THE HOME BOOK OF

SHAKESPEARE QUOTATIONS

STEVENSON'S BOOK OF SHAKESPEARE QUOTATIONS

Being also a Concordance & a Glossary of the Unique Words & Phrases in the Plays & Poems

ARRANGED AND EDITED BY

BURTON STEVENSON

CASSELL • LONDON

CASSELL & COMPANY LTD.
35 Red Lion Square, London, WC1
Melbourne, Sydney, Toronto
Johannesburg, Auckland

This edition first published in Great Britain 1969

S.B.N. 304 93496 8

Yet be most proud of that which I compile,
Whose influence is thine and born of thee.

Sonnets. No. lxxviii.

PREFATORY NOTE

THE text used in the preparation of this book is that of the revised (1911) *Globe* edition, which seemed to the editor the best for his purpose, and which has the added advantage of being the one used in an earlier revision (1891) by Mr. John Bartlett for his *Concordance.* Therefore, since the original numbering was not changed in the later edition, the lines as given here will be found to correspond with Bartlett, except in the infrequent instances where a careful count showed Bartlett to be in error.

The arrangement is alphabetically by subject, and under each subject alphabetically by play or poem, except that nearly identical phrases, and similar ideas varying only slightly in expression, are grouped together in the chronological order of the plays. The more important subjects are divided into sections in order to throw cognate quotations closely together, and the result is often a juxtaposition which is both interesting and amusing.

The chronological order followed is that of Mr. E. K. Chambers, as given in his *William Shakespeare,* vol. i, ch. 8, beginning with *II Henry VI,* in 1590, and ending with *The Two Noble Kinsmen* in 1613. It was selected because Shakespeare scholars seem to take fewer exceptions to it than to any other, and will be found in full on the following page. All the plays and poems listed in it are included here with the exception of *The Two Noble Kinsmen,* which was not included in the *Globe* edition, and with which Shakespeare's connection is extremely nebulous.

As the editor proceeded with the arrangement of this book, he was struck by the astonishing number of words and phrases which Shakespeare used only once—not only unusual and coined words, but such ordinary ones as "fidelity," "gallantry," "decent," "difficult," "dreary," "friendless," and "improbable." Some passages, especially of vituperation, consist almost entirely of unique words. In *The Tempest,* i, 1, 43, three such words occur in a single line, "bawling," "blasphemous," and "incharitable." Various eccentricities of diction also developed. "Gobbets," for example, occurs twice in the first play and never in any later one, while "manacled" occurs twice in the last play and never in any earlier one. "Emulous" is used four times in *Troilus and Cressida,* and nowhere else. What is true of words is true also of phrases. "Turned to stone" occurs in the first play and is never repeated. "Swim like a duck" is used for the first time in the next to the last one. Only once does any character in Shakespeare say "above compare," or "all at once," or "boy's play," or "cheek by jole," or "good riddance," or "against the grain," or "ill at ease." There are literally hundreds of such expressions, and these grew so deeply interesting to the editor that he decided to indicate all unique words and phrases, and also all familiar ones which were used only twice or thrice. Mr. Chambers notes that a small corner of this field was explored by Professor Sarrazin in his vocabulary tests to determine the chronology of the plays, but for the most part it is apparently virgin soil.

The range of use of the principal adjectives as applied to different nouns (good boy, good girl, good man, good woman) is given by Bartlett and so is not repeated here, but the variations in the use of the minor adjectives not covered by Bartlett are given, and also the play of different adjectives on the same noun (dear boy, little boy, poor boy, unbridled boy), which, so far as the editor is aware, has never before been attempted. He has leaned heavily upon Bartlett in his indication of unique words, and upon Onions's *Shakespeare Glossary* for the definition of such of them as are in any way obscure.

Special effort has been made to render the book easy to use. Great care has been taken with the arrangement, cross-references have been inserted wherever they would be of assistance, and the INDEX AND CONCORDANCE at the end of the volume will be found unusually complete. Detailed suggestions for its use are given on the page preceding it, and should be carefully read. Some general suggestions will be found on page xl.

Chillicothe, Ohio, May 1, 1937

CHRONOLOGY OF THE PLAYS

NO.	NAME OF PLAY	DATE
1	II Henry VI	1590–1
2	III Henry VI	"
3	I Henry VI	1591–2
4	Richard III	1592–3
5	The Comedy of Errors	"
6	Titus Andronicus	1593–4
7	The Taming of the Shrew	"
8	The Two Gentlemen of Verona	1594–5
9	Love's Labour 's Lost	"
10	Romeo and Juliet	"
11	Richard II	1595–6
12	A Midsummer-Night's Dream	"
13	King John	1596–7
14	The Merchant of Venice	"
15	I Henry IV	1597–8
16	II Henry IV	"
17	Much Ado about Nothing	1598–9
18	Henry V	"
19	Julius Cæsar	1599–1600
20	As You Like It	"
21	Twelfth Night	1599–1600
22	Hamlet	1600–1
23	The Merry Wives of Windsor	"
24	Troilus and Cressida	1601–2
25	All 's Well That Ends Well	1602–3
		1603–4 *
26	Measure for Measure	1604–5
27	Othello	"
28	King Lear	1605–6
29	Macbeth	"
30	Antony and Cleopatra	1606–7
31	Coriolanus	1607–8
32	Timon of Athens	"
33	Pericles	1608–9
34	Cymbeline	1609–10
35	The Winter's Tale	1610–11
36	The Tempest	1611–12
37	Henry VIII	1612–13
38	The Two Noble Kinsmen	"

CHRONOLOGY OF THE POEMS

1	Venus and Adonis	1593
2	The Rape of Lucrece	1594
3	The Passionate Pilgrim	1599
4	The Phœnix and Turtle	1601
5	Sonnets	1609
6	A Lover's Complaint	1609

* The London theatres were closed from March, 1603, to April, 1604, on account of the plague, and during this period Shakespeare apparently wrote no plays.

TABLE OF CONTENTS

B

C

D

E

F

G

H

I

J

K

L

M

N

O

P

Q

R

S

T

U

V

W

Y

Z

THE HOME BOOK OF SHAKESPEARE QUOTATIONS

NOTE TO READER

THE quotations in this book are arranged alphabetically by subject, and under each subject alphabetically by play or poem, except that phrases which are identical or nearly so, and turns of thought which are essentially similar, are grouped together in the chronological order of the plays. The order followed is given in full on page ix.

To bring cognate quotations closely together, the longer subjects are divided into sections. Under "Age," for example, the sub-heads are (1) "Age and Youth," (2) "Age: Its Compensations," (3) "Age: Its Penalties," (4) "Age and Beauty," (5) "Age and Love," (6) "Age and Wisdom," (7) "Age: Its Silver Livery," (8) "Middle Age," (9) "Old Age," (10) "The Age." A full list of both subjects and sub-divisions will be found in the TABLE OF CONTENTS, beginning on page xi. The purpose has been to present to the reader all closely related quotations in a single group, which not only makes it more easy to compare them, but which also adds greatly to their interest.

In order to save space, portions of two lines of verse are sometimes run in one, but a capital always indicates the beginning of the second line. After every quotation, not only the play is given, but the act, scene and line, and the name of the speaker, but in the case of simple phrases the name of the speaker is omitted and the act, scene and line are indicated by numerals only.

The book should be easy to use, once the principles of arrangement are understood. In order to see what Shakespeare has to say on any subject, the reader will, of course, turn to the subject itself and run through the quotations under it, but in looking for a particular quotation the easier way is to consult the CONCORDANCE at the back of the book, where every quotation is listed by its keywords. "To make a virtue of necessity," for example, will be found entered under both "virtue" and "necessity," with a reference not only to the page on which the quotation may be found, but to its number on the page. All quotations are numbered in this way, so that they may be instantly turned to. Detailed suggestions for the use of the CONCORDANCE will be found on the page preceding it, and should be carefully read, for the CONCORDANCE is the key to the volume.

A

ABILITY

1
I know you . . . have ability enough to make such knaveries yours.
All's Well that Ends Well. Act i, sc. 3, l. 12. [Countess]

Be able for thine enemy.—*All's Well that Ends Well,* i, 1, 74.
More able.—*As You Like It,* ii, 4, 77.
So able.—*Hamlet,* v, 2, 211.
Abler than yourself.—*Julius Cæsar,* iv, 3, 31. The only use of "abler."

2
To-morrow, Cæsar,
I shall be furnish'd to inform you rightly
Both what by sea and land I can be able
To front this present time.
Antony and Cleopatra. Act i, sc. 4, l. 76. [Lepidus]

3
None of you but is
Able to bear against the great Aufidius
A shield as hard as this.
Coriolanus. Act i, sc. 6, l. 78. [Marcius]

Able to bear.—*The Merry Wives of Windsor,* iv, 5, 111.
He is able to pierce a corslet with his eye.
Coriolanus. Act v, sc. 4, l. 20. [Menenius] The only use of "corslet."

4
[We should] know our own estate,
How able such a work to undergo.
II Henry IV. Act i, sc. 3, l. 53. [Bardolph]

5
You can do it, sir; you can do it.
II Henry IV. Act iii, sc. 2, l. 157. [Shallow]

I know I can do it.
Twelfth Night. Act ii, sc. 3, l. 148. [Maria]

If we fail, We then can do 't at land.
Antony and Cleopatra. Act iii, sc. 7, l. 54. [Antony] The only uses of "can do it."

6
Would I were able to load him with his desert!
Henry V. Act iii, sc. 7, l. 85. [Dauphin]

Henry is able to enrich his queen,
And not to seek a queen to make him rich.
I Henry VI. Act v, sc. 5, l. 51. [Suffolk]

7
I am able to endure much.
II Henry VI. Act iv, sc. 2, l. 60. [Cade]

I am able now, methinks,
Out of a fortitude of soul I feel,
To endure more miseries and greater far
Than my weak-hearted enemies dare offer.
Henry VIII. Act iii, sc. 2, l. 387. [Wolsey] The only use of "weak-hearted."

I am able.—*Two Gentlemen of Verona,* ii, 3, 58.
Able to endure.—*Henry VIII,* v, 4, 66.
Able to breathe life into a stone.—*All's Well that Ends Well,* ii, 1, 76. See under MEDICINE.
Able to corrupt a saint.—*I Henry IV,* i, 2, 102.
Able to freeze the god Priapus.—*Pericles,* iv, 6, 3. The only mention of Priapus.
Able to instruct.—*I Henry VI,* iv, 1, 159.
Able . . . to kill and cure.—*II Henry VI,* v, 1, 101.
Able to lead her a coranto.—*All's Well that Ends Well,* ii, 3, 49. Coranto (a kind of dance consisting of a time, a step, a balance, and a bow) is mentioned again in *Twelfth Night,* i, 3, 137, and in *Henry V,* iii, 5, 33.
Able to maintain it.—*The Taming of the Shrew,* v, 1, 78.
Able to maintain you.—*III Henry VI,* iii, 3, 154.
Able to overtake.—*The Merry Wives of Windsor,* i, 1, 54.
Able to perform.—*Henry VIII,* i, 1, 161.
Able to ravish.—*I Henry VI,* v, 5, 15.
Able to speak for himself.—*II Henry IV,* v, 1, 50.
Able to woo.—*The Merry Wives of Windsor,* v, 5, 142.

8
Would it not grieve an able man to leave
So sweet a bedfellow?
Henry VIII. Act ii, sc. 2, l. 142. [King]

Able body.—*II Henry IV,* ii, 4, 274; *All's Well that Ends Well,* iv, 5, 86.
Able means.—*Henry VIII,* iv, 2, 153.
Able spirit.—*Sonnets,* lxxxv.

9
I'll able 'em.
King Lear. Act iv, sc. 6, l. 172. [King Lear]

10
Is he not able to discharge the money?
The Merchant of Venice. Act iv, sc. 1, l. 208. [Portia]

Pay . . . when he was able.—*The Merchant of Venice,* i, 2, 88.

11
You have not a man in all Athens able to discharge
Pyramus but he.
A Midsummer-Night's Dream. Act iv, sc. 2, l. 8. [Quince]

Another of his fathom they have none
To lead their business.
Othello. Act i, sc. 1, l. 153. [Iago] The only use of "fathom" in the sense of ability.

12
Time hath not yet so dried this blood of mine,
Nor age so eat up my invention,
Nor fortune made such havoc of my means,
Nor my bad life reft me so much of friends,
But they shall find, awaked in such a kind,
Both strength of limb and policy of mind,
Ability in means and choice of friends,
To quit me of them throughly.
Much Ado about Nothing. Act iv, sc. 1, l. 195. [Leonato] "Throughly" is used thirteen times in the plays, and "thoroughly" only four times.

13
I will do All my abilities in thy behalf.
Othello. Act iii, sc. 3, l. 1. [Desdemona]

1
He fills it up with great ability.
Othello. Act iii, sc. 3, l. 247. [Iago]
Wish'd ability.—*The Winter's Tale,* v, 1, 143.
Ability of life.—*Hamlet,* v, 2, 384.
2
I am as able and as fit as thou.
Titus Andronicus. Act ii, sc. 1, l. 33. [Chiron]
See also under FITNESS.

II—Lack of Ability

3 A Syracusian merchant, . . .
Not being able to buy out his life, . . .
Dies ere the weary sun set in the west.
The Comedy of Errors. Act i, sc. 2, l. 5. [Merchant] "Syracusian" is used seven times in this play, and in no other.
Not able to maintain
The many to them 'longing.
Henry VIII, i, 2, 31. See under REBELS. "'Longing" (for belonging) is used again in *All's Well that Ends Well,* iv, 2, 42.
Not able to maintain.—*Henry VIII,* i, 2, 31.
Not able to endure.—*Richard II,* iii, 2, 52.
Not able to invent.—*II Henry IV,* i, 2, 9.
Not able to produce.—*Winter's Tale,* ii, 3, 118.
Not able to taste.—*A Midsummer-Night's Dream,* iv, 1, 218.
Not able.—*The Winter's Tale,* ii, 3, 118.
Cannot be able.—*The Winter's Tale,* v, 2, 27.
Should not be able.—*III Henry VI,* iv, 8, 36.
Am not able.—*I Henry VI,* iii, 1, 12. "Inability" does not occur in the plays.
Able to do least.—*Romeo and Juliet,* v, 3, 223.
As well as I am able.—*Henry VIII,* iv, 1, 62.
4
Your abilities are too infant-like for doing much alone.
Coriolanus. Act ii, sc. 1, l. 40. [Menenius] The only use of "infant-like."
Alas! what poor ability 's in me
To do him good?
Measure for Measure. Act i, sc. 4, l. 75. [Isabella]
Altogether lacks the abilities.—*Othello,* i, 3, 25.
My lean and low ability.—*Twelfth Night,* iii, 4, 378.
5
I shall never be able to fight a blow.
II Henry VI. Act i, sc. 3, l. 220. [Peter]
I can no more.—*II Henry VI,* iii, 2, 120; *Hamlet,* v, 2, 331; *Antony and Cleopatra,* iv, 15, 59; *Henry VIII,* iv, 2, 173.
6
I am never able to deal with my master.
II Henry VI. Act ii, sc. 3, l. 78. [Peter]
I am not able.—*Timon of Athens,* iii, 2, 54.
I am not able to answer the Welsh flannel.
The Merry Wives of Windsor. Act v, sc. 5, l. 171. [Falstaff] The only use of "flannel"; referring to Evans, a Welshman of uncouth manners.
Poor men . . . not able to answer.—*III Henry VI,* iv, 7, 46.
7
I am not able to stand alone.
II Henry VI. Act ii, sc. 1, l. 145. [Simpcox]
I am almost afraid to stand alone.
Romeo and Juliet. Act v, sc. 3, l. 10. [Page]
Then she could stand alone.
Romeo and Juliet. Act i, sc. 3, l. 36. [Nurse]
He . . . stands alone.—*Troilus and Cressida,* i, 2, 16. The only uses of "stand alone."
Me they shall feel while I am able to stand.
Romeo and Juliet. Act i, sc. 1, l. 33. [Sampson]
8
Now of late, not able to travel with her furred pack, she washes bucks here at home.
II Henry VI. Act iv, sc. 2, l. 50. [Smith] The only use of "bucks" in the sense of a quantity of clothes put through the buck or lye, though Ford has a play upon the word in *The Merry Wives of Windsor,* iii, 3, 167, when his wife remarks, "You were best meddle with buck-washing," and he retorts, referring to Falstaff, "Buck! I would I could wash myself of the buck!"
Furred gown.—*Measure for Measure,* iii, 2, 8; *King Lear,* iv, 6, 169.
Furr'd moss.—*Cymbeline,* iv, 2, 228.
Furred with fox.—*Measure for Measure,* iii, 2, 9. The only uses of "furred."
9
We are unable to resist.
Pericles. Act i, sc. 4, l. 84. [Cleon]
Unable for itself.—*Measure for Measure,* ii, 4, 21.
All-unable.—*Henry V,* Epil., 1. The only use of the phrase.

ABSENCE

10
Herself most chastely absent.
All's Well that Ends Well. Act iii, sc. 7, l. 34. [Helena]
Long absent.—*Twelfth Night,* i, 5, 18.
Long absence.—*Cymbeline,* iii, 6, 74; *Henry VIII,* ii, 3, 106.
11
My absence was not six months old.
The Comedy of Errors. Act i, sc. 1, l. 45. [Ægeon]
Defend yourself . . . by absence.—*Coriolanus,* iii, 2, 95.
A fever with the absence of her son.
Cymbeline. Act iv, sc. 3, l. 2. [Cymbeline]
Absence of the cat.—*Henry V,* i, 2, 172.
Absence of the duke.—*Measure for Measure,* v, 1, 331.
Absence of your king.—*Pericles,* ii, 4, 46.
Absence of your lord.—*The Merchant of Venice,* iii, 4, 4.
Absence of the needer.—*Coriolanus,* iv, 1, 44. The only use of "needer."
Absence of the sun.—*The Merchant of Venice,* v, 1, 128.
Ulysses' absence.—*Coriolanus,* i, 3, 93.
12 Your nobles, jealous of your absence,
Seek through your camp to find you.
Henry V. Act iv, sc. 1, l. 302. [Erpingham]
Impatient of my absence.—*Julius Cæsar,* iv, 3, 152.
13
I am combined by a sacred vow
And shall be absent.
Measure for Measure. Act iv, sc. 3, l. 149. [Duke]
Take No note at all of our being absent hence.
The Merchant of Venice. Act v, sc. 1, l. 119. [Portia]

There is not one among them but I dote on his very absence.
The Merchant of Venice. Act i, sc. 2, l. 119. [Portia]

1
I am gone, though I am here.
Much Ado about Nothing. Act iv, sc. 1, l. 295. [Beatrice]

These present-absent with quick motion slide.
Sonnets. No. xlv. The only use of "present-absent."

2
I hope,
My absence doth neglect no great designs,
Which by my presence might have been concluded.
Richard III. Act iii, sc. 4, l. 24. [Gloucester]

3
Our absence makes us unthrifty to our knowledge.
Winter's Tale. Act v, sc. 2, l. 120. [Gentleman] "Unthrifty" is repeated in *The Merchant of Venice,* i, 3, 177: "Unthrifty knave"; in *Richard II,* v, 3, 1: "Unthrifty son"; and in *Sonnets,* iv: "Unthrifty loveliness."

II—Absence and Love

4
I am undone: there is no living, none,
If Bertram be away.
All's Well that Ends Well. Act i, sc. 1, l. 95. [Helena]

But now he 's gone, and my idolatrous fancy
Must sanctify his reliques.
All's Well that Ends Well. Act i, sc. 1, l. 108. [Helena] The only use of "idolatrous." "Reliques" occurs again in *Twelfth Night,* iii, 3, 19.

This dull world, which in thy absence is
No better than a sty.
Antony and Cleopatra. Act iv, sc. 15, l. 61. [Cleopatra]

5
Where have you been all this while?
As You Like It. Act iv, sc. 1, l. 39. [Rosalind]

Orlando: For these two hours, Rosalind, I will leave thee.
Rosalind: Alas! dear love, I cannot lack thee two hours.
As You Like It. Act iv, sc. 1, l. 181.

What, keep a week away? seven days and nights?
Eight score eight hours? and lovers' absent hours,
More tedious than the dial eight score times?
O weary reckoning!
Othello. Act iii, sc. 4, l. 173. [Bianca]

6
Thou 'lt forget me when I am gone.
II Henry IV. Act ii, sc. 4, l. 300. [Falstaff]

What, out of hearing? gone? no sound, no word?
A Midsummer-Night's Dream. Act ii, sc. 2, l. 152. [Hermia]

7
When you depart from me, sorrow abides and happiness takes his leave.
Much Ado about Nothing. Act i, sc. 1, l. 101. [Leonato]

8
I a heavy interim shall support
By his dear absence.
Othello. Act i, sc. 3, l. 260. [Desdemona]

To the felt absence now I feel a cause.
Othello. Act iii, sc. 4, l. 182. [Bianca]

Strange absence.—*Cymbeline,* v, 5, 57.

9
O absence, what a torment wouldst thou prove
Were it not thy sour leisure gave sweet leave
To entertain the time with thoughts of love!
Sonnets. No. xxxix.

Nor think the bitterness of absence sour
When you have bid your servant once adieu.
Sonnets. No. lvii.

How like a winter hath my absence been
From thee, the pleasure of the fleeting year!
What freezings have I felt, what dark days seen!
What old December's bareness everywhere! . . .
For summer and his pleasures wait on thee,
And, thou away, the very birds are mute;
Or, if they sing, 'tis with so dull a cheer
That leaves look pale, dreading the winter 's near.
Sonnets. No. xcvii. The only use of "freezings." "Freezing" occurs in *Cymbeline,* iii, 3, 39: "Freezing hours"; and in *The Rape of Lucrece,* l. 1145: "Freezing cold."

From you have I been absent in the spring,
When proud-pied April dress'd in all his trim
Hath put a spirit of youth in every thing,
That heavy Saturn laugh'd and leap'd with him. . . .
Yet seem'd it winter still, and, you away,
As with your shadow I with these did play.
Sonnets. No. xcviii. The only use of "proud-pied."

Absent from thy heart.—*Sonnets,* xli.

Absent from thy walks.—*Sonnets,* lxxxix.

10
O thou that dost inhabit in my breast,
Leave not the mansion so long tenantless,
Lest, growing ruinous, the building fall
And leave no memory of what it was!
The Two Gentlemen of Verona. Act v, sc. 4, l. 7. [Valentine] "Tenantless" is used again in *Hamlet,* v, 4, 8.

ABSTINENCE

See also Temperance

11
Refrain to-night,
And that shall lend a kind of easiness
To the next abstinence.
Hamlet. Act iii, sc. 4, l. 165. [Hamlet] "Easiness" is repeated in v, 1, 76, and in *Henry VIII,* v, 3, 25.

12
Abstinence engenders maladies.
Love's Labour 's Lost. Act iv, sc. 3, l. 295. [Biron]

13
A man of stricture and firm abstinence.
Measure for Measure. Act i, sc. 3, l. 12. [Duke] The only use of "stricture."

He doth with holy abstinence subdue
That in himself which he spurs on his power
To qualify in others.
Measure for Measure. Act iv, sc. 2, l. 84. [Duke]

Who abstains from meat that is not gaunt?
Richard II. Act ii, sc. 1, l. 76. [King Richard]

1
Be more abstemious.
The Tempest. Act iv, sc. 1, l. 53. [Prospero] The only use of "abstemious."

ABUSE

2
You are abused
Beyond the mark of thought: and the high gods,
To do you justice, make them ministers
Of us and those that love you.
Antony and Cleopatra. Act iii, sc. 6, l. 86. [Cæsar]

There was never man thus abused.
Twelfth Night. Act iv, sc. 2, l. 51. [Malvolio]

Abused extremely.—*Henry VIII,* Epil., 6.
A great deal abused.—*Cymbeline,* i, 4, 124.
Abused and dishonour'd.—*The Comedy of Errors,* v, 1, 199.
Haled and abused.—*The Taming of the Shrew,* v, 1, 111.
Mightily abused.—*Much Ado about Nothing,* v, 2, 100; *Titus Andronicus,* ii, 3, 87; *King Lear,* iv, 7, 53.
Much abused.—*Romeo and Juliet,* iv, 1, 29.
Notoriously abused.—*Twelfth Night,* iv, 2, 95; v, 1, 388. "Notoriously" occurs in no other play.
Rankly abused.—*Hamlet,* i, 5, 38.
So abused.—*As You Like It,* iii, 5, 80.
Too much abused.—*Richard II,* ii, 3, 137.

3
Abuses me to damn me.
Hamlet. Act ii, sc. 2, l. 632. [Hamlet]
Is it some abuse?—*Hamlet,* iv, 7, 51.

4
The poor abuses of the time want countenance.
I Henry IV. Act i, sc. 2, l. 174. [Falstaff]
Poor abuses.—*The Rape of Lucrece,* l. 269.
The time's abuse.—*Julius Cæsar,* ii, 1, 116.
Growth's abuse.—*Venus and Adonis,* l. 166.
Lust's abuse.—*Venus and Adonis,* l. 792.
Men's abuses.—*The Rape of Lucrece,* l. 1259.
Night's abuses.—*The Rape of Lucrece,* l. 1075.
Abuse of greatness.—*Julius Cæsar,* ii, 1, 18.

5
Cries out upon abuses, seems to weep
Over his country's wrongs.
I Henry IV. Act iv, sc. 3, l. 81. [Hotspur]

6
Prince: I shall drive you then to confess the wilful abuse. . . .
Falstaff: No abuse, Hal, o' my honour; no abuse.
Prince: Not to dispraise me, and call me pantler and bread-chipper and I know not what?
Falstaff: No abuse, Hal.
Prince: No abuse?
Falstaff: No abuse, Ned, i' the world; honest Ned, none.
II Henry IV. Act ii, sc. 4, l. 339. The only use of "bread-chipper." "Pantler" occurs four times. See under CHARACTER.

7
It was ourself thou didst abuse.
Henry V. Act iv, sc. 8, l. 52. [King Henry]
Abuse myself.—*Twelfth Night,* iii, 1, 124.

8
Pardon my abuse.
I Henry VI. Act ii, sc. 3, l. 67. [Count]
Give him chastisement for this abuse.
I Henry VI. Act iv, sc. 1, l. 67. [King Henry]

9
This is a strange abuse.
Measure for Measure. Act v, sc. 1, l. 205. [Angelo]
Lend him your kind pains To find out this abuse.
Measure for Measure. Act v, sc. 1, l. 247. [Duke Vincentio]
Hark, how the villain would close now, after his treasonable abuses!
Measure for Measure. Act v, sc. 1, l. 347. [Angelo] The only use of "treasonable."

10
I therefore apprehend and do attach thee
For an abuser of the world.
Othello, i, 2, 77. See under MAGIC. The only use of "abuser."
It is my nature's plague To spy into abuses.
Othello. Act iii, sc. 3, l. 146. [Iago]

11
They that level
At my abuses reckon up their own.
Sonnets. No. cxxi.

12
So him I lose through my unkind abuse.
Sonnets. No. cxxxiv.
Gross abuse.—*The Rape of Lucrece,* l. 1315.

13
Hang him, he 'll abuse us.
Timon of Athens. Act ii, sc. 2, l. 49. [Servant]
Do not abuse me.—*King Lear,* iv, 7, 77.
Abuse your bosom.—*Othello,* iv, 2, 14.
Abuse our ears.—*All's Well that Ends Well,* v, 3, 295.
His ear abused.—*King Lear,* ii, 4, 310.
Abuse their husbands.—*Othello,* iv, 3, 62.
Abuse your soul.—*Pericles,* i, 1, 126.

ACCENT

14
Your accent is something finer than you could purchase in so removed a dwelling.
As You Like It. Act iii, sc. 2, l. 259. [Orlando]
Do not take
His rougher accents for malicious sounds.
Coriolanus. Act ii, sc. 3, l. 55. [Menenius]

15
Breathe short-winded accents of new broils.
I Henry IV. Act i, sc. 1, l. 3. [King Henry] "Short-winded" is repeated in *II Henry IV,* ii, 2, 136.
Many accents.—*The Rape of Lucrece,* l. 1719.
Other accents.—*King Lear,* i, 4, 1.
Plain accent.—*King Lear,* ii, 2, 117.
Second accent.—*Henry V,* ii, 4, 126.
Timorous accent.—*Othello,* i, 1, 75.
Accents terrible.—*Macbeth,* ii, 3, 62.
Accents yet unknown.—*Julius Cæsar,* iii, 1, 113.

16
The accent of his tongue affecteth him.
King John. Act i, sc. 1, l. 86. [Elinor] See LIKENESS, 872:13, for full quotation.

Brave soldier, pardon me,
That any accent breaking from my tongue
Should 'scape the true acquaintance of mine ear.
King John. Act v, sc. 6, l. 13. [Hubert de Burgh]

1 You find not the apostraphas, and so miss the accent.
Love's Labour's Lost. Act iv, sc. 2, l. 123. [Holofernes] The only use of "apostraphas."

Action and accent did they teach him there;
'Thus must thou speak,' and 'thus thy body bear.'
Love's Labour's Lost. Act v, sc. 2, l. 99. [Boyet]

2 Throttle their practised accent in their fears.
A Midsummer-Night's Dream. Act v, sc. 1, l. 97. [Theseus] The only use of "throttle."

These new tuners of accents.
Romeo and Juliet. Act ii, sc. 4, l. 31. [Mercutio] See under Fop for full quotation. The only use of "tuners."

With an accent tuned in selfsame key
Retorts to chiding fortune.
Troilus and Cressida. Act i, sc. 3, l. 53. [Agamemnon]

ACCIDENT

See also Chance

3 Accidents unpurposed.
Antony and Cleopatra. Act iv, sc. 14, l. 84. [Antony] The only use of "unpurposed."

These happen'd accidents.
The Tempest. Act v, sc. 1, l. 250. [Prospero]

4 Accidentally are met together.
The Comedy of Errors. Act v, 1, 361. [Duke]

I am most fortunate thus accidentally to encounter you.
Coriolanus. Act iv, sc. 3, l. 40. [Volscian]

Accidentally . . . hath miscarried.—*Love's Labour's Lost*, iv, 2, 143. The only uses of "accidentally."

5 All solemn things
Should answer solemn accidents.
Cymbeline. Act iv, sc. 2, l. 191. [Guiderius]

Be not with mortal accidents oppressed.
Cymbeline. Act v, sc. 4, l. 99. [Jupiter]

Particular accidents.—*The Tempest*, v, 1, 305.

Slender accident.—*Hamlet*, iii, 2, 209.

6 The day Was yours by accident.
Cymbeline. Act v, sc. 5, l. 76. [Lucius]

As 'twere by accident.
Hamlet. Act iii, sc. 1, l. 30. [King Claudius]

By accident.—*Romeo and Juliet*, v, 3, 251; *Cymbeline*, v, 5, 278.

By some accident.—*Othello*, iv, 2, 231.

7 And for his death no wind of blame shall breathe,
But even his mother shall uncharge the practice
And call it accident.
Hamlet. Act iv, sc. 7, l. 67. [King] The only use of "uncharge."

Let my disclaiming from a purposed evil
Free me so far in your most generous thoughts,
That I have shot mine arrow o'er the house,
And hurt my brother.
Hamlet. Act v, sc. 2, l. 252. [Hamlet] "Disclaiming" is repeated in *Richard II*, i, 1, 70.

8 Nothing pleaseth but rare accidents.
I Henry IV. Act i, sc. 2, l. 230. [Prince]

Dismay not, princes, at this accident.
I Henry VI. Act iii, sc. 3, l. 1. [La Pucelle]

Accidental evils.—*Julius Cæsar*, iv, 3, 146.

Accidental judgements.—*Hamlet*, v, 2, 393.

9 The accident which brought me to her eye
Upon the moment did her force subdue.
A Lover's Complaint, l. 247.

10 O, 'tis an accident that heaven provides!
Measure for Measure. Act iv, 3, 81. [Duke]

This is an accident of hourly proof.
Much Ado about Nothing. Act ii, sc. 1, l. 188. [Claudio]

11 Think no more of this night's accidents.
A Midsummer-Night's Dream. Act iv, sc. 1, l. 71. [Oberon]

This accident is not unlike my dream:
Belief of it oppresses me already.
Othello. Act i, sc. 1, l. 143. [Brabantio]

Accident most strange.—*The Tempest*, i, 2, 178.

12 Moving accidents by flood and field.
Othello. Act i, sc. 3, l. 135. [Othello]

13 'Tis not a visitation framed, but forced
By need and accident.
Winter's Tale. Act v, sc. 1, l. 91. [Leontes]

ACCOMPLICE

14 I am your accessary.
All's Well that Ends Well. Act ii, sc. 1, l. 35. [Second Lord]

To both their deaths thou shalt be accessary.
Richard III. Act i, sc. 2, l. 192. [Gloucester]

An accessary by thine inclination
To all sins past, and all that are to come,
From the creation to the general doom.
The Rape of Lucrece, l. 922.

I an accessary needs must be.
Sonnets, xxxv. See under Love and Hate.

Accessary yieldings.—*The Rape of Lucrece*, l. 1658. "Accessary" is used a fifth time in *Sonnets*, xxxv.

15 Art thou a feodary for this act, and look'st
So virgin-like without?
Cymbeline. Act iii, sc. 2, l. 21. [Pisanio] The only use of "virgin-like." "Feodary" (accomplice) is repeated in *Measure for Measure*, ii, 4, 122.

16 Happiness to his accomplices!
I Henry VI. Act v, sc. 2, l. 9. [Scout] The only use of "accomplices."

17 One incorporate To our attempts.
Julius Cæsar. Act i, sc. 3, l. 135. [Cassius]

Three parts of him
Is ours already, and the man entire
Upon the next encounter yields him ours.
Julius Cæsar. Act i, sc. 3, l. 154. [Cassius]

I think he will stand very strong with us.
Julius Cæsar. Act ii, sc. 1, l. 142. [Casca]

1 Their complices,
The caterpillars of the commonwealth.
Richard II, ii, 3, 165. See under PARASITE.
All thy complices.—*III Henry VI*, iv, 3, 44.
Glendower and his complices.—*Richard II*, iii, 1, 43.
The rebels and their complices.—*II Henry VI*, v, 1, 212.
Loving complices.—*II Henry IV*, i, 1, 163. The only uses of "complices."

2
Thy brother was a furtherer in the act.
The Tempest. Act v, sc. 1, l. 73. [Prospero] The only use of "furtherer."

ACCUSATION

3
King: Wherefore hast thou accused him all this while?
Diana: Because he 's guilty.
All 's Well that Ends Well. Act v, sc. 3, l. 289.
Who does he accuse?—*Antony and Cleopatra*, iii, 6, 23.
Accuse me thus.—*Sonnets*, cxvii.
I accuse thee.—*Sonnets*, clii.
I accuse them not.—*Pericles*, iv, 2, 76.

4
I need not be barren of accusations.
Coriolanus. Act i, sc. 1, l. 46. [First Citizen]
They are prepared
With accusations, as I hear, more strong
Than are upon you yet.
Coriolanus. Act iii, sc. 2, l. 140. [Cominius]

5
I could accuse me of such things that it were better my mother had not borne me.
Hamlet, iii, 1, 124. See under HONESTY.
Accuse myself.—*Richard III*, i, 2, 85; *Cymbeline*, ii, 3, 115.

6
It warms the very sickness in my heart,
That I shall live and tell him to his teeth,
'Thus didest thou.'
Hamlet. Act iv, sc. 7, l. 56. [Laertes]

7 Let not his report
Come current for an accusation.
I Henry IV. Act i, sc. 3, l. 67. [Hotspur]
Do not cast away an honest man for a villain's accusation.
II Henry VI. Act i, sc. 3, l. 205. [Horner]

8 If thou canst accuse,
Or aught intend'st to lay unto my charge,
Do it without invention, suddenly.
I Henry VI. Act iii, sc. 1, l. 3. [Winchester]
Let them accuse me by invention, I
Will answer in mine honour.
Coriolanus. Act iii, sc. 2, l. 143. [Coriolanus]

9
Suffolk: Here is a man accused of treason:
Pray God the Duke of York excuse himself!
York: Doth any one accuse York for a traitor?
Suffolk: . . . This is the man
That doth accuse his master of high treason.
II Henry VI. Act i, sc. 3, l. 180.
Accused of high treason.—*The Winter's Tale*, iii, 2, 13. See under TREASON.
Accused of folly.—*Coriolanus*. i, 1, 92.
Accused a crafty murderer.—*II Henry VI*, iii, 1, 254.

Accusing you of injury.—*Sonnets*, lviii.

10
By false accuse doth level at my life.
II Henry VI. Act iii, sc. 1, l. 160. [Gloucester] "False accuse" was never used after the first play.
False accusation.—*Much Ado about Nothing*, v, 1, 249; *The Winter's Tale*, iii, 2, 32.

11
Reprove my allegation, if you can;
Or else conclude my words effectual.
II Henry VI. Act iii, sc. 1, l. 40. [Queen]
Swear
False allegations to o'erthrow his state.
II Henry VI. Act iii, sc. 1, l. 181. [Suffolk] "Allegation" is used twice in this scene and nowhere else in the plays.

12 To his accusations
He pleaded still not guilty.
Henry VIII. Act ii, sc. 1, l. 12. [Gentleman]
We come not by the way of accusation,
To taint that honour every good tongue blesses.
Henry VIII. Act iii, sc. 1, l. 54. [Wolsey]

13
Suffolk: No man dare accuse you. . . .
Gardiner: You shall know many dare accuse you boldly,
More than, I fear, you are provided for.
Henry VIII. Act v, sc. 3, l. 50.
All these accused him strongly.
Henry VIII. Act ii, sc. 1, l. 25. [Gentleman]

14
It ill beseems this presence to cry aim
To these ill-tuned repetitions.
King John. Act ii, sc. 1, l. 196. [King Philip] The only use of "ill-tuned."

15
Accuse him home and home.
Measure for Measure. Act iv, sc. 3, l. 148. [Duke]
He will avoid your accusation.
Measure for Measure. Act iii, sc. 1, l. 201. [Duke]
So vulgarly and personally accused.
Measure for Measure. Act v, sc. 1, l. 160. [Friar Peter] The only use of "vulgarly."

16
I would say the truth; but to accuse him so,
That is your part: yet I am advised to do it.
Measure for Measure. Act iv, sc. 6, l. 2. [Isabella]
Accuses him of fornication.—*Measure for Measure*, v, 1, 196.
Accused in fornication.—*Measure for Measure*, ii, 1, 82.
Accuse him of incontinency.—*Cymbeline*, iii, 4, 49.

17
Be you constant in the accusation, and my cunning shall not shame me.
Much Ado about Nothing. Act ii, sc. 2, l. 55. [Borachio]
Friar: What man is he you are accused of?
Hero: They know that do accuse me: I know none.
Much Ado about Nothing. Act iv, sc. 1, l. 178.
Then shall he mourn, . . .
And wish he had not so accused her,
No, though he thought his accusation true.
Much Ado about Nothing. Act iv, sc. 1, l. 232. [Friar]

With public accusation, uncovered slander, unmitigated rancour.
Much Ado about Nothing. Act iv, sc. 1, l. 307. [Beatrice] The only use of "unmitigated."
Publicly accused.—*The Winter's Tale,* ii, 3, 204.

1
Hero was in this manner accused, in this very manner refused, and upon the grief of this suddenly died.
Much Ado about Nothing. Act iv, sc. 2, l. 63. [Sexton]
My Lady Hero hath been falsely accused.
Much Ado about Nothing. Act v, sc. 2, l. 99. [Ursula]
Falsely accused.—*II Henry VI,* i, 3, 192.
Wrongfully accused.—*Measure for Measure,* v, 1, 140.
Accusing . . . wrongfully.—*Much Ado about Nothing,* iv, 2, 50.

2
If she be accused in true report,
Bear with her weakness.
Richard III, i, 3, 27. See under WEAKNESS.

3
Accuse some innocent and forswear myself.
Titus Andronicus. Act v, sc. 1, l. 130. [Aaron]
Accuse your mothers.—*All's Well that Ends Well,* i, 1, 149.
Accuse the thunderer.—*Cymbeline,* v, 4, 95.

II—The Accuser

4
What monster 's her accuser?
Cymbeline. Act iii, sc. 2, l. 2. [Pisanio]
My accuser is my 'prentice.
II Henry VI. Act i, sc. 3, l. 201. [Horner]
Botcher's 'prentice.—*All's Well that Ends Well,* iv, 3, 211. "'Prentice" is repeated in *II Henry IV,* ii, 2, 194, and in *II Henry VI,* ii, 3, 71.

5
I should have ta'en some pains to bring together
Yourself and your accusers.
Henry VIII. Act v, sc. 1, l. 119. [King Henry]
I do beseech your lordships,
That, in this case of justice, my accusers
Be what they will, may stand forth face to face,
And freely urge against me.
Henry VIII. Act v, sc. 3, l. 45. [Cranmer]
Yet I am richer than my base accusers,
That never knew what truth meant.
Henry VIII. Act ii, sc. 1, l. 104. [Buckingham]
False accusers.—*Richard III,* i, 3, 26.

6
Sexton: Master constable, you go not the way to examine: you must call forth the watch that are their accusers.
Dogberry: Yea, marry, that 's the eftest way. Let the watch come forth. Masters, I charge you, in the prince's name, accuse these men.
Much Ado about Nothing. Act iv, sc. 2, l. 35. The only use of "eftest."

7
Frowning brow to brow, ourselves will hear
The accuser and the accused freely speak.
Richard II. Act i, sc. 1, l. 16. [King Richard]

ACQUAINTANCE

8
Art not acquainted with him?
All's Well that Ends Well. Act iv, sc. 1, l. 10. [Lord]
Are you acquainted?—*The Merchant of Venice,* iv, 1, 171.
Ne'er acquainted.—*Timon of Athens,* iii, 3, 38.
Nothing acquainted.—*All's Well that Ends Well,* iii, 7, 5.

9
Well acquainted with yourself.
All's Well that Ends Well. Act v, sc. 3, l. 106. [King]
I am as well acquainted here as I was in our house of profession.
Measure for Measure. Act iv, sc. 3, l. 1. [Pompey]
We are too well acquainted.—*Troilus and Cressida,* ii, 3, 122.
Well acquainted.—*II Henry IV,* ii, 1, 120.
Best acquainted.—*Richard III,* iv, 4, 269; *Sonnets,* lxxxviii.

10
Have you not been acquainted with goldsmiths' wives?
As You Like It, iii, 2, 288. See under RING.
I did not think he had been acquainted with her.
Othello. Act iii, sc. 3, l. 99. [Iago]
What need she be acquainted?—*The Comedy of Errors,* iii, 2, 15.

11
Is 't possible that on so little acquaintance you should like her?
As You Like It, v, 2, 1. See under LOVE.
Small acquaintance.—*As You Like It,* v, 2, 7.

12
Hereafter, in a better world than this,
I shall desire more love and knowledge of you.
As You Like It. Act i, sc. 2, l. 296. [Le Beau]
I prithee, pretty youth, let me be better acquainted with thee.
As You Like It. Act iv, sc. 1, l. 1. [Jaques]
How creeps acquaintance?
Cymbeline. Act i, sc. 4, l. 25. [Iachimo]

13
I 'll be acquainted with him, if I return.
II Henry IV. Act iii, sc. 2, l. 353. [Falstaff]
Be Acquainted with this stranger.
Henry VIII. Act v, sc. 1, l. 168. [Lady]
I pray you, be acquainted with this maid.
Measure for Measure. Act iv, sc. 1, l. 51. [Duke] See under MAID.
There 's one Master Brook below would fain speak with you, and be acquainted with you.
The Merry Wives of Windsor. Act ii, sc. 2, l. 150. [Bardolph]
Be acquainted.—*The Merry Wives of Windsor,* iii, 1, 68; *The Taming of the Shrew,* iv, 1, 2.
Craves acquaintance.—*Romeo and Juliet,* iii, 3, 5.
Hold acquaintance.—*Twelfth Night,* i, 2, 16.

14
What, old acquaintance!
I Henry IV. Act v, sc. 4, l. 102. [Prince]
How many of my old acquaintance are dead!
II Henry IV. Act iii, sc. 2, l. 38. [Shallow]
Let our old acquaintance be renewed.
II Henry IV. Act iii, sc. 2, l. 314. [Shallow]
How does my old acquaintance of this isle?
Othello. Act ii, sc. 1, l. 205. [Othello]

I urged our old acquaintance.
Coriolanus. Act v, sc. 1, l. 10. [Cominius]
New acquaintance.—*Sonnets,* lxxvii.
True acquaintance.—*I Henry IV*, i, 1, 16.

1
Must Perforce be their acquaintance.
Henry VIII. Act i, sc. 2, l. 46. [Queen Katharine]
Utterly Grow from the King's acquaintance.
Henry VIII. Act iii, sc. 1, l. 160. [Wolsey]

2 You shall not grieve
Lending me this acquaintance.
King Lear. Act iv, sc. 3, l. 55. [Kent]

3
I would not have you acquainted with tapsters.
Measure for Measure. Act ii, sc. 1, l. 214. [Escalus]

4
I 'll entertain myself like one I am not acquainted withal.
The Merry Wives of Windsor. Act ii, sc. 1, l. 87. [Mrs. Page]

5
I shall desire you of more acquaintance.
A Midsummer-Night's Dream. Act iii, sc. 1, l. 185. [Bottom]
I desire better acquaintance.
Twelfth Night. Act i, sc. 3, l. 55. [Sir Andrew]
I desire more acquaintance of you.
The Merry Wives of Windsor. Act ii, sc. 2, l. 168. [Falstaff]
I have a desire to hold my acquaintance with thee, or rather my knowledge, that I may say in the default, he is a man I know.
All's Well that Ends Well. Act ii, sc. 3, l. 240. [Lafeu]
I pray you, be better acquainted.
Cymbeline. Act i, sc. 4, l. 131. [Philario]
I am blest in your acquaintance.
The Merry Wives of Windsor. Act ii, sc. 2, l. 279. [Ford]

6 We 'll talk with Margaret,
How her acquaintance grew with this lewd fellow.
Much Ado about Nothing. Act v, sc. 1, l. 241. [Leonato]

7
'Faith, my acquaintance lies little amongst them.
Pericles. Act iv, sc. 6, l. 206. [Boult]

8
I will make them acquainted.
Pericles. Act iv, sc. 6, l. 209. [Boult]
Make me acquainted.—*Julius Cæsar,* ii, 1, 256.
Made me acquainted.—*The Taming of the Shrew,* iv, 4, 26.
Make myself acquainted.—*The Merry Wives of Windsor,* ii, 2, 189.
Acquainted with the smell.—*The Two Gentlemen of Verona,* iv, 4, 25.

9 To my knowledge
I never in my life did look on him.
Richard II. Act ii, sc. 3, l. 38. [Percy]
Diana: Know you such a one?
Helena: But by the ear, that hears most nobly of him:
His face I know not.
All's Well that Ends Well. Act iii, sc. 5, l. 52.
Æneas: We know each other well.
Diomedes: We do; and long to know each other worse.
Troilus and Cressida. Act iv, sc. 1, l. 30.

10
Your eld'st acquaintance cannot be three hours.
The Tempest. Act v, sc. 1, l. 186. [Alonso]

11
Taught him to face me out of his acquaintance.
Twelfth Night, v, 1, 91. See under CUNNING.

ACT, ACTION

See also Deed; Thought and Act

12 Thyself art coming
To see perform'd the dreaded act which thou
So sought'st to hinder.
Antony and Cleopatra. Act v, sc. 2, l. 334. [Dolabella]
Cruel act.—*King John,* iv, 3, 126.
Horrid act.—*King Lear,* iii, 7, 87; *Cymbeline,* ii, 1, 66.
Monstrous act.—*Othello,* v, 2, 190.

13
How many actions most ridiculous
Hast thou been drawn to by thy fantasy?
As You Like It. Act ii, sc. 4, l. 30. [Silvius]

14
Action is eloquence.
Coriolanus. Act iii, sc. 2, l. 76. [Volumnia]

15
He hath in this action outdone his former deeds doubly.
Coriolanus. Act ii, sc. 1, l. 149. [Volumnia] The only use of "outdone."

16
It is no act of common passage, but
A strain of rareness.
Cymbeline. Act iii, sc. 4, l. 94. [Imogen]

17
Her pretty action did outsell her gift,
And yet enrich'd it too.
Cymbeline. Act ii, sc. 4, l. 102. [Iachimo] "Outsell" is repeated in iii, 5, 74, and occurs in no other play.

18
If you will make 't an action, call witness to 't.
Cymbeline. Act ii, sc. 3, l. 156. [Imogen] See also under LAW.
I 'll bring mine action on the proudest he
That stops my way in Padua.
The Taming of the Shrew. Act iii, sc. 2, l. 236. [Petruchio]
He upon some action Is now in durance.
Twelfth Night. Act v, sc. 1, l. 282. [Viola]
Bring action.—*Troilus and Cressida,* ii, 3, 145.

19 Some act
That has no relish of salvation in 't.
Hamlet. Act iii, sc. 3, l. 91. [Hamlet] See under HELL for full quotation.

An act
That blurs the grace and blush of modesty,
Calls virtue hypocrite, takes off the rose
From the fair forehead of an innocent love
And sets a blister there.
Hamlet. Act iii, sc. 4, l. 40. [Hamlet]

Carnal, bloody, and unnatural acts.
Hamlet. Act v, sc. 2, l. 392. [Horatio]

1 What act,
That roars so loud, and thunders in the index?
Hamlet. Act iii, sc. 4, l. 51. [Queen]

An act hath three branches; it is, to act, to do, and to perform.
Hamlet. Act v, sc. 1, l. 11. [First Clown]

2
Simply the most active fellow in Europe.
II Henry IV. Act iv, sc. 3, l. 24. [Falstaff]

Simply the most active gentleman of France.
Henry V. Act iii, sc. 7, l. 105. [Orlando]

3
As many arrows, loosed several ways,
Come to one mark; as many ways meet in one town;
As many fresh streams meet in one salt sea;
As many lines close in the dial's centre;
So may a thousand actions, once afoot,
End in one purpose.
Henry V. Act i, sc. 2, l. 207. [Canterbury]

4
We must not stint Our necessary actions.
Henry VIII. Act i, sc. 2, l. 77. [Wolsey]

The instant action.—*II Henry IV*, i, 3, 37.
In heat of action.—*Troilus and Cressida*, iv, 5, 106.

5
Between the acting of a dreadful thing
And the first motion, all the interim is
Like a phantasma, or a hideous dream.
Julius Cæsar. Act ii, sc. 1, l. 63. [Brutus]
The only use of "phantasma."

His act did not o'ertake his bad intent,
And must be buried but as an intent
That perish'd by the way.
Measure for Measure. Act v, sc. 1, l. 456. [Isabella]

6
Who hath read or heard
Of any kindred action like to this?
King John. Act iii, sc. 4, l. 13. [Lewis]

This act so evilly born shall cool the hearts
Of all his people and freeze up their zeal.
King John. Act iii, sc. 4, l. 149. [Pandulph]

It is a damned and a bloody work;
The graceless action of a heavy hand.
King John. Act iv, sc. 3, l. 57. [Bastard]

This act is as an ancient tale new told.
King John. Act iv, sc. 2, l. 18. [Pembroke]

7 Long-during action tires
The sinewy vigour of the traveller.
Love's Labour's Lost. Act iv, sc. 3, l. 307. [Biron] The only use of "long-during."

8
Doctor: Look, how she rubs her hands.
Gentleman: It is an accustomed action with her.
Macbeth. Act v, sc. 1, l. 31.

Continual action.—*Pericles*, iv, 2, 9.
Ended action.—*Much Ado about Nothing*, i, 1, 299.
Human action.—*Coriolanus*, ii, 1, 265; *The Winter's Tale*, iii, 2, 30.
Living actions.—*Henry VIII*, iv, 2, 70.
Last action.—*I Henry IV*, iii, 3, 2.
Leaner action.—*Antony and Cleopatra*, ii, 2, 19.
Outward actions.—*Richard III*, i, 3, 66.
Particular action.—*All's Well that Ends Well*, iii, 6, 18.
Personal action.—*Julius Cæsar*, i, 3, 77.
Present action.—*Coriolanus*, i, 1, 283; iv, 3, 53.
Private actions.—*Pericles*, i, 1, 153.
Rarer action.—*The Tempest*, v, 1, 27.

9
So then it seems your most offenceful act
Was mutually committed?
Measure for Measure. Act ii, sc. 3, l. 26. [Duke] The only use of "offenceful."

She with Cassio hath the act of shame
A thousand times committed.
Othello. Act v, sc. 2, l. 211. [Othello]

Act of darkness.—*King Lear*, iii, 4, 90.
Act of fornication.—*Measure for Measure*, v, 1, 70.
Act of lust.—*The Rape of Lucrece*, l. 1636.
Act of sport.—*Othello*, ii, 1, 230.
Bodily act.—*Coriolanus*, i, 2, 5.
Body's action.—*Coriolanus*, iii, 2, 122.

10
My outward action doth demonstrate
The native act and figure of my heart.
Othello. Act i, sc. 1, l. 61. [Iago]

I know this act shows horrible and grim.
Othello. Act v, sc. 2, l. 203. [Othello]

Myself will straight aboard; and to the state
This heavy act with heavy heart relate.
Othello. Act v, sc. 2, l. 370. [Lodovico]

11
I am bound to every act of duty.
Othello. Act iii, sc. 3, l. 134. [Iago]

Acts of death.—*King John*, ii, 1, 376.
Act of fear.—*Hamlet*, i, 2, 205.
Act of grace.—*Antony and Cleopatra*, ii, 2, 149.
Act of hares.—*Troilus and Cressida*, iii, 2, 96.
Act of men.—*All's Well that Ends Well*, ii, 1, 155.
Man's act.—*Macbeth*, ii, 4, 5.
Men's acts.—*Pericles*, i, 1, 73.
Act of order.—*Henry V*, i, 2, 189.
Act of rage.—*Julius Cæsar*, ii, 1, 176.
Act of seizure.—*The Passionate Pilgrim*, l. 152.

12
O impious act, including all foul harms!
The Rape of Lucrece, l. 199. The only use of "including."

This act will be
My fame and thy perpetual infamy.
The Rape of Lucrece, l. 1637.

The blood of English shall manure the ground,
And future ages groan for this foul act.
Richard II. Act iv, sc. 1, l. 137. [Carlisle] The only use of "manure." "Manured" occurs in *II Henry IV*, iv, 3, 129, and *Othello*, i, 3, 328.

Foul act.—*The Rape of Lucrece*, l. 1824.

An act of tragic violence.
Richard III. Act ii, sc. 2, l. 39. [Queen]

13
Send her a story of thy noble acts.
Richard III. Act iv, sc. 4, l. 280. [Queen]

Noble act.—*Antony and Cleopatra*, v, 2, 288.
Brave acts.—*II Henry IV*, ii, 3, 21.

14
So smile the heavens upon this holy act,
That after hours with sorrow chide us not!
Romeo and Juliet. Act ii, sc. 6, l. 1. [Friar Laurence]

Best act.—*Henry VIII*, i, 2, 85.
Better act.—*King John*, iii, 1, 274.

Fair act.—*Cymbeline,* iii, 3, 53.
Good acts.—*Coriolanus,* iv, 2, 15.
Lawful act.—*All's Well that Ends Well,* iii, 7, 46.
Lingering act.—*II Henry IV,* i, 1, 156.
Loving act.—*Antony and Cleopatra,* i, 2, 148.
Mutual act.—*Troilus and Cressida,* i, 3, 348.
Particular act.—*Hamlet,* i, 3, 26.
Present act.—*Julius Cæsar,* iii, 1, 166.
Wholesome act.—*Coriolanus,* i, 1, 85.

1

Thy wild acts denote
The unreasonable fury of a beast.
Romeo and Juliet, iii, 3, 110. See under MAN.

Wild action.—*Troilus and Cressida,* i, 3, 340.
Dangerous action.—*II Henry IV,* i, 2, 238.
Fearful action.—*King John,* iv, 2, 191.
Odd action.—*The Rape of Lucrece,* l. 1433.
Piteous action.—*Hamlet,* iii, 4, 128.
Unchaste action.—*King Lear,* i, 1, 231.
Waspish action.—*As You Like It,* iv, 3, 9.
Actions blacker than the night.
Pericles, i, 1, 135. See under MAN.

2

Tell him from me, as he will win my love,
He bear himself with honourable action.
The Taming of the Shrew. Induction, sc. 1, l. 109. [Lord]

So honourable an action.—*I Henry IV,* ii, 3, 36.
Courteous action.—*Hamlet,* i, 4, 60.
Dearest action.—*Othello,* i, 3, 85.
Fair action.—*Henry V,* i, 2, 310.
Great action.—*Coriolanus,* v, 6, 48.
Honest action.—*Othello,* ii, 3, 146.
Pious action.—*Hamlet,* iii, 1, 48.
Sober action.—*The Rape of Lucrece,* l. 1403.
Stiff-borne action.—*II Henry IV,* i, 1, 177. The only use of "stiff-borne."
Action glorious.—*Othello,* ii, 3, 186.

3

An act whereof what's past is prologue.
The Tempest. Act ii, sc. 1, l. 252. [Antonio]

An act that very chance doth throw upon him.
Troilus and Cressida. Act iii, sc. 3, l. 131. [Ulysses]

4

I must talk of murders, rapes and massacres,
Acts of black night, abominable deeds,
Complots of mischief, treason, villanies
Ruthful to hear, yet piteously perform'd.
Titus Andronicus. Act v, sc. 1, l. 63. [Aaron]

5

They . . . esteem no act But that of hand.
Troilus and Cressida. Act i, sc. 3, l. 197. [Ulysses]

We may not think the justness of each act
Such and no other than event doth form it.
Troilus and Cressida. Act ii, sc. 2, l. 119. [Troilus] The only use of "justness."

6

It shall become thee well to act my woes.
Twelfth Night. Act i, sc. 4, l. 26. [Duke]

Act The deed.—*King John,* iv, 2, 240.
Act the woman.—*Coriolanus,* ii, 2, 100.
Act in safety.—*Macbeth,* iii, 1, 54.

7

He finished indeed his mortal act
That day that made my sister thirteen years.
Twelfth Night. Act v, sc. 1, l. 254. [Sebastian]

8

What dangerous action, stood it next to death,
Would I not undergo for one calm look!
The Two Gentlemen of Verona. Act v, sc. 4, l. 41. [Proteus]

9

For in an act of this importance 'twere
Most piteous to be wild.
The Winter's Tale. Act ii, sc. 1, l. 181. [Leontes]

Act of parliament.—*III Henry VI,* i, 1, 249; ii, 2, 91.

ACTING AND ACTOR

See also Part: Playing a Part; Play; Stage.

I—Acting

10

Look, whether he has not turned his colour and has tears in 's eyes.
Hamlet. Act ii, sc. 2, l. 542. [Polonius]

Is it not monstrous that this player here,
But in a fiction, in a dream of passion,
Could force his soul so to his own conceit
That from her working all his visage wann'd,
Tears in his eyes, distraction in 's aspect,
A broken voice, and his whole function suiting
With forms to his conceit? and all for nothing!
For Hecuba!
What 's Hecuba to him, or he to Hecuba,
That he should weep for her? What would he do,
Had he the motive and the cue for passion
That I have? He would drown the stage with tears
And cleave the general ear with horrid speech,
Make mad the guilty and appal the free,
Confound the ignorant, and amaze indeed
The very faculties of eyes and ears.
Hamlet. Act ii, sc. 2, l. 577. [Hamlet] The only use of "wann'd" and "suiting."

Well acted.—*Antony and Cleopatra,* v, 2, 45.

11

Speak the speech, I pray you, as I pronounced it to you, trippingly on the tongue: but if you mouth it, as many of your players do, I had as lief the town-crier spoke my lines. Nor do not saw the air too much with your hand, thus, but use all gently; for in the very torrent, tempest, and, as I may say, the whirlwind of passion, you must acquire and beget a temperance that may give it smoothness. O, it offends me to the soul to hear a robustious periwig-pated fellow tear a passion to tatters, to very rags, to split the ears of the groundlings.
Hamlet. Act iii, sc. 2, l. 1. [Hamlet] The only use of "town-crier," "periwig-pated," and "groundlings." "Trippingly" is repeated in *A Midsummer-Night's Dream,* v, 1, 403; and "robustious" in *Henry V,* iii, 7, 159.

Be not too tame, neither, but let your own discretion be your tutor: suit the action to the word, the word to the action; with this special observance, that you overstep not the modesty of nature; for any thing so overdone is from the purpose of playing, whose end, both at the first and now, was and is, to hold, as 'twere, the mirror up to nature; to show virtue her own feature, scorn her own image, and the very age and body of the time his form and pressure. Now this overdone, or come tardy off, though it make the unskilful laugh, cannot but make the judicious grieve; the censure of the which one must in your allowance o'erweigh a whole theatre of others. O, there be players that I have seen play, and heard others praise, and that highly, not to speak it profanely, that, neither having the accent of Christians nor the gait of Christian, pagan, nor man, have so strutted and bellowed that I have thought some of nature's journeymen had made men and not made them well, they imitated humanity so abominably.

Hamlet. Act iii, sc. 2, l. 19. [Hamlet] The only use of "profanely," "strutted," "journeymen," and "abominably." "Journeyman" occurs in *Richard II,* i, 3, 274: "A journeyman to grief."

Let those that play your clowns speak no more than is set down for them; for there be of them that will themselves laugh, to set on some quantity of barren spectators to laugh too; though, in the meantime, some necessary question of the play be then to be considered: that 's villanous, and shows a most pitiful ambition in the fool that uses it.

Hamlet. Act iii, sc. 2, l. 42. [Hamlet]

1
What scene of death hath Roscius now to act?

III Henry VI. Act v, sc. 6, l. 10. [King Henry] Roscius is mentioned again in *Hamlet,* ii, 2, 410: "When Roscius was an actor."

Bottom: Name what part I am for, and proceed.
Quince: You, Nick Bottom, are set down for Pyramus.
Bottom: What is Pyramus? a lover, or a tyrant?
Quince: A lover that kills himself most gallant for love.
Bottom: That will ask some tears in the true performing of it; if I do it, let the audience look to their eyes; I will move storms, I will condole in some measure. . . . Yet my chief humour is for a tyrant: I could play Ercles rarely, or a part to tear a cat in, to make all split.

The raging rocks
And shivering shocks
Shall break the locks
  Of prison gates;
And Phibbus' car
Shall shine from far
And make and mar
  The foolish Fates.

This was lofty! . . . This is Ercles' vein, a tyrant's vein; a lover is more condoling.

A Midsummer-Night's Dream. Act i, sc. 2, l. 21. The only use of "performing" and Ercles (Hercules). On the stage the part of Hercules was always a ranting one.

I must speak in passion, and I will do it in King Cambyses' vein.

I Henry IV. Act ii, sc. 4, l. 424. [Falstaff] Cambyses was a pompous, ranting character in Thomas Preston's "lamentable tragedy" of that name. This is the only reference to him.

O Jesu, he doth it as like one of these harlotry players as ever I see!

I Henry IV. Act ii, sc. 4, l. 435. [Hostess]

2
But, masters, here are your parts: and I am to entreat you, request you and desire you, to con them by to-morrow night.

A Midsummer-Night's Dream. Act i, sc. 2, l. 101. [Quince]

There we may rehearse most obscenely and courageously.

A Midsummer-Night's Dream. Act i, sc. 2, l. 110. [Bottom]

3
Thus play I in one person many people,
And none contented.

Richard II. Act v, sc. 5, l. 31. [King Richard]

Tut, I can counterfeit the deep tragedian;
Speak and look back, and pry on every side,
Tremble and start at wagging of a straw,
Intending deep suspicion: ghastly looks
Are at my service, like enforced smiles;
And both are ready in their offices,
At any time, to grace my stratagems.

Richard III. Act iii, sc. 5, l. 5. [Buckingham]

4
You come upon your cue.

Richard III. Act iii, sc. 4, l. 27. [Buckingham]

So every one according to his cue.

A Midsummer-Night's Dream. Act iii, sc. 1, l. 78. [Quince]

When my cue comes, call me, and I will answer.

A Midsummer-Night's Dream. Act iv, sc. 1, l. 204. [Bottom]

Speak, count, 'tis your cue.

Much Ado about Nothing. Act ii, sc. 1, l. 316. [Beatrice]

You speak all your part at once, cues and all.

A Midsummer-Night's Dream. Act iii, sc. 1, l. 102. [Quince]

Mrs. Ford: Remember you your cue.
Mrs. Page: I warrant thee.

The Merry Wives of Windsor. Act iii, sc. 3, l. 38.

5
My dismal scene I needs must act alone.

Romeo and Juliet. Act iv, sc. 3, l. 19. [Juliet]

If I do not act it, hiss me.

The Merry Wives of Windsor. Act iii, sc. 3, l. 40. [Mrs. Page]

6
Go, play, boy, play: thy mother plays, and I
Play too, but so disgraced a part, whose issue
Will hiss me to my grave.

Winter's Tale. Act i, sc. 2, l. 187. [Leontes]

II—Actor

7
A showing of a heavenly effect in an earthly actor.

All's Well that Ends Well. Act ii, sc. 3, l. 27. [Lafeu]

The king 's a beggar, now the play is done.

All's Well that Ends Well. Epilogue, l. 335. [King]

8
When good will is show'd though 't come too short
The actor may plead pardon.

Antony and Cleopatra. Act ii, sc. 5, l. 8. [Cleopatra]

1
I 'll prove a busy actor in their play.
As You Like It. Act iii, sc. 4, l. 62. [Rosalind]
Like a dull actor now,
I have forgot my part, and I am out,
Even to a full disgrace.
Coriolanus. Act v, sc. 3, l. 40. [Coriolanus]
As an unperfect actor on the stage
Who with his fear is put besides his part.
Sonnets. No. xxiii. The only use of "unperfect."
2
Hamlet: What players are they?
Rosencrantz: Even those you were wont to take delight in, the tragedians of the city.
Hamlet. Act ii, sc. 2, l. 340.
The English tragedians.—*All's Well that Ends Well*, iv, 3, 299.
The deep tragedian.—*Richard III*, iii, 5, 5. The only uses of "tragedian." See under TRAGEDY.
3
Hamlet: Then came each actor on his ass,—
Polonius: The best actors in the world, either for tragedy, comedy, history, pastoral, pastoral-comical, historical-pastoral, tragical-historical, tragical-comical-historical-pastoral, scene individable, or poem unlimited. Seneca cannot be too heavy, nor Plautus too light.
Hamlet. Act ii, sc. 2, l. 414. The only use of the hyphenated phrases, and also of "individable," "poem," and "unlimited." The only mention of Seneca and Plautus.
Accounted a good actor.
Hamlet. Act iii, sc. 2, l. 106. [Polonius]
4
Good my lord, will you see the players well bestowed? Do you hear, let them be well used; for they are the abstract and brief chronicles of the time: after your death you were better have a bad epitaph than their ill report while you live.
Hamlet. Act ii, sc. 2, l. 546. [Hamlet]
The players cannot keep counsel; they 'll tell all.
Hamlet. Act iii, sc. 2, l. 151. [Hamlet]
5
I 'll have these players
Play something like the murder of my father.
Hamlet. Act ii, sc. 2, l. 623. [Hamlet]
Common players.—*Hamlet*, ii, 2, 365.
Players in the theatre.—*Julius Cæsar*, i, 2, 263.
6
The actors are at hand and by their show
You shall know all that you are like to know.
A Midsummer-Night's Dream. Act v, sc. 1, l. 116. [Quince]
When the players are all dead, there need none to be blamed.
A Midsummer-Night's Dream. Act v, sc. 1, l. 364. [Theseus]
7
As in a theatre, the eyes of men,
After a well-graced actor leaves the stage,
Are idly bent on him that enters next,
Thinking his prattle to be tedious.
Richard II. Act v, sc. 2, l. 23. [York] The only use of "well-graced."
Counterfeiting actors.—*III Henry VI*, ii, 3, 28.

8
A strutting player, whose conceit
Lies in his hamstring, and doth think it rich
To hear the wooden dialogue and sound
'Twixt his stretch'd footing and the scaffoldage.
Troilus and Cressida. Act i, sc. 3, l. 153. [Ulysses] "Strutting chanticleer" occurs in *The Tempest*, i, 2, 385. The only use of "hamstring" and "scaffoldage."
9
Olivia: Are you a comedian?
Viola: No, my profound heart: and yet, by the very fangs of malice, I swear, I am not that I play.
Twelfth Night. Act i, sc. 5, l. 194. [This and the following quotation show the only uses of "comedian."]
The quick comedians
Extemporally will stage us, and present
Our Alexandrian revels.
Antony and Cleopatra. Act v, sc. 2, l. 216. [Cleopatra] The only use of "extemporally." "Alexandrian" is repeated in ii, 7, 102: "Alexandrian feast"; and occurs in no other play. See under COMEDY.

ADAM

10
Here feel we but the penalty of Adam.
As You Like It. Act ii, sc. 1, l. 5. [Duke]
11
Dromio of Syracuse: What, have you got the picture of old Adam new-apparelled?
Antipholus of Syracuse: What gold is this? What Adam dost thou mean?
Dromio of Syracuse: Not that Adam that kept the Paradise but that Adam that keeps the prison: he that goes in the calf's skin that was killed for the Prodigal.
The Comedy of Errors. Act iv, sc. 3, l. 13. The only use of "new-apparelled."
12
First Clown: There is no ancient gentlemen but gardeners, ditchers, and grave-makers: they hold up Adam's profession.
Second Clown: Was he a gentleman?
First Clown: A' was the first that ever bore arms.
Second Clown: Why, he had none.
First Clown: What, art a heathen? How dost thou understand the Scripture? The scripture says "Adam digged"; could he dig without arms?
Hamlet. Act v, sc. 1, l. 33. The only use of "ditchers." "Grave-makers" is repeated twice more in this act, and occurs nowhere else.
And Adam was a gardener.
II Henry VI. Act iv, sc. 2, l. 142. [Cade]
13
The old days of goodman Adam.
I Henry IV. Act ii, sc. 4, l. 106. [Prince]
Thou knowest in the state of innocency Adam fell.
I Henry IV. Act iii, sc. 3, l. 185. [Falstaff]
1
Consideration, like an angel, came
And whipp'd the offending Adam out of him,

Leaving his body as a paradise,
To envelope and contain celestial spirits.
Henry V. Act i, sc. 1, l. 28. [Canterbury] "Envelope" is repeated in *Measure for Measure*, iv, 2, 77.

1 Had he been Adam, he had tempted Eve.
Love's Labour's Lost. Act v, sc. 2, l. 322. [Biron]

Thou, old Adam's likeness, set to dress this garden, . . .
What Eve, what serpent, hath suggested thee
To make a second fall of cursed man?
Richard II. Act iii, sc. 4, l. 73. [Queen]

Endowed with all that Adam had left him before he transgressed.
Much Ado about Nothing. Act ii, sc. 1, l. 259. [Benedick]

He that hits me, let him be clapped on the shoulder, and called Adam.
Much Ado about Nothing. Act i, sc. 1, l. 261. [Benedick]

Adam's sons are my brethren.
Much Ado about Nothing. Act ii, sc. 1, l. 66. [Beatrice]

ADDER

See also Serpent, Snake

2 It is the bright day that brings forth the adder.
Julius Cæsar. Act ii, sc. 1, l. 14. [Brutus]

3 A lurking adder
Whose double tongue may with a mortal touch
Throw death upon thy sovereign's enemies.
Richard II. Act iii, sc. 2, l. 20. [King]

Sometime am I
All wound with adders who with cloven tongues
Do hiss me into madness.
The Tempest. Act ii, sc. 2, l. 12. [Caliban]

The adder hisses where the sweet birds sing.
The Rape of Lucrece, l. 871.

The adder blue.—*Timon of Athens*, iv, 3, 181.

4 Even as an adder when she doth unroll
To do some fatal execution.
Titus Andronicus. Act ii, sc. 3, l. 35. [Aaron] The only use of "unroll."

One that spies an adder
Wreathed up in fatal folds just in his way.
Venus and Adonis, l. 878.

ADDITION

5 Where great additions swell 's, and virtue none,
It is a dropsied honour.
All's Well that Ends Well, ii, 3, 134. See under Deed. The only use of "dropsied."

Great addition.—*Troilus and Cressida*, iv, 5, 141.

6 Cominius: Call him . . .
Caius Marcius Coriolanus! Bear
The addition nobly ever! . . .
Coriolanus: I thank you.
I mean to stride your steed, and at all times
To undercrest your good addition
To the fairness of my power.
Coriolanus. Act i, sc. 9, l. 63. The only use of "undercrest," to wear as a crest.

He bade me, from him, call thee thane of Cawdor:
In which addition, hail, most worthy thane!
Macbeth. Act i, sc. 3, l. 106. [Ross] "Thane" is used twenty-seven times, and Cawdor nineteen times, in *Macbeth*, and occur in no other play.

Iago: How do you now, lieutenant?
Cassio: The worser that you give me the addition
Whose want even kills me.
Othello. Act iv, sc. 1, l. 104.

7 This addition more,
Full thirty thousand marks of English coin.
King John. Act ii, sc. 1, l. 529. [King John]

8 We still retain . . . all the additions to a king.
King Lear. Act i, sc. 1, l. 138. [King Lear]

With boot, and such addition as your honours
Have more than merited.
King Lear. Act v, sc. 3, l. 301. [Albany]

With addition!—*All's Well that Ends Well*, iv, 2, 3.

With what addition?—*Julius Cæsar*, iv, 3, 172.

With no addition.—*Hamlet*, iv, 4, 17.

Without addition.—*Comedy of Errors*, ii, 2, 130.

9 All aids, themselves made fairer by their place,
Came for additions.
A Lover's Complaint, l. 117.

10 Whereby he doth receive
Particular addition, from the bill
That writes them all alike.
Macbeth. Act iii, sc. 1, l. 99. [Macbeth]

Particular additions.—*Troilus and Cressida*, i, 2, 20.

Shrill addition.—*I Henry IV*, ii, 4, 29.

Devils' additions.—*The Merry Wives of Windsor*, ii, 2, 312.

11 By my troth, it is no addition to her wit.
Much Ado about Nothing. Act ii, sc. 3, l. 242. [Benedick]

12 And by addition me of thee defeated,
By adding one thing to my purpose nothing.
Sonnets. No. xx.

Adding but one more.—*Love's Labour's Lost*, iv, 2, 63.

Adding four.—*Love's Labour's Lost*, iii, 1, 93.

Adding to clouds more clouds.—*Romeo and Juliet*, i, 1, 139.

Adding a tongue.—*Love's Labour's Lost*, ii, 1, 252.

13 To thy sweet will making addition thus.
Sonnets. No. cxxxv. See under Will.

His addition shall be humble.—*Troilus and Cressida*, iii, 2, 102.

ADMIRATION

See also Wonder

14 Bring in the admiration; that we with thee
May spend our wonder too, or take off thine
By wondering how thou took'st it.
All's Well that Ends Well. Act ii, sc. 1, l. 91. [King]

Fair and admired.—*Antony and Cleopatra,* i, 1, 51.
So admired.—*As You Like It,* iii, 2, 412.

1
Where great patricians shall attend and shrug,
I' the end admire.
Coriolanus. Act i, sc. 9, l. 4. [Cominius]

2
I could then have looked on him without the help of admiration, though the catalogue of his endowments had been tabled by his side.
Cymbeline. Act i, sc. 4, l. 4. [Iachimo] The only use of "tabled."
What makes your admiration?
Cymbeline. Act i, sc. 6, l. 38. [Imogen]

3
Season your admiration for a while.
Hamlet. Act i, sc. 2, l. 192. [Horatio]
But is there no sequel at the heels of this mother's admiration?
Hamlet. Act iii, sc. 2, l. 341. [Hamlet]

4
Admiration did not hoop at them.
Henry V. Act ii, sc. 2, l. 108. [King Henry] The only use of "hoop" in the sense of whoop.
It is the greatest admiration in the universal world.
Henry V, iv, 1, 66. See under WAR.

5
All the court admired him.
II Henry VI, iii, 1, 12. See under CHARACTER.
Admired of lewd unhallowed eyes.—*The Rape of Lucrece,* l. 392.
Most admired.—*III Henry VI,* i, 4, 130; *Macbeth,* iii, 4, 110.

6 Ever since a fresh admirer
Of what I saw there.
Henry VIII. Act i, sc. 1, l. 3. [Norfolk] The only use of "admirer."
Great in admiration.—*Henry VIII,* v, 5, 43.

7
This admiration, sir, is much o' the savour
Of other your new pranks.
King Lear. Act i, sc. 4, l. 258. [Goneril]

8
With more than admiration he admired
Her azure veins, her alabaster skin,
Her coral lips, her snow-white dimpled chin.
The Rape of Lucrece, l. 418. "Azure" is repeated in *Cymbeline,* ii, 2, 22.
I thy parts admire.—*Love's Labour 's Lost,* iv, 2, 118; *The Passionate Pilgrim,* l. 66.
Admiring of his qualities.—*A Midsummer-Night's Dream,* i, 1, 231.
Admiring thy renown.—*I Henry VI,* ii, 2, 39.
Admiring the nothing of it.—*The Winter's Tale,* iv, 4, 625.

9 We do admire
This virtue and this moral discipline.
The Taming of the Shrew. Act i, sc. 1, l. 29. [Tranio]
Do so much admire.—*The Tempest,* v, 1, 154.
Admire our sufferance.—*Henry V,* iii, 6, 132.
Admire not in thy mind.—*Twelfth Night,* iii, 4, 165.

10
Indeed the top of admiration!
Tempest. Act iii, sc. 1, l. 38. [Ferdinand]
Very notes of admiration.
Winter's Tale. Act v, sc. 2, l. 12. [Gentleman]

ADORATION, see Worship

ADULTERY

See also Cuckold, Lechery, Wantonness

11
Adulterers, by an enforced obedience of planetary influence.
King Lear, i, 2, 135. See under PROVIDENCE. The only use of "adulterers." "Planetary" occurs again in *Timon of Athens,* iv, 3, 108: "Planetary plague."

12
What was thy cause? Adultery?
Thou shalt not die: die for adultery! No:
The wren goes to 't, and the small gilded fly
Does lecher in my sight.
King Lear. Act iv, sc. 6, l. 111. [King Lear] The only use of "lecher" as a verb.
Committing adultery.—*Winter's Tale,* iii, 2, 15.
Wilful adultery.—*Henry V,* ii, 1, 40.

13
Desdemona: Wouldst thou do such a deed for all the world?
Emilia: Why, would not you?
Desdemona: No, by this heavenly light!
Emilia: Nor I neither by this heavenly light;
I might do 't as well i' the dark.
Othello. Act iv, sc. 3, l. 64. See also "act of darkness" under ACT.

14 They call'd me foul adulteress,
Lascivious Goth.
Titus Andronicus. Act ii, sc. 3, l. 109. [Tamora]
She 's an adulteress; I have said with whom:...
A bed-swerver, even as bad as those
That vulgars give bold'st titles.
The Winter's Tale. Act ii, sc. 1, l. 88. [Leontes] The only use of "bed-swerver."
When you have said 'she 's goodly,' come between
Ere you can say 'she 's honest': but be 't known,
From him that has most cause to grieve it should be,
She 's an adulteress.
Winter's Tale. Act ii, sc. 1, l. 75. [Leontes]
He thinks, nay, with all confidence he swears,
As he had seen 't or been an instrument
To vice you to 't, that you have touch'd his queen
Forbiddenly.
The Winter's Tale. Act i, sc. 2, l. 414. [Camillo] The only use of "forbiddenly."

ADVANTAGE

15
Vantage like a pair of twins appear'd.
Antony and Cleopatra, iii, 10, 12. See under FLIGHT.
Our advantage serves For a fair victory.
Antony and Cleopatra. Act iv, sc. 7, l. 11. [Eros]

16
If, as his nature is, he fall in rage, . . .
Observe and answer The vantage of his anger.
Coriolanus. Act ii, sc. 3, l. 266. [Brutus]

1
And lose advantage, which doth ever cool
I' the absence of the needer.
Coriolanus. Act iv, sc. 1, l. 43. [Cominius] The only use of "needer."

2
We have the advantage of the ground.
Cymbeline. Act v, sc. 2, l. 11. [Belarius]
Vantage of ground.—*II Henry IV*, ii, 1, 85.

3
Colleagued with the dream of his advantage.
Hamlet. Act i, sc. 2, l. 21. [King] The only use of "colleagued."

4
Advantage feeds him fat, while men delay.
I Henry IV. Act iii, sc. 2, l. 180. [King]
Lets go by no vantages.—*Cymbeline*, ii, 3, 50.

5
We 'll read it at more advantage.
I Henry IV. Act ii, sc. 4, l. 594. [Prince]
Upon advantage.—*King John*, v, 7, 62.
With advantage.—*King John*, iii, 3, 22.
With all advantages.—*Henry V*, i, 2, 139.
With like advantage.—*I Henry IV*, iii, 1, 109.
With most advantage.—*I Henry VI*, i, 4, 12.
With no more advantage.—*Cymbeline*, i, 4, 140.

6
You give him then advantage.
I Henry IV. Act iv, sc. 3, l. 2. [Douglas]

7
If they get ground and vantage of the king,
Then join you with them.
II Henry IV. Act ii, sc. 4, l. 53. [Lady Percy]
Vantage of a king.—*Henry V*, iv, 1, 297.

8
Advantage is a better soldier than rashness.
Henry V. Act iii, sc. 6, l. 127. [Montjoy]

9
Clarence: I fear her not, unless she chance to fall.
Gloucester: God forbid that! for he 'll take vantages.
III Henry VI. Act iii, sc. 2, l. 24.
Take all the swift advantage of the hours.
Richard III. Act iv, sc. 1, l. 49. [Stanley]
To take an ill advantage of his absence.
The Merry Wives of Windsor. Act iii, sc. 3, l. 116. [Mrs. Page]
Advantage of his absence took the king.
King John. Act i, sc. 1, l. 102. [Robert]
Thus I took the vantage of those few.
Richard III. Act iii, sc. 7, l. 37. [Buckingham]
You should have ta'en the advantage of his choler.
Coriolanus. Act ii, sc. 3, l. 206. [Sicinius]
The next advantage will we take throughly.
The Tempest. Act iii, sc. 3, l. 13. [Sebastian]
Take vantage.—*King Lear*, ii, 2, 178.
Take all vantages.—*III Henry VI*, i, 4, 59.
Claim my vantage.—*Hamlet*, v, 2, 401.
Forego this vantage.—*Troilus and Cressida*, v, 8, 9.
Gain Advantage.—*Sonnets*, lxiv.
Spy advantage.—*II Henry VI*, i, 1, 242.
Win some vantage.—*Coriolanus*, i, 1, 164.

10
This advantage, this vile-drawing bias.
King John. Act ii, sc. 1, l. 577. [Bastard] The only use of "vile-drawing."
Turn'd another way To our own vantage.
King John, ii, 1, 550. See under Right.

11
You have now the good advantage of the night.
King Lear. Act ii, sc. 1, l. 24. [Edmund]
Good advantage.—*II Henry IV*, iv, 4, 28.
Best advantage.—*Richard III*, v, 3, 92; *Henry V*, iv, 1, 301; *King John*, ii, 1, 40; *Othello*, i, 3, 298; *Antony and Cleopatra*, iv, 11, 4.
Better vantage.—*Coriolanus*, iii, 2, 31.
Fair advantage.—*The Two Gentlemen of Verona*, ii, 4, 68; *The Merchant of Venice*, ii, 7, 19; *I Henry IV*, v, 1, 55.
False vantage.—*The Two Gentlemen of Verona*, iv, 1, 29.
Happy vantage.—*Richard II*, v, 3, 132.
Least advantage.—*Othello*, iv, 2, 179.
Rich advantage.—*Troilus and Cressida*, ii, 2, 204.

12
Let it . . . be my vantage to exclaim on you.
The Merchant of Venice. Act iii, sc. 2, l. 175. [Portia]
Coign of vantage.—*Macbeth*, i, 6, 7. The only use of the phrase.

13
But little vantage shall I reap thereby.
Richard II. Act i, sc. 3, l. 218. [Gaunt]

14
You have all the vantage.
Richard III. Act i, sc. 3, l. 310. [Gloucester]
Have such vantage.—*Measure for Measure*, iv, 6, 11.
Having some advantage.—*Julius Cæsar*, v, 4, 6.
Having thee at vantage.—*Venus and Adonis*, l. 635.

15
I 'll use the vantage of my power.
Richard II, iii, 3, 42. See under Blood.

16
All for our vantage.
Richard III. Act v, sc. 2, l. 22. [Richmond]
For our advantage.—*I Henry IV*, i, 1, 27.
For his own advantage.—*Henry VIII*, i, 1, 193.

17
Let us survey the vantage of the field.
Richard III, v, 3, 15. See under Field.
Speed then, to take advantage of the field.
King John. Act ii, sc. 1, l. 297. [Bastard]

18
We mean to . . . watch our vantage.
The Taming of the Shrew. Act iii, sc. 2, l. 146. [Tranio]

19
Perchance some single vantages you took,
When my indisposition put you back.
Timon of Athens. Act ii, sc. 2, l. 139. [Timon] The only use of "indisposition."

20
It shall advantage more than do us wrong.
Julius Cæsar. Act iii, sc. 1, l. 242. [Brutus]
It shall advantage thee more than ever.
Twelfth Night. Act iv, sc. 2, l. 119. [Malvolio]
Doing thee vantage.—*Sonnets*, lxxxviii.

21
Let not advantage slip.
Venus and Adonis, l. 129. See also under Opportunity.
Take advantage on presented joy.
Venus and Adonis, l. 405.

ADVENTURE

1
Fear of your adventure would counsel you to a more equal enterprise.
As You Like It. Act i, sc. 2, l. 187. [Celia]
Hard adventure.—*As You Like It,* ii, 4, 45.

2
If you fall in the adventure, our crows shall fare the better for you.
Cymbeline. Act iii, sc. 1, l. 82. [Cloten].

3 The over-daring Talbot
Hath sullied all his gloss of former honour
By this unheedful, desperate, wild adventure.
I Henry VI. Act iv, sc. 4, l. 5. [Somerset] The only use of "over-daring" and "sullied." "Unheedful" occurs again in *The Two Gentlemen of Verona,* ii, 6, 11.

4
Our scouts have found the adventure very easy.
III Henry VI. Act iv, sc. 2, l. 18. [Warwick]

5
And all the unsettled humours of the land,
Rash, inconsiderate, fiery voluntaries,
With ladies' faces and fierce dragons' spleens,
Have sold their fortunes at their native homes,
Bearing their birthrights proudly on their backs,
To make a hazard of new fortunes here:
In brief, a braver choice of dauntless spirits
Than now the English bottoms have waft o'er
Did never float upon the swelling tide,
To do offence and scathe in Christendom.
King John. Act ii, sc. 1, l. 66. [Chatillon] The only use of "voluntaries." "Inconsiderate" occurs again in *Love's Labour's Lost,* iii, 1, 79, and "float" in *Macbeth,* iv, 2, 21. For "scathe" see under INJURY.
And cull'd these fiery spirits from the world,
To outlook conquest and to win renown.
King John. Act v, sc. 2, l. 114. [Dauphin] The only use of "outlook."
Drawn by report, adventurous by desire.
Pericles. Act i, sc. 1, l. 35. [Antiochus]

The day shall not be up so soon as I,
To try the fair adventure of to-morrow.
King John. Act v, sc. 5, l. 21. [Dauphin]
I dare adventure.—*Richard III,* i, 3, 116.

Wherein I spake of most disastrous chances,
Of moving accidents by flood and field,
Of hair-breadth scapes i' the imminent deadly breach,
Of being taken by the insolent foe
And sold to slavery, of my redemption thence
And portance in my travels' history:
Wherein of antres vast and deserts idle,
Rough quarries, rocks and hills whose heads touch heaven,
It was my hint to speak,—such was the process:
And of the Cannibals that each other eat,
The Anthropophagi and men whose heads
Do grow beneath their shoulders.
Othello. Act i, sc. 3, l. 134. [Othello] The only use of "disastrous," "hair-breadth," "antres," and "Anthropophagi." "Portance" is repeated in *Coriolanus,* ii, 3, 232.

8
What will you adventure?
Winter's Tale. Act ii, sc. 3, l. 162. [Leontes]
Will you adventure?—*Winter's Tale,* ii, 3, 162.
Wouldst adventure?—*Winter's Tale,* iv, 4, 470.
I will adventure.—*Romeo and Juliet,* v, 3, 11.
I would adventure.—*Cymbeline,* iii, 4, 156.
Then will they adventure.—*I Henry IV,* i, 2, 192.
At all adventures.—*Henry V,* iv, 1, 121.
Adventuring both.—*The Merchant of Venice,* i, 1, 143. The only use of "adventuring."

ADVERSARY, see Enemy

ADVERSITY

See also Disaster; Extremity; Friends and Adversity; Mischance; Misfortune; Prosperity

9
Sweet are the uses of adversity,
Which, like the toad, ugly and venomous,
Wears yet a precious jewel in his head.
As You Like It. Act ii, sc. 1, l. 12. [Duke]

10
You have look'd on better days.
As You Like It. Act ii, sc. 7, l. 113. [Orlando]
True is it that we have seen better days.
As You Like It. Act ii, sc. 7, l. 120. [Duke]
Let 's shake our heads, and say, . . .
'We have seen better days.'
Timon of Athens. Act iv, sc. 2, l. 25. [Flavius]

11
A wretched soul, bruised with adversity.
Comedy of Errors, ii, 1, 34. See under SOUL.
Nay, 'tis for me to be patient; I am in adversity.
The Comedy of Errors. Act iv, sc. 4, l. 21. [Dromio of Ephesus]

12
Ring'd about with bold adversity.
I Henry VI. Act iv, sc. 4, l. 14. [Lucy]
Like one lost in a thorny wood,
That rends the thorns and is rent with the thorns,
Seeking a way and straying from the way;
Not knowing how to find the open air,
But toiling desperately to find it out.
III Henry VI. Act iii, sc. 2, l. 174. [Gloucester]

13
Let me embrace thee, sour adversity,
For wise men say it is the wisest course.
III Henry VI. Act iii, sc. 1, l. 24. [King Henry]

14
Let . . . all indign and base adversities
Make head against my estimation.
Othello. Act i, sc. 3, l. 273. [Othello] The only use of "indign."
Well said, adversity!—*Troilus and Cressida,* v, 1, 14.

15
A man I am cross'd with adversity.
The Two Gentlemen of Verona. Act iv, sc. 1, l. 12. [Valentine]

Who gives anything to poor Tom? whom the foul fiend hath led through fire and through flame, through ford and whirlipool, o'er bog and quagmire; that hath laid knives under his pillow, and halters in his pew; set ratsbane by his porridge; made him proud of heart, to ride on a bay trotting-horse over four-inched bridges, to course his own shadow for a traitor. Bless thy five wits! Tom 's a-cold.
King Lear. Act iii, sc. 4, l. 51. [Edgar] The only use of "whirlipool," "trotting-horse" and "four-inched."

What freezings have I felt, what dark days seen!
Sonnets. No. xcvii. The only use of "freezings." "Freezing" occurs in *The Rape of Lucrece,* l. 1145: "Freezing cold"; and in *Cymbeline,* iii, 3, 39: "Freezing hours."

ADVERTISEMENT

1
That is an advertisement to a proper maid in Florence.
All's Well that Ends Well. Act iv, sc. 3, l. 240. [Parolles]

This advertisement is five days old.
I Henry IV. Act iii, sc. 2, l. 172. [King Henry]

Yet doth he give us bold advertisement.
I Henry IV. Act iv, sc. 1, l. 36. [Hotspur]

2
Please it your grace to be advertised
The Duke of York is newly come from England.
II Henry VI. Act iv, sc. 9, l. 23. [Messenger]

I was advertised That she was coming.
III Henry VI. Act ii, sc. 1, l. 116. [Warwick]

3
We are advertised by our loving friends.
III Henry VI. Act v, sc. 3, l. 18. [King Henry]

I by friends am well advertised.
Richard III. Act iv, sc. 4, l. 501. [Messenger]

I was then Advertising.
Measure for Measure. Act v, sc. 1, l. 387. [Duke]

ADVICE

See also Counsel, Direction

4
Share the advice betwixt you.
All's Well that Ends Well. Act ii, sc. 1, l. 3. [King]

You did never lack advice so much.
All's Well that Ends Well. Act iii, sc. 4, l. 19. [Count]

He wants advice.—*Measure for Measure,* iv, 2, 154.

Ask advice.—*Pericles,* i, 1, 62.

I hope I need not to advise you further.
All's Well that Ends Well. Act iii, sc. 5, l. 27.

I shall anon advise you Further.
Henry VIII. Act i, sc. 2, l. 107. [Wolsey]

5 Make yourself some comfort
Out of your best advice.
Cymbeline. Act i, sc. 1, l. 155. [Queen] The only use of "best advice."

6
Go, bid thy master well advise himself.
Henry V. Act iii, sc. 6, l. 168. [King Henry]

Gramercies, Tranio, well dost thou advise.
The Taming of the Shrew. Act i, sc. 1, l. 41. [Lucentio]

Were you well advised?—*Love's Labour's Lost,* v, 2, 434.

Be well advised.—*King John,* iii, 1, 5; *The Merchant of Venice,* v, 1, 234.

Being well advised.—*Richard III,* i, 3, 318.
"Well-advised" (sometimes hyphenated, sometimes not) is used six times in the plays.

7 Not a man in England
Can advise me like you.
Henry VIII. Act i, sc. 1, l. 135. [Norfolk]

You advise me well.—*Othello,* ii, 3, 332.

Well hast thou advised.—*The Two Gentlemen of Verona,* i, 3, 34.

8
For when we rage, advice is often seen
By blunting us to make our wits more keen.
A Lover's Complaint, l. 160. "Blunting" is repeated in *Sonnets,* iii.

9
If you will take a homely man's advice,
Be not found here.
Macbeth. Act iv, sc. 2, l. 68. [Messenger]

Your good advice,
Which still hath been both grave and prosperous.
Macbeth. Act iii, sc. 1, l. 21. [Macbeth]

We will prosecute by good advice
Mortal revenge upon these traitorous Goths,
And see their blood, or die with this reproach.
Titus Andronicus. Act iv, sc. 1, l. 92. [Marcus Andronicus]

Thy good advice.—*The Two Gentlemen of Verona,* iii, 2, 94.

With good advice.—*II Henry IV,* iii, 1, 43.

Upon good advice.—*Richard II,* i, 3, 233.

Upon advice.—*The Taming of the Shrew,* i, 1, 117; *The Two Gentlemen of Verona,* iii, 1, 73; *Titus Andronicus,* i, 1, 379.

Upon more advice.—*The Merchant of Venice,* iv, 2, 6.

After more advice.—*Measure for Measure,* v, 1, 469.

By advice—*I Henry IV,* i, 2, 109.

By my advice.—*Hamlet,* i, 1, 168; *Titus Andronicus,* i, 1, 228; 472.

By thy advice.—*Richard III,* iv, 2, 3.

On his more advice.—*Henry V,* ii, 2, 43.

10
Fasten your ear on my advisings.
Measure for Measure. Act iii, sc. 1, l. 203. [Duke] The only use of "advisings."

11
I will give him a present shrift and advise him for a better place.
Measure for Measure, iv, 2, 222. [Duke]

Advise him.—*All's Well that Ends Well,* i, 1, 81.

Friar, advise him.—*Measure for Measure,* v, 1, 490.

Let the friar advise you.—*Much Ado about Nothing,* iv, 1, 246.

Advise him to a caution.—*Macbeth,* iii, 6, 44.

Advise your fellows so.—*King Lear,* i, 3, 23.

1 This advice is free I give and honest,
Probal to thinking.
Othello. Act ii, sc. 3, l. 343. [Iago] The only use of "probal."

2
Advice is sporting while infection breeds.
The Rape of Lucrece, l. 907. The only use of "sporting."

3
Who sued to me for him? who, in my rage,
Kneel'd at my feet, and bade me be advised?
Richard III. Act ii, sc. 1, l. 106. [King Edward] "Be advised" occurs five times in the plays.

Be first advised.—*Love's Labour's Lost,* iv, 3, 368.
Bid me be advised.—*II Henry VI,* ii, 4, 36.
Are ye advised?—*II Henry VI,* ii, 1, 48.
Art thou not advised?—*The Taming of the Shrew,* i, 1, 191.

4
Be gone, or talk not, I advise you.
The Taming of the Shrew. Act i, sc. 2, l. 44. [Petruchio] "I advise you" is repeated frequently.

I advise you to the best.—*King Lear,* i, 2, 188.
I do advise you.—*King Lear,* iv, 5, 29.
I am come to advise you.—*Measure for Measure,* iv, 3, 55.
I will advise you.—*Macbeth,* iii, 1, 129.
This I will advise you.—*The Taming of the Shrew,* iv, 2, 92.
I would advise you.—*Cymbeline,* i, 2, 1.
Advise thee.—*Titus Andronicus,* iv, 2, 129; *Pericles,* i, 1, 39.
Advise yourself.—*King Lear,* ii, 1, 29.
I am advised to do it.—*Measure for Measure,* iv, 6, 3.
I am advised what I say.—*The Comedy of Errors,* v, 1, 214.

5
We will all subscribe to thy advice.
Titus Andronicus. Act iv, sc. 2, l. 130. [Demetrius]

Thy advice this night I'll put in practice.
The Two Gentlemen of Verona. Act iii, sc. 2, l. 89. [Thurio]

She took the fruits of my advice.
Hamlet. Act ii, sc. 2, l. 145. [Polonius]

Now I begin to relish thy advice.
Troilus and Cressida. Act i, sc. 3, l. 388. [Nestor]

Thou dost advise me
Even so as I mine own course have set down.
Winter's Tale. Act i, sc. 2, l. 339. [Leontes]

I'll go along By your prescription.
Henry VIII. Act i, sc. 1, l. 150. [Buckingham] See under MEDICINE.

You'll do as I advise.—*Pericles,* iv, 3, 51.

6
She shall file our engines with advice.
Titus Andronicus. Act ii, sc. 1, l. 123. [Aaron]

She thus advises thee that sighs for thee.
Twelfth Night. Act ii, sc. 5, l. 165. [Malvolio, reading]

7
How shall I dote on her with more advice,
That thus without advice begin to love her!
The Two Gentlemen of Verona. Act ii, sc. 4, l. 207. [Proteus]

8 As thou art a gentleman of blood,
Advise me.
The Two Gentlemen of Verona. Act iii, sc. 1, l. 121. [Duke]

Advise me.—*Coriolanus,* v, 3, 197; *Antony and Cleopatra,* v, 2, 137.
Can you advise me?—*Hamlet,* iv, 7, 54.

9
I would your spirit were easier for advice.
Winter's Tale. Act iv, sc. 4, l. 516. [Camillo]

10 Why need we
Commune with you of this, but rather follow
Our forceful instigation? Our prerogative
Calls not your counsels, . . .
We need no more of your advice.
The Winter's Tale. Act ii, sc. 1, l. 161. [Leontes] The only use of "forceful."

AFFABILITY, see Courtesy

AFFAIRS

See also Business

11
My affairs Are servanted to others.
Coriolanus. Act v, sc. 2, l. 88. [Coriolanus] The only use of "servanted."

12
What is your affair in Elsinore?
Hamlet. Act i, sc. 2, l. 174. [Hamlet]

What's your affair?—*Troilus and Cressida,* i, 3, 247.
God prosper your affairs.—*II Henry IV,* iii, 2, 313.

13 Affairs, that walk,
As they say spirits do, at midnight, have
In them a wilder nature than the business
That seeks dispatch by day.
Henry VIII. Act v, sc. 1, l. 13. [Gardiner]

From your affairs I hinder you too long.
Henry VIII. Act v, sc. 1, l. 53. [Gardiner]

Their affairs are righteous.—*Henry VIII,* iii, 1, 22.

14
Sweet friends, your patience for my long abode;
Not I, but my affairs, have made you wait.
The Merchant of Venice. Act ii, sc. 6, l. 21. [Lorenzo]

Let's to our affairs.—*Othello,* ii, 3, 115.
Affairs in hand.—*Richard II,* i, 4, 47.
Affairs to heaven.—*Measure for Measure,* iii, 1, 57.

15
My affairs Do even drag me homeward.
The Winter's Tale. Act i, sc. 2, l. 23. [Polixenes]

Home affairs.—*The Two Gentlemen of Verona,* ii, 4, 119.

16
What his happier affairs may be, are to me unknown.
Winter's Tale. Act iv, sc. 2, l. 34. [Camillo]

Chief affairs.—*III Henry VI,* iv, 6, 58.
Commonwealth affairs.—*II Henry VI,* i, 3, 157; *Henry V,* i, 1, 41.
Great affairs.—*II Henry VI,* iii, 1, 224; *Richard III,* i, 3, 122; *II Henry IV,* iv, 1, 6; *Richard II,* ii, 1, 159.
High affairs.—*King John,* i, 1, 101.

Reasonable affairs.—*Winter's Tale,* iv, 4, 409.
Worthiest affairs.—*All's Well that Ends Well,* iii, 2, 99.
Mine own affairs.—*II Henry VI,* iii, 1, 320.
Rough affairs.—*II Henry IV,* ii, 3, 2.
Affairs of death.—*Macbeth,* iii, 5, 5.
Affairs of love.—*Much Ado about Nothing,* ii, 1, 183; *As You Like It,* iv, 1, 47.
Affairs of men.—*Julius Cæsar,* iv, 3, 218; v, 1, 96.
Affairs of state.—*Othello,* i, 3, 220.

AFFECTATION

1
He is too picked, too spruce, too affected, too odd.
Love's Labour's Lost. Act v, sc. 1, l. 14. [Holofernes]
Spruce affectation.
Love's Labour's Lost. Act v, sc. 2, l. 407. [Biron] See under RHETORIC for full quotation.

2
What phrase is this, 'He hears with ear'? why, it is affectations.
The Merry Wives of Windsor. Act i, sc. 1, l. 151. [Evans]

3
An affectioned ass.
Twelfth Night. Act ii, sc. 3, l. 160. [Maria] See CHARACTER, 177:3, for full quotation.

AFFECTION

See also Love

4
Yet have I fierce affections, and think
What Venus did with Mars.
Antony and Cleopatra. Act i, sc. 5, l. 17. [Mardian, the eunuch]
Affections dark as Erebus.
The Merchant of Venice. Act v, sc. 1, l. 87. [Lorenzo] Erebus is mentioned also in *II Henry IV,* ii, 4, 171, and in *Julius Cæsar,* ii, 1, 84.

5
Your affections are
A sick man's appetite, who desires most that
Which would increase his evil.
Coriolanus. Act i, sc. 1, l. 181. [Marcius]
But, out, affection!
All bond and privilege of nature, break!
Coriolanus. Act v, sc. 3, l. 24. [Coriolanus]
The pangs of barr'd affections.
Cymbeline. Act i, sc. 1, l. 82. [Queen]

6
And will continue fast in your affection,
Still close as sure.
Cymbeline. Act i, sc. 6, l. 138. [Iachimo]
True affection.—*Coriolanus,* i, 3, 239; *The Rape of Lucrece,* l. 1060.

7
Keep you in the rear of your affection,
Out of the shot and danger of desire.
Hamlet. Act i, sc. 3, l. 34. [Laertes]
Ophelia: He hath, my lord, of late made many tenders
Of his affection to me.
Polonius: Affection! pooh! you speak like a green girl,
Unsifted in such perilous circumstance.
Hamlet. Act i, sc. 3, l. 99. The only use of "pooh" and "unsifted."
Love! his affections do not that way tend.
Hamlet. Act iii, sc. 1, l. 170. [King]
His salt and most hidden loose affection.
Othello. Act ii, sc. 1, l. 245. [Iago]

8
Thy affections which do hold a wing
Quite from the flight of all thy ancestors.
I Henry IV. Act iii, sc. 2, l. 30. [King Henry]
When his headstrong riot hath no curb,
When rage and hot blood are his counsellors,
When means and lavish manners meet together,
O, with what wings shall his affection fly
Towards fronting peril and opposed decay!
II Henry IV. Act iv, sc. 4, l. 62. [King Henry] "Fronting" is repeated in *Troilus and Cressida,* iii, 3, 122.
Though his affections are higher mounted than ours, yet, when they stoop, they stoop with the like wing.
Henry V. Act iv, sc. 1, l. 110. [King Henry]

9
Thou hast a better place in his affection
Than all my brothers: cherish it, my boy.
II Henry IV. Act iv, sc. 4, l. 22. [King Henry]
It shows my earnestness of affection.
II Henry IV. Act v, sc. 5, l. 17. [Falstaff]
A mountain of affection.
Much Ado about Nothing. Act ii, sc. 1, l. 382. [Don Pedro]
Fair encounter Of two most rare affections!
The Tempest. Act iii, sc. 1, l. 74. [Prospero]

10
My king is tangled in affection to
A creature of the queen's.
Henry VIII. Act iii, sc. 2, l. 35. [Surrey]
Enraged affection.—*Much Ado about Nothing,* ii, 3, 106.
Entire affection.—*The Taming of the Shrew,* iv, 2, 23.
Forced affection.—*Julius Cæsar,* iv, 3, 205.
Full affection.—*Henry VIII,* iii, 1, 129.
Ill-composed affection.—*Macbeth,* iv, 3, 77. The only use of "ill-composed."
Least affection.—*II Henry IV,* iv, 5, 173.
Vain though apt affection.—*Measure for Measure,* i, 4, 49.
Affections hot.—*A Lover's Complaint,* l. 218.
Affections new.—*Sonnets,* cx.

11
Your fore-vouch'd affection Fall'n into taint.
King Lear. Act i, sc. 1, l. 223. [France] The only use of "fore-vouch'd."
To my judgement, your highness is not entertained with the ceremonious affection as you were wont.
King Lear. Act i, sc. 4, l. 62. [Knight]
And nice affections wavering stood in doubt.
A Lover's Complaint, l. 97.

12
Affection,
Mistress of passion, sways it to the mood
Of what it likes or loathes.
The Merchant of Venice. Act iv, sc. 1, l. 50. [Shylock]
Believe me, sir, had I such venture forth,
The better part of my affections would
Be with my hopes abroad.
The Merchant of Venice. Act i, sc. 1, l. 15. [Salanio]

1
What warmth is there in your affection?
The Merchant of Venice. Act i, sc. 2, l. 37. [Nerissa]
Tender me, forsooth, affection.
A Midsummer-Night's Dream. Act iii, sc. 2, l. 230. [Helena]
First affection.—*Measure for Measure,* iii, 1, 249.
2
Claudio: How do you know he loves her?
Don John: I heard him swear his affection.
Much Ado about Nothing. Act ii, sc. 1, l. 174.
I would have thought her spirit had been invincible against all assaults of affection.
Much Ado about Nothing. Act ii, sc. 3, l. 119. [Don Pedro]
It seems her affections have their full bent.
Much Ado about Nothing. Act ii, sc. 3, l. 231. [Benedick]
Hath she made her affection known?
Much Ado about Nothing. Act ii, sc. 3, l. 127. [Don Pedro]
She will rather die than give any sign of affection.
Much Ado about Nothing. Act ii, sc. 3, l. 236. [Benedick]
3
To wish him wrestle with affection.
Much Ado about Nothing. Act iii, sc. 1, l. 42. [Hero]
Wrestle with thy affections.
As You Like It. Act i, sc. 3, l. 21. [Celia]
4
Affection is my captain, and he leadeth;
And when his gaudy banner is display'd,
The coward fights and will not be dismay'd.
The Rape of Lucrece, l. 271.
Nothing can affection's course control,
Or stop the headlong fury of his speed.
The Rape of Lucrece, l. 500.
5
Measuring his affections by my own,
That most are busied when they 're most alone.
Romeo and Juliet. Act i, sc. 1, l. 133. [Benvolio]
Affection makes him false; he speaks not true.
Romeo and Juliet. Act iii, sc. 1, l. 182. [Lady Capulet]
6
Had she affections and warm youthful blood,
She would be as swift in motion as a ball.
Romeo and Juliet. Act ii, sc. 5, l. 12. [Juliet]
7
Affection is not rated from the heart.
The Taming of the Shrew. Act i, sc. 1, l. 165. [Tranio]
Affection's edge.—*The Taming of the Shrew,* i, 2, 73.
8
My affections Are then most humble.
The Tempest. Act i, sc. 2, l. 481. [Miranda]
I weigh my friend's affection with mine own.
Timon of Athens. Act i, sc. 2, l. 222. [Timon]
9
Valentine: In conclusion, I stand affected to her.
Speed: I would you were set, so your affection would cease.
Two Gentlemen of Verona. Act ii, sc. 1, l. 90.
Ill affected.—*King Lear,* ii, 1, 100.
10
Affection is a coal that must be cool'd;
Else, suffer'd, it will set the heart on fire.
Venus and Adonis, l. 387.
Affection faints not like a pale-faced coward,
But then woos best when most his choice is froward.
Venus and Adonis, l. 569.
11
Affection! thy intention stabs the centre:
Thou dost make possible things not so held,
Communicatest with dreams.
The Winter's Tale. Act i, sc. 2, l. 138. [Leontes] "Intention" is used only once more, in *The Winter's Tale,* i, 2, 138.
This shows a sound affection.
Winter's Tale. Act iv, sc. 4, l. 389. [Camillo]
Such an affection, which cannot choose but branch.
The Winter's Tale, i, 1, 26. See under ROOT.
With all greediness of affection.
The Winter's Tale. Act v, sc. 2, l. 111. [Third Gentleman]

AFFLICTION

See also Adversity, Disaster, Misfortune

12 Gentle, but unfortunate;
Dishonestly afflicted, but yet honest.
Cymbeline. Act iv, sc. 2, l. 39. [Guiderius]
Happier much by his affliction made.
Cymbeline. Act v, sc. 4, l. 108. [Jupiter]
13
In most great affliction of spirit.
Hamlet. Act iii, sc. 2, l. 324. [Guildenstern]
How sad he looks! sure, he is much afflicted.
Henry VIII. Act ii, sc. 2, l. 63. [Suffolk]
14
O fair affliction, peace!
King John. Act iii, sc. 4, l. 36. [King Philip]
Biting affliction.—*The Merry Wives of Windsor,* v, 5, 178.
15 Man's nature cannot carry
The affliction nor the fear.
King Lear. Act iii, sc. 2, l. 49. [Kent]
O you mighty gods!
This world I do renounce, and in your sights,
Shake patiently my great affliction off.
King Lear. Act iii, sc. 5, l. 35. [Gloucester]
Henceforth I 'll bear
Affliction till it do cry out itself
'Enough, enough,' and die.
King Lear. Act iv, sc. 6, l. 75. [Gloucester]
Had it pleased heaven
To try me with affliction; had they rain'd
All kinds of sores and shames on my bare head,
Steep'd me in poverty to the very lips,
Given to captivity me and my utmost hopes,
I should have found in some place of my soul
A drop of patience.
Othello. Act iv, sc. 2, l. 47. [Othello]
16
Affliction is enamour'd of thy parts,
And thou art wedded to calamity.
Romeo and Juliet. Act iii, sc. 3, l. 2. [Friar Laurence]

1
The affliction of my mind amends.
The Tempest. Act v, sc. 1, l. 115. [Alonso]
I think affliction may subdue the cheek,
But not take in the mind.
Winter's Tale. Act iv, sc. 4, l. 586. [Perdita]
2
I count it one of my greatest afflictions, say, that I cannot pleasure such an honourable gentleman.
Timon of Athens. Act iii, sc. 2, l. 62. [Lucius]
Chief afflictions.—*Timon of Athens,* iv, 2, 44.
3
This affliction has a taste as sweet
As any cordial comfort.
Winter's Tale. Act v, sc. 3, l. 76. [Leontes]

AGE

I—Age and Youth

See also Man: Old and Young Men

4
'Let me not live,' quoth he,
'After my flame lacks oil, to be the snuff
Of younger spirits, whose apprehensive senses
All but new things disdain; whose judgements are
Mere fathers of their garments; whose constancies
Expire before their fashions.'
All's Well that Ends Well, i, 2, 58. [King]
Young boys and girls Are level now with men.
Antony and Cleopatra, iv, 15, 65. [Cleopatra]
With his Amazonian chin he drove
The bristled lips before him.
Coriolanus. Act ii, sc. 2, l. 95. [Cominius]
"Amazonian" is repeated in *III Henry VI,* i, 4, 114: "Amazonian trull"; and "bristled" in *A Midsummer-Night's Dream,* ii, 2, 31: "Bristled hair."
5
Though grey
Do something mingle with our younger brown, yet ha' we
A brain that nourishes our nerves, and can
Get goal for goal of youth.
Antony and Cleopatra, iv, 8, 19. [Antony]
6
At seventeen years many their fortunes seek;
But at fourscore it is too late a week.
As You Like It. Act ii, sc. 3, l. 73. [Adam]
The oldest hath borne most: we that are young
Shall never see so much, nor live so long.
King Lear. Act v, sc. 3, l. 325. [Albany]
He that no more must say is listen'd more
Than they whom youth and ease have taught to glose.
Richard II. Act ii, sc. 1, l. 9. [John of Gaunt]
7
By heaven, it is as proper to our age
To cast beyond ourselves in our opinions
As it is common for the younger sort
To lack discretion.
Hamlet. Act ii, sc. 1, l. 114. [Polonius]
A very riband in the cap of youth,
Yet needful too; for youth no less becomes
The light and careless livery that it wears
Than settled age his sables and his weeds,
Importing health and graveness.
Hamlet. Act iv, sc. 7, l. 78. [King] The only use of "graveness."
8
An old man is twice a child.
Hamlet. Act ii, sc. 2, l. 403. [Rosencrantz]
Old men fool and children calculate.
Julius Cæsar. Act i, sc. 3, l. 65. [Cassius]
Old fools are babes again; and must be used
With checks as flatteries.
King Lear. Act i, sc. 3, l. 19. [Goneril]
Grandsires, babies and old women,
Either past or not arrived to pith and puissance.
Henry V, iii, Prol., l. 19.
9
Your lordship, though not clean past your youth, hath yet some smack of age in you, some relish of the saltness of time.
II Henry IV. Act i, sc. 2, l. 110. [Falstaff] The only use of "saltness."
Falstaff: You that are old consider not the capacities of us that are young; you do measure the heat of our livers with the bitterness of your galls: and we that are in the vaward of our youth, I must confess are wags too.
Chief Justice: Do you set down your name in the scroll of youth, that are written down old with all the characters of age? Have you not a moist eye? a dry hand? a yellow cheek? a white beard? a decreasing leg? an increasing belly? is not your voice broken? your wind short? your chin double? your wit single? and every part about you blasted with antiquity? and will you yet call yourself young? Fie, fie, fie, Sir John!
II Henry IV. Act i, sc. 2, l. 196. "Vaward" occurs five times in the plays. The only use of "decreasing."
Moth: Why tender juvenal? why tender juvenal?
Armado: I spoke it, tender juvenal, as a congruent epitheton appertaining to thy young days, which we may nominate tender.
Moth: And I, tough senior, as an appertinent title to your old time, which we may name tough.
Love's Labour's Lost. Act i, sc. 2, l. 12. The only use of "epitheton," an earlier form of epithet. "Congruent" is repeated in v, 1, 97, and in no other play. "Appertinent" occurs three times.
10
The blood of youth burns hot with such excess
As gravity's revolt to wantonness.
Love's Labour's Lost. Act v, sc. 2, l. 73. [Rosaline]
11
Young in limbs, in judgement old.
The Merchant of Venice. Act ii, sc. 7, l. 71. [Prince of Morocco, reading scroll]
I never knew so young a body with so old a head.
The Merchant of Venice. Act iv, sc. 1, l. 163. [Clerk]
How much more elder art thou than thy looks!
The Merchant of Venice. Act iv, sc. 1, l. 251. [Shylock]
12
Crabbed age and youth cannot live together:
Youth is full of pleasance, age is full of care;
Youth like summer morn, age like winter weather;

Youth like summer brave, age like winter bare.
Youth is full of sport, age's breath is short;
Youth is nimble, age is lame;
Youth is hot and bold, age is weak and cold;
Youth is wild, and age is tame.
Age, I do abhor thee; youth, I do adore thee.
The Passionate Pilgrim, l. 157.

1
My glass shall not persuade me I am old,
So long as youth and thou are of one date.
Sonnets. No. xxii.

Nativity, once in the main of light,
Crawls to maturity.
Sonnets. No. lx. "Maturity" is used only once again, in *Troilus and Cressida,* i, 3, 317.

When hours have drain'd his blood and fill'd his brow
With lines and wrinkles; when his youthful morn
Hath travell'd on to age's steepy night.
Sonnets. No. lxiii. "Steepy" is repeated in *Timon of Athens,* i, 1, 75.

2
Gremio: 'Tis age that nourisheth.
Tranio: But youth in ladies' eyes that flourisheth.
The Taming of the Shrew. Act ii, sc. 1, l. 341.

II—Age: Its Compensations

3
Though age from folly could not give me freedom,
It does from childishness.
Antony and Cleopatra. Act i, sc. 3, l. 57. [Cleopatra]

Age cannot wither her.—*Antony and Cleopatra,* ii, 2, 240. See Woman: 1699:12.

4
Though I look old, yet I am strong and lusty;
For in my youth I never did apply
Hot and rebellious liquors in my blood,
Nor did not with unbashful forehead woo
The means of weakness and debility;
Therefore my age is as a lusty winter,
Frosty but kindly.
As You Like It. Act ii, sc. 3, l. 47. [Adam] The only use of "unbashful" and "debility."

Though now this grained face of mine be hid
In sap-consuming winter's drizzled snow
And all the conduits of my blood froze up,
Yet hath my night of life some memory,
My wasting lamps some fading glimmer left,
My dull deaf ears a little use to hear.
The Comedy of Errors. Act v, sc. 1, l. 311. [Ægeon] The only use of "sap-consuming."

I am only old in judgement and understanding; and he that will caper with me for a thousand marks, let him lend me the money, and have at him!
II Henry IV. Act i, sc. 2, l. 215. [Falstaff]

If to be old and merry be a sin, then many an old host that I know is damned.
I Henry IV. Act ii, sc. 4, l. 518. [Falstaff]

5
The elder I wax, the better I shall appear.
Henry V. Act v, sc. 2, l. 246. [King Henry]

A gracious aged man,
Whose reverence even the head-lugg'd bear would lick.
King Lear. Act iv, sc. 2, l. 41. [Albany] The only use of "head-lugg'd."

Whose age has charms in it.
King Lear, v, 3, 48. See under Bosom.

6
Privileged by age.
A Lover's Complaint, l. 62.

Hadst thou not the privilege of antiquity upon thee.
All's Well that Ends Well. Act ii, sc. 3, l. 220. [Parolles]

Under privilege of age to brag
What have I done being young, or what would do
Were I not old.
Much Ado about Nothing. Act v, sc. 1, l. 60. [Leonato]

Prerogative of age.
Troilus and Cressida. Act i, sc. 3, l. 107. [Ulysses]

7
That which should accompany old age,
As honour, love, obedience, troops of friends.
Macbeth. Act v, sc. 3, l. 24. [Macbeth]

Respect and reason, wait on wrinkled age!
The Rape of Lucrece, l. 275.

8
You shall more command with years
Than with your weapons.
Othello. Act i, sc. 2, l. 60. [Othello]

I am too old to fawn upon a nurse,
Too far in years to be a pupil now.
Richard II. Act i, sc. 3, l. 170. [Mowbray]

9
I do hope good days and long to see.
The Taming of the Shrew. Act i, sc. 2, l. 193. [Petruchio]

The gods to-day stand friendly, that we may,
Lovers in peace, lead on our days to age!
Julius Cæsar. Act v, sc. 1, l. 94. [Cassius]

10
Let me embrace thine age, whose honour cannot
Be measured or confined.
The Tempest. Act v, sc. 1, l. 121. [Prospero]

Let me embrace thee, good old chronicle,
That hast so long walk'd hand in hand with time.
Troilus and Cressida. Act iv, sc. 5, l. 202. [Hector]

This good old man.
Titus Andronicus. Act i, sc. 1, l. 457. [Tamora]

11
Thou most reverent for thy stretch'd-out life.
Troilus and Cressida. Act i, sc. 3, l. 61. [Ulysses] The only use of "stretch'd-out."

Reverend age.—*The Taming of the Shrew,* iv, 5, 60; *Timon of Athens,* iii, 5, 80.
Honourable age.—*II Henry VI,* v, 1, 170.
Perfect age.—*King Lear,* i, 2, 77.
Pretty age.—*Romeo and Juliet,* i, 3, 10.
Valiant age.—*I Henry VI,* iii, 2, 54.

III—Age: Its Penalties

12
On us both did haggish age steal on.
All's Well that Ends Well. Act i, sc. 2, l. 29. [King] The only use of "haggish."

But age, with his stealing steps,
Hath claw'd me in his clutch.
Hamlet. Act v, sc. 1, l. 79. [First Clown]

Old I do wax.
Henry V. Act v, sc. 1, l. 89. [Pistol]

Wherefore say not I that I am old?
The Passionate Pilgrim, l. 10.

1 The sixth age shifts
Into the lean and slipper'd pantaloon,
With spectacles on nose and pouch on side,
His youthful hose, well saved, a world too wide
For his shrunk shank; and his big manly voice,
Turning again toward childish treble, pipes
And whistles in his sound.
As You Like It. Act ii, sc. 7, l. 157. [Jaques] The only use of "slipper'd."

That we might beguile the old pantaloon.
The Taming of the Shrew, iii, 1, 37. The only uses of "pantaloon."

2
I see thy age and dangers make thee dote.
The Comedy of Errors. Act v, sc. 1, l. 329. [Duke]

The old folk, time's doting chronicles.
II Henry IV. Act iv, sc. 4, l. 126. [Clarence]

3
Impotent and bed-rid.
Hamlet. Act i, sc. 1, l. 29. [King]

Age and impotence.
Hamlet. Act ii, sc. 2, l. 66. [Voltimand] The only use of "impotence" in the plays.

4
The satirical rogue says here that old men have grey beards, that their faces are wrinkled, their eyes purging thick amber and plum-tree gum and that they have a plentiful lack of wit, together with most weak hams: all which, sir, though I most powerfully and potently believe, yet I hold it not honesty to have it thus set down, for yourself, sir, should be as old as I am, if like a crab you could go backward.
Hamlet. Act ii, sc. 2, l. 198. [Hamlet] The only use of "satirical," and "powerfully." "Potently" occurs again in *Henry VIII,* v, 1, 134, and "plum-tree" in *II Henry VI,* ii, 1, 97.

5
A man can no more separate age and covetousness than a' can part young limbs and lechery: but the gout galls the one, and the pox pinches the other; and so both the degrees prevent my curses.
II Henry IV. Act i, sc. 2, l. 256. [Falstaff]

Lord, Lord, how subject we old men are to this vice of lying!
II Henry IV. Act iii, sc. 2, l. 325. [Falstaff]

Old men of less truth than tongue.
Sonnets. No. xvii.

6
My weak decaying age.
I Henry VI. Act ii, sc. 5, l. 1. [Mortimer] The only use of "decaying."

Crazy age.—*I Henry VI,* iii, 2, 89. Shakespeare used "crazy" in this his third play, and never again.
Endless age.—*Sonnets,* cvii.
Feeble age.—*Venus and Adonis,* l. 941.
Growing age.—*Sonnets,* xxxii.
Outworn buried age.—*Sonnets,* lxiv.
Sapless age.—*I Henry VI,* iv, 5, 4.
Unregarded age.—*As You Like It,* ii, 3, 42.
Waning age.—*The Taming of the Shrew,* ii, 1, 403; *The Rape of Lucrece,* l. 142.
Weak age.—*Henry V,* i, 1, 15.
Wretched age.—*Richard III,* iii, 4, 107.
Yellow'd with their age.—*Sonnets,* xvii. The only use of "yellow'd."

7
'Tis the infirmity of his age.
King Lear. Act i, sc. 1, l. 296. [Regan]

Then must we look to receive from his age, not alone the imperfections of long-engraffed condition, but therewithal the unruly waywardness that infirm and choleric years bring with them.
King Lear. Act i, sc. 1, l. 299. [Goneril] The only use of "long-engraffed" and "waywardness."

This policy and reverence of age makes the world bitter to the best of our times; keeps our fortunes from us till our oldness cannot relish them.
King Lear. Act i, sc. 2, l. 50. [Gloucester] The only use of "oldness."

8
Dear daughter, I confess that I am old;
Age is unnecessary: on my knees I beg
That you'll vouchsafe me raiment, bed, and food.
King Lear. Act ii, sc. 4, l. 156. [King Lear]

O heavens,
If you do love old men, if your sweet sway
Allow obedience, if yourselves are old,
Make it your cause; send down, and take my part!
King Lear. Act ii, sc. 4, l. 192. [King Lear]

For those that mingle reason with your passion
Must be content to think you old.
King Lear. Act ii, sc. 4, l. 237. [Regan]

9
You see me here, you gods, a poor old man,
As full of grief as age; wretched in both!
King Lear. Act ii, sc. 4, l. 275. [King Lear]

A poor, infirm, weak, and despised old man.
King Lear. Act iii, sc. 2, l. 20. [King Lear]

I am a very foolish fond old man,
Fourscore and upward, not an hour more nor less.
King Lear. Act iv, sc. 7, l. 60. [King Lear]

This is a man, old, wrinkled, faded, wither'd.
The Taming of the Shrew. Act iv, sc. 5, l. 43. [Petruchio]

10 When thou art old and rich,
Thou hast neither heat, affection, limb, nor beauty,
To make thy riches pleasant.
Measure for Measure. Act iii, sc. 1, l. 36. [Duke]

When the age is in, the wit is out.
Much Ado about Nothing. Act iii, sc. 5, l. 37. [Dogberry] A play upon the proverb, "When the wine is in, the wit is out."

11
The superstitious idle-headed eld.
Merry Wives of Windsor. Act iv, sc. 4, l. 36. [Mrs. Page] The only use of "idle-headed."

Palsied eld.—*Measure for Measure,* iii, 1, 36.
Wrinkled eld.—*Troilus and Cressida,* ii, 2, 104. The only uses of "eld."

1
Old Gaunt indeed, and gaunt in being old.
Richard II. Act ii, sc. 1, l. 74. [Gaunt]
Here am I left to underprop his land.
Who, weak with age, cannot support myself.
Richard II. Act ii, sc. 2, l. 82. [York] "Underprop" is repeated in *King John,* v, 2, 99.
2
Thy age confirm'd, proud, subtle, bloody, treacherous,
More mild, but yet more harmful, kind in hatred.
Richard III. Act iv, sc. 4, l. 171. [Duchess of York]
Confounding age's cruel knife.
Sonnets. No. lxiii.
3 'Tis not hard, I think,
For men so old as we to keep the peace.
Romeo and Juliet. Act i, sc. 2, l. 2. [Capulet]
But old folks, many feign as they were dead;
Unwieldy, slow, heavy and pale as lead.
Romeo and Juliet. Act ii, sc. 5, l. 16. [Juliet] "Unwieldy" is repeated in *Richard II,* iii, 2, 115; iv, 1, 205.
Leaden age.—*I Henry VI,* iv, 6, 12.
4 These old fellows
Have their ingratitude in them hereditary:
Their blood is caked, 'tis cold, it seldom flows;
'Tis lack of kindly warmth they are not kind;
And nature, as it grows again toward earth,
Is fashion'd for the journey, dull and heavy.
Timon of Athens. Act ii, sc. 2, l. 223. [Timon] The only use of "caked."
Now the gods keep you old enough; that you may live
Only in bone, that none may look on you!
Timon of Athens. Act iii, sc. 5, l. 104. [Alcibiades]
5
For pity of mine age, whose youth was spent
In dangerous wars, whilst you securely slept.
Titus Andronicus. Act iii, sc. 1, l. 2. [Titus]
I have seen the day, with my good biting falchion
I would have made them skip: I am old now,
And these same crosses spoil me.
King Lear. Act v, sc. 3, l. 276. [King Lear]
6 The faint defects of age
Must be the scene of mirth; to cough and spit,
And, with a palsy-fumbling on his gorget,
Shake in and out the rivet.
Troilus and Cressida. Act i, sc. 3, l. 172. [Ulysses] The only use of "palsy-fumbling" and "gorget."
7
They that went on crutches ere he was born
desire yet their life to see him a man.
Winter's Tale. Act i, sc. 1, l. 44. [Camillo]
Is not your father grown incapable
Of reasonable affairs? is he not stupid
With age and altering rheums? can he speak? hear?
Know man from man? dispute his own estate?
Lies he not bed-rid? and again does nothing
But what he did being childish?
The Winter's Tale. Act iv, sc. 4, l. 407. [Polixenes] The only use of "stupid" (stupidity does not occur in the plays) and "altering." "Bed-rid" is repeated in *Love's Labour's Lost,* i, 1, 139, and in *Hamlet,* i, 2, 29.
You have undone a man of fourscore three,
That thought to fill his grave in quiet, yea,
To die upon the bed my father died,
To lie close by his honest bones.
The Winter's Tale, iv, 4, 463. [Shepherd]

IV—Age and Beauty

8
Hath homely age the alluring beauty took
From my poor cheek?
The Comedy of Errors. Act ii, sc. 1, l. 89. [Adriana] The only use of "alluring."
9
Shallow: Doth she hold her own well?
Falstaff: Old, old, Master Shallow.
II Henry IV. Act iii, sc. 2, l. 218.
An old trot with ne'er a tooth in her head, though she have as many diseases as two and fifty horses.
Taming of the Shrew. Act i, sc. 2, l. 80. [Grumio] The only use of "trot" in this sense.
Old age, that ill layer up of beauty.
Henry V. Act v, sc. 2, l. 248. [King]
10
Time had not scythed all that youth begun,
Nor youth all quit; but, spite of heaven's fell rage,
Some beauty peep'd through lattice of sear'd age.
A Lover's Complaint, l. 12. The only use of "scythed." "Lattice" is repeated in *All's Well that Ends Well,* ii, 3, 225.
11
When forty winters shall besiege thy brow,
And dig deep trenches in thy beauty's field,
Thy youth's proud livery, so gazed on now,
Will be a tatter'd weed, of small worth held.
Sonnets. No. ii.
To me, fair friend, you never can be old,
For as you were when first your eye I eyed,
Such seems your beauty still.
Sonnets. No. civ.
Counting no old thing old.—*Sonnets,* cviii.
12
And as with age his body uglier grows,
So his mind cankers.
The Tempest. Act iv, sc. 1, l. 191. [Prospero]

V—Age and Love

13
You cannot call it love; for at your age
The hey-day in the blood is tame, it 's humble,
And waits upon the judgement.
Hamlet. Act iii, sc. 4, l. 68. [Hamlet] "Hey-day" occurs only once again, in *The Tempest,* ii, 2, 190.
Why then, say an old man can do somewhat.
II Henry IV. Act v, sc. 3, l. 82. [Silence]
A little fire in a wild field were like an old lecher's heart; a small spark, all the rest on 's body cold.
King Lear. Act iii, sc. 4, l. 116. [Fool]
One that is well nigh worn to pieces with age to show himself a young gallant!
The Merry Wives of Windsor. Act ii, sc. 1, l. 21. [Mrs. Page]

1
Age, in love, loves not to have years told.
The Passionate Pilgrim, l. 12. Repeated in *Sonnets,* cxxxviii.

VI—Age and Wisdom

2
Why art thou old and want'st experience?
II Henry VI. Act v, sc. 1, l. 171. [King]

3
As you are old and reverend, you should be wise.
King Lear. Act i, sc. 4, l. 261. [Goneril]

Thou shouldst not have been old till thou hadst been wise.
King Lear. Act i, sc. 5, l. 48. [Fool]

Why art thou old and yet not wise?
The Rape of Lucrece, l. 1550.

VII—Age: Its Silver Livery

4
This grizzled head.
Antony and Cleopatra. Act iii, sc. 13, l. 17. [Antony]

His beard was grizzled.—*Hamlet,* i, 2, 240. The only uses of "grizzled."

5
That he is old, the more the pity, his white hairs do witness it.
I Henry IV. Act ii, sc. 4, l. 514. [Falstaff]

I know thee not, old man: fall to thy prayers;
How ill white hairs become a fool and jester!
II Henry IV. Act v, sc. 5, l. 51. [King Henry V]

6
The silver livery of advised age.
II Henry VI. Act v, sc. 2, l. 47. [Young Clifford]

Grey locks, the pursuivants of death.
I Henry VI. Act ii, sc. 5, l. 5. [Edmund Mortimer]

A head So old and white as this.
King Lear. Act iii, sc. 2, l. 23. [King Lear]

7
White-beards have arm'd their thin and hairless scalps.
Richard II. Act iii, sc. 2, l. 112. [Scroop] "Hairless" is used only once again, in *Venus and Adonis,* l. 487.

Pity not honour'd age for his white beard;
He is an usurer.
Timon of Athens. Act iv, sc. 3, l. 111. [Timon]

VIII—Age: Middle Age

8
Touchstone: How old are you, friend?
William: Five and twenty, sir.
Touchstone: A ripe age.
As You Like It. Act v, sc. 1, l. 20.

King Lear: How old art thou?
Kent: Not so young, sir, to love a woman for singing, nor so old to dote on her for any thing: I have years on my back forty eight.
King Lear. Act i, sc. 4, l. 49.

I have looked upon the world for four times seven years.
Othello. Act i, sc. 3, l. 312. [Iago]

His age some fifty, or, by 'r lady, inclining to three score.
I Henry IV. Act ii, sc. 4, l. 466. [Falstaff]

9
Octavius, I have seen more days than you.
Julius Cæsar. Act iv, sc. 1, l. 18. [Antony]

I have seen more years, I 'm sure, than ye.
Julius Cæsar. Act iv, sc. 3, l. 132. [Poet]

10
Thou hast nor youth nor age,
But, as it were, an after-dinner's sleep,
Dreaming on both.
Measure for Measure. Act iii, sc. 1, l. 32. [Duke] "After-dinner" is repeated in *Troilus and Cressida,* ii, 3, 121: "After-dinner's breath."

11
I am declined into the vale of years.
Othello. Act iii, sc. 3, l. 265. [Othello]

I know my years be past the best.
The Passionate Pilgrim, l. 6.

Myself am struck in years.
The Taming of the Shrew. Act ii, sc. 1, l. 362. [Gremio]

12
I am of age To keep mine own.
Titus Andronicus. Act iv, sc. 2, l. 104. [Aaron]

I will not compare with an old man.
Twelfth Night. Act 1, sc. 3, l. 126. [Sir Andrew]

IX—Age: Old Age

13
Is second childishness and mere oblivion,
Sans teeth, sans eyes, sans taste, sans every thing.
As You Like It, ii, 7, 165. See under MAN.

14
Indigent faint souls past corporal toil.
Henry V. Act i, sc. 1, l. 16. [Canterbury] The only use of "indigent."

15
If I to-day die not with Frenchmen's rage,
To-morrow I shall die with mickle age.
I Henry VI. Act iv, sc. 6, l. 34. [Talbot]

For shame! in duty bend thy knee to me
That bows unto the grave with mickle age.
II Henry VI. Act v, sc. 1, l. 173. [King Henry]

16
Even in the downfall of his mellow'd years,
When nature brought him to the door of death.
III Henry VI. Act iii, sc. 3, l. 104. [Oxford]

Mellow'd by the stealing hours of time.
Richard III, iii, 7, 168. The only uses of "mellow'd."

17
O, sir, you are old;
Nature in you stands on the very verge
Of her confine.
King Lear. Act ii, sc. 4, l. 148. [Regan]

Threescore and ten I can remember well:
Within the volume of which time I have seen
Hours dreadful and things strange.
Macbeth. Act ii, sc. 4, l. 1. [Old Man]

18
Beated and chopp'd with tann'd antiquity.
Sonnets. No. lxii. The only use of "beated." "Tann'd" is repeated in *Hamlet,* v, 1, 186.

That time of year thou mayst in me behold
When yellow leaves, or none, or few, do hang
Upon those boughs which shake against the cold,
Bare ruin'd choirs, where late the sweet birds sang.
In me thou see'st the twilight of such day
As after sunset fadeth in the west,

Which by and by black night doth take away,
Death's second self, that seals up all in rest.
Sonnets. No. lxxiii. The only use of "twilight."

1 The remnant of mine age
Should have been cherish'd by her child-like duty.
The Two Gentlemen of Verona. Act iii, sc. 1, l. 74. [Duke] "Child-like" is repeated in *King Lear,* ii, 1, 108: "Child-like office."

Extreme age.—*Richard III,* iv, 4, 185.
Old age.—*Henry V,* iv, 3, 44; v, 2, 248; *Romeo and Juliet,* v, 3, 207; *Macbeth,* v, 3, 24; *Twelfth Night,* ii, 4, 49; *The Rape of Lucrece,* l. 1759; *Sonnets,* cxxvii.

X—Age: The Age

See also Time: The Times

2
The age is grown so picked that the toe of the peasant comes so near the heel of the courtier, he galls his kibe.
Hamlet. Act v, sc. 1, l. 151. [Hamlet] "Kibe" (a chilblain in the heel) is used four times.

The drossy age.—*Hamlet,* v, 2, 197. The only use of "drossy."

3
O miserable age!
II Henry VI. Act iv, sc. 2, l. 11. [Bevis]

O, pity, God, this miserable age!
III Henry VI. Act ii, sc. 5, l. 88. [Father]

This iron age.—*King John,* iv, 1, 60.
This pattern of the worn-out age.—*The Rape of Lucrece,* l. 1350. The only use of "worn-out."
The grossness of this age.—*Richard III,* iii, 1, 46.
To see this age!—*Twelfth Night,* iii, 1, 12.
Filching age.—*Sonnets,* lxxv.
Woeful ages.—*Richard II,* v, 1, 42.
Age of discord.—*I Henry VI,* v, 3, 63.

4
Groaning underneath this age's yoke.
Julius Cæsar. Act i, sc. 2, l. 61. [Cassius]

When went there by an age, since the great flood,
But it was famed with more than with one man?
Julius Cæsar. Act i, sc. 2, l. 152. [Cassius]

5 This long age of three hours
Between our after-supper and bed-time.
A Midsummer-Night's Dream. Act v, sc. 1, l. 33. [Theseus] The only use of "after-supper." "Bed-time" is repeated in *The Comedy of Errors,* i, 2, 28, and in *I Henry IV,* v, 1, 125.

6
Successively from age to age.
Richard III. Act iii, sc. 1, l. 75. [Prince] "From age to age" is repeated in l. 76 of the same scene, and appears nowhere else.

The age to come.—*Sonnets,* xvii.
Ensuing age.—*Coriolanus,* v, 3, 148.
Succeeding ages.—*Richard III,* iii, 1, 71. See also FUTURE.

7
I would . . . excel the golden age.
The Tempest, ii, 1, 168. See under GOVERNMENT. "Golden age" is used only once again, in *The Rape of Lucrece,* l. 60. "Former golden days" occurs in *Richard III,* i, 2, 248.

This fine age.—*I Henry IV,* iv, 1, 2.
This latter age.—*I Henry IV,* v, 1, 92.

AGREEMENT

8
'Twere pregnant they should square between themselves.
Antony and Cleopatra. Act ii, sc. 1, l. 45. [Pompey]

We have cause to be glad that matters are so well digested.
Antony and Cleopatra. Act ii, sc. 2, l. 178. [Macænas]

9
I crave our composition may be written,
And seal'd between us.
Antony and Cleopatra. Act ii, sc. 6, l. 60. [Pompey]

Come not to composition.—*Measure for Measure,* i, 2, 2.
Short of composition.—*Measure for Measure,* v, 1, 220.
Mad composition!—*King John,* ii, 1, 561.
Unchaste composition.—*All's Well that Ends Well,* iv, 3, 22.

10
What is the course and drift of your compact?
The Comedy of Errors. Act ii, sc. 2, l. 163. [Antipholus of Syracuse]

A seal'd compact,
Well ratified by law and heraldry.
Hamlet. Act i, sc. 1, l. 86. [Horatio]

The compact is firm and true in me.
Richard III. Act ii, sc. 2, l. 133. [Gloucester]

Confirm'd, sign'd, ratified by you.
The Merchant of Venice. Act iii, sc. 2, l. 149. [Bassanio]

11
This gentle and unforced accord . . .
Sits smiling to my heart.
Hamlet. Act i, sc. 2, l. 123. [King]

Be at accord.—*As You Like It,* i, 1, 67.
Christian-like accord.—*Henry V,* v, 2, 381.
Full accord.—*Henry V,* v, 2, 71.
Jove's accord.—*Troilus and Cressida,* i, 3, 238.

12
To cry amen to that.
Henry V. Act v, sc. 2, l. 21. [King Henry] "Cry amen" is repeated in *Much Ado about Nothing,* ii, 1, 110, and in *Richard II,* i, 3, 102.

I say, Amen.
The Tempest. Act v, sc. 1, l. 204. [Alonso] To "say amen" is used forty times.

13
Agree to any covenants.
I Henry VI. Act v, sc. 5, l. 88. [King]

Let there be covenants drawn between 's.
Cymbeline. Act i, sc. 4, l. 155. [Posthumus]

My heart this covenant makes.
Richard II, ii, 3, 50. See HEART and HAND.

Covenants may be kept.—*The Taming of the Shrew,* ii, 1, 128.
Keep covenant.—*Cymbeline,* ii, 4, 50.
Strict and severe covenants.—*I Henry VI,* v, 4, 114.

14
It is further agreed between them.
II Henry VI. Act i, sc. 1, l. 57. [Beaufort, reading]

It stands agreed, I take it, by all voices.
Henry VIII. Act v, sc. 3, l. 87. [Lord Chancellor]
All agreeing.—*Coriolanus,* ii, 1, 228.
Thus we are agreed.—*Antony and Cleopatra,* ii, 6, 58.
Agreed upon.—*Much Ado about Nothing,* i, 3, 64.

1 That they may agree like brothers.
II Henry VI. Act iv, sc. 2, l. 82. [Cade]
The gentlemen do not agree with the gentlewomen.
II Henry IV, Epilogue, l. 24.
How dost thou and thy master agree?
The Merchant of Venice. Act ii, sc. 2, l. 105. [Gobbo]
How can these contrarieties agree?
I Henry VI, ii, 3, 59. See under RIDDLE. The only use of "contrarieties." "Contrariety" occurs in *Coriolanus,* iv, 6, 73.
How ill agrees it.—*Comedy of Errors,* ii, 2, 70.

2 I agree, and thank you for your motion.
III Henry VI. Act iii, sc. 3, l. 244. [Queen]
Agree with his demands to the point.
Measure for Measure. Act iii, sc. 1, l. 256. [Duke]

3 To say 'ay' and 'no' to every thing that I said!—
'Ay' and 'no' too was no good divinity.
King Lear. Act iv, sc. 6, l. 100. [King Lear]

4 Are you agreed?
Measure for Measure. Act iv, sc. 2, l. 51. [Provost]
Are you all agreed?—*Henry VIII,* v, 3, 91.
I am agreed.
The Taming of the Shrew. Act i, sc. 1, l. 147. [Gremio]
Unwilling I agreed.
Comedy of Errors. Act i, sc. 1, l. 61. [Ægeon]
At last, though long, our jarring notes agree.
The Taming of the Shrew. Act v, sc. 2, l. 1. [Lucentio]

5 Upon agreement.
The Taming of the Shrew. Act i, sc. 2, l. 183; *I Henry IV,* i, 3, 103.

6 As he saith, so say we all with him.
Titus Andronicus. Act v, sc. 1, l. 17. [Goths]
And be it moon, or sun, or what you please:
An if you please to call it a rush-candle,
Henceforth I vow it shall be so for me.
The Taming of the Shrew. Act iv, sc. 5, l. 13. [Katharina] The only use of "rush-candle."

AID

See also Help

7 The Florentine will move us For speedy aid.
All's Well that Ends Well. Act i, sc. 2, l. 6. [King]
Swift aid.—*Venus and Adonis,* l. 1190.

8 But think you, Helen,
If you should tender your supposed aid,
He would receive it?
All's Well that Ends Well. Act i, sc. 3, l. 241. [Countess]
You cannot,
By the good aid that I of you shall borrow,
Err in bestowing it.
All's Well that Ends Well. Act iii, sc. 7, l. 10. [Helena]
Aid me with that store of power you have.
All's Well that Ends Well. Act v, sc. 1, l. 20. [Helena]

9 If I do send, dispatch
Those centuries to our aid
Coriolanus. Act i, sc. 7, l. 2. [Lartius]
If you refuse your aid
In this so never-needed help, yet do not
Upbraid 's with our distress.
Coriolanus. Act v, sc. 1, l. 33. [Sicinius] The only use of "never-needed."
Aidless came off.—*Coriolanus,* ii, 2, 116. The only use of "aidless."

10 Lucina lent not me her aid.
Cymbeline. v, 4, 43. See under LABOUR.
Lend him aid.—*I Henry VI,* iv, 4, 23.
Lend thee aid.—*Richard III,* v, 3, 173.

11 Her aid she promised and assured success.
I Henry VI. Act i, sc. 2, l. 82. [La Pucelle]
Promise aid.—*The Rape of Lucrece,* l. 1696.

12 Come, go; I will dispatch the horsemen straight:
Within six hours they will be at his aid.
I Henry VI. Act iv, sc. 4, l. 40. [Somerset]
Wanting aid.—*I Henry VI,* i, 1, 43.
I cannot aid the man.—*I Henry VI,* iv, 3, 44.
Sent him aid.—*I Henry VI,* iv, 4, 29.

13 You speedy helpers . . .
Appear and aid me in this enterprise.
I Henry VI. Act v, sc. 3, l. 5. [La Pucelle]
Be my aid.—*Twelfth Night,* i, 2, 53.

14 Such aid as I can spare you shall command.
II Henry VI. Act iv, sc. 5, l. 7. [Scales]

15 I . . .
Am come to crave thy just and lawful aid.
III Henry VI. Act iii, sc. 3, l. 32. [Queen Margaret]
Craves aid.—*II Henry VI,* iv, 5, 4.
Craving aid.—*III Henry VI,* iii, 1, 43.

16 Therefore at last I firmly am resolved
You shall have aid.
III Henry VI. Act iii, sc. 3, l. 219. [King Lewis]
Giving aid.—*III Henry VI,* iii, 3, 148.
Giving him aid.—*Sonnets,* lxxxvi.
Never seek for aid.—*Henry VIII,* i, 2, 114.

17 Be aidant and remediate
In the good man's distress.
King Lear. Act iv, sc. 4, l. 17. [Cordelia] The only use of "aidant" and "remediate."

18 We all have strongly sworn to give him aid.
Richard II. Act ii, sc. 3, l. 150. [Northumberland]
We swore our aid.—*I Henry IV,* v, 1, 46.

19 Every hour more competitors
Flock to their aid.
Richard III. Act iv, sc. 4, l. 506. [Messenger]
I, as I may—that which I would I cannot,—
With best advantage will deceive the time,

And aid thee in this doubtful shock of arms.
Richard III. Act v, sc. 3, l. 91. [Derby]
How can we aid you?—*Richard III*, ii, 2, 63.

1 I alone did call upon thy aid.
Sonnets. No. lxxix.

2 I have her sovereign aid
And rest myself content.
The Tempest. Act v, sc. 1, l. 143. [Prospero]
Determined aid.—*King John*, ii, 1, 584.
Further aid.—*Hamlet*, iv, 1, 33.
Honest aid.—*All's Well that Ends Well*, v, 3, 329.
Metaphysical aid.—*Macbeth*, i, 5, 30. The only use of "metaphysical."
Present aid.—*Richard III*, iv, 5, 5.

AIM

See also Purpose

3 I am not an impostor that proclaim
Myself against the level of mine aim.
All's Well that Ends Well. Act ii, sc. 1, l. 158. [Helena]

4 In faith, it is exceedingly well aim'd.
I Henry IV. Act i, sc. 3, l. 282. [Hotspur]
Well aim'd of such a young one.
The Taming of the Shrew. Act ii, sc. 1, l. 236. [Katharina]
Aim'd so high.—*Pericles*, ii, v, 47.
Aim'd so near.—*Romeo and Juliet*, i, 1, 211.

5 Howe'er unfortunate I miss'd my aim.
I Henry VI. Act i, sc. 4, l. 4. [Boy]

6 Here stand we both, and aim we at the best.
III Henry VI. Act iii, sc. 1, l. 8. [Keeper]
Hunter's aim.—*As You Like It*, ii, 1, 34.

7 What you would work me to, I have some aim.
Julius Cæsar, i, 2, 163. See UNDERSTANDING.

8 I will watch the aim.
The Merchant of Venice. Act i, sc. 1, l. 150. [Bassanio]
A certain aim he took.
A Midsummer-Night's Dream. Act ii, sc. 1, l. 157. [Oberon]
They aim at it.—*Hamlet*, iv, 5, 9.

9 All my neighbours shall cry aim.
The Merry Wives of Windsor. Act iii, sc. 2, l. 45. [Ford] "Cry aim" (to applaud) is repeated in *King John*, ii, 1, 196.
Give me aim awhile.—*Titus Andronicus*, v, 3, 149.

10 If all aim but this be levell'd false.
Much Ado about Nothing. Act iv, sc. 1, l. 239. [Friar]
False aim.—*All's Well that Ends Well*, iii, 2, 113.
Chief aim.—*Henry VIII*, v, 3, 118.
Near aim.—*II Henry IV*, iii, 1, 83.

11 The aim of all is but to nurse the life
With honour, wealth, and ease, in waning age.
The Rape of Lucrece, l. 141.
End thy ill aim before thy shoot be ended.
The Rape of Lucrece, l. 579.
All-hurting aim.—*A Lover's Complaint*, l. 310. The only use of "all-hurting."

12 Canst thou guess that he doth aim at it?
Richard III. Act iii, sc. 2, l. 45. [Hastings]

13 In fellest manner execute your aims.
Troilus and Cressida. Act v, sc. 7, l. 6. [Achilles]
Fearing lest my jealous aim might err.
The Two Gentlemen of Verona. Act iii, sc. 1, l. 28. [Duke]

AIR

14 The air of paradise did fan the house
And angels officed all.
All's Well that Ends Well. Act iii, sc. 2, l. 128. [Helena]

15 Where air comes out, air comes in: there's none abroad so wholesome as that you vent.
Cymbeline. Act i, sc. 2, l. 3. [First Lord]
Air yourself.—*Cymbeline*, i, 1, 110.

16 A wonderful sweet air, with admirable rich words to it.
Cymbeline. Act ii, sc. 3, l. 18. [Cloten]
Sweet airs, that give delight and hurt not.
The Tempest. Act iii, sc. 2, l. 145. [Caliban]
Sweet air.—*Love's Labour's Lost*, iii, 1, 4; *A Midsummer-Night's Dream*, i, 1, 183; *Tempest*, i, 2, 393. Always with reference to music.
Divine air.—*Much Ado about Nothing*, ii, 3, 60.
Light airs.—*Twelfth Night*, ii, 4, 5.
Solemn air.—*The Tempest*, v, 1, 58.
Air of music.—*Merchant of Venice*, v, 1, 76.

17 Be embraced by a piece of tender air.
Cymbeline. Act v, sc. 4, l. 140. [Posthumus, reading] Repeated in act v, sc. 5, l. 437.
The piece of tender air, thy virtuous daughter,
What we call 'mollis aer.'
Cymbeline. Act v, sc. 5, l. 446. [Soothsayer] "Mollis aer" is used twice in this scene and nowhere else. "Tender air" is repeated a fourth time in l. 452.

18 But, soft! methinks I scent the morning air.
Hamlet. Act i, sc. 5, l. 58. [Ghost]
Morning air.—*The Rape of Lucrece*, l. 778.

19 This most excellent canopy, the air.
Hamlet. Act ii, sc. 2, l. 311. [Hamlet]

20 The chameleon's dish: I eat the air, promise-crammed: you cannot feed capons so.
Hamlet. Act iii, sc. 2, l. 98. [Hamlet] The only use of "promise-crammed."
The chameleon . . . can feed on air.
The Two Gentlemen of Verona, ii, 2, 178. The chameleon is referred to a third time in *III Henry VI*, iii, 2, 191.

21 Stand from him, give him air; he'll straight be well.
II Henry IV. Act iv, sc. 4, l. 116. [Warwick]
Give her air.—*Pericles*, iii, 2, 91.

22 Welcome then,
Thou unsubstantial air that I embrace!

The wretch that thou hast blown unto the worst,
Owes nothing to thy blasts.
King Lear. Act iv, sc. 1, l. 6. [Edgar] "Unsubstantial" is repeated in *Romeo and Juliet,* v, 3, 103.

Incorporal air.—*Hamlet,* iii, 4, 118. The only use of "incorporal."
Intrenchant air.—*Macbeth,* v, 8, 9. The only use of "intrenchant" (incapable of being cut).

1
I did commend the black-oppressing humour to the most wholesome physic of thy health-giving air.
Love's Labour's Lost. Act i, sc. 1, l. 234. [King Ferdinand] The only use of "black-oppressing" and "health-giving."

Healthsome air.—*Romeo and Juliet,* iv, 3, 34. The only use of "healthsome."
Summer air.—*Love's Labour's Lost,* v, 2, 293.

2
Playing in the wanton air.
Love's Labour's Lost. Act iv, sc. 3, l. 104. [Dumain, reading]

Wanton summer air.—*Romeo and Juliet,* ii, 6, 19.
Common air.—*Richard II,* i, 3, 157.
Desert air.—*Macbeth,* iv, 3, 194.
Filthy air.—*Macbeth,* i, 1, 12.
Sick air.—*Timon of Athens,* iv, 3, 110.
Vulgar air.—*King John,* ii, 1, 387.

3
They made themselves air, into which they vanished.
Macbeth. Act i, sc. 5, l. 5. [Lady Macbeth]

Melted into air, into thin air.
The Tempest, iv, 1, 150. See under VISION.

4
The heaven's breath Smells wooingly here.
Macbeth. Act i, sc. 6, l. 5. [Banquo]

Heaven's air.—*Sonnets,* xxi. Used twice.
Heaven's sweetest air.—*Sonnets,* lxx.
Airs from heaven.—*Hamlet,* i, 4, 41.
The air is delicate.—*Macbeth,* i, 6, 10.
I am for the air.—*Macbeth,* iii, 5, 20.
Good air.—*II Henry IV,* v, 3, 9.
Pure air.—*Henry V,* iii, 7, 22.
Purer air.—*Pericles,* iv, 6, 109.
The spiced Indian air.—*A Midsummer-Night's Dream,* ii, 1, 124. The only use of "spiced."

5
As broad and general as the casing air.
Macbeth, iii, 4, 23. See under PERFECTION. The only use of "casing."

Appalled air.—*Troilus and Cressida,* iv, 5, 4.
Dispersed air.—*The Rape of Lucrece,* l. 1805.
Listening air.—*Pericles,* i, 2, 87.
Midway air.—*King Lear,* iv, 6, 13.
Pendulous air.—*King Lear,* iii, 4, 69. The only use of "pendulous."

6
The empty vast and wandering air.
Richard III. Act i, sc. 4, l. 39. [Clarence]

7
In to our tent; the air is raw and cold.
Richard III. Act v, sc. 3, l. 46. [Richmond]

Hamlet: The air bites shrewdly; it is very cold.
Horatio: It is a nipping and an eager air.
Hamlet. Act i, sc. 4, l. 1.

The air is quick there,
And it pierces and sharpens the stomach.
Pericles. Act iv, sc. 1, l. 28. [Dionyza]

8
Adrian: The air breathes upon us here most sweetly.
Sebastian: As if it had lungs and rotten ones.
Antonio: Or as 'twere perfumed by a fen.
The Tempest. Act ii, sc. 1, l. 46.

The climate's delicate, the air most sweet.
The Winter's Tale. Act iii, sc. 1, l. 1. [Cleomenes]

9
Well are you welcome to the open air.
Richard III. Act i, sc. 1, l. 124. [Gloucester]

Open air.—*Winter's Tale,* iii, 2, 106; *King John,* v, 7, 7; *King Lear,* iii, 6, 1.
Free air.—*Timon of Athens,* i, 1, 83.
Fresher air.—*Henry VIII,* i, 4, 101.

10
Why will he not upon our fair request
Untent his person and share the air with us?
Troilus and Cressida. Act ii, sc. 3, l. 177. [Agamemnon] The only use of "untent."

11
What, think'st
That the bleak air, thy boisterous chamberlain,
Will put thy shirt on warm?
Timon of Athens. Act iv, sc. 3, l. 221. [Apemantus]

Bleak air.—*As You Like It,* ii, 6, 16.

ALE

See also Beer

12
I would have him poison'd with a pot of ale.
I Henry IV. Act i, sc. 3, l. 233. [Hotspur]

And on her wither'd dewlap pour the ale.
A Midsummer-Night's Dream. Act ii, sc. 1, l. 50. [Puck] The only use of "dewlap."

13
Would I were in an alehouse in London! I would give all my fame for a pot of ale and safety.
Henry V. Act iii, sc. 2, l. 12. [Boy] See also under INN.

14
In his ales and his angers. . . . In his ales and his cups.
Henry V, iv, 7, 40. See under ALEXANDER.

15
Were he not warm'd with ale,
This were a bed but cold to sleep so soundly.
The Taming of the Shrew. Induction, sc. 1, l. 32. [Second Huntsman]

16
For God's sake, a pot of small ale.
The Taming of the Shrew. Induction, sc. 2, l. 1. [Sly]

And once again, a pot o' the smallest ale.
The Taming of the Shrew. Induction, sc. 2, l. 77. [Sly]

17
Sir Toby: Dost thou think, because thou art virtuous, there shall be no more cakes and ale?
Clown: Yes, by Saint Anne, and ginger shall be hot i' the mouth too.
Twelfth Night. Act ii, sc. 3, l. 123.

Do you look for ale and cakes here, you rude rascals?
Henry VIII. Act v, sc. 4, l. 11. [Porter]

1
Speed: 'Item: She brews good ale.'
Launce: And thereof comes the proverb: 'Blessing of your heart, you brew good ale.'
The Two Gentlemen of Verona. Act iii, sc. 1, l. 304.

2
A quart of ale is a dish for a king.
Winter's Tale. Act iv, sc. 3, l. 8. [Autolycus]

ALEHOUSE, see Inn

ALEXANDER THE GREAT

3
Hamlet: Dost thou think Alexander looked o' this fashion i' the earth?
Horatio: E'en so.
Hamlet: And smelt so? pah!
Horatio: E'en so, my lord.
Hamlet: To what base uses we may return, Horatio! Why may not imagination trace the noble dust of Alexander, till he find it stopping a bung-hole? . . . Alexander died, Alexander was buried, Alexander returneth into dust; the dust is earth; of earth we make loam; and why of that loam, whereto he was converted, might they not stop a beer-barrel?
Hamlet. Act v, sc. 1, l. 218. The only use of "bung-hole" and "beer-barrel." "Pah" is repeated in *King Lear,* iv, 6, 132.

4 Like so many Alexanders,
Have in these parts from morn till even fought.
Henry V. Act iii, sc. 1, l. 19. [King Henry]

5
Fluellen: What call you the town's name where Alexander the Pig was born? . . .
Gower: I think Alexander the Great was born in Macedon.
Henry V. Act iv, sc. 7, l. 13.

Alexander, God knows, and you know, in his rages, and his furies, and his wraths, and his cholers, and his moods, and his displeasures, and his indignations, and also being a little intoxicates in his prains, did, in his ales and his angers, look you, kill his best friend, Cleitus. . . . Alexander killed his friend Cleitus, being in his ales and his cups.
Henry V. Act iv, sc. 7, l. 37. [Fluellen] The only mention of Cleitus, and use of "intoxicates."

6
When in the world I lived, I was the world's commander;
By east, west, north, and south, I spread my conquering might:
My scutcheon plain declares that I am Alisander.
Love's Labour's Lost. Act v, sc. 2, l. 565. [Sir Nathaniel] "East, west, north, and south," always in the same order, occurs four times in the plays: *II Henry IV,* iv, 2, 104; *Coriolanus,* iv, 2, 104; *The Winter's Tale,* i, 2, 203.

O, sir, you have overthrown Alisander the conqueror!
Love's Labour's Lost. Act v, sc. 2, l. 575. [Costard] "Alisander" is used six times in this scene and nowhere else.

Good Alexander.—*Love's Labour's Lost,* v, 2, 570.

7
The crown will find an heir: great Alexander
Left his to the worthiest; so his successor
Was like to be the best.
Winter's Tale. Act v, sc. 1, l. 47. [Paulina]

ALLEGIANCE

See also Loyalty

8
Sworn allegiance.
II Henry VI, v, 1, 179; *III Henry VI,* iii, 1, 70.

True allegiance.—*II Henry VI,* v, 1, 20.

Owe allegiance.—*III Henry VI,* iv, 7, 19.

9
Don Pedro: I charge thee on thy allegiance. . . .
Benedick: On my allegiance, mark you this, on my allegiance.
Much Ado about Nothing. Act i, sc. 1, l. 210.

On your allegiance,
Out of the chamber with her!
Winter's Tale. Act ii, sc. 3, l. 121. [Leontes]

10
Allegiance and true faith of heart.
Richard II. Act iii, sc. 3, l. 37. [Bolingbroke]

Contrary to the faith and allegiance of a true subject.
Winter's Tale. Act iii, sc. 2, l. 20. [Officer]

ALLIANCE

See also League

11 This dear conjunction
Plant neighbourhood and Christian-like accord
In their sweet bosoms.
Henry V. Act v, sc. 2, l. 380. [French King] "Neighbourhood" is repeated in i, 2, 154: "Ill neighbourhood"; and in *Timon of Athens,* iv, 1, 17.

List to this conjunction, make this match.
King John. Act ii, sc. 1, l. 468. [Elinor] See also under MATCH.

Conjunction of our inward souls.
King John, iii, 1, 227. See under LEAGUE.

Smile heaven upon this fair conjunction,
That long have frown'd upon their enmity!
Richard III. Act v, sc. 5, l. 20. [Richmond]

Married in conjunction.—*II Henry IV,* v, 1, 77.

In conjunction.—*II Henry IV,* iv, 1, 37.

Small conjunction.—*I Henry IV,* iv, 1, 37.

12
His alliance will confirm our peace
And keep the Frenchmen in allegiance.
I Henry VI. Act v, sc. 5, l. 42. [Suffolk]

Join we together, for the public good.
II Henry VI. Act i, sc. 1, l. 199. [Salisbury]

So shalt thou sinew both these lands together.
III Henry VI. Act ii, sc. 6, l. 91. [Warwick]

Is this the alliance that he seeks with France?
III Henry VI. Act iii, sc. 3, l. 177. [King]

Yet, to have join'd with France in such alliance
Would more have strengthen'd this our commonwealth
'Gainst foreign storms than any home-bred marriage.
III Henry VI. Act iv, sc. 1, l. 36. [Montague] "Home-bred" is repeated in *Richard II,* i, 3, 187: "Home-bred hate."

1 This last costly treaty, the interview,
That swallow'd so much treasure, and like a glass
Did break i' the rinsing.
Henry VIII. Act i, sc. 1, l. 165. [Buckingham] The only use of "rinsing."

What good condition can a treaty find?
Coriolanus, i, 10, 6. See under CONDITION.

We are convented Upon a pleasing treaty.
Coriolanus, ii, 2, 59. See under HEART. "Convented" is repeated in *Measure for Measure,* v, 1, 158, and in *Henry VIII,* v, 1, 52.

Making a treating where There was a yielding.
Coriolanus. Act v, sc. 6, l. 68. [Lord]

Thy father, Pompey, would ne'er have made this treaty.
Antony and Cleopatra. Act ii, sc. 6, l. 85. [Menas]

Friendly treaty.—*King John,* ii, 1, 481.

Humble treaties.—*Antony and Cleopatra,* iii, 11, 62.

2 King Richard: Infer fair England's peace by this alliance.
Queen Elizabeth: Which she shall purchase with still lasting war.
Richard III. Act iv, sc. 4, l. 343.

3 This alliance may so happy prove,
To turn your households' rancour to pure love.
Romeo and Juliet. Act ii, sc. 3, l. 91. [Friar Laurence]

Dear alliance.—*Henry V,* v, 2, 273.

For alliance sake.—*I Henry VI,* ii, 5, 53.

ALMANAC

4 Here comes the almanac of my true date.
The Comedy of Errors. Act i, sc. 2, l. 41. [Antipholus of Syracuse]

5 Saturn and Venus this year in conjunction! what says the almanac to that?
II Henry IV. Act ii, sc. 4, l. 286. [Prince of Wales]

6 Is not to-morrow, boy, the ides of March?
. . . Look in the calendar, and bring me word.
Julius Cæsar. Act ii, sc. 1, l. 40. [Brutus]

A calendar, a calendar! look in the almanac.
A Midsummer-Night's Dream. Act iii, sc. 1, l. 54. [Bottom]

Give me a calendar.—*Richard III,* v, 3, 276.

Search out of the calendar.—*Pericles,* ii, 1, 58.

Calendar of gentry.—*Hamlet,* v, 2, 114.

ALMS, see under Beggar

AMAZEMENT

7 You amaze me.
As You Like It, i, 2, 115; *Much Ado about Nothing,* ii, 3, 118.

You do amaze her.—*The Merry Wives of Windsor,* v, 5, 233.

It doth amaze me.—*Julius Cæsar,* i, 2, 128.

I am amazed.—*A Midsummer-Night's Dream,* iii, 2, 220; 344; *King John,* iv, 3, 140.

I was amazed.—*King John,* iv, 2, 137.

I am amazed with matter.
Cymbeline. Act iv, sc. 3, l. 28. [Cymbeline]

It would have much amazed you.
Hamlet. Act i, sc. 2, l. 236. [Horatio]

I stood amazed.—*The Taming of the Shrew,* ii, 1, 156.

Yet you are amazed.—*Measure for Measure,* iv, 2, 224.

You are all amazed.—*The Merchant of Venice,* v, 1, 266.

Thou hast amazed me.—*Romeo and Juliet,* iii, 3, 114.

We are amazed.—*Richard II,* iii, 3, 72.

Thou art amazed.—*Richard II,* v, 2, 85.

You are amazed.—*Troilus and Cressida,* v, 3, 91.

You stand amazed; But be of comfort.
Twelfth Night. Act iii, sc. 4, l. 371. [Antonio]

All-amazed.—*The Taming of the Shrew,* iii, 2, 163. The only use of "all-amazed."

In great amazedness.—*The Merry Wives of Windsor,* iv, 4, 55. "Amazedness" is repeated in *The Winter's Tale,* v, 2, 5.

8 Am I in earth, in heaven, or in hell?
Sleeping or waking? mad or well-advised?
The Comedy of Errors. Act ii, sc. 2, l. 214. [Antipholus of Syracuse]

How come these staggers on me?
Cymbeline. Act v, sc. 5, l. 233. [Posthumus]

9 Amazement on thy mother sits.
Hamlet. Act iii, sc. 4, l. 112. [Ghost]

10 Be not amazed.
I Henry VI, i, 2, 6; *The Merry Wives of Windsor,* iii, 3, 123; v, 3, 19; *Twelfth Night,* v, 1, 271.

Stand not amazed.
Merry Wives of Windsor, v, 5, 244; *Romeo and Juliet,* iii, 1, 139; *Othello,* iv, 2, 246.

Be collected: No more amazement.
The Tempest. Act i, sc. 2, l. 13. [Prospero]

11 Wild amazement hurries up and down.
King John. Act v, sc. 1, l. 35. [Bastard]

I flamed amazement.—*The Tempest,* i, 2, 198. The only use of "flamed."

12 Amazed, my lord? why looks your highness sad?
Love's Labour's Lost. Act v, sc. 2, l. 391. [Princess of France]

My mind she has mated, and amazed my sight.
Macbeth. Act v, sc. 1, l. 86. [Doctor]

Put not yourself into amazement how these things should be.
Measure for Measure. Act iv, sc. 2, l. 220. [Duke]
All this amazement can I qualify.
Much Ado about Nothing, v, 4, 67. [Friar]

1 I shall reply amazedly.
A Midsummer-Night's Dream. Act iv, sc. 1, l. 151. [Lysander]
I speak amazedly.
Winter's Tale. Act v, sc. 1, l. 187. [Lord]
Saw amazedly.—*The Rape of Lucrece,* l. 1591.
Stands . . . amazedly.—*Macbeth,* iv, 1, 126. The only uses of "amazedly."

2 Amazement shall drive courage from the state.
Pericles. Act i, sc. 2, l. 26. [Pericles]
Stone-still, astonish'd.—*The Rape of Lucrece,* l. 1730. "Stone-still" is repeated in *King John,* iv, 1, 77.
I' the name of something holy, sir, why stand you
In this strange stare?
The Tempest. Act iii, sc. 3, l. 94. [Gonzalo]

3 All torment, trouble, wonder and amazement
Inhabits here.
The Tempest. Act v, sc. 1, l. 104. [Gonzalo]
I perceive, these lords
At this encounter do so much admire
That they devour their reason and scarce think
Their eyes do offices of truth, their words
Are natural breath.
The Tempest. Act v, sc. 1, l. 153. [Prospero]

4 Amazed, as one that unaware
Hath dropp'd a precious jewel in the flood,
Or stonish'd as night-wanderers often are,
Their light blown out in some mistrustful wood,
Even so confounded in the dark she lay,
Having lost the fair discovery of her way.
Venus and Adonis, l. 823. The only use of "stonish'd." "Night-wanderers" is repeated in *A Midsummer-Night's Dream,* ii, 1, 39; and "mistrustful" in *III Henry VI,* iv, 2, 8.
Resolve you For more amazement.
Winter's Tale. Act v, sc. 3, l. 86. [Paulina]

AMBASSADOR

5 Ambassadors from Harry King of England
Do crave admittance.
Henry V. Act ii, sc. 4, l. 65. [Messenger]
We come ambassadors from the king
Unto the commons whom thou hast misled.
II Henry VI. Act iv, sc. 7, l. 7. [Buckingham]
I came from Edward as ambassador.
III Henry VI. Act iii, sc. 3, l. 256. [Warwick]
Ambassadors of England.—*Hamlet,* v, 2, 362.
Ambassador from the French.—*Henry V,* iii, Prol., 28.
French ambassador.—*Henry VIII,* ii, 4, 172.
Ambassadors from Norway.—*Hamlet,* ii, 2, 40.
Ambassadors from Rome.—*Cymbeline,* ii, 3, 59.

6 Call the ambassadors; and, as you please,
So let them have their answers every one.
I Henry VI. Act v, sc. 1, l. 24. [King Henry]

7 He was the lord ambassador
Sent from a sort of tinkers to the king.
II Henry VI. Act iii, sc. 2, l. 276. [Suffolk]
Lord ambassador.—*III Henry VI,* iii, 3, 163; *Henry VIII,* iv, 2, 109.
Lords ambassadors.—*I Henry VI,* v, 1, 34.

8 Alas! how should you govern any kingdom,
That know not how to use ambassadors.
III Henry VI. Act iv, sc. 3, l. 35. [Warwick]

9 When you went
Ambassador to the emperor, you made bold
To carry into Flanders the great seal.
Henry VIII. Act iii, sc. 2, l. 318. [Suffolk]
Is it therefore The ambassador is silenced?
Henry VIII, i, 1, 97. [Abergavenny]

10 A message well sympathized; a horse to be ambassador for an ass.
Love's Labour's Lost. Act iii, sc. 1, l. 52. [Moth]

11 Lord Angelo, having affairs to heaven,
Intends you for his swift ambassador,
Where you shall be an everlasting leiger.
Measure for Measure. Act iii, sc. 1, l. 57. [Isabella] "Leiger" (or lieger, ledger) is repeated in *Cymbeline,* i, v, 80.
Go thou before, be our ambassador.
Titus Andronicus, iv, 4, 100. [Tamora]
Ambassadors of love.
Love's Labour's Lost, v, 2, 788; *The Merchant of Venice,* ii, 9, 92.
Great ambassadors.—*Henry VIII,* i, 4, 55.
Late ambassadors.—*Henry V,* ii, 4, 31.

AMBITION

12 His humble ambition, proud humility.
All's Well that Ends Well. Act i, sc. 1, l. 185. [Helena]
Tongue-tied ambition.—*Richard III,* iii, 7, 145.
Pitiful ambition.—*Hamlet,* iii, 2, 49.

13 Ambition,
The soldier's virtue, rather makes choice of loss,
Than gain which darkens him.
Antony and Cleopatra. Act iii, sc. 1, l. 22. [Ventidius]
Divine ambition.—*Hamlet,* iv, 4, 49.

14 Who doth ambition shun
And loves to live i' the sun,
Seeking the food he eats
And pleased with what he gets,
Come hither, come hither, come hither.
As You Like It. Act ii, sc. 5, l. 40. [Song]

15 You are ambitious for poor knaves' caps and legs.
Coriolanus. Act ii, sc. 1, l. 76. [Menenius]
Ambitious past all thinking.
Coriolanus. Act iv, sc. 6, l. 31. [Brutus]
Full of ambition.—*As You Like It,* i, 1, 149.

16 Cæsar's ambition,
Which swell'd so much that it did almost stretch
The sides o' the world.
Cymbeline, iii, 1, 49. See under CÆSAR.

Cæsar's ambition.—*Julius Cæsar,* i, 2, 324.
Somerset's ambition.—*II Henry VI,* ii, 2, 71.

1
I hold ambition of so airy and light a quality that it is but a shadow's shadow.
Hamlet. Act ii, sc. 2, l. 267. [Hamlet]

2
Ill-weaved ambition, how much art thou shrunk!
When that this body did contain a spirit,
A kingdom for it was too small a bound;
But now two paces of the vilest earth
Is room enough.
I Henry IV. Act v, sc. 4, l. 88. [Prince of Wales] The only use of "ill-weaved."

Go forward and be choked with thy ambition!
I Henry VI. Act ii, sc. 4, l. 112. [Suffolk]

Yet their ambition makes them still to fight.
The Rape of Lucrece, l. 68.

Ambition's debt is paid.—*Julius Cæsar,* iii, 1, 83.

3
Banish the canker of ambitious thoughts.
II Henry VI. Act i, sc. 2, l. 18. [Gloucester]

Fie on ambition!—*II Henry VI,* iv, 10, 1.

I would not be ambitious in my wish.
The Merchant of Venice. Act iii, sc. 2, l. 152. [Portia]

This is the period of my ambition.
The Merry Wives of Windsor. Act iii, sc. 3, l. 47. [Falstaff]

4
Were I a man, a duke, and next of blood,
I would remove these tedious stumbling-blocks
And smooth my way upon their headless necks.
II Henry VI. Act i, sc. 2, l. 63. [Duchess of Gloucester] The only use of "stumbling-blocks."

Buz these conjurations in her brain.
II Henry VI. Act i, sc. 2, l. 99. [Hume]

To see how God in all his creatures works!
Yea, man and birds are fain of climbing high
II Henry VI. Act ii, sc. 1, l. 7. [King]

Thy heaven is on earth; thine eyes and thoughts
Beat on a crown, the treasure of thy heart.
II Henry VI. Act ii, sc. 1, l. 19. [Beaufort]

5
Virtue is choked with foul ambition.
II Henry VI. Act iii, sc. 1, l. 143. [Gloucester]

Mark but my fall, and that that ruin'd me.
Cromwell, I charge thee, fling away ambition:
By that sin fell the angels; how can man, then,
The image of his Maker, hope to win by it?
Henry VIII. Act iii, sc. 2, l. 439. [Wolsey]

Out of mere ambition, you have caused
Your holy hat to be stamp'd on the king's coin.
Henry VIII. Act iii, sc. 2, l. 324. [Suffolk]

6
Lowliness is young ambition's ladder,
Whereto the climber-upward turns his face;
But when he once attains the upmost round.
He then unto the ladder turns his back,
Looks in the clouds, scorning the base degrees
By which he did ascend.
Julius Cæsar. Act ii, sc. 1, l. 22. [Brutus] The only use of "climber-upward" and "upmost."

7
No blown ambition doth our arms incite,
But love, dear love, and our aged father's right.
King Lear. Act iv, sc. 4, l. 27. [Cordelia]

8 Thou wouldst be great;
Art not without ambition, but without
The illness should attend it.
Macbeth. Act i, sc. 4, l. 19. [Lady Macbeth] The only use of "illness" in the plays.

Ambition should be made of sterner stuff.
Julius Cæsar. Act iii, sc. 2, l. 97. [Antony] "Sterner" is repeated in *As You Like It,* iii, 5, 6.

9 I have no spur
To prick the sides of my intent, but only
Vaulting ambition, which o'erleaps itself
And falls on the other.
Macbeth. Act i, sc. 7, l. 25. [Macbeth] "Vaulting" is repeated in *Henry V,* v, 2, 142, and in *Cymbeline,* i, 6, 134.

Thriftless ambition, that wilt ravin up
Thine own life's means!
Macbeth. Act ii, sc. 4, l. 28. [Ross]

10 Flesh and blood,
You, brother mine, that entertain'd ambition.
The Tempest. Act v, sc. 1, l. 75. [Prospero]

A beastly ambition, which the gods grant thee t' attain to!
Timon of Athens. Act iv, sc. 3, l. 329. [Timon]

11
Strive by factions and by friends
Ambitiously for rule and empery.
Titus Andronicus. Act i, sc. 1, l. 18. [Marcus Andronicus] "Ambitiously" is repeated in *II Henry IV,* ii, 3, 36.

Proud and ambitious tribune.—*Titus Andronicus,* i, 1, 202.

His ambition is dry.—*Troilus and Cressida,* ii, 3, 233

12
Wilt thou aspire to guide the heavenly car
And with thy daring folly burn the world?
Wilt thou reach stars, because they shine on thee?
The Two Gentlemen of Verona. Act iii, sc. 1, l. 154. [Duke]

Reaches at the moon.—*II Henry VI,* iii, 1, 158.

Who digs hills because they do aspire
Throws down one mountain to cast up a higher.
Pericles. Act i, sc. 4, l. 5. [Dionyza]

AMENDS, see under Repentance

AMITY

See also Friendship

13
To hold you in perpetual amity,
To make you brothers.
Antony and Cleopatra. Act ii, sc. 2, l. 127. [Agrippa]

Love and amity.—*II Henry IV,* iv, 2, 65; *I Henry VI,* iii, 1, 68.

14 The sooner to effect
And surer bind this knot of amity.
I Henry VI. Act v, sc. 1, l. 15. [Gloucester]

I come . . . to crave a league of amity,
And lastly to confirm that amity

With nuptial knot.
III Henry VI. Act iii, sc. 3, l. 51. [Warwick]
I will pursue the amity.—*All's Well that Ends Well,* ii, 5, 15.

1
Let in that amity which you have made.
King John. Act ii, sc. 1, l. 537. [King Philip]
We swore to you
Dear amity and everlasting love.
King John. Act v, sc. 4, l. 19. [Melun]

2 How, in one house,
Should many people, under two commands,
Hold amity?
King Lear. Act ii, sc. 4, l. 243. [Regan]

3
Madam, although I speak it in your presence,
You have a noble and a true conceit
Of god-like amity.
The Merchant of Venice. Act iii, sc. 4, l. 1. [Lorenzo]
Now thou and I are new in amity.
A Midsummer-Night's Dream. Act iv, sc. 1, l. 91. [Oberon]

4
The amity that wisdom knits not, folly may easily untie.
Troilus and Cressida. Act ii, sc. 3, l. 109. [Ulysses]

AMOROUSNESS, see Wantonness

ANCESTRY

See also Nobility

5
Though my estate be fallen, I was well born.
All's Well that Ends Well. Act iii, sc. 7, l. 4. [Widow]
Well-born bloods.—*King John,* ii, 1, 278. The only uses of "well-born."
This youth, howe'er distress'd, appears he hath had
Good ancestors.
Cymbeline. Act iv, sc. 2, l. 48. [Belarius]
Great ancestor.—*Coriolanus,* ii, 3, 253; *Julius Cæsar,* i, 2, 112.
Many ancestors.—*All's Well that Ends Well,* iv, 2, 43; 47.
Noble ancestors.—*Richard II,* ii, 1, 254.
Preceding ancestors.—*All's Well that Ends Well,* v, 3, 196.
He is true bred.—*II Henry IV,* v, 3, 71. "True-bred" (hyphenated) occurs also in *II Henry IV,* v, 3, 71; *Twelfth Night,* ii, 3, 195; and *Coriolanus,* i, 1, 247.

6
Cowards father cowards and base things sire base:
Nature hath meal and bran, contempt and grace.
Cymbeline. Act iv, sc. 2, l. 26. [Belarius]
Meal and bran.—*Coriolanus,* iii, 1, 322.
Bran and water.—*Love's Labour's Lost,* i, 1, 303.
Chaff and bran!—*Troilus and Cressida,* i, 2, 263.
Water and bran.—*Measure for Measure,* iv, 3, 160.
Leave me but the bran.—*Coriolanus,* i, 1, 150. The only uses of "bran."

7
He himself is subject to his birth:
He may not, as unvalued persons do,
Carve for himself.
Hamlet. Act i, sc. 3, l. 18. [Laertes]
Will have a wild trick of his ancestors.
I Henry IV. Act v, sc. 2, l. 11. [Worcester]

8
Honest gentlemen, I know not your breeding.
II Henry IV. Act v, sc. 3, l. 111. [Shallow]
She is as forward of her breeding as
She is i' the rear our birth.
The Winter's Tale. Act iv, sc. 4, l. 590. [Florizel] See also under MANNERS.

9
When I am sleeping with my ancestors.
II Henry IV. Act iv, sc. 4, l. 61. [King]
Give him a statue with his ancestors.
Julius Cæsar. Act iii, sc. 2, l. 55. [Citizen]
She lies buried with her ancestors.
Much Ado about Nothing. Act v, sc. 1, l. 69. [Leonato]
Burial among their ancestors.
Titus Andronicus. Act i, sc. 1, l. 84. [Titus]
Buried ancestors.—*Romeo and Juliet,* iv, 3, 41.

10
Look back into your mighty ancestors.
Henry V. Act i, sc. 2, l. 102. [Canterbury]
The blood and courage that renowned them
Runs in your veins.
Henry V. Act i, sc. 2, l. 118. [Ely]
Come they of noble family? Why, so didst thou.
Henry V. Act ii, sc. 2, l. 129. [King Henry]
He is bred out of that bloody strain
That haunted us in our familiar paths.
Henry V. Act ii, sc. 4, l. 51. [French King]

11 On, on, you noblest English,
Whose blood is fet from fathers of war-proof!
Henry V. Act iii, sc. 1, l. 17. [King Henry] Only use of "fet" (fetched, derived), and "war-proof."
Show us here
The mettle of your pasture; let us swear
That you are worth your breeding.
Henry V. Act iii, sc. 1, l. 26. [King Henry]

12 Like a hedge-born swain
That doth presume to boast of gentle blood.
I Henry VI. Act iv, sc. 1, l. 43. [Talbot] The only use of "hedge-born."
To tell thee whence thou camest, of whom derived,
Were shame enough to shame thee, wert thou not shameless.
III Henry VI. Act i, sc. 4, l. 119. [York]
Villain, thy father was a plasterer.
II Henry VI. Act iv, sc. 2, l. 140. [Stafford] The only use of "plasterer."
Your predecessors, . . . though peradventure some of the best of 'em were hereditary hangmen.
Coriolanus. Act ii, sc. 1, l. 101. [Menenius]
The sacred storehouse of his predecessors.
Macbeth, ii, 4, 34. See under GRAVE.
Great predecessors.—*Henry V,* i, 2, 248. "Predecessors" is also used in *Henry V,* i, 1, 81, and in *Coriolanus,* ii, 2, 147.

1
Sons of your progenitors.
I Henry VI. Act iv, sc. 1, l. 166. [King Henry]
Children pre-decease progenitors.—*The Rape of Lucrece,* l. 1756. The only use of "pre-decease." "Predeceased" occurs in *Henry V,* v, 1, 76.
Great progenitors.—*I Henry VI,* v, 4, 110.
Your progenitors.—*Henry V,* i, 2, 95. The only uses of "progenitors."
2
By reputing of his high descent.
II Henry VI. Act iii, sc. 1, l. 48. [Suffolk] The only use of "reputing."
Was 't you that revell'd in our parliament,
And made a preachment of your high descent?
III Henry VI. Act i, sc. 4, l. 7. [Queen] The only use of "preachment."
The house of York
From whence you spring by lineal descent.
I Henry VI. Act iii, sc. 1, l. 165. [King]
From these our Henry lineally descends.
III Henry VI. Act iii, sc. 3, l. 87. [Oxford] The only use of "lineally."
3
Nay, if thou be that princely eagle's bird,
Show thy descent by gazing 'gainst the sun.
III Henry VI. Act ii, sc. 1, l. 91. [Richard]
Do me but right, and you must all confess
That I was not ignoble of descent.
III Henry VI. Act iv, sc. 1, l. 69. [Queen]
4
But for the rest, you tell a pedigree
Of threescore and two years; a silly time
To make prescription for a kingdom's worth.
III Henry VI. Act iii, sc. 3, l. 92. [Warwick]
He
From John of Gaunt doth bring his pedigree,
Being but fourth of that heroic line.
I Henry VI. Act ii, sc. 5, l. 76. [Mortimer] The only use of "heroic."
Buckler falsehood with a pedigree.—*III Henry VI,* iii, 3, 99.
Overlook this pedigree.—*Henry V,* ii, 4, 90. The only uses of "pedigree."
5
Ancestry, whose grace
Chalks successors their way.
Henry VIII. Act i, sc. 1, l. 59. [Norfolk] The only use of "chalks." "Chalked forth the way" occurs in *The Tempest,* v, 1, 203.
All his successors gone before him hath done 't; and all his ancestors that come after him may.
The Merry Wives of Windsor. Act i, sc. 1, l. 14. [Slender]
His successor Was like to be the best.
The Winter's Tale. Act v, sc. 1, l. 48. [Paulina] The only uses of "successor."
6
My ancestors did from the streets of Rome
The Tarquin drive, when he was call'd a king.
Julius Cæsar. Act ii, sc. 1, l. 53. [Brutus]
7
Brother, adieu: good fortune come to thee!
For thou wast got i' the way of honesty.
King John. Act i, sc. 1, l. 180. [Bastard]
I am too high-born to be propertied,
To be a secondary at control,
Or useful serving man and instrument,
To any sovereign state throughout the world.
King John. Act v, sc. 2, l. 79. [Dauphin] "High-born" is repeated in *Love's Labour's Lost,* i, 1, 173; "secondary" in *Measure for Measure,* i, 1, 47; "useful" in *Antony and Cleopatra,* iv, 14, 80; and "propertied" in *Twelfth Night,* iv, 2, 99, and in *Antony and Cleopatra,* v, 2, 83.
8
I fetch my life and being
From men of royal siege, and my demerits
May speak unbonneted to as proud a fortune
As this I have reach'd.
Othello. Act i, sc. 2, l. 21. [Othello] "Unbonneted" is repeated in *King Lear,* iii, 1, 14.
My derivation was from ancestors
Who stood equivalent with mighty kings.
Pericles. Act v, sc. 1, l. 91. [Marina] The only use of "equivalent" in the plays.
Derivation of my birth.—*Henry V,* iii, 2, 141. The only uses of "derivation."
9
One vial full of Edward's sacred blood,
One flourishing branch of his most royal root.
Richard II. Act i, sc. 2, l. 17. [Duchess]
The royalties of both your bloods,
Currents that spring from one most gracious head.
Richard II. Act iii, sc. 3, l. 107. [Northumberland]
Draw forth your noble ancestry.
Richard III. Act iii, sc. 7, l. 198. [Buckingham]
We came in with Richard Conqueror.
Taming of the Shrew. Ind., sc. 1, l. 4. [Sly] The only mention of Richard the Conqueror.
Touch not the boy: he is of royal blood.
Titus Andronicus, Act v, sc. 1, l. 49. [Aaron]
10
Where the bull and cow are both milk-white,
They never do beget a coal-black calf.
Titus Andronicus. Act v, sc. 1, l. 31. [Goth]
11
Thurio: What says she to my birth?
Proteus: That you are well derived.
Two Gentlemen of Verona. Act v, sc. 2, l. 22.
A gentleman and well derived.
The Two Gentlemen of Verona, v, 4, 146. See under GENTLEMAN.
As well derived as he.—*A Midsummer-Night's Dream,* i, 1, 99.
Evenly derived
From his most famed of famous ancestors.
Henry V. Act ii, sc. 4, l. 91. [Exeter] "Evenly" is used only twice more, in *I Henry IV,* iii, 1, 103, and in *Much Ado about Nothing,* ii, 2, 7.
Derived from honourable loins.
Julius Cæsar, ii, 1, 322. See under SON.
12
Now, by the honour of my ancestry.
The Two Gentlemen of Verona. Act v, sc. 4, l. 139. [Duke of Milan]

ANCHOR

13
Posthumus anchors upon Imogen.
Cymbeline. Act v, sc. 5, l. 393. [Cymbeline]
Anchors in the Downs.—*II Henry VI,* iv, 1, 9. The only mention of the Downs.

Anchor'd in the bay.—*Sonnets,* cxxxvii.
Now at anchor.—*Pericles,* iv, Gower, 16.

1
Say Warwick was our anchor; what of that? . . .
Why, is not Oxford here another anchor?
III Henry VI. Act v, sc. 4, l. 13. [Queen]

The anchor is deep: will that humour pass?
The Merry Wives of Windsor. Act i, sc. 3, l. 56. [Nym]

2
You had much ado to make his anchor hold:
When you cast out, it still came home.
Winter's Tale. Act i, sc. 2, l. 213. [Camillo]

Nothing so certain as your anchors, who
Do their best office, if they can but stay you
Where you 'll be loath to be.
Winter's Tale. Act iv, sc. 4, l. 580. [Camillo]

ANGEL

3
What angel shall
Bless this unworthy husband?
All's Well that Ends Well. Act iii, sc. 4, l. 25. [Countess]

4
By Jupiter, an angel! or, if not,
An earthly paragon! Behold divineness!
Cymbeline. Act iii, sc. 6, l. 43. [Belarius] The only use of "divineness."

Valentine: Is she not a heavenly saint?
Proteus: No; but she is an earthly paragon.
Two Gentlemen of Verona. Act ii, sc. 4, l. 145.

An angel is like you, Kate, and you are like an angel.
Henry V. Act v, sc. 2, l. 110. [King Henry]

Few are angels.—*Henry VIII,* v, 3, 12.

5
Angels and ministers of grace defend us!
Hamlet. Act i, sc. 4, l. 39. [Hamlet]

Help, angels! Make assay!
Hamlet. Act iii, sc. 3, l. 69. [King]

Flights of angels sing thee to thy rest!
Hamlet. Act v, sc. 2, l. 371. [Horatio]

6
A ministering angel shall my sister be.
Hamlet, v, 1, 264. See under SISTER. The only use of "ministering."

Heavenly angel.—*Cymbeline,* ii, 2, 50.
Holy angel.—*Macbeth,* iii, 6, 45.
Radiant angel.—*Hamlet,* i, 5, 55.

7
And even there, methinks, an angel spake.
King John. Act v, sc. 2, l. 64. [Lewis]

8
'For,' quoth the king, 'an angel shalt thou see:
Yet fear not thou, but speak audaciously.'
The boy replied, 'An angel is not evil;
I should have fear'd her had she been a devil.'
Love's Labour's Lost. Act v, sc. 2, l. 103. [Boyet] "Audaciously" is repeated in *The Rape of Lucrece,* l. 1223.

Art thou some god, some angel, or some devil?
Julius Cæsar. Act iv, sc. 3, l. 279. [Brutus]

O, the more angel she,
And you the blacker devil!
Othello. Act v, sc. 2, l. 130. [Emilia]

9
Brutus, as you know, was Cæsar's angel.
Julius Cæsar. Act iii, sc. 2, l. 185. [Antony]

10
What angel wakes me from my flowery bed?
A Midsummer-Night's Dream. Act iii, sc. 1, l. 132. [Titania]

11
God for his Richard hath in heavenly pay
A glorious angel: then, if angels fight,
Weak men must fall, for heaven still guards the right.
Richard II. Act iii, sc. 2, l. 60. [King Richard]

Wonderful, when angels are so angry.
Richard III. Act i, sc. 2, l. 74. [Gloucester]

God's angel.—*I Henry IV,* iii, 3, 40.

12
O, speak again, bright angel! for thou art
As glorious to this night, being o'er my head,
As is a winged messenger of heaven
Unto the white-upturned wondering eyes
Of mortals that fall back to gaze on him
When he bestrides the lazy-pacing clouds
And sails upon the bosom of the air.
Romeo and Juliet. Act ii, sc. 2, l. 26. [Romeo] The only use of "white-upturned" and "lazy-pacing."

Angels are bright still, though the brightest fell.
Macbeth. Act iv, sc. 3, l. 22. [Malcolm]

13
At last I spied
An ancient angel coming down the hill.
The Taming of the Shrew. Act iv, sc. 2, l. 60. [Biondello]

Bending angels.—*Troilus and Cressida,* i, 3, 236.

II—Angels Good and Bad

14
He that came behind you, sir, like an evil angel.
The Comedy of Errors. Act iv, sc. 3, l. 19. [Dromio of Syracuse]

Evil angel.—*Love's Labour's Lost,* i, 2, 178.

You follow the young prince up and down, like his ill angel.
II Henry IV. Act i, sc. 2, l. 186. [Chief Justice]

Croak not, black angel; I have no food for thee.
King Lear. Act iii, sc. 6, l. 33. [Edgar]

15
O, my sweet beef, I must still be good angel to thee.
I Henry IV. Act iii, sc. 3, l. 199. [Prince]

There is a good angel about him; but the devil outbids him too.
II Henry IV. Act ii, sc. 4, l. 363. [Falstaff]

Go with me, like good angels, to my end.
Henry VIII. Act ii, sc. 1, l. 75. [Buckingham]

Good angels keep it from us!
Henry VIII. Act ii, sc. 1, l. 142. [Gentleman]

Now, good angels
Fly o'er thy royal head, and shade thy person
Under their blessed wings!
Henry VIII. Act v, sc. 1, l. 159. [Old Lady]

16
Good angels guard thy battle!
Richard III. Act v, sc. 3, l. 138. [Ghost of the Duke of Clarence]

Good angels guard thee from the boar's annoy!
Richard III. Act v, sc. 3, l. 156. [Ghosts of the two young Princes]

Good angels guard thee!—*Richard III*, iv, 1, 93.

God and good angels fight on Richmond's side.
Richard III. Act v, sc. 3, l. 175. [Ghost]

Good angels Preserve the king.
The Tempest. Act ii, sc. 1, l. 307. [Gonzalo]

III—Guardian Angel

1
Thy demon, that's thy spirit which keeps thee, is
Noble, courageous, high, unmatchable,
Where Cæsar's is not; but, near him, thy angel
Becomes a fear, as being o'erpower'd.
Antony and Cleopatra. Act ii, sc. 3, l. 19. [Soothsayer]

Thy spirit
Is all afraid to govern thee near him.
Antony and Cleopatra. Act ii, sc. 3, l. 28. [Soothsayer]

2
One of these men is Genius to the other.
The Comedy of Errors. Act v, sc. 1, l. 332. [Duke]

The Genius and the mortal instruments
Are then in counsel.
Julius Cæsar. Act ii, sc. 1, l. 66. [Brutus]

Under him, My Genius is rebuked.
Macbeth. Act iii, sc. 1, l. 55. [Macbeth]

Hark! you are call'd: some day the Genius so
Cries 'come' to him that instantly must die.
Troilus and Cressida. Act iv, sc. 4, l. 52. [Troilus]

Our worser genius.—*The Tempest*, iv, 1, 27.

3
Save me, and hover o'er me with your wings,
You heavenly guards!
Hamlet. Act iii, sc. 4, l. 103. [Hamlet]

4
Yea, curse his better angel from his side,
And fall to reprobation.
Othello. Act v, sc. 2, l. 208. [Gratiano] The only use of "reprobation."

The better angel is a man right fair,
The worser spirit a woman colour'd ill.
To win me soon to hell, my female evil
Tempteth my better angel from my side,
And would corrupt my saint to be a devil,
Wooing his purity with her foul pride.
Sonnets. No. cxliv. Also *The Passionate Pilgrim*, l. 17.

I guess one angel in another's hell:
Yet this shall I ne'er know, but live in doubt,
Till my bad angel fire my good one out.
Sonnets. No. cxliv. Also *The Passionate Pilgrim*, l. 27.

5
O, a cherubin
Thou wast that did preserve me.
The Tempest. Act i, sc. 2, l. 152. [Prospero]

IV—Angel: An English Coin

6
They have in England
A coin that bears the figure of an angel
Stamped in gold.
The Merchant of Venice. Act ii, sc. 7, l. 55. [Prince of Morocco]

7
Here are the angels that you sent for.
The Comedy of Errors. Act iv, sc. 3, l. 41. [Dromio of Syracuse]

8
See thou shake the bags
Of hoarding abbots; imprisoned angels
Set at liberty.
King John. Act iii, sc. 3, l. 7. [King John]

His fair angels would salute my palm.
King John, ii, 1, 590. See under PALM.

9
Falstaff: He hath a legion of angels. . . .
Nym: Humour me with angels.
Merry Wives of Windsor. Act i, sc. 3, l. 60.

I had myself twenty angels given me this morning; but I defy all angels, in any such sort, as they say, but in the way of honesty.
The Merry Wives of Windsor. Act ii, sc. 2, l. 73. [Mistress Quickly]

ANGER

See also Annoyance, Choler, Frown, Fury, Rage, Spleen, Wrath

10
He makes me angry with him; for he seems
Proud and disdainful, harping on what I am,
Not what he knew I was.
Antony and Cleopatra. Act iii, sc. 13, l. 141. [Antony]

11
Never anger Made good guard for itself.
Antony and Cleopatra. Act iv, sc. 1, l. 9 [Mecænas]

12
She'll fall in love with my anger.
As You Like It. Act iii, sc. 5, l. 67. [Rosalind]

I will be bitter with him and passing short.
As You Like It. Act iii, sc. 5, l. 138. [Phebe]

It bears an angry tenour.
As You Like It. Act iv, sc. 3, l. 11. [Silvius]

13
It would make a man mad as a buck, to be so bought and sold.
The Comedy of Errors. Act iii, sc. 1, l. 72. [Dromio of Ephesus]

Wherefore dost thou mad me?
The Comedy of Errors, iv, 4, 129.

Would mad or man or beast.
The Comedy of Errors, v, 1, 84.

God's bread! It makes me mad.
Romeo and Juliet. Act iii, sc. 5, l. 177. [Capulet]

An 'twere to me, I should be mad at it.
The Merchant of Venice. Act v, sc. 1, l. 176. [Portia]

He made me mad.—*I Henry IV*, i, 3, 53.

Peace, cousin Percy; you will make him mad.
I Henry IV. Act iii, sc. 1, l. 52. [Mortimer]

It will inflame you, it will make you mad.
Julius Cæsar. Act iii, sc. 2, l. 149. [Antony]

He'll find the young man there and be mad!
The Merry Wives of Windsor. Act i, sc. 4, l. 69. [Mistress Quickly]

O, he is more mad
Than Telamon for his shield; the boar of Thessaly

Was never so emboss'd.
Antony and Cleopatra. Act iv, sc. 13, l. 1. [Cleopatra]

He is very courageous mad about his throwing into the water.
The Merry Wives of Windsor. Act iv, sc. 1, l. 4. [Mistress Quickly]

He would have been horn-mad.—*The Merry Wives of Windsor,* i, 4, 51. "Horn-mad" is also in *The Comedy of Errors,* ii, 1, 57; *The Merry Wives of Windsor,* iii, 5, 155; and *Much Ado about Nothing,* i, 1, 272. It means mad enough to horn any one—stark mad.

1
Give your dispositions the reins, and be angry at your pleasures.
Coriolanus. Act ii, sc. 1, l. 33. [Menenius]

Anger 's my meat; I sup upon myself,
And so shall starve with feeding.
Coriolanus. Act iv, sc. 2, l. 52. [Volumnia]

All 's in anger.—*Coriolanus,* iii, 2, 95.

2
For more is to be said and to be done
Than out of anger can be uttered.
I Henry IV. Act i, sc. 1, l. 106. [King Henry]

To keep his anger still in motion.
I Henry IV. Act i, sc. 3, l. 226. [Hotspur]

'Tis not for fear but anger that my cheeks Blush.
I Henry VI. Act ii, sc. 4, l. 65. [Somerset]

3
Who struck this heat up?
I Henry IV. Act i, sc. 3, l. 139. [Worcester]

Take heed, lest by your heat you burn yourselves.
II Henry VI. Act v, sc. 1, l. 160. [Clifford]

You 'll heat my blood.—*Antony and Cleopatra,* i, 3, 80.

4
Now ye grow too hot.
II Henry VI. Act i, sc. 1, l. 137. [Beaufort]

Are you so hot?—*I Henry VI,* iii, 2, 58; *Romeo and Juliet,* ii, 5, 64.

Finds the testy gentleman so hot.
Richard III. Act iii, sc. 4, l. 39. [Gloucester]

You are too hot.—*Romeo and Juliet,* iii, 5, 176.

Be not so hot.—*Measure for Measure,* v, 1, 315.

Not so hot, good sir.—*Winter's Tale,* ii, 3, 32.

5
Nay, be not angry.
II Henry VI. Act i, sc. 2, l. 55. [Gloucester]
Repeated a dozen times in later plays.

Nay, do not fright us with an angry look.
II Henry VI. Act v, sc. 1, l. 126. [York]

6
It angered him to the heart.
II Henry IV. Act ii, sc. 4, l. 9. [Drawer]

By the mass, I could anger her to the heart.
II Henry IV. Act iii, sc. 2, l. 216. [Shallow]

7
Pistol's cock is up,
And flashing fire will follow.
Henry V. Act ii, sc. 1, l. 55. [Pistol]

8
Here comes the queen, whose looks bewray her anger.
III Henry VI. Act i, sc. 1, l. 211. [Exeter]

By some of these The queen is put in anger.
Henry VIII. Act ii, sc. 4, l. 160. [King Henry]

Red cheeks and fiery eyes blaze forth her wrong.
Venus and Adonis, l. 219.

She is sad and passionate at your highness' tent.
King John. Act ii, sc. 1, l. 544. [Dauphin]

9
He knits his brow and shows an angry eye
And passeth by with stiff unbowed knee,
Disdaining duty that to us belongs.
II Henry VI. Act iii, sc. 1, l. 15. [Queen]
"Unbowed" is repeated in *Tempest,* i, 2, 115.

10
O, I could hew up rocks and fight with flint,
I am so angry at these abject terms.
II Henry VI. Act v, sc. 1, l. 24. . [York]

My heart for anger burns; I cannot brook it.
III Henry VI. Act i, sc. 1, l. 60. [Westmoreland]

Stamp, rave, and fret, that I may sing and dance.
III Henry VI. Act i, sc. 4, l. 91. [Queen]

Why, how now, kinsman! wherefore storm you so?
Romeo and Juliet. Act i, sc. 5, l. 62. [Capulet]

11
Anger is like
A full-hot horse, who being allow'd his way,
Self-mettle tires him.
Henry VIII. Act i, sc. 1, l. 132. [Norfolk]
The only use of "full-hot" and "self-mettle."

12
Suffolk: I do assure you
The king cried Ha! at this.
Lord Chamberlain: Now, God incense him,
And let him cry Ha! louder!
Henry VIII. Act iii, sc. 2, l. 60.

The king Does whet his anger to him.
Henry VIII. Act iii, sc. 2, l. 91. [Suffolk]

The king is angry: see, he bites the lip.
Richard III. Act iv, sc. 2, l. 27. [Catesby]

13
What should this mean?
What sudden anger 's this? how have I reap'd it?
He parted frowning from me, as if ruin
Leap'd from his eyes; so looks the chafed lion
Upon the daring huntsman that has gall'd him;
Then makes him nothing.
Henry VIII. Act iii, sc. 2, l. 203. [Wolsey]

14
The angry spot doth glow on Cæsar's brow.
Julius Cæsar. Act i, sc. 2, l. 183. [Brutus]

Must I budge?
Must I observe you? must I stand and crouch
Under your testy humour?
Julius Cæsar. Act iv, sc. 3, l. 44. [Brutus]

Be angry when you will, it shall have scope.
Julius Cæsar. Act iv, sc. 3, l. 108. [Brutus]

You are yoked with a lamb
That carries anger as the flint bears fire;
Who, much enforced, shows a hasty spark,
And straight is cold again.
Julius Cæsar. Act iv, sc. 3, l. 110. [Brutus]

I did not think you could have been so angry.
Julius Cæsar. Act iv, sc. 3, l. 143. [Cassius]

15
Nor look upon the iron angerly.
King John. Act iv, sc. 1, l. 82. [Arthur]

How angerly I taught my brow to frown.
The Two Gentlemen of Verona. Act i, sc. 2, l. 62. [Julia]

You look angerly.—*Macbeth,* iii, 5, 1. The only uses of "angerly."

1
Anger hath a privilege.
King Lear. Act ii, sc. 2, l. 76. [Kent]
Touch me with noble anger.
King Lear. Act ii, sc. 4, l. 279. [King Lear]
Nay, then, come on, and take the chance of anger.
King Lear. Act iii, sc. 7, l. 79. [First Servant]
Red-look'd anger.—*The Winter's Tale,* ii, 2, 34. The only use of "red-look'd."
2
I beseech you, be not so phlegmatic.
The Merry Wives of Windsor. Act i, sc. 4, l. 79. [Mistress Quickly] The only use of "phlegmatic."
3
Don Pedro: I think he be angry indeed.
Claudio: If he be, he knows how to turn his girdle.
Much Ado about Nothing. Act v, sc. 1, l. 141.
There 's matter in 't indeed, if he be angry.
Othello. Act iii, sc. 4, l. 139. [Iago]
Something . . . Hath puddled his clear spirit.
Othello. Act iii, sc. 4, l. 140. [Desdemona] "Puddled" is repeated in *The Comedy of Errors,* v, 1, 173.
4
I have rubb'd this young quat almost to the sense,
And he grows angry.
Othello. Act v, sc. 1, l. 11. [Iago] The only use of "quat" (pimple).
5
And, being anger'd, puffs away from thence.
Romeo and Juliet. Act i, sc. 4, l. 102. [Romeo]
You part in anger.
Troilus and Cressida. Act v, sc. 2, l. 45. [Cressida]
6
The bloody spur cannot provoke him on
That sometimes anger thrusts into his side.
Sonnets. No. 1.
7
They say, my lords, 'ira furor brevis est'; but yond man is ever angry.
Timon of Athens. Act i, sc. 2, l. 28. [Timon] The only use of the Latin proverb.
He did behave his anger, ere 'twas spent,
As if he had but proved an argument.
Timon of Athens. Act iii, sc. 5, l. 22. [Alcibiades] The only use of "behave."
To be in anger is impiety;
But who is man that is not angry?
Timon of Athens. Act iii, sc. 5, l. 54. [Alcibiades]
Do you dare our anger?
'Tis in few words, but spacious in effect.
Timon of Athens. Act iii, sc. 5, l. 96. [Senator]
8
The knight is incensed against you, even to a mortal arbitrement.
Twelfth Night. Act iii, sc. 4, l. 285. [Fabian]

ANGLING, see Fishing

ANIMAL

See also Beast

9
The wretched animal heaved forth such groans
That their discharge did stretch his leathern coat
Almost to bursting, and the big round tears
Coursed one another down his innocent nose
In piteous chase.
As You Like It. Act ii, sc. 1, l. 36. [First Lord] The only use of "bursting."
To fright the animals and kill them up
In their assign'd and native dwelling-place.
As You Like It. Act iii, sc. 1, l. 62. [Lord]
Animals on his dunghills.—*As You Like It,* i, 1, 16.
Forked animal.—*King Lear,* iii, 4, 113.
Pamper'd animals.—*Much Ado about Nothing,* iv, 1, 61.
The paragon of animals!—*Hamlet,* ii, 2, 320.
10
Coward hares, hot goats, and venison.
Cymbeline. Act iv, sc. 4, l. 37. [Arviragus]
To be a dog, a mule, a cat, a fitchew, a toad, a lizard, an owl, a puttock, or a herring without a roe, I would not care.
Troilus and Cressida, v, 1, 67. [Thersites]
11
He is only an animal, only sensible in the duller parts.
Love's Labour 's Lost. Act iv, sc. 2, l. 27. [Sir Nathaniel]

ANNOYANCE

See also Anger, Choler, Gall, Rage, Vexation, Worry

12
How this Herculean Roman does become
The carriage of his chafe.
Antony and Cleopatra. Act i, sc. 3, l. 84. [Cleopatra] The only use of "Herculean."
Being once chafed, he cannot
Be rein'd again to temperance.
Coriolanus. Act iii, sc. 3, l. 27. [Brutus]
I chafe you, if I tarry: let me go.
The Taming of the Shrew. Act ii, sc. 1, l. 243. [Katharina]
Do not chafe thee, cousin.
Troilus and Cressida. Act iv, sc. 5, l. 260. [Ajax]
What, are you chafed?—*Henry VIII,* i, 1, 123.
All swoln with chafing.—*Venus and Adonis,* l. 325. "Chafing" is used only once in the plays, in *Julius Cæsar,* i, 2, 101.
13
His means
If he improve them, may well stretch so far
As to annoy us all.
Julius Cæsar. Act ii, sc. 1, l. 158. [Cassius] The only use of "improve."
14
Remove from her the means of all annoyance.
Macbeth. Act v, sc. 1, l. 84. [Doctor]
Doing annoyance.—*Richard II,* iii, 2, 16.
Annoy my finger.—*Henry V,* ii, 2, 103.
Annoy our foot.—*II Henry VI,* iii, 1, 67.
She will not be annoy'd with suitors.
The Taming of the Shrew, i, 1, 189. See under SUITOR. The only use of "annoyed."
15
Why art thou then exasperate?
Troilus and Cressida, v, 1, 34. [Thersites]
To exasperate you.—*Twelfth Night,* iii, 2, 20.

1 Worse than Tantalus' is her annoy,
To clip Elysium and to lack her joy.
Venus and Adonis, l. 599.

Still-pining Tantalus.—*The Rape of Lucrece*, l. 858. The only references to Tantalus, and the only use of "still-pining."

Why lovest thou that which thou receivest not gladly,
Or else receivest with pleasure thine annoy?
Sonnets. No. viii.

ANSWER

See also Question, Reply

2
To answer you as you would be understood.
All's Well that Ends Well. Act iv, sc. 3, l. 123. [Lord]

Soldier: Shall I set down your answer so?
Parolles: Do: I'll take the sacrament on't, how and which way you will.
All's Well that Ends Well. Act iv, sc. 3, l. 155.

Clown: I have an answer will serve all men.
Countess: Marry, that's a bountiful answer that fits all questions. . . . Will your answer serve fit to all questions?
Clown: As fit as ten groats is for the hand of an attorney, as your French crown for your taffeta punk, as Tib's rush for Tom's forefinger, as a pancake for Shrove Tuesday, a morris for May-day, as the nail to his hole, the cuckold to his horn, as a scolding quean to a wrangling knave, as the nun's lip to the friar's mouth, nay, as the pudding to his skin.
All's Well that Ends Well. Act ii, sc. 2, l. 14. "Forefinger" is repeated in *Romeo and Juliet*, i, 4, 56, and "morris" in *A Midsummer-Night's Dream*, ii, 1, 98. Tib is mentioned again in *Pericles*, iv, 6, 176, and May-day in *Henry VIII*, v, 4, 15. The only reference to Shrove Tuesday. "Pancake" is used four times. For "quean" see under WHORE.

3
You have answered to his reputation with the duke.
All's Well that Ends Well. Act iv, sc. 3, l. 277. [Soldier]

Answer'd my affection.—*The Merry Wives of Windsor*, iv, 6, 10.

Answer'd for his deed.—*Measure for Measure*, ii, 2, 93.

Answer'd their cries.—*The Rape of Lucrece*, l. 1806.

I must be answer'd.—*Winter's Tale*, i, 2, 399.

What, are you answer'd yet?—*The Merchant of Venice*, iv, 1, 46.

Are you answer'd?—*The Merchant of Venice*, iv, 1, 62.

Darkly answer'd.—*Measure for Measure*, iii, 2, 198.

Quickly answer'd.—*III Henry VI*, iii, 1, 133.

Surest answered.—*Julius Cæsar*, iv, 1, 47.

4
I cannot answer thee acutely.
All's Well that Ends Well. Act i, sc. 1, l. 220. [Parolles] The only use of "acutely."

I could not answer in that course of honour
As she had made the overture.
All's Well that Ends Well. Act v, sc. 3, l. 98. [Bertram]

5
No more light answers.
Antony and Cleopatra. Act i, sc. 2, l. 183. [Antony]

Heaviest answer.—*Timon of Athens*, v, 4, 63.

Present answer.—*All's Well that Ends Well*, ii, 2, 67.

Stubborn answer.—*Henry VIII*, ii, 2, 346.

6
I shall entreat him To answer like himself.
Antony and Cleopatra. Act ii, sc. 2, l. 3. [Enobarbus]

7
Le Beau: How shall I answer you?
Rosalind: As wit and fortune will.
As You Like It. Act i, sc. 2, l. 109.

How answer you?—*Henry V*, v, 2, 230.

How is that answer'd?—*I Henry IV*, iii, 3, 198.

8
Answer me in one word.
As You Like It. Act iii, sc. 2, l. 237. [Rosalind]

To say ay and no to these particulars is more than to answer in a catechism.
As You Like It. Act iii, sc. 2, l. 240. [Celia] "Catechism" is repeated in *I Henry IV*, v, 1, 144: "So ends my catechism."

Lady Grey: Please you dismiss me, either with 'ay' or 'no.'
King Edward: Ay, if thou wilt say 'ay' to my request;
No, if thou dost say 'no' to my demand.
III Henry VI. Act iii, sc. 2, l. 78.

9
You are full of pretty answers.
As You Like It. Act iii, sc. 2, l. 287. [Jaques]

They laughed not so much at the hair as at his pretty answer.
Troilus and Cressida. Act i, sc. 2, l. 168. [Pandar]

10
Why pratest thou to thyself and answer'st not?
The Comedy of Errors. Act ii, sc. 2, l. 195. [Luciana]

Thou answerest me not to the purpose
Hamlet. Act v, sc. 1, l. 43. [Hamlet]

Thou answer'st, 'she is fair.'
Troilus and Cressida, i, 1, 52. The only uses of "answerest."

11
Second Merchant: Good sir, say whether you'll answer me or no. . . .
Antipholus of Ephesus: I answer you! what should I answer you?
The Comedy of Errors. Act iv, sc. 1, l. 60.

Wilt thou not answer?—*Antony and Cleopatra*, iv, 14, 115.

12
He is himself alone To answer all the city.
Coriolanus. Act i, sc. 4, l. 51. [Soldier]

13
Deliver with more openness your answers.
Cymbeline. Act i, sc. 6, l. 88. [Imogen]

14
There's no answer
That will be given to the loudest noise we make.
Cymbeline. Act iii, sc. 5, l. 43. [Attendant]

No answer?—*Cymbeline*, iii, 6, 24.

There is no answer made.—*Henry V*, v, 2, 75.
Answer made it none.—*Hamlet*, i, 2, 215.
Answer have I none.—*Othello*, iv, 2, 103.
Answer none.—*Measure for Measure*, ii, 1, 39.

Give answer to this boy, and do it freely.
Cymbeline. Act v, sc. 5, l. 131. [Cymbeline]
Shall I give him answer?—*I Henry IV*, ii, 4, 326.
Give answer.—*A Midsummer-Night's Dream*, iv, 1, 141.

2
Out of my grief and my impatience,
Answer'd neglectingly I know not what.
I Henry IV. Act i, sc. 3, l. 51. [Hotspur]
The only use of "neglectingly."
If thou love me, practise an answer.
I Henry IV. Act ii, sc. 4, l. 411. [Falstaff]

3
Shall I return this answer to the king?
I Henry IV. Act iv, sc. 3, l. 106. [Blunt]
Bear my former answer back.—*Henry V*, iv, 3, 90.
He himself will answer.—*II Henry IV*, i, 1, 6.
Answer royally.—*Henry V*, ii, 4, 3.

4
I pray ye, since my exion is entered and my case so openly known to the world, let him be brought in to his answer.
II Henry IV, ii, 1, 32. The only use of "exion" (blunder).
Put us to our answer.—*Cymbeline*, iv, 2, 161.
The answer is ready as a borrower's cap.
II Henry IV. Act ii, sc. 2, l. 124. [Poins]
I do say thou art quick in answers.
Love's Labour's Lost. Act i, sc. 2, l. 31. [Armado]

5
Answer, thou dead elm, answer.
II Henry IV. Act ii, sc. 4, l. 358. [Poins]
Give me your answer.—*Henry V*, v, 2, 133.
Answer, if you can.—*II Henry VI*, iv, 2, 179.
Do but answer this.—*III Henry VI*, v, 1, 40.
Answer to this.—*Measure for Measure*, ii, 4, 60; *Much Ado about Nothing*, iv, 1, 86.
Your answer to that.—*The Merchant of Venice*, i, 3, 11.
Answer to that.—*Romeo and Juliet*, ii, 5, 35.
Let him answer me.—*Much Ado about Nothing*, v, 1, 82.
Let me answer.—*All's Well that Ends Well*, iv, 2, 206.
Answer me directly.—*Julius Cæsar*, i, 1, 12.
You shall answer it.—*Richard III*, iv, 2, 96.

6
Thou wilt answer this before the pope.
I Henry VI. Act i, sc. 3, l. 52. [Winchester]
Let them have their answers every one.
I Henry VI, v, 1, 25. See under AMBASSADOR.
I would that you would answer me.
I Henry VI. Act v, sc. 3, l. 87. [Margaret]
Answer of thy just demand.—*I Henry VI*, v, 3, 144.

7 Pardon me,
That I have given no answer all this while.
II Henry VI. Act v, sc. 1, l. 32. [York]
What canst thou answer?—*II Henry VI*, iv, 7, 29.

8
Ay, crook-back, here I stand to answer thee,
Or any he the proudest of thy sort.
III Henry VI. Act ii, sc. 2, l. 96. [Clifford]
"Crook-back" is repeated in i, v, 75, and in v, 5, 30, and occurs in no other play.
Thus did he answer me.—*Cymbeline*, iv, 2, 41.

9 How to make ye suddenly an answer,
In such a point of weight, . . . In truth, I know not.
Henry VIII. Act iii, sc. 1, l. 70. [Queen]
Make thee answer.—*Romeo and Juliet*, iii, 2, 49.
I dare make his answer.—*Much Ado about Nothing*, iv, 1, 18.
I'll make answer.—*Antony and Cleopatra*, ii, 7, 107.
What answer makes your grace?—*I Henry VI*, v, 3, 150; *II Henry VI*, iv, 4, 7.
Let me make answer.—*King John*, ii, 1, 121.
Make answer.—*II Henry VI*, i, 2, 80.

10
Lacking wit To make a seemly answer.
Henry VIII, iii, 1, 177. The only use of "seemly."
Fairly answer'd.—*Henry VIII*, iii, 2, 179.

11
Second Citizen: Answer every man directly.
First Citizen: Ay, and briefly.
Fourth Citizen: Ay, and wisely.
Third Citizen: Ay, and truly, you were best.
Julius Cæsar. Act iii, sc. 3, l. 10.
To answer every man directly and briefly, wisely and truly.
Julius Cæsar. Act iii, sc. 3, l. 16. [Cinna]
Answer them directly.—*II Henry IV*, iv, 2, 52.
That matter is answered directly.
Julius Cæsar. Act iii, sc. 3, l. 25. [Citizen]
Answer'd indirectly.—*I Henry IV*, i, 3, 66.
Come, sir, leave me your snatches, and yield me a direct answer.
Measure for Measure. Act iv, sc. 2, l. 6. [Provost] The only use of "direct answer."

12
Should I have answer'd Caius Cassius so?
Julius Cæsar. Act iv, sc. 3, l. 78. [Brutus]

13
Answering before we do demand of them.
Julius Cæsar. Act v, sc. 1, l. 6. [Octavius]
Answering us with our own charge.
Coriolanus. Act v, sc. 6, l. 67. [Lord]
Answering the aim.—*Troilus and Cressida*, i, 3, 15.
Answering every call.—*Venus and Adonis*, l. 849.
Answering the most strange inquire.—*Pericles*, iii, Gower, 22.
Answering the letter.—*Cymbeline*, v, 5, 450.
Answering A slave.—*Cymbeline*, iv, 2, 73.
Answering to the weight.—*Antony and Cleopatra*, v, 2, 102.
Answering one foul wrong.—*Measure for Measure*, ii, 2, 103.

14
We will answer on their charge.
Julius Cæsar. Act v, sc. 1, l. 24. [Antony]
Answer to my just belief.—*Pericles*, v, 1, 239.
Answer to your embassy.—*King John*, ii, 1, 44.
Answer to my lust.—*Troilus and Cressida*, iv, 4, 134.
Answer to his part.—*Winter's Tale*, v, 3, 153.

15
When I have said, make answer to us both.
King John. Act ii, sc. 1, l. 235. [King Philip]
Thou canst not, cardinal, devise a name
So slight, unworthy and ridiculous,

To charge me to an answer.
King John. Act iii, sc. 1, l. 149. [King John]
This must be answer'd either here or hence.
King John. Act iv, sc. 2, l. 89. [Pembroke]

1 O, be removed from him, and answer well!
King John. Act iii, sc. 1, l. 218. [Constance]
Answer well.—*Hamlet,* iii, 4, 176.
Answered him well.—*The Comedy of Errors,* iii, 1, 54.

2 Heaven he knows how we shall answer him.
King John. Act v, sc. 7, l. 60. [Bastard]
Now we shall know some answer.—*Timon of Athens,* iii, 4, 67.
Shall I know your answer?—*The Merchant of Venice,* 1, 3, 8.
Know her answer.—*The Taming of the Shrew,* v, 2, 97.
Know your answer.—*The Merchant of Venice,* iv, 1, 146.

3 He answered me in the roundest manner.
King Lear. Act i, sc. 4, l. 58. [Knight] The only use of "roundest."
Peremptory answer.—*Henry V,* v, 2, 82.

4 Fetch me a better answer.
King Lear. Act ii, sc. 4, l. 82. [King Lear]
Better answer.—*Much Ado about Nothing,* iii, 3, 49.

5 Lady, I am not well; else I should answer
From a full-flowing stomach.
King Lear. Act v, sc. 3, l. 73. [Regan] The only use of "full-flowing."

6 The cloudy messenger turns me his back,
And hums, as who would say 'You 'll rue the time
That clogs me with this answer.'
Macbeth. Act iii, sc. 6, l. 41. [Lord]

7 Macbeth: Answer me To what I ask you.
First Witch: Speak.
Second Witch: Demand.
Third Witch: We 'll answer.
Macbeth. Act iv, sc. 1, l. 60.
Answer me one doubt.—*III Henry VI,* iii, 3, 238.
Answer me to that.—*I Henry IV,* ii, 4, 157.

8 Let me desire you to make your answer before him.
Measure for Measure. Act iii, sc. 2, l. 164. [Duke]
Answer me to-morrow.—*Measure for Measure,* ii, 4, 167.
Answer it at your peril.—*Measure for Measure,* iv, 2, 130.
You 'll answer this one day.
Measure for Measure. Act iv, sc. 3, l. 172. [Duke]

9 We shall expect a gentle answer, Jew.
The Merchant of Venice. Act iv, sc. 1, l. 34. [Duke]
Now for your answer.—*The Merchant of Venice,* iv, 1, 52.
This is no answer, thou unfeeling man.
The Merchant of Venice. Act iv, sc. 1, l. 63. [Bassanio]
This is no answer.—*Cymbeline,* ii, 3, 98.
I am not bound to please thee with my answers.
The Merchant of Venice. Act iv, sc. 1, l. 65. [Shylock]

10 Tut, a pin! this shall be answered.
The Merry Wives of Windsor. Act i, sc. 1, l. 117. [Shallow]
It is a fery discretion answer.
The Merry Wives of Windsor. Act i, sc. 1, l. 261. [Evans]
This day we shall have our answer.
The Merry Wives of Windsor. Act iii, sc. 2, l. 60. [Shallow]

11 What, will you tear
Impatient answers from my gentle tongue?
A Midsummer-Night's Dream. Act iii, sc. 2, l. 286. [Helena]

12 Mark how short his answer is.
Much Ado about Nothing. Act i, sc. 1, l. 215. [Benedick]
You know your answer.—*Much Ado about Nothing,* ii, 1, 71.
I knew it would be your answer.
Much Ado about Nothing. Act iii, sc. 3, l. 19. [Dogberry]
I will owe thee an answer for that.
Much Ado about Nothing. Act iii, sc. 3, l. 108. [Conrade]
Bid her answer truly.
. . . Answer truly to your name.
Much Ado about Nothing. Act iv, sc. 1, l. 76. [Claudio]

13 Thus answer I in name of Benedick.
Much Ado about Nothing. Act ii, sc. 1, l. 179. [Claudio]
I answer to that name.—*Much Ado about Nothing,* v, 4, 73.
Answer . . . in our name.—*Antony and Cleopatra,* v, 2, 178.

14 Let me go no farther to mine answer.
Much Ado about Nothing. Act v, sc. 1, l. 237. [Borachio]
I know no answer.—*King Lear,* i, 1, 204.
Stand not to answer.—*Julius Cæsar,* v, 3, 43.
Dares not answer nay.—*A Midsummer-Night's Dream,* iii, 1, 136.
Answer nay.—*Richard III,* iii, 7, 51.

15 How answer you for yourselves?
Much Ado about Nothing. Act iv, sc. 2, l. 25. [Dogberry]
How answer you that?—*A Midsummer-Night's Dream,* iii, 1, 12.

16 Your answer, sir, is enigmatical.
Much Ado about Nothing. Act v, sc. 4, l. 27. [Benedick] The only use of "enigmatical."
Is that an answer?
The Taming of the Shrew. Act v, sc. 2, l. 83. [Petruchio]
We cannot take this for an answer.
Timon of Athens. Act iii, sc. 4, l. 78. [Titus]
I cannot be so answer'd.
Twelfth Night. Act ii, sc. 4, l. 91. [Duke]
Had I as many mouths as Hydra, such an answer would stop them all.
Othello. Act ii, sc. 3, l. 307. [Cassio]

1 At length address'd to answer his desire.
The Rape of Lucrece, l. 1606.
I come To answer thy best pleasure.
The Tempest. Act i, sc. 2, l. 190. [Ariel]
Answer all things faithfully.—*The Merchant of Venice,* v, 1, 299.
Answer as I call you.—*A Midsummer-Night's Dream,* i, 2, 18.
Answer every strain.—*Much Ado about Nothing,* v, 1, 12.
Answer his demand.—*III Henry VI,* iii, 3, 259.
Answer his emptiness!—*Antony and Cleopatra,* iii, 13, 36.
Answer his requiring.—*Measure for Measure,* iii, 1, 253.
Answer my distress.—*Titus Andronicus,* iii, 1, 38.
Answer my good will.—*The Comedy of Errors,* iii, 1, 20.
Answer my mind.—*Much Ado about Nothing,* ii, 1, 376.
Answer other business.—*The Tempest,* i, 2, 367.
Answer our hope.—*I Henry VI,* v, 5, 72.
Answer your master.—*The Merry Wives of Windsor,* iv, 1, 20.
Answer your summons.—*Tempest,* iv, 1, 131.

2 What answer shall I make to this base man?
Richard II. Act iv, sc. 1, l. 20. [Aumerle]
Who shall answer him?—*Troilus and Cressida,* ii, 1, 139.

3 Definitely thus I answer you.
Richard III. Act iii, sc. 7, l. 153. [Gloucester] The only use of "definitely."
I answer you for that.—*Henry V,* v, 2, 319.
I will answer it straight.—*The Merry Wives of Windsor,* i, 1, 118.
I will answer any thing.
Othello. Act i, sc. 1, l. 121. [Roderigo]

4 Speak not, reply not, do not answer me.
Romeo and Juliet. Act iii, sc. 5, l. 164. [Capulet]
I may not answer.—*The Winter's Tale,* i, 2, 397.

5 Answer me like men.
Romeo and Juliet. Act iv, sc. 5, l. 127. [Peter]
Answers with a groan.—*Sonnets,* l.
Answers with surmise.—*Rape of Lucrece,* l. 83.

6 Would I had a rod in my mouth, that I might answer thee profitably.
Timon of Athens. Act ii, sc. 2, l. 80. [Apemantus] "Profitably" is repeated in *Othello,* ii, 1, 286.

7 Servant: Ay, but this answer will not serve.
Flavius: If 'twill not serve, 'tis not so base as you:
For you serve knaves.
Timon of Athens. Act iii, sc. 4, l. 57.
Never yields us kind answer.
The Tempest. Act i, sc. 2, l. 309. [Prospero]

8 He'll answer nobody; he professes not answering.
Troilus and Cressida. Act iii, sc. 3, l. 269. [Thersites]
Answer not.—*Two Gentlemen of Verona,* ii, 2, 13; ii, 7, 89; *King John,* ii, 1, 480; iv, 2, 267.
Answer no more.—*III Henry VI,* iii, 2, 106.

9 We are too well acquainted with these answers.
Troilus and Cressida. Act ii, sc. 3, l. 122. [Agamemnon]

10 A good lenten answer.
Twelfth Night. Act i, sc. 5, l. 9. [Maria] "Lenten" is repeated in *Romeo and Juliet;* ii, 4, 139: "Lenten-pie"; and in *Hamlet,* ii, 2, 329: "Lenten entertainment."
A good answer.—*As You Like It,* v, 1, 27. The only use of the phrase in the plays.
A silly answer and fitting well a sheep.
The Two Gentlemen of Verona. Act i, sc. 1, l. 81. [Proteus]

11 I shall answer for her.
Twelfth Night. Act i, sc. 5, l. 179. [Olivia]
Answer for her.—*Henry VIII,* v, 3, 163.
Answer for his love.—*Troilus and Cressida,* i, 3, 295.
Answer for your raising.—*All's Well that Ends Well,* ii, 3, 120.

12 He might have took his answer long ago.
Twelfth Night. Act i, sc. 5, l. 282. [Olivia]
I will answer you with gait and entrance.
Twelfth Night. Act iii, sc. 1, l. 93. [Viola]

13 She answers him as if she knew his mind.
Venus and Adonis, l. 308.
You shall never take her without her answer, unless you take her without her tongue.
As You Like It. Act iv, sc. 1, l. 175. [Rosalind]

ANTICIPATION, see Expectation

ANTIPATHY, see Dislike

ANTIQUITY, see Past

APE

See also Monkey

14 More new-fangled than an ape.
As You Like It. Act iv, sc. 1, l. 153. [Rosalind]
I am an ape.—*The Comedy of Errors,* ii, 2, 200.
Angry ape.—*Measure for Measure,* ii, 2, 120.
John ape.—*Merry Wives of Windsor,* iii, 1, 86.
Poor ape.—*II Henry IV,* ii, 4, 234.
Ape of death.—*Cymbeline,* ii, 2, 31.
Apes of idleness!—*II Henry IV,* iv, 5, 123.

15 For apes and monkeys
'Twixt two such shes would chatter this way and
Contemn with mows the other.
Cymbeline. Act i, sc. 6, l. 39. [Iachimo]

16 Like the famous ape,
To try conclusions, in the basket creep,
And break your own neck down.
Hamlet. Act iii, sc. 4, l. 194. [Hamlet] The fable alluded to by Shakespeare has not been identified.
He keeps them, like an ape, in the corner of his jaw; first mouthed, to be last swallowed.
Hamlet. Act iv, sc. 2, l. 19. [Hamlet]

1
Out, you mad-headed ape!
A weasel hath not such a deal of spleen
As you are toss'd with.
I Henry IV. Act ii, sc. 3, l. 80. [Lady Percy] The only use of "mad-headed."
A' had him from me Christian; and look, if the fat villain have not transformed him ape.
II Henry IV. Act ii, sc. 2, l. 76. [Prince]

2
I will even take six-pence in earnest of the bear-ward, and lead his apes into hell.
Much Ado about Nothing. Act ii, sc. 1, l. 42. [Beatrice] "Bear-ward" is used three times.
I must dance bare-foot on her wedding day
And for your love to her lead apes in hell.
The Taming of the Shrew. Act ii, sc. 1, l. 33. [Katharina] The reference is to the proverb, which appears first in George Gascoigne's *Posies* (1575), that girls who die unmarried will lead apes in hell.

3
He is then a giant to an ape; but then is an ape a doctor to such a man.
Much Ado about Nothing. Act v, sc. 1, l. 205. [Claudio]

4
Sometime like apes that mow and chatter at me.
The Tempest. Act ii, sc. 2, l. 9. [Caliban]
Apes With foreheads villanous low.
The Tempest. Act iv, sc. 1, l. 249. [Caliban]

APOLOGY, see Excuse

APPAREL, see Dress

APPEARANCE

See also Look, Presence, Pretence, Seeming, Semblance, Shape

5
I will never trust a man again for keeping his sword clean, nor believe he can have every thing in him by wearing his apparel neatly.
All's Well that Ends Well. Act iv, sc. 3, l. 166. [Lord] The only use of "neatly."

6
For her own person,
It beggar'd all description: she did lie
In her pavilion—cloth-of-gold of tissue—
O'er-picturing that Venus where we see
The fancy outwork nature.
Antony and Cleopatra. Act ii, sc. 2, l. 202. [Enobarbus] The only use of "o'er-picturing" and "outwork." "Cloth-o'-gold" is repeated in *Much Ado about Nothing,* iii, 4, 19.

7
We 'll have a swashing and a martial outside,
As many other mannish cowards have
That do outface it with their semblances.
As You Like It. Act i, sc. 3, l. 122. [Rosalind] "Swashing" is repeated in *Romeo and Juliet,* i, 1, 70: "Swashing blow"; and "mannish" in *Troilus and Cressida,* iii, 3, 217, and in *Cymbeline,* iv, 2, 236.
In such a habit,
That they shall think we are accomplished
With that we lack.
The Merchant of Venice. Act iii, sc. 4, l. 61. [Portia]

8
Looks he as freshly as he did the day he wrestled?
As You Like It. Act iii, sc. 2, l. 243. [Rosalind]
Look'd he or red or pale, or sad or merrily?
The Comedy of Errors. Act iv, sc. 2, l. 4. [Adriana]
Alas, how fiery and how sharp he looks!
The Comedy of Errors. Act iv, sc. 4, l. 53. [Luciana]

9
Who 's yonder,
That does appear as he were flay'd?
Coriolanus. Act i, sc. 6, l. 22. [Cominius]
Appear As huge as high Olympus.
Julius Cæsar, iv, 3, 91. See under FAULT.
Let him be but testimonied in his own bringings-forth, and he shall appear to the envious a scholar, a statesman, and a soldier.
Measure for Measure. Act iii, sc. 2, l. 52. [Duke] The only use of "testimonied" and "bringings-forth."
Appear bloody and cruel.—*Julius Cæsar,* iii, 1, 165.
Appear foul!—*Timon of Athens,* iii, 3, 32.
Appear fresh.—*Twelfth Night,* ii, 5, 162.
Appear a gentleman.—*Pericles,* ii, 1, 147.
Appear honest.—*The Merry Wives of Windsor,* ii, 2, 230.
Appear more wise and modest.—*II Henry IV,* v, 5, 107.
Appear most ugly.—*Antony and Cleopatra,* ii, 5, 97.
Appear plain and free.—*The Two Gentlemen of Verona,* v, 4, 82.
Appear not plain.—*All's Well that Ends Well,* v, 3, 318.
Appear soul-vex'd.—*The Winter's Tale,* v, 1, 59. The only use of "soul-vex'd."
Appear stubborn.—*Twelfth Night,* iii, 4, 78.
Appear unkinglike.—*Cymbeline,* iii, 5, 7. The only use of "unkinglike."
Appear well.—*Coriolanus,* iv, 3, 35.
Well appear.—*Henry V,* i, 2, 54; *Hamlet,* iv, 7, 5.
Well appeared.—*Richard III,* iii, 5, 91.
Well appeareth.—*Richard II,* i, 1, 26. "Appeareth" is used only once more, in *The Merchant of Venice,* iv, 1, 249.

10
Bear a fair presence, though your heart be tainted.
The Comedy of Errors. Act iii, sc. 2, l. 13. [Luciana] See under PRESENCE.

11
Thou hast a grim appearance, and thy face
Bears a command in 't; though thy tackle's torn,
Thou show'st a noble vessel.
Coriolanus. Act iv, sc. 5, l. 66. [Aufidius]

12
These blazes, daughter,
Giving more light than heat, extinct in both,
Even in their promise, as it is a-making,
You must not take for fire.
Hamlet. Act i, sc. 3, l. 117. [Polonius] "A-making" is repeated in *Macbeth,* iii, 4, 34, and "extinct" in *Richard II,* i, 3, 222.

13
See, what a grace was seated on this brow;
Hyperion's curls; the front of Jove himself;

An eye like Mars, to threaten and command;
A station like the herald Mercury
New-lighted on a heaven-kissing hill;
A combination and a form indeed,
Where every god did seem to set his seal,
To give the world assurance of a man.
Hamlet. Act iii, sc. 4, l. 55. [Hamlet] The only use of "heaven-kissing." "New-lighted" occurs again in *I Henry IV,* i, 1, 63.

1 By my troth, you like well and bear your years very well.
II Henry IV. Act iii, sc. 2, l. 92. [Shallow]

A good-limbed fellow; young, strong, and of good friends.
II Henry IV. Act iii, sc. 2, l. 113. [Shallow] The only use of "good-limbed."

2 You see what a ragged appearance it is.
II Henry IV. Act iii, sc. 2, l. 279. [Falstaff]

A semblance That very dogs disdain'd.
King Lear. Act v, sc. 3, l. 187. [Edgar]

3 He is not the man that he would gladly make show to the world he is.
Henry V. Act iii, sc. 6, l. 87. [Fluellen]

4 His ceremonies laid by, in his nakedness he appears but a man.
Henry V, iv, 1, 110. See under KING.

You appeared to me but as a common man.
Henry V, iv, 8, 54. See under MAN.

Appear there for a man.—*Antony and Cleopatra,* iii, 7, 19.

5 If my legs were two such riding-rods,
My arms such eel-skins stuff'd, my face so thin
That in mine ear I durst not stick a rose
Lest men should say 'Look, where three-farthings goes!'
And, to his shape, were heir to all this land,
Would I might never stir from off this place,
I would give it every foot to have this face;
I would not be sir Nob in any case.
King John. Act i, sc. 1, l. 140. [Bastard] The only use of "riding-rods," "sir Nob," and "three-farthings" as a hyphenated phrase. "Eel-skin" is repeated in *II Henry IV,* iii, 2, 351.

6 You look but on the outside of this work.
King John. Act v, sc. 2, l. 109. [Pandulph]

I am much more Than my out-wall.
King Lear. Act iii, sc. 1, l. 44. [Kent] The only use of "out-wall."

Thy outside looks so fair and warlike.
King Lear. Act v, sc. 3, l. 142. [Edmund]

7 One by nature's outwards so commended,
That maidens' eyes stuck over all his face.
A Lover's Complaint, l. 80.

They have a good cover; they show well outward.
Much Ado about Nothing. Act i, sc. 2, l. 7. [Antonio]

O Hero, what a Hero hadst thou been,
If half thy outward graces had been placed
About thy thoughts and counsels of thy heart!
Much Ado about Nothing. Act iv, sc. 1, l. 101. [Claudio]

The outward face of royalty.
The Tempest. Act i, sc. 2, l. 104. [Prospero]

8 I' the name of truth,
Are ye fantastical, or that indeed
Which outwardly ye show?
Macbeth. Act i, sc. 3, l. 52. [Banquo]

9 O what may man within him hide,
Though angel on the outward side!
Measure for Measure, iii, 2, 285. [Duke]

One, the wicked'st caitiff on the ground,
May seem as shy, as grave, as just, as absolute
As Angelo; even so may Angelo,
In all his dressings, characts, titles, forms,
Be an arch-villain.
Measure for Measure. Act v, sc. 1, l. 53. [Isabella] The only use of "wicked'st," "dressings," and "characts" (distinctive marks). "Arch-villain" is repeated in *Timon of Athens,* v, 1, 111.

10 Do I look like a cudgel or a hovel-post, a staff or a prop?
The Merchant of Venice. Act ii, sc. 2, l. 71. [Launcelot] The only use of "hovel-post."

11 All that glisters is not gold;
Often have you heard that told.
The Merchant of Venice. Act ii, sc. 7, l. 65. [Prince of Morocco] Quoting a Latin proverb, "Non teneas aurum totum quod splendet ut aurum." (Alanus de Insulis, *Parabolæ,* c. iii. c. 1290.) "Glisters" is used again in *King John,* v, 1, 54; in *The Winter's Tale,* ii, 2, 171; and in *Venus and Adonis,* l. 275.

12 God defend the lute should be like the case!
Much Ado about Nothing, ii, 1, 97. [Hero]

13 There is no appearance of fancy in him.
Much Ado about Nothing, iii, 2, 31. See under FANCY.

Appearance of fear.—*Henry V,* iv, 1, 116.
Fair appearance.—*Sonnets,* xlvi.
Frank appearance.—*Othello,* i, 3, 38.
Reverend appearer.—*Pericles,* v, 3, 18. The only use of "appearer."

14 They are not the men you took them for.
Much Ado about Nothing. Act iii, sc. 3, l. 50. [Dogberry]

I am not what I am.
Othello. Act i, sc. 1, l. 65. [Iago]

15 I was mortally brought forth, and am
No other than I appear.
Pericles. Act v, sc. 1, l. 104. [Marina]

Appear in his true likeness.—*Henry V,* v, 2, 317; 321.
Appear itself.—*Cymbeline,* iii, 4, 148.
Thus thou wilt appear.—*King Lear,* i, 1, 183.
Thus we appear.—*Henry V,* v, 2, 21.
It appears so.—*I Henry IV,* iii, 3, 191.

16 Of what she was no semblance did remain.
The Rape of Lucrece, l. 1453. See also under SEMBLANCE.

So fair a form lodged not a mind so ill.
The Rape of Lucrece, l. 1530.

1
We say that Shore's wife hath a pretty foot,
A cherry lip, a bonny eye, a passing pleasing tongue.
Richard III. Act i, sc. 1, l. 93. [Gloucester]

There 's language in her eye, her cheek, her lip,
Nay, her foot speaks; her wanton spirits look out
At every joint and motive of her body.
Troilus and Cressida, iv, 5, 55. [Ulysses]

Thy tongue, thy face, thy limbs, actions and spirit,
Do give thee five-fold blazon.
Twelfth Night. Act i, sc. 5, l. 311. [Olivia] The only use of "five-fold."

2
Nor more can you distinguish of a man
Than of his outward show; which, God he knows,
Seldom or never jumpeth with the heart.
Richard III. Act iii, sc. 1, l. 9. [Gloucester]

A dream of what thou wert, a breath, a bubble,
A sign of dignity, a garish flag,
To be the aim of every dangerous shot.
Richard III. Act iv, sc. 4, l. 88. [Queen Margaret] "Garish" is repeated in *Romeo and Juliet,* iii, 2, 25: "Garish sun."

3
Appear thou in the likeness of a sigh.
Romeo and Juliet, ii, 1, 8. See CONJURING.

Appear like death.—*Romeo and Juliet,* iv, 1, 103.

Appears like a lord.—*Timon of Athens,* ii, 2, 115.

Appear like mice.—*King Lear,* iv, 6, 18.

Appear like unshorn velvet.—*A Lover's Complaint,* l. 93. The only use of "unshorn."

Appear not like a guest.—*Coriolanus,* iv, 5, 6.

4
O, what a mansion have those vices got
Which for their habitation chose out thee,
Where beauty's veil doth cover every blot,
And all things turn to fair that eyes can see!
Sonnets. No. xcv.

5
There 's nothing ill can dwell in such a temple:
If the ill spirit have so fair a house,
Good things will strive to dwell with 't.
The Tempest. Act i, sc. 2, l. 457. [Miranda]

6 Nature, what things there are
Most abject in regard and dear in use!
What things again most dear in the esteem
And poor in worth!
Troilus and Cressida. Act iii, sc. 3, l. 127. [Ulysses]

Nature with a beauteous wall
Doth oft close in pollution.
Twelfth Night. Act i, sc. 2, l. 48. [Viola]

7
Most putrefied core, so fair without,
Thy goodly armour thus hast cost thy life.
Troilus and Cressida. Act v, sc. 8, l. 1. [Hector] "Putrefied" is repeated in *The Rape of Lucrece,* l. 1750. "Putrefy" occurs in *I Henry VI,* iv, 7, 90.

8
Fortune forbid my outside have not charm'd her!
Twelfth Night. Act ii, sc. 2, l. 19. [Viola]

How easy is it for the proper-false
In women's waxen hearts to set their forms!
Twelfth Night. Act ii, sc. 2, l. 30. [Viola] The only use of "proper-false."

II—Appearance: Well-favoured and Ill-favoured

See also Beauty, Ugliness

9
To be a well-favoured man is a gift of fortune.
Much Ado about Nothing. Act iii, sc. 3, l. 15. [Dogberry]

He is very well-favoured.—*Twelfth Night,* i, 5, 169.

His wife seems to me well-favoured.
The Merry Wives of Windsor. Act ii, sc. 2, l. 285. [Falstaff]

Those wicked creatures yet do look well-favour'd,
When others are more wicked.
King Lear. Act ii, sc. 4, l. 259. [King Lear]

You are well favour'd, and your looks foreshow
You have a gentle heart.
Pericles. Act iv, sc. 1, l. 86. [Marina] The only use of "foreshow."

10
Well, for your favour, sir, why, give God thanks, and make no boast of it.
Much Ado about Nothing. Act iii, sc. 3, l. 19. [Dogberry]

By your good favour,—for surely, sir, a good favour you have.
Measure for Measure. Act iv, sc. 2, l. 33. [Pompey]

Sickness is catching: O, were favour so,
Yours would I catch, fair Hermia, ere I go.
A Midsummer-Night's Dream. Act i, sc. 1, l. 186. [Helena]

I know your favour well.—*Twelfth Night,* iii, 4, 363; *Troilus and Cressida,* iv, 5, 213.

I do know your outward favour.—*Julius Cæsar,* i, 2, 91.

Of female favour.—*As You Like It,* iv, 3, 87.

11
That will be ill-favoured.
The Two Gentlemen of Verona. Act ii, sc. 7, l. 54. [Julia]

12
Hard-favour'd, foul, or wrinkled-old,
Ill-nurtured, crooked, churlish, harsh in voice,
O'erworn, despised, rheumatic and cold,
Thick-sighted, barren, lean and lacking juice.
Venus and Adonis, l. 133. The only use of "wrinkled-old" and "thick-sighted." "Ill-nurtured" is repeated in *II Henry VI,* i, 2, 42, and "o'erworn" in *Richard III,* i, 1, 81, and in *Twelfth Night,* iii, 1, 66.

Valentine: But tell me, dost thou know my lady Silvia? . . .
Speed: Is she not hard-favoured, sir?
Valentine: Not so fair, boy, as well-favoured.
Speed: Sir, I know that well enough.
Valentine: What dost thou know?
Speed: That she is not so fair as, of you, well-favoured.
Valentine: I mean that her beauty is exquisite, but her favour infinite.

Speed: That's because the one is painted and the other out of all count.
Two Gentlemen of Verona. Act ii, sc. 1, l. 47.
Some hard-favour'd groom.
The Rape of Lucrece, l. 1632.
Hard-favour'd Richard.
III Henry VI. Act v, sc. 5, l. 78. [Queen]

APPETITE

See also Eating, Stomach

1 Epicurean cooks
Sharpen with cloyless sauce his appetite;
That sleep and feeding may prorogue his honour
Even till a Lethe'd dulness!
Antony and Cleopatra. Act ii, sc. 1, l. 24. [Pompey] The only use of "cloyless" and "Lethe'd." "Epicurean" is repeated in *The Merry Wives of Windsor,* ii, 2, 300, and "prorogue" in *Romeo and Juliet,* iv, 1, 48, and in *Pericles,* v, 1, 26.

2
I am weak with toil, yet strong in appetite.
Cymbeline. Act iii, sc. 6, l. 37. [Arviragus]

3 She would hang on him,
As if increase of appetite had grown
By what it fed on.
Hamlet. Act i, sc. 2, l. 143. [Hamlet]

4
To breakfast with What appetite you have.
Henry VIII. Act iii, sc. 2, l. 202. [King Henry] "Breakfast" is used fifteen times in the plays.

5
O appetite, from judgement stand aloof!
The one a palate hath that needs will taste,
Though Reason weep, and cry "It is thy last."
A Lover's Complaint, l. 166.
To please the palate of my appetite.
Othello. Act i, sc. 3, l. 263. [Othello]
To make our appetites more keen,
With eager compounds we our palate urge.
Sonnets. No. cxviii.

6
Now, good digestion wait on appetite,
And health on both!
Macbeth. Act iii, sc. 4, l. 38. [Macbeth]
A good digestion to you all.
Henry VIII. Act i, sc. 4, l. 62. [Wolsey]
Unquiet meals make ill digestions.
The Comedy of Errors. Act v, sc. 1, l. 74. [Abbess]
Things sweet to taste prove in digestion sour.
Richard II, i, 3, 236. See SWEET and SOUR.
For your health and your digestion sake,
An after-dinner's breath.
Troilus and Cressida, ii, 3, 120. See under DINING.
Art thou come? why, my cheese, my digestion.
Troilus and Cressida, ii, 3, 44. See under CHEESE.
Hot digestion.—*Troilus and Cressida,* ii, 2, 6. The only uses of "digestion." Out of the seven instances in the plays, three are in *Troilus and Cressida.*

7
Doth not the appetite alter? a man loves the meat in his youth that he cannot endure in his age.
Much Ado about Nothing. Act ii, sc. 3, l. 247. [Benedick]
But, like in sickness, did I loathe this food;
But, as in health, come to my natural taste.
A Midsummer-Night's Dream. Act iv, sc. 1, l. 177. [Demetrius]
Sick man's appetite.—*Coriolanus,* i, 1, 182.

8
Or cloy the hungry edge of appetite
By bare imagination of a feast?
Richard II. Act i, sc. 3, l. 296. [Bolingbroke]
Cloy the appetites.—*Antony and Cleopatra,* ii, 2, 242.
Gorge his appetite.—*King Lear,* i, 1, 120.
Who riseth from a feast
With that keen appetite that he sits down?
The Merchant of Venice. Act ii, sc. 6, l. 8. [Gratiano]
Sweet love, renew thy force; be it not said
Thy edge should blunter be than appetite,
Which but to-day by feeding is allay'd,
To-morrow sharpen'd in his former might.
Sonnets. No. lvi. The only use of "blunter" and "sharpen'd."
Leaden appetite, unapt to toy.
Venus and Adonis, l. 34.

9
Every thing includes itself in power,
Power into will, will into appetite;
And appetite, an universal wolf,
So doubly seconded with will and power,
Must make perforce an universal prey,
And last eat up himself.
Troilus and Cressida. Act i, sc. 3, l. 119. [Ulysses]

10 Threw off . . . his appetite . . .
And downright languish'd.
Winter's Tale, ii, 3, 16. See under SICKNESS.
Bestial appetite.—*Richard III,* iii, 5, 81.
Better appetite.—*Julius Cæsar,* i, 2, 306.
Distempered appetite.—*Twelfth Night,* i, 5, 98.
Dry appetite.—*Titus Andronicus,* iii, 1, 14.
Raging appetites.—*Troilus and Cressida,* ii, 2, 181.
Riotous appetite.—*King Lear,* iv, 6, 125.
Sharp appetite.—*Measure for Measure,* ii, 4, 161.

APPLAUSE

See also Praise, Shouting

11 They threw their caps
As they would hang them on the horns o' the moon,
Shouting their emulation.
Coriolanus. Act i, sc. 1, l. 216. [Marcius]
I have seen the dumb men throng to see him and
The blind to hear him speak: matrons flung gloves,
Ladies and maids their scarfs and handkerchers,
Upon him as he pass'd: the nobles bended,
As to Jove's statue, and the commons made
A shower and thunder with their caps and shouts:
I never saw the like.
Coriolanus. Act ii, sc. 1, l. 278. [Messenger]

O thou fond many, with what loud applause
Didst thou beat heaven.
II Henry IV. Act i, sc. 3, l. 91. [Archbishop]

Caps, hands, and tongues, applaud it to the clouds.
Hamlet. Act iv, sc. 5, l. 107. [Gentleman]

1 Call ye the warlike Talbot, for his acts
So much applauded through the realm of France.
I Henry VI. Act ii, sc. 2, l. 35. [Messenger]

2 Clapping their hands, and crying with loud voice,
'Jesu maintain your royal excellence!'
II Henry VI. Act i, sc. 1, l. 160. [Beaufort]

You all clapp'd your hands,
And cried 'Inestimable!'
Troilus and Cressida. Act ii, sc. 2, l. 87. [Troilus]

Your gentle hands lend us, and take our hearts.
All's Well that Ends Well, Epil., l. 340.

Clapped their chopped hands.—*Julius Cæsar*, i, 2, 246.

3 I do believe that these applauses are
For some new honours.
Julius Cæsar. Act i, sc. 2, l. 133. [Brutus] The only use of "applauses."

4 I would applaud thee to the very echo,
That should applaud again.
Macbeth. Act v, sc. 3, l. 53. [Macbeth]

Applaud my choice.—*Titus Andronicus*, i, 1, 321.

Applaud his courage.—*Pericles*, ii, 5, 58.

Applaud our loves!—*The Two Gentlemen of Verona*, i, 3, 48.

Applaud thy spirit.—*The Two Gentlemen of Verona*, v, 4, 140.

Applaud our sport!—*I Henry IV*, i, 3, 302.

5 This general applause and loving shout
Argues your wisdoms and your love to Richard.
Richard III. Act iii, sc. 7, l. 39. [Buckingham]

Applause and universal shout.
The Merchant of Venice. Act iii, sc. 2, l. 144. [Bassanio]

With voices and applause of every sort.
Titus Andronicus. Act i, sc. 1, l. 230. [Marcus]

With all the applause and clamour of the host.
Coriolanus. Act i, sc. 9, l. 64. [Cominius]

Applause and approbation.—*Troilus and Cressida*, i, 3, 59.

6 From his deep chest laughs out a loud applause.
Troilus and Cressida. Act i, sc. 3, l. 163. [Ulysses]

Who broils in loud applause.
Troilus and Cressida. Act i, sc. 3, l. 379. [Ulysses]

How his silence drinks up this applause!
Troilus and Cressida. Act ii, sc. 3, l. 211. [Diomedes]

APPOINTMENT

7 Where their appointment we may best discover,
And look on their endeavour.
Antony and Cleopatra. Act iv, sc. 10, l. 8. [Antony]

8 My lords, you are appointed for that office.
Cymbeline. Act iii, sc. 5, l. 10. [Cymbeline]

Appointed to direct these fair designs.
Richard II. Act i, sc. 3, l. 45. [Marshal]

Appointed Master of this design.—*The Tempest*, i, 2, 162.

Appointed for the place.—*II Henry VI*, i, 3, 170.

Appointed justices of peace.—*II Henry VI*, iv, 7, 45.

Appointed . . . to murder you.—*The Winter's Tale*, i, 2, 412.

9 Appoint some of your council presently.
Henry V. Act v, sc. 2, l. 79. [French King]

Why the devil . . . took he upon him,
Without the privity o' the king, to appoint
Who should attend on him?
Henry VIII. Act i, sc. 1, l. 72. [Buckingham] The only use of "privity."

10 We shall advise this wronged maid to stead up your appointment, go in your place.
Measure for Measure. Act iii, sc. 1, l. 260. [Duke]

11 I have appointed mine host of de Jarteer to measure our weapon.
The Merry Wives of Windsor. Act i, sc. 4, l. 124. [Caius]

I was at her house the hour she appointed me.
The Merry Wives of Windsor. Act iii, sc. 5, l. 64. [Falstaff]

We have appointed to dine with Mistress Anne.
The Merry Wives of Windsor. Act iii, sc. 2, l. 55. [Slender]

12 I shall be with her, I may tell you, by her own appointment.
The Merry Wives of Windsor. Act ii, sc. 2, l. 272. [Falstaff]

I will then address me to my appointment.
The Merry Wives of Windsor. Act iii, sc. 5, l. 135. [Falstaff]

13 I'll appoint my men to carry the basket again.
The Merry Wives of Windsor. Act iv, sc. 2, l. 94. [Mrs. Ford]

Appoint her to look out.—*Much Ado about Nothing*, ii, 2, 17.

Appoint him an encounter.—*All's Well that Ends Well*, iii, 7, 32.

Appoint him store of provender.—*Julius Cæsar*, iv, 1, 30.

Appoint a meeting.—*The Merry Wives of Windsor*, iv, 4, 15. See under MEETING.

Appoint myself.—*The Winter's Tale*, i, 2, 326.

14 Here art thou in appointment fresh and fair,

Anticipating time with startling courage.
Troilus and Cressida. Act iv, sc. 5, l. 1. [Agamemnon] The only use of "anticipating."

Therefore your best appointment make with speed;
To-morrow you set on.
Measure for Measure, iii, 1, 60. [Isabella]

In best appointments.—*King John,* ii, 1, 296.
Fair appointments.—*Richard II,* iii, 3, 53.
Warlike appointment.—*Hamlet,* iv, 6, 16.

1 It shall so be my care
To have you royally appointed.
Winter's Tale. Act iv, sc. 4, l. 601. [Camillo]

Appointed well.—*Titus Andronicus,* iv, 2, 16.
Well appointed.—*I Henry VI,* iv, 2, 21.

APPREHENSION

2 Being scarce made up,
I mean, to man, he had not apprehension
Of roaring terrors.
Cymbeline. Act iv, sc. 2, l. 109. [Belarius]

3
In apprehension how like a god.
Hamlet. Act ii, sc. 2, l. 319. [Hamlet] See under MAN for full quotation.

This brainish apprehension.
Hamlet. Act iv, sc. 1, l. 11. [Queen] The only use of "brainish."

4
Think how such an apprehension
May turn the tide of fearful faction
And breed a kind of question in our cause.
I Henry IV. Act iv, sc. 1, l. 66. [Worcester]

5
Where 's that palace whereinto foul things
Sometimes intrude not? who has a breast so pure,
But some uncleanly apprehensions
Keep leets and law-days and in session sit
With meditations lawful?
Othello. Act iii, sc. 3, l. 137. [Iago] The only use of "law-days." "Leet" is repeated in *The Taming of the Shrew,* Ind., 2, 89. "Leets and law-days" is tautological, for they are the same thing. The leet was a special court of record, and the days when it was in session were the "leets" or "law-days."

O, no! the apprehension of the good
Gives but the greater feeling to the worse.
Richard II, i, 3, 300. [Bolingbroke]

6
But his evasion, wing'd thus swift with scorn,
Cannot outfly our apprehensions.
Troilus and Cressida. Act ii, sc. 3, l. 123. [Agamemnon] The only use of "outfly."

APPROBATION, see Commendation

APRIL

See also Spring

7
The April 's in her eyes: it is love's spring.
Antony and Cleopatra. Act iii, sc. 2, l. 43. [Antony]

8 Well-apparell'd April on the heel
Of limping winter treads.
Romeo and Juliet. Act i, sc. 2, l. 27. [Capulet] The only use of "well-apparell'd."

9 Proud-pied April dress'd in all his trim
Hath put a spirit of youth in every thing.
Sonnets. No. xcviii. Only use of "proud-pied."

Lovely April.—*Sonnets,* iii.

10
Thy banks with pioned and twilled brims,
Which spongy April at thy hest betrims.
The Tempest. Act iv, sc. 1, l. 64. [Iris] The only use of "pioned," "twilled," and "betrims." "Spongy" occurs also in *Troilus and Cressida,* ii, 2, 12; *Macbeth,* i, 7, 91; and *Cymbeline,* iv, 2, 349.

APTNESS, see Intelligence

ARGUMENT

See also Debate, Dispute, Reason

11
Why, 'tis the rarest argument of wonder that hath shot out in our latter times.
All's Well that Ends Well. Act ii, sc. 3, l. 7. [Parolles]

Cut off the argument.—*As You Like It,* i, 2, 50.
Absent argument.—*As You Like It,* iii, 1, 3.

12
It was much like an argument that fell out last night.
Cymbeline. Act i, sc. 4, l. 60. [Frenchman]

13 To expostulate
What majesty should be, what duty is,
Why day is day, night night, and time is time,
Were nothing but to waste night, day and time.
Hamlet. Act ii, sc. 2, l. 86. [Polonius]

There has been much to do on both sides.
Hamlet. Act ii, sc. 2, l. 369. [Rosencrantz]

There was, for a while, no money bid for argument, unless the poet and the player went to cuffs in the question.
Hamlet. Act ii, sc. 2, l. 371. [Rosencrantz]

There has been much throwing about of brains.
Hamlet. Act ii, sc. 2, l. 375. [Guildenstern]

Argument for a week.—*I Henry IV,* ii, 2, 100.
Argument for them all.—*Henry V,* iii, 7, 37.

14 Our argument
Is all too heavy to admit much talk.
II Henry IV. Act v, sc. 2, l. 23. [Warwick]

Inferreth arguments of mighty strength.
III Henry VI. Act iii, sc. 1, l. 49. [King Henry] The only use of "inferreth."

Good argument.—*Henry V,* iv, 3, 113; *Troilus and Cressida,* iv, 5, 26.
Great argument.—*Hamlet,* iv, 4, 54; *Love's Labour's Lost,* i, 2, 175; *Much Ado about Nothing,* ii, 3, 243; *Twelfth Night,* iii, 2, 12.
Weighty arguments.—*Richard III,* i, 1, 148.

15
And sheathed their swords for lack of argument.
Henry V. Act iii, sc. 1, l. 21. [King Henry]

I cannot fight upon this argument;
It is too starved a subject for my sword.
Troilus and Cressida, i, 1, 95. [Troilus]

16
Unless my study and my books be false,
The argument you held was wrong in you.
I Henry VI. Act ii, sc. 4, l. 56. [Lawyer]

We have but trivial argument.
II Henry VI. Act iii, sc. 1, l. 241. [Suffolk]

1
My lord, you do not well in obstinacy
To cavil in the course of this contract.
I Henry VI. Act v, sc. 4, l. 155. [Reignier]
You cavil, widow.—*III Henry VI,* iii, 2, 99.
I 'll cavil on the ninth part of a hair.
I Henry IV, iii, 1, 140. See under BARGAIN.
In vain I cavil with mine infamy.
The Rape of Lucrece, l. 1025.
That 's but a cavil.—*The Taming of the Shrew,* ii, 1, 392.
'Tis love you cavil at.—*The Two Gentlemen of Verona,* i, 1, 38. The only uses of "cavil."

2 If arguing make us sweat,
The proof of it will turn to redder drops.
Julius Cæsar. Act v, sc. 1, l. 48. [Octavius] The only use of "redder."

3
Doth move the murmuring lips of discontent
To break into this dangerous argument.
King John. Act iv, sc. 2, l. 53. [Pembroke]

4
They are yet but ear-kissing arguments.
King Lear. Act ii, sc. 1, l. 9. [Curan] The only use of "ear-kissing."

5
How did this argument begin?
Love's Labour 's Lost. Act iii, sc. 1, l. 106. [Armado]
Thus came your argument in.
Love's Labour 's Lost, iii, 1, 109. [Costard]
He draweth out the thread of his verbosity finer than the staple of his argument.
Love's Labour 's Lost. Act v, sc. 1, l. 18. [Holofernes] The only use of "verbosity" and of "staple" in this sense.
I 'll darkly end the argument.
Love's Labour 's Lost, v, 2, 23. [Katharine]
Hold argument.—*Love's Labour 's Lost,* iv, 3, 61.
Armed in arguments.—*Love's Labour 's Lost,* v, 2, 84.

6
So on the tip of his subduing tongue
All kind of arguments and question deep,
All replication prompt, and reason strong.
A Lover's Complaint, l. 120. The only use of "subduing."
He will maintain his argument as well as any military man in the world.
Henry V. Act iii, sc. 2, l. 85. [Fluellen]
Claim this argument.—*Macbeth,* ii, 3, 126.
Proved an argument.—*Timon of Athens,* iii, 5, 23.

7
It were a goot motion if we leave our pribbles and prabbles.
The Merry Wives of Windsor. Act i, sc. 1, l. 55. [Evans]
Leave your prabbles, 'oman.
The Merry Wives of Windsor. Act iv, sc. 1, l. 52. [Evans]
Pribbles and prabbles.—*The Merry Wives of Windsor,* v, 5, 169.
Prawls and prabbles.—*Henry V,* iv, 8, 69. The only use of "prabbles" and "pribbles."

8
If you have any pity, grace, or manners,
You would not make me such an argument.
A Midsummer-Night's Dream. Act iii, sc. 2, l. 241. [Helena]

9
Well, if ever thou dost fall from this faith, thou wilt prove a notable argument.
Much Ado about Nothing. Act i, sc. 1, l. 257. [Don Pedro]
If thou wilt hold longer argument,
Do it in notes.
Much Ado about Nothing. Act ii, sc. 3, l. 55. [Don Pedro]

10 I force not argument a straw,
Since that my case is past the help of law.
The Rape of Lucrece, l. 1021.

11
As near as I could sift him on that argument.
Richard II. Act i, sc. 1, l. 12. [Gaunt]
Well have you argued, sir.
Richard II. Act iv, sc. 1, l. 150. [Northumberland]
Argue like a father.—*Richard II,* i, 3, 238.

12
How now, how now, chop-logic!
Romeo and Juliet. Act iii, sc. 5, l. 150. [Capulet] The only use of "chop-logic."
I . . . meant, indeed, to occupy the argument no longer.
Romeo and Juliet. Act ii, sc. 4, l. 104. [Mercutio]

13
Thine own sweet argument, too excellent
For every vulgar paper to rehearse.
Sonnets. No. xxxviii.
You and love are still my argument.
Sonnets. No. lxxvi.
I grant, sweet love, thy lovely argument
Deserves the travail of a worthier pen,
Yet what of thee thy poet doth invent
He robs thee of and pays it thee again.
Sonnets. No. lxxix.
The argument all bare is of more worth
Than when it hath my added praise beside!
Sonnets. No. ciii.

14
I should be arguing still upon that doubt.
The Taming of the Shrew. Act iii, sc. 1, l. 55. [Bianca]
You have both said well,
And on the cause and question now in hand
Have glozed, but superficially.
Troilus and Cressida. Act ii, sc. 2, l. 163. [Hector] "Superficially" occurs again in iii, 1, 10, and in no other play. The only use of "glozed."
All the argument is a cuckold and a whore.
Troilus and Cressida. Act ii, sc. 3, l. 78. [Thersites]
Nestor: Then will Ajax lack matter, if he have lost his argument.
Ulysses: No, you see, he is his argument that has his argument, Achilles.
Troilus and Cressida. Act ii, sc. 3, l. 103.

15
The quality of the time and quarrel
Might well have given us bloody argument.
Twelfth Night. Act iii, sc. 3, l. 31. [Antonio]
Arguments of fear.—*Twelfth Night,* iii, 3, 12.
Argument of hearts.—*Timon of Athens,* ii, 2, 187.
Arguments of love.—*King John,* i, 1, 36; *Twelfth Night,* iii, 2, 12.
Love's argument.—*Love's Labour 's Lost,* v, 2, 757.

Argument of the play.—*Hamlet,* iii, 2, 149.
Argument of your praise.—*King Lear,* i, 1, 218.
Argument of his own scorn.—*Much Ado about Nothing,* ii, 3, 11.
Arguments of state.—*Twelfth Night,* ii, 5, 163; iii, 4, 78.
Argument of Time.—*Winter's Tale,* iv, 1, 29.

1
Nor need'st thou much importune me to that
Whereon this month I have been hammering.
The Two Gentlemen of Verona. Act i, sc. 3, l. 17. [Antonio]
Wilt thou still be hammering treachery?
II Henry VI, i, 2, 47. See under TREACHERY.
Hammering in my head.—*Titus Andronicus,* ii, 3, 39. The only use of "hammering."

ARITHMETIC

2
Spare your arithmetic: never count the turns;
Once, and a million!
Cymbeline. Act ii, sc. 4, l. 142. [Posthumus]

3
To divide him inventorially would dizzy the arithmetic of memory, and yet but yaw neither, in respect of his quick sail.
Hamlet. Act v, sc. 2, l. 118. [Hamlet] The only use of "inventorially" and "yaw."

4
A tapster's arithmetic.
Troilus and Cressida. Act i, sc. 2, l. 123. [Cressida]
No arithmetic but her brain.
Troilus and Cressida. Act iii, sc. 3, l. 253. [Thersites]
A great arithmetician.—*Othello,* i, 1, 9. The only use of "arithmetician."

ARM

See also Limb

5
Lend me an arm; the rest have worn me out.
All's Well that Ends Well. Act i, sc. 2, l. 73. [King of France]
Give me thy arm.—*King Lear,* iv, 1, 81.
Give me your arm.—*King Lear,* iii, 7, 98.
Support him by the arm.—*As You Like It,* ii, 7, 199.
Take her by the arm.—*Pericles,* iv, 1, 30.
Take him by the arm.—*As You Like It,* iv, 3, 163.
My arm shall give thee help to bear thee hence.
King John. Act v, sc. 4, l. 58. [Salisbury]

6
The arm And burgonet of men.
Antony and Cleopatra, i, 5, 23. See under PERFECTION.
His rear'd arm crested the world.
Antony and Cleopatra, v, 2, 82. See MAN: GREAT MEN, 948:4.

7
Though others have the arm, show us the sleeve.
The Comedy of Errors. Act iii, sc. 2, l. 23. [Luciana]
I come to lose my arm or win my sleeve.
Troilus and Cressida. Act v, sc. 3, l. 96. [Troilus] Referring to the token which he had given Cressida, which she had carried with her into the Grecian camp, and which Diomed was wearing in his helmet.

8
Death, that dark spirit, in 's nervy arm doth lie;
Which, being advanced, declines, and then men die.
Coriolanus. Act ii, sc. 1, l. 177. [Volumnia] The only use of "nervy."
What an arm he has! he turned me about with his finger and his thumb, as one would set up a top.
Coriolanus. Act iv, sc. 5, l. 159. [Servant]
Have not I An arm as big as thine?
Cymbeline. Act iv, sc. 2, l. 77. [Guiderius]
Put the world's whole strength
Into one giant arm.
II Henry IV. Act iv, sc. 5, l. 45. [Prince]
Powerful arm.—*Richard III,* i, 4, 223.
Strong arm.—*I Henry V,* i, 3, 298; *The Rape of Lucrece,* l. 1834.
Good arms.—*The Tempest,* ii, 1, 119; *Troilus and Cressida,* i, 3, 238.
Free arms.—*The Winter's Tale,* iv, 4, 559.
Straight arms.—*Cymbeline,* iii, 1, 38.

9
Let me twine Mine arms about that body.
Coriolanus, iv, 5, 113. See under BODY.
Twining arms.—*Venus and Adonis,* l. 256.

10
Whose arms were moulded in their mothers' womb.
I Henry IV. Act i, sc. 1, l. 23. [King]

11
I will embrace him with a soldier's arm.
I Henry IV. Act v, sc. 2, l. 74. [Hotspur]
Achilles' arm.—*Troilus and Cressida,* i, 3, 220.
Arm of peace.—*II Henry IV,* iv, 1, 177.
Cæsar's arm.—*Julius Cæsar,* ii, 1, 182.
Desdemona's arms.—*Othello,* ii, 1, 80.
Fortune's tender arm.—*Timon of Athens,* iv, 3, 250.
God's arm.—*Henry V,* iv, 3, 5.
Keeper's arms.—*II Henry IV,* i, 1, 143.
Love's arms.—*A Lover's Complaint,* l. 271.
Murder's arms.—*King John,* iv, 3, 47.
Neptune's arms.—*King John,* v, 2, 34.
Nurse's arms.—*As You Like It,* ii, 7, 144.

12
Katharine: Dites-moi l'Anglois pour le bras.
Alice: De arm, madame.
Henry V. Act iii, sc. 4, l. 21. "Bras" is repeated in iv, 4, 18, and occurs in no other play.

13
Over Suffolk's neck
He threw his wounded arm.
Henry V. Act iv, sc. 6, l. 24. [Exeter]
My arm is sore.—*Antony and Cleopatra,* ii, 5, 4.

14
From my shoulders crack my arms asunder.
I Henry VI. Act i, sc. 5, l. 11. [Talbot]

15
Coward of France! how much he wrongs his fame,
Despairing of his own arm's fortitude.
I Henry VI. Act ii, sc. 1, l. 16. [Bedford]

16
And pithless arms, like to a wither'd vine
That droops his sapless branches to the ground.
I Henry VI. Act ii, sc. 5, l. 11. [Mortimer]

The only use of "pithless." "Sapless" occurs again in the same play, iv, 5, 4, and in no other.

Shrink mine arm up like a wither'd shrub.
III Henry VI. Act iii, sc. 2, l. 156. [Gloucester]

This arm of mine, Now prisoner to the palsy.
Richard II. Act ii, sc. 3, l. 103. [York]

Behold mine arm
Is, like a blasted sapling, wither'd up.
Richard III. Act iii, sc. 4, l. 70. [Gloucester]

Little arm.—*Othello,* v, 2, 262.
Old arms.—*Coriolanus,* iv, 1, 56.
Stiff unwieldy arms.—*Richard II,* iii, 2, 115.
Weak arm.—*Richard II,* iii, 2, 65.

1
This arm, that hath reclaim'd
To your obedience fifty fortresses,
Twelve cities and seven walled towns of strength.
I Henry VI. Act iii, sc. 4, l. 5. [Talbot]

2
Come, come and lay him in his father's arms.
I Henry VI, iv, 7, 29. See Father, 511:12.

See, where he lies inhearsed in the arms
Of the most bloody nurser of his harms!
I Henry VI, iv, 7, 45. See under Knighthood. The only use of "inhearsed."

3
He marcheth with us arm in arm.
II Henry VI. Act v, sc. 1, l. 57. [King Henry]

Arm in arm they both came swiftly running.
I Henry VI. Act ii, sc. 2, l. 29. [Burgundy] The only uses of "arm in arm."

4 Dogged York, that reaches at the moon,
Whose overweening arm I have pluck'd back.
II Henry VI. Act iii, sc. 1, l. 158. [Gloucester]

5
These arms of mine shall be thy winding-sheet.
III Henry VI. Act ii, sc. 5, l. 114. [Father] "Winding-sheet" is repeated in i, 1, 129, and occurs in no other play.

Sleep thou, and I will wind thee in my arms.
A Midsummer-Night's Dream. Act iv, sc. 1, l. 43. [Titania]

6 Our arms . . . do receive you
With all kind love.
Julius Cæsar. Act iii, sc. 1, l. 174. [Brutus]

7
Good friend, I prithee, take him in thy arms.
King Lear. Act iii, sc. 6, l. 95. [Gloucester]

Take in your arms this piece
Of your dead queen.
Pericles. Act iii, sc. 1, l. 17. [Lychorida]

In thy dead arms do I mean to place him.
The Rape of Lucrece, l. 517.

8
Bind fast his corky arms.
King Lear. Act iii, sc. 7, l. 29. [Cornwall] The only use of "corky."

Let his arms alone;
They were not born for bondage.
Cymbeline. Act v, sc. 5, l. 305. [Belarius]

9 With his strong arms
He fasten'd on my neck.
King Lear. Act v, sc. 3, l. 211. [Edgar]

And on his neck her yoking arms she throws.
Venus and Adonis, l. 592. The only use of "yoking."

10
With your arms crossed on your thin-belly doublet like a rabbit on a spit.
Love's Labour's Lost. Act iii, sc. 1, l. 18. [Moth] The only use of thin-belly." For "doublet" see under Dress.

Nor never lay his wreathed arms athwart
His loving bosom to keep down his heart.
Love's Labour's Lost. Act iv, sc. 3, l. 135. [King]

To cross their arms and hang their heads with mine.
The Rape of Lucrece, l. 793.

With sad set eyes, and wretched arms across.
The Rape of Lucrece, l. 1662.

With your arms across.—*Julius Cæsar,* ii, 1, 240.

Sitting, His arms in this sad knot.
The Tempest, i, 2, 224. See under Sigh.

Wreath your arms like a malcontent.
The Two Gentlemen of Verona, ii, 1, 20. See under Love.

Folded arms.—*Love's Labour's Lost,* iii, 1, 183; *Titus Andronicus,* iii, 2, 7.
Pleach'd arms.—*Antony and Cleopatra,* iv, 14, 73. The only use of "pleach'd" in the sense of folded.
Traversed arms.—*Timon of Athens,* v, 4, 7. The only use of "traversed" (folded).

11
For since these arms of mine had seven years' pith,
Till now some nine moons wasted, they have used
Their dearest action in the tented field.
Othello. Act i, sc. 3, l. 83. [Othello] The only use of "tented."

Or do but lift this arm, the best of you
Shall sink in my rebuke.
Othello. Act ii, sc. 3, l. 208. [Othello]

12
By the grace of God and this mine arm.
Richard II. Act i, sc. 3, l. 22. [Mowbray]

I heard you say, 'Is not my arm of length?'
Richard II. Act iv, sc. 1, l. 11. [Bagot]

His hell-govern'd arm.
Richard III. Act i, sc. 2, l. 67. [Lady Anne] The only use of "hell-govern'd."

Angry arm.—*Richard II,* i, 2, 41.
Ireful arm.—*III Henry VI,* ii, 1, 57.
Ruthless arm.—*II Henry V,* i, 4, 31.

13
From her jealous arms pluck him perforce.
Richard III. Act iii, sc. 1, l. 36. [Buckingham]

Girdling one another
Within their innocent alabaster arms.
Richard III. Act iv, sc. 3, l. 10. [Tyrrel] The only use of "girdling."

Bare arms.—*King Lear,* ii, 3, 15.
Fair arms.—*Venus and Adonis,* l. 812.

14 This arm of mine hath chastised
The petty rebel.
Richard III. Act iv, sc. 4, l. 331. [King Richard]

15
His agile arm beats down their fatal points.
Romeo and Juliet. Act iii, sc. 1, l. 171. [Benvolio] The only use of "agile."

Arms, take your last embrace!
Romeo and Juliet. Act v, sc. 3, l. 113. [Romeo]

1
His right arm might purchase his own time
And be in debt to none.
Timon of Athens. Act iii, sc. 5, l. 77. [Alcibiades] The only use of "right arm."
Left arm.—*The Comedy of Errors,* iii, 2, 148; *Coriolanus,* ii, 1, 163. The only uses.

2
For what, alas, can these my single arms?
Troilus and Cressida, ii, 2, 135. [Paris]
By him that thunders, thou hast lusty arms.
Troilus and Cressida, iv, 5, 136. [Hector]
Nestor: I would my arms could match thee in contention,
As they contend with thee in courtesy.
Hector: I would they could.
Troilus and Cressida. Act iv, sc. 5, l. 205.

3
With his arms outstretch'd as he would fly.
Troilus and Cressida, iii, 3, 167. See under TIME.
Outstretched arms.—*III Henry VI,* i, 4, 68.
Oped their arms.—*Titus Andronicus,* v, 3, 108.
Arm 'gainst arm.—*Macbeth,* i, 2, 56.
At arms' end.—*The Two Gentlemen of Verona,* v, 4, 57; *As You Like It,* ii, 6, 10.

4
Over one arm the lusty courser's rein,
Under her other was the tender boy.
Venus and Adonis, l. 31.
Look, how a bird lies tangled in a net,
So fasten'd in her arms Adonis lies.
Venus and Adonis, l. 67.
Making my arms his field.
Venus and Adonis, l. 108.

II—Arms: Weapons
See also Weapon

5
He whose sable arms,
Black as his purpose, did the night resemble.
Hamlet. Act ii, sc. 2, l. 474. [Hamlet]

6
All furnish'd, all in arms:
All plumed like estridges that with the wind
Baited like eagles having lately bathed.
I Henry IV. Act iv, sc. 1, l. 97. [Vernon] "Estridge" is repeated in *Antony and Cleopatra,* iii, 13, 197.

7
Now is it time to arm: come, shall we about it?
Henry V. Act iii, sc. 7, l. 167. [Constable]
I'll go arm myself.—*Henry V,* iii, 7, 97.
Arm yourself.—*Coriolanus,* iii, 2, 138; *A Midsummer-Night's Dream,* i, 1, 117.
Put himself in arms.—*King John,* ii, 1, 57.
Take arms.—*Hamlet,* iii, 1, 59.
Take up arms.—*I Henry VI,* iii, 2, 70.

8
Villain, thou know'st the law of arms is such
That whoso draws a sword, 'tis present death.
I Henry VI. Act iii, sc. 4, l. 38. [Basset]
I crave the benefit of law of arms.
I Henry VI. Act iv, sc. 1, l. 100. [Vernon]
By the law of arms thou wast not bound to answer
An unknown opposite.
King Lear. Act v, sc. 3, l. 152. [Goneril]
Lay down thy arms.—*King John,* ii, 1, 154; v, 1, 24; v, 2, 126.

9
Will I not think of home, but follow arms.
King John. Act ii, sc. 1, l. 31. [Austria]
Upon my knee I beg, go not to arms.
King John. Act iii, sc. 1, l. 308. [Blanch]

10
Arm, arm, you heavens, against these perjured kings!
King John, iii, 1, 107. See under HEAVEN.
Arm you against your other enemies.
King John, iv, 2, 249. See under PEACE.
Arm, wenches, arm! encounters mounted are
Against your peace.
Love's Labour's Lost, v, 2, 82. [Boyet]
Arm, arm, my lord; the foe vaunts in the field.
Richard III. Act v, sc. 3, l. 288. [Norfolk]
Arm, arm, my lord.—*Titus Andronicus,* iv, 4, 62.
Arm, arm, and out!—*Macbeth,* v, 5, 46.
Arm, arm, with speed.—*I Henry IV,* v, 2, 76.
Arm, arm!—*I Henry VI,* ii, 1, 38, and frequently in later plays.
Arms, arms, sword, fire!—*King Lear,* iii, 6, 58.

11
To arms let 's hie!
King John. Act iii, sc. 1, l. 347. [King John]
Let us, my liege, to arms.
King John. Act v, sc. 1, l. 73. [Bastard]
To arms!—*III Henry VI,* i, 2, 28, and frequently in later plays.
Now arms must rule.—*III Henry VI,* iv, 7, 61.

12
Travelling along this coast, I here am come by chance,
And lay my arms before the legs of this sweet lass of France.
Love's Labour's Lost, v, 2, 557. [Costard]
I bepray you, let me borrow my arms again.
Love's Labour's Lost, v, 2, 702. See under CHALLENGE. The only use of "bepray."
Lend me arms.—*Antony and Cleopatra,* ii, 2, 88.

13
He'll fill the land with arms.
Pericles. Act i, sc. 2, l. 90. [Pericles]
Arms invasive.—*King John,* v, 1, 69. The only use of "invasive."
Civil and uncivil arms.—*Richard II,* iii, 3, 102.
Confederate arms.—*Coriolanus,* v, 3, 208.
Despised arms.—*Richard II,* ii, 3, 95.
Haughty arms.—*I Henry IV,* v, 2, 41.
Hostile arms.—*Richard III,* iv, 4, 399.
Ill-beseeming arms.—*II Henry IV,* iv, 1, 84.
Just-borne arms.—*King John,* ii, 1, 345. The only use of "just-borne."
Pigmy arms.—*King John,* v, 2, 135.
Revengeful arms.—*III Henry VI,* ii, 1, 164; *The Rape of Lucrece,* l. 1693.
Self-born arms.—*Richard II,* ii, 3, 80. "Self-born" is repeated in *The Winter's Tale,* iv, 1, 8: "Self-born hour."
Uplifted arms.—*Richard II,* ii, 2, 50.
Wrathful iron arms.—*Richard II,* i, 3, 136.
Foul rebellion's arms.—*Richard II,* iii, 2, 26.
Rebels' arms.—*I Henry IV,* v, 4, 14.
Traitors' arms.—*Julius Cæsar,* iii, 2, 189.

14
Say who thou art
And why thou comest thus knightly clad in arms.
Richard II. Act i, sc. 3, l. 11. [Marshal]

Flourishing in arms.—*Titus Andronicus,* i, 1, 38.
Furbish'd arms.—*Macbeth,* i, 2, 32.
Gilded arms.—*Cymbeline,* v, 5, 4.
Shining arms.—*The Rape of Lucrece,* l. 197.

1
Our bruised arms hung up for monuments.
Richard III, i, 1, 6. See under PEACE.
Bruised arms.—*The Rape of Lucrece,* l. 110.
Bruising arms.—*I Henry IV,* iii, 2, 105.
Arms torn and defaced.—*II Henry VI,* iv, 1, 42.

2
Hector, by this, is arming him in Troy.
Troilus and Cressida. Act v, sc. 2, l. 183. [Æneas]
Great Achilles Is arming.—*Troilus and Cressida,* v, 5, 31.
Arming myself.—*Julius Cæsar,* v, 1, 106.

3
Be happy that my arms are out of use.
Troilus and Cressida. Act v, sc. 6, l. 16. [Achilles]

ARMOUR

4
Cleopatra: Go put on thy defences. . . . Is not this buckled well?
Antony: Rarely, rarely:
He that unbuckles this, till we do please
To daff 't for our repose, shall hear a storm.
Antony and Cleopatra. Act iv, sc. 4, l. 10.
Unbuckle, unbuckle.—*The Winter's Tale,* iv, 4, 661. The only uses of "unbuckle."
Canst thou so daff me?—*Much Ado about Nothing,* v, 1, 78. The only uses of "daff."
Cleopatra: I 'll give thee, friend,
An armour all of gold; it was a king's.
Antony: He has deserved it, were it carbuncled
Like holy Phœbus' car.
Antony and Cleopatra. Act iv, sc. 8, l. 26. The only use of "carbuncled."
Come, mine armour.—*Antony and Cleopatra,* iv, 4, 2.
Give me my (mine) armour.—*Macbeth,* v, 3, 33; 36.

5
Such was the very armour he had on
When he the ambitious Norway combated.
Hamlet. Act i, sc. 1, l. 60. [Horatio]

6
Hence, therefore, thou nice crutch!
A scaly gauntlet now with joints of steel
Must glove this hand.
II Henry IV. Act i, sc. 1, l. 145. [Northumberland] The only use of "scaly."
Thus plated in habiliments of war.
Richard II. Act i, sc. 3, l. 28. [King Richard] "Plated" is repeated in *Antony and Cleopatra,* i, 1, 4: "Plated Mars."
Crush our old limbs in ungentle steel.—*I Henry IV,* v, 1, 13.
Clothed in steel.—*Pericles,* ii, 1, 160.
Complete armour.—*Richard III,* iv, 4, 189.

7
The armourers, accomplishing the knights,
With busy hammers closing rivets up,
Give dreadful note of preparation.
Henry V, iv, Prol., 12. The only use of "accomplishing."
Now thrive the armourers.—*Henry V,* ii, Prol., 3.
Thou art The armourer of my heart.
Antony and Cleopatra. Act iv, sc. 4, l. 7. [Antony]
He . . . struck his armourer.—*Troilus and Cressida,* i, 2, 6.
The armourer and his man.—*II Henry VI,* ii, 3, 50.
The servant of the armourer.—*II Henry VI,* ii, 3, 58. The only uses of "armourer."

8
Their armours, that march'd hence so silver-bright,
Hither return all gilt with Frenchmen's blood.
King John. Act ii, sc. 1, l. 315. [English Herald] The only use of "silver-bright."

9
Before my body I throw my warlike shield.
Macbeth. Act v, sc. 8, l. 32. [Macbeth]
Sword and shield.—*Henry V,* iii, 2, 9.
Targe and shield.—*Love's Labour's Lost,* v, 2, 556.
Targes of proof.—*Cymbeline,* v, 5, 5.
Targes undinted.—*Antony and Cleopatra,* ii, 6, 39. The only uses of "targe."

10
I am arm'd and well prepared.
The Merchant of Venice. Act iv, sc. 1, l. 264. [Antonio]
Armed at point exactly, cap-a-pe.
Hamlet. Act i, sc. 2, l. 200. [Horatio] "Cap-a-pe" is repeated in *Winter's Tale,* iv, 4, 761.

11
He would have walked ten mile a-foot to see a good armour.
Much Ado about Nothing. Act ii, sc. 3, l. 17. [Benedick]
Armour forged for proof eterne.—*Hamlet,* ii, 2, 512. "Eterne" is repeated in *Macbeth,* iii, 2, 38.

12
Put armour on thine ears and on thine eyes;
Whose proof, nor yells of mothers, maids, nor babes,
Nor sight of priests in holy vestments bleeding,
Shall pierce a jot.
Timon of Athens. Act iv, sc. 3, l. 123. [Timon]

13
I like thy armour well;
I 'll frush it and unlock the rivets all,
And I 'll be master of it.
Troilus and Cressida. Act v, sc. 6, l. 28. [Hector] The only use of "frush" (shatter).

ARMY

See also Soldier, Troop

14
Your army, which doth most consist
Of war-mark'd footmen.
Antony and Cleopatra. Act iii, sc. 7, l. 44. [Enobarbus] The only use of "war-mark'd."
'Tis a brave army, And full of purpose.
Antony and Cleopatra. Act iv, sc. 3, l. 11. [Third Soldier]
A fearful army.—*Coriolanus,* iv, 6, 75.
A mighty army.—*I Henry VI,* iv, 3, 2.

A treacherous army.—*The Tempest,* i, 2, 128.
Christian armies.—*King John,* v, 2, 37.
Huge army.—*Love's Labour 's Lost,* i, 1, 10.
Armies of pestilence.—*Richard II,* iii, 3, 87.

1
Roman: Have you an army ready, say you?
Volsce: A most royal one; . . . to be on foot at an hour's warning.
Coriolanus. Act iv, sc. 3, l. 46.

Instant army.—*Coriolanus,* v, 1, 37.

2 Our army is dispersed already:
Like youthful steers unyoked, they take their courses
East, west, north, south; or, like a school broke up,
Each hurries toward his home and sporting-place.
II Henry IV. Act iv, sc. 2, l. 103. [Lord Hastings] The only use of "sporting-place."

The army is discharged and all are gone.
II Henry IV. Act iv, sc. 3, l. 137. [Bardolph]

The army broken.—*Cymbeline,* v, 3, 5.
Cloven army.—*Coriolanus,* i, 4, 21.

3
For lo! within a ken our army lies,
Upon mine honour, all too confident
To give admittance to a thought of fear.
Our battle is more full of names than yours,
Our men more perfect in the use of arms,
Our armour all as strong, our cause the best.
II Henry IV. Act iv, sc. 1, l. 151. [Westmoreland]

Our army 's in the field.—*Coriolanus,* i, 2, 17.

4
Upon his royal face there is no note
How dread an army hath enrounded him.
Henry V. Act iv, Prologue, l. 36. [Chorus] The only use of "enrounded."

An army have I muster'd in my thoughts.
I Henry VI. Act i, sc. 1, l. 101. [Bedford]

5
The English army is grown weak and faint.
I Henry VI. Act i, sc. 1, l. 158. [Messenger]

The English army, that divided was
Into two parties, is now conjoin'd in one.
I Henry VI. Act v, sc. 2, l. 11. [Scout]

The army of France is landed.—*King Lear,* iii, 7, 2.

6
His army is a ragged multitude
Of hinds and peasants, rude and merciless.
II Henry VI. Act iv, sc. 4, l. 32. [Messenger]

With a puissant and a mighty power
Of gallowglasses and stout kerns
Is marching hitherward in proud array.
II Henry VI. Act iv, sc. 9, l. 25. [Messenger] "Gallowglasses" (armed retainers of ancient Irish chieftains) occurs again in *Macbeth,* i, 2, 13.

Cheer'd up the drooping army.
III Henry VI. Act i, sc. 1, l. 6. [Warwick]

7
York: The army of the queen mean to besiege us.
Mortimer: She shall not need; we 'll meet her in the field.
III Henry VI. Act i, sc. 2, l. 64.

The army of the queen hath got the field.
III Henry VI. Act i, sc. 4, l. 1. [York]

8 If but a dozen French
Were there in arms, they would be as a call
To train ten thousand English to their side,
Or as a little snow, tumbled about,
Anon becomes a mountain.
King John. Act iii, sc. 4, l. 173. [Pandulph]

Rash-levied army.—*Richard III,* iv, 3, 50. The only use of "rash-levied."

ARROGANCE

See also Pride

9
You 're meek and humble-mouth'd;
You sign your place and calling, in full seeming,
With meekness and humility; but your heart
Is cramm'd with arrogancy, spleen, and pride.
Henry VIII. Act ii, sc. 4, l. 107. [Queen Katharine] The only use of "humble-mouth'd" and "arrogancy."

Can ye endure to hear this arrogance,
And from this fellow?
Henry VIII. Act iii, sc. 2, l. 278. [Surrey]

10
I hate not you for her proud arrogance.
Richard III. Act i, sc. 3, l. 24. [Queen]

O monstrous arrogance!—*The Taming of the Shrew,* iv, 3, 106.

11 The proud lord
That bastes his arrogance with his own seam.
Troilus and Cressida. Act ii, sc. 3, l. 194. [Ulysses] The only use of "bastes." "Seam" is repeated in *Pericles,* ii, 1, 156.

ART

See also Painting

12 Those arts they have as I
Could put into them.
Cymbeline. Act v, sc. 5, l. 337. [Belarius]

Arts and arms.—*Pericles,* ii, 3, 82.
Arts and exercise.—*Troilus and Cressida,* iv, 4, 80; *Hamlet,* iv, 7, 98.
Arts and martial exercises.—*II Henry IV,* iv, 5, 74.

13
Queen: More matter, with less art.
Polonius: Madam, I swear I use no art at all.
Hamlet. Act ii, sc. 2, l. 95.

I will use no art.—*Hamlet,* ii, 2, 99.

14
Trace me in the tedious ways of art.
I Henry IV. Act iii, sc. 1, l. 48. [Glendower]

The art and practic part of life.
Must be the mistress to this theoric.
Henry V. Act i, sc. 1, l. 51. [Canterbury] The only use of "practic." "Theoric" occurs twice more, in *All 's Well that Ends Well,* iv, 3, 162, and in *Othello,* i, 1, 24.

Temper him with all the art I have.
Titus Andronicus. Act iv, sc. 4, l. 109. [Tamora]

So excellent in art, and still so rising,
Henry VIII. Act iv, sc. 2, l. 62. [Griffith]

1 Nature 's above art.
King Lear. Act iv, sc. 6, l. 86. [King Lear]

In scorn of nature, art gave lifeless life.
The Rape of Lucrece, l. 1374.

Now art thou what thou art, by art as well as by nature.
Romeo and Juliet, ii, 4, 94. [Mercutio]

Nature is made better by no mean
But nature makes that mean: so, over that art
Which you say adds to nature, is an art
That nature makes. You see, sweet maid, we marry
A gentler scion to the wildest stock,
And make conceive a bark of baser kind
By bud of nobler race: this is an art
Which does mend nature, change it rather, but
The art itself is nature.
The Winter's Tale. Act iv, sc. 4, l. 87. [Polixenes]

2 Other slow arts entirely keep the brain.
Love's Labour 's Lost. Act iv, sc. 3, l. 324. [Biron]

What with his art in youth, and youth in art,
Threw my affections in his charmed power.
A Lover's Complaint, l. 145.

3 In framing an artist, art hath thus decreed,
To make some good, but others to exceed.
Pericles. Act ii, sc. 3, l. 15. [Simonides] The only use of "framing."

O, had I but followed the arts!
Twelfth Night. Act i, sc. 3, l. 99. [Sir Andrew]

4 In others' works thou dost but mend the style,
And arts with thy sweet graces graced be;
But thou art all my art and dost advance
As high as learning my rude ignorance.
Sonnets. No. lxxviii.

5 Fair Padua, nursery of arts.
The Taming of the Shrew. Act i, sc. 1, l. 2. [Lucentio]

The liberal arts.—*The Tempest,* i, 2, 73.

Living art.—*Love's Labour 's Lost,* i, 1, 14.

6 Lucentio: I profess, the Art to Love.
Bianca: And may you prove, sir, master of your art!
The Taming of the Shrew. Act iv, sc. 2, l. 8.

Art of wooing.—*The Merry Wives of Windsor,* ii, 2, 244.

7 His art is of such power,
It would control my dam's god, Setebos.
The Tempest. Act i, sc. 2, l. 372. [Caliban] Setebos is mentioned again in v, 1, 261.

My art is not past power.—*All's Well that Ends Well,* ii, 1, 161.

8 It was mine art . . . that made gape
The pine.
The Tempest. Act i, sc. 2, l. 291. [Prospero]

Some vanity of mine art.—*Tempest,* iv, 1, 41.

False art.—*Sonnets,* lxviii.

Plastering art.—*Hamlet,* iii, 1, 51. The only use of "plastering."

Potent art.—*The Tempest,* v, 1, 50.

Prosperous art.—*Measure for Measure,* i, 2, 189.

Secret art.—*Pericles,* iii, 2, 32.

Pleasure's art.—*Pericles,* i, 2, 9.

Wise man's art.—*Twelfth Night,* iii, 1, 73.

Art of beauty.—*Sonnets,* liii.

Art of craft.—*A Lover's Complaint,* l. 295.

Art to enchant.—*The Tempest,* Epil., 14.

ASPIRATION, see Ambition

ASS

9 Luciana: If thou art changed to aught, 'tis to an ass.
Dromio of Syracuse: 'Tis true; she rides me and I long for grass.
'Tis so, I am an ass.
The Comedy of Errors, Act ii, sc. 2, l. 201.

Antipholus of Ephesus: I think thou art an ass.
Dromio of Ephesus: Marry, so it doth appear
By the wrongs I suffer and the blows I bear.
I should kick, being kick'd; and, being at that pass,
You would keep from my heels and beware of an ass.
The Comedy of Errors. Act iii, sc. 1, l. 15.

Antipholus of Ephesus: Thou art sensible in nothing but blows, and so is an ass.
Dromio of Ephesus: I am an ass, indeed; you may prove it by my long ears.
The Comedy of Errors. Act iv, sc. 4, l. 29.

O this woodcock, what an ass it is!
The Taming of the Shrew. Act i, sc. 2, l. 61. [Grumio]

What an ass it is!—*Coriolanus,* iv, 5, 47.

What an ass art thou!—*The Two Gentlemen of Verona,* ii 5, 25.

10 Why, what an ass am I!
Hamlet. Act ii, sc. 2, l. 611. [Hamlet]

What a thrice-double ass was I.
The Tempest, v, 1, 295. The only use of "thrice-double."

I am such a tender ass, if my hair do but tickle me, I must scratch.
A Midsummer-Night's Dream. Act iv, sc. 1, l. 27. [Bottom]

O that he were here to write me down an ass!
But, masters, remember that I am an ass; though it be not written down, yet forget not that I am an ass.
Much Ado about Nothing. Act iv, sc. 2, l. 77. [Dogberry]

This plaintiff here, the offender, did call me ass:
I beseech you, let it be remembered in his punishment.
Much Ado about Nothing. Act v, sc. 1, l. 315. [Dogberry] "Plaintiff" is repeated in l. 261, and in *Twelfth Night,* v, 1, 362.

I am not altogether an ass.
The Merry Wives of Windsor. Act i, sc. 1, l. 175. [Slender]

11 Your dull ass will not mend his pace with beating.
Hamlet. Act v, sc. 1, l. 64. [First Clown]

1
He is an ass, as is the world: I will verify as much in his beard.
Henry V. Act iii, sc. 2, l. 75. [Fluellen]
He is an ass.—*Love's Labour 's Lost,* v, 2, 628.
Page is an ass, a secure ass.
The Merry Wives of Windsor. Act ii, sc. 2, l. 315. [Ford]
Man is but an ass.—*A Midsummer-Night's Dream,* iv, 1, 212. See under MAN.
Egregiously an ass.—*Othello,* ii, 1, 318. The only use of "egregiously."
An ass, a madman.—*Measure for Measure,* v, 1, 506.
Preposterous ass.—*The Taming of the Shrew,* iii, 1, 9.
Virtuous ass.—*II Henry IV,* ii, 2, 80.
Young Trojan ass.—*Troilus and Cressida,* v, 4, 6.

2
Like to the empty ass, to shake his ears,
And graze in commons.
Julius Cæsar. Act iv, sc. 1, l. 26. [Antony]

3
May not an ass know when the cart draws the horse?
King Lear. Act i, sc. 4, l. 244. [Fool]

4
I do begin to perceive that I am made an ass.
The Merry Wives of Windsor. Act v, sc. 5, l. 124. [Falstaff]
I see their knavery: this is to make an ass of me.
A Midsummer-Night's Dream. Act iii, sc. 1, l. 123. [Bottom]
'Slight, will you make an ass o' me?
Twelfth Night. Act iii, sc. 2, l. 14. [Sir Andrew] "'Slight" (by God's light) is used a second time in ii, 5, 38, and appears in no other play. It is peculiar to Sir Andrew Aguecheck.

5
Snout: What do I see on thee?
Bottom: What do you see? you see an ass-head of your own, do you?
A Midsummer-Night's Dream. Act iii, sc. 1, l. 119.
An ass's nole I fixed on his head.
A Midsummer-Night's Dream. Act iii, sc. 2, l. 17. [Puck] The only use of "nole."
An ass-head and a coxcomb.
Twelfth Night. Act v, sc. 1, l. 212. [Sir Toby] The only uses of "ass-head."

6
When in that moment, so it came to pass,
Titania waked and straightway loved an ass.
A Midsummer-Night's Dream. Act iii, sc. 2, l. 33. [Puck]
Methought I was enamour'd of an ass.
A Midsummer-Night's Dream. Act iv, sc. 1, l. 80. [Titania]

7
Theseus: I wonder if the lion be to speak.
Demetrius: No wonder, my lord: one lion may, when many asses do.
A Midsummer-Night's Dream. Act v, sc. 1, l. 153.
Lysander: He is dead; he is nothing.
Theseus: With the help of a surgeon he might yet recover, and prove an ass.
A Midsummer-Night's Dream. Act v, sc. 1, l. 316.

8
Away! you are an ass, you are an ass.
Much Ado about Nothing. Act iv, sc. 2, l. 75. [Conrade]
Away, away, mad ass!
The Taming of the Shrew. Act v, sc. 1, l. 87. [Pedant]
An assinego may tutor thee: thou scurvy-valiant ass!
Troilus and Cressida. Act ii, sc. 1, l. 49. [Thersites] The only use of "assinego" (little ass) and "scurvy-valiant."
Thou whoreson ass.—*The Two Gentlemen of Verona,* ii, 5, 49.

9
I bear a burthen like an ass,
Spur-gall'd and tired by jauncing Bolingbroke.
Richard II. Act v, sc. 5, l. 94. [King Richard] The only use of "spur-gall'd" and "jauncing."
Asses are make to bear, and so are you.
The Taming of the Shrew. Act ii, sc. 1, l. 200. [Katharina]

10
Servants: What are we, Apemantus?
Apemantus: Asses.
Servants: Why?
Apemantus: That you ask what you are, and do not know yourselves.
Timon of Athens. Act ii, sc. 2, l. 63.

11
The ass more captain than the lion.
Timon of Athens. Act iii, sc. 5, l. 49. [Alcibiades]
Apemantus: The commonwealth of Athens is become a forest of beasts.
Timon: How has the ass broke the wall, that thou art out of the city?
Timon of Athens. Act iv, sc. 3, l. 354.

12
Now, what a thing it is to be an ass!
Titus Andronicus. Act iv, sc. 2, l. 25. [Aaron]
Asses, fools, dolts! chaff and bran, chaff and bran! porridge after meat!
Troilus and Cressida. Act i, sc. 2, l. 262. [Pandarus] "Dolt" is used only once again, in *Othello,* v, 2, 163.

13
To [be] an ass, were nothing; he is both ass and ox: to [be] an ox, were nothing; he is both ox and ass.
Troilus and Cressida. Act v, sc. 1, l. 65. [Thersites]

ASSAULT

14
The assault you have made to her chastity you shall answer me with your sword.
Cymbeline. Act i, sc. 4, l. 176. [Posthumus]
Undergoes . . . such assaults
As would take in some virtue.
Cymbeline, iii, 2, 7. See under PUNISHMENT.

15
Arm! arm! the enemy doth make assault!
I Henry VI. Act ii, sc. 1, l. 38. [Sentinel]

Say, where will you assault?
King John. Act ii, sc. 1, l. 408. [King Philip]

1 The Norweyan lord surveying vantage,
With furbish'd arms and new supplies of men
Began a fresh assault.
Macbeth. Act i, sc. 1, l. 31. [Sergeant] The only use of "surveying" and "furbish'd." "Furbish" occurs in *Richard II,* i, 3, 76. "Norweyan" is repeated in i, 2, 49: "Norweyan banners"; and in i, 3, 95: "Norweyan ranks"; and occurs in no other play.

First assault.—*All's Well that Ends Well,* i, 3, 121.
General assault.—*Hamlet,* ii, 1, 35.
Rude assault.—*Richard II,* v, 5, 106.
Strong assault.—*The Rape of Lucrece,* l. 835.
Vain assault.—*All's Well that Ends Well,* iv, 2, 51.

2 The assault which Angelo hath made to you, fortune hath conveyed to my understanding.
Measure for Measure. Act iii, sc. 1, l. 188. [Duke]

Assaults of affection.—*Much Ado about Nothing,* ii, 3, 120.

3 Speak with me,
Or, naked as I am, I will assault thee.
Othello. Act v, sc. 2, l. 257. [Othello]

4 I will make a complimental assault upon him.
Troilus and Cressida. Act iii, sc. 1, l. 42. [Pandarus] The only use of "complimental."

ASSISTANCE, see Help

ASSURANCE

5 I know not how I shall assure you further.
All's Well that Ends Well. Act iii, sc. 7, l. 2. [Helena]

What can you assure her?—*The Taming of the Shrew,* ii, 1, 347.
These I will assure her.—*The Taming of the Shrew,* ii, 1, 381.
I assure thee.—*As You Like It,* i, 1, 159; *The Merry Wives of Windsor,* ii, 2, 109; *King Lear,* ii, 1, 106.
Assure thee.—*Titus Andronicus,* v, 1, 61; *Othello,* iii, 3, 20.
I can assure thee.—*II Henry IV,* v, 3, 70.
I dare assure thee.—*Julius Cæsar,* v, 4, 21.
I do assure thee.—*The Taming of the Shrew,* iv, 5, 74, and five times in later plays.
I assure ye.—*Love's Labour 's Lost,* iv, 2, 10; *Sonnets,* cxi.
I assure you.—*A Midsummer-Night's Dream,* i, 2, 14, and nine times in later plays.
I can assure you.—*Love's Labour 's Lost,* v, 2, 490; *I Henry IV,* v, 4, 146; *II Henry IV,* i, 2, 33; *Pericles,* iv, 6, 46.
I dare assure you.—*The Taming of the Shrew,* iv, 3, 191.
I do assure you.—*Twelfth Night,* iii, 4, 342.
I 'll assure you.—*Henry V,* iii, 6, 66; *Henry VIII,* i, 3, 54; iv, 1, 12.
Remain assured.—*Timon of Athens,* v, 1, 100.
Rest assured.—*Julius Cæsar,* v, 3, 17.
Stand you so assured.—*The Taming of the Shrew,* i, 2, 156.

6 You should procure him better assurance.
II Henry IV. Act i, sc. 2, l. 36. [Page]

Better assurance.—*A Midsummer-Night's Dream,* iii, 1, 21.

7 This I do assure myself.
II Henry VI. Act ii, sc. 2, l. 79. [York]

Assure thyself.—*Twelfth Night,* iii, 2, 38.
Assure yourself.—*Twelfth Night,* i, 2, 9; *Othello,* iv, 2, 202.
Assure yourselves.—*II Henry VI,* iv, 9, 19.

8 Give me assurance with some friendly vow
That I may never have you in suspect.
III Henry VI, iv, 1, 141. See under Obedience.

Give assurance.—*The Taming of the Shrew,* iv, 2, 69.
Make assurance.—*The Taming of the Shrew,* iii, 2, 136.
Make her the assurance.—*The Taming of the Shrew,* ii, 1, 389.
Make this assurance.—*The Taming of the Shrew,* ii, 1, 398.
Pass assurance.—*The Taming of the Shrew,* iv, 2, 117.
Take you assurance.—*The Taming of the Shrew,* iv, 4, 92.
Assurance of equal friendship.—*Henry VIII,* ii, 4, 17.
Assurance of a man.—*Hamlet,* iii, 4, 62.

9 Would I were assured of my condition!
King Lear. Act iv, sc. 7, l. 56. [King Lear]

Assured of thy fair health.
Sonnets. No. xlv.
Be assured.—*Richard III,* i, 3, 352, and frequently in later plays.
Be well assured.—*II Henry VI,* iii, 1, 346; iii, 2, 349; *III Henry VI,* v, 3, 16.
Be you well assured.—*Othello,* iii, 3, 11; iv, 1, 30.
I am well assured.—*King John,* ii, 1, 534.
Well I am assured.—*Richard III,* v, 3, 36.
I am assured.—*II Henry IV,* v, 2, 64; *I Henry VI,* v, 5, 83.
Well assured.—*Richard II,* ii, 4, 17; *Coriolanus,* iii, 1, 121; *Pericles,* v, 1, 67.
Most assured.—*Richard III,* ii, 1, 37.

10 But yet I 'll make assurance double sure,
And take a bond of fate.
Macbeth. Act iv, sc. 1, l. 83. [Macbeth]

11 My assurance bids me search.
The Merry Wives of Windsor. Act iii, sc. 2, l. 46. [Ford]

12 Such assurance ta'en
As shall with either part's agreement stand?
The Taming of the Shrew. Act iv, sc. 4, l. 49. [Tranio]

13 More assurance than a living prince
Does now speak to thee.
The Tempest. Act v, sc. 1, l. 98. [Prospero]

14 Assurance bless your thoughts!
Timon of Athens. Act ii, sc. 2, l. 189. [Flavius]

1
Give me modest assurance if you be the lady of the house.
Twelfth Night. Act i, sc. 5, l. 192. [Viola]
You should put your lord into a desperate assurance she will none of him.
Twelfth Night. Act ii, sc. 2, l. 7. [Malvolio]
Auricular assurance.—*King Lear,* i, 2, 99. The only use of "auricular."
Counterfeit assurance.—*Taming of the Shrew,* iv, 4, 92. Of the twenty-nine times that "assurance" is used in the plays, nine, or nearly one third, occur in *The Taming of the Shrew.*
Full assurance.—*Twelfth Night,* iv, 3, 26.
Unsured assurance.—*King John,* ii, 1, 471. The only use of "unsured."

ASTONISHMENT, see Amazement

ATTEMPT

2
I know not what the success will be, my lord; but the attempt I vow.
All's Well that Ends Well. Act iii, sc. 6, l. 86. [Bertram]
3
A man may, if he were of a fearful heart, stagger in this attempt.
As You Like It. Act iii, sc. 3, l. 48. [Touchstone]
Give over this attempt.
As You Like It. Act i, sc. 2, l. 190. [Celia]
This attempt
I am soldier to, and will abide it with
A prince's courage.
Cymbeline. Act iii, sc. 4, l. 185. [Imogen]
4
I have attempted . . . and led your wars.
Coriolanus, v, 6, 75. See under War.
Falsely attempted.—*Love's Labour's Lost,* i, 2, 177. The only uses of "attempted."
5
The quality and hair of our attempt
Brooks no division.
I Henry IV. Act iv, sc. 1, l. 61. [Worcester]
This haughty great attempt.—*I Henry VI,* ii, 5, 79.
Bold attempt.—*Richard III,* v, 3, 265.
Dangerous attempt.—*Richard III,* iv, 4, 398.
Direct or indirect attempts.—*The Merchant of Venice,* iv, 1, 350.
Last attempt.—*Coriolanus,* v, 3, 146.
6
Never attempt anything on him.
Henry VIII. Act iii, sc. 2, l. 17. [Lord Chamberlain]
7
The attempt and not the deed Confounds us.
Macbeth. Act ii, sc. 2, l. 11. [Lady Macbeth]
8
I must attempt you further.
The Merchant of Venice. Act iv, sc. 1, l. 421. [Bassanio]
He will never, I think, in the way of waste, attempt us again.
The Merry Wives of Windsor. Act iv, sc. 2, l. 226. [Mrs. Page]
I durst attempt it against any lady in the world.
Cymbeline. Act i, sc. 4, l. 123. [Iachimo]
9
I will attempt the doing it.
***Othello,* iii, 4, 22.** See under Deed.
I will be near to second your attempt.
Othello. Act iv, sc. 2, l. 244. [Iago]
If thou attempt it, it will cost thee dear.
Othello. Act v, sc. 2, l. 255. [Gratiano]

ATTENDANCE

10
Last time, I danced attendance on his will
Till Paris was besieged, famish'd, and lost.
II Henry VI. Act i, sc. 3, l. 174. [York]
I dance attendance here.
Richard III. Act iii, sc. 7, l. 56. [Buckingham]
Dance attendance on their lordships' pleasures.
Henry VIII. Act v, sc. 2, l. 31. [King Henry]
11
Why might not you, my lord, receive attendance
From those that she calls servants or from mine?
King Lear. Act ii, sc. 4, l. 246. [Regan]
What, no attendance? no regard? no duty?
The Taming of the Shrew. Act iv, sc. 1, l. 129. [Petruchio]
12
Wait attendance
Till you hear further from me.
Timon of Athens. Act i, sc. 1, l. 161. [Timon]
On your attendance.—*Twelfth Night,* i, 4, 11.

ATTENTION

13
Vex not his prescience; be attentive.
Antony and Cleopatra. Act i, sc. 2, l. 20. [Alexas]
Be you silent and attentive too,
For he that interrupts him shall not live.
III Henry VI. Act i, sc. 1, l. 122. [Warwick]
The very minute bids thee ope thine ear;
Obey and be attentive.
The Tempest. Act i, sc. 2, l. 37. [Prospero]
Set his sense on the attentive bent.
Troilus and Cressida. Act i, sc. 3, l. 252. [Æneas]
Your spirits are attentive.—*The Merchant of Venice,* v, 1, 70. The only uses of "attentive."
Attentiveness wounded his daughter.
The Winter's Tale. Act v, sc. 2, l. 94. [Gentleman] The only use of "attentiveness."
14
Imogen: Give me hearing.
Cymbeline: Ay, with all my heart,
And lend my best attention.
Cymbeline. Act v, sc. 5, l. 117.
Prospero: Dost thou attend me?
Miranda: Sir, most heedfully.
The Tempest. Act i, sc. 2, l. 78.
15
Falstaff: Dost thou hear me, Hal?
Prince: Ay, and mark thee too, Jack.
Falstaff: Do so, for it is worth the listening to.
I Henry IV. Act ii, sc. 4, l. 233.
Falstaff: It is the disease of not listening, the malady of not marking, that I am troubled withal.
Chief Justice: To punish you by the heels would amend the attention of your ears.
II Henry IV. Act i, sc. 2, l. 138.
16
I will be bold with time and your attention.
Henry VIII. Act ii, sc. 4, l. 168. [King Henry]

1
King: Will you hear this letter with attention?
Biron: As we would hear an oracle.
Love's Labour's Lost. Act i, sc. 1, l. 217.

With sad attention long to hear her words.
The Rape of Lucrece, l. 1610.

Beguiled attention.—*Rape of Lucrece,* l. 1404.

Enforce attention.—*Richard II,* ii, 1, 6.

ATTIRE, see Dress

AUDACITY, see Boldness

AUNT

2
Ford: Old woman! what old woman 's that?
Mrs. Ford: Why, it is my maid's aunt of Brentford.
Merry Wives of Windsor. Act iv, sc. 2, l. 178.

A widow aunt, a dowager.
A Midsummer-Night's Dream, i, 1, 157. [Lysander] "Dowager" is used five times.

3
The wisest aunt, telling the saddest tale.
A Midsummer-Night's Dream. Act ii, sc. 1, l. 51. [Puck]

Make my aunt merry with some pleasing tale.
Titus Andronicus. Act iii, sc. 2, l. 47. [Boy]

4
Their aunt I am in law, in love their mother.
Richard III. Act iv, sc. 1, l. 24. [Duchess of York]

Aunt-mother.—*Hamlet,* ii, 2, 394. The only use of the phrase.

5
An old aunt whom the Greeks held captive.
Troilus and Cressida. Act ii, sc. 2, l. 77. [Troilus]

Good aunt.—*Richard III,* ii, 2, 62.

Kind aunt.—*III Henry VI,* ii, 1, 146; *Richard III,* iv, 1, 2.

Noble aunt.—*Titus Andronicus,* iv, 1, 22.

Sweet aunt.—*II Henry VI,* i, 3, 146; *Titus Andronicus,* iv, 1, 4.

My aunt Lavinia.—*Titus Andronicus,* iv, 1, 1.

My aunt Percy.—*I Henry IV,* iii, 1, 196.

My sacred aunt.—*Troilus and Cressida,* iv, 5, 134.

AUTHOR, see Writer

AUTHORITY

6
There is no fettering of authority.
All's Well that Ends Well. Act ii, sc. 3, l. 251. [Parolles] The only use of "fettering."

Authority melts from me.
Antony and Cleopatra. Act iii, sc. 13, l. 90. [Antony]

7
Behold, these are the tribunes of the people,
The tongues o' the common mouth: I do despise them;
For they do prank them in authority,
Against all noble sufferance.
Coriolanus. Act iii, sc. 1, l. 21. [Coriolanus]

When two authorities are up,
Neither supreme, how soon confusion
May enter 'twixt the gap of both and take
The one by the other.
Coriolanus. Act iii, sc. 1, l. 109. [Coriolanus]

Or let us stand to our authority,
Or let us lose it.
Coriolanus. Act iii, sc. 1, l. 208. [Brutus]

8
I gave bold way to my authority.
II Henry IV. Act v, sc. 2, l. 82. [Chief Justice]

9
A man of great authority in France.
I Henry VI. Act v, sc. 1, l. 18. [Gloucester]

Of such great authority in France.
I Henry VI. Act v, sc. 5, l. 41. [Suffolk]

10
Our authority is his consent,
And what we do establish he confirms.
II Henry VI. Act iii, sc. 1, l. 316. [Suffolk]

The winking of authority.—*King John,* iv, 2, 211.

Sovereign greatness and authority.—*King John,* v, 1, 4.

11
Idle old man,
That still would manage those authorities
That he hath given away!
King Lear. Act i, sc. 3, l. 16. [Goneril]

Kent: You have that in your countenance which I would fain call master.
King Lear: What 's that?
Kent: Authority.
King Lear. Act i, sc. 4, l. 29.

12
Thou hast seen a farmer's dog bark at a beggar? . . . And the creature run from the cur?
There thou mightst behold the great image of authority: a dog 's obeyed in office.
King Lear. Act iv, sc. 6, l. 158. [King Lear]

Drest in a little brief authority.
Measure for Measure. Act ii, sc. 2, l. 118. [Isabella]

13
More authority, dear boy, name more.
Love's Labour's Lost. Act i, sc. 2, l. 70. [Armado]

Some authority how to proceed.—*Love's Labour's Lost,* iv, 3, 287.

Some authority.—*II Henry IV,* v, 3, 117.

14
Thus can the demigod Authority
Make us pay down for our offence by weight
The words of heaven; on whom it will, it will;
On whom it will not, so; yet still 'tis just.
Measure for Measure. Act i, sc. 2, l. 124. [Claudio]

Authority, though it err like others,
Hath yet a kind of medicine in itself,
That skins the vice o' the top.
Measure for Measure. Act ii, sc. 2, l. 134. [Isabella]

My authority bears of a credent bulk,
That no particular scandal once can touch
But it confounds the breather.
Measure for Measure. Act iv, sc. 4, l. 29. [Angelo]

15
Wrest once the law to your authority.
The Merchant of Venice. Act iv, sc. 1, l. 215. [Bassanio]

Art made tongue-tied by authority.
Sonnets. No. lxiv.

Bi-fold authority! where reason can revolt
Without perdition, and loss assume all reason
Without revolt.
Troilus and Cressida. Act v, sc. 2, l. 144. [Troilus] The only use of "bi-fold."

1 His great authority;
Which often hath no less prevail'd than so
On your command.
The Winter's Tale. Act ii, sc. 1, l. 53. [Lord]

He seems to be of great authority: close with him, give him gold; and though authority be a stubborn bear, yet he is oft led by the nose with gold.
The Winter's Tale. Act iv, sc. 4, l. 830. [Clown]

Base authority.—*Love's Labour 's Lost,* i, 1, 87.
Corrigible authority.—*Othello,* i, 3, 329. "Corrigible" is repeated in *Antony and Cleopatra,* iv, 14, 74: "Corrigible neck."
High authority.—*Antony and Cleopatra,* iii, 6, 33.
Strong authority.—*King John,* ii, 1, 113.
Usurp'd authority.—*King John,* iii, 1, 160.
Authority of manners.—*Timon of Athens,* ii, 2, 147.
Authority of . . . merit.—*Othello,* ii, 1, 147.

AUTUMN, see Seasons

AVARICE, see Covetousness

AWE

2
Thy free awe Pays homage to us.
Hamlet. Act iv, sc. 3, l. 63. [King]

3
We 'll bend it to our awe.
Henry V, i, 2, 224. See under FRANCE.

4
She holdeth thee in awe.
I Henry VI, i, 1, 39. See under WIFE.

Wrench awe from fools!
Measure for Measure, ii, 4, 14. See under PLACE.

5
I will awe him with my cudgel.
The Merry Wives of Windsor, ii, 2, 291. See under CUCKOLD.

6
Shall by a painted cloth be kept in awe.
The Rape of Lucrece, l. 245.

Kept in awe.—*II Henry VI,* i, 1, 92.
Keep . . . men in awe.—*Pericles,* i, Gower, 36.
Keep the strong in awe.—*Richard III,* v, 3, 310.
Keep you in awe.—*Coriolanus,* i, 1, 191.
Kept the world in awe.—*Hamlet,* v, 1, 238.
Awe the world.—*Julius Cæsar,* i, 2, 123.
Awe a man.—*Much Ado about Nothing,* ii, 3, 250.
One man's awe.—*Julius Cæsar,* ii, 1, 52.
Sceptre's awe.—*Richard II,* i, 1, 118.
Domestic awe.—*Timon of Athens,* iv, 1, 17.
Awe and fear.—*Henry V,* iv, 1, 264.
Awe and majesty.—*The Merchant of Venice,* iv, 1, 191.
Awe and terror.—*II Henry IV,* iv, 5, 177.

B

BABY

See also Infancy

7
So holy writ in babes hath judgement shown,
When judges have been babes.
All's Well that Ends Well. Act ii, sc. 1, l. 141. [Helena]

8
Dost thou not see my baby at my breast,
That sucks the nurse asleep?
Antony and Cleopatra. Act v, sc. 2, l. 312. [Cleopatra]

At their mothers' moist eyes babes shall suck.
I Henry VI, i, 1, 49. See under POSTERITY.

I have given suck, and know
How tender 'tis to love the babe that milks me.
Macbeth. Act i, sc. 7, l. 54. [Lady Macbeth]

9 Think yourself a baby
That you have ta'en these tenders for true pay,
Which are not sterling.
Hamlet. Act i, sc. 3, l. 105. [Polonius] "Sterling" is repeated in *II Henry IV,* ii, 1, 131: "Sterling money"; and in *Richard II,* iv, 1, 264: "If my word be sterling."

10
That great baby you see there is not yet out of his swaddling-clouts.
Hamlet. Act ii, sc. 2, l. 400. [Hamlet] The only use of "swaddling-clouts."

I' the swathing-clothes the other.—*Cymbeline,* i, 1, 59.
Mars in swathling clothes.—*I Henry IV,* iii, 2, 112.

11 From her derogate body never spring
A babe to honour her!
King Lear, i, 4, 303. See under CURSE.

12 Birth-strangled babe
Ditch-deliver'd by a drab.
Macbeth. Act iv, sc. 1, l. 30. [Third Witch] The only use of either phrase.

Baby of a girl.—*Macbeth,* iii, 4, 106.

13 Those that do teach young babes
Do it with gentle means and easy tasks.
Othello, iv, 2, 111. See under CHIDING.

14
Pity, you ancient stones, those tender babes
Whom envy hath immured within your walls!
Rough cradle for such little pretty ones!
Rude ragged nurse, old sullen playfellow
For tender princes, use my babies well!
So foolish sorrow bids your stones farewell.
Richard III. Act iv, sc. 1, l. 99. [Queen] "Immured" is used four times.

Ah, my tender babes!
My unblown flowers, new-appearing sweets!
If yet your gentle souls fly in the air
And be not fix'd in doom perpetual

Hover about me with your airy wings
And hear your mother's lamentation!
Richard III. Act iv, sc. 4, l. 9. [Queen Elizabeth] The only use of "unblown." "New-appearing" is repeated in *Sonnets*, vii: "New-appearing sun." "Tender babes" is used a third time in iv, 3, 9, and occurs in no other play.

Think that thy babes were fairer than they were,
And he that slew them fouler than he is.
Richard III. Act iv, sc. 4, l. 120. [Queen]

1
Thou wast the prettiest babe that e'er I nursed.
Romeo and Juliet. Act i, sc. 3, l. 60. [Nurse]

The baby beats the nurse.
Measure for Measure. Act i, sc. 4, l. 30. [Duke]

2 Spare not the babe,
Whose dimpled smiles from fools exhaust their mercy;
Think it a bastard, whom the oracle
Hath doubtfully pronounced thy throat shall cut,
And mince it sans remorse.
Timon of Athens. Act iv, sc. 3, l. 118. [Timon] The only use of "exhaust."

Ho, ho! I laugh to think that babe a bastard.
Timon of Athens, i, 2, 117. See under Bastard.

Here is the babe, as loathsome as a toad
Amongst the fairest breeders of our clime:
The empress sends it thee, thy stamp, thy seal,
And bids thee christen it with thy dagger's point.
Titus Andronicus. Act iv, sc. 2, l. 67. [Nurse]

I 'll broach the tadpole on my rapier's point.
Titus Andronicus. Act iv, sc. 2, l. 85. [Demetrius] "Tadpole" is repeated in *King Lear*, iii, 4, 135.

3 Come on, poor babe:
Some powerful spirit instruct the kites and ravens
To be thy nurses! Wolves and bears, they say,
Casting their savageness aside have done
Like offices of pity.
The Winter's Tale. Act ii, sc. 3, l. 185. [Antigonus]

Come, poor babe.—*The Winter's Tale*, iii, 3, 15.

4
Look to your babe, my lord; 'tis yours.
Winter's Tale. Act ii, sc. 3, l. 126. [Paulina]

His innocent babe truly begotten.
Winter's Tale. Act iii, sc. 2, l. 135. [Officer]

5 And for the babe
Is counted lost for ever, Perdita,
I prithee, call 't.
Winter's Tale. Act iii, sc. 3, l. 32. [Antigonus]

My gentle babe Marina, whom,
For she was born at sea, I have named so.
Pericles. Act iii, sc. 3, l. 12. [Pericles]

Crying babe.—*Titus Andronicus*, v, 1, 26; *The Rape of Lucrece*, l. 814.
Goodly babe.—*The Winter's Tale*, ii, 2, 26.
Little babe.—*The Winter's Tale*, ii, 2, 37.
Lowly babe.—*I Henry VI*, iii, 3, 47.
New-born babe.—*Hamlet*, iii, 3, 71.
Naked new-born babe.—*Macbeth*, i, 7, 21.
Pretty babes.—*The Comedy of Errors*, i, 1, 73.
Sweet babe.—*III Henry VI*, v, 7, 29; *Richard III*, iv, 4, 87; *The Rape of Lucrece*, l. 1161.
Testy babe.—*The Two Gentlemen of Verona*, i, 2, 58.
Empress' babe.—*Titus Andronicus*, v, 1, 35.
Babe of clouts.—*King John*, iii, 4, 58.

BACHELOR, see Marriage and Celibacy

BACK

6 Let us score their backs,
And snatch 'em up, as we take hares, behind.
Antony and Cleopatra. Act iv, sc. 7, l. 12. [Scarus]

Show'd his back.—*Antony and Cleopatra*, v, 2, 89.

7
Twice did he turn his back.
As You Like It. Act iv, sc. 3, l. 128. [Oliver]

Turns his back.—*Julius Cæsar*, ii, 1, 23.
Turns me his back.—*Macbeth*, iii, 6, 41.
Thus I turn my back.—*Coriolanus*, iii, 3, 134.
Turn my back.—*A Midsummer-Night's Dream*, iii, 2, 238.
Turn our backs.—*Timon of Athens*, iv, 2, 8.
Turn'd their backs.—*II Henry IV*, i, 1, 130.
Turn thy hated back.—*King Lear*, i, 1, 178.
For "turn back" see under Turn.

8
Backs red . . . With flight and agued fear!
Coriolanus. Act i, sc. 4, l. 37. [Marcius]

But the backs of Britons seen, all flying.
Cymbeline. Act v, sc. 3, l. 6. [Posthumus]

9
Well, I will back him straight.
I Henry IV. Act ii, sc. 3, l. 74. [Hotspur]

Sampson: I will back thee.
Gregory: How! turn thy back and run?
Romeo and Juliet. Act i, sc. 1, l. 39.

Back thy quarrels.—*Titus Andronicus*, ii, 3, 54.
Back my ring.—*Cymbeline*, ii, 4, 118.
Back my suit.—*Richard III*, i, 2, 236.

10
You are straight enough in the shoulders, you care not who sees your back.
I Henry IV, ii, 4, 165. See under Running.

A straight back will stoop.
Henry V, v, 2, 168. See under Heart.

11
He leaves his back unarm'd.
II Henry IV. Act i, sc. 3, l. 79. [Hastings]

Strip thine own back.—*King Lear*, iv, 6, 165.

12
You knew I was at your back.
II Henry IV. Act ii, sc. 4, l. 334. [Prince]

At his back.—*Troilus and Cressida*, iii, 3, 145.
At my back.—*I Henry IV*, ii, 4, 247.
At our backs.—*III Henry VI*, ii, 5, 133; *Julius Cæsar*, iv, 3, 212.

13
She bears a duke's revenues on her back.
II Henry VI. Act i, sc. 3, l. 83. [Queen]

On her back.—*Titus Andronicus*, iv, 1, 99.

He hath borne me on his back a thousand times.
Hamlet. Act v, sc. 1, l. 205. [Hamlet]

On his back doth lie
An image like thyself, all stain'd with gore.
Venus and Adonis, l. 663.

On his back.—*As You Like It*, iv, 3, 108; *Merchant of Venice*, iv, 1, 28; *Richard II*, v, 5, 84.

The things that threaten'd me
Ne'er look'd but on my back.
Julius Cæsar, ii, 2, 11. See under THREAT.
On my back.—*Henry V,* v, 2, 143; *Richard III,* iii, 7, 228; *King Lear,* i, 4, 42.
On our back.—*Macbeth,* v, 5, 52.
On their backs.—*King John,* ii, 1, 70; *Romeo and Juliet,* i, 4, 92.
On your back.—*I Henry IV,* v, 4, 160; *Timon of Athens,* ii, 2, 57.

1
Leaves Love upon her back deeply distress'd.
Venus and Adonis, l. 814.
Upon my back.—*Troilus and Cressida,* i, 2, 284.
Upon our backs.—*III Henry VI,* v, 1, 61.
Upon thy back.—*Romeo and Juliet,* iii, 3, 141; v, 1, 71.

2 Many
Have broke their backs with laying manors on 'em.
Henry VIII. Act i, sc. 1, l. 84. [Buckingham]
Break his foaming courser's back.
Richard II, i, 2, 51. See under SIN.
I love and honour him,
But must not break my back to heal his finger.
Timon of Athens. Act ii, sc. 1, l. 23. [Senator]
Break my back.—*III Henry VI,* v, 7, 24; *The Tempest,* iii, 1, 26.
Break some gallows' back.—*II Henry IV,* iv, 3, 32.
Break the back of man.—*The Winter's Tale,* iv, 4, 797.

3
The back is sacrifice to the load.
Henry VIII, i, 2, 50. See under TAXATION.
If your back
Cannot vouchsafe this burthen, 'tis too weak
Ever to get a boy. . . . By this time
I know your back will bear a duchess.
Henry VIII. Act ii, sc. 3, l. 42. [Lady]

4
Stand between her back, sir, and the fire.
Love's Labour 's Lost. Act v, sc. 2, l. 476. [Biron]
Hot backs.—*The Merry Wives of Windsor,* v, 5, 13.
Bat's back.—*The Tempest,* v, 1, 91.
Dolphin's back.—*Midsummer-Night's Dream,* ii, 1, 150; *Twelfth Night,* i, 2, 15.
Neptune's back.—*Antony and Cleopatra,* iv, 14, 58.
Raven's back.—*Romeo and Juliet,* iii, 2, 19.
Back of his hand.—*Julius Cæsar,* i, 2, 221.

5
My back o' t' other side,—O, my back, my back!
Romeo and Juliet. Act ii, sc. 5, l. 51. [Nurse]

6 It will be of more price,
Being spoke behind your back. than to your face.
Romeo and Juliet. Act iv, sc. 1, l. 27. [Juliet]
Behind her back.—*The Merchant of Venice,* iv, 1, 293.

7
Swayed in the back and shoulder-shotten.
The Taming of the Shrew, iii, 2, 56. See under HORSE.
Loads o' gravel i' the back.
Troilus and Cressida, v, 1, 22. See under DISEASE.

8 Steel to the very back,
Yet wrung with wrongs more than our backs can bear.
Titus Andronicus. Act iv, sc. 3, l. 47. [Titus]
So proud a back.—*Venus and Adonis,* l. 300.

BADGE

9
Wearing leeks in their Monmouth caps; which, your majesty know, to this hour is an honourable badge of the service.
Henry V. Act iv, sc. 7, l. 104. [Fluellen]

10
He first took exceptions at this badge,
Pronouncing that the paleness of this flower
Bewray'd the faintness of my master's heart.
I Henry VI. Act iv, sc. 1, l. 105. [Vernon]

11
Now, by my father's badge, old Nevil's crest,
The rampant bear chain'd to the ragged staff,
This day I 'll wear aloft my burgonet.
II Henry VI. Act v, sc. 1, l. 202. [Warwick]
The only use of "rampant." "Burgonet" (light casque of steel) is repeated in l. 200 and l. 208, and in *Antony and Cleopatra,* i, 5, 24.
Badge of pusillanimity.—*II Henry VI,* iv, 3, 113.
Badge of hell.—*Love's Labour 's Lost,* iv, 3, 254.
Badge of faith.—*A Midsummer-Night's Dream,* iii, 2, 127.
Badge of bitterness.—*Much Ado about Nothing,* i, 1, 23.
A badge of fame to slander's livery.
The Rape of Lucrece, l. 1054.

BADNESS

See also Good and Evil; Vileness; Villainy; Wickedness

12
He that hath miss'd the princess is a thing
Too bad for bad report.
Cymbeline. Act i, sc. 1, l. 16. [Gentleman]
Thou art too bad to curse.
Timon of Athens. Act iv, sc. 3, l. 365. [Apemantus]
'Tis too bad, too bad.
King Lear. Act ii, sc. 1, l. 98. [Gloucester]
The only uses of "too bad."

13
Thus bad begins and worse remains behind.
Hamlet. Act iii, sc. 4, l. 179. [Hamlet]

14
Counting myself but bad till I be best.
III Henry VI. Act v, sc. 6, l. 91. [Gloucester]

15
Creating every bad a perfect best.
Sonnets. No. cxiv.
Bad in the best.—*Passionate Pilgrim,* l. 102.
Exchange the bad for better.
The Two Gentlemen of Verona, ii, 6, 13. See under WIT.
A little bad.—*Measure for Measure,* v, 1, 446.

16 Heaven me such uses send,
Not to pick bad from bad, but by bad mend!
Othello. Act iv, sc. 3, l. 105. [Desdemona]

1
Neither of these are so bad as thou art.
Pericles. Act iv, sc. 6, l. 171. [Marina]

2
Bad is the world; and all will come to nought,
When such bad dealing must be seen in thought.
Richard III. Act iii, sc. 6, l. 13. [Scrivener]

Bad world the while!—*King John,* iv, 2, 100. See under WORLD.
Bad child.—*Pericles,* i, Gower, 27.
Bad friends.—*Richard III,* iv, 4, 216.
Bad men.—*Richard II,* v, 1, 71.
Bold bad man.—*Henry VIII,* ii, 2, 44.
Bad neighbour.—*Henry V,* iv, 1, 6.
Bad sons.—*The Tempest,* i, 2, 120.
Bad woman.—*Measure for Measure,* ii, 1, 64.

3
All men are bad, and in their badness reign.
Sonnets. No. cxxi. See MAN, 947:9.

As duteous to the vices of thy mistress
As badness would desire.
King Lear, iv, 6, 259. See LUST, 926:8.

Reproveable badness.—*King Lear,* iii, 5, 9. The only use of "reproveable."
Name for badness.—*Measure for Measure,* v, 1, 59. The only uses of "badness."

4
As bad as those
That vulgars give bold'st titles.
The Winter's Tale, ii, 1, 93. See under ADULTERY.

BAG AND BAGGAGE

5
Though not with bag and baggage, let with scrip and scrippage.
As You Like It. Act iii, sc. 2, l. 170. [Touchstone] The only use of "scrippage." "Scrip" occurs again in *A Midsummer-Night's Dream,* i, 2, 3.

With bag and baggage.—*The Winter's Tale,* i, 2, 206.

6
Thou baggage, let me in.
The Comedy of Errors. Act iii, sc. 1, l. 57. [Antipholus of Ephesus]

Ye are a baggage.
The Taming of the Shrew. Induction, sc. 1, l. 3. [Sly]

Hang thee, young baggage, disobedient wretch!
Romeo and Juliet. Act iii, sc. 5, l. 161. [Capulet]

Pandar: The poor Transylvanian is dead, that lay with the little baggage.
Boult: Ay, she quickly pooped him; she made him roast meat for worms.
Pericles. Act iv, sc. 1, l. 23. The only use of "Transylvanian" and "pooped."

7
The clergy's bags Are lank and lean.
II Henry VI. Act i, sc. 3, l. 131. [Beaufort]

8
See thou shake the bags Of hoarding abbots.
King John, iii, 3, 7. See under ANGEL.

Look to your house, your daughter and your bags!
Othello. Act i, sc. 1, l. 80. [Iago]

Sealed bags.—*The Merry Wives of Windsor,* iii, 4, 16.

BAIL, see Surety

BAIT, see Fish and Fishing

BALANCE

9
Hung . . . tottering in the balance.
All's Well that Ends Well. Act i, sc. 3, l. 131. [Steward]

10
Are there balance here to weigh The flesh?
The Merchant of Venice. Act iv, sc. 1, l. 255. [Portia]

11
A mote will turn the balance.
A Midsummer-Night's Dream. Act v, sc. 1, l. 324. [Hippolyta]

12
If the balance of our lives had not one scale of reason to poise another of sensuality, the blood and baseness of our natures would conduct us to most preposterous conclusions.
Othello. Act i, sc. 3, l. 330. [Iago]

BALDNESS, see Hairlessness

BALLAD

See also Song

13
Scald rhymers Ballad us out o' tune.
Antony and Cleopatra. Act v, sc. 2, l. 215. [Cleopatra] The only use of "rhymers."

14
An I have not ballads made on you all and sung to filthy tunes, let a cup of sack be my poison.
I Henry IV. Act ii, sc. 2, l. 48. [Falstaff]

I will have it in a particular ballad else, with mine own picture on the top on 't, Colevile kissing my foot.
II Henry IV. Act iv, sc. 3, l. 52. [Falstaff]

Odious ballads.—*All's Well that Ends Well,* ii, 1, 175.

15
I had rather be a kitten and cry mew
Than one of these same metre ballad-mongers;
I had rather hear a brazen canstick turn'd,
Or a dry wheel grate on the axle-tree;
And that would set my teeth nothing on edge,
Nothing so much as mincing poetry:
'Tis like the forced gait of a shuffling nag.
I Henry IV. Act iii, sc. 1, l. 129. [Hotspur] The only use of "kitten," "ballad-mongers," and "canstick." "Axle-tree" occurs again in *Troilus and Cressida,* i, 3, 66. "Canstick" is short for candlestick.

16
Armado: Is there not a ballad, boy, of the King and the Beggar?
Moth: The world was very guilty of such a ballad some three ages since.
Love's Labour's Lost. Act i, sc. 2, l. 114. The ballad, *King Cophetua and the Beggar Maid,* may be found in Percy's *Reliques of Ancient English Poetry,* ser. I, bk. ii, no. 6.

The magnanimous and most illustrate king Cophetua set eye upon the pernicious and indubitate beggar Zenelophon.
Love's Labour's Lost. Act iv, sc. 1, l. 65.

[Boyet] The beggar-maid's name, as given in the old ballad, was Penelophon. "Zenelophon" is probably a corruption. Shakespeare also refers to the ballad in *Romeo and Juliet*, i, 2, 13 (see under CUPID); *II Henry VI*, v, 3, 106 (see under NEWS); and in *Richard II*, v, 3, 80. The only use of "indubitate." "Illustrate" is repeated in v, 1, 128, and occurs in no other play. "Illustrious" is used three times.

1
I love a ballad but even too well, if it be doleful matter merrily set down, or a very pleasant thing indeed and sung lamentably.
The Winter's Tale. Act iv, sc. 4, l. 188. [Clown] The only instance of the use of the phrase "even too well" in the plays.
Mopsa: I love a ballad in print o' life, for then we are sure they are true.
Autolycus: Here 's one to a very doleful tune, how a usurer's wife was brought to bed of twenty money-bags at a burthen and how she longed to eat adder's heads and toads carbonadoed.
Mopsa: Is it true, think you?
Autolycus: Very true, and but a month old.
The Winter's Tale. Act iv, sc. 4, l. 263.
Here 's another ballad of a fish, that appeared upon the coast on Wednesday the fourscore of April, forty thousand fathom above water, and sung this ballad against the hard hearts of maids: it was thought she was a woman and was turned into a cold fish for she would not exchange flesh with one that loved her: the ballad is very pitiful and as true.
The Winter's Tale. Act iv, sc. 4, l. 279. [Autolycus]
Autolycus: This is a merry ballad, but a very pretty one.
Mopsa: Let 's have some merry ones.
Autolycus: Why, this is a passing merry one and goes to the tune of 'Two maids wooing a man': there 's scarce a maid westward but she sings it; 'tis in request, I can tell you.
The Winter's Tale. Act iv, sc. 4, l. 291.

2
The ballad-makers cannot be able to express it.
The Winter's Tale. Act v, sc. 2, l. 27. [Gentleman] "Ballad-maker" is repeated in *Much Ado about Nothing*, i, 1, 254, and *Coriolanus*, iv, 5, 235.

BALM

3
As sweet as balm, as soft as air.
Antony and Cleopatra. Act v, sc. 2, l. 314. [Cleopatra]

4
I could wish
You were conducted to a gentle bath
And balms applied to you.
Coriolanus. Act i, sc. 6, l. 62. [Cominius]
Juice of balm and every precious flower.
The Merry Wives of Windsor. Act v, sc. 5, l. 67. [Mistress Quickly]

5
Thy balm wash'd off wherewith thou wast anointed.
III Henry VI. Act iii, sc. 1, l. 17. [King Henry] See also under KING.

6
Balm his foul head in warm distilled waters.
The Taming of the Shrew, Ind., 1, 48. [Lord]
And drop sweet balm in Priam's painted wound.
The Rape of Lucrece, l. 1466.
Is this the balsam that the usuring senate
Pours into captains' wounds?
Timon of Athens. Act iii, sc. 5, l. 110. [Alcibiades] The only use of "balsam." "Balsamum" occurs in *Comedy of Errors*, iv, 1, 89.
We sent to thee, to give thy rages balm.
Timon of Athens. Act v, sc. 4, l. 16. [Senator]

7
Balm'd and entreasured
With full bags of spices.
Pericles. Act iii, sc. 2, l. 65. [Cerimon] "Balm'd" is repeated in *King Lear*, iii, 6, 105. The only use of "entreasured."
Balmy breath.—*Othello*, v, 2, 16.
Balmy slumbers.—*Othello*, ii, 3, 258.
Balmy time.—*Sonnets*, cvii.

BANISHMENT

See also Exile

8
Push him out of doors; . . . turn him going.
As You Like It. Act iii, sc. 1, l. 15. [Duke]

9
Sicinius: In the name o' the people
And in the power of us the tribunes, we,
Even from this instant, banish him our city,
In peril of precipitation
From off the rock Tarpeian. . . .
Citizens: He 's banish'd, and it shall be so.
Brutus: . . . He is banish'd,
As enemy to the people and the country:
It shall be so.
Citizens: It shall be so, it shall be so.
Coriolanus: You common cry of curs! . . .
Have the power still
To banish your defenders. . . . Despising,
For you, the city, thus I turn my back.
Coriolanus. Act iii, sc. 3, l. 99. "Precipitation" is repeated in iii, 2, 4, and occurs in no other play. The Tarpeian rock is mentioned five times, only in *Coriolanus*.
Banish your defenders.—*Coriolanus*, iii, 3, 128.

10
Heaven and my conscience knows
Thou didst unjustly banish me.
Cymbeline. Act iii, sc. 3, l. 99. [Belarius]

11
For what offence have I this fortnight been
A banish'd woman from my Harry's bed?
I Henry IV, ii, 3, 42. See under BED.
I banish her my bed and company.
II Henry VI, ii, 1, 197. See under WIFE.
Banish'd me his bed.—*Henry VIII*, iii, 1, 119.
His lady banish'd.—*II Henry VI*, ii, 3, 42.

12
No, my good lord; banish Peto, banish Bardolph, banish Poins: but for sweet Jack Falstaff, kind Jack Falstaff, true Jack Falstaff, valiant Jack Falstaff, and therefore more valiant, being, as he is, old Jack Falstaff, banish not him thy Harry's company, banish not him thy Harry's company: banish plump Jack, and banish all the world.
I Henry IV. Act ii, sc. 4, l. 521. [Falstaff] "Plump" is repeated in *Venus and Adonis*, l. 142: "Plump flesh."

1
I banish thee, on pain of death.
II Henry IV. Act v, sc. 5, l. 67. [King Henry]
Out of my sight, and never see me more!
King John. Act iv, sc. 2, l. 242. [King John]
Five days we do allot thee, for provision
To shield thee from diseases of the world;
And on the sixth to turn thy hated back
Upon our kingdom.
King Lear. Act i, sc. 1, l. 176. [King Lear]
The hopeless word of 'never to return'
Breathe I against thee, upon pain of life.
Richard II. Act i, sc. 3, l. 152. [King]
First Senator: We banish thee for ever.
Alcibiades: Banish me!
Banish your dotage; banish usury,
That makes the senate ugly. . . . Banishment!
It comes not ill; I hate not to be banish'd;
It is a cause worthy my spleen and fury,
That I may strike at Athens.
Timon of Athens. Act iii, sc. 5, l. 98.

2
Welcome is banishment; welcome were my death.
II Henry VI. Act ii, sc. 3, l. 14. [Duchess]
I will repeal thee, or, be well assured,
Adventure to be banished myself:
And banished I am, if but from thee.
II Henry VI. Act iii, sc. 2, l. 349. [Queen]
Ten times banished;
Once by the king, and three times thrice by thee.
II Henry VI. Act iii, sc. 2, l. 357. [Suffolk]

3
Banished fair England's territories.
II Henry VI. Act iii, sc. 2, l. 245. [Salisbury]
Banish'd the kingdom!—*Henry VIII,* iv, 2, 127.

4
A banish'd man,
And forced to live in Scotland a forlorn.
III Henry VI. Act iii, sc. 3, l. 25. [Queen]
Here stands my other son, a banish'd man.
Titus Andronicus. Act iii, sc. 1, l. 99. [Titus]
Poor banish'd man.—*King Lear,* iii, 4, 169.
Thou art a banish'd man.—*Richard II,* ii, 3, 110.
See also under MAN.
That same banish'd runagate.—*Romeo and Juliet,* iii, 5, 90.

5
Freedom lives hence, and banishment is here.
King Lear. Act i, sc. 1, l. 184. [Kent]
Banishment of friends.—*King Lear,* i, 2, 161.

6
O, banish me, my lord, but kill me not.
Othello, v, 2, 78. See under KILLING.

7
Then thus I turn me from my country's light,
To dwell in solemn shades of endless night.
Richard II. Act i, sc. 3, l. 176. [Mowbray]
Embrace each other's love in banishment.
Richard II. Act i, sc. 3, l. 184. [King Richard]
Six frozen winters spent,
Return with welcome home from banishment.
Richard II. Act i, sc. 3, l. 211. [King Richard]
John of Gaunt: The sullen passage of thy weary steps
Esteem as foil wherein thou art to set
The precious jewel of thy home return.
Bolingbroke: Nay, rather, every tedious stride I make
Will but remember me what a deal of world
I wander from the jewels that I love.
Richard II. Act i, sc. 3, l. 265.
When time shall call him home from banishment.
Richard II. Act i, sc. 4, l. 21. [King Richard]
Short banishment.—*Richard II,* i, 4, 17

8
Banish'd this frail sepulchre of our flesh,
As now our flesh is banish'd from this land.
Richard II, i, 3, 196. See under SOUL.
From heaven banish'd!—*Richard II,* i, 2, 203.

9
Eating the bitter bread of banishment;
Whilst you have fed upon my signories,
Dispark'd my parks and fell'd my forest woods,
From my own windows torn my household coat,
Razed out my imprese, leaving me no sign,
Save men's opinions and my living blood,
To show the world I am a gentleman.
Richard II. Act iii, sc. 1, l. 21. [Bolingbroke] The only use of "dispark'd" and "imprese" (device, emblem).

10
Gloucester: Wert thou not banished on pain of death?
Queen Margaret: I was; but I do find more pain in banishment
Than death can yield me here by my abode.
Richard III. Act i, sc. 3, l. 167.
Deadly banishment.—*The Two Gentlemen of Verona,* iii, 1, 173.
Everlasting banishment.—*The Rape of Lucrece,* l. 1855.
Reputeless banishment.—*I Henry IV,* iii, 2, 44.
Woful banishment.—*Richard III,* i, 3, 193.

11
That 'banished,' that one word 'banished.'
Romeo and Juliet, iii, 2, 113. [Juliet]
Friar Laurence: A gentler judgement vanish'd from his lips,
Not body's death, but body's banishment.
Romeo: Ha, banishment! be merciful, say 'death';
For exile hath more terror in his look,
Much more than death: do not say 'banishment.'
Friar Laurence: Hence from Verona art thou banished:
Be patient, for the world is broad and wide.
Romeo: There is no world without Verona walls,
But purgatory, torture, hell itself.
Hence-banished is banish'd from the world,
And world's exile is death: then banished
Is death mis-termed: calling death banishment,
Thou cutt'st my head off with a golden axe,
And smilest upon the stroke that murders me.
Romeo and Juliet. Act iii, sc. 3, l. 10. The only use of "hence-banished" and "mis-termed."

12
'Banished'?
O friar, the damned use that word in hell.
Romeo and Juliet, iii, 3, 46. [Romeo]

13
She at least is banish'd from your eye,
Who hath cause to wet the grief on 't.
The Tempest. Act ii, sc. 1, l. 126. [Sebastian]
Banish'd from her sight.—*The Two Gentlemen of Verona,* iii, 2, 2.

1 The judges have pronounced
My everlasting doom of banishment.
Titus Andronicus. Act iii, sc. 1, l. 50. [Lucius]
How happy art thou, then,
From these devourers to be banished!
Titus Andronicus, iii, 1, 57. See under TIGER. The only use of "devourers."
Unkindly banished,
The gates shut on me, and turn'd weeping out.
Titus Andronicus. Act v, sc. 3, l. 104. [Lucius]

2
To die is to be banish'd from myself;
And Silvia is myself: banish'd from her
Is self from self: a deadly banishment!
The Two Gentlemen of Verona. Act iii, sc. 1, l. 171. [Valentine]
That thou art banished—O, that 's the news!—
From hence, from Silvia and from me thy friend.
The Two Gentlemen of Verona. Act iii, sc. 1, l. 217. [Proteus]

3
What, were you banish'd thence?
The Two Gentlemen of Verona. Act iv, sc. 1, l. 23. [Outlaw]
Were you banish'd for so small a fault?
The Two Gentlemen of Verona. Act iv, sc. 1, l. 31. [Outlaw]
Myself was from Verona banished
For practising to steal away a lady.
Two Gentlemen of Verona, iv, 1, 47.

BANKRUPTCY

4 Wherefore do you look
Upon that poor and broken bankrupt there?
As You Like It. Act ii, sc. 1, l. 56. [First Lord]
Poor bankrupt.—*Romeo and Juliet,* iii, 2, 57.

5
There came divers of Antonio's creditors in my company to Venice, that swear he cannot choose but break.
The Merchant of Venice. Act iii, sc. 1, l. 118. [Tubal]

6
The king 's grown bankrupt, like a broken man.
Richard II. Act ii, sc. 1, l. 257. [Willoughby]

7 Bankrupts, hold fast;
Rather than render back, out with your knives,
And cut your trusters' throats.
Timon of Athens. Act iv, sc. 1, l. 8. [Timon] "Truster" is repeated in *Hamlet,* i, 2, 172.
Blessed bankrupt.—*Venus and Adonis,* l. 466.

BANNER, see Flag

BANQUET, see Feast

BAR, see Impediment

BARBER

8
It is like a barber's chair that fits all buttocks, the pin-buttock, the quatch-buttock, the brawn buttock, or any buttock.
All's Well that Ends Well. Act ii, sc. 2, l. 17. [Clown] The only use of "pin-buttock" and "quatch-buttock," thin and fat.

9
Being barber'd ten times o'er.
Antony and Cleopatra. Act ii, sc. 2, l. 229. [Enobarbus]
I must to the barber's, mounsieur; for methinks I am marvellous hairy about the face.
A Midsummer-Night's Dream. Act iv, sc. 1, l. 25. [Bottom]
It shall to the barber's, with your beard.
Hamlet. Act ii, sc. 2, l. 521. [Hamlet]

10
Don Pedro: Hath any man seen him at the barber's?
Claudio: No, but the barber's man hath been seen with him.
Much Ado about Nothing. Act iii, sc. 2, l. 44.

BARGAIN

11 In the way of bargain, mark ye me,
I 'll cavil on the ninth part of a hair.
I Henry IV. Act iii, sc. 1, l. 139. [Hotspur]

12
Clap hands and a bargain.
Henry V. Act v, sc. 2, l. 134. [King Henry]
Clap this royal bargain up.
King John. Act iii, sc. 1, l. 235. [King Philip]
Take hands, a bargain!
And, friends unknown, you shall bear witness to 't.
Winter's Tale. Act iv, sc. 4, l. 393. [Shepherd]
There 's a bargain made.
Julius Cæsar. Act i, sc. 3, l. 120. [Cassius]
So is the bargain.—*As You Like It,* v, 4, 15.
By bargain.—*Henry V,* iv, 7, 182.

13
The boy hath sold him a bargain.
Love's Labour 's Lost. Act iii, sc. 1, l. 102. [Costard]
To sell a bargain well is as cunning as fast and loose.
Love's Labour 's Lost. Act iii, sc. 1, l. 104. [Costard]
A world-without-end bargain.
Love's Labour 's Lost. Act v, sc. 2, l. 799. [Princess of France] The only use of "world-without-end."

14
My bargains and my well-won thrift,
Which he calls interest.
The Merchant of Venice. Act i, sc. 3, l. 51. [Shylock] The only use of "well-won."
Solemnize The bargain of your faith.
The Merchant of Venice. Act iii, sc. 2, l. 194. [Gratiano]
Thwarted my bargains.—*The Merchant of Venice,* iii, 1, 59.

15
She was too fond of her most filthy bargain.
Othello. Act v, sc. 2, l. 157. [Emilia]
A dateless bargain to engrossing death!
Romeo and Juliet. Act v, sc. 3, l. 115. [Romeo] "Dateless" is repeated in *Richard II,* i, 3, 151, and in *Sonnets,* xxx and cliii.

16
'Tis bargain'd 'twixt us twain.
The Taming of the Shrew. Act ii, sc. 1, l. 306. [Petruchio]
Bargain'd for and sold.—*II Henry VI,* i, 1, 231.
I have bargained for the joint.—*Pericles,* iv, 2, 141. The only uses of "bargained."

1 Go to, a bargain made: seal it, seal it; I 'll be the witness.
Troilus and Cressida. Act iii, sc. 2, l. 204. [Pandarus]

And seal the bargain with a holy kiss.
The Two Gentlemen of Verona. Act ii, sc. 2, l. 7. [Julia]

BARK

See also Dogs: Bark and Bite; Ship

2 There is a bark of Epidamnum
That stays but till her owner comes aboard.
Comedy of Errors. Act iv, sc. 1, l. 85. [Dromio of Syracuse] Epidamnum is mentioned seven times in this play, and in no other.

The bark Expedition.—*The Comedy of Errors,* iv, 3, 38.

Their bark . . . very slow of sail.—*The Comedy of Errors,* i, 1, 117.

Swim bark!—*Julius Cæsar,* v, 1, 67.

3 The bark is ready, and the wind at help.
Hamlet. Act iv, sc. 3, l. 46. [King]

How like a younker or a prodigal
The scarfed bark puts from her native bay,
Hugg'd and embraced by the strumpet wind!
How like the prodigal doth she return,
With over-weather'd ribs and ragged sails,
Lean, rent and beggar'd by the strumpet wind!
The Merchant of Venice. Act ii, sc. 6, l. 14. [Gratiano] The only use of "over-weather'd." "Scarfed" is repeated in *Hamlet,* v, 2, 13.

4 Montano: Is he well shipp'd?
Cassio: His bark is stoutly timber'd.
Othello. Act ii, sc. 1, l. 47. "Timber'd" is repeated in *Hamlet,* iv, 7, 22: "Slightly timber'd."

Let the labouring bark climb hills of seas
Olympus-high and duck again as low
As hell 's from heaven!
Othello, ii, 1, 189. See under TEMPEST. The only use of "Olympus-high."

Though his bark cannot be lost,
Yet it shall be tempest-tost.
Macbeth. Act i, sc. 3, l. 24. [First Witch] "Tempest-tossed" occurs again in *Romeo and Juliet,* iii, 5, 138: "Tempest-tossed body."

5 We at time of year
Do wound the bark, the skin of our fruit-trees.
Richard II, iii, 4, 58. See under PRUDENCE. "Fruit-trees" is repeated in l. 45 of the same scene, and in *Romeo and Juliet,* ii, 2, 108.

Mine, as sure as bark on tree.
Love's Labour 's Lost. Act v, sc. 2, l. 285. [Maria]

Bark of a tree.—*The Tempest,* ii, 2, 127; *Titus Andronicus,* v, 1, 138; *Antony and Cleopatra,* i, 4, 66.

Bark of baser kind.—*Winter's Tale,* iv, 4, 94.

Bark peel'd from the lofty pine.—*The Rape of Lucrece,* l. 1167.

Her bark being peel'd away.—*The Rape of Lucrece,* l. 1169.

6 Being a bark to brook no mighty sea.
Richard III, iii, 7, 162. See under MODESTY.

A poor bark, of sails and tackling reft.
Richard III, iv, 4, 233. See under ROCK.

Poor bark.—*III Henry VI,* v, 4, 28.

Sea-sick weary bark!—*Romeo and Juliet,* v, 3, 118.

Splitted bark.—*II Henry VI,* iii, 2, 411.

Tall anchoring bark.—*King Lear,* iv, 6, 18.

Wandering bark.—*Sonnets,* cxvi.

My saucy bark inferior far to his.
Sonnets. No. lxxx.

7 In few, they hurried us aboard a bark.
The Tempest. Act i, sc. 2, l. 144. [Prospero]

8 Leak'd is our bark,
And we, poor mates, stand on the dying deck,
Hearing the surges threat.
Timon of Athens. Act iv, sc. 2, l. 19. [Servant]

9 The bark, that hath discharged her fraught,
Returns with precious lading to the bay
From whence at first she weigh'd her anchorage.
Titus Andronicus. Act i, sc. 1, l. 71. [Titus] The only use of "anchorage."

Deep-drawing barks do there disgorge
Their warlike fraughtage.
Troilus and Cressida, Prol., l. 12. The only use of "deep-drawing."

Our fraughtage I have convey'd aboard.—*The Comedy of Errors,* iv, 1, 87. The only uses of "fraughtage" (freight, cargo).

10 Behold
The strong-ribb'd bark through liquid mountains cut,
Bounding between the two moist elements.
Troilus and Cressida. Act i, sc. 3, l. 39. [Nestor] The only use of "strong-ribb'd."

Look to thy bark.—*The Winter's Tale,* iii, 3, 8.

BASENESS

See also Vileness, Villainy

11 Profane fellow!
Wert thou the son of Jupiter and no more
But what thou art besides, thou wert too base
To be his groom.
Cymbeline. Act ii, sc. 3, l. 129. [Imogen]

From whose so many weights of baseness cannot
A dram of worth be drawn.
Cymbeline. Act iii, sc. 5, l. 88. [Cloten]

This proves me base.—*Antony and Cleopatra,* v, 2, 303.

O rarely base!—*Antony and Cleopatra,* v, 2, 158.

Base and abject.—*II Henry IV,* iv, 1, 33.

Base and bloody.—*II Henry IV,* iv, 1, 40.

Base and envious.—*I Henry VI,* iii, 1, 194.

Base and humble.—*II Henry VI,* i, 2, 62.

Base and ignominious.—*II Henry VI,* iv, 8, 66.

Base And misbegotten.—*I Henry VI,* iv, 6, 21.

Base and poor.—*I Henry VI,* v, 5, 49.

Base and rotten.—*I Henry IV,* i, 3, 108.

Base and unlustrous.—*Cymbeline,* i, 6, 109. The only use of "unlustrous."

Base and vile.—*A Midsummer-Night's Dream,* i, 1, 232.

Base, fearful and despairing.—*III Henry VI,* i, 1, 178.
Base, proud, shallow.—*King Lear,* ii, 2, 16.
Mean and base.—*Henry V,* iii, 1, 29.
Most base.—*All's Well that Ends Well,* ii, 3, 178; *King John,* ii, 1, 586.
Worldlings base.—*II Henry IV,* v, 3, 103. "Worldlings" is repeated in *As You Like It,* ii, 1, 48.

1 Contemptuous base-born callet as she is.
II Henry VI. Act i, sc. 3, l. 86. [Queen]
Base-born Cades.—*II Henry VI,* iv, 8, 49.
Base-born heart.—*III Henry VI,* ii, 2, 143. The only uses of "base-born." See also under ANCESTRY.
Civet is of baser birth than tar, the very uncleanly flux of a cat.
As You Like It. Act iii, sc. 2, l. 69. [Touchstone] Civet is mentioned four times in the plays. Tar is repeated in *Tempest,* ii, 2, 54.

2 Who is here so base that would be a bondman?
Julius Cæsar, iii, 2, 31. See under OFFENCE.

3 Thou art not noble;
For all the accommodations that thou bear'st
Are nursed by baseness.
Measure for Measure. Act iii, sc. 1, l. 13. [Duke]

4 For who so base would such an office have
As slanderous deathsman to so base a slave?
The Rape of Lucrece, l. 1000.
The baser is he, coming from a king,
To shame his hope with deeds degenerate.
The Rape of Lucrece, l. 1002.

5 We do debase ourselves, cousin, do we not,
To look so poorly and to speak so fair?
Richard II. Act iii, sc. 3, l. 127. [King Richard]
Thus we debase The nature of our seats.
Coriolanus. Act iii, sc. 1, l. 135. [Coriolanus]
Debase her eyes.—*Richard III,* i, 2, 247.
Debase your princely knee.—*Richard II,* iii, 3, 190. The only uses of "debase."

6 Some kinds of baseness
Are nobly undergone.
The Tempest. Act iii, sc. 1, l. 2. [Ferdinand]
Such baseness Had never like executor.
The Tempest. Act iii, sc. 1, l. 12. [Ferdinand]
They have all been touch'd and found base metal.
Timon of Athens. Act iii, sc. 3, l. 6. [Servant]

7 It could not else be, I should prove so base,
To sue, and be denied such common grace.
Timon of Athens. Act iii, sc. 5, l. 94. [Alcibiades]
'Tis not so base as you.—*Timon of Athens,* iii, 4, 58.

8 Base men that use them to so base effect!
The Two Gentlemen of Verona. Act ii, sc. 7, l. 73. [Julia] "Base men" is repeated four times in other plays.
Forced baseness.—*The Winter's Tale,* ii, 3, 78.
Basely die.—*Antony and Cleopatra,* iv, 15, 55.
Basely fled.—*I Henry VI,* iv, 5, 17.
Basely fly.—*Venus and Adonis,* l. 894.
Basely slain.—*Titus Andronicus,* i, 1, 353.
Basely yielded.—*Richard II,* ii, 1, 253.

9 The more degenerate and base art thou.
The Two Gentlemen of Verona. Act v, sc. 4, l. 136. [Duke]

10 Thou art too base To be acknowledged.
The Winter's Tale, iv, 4, 429. See under SON.

BASTARD

11 We are all bastards;
And that most venerable man which I
Did call my father, was I know not where
When I was stamp'd; some coiner with his tools
Made me a counterfeit: yet my mother seem'd
The Dian of that time.
Cymbeline. Act ii, sc. 5, l. 2. [Posthumus] The only use of "coiner."

12 That drop of blood that 's calm proclaims me bastard,
Cries cuckold to my father, brands the harlot
Even here, between the chaste unsmirched brow
Of my true mother.
Hamlet. Act iv, sc. 5, l. 117. [Laertes] The only use of "unsmirched."
We 'll have no bastards live.—*I Henry VI,* v, 4, 70.
I wish the bastards dead.—*Richard III,* iv, 2, 18.

13 If ever lady wrong'd her lord so much,
Thy mother took into her blameful bed
Some stern untutor'd churl, and noble stock
Was graft with crab-tree slip.
II Henry VI. Act iii, sc. 2, l. 211. [Suffolk] "Graft" is repeated in *Richard III,* iii, 7, 127; and "crab-tree" in *Coriolanus,* ii, 1, 205, and in *Henry VIII,* v, 4, 8.
Thou thyself wast born in bastardy.
II Henry VI. Act iii, sc. 2, l. 223. [Warwick]

14 Once he slander'd me with bastardy:
But whether I be as true begot or no,
That still I lay upon my mother's head.
King John. Act i, sc. 1, l. 74. [Bastard]
Large lengths of seas and shores
Between my father and my mother lay,
As I have heard my father speak himself,
When this same lusty gentleman was got.
King John. Act i, sc. 1, l. 105. [Faulconbridge]
My boy a bastard! By my soul, I think
His father never was so true begot.
King John. Act ii, sc. 1, l. 129. [Constance]

15 Thy bastard shall be king.
King John, ii, 1, 122. See under QUEEN.
A bastard of the king's.—*King John,* ii, 1, 65.
A bastard son of the king's?—*II Henry IV,* ii, 4, 307.
A bastard, and a knave.—*Henry V,* iii, 2, 133.
Thou bastard of my grandfather!—*I Henry VI,* iii, 1, 42.
Bastard children.—*Coriolanus,* iv, 5, 240.

Bastard son.—*King Lear,* iv, 6, 116; iv, 7, 89.
Bastard Bretons.—*Richard III,* v, 3, 333.
Bastard Normans, Norman bastards!—*Henry V,* iii, 5, 10.
Fruit of bastardy.—*Titus Andronicus,* v, 1, 48.
Guilty of a several bastardy.—*Julius Cæsar,* ii, 1, 138.

1 Why bastard? wherefore base?
When my dimensions are as well compact,
My mind as generous, and my shape as true,
As honest madam's issue? Why brand they us
With base? with baseness? bastardy? base, base?
Who, in the lusty stealth of nature, take
More composition and fierce quality
Than doth, within a dull, stale, tired bed,
Go to the creating a whole tribe of fops,
Got 'tween asleep and wake?
King Lear. Act i, sc. 2, l. 6. [Edmund] The only use of "fops."

Now, gods, stand up for bastards!
King Lear. Act i, sc. 2, l. 22. [Edmund]

Degenerate bastard! I'll not trouble thee:
Yet have I left a daughter.
King Lear. Act i, sc. 4, l. 275. [King Lear]

Thou unpossessing bastard!—*King Lear,* ii, 1, 69. The only use of "unpossessing."

2
O, an the heavens were so pleased that thou wert but my bastard, what a joyful father wouldst thou make me!
Love's Labour's Lost. Act v, sc. 1, l. 78. [Costard]

Thy issue blurr'd with nameless bastardy.
The Rape of Lucrece, l. 522. "Blurr'd" is repeated in *Cymbeline,* iv, 2, 104.

Thought characters and words merely but art,
And bastards of his foul adulterate heart.
A Lover's Complaint, l. 174.

3
This bastard graff shall never come to growth.
The Rape of Lucrece, l. 1062.

4 Thou dost suspect
That I have been disloyal to thy bed,
And that he is a bastard, not thy son.
Richard II. Act v, sc. 2, l. 104. [Duchess of York]

My princely father . . . by just computation of the time,
Found that the issue was not his begot.
Richard III. Act iii, sc. 5, l. 88. [Gloucester] "Computation" is repeated in *The Comedy of Errors,* ii, 2, 4.

5
Ho, ho! I laugh to think that babe a bastard.
Timon of Athens. Act i, sc. 2, l. 117. [Apemantus]

Thou wast born a bastard, and thou 't die a bawd.
Timon of Athens. Act ii, sc. 2, l. 88. [Apemantus]

What, wouldst thou have me prove myself a bastard?
Titus Andronicus. Act ii, sc. 3, l. 148. [Chiron]

6
I love bastards: I am a bastard begot, bastard instructed, bastard in mind, bastard in valour, in every thing illegitimate. One bear will not bite another, and wherefore should one bastard?
Troilus and Cressida. Act v, sc. 7, l. 16. [Thersites] "Illegitimate" is repeated in *Much Ado about Nothing,* iii, 4, 50.

7
'Tis a bastard, So sure as this beard 's grey.
Winter's Tale. Act ii, sc. 3, l. 161. [Leontes]

He 's a bastard.—*The Tempest,* v, 1, 273.
Female bastard.—*The Winter's Tale,* ii, 3, 175.
Fortune's bastard.—*Sonnets,* cxxiv.
A pint of bastard, see under Wine.

8
Shall I live on to see this bastard kneel
And call me father?
Winter's Tale. Act ii, sc. 3, l. 155. [Leontes]

BATTLE

See also War

9 To-morrow the last of many battles
We mean to fight.
Antony and Cleopatra. Act iv, sc. 1, l. 11. [Cæsar]

They say we shall embattle
By the second hour i' the morn.
Antony and Cleopatra. Act iv, sc. 8, l. 3. [First Soldier] The only use of "embattle."

Wage this battle at Pharsalia,
Where Cæsar fought with Pompey.
Antony and Cleopatra. Act iii, sc. 7, l. 32. [Canidius] The only mention of Pharsalia.

Cæsar's battle.—*Antony and Cleopatra,* iii, 9, 2.
Provoke not battle.—*Antony and Cleopatra,* iii, 8, 3.
At the point of battle.—*Coriolanus,* i, 1, 166.

10
Battles thrice six I have seen and heard of.
Coriolanus. Act ii, sc. 3, l. 135. [Coriolanus]

11
The king will bid you battle presently.
I Henry IV, v, 2, 31. See under King.

Bid false Edward battle.—*III Henry VI,* iii, 3, 235.
Bid his brother battle.—*III Henry VI,* v, 1, 77.
Bid thee battle.—*III Henry VI,* v, 1, 111.
Bid them battle.—*III Henry VI,* i, 2, 71.
Bid us battle.—*III Henry VI,* v, 1, 63.

12
What may the king's whole battle reach unto?
I Henry IV. Act iv, sc. 1, l. 129. [Hotspur]

Our battle is more full of names than yours.
II Henry IV. Act iv, sc. 1, l. 154. [Westmoreland] See also under Army.

How lies their battles?—*Coriolanus,* i, 6, 51.
Their battles are at hand.—*Julius Cæsar,* v, 1, 4.
Set our battles on.—*Julius Cæsar,* v, 3, 108.

13
We would not seek a battle, as we are;
Nor, as we are, we say we will not shun it.
Henry V. Act iii, sc. 6, l. 173. [King Henry]

14
Fire answers fire, and through their paly flames
Each battle sees the other's umber'd face.
Henry V. Act iv, Prologue, l. 8. [Chorus] The only use of "umber'd." "Paly" is repeated in *II Henry VI,* iii, 2, 141: "Paly

lips"; and in *Romeo and Juliet,* iv, 1, 100: "Paly ashes."

I am afeard there are few die well that die in battle; for how can they charitably dispose of any thing, when blood is their argument?
Henry V. Act iv, sc. 1, l. 148. [Williams] The only use of "charitably."

When, without stratagem,
But in plain shock and even play of battle,
Was ever known so great and little loss
On one part and on the other?
Henry V. Act iv, sc. 8, l. 113. [King Henry]

1
The battles of the Lord of hosts he fought.
I Henry VI. Act i, sc. 1, l. 31. [Bishop of Winchester] The only use of "Lord of hosts."

2
Rush'd into the bowels of the battle.
I Henry VI. Act i, sc. 1, l. 129. [Messenger]

Give battle.—*I Henry VI,* v, 2, 13; *As You Like It,* iv, 3, 131.

3
Saint Alban's battle won by famous York
Shall be eternized in all age to come.
II Henry VI. Act v, sc. 3, l. 31. [Warwick] The only use of "eternized."

We at Saint Alban's met, Our battles join'd.
III Henry VI, ii, 1, 121. See under FIGHTING. Saint Alban is referred to seventeen times.

Battle of Saint Alban's.—*Richard III,* i, 3, 130.

Cressy battle.—*Henry V,* ii, 4, 54. The only mention of Cressy.

Battle of Patay.—*I Henry VI,* iv, 1, 19. The only mention of Patay.

Battle of the Centaurs.—*A Midsummer-Night's Dream,* v, 1, 44.

4
Darraign your battle, for they are at hand.
III Henry VI. Act ii, sc. 2, l. 72. [Messenger] The only use of "darraign," to set in array.

Their bloody sign of battle is hung out.
Julius Cæsar. Act v, sc. 1, l. 14. [Messenger]

This battle fares like to the morning's war, . . .
Now sways it this way, like a mighty sea
Forced by the tide to combat with the wind;
Now sways it this way, like the selfsame sea
Forced to retire by fury of the wind.
III Henry VI. Act ii, sc. 5, l. 1. [King Henry]

Now the battle's ended.—*III Henry VI,* ii, 6, 44.

The battle done.—*King Lear,* v, 1, 67.

5
Edgar: Do you hear aught, sir, of a battle toward?
Gentleman: Most sure and vulgar: every one hears that,
Which can distinguish sound.
King Lear. Act iv, sc. 6, l. 213.

6
I 'll draw the form and model of our battle.
Richard III. Act v, sc. 3, l. 24. [Richmond]

Prepare thy battle early in the morning.
Richard III. Act v, sc. 3, l. 88. [Derby]

Thus my battle shall be ordered.
Richard III. Act v, sc. 3, l. 292. [King Richard]

Bloody battle.—*Richard III,* v, 3, 147.
Clustering battle.—*I Henry VI,* iv, 7, 13.
Cruel battle.—*Troilus and Cressida,* i, 1, 3.
Dreadful battles.—*King John,* iv, 2, 78.
Enemy's battle.—*II Henry IV,* iii, 2, 165.
Fearful battle.—*Henry V,* i, 1, 44.
Fell battle.—*The Rape of Lucrece,* l. 145.
High engender'd battles.—*King Lear,* iii, 2, 23. The only use of "high engender'd."
Main battle.—*Richard III,* v, 3, 299.
Pitch'd battle.—*III Henry VI,* iv, 4, 4; *The Taming of the Shrew,* i, 2, 206.
Puny battle.—*Coriolanus,* iv, 4, 6.
Royal battle.—*Richard III,* iv, 4, 538; *Henry V,* iv, 3, 75.
Ruffian battle.—*II Henry VI,* v, 2, 49.
Scarce-cold battle.—*Cymbeline,* v, 5, 469. "Scarce cold" is repeated in *I Henry VI,* iv, 3, 50: "Scarce cold conqueror."
To-morrow's battle.—*Troilus and Cressida,* v, 1, 43.
Squares of battle.—*Henry V,* iv, 2, 28.

7
A maiden battle, then? O, I perceive you.
Troilus and Cressida. Act iv, sc. 5, l. 87. [Achilles]

BAWD

See also Pandar

8
To get your living by the copulation of cattle; to be bawd to a bell-wether, and to betray a she-lamb of a twelvemonth to a crooked-pated, old cuckoldly ram.
As You Like It. Act ii, sc. 2, l. 84. [Touchstone] The only use of "she-lamb" and "crooked-pated." "Copulation" is repeated in *King Lear,* iv, 6, 116: "Let copulation thrive."

9
It will be thought we keep a bawdy house.
Henry V, ii, 1, 37. "Bawdy-house" (always hyphenated except in the above instance) is used six times in the plays.

Bawdy hand.—*Romeo and Juliet,* ii, 4, 118.
Bawdy planet.—*The Winter's Tale,* i, 2, 201.
Bawdy play.—*Henry VIII,* Prol., 14.
Bawdy song.—*I Henry IV,* iii, 3, 15.
Bawdy talk.—*Measure for Measure,* iv, 3, 188.
Bawdy veins.—*Troilus and Cressida,* iv, 1, 69.
Bawdy villain.—*Hamlet,* ii, 2, 608.
Bawdy wind.—*Othello,* iv, 2, 78.

10
One that wouldst be a bawd, in way of good service.
King Lear, ii, 2, 21. See under KNAVE.

Bawd I 'll turn.—*Henry V,* v, 1, 90.

11
Bawd is he doubtless, and of antiquity too; bawd-born.
Measure for Measure. Act iii, sc. 2, l. 71. [Lucio] The only use of "bawd-born."

A bawd of eleven years' continuance.
Measure for Measure. Act iii, sc. 2, l. 208. [Provost]

I have been an unlawful bawd time out of mind.
Measure for Measure. Act iv, sc. 2, l. 16. [Pompey]

A bawd, a wicked bawd!—*Measure for Measure,* iii, 2, 20.
A bawd, a bawd, a bawd! So ho!—*Romeo and Juliet,* ii, 4, 136.
Cursed bawd.—*Pericles,* v, Gower, 11.
Powdered bawd.—*Measure for Measure,* iii, 2, 62.
Vice's bawd.—*Richard II,* v, 3, 67.

Bawds between gold and want.—*Timon of Athens,* ii, 2, 61.
This bawd, the broker.—*King John,* ii, 1, 582.
A bawd, a cutpurse.—*Henry V,* iii, 6, 65.

1

Strike me the counterfeit matron;
It is her habit only that is honest,
Herself 's a bawd.
Timon of Athens. Act iv, sc. 3, l. 112. [Timon]

By the same token, you are a bawd.
Troilus and Cressida. Act i, sc. 2, l. 307. [Cressida]

Thou 't die a bawd.—*Timon of Athens,* ii, 2, 89.

BEAM

2 But to the brightest beams
Distracted clouds give way.
All 's Well that Ends Well, v, 3, 34. See under WEATHER.

Blest beams.—*Cymbeline,* iv, 4, 42.
Bright out-shining beams.—*Richard III,* i, 2, 268. The only use of "out-shining."
Comfortable beams.—*King Lear,* ii, 2, 171.
Counterfeited beam.—*I Henry VI,* v, 3, 63.
Fair blessed beams.—*A Midsummer-Night's Dream,* iii, 2, 392.
Golden beams.—*Richard II,* i, 3, 146.
Thousand beams.—*Henry VIII,* iv, 2, 89.

3

Like to the glorious sun's transparent beams.
II Henry VI, iii, 1, 353. See under TEMPEST.

Sun's beams.—*Romeo and Juliet,* ii, 5, 5.
Sun's hot beams.—*II Henry VI,* iii, 1, 223.
Sunny beams.—*A Midsummer-Night's Dream,* v, 1, 277.
Beams o' the sun.—*Cymbeline,* v, 5, 472.
Beams of life.—*III Henry VI,* ii, 6, 62.

4

The very beams will dry these vapours up.
III Henry VI. Act v, sc. 3, l. 12. [Clarence]

5

A rush will be a beam To hang thee on.
King John, iv, 3, 129. See under HANGING.

Turn the beam.—*Hamlet,* iv, 5, 157.
Weigh thee to the beam.—*All 's Well that Ends Well,* ii, 3, 162.
Weaver's beam.—*The Merry Wives of Windsor,* v, 1, 24.

6

You found his mote; the king your mote did see;
But I a beam do find in each of three.
Love's Labour 's Lost. Act iv, sc. 3, l. 161. [Biron]

7

Sometimes the beam of her view gilded my foot, sometimes my portly belly.
The Merry Wives of Windsor, i, 3, 68. See under COQUETRY.

Beam of sight.—*Coriolanus,* iii, 2, 5.

8

Chaste beams of the watery moon.
A Midsummer-Night's Dream, ii, 1, 162. See under MOON.

Moonshine's watery beams.—*Romeo and Juliet,* i, 4, 62.

9

Mock with thy tickling beams eyes that are sleeping.
The Rape of Lucrece, l. 1090.

BEAR

10

Are these thy bears? we 'll bait thy bears to death,
And manacle the bear-ward in their chains.
II Henry VI. Act v, sc. 1, l. 148. [Clifford]

Call hither to the stake my two brave bears,
That with the very shaking of their chains
They may astonish these fell-lurking curs.
II Henry VI. Act v, sc. 1, l. 144. [York] The only use of "fell-lurking."

From thy burgonet I 'll rend thy bear
And tread it under foot with all contempt,
Despite the bear-ward that protects the bear.
II Henry VI. Act v, sc. 1, l. 208. [Clifford] "Bear-ward" is used a third time in *Much Ado about Nothing,* ii, 1, 43.

11

Whose hand is that the forest bear doth lick?
Not his that spoils her young before her face.
III Henry VI. Act ii, sc. 2, l. 13. [Clifford]

Like to a chaos, or an unlick'd bear-whelp
That carries no impression like the dam.
III Henry VI. Act iii, sc. 2, l. 161. [Gloucester] The only use of "unlick'd" and "bear-whelp."

But if you hunt these bear-whelps, then beware:
The dam will wake.
Titus Andronicus. Act iv, sc. 1, l. 96. [Titus] The only use of "bear-whelps."

12 The two brave bears, . . .
That in their chains fetter'd the kingly lion
And made the forest tremble when they roar'd.
III Henry VI. Act v, sc. 7, l. 10. [King Edward]

Chain me with roaring bears.
Romeo and Juliet. Act iv, sc. 1, l. 80. [Juliet]

Angry bears.—*The Tempest,* i, 2, 289.
Muzzled bear.—*King John,* ii, 1, 249.
Roman bear.—*Julius Cæsar,* iv, 3, 188.
Russian bear.—*Henry V,* iii, 7, 154.
Stubborn bear.—*The Winter's Tale,* iv, 4, 832

13

Why do your dogs bark so? be there bears i' the town? . . . You are afraid, if you see the bear loose, are you not?
The Merry Wives of Windsor. Act i, sc. 1, l. 298. [Slender]

They are very ill favoured rough things.
The Merry Wives of Windsor. Act i, sc. 1, l. 311. [Slender]

The two bears will not bite one another when they meet.
Much Ado about Nothing. Act iii, sc. 2, l. 80. [Claudio]

14

Fabian: He brought me out o' favour with my lady about a bear-baiting here.
Sir Toby: To anger him we 'll have the bear again.
Twelfth Night. Act ii, sc. 5, l. 8. "Bear-baiting" is repeated in i, 3, 98; and in *The Winter's Tale,* iv, 3, 109.

BEARD

1
Were I the wearer of Antonius' beard,
I would not shave 't to-day.
Antony and Cleopatra. Act ii, sc. 2, l. 7. [Enobarbus]

2
Stroke your chins, and swear by your beards that I am a knave.
As You Like It. Act i, sc. 2, l. 76. [Touchstone]

Stroke his beard.—*Much Ado about Nothing,* v, 1, 15.
Stroke thy beard.—*Troilus and Cressida,* i, 3, 165.
Scratch his beard.—*Winter's Tale,* iv, 4, 728.

3
Bearded like a pard.
As You Like It. Act ii, sc. 7, l. 150. [Jaques] See under LIFE.

Beard of formal cut.
As You Like It. Act ii, sc. 7, l. 155. [Jaques] See under LIFE.

I did dislike the cut of a certain courtier's beard.
As You Like It. Act v, sc. 4, l. 73. [Touchstone]

What a beard of the general's cut and a horrid suit of the camp will do among foaming bottles and ale-washed wits, is wonderful to be thought on.
Henry V. Act iii, sc. 6, l. 81. [Gower] The only use of "ale-washed."

4
Beaten the maids a-row and bound the doctor,
Whose beard they have singed off with brands of fire.
The Comedy of Errors. Act v, sc. 1, l. 170. [Servant] The only use of "a-row."

5
If e'er again I meet him beard to beard,
He 's mine, or I am his.
Coriolanus. Act i, sc. 10, l. 11. [Aufidius]

We might have met them dareful, beard to beard.
Macbeth. Act v, sc. 5, l. 6. [Macbeth] The only use of "dareful."

6
You had more beard when I last saw you.
Coriolanus. Act iv, sc. 3, l. 8. [A Volsce]

Claudio: The old ornament of his cheek hath already stuffed tennis-balls.
Leonato: Indeed, he looks younger than he did, by the loss of a beard.
Much Ado about Nothing. Act iii, sc. 2, l. 46.

7
Hamlet: His beard was grizzled,—no?
Horatio: It was, as I have seen it in his life,
A sable silver'd.
Hamlet. Act i, sc. 2, l. 240. "Grizzled" is repeated in *Antony and Cleopatra,* iii, 13, 17.

His beard was as white as snow,
All flaxen was his poll.
Hamlet. Act iv, sc. 5, l. 195. [Ophelia] The only use of "flaxen" in the plays.

Thy father's beard is turned white with the news.
I Henry IV. Act ii, sc. 4, l. 393. [Falstaff]

Whose beard the silver hand of peace hath touch'd.
II Henry IV, iv, 1, 43. [Westmoreland]

[They] told me I had white hairs in my beard ere the black ones were there.
King Lear. Act iv, sc. 6, l. 98. [King Lear]

I 'll hide my silver beard in a gold beaver.
Troilus and Cressida. Act i, sc. 3, l. 296. [Nestor]

White beard.—*II Henry IV,* i, 2, 204, and six times in later plays.
White-bearded.—*I Henry IV,* ii, 4, 509; *Much Ado about Nothing,* ii, 3, 124.
White and bristly beard.—*Sonnets,* xii.

8
Thy face is valanced since I saw thee last:
comest thou to beard me?
Hamlet. Act ii, sc. 2, l. 442. [Hamlet] The only use of "valanced."

9
Plucks off my beard and blows it in my face.
Hamlet, ii, 2, 600. See under COWARDICE.

10
Winchester: Do what thou darest: I beard thee to thy face.
Gloucester: What! am I dared and bearded to my face?
I Henry VI. Act i, sc. 3, l. 44.

Brave thee! ay, by the best blood that ever was broached, and beard thee too.
II Henry VI. Act iv, sc. 10, l. 39. [Cade]

I will beard him.—*I Henry IV,* iv, 1, 12.

11
You must not think
That we are made of stuff so flat and dull
That we can let our beard be shook with danger
And think it pastime.
Hamlet. Act iv, sc. 7, l. 30. [King]

12
'Tis merry in hall when beards wag all.
II Henry IV. Act v, sc. 3, l. 37. [Silence] First used by an unknown writer about 1310 in *King Alisaunder* (l. 1163); and in 1546, included by John Heywood in his collection of *Proverbs* (Pt. ii, ch. 8).

His beard, all silver white, Wagg'd up and down.
The Rape of Lucrece, l. 1405.

When you speak best unto the purpose, it is not worth the wagging of your beards; and your beards deserve not so honourable a grave as to stuff a botcher's cushion, or to be entombed in an ass's pack-saddle.
Coriolanus. Act ii, sc. 1, l. 95. [Menenius Agrippa] The only use of "pack-saddle."

13
Takes him by the beard.
Henry V. Act iv, sc. 6, l. 13. [Exeter]

Take our goodly aged men by the beards.
Timon of Athens. Act v, sc. 1, l. 175.

Go to Constantinople and take the Turk by the beard.
Henry V. Act v, sc. 2, l. 223. [King Henry] The only mention of Constantinople.

The great Cham's beard.—*Much Ado about Nothing,* ii, 1, 277. The only reference to the great Cham.

Dutchman's beard.—*Twelfth Night,* iii, 2, 30.

14
Priest, beware your beard;
I mean to tug it and to cuff you soundly.
I Henry VI. Act i, sc. 3, l. 47. [Gloucester]

'Tis most ignobly done
To pluck me by the beard.
King Lear. Act iii, sc. 7, l. 35. [Gloucester]

1
His well-proportion'd beard made rough and rugged,
Like to the summer's corn by tempest lodged.
II Henry VI. Act iii, sc. 2, l. 175. [Warwick] The only use of "well-proportion'd."

2
Spare my gray beard, you wagtail?
King Lear. Act ii, sc. 2, l. 72. [Kent] The only use of "wagtail."

Gray beard.—*King Lear,* ii, 2, 68. "Gray" is so spelled three times in *King Lear,* once in *Julius Cæsar* and once in *A Midsummer-Night's Dream.*

He 'll over-reach the greybeard, Gremio.
The Taming of the Shrew. Act iii, sc. 2, l. 147. [Lucentio] "Greybeard" is repeated in ii, 1, 340, and in *I Henry VI,* iii, 2, 50, and *III Henry VI,* v, 6, 81. In *Julius Cæsar,* ii, 2, 67, it is "graybeard."

3
Art not ashamed to look upon this beard?
King Lear. Act ii, sc. 4, l. 196. [King Lear]

God's blessings on your beard!
Love's Labour's Lost. Act ii, sc. 1, l. 203. [Longaville]

With his royal finger, thus, dally with my excrement, with my mustachio.
Love's Labour's Lost. Act v, sc. 1, l. 109. [Armado] "Mustachio" occurs again in *I Henry IV,* ii, 1, 83.

4
You should be women,
And yet your beards forbid me to interpret
That you are so.
Macbeth. Act i, sc. 3, l. 45. [Banquo]

5
What a beard hast thou got! thou hast got more hair on thy chin than Dobbin my fill-horse has on his tail.
The Merchant of Venice. Act ii, sc. 2, l. 99. [Gobbo] The only mention of Dobbin and use of "fill-horse" which is Gobbo's rendering of thill-horse (shaft-horse).

Good beards.—*As You Like It,* Epil., 22.

6
Bottom: What beard were I best to play it in?
Quince: Why, what you will.
Bottom: I will discharge it in either your straw-colour beard, your orange-tawny beard, your purple-in-grain beard, or your French-crown-colour beard, your perfect yellow.
A Midsummer-Night's Dream. Act i, sc. 2, l. 92. The only use of "straw-colour," "purple-in-grain," and "French-crown-colour." "Orange-tawny" occurs again in iii, i, 129.

7
Beatrice: Lord, I could not endure a husband with a beard on his face: I had rather lie in the woollen.
Leonato: You may light on a husband that hath no beard.
Beatrice: What should I do with him? dress him in my apparel and make him my waiting-gentlewoman?
Much Ado about Nothing. Act ii, sc. 1, l. 31.

He that hath a beard is more than a youth, and he that hath no beard is less than a man.
Much Ado about Nothing. Act ii, sc. 1, l. 38. [Beatrice]

Defeat thy favour with an usurped beard.
Othello. Act i, sc. 3, l. 346. [Iago]

8
By this white beard, I'ld fight with thee to-morrow.
Troilus and Cressida. Act iv, sc. 5, l. 209. [Nestor]

By my old beard, And every hair that 's on it.
All's Well that Ends Well. Act v, sc. 3, l. 76. [Lafeu]

By my white beard.—*The Winter's Tale,* iv, 4, 414.

Ay, by my beard.—*The Two Gentlemen of Verona,* iv, 1, 10.

II—Beardlessness

9
Rosalind: Is his head worth a hat, or his chin worth a beard?
Celia: Nay, he hath but a little beard.
Rosalind: Why, God will send more, if the man will be thankful: let me stay the growth of his beard, if thou delay me not the knowledge of his chin.
As You Like It. Act iii, sc. 2, l. 217.

Mistress Quickly: Master Slender 's your master?
Simple: Ay, forsooth.
Mistress Quickly: Does he not wear a great round beard, like a glover's paring-knife?
Simple: No, forsooth: he hath but a little wee face, with a little yellow beard, a Cain-coloured beard.
The Merry Wives of Windsor. Act i, sc. 4, l. 18. The only use of "glover," "paring-knife," and "Cain-coloured."

Little beard.—*All's Well that Ends Well,* ii, 3, 67.

10
Your master, whose chin is not yet fledged.
I will sooner have a beard grow in the palm of my hand than he shall get one on his cheek.
II Henry IV. Act i, sc. 2, l. 23. [Falstaff] "Fledged" is repeated in *The Merchant of Venice,* iii, 2, 32.

Whose chin is but enrich'd
With one appearing hair.
Henry V. Act iii, Prologue, l. 22. [Chorus]

If you did wear a beard upon your chin,
I 'd shake it on this quarrel.
King Lear. Act iii, sc. 7, l. 76. [Servant]

A beardless boy.—*King John,* v, 1, 69. "Beardless" is repeated in *I Henry IV,* iii, 2, 67.

11
A beard, fair health, and honesty;
With three-fold love I wish you all these three.
Love's Labour's Lost. Act v, sc. 2, l. 834. [Katharine]

Clown: Now Jove, in his next commodity of hair, send thee a beard!
Viola: By my troth, I 'll tell thee, I am almost sick for one; though I would not have it grow on my chin.
Twelfth Night. Act iii, sc. 1, l. 50.

My Lord Lackbeard.
Much Ado about Nothing. Act v, sc. I, l. 195. [Benedick] The only use of the phrase.

His beard grew thin and hungerly.
The Taming of the Shrew. Act iii, sc. 2, l. 177. [Gremio]

1 Till new-born chins Be rough and razorable.
The Tempest. Act ii, sc. I, l. 249. [Antonio] The only use of "razorable."

Alas, poor chin! many a wart is richer.
Troilus and Cressida. Act i, sc. 2, l. 155. [Cressida]

Pandarus: He has not past three or four hairs on his chin,—
Cressida: Indeed, a tapster's arithmetic may soon bring his particulars therein to a total.
Troilus and Cressida. Act i, sc. 2, l. 121. "Total" is used only once again, in *Hamlet*, ii, 2, 479: "Total gules."

Here 's but two and fifty hairs on your chin, and one of them is white.
Troilus and Cressida. Act i, sc. 2, l. 171. [Pandarus]

2 The tender spring upon thy tempting lip
Shows thee unripe.
Venus and Adonis, l. 127.

Small show of man was yet upon his chin;
His phœnix down began but to appear
Like unshorn velvet on that termless skin
Whose bare out-bragg'd the web it seem'd to wear.
A Lover's Complaint, l. 92. The only use of "unshorn," "termless," and "out-bragg'd."

BEAST

See also Animal

3 A pair of very strange beasts.
As You Like It, v, 4, 37. See under Fool.

Strange beast.—*The Tempest*, ii, 2, 32.

4 Nature teaches beasts to know their friends.
Coriolanus. Act ii, sc. I, l. 6. [Sicinius]

5 A beast, that wants discourse of reason.
Hamlet. Act i, sc. 2, l. 150. [Hamlet]

That incestuous, that adulterate beast.
Hamlet. Act i, sc. 5, l. 41. [Ghost]

Bloody beast.—*Venus and Adonis*, l. 999.
Brutish beasts.—*Julius Cæsar*, iii, 2, 109.
Grisly beast.—*A Midsummer-Night's Dream*, v, I, 140.
Horn-beasts.—*As You Like It*, iii, 3, 51. The only use of "horn-beasts."
Hyrcanian beast.—*Hamlet*, ii, 2, 472. "Hyrcanian" is repeated in *The Merchant of Venice*, ii, 7, 41. Hyrcania, the ancient name of a country south of the Caspian Sea, is used once, in *III Henry VI*, i, 4, 155.
Ill-beseeming beast.—*Romeo and Juliet*, iii, 3, 113.
Mere beasts.—*Hamlet*, iv, 5, 86.
Poor beast.—*Sonnets*, xl.
Rude beast.—*Measure for Measure*, iii, 2, 34.
Ruthless beasts.—*Passionate Pilgrim*, l. 394.
Sick-fall'n beast.—*King John*, iv, 3, 153. The only use of "sick-fall'n."
Unkindest beast.—*Timon of Athens*, iv, I, 36.
Unruly beast.—*Venus and Adonis*, l. 326.

6 Let a beast be lord of beasts, and his crib shall stand at the king's mess.
Hamlet. Act v, sc. 2, l. 87. [Hamlet]

7 Falstaff: Setting thy womanhood aside, thou art a beast to say otherwise.
Hostess: Say, what beast, thou knave, thou?
Falstaff: What beast! why, an otter.
Prince of Wales: An otter, Sir John! why an otter?
Falstaff: Why, she 's neither fish nor flesh; a man knows not where to have her.
I Henry IV. Act iii, sc. 3, l. 139. The only mention of otter.

8 It is a beast for Perseus.
Henry V, iii, 7, 22. See under Horse.

A beast without a heart.—*Julius Cæsar*, ii, 2, 42.

9 What beast was 't, then,
That made you break this enterprise to me?
Macbeth. Act i, sc. 7, l. 47. [Lady Macbeth]

10 It is a familiar beast to man, and signifies love.
The Merry Wives of Windsor. Act i, sc. I, l. 20. [Evans] Referring to the louse.

11 What a beast am I to slack it!
The Merry Wives of Windsor. Act iii, sc. 4, l. 115. [Mistress Quickly]

Alcibiades: What art thou there? speak.
Timon: A beast, as thou art.
Timon of Athens. Act iv, sc. 3, l. 48.

12 Demetrius: I 'll . . . leave thee to the mercy of wild beasts.
Helena: The wildest hath not such a heart as you.
A Midsummer-Night's Dream. Act ii, sc. I, l. 227. [Theseus]

Here come two noble beasts in, man and lion.
A Midsummer-Night's Dream. Act v, sc. I, l. 220. [Theseus]

Noble beast.—*Much Ado about Nothing*, v, 4, 47.

Theseus: A very gentle beast, and of a good conscience.
Demetrius: The very best at a beast, my lord, that e'er I saw.
A Midsummer-Night's Dream. Act v, sc. I, l. 231.

Gentle beast.—*Love's Labour 's Lost*, ii, I, 222.
Bonny beast.—*II Henry VI*, v, 2, 12.
Brave beast.—*Hamlet*, iv, 7, 89.

13 There 's many a beast then in a populous city.
Othello, iv, I, 64. See under Cuckold.

14 Beasts did leap, and birds did sing.
The Passionate Pilgrim, l. 377.

Beasts and birds and fishes.—*Timon of Athens*, iv, 3, 426.
Beasts and birds of prey.—*Titus Andronicus*, v, 3, 198.

15 The rough beast that knows no gentle right,
Nor aught obeys but his foul appetite.
The Rape of Lucrece, l. 545.

Since men prove beasts, let beasts bear gentle minds.
The Rape of Lucrece, l. 1148.

1 The beast that bears me, tired with my woe,
Plods dully on.
Sonnets. No. l.

2 O monstrous beast! how like a swine he lies!
The Taming of the Shrew. Induction, sc. 1, l. 34. [Lord]

You beasts!—*Romeo and Juliet*, i, 1, 90.
The more beast, I say.—*Timon of Athens*, iii, 2, 55.
A beast, no more.—*Hamlet*, iv, 4, 35.
Meaning me a beast.—*As You Like It*, iv, 3, 49.
Transform ourselves into beasts!—*Othello*, ii, 3, 294.

3 Away, you three-inch fool! I am no beast.
The Taming of the Shrew. Act iv, sc. 1, l. 28. [Curtis] The only use of "three-inch." "Three inches" occurs in the same scene, l. 29, and in *The Tempest*, ii, 1, 283.

4 Wouldst thou have thyself fall in the confusion of men, and remain a beast with the beasts?
Timon of Athens. Act iv, sc. 3, l. 326. [Timon]

If thou wert the lion, the fox would beguile thee: if thou wert the lamb, the fox would eat thee: if thou wert the fox, the lion would suspect thee, when peradventure thou wert accused by the ass: if thou wert the ass, thy dulness would torment thee, and still thou livedst but as a breakfast to the wolf: if thou wert the wolf, thy greediness would afflict thee, and oft thou shouldst hazard thy life for thy dinner: wert thou the unicorn, pride and wrath would confound thee and make thine own self the conquest of thy fury: wert thou a bear, thou wouldst be killed by the horse: wert thou a horse, thou wouldst be seized by the leopard: wert thou a leopard, thou wert german to the lion and the spots of thy kindred were jurors on thy life: all thy safety were remotion and thy defense absence. What beast couldst thou be, that were not subject to a beast? and what a beast art thou already, that seest not thy loss in transformation!
Timon of Athens. Act iv, sc. 3, l. 330. [Timon] "Juror" is repeated in *Henry VIII*, v, 3, 60; and "remotion" (keeping aloof) in *King Lear*, ii, 4, 115.

5 Wilt thou not, beast, abide?
Why, then fly on, I'll hunt thee for thy hide.
Troilus and Cressida. Act v, sc. 6, l. 30. [Hector]

BEATING

See also Scourge, Whipping

6 I'll beat him, by my life, if I can meet him with any convenience, an he were double and double a lord.
All's Well that Ends Well. Act ii, sc. 3, l. 252. [Parolles]

By mine honour, if I were but two hours younger, I'ld beat thee: methinks thou art a general offence, and every man should beat thee.
All's Well that Ends Well. Act ii, sc. 3, l. 268. [Lafeu]

You were beaten in Italy for picking a kernel out of a pomegranate.
All's Well that Ends Well. Act ii, sc. 3, l. 275. [Lafeu] Only use of "pomegranate."

In conclusion, he did beat me there.
The Comedy of Errors. Act ii, sc. 1, l. 74. [Dromio of Ephesus]

7 We'll beat 'em into bench-holes.
Antony and Cleopatra. Act iv, sc. 7, l. 9. [Scarus] The only use of "bench-holes" (privies). See also under Victory.

He beats thee against the odds.—*Antony and Cleopatra*, ii, 3, 27. See under Odds.

I shall beat you to your tent, and prove a shrewd Cæsar to you; in plain dealing, Pompey, I shall have you whipt.
Measure for Measure. Act ii, sc. 1, l. 262. [Escalus]

8 Dromio of Syracuse: But, I pray, sir, why am I beaten?
Antipholus of Syracuse: Dost thou not know?
Dromio: Nothing, sir, but that I am beaten.
The Comedy of Errors. Act ii, sc. 2, l. 39.

Was there any man thus beaten out of season?
The Comedy of Errors. Act ii, sc. 2, l. 48. [Dromio of Syracuse]

Was ever man so beaten?—*The Taming of the Shrew*, iv, 1, 3.

So is Alcides beaten by his page.
The Merchant of Venice. Act ii, sc. 1, l. 35. [Morocco] Alcides is mentioned seven times.

Let us be beaten, if we cannot fight.
Macbeth, v, 6, 8. See under Fighting.

I did think to have beaten thee.—*Much Ado about Nothing*, v, 4, 111.
You have beaten my men.—*The Merry Wives of Windsor*, i, 1, 114.
They are beaten, sir.—*Antony and Cleopatra*, iv, 7, 11.
Beaten, bobb'd, and thump'd.—*Richard III*, v, 3, 334. "Thump'd" is repeated in *Love's Labour's Lost*, iv, 3, 23.
Beaten for loyalty.—*Cymbeline*, v, 5, 344.
Beaten from Modena.—*Antony and Cleopatra*, i, 4, 57.
Beaten out of door.—*The Taming of the Shrew*, Ind., 2, 87.
Beaten with brains.—*Much Ado about Nothing*, v, 4, 104.
Twice beaten.—*Cymbeline*, iii, 1, 26.

9 You'll cry for this, minion, if I beat the door down.
The Comedy of Errors. Act iii, sc. 1, l. 59. [Antipholus of Ephesus]

Will you beat down the door?—*Troilus and Cressida*, iv, 2, 44.
Beat down the gate.—*The Taming of the Shrew*, v, 1, 17.
Beat at this gate.—*King Lear*, i, 4, 293.
Beat down Alencon.—*I Henry VI*, iv, 6, 14.
Beat down Edward's guard.—*III Henry VI*, iv, 2, 23.
Beat down our foes.—*Troilus and Cressida*, ii, 2, 201.

Beat down The Never-daunted Percy.—*II Henry IV*, i, 1, 109.
Beaten down young Hotspur.—*II Henry IV*, Ind., 25.
Beat down these rebels.—*Richard III*, iv, 4, 532.
Beat down with storms.—*Titus Andronicus*, iv, 4, 71.
To beat us down, the which are down already.
Pericles. Act i, sc. 4, l. 68. [Cleon]
But our great Ajax bravely beat down him.
Troilus and Cressida. Act iii, sc. 3, l. 213. [Ulysses]
The fierce Polydamus Hath beat down Menon.
Troilus and Cressida. Act v, sc. 5, l. 7. [Agamemnon] The only mention of either Polydamus or Menon.
Beats it down.—*The Passionate Pilgrim*, l. 328.
Beat it dead.—*The Rape of Lucrece*, l. 489.
Beat love down.—*Romeo and Juliet*, i, 4, 28.
Beat them down!—*Romeo and Juliet*, i, 1, 80.
Beat usurping down.—*King John*, ii, 1, 119.

1
That you beat me at the mart, I have your hand to show.
The Comedy of Errors. Act iii, sc. 1, l. 12. [Dromio of Ephesus]
I have served him from the hour of my nativity to this instant, and have nothing at his hands for my service but blows. When I am cold, he heats me with beating; when I am warm, he cools me with beating; I am waked with it when I sleep; raised with it when I sit; driven out of doors with it when I go from home; welcomed home with it when I return: nay, I bear it on my shoulders, as a beggar wont her brat; and, I think, when he hath lamed me, I shall beg with it from door to door.
The Comedy of Errors. Act iv, sc. 4, l. 31. [Dromio of Ephesus]

2
If you 'll stand fast, we 'll beat them to their wives,
As they us to our trenches followed.
Coriolanus. Act i, sc. 4, l. 41. [Marcius]
Beat you to your trenches.—*Coriolanus*, i, 6, 40.

3
Five times, Marcius,
I have fought with thee; so often hast thou beat me,
And wouldst do so, I think, should we encounter
As often as we eat.
Coriolanus. Act i, sc. 10, l. 7. [Aufidius]
Thou hast beat me out
Twelve several times, and I have nightly since
Dreamt of encounters 'twixt thyself and me;
We have been down together in my sleep,
Unbuckling helms, fisting each other's throat,
And waked half dead with nothing.
Coriolanus. Act iv, sc. 5, l. 127. [Aufidius] The only use of "unbuckling."
On fair ground I could beat forty of them.
Coriolanus. Act iii, sc. 1, l. 242. [Coriolanus]

4
I prithee, Tom, beat Cut's saddle, put a few flocks in the point.
I Henry IV. Act ii, sc. 1, l. 6. [Carrier] The only use of "flocks" in the sense of tufts of wool.
Beat my bones.—*Troilus and Cressida*, ii, 1, 76.
Beats cold death aside.—*Romeo and Juliet*, iii, 1, 166.

Beat his offenceless dog.—*Othello*, ii, 3, 275. The only use of "offenceless."
Beat the drum, see under DRUM.
Beat the ground.—*The Tempest*, iv, 1, 173.
Beat heaven.—*II Henry IV*, i, 3, 92.
Beat her husband!—*The Winter's Tale*, ii, 3, 91.
Beat the messenger.—*Coriolanus*, iv, 6, 54.
Beat his own name.—*II Henry IV*, iii, 2, 349.
Beats the nurse.—*Measure for Measure*, i, 3, 30.
Beating your officers.—*Coriolanus*, iii, 3, 78.
Beat the stones.—*III Henry VI*, v, 1, 108.
Beat the surges.—*The Tempest*, ii, 1, 114.
Beat my tabor.—*The Tempest*, iv, 1, 175.
Beat our watch.—*Richard II*, v, 3, 9.
Beat into clamorous whining.—*King Lear*, ii, 2, 24.
Beat me out of Egypt.—*Antony and Cleopatra*, iv, 1, 2.
Beat us out of it.—*Cymbeline*, iii, 1, 81.

5
The man is dead that you and Pistol beat amongst you.
II Henry IV. Act v, sc. 4, l. 18. [Beadle]

6
A rope! a rope! Now beat them hence.
I Henry VI. Act i, sc. 3, l. 53. [Gloucester]
I am loathe to beat thee.—*Cymbeline*, iv, 2, 86.

7
See thou thump thy master well.
II Henry VI. Act ii, sc. 3, l. 85. [Salisbury]
Thump then and I flee.
Love's Labour 's Lost. Act iii, sc. 1, l. 66. [Moth] The only use of "flee."
Jump her and thump her.—*The Winter's Tale*, iv, 4, 196.
Thus I thump it down.—*Titus Andronicus*, iii, 2, 11. The only uses of "thump."

8
If thou wert my fool, nuncle, I 'ld have thee beaten for being old before thy time.
King Lear. Act i, sc. 5, l. 46. [Fool]

9
[He] forbade her my house and hath threatened to beat her.
The Merry Wives of Windsor. Act iv, sc. 2, l. 85. [Mrs. Ford]

10
Mrs. Page: Trust me, he beat him most pitifully.
Mrs. Ford: Nay, by the mass, that he did not; he beat him most unpitifully, methought.
The Merry Wives of Windsor. Act iv, sc. 2, l. 212. The only use of "unpitifully." "Pitifully" occurs four times.
Mistress Quickly: Mistress Ford, good heart, is beaten black and blue, that you cannot see a white spot about her.
Falstaff: What tellest thou me of black and blue? I was beaten myself into all the colours of the rainbow.
The Merry Wives of Windsor. Act iv, sc. 5, l. 114.
He beat me grievously.—*The Merry Wives of Windsor*, v, 1, 21.
Since I plucked geese, played truant and whipped top, I knew not what 'twas to be beaten till lately.
The Merry Wives of Windsor. Act v, sc. 1, l. 26. [Falstaff]

1
I swear I 'll cuff you, if you strike again.
The Taming of the Shrew. Act ii, sc. 1, l. 221. [Petruchio]
This cuff was but to knock at your ear, and beseech listening.
The Taming of the Shrew. Act iv, sc. 1, l. 67. [Grumio]
Took him such a cuff.—*The Taming of the Shrew,* iii, 2, 165.
Sir Andrew: 'Slid, I 'll after him again and beat him.
Sir Toby: Do; cuff him soundly.
Twelfth Night. Act iii, sc. 4, l. 426. "'Slid" (by God's lid) is repeated in *The Merry Wives of Windsor,* iii, 4, 24.
Cuff you soundly.—*I Henry VI,* i, 3, 48.
Went to cuffs.—*Hamlet,* ii, 2, 373. The only uses of "cuff" and "cuffs" in the sense of strike. As an article of dress it is referred to once, in *The Taming of the Shrew,* iv, 3, 56: "Ruffs and cuffs."

2
How he beat me because her horse stumbled.
The Taming of the Shrew, iv, 1, 79.
Beat me to death with a bottom of brown thread.
The Taming of the Shrew. Act iv, sc. 3, l. 137. [Grumio]

3
Beat him enough: after a little time
I 'll beat him too.
The Tempest. Act iii, sc. 2, l. 93. [Caliban]
I could find it in my heart to beat him.
The Tempest. Act ii, sc. 2, l. 160. [Trinculo]
I 'ld beat thee, but I should infect my hands.
Timon of Athens. Act iv, sc. 3, l. 369. [Timon]

4
Ajax: I will beat thee into handsomeness.
Thersites: I shall sooner rail thee into wit and holiness.
Troilus and Cressida. Act ii, sc. 1, l. 16. The only use of "handsomeness."
He beats me, and I rail at him: O, worthy satisfaction! would it were otherwise; that I could beat him whilst he railed at me.
Troilus and Cressida. Act ii, sc. 3, l. 3. [Thersites]

5
'Slight, I could so beat the rogue!
Twelfth Night. Act ii, sc. 5, l. 38. [Sir Andrew] Sir Andrew repeats "'slight" (by God's light) in iii, 2, 14. It is used nowhere else.
Beat him like a dog.
Twelfth Night. Act ii, sc. 3, l. 153. [Sir Andrew]
I 'ld have beaten him like a dog.
Coriolanus. Act iv, sc. 5, l. 56. [Second Servant]
Beat forth our brains.—*Titus Andronicus,* v, 3, 133.
Beat out his brains.—*Timon of Athens,* iv, 1, 15.
Beat out my brains.—*Measure for Measure,* iv, 3, 58.
Beat your breast.—*Richard III,* ii, 2, 3.
Beating on her breast.—*The Rape of Lucrece,* l. 759.
Beats her heart.—*Much Ado about Nothing,* ii, 3, 153; *Hamlet,* iv, 5, 5; *Venus and Adonis,* l. 829.

6
Say this to him,
He 's beat from his best ward.
Winter's Tale. Act i, sc. 2, l. 32. [Hermione]

7
Autolycus: Stripes I have received, which are mighty ones and millions.
Clown: Alas, poor man! a million of beating may come to a great matter.
The Winter's Tale. Act iv, sc. 3, l. 60.
Whom stripes may move, not kindness!
The Tempest. Act i, sc. 2, l. 345. [Prospero]
Wears my stripes impress'd upon him.—*Coriolanus,* v, 6, 108.
Hence with thy stripes, begone!—*Antony and Cleopatra,* iii, 13, 152. The only uses of "stripes."

BEAUTY

I—Familiar Phrases

8
Beauty provoketh thieves sooner than gold.
As You Like It. Act i, sc. 3, l. 112. [Rosalind]
Here 's metal more attractive.
Hamlet. Act iii, sc. 2, l. 116. [Hamlet]
In this book of beauty read 'I love.'
King John. Act ii, sc. 1, l. 485. [King John]
Pretty and apt.—*Love's Labour 's Lost,* i, 2, 19.

9
And beauty's crest becomes the heavens well.
Love's Labour 's Lost. Act iv, sc. 3, l. 256. [King]

10
Thou hast the right arched beauty of the brow.
The Merry Wives of Windsor, iii, 3, 59. See under BROW.
Beauty of a fair queen's cheeks.—*Richard II,* iii, 1, 14.
Beauty of thy days.—*Sonnets,* lxii.
Day's beauty.—*I Henry IV,* i, 2, 28.
Beauty of your eyes.—*Sonnets,* xvii.
Beauty of a woman's face.—*Love's Labour 's Lost,* iv, 3, 301.
Beauty of my glass.—*Rape of Lucrece,* l. 1763.
Beauty of this kingdom.—*Henry VIII,* iv, 2, 144.
Beauty of thy mind.—*Sonnets,* lxix.
Beauty of her person.—*Henry VIII,* iv, 2, 144.
Beauty of the soul.—*Henry VIII,* iv, 2, 144.
Beauty of the sun.—*The Two Gentlemen of Verona,* i, 3, 86.
Beauty of the world!—*Hamlet,* ii, 2, 319.
Helen's beauty.—*Midsummer-Night's Dream,* v, 1, 11.
Proserpina's beauty.—*Troilus and Cressida,* ii, 1, 37.

11
He hath a daily beauty in his life
That makes me ugly.
Othello. Act v, sc. 1, l. 19. [Iago]

12
And what this fourteen years no razor touch'd,
To grace thy marriage-day, I 'll beautify.
Pericles. Act v, sc. 3, l. 75. [Pericles]
Beautify him.—*Romeo and Juliet,* i, 3, 88.
Beautify the cheek.—*II Henry VI,* iii, 2, 167.
Beautify thy triumphs.—*Titus Andronicus,* i, 1, 110.

Themselves so beautify.—*The Rape of Lucrece,* l. 404. The only uses of "beautify."

1
Beauty 's red and virtue 's white.
The Rape of Lucrece, l. 65.
Desire my pilot is, beauty my prize.
The Rape of Lucrece, l. 279.
Beauty's pattern.—*Sonnets,* xix.
Beauty 's a flower.—*Twelfth Night,* i, 5, 57.

2
The ornament of beauty is suspect,
A crow that flies in heaven's sweetest air.
Sonnets. No. lxx.

3
If beauty have a soul, this is not she.
Troilus and Cressida. Act v, sc. 2, l. 138. [Troilus]

4
Seeing you are beautified with goodly shape.
The Two Gentlemen of Verona. Act iv, sc. 1, l. 55. [First Outlaw]
"Beautified" is a vile phrase.—*Hamlet,* ii, 2, 110. The only uses of "beautified."

5
Marry, sir, so painted, to make her fair, that no man counts of her beauty.
The Two Gentlemen of Verona. Act ii, sc. 1, l. 64. [Speed]
Painted beauty.—*Sonnets,* xxi.

6
Is she not passing fair?
The Two Gentlemen of Verona. Act iv, sc. 4, l. 153. [Silvia]
Passing fair.—*Love's Labour 's Lost,* iv, 3, 103; *Romeo and Juliet,* i, 1, 240; 242. The only uses of this phrase.
As fair as day.
Love's Labour 's Lost, iv, 3, 90. The only use of this phrase in the plays.
O happy fair!—*A Midsummer-Night's Dream,* i, 1, 182.

7
True-sweet beauty lived and died with him.
Venus and Adonis, l. 1080. The only use of "true-sweet."

II—Beauty: Its Power

8
Ay, beauty's princely majesty is such,
Confounds the tongue and makes the senses rough.
I Henry VI. Act v, sc. 3, l. 70. [Suffolk]
Beauty that the tyrant oft reclaims
Shall to my flaming wrath be oil and flax.
II Henry VI. Act v, sc. 2, l. 54. [Young Clifford] "Reclaims" was used in the first play and never again.
O beauty, Till now I never knew thee!
Henry VIII, i, 4, 75. See under HAND.

9
Upon my knees,
I charm you, by my once-commended beauty.
Julius Cæsar. Act ii, sc. 1, l. 270. [Portia] The only use of "once-commended."

10 Thou art fair, and at thy birth, dear boy,
Nature and Fortune join'd to make thee great:
Of Nature's gifts thou mayst with lilies boast
And with the half-blown rose.
King John. Act iii, sc. 1, l. 51. [Constance] The only use of "half-blown."

11
Beauty doth varnish age, as if new-born,
And gives the crutch the cradle's infancy.
Love's Labour 's Lost. Act iv, sc. 3, l. 244. [Biron]
Your beauty, ladies, Hath much deform'd us.
Love's Labour 's Lost. Act v, sc. 2, l. 766. [Biron]

12
Beauty is a witch
Against whose charms faith melteth into blood.
Much Ado about Nothing. Act ii, sc. 1, l. 186. [Claudio]
Beauty hath his power and will,
Which can as well inflame as it can kill.
Pericles. Act ii, sc. 2, l. 34. [Thaisa]
Alluring beauty.—*Comedy of Errors,* ii, 1, 89.
Bright beauty.—*The Rape of Lucrece,* l. 490.
Delighted beauty.—*Othello,* i, 3, 290.
Fresh beauty.—*Venus and Adonis,* l. 796.
Glorious beauty.—*Pericles,* i, 2, 72.
Good beauties.—*Hamlet,* iii, 1, 99; *Twelfth Night,* i, 5, 186.
Indian beauty.—*Merchant of Venice,* iii, 2, 99.
Native beauty.—*King John,* iii, 4, 83.
Pure and princely beauty.—*King John,* iv, 3, 35.
Sacred beauty.—*Sonnets,* cxv.
Summer beauty.—*Richard III,* iv, 3, 13.

13
Beauty itself doth of itself persuade
The eyes of men without an orator.
The Rape of Lucrece, l. 29.
All orators are dumb when beauty pleadeth.
The Rape of Lucrece, l. 268.
Thy beauty hath ensnared thee to this night.
The Rape of Lucrece, l. 485.
My poor beauty had purloin'd his eyes.
The Rape of Lucrece, l. 1651.

14
Your beauty, which did haunt me in my sleep
To undertake the death of all the world,
So I might live one hour in your sweet bosom.
Richard III. Act i, sc. 2, l. 122. [Gloucester]
These eyes could never endure sweet beauty's wreck;
You should not blemish it, if I stood by:
As all the world is cheered by the sun,
So I by that; it is my day, my life.
Richard III. Act i, sc. 2, l. 127. [Gloucester]
And what these sorrows could not thence exhale,
Thy beauty hath, and made them blind with weeping.
Richard III. Act i, sc. 2, l. 166. [Gloucester]
But, now thy beauty is proposed my fee,
My proud heart sues and prompts my tongue to speak.
Richard III. Act i, sc. 2, l. 170. [Gloucester]
'Twas thy beauty that provoked me.
Richard III. Act i, sc. 2, l. 181. [Gloucester]

15
Thy beauty hath made me effeminate
And in my temper soften'd valour's steel!
Romeo and Juliet. Act iii, sc. 1, l. 119. [Romeo]
Her beauty makes
This vault a feasting presence full of light.
Romeo and Juliet, v, 3, 85. See under GRAVE.

1
Since brass, nor stone, nor earth, nor boundless sea,
But sad mortality o'er-sways their power,
How with this rage shall beauty hold a plea,
Whose action is no stronger than a flower?
Sonnets. No. lxv.

And beauty making beautiful old rhyme
In praise of ladies dead and lovely knights.
Sonnets. No. cvi.

2 Upon the altar of her beauty
You sacrifice your tears, your sighs, your heart.
The Two Gentlemen of Verona. Act iii, sc. 2, l. 73. [Proteus]

3
Were beauty under twenty locks kept fast,
Yet love breaks through and picks them all at last.
Venus and Adonis, l. 575.

4
Would she begin a sect, might quench the zeal
Of all professors else, make proselytes
Of who she but bid follow.
The Winter's Tale. Act v, sc. 1, l. 107. [Gentleman] The only use of "proselytes."

III—Beauty: Its Penalties

5
Those that she makes fair she scarce makes honest, and those that she makes honest she makes very ill-favouredly.
As You Like It. Act i, sc. 2, l. 40. [Celia]

Hamlet: If you be honest and fair, your honesty should admit no discourse to your beauty.
Ophelia: Could beauty, my lord, have better commerce than with honesty?
Hamlet: Ay, truly; for the power of beauty will sooner transform honesty from what it is to a bawd than the force of honesty can translate beauty into his likeness.
Hamlet. Act iii, sc. 1, l. 107.

6
Since that my beauty cannot please his eye,
I 'll weep what 's left away, and weeping die.
The Comedy of Errors. Act ii, sc. 1, l. 114. [Adriana]

7
Her beauty and her brain go not together: she 's a good sign, but I have seen small reflection of her wit.
Cymbeline. Act i, sc. 2, l. 31. [First Lord]

All of her that is out of door most rich!
If she be furnish'd with a mind so rare,
She is alone the Arabian bird.
Cymbeline. Act i, sc. 6, l. 15. [Iachimo]

Let her beauty
Look through a casement to allure false hearts
And be false with them.
Cymbeline. Act ii, sc. 4, l. 33. [Posthumus]

8 Look on beauty,
And you shall see 'tis purchased by the weight.
The Merchant of Venice. Act iii, sc. 2, l. 88. [Bassanio]

9
Beauty is but a vain and doubtful good;
A shining gloss that vadeth suddenly;
A flower that dies when first it gins to bud;
A brittle glass that 's broken presently:
A doubtful good, a gloss, a glass, a flower,
Lost, vaded, broken, dead within an hour.
The Passionate Pilgrim, l. 171. The only use of "vadeth" (fadeth). "Vaded" occurs three times in this poem and nowhere else.

So beauty blemish'd once 's for ever lost,
In spite of physic, painting, pain and cost.
The Passionate Pilgrim, l. 179.

Tainted beauty.—*Sonnets,* xxi.

1
Since sweets and beauties do themselves forsake
And die as fast as they see others grow.
Sonnets. No. xii.

And every fair from fair sometime declines,
By chance or nature's changing course untrimm'd.
Sonnets. No. xviii. "Untrimm'd" is repeated in *King John,* iii, 1, 209.

Why should poor beauty indirectly seek
Roses of shadow, since his rose is true?
Sonnets. No. lxvii.

How like Eve's apple doth thy beauty grow,
If thy sweet virtue answer not thy show!
Sonnets. No. xciii.

Ah! yet doth beauty, like a dial-hand,
Steal from his figure and no pace perceived.
Sonnets. No. civ. The only use of "dial-hand."

Sweet beauty hath no name, no holy bower,
But is profaned, if not lives in disgrace.
Sonnets. No. cxxvii.

IV—Beauty: Its Use

11
If she be fair and wise, fairness and wit,
The one 's for use, the other useth it.
Othello. Act ii, sc. 1, l. 130. [Iago]

12
From fairest creatures we desire increase,
That thereby beauty's rose might never die.
Sonnets. No. i.

Then being ask'd where all thy beauty lies,
Where all the treasure of thy lusty days,
To say, within thine own deep-sunken eyes,
Were an all-eating shame and thriftless praise.
Sonnets. No. ii. The only use of "deep-sunken" and "all-eating."

Unthrifty loveliness, why dost thou spend
Upon thyself thy beauty's legacy?
Sonnets. No. iv. "Loveliness" is used only once more, in *Othello,* ii, 1, 232.

Thy unused beauty must be tomb'd with thee,
Which, used, lives th' executor to be.
Sonnets, No. iv. The only use of "tomb'd."

Make sweet some vial; treasure thou some place
With beauty's treasure, ere it be self-kill'd.
Sonnets. No. vi. The only use of "self-kill'd."

Thou art much too fair
To be death's conquest and make worms thine heir.
Sonnets. No. vi.

13
Beauty within itself should not be wasted.
Venus and Adonis, l. 130.

Torches are made to light, jewels to wear,
Dainties to taste, fresh beauty for the use.
Venus and Adonis, l. 163.

Seeds spring from seeds and beauty breedeth beauty.
Venus and Adonis, l. 167.

1
He being dead, with him is beauty slain,
And, beauty dead, black chaos comes again.
Venus and Adonis, l. 1019.

The flowers are sweet, their colours fresh and trim;
But true-sweet beauty lived and died with him.
Venus and Adonis, l. 1079. The only use of "true-sweet."

V—Beauty in Women

2
She 's a fair creature.
All's Well that Ends Well. Act iii, sc. 6, l. 124. [Bertram]

You shall be yet far fairer than you are.
Antony and Cleopatra. Act i, sc. 1, l. 16. [Soothsayer]

And she is fair and, fairer than that word,
Of wondrous virtues.
The Merchant of Venice. Act i, sc. 1, l. 162. [Bassanio]

I am as fair now as I was erewhile.
A Midsummer-Night's Dream. Act iii, sc. 2, l. 274. [Hermia]

Fairer than tongue can name thee.
Richard III. Act i, sc. 2, l. 81. [Gloucester]

My love is as fair As any mother's child.
Sonnets. No. xxi.

But, if you were the devil, you are fair.
Twelfth Night. Act i, sc. 5, l. 270. [Viola]

The fairest I have yet beheld.
The Winter's Tale. Act v, sc. 1, l. 87. [Gentleman]

3
For beauty that made barren the swell'd boast
Of him that best could speak.
Cymbeline. Act v, sc. 5, l. 162. [Iachimo]

4
As plays the sun upon the glassy streams,
Twinkling another counterfeited beam,
So seems this gorgeous beauty to mine eyes.
I Henry VI. Act v, sc. 3, l. 62. [Suffolk]

And, whereas I was black and swart before,
With those clear rays which she infused on me
That beauty am I bless'd with which you see.
I Henry VI. Act i, sc. 2, l. 84. [La Pucelle]

O fairest beauty, do not fear nor fly!
For I will touch thee but with reverent hands.
I Henry VI. Act v, sc. 3, l. 46. [Suffolk]

Beauty and honour in her are so mingled
That they have caught the king.
Henry VIII. Act ii, sc. 3, l. 76. [Lord Chamberlain]

She 's beautiful.—*I Henry VI*, v, 3, 77.

5
See, see, my beauty will be saved by merit!
Love's Labour 's Lost. Act iv, sc. 1, l. 21. [Princess of France]

My continent of beauty.
Love's Labour 's Lost. Act iv, sc. 1, l. 111. [Boyet]

Moth: All hail, the richest beauties on the earth.
Boyet: Beauties no richer than rich taffeta.
Moth: A holy parcel of the fairest dames . . .
That ever turn'd their eyes to mortal views!
Love's Labour 's Lost. Act v, sc. 2, l. 158.

6
She in beauty, education, blood,
Holds hand with any princess of the world.
King John. Act ii, sc. 1, l. 493. [King John]

7
By heaven, that thou art fair, is most infallible; true, that thou art beauteous; truth itself, that thou art lovely. More fairer than fair, beautiful than beauteous.
Love's Labour 's Lost. Act iv, sc. 1, l. 60. [Boyet]

She is too bright to be looked against.
The Merry Wives of Windsor. Act ii, sc. 2, l. 254. [Ford]

There 's her cousin, an she were not possessed with a fury, exceeds her as much in beauty as the first of May doth the last of December.
Much Ado about Nothing. Act i, sc. 1, l. 192. [Benedick]

8
That whiter skin of hers than snow,
And smooth as monumental alabaster.
Othello. Act v, sc. 2, l. 4. [Othello]

Alabaster skin.—*The Rape of Lucrece*, l. 419.

Beauty, in that white intituled,
From Venus' doves doth challenge that fair field.
The Rape of Lucrece, l. 57. "Intituled" (designated) is repeated in *Love's Labour 's Lost*, v, 1, 8.

9
O, she is rich in beauty, only poor,
That when she dies with beauty dies her store.
Romeo and Juliet. Act i, sc. 1, l. 221. [Romeo]

She is too fair, too wise, wisely too fair,
To merit bliss by making me despair.
Romeo and Juliet. Act i, sc. 1, l. 227. [Romeo]

Benvolio: By giving liberty unto thine eyes;
Examine other beauties.
Romeo: 'Tis the way
To call hers exquisite, in question more.
Romeo and Juliet. Act i, sc. 1, l. 233.

10
Show me a mistress that is passing fair,
What doth her beauty serve but as a note
Where I may read who pass'd that passing fair?
Romeo and Juliet. Act i, sc. 1, l. 240. [Romeo]

One fairer than my love! the all-seeing sun
Ne'er saw her match since first the world begun.
Romeo and Juliet. Act i, sc. 2, l. 97. [Romeo] "All-seeing" is repeated in *Richard III*, ii, 1, 82. "All-seeing heaven."

'Tis much pride
For fair without the fair within to hide.
Romeo and Juliet. Act i, sc. 3, l. 89. [Lady Capulet]

11
O, she doth teach the torches to burn bright!
It seems she hangs upon the cheek of night
Like a rich jewel in an Ethiope's ear;
Beauty too rich for use, for earth too dear!
Romeo and Juliet. Act i, sc. 5, l. 46. [Romeo]

Thou for whom Jove would swear
Juno but an Ethiope were.
Love's Labour 's Lost. Act iv, sc. 3, l. 117. [Dumain]

1
Did my heart love till now? forswear it, sight!
For I ne'er saw true beauty till this night.
Romeo and Juliet. Act i, sc. 5, l. 54. [Romeo] "True beauty" is repeated in *Henry VIII,* iv, 2, 144.

Death, that hath suck'd the honey of thy breath,
Hath had no power yet upon thy beauty:
Thou art not conquer'd; beauty's ensign yet
Is crimson in thy lips and in thy cheeks,
And death's pale flag is not advanced there.
Romeo and Juliet. Act v, sc. 3, l. 92. [Romeo]

The blazon of sweet beauty's best,
Of hand, of foot, of lip, of eye, of brow.
Sonnets. No. cvi.

2
I saw sweet beauty in her face.
The Taming of the Shrew. Act i, sc. 1, l. 172. [Lucentio]

I see thy beauty,
Thy beauty, that doth make me like thee well.
The Taming of the Shrew. Act ii, sc. 1, l. 275. [Petruchio]

Embrace her for her beauty's sake.
The Taming of the Shrew. Act iv, sc. 5, l. 34. [Petruchio]

3
Sweet blowse, you are a beauteous blossom, sure.
Titus Andronicus. Act iv, sc. 2, l. 72. [Aaron] The only use of "blowse" (ruddy-faced wench).

4
She looked yesternight fairer than ever I saw her look, or any woman else.
Troilus and Cressida. Act i, sc. 1, l. 32. [Pandarus]

Let her be as she is: if she be fair, 'tis the better for her; an she be not, she has the mends in her own hands.
Troilus and Cressida. Act i, sc. 1, l. 66. [Pandarus]

An she were not kin to me, she would be as fair on Friday as Helen is on Sunday.
Troilus and Cressida. Act i, sc. 1, l. 76. [Pandarus]

5
The beauty that is born here in the face
The bearer knows not, but commends itself
To others' eyes.
Troilus and Cressida. Act iii, sc. 3, l. 103. [Achilles]

The lustre in your eye, heaven in your cheek,
Pleads your fair usage.
Troilus and Cressida. Act iv, sc. 4, l. 120. [Diomedes]

Most radiant, exquisite and unmatchable beauty.
Twelfth Night. Act i, sc. 5, l. 181. [Viola]

6
Viola: Good madam, let me see your face.
Olivia: . . . We will draw the curtain and show you the picture. Look you, sir, such a one I was this present: is 't not well done?
Viola: Excellently done, if God did all.
Olivia: 'Tis in grain, sir; 'twill endure wind and weather.
Viola: 'Tis beauty truly blent, whose red and white
Nature's own sweet and cunning hand laid on.
Twelfth Night. Act i, sc. 5, l. 248.

I will give out divers schedules of my beauty: it shall be inventoried, and every particle and utensil labelled to my will: as, item, two lips, indifferent red; item, two grey eyes, with lids to them; item, one neck, one chin, and so forth.
Twelfth Night. Act i, sc. 5, l. 262. [Olivia] The only use of "inventoried."

A lady, sir, though it was said she much resembled me, was yet of many accounted beautiful.
Twelfth Night, ii, 1, 26. [Sebastian]

7
I have loved her ever since I saw her; and still I see her beautiful.
The Two Gentlemen of Verona. Act ii, sc. 1, l. 73. [Valentine]

She is as white as a lily and as small as a wand.
The Two Gentlemen of Verona. Act ii, sc. 3, l. 22. [Launce]

When to her beauty I commend my vows,
She bids me think how I have been forsworn.
The Two Gentlemen of Verona. Act iv, sc. 2, l. 9. [Proteus]

8
My beauty as the spring doth yearly grow.
Venus and Adonis, l. 141.

VI—Lack of Beauty

See also Ugliness

9 What, though you have no beauty,
As, by my faith, I see no more in you
Than without candle may go dark to bed.
As You Like It, iii, 5, 37. [Rosalind]

10
'Tis beauty that doth oft make women proud;
But, God he knows, thy share thereof is small.
III Henry VI. Act i, sc. 4, l. 128. [York]

11 My beauty, though but mean,
Needs not the painted flourish of your praise:
Beauty is bought by judgement of the eye,
Not utter'd by base sale of chapmen's tongues.
Love's Labour's Lost. Act ii, sc. 1, l. 13. [Princess of France] "Chapmen" is repeated in *Troilus and Cressida,* iv, 1, 75. A chapman was a trader, and in the instance given above he figures as a seller; in *Troilus* as a buyer: "You do as chapmen do, Dispraise the thing that you desire to buy."

Princess of France: Beauteous as ink. . . .
Katharine: Fair as text B in a copy-book.
Love's Labour's Lost. Act v, sc. 2, l. 41. The only use of "copy-book."

12
For all that beauty that doth cover thee
Is but the seemly raiment of my heart.
Sonnets. No. xxii. "Seemly" is used only once again, in *Henry VIII,* iii, 1, 178: "Seemly answer."

If that be fair whereon my false eyes dote,
What means the world to say it is not so?
Sonnets. No. cxlviii.

Bereft of beauty.—*The Taming of the Shrew,* v, 2, 143.

BED

See also Couch

1
Blessing upon your vows! and in your bed
Find fairer fortune, if you ever wed!
All's Well that Ends Well. Act ii, sc. 3, l. 97. [Helena]
Give their bed joy and prosperity.
A Midsummer-Night's Dream. Act ii, sc. 1, l. 73. [Titania]
To the best bride-bed will we,
Which by us shall blessed be;
And the issue there create
Ever shall be fortunate.
A Midsummer-Night's Dream. Act v, sc. 1, l. 410. [Oberon]
I thought thy bride-bed to have deck'd, sweet maid.
Hamlet. Act v, sc. 1, l. 268. [Queen] The only uses of "bride-bed."
Make the bridal bed
In that dim monument where Tybalt lies.
Romeo and Juliet. Act iii, sc. 5, l. 202. [Juliet]
Bridal bed.—*King John,* ii, 1, 491; *Romeo and Juliet,* v, 3, 12. The only uses of "bridal bed."
Bed of blessed marriage.—*Henry V,* v, 2, 392.
Nuptial bed.—*I Henry VI,* v, 5, 58.
Wedding bed.—*Romeo and Juliet,* i, 5, 137.

2
Although before the solemn priest I have sworn,
I will not bed with her.
All's Well that Ends Well. Act ii, sc. 3, l. 286. [Bertram]
I'll . . . never bed her.—*All's Well that Ends Well,* ii, 3, 290.
Bed her.—*The Taming of the Shrew,* i, 1, 149.

3
When you have conquer'd my yet maiden bed,
Remain there but an hour.
All's Well that Ends Well. Act iv, sc. 2, l. 57. [Diana]
You shall as easy prove
That I husbanded her bed.
All's Well that Ends Well. Act v, sc. 3, l. 125. [Bertram]

4
I knew of their going to bed.
All's Well that Ends Well, v, 3, 264. See under Marriage.
Going to bed.—*The Winter's Tale,* iv, 4, 247.

5
It is not
Amiss to tumble on the bed of Ptolemy.
Antony and Cleopatra. Act i, sc. 4, l. 16. [Cæsar]
The beds i' the east are soft.
Antony and Cleopatra. Act ii, sc. 6, l. 51. [Antony]
Let their beds Be made as soft as yours.
The Merchant of Venice. Act iv, sc. 1, l. 95. [Shylock]
Soft beds.—*Cymbeline,* v, 3, 71.

6
They found the bed untreasured of their mistress.
As You Like It. Act ii, sc. 2, l. 7. [First Lord] The only use of "untreasured."

7
So he would keep fair quarter with his bed!
The Comedy of Errors. Act ii, sc. 1, l. 108. [Adriana]
Keep then fair league and truce with thy true bed;
I live unstain'd, thou undishonoured.
Comedy of Errors. Act ii, sc. 2, l. 147. [Adriana] "True bed" is repeated in *II Henry IV,* iv, 2, 123. The only use of "undishonoured."
'Tis double wrong to truant with your bed
And let her read it in thy looks at board.
The Comedy of Errors. Act iii, sc. 2, l. 17. [Luciana]
That runagate to your bed.
Cymbeline. Act i, sc. 6, l. 137. [Iachimo]

8
Let not the royal bed of Denmark be
A couch for luxury and damned incest.
Hamlet. Act i, sc. 5, l. 82. [Ghost]
Nay, but to live
In the rank sweat of an enseamed bed,
Stew'd in corruption, honeying and making love
Over the nasty sty.
Hamlet. Act iii, sc. 4, l. 91. [Hamlet] The only use of "enseamed" (loaded with grease), and of "honeying."

9
For what offence have I this fortnight been
A banish'd woman from my Harry's bed?
I Henry IV. Act ii, sc. 3, l. 41. [Lady Percy]
Abandon'd from your bed.—*The Taming of the Shrew,* Ind., 2, 117.
Absent me from your bed.—*The Taming of the Shrew,* Ind., 2, 125.
Banish'd me his bed.—*Henry VIII,* iii, 1, 119.
See under Banishment.

10
I prithee, tell me, doth he keep his bed?
I Henry IV. Act iv, sc. 1, l. 13. [Worcester]

11
I would 'twere bed-time, Hal, and all well.
I Henry IV. Act v, sc. 1, l. 125. [Falstaff] "Bed-time" is repeated in *The Comedy of Errors,* i, 2, 28, and in *A Midsummer-Night's Dream,* v, 1, 34.

12
Please it your grace To go to bed.
II Henry IV. Act iii, sc. 1, l. 99. [Warwick]
You were best to go to bed and dream again.
II Henry VI, v, 1, 196.
He hath commanded me to go to bed.
Othello. Act iv, sc. 3, l. 13. [Desdemona]
Go to bed.—*The Merry Wives of Windsor,* ii, 2, 124; *Henry VIII,* v, 1, 9.
Go to bed, and sleep.—*Othello,* i, 3, 305.
Go to bed to work.—*Othello,* ii, 1, 116.
Go dark to bed.—*As You Like It,* iii, 5, 39.
Go not to mine uncle's bed.—*Hamlet,* iii, 4, 159.
Ere he go to bed.—*The Rape of Lucrece,* l. 776.
Ere you go to bed.—*Hamlet,* iii, 2, 344; iii, 3, 34.
Goes to bed.—*Troilus and Cressida,* v, 8, 20.
Goes to bed wi' the sun.—*The Winter's Tale,* iv, 4, 105.
Gone to bed.—*King Lear,* iii, 3, 18.
Went to bed.—*Henry VIII,* iv, 2, 24.
He . . . would to bed.—*Henry V,* ii, 1, 87.

13
If I did but stir out of my bed,
Ready they were to shoot me to the heart.
I Henry VI. Act i, sc. 4, l. 55. [Talbot]
Leave our beds.—*I Henry VI,* ii, 1, 41.

Leap'd from his bed.—*Rape of Lucrece,* l. 169.
Raised me from my bed.—*Othello,* i, 3, 54.

1
Rousèd on a sudden from their drowsy beds.
I Henry VI. Act ii, sc. 2, l. 23. [Bedford]
Blameful bed.—*II Henry VI,* iii, 2, 29.
Celestial bed.—*Hamlet,* i, 5, 56.
Clear bed.—*The Rape of Lucrece,* l. 382.
Curious bed.—*III Henry VI,* ii, 5, 53.
Dark beds.—*Venus and Adonis,* l. 1050.
Desperate bed.—*Cymbeline,* iv, 3, 6.
Flowery bed.—*A Midsummer-Night's Dream,* iii, 1, 132; v, 1, 1.
Golden bed.—*The Merchant of Venice,* ii, 7, 58.
Lawful bed.—*The Rape of Lucrece,* l. 938.
Loathsome beds.—*II Henry IV,* iii, 1, 16.
Naked bed.—*Venus and Adonis,* l. 397.
Oozy bed.—*The Tempest,* v, 1, 151. The only use of "oozy."
Paved bed.—*Measure for Measure,* v, 1, 440.
Pendent bed.—*Macbeth,* i, 6, 8.
Quiet beds.—*I Henry VI,* ii, 1, 6.
Sickly bed.—*All's Well that Ends Well,* ii, 3, 118.
So pure a bed!—*The Rape of Lucrece,* l. 684.
Unlawful bed.—*Richard III,* iii, 7, 190.
Well-deserved bed.—*As You Like It,* v, 4, 196. The only use of "well-deserved."
Western bed.—*III Henry VI,* v, 3, 6.
Wholesome bed.—*Julius Cæsar,* ii, 1, 264.
Woful bed.—*Richard III,* i, 2, 249.
Weary beds.—*Love's Labour's Lost,* v, 2, 832.
Wormy beds.—*A Midsummer-Night's Dream,* iii, 2, 384.

2
Have you laid fair the bed?
II Henry VI. Act iii, sc. 2, l. 11. [Suffolk]
Make his bed.—*Cymbeline,* iv, 2, 357.
Make the beds.—*The Merry Wives of Windsor,* i, 4, 102.

3
Every man hence to his idle bed.
Julius Cæsar. Act ii, sc. 1, l. 117. [Brutus]
Lovers, to bed. . . . Sweet friends, to bed.
A Midsummer-Night's Dream. Act v, sc. 1, l. 371. [Theseus]
For this night, to bed, and dream on the event.
Twelfth Night. Act ii, sc. 3, l. 191. [Maria]
To bed, to bed!—*Macbeth,* v, 1, 73; 76; *Troilus and Cressida,* iv, 2, 4; *Cymbeline,* ii, 2, 4; iii, 4, 103.
All to bed.—*Much Ado about Nothing,* iii, 3, 96.
Prithee now, to bed.—*Troilus and Cressida,* iv, 2, 7; *Henry VIII,* v, 1, 73.
To bed with him.—*Taming of Shrew,* Ind., 2, 72.
I must to bed.—*Henry VIII,* iv, 2, 166.
Return to bed.—*Macbeth,* v, 1, 8.

4
You 've ungently, . . . Stole from my bed.
Julius Cæsar. Act ii, sc. 1, l. 237. [Portia]
I have forsworn his bed and company.
A Midsummer-Night's Dream. Act ii, sc. 1, l. 62. [Titania]

5 From their fixed beds of lime
Had been dishabited.
King John. Act ii, sc. 1, l. 219. [King John] The only use of "dishabited."
Bed of blackness.—*Pericles,* i, 2, 89.
Bed of death.—*Richard III,* iv, 1, 54; *All's Well that Ends Well,* ii, 1, 107; *Romeo and Juliet,* v, 3, 28.
Bed of down.—*Othello,* i, 3, 232.
Beds of lust.—*Timon of Athens,* iv, 3, 257.
Bed of roses.—*The Passionate Pilgrim,* l. 361.

6
His bed my gaol; from the loathed warmth whereof deliver me, and supply the place for your labour.
King Lear. Act iv, sc. 6, l. 272. [Edgar, reads]

7
Decrepit, sick and bedrid.
Love's Labour's Lost. Act i, sc. 1, l. 139. [Biron] "Decrepit" is repeated in *I Henry VI,* v, 4, 7.
Lies he not bed-rid?
Winter's Tale. Act iv, sc. 4, l. 411. [Polixenes]
Impotent and bedrid.—*Hamlet,* i, 2, 29. The only uses of "bedrid."

8
Get on your nightgown.
Macbeth. Act ii, sc. 2, l. 70. [Lady Macbeth]
Put on your nightgown.—*Macbeth,* v, 1, 69.
Throw her nightgown upon her.—*Macbeth,* v, 1, 5.
Shall I go fetch your nightgown?—*Othello,* iv, 3, 34.
A night-gown in respect of yours.—*Much Ado about Nothing,* iii, 4, 18. The only uses of "nightgown."

9
If for this night he entreat you to his bed, give him promise of satisfaction.
Measure for Measure. Act iii, sc. 1, l. 275. [Duke]

10
Whether till the next night she had rather stay
Or go to bed now, being two hours to day.
The Merchant of Venice. Act v, sc. 1, l. 302. [Gratiano]

Iago: You have not been a-bed, then?
Cassio: Why, no; the day had broke
Before we parted.
Othello. Act iii, sc. 1, l. 33.

Here I hit it right,
Our Romeo hath not been in bed to-night.
Romeo and Juliet. Act ii, sc. 3, l. 41. [Friar Laurence]
I 'll not to bed to-night.—*Romeo and Juliet,* iv, 2, 42.
What, will he not to bed?—*III Henry VI,* iv, 3, 3.
What, is he in bed?—*Richard III,* i, 1, 142.

11
Hermia: Find you out a bed;
For I upon this bank will rest my head.
Lysander: One turf shall serve as pillow for us both;
One heart, one bed, two bosoms and one troth.
Hermia: Nay, good Lysander; for my sake, my dear,
Lie further off yet, do not lie so near.
Lysander: O, take the sense, sweet, of my innocence!
Love takes the meaning in love's conference.
I mean, that my heart unto yours is knit
So that but one heart we can make of it;
Two bosoms interchained with an oath;

So then two bosoms and a single troth.
Then by your side no bed-room me deny;
For lying so, Hermia, I do not lie.
Hermia: Lysander riddles very prettily: . . .
But, gentle friend, for love and courtesy
Lie further off. . . .
Lysander: Here is my bed: sleep give thee all his rest!
A Midsummer-Night's Dream. Act ii, sc. 2, l. 39. The only use of "interchained," "bed-room," and "riddles" as a verb.

To have my love to bed and to arise.
A Midsummer-Night's Dream. Act iii, sc. 1, l. 174. [Titania]

1 Doth not the gentleman
Deserve as full as fortunate a bed
As ever Beatrice shall couch upon?
Much Ado about Nothing. Act iii, sc. 1, l. 44. [Ursula]

She knows the heat of a luxurious bed.
Much Ado about Nothing. Act iv, sc. 1, l. 42. [Claudio]

Lustful bed.—*Taming of the Shrew,* Ind., 2, 39.

2 There 's millions now alive
That nightly lie in those unproper beds
Which they dare swear peculiar.
Othello. Act iv, sc. 1, l. 68. [Iago] The only use of "unproper."

Devesting them for bed.—*Othello,* ii, 3, 181. The only use of "devesting."

3
Strangle her in her bed, even the bed she hath contaminated.
Othello, iv, 1, 220. See Poison, 1174:12.

Thy bed, lust-stain'd, shall with lust's blood be spotted.
Othello, v, 1, 36. See under Threat. The only use of "lust-stain'd."

4
Hymen hath brought the bride to bed.
Pericles. Act iii, Gower, l. 9.

He went to bed to her very description.
Pericles. Act iv, sc. 2, l. 109. [Bawd]

The beauty of this sinful dame
Made many princes thither frame,
To seek her as a bed-fellow,
In marriage-pleasures play-fellow.
Pericles. Act i, Gower, l. 33. The only use of "marriage-pleasures."

5
To his borrow'd bed he made retire.
The Rape of Lucrece, l. 573.

I mean to bear thee
Unto the base bed of some rascal groom.
The Rape of Lucrece, l. 670.

6
Convey me to my bed, then to my grave.
Richard II, ii, 1, 137. See under Grave.

Convey'd to bed.—*The Taming of the Shrew,* Ind., 1, 37.

Help him to bed.—*Cymbeline,* v, 4, 179.

7
Broke the possession of a royal bed.
Richard II. Act iii, sc. 1, l. 13. [Bolingbroke]

Royal bed.—*The Winter's Tale,* iii, 2, 39.

Bed majestical.—*Henry V,* iv, 1, 284.

Bed of majesty.—*The Winter's Tale,* v, 1, 33.

8
Let 's to bed . . . it waxes late:
I 'll to my rest.
Romeo and Juliet. Act i, sc. 5, l. 127. [Capulet]

I 'll to my truckle-bed;
This field-bed is too cold for me to sleep.
Romeo and Juliet. Act ii, sc. 1, l. 39. [Mercutio] "Truckle-bed" is repeated in *The Merry Wives of Windsor,* iv, 5, 7. The only use of "field-bed."

I 'll to bed.—*King Lear,* iii, 6, 92.

9 He is wise;
And, on my life, hath stol'n him home to bed.
Romeo and Juliet. Act ii, sc. 1, l. 3. [Mercutio]

My will is even this:
That presently you hie you home to bed.
The Two Gentlemen of Verona. Act iv, sc. 2, l. 93. [Silvia]

Go home to bed.—*III Henry VI,* v, 4, 56.

10
Bid her hasten all the house to bed.
Romeo and Juliet. Act iii, sc. 3, l. 156. [Friar Laurence]

I haste me to my bed.—*Sonnets,* xxvii.

11
Get thee to bed, and rest; for thou hast need.
Romeo and Juliet. Act iv, sc. 3, l. 13. [Lady Capulet]

Get thee to bed.—*Macbeth,* ii, 1, 32; *Hamlet,* i, 1, 7.

Get them to bed.—*Much Ado about Nothing,* iii, 3, 46.

Get you to bed again; it is not day.
Julius Cæsar. Act ii, sc. 1, l. 39. [Brutus]

Get you to bed on the instant.
Othello. Act iv, sc. 3, l. 7.

Get you to bed.—*Romeo and Juliet,* iv, 4, 7; *Pericles,* ii, 5, 93.

12
Ay, let the county take you in your bed;
He 'll fright you up, i' faith.
Romeo and Juliet. Act iv, sc. 5, l. 10. [Nurse]

Rouse thee from thy bed.—*Romeo and Juliet,* iv, 1, 108.

13
Robb'd others' beds' revenues of their rents.
Sonnets. No. cxlii.

14
Go to thy cold bed, and warm thee.
The Taming of the Shrew. Induction, sc. 1, l. 9. [Sly] The same sentence is repeated in *King Lear,* iii, 4, 48.

Cold bed.—*A Midsummer-Night's Dream,* iii, 2, 429.

Katharina: Keep you warm.
Petruchio: Marry, so I mean, sweet Katharine, in thy bed.
Taming of the Shrew. Act ii, sc. 1, l. 268.

Olivia: Wilt thou go to bed, Malvolio?
Malvolio: To bed! ay, sweet-heart, and I 'll come to thee.
Twelfth Night. Act iii, sc. 4, l. 32.

15
Madam, undress you and come now to bed.
The Taming of the Shrew. Induction, sc. 2, l. 119. [Sly] The only use of "undress."

Come away to bed.—*Othello,* ii, 3, 252.

Come to my bed.—*Hamlet,* iv, 5, 66.

Will you come to bed, my lord?—*Othello,* v, 2, 24.

1 Some undeserved fault
I 'll find about the making of the bed;
And here I 'll fling the pillow, there the bolster,
This way the coverlet, another way the sheets.
The Taming of the Shrew. Act iv, sc. 1, l. 202. [Petruchio] "Bolster" is repeated in *Othello,* iii, 3, 399, and "coverlet" in *The Rape of Lucrece,* l. 394. See also SHEETS.

2 Come, Kate, we 'll to bed.
We three are married, but you two are sped.
The Taming of the Shrew. Act v, sc. 2, l. 184. [Petruchio]

We 'll to bed.—*II Henry IV,* ii, 4, 229.

3
Maid, to thy master's bed.
Timon of Athens, iv, 1, 12. See under MISTRESS.

Here was my father's bed.
Venus and Adonis, l. 1183.

Conqueror's bed.—*Richard III,* iv, 4, 334.
Honour's bed.—*Titus Andronicus,* i, 1, 178.
Honour's lofty bed.—*Titus Andronicus,* iii, 1, 11.
Husband's bed.—*Merchant of Venice,* v, 1, 228.
Lover's bed.—*Antony and Cleopatra,* iv, 14, 101.
Neighbour's bed.—*As You Like It,* iv, 1, 171.
Parent's bed.—*Pericles,* i, 1, 131.
Aurora's bed.—*Romeo and Juliet,* i, 1, 142.
Edward's bed.—*Richard III,* iv, 4, 207.
Hymen's purest bed.—*Timon of Athens,* iv, 3, 384.
Lucrece's bed.—*The Rape of Lucrece,* l. 301; *Titus Andronicus,* iv, 1, 64.

4
Upon a lazy bed the livelong day.
Troilus and Cressida. Act i, sc. 3, l. 147. [Ulysses]

Livelong day.—*Julius Cæsar,* i, 1, 46.
Livelong night.—*Macbeth,* ii, 3, 65. The only uses of "livelong."

Had I so good occasion to lie long
As you, Prince Paris, nothing but heavenly business
Should rob my bed-mate of my company.
Troilus and Cressida. Act iv, sc. 1, l. 3. [Æneas] The only use of "bed-mate."

On his press'd bed lolling.—*Troilus and Cressida,* i, 3, 162.

5
I will show you a chamber with a bed; which bed, because it shall not speak of your pretty encounters, press it to death.
Troilus and Cressida. Act iii, sc. 2, l. 215. [Pandarus]

6
To be up after midnight and to go to bed then, is early: so that to go to bed after midnight is to go to bed betimes.
Twelfth Night. Act ii, sc. 3, l. 7. [Sir Toby Belch]

Having come from a day-bed, where I have left Olivia sleeping.
Twelfth Night. Act ii, sc. 5, l. 54. [Malvolio]

He is not lolling on a lewd day-bed.
Richard III. Act iii, sc. 7, l. 72. [Buckingham] See under MEDITATION. The only uses of "day-bed."

7
I was in love with my bed.
The Two Gentlemen of Verona. Act ii, sc. 1, l. 87. [Speed]

BEE

8
'Tis seldom when the bee doth leave her comb
In the dead carrion.
II Henry IV. Act iv, sc. 4, l. 79. [King Henry] The only use of "comb" in this sense.

Like the bee, culling from every flower
The virtuous sweets,
Our thighs pack'd with wax, our mouths with honey,
We bring it to the hive, and, like the bees,
Are murdered for our pains.
II Henry IV. Act iv, sc. 5, l. 75. [King]

9 So work the honey-bees,
Creatures that by a rule in nature teach
The act of order to a peopled kingdom.
They have a king and officers of sorts;
Where some, like magistrates, correct at home,
Others, like merchants, venture trade abroad,
Others, like soldiers, armed in their stings,
Make boot upon the summer's velvet buds,
Which pillage they with merry march bring home
To the tent-royal of their emperor;
Who, busied in his majesty, surveys
The singing masons building roofs of gold,
The civil citizens kneading up the honey,
The poor mechanic porters crowding in
Their heavy burdens at his narrow gate,
The sad-eyed justice, with his surly hum,
Delivering o'er to executors pale
The lazy yawning drone.
Henry V. Act i, sc. 2, l. 187. [Archbishop of Canterbury] The only use of "honey-bees," "tent-royal," and "sad-eyed." "Kneading" is repeated in *Troilus and Cressida,* i, 1, 23.

10
So bees with smoke and doves with noisome stench
Are from their hives and houses driven away.
I Henry VI. Act i, sc. 5, l. 23. [Talbot]

Angry hive of bees.—*II Henry VI,* iii, 2, 125.

11
Some say the bee stings: but I say, 'tis the bee's wax.
II Henry VI, iv, 2, 88. See under LAWYER. The only use of "bee's wax."

12
The honey-bags steal from the humble-bees,
And for night-tapers crop their waxen thighs
And light them at the fiery glow-worm's eyes.
A Midsummer-Night's Dream. Act iii, sc. 1, l. 171. [Titania] Only use of "night-tapers."

Kill me a red-hipped humble-bee on the top of a thistle.
A Midsummer-Night's Dream. Act iv, sc. 1, l. 11. [Bottom] The only use of "red-hipped."

Full merrily the humble-bee doth sing,
Till he hath lost his honey and his sting;
And being once subdued in armed tail,
Sweet honey and sweet notes together fail.
Troilus and Cressida. Act v, sc. 10, l. 42. [Pandarus]

That red-tailed humble-bee.—*All's Well that Ends Well,* iv, 5, 7. The only use of "red-tailed."

The fox, the ape and the humble-bee.—*Love's Labour's Lost,* iii, 1, 96.

Chaste bee.—*The Rape of Lucrece,* l. 840.

Drone-like bee.—*The Rape of Lucrece,* l. 836. The only use of "drone-like."

Hybla bees.—*Julius Cæsar,* v, 1, 34. Hybla is mentioned again in *I Henry IV,* i, 2, 47: "Honey of Hybla."

Stinging bees.—*Titus Andronicus,* v, 1, 14.

1 The old bees die, the young possess their hive.
The Rape of Lucrece, l. 1769.

2 Where the bee sucks, there suck I:
In a cowslip's bell I lie.
The Tempest, v, 1, 88. See under FAIRY.

BEER

See also Ale

3 Prince: Doth it not show vilely in me to desire small beer?
Poins: Why, a prince should not be so loosely studied as to remember so weak a composition.
Prince: Belike then my appetite was not princely got; for, by my troth, I do now remember the poor creature, small beer.
II Henry IV. Act ii, sc. 2, l. 7.

I will make it felony to drink small beer.
II Henry VI. Act iv, sc. 2, l. 73. [Jack Cade] "Felony" is used only once again in the plays, in *The Tempest,* iv, 2, 73. It is perhaps worth noting that one was his first play and the other his last completed one.

Chronicle small beer.—*Othello,* ii, 1, 161. The only uses of "small beer."

4 Here's a pot of good double beer, neighbour: drink, and fear not.
II Henry VI. Act ii, sc. 3, l. 65. [Neighbour] The only use of "double beer." Beer is mentioned only five times in the plays.

Stop a beer-barrel.—*Hamlet,* v, 1, 235. The only use of "beer-barrel."

5 Let me see thee froth and lime.
The Merry Wives of Windsor. Act i, sc. 3, l. 15. [Host]

A tapster is a good trade: an old cloak makes a new jerkin; a withered serving-man a fresh tapster.
The Merry Wives of Windsor. Act i, sc. 3, l. 17. [Falstaff]

Though you change your place, you need not change your trade; I'll be your tapster still.
Measure for Measure. Act i, sc. 2, l. 110. [Pompey]

Escalus: So. What trade are you of, sir?
Pompey: A tapster; a poor widow's tapster.
Measure for Measure. Act ii, sc. 1, l. 206.

I would not have you acquainted with tapsters: they will draw you, Master Froth, and you will hang them.
Measure for Measure. Act ii, sc. 1, l. 214. [Escalus]

Shrill-tongued tapsters answering every call,
Soothing the humour of fantastic wits.
Venus and Adonis, l. 849. "Shrill-tongued" is repeated twice in *Antony and Cleopatra,* i, 1, 32, and iii, 3, 15.

6 O base Hungarian wight! wilt thou the spigot wield?
The Merry Wives of Windsor. Act i, sc. 3, l. 23. [Pistol] The only use of "Hungarian" and "spigot."

BEGGAR

See also King and Beggar

7 Wilt thou needs be a beggar?
All's Well that Ends Well. Act i, sc. 3, l. 22. [Countess]

What, wouldst thou have me go and beg my food?
As You Like It. Act ii, sc. 3, l. 31. [Orlando]

I am not furnished like a beggar, therefore to beg will not become me.
As You Like It. Epilogue, l. 10. [Rosalind]

Beg thou, or borrow.—*The Comedy of Errors,* i, 1, 154.

Begg'd or borrow'd.—*Twelfth Night,* iii, 4, 3.

8 I, that now
Refused most princely gifts, am bound to beg.
Coriolanus. Act i, sc. 9, l. 79. [Coriolanus]

Beggar that I am.—*Hamlet,* ii, 2, 280.

9 'Twas never my desire yet to trouble the poor with begging.
Coriolanus. Act ii, sc. 3, l. 75. [Coriolanus]

Better it is to die, better to starve,
Than crave the hire which first we do deserve.
Why in this woolvish toge should I stand here,
To beg of Hob and Dick?
Coriolanus. Act ii, sc. 3, l. 120. [Coriolanus] The only use of "woolvish," "toge" (toga), and "Hob and Dick." "Toged" occurs in *Othello,* i, 1, 25: "Toged consuls."

10 One bred of alms and foster'd with cold dishes.
Cymbeline. Act ii, sc. 3, l. 119. [Cloten]

One that by alms doth live,
Disdain to him disdained scraps to give.
The Rape of Lucrece, l. 986.

Have their alms out of the empress' chest.
Titus Andronicus. Act ii, sc. 3, l. 9. [Aaron]

I have your alms.—*Coriolanus,* ii, 3, 87.

Received an alms.—*Coriolanus,* iii, 2, 120.

Give alms.—*The Winter's Tale,* iv, 4, 138.

Fortune's alms.—*King Lear,* i, 1, 281; *Othello,* iii, 4, 122.

Alms for oblivion.—*Troilus and Cressida,* iii, 3, 146.

Alms Of palsied eld.—*Measure for Measure,* iii, 1, 35. Although "alms" is used thirteen times, it is worth noting that it does not occur in any of the historical plays.

1
What wouldst thou beg, Laertes,
That shall not be my offer, not thy asking?
Hamlet. Act i, sc. 2, l. 45. [King]

2
What! a young knave, and begging! Is there not wars? is there not employment? doth not the king lack subjects? do not the rebels need soldiers? Though it be a shame to be on any side but one, it is worse shame to beg than to be on the worst side, were it worse than the name of rebellion can tell how to make it.
II Henry IV. Act i, sc. 2, l. 84. [Falstaff]

Never shall you see that I will beg
A ragged and forestall'd remission.
II Henry IV. Act v, sc. 2, l, 37. [Chief Justice]

3
Beggars all, beggars all.
II Henry IV. Act v, sc. 3, l. 8. [Shallow]

Bedlam beggars, who, with roaring voices,
Strike in their numb'd and mortified bare arms
Pins, wooden pricks, nails, sprigs of rosemary;
And with this horrible object, from low farms,
Poor pelting villages, sheep-cotes, and mills,
Sometime with lunatic bans, sometime with prayers,
Enforce their charity.
King Lear. Act ii, sc. 3, l. 14. [Edgar] The only use of "numb'd" and "sprigs."

Your beggar of fifty.—*Measure for Measure,* iii, 2, 133.

A beggar, that was used to come so smug upon the mart.
The Merchant of Venice. Act iii, sc. 1, l. 48. [Shylock]

These famish'd beggars, weary of their lives.
Richard III. Act v, sc. 3, l. 329. [King]

A poor and loathsome beggar.
The Taming of the Shrew. Induction, sc. 1, l. 123. [Lord]

Poor beggar.—*King John,* ii, 1, 592.

Lean beggar.—*Hamlet,* iv, 3, 23.

Beggars of the world.—*Timon of Athens,* i, 1, 138.

4
Most humbly on my knee I beg.
Henry V, iv, 3, 129. See LEADER, 847:2.

Upon my knee I beg.—*King John,* iii, 1, 308; *King Lear,* ii, 4, 157.

On our knees we beg.—*Winter's Tale,* ii, 3, 149.

Beg during life.—*I Henry IV,* v, 3, 39.

She 's come to beg.—*III Henry VI,* iii, 1, 42.

5
Beggary is valiant.
II Henry VI. Act iv, sc. 2, l. 58. [Smith]

Beggary
Is crept into the palace of our king.
II Henry VI, iv, 1, 101. See under REPROACH.

Beggary hangs upon thy back.
Romeo and Juliet, v, 1, 71. See under CONTEMPT.

Usurp the beggary he was never born to.
Measure for Measure. Act iii, sc. 2, l. 99. [Lucio]

Snail-paced beggary.—*Richard III,* iv, 3, 53.

Deceased in beggary.—*A Midsummer-Night's Dream,* v, 1, 53.

Brats and beggary.—*Cymbeline,* ii, 3, 124.

6
The adage must be verified,
That beggars mounted run their horse to death.
III Henry VI. Act i, sc. 4, l. 126. [York]

7
A beggar's book Outworths a noble's blood.
Henry VIII. Act i, sc. 1, l. 122. [Buckingham] The only use of "outworths."

8
When beggars die, there are no comets seen;
The heavens themselves blaze forth the death of princes.
Julius Cæsar. Act ii, sc. 2, l. 30. [Calpurnia]

9
Gloucester: Is it a beggar-man?
Old Man: Madman and beggar too.
Gloucester: He has some reason, else he could not beg.
King Lear. Act iv, sc. 1, l. 31. The only use of "beggar-man."

The elder of them, being put to nurse,
Was by a beggar-woman stolen away.
II Henry VI. Act iv, sc. 2, l. 150. [Cade] The only use of "beggar-woman."

10
Thou bid'st me beg: this begging is not strange.
Love's Labour's Lost. Act v, sc. 2, l. 210. [King]

You taught me first to beg; and now methinks
You teach me how a beggar should be answer'd.
The Merchant of Venice. Act iv, sc. 1, l. 439. [Portia]

Being so great, I have no need to beg.
Richard II. Act iv, sc. 1, l. 309. [King]

You cannot beg us.—*Love's Labour's Lost,* v, 2, 490.

More I beg not.—*Macbeth,* v, 7, 23.

11
Second Fisherman: Hark you, my friend; you said you could not beg.
Pericles: I did but crave.
Second Fisherman: But crave! Then I'll turn craver too, and so I shall 'scape whipping.
Pericles: Why, are all your beggars whipped, then?
Second Fisherman: O, not all, my friend, not all; for if all your beggars were whipped, I would wish no better office than to be beadle.
Pericles. Act ii, sc. 1, l. 90. The only use of "craver."

12
What fond beggar, but to touch the crown,
Would with the sceptre straight be strucken down?
The Rape of Lucrece, l. 216.

Let him have time a beggar's orts to crave.
The Rape of Lucrece, l. 985.

13
A beggar begs that never begg'd before.
Richard II. Act v, sc. 3, l. 78. [Duchess of York]

14
They are but beggars that can count their worth.
Romeo and Juliet, ii, 6, 32. See under WORTH.

There 's beggary in the love that can be reckon'd.
Antony and Cleopatra, i, 1, 15. See LOVE: PROTESTATIONS, 904:8.

1 Would not the beggar then forget himself?
The Taming of the Shrew. Induction, sc. 1, l. 41. [Lord]
Beggars, that come unto my father's door
Upon entreaty have a present alms:
If not, elsewhere they meet with charity.
The Taming of the Shrew. Act iv, sc. 3, l. 4. [Katharina]

2 The rest were ragged, old, and beggarly.
The Taming of the Shrew. Act iv, sc. 1, l. 140. [Grumio]
Beggarly, lousy.—*Henry V,* iv, 8, 36; v, 1, 5.
Beggarly, three-suited.—*King Lear,* ii, 2, 16.
The only use of "three-suited," having three suits of clothes a year, a servant's allowance.
Too beggarly.—*I Henry IV,* iv, 2, 75.

3 Beg at the gates, like Tarquin and his queen.
Titus Andronicus. Act iii, sc. 1, l. 299. [Lucius]

4 Viola: I understand you, sir; 'tis well begged.
Clown: The matter, I hope, is not great, sir, begging but a beggar.
Twelfth Night. Act iii, sc. 1, l. 60.
Well begg'd!—*Coriolanus,* i, 9, 87.

BEGINNING

5 This was an ill beginning of the night.
Julius Cæsar. Act iv, sc. 3, l. 234. [Cassius]
Weak beginnings.—*II Henry IV,* iii, 1, 85.
Things bad begun make strong themselves by ill.
Macbeth. Act iii, sc. 2, l. 55. [Macbeth]

6 Thus, leaning on my elbow, I begin.
King John. Act i, sc. 1, l. 194. [Bastard]
I 'll begin it.—*Merchant of Venice,* iii, v, 271.
Now will I begin.—*Love's Labour 's Lost,* iii, 1, 94.
Then I will begin.—*Titus Andronicus,* v, 1, 70.
Begin, sir; you are my elder.—*Love's Labour 's Lost,* v, 2, 609.
Brother, begin.—*Cymbeline,* iv, 2, 254.
Come, begin.—*Hamlet,* v, 2, 289.
Who shall begin?—*The Taming of the Shrew,* v, 2, 75.
Let them begin.—*Romeo and Juliet,* i, 1, 45.
There it begins.—*Cymbeline,* v, 5, 179.
At last she thus begins.—*The Rape of Lucrece,* l. 1303.
Twice she doth begin.—*The Rape of Lucrece,* l. 567.
Begin again.—*Richard III,* iii, 5, 3; *The Tempest,* i, 2, 395.
First begin.—*Richard III,* i, 3, 324; *The Comedy of Errors,* iv, 1, 51; *Henry V,* i, 2, 168; *Sonnets,* cxiv; *The Tempest,* ii, 1, 28.

7 Beginning in the middle, starting thence away
To what may be digested in a play
Troilus and Cressida, Prol., 28.

8 Sir Andrew: Begin, fool: it begins Hold thy peace.'
Clown: I shall never begin if I hold my peace.
Twelfth Night. Act ii, sc. 3, l. 72.
First beginners.—*Cymbeline,* v, 3, 37.
Vile beginners.—*Romeo and Juliet,* iii, 1, 146.
The only uses of "beginners."

II—Beginning and End

9 O make an end Of what I have begun.
Antony and Cleopatra. Act iv, sc. 14, l. 106. [Antony]
But there to end Where he was to begin.
Coriolanus. Act v, sc. 6, l. 66. [First Lord]
End ere I do begin.—*All's Well that Ends Well,* ii, 5, 29.
Begin and end.—*Coriolanus,* ii, 1, 241.

10 But, orderly to end where I begun.
Hamlet. Act iii, sc. 2, l. 220. [Player King]
Let this end where it begun.
Richard II. Act i, sc. 1, l. 158. [King Richard]

11 Where I did begin, there shall I end.
Julius Cæsar, v, 3, 24. See under LIFE.

12 I will tell you the beginning; and . . . you may see the end.
As You Like It. Act i, sc. 2, l. 119. [Le Beau]
The end of it Unknown to the beginning.
Coriolanus. Act iii, sc. 1, l. 328. [Senator]

13 To the latter end of a fray and the beginning of a feast
Fits a dull fighter and a keen guest.
I Henry IV. Act iv, sc. 2, l. 84. [Falstaff]
Falstaff is paraphrasing an old proverb, "It is ill coming to the end of a feast and beginning of a fray." [John Heywood, *Proverbs.* Pt. ii, ch. 8, 1546.]

14 We see yonder the beginning of the day, but I think we shall never see the end of it.
Henry V. Act iv, sc. 1, l. 91. [Williams]
That is the true beginning of our end.
A Midsummer-Night's Dream. Act v, sc. 1, l. 111. [Quince]

15 You, my origin and ender.
A Lover's Complaint, l. 222. The only use of "ender."

16 The latter end . . . forgets the beginning.
The Tempest. Act ii, sc. 1, l. 157. [Antonio]
You always end ere you begin.
The Two Gentlemen of Verona. Act ii, sc. 4, l. 31. [Valentine]

17 And where she ends she doth anew begin.
Venus and Adonis, l. 60.

BEHAVIOUR

See also Manners

18 Love all, trust a few,
Do wrong to none: be able for thine enemy
Rather in power than use, and keep thy friend

Under thy own life's key: be check'd for silence,
But never tax'd for speech.
All's Well that Ends Well. Act i, sc. 1, l. 73. [Countess]

Love thy husband, look to thy servants, cherish thy guests.
I Henry IV. Act iii, sc. 3, l. 193. [Falstaff]

Love thyself last: cherish those hearts that hate thee.
Henry VIII. Act iii, sc. 2, l. 443. [Wolsey]

1
You must not marvel, Helen, at my course,
Which holds not colour with the time.
All's Well that Ends Well. Act ii, sc. 5, l. 63. [Bertram]

Read not my blemishes in the world's report:
I have not kept my square; but that to come
Shall all be done by the rule.
Antony and Cleopatra. Act ii, sc. 3, l. 5. [Antony]

2
Fashion your demeanour to my looks.
Comedy of Errors, ii, 2, 33. See under JEST.

A deep demeanour in great sorrow.
II Henry IV. Act iv, sc. 5, l. 85. [Warwick]

Cold demeanour.—*Julius Cæsar,* v, 2, 4.
Dumb demeanour.—*Rape of Lucrece,* l. 474.
Ignoble in demeanour.—*II Henry VI,* iii, 2, 210.
The only uses of "demeanour."

3
Oft have I seen the haughty cardinal,
More like a soldier than a man o' the church,
As stout and proud as he were lord of all,
Swear like a ruffian and demean himself
Unlike the ruler of a commonweal.
II Henry VI. Act i, sc. 1, l. 185. [Salisbury] "Demean himself" is repeated in *The Comedy of Errors,* iv, 3, 83; the only uses of "demean."

They have demean'd themselves Like men.
III Henry VI, i, 4, 7. See under SON.

He demean'd himself rough, rude and wildly.
The Comedy of Errors. Act v, sc. 1, l. 88. [Luciana]

Ill demean'd himself.—*II Henry VI,* i, 3, 106.

4
Could such inordinate and low desires,
Such poor, such bare, such lewd, such mean attempts,
Such barren pleasures, rude society,
As thou art match'd withal and grafted to,
Accompany the greatness of thy blood
And hold their level with thy princely heart?
I Henry IV. Act iii, sc. 2, l. 12. [King Henry] "Inordinate" is repeated in *Othello,* ii, 3, 311, and in *The Rape of Lucrece,* l. 94.

5
Omit him not; blunt not his love,
Nor lose the good advantage of his grace
By seeming cold or careless of his will.
II Henry IV. Act iv, sc. 4, l. 27. [King Henry]

Chide him for faults, and do it reverently,
When you perceive his blood inclined to mirth;
But, being moody, give him line and scope,
Till that his passions, like a whale on ground,
Confound themselves with working.
II Henry IV. Act iv, sc. 4, l. 37. [King Henry]

6
Some swearing, some crying for a surgeon, some upon their wives left poor behind them, some upon the debts they owe, some upon their children rawly left.
Henry V. Act iv, sc. 1, l. 143. [Williams] The only use of "rawly."

7
To serve him truly that will put me in trust; to love him that is honest; to converse with him that is wise, and says little; to fear judgement; to fight when I cannot choose; and to eat no fish.
King Lear. Act i, sc. 4, l. 15. [Kent]

8
Have more than thou showest,
Speak less than thou knowest,
Lend less than thou owest,
Ride more than thou goest,
Learn more than thou trowest,
Set less than thou throwest;
Leave thy drink and thy whore,
And keep in-a-door,
And thou shalt have more
Than two tens to a score.
King Lear. Act i, sc. 4, l. 131. [Fool] The only use of "in-a-door."

Keep thy foot out of brothels, thy hand out of plackets, thy pen from lenders' books, and defy the foul fiend.
King Lear. Act iii, sc. 4, l. 99. [Edgar]

9
Why, all his behaviours did make their retire
To the court of his eye, peeping thorough desire.
Love's Labour's Lost. Act ii, sc. 1, l. 234. [Boyet] The only use of "peeping."

Behaviour, what wert thou
Till this madman show'd thee?
Love's Labour's Lost. Act v, sc. 2, l. 337. [Biron]

Mark his behaviour.—*Coriolanus,* ii, 3, 45.

10
If I do not put on a sober habit,
Talk with respect and swear but now and then,
Wear prayer-books in my pocket, look demurely,
Nay more, while grace is saying, hood mine eyes
Thus with my hat, and sigh and say 'amen,'
Use all the observance of civility,
Like one well studied in a sad ostent
To please his grandam, never trust me more.
The Merchant of Venice. Act ii, sc. 2, l. 199. [Gratiano] "Prayer-book" is repeated in *Richard III,* iii, 7, 47, and "demurely" in *Antony and Cleopatra,* iv, 9, 31.

11
I will keep the haviour of reputation.
The Merry Wives of Windsor, i, 3, 86. See under REPUTATION.

Thou mayst think my 'haviour light.
Romeo and Juliet. Act ii, sc. 2, l. 99. [Juliet]

Neighbour'd to his haviour.—*Hamlet,* ii, 2, 12.
Dejected 'haviour.—*Hamlet,* i, 2, 81.
Lusty haviour.—*Richard II,* i, 3, 77.
The same 'haviour.—*Twelfth Night,* iii, 4, 226.
Haviour of less fear.—*Cymbeline,* iii, 4, 9. The uses of "haviour."

1
What an unweighed behaviour hath this Flemish drunkard picked—with the devil's name!—out of my conversation, that he dares in this manner assay me?
The Merry Wives of Windsor. Act ii, sc. 1, l. 23. [Mrs. Page] The only use of "unweighed," and "Flemish."
I will teach the children their behaviours.
The Merry Wives of Windsor. Act iv, sc. 4, l. 66. [Evans]
2
Her sad behaviour feeds his vulture folly.
The Rape of Lucrece, l. 556.
Outward behaviours.—*Much Ado about Nothing,* ii, 3, 100.
Rude behaviour.—*Henry VIII,* iv, 2, 103.
Wild behaviour.—*Merchant of Venice,* ii, 2, 196.
3
Well, bear you well in this new spring of time,
Lest you be cropp'd before you come to prime.
Richard II. Act v, sc. 2, l. 50. [York]
He has borne all things well.
Macbeth. Act iii, sc. 6, l. 17. [Lennox]
4
Over-eyeing of his odd behaviour.
Taming of the Shrew. Induction, sc. 1, l. 95. [A Player] The only use of "over-eyeing."
Your behaviour hath struck her into amazement and admiration.
Hamlet. Act iii, sc. 2, l. 338. [Rosencrantz]
5
There is a fair behaviour in thee, captain.
Twelfth Night. Act i, sc. 2, l. 47. [Viola]
He has been yonder i' the sun practising behaviour to his own shadow this half hour.
Twelfth Night. Act ii, sc. 5, l. 19. [Maria]
6
Be opposite with a kinsman, surly with servants; let thy tongue tang arguments of state; put thyself into the trick of singularity.
Twelfth Night. Act ii, sc. 5, l. 162. [Malvolio] "Singularity" is repeated in *Coriolanus,* i, 1, 281, and "singularities" occurs in *The Winter's Tale,* v, 3, 12.
Let thy tongue tang with arguments of state. —*The Winter's Tale,* iii, 4, 78.
A tongue with a tang.—*The Tempest,* ii, 2, 52. The only uses of "tang." See under TONGUE.
7
I will be proud, I will read politic authors, I will baffle Sir Toby, I will wash off gross acquaintance, I will be point-devise the very man.
Twelfth Night. Act ii, sc. 5, l. 175. [Malvolio]
Point-device in your accoutrements.—*As You Like It,* iii, 2, 401.
Point-devise companions.—*Love's Labour's Lost,* v, 1, 21. The only uses of "point-devise."
8
The behaviour of the young gentleman gives him out to be of good capacity and breeding.
Twelfth Night. Act iii, sc. 4, l. 203. [Sir Toby]
A smooth, discreet and stable bearing.
Twelfth Night. Act iv, sc. 3, l. 19. [Sebastian]
9
Valentine: You'll still be too forward.
Speed: And yet I was last chidden for being too slow.
Two Gentlemen of Verona. Act ii, sc. 1, l. 11.

BELIEF

See also Faith, Trust, Unbelief

10
Believe not all; or, if you must believe, Stomach not all.
Antony and Cleopatra. Act iii, sc. 4, l. 11. [Octavia]
He that will believe all that they say, shall never be saved by half that they do.
Antony and Cleopatra, v, 2, 256. [Clown]
11
I sometimes do believe, and sometimes do not.
As You Like It. Act v, sc. 4, l. 3. [Orlando]
12
Many likelihoods informed me of this before, which hung so tottering in the balance that I could neither believe nor misdoubt.
All's Well that Ends Well. Act i, sc. 3, l. 128. [Count]
In time I may believe, yet I mistrust.
The Taming of the Shrew. Act iii, sc. 1, l. 51. [Bianca]
13
Whatsoever a man denies, you are now bound to believe him.
The Comedy of Errors. Act v, sc. 1, l. 305. [Dromio of Ephesus]
Make us but believe.—*The Comedy of Errors,* iii, 2, 21.
You make me believe so.—*Hamlet,* iii, 1, 117.
He believes it is a thing most precious.
Cymbeline. Act iii, sc. 5, l. 58. [Queen]
I could not but believe.—*Cymbeline,* i, 4, 80.
Wounding his belief in her renown
With tokens thus, and thus.
Cymbeline. Act v, sc. 5, l. 202. [Iachimo]
14
Believe so much in him, that he is young.
Hamlet, i, 3, 124. See under YOUTH.
I most powerfully and potently believe.
Hamlet, ii, 2, 204. See under AGE.
15
Wilt thou believe me, Hal?
I Henry IV. Act iii, sc. 3, l. 116. [Falstaff]
And you, base peasants, do you believe him?
II Henry VI. Act iv, sc. 8, l. 22. [Cade]
16
If I may be believed, so; if not, let them that should reward valour bear the sin upon their own heads.
I Henry IV. Act v, sc. 4, l. 152. [Falstaff]
17
Believe me, Cousin Gloucester.
II Henry VI. Act ii, sc. 1, l. 44. [Cardinal] "Believe me" was used twice in the first play, and very frequently thereafter.
Dear lad, believe it.
Twelfth Night. Act i, sc. 4, l. 29. [Duke] "Believe it" was not used until the twenty-first play, written in 1600, but thereafter in nearly every one.
I do believe it.
Troilus and Cressida. Act iii, sc. 3, l. 142. [Achilles] Used for the first time in this,

the twenty-fourth play; once in *Troilus and Cressida,* and once in *The Winter's Tale.*

Believe this of me.
All's Well that Ends Well. Act ii, sc. 5, l. 46. [Lafeu] This expression was first used in the twenty-fifth play, written in 1602. It was used twice in the next play, *Measure for Measure,* and never again.

I do well believe it.
Othello. Act ii, sc. 1, l. 295. [Iago] First used in this, the twenty-seventh play, and afterwards in *Cymbeline, The Winter's Tale,* and *The Tempest.*

So have I heard and do in part believe it.
Hamlet. Act i, sc. 1, l. 165. [Horatio]

I do constantly believe you.
Measure for Measure. Act iv, sc. 1, l. 21. [Duke]

I do believe it Against an oracle.
The Tempest. Act iv, sc. 1, l. 11. [Ferdinand]

Well believe.—*King John,* v, 6, 7.

I do make myself believe.—*Measure for Measure,* iii, 1, 205.

We did believe no less.—*Measure for Measure,* v, 1, 142.

1 Let belief and life encounter so
As doth the fury of two desperate men
Which in the very meeting fall and die.
King John. Act iii, sc. 1, l. 31. [Constance]

2 What I believe I'll wail,
What know believe, and what I can redress.
Macbeth. Act iv, sc. 3, l. 8. [Malcolm]

3 Nerissa teaches me what to believe.
The Merchant of Venice. Act v, sc. 1, l. 207. [Portia]

4 The guiltiness of my mind, the sudden surprise of my powers, drove the grossness of the foppery into a received belief.
The Merry Wives of Windsor. Act v, sc. 5, l. 130. [Falstaff]

5 I have greater reason to believe now than ever.
Othello. Act iv, sc. 2, l. 217. [Iago]

6 See how belief may suffer by foul show!
Pericles. Act iv, sc. 4, l. 23. [Gower]

Just beliefs.—*Pericles,* v, 1, 239.

7 I will believe you by the syllable
Of what you shall deliver.
Pericles. Act v, sc. 1, l. 169. [Pericles]

I will believe thee.—*Pericles,* v, 1, 123.

You said you would believe me.—*Pericles,* v, 1, 152.

I do believe her.—*Sonnets,* cxxxviii; *The Passionate Pilgrim,* l. 2.

I do believe thee.—*Troilus and Cressida,* v, 4, 32.

I must believe you.—*Winter's Tale,* i, 2, 333.

Would you imagine, or almost believe?
Richard III. Act iii, sc. 5, l. 35. [Buckingham]

8 Now I will believe That there are unicorns.
The Tempest. Act iii, sc. 3, l. 21. [Sebastian] Unicorns are mentioned also in *Timon of Athens,* iv, 3, 339; in *Julius Cæsar,* ii, 1, 204; and in *The Rape of Lucrece,* l. 956.

9 Credulous in this mad thought.
Titus Andronicus. Act v, sc. 2, l. 74. [Tamora]

Credulous to false prints.—*Measure for Measure,* ii, 4, 130.

Credulous of cure.—*All's Well that Ends Well,* ii, 1, 118.

Got credit.—*Henry VIII,* i, 1, 37. The only use of this phrase in the plays.

10 No Christian, that means to be saved by believing rightly, can ever believe such impossible passages of grossness.
Twelfth Night. Act iii, sc. 2, l. 75. [Maria]

A comfortable doctrine, and much may be said of it.
Twelfth Night. Act i, sc. 5, l. 239. [Olivia]

11 Will you make me believe that I am not sent for you?
Twelfth Night. Act iv, sc. 1, l. 1. [Clown]

He believes himself.—*Twelfth Night,* iii, 4, 408.

12 Valentine: No, believe me.
Speed: No believing you, indeed, sir.
Two Gentlemen of Verona. Act ii, sc. 1, l. 161.

13 So I believe; but Thurio thinks not so.
The Two Gentlemen of Verona. Act iii, sc. 2, l. 16. [Duke]

14 And I'll be sworn you would believe my saying,
Howe'er you lean to the nayward.
The Winter's Tale. Act ii, sc. 1, l. 63. [Hermione] The only use of "nayward."

II—Lack of Belief

15 Nothing, but to close
Her eyes myself, could win me to believe.
All's Well that Ends Well. Act v, sc. 3, l. 118. [King]

Beyond belief.—*Antony and Cleopatra,* iii, 7, 76.

This is not strong enough to be believed.
Cymbeline. Act ii, sc. 4, l. 131. [Philario]

16 Before my God, I might not this believe
Without the sensible and true avouch
Of mine own eyes.
Hamlet. Act i, sc. 1, l. 56. [Horatio]

17 Believe me, I do not believe thee, man;
I have a king's oath to the contrary.
King John. Act iii, sc. 1, l. 9. [Constance]

An if an angel should have come to me
And told me Hubert should put out mine eyes,
I would not have believed him.
King John. Act iv, sc. 1, l. 68. [Arthur]

I'll believe as soon
The whole earth may be bored and that the moon
May through the centre creep and so displease
Her brother's noontide with the Antipodes.
A Midsummer-Night's Dream. Act iii, sc. 2, l. 52. [Hermia]

18 I can hardly believe that, since you know not what you speak.
Measure for Measure. Act iii, sc. 2, l. 162. [Duke]

I cannot believe that.—*Othello,* ii, 1, 254.
I 'll ne'er believe that.—*The Merry Wives of Windsor,* ii, 1, 37.
I 'll not believe.—*Richard III,* i, 3, 287.
I 'll not believe 't.—*Othello,* iii, 3, 279.
I 'ld not believe thee.—*Troilus and Cressida,* iv, 5, 253.
I must not believe you.—*Troilus and Cressida,* iv, 5, 221.

1 I will not believe such a Cataian, though the priest o' the town commended him for a true man.
The Merry Wives of Windsor. Act ii, sc. 1, l. 148. [Page] "Cataian" (a native of Cathay, a Chinaman, a scoundrel) is repeated in *Twelfth Night,* ii, 3, 80.

2 They will scarcely believe this without trial.
Much Ado about Nothing. Act ii, sc. 2, l. 41. [Borachio]

3 This would not be believed in Venice,
Though I should swear I saw 't.
Othello. Act iv, sc. 1, l. 253. [Lodovico]

If in Naples
I should report this now, would they believe me?
The Tempest. Act iii, sc. 3, l. 27. [Gonzalo]

Did I tell this, who would believe me?
Measure for Measure. Act ii, sc. 4, l. 172. [Isabella]

4 Believe not this hard-hearted man!
Richard II. Act v, sc. 3, l. 87. [Duchess]

Believe not.—*All 's Well that Ends Well,* ii, 3, 166; *II Henry IV,* iv, 3, 59.
Believe not so.—*Julius Cæsar,* v, 1, 90.
Believe 't not lightly.—*Coriolanus,* iv, 1, 29.
Believe him not.—*Richard III,* i, 4, 152.
Believe me not.—*Much Ado about Nothing,* iv, 1, 273.
Believe none of us.—*Hamlet,* iii, 1, 131.
Do not believe.—*A Midsummer-Night's Dream,* ii, 1, 236; *Hamlet,* i, 3, 127.

Do not believe it.
Hamlet. Act iv, sc. 2, l. 10. [Hamlet] Used for the first time in this, the twenty-second play; once in *Measure for Measure,* and once in *Timon of Athens.*

Do not believe That.—*Othello,* i, 1, 131.
Never believe.—*Sonnets,* cix.
Never believe it.—*Hamlet,* v, 2, 351.
Never believe me.—*Richard II,* ii, 2, 111.

BELL

5 Let 's mock the midnight bell.
Antony and Cleopatra. Act iii, sc. 13, l. 185. [Antony]

The midnight bell
Did, with his iron tongue and brazen mouth,
Sound on into the drowsy race of night.
King John. Act iii, sc. 3, l. 37. [King John] The only uses of "midnight bell."

The bell have told eleven.—*Othello,* ii, 2, 11.
The bell then beating one.—*Hamlet,* i, 1, 39.

6 Bells have knoll'd to church.
As You Like It. Act ii, sc. 7, l. 114. [Orlando]

Have with holy bell been knoll'd to church.
As You Like It. Act ii, sc. 7, l. 121. [Duke]

Funeral bell.—*III Henry VI,* ii, 5, 117.
Melancholy bells.—*Romeo and Juliet,* iv, 5, 86.
Sullen bell.—*II Henry IV,* i, 1, 102.
Surly sullen bell.—*Sonnets,* lxxi.

7 Like sweet bells jangled, out of tune and harsh.
Hamlet. Act iii, sc. 1, l. 166. [Ophelia] The only use of "jangled." For full quotation, see under MADNESS. "Jangling" is used three times. See *Pericles,* ii, 1, 38, under BELLY.

8 Bid the merry bells ring to thine ear.
II Henry IV. Act iv, sc. 5, l. 112. [King Henry]

Why ring not out the bells aloud throughout the town?
I Henry VI. Act i, sc. 6, l. 11. [Reignier]

Ring, bells, aloud; burn, bonfires, clear and bright.
II Henry VI. Act v, sc. 1, l. 3. [York]

9 A warning bell
Sings heavy music to thy timorous soul.
I Henry VI. Act iv, sc. 2, l. 39. [General]

Silence that dreadful bell: it frights the isle
From her propriety.
Othello. Act ii, sc. 3, l. 175. [Othello] "Propriety" occurs again in *Twelfth Night,* v, 1, 150.

I 'll startle you Worse than the sacring bell.
Henry VIII. Act iii, sc. 2, l. 294. [Surrey] The only use of "sacring bell" (sounded at the elevation of the Host).

10 Bell, book, and candle shall not drive me back,
When gold and silver becks me to come on.
King John. Act iii, sc. 3, l. 12. [Bastard]

11 Go, bid thy mistress, when my drink is ready,
She strike upon the bell.
Macbeth. Act ii, sc. 1, l. 31. [Macbeth]

12 Let us all ring fancy's knell:
I 'll begin it,—Ding, dong, bell.
Ding, dong, bell.
The Merchant of Venice, iii, 2, 70. See under FANCY.

Ding-dong. . . . Ding-dong, bell.
The Tempest. Act i, sc. 2, l. 403. [Ariel]

13 Who 's that which rings the bell?
Othello. Act ii, sc. 3, l. 161. [Iago]

Ring the bell.—*Macbeth,* ii, 3, 85.
Ring your bells.—*King John,* ii, 1, 312.
Shake his bells.—*III Henry VI,* i, 1, 47.

14 My wether's bell rings doleful knell.
The Passionate Pilgrim, l. 272. "Wether" is repeated in *The Merchant of Venice,* iv, 1, 114, and in *The Winter's Tale,* iv, 3, 33.

Cowslip's bell.—*The Tempest,* v, 1, 89.
Falcon's bells.—*The Rape of Lucrece,* l. 511.

15 The curfew-bell has rung.
Romeo and Juliet. Act iv, sc. 4, l. 4. [Capulet] The only use of "curfew-bell."

Since the curfew rung.—*Measure for Measure,* iv, 2, 78.

He begins at curfew.—*King Lear,* iii, 4, 121.
Solemn curfew.—*The Tempest,* v, 1, 40. The only uses of "curfew."

1
The bells of Saint Bennet, sir, may put you in mind; one, two, three.
Twelfth Night. Act v, sc. 1, l. 42. [Clown]
The Windsor bell hath struck twelve.
The Merry Wives of Windsor. Act v, sc. 5, l. 1. [Falstaff]

BELLY

2
In fair round belly with good capon lined.
As You Like It. Act ii, sc. 7, l. 154. [Jaques]
With . . . something a round belly.
II Henry IV. Act i, sc. 2, l. 212. [Falstaff]
Fat belly.—*II Henry IV,* ii, 1, 82.
An increasing belly.—*II Henry IV,* i, 2, 205.
Portly belly.—*The Merry Wives of Windsor,* i, 3, 69.

3
You may put a man in your belly.
As You Like It. Act iii, sc. 2, l. 215. [Celia]
No barricado for a belly; know 't;
It will let in and out the enemy
With bag and baggage.
The Winter's Tale. Act i, sc. 2, l. 204. [Leontes] "Barricado" is repeated in *All's Well that Ends Well,* i, 1, 124, and in *Twelfth Night,* iv, 2, 41.

4
There was a time when all the body's members
Rebell'd against the belly, thus accused it:
That only like a gulf it did remain
I' the midst o' the body, idle and unactive,
Still cupboarding the viand, never bearing
Like labour with the rest, where the other instruments
Did see and hear, devise, instruct, walk, feel,
And, mutually participate, did minister
Unto the appetite and affection common
Of the whole body.
Coriolanus. Act i, sc. 1, l. 99. [Menenius] This is taken bodily from Plutarch (*Coriolanus,* sec. 6), who tells how Menenius Agrippa related this "celebrated fable." The only use of "unactive," and "cupboarding." "Participate" is repeated in *Twelfth Night,* v, 1, 245.
Your most grave belly was deliberate,
Not rash like his accusers, and thus answer'd:
'True is it, my incorporate friends,' quoth he,
'That I receive the general food at first,
Which you do live upon; and fit it is,
Because I am the store-house and the shop
Of the whole body: but, if you do remember,
I send it through the rivers of your blood,
Even to the court, the heart, to the seat o' the brain;
And, through the cranks and offices of man,
The strongest nerves and small inferior veins
From me receive that natural competency
Whereby they live.
Coriolanus. Act i, sc. 1, l. 132. [Menenius] "Cranks" is repeated in *Venus and Adonis,* l. 682.
For, look you, I may make the belly smile
As well as speak.
Coriolanus. Act i, sc. 1, l. 113. [Menenius]
The cormorant belly . . .
Who is the sink o' the body.
Coriolanus. Act i, sc. 1, l. 125. [Citizen]
Good belly.—*Coriolanus,* i, 1, 152.

5
An I had but a belly of any indifferency, I were simply the most active fellow in Europe: my womb, my womb, my womb, undoes me.
II Henry IV. Act iv, sc. 3, l. 22. [Falstaff] "Indifferency" is repeated in *King John,* ii, 1, 579.
My belly 's as cold as if I had swallowed snowballs for pills to cool the reins.
The Merry Wives of Windsor. Act iii, sc. 5, l. 23. [Falstaff]
Cold as a snowball.—*Pericles,* iv, 6, 149. The only uses of "snowball."
Mistress Ford! I have had ford enough; I was thrown into the ford; I have my belly full of ford.
The Merry Wives of Windsor. Act iii, sc. 5, l. 36. [Falstaff]

6
The getting up of the negro's belly.
The Merchant of Venice, iii, 5, 41. See under PREGNANCY.
Tom's belly.—*King Lear,* iii, 6, 33.
Belly of their steeds.—*III Henry VI,* ii, 3, 20.

7
When I had been in his belly, I would have kept such a jangling of the bells, that he should never have left, till he cast bells, steeple, church, and parish, up again.
Pericles. Act ii, sc. 1, l. 38. [Fisherman] "Jangling" is repeated in *Love's Labour's Lost,* ii, 1, 225, and in *A Midsummer-Night's Dream,* iii, 2, 353.

BENEFIT

See also Gift, Injury, Kindness, Office

8
You shall find A benefit in this change.
Antony and Cleopatra. Act v, sc. 2, l. 128. [Cæsar]

9
Her benefits are mightily misplaced.
As You Like It. Act i, sc. 2, l. 37. [Rosalind] "Misplaced" is repeated in *King John,* iii, 4, 133, and in *Richard III,* iii, 2, 44.
When these so noble benefits shall prove
Not well disposed, the mind growing once corrupt,
They turn to vicious forms, ten times more ugly
Than ever they were fair.
Henry VIII. Act i, sc. 2, l. 115. [King Henry]

10
Freeze, freeze, thou bitter sky,
That dost not bite so nigh
As benefits forgot.
As You Like It. Act ii, sc. 7, l. 184. [Amiens]

11
Disable all the benefits of your own country.
As You Like It, iv, 1, 34. See under TRAVEL. "Disable" is repeated in *I Henry VI,* v, 3, 67: "Disable not thyself."
Country's benefit.—*I Henry VI,* v, 4, 106.
Give away The benefit of our levies.
Coriolanus. Act v, sc. 6, l. 68. [Lord]
Benefit o' the wind.—*Cymbeline,* iv, 2, 342.

1 By the benefit of his wished light,
The seas waxed calm.
Comedy of Errors. Act i, sc. 1, l. 91. [Ægeon]

2
No public benefit which you receive
But it proceeds or comes from them to you
And no way from yourselves.
Coriolanus. Act i, sc. 1, l. 156. [Menenius]
The benefit
Which thou shalt thereby reap is such a name,
Whose repetition will be dogg'd with curses.
Coriolanus. Act v, sc. 3, l. 142. [Volumnia]

3
I 'll lop a member off and give it you
In earnest of a further benefit.
I Henry VI. Act v, sc. 3, l. 15. [La Pucelle]
Give benefit.—*Hamlet,* i, 3, 2.
Come, Pistol, utter more to me; and withal devise something to do thyself good.
II Henry IV. Act v, sc. 3, l. 139. [Falstaff]

4
Benefit no further Than vainly longing.
Henry VIII. Act i, sc. 2, l. 80. [Wolsey]
Receive the benefit.—*Julius Cæsar,* iii, 2, 47.

5
A man, a prince, by him so benefited!
King Lear. Act iv, sc. 2, l. 45. [Albany] The only use of "benefited."

6
What benefactors are they? are they not malefactors?
Measure for Measure. Act ii, sc. 1, l. 51. [Angelo]
You great benefactors, sprinkle our society with thankfulness.
Timon of Athens. Act iii, sc. 6, l. 79. [Timon] The only uses of "benefactors."

7
You may most uprighteously do a poor wronged lady a merited benefit.
Measure for Measure. Act iii, sc. 1, l. 207. [Duke] The only use of "uprighteously."
The doubleness of the benefit defends the deceit from reproof.
Measure for Measure. Act iii, sc. 1, l. 270. [Duke] The only use of "doubleness."
I am half afraid he will have need of washing; so throwing him into the water will do him a benefit.
The Merry Wives of Windsor. Act iii, sc. 3, 193. [Mrs. Ford]

8 Take to your royal self
This proffer'd benefit of dignity.
Richard III. Act iii, sc. 7, l. 195. [Buckingham]
Benefit of access.—*The Winter's Tale,* v, 2, 119.
Benefit of ill.—*Venus and Adonis,* l. 618.
Benefit of law.—*I Henry VI,* iv, 1, 100.
Benefit of rest.—*Sonnets,* xxviii.
Benefit of my senses.—*Twelfth Night,* v, 1, 313.
Benefit of seniory.—*Richard III,* iv, 4, 36. The only use of "seniory."
Benefit of silence.—*Measure for Measure,* v, 1, 190.
Benefit of sleep.—*Macbeth,* v, 1, 11.
Benefit of time.—*The Two Gentlemen of Verona,* ii, 4, 65. See under STUDY.

9
We are born to do benefits.
Timon of Athens. Act i, sc. 2, l. 106. [Timon]

I do beseech you, as in way of taste,
To give me now a little benefit,
Out of those many register'd in promise.
Troilus and Cressida. Act iii, sc. 3, l. 13. [Calchas]

BENISON, see Blessing

BETRAYAL

See also Deceit, Treachery

10
If he do not . . . offer to betray you, . . . never trust my judgement in any thing.
All's Well that Ends Well. Act iii, sc. 6, l. 30. [Lord]
Soldier: If your life be saved, will you undertake to betray the Florentine?
Parolles: Ay, and the captain of his horse.
All's Well that Ends Well. Act iv, sc. 3, l. 325.

11
A' will betray us all unto ourselves.
All's Well that Ends Well. Act iv, sc. 1, l. 102. [Second Lord]
Betray themselves.—*As You Like It,* iv, 1, 6.

12
Betray'd I am: O this false soul of Egypt!
Antony and Cleopatra. Act iv, sc. 10, l. 24. [Antony]
All is lost; This foul Egyptian hath betrayed me:
My fleet hath yielded to the foe; and yonder
They cast their caps up and carouse together
Like friends long lost.
Antony and Cleopatra. Act iv, sc. 12, l. 9. [Antony]
She hath betray'd me and shall die the death.
Antony and Cleopatra. Act iv, sc. 14, l. 26. [Antony]
She did betray me to my own reproof.
The Comedy of Errors. Act v, sc. 1, l. 90. [Adriana]
She must die, else she 'll betray more men.
Othello. Act v, sc. 2, l. 6. [Othello]

13 Some jay of Italy
Whose mother was her painting, hath betray'd him:
Poor I am stale, a garment out of fashion.
Cymbeline. Act iii, sc. 4, l. 51. [Imogen]

14
Who, on my soul, hath wilfully betray'd
The lives of those that he did lead to fight.
I Henry IV. Act i, sc. 3. l. 81. [King Henry]
He hath betrayed his followers, whose condemnation is pronounced.
Henry V. Act iii, sc. 6, l. 143. [Montjoy]
Perfidiously He hath betray'd your business.
Coriolanus. Act v, sc. 6, l. 91. [Aufidius] The only use of "perfidiously."
Ah, villain, thou wilt betray me, and get a thousand crowns of the king by carrying my head to him.
II Henry VI. Act iv, sc. 10, l. 28. [Cade]

15
If I be ta'en, I 'll peach for this.
I Henry IV. Act ii, sc. 2, l. 48. [Falstaff]
Peach-coloured satin, which now peaches him a beggar.
Measure for Measure, iv, 3, 12. The only uses of "peach." The fruit is not referred to in

the plays, except in the compound, "peach-coloured," which is used twice, as above, in *II Henry IV*, ii, 2, 19.

1
The fraud of England, not the force of France,
Hath now entrapp'd the noble-minded Talbot:
Never to England shall he bear his life;
But dies, betray'd to fortune by your strife.
I Henry VI. Act iv, sc. 4, l. 36. [Lucy] The only use of "entrapp'd." "Noble-minded" is repeated in *Titus Andronicus*, i, 1, 209: "Noble-minded Titus."

2
My noble father . . . was by that wretch betray'd.
Henry VIII. Act ii, sc. 1, l. 107. [Buckingham]

3 We come not . . .
To betray you any way to sorrow,
You have too much, good lady.
Henry VIII. Act iii, sc. 1, l. 54. [Wolsey]

4
These betray nice wenches, that would be betrayed without these.
Love's Labour's Lost. Act iii, sc. 1, l. 23. [Moth]

5
King: Are we betray'd thus to thy over-view?
Biron: Not you to me, but I betray'd by you.
Love's Labour's Lost. Act iv, sc. 3, l. 174. The only use of "over-view."

I am betray'd, by keeping company
With men like men of inconstancy.
Love's Labour's Lost. Act iv, sc. 3, l. 179. [Biron]

6
At no time broke my faith, would not betray
The devil to his fellow and delight
No less in truth than life.
Macbeth. Act iv, sc. 3, l. 128. [Malcolm]

7
Alas! he is betray'd and I undone.
Othello. Act v, sc. 2, l. 76. [Desdemona]

We'll betray him finely.—*The Merry Wives of Windsor*, v, 3, 22.

Do not betray me, sir.—*The Merry Wives of Windsor*, iii, 3, 82.

8 Thou art like the harpy,
Which, to betray, dost, with thine angel's face,
Seize with thine eagle's talons.
Pericles. Act iv, sc. 3, l. 47. [Dionyza] "Harpy" occurs again in *Much Ado about Nothing*, ii, 1, 279, and *Tempest*, iii, 3, 83.

9
For, thou betraying me, I do betray
My nobler part to my gross body's treason;
My soul doth tell my body that he may
Triumph in love; flesh stays no farther reason.
Sonnets. No. cli.

10 By oppressing and betraying me,
Thou mightst have sooner got another service.
Timon of Athens. Act iv, sc. 3, l. 510. [Flavius] The only use of "oppressing."

11
Wilt thou betray thy noble mistress thus?
Titus Andronicus, iv, 2, 106. See under MISTRESS.

Wouldst thou betray me?—*Richard III*, i, 1, 102.

Betray the fore-betray'd!—*A Lover's Complaint*, l. 328. The only use of "fore-betray'd."

Betray thy foes.—*Titus Andronicus*, v, 2, 147.

Betray Mine interest.—*Cymbeline*, i, 3, 29.

Betray my life.—*The Rape of Lucrece*, l. 233.

BETROTHAL

See also Match

12
Thou didst swear to me upon a parcel-gilt goblet, sitting in my Dolphin-chamber, at the round table, by a sea-coal fire, upon Wednesday in Wheeson week, when the prince broke thy head for liking his father to a singing-man of Windsor, thou didst swear to me then, as I was washing thy wound, to marry me and make me my lady thy wife.
II Henry IV. Act ii, sc. 1, l. 93. [Hostess] The only use of "parcel-gilt," "Dolphin-chamber," "Wheeson" and "singing-man." "Sea-coal fire" is repeated in *The Merry Wives of Windsor*, i, 4, 9.

13
You were troth-plight to her.
Henry V. Act ii, sc. 1, l. 21. [Bardolph]

This is your son-in-law
And son unto the king, who, heavens directing,
Is troth-plight to your daughter.
The Winter's Tale. Act v, sc. 3, l. 149. [Leontes] The only use of "directing." "Troth-plight" is repeated in i, 2, 278.

14
You know, my lord, your highness is betroth'd
Unto another lady of esteem:
How shall we then dispense with that contract,
And not deface your honour with reproach?
I Henry VI. Act v, sc. 5, l. 26. [Gloucester]

Betrothed lovers.—*Henry V*, ii, 4, 108.

15
Affianced to her by oath, and the nuptial appointed.
Measure for Measure. Act iii, sc. 1, l. 222. [Duke]

As there comes light from heaven and words from breath,
As there is sense in truth and truth in virtue,
I am affianced this man's wife as strongly
As words could make up vows.
Measure for Measure. Act v, sc. 1, l. 225. [Mariana] The only uses of "affianced."

16
The sealing-day betwixt my love and me.
A Midsummer-Night's Dream. Act i, sc. 1, l. 84. [Theseus] Only use of "sealing-day."

17
Betroth'd and would have married her perforce.
Romeo and Juliet. Act v, sc. 3, l. 238. [Friar Laurence]

Him that justly may
Bear his betroth'd from all the world away.
Titus Andronicus. Act i, sc. 1, l. 285. [Bassianus]

1
A contract of eternal bond of love,
Confirm'd by mutual joinder of your hands,
Attested by the holy close of lips,
Strengthen'd by interchangement of your rings;
And all the ceremony of this compact
Seal'd in my function, by my testimony.
Twelfth Night. Act v, sc. 1, l. 159. [Priest] The only use of "joinder" and "interchangement."

The contract you pretend with this base wretch,
One bred of alms and foster'd with cold dishes,
With scraps o' the court, it is no contract, none.
Cymbeline. Act ii, sc. 3, l. 118. [Cloten]

Come on, Contract us 'fore these witnesses.
The Winter's Tale. Act iv, sc. 4, l. 401. [Florizel]

True contract.—*Measure for Measure,* i, 2, 149.
Vow'd contract.—*Measure for Measure,* v, 1, 209.
Contract of her marriage.—*As You Like It,* iii, 2, 332.

Wast thou e'er contracted to this woman?
Measure for Measure. Act v, sc. 1, l. 380. [Duke]

She and I, long since contracted,
Are now so sure that nothing can dissolve us.
The Merry Wives of Windsor. Act v, sc. 5, l. 236. [Fenton]

I was contracted to them both.
King Lear. Act v, sc. 3, l. 228. [Edmund]

You would have been contracted to a maid;
Nor are you therein, by my life, deceived,
You are betroth'd both to a maid and man.
Twelfth Night. Act v, sc. 1, l. 266. [Sebastian]

We are betrothed: nay, more, our marriage-hour . . . Determined of.
The Two Gentlemen of Verona. Act ii, sc. 4, l. 179. [Valentine] The only use of "marriage-hour."

2
Three crabbed months had sour'd themselves to death,
Ere I could make thee open thy white hand
And clap thyself my love: then didst thou utter
'I am yours for ever.'
Winter's Tale. Act i, sc. 2, l. 102. [Leontes] The only use of "sour'd."

BILLOW, see Wave

BIRD

See also Lark, Nightingale, Raven, Sparrow, Wren

3
Show the world what the bird hath done to her own nest.
As You Like It. Act iv, sc. 1, l. 207. [Celia] "It's an ill bird that fouls its own nest" was referred to by Thomas Hoccleve, as early as 1400, as an "old proverb." (*Minor Poems,* p. 80.) See also under NEST.

4
Far from her nest the lapwing cries away.
The Comedy of Errors. Act iv, sc. 2, l. 27. [Adriana]

This lapwing runs away with the shell on his head.
Hamlet. Act v, sc. 2, l. 193. [Horatio]

Like a lapwing, runs Close by the ground.
Much Ado about Nothing. Act iii, sc. 1, l. 24. [Hero]

With maids to seem the lapwing.
Measure for Measure, i, 4, 32. See under VIRGIN. The only references to the lapwing.

5
The bird is dead
That we have made so much on.
Cymbeline. Act iv, sc. 2, l. 197. [Arviragus]

Dead birds.—*The Phœnix and the Turtle,* l. 67.

6
His royal bird
Prunes the immortal wing and cloys his beak,
As when his god is pleased.
Cymbeline. Act v, sc. 4, l. 117. [Sicilius]

Jove's bird.—*Cymbeline,* iv, 2, 348.
Princely eagle's bird.—*III Henry VI,* ii, 1, 91. See under EAGLE.

7
The bird of dawning singeth all night long.
Hamlet, i, 1, 160. See under COCK.

The obscure bird Clamour'd the livelong night.
Macbeth, ii, 3, 64. See under OMEN.

Bird of night.—*Julius Cæsar,* i, 3, 26.
Bird of peace.—*Henry VIII,* iv, 1, 89.
Birds of prey.—*Measure for Measure,* ii, 1, 2; *Titus Andronicus,* v, 3, 198.
Bird of wonder.—*Henry VIII,* v, 5, 41.

8
Thou art a summer bird,
Which ever in the haunch of winter sings
The lifting up of day.
II Henry IV. Act iv, sc. 4, l. 91. [King Henry] "Haunch" is repeated in *As You Like It,* ii, 1, 25, and in *The Merry Wives of Windsor,* v, 5, 28; and "lifting" in *King Lear,* iii, 4, 16.

I heard a bird so sing,
Whose music, to my thinking, pleased the king.
II Henry IV. Act v, sc. 5, l. 113. [Lancaster]

As duly, but not as truly,
As bird doth sing on bough.
Henry V. Act iii, sc. 2, l. 19. [Boy]

9
Of their feather many moe proud birds.
III Henry VI. Act ii, sc. 1, l. 170. [Warwick]

Both of you are birds of selfsame feather.
III Henry VI. Act ii, sc. 3, l. 161. [Queen Margaret]

10
Ay, such a pleasure as incaged birds
Conceive when after many moody thoughts
At last by notes of household harmony
They quite forget their loss of liberty.
III Henry VI. Act iv, sc. 6, l. 12. [King Henry] "Incaged" is repeated in *Richard II,* ii, 1, 102.

11
The bird that hath been limed in a bush,
With trembling wings misdoubteth every bush.
III Henry VI. Act v, sc. 6, l. 13. [King Henry] The only use of "misdoubteth."

Birds never limed no secret bushes fear.
The Rape of Lucrece, l. 88.

Lady Macduff: How will you live?
Son: As birds do, mother.
Lady Macduff: What, with worms and flies?
Son: With what I get, I mean; and so do they.
Lady Macduff: Poor bird! thou 'ldst never fear the net nor lime,
The pitfall nor the gin.
Macbeth. Act iv, sc. 2, l. 31. The only use of "pitfall."

1 This guest of summer,
The temple-haunting martlet, does approve
By his loved mansionry, that the heaven's breath
Smells wooingly here; no jutty, frieze,
Buttress, nor coign of vantage, but this bird
Hath made his pendent bed and procreant cradle:
Where they most breed and haunt, I have observed,
The air is delicate.
Macbeth. Act i, sc. 6, l. 3. [Banquo] The only use of "temple-haunting," "mansionry," "frieze" and "buttress." The martlet is mentioned again in *Merchant of Venice,* ii, 9, 28.

2
The bird was fledged; and then it is the complexion of them all to leave the dam.
The Merchant of Venice. Act iii, sc. 1, l. 32. [Salanio]

3
Melodious birds sing madrigals—.
The Merry Wives of Windsor. Act iii, sc. 1, l. 23. [Evans] Quoting a line from a famous song by Christopher Marlowe, *The Passionate Shepherd to His Love,* included in *The Passionate Pilgrim* in 1599, a year before *The Merry Wives of Windsor* was written.

All thy fellow birds do sing.
The Passionate Pilgrim, l. 397.

Birds did sing.—*The Passionate Pilgrim,* l. 377.

The little birds that tune their morning's joy.
The Rape of Lucrece, l. 1107.

Little birds.—*Titus Andronicus,* iv, 4, 83.

The birds chant melody on every bush.
Titus Andronicus. Act ii, sc. 3, l. 12. [Tamora]

With heigh! the sweet birds, O, how they sing!
The Winter's Tale. Act iv, sc. 3, l. 6. [Autolycus]

Singing birds.—*Richard II,* i, 3, 288.

Sweet melodious birds.—*Titus Andronicus,* ii, 3, 27; iii, 1, 85.

Sweet bird.—*III Henry VI,* v, 6, 15; *As You Like It,* ii, 5, 4; *The Rape of Lucrece,* l. 871; *Sonnets,* lxxiii.

Enticing birds.—*II Henry VI,* i, 3, 92.

New-kill'd bird.—*The Rape of Lucrece,* l. 457. "New killed," unhyphenated, is used in *Romeo and Juliet,* v, 3, 197.

Prison'd bird.—*Cymbeline,* iii, 3, 43.

Sneaped birds.—*The Rape of Lucrece,* l. 333. The only use of "sneaped" (pinched with cold).

4
The ousel cock so black of hue,
With orange-tawny bill,
The throstle with his note so true,
The wren with little quill.
A Midsummer-Night's Dream. Act iii, sc. 1, l. 128. [Bottom] The ousel is mentioned again in *II Henry IV,* iii, 2, 9; "orange-tawny" is repeated in *A Midsummer-Night's Dream,* iii, 1, 129 ("orange-tawny beard"), and occurs in no other play; the throstle is referred to again in *The Merchant of Venice,* i, 2, 65; and the wren is mentioned eight times in the plays. See under WREN.

The finch, the sparrow and the lark.
A Midsummer-Night's Dream. Act iii, sc. 1, l. 133. [Bottom] The only use of "finch."

5
Russet-pated choughs, many in sort,
Rising and cawing at the gun's report.
A Midsummer-Night's Dream. Act iii, sc. 2, l. 21. [Puck] The only use of "russet-pated" and "cawing."

Scared my choughs from the chaff.
The Winter's Tale, iv, 4, 630. "Chough" (jackdaw) is used seven times in the plays.

6
A bird of my tongue is better than a beast of yours.
Much Ado about Nothing. Act i, sc. 1, l. 140. [Beatrice]

The meanest bird That flies i' the purer air!
Pericles, iv, 6, 108. See under MAID.

7
Let the bird of loudest lay,
On the sole Arabian tree,
Herald sad and trumpet be,
To whose sound chaste wings obey.

But thou shrieking harbinger,
Foul precurrer of the fiend,
Augur of the fever's end,
To this troop come thou not near!
The Phœnix and the Turtle, l. 1. The only use of "precurrer."

Arabian bird.—*Antony and Cleopatra,* iii, 2, 12; *Cymbeline,* i, 6, 17. The Arabian bird was the phœnix.

8
'You mocking birds,' quoth she, 'your tombs entomb
Within your hollow-swelling feather'd breasts,
And in my hearing be you mute and dumb.'
The Rape of Lucrece, l. 1121. The only use of "hollow-swelling."

Poor bird, thou sing'st not in the day,
As shaming any eye should thee behold.
The Rape of Lucrece, l. 1142. The only use of "shaming."

Poor birds.—*Venus and Adonis,* l. 601; 604. *The Passionate Pilgrim,* l. 381; 399.

9
Juliet: I would have thee gone:
And yet no further than a wanton's bird. . . .
Romeo: I would I were thy bird.
Juliet: Sweet, so would I:
Yet I should kill thee with much cherishing.
Romeo and Juliet. Act ii, sc. 2, l. 177.

10
Thou away, the very birds are mute.
Sonnets, xcvii. See under ABSENCE.

Sweet birds sing not.—*The Passionate Pilgrim,* l. 282.

1
Am I your bird? I mean to shift my bush;
And then pursue me as you draw your bow.
The Taming of the Shrew. Act v, sc. 2, l. 46. [Bianca]

This bird you aim'd at, though you hit her not.
The Taming of the Shrew. Act v, sc. 2, l. 50. [Petruchio]

2
When he was by, the birds such pleasure took,
That some would sing, some other in their bills
Would bring him mulberries and ripe-red cherries;
He fed them with his sight, they him with berries.
Venus and Adonis, l. 1101. The only use of "ripe-red."

Like a wild bird being tamed with too much handling.
Venus and Adonis, l. 560.

BIRTH

See also Ancestry, Pregnancy

3
Helena: You were born under a charitable star.
Parolles: Under Mars, I.
All's Well that Ends Well, i, 1, 205. See under STAR. Mars is mentioned thirty-six times.

Beatrice: I was born to speak all mirth and no matter.
Don Pedro: Out of question, you were born in a merry hour.
Beatrice: No, sure, my lord, my mother cried; but then there was a star danced, and under that I was born.
Much Ado about Nothing. Act ii, sc. 1, l. 343. See also under STAR.

King Richard: Her life is only safest in her birth.
Queen Elizabeth: And only in that safety died her brothers.
King Richard: Lo, at their births good stars were opposite.
Richard III. Act iv, sc. 4, l. 213.

I was not born under a rhyming planet.
Much Ado about Nothing, v, 2, 40. See under RHYME.

Born under Saturn.—*Much Ado about Nothing,* i, 3, 12. Saturn is mentioned five times.

Were we not born under Taurus?—*Twelfth Night,* i, 3, 147. Taurus is mentioned five times.

My nativity was under Ursa major.—*King Lear,* i, 2, 140. The only mention of Ursa major.

4
Wast born i' the forest here?
As You Like It. Act v, sc. 1, l. 24. [Touchstone]

5
That very hour and in the self-same inn
A meaner woman was delivered
Of such a burden, male twins, both alike.
The Comedy of Errors. Act i, sc. 1, l. 54. [Ægeon]

Thou hadst a wife once call'd Æmilia
That bore thee at a burden two fair sons.
The Comedy of Errors. Act v, sc. 1, l. 342. [Abbess]

Birth of three.—*Cymbeline,* v, 5, 369.

6
Their birth—wherein they are not guilty,
Since nature cannot choose his origin.
Hamlet. Act i, sc. 4, l. 25. [Hamlet]

7
I am by birth a shepherd's daughter.
I Henry VI. Act i, sc. 2, l. 72. [La Pucelle] See under DAUGHTER.

By birth a pedlar.—*The Taming of the Shrew,* Ind., 2, 20.

8
I was the next by birth and parentage.
I Henry VI. Act ii, sc. 5, l. 73. [Mortimer]

Ignorant of his birth and parentage.
II Henry VI. Act iv, sc. 2, l. 152. [Cade]

9
At my nativity
The front of heaven was full of fiery shapes,
Of burning cressets; and at my birth
The frame and huge foundation of the earth
Shaked like a coward.
I Henry IV. Act iii, sc. 1, l. 13. [Glendower] The only use of "cressets" (fire-baskets).

Glendower: I say the earth did shake when I was born . . .
The heavens were all on fire, the earth did tremble.
Hotspur: O, then the earth shook to see the heavens on fire.
I Henry IV. Act iii, sc. 1, l. 21.

At my birth
The front of heaven was full of fiery shapes,
The goats ran from the mountains, and the herds
Were strangely clamorous to the frighted fields.
I Henry IV. Act iii, sc. 1, l. 37. [Glendower]

The owl shriek'd at thy birth,—an evil sign;
The night-crow cried, aboding luckless time;
Dogs howl'd, and hideous tempest shook down trees;
The raven rook'd her on the chimney's top,
And chattering pies in dismal discords sung.
III Henry VI. Act v, sc. 6, l. 44. [King Henry] The only use of "night-crow," "aboding," "rook'd" and "pies."

10
I was born about three of the clock in the afternoon, with a white head and something a round belly.
II Henry IV. Act i, sc. 2, l. 210. [Falstaff]

The field is honourable; and there was he born, under a hedge, for his father had never a house but the cage.
II Henry VI. Act iv, sc. 2, l. 54. [Dick]

Some report a sea-maid spawned him; some, that he was begot between two stock-fishes.
Measure for Measure. Act iii, sc. 2, l. 115. [Lucio] The only use of "spawned." "Stock-fish" (dried codfish) occurs four times. "Sea-maid" is repeated in *A Midsummer-Night's Dream,* ii, 1, 154.

He was gotten in drink: is not the humour conceited?
Merry Wives of Windsor, i, 3, 25. [Nym]

I was bred and born
Not three hours' travel from this very place.
Twelfth Night. Act i, sc. 2, l. 22. [Captain]

1
I pray God the fruit of her womb miscarry!
II Henry IV. Act v, sc. 4, l. 15. [Hostess]
Murder not then the fruit within my womb.
I Henry VI. Act v, sc. 4, l. 63. [La Pucelle]
Why should I joy in any abortive birth?
Love's Labour's Lost. Act i, sc. 1, l. 104. [Biron]
If ever he have child, abortive be it.
Richard III. Act i, sc. 2, l. 21. [Anne]
Macduff was from his mother's womb
Untimely ripp'd.
Macbeth. Act v, sc. 8, l. 15. [Macduff]
Sent before my time
Into this breathing world, scarce half made up.
Richard III. Act i, sc. 1, l. 20. [Gloucester]

2 Salute our rightful sovereign
With honour of his birthright to the crown.
II Henry VI. Act ii, sc. 3, l. 61. [Warwick]
Hath he deserved to lose his birthright thus?
III Henry VI. Act i, sc. 1, l. 219. [Queen Margaret]
Were it not pity that this goodly boy
Should lose his birthright by his father's fault?
III Henry VI. Act ii, sc. 2, l. 34. [Clifford]
Bearing their birthrights proudly on their backs.
King John. Act ii, sc. 1, l. 70. [Chatillon] See under ADVENTURE.

3
Thy mother felt more than a mother's pain,
And yet brought forth less than a mother's hope,
To wit, an indigested and deformed lump,
Not like the fruit of such a goodly tree.
III Henry VI. Act v, sc. 6, l. 49. [King Henry]
Foul indigested lump,
As crooked in thy manners as thy shape!
II Henry VI. Act v, sc. 1, l. 157. [Clifford] The only uses of "indigested."

4
For I have often heard my mother say
I came into the world with my legs forward.
III Henry VI. Act v, sc. 6, l. 70. [Gloucester]

5
God safely quit her of her burthen, and
With gentle travail, to the gladding of
Your highness with an heir!
Henry VIII. Act v, sc. 1, l. 70. [Suffolk] The only use of "gladding." For "travail" see LABOUR.
Happy birth.—*Julius Cæsar,* v, 3, 70.
Joyful births.—*Henry V,* v, 2, 35.
True birth.—*Romeo and Juliet,* ii, 3, 20.
Birth of love.—*Romeo and Juliet,* i, 5, 142.
Birth of Cain.—*King John,* iii, 4, 79.
Cain's birth.—*Love's Labour's Lost,* iv, 2, 36.
Saviour's birth.—*Hamlet,* i, 1, 159.

6
I was not born to die on Brutus' sword.
Julius Cæsar. Act v, sc. 1, l. 57. [Octavius]
Well, we were born to die.
Romeo and Juliet, iii, 4, 4. See under DEATH.

7
This is my birth-day; as this very day
Was Cassius born.
Julius Cæsar. Act v, sc. 1, l. 72. [Cassius]
It is my birth-day:
I had thought to have held it poor.
Antony and Cleopatra. Act iii, sc. 13, l. 185. [Cleopatra]
To-morrow is her birth-day.
Pericles, ii, 1, 114. The only uses of "birth-day."
My birth-place hate I.—*Coriolanus,* iv, 4, 23. The only use of "birth-place."

8 Better thou
Hadst not been born than not to have pleased me better.
King Lear. Act i, sc. 1, l. 236. [King Lear]
Thou hadst been better have been born a dog.
Othello. Act iii, sc. 3, l. 362. [Othello] See under WHORE.

9 We came crying hither:
Thou know'st, the first time that we smell the air,
We wawl and cry. . . .
When we are born, we cry that we are come
To this great stage of fools.
King Lear. Act iv, sc. 6, l. 182. [King Lear] The only use of "wawl."

10 What's the boy Malcolm?
Was he not born of woman? The spirits that know
All mortal consequences have pronounced me thus:
'Fear not, Macbeth; no man that's born of woman
Shall e'er have power upon thee.'
Macbeth. Act v, sc. 3, l. 4. [Macbeth]
What's he That was not born of woman?
Macbeth, v, 7, 2. See under WOMAN.
Thou wast born of woman.
But swords I smile at, weapons laugh to scorn,
Brandish'd by man that's of a woman born.
Macbeth. Act v, sc. 7, l. 11. [Macbeth]
Born of woman.—*Timon of Athens,* iv, 3, 501.
Of woman born.—*Macbeth,* iv, 1, 80.
One of woman born.—*Macbeth,* 5, 8, 13.
Born of madness.—*As You Like It,* iv, 1, 218.

11
And so in progress to be hatch'd and born.
Measure for Measure. Act ii, sc. 2, l. 97. [Angelo]
'Tis hatch'd and shall be so.
The Taming of the Shrew. Act i, sc. 1, l. 211. [Lucentio]
In wisdom hatch'd.—*Love's Labour's Lost,* v, 2, 70.
New hatch'd.—*Macbeth,* ii, 3, 64.

12 Mark what Jacob did.
When Laban and himself were compromised
That all the eanlings that were streaked and pied
Should fall as Jacob's hire, the ewes, being rank,
In the end of autumn turned to the rams,
And, when the work of generation was
Between these woolly breeders in the act,
The skilful shepherd peel'd me certain wands
And, in the doing of the deed of kind,
He stuck them up before the fulsome ewes,
Who then conceiving did in eaning time

Fall parti-colour'd lambs, and those were Jacob's.
The Merchant of Venice. Act i, sc. 3, l. 78. [Shylock] This story of pre-natal influence is told in *Genesis,* xxx, 37–39. The only use of "compromised," "eanlings," and "parti-colour'd." "Eaning time" occurs again in *Pericles,* iii, 4, 6. Laban is mentioned again in l. 72 of the same scene, and nowhere else. Jacob is referred to seven times.

1 Hell and night
Must bring this monstrous birth to the world's light.
Othello. Act i, sc. 3, l. 409. [Iago]

Abhorred births.—*Timon of Athens,* iv, 3, 183.
Loathly births.—*II Henry IV,* iv, 4, 122. "Loathly" is repeated in *King Lear,* ii, 1, 51, and in *The Tempest,* iv, 1, 21.

2
A more blustrous birth had never babe.
Pericles. Act iii, sc. 1, l. 28. [Pericles] The only use of "blustrous."

Violent birth.—*Hamlet,* iii, 2, 199.

3
A terrible childbed hast thou had, my dear;
No light, no fire: the unfriendly elements
Forgot thee utterly.
Pericles. Act iii, sc. 1, l. 57. [Pericles] The only use of "unfriendly," in a scene probably not by Shakespeare.

At sea in childbed died she, but brought forth
A maid-child.
Pericles. Act v, sc. 3, l. 6. [Pericles] The only use of "maid-child." "Childbed" occurs a third time in *The Winter's Tale,* iii, 2, 104: "Child-bed privilege."

4
Born in a tempest, when my mother died.
Pericles. Act iv, sc. 1, l. 19. [Marina]

Pericles: Where were you born?
And wherefore call'd Marina?
Marina: Call'd Marina
For I was born at sea.
Pericles. Act v, sc. 1, l. 156.

Born at sea.—*Pericles,* iii, 3, 13; v, 1, 198.

5 I was born so high,
Our aery buildeth in the cedar's top,
And dallies with the wind and scorns the sun.
Richard III. Act i, sc. 3, l. 263. [Gloucester]

Your right of birth, your empery, your own.
Richard III. Act iii, sc. 7, l. 136. [Buckingham]

The primogenitive and due of birth.
Troilus and Cressida. Act i, sc. 3, l. 106. [Ulysses] The only use of "primogenitive."

Due of birth.—*Richard III,* iii, 7, 120; 158; *Macbeth,* iii, 6, 25.
Above him in birth.—*Cymbeline,* iv, 1, 13.
Thy betters in their birth.—*II Henry VI,* v, 1, 119.

6
Wrong not her birth, she is of royal blood.
Richard III. Act iv, sc. 4, l. 211. [King Richard]

High birth.—*Troilus and Cressida,* iii, 3, 172.
Royal birth.—*I Henry VI,* iii, 1, 95.
Great of birth.—*The Merry Wives of Windsor,* iii, 4, 4.
Nobleness of birth.—*The Two Gentlemen of Verona,* i, 3, 33.
Of noble birth.—*I Henry VI,* iv, 1, 35; v, 4, 22.
Of fair birth.—*II Henry IV,* i, 3, 63.
Of worthy birth.—*The Taming of the Shrew,* iv, 5, 65.

7
A grievous burthen was thy birth to me.
Richard III. Act iv, sc. 4, l. 167. [Duchess of York]

8
O, well-a-day, that ever I was born!
Romeo and Juliet. Act iv, sc. 5, l. 15. [Nurse]

O that ever I was born!
Winter's Tale. Act iv, sc. 3, l. 53. [Autolycus]

Wherefore was I born?—*Richard II,* ii, 3, 122.
What, was I born to this?—*Richard II,* iii, 4, 98.

Why rail'st thou on thy birth, the heaven, and earth?
Since birth, and heaven, and earth, all three do meet
In thee at once; which thou at once wouldst lose.
Romeo and Juliet. Act iii, sc. 3, l. 119. [Friar Laurence]

9
He was not born to shame.
Romeo and Juliet, iii, 2, 91. See under SHAME.

Born to do me shame.—*Love's Labour's Lost,* iv, 3, 204.
Born to do benefits.—*Timon of Athens,* i, 2, 105.
Born to bear.—*Richard II,* v, 5, 92. See also under DESTINY.
Born to conquer.—*Timon of Athens,* iv, 3, 106.
Born to fears.—*King John,* iii, 1, 15.
Born to honour.—*Pericles,* iv, 6, 99.
Born to make black fair.—*Love's Labour's Lost,* iv, 3, 261.
Born to undo us.—*Pericles,* iv, 6, 158.
Born blind.—*II Henry VI,* ii, 1, 77; 126.
Born fair.—*Sonnets,* cxxvii.
Born free.—*Julius Cæsar,* i, 2, 97.
Born great.—*Twelfth Night,* ii, 5, 157; iii, 4, 45; v, 1, 378.
Born a bastard.—*Timon of Athens,* ii, 2, 88.
Born a fool.—*The Winter's Tale,* ii, 1, 174.
Born for bondage.—*Cymbeline,* v, 5, 306.
Born in April.—*Troilus and Cressida,* i, 2, 189.
Born of love.—*Sonnets,* cli.
Born with teeth!—*III Henry VI,* v, 6, 75.
Born your vassal.—*Cymbeline,* v, 5, 113.
Better born.—*II Henry VI,* v, 1, 28.
Evilly born.—*King John,* iii, 4, 149.
Lowly born.—*Henry VIII,* ii, 3, 19.
New born.—*The Rape of Lucrece,* l. 1759.
Newly born.—*Timon of Athens,* iii, 5, 30.
Noble born.—*Henry VIII,* ii, 4, 141.
Nobly born.—*II Henry VI,* ii, 3, 9.
Northward born.—*Merchant of Venice,* ii, 1, 4.
Unlawfully born.—*Measure for Measure,* iii, 1, 196.
Well born.—*All's Well that Ends Well,* iii, 7, 4; *King John,* ii, 1, 278.
To the manner born.—*Hamlet,* i, 4, 15.

10
Prospero: Where was she born? speak; tell me.
Caliban: Sir, in Argier.
The Tempest. Act i, sc. 2, l. 260. Argier (Algiers) is mentioned again in l. 265.

King Henry: Where wert thou born?
Simpcox: At Berwick in the north.
II Henry VI. Act ii, sc. 1, l. 83.

A Bohemian born, but here nursed up and bred.
Measure for Measure. Act iv, sc. 2, l. 134. [Provost] The only use of "Bohemian." Bohemia is mentioned twenty-four times in *The Winter's Tale,* and nowhere else. "Bohemian-Tartar" occurs in *The Merry Wives of Windsor,* iv, 5, 21.

Esaclus: Where were you born, friend?
Froth: Here in Vienna, sir.
Measure for Measure. Act ii, sc. 1, l. 202.

In Cambria are we born.—*Cymbeline,* xv, 5, 17.
Born at Ephesus.—*The Comedy of Errors,* i, 1, 17.
Born in Macedon.—*Henry V,* iv, 7, 20.
Born at Monmouth.—*I Henry VI,* iii, 1, 198.
Born in Northamptonshire.—*King John,* i, 1, 51. The only mention of Northamptonshire.
Born in Rome.—*Coriolanus,* i, 3, 37.
In Syracusa was I born.—*The Comedy of Errors,* i, 1, 37. Syracusa is mentioned five times in this play, and in no other. Syracuse is used once.
Born at Windsor.—*I Henry VI,* iii, 1, 199.

1 Nurse: She is deliver'd, lords; she is deliver'd.
Aaron: To whom?
Nurse: I mean, she is brought a-bed.
Titus Andronicus. Act iv, sc. 2, l. 61.

And from that womb where you imprison'd were
He is enfranchised and come to light.
Titus Andronicus. Act iv, sc. 2, l. 124. [Aaron]

His wife but yesternight was brought to bed.
Titus Andronicus. Act iv, sc. 2, l. 153. [Aaron]

Emilia: She is something before her time deliver'd.
Paulina: A boy?
Emilia: A daughter, and a goodly babe,
Lusty and like to live: the queen receives
Much comfort in 't.
The Winter's Tale. Act ii, sc. 2, l. 25.

There shall not at your father's house these seven years
Be born another such.
Winter's Tale. Act iv, sc. 4, l. 588. [Camillo]

2 Would thou hadst ne'er been born!
Troilus and Cressida. Act iv, sc. 2, l. 89. [Pandarus]

Would thou hadst ne'er been born!
Othello. Act iv, sc. 2, l. 69. [Othello]

BITTERNESS

See also Gall

3 The bitterness of it I now belch from my heart.
Cymbeline. Act iii, sc. 5, l. 137. [Cloten]

4 The bitterness of your galls.
II Henry IV. Act i, sc. 2, l. 198. [Falstaff] For full quotation, see under AGE AND YOUTH.

Bitterness of absence.—*Sonnets,* lvii.
Bitterness of soul.—*Richard III,* i, 3, 179.

5 This bitter taste.
II Henry IV. Act iv, sc. 5, l. 79. [King]

How tastes it? is it bitter?
Henry VIII. Act ii, sc. 3, l. 89. [Old Lady]

6 Weed this wormwood from your fruitful brain.
Love's Labour 's Lost. Act v, sc. 2, l. 857. [Rosaline]

Bitter wormwood.—*Rape of Lucrece,* l. 893.
Wormwood, wormwood.—*Hamlet,* iii, 2, 191. "Wormwood" is also used twice in *Romeo and Juliet,* i, 3, 26; 30.

7 Do not be so bitter with me.
A Midsummer-Night's Dream. Act iii, sc. 2, l. 306. [Helena]

Paris: You are too bitter to your countrywoman.
Diomedes: She 's bitter to her country.
Troilus and Cressida. Act iv, sc. 1, l. 67.

8 What 's to come of my despised time
Is nought but bitterness.
Othello. Act i, sc. 1, l. 162. [Brabantio]

Bitter as coloquintida.—*Othello,* i, 3, 355. See under FOOD for full quotation. The only use of "coloquintida" (the colocynth or bitter apple).

No bitterness that I will bitter think.
Sonnets. No. cxi.

BLACKNESS

9 Think on me,
That am with Phœbus' amorous pinches black,
And wrinkled deep in time.
Antony and Cleopatra. Act i, sc. 5, l. 27. [Cleopatra]

The shadow'd livery of the burnish'd sun.
The Merchant of Venice, ii, 1, 2. See under COMPLEXION.

10 He, my lady,
Hath into monstrous habits put the graces
That once were his, and is become as black
As if besmear'd in hell.
Henry VIII. Act i, sc. 2, l. 121. [King Henry]

Black, fearful, comfortless and horrible.
King John, v, 6, 20. See under NEWS.

Black and damned.—*A Lover's Complaint,* l. 54.
Black and fearful.—*All 's Well that Ends Well,* iii, 1, 5.
Black and grim.—*Venus and Adonis,* l. 920.
Black and portentous.—*Romeo and Juliet,* i, 1, 147.
Black and swart.—*I Henry VI,* i, 2, 84.
Black and tragical.—*Richard III,* iv, 4, 7.
Begrimed and black.—*Othello,* iii, 3, 387.
Black in my mind.—*Twelfth Night,* iii, 4, 28.
Black of hue.—*A Midsummer-Night's Dream,* iii, 1, 128.
Hue so black!—*A Midsummer-Night's Dream,* v, 1, 171.

11 King: By heaven, thy love is black as ebony.
Biron: Is ebony like her? O wood divine!
A wife of such wood were felicity.
O, who can give an oath? where is a book?
That I may swear beauty doth beauty lack,

If that she learn not of her eyes to look:
No face is fair that is not full so black.
King: O paradox! Black is the badge of hell,
The hue of dungeons and the suit of night. . . .
Biron: O, if in black my lady's brows be deck'd,
It mourns that painting and usurping hair
Should ravish doters with a false aspect;
And therefore is she born to make black fair.
Her favour turns the fashion of the days,
For native blood is counted painting now;
And therefore red, that would avoid dispraise,
Paints itself black to imitate her brow.
Dumain: To look like her are chimney-sweepers black.
Longaville: And since her time are colliers counted bright.
King: And Ethiopes of their sweet complexion crack. . . .
I 'll find a fairer face not wash'd to-day.

Love's Labour 's Lost. Act iv, sc. 3, l. 247. The only use of "doters." "Chimney-sweepers" is repeated in *Cymbeline,* iv, 2, 263, and "ebony" in *Twelfth Night,* iv, 2, 42: "Lustrous as ebony."

'Tis not your inky brows, your black silk hair,
Your bugle eyeballs, nor your cheek of cream,
That can entame my spirits to your worship.

As You Like It. Act iii, sc. 5, l. 46. [Rosalind] The only use of "entame."

If she be black, and thereto have a wit,
She 'll find a white that shall her blackness fit.

Othello. Act ii, sc. 1, l. 133. [Iago]

1
In black mourn I.

The Passionate Pilgrim, l. 263.

Mourning black.—*The Rape of Lucrece,* l. 1585. See under MOURNING.

All in black.—*Romeo and Juliet,* iii, 2, 11.

Solemn black.—*Hamlet,* i, 2, 78.

2
In the old age black was not counted fair,
Or if it were, it bore not beauty's name;
But now is black beauty's successive heir,
And beauty slander'd with a bastard shame.

Sonnets. No. cxxvii.

Thinking on thy face, . . .
Thy black is fairest in my judgement's place.
In nothing art thou black save in thy deeds,
And thence this slander, as I think, proceeds.

Sonnets. No. cxxxi.

3
'Zounds, ye whore! is black so base a hue?

Titus Andronicus. Act iv, sc. 2, l. 71. [Aaron]

Ye white-limed walls! ye alehouse painted signs!
Coal-black is better than another hue,
In that it scorns to bear another hue.

Titus Andronicus. Act iv, sc. 2, l. 98. [Aaron] The only use of "white-limed." "Coal-black" occurs six times in the plays and twice in the poems.

Coal-black as jet.
II Henry VI, ii, 1, 112; *Titus Andronicus,* v, 2, 50.

Black as Acheron.—*A Midsummer Night's Dream,* iii, 2, 357.

Black as death.—*Hamlet,* iii, 3, 67.

Black as hell.—*Hamlet,* iii, 2, 94; *Sonnets,* cxlvii.

Black as ink.—*The Two Gentlemen of Verona,* iii, 1, 288.

Black as Vulcan.—*Twelfth Night,* v, 1, 56. It is perhaps worth noting that Shakespeare used only one of these comparisons more than once.

Black as e'er was crow.—*The Winter's Tale,* iv, 4, 221.

4
Black men are pearls in beauteous ladies' eyes.

The Two Gentlemen of Verona. Act v, sc. 2, l. 12. [Proteus] Quoting an old proverb.

5
The raven chides blackness.

Troilus and Cressida. Act ii, sc. 3, l. 221. [Ulysses]

Raven black.—*Sonnets,* cxxvii.

Sullen black.—*Richard II,* v, 6, 48.

O'er-dyed blacks.—*The Winter's Tale,* i, 2, 132. The only use of "o'er-dyed."

BLAME

See also Reproach

6
Since you are like to see the king before me,
Commend the paper to his gracious hand,
Which I presume shall render you no blame
But rather make you thank your pains for it.

All's Well that Ends Well. Act v, sc. 1, l. 30. [Helena]

Whether I have been to blame or no, I know not.

All's Well that Ends Well. Act v, sc. 3, l. 129. [Gentleman]

My high-repented blames,
Dear sovereign, pardon to me.

All's Well that Ends Well. Act v, sc. 3, l. 36. [Bertram] The only use of "high-repented."

7
Phebe: If this be so, why blame you me to love you?
Silvius: If this be so, why blame you me to love you?
Orlando: If this be so, why blame you me to love you?
Rosalind: Who do you speak to, 'Why blame you me to love you?'
Orlando: To her that is not here, nor doth her hear.
Rosalind: Pray you, no more of this; 'tis like the howling of Irish wolves against the moon.

As You Like It. Act v, sc. 2, l. 109.

8
Some men are much to blame.

Cymbeline. Act i, sc. 6, l. 77. [Iachimo]

I feel me much to blame.—*II Henry IV,* ii, 4, 390.

I am much to blame.—*Othello,* iii, 3, 211.

I am to blame.—*Othello,* iii, 3, 282.

You are to blame, my lord, to rate her so.
Romeo and Juliet. Act iii, sc. 5, l. 170. [Nurse]

In sooth, you are to blame.—*Othello,* iii, 4, 97; *Henry VIII,* iv, 2, 101.

'Tis much to blame.—*Timon of Athens,* i, 2, 27.

We are oft to blame in this.—*Hamlet,* iii, 1, 46.

By cock, they are to blame.—*Hamlet,* iv, 5, 62.

Full of blame.—*Sonnets,* 129, 3.

Truly, the more to blame he.—*The Merchant of Venice,* iii, 5, 23; *The Rope of Lucrece,* l. 1278.

Worthy blame.—*III Henry VI,* v, 5, 54.

Mickle blame.—*The Comedy of Errors,* iii, 1, 45.

Ever-during blame.—*Rape of Lucrece,* 224.
The only use of "ever-during."

1
Nay, then I cannot blame this cousin king,
That wish'd him on the barren mountains starve.
I Henry IV. Act i, sc. 3, l. 158. [Hotspur]

I cannot blame them all: what is 't to them?
'Tis thine they give away, and not their own.
II Henry VI. Act i, sc. 1, l. 220. [York]

I cannot blame her.—*Richard III,* i, 3, 306.

I cannot blame thee.—*The Taming of the Shrew,* iii, 2, 27; *The Tempest,* iii, 3, 4.

Clears her from all blame.—*King Lear,* ii, 4, 147.

2
Yet in this one thing let me blame your grace,
For choosing me when Clarence is in place.
III Henry VI. Act iv, sc. 6, l. 30. [Warwick]

You were to blame, I must be plain with you.
Merchant of Venice, v, 1, 166. [Portia]

I am to blame to be thus waited for.
Julius Cæsar. Act ii, sc. 2, l. 119. [Cæsar]

3 For even now I . . .
Unspeak mine own detraction, here abjure
The taints and blames I laid upon myself,
For strangers to my nature.
Macbeth. Act iv, sc. 3, l. 121. [Malcolm]
The only use of "unspeak."

4
If she confess that she was half the wooer,
Destruction on my head, if my bad blame
Light on the man!
Othello Act i, sc. 3, l. 176. [Brabantio]

5
The king my uncle is to blame for this.
Richard III. Act ii, sc. 2, l. 13. [Boy]

I 'll bear thy blame
And take thy office from thee, on my peril.
Richard III. Act iv, sc. 1, l. 25. [Anne]

6 Ingeniously I speak
No blame belongs to thee.
Timon of Athens. Act ii, sc. 2, l. 230. [Timon] The only use of "ingeniously."

Who is 't can blame him?—*Coriolanus,* iv, 6, 105.

No blame be to you, sir.—*Cymbeline,* v, 3, 3.

Blame him not.—*I Henry VI,* iv, 1, 178.

Blame me not.—*III Henry VI,* ii, 1, 157.

I blame not her.—*III Henry VI,* iv, 1, 101.

Poor knave, I blame thee not.—*Julius Cæsar,* iv, 3, 241.

Canst thou blame him?—*King Lear,* iii, 4, 167:

Blame us not.—*King Lear,* iv, 6, 264.

Who let us not therefore blame.—*Othello,* ii, 3, 16.

Lay not your blame on me.—*Othello,* iv, 2, 46.

Let nobody blame him.—*Othello,* iv, 3, 52.

Alas, I blame you not.—*Richard III,* i, 2, 44; *Henry V,* iv, 6, 32; *Cymbeline,* v, 5, 267.

O, blame me not.—*Sonnets,* 103, 5.

BLASPHEMY

7
Blaspheming God and cursing men on earth.
II Henry VI. Act iii, sc. 2, l. 372. [Vaux]

I would speak blasphemy ere bid you fly.
II Henry VI. Act v, sc. 2, l. 85. [Young Clifford]

Flat blasphemy.—*Measure for Measure,* ii, 2, 131.

8
Brother of England, you blaspheme in this.
King John. Act iii, sc. 1, l. 161. [King Philip]

You do blaspheme the good in mocking me.
Measure for Measure. Act i, sc. 4, l. 38. [Isabella]

Stands accursed And does blaspheme his breed.
Macbeth. Act iv, sc. 3, l. 108. [Macduff]

9 Now, blasphemy,
That swear'st grace o'erboard.
The Tempest. Act v, sc. 1, l. 218. [Gonzalo]

BLEMISH, see Fault

BLESSING

10 I 'll stay at home
And pray God's blessing into thy attempt.
All's Well that Ends Well. Act i, sc. 3, l. 259. [Countess]

Blessing of God.—*All's Well that Ends Well,* i, 3, 27.

God bless you, see under GOD.

Bless him at home in peace.
All's Well that Ends Well. Act iii, sc. 4, l. 10. [Steward]

11
Let all the number of the stars give light
To thy fair way!
Antony and Cleopatra. Act iii, sc. 2, l. 65. [Lepidus]

12
It is said, 'many a man knows no end of his goods.'
As You Like It. Act iii, sc. 3, l. 52. [Touchstone]

13
Be blest For making up this peace!
Coriolanus. Act v, sc. 3, l. 139. [Volumnia]

Let me be blest to make this happy close.
The Two Gentlemen of Verona. Act v, sc. 4, l. 117. [Valentine]

Be blest!—*As You Like It,* ii, 7, 135; *The Winter's Tale,* v, 1, 71.

Be thou blest!—*All's Well that Ends Well,* i, 1, 70.

Be you blest!—*The Winter's Tale,* ii, 2, 54.

Blest pray you be!—*Cymbeline,* v, 5, 370.

Evermore be blest!—*The Merry Wives of Windsor,* v, 5, 68.

How blest am I!—*The Winter's Tale,* ii, 1, 36.

I am blest.—*The Merry Wives of Windsor,* ii, 2, 279.

We are blest.—*Julius Cæsar*, iii, 2, 75; *The Winter's Tale*, iv, 4, 58.
We shall be blest.—*King John*, iii, 1, 251; *Coriolanus*, ii, 2, 62.
O blest!—*Cymbeline*, i, 1, 139.
O stand up blest!—*Coriolanus*, v, 3, 52.
Blest and free.—*Timon of Athens*, iv, 3, 542.
Blest, and mine own!—*Pericles*, v, 3, 48.
Twice blest.—*Merchant of Venice*, iv, 1, 186.

1 Blest be those,
How mean soe'er, that have their honest wills.
Cymbeline. Act i, sc. 6, l. 7. [Imogen]
May the gods Direct you to the best!
Cymbeline. Act iii, sc. 4, l. 195. [Pisanio]
Flow, flow, You heavenly blessings, on her!
Cymbeline. Act iii, sc. 5, l. 167. [Pisanio]
The dews of heaven fall thick as blessings on her!
Henry VIII. Act iv, sc. 2, l. 133. [Katharine]
Heaven bless you, see under HEAVEN.

2
A double blessing is a double grace.
Hamlet. Act i, sc. 3, l. 53. [Laertes]
My blessing season this in thee!
Hamlet. Act i, sc. 3, l. 81. [Polonius]
And when you are desirous to be bless'd,
I'll blessing beg of you.
Hamlet. Act iii, sc. 4, l. 171. [Hamlet]

3
The heavens thee guard and keep, most royal imp of fame!
II Henry IV. Act v, sc. 5, l. 45. [Pistol]
Now, the Lord bless that sweet face of thine!
II Henry IV. Act ii, sc. 4, l. 316. [Hostess]
The Lord bless you! God prosper your affairs!
II Henry IV, Act iii, sc. 2, l. 312. [Shallow]
The Lord in heaven bless thee, noble Harry!
Henry V. Act iv, sc. 1, l. 33. [Erpingham]
O Lord bless me! I pray God!
II Henry VI. Act ii, sc. 3, l. 77. [Peter]
Jesus bless us!—*III Henry VI*, v, 6, 75.

4
Kneel down and take my blessing, good my girl.
I Henry VI. Act v, sc. 4, l. 25. [Shepherd]
Give me your blessing.—*The Merchant of Venice*, ii, 2, 83; ii, 2, 89.

5 Blessings on him; may he live
Longer than I have time to tell his years!
Henry VIII. Act ii, sc. 1, l. 90. [Buckingham]
From her Will fall some blessing to this land.
Henry VIII. Act iii, sc. 2, l. 50. [Suffolk]
Upon this land a thousand thousand blessings.
Henry VIII. Act v, sc. 5, l. 20. [Cranmer]

6
My blessing go with thee!
King John. Act iii, sc. 3, l. 71. [Elinor]
My blessing with thee!—*Hamlet*, i, 3, 57.

7
Good king, that must approve the common saw,
Thou out of heaven's benediction comest
To the warm sun!
King Lear. Act ii, sc. 2, l. 167. [Kent] "Out of Christ's blessing into the warm sun" was used by John Palsgrave (*Acolastus*, sig. H3), in 1540. It refers to the haste of the congregation to leave the church after the benediction has been pronounced, and is equivalent of "from better to worse."
Hold your hands in benediction o'er me.
King Lear. Act iv, sc. 7, l. 58. [Cordelia]
The benediction of these covering heavens
Fall on their heads like dew!
Cymbeline. Act v, sc. 5, l. 350. [Belarius]
Brought a benediction.—*The Winter's Tale*, iv, 4, 614.
Healing benediction.—*Macbeth*, iv, 3, 156.
Stripped her from his benediction.—*King Lear*, iv, 3, 45. The only uses of "benediction."

8
Good nuncle, in, and ask thy daughters' blessing.
King Lear. Act iii, sc. 2, l. 12. [Fool]
I ask'd his blessing.—*King Lear*, v, 3, 195.

9
Bless thee from whirlwinds, star-blasting, and taking!
King Lear. Act iii, sc. 4, l. 60. [Edgar] The only use of "star-blasting."

10
The bounty and the benison of heaven
To boot, and boot!
King Lear. Act iv, sc. 6, l. 229. [Gloucester]
God's benison go with you.—*Macbeth*, ii, 4, 40.
I give my benison.—*Pericles*, ii, Gower, 10.
Without . . . our benison.—*King Lear*, i, 1, 268. The only uses of "benison."

11
I had most need of blessing, and 'Amen'
Stuck in my throat.
Macbeth. Act ii, sc. 2, l. 32. [Macbeth]

12
Grace go with you, Benedicite!
Measure for Measure. Act ii, sc. 3, l. 39. [Duke] "Benedicite" is used once again in *Romeo and Juliet*, ii, 3, 31.
Bliss and goodness on you!
Measure for Measure. Act iii, sc. 2, l. 228. [Duke]
Bliss be upon you!—*Romeo and Juliet*, v, 3, 124.

13
Blessed be your royal grace!
Measure for Measure. Act v, sc. 1, l. 137. [Friar Peter]
Blessed live you long!
Cymbeline. Act i, sc. 6, l. 159. [Iachimo]
Blessed are you.—*Sonnets*, lii.
Blessing on thee!—*Pericles*, v, 1, 215.
Blessing upon you!—*Macbeth*, iv, 2, 26.
Blessing on your heart.—*The Merry Wives of Windsor*, ii, 2, 112; iv, 1, 13.
God's blessing of your good heart!
II Henry IV. Act ii, sc. 4, l. 329. [Hostess]
Blessing of your heart.—*The Two Gentlemen of Verona*, iii, 1, 306.
A pack of blessings lights upon thy back.
Romeo and Juliet. Act iii, sc. 3, l. 141. [Friar Laurence]
Bless you, sir!—*The Merry Wives of Windsor*, ii, 2, 160; iii, 5, 61.
Bless thee, bully doctor!—*The Merry Wives of Windsor*, ii, 3, 18.
Bless thee, Bottom! bless thee!—*A Midsummer-Night's Dream*, iii, 1, 121.
Bless you, my fortunate lady.—*All's Well that Ends Well*, ii, 4, 14.

1
I feel too much thy blessing: make it less.
The Merchant of Venice, iii, 2, 114. See LOVE: ITS MANIFESTATIONS, 902:8.

2
Hand in hand, with fairy grace,
Will we sing, and bless the place.
A Midsummer-Night's Dream. Act v, sc. 1, l. 406. [Titania]

And each several chamber bless,
Through this palace, with sweet peace;
And the owner of it blest
Ever shall in safety rest.
A Midsummer-Night's Dream. Act v, sc. 1, l. 424. [Oberon]

Bless it to all fair prosperity.
A Midsummer-Night's Dream. Act iv, sc. 1, l. 94. [Oberon]

3
Ye men of Cyprus, let her have your knees.
Hail to thee, lady! and the grace of heaven,
Before, behind thee and on every hand,
Enwheel thee round!
Othello. Act ii, sc. 1, l. 84. [Cassio] The only use of "enwheel."

4
With thy blessings steel my lance's point.
Richard II. Act i, sc. 3, l. 74. [Bolingbroke]

Blessing on his heart that gives it me!
For 'tis a sign of love.
Richard II. Act v, sc. 5, l. 64. [King Richard]

5
Now fair befall thee and thy noble house!
Richard III. Act i, sc. 3, l. 282. [Queen Margaret]

6
I, by attorney, bless thee from thy mother.
Richard III, v, 3, 83. See under MOTHER.

That is the butt-end of a mother's blessing.
Richard III. Act ii, sc. 2, l. 110. [Gloucester] The only use of "butt-end."

Kneel And pray your mother's blessing.
Winter's Tale. Act v, sc. 3, l. 119. [Paulina]

Humbly on my knee I crave your blessing.
Richard III. Act ii, sc. 2, l. 106. [Gloucester]

7
Steal immortal blessing from her lips.
Romeo and Juliet, iii, 3, 37. See under LIP.

Heavenly blessings.—*Henry VIII,* ii, 3, 57.

Earthly blessings.—*II Henry VI,* i, 1, 22.

8
Honour, riches, marriage-blessing,
Long continuance, and increasing,
Hourly joys be still upon you!
Juno sings her blessings on you.
The Tempest. Act iv, sc. 1, l. 106. [Juno] The only use of "marriage-blessing."

Spring come to you at the farthest
In the very end of harvest!
Scarcity and want shall shun you;
Ceres' blessing so is on you.
The Tempest. Act iv, sc. 1, l. 114. [Ceres]

Now all the blessings
Of a glad father compass thee about!
The Tempest. Act v, sc. 1, l. 179. [Alonso]

Look down, you gods,
And on this couple drop a blessed crown!
The Tempest. Act v, sc. 1, l. 201. [Gonzalo]

Heavens rain grace
On that which breeds between 'em!
The Tempest. Act iii, sc. 1, l. 75. [Prospero]

9
The best of happiness,
Honour and fortunes, keep with you.
Timon of Athens. Act i, sc. 2, l. 234. [Lord]

The gentleness of all the gods go with thee!
Twelfth Night. Act ii, sc. 1, l. 45. [Antonio]

10
Tell me what blessings I have here alive,
That I should fear to die?
The Winter's Tale. Act iii, sc. 2, l. 108. [Hermione]

Now bless thyself: thou mettest with things dying, I with things new-born.
The Winter's Tale. Act iii, sc. 3, l. 116. [Shepherd] The only use of "mettest." "Met'st" occurs in *Antony and Cleopatra,* i, 5, 61.

We are blest in this man, as I may say, even blest.
The Winter's Tale. Act iv, sc. 4, l. 857. [Clown]

You gods, look down
And from your sacred vials pour your graces
Upon my daughter's head!
The Winter's Tale. Act v, sc. 3, l. 121. [Hermione]

BLINDNESS

11
Forsooth, a blind man at Saint Alban's shrine,
Within this half hour, hath received his sight;
A man that ne'er saw in his life before.
II Henry VI. Act ii, sc. 1, l. 63. [Townsman]

Gloucester: What, hast thou been long blind and now restored?
Simpcox: Born blind, an 't please your grace.
II Henry VI. Act ii, sc. 1, l. 76.

12
Blind with weeping.
II Henry VI, iii, 2, 62; *Richard III,* i, 2, 67.

Blind with tears.
Titus Andronicus, iii, 1, 270; v, 3, 49.

13
'Tis the times' plague, when madmen lead the blind.
King Lear. Act iv, sc. 1, l. 48. [Gloucester]

14
Met I my father with his bleeding rings,
Their precious stones new lost.
King Lear. Act v, sc. 3, l. 189. [Edgar]

Sightless eyes.—*Sonnets,* xliii.

Sightless view.—*Sonnets,* xxvii.

15
Strucken blind,
Kisses the base ground with obedient breast.
Love's Labour 's Lost. Act iv, sc. 3, l. 224. [Biron]

He that is strucken blind cannot forget
The precious treasure of his eyesight lost.
Romeo and Juliet. Act i, sc. 1, l. 238. [Romeo]

16
Blind they are, and keep themselves enclosed.
The Rape of Lucrece, l. 378.

More than sand-blind, high-gravel blind.
The Merchant of Venice. Act ii, sc. 2, l. 37. [Launcelot] The only use of "high-gravel." "Sand-blind" (half-blind) occurs again in the same scene, l. 77, and nowhere else.

"High-gravel blind" is a jocular intensive of "sand-blind."

Nay, then he should be blind; and, being blind,
How could he see his way?

The Two Gentlemen of Verona. Act ii, sc. 4, l. 93. [Silvia]

1 Lower messes
Perchance are to this business purblind? say.

The Winter's Tale. Act i, sc. 2, l. 227. [Leontes]

Purblind Argus, all eyes and no sight.

Troilus and Cressida. Act i, sc. 2, l. 30. [Alexander]

Purblind boy.—*Love's Labour's Lost,* iii, 1, 181.

Purblind eye.—*I Henry VI,* ii, 4, 21.

Purblind son.—*Romeo and Juliet,* ii, 1, 12. The only uses of "purblind."

BLISS, see Joy

BLOOD

See also Flesh and Blood

2 Strange is it that our bloods,
Of colour, weight and heat, pour'd all together,
Would quite confound distinction, yet stand off
In differences so mighty.

All's Well that Ends Well. Act ii, sc. 3, l. 125. [King]

There is more difference . . . between your bloods than there is between red wine and rhenish.

The Merchant of Venice. Act iii, sc. 1, l. 41. [Salarino] For "rhenish" see under WINE.

3
Now his important blood will nought deny
That she'll demand.

All's Well that Ends Well. Act iii, sc. 7, l. 21. [Helena]

4
Many will swoon when they do look on blood.

As You Like It. Act iv, sc. 3, l. 159. [Oliver]

Scarce ever look'd on blood,
But that of coward hares, hot goats, and venison!

Cymbeline. Act iv, sc. 4, l. 36. [Arviragus]

5
His bloody brow! O Jupiter, no blood!

Coriolanus. Act i, sc. 3, l. 41. [Virgilia]

The blood I drop is rather physical
Than dangerous to me.

Coriolanus. Act i, sc. 5, l. 19. [Marcius]

'Tis not my blood
Wherein thou seest me mask'd.

Coriolanus. Act i, sc. 8, l. 9. [Marcius]

The blood upon your visage dries; 'tis time
It should be look'd to.

Coriolanus. Act i, sc. 9, l. 93. [Cominius]

6
From face to foot He was a thing of blood.

Coriolanus, ii, 2, 113. See under MOTION.

Head to foot
Now is he total gules; horridly trick'd
With blood of fathers, mothers, daughters, sons,
Baked and impasted with the parching streets,
That lend a tyrannous and damned light
To their lord's murder.

Hamlet. Act ii, sc. 2, l. 478. [Hamlet] The only use of "impasted."

With man's blood paint the ground, gules, gules.

Timon of Athens, iv, 3, 59. See under WAR. The only uses of "gules," the heraldic name for red.

King Henry: From helmet to the spur all blood he was.
Exeter: In which array, brave soldier, doth he lie,
Larding the plain.

Henry V. Act iv, sc. 6, l. 6.

Their hands and faces were all badged with blood.

Macbeth. Act ii, sc. 3, l. 107. [Lennox] The only use of "badged."

There's blood upon thy face.

Macbeth. Act iii, sc. 4, l. 13 [Macbeth]

O blood-bespotted Neapolitan.

II Henry VI. Act v, sc. 1, l. 117. [York] The only use of "blood-bespotted."

The blood-bolter'd Banquo smiles upon me.

Macbeth. Act iv, sc. 1, l. 122. [Macbeth] The only use of "blood-bolter'd" (having the hair matted with blood).

Dabbled in blood.—*Richard III,* i, 4, 54. The only use of "dabbled."

All bedaub'd in blood, All in gore-blood.

Romeo and Juliet. Act iii, sc. 2, l. 55. [Nurse] The only use of "gore-blood."

7 Our bloods
No more obey the heavens than our courtiers
Still seem as does the king.

Cymbeline. Act i, sc. 1, l. 1. [Gentleman]

8
Give colour to my pale cheek with thy blood,
That we the horrider may seem to those
Which chance to find us.

Cymbeline. Act iv, sc. 2, l. 330. [Imogen] The only use of "horrider."

9 O the blood more stirs
To rouse a lion than to start a hare.

I Henry IV. Act i, sc. 3, l. 197. [Hotspur]

Stir men's blood.—*Julius Cæsar,* iii, 2, 227.

10 The tide of blood in me
Hath proudly flow'd in vanity till now:
Now doth it turn and ebb back to the sea,
Where it shall mingle with the state of floods
And flow henceforth in formal majesty.

II Henry IV. Act v, sc. 2, l. 129. [King Henry V]

11
For never two such kingdoms did contend
Without much fall of blood; whose guiltless drops
Are every one a woe, a sore complaint
'Gainst him whose wrongs give edge unto the swords
That make such waste in brief mortality.

Henry V. Act i, sc. 2, l. 24. [King Henry]

Stain'd with the guiltless blood of innocents.

I Henry VI. Act v, sc. 4, l. 44. [La Pucelle]

We give thee up our guiltless blood to drink.

Richard III. Act iii, sc. 3, l. 14. [Rivers]

My guiltless blood must cry against 'em.
Henry VIII. Act ii, sc. 1, l. 68. [Buckingham]

Guiltless blood-shedding.—*II Henry VI*, iv, 7, 108. The only use of "blood-shedding."

1 Stiffen the sinews, summon up the blood.
Henry V. Act iii, sc. 1, l. 7. [King Henry]

2 Scarce blood enough in all their sickly veins
To give each naked curtle-axe a stain.
Henry V. Act iv, sc. 2, l. 20. [Constable] "Curtle-axe" (cutlass) is repeated in *As You Like It*, i, 3, 119.

For Andrew, if he were opened, and you find so much blood in his liver as will clog the foot of a flea, I 'll eat the rest of the anatomy.
Twelfth Night. Act iii, sc. 2, l. 65. [Sir Toby]

3 We shall your tawny ground with your red blood
Discolour.
Henry V. Act iii, sc. 6, l. 170. [King Henry] "Red blood" occurs also in *Julius Cæsar*, v, 3, 61; *The Winter's Tale*, iv, 3, 4; and *The Rape of Lucrece*, l. 1377, and l. 1437.

Drown'd and soak'd in mercenary blood.
Henry V. Act iv, sc. 7, l. 79. [Montjoy] The only use of "soak'd."

Stain'd
With heart-blood of the house of Lancaster.
I Henry VI. Act ii, sc. 3, l. 65. [York]

Thy heart-blood I will have for this day's work.
I Henry VI, i, 3, 83. See under THREAT.

No balm can cure but his heart-blood.
Richard II, i, 1, 172. See under SLANDER.

I . . . will maintain what thou hast said is false
In thy heart-blood.
Richard II, iv, 1, 28. See under LIE.

In my heart-blood warm'd.—*Richard II*, iii, 2, 131.

Dearest heart-blood.—*III Henry VI*, i, 1, 223.

Heart-blood of beauty.—*Troilus and Cressida*, iii, 1, 34. The only uses of "heart-blood."

4 The world will say, he is not Talbot's blood,
That basely fled when noble Talbot stood.
I Henry VI. Act iv, sc. 5, l. 16. [John Talbot]

5 Contaminated, base
And misbegotten blood I spill of thine,
Mean and right poor, for that pure blood of mine.
I Henry VI. Act iv, sc. 6, l. 21. [Talbot] "Pure blood" is repeated in *Julius Cæsar*, ii, 2, 78.

False blood to false blood join'd!
King John. Act iii, sc. 1, l. 2. [Constance]

O false blood, thou register of lies,
What unapproved witness dost thou bear!
Ink would have seem'd more black and damned here!
A Lover's Complaint, l. 52. The only use of "unapproved."

False bloods!—*Timon of Athens*, iv, 3, 539.

Distemper'd blood.—*Troilus and Cressida*, ii, 2, 169.

Diverted blood.—*As You Like It*, ii, 3, 37.

Drowsy blood.—*Troilus and Cressida*, v, 5, 32.

Foul-defiled blood.—*The Rape of Lucrece*, l. 1029. The only use of "foul-defiled."

Grosser blood.—*Henry V*, iii, 1, 24.

Stained blood.—*The Rape of Lucrece*, l. 1181.

Unreprievable condemned blood.—*King John*, v, 7, 48. The only use of "unreprievable."

Usurping blood.—*III Henry VI*, i, 1, 169.

Wretched blood.—*The Rape of Lucrece*, l. 999.

Blood ill-temper'd.—*Julius Cæsar*, iv, 3, 115. "Ill-temper'd" is repeated in l. 116, and occurs nowhere else.

6 In that sea of blood my boy did drench
His over-mounting spirit.
I Henry VI. Act iv, sc. 7, l. 14. [Talbot] The only use of "sea of blood," and "over-mounting."

7 He is the next of blood, And heir apparent.
II Henry VI, i, 1, 151. See under HEIR.

Thou art the next of blood.
Venus and Adonis, l. 1184.

Next of blood.—*II Henry VI*, i, 2, 63.

The near in blood, The nearer bloody.
Macbeth. Act ii, sc. 3, l. 146. [Donalbain]

8 See how the blood is settled in his face.
II Henry VI. Act iii, sc. 2, l. 160. [Warwick]

Behold his blood.—*III Henry VI*, i, 1, 13.

9 By the best blood that ever was broached.
II Henry VI, iv, 10, 39. See BEARD, 73:10.

Stain With the best blood.
I Henry IV, v, 2, 95. See under SWORD.

The best blood chamber'd in his bosom.
Richard II. Act i, sc. 1, l. 149. [Mowbray] The only use of "chamber'd."

O, then my best blood turn
To an infected jelly!
The Winter's Tale. Act i, sc. 2, l. 417. [Polixenes] The only uses of "best blood."

10 This thy son's blood cleaving to my blade
Shall rust upon my weapon, till thy blood
Congeal'd with this, do make me wipe off both.
III Henry VI. Act i, sc. 3, l. 50. [Clifford]

Brother's blood.—*III Henry VI*, ii, 3, 15; *Richard III*, v, 5, 24; *Hamlet*, iii, 3, 44.

Children's blood.—*I Henry IV*, i, 1, 6.

Sons' sweet blood.—*Titus Andronicus*, iii, 1, 15.

Dead men's blood.—*Henry V*, ii, 4, 107.

Lust's blood.—*Othello*, v, 1, 36.

Noble's blood.—*Henry VIII*, i, 1, 123.

Princes' bloods.—*Pericles*, i, 2, 88.

Baboon's blood.—*Macbeth*, iv, 1, 37.

Eagles' blood.—*II Henry VI*, iv, 1, 109.

Horses' blood.—*Henry V*, iv, 2, 12.

Sow's blood.—*Macbeth*, iv, 1, 64.

Clotens blood.—*Cymbeline*, iv, 2, 168.

Pompey's blood.—*Julius Cæsar*, i, 1, 56.

11 How couldst thou drain the life-blood of the child,
To bid the father wipe his eyes withal?
III Henry VI. Act i, sc. 4, l. 138. [York]

Draw life-blood from my heart.—*I Henry VI*, iv, 6, 43.

Issuing life-blood.—*The Merchant of Venice*, iii, 2, 269.

Thy life-blood out.—*Titus Andronicus,* iv, 4, 37.
The life-blood of thee.—*Henry VIII,* iii, 2, 277.
Life-blood of our enterprise.—*I Henry IV,* iv, 1, 29. The only uses of "life-blood."

1
In vain thou speak'st, poor boy; my father's blood
Hath stopp'd the passage where they words should enter.
Rutland: Then let my father's blood open it again.
III Henry VI. Act i, sc. 3, l. 21.

2 I stain'd this napkin with the blood
That valiant Clifford, with his rapier's point,
Made issue from the bosom of the boy.
III Henry VI. Act i, sc. 4, l. 79. [Queen Margaret]

Stain'd with blood.—*III Henry VI,* i, 5, 153; *A Midsummer-Night's Dream,* v, 1, 288.
This cloth thou dip'dst in blood of my sweet boy.
III Henry VI, i, 4, 157. See under TEAR. "Dip'dst" was, wisely, used only once.

3
My blood upon your heads!
III Henry VI. Act i, sc. 4, l. 168. [York]
Their blood upon thy head.
III Henry VI. Act ii, sc. 2, l. 129. [Warwick]

4
Thy brother's blood the thirsty earth hath drunk
Broach'd with the steely point of Clifford's lance.
III Henry VI. Act ii, sc. 3, l. 15. [Richard] "Steely" is repeated in *All's Well that Ends Well,* i, 1, 114.
Then let the earth be drunken with our blood.
III Henry VI. Act ii, sc. 3, l. 23. [Warwick]

5
Tied by blood and favour to her.
Henry VIII. Act ii, sc. 2, l. 90. [Wolsey]

6 Be not fond,
To think that Cæsar bears such rebel blood
That will be thaw'd from the true quality
With that which melteth fools.
Julius Cæsar. Act iii, sc. 1, l. 39. [Cæsar]
Rebels' blood.—*II Henry IV,* Ind., 27.
And as he pluck'd his cursed steel away,
Mark how the blood of Cæsar follow'd it.
Julius Cæsar. Act iii, sc. 2, l. 181. [Antony]

7
And let us bathe our hands in Cæsar's blood
Up to the elbows.
Julius Cæsar. Act iii, sc. 1, l. 106. [Brutus]
Dip their napkins in his sacred blood.
Julius Cæsar. Act iii, sc. 2, l. 138. [Antony] "Sacred blood" occurs also in *Richard II,* i, 2, 12, and 17.
Wash their hands in Bassianus' blood.
Titus Andronicus. Act ii, sc. 3, l. 45. [Aaron]
To wash your blood
From off my hands, here in the view of men
I will unfold some causes of your deaths.
Richard II. Act iii, sc. 1, l. 5. [Bolingbroke]
Scarce the blood was well wash'd from his hands
Which issued from my other angel husband.
Richard III. Act iv, sc. 1, l. 68. [Anne]

Issuing blood.—*III Henry VI,* ii, 6, 82.

8 We shall repent each drop of blood
That hot rash haste so indirectly shed.
King John. Act ii, sc. 1, l. 48. [Constance]
An Ate, stirring him to blood and strife.
King John. Act ii, sc. 1, l. 63. [Chatillon] Ate, the goddess of evil, is mentioned four times.
Blood and death!—*III Henry VI,* ii, 1, 127; *King John,* ii, 1, 360; *Macbeth,* v, 6, 10; *Titus Andronicus,* ii, 3, 216.
Blood and destruction.—*Julius Cæsar,* iii, 1, 265.
Blood and life.—*Antony and Cleopatra,* i, 2, 197.

9
Living blood doth in these temples beat.
King John, ii, 1, 108. See under KING.
Living blood.—*Richard II,* iii, 1, 26.

10
Whose veins bound richer blood than Lady Blanch?
King John, ii, 1, 431. See LOVE, 906:4.

11
And baked thy blood and made it heavy thick,
Which else runs tickling up and down the veins.
King John. Act iii, sc. 3, l. 43. [King John]
Curd thy blood.—*All's Well that Ends Well,* i, 3, 155. The only use of the phrase.
Thick my blood.—*Macbeth,* i, 5, 44; *The Winter's Tale,* i, 2, 171.

12
For he that steeps his safety in true blood
Shall find but bloody safety and untrue.
King John. Act iii, sc. 4, l. 147. [Pandulph]
Be satisfied, dear God, with our true blood,
Which, as thou know'st, unjustly must be spilt.
Richard III. Act iii, sc. 3, l. 21. [Lord Rivers] "True blood" is used a third time in *The Winter's Tale,* iv, 4, 148.

13
That blood which owed the breadth of all this isle,
Three foot of it doth hold.
King John, iv, 2, 99. See under GRAVE.

14
There is no sure foundation set on blood,
No certain life achieved by others' death.
King John. Act iv, sc. 2, l. 104. [King John]
Where is that blood
That I have seen inhabit in those cheeks?
King John. Act iv, sc. 2, l. 106. [King John]
Combine
The blood of malice in a vein of league,
And not to spend it so unneighbourly!
King John. Act v, sc. 2, l. 37. [Salisbury] The only use of "unneighbourly."
Blood of enemies.—*III Henry VI,* v, 7, 2.
Blood of hearts.—*Antony and Cleopatra,* v, 1, 41.
Blood of man.—*Hamlet,* i, 5, 65.
Blood of true men.—*I Henry IV,* ii, 4, 342.
Blood of princes.—*Henry V,* iv, 7, 81.
Blood of youth.—*Love's Labour's Lost,* v, 2, 73.
Blood of your begetting.—*Cymbeline,* v, 5, 331.

15 Fie, foh, and fum,
I smell the blood of a British man.
King Lear. Act iii, sc. 4, l. 188. [Edgar] The only use of "fum." "Foh" occurs nine times.

Blood of Englishmen.—*II Henry VI,* iii, 1, 311.

1
I am no less in blood that thou art, Edmund.
King Lear. Act v, sc. 3, l. 166. [Edgar]

As great in blood as I myself.
Pericles. Act ii, sc. 5, l. 80. [Simonides]

2
Native blood is counted painting now.
Love's Labour 's Lost. Act iv, sc. 3, l. 263. [Biron]

3
I am in blood
Stepp'd in so far that, should I wade no more,
Returning were as tedious as go o'er.
Macbeth. Act iii, sc. 4, l. 136. [Macbeth]

And make us wade even in our kindred's blood.
Richard II. Act i, sc. 3, l. 138. [King Richard]

Wade to the market-place in Frenchmen's blood.
King John. Act ii, sc. 1, l. 42. [King Philip]

Frenchmen's blood.—*I Henry VI,* iv, 7, 36.

O'er shoes in blood.—*A Midsummer-Night's Dream,* iii, 2, 48.

Up to the ears in blood.—*I Henry IV,* iv, 1, 117.

4
Blood will have blood.
Macbeth, iii, 4, 122. See under Retribution.

Blood, thou art blood.—*Measure for Measure,* ii, 4, 15.

From blood to blood.—*Richard III,* iii, 7, 135.

Blood against blood.—*Richard III,* ii, 4, 62.

O, blood, blood, blood!
Othello. Act iii, sc. 3, l. 451. [Othello]

5
Who would have thought the old man to have had so much blood in him.
Macbeth. Act v, sc. 1, l. 44. [Lady Macbeth]

Gouts of blood.—*Macbeth,* ii, 1, 46. The only use of "gouts."

My soul is too much charged
With blood of thine already.
Macbeth. Act v, sc. 8, l. 5. [Macbeth]

6
The resolute acting of your blood.
Measure for Measure. Act ii, sc. 1, l. 12. [Escalus]

Why does my blood thus muster to my heart,
Making both it unable for itself,
And dispossessing all my other parts
Of necessary fitness?
Measure for Measure. Act ii, sc. 4, l. 20. [Angelo] The only use of "dispossessing."

7
And let us make incision for your love,
To prove whose blood is reddest, his or mine.
The Merchant of Venice. Act ii, sc. 1, l. 6. [Morocco] The only use of "reddest."

My blood speaks to you in my veins.
The Merchant of Venice. Act iii, sc. 2, l. 178. [Bassanio]

8
Wisdom and blood combating in so tender a body, we have ten proofs to one that blood hath the victory.
Much Ado about Nothing. Act ii, sc. 3, l. 170. [Leonato]

Could she here deny
The story that is printed in her blood?
Much Ado about Nothing. Act iv, sc. 1, l. 123. [Leonato]

9
The blood is made dull with the act of sport.
Othello, ii, 1, 229. See under Lust.

My blood begins my safer guides to rule.
Othello. Act ii, sc. 3, l. 205. [Othello]

10
We 'll mingle our bloods together in the earth,
From whence we had our being and our birth.
Pericles. Act i, sc. 2, l. 113. [Helicanus]

11
My blood shall wash the slander of mine ill.
The Rape of Lucrece, l. 1207.

Her blue blood changed to black in every vein.
The Rape of Lucrece, l. 1454. The only use of "blue blood."

The crimson blood
Circles her body on every side.
The Rape of Lucrece, l. 1738.

Crimson blood.—*II Henry VI,* iii, 1, 259; *Henry V,* iv, 4, 16.

Crimson spots of blood.—*King John,* iv, 2, 253.

12
The red blood reek'd, to show the painter's strife.
The Rape of Lucrece, l. 1377. The only use of "reek'd."

To Simois' reedy banks the red blood ran.
The Rape of Lucrece, l. 1437. Simois is used twice in *The Taming of the Shrew,* iii, 1, 28 and 31: "Hic ibat Simois," from Ovid's *Heroides,* i, 33.

Some of her blood still pure and red remain'd,
And some look'd black.
The Rape of Lucrece, l. 1742.

Corrupted blood some watery token shows;
And blood untainted still doth red abide,
Blushing at that which is so putrified.
The Rape of Lucrece, l. 1748. "Putrified" is used once again in *Troilus and Cressida,* v, 8, 1: "Putrified within."

Corrupted blood.—*King Lear,* ii, 4, 28.

Corrupt blood.—*II Henry IV,* ii, 4, 320.

13
Sluiced out his innocent soul through streams of blood:
Which blood, like sacrificing Abel's, cried,
To me for justice and rough chastisement.
Richard II. Act i, sc. 1, l. 103. [Bolingbroke] "Sluiced" is repeated in *The Winter's Tale,* i, 2, 194.

14
Thy fierce hand
Hath with the king's blood stain'd the king's own land.
Richard II. Act v, sc. 5, l. 110. [King Richard]

They never prick their finger but they say, "There 's some of the king's blood spilt."
II Henry IV. Act ii, sc. 2, l. 121. [Poins]

King's blood!—*Richard III,* i, 2, 66.

Rich blood of kings.—*King John,* ii, 1, 351.

15
Thou bloodless remnant of that royal blood!
Richard III. Act i, sc. 2, l. 7. [Lady Anne] "Royal blood" is repeated seven times in later plays. For "bloodless" see under Paleness.

To royalise his blood I spilt mine own.
Richard III. Act i, sc. 3, l. 125. [Gloucester] The only use of "royalise."

Thou camest not of the blood royal, if thou darest not stand for ten shillings.
I Henry IV. Act i, sc. 2, l. 156. [Falstaff]

1
For 'tis thy presence that exhales this blood
From cold and empty veins, where no blood dwells.
Richard III. Act i, sc. 2, l. 58. [Lady Anne]

As it was won with blood, lost be it so!
Richard III. Act i, sc. 3, l. 272. [Queen Margaret]

Thy garments are not spotted with our blood.
Richard III. Act i, sc. 3, l. 283. [Queen Margaret]

Nearer in bloody thoughts, but not in blood.
Richard III. Act ii, sc. 1, l. 92. [Gloucester]

Of your very blood.—*Richard III,* iv, 4, 302.

2
A knot you are of damned blood-suckers.
Richard III. Act iii, sc. 3, l. 6. [Lord Grey] "Blood-sucker" occurs again in *II Henry VI,* iii, 2, 226.

3
Unlawfully made drunk with innocents' blood!
Richard III. Act iv, sc. 4, l. 30. [Duchess of York]

4
Civil blood makes civil hands unclean.
Romeo and Juliet, Prologue, l. 4. See also WAR: CIVIL WAR.

5 Quench the fire of your pernicious rage
With purple fountains issuing from your veins.
Romeo and Juliet. Act i, sc. 1, l. 91. [Verona]

Purple fountain.—*The Rape of Lucrece,* l. 1735.
Purple blood.—*III Henry VI,* ii, 5, 99.
Purple sap.—*Richard III,* iv, 4, 276.

6
Now, these hot days, is the mad blood stirring.
Romeo and Juliet. Act iii, sc. 1, l. 4. [Benvolio] The only use of "mad blood."

Hood my unmann'd blood, bating in my cheeks.
Romeo and Juliet. Act iii, sc. 2, l. 14. [Juliet] The only use of "bating." "Unmann'd" occurs again in *Macbeth,* iii, 4, 73.

Lusty blood.—*King John,* ii, 1, 255; ii, 1, 461.
Sportive blood.—*Sonnets.* No. cxxi.
Wanton blood.—*Romeo and Juliet,* ii, 5, 72. See BLUSHING, 115:12.

7
Romeo slew him, he slew Mercutio;
Who now the price of his dear blood doth owe?
Romeo and Juliet. Act iii, sc. 1, l. 187. [Prince]

Shed my dear blood.—*I Henry IV,* i, 3, 134.
Christ's dear blood.—*Richard III,* i, 4, 195. "Dear blood" is used a fourth time in *Richard II,* i, 3, 126.
Dearest blood.—*I Henry VI,* iii, 4, 40; *III Henry VI,* v, 1, 69.

8
Her blood is settled, and her joints are stiff.
Romeo and Juliet, iv, 5, 26. See under DEATH.

Alack, alack, what blood is this, which stains
The stony entrance of this sepulchre? . . .
Romeo! O pale! Who else? what, Paris, too?
And steep'd in blood?
Romeo and Juliet. Act v, sc. 3, l. 140. [Friar Laurence]

Steep'd in blood.—*III Henry VI,* ii, 1, 62; *Richard III,* i, 3, 178; iv, 4, 275.
Bathed in maiden blood.—*Titus Andronicus,* ii, 3, 232.

9
And that fresh blood which youngly thou bestowest
Thou mayst call thine when thou from youth convertest.
Sonnets. No. xi. "Youngly" is repeated in *Coriolanus,* ii, 3, 244.

Drops of new-shed blood
As fresh as morning dew distill'd on flowers.
Titus Andronicus. Act ii, sc. 3, l. 200. [Quintus] The only use of "new-shed."

Fresh blood.—*I Henry IV,* ii, 3, 47; *A Midsummer-Night's Dream,* iii, 2, 97.

10 Lavinia 'tween her stumps doth hold
The basin that receives your guilty blood.
Titus Andronicus. Act v, sc. 2, l. 183. [Titus] The only use of "guilty blood."

11
I'll prove this truth with my three drops of blood.
Troilus and Cressida, i, 3, 299. [Nestor]

Is your blood
So madly hot that no discourse of reason,
Nor fear of bad success in a bad cause,
Can qualify the same?
Troilus and Cressida. Act ii, sc. 2, l. 115. [Hector]

Let thy blood be thy direction till thy death!
Troilus and Cressida. Act ii, sc. 3, l. 33. [Thersites]

12
I would not wish a drop of Trojan blood
Spent more in her defence.
Troilus and Cressida. Act ii, sc. 2, l. 197. [Troilus]

For every false drop in her bawdy veins
A Grecian's life hath sunk.
Troilus and Cressida. Act iv, sc. 1, l. 69. [Diomedes]

The fall of every Phrygian stone will cost
A drop of Grecian blood.
Troilus and Cressida. Act iv, sc. 5, l. 223. [Hector]

13
Our bloods are now in calm; and, so long, health!
Troilus and Cressida. Act iv, sc. 1, l. 15. [Diomedes]

14
The obligation of our blood forbids
A gory emulation 'twixt us twain:
. . . my mother's blood
Runs on the dexter cheek, and this sinister
Bounds in my father's.
Troilus and Cressida. Act iv, sc. 5, l. 122. [Hector] The only use of "dexter."

Too little blood.—*Troilus and Cressida,* v, 1, 55.
Too much blood.—*Troilus and Cressida,* v, 1, 53.
Much blood.—*Coriolanus,* iii, 2, 61.

1
Am not I consanguineous? am I not of her blood?
Twelfth Night. Act ii, sc. 3, l. 82. [Sir Toby] The only use of "consanguineous."
Kindred blood.—*Richard II,* ii, 1, 182.

2
Right noble is his blood.
Twelfth Night. Act v, sc. 1, l. 271. [Duke]
Noble blood.—*Antony and Cleopatra,* v, 1, 26; *Julius Cæsar,* i, 2, 151; iii, 1, 156; *Richard II,* ii, 1, 240.
The princely blood flows in his cheek.
Cymbeline. Act iii, sc. 3, l. 93. [Belarius]
Aspiring blood.—*III Henry VI,* v, 6, 61.
Chaste blood.—*The Rape of Lucrece,* l. 1836.
Costly blood.—*Julius Cæsar,* iii, 1, 258.
Faultless blood.—*Richard III,* i, 3, 178.
Frail blood.—*Twelfth Night,* iii, 4, 391.
Gentle blood.—*I Henry VI,* iv, 1, 44; *Richard III,* iv, 4, 50.
Golden blood.—*Macbeth,* ii, 3, 118.
High blood.—*II Henry IV,* ii, 2, 3; *Richard II,* i, 1, 58; *Troilus and Cressida,* Prol., 2.
Honourable blood.—*II Henry VI,* iv, 1, 50.
Old blood.—*Richard II,* i, 2, 10.
Reviving blood.—*Julius Cæsar,* ii, 2, 85.
Stranger blood.—*King John,* v, 1, 11.
Stronger blood.—*The Winter's Tale,* i, 2, 73.
Subtle blood.—*Timon of Athens,* iv, 3, 432.
Sweet blood.—*Titus Andronicus,* iii, 1, 15.
Sweet bloods.—*Love's Labour's Lost,* v, 2, 714.
Well-born bloods.—*King John,* ii, 1, 278.
Wholesome blood.—*Hamlet,* i, 5, 70.

3
An image like thyself, all stain'd with gore;
Whose blood upon the fresh flowers being shed
Doth make them droop with grief and hang the head.
Venus and Adonis, l. 664.
Lay them in gore.—*Midsummer Night's Dream,* v, 1, 346.
In gore he lay insteep'd.—*Henry V,* iv, 6, 12. The only use of "insteep'd."
Streams of foreign gore.—*I Henry VI,* iii, 3, 55.
Valiant gore.—*Timon of Athens,* iii, 5, 84.
Coagulate gore.—*Hamlet,* ii, 2, 484. The only use of "coagulate."

4
No flower was nigh, no grass, herb, leaf, or weed,
But stole his blood and seem'd with him to bleed.
Venus and Adonis, l. 1055.
I'll pawn the little blood which I have left
To save the innocent.
Winter's Tale, ii, 3, 166. [Antigonus]

5
He tells her something
That makes her blood look out.
Winter's Tale. Act iv, sc. 4, l. 160. [Camillo]

II—Cold Blood

6
Cold in blood, To say as I said then!
Antony and Cleopatra, i, 5, 74. [Cleopatra]
Our blood is cold.—*Coriolanus,* v, 1, 51.
Thy blood is cold.—*Macbeth,* iii, 4, 94.
When the blood was cool.—*Cymbeline,* v, 5, 77.

7
My blood hath been too cold and temperate,
Unapt to stir at these indignities.
I Henry IV. Act i, sc. 3, l. 1. [King Henry]

8
Cold blood he did naturally inherit of his father.
II Henry IV. Act iv, sc. 3, l. 128. [Falstaff] See under Sack.
Cold blood.—*III Henry VI,* i, 1, 184; *Much Ado about Nothing,* i, 1, 131; *Timon of Athens,* iii, 5, 53.
Cold congealed blood.—*III Henry VI,* v, 2, 37.
Congeal'd your blood.—*The Taming of the Shrew,* Ind., ii, 134.

9
Where have they this mettle? . . . Can sodden water,
A drench for sur-rein'd jades, their barley-broth,
Decoct their cold blood to such valiant heat?
And shall our quick blood, spirited with wine,
Seem frosty? O, for honour of our land,
Let us not hang like roping icicles
Upon our houses' thatch, whiles a more frosty people
Sweat drops of gallant blood in our rich fields!
Henry V. Act iii, sc. 5, l. 15. [Constable] The only use of "sur-rein'd" (over-ridden), "barley-broth," "decoct," "spirited," and "roping" (hanging down like a rope). "Sodden" is repeated in *Troilus and Cressida,* iii, 1, 44: "Sodden business"; and in *Pericles,* iv, 2, 21: "Pitifully sodden."

10
A man whose blood Is very snow-broth.
Measure for Measure. Act i, sc. 4, l. 57. [Lucio] The only use of "snow-broth."
Lukewarm blood.—*III Henry VI,* i, 2, 34. "Luke-warm" (hyphenated) is repeated in *Timon of Athens,* iii, 6, 99: "Luke-warm water."

III—Hot Blood

11
Make incision in their hides,
That their hot blood may spin in English eyes.
Henry V. Act iv, sc. 2, l. 9. [Dauphin]
Hot blood.—*II Henry VI,* i, 1, 118, and six times in later plays.
Hot-blooded.—*The Merry Wives of Windsor,* v, 5, 2; *King Lear,* ii, 4, 215.

12
Thou heatest my blood.
Love's Labour's Lost. Act i, sc. 2, l. 32. [Armado]
I'll heat this blood with Greekish wine to-night,
Which with my scimitar I'll cool to-morrow.
Troilus and Cressida. Act v, sc. 1, l. 1. [Achilles]
Do not heat your blood.
Pericles. Act iv, sc. 1, l. 49. [Dionyza]
Heated bloods.—*III Henry VI,* ii, 2, 169.
Heat of blood.—*Love's Labour's Lost,* v, 2, 810; *Measure for Measure,* v, 1, 477; *I Henry IV,* v, 2, 17.

Heating of the blood.—*Venus and Adonis,* l. 742.
Fire the blood.—*Julius Cæsar,* iii, 1, 37. See under SERVILITY.
Her blood doth boil.—*Venus and Adonis,* l. 555.
Smoking blood.—*III Henry VI,* ii, 3, 21.
The hectic in my blood.—*Hamlet,* iv, 3, 68. The only use of "hectic."

1 The blood is hot that must be cool'd for this.
Richard II. Act i, sc. 1, l. 51. [Mowbray]

2 Alas, a crimson river of warm blood,
Like to a bubbling fountain stirr'd with wind,
Doth rise and fall between those rosed lips.
Titus Andronicus. Act ii, sc. 4, l. 22. [Martius] "Rosed" repeated in *Henry V,* v, 2, 323.

A man, whose blood is warm within.
The Merchant of Venice, i, 1, 83.
Warm blood.—*Richard III,* v, 2, 9; *King John,* v, 2, 59.
Warm youthful blood.—*Romeo and Juliet,* ii, 5, 12.

IV—Shedding Blood

3 By the blood we have shed together.
Coriolanus. Act i, sc. 6, l. 57. [Marcius]
For my country I have shed my blood.
Coriolanus, iii, 1, 76. See under DISEASE.
All my blood in Rome's great quarrel shed.
Titus Andronicus. Act iii, sc. 1, l. 4. [Titus]

4 Shed Thy wife and children's blood.
Coriolanus. Act v, sc. 3, l. 117. [Volumnia]
Thou shalt be waking while I shed thy blood.
II Henry VI. Act iii, sc. 2, l. 227. [Suffolk]
Yet I'll not shed her blood.
Othello. Act v, sc. 2, l. 3. [Othello]
Sheds his blood.—*Henry V,* iv, 3, 61.

5 Killing our enemies, the blood he hath lost—
Which, I dare vouch, is more than that he hath,
By many an ounce—he dropp'd it for his country.
Coriolanus. Act iii, sc. 1, l. 299. [Menenius]
Loss of blood.—*Titus Andronicus,* ii, 4, 29.

6 I have . . .
Drawn tuns of blood out of thy country's breast.
Coriolanus. Act iv, sc. 5, l. 105. [Coriolanus]
Tun of man.—*I Henry IV,* ii, 4, 493.
Tuns of oil.—*The Merry Wives of Windsor,* ii, 1, 65.
Tun of treasure.—*Henry V,* i, 2, 255. The only uses of "tun."

7 Back, I say, go; lest I let forth your half-pint of blood.
Coriolanus. Act v, sc. 2, l. 61. [Senator] The only use of "half-pint."
Let blood.—*Richard III,* iii, 1, 183; *Julius Cæsar,* iii, 1, 152.
Letting blood.—*Richard II,* i, 1, 153.

8 Blood will I draw on thee.
I Henry VI, i, 5, 6. See under WITCH.
Draws blood.—*Hamlet,* iv, 7, 144.
Drew blood.—*I Henry VI,* iv, 6, 16.

Thirst for blood.—*I Henry VI,* iii, 1, 117.
Blood-thirsty lord.—*I Henry VI,* ii, 3, 34. The only use of "blood-thirsty."

9 With their blood stain this discolour'd shore.
II Henry VI. Act iv, sc. 1, l. 11. [Captain]

10 You came in arms to spill mine enemies' blood,
But now in arms you strengthen it with yours.
King John. Act iii, sc. 1, l. 102. [Constance]
To-morrow,
Before the sun shall see 's, we 'll spill the blood
That has to-day escaped.
Antony and Cleopatra, iv, 8, 2. [Antony]
O, the blood is spilt
Of my dear kinsman! Prince, as thou art true,
For blood of ours, shed blood of Montague.
Romeo and Juliet. Act iii, sc. 1, l. 152. [Lady Capulet]
He forfeits his own blood that spills another.
Timon of Athens, iii, 5, 88. See under RETRIBUTION.

11 If thou dost shed
One drop of Christian blood, thy lands and goods
Are, by the laws of Venice, confiscate.
The Merchant of Venice. Act iv, sc. 1, l. 309. [Portia]
Shed thou no blood.—*The Merchant of Venice,* iv, 1, 325.
Christian blood.—*I Henry VI,* v, 1, 9.

12 Farewell, my blood; which if to-day thou shed,
Lament we may, but not revenge thee dead.
Richard II, i, 3, 57. [King Richard]
That blood already, like the pelican,
Hast thou tapp'd out and drunkenly carousèd.
Richard II. Act ii, sc. 1, l. 126. [John of Gaunt] The only use of "tapp'd" and "drunkenly." The pelican is referred to again in *Hamlet,* iv, 5, 146: "Kind life-rendering pelican"; and in *King Lear,* iii, 4, 77: "Pelican daughters."
But now the blood of twenty thousand men
Did triumph in my face, and they are fled;
And, till so much blood thither come again,
Have I not reason to look pale and dead?
Richard II, iii, 2, 76. [King Richard]
I 'll . . . lay the summer's dust with showers of blood
Rain'd from the wounds of slaughter'd Englishmen.
Richard II. Act iii, sc. 3, l. 42. [Bolingbroke]
Lords, I protest, my soul is full of woe,
That blood should sprinkle me to make me grow.
Richard II. Act v, sc. 6, l. 45. [Bolingbroke]

13 Juliet: O God! did Romeo's hand shed Tybalt's blood?
Nurse: It did, it did; alas the day, it did!
Romeo and Juliet. Act iii, sc. 2, l. 71.
Drain'd his blood.—*Sonnets,* lxiii.
Beggar'd of blood.—*Sonnets,* lxvii.
Lack blood.—*Antony and Cleopatra,* i, 4, 52. For "bloodless" see PALENESS.
Tell out my blood.—*Timon of Athens,* iii, 4, 95.

BLOSSOM, see Flower

BLOW

See also Word and Blow

1 The blow thou hadst
Shall make thy peace for moving me to rage.
Antony and Cleopatra. Act ii, sc. 5, l. 69. [Cleopatra]

2
Nay, he struck so plainly, I could too well feel his blows.
The Comedy of Errors. Act ii, sc. 1, l. 53. [Dromio of Ephesus]
There was blow for blow.—*The Comedy of Errors,* iii, 1, 56.
Blows have answer'd blows.—*King John,* ii, 1, 329.

3
Come, leave your drinking, and fall to blows.
II Henry VI. Act ii, sc. 3, l. 80. [Salisbury] Shakespeare used the phrase "fall to blows" in his first play and never again.
Have at thee with a downright blow!
II Henry VI. Act ii, sc. 3, l. 93. [Horner]
I cleft his beaver with a downright blow.
III Henry VI. Act i, sc. 1, l. 12. [Edward] The only uses of "downright blow."
Noble blows.—*Coriolanus,* iv, 2, 21.
Quick blows.—*Timon of Athens,* i, 1, 91.
Sharpest blow.—*Pericles,* i, 1, 55.
Sore blows.—*Coriolanus,* ii, 1, 268.
Vain blows.—*Hamlet,* i, 1, 146.

4
When struck'st thou one blow in the field?
II Henry VI. Act iv, sc. 7, l. 84. [Cade]

5
Fight closer, or, good faith, you 'll catch a blow.
III Henry VI, iii, 2, 23. See under PLEASING.
Blows, blood and death!—*King John,* ii, 1, 360.
Blow of justice.—*Measure for Measure,* ii, 2, 30.
Blow of the law.—*Twelfth Night,* iii, 4, 169.
Fortune's blows.—*King Lear,* iv, 6, 225.
War's blow.—*Pericles,* i, 2, 93.
Civil blows.—*II Henry IV,* iv, 5, 134.

6 I found them close together
At blow and thrust.
Othello. Act ii, sc. 3, l. 238. [Iago]
At blows.—*Antony and Cleopatra,* ii, 6, 45.

7
'Tis but a blow that never shall be known.
Pericles. Act iv, sc. 1, l. 2. [Dionyza]

8
Alas, how many bear such shameful blows,
Which not themselves, but he that gives them knows!
The Rape of Lucrece, l. 832.
Give thyself a blow.—*Rape of Lucrece,* l. 1823.

9
And let thy blows, doubly redoubled,
Fall like amazing thunder on the casque
Of thy adverse pernicious enemy.
Richard II. Act i, sc. 3, l. 80. [John of Gaunt] The only use of "amazing."
I come
To change blows with thee for our day of doom.
Richard II. Act iii, sc. 2, l. 188. [King Richard]

10
I 'll knock you o'er the mazzard.
Othello. Act ii, sc. 3, l. 155. [Cassio]
Knocked about the mazzard.—*Hamlet,* v, 1, 97. See also under KNOCKING. The only uses of "mazzard."

11
There is my purse to cure that blow of thine.
Richard III, iv, 4, 516. [King Richard]

12
What a blow was there given!
The Tempest. Act ii, sc. 1, l. 180. [Antonio]
I do beseech thy greatness, give him blows.
The Tempest. Act iii, sc. 2, l. 72. [Caliban]
His blows are well disposed.
Troilus and Cressida. Act iv, sc. 5, l. 116. [Agamemnon]

13
Look you what hacks are on his helmet! look you yonder, do you see? look you there: there 's no jesting; there 's laying on, take 't off who will, as they say: there be hacks!
Troilus and Cressida, i, 2, 222. [Pandarus]
These knights will hack.—*The Merry Wives of Windsor,* ii, 1, 52.
Hack their bones asunder.—*I Henry VI,* iv, 7, 47.
Hack our English.—*The Merry Wives of Windsor,* iii, 1, 79.
To hick and to hack.—*The Merry Wives of Windsor,* iv, 1, 68. The only use of "hick."
Hack the limbs.—*Julius Cæsar,* ii, 1, 163.
Hack thy sword.—*I Henry IV,* ii, 4, 288. The only uses of "hack."

14
You fillip me o' the head.
Troilus and Cressida, iv, 5, 45. [Menelaus]
Fillip me with a three-man beetle.
II Henry IV, i, 2, 255. The only use of "three-man beetle," a mallet used in ramming paving-stones, and so heavy that it required three men to lift it. "Fillip" occurs a third time in *Coriolanus,* v, 3, 59.

BLUNTNESS, see Candour

BLUSHING

15
The blushes in my cheeks thus whisper me,
'We blush that thou shouldst choose; but, be refused.'
All's Well that Ends Well. Act ii, sc. 3, l. 75. [Helena]
Cool, blushes!—*All's Well that Ends Well,* iv, 3, 373.

16
Thou blushest, Antony; and that blood of thine
Is Cæsar's homager.
Antony and Cleopatra. Act i, sc. 1, l. 30. [Cleopatra] The only use of "homager."
I follow'd that I blush to look upon.
Antony and Cleopatra, iii, 11, 12. [Antony]
Blush not.—*Antony and Cleopatra,* v, 2, 149.

17
His heart's meteors tilting in his face.
The Comedy of Errors. Act iv, sc. 2, l. 6. [Adriana] "Tilting" is repeated in *Love's Labour's Lost,* v, 2, 483, and in *Othello,* ii, 3, 183.
Heaven's face doth glow.
Hamlet. Act iii, sc. 4, l. 48. [Hamlet]

1 I will go wash;
And when my face is fair, you shall perceive
Whether I blush or no.
Coriolanus. Act i, sc. 9, l. 68. [Coriolanus]

It is a part That I shall blush in acting.
Coriolanus. Act ii, sc. 2, l. 148. [Coriolanus]

Here do we make his friends
Blush that the world goes well.
Coriolanus. Act iv, sc. 6, l. 4. [Sicinius]

2
I blushed to hear his monstrous devices.
I Henry IV. Act ii, sc. 4, l. 344. [Bardolph]

Ever since thou hast blushed extempore.
I Henry IV. Act ii, sc. 4, l. 347. [Prince of Wales]

Come, you virtuous ass, you bashful fool, must you be blushing? wherefore blush you now?
II Henry IV. Act ii, sc. 2, l. 80. [Bardolph]

3
I must not blush to affirm it.
Henry V. Act v, sc. 2, l. 116. [King Henry]

I blush to say it.—*All's Well that Ends Well,* v, 3, 140.

Blush for shame.—*I Henry VI,* ii, 4, 66; *King John,* v, 2, 153; *The Rape of Lucrece,* l. 54. See also under SHAME.

4
I would assay, proud queen, to make thee blush.
III Henry VI. Act i, sc. 4, l. 118. [York]

Bewray thy treason with a blush.
III Henry VI. Act iii, sc. 3, l. 97. [Oxford]

I do betray myself with blushing.
Love's Labour's Lost. Act i, sc. 2, l. 138. [Armado]

5
To my brother turn my blushing cheeks.
III Henry VI. Act v, sc. 1, l. 99. [Clarence]

Thou shalt not see me blush
Nor change my countenance.
II Henry VI. Act iii, sc. 1, l. 98. [Gloucester]

Surrey: Now, if you can blush and cry 'guilty,' cardinal,
You'll show a little honesty. . . .
Wolsey: If I blush,
It is to see a nobleman want manners.
Henry VIII. Act iii, sc. 2, l. 305.

6
If she be made of white and red,
Her faults will ne'er be known,
For blushing cheeks by faults are bred
And fears by pale white shown:
Then if she fear, or be to blame,
By this you shall not know,
For still her cheeks possess the same
Which native she doth owe.
Love's Labour's Lost. Act i, sc. 2, l. 104. [Moth]

To blush at speeches rank, to weep at woes,
Or to turn white and swoon at tragic shows.
A Lover's Complaint, l. 307.

The fighting conflict of her hue,
How white and red each other did destroy!
But now her cheek was pale, and by and by
It flash'd forth fire, as lightning from the sky.
Venus and Adonis, l. 345.

Their silent war of lilies and of roses.
The Rape of Lucrece, l. 71.

7
I have been closely shrouded in this bush
And mark'd you both and for you both did blush.
Love's Labour's Lost, iv, 3, 137. [King]

Lay by all nicety and prolixious blushes,
That banish what they sue for.
Measure for Measure. Act ii, sc. 4, l. 162. [Angelo] The only use of "nicety" and "prolixious."

Burning blushes.—*A Lover's Complaint,* l. 304.

8
Behold how like a maid she blushes here!
Much Ado about Nothing. Act iv, sc. 1, l. 35. [Claudio]

Comes not that blood as modest evidence
To witness simple virtue?
Much Ado about Nothing. Act iv, sc. 1, l. 38. [Claudio]

Blush of modesty.—*Hamlet,* iii, 4, 41.

Her blush is guiltiness, not modesty.
Much Ado about Nothing. Act iv, sc. 1, l. 43. [Claudio]

By noting of the lady I have mark'd
A thousand blushing apparitions
To start into her face, a thousand innocent shames
In angel whiteness beat away those blushes.
Much Ado about Nothing. Act iv, sc. 1, l. 160. [Friar Francis]

Blush'd at herself.—*Othello,* i, 3, 96.

These blushes of hers must be quenched with some present practice.
Pericles. Act iv, sc. 2, l. 135. [Boult]

9
Two red fires in both their faces blazed.
The Rape of Lucrece, l. 1353.

She thought he blush'd, . . .
And, blushing with him, wistly on him gazed.
The Rape of Lucrece, l. 1354. "Wistly" is repeated in *Richard II,* v, 4, 7: "He wistly look'd on me."

The more she saw the blood his cheeks replenish,
The more she thought he spied in her some blemish.
The Rape of Lucrece, l. 1357.

10
Here are the beetle brows shall blush for me.
Romeo and Juliet. Act i, sc. 4, l. 32. [Mercutio] The only use of "beetle brows."

Thou know'st the mask of night is on my face,
Else would a maiden blush bepaint my cheek.
Romeo and Juliet. Act ii, sc. 2, l. 85. [Juliet] The only use of "bepaint." "Bepainted" occurs in *Venus and Adonis,* l. 901.

Put off your maiden blushes.
Henry V. Act v, sc. 2, l. 253. [King Henry]

Yet will she blush, here be it said,
To hear her secrets so bewray'd.
The Passionate Pilgrim, l. 351.

11
Why should he live, now Nature bankrupt is,
Beggar'd of blood to blush through lively veins?
Sonnets. No. lxvii.

12
And, notwithstanding all this loss of blood,
As from a conduit with three issuing spouts,
Yet do thy cheeks look red as Titan's face
Blushing to be encounter'd with a cloud.
Titus Andronicus. Act ii, sc. 4, l. 29. [Marcus]

Now comes the wanton blood up in your cheeks,
They 'll be in scarlet straight at any news.
Romeo and Juliet. Act ii, sc. 5, l. 72. [Nurse]

And bid the cheek be ready with a blush
Modest as morning.
Troilus and Cressida. Act i, sc. 3, l. 228. [Æneas]

1 Chiron: I blush to think upon this ignomy.
Aaron: Why, there 's the privilege your beauty bears:
Fie, treacherous hue, that will betray with blushing
The close enacts and counsels of the heart!
Titus Andronicus. Act iv, sc. 2, l. 115. The only use of "enacts" as a noun.

First Goth: What, canst thou say all this, and never blush?
Aaron: Ay, like a black dog, as the saying is.
Titus Andronicus. Act v, sc. 1, l. 121.

2 Let this habit make thee blush!
The Two Gentlemen of Verona. Act v, sc. 4, l. 104. [Julia]

I think the boy hath grace in him; he blushes.
The Two Gentlemen of Verona. Act v, sc. 4, l. 165. [Duke]

3 Blush'd and pouted in a dull disdain.
Venus and Adonis, l. 33.

4 Come, quench your blushes.
The Winter's Tale. Act iv, sc. 4, l. 67. [Shepherd]

He tells her something
That makes her blood look out.
The Winter's Tale. Act iv, sc. 4, l. 159. [Camillo]

For this I 'll blush you thanks.
The Winter's Tale. Act iv, sc. 4, l. 593. [Perdita]

BOAR

5 Where sups he? doth the old boar feed in the old frank?
II Henry IV. Act ii, sc. 2, l. 159. [Prince of Wales]

Pard, or boar with bristled hair.
A Midsummer-Night's Dream. Act ii, sc. 2, l. 32. [Oberon]

The sty of this most bloody boar.
Richard III. Act iv, sc. 5, l. 2. [Derby]

The wretched, bloody, and usurping boar,
That spoil'd your summer fields and fruitful vines,
Swills your warm blood like wash, and makes his trough
In your embowell'd bosoms.
Richard III. Act v, sc. 2, l. 7. [Richmond] The only use of "swills" and "trough."

6 Where is your boar-spear, man?
Fear you the boar, and go so unprovided?
Richard III. Act iii, sc. 2, l. 74. [Hastings]

A boar-spear in my hand.—*As You Like It,* i, 3, 120. The only uses of "boar-spear."

7 An angry-chafing boar,
Under whose sharp fangs on his back doth lie
An image like thyself.
Venus and Adonis, l. 662. The only use of "angry-chafing."

The boar, that bloody beast,
Which knows no pity, but is still severe.
Venus and Adonis, l. 999.

This foul, grim, and urchin-snouted boar,
Whose downward eye still looketh for a grave.
Venus and Adonis, l. 1105. The only use of "urchin-snouted."

Blunt boar.—*Venus and Adonis,* l. 884.
Foul boar.—*Venus and Adonis,* l. 1030.
Hunted boar.—*Venus and Adonis,* l. 900.
Hunt the boar, see under HUNTING.

BOASTING

8 We wound our modesty and make foul the clearness of our deservings, when of ourselves we publish them.
All's Well that Ends Well. Act i, sc. 3, l. 5. [Steward]

Who knows himself a braggart,
Let him fear this, for it will come to pass
That every braggart shall be found an ass.
All's Well that Ends Well. Act iv, sc. 3, l. 370. [Parolles]

This unholy braggart.—*Coriolanus,* v, 6, 119.

Rating myself at nothing, you shall see
How much I was a braggart.
The Merchant of Venice. Act iii, sc. 2, l. 260. [Bassanio] The only use of "rating."

Braggart with my tongue!—*Macbeth,* iv, 3, 231.

9 To brag unto them, thus I did, and thus;
Show them the unaching scars which I should hide,
As if I had received them for the hire
Of their breath only.
Coriolanus. Act ii, sc. 2, l. 151. [Coriolanus] The only use of "unaching."

Thou coward, art thou bragging to the stars?
A Midsummer-Night's Dream. Act iii, sc. 2, l. 407. [Puck]

May be the knave bragged of that he could not compass.
The Merry Wives of Windsor. Act iii, sc. 3, l. 211. [Ford]

Bragging and telling her fantastical lies.
Othello. Act ii, sc. 1, l. 225. [Iago]

Our brags Were crack'd of kitchen-trulls.
Cymbeline. Act v, sc. 5, l. 176. [Iachimo] The only use of "kitchen-trulls."

Forgive me, God,
That I do brag thus! This your air of France
Hath blown that vice in me; I must repent.
Henry V. Act iii, sc. 6, l. 159. [King Henry]

Pardon me this brag.
Troilus and Cressida. Act iv, sc. 5, l. 257. [Hector]

Brag and stamp and swear.
King John. Act iii, sc. 1, l. 122. [Constance] See under Cæsar for "thrasonical brag."

What braggardism is this?
The Two Gentlemen of Verona. Act ii, sc. 4, l. 164. [Proteus] The only use of "braggardism."

Thou shalt not live to brag what we have offer'd.
The Two Gentlemen of Verona. Act iv, sc. 1, l. 69. [Outlaw]

Bragless let it be.—*Troilus and Cressida,* v, 9, 5. The only use of "bragless."

1 That 's more Than some . . .
Can justly boast of.
Cymbeline. Act ii, sc. 3, l. 85. [Lady]

Swell'd boast.—*Cymbeline,* v, 5, 162.

Gleeful boast.—*Titus Andronicus,* ii, 3, 11.

2
How now, my sweet creature of bombast!
I Henry IV. Act ii, sc. 4, l. 359. [Prince of Wales]

As bombast and as lining to the time.
Love's Labour 's Lost. Act v, sc. 2, l. 791. [Princess of France] "Lining" is repeated in *Richard II,* i, 4, 61: "Lining of his coffers."

A bombast circumstance
Horribly stuff'd with epithets of war.
Othello. Act i, sc. 1, l. 13. [Iago] The only uses of "bombast."

3
If he swagger, let him not come here. I must live among my neighbours: I 'll no swaggerers: shut the door; there comes no swaggerers here: I have not lived all this while to have swaggering now.
II Henry IV. Act ii, sc. 4, l. 79. [Hostess]

Hostess: 'Receive,' says he, 'no swaggering companions.' There comes none here: . . . no, I 'll no swaggerers.
Falstaff: He 's no swaggerer, hostess; a tame cheater, i' faith; you may stroke him as gently as a puppy greyhound: he 'll not swagger with a Barbary hen, if her feathers turn back in any show of resistance.
Hostess: Cheater, call you him? I will bar no honest man my house, nor no cheater: but I do not love swaggering, by my troth; I am the worse, when one says swagger. . . . I cannot abide swaggerers.
II Henry IV. Act ii, sc. 4, l. 101.

A rascal that swaggered with me last night.
Henry V. Act iv, sc. 7, l. 131. [Williams]

Will he swagger himself out on 's own eyes?
Troilus and Cressida. Act v, sc. 2, l. 136. [Thersites]

By swaggering could I never thrive.
Twelfth Night. Act v, sc. 1, l. 408. [Clown]

4 Be it death proclaimed through our host
To boast of this or take that praise from God
Which is his only.
Henry V. Act iv, sc. 8, l. 119. [King Henry]

5
She vaunted 'mongst her minions t' other day,
The very train of her worst wearing gown
Was better worth than all my father's lands.
II Henry VI. Act i, sc. 3, l. 87. [Queen] The only use of "vaunted."

Such high vaunts of his nobility.
II Henry VI. Act iii, sc. 1, l. 50. [Suffolk]

The foe vaunts in the field.
Richard III, v, 3, 288. See under Foe.

Vaunt in their youthful sap.—*Sonnets,* xv.

Vaunt That golden hap.—*The Rape of Lucrece,* l. 41. "Vaunt" is used a fifth time in *Troilus and Cressida,* Prol., 27.

Alas, you know I am no vaunter, I.
Titus Andronicus. Act v, sc. 3, l. 113. [Lucius] The only use of "vaunter."

Vauntingly thou spakest it.
Richard II. Act iv, sc. 1, l. 36. [Fitzwater] The only use of "vauntingly."

Make your vaunting true,
And it shall please me well.
Julius Cæsar. Act iv, sc. 3, l. 52. [Brutus]

Vaunting enemies.—*I Henry IV,* v, 3, 43.

Vaunting veins.—*Henry V,* ii, 3, 4. The only uses of "vaunting."

6
What cracker is this same that deafs our ears
With this abundance of superfluous breath?
King John. Act ii, sc. 1, l. 147. [Austria] The only use of "cracker."

7 Here 's a stay
That shakes the rotten carcass of old Death
Out of his rags! Here 's a large mouth, indeed,
That spits forth death and mountains, rocks and seas!
King John. Act ii, sc. 1, l. 455. [Bastard]

The Hotspur of the north; he that kills me some six or seven dozen of Scots at a breakfast, washes his hands, and says to his wife 'Fie upon this quiet life! I want work.' 'O my sweet Harry,' says she, 'how many hast thou killed to-day?' 'Give my roan horse a drench,' says he; and answers 'Some fourteen,' an hour after; 'a trifle, a trifle.'
I Henry IV. Act ii, sc. 4, l. 114. [Prince of Wales]

8
Of Nature's gifts thou mayst with lilies boast.
King John, iii, 1, 53. See under Beauty.

9
I know that boasting is an honour.
Othello. Act i, sc. 2, l. 20. [Othello]

Make no boast of it.—*Much Ado about Nothing,* ii, 3, 20; *As You Like It,* iv, 3, 91.

No boasting like a fool.—*Macbeth,* iv, 1, 153.

Topping all others in boasting.—*Coriolanus,* ii, 1, 23. The only use of "topping."

10
He shall not boast who did thy stock pollute
That thou art doting father of his fruit.
The Rape of Lucrece, l. 1063.

11 Boast of this I can,
Though banish'd, yet a trueborn Englishman.
Richard II, i, 3, 308. See under England.

Do not smile at me that I boast her off.
The Tempest. Act v, sc. 1, l. 9. [Prospero]

12
Full of protest, of oath and big compare.
Troilus and Cressida. Act iii, sc. 2, l. 182. [Troilus]

This fusty stuff.—*Troilus and Cressida,* i, 3, 161. "Fusty" is repeated in ii, 1, 111: "Fusty nut"; and in *Coriolanus,* i, 9, 7: "Fusty plebeians."

13 What canst thou boast
Of things long since, or any thing ensuing?
Venus and Adonis, l. 1077.

BOAT, see Ship

BODY

See also Form; Mind and Body

1
Of as able body as when he numbered thirty.
All's Well that Ends Well. Act iv, sc. 5, l. 86. [Lafeu]
A weak mind and an able body.
II Henry IV. Act ii, sc. 4, l. 275. [Falstaff] For full quotation see under CHARACTER. The only uses of "able body."

2
This common body,
Like to a vagabond flag upon the stream,
Goes to and back, lackeying the varying tide,
To rot itself with motion.
Antony and Cleopatra. Act i, sc. 4, l. 44. [Cæsar] See also under PEOPLE. The only use of "lackeying."
Common body.—*Coriolanus,* ii, 2, 57; *Pericles,* iii, 3, 21.
The body public be
A horse whereon the governor doth ride.
Measure for Measure, i, 2, 163. See under PEOPLE.
Public body.—*Timon of Athens,* v, 1, 148.

3
Bear the king's son's body Before our army.
Antony and Cleopatra. Act iii, sc. 1, l. 3. [Ventidius]
Bear from hence his body.—*Coriolanus,* v, 6, 143.
Bear hence his body; I will help to bury it.
I Henry VI. Act i, sc. 4, l. 87. [Talbot]
If thou wilt ever thrive, bury my body.
King Lear. Act iv, sc. 6, l. 253. [Oswald]
His body will I bear unto the king.
II Henry VI. Act iv, sc. 1, l. 145. [Gentleman]
Rear up his body.—*II Henry VI,* iii, 2, 34.
Bring the body into the chapel.
Hamlet. Act iv, sc. 1, l. 36. [Queen]
I 'll bring the body presently.
Pericles. Act iii, sc. 1, l. 82. [Pericles]

4
She shows a body rather than a life,
A statue than a breather.
Antony and Cleopatra. Act iii, sc. 3, l. 23. [Messenger]
I will chide no breather in the world but myself.
As You Like It, iii, 2, 297. "Breather" occurs again in *Measure for Measure,* iv, 4, 31.

5
A body would think this was well counterfeited.
As You Like It, iv, 3, 166. See also *The Comedy of Errors,* iii, 2, 91; *Titus Andronicus,* ii, 3, 103.
Hath any body inquired for me here to-day?
Measure for Measure, iv, 1, 16. See also *The Merry Wives of Windsor,* i, 4, 4; *Henry V,* iii, 7, 121.
Cough, or cry "hem," if any body come.
Othello, iv, 2, 29.
Body o' me, where is it?
Henry VIII. Act v, sc. 2, l. 22. [King Henry]

6
Bear your body more seeming, Audrey.
As You Like It. Act v, sc. 4, l. 72. [Touchstone]

7
This mould of Marcius, they to dust should grind it
And throw 't against the wind.
Coriolanus. Act iii, sc. 2, l. 103. [Coriolanus]
Men of mould.—*Henry V,* iii, 2, 23.
Nature's mould.—*King Lear,* iii, 2, 8.

8
Let me twine
Mine arms about that body, where against
My grained ash an hundred times hath broke,
And scarr'd the moon with splinters.
Coriolanus. Act iv, sc. 5, l. 112. [Aufidius] The only use of "ash."

9
His body 's a passable carcass.
Cymbeline. Act i, sc. 2, l. 10. [First Lord]
Dead carcasses.—*Coriolanus,* iii, 3, 122.
Rotten carcass.—*King John,* ii, 1, 456; *The Tempest,* i, 2, 146.
Saved their carcases.—*Cymbeline,* v, 3, 67.

10
My body 's mark'd with Roman swords.
Cymbeline. Act iii, sc. 3, l. 56. [Belarius]

11
Thersites' body is as good as Ajax',
When neither are alive.
Cymbeline. Act iv, sc. 2, l. 252. [Guiderius]
The lines of my body are as well drawn as his.
Cymbeline. Act iv, sc. 1, l. 10. [Cloten]

12
Most holy and religious fear it is
To keep those many many bodies safe
That live and feed upon your majesty.
Hamlet. Act iii, sc. 3, l. 8. [Guildenstern]

13
And as the soldiers bore dead bodies by,
He call'd them untaught knaves, unmannerly,
To bring a slovenly unhandsome corse
Betwixt the wind and his nobility.
I Henry IV. Act i, sc. 3, l. 42. [Hotspur] The only use of "slovenly." "Dead bodies" or "dead body" is used nine times.
My lord, your son had only but the corpse,
But shadows and the shows of men, to fight.
II Henry IV. Act i, sc. 1, l. 192. [Morton]
Thou shalt not back till I have borne this corse
Into the market-place.
Julius Cæsar. Act iii, sc. 1, l. 291. [Antony]
Corpse of Cæsar.—*Julius Cæsar,* iii, 2, 162.
Cæsar's corpse.—*Julius Cæsar,* iii, 2, 62.
O you most potent gods! what 's here? a corse!
Pericles. Act iii, sc. 2, l. 63. [Cerimon]
Stay, you that bear the corse, and set it down.
. . . Set down the corse; or, by Saint Paul,
I 'll make a corse of him that disobeys.
Richard III. Act i, sc. 2, l. 33. [Gloucester] See also *Hamlet,* i, 4, 85, under GHOST.
Take up the corse.—*Richard III,* i, 2, 226.
Dead Henry's corse.—*I Henry VI,* i, 1, 62.
Henry's corse.—*Richard III,* iv, 1, 67.
A piteous corse, a bloody piteous corse;
Pale, pale as ashes, all bedaub'd in blood.
Romeo and Juliet. Act iii, sc. 2, l. 54. [Nurse] The only use of "bedaub'd."
Poor living corse, closed in a dead man's tomb.
Romeo and Juliet. Act v, sc. 2, l. 28. [Friar Laurence]
Tybalt's corse.—*Romeo and Juliet,* iii, 2, 128.

And stands colossus-wise, waving his beam,
Upon the pashed corses of the kings.
Troilus and Cressida. Act v, sc. 5, l. 9. [Agamemnon] The only use of "colossus-wise" and "pashed."

The most noble corse that ever herald
Did follow to his urn.
Coriolanus. Act v, sc. 6, l. 145. [First Lord]

Breathless corpse.—*II Henry VI,* iii, 2, 132.
Buried corse.—*Romeo and Juliet,* iv, 5, 89.
Dead corpse.—*I Henry IV,* i, 1, 43.
Dead corse.—*Hamlet,* i, 4, 52.
Fair corse.—*Romeo and Juliet,* iv, 5, 80; 93; *Troilus and Cressida,* ii, 3, 35.
Pocky corses.—*Hamlet,* v, 1, 181.
Poor corpse.—*Twelfth Night,* ii, 4, 63.

1 But what need I thus
My well-known body to anatomize?
II Henry IV. Induction, l. 20. [Rumour] The only use of "well-known." "Anatomize" is repeated in *As You Like It,* i, 1, 162, and in *King Lear,* iii, 6, 80.

I think we are a body strong enough,
Even as we are, to equal with the king.
II Henry IV. Act i, sc. 3, l. 66. [Hastings]

Make less thy body hence, and more thy grace.
II Henry IV, v, 5, 56. See under Fasting.

Here I commit my body to your mercies.
II Henry IV. Epilogue, l. 15.

2
What is the body when the head is off?
III Henry VI. Act v, sc. 1, l. 41. [King Edward]

I must yield my body to the earth.
III Henry VI. Act v, sc. 2, l. 9. [Warwick]

What can we bequeath
Save our deposed bodies to the ground?
Richard II. Act iii, sc. 2, l. 149. [King Richard]

3
Produce his body to the market-place.
Julius Cæsar. Act iii, sc. 1, l. 228. [Antony]

Prepare the body then, and follow us.
Julius Cæsar. Act iii, sc. 1, l. 253. [Brutus]

Here comes his body.—*Julius Cæsar,* iii, 2, 45.
Cæsar's body.—*Julius Cæsar,* iii, 1, 244.

We 'll burn his body in the holy place,
And with the brands fire the traitors' houses.
Take up the body.
Julius Cæsar. Act iii, sc. 2, l. 259. [Citizen]

4
Which had you rather, that the most just law
Now took your brother's life; or, to redeem him,
Give up your body to such sweet uncleanness
As she that he hath stain'd?
Measure for Measure. Act ii, sc. 4, l. 52. [Angelo] The only use of "uncleanness."

[He] thinks he knows that he ne'er knew my body,
But knows he thinks that he knows Isabel's.
Measure for Measure. Act v, sc. 1 l. 203. [Mariana]

This is the body
That took away the match from Isabel,
And did supply thee at thy garden-house
In her imagined person.
Measure for Measure. Act v, sc. 1, l. 210. [Mariana] "Garden-house" is used again in l. 229, and nowhere else.

5
My little body is aweary of this great world.
The Merchant of Venice. Act i, sc. 2, l. 1. [Portia]

I once did lend my body for his wealth.
The Merchant of Venice. Act v, sc. 1, l. 249. [Antonio]

I 'll make more of thy old body than I have done.
The Merry Wives of Windsor. Act ii, sc. 2, l. 145. [Falstaff]

Adventurous body.—*Titus Andronicus,* v, 3, 112.
Anointed body.—*Richard III,* v, 3, 124; *Richard II,* ii, 1, 98.
Damned'st body.—*Measure for Measure,* iii, 1, 96. The only use of "damned'st."
Derogate body.—*King Lear,* i, 4, 302.
Eminent body.—*Measure for Measure,* iv, 4, 25.
Feeble body.—*II Henry VI,* v, 3, 13.
Foul body.—*As You Like It,* ii, 7, 60.
Glorious body.—*Timon of Athens,* i, 1, 187.
Great body.—*II Henry IV,* v, 2, 136.
Gross body.—*Sonnets,* cli.
Idle body.—*Richard III,* iii, 7, 77.
Lifeless body.—*II Henry VI,* iv, 1, 142.
Lively body.—*Titus Andronicus,* iii, 1, 105.
Poor bodies.—*Henry V,* iv, 3, 87.
Poor body.—*All 's Well that Ends Well,* i, 3, 30.
Smooth body.—*Hamlet,* i, 5, 73.
Sweet body.—*Othello,* iii, 5, 346.
Tortured body.—*All 's Well that Ends Well,* ii, 1, 37.
Uncovered body.—*King Lear,* iii, 4, 106.
Unprovided body.—*King Lear,* ii, 1, 54.
Unworthy body.—*The Two Gentlemen of Verona,* i, 2, 18.
So tender a body.—*Much Ado about Nothing,* ii, 3, 171.
So young a body.—*The Merchant of Venice,* iv, 1, 164.
Nature's fragile vessel.—*Timon of Athens,* v, 1, 204. The only use of "fragile."

6
Who cannot abuse a body dead?
The Rape of Lucrece, l. 1267.

Life imprison'd in a body dead.
The Rape of Lucrece, l. 1456.

The prey of worms, my body being dead.
Sonnets. No. lxxiv. See also under Worm.

Whoreson dead body.—*Hamlet,* v, 1, 190.
Is this thy body's end?—*Sonnets,* cxlvi.

7 Lucrece' father, that beholds her bleed,
Himself on her self-slaughter'd body threw.
The Rape of Lucrece, l. 1732. The only use of "self-slaughter'd."

They did conclude to bear dead Lucrece thence,
To show her bleeding body thorough Rome.
The Rape of Lucrece, l. 1850.

8 In one little body
Thou conterfeit'st a bark, a sea, a wind;
For still thy eyes, which I may call the sea,
Do ebb and flow with tears; the bark, thy body is,
Sailing in this salt flood; the winds, thy sighs;
Who, raging with thy tears, and they with them,
Without a sudden calm, will overset

Thy tempest-tossed body.
Romeo and Juliet. Act iii, sc. 5, l. 131. [Capulet] "Tempest-tost" is used in *Macbeth*, i, 3, 25.

1 Serving of becks and jutting-out of bums!
Timon of Athens. Act i, sc. 2, l. 237. [Apemantus] The only use of "jutting-out."

Your bum is the greatest thing about you.
Measure for Measure. Act ii, sc. 1, l. 228. [Escalus]

Then slip I from her bum.
A Midsummer-Night's Dream. Act ii, sc. 1, l. 53. The only uses of "bum."

2 Come, tie his body to my horse's tail;
Along the field I will the Trojan trail.
Troilus and Cressida. Act v, sc. 8, l. 21. [Achilles]

II—Body and Soul

3 This case of that huge spirit now is cold.
Antony and Cleopatra. Act iv, sc. 15, l. 89. [Cleopatra]

4 My body shall
Pay recompense, if you will grant my suit.
Cannot my body nor blood-sacrifice
Entreat you to your wonted furtherance?
Then take my soul, my body, soul and all.
I Henry VI. Act v, sc. 3, l. 18. [La Pucelle] The only use of "blood-sacrifice."

5 As I thrust thy body in with my sword,
So wish I, I might thrust thy soul to hell.
II Henry VI, iv, 10, 84. See under CURSE.

My soul and body on the action both!
II Henry VI. Act v, sc. 2, l. 26. [Clifford]

6 Now my soul's palace is become a prison:
Ah, would she break from hence, that this my body
Might in the ground be closed up in rest!
III Henry VI. Act ii, sc. 1, l. 74. [Edward]

7 Within this wall of flesh
There is a soul counts thee her creditor.
King John. Act iii, sc. 3, l. 20. [King John]

Look, who comes here! a grave unto a soul;
Holding the eternal spirit, against her will,
In the vile prison of afflicted breath.
King John. Act iii, sc. 4, l. 17. [King Philip]

8 I had rather give my body than my soul.
Measure for Measure. Act ii, sc. 4, l. 56. [Isabella]

9 He is a curer of souls, and you a curer of bodies.
The Merry Wives of Windsor. Act ii, sc. 3, l. 40. [Shallow]

Soul-curer and body-curer!
The Merry Wives of Windsor. Act iii, sc. 1, l. 100. [Host] The only use of either phrase.

10 It were pity but they should suffer salvation body and soul.
Much Ado about Nothing. Act iii, sc. 3, l. 3. [Verges]

I will deal in this
As secretly and justly as your soul
Should with your body.
Much Ado about Nothing. Act iv, sc. 1, l. 249. [Benedick]

11 His soul's fair temple is defaced.
The Rape of Lucrece, l. 719.

My body or my soul, which was the dearer,
When the one pure, the other made divine?
The Rape of Lucrece, l. 1163.

12 I will not vex your souls—
Since presently your souls must part your bodies.
Richard II. Act iii, sc. 1, l. 2. [Bolingbroke]

I have given here my soul's consent
To undeck the pompous body of a king.
Richard II. Act iv, sc. 1, l. 249. [King Richard] The only use of "undeck."

13 Mount, mount, my soul! thy seat is up on high;
Whilst my gross flesh sinks downward, here to die.
Richard II. Act v, sc. 5, l. 112. [King Richard]

O me! my uncle's spirit is in these stones:
Heaven take my soul, and England keep my bones!
King John. Act iv, sc. 3, l. 9. [Arthur]

My soul and body to the skies and ground.
The Rape of Lucrece, l. 1199.

Her body sleeps in Capels' monument,
And her immortal part with angels lives.
Romeo and Juliet. Act v, sc. 1, l. 18. [Balthasar]

14 Thou hadst but power over his mortal body,
His soul thou canst not have.
Richard III. Act i, sc. 2, l. 47. [Lady Anne] "Mortal body" is repeated in *Titus Andronicus,* ii, 3, 103.

Methought their souls, whose bodies Richard murder'd,
Came to my tent, and cried on victory.
Richard III. Act v, sc. 3, l. 230. [Richmond]

Souls and bodies hath he divorced three.
Twelfth Night. Act iii, sc. 4, l. 259. [Sir Toby] See under DUELLING for full quotation.

15 I do in justice charge thee,
On thy soul's peril and thy body's torture.
The Winter's Tale. Act ii, sc. 3, l. 180. [Leontes]

BOLDNESS

See also Rashness

16 'Tis but the boldness of his hand, haply, which his heart was not consenting to.
All's Well that Ends Well. Act iii, sc. 2, l. 79. [Gentleman]

Boldness of his speech.—*The Winter's Tale,* iii, 2, 219.

Boldness of a wife.—*Winter's Tale,* i, 2, 184.

17 Thou art, if thou darest be, the earthly Jove:
Whate'er the ocean pales, or sky inclips,
Is thine, if thou wilt ha 't.
Antony and Cleopatra. Act ii, sc. 7, l. 73. [Menas] The only use of "inclips."

1
'Tis for the followers fortune widens them,
Not for the fliers.
Coriolanus. Act i, sc. 4, l. 44. [Caius Marcius] The only use of "widens."

2
I will be bold to take my leave of you.
Coriolanus. Act ii, sc. 1, l. 106. [Menenius]
I will be bold with time and your attention.
Henry VIII, ii, 4, 168. See under ATTENTION.
Thy words are but as thoughts; therefore, be bold.
Richard II. Act ii, sc. 1, l. 276. [Lord Ross]
Be bold and take thy stand.
Othello. Act v, sc. 1, l. 7. [Iago]
O, then be bold!—*The Merchant of Venice,* iii, 2, 187.
Be bold in us.—*Titus Andronicus,* v, 1, 13.
May I be bold to say so?—*The Merry Wives of Windsor,* iv, 5, 54.
To be bold with you.—*Othello,* iii, 3, 228.

3 Boldness be my friend!
Arm me, audacity, from head to foot!
Cymbeline. Act i, sc. 6, l. 18. [Iachimo] "Audacity" is used again in *I Henry VI,* i, 2, 36.

4
I will make bold To send them to you.
Cymbeline. Act i, sc. 6, l. 197. [Iachimo]
I shall make bold with you.
A Midsummer-Night's Dream. Act iii, sc. 1, l. 187. [Bottom]
I will make bold.—*The Merry Wives of Windsor,* ii, 2, 162; ii, 2, 262.
I'll make bold.—*Cymbeline,* v, 5, 89.
I'll make so bold to call.—*Macbeth,* ii, 3, 56.
Make bold.—*Romeo and Juliet,* iii, 1, 81.
Making so bold.—*Hamlet,* v, 2, 16.

5
To hell, allegiance! vows, to the blackest devil!
Conscience and grace, to the profoundest pit!
I dare damnation.
Hamlet. Act iv, sc. 5, l. 131. [Laertes] The only use of "profoundest."

6
O, sir, your presence is too bold and peremptory.
I Henry IV. Act i, sc. 3, l. 17. [King Henry]
You are a great deal abused in too bold a persuasion.
Cymbeline. Act i, sc. 4, l. 124. [Posthumus]
I think we are too bold upon your rest.
Julius Cæsar. Act ii, sc. 1, l. 86. [Cassius]
I am too bold.—*Romeo and Juliet,* ii, 2, 14.
Too bold.—*Hamlet,* iii, 2, 363.

7
It lends a lustre and more great opinion,
A larger dare to our great enterprise.
I Henry IV. Act iv, sc. 1, l. 77. [Hotspur]

8
Boldly did outdare The dangers of the time.
I Henry IV. Act v, sc. 1, l. 40. [Worcester]
Sensibly outdares.—*Coriolanus,* i, 4, 53. The only uses of "outdare." "Out-dared" occurs in *Richard II,* i, 1, 190.

9
You call honourable boldness impudent sauciness.
II Henry IV. Act ii, sc. 1, l. 134. [Falstaff]

10
Therefore am I bold and resolute.
II Henry VI, iv, 4, 60. See under INNOCENCE.
I am bold.—*II Henry VI,* i, 3, 96.
I have been bold.—*I Henry VI,* ii, 3, 25; *Timon of Athens,* ii, 2, 208.
May I be bold?—*The Tempest,* iv, 1, 119.
Bold as an oracle.—*Troilus and Cressida,* i, 3, 192.
Bold in the quarrel's right.—*King Lear,* ii, 1, 56.
Bold in war.—*III Henry VI,* ii, 1, 155; iv, 8, 10.
Bold of voice.—*Merchant of Venice,* ii, 2, 190.

11
Becomes it thee to be so bold in terms?
III Henry VI, ii, 2, 85. See under KING.
Be so bold.—*The Rape of Lucrece,* l. 1282.
This bold bad man.—*Henry VIII,* ii, 2, 44.

12
And I will set this foot of mine as far
As who goes farthest.
Julius Cæsar. Act i, sc. 3, l. 119. [Casca]
Fire enough
To kindle cowards and to steel with valour
The melting spirits of women.
Julius Cæsar. Act ii, sc. 1, l. 120. [Brutus]
The insuppressive mettle of our spirits.
Julius Cæsar. Act ii, sc. 1, l. 134. [Brutus] The only use of "insuppressive."
It is more worthy to leap in ourselves,
Than tarry till they push us.
Julius Cæsar. Act v, sc. 5, l. 24. [Brutus]

13
O, he is bold and blushes not at death.
King John. Act iv, sc. 3, l. 76. [Salisbury]
Be stirring as the time; be fire with fire;
Threaten the threatener and outface the brow
Of bragging horror.
King John. Act v, sc. 1, l. 48. [Bastard] The only use of "threatener."
Show boldness and aspiring confidence.
King John. Act v, sc. 1, l. 56. [Bastard]

14
He is bold in his defence.
King Lear, v, 3, 114. See under DEFENCE.

15
But pardon me, I am too sudden-bold.
Love's Labour's Lost. Act ii, sc. 1, l. 107. [Princess of France] The only use of "sudden-bold."
Over-boldly we have borne ourselves.
Love's Labour's Lost. Act v, sc. 2, l. 744. [Princess] The only use of "over-boldly."

16
That which hath made them drunk hath made me bold;
What hath quench'd them hath given me fire.
Macbeth. Act ii, sc. 2, l. 1. [Lady Macbeth]

17 'Tis much he dares;
And, to that dauntless temper of his mind,
He hath a wisdom that doth guide his valour
To act in safety.
Macbeth. Act iii, sc. 1, l. 51. [Macbeth]
He shall spurn fate, scorn death, and bear
His hopes 'bove wisdom, grace and fear.
Macbeth. Act iii, sc. 5, l. 30. [Hecate]

18
Be bloody, bold, and resolute; laugh to scorn
The power of man.
Macbeth. Act iv, sc. 1, l. 79. [Second Apparition] The phrase "laugh to scorn" occurs

twice more in *Macbeth* (v, 5, 3, and v, 7, 12) and in *As You Like It,* iv, 2, 19. "Bold and resolute" is repeated in *II Henry VI,* iv, 4, 60. See under RESOLUTION.

Be lion-mettled, proud; and take no care
Who chafes, who frets, or where conspirers are.
Macbeth. Act iv, sc. 1, l. 90. [Third Apparition] The only use of "lion-mettled" and "conspirer."

1
Ginger was not much in request.
Measure for Measure. Act iv, sc. 3, l. 8. [Pompey]

Ginger shall be hot i' the mouth.
Twelfth Night, ii, 3, 126.

He 's of the heat of ginger.
Henry V, iii, 7, 21.

2
I know not by what power I am made bold,
Nor how it may concern my modesty,
In such a presence here to plead my thoughts.
A Midsummer-Night's Dream. Act i, sc. 1, l. 59. [Hermia] "Made bold" is repeated in *Othello,* ii, 1, 35.

3
If in thy hope thou darest do such outrage,
What darest thou not when once thou art a king?
The Rape of Lucrece, l. 605.

4
A jewel in a ten-times-barr'd-up chest
Is a bold spirit in a loyal breast.
Richard II. Act i, sc. 1, l. 180. [Mowbray] The only use of the hyphenated phrase.

On pain of death, no person be so bold
Or daring-hardy as to touch the lists.
Richard II. Act i, sc. 3, l. 42. [Lord Marshall] The only use of "daring-hardy."

Sprightfully and bold.—*Richard II,* i, 3, 3. The only use of "sprightfully."

5
Out with it boldly, man.
Richard II. Act ii, sc. 1, l. 233. [Willoughby]

Out with it boldly.—*Henry VIII,* iii, 1, 39.

6
Than my Lord Hastings no man might be bolder.
Richard III. Act iii, sc. 4, l. 30. [Gloucester]

Grown bold.—*Romeo and Juliet,* iii, 2, 15.

7
To say they err I dare not be so bold.
Sonnets. No. cxxxi.

Dare any be so bold?—*II Henry VI,* iv, 8, 4.
Dare you be so bold?—*II Henry VI,* iii, 2, 238.
I dare be bold.—*The Two Gentlemen of Verona,* v, 4, 162.
Dare be bold.—*Henry VIII,* ii, 1, 72.
I 'll be so bold.—*I Henry VI,* ii, 1, 78; *Henry V,* iii, 2, 162; *The Merry Wives of Windsor,* iv, 5, 13; *The Two Gentlemen of Verona,* iii, 1, 139; *Much Ado about Nothing,* iii, 2, 8.
If I may be so bold.—*The Taming of the Shrew,* i, 2, 219.
May I be so bold?—*The Taming of the Shrew,* ii, 1, 88; *All 's Well that Ends Well,* iii, 6, 84.

8
Let me be thus bold with you.
The Taming of the Shrew. Act i, sc. 2, l. 104. [Petruchio]

Let me be bold.—*The Taming of the Shrew,* i, 2, 251; *Measure for Measure,* ii, 4, 133.

9
With the little skill I have,
Full well shalt thou perceive how much I dare.
Titus Andronicus. Act ii, sc. 1, l. 43. [Chiron]

He dares, being dared.
Romeo and Juliet. Act ii, sc. 4, l. 12. [Benvolio]

I will make it good how you dare, with what you dare, and when you dare.
Much Ado about Nothing. Act v, sc. 1, l. 147. [Benedick]

What I dare too well do, I dare not do.
All's Well that Ends Well. Act ii, sc. 3, l. 210. [Parolles]

What man dare, I dare.
Macbeth. Act iii, sc. 4, l. 99. [Macbeth]

10
Boldness comes to me now, and brings me heart.
Troilus and Cressida. Act iii, sc. 2, l. 121. [Cressida]

I do not speak of flight, of fear, of death,
But dare all imminence that gods and men
Address their dangers in.
Troilus and Cressida. Act v, sc. 10, l. 12. [Troilus] The only use of "imminence."

11
What foolish boldness brought thee to their mercies,
Whom thou, in terms so bloody and so dear,
Hast made thine enemies?
Twelfth Night. Act v, sc. 1, l. 73. [Duke]

Ridiculous boldness.—*Twelfth Night,* iii, 4, 41.

12
Who is so faint, that dares not be so bold
To touch the fire, the weather being cold?
Venus and Adonis, l. 401.

Things out of hope are compass'd oft with venturing,
Chiefly in love, whose leave exceeds commission.
Venus and Adonis, l. 567.

'Slid, 'tis but venturing.—*The Merry Wives of Windsor,* iii, 4, 25. The only uses of "venturing." See also under ADVENTURE.

BOND
See also Surety, Word

13
I knew it for my bond.
Antony and Cleopatra. Act i, sc. 4, l. 84. [Cæsar]

14
I will discharge my bond and thank you too.
The Comedy of Errors. Act iv, sc. 1, l. 13. [Angelo]

I am here enter'd in bond for you.
The Comedy of Errors. Act iv, sc. 4, l. 128. [Dromio of Ephesus]

I would I had your bond, for I perceive
A weak bond holds you.
A Midsummer-Night's Dream. Act iii, sc. 2, l. 267. [Demetrius]

15
If you will take this audit, take this life,
And cancel these cold bonds.
Cymbeline. Act iv, sc. 4, l. 27. [Posthumus]

Cancel and tear to pieces that great bond
Which keeps me pale!
Macbeth, iii, 2, 49. See NIGHT, 1067:3.
Cancel his bond of life, dear God, I pray.
Richard III, iv, 4, 77. See under DOG.

1
Our indentures tripartite are drawn.
I Henry IV. Act iii, sc. 1, l. 80. [Mortimer] The only use of "tripartite."
Are the indentures drawn?—*I Henry IV,* iii, 1, 141.
An the indentures be drawn, I 'll away within these two hours.
I Henry IV. Act iii, sc. 1, l. 265. [Hotspur]
Indenture of my love.—*King John,* ii, 1, 20.
Indenture of his oath.—*Pericles,* i, 3, 9.
Pair of indentures.—*Hamlet,* v, 1, 119.
Serve by indenture.—*Pericles,* iv, 6, 187.
Play the coward with thy indenture.—*I Henry IV,* ii, 4, 53. The only uses of "indenture."

2
I 'll take a bond of fate.
Macbeth, iv, 1, 84. See ASSURANCE, 58:10.

3
The man is notwithstanding sufficient. Three thousand ducats. I think I may take his bond.
The Merchant of Venice. Act i, sc. 3, l. 26. [Shylock]
Go with me to a notary, seal me there
Your single bond.
The Merchant of Venice. Act i, sc. 3, l. 146. [Shylock]
Antonio: Content, i' faith: I 'll seal to such a bond. . . .
Yes, Shylock, I will seal unto this bond.
Shylock: Then meet me forthwith at the notary's;
Give him direction for this merry bond.
The Merchant of Venice. Act i, sc. 3, l. 153. The only uses of "notary."
For the Jew's bond which he hath of me,
Let it not enter in your mind of love.
The Merchant of Venice. Act ii, sc. 8, l. 41. [Antonio]
Let him look to his bond: he was wont to call me usurer; let him look to his bond: he was wont to lend money for a Christian courtesy; let him look to his bond.
The Merchant of Venice. Act iii, sc. 1, l. 49. [Shylock]
Pay him six thousand, and deface his bond.
The Merchant of Venice. Act iii, sc. 2, l. 302. [Portia]
My bond to the Jew is forfeit.
The Merchant of Venice. Act iii, sc. 2, l. 319. [Antonio]
I 'll have my bond; speak not against my bond:
I have sworn an oath that I will have my bond.
The Merchant of Venice. Act iii, sc. 3, l. 4. [Shylock]
By our holy Sabbath have I sworn
To have the due and forfeit of my bond.
The Merchant of Venice. Act iv, sc. 1, l. 36. [Shylock]
I would have my bond.—*The Merchant of Venice,* iv, 1, 87.
Is it so nominated in the bond?
The Merchant of Venice. Act iv, sc. 1, l. 259. [Shylock] "Nominated" is repeated in i, 3, 150, and in *Love's Labour 's Lost,* v, 1, 8.
According to my bond.—*King Lear,* i, 1, 95.
Portia: I pray you, let me look upon the bond.
Shylock: Here 'tis, most reverend doctor, here it is. . . .
Portia: Why, this bond is forfeit;
And lawfully by this the Jew may claim
A pound of flesh, to be by him cut off
Nearest the merchant's heart. Be merciful:
Take thrice thy money; bid me tear the bond.
Shylock: When it is paid according to the tenour.
. . . I stay here on my bond. . . .
Portia: Tarry a little: there is something else.
This bond doth give thee here no jot of blood;
The words expressly are 'a pound of flesh:'
Take then thy bond, take thou thy pound of flesh;
But, in the cutting it, if thou dost shed
One drop of Christian blood, thy lands and goods
Are, by the laws of Venice, confiscate. . . .
Therefore prepare thee to cut off the flesh.
Shed thou no blood, nor cut thou less nor more
But just a pound of flesh: if thou cut'st more
Or less than just a pound, be it but so much
As makes it light or heavy in the substance,
Or the division of the twentieth part
Of one poor scruple, nay, if the scale do turn
But in the estimation of a hair,
Thou diest and all thy goods are confiscate.
The Merchant of Venice. Act iv, sc. 1, l. 225.

4
Inky blots and rotten parchment bonds.
Richard II. Act ii, sc. 1, l. 64. [Gaunt]
Duchess of York: 'Tis nothing but some bond, that he is enter'd into. . . .
York: Bound to himself! what doth he with a bond
That he is bound to?
Richard II. Act v, sc. 2, l. 65.

5
My bonds in thee are all determinate.
Sonnets. No. lxxxvii. See FAREWELL, 503:4.
Seal'd false bonds.—*Sonnets,* cxlii.
Three or four bonds of forty pound a-piece.
I Henry IV. Act iii, sc. 3, l. 117. [Falstaff]

6
Take the bonds along with you,
And have the dates in compt.
Timon of Athens. Act ii, sc. 1, l. 34. [Senator]
Date-broke bonds.—*Timon of Athens,* ii, 2, 38. The only use of "date-broke."

BONDAGE

See also Slavery

7
Thou shalt find what it is to be proud of thy bondage.
All's Well that Ends Well. Act ii, sc. 3, l. 239. [Lafeu]
Most welcome, bondage! for thou art a way,
I think, to liberty.
Cymbeline. Act v, sc. 4, l. 3. [Posthumus]
Increase your bondage.—*Measure for Measure,* iii, 2, 79.
Chains of bondage.—*Richard II,* i, 3, 89.

8
Bondage is hoarse, and may not speak aloud.
Romeo and Juliet. Act ii, sc. 2, l. 161. [Juliet]

9
If I were not in love with Mopsa, thou

shouldst take no money of me; but being enthralled as I am, it will also be the bondage of certain ribbons and gloves.
Winter's Tale. Act iv, sc. 4, l. 233. [Clown]
Assured bondage.—*Cymbeline,* i, 6, 73.
Fond bondage.—*King Lear,* i, 2, 52.
Hard bondage.—*All's Well that Ends Well,* iii, 5, 67.
Obsequious bondage.—*Othello,* i, 1, 46.
Petty bondage.—*Venus and Adonis,* l. 391.

II—The Bondman

1
Ægeus: Is not that your bondman, Dromio?
Dromio of Ephesus: Within this hour I was his bondman, sir,
But he, I thank him, gnaw'd in two my cords:
Now am I Dromio and his man unbound.
The Comedy of Errors. Act v, sc. 1, l. 287.

2
Who is here so base that he would be a bondman?
Julius Cæsar. Act iii, sc. 2, l. 32. [Brutus]
Go show your slaves how choleric you are,
And make your bondmen tremble.
Julius Cæsar. Act iv, sc. 3, l. 43. [Brutus]
Check'd like a bondman.—*Julius Cæsar,* iv, 3, 97.
Bad bondmen.—*Titus Andronicus,* iv, 1, 109.
Enfranchised bondman.—*Antony and Cleopatra,* iii, 13, 149.
Willing bondman.—*Julius Cæsar,* i, 3, 113.
Bowed like bondmen.—*Julius Cæsar,* v, 1, 42. See under SERVILITY.
Bondmen to thy sovereignty.—*II Henry VI,* i, 3, 130.

3 If such actions may have passage free,
Bond-slaves and pagans shall our statesmen be.
Othello. Act i, sc. 2, l. 98. [Brabantio]
Shall I play my freedom at tray-trip, and become thy bond-slave?
Twelfth Night. Act ii, sc. 5, l. 209. [Sir Toby] The only use of "tray-trip," a game of dice.
Bondslave to the law.—*Richard II,* ii, 1, 114. The only uses of "bondslave."

4
Good sister, wrong not me, nor wrong yourself,
To make a bondmaid and a slave of me.
The Taming of the Shrew. Act ii, sc. 1, l. 1. [Bianca] The only use of "bondmaid."

BONDS

5
Blessed bond of board and bed!
As You Like It, v, 4, 148. See under WEDLOCK.
Bond of chastity.—*Cymbeline,* v, 5, 207.
Bond of childhood.—*King Lear,* ii, 4, 181.
Bonds of death!—*Cymbeline,* i, 1, 117.
Bond of duty.—*Henry VIII,* iii, 2, 188.
Bond of faith.—*Richard II,* iv, 1, 76.
Bond of love.—*Twelfth Night,* v, 1, 159; *The Winter's Tale,* iv, 4, 584.
Bond of marriage.—*Julius Cæsar,* ii, 1, 280.
Natural bond of sisters.—*As You Like It,* i, 2, 288.
Bond to wedlock.—*Henry VIII,* ii, 4, 40.
Love's bonds.—*The Merchant of Venice,* ii, 6, 6.

6
Whoever bound him, I will loose his bonds.
The Comedy of Errors. Act v, sc. 1, l. 339. [Abbess]

7
Coupled in bonds of perpetuity.
I Henry VI. Act iv, sc. 7, l. 20. [Talbot]

8
To grace in captive bonds his chariot-wheels.
Julius Cæsar, i, 1, 39. See under CONQUEST.
Dangerous bonds.—*Cymbeline,* iii, 2, 37.

9
I tore them from their bonds, . . .
But now I envy at their liberty,
And will again commit them to their bonds.
King John, ii, 4, 70. See under HAIR.
You make my bonds still greater.
Measure for Measure. Act v, sc. 1, l. 8. [Angelo]

10 A bond of air, strong as the axle-tree
On which heaven rides.
Troilus and Cressida. Act i, sc. 3, l. 66. [Ulysses]
Cressid is mine, tied with the bonds of heaven:
Instance, O instance! strong as heaven itself;
The bonds of heaven are slipp'd, dissolved, and loosed.
Troilus and Cressida. Act v, sc. 2, l. 154. [Troilus]

BONES

11 My bones bear witness,
That since have felt the vigour of his rage.
The Comedy of Errors. Act iv, sc. 4, l. 80. [Dromio of Ephesus]
He has beat my bones.—*Troilus and Cressida,* ii, 1, 76.

12 Thy canonised bones, hearsed in death,
Have burst their cerements.
Hamlet, i, 4, 47. See SPIRIT, 1432:16. "Hearsed" is repeated in *The Merchant of Venice,* iii, 1, 93. The only use of "cerements."
Did these bones cost no more the breeding, but to play at loggats with 'em? Mine ache to think on 't.
Hamlet. Act v, sc. 1, l. 99. [Hamlet] The only use of "loggats" (a pitching game).
Thy bones are marrowless.—*Macbeth,* iii, 4, 94. See under GHOST.
Hollow bones of man.—*Timon of Athens,* iv, 3, 152.

13
Lay these bones in an unworthy urn,
Tombless, with no remembrance over them.
Henry V. Act i, sc. 2, l. 228. [King Henry] The only use of "tombless."
I desire to lay my bones there.
The Winter's Tale, iv, 2, 6. See under PATRIOTISM.

14
Bid them achieve me and then sell my bones.
Henry V. Act iv, sc. 3, l. 91. [King Henry]
How now! what means this, herald? know'st thou not
That I have fined these bones of mine for ransom?
Henry V. Act iv, sc. 7, l. 71. [King Henry]

1
By these ten bones, my lords, he did speak to me in the garret one night.
II Henry VI. Act i, sc. 3, l. 193. [Peter]
The only use of "garret" in the plays.

2 His bones,
When he has run his course and sleeps in blessings,
May have a tomb of orphans' tears wept on 'em!
Henry VIII. Act iii, sc. 2, l. 397. [Wolsey]

Within my tent his bones to-night shall lie,
Most like a soldier, order'd honourably.
Julius Cæsar. Act v, sc. 5, l. 78. [Octavius]

Now unto thy bones good night!
Much Ado about Nothing, v, 2, 22. [Claudio]

Fair fall the bones that took the pains for me!
King John. Act i, sc. 1, l. 78. [Bastard]

3
Beat not the bones of the buried.
Love's Labour's Lost, v, 2, 667. [Armado]

4
Let 's have the tongs and the bones.
A Midsummer-Night's Dream. Act iv, sc. 1, l. 32. [Bottom]

5
Nurse: Fie, how my bones ache!
Juliet: I would thou hadst my bones, and I thy news.
Romeo and Juliet. Act ii, sc. 5, l. 26.

My aching bones.
Romeo and Juliet. Act ii, sc. 5, l. 65. [Nurse]
Also, *Troilus and Cressida,* v, 10, 35; 51.

My old bones ache.
The Tempest. Act iii, sc. 3, l. 2. [Gonzalo]

Fill his bones with aches.—*The Tempest,* i, 2, 370.

Such an ache in my bones.
Troilus and Cressida, v, 3, 106. See under DISEASE.

Incurable bone-ache.—*Troilus and Cressida,* v, 1, 26. "Bone-ache" is repeated in ii, 3, 20, and occurs in no other play.

6 Shut me nightly in a charnel-house,
O'er-cover'd quite with dead men's rattling bones,
With reeky shanks and yellow chapless skulls.
Romeo and Juliet. Act iv, sc. 1, l. 81. [Juliet]
The only use of "reeky." "Charnel-houses" occurs in *Macbeth,* iii, 4, 71, and "chapless" is repeated in *Hamlet,* v, 1, 97.

O, their bones, their bones!—*Romeo and Juliet,* ii, 4, 37.

7
In this rage, with some great kinsman's bone,
As with a club, dash out my desperate brains.
Romeo and Juliet. Act iv, sc. 3, l. 53. [Juliet]

8
Of his bones are coral made.
The Tempest, i, 2, 397. See under FATHER.

Bare-pick'd bone.—*King John,* iv, 3, 148. The only use of "bare-pick'd."
Detestable bones.—*King John,* iii, 4, 29.
Honest bones.—*The Winter's Tale,* iv, 4, 467.
Honour'd bones.—*All 's Well that Ends Well,* ii, 3, 148.
Steely bones.—*All 's Well that Ends Well,* i, 1, 114. "Steely" is repeated in *III Henry VI,* ii, 3, 16.
Valiant bones.—*Henry V,* iv, 3, 98.
Weary bones.—*Henry VIII,* iv, 2, 22.
Cricket's bone.—*Romeo and Juliet,* i, 4, 63.
Royal grandsire's bones.—*Richard II,* iii, 3, 106.
Matron's bones.—*Hamlet,* iii, 4, 83.
Mutius' bones.—*Titus Andronicus,* i, 1, 369.
Traveller's bones.—*Measure for Measure,* iv, 2, 70.
Warwick's bones.—*III Henry VI,* v, 2, 4.
Whale's bone.—*Love's Labour 's Lost,* v, 2, 332.
Bone of Greece.—*Troilus and Cressida,* i, 3, 55.

9
I feel 't upon my bones.
Timon of Athens. Act iii, sc. 6, l. 130. [Lord]

10
There lie thy bones, sweet Mutius, with thy friends.
Titus Andronicus. Act i, sc. 1, l. 387. [Lucius]

11
Hark, villains! I will grind your bones to dust.
Titus Andronicus. Act v, sc. 2, l. 187. [Titus]

Let me go grind their bones to powder small.
Titus Andronicus, v, 2, 199. See under THREAT.

Hack their bones asunder.—*I Henry VI,* iv, 7, 47.

BONNET, see Hat

BOOK

See also Reading

12
Books in the running brooks.
As You Like It, ii, 1, 16. See LIFE, 866:10.

Nature's infinite book of secrecy.—*Antony and Cleopatra,* i, 2, 9. See under NATURE.

13
Thy general is my lover: I have been
The book of his good acts, whence men have read
His fame unparallell'd, haply amplified.
Coriolanus. Act v, sc. 2, l. 14. [Menenius]
The only use of "amplified."

Book of beauty.—*King John,* ii, 1, 485.
Book of fate.—*II Henry IV,* iii, 1, 45.
Book of honour.—*Sonnets,* xxv.
Book of life.—*Richard II,* i, 3, 202.
Book of memory.—*I Henry VI,* ii, 4, 101; *II Henry VI,* i, 1, 100.
Book of Riddles.—*The Merry Wives of Windsor,* i, 1, 209.
Book of sport.—*Troilus and Cressida,* iv, 5, 239.
Book of virtue.—*The Winter's Tale,* iv, 3, 131.
Book of words.—*Much Ado about Nothing,* i, 1, 309.
Lenders' books.—*King Lear,* iii, 4, 101.
Greek and Latin books.—*The Taming of the Shrew,* ii, 1, 101.

14 A book? O rare one!
Be not, as is our fangled world, a garment
Nobler than that it covers.
Cymbeline. Act v, sc. 4, l. 134. [Posthumus]
The only use of "fangled."

Was ever book containing such vile matter
So fairly bound?
Romeo and Juliet, iii, 2, 83. See under DECEIT.

15
And now I will unclasp a secret book,

And to your quick-conceiving discontents
I'll read you matter deep and dangerous,
As full of peril and adventurous spirit
As to o'er-walk a current roaring loud
On the unsteadfast footing of a spear.
I Henry IV. Act i, sc. 3, l. 188. [Earl of Worcester] The only use of "quick-conceiving," "o'er-walk" and "unsteadfast."

I have unclasp'd
To thee the book even of my secret soul.
Twelfth Night. Act i, sc. 4, l. 13. [Duke]

A book . . . with red letters in 't.
II Henry VI, iv, 2, 97. See under EDUCATION.

1 A volume of enticing lines,
Able to ravish any dull conceit.
I Henry VI. Act v, sc. 5, l. 14. [Suffolk] See under PERFECTION.

Volumes in folio.—*Love's Labour 's Lost,* i, 2, 191.

A title-leaf,
Fortells the nature of a tragic volume.
II Henry IV. Act i, sc. 1, l. 61. [Northumberland] The only use of "title-leaf."

Fair volume.—*Romeo and Juliet,* i, 3, 81.

World's volume.—*Cymbeline,* iii, 4, 140.

2 What, at your book so hard?
III Henry VI. Act v, sc. 6, l. 1. [Gloucester]

I 'll to my book.—*The Tempest,* iii, 1, 94.

Book of arithmetic.—*Romeo and Juliet,* iii, 1, 106.

Learned books.—*The Rape of Lucrece,* l. 811.

3 Here 's the book I sought for so;
I put it in the pocket of my gown.
Julius Cæsar. Act iv, sc. 3, l. 252. [Brutus]

In my chamber-window lies a book: bring it hither to me in the orchard.
Much Ado about Nothing. Act ii, sc. 3, l. 3. [Benedick]

Some book there is that she desires to see.
Titus Andronicus. Act iv, sc. 1, l. 31. [Titus]

4 You two are book-men.
Love's Labour 's Lost. Act iv, sc. 2, l. 35. [Dull] "Book-men" was used once again in the same play, ii, 1, 227.

We turned o'er many books together.
The Merchant of Venice. Act iv, sc. 1, l. 156. [Clerk]

The bookish theoric.—*Othello,* i, 1, 24. "Theoric" is repeated in *All 's Well that Ends Well,* iv, 3, 162; and in *Henry V,* i, 1, 52.

5 I had rather than forty shillings I had my Book of Songs and Sonnets here.
The Merry Wives of Windsor. Act i, sc. 1, l. 205. [Slender]

6 I see, lady, the gentleman is not in your books.
Much Ado about Nothing. Act i, sc. 1, l. 78. [Messenger]

A herald, Kate? O, put me in thy books!
The Taming of the Shrew. Act ii, sc. 1, l. 225. [Petruchio]

7 Who has a book of all that monarchs do,
He 's more secure to keep it shut than shown.
Pericles. Act i, sc. 1, l. 94. [Pericles]

Shut the book.—*II Henry IV,* iii, 1, 56.

8 To blot old books and alter their contents.
The Rape of Lucrece, l. 948.

Antique book.—*Sonnets,* lix.

9 My book, wherein my soul recorded
The history of all her secret thoughts.
Richard III. Act iii, sc. 5, l. 27. [Gloucester]

10 And see, a book of prayer in his hand.
Richard III. Act iii, sc. 7, l. 98. [Buckingham]

A book of prayers on their pillow lay.
Richard III. Act iv, sc. 3, l. 14. [Tyrrel]

Books of God.—*II Henry IV,* iv, 2, 17. See under PREACHER.

God's book.—*II Henry VI,* ii, 3, 4.

Goodly book.—*Othello,* iv, 2, 71.

Jove's own book.—*Coriolanus,* iii, 1, 293.

Book of heaven.—*Richard II,* iv, 1, 236.

Book of Numbers.—*Henry V,* i, 2, 98. See under INHERITANCE.

11 This precious book of love, this unbound lover,
To beautify him, only lacks a cover.
Romeo and Juliet. Act i, sc. 3, l. 87. [Lady Capulet]

Love's richest book.—*A Midsummer-Night's Dream,* ii, 2, 122.

That book in many's eyes doth share the glory,
That in gold clasps locks in the golden story.
Romeo and Juliet. Act i, sc. 3, l. 91. [Lady Capulet]

Sour misfortune's book.—*Romeo and Juliet,* v, 3, 82. See under MISFORTUNE.

12 O, let my books be then the eloquence
And dumb presagers of my speaking breast.
Sonnets. No. xxiii. The only use of "presagers."

13 My books and instruments shall be my company.
The Taming of the Shrew. Act i, sc. 1, l. 82. [Bianca]

I 'll have them very fairly bound:
All books of love.
The Taming of the Shrew. Act i, sc. 2, l. 146. [Gremio]

Set of books.—*Taming of the Shrew,* ii, 1, 107.

14 Your father prays you leave your books.
The Taming of the Shrew. Act iii, sc. 1, l. 82. [Servant]

Ply his book.—*Taming of the Shrew,* i, 1, 201.

15 Knowing I loved my books, he furnish'd me
From mine own library with volumes that
I prize above my dukedom.
The Tempest. Act i, sc. 2, l. 166. [Prospero]

My library Was dukedom large enough.
The Tempest. Act i, sc. 2, l. 109. [Prospero]

Come, and take choice of all my library,
And so beguile thy sorrow.
Titus Andronicus. Act iv, sc. 1, l. 34. [Titus] The only uses of "library."

16 Remember
First to possess his books; for without them

He 's but a sot, as I am . . . Burn but his books.
The Tempest. Act iii, sc. 2, l. 99. [Caliban]
And deeper than did ever plummet sound
I 'll drown my book.
The Tempest. Act v, sc. 1, l. 56. [Prospero]
The devil's book. *II Henry IV,* ii, 2, 49.
Lawless bloody book.—*II Henry IV,* iv, 1, 91. See under REBELLION.
Bloody book of law.—*Othello,* i, 3, 67. See under LAW.

1
Painter: When comes your book forth?
Poet: Upon the heels of my presentment, sir.
Timon of Athens. Act i, sc. 1, l. 26. "Presentment is used only once again, in *Hamlet,* iii, 4, 54: "Counterfeit presentment."

2
Titus: What book is that she tosseth so?
Young Lucius: Grandsire, 'tis Ovid's Metamorphoses.
Titus Andronicus. Act iv, sc. 1, l. 41. This is the only mention of the *Metamorphoses,* but Ovid is referred to in *The Taming of the Shrew,* i, 1, 33, and *As You Like It,* iii, 3, 8.

BOON

See also Gift

3
Ask of Cymbeline what boon thou wilt,
Fitting my bounty and thy state, I 'll give it.
Cymbeline. Act v, sc. 5, l. 97. [Cymbeline]

4
King Edward: But you will take exceptions to my boon.
Lady Grey: No, gracious lord, except I cannot do it.
III Henry VI. Act iii, sc. 2, l. 46.

5
My boon I make it, that you know me not
Till time and I think meet.
King Lear. Act iv, sc. 7, l. 10. [Kent]
Why, this is not a boon;
'Tis as I should entreat you wear your gloves,
Or feed on nourishing dishes, or keep you warm.
Othello. Act iii, sc. 3, l. 76. [Desdemona] The only use of "nourishing."

6
I 'll beg one boon,
And then be gone and trouble you no more.
Richard II. Act iv, sc. 1, l. 302. [King Richard]
Gloucester: For divers unknown reasons, I beseech you,
Grant me this boon.
Anne: With all my heart.
Richard III. Act i, sc. 2, l. 219.
Upon my feeble knee
I beg this boon, with tears not lightly shed.
Titus Andronicus. Act ii, sc. 3, l. 288. [Titus]
I now beseech you, for your daughter's sake,
To grant one boon that I shall ask of you.
The Two Gentlemen of Verona. Act v, sc. 4, l. 149. [Valentine]
This, my last boon, give me,
For such kindness must relieve me.
Pericles. Act v, sc. 2, l. 3. [Gower]

BOOT, see under Shoe

BORROWING

I—Borrowing

7
Shut his bosom
Against our borrowing prayers.
All's Well that Ends Well, iii, 1, 8. [Duke]

8
Coming in to borrow a mess of vinegar.
II Henry IV. Act ii, sc. 1, l. 103. [Hostess]
By this heavenly ground I tread on, I must be fain to pawn both my plate and the tapestry of my dining-chambers.
II Henry IV. Act ii, sc. 1, l. 152. [Hostess] "Dining-chamber" is repeated in *The Two Gentlemen of Verona,* iv, 4, 9.

9
When men come to borrow of your masters, they approach sadly, and go away merry.
Timon of Athens. Act ii, sc. 2, l. 105. [Fool]
'Tis much to borrow, and I will not owe it.
Venus and Adonis, l. 411.

II—Borrowing and Lending

10
Neither a borrower nor a lender be;
For loan oft loses both itself and friend,
And borrowing dulls the edge of husbandry.
Hamlet. Act i, sc. 3, l. 75. [Polonius] "Loan" is repeated in *Richard III,* iv, 4, 323, and in *Sonnets,* vi.
Keep . . . thy pen from lenders' books.
King Lear, iii, 4, 100. See under BEHAVIOUR.
I must become a borrower.—*Macbeth,* iii, 1, 27. "Borrower" is used a third time in *II Henry IV,* ii, 2, 125: "Borrower's cap."

11 I neither lend nor borrow
By taking nor by giving of excess.
The Merchant of Venice, i, 3, 62. [Antonio]
Methought you said you neither lend nor borrow
Upon advantage.
The Merchant of Venice, i, 3, 70. [Shylock]

12
Borrows money in God's name, the which he hath used so long and never paid that now men grow hard-hearted and will lend nothing for God's sake.
Much Ado about Nothing. Act v, sc. 1, l. 220. [Dogberry]

13
She lends them words, and she their looks doth borrow.
The Rape of Lucrece, l. 1498.

14
Lend to each man enough, that one need not lend to another; for, were your godheads to borrow of men, men would forsake the gods.
Timon of Athens. Act iii, sc. 6, l. 82. [Timon]
Stay, I will lend thee money, borrow none.
Timon of Athens. Act iii, sc. 6, l. 111. [Timon]

BOSOM

15
Whose bosom was my crownet and chief end.
Antony and Cleopatra. Act iv, sc. 12, l. 27. [Antony] "Crownet" (coronet) is repeated in v, 2, 91; and in *Troilus and Cressida,* Prol., 6.

1
In her excellent white bosom.
Hamlet. Act ii, sc. 2, l. 113. [Hamlet]
The milk-white bosom of thy love.
The Two Gentlemen of Verona. Act iii, sc. 1, l. 250. [Proteus]
Pure bosom.—*The Two Gentlemen of Verona*, iii, 1, 144.
2
O bosom black as death!
Hamlet. Act iii, sc. 3, l. 67. [King]
Black bosom.—*The Rape of Lucrece*, l. 788.
Covert bosom.—*Measure for Measure*, v, 1, 10.
Flint bosom.—*Richard II*, v, 1, 3.
Flinty bosom.—*All's Well that Ends Well*, iv, 4, 7.
Frozen bosom.—*II Henry VI*, v, 2, 35; *Romeo and Juliet*, i, 4, 101.
Glutton bosom.—*II Henry IV*, i, 3, 98.
Harder bosoms!—*The Winter's Tale*, i, 2, 153.
Hollow bosoms.—*Henry V*, ii, Prol., 21.
Rocky bosom.—*Richard III*, iv, 4, 234.
3
Whose bosom burns
With an incensed fire of injuries.
II Henry IV. Act i, sc. 3, l. 13. [Hastings]
Burn'd bosom.—*King John*, v, 7, 39. See under DISEASE: FEVER.
4
I stabb'd your fathers' bosoms, split my breast.
III Henry VI. Act ii, sc. 6, l. 30. [Clifford]
Portia: You must prepare your bosom for the knife. . . .
Therefore lay bare your bosom.
Shylock: Ay, his breast: So says the bond: . . .
'Nearest his heart:' those are the very words.
The Merchant of Venice. Act iv, sc. 1, l. 245.
Wounded bosoms.—*Sonnets*, cxx.
5
I am in their bosoms.
Julius Cæsar. Act v, sc. 1, l. 7. [Antony] See under KNOWLEDGE.
I know you are of her bosom.
King Lear. Act iv, sc. 5, l. 26. [Regan]
He shall not perceive
But that you have your father's bosom there
And speak his very heart.
The Winter's Tale. Act iv, sc. 4, l. 572. [Camillo]
Shut his bosom.—*All's Well that Ends Well*, iii, 1, 8.
6
Whose age has charms in it, whose title more,
To pluck the common bosom on his side.
King Lear. Act v, sc. 3, l. 48. [Edmund]
He did in the general bosom reign
Of young, of old; and sexes both enchanted.
A Lover's Complaint, l. 127.
7
The broken bosoms that to me belong
Have emptied all their fountains in my well,
And mine I pour your ocean all among.
A Lover's Complaint, l. 254.
Sad bosoms.—*Macbeth*, iv, 3, 2.
8
Sweet peace conduct his sweet soul to the bosom
Of good old Abraham!
Richard II. Act iv, sc. 1, l. 103. [Bolingbroke]
The sons of Edward sleep in Abraham's bosom.
Richard III. Act iv, sc. 3, l. 38. [King Richard]
Nay, sure he's not in hell: he's in Arthur's bosom, if ever man went to Arthur's bosom.
Henry V. Act ii, sc. 3, l. 9. [Hostess]
Richard's bosom.—*Richard III*, v, 3, 144.
Bosom of the air.—*Romeo and Juliet*, ii, 2, 32.
Bosom of my child.—*A Midsummer-Night's Dream*, i, 1, 27.
Bosom of my conscience.—*Henry VIII*, ii, 4, 182.
Bosom of the earth.—*Richard II*, iii, 2, 147.
Bosom of the ground.—*King John*, iv, 1, 3.
Bosom of the ocean.—*Richard III*, i, 1, 4.
Bosom of the sea.—*II Henry VI*, iv, 1, 2.
9
Thou and my bosom henceforth shall be twain.
Romeo and Juliet. Act iii, sc. 5, l. 240. [Juliet]
10
No love toward others in that bosom sits
That on itself such murderous shame commits.
Sonnets. No. ix.
11
Thy bosom is endeared with all hearts,
Which I by lacking have supposed dead.
Sonnets. No. xxxi.
My bosom is full of kindness.
Twelfth Night, ii, 1, 40. See under KINDNESS.
Generous bosoms.—*Troilus and Cressida*, ii, 2, 155.
Loyal bosom.—*Richard II*, ii, 3, 98.
12
And by her fair immortal hand she swears,
From his soft bosom never to remove.
Venus and Adonis, l. 80.
Complete bosom.—*Measure for Measure*, i, 3, 3.
Gentle bosom.—*Henry V*, iv, 1, 174; *King John*, v, 2, 28.
Loving bosom.—*Love's Labour's Lost*, iv, 3, 136.
Melting bosoms.—*Titus Andronicus*, iii, 1, 214.
Peaceful bosom.—*Richard II*, ii, 3, 93.
Plenteous bosom.—*Timon of Athens*, i, 2, 131; iv, 3, 186.
Sweet bosom.—*Richard III*, i, 2, 124; *Henry V*, v, 2, 382.

BOTTOM

13
Now I see The bottom of your purpose.
All's Well that Ends Well. Act iii, sc. 7, l. 29. [Widow] See also under PURPOSE.
I do see the bottom of Justice Shallow.
II Henry IV. Act iii, sc. 2, l. 324. [Falstaff]
We then should see the bottom
Of all our fortunes.
II Henry VI. Act v, sc. 2, l. 78. [Queen]
I myself see not the bottom of it.
Troilus and Cressida, iii, 3, 312. See under MIND.
Bottom of annoy.—*The Rape of Lucrece*, l. 1109.
Bottom of a cowslip.—*Cymbeline*, ii, 2, 39.
Bottom of the deep.—*I Henry IV*, i, 2, 203.
Slimy bottom of the deep.—*Richard III*, i, 4, 32.
Bottom of my grief.—*Romeo and Juliet*, iii, 5, 199.
Bottom of the news.—*Coriolanus*, iv, 5, 209.

Bottom of the sea.—*Henry V*, i, 2, 164; *Richard III*, i, 4, 28.
The very bottom of my soul.—*Henry V*, ii, 2, 97.
Bottom of your story.—*Pericles*, v, 1, 166.
Bottom of his success.—*All's Well that Ends Well*, iii, 6, 38.
Bottom of brown thread.—*The Taming of the Shrew*, iv, 3, 138.
Bottom of a tomb.—*Romeo and Juliet*, iii, 5, 56.
Bottom of the worst.—*Troilus and Cressida*, ii, 2, 17.

1
Down in the neighbour bottom.
As You Like It. Act iv, sc. 3, l. 79. [Celia] The only use of "bottom" in the sense of low-lying land.

2
The very bottom and the soul of hope.
I Henry IV, iv, 1, 50. See under HOPE.

3 There 's no bottom, none,
In my voluptuousness.
Macbeth, iv, 3, 60. See under WANTONNESS.
It hath no bottom.—*A Midsummer-Night's Dream*, iv, 1, 221.
Having no bottom.—*Titus Andronicus*, iii, 1, 217.
Unknown bottom.—*As You Like It*, iv, 1, 212.
Then be my passions bottomless.
Titus Andronicus, iii, 1, 218. See under SORROW. "Bottomless" is repeated in *The Rape of Lucrece*, l. 701: "Bottomless conceit."

4 It concerns me
To look into the bottom of my place.
Measure for Measure. Act i, sc. 1, l. 79. [Escalus]
Sound the bottom.—*II Henry IV*, iv, 2, 51.

5
If the bottom were as deep as hell, I should down.
The Merry Wives of Windsor, iii, 5, 13. See under DROWNING.

6
Now to the bottom dost thou search my wound.
Titus Andronicus, ii, 3, 262. See under WOUND.
Near the bottom.—*The Tempest*, ii, 1, 227.

7
Finds bottom in the uncomprehensive deeps.
Troilus and Cressida, iii, 3, 198. See under PROVIDENCE. The only use of "uncomprehensive."

8
The most noble bottom of our fleet.
Twelfth Night, v, 1, 60. See FAME, 470:14.

BOUNTY

See also Generosity, Gift

9
Thou mine of bounty, how wouldst thou have paid
My better service, when my turpitude
Thou dost so crown with gold!
Antony and Cleopatra. Act iv, sc. 6, l. 32. [Enobarbus] "Turpitude" is used only once again, in *Troilus and Cressida*, v, 2, 112: "Full of turpitude."

For his bounty,
There was no winter in't; an autumn 'twas
That grew the more by reaping.
Antony and Cleopatra. Act v, sc. 2, l. 86. [Cleopatra]

10
To you This honourable bounty shall belong.
I Henry IV. Act v, sc. 5, l. 26. [Prince of Wales]
May Iden live to merit such a bounty,
And never live but true unto his liege!
II Henry VI. Act v, sc. 1, l. 81. [Iden]

11 I have not alone
Employ'd you where high profits might come home,
But pared my present havings, to bestow
My bounties upon you.
Henry VIII. Act iii, sc. 2, l. 157. [King Henry]
As my hand has open'd bounty to you,
My heart dropp'd love, my power rain'd honour.
Henry VIII. Act iii, sc. 2, l. 184. [King Henry]

12
Which of you shall we say doth love us most?
That we our largest bounty may extend
Where nature doth with merit challenge.
King Lear. Act i, sc. 1, l. 52. [King Lear] The only use of "largest."

13
She is a region in Guiana, all gold and bounty.
The Merry Wives of Windsor. Act i, sc. 3, l. 77. The only mention of Guiana.
As bountiful As mines of India.
I Henry IV. Act iii, sc. 1, l. 168. [Mortimer]
Bountiful good lord and master.
Timon of Athens. Act iii, sc. 1, l. 10. [Lucullus]

14
My bounty is as boundless as the sea.
Romeo and Juliet. Act ii, sc. 2, l. 133. [Juliet] See under LOVE for full quotation.

I thank thee, king,
For thy great bounty, that not only givest
Me cause to wail but teachest me the way
How to lament the cause.
Richard II. Act iv, sc. 1, l. 299. [King Richard]

15
Magic of bounty! all these spirits thy power
Hath conjured to attend.
Timon of Athens. Act i, sc. 1, l. 6. [Poet]

Come, shall we in,
And taste Lord Timon's bounty?
Timon of Athens. Act i, sc. 1, l. 283. [Lord]
Hail to thee, worthy Timon, and to all
That of his bounties taste!
Timon of Athens. Act i, sc. 2, l. 128. [Cupid]
I never tasted Timon in my life,
Nor came any of his bounties over me.
Timon of Athens. Act iii, sc. 2, l. 85. [Stranger]
Having often of your open bounty tasted.
Timon of Athens. Act v, sc. 1, l. 61. [Poet]

16
'Tis pity bounty had not eyes behind,
That man might ne'er be wretched for his mind.
Timon of Athens. Act i, sc. 2, l. 169. [Flavius]
Heavens, have I said, the bounty of this lord!

How many prodigal bits have slaves and peasants
This night englutted!
Timon of Athens. Act ii, sc. 2, l. 173. [Flavius]
So near the gulf, Thou needs must be englutted.
Henry V, iv, 3, 83. The only uses of "englutted." "Englut" occurs in *Othello,* i, 3, 57.

1
O, he 's the very soul of bounty!
Timon of Athens. Act i, sc. 2, l. 215. [Lord]
No villanous bounty yet hath pass'd my heart;
Unwisely, not ignobly, have I given.
Timon of Athens. Act ii, sc. 2, l. 182. [Timon]
Bounty, that makes gods, does still mar men.
Timon of Athens. Act iv, sc. 2, l. 41. [Flavius]

2
His heart and hand both open and both free;
For what he has he gives, what thinks he shows;
Yet gives he not till judgement guide his bounty.
Troilus and Cressida. Act iv, sc. 5, l. 100. [Ulysses]

3
Duke: It may awake my bounty further.
Clown: Marry, sir, lullaby to your bounty till I come again. . . . Let your bounty take a nap.
Twelfth Night. Act v, sc. 1, l. 47.
To testify your bounty, I thank you, you have testerned me.
The Two Gentlemen of Verona. Act i, sc. 1, l. 152. [Speed] The only use of "testerned" (to give a tester, or sixpence, to).

BOW

4
My arrows,
Too slightly timber'd for so loud a wind,
Would have reverted to my bow again,
And not where I had aim'd them.
Hamlet. Act iv, sc. 7, l. 21. [King]
Stoutly timber'd.—*Othello,* ii, 1, 48. The only uses of "timber'd."

5
A' drew a good bow; a' shot a fine shoot.
II Henry IV. Act iii, sc. 2, l. 48. [Shallow]
That fellow handles his bow like a crow-keeper: draw me a clothier's yard.
King Lear. Act iv, sc. 6, l. 87. [King Lear]
Scaring the ladies like a crow-keeper.—*Romeo and Juliet,* i, 4, 6. The only uses of "crow-keeper."

6
King Lear: The bow is bent and drawn, make from the shaft.
Kent: Let it fall rather, though the fork invade
The region of my heart.
King Lear. Act i, sc. 1, l. 145.
Bows Of double-fatal yew.—*Richard II,* iii, 2, 116. The only use of "double-fatal."
Cupid's bow.—*Venus and Adonis,* l. 581.
Cupid's strongest bow.—*A Midsummer-Night's Dream,* i, 1, 169.
A silver bow.—*A Midsummer-Night's Dream,* i, 1, 9; *Pericles,* v, 1, 249.
Tartar's bow.—*A Midsummer-Night's Dream,* iii, 2, 101.

7
A well-experienced archer hits the mark
His eye doth level at.
Pericles. Act i, sc. 1, l. 164. [Antiochus] The only use of "well-experienced."
Good archer.—*Titus Andronicus,* iv, 3, 52.

8
Draw, archers, draw your arrows to the head!
Richard III. Act v, sc. 3, l. 339. [King Richard]
Draw your bow.—*The Taming of the Shrew,* v, 2, 47.
Bend his bow.—*The Rape of Lucrece,* l. 580.
Sir boy, now let me see your archery;
Look ye draw home enough, and 'tis there straight.
Titus Andronicus. Act iv, sc. 3, l. 2. [Titus]
Cupid's archery.—*Midsummer-Night's Dream,* iii, 2, 103. The only uses of "archery."

BOWELS

See also Guts

9
In the bowels of the Lord.
Henry V. Act ii, sc. 4, l. 102. [Exeter]
Bowels of the battle.—*I Henry IV,* i, 1, 129.
Bowels of the deep.—*Richard III,* iii, 4, 103.
Bowels of the earth.—*I Henry IV,* i, 3, 61.
Brinish bowels.—*Titus Andronicus,* iii, 1, 97. "Brinish" is repeated in *III Henry VI,* iii, 1, 41: "Brinish tears."

10
For thine own bowels, which do call thee sire,
The mere effusion of thy proper loins,
Do curse the gout, serpigo, and the rheum,
For ending thee no sooner.
Measure for Measure. Act iii, sc. 1, l. 29. [Duke]
Dry serpigo.—*Troilus and Cressida,* ii, 3, 81. The only uses of "serpigo" (shingles).

11 With thy treacherous blade
Unrip'dst the bowels of thy sovereign's son.
Richard III. Act i, sc. 4, l. 212. [Murderer] The only use of "unrip'dst."

12
Thou thing of no bowels!
Troilus and Cressida. Act ii, sc. 1, l. 54. [Thersites] For "embowell'd" see under THREAT.

BOY

See also Child, Lad, Son, Youth

13
These boys are boys of ice.
All's Well that Ends Well. Act ii, sc. 3, l. 99. [Lafeu]
Boys of art.—*The Merry Wives of Windsor,* iii, 1, 109.
Boy of tears!—*Coriolanus,* v, 6, 101.

14
Proud scornful boy, unworthy this good gift;
That dost in vile misprision shackle up
My love and her desert.
All's Well that Ends Well. Act ii, sc. 3, l. 158. [King]
Go, rate thy minions, proud insulting boy!
III Henry VI. Act ii, sc. 2, l. 84. [Queen Margaret]

Dishonourable boy!—*Richard II,* iv, 1, 65.
Faint-hearted boy.—*Titus Andronicus,* iii, 1, 65. "Faint-hearted" is repeated in *I Henry VI,* i, 3, 22; and in *III Henry VI,* i, 1, 183.
Flint-hearted boy!—*Venus and Adonis,* l. 95. The only use of "flint-hearted."
Gibing boys.—*I Henry IV,* iii, 2, 66.
Hangman boys.—*The Two Gentlemen of Verona,* iv, 4, 60.
Peevish boy.—*I Henry VI,* ii, 4, 76; *As You Like It,* iii, 5, 110.
Rascally boy.—*As You Like It,* iv, 1, 218.
Rash and unbridled boy.—*All's Well that Ends Well,* iii, 2, 30. "Unbridled" is repeated in *Troilus and Cressida,* iii, 2, 130: "Unbridled children."
Rude boys.—*All's Well that Ends Well,* iii, 2, 84.
Scurvy young boy.—*II Henry IV,* ii, 4, 296.
Transgressing boy.—*Richard II,* v, 3, 96. "Transgressing" is repeated in *Love's Labour's Lost,* i, 2, 159: "Transgressing slave."
Ungracious boy.—*I Henry IV,* ii, 4, 490.
Unreverend boy.—*King John,* i, 1, 227.
Unruly boys.—*Comedy of Errors,* iii, 1, 62.
Waggish boys.—*A Midsummer-Night's Dream,* i, 1, 241. "Waggish" is repeated in *Cymbeline,* iii, 4, 160: "Waggish courage."
Wayward boy.—*Venus and Adonis,* l. 344.
Wilful boy.—*III Henry VI,* v, 5, 31.
Wretched boy.—*Romeo and Juliet,* iii, 1, 135.

1
A foolish idle boy, but for all that very ruttish . . . a dangerous and lascivious boy, who is a whale to virginity and devours up all the fry it finds.
All's Well that Ends Well. Act iv, sc. 3, l. 242. [Parolles] The only use of "ruttish."
Lascivious young boy.—*All's Well that Ends Well,* iv, 3, 333.
The boy is foolish, and I fear not him.
Richard III. Act iv, sc. 2, l. 55. [King Richard]
Foolish boy.—*Richard II,* ii, 3, 97.
Silly boy.—*Venus and Adonis,* l. 467.

2
The boy is fair,
Of female favour, and bestows himself
Like a ripe sister.
As You Like It. Act iv, sc. 3, l. 86. [Oliver]
Fair boy.—*King John,* ii, 1, 30.

3
This boy is forest-born.
As You Like It. Act v, sc. 4, l. 30. [Orlando] The only use of "forest-born."

4
As we rate boys, who, being mature in knowledge,
Pawn their experience to their present pleasure,
And so rebel to judgement.
Antony and Cleopatra. Act i, sc. 4, l. 31. [Cæsar]
Pretty dimpled boys, like smiling Cupids.
Antony and Cleopatra. Act ii, sc. 2, l. 207. [Enobarbus]
Volumnia: He had rather see the swords, and hear a drum, than look upon his schoolmaster.
Valeria: O' my word, the father's son: I'll swear, 'tis a very pretty boy.
***Coriolanus.* Act i, sc. 3, l. 60.**

Speak thou, boy:
Perhaps thy childishness will move him more
Than can our reasons.
Coriolanus. Act v, sc. 3, l. 156. [Volumnia] "Childishness" is repeated in *As You Like It,* ii, 7, 165: "Second childishness"; and in *Antony and Cleopatra,* i, 3, 58.
My young boy
Hath an aspect of intercession, which
Great nature cries 'Deny not.'
Coriolanus. Act v, sc. 3, l. 31. [Coriolanus]
Young boy.—*King John,* iii, 3, 60; iv, 1, 40; *Antony and Cleopatra,* iv, 15, 65.
Young sober-blooded boy.—*II Henry IV,* iv, 3, 94. The only use of "sober-blooded."

5
That brought you forth this boy, to keep your name
Living to time.
Coriolanus. Act v, sc. 3, l. 126. [Virgilia]
This boy, that cannot tell what he would have.
Coriolanus. Act v, sc. 3, l. 174. [Volumnia]

6
Thou divine Nature, how thyself thou blazon'st
In these two princely boys!
Cymbeline. Act iv, sc. 2, l. 171. [Belarius] The only use of "blazon'st."
Two boys, an old man twice a boy, a lane,
Preserved the Britons, was the Romans' bane.
Cymbeline. Act v, sc. 3, l. 57. [Posthumus]

7
Hath my poor boy done aught but well,
Whose face I never saw?
I died whilst in the womb he stay'd
Attending nature's law.
Cymbeline. Act v, sc. 4, l. 35. [Sicilius] "Poor boy" occurs seven times in the plays.

8
O, this boy Lends mettle to us all!
I Henry IV. Act v, sc. 4, l. 23. [Prince of Wales]
The boy hath taught us manly duties.
Cymbeline. Act iv, sc. 2, l. 397. [Lucius]
Ay, that's my boy!—*Titus Andronicus,* iv, 1, 110.
That's my brave boy!—*Coriolanus,* v, 3, 76. "Brave boy" is repeated in *I Henry VI,* iv, 6, 24; *Titus Andronicus,* ii, 1, 129; *Troilus and Cressida,* v, 3, 33.

9
Nay, you shall find no boy's play here, I can tell you.
I Henry IV. Act v, sc. 4, l. 75. [Falstaff] The only use of "boy's play."
Thou whoreson mandrake, thou art fitter to be worn in my cap than to wait at my heels.
II Henry IV. Act i, sc. 2, l. 17. [Falstaff]
There's never none of these demure boys come to any proof.
II Henry IV. Act iv, sc. 3, l. 97. [Falstaff] "Demure" is repeated in *Twelfth Night,* ii, 5, 89: "Demure travel of regard"; and in *Henry VIII,* i, 2, 167: "Demure confidence."

10
God save thee, my sweet boy!
II Henry IV. Act v, sc. 5, l. 47. [Falstaff]
Sweet boy.—*III Henry VI,* i, 4, 157; ii, 5, 115; v, 6, 23. *Titus Andronicus,* iv, 1, 88.

11
Shall not thou and I, between Saint Denis

and Saint George, compound a boy, half French, half English, that shall go to Constantinople and take the Turk by the beard? shall we not? what sayest thou, my fair flower-de-luce?

Henry V. Act v, sc. 2, l. 220. [King Henry]

We 'll play with them the first boy for a thousand ducats.

The Merchant of Venice. Act iii, sc. 2, l. 216. [Gratiano]

If my lord get a boy of you, you 'll give him me.

Troilus and Cressida. Act iii, sc. 2, l. 112. [Pandarus]

1 Look on the boy;
And let his manly face, which promiseth
Successful fortune, steel thy melting heart.

III Henry VI. Act ii, sc. 2, l. 39. [Clifford]

O boy, thy father gave thee life too soon,
And hath bereft thee of thy life too late!

III Henry VI. Act ii, sc. 5, l. 92. [Father]

I have heard you say
That we shall see and know our friends in heaven:
If that be true, I shall see my boy again.

King John. Act iii, sc. 4, l. 76. [Constance]

2
Yon green boy shall have no sun to ripe
The bloom that promiseth a mighty fruit.

King John. Act ii, sc. 1, l. 472. [Elinor]

A beardless boy, A cocker'd silken wanton.

King John. Act v, sc. 1, l. 69. [Bastard] The only use of "cocker'd" (pampered).

Young wanton and effeminate boy.

Richard II. Act v, sc. 3, l. 10. [Bolingbroke]

Wanton boys.—*King Lear,* iv, 1, 38.

Little wanton boys.—*Henry VIII,* iii, 2, 359.

Little boy.—*Love's Labour 's Lost,* iv, 1, 123.

A little peevish boy.—*Richard III,* iv, 2, 100.

Little tiny boy.—*Twelfth Night,* v, 1, 398.

Bastard boys.—*II Henry VI,* v, 1, 115.

3 Of my land,
Loyal and natural boy, I 'll work the means
To make thee capable.

King Lear. Act ii, sc. 1, l. 85. [Gloucester]

4
The boy was the very staff of my age, my very prop.

The Merchant of Venice. Act ii, sc. 2, l. 69. [Gobbo]

Is my boy, God rest his soul, alive or dead?

The Merchant of Venice. Act ii, sc. 2, l. 74. [Gobbo]

Your boy that was, your son that is, your child that shall be.

The Merchant of Venice. Act ii, sc. 2, l. 90. [Launcelot]

5 Cupid himself would blush
To see me thus transformed to a boy.

The Merchant of Venice. Act ii, sc. 6, l. 38. [Jessica]

A kind of boy, a little scrubbed boy,
No higher than thyself, the judge's clerk,
A prating boy.

The Merchant of Venice. Act v, sc. 1, l. 162. [Gratiano]

That same scrubbed boy.—*The Merchant of Venice,* v, 1, 261. The only uses of "scrubbed."

6
'Tis a postmaster's boy.

The Merry Wives of Windsor, v, 5, 199; 211. The only uses of "postmaster."

Peasant boys.—*I Henry VI,* iv, 6, 48.

Shepherd boy.—*As You Like It,* v, 4, 26.

A great lubberly boy.—*Merry Wives of Windsor,* v, 5, 195. The only use of "lubberly."

7
A lovely boy, stolen from an Indian king.

A Midsummer-Night's Dream. Act ii, sc. 1, l. 22. [Puck]

But she perforce withholds the loved boy,
Crowns him with flowers and makes him all her joy.

A Midsummer-Night's Dream. Act ii, sc. 1, l. 26. [Puck]

I do but beg a little changeling boy,
To be my henchman.

A Midsummer-Night's Dream. Act ii, sc. 1, l. 120. [Oberon] The only use of "henchman."

Whiles I in this affair do thee employ,
I 'll to my queen and beg her Indian boy.

A Midsummer-Night's Dream. Act iii, sc. 2, l. 375. [Oberon]

8
The flat transgression of a school-boy.

Much Ado about Nothing. Act ii, sc. 1, l. 229. [Benedick] "School-boy" occurs nine times in the plays.

Scambling, out-facing, fashion-monging boys,
That lie and cog and flout, deprave and slander,
Go anticly, show outward hideousness,
And speak off half a dozen dangerous words,
How they might hurt their enemies, if they durst.

Much Ado about Nothing. Act v, sc. 1, l. 94. [Antonio] "Out-facing" is repeated in *The Comedy of Errors,* v, 1, 244, and in *Passionate Pilgrim,* l. 8. The only use of "fashion-monging," "anticly," and "hideousness."

Boys, with women's voices,
Strive to speak big and clap their female joints
In stiff unwieldy arms.

Richard II. Act iii, sc. 2, l. 113. [Scroop]

9
A parlous boy: go to, you are too shrewd.

Richard III. Act ii, sc. 4, l. 35. [Queen Elizabeth]

O, 'tis a parlous boy;
Bold, quick, ingenious, forward, capable:
He is all the mother's, from the top to toe.

Richard III. Act iii, sc. 1, l. 154. [Gloucester]

A saucy boy.—*Romeo and Juliet,* i, 5, 85. See also SAUCINESS.

A boy right out.—*The Tempest,* iv, 1, 101.

10 What, villain boy!
Barr'st me my way in Rome?

Titus Andronicus. Act i, sc. 1, l. 290. [Titus]

Marcus: Alas, the tender boy, in passion moved,
Doth weep to see his grandsire's heaviness.
Titus: Peace, tender sapling.

Titus Andronicus. Act iii, sc. 2, l. 48.

Foolish young sapling.—*Pericles,* iv, 2, 93.

Blasted sapling.—*Richard III,* iii, 4, 71. The only uses of "sapling."

11
Ye sanguine, shallow-hearted boys!

Titus Andronicus. Act iv, sc. 2, l. 97. [Aaron] The only use of "shallow-hearted."

1
Save my boy, to nourish and bring him up;
Or else I will discover nought to thee.
Titus Andronicus. Act v, sc. 1, l. 84. [Aaron]
Dear boy.—*I Henry VI,* iv, 5, 9; *King John,* iii, 1, 51; *Love's Labour's Lost,* i, 2, 71.
Fond boy.—*The Winter's Tale,* iv, 4, 437.
Gentle boy.—*Venus and Adonis,* l. 403.
Good boy.—*I Henry IV,* ii, 4, 13, and seven times in later plays.
Lovely boy.—*Sonnets,* cxxvi; *Henry VIII,* v, 1, 163.
A most rare boy.—*Cymbeline,* iv, 2, 208.
Sweet boy.—*Venus and Adonis,* l. 155; 583; *Sonnets,* cviii.

2
One would think his mother's milk were scarce out of him.
Twelfth Night. Act i, sc. 5, l. 170. [Malvolio] The only use of "mother's milk."
Did she see thee the while, old boy? tell me that.
Twelfth Night. Act iii, sc. 2, l. 9. [Sir Toby Belch] This is the only time that "old boy," as a term of affection, is used in the plays.
That most ingrateful boy there by your side,
From the rude sea's enraged and foamy mouth
Did I redeem; a wreck past hope he was.
Twelfth Night. Act v, sc. 1, l. 80. [Antonio]

3 Looking on the lines
Of my boy's face, methoughts I did recoil
Twenty-three years, and saw myself unbreech'd,
In my green velvet coat, my dagger muzzled,
Lest it should bite its master, and so prove,
As ornaments oft do, too dangerous.
The Winter's Tale. Act i, sc. 2, l. 153. [Leontes] The only use of "unbreech'd." "Muzzled" is repeated in *King John,* ii, 1, 249: "Muzzled bear."

4
Take the boy to you: he so troubles me,
'Tis past enduring.
The Winter's Tale. Act ii, sc. 1, l. 1. [Hermione]
Give me the boy: I am glad you did not nurse him
Though he does bear some signs of me, yet you
Have too much blood in him.
The Winter's Tale. Act ii, sc. 1, l. 56. [Leontes]

BRAGGING, see Boasting

BRAIN

See also Heart and Brain; Mind

5
It's a monstrous labour, when I wash my brain,
And it grows fouler.
Antony and Cleopatra. Act ii, sc. 7, l. 105. [Cæsar]
A brain that nourishes our nerves.
Antony and Cleopatra, iv, 8, 21. See under Age and Youth.

6 And in his brain,
Which is as dry as the remainder biscuit
After a voyage, he hath strange places cramm'd
With observation, the which he vents
In mangled forms.
As You Like It. Act ii, sc. 7, l. 38. [Jaques]

7 This brain of mine
Hunts not the trail of policy so sure
As it hath used to do.
Hamlet. Act ii, sc. 2, l. 46. [Polonius]
Whereupon his brains still beating puts him thus
From fashion of himself.
Hamlet. Act iii, sc. 1, l. 182. [King]

8
Cudgel thy brains no more about it.
Hamlet. Act v, sc. 1, l. 63. [First Clown]

9
My brain more busy than the labouring spider
Weaves tedious snares to trap mine enemies.
II Henry VI. Act iii, sc. 1, l. 339. [York]

10 Some strange commotion
Is in his brain: he bites his lip, and starts;
Stops on a sudden, looks upon the ground,
Then lays his finger on his temple; straight
Springs out into fast gait; then stops again,
Strikes his breast hard, and anon he casts
His eye against the moon.
Henry VIII. Act iii, sc. 2, l. 112. [Norfolk]

11 His pure brain,
Which some suppose the soul's frail dwelling-house,
Doth by the idle comments that it makes
Foretell the ending of mortality.
King John. Act v, sc. 7, l. 2. [Prince Henry] The only use of "dwelling-house."
Pure brain.—*Much Ado about Nothing,* v, 4, 87.
My dull brain was wrought
With things forgotten.
Macbeth. Act i, sc. 3, l. 149. [Macbeth]
Gross brain.—*Henry V,* iv, 1, 299.
Idle brain.—*Romeo and Juliet,* i, 4, 97.

12
If a man's brains were in 's heels, were 't not in danger of kibes?
King Lear. Act i, sc. 5, l. 8. [Fool]
Brains of men.—*Julius Cæsar,* ii, 1, 232.
Brain of Britain.—*Cymbeline,* v, 5, 14.
Italian brain.—*Cymbeline,* v, 5, 196.
Lovers' brains.—*Romeo and Juliet,* i, 4, 71.

13
I 'll look no more; Lest my brain turn.
King Lear, iv, 6, 23. See under Distance.

14
The brain may devise laws for the blood.
The Merchant of Venice, i, 2, 19. See under Temper.

15
Have I laid my brain in the sun and dried it?
The Merry Wives of Windsor. Act v, sc. 5, l. 143. [Falstaff]

16
If a man will be beaten with brains, a' shall wear nothing handsome about him.
Much Ado about Nothing. Act v, sc. 4, l. 104. [Benedick]

17
I have very poor and unhappy brains for drinking.
Othello, ii, 3, 35. See under Drinking.
Is he not light of brain?—*Othello,* iv, 1, 280.

Has Page any brains?—*The Merry Wives of Windsor,* iii, 2, 30.
Nay, I do bear a brain.
Romeo and Juliet. Act i, sc. 3, l. 29. [Nurse]
Fruitful brain.—*Love's Labour's Lost,* v, 2, 857.
Unstuff'd brain.—*Romeo and Juliet,* ii, 3, 37. The only use of "unstuff'd."

1
My brain I 'll prove the female to my soul,
My soul the father.
Richard II. Act v, sc. 5, l. 6. [King Richard]

2
What 's in the brain that ink may character?
Sonnets. No. cviii.

3
My old brain is troubled.
The Tempest. Act iv, sc. 1, l. 159. [Prospero]
Thy brains,
Now useless, boil'd within thy skull!
The Tempest. Act v, sc. 1, l. 59. [Prospero] This is the only use of "useless" in the plays, but it occurs again in *The Rape of Lucrece,* l. 859: "And useless barns the harvest of his wits."
The disposing of her troubled brain.
Venus and Adonis, l. 1039. "Troubled brain" is repeated in *As You Like It,* iv, 3, 4.
Here is more matter for a hot brain.
The Winter's Tale. Act iv, sc. 4, l. 699. [Autolycus] The only use of "hot brain."
Heat-oppressed brain.—*Macbeth,* ii, 1, 39.
Seething brain.—*A Midsummer-Night's Dream,* v, 1, 4.
A mad-brain rudesby.—*The Taming of the Shrew,* iii, 2, 10. The only use of "mad-brain." "Mad-brain'd" occurs three times in the plays: *I Henry VI,* i, 2, 15; *The Taming of the Shrew,* iii, 2, 165; *Timon of Athens,* v, 1, 177. "Rudesby" is repeated in *Twelfth Night,* iv, 1, 55: "Rudesby, be gone!"

4
Thou . . . Scorn'dst our brain's flow.
Timon of Athens. Act v, sc. 4, l. 76. [Alcibiades]

5
His brain as barren As banks of Libya.
Troilus and Cressida. Act i, sc. 3, l. 327. [Nestor]

6
Thou hast no more brain than I have in mine elbows.
Troilus and Cressida. Act ii, sc. 1, l. 48. [Thersites]
He has not so much brain as ear-wax.
Troilus and Cressida. Act v, sc. 1, l. 58. [Thersites] The only use of "ear-wax."

7
I have bobbed his brain more than he has beat my bones: I will buy nine sparrows for a penny, and his pia mater is not worth the ninth part of a sparrow.
Troilus and Cressida. Act ii, sc. 1, l. 76. [Thersites]
Whose skull Jove cram with brains! for,—here he comes,—one of thy kin has a most weak pia mater.
Twelfth Night. Act i, sc. 5, l. 122. [Clown]
Nourished in the womb of pia mater.—*Love's Labour's Lost,* iv, 2, 71. The only uses of "pia mater."

8
Cucullus non facit monachum; that 's as much to say as I wear not motley in my brain.
Twelfth Night. Act i, sc. 5, l. 62. [Clown] The only use of "Cucullus non facit monachum," a Latin proverb, meaning, "A cowl does not make a monk." Shakespeare puts it into English in *Henry VIII,* iii, 1, 23: "All hoods make not monks."

9
Like the proceedings of a drunken brain.
Venus and Adonis, l. 910.

II—Knocking out the Brains

10
I know his brains are forfeit to the next tile that falls.
All's Well that Ends Well. Act iv, sc. 3, l. 216. [Bertram] The only use of "tile."

11
Troilus had his brains dashed out with a Grecian club.
As You Like It. Act iv, sc. 1, l. 98. [Rosalind]
Dash'd the brains out.—*Macbeth,* i, 7, 58.
Dash out my desperate brains.—*Romeo and Juliet,* iv, 3, 54.
The bastard brains with these my proper hands
Shall I dash out.
The Winter's Tale. Act ii, sc. 3, l. 140. [Leontes]

12
I could brain him with a lady's fan.
I Henry IV, ii, 3, 24. See under Fan.
Brain him.—*The Tempest,* iii, 2, 96. See under Murder.

13
Many have their giddy brains knock'd out.
I Henry VI. Act iii, sc. 1, l. 83. [Mayor]
My brain is giddy.—*II Henry IV,* iv, 4, 110.
The brains of my Cupid 's knocked out.
All's Well that Ends Well, iii, 2, 16. See under Love.
Knocking out his brains.—*Othello,* iv, 2, 236.
Timon: Whither art going?
Apemantus: To knock out an honest Athenian's brains.
Timon of Athens. Act i, sc. 1, l. 191.

14
Hector shall have a great catch, if he knock out either of your brains: a' were as good crack a fusty nut with no kernel.
Troilus and Cressida. Act ii, sc. 1, l. 110. [Thersites] "Fusty" is repeated in i, 3, 161: "Fusty stuff"; and in *Coriolanus,* i, 9, 7: "Fusty plebeians."
Not Hercules
Could have knock'd out his brains, for he had none.
Cymbeline. Act iv, sc. 2, l. 114. [Guiderius]

15
The time has been,
That, when the brains were out, the man would die.
Macbeth, iii, 4, 79. See under Ghost.

16
They shall beat out my brains with billets.
Measure for Measure. Act iv, sc. 3, l. 58. [Barnardine] The only use of "billets."
Pluck the lined crutch from thy old limping sire,

With it beat out his brains!
Timon of Athens. Act iv, sc. 1, l. 14. [Timon] "Limping" is repeated in *Romeo and Juliet,* i, 2, 28: "Limping winter."

Hand in hand, all headlong cast us down,
And on the ragged stones beat forth our brains.
Titus Andronicus, v, 3, 132. [Marcus]

BRAVERY, see Courage

BRAWL, see Fighting

BREAD

1
O monstrous! but one half-penny-worth of bread to this intolerable deal of sack!
I Henry IV. Act ii, sc. 4, l. 592. [Prince of Wales] Referring to the bill for supper found in Falstaff's pocket: "A capon, 2s. 2d.; sauce, 4d.; sack, two gallons, 5s. 8d.; anchovies and sack after supper, 2s. 6d.; bread, ob." The only mention of anchovies, and use of "half-penny-worth."

2
Cramm'd with distressful bread.
Henry V, iv, 1, 287. See under KING.

Full of bread.—*Hamlet,* iii, 3, 80.

3
Those palates who, not yet two summers younger,
Must have inventions to delight the taste,
Would now be glad of bread, and beg for it.
Pericles. Act i, sc. 4, l. 39. [Cleon]

Needy bread.—*Pericles,* i, 4, 95. See under CORN.

4
I live with bread like you.
Richard II, iii, 2, 175. See under KING.

Brown bread.—*Measure for Measure,* iii, 2, 195.
Bread and cheese.—*The Merry Wives of Windsor,* ii, 1, 140.
Bread and clothes.—*Othello,* iv, 1, 96.
The bitter bread of banishment.—*Richard II,* iii, 1, 21.
God's bread!—*Romeo and Juliet,* iii, 5, 177.
Holy bread.—*As You Like It,* iii, 4, 15.

5
That jade hath eat bread from my royal hand.
Richard II. Act v, sc. 5, l. 85. [King Richard]

His appetite Is more to bread than stone.
Measure for Measure, i, 3, 53. See under CHARACTER.

Hunger for bread.—*Coriolanus,* i, 1, 25.
Taste bread.—*King Lear,* v, 3, 94.
Work for bread.—*A Midsummer-Night's Dream,* iii, 2, 10.
Parts bread with him.—*Timon of Athens,* i, 2, 49.

BREAKFAST, see Eating

BREAST

6
Till we call'd
Both field and city ours, he never stood
To ease his breast with panting.
Coriolanus. Act ii, sc. 2, l. 124. [Cominius]

Whose naked breast
Stepp'd before targes of proof.
Cymbeline. Act v, sc. 5, l. 4. [Cymbeline] "Naked breast" occurs again in *Julius Cæsar,* iv, 3, 101.

Bloody breast.—*Love's Labour 's Lost,* v, i, 148.
Dying breast!—*I Henry VI,* iii, 2, 99.
Forward breast.—*All's Well that Ends Well,* iii, 2, 116.
O'er-fed breast.—*Pericles,* iii, Gower, 3. The only use of "o'er-fed."
Breast to breast.—*III Henry VI,* ii, 5, 11.

7
Nothing could have stayed
My father from the breast of Bolingbroke.
II Henry IV. Act iv, sc. 1, l. 124. [Mowbray]

Man but a rush against Othello's breast,
And he retires.
Othello, v, 2, 270. See under DISMAY.

Brave Hector's breast.—*Troilus and Cressida,* iii, 3, 140.
Mercutio's breast.—*Romeo and Juliet,* iii, 1, 164.
Butcher Mowbray's breast!—*Richard II,* i, 2, 48.
Volscian breasts.—*Coriolanus,* v, 2, 91.
Country's breast.—*Coriolanus,* iv, 5, 105.
Breast of heaven.—*Julius Cæsar,* i, 3, 51.

8
My sighing breast shall be thy funeral bell.
III Henry VI. Act ii, sc. 5, l. 117. [Father]

Troubled breast.—*King John,* iv, 2, 73.
Woful breast.—*I Henry VI,* iii, 3, 51.

9
Take notice, lords, he has a loyal breast,
For you have seen him open 't.
Henry VIII. Act iii, sc. 2, l. 200. [King Henry] "Loyal breast" is repeated in *The Phœnix and the Turtle,* l. 57.

10
What breast so cold that is not warmed here?
A Lover's Complaint, l. 292.

Cold breast.—*A Lover's Complaint,* l. 259.
Quailing breasts.—*III Henry VI,* ii, 3, 54. "Quailing" is repeated in *I Henry IV,* iv, 1, 39: "No quailing now."

11
Why do your wring your hands, and beat your breast?
Richard III. Act ii, sc. 2, l. 3. [Boy]

Strikes his breast hard.—*Henry VIII,* iii, 2, 117.

12
Within the gentle closure of my breast,
From whence at pleasure thou mayst come and part.
Sonnets. No. xlviii.

The quiet closure of my breast.—*Venus and Adonis,* l. 782. "Closure" is repeated in *Richard III,* iii, 3, 11: "Closure of thy walls"; and in *Titus Andronicus,* v, 3, 134: "Closure of our house."

13
Then give me welcome, next my heaven the best,
Even to thy pure and most most loving breast.
Sonnets. No. cx.

Gentle breast.—*The Rape of Lucrece,* l. 851.
Harmless breast.—*The Rape of Lucrece,* l. 1723.
Infinite breast.—*Timon of Athens,* iv, 3, 178.
Obedient breast.—*Love's Labour 's Lost,* iv, 3, 225.
Patient breast.—*Troilus and Cressida,* i, 3, 36.
Quiet breast.—*Richard II,* i, 3, 96.
Sacred breast.—*Pericles,* i, 2, 33.

Silver breast.—*Venus and Adonis,* l. 855.
Single breast.—*Macbeth,* iv, 3, 197.
Speaking breast.—*Sonnets,* xxiii.
Throbbing breast.—*II Henry VI,* iv, 4, 5.

1
In whose breast
Doubt and suspect, alas, are placed too late.
Timon of Athens. Act iv, sc. 3, l. 518. [Flavius]

2
By my troth, the fool has an excellent breast.
Twelfth Night. Act ii, sc. 3, l. 19. [Sir Andrew]

Broad breast.—*Venus and Adonis,* l. 296.
Manly breast.—*Romeo and Juliet,* iii, 2, 53.

II—Women's Breasts

3
The breasts of Hecuba,
When she did suckle Hector, look'd not lovelier.
Coriolanus. Act i, sc. 3, l. 43. [Volumnia]

4
Her breasts, like ivory globes circled with blue.
A pair of maiden worlds unconquered,
Save of their lord no bearing yoke they knew,
And him by oath they truly honoured.
These worlds in Tarquin new ambition bred.
The Rape of Lucrece, l. 407.

His hand . . . march'd on to make his stand
On her bare breast, the heart of all her land;
Whose ranks of blue veins, as his hand did scale,
Left their round turrets destitute and pale.
The Rape of Lucrece, l. 438.

If snow be white, why then her breasts are dun.
Sonnets. No. cxxx.

The boy for trial needs would touch my breast.
Sonnets. No. cliii.

5
From my dugs he drew not this deceit.
Richard III, ii, 2, 30. See under DECEIT.

He did comply with his dug, before he sucked it.
Hamlet. Act v, sc. 2, l. 195. [Hamlet]

Never palates more the dug.
Antony and Cleopatra, v, 2, 7.

Mother's dug.—*II Henry VI,* iii, 2, 393.
Old dugs.—*Richard II,* v, 3, 90.
Swelling dugs.—*Venus and Adonis,* l. 875.
Cow's dugs.—*As You Like It,* ii, 4, 50.

6
For I had then laid wormwood to my dug.
Romeo and Juliet. Act i, sc. 3, l. 26. [Nurse]

It did taste the wormwood on the nipple
Of my dug.
Romeo and Juliet. Act i, sc. 3, l. 31. [Nurse]

Pluck'd my nipple from his boneless gums.
Macbeth, i, 7, 57. The only uses of "nipple."

7
Feed where thou wilt, on mountain or in dale:
Graze on my lips; and if those hills be dry,
Stray lower, where the pleasant fountains lie.
Venus and Adonis, l. 232.

BREATH

See also Wind

I—Familiar Phrases

8
Never man Sigh'd truer breath.
Coriolanus. Act iv, sc. 5, l. 120. [Aufidius]

9
Hark, how hard he fetches breath.
I Henry IV. Act ii, sc. 4, l. 579. [Prince]

Draw my breath in pain.—*Hamlet,* v, 2, 359.
Afflicted breath.—*King John,* iii, 4, 19.
Labouring breath.—*Troilus and Cressida,* iv, 4, 40.

10
O, . . . That no man might draw short breath to-day
But I and Harry Monmouth!
I Henry IV. Act v, sc. 2, l. 49. [Hotspur]

Draws breath.—*The Merchant of Venice,* iii, 2, 298.
Hold hard the breath.—*Henry V,* iii, 1, 16.

11
God witness with me, when I here came in,
And found no course of breath within your majesty,
How cold it struck my heart!
II Henry IV. Act iv, sc. 5, l. 150. [Prince]

And may that thought, when I imagine ill . . .
Be my last breathing in this mortal world!
II Henry VI. Act i, sc. 2, l. 21. [Gloucester]

Even this ill night, your breathing shall expire.
King John. Act v, sc. 4, l. 36. [Melun]

Come, you shake the head at so long a breathing.
Much Ado about Nothing. Act ii, sc. 1, l. 378. [Don Pedro]

12
It was my breath that blew this tempest up.
King John. Act v, sc. 1, l. 17. [Pandulph]

Art thou the slave that with thy breath hast kill'd
Mine innocent child?
Much Ado about Nothing. Act v, sc. 1, l. 273. [Leonato] See also under CALUMNY.

13
Saint Denis to Saint Cupid! What are they
That charge their breath against us? say, scout, say.
Love's Labour's Lost. Act v, sc. 2, l. 87. [Prince]

Breath a vapour is.—*Love's Labour's Lost,* iv, 3, 68.

14
I breathe free breath.
Love's Labour's Lost. Act v, sc. 2, l. 732. [Armado]

Cheerly drawing breath.—*Richard II,* i, 3, 66.

15
Never did mockers waste more idle breath.
A Midsummer-Night's Dream. Act iii, sc. 2, l. 168. [Helena]

All-obeying breath.—*Antony and Cleopatra,* iii, 13, 77. The only use of "all-obeying."
Bate one breath.—*Much Ado about Nothing,* ii, 3, 184.
Bated breath.—*The Merchant of Venice,* i, 3, 125. The only use of the phrase.
Courteous breath.—*The Merchant of Venice,* ii, 9, 90.
Gentle breath.—*Romeo and Juliet,* iii, 1, 161.

Holy breath.—*King John,* v, 2, 68.
Natural breath.—*The Tempest,* v, 1, 157.
Pious breath.—*Timon of Athens,* iv, 3, 140.
Scandalous breath.—*Measure for Measure,* v, 1, 122.
Servile breath.—*Richard II,* iii, 2, 185.
Superfluous breath.—*King John,* ii, 1, 148.
Vain breath.—*King John,* iii, 1, 8.
Windy breath.—*King John,* ii, 1, 477.

1
They met so near with their lips that their breaths embraced together.
Othello. Act ii, sc. 1, l. 265. [Iago]

2
What he breathes out his breath drinks up again.
The Rape of Lucrece, l. 1666.

3
Friar Laurence: Arise; one knocks; good Romeo, hide thyself.
Romeo: Not I; unless the breath of heart-sick groans,
Mist-like, infold me from the search of eyes.
Romeo and Juliet. Act iii, sc. 3, l. 71. "Heart-sick" is repeated in *Cymbeline,* iv, 2, 37. The only use of "mist-like."

4
Gentle breath of yours my sails
Must fill, or else my project fails.
The Tempest: Epilogue, l. 11. [Prospero]
Your breath of full consent bellied his sails.
Troilus and Cressida. Act ii, sc. 2, l. 74. The only use of "bellied."

5
Strike not a stroke, but keep yourselves in breath.
Troilus and Cressida. Act v, sc. 7, l. 3. [Achilles]

6
Fly away, fly away, breath;
I am slain by a fair cruel maid.
Twelfth Night. Act ii, sc. 4, l. 54. [Clown]

7
Here 's my mother's breath up and down.
The Two Gentlemen of Verona. Act ii, sc. 3, l. 32. [Launce]
His breath breatheth life in her again.
Venus and Adonis, l. 474.
Put breath into his work.—*The Winter's Tale,* v, 2, 107.

II—Sweet Breath

8 'Tis her breathing that
Perfumes the chamber thus.
Cymbeline. Act ii, sc. 2, l. 18. [Iachimo]

9
Odours savours sweet: So hath thy breath.
A Midsummer-Night's Dream. Act iii, sc. 1, l. 87. [Bottom]
Ah, balmy breath, that dost almost persuade
Justice to break her sword!
Othello. Act v, sc. 2, l. 16. [Othello]

10 Then sweeten with thy breath
This neighbour air.
Romeo and Juliet. Act ii, sc. 6, l. 26. [Romeo]
With her breath she did perfume the air.
The Taming of the Shrew. Act i, sc. 1, l. 180. [Lucentio]

11
Coming and going with thy honey breath.
Titus Andronicus. Act ii, sc. 4, l. 25. [Marcus]
The honey of thy breath.—*Romeo and Juliet,* v, 3, 92.
Sweet thief, whence didst thou steal thy sweet that smells,
If not from my love's breath?
Sonnets. No. xcix.
Heaven's breath.—*Love's Labour 's Lost,* iv, 3, 108.
Adonis' breath.—*Venus and Adonis,* l. 1172.
Sugar breath.—*The Merchant of Venice,* iii, 2, 119.
Sweet breath.—*The Comedy of Errors,* iii, 2, 28; *Love's Labour 's Lost,* v, 2, 267; 524; *A Midsummer-Night's Dream,* iv, 2, 44; *As You Like It,* Epil., 22; *King John,* iv, 3, 136.
Sweet infant breath.—*Richard II,* i, 3, 133.

12
Sir Toby: A contagious breath.
Sir Andrew: Very sweet and contagious, i' faith.
Sir Toby: To hear by the nose, it is dulcet in contagion.
Twelfth Night. Act ii, sc. 3, l. 56.
Black contagious breath.—*King John,* v, 4, 33.
The plague is banish'd by thy breath.
Venus and Adonis, l. 510.

13
She feedeth on the steam as on a prey,
And calls it heavenly moisture, air of grace.
Venus and Adonis, l. 63. The only use of "steam."
I 'll sigh celestial breath, whose gentle wind
Shall cool the heat of this descending sun.
Venus and Adonis, l. 189.
For from the stillitory of thy face excelling
Comes breath perfumed that breedeth love by smelling.
Venus and Adonis, l. 443. Shakespeare used "stillitory" only once—an erroneous spelling of stillatory (alembic).
His breath and beauty set
Gloss on the rose, smell to the violet.
Venus and Adonis, l. 935.

III—Bad Breath

14 In their thick breaths,
Rank of gross diet, shall we be enclouded,
And forced to drink their vapour.
Antony and Cleopatra. Act v, sc. 2, l. 211. [Cleopatra] The only use of "enclouded."
Why do we wrap the gentleman in our more rawer breath?
Hamlet. Act v, sc. 2, l. 128. [Hamlet] The only use of "rawer."

15 Whose breath I hate
As reeks o' the rotten fens.
Coriolanus. Act iv, sc. 1, l. 120. [Coriolanus]
His celestial breath Was sulphurous to smell.
Cymbeline. Act v, sc. 4, l. 114. [Sicilius]

16
His breath stinks with eating toasted cheese.
II Henry VI. Act iv, sc. 7, l. 13. [Smith]
Eat no onions nor garlic, for we are to utter sweet breath.
A Midsummer-Night's Dream. Act iv, sc. 2, l. 43. [Bottom]

The breath of garlic-eaters!—*Coriolanus,* iv, 6, 98. See under PEOPLE.

1
If her breath were as terrible as her terminations, there were no living near her; she would infect to the north star.
Much Ado about Nothing. Act ii, sc. 1, l. 256. [Benedick] The only use of "terminations."

And in some perfumes is there more delight
Than in the breath that from my mistress reeks.
Sonnets. No. cxxx.

Speed: She is not to be kissed fasting, in respect of her breath.
Launce: Well, that fault may be mended with a breakfast.
Speed: She hath a sweet mouth.
Launce: That makes amends for her sour breath.
The Two Gentlemen of Verona. Act iii, sc. 1, l. 326.

Cold breath.—*Macbeth,* ii, 1, 61.

2
Let their exhaled unwholesome breaths make sick
The life of purity.
The Rape of Lucrece, l. 779.

Their breaths with sweetmeats tainted are.
Romeo and Juliet. Act i, sc. 4, l. 76. [Mercutio] "Sweetmeats" is repeated in *A Midsummer-Night's Dream,* i, 1, 34.

3
Breath infect breath,
That their society, as their friendship, may
Be merely poison!
Timon of Athens. Act iv, sc. 1, l. 30. [Timon]

IV—Breathlessness

4
Having lost her breath, she spoke, and panted.
Antony and Cleopatra. Act ii, sc. 2, l. 235. [Enobarbus] The only use of "panted."

5
I grant you I was down and out of breath.
I Henry IV. Act v, sc. 4, l. 150. [Falstaff]

O, I am out of breath in this fond chase!
A Midsummer-Night's Dream. Act ii, sc. 2, l. 88. [Helena]

How art thou out of breath, when thou hast breath
To say to me that thou art out of breath?
Romeo and Juliet. Act ii, sc. 5, l. 31. [Juliet]

Out of breath.—*Antony and Cleopatra,* iii, 10, 25; *The Comedy of Errors,* iv, 1, 57; *Coriolanus,* iii, 1, 189; *Twelfth Night,* iii, 4, 152.

Discharged of breath.—*Romeo and Juliet,* v, 1, 63.

Scant of breath.—*Hamlet,* v, 2, 298.

I am scarce in breath.—*King Lear,* ii, 2, 57.

The breath is gone.—*Pericles,* i, 1, 99.

Wanting breath to speak.—*Pericles,* i, 4, 19.

6
Luciana: How hast thou lost thy breath?
Dromio of Syracuse: By running fast.
The Comedy of Errors. Act iv, sc. 2, l. 30.

Direct not him whose way himself will choose:
'Tis breath thou lack'st, and that breath wilt thou lose.
Richard II. Act ii, sc. 1, l. 29. [York]

7
Here breathless lies the king.
I Henry IV, v, 3, 16. See under KING.

Herein all breathless lies
The mightiest of thy greatest enemies.
Richard II, v, 6, 31. See under ENEMY.

Why are you breathless? and why stare you so?
Julius Cæsar. Act i, sc. 3, l. 2. [Cicero]

Breathless, he disjoin'd, and backward drew.
Venus and Adonis, l. 541.

Breathless and bleeding.—*I Henry IV,* v, 4, 137.

Breathless and faint.—*I Henry IV,* i, 3, 32.

Half breathless.—*King Lear,* ii, 4, 31.

8
The breath no sooner left his father's body.
Henry V. Act i, sc. 1, l. 25. [Canterbury]

Fading breath.—*I Henry VI,* ii, 5, 61.

Last breath.—*All's Well that Ends Well,* iv, 3, 62.

Weak breath.—*Coriolanus,* v, 2, 50.

Yield thy breath!—*I Henry VI,* iv, 7, 24; *Richard III,* v, 3, 172.

Steal his breath.—*Venus and Adonis,* l. 934.

9
If that her breath will mist or stain the stone,
Why, then she lives.
King Lear. Act v, sc. 3, l. 262. [King Lear]

No warmth, no breath, shall testify thou livest.
Romeo and Juliet. Act iv, sc. 1, l. 98. [Friar Laurence]

10
Who, almost dead for breath, had scarcely more
Than would make up his message.
Macbeth. Act i, sc. 5, l. 37. [Messenger]

Let your breath cool yourself, telling your haste.
Pericles. Act i, sc. 1, l. 161. [Antiochus]

Recover breath.—*Richard II,* v, 3, 47.

11
There lies your niece,
Whose breath, indeed, these hands have newly stopp'd.
Othello. Act v, sc. 2, l. 201. [Othello]

Stop my breath.—*The Rape of Lucrece,* l. 1180.

Stopp'd her breath.—*Romeo and Juliet,* v, 3, 211.

12
From his lips did fly
Thin winding breath, which purl'd up the sky.
Rape of Lucrece, l. 1406. Only use of "purl'd."

13
Give me some breath, some little pause, my lord.
Richard III. Act iv, sc. 2, l. 24. [Buckingham] See also under PAUSE.

Give me breath.—*Timon of Athens,* ii, 2, 34.

Give it breath.—*Hamlet,* iii, 2, 74.

Givest them breath.—*Othello,* iii, 3, 119.

Hath he so long held out with me untired,
And stops he now for breath?
Richard III. Act iv, sc. 2, l. 44. [King Richard] "Untired" is repeated in *Julius Cæsar,* ii, 1, 227: "Untired spirits."

BREEDING, see Manners

BREVITY

14
She told me, In a sweet verbal brief.
All's Well that Ends Well. Act v, sc. 3, l. 136. [Gentleman]

Leave nothing out for length.
Coriolanus. Act ii, sc. 2, l. 53. [Senator]

1
Therefore, since brevity is the soul of wit,
And tediousness the limbs and outward flourishes,
I will be brief.
Hamlet. Act ii, sc. 2, l. 90. [Polonius]
A short tale to make.—*Hamlet,* ii, 2, 146. See under TALE.
It will be short: the interim is mine.
Hamlet. Act v, sc. 2, l. 73. [Hamlet]
2
But to the purpose, and so to the venture.
II Henry IV. Epilogue, l. 7. See PURPOSE.
'I will imitate the honourable Romans in brevity:' he sure means brevity in breath, short-winded.
II Henry IV. Act ii, sc. 2, l. 134. [Poins]
Short-winded accents.—*I Henry IV,* i, 1, 3. The only uses of "short-winded."
3
Speak on; but be not over-tedious.
I Henry VI. Act iii, sc. 3, l. 43. [Burgundy] The only use of "over-tedious."
Northumberland: Only to be brief,
Left I his title out.
York: The time hath been,
Would you have been so brief with him, he would
Have been so brief with you.
Richard II. Act iii, sc. 3, l. 10.
4
Briefness and fortune, work!
King Lear. Act ii, sc. 1, l. 20. [Edmund]
Briefness of your answer.—*Cymbeline,* ii, 4, 30.
Feather'd briefness.—*Pericles,* v, 2, 280. The only uses of "briefness."
5
Fewness and truth, 'tis thus.
Measure for Measure. Act i, sc. 4, l. 39. [Lucio] The only use of "fewness."
In few.—*The Tempest,* i, 2, 144.
6
It is better to be brief than tedious.
Richard III. Act i, sc. 4, l. 88. [Second Murderer] See also "short and long of it," under FAMILIAR PHRASES.
What sayest thou? speak suddenly; be brief.
Richard III. Act iv, sc. 2, l. 20. [King]
And brief, good mother; for I am in haste.
Richard III. Act iv, sc. 4, l. 161. [King]
If you have reason, be brief.
Twelfth Night. Act i, sc. 5, l. 212. [Olivia]
Be curst and brief.—*Twelfth Night,* iii, 2, 45.
Very brief, and to exceeding good sense—less.
Twelfth Night. Act iii, sc. 4, l. 174. [Fabian]
7
Speak briefly.
Romeo and Juliet, i, 3, 96; *Coriolanus,* iii, 1, 285. "Briefly," "Be brief," and "In brief" occur frequently throughout the plays.
I will be brief, for my short date of breath
Is not so long as is a tedious tale.
Romeo and Juliet. Act v, sc. 3, l. 229. [Friar]

BRIBERY

8
For a quart d'ecu he will sell the fee-simple of his salvation, the inheritance of it; and cut the entail from all remainders, and a perpetual succession for it perpetually.
All's Well that Ends Well. Act iv, sc. 3, l. 311. [Parolles] "Quart d'ecu" is repeated in v, 2, 35, and occurs in no other play. "Fee-simple" is used five times and "entail" and "perpetually" thrice.
9
I . . . cannot make my heart consent to take
A bribe to pay my sword.
Coriolanus. Act i, sc. 9, l. 36. [Marcius]
There is gold for you;
Sell me your good report.
Cymbeline. Act ii, sc. 3, l. 87. [Cloten]
Hold, there's money for thee; let me have thy voice in my behalf.
The Merry Wives of Windsor. Act i, sc. 4, l. 166. [Fenton]
10
A nest of hollow bosoms, which he fills
With treacherous crowns.
Henry V. Act ii. Prologue, l. 21. [Chorus]
Join'd with an enemy proclaim'd and from his coffers
Received the golden earnest of our death.
Henry V. Act ii, sc. 2, l. 168. [King Henry]
11
Foul subornation is predominant
And equity exiled your highness' land.
II Henry VI. Act iii, sc. 1, l. 145. [Gloucester]
Guilty of subornation.—*Rape of Lucrece,* l. 919.
Murderous subornation.—*I Henry IV,* i, 3, 163.
Subornation, Upon my life.—*II Henry VI,* iii, 1, 45. The only uses of "subornation."
12
You have suborn'd this man.
I Henry VI. Act v, sc. 4, l. 21. [La Pucelle]
Suborned . . . to swear False allegations.
II Henry VI. Act iii, sc. 1, l. 180. [Suffolk] "Allegation" is repeated in l. 40, and occurs in no other scene.
Suborned the witness.—*Othello.* Act iii, sc. 4, l. 153.
Whom I did suborn
To do this ruthless piece of butchery.
Richard III. Act iv, sc. 3, l. 4. [Tyrrel] The only use of "suborn."
Thou hast suborn'd the goldsmith to arrest me.
The Comedy of Errors. Act iv, sc. 4, l. 85. [Antipholus of Ephesus]
Is 't not enough thou hast suborn'd these women
To accuse this worthy man?
Measure for Measure. Act v, sc. 1, l. 308. [Escalus]
What peer hath been suborn'd to grate on you?
II Henry IV, iv, 1, 90. See under REBELLION.
They were suborn'd.—*Macbeth,* ii, 4, 24.
Thou art suborn'd.—*Measure for Measure,* v, 1, 106.
Suborn'd informer.—*Sonnets,* cxxv. The only uses of "suborn'd."
13
She did corrupt frail nature with some bribe.
III Henry VI. Act iii, sc. 2, l. 155. [Gloucester]
Know'st thou not any whom corrupting gold
Would tempt unto a close exploit of death?
Richard III. Act iv, sc. 2, l. 34. [King Richard]
I will corrupt the Grecian sentinels.
Troilus and Cressida, iv, 4, 74.

I need not ask you if gold will corrupt him.
All's Well that Ends Well, iv, 3, 309.

1 You yourself
Are much condemn'd to have an itching palm;
To sell and mart your offices for gold
To undeservers.
Julius Cæsar. Act iv, sc. 3, l. 9. [Brutus] The only use of "itching." "Undeserver" is repeated in *II Henry IV*, ii, 4, 406, and in *Henry VIII*, iii, 2, 175. See under DESERVING.

Shall we now
Contaminate our fingers with base bribes,
And sell the mighty space of our large honours
For so much trash as may be grasped thus?
Julius Cæsar. Act iv, sc. 3, l. 23. [Brutus]

2
Isabella: Hark how I'll bribe you: good my lord, turn back.
Angelo: How! bribe me?
Isabella: Ay, with such gifts that heaven shall share with you.
Measure for Measure. Act ii, sc. 2, l. 145.

3
When they have lined their coats.
Othello. Act i, sc. 1, l. 53. [Iago]
What If I do line one of their hands?
Cymbeline. Act ii, sc. 3, l. 71. [Cloten]
He will line your apron with gold.
Pericles. Act iv, sc. 6, l. 63. [Bawd]

BRIDE AND BRIDEGROOM

See also Marriage

I—Bride

4 To-night,
When I should take possession of the bride,
End ere I do begin.
All's Well that Ends Well. Act ii, sc. 5, l. 27. [Bertram]
'Tis not his new-made bride shall succour him.
III Henry VI. Act iii, sc. 3, l. 207. [Warwick]
New bride.—*II Henry VI*, i, 1, 252.
A new untrimmed bride.—*King John*, iii, 1, 209. The only use of "untrimmed."
Well-chosen bride.—*III Henry VI*, iv, 1, 7. "Well chosen" (unhyphenated) occurs again in *Henry VIII*, ii, 2, 2.

5
In your bride you bury brotherhood.
III Henry VI. Act iv, sc. 1, l. 55. [Gloucester]

6
Hymen hath brought the bride to bed,
Where, by the loss of maidenhead,
A babe is moulded.
Pericles. Act iii, Prelude. [Gower]
Bawd: Your bride goes to that with shame which is her way to go with warrant.
Boult: 'Faith, some do, and some do not.
Pericles. Act iv, sc. 2, l. 138.

7
My child is yet a stranger in the world;
She hath not seen the change of fourteen years;
Let two more summers wither in their pride,
Ere we may think her ripe to be a bride.
Romeo and Juliet. Act i, sc. 2, l. 8. [Capulet]

Lady Capulet: The gallant, young, and noble gentleman,
The County Paris, at Saint Peter's Church,
Shall happily make thee there a joyful bride.
Juliet: Now, by Saint Peter's Church and Peter too,
He shall not make me there a joyful bride.
Romeo and Juliet. Act iii, sc. 5, l. 114.

8
Where is my lovely bride?
The Taming of the Shrew. Act iii, sc. 2, l. 94. [Petruchio]
Loving bride.—*III Henry VI*, iv, 1, 53.
See not your bride in these unreverant robes.
The Taming of the Shrew. Act iii, sc. 2, l. 114. [Tranio]

9
But what a fool am I to chat with you,
When I should bid good morrow to my bride,
And seal the title with a lovely kiss!
The Taming of the Shrew. Act iii, sc. 2, l. 123. [Petruchio]

10 On the Sunday following shall Bianca
Be bride to you.
The Taming of the Shrew. Act ii, sc. 1, l. 397. [Baptista]
Shall sweet Bianca practise how to bride it?
The Taming of the Shrew. Act iii, sc. 2, l. 253. [Tranio]
Vincentio: Ay, mistress bride, hath that awaken'd you?
Bianca: Ay, but not frighted me; therefore I'll sleep again.
Taming of the Shrew. Act v, sc. 2, l. 42.

11
Obey the bride, you that attend on her.
The Taming of the Shrew. Act iii, sc. 2, l. 225. [Petruchio]
I am not bid to wait upon this bride.
Titus Andronicus. Act i, sc. 1, l. 338. [Titus]

12
If thou be pleased with this my sudden choice,
Behold, I choose thee, Tamora, for my bride. . . .
Ascend, fair queen, Pantheon. Lords, accompany
Your noble emperor and his lovely bride,
Sent by the heavens for Prince Saturnine,
Whose wisdom hath her fortune conquered:
There shall we consummate our spousal rites.
Titus Andronicus. Act i, sc. 1, l. 318. [Saturninus] "Spousal" is repeated in *Henry V*, v, 2, 390.
And in the sacred Pantheon her espouse.
Titus Andronicus. Act i, sc. 1, l. 242. [Saturninus] The Pantheon is mentioned nowhere else.

13
God give you joy, sir, of your gallant bride!
Titus Andronicus. Act i, sc. 1, l. 400. [Saturninus]
Somewhat too early for new-married ladies.
Titus Andronicus. Act ii, sc. 2, l. 15. [Saturninus]
New-married wife.—*Henry V*, v, 2, 190. "New-married" is used a third time in *Measure for Measure*, v, 1, 405. See under BRIDEGROOM.

II—Bridegroom

1 Bellona's bridegroom, lapp'd in proof,
Confronted him.

Macbeth, i, 2, 54. See under WAR. The only mention of Bellona. "Lapp'd" is repeated in *Cymbeline,* v, 5, 360: "Lapp'd In a most curious mantle."

2 Those dulcet sounds in break of day
That creep into the dreaming bridegroom's ear
And summon him to marriage.

The Merchant of Venice. Act iii, sc. 2, l. 51. [Portia]

3
Now, when the bridegroom in the morning comes
To rouse thee from thy bed, there art thou dead.

Romeo and Juliet. Act iv, sc. 1, l. 107. [Friar Laurence]

New-made bridegroom.—*Romeo and Juliet,* v, 3, 235.

4
What will be said? what mockery will it be,
To want the bridegroom when the priest attends
To speak the ceremonial rites of marriage!

The Taming of the Shrew. Act iii, sc. 2, l. 4. [Baptista] The only use of "ceremonial."

New-married man.—*Measure for Measure,* v, 1, 405.

III—Bride and Bridegroom

5
Play, music! and you, brides and bridegrooms all,
With measure heap'd in joy, to the measures fall.

As You Like It. Act v, sc. 4, l. 184. [Duke]

6
Bride and groom Devesting them for bed.

Othello, ii, 3, 180. See under FRIEND. The only use of "devesting."

7
Tranio: And is the bride and bridegroom coming home?
Gremio: A bridegroom say you? 'tis a groom indeed,
A grumbling groom, and that the girl shall find.

The Taming of the Shrew. Act iii, sc. 2, l. 153. See also GROOM.

Bride and bridegroom wants
For to supply the places at the table.

The Taming of the Shrew. Act iii, sc. 2, l. 250. [Baptista]

BRIER, see Thorn

BRITAIN, see England

BROOK

8
The brook that brawls along this wood.

As You Like It. Act ii, sc. 1, l. 32. [Lord]

By rushy brook.—*A Midsummer-Night's Dream,* ii, 1, 84. The only use of "rushy."

Running brooks.—*As You Like It,* ii, 1, 16; *The Taming of the Shrew,* Ind., 2, 52.

Small brooks.—*III Henry VI,* iv, 8, 54.

Swift brook.—*As You Like It,* ii, 1, 42.

Windring brooks.—*The Tempest,* iv, 1, 128. The only use of "windring" (wand'ring[?]).

9
When down her weedy trophies and herself
Fell in the weeping brook.

Hamlet. Act iv, sc. 7, l. 175. [Queen] The only use of "weedy."

10
Empties itself, as doth the inland brook,
Into the main of waters.

The Merchant of Venice. Act v, sc. 1, l. 96. [Portia]

11
Such Brooks are welcome to me, that o'er flow such liquor.

The Merry Wives of Windsor. Act ii, sc. 2, l. 156. [Falstaff] The liquor having been provided by Master Brook.

12 Will the cold brook,
Candied with ice, caudle thy morning taste?

Timon of Athens. Act iv, sc. 3, l. 225. [Apemantus] "Candied" is repeated in *Hamlet,* iii, 2, 65, and in *The Tempest,* ii, 1, 279; "Caudle" is repeated in *II Henry VI,* iv, 7, 95, and in *Love's Labour's Lost,* iv, 3, 174.

BROTHER

13
I know you are my eldest brother; and in the gentle condition of blood, you should so know me.

As You Like It. Act i, sc. 1, l. 47. [Orlando]

Elder brother.—*III Henry VI,* iii, 3, 102, and five times in later plays.

14
Your brother is but young and tender.

As You Like It. Act i, sc. 1, l. 135. [Charles]

The worst that they can say of me is that I am a second brother.

II Henry IV. Act ii, sc. 2, l. 70. [Poins]

Younger brothers.—*I Henry IV,* iv, 2, 31, and five times in later plays.

Youngest brother!—*Troilus and Cressida,* v, 6, 12.

15
I rather will subject me to the malice
Of a diverted blood and bloody brother.

As You Like It. Act ii, sc. 3, l. 36. [Orlando]

False brother.—*The Tempest,* i, 2, 92.

Tyrant brother.—*As You Like It,* i, 2, 300.

Unworthy brother.—*As You Like It,* i, 1, 36; *Titus Andronicus,* i, 1, 346.

Wretched brother.—*Richard II,* i, 2, 27.

16
Find out thy brother, wheresoe'er he is;
Seek him with candle; bring him dead or living
Within this twelvemonth, or turn thou no more
To seek a living in our territory.

As You Like It. Act iii, sc. 1, l. 5. [Duke]

Oliver: Orlando did approach the man
And found it was his brother, his elder brother.
Celia: O, I have heard him speak of that same brother;
And he did render him the most unnatural
That lived mongst men.

Oliver: And well he might so do,
For well I know he was unnatural.
As You Like It. Act iv, sc. 3, l. 120.

1
Embrace thy brother there; rejoice with him.
The Comedy of Errors. Act v, sc. 1, l. 413. [Antipholus of Syracuse]

You call'd me brother,
When I was but your sister; I you brothers,
When ye were so indeed.
Cymbeline. Act v, sc. 5, l. 376. [Imogen]

2
Forty thousand brothers
Could not, with all their quantity of love,
Make up my sum.
Hamlet. Act v, sc. 1, l. 292. [Hamlet]

A hoop of gold to bind thy brothers in.
II Henry IV. Act iv, sc. 4, l. 43. [King Henry]

Agree like brothers.—*II Henry VI,* iv, 2, 81.
This is brother-like.—*III Henry VI,* v, 1, 105.
The only use of "brother-like."

3
How to use your brothers brotherly.
III Henry VI. Act iv, sc. 3, l. 38. [Warwick]

I speak but brotherly of him.
As You Like It, i, 1, 163.

I love thee brotherly.
Cymbeline, iv, 2, 158. The only uses of "brotherly."

4
I have no brother, I am like no brother.
III Henry VI. Act v, sc. 6, l. 80. [Gloucester]

I never had a brother;
Nor can there be that deity in my nature,
Of here and every where.
Twelfth Night. Act v, sc. 1, l. 233. [Sebastian]

Reft of his brother.—*The Comedy of Errors,* i, 1, 129.
Banish'd brother.—*As You Like It,* v, 4, 169.
I had a brother, then.—*Measure for Measure,* ii, 2, 42.

5
Sirrah, your brother is legitimate;
Your father's wife did after wedlock bear him,
And if she did play false, the fault was hers;
Which fault lies on the hazards of all husbands
That marry wives.
King John. Act i, sc. 1, l. 116. [King John]

Legitimation, name and all is gone.
King John. Act i, sc. 1, l. 248. [Bastard]
The only use of "legitimation."

Brother by the mother's side, give me your hand.
King John. Act i, sc. 1, l. 163. [Bastard]

Natural brother.—*As You Like It,* i, 1, 151.

I am sworn brother to a leash of drawers.
I Henry IV. Act ii, sc. 4, l. 7. [Prince of Wales] See under BROTHERHOOD.

6
How fares my brother? why is he so sad?
III Henry VI. Act ii, sc. 1, l. 8. [Edward]

Prince: How fares our loving brother?
York: Well, my dread lord; so must I call you now.
Richard III. Act iii, sc. 1, l. 96.

What cheer? how is 't with you, best brother?
The Winter's Tale. Act i, sc. 2, l. 148. [Polixenes]

7
I have a brother is condemn'd to die:
I do beseech you, let it be his fault,
And not my brother.
Measure for Measure. Act ii, sc. 2, l. 34. [Isabella]

Be satisfied;
Your brother dies to-morrow; be content.
Measure for Measure. Act ii, sc. 2, l. 105. Angelo]

Your brother cannot live.—*Measure for Measure,* ii, 4, 33.
Your brother is to die.—*Measure for Measure,* ii, 4, 83.
Poor brother.—*Measure for Measure,* i, 4, 71; ii, 4, 99; v, 1, 77.

8
I, now the voice of the recorded law,
Pronounce a sentence on your brother's life:
Might there not be a charity in sin
To save this brother's life?
Measure for Measure. Act ii, sc. 4, l. 61. [Angelo]

We cannot weigh our brother with ourself.
Measure for Measure. Act ii, sc. 2, l. 126. [Isabella]

Better it were a brother dies at once,
Than that a sister, by redeeming him,
Should die for ever.
Measure for Measure. Act ii, sc. 4, l. 106. [Isabella]

Redeem thy brother
By yielding up thy body to my will.
Measure for Measure. Act ii, sc. 4, l. 163. [Angelo]

Redeem your brother from the angry law.
Measure for Measure. Act iii, sc. 1, l. 207. [Duke]

I had rather my brother die by the law than my son should be unlawfully born.
Measure for Measure. Act iii, sc. 1, l. 195. [Isabella]

9
I am a brother Of gracious order.
Measure for Measure. Act iii, sc. 2, l. 231. [Duke]

A brother of your order.—*Measure for Measure,* i, 3, 44.
Bare-foot brother.—*Romeo and Juliet,* v, 2, 5.

10
You have of late stood out against your brother.
Much Ado about Nothing. Act i, sc. 3, l. 23. [Conrade]

You are very near my brother in his love.
Much Ado about Nothing. Act ii, sc. 1, l. 169. [Don John]

Hath your grace ne'er a brother like you?
Much Ado about Nothing. Act ii, sc. 1, l. 336. [Beatrice]

11
His blood was thine! that bed, that womb,
That metal, that self mould, that fashion'd thee
Made him a man.
Richard II. Act i, sc. 2, l. 22. [Duchess of Gloucester]

Twinn'd brothers of one womb,
Whose procreation, residence, and birth,
Scarce is dividant.
Timon of Athens. Act iv, sc. 3, l. 3. [Timon] The only use of "procreation" and "dividant."

Brother born.—*II Henry IV,* iv, 1, 95; *King John,* ii, 1, 104.

1
Oh, if you love my brother, hate not me;
I am his brother, and I love him well.
Richard III. Act i, sc. 4, l. 232. [Clarence]

2
That a brother should Be so perfidious!
The Tempest. Act i, sc. 2, l. 67. [Prospero]

Here lies your brother,
No better than the earth he lies upon,
If he were that which now he 's like, that 's dead;
Whom I, with this obedient steel, three inches of it,
Can lay to bed for ever.
The Tempest. Act ii, sc. 1, l. 280. [Antonio]

You, most wicked sir, whom to call brother
Would even infect my mouth.
The Tempest. Act v, sc. 1, l. 130. [Prospero]

3
Brother, for in that name doth nature plead.
Titus Andronicus. Act i, sc. 1, l. 370. [Marcus]

Dear brother.—*III Henry VI,* iii, 3, 212, and five times in later plays.
Gentle brother.—*The Comedy of Errors,* iii, 2, 25; *Cymbeline,* v, 5, 374.
Good brother.—*II Henry IV,* v, 2, 49; v, 2, 54; *Julius Cæsar,* iv, 3, 212; iv, 3, 237; *King Lear,* iv, 2, 44; *Cymbeline,* iv, 2, 20.
Noble brother.—*Julius Cæsar,* iv, 2, 37.
Own brother.—*Othello,* iii, 4, 137.
Sweet brother.—*III Henry VI,* v, 2, 34; *Richard III,* iv, 4, 277; *Troilus and Cressida,* v, 3, 14.
Worthy brother.—*III Henry VI,* v, 7, 30.

4
Remember, boys, I pour'd forth tears in vain,
To save your brother from the sacrifice.
Titus Andronicus. Act ii, sc. 3, l. 163. [Tamora]

And here my brother, weeping at my woes.
Titus Andronicus. Act iii, sc. 1, l. 100. [Titus]

Lucius: Sweet father, if I shall be thought thy son,
Let me redeem my brothers both from death.
Marcus: And, for our father's sake and mother's care,
Now let me show a brother's love to thee.
Titus Andronicus. Act iii, sc. 1, l. 180.

Brother-love.—*Henry VIII,* v, 3, 173. The only instance of the use of this phrase.

5
Stay, murderous villains! will you kill your brother?
Titus Andronicus. Act iv, sc. 2, l. 88. [Aaron]

He is your brother, lords, sensibly fed
Of that self-blood that first gave life to you.
Titus Andronicus. Act iv, sc. 2, l. 122. [Aaron] The only use of "self-blood."

Nay, he is your brother by the surer side,
Although my seal be stamped in his face.
Titus Andronicus. Act iv, sc. 2, l. 126. [Aaron]

My spritely brethren.—*Troilus and Cressida,* ii, 2, 190.
You brace of warlike brothers.—*Troilus and Cressida,* iv, 5, 175.
Valiant brother.—*III Henry VI,* v, 2, 42; *Hamlet,* i, 2, 25.

6
Viola: My brother he is in Elysium.
Perchance he is not drown'd: what think you, sailors?
Captain: It is perchance that you yourself were saved.
Viola: O my poor brother; and so perchance may he be.
Captain: . . . I saw your brother,
Most provident in peril, bind himself,
Courage and hope both teaching him the practice,
To a strong mast that lived upon the sea;
Where, like Arion on the dolphin's back,
I saw him hold acquaintance with the waves
As long as I could see.
Twelfth Night. Act i, sc. 2, l. 4. The only mention of Arion.

I my brother know
Yet living in my glass; even such and so
In favour was my brother, and he went
Still in this fashion, colour, ornament,
For him I imitate.
Twelfth Night. Act iii, sc. 4, l. 413. [Viola]

But, had it been the brother of my blood,
I must have done no less with wit and safety.
Twelfth Night. Act v, sc. 1, l. 217. [Sebastian]

7
No honest man, neither to his father nor to me, to go about to make me the king's brother-in-law.
The Winter's Tale. Act iv, sc. 4, l. 718. [Shepherd]

Our trusty brother-in-law.—*Richard II,* v, 3, 137.
Ransom straight His brother-in-law.—*I Henry IV,* i, 3, 80. The only uses of "brother-in-law."

BROTHERHOOD

See also Comradeship, Fellowship

8
Further this act of grace; and from this hour
The heart of brothers govern in our loves
And sway our great designs!
Antony and Cleopatra. Act ii, sc. 2, l. 149. [Antony]

They shook hands and swore brothers.
As You Like It. Act v, sc. 4, l. 107. [Touchstone]

Sworn brother.—*I Henry IV,* ii, 4, 7, and seven times in later plays.

9
We came into the world like brother and brother;
And now let 's go hand in hand, not one before another.
The Comedy of Errors. Act v, sc. 1, l. 424.

1
Arviragus: Are we not brothers?
Imogen: So man and man should be:
But clay and clay differs in dignity,
Whose dust is both alike.
Cymbeline. Act iv, sc. 2, l. 2.

2
A noble shalt thou have, and present pay;
And liquor likewise will I give to thee,
And friendship shall combine, and brotherhood:
I 'll live by Nym, and Nym shall live by me;
Is not this just? for I shall sutler be
Unto the camp, and profits will accrue.
Give me thy hand.
Henry V. Act ii, sc. 1, l. 112. [Pistol] The only use of "sutler."

3
For forth he goes and visits all his host,
Bids them good morrow with a modest smile
And calls them brothers, friends and countrymen.
Henry V. Act iv, Prol., l. 32.

We few, we happy few, we band of brothers;
For he to-day that sheds his blood with me
Shall be my brother; be he ne'er so vile,
This day shall gentle his condition.
Henry V. Act iv, sc. 3, l. 60. [King Henry]

4
Finds brotherhood in thee no sharper spur?
Richard II. Act i, sc. 2, l. 9. [Duchess of Gloucester]

Meantime, this deep disgrace in brotherhood
Touches me deeper than you can imagine.
Richard III. Act i, sc. 1, l. 111. [Gloucester]

Who spake of brotherhood?—*Richard III*, ii, 1, 108.
Bury brotherhood.—*III Henry VI*, iv, 1, 55.
Brotherhoods in cities.—*Troilus and Cressida*, i, 3, 104.

5 I am sworn brother, sweet,
To grim Necessity.
Richard II. Act v, sc. 1, l. 20. [King Richard]

I am sworn brother to a leash of drawers.
I Henry IV. Act ii, sc. 4, l. 7. [Prince of Wales]

Sworn brothers to France.—*Henry V*, ii, 1, 13.
Sworn brothers in filching.—*Henry V*, iii, 2, 47.
My sworn brother, the people.—*Coriolanus*, ii, 3, 102.
His sworn brother, a very simple gentleman.—*The Winter's Tale*, iv, 4, 607.

6
The king's son took me by the hand, and called me brother; and then the two kings called my father brother; and then the prince my brother and the princess my sister called my father father.
Winter's Tale. Act v, sc. 2, l. 152. [Clown]

BROW

See also Eye

7
The chaste unsmirched brow of my true mother.
Hamlet, iv, 5, 119. See under BASTARD. The only use of "unsmirched."

Gentle brow.—*King John*, iii, 1, 247.
Living brow.—*Sonnets*, lxviii.
Smoothed brow.—*I Henry VI*, iii, 1, 124.
Sober brow.—*Merchant of Venice*, iii, 2, 78.

8
Yea, this man's brow, like to a title-leaf,
Foretells the nature of a tragic volume.
II Henry IV, i, 1, 60. See under PROPHECY. The only use of "title-leaf."

Beauty's brow.—*Sonnets*, lx.
Cynthia's brow.—*Romeo and Juliet*, iii, 5, 20.
Fair ladies' brows.—*Romeo and Juliet*, i, 1, 236.

9
Now bind my brows with iron.
II Henry IV. Act i, sc. 1, l. 150. [Northumberland]

He whose brow with homely biggen bound
Snores out the watch of night.
II Henry IV, iv, 5, 27. See under CROWN. The only use of "biggen" (nightcap).

10
Now are our brows bound with victorious wreaths.
Richard III, i, 1, 5. See under PEACE.

His brows bound with oak.—*Coriolanus*, i, 3, 16.
Gold-bound brow.—*Macbeth*, iv, 1, 114. The only use of "gold-bound."

11
These brows, were moulded out of his.
King John, ii, 1, 100. See under FACE.

12
Why do you bend such solemn brows on me?
King John. Act iv, sc. 2, l. 90. [King John]

Bent his brow.—*III Henry VI*, v, 2, 22.
Cloudy brow.—*II Henry VI*, iii, 1, 155.
Cunning brow.—*The Rape of Lucrece*, l. 749.
Dangerous brow.—*Julius Cæsar*, ii, 1, 78.
Serious brow.—*Henry VIII*, Prol., 2.
Wrinkled brows.—*King John*, iv, 2, 192; *The Merchant of Venice*, iv, 1, 270.

13
The heaven of her brow.
Love's Labour's Lost. Act iv, sc. 3, l. 227. [Biron]

Velvet brow.—*Love's Labour's Lost*, iii, 1, 198.
Brows of grace.—*Macbeth*, iv, 3, 23.
Brow of justice.—*I Henry IV*, iv, 3, 83.
Brow of youth.—*II Henry VI*, v, 3, 4; *King Lear*, i, 4, 306.
Bare brow of a bachelor.—*As You Like It*, iii, 3, 62.
Mourning brow of progeny.—*Love's Labour's Lost*, v, 2, 754.

14
O, if in black my lady's brows be deck'd,
It mourns that painting and usurping hair
Should ravish doters with a false aspect;
And therefore is she born to make black fair.
Love's Labour's Lost. Act iv, sc. 3, l. 258. [Biron] The only use of "doters."

Your brows are blacker; yet black brows, they say,
Become some women best, so that there be not
Too much hair there, but in a semicircle,
Or a half-moon made with a pen.
The Winter's Tale. Act ii, sc. 1, l. 8. [Mamillius] The only use of "semicircle."

"Semi-circled" occurs in *The Merry Wives of Windsor,* iii, 3, 68.
Black brow.—*King John,* v, 6, 17.
Inky brows.—*As You Like It,* iii, 5, 46.
Brow of Egypt.—*A Midsummer-Night's Dream,* v, 1, 11.

1
Thou hast the right arched beauty of the brow that becomes the ship-tire, the tire-valiant, or any tire of Venetian admittance.
The Merry Wives of Windsor. Act iii, sc. 3, l. 60. [Falstaff] The only use of "ship-tire" and "tire-valiant," a woman's head-dress of extravagant form, resembling a ship.
Arched brows.—*All's Well that Ends Well,* i, 1, 105.
Vaulty brows.—*King John,* iii, 4, 30.
Square brows.—*Pericles,* v, 1, 109.

2
A brow unbent, that seem'd to welcome woe.
The Rape of Lucrece, l. 1509.
Sad brow.—*II Henry IV,* v, 1, 92; *Much Ado about Nothing,* i, 1, 185; *Julius Cæsar,* ii, 1, 308; *As You Like It,* iii, 2, 227.
Servant brow.—*I Henry IV,* i, 3, 19.

3
Mamillius: What color are your eyebrows?
First Lady: Blue, my lord.
Mamillius: Nay, that 's a mock: I have seen a lady's nose
That has been blue, but not her eyebrows.
The Winter's Tale. Act ii, sc. 1, l. 13.

II—The Angry Brow

4
The stern brow and waspish action.
As You Like It. Act iv, sc. 3, l. 9. [Silvius]
Angry brow.—*Pericles,* i, 2, 52; *Venus and Adonis,* l. 339.

5
Prepare thy brow to frown.
Coriolanus. Act iv, sc. 5, l. 69. [Coriolanus]
What though her frowning brows be bent,
Her cloudy looks will calm ere night.
The Passionate Pilgrim, l. 311.
Frowning brow to brow.—*Richard II,* i, 1, 16.

6 Let the brow o'erwhelm it
As fearfully as doth a galled rock
O'erhang and jutty his confounded base.
Henry V. Act iii, sc. 1, l. 11. [King Henry] The only use of "o'erhang." "Jutty" occurs again in *Macbeth,* i, 6, 6.

7 Knit his brows,
As frowning at the favours of the world.
II Henry VI. Act i, sc. 2, l. 3. [Duchess] Shakespeare used the phrase, "knit his brows," twice in this play (iii, 1, 15), his first one; and twice in his second one, *III Henry VI* (ii, 2, 20; iii, 2, 82), and never after that. The nearest to it is "purse thy brow together," *Othello,* iii, 3, 114. The phrase "knit brow" occurs in *The Rape of Lucrece,* l. 709.
Fie, fie! unknit that threatening unkind brow.
The Taming of the Shrew. Act v, sc. 2, l. 136. [Katharina] For the three other uses of "unknit" see under KNOT.

8
His louring brows o'erwhelming his fair sight,
Like misty vapours when they blot the sky.
Venus and Adonis, l. 183.
Overwhelming brows.—*Romeo and Juliet,* v, 1, 39. The only uses of "overwhelming."
Warlike brows.—*Richard III,* i, 3, 175.

BUILDING

9 I have lived To see . . .
The buildings of my fancy.
Coriolanus. Act ii, sc. 1, l. 214. [Volumnia]
Sumptuous buildings.—*II Henry VI,* i, 3, 133.
Wasted building.—*Titus Andronicus,* v, 1, 23.
Worthy building.—*Cymbeline,* iv, 2, 355.

10 When we mean to build,
We first survey the plot, then draw the model;
And when we see the figure of the house,
Then must we rate the cost of the erection;
Which if we find outweighs ability,
What do we then but draw anew the model
In fewer offices, or at least desist
To build at all?
II Henry IV. Act i, sc. 3, l. 41. [Bardolph]
Much more, in this great work, . . . should we survey
The plot of situation and the model,
Consent upon a sure foundation,
Question surveyors, know our own estate,
How able such a work to undergo.
II Henry IV. Act i, sc. 3, l. 48. [Bardolph]

11 Like the martlet,
Builds in the weather on the outward wall,
Even in the force and road of casualty.
The Merchant of Venice. Act ii, sc. 9, l. 28. [Arragon] The only use of "casualty."

12
Thou shalt build from men.—*Timon of Athens,* iv, 3, 533.
Build there, carpenter.—*Troilus and Cressida,* iii, 2, 53.
Build churches.—*Hamlet,* iii, 2, 142.
Churches build.—*King Lear,* iii, 2, 90.

BULL

13
Rages like a chafed bull.
III Henry VI. Act ii, sc. 5, l. 126. [Prince of Wales]
Well, as time shall try:
'In time the savage bull doth bear the yoke.'
Much Ado about Nothing. Act i, sc. 1, l. 262. [Don Pedro]
Savage bull.—*Much Ado about Nothing,* v, 1, 184; v, 4, 43.

14
Bull Jove, sir, had an amiable low;
And some such strange bull leap'd your father's cow,
And got a calf in that same noble feat
Much like to you, for you have just his bleat.
Much Ado about Nothing. Act v, sc. 4, l. 48. [Benedick]
Remember, Jove, thou wast a bull for thy Europa.
The Merry Wives of Windsor. Act v, sc. 5, l. 3. [Falstaff] Europa is mentioned again in *Much Ado about Nothing,* v, 4, 45.

Jupiter became a bull, and bellow'd.
The Winter's Tale. Act iv, sc. 4, l. 27. [Perdita]
The goodly transformation of Jupiter there, his brother, the bull.
Troilus and Cressida. Act v, sc. 1, l. 59. [Thersites]
From a god to a bull? a heavy declension! it was Jove's case.
II Henry IV. Act ii, sc. 2, l. 192. [Prince Henry]

1
The bull has the game: ware horns, ho!
Troilus and Cressida. Act v, sc. 7, l. 12. [Thersites]
Bull-calf.—*I Henry IV,* ii, 4, 287. The only use of the word except as a man's name.
Young bulls.—*II Henry IV,* iv, 1, 103.
Thessalian bulls.—*Midsummer-Night's Dream,* iv, 1, 127. The only use of "Thessalian."

BURDEN

See also Load, Weight

2
I would sing my song without a burden.
As You Like It. Act iii, sc. 2, l. 261. [Celia]
Clap 's into 'Light o' love;' that goes without a burden.
Much Ado about Nothing. Act iii, sc. 4, l. 44. [Margaret]
Julia: Best sing it to the tune of 'Light o' love.'
Lucetta: It is too heavy for so light a tune.
Julia: Heavy! belike it hath some burden then?
The Two Gentlemen of Verona, i, 2, 83. See under SONG.

3
O heavy burthen!
Hamlet. Act iii, sc. 1, l. 54. [King]
Heavy burthen.—*Comedy of Errors,* v, 1, 402; *Henry V,* i, 2, 201; *Romeo and Juliet,* i, 4, 22.
Clogging burthen.—*Richard II,* i, 3, 200. The only use of "clogging."
Goodly burthen.—*The Tempest,* iv, 1, 113.
Great burthen.—*III Henry VI,* ii, 1, 81.
Grievous burthen.—*Richard III,* iv, 4, 167.
Joint burden.—*II Henry IV,* v, 2, 55.
Venerable burden.—*As You Like It,* ii, 7, 167.

4
Take heed, lest at once
The burthen of my sorrows fall upon ye.
Henry VIII. Act iii, sc. 1, l. 110. [Queen Katharine]
But, ass, I 'll take that burthen from your back,
Or lay on that shall make your shoulders crack.
King John. Act ii, sc. 1, l. 145. [Bastard]

5
Why sweat they under burthens?
The Merchant of Venice. Act iv, sc. 1, l. 95. [Shylock]
Under my burthen groaned.—*The Tempest,* i, 2, 156.

6
Now thy proud neck bears half my burthen'd yoke;
From which even here I slip my weary neck,
And leave the burthen of it all on thee.
Richard III. Act iv, sc. 4, l. 111. [Queen Margaret] See under YOKE.
I will not burden thee.—*The Taming of the Shrew,* ii, 1, 203.

7
I am the drudge and toil in your delight,
But you shall bear the burden soon at night.
Romeo and Juliet. Act ii, sc. 5, l. 77. [Nurse]
I, to bear this,
That never knew but better, is some burden.
Timon of Athens. Act iv, sc. 3, l. 266. [Timon]
'Tis a burden Which I am proud to bear.
Troilus and Cressida. Act iii, sc. 3, l. 36. [Diomedes]
Bear her burthen.—*Richard III,* iii, 7, 229.

8
Your affairs there, what, with whom, the condition of that fardel, the place of your dwelling, your names, your ages, of what having, breeding, and any thing that is fitting to be known, discover.
The Winter's Tale. Act iv, sc. 4, l. 737. [Autolycus]
Autolycus: The fardel there? what 's i' the fardel? Wherefore that box?
Shepherd: Sir, there lies such se-rets in this fardel.
The Winter's Tale. Act iv, sc. 4, l. 780.
There is that in this fardel will make him scratch his beard.
Winter's Tale. Act iv, sc. 4, l. 728. [Shepherd]
I was by at the opening of the fardel.
The Winter's Tale. Act v, sc. 2, l. 4. [Gentleman]
I heard them talk of a fardel.
The Winter's Tale. Act v, sc. 2, l. 125. [Autolycus]
Who would fardels bear?—*Hamlet,* iii, 1, 76. See under SUICIDE. The only uses of "fardel," all but one in *The Winter's Tale.*

BURIAL

9
Buried in highways out of all sanctified limit.
All's Well that Ends Well. Act i, sc. 1, l. 151. [Parolles]

10
First Clown: Is she to be buried in Christian burial that wilfully seeks her own salvation?
Second Clown: I tell thee she is; and therefore make her grave straight.
Hamlet. Act v, sc. 1, l. 1.
If this had not been a gentlewoman, she should have been buried out o' Christian burial.
Hamlet. Act v, sc. 1, l. 26. [Second Clown] "Christian burial" is repeated in l. 5, and occurs in no other scene.
She should in ground unsanctified have lodged
Till the last trumpet.
Hamlet. Act v, sc. 1, l. 252. [First Priest]

11
To look our dead, and then to bury them.
Henry V. Act iv, sc. 7, l. 76. [King Henry]
Give them burial.—*I Henry VI,* iv, 7, 86. Repeated five times in later plays.
Groaning for burial.—*Julius Cæsar,* iii, 1, 275.

12
She shall be buried with her face upwards.
Much Ado about Nothing. Act iii, sc. 2, l. 70. [Don Pedro]
These two days buried.—*Romeo and Juliet,* v, 3, 176.

Lie buried.—*The Merchant of Venice,* iii, 1, 6; *Henry V,* iii, 3, 9.

1 Do all rites That appertain unto a burial.
Much Ado about Nothing. Act iv, sc. 1, l. 209. [Friar]

2 Now must I hide his body in some hole,
Until the duke take order for his burial.
Richard III. Act i, sc. 4, l. 287. [Murderer]

3 Inter their bodies as becomes their births.
Richard III. Act v, sc. 5, l. 15. [Richmond]

Remaineth nought, but to inter our brethren.
Titus Andronicus. Act i, sc. 1, l. 146. [Lucius]

We have done but greenly,
In hugger-mugger to inter him.
Hamlet. Act iv, sc. 5, l. 83. [King] The only use of "hugger-mugger" (secretly). "Greenly" (foolishly) is repeated in *Henry V,* v, 2, 149.

Like A queen . . . inter me.
Henry VIII, iv, 2, 171. See under QUEEN.

4 Bury him where you can; he comes not here.
Titus Andronicus. Act i, sc. 1, l. 354. [Titus]

Well, bury him, and bury me the next.
Titus Andronicus. Act i, sc. 1, l. 386. [Titus]

Bury him as a prince.—*Cymbeline,* v, 2, 251.

Bury the dead.—*Midsummer-Night's Dream,* v, 1, 355.

BUSINESS

See also Affairs, Commerce, Merchant, Trade

5 I am so full of businesses, I cannot answer thee acutely.
All's Well that Ends Well. Act i, sc. 1, l. 220. [Parolles] The only use of "acutely."

I have to-night dispatched sixteen businesses, a month's length a-piece, by an abstract of success.
All's Well that Ends Well. Act iv, sc. 3, l. 98. [Bertram]

6 Will you see her,
For that is her demand, and know her business?
All's Well that Ends Well. Act ii, sc. 1, l. 88. [Lafeu]

Know his business of him.—*Measure for Measure,* i, 4, 8.

I know my business.—*All's Well that Ends Well,* ii, 2, 4.

7 Now, fair one, does your business follow us?
All's Well that Ends Well. Act ii, sc. 1, l. 102. [King]

To your business.—*All's Well that Ends Well,* ii, 2, 65.

Undertake this business.—*All's Well that Ends Well,* iii, 6, 94, *The Winter's Tale,* iv, 4, 835.

8 A very serious business calls on him.
All's Well that Ends Well. Act ii, sc. 4, l. 41. [Parolles]

Serious business, craving quick dispatch.
Love's Labour's Lost. Act ii, sc. 1, l. 31. [Princess]

If the business be of any difficulty . . . it requires haste of your lordship.
All's Well that Ends Well. Act iv, sc. 3, l. 107. [Second Lord]

I am for other business.—*All's Well that Ends Well,* v, 2, 36.

Her business looks in her
With an importing visage.
All's Well that Ends Well. Act v, sc. 3, l. 135. [Gentleman]

9 You do mistake your business.
Antony and Cleopatra. Act ii, sc. 2, l. 45. [Antony]

Yet, ere we put ourselves in arms, dispatch we
The business we have talk'd of.
Antony and Cleopatra. Act ii, sc. 2, l. 168. [Antony]

Our graver business Frowns at this levity.
Antony and Cleopatra. Act ii, sc. 7, l. 127. [Cæsar]

I find thee Most fit for business.
Antony and Cleopatra. Act iii, sc. 3, l. 39. [Cleopatra]

The business of this man looks out of him.
Antony and Cleopatra. Act v, sc. 1, l. 50. [Cæsar]

10 To business that we love we rise betime,
And go to 't with delight.
Antony and Cleopatra. Act iv, sc. 4, l. 20. [Antony]

11 My present business calls me from you now.
The Comedy of Errors. Act i, sc. 2, l. 29. [Merchant]

Some present business of the state.
Othello. Act i, sc. 2, l. 90. [Othello]

Business of the state.—*Othello,* iv, 2, 166.

Business of estate.—*Henry VIII,* ii, 2, 70.

I 'll bring thee to the present business
Which now 's upon 's.
The Tempest. Act i, sc. 2, l. 136. [Prospero]

Present business.—*King Lear,* v, 3, 318.

Business present.—*Henry VIII,* i, 1, 206.

12 Our business is not unknown to the senate.
Coriolanus. Act i, sc. 1, l. 58. [Citizen]

You are like to do such business.
Coriolanus. Act iii, sc. 1, l. 48. [Cominius]

13 O, if he had borne the business!
Coriolanus. Act i, sc. 1, l. 273. [Brutus]

You must report to the Volscian lords, how plainly
I have borne this business.
Coriolanus. Act v, sc. 3, l. 3. [Coriolanus]

Bear the business.—*Coriolanus,* i, 6, 82.

14 Myself and other noble friends
Are partners in the business.
Cymbeline. Act i, sc. 6, l. 183. [Iachimo] For "partner" see under WIFE.

15 There 's business in these faces.
Cymbeline. Act v, sc. 5, l. 23. [Cymbeline]

'Tis not sleepy business.—*Cymbeline,* iii, 5, 26.

16 Thus much the business is.
Hamlet. Act i, sc. 2, l. 27. [King]

For every man has business and desire,
Such as it is.
Hamlet. Act i, sc. 5, l. 130. [Hamlet]

1
We 'll . . . think upon this business.
Hamlet. Act ii, sc. 2, l. 82. [King]

2
This business is well ended.
Hamlet. Act ii, sc. 2, l. 85. [Polonius]
End of my business.—*Hamlet*, iii, 2, 330.
End the business.—*The Winter's Tale*, iii, 1, 18.
The business is not ended.—*All's Well that Ends Well*, iv, 3, 110.
I am glad at heart
To be so rid o' the business.
The Winter's Tale. Act iii, sc. 3, l. 14. [Mariner]

3
Now, my masters, happy man be his dole, say I: every man to his business.
I Henry IV. Act ii, sc. 2, l. 80. [Falstaff]
About thy business.—*II Henry IV*, v, 1, 39; *Richard III*, i, 3, 355.
About your own business.—*Much Ado about Nothing*, ii, 1, 195.

4
Some heavy business hath my lord in hand.
I Henry IV. Act ii, sc. 3, l. 66. [Lady Percy]
Our hands are full of business.
I Henry IV. Act iii, sc. 2, l. 179. [King Henry]
A thousand businesses are brief in hand.
King John. Act iv, sc. 3, l. 158. [Bastard]
You have mighty business in hand.
King Lear. Act iii, sc. 5, l. 17. [Edmund]
You have your hands full all,
In this so sudden business.
Romeo and Juliet. Act iv, sc. 3, l. 12. [Juliet]

5
This weighty business will not brook delay.
II Henry VI. Act i, sc. 1, l. 170. [Beaufort]
There ye shall meet about this weighty business.
Henry VIII. Act ii, sc. 2, l. 140. [King Henry]
Weighty business.—*Richard III*, ii, 2, 144.

6
I would your highness
Would give it quick consideration, for
There is no primer business.
Henry VIII. Act i, sc. 2, l. 65. [Queen Katharine] The only use of "primer."
How holily he works in all his business!
And with what zeal!
Henry VIII. Act ii, sc. 2, l. 24. [Norfolk] "Holily" is also used twice in *Macbeth*, i, 5, 22; v, 1, 67.

7
Let 's in;
And with some other business put the king
From these sad thoughts.
Henry VIII. Act ii, sc. 2, l. 56. [Norfolk]
Business with the king.—*Hamlet*, i, 2, 37.
King's business.—*Henry VIII*, iii, 2, 73.

8
It was a gentle business, and becoming
The action of good women.
Henry VIII. Act ii, sc. 3, l. 54. [Lord Chamberlain]
How goes her business?—*Henry VIII*, iv, 1, 23.
You ever
Have wish'd the sleeping of this business.
Henry VIII. Act ii, sc. 4, l. 163. [King Henry]

9
What can be their business?
Henry VIII. Act iii, sc. 1, l. 19. [Queen Katharine]
What 's the business,
That such a hideous trumpet calls to parley
The sleepers of the house?
Macbeth. Act ii, sc. 3, l. 86. [Lady Macbeth]
Now, what 's the business?—*Othello*, i, 3, 13.
What business, lord, so early?
Troilus and Cressida. Act iv, sc. 1, l. 34. [Paris]

10
Speak to the business, master secretary.
Henry VIII. Act v, sc. 3, l. 1. [Chancellor]
My lord, because we have business of more moment,
We will be short with you.
Henry VIII. Act v, sc. 3, l. 51. [Gardiner]

11
To groan and sweat under the business,
Either led or driven.
Julius Cæsar. Act iv, sc. 1, l. 22. [Antony]
To consummate this business happily.
King John. Act v, sc. 7, l. 95. [Salisbury]

12
Hath he never heretofore sounded you in this business?
King Lear. Act i, sc. 2, l. 74. [Gloucester] The only use of "heretofore."

13
I see the business.
King Lear. Act i, sc. 2, l. 198. [Edmund]
I understand the business, I hear it.
The Winter's Tale. Act iv, sc. 4, l. 683. [Autolycus]

14
It is thy business that I go about.
King Lear. Act iv, sc. 4, l. 24. [Cordelia]
For this business, It toucheth us.
King Lear. Act v, sc. 1, l. 24. [Albany]
It is my business too.—*Antony and Cleopatra*, i, 4, 80.
No man's business.—*Much Ado about Nothing*, i, 3, 18.

15
To things of sale a seller's praise belongs.
Love's Labour's Lost. Act iv, sc. 3, l. 240. [Biron] The only use of "seller."
You do as chapmen do,
Dispraise the thing that you desire to buy:
But we in silence hold this virtue well,
We 'll but commend what we intend to sell.
Troilus and Cressida. Act iv, sc. 1, l. 75. [Paris]
Base sale of chapmen's tongues.
Love's Labour's Lost, ii, 1, 16. The only uses of "chapmen." See under BEAUTY.

16
You shall put
This night's business into my dispatch;
Which shall to all our nights and days to come
Give solely sovereign sway and masterdom.
Macbeth. Act i, sc. 5, l. 68. [Lady Macbeth] The only use of "masterdom."
We will proceed no further in this business.
Macbeth. Act i, sc. 7, l. 31. [Macbeth]
It is the bloody business which informs
Thus to mine eyes.
Macbeth. Act ii, sc. 1, l. 48. [Macbeth]
What bloody business.—*Othello*, iii, 3, 469.

Bleeding business.—*Julius Cæsar,* iii, 1, 168.
Bitter business.—*Hamlet,* iii, 3, 409.

1
I will put that business in your bosoms.
Macbeth. Act iii, sc. 1, l. 104. [Macbeth]

Masking the business from the common eye
For sundry weighty reasons.
Macbeth. Act iii, sc. 1, l. 125. [Macbeth] The only use of "masking." "Masquing" occurs twice, in *The Merchant of Venice,* ii, 6, 59, and in *The Taming of the Shrew,* iv, 3, 87.

2
Great business must be wrought ere noon.
Macbeth. Act iii, sc. 5, l. 22. [Hecate]

Great and trusty business.—*All's Well that Ends Well,* iii, 6, 16.
Importunate business.—*Timon of Athens,* iii, 6, 16.
Special business.—*Measure for Measure,* iii, 2, 233.

3
My business is a word or two with Claudio.
Measure for Measure. Act iii, sc. 1, l. 48. [Isabella]

That's my pith of business.—*Measure for Measure,* i, 4, 70.
That, indeed, Sir John, is my business.—*The Merry Wives of Windsor,* iii, 5, 64.
That's my business to you.—*The Tempest,* iii, 3, 69.

4 When you have
A business for yourself, pray heaven you then
Be perfect.
Measure for Measure. Act v, sc. 1, l. 80. [Duke]

I have some business.—*The Merchant of Venice,* ii, 2, 213.

5
Slubber not business for my sake, Bassanio.
The Merchant of Venice. Act ii, sc. 8, l. 39. [Salarino]

You must therefore be content to slubber the gloss of your new fortunes with this more stubborn and boisterous expedition.
Othello. Act i, sc. 3, l. 227. [Duke] The only uses of "slubber."

6
O love, dispatch all business, and be gone!
The Merchant of Venice. Act iii, sc. 2, l. 325. [Portia]

It is a business of some heat.
Othello. Act i, sc. 2, l. 40. [Cassio]

My business asketh haste.
The Taming of the Shrew. Act ii, sc. 1, l. 115. [Petruchio]

I have important business,
The tide whereof is now.
Troilus and Cressida. Act v, sc. 1, l. 89. [Diomedes]

7
O, full of careful business are his looks!
Richard II. Act ii, sc. 2, l. 75. [Queen]

Let's look to our business.—*Othello,* ii, 3, 116.

Effect this business soundly.
Richard III. Act iii, sc. 1, l. 186. [Buckingham]

Do my business.—*The Two Gentlemen of Verona,* iv, 4, 70.
It is a busy time with me.—*Much Ado about Nothing.* Act iii, sc. 5, l. 6. [Leonato]

Soft! see how busily she turns the leaves!
Titus Andronicus. Act iv, sc. 1, l. 45. [Titus] "Busily" is repeated in *I Henry IV,* v, 5, 38.

8
Let us consult upon to-morrow's business.
Richard III. Act v, sc. 3, l. 45. [Richmond]

9
You shall hop without my custom, sir.
The Taming of the Shrew. Act iv, sc. 3, l. 99. [Petruchio]

What with the war, what with the sweat, what with the gallows and what with poverty, I am custom-shrunk.
Measure for Measure. Act i, sc. 2, l. 83. [Mrs. Overdone] The only use of "custom-shrunk."

10 There, this night,
We'll pass the business privately and well.
The Taming of the Shrew. Act iv, sc. 4, l. 56. [Tranio]

So shall you stay
Till you have done your business in the city.
The Taming of the Shrew. Act iv, sc. 2, l. 109. [Tranio]

11 There's other business for thee:
Come, thou tortoise!
The Tempest. Act i, sc. 2, l. 315. [Prospero] "Tortoise" is repeated in *Romeo and Juliet,* v, 1, 42.

Be quick, thou'rt best,
To answer other business.
The Tempest. Act i, sc. 2, l. 366. [Prospero]

For yet ere supper-time must I perform
Much business appertaining.
The Tempest. Act iii, sc. 1, l. 95. [Prospero] "Appertaining" is used twice more, in *Love's Labour's Lost,* i, 2, 15, and in *Romeo and Juliet,* iii, 1, 66.

12
One business does command us all; for mine
Is money.
Timon of Athens. Act iii, sc. 4, l. 4. [Servant]

Caphis: What, You come for money?
Servant: Is't not your business too?
Timon of Athens. Act ii, sc. 2, l. 9.

Set abroad new business for you all.
Titus Andronicus. Act i, sc. 1, l. 192. [Titus]

13 This Antenor,
I know, is such a wrest in their affairs
That their negotiations all must slack,
Wanting his manage.
Troilus and Cressida. Act iii, sc. 3, l. 24. [Calchas]. The only use of "wrest" in this sense (a key for tuning a harp) and of "negotiations."

14
Business, my lord! I think most understand.
Winter's Tale. Act i, sc. 2, l. 229. [Camillo]

This business Will raise us all.
Winter's Tale. Act ii, sc. 1, l. 197. [Leontes]

Are you a party in this business?
The Winter's Tale. Act iv, sc. 4, l. 842. [Autolycus]

Leontes: What is the business?
Servant: O sir, I shall be hated to report it!
The Winter's Tale. Act iii, sc. 2, l. 143.

This ungentle business, Put on thee by my lord.
The Winter's Tale. Act iii, sc. 3, l. 34. [Antigonus]

Those who think it is unlawful business
I am about, let them depart.
Winter's Tale. Act v, sc. 3, l. 96. [Paulina]

II—Business and Pleasure

1
Now, for the love of Love and her soft hours,
Let 's not confound the time with conference harsh.
Antony and Cleopatra. Act i, sc. 1, l. 44. [Antony]

Antony: The business she hath broached in the state cannot endure my absence.
Enobarbus: And the business you have broached here cannot be without you.
Antony and Cleopatra. Act i, sc. 2, l. 178.

Broach this business.—*Henry VIII,* ii, 4, 149.

2
Adriana: Why should their liberty than ours be more?
Luciana: Because their business still lies out o' door.
The Comedy of Errors. Act ii, sc. 1, l. 10.

3
Go to; I 'll make you know your times of business:
Is this an hour for temporal affairs?
Henry VIII. Act ii, sc. 2, l. 72. [King Henry]

4
Heaven defend your good souls, that you think
I will your serious and great business scant
For she is with me: no, when light-wing'd toys
Of feather'd Cupid seel with wanton dullness
My speculative and officed instruments,
That my disports corrupt and taint my business,
Let housewives make a skillet of my helm,
And all indign and base adversities
Make head against my estimation!
Othello. Act i, sc. 3, l. 268. [Othello] The only use of "light-wing'd," "skillet," and "indign." "Feather'd" is repeated in *I Henry IV:* "Feather'd Mercury"; and in *Pericles,* v, 2, 280: "Feather'd briefness." "Seel" occurs again in iii, 3, 210, and in *Antony and Cleopatra,* iii, 13, 112; "speculative" in *Macbeth,* v, 4, 19; "officed" in *All's Well that Ends Well,* iii, 2, 129, and in *Winter's Tale,* i, 2, 172. The only use of "disports" as a noun, though as a verb it occurs in *III Henry VI,* iv, 5, 8, and in *Timon of Athens,* i, 2, 141.

5
Pandarus: My business seethes.
Servant: Sodden business! there 's a stewed phrase indeed!
Troilus and Cressida. Act iii, sc. 1, l. 42.

BUTCHER

6
Herod's bloody-hunting slaughtermen.
Henry V. Act iii, sc. 3, l. 41. [King Henry] The only use of "bloody-hunting."

Slaughter-man to all my kin.—*III Henry VI,* i, 4, 169.

I 'll be thy slaughter-man.—*Titus Andronicus,* iv, 4, 58.

Will be thy slaughter-men.—*I Henry VI,* iii, 3, 75.

Each one the slaughter-man of twenty.—*Cymbeline,* v, 3, 49. The only uses of "slaughter-man."

7
And as the butcher takes away the calf
And binds the wretch and beats it when it strays,
Bearing it to the bloody slaughter-house,
Even so remorseless have they borne him hence.
II Henry VI. Act iii, sc. 1, l. 210. [King Henry]

They fell before thee like sheep and oxen, and thou behavedst thyself as if thou hadst been in thine own slaughter-house.
II Henry VI. Act iv, sc. 3, l. 4. [Cade]

His realm a slaughter-house.—*III Henry VI,* v, 4, 78. See under SOVEREIGN.

Loath to bear me to the slaughter-house. *Richard III,* iii, 4, 88. See under OMEN.

Go, hie thee, hie thee from this slaughter-house,
Lest thou increase the number of the dead.
Richard III. Act iv, sc. 1, l. 44. [Queen Elizabeth] See also under HASTE.

The uncleanly savours of a slaughter-house.—*King John,* iv, 3, 112. The only uses of "slaughter-house."

8
Are you there, butcher?
III Henry VI. Act ii, sc. 2, l. 95. [Richard]

Where is that devil's butcher?
III Henry VI. Act v, sc. 5, l. 77. [Queen Margaret]

Butcher of my son.—*Coriolanus,* i, 9, 88.

Butcher of an innocent child.—*King John,* iv, 2, 259.

Butchers of his life.—*Richard II,* i, 2, 3.

Butcher to the sire.—*Richard III,* v, 5, 26.

9
O, pardon me, thou bleeding piece of earth,
That I am meek and gentle with these butchers!
Julius Cæsar. Act iii, sc. 1, l. 254. [Antony]

Butchers and villains!—*III Henry VI,* v, 5, 61.

10
This good king's blood,
Which his hell-govern'd arm hath butchered!
Richard III. Act i, sc. 2, l. 66. [Anne] The only use of "hell-govern 'd."

They at Pomfret bloodily were butcher 'd.
Richard III. Act iii, sc. 4, l. 92. [Hastings]

A thousand of his people butchered.
I Henry IV. Act i, sc. 1, l. 42. [Westmoreland]

Butcher'd wrongfully!—*Titus Andronicus,* iv, 4, 55.

11
This ruthless piece of butchery.
Richard III. Act iv, sc. 3, l. 5. [Tyrrel]

This house is but a butchery.
As You Like It. Act ii, sc. 3, l. 27. [Adam]

Civil butchery.—*I Henry IV,* i, 1, 13. The only uses of "butchery."

12
Like to a mortal butcher bent to kill.
Venus and Adonis, l. 618.

Lay on like a butcher.—*Henry V,* v, 2, 147.
The very butcher of a silk button.
Romeo and Juliet. Act ii, sc. 4, l. 24. [Mercutio] See also under DUELLING.

BUTTERFLY

1
I saw him run after a gilded butterfly; and when he caught it, he let it go again.
Coriolanus. Act i, sc. 3, l. 66. [Valeria]
Laugh at gilded butterflies.—*King Lear,* v, 3, 13.
Summer butterflies.—*Coriolanus,* iv, 6, 94.

2
There is differency between a grub and a butterfly; yet your butterfly was a grub.
Coriolanus. Act v, sc. 4, l. 11. [Menenius] The only use of "differency."

3
And pluck the wings from painted butterflies
To fan the moonbeams from his sleeping eyes.
A Midsummer-Night's Dream. Act iii, sc. 1, l. 175. [Titania] The only use of "moonbeams."

C

CÆSAR

4
Cæsar gets money where He loses hearts.
Antony and Cleopatra. Act ii, sc. 1, l. 13. [Pompey]

I cannot hope
Cæsar and Antony shall well greet together:
His wife that 's dead did trespasses to Cæsar;
His brother warr'd upon him.
Antony and Cleopatra. Act ii, sc. 1, l. 38. [Menecrates]

Julius Cæsar,
Who at Philippi the good Brutus ghosted.
Antony and Cleopatra. Act ii, sc. 6, l. 12. [Pompey] The only use of "ghosted."

Pompey: Apollodorus carried— . . .
Enobarbus: A certain queen to Cæsar in a mattress.
Antony and Cleopatra. Act ii, sc. 6, l. 69. The only mention of Apollodorus and use of "mattress."

5
The scarce-bearded Cæsar.
Antony and Cleopatra. Act i, sc. 1, l. 21. [Cleopatra] The only use of "scarce-bearded."
Blossoming Cæsar.—*Antony and Cleopatra,* iv, 12, 23.
O that brave Cæsar!—*Antony and Cleopatra,* i, 5, 67.
Broad-fronted Cæsar.—*Antony and Cleopatra,* i, 5, 29. The only use of "broad-fronted."
Great Cæsar.—*Antony and Cleopatra,* iii, 13, 74.
Imperial Cæsar.—*Cymbeline,* v, 5, 474.
Most noble Cæsar!—*Julius Cæsar,* iii, 2, 248; *Antony and Cleopatra,* i, 4, 35.
O noble Cæsar!—*Julius Cæsar,* iii, 2, 203.
O royal Cæsar!—*Julius Cæsar,* iii, 2, 248.
Valiant Cæsar!—*Antony and Cleopatra,* i, 5, 69.

6
Enobarbus: Cæsar? Why, he 's the Jupiter of men.
Agrippa: What 's Antony? The god of Jupiter.
Enobarbus: Spake you of Cæsar? How! the nonpareil! . . .
Would you praise Cæsar, say 'Cæsar:' go no further.
Antony and Cleopatra. Act iii, sc. 2, l. 9. For "nonpareil" see under PERFECTION.

But as for Cæsar,
Kneel down, kneel down, and wonder.
Antony and Cleopatra. Act iii, sc. 2, l. 18. [Enobarbus]

Hail, Cæsar, and my lord! hail, most dear Cæsar!
Antony and Cleopatra. Act iii, sc. 6, l. 39. [Octavia]

This speed of Cæsar's Carries beyond belief.
Antony and Cleopatra. Act iii, sc. 7, l. 75. [Canidius]

To Cæsar will I render
My legions and my horse: six kings already
Show me the way of yielding.
Antony and Cleopatra. Act iii, sc. 10, l. 33. [Canidius]

Yes, like enough, high-battled Cæsar will
Unstate his happiness, and be staged to the show,
Against a sworder!
Antony and Cleopatra. Act iii, sc. 13, l. 29. [Enobarbus] The only use of "high-battled" and "staged." "Unstate" is used again in *King Lear,* i, 2, 108; and "sworder" in *II Henry VI,* iv, 1, 135: "A Roman sworder."

7
Thus then, thou most renown'd: Cæsar entreats,
Not to consider in what case thou stand'st,
Further than he is Cæsar.
Antony and Cleopatra. Act iii, sc. 13, l. 53. [Thyreus]

Be thou sorry
To follow Cæsar in his triumph, since
Thou hast been whipp'd for following him.
Antony and Cleopatra. Act iii, sc. 13, l. 136. [Antony]

Not the imperious show
Of the full-fortuned Cæsar ever shall
Be brooch'd with me.
Antony and Cleopatra. Act iv, sc. 15, l. 23. [Cleopatra] The only use of "full-fortuned."

'Tis paltry to be Cæsar;
Not being Fortune, he 's but Fortune's knave,
A minister of her will.
Antony and Cleopatra. Act v, sc. 2, l. 2. [Cleopatra]

8
Cæsar cannot live To be ungentle.
Antony and Cleopatra. Act v, sc. 1, l. 59. [Cæsar]

Cæsar 's no merchant, to make prize with you
Of things that merchants sold.
Antony and Cleopatra. Act v, sc. 2, l. 183. [Cæsar]

O, couldst thou speak,
That I might hear thee call great Cæsar ass
Unpoliced!
Antony and Cleopatra. Act v, sc. 2, l. 309. [Cleopatra] The only use of "unpoliced."

A way there, a way for Cæsar!
Antony and Cleopatra, act v, sc. 2, l. 335.

1 Cæsar's thrasonical brag of 'I came, saw, and overcame.'
As You Like It. Act v, sc. 2, l. 34. [Rosalind] "Thrasonical" (after Thraso, a bragging character in Terence's *Eunuchus*) is repeated in *Love's Labour 's Lost,* v, 1, 14.

Veni, vidi, vici; which to annothanize in the vulgar,—O base and obscure vulgar!—videlicet, He came, saw, and overcame.
Love's Labour 's Lost. Act iv, sc. 1, l. 68. [Boyet, reading.] The only use of "veni, vidi, vici," and of "annothanize" (probably for anatomize, interpret). "Videlicet" occurs four times in the plays.

A kind of conquest
Cæsar made here; but made not here his brag
Of 'came' and 'saw' and 'overcame:' with shame—
The first that ever touch'd him—he was carried
From off our coast, twice beaten; and his shipping—
Poor ignorant baubles!—on our terrible seas,
Like egg-shells moved upon their surges, crack'd
As easily 'gainst our rocks.
Cymbeline. Act iii, sc. 1, l. 22. [Queen] "Egg-shell" is repeated in *Hamlet,* iv, 4, 53.

2 Julius Cæsar, whose remembrance yet
Lives in men's eyes and will to ears and tongues
Be theme and hearing ever.
Cymbeline. Act iii, sc. 1, l. 2. [Caius Lucius]

There be many Cæsars, Ere such another Julius.
Cymbeline. Act iii, sc. 1, l. 11. [Cloten]

There is no moe such Cæsars: other of them may have crook'd noses, but to owe such straight arms, none.
Cymbeline. Act iii, sc. 1, l. 36. [Cloten]

Antony: Here was a Cæsar! when comes such another?
First Citizen: Never, never. Come, away, away!
We 'll burn his body in the holy place.
Julius Cæsar. Act iii, sc. 2, l. 257.

3 If Cæsar can hide the sun from us with a blanket, or put the moon in his pocket, we will pay him tribute for light.
Cymbeline. Act iii, sc. 1, l. 43. [Cloten]

Cæsar, that hath more kings his servants than
Thyself domestic officers.
Cymbeline. Act iii, sc. 1, l. 64. [Lucius]

4 Polonius: I did enact Julius Cæsar: I was killed i' the Capitol; Brutus killed me.
Hamlet: It was a brute part of him to kill so capital a calf there.
Hamlet. Act iii, sc. 2, l. 110. The only use of "brute."

Brutus' bastard hand Stabb'd Julius Cæsar.
II Henry VI. Act iv, sc. 1, l. 136.

Et tu, Brute! Then fall, Cæsar!
Julius Cæsar. Act iii, sc. 1, l. 77. [Cæsar] The only use of the Latin phrase.

They that stabb'd Cæsar shed no blood at all,
Did not offend, nor were not worthy blame,
If this foul deed were by to equal it.
III Henry VI. Act v, sc. 5, l. 53. [Queen Margaret]

5 Imperious Cæsar, dead and turn'd to clay,
Might stop a hole to keep the wind away:
O, that that earth, which kept the world in awe,
Should patch a wall to expel the winter's flaw!
Hamlet. Act v, sc. 1, l. 236. [Hamlet]

6 Go forth and fetch their conquering Cæsar in.
Henry V. Act v, Prologue, l. 28. [Chorus]

Now am I like that proud insulting ship
Which Cæsar and his fortune bare at once.
I Henry VI. Act i, sc. 2, l. 138. [La Pucelle]

7 These growing feathers pluck'd from Cæsar's wing
Will make him fly an ordinary pitch,
Who else would soar above the view of men
And keep us all in servile fearfulness.
Julius Cæsar. Act i, sc. 1, l. 77. [Flavius] The only use of "fearfulness."

What means this shouting? I do fear, the people
Choose Cæsar for their king.
Julius Cæsar. Act i, sc. 2, l. 79. [Brutus]

8 Cassius: But, soft, I pray you: what, did Cæsar swound?
Casca: He fell down in the market-place, and foamed at mouth, and was speechless.
Brutus: 'Tis very like: he hath the falling sickness.
Cassius: No, Cæsar hath it not; but you and I
And honest Casca, we have the falling sickness.
Julius Cæsar. Act i, sc. 2, l. 252. The only uses of "falling sickness," i.e., epilepsy, with which Cæsar is said to have been afflicted.

9 O, that we then could come by Cæsar's spirit,
And not dismember Cæsar! But, alas,
Cæsar must bleed for it!
Julius Cæsar. Act ii, sc. 1, l. 169. [Brutus] "Dismember" is repeated in *King John,* iii, 1, 330.

And for Mark Antony, think not of him:
For he can do no more than Cæsar's arm
When Cæsar's head is off.
Julius Cæsar. Act ii, sc. 1, l. 181. [Brutus]

10 Cæsar should be a beast without a heart,
If he should stay at home to-day for fear.
Julius Cæsar. Act ii, sc. 2, l. 42. [Cæsar]

If Cæsar hide himself, shall they not whisper
'Lo, Cæsar is afraid'?
Julius Cæsar. Act ii, sc. 2, l. 100. [Decius]
How foolish do your fears seem now, Calpurnia!
I am ashamed I did yield to them.
Julius Cæsar. Act ii, sc. 2, l. 105. [Cæsar]

1 Most high, most mighty, and most puissant Cæsar.
Julius Cæsar. Act iii, sc. 1, l. 33. [Metellus]
Know, Cæsar doth not wrong, nor without cause
Will he be satisfied.
Julius Cæsar. Act iii, sc. 1, l. 47. [Cæsar]

2 Cæsar was mighty, bold, royal, and loving.
Julius Cæsar. Act iii, sc. 1, l. 127. [Servant]
Say I fear'd Cæsar, honour'd him and loved him.
Julius Cæsar. Act iii, sc. 1, l. 129. [Servant]
That I did love thee, Cæsar, O, 'tis true.
Julius Cæsar. Act iii, sc. 1, l. 194. [Antony]

3 How many times shall Cæsar bleed in sport,
That now on Pompey's basis lies along
No worthier than the dust!
Julius Cæsar. Act iii, sc. 1, l. 114. [Brutus]
But yesterday the word of Cæsar might
Have stood against the world; now lies he there,
And none so poor to do him reverence.
Julius Cæsar. Act iii, sc. 2, l. 123. [Antony]
O mighty Cæsar! dost thou lie so low?
Are all thy conquests, glories, triumphs, spoils,
Shrunk to this little measure?
Julius Cæsar. Act iii, sc. 1, l. 148. [Antony]
No bending knee will call thee Cæsar now.
III Henry VI. Act iii, sc. 1, l. 18. [King Henry]

4 And Cæsar's spirit, ranging for revenge,
With Ate by his side come hot from hell.
Julius Cæsar. Act iii, sc. 1, l. 270. [Antony]
Ate is mentioned also in *Love's Labour's Lost,* v, 2, 694; *King John,* ii, 1, 63; and *Much Ado about Nothing,* ii, 1, 263.

5 As Cæsar loved me, I weep for him; as he was fortunate, I rejoice at it; as he was valiant, I honour him; but as he was ambitious, I slew him. There is tears for his love; joy for his fortune; honour for his valour; and death for his ambition.
Julius Cæsar. Act iii, sc. 2, l. 26. [Brutus]
The noble Brutus
Hath told you Cæsar was ambitious:
If it were so, it was a grievous fault,
And grievously hath Cæsar answer'd it.
Julius Cæsar. Act iii, sc. 2, l. 82. [Antony]
Cæsar's ambition,
Which swell'd so much that it did almost stretch
The sides o' the world.
Cymbeline. Act iii, sc. 1, l. 49. [Cymbeline]

6 Had you rather Cæsar were living and die all slaves, than that Cæsar were dead, to live all free men?
Julius Cæsar. Act iii, sc. 2, l. 24. [Brutus]
First Citizen: This Cæsar was a tyrant.
Third Citizen: Nay, that's certain:
We are blest that Rome is rid of him.
Julius Cæsar. Act iii, sc. 2, l. 74.
And why should Cæsar be a tyrant then?
Julius Cæsar. Act i, sc. 3, l. 103. [Cassius]

7 I come to bury Cæsar, not to praise him.
Julius Cæsar. Act iii, sc. 2, l. 79. [Antony]
If thou consider rightly of this matter,
Cæsar has had great wrong.
Julius Cæsar. Act iii, sc. 2, l. 114. [Citizen]

8 Cæsar, thou art revenged,
Even with the sword that kill'd thee.
Julius Cæsar. Act v, sc. 3, l. 45. [Cassius]
O Julius Cæsar, thou art mighty yet!
Thy spirit walks abroad, and turns our swords
In our own proper entrails.
Julius Cæsar. Act v, sc. 3, l. 94. [Brutus]

9 Thou 'rt an emperor, Cæsar, Keisar, and Pheezar.
The Merry Wives of Windsor. Act i, sc. 3, l. 9. [Host] The only use of "Keisar" and "Pheezar."

10 That Julius Cæsar was a famous man;
With what his valour did enrich his wit,
His wit set down to make his valour live.
Richard III. Act iii, sc. 1, l. 84. [Prince of Wales]

11 Cæsarion, whom they call my father's son.
Antony and Cleopatra. Act iii, sc. 6, l. 6. [Cæsar]
The next Cæsarion.—*Antony and Cleopatra,* iii, 13, 162. The only references to Cæsarion, the son of Cæsar by Cleopatra, executed by order of Augustus.

CAITIFF, see Cowardice

CALAMITY, see Adversity

CALENDAR, see Almanac

CALLING, see Profession

CALUMNY

See also Slander

12 Virtue itself 'scapes not calumnious strokes.
Hamlet. Act i, sc. 3, l. 38. [Lærtes]
There 's none stands under more calumnious tongues
Than I myself, poor man.
Henry VIII. Act v, sc. 1, l. 112. [Cranmer]
Calumnious knave.—*All's Well that Ends Well,* i, 3, 61. The only uses of "calumnious."

13 If thou dost marry, I 'll give thee this plague for thy dowry: be thou as chaste as ice, as pure as snow, thou shalt not escape calumny.
Hamlet. Act iii, sc. 1, l. 139. [Hamlet]

14 No might nor greatness in mortality
Can censure 'scape; back-wounding calumny
The whitest virtue strikes. What king so strong
Can tie the gall up in the slanderous tongue?
Measure for Measure. Act iii, sc. 2, l. 196.

[Duke] The only use of "back-wounding." "Whitest" is repeated in *Henry VIII*, i, 1, 209.

Smell of calumny.—*Measure for Measure*, ii, 4, 159.

The shrug, the hum or ha, these petty brands
That calumny doth use—O, I am out—
That mercy does, for calumny will sear
Virtue itself: these shrugs, these hums and ha's.
Winter's Tale. Act ii, sc. 1, l. 71. [Leontes]

CANDLE

1
Chief Justice: What! you are as a candle, the better part burnt out.
Falstaff: A wassail candle, my lord, all tallow.
II Henry IV. Act i, sc. 2, l. 177.

Here burns my candle out; ay, here it dies.
III Henry VI. Act ii, sc. 6, l. 1. [Clifford]

Out, out, brief candle!
Macbeth. Act v, sc. 5, l. 23. [Macbeth]

2
This candle burns not clear: 'tis I must snuff it;
Then out it goes.
Henry VIII. Act iii, sc. 2, l. 96. [Wolsey]

Out went the candle, and we were left darkling.
King Lear. Act i, sc. 4, l. 237. [Fool]

Dark needs no candles now, for dark is light.
Love's Labour's Lost. Act iv, sc. 3, l. 269. [Dumain]

3
Thus hath the candle singed the moth.
The Merchant of Venice. Act ii, sc. 9, l. 79. [Portia]

4
How far that little candle throws his beams!
So shines a good deed in a naughty world.
The Merchant of Venice. Act v, sc. 1, l. 90. [Portia]

When the moon shone, we did not see the candle.
The Merchant of Venice. Act v, sc. 1, l. 92. [Nerissa]

5
Night's candles are burnt out.
Romeo and Juliet, iii, 5, 9. See under DAY.

There's husbandry in heaven;
Their candles are all out.
Macbeth, ii, 1, 5. See under STAR.

Blessed candles of the night.—*The Merchant of Venice*, v, 1, 220.

6
Help me to a candle.
Twelfth Night. Act iv, sc. 2, l. 87. [Malvolio]

CANDOUR

7
A common and an outward man.
All's Well that Ends Well. Act iii, sc. 1, l. 11. [Second Lord]

8
Speak to me home, mince not the general tongue.
Antony and Cleopatra. Act i, sc. 2, l. 109. [Antony]

9
Enjoy thy plainness,
It nothing ill becomes thee.
Antony and Cleopatra. Act ii, sc. 6, l. 80. [Pompey]

Thy plainness . . .
Hath won the greatest favour.
I Henry VI, i, 1, 191. See DEED, 316:5.

Your plainness and your shortness please me well.
The Taming of the Shrew. Act iv, sc. 4, l. 39. [Baptista]

Therefore with frank and uncurbed plainness
Tell us the Dauphin's mind.
Henry V. Act i, sc. 2, l. 244. [King Henry] The only use of "uncurbed."

Pride, which she calls plainness.
King Lear, i, 1, 131. See under PRIDE.

To plainness honour's bound.
King Lear, i, 1, 150. See under MAJESTY.

In this plainness
Harbour more craft and more corrupter ends
Than twenty silly ducking observants.
King Lear, ii, 2, 107. See under HYPOCRISY.

Whilst some with cunning gild their copper crowns,
With truth and plainness I do wear mine bare.
Troilus and Cressida. Act iv, sc. 4, l. 107. [Troilus]

In plainness do confess.—*The Taming of the Shrew*, i, 1, 157.

Plainness of the case.—*I Henry VI*, ii, 4, 46.

Honest plainness.—*Othello*, i, 1, 97. The only uses of "plainness."

10
Give me leave To speak my mind.
As You Like It. Act ii, sc. 7, l. 58. [Jaques]

Your betters have endured me say my mind,
And if you cannot, best you stop your ears.
The Taming of the Shrew. Act iv, sc. 3, l. 75. [Katharina]

11
Am I so round with you as you with me,
That like a football you do spurn me thus?
The Comedy of Errors. Act ii, sc. 1, l. 82. [Dromio of Ephesus] "Foot-ball" (hyphenated) is repeated in *King Lear*, i, 4, 95: "Foot-ball player."

Be round with him.—*Hamlet*, iii, 4, 5.

Let her be round with him.—*Hamlet*, iii, 1, 191.

I must be round with him.—*Timon of Athens*, ii, 2, 8.

I must be round with you.—*Twelfth Night*, ii, 3, 102.

12
What I think I utter, and spend my malice in my breath.
Coriolanus. Act ii, sc. 1, l. 58. [Menenius]

If the drink you give me touch my palate adversely,
I make a crooked face at it.
Coriolanus. Act ii, sc. 1, l. 58. [Menenius] The only use of "adversely."

We call a nettle but a nettle and
The faults of fools but folly.
Coriolanus. Act ii, sc. 1, l. 207. [Menenius]

13
His heart's his mouth:
What his breast forges, that his tongue must vent;
And, being angry, does forget that ever
He heard the name of death.
Coriolanus. Act iii, sc. 1, l. 257. [Menenius]

He . . . is ill school'd
In bolted language; meal and bran together
He throws without distinction.
Coriolanus. Act iii, sc. 1, l. 320. [Menenius]

"Bolted" is repeated in *Henry V*, ii, 2, 137: "Finely bolted"; and in *The Winter's Tale*, iv, 4, 375: "Bolted By the northern blasts twice o'er." See HAND, 664:15.

He speaks What 's in his heart.
Coriolanus. Act iii, sc. 3, l. 28. [Junius Brutus]

He speaks home, madam: you may relish him more in the soldier than in the scholar.
Othello. Act ii, sc. 1, l. 166. [Cassio]

1
I am too blunt and saucy.
Cymbeline. Act v, sc. 5, l. 325. [Belarius]

Base slave, thy words are blunt and so art thou.
II Henry VI. Act iv, sc. 1, l. 67. [Suffolk]

What a blunt fellow is this grown to be!
Julius Cæsar. Act i, sc. 2, l. 299. [Brutus]

A good blunt fellow.—*King John*, i, 1, 71.

You are too blunt.—*The Taming of the Shrew*, ii, 1, 45.

2
Let me conjure you, by the rights of our fellowship, by the consonancy of our youth, by the obligation of our ever-preserved love, and by what more dear a better proposer could charge you withal, be even and direct with me.
Hamlet. Act ii, sc. 2, l. 293. [Hamlet] "Consonancy" is repeated in *Twelfth Night*, ii, 5, 141. The only use of "ever-preserved" and "proposer."

To be direct and honest is not safe.
Othello, iii, 3, 378. See under HONESTY.

3
I do believe you think what now you speak.
Hamlet. Act iii, sc. 2, l. 196. [Player King]

I mind to tell him plainly what I think.
III Henry VI. Act iv, sc. 1, l. 8. [Clarence]

Speak freely what you think.
III Henry VI. Act iv, sc. 1, l. 28. [King Edward]

4
Pardon the frankness of my mirth.
Henry V. Act v, sc. 2, l. 318. [Burgundy] The only use of "frankness."

5
And since you know you cannot see yourself
So well as by reflection, I, your glass,
Will modestly discover to yourself
That of yourself which you yet know not of.
Julius Cæsar. Act i, sc. 2, l. 67. [Cassius]

All my engagements I will construe to thee,
All the charactery of my sad brows.
Julius Cæsar. Act ii, sc. 1, l. 307. [Brutus] The only use of "engagements." "Charactery" is repeated in *The Merry Wives of Windsor*, v, 5, 77.

6
Now to plain-dealing; lay these glozes by.
Love's Labour 's Lost. Act iv, sc. 3, l. 370. [Longaville] For "gloze" see under DECEIT.

Plain-dealing, which will not cost a man a doit.
Timon of Athens. Act i, sc. 1, l. 216. [Apemantus]

In plain-dealing.—*Measure for Measure*, ii, 1, 263.

An honest plain-dealing man.—*II Henry VI*, iv, 2, 111.

Plain-dealing villain.—*Much Ado about Nothing*, i, 3, 33. The only uses of "plain-dealing."

7
Lo, he is tilting straight!
Love's Labour 's Lost. Act v, sc. 2, l. 483. [Biron] "Tilting" is repeated in *The Comedy of Errors*, iv, 2, 6, and in *Othello*, ii, 3, 183.

8
I cannot cog, I cannot prate.
The Merry Wives of Windsor. Act iii, sc. 3, l. 50. [Falstaff] "I cannot cog" is repeated in l. 76. See under CHEATING.

9
I cannot hide what I am: I must be sad when I have cause and smile at no man's jests, eat when I have stomach and wait for no man's leisure, sleep when I am drowsy and tend on no man's business, laugh when I am merry and claw no man in his humour.
Much Ado about Nothing. Act i, sc. 3, l. 14. [Don John]

It better fits my blood to be disdained of all than to fashion a carriage to rob love from any: in this, though I cannot be said to be a flattering honest man, it must not be denied but I am a plain-dealing villain.
Much Ado about Nothing. Act i, sc. 3, l. 29. [Don John]

10
The Moor is of a free and open nature,
That thinks men honest that but seem to be so.
Othello. Act i, sc. 3, l. 405. [Iago]

Your free and noble nature.—*Othello*, iii, 3, 199.

Frank nature.—*All's Well that Ends Well*, i, 2, 20.

Frank appearance.—*Othello*, i, 3, 38.

Frank donation.—*Coriolanus*, iii, 1, 130.

Frank election.—*All 's Well that Ends Well*, ii, 3, 61.

Frank heart.—*King Lear*, iii, 4, 20.

But to be frank.—*Romeo and Juliet*, ii, 2, 131.

11
Now I shall have reason
To show the love and duty that I bear you
With franker spirit.
Othello. Act iii, sc. 3, l. 195. [Iago] The only use of "franker."

12
I think there 's never a man in Christendom
That can less hide his love or hate than he.
Richard III. Act iii, sc. 4, l. 53. [Hastings]

13
Shall I be plain?
Richard III. Act iv, sc. 2, l. 18. [King Richard]

Be plain, good son, and homely in thy drift;
Riddling confession finds but riddling shrift.
Romeo and Juliet. Act ii, sc. 3, l. 55. [Friar Laurence]

I was always plain with you, and so now I speak my agitation of the matter.
The Merchant of Venice. Act iii, sc. 5, l. 3. [Launcelot] "Agitation" is repeated in *Macbeth*, v, 1, 12.

He was wont to speak plain and to the purpose, like an honest man and a soldier.
Much Ado about Nothing. Act ii, sc. 3, l. 19. [Benedick]

Sir, 'tis my occupation to be plain.
King Lear. Act ii, sc. 2, l. 98. [Kent]

14
To be generous, guiltless and of free dispo-

sition, is to take those things for bird-bolts that you deem cannon-bullets.
Twelfth Night. Act i, sc. 5, l. 98. [Olivia] The only use of "cannon-bullets." "Bird-bolts" is repeated in *Love's Labour's Lost,* iv, 3, 25, and in *Much Ado about Nothing,* i, 1, 42.

1
Why, this is evident to any formal capacity; there is no obstruction in this.
Twelfth Night. Act ii, sc. 5, l. 128. [Malvolio]

Daylight and champain discovers not more: this is open.
Twelfth Night. Act ii, sc. 5, l. 174. [Malvolio] "Champains" (open fields) is repeated in *King Lear,* i, 1, 65.

Lay open all proceedings.—*I Henry IV,* ii, 3, 34.

Deliver with more openness your answers.
Cymbeline. Act i, sc. 6, l. 88. [Imogen] The only use of "openness."

Be intelligent to me.—*Winter's Tale,* i, 2, 378.

Swift and intelligent.—*King Lear,* iii, 7, 12. See under INTELLIGENCE.

2
Speak frankly as the wind.
Troilus and Cressida. Act i, sc. 3, l. 253. [Agamemnon]

I will begin at thy heel, and tell what thou art by inches, thou thing of no bowels, thou!
Troilus and Cressida. Act ii, sc. 1, l. 53. [Thersites]

CANKER

3
The canker galls the infants of the spring,
Too oft before their buttons be disclosed.
Hamlet, i, 3, 39. See under YOUTH.

4
The cankers of a calm world and a long peace.
I Henry IV, iv, 2, 32. See under KNAVE.

5
O, that this good blossom could be kept from cankers!
II Henry IV. Act ii, sc. 2, l. 101. [Poins]

Hath not thy rose a canker?
I Henry VI, ii, 4, 68. See under ROSE.

6
Banish the canker of ambitious thoughts.
II Henry VI, i, 2, 18. See under AMBITION.

Canker of our nature.—*Hamlet,* v. 2, 69.

Beauty's canker.—*The Tempest,* i, 2, 415.

7
Now will canker sorrow eat my bud.
King John, iii, 4, 82. See under SORROW.

Canker vice the sweetest buds doth love.
Sonnets. No. lxx. See under VICE.

8
I had rather be a canker in a hedge than a rose in his grace.
Much Ado about Nothing. Act i, sc. 3, l. 28. [Don John]

9
Full soon the canker death eats up that plant.
Romeo and Juliet, ii, 3, 30. See under GOOD AND EVIL.

10
Loathsome canker lives in sweetest bud.
Sonnets. No. xxxv. See under IMPERFECTION.

Consuming canker.—*I Henry VI,* ii, 4, 71.

Inveterate canker.—*King John,* v, 2, 14.

11
Like a canker in the fragrant rose.
Sonnets. No. xcv. See under SHAME.

Cankers in the musk-rose buds.—*Midsummer-Night's Dream,* ii, 2, 3. "Musk-rose" is used three times in this play, and nowhere else.

12
In pride of all his growth,
A vengeful canker eat him up to death.
Sonnets. No. xcix.

13
The canker gnaw thy heart
For showing me again the eyes of man!
Timon of Athens. Act iv, sc. 3, l. 49. [Timon]

14
In the sweetest bud
The eating canker dwells.
The Two Gentlemen of Verona, i, 1, 43. See under LOVE.

The most forward bud
Is eaten by the canker ere it blows.
The Two Gentlemen of Verona, i, 1, 46. See under DEATH AND YOUTH.

15
This canker that eats up Love's tender spring.
Venus and Adonis, l. 656. See under JEALOUSY.

You canker-blossom!—*A Midsummer-Night's Dream,* iii, 2, 282. The only use of the phrase.

Bare-gnawn and canker-bit.—*King Lear,* v, 3, 122. The only use of either phrase.

CANNON

16
No jocund health that Denmark drinks to-day,
But the great cannon to the clouds shall tell,
And the king's rouse the heavens shall bruit again,
Re-speaking earthly thunder.
Hamlet. Act i, sc. 2, l. 125. [King] The only use of "re-speaking." "Rouse" in this sense is used twice more in *Hamlet,* i, 4, 8, and ii, 1, 58, and in *Othello,* ii, 3, 66.

And let the kettle to the trumpet speak,
The trumpet to the cannoneer without,
The cannons to the heavens, the heavens to earth.
Hamlet. Act v, sc. 2, l. 286. [King] The only use of "kettle." "Cannoneer" is repeated in *King John,* ii, 1, 461.

17
Telling me . . . it was great pity, so it was,
This villanous salt-petre should be digg'd
Out of the bowels of the harmless earth,
Which many a good tall fellow had destroy'd
So cowardly; and but for these vile guns,
He would himself have been a soldier.
I Henry IV. Act i, sc. 3, l. 59. [Hotspur] The only mention of salt-petre.

Overcharged gun.—*II Henry VI,* iii, 2, 331.

18
Thou hast talk'd . . . of cannon, culverin.
I Henry IV, ii, 3, 56. See under WAR. The only use of "culverin."

19
The nimble gunner
With linstock now the devilish cannon touches.
Henry V. Act iii, Prologue, l. 33. [Chorus] The only use of "linstock."

The gunner and his mate.
The Tempest, ii, 2, 49. The only uses of "gunner."
Sweep 'em from the door with cannons.
Henry VIII. Act v, sc. 4, l. 13. [Man]
1
The thunder of my cannon shall be heard.
King John. Act i, sc. 1, l. 26. [King John]
Our thunder from the south
Shall rain their drift of bullets on this town.
King John. Act ii, sc. 1, l. 411. [King Philip]
Our cannon shall be bent
Against the brows of this resisting town.
King John. Act ii, sc. 1, l. 37. [King Philip]
The cannons have their bowels full of wrath,
And ready mounted are they to spit forth
Their iron indignation 'gainst your walls.
King John. Act ii, sc. 1, l. 210. [King John]
Our arms, like to a muzzled bear,
Save in aspect, hath all offence seal'd up;
Our cannons' malice vainly shall be spent
Against the invulnerable clouds of heaven.
King John. Act ii, sc. 1, l. 249. [King Philip] "Invulnerable" is repeated in *Hamlet*, i, 1, 145, and in *The Tempest*, iii, 3, 66.
Cannon fire.—*King John*, ii, 1, 462.
Roaring cannon-shot.—*I Henry VI*, iii, 3, 79. The only use of the phrase.
Cannon's mouth.—*As You Like It*, ii, 7, 153.
2
By east and west let France and England mount
Their battering cannon charged to the mouths,
Till their soul-fearing clamours have brawl'd down
The flinty ribs of this contemptuous city:
I 'ld play incessantly upon these jades,
Even till unfenced desolation
Leave them as naked as the vulgar air.
King John. Act ii, sc. 1, l. 381. [Bastard] The only use of "soul-fearing," "incessantly" and "unfenced." "Contemptuous" occurs again in *II Henry VI*, i, 3, 86, and "contemptuously" in *The Two Gentlemen of Verona*, i, 2, 112.
An if thou hast the mettle of a king,
Being wrong'd as we are by this peevish town,
Turn thou the mouth of thy artillery,
As we will ours, against these saucy walls.
King John. Act ii, sc. 1, l. 401. [Bastard]
I 'll to the Tower with all the haste I can
To view the artillery.
I Henry VI. Act i, sc. 1, l. 168. [Gloucester]
Discharge of their artillery.—*I Henry IV*, i, 1, 57.
Dangerous artillery.—*I Henry VI*, iv, 2, 29.
Heaven's artillery.—*The Taming of the Shrew*, i, 2, 205. The only uses of "artillery."
3
If I say sooth, I must report they were
As cannons overcharged with double cracks.
Macbeth. Act i, sc. 2, l. 36. [Sergeant]
I have seen the cannon,
When it hath blown his ranks into the air,
And, like the devil, from his very arm
Puff'd his own brother.
Othello. Act iii, sc. 4, l. 134. [Iago]
Brass cannon.—*Henry V*, iii, 1, 11.
Brazen cannon.—*Hamlet*, i, 1, 73.
Fatal cannon.—*Romeo and Juliet*, v, 1, 65.
4
And, O you mortal engines, whose rude throats
The immortal Jove's dread clamours counterfeit,
Farewell!
Othello. Act iii, sc. 3, l. 355. [Othello]
5
Have I not heard great ordnance in the field?
The Taming of the Shrew, i, 2, 204. See under WOOING for full quotation.
Let all the battlements their ordnance fire.
Hamlet. Act. v, sc. 2, l. 281. [King]
Return your mock
In second accent of his ordnance.
Henry V, ii, 4, 126. See under RETRIBUTION.
Behold the ordnance on their carriages,
With fatal mouths gaping on girded Harfleur.
Henry V. Act iii, Prologus, l. 26. [Chorus] "Girded" is repeated in *Sonnets*, xii.
A piece of ordnance 'gainst it I have placed.
I Henry VI. Act i, sc. 4, l. 15. [Gunner] The only uses of "ordnance."

CAP

See also Hat

6
Wears her cap out of fashion: richly suited, but unsuitable.
All's Well that Ends Well, i, 1, 170. See under VIRGINITY.
So unsuitable to her disposition.
Twelfth Night, ii, 5, 222. The only uses of "unsuitable."
7
I have ever held my cap off to thy fortunes.
Antony and Cleopatra. Act ii, sc. 7, l. 63. [Menas]
Ho! says a'. There 's my cap.
Antony and Cleopatra. Act ii, sc. 7, l. 141. [Enobarbus]
Put off 's cap.—*All's Well that Ends Well*, ii, 2, 10.
Cap in hand.—*Henry V*, iv, 5, 13.
Off-capp'd to him.—*Othello*, i, 1, 10. The only use of "off-capp'd."
8
They threw their caps
As they would hang them on the horns o' the moon,
Shouting their emulation.
Coriolanus. Act i, sc. 1, l. 216. [Marcius]
Cast their caps up.—*Antony and Cleopatra*, iv, 12, 12.
Fling up his cap.—*II Henry VI*, iv, 8, 15.
Borrower's cap.—*II Henry IV*, ii, 2, 125.
Knaves' caps.—*Coriolanus*, ii, 1, 77.
Monmouth caps.—*Henry V*, iv, 7, 104.
Silken caps.—*Taming of the Shrew*, iv, 3, 55.
Stinking greasy caps.—*Coriolanus*, iv, 6, 131.
A cap of flowers.—*Passionate Pilgrim*, l. 363.
9
Take my cap, Jupiter, and I thank thee.
Coriolanus. Act ii, sc. 1, l. 115. [Menenius]
Such gain the cap of him that makes 'em fine.
Cymbeline, iii, 3, 25. See LIFE, 865:15.
10
Thou sickly quoif!
Thou art a guard too wanton for the head.
II Henry IV. Act i, sc. 1, l. 147. [Northum-

berland] "Quoif" (close-fitting cap) occurs again in *The Winter's Tale,* iv, 4, 226.
I . . . shalt have a cap to-morrow.—*II Henry IV,* ii, 4, 98.
1
This also will I wear in my cap.
Henry V. Act iv, sc. 1, l. 230. [Williams]
I will be so bold as to wear it in my cap.
Henry V. Act v, sc. 1, l. 13. [Fluellen]
Wear it in your cap.—*Much Ado about Nothing,* iii, 4, 72.
Worn in my cap.—*II Henry IV,* i, 2, 17.
Worn in the cap.—*Love's Labour's Lost,* v, 2, 622.
Wear his cap with suspicion.—*Much Ado about Nothing,* i, 1, 200.
2
Haberdasher: Here is the cap your worship did bespeak.
Petruchio: Why, this was moulded on a porringer;
A velvet dish: fie, fie! 'tis lewd and filthy:
Why, 'tis a cockle or a walnut-shell,
A knack, a toy, a trick, a baby's cap:
Away with it! come, let me have it bigger.
Katharina: I 'll have no bigger: this doth fit the time,
And gentlewomen wear such caps as these.
Petruchio: When you are gentle, you shall have one too,
And not till then.
The Taming of the Shrew. Act iv, sc. 3, l. 63. The only use of "walnut-shell."
Her pinked porringer fell off her head.
Henry VIII, v, 4, 50. The only use of "pinked" (ornamented with perforations), and of "porringer."
Petruchio: Why, thou say'st true; it is a paltry cap,
A custard-coffin, a bauble, a silken pie:
I love thee well, in that thou likest it not.
Katharina: Love me or love me not, I like the cap;
And it I will have, or I will have none.
The Taming of the Shrew. Act iv, sc. 3, l. 81. The only use of "custard-coffin" (crust over a custard).
Katharine, that cap of yours becomes you not:
Off with that bauble, throw it under-foot.
The Taming of the Shrew. Act v, sc. 2, l. 121. [Petruchio] The only use of "under-foot."
3
The cap Plays in the right hand, thus.
Timon of Athens. Act ii, sc. 1, l. 18. [Senator]
Faith, I perceive our masters may throw their caps at their money.
Timon of Athens. Act iii, sc. 4, l. 102. [Hortensius]
4
Thou art the cap of all the fools alive.
Timon of Athens. Act iv, sc. 3, l. 363. [Apemantus]
The cap of the time.—*All's Well that Ends Well,* ii, 1, 55.
Fortune's cap.—*Hamlet,* ii, 2, 233.
Cap that proverb.—*Henry V,* iii, 7, 124.

CAPTAIN, see Soldier: Officers

CAPTIVITY

See also Prison

5
Beware of being captives Before you serve.
All's Well that Ends Well. Act ii, sc. 1, l. 21. [King]
Abated captives to some nation
That won you without blows!
Coriolanus. Act iii, sc. 3, l. 132. [Coriolanus]
6
Like captives bound to a triumphant car.
I Henry VI. Act i, sc. 1, l. 22. [Exeter]
Smear'd with captivity.—*I Henry VI,* iv, 7, 3.
7
Kept him in captivity till he died.
II Henry VI. Act ii, sc. 2, l. 42. [Salisbury]
Set him free from his captivity.
III Henry VI. Act iv, sc. 5, l. 13. [Gloucester]
8
Every bondman in his own hand bears
The power to cancel his captivity.
Julius Cæsar, i, 3, 102. See under SUICIDE.
9
He hath brought many captives home to Rome,
Whose ransoms did the general coffers fill.
Julius Cæsar. Act iii, sc. 2, l. 93. [Antony]
You have the captives
That were the opposites of this day's strife:
We do require them of you, so to use them
As we shall find their merits and our safety
May equally determine.
King Lear. Act v, sc. 3, l. 41. [Albany]
The captive is enriched.—*Love's Labour's Lost,* iv, 1, 76.
10
Given to captivity me and my utmost hopes.
Othello, iv, 2, 51. See under AFFLICTION.
Held captive.—*Troilus and Cressida,* ii, 2, 77.
All our princes captived.—*Henry V,* ii, 4, 55. The only use of "captived."
11
The coward captive vanquished doth yield
To these two armies.
The Rape of Lucrece, l. 75.
A captive victor that hath lost in gain.
The Rape of Lucrece, l. 730.
12
Never did captive with a freer heart
Cast off his chains of bondage and embrace
His golden uncontroll'd enfranchisement.
Richard II. Act i, sc. 3, l. 88. [Mowbray]
13
Captive to thee and to thy Roman yoke.
Titus Andronicus. Act i, sc. 1, l. 111. [Tamora]
Captive to his honey words.—*Richard III,* iv, 1, 80.
Captive good.—*Sonnets,* lxvi.
Captive state.—*III Henry VI,* iv, 6, 3.
Captive Grecian.—*Troilus and Cressida,* v, 3, 40.
Roman captive.—*Cymbeline,* v, 5, 385.
14
Yet hath he been my captive and my slave,
And begg'd for that which thou unask'd shalt have.
Venus and Adonis, l. 101. The only use of "unask'd."

CARD

1
Pack'd cards with Cæsar, and false-play'd my glory.
Antony and Cleopatra. Act iv, sc. 14, l. 19. [Antony] The only use of "false-play'd."
2
He is the card or calendar of gentry.
Hamlet, v, 2, 114. See under GENTLEMAN.
There all is marr'd; there lies a cooling card.
I Henry VI. Act v, sc. 3, l. 84. [Suffolk]
Shipman's card.—*Macbeth,* i, 3, 17.
3
But, whiles he thought to steal the single ten,
The king was slily finger'd from the deck!
III Henry VI. Act v, sc. 1, l. 43. [Gloucester]
Yet I have faced it with a card of ten.
The Taming of the Shrew. Act ii, sc. 1, l. 407. [Tranio] That is, put on a bold front.
4
Have I not here the best cards for the game,
To win this easy match play'd for a crown?
King John. Act v, sc. 2, l. 105. [Dauphin]
As sure a card as ever won the set.
Titus Andronicus. Act v, sc. 1, l. 100. [Aaron]

CARE

5
I will throw thee from my care for ever.
All's Well that Ends Well. Act ii, sc. 3, l. 169. [King]
Take thou no care.—*Antony and Cleopatra,* v, 2, 269.
Take no care.—*Macbeth,* iv, 1, 90.
No care of yours it is.—*Cymbeline,* v, 4, 100.
Hast thou no care of me?—*Antony and Cleopatra,* iv, 15, 60.
Noble carelessness.—*Coriolanus,* ii, 2, 16. The only use of "carelessness."
6
I tell you, friends, most charitable care
Have the patricians of you.
Coriolanus. Act i, sc. 1, l. 67. [Menenius]
Fear not our care.—*Coriolanus,* i, 7, 5.
So much For my peculiar care.
Cymbeline. Act v, sc. 5, l. 82. [Lucius]
Busy care.—*Julius Cæsar,* ii, 1, 232; *Venus and Adonis,* l. 383.
Chief care.—*The Merchant of Venice,* i, 1, 127.
Dear care.—*Henry V,* ii, 2, 58.
Eldest care.—*The Comedy of Errors,* i, 1, 125.
Human care.—*The Tempest,* i, 2, 346.
Incessant care.—*II Henry IV,* iv, 4, 118.
Princely care.—*Henry VIII,* v, 1, 49.
Studious care.—*I Henry VI,* ii, 5, 97.
Tender care.—*III Henry VI,* iv, 6, 66.
7
So wan with care.
I Henry IV. Act i, sc. 1, l. 1. [King Henry]
Dull with care.—*The Comedy of Errors,* i, 2, 20.
Full of care.—*The Rape of Lucrece,* l. 1503; *Sonnets,* lvi.
Much overgone with care.—*III Henry VI,* ii, 5, 123.
Broke . . . their brains with care.—*II Henry IV,* iv, 5, 69.
8
'The care on thee depending
Hath fed upon the body of my father.'
II Henry IV. Act iv, sc. 5, l. 159. [Prince]
9
His cares are now all ended.
II Henry IV. Act v, sc. 2, l. 3. [Warwick]
Deadly cares.—*The Rape of Lucrece,* l. 1593.
Grim care.—*The Rape of Lucrece,* l. 1451.
Grisly care.—*The Rape of Lucrece,* l. 926.
Killing care.—*Henry VIII,* iii, 1, 13.
Restless cares.—*Richard III,* i, 4, 81.
Untuned cares.—*Comedy of Errors,* v, 1, 310.
10
Care is no cure, but rather corrosive,
For things that are not to be remedied.
I Henry VI. Act iii, sc. 3, l. 3. [La Pucelle] "Corrosive" is repeated in *II Henry VI,* iii, 2, 403.
11
The care you have of us,
To mow down thorns that would annoy our foot,
Is worthy praise.
II Henry VI. Act iii, sc. 1, l. 66. [King Henry]
In care of your most royal person.
II Henry VI. Act iii, sc. 2, l. 254. [Salisbury]
Dear care
And tender preservation of our person.
Henry V. Act ii, sc. 2, l. 58. [King Henry]
12
I thank them for their tender loving care.
II Henry VI. Act iii, sc. 2, l. 280. [King Henry]
I thank you for your honest care.
All's Well that Ends Well. Act i, sc. 3, l. 132. [Countess]
My life itself, and the best heart of it,
Thanks you for this great care.
Henry VIII. Act i, sc. 2, l. 1. [King Henry]
Great care.—*The Comedy of Errors,* i, 1, 43; ii, 1, 56; *Henry VIII,* ii, 2, 78.
13
Pray, look to 't; I put it to your care.
Henry VIII. Act i, sc. 2, l. 101. [King Henry]
None here, he hopes,
In all this noble bevy, has brought with her
One care abroad.
Henry VIII. Act i, sc. 4, l. 3. [Guildford] The only use of "bevy."
With all the care I had.—*Henry VIII,* ii, 2, 2.
That 's Christian care enough.—*Henry VIII,* ii, 2, 131.
Christian care.—*II Henry IV,* iv, 2, 115.
14
What watchful cares do interpose themselves
Betwixt your eyes and night?
Julius Cæsar. Act ii, sc. 1, l. 98. [Brutus] "Interpose" is repeated in *The Winter's Tale,* v, 3, 119.
15
Keep . . . good care to-night.
King John. Act v, sc. 5, l. 20. [Lewis]
We will take some care.
Love's Labour 's Lost. Act v, sc. 2, l. 511. [Costard]
He took some care.—*The Taming of the Shrew,* i, 1, 191.
Take care.—*The Tempest,* v, 1, 257.
I 'll take the better care.—*Cymbeline,* iv, 4, 45.
16
'Tis our fast intent
To shake all cares and business from our age;

Conferring them on younger strengths, while we
Unburthen'd crawl toward death.
King Lear. Act i, sc. 1, l. 39. [King Lear] The only use of "unburthen'd." "Crawl" is repeated in *A Midsummer-Night's Dream,* iii, 2, 444.

Cares of state.—*King Lear,* i, 1, 51.

1
Here I disclaim all my paternal care,
Propinquity and property of blood,
And as a stranger to my heart and me
Hold thee, from this, for ever.
King Lear. Act i, sc. 1, l. 115. [King Lear] The only use of "paternal" and "propinquity."

In a good father's care.—*The Taming of the Shrew,* iv, 4, 31.
Thy father's care.—*I Henry VI,* iv, 6, 26.

Yet I express to you a mother's care.
All's Well that Ends Well. Act i, sc. 3, l. 154. [Countess]

Mother's care.—*King John,* iv, 2, 117; *Titus Andronicus,* iii, 1, 182.

2
O, I have ta'en Too little care of this!
King Lear. Act iii, sc. 4, l. 33. [King Lear]

3
Effect it with some care.
A Midsummer-Night's Dream. Act ii, sc. 1, l. 265. [Oberon]

With some care.—*The Winter's Tale,* iv, 2, 40.
More care.—*Romeo and Juliet,* iii, 5, 23.
Much care.—*Henry V,* iv, 1, 86; *The Merchant of Venice,* i, 1, 75.

4
What though care killed a cat, thou hast mettle enough in thee to kill care.
Much Ado about Nothing. Act v, sc. 1, l. 132. [Claudio] The proverb, "Care will kill a cat," was quoted in the *Shirburn Ballads* in 1585, and by Ben Jonson in *Every Man in His Humour,* i, 3, produced in 1598, with Shakespeare in the cast. *Much Ado about Nothing* was written the same year.

Nor doth the general care Take hold on me.
Othello. Act i, sc. 3, l. 54. [Brabantio]

The care I had and have of subjects good
On thee I lay, whose wisdom's strength can bear it.
Pericles. Act i, sc. 2, l. 118. [Pericles]

5
Deep-drenched in a sea of care.
The Rape of Lucrece, l. 1100. The only use of "deep-drenched."

6
Say, is my kingdom lost? why, 'twas my care;
And what loss is it to be rid of care?
Richard II. Act iii, sc. 2, l. 95. [King Richard]

Drive away the heavy thought of care.
Richard II. Act iii, sc. 4, l. 2. [Queen]

Bolingbroke: Part of your cares you give me with your crown.
King Richard: Your cares set up do not pluck my cares down.
My care is loss of care, by old care done;
Your care is gain of care, by new care won:
The cares I give I have, though given away;
They tend the crown, yet still with me they stay.
Richard II. Act iv, sc. 1, l. 194.

7
Alas, why should you heap these cares on me?
Richard III. Act iii, sc. 7, l. 204. [Gloucester]

Would you enforce me to a world of care?
Richard III. Act iii, sc. 7, l. 223. [Gloucester]

Full of wise care.—*Richard III,* iv, 1, 48.

A very caitiff crown'd with care.
Richard III. Act iv, sc. 4, l. 100. [Queen Margaret]

8
Care keeps his watch in every old man's eye,
And where care lodges, sleep will never lie.
Romeo and Juliet. Act ii, sc. 3, l. 35. [Friar Laurence]

9
Ay, and amid this hurly I intend
That all is done in reverend care of her.
The Taming of the Shrew. Act iv, sc. 1, l. 206. [Petruchio]

Reverent care.—*II Henry VI,* iii, 1, 34; *II Henry IV,* i, 2, 113.

10
Why this spade, this place?
This slave-like habit? and these looks of care?
Timon of Athens. Act iv, sc. 3, l. 204. [Apemantus] The only use of "slave-like."

Care of your food and living.
Timon of Athens. Act iv, sc. 3, l. 524. [Flavius]

Be 't not in thy care.—*Timon of Athens,* iii, 4, 117.
It shall be so my care.—*The Winter's Tale,* iv, 4, 602.

11
Care 's an enemy to life.
Twelfth Night. Act i, sc. 3, l. 3. [Sir Toby]

12
Let some of my people have a special care of him.
Twelfth Night. Act iii, sc. 4, l. 69. [Olivia]

Special care.—*Richard II,* iii, 1, 39.
Care for something.—*Twelfth Night,* iii, 1, 32.
Care for nothing.—*Twelfth Night,* iii, 1, 34.
Nobody cares.—*II Henry IV,* ii, 4, 73.

CASEMENT, see Window

CASTLE

13
And this worm-eaten hold of ragged stone.
II Henry IV. Induction, l. 35. [Rumour] "Worm-eaten" is repeated in *As You Like It,* iii, 4, 27: "Worm-eaten nut"; and in *Much Ado about Nothing,* iii, 3, 145: "Worm-eaten tapestry."

14
King Henry: What is this castle call'd that stands hard by?
Montjoy: They call it Agincourt.
King Henry: Then call we this the field of Agincourt,
Fought on the day of Crispin Crispianus.
Henry V. Act iv, sc. 7, l. 91.

Barkloughly castle call they this at hand?
Richard II, iii, 2, 1. [King Richard]

But we must win your grace to go with us
To Bristol castle, which they say is held
By Bushy, Bagot and their complices.
Richard II. Act ii, sc. 3, l. 163. [Bolingbroke] "Bristol castle" is repeated in ii, 2, 135.
Baynard's Castle.—*Richard III*, iii, 5, 98; iii, 5, 105.
Dover castle.—*King John*, v, 1, 31.
Flint castle.—*Richard II*, iii, 2, 209.
Hames Castle.—*III Henry VI*, v, 5, 2.
Pomfret-castle.—*Richard III*, iii, 1, 183.
Windsor castle.—*The Merry Wives of Windsor*, iii, 3, 232; v, 5, 60.

1
This castle hath a pleasant seat; the air
Nimbly and sweetly recommends itself
Unto our gentle senses.
Macbeth. Act i, sc. 6, l. 1. [Duncan]
Your castle is surprised.—*Macbeth*, iv, 3, 204.
Our castle's strength
Will laugh a siege to scorn.
Macbeth. Act v, sc. 5, l. 2. [Macbeth]
The castle's gently render'd.—*Macbeth*, v, 7, 24.

2
The rude ribs of that ancient castle.
Richard II. Act iii, sc. 3, l. 32. [Bolingbroke]
There stands the castle, by yon tuft of trees,
Mann'd with three hundred men, as I have heard.
Richard II. Act ii, sc. 3, l. 53. [Percy]

3
And all your northern castles yielded up.
Richard II. Act iii, sc. 2, l. 201. [Scroop]
Bolingbroke: What, will not this castle yield?
Percy: The castle royally is mann'd, my lord,
Against thy entrance.
Bolingbroke: Royally!
Why, it contains no king?
Richard II. Act iii, sc. 3, l. 20.
From this castle's tatter'd battlements.
Richard II. Act iii, sc. 3, l. 52. [Bolingbroke]
Enemy's castle.—*Titus Andronicus*, iii, 1, 170.

CAT

4
I could endure any thing before but a cat, and now he's a cat to me.
All's Well that Ends Well. Act iv, sc. 3, l. 266. [Bertram]
A pox upon him for me, he's more and more a cat.
All's Well that Ends Well. Act iv, sc. 3, l. 295. [Bertram]
He's a cat still.—*All's Well that Ends Well*, iv, 3, 307.

5
If the cat will after kind,
So be sure will Rosalind.
As You Like It. Act iii, sc. 2, l. 109. [Touchstone]

6
Let Hercules himself do what he may,
The cat will mew and dog will have his day.
Hamlet. Act v, sc. 1, l. 314. [Hamlet]

7
I am as vigilant as a cat to steal cream.
I Henry IV. Act iv, sc. 2, l. 64. [Falstaff]
As a cat laps milk.—*The Tempest*, ii, 1, 288.

8
Westmoreland: Playing the mouse in absence of the cat,
To tear and havoc more than she can eat.
Exeter: It follows then the cat must stay at home.
Henry V. Act i, sc. 2, l. 172.
The cat, with eyne of burning coal,
Now crouches fore the mouse's hole.
Pericles. Act iii, Prologue, l. 5. [Gower]

9
Pur! the cat is gray.
King Lear. Act iii, sc. 6, l. 47. [Edgar]
Thrice the brinded cat hath mew'd.
Macbeth. Act iv, sc. 1, l. 1. [First Witch] The only use of "brinded."

10
Hang me in a bottle like a cat and shoot at me.
Much Ado about Nothing. Act i, sc. 1, l. 259. [Benedick]

11
More than prince of cats, I can tell you.
Romeo and Juliet. Act ii, sc. 4, l. 19. [Mercutio]
Tybalt: What wouldst thou have with me?
Mercutio: Good king of cats, nothing but one of your nine lives.
Romeo and Juliet. Act iii, sc. 1, l. 79.

12
Some, that are mad if they behold a cat.
The Merchant of Venice. Act iv, sc. 1, l. 48. [Shylock]
A harmless necessary cat.—*The Merchant of Venice*, iv, 1, 55.
Foul night-waking cat.—*The Rape of Lucrece*, l. 554. The only use of "night-waking."
Gib cat.—*I Henry IV*, i, 2, 83. The only use of "gib cat" (tom cat).
Poor cat.—*Macbeth*, i, 7, 45.
Ramping cat.—*I Henry IV*, iii, 1, 153.

CAUSE

I—Cause: Object

13
I cannot project mine own cause so well
To make it clear.
Antony and Cleopatra. Act v, sc. 2, l. 121. [Cleopatra]
Served the cause.—*Antony and Cleopatra*, iv, 8, 6.

14
You wear out a good wholesome forenoon in hearing a cause between an orange-wife and a fosset-seller.
Coriolanus, ii, 1, 77. See under LAW. The only use of "orange-wife" and "fosset-seller" (a seller of faucets or taps).
Thus you have heard our cause.
II Henry IV. Act i, sc. 3, l. 1. [Archbishop of York]
Give me hearing in a cause.—*I Henry VI*, v, 3, 106.
I'll . . . leave you to the hearing of the cause;
Hoping you'll find good cause to whip them all.
Measure for Measure. Act ii, sc. 1, l. 141. [Angelo]
He's hearing of a cause.—*Measure for Measure*, ii, 2, 1.
Plead your cause.—*Henry VIII*, ii, 4, 61.
Poor men's causes.—*II Henry VI*, iv, 7, 93.

Pray you, Stand to me in this cause.
Coriolanus. Act v, sc. 3, l. 198. [Coriolanus]

1 Your cause doth strike my heart
With pity, that doth make me sick.
Cymbeline. Act i, sc. 6, l. 118. [Iachimo]

2
And God befriend us, as our cause is just!
I Henry IV. Act v, sc. 1, l. 120. [King Henry]

His cause being just and his quarrel honourable.
Henry V. Act iv, sc. 1, l. 133. [King Henry]

Just cause.—*II Henry IV,* v, 2, 66; v, 2, 144; *Much Ado about Nothing,* ii, 3, 173; *The Winter's Tale,* v, 1, 61.

Depose him in the justice of his cause.
Richard II. Act i, sc. 3, l. 30. [King Richard]

Our cause the best.—*II Henry IV,* iv, 1, 156.

3
Bates: If his cause be wrong, our obedience to the king wipes the crime of it out of us.
Williams: But if the cause be not good, the king himself hath a heavy reckoning to make, when all those legs and arms and heads, chopped off in a battle, shall join together at the latter day and cry all 'We died at such a place.'
Henry V. Act iv, sc. 1, l. 138.

His cause never so spotless.—*Henry V,* iv, 1, 169.

4
Left the cause of the king unhandled.
Henry VIII. Act iii, sc. 2, l. 58. [Suffolk]

I take my cause
Out of the gripes of cruel men, and give it
To a most noble judge, the king my master.
Henry VIII. Act v, sc. 3, l. 99. [Cranmer]

5
What need we any spur but our own cause,
To prick us to redress?
Julius Cæsar. Act ii, sc. 1, l. 123. [Brutus]

Hear me for my cause, and be silent, that you may hear.
Julius Cæsar. Act iii, sc. 2, l. 13. [Brutus]

Our cause is ripe.—*Julius Cæsar,* iv, 3, 215.

Bad causes.—*Julius Cæsar,* ii, 1, 131.

6 Some dear cause
Will in concealment wrap me up awhile.
King Lear. Act iv, sc. 3, l. 53. [King Lear]

Give your cause to heaven.—*Measure for Measure,* iv, 3, 129.

Cause in controversy.—*The Merchant of Venice,* iv, 1, 155.

7 For mine own good,
All causes shall give way.
Macbeth. Act iii, sc. 4, l. 136. [Macbeth]

Their dear causes
Would to the bleeding and the grim alarm
Excite the mortified man.
Macbeth. Act v, sc. 2, l. 3. [Menteith]

He cannot buckle his distemper'd cause
Within the belt of rule.
Macbeth. Act v, sc. 2, l. 15. [Caithness]

8
Her cause and yours I 'll perfect him withal.
Measure for Measure. Act iv, sc. 3, l. 145. [Duke]

Make it your cause.—*King Lear,* ii, 4, 195.

9
Mine 's not an idle cause.
Othello. Act i, sc. 2, l. 95. [Brabantio]

My cause is hearted.—*Othello,* i, 3, 373.

Be merry, Cassio,
For thy solicitor shall rather die
Than give thy cause away.
Othello. Act iii, sc. 3, l. 26. [Desdemona]

But, sith I am enter'd in this cause so far,
Prick'd to 't by foolish honesty and love,
I will go on.
Othello. Act iii, sc. 3, l. 411. [Iago]

The cause craves haste.—*The Rape of Lucrece,* l. 1295.

10 As thy cause is right,
So be thy fortune in his royal fight!
Richard II. Act i, sc. 3, l. 55. [King Richard]

God in thy good cause make thee prosperous!
Richard II. Act i, sc. 3, l. 78. [Gaunt]

God and our good cause fight upon our side.
Richard III. Act v, sc. 3, l. 240. [Richmond] "Good cause" is repeated in *Measure for Measure,* ii, 1, 142, and *As You Like It,* iii, 4, 5.

Better cause.—*Cymbeline,* iii, 4, 74.

General cause.—*Macbeth,* iv, 3, 196.

Great cause.—*Henry V,* ii, 2, 32; iv, 1, 90; *As You Like It,* iii, 2, 29; *Coriolanus,* v, 4, 63; *Antony and Cleopatra,* i, 2, 143.

Happy cause.—*Hamlet,* iii, 1, 39.

Lawful cause.—*Taming of the Shrew,* i, 2, 29.

Malignant cause.—*All's Well that Ends Well,* ii, 1, 114.

Mighty cause.—*King John,* iv, 2, 205.

Notable cause.—*Twelfth Night,* ii, 3, 166.

Rightful cause.—*II Henry VI,* ii, 1, 204.

Special cause.—*King Lear,* iv, 6, 219.

Weighty cause.—*II Henry VI,* i, 2, 86; iii, 1, 289; *The Taming of the Shrew,* iv, 4, 26.

Well-hallow'd cause.—*Henry V,* i, 2, 293. The only use of the phrase.

So fierce a cause.—*King John,* iii, 4, 12.

Causes now in hand.—*Henry V,* i, 1, 77.

Cause of Rome.—*Titus Andronicus,* i, 1, 32.

Cause of state.—*Macbeth,* iii, 1, 34.

Country's cause.—*Titus Andronicus,* i, 1, 113; *Cymbeline,* v, 4, 71.

French causes.—*Henry* V, ii, 2, 60.

Grecians' cause.—*Troilus and Cressida,* iv, 5, 268.

Lavinia's cause.—*Titus Andronicus,* i, 1, 377.

Virtue's cause.—*Titus Andronicus,* i, 1, 390.

11
It is a cause worthy my spleen and fury.
Timon of Athens, iii, 5, 113. See under BANISHMENT.

Worthy cause.—*Julius Cæsar,* iv, 2, 8; *Othello,* iii, 3, 254.

12
And to my fortunes and the people's favour
Commit my cause in balance to be weigh'd.
Titus Andronicus. Act i, sc. 1, l. 54. [Bassianus]

For 'tis a cause that hath no mean dependance
Upon our joint and several dignities.
Troilus and Cressida. Act ii, sc. 2, l. 192. [Hector] The only use of "dependance."

II—Cause: Source, Reason

1
That which is the strength of their amity shall prove the immediate author of their variance.
Antony and Cleopatra. Act ii, sc. 6, l. 136. [Enobarbus] The only use of "variance."
You shall not find,
Though you be therein curious, the least cause
For what you seem to fear.
Antony and Cleopatra. Act iii, sc. 2, l. 34. [Antony]
I have savage cause.—*Antony and Cleopatra,* iii, 13, 128.
Lesser cause.—*Romeo and Juliet,* iv, 4, 10.
More cause.—*Richard III,* i, 2, 212.
Cause of anger.—*Troilus and Cressida,* i, 2, 11.
Cause of Fear.—*Timon of Athens,* v, 4, 15; *Venus and Adonis,* l. 1153; *Cymbeline,* iv, 2, 112.
Cause for fear.—*Much Ado about Nothing,* v, 1, 56.
Cause of grief.—*Julius Cæsar,* ii, 1, 256; *The Merchant of Venice,* v, 1, 175.
Cause to grieve.—*The Winter's Tale,* ii, 1, 77.
Cause of hate.—*Sonnets,* cl.
Cause of sorrow.—*The Two Gentlemen of Verona,* iv, 4, 152; *Macbeth,* v, 8, 44.
Cause of suspicion!—*The Merry Wives of Windsor,* iii, 3, 108.
Cause of thankfulness.—*Henry V,* ii, 2, 32.
Cause of thunder.—*King Lear,* iii, 4, 160.
Cause of war.—*Venus and Adonis,* l. 1159.
Cause of weeping.—*King Lear,* ii, 4, 287.
Cause to be glad.—*Antony and Cleopatra,* ii, 2, 178.
Cause to be proud.—*Coriolanus,* ii, 1, 161.
Cause to complain.—*Measure for Measure,* ii, 1, 121.
Cause to curse.—*Henry V,* i, 2, 288.
Cause to fear.—*Richard II,* v, 3, 42.
Cause to plain.—*King Lear,* iii, 1, 39.
Cause to rue.—*Titus Andronicus,* v, 1, 109.
Cause to sigh.—*The Taming of the Shrew,* v, 2, 123.
Cause to sing.—*The Rape of Lucrece,* l. 333.
Cause to speak.—*Hamlet,* v, 2, 402.

2
Say that I wish he never find more cause
To change a master.
Antony and Cleopatra. Act iv, sc. 5, l. 15. [Antony]
Find cause.—*Antony and Cleopatra,* v, 2, 64.
I have found The very cause of Hamlet's lunacy.
Hamlet. Act ii, sc. 2, l. 49. [Polonius]

3
The 'why' is plain as way to parish church.
As You Like It. Act ii, sc. 7, l. 52. [Jaques]
Antipholus of Syracuse: Shall I tell you why?
Dromio of Syracuse: Ay, sir, and wherefore; for they say every why hath a wherefore.
The Comedy of Errors. Act ii, sc. 2, l. 43.
In the why and the wherefore is neither rhyme nor reason.
The Comedy of Errors. Act ii, sc. 2, l. 49. [Dromio of Syracuse]
I 'll tell you when, an you 'll tell me wherefore.
The Comedy of Errors. Act iii, sc. 1, l. 39. [Dromio of Syracuse]
There is occasions and causes why and wherefore in all things.
Henry V. Act v, sc. 1, l. 3. [Fluellen]
There is reasons and causes for it.
The Merry Wives of Windsor. Act iii, sc. 1, l. 48. [Evans]

4
Her sober virtue, years and modesty,
Plead on her part some cause to you unknown.
The Comedy of Errors. Act iii, sc. 1, l. 90. [Balthazar]

5
You know the cause, sir, of my standing here.
Coriolanus. Act ii, sc. 3, l. 68. [Coriolanus]
Do you know the cause?—*Romeo and Juliet,* i, 1, 149.
I know no personal cause to spurn at him.
Julius Cæsar. Act ii, sc. 1, l. 11. [Brutus]
Cæsar: Go tell them Cæsar will not come.
Decius: Most mighty Cæsar, let me know some cause,
Lest I be laugh'd at when I tell them so.
Cæsar: The cause is in my will: I will not come.
Julius Cæsar. Act ii, sc. 2, l. 68.
Lucio: I believe I know the cause of his withdrawing.
Duke: What, I prithee, might be the cause?
Measure for Measure. Act iii, sc. 2, l. 139.
Yet once more
Let me entreat to know at large the cause
Of your king's sorrow.
Pericles. Act v, sc. 1, l. 61. [Lysimachus]
May I be so bold to know the cause of your coming?
The Taming of the Shrew. Act ii, sc. 1, l. 88. [Baptista]
Know the cause.—*The Taming of the Shrew,* iii, 1, 10; *Troilus and Cressida,* i, 2, 57.
Know you not the cause?—*The Taming of the Shrew,* iv, 2, 82.
On what cause I know not.—*Pericles,* i, 3, 20.

6
I wish I had a cause to seek him there.
Coriolanus. Act iii, sc. 1, l. 19. [Coriolanus]
I would he had some cause
To prattle for himself.
Measure for Measure. Act v, sc. 1, l. 181. [Duke]

7
What cause, do you think, I have to swoon?
Coriolanus, v, 2, 106. See under SWOONING.
Upon what cause?—*Richard III,* i, 1, 46.
What 's the cause?—*Henry VIII,* ii, 2, 16.
What is the cause?—*Hamlet,* iv, 5, 120.
What was thy cause?—*King Lear,* iv, 6, 111.

8
It honours us
That we have given him cause.
Cymbeline. Act iii, sc. 5, l. 19. [Queen]
We shall give you
The full cause of our coming.
Henry VIII. Act iii, sc. 1, l. 29. [Wolsey]
Given me cause.—*Midsummer-Night's Dream,* iii, 2, 46.
Givest Me cause.—*Richard II,* iv, 1, 301.
Give us cause.—*Love's Labour 's Lost,* i, 1, 202.
Give you cause.—*King John,* iii, 1, 28.
Give cause.—*Cymbeline,* i, 1, 93.
I never gave him cause.—*Othello,* iii, 4, 158.
I never gave you cause.—*Othello,* v, 2, 299.

1
Mad let us grant him, then: and now remains
That we find out the cause of this effect,
Or rather say, the cause of this defect,
For this effect defective comes by cause.
Hamlet. Act ii, sc. 2, l. 100. [Polonius]
Thou art the cause, and most accursed effect.
Richard III. Act i, sc. 2, l. 120. [Lady Anne]
Cause of his effects.—*II Henry IV*, i, 2, 133.

2
Every slight and false-derived cause.
II Henry IV. Act iv, sc. 1, l. 190. [Mowbray] The only use of "false-derived."
Frivolous cause.—*I Henry VI*, iv, 1, 112.
Chief cause.—*Henry VIII*, v, 3, 3.
Main cause.—*Henry VIII*, iii, 1, 93.
Natural cause.—*Henry V*, ii, 2. 107; *King John*, iii, 4, 156.
True cause.—*II Henry IV*, ii, 1, 121; *Julius Cæsar*, i, 3, 62.
Unaccustom'd cause.—*Romeo and Juliet*, iii, 5, 68.

3
Plantagenet: Declare the cause
My father, Earl of Cambridge, lost his head.
Mortimer: That cause, fair nephew, that imprison'd me
And hath detained me all my flowering youth
Within a loathsome dungeon, there to pine,
Was cursed instrument of his decease.
Plantagenet: Discover more at large what cause that was.
I Henry VI. Act ii, sc. 5, l. 53.

4
Causeless have laid disgraces on my head.
II Henry VI, iii, 1, 162. See under DISGRACE. "Causeless" is repeated in *All's Well that Ends Well*, ii, 3, 3, in *Titus Andronicus*, iv, 1, 26, and in *Venus and Adonis*, l. 897.
Without cause.—*Troilus and Cressida*, i, 2, 27, *Twelfth Night*, v, 1, 191.

5
Thou shalt have cause to fear before I leave thee.
II Henry VI. Act iv, sc. 1, l. 118. [Whitmore]
I have cause.—*Much Ado about Nothing*, i, 3, 15.
I have more cause.—*As You Like It*, i, 3, 95.
I have the most cause.—*Coriolanus*, iv, 3, 56.
You have cause.—*Coriolanus*, iv, 2, 49; *The Tempest*, ii, 1, 1.
Have cause.—*Timon of Athens*, iv, 3, 102.
'Tis well that thou hast cause.—*Richard II*, iii, 4, 19.

6
Such a cause as fills mine eyes with tears
And stops my tongue, while heart is drown'd in cares.
III Henry VI. Act iii, sc. 3, l. 13. [Queen]

7
Nor without cause will he be satisfied.
Julius Cæsar. Act iii, sc. 1, l. 47. [Cæsar]
Not without cause.—*Julius Cæsar*, iii, 2, 107.

8 You shall have no cause
To curse the fair proceedings of this day.
King John. Act iii, sc. 1, l. 96. [King Philip]
Thou hast no cause to say so yet.
King John, iii, 3, 30. See under REWARD.
Thou therefore hast no cause.—*Twelfth Night*, iii, 1, 166.
Nor have you cause.—*Antony and Cleopatra*, iii, 6, 41.
You have no cause.—*Richard III*, ii, 4, 68; iv, 4, 493.
There is no cause.—*Winter's Tale*, ii, 1, 119.
No such cause.—*Love's Labour's Lost*, v, 2, 802.

9
Never afflict yourself to know the cause.
King Lear. Act i, sc. 4, l. 313. [Goneril]
King Lear: You have some cause, they have not.
Cordelia: No cause, no cause.
King Lear. Act iv, sc. 7, l. 75.
Others, whom, I fear,
Most just and heavy causes make oppose.
King Lear. Act v, sc. 1, l. 26. [Albany]

10
We cannot cross the cause why we were born.
Love's Labour's Lost. Act iv, sc. 3, l. 218. [Biron]

11
You have little cause to say so.
Othello. Act ii, sc. 1, l. 109. [Emilia]
It is the cause, it is the cause, my soul,—
Let me not name it to you, you chaste stars!—
It is the cause.
Othello. Act v, sc. 2, l. 1. [Othello]

12 Demand of yonder champion
The cause of his arrival here in arms.
Richard II. Act i, sc. 3, l. 7. [King Richard]

13
God pardon them that are the cause of it!
Richard III. Act i, sc. 3, l. 315. [Gloucester]

14 The cause why we are met
Is, to determine of the coronation.
Richard III. Act iii, sc. 4, l. 1. [Hastings]
The cause of this fair gift in me is wanting.
Sonnets. No. lxxxvii.
Let him show us the cause.—*Troilus and Cressida*, ii, 3, 96.
Now Jove afford you cause!—*The Winter's Tale*, iv, 4, 16.

CAUTION

See also Prudence

15 My caution was more pertinent
Than the rebuke you give it.
Coriolanus. Act ii, sc. 2, l. 67. [Brutus] "Pertinent" is repeated in *The Winter's Tale*, i, 2, 221.
In way of caution.—*Hamlet*, i, 3, 95.

16
But yet be wary in thy studious care.
I Henry VI. Act ii, sc. 5, l. 97. [Mortimer]
Be wary then; best safety lies in fear.
Hamlet. Act i, sc. 3, l. 43. [Lærtes]
It behoves men to be wary.
The Winter's Tale. Act iv, sc. 4, l. 257. [Autolycus]
Let us be wary.—*Othello*, iii, 3, 420.
Be wary.—*I Henry VI*, iii, 2, 3; *Romeo and Juliet*, iii, 5, 40.
Bear a wary eye.—*Hamlet*, v, 2, 290.
O, therefore, love, be of thyself so wary
As I, not for myself, but for thee will.
Sonnets. No. xxii.

I have ta'en a due and wary note upon 't.
Measure for Measure. Act iv, sc. 1, l. 38. [Isabella]

1
Whate'er thou art, for thy good caution, thanks.
Macbeth. Act iv, sc. 1, l. 73. [Macbeth]
See also WARNING.

That well might
Advise him to a caution, to hold what distance
His wisdom can provide.
Macbeth. Act iii, sc. 6, l. 43. [Lennox]

2
Have a care this busy time.
Much Ado about Nothing. Act i, sc. 2, l. 28. [Leonato]

Have care.—*The Tempest,* i, 1, 10.
Take care.—*The Winter's Tale,* iv, 4, 459.

3
Touch this sparingly, as 'twere far off.
Richard III. Act iii, sc. 5, l. 93. [Gloucester]
"Sparingly" is repeated in *Henry V*, i, 2, 239.

'Tis best we stand upon our guard.
The Tempest. Act ii, sc. 1, l. 321. [Gonzalo]

4
Advantageous care
Withdrew me from the odds of multitude.
Troilus and Cressida. Act v, sc. 4, l. 22. [Diomedes]

5
Not too fast: soft, soft!
Twelfth Night. Act i, sc. 5, l. 312. [Olivia]

Go to, go to; peace, peace; we must deal gently with him.
Twelfth Night. Act iii, sc. 4, l. 105. [Sir Toby]

CEDAR

6
Thus yields the cedar to the axe's edge,
Whose arms gave shelter to the princely eagle,
Under whose shade the ramping lion slept,
Whose top-branch overpeer'd Jove's spreading tree
And kept low shrubs from winter's powerful wind.
III Henry VI. Act v, sc. 2, l. 11. [Warwick]
The only use of "top-branch" and "overpeer'd." "Ramping" occurs in *King John,* iii, 1, 122: "ramping fool"; and in *I Henry IV,* iii, 1, 153: "ramping cat."

Proud cedars.—*Coriolanus,* v, 3, 60.
Lofty cedar.—*Cymbeline,* v, 5, 453.
Majestic cedar.—*Cymbeline,* v, 5, 457.
Pine and cedar.—*The Tempest,* v, 1, 48.

7
Like a mountain cedar, reach his branches
To all the plains about him.
Henry VIII. Act v, sc. 5, l. 54. [Cranmer]

Upright as the cedar.—*Love's Labour's Lost,* iv, 3, 89.

8
The cedar stoops not to the base shrub's foot,
But low shrubs wither at the cedar's root.
The Rape of Lucrece, l. 664.

CELIBACY, see Marriage and Celibacy

CENSURE

See also Criticism, Judgement

9
Betray themselves to every modern censure worse than drunkards.
As You Like It. Act iv, sc. 1, l. 7. [Rosalind]

Beware my censure.—*As You Like It,* iv, 1, 200.
Fear not . . . censure rash.—*Cymbeline,* iv, 2, 272.

10
Censure me by what you were,
Not what you are.
I Henry VI. Act v, sc. 5, l. 97. [King Henry]

Censure me in your wisdom, and awake your senses, that you may the better judge.
Julius Cæsar. Act iii, sc. 2, l. 16. [Brutus]

Censure well the deed.—*II Henry VI,* iii, 1, 275.
Give his censure.—*II Henry VI,* i, 3, 120.
Give your censures.—*Richard III,* ii, 2, 144.

11
No discerner
Durst wag his tongue in censure.
Henry VIII. Act i, sc. 1, l. 32. [Norfolk]
The only use of "discerner."

Forgetting, like a good man, your late censure
Both of his truth and him.
Henry VIII. Act iii, sc. 1, l. 64. [Campeius]

12
Let our just censures Attend the true event.
Macbeth. Act v, sc. 4, l. 14. [Macduff]

General censure.—*Hamlet,* i, 4, 35.
Giddy censure.—*Coriolanus,* i, 1, 272.
Heaviest censure.—*Coriolanus,* v, 6, 143.
Wisest censure.—*Othello,* ii, 3, 193.

13
I hear how I am censured.
Much Ado about Nothing. Act ii, sc. 3, l. 233. [Benedick]

Why, how are we censured?
Coriolanus. Act ii, sc. 1, l. 27. [Tribunes]

I may not breathe my censure.—*Othello,* iv, 1, 281.

14
The carping censures of the world.
Richard III. Act iii, sc. 5, l. 68. [Gloucester]

15
How blest am I
In my just censure, in my true opinion!
The Winter's Tale. Act ii, sc. 1, l. 37. [Leontes]

CEREMONY

16
Use a more spacious ceremony to the noble lords.
All's Well that Ends Well. Act ii, sc. 1, l. 51. [Parolles]

Enforced ceremony.—*Julius Cæsar,* iv, 2, 21.
United ceremony.—*The Merry Wives of Windsor,* iv, 6, 51.

Neither will they bate One jot of ceremony.
Coriolanus. Act ii, sc. 2, l. 145. [Sicinius]

17
And what have kings, that privates have not too,
Save ceremony, save general ceremony?
And what art thou, thou idol ceremony?
What kind of god art thou, that suffer'st more
Of mortal griefs than do thy worshippers?

What are thy rents? what are thy comings in?
O ceremony, show me but thy worth!
What is thy soul of adoration?
Art thou aught else but place, degree and form,
Creating awe and fear in other men?
Henry V. Act iv, sc. 1, l. 255. [King Henry]
O, be sick, great greatness,
And bid thy ceremony give thee cure!
Henry V. Act iv, sc. 1, l. 268. [King Henry]

1 Set on; and leave no ceremony out.
Julius Cæsar. Act i, sc. 2, l. 11. [Cæsar]
I never stood on ceremonies,
Yet now they fright me.
Julius Cæsar. Act ii, sc. 2, l. 13. [Calpurnia]
Deck'd with ceremonies.—*Julius Cæsar*, i, 1, 70.
Lawful ceremonies.—*Julius Cæsar*, iii, 1, 241.
Ceremonies of the wars.—*Henry V*, iv, 1, 73.

2 The sauce to meat is ceremony.
Macbeth, iii, 4, 36. See FEEDING, 528:3.

3 Let us take a ceremonious leave.
Richard II. Act i, sc. 3, l. 50. [Bolingbroke]
Ceremonious affection.—*King Lear*, i, 4, 63.
Ceremonious courtiers.—*Troilus and Cressida*, i, 3, 234.
Ceremonious duty.—*Richard II*, iii, 2, 173.
Ceremonious vows.—*Richard III*, v, 3, 98.

4 The perfect ceremony of love's rite.
Sonnets. No. xxiii.

5 Ceremony was but devised at first
To set a gloss on faint deeds, hollow welcomes,
Recanting goodness, sorry ere 'tis shown;
But where there is true friendship, there needs none.
Timon of Athens. Act i, sc. 2, l. 15. [Timon]
I am so fraught with curious business that
I leave out ceremony.
The Winter's Tale. Act iv, sc. 4, l. 524. [Florizel]

CERTAINTY

6 'Tis most credible; we here receive it
A certainty.
All's Well that Ends Well. Act i, sc. 2, l. 5. [King] The only use of "credible."
Encourage myself in my certainty.
All's Well that Ends Well. Act iii, sc. 6, l. 81. [Parolles]
Certain it is.—*All's Well that Ends Well*, iii, 6, 98; v, 3, 210.
This is most certain.—*Antony and Cleopatra*, ii, 1, 28.
Certain and unfallible.—*I Henry VI*, i, 2, 59. The only use of "unfallible." "Infallible" occurs five times.
'Tis certain so.—*Much Ado about Nothing*, ii, 1, 181.
'Tis now too certain.—*Henry VIII*, v, 3, 107.
That's certain.—*The Merchant of Venice*, iii, 1, 29, and twelve times in later plays.
That's most certain.—*Hamlet*, v, 2, 11; *King Lear*, i, 1, 289; *The Tempest*, iii, 2, 64.
'Tis certain.—*Henry V*, iii, 5, 1; iv, 1, 197; iv, 7, 5.
'Tis most certain.—*The Merry Wives of Windsor*, iii, 3, 120; *Antony and Cleopatra*, v, 2, 214; *Pericles*, v, 3, 20.
Most certain.—*King John*, i, 1, 59; *Twelfth Night*, i, 5; *Antony and Cleopatra*, iii, 6; iv, 5; *King Lear*, iv, 7; *Winter's Tale*, iv, 4.

7 Cleopatra: Is this certain?
Messenger: Or I have no observance.
Antony and Cleopatra. Act iii, sc. 3, l. 24.
As certain as I know the sun is fire.
Coriolanus. Act v, sc. 4, l. 48. [Messenger]

8 I speak from certainties.
Coriolanus. Act i, sc. 2, l. 31. [Aufidius]
Certainties
Either are past remedies, or, timely knowing,
The remedy then born.
Cymbeline. Act i, sc. 6, l. 96. [Imogen]
He is furnish'd with no certainties.
II Henry IV. Act i, sc. 1, l. 31. [Bardolph] The only uses of "certainties."

9 Hath there been such a time—I'd fain know that—
That I have positively said ' 'Tis so,'
When it proved otherwise?
Hamlet. Act ii, sc. 2, l. 153. [Polonius] "Positively" is repeated in *Richard III*, iv, 2, 25.

10 'Tis positive 'gainst all exceptions.
Henry V. Act iv, sc. 2, l. 25. [Constable]
It is as positive as the earth is firm.
The Merry Wives of Windsor. Act iii, sc. 2, l. 49. [Ford]
Fool positive.—*Troilus and Cressida*, ii, 3, 70. The only uses of "positive."
Well I wot.—*I Henry VI*, iv, 6, 32, and nine times in later plays.

11 This from a dying man receive as certain.
Henry VIII. Act ii, sc. 1, l. 125. [Buckingham]
Be certain, nothing truer.—*A Midsummer-Night's Dream*, iii, 2, 280. [Lysander]
Hear for certain.—*II Henry IV*, i, 1, 188.
Held for certain.—*Henry VIII*, ii, 1, 155.
Know for certain.—*The Tempest*, v, 1, 158.
Read for certain.—*The Merchant of Venice*, v, 1, 287.

12 As sure as bark on tree.
Love's Labour's Lost. Act v, sc. 2, l. 285. [Maria]
As sure as his guts are made of puddings.
The Merry Wives of Windsor, ii, 1, 31.
Yea, as sure as I have a thought or a soul.
Much Ado about Nothing. Act iv, sc. 1, l. 333. [Beatrice]
Sure as day.—*I Henry IV*, iii, 1, 255.
Sure as death.—*Titus Andronicus*, i, 1, 487.
Sure as I live.—*The Two Gentlemen of Verona*, iv, 4, 17.
Sure enough.—*Timon of Athens*, iii, 4, 48; *Titus Andronicus*, iv, 1, 95; *The Two Gentlemen of Verona*, v, 1, 12.
Most sure and vulgar.—*King Lear*, iv, 6, 214.

1 Thou art not certain;
For thy complexion shifts to strange effects,
After the moon.
Measure for Measure. Act iii, sc. 1, l. 23. [Duke]

Not a resemblance, but a certainty.
Measure for Measure. Act iv, sc. 2, l. 203. [Duke]

2
I was certain o'er incertainty.
Sonnets. No. cxv.

Be not uncertain.—*The Winter's Tale,* i, 2, 441.

CHAFING, see Annoyance

CHALLENGE

See also Duelling

3
The Prince of Wales stepp'd forth before the king,
And, nephew, challenged you to single fight.
I Henry IV. Act v, sc. 2, l. 46. [Worcester]

I never in my life
Did hear a challenge urged more modestly,
Unless a brother should a brother dare
To gentle exercise and proof of arms.
I Henry IV. Act v, sc. 2, l. 52. [Vernon]

4
Gloucester: In thine own person answer thy abuse.
Beaufort: Ay, where thou darest not peep.
II Henry VI. Act ii, sc. 1, l. 41.

5
By this I challenge him to single fight.
III Henry VI. Act iv, sc. 7, l. 75. [Montague]

Challenged The noble spirits to arms.
Henry VIII. Act i, sc. 1, l. 34. [Norfolk]

Read thou this challenge; mark but the penning of it.
King Lear. Act iv, sc. 6, l. 141. [King Lear] The only use of "penning."

6
Come, challenge me, challenge me by these deserts.
Love's Labour's Lost. Act v, sc. 2, l. 815. [Princess]

Armado: By the north pole, I do challenge thee.
Costard: I will not fight with a pole, like a northern man: I'll slash; I'll do it by the sword. I bepray you let me borrow my arms again.
Love's Labour's Lost. Act v, sc. 2, l. 699. The only use of "bepray."

7
I am forced to lay my reverence by
And, with grey hairs and bruise of many days,
Do challenge thee to trial of a man.
Much Ado about Nothing. Act v, sc. 1, l. 64. [Leonato]

Enough, I am engaged; I will challenge him.
Much Ado about Nothing. Act iv, sc. 1, l. 335. [Benedick]

God bless me from a challenge!
Much Ado about Nothing. Act v, sc. 1, l. 145. [Claudio]

8
Pale trembling coward, there I throw my gage.
Richard II. Act i, sc. 1, l. 69. [Bolingbroke]

Hurl down my gage.—*Richard II,* i, 1, 146.

There is my gage, the manual seal of death,
That marks thee out for hell.
Richard II. Act iv, sc. 1, l. 25. [Aumerle]

There I throw my gage,
To prove it on thee to the extremest point
Of mortal breathing: seize it, if thou darest.
Richard II. Act iv, sc. 1, l. 46. [Henry Percy] "Gage" is used eleven times in *Richard II,* and only three times in all the other plays.

If guilty dread have left thee so much strength
As to take up mine honour's pawn, then stoop.
Richard II. Act i, sc. 1, l. 73. [Bolingbroke]

9 He would unto the stews,
And from the common'st creature pluck a glove,
And wear it as a favour; and with that
He would unhorse the lustiest challenger.
Richard II. Act v, sc. 3, l. 16. [Henry Percy] The only use of "common'st," "unhorse," and "lustiest." "Stews" is repeated in *II Henry IV,* i, 2, 60.

Stood challenger.—*Hamlet,* iv, 7, 28.

10
I have a roisting challenge sent amongst
The dull and factious nobles of the Greeks
Will strike amazement to their drowsy spirits.
Troilus and Cressida. Act ii, sc. 2, l. 208. [Hector] The only use of "roisting" (bullying).

11
I'll write thee a challenge; or I'll deliver thy indignation to him by word of mouth.
Twelfth Night. Act ii, sc. 3, l. 139. [Sir Toby]

Challenge me the count's youth to fight with him; hurt him in eleven places.
Twelfth Night. Act iii, sc. 2, l. 36. [Sir Toby]

Here's the challenge, read it: I warrant there's vinegar and pepper in 't.
Twelfth Night. Act iii, sc. 4, l. 157. [Sir Andrew] The only mention of pepper. "Pepper-box" occurs in *The Merry Wives of Windsor,* iii, 5, 148, and "peppercorn" in *I Henry IV,* iii, 3, 9. "Peppered" is used three times.

I will deliver his challenge by word of mouth; set upon Aguecheek a notable report of valour; and drive the gentleman, as I know his youth will aptly receive it, into a most hideous opinion of his rage, skill, fury and impetuosity. This will so fright them both that they will kill one another by the look, like cockatrices.
Twelfth Night. Act iii, sc. 4, l. 209. [Sir Toby] The only use of "impetuosity."

I will meditate the while upon some horrid message for a challenge.
Twelfth Night. Act iii, sc. 4, l. 219. [Sir Toby]

CHAMBER

See also Room

12
Go with me to my chamber, and advise me.
All's Well that Ends Well. Act ii, sc. 3, l. 311. [Bertram]

Go with me to my chamber.
The Two Gentlemen of Verona, ii, 4, 184. See under COUNSEL. The phrase is repeated in ii, 7, 83.

1
Lead me to my chamber.
Antony and Cleopatra. Act ii, sc. 5, l. 119. [Cleopatra]
Come, I 'll to my chamber.
Cymbeline. Act i, sc. 2, l. 36. [Cloten]

2
Keep close within your chamber.
Hamlet. Act iv, sc. 7, l. 130. [King]
Servilius: He 's much out of health, and keeps his chamber.
Servant: Many do keep their chambers are not sick.
Timon of Athens. Act iii, sc. 4, l. 72.
Keep her chamber.—*Cymbeline,* ii, 3, 87.

3
Now get you to my lady's chamber.
Hamlet. Act v, sc. 1, l. 213. [Hamlet]
Lady's chamber.—*Richard III,* i, 1, 12; *The Winter's Tale,* iv, 4, 225.

4
To venture upon the charged chambers bravely.
II Henry IV. Act ii, sc. 4, l. 56. [Falstaff]

5
The perfumed chambers of the great.
II Henry IV, iii, 1, 12. See under SLEEP.

6
Bear me hence Into some other chamber.
II Henry IV. Act iv, sc. 4, l. 132. [King Henry]
Bear me to that chamber; there I 'll lie.
II Henry IV. Act iv, sc. 5, l. 240. [King Henry]
To the next chamber bear her.
Pericles. Act iii, sc. 2, l. 108. [Cerimon]
Next chamber.—*Henry VIII,* i, 4, 102.

7
May it please you, noble madam, to withdraw
Into your private chamber?
Henry VIII. Act iii, sc. 1, l. 28. [Wolsey]
Privy chamber.—*Henry VIII,* i, 4, 99.
Private in his chamber.—*Romeo and Juliet,* i, 1, 144.

8
Why have you left the chamber?
Macbeth. Act i, sc. 7, l. 29. [Lady Macbeth]
Who lies in the second chamber?
Macbeth. Act ii, sc. 2, l. 20. [Macbeth]
Retire we to our chamber.
Macbeth. Act ii, sc. 2, l. 66. [Lady Macbeth]
Approach the chamber.—*Macbeth,* ii, 3, 76.

9
I hope the days are near at hand
That chambers will be safe.
Macbeth. Act v, sc. 4, l. 1. [Malcolm]

10
Would I might never come in mine own great chamber again else.
The Merry Wives of Windsor, i, 1, 157. See under PURSE.
You are looked for and called for . . . in the great chamber.
Romeo and Juliet. Act i, sc. 5, l. 14. [Servant]
Great chamber.—*Midsummer-Night's Dream,* iii, 1, 58.
Goodly chamber.—*The Taming of the Shrew,* Ind., 2, 86.

11
Here be my keys: ascend my chambers.
The Merry Wives of Windsor. Act iii, sc. 3, l. 173. [Ford]
Ascend her chamber.—*Romeo and Juliet,* iii, 3, 147.

12
There 's his chamber, his house, his castle,
The Merry Wives of Windsor. Act iv, sc. 5, l. 6. [Host] See under HOUSE.

13
My chambers are honourable: fie! privacy? fie!
The Merry Wives of Windsor. Act iv, sc. 5, l. 23. [Host]

14
Withdraw into a chamber by yourselves.
Much Ado about Nothing. Act v, sc. 4, l. 11. [Leonato]
Depart the chamber.—*II Henry IV,* iv, 5, 91.

15
Now he tells how she plucked him to my chamber.
Othello. Act iv, sc. 1, l. 145. [Othello]

16
You are of our chamber, and our mind partakes
Her private actions to your secrecy.
Pericles. Act i, sc. 1, l. 152. [Antiochus]

17
She hath so strictly tied Her to her chamber.
Pericles. Act ii, sc. 5, l. 8. [Simonides]

18
Into the chamber wickedly he stalks.
The Rape of Lucrece, l. 365. The only use of "wickedly."
Enter his chamber.—*II Henry VI,* iii, 2, 132.

19
Carry him gently to my fairest chamber
And hang it round with all my wanton pictures.
The Taming of the Shrew. Induction, sc. 1, l. 46. [Lord]
Conduct him to the drunkard's chamber.
The Taming of the Shrew. Induction, sc. 1, l. 107. [Lord]

20
Come, I will bring thee to thy bridal chamber.
The Taming of the Shrew. Act iv, sc. 1, l. 181. [Petruchio]
I will show you a chamber with a bed.
Troilus and Cressida. Act iii, sc. 2, l. 216. [Pandarus]

21
My lord, come you again into my chamber.
Troilus and Cressida. Act iv, sc. 2, l. 37. [Cressida]
Come by and by to my chamber.
Twelfth Night. Act iv, sc. 2, l. 77. [Sir Toby]
Come up into my chamber.—*The Merry Wives of Windsor,* iv, 5, 131.

22
Her chamber is aloft, far from the ground,
And built so shelving that one cannot climb it
Without apparent hazard of his life.
The Two Gentlemen of Verona. Act iii, sc. 1, l. 114. [Duke] The only use of "shelving."

That 's her chamber.—*The Two Gentlemen of Verona,* iv, 4, 91.

1
Hie home unto my chamber.
The Two Gentlemen of Verona. Act iv, sc. 4, l. 93. [Proteus]

Hie to your chamber.—*Romeo and Juliet,* iii, 2, 138.

Go to my chamber.—*The Taming of the Shrew,* iii, 2, 115.

2
Out of the chamber with her!
Winter's Tale. Act ii, sc. 3, l. 122. [Leontes]

We were all commanded out of the chamber.
Winter's Tale. Act v, sc. 2, l. 6. [Gentleman]

CHAMPION

See also Knighthood

3
A stouter champion never handled sword.
I Henry VI. Act iii, sc. 4, l. 19. The only use of "stouter."

4
His champions are the prophets and apostles.
II Henry VI, i, 3, 60. See under HOLINESS.

5
By my valour, the most complete champion that ever I heard!
II Henry VI. Act iv, sc. 10, l. 58. [Cade]

Hardy and undoubted champions.
III Henry VI. Act v, sc. 7, l. 6. [King Edward]

6
And now will I be Edward's champion.
III Henry VI. Act iv, sc. 7, l. 68. [Montgomery]

7
Thou Fortune's champion that dost never fight
But when her humorous ladyship is by
To teach thee safety!
King John. Act iii, sc. 1, l. 118. [Constance]

Champion of our church.—*King John,* iii, 1, 255.

The widow's champion.—*Richard II,* i, 2, 43.

8
Wretched though I seem,
I can produce a champion that will prove
What is avouched there.
King Lear. Act v, sc. 1, l. 42. [Edgar] The only use of "avouched."

9
Like a bold champion, I assume the lists.
Pericles, i, 1, 61. See under FIDELITY.

10
Aumerle: The champions are prepared, and stay
For nothing but his majesty's approach.
King Richard: Marshal, demand of yonder champion
The cause of his arrival here in arms.
Richard II. Act i, sc. 3, l. 5.

New-come champion.—*I Henry VI,* ii, 2, 20.

11
Rome's readiest champions, repose you here in rest,
Secure from worldly chances and mishaps!
Titus Andronicus. Act i, sc. 1, l. 150. [Titus]

Rome's best champion.—*Titus Andronicus,* i, 1, 65.

12
Her champion mounted for the hot encounter.
Venus and Adonis, l. 596. See under LOVE.

CHANCE

See also Accident, Hazard

13
Give up yourself merely to chance and hazard,
From firm security.
Antony and Cleopatra. Act iii, sc. 7, l. 48. [Enobarbus]

I 'll yet follow The wounded chance of Antony.
Antony and Cleopatra. Act iii, sc. 10, l. 35. [Enobarbus]

Things but done by chance.—*Antony and Cleopatra,* v, 2, 120.

14
Wilt take thy chance with me?
Cymbeline. Act iv, sc. 2, l. 382. [Lucius]

15
Think what a chance thou changest on.
Cymbeline. Act i, sc. 5, l. 68. [Queen]

We grieve at chances here.—*Cymbeline,* iv, 3, 35.

This was strange chance.—*Cymbeline,* v, 3, 51.

This golden chance.—*Cymbeline,* v, 4, 132.

From chance to chance.—*Cymbeline,* v, 5, 391.

16
You that look pale and tremble at this chance.
Hamlet. Act v, sc. 2, l. 345. [Hamlet]

17
Chance of war.
I Henry IV, i, 3, 95; *Troilus and Cressida,* Prologue, 31; *Titus Andronicus,* i, 1, 264; *Cymbeline,* v, 5, 75.

Chance of anger.—*King Lear,* iii, 7, 79.

Chance of goodness.—*Macbeth,* iv, 3, 136.

18
Against ill chances men are ever merry;
But heaviness foreruns the good event.
II Henry IV. Act iv, sc. 2, l. 81. [Archbishop of York]

Disastrous chances.—*Othello,* i, 3, 134.

Woful chances.—*III Henry VI,* ii, 5, 107.

Worldly chances.—*Titus Andronicus,* i, 1, 152.

19
What chance is this that suddenly hath cross'd us?
I Henry VI. Act i, sc. 4, l. 72. [Talbot]

20
Now it is my chance to find thee out.
I Henry VI. Act v, sc. 4, l. 4. [Shepherd]

By chance.—*II Henry VI,* ii, 1, 87, and frequently in later plays.

By some chance.—*Coriolanus,* iv, 4, 20.

21
Brother, take you my land, I 'll take my chance.
King John. Act i, sc. 1, l. 151. [Bastard]

You must take your chance.—*The Merchant of Venice,* ii, 1, 38.

22
This feather stirs; she lives! if it be so,
It is a chance which does redeem all sorrows
That ever I have felt.
King Lear. Act v, sc. 3, l. 265. [King Lear]

1
If chance will have me king, why, chance may crown me,
Without my stir.
Macbeth. Act i, sc. 3, l. 143. [Macbeth]
Come, bring me unto my chance.
The Merchant of Venice. Act ii, sc. 1, l. 43. [Morocco]
May any terms acquit me from this chance?
The Rape of Lucrece, l. 1706.
Chance it as it may.—*Timon of Athens,* iv, 1, 129.
Triumphs over chance.—*Titus Andronicus,* i, 1, 178.

2 In the reproof of chance
Lies the true proof of men.
Troilus and Cressida. Act i, sc. 3, l. 33. [Nestor]
Seld I have the chance.—*Troilus and Cressida,* iv, 5, 150. The only use of "seld" (for seldom).
To comfort you with chance.
Twelfth Night. Act i, sc. 2, l. 8. [Captain]

3
But as the unthought-on accident is guilty
To what we wildly do, so we profess
Ourselves to be the slaves of chance and flies
Of every wind that blows.
The Winter's Tale. Act iv, sc. 4, l. 548. [Florizel] The only use of "unthought-on." See also under ACCIDENT.

CHANGE

See also Transformation

4
He changed almost into another man.
All's Well that Ends Well. Act iv, sc. 3, l. 5. [Lord]

5
Do not seek to take your change upon you.
As You Like It, i, 3, 104. See under GRIEF.
There is a change upon you.—*Antony and Cleopatra,* ii, 6, 54.
He changes much.—*II Henry IV,* iv, 5, 6.
Change his nature.—*Julius Cæsar,* ii, 1, 13.

6 His humour
Was nothing but mutation, ay, and that
From one bad thing to worse.
Cymbeline. Act iv, sc. 2, l. 132. [Belarius]
Strange mutations.—*King Lear,* iv, 1, 11. The only uses of "mutation."

7
I 'll change that name with you.
Hamlet, i, 2, 163. See under NAME.
Change their names.—*Measure for Measure,* i, 4, 47.

8
Nor the exterior nor the inward man
Resembles that it was.
Hamlet. Act ii, sc. 2, l. 6. [King]
I have of late . . . lost all my mirth, forgone all custom of exercises.
Hamlet. Act ii, sc. 2, l. 307. [Hamlet]

9
Of fickle changelings and poor discontents,
Which gape and rub the elbow at the news
Of hurlyburly innovation.
I Henry IV. Act v, sc. 1, l. 76. [King Henry] "Hurlyburly" occurs again in *Macbeth,* i, 1, 3: "When the hurlyburly 's done."
Behold, what innovation it makes here.
Othello. Act ii, sc. 3, l. 41. [Cassio]
Late innovation.—*Hamlet,* ii, 2, 347.
Traitorous innovator.—*Coriolanus,* iii, 1, 175. The only use of "innovator."

10 How chances mock,
And changes fill the cup of alteration
With divers liquors!
II Henry IV. Act iii, sc. 1, l. 51. [King Henry]
The noble change that I have purposed!
II Henry IV. Act iv, sc. 5, l. 155. [Prince of Wales]
He 's full of alteration And self-reproving.
King Lear. Act v, sc. 1, l. 3. [Edmund] The only use of "self-reproving."

11
We are blessed in the change.
Henry V. Act i, sc. 1, l. 37. [Ely]
What makes you in this sudden change?
III Henry VI. Act iv, sc. 4, l. 1. [Rivers]
What makes this change.—*Coriolanus,* iii, 1, 27.
Desperate change.—*Antony and Cleopatra,* i, 3, 54.
Desired change.—*Sonnets,* lxxxix.
Fearful change.—*Richard II,* ii, 4, 11.
Quick change.—*Sonnets,* lxxvi.
Shifting change.—*Sonnets,* xx.

12 Henry was well pleased
To change two dukedoms for a duke's fair daughter.
II Henry VI. Act i, sc. 1, l. 218. [York]

13
Change misdoubt to resolution.
II Henry VI, iii, 1, 332. See under RESOLUTION.
Change command into obedience.—*Cymbeline* iii, 4, 157.
Changes right or wrong.—*Sonnets,* cxii.

14
Ay, but the case is alter'd.
III Henry VI. Act iv, sc. 3, l. 31. [Warwick]
The times and titles now are alter'd strangely
With me since first you knew me.
Henry VIII. Act iv, sc. 2, l. 112. [Katharine]
Life is alter'd now.—*The Two Gentlemen of Verona,* ii, 4, 128.

15
All these things change from their ordinance
Their natures and performed faculties
To monstrous quality.
Julius Cæsar. Act i, sc. 3, l. 66. [Cassius]
It is but change.—*Julius Cæsar,* v, 3, 51.

16
Kiss the lips of unacquainted change.
King John. Act iii, sc. 4, l. 166. [Pandulph] "Unacquainted" is repeated in v, 2, 32: "Unacquainted colours"; and in *Troilus and Cressida,* iii, 3, 12: "Strange, unacquainted."
Change of cheer.—*Titus Andronicus,* i, 1, 264.
Change of mood.—*Timon of Athens,* i, 1, 84.

17
You see how full of changes his age is.
King Lear. Act i, sc. 1, l. 291. [Goneril]
Never man so changed.
King Lear. Act iv, sc. 2, l. 3. [Oswald]

You 're much deceived: in nothing am I changed
But in my garments.
King Lear. Act iv, sc. 6, l. 9. [Edgar]

May I change these garments?
Coriolanus. Act ii, sc. 3, l. 154. [Coriolanus]

Change garments with the gentleman.
Winter's Tale. Act iv, sc. 4, l. 648. [Camillo]

1 To be worst,
The lowest and most dejected thing of fortune,
Stands still in esperance, lives not in fear:
The lamentable change is from the best;
The worst returns to laughter.
King Lear. Act iv, sc. 1, l. 2. [Edgar]

Things might change or cease.—*King Lear,* iii, 1, 7.

2
Thus change I like the moon.
Love's Labour 's Lost. Act v, sc. 2, l. 212. [Rosaline] See also under MOON.

No, Time, thou shalt not boast that I do change.
Sonnets. No. cxxiii.

3
Here 's a change indeed!
Measure for Measure, i, 2, 107; *Othello,* iv, 2, 106.

What change is this?—*A Midsummer-Night's Dream,* iii, 2, 262.

Holy Saint Francis, what a change is here!
Romeo and Juliet. Act ii, sc. 3, l. 65. [Friar Laurence]

All things change them to the contrary.
Romeo and Juliet. Act iv, sc. 5, l. 90. [Friar Laurence]

4
Believe me, you are marvellously changed.
The Merchant of Venice. Act i, sc. 1, l. 76. [Gratiano]

Lord, how art thou changed!
The Merchant of Venice. Act ii, sc. 2, l. 106. [Gobbo]

O Bottom, thou art changed!
A Midsummer-Night's Dream. Act iii, sc. 1, l. 117. [Snout]

Bless thee, Bottom! bless thee! thou art translated.
A Midsummer-Night's Dream. Act iii, sc. 1, l. 121. [Quince]

Thou hast metamorphosed me.
The Two Gentlemen of Verona. Act i, sc. 1, l. 66. [Proteus] "Metamorphosed" is used again in ii, 1, 32, and in no other play.

Suffer a sea-change.—*The Tempest,* i, 2, 396. See under FATHER. The only use of "sea-change."

5 I would not change this hue,
Except to steal your thoughts, my gentle queen.
The Merchant of Venice. Act ii, sc. 1, l. 11. [Morocco]

I would not change it.—*As You Like It,* ii, 1, 18.

Change no more.—*III Henry VI,* v, 1, 57.

6
Gallants, I am not as I have been.
Much Ado about Nothing. Act iii, sc. 2, l. 15. [Benedick]

O, would thou wert as thou tofore hast been!
Titus Andronicus. Act iii, sc. 1, l. 294. [Lucius] "Tofore" is used once again in *Love's Labour 's Lost,* iii, 1, 83.

To inure thyself to what thou art like to be, cast thy humble slough and appear fresh.
Twelfth Night. Act ii, sc. 5, l. 160. [Malvolio] The only use of "inure." "Inured" occurs in *The Rape of Lucrece,* l. 321.

7
She must have change, she must.
Othello. Act i, sc. 3, l. 358. [Iago]

She must change for youth.—*Othello,* i, 3, 356.

How say you by this change?—*Othello,* i, 3, 17.

She is changed as she had never been.
The Taming of the Shrew. Act v, sc. 2, l. 115. [Baptista]

Change you, madam?—*Cymbeline,* i, 6, 11.

8 What is it that they do
When they change us for others?
Othello, iv, 3, 98. See under WIFE.

9
O change thy thought, that I may change my mind!
Sonnets. No. x.

Change of thoughts.—*Pericles,* i, 2, 1.

Change your mind.—*Much Ado about Nothing,* iii, 2, 119; *The Two Gentlemen of Verona,* iii, 2, 59. See also under MIND.

Change my countenance.—*II Henry VI,* iii, 1, 99.

Change the course.—*King Lear,* v, 1, 3.

Change her determination.—*The Merry Wives of Windsor,* iii, 5, 69.

Change his nature.—*The Merchant of Venice,* v, 1, 82.

Change my disposition.—*The Winter's Tale,* iv, 4, 135.

Change my shape.—*I Henry VI,* v, 3, 35.

Change their shapes.—*The Two Gentlemen of Verona,* v, 4, 109.

Change their state.—*Sonnets,* cxxviii.

Change of fortune.—*Timon of Athens,* iv, 3, 204.

Change of honours.—*Coriolanus,* ii, 1, 214.

Change of prides.—*Cymbeline,* ii, 5, 25.

Change of time.—*Cymbeline,* ii, 4, 4.

Change arms.—*King Lear,* iv, 2, 17.

Change eyes.—*Romeo and Juliet,* iii, 5, 31.

Change favours.—*Love's Labour 's Lost,* v, 2, 292; 468.

Change your favours.—*Love's Labour 's Lost,* v, 2, 134.

Change habits.—*Love's Labour 's Lost,* v, 2, 542.

Change places.—*King Lear,* iv, 6, 156; *Cymbeline,* v, 4, 180.

Change this purpose.—*The Winter's Tale,* iv, 4, 39.

Change your purpose.—*The Winter's Tale,* ii, 3, 151; iv, 4, 553.

Change a word.—*Love's Labour 's Lost,* v, 2, 238.

Double change of bravery.—*The Taming of the Shrew,* iv, 3, 57.

There will come some change.—*Troilus and Cressida,* v, 1, 101.

Turn and change together.—*Troilus and Cressida,* v, 3, 110.

10
Silva: Do you change colour?
Valentine: Give him leave, madam; he is a kind of chameleon.

Thurio: That hath more mind to feed on your blood than live in your air.
The Two Gentlemen of Verona. Act ii, sc. 4, l. 23.

I can add colours to the chameleon.
III Henry VI. Act iii, sc. 2, l. 191. See also *As You Like It,* iii, 2, 192; *Henry V,* ii, 2, 73; *Richard III,* iii, 5, 1.

By this light, he changes more and more.
Much Ado about Nothing. Act v, sc. 1, l. 140. [Don Pedro]

1
The changes I perceived in the king and Camillo were very notes of admiration.
The Winter's Tale. Act v, sc. 2, l. 12. [Gentleman]

CHAOS

2 Let not Nature's hand
Keep the wild flood confined! let order die!
And let this world no longer be a stage
To feed contention in a lingering act;
But let one spirit of the first-born Cain
Reign in all bosoms, that, each heart being set
On bloody courses, the rude scene may end,
And darkness be the burier of the dead!
II Henry IV. Act i, sc. 1, l. 153. [Northumberland] The only use of "burier."

3 Had I power, I should
Pour the sweet milk of concord into hell,
Uproar the universal peace, confound
All unity on earth.
Macbeth. Act iv, sc. 3, l. 97. [Malcolm]

4
Chaos is come again.
Othello, iii, 3, 92. See under LOVE.

Black chaos comes again.—*Venus and Adonis,* l. 1020.

Mis-shapen chaos of well-seeming forms!
Romeo and Juliet. Act i, sc. 1, l. 185. [Romeo] "Well-seeming" is repeated in *Measure for Measure,* iii, 1, 232.

Vast sin-concealing chaos! nurse of blame!
The Rape of Lucrece, l. 767. The only use of "sin-concealing."

This chaos follows.—*Troilus and Cressida,* i, 3, 128.

Like to a chaos.—*III Henry VI,* iii, 2, 161. The only uses of "chaos."

5 Piety and fear,
Religion to the gods, peace, justice, truth,
Domestic awe, night-rest, and neighbourhood,
Instruction, manners, mysteries, and trades,
Degrees, observances, customs, and laws,
Decline to your confounding contraries,
And let confusion live!
Timon of Athens. Act iv, sc. 1, l. 15. [Timon] The only use of "night-rest." See also CONFUSION.

6 When the planets
In evil mixture to disorder wander,
What plagues and what portents! what mutiny!
What raging of the sea! shaking of earth!
Commotion in the winds! frights, changes, horrors,
Divert and crack, rend and deracinate
The unity and married calm of states.
Troilus and Cressida. Act i, sc. 3, l. 94. [Ulysses] "Deracinate" is used once again in *Henry V,* v, 2, 47.

CHARACTER

See also Disposition, Nature

I—Good Character

7
So like a courtier, contempt nor bitterness
Were in his pride or sharpness.
All's Well that Ends Well. Act i, sc. 2, l. 36. [King]

He 's gentle, never schooled and yet learned, full of noble device, of sorts enchantingly beloved.
As You Like It. Act i, sc. 1, l. 176. [Oliver] The only use of "enchantingly."

And wherefore are you gentle, strong and valiant?
As You Like It. Act ii, sc. 3, l. 6. [Adam]

8
The duke is humorous: what he is indeed,
More suits you to conceive than I to speak of.
As You Like It. Act i, sc. 2, l. 278. [Le Beau]

He was full of jests, and gipes, and knaveries, and mocks.
Henry V. Act iv, sc. 7, l. 51. [Fluellen] The only use of "gipes."

Being incensed, he 's flint,
As humorous as winter and as sudden
As flaws congealed in the spring of day.
II Henry IV. Act iv, sc. 4, l. 33. [King Henry]

Lofty and sour to them that loved him not;
But to those men that sought him sweet as summer.
Henry VIII. Act iv, sc. 2, l. 53. [Griffith]

9
A very reverent body; ay, such a one as a man may not speak of without he say 'Sir-reverence.'
The Comedy of Errors. Act iii, sc. 2, l. 91. [Dromio of Syracuse]

10 He is one
The truest manner'd; such a holy witch
That he enchants societies into him;
Half all men's hearts are his . . .
He sits 'mongst men like a descended god:
He hath a kind of honour sets him off,
More than a mortal seeming.
Cymbeline. Act i, sc. 6, l. 165. [Iachimo]

They are as gentle
As zephyrs blowing below the violet,
Not wagging his sweet head; and yet as rough,
Their royal blood enchafed, as the rudest wind,
That by the top doth take the mountain pine,
And make him stoop to the vale.
Cymbeline. Act iv, sc. 2, l. 171. [Belarius] The only use of "zephyrs." "Enchafed" is repeated in *Othello,* ii, 1, 17.

11
A man faithful and honourable.
Hamlet. Act ii, sc. 2, l. 130. [King]

As just a man
As e'er my conversation coped withal.
Hamlet. Act iii, sc. 2, l. 59. [Hamlet]

Thou hast been
As one, in suffering all, that suffers nothing,
A man that fortune's buffets and rewards
Hast ta'en with equal thanks.
Hamlet. Act iii, sc. 2, l. 70. [Hamlet]

He is the brooch indeed
And gem of all the nation.
Hamlet. Act iv, sc. 7, l. 94. [Laertes]

I have known thee these twenty nine years, come peascod-time; but an honester and truer-hearted man—.
II Henry IV. Act ii, sc. 4, l. 412. [Hostess] The only use of "peascod-time" (season for peas) and "truer-hearted."

1
His looks are full of peaceful majesty,
His head by nature framed to wear a crown,
His hand to wield a sceptre, and himself
Likely in time to bless a regal throne.
III Henry VI. Act iv, sc. 6, l. 71. [King Henry]

2 Are they spare in diet,
Free from gross passion or of mirth or anger,
Constant in spirit, not swerving with the blood,
Garnish'd and deck'd in modest complement,
Not working with the eye without the ear,
And but in purged judgement trusting neither?
Such and so finely bolted didst thou seem.
Henry V. Act ii, sc. 2, l. 131. [King Henry] "Swerving" is used again in *Antony and Cleopatra,* iii, 11, 50.

3
Men of singular integrity and learning,
Yea, the elect o' the land.
Henry VIII. Act ii, sc. 4, l. 58. [Wolsey]

Men of gravity and learning.
Henry VIII. Act iii, sc. 1, l. 73. [Queen Katharine]

4
Since the birth of Cain, the first male child,
To him that did but yesterday suspire,
There was not such a gracious creature born.
King John. Act iii, sc. 4, l. 79. [Constance] "Suspire" is repeated in *II Henry IV,* iv, 5, 33.

A brother noble,
Whose nature is so far from doing harms,
That he suspects none; on whose foolish honesty
My practices ride easy!
King Lear. Act i, sc. 2, l. 195. [Edmund]

My train are men of choice and rarest parts,
That all particulars of duty know,
And in the most exact regard support
The worships of their name.
King Lear. Act i, sc. 4, l. 285. [King Lear]

5
A man of good repute, carriage, bearing, and estimation.
Love's Labour's Lost. Act i, sc. 1, l. 271. [King]

Let them be men of good repute and carriage.
Love's Labour's Lost. Act i, sc. 2, l. 71. [Armado]

A man of sovereign parts he is esteem'd;
Well fitted in arts, glorious in arms:
Nothing becomes him ill that he would well.
Love's Labour's Lost. Act ii, sc. 1, l. 44. [Maria]

6
The dearest friend to me, the kindest man,
The best-condition'd and unwearied spirit
In doing courtesies, and one in whom
The ancient Roman honour more appears
Than any that draws breath in Italy.
The Merchant of Venice. Act iii, sc. 2, l. 295. [Bassanio] The only use of "best-conditioned" and "unwearied."

7
A softly-sprighted man, is he not?
The Merry Wives of Windsor. Act i, sc. 4, l. 25. [Mistress Quickly] The only use of "softly-sprighted."

Messenger: And a good soldier too, lady.
Beatrice: And a good soldier to a lady: but what is he to a lord?
Messenger: A lord to a lord, a man to a man; stuffed with all honourable virtues.
Much Ado about Nothing. Act i, sc. 1, l. 53.

8
A constant, loving, noble nature.
Othello. Act ii, sc. 1, l. 298. [Iago]

For if he be not one that truly loves you,
That errs in ignorance and not in cunning,
I have no judgement in an honest face.
Othello. Act iii, sc. 3, l. 48. [Desdemona]

9
O, he was gentle, mild, and virtuous!
Richard III. Act i, sc. 2, l. 104. [Lady Anne]

10
He plays o' the viol-de-gamboys, and speaks three or four languages word for word without book, and hath all the good gifts of nature.
Twelfth Night. Act i, sc. 3, l. 26. [Sir Toby] The only use of "viol-de-gamboys" ('cello).

Yet I suppose him virtuous, know him noble,
Of great estate, of fresh and stainless youth;
In voices well divulged, free, learn'd and valiant;
And in dimension and the shape of nature
A gracious person.
Twelfth Night. Act i, sc. 5, l. 277. [Olivia]

11 A gracious, innocent soul,
More free than he is jealous.
The Winter's Tale. Act ii, sc. 3, l. 29. [Paulina]

A man of truth, of mercy.
The Winter's Tale. Act iii, sc. 2, l. 158. [Leontes]

II—Bad Character

12
First Lord: If your lordship find him not a hilding, hold me no more in your respect.
Second Lord: On my life, my lord, a bubble.
Bertram: Do you think I am so far deceived in him?
Second Lord: Believe it, my lord, in mine own direct knowledge, without any malice, but to speak of him as my kinsman, he's a

most notable coward, an infinite and endless liar, an hourly promise-breaker, the owner of no one good quality worthy your lordship's entertainment.

All's Well that Ends Well. Act iii, sc. 6, l. 3. "Promise-breaker" is repeated in *Coriolanus,* i, 8, 2.

A snipt-taffeta fellow there, whose villanous saffron would have made all the unbaked and doughy youth of a nation in his colour.

All's Well that Ends Well. Act iv, sc. 5, l. 2. [Lafeu] The only use of "snipt-taffeta" (wearing slashed garments of taffeta), "unbaked" and "doughy."

It is the stubbornest young fellow of France, full of ambition, an envious emulator of every man's good parts, a secret and villanous contriver.

As You Like It. Act i, sc. 1, l. 149. [Oliver] The only use of "stubbornest" and "emulator." For "contriver" see CUNNING.

1

He is deformed, crooked, old and sere,
Ill-faced, worse bodied, shapeless everywhere;
Vicious, ungentle, foolish, blunt, unkind,
Stigmatical in making, worse in mind.

The Comedy of Errors. Act iv, sc. 2, l. 19. [Adriana] The only use of "ill-faced" and "stigmatical" (deformed).

A mere anatomy, a mountebank,
A threadbare juggler and a fortune-teller,
A needy, hollow-eyed, sharp-looking wretch,
A living-dead man.

The Comedy of Errors. Act v, sc. 1, l. 238. [Antipholus Ephesus] The only use of "fortune-teller," "hollow-eyed," "sharp-looking," and "living-dead." "Threadbare" appears again in *II Henry VI,* iv, 2, 8.

2

If you see this in the map of my microcosm, follows it that I am known well enough too? what harm can your bisson conspectuities glean out of this character, if I be known well enough too?

Coriolanus. Act ii, sc. 1, l. 68. [Menenius] The only use of "microcosm" and "conspectuities." "Bisson" (blind, or blinding) is used again in *Coriolanus,* iii, 1, 131: "Bisson multitude"; and in *Hamlet,* ii, 2, 529: "Bisson rheum."

Why did you wish me milder? would you have me
False to my nature? Rather say I play
The man I am.

Coriolanus. Act iii, sc. 2, l. 14. [Coriolanus] See also NATURE.

3

We are beastly, subtle as the fox for prey,
Like warlike as the wolf for what we eat.

Cymbeline. Act iii, sc. 3, l. 40. [Arviragus]

4

I am very proud, revengeful, ambitious, with more offences at my beck than I have thoughts to put them in, imagination to give them shape, or time to act them in.

Hamlet. Act iii, sc. 1, l. 126. [Hamlet]

I prithee, take thy fingers from my throat;
For, though I am not splenitive and rash,
Yet have I something in me dangerous,
Which let thy wiseness fear.

Hamlet. Act v, sc. 1, l. 283. [Hamlet] The only use of "splenitive" (hot-headed) and "wiseness."

5

Thou art so fat-witted, with drinking of old sack and unbuttoning thee after supper and sleeping upon benches after noon, that thou hast forgotten to demand that truly which thou wouldst truly know.

I Henry IV. Act i, sc. 2, l. 2. [Prince of Wales] The only use of "fat-witted" and "unbuttoning."

A' plays at quoits well, and eats conger and fennel, and drinks off candles' ends for flap-dragons, and rides the wild-mare with the boys, and jumps upon joined-stools, and swears with a good grace, and wears his boots very smooth, like unto the sign of the leg, and breeds no bate with telling of discreet stories; and such other gambol faculties a' has, that show a weak mind and an able body.

II Henry IV. Act ii, sc. 4, l. 266. [Falstaff] "Quoit" occurs again in i, 4, 206, and "conger" in ii, 4, 58; neither is used in any other play. "Fennel" is repeated in *Hamlet,* iv, 6, 180. The only use of "flap-dragons" and "wild-mare." Flap-dragons (snap-dragons) are plums or raisins snatched out of burning brandy or spirits, and eaten.

Why dost thou converse with that trunk of humours, that bolting-hutch of beastliness, that swollen parcel of dropsies, that huge bombard of sack, that stuffed cloak-bag of guts, that roasted Manning-tree ox with the pudding in his belly, that reverend vice, that grey iniquity, that father ruffian, that vanity in years? Wherein is he good, but to taste sack and drink it? wherein neat and cleanly, but to carve a capon and eat it? wherein cunning, but in craft? wherein crafty, but in villany? wherein villanous, but in all things? wherein worthy, but in nothing?

I Henry IV. Act ii, sc. 4, l. 494. [Prince of Wales] The only use of "bolting-hutch," "beastliness," and "manning-tree ox." "Cloak-bag" (portmanteau) is repeated in *Cymbeline,* iii, 4, 172.

A man made after supper of a cheese-paring: when a' was naked, he was, for all the world, like a forked radish, with a head fantastically carved upon it with a knife: a' was so forlorn, that his dimensions to any thick sight were invincible: a' was the very genius of famine; yet lecherous as a monkey, and the whores called him mandrake: a' came ever in the rearward of the fashion, and sung those tunes to the overscutched huswives that he heard the carmen whistle, and sware they were his fancies or his good-nights.

II Henry IV. Act iii, sc. 2, l. 332. [Falstaff] The only use of "cheese-paring," "overscutched" and "carmen." "Radish" occurs again in *I Henry IV,* ii, 4, 206, and "carman" in *Measure for Measure,* ii, 1, 269.

6

His hours fill'd up with riots, banquets, sports,
And never noted in him any study,

Any retirement, any sequestration
From open haunts and popularity.
Henry V. Act i, sc. 1, l. 56. [Canterbury] "Sequestration" is repeated in *I Henry VI,* ii, 5, 25: "Loathsome sequestration"; and in *Othello,* i, 3, 351: "Answerable sequestration."

He 's a sworn rioter: he has a sin that often
Drowns him, and takes his valour prisoner:
If there were no foes, that were enough
To overcome him: in that beastly fury
He has been known to commit outrages,
And cherish factions: 'tis inferr'd to us,
His days are foul and his drink dangerous.
Timon of Athens. Act iii, sc. 5, l. 68. [Senator]

1
I, that have neither pity, love, nor fear.
III Henry VI. Act v, sc. 6, l. 68. [Gloucester]

Wolf in greediness, dog in madness, lion in prey.
King Lear. Act iii, sc. 4, l. 97. [Edgar]

I have many ill qualities.
Much Ado about Nothing. Act ii, sc. 1, l. 106. [Margaret]

2
A barren-spirited fellow; one that feeds
On abjects, orts and imitations,
Which, out of use and staled by other men,
Begin his fashion: do not talk of him,
But as a property.
Julius Cæsar. Act iv, sc. 1, l. 36. [Antony] The only use of "barren-spirited" and "staled."

3
Men so disorder'd, so debosh'd and bold,
That this our court, infected with their manners,
Shows like a riotous inn: epicurism and lust
Make it more like a tavern or a brothel
Than a graced palace.
King Lear. Act i, sc. 4, l. 263. [Goneril] The only use of "epicurism."

4
It is myself I mean: in whom I know
All the particulars of vice so grafted
That, when they shall be open'd, black Macbeth
Will seem as pure as snow, and the poor state
Esteem him as a lamb, being compared
With my confineless harms.
Macbeth. Act iv, sc. 3, l. 50. [Malcolm] The only use of "confineless."

I grant him bloody,
Luxurious, avaricious, false, deceitful,
Sudden, malicious, smacking of every sin
That has a name.
Macbeth. Act iv, sc. 3, l. 57. [Malcolm] The only use of "avaricious" and "smacking."

The king-becoming graces,
As justice, verity, temperance, stableness,
Bounty, perseverance, mercy, lowliness,
Devotion, patience, courage, fortitude,
I have no relish of them, but abound
In the division of each several crime.
Macbeth. Act iv, sc. 3, l. 91. [Malcolm] The only use of "king-becoming," and "stableness."

5
Lord Angelo is precise;
Stands at a guard with envy; scarce confesses
That his blood flows, or that his appetite
Is more to bread than stone.
Measure for Measure. Act i, sc. 3, l. 50. [Duke]

6
A very superficial, ignorant, unweighing fellow.
Measure for Measure. Act iii, sc. 2, l. 147. [Lucio] The only use of "unweighing." "Superficial" occurs again in *I Henry VI,* v, 5, 10.

A paltry fellow.—*Richard III,* v, 3, 323. See also under Fellow.

A man that apprehends death no more dreadfully but as a drunken sleep; careless, reckless, and fearless of what 's past, present, or to come; insensible of mortality, and desperately mortal.
Measure for Measure. Act iv, sc. 2, l. 149. [Provost]

Given to fornications, and to taverns and sack and wine and metheglins, and to drinkings and swearings and starings, pribbles and prabbles?
The Merry Wives of Windsor. Act v, sc. 5, l. 166. [Evans] Metheglin, a spiced drink of Welsh origin, is mentioned again in *Love's Labour 's Lost,* v, 2, 233. "Pribbles and prabbles" is used again in i, 1, 56, and in no other play.

7
The man, as you know all, hath a contemptible spirit.
Much Ado about Nothing. Act ii, sc. 3, l. 187. [Don Pedro]

A drayman, a porter, a very camel.
Troilus and Cressida. Act i, sc. 2, l. 270. [Pandarus]

III—Eccentric and Crotchety Character

8
Will this capriccio hold in thee? art sure?
All's Well that Ends Well. Act ii, sc. 3, l. 310. [Parolles] The only use of "capriccio."

His pettish lunes, his ebbs, his flows.
Troilus and Cressida. Act ii, sc. 3, l. 139. [Agamemnon] "Lunes" (fits of lunacy) is repeated in *The Merry Wives of Windsor,* iv, 2, 22, and in *The Winter's Tale,* ii, 2, 30. The only use of "pettish."

9
Indeed, good lady,
The fellow has a deal of that too much,
Which holds him much to have.
All's Well that Ends Well. Act iii, sc. 2, l. 91. [First Gentleman]

10
Should I anatomize him to thee as he is, I must blush and weep and thou must look pale and wonder.
As You Like It. Act i, sc. 1, l. 164. [Oliver]

Let them anatomize Regan; see what breeds about her heart.
King Lear. Act iii, sc. 6, l. 80. [King Lear]

My well-known body to anatomize.
II Henry IV, Ind., 21. The only uses of "anatomize."

11
I, being but a moonish youth, [would]

grieve, be effeminate, changeable, longing and liking, proud, fantastical, apish, shallow, inconstant, full of tears, full of smiles.

As You Like It. Act iii, sc. 2, l. 430. [Rosalind] The only use of "moonish."

1
I paint him in the character.

Coriolanus. Act v, sc. 4, l. 28. [Menenius]

See thou character.—*Hamlet,* i, 3, 59.
Outward character.—*Twelfth Night,* i, 2, 51.
With character too gross.—*Measure for Measure,* i, 2, 159. See also WRITING: HANDWRITING.

2
Hasty and tinder-like upon too trivial motion.

Coriolanus. Act ii, sc. 1, l. 55. [Menenius] The only use of "tinder-like."

3
In the verity of extolment, I take him to be a soul of great article; and his infusion of such dearth and rareness, as, to make true diction of him, his semblable is his mirror; and who else would trace him, his umbrage, nothing more.

Hamlet. Act v, sc. 2, l. 121. [Hamlet] The only use of "extolment," "diction," and "umbrage."

4
I am no proud Jack, like Falstaff, but a Corinthian, a lad of mettle, a good boy.

I Henry IV. Act ii, sc. 4, l. 12. [Prince of Wales] The only use of "Corinthian" (spirited fellow).

5
How insolent of late he is become,
How proud, how peremptory, and unlike himself?
We know the time since he was mild and affable,
And if we did but glance a far-off look,
Immediately he was upon his knee,
That all the court admired him for submission.

II Henry VI. Act iii, sc. 1, l. 7. [Queen Margaret]

6
I am no orator, as Brutus is;
But, as you know me all, a plain blunt man,
That love my friend.

Julius Cæsar. Act iii, sc. 2, l. 221. [Antony]

7
A phantasime, a Monarcho, and one that makes sport
To the prince and his bookmates.

Love's Labour's Lost. Act iv, sc. 1, l. 101. [Boyet] The only use of "monarcho" and "bookmates." "Phantasime" (fantastic) is repeated in v, 1, 20, and occurs in no other play.

His humour is lofty, his discourse peremptory, his tongue filed, his eye ambitious, his gait majestical, and his general behaviour vain, ridiculous, and thrasonical. He is too picked, too spruce, too affected, too odd as it were, too peregrinate, as I may call it.

Love's Labour's Lost. Act v, sc. 1, l. 10. [Holofernes] The only use of "peregrinate." "Thrasonical" (bragging, from Thraso, a boastful character in Terence's *Eunuchus*) occurs again in *As You Like It,* iv, 2, 34.

The world 's large tongue
Proclaims you for a man replete with mocks,
Full of comparisons and wounding flouts.

Love's Labour's Lost. Act v, sc. 2, l. 852. [Rosaline]

8
There is a kind of character in thy life,
That to the observer doth thy history
Fully unfold.

Measure for Measure. Act i, sc. 1, l. 28 [Duke]

9
The duke had crotchets in him.

Measure for Measure. Act iii, sc. 2, l. 135. [Lucio]

Thou hast some crotchets in thy head.

The Merry Wives of Windsor. Act ii, sc. 1, l. 159. [Mrs. Ford]

These are very crotchets.—*Much Ado about Nothing,* ii, 3, 58.
I will carry no crotchets.—*Romeo and Juliet,* iv, 5, 120. The only uses of "crotchets."

10
Some that will evermore peep through their eyes
And laugh like parrots at a bag-piper,
And other of such vinegar aspect
That they 'll not show their teeth in way of smile,
Though Nestor swear the jest be laughable.

The Merchant of Venice. Act i, sc. 1, l. 52. [Salarino] The only use of "bag-piper" and "laughable." "Vinegar aspect" is also unique, but "vinegar" occurs twice more in the plays, in *II Henry IV,* ii, 1, 103, and *Twelfth Night,* iii, 4, 158.

When he is best, he is a little worse than a man, and when he is worst, he is little better than a beast.

The Merchant of Venice. Act i, sc. 2, l. 94. [Portia]

You have it full, Benedick: we may guess by this what you are, being a man.

Much Ado about Nothing. Act i, sc. 1, l. 110. [Don Pedro]

11
Is this the nature
Whom passion could not shake? whose solid virtue
The shot of accident, nor dart of chance,
Could neither graze nor pierce?

Othello. Act iv, sc. 1, l. 276. [Lodovico]

12
High-stomach'd are they both, and full of ire,
In rage deaf as the sea, hasty as fire.

Richard II. Act i, sc. 1, l. 18. [King Richard] The only use of "high-stomach'd."

Not soon provoked nor being provoked soon calm'd.

Troilus and Cressida. Act iv, sc. 5, l. 99. [Ulysses]

But what thou art, God, thou, and I do know.

Richard II. Act i, sc. 3, l. 204. [Mowbray]

13
Let 's be no stoics nor no stocks, I pray;
Or so devote to Aristotle's checks

As Ovid be an outcast quite abjured.
The Taming of the Shrew. Act i, sc. 1, l. 31. [Tranio] The only use of "stoics."

1
He is as valiant as the lion, churlish as the bear, slow as the elephant: a man into whom nature hath so crowded humours that his valour is crushed into folly, his folly sauced with discretion: there is no man hath a virtue that he hath not a glimpse of, nor any man an attaint but he carries some stain of it.
Troilus and Cressida. Act i, sc. 2, l. 19. [Alexander] The only use of "crowded."

2
Belike this is a man of that quirk.
Twelfth Night. Act iii, sc. 4, l. 268. [Viola]
She has me her quirks.—*Pericles,* iv, 6, 8.
Quirks of blazoning pens.—*Othello,* ii, 1, 63.
Quirks of joy.—*All's Well that Ends Well,* iii, 2, 51.
Odd quirks.—*Much Ado about Nothing,* ii, 3, 245. The only uses of "quirks."

3
Sir Toby: Possess us, possess us; tell us something of him.
Maria: Marry, sir, sometimes he is a kind of puritan.
Sir Andrew: O, if I thought that, I 'ld beat him like a dog!
Sir Toby: What, for being a puritan? thy exquisite reason, dear knight?
Sir Andrew: I have no exquisite reason for 't, but I have reason good enough.
Maria: The devil a puritan that he is, or anything constantly, but a time-pleaser; an affectioned ass, that cons state without book and utters it by great swarths: the best persuaded of himself, so crammed, as he thinks, with excellencies, that it is his grounds of faith that all that look on him love him.
Twelfth Night. Act ii, sc. 3, l. 149. The only use of "affectioned" and "swarths." "Time-pleaser" is repeated in *Coriolanus,* iii, 1, 45.
Young Charbon the puritan.—*All's Well that Ends Well,* i, 3, 56.
No puritan.—*All's Well that Ends Well,* i, 3, 98.
But one puritan amongst them.—*The Winter's Tale,* iv, 3, 46.
Make a puritan of the devil.—*Pericles,* iv, 6, 9. The only uses of "puritan."

4
Viola: What manner of man is he?
Fabian: Nothing of that wonderful promise, to read him by his form, as you are like to find him in the proof of his valour. He is, indeed, sir, the most skilful, bloody and fatal opposite that you could possibly have found in any part of Illyria.
Twelfth Night. Act iii, sc. 4, l. 288.

IV—Woman's Character

5
Her disposition she inherits, which makes fair gifts fairer; for where an unclean mind carries virtuous qualities, there commendations go with pity; they are virtues and traitors too: in her they are the better for their simpleness; she derives her honesty and achieves her goodness.
All's Well that Ends Well. Act i, sc. 1, l. 46. [Countess]

I have spoke
With one that, in her sex, her years, profession,
Wisdom and constancy, hath amazed me more
Than I dare blame my weakness.
All's Well that Ends Well. Act ii, sc. 1, l. 85. [Lafeu]

Women are soft, mild, pitiful and flexible;
Thou stern, obdurate, flinty, rough, remorseless.
III Henry VI. Act i, sc. 4, l. 141. [York] "Flexible" is repeated in *Troilus and Cressida,* i, 3, 5.

6
She is fair and virtuous.
III Henry VI. Act iii, sc. 3, l. 245. [Queen]
She never knew harm-doing.
Henry VIII. Act ii, sc. 3, l. 5. [Anne] The only use of "harm-doing."

Beshrew me but I love her heartily;
For she is wise, if I can judge of her,
And fair she is, if that mine eyes be true,
And true she is, as she hath proved herself,
And therefore, like herself, wise, fair and true,
Shall she be placed in my constant soul.
The Merchant of Venice. Act ii, sc. 6, l. 52. [Lorenzo]

7
Rich she shall be, that 's certain; wise, or I 'll none; virtuous, or I 'll never cheapen her; fair, or I 'll never look on her; mild, or come not near me; noble, or not I for an angel; of good discourse, an excellent musician, and her hair shall be of what colour it please God.
Much Ado about Nothing. Act ii, sc. 3, l. 32. [Benedick]

They say the lady is fair; 'tis a truth, I can bear them witness; and virtuous; 'tis so, I cannot reprove it; and wise, but for loving me.
Much Ado about Nothing. Act ii, sc. 3, l. 239. [Benedick]

8
Iago: She that was ever fair and never proud,
Had tongue at will and yet was never loud,
Never lack'd gold and yet went never gay,
Fled from her wish and yet said 'Now I may,'
She that being anger'd, her revenge being nigh,
Bade her wrong stay and her displeasure fly,
She that in wisdom never was so frail
To change the cod's head for the salmon's tail,
She that could think and ne'er disclose her mind,
See suitors following and not look behind,
She was a wight, if ever such wight were,—
Desdemona: To do what?
Iago: To suckle fools and chronicle small beer.
Othello. Act ii, sc. 1, l. 149. "Suckle" is repeated in *Coriolanus,* i, 3, 44.

1
She is of so free, so kind, so apt, so blessed a disposition, she holds it a vice in her goodness not to do more than she is requested.
Othello. Act ii, sc. 3, l. 326. [Iago]
She 's framed as fruitful As the free elements.
Othello. Act ii, sc. 3, l. 347. [Iago]

2
Fair is my love, but not so fair as fickle;
Mild as a dove, but neither true nor trusty;
Brighter than glass, and yet, as glass is, brittle;
Softer than wax, and yet, as iron, rusty.
A lily pale, with damask dye to grace her,
None fairer, nor none falser to deface her.
The Passionate Pilgrim, l. 85. The only use of "brighter."

3 Her beauty and her wit,
Her affability and bashful modesty,
Her wondrous qualities and mild behaviour.
The Taming of the Shrew. Act ii, sc. 1, l. 48. [Petruchio]
For thou art pleasant, gamesome, passing courteous,
But slow in speech, yet sweet as spring-time flowers:
Thou canst not frown, thou canst not look askance,
Nor bite the lip, as angry wenches will,
Nor hast thou pleasure to be cross in talk,
But thou with mildness entertain'st thy wooers,
With gentle conference, soft and affable.
The Taming of the Shrew. Act ii, sc. 1, l. 247. [Petruchio]
So merry and so gamesome.—*Cymbeline,* i, 6, 60.
I am not gamesome.—*Julius Cæsar,* i, 2, 28. The only uses of "gamesome."
Kate like the hazel-twig
Is straight and slender and as brown in hue
As hazel nuts and sweeter than the kernels.
Taming of the Shrew. Act ii, sc. 1, l. 255. [Petruchio] The only use of "hazel-twig."

4 Be but about
To say 'she is a goodly lady,' and
The justice of your hearts will thereto add
''Tis pity she 's not honest, honourable.'
The Winter's Tale. Act ii, sc. 1, l. 65. [Leontes]

CHARITY

5 A man by his own alms empoison'd,
And with his charity slain.
Coriolanus. Act v, sc. 6, l. 11. [Aufidius] The only use of "empoison'd."
Charity chased hence by rancour's hand.
II Henry VI. Act iii, sc. 1, l. 144. [Gloucester]

6
He hath a tear for pity and a hand
Open as day for melting charity.
II Henry IV. Act iv, sc. 4, l. 31. [King Henry]
Learned charity.—*Pericles,* v, 3, 94.

7
'Twas sin before, but now 'tis charity.
III Henry VI. Act v, sc. 5, l. 76. [Queen Margaret]
Might there not be a charity in sin?
Measure for Measure. Act ii, sc. 4, l. 63. [Angelo]
It is no sin at all, but charity.
Measure for Measure. Act ii, sc. 4, l. 66. [Isabella]

8
Deliver all with charity.
Henry VIII. Act i, sc. 2, l. 143. [Queen Katharine]
I have more charity.—*Henry VIII,* iii, 1, 109.

9
Ransacking the church, Offending charity.
King John. Act iii, sc. 4, l. 172. [Pandulph] The only use of "ransacking."

10
Do poor Tom some charity, whom the foul fiend vexes.
King Lear. Act iii, sc. 4, l. 61. [Edgar]
Let 's exchange charity.—*King Lear,* v, 3, 166.

11
For charity itself fulfils the law,
And who can sever love from charity?
Love's Labour 's Lost. Act iv, sc. 3, l. 364. [Biron]

12
Let her have needful, but not lavish, means.
Measure for Measure. Act ii, sc. 2, l. 24. [Angelo]
'Twere good you do so much for charity.
The Merchant of Venice. Act iv, sc. 1, l. 261. [Portia]

13
And finding little comfort to relieve them,
I thought it princely charity to grieve them.
Pericles. Act i, sc. 2, l. 99. [Pericles]
The gods requite his charity!
Pericles. Act iii, sc. 2, l. 75. [Cerimon]

14
Lady, you know no rules of charity,
Which renders good for bad, blessings for curses.
Richard III. Act i, sc. 2, l. 68. [Gloucester]
My charity is outrage.—*Richard III,* i, 3, 277.

15
We have done deeds of charity.
Richard III. Act ii, sc. 1, l. 49. [King Edward]
This was but a deed of charity
To that which thou shalt hear of me anon.
Titus Andronicus. Act v, sc. 1, l. 89. [Aaron]
Charitable deeds.—*Richard III,* i, 2, 35; *Titus Andronicus,* iii, 2, 70.
You ha' done me a charitable office.
Winter's Tale. Act iv, sc. 3, l. 80. [Autolycus]

16
Thou hast not so much charity in thee as to go to the ale with a Christian.
The Two Gentlemen of Verona. Act ii, sc. 5, l. 60. [Launce]
Lack of charity.—*Cymbeline,* ii, 3, 114.
Show charity to none.—*Timon of Athens,* iv, 3, 534.

CHARM

See also Conjuring, Magic, Omen

17
Amiens: What 's that 'ducdame'?
Jaques: 'Tis a Greek invocation, to call fools into a circle.
As You Like It. Act ii, sc. 5, l. 60. "Duc-

dame" is used only in this scene, probably, in spite of the conjectures of learned commentators, merely a bit of doggerel.

1
Guiderius: No exorciser harm thee!
Arviragus: Nor no witchcraft charm thee!
Guiderius: Ghost unlaid forbear thee!
Arviragus: Nothing ill come near thee!
Both: Quiet consummation have;
And renowned be thy grave!

Cymbeline. Act iv, sc. 2, l. 276. The only use of "exorciser." *II Henry VI,* i, 4, 5, has "exorcism"; and "exorcist" occurs twice, in *All's Well that Ends Well,* v, 3, 305, and *Julius Cæsar,* ii, 1, 323. "Consummation" is used only once again, in *Hamlet,* iii, 1, 63: "A consummation Devoutly to be wish'd."

2
Unchain your spirits now with spelling charms.

I Henry VI. Act v, sc. 3, l. 31. [York] The only use of "unchain" and "spelling."

Airy charm.—*The Tempest,* v, 1, 54.
Grave charm.—*Antony and Cleopatra,* iv, 12, 25.
Hellish charms.—*Richard III,* iii, 4, 64.
Wicked charms.—*King Lear,* ii, 1, 41.

3
The weird sisters, hand in hand,
Posters of the sea and land,
Thus do go about, about:
Thrice to thine and thrice to mine
And thrice again, to make up nine.
Peace! the charm 's wound up.

Macbeth. Act i, sc. 3, l. 32. [Witches] The only use of "posters."

How did you dare
To trade and traffic with Macbeth
In riddles and affairs of death;
And I, the mistress of your charms,
The close contriver of all harms,
Was never call'd to bear my part,
Or show the glory of our art?

Macbeth. Act iii, sc. 5, l. 3. [Hecate]

Your vessels and your spells provide,
Your charms and every thing beside.

Macbeth. Act iii, sc. 5, l. 18. [Hecate]

4
Double, double toil and trouble;
Fire burn, and cauldron bubble.

Macbeth. Act iv, sc. 1, l. 10. [Witches]

Eye of newt and toe of frog,
Wool of bat and tongue of dog,
Adder's fork and blind-worm's sting,
Lizard's leg and howlet's wing,
For a charm of powerful trouble,
Like a hell-broth boil and bubble.

Macbeth. Act iv, sc. 1, l. 14. [Second Witch] The only use of "howlet" (owl) and "hell-broth." "Newt" is repeated in *A Midsummer-Night's Dream,* ii, 2, 11, and in *Timon of Athens,* iv, 3, 182: "Gilded newt." "Blind-worm" occurs again in *A Midsummer-Night's Dream,* ii, 2, 11. "Frog" is used only once again, in *King Lear,* iii, 4, 134.

Cool it with a baboon's blood,
Then the charm is firm and good.

Macbeth. Act iv, sc. 1, l. 37. [Second Witch]

5
As easy may'st thou the intrenchant air
With thy keen sword impress as make me bleed:
Let fall thy blade on vulnerable crests;
I bear a charmed life, which must not yield
To one of woman born.

Macbeth. Act v, sc. 8, l. 9. [Macbeth] The only use of "intrenchant" (incapable of being cut), and "vulnerable."

Despair thy charm.—*Macbeth,* v, 8, 13.

6
Mistress Quickly: Surely I think you have charms, la; yes, in truth.
Falstaff: Not I, I assure thee: setting the attraction of my good parts aside, I have no other charms.

Merry Wives of Windsor. Act ii, sc. 2, l. 106.

Loving charms.—*Passionate Pilgrim,* l. 150.
Charms of love.—*Antony and Cleopatra,* ii, 1, 20.
Charm of looks.—*Romeo and Juliet,* ii, Prol., 6.

7
Never harm, Nor spell nor charm,
Come our lovely lady nigh.

A Midsummer-Night's Dream. Act ii, sc. 2, l. 16. [Fairies' Song]

Churl, upon thy eyes I throw
All the power this charm doth owe.

A Midsummer-Night's Dream. Act ii, sc. 2, l. 78. [Puck]

8
Charm ache with air and agony with words.

Much Ado about Nothing. Act v, sc. 1, l. 26. [Leonato]

9
Judge me the world, if 'tis not gross in sense
That thou hast practised on her with foul charms,
Abused her delicate youth with drugs or minerals
That weaken motion.

Othello. Act i, sc. 2, l. 72. [Brabantio]

She was a charmer, and could almost read
The thoughts of people.

Othello. Act iii, sc. 4, l. 57. [Othello] The only use of "charmer."

10
Have done thy charm, thou hateful wither'd hag!

Richard III. Act i, sc. 3, l. 215. [Gloucester]

11
My high charms work.

The Tempest. Act iii, sc. 3, l. 88. [Prospero]

My charms crack not.—*The Tempest,* v, 1, 2.

Your charm so strongly works 'em
That if you now beheld them, your affections
Would become tender.

The Tempest. Act v, sc. 1, l. 17. [Ariel]

12
Here thought they to have done
Some wanton charm upon this man and maid.

The Tempest. Act iv, sc. 1, l. 95. [Ceres]

13
Hush, and be mute,
Or else our spell is marr'd.

The Tempest. Act iv, sc. 1, l. 127. [Prospero]

Untie the spell.—*The Tempest,* v, 1, 253.

O, fear him not;
His spell in that is out.

Henry VIII. Act iii, sc. 2, l. 19. [Norfolk]

My spell is lawful.—*Winter's Tale,* v, 3, 105.
'Tis a spell, you see, of much power.
Coriolanus. Act v, sc. 2, l. 102. [Senator]
Charming spells.—*I Henry VI,* v, 3, 2.
You are spell-stopp'd.—*The Tempest,* v, 1, 61. The only use of the phrase.

1
My charms I 'll break.
The Tempest. Act v, sc. 1, l. 31. [Prospero]
The charm dissolves apace.—*The Tempest,* v, 1, 64.
Now my charms are all o'erthrown.—*The Tempest,* Epil. 1.

2
Sit fas aut nefas, till I find the stream
To cool this heat, a charm to calm these fits.
Titus Andronicus. Act ii, sc. 1, l. 133. [Demetrius] "Sit fas aut nefas" (be it right or wrong), a common Latin phrase used only once.

CHASE, see Hunting

CHASTITY

See also Honour: Woman's Honour

3
My chastity 's the jewel of our house,
Bequeathed down from many ancestors;
Which were the greatest obloquy i' the world
In me to lose.
All's Well that Ends Well. Act iv, sc. 2, l. 46. [Diana] "Obloquy" is repeated in *I Henry VI,* ii, 5, 49.
Of a most chaste renown.
All's Well that Ends Well. Act iv, sc. 3, l. 18. [Second Lord]
First Lord: But you say she 's honest.
Bertram: That 's all the fault.
All's Well that Ends Well. Act iii, sc. 6, l. 119.

4
There 's a palm presages chastity, if nothing else.
Antony and Cleopatra. Act i, sc. 2, l. 47. [Iras]

5
The fair, the chaste and unexpressive she.
As You Like It. Act iii, sc. 2, l. 10. [Orlando] The only use of "unexpressive."
Audrey: Well, I am not fair; and therefore I pray the gods make me honest.
Touchstone: Truly, and to cast away honesty upon a foul slut were to put good meat into an unclean dish.
As You Like It. Act iii, sc. 3, l. 33.

6
The very ice of chastity.
As You Like It. Act iii, sc. 4, l. 18. [Celia]
Chaste as ice.—*Hamlet,* iii, 1, 140.
Chaste as the icicle
That 's curdied by the frost from purest snow.
Coriolanus. Act v, sc. 3, l. 65. [Coriolanus] The only use of "curdied."
More fair, virtuous, wise, chaste, constant-qualified and less attemptable than any the rarest of our ladies in France.
Cymbeline. Act i, sc. 4, l. 64. [Frenchman] The only use of "constant-qualified" and "attemptable."

As chaste as unsunn'd snow.—*Cymbeline,* ii, 5, 13. The only use of "unsunn'd."
Cold, cold, my girl! Even like thy chastity.
Othello. Act v, sc. 2, l. 275. [Othello]
Cold chastity.—*A Lover's Complaint,* l. 315.

7
Should he make me
Live, like Diana's priest, betwixt cold sheets,
Whiles he is vaulting variable ramps?
Cymbeline. Act i, sc. 6, l. 132. [Iachimo] The only use of "ramps." See under SHEETS.
Our Tarquin thus
Did softly press the rushes, ere he waken'd
The chastity he wounded.
Cymbeline. Act ii, sc. 2, l. 12. [Iachimo]

8
Your daughter's chastity—there it begins.
He spake of her, as Dian had hot dreams,
And she alone were cold.
Cymbeline. Act v, sc. 5, l. 179. [Iachimo]
I was taught
Of your chaste daughter the wide difference
'Twixt amorous and villanous.
Cymbeline. Act v, sc. 5, l. 193. [Iachimo]
He could not
But think her bond of chastity quite crack'd,
I having ta'en the forfeit.
Cymbeline. Act v, sc. 5, l. 206. [Iachimo]

9
Then weigh what loss your honour may sustain,
If with too credent ear you list his songs,
Or lose your heart, or your chaste treasure open
To his unmaster'd importunity.
Hamlet. Act i, sc. 3, l. 29. [Laertes] The only use of "unmaster'd."

10
There my white stole of chastity I daff'd.
A Lover's Complaint, l. 297. The only use of "stole" in the sense of robe.
Maiden virtue rudely strumpeted.—*Sonnets,* lxvi.

11
I am yet Unknown to woman.
Macbeth. Act iv, sc. 3, l. 125. [Malcolm]

12
The treasures of your body.
Measure for Measure. Act ii, sc. 4, l. 96. [Angelo]
The impression of keen whips I 'ld wear as rubies,
And strip myself to death, as to a bed
That longing have been sick for, ere I 'ld yield
My body up to shame.
Measure for Measure. Act ii, sc. 4, l. 101. [Isabella]
Then, Isabel, live chaste, and brother, die:
More than our brother is our chastity.
Measure for Measure. Act ii, sc. 4, l. 184. [Isabella]

13
If I live to be as old as Sibylla, I will die as chaste as Diana.
The Merchant of Venice. Act i, sc. 2, l. 116. [Portia] The only mention of Sibylla.
If she be less than an honest woman, she is indeed more than I took her for.
The Merchant of Venice. Act iii, sc. 5, l. 45. [Launcelot] "Honest woman" occurs eleven times. See under WOMAN: HER VIRTUES.

1
Well, I will find you twenty lascivious turtles ere one chaste man.
The Merry Wives of Windsor. Act ii, sc. 1, l. 82. [Mrs. Page] It should be remembered that in Shakespeare "turtle" always refers to turtle-dove.

2
If I know more of any man alive
Than that which maiden modesty doth warrant,
Let all my sins lack mercy!
Much Ado about Nothing. Act iv, sc. 1, l. 180. [Hero]

Out of all suspicion, she is virtuous.
Much Ado about Nothing. Act ii, sc. 3, l. 166. [Don Pedro]

3
I durst, my lord, to wager she is honest,
Lay down my soul at stake: if you think other,
Remove your thought; it doth abuse your bosom.
Othello. Act iv, sc. 2, l. 12. [Emilia]

For, if she be not honest, chaste, and true,
There's no man happy; the purest of their wives
Is foul as slander.
Othello. Act iv, sc. 2, l. 17. [Emilia]

Desdemona: I hope my noble lord esteems me honest.
Othello: O, ay; as summer flies are in the shambles,
That quicken even with blowing.
Othello. Act iv, sc. 2, l. 65. "Shambles" is repeated in *III Henry VI*, i, 1, 71.

4
Touches so soft still conquer chastity.
The Passionate Pilgrim, l. 50.

5
Your peevish chastity, which is not worth a breakfast in the cheapest country under the cope, shall undo a whole household.
Pericles. Act iv, sc. 6, l. 130. [Boult] The only use of "cope" in the sense of sky.

Will you not go the way of women-kind? Marry, come up, my dish of chastity with rosemary and bays!
Pericles. Act iv, sc. 6, l. 158. [Bawd] The only use of "women-kind."

6
Haply that name of 'chaste' unhappily set
This bateless edge on his keen appetite.
The Rape of Lucrece, l. 8. The only use of "bateless."

Honour and beauty, in the owner's arms,
Are weakly fortress'd from a world of harms.
The Rape of Lucrece, l. 27. The only use of "fortress'd."

7
But she hath lost a dearer thing than life,
And he hath won what he would lose again.
The Rape of Lucrece, l. 687.

That more dear
Than hands or tongue, her spotless chastity.
Titus Andronicus. Act v, sc. 2, l. 176. [Titus]

8
Pure Chastity is rifled of her store,
And Lust, the thief, far poorer than before.
The Rape of Lucrece, l. 692.

My honey lost, and I, a drone-like bee,
Have no perfection of my summer left.
The Rape of Lucrece, l. 836. The only use of "drone-like."

9
And, in strong proof of chastity well arm'd,
From love's weak childish bow she lives unharm'd.
Romeo and Juliet. Act i, sc. 1, l. 216. [Romeo]

Benvolio: Then she hath sworn that she will still live chaste?
Romeo: She hath, and in that sparing makes huge waste,
For beauty starved with her severity
Cuts beauty off from all posterity.
Romeo and Juliet. Act i, sc. 1, l. 223.

Fruitless chastity,
Love-lacking vestals and self-loving nuns,
That on the earth would breed a scarcity
And barren dearth of daughters and of sons.
Venus and Adonis, l. 751. The only use of "love-lacking." "Self-loving" is repeated in *Coriolanus,* iv, 6, 32.

10
Roman Lucrece for her chastity.
The Taming of the Shrew. Act ii, sc. 1, l. 298. [Petruchio]

She is stubborn-chaste against all suit.
Troilus and Cressida. Act i, sc. 1, l. 100. [Troilus] The only use of "stubborn-chaste."

Whose vows are, that no bed-right shall be paid
Till Hymen's torch be lighted.
The Tempest. Act iv, sc. 1, l. 96. [Iris] The only use of "bed-right."

11
Grumio: Where is he?
Curtis: In her chamber, making a sermon of continency to her.
Taming of the Shrew. Act iv, sc. 1, l. 184.

This ungenitured agent will unpeople the province with continency.
Measure for Measure. Act iii, sc. 2, l. 184. [Lucio] The only use of "ungenitured" (impotent).

My past life
Hath been as continent, as chaste, as true,
As I am now unhappy.
The Winter's Tale. Act iii, sc. 2, l. 34. [Hermione]

Chaste life.—*Sonnets,* cliv.

12
Thy sons make pillage of her chastity.
Titus Andronicus. Act ii, sc. 3, l. 44. [Aaron]

Demetrius: This minion stood upon her chastity,
Upon her nuptial vow, her loyalty,
And with that painted hope braves your mightiness:
And shall she carry this unto her grave?
Chiron: An if she do, I would I were an eunuch.
Titus Andronicus. Act ii, sc. 3, l. 124.

Married chastity.—*The Phœnix and the Turtle,* l. 61.

Now perforce we will enjoy
That nice-preserved honesty of yours.
Titus Andronicus. Act ii, sc. 3, l. 134. [Chiron] The only use of "nice-preserved."

That chaste dishonour'd dame.
Titus Andronicus. Act iv, sc. 1, l. 90. [Marcus]

1 My lady
Was fairer than his grandam and as chaste
As may be in the world.
Troilus and Cressida. Act i, sc. 3, l. 298. [Nestor]

Upon whose grave thou vow'dst pure chastity.
The Two Gentlemen of Verona. Act iv, sc. 3, l. 21. [Silvia]

Sacred chastity.—*Measure for Measure,* v, 1, 410.

CHAT, see Conversation

CHEATING

2 I hope you do not mean to cheat me so.
The Comedy of Errors. Act iv, sc. 3, l. 79. [Courtezan]

Cheated of our lives.—*The Tempest,* i, 1, 59.

Cheating, lack-linen mate!—*II Henry IV,* ii, 4, 133. The only use of "cheating" and "lack-linen."

3 They say this town is full of cozenage.
The Comedy of Errors. Act i, sc. 2, l. 97. [Antipholus of Syracuse]

Out, alas, sir! cozenage, mere cozenage!
The Merry Wives of Windsor. Act iv, sc. 5, l. 64. [Bardolph]

Such cozenage.—*Hamlet,* v, 2, 67. The only uses of "cozenage."

I would all the world might be cozened; for I have been cozened and beaten too.
The Merry Wives of Windsor. Act iv, sc. 5, l. 95. [Falstaff]

Thou art not vanquish'd,
But cozen'd and beguiled.
King Lear. Act v, sc. 3, l. 153. [Goneril]

Lay hands on the villain: I believe a' means to cozen somebody in this city under my countenance.
The Taming of the Shrew. Act v, sc. 1, l. 39. [Pedant]

I think 't no sin
To cozen him that would unjustly win.
All's Well that Ends Well. Act iv, sc. 2, l. 75. [Diana]

4 Some tricks, some quillets, how to cheat the devil.
Love's Labour's Lost. Act iv, sc. 3, l. 288. [Longaville]

Prithee, keep up thy quillets.
Othello. Act iii, sc. 1, l. 25. [Cassio]

Do not stand on quillets.—*II Henry VI,* iii, 1, 261.

Sound his quillets shrilly.—*Timon of Athens,* iv, 3, 155.

Where be . . . his quillets?—*Hamlet,* v, 1, 108.

Sharp quillets.—*I Henry VI,* ii, 4, 17. The only uses of "quillets" (quibbles).

5 Since you can cog, I 'll play no more with you.
Love's Labour's Lost. Act v, sc. 2, l. 235. [Princess of France] Biron has mentioned dice, and the Princess is playing with the idea of cogged dice.

I cannot . . . cog.—*Richard III,* i, 3, 48; *The Merry Wives of Windsor,* iii, 3, 50; 76.

You hear him cog.—*Timon of Athens,* v, 1, 98. "Cog" (cheat) occurs also in *Much Ado about Nothing,* v, 1, 95, and in *Coriolanus,* iii, 2, 133.

6 I will be cheater to them both, and they shall be exchequers to me.
The Merry Wives of Windsor. Act i, sc. 3, l. 77. [Falstaff]

I will bar . . . no cheater.
II Henry IV. Act ii, sc. 4, l. 111. [Hostess]

I play'd the cheater for thy father's hand.
Titus Andronicus. Act v, sc. 1, l. 111. [Aaron]

Damned cheater.—*II Henry IV,* ii, 4, 152.

Disguised cheaters.—*The Comedy of Errors,* i, 2, 101.

Gentle cheater.—*Sonnets,* cli.

Tame cheater.—*II Henry IV,* ii, 4, 106. The only uses of "cheater."

7 Cousins, indeed; and by their uncle cozen'd
Of comfort, kingdom, kindred, freedom, life.
Richard III. Act iv, sc. 4, l. 222. [Queen Elizabeth]

There is three cozen-germans that has cozened all the hosts of Readins. . . . 'Tis not convenient you should be cozened.
The Merry Wives of Windsor. Act iv, sc. 5, l. 79. [Evans] The only use of "cozen-germans." "Cousin-german" occurs in *Troilus and Cressida,* iv, 5, 121.

8 Take heed, Signior Baptista, lest you be cony-catched in this business.
The Taming of the Shrew. Act v, sc. 1, l. 101. [Gremio] The only use of "cony-catched." "Cony-catching" occurs twice, in *The Taming of the Shrew,* iv, 1, 45, and *The Merry Wives of Windsor,* i, 1, 128.

9 Clown: I was cozened by the way and lost all my money.
Autolycus: And indeed, sir, there are cozeners abroad; therefore it behoves men to be wary.
The Winter's Tale. Act iv, sc. 4, l. 254.

The devil take such cozeners!—*I Henry IV,* i, 3, 255.

The usurer hangs the cozener.—*King Lear,* iv, 6, 167. The only uses of "cozener."

CHEEK

See also Face

10 His left cheek is a cheek of two pile and a half, but his right cheek is worn bare.
All's Well that Ends Well. Act iv, sc. 5, l. 102. [Clown] The only use of "left cheek." "Right cheek" occurs again in *Cymbeline,* iv, 2, 211.

My mother's blood
Runs on the dexter cheek, and this sinister
Bounds in my father's.
Troilus and Cressida. Act iv, sc. 5, l. 127 [Hector] The only use of "dexter."

Sinister cheek.—*All's Well that Ends Well,* ii, 1, 44.

11 We have burnt our cheeks.
Antony and Cleopatra, ii, 7, 129. See under DRINKING.

1
Put colour in thy cheek.
Antony and Cleopatra. Act iv, sc. 14, l. 69. [Antony]
The silly boy, believing she is dead,
Claps her pale cheek, till clapping makes it red.
Venus and Adonis, l. 467.
2 Nature presently distill'd
Helen's cheek, but not her heart.
As You Like It. Act iii, sc. 2, l. 152. [Celia]
3 Our veil'd dames
Commit the war of white and damask in
Their nicely-gawded cheeks to the wanton spoil
Of Phœbus' burning kisses.
Coriolanus. Act ii, sc. 1, l. 231. [Brutus] The only use of "nicely-gawded."
Forget that rarest treasure of your cheek,
Exposing it—but, O, the harder heart!
Alack, no remedy!—to the greedy touch
Of common-kissing Titan.
Cymbeline. Act iii, sc. 4, l. 163. [Pisanio] The only use of "common-kissing." Titan is mentioned six times.
4 Your cheeks do counterfeit our roses;
For pale they look with fear.
I Henry VI. Act ii, sc. 4, l. 62. [Plantagenet]
Their cheeks are paper.—*Henry V,* ii, 2, 74.
These cheeks are pale for watching for your good.
II Henry VI. Act iv, sc. 7, l. 90. [Say]
Why is your cheek so pale?
How chance the roses there do fade so fast?
A Midsummer-Night's Dream. Act i, sc. 1, l. 128. [Lysander]
Pale and pined cheek.—*A Lover's Complaint,* l. 32.
But now her cheek was pale and by and by
It flashed forth fire.
Venus and Adonis, l. 347.
Calpurnia's cheek is pale.—*Julius Cæsar,* i, 2, 185.
Make pale our cheek.—*Richard II,* ii, 1, 118.
Pale cheeks.—*Venus and Adonis,* l. 1169.
5
The sanguine colour of the leaves
Did represent my master's blushing cheeks.
I Henry VI. Act iv, sc. 1, l. 92. See also under BLUSHING.
Red cheeks.—*Venus and Adonis,* l. 219.
Rosy cheek.—*The Rape of Lucrece,* l. 386; *Sonnets,* cxvi.
6
Thou bear'st a cheek for blows.
King Lear, iv, 2, 51. See under COWARDICE.
Threaten'd cheeks.—*King John,* ii, 1, 225.
Sphered bias cheek.—*Troilus and Cressida,* iv, 5, 8. "Sphered" is used again in i, 3, 90, and in no other play.
Welkin's cheek.—*The Tempest,* i, 2, 4.
7
While I thy amiable cheeks do coy.
A Midsummer-Night's Dream. Act iv, sc. 1, l. 2. [Titania]
She strokes his cheek!—*Troilus and Cressida,* v, 2, 51.
His tenderer cheek receives her soft hand's print,
As apt as new-fall'n snow takes any dint.
Venus and Adonis, l. 353. The only use of "tenderer."
Delicate cheek.—*Antony and Cleopatra,* ii, 2, 209; *King Lear,* iv, 3, 15.
Fresh cheek.—*As You Like It,* iii, 5, 29.
Gentle cheeks.—*II Henry IV,* iv, 5, 84.
Praised cheeks.—*Troilus and Cressida,* iv, 2, 113.
Smiling cheek.—*Merchant of Venice,* i, 3, 101.
Soft cheek.—*Sonnets,* xcix.
Cheek of night.—*Romeo and Juliet,* i, 5, 47.
Cloudy cheeks of heaven.—*Richard II,* iii, 3, 57.
Wide cheeks o' the air.—*Coriolanus,* v, 3, 151.
8
Her fair cheeks over-wash'd with woe.
The Rape of Lucrece, l. 1225. The only use of "over-wash'd."
Fair cheek.—*Love's Labour 's Lost,* iv, 3, 235; *Henry VIII,* i, 4, 44.
9
Her cheeks with chops and wrinkles were disguised.
The Rape of Lucrece, l. 1452. The only use of "chops" for chaps.
Grey cheeks.—*Sonnets,* cxxxii.
Lank-lean cheeks.—*Henry V,* iv, Prol., 26. The only use of "lank-lean."
With lank and lean discolour'd cheek.—*The Rape of Lucrece,* 708.
Sallow cheeks.—*Romeo and Juliet,* ii, 3, 70. The only use of "sallow."
Yellow cheek.—*II Henry IV,* i, 2, 204.
10
Cheeks neither red nor pale, but mingled so
That blushing red no guilty instance gave,
Nor ashy pale the fear that false hearts have.
The Rape of Lucrece, l. 1510.
11
Two of the fairest stars in all the heaven,
Having some business, do entreat her eyes
To twinkle in their spheres till they return.
What if her eyes were there, they in her head?
The brightness of her cheek would shame those stars,
As daylight doth a lamp.
Romeo and Juliet. Act ii, sc. 2, l. 15. [Romeo] The only use of "twinkle."
See, how she leans her cheek upon her hand!
O, that I were a glove upon that hand,
That I might touch that cheek!
Romeo and Juliet. Act ii, sc. 2, l. 23. [Romeo]
12
I have seen roses damask'd, red and white,
But no such roses see I in her cheeks.
Sonnets. No. cxxx. The only use of "damask'd."
Such war of white and red within her cheeks!
The Taming of the Shrew. Act iv, sc. 5, l. 30. [Petruchio]
Damask cheek.—*Twelfth Night,* ii, 4, 115.
13
Thus is his cheek the map of days outworn,
When beauty lived and died as flowers do now,
Before these bastard signs of fair were born,

Or durst inhabit on a living brow.
Sonnets. No. lxviii.

1 Let not the virgin's cheek
Make soft thy trenchant sword.
Timon of Athens, iv, 3, 114. See under VIRGIN.

2 Behold our cheeks
How they are stain'd, as meadows, yet not dry,
With miry slime left on them by a flood.
Titus Andronicus. Act iii, sc. 1, l. 124. [Titus] "Miry" is repeated in *Titus Andronicus,* iii, 1, 126.

Each cheek a river running from a fount.
A Lover's Complaint, l. 283.

Wet cheeks.—*Cymbeline,* v, 5, 35.

3
Wishing her cheeks were gardens full of flowers,
So they were dew'd with such distilling showers.
Venus and Adonis, l. 65. The only use of "dew'd" and "distilling."

CHEERFULNESS

See also Happiness, Mirth

4
I prithee, lady, have a better cheer.
All's Well that Ends Well. Act iii, sc. 2, l. 67. [Countess]

Show a merry cheer.—*The Merchant of Venice,* iii, 2, 314.

Cheer your heart.—*III Henry VI,* ii, 2, 4; *Richard III,* v, 3, 174; *Titus Andronicus,* i, 1, 457; *Antony and Cleopatra,* iii, 6, 81.

This cheers my heart.—*III Henry VI,* v, 4, 65.

Cheerer of the heart.—*Henry V,* v, 2, 41. The only use of "cheerer."

5
My sovereign lord, cheer up yourself, look up.
II Henry IV. Act iv, sc. 4, l. 113. [Westmoreland]

Cheer thy spirit with this comfort.
I Henry VI. Act i, sc. 4, l. 90. [Talbot]

Then cheer thy spirit.—*Titus Andronicus,* iv, 4, 88.

Cheer our drooping spirits.—*I Henry VI,* v, 2, 1.

Cheer up your spirits.—*III Henry VI,* ii, 2, 56.

Cheer we up his sprites.—*Macbeth,* iv, 1, 127.

6
To lay aside life-harming heaviness
And entertain a cheerful disposition.
Richard II. Act ii, sc. 2, l. 3. [Bushy] The only use of "life-harming."

Be of good cheer.—*Richard III,* iv, 1, 36; *Merchant of Venice,* iii, 5, 6; *Henry V,* ii, 3, 19; *As You Like It,* iv, 3, 164; *Antony and Cleopatra,* v, 2, 21; *Henry VIII,* v, 1, 142.

Be cheerful.—*Richard III,* v, 3, 121; *As You Like It,* i, 3, 96; *Merry Wives of Windsor,* v, 5, 179; *Cymbeline,* iv, 2, 402; *The Tempest,* iv, 1, 147; v, 1, 250; *Pericles,* iv, 1, 40.

7
In God's name, cheerly on, courageous friends.
Richard III. Act v, sc. 2, l. 14. [Richmond]

Well said! thou lookest cheerly.—*As You Like It,* ii, 6, 14.

Prithee, man, look cheerly.—*Timon of Athens,* ii, 2, 223.

Cheerly, my hearts!—*Romeo and Juliet,* i, 5, 90; *The Tempest,* i, 1, 6; i, 1, 29. See also *As You Like It,* ii, 6, 19; *I Henry IV,* iv, 4, 44; *Henry V,* ii, 2, 192; *Romeo and Juliet,* i, 5, 16; *III Henry VI,* v, 4, 2; *Richard II,* i, 3, 66. The only uses of "cheerly."

8
His grace looks cheerfully and smooth today;
There 's some conceit or other likes him well,
When he doth bid good morrow with such a spirit.
Richard III. Act iii, sc. 4, l. 50. [Hastings]

Look cheerfully upon me.—*The Taming of the Shrew,* iv, 3, 38.

God-a-mercy, old heart! thou speak'st cheerfully.—*Henry V,* iv, 1, 34.

Madam, good hope; his grace speaks cheerfully.—*Richard III,* i, 3, 34.

How cheerfully my mother looks.—*Hamlet,* iii, 2, 134.

How cheerfully on the false trail they cry.—*Hamlet,* iv, 5, 109.

Fight cheerfully.—*Henry V,* iv, 1, 204.

Go cheerfully.—*I Henry VI,* iv, 1, 167.

Boldly and cheerfully.—*Richard III,* v, 3, 269. The only uses of "cheerfully."

9
I have not that alacrity of spirit,
Nor cheer of mind, that I was wont to have.
Richard III. Act v, sc. 3, l. 73. [King Richard]

What cheer?—*The Tempest,* i, 1, 2.

CHEESE

10
You Banbury cheese.
The Merry Wives of Windsor. Act i, sc. 1, l. 130. [Bardolph] The taunt is addressed to Slender, and refers to the proverb, "As thin as a Banbury cheese."

Made after supper of a cheese-paring.
II Henry IV, iii, 2, 332. See under CHARACTER. The only use of "cheese-paring."

11
There 's pippins and cheese to come.
The Merry Wives of Windsor. Act i, sc. 2. l. 13. [Evans] "Pippin" is repeated in *II Henry IV,* v, 3, 2.

12
I love not the humour of bread and cheese.
The Merry Wives of Windsor. Act ii, sc. 1, l. 140. [Nym]

'Tis time I were choked with a piece of toasted cheese.
The Merry Wives of Windsor. Act v, sc. 5, l. 146. [Falstaff] "Toasted cheese" is repeated in *II Henry VI,* iv, 7, 13; and *King Lear,* iv, 6, 90. "Toast cheese" occurs in *Henry V,* ii, 1, 9.

13
Why, my cheese, my digestion, why hast thou not served thyself in to my table so many meals?
Troilus and Cressida. Act ii, sc. 3, l. 44. [Achilles]

That stale old mouse-eaten dry cheese.
Troilus and Cressida. Act v, sc. 4, l. 11. [Thersites] The only use of "mouse-eaten."

CHIDING

See also Reproof

1
Sweet youth, I pray you, chide a year together:
I had rather hear you chide than this man woo.
As You Like It. Act iii, sc. 5, l. 64. [Phebe]
Call you this chiding?—*As You Like It,* iv, 3, 67.
Churlish chiding.—*As You Like It,* ii, 1, 7.
2
Thou wilt be horribly chid to-morrow when thou comest to thy father.
I Henry IV. Act ii, sc. 4, l. 410. [Falstaff]
I should have chid you.—*The Comedy of Errors,* iv, 1, 50.
And chid the painter for his wondrous skill.
The Rape of Lucrece, l. 1528.
How churlishly I chid Lucetta hence.
The Two Gentlemen of Verona. Act i, sc. 2, l. 60. [Julia] The only use of "churlishly."
3
Then must I chide outright.
II Henry VI. Act i, sc. 2, l. 41. [Gloucester]
Sweetly chide thee.—*Sonnets,* viii.
Chide as loud As thunder.—*The Taming of the Shrew,* i, 2, 95.
Chide your trespass.—*Henry V,* ii, 4, 125.
Chide my fortune.—*Richard III,* ii, 2, 35.
Chide away this shame.—*Romeo and Juliet,* iv, 1, 74.
Chide the cripple tardy-gaited night.—*Henry V,* iv, Prol., 20. Only use of "tardy-gaited."
Chides the dice.—*Love's Labour 's Lost,* v, 2, 326.
Chides the sea.—*III Henry VI,* iii, 2, 138.
4
You chide at him, offending twice as much.
Love's Labour 's Lost. Act iv, sc. 3, l. 132. [King]
Better a little chiding than a great deal of heart-break.
The Merry Wives of Windsor. Act v, sc. 3, l. 11. [Mrs. Page] The only use of "heart-break." "Heart-breaking" occurs in *Antony and Cleopatra,* i, 2, 74.
5
We shall chide downright, if I longer stay.
A Midsummer-Night's Dream. Act ii, sc. 1, l. 145. [Titania]
Now I but chide; but I should use thee worse.
A Midsummer-Night's Dream. Act iii, sc. 2, l. 45. [Hermia]
6
Those that do teach young babes
Do it with gentle means and easy tasks:
He might have chid me so; for, in good faith,
I am a child to chiding.
Othello. Act iv, sc. 2, l. 111. [Desdemona]
He does chide with you.—*Othello,* iv, 2, 167.
O what a beast was I to chide at him!
Romeo and Juliet. Act iii, sc. 2, l. 95. [Juliet]
Bid my sweet prepare to chide.
Romeo and Juliet. Act iii, sc. 3, l. 162. [Romeo]
I pray thee, chide not.—*Romeo and Juliet,* ii, 3, 85.
Chide me no more.—*Coriolanus,* iii, 2, 132.
Do not you chide.—*Othello,* iii, 3, 301.
I 'll not chide thee.—*King Lear,* ii, 4, 228.
I will no further chide you.—*Twelfth Night,* iii, 3, 3.
It is no time to chide you now.
The Taming of the Shrew. Act i, sc. 1, l. 164. [Tranio]
I love no chiders, sir.
The Taming of the Shrew. Act i, sc. 2, l. 228. [Tranio] The only use of "chiders."
7
If he flinch, chide me for it.
Troilus and Cressida. Act iii, sc. 2, l. 114. [Pandarus] Also v, 3, 39. "Flinch" is repeated in *All 's Well that Ends Well,* ii, 1, 190.
By and by intend to chide myself.—*The Two Gentlemen of Verona,* iv, 2, 103.
8
Chide me, dear stone, that I may say indeed
Thou art Hermione.
Winter's Tale. Act v, sc. 3, l. 24. [Leontes]
Thou chidest me well.—*Richard II,* iii, 2, 188.

CHILD

See also Boy, Girl, Infancy, Issue, Son, Youth

9
His sole child, my lord, and bequeathed to my overlooking.
All 's Well that Ends Well. Act i, sc. 1, l. 44. [Countess] "O'er-looking" occurs in *King Lear,* i, 2, 40.
Second Gentleman: Is she sole child to the king?
First Gentleman: His only child.
Cymbeline. Act i, sc. 1, l. 56.
Thou art all my child.—*All 's Well that Ends Well,* iii, 2, 71.
10
I . . . put you in the catalogue of those
That were enwombed mine.
All 's Well that Ends Well. Act i, sc. 3, l. 148. [Countess] The only use of "enwombed."
My dear wife 's estimate, her womb's increase,
And treasure of my loins.
Coriolanus. Act iii, sc. 3, l. 114. [Cominius]
My flesh, my child!—*Cymbeline,* v, 5, 264.
11
Let me have a child at fifty, to whom Herod of Jewry may do homage.
Antony and Cleopatra. Act i, sc. 2, l. 27. [Charmian]
Charmian: How many boys and wenches must I have?
Soothsayer: If every of your wishes had a womb,
And fertile every wish, a million.
Antony and Cleopatra. Act i, sc. 2, l. 36.
Royal wench!
She made great Cæsar lay his sword to bed:
He plough'd her, and she cropp'd.
Antony and Cleopatra. Act ii, sc. 2, l. 231. [Agrippa]
12
'Tis such fools as you
That makes the world full of ill-favour'd children.
As You Like It. Act iii, sc. 5, l. 52. [Rosalind]
Forlorn children.—*Titus Andronicus,* ii, 3, 153.
Poor children!—*Richard III,* i, 4, 72.
Poor child.—*King John,* iv, 2, 97.

Unbridled children.—*Troilus and Cressida,* iii, 2, 130.
Unconstant children.—*King John,* iii, 1, 243.

1
Valeria: Indeed, la, 'tis a noble child.
Virgilia: A crack, madam.
Coriolanus. Act i, sc. 3, l. 74.
When a' was a crack not thus high.
II Henry IV. Act iii, sc. 2, l. 34. [Shallow] The only uses of "crack" in the sense of a pert boy.
Active child.—*Sonnets,* xxxvii.
Christom child.—*Henry V,* ii, 3, 12. The only use of "christom" (child in its christening-robe, innocent).
Pretty child.—*King John,* iv, 1, 130.
Proud child.—*Timon of Athens,* iv, 3, 180.

2
There is, sir, an aery of children, little eyases, that cry out on the top of question, and are most tyrannically clapped for 't.
Hamlet. Act ii, sc. 2, l. 354. [Rosencrantz] The only use of "eyases." It is a term in falconry, meaning a hawk which has been brought up from the nest, as distinguished from one caught and trained. In *The Merry Wives of Windsor,* iii, 3, 22, is the phrase, "How now, my eyas-musket!" an eyas-musket being an unfledged male hawk. The term is applied by Mrs. Ford to the boy Robin. Also the only use of "tyrannically."
The indifferent children of the earth.
Hamlet. Act ii, sc. 2, l. 231. [Rosencrantz]
Children rawly left.—*Henry V,* iv, 1, 147.

3 O that it could be proved
That some night-tripping fairy had exchanged
In cradle-clothes our children where they lay.
I Henry IV. Act i, sc. 1, l. 86. [King Henry] The only use of "night-tripping" and "cradle-clothes."

4
The midwives say the children are not in the fault; whereupon the world increases, and kindreds are mightily strengthened.
II Henry IV. Act ii, sc. 2, l. 29. [Prince of Wales]
An the child I now go with do miscarry, thou wert better thou hadst struck thy mother, thou paper-faced villain.
II Henry IV. Act v, sc. 4, l. 10. [Doll Tearsheet] The only use of "paper-faced."
Shalt not thou and I, between Saint Denis and Saint George, compound a boy, half French, half English, that shall go to Constantinople and take the Turk by the beard? shall we not? what sayest thou, my fair flower-de-luce?
Henry V. Act v, sc. 2, l. 219. [King Henry]

5
'Tis much when sceptres are in children's hands.
I Henry VI. Act iv, sc. 1, l. 192. [Exeter]
What, shall a child instruct you what to do?
I Henry VI. Act iii, sc. 1, l. 133. [Warwick]
Woe to that land that 's govern'd by a child!
Richard III. Act ii, sc. 3, l. 11. [Citizen]
Your children shall be kings.
Macbeth. Act i, sc. 3, l. 86. [Macbeth]

6
Happy for so sweet a child.
I Henry VI. Act v, sc. 3, l. 148. [Suffolk]
Sweet child.—*King John,* iv, 2, 81.

7
Not me begotten of a shepherd swain,
But issued from the progeny of kings.
I Henry VI. Act v, sc. 4, l. 37. [La Pucelle]
Bragg'd progeny.—*Coriolanus,* i, 8, 12.
Lawful progeny.—*I Henry VI,* iii, 3, 61.
Brow of progeny.—*Love's Labour 's Lost,* v, 2, 754.
Progeny of evils.—*A Midsummer-Night's Dream,* ii, 1, 115. The only uses of "progeny."

8 Murder not this innocent child,
Lest thou be hated both of God and man!
III Henry VI. Act i, sc. 3, l. 8. [Tutor]
Innocent child.—*King John,* iv, 2, 259; *Much Ado about Nothing,* v, 1, 63; 67; 274; *The Tempest,* iii, 3, 72.
Incapable and shallow innocents.
Richard III. Act ii, sc. 2, l. 18. [Duchess of York]

9
Unreasonable creatures feed their young;
And though man's face be fearful to their eyes,
Yet, in protection of their tender ones,
Who hath not seen them, even with those wings
Which sometime they have used with fearful flight,
Make war with him that climb'd unto their nest,
Offering their own lives in their young's defence?
III Henry VI. Act ii, sc. 2, l. 26. [Clifford]

10
Clarence: I think he means to beg a child of her.
Gloucester: Nay, whip me then: he'll rather give her two.
III Henry VI. Act iii, sc. 2, l. 27.
King Edward: Now tell me, madam, do you love your children?
Lady Grey: Ay, full as dearly as I love myself.
III Henry VI. Act iii, sc. 2, l. 36.
Lady Grey: 'Twill grieve your grace my sons should call you father.
King Edward: No more than when my daughters call thee mother.
III Henry VI. Act iii, sc. 2, l. 100.
Thou art a widow, and thou hast some children;
And, by God's mother, I, being but a bachelor,
Have other some.
III Henry VI. Act iii, sc. 2, l. 102. [King Edward]

11
And I the rather wean me from despair
For love of Edward's offspring in my womb.
III Henry VI. Act iv, sc. 4, l. 17. [Queen Elizabeth]
Wean them from themselves.—*Titus Andronicus,* i, 1, 211.
Take all, and wean it.—*Love's Labour 's Lost,* v, 2, 250. The only uses of "wean."
She was wean'd.—*Romeo and Juliet,* i, 3, 24. The only use of "wean'd."
Lest with my sighs or tears I blast or drown

King Edward's fruit, true heir to the English crown.
III Henry VI. Act iv, sc. 4, l. 23. [Queen Elizabeth]

1
Men ne'er spend their fury on a child.
III Henry VI. Act v, sc. 5, l. 57. [Queen Margaret]

2
But from this lady may proceed a gem
To lighten all this isle.
Henry VIII. Act ii, sc. 3, l. 78. [Lord Chamberlain]

3
The jewels of our father.
King Lear. Act i, sc. 1, l. 271. [Cordelia]
Jewel of children.—*Winter's Tale,* v, 1, 116.

4
How sharper than a serpent's tooth it is
To have a thankless child!
King Lear. Act i, sc. 4, l. 310. [King Lear]
Bad child.—*Pericles,* i, Gower, 27.
Forward child.—*As You Like It,* iii, 3, 14.
Impatient child.—*Romeo and Juliet,* iii, 2, 30.
Neglected child.—*Sonnets,* cxliii.
Oppressed child.—*King John,* ii, 1, 245.
Child of fancy.—*Love's Labour's Lost,* i, 1, 171.
Child of hell.—*Henry V,* iv, 1, 288.
Child of honour.—*I Henry IV,* iii, 2, 139; *Henry VIII,* iv, 2, 6.
Child of integrity.—*Macbeth,* iv, 3, 115.
Child of spleen.—*King Lear,* i, 4, 304.
Child of state.—*Sonnets,* cxxiv.
Child of our grandmother Eve.—*Love's Labour's Lost,* i, 1, 266.
Be a child o' the time.—*Antony and Cleopatra,* ii, 7, 106.

5 Bring forth men-children only;
For thy undaunted mettle should compose
Nothing but males.
Macbeth. Act i, sc. 7, l. 72. [Macbeth] The only use of "men-children."
Male child.—*King John,* iii, 4, 79; *Henry VIII,* ii, 4, 189.

6 All my pretty ones?
Did you say all? O hell-kite! All?
What, all my pretty chickens and their dam
At one fell swoop?
Macbeth. Act iv, sc. 3, l. 216. [Macduff] The only use of "hell-kite" and "fell swoop."

7
His child is a year and a quarter old, come Philip and Jacob.
Measure for Measure. Act iii, sc. 2, l. 213. [Mrs. Overdone] The festival of St. Philip and St. Jacob (or St. James) is May 1st.
My father's child!—*The Merchant of Venice,* ii, 3, 17.

8
'Tis not good that children should know any wickedness.
The Merry Wives of Windsor. Act ii, sc. 2, l. 133. [Mistress Quickly]

9
I then did ask of her her changeling child.
A Midsummer-Night's Dream. Act iv, sc. 1, l. 64. [Oberon]
So sweet a changeling.—*A Midsummer-Night's Dream,* ii, 1, 23. See also under Boy.
This is some changeling.—*The Winter's Tale,* iii, 3, 122.
She's a changeling and none of your flesh and blood.
The Winter's Tale. Act iv, sc. 4, l. 704. [Clown]
No changeling.—*Coriolanus,* iv, 7, 11.
The changeling never known.—*Hamlet,* v, 2, 53.
Changeling boy.—*Midsummer-Night's Dream,* ii, 1, 120.
Fickle changelings.—*I Henry IV,* v, 1, 76. The only uses of "changeling."

10
Never mole, hare-lip, nor scar,
Nor mark prodigious, such as are
Despised in nativity,
Shall upon their children be.
A Midsummer-Night's Dream. Act v, sc. 1, l. 418. [Oberon] "Hare-lip" is repeated in *King Lear,* iii, 4, 123.

11
The world must be peopled.
Much Ado about Nothing. Act ii, sc. 3, l. 251. [Benedick]
Thou wast begot; to get it is thy duty.
Venus and Adonis, l. 168.
I had rather to adopt a child than get it.
Othello. Act i, sc. 3, l. 191. [Brabantio]
She never yet was foolish that was fair;
For even her folly help'd her to an heir.
Othello. Act ii, sc. 1, l. 137. [Iago]

12
This bastard graff shall never come to growth.
The Rape of Lucrece, l. 1062.
Bastard children.—*Coriolanus,* iv, 5, 240. See also Bastard.

13
If children pre-decease progenitors,
We are their offspring, and they none of ours.
The Rape of Lucrece, l. 1756. The only use of "pre-decease."
Give his offspring life.—*King John,* ii, 1, 13.
Edward's offspring.—*III Henry VI,* iv, 4, 18.
Hagar's offspring.—*The Merchant of Venice,* ii, 5, 44. The only mention of Hagar.
Accursed the offspring of so foul a fiend!
Titus Andronicus. Act iv, sc. 2, l. 79. [Demetrius]
Offspring of the house of Lancaster.—*Richard III,* v, 3, 136.
Valiant offspring.—*Troilus and Cressida,* ii, 2, 207. The only uses of "offspring."

14
The pleasure that some fathers feed upon,
Is my strict fast; I mean, my children's looks.
Richard II. Act ii, sc. 1, l. 79. [Gaunt]

15
If ever he have child, abortive be it,
Prodigious, and untimely brought to light,
Whose ugly and unnatural aspect
May fright the hopeful mother at the view.
Richard III. Act i, sc. 2, l. 21. [Lady Anne]
Thou slander of thy mother's heavy womb!
Thou loathed issue of thy father's loins!
Richard III. Act i, sc. 3, l. 231. [Queen Margaret]

1
I am too childish-foolish for this world.
Richard III. Act i, sc. 3, l. 142. [Gloucester] The only use of "childish-foolish."

You'll turn a child again.—*Pericles,* iv, 3, 4.

Make the young old, and the old become a child.
Venus and Adonis, l. 1152. See under LOVE.

I am no child.—*The Taming of the Shrew,* iv, 3, 74.

2
Where are thy children? wherein dost thou joy?
Richard III. Act iv, sc. 4, l. 93. [Queen Margaret]

Tell me, thou villain slave, where are my children?
Richard III. Act iv, sc. 4, l. 144. [Queen Elizabeth]

If I have kill'd the issue of your womb,
To quicken your increase, I will beget
Mine issue of your blood upon your daughter.
Richard III. Act iv, sc. 4, l. 296. [King Richard]

Your children were vexation to your youth,
But mine shall be a comfort to your age.
Richard III. Act iv, sc. 4, l. 305. [King Richard]

Queen Elizabeth: But thou didst kill my children.
King Richard: But in your daughter's womb I bury them:
Where in that nest of spicery they shall breed
Selves of themselves, to your recomforture.
Richard III. Act iv, sc. 4, l. 422. The only use of "spicery" and "recomforture."

If you do free your children from the sword,
Your children's children quit it in your age.
Richard III. Act v, sc. 3, l. 261. [Richmond]

Our children's children.—*Henry VIII,* v, 5, 55.

Child, child's children.—*Richard II,* iv, 1, 149.

Children yet unborn.—*Richard II,* iv, 1, 322.

3 Wife, we scarce thought us blest
That God had lent us but this only child;
But now I see this one is one too much,
And that we have a curse in having her.
Romeo and Juliet. Act iii, sc. 5, l. 165. [Capulet]

Grieved I, I had but one?
Chid I for that at frugal nature's frame?
O, one too much by thee! Why had I one?
Much Ado about Nothing. Act iv, sc. 1, l. 129. [Leonato]

For your sake, jewel,
I am glad at soul I have no other child;
For thy escape would teach me tyranny,
To hang clogs on them.
Othello. Act i, sc. 3, l. 195. [Brabantio]

4
O me, O me! My child, my only life,
Revive, look up, or I will die with thee!
Romeo and Juliet. Act iv, sc. 5, l. 19. [Lady Capulet]

But one, poor one, one poor and loving child,
But one thing to rejoice and solace in,
And cruel death hath catch'd it from my sight!
Romeo and Juliet. Act iv, sc. 5, l. 46. [Lady Capulet] "Loving child" is repeated in *Titus Andronicus,* v, 3, 166.

O child! O child! my soul, and not my child!
Dead art thou! Alack! my child is dead;
And with my child my joys are buried.
Romeo and Juliet. Act iv, sc. 5, l. 62. [Capulet]

O, in this love, you love your child so ill,
That you run mad, seeing that she is well.
Romeo and Juliet. Act iv, sc. 5, l. 75. [Friar Laurence]

5
If thou couldst answer 'This fair child of mine,
Shall sum my count and make my old excuse,'
Proving his beauty by succession thine!
This were to be new made when thou art old,
And see thy blood warm when thou feel'st it cold.
Sonnets. No. ii.

That's for thyself to breed another thee,
Or ten times happier, be it ten for one;
Ten times thyself were happier than thou art,
If ten of thine ten times refigured thee.
Sonnets. No. vi. The only use of "refigured."

Let those whom Nature hath not made for store,
Harsh, featureless and rude, barrenly perish. . . .
She carved thee for her seal, and meant thereby
Thou shouldst print more, not let that copy die.
Sonnets. No. xi. The only use of "featureless" and "barrenly."

Against this coming end you should prepare,
And your sweet semblance to some other give.
So should that beauty which you hold in lease
Find no determination.
Sonnets. No. xiii.

Upon the earth's increase why shouldst thou feed,
Unless the earth with thy increase be fed?
By law of nature thou art bound to breed,
That thine may live when thou thyself art dead;
And so, in spite of death, thou dost survive,
In that thy likeness still is left alive.
Venus and Adonis, l. 169.

'Tis a good hearing when children are toward.
The Taming of the Shrew. Act v, sc. 2, l. 182. [Vincentio]

6
She will become thy bed, I warrant,
And bring thee forth brave brood.
The Tempest. Act iii, sc. 2, l. 112. [Caliban]

Pandarus: He! no, she'll none of him; they two are twain.
Helen: Falling in, after falling out, may make them three.
Troilus and Cressida. Act iii, sc. 1, l. 111.

7 Let no man but I
Do execution on my flesh and blood.
Titus Andronicus. Act iv, sc. 2, l. 83. [Aaron] See also under FLESH.

8
Save thou the child, so we may all be safe.
Titus Andronicus. Act iv, sc. 2, l. 131. [Demetrius]

His child is like to her, fair as you are.
Titus Andronicus. Act iv, sc. 2, l. 154. [Aaron]

First hang the child, that he may see it sprawl;
A sight to vex the father's soul withal.
Titus Andronicus. Act v, sc. 1, l. 51. [Lucius] The only use of "sprawl."

Thy child shall live, and I will see it nourish'd.
Titus Andronicus. Act v, sc. 1, l. 60. [Lucius]

1
It is a gallant child; one that indeed physics the subject, makes old hearts fresh.
The Winter's Tale. Act i, sc. 1, l. 42. [Camillo]

A very pretty barne! A boy or a child, I wonder? A pretty one; a very pretty one.
The Winter's Tale. Act iii, sc. 3, l. 71. [Shepherd]

They say barnes are blessings.
All's Well that Ends Well, i, 3, 28. The only use of "barnes" (bairns).

2
This brat is none of mine; . . .
Hence with it, and together with the dam
Commit them to the fire!
The Winter's Tale. Act ii, sc. 3. l. 92. [Leontes]

Thy brat hath been cast out, like to itself,
No father owning it.
The Winter's Tale. Act iii, sc. 2. l. 88. [Leontes]

That peevish brat.—*Richard III,* i, 3, 194.

Brats and beggary.—*Cymbeline,* ii, 3, 124.

3
My child? away with 't! Even thou, that hast
A heart so tender o'er it, take it hence
And see it instantly consumed with fire.
The Winter's Tale, Act ii, sc. 3, l. 132. [Leontes]

What might I have been,
Might I a son and daughter now have look'd on,
Such goodly things as you!
The Winter's Tale. Act v, sc. 1, l. 176. [Leontes]

I am past moe children, but thy sons and daughters will be all gentlemen born.
The Winter's Tale. Act v, sc. 2, l. 138. [Shepherd]

CHIN

See also Beard

4
His chin new reap'd
Show'd like a stubble-land at harvest-home.
I Henry IV. Act i, sc. 2, l. 34. [Hotspur] The only use of "stubble-land." "Harvest-home" is repeated in *The Merry Wives of Windsor,* ii, 2, 287.

5
Is not . . . your chin double?
II Henry IV. Act i, sc. 2, l. 206. [Chief Justice]

Amazonian chin.—*Coriolanus,* ii, 2, 95.

Her snow-white dimpled chin.—*The Rape of Lucrece,* l. 420.

Cloven chin.—*Troilus and Cressida,* i, 2, 132.

6
Whose chin is but enrich'd
With one appearing hair.
Henry V. Act iii, Prol., l. 22. [Chorus]

Whose chin is not yet fledged.—*II Henry IV,* i, 2, 23.

Alas, poor chin! many a wart is richer.
Troilus and Cressida. Act i, sc. 2, l. 155. [Cressida]

Is . . . his chin worth a beard?—*As You Like It,* iii, 2, 217.

7
Till new-born chins Be rough and razorable.
The Tempest. Act ii, sc. 1, l. 249. [Antonio] The only use of "razorable."

Stroke your chins.—*As You Like It,* i, 2, 76.

Up to the chins.—*The Tempest,* iv, 1, 183.

CHIVALRY

See also Knighthood

8
For my part, I may speak it to my shame,
I have a truant been to chivalry.
I Henry IV. Act v, sc. 1, l. 93. [Prince of Wales]

9
Did all the chivalry of England move
To do brave acts.
II Henry IV. Act ii, sc. 3, l. 20. [Lady Percy]

10
With one appearing hair, that will not follow
These cull'd and choice-drawn cavaliers to France?
Henry V. Act iii, Prol., l. 24. [Chorus] The only use of "choice-drawn" and "cavaliers."

11
Break a lance, and run a tilt at death.
I Henry VI. Act 3, sc. 2, l. 50. [La Pucelle]

Ran'st a tilt in honour of my love.
II Henry VI. Act i, sc. 3, l. 54. [Queen]

There shall he practise tilts and tournaments.
The Two Gentlemen of Verona. Act i, sc. 3, l. 30. [Panthino] The only mention of tournaments.

He tilts With piercing steel.—*Romeo and Juliet,* iii, 1, 163.

Lo, he is tilting straight!
Love's Labour's Lost. Act v, sc. 2, l. 483. [Biron]

Tilting one at other's breast,
In opposition bloody.
Othello, ii, 3, 183. See FRIEND, 591:8.

A puisny tilter, that spurs his horse but on one side.
As You Like It. Act iii, sc. 4, l. 46. [Celia] The only use of "puisny" (paltry). "Tilter" is repeated in *Measure for Measure,* iv, 3, 17.

I'll be sworn a' ne'er saw him but once in the Tilt-yard.
II Henry IV. Act iii, sc. 2, l. 347. [Falstaff]

His study is his tilt-yard.
II Henry VI, i, 3, 62. The only uses of "tilt-yard."

12
Thou art seal'd the son of chivalry.
I Henry VI. Act iv, sc. 6, l. 29. [Talbot]

The prince of chivalry!—*Troilus and Cressida,* i, 2, 249.

13
Thou hast slain
The flower of Europe for his chivalry.
III Henry VI. Act ii, sc. 1, l. 70. [Edward]

14
And his device, a wreath of chivalry;
The word, 'me pompæ provexit apex.'
Pericles. Act ii, sc. 2, l. 29. [Thaisa] The

only use of this Latin motto, "The crown of honour has led me on." Its origin is unknown. See under KNIGHTHOOD for full quotation.

1
Made glorious by his manly chivalry.
The Rape of Lucrece, l. 109.

Single chivalry.—*Troilus and Cressida*, iv, 4, 150.
True chivalry.—*Richard II*, ii, 1, 54.

2
I 'll answer thee in any fair degree,
Or chivalrous design of knightly trial.
Richard II. Act i, sc. 1, l. 80. [Mowbray] The only use of "chivalrous."

3
I am to-day i' the vein of chivalry.
Troilus and Cressida. Act v, sc. 3, l. 32. [Hector]

Troilus: When many times the captive Grecian falls,
Even in the fan and wind of your fair sword,
You bid them rise, and live.
Hector: O, 'tis fair play.
Troilus: Fool's play, by heaven, Hector.
Troilus and Cressida. Act v, sc. 3, l. 40.

CHOICE

See also Election

4
I had rather be in this choice than throw ames-ace for my life.
All's Well that Ends Well. Act ii, sc. 3, l. 84. [Lafeu] The only use of "ames-ace" (two aces, the lowest possible throw).

I stuck my choice upon her, ere my heart
Durst make too bold a herald of my tongue.
All's Well that Ends Well. Act v, sc. 3, l. 45. [Bertram]

Of their own choice.—*Coriolanus*, i, 1, 220.
Your only choice.—*Coriolanus*, i, 9, 36.

5
He may not, as unvalued persons do,
Carve for himself; for on his choice depends
The safety and health of this whole state;
And therefore must his choice be circumscribed.
Hamlet. Act i, sc. 3, l. 19. [Laertes] "Unvalued" is repeated in *Richard III*, i, 4, 27: "Unvalued jewels"; and "circumscribed" in *Titus Andronicus*, i, 1, 68.

Madness would not err,
Nor sense to ecstasy was ne'er so thrall'd
But it reserved some quantity of choice.
Hamlet. Act iii, sc. 4, l. 73. [Hamlet] "Thrall'd" is repeated in *The Taming of the Shrew*, i, 1, 225: "Thrall'd my wounded eye."

6
The commonwealth is sick of their own choice.
II Henry IV. Act i, sc. 3, l. 87. [Archbishop of York]

Of your choice.—*Henry VIII*, ii, 4, 58.
Choice of all delights.—*I Henry IV*, v, 5, 17.
My father's choice.—*The Merry Wives of Windsor*, iii, 4, 31.

7
I shall be well content with any choice
Tends to God's glory and my country's weal.
I Henry VI. Act v, sc. 1, l. 26. [King Henry]

How like you our choice,
That you stand pensive, as half malcontent?
III Henry VI. Act iv, sc. 1, l. 9. [King Edward] "Pensive" is used only once again, in *Romeo and Juliet*, iv, 1, 39.

Hath not our brother made a worthy choice?
III Henry VI. Act iv, sc. 1, l. 3. [Gloucester]

Your choice is not so rich in worth as beauty.
The Winter's Tale. Act v, sc. 1, l. 214. [Leontes]

8
We have with a leaven'd and prepared choice
Proceeded to you.
Measure for Measure. Act i, sc. 1, l. 52. [Duke] The only use of "leaven'd."

9
I 'll make My royal choice.
Henry VIII. Act i, sc. 4, l. 86. [Wolsey]

Braver choice.—*King John*, ii, 1, 72.
Rich choice.—*All's Well that Ends Well*, iii, 7, 26.
Sudden choice.—*Titus Andronicus*, i, 1, 318.

10
As they are chosen, they are glad to choose me for them.
Measure for Measure. Act ii, sc. 1, l. 283. [Elbow]

11
Is it not hard, Nerissa, that I cannot choose one nor refuse none?
The Merchant of Venice. Act i, sc. 2, l. 27. [Portia]

Portia: Go draw aside the curtains and discover
The several caskets to this noble prince.
Now make your choice.
Prince of Morocco: The first, of gold, who this inscription bears,
'Who chooseth me shall gain what many men desire;'
The second silver, which this promise carries,
'Who chooseth me shall get as much as he deserves;'
This third, dull lead, with warning all as blunt,
'Who chooseth me must give and hazard all he hath.'
How shall I know if I do choose the right?
The Merchant of Venice. Act ii, sc. 7, l. 1. "Inscription" is repeated in l. 14 of the same scene, and occurs nowhere else.

Make choice.—*A Midsummer-Night's Dream*, v, 1, 43; *All's Well that Ends Well*, ii, 1, 206; ii, 3, 78; *Hamlet*, iv, 5, 204; *King Lear*, i, 1, 7; *Antony and Cleopatra*, iii, 1, 23.
Make his choice.—*A Midsummer-Night's Dream*, iii, 2, 43.
Choice of friends.—*A Midsummer-Night's Dream*, i, 1, 139; *Much Ado about Nothing*, iv, 1, 201.

12
I will not choose what many men desire,
Because I will not jump with common spirits
And rank me with the barbarous multitudes.
The Merchant of Venice. Act ii, sc. 9, l. 31. [Arragon]

By cock and pie, you shall not choose, sir! come, come.
The Merry Wives of Windsor. Act i, sc. 1, l. 316. [Mistress Page]

1
Or, if there were a sympathy in choice,
War, death, or sickness did lay siege to it.
A Midsummer-Night's Dream. Act i, sc. 1, l. 141. [Lysander]

2
When she is sated with his body, she will find the error of her choice.
Othello. Act i, sc. 3, l. 357. [Iago] The only use of "sated."

Very nature will instruct her in it and compel her to some second choice.
Othello. Act ii, sc. 1, l. 238. [Iago] The only use of "second choice."

Pedlar, let 's have the first choice.
The Winter's Tale. Act iv, sc. 4, l. 319. [Clown] The only use of "first choice."

3
Your choice agrees with mine.
Pericles. Act ii, sc. 5, l. 18. [Simonides]

I do commend her choice.
Pericles. Act ii, sc. 5, l. 21. [Simonides]

I 'ld wish no better choice.
Pericles. Act v, sc. 1, l. 69. [Lysimachus] The only use of "better choice."

4
Well, you have made a simple choice; you know not how to choose a man.
Romeo and Juliet. Act ii, sc. 5, l. 38. [Nurse]

She had eyes, and chose me.
Othello. Act iii, sc. 3, l. 189. [Othello]

5
There 's small choice in rotten apples.
The Taming of the Shrew. Act i, sc. 1, l. 138. [Hortensio]

6
Why, gentlemen, you do me double wrong,
To strive for that which resteth in my choice.
The Taming of the Shrew. Act iii, sc. 1, l. 16. [Bianca]

Fight for freedom in your choice.
Titus Andronicus. Act i, sc. 1, l. 17. [Bassianus]

7
Dost thou applaud my choice?
Titus Andronicus. Act i, sc. 1, l. 321. [Saturninus]

Youngling, learn thou to make some meaner choice.
Titus Andronicus. Act ii, sc. 1, l. 73. [Demetrius] "Youngling" is repeated in iv, 2, 93, and in *The Taming of the Shrew,* ii, 1, 339.

Woe to her chance, and damn'd her loathed choice!
Titus Andronicus. Act iv, sc. 2, l. 78. [Demetrius]

8
Had I a sister were a grace, or a daughter a goddess, he should take his choice.
Troilus and Cressida. Act i, sc. 2, l. 257. [Pandarus]

Take your choice.—*Coriolanus,* i, 6, 65.

At thy choice.—*Coriolanus,* iii, 2, 123; *King Lear,* ii, 4, 220.

9
And choice, being mutual act of all our souls,
Makes merit her election.
Troilus and Cressida. Act i, sc. 3, l. 348. [Nestor]

CHOLER

See also Anger, Rage

10
Plunge him . . . into choler.
Hamlet, iii, 2, 319. See under KING.

Put him to choler straight.—*Coriolanus,* iii, 3, 25.

Touch'd with choler, hot as gunpowder.
Henry V. Act iv, sc. 7, l. 188. [King Henry] "Gunpowder" is repeated in *I Henry IV,* v, 4, 123; and in *II Henry IV,* iv, 4, 48: "Rash gunpowder."

Sudden in choler.—*Othello,* ii, 1, 279.

Wilful choler.—*Romeo and Juliet,* i, 5, 91.

11
What, drunk with choler?
I Henry IV. Act i, sc. 3, l. 129. [Northumberland]

What, what, my lord! are you so choleric?
II Henry VI. Act i, sc. 2, l. 51. [Duchess of Gloucester]

How choleric you are.—*Julius Cæsar,* iv, 3, 43. See also under SLAVE.

Make you choleric.—*The Comedy of Errors,* ii, 2, 63.

You were so choleric.—*The Comedy of Errors,* ii, 2, 68.

12
I beseek you now, aggravate your choler.
II Henry IV. Act ii, sc. 4, l. 175. [Hostess] The only use of "beseek."

Go cheerfully together and digest
Your angry choler on your enemies.
I Henry VI. Act iv, sc. 1, l. 167. [King Henry]

Throw cold water on thy choler.
The Merry Wives of Windsor. Act ii, sc. 3, l. 89. [Host]

My choler being over-blown.—*II Henry VI,* i, 3, 155.

Clean over-blown.—*Richard III,* ii, 4, 61. "Over-blown" is repeated in *Richard II,* iii, 2, 190; *The Taming of the Shrew,* v, 2, 3; *The Tempest,* ii, 2, 114.

Nay, my choler is ended.—*Love's Labour 's Lost,* ii, 1, 206.

13
Boiling choler chokes
The hollow passage of my poison'd voice.
I Henry VI. Act v, sc. 4, l. 120. [York]

Choler does kill me.—*Timon of Athens,* iv, 3, 372.

Spoke in choler.—*Henry VIII,* ii, 1, 34.

In choler parted!—*King Lear,* i, 2, 23.

How full of chollors I am, and trempling of mind!
The Merry Wives of Windsor. Act iii, sc. 1, l. 11. [Evans] The only use of "chollors."

14
Must I give way and room to your rash choler?
Julius Cæsar. Act iv, sc. 3, l. 39. [Brutus]

15
Wrath-kindled gentlemen, be ruled by me;
Let 's purge this choler without letting blood.
Richard II. Act i, sc. 1, l. 152. [King Richard] The only use of "wrath-kindled."

16
Since, of ourselves, ourselves are choleric.
The Taming of the Shrew, iv, 1, 177. See MEAT, 973:1.

I fear 'tis choleric.—*The Taming of the Shrew,* iv, 3, 22.
Engenders choler.—*The Taming of the Shrew,* iv, 1, 175.

CHRIST

1
As far as to the sepulchre of Christ,
Whose soldier now, under whose blessed cross
We are impressed and engaged to fight.
I Henry IV. Act i, sc. 1, l. 19. [King Henry]
The sepulchre in stubborn Jewry
Of the world's ransom, blessed Mary's son.
Richard II. Act ii, sc. 1, l. 55. [Gaunt]
Those holy fields
Over whose acres walk'd those blessed feet
Which fourteen hundred years ago were nail'd
For our advantage on the bitter cross.
I Henry IV. Act i, sc. 1, l. 24. [King Henry] The only use of "nail'd."
Him that died for all.—*II Henry VI,* i, 1, 113.
2
Through all the kingdoms that acknowledge Christ.
I Henry IV. Act iii, sc. 2, l. 111. [King Henry]
Christian kingdoms.—*Henry VIII,* ii, 2, 93.
Christian land.—*Richard III,* iii, 7, 116.
The states of Christendom.—*I Henry VI,* v, 4, 96. "Christendom" is used eighteen times.
The Christian world.—*All's Well that Ends Well,* iv, 4, 2.
3
Jesus preserve your royal majesty!
II Henry VI. Act i, sc. 2, l. 70. [Hume]
Jesus bless us!—*III Henry VI,* v, 6, 75; *I Henry IV,* ii, 2, 86. The only uses of "Jesus."
In the name of Jesu Christ.—*Henry V,* iv, 1, 65. "Jesu Christ" is used again in *II Henry VI,* v, 1, 214, and in *Richard II,* iv, 1, 93.
Captain Christ.—*Richard II,* iv, 1, 99.
By Chrish, la!—*Henry V,* iii, 2, 93. "Chrish" is used five times in this scene, always by Macmorris, and occurs nowhere else.

CHRISTIAN

4
Yet he most Christian-like laments his death.
II Henry VI, iii, 2, 58. "Christian-like" is repeated in *Richard III,* i, 3, 316; *Henry V,* v, 2, 381; *Much Ado about Nothing,* ii, 3, 199.
Like a Christian.—*I Henry IV,* v, 5, 9.
As I am a Christian.—*The Comedy of Errors,* i, 2, 77; *Othello,* iv, 2, 82.
As I am a Christian soul.—*The Merry Wives of Windsor,* iii, 1, 96.
5
I long
To have this young one made a Christian.
Henry VIII. Act v, sc. 3, l. 180. [King Henry]
Jessica: I shall be saved by my husband, he hath made me a Christian.
Launcelot: Truly, the more to blame he; we were Christians enow before; e'en as many as could well live, one by another. This making of Christians will raise the price of hogs.
The Merchant of Venice. Act ii, sc. 3, l. 21.
Become a Christian.—*The Merchant of Venice,* ii, 3, 21; iv, 1, 387.
6
Void of all profanation in the world that good
Christians ought to have.
Measure for Measure. Act ii, sc. 1, l. 55. [Elbow]
7
I hate him for he is a Christian.
The Merchant of Venice. Act i, sc. 3, l. 43. [Shylock]
O father Abram, what these Christians are,
Whose own hard dealings teaches them suspect
The thoughts of others!
The Merchant of Venice. Act i, sc. 3, l. 161. [Shylock]
Prodigal Christian.—*The Merchant of Venice,* ii, 5, 15.
There will come a Christian by,
Will be worth a Jewess' eye.
The Merchant of Venice. Act ii, sc. 5, l. 42. [Launcelot]
8
Thou art as foolish Christian creatures as I would desires.
The Merry Wives of Windsor. Act iv, sc. 1, l. 73. [Evans]
Not worth the name of a Christian.—*The Two Gentlemen of Verona,* ii, 5, 58.
Bare Christian.—*The Two Gentlemen of Verona,* iii, 1, 272.

CHURCH

See also Temple

9
Winchester: The church's prayers made him so prosperous.
Gloucester: The church! where is it? Had not churchmen pray'd,
His thread of life had not so soon decay'd.
I Henry VI. Act i, sc. 1, l. 32.
10
Name not religion, for thou lovest the flesh,
And ne'er throughout the year to church thou go'st
Except it be to pray against thy foes.
I Henry VI. Act i, sc. 1, l. 41. [Gloucester]
An I have not forgotten what the inside of a church is made of, I am a peppercorn, a brewer's horse: the inside of a church!
I Henry IV. Act iii, sc. 3, l. 8. [Falstaff] The only use of "peppercorn."
Should I go to church
And see the holy edifice of stone?
The Merchant of Venice. Act i, sc. 1, l. 29. [Salarino]
Go with me to church.—*The Merchant of Venice,* iii, 2, 305.
Why dost thou not go to church in a galliard and come home in a coranto?
Twelfth Night. Act i, sc. 3, l. 136. [Sir Toby Belch] A galliard and a coranto are both lively dances.
11
The cathedral church of Westminister.—*II Henry VI,* i, 2, 37.
Saint Luke's church.—*The Taming of the Shrew,* iv, 4, 88.
Saint Peter's Church.—*Romeo and Juliet,* iii, 5, 115; iii, 5, 117; iii, 5, 155.

Parish church.—*As You Like It*, ii, 7, 52. The only use of the phrase.
Holy church.—*Henry V*, i, 1, 23; *King John*, v, 2, 71; *Romeo and Juliet*, ii, 6, 37.
And thank the holy conclave for their loves.
Henry VIII. Act ii, sc. 2, l. 100. The only use of "conclave."

1
One that, in all obedience, makes the church
The chief aim of his honour.
Henry VIII. Act v, sc. 3, l. 117. [Gardiner]

2
Therefore to arms! be champion of our church,
Or let the church, our mother, breathe her curse,
A mother's curse, on her revolting son.
King John. Act iii, sc. 1, l. 255. [Pandulph]

3
I can see a church by daylight.
Much Ado about Nothing, ii, 1, 86. See under EYE.

4 Get thee to church o' Thursday,
Or never after look me in the face.
Romeo and Juliet. Act iii, sc. 5, l. 162. [Capulet]
We 'll to church to-morrow.—*Romeo and Juliet*, iv, 2, 37.
As the custom is,
In all her best array bear her to church.
Romeo and Juliet. Act iv, sc. 5, l. 80. [Friar Laurence]
'Tis time we were at church.—*The Taming of the Shrew*, iii, 2, 113.

5
I have seen them in the church together.
The Taming of the Shrew. Act v, sc. 1, l. 42. [Biondello]
I 'll see the church o' your back.—*The Taming of the Shrew*, v, 1, 5.
Came you from the church?—*The Taming of the Shrew*, iii, 2, 151.
Stay for me at church.—*The Merry Wives of Windsor*, iv, 6, 49.

6
Viola: Save thee, friend, and thy music: dost thou live by thy tabor?
Clown: No, sir, I live by the church.
Viola: Art thou a churchman?
Clown: No such matter, sir: I do live by the church; for I do live at my house, and my house doth stand by the church.
Twelfth Night. Act iii, sc. 1, l. 1.
The church stands by thy tabor, if thy tabor stand by the church.
Twelfth Night. Act iii, sc. 1, l. 10. [Viola]
That consecrated roof.—*Twelfth Night*, i, v, 3, 25.

CHURCHMAN, see Priest

CIRCUMSTANCE

7 My circumstances,
Being so near the truth as I will make them,
Must first induce you to believe.
Cymbeline. Act ii, sc. 4, l. 61. [Iachimo]

8
In our circumstance and course of thought,
'Tis heavy with him.
Hamlet. Act iii, sc. 3, l. 83. [Hamlet]

9
You do remember all the circumstance?
Hamlet. Act v, sc. 2, l. 2. [Hamlet]
Drift of circumstance.—*Hamlet*, iii, 1, 1.

10
Mark every circumstance.
I Henry VI. Act iii, sc. 1, l. 153. [Gloucester]
The circumstance consider'd.—*I Henry IV*, i, 3, 70.
By circumstance.—*II Henry VI*, v, 2, 39; *Richard III*, i, 2, 77; i, 2, 80; *The Winter's Tale*, iii, 2, 18.

11
Tell us here the circumstance.
II Henry VI. Act ii, sc. 1, l. 74. [King Henry]

12
Being constrain'd with dreadful circumstance.
The Rape of Lucrece, l. 1703.
Bombast circumstance.—*Othello*, i, 1, 13.
Frivolous circumstances.—*The Taming of the Shrew*, v, 1, 28.
Other circumstance.—*Measure for Measure*, iv, 2, 108.
Perilous circumstance.—*Hamlet*, i, 3, 102.
Potent circumstances.—*Henry VIII*, ii, 4, 76.
Circumstances strong.—*The Rape of Lucrece*, l. 1262.

13
I 'll stay the circumstance.
Romeo and Juliet. Act ii, sc. 5, l. 36. [Juliet]
Circumstances shortened.—*Much Ado about Nothing*, iii, 2, 105.

14
In all these circumstances I 'll instruct you.
The Taming of the Shrew. Act iv, sc. 2, l. 119. [Tranio]
The circumstance I 'll tell you more at large.
I Henry VI. Act i, sc. 1, l. 109. [Messenger]
And tell them both the circumstance of all.
Titus Andronicus. Act iv, sc. 2, l. 156. [Aaron]

15
I know . . . nothing of the circumstance.
Twelfth Night. Act iii, sc. 2, l. 287. [Fabian]

16
Do not embrace me till each circumstance
Of place, time, fortune, do cohere and jump.
Twelfth Night. Act v, sc. 1, l. 258. [Viola] The only use of "cohere."

17
That I can deny by a circumstance.
The Two Gentlemen of Verona. Act i, sc. 1, l. 84. [Speed]
By your circumstance.—*The Two Gentlemen of Verona*, i, 1, 36; 37.

18
It must with circumstance be spoken.
The Two Gentlemen of Verona. Act iii, sc. 2, l. 36. [Proteus]
With circumstance.—*The Comedy of Errors*, v, 1, 16; *The Merchant of Venice*, i, 1, 154.
Without circumstance.—*Romeo and Juliet*, v, 3, 181.
Without more circumstance.—*Hamlet*, i, 5, 127.

19 All other circumstances
Made up to the deed.
Winter's Tale. Act ii, sc. 1, l. 178. [Leontes]

So out of circumstance and sudden.
Winter's Tale. Act v, sc. 1, l. 90. [Leontes]
Out of circumstance.—*Othello,* iii, 3, 16.

CITIZEN

1
Sweep on, you fat and greasy citizens.
As You Like It. Act ii, sc. 1, l. 55. [First Lord]
Snorting citizens.—*Othello,* i, 1, 90.
We are accounted poor citizens.—*Coriolanus,* i, 1, 15.
Poor citizen.—*The Rape of Lucrece,* l. 465.

2
The civil citizens kneading up the honey.
Henry V. Act i, sc. 2, l. 199. [Canterbury]
Duteous citizens.—*Richard III,* iii, 5, 65.
Gentle citizens.—*Richard III,* iii, 7, 38.
Kind citizens.—*King John,* ii, 1, 231.

3
The citizens fly and forsake their houses.
II Henry VI. Act iv, sc. 4, l. 50. [Messenger]
The citizens are up.—*Romeo and Juliet,* iii, 1, 138.
The generous and gravest citizens
Have bent the gates.
Measure for Measure. Act iv, sc. 6, l. 13. [Friar Peter] The only use of "gravest."
Grave citizens.—*The Taming of the Shrew,* i, 1, 10; iv, 2, 95.

4
The citizens,
I am sure, have shown at full their royal minds—
As, let 'em have their rights, they are ever forward.
Henry VIII. Act iv, sc. 1, l. 7. [Gentleman]

5
He wonders to what end you have assembled
Such troops of citizens to speak with him.
Richard III. Act iii, sc. 7, l. 85. [Catesby]
What say the citizens?—*Richard III,* iii, 7, 1.
The citizens are mum and speak not a word.—*Richard III,* iii, 7, 3.
Consorted with the citizens.—*Richard III,* iii, 7, 137.

6
Ancient citizens
Cast by their grave beseeming ornaments,
To wield old partisans, in hands as old.
Romeo and Juliet. Act i, sc. 1, l. 99. [Prince]
Rome's best citizens.—*Titus Andronicus,* i, 1, 164.
Roman citizen.—*Julius Cæsar,* iii, 2, 246.
Citizens of Angiers.—*King John,* ii, 1, 536.
Citizens of Corioli.—*Coriolanus,* i, 6, 10.

CITY

See also Town

7
The city cast Her people out upon her.
Antony and Cleopatra. Act ii, sc. 2, l. 218. [Enobarbus]

8
Sicinius: What is the city but the people?
Citizens: True, The people are the city.
Coriolanus. Act iii, sc. 1, l. 199.
I' the city of kites and crows!—*Coriolanus,* iv, 5, 45.
Desert city.—*As You Like It,* ii, 1, 23.
Poor city.—*Coriolanus,* v, 4, 31.

9
Did you but know the city's usuries
And felt them knowingly.
Cymbeline. Act iii, sc. 3, l. 45. [Belarius] "Knowingly" is repeated in *All's Well that Ends Well,* i, 3, 256.

10
For aught I see, this city must be famish'd,
Or with light skirmishes enfeebled.
I Henry VI. Act i, sc. 4, l. 68. [Talbot]

11
Razeth your cities and subverts your towns
And in a moment makes you desolate.
I Henry VI. Act ii, sc. 3, l. 65. [Talbot] The only use of "razeth" and "subverts."
See the cities and the towns defaced
By wasting ruin of the cruel foe.
I Henry VI. Act iii, sc. 3, l. 45. [La Pucelle]
That is the way to lay the city flat;
To bring the roof to the foundation,
And bury all, which yet distinctly ranges,
In heaps and piles of ruin.
Coriolanus. Act iii, sc. 1, l. 204. [Cominius]
Sack the city.—*I Henry VI,* iii, 2, 10; *I Henry IV,* v, 3, 56.
Spoil the city.—*II Henry VI,* iv, 4, 53.

12
In the famous ancient city of Tours.
II Henry VI. Act i, sc. 1, l. 5. [Suffolk] Repeated in i, 3, 53.
A fair French city.—*Henry V,* v, 2, 345.
A goodly city is this Antium. City,
'Tis I that made thy widows.
Coriolanus. Act iv, sc. 4, l. 1. [Coriolanus]
Good city.—*Coriolanus,* iii, 2, 27.
This Tarsus, o'er which I have the government,
A city on whom plenty held full hand,
For riches strew'd herself even in the streets;
Whose towers bore heads so high they kiss'd the clouds,
And strangers ne'er beheld but wonder'd at;
Whose men and dames so jetted and adorn'd,
Like one another's glass to trim them by;
Their tables were stored full, to glad the sight,
And not so much to feed on as delight;
All poverty was scorn'd, and pride so great,
The name of help grew odious to repeat.
Pericles. Act i, sc. 4, l. 21. [Cleon] The only use of "jetted."
High-viced city.—*Timon of Athens,* iv, 3, 109. The only use of "high-viced."
Maiden cities.—*Henry V,* v, 2, 353.
Peaceful city.—*Henry V,* v, Prol., 33.
Populous cities.—*Othello,* i, 1, 77; iv, 1, 64; *Cymbeline,* iv, 6, 197.

13
And are the cities, that I got with wounds,
Deliver'd up again with peaceful words?
II Henry VI. Act i, sc. 1, l. 121. [Warwick]
The city being but of small defence,
We'll quickly rouse the traitors in the same.
III Henry VI. Act v, sc. 1, l. 64. [King Edward]

14
Dwell I but in the suburbs?
Julius Cæsar. Act ii, sc. 1, l. 285. [Portia]
In the south suburbs.—*Twelfth Night,* iii, 3, 39. "In the suburbs" occurs six times in the plays.

1
Save unscratch'd your city's threaten'd cheeks.
King John. Act iii, sc. 1, l. 225. [King John] The only use of "unscratch'd."
Make the breach and enter this sweet city.
The Rape of Lucrece, l. 469.
Why should you fear? is not your city strong?
Titus Andronicus. Act iv, sc. 4, l. 78. [Tamora]
2
O, let those cities that of plenty's cup
And her prosperities so largely taste,
With their superfluous riots, hear these tears!
Pericles. Act i, sc. 4, l. 52. [Cleon]
3
All our whole city is much bound to him.
Romeo and Juliet. Act iv, sc. 2, l. 32. [Capulet]
4
I wonder now how yonder city stands
When we have here her base and pillar by us.
Troilus and Cressida. Act iv, sc. 5, l. 211. [Ulysses]

CIVILITY

See also Courtesy

5
In civility thou seem'st so empty.
As You Like It. Act ii, sc. 7, l. 93. [Duke Senior]
Smooth civility.—*As You Like It,* ii, 7, 96.
6
Use all the observance of civility.
The Merchant of Venice, ii, 2, 204. See under BEHAVIOUR.
Civility and patience.—*The Merry Wives of Windsor,* iv, 2, 28.
Sense of all civility.—*Othello,* i, 1, 132.
7
The count is neither sad, nor sick, nor merry, nor well; but civil count, civil as an orange, and something of that jealous complexion.
Much Ado about Nothing. Act ii, sc. 1, l. 303. [Beatrice]
He is sad and civil.—*Twelfth Night,* iii, 4, 5.
8
You were wont be civil.
Othello. Act ii, sc. 3, l. 190. [Othello]
Civil, full of good.—*The Two Gentlemen of Verona,* v, 4, 156.

CLAMOUR

9
More clamorous than a parrot against rain.
As You Like It. Act iv, sc. 1, l. 152. [Rosalind]
Be clamorous and leap all civil bounds.
Twelfth Night. Act i, sc. 4, l. 21. [Duke]
Strangely clamorous.—*I Henry IV,* iii, 1, 40.
10
The instant burst of clamour that she made, . . .
Would have made milch the burning eyes of heaven.
Hamlet. Act ii, sc. 2, l. 538. [First Player] The only use of "milch." "Milch-kine" occurs in *The Taming of the Shrew,* ii, 1, 359, and in *Merry Wives of Windsor,* iv, 4, 33, and "milch-doe" in *Venus and Adonis,* l. 875.
With clamours fill'd The dispersed air.
The Rape of Lucrece, l. 1804.
Clamour Will be my knell.—*The Winter's Tale,* i, 2, 189.
11
Why, what tumultuous clamour have we here?
II Henry VI. Act iii, sc. 2, l. 239. [King]
Peace, you ungracious clamours! peace, rude sounds!
Troilus and Cressida. Act i, sc. 1, l. 92. [Troilus]
Piteous clamours.—*Rape of Lucrece,* l. 681.
Savage clamour!—*Winter's Tale,* iii, 3, 56.
Venom clamours.—*Comedy of Errors,* v, 1, 69.
Clamours of hell.—*King John,* iii, 1, 304.
Clamour of the host.—*Coriolanus,* i, 9, 64.
12 We 'll bring him to his house
With shouts and clamours.
Julius Cæsar. Act iii, sc. 2, l. 58. [Citizen]
By this great clatter, one of greatest note
Seems bruited.
Macbeth. Act v, sc. 7, l. 21. [Macduff] The only use of "clatter."
13
An hour in clamour and a quarter in rheum.
Much Ado about Nothing. Act v, sc. 2, l. 84. [Benedick]
14
If she chance to nod, I 'll rail and brawl
And with the clamour keep her still awake.
The Taming of the Shrew. Act iv, sc. 1, l. 209. [Petruchio]

CLERGY, see Preacher

CLOAK

See also Dress

15
Gloucester: What colour is this cloak of?
Simpcox: Red, master; red as blood.
II Henry VI, ii, 1, 109. See under COLOUR.
16
You pull'd me by the cloak; would you speak with me?
Julius Cæsar, i, 2, 215. See under SPEECH.
17
We will not line his thin bestained cloak
With our pure honours.
King John. Act iv, sc. 3, l. 24. [Salisbury] The only use of "bestained."
18
An old cloak makes a new jerkin.
The Merry Wives of Windsor. Act i, sc. 3, l. 18. [Falstaff]
Take thine auld cloak about thee.
Othello, ii, 3, 99. See under PRIDE.
19
The fashion of . . . a cloak, is nothing to a man.
Much Ado about Nothing, iii, 3, 126. See under FASHION.
20
I have night's cloak to hide me from their sight.
Romeo and Juliet. Act ii, sc. 2, l. 75. [Romeo]
Cloak of night.—*Richard II,* iii, 2, 45.
Black all-hiding cloak.—*The Rape of Lucrece,* l. 801. The only use of "all-hiding."
Inky cloak.—*Hamlet,* i, 2, 77.
Short cloak.—*II Henry IV* i, 2, 34.

Wet cloak.—*II Henry IV,* v, 1, 95.

1
Make me travel forth without my cloak.
Sonnets. No. xxxiv. See under Cloud.

2
What hast thou there under thy cloak?
Timon of Athens. Act iii, sc. 1, l. 14. [Lucullus]

Get on your cloak.—*Timon of Athens,* ii, 1, 15.
Lend me thy cloak.—*Henry V,* iv, 1, 24.

3
Uncase thee; take my colour'd hat and cloak.
The Taming of the Shrew. Act i, sc. 1, l. 212. [Lucentio] The only use of "uncase."

A scarlet cloak!—*The Taming of the Shrew,* v, 1, 69.

4
Duke: How shall I best convey the ladder thither?
Valentine: It will be light, my lord, that you may bear it
Under a cloak that is of any length.
Duke: A cloak as long as thine will serve the turn?
Valentine: Ay, my good lord.
Duke: Then let me see thy cloak:
I 'll get me one of such another length.
Valentine: Why, any cloak will serve the turn, my lord.
Duke: How shall I fashion me to wear a cloak?
I pray thee, let me feel thy cloak upon me.
The Two Gentlemen of Verona. Act iii, sc. 1, l. 128.

CLOCK

5
Rosalind: I pray you, what is 't o'clock?
Orlando: You should ask me what time o' day: there 's no clock in the forest.
As You Like It. Act iii, sc. 2, l. 317.

What 's o'clock?—*II Henry VI,* ii, 4, 5; *Richard III,* iv, 2, 114; *Measure for Measure,* ii, 1, 290.
What is 't o'clock?—*Richard III,* iii, 2, 4; *Julius Cæsar,* ii, 2, 114; ii, 4, 23.
Tell the clock there.—*Richard III,* v, 3, 276; *The Tempest,* ii, 1, 289.

6
The clock hath strucken twelve upon the bell.
The Comedy of Errors. Act i, sc. 2, l. 45. [Dromio of Ephesus]

Now the clock strikes one.—*The Comedy of Errors,* iv, 2, 54.

Brutus: Peace! count the clock.
Cassius: The clock hath strucken three.
Julius Cæsar. Act ii, sc. 1, l. 192.

The clock struck nine.—*Romeo and Juliet,* ii, 5, 1.

7 Unhappy was the clock
That struck the hour!
Cymbeline. Act v, sc. 5, l. 153. [Iachimo]

The clocks do toll.—*Henry V,* iv, Prol., 15.

8 A German clock,
Still a-repairing, ever out of frame.
Love's Labour 's Lost, iii, 1, 192. See under Woman.

Ploughmen's clocks.—*Love's Labour 's Lost,* v, 2, 914.
Shrewsbury clock.—*I Henry IV,* v, 4, 152.

9
The clock gives me my cue.
The Merry Wives of Windsor. Act iii, sc. 2, l. 46. [Ford]

I do count the clock that tells the time.
Sonnets. No. xii.

Whilst I, my sovereign, watch the clock for you.
Sonnets. No. lvii.

10
The clock upbraids me with the waste of time.
Twelfth Night. Act iii, sc. 1, l. 141. [Olivia]

CLOTHES, see Dress

CLOUD

11
Sometime we see a cloud that 's dragonish;
A vapour sometime like a bear or lion,
A tower'd citadel, a pendent rock,
A forked mountain, or blue promontory
With trees upon 't, that nod unto the world,
And mock our eyes with air: thou hast seen these signs;
They are black vesper's pageants . . .
That which is now a horse, even with a thought
The rack dislimns, and makes it indistinct,
As water is in water.
Antony and Cleopatra. Act iv, sc. 14, l. 2. [Antony] The only use of "dragonish" ("dragon-like" occurs in *Coriolanus,* iv, 7, 23), "tower'd," "vesper," and "dislimns."

Hamlet: Do you see yonder cloud that 's almost in shape of a camel?
Polonius: By the mass, and 'tis a camel, indeed.
Hamlet: Methinks it is like a weasel.
Polonius: It is backed like a weasel.
Hamlet: Or like a whale?
Polonius: Very like a whale.
Hamlet. Act iii, sc. 2, l. 393.

12
He would be above the clouds.
II Henry VI. Act ii, sc. 1, l. 15. [Cardinal]

He has a cloud in 's face.—*Antony and Cleopatra,* iii, 2, 51.

13
But, in the midst of this bright-shining day,
I spy a black, suspicious and threatening cloud,
That will encounter with our glorious sun,
Ere he attain his easeful western bed.
III Henry VI. Act v, sc. 3, l. 3. [King Edward] The only use of "bright-shining" and "easeful."

Base contagious clouds.—*I Henry IV,* i, 2, 222.
Filthy and contagious clouds.—*Henry V,* iii, 3, 31.
Darkest clouds.—*The Taming of the Shrew,* iv, 3, 175.
Foggy cloud.—*Macbeth,* iii, 5, 36.
Racking clouds.—*III Henry VI,* ii, 1, 27.
Slippery clouds.—*II Henry IV,* iii, 1, 24.
Thick cloud.—*Antony and Cleopatra,* v, 2, 302.
Threatening clouds.—*Julius Cæsar,* i, 3, 8.

1
A little gale will soon disperse that cloud
And blow it to the source from whence it came.
III Henry VI. Act v, sc. 3, l. 10. [Clarence]
Every cloud engenders not a storm.
III Henry VI. Act v, sc. 3, l. 13. [Clarence]
But when a black-faced cloud the world doth threat,
In his dim mist the aspiring mountains hiding,
From earth's dark womb some gentle gust doth get,
Which blows these pitchy vapours from their biding.
The Rape of Lucrece, l. 547. "Black-faced" is repeated in *Richard III,* i, 2, 159.
Coal-black clouds that shadow heaven's light.
Venus and Adonis, l. 533.
Curl'd clouds.—*The Tempest,* i, 2, 192.
Lazy-pacing clouds.—*Romeo and Juliet,* ii, 2, 31. The only use of "lazy-pacing."
Meeting clouds.—*Venus and Adonis,* l. 820.
Severing clouds.—*Romeo and Juliet,* iii, 5, 8. "Severing" is repeated in *Henry VIII,* ii, 3, 16.

2
Since the more fair and crystal is the sky,
The uglier seem the clouds that in it fly.
Richard II. Act i, sc. 1, l. 41. [Bolingbroke] "Uglier" is used again in *The Tempest,* iv, 1, 191.

3
When clouds appear, wise men put on their cloaks.
Richard III. Act ii, sc. 3, l. 32. [Citizen]
Why didst thou promise such a beauteous day
And make me travel forth without my cloak,
To let base clouds o'ertake me in my way,
Hiding thy bravery in their rotten smoke?
Sonnets. No. xxxiv.
Many clouds consulting for foul weather.
Venus and Adonis, l. 972. "Consulting" is repeated in *Henry VIII,* i, 1, 91.

4
Yond same black cloud, yond huge one, looks like a foul bombard that would shed his liquor.
The Tempest. Act ii, sc. 2, l. 20. [Trinculo] "Bombard" (a leather jug for liquor, roughly resembling the cannon formerly so-called) is repeated in *I Henry IV,* ii, 4, 497: "That huge bombard of sack"; and in *Henry VIII,* v, 4, 85.
Yond same cloud cannot choose but fall by pailfuls.
The Tempest. Act ii, sc. 2, l. 24. [Trinculo] The only use of "pailfuls."
Weeping clouds.—*II Henry IV,* i, 3, 61.

CLOWN

5 The roynish clown, at whom so oft
Your grace was wont to laugh.
As You Like It. Act ii, sc. 2, l. 8. [Second Lord] The only use of "roynish" (mangy).
The clown shall make those laugh whose lungs are tickle o' the sere.
Hamlet. Act ii, sc. 2, l. 336. [Hamlet] "Sere" is repeated in *The Comedy of Errors,* iv, 2, 19: "Old and sere."

6
Touchstone: Holla, you clown!
Rosalind: Peace, fool: he 's not thy kinsman.
As You Like It. Act ii, sc. 4, l. 66.
Therefore, you clown, abandon,—which is in the vulgar leave.
As You Like It. Act v, sc. 1, l. 51. [Touchstone]

7
By my soul, a swain! a most simple clown!
Love's Labour 's Lost. Act iv, sc. 1, l. 142. [Costard]
Burly-boned clown.—*II Henry VI,* iv, 10, 60. The only use of "burly-boned."
Sweet clown.—*Love's Labour 's Lost,* iv, 3, 17.

COAL

8
If he should burn us all into one coal,
We have deserved it.
Coriolanus. Act iv, sc. 6, l. 137. [Menenius]

9
A pair of tribunes that have rack'd for Rome,
To make coals cheap,—a noble memory!
Coriolanus. Act v, sc. 1, l. 16. [Menenius]

10
Throw in the frozen bosoms of our part
Hot coals of vengeance!
II Henry VI, v, 2, 36. See under War.

11 Coals that fires all my breast,
And burns me up with flames.
III Henry VI, ii, 1, 83.
Coal of fire.—*Coriolanus,* i, 1, 177; *Henry V,* iii, 6, 110.
Coals of glowing fire.—*Venus and Adonis,* l. 35.
Burning coal.—*King John,* iv, 1, 109; *Pericles,* iii, Gower, 5.

12
Queen Katharine: It is you
Have blown this coal betwixt my lord and me;
Which God's dew quench! . . .
Wolsey: You charge me
That I have blown this coal: I do deny it.
Henry VIII. Act ii, sc. 4, l. 78.
Your breath first kindled the dead coal of wars.
King John, v, 2, 83. See under War.
Dead coals!—*The Winter's Tale,* v, 1, 68.

13 With swift intent he goes
To quench the coal which in his liver glows.
The Rape of Lucrece, l. 46.

14
Sampson: O' my word, we'll not carry coals.
Gregory: No, for then we should be colliers.
Romeo and Juliet. Act i, sc. 1, l. 1.
Since her time are colliers counted bright.
Love's Labour 's Lost. Act iv, sc. 3, l. 267. [Longaville]
Foul collier!—*Twelfth Night,* iii, 4, 130. The only uses of "collier."
Carry coals.—*Henry V,* iii, 2, 50.

15
That were to . . . add more coals to Cancer when he burns
With entertaining great Hyperion.
Troilus and Cressida. Act ii, sc. 3, l. 206. [Ulysses]

1
He sees her coming, and begins to glow,
Even as a dying coal revives with wind.
Venus and Adonis, l. 337.
Dying coals burnt out in tedious nights.
The Rape of Lucrece, l. 1379.
Coal-black, see under BLACKNESS.

COAST

2
See the coast clear'd, and then we will depart.
I Henry VI. Act i, sc. 3, l. 89. [Mayor]
3
Losing ken of Albion's wished coast.
II Henry VI. Act iii, sc. 2, l. 113. [Queen]
Native coast.—*II Henry VI,* iv, 8, 52.
Our coast.—*III Henry VI,* iii, 3, 205; v, 3, 8.
Your coast.—*Cymbeline,* iv, 3, 25.
Rebelling coasts.—*Cymbeline,* v, 4, 96.
Western coast.—*Richard III,* iv, 4, 433.
4
Mariner, say what coast is this?
Pericles. Act iii, sc. 1, l. 73. [Pericles]
Along this coast.—*Love's Labour's Lost,* v, 2, 557.
From another coast.—*II Henry VI,* i, 2, 93.
From coast to coast.—*Pericles,* ii, Gower, 34.
From every coast.—*The Merchant of Venice,* i, 1, 168.
From off our coast.—*Cymbeline,* iii, 1, 26.
On this coast.—*Pericles,* v, Gower, 15.
Upon this coast.—*Richard II,* iii, 3, 4; *The Winter's Tale,* iv, 4, 280; *Pericles,* v, 3, 20.
Upon your coast.—*Pericles,* ii, 1, 60.

COAT

See also Dress

5
I am ambitious for a motley coat.
As You Like It. Act ii, sc. 7, l. 43. [Jaques]
6
Glittering in golden coats, like images.
I Henry IV. Act iv, sc. 1, l. 100. [Vernon]
Golden coat.—*The Rape of Lucrece,* l. 205.
Gold coats.—*A Midsummer-Night's Dream,* ii, 1, 11.
Blue coats.—*Taming of the Shrew,* iv, 1, 94.
Green velvet coat.—*Winter's Tale,* i, 2, 156.
Richest coat.—*A Lover's Complaint,* l. 236.
Silken coats.—*Taming of the Shrew,* iv, 3, 55.
Coat of worth.—*Pericles,* ii, 1, 142.
Coat of folly.—*Henry V,* ii, 4, 38.
7
Doth, like a miser, spoil his coat with scanting
A little cloth.
Henry V. Act ii, sc. 4, l. 47. [Dauphin] The only use of "scanting."
8
If I find a hole in his coat, I will tell him my mind.
Henry V. Act iii, sc. 6, l. 88. [Fluellen]
There's a hole made in your best coat, Master Ford.
The Merry Wives of Windsor. Act iii, sc. 5, l. 143. [Ford]
9
They will pluck
The gay new coats o'er the French soldiers' heads.
Henry V. Act iv, sc. 3, l. 118. [King Henry]
New coat.—*Much Ado about Nothing,* iii, 2, 7.
A herald's coat.—*II Henry VI,* iv, 10, 75.
A herald's coat without sleeves.—*I Henry IV,* iv, 2, 49.
Coats in heraldry.—*A Midsummer-Night's Dream,* iii, 2, 213.
10
Cropp'd are the flower-de-luces in your arms;
Of England's coat one half is cut away.
I Henry VI. Act i, sc. 1, l. 80. [Messenger] "Flower-de-luce" is used five times.
Hark, countrymen! either renew the fight,
Or tear the lions out of England's coat.
I Henry VI. Act i, sc. 5, l. 27. [Talbot]
Slender: They may give the dozen white luces in their coat.
Shallow: It is an old coat.
Evans: The dozen white louses do become an old coat well. . . .
Slender: I may quarter, coz.
Shallow: You may, by marrying.
Evans: It is marring indeed, if he quarter it.
Shallow: Not a whit.
Evans: Yes, py'r lady; if he has a quarter of your coat, there is but three skirts for yourself, in my simple conjectures.
The Merry Wives of Windsor. Act i, sc. 1, l. 16. "Luce" is repeated in l. 22, and occurs nowhere else. "Louse" is used again in *King Lear,* iii, 2, 29, and in *Troilus and Cressida,* v, 1, 72.
Each fair instalment, coat, and several crest,
With loyal blazon, evermore be blest!
The Merry Wives of Windsor. Act v, sc. 5, l. 67. [Mistress Quickly]
11
He need not fear the sword; for his coat is of proof.
II Henry VI. Act iv, sc. 2, l. 65. [Smith]
That thrust had been mine enemy indeed,
But that my coat is better than thou know'st.
Othello. Act v, sc. 1, l. 25. [Cassio]
Steeled coat.—*I Henry VI,* i, 1, 85.
Coats of steel.—*III Henry VI,* ii, 1, 160.
12 War with rere-mice for their leathern wings,
To make my small elves coats.
A Midsummer-Night's Dream. Act ii, sc. 2, l. 4. [Titania] The only use of "rere-mice" (bats).
13
The lining of his coffers shall make coats
To deck our soldiers for these Irish wars.
Richard II. Act i, sc. 4, l. 61. [King Richard]
Give the soldiers coats.—*II Henry IV,* iii, 2, 311.
Lined their coats.—*Othello,* i, 1, 53.
14
Nathaniel's coat, sir, was not fully made.
The Taming of the Shrew. Act iv, sc. 1, l. 135. [Grumio]
15
I would not be in some of your coats for two pence.
Twelfth Night. Act iv, sc. 1, l. 32. [Clown]
16
If this be a horseman's coat, it hath seen very hot service.
Winter's Tale. Act iv, sc. 3, l. 70. [Clown]

Leathern coat.—*As You Like It,* ii, 1, 37.
War-worn coats.—*Henry V,* iv, Prol., 26. The only use of "war-worn."
Waxen coat.—*Richard II,* i, 3, 75.

COCK

1
His cocks do win the battle still of mine,
When it is all to nought.
Antony and Cleopatra. Act ii, sc. 3, l. 36. [Antony]

2
Of what kind should this cock come of?
As You Like It. Act ii, sc. 7, l. 90. [Jaques]

Cloten: I must go up and down like a cock that nobody can match.
Second Lord: You are cock and capon too; and you crow, cock, with your comb on.
Cymbeline. Act ii, sc. 1, l. 24.

3
The cock, that is the trumpet to the morn,
Doth with his lofty and shrill-sounding throat
Awake the god of day; and, at his warning,
Whether in sea or fire, in earth or air,
The extravagant and erring spirit hies
To his confine.
Hamlet. Act i, sc. 1, l. 150. [Horatio] The only use of "shrill-sounding." "Extravagant" is used only twice again; "A foolish extravagant spirit," *Love's Labour 's Lost,* iv, 2, 68; and "An extravagant and wheeling stranger," *Othello,* i, 1, 137.

Some say that ever 'gainst that season comes
Wherein our Saviour's birth is celebrated,
The bird of dawning singeth all night long.
Hamlet. Act i, sc. 1, l. 158. [Marcellus] The only use of the word Saviour in the plays.

Even then the morning cock crew loud.
Hamlet. Act i, sc. 2, l. 218. [Horatio]

4
Pistol's cock is up,
And flashing fire will follow.
Henry V. Act ii, sc. 1, l. 55. [Pistol] The only use of "flashing."

5
The country cocks do crow, the clocks do toll,
And the third hour of drowsy morning name.
Henry V. Act iv. Prologue, l. 15. [Chorus]

The early village cock
Hath twice done salutation to the morn.
Richard III. Act v, sc. 3, l. 209. [Ratcliff]

6
Look thou meet me ere the first cock crow.
A Midsummer-Night's Dream. Act ii, sc. 1, l. 267. [Oberon] "First cock" is repeated in *I Henry IV,* ii, 1, 20, and in *King Lear,* iii, 4, 121.

The second cock hath crow'd.
Romeo and Juliet. Act iv, sc. 4, l. 3. [Capulet] "Second cock" is repeated in *Macbeth,* ii, 3, 27. The only use of "crow'd."

7
Katharina: What is your crest? a coxcomb?
Petruchio: A combless cock, so Kate will be my hen.
Katharina: No cock of mine; you crow too like a craven.
The Taming of the Shrew. Act ii, sc. 1, l. 226. The only use of "combless."

8
Hark, hark! I hear
The strain of strutting chanticleer
Cry, Cock-a-diddle-dow.
The Tempest. Act i, sc. 2, l. 384. [Ariel] "Chanticleer" is repeated in *As You Like It,* ii, 7, 30: "Crow like chanticleer." The only use of "cock-a-diddle-dow."

Crow like a cock.—*The Two Gentlemen of Verona,* ii, 1, 28.

Antonio: Which . . . first began to crow?
Sebastian: The old cock.
Antonio: The cockerel.
The Tempest. Act ii, sc. 1, l. 29. "Cockerel" is repeated in *Romeo and Juliet,* i, 3, 53.

9
Can this cockpit hold
The vasty fields of France?
Henry V, Prol., 11. Only use of "cockpit."

CODPIECE

10
The cod-piece that will house
Before the head has any,
The head and he shall louse;
So beggars marry many.
King Lear. Act iii, sc. 2, l. 27. [Fool]

Marry, here 's a grace and a cod-piece; that 's a wise man and a fool.
King Lear. Act iii, sc. 2, l. 40. [Fool]

11
For the rebellion of a codpiece to take away the life of a man!
Measure for Measure. Act iii, sc. 2, l 122. [Lucio]

His codpiece seems as massy as his club.
Much Ado about Nothing. Act iii, sc. 3, l. 146. See under FASHION for full quotation.

12
Lucetta: What fashion, madam, shall I make your breeches? . . .
Julia: Why even what fashion thou best likest, Lucetta.
Lucetta: You must needs have them with a codpiece, madam.
Julia: Out, out, Lucetta! that will be ill-favour'd.
Lucetta: A round hose, madam, now 's not worth a pin,
Unless you have a codpiece to stick pins on.
Two Gentlemen of Verona. Act ii, sc. 7, l. 49.

To geld a codpiece.—*Winter's Tale,* iv, 4, 623.

COG, see Cheating

COLDNESS

See also Blood: Cold Blood; Heat and Cold

13
I spoke with her but once
And found her wondrous cold.
All's Well that Ends Well. Act iii, sc. 6, l. 120. [Bertram]

When you are dead, you should be such a one
As you are now, for you are cold and stern.
All's Well that Ends Well. Act iv, sc. 2, l. 7. [Bertram]

Cold and sickly.—*Antony and Cleopatra,* iii, 4, 7.
Cold and temperate.—*I Henry IV,* i, 3, 1.

Cold in blood.—*Antony and Cleopatra,* i, 5, 74. For "cold blood" see under Blood.
Cold in zeal.—*Richard III,* ii, 1, 40.
As cold as can be.—*The Taming of the Shrew,* iv, 3, 37.
As cold as if I had swallowed snowballs.—*The Merry Wives of Windsor,* ii, 5, 24.
Cold as a snowball.—*Pericles,* iv, 6, 149. The only uses of "snowball."
Cold blood.—*III Henry VI,* i, 1, 184, and four times in later plays. See under Blood.
Cold comfort.—*The Taming of the Shrew,* iv, 1, 33; *King John,* v, 7, 42.
Cold heart.—*I Henry IV,* ii, 3, 33; iv, 3, 7; *Antony and Cleopatra,* iii, 13, 159; *Henry VIII,* i, 2, 61.
Cold looks.—*King Lear,* ii, 4, 37.

1
Antony: Cold-hearted toward me?
Cleopatra: Ah, dear, if I be so,
From my cold heart let heaven engender hail,
And poison it in the source; and the first stone
Drop in my neck.
Antony and Cleopatra. Act iii, sc. 13, l. 158. The only use of "cold-hearted."

2
Let him walk from whence he came, lest he catch cold on 's feet.
Comedy of Errors. Act iii, sc. 1, l. 37. [Dromio of Syracuse] See also under Disease.

3
'Tis bitter cold, And I am sick at heart.
Hamlet. Act i, sc. 1, l. 8. [Francisco]
It is very cold.—*Hamlet,* i, 4, 1; v, 2, 98.
It is indifferent cold.—*Hamlet,* v, 2, 98.
Biting cold.—*II Henry VI,* iii, 2, 337.
Nipping cold.—*II Henry VI,* ii, 4, 3.

4
In winter's cold and summer's parching heat.
II Henry VI. Act i, sc. 1, l. 81. [Gloucester] See also Heat and Cold.
Winter's cold.—*Julius Cæsar,* i, 2, 99.

5
My lord is cold in great affairs.
II Henry VI. Act iii, sc. 1, l. 224. [Queen]
I muse your majesty doth seem so cold,
When such profound respects do pull you on.
King John. Act iii, sc. 1, l. 317. [Dauphin]
You may
Convey your pleasures in a spacious plenty,
And yet seem cold.
Macbeth. Act iv, sc. 3, l. 70. [Macduff]
If he be leaden, icy-cold, unwilling,
Be thou so too.
Richard III. Act iii, sc. 1, l. 176. [Buckingham] The only use of "icy-cold."

6
How dost, my boy? art cold? I am cold myself.
King Lear. Act iii, sc. 2, l. 68. [King Lear]
Poor Tom 's a-cold.
King Lear. Act iii, sc. 4, l. 152. [Edgar] "A-cold" is repeated in l. 59, and occurs in no other scene.
Shivering cold.—*Richard II,* v, 1, 77.
Shrink with cold.—*As You Like It,* ii, 1, 9.
Endure cold.—*Henry V,* ii, 1, 10.

7
This place is too cold for hell.
Macbeth. Act ii, sc. 3, l. 19. [Porter]
You are too cold.—*Measure for Measure,* ii, 2, 45.
Most coldest.—*Cymbeline,* ii, 3, 2.

8
Dull not device by coldness and delay.
Othello, ii, 3, 394. See under Delay.
Coldness of the king.—*III Henry VI,* ii, 1, 122. The only uses of "coldness."

9
When we both lay in the field
Frozen almost to death, how he did lap me
Even in his own garments, and gave himself,
All thin and naked, to the numb cold night.
Richard III. Act ii, sc. 1, l. 114. [King Edward]

10
Alas! she 's cold.
Romeo and Juliet, iv, 5, 25. See under Death.
Cold and numb.—*Titus Andronicus,* iii, 1, 259.
Of an earthly cold.—*Henry VIII,* iv, 2, 98.
Death's eternal cold.—*Sonnets,* xiii.
The men are not yet cold.—*The Winter's Tale,* iii, 3, 107.

11
Who, moving others, are themselves as stone,
Unmoved, cold, and to temptation slow,
They rightly do inherit heaven's graces
And husband nature's riches from expense;
They are the lords and owners of their faces,
Others but stewards of their excellence.
Sonnets. No. xciv.
As cold as any stone.—*Henry V,* ii, 3, 26.
Cold and senseless stone.—*Venus and Adonis,* l. 211.

12
You, sir, Charge him too coldly.
The Winter's Tale. Act i, sc. 2, l. 29. [Hermione]
Bear it coldly.—*Much Ado about Nothing,* iii, 2, 132.
We coldly pause for thee.—*King John,* ii, 1, 53.
Reason coldly.—*Romeo and Juliet,* iii, 1, 55.

COLOUR

13
Nay, pray you, seek no colour for your going.
Antony and Cleopatra, i, 3, 32. See under Parting.
What I have to do Will want true colour.
Hamlet. Act iii, sc. 4, l. 129. [Hamlet] The only use of "true colour."
Yet we want a colour for his death.
II Henry VI, iii, 1, 236. See under Death.
Under the colour of his usual game.
III Henry VI. Act iv, sc. 5, l. 11. [Gloucester]
Under the colour of commending him,
I have access my own love to prefer.
The Two Gentlemen of Verona. Act iv, sc. 2, l. 3. [Proteus]
If I find not what I seek, show no colour for my extremity.
The Merry Wives of Windsor. Act iv, sc. 2, l. 169. [Ford]
Why hunt I then for colour or excuses?
Rape of Lucrece, l. 267. See under Excuse.

But she with vehement prayers urgeth still
Under what colour he commits this ill.
The Rape of Lucrece, l. 475.
What colour for my visitation shall I
Hold up before him?
Winter's Tale. Act iv, sc. 4, l. 565. [Florizel]
Against all colour.—*Cymbeline,* iii, 1, 51.

1
Your chestnut was ever the only colour.
As You Like It. Act iii, sc. 4, l. 12. [Celia]
A' could never abide carnation; 'twas a colour he never liked.
Henry V. Act ii, sc. 3, l. 35. [Hostess]
Green indeed is the colour of lovers.
Love's Labour 's Lost. Act i, sc. 2, l. 90. [Armado]
Yellow . . . a colour she abhors.
Twelfth Night, ii, 5, 220.
'Mongst all colours no yellow in 't!
The Winter's Tale, ii, 3, 106.

2
Give colour to my pale cheek with thy blood.
Cymbeline. Act iv, sc. 2, l. 330. [Imogen]

3
Yea, bloody cloth, I 'll keep thee, for I wish'd
Thou shouldst be colour'd thus.
Cymbeline. Act v, sc. 1, l. 1. [Posthumus]
Colour'd with his high estate.
The Rape of Lucrece, l. 92.
Diversely coloured.—*Coriolanus,* ii, 3, 22. The only use of "diversely."
Well coloured.—*I Henry VI,* iv, 2, 37.

4
Look, whether he has not turned his colour.
Hamlet, ii, 2, 542. See under Acting.
Change thy colour.—*Richard III,* iii, 5, 1.
Change you colour?—*As You Like It,* iii, 2, 192.
Do you change colour?—*The Two Gentlemen of Verona,* ii, 4, 24.
Changed colour.—*The Winter's Tale,* v, 2, 98.

5
How might we see Falstaff bestow himself to-night in his true colours?
II Henry IV. Act ii, sc. 2, l. 186. [Prince of Wales] The only use of "true colours."

6
Your colour, I warrant you, is as red as any rose, in good truth, la!
II Henry IV. Act i, sc. 4, l. 27. [Hostess]
Of colour like the red rose on triumphant brier.
A Midsummer-Night's Dream. Act iii, sc. 1, l. 96. [Flute]
My red dominical, my golden letter.
Love's Labour 's Lost. Act v, sc. 2, l. 44. [Rosaline] The only use of "dominical."

7
Falstaff: This that you heard was but a colour.
Shallow: A colour that I fear you will die in, Sir John.
Falstaff: Fear no colours.
II Henry IV. Act v, sc. 5, l. 91.
I love no colours, and without all colour
Of base insinuating flattery,
I pluck this white rose with Plantagenet.
I Henry VI. Act ii, sc. 4, l. 34. [Warwick]

8
Advance our waving colours on the walls.
I Henry VI, i, 6, 1. See also under Flag.
Wear his colours like a tumbler's hoop!
Love's Labour 's Lost. Act iii, sc. 1, l. 190. [Biron] The only use of "tumbler."

9
Gloucester: What colour is this cloak of?
Simpox: Red, master; red as blood.
Gloucester: Why, that 's well said. What colour is my gown of?
Simpox: Black, forsooth: coal-black as jet.
King Henry: Why, then, thou know'st what colour jet is of?
Suffolk: And yet, I think, jet did he never see.
II Henry VI. Act ii, sc. 1, l. 108.

10
Add colours to the chameleon.
III Henry VI, iii, 2, 191. See under Cunning.
Dissembling colour.—*As You Like It,* iii, 4, 8.
Fair colour.—*The Rape of Lucrece,* l. 1600.
Fine colour.—*I Henry IV,* v, 1, 75.
Mingled colours.—*King John,* ii, 1, 389.
Native colours.—*Henry V,* i, 2, 17.
Nighted colour.—*Hamlet,* i, 2, 68. "Nighted" is repeated in *King Lear,* iv, 5, 13: "Nighted life."

11
All the colours of the rainbow.—*The Merry Wives of Windsor,* iv, 5, 118.
All the colours i' the rainbow.—*The Winter's Tale,* iv, 4, 205.

12
I do fear colourable colours.
Love's Labour 's Lost. Act iv, sc. 2, l. 153. [Holofernes] The only use of "colourable."
Being rather new-dyed.—*The Tempest,* ii, 1, 63. The only use of "new-dyed."

13
Steep'd in the colours of their trade.
Macbeth, ii, 3, 121. See under Murderer.
Colour of his beard.—*Twelfth Night,* ii, 3, 169.
Colour of her hair.—*Pericles,* iv, 2, 62.
Just of his colour.—*Measure for Measure,* iv, 3, 77.
'Twas indeed his colour.—*Henry VIII,* i, 1, 178.
He having colour enough.—*Troilus and Cressida,* i, 2, 112.
Of what colour?—*As You Like It,* i, 2, 107.
The colour 's Not dry.—*Winter's Tale,* v, 3, 47.

14
There are some shrewd contents in yon same paper,
That steals the colour from Bassanio's cheek.
The Merchant of Venice. Act iii, sc. 2, l. 246. [Portia]

15
Her lively colour kill'd with deadly cares.
The Rape of Lucrece, l. 1593.
His red colour hath forsook his cheeks.
Richard III. Act ii, sc. 1, l. 85. [Dorset]
Lose some colour.—*Othello,* i, 1, 73.

COMBAT

See also Duelling, Fighting

16
Dares me to personal combat.
Antony and Cleopatra. Act iv, sc. 1, l. 3. [Cæsar]
Dared to the combat.—*Hamlet,* i, 1, 84.

1
In single combat thou shalt buckle with me.
I Henry VI. Act i, sc. 2, l. 95. [Charles]
Vernon: Grant me the combat, gracious sovereign.
Basset: And me, my lord, grant me the combat too. . . .
King: Say, gentlemen, what makes you thus exclaim?
And wherefore crave you combat? or with whom?
Vernon: With him, my lord; for he hath done me wrong.
I Henry VI. Act iv, sc. 1, l. 78.
Gloucester: And let these have a day appointed them
For single combat in convenient place. . . .
Somerset: I humbly thank your royal majesty.
Horner: And I accept the combat willingly. . . .
King Henry: The day of combat shall be the last of next month.
II Henry VI. Act i, sc. 3, l. 211.
By combat.—*I Henry VI,* i, 2, 89; *The Winter's Tale,* ii, 3, 60.

2
Combat with adverse planets in the heavens!
I Henry VI. Act i, sc. 1, l. 54. [Bedford]
Combat with the wind.—*III Henry VI,* ii, 5, 6.

3
King Henry: Come hither, you that would be combatants.
I Henry VI. Act iv, sc. 1, l. 134.
Set forward, combatants.—*Richard II,* i, 3, 117.
The combatants being kin,
Half stints their strife before their strokes begin.
Troilus and Cressida. Act iv, sc. 5, l. 92. [Agamemnon]
Great combatant.—*Troilus and Cressida,* iv, 5, 5.
Valiant combatants.—*I Henry IV,* i, 3, 107.

4
O, what a noble combat hast thou fought
Between compulsion and a brave respect!
King John. Act v, sc. 2, l. 43. [Dauphin]
Eager combat.—*The Rape of Lucrece,* l. 1298.

5
Do you not see that Pompey is uncasing for the combat?
Love's Labour's Lost. Act v, sc. 2, l. 707. The only use of "uncasing."

6
Long was the combat doubtful that love with love did fight,
To leave the master loveless, or kill the gallant knight:
To put in practice either, alas, it was a spite
Unto the silly damsel.
The Passionate Pilgrim, l. 215. Probably not by Shakespeare. The only use of "loveless."

7
Though 't be a sportful combat,
Yet in the trial much opinion dwells.
Troilus and Cressida. Act i, sc. 3, l. 335. [Nestor]
This beauteous combat, wilful and unwilling,
Show'd like two silver doves that sit a-billing.
Venus and Adonis, l. 365. The only use of "a-billing."

COMEDY

See also Play, Tragedy

8
Marry, our play is, The most lamentable comedy, and most cruel death of Pyramus and Thisby.
A Midsummer-Night's Dream. Act i, sc. 2, l. 11. [Quince]
There are things in this comedy of Pyramus and Thisby that will never please.
A Midsummer-Night's Dream. Act iii, sc. 1, l. 9. [Bottom]
I do not doubt to hear them say, it is a sweet comedy.
A Midsummer-Night's Dream. Act iv, sc. 2, l. 45. [Bottom]
Christmas comedy.—*Love's Labour's Lost,* v, 2, 462.

9
Messenger: Your honour's players, hearing your amendment,
Are come to play a pleasant comedy;
For so your doctors hold it very meet . . .
You hear a play And frame your mind to mirth. . . .
Sly: Marry, I will, let them play it. Is not a comonty a Christmas gambold or a tumbling-trick?
Page: No, my good lord; it is more pleasing stuff.
Sly: What, household stuff?
Page: It is a kind of history.
The Taming of the Shrew. Ind., sc. 2, l. 131. The only use of "comonty" (comedy), "gambold" (gambol), and "tumbling-trick."

10
Are you a comedian?
Twelfth Night. Act i, sc. 5, l. 194. [Olivia]
Quick comedians.—*Antony and Cleopatra,* v, 2, 216. The only uses of "comedian."

COMFORT

11
Be comfortable to my mother, your mistress, and make much of her.
All's Well that Ends Well. Act i, sc. 1, l. 86. [Bertram]
For my sake be comfortable.
As You Like It. Act ii, sc. 6, l. 9. [Orlando]
So true, so just, and now so comfortable?
Timon of Athens. Act iv, sc. 3, l. 498. [Timon]

12
Nay, there is some comfort in the news, some comfort.
All's Well that Ends Well. Act iii, sc. 2, l. 38. [Clown]
Nay, there's comfort in 't.—*The Winter's Tale,* i, 2, 196.
Why, that's some comfort.—*The Winter's Tale,* i, 2, 208.

13
Her head's declined, and death will seize her, but
Your comfort makes the rescue.
Antony and Cleopatra. Act iii, sc. 11, l. 47. [Eros]
Best of comfort.—*Antony and Cleopatra,* iii, 6, 89.

All strange and terrible events are welcome,
But comforts we despise.
Antony and Cleopatra. Act iv, sc. 15, l. 3. [Cleopatra]

Give her what comforts
The quality of her passion shall require.
Antony and Cleopatra. Act v, sc. 1, l. 62. [Cæsar]

1 He that doth the ravens feed,
Yea, providently caters for the sparrow,
Be comfort to my age!
As You Like It. Act ii, sc. 3, l. 43. [Adam] The only use of "providently" and "caters."

2
I must comfort the weaker vessel.
As You Like It, ii, 4, 6. For "weaker vessel" see under WOMAN.

Comfort my sister.—*The Comedy of Errors,* iii, 2, 26.

Go, comfort your cousin.—*Much Ado about Nothing,* iv, 1, 339.

3
In that there's comfort.
Coriolanus. Act ii, sc. 1, l. 242. [Brutus]

His comforts thrive.—*Cymbeline.* v, 4, 104.

They shall taste our comfort.—*Cymbeline,* v, 5, 403.

4 Thou art all the comfort
The gods will diet me with.
Cymbeline. Act iii, sc. 4, l. 182. [Imogen]

It strikes me, past The hope of comfort.
Cymbeline. Act iv, sc. 3, l. 8. [Cymbeline]

Plucks comfort from his looks.
Henry V. Act iv, Prologue, l. 42. [Chorus]

5
God comfort him in his necessity!
I Henry VI. Act iv, sc. 3, l. 15. [York]

God comfort thee!
Twelfth Night. Act iii, sc. 4, l. 34. [Olivia]

God comfort thy capacity!—*Love's Labour's Lost,* iv, 2, 44.

Heaven give your spirits comfort!
Measure for Measure. Act iv, sc. 2, l. 73. [Provost]

6
Great is his comfort in this earthly vale,
Although by his sight his sin be multiplied.
II Henry VI. Act ii, sc. 1, l. 70. [King Henry] "Multiplied" is repeated in i, 2, 73, and occurs in no other play.

Suffolk: Comfort, my sovereign! gracious Henry, comfort!
King: What, doth my Lord of Suffolk comfort me?
Came he right now to sing a raven's note,
Whose dismal tune bereft my vital powers;
And thinks he that the chirping of a wren,
By crying comfort from a hollow breast,
Can chase away the first-conceived sound?
II Henry VI. Act iii, sc. 2, l. 40. [King Henry] The only use of "chirping."

Comfort, my liege.—*Richard II,* iii, 2, 75; 82.

Comfort, my lord.—*III Henry VI,* iv, 8, 28.

Comfort, your majesty!—*II Henry IV,* iv, 4, 112.

Comfort, dear mother.—*Richard III,* ii, 2, 89.

7
Is all thy comfort shut in Gloucester's tomb?
II Henry VI. Act iii, sc. 2, l. 78. [Queen]

You muddy rascal, is that all the comfort you give me?
II Henry IV. Act ii, sc. 4. l. 43. [Doll Tearsheet]

Is this your comfort?
The cordial that ye bring a wretched lady,
A woman lost among ye, laugh'd at, scorn'd?
Henry VIII. Act iii, sc. 1, l. 105. [Queen Katharine]

That comfort comes too late;
'Tis like a pardon after execution.
Henry VIII. Act iv, sc. 2, l. 120. [Queen Katharine]

8
And in thy need such comfort come to thee
As now I reap at thy too cruel hand!
III Henry VI. Act i, sc. 4, l. 165. [York]

9
I beg cold comfort; and you are so strait
And so ingrateful, you deny me that.
King John. Act v, sc. 7, l. 42. [King John] "Cold comfort" is repeated in *The Taming of the Shrew,* iv, 1, 33.

Comfort me with cold.—*King John,* v, 7, 41.

10 Our good old friend,
Lay comforts to your bosom.
King Lear. Act ii, sc. 1, l. 127. [Regan]

I will piece out the comfort with what addition I can.
King Lear. Act iii, sc. 6, l. 2. [Gloucester]

Thy comforts can do me no good at all;
Thee they may hurt.
King Lear. Act iv, sc. 1, l. 17. [Gloucester]

'Twas yet some comfort,
When misery could beguile the tyrant's rage,
And frustrate his proud will.
King Lear. Act iv, sc. 6, l. 62. [Gloucester]

11
As whence the sun 'gins his reflection
Shipwrecking storms and direful thunders break,
So from that spring whence comfort seem'd to come
Discomfort swells.
Macbeth. Act i, sc. 2, l. 25. [Sergeant] The only use of "shipwrecking."

There's comfort yet.—*Macbeth,* iii, 2, 39.

Would I could answer
This comfort with the like!
Macbeth. Act iv, sc. 3, l. 193. [Ross]

12
Here comes newer comfort.
Macbeth. Act v, sc. 8, l. 53. [Siward]

I spy comfort.—*Measure for Measure,* iii, 2, 43.

Here's my comfort.—*The Tempest,* ii, 2, 47; ii, 2, 57.

13
I am come to . . . comfort you.
Measure for Measure. Act iv, sc. 3, l. 55. [Duke]

I could put thee in comfort.—*Love's Labour's Lost,* iv, 3, 52.

I will keep her ignorant of her good,
To make her heavenly comforts of despair,
When it is least expected.
Measure for Measure. Act iv, sc. 3, l. 113. [Duke]

There is another comfort than this world.
Measure for Measure. Act v, sc. 1, l. 49. [Isabella]

Make it your comfort,
So happy is your brother.
Measure for Measure. Act v, sc. 1, l. 403. [Duke]

1
Let 's . . . give him a show of comfort in his suit and lead him on.
The Merry Wives of Windsor. Act ii, sc. 1, l. 97. [Mrs. Page]

2
Nor let no comforter delight mine ear.
Much Ado about Nothing. Act v, sc. 1, l. 6. [Leonato]

Be your comforter.—*Richard III,* i, 3, 10.
It is a comforter.—*The Tempest,* ii, 1, 196.
The best comforter.—*The Tempest,* v, 1, 58.
World's comforter.—*Venus and Adonis,* l. 529.
The only uses of "comforter."

3
Our . . . comforts should increase,
Even as our days do grow!
Othello. Act ii, sc. 1, l. 196. [Desdemona]

I dote In mine own comforts.
Othello. Act ii, sc. 1, l. 208. [Othello]

4
Queen: Uncle, for God's sake, speak comfortable words.
York: Should I do so, I should belie my thoughts:
Comfort 's in heaven; and we are on the earth,
Where nothing lives but crosses, cares and grief.
Richard II. Act ii, sc. 2, l. 76.

Speak comfort.—*Much Ado about Nothing,* v, 1, 21.
Comfort me, boy.—*Love's Labour 's Lost,* i, 2, 67.
Comfort me, counsel me.—*Romeo and Juliet,* iii, 5, 210.
Some comfort, nurse.—*Romeo and Juliet,* iii, 5, 214.
Be my comfort still.—*Sonnets,* cxxxiv.
Men must comfort you.—*Pericles,* iv, 2, 97.
In him your comfort lives.—*Richard III,* ii, 2, 98.

5
Yet this good comfort bring I to your grace.
Richard III. Act iv, sc. 4, l. 522. [Messenger]

Claudio: Now, sister, what 's the comfort?
Isabella: Why,
As all comforts are; most good, most good indeed.
Measure for Measure. Act iii, sc. 1, l. 54.

My clerk hath some good comforts too for you.
The Merchant of Venice, v, 1, 289. [Portia]

Entertain good comfort.—*Richard III,* i, 3, 4.
Be of good comfort.—*King John,* v, 3, 9; v, 7, 25.
Take good comfort.—*Henry VIII,* iv, 2, 119.
Be blest for your good comfort!—*As You Like It,* ii, 7, 135.
I thank you for that good comfort.—*The Merry Wives of Windsor,* iii, 4, 54; *Measure for Measure,* iii, 1, 280.
Comfort, good comfort!—*The Winter's Tale,* iv, 4, 847.

6
Have comfort.
Richard III, ii, 2, 101; *Much Ado about Nothing,* iv, 1, 119; *Anthony and Cleopatra,* v, 2, 33; *The Tempest,* i, 2, 25.

Be comforted.—*King Lear,* iv, 7, 78; *Macbeth,* iv, 3, 213; *Antony and Cleopatra,* iv, 15, 2.
Be of comfort.—*Twelfth Night,* iii, 4, 372; *The Tempest,* i, 2, 495.
Cheer thy spirit with this comfort.—*I Henry VI,* i, 4, 90.
Keep comfort to you.—*Henry VIII,* v, 1, 144.
Take comfort.—*A Midsummer-Night's Dream,* i, 1, 202.
Be manly, and take comfort.—*Pericles,* iii, 1, 22.

7
All comfort that the dark night can afford
Be to thy person.
Richard III. Act v, sc. 3, l. 80. [Richmond]

First Lord: Joy and all comfort in your sacred breast!
Second Lord: And keep your mind, till you return to us,
Peaceful and comfortable!
Pericles. Act i, sc. 2, l. 35.

8
Of comfort no man speak.
Richard II. Act iii, sc. 2, l. 144. [King Richard]

What say you now? what comfort have we now?
By heaven, I 'll hate him everlastingly
That bids me be of comfort any more.
Richard II. Act iii, sc. 2, l. 206. [King Richard]

Comfort forswear me!—*Othello,* iv, 2, 159.

He receives comfort like cold porridge.
The Tempest. Act ii, sc. 1, l. 10. [Sebastian]

9
Such comfort as do lusty young men feel
When well-apparell'd April on the heel
Of limping winter treads.
Romeo and Juliet. Act i, sc. 2, l. 26. [Capulet] The only use of "well-apparell'd."

All this is comfort; wherefore weep I then?
Romeo and Juliet. Act iii, sc. 2, l. 107. [Juliet]

How well my comfort is revived by this!
Romeo and Juliet. Act iii, sc. 3, l. 165. [Romeo]

10
I have great comfort from this fellow.
The Tempest. Act i, sc. 1, l. 30. [Gonzalo]

O grave and good Paulina, the great comfort
That I have had of thee!
Winter's Tale. Act v, sc. 3, l. 1, [Leontes]

Comfort of my life.—*Winter's Tale,* iii, 2, 95.
Great comfort.—*The Merry Wives of Windsor,* ii, 1, 73.
Cordial comfort.—*The Winter's Tale,* v, 3, 77.
Spritely comfort.—*Antony and Cleopatra,* iv, 7, 15.
Unspeakable comfort.—*Winter's Tale,* i, 1, 38.
Most worthy comfort.—*Sonnets,* xlviii.

11
Why dost not comfort me, and help me out?
Titus Andronicus. Act ii, sc. 3, l. 209. [Martius]

COMMAND

See also Obedience, Order

I—Command

1
I must attend his majesty's command.
All's Well that Ends Well. Act i, sc. 1, l. 5. [Bertram]
At your majesty's command.—*All's Well that Ends Well,* v, 3, 252.
At your command.—*The Taming of the Shrew,* iv, 4, 89.
At your best command.—*King John,* i, 1, 197.
2
Leave me, I pray, a little: pray you now:
Nay, do so; for, indeed, I have lost command.
Antony and Cleopatra. Act iii, sc. 11, l. 22. [Antony]
3
I have left you commands.
As You Like It. Act v, sc. 2, l. 131. [Rosalind]
There was excellent command.—*All's Well that Ends Well,* iii, 6, 51.
Fair commands.—*The Merchant of Venice,* iii, 4, 36.
4
Hear you this Triton of the minnows? mark you
His absolute 'shall'?
Coriolanus. Act iii, sc. 1, l. 89. [Coriolanus]
The only mention of Triton. "Minnow" is repeated in *Love's Labour's Lost,* i, 1, 251.
'And shall!' what villain was it spake that word?
Titus Andronicus. Act i, sc. 1, l. 359. [Titus]
His peremptory 'shall.'—*Coriolanus,* iii, 1, 94.
See also under OBSTINACY.
5
Still subsisting Under your great command.
Coriolanus. Act v, sc. 6, l. 73. [Coriolanus]
Great command o'ersways the order.
Hamlet. Act v, sc. 1, l. 251. [Priest]
Good command.—*II Henry IV,* iii, 2, 84.
6
You have done Not after our command.
Cymbeline. Act i, sc. 1, l. 152. [Queen]
7
An exact command,
Larded with many several sorts of reasons.
Hamlet. Act v, sc. 2, l. 19. [Hamlet]
Hard commands.—*King Lear,* iii, 4, 154.
Just command.—*Pericles,* v, 3, 1.
Received command.—*Cymbeline,* iii, 4, 102.
Command of Cæsar.—*Antony and Cleopatra,* iii, 13, 25.
A mistress's command.—*King Lear,* iv, 2, 21.
8
Will you command me to use my legs?
II Henry IV. Epilogue, l. 19.
My heels are at your command.
The Merchant of Venice. Act ii, sc. 2, l. 33. [Launcelot]
9
Dost thou command me to be shut out?
I Henry VI. Act i, sc. 3, l. 30. [Gloucester]
Command in Anjou what your honour pleases.
I Henry VI. Act v, sc. 3, l. 147. [Reignier]
10
We charge and command you, in his highness' name.
I Henry VI. Act i, sc. 3, l. 76. [Officer]
I charge and command.—*II Henry VI,* iv, 6, 3.
We charge and command.—*II Henry VI,* iv, 7, 132.
11
She is content to be at your command;
Command, I mean, of virtuous chaste intents.
I Henry VI. Act v, sc. 5, l. 19. [Suffolk]
12
Stern Falconbridge commands the narrow seas.
III Henry VI. Act i, sc. 1, l. 239. [Queen Margaret]
Sextus Pompeius
Hath given the dare to Cæsar, and commands
The empire of the sea.
Antony and Cleopatra. Act i, sc. 2, l. 191. [Antony]
13
Go where you will, the king shall be commanded;
And be you kings, command, and I 'll obey.
III Henry VI. Act iii, sc. 1, l. 92. [King Henry]
14
Let your highness Command upon me.
Macbeth. Act iii, sc. 1, l. 16. [Banquo]
What I am truly,
Is thine and my poor country's to command.
Macbeth. Act iv, sc. 3, l. 132. [Malcolm]
'Tis her command.—*Macbeth,* v, 1, 27.
15
Those he commands move only in command,
Nothing in love.
Macbeth. Act v, sc. 2, l. 19. [Angus]
16
See this be done,
And sent according to command.
Measure for Measure. Act iv, sc. 3, l. 84. [Duke]
Commands shall be executed.—*Twelfth Night,* iii, 4, 29.
17
How many be commanded that command!
The Merchant of Venice. Act ii, sc. 9, l. 45. [Arragon]
I was commanded from you.
All's Well that Ends Well. Act ii, sc. 5, l. 59. [Helena]
I am commanded here.—*All's Well that Ends Well,* ii, 1, 27.
It was commanded so.—*Measure for Measure,* v, 1, 463.
18
Hast thou command? by him that gave it thee,
From a pure heart command thy rebel will.
The Rape of Lucrece, l. 624.
19
We were not born to sue, but to command.
Richard II. Act i, sc. 1, l. 196. [King Richard]
20
Unmanner'd dog! stand thou, when I command.
Richard III. Act i, sc. 2, l. 39. [Gloucester]
Do as I command ye.—*II Henry VI,* iv, 7, 125.
I command thee go.—*I Henry VI,* iv, 5, 36.
Command him away.—*The Comedy of Errors,* v, 1, 335.
Keep close, I thee command.—*Henry V,* ii, 3, 65.

1
First Murderer: What we will do, we do upon command.
Second Murderer: And he that hath commanded is the king.
Richard III. Act i, sc. 4, l. 198.
At the king's command.—*Love's Labour's Lost,* v, 1, 128.
2
For one commanding all, obey'd of none.
Richard III. Act iv, sc. 4, l. 104. [Queen Margaret]
3
'I may command where I adore.' Why, she may command me: I serve her; she is my lady.
Twelfth Night. Act ii, sc. 5, l. 126. [Malvolio]
4
What is it your honour will command?
The Taming of the Shrew. Ind., sc. 1, l. 54. [Lord] Repeated in the same scene, l. 115.
What you will command me will I do.
The Taming of the Shrew. Act ii, sc. 1, l. 6. [Bianca]
You may command us, sir.—*Henry VIII,* iv, 1, 117.
You shall command me.—*Troilus and Cressida,* iv, 5, 286.
Please you command.—*The Two Gentlemen of Verona,* ii, 1, 120.
Command me while I live.—*The Two Gentlemen of Verona,* iii, 1, 23.
Command me any service.—*Love's Labour's Lost,* v, 2, 312.
5
One that attends your ladyship's command.
The Two Gentlemen of Verona. Act iv, sc. 3, l. 5. [Eglamour]
By his master's command.—*The Two Gentlemen of Verona,* iv, 2, 79.
6 The good mind of Camillo tardied
My swift command.
The Winter's Tale. Act iii, sc. 2, l. 163. [Leontes] The only use of "tardied."
Abhorr'd commands.—*The Tempest,* i, 2, 273.
Dread command.—*Hamlet,* iii, 4, 108.
Vain command.—*Henry V,* iii, 3, 24.

II—Commandment

7
And thy commandment all alone shall live,
Within the book and volume of my brain.
Hamlet. Act i, sc. 5, l. 102. [Hamlet]
Tell him his commandment is fulfill'd.
Hamlet. Act v, sc. 2, l. 381. [Fortinbras]
He never gave commandment for their death.
Hamlet. Act v, sc. 2, l. 385. [Horatio]
8
Ten commandments.
II Henry VI, i, 3, 145. The only reference to the Scriptural commandents.
Ten Commandments.—*Measure for Measure,* i, 2, 8. Referring to the finger-nails.
9
Have I commandment on the pulse of life?
King John. Act iv, sc. 2, l. 92. [King John]
10
'Twas a commandment to command the captain and all the rest from their functions: they put forth to steal.
Measure for Measure. Act i, sc. 2, l. 13. [First Gentleman]
Commandment of a king.—*Troilus and Cressida,* i, 3, 93.
Stern commandment.—*As You Like It,* ii, 7, 109.
Your mother's commandment.—*Hamlet,* iii, 2, 239.
Your wife's commandment.—*The Merchant of Venice,* iv, 1, 451.
11
To the contrary, I have express commandment.
The Winter's Tale. Act ii, sc. 2, l. 8. [Gaoler]
Express commandment.—*I Henry VI,* i, 3, 20.
Express command.—*Measure for Measure,* iv, 2, 176.

III—Commander

12
The commanders [are] very poor rogues, upon my reputation and credit and as I hope to live.
All's Well that Ends Well. Act iv, sc. 3, l. 153. [Parolles]
13
A good old commander and a most kind gentleman.
Henry V. Act iv, sc. 1, l. 97. [Williams]
I will rather sue to be despised than to deceive so good a commander.
Othello. Act ii, sc. 3, l. 279. [Cassio]
14
Commander of this hot malicious day.
King John. Act ii, sc. 1, l. 314. [English Herald]
Commander of our commonweal.—*Titus Andronicus,* i, 1, 247.
Commander of my thoughts.—*Titus Andronicus,* iv, 4, 28.
15
In great commanders grace and majesty
You might behold, triumphing in their faces.
The Rape of Lucrece, l. 1387.
Great commanders.—*I Henry VI,* iv, 3, 48; *Henry V,* iii, 6, 74; *Troilus and Cressida,* i, 3, 55.
Greatest commander.—*All's Well that Ends Well,* iii, 5, 6.
World's commander.—*Love's Labour's Lost,* v, 2, 565.
Royal commanders.—*III Henry VI,* ii, 2, 67.

COMMENDATION

See also Applause, Praise

16
The duke hath offered him letters of commendations.
All's Well that Ends Well. Act iv, sc. 3, l. 91. [Servant]
I have your commendation.—*Cymbeline,* i, 4, 166.
17
With most prosperous approbation.
Coriolanus. Act ii, sc. 1, l. 113. [Volumnia]
Give them . . . approbation.—*Timon of Athens,* iv, 3, 36.
Receive her approbation.—*Measure for Measure,* i, 2, 183.

Seal'd in approbation.—*Measure for Measure,* v, 1, 245.
Upon your approbation.—*Coriolanus,* ii, 3, 152.
Learned approbation.—*Henry VIII,* i, 2, 71.
Applause and approbation.—*Troilus and Cressida,* i, 3, 59.

1
The approbation of those that weep this lamentable divorce.
Cymbeline. Act i, sc. 4, l. 19. [Iachimo]
Would I had put my estate and my neighbour's on the approbation of what I have spoke!
Cymbeline. Act i, sc. 4, l. 133. [Iachimo]
To such proceeding
Who ever but his approbation added,
Though not his prime consent, he did not flow
From honourable sources.
Pericles. Act iv, sc. 3, l. 25. [Cleon] See also CONSENT.
Revoke Your sudden approbation.—*Coriolanus,* ii, 3, 259.
Nought for approbation.—*The Winter's Tale,* ii, 1, 177.

2
His majesty commended him to you.
Hamlet. Act v, sc. 2, l. 203. [Lord]
Commended him a true man.—*The Merry Wives of Windsor,* ii, 1, 149.
Much commended.—*The Two Gentlemen of Verona,* ii, 4, 123.
Commended to his goodness.—*Henry VIII,* iv, 2, 131.
Commended to our master.—*Pericles,* i, 3, 38.

3
Beguiling them of commendation.
I Henry IV. Act iii, sc. 1, l. 189. [Worcester] "Beguiling" is repeated in *Henry V,* iv, 1, 171.
High commendation.—*As You Like It,* i, 2, 275.

4
I commend me to thee, I commend thee, and I leave thee.
II Henry IV. Act ii, sc. 2, l. 136. [Poins]
Biron: Lady, I will commend you to mine own heart.
Rosaline: Pray you, do my commendations; I would be glad to see it.
Love's Labour's Lost. Act ii, sc. 1, l. 180.
I'll commend you to my master.
The Two Gentlemen of Verona. Act i, sc. 1, l. 155. [Speed]
O, well done! I commend your pains.
Macbeth. Act iv, sc. 1, l. 39. [Hecate]

5
Suffolk: Farewell, sweet madam: but hark you, Margaret;
No princely commendations to my king?
Margaret: Such commendations as becomes a maid,
A virgin and his servant, say to him.
I Henry VI. Act v, sc. 3, l. 177.
Princely commendations.—*Henry VIII,* iv, 2, 118.
You were ever good at sudden commendations.
Henry VIII. Act v, sc. 3, l. 122. [King Henry]

6
And in his commendations I am fed;
It is a banquet to me.
Macbeth. Act i, sc. 4, l. 55. [Duncan]

7
As thou seest her before me, commend me.
The Merry Wives of Windsor. Act i, sc. 4, l. 168. [Fenton]
Commend me bountifully to his good lordship.
Timon of Athens. Act iii, sc. 2, l. 58. [Lucius]
Commend me.—*III Henry VI,* v, 2, 42, and twenty-five times in later plays.
Kind commends.—*Richard II,* iii, 1, 38.
Commends and courteous breath.—*The Merchant of Venice,* ii, 9, 90.

8
Only this commendation I can afford her, that were she other than she is, she were unhandsome.
Much Ado about Nothing. Act i, sc. 1, l. 175. [Benedick] "Unhandsome" is repeated in *As You Like It,* Epil., 2; *I Henry IV,* i, 3, 44; *Othello,* iii, 4, 151.
The commendation is not in his wit, but in his villany.
Much Ado about Nothing. Act ii, sc. 1, l. 145. [Beatrice]

9
It pleaseth you, my royal father, to express
My commendations great, whose merit 's less.
Pericles. Act ii, sc. 2, l. 8. [Thaisa]
Man's commendation.—*Twelfth Night,* iii, 2, 40.

10
'Tis a word or two Of commendations.
The Two Gentlemen of Verona. Act i, sc. 3, l. 53. [Proteus]
Well, sir, this gentleman is come to me,
With commendation from great potentates.
The Two Gentlemen of Verona. Act ii, sc. 4, l. 78. [Duke] "Potentates" is repeated in *I Henry VI,* iii, 2, 136; and in *Love's Labour's Lost,* v, 2, 684.
Hearty commendations.—*The Merry Wives of Windsor,* ii, 2, 99.

11
Who is Silvia? what is she,
That all our swains commend her?
Holy, fair and wise is she;
The heaven such grace did lend her,
That she might admired be.
The Two Gentlemen of Verona. Act iv, sc. 2, l. 39. [Host]

COMMERCE, see Trade

COMMISSION

12
You must to Parthia: your commission 's ready.
Antony and Cleopatra. Act ii, sc. 3, l. 41. [Antony]
I might ask you for your commission.
As You Like It. Act iv, sc. 1, l. 138. [Rosalind]
Commission of your birth.—*All's Well that Ends Well,* ii, 3, 279.

13
Take your commission; hie you to your bands.
Coriolanus. Act i, sc. 2, l. 26. [Senator]
Take The one half of my commission.
Coriolanus. Act iv, sc. 5, l. 144. [Aufidius]
Yet I wish, sir,—
I mean for your particular,—you had not

Join'd in commission with him; but either
Had borne the action of yourself, or else
To him had left it solely.
Coriolanus. Act iv, sc. 7, l. 12. [Lieutenant]

1 He creates
Lucius proconsul: and to you the tribunes,
For this immediate levy, he commends
His absolute commission.
Cymbeline. Act iii, sc. 7, l. 7. [Senator] The only use of "proconsul."
Full commission.—*II Henry IV,* iv, 1, 162; *Othello,* ii, 1, 29.

2
I your commission will forthwith dispatch.
Hamlet. Act iii, sc. 3, l. 3. [King]
Give him . . . his commission.—*Hamlet,* ii, 2, 74.
Hamlet: Making so bold,
My fears forgetting manners, to unseal
Their grand commission; where I found . . .
An exact command . . . My head should be struck off.
Horatio: Is 't possible?
Hamlet: Here 's the commission: read it at more leisure.
But wilt thou hear me how I did proceed?
Horatio: I beseech you.
Hamlet: I sat me down,
Devised a new commission, wrote it fair:
I once did hold it, as our statists do,
A baseness to write fair and labour'd much
How to forget that learning, but, sir, now
It did me yeoman's service.
Hamlet. Act v, sc. 2, l. 16. "Statist" is repeated in *Cymbeline,* ii, 4, 16.

3
Who are the late commissioners?
Henry V. Act ii, sc. 2, l. 61. [King Henry] The only use of "commissioners."

4 I do greet your excellence
With letters of commission from the king.
I Henry VI. Act v, sc. 4, l. 94. [Cardinal]
King's commission.—*II Henry VI,* ii, 4, 75.

5
Here my commission stays.
II Henry VI. Act ii, sc. 4, l. 76. [Sheriff]

6 Your subjects
Are in great grievance; there have been commissions
Sent down among 'em, which hath flaw'd the heart
Of all their loyalties: . . . commissions, which compel from each
The sixth part of his substance.
Henry VIII. Act i, sc. 2, l. 19. [Queen Katharine] "Flaw'd" is repeated in i, 1, 95: "Flaw'd the league"; and in *King Lear,* v, 3, 196: "Flaw'd heart."
By commission.—*Henry VIII,* ii, 2, 6.

7
To your highness' hand I tender my commission.
Henry VIII. Act ii, sc. 2, l. 103. [Campeius]
Commission from Rome.—*Henry VIII,* ii, 4, 1.
Commission from the consistory.—*Henry VIII,* ii, 4, 91.

8
Where 's your commission, lords? words cannot carry
Authority so weighty.
Henry VIII. Act iii, sc. 2, l. 233. [Wolsey]
Item, you sent a large commission
To Gregory de Cassado.
Henry VIII. Act iii, sc. 2, l. 320. [Surrey] The only mention of Cassado.

9
From whom hast thou this great commission?
King John. Act ii, sc. 1, l. 110. [King John]
Use our commission in his utmost force.
King John. Act iii, sc. 3, l. 11. [King John]

10 He led our powers;
Bore the commission of my place and person;
The which immediacy may well stand up,
And call itself your brother.
King Lear. Act v, sc. 3, l. 63. [Regan] The only use of "immediacy."
He hath commission from my wife and me
To hang Cordelia in the prison, and
To lay the blame upon her own despair,
That she fordid herself.
King Lear. Act v, sc. 3, l. 252. [Edmund] The only use of "fordid."

11 This is our commission,
From which we would not have you warp.
. . . Take thy commission. . . .
To the hopeful execution do I leave you
Of your commissions.
Measure for Measure. Act i, sc. 1, l. 14. [Duke]
Take thy commission.—*Measure for Measure,* i, 1, 48.

12
There is especial commission come from Venice.
Othello. Act iv, sc. 2, l. 225. [Iago]

13
His seal'd commission, left in trust with me,
Doth speak sufficiently he 's gone to travel.
Pericles. Act i, sc. 3, l. 13. [Helicanus]
Seals a commission.—*Troilus and Cressida,* iii, 3, 231.
My commission
Is not to reason of the deed, but do it.
Pericles. Act iv, sc. 1, l. 83. [Leonine]
Shew him our commission.—*Richard III,* i, 4, 90.

14
But this is from my commission.
Twelfth Night. Act i, sc. 5, l. 202. [Viola]
Have you any commission from your lord to negotiate with my face? You are now out of your text.
Twelfth Night. Act i, sc. 5, l. 249. [Olivia]

15
I 'll give him my commission.
The Winter's Tale. Act i, sc. 2, l. 40. [Hermione]
Beyond commission.—*Winter's Tale,* i, 2, 144.

COMMONNESS, see Vulgarity

COMMONWEALTH

See also Government, State

16
The commonwealth doth stand, and so would do,
Were he more angry at it.
Coriolanus. Act iv, sc. 6, l. 14. [Sicinius]

The commonwealth of Athens.—*Timon of Athens,* iv, 3, 352.
The commonwealth of Rome.—*Titus Andronicus,* i, 1, 313.
Commonwealth of nature.—*All's Well that Ends Well,* i, 1, 137.

1
Gadshill: They pray continually to their saint, the commonwealth; or rather, not pray to her, but prey on her, for they ride up and down on and make her their boots.
Chamberlain: What, the commonwealth their boots? will she hold out water in foul way?
Gadshill: She will, she will: justice hath liquored her.
I Henry IV. Act ii, sc. 1, l. 89. The only use of "liquored."

2
Whiles I was busy for the commonwealth,
Your highness pleased to forget my place.
II Henry IV. Act v, sc. 2, l. 76. [Chief Justice]

3
So kind a father of the commonweal.
I Henry VI. Act iii, sc. 1, l. 98. [Third Servant]
King and commonweal.—*II Henry VI,* i, 4, 46; ii, 1, 22; ii, 1, 191; *Titus Andronicus,* i, 1, 114.
King and commander of our commonweal.—*Titus Andronicus,* i, 1, 247.

4
Since thou wert king—as who is king but thou?—
The commonwealth hath daily run to wreck.
II Henry VI. Act i, sc. 3, l. 127. [Suffolk]
Commonwealth affairs.—*II Henry VI,* i, 3, 157. *Henry V,* i, 1, 41.

5
The clothier means to dress the commonwealth, and turn it, and set a new nap upon it.
II Henry VI. Act iv, sc. 2, l. 6. [Bevis]
"Clothier" is repeated in *King Lear,* iv, 6, 88; and in *Henry VIII,* i, 2, 31.
Lord Say hath gelded the commonwealth, and made it an eunuch.
II Henry VI. Act iv, sc. 2, l. 177. [Cade]

6
Here comes a member of the commonwealth.
Love's Labour 's Lost. Act iv, sc. 1, l. 41. [Boyet]
You are a good member of the commonwealth.
Love's Labour 's Lost. Act iv, sc. 2, l. 79. [Sir Nathaniel]
You are no good member of the commonwealth.
The Merchant of Venice. Act iii, sc. 5, l. 37. [Jessica]

7
I' the commonwealth I would by contraries
Execute all things; for no kind of traffic
Would I admit; no name of magistrate;
Letters should not be known; riches, poverty,
And use of service, none; contract, succession,
Bourn, bound of land, tilth, vineyard, none;
No use of metal, corn, or wine, or oil.
The Tempest. Act ii, sc. 1, l. 147. [Gonzalo]
"Tilth" is used only once again, in *Measure for Measure,* i, 4, 44: "Tilth and husbandry."

COMPANION

See also Comradeship

8
Did this companion with the saffron face
Revel and feast it at my house to-day,
Whilst upon me the guilty doors were shut
And I denied to enter in my house?
The Comedy of Errors. Act iv, sc. 4, l. 64. [Antipholus of Ephesus]
Companionship in peace.—*Coriolanus,* iii, 2, 49.
All of companionship.—*Timon of Athens,* i, 1, 251. The only uses of "companionship."

9
I 'ld change my sex to be companion with them.
Cymbeline. Act iii, sc. 6, l. 88. [Imogen]
Two of the sweet'st companions in the world.
Cymbeline. Act v, sc. 5, l. 349. [Belarius]
The sweet'st companion that e'er man
Bred his hopes out of.
The Winter's Tale. Act v, sc. 1, l. 11. [Leontes]
Companion of his nuptial bed.
I Henry VI. Act v, sc. 5, l. 58. [Suffolk] See under WIFE.
Fit to be made companion with a king.
I Henry VI. Act v, sc. 3. l. 149. [Suffolk]

10
There is a devil haunts thee in the likeness of an old fat man; a tun of man is thy companion.
I Henry IV. Act ii, sc. 4, l. 492. [Prince of Wales]
Grew a companion to the common streets.
I Henry IV, iii, 2, 68. See under KING.

11
The prince but studies his companions
Like a strange tongue, wherein, to gain the language,
'Tis needful that the most immodest word
Be look'd upon and learn'd; which once attain'd,
Your highness knows, comes to no further use
But to be known and hated.
II Henry IV. Act iv, sc. 4, l. 68. [Warwick]
Chief Justice: Well, God send the prince a better companion!
Falstaff: God send the companion a better prince!
II Henry IV. Act i, sc. 2, l. 223.

12
Why, rude companion, whatso'er thou be,
I know thee not.
II Henry VI. Act iv, sc. 10, l. 33. [Iden]
I scorn you, scurvy companion.—*II Henry IV,* ii, 4, 132.
Mild companion.—*Pericles,* i, 1, 18.
Pale companion.—*A Midsummer-Night's Dream,* i, 1, 16.
Sad companion.—*Pericles,* i, 2, 2.
Spruce companions.—*The Taming of the Shrew,* iv, 1, 116.

1
I abhor such fanatical phantasimes, such insociable and point-devise companions.
Love's Labour's Lost. Act v, sc. 1, l. 19. [Holofernes] The only use of "fanatical." "Phantisime" (fantastic person) is used again in iv, 1, 101 (see below), and in no other play. "Insociable" is repeated in v, 2, 809, and nowhere else.
You are rather point-device.—*As You Like It,* iii, 2, 401.
Point-devise the very man.—*Twelfth-Night,* ii, 5, 177. The only uses of "point-devise."
A phantasime, a Monarcho.—*Love's Labour's Lost,* iv, 1, 101. The only use of "Monarcho," a title assumed by an insane Italian, who fancied himself emperor of the world.
2
Companions
That do converse and waste the time together,
Whose souls do bear an equal yoke of love,
There must be needs a like proportion
Of lineaments, of manners and of spirit.
The Merchant of Venice. Act iii, sc. 4, l. 11. [Portia]
3
Who is his companion now? He hath every month a new sworn brother.
Much Ado about Nothing. Act i, sc. 1, l. 72. [Beatrice] See under BROTHERHOOD.
Who is his companion?—*Much Ado about Nothing,* i, 1, 81.
Co-partners in my claim.—*The Rape of Lucrece,* l. 789. The only use of "co-partners."
4
Inquire at London, 'mongst the taverns there,
For there, they say, he daily doth frequent,
With unrestrained loose companions.
Richard II. Act v, sc. 3, l. 5. [Bolingbroke] The only use of "unrestrained."
His companies unletter'd, rude and shallow.
Henry V. Act i, sc. 1, l. 55. [Canterbury]
5
I would not wish
Any companion in the world but you.
The Tempest. Act iii, sc. 1, l. 54. [Miranda]

COMPANY

See also Society

6
I would gladly have him see his company anatomized.
All's Well that Ends Well. Act iv, sc. 3, l. 37. [First Lord] "Anatomized" is repeated in *As You Like It,* ii, 7, 56. "Anatomize" is used three times.
7
Antony: Let us, Lepidus,
Not lack your company.
Lepidus: Noble Antony,
Not sickness should detain me.
Antony and Cleopatra. Act ii, sc. 2, l. 172.
Choose your own company.—*Antony and Cleopatra,* iii, 4, 37.
8
I cannot live out of her company.
As You Like It. Act i, sc. 3. l. 88. [Celia]
If thou hast not broke trom company
Abruptly, as my passion now makes me,
Thou hast not loved.
As You Like It. Act ii, sc. 4, l. 40. [Silvius] The only use of "abruptly."
Why, how now, monsieur! what a life is this,
That your poor friends must woo your company?
As You Like It. Act ii, sc. 7, l. 9. [Duke]
Jaques: I thank you for your company; but, good faith, I had as lief have been myself alone.
Orlando: And so had I; but yet, for fashion sake, I thank you too for your society.
As You Like It. Act iii, sc. 2, l. 268.
9
Here comes more company.
As You Like It. Act iv, sc. 3, l. 75. [Rosalind]
More company!—*The Comedy of Errors,* iv, 4, 110.
Here's company.—*The Merry Wives of Windsor,* ii, 3, 17.
Is all our company here?—*A Midsummer-Night's Dream,* i, 2, 1.
Company! stay.—*Love's Labour's Lost,* iv, 3, 77.
10
Guiderius: What company Discover you abroad?
Belarius: No single soul Can we set eye on.
Cymbeline. Act iv, sc. 2, l. 129.
What company is this?—*The Taming of the Shrew,* i, 1, 46.
11
I am joined with no foot land-rakers, no long-staff sixpenny strikers, none of these mad mustachio purple-hued malt-worms; but with nobility and tranquillity, burgomasters and great oneyers.
I Henry IV. Act ii, sc. 1, l. 80. [Gadshill] The only use of "land-rakers," "long-staff," "sixpenny," "strikers," "purple-hued," "malt-worms," "tranquillity," "burgomasters" and "oneyers" (meaning unknown). Shakespeare's fertility of invention in invective of this sort is notable throughout the plays. "Purple-coloured" occurs in *Venus and Adonis,* l. 1.
I have forsworn his company hourly any time this two and twenty years, and yet I am bewitched with the rogue's company.
I Henry IV. Act ii, sc. 2, l. 16. [Falstaff]
12
There is a thing, Harry, which thou hast often heard of and it is known to many in our land by the name of pitch: this pitch, as ancient writers do report, doth defile; so doth the company thou keepest.
I Henry IV. Act ii, sc. 4, l. 452. [Falstaff]
It is certain that either wise bearing or ignorant carriage is caught, as men take diseases, one of another: therefore let men take heed of their company.
II Henry IV. Act v, sc. 1, l. 84. [Falstaff]
13
Company, villanous company, hath been the spoil of me.
I Henry IV. Act iii, sc. 3, l. 10. [Falstaff]
Keeping such vile company as thou art hath in reason taken from me all ostentation of sorrow.
II Henry IV. Act ii, sc. 2, l. 52. [Prince of Wales]

Too familiar
Is my dear son with such sour company.
Romeo and Juliet. Act iii, sc. 3, l. 6. [Friar Laurence]
What, hath your grace no better company?
King Lear. Act iii, sc. 4, l. 147. [Gloucester]
Curst company.—*A Midsummer-Night's Dream,* iii, 2, 341.
Scandal'd company.—*The Tempest,* iv, 1, 90.
Thief's company.—*I Henry IV,* ii, 2, 10.
Vulgar company.—*I Henry IV,* iii, 2, 41.

1
Prince of Wales: What company?
Page: Ephesians, my lord, of the old church.
II Henry IV. Act ii, sc. 2, l. 163. "Ephesian" (boon companion) is repeated in *The Merry Wives of Windsor,* iv, 5, 19.
Discharge yourself of our company, Pistol.
II Henry IV. Act ii, sc. 4, l. 147. [Falstaff] See under DISMISSAL.

2
Talbot: Will not your honours bear me company?
Bedford: No, truly; it is more than manners will.
I Henry VI. Act ii, sc. 2, l. 53.
Bear me company and go with me.
The Two Gentlemen of Verona. Act iv, sc. 3, l. 34. [Eglamour]
Bear him company.—*The Comedy of Errors,* i, 1, 130.
Bear you company.—*III Henry VI,* i, 3, 6; *Richard III,* ii, 3, 47; *The Taming of the Shrew,* iv, 3, 49; *Henry VIII,* i, 1, 212; ii, 2, 59.

3
A wilderness is populous enough,
So Suffolk had thy heavenly company.
II Henry VI. Act iii, sc. 2, l. 360. [Suffolk] See under LOVE.
Nor doth this wood lack worlds of company,
For you in my respect are all the world.
A Midsummer-Night's Dream. Act ii, sc. 1, l. 223. [Helena]
Godly company.—*The Merry Wives of Windsor,* i, 1, 187.
Good company.—*The Taming of the Shrew,* i, 1, 6, and four times in later plays.
Goodly company.—*The Taming of the Shrew,* iii, 2, 96.
Honest company.—*The Taming of the Shrew,* iii, 2, 195.
Merry company.—*The Rape of Lucrece,* l. 1110.
Wise company.—*Timon of Athens,* ii, 2, 77.

4
A noble company! what are their pleasures?
Henry VIII. Act i, sc. 4, l. 64. [Wolsey]
Noble company.—*Othello,* i, 3, 179.
Courtly company.—*II Henry VI,* i, 1, 27.
Valiant company.—*I Henry VI,* iii, 2, 125.

5
Given To . . . much company.
Julius Cæsar. Act ii, sc. 1, l. 189. [Brutus]
Loves company.—*Othello,* iii, 3, 184.

6
King: Prize you yourselves: what buys your company?
Rosaline: Your absence only.
King: That can never be.
Rosaline: Then cannot we be bought: and so, adieu;
Twice to your visor and half once to you.
Love's Labour's Lost. Act v, sc. 2, l. 224.

7
Your company is fairer than honest.
Measure for Measure. Act iv, sc. 3, l. 185. [Duke]
Fair company.—*Troilus and Cressida,* iii, 1, 47; *Henry VIII,* i, 4, 8.

8
He kept company with the wild prince.
The Merry Wives of Windsor. Act iii, sc. 2, l. 73. [Page]
Keep company.—*Henry V,* iv, 6, 16; *Twelfth Night,* v, 1, 99.
Keep her company.—*Othello,* iv, 2, 137.
Keep him company.—*Romeo and Juliet,* iii, 1, 133; *Macbeth,* iii, 1, 135; *Timon of Athens,* v, 1, 111.
Keep me company.—*The Merchant of Venice,* i, 1, 108.
Keep us company.—*The Comedy of Errors,* v, 1, 398.
Keep you company.—*II Henry VI,* iii, 2, 302; *Troilus and Cressida,* v, 1, 93; i, 1, 294; *Coriolanus,* ii, 3, 157.
Kept me company.—*II Henry IV,* v, 5, 63.

9
We shall be dogged with company.
A Midsummer-Night's Dream. Act i, sc. 2, l. 106. [Quince]

10
I offered him my company to a willow-tree, either to make him a garland, as being forsaken, or to bind him up a rod, as being worthy to be whipped.
Much Ado about Nothing. Act ii, sc. 1, l. 225. [Benedick] The only use of "willow-tree."

11
I must discontinue your company.
Much Ado about Nothing. Act v, sc. 1, l. 192. [Benedick] The only use of "discontinue."
Steal out of your company.—*Much Ado about Nothing,* iii, 3, 63.
I have forsworn his . . . company.—*A Midsummer-Night's Dream,* ii, 1, 62.
Well, I must leave her company.—*Othello,* iv, 1, 148.
They that fawn'd on him before
Use his company no more.
The Passionate Pilgrim, l. 422.

12
Your company,
Which, I protest, hath very much beguiled
The tediousness and process of my travel.
Richard II. Act ii, sc. 3, l. 10. [Northumberland]
Northumberland: By this the weary lords
Shall make their way seem short, as mine hath done
By sight of what I have, your noble company.
Bolingbroke: Of much less value is my company
Than your good words.
Richard II. Act ii, sc. 3, l. 16.
Withal make known
Which way thou travellest: if along with us,

We shall be joyful of thy company.
The Taming of the Shrew. Act iv, sc. 5, l. 50. [Petruchio]

How I love thy company.
Romeo and Juliet. Act ii, sc. 2, l. 174. [Juliet]

1
You like not of my company.
The Taming of the Shrew, Act ii, sc. 1, l. 65. [Petruchio]

2
But, soft! company is coming here.
The Taming of the Shrew. Act iv, sc. 5, l. 26. [Petruchio]

3
Go, let him have a table by himself, for he does neither affect company, nor is he fit for 't, indeed.
Timon of Athens. Act i, sc. 2, l. 29. [Timon]

The plague of company light upon thee!
Timon of Athens. Act iv, sc. 3, l. 357. [Apemantus]

Get thee gone;
I see thou art not for my company.
Titus Andronicus. Act iii, sc. 2, l. 57. [Titus]

I myself am best When least in company.
Twelfth Night. Act i, sc. 4, l. 37. [Duke]

Leave me alone;
For I must think of that which company
Would not be friendly to.
Henry VIII. Act v, sc. 1, l. 74. [King]

4
Troilus: What offends you, lady?
Cressida: Sir, mine own company.
Troilus: You cannot shun Yourself.
Cressida: Let me go and try.
Troilus and Cressida. Act iii, sc. 2, l. 152.

Mine own company.—*A Midsummer-Night's Dream,* iii, 2, 436; *All's Well that Ends Well,* iv, 3, 187.

5
I do desire thy worthy company.
The Two Gentlemen of Verona. Act iv, sc. 3, l. 25. [Silvia]

Entreats your company.—*Timon of Athens,* i, 2, 194.

Let 's have your company.—*Troilus and Cressida,* iv, 1, 39.

Please 't your highness
To grace us with your royal company.
Macbeth. Act iii, sc. 4, l. 45. [Ross]

Doth entreat Your company at dinner.
The Merchant of Venice. Act iv, sc. 2, l. 8. [Gratiano] See under DINING.

Say, by this token, I desire his company.
Measure for Measure. Act iv, sc. 3, l. 144. [Duke]

Let me desire your company.—*Coriolanus,* iii, 1, 335.

Crave my company.—*II Henry IV,* ii, 3, 68.

Craves your company.—*III Henry VI,* ii, 1, 208.

COMPARISON

6
Lay his gay comparisons apart.
Antony and Cleopatra. Act iii, sc. 13, l. 26. [Antony]

As fair and as good—a kind of hand-in-hand comparison.
Cymbeline. Act i, sc. 4, l. 75. [Iachimo] The only use of the hyphenated phrase "hand-in-hand." "Hand in hand," unhyphenated, is used eleven times.

7
When thou hast tired thyself in base comparisons, hear me speak but this.
I Henry IV. Act ii, sc. 4, l. 276. [Prince of Wales]

Comparisons with dirt.—*Troilus and Cressida,* i, 3, 194.

8
Stand'st thou aloof upon comparison?
I Henry VI. Act v, sc. 4, l. 150. [York]

So stands the comparison.—*Love's Labour 's Lost,* iv, 1, 80.

That the comparison May stand more proper.
The Merchant of Venice. Act iii, sc. 2, l. 45. [Portia]

9
Compare our faces and be judge yourself.
King John. Act i, sc. 1, l. 78. [Bastard]

I am compared to twenty thousand fairs.
Love's Labour 's Lost. Act v, sc. 2, l. 37. [Rosaline]

What wicked and dissembling glass of mine
Made me compare with Hermia's sphery eyne?
A Midsummer-Night's Dream. Act ii, sc. 2, l. 98. [Helena] The only use of "sphery."

10
He 'll break a comparison or two on me.
Much Ado about Nothing. Act ii, sc. 1, l. 152. [Beatrice]

Full of comparisons.—*Love's Labour 's Lost,* v, 2, 854.

Comparisons of truth.—*Troilus and Cressida,* iii, 2, 187.

11
Comparisons are odorous.
Much Ado about Nothing. Act iii, sc. 5, l. 18. [Dogberry] "Odorous" is repeated in *A Midsummer-Night's Dream,* ii, 1, 110: "Odorous chaplet."

12
Compare dead happiness with living woe.
Richard III. Act iv, sc. 4, l. 119. [Queen Margaret]

Above compare.—*Romeo and Juliet,* iii, 5, 238; *Venus and Adonis,* l. 8.

Past compare.—*The Taming of the Shrew,* v, 2, 174; *Romeo and Juliet,* ii, 5, 43.

Braving compare.—*The Rape of Lucrece,* l. 40.

Big compare.—*Troilus and Cressida,* iii, 2, 182.

13
Shall I compare thee to a summer's day?
Thou art more lovely and more temperate.
Sonnets. No. xviii.

Making a couplement of proud compare,
With sun and moon, with earth and sea's rich gems,
With April's first-born flowers, and all things rare
That heaven's air in this huge rondure hems.
Sonnets. No. xxi. "Couplement" is repeated in *Love's Labour 's Lost,* v, 2, 535. The only use of "rondure."

Belied with false compare.—*Sonnets,* cxxx.

O, but with mine compare thou thine own state,
And thou shalt find it merits not reproving.
Sonnets. No. cxlii.

14
An her hair were not somewhat darker than

Helen's—well, go to—there were no more comparison between the women.
Troilus and Cressida. Act i, sc. 1, l. 41. [Pandarus]
Pandarus: Troilus is the better man of the two.
Cressida: O Jupiter! there 's no comparison.
Troilus and Cressida. Act i, sc. 2, l. 63.

II—Some Examples

1 Which of them both
Is dearest to me, I have no skill in sense
To make distinction.
All's Well that Ends Well. Act iii, sc. 4, l. 38. [Countess]

2
This was but as a fly by an eagle.
Antony and Cleopatra. Act ii, sc. 2, l. 186. [Enobarbus]
Even such a man, so faint, so spiritless,
So dull, so dead in look, so woe-begone,
Drew Priam's curtain, in the dead of night.
II Henry IV. Act i, sc. 1, l. 70. [Northumberland] The only use of "spiritless" and "woe-begone."

3 Shall pack-horses
And hollow pamper'd jades of Asia,
Which cannot go but thirty mile a-day,
Compare with Cæsars, and with Cannibals.
II Henry IV. Act ii, sc. 4, l. 177. [Pistol] "Pack-horse" is repeated in *Richard III,* i, 3, 122; and "a-day" in *Henry V,* iv, 1, 316: "Twice a-day."
Thy hand is but a finger to my fist,
Thy leg a stick compared with this truncheon.
II Henry VI. Act iv, sc. 10, l. 51. [Iden]

4
We both have fed as well, and we can both
Endure the winter's cold as well as he.
Julius Cæsar. Act i, sc. 2, l. 98. [Cassius]

5
If he had been as you and you as he,
You would have slipt like him; but he, like you,
Would not have been so stern.
Measure for Measure. Act ii, sc. 2, l. 64. [Isabella]
Why, if two gods should play some heavenly match
And on the wager lay two earthly women,
And Portia one, there must be something else
Pawn'd with the other, for the poor rude world
Hath not her fellow.
The Merchant of Venice. Act iii, sc. 5, l. 84. [Jessica]

6
Tut, you saw her fair, none else being by,
Herself poised with herself in either eye:
But in that crystal scales let there be weigh'd
Your lady's love against some other maid
That I will show you shining at this feast,
And she shall scant show well that now shows best.
Romeo and Juliet. Act i, sc. 2, l. 99. [Benvolio]
Dido a dowdy; Cleopatra a gypsy; Helen and Hero hildings and harlots; Thisbe a grey eye or so, but not to the purpose.
Romeo and Juliet. Act ii, sc. 4, l. 44. [Mercutio] The only use of "dowdy."

7
Ajax: What is he more than another?
Agamemnon: No more than what he thinks he is.
Ajax: Is he so much? Do you not think he thinks himself a better man than I am?
Agamemnon: No question.
Ajax: Will you subscribe his thought, and say he is?
Agamemnon: No, noble Ajax; you are as strong, as valiant, as wise, no less noble, much more gentle, and altogether more tractable.
Troilus and Cressida. Act ii, sc. 3, l. 151.
He, like a puling cuckold, would drink up
The lees and dregs of a flat tamed piece;
You, like a lecher, out of whorish loins
Are pleased to breed out your inheritors:
Both merits poised, each weighs nor less nor more;
But he as he, the heavier for a whore.
Troilus and Cressida. Act iv, sc. 1, l. 61. [Diomedes] The only use of "whorish."

8 How he glisters
Thorough my rust! and how his piety
Does my deeds make the blacker!
The Winter's Tale. Act iii, sc. 2, l. 171. [Leontes]

COMPASSION

See also Pity

9 It is no little thing to make
Mine eyes to sweat compassion.
Coriolanus. Act v, sc. 3, l. 195. [Coriolanus]

10
Moved with compassion of my country's wreck.
I Henry VI. Act iv, sc. 1, l. 56. [Gloucester, reading]
Consent Of mere compassion and of lenity.
I Henry VI. Act v, sc. 4, l. 124. [Beaufort]
His compassion may Give life to yours.
King John. Act iv, sc. 1, l. 89. [Arthur]

11
O, if no harder than a stone thou art,
Melt at my tears, and be compassionate!
The Rape of Lucrece, l. 593.
It boots thee not to be compassionate.
Richard II. Act i, sc. 3, l. 174. [King Richard] "Compassionate" is repeated in *Titus Andronicus,* ii, 3, 217: "Compassionate heart."

12
The senseless brands will sympathise
The heavy accent of thy moving tongue
And in compassion weep the fire out.
Richard II. Act v, sc. 1, l. 46. [King Richard]
Kind compassion.—*Richard III,* iv, 3, 7.
The very virtue of compassion.—*The Tempest,* i, 2, 27.

COMPENSATION

13
One fire drives out one fire; one nail, one nail;
Rights by rights falter, strengths by strengths do fail.
Coriolanus. Act iv, sc. 7, l. 54. [Aufidius]

Thought and affliction, passion, hell itself,
She turns to favour and to prettiness.
Hamlet. Act iv, sc. 5, l. 188. [Laertes]
The only use of "prettiness."

1
Of sufferance comes ease.
II Henry IV. Act v, sc. 4, l. 28. [Hostess]

2
The strawberry grows underneath the nettle
And wholesome berries thrive and ripen best
Neighbour'd by fruit of baser quality.
Henry V. Act i, sc. 1, l. 60. [Bishop of Ely]

3
Thus sometimes hath the brightest day a cloud;
And after summer evermore succeeds
Barren winter, with his wrathful nipping cold:
So cares and joys abound, as seasons fleet.
II Henry VI. Act ii, sc. 4, l. 1. [Gloucester]
"Nipping" is repeated in *Hamlet*, i, 4, 2: "Nipping air."

4
Not being the worst
Stands in some rank of praise.
King Lear. Act ii, sc. 4, l. 260. [King Lear]
Biron: This is not so well as I looked for, but the best that ever I heard.
King Ferdinand: Ay, the best for the worst.
Love's Labour's Lost. Act i, sc. 1, l. 282.
Things at the worst will cease, or else climb upward
To what they were before.
Macbeth. Act iv, sc. 2, l. 24. [Ross]

5
Haste still pays haste, and leisure answers leisure;
Like doth quit like, and MEASURE still FOR MEASURE.
Measure for Measure, v, 1, 415. [Duke]

6
So I return rebuked to my content
And gain by ill thrice more than I have spent.
Sonnets. No. cxix.
By foul play, as thou say'st, were we heaved thence,
But blessedly holp hither.
The Tempest. Act i, sc. 2, l. 62. [Prospero]

7
If I have too austerely punish'd you,
Your compensation makes amends, for I
Have given you here a thrid of mine own life,
Or that for which I live.
The Tempest. Act iv, sc. 1, l. 1. [Prospero]
The only use of "compensation" and "thrid" (thread).

COMPETITION, see Rivalry

COMPLAINT

8
The complaints I have heard of you I do not all believe: 'tis my slowness that I do not; for I know you lack not folly to commit them, and have ability enough to make such knaveries yours.
All's Well that Ends Well. Act i, sc. 3, l. 10. [Countess] "Slowness" is repeated in *Cymbeline*, iii, 5, 168: "Cross'd with slowness."

9
With these shreds
They vented their complainings.
Coriolanus. Act i, sc. 1, l. 212. [Marcius]
"Shreds" is repeated in *Hamlet*, iii, 4, 102: "A king of shreds and patches."
Lack, good youth!
Thou movest no less with thy complaining than
Thy master in bleeding.
Cymbeline. Act iv, sc. 2, l. 374. [Lucius]

10
Dost thou come here to whine?
Hamlet. Act v, sc. 1, l. 300. [Hamlet]
Whine aloud for mercy.—*Antony and Cleopatra*, iii, 13, 101. The only uses of "whine."
He whined away your victory.—*Coriolanus*, v, 6, 98. "Whined" is repeated in *Macbeth*, iv, 1, 2.
Clamorous whining.—*King Lear*, ii, 2, 25.
Whining . . . boy.—*Love's Labour's Lost*, iii, 1, 181.
Whining mammet.—*Romeo and Juliet*, iii, 5, 186. "Mammet" (doll) is repeated in *I Henry IV*, ii, 3, 95: "Play with mammets."
Whining school-boy.—*As You Like It*, ii, 7, 145. The only uses of "whining."

11
Prince: The complaints I hear of thee are grievous.
Falstaff: 'Sblood, my lord, they are false.
I Henry IV. Act ii, sc. 4, l. 486.
I have, and most unwillingly, of late
Heard many grievous, I do say, my lord,
Grievous complaints of you.
Henry VIII. Act v, sc. 1, l. 97. [King Henry]

12
This late complaint
Will make but little for his benefit.
II Henry VI. Act i, sc. 3, l. 100. [Suffolk]
Pitiful complaints.—*I Henry VI*, iv, 1, 57.
Sore complaint.—*Henry V*, i, 2, 26.

13
Bootless are plaints.
III Henry VI. Act ii, sc. 6, l. 23. [Clifford]
She her plaints a little while doth stay.
The Rape of Lucrece, l. 1364.
Plaints and prayers.—*Richard II*, v, 3, 127.
See her plaints.—*III Henry VI*, iii, 1, 41.
Overgo thy plaints.—*Richard III*, ii, 2, 61. The only uses of "plaints."
After our sentence plaining comes too late.
Richard II. Act i, sc. 3, l. 175. [Richard]
Piteous plainings.—*The Comedy of Errors*, i, 1, 73. "Plaining" occurs again in *The Rape of Lucrece*, l. 559.

14
Unite in your complaints,
And force them to a constancy.
Henry VIII. Act iii, sc. 2, l. 1. [Norfolk]
Given ear to our complaint.
Henry VIII, Act v, sc. 1, l. 48. [Gardiner]
Each buzz, each fancy, each complaint.
King Lear. Act i, sc. 4, l. 348. [Goneril]

15
Let us complain to them what fools were here.
Love's Labour's Lost. Act v, sc. 2, l. 302. [Rosaline]
He hath cause to complain.—*Measure for Measure*, ii, 1, 121.
To whom should I complain?—*Measure for Measure*, ii, 4, 171.

You'll complain of me.—*The Merry Wives of Windsor,* i, 1, 112.
Shall I complain on thee?—*The Taming of the Shrew,* iv, 1, 31.
Complain on drouth.—*Venus and Adonis,* l. 544.
Complain on theft.—*Venus and Adonis,* l. 160.

1
Let me not find you before me again upon any complaint whatsoever.
Measure for Measure. Act ii, sc. 1, l. 260. [Escalus]

For he indeed
Hath set the women on to this complaint.
Measure for Measure. Act v, sc. 1, l. 250. [Friar Peter]

2
That to hear her so complain,
Scarce I could from tears refrain;
For her griefs, so lively shown,
Made me think upon mine own.
The Passionate Pilgrim, l. 387.

3
Humbly complaining to her deity.
Richard III. Act i, sc. 1, l. 76. [Gloucester]
Duchess of Gloucester: Where then, alas, may I complain myself?
Gaunt: To God, the widow's champion and defence.
Richard II. Act i, sc. 2, l. 42.
To all the host of heaven I complain me.
The Rape of Lucrece, l. 598.

4 His royal person, . . .
Cannot be quiet scarce a breathing-while,
But you must trouble him with lewd complaints.
Richard III. Act i, sc. 3, l. 59. [Gloucester] The only use of "breathing-while."
I am not barren to bring forth complaints.
Richard III. Act ii, sc. 2, l. 67. [Queen Elizabeth]
Poor heart, adieu! I pity thy complaining.
Richard III. Act iv, sc. 1, l. 88. [Queen Elizabeth]

5
What, do you grumble?
The Taming of the Shrew. Act iv, sc. 1, l. 170. [Petruchio]
What art thou that dost grumble there i' the straw?
King Lear. Act iii, sc. 4, l. 44. [Kent]
Thou grumblest and railest every hour.
Troilus and Cressida. Act ii, sc. 1, l. 35. [Thersites] The only use of "grumblest."
Without or grudge or grumblings.
The Tempest. Act i, sc. 2, l. 249. [Ariel]
Grumbling groom.—*The Taming of the Shrew,* iii, 2, 155.
Grumbling voice.—*III Henry VI,* i, 4, 76.
Grumbling York.—*II Henry VI,* i, 3, 73. The only uses of "grumbling."

COMPLEXION

6
Good my complexion!
As You Like It. Act iii, sc. 2, l. 204. [Rosalind]
The best thing in him Is his complexion.
As You Like It. Act iii, sc. 5, l. 115. [Phebe]

7
Antipholus of Syracuse: What complexion is she of?
Dromio of Syracuse: Swart, like my shoe, but her face nothing like so clean kept.
The Comedy of Errors. Act iii, sc. 2, l. 103. "Swart" is repeated in *I Henry VI,* i, 2, 84, and in *King John,* iii, 1, 46.
A swarthy Ethiope.—*The Two Gentlemen of Verona,* ii, 6, 26. The only use of "swarthy."
Moth: A woman, master.
Armado: Of what complexion?
Moth: Of all the four, of the three, or the two, or one of the four.
Armado: Tell me precisely of what complexion.
Moth: Of the sea-water green, sir.
Armado: Is that one of the four complexions?
Moth: As I have read, sir; and the best of them too.
Love's Labour's Lost. Act i, sc. 2, l. 81. "Sea-water" is repeated in *Tempest,* i, 2, 462.
Variable complexions.—*Coriolanus,* ii, 1, 228.
Pale complexion.—*As You Like It,* iii, 4, 56.

8
The red rose and the white are on his face.
III Henry VI. Act ii, sc. 5, l. 97. [King Henry]

The colour in thy face,
That even for anger makes the lily pale,
And the red rose blush at her own disgrace.
The Rape of Lucrece, l. 477.
Such war of white and red within her cheeks!
The Taming of the Shrew. Act iv, sc. 5, l. 30. [Petruchio]

The war of white and damask in
Their nicely-gawded cheeks.
Coriolanus, ii, 1, 232. See under CHEEK.

Whose red and white
Nature's own sweet and cunning hand laid on.
Twelfth Night, i, 5, 257. See under BEAUTY.
More white and red than doves or roses are.
Venus and Adonis, l. 10.
Immaculate white and red.—*Love's Labour's Lost,* i, 2, 95.
Made of white and red.—*Love's Labour's Lost,* i, 2, 104.

9 The complexion of the element
In favour's like the work we have in hand.
Julius Cæsar, i, 3, 128. See under NIGHT.
Change the complexion of her maid-pale peace.
Richard II, iii, 3, 98. See under ENGLAND. The only use of "maid-pale.".
The complexion of a devil.—*The Merchant of Venice,* i, 2, 143.
Complexion of a goose!—*The Merry Wives of Windsor,* v, 5, 9.
Complexion of my greatness.—*II Henry IV,* ii, 2, 6.
Complexion of the sky.—*Richard II,* iii, 2, 194.
Complexion of them all.—*The Merchant of Venice,* iii, 1, 32.

10
Of all complexions the cull'd sovereignty
Do meet, as at a fair, in her fair cheek.
Love's Labour's Lost. Act iv, sc. 3, l. 234. [Biron]
Your mistresses dare never come in rain,
For fear their colours should be wash'd away.
Love's Labour's Lost. Act iv, sc. 3, l. 270. [Biron]
Soft as our complexions are.—*Measure for Measure,* ii, 4, 129.

Thou painted maypole.—*A Midsummer-Night's Dream,* iii, 2, 296. The only use of "maypole." See FACE: THE PAINTED FACE.

1
Mislike me not for my complexion,
The shadow'd livery of the burnish'd sun.
The Merchant of Venice. Act ii, sc. 1, l. 1. [Prince of Morocco]

His complexion is perfect gallows.—*The Tempest.* Act i, sc. 1, l. 32. See under HANGING for full quotation.

Black complexion.—*Hamlet,* ii, 2, 477.

Smirch'd complexion.—*Henry V,* iii, 3, 17.

Beauty herself is black
And all they foul that thy complexion lack.
Sonnets. No. cxxxii.

2
That excellent complexion, which did steal
The eyes of young and old.
Pericles. Act iv, sc. 1, l. 41. [Dionyza]

3
A goodly lady, trust me; of the hue
That I would choose, were I to choose anew.
Titus Andronicus. Act i, sc. 1, l. 261. [Saturninus]

4
Pandarus: She praised his complexion above Paris.
Cressida: Why, Paris hath colour enough.
Pandarus: So he has.
Cressida: Then Troilus should have too much: if she praised him above, his complexion is higher than his; he having colour enough, and the other higher, is too flaming a praise for a good complexion.
Troilus and Cressida. Act i, sc. 2, l. 107.

5
Duke: What kind of woman is 't?
Viola: Of your complexion.
Twelfth Night. Act ii, sc. 4, l. 27.

Maria once told me she did affect me: and I have heard herself come thus near, that, should she fancy, it should be one of my complexion.
Twelfth Night. Act ii, sc. 5, l. 27. [Malvolio]

Of a man's complexion.—*Venus and Adonis,* l. 215.

Of his complexion.—*The Merchant of Venice,* ii, 7, 79.

Of what complexion soever.—*The Merry Wives of Windsor,* iv, 2, 25.

6
Your changed complexions are to me a mirror
Which shows me mine changed.
The Winter's Tale. Act i, sc. 2, l. 381. [Polixenes]

COMPLIMENT

7 Rebukeable
And worthy shameful cheek it were, to stand
On mere mechanic compliment.
Antony and Cleopatra. Act iv, sc. 5, l. 31. [Antony] The only use of "rebukeable."

That they call compliment is like the encounter of two dog-apes.
As You Like It. Act ii, sc. 5, l. 26. [Jaques] The only use of "dog-apes."

8
The time will not allow the compliment
Which very manners urges.
King Lear. Act v, sc. 3, l. 233. [Albany]

Fain would I dwell on form, fain, fain deny
What I have spoke: but farewell compliment!
Romeo and Juliet. Act ii, sc. 2, l. 88. [Juliet]

Sans compliment.—*King John,* v, 6, 16.

Stay not thy compliment.—*Love's Labour's Lost,* iv, 2, 147.

9 Even now I met him
With customary compliment.
The Winter's Tale. Act i, sc. 2, l. 370. [Polixenes]

COMPROMISE

10 Noble offices thou mayst effect
Of mediation, after I am dead.
II Henry IV. Act iv, sc. 4, l. 24. [King Henry]

Induce Their mediation.—*Antony and Cleopatra,* v, 2, 170. The only uses of "mediation."

To trembling clients be you mediators!
The Rape of Lucrece, l. 1020.

Nonsuits my mediators.—*Othello,* i, 1, 16. The only uses of "nonsuits" and "mediators."

11
Now the matter grows to compromise.
I Henry VI. Act v, sc. 4, l. 149. [York]

12 O inglorious league!
Shall we, upon the footing of our land,
Send fair-play orders and make compromise,
Insinuation, parley and base truce
To arms invasive?
King John. Act v, sc. 1, l. 66. [Bastard] The only use of "inglorious" and "invasive." "Fair-play" occurs five times.

13
I am of the church, and will be glad to do my benevolence to make atonements and compremises between you.
The Merry Wives of Windsor. Act i, sc. 1, l. 32. [Evans] "Benevolence" is used only once again in the plays, in *Richard II,* ii, 1, 250. The only use of "compremises."

14 Basely yielded upon compromise
That which his noble ancestors achieved with blows.
Richard II. Act ii, sc. 1, l. 253. [Northumberland]

COMPULSION

See also Necessity

15
The king that loved him, as the state stood then,
Was force perforce compell'd to banish him.
II Henry IV. Act iv, sc. 1, l. 115. [Mowbray] For "force perforce" see FORCE.

16
If requiring fail, he will compel.
Henry V. Act ii, sc. 4, l. 101. [Exeter]

Answer his requiring.—*Measure for Measure,* iii, 1, 253.

Fetch in firing At requiring.—*The Tempest,* ii, 2, 186. The only uses of "requiring."

17
By the compulsion of their ordinance.
King John. Act ii, sc. 1, l. 218. [King John]

The highest compulsion of base fear.
All's Well that Ends Well. Act iii, sc. 6, l. 31. [Second Lord]

1
It may compel him to her recompense.
Measure for Measure. Act iii, sc. 1, l. 262. [Duke]

2
Portia: Then must the Jew be merciful.
Shylock: On what compulsion must I? tell me that.
The Merchant of Venice. Act v, sc. 1, l. 182.

Heavenly compulsion.—*King Lear,* i, 2, 133.

3
Demetrius: If she cannot entreat, I can compel.
Lysander: Thou canst compel no more than she entreat.
A Midsummer-Night's Dream. Act iii, sc. 2, l. 248.

COMRADESHIP

See also Brotherhood, Companion

4
But he loves Cæsar best; yet he loves Antony: . . .
They are his shards, and he their beetle.
Antony and Cleopatra. Act iii, sc. 2, l. 15. [Enobarbus] "Shards" is repeated in *Hamlet,* v, 1, 254.

My brother, my competitor
In top of all design, my mate in empire,
Friend and companion in the front of war,
The arm of mine own body, and the heart
Where mine his thoughts did kindle.
Antony and Cleopatra. Act v, sc. 1, l. 42. [Cæsar]

5
Being ever from their cradles bred together.
As You Like It. Act i, sc. 1, l. 113. [Charles]

We still have slept together,
Rose at an instant, learn'd, play'd, eat together,
And wheresoe'er we went, like Juno's swans,
Still we went coupled and inseparable.
As You Like It. Act i, sc. 3, l. 75. [Celia]

True, inseparable, faithful loves.
King John, iii, 4, 66. The only uses of "inseparable."

Thou and I am one.—*As You Like It,* i, 3, 99.

Co-mates and brothers in exile.—*As You Like It,* ii, 1, 1. The only use of "co-mates."

6
New-hatch'd, unfledged comrade.
Hamlet, i, 3, 65. See under FRIEND. "New-hatch'd" is repeated in *Macbeth,* ii, 3, 64.

Comrade with the wolf and owl.—*King Lear,* ii, 4, 213.

7
Yoke-fellows in arms,
Let us to France; like horse-leeches, my boys,
To suck, to suck, the very blood to suck!
Henry V. Act ii, sc. 3, l. 56. [Pistol] The only use of "horse-leeches."

By his bloody side, Yoke-fellow.—*Henry V,* iv, 6, 9.

His yoke-fellow of equity.—*King Lear,* iii, 6, 39. The only uses of "yoke-fellow."

We'll yoke together, like a double shadow.
III Henry VI. Act iv, sc. 6, l. 49. [Warwick]

8
Like to a pair of loving turtle-doves
That could not live asunder day or night.
I Henry VI. Act ii, sc. 2, l. 30. [Burgundy] The only use of "turtle-doves." "Turtle" is used eight times, always referring to the dove.

We, Hermia, like two artificial gods,
Have with our needles created both one flower,
Both on one sampler, sitting on one cushion,
Both warbling of one song, both in one key,
As if our hands, our sides, voices and minds,
Had been incorporate. So we grew together,
Like to a double cherry, seeming parted,
But yet an union in partition;
Two lovely berries molded on one stem;
So, with two seeming bodies, but one heart.
A Midsummer-Night's Dream. Act iii, sc. 2, l. 203. [Helena] "Warbling" is repeated in v, 1, 405, and occurs in no other play. "Sampler" is used again in *Titus Andronicus,* ii, 4, 39.

We were as twinn'd lambs that did frisk i' the sun,
And bleat the one at the other: what we changed
Was innocence for innocence; we knew not
The doctrine of ill-doing, nor dream'd
That any did.
The Winter's Tale. Act i, sc. 2, l. 67. [Polixenes] The only use of "frisk" and "ill-doing."

9
Who is most inward with the noble duke?
Richard III. Act iii, sc. 4, l. 8. [Buckingham]

I was an inward of his.—*Measure for Measure,* iii, 2, 138. The only uses of "inward" with this meaning.

The neighbour to my counsel.—*Richard III,* iv, 2, 43.

10
Wish me partaker in thy happiness
When thou dost meet good hap; and in thy danger,
If ever danger do environ thee.
The Two Gentlemen of Verona. Act i, sc. 1, l. 14. [Proteus] "Environ" is repeated in *I Henry VI,* v, 4, 90, and in *II Henry IV,* iv, 3, 106.

Make us partakers.—*I Henry VI,* ii, 1, 52.

Let me be partaker.—*Antony and Cleopatra,* i, 4, 83.

For your partaker.—*I Henry VI,* ii, 4, 100. The only uses of "partaker."

11
I know him as myself; for from our infancy
We have conversed and spent our hours together.
The Two Gentlemen of Verona. Act ii, sc. 4, l. 62. [Valentine]

We are fellows still, Serving alike in sorrow.
Timon of Athens. Act iv, sc. 2, l. 18. [Servant]

12
They have seemed to be together, though absent, shook hands, as over a vast, and embraced, as it were, from the ends of opposed winds.
Winter's Tale. Act i, sc. 1, l. 31. [Camillo]

CONCEALMENT

See also Secrecy

1
'Tis he: slink by, and note him.
As You Like It. Act iii, sc. 2, l. 267. [Rosalind]

Nay, we will slink away in supper-time,
Disguise us at my lodging and return,
All in an hour.
The Merchant of Venice. Act ii, sc. 4, l. 1. [Lorenzo]

Slink all away.—*Timon of Athens,* iv, 2, 11. The only uses of "slink."

2
'Twere a concealment
Worse than a theft, no less than a traducement,
To hide your doings.
Coriolanus. Act i, sc. 9, l. 21. [Cominius] The only use of "traducement."

3
Go, hide thee behind the arras.
I Henry IV. Act ii, sc. 4, l. 549. [Prince of Wales] "Behind the Arras" is repeated in ii, 4, 577, and iii, 3, 113.

Stand Within the arras.—*King John,* iv, 1, 2.

Behind the arras I 'll convey myself.
Hamlet. Act iii, sc. 3, l. 28. [Polonius] "Behind the arras" is repeated in ii, 2, 163, and iv, 1, 9.

I will ensconce me behind the arras.
The Merry Wives of Windsor. Act iii, sc. 3, l. 96. [Falstaff]

I whipt me behind the arras.
Much Ado about Nothing. Act i, sc. 3, l. 63. [Borachio]

Do but encave yourself.—*Othello,* iv, 1, 82. The only use of "encave."

4
Profited In strange concealments.
I Henry IV. Act iii, sc. 1, l. 166. [Mortimer]

5
Lurk, lurk.
King Lear. Act iii, sc. 6, l. 122. [Edgar]

Bid me lurk.—*Romeo and Juliet,* iv, 1, 79.

Lurk I in a gossip's bowl.—*A Midsummer-Night's Dream,* ii, 1, 47.

6
In concealment wrap me up awhile.
King Lear. Act iv, sc. 3, l. 54. [Kent]

Let it be concealed awhile.—*All 's Well that Ends Well,* ii, 3, 283.

7
He cannot creep into a halfpenny purse, nor into a pepper-box.
Merry Wives of Windsor. Act iii, sc. 5, l. 148. [Ford] The only use of "pepper-box."

8
Thou art sworn as deeply to effect what we intend
As closely to conceal what we impart.
Richard III. Act iii, sc. 1, l. 158. [Buckingham]

9
And all the more it seeks to hide itself,
The bigger bulk it shows.
The Tempest. Act iii, sc. 1, l. 80. [Miranda]

Seeking to hide herself, as doth the deer
That hath received some unrecuring wound.
Titus Andronicus. Act iii, sc. 1, l. 89. [Marcus] The only use of "unrecuring."

10
She never told her love,
But let concealment, like a worm i' the bud,
Feed on her damask cheek.
Twelfth Night. Act ii, sc. 4, l. 113. [Viola]

Conceal me what I am.—*Twelfth Night,* i, 2, 53.

11
If you know aught which does behove my knowledge
Thereof to be inform'd, imprison 't not
In ignorant concealment.
The Winter's Tale. Act i, sc. 2, l. 395. [Polixenes]

CONCEIT

See also Thought

12
Thy conceit is nearer death than thy powers.
As You Like It. Act ii, sc. 6, l. 8. [Orlando]

Of good conceit.—*As You Like It,* v, 2, 59.

13
My earthy-gross conceit,
Smother'd in errors, feeble, shallow, weak.
The Comedy of Errors. Act iii, sc. 2, l. 34. [Antipholus of Syracuse] The only use of "earthy-gross."

I am press'd down with conceit—
Conceit, my comfort and my injury.
The Comedy of Errors. Act iv, sc. 2, l. 65. [Adriana]

14
Conceit in weakest bodies strongest works.
Hamlet. Act iii, sc. 4, l. 114. [Ghost]

15
There's no more conceit in him than is in a mallet.
II Henry IV. Act ii, sc. 4, l. 263. [Falstaff] The only use of "mallet."

Dull conceit.—*I Henry VI,* v, 5, 15.

16
I shall not fail to approve the fair conceit
The king hath of you.
Henry V. Act ii, sc. 3, l. 74. [Chamberlain]

The good conceit I hold of thee.—*The Two Gentlemen of Verona,* iii, 2, 17.

17
With forged quaint conceit
To set a gloss upon his bold intent.
I Henry VI. Act iv, sc. 1, l. 102. [Vernon]

18
Using conceit alone,
Without eyes, ears and harmful sound of words.
King John. Act iii, sc. 3, l. 50. [King John]

Of very liberal conceit.—*Julius Cæsar,* v, 2, 160.

19
I know not how conceit may rob
The treasury of life, when life itself
Yields to the theft.
King Lear. Act iv, sc. 6, l. 42. [Edgar]

20
A good lustre of conceit in a turf of earth.
Love's Labour 's Lost. Act iv, sc. 2, l. 88. [Holofernes]

Their conceits have wings
Fleeter than arrows, bullets, wind, thought, swifter things.
Love's Labour 's Lost. Act v, sc. 2, l. 260. [Boyet]

Keen conceit.—*Love's Labour 's Lost,* v, 2, 399.

True conceit.—*Merchant of Venice,* iii, 4, 2.

1 Dress'd in an opinion
Of wisdom, gravity, profound conceit,
As who should say 'I am Sir Oracle,
And when I ope my lips let no dog bark!'
The Merchant of Venice. Act i, sc. 1, l. 91. [Gratiano]

2
Dangerous conceits are, in their natures, poisons,
Which at the first are scarce found to distaste,
But with a little act upon the blood,
Burn like the mines of sulphur.
Othello. Act iii, sc. 3, l. 326. [Iago]
His conceit is false.—*Much Ado about Nothing,* ii, 1, 309.

3
Conceit and grief an eager combat fight.
The Rape of Lucrece, l. 1298.
Conceit deceitful.—*Rape of Lucrece,* l. 1423.

4
Bushy: 'Tis nothing but conceit, my gracious lady.
Queen: 'Tis nothing less; conceit is still derived
From some forefather grief.
Richard II. Act ii, sc. 2, l. 33.
Self and vain conceit.—*Richard II.* Act iii, sc. 2, l. 166. See under KING for full quotation.

5
Conceit, more rich in matter than in words,
Brags of his substance, not of ornament.
Romeo and Juliet. Act ii, sc. 6, l. 30. [Juliet]
Horrible conceit of death and night.—*Romeo and Juliet,* iv, 3, 37.
Horrible conceit.—*Othello,* iii, 3, 115. See under THOUGHT.

6
Petruchio: Why, sir, what 's your conceit in that?
Grumio: O, sir, the conceit is deeper than you think for.
Taming of the Shrew. Act iv, sc. 3, l. 162.

7 Rich conceit
Taught thee to make vast Neptune weep for aye
On this low grave, on faults forgiven.
Timon of Athens. Act v, sc. 4, l. 77. [Alcibiades]
Mere conceit.—*Timon of Athens,* v, 4, 14; *The Winter's Tale,* iii, 2, 145.

8
Thy conceit is soaking, will draw in
More than the common blocks.
The Winter's Tale. Act i, sc. 2, l. 224. [Leontes] "Soaking" is repeated in *Titus Andronicus,* iii, 2, 19.

9
An admirable conceited fellow.
The Winter's Tale. Act iv, sc. 4, l. 203. [Clown]
Horribly conceited.—*Twelfth Night,* iii, 4, 322.
Well conceited.—*II Henry IV,* v, 1, 39; *Julius Cæsar,* i, 3, 162.

CONCEPTION

See also Idea

10
Conceptions only proper to myself,
Which give some soil perhaps to my behaviours.
Julius Cæsar. Act i, sc. 2, l. 41. [Brutus]

11
Thou but rememberest me of mine own conception.
King Lear. Act i, sc. 4, l. 72. [King Lear]
Dangerous conception.—*Henry VIII,* i, 2, 139.
First conception.—*Pericles,* i, 2, 12.
Like conception.—*Timon of Athens,* i, 2, 115.
Strong conception.—*Othello,* v, 2, 55.

12
I have a young conception in my brain.
Troilus and Cressida. Act i, sc. 3, l. 312. [Ulysses]
Faith, thou hast some crotchets in thy head.
The Merry Wives of Windsor. Act ii, sc. 1, l. 159. [Mrs. Ford]

13
Conception is a blessing.
Hamlet, ii, 2, 185. See under PREGNANCY.

CONCLUSION

See also Result

14
'Tis I must make conclusion
Of these most strange events.
As You Like It. Act v, sc. 4, l. 132. [Hymen]
I knew 'twould be a bald conclusion.
The Comedy of Errors. Act ii, sc. 2, l. 110. [Antipholus of Syracuse]

15
To try conclusions.
Hamlet. Act iii, sc. 3, l. 195. [Hamlet]
There must be conclusions.
Henry V. Act ii, sc. 1, l. 27. [Nym]

16
Concluded by consent.
II Henry VI. Act i, sc. 1, l. 42. [Suffolk]
'Tis so concluded on.—*Hamlet,* iii, 4, 201.
It is concluded.—*Macbeth,* iii, 1, 141.
Concluded with a sigh.—*Much Ado about Nothing,* v, 1, 173.
Is it concluded?—*Richard III,* i, 3, 14.
Is it so concluded?—*Troilus and Cressida,* iv, 2, 68.
Be it concluded.—*The Winter's Tale,* i, 2, 203.

17
And, to conclude.
II Henry VI, iv, 1, 101; repeated in seven later plays.
But, to conclude.—*III Henry VI,* ii, 1, 128.
Conclude with me.—*I Henry VI,* v, 5, 77.
Conclude and be agreed.—*Richard II,* i, 1, 156.

18 The vile conclusion
I now begin with grief and shame to utter.
Measure for Measure. Act v, sc. 1, l. 95. [Isabella]

19
The conclusion shall be crowned with your enjoying her.
The Merry Wives of Windsor. Act iii, sc. 5, l. 138. [Falstaff]
And the conclusion is, she shall be thine.
Much Ado about Nothing. Act i, sc. 1, l. 329. [Don Pedro]
This is my conclusion.—*Much Ado about Nothing,* v, 4, 110.
The conclusion is victory.—*Love's Labour 's Lost,* iv, 1, 75.

A good conclusion.—*Love's Labour's Lost,* v, 2, 41.

1
O most lame and impotent conclusion!
Othello. Act ii, sc. 1, l. 162. [Desdemona]

Most preposterous conclusions.—*Othello,* i, 3, 333.

Incorporate conclusion.—*Othello,* ii, 1, 269.

A foregone conclusion.—*Othello,* iii, 3, 428.

2
A false conclusion: I hate it as an unfilled can.
Twelfth Night. Act ii, sc. 3, l. 6. [Sir Toby]
"Unfilled" is repeated in *Coriolanus,* v, 1, 51.

Merciless conclusion.—*The Rape of Lucrece,* l. 1160.

3
Of this make no conclusion.
The Winter's Tale. Act i, sc. 2, l. 81. [Hermione]

Read the conclusion.—*Pericles,* i, 1, 56.

CONCORD, see Discord

CONDEMNATION

See also Punishment

4
Therefore by law thou art condemn'd to die.
The Comedy of Errors. Act i, sc. 1, l. 26. [Duke]

Condemn'd to die.—*I Henry VI,* ii, 4, 97; *Measure for Measure,* ii, 2, 34.

Condemns you to the death.—*Richard II,* iii, 1, 29.

Condemn'd to burn.—*I Henry VI,* v, 4, 1.

Condemned . . . To lose his head.—*Measure for Measure,* v, 1, 70.

Condemned to loss!—*The Winter's Tale,* ii, 3, 192.

5
As with a man busied about decrees:
Condemning some to death, and some to exile.
Coriolanus. Act i, sc. 6, l. 35. [Marcius]
"Condemning" is repeated in *Antony and Cleopatra,* v, 2, 100.

6
Prepare for your execution: you are condemned, our general has sworn you out of reprieve and pardon.
Coriolanus. Act v, sc. 2, l. 51. [Sentinel]
You might condemn us
As poisonous of your honour.
Coriolanus. Act v, sc. 3, l. 134. [Volumnia]

7
Condemnation is pronounced.
Henry V. Act iii, sc. 6, l. 143. [Montjoy]
"Condemnation" is repeated in *Measure for Measure,* ii, 4, 174, and *Cymbeline,* iii, 5, 98.

8
'Tis meet he be condemn'd by course of law.
II Henry VI. Act iii, sc. 1, l. 237. [Cardinal]

9
We do condemn thee to the very block
Where Claudio stoop'd to death, and with like haste.
Measure for Measure. Act v, sc. 1, l. 419. [Duke]

Thou 'rt condemned.—*Measure for Measure,* v, 1, 487.

10
Stand I condemn'd for pride and scorn so much?
Much Ado about Nothing. Act iii, sc. 1, l. 108. [Beatrice]

Wherein the king stands generally condemn'd.
Richard II. Act ii, sc. 2, l. 132. [Bushy]

I stand condemn'd for this.
Troilus and Cressida. Act iii, sc. 3, l. 219. [Patroclus]

Stand condemn'd.—*Richard II,* ii, 3, 119; *King Lear,* i, 4, 5.

11
Thou wilt be condemned into everlasting redemption for this.
Much Ado about Nothing. Act iv, sc. 2, l. 58. [Dogberry]

12
And here I stand, both to impeach and purge
Myself condemned and myself excused.
Romeo and Juliet. Act v, sc. 3, l. 227. [Friar Laurence]

13
For that vile fault
Two of her brothers were condemn'd to death.
Titus Andronicus. Act v, sc. 2, l. 173. [Titus]

Condemned for a fault alone.—*Measure for Measure,* ii, 1, 40.

Condemned for untrussing.—*Measure for Measure,* iii, 2, 190. The only use of "untrussing."

Condemn'd of treason.—*Venus and Adonis,* l. 729.

14
Condemn'd by the king's own mouth, thereon
His execution sworn.
The Winter's Tale. Act i, sc. 2, l. 445. [Camillo]

Condemn'd Upon surmises.—*The Winter's Tale,* iii, 2, 112.

CONDITION

I—Condition: Circumstances

15
Demand of him my condition.
All's Well that Ends Well. Act iv, sc. 3, l. 196. [First Lord]

I will forget the condition of my estate, to rejoice in yours.
As You Like It. Act i, sc. 2, l. 16. [Rosalind]

16
Is 't possible that so short a time can alter the condition of a man?
Coriolanus. Act v, sc. 4, l. 9. [Sicinius]

Of what condition are you?—*II Henry IV,* iv, 3, 1.

O hard condition.—*Henry V,* iv, 1, 250.

My condition is not smooth.—*Henry V,* v, 2, 314.

Of mean condition.—*II Henry VI,* v, 1, 64.

Of true condition.—*Henry VIII,* i, 2, 19.

Weak condition.—*Julius Cæsar,* ii, 1, 236.

17
Would I were assured Of my condition!
King Lear. Act iv, sc. 7, l. 57. [King Lear]

18
A light condition in a beauty dark.
Love's Labour's Lost. Act v, sc. 2, l. 20. [Katharine]

Roderigo: She's full of most blessed condition.
Iago: Blessed fig's-end! . . . Blessed pudding!
Othello. Act ii, sc. 1, l. 254. The only use of "fig's-end."
The condition of a saint.—*The Merchant of Venice,* i, 2, 143.
Unhoused free condition.—*Othello,* i, 2, 26.

1
Othello: And then, of so gentle a condition!
Iago: Ay, too gentle.
Othello. Act iv, sc. 1, l. 203.
Gentle condition of blood.—*As You Like It,* i, 1, 48.
Hot condition of their blood.—*The Merchant of Venice,* v, 1, 74.

2
Bolingbroke: My gracious uncle, let me know my fault:
On what condition stands it and wherein?
York: Even in condition of the worst degree.
Richard II. Act ii, sc. 3, l. 106.
Mark his condition.—*The Tempest,* i, 2, 117.
I have a touch of your condition.—*Richard III,* iv, 4, 157.

3
Here is the cate-log of her condition.
Two Gentlemen of Verona. Act iii, sc. 1, l. 273. [Launce] The only use of "cate-log."

4
I am in my condition
A prince, Miranda; I do think, a king.
The Tempest. Act iii, sc. 1, l. 59. [Ferdinand]

II—Condition: Stipulation

5
First Soldier: 'Twill be deliver'd back on good condition.
Aufidius: Condition! . . . Condition!
What good condition can a treaty find
I' the part that is at mercy?
Coriolanus. Act i, sc. 10, l. 2.
On like condition.—*Coriolanus,* v, 3, 205.
Upon condition.—*I Henry VI,* v, 3, 153; v, 4, 129.

6
I embrace these conditions; let us have articles betwixt us.
Cymbeline. Act i, sc. 4, l. 168. [Posthumus]

7
You shall be soon dispatch'd with fair conditions.
Henry V. Act ii, sc. 4, l. 144. [French King]
Conditions we shall stand upon.—*II Henry IV,* iv, 1, 165.
Shall our condition stand?—*I Henry VI,* v, 4, 165.

8
It were, my lord, a hard condition for a maid to consign to.
Henry V. Act v, sc. 2, l. 326. [Burgundy]
Hard conditions.—*Julius Cæsar,* i, 2, 174.
Make conditions.—*Julius Cæsar,* iv, 3, 32.
Gentle thy conditions!—*Pericles,* iii, 1, 29.
Now the condition.—*The Tempest,* i, 2, 120.
Slight conditions.—*The Two Gentlemen of Verona,* v, 4, 138.

CONDUCT, see Behaviour, Manners

CONFERENCE

See also Council

9
Let's not confound the time with conference harsh.
Antony and Cleopatra. Act i, sc. 1, l. 45. [Antony]

10
I cannot speak to her, yet she urged conference.
As You Like It. Act i, sc. 2, l. 270. [Orlando]

11
I'll be placed, so please you, in the ear
Of all their conference.
Hamlet. Act iii, sc. 1, l. 192. [Polonius]

12
Not willing any longer conference.
III Henry VI. Act ii, sc. 2, l. 171. [Edward]
Vouchsafe, at our request, to stand aside
While I use further conference.
III Henry VI. Act iii, sc. 3, l. 110. [King Lewis]

13
Let no man
Come to our tent till we have done our conference.
Julius Cæsar. Act iv, sc. 2, l. 50. [Brutus]
Women and fools, break off your conference.
King John. Act ii, sc. 1, l. 150. [King Philip]
So sensible Seemeth their conference.
Love's Labour's Lost. Act v, sc. 2, l. 259. [Boyet]

14
I am invisible;
And I will overhear their conference.
A Midsummer-Night's Dream. Act ii, sc. 1, l. 186. [Oberon]
Overhear The speech.—*Hamlet,* iii, 3, 32.
Overheard what you shall overhear.—*Love's Labour's Lost,* v, 2, 93. The only uses of "overhear." "Overheard" occurs ten times.
Hear our conference.—*Much Ado about Nothing,* iii, 1, 25.

15
Comes me the prince and Claudio, hand in hand, in sad conference.
Much Ado about Nothing. Act i, sc. 3, l. 61. [Borachio]
The conference was sadly borne.
Much Ado about Nothing. Act ii, sc. 3, l. 229. [Benedick]

16
I do beseech your majesty
To have some conference with your grace alone.
Richard II. Act v, sc. 3, l. 26. [Aumerle]

17
His majesty hath straitly given in charge
That no man shall have private conference,
Of what degree soever, with his brother.
Richard III. Act i, sc. 1, l. 85. [Brakenbury]
"Straitly" is repeated in iv, 1, 17, and occurs in no other play.
Private conference.—*I Henry IV,* iii, 2, 2; *Henry VIII,* ii, 2, 81; *Pericles,* ii, 4, 17.

18
Forbear your conference with the noble duke.
Richard III. Act i, sc. 1, l. 104. [Brakenbury]

The mayor and citizens, . . .
Are come to have some conference with his grace.
Richard III. Act iii, sc. 7, l. 66. [Buckingham]

1
Gentle conference, soft and affable.
The Taming of the Shrew, ii, 1, 253. See under CHARACTER.

Free and friendly conference.—*Julius Cæsar,* iv, 2, 17.
Last conference.—*Macbeth,* iii, 1, 80.
Love's conference.—*A Midsummer-Night's Dream,* ii, 2, 46.
Needful conference.—*Winter's Tale,* ii, 3, 40.
Personal conference.—*Love's Labour's Lost,* ii, 1, 32.
Second conference.—*Cymbeline,* i, 4, 141.
Three words' conference.—*Much Ado about Nothing,* ii, 1, 279.

2
I must be present at your conference.
Winter's Tale. Act ii, sc. 2, l. 17. [Gaoler]

CONFESSION

3
Thy cheeks
Confess it, th' one to th' other; and thine eyes
See it so grossly shown in thy behaviours
That in their kind they speak it.
All's Well that Ends Well. Act i, sc. 3, l. 182. [Countess]

There is a kind of confession in your looks which your modesties have not craft enough to colour.
Hamlet. Act ii, sc. 2, l. 288. [Hamlet]

I see a strange confession in thine eye.
II Henry IV. Act i, sc. 1, l. 94. [Morton]

4
I confess,
Here on my knee, before high heaven and you.
All's Well that Ends Well. Act i, sc. 3, l. 197. [Helena]

Confess yourself to heaven.
Hamlet. Act iii, sc. 4, l. 149. [Hamlet]

5
His confession is taken, and it shall be read to his face.
All's Well that Ends Well. Act iv, sc. 3, l. 130. [Second Lord]

He hath confessed.—*II Henry VI,* iv, 2, 114; *Othello,* v, 2, 68.
She hath confess'd it.—*King Lear,* v, 3, 227.
Bravely confessed.—*Winter's Tale,* v, 2, 93.

6
I will confess what I know without constraint: if ye pinch me like a pasty, I can say no more.
All's Well that Ends Well. Act iv, sc. 3, l. 139. [Parolles] "Pasty" is repeated in *The Merry Wives of Windsor,* i, 1, 202: "A hot venison pasty."

I will confess it to all the 'orld.
Henry V. Act iv, sc. 7, l. 117. [Fluellen]

I will hereupon confess.—*Love's Labour's Lost,* i, 2, 60.
I will confess.—*II Henry VI,* iii, 3, 11; *Richard III,* iv, 4, 210; *The Merry Wives of Windsor,* iii, 4, 13.
Hold! I confess, I confess.—*II Henry VI,* ii, 3, 96.
I must confess.—*III Henry VI,* iii, 3, 6, and sixteen times in later plays.
I must needs confess.—*Richard II,* ii, 3, 153; *Timon of Athens,* iii, 2, 22.
I will tell you every thing, right as it fell out.
A Midsummer-Night's Dream. Act iv, sc. 2, l. 31. [Bottom]

7
I have heard
That guilty creatures sitting at a play
Have by the very cunning of the scene
Been struck so to the soul that presently
They have proclaim'd their malefactions.
Hamlet. Act ii, sc. 2, l. 617. [Hamlet] The only use of "malefactions."

8
He made a blushing cital of himself;
And chid his truant youth with such a grace
As if he master'd there a double spirit
Of teaching and of learning instantly.
I Henry IV. Act v, sc. 2, l. 62. [Vernon] The only use of "cital."

9
I do confess my fault;
And do submit me to your highness' mercy.
Henry V. Act ii, sc. 2, l. 76. [Cambridge]

I do confess.—*All's Well that Ends Well,* v, 3, 231; *Hamlet,* v, 2, 297; *Othello,* i, 3, 123; *The Winter's Tale,* iii, 2. 63.
Most freely I confess.—*Twelfth Night,* v, 1, 367.
I am to blame.—*Othello,* iii, 3, 282. See under BLAME.

10
I'll hear him his confessions justify.
Henry VIII. Act i, sc. 2, l. 6. [King Henry]

Let my trial be mine own confession.
Measure for Measure. Act v, sc. 1, l. 377. [Angelo]

Thine own confession.—*Measure for Measure,* i, 2, 39.

11
Let us confess and turn it to a jest.
Love's Labour's Lost. Act v, sc. 2, l. 390. [Dumain]

King Ferdinand: Teach us, sweet madam, for our rude transgression
Some fair excuse.
Princess of France: The fairest is confession.
Love's Labour's Lost. Act v, sc. 2, l. 431.

12
Confess the truth, and say by whose advice
Thou camest here to complain.
Measure for Measure. Act v, sc. 1, l. 113. [Duke]

Bassanio: Promise me life, and I'll confess the truth.
Portia: Well then, confess and live.
Bassanio: 'Confess' and 'love'
Had been the very sum of my confession.
The Merchant of Venice. Act iii, sc. 2, l. 34.

Desdemona: Let him confess a truth.
Othello: He hath confess'd.
Desdemona: What, my lord?
Othello: That he hath used thee.
Othello. Act v, sc. 2, l. 68.

13
If it be confessed, it is not redressed.
The Merry Wives of Windsor. Act i, sc. 1, l. 106. [Shallow]

1
I confess nothing, nor I deny nothing.
Much Ado about Nothing. Act iv, sc. 1, l. 274. [Beatrice]
Slender: You 'll not confess, you 'll not confess.
Shallow: That he will not.
Merry Wives of Windsor. Act i, sc. 1, l. 94.
I dare not confess.—*Hamlet,* v, 2, 145.
2
To confess, and be hanged for his labour;—first, to be hanged, and then to confess.—I tremble at it.
Othello. Act iv, sc. 1, l. 38. [Othello]
3 Confess thee freely of thy sin;
For to deny each article with oath
Cannot remove nor choke the strong conception
That I do groan withal.
Othello. Act v, sc. 2, l. 52. [Othello]
Confess yourself freely to her.—*Othello,* ii, 3, 323.
Timorously confess.—*Richard III,* iii, 5, 57. The only use of "timorously."
4
Ere I last received the sacrament
I did confess it.
Richard II. Act i, sc. 1, l. 139. [Mowbray] "Receive the sacrament" is repeated in *Richard III,* i, 4, 208. "Take the sacrament" occurs six times.
Go in; and tell my lady I am gone . . .
To make confession and to be absolved.
Romeo and Juliet. Act iii, sc. 5, l. 233. [Juliet]
Paris: Come you to make confession to this father?
Juliet: To answer that, I should confess to you.
Romeo and Juliet. Act iv, sc. 1, l. 22.
She did intend confession
At Patrick's cell this even.
The Two Gentlemen of Verona. Act v, sc. 2, l. 41. [Duke]
Holy confession.—*The Two Gentlemen of Verona,* iv, 3, 44.
5
Good even to my ghostly confessor.
Romeo and Juliet. Act ii, sc. 6, l. 21. [Juliet]
A ghostly confessor.—*Romeo and Juliet,* iii, 3, 49.
Bring him his confessor.—*Measure for Measure,* ii, 1, 35. "Confessor" occurs ten times in the plays.
6
And now in plainness do confess to thee.
The Taming of the Shrew. Act i, sc. 1, l. 157. [Lucentio]
7
Fell so roundly to a large confession,
To angle for your thoughts.
Troilus and Cressida. Act iii, sc. 2, l. 161. [Cressida]

CONFIDENCE

See also Trust

8
Art thou so confident?
All's Well that Ends Well. Act ii, sc. 1, l. 162. [King]
Confident I am.—*Cymbeline,* ii, 3, 150.
I am confident.—*Titus Andronicus,* i, 1, 61; *Henry VIII,* ii, 1, 146.
We are confident.—*Troilus and Cressida,* i, 3, 72.
Secure And confident.—*King John,* ii, 1, 28.
Confident against the world in arms.
I Henry IV. Act v, sc. 1, l. 117. [Prince of Wales]
As confident as is the falcon's flight
Against a bird, do I with Mowbray fight.
Richard II. Act i, sc. 3, l. 61. [Bolingbroke]
A man may be too confident.
The Merry Wives of Windsor. Act ii, sc. 1, l. 193. [Ford]
9
Upon thy certainty and confidence
What darest thou venture?
All's Well that Ends Well. Act ii, sc. 1, l. 172. [King]
Confidently undertake.—*All's Well that Ends Well,* iii, 6, 21; iii, 6, 93. The only uses of "confidently."
10
Your wisdom is consumed in confidence.
Julius Cæsar. Act ii, sc. 2, l. 49. [Calpurnia]
With demure confidence.—*Henry VIII,* i, 2, 167.
11
Marry, sir, I would have some confidence with you that decerns you nearly.
Much Ado about Nothing. Act iii, sc. 5, l. 3. [Dogberry] The only use of "decerns."
I will tell your worship more of the wart the next time we have confidence.
The Merry Wives of Windsor. Act i, sc. 4, l. 171. [Mistress Quickly]
I desire some confidence with you.—*Romeo and Juliet,* ii, 4, 133.
In all confidence.—*Othello,* i, 3, 31.
With all confidence.—*Winter's Tale,* i, 2, 414.
I renounce all confidence.—*I Henry VI,* i, 2, 97.
12
The king reposeth all his confidence in thee
Richard II. Act ii, sc. 4, l. 6. [Salisbury]
A confidence sans bound.
The Tempest. Act i, sc. 2, l. 97. [Prospero]
Your master's confidence was above mine.
Timon of Athens. Act iii, sc. 4, l. 31. [First Varro Servant]

CONFUSION

13
Peace, ho! I bar confusion.
As You Like It. Act v, sc. 4, l. 131. [Hymen]
Confusion 's near.—*Coriolanus,* iii, 1, 190.
14
And can you, by no drift of circumstance,
Get from him why he puts on this confusion?
Hamlet. Act iii, sc. 1, l. 1. [King]
15
Shame and confusion! all is on the rout;
Fear frames disorder, and disorder wounds
Where it should guard.
II Henry VI. Act v, sc. 2, l. 31. [Young Clifford]
These fellows ran about the streets,
Crying confusion.
Coriolanus. Act iv, sc. 6, l. 28. [Sicinius]
16
Disorder, that hath spoil'd us, friend us now!
Let us on heaps go offer up our lives.
Henry V. Act iv, sc. 5, l. 17. [Constable]

You have displaced the mirth, broke the good meeting,
With most admired disorder.
Macbeth. Act iii, sc. 4, l. 109. [Lady Macbeth]
The disorder 's such As war were hoodwink'd.
Cymbeline. Act v, sc. 2. l. 15. [Lucius]
Ruinous disorders.—*King Lear,* i, 2, 123.

1 Vast confusion waits,
As doth a raven on a sick-fall'n beast,
The imminent decay of wrested pomp.
King John. Act iv, sc. 3, l. 152. [Bastard] The only use of "sick-fall'n."
Confusion thick.—*Cymbeline,* v, 3, 41.
Great confusion.—*King Lear,* iii, 2, 92.

2
Confusion now hath made his masterpiece!
Macbeth. Act ii, sc. 3, l. 71. [Macduff] The only use of "masterpiece" in the plays.
Draw him on to his confusion.
Macbeth. Act iii, sc. 5, l. 29. [Hecate]
To our confusion.—*Antony and Cleopatra,* iii, 13, 115.
To thy mere confusion.—*Cymbeline,* iv, 2, 92.

3
So quick bright things come to confusion.
A Midsummer-Night's Dream, i, 1, 149. See under LOVE for full quotation.
Musical confusion.—*A Midsummer-Night's Dream,* iv, 1, 115.
Confusion of their cries.—*The Rape of Lucrece,* l. 445.
Swallow'd in confusion.—*The Rape of Lucrece,* l. 1159.

4 Confusion's cure lives not
In these confusions.
Romeo and Juliet. Act iv, sc. 5, l. 65. [Friar Laurence]

5
Make large confusion: and, thy fury spent,
Confounded be thyself!
Timon of Athens. Act iv, sc. 3, l. 127. [Timon]
Work confusion.—*Titus Andronicus,* v, 2, 8.

CONJECTURE, see Imagination

CONJUNCTION, see Alliance

CONJURING

See also Charm, Magic, Witchcraft

6
My way is to conjure you.
As You Like It. Epilogue, l. 12. [Rosalind]
Let me conjure you.—*Hamlet,* ii, 2, 294.
I do conjure thee.—*The Two Gentlemen of Verona,* ii, 7, 2.
I 'll conjure you.—*The Merry Wives of Windsor,* iv, 2, 195.
I 'll conjure thee.—*I Henry VI,* i, 5, 5; *The Comedy of Errors,* iv, 3, 68; iv, 4, 60; *Measure for Measure,* v, 1, 48; *The Winter's Tale,* i, 2, 400; *King John,* iv, 2, 269.
I must conjure him.—*Romeo and Juliet,* ii, 1, 16.
You cannot conjure me.—*Henry V,* ii, 1, 57.
I cannot conjure.—*Troilus and Cressida,* v, 2, 125.

7
And sure, unless you send some present help,
Between them they will kill the conjurer.
The Comedy of Errors. Act v, sc. 1, l. 176. [Servant]
This pernicious slave,
Forsooth, took on him as a conjuror.
The Comedy of Errors. Act v, sc. 1, l. 241. [Antipholus of Ephesus]
He is a conjurer.—*II Henry VI,* iv, 2, 99.
You are a conjurer.—*The Comedy of Errors,* iv, 4, 50.
Dealing with . . . conjurers.—*II Henry VI,* ii, 1, 172.
Bolingbroke, the conjurer.—*II Henry VI,* i, 2, 76.
French Conjurers.—*I Henry VI,* i, 1, 26. The only uses of "conjurer."

8
If you would conjure in her, you must make a circle.
Henry V. Act v, sc. 2, l. 319. [Burgundy]
I would to God some scholar would conjure her.
Much Ado about Nothing, ii, 1, 264.
She conjures: away with her!
Pericles. Act iv, sc. 6, l. 156. [Bawd]

9
Here stood he in the dark, his sharp sword out,
Mumbling of wicked charms, conjuring the moon
To stand auspicious mistress.
King Lear. Act ii, sc. 1, l. 40. [Edmund] The only use of "conjuring." "Mumbling" is repeated in *Romeo and Juliet,* iii, 5, 174: "Mumbling fool."
With some mixtures powerful o'er the blood,
Or with some dram conjured to this effect,
He wrought upon her.
Othello. Act ii, sc. 1, l. 104. [Brabantio]

10 Nay, I 'll conjure too.
Romeo! humours! madman! passion! lover!
Appear thou in the likeness of a sigh. . . .
He heareth not, he stirreth not, he moveth not;
The ape is dead, and I must conjure him.
I conjure thee by Rosaline's bright eyes,
By her high forehead and her scarlet lip,
By her fine foot, straight leg and quivering thigh
And the demesnes that there adjacent lie,
That in thy likeness thou appear to us! . . .
This cannot anger him: . . . my invocation
Is fair and honest, and in his mistress' name.
I conjure only but to raise up him.
Romeo and Juliet. Act ii, sc. 1, l. 6. [Mercutio] The only use of "quivering." "Demesnes" is repeated in iii, 5, 182: "Fair demesnes"; and in *Cymbeline,* iii, 3, 70: "These desmesnes have been my world."
I do defy thy conjurations.
Romeo and Juliet. Act v, sc. 3, l. 68. [Paris]
Earnest conjuration.—*Hamlet,* v, 2, 38.
Senseless conjuration.—*Richard II,* iii, 2, 23.

11
He hath conjured me beyond them, and I must needs appear.
Timon of Athens. Act iii, sc. 6, l. 12. [First Lord]

1
'Sfoot, I 'll learn to conjure and raise devils.
Troilus and Cressida. Act ii, sc. 3, l. 6. [Thersites] The only use of "'Sfoot" (God's foot).

Conjured the devil.—*The Merchant of Venice,* i, 3, 35.

CONQUEST

2
So it should be, that none but Antony
Should conquer Antony; but woe 'tis so.
Antony and Cleopatra. Act iv, sc. 15, l. 16. [Cleopatra]

We Have used to conquer, standing on the earth,
And fighting foot to foot.
Antony and Cleopatra. Act iii, sc. 7, l. 65. [Soldier] The only use of the phrase "foot to foot" in the plays.

These three world-sharers.—*Antony and Cleopatra,* ii, 7, 76. The only use of "world-sharers."

3 He that can endure
To follow with allegiance a fall'n lord
Does conquer him that did his master conquer,
And earns a place i' the story.
Antony and Cleopatra. Act iii, sc. 13, l. 43. [Enobarbus]

4
It is a conquest for a prince to boast of.
I Henry IV. Act i, sc. 1, l. 77. [Westmoreland]

Command the conquest, Charles, it shall be thine,
Let Henry fret and all the world repine.
I Henry IV. Act v, sc. 2, l. 19. [La Pucelle] The only use of "repine."

5
I may justly say, with the hook-nosed fellow of Rome, 'I came, saw, and overcame.'
II Henry IV. Act iv, sc. 3, l. 45. [Falstaff] See also under CÆSAR.

He it was that might rightly say, Veni, vidi, vici; which to annothanize in the vulgar,—O base and obscure vulgar!—videlicet, He came, saw and overcame; he came, one; saw, two; overcame, three.
Love's Labour 's Lost. Act iv, sc. 1, l. 67. [Boyet] The only use of "annothanize" (anatomize, interpret).

6
He ne'er lift up his hand but conquered.
I Henry VI. Act i, sc. 1, l. 16. [Gloucester]

This conquering vein.—*I Henry VI,* iv, 7, 95.

7
My mind presageth happy gain and conquest.
III Henry VI. Act v, sc. 1, l. 71. [King Edward]

What conquest brings he home?
What tributaries follow him to Rome,
To grace in captive bonds his chariot wheels?
Julius Cæsar. Act i, sc. 1, l. 37. [Marullus]

The coward conquest of a wretch's knife.
Sonnets. No. lxxiv.

Vile conquest.—*Julius Cæsar,* v, 5, 38.

8
And better conquest never canst thou make
Than arm thy constant and thy nobler parts
Against these giddy loose suggestions.
King John. Act iii, sc. 1, l. 290. [Pandulph]

And make a conquest of unhappy me,
Whereas no glory 's got to overcome.
Pericles. Act i, sc. 4, l. 69. [Cleon]

9
If we be conquer'd, let men conquer us,
And not these bastard Bretons; whom our fathers
Have in their own land beaten, bobb'd, and thump'd.
Richard III. Act v, sc. 3, l. 332. [King Richard]

Conquer'd by a lady.—*Pericles,* ii, 2, 26.

10
The gods confound them all in thy conquest;
And thee after, when thou hast conquer'd!
Timon of Athens. Act iv, sc. 3, l. 103. [Timon]

Conquer my country.—*Timon of Athens,* iv, 3, 106.

Conquer the kingdom.—*Henry V,* v, 2, 195.

Conquer France.—*II Henry VI,* i, 1, 82.

Conquer Rome.—*Coriolanus,* v, 3, 142.

II—The Conqueror

11 You did know
How much you were my conqueror; and that
My sword, made weak by my affection, would
Obey it on all cause.
Antony and Cleopatra. Act iii, sc. 11, l. 65. [Antony]

A conqueror that will pray in aid for kindness,
Where he for grace is kneel'd to.
Antony and Cleopatra. Act v, sc. 2, l. 27. [Proculeis]

12 Henry, son unto a conqueror,
Is likely to beget more conquerors.
I Henry VI. Act v, sc. 5, l. 73. [Suffolk]

13
There is nothing done, if he return the conqueror.
King Lear. Act iv, sc. 6, l. 271. [Edgar]

14
Therefore, brave conquerors,—for so you are,
That war against your own affections
And the huge army of the world's desires.
Love's Labour 's Lost. Act i, sc. 1, l. 8. [King Ferdinand]

15
A conqueror and afeard to speak.
Love's Labour 's Lost. Act v, sc. 2, l. 580. [Costard]

The conqueror is dismay'd.—*Love's Labour 's Lost,* v, 2, 570.

Take away the conqueror.—*Love's Labour 's Lost,* v, 2, 575.

16 Themselves, the conquerors,
Make war upon themselves; blood against blood,
Self against self.
Richard III. Act ii, sc. 4, l. 61. [Duchess of York]

17
Virtuous and holy, be thou conqueror!
Richard III. Act v, sc. 3, l. 128. [Ghost of Henry VI]

Turn a conqueror.—*Richard III,* iv, 4, 184.
Gracious conqueror.—*Titus Andronicus,* i, 1, 104.
Roman conqueror.—*As You Like It,* iv, 2, 4.
Richard Conqueror.—*The Taming of the Shrew,* Ind., 1, 5.

CONSCIENCE

1
Soft conscienced men.
Coriolanus. Act i, sc. 1, l. 37. [Citizen] The only use of "conscienced."
Your soft cheveril conscience.
Henry VIII. Act ii, sc. 3, l. 32. [Old Lady] A popular phrase in Shakespeare's day. It had been used in *Discoverie of Knights of the Poste* (Sig. B4) in 1597: "Their consciences are like chiverell skins, that will stretch every way." In *Twelfth Night* (iii, 1, 13), Shakespeare says, "A sentence is but a cheveril glove to good wit," and in *Romeo and Juliet* (ii, 4, 87), "O, here's a wit of cheveril, that stretches from an inch narrow to an ell broad!" Cheveril was kidskin, used especially for making gloves because of its flexibility.

2
For conscience sake.
Coriolanus. Act ii, sc. 3, l. 36. [Citizen]
My conscience bids me ask.—*Cymbeline,* i, 5, 7.
Thy conscience witness.—*Cymbeline,* iii, 4, 48.

3 My conscience, thou art fetter'd
More than my shanks and wrists.
Cymbeline. Act v, sc. 4, l. 8. [Posthumus] "Shanks" is repeated in *Romeo and Juliet,* iv, 1, 83: "Reeky shanks"; and in *King Lear,* ii, 2, 41: "Carbonado your shanks." "Shank" is used once, in *As You Like It,* ii, 7, 161: "Shrunk shank."
Now my heavy conscience sinks my knee.
Cymbeline. Act v, sc. 5, l. 413. [Iachimo]
How smart a lash that speech doth give my conscience!
Hamlet. Act iii, sc. 1, l. 50. [King]

4
Conscience does make cowards of us all.
Hamlet. Act iii, sc. 1, l. 83. [Hamlet]
Now must your conscience my acquittance seal.
Hamlet. Act iv, sc. 7, l. 1. [King]
They are not near my conscience.
Hamlet. Act v, sc. 2, l. 58. [Hamlet]
'Tis almost 'gainst my conscience.
Hamlet. Act v, sc. 2, l. 307. [Lærtes]

5
Now, my masters, for a true face and good conscience.
I Henry IV, ii, 4, 550. [Prince of Wales]
A good conscience will make any possible satisfaction.
II Henry IV. Epilogue, l. 22.
The witness of a good conscience.
The Merry Wives of Windsor. Act iv, sc. 2, l. 221. [Mrs. Ford]
Done in the testimony of a good conscience.
Love's Labour's Lost. Act iv, sc. 2, l. 1. [Sir Nathaniel]
Of a good conscience.—*A Midsummer-Night's Dream,* v, 1, 230.

6
Could not keep quiet in his conscience.
Henry V. Act i, sc. 2, l. 79. [Canterbury]
I speak my conscience.—*II Henry VI,* iii, 1, 68; *Henry V,* iv, 1, 123.
In (on) my conscience.—*II Henry VI,* v, 1, 177; and twelve times in later plays.

7
My conscience tells me you are innocent.
II Henry VI. Act iii, sc. 1, l. 141. [King Henry]
My conscience tells me he is lawful king.
III Henry VI. Act i, sc. 1, l. 150. [Exeter]
Upon thy conscience.—*III Henry VI,* iii, 3, 113.

8
If I have a conscience, let it sink me,
Even as the axe falls, if I be not faithful.
Henry VIII. Act ii, sc. 1, l. 60. [Buckingham]
Lord Chamberlain: It seems the marriage with his brother's wife.
Has crept too near his conscience.
Suffolk: No, his conscience
Has crept too near another lady.
Henry VIII. Act ii, sc. 2, l. 17.

9
The quiet of my wounded conscience.
Henry VIII. Act ii, sc. 2, l. 75. [King Henry]
Conscience, conscience! O, 'tis a tender place.
Henry VIII. Act ii, sc. 2, l. 143. [King Henry]
My conscience first received a tenderness,
Scruple and prick.
Henry VIII. Act ii, sc. 4, l. 170. [King Henry]
Wringing of the conscience.—*Henry VIII,* ii, 2, 28.

10 This respite shook
The bosom of my conscience, enter'd me,
Yea, with a splitting power, and made to tremble
The region of my breast.
Henry VIII. Act ii, sc. 4, l. 181. [King Henry]
The wild sea of my conscience.—*Henry VIII,* ii, 4, 200.
I meant to rectify my conscience,—which
I then did feel full sick, and yet not well.
Henry VIII. Act ii, sc. 4, l. 203. [King Henry] "Rectify" is repeated in *Henry VIII,* ii, 4, 63, and in *The Tempest,* v, 1, 245: "Rectify our knowledge."
I leave to your own conscience.—*Henry VIII,* iii, 2, 327.
I know myself now; and I feel within me
A peace above all earthly dignities,
A still and quiet conscience.
Henry VIII. Act iii, sc. 2, l. 378. [Wolsey]
I cannot blame his conscience.
Henry VIII. Act iv, sc. 1, l. 47. [Second Gentleman]
Private conscience.—*Henry VIII,* v, 3, 40.
Christian conscience.—*Henry VIII,* v, 4, 37.
Safe conscience.—*Julius Cæsar,* i, 1, 14.

11
So much my conscience whispers in your ear,
Which none but heaven and you and I shall hear.
King John. Act i, sc. 1, l. 42. [Queen Elinor]
Awakes my conscience.—*King John,* v, 4, 43.

1
Consciences, that will not die in debt.
Love's Labour's Lost. Act v, sc. 2, l. 333. [Biron]

2
Certainly my conscience will serve me to run from this Jew my master. The fiend is at mine elbow and tempts me saying to me 'Gobbo, . . . use your legs, take the start, run away.' My conscience says 'No; take heed, honest Launcelot; . . . do not run; scorn running with thy heels.' Well, the most courageous fiend bids me pack. . . . My conscience, hanging about the neck of my heart, says very wisely to me . . . 'Launcelot, budge not.' 'Budge,' says the fiend. 'Budge not,' says my conscience. 'Conscience,' say I, 'you counsel well;' 'Fiend,' say I, 'you counsel well;' to be ruled by my conscience, I should stay with the Jew my master, who, God bless the mark, is a kind of devil; . . . my conscience, my conscience is but a kind of hard conscience, to offer to counsel me to stay with the Jew. . . . I will run, fiend.
The Merchant of Venice. Act ii, sc. 2, l. 1. [Launcelot]

3
You suffer for a pad conscience.
The Merry Wives of Windsor. Act iii, sc. 3, l. 235. [Evans]

Examine your conscience.—*Much Ado about Nothing,* i, 1, 291.

4
Let not conscience,
Which is but cold, inflaming love i' thy bosom,
Inflame too nicely.
Pericles. Act iv, sc. 1, l. 4. [Dionyza]

5
The guilt of conscience take thou for thy labour.
Richard II. Act v, sc. 6, l. 41. [Bolingbroke]

Clog of conscience.—*Richard II,* v, 6, 20.

6
The worm of Conscience still begnaw thy soul!
Richard III. Act i, sc. 3, l. 222. [Queen Margaret] The only use of "begnaw."

Don Worm, his conscience.—*Much Ado about Nothing,* v, 2, 86. See under PRAISE: SELF-PRAISE for full quotation.

Against my conscience and my soul.
Richard III. Act iii, sc. 7, l. 226. [Gloucester]

7
Some certain dregs of conscience are yet within me.
Richard III. Act i, sc. 4, l. 124. [Second Murderer]

First Murderer: Where is thy conscience now?
Second Murderer: In the Duke of Gloucester's purse.
First Murderer: So when he opens his purse to give us our reward, thy conscience flies out.
Second Murderer: Let it go; there's few or none will entertain it.
First Murderer: How if it come to thee again?
Second Murderer: I'll not meddle with it: it is a dangerous thing: it makes a man a coward: a man cannot steal, but it accuseth him; he cannot swear, but it checks him; he cannot lie with his neighbour's wife, but it detects him: 'tis a blushing shamefast spirit that mutinies in a man's bosom; it fills one full of obstacles: it made me once restore a purse of gold that I found; it beggars any man that keeps it: it is turned out of all towns and cities for a dangerous thing; and every man that means to live well endeavours to trust to himself and to live without it.
Richard III. Act i, sc. 4, l. 130. The only use of "shamefast."

8
This argues conscience in your grace.
Richard III. Act iii, sc. 7, l. 174. [Buckingham]

Every man's conscience is a thousand swords.
Richard III. Act v, sc. 2, l. 17. [Oxford]

O coward conscience, how dost thou afflict me!
Richard III. Act v, sc. 3, l. 179. [King Richard]

My conscience hath a thousand several tongues,
And every tongue brings in a several tale,
And every tale condemns me for a villain.
Richard III. Act v, sc. 3, l. 193. [King Richard]

9
Conscience is but a word that cowards use,
Devised at first to keep the strong in awe:
Our strong arms be our conscience, swords our law.
Richard III. Act v, sc. 3, l. 309. [King Richard]

10
Love is too young to know what conscience is;
Yet who knows not conscience is born of love.
Sonnets. No. cli.

Want of conscience.—*Sonnets,* cli.

11
Sebastian: But, for your conscience?
Antonio: Ay, sir; where lies that? if 'twere a kibe,
'Twould put me to my slipper: but I feel not
This deity in my bosom: twenty consciences,
That stand 'twixt me and Milan, candied be they
And melt ere they molest!
The Tempest. Act ii, sc. 1, l. 275. "Molest" is repeated in *Titus Andronicus,* v, 2, 9. "Kibe" (chilblain) is used four times.

12
I'll haunt thee like a wicked conscience still,
That mouldeth goblins swift as frenzy's thoughts.
Troilus and Cressida. Act v, sc. 10, l. 28. [Troilus]

I appeal To your own conscience.—*The Winter's Tale,* iii, 2, 47.

CONSENT

13
Consent with both that we may enjoy each other.
As You Like It. Act v, sc. 2, l. 10. [Oliver]

Let in her fine consent.—*All's Well that Ends Well,* iii, 7, 19.

You have my consent.—*As You Like It,* v, 2, 15.

1
Though we willingly consented to his banishment, yet it was against our will.
Coriolanus. Act iv, sc. 6, l. 144. [Citizen]

The Romans plausibly did give consent
To Tarquin's everlasting banishment.
The Rape of Lucrece, l. 1854. The only use of "plausibly."

2
Do you consent we shall acquaint him with it,
As needful in our loves, fitting our duty?
Hamlet. Act i, sc. 1, l. 172. [Horatio]

Upon his will I seal'd my hard consent.
Hamlet. Act i, sc. 2, l. 60. [Polonius]

3
Consent, and for thy honour give consent.
I Henry VI. Act v, sc. 3, l. 136. [Suffolk]

Give consent.—*All's Well that Ends Well,* ii, 1, 156; *Romeo and Juliet,* iv, 1, 89.

I yield thee my free consent.
III Henry VI. Act iv, sc. 6, l. 36. [Clarence]

Fair consent.—*Henry V,* ii, 2, 22.

4
We have consented to all terms of reason.
Henry V. Act v, sc. 2, l. 357. [French King]

You all consented.—*I Henry VI,* i, 5, 34.

5
And my consent ne'er ask'd herein before!
II Henry VI. Act ii, sc. 4, l. 72. [Gloucester]

Say you consent.—*II Henry VI,* iii, 1, 275.

He swore consent.—*III Henry VI,* ii, 1, 172.

Yield consent.—*III Henry VI,* ii, 2, 24.

6
Then be it as you will.
III Henry VI. Act iv, sc. 7, l. 65. [King Edward]

As red as fire! nay, then her wax must melt.
III Henry VI. Act iii, sc. 2, l. 51. [Clarence]

7
But by particular consent proceeded
Under your hands and seals.
Henry VIII. Act ii, sc. 4, l. 221. [King Henry]

8
Octavius: Consent you, Lepidus?
Lepidus: I do consent.
Julius Cæsar. Act iv, sc. 1, l. 2.

Let thy heart consent.—*King John,* iv, 2, 239.

9
If you say ay, the king will not say no.
King John. Act iii, sc. 4, l. 183. [Dauphin]

10
Fit thy consent to my sharp appetite.
Measure for Measure. Act ii, sc. 4, l. 161. [Angelo]

You consenting to 't,
Would bark your honour from that trunk you bear,
And leave you naked.
Measure for Measure. Act iii, sc. 1, l. 71. [Isabella]

Consenting to the safeguard of your honour.
Measure for Measure. Act v, sc. 1, l. 424. [Duke]

Sudden consenting.—*As You Like It,* v, 2, 8.

11
The wealth I have waits on my consent, and my consent goes not that way.
The Merry Wives of Windsor. Act iii, sc. 2, l. 78. [Page]

Not by my consent.—*The Merry Wives of Windsor,* iii, 2, 72.

I will not consent.—*Measure for Measure,* iv, 3, 59.

Not having my consent.—*Pericles,* ii, 5, 76.

Do not consent.—*Troilus and Cressida,* i, 3, 362.

Say, have I thy consent?—*Richard III,* iv, 2, 23.

This man hath my consent.—*A Midsummer-Night's Dream,* i, 1, 25.

By your consent.—*A Midsummer-Night's Dream,* iii, 2, 231; *The Merry Wives of Windsor,* iii, 3, 116.

By the consent of all.—*Troilus and Cressida,* iii, 1, 201.

12
If 't be your pleasure and most wise consent.
Othello. Act i, sc. 1, l. 122. [Roderigo]

Prime consent.—*Pericles,* iv, 3, 27.

13
For I have given here my soul's consent.
Richard II. Act iv, sc. 1, l. 249. [King Richard]

My soul consents.—*A Midsummer-Night's Dream,* i, 1, 82.

Never, my soul, consent!—*Hamlet,* iii, 2, 417.

14
Tell him the queen hath heartily consented.
Richard III. Act iv, sc. 5, l. 17. [Derby]

She hath consented.—*The Merry Wives of Windsor,* iv, 6, 25.

Your father hath consented.—*The Taming of the Shrew,* ii, 1, 271.

'Tis well consented.—*Much Ado about Nothing,* iv, 1, 253.

15
Within her scope of choice
Lies my consent and fair according voice.
Romeo and Juliet. Act i, sc. 2, l. 18. [Capulet]

With one consent.—*The Taming of the Shrew,* iv, 4, 35; *Troilus and Cressida,* iii, 3, 176; *Timon of Athens,* v, 1, 143.

With the consent of supreme Jove.—*Troilus and Cressida,* v, 3, 71.

By his consent.—*III Henry VI,* ii, 2, 88.

By my consent.—*The Winter's Tale,* v, 3, 136.

By your consent and voice.—*Troilus and Cressida,* v, 3, 74.

16
Your breath of full consent bellied his sails.
Troilus and Cressida. Act ii, sc. 2, l. 74. [Troilus] The only use of "bellied."

Your full consent
Gave wings to my propension.
Troilus and Cressida. Act ii, sc. 2, l. 132. [Paris] The only use of "propension" (inclination).

CONSEQUENCE

See also Event, Result

17
The consequence is then thy jealous fits
Have scared thy husband from the use of wits.
The Comedy of Errors, v, 1, 85. See under JEALOUSY.

Joy be the consequence!—*The Merchant of Venice,* iii, 2, 107.

1 Polonius: Be assured
He closes with you in this consequence. . . .
He does—what was I about to say? By the mass, I was about to say something: where did I leave?
Reynaldo: At 'closes in the consequence.' . . .
Polonius: At 'closes in the consequence,' ay, marry.
Hamlet. Act ii, sc. 1, l. 44.

2 If consequence do but approve my dream,
My boat sails freely, both with wind and stream.
Othello. Act ii, sc. 3, l. 64. [Iago]

3 It is a matter of small consequence.
Richard II, v, 2, 61. See under TRIFLE.

Matter of heavy consequence.—*All's Well that Ends Well,* ii, 5, 49.

Matters of this consequence.—*Henry V,* ii, 4, 146.

4 The consequence
Will prove as bitter, black, and tragical.
Richard III. Act iv, sc. 4, l. 6. [Queen Margaret]

O bitter consequence!—*Richard III,* iv, 2, 15.

Deepest consequence.—*Macbeth,* i, 3, 126.

Honourable-dangerous consequence.—*Julius Cæsar,* i, 3, 124. The only use of "honourable-dangerous."

Mortal consequences.—*Macbeth,* v, 3, 5.

Petty consequence.—*Hamlet,* iii, 3, 21.

An unshunned consequence.—*Measure for Measure,* iii, 2, 62. The only use of "unshunned."

Consequence o' the crown.—*Cymbeline,* ii, 3, 126.

Consequence of dread.—*Henry VIII,* ii, 4, 214.

5 Some consequence yet hanging in the stars
Shall bitterly begin his fearful date
With this night's revels.
Romeo and Juliet. Act i, sc. 4, l. 107. [Romeo]

6 Consequently sets down the manner how.
Twelfth Night. Act iii, sc. 4, l. 79. [Malvolio] "Consequently" is repeated in *King John,* iv, 2, 240, and in *Richard II,* i, 1, 102.

CONSIDERATION

See also Reflection

7 If thou hast consider'd, let us know.
Antony and Cleopatra. Act ii, sc. 6, l. 5. [Cæsar]

I have consider'd of a course.
Cymbeline. Act iii, sc. 4, l. 114. [Pisanio]

Have you consider'd?—*Macbeth,* iii, 1, 76.

8 Let 's to supper, come,
And drown consideration.
Antony and Cleopatra. Act iv, sc. 2, l. 44. [Antony]

9 Madam, you 're best consider.
Cymbeline. Act iii, sc. 2, l. 79. [Pisanio]

Better consider.—*I Henry IV,* v, 2, 77.

Let her consider.—*The Merry Wives of Windsor,* iii, 5, 51; *Cymbeline,* ii, 3, 20.

10 Let 's further think of this.
Hamlet. Act iv, sc. 7, l. 149. [King]

For us, we will consider of this further.
Henry V. Act ii, sc. 4, l. 113. [French King]

Consider further.—*Coriolanus,* iii, 3, 52; *Henry VIII,* i, 1, 106.

'Twere to consider too curiously, to consider so.
Hamlet. Act v, sc. 1, l. 227. [Horatio]

11 Considerations infinite.
I Henry IV. Act v, sc. 1, l. 102. [King Henry]

Humble considerations.—*II Henry IV,* ii, 2, 14.

12 After this cold considerance, sentence me.
II Henry IV. Act v, sc. 2, l. 98. [Chief Justice] The only use of "considerance."

13 Widow, we will consider of your suit.
III Henry VI. Act iii, sc. 2, l. 16. [King Edward]

Consider of it.—*Coriolanus,* i, 2, 17.

Well consider of them.—*II Henry IV,* iii, 1, 3.

Consider how it stands.—*The Comedy of Errors,* iv, 1, 68.

Consider, lords.—*II Henry VI,* i, 1, 151.

Consider rightly.—*Julius Cæsar,* iii, 2, 114.

Consider then.—*A Midsummer-Night's Dream,* v, 1, 112.

Consider this.—*The Merchant of Venice,* iv, 1, 198; *Coriolanus,* iii, 1, 320.

Consider.—*Richard III,* i, 4, 261, and frequently in later plays.

Therefore consider.—*Henry V,* iii, 6, 133.

For goodness' sake, consider what you do.
Henry VIII. Act iii, sc. 1, l. 159. [Wolsey]

14 Many mazed considerings did throng
And press'd in with this caution.
Henry VIII. Act ii, sc. 4, l. 185. [King] "Mazed" is repeated in *I Henry VI,* iv, 2, 47, and in *Midsummer-Night's Dream,* ii, 1, 113.

Startles and frights consideration.
King John. Act iv, sc. 2, l. 25. [Salisbury]

Best consideration.—*King Lear,* i, 1, 152.

Consideration, like an angel, came.
Henry V, i, 1, 28. See under ADAM for full quotation.

15 You that have worn your eyes almost out in the service, you will be considered.
Measure for Measure. Act i, sc. 2, l. 114. [Pompey]

Being consider'd.—*Henry VIII,* v, 1, 99.

16 You ought to consider with yourselves.
A Midsummer-Night's Dream. Act iii, sc. 1, l. 30. [Bottom]

I have consider'd with myself.—*II Henry VI,* v, 1, 175.

I hope you will consider.—*Othello,* iii, 3, 216.

I will consider.—*Cymbeline,* ii, 3, 32.

Consider it not so deeply.—*Macbeth,* ii, 2, 30.

Consider little.—*The Winter's Tale,* v, 1, 26.

17 All circumstance well considered.
Richard III. Act iii, sc. 7, l. 176. [Buckingham]

I have consider'd in my mind
The late demand which you did sound me in.
Richard III. Act iv, sc. 2, l. 86. [Buckingham]

I have consider'd well.—*The Two Gentlemen of Verona,* i, 3, 19.

I have considered so much, Camillo, and with some care.
The Winter's Tale. Act iv, sc. 2, l. 39. [Polixenes]

Gently considered.—*Winter's Tale,* iv, 4, 825.

Serious considering.—*Henry VIII,* iii, 2, 135.

CONSPIRACY

See also Plot

1
Much is breeding,
Which, like the courser's hair, hath yet but life,
And not a serpent's poison.
Antony and Cleopatra. Act i, sc. 2, l. 199. [Antony]

2
This man
Hath, for a few light crowns, lightly conspired.
Henry V. Act ii, sc. 2, l. 88. [King Henry]

You have conspired against our royal person.
Henry V. Act iii, sc. 2, l. 167. [King Henry]

3
Stand back, thou manifest conspirator,
Thou that contrivedst to murder our dead lord.
I Henry VI. Act i, sc. 3, l. 33. [Gloucester]

Grand conspirator.—*Richard II,* v, 6, 19.

Whispering conspirator.—*The Rape of Lucrece,* l. 769.

Conspirant 'gainst this high-illustrious prince.
King Lear. Act v, sc. 3, l. 135. [Edgar] The only use of "conspirant" and "high-illustrious."

4
What mutter you, or what conspire you?
III Henry VI. Act i, sc. 1, l. 165. [York]

5
O conspiracy,
Shamest thou to show thy dangerous brow by night,
When evils are most free? O, then by day
Where wilt thou find a cavern dark enough
To mask thy monstrous visage? Seek none, conspiracy;
Hide it in smiles and affability.
Julius Cæsar. Act ii, sc. 1, l. 77. [Brutus]

6
Away, then! come, seek the conspirators.
Julius Cæsar. Act iii, sc. 2, l. 237. [Citizen]

Some six or seven, who did hide their faces
Even from darkness.
Julius Cæsar. Act ii, sc. 1, l. 277. [Portia]

Tear him to pieces; he's a conspirator.
Julius Cæsar. Act iii, sc. 3, l. 30. [Citizen]

I draw a sword against conspirators.
Julius Cæsar. Act v, sc. 1, l. 51. [Octavius]

The old fantastical duke of dark corners.
Measure for Measure. Act iv, sc. 3, l. 163. [Lucio]

7
Hast thou conspired with thy brother too,
That for thine own gain shouldst defend mine honour?
King John. Act i, sc. 1, l. 241. [Lady Faulconbridge]

They have conspired together.—*The Merchant of Venice,* ii, 5, 22.

8
There 's a knot, a ging, a pack, a conspiracy against me.
The Merry Wives of Windsor. Act iv, sc. 2, l. 123. [Ford] The only use of "ging" (gang) in the plays.

Confirm'd conspiracy.—*Henry V,* ii, Prol., 27.

I had forgot that foul conspiracy.
Tempest. Act iv, sc. 1, l. 139. [Prospero]

9
Thou dost conspire against thy friend, Iago,
If thou but think'st him wrong'd and makest his ear
A stranger to thy thoughts.
Othello. Act iii, sc. 3, l. 142. [Othello]

Conspire my death.—*Richard III,* iii, 4, 62.

10
Thou fond mad woman,
Wilt thou conceal this dark conspiracy?
Richard II. Act v, sc. 2, l. 95. [York]

O heinous, strong and bold conspiracy!
Richard II. Act v, sc. 3, l. 59. [Bolingbroke]

11
While you here do snoring lie,
Open-eyed conspiracy His time doth take.
The Tempest. Act ii, sc. 1, l. 300. [Ariel] The only use of "snoring" and "open-eyed."

12
Dare you presume to harbour wanton lines?
To whisper and conspire against my youth?
The Two Gentlemen of Verona. Act i, sc. 2, l. 42. [Julia]

13
Now, for conspiracy,
I know not how it tastes; though it be dish'd
For me to try how.
The Winter's Tale. Act iii, sc. 2, l. 72. [Hermione] The only use of "dish'd."

CONSTABLE

14
When I came hither, I was lord high constable.
Henry VIII. Act ii, sc. 1, l. 102. [Buckingham]

Lord high constable.—*Henry V,* ii, 4, 41; iii, 7, 8; iii, 7, 135.

Lord constable.—*Henry V,* iii, 5, 61; 67; iii, 7, 73; iv, 2, 7.

The Constable of France.—*Henry V,* iv, 3, 89.

15
If it please your honour, I am the poor duke's constable, and my name is Elbow: I do lean upon justice, sir.
Measure for Measure. Act ii, sc. 1, l. 48. [Elbow]

The knave constable had set me i' the stocks, i' the common stocks, for a witch.
The Merry Wives of Windsor. Act v, sc. 5, l. 122. [Falstaff]

16
Dogberry: First, who think you the most desartless man to be constable?
First Watchman: Hugh Otecake, sir, or

George Seacole; for they can write and read.
Much Ado about Nothing. Act iii, sc. 3, l. 10. The only use of "desartless."

You are thought here to be the most senseless and fit man for the constable of the watch; therefore bear you the lantern.
Much Ado about Nothing. Act iii, sc. 3, l. 23. [Dogberry]

1 Call up the right master constable.
Much Ado about Nothing. Act iii, sc. 3, l. 178. [Second Witch]

Master constable.—*Much Ado about Nothing,* iv, 2, 8; 35; 45; 66.

This learned constable is too cunning to be understood.
Much Ado about Nothing. Act v, sc. 1, l. 233. [Don Pedro]

A night-watch constable.—*Love's Labour's Lost,* iii, 1, 178. The only use of "night-watch."

2 I am in case to justle a constable.
The Tempest. Act iii, sc. 2, l. 28. [Trinculo] "Justle" is repeated in *Love's Labour's Lost,* v, 2, 758; and in *Troilus and Cressida,* iv, 4, 36.

CONSTANCY

See also Fidelity; Love: Constant and Inconstant; Loyalty; Woman

3 Why should I think you can be mine and true?
Antony and Cleopatra. Act i, sc. 3, l. 27. [Cleopatra]

My resolution's placed, and I have nothing
Of woman in me: now from head to foot
I am marble-constant; now the fleeting moon
No planet is of mine.
Antony and Cleopatra. Act v, sc. 2, l. 238. [Cleopatra] The only use of "marble-constant."

4 Adriana: How if your husband start some other where?
Luciana: Till he come home again, I would forbear.
The Comedy of Errors. Act ii, sc. 1, l. 30.

I am constant.—*Coriolanus,* i, 1, 243.

Be you constant.—*Much Ado about Nothing,* ii, 2, 55.

5 Take a fellow of plain and uncoined constancy; for he perforce must do thee right, because he hath not the gift to woo in other places.
Henry V. Act v, sc. 2, l. 161. [King Henry] The only use of "uncoined."

6 I have made strong proof of my constancy.
Julius Cæsar. Act ii, sc. 1, l. 299. [Portia]

Formal constancy.—*Julius Cæsar,* ii, 1, 227.

Honesty and constancy.—*Measure for Measure,* iv, 2, 163.

Wisdom and constancy.—*All's Well that Ends Well,* ii, 1, 87.

7 O constancy be strong upon my side,
Set a huge mountain 'tween my heart and tongue!
Julius Cæsar. Act ii, sc. 4, l. 6. [Portia]

But I am constant as the northern star,
Of whose true-fix'd and resting quality
There is no fellow in the firmament.
Julius Cæsar. Act iii, sc. 1, l. 60. [Cæsar] The only use of "true-fix'd."

8 Your constancy Hath left you unattended.
Macbeth. Act ii, sc. 2, l. 68. [Lady Macbeth] The only use of "unattended."

9 It is as dangerous to be aged in any kind of course, as it is virtuous to be constant in any undertaking.
Measure for Measure. Act iii, sc. 2, l. 238. [Duke]

10 God join'd my heart and Romeo's, thou our hands,
And ere this hand, by thee to Romeo seal'd,
Shall be the label to another deed,
Or my true heart with treacherous revolt
Turn to another, this shall slay them both.
Romeo and Juliet. Act iv, sc. 1, l. 55. [Juliet] "Label" is repeated in *Cymbeline,* v, 5, 430.

11 In all external grace you have some part,
But you like none, none you, for constant heart.
Sonnets. No. liii.

This I do vow and this shall ever be;
I will be true, despite thy scythe and thee.
Sonnets. No. cxxiii.

12 Persistive constancy in men:
The fineness of which metal is not found
In fortune's love.
Troilus and Cressida. Act i, sc. 3, l. 21. [Agamemnon] The only use of "persistive."

13 Our kindred, though they be long ere they are wooed, they are constant being won: they are burs, I can tell you; they'll stick where they are thrown.
Troilus and Cressida. Act iii, sc. 2, l. 18. [Pandarus]

I am a kind of burr; I shall stick.
Measure for Measure. Act iv, sc. 3, l. 189. [Lucio]

They are but burs, cousin, thrown upon thee in holiday foolery.
As You Like It. Act i, sc. 3, l. 13. [Celia]

These burs are in my heart.—*As You Like It,* i, 3, 17.

Thou burr!—*A Midsummer-Night's Dream,* iii, 2, 260.

Kecksies, burs.—*Henry V,* v, 2, 52. The only uses of "burr."

14 What truth can speak truest not truer than Troilus.
Troilus and Cressida. Act iii, sc. 2, l. 105. [Troilus]

True swains in love shall in the world to come
Approve their truths by Troilus: when their rhymes,
Full of protest, of oath and big compare,
Want similes, truth tired with iteration,

As true as steel, as plantage to the moon,
As sun to day, as turtle to her mate,
As iron to adamant, as earth to the centre,
Yet, after all comparisons of truth,
As truth's authentic author to be cited,
'As true as Troilus' shall crown up the verse,
And sanctify the numbers.
Troilus and Cressida. Act iii, sc. 2, l. 180. [Troilus] The only use of "plantage."

I speak not 'be thou true,' as fearing thee,
For I will throw my glove to Death himself,
That there 's no maculation in thy heart.
Troilus and Cressida. Act iv, sc. 4, l. 64. [Troilus] The only use of "maculation" (stain of impurity).

Cressida: My lord, will you be true?
Troilus: Who, I? alas, it is my vice, my fault.
Troilus and Cressida. Act iv, sc. 4, l. 103.

Never did young man fancy
With so eternal and so fix'd a soul.
Troilus and Cressida. Act v, sc. 2, l. 165. [Troilus]

Who shall be true to us,
When we are so unsecret to ourselves?
Troilus and Cressida. Act iii, sc. 2, l. 132. [Cressida] The only use of "unsecret."

1
I would have men of such constancy put to sea, that their business might be every thing and their intent every where; for that 's it that always makes a good voyage of nothing.
Twelfth Night. Act ii, sc. 4, l. 77. [Clown]

2
Here is my hand for my true constancy.
The Two Gentlemen of Verona. Act ii, sc. 2, l. 8. [Proteus]

I would always have one play but one thing.
The Two Gentlemen of Verona. Act iv, sc. 2, l. 72. [Julia]

O Heaven! were man
But constant, he were perfect. That one error
Fills him with faults; makes him run through all the sins.
The Two Gentlemen of Verona. Act v, sc. 4, l. 110. [Proteus]

3 To this I am most constant
Though destiny say no.
The Winter's Tale. Act iv, sc. 4, l. 45. [Florizel]

I am but sorry, not afeard; delay'd,
But nothing alter'd: what I was, I am;
More straining on for plucking back, not following
My leash unwillingly.
The Winter's Tale. Act iv, sc. 4, l. 474. [Florizel] "Leash" is repeated in *I Henry IV,* ii, 4, 7, and in *Coriolanus,* i, 6, 38." "Leashed" is used once, in *Henry V,* Prol., 7.

CONTAGION, see Infection

CONTEMPLATION

See also Meditation

4
So many hours must I contemplate.
III Henry VI, ii, 5, 33. The only use of "contemplate."

What serious contemplation are you in?
King Lear. Act i, sc. 2, l. 150. [Edgar]

Leaden contemplation.—*Love's Labour 's Lost,* iv, 3, 321.

Sundry contemplation.—*As You Like It,* iv, 1, 18.

5 The prince obscured his contemplation
Under the veil of wildness.
Henry V. Act i, sc. 1, l. 63. [Bishop of Ely]

His contemplation were above the earth,
And fix'd on spiritual object.
Henry VIII. Act iii, sc. 2, l. 131. [King]

6
When holy and devout religious men
Are at their beads, 'tis hard to draw them thence,
So sweet is zealous contemplation.
Richard III. Act iii, sc. 7, l. 92. [Buckingham]

Who doth molest my contemplation?
Titus Andronicus. Act v, sc. 2, l. 9. [Titus]

CONTEMPT

See also Scorn

7
Check thy contempt.
All's Well that Ends Well. Act ii, sc. 3, l. 164. [King]

Contempt his scornful perspective did lend me,
Which warp'd the line of every other favour;
Scorn'd a fair colour, or express'd it stolen;
Extended or contracted all proportions
To a most hideous object.
All's Well that Ends Well. Act v, sc. 3, l. 48. [Bertram]

8
What our contempt doth often hurl from us,
We wish it ours again.
Antony and Cleopatra. Act i, sc. 2, l. 127. [Antony]

9
I see no more in you than in the ordinary
Of nature's sale-work.
As You Like It. Act iii, sc. 5, l. 42. [Rosalind] The only use of "sale-work."

Wouldst thou not spit at me and spurn at me?
The Comedy of Errors. Act ii, sc. 2, l. 136. [Adriana]

10
He did solicit you in free contempt
When he did need your loves, and do you think
That his contempt shall not be bruising to you,
When he hath power to crush?
Coriolanus. Act ii, sc. 3, l. 208. [Brutus]

Forget not
With what contempt he wore the humble weed,
How in his suit he scorn'd you.
Coriolanus. Act ii, sc. 3, l. 229. [Sicinius]

11 Despising,
For you, the city, thus I turn my back.
Coriolanus. Act iii, sc. 3, l. 133. [Coriolanus] See also under Back.

Despising many forfeits.—*Troilus and Cressida,* iv, 5, 187.

Myself almost despising.—*Sonnets,* xxix. The only uses of "despising."

12
How Can her contempt be answer'd?
Cymbeline. Act iii, sc. 5, l. 42. [Cymbeline]

Jeering and disdain'd contempt.
I Henry IV. Act i, sc. 3, l. 183. [Hotspur] The only use of "jeering."

1
Falstaff: Go, you thing, go.
Hostess: Say, what thing? what thing?
Falstaff: What thing! why, a thing to thank God on.
Hostess: I am no thing to thank God on, I would thou shouldst know it.
I Henry IV. Act iii, sc. 3, l. 131.
Nym: Pish!
Pistol: Pish for thee, Iceland dog! thou prick-ear'd cur of Iceland!
Henry V. Act ii, sc. 1, l. 42. The only use of "prick-ear'd" and mention of Iceland.
Pish!—*Othello*, ii, 1, 270; iv, 1, 42. The only uses of "pish."

2
Scorn and defiance; slight regard, contempt,
And any thing that may not misbecome
The mighty sender, doth he prize you at.
Henry V. Act ii, sc. 4, l. 117. [Exeter] The only use of "misbecome."
It cannot be this weak and writhled shrimp
Should strike such terror to his enemies.
I Henry VI. Act ii, sc. 3, l. 23. [Countess of Auvergne] The only use of "writhled" (wrinkled). "Shrimp" is repeated in *Love's Labour's Lost*, v, 2, 594.

3 Let the foul'st contempt
Shut door upon me, and so give me up
To the sharp'st kind of justice.
Henry VIII. Act ii, sc. 4, l. 42. [Queen Katharine]
Foul contempt.—*Titus Andronicus*, v, 1, 12.
Proud contempt.—*King John*, ii, 1, 88.

4 Methinks, I could despise this man,
But that I am bound in charity against it!
Henry VIII. Act iii, sc. 2, l. 297. [Wolsey]
Despise me, when I break this oath of mine.
Love's Labour's Lost. Act v, sc. 2, l. 441. [King]
I am so far from granting thy request
That I despise thee for thy wrongful suit.
The Two Gentlemen of Verona. Act iv, sc. 2, l. 101. [Silvia] "Wrongful" is used once again in *Titus Andronicus*, i, 1, 293: "Wrongful quarrel."
I do despise them.—*Coriolanus*, iii, 1, 22.
Despise me.—*Othello*, i, 1, 8.
Despise myself.—*Othello*, ii, 3, 299.
Despiseth me.—*The Two Gentlemen of Verona*, iv, 4, 99; 100. "Despiseth" occurs in no other scene.

5
Why, that contempt will kill the speaker's heart,
And quite divorce his memory from his part.
Love's Labour's Lost. Act v, sc. 2, l. 149. [Boyet]
Contempt, farewell! and maiden pride, adieu!
Much Ado about Nothing. Act iii, sc. 1, l. 109. [Beatrice]

6
Canst thou so daff me?
Much Ado about Nothing. Act v, sc. 1, l. 78. [Leonato] The only use of "daff" in the sense of thrust aside. "Daff'd the world aside" occurs in *I Henry IV*, iv, 1, 96.
Every day thou daffest me with some device.
Othello. Act iv, sc. 2, l. 176. [Roderigo] The only use of "daffest."

7
Contempt and beggary hangs upon thy back.
Romeo and Juliet. Act v, sc. 1, l. 71. [Romeo]

8 Rewards he my true service
With such deep contempt?
Richard III. Act iv, sc. 2, l. 123. [Buckingham]
Held in contempt.—*Richard III*, i, 3, 80.

9
The senator shall bear contempt hereditary,
The beggar native honour.
Timon of Athens. Act iv, sc. 3, l. 10. [Timon]
For the extent
Of egal justice, used in such contempt.
Titus Andronicus. Act iv, sc. 4, l. 3. [Saturninus] The only use of "egal" (equal).

10
It cannot but turn him into a notable contempt.
Twelfth Night. Act ii, sc. 5, l. 224. [Maria]
Placed in contempt.—*Twelfth Night*, i, 5, 307.
Put into contempt.—*Cymbeline*, iii, 4, 92.
Contempt and anger.—*Twelfth Night*, iii, 1, 158.
Contempt of empire.—*All's Well that Ends Well*, iii, 2, 34.
Contempt of love.—*The Two Gentlemen of Verona*, ii, 4, 133.
Contempt of man.—*King Lear*, ii, 3, 8.
Contempt of nature.—*Timon of Athens*, iv, 3, 8.
Contempt of question.—*Twelfth Night*, ii, 5, 97.

CONTENT

11
And ere we have thy youthful wages spent,
We'll light upon some settled low content.
As You Like It. Act ii, sc. 3, l. 67. [Orlando]
I will content you, if what pleases you contents you.
As You Like It. Act v, sc. 2, l. 126. [Rosalind]
I will content you.—*Richard III*, iii, 2, 113.
I will content your pains.—*Othello*, iii, 1, 1.
We will content you.—*The Taming of the Shrew*, v, 1, 138.
It shall content me best.—*Antony and Cleopatra*, v, 2, 68.

12
He that commends me to mine own content
Commends me to the thing I cannot get.
The Comedy of Errors. Act i, sc. 2, l. 33. [Antipholus of Syracuse]

13 Our spoils he kick'd at,
And look'd upon things precious as they were
The common muck of the world: he covets less
Than misery itself would give; rewards
His deeds with doing them, and is content
To spend the time to end it.
Coriolanus. Act ii, sc. 2, l. 128. [Cominius] The only use of "muck."

14
Be you content to lend your patience to us,

And we shall jointly labour with your soul
To give it due content.
Hamlet. Act iv, sc. 5, l. 210. [King]
Be content.—*Richard II,* v, 2, 82, and ten times in later plays.
Be you content.—*Julius Cæsar,* i, 3, 142; *Measure for Measure,* ii, 2, 79.
Content thee (thyself).—*III Henry VI,* i, 1, 85, and ten times in later plays.
Be contented.—*Merry Wives of Windsor,* iii, 3, 177; *King Lear,* iii, 4, 115; *Sonnets,* lxxiv.
Be you contented.—*II Henry IV,* v, 2, 84.
Be well contented.—*Henry VIII,* v, 1, 105.

1 It doth much content me
To hear him so inclined.
Hamlet. Act iii, sc. 1, l. 24. [King]
With very much content.—*All's Well that Ends Well,* iv, 5, 83.
Not without much content.—*The Winter's Tale,* v, 3, 11.

2 I could be well content
To entertain the lag-end of my life
With quiet hours.
I Henry IV. Act v, sc. 1, l. 23. [Worcester] "Lag-end" occurs once again in the plays, in *Henry VIII,* i, 3, 35.
I could be well content.—*I Henry VI,* v, 3, 165.
I shall be well content.—*I Henry VI,* v, 1, 26.
Well content.—*III Henry VI,* iv, 7, 24.
Well contented.—*Macbeth,* ii, 3, 140.

3
Suffolk: How say you, madam, are ye so content?
Margaret: An if my father please, I am content.
I Henry VI. Act v, sc. 3, l. 126. "I am content" is repeated seven times in later plays.
Are you content?—*The Two Gentlemen of Verona,* iv, 1, 61.
I will be content.—*Measure for Measure,* iv, 2, 17.
I must be content.—*Coriolanus,* ii, 1, 65.
Gives me content.—*Measure for Measure,* iii, 1, 270.

4
Such is the fulness of my heart's content.
II Henry VI. Act i, sc. 1, l. 35. [King Henry]
I wish your ladyship all heart's content.
The Merchant of Venice. Act iii, sc. 4, l. 42. [Jessica]
Heart's content.—*Troilus and Cressida,* i, 2, 320.

5
Lord, who would live turmoiled in the court,
And may enjoy such quiet walks as these?
This small inheritance my father left me
Contenteth me, and worth a monarchy.
I seek not to wax great by others' waning,
Or gather wealth, I care not, with what envy:
Sufficeth that I have maintains my state
And sends the poor well pleased from my gate.
II Henry VI. Act iv, sc. 10, l. 18. [Iden] The only use of "turmoiled."

6
Second Keeper: If thou be a king, where is thy crown?
King Henry: My crown is in my heart, and not on my head;
Not deck'd with diamonds and Indian stones,
Nor to be seen: my crown is called content:
A crown it is that seldom kings enjoy.
Second Keeper: Well, if you be a king crown'd with content,
Your crown content and you must be contented.
III Henry VI. Act iii, sc. 1, l. 61.
Though loath, yet must I be content.
III Henry VI. Act iv, sc. 6, l. 48. [Warwick]

7
This night he dedicates to fair content.
Henry VIII. Act i, sc. 4, l. 2. [Guildford]
Shut up In measureless content.
Macbeth. Act ii, sc. 1, l. 16. [Banquo]
Full content.—*II Henry VI,* i, 3, 70.
Sweet content.—*The Passionate Pilgrim,* l. 295.
Calm contents.—*Richard II,* v, 2, 38.
Our content Is our best having.
Henry VIII. Act ii, sc. 3, l. 22. [Old Lady]

8
He that has and a little tiny wit,—
With hey, ho, the wind and the rain,—
Must make content with his fortunes fit,
For the rain it raineth every day.
King Lear. Act iii, sc. 2, l. 74. [Fool]

9
Portia: Art thou contented, Jew? what dost thou say?
Shylock: I am content.
The Merchant of Venice. Act iv, sc. 1, l. 393.
Are you contented?—*Richard II,* iv, 1, 200.
We are contented.—*Julius Cæsar,* iii, 1, 240.
You are contented.—*Julius Cæsar,* v, 1, 109.

10
Poor and content is rich and rich enough.
Othello. Act iii, sc. 3, l. 172. [Iago]

11
Farewell the tranquil mind! farewell content!
Othello. Act iii, sc. 3, l. 348. [Othello] The only use of "tranquil."
So shall I clothe me in a forced content,
And shut myself up in some other course,
To fortune's alms.
Othello. Act iii, sc. 4, l. 120. [Cassio]

12
That contented hap which I enjoy'd.
Richard III. Act i, sc. 3, l. 84. [Queen Elizabeth]
None contented.—*Richard II,* v, 5, 32.

13
Petruchio: I am content.
Katharina: Are you content to stay?
Petruchio: I am content you shall entreat me stay;
But yet not stay, entreat me how you can.
Taming of the Shrew. Act iii, sc. 2, l. 203.
If you were so contented.—*The Taming of the Shrew,* iv, 1, 172.
If you be so contented.—*The Taming of the Shrew,* iv, 2, 25.
If she be so contented.—*The Taming of the Shrew,* iv, 4, 106.

14
And all the ruins of distressful times

Repair'd with double riches of content.
Richard III. Act iv, sc. 4, l. 318. [King Richard]

1 And how does your content
Tender your own good fortune?
The Tempest. Act ii, sc. 1, l. 269. [Antonio]

I . . . rest myself content.—*The Tempest,* v, 1, 144.

2
Forced to content, but never to obey,
Panting he lies and breatheth in her face.
Venus and Adonis, l. 61.

To sell myself I can be well contented,
So thou wilt buy and pay and use good dealing.
Venus and Adonis, l. 513.

3 What you can make her do,
I am content to look on: what to speak,
I am content to hear.
The Winter's Tale. Act v, sc. 3, l. 91. [Leontes]

Content to die.—*The Winter's Tale,* i, 1, 46.

CONTENTION

See also Combat, Discord, Fighting, Quarrel

4
The very heat and pride of their contention.
I Henry IV. Act i, sc. 1, l. 59. [Westmoreland]

5 Contention, like a horse
Full of high feeding, madly hath broke loose
And bears down all before him.
II Henry IV. Act i, sc. 1, l. 9. [Northumberland]

Feed contention.—*II Henry IV,* i, 1, 156.

I could not breed no contention with him.
Henry V. Act v, sc. 1, l. 11. [Fluellen]

6
Sometime the flood prevails, and then the wind;
Now one the better, then another best;
Both tugging to be victors, breast to breast,
Yet neither conqueror nor conquered.
III Henry VI. Act ii, sc. 5, l. 9. [King Henry]

7
My liege, here is the strangest controversy . . .
That e'er I heard.
King John. Act i, sc. 1, l. 44. [Essex]

I acquainted him with the cause in controversy.
The Merchant of Venice. Act iv, sc. 1, l. 155. [Clerk, reading]

Let's stand aside and see the end of this controversy.
The Taming of the Shrew. Act v, sc. 1, l. 63. [Petruchio]

CONTRADICTION

8 He hath been used
Ever to conquer, and to have his worth
Of contradiction.
Coriolanus. Act iii, sc. 3, l. 27. [Sicinius]

Of this contradiction you shall now be quit.
Cymbeline. Act v, sc. 4, l. 169. [First Gaoler]

9
Many things, having full reference
To one consent, may work contrariously.
Henry V. Act i, sc. 2, l. 205. [Canterbury] The only use of "contrariously."

These contraries such unity do hold,
Only to flatter fools and make them bold.
The Rape of Lucrece, l. 1558.

10
I prithee, contradict thyself.
Macbeth. Act ii, sc. 3, l. 94. [Banquo]

Fair is foul, and foul is fair.
Macbeth. Act i, sc. 1, l. 11. [The Witches]

11
All the number of his fair demands
Shall be accomplish'd without contradiction.
Richard II. Act iii, sc. 3, l. 123. [King Richard]

Without contradiction.—*Antony and Cleopatra,* ii, 7, 41; *Cymbeline,* i, 4, 59.

12
Feather of lead, bright smoke, cold fire, sick health!
Romeo and Juliet. Act i, sc. 1, l. 186. [Romeo]

Beautiful tyrant! fiend angelical!
Dove-feather'd raven! wolvish-ravening lamb!
Despised substance of divinest show!
Just opposite to what thou justly seem'st,
A damned saint, an honourable villain!
Romeo and Juliet. Act iii, sc. 2, l. 75. [Juliet] The only use of "angelical," "dove-feather'd," and "wolvish-ravening."

13
Look, what I speak, or do, or think to do,
You are still crossing it.
The Taming of the Shrew. Act iv, sc. 3, l. 194. [Petruchio]

Evermore cross'd and cross'd; nothing but cross'd!
The Taming of the Shrew. Act iv, sc. 5, l. 10. [Petruchio]

I love not to be crossed.
Love's Labour's Lost. Act i, sc. 1, l. 34. [Armado]

You are so crossed.—*The Merry Wives of Windsor,* iv, 5, 130.

CONVERSATION

See also Discourse, Talk

14
More of your conversation would infect my brain, being the herdsmen of the beastly plebeians.
Coriolanus. Act ii, sc. 1, l. 104. [Menenius]

With five times so much conversation, I should get ground of your fair mistress.
Cymbeline. Act i, sc. 4, l. 113. [Iachimo]

15
This bald unjointed chat.
I Henry IV. Act i, sc. 3, l. 65. [Hotspur] The only use of "unjointed."

Come, come, no more of this unprofitable chat.
I Henry IV. Act iii, sc. 1, l. 63. [Mortimer]

You muse what chat we two have had.
III Henry VI. Act iii, sc. 2, l. 109. [King Edward]

If you deny to dance, let's hold more chat.
Love's Labour's Lost. Act v, sc. 2, l. 228. [King]

O, how I long to have some chat with her!
The Taming of the Shrew. Act ii, sc. 1, l. 163. [Petruchio]

Setting all this chat aside.
The Taming of the Shrew. Act ii, sc. 1, l. 270. [Petruchio]

Now we sit to chat as well as eat.
The Taming of the Shrew. Act v, sc. 2, l. 11. [Lucentio]

I myself could make A chough of as deep chat.
The Tempest. Act ii, sc. 1, l. 265. [Antonio]

Leave this idle theme, this bootless chat.
Venus and Adonis, l. 422.

1
Full often, like a shag-hair'd crafty kern,
Hath he conversed with the enemy.
II Henry VI. Act iii, sc. 1, l. 367. [York] "Shag-hair'd" is repeated in *Macbeth,* iv, 2, 83: "Shag-hair'd villain."

Conversed At hours unmeet.—*Much Ado about Nothing,* iv, 1, 183.

Conversed with a magician.—*As You Like It,* v, 2, 66.

Conversing with him.—*I Henry VI,* ii, 4, 81.

Conversing with them.—*II Henry IV,* v, 1, 75. The only uses of "conversing."

2
But all are banish'd till their conversations
Appear more wise and modest to the world.
II Henry IV. Act v, sc. 5, l. 106. [Lancaster]

Of a holy, cold, and still conversation.—*Antony and Cleopatra,* ii, 6, 131.

3
I . . . have not those soft parts of conversation
That chamberers have.
Othello. Act iii, sc. 3, l. 264. [Othello] The only use of "chamberers" (frequenters of ladies' chambers, gallants).

4
The good in conversation,
To whom I give my benison.
Pericles. Act ii, Gower, l. 9.

5
I will converse with iron-witted fools
And unrespective boys.
Richard III. Act iv, sc. 2, l. 28. [King Richard] The only use of "iron-witted" in the plays. "Unrespective" is used once again in *Troilus and Cressida,* ii, 2, 71.

Who can converse with a dumb-show?
The Merchant of Venice. Act i, sc. 2, l. 78. [Portia] "Dumb-show" is used four times.

Converse With groaning wretches.—*Love's Labour's Lost,* v, 2, 861.

Converse with spirits.—*I Henry VI,* ii, 1, 25.

COOKERY

6 Your fine Egyptian cookery
Shall have the fame. I have heard that Julius Cæsar
Grew fat with feasting there.
Antony and Cleopatra. Act ii, sc. 6, l. 64. [Pompey]

He will to his Egyptian dish again.
Antony and Cleopatra. Act ii, sc. 6, l. 134. [Enobarbus]

7
The capon burns, the pig falls from the spit.
The Comedy of Errors. Act i, sc. 2, l. 44. [Dromio of Ephesus]

You are well cooked.—*Cymbeline,* v, 4, 156.

8
But his neat cookery! he cut our roots
In characters,
And sauced our broths, as Juno had been sick
And he her dieter.
Cymbeline. Act iv, sc. 2, l. 49. [Guiderius] "Broth" is repeated in *The Merchant of Venice,* i, 1, 22. The only use of "dieter."

9
The cook help to make the gluttony.
II Henry IV. Act ii, sc. 4, l. 48. [Falstaff] "Gluttony" occurs two lines above this quotation, and nowhere else in the plays. "Glutton" is used three times, once in *I Henry IV* (iv, 2, 28), and twice in *II Henry IV* (i, 2, 39; i, 3, 98). "Gluttonous" occurs but once, in *Timon of Athens,* iii, 4, 52.

Epicurean cooks.—*Antony and Cleopatra,* ii, 1, 24.

Rascal cook.—*Taming of the Shrew,* iv, 1, 165.

Cook to honest creatures.—*Cymbeline,* iv, 2, 299.

10
Would the cook were of my mind!
Much Ado about Nothing. Act i, sc. 3, l. 74. [Don John]

11
Capulet: Sirrah, go hire me twenty cunning cooks.
Second Servant: You shall have none ill, sir; for I 'll try if they can lick their fingers.
Capulet: How canst thou try them so?
Second Servant: Marry, sir, 'tis an ill cook that cannot lick his own fingers.
Romeo and Juliet. Act iv, sc. 2, l. 2.

I 'll play the cook.—*Titus Andronicus,* v, 2, 205; *Cymbeline,* iii, 6, 30; iv, 2, 164.

COQUETRY

12
She knew her distance and did angle for me,
Madding my eagerness with her restraint,
As all impediments in fancy's course
Are motives of more fancy; and, in fine,
Her infinite cunning, with her modern grace,
Subdued me to her rate.
All's Well that Ends Well. Act v, sc. 3, l. 212. [Bertram] The only use of "eagerness." "Madding" is repeated in *II Henry VI,* iii, 2, 117, and in *Cymbeline,* ii, 2, 37.

13
I spy entertainment in her; she discourses, she carves, she gives the leer of invitation.
The Merry Wives of Windsor. Act i, sc. 3, l. 48. [Falstaff] The only use of "invitation."

Page's wife, who even now gave me good eyes too, examined my parts with most judicious œillades; sometimes the beam of her view gilded my foot, sometimes my portly belly.
The Merry Wives of Windsor. Act i, sc. 3, l. 66. [Falstaff]

Strange œillades and most speaking looks.
King Lear. Act iv, sc. 5, l. 25. [Regan] The only uses of "œillades."

O, she did so course o'er my exteriors with such a greedy intention, that the appetite of her eye did seem to scorch me up like a burning-glass!
Merry Wives of Windsor. Act i, sc. 3, l. 72. [Falstaff] The only use of "burning-glass."

1
O, these encounterers, so glib of tongue,
That give accosting welcome ere it comes,
And wide unclasp the tables of their thoughts
To every ticklish reader! set them down
For sluttish spoils of opportunity
And daughters of the game.
Troilus and Cressida. Act iv, sc. 5, l. 58. [Ulysses] The only use of "encounterers," "accosting," "ticklish" and "reader."

2
If she do frown, 'tis not in hate of you,
But rather to beget more love in you:
If she do chide, 'tis not to have you gone;
For why, the fools are mad, if left alone.
Take no repulse, whatever she doth say;
For 'get you gone,' she doth not mean 'away!'
The Two Gentlemen of Verona. Act iii, sc. 1, l. 96. [Valentine]

3
How she holds up the neb, the bill to him!
And arms her with the boldness of a wife
To her allowing husband!
The Winter's Tale. Act i, sc. 2, l. 183. [Leontes] The only use of "neb" (beak, mouth).

Is whispering nothing?
Is leaning cheek to cheek? is meeting noses?
Kissing with inside lip? stopping the career
Of laughter with a sigh?—a note infallible
Of breaking honesty—horsing foot on foot?
Skulking in corners? wishing clocks more swift?
Hours, minutes? noon, midnight? and all eyes
Blind with the pin and web but theirs, theirs only,
That would unseen be wicked? is this nothing?
Why, then the world and all that 's in't is nothing;
The covering sky is nothing; Bohemia nothing;
My wife is nothing; nor nothing have these nothings,
If this be nothing.
The Winter's Tale. Act i, sc. 2, l. 284. [Leontes] The only use of "horsing" and "skulking."

CORN

4
Let us kill him, and we 'll have corn at our own price.
Coriolanus. Act i, sc. 1, l. 10. [Citizen]

The Volsces have much corn; take these rats thither
To gnaw their garners.
Coriolanus. Act i, sc. 1, l. 253. [Marcius]

Tell me of corn!—*Coriolanus,* iii, 1, 61.
Corn o' the storehouse.—*Coriolanus,* iii, 1, 114.

5
Good morrow, gallants! want ye corn for bread?
I Henry VI. Act iii, sc. 2, l. 41. [La Pucelle]

With corn to make your need bread,
And give them life whom hunger starved half dead.
Pericles. Act i, sc. 4, l. 95. [Pericles]

Autumn's corn.—*III Henry VI,* v, 7, 3.
Summer corn.—*Richard II,* iii, 3, 162.
Summer's corn.—*II Henry VI,* iii, 2, 176.
Beaten corn.—*Henry VIII,* v, 5, 32.
Bladed corn.—*Macbeth,* iv, 1, 55.
Green corn.—*A Midsummer-Night's Dream,* ii, 1, 94.
Green corn-field.—*As You Like It,* v, 3, 19. The only use of "corn-field."
Sustaining corn.—*King Lear,* iv, 4, 6.
A corn o'ergrown by weeds.—*The Rape of Lucrece,* l. 281.

6
First thrash the corn, then after burn the straw.
Titus Andronicus. Act ii, sc. 3, l. 123. [Demetrius] "Thrash" is repeated in *Troilus and Cressida,* ii, 1, 50: "Thrash Trojans."

O, let me teach you how to knit again
This scatter'd corn into one mutual sheaf.
Titus Andronicus. Act v, sc. 3, l. 70. [Marcus]

Our corn's to reap.—*Measure for Measure,* iv, 1, 76.
Reap'd no corn.—*Love's Labour 's Lost,* iv, 3, 383.

7
The man that makes his toe
What he his heart should make
Shall of a corn cry woe,
And turn his sleep to wake.
King Lear. Act iii, sc. 2, l. 31. [Fool]

Ladies that have their toes
Unplagued with corns will have a bout with you.
Ah ha, my mistresses! which of you all
Will now deny to dance? she that makes dainty,
She, I 'll swear, hath corns; am I come near ye now?
Romeo and Juliet. Act i, sc. 5, l. 18. [Capulet] The only use of "unplagued."

CORNER

8
I 'll to yond corner.
I Henry VI. Act ii, sc. 1, l. 33. [Bedford]

Sit in a corner.—*Much Ado about Nothing,* ii, 1, 332.
Skulking in corners?—*The Winter's Tale,* i, 2, 289. The only use of "skulking."
Dark corners.—*Measure for Measure,* iv, 3, 164.
Saint Magnus' Corner!—*II Henry VI,* iv, 8, 2.

9
There 's nothing I have done yet, o' my conscience,
Deserves a corner.
Henry VIII, iii, 1, 31. See under DESERVING.

10
That utmost corner of the west.
King John, ii, 1, 29. See under ENGLAND.

The west corner of thy curious-knotted garden.
Love's Labour 's Lost, i, 1, 249. See under

GARDEN. The only use of "curious-knotted" (laid out in intricate designs).
Corner of the orchard.—*Twelfth Night*, iii, 4, 194.
Corner of his jaw.—*Hamlet*, iv, 2, 19.
Corner of the moon.—*Macbeth*, iii, 5, 23.

1
Thou makest the triumviry, the corner-cap of society.
Love's Labour's Lost. Act iv, sc. 3, l. 53. [Biron] The only use of "triumviry" and "corner-cap" (a three-cornered cap).

See you yon . . . corner-stone?
Coriolanus, v, 4, 2. The only use of "corner-stone." See under STONE.

2
I had rather be a toad,
And live upon the vapour of a dungeon,
Than keep a corner in the thing I love
For others' uses.
Othello. Act iii, sc. 3, l. 270. [Othello]

3
All corners else o' the earth
Let liberty make use of.
The Tempest, i, 2, 491. See under PRISON.

All corners of the world.—*Cymbeline*, iii, 4, 39.
All the corners.—*Cymbeline*, ii, 4, 28.
At every corner.—*II Henry VI*, iv, 7, 145.
Four corners of the earth.—*The Merchant of Venice*, ii, 7, 39.
Three corners of the world.—*King John*, v, 7, 116.

CORONET, see Crown

CORPSE, see Body

CORRECTION

See also Punishment

4
Rebuke and dread correction wait on us
And they shall do their office.
I Henry IV. Act v, sc. 1, l. 111. [King Henry]

Correct correction.—*Sonnets*, cxi.
Resolved correction.—*II Henry IV*, iv, 1, 213.
Strong correction.—*Richard II*, iv, 1, 77.

5
Brought to the correction of your law.
II Henry IV. Act iv, sc. 4, l. 85. [Westmoreland]

6
You filthy famished correctioner.
II Henry IV. Act v, sc. 4, l. 22. [Doll] The only use of "correctioner" (one who administers correction). Doll is speaking to a beadle.

7
You show great mercy if you give him life,
After the taste of much correction.
Henry V. Act ii, sc. 2, l. 50. [Grey]

8
Henceforth let a Welsh correction teach you a good English condition.
Henry V. Act 5, sc. 1, l. 83. [Gower]

9
Under the correction of bragging be it spoken.
Henry V, v, 2, 144. See under WOOING.

Under correction.—*Love's Labour's Lost*, v, 2, 489; 493.
Under your correction.—*Henry V*, iii, 2, 130.
Under your good correction.—*Measure for Measure*, ii, 2, 10.

10
Your purposed low correction
Is such as basest and contemned'st wretches
For pilferings and most common trespasses
Are punish'd with.
King Lear. Act ii, sc. 2, l. 149. [Gloucester] The only use of "contemned'st." "Pilfering" is repeated in *Henry V*, i, 2, 142: "Pilfering borderers."

Correction and instruction both must work
Ere this rude beast will profit.
Measure for Measure. Act iii, sc. 2, l. 215. [Duke]

11
Correction lieth in those hands
Which made the fault which we cannot correct.
Richard II. Act i, sc. 2, l. 3. [Gaunt]

Chastise thee
And minister correction to thy fault!
Richard II. Act ii, sc. 3, l. 104. [York]

Wilt thou, pupil-like,
Take thy correction mildly, kiss the rod?
Richard II, v, 1, 32. See KING, 805:1. The only use of "pupil-like."

12
There is no woe to his correction.
The Two Gentlemen of Verona, ii, 4, 138. See under LOVE.

I 'll after, to rejoice in the boy's correction.
The Two Gentlemen of Verona. Act v, sc. 1, l. 394. [Launce]

CORRUPTION

13
My son corrupts a well-derived nature
With his inducement.
All's Well that Ends Well. Act iii, sc. 2, l. 90. [Countess] The only use of "well-derived" as a hyphenated phrase. "Well derived" occurs three times.

Corrupt our hope.—*All's Well that Ends Well*, ii, 1, 123.
Corrupt my air.—*Coriolanus*, iii, 3, 123.
Corrupted honest men!—*Antony and Cleopatra*, iv, 5, 17.
Three corrupted men.—*Henry V*, ii, Prol., 22.
Corrupted the youth of the realm.—*II Henry VI*, iv, 7, 36.

14
Away, away,
Corrupters of my faith! you shall no more
Be stomachers to my heart.
Cymbeline. Act iii, sc. 4, l. 84. [Imogen] "Stomachers" is repeated in *The Winter's Tale*, iv, 4, 226.

Corrupter of words.—*Twelfth Night*, iii, 1, 41.

15
Lay not that flattering unction to your soul,
That not your trespass, but my madness speaks:
It will but skin and film the ulcerous place,
Whiles rank corruption, mining all within,
Infects unseen.
Hamlet. Act iii, sc. 4, l. 145. [Hamlet] "Unction" is repeated in iv, 7, 142, and occurs in no other play. "Film" is used again in *Romeo and Juliet*, i, 4, 63. The only use of "mining."

1
Corrupted, and exempt from ancient gentry.
I Henry VI. Act ii, sc. 4, l. 93. [Somerset]
Corrupt and tainted.—*I Henry VI,* v, 4, 45.
Corrupt and treasonous.—*Henry VIII,* i, 1, 156.

2
Corruption wins not more than honesty.
Henry VIII. Act iii, sc. 2, l. 444. [Wolsey]
Simony was fair-play.—*Henry VIII,* iv, 2, 36.
The only mention of simony.

3
The foul corruption of a sweet child's death.
King John. Act iv, sc. 2, l. 81. [Pembroke]
The life of all his blood Is touch'd corruptibly.
King John. Act v, sc. 7, l. 1. [Prince Henry]
The only use of "corruptibly."
Corruption in the place!
King Lear. Act iii, sc. 6, l. 58. [King Lear]

4
She is corrupted, changed and won from thee.
King John. Act iii, sc. 1, l. 55. [Constable]
Angelo had never the purpose to corrupt her.
Measure for Measure. Act iii, sc. 1, l. 163. [Duke]
Corrupt the tender honour of a maid.—*All's Well that Ends Well,* iii, 5, 75.
Corrupt frail nature.—*III Henry VI,* iii, 2, 155.
Corrupted By spells.—*Othello,* i, 3, 60.
Corrupted through affection.—*Troilus and Cressida,* ii, 2, 177.

5
What corruption in this life, that it will let this man live!
Measure for Measure. Act iii, sc. 1, l. 241. [Isabella]
I have seen corruption boil and bubble
Till it o'er-run the stew.
Measure for Measure. Act v, sc. 1, l. 320. [Duke] "Stew" is repeated in *Cymbeline,* i, 6, 152: "Romish stew."

6
Corrupt, corrupt, and tainted in desire!
The Merry Wives of Windsor. Act v, sc. 5, l. 94. [Mistress Quickly]
Corrupt minds.—*Henry VIII,* v, 1, 133.
Corrupt and taint my business.—*Othello,* i, 3, 272.
I'll corrupt her manners.—*Richard III,* iv, 4, 206.
I will corrupt the Grecian sentinels.—*Troilus and Cressida,* iv, 4, 74. See under BRIBERY.

7
Spotted, spoil'd, corrupted,
Grossly engirt with daring infamy.
The Rape of Lucrece, l. 1172.

8
The corruption of a blemish'd stock.
Richard III. Act iii, sc. 7, l. 122. [Buckingham]
The corruption of abusing times.
Richard III. Act iii, sc. 7, l. 199. [Buckingham]
Strong corruption.—*Twelfth Night,* iii, 4, 390.

COST

9
Command what cost Your heart has mind to.
Antony and Cleopatra. Act iii, sc. 4, l. 37. [Antony]
Spare not for cost.—*Romeo and Juliet,* iv, 4, 6.
Rate the cost.—*II Henry IV,* i, 3, 44.

10
His bravery is not on my cost.
As You Like It, ii, 7, 80. See under FOLLY.
At my proper cost.—*Twelfth Night,* v, 1, 327.
Proper cost.—*II Henry VI,* i, 1, 61.
At our mother's cost.—*Richard III,* v, 3, 324.
To my cost.—*II Henry IV,* iii, 2, 13.
To thy cost.—*I Henry VI,* i, 3, 82; iii, 4, 43.
Upon my cost.—*Henry V,* iv, 3, 25.
Costs and charges!—*II Henry VI,* i, 1, 134.
City's cost.—*II Henry VI,* iv, 6, 3.
Cost of princes.—*As You Like It,* ii, 7, 76.

11
It may chance cost some of us our lives.
II Henry IV, ii, 1, 12. See under LIFE.
Cost thy life.—*Troilus and Cressida,* v, 8, 2.
Cost The death of all.—*Rape of Lucrece,* l. 146.

12
Thy sumptuous buildings and thy wife's attire
Have cost a mass of public treasury.
II Henry VI. Act i, sc. 3, l. 133. [Somerset]

13
How little is the cost I have bestow'd
In purchasing the semblance of my soul
From out the state of hellish misery!
Merchant of Venice, iii, 4, 19. [Portia]
Little cost.—*I Henry VI,* i, 1, 74.
Some little cost.—*Richard III,* i, 2, 260.
Not cost a man a doit.—*Timon of Athens,* i, 1, 217.
One penny cost.—*I Henry IV,* i, 3, 91.

14
It will cost him a thousand pound.
Much Ado about Nothing, i, 1, 90. See under DISEASE.
Cost me an hundred crowns.—*The Taming of the Shrew,* v, 2, 128.
Cost him but a crown.—*Othello,* ii, 3, 93.
Cost my crown.—*III Henry VI,* i, 1, 268.
Cost me two shilling and two pence.—*The Merry Wives of Windsor,* i, 1, 159.
Cost me two thousand ducats!—*The Merchant of Venice,* iii, 1, 88.
Cost me some expense.—*The Comedy of Errors,* iii, 1, 123.
Cost me the dearest groans of a mother.—*All's Well that Ends Well,* iv, 5, 11.
Cost you a groaning.—*Hamlet,* iii, 2, 259.
Cost him his eyes.—*King Lear,* v, 3, 173.
Cost ten thousand lives.—*III Henry VI,* ii, 2, 177.

15
The fashion of the world is to avoid cost, and you encounter it.
Much Ado about Nothing, i, 1, 97. See under TROUBLE.
I am for you, though it cost me ten nights' watchings.
Much Ado about Nothing. Act ii, sc. 1, l. 386. [Leonato]

16
Your grace is too costly to wear every day.
Much Ado about Nothing. Act ii, sc. 1, l. 341. [Beatrice]
Costly thy habit as thy purse can buy.
Hamlet, i, 3, 70. See under DRESS.
Costly apparel.—*Taming of the Shrew,* ii 1, 354.
Costly suit.—*Taming of the Shrew,* Ind., 1, 59.
Garments' cost.—*Sonnets,* xci.
Costly gay.—*Sonnets,* cxlvi.

1
Othello: Uncle, I must come forth.
Gratiano: If thou attempt it, it will cost thee dear.
Othello. Act v, sc. 2, l. 254.
Costs . . . dear.—*Midsummer-Night's Dream,* iii, 2, 97.
2
The rich proud cost of outworn buried age.
Sonnets. No. lxiv. See under TIME.
Why so large cost, having so short a lease?
Sonnets. No. cxlvi.
Dearest cost.—*Timon of Athens,* i, 1, 124.
Mundane cost.—*Pericles,* iii, 2, 71. The only use of "mundane."
Part-created cost.—*II Henry IV,* i, 3, 60. The only use of the phrase.
3
The fall of every Phrygian stone will cost
A drop of Grecian blood.
Troilus and Cressida. Act iv, sc. 5, l. 223. [Hector] "Phrygian" is repeated in iv, 5, 186: "Phrygian steed"; in v, 10, 24: "Phrygian plains"; and in *The Merry Wives of Windsor,* i, 3, 97: "Base Phrygian Turk."

COUCH

See also Bed

4
Couching with the doctor's clerk.
The Merchant of Venice, v, 1, 305. See DAY AND NIGHT, 296:11.
Lay couching.—*As You Like It,* iv, 3, 116.
Couching lion.—*I Henry IV,* iii, 1, 153. The only uses of "couching."
Couchings and lowly courtesies.—*Julius Cæsar,* iii, i, 36. The only use of "couchings."
Coucheth the fowl below.—*The Rape of Lucrece,* l. 507. The only use of "coucheth."
5
We 'll couch i' the castle-ditch.
The Merry Wives of Windsor. Act v, sc. 2, l. 1. [Page] The only use of "castle-ditch."
Couch we awhile.—*Hamlet,* v, 1, 245.
I 'll wink and couch.—*The Merry Wives of Windsor,* v, 5, 52.
There I couch.—*The Tempest,* v, 1, 90.
Couch his limbs.—*Romeo and Juliet,* ii, 3, 38.
Couch on flowers.—*Antony and Cleopatra,* iv, 14, 51.
Couch down in fear.—*Henry V,* iv, 2, 37.
Couch for fear.—*Titus Andronicus,* v, 2, 38.
Couch, ho!—*All's Well that Ends Well,* iv, 1, 24.
6
They are all couched in a pit hard by.
The Merry Wives of Windsor. Act v, sc. 3, l. 14. [Mrs. Page]
Couched in a curious bed.—*III Henry VI,* ii, 5, 53.
Couched in thine eye.—*Richard II,* i, 3, 98.
Couch'd in seeming gladness.—*Troilus and Cressida,* i, 1, 39.
Couched in the ominous horse.—*Hamlet,* ii, 2, 476.
Couched in the woodbine coverture.—*Much Ado about Nothing,* iii, 1, 30.
Clerkly couch'd.—*II Henry VI,* iii, 1, 179.
These flies are couch'd.—*Timon of Athens,* ii, 2, 181.
Couched lance.—*I Henry VI,* iii, 2, 134. The only uses of "couched."
7
Flinty and steel couch of war.
Othello, i, 3, 231. See under CUSTOM.
Be-tumbled couch.—*The Rape of Lucrece,* l. 1037. The only use of "be-tumbled."
Kingly couch.—*II Henry IV,* iii, 1, 16.
Secure couch.—*Othello,* iv, 1, 72.
Couch for luxury.—*Hamlet,* i, 5, 83.
Couch of lasting night.—*King John,* iii, 4, 27.
8
You 'll couch with moe men.
Othello, iv, 3, 57. See LOVE, 904:2.
9
We 'll have thee to a couch
Softer and sweeter than the lustful bed
On purpose trimm'd up for Semiramis.
The Taming of the Shrew, Induction. Sc. 2, l. 39. [Lord] Semiramis is mentioned also in *Titus Andronicus,* ii, 1, 22; ii, 3, 118.
Soft couch.—*Merry Wives of Windsor,* i, 3, 108.

COUNCIL

10
And to that end
Assemble we immediate council.
Antony and Cleopatra. Act i, sc. 4, l. 74. [Cæsar]
Why are we met in council?—*Henry VIII,* v, 3, 2.
Learned council.—*II Henry VI,* i, 1, 89.
Maiden council.—*Love's Labour 's Lost,* v, 2, 789.
Private conference Or council.—*Pericles,* ii, 4, 18. See also CONFERENCE.
Wise council.—*Henry VIII,* ii, 4, 51.
French council.—*Henry V,* v, 2, 304.
11
Rated mine uncle from the council-board.
I Henry IV. Act iv, sc. 3, l. 99. [Hotspur]
To-morrow morning to the council-board.
Henry VIII. Act v, sc. 1, l. 51. [Gardiner] The only uses of "council-board."
Sat in the council-house Early and late.
II Henry VI, i, 1, 90. "Council-house" is repeated in *Richard III,* iii, 5, 38.
12
The king's council are no good workmen.
II Henry VI. Act iv, sc. 2, l. 15. [Bevis]
13
Shallow: The council shall hear it; it is a riot.
Evans: It is not meet the council hear a riot; there is no fear of Got in a riot; the council, look you, shall desire to hear the fear of Got, and not to hear a riot.
Merry Wives of Windsor. Act i, sc. 1, l. 35.
Shallow: The council shall know this.
Falstaff: 'Twere better for you if it were known in counsel.
Merry Wives of Windsor. Act i, sc. 1, l. 120.
14
We to-morrow hold divided councils.
Richard III. Act iii, sc. 1, l. 179. [Buckingham]
There are two councils held;
And that may be determined at the one
Which may make you and him to rue at the other.
Richard III. Act iii, sc. 2, l. 12. [Messenger]
Bid him not fear the separated councils.
Richard III. Act iii, sc. 2, l. 20. [Hastings]

You may jest on, but, by the holy rood,
I do not like these several councils, I.
Richard III. Act iii, sc. 2, l. 77. [Stanley]

COUNSEL

See also Advice

1
Thou will be capable of a courtier's counsel.
All's Well that Ends Well. Act i, sc. 1, l. 224. [Parolles]
Very courtly counsel.—*Troilus and Cressida,* iv, 5, 22.

2
For we intend so to dispose you as
Yourself shall give us counsel.
Antony and Cleopatra. Act v, sc. 2, l. 187. [Cæsar]

3
Good sir, I do in friendship counsel you.
As You Like It. Act i, sc. 2, l. 273. [Le Beau]
Let me counsel thee.—*As You Like It,* iii, 3, 96.
I am bold to counsel you.—*II Henry VI,* i, 3, 96.

4
I would give him some good counsel.
As You Like It. Act iii, sc. 2, l. 383. [Rosalind]
This man hath had good counsel.
King Lear. Act i, sc. 4, l. 345. [Goneril]
I thank you for your good counsel.
Hamlet. Act iv, sc. 5, l. 72. [Ophelia]
I thank your worship for your good counsel: [Aside] but I shall follow it as the flesh and fortune shall better determine.
Measure for Measure. Act ii, sc. 1, l. 266. [Pompey]
Let her wear it out with good counsel.
Much Ado about Nothing. Act ii, sc. 3, l. 207. [Claudio]
Good counsel, marry: learn it, learn it, marquess.
Richard III. Act i, sc. 3, l. 261. [Gloucester]
O Lord, I could have stay'd here all the night
To hear good counsel.
Romeo and Juliet. Act iii, sc. 3, l. 159. [Nurse]
Cast your good counsels Upon his passion.
The Winter's Tale. Act iv, sc. 4, l. 505. [Florizel]
Learned counsel.—*II Henry IV,* i, 2, 153.
Seal'd-up counsel.—*Love's Labour's Lost,* iii, 1, 170. "Seal'd-up" is repeated in *The Winter's Tale,* iii, 2, 128: "Seal'd-up oracle."
Speedy counsel.—*III Henry VI,* ii, 1, 208.
Spiritual counsel.—*Winter's Tale,* ii, 1, 186.
Sworn counsel.—*All's Well that Ends Well,* iii, 7, 9.

5
Pray, be counsell'd.
Coriolanus. Act iii, sc. 2, l. 28. [Volumnia]
Examine Their counsels.—*Coriolanus,* i, 1, 154.
I shall be counsell'd.—*Macbeth,* ii, 1, 29.

6
We will have these things set down by lawful counsel.
Cymbeline. Act i, sc. 4, l. 178. [Iachimo]

7
You do not counsel well.
I Henry IV. Act iv, sc. 3, l. 6. [Douglas]
You give me ill counsel.—*Twelfth Night,* v, 1, 34.
Ill counsel.—*A Midsummer-Night's Dream,* ii, 1, 218.

8
His note-book, his counsel-keeper.
II Henry IV. Act ii, sc. 4, l. 290. [Poins]
The only use of "counsel-keeper."
Set in a note-book.—*Julius Cæsar,* iv, 3, 98.
I will make a prief of it in my note-book.—*The Merry Wives of Windsor,* i, 1, 147. The only uses of "note-book."

9
The very latest counsel
That ever I shall breathe.
II Henry IV. Act iv, sc. 5, l. 183. [King Henry]
And let us choose such limbs of noble counsel,
That the great body of our state may go
In equal rank with the best govern'd nation.
II Henry IV. Act v, sc. 2, l. 135. [King Henry V]

10
Friendly counsel cuts off many foes.
I Henry VI. Act iii, sc. 1, l. 185. [King Henry]
They that thrive well take counsel of their friends.
Venus and Adonis, l. 640.
The fiend gives the more friendly counsel.
The Merchant of Venice. Act ii, sc. 2, l. 31. [Launcelot]

11
What counsel give you in this weighty cause?
II Henry VI. Act iii, sc. 1, l. 289. [Beaufort]
What counsel give you?—*III Henry VI,* ii, 3, 11.
Give me some counsel.—*The Merry Wives of Windsor,* ii, 1, 42.

12
Bosom up my counsel,
You'll find it wholesome.
Henry VIII. Act i, sc. 1, l. 112. [Norfolk]
For in thy shoulder do I build my seat,
And never will I undertake the thing
Wherein thy counsel and consent is wanting.
III Henry VI. Act ii, sc. 6, l. 100. [Edward]

13
Heaven hath an end in all: yet, you that hear me,
This from a dying man receive as certain:
Where you are liberal of your loves and counsels
Be sure you be not loose.
Henry VIII. Act ii, sc. 1, l. 124. [Buckingham]
Heaven keep me from such counsel!
Henry VIII. Act ii, sc. 2, l. 38. [Chamberlain]

14
Let me have time and counsel for my cause.
Henry VIII. Act iii, sc. 1, l. 79. [Queen Katharine]
Can you think, lords,
That any Englishman dare give me counsel?
Henry VIII. Act iii, sc. 1, l. 84. [Queen Katharine]
Is this your Christian counsel? out upon ye!
Henry VIII. Act iii, sc. 1, l. 99. [Queen Katharine]

Come, reverend fathers,
Bestow your counsels on me.
Henry VIII. Act iii, sc. 1, l. 181. [Queen Katharine]

I committed
The daring'st counsel which I had to doubt.
Henry VIII, iii, 1, 214. See under QUESTION.

1 I would your grace
Would leave your griefs, and take my counsel.
Henry VIII. Act iii, sc. 1, l. 92. [Campeius]

I will take your counsel.—*II Henry IV,* iii, 1, 106.

Take counsel of some wiser head,
Neither too young nor yet unwed.
The Passionate Pilgrim, l. 303.

2
How like you this wild counsel, mighty states?
Smacks it not something of the policy?
King John. Act ii, sc. 1, l. 395. [Bastard]

No, I defy all counsel, all redress,
But that which ends all counsel, true redress.
King John. Act iii, sc. 4, l. 23. [Constance]

We breathed our counsel: but it pleased your highness
To overbear it.
King John. Act iv, sc. 2, l. 36. [Salisbury]

3 Bestow
Your needful counsel to our business,
Which craves the instant use.
King Lear. Act ii, sc. 1, l. 128. [Regan]

When a wise man gives thee better counsel, give me mine again: I would have none but knaves follow it, since a fool gives it.
King Lear. Act ii, sc. 4, l. 76. [Fool]

My Regan counsels well.—*King Lear,* ii, 4, 312.

4
Their several counsels they unbosom shall
To loves mistook, and so be mock'd withal.
Love's Labour 's Lost. Act v, sc. 2, l. 141. [Princess]

5
The counsel that we two have shared.
A Midsummer-Night's Dream. Act iii, sc. 2, l. 198. [Helena]

Counsels of the heart.—*Titus Andronicus,* iv, 2, 118.

Counsels of thy heart!—*Much Ado about Nothing,* iv, 1, 103.

6 Pause awhile,
And let my counsel sway you in this case.
Much Ado about Nothing. Act iv, sc. 1, l. 203. [Friar]

Counsel may stop awhile what will not stay.
A Lover's Complaint, l. 159.

7
I pray thee, cease thy counsel,
Which falls into mine ears as profitless
As water in a sieve.
Much Ado about Nothing. Act v, sc. 1, l. 3. [Leonato] "Profitless" is repeated in *Othello,* i, 3, 30.

Give not me counsel.—*Much Ado about Nothing,* v, 1, 5.

Give me no counsel.—*Much Ado about Nothing,* v, 1, 31.

8 Men
Can counsel and speak comfort to that grief
Which they themselves not feel; but, tasting it,
Their counsel turns to passion.
Much Ado about Nothing. Act v, sc. 1, l. 20. [Leonato]

9
We lack'd your counsel and your help to-night.
Othello. Act i, sc. 3, l. 51. [Duke]

10
Gaunt: Will the king come, that I may breathe my last
In wholesome counsel to his unstaid youth?
York: Vex not yourself, nor strive not with your breath;
For all in vain comes counsel to his ear.
Gaunt: O, but they say the tongues of dying men
Enforce attention like deep harmony: . . .
Though Richard my life's counsel would not hear,
My death's sad tale may yet undeaf his ear.
Richard II. Act ii, sc. 1, l. 1. The only use of "undeaf."

Then all too late comes counsel to be heard,
Where will doth mutiny with wit's regard.
Richard II. Act ii, sc. 1, l. 27. [York]

Let no man speak again
To alter this, for counsel is but vain.
Richard II. Act iii, sc. 2, l. 213. [King Richard]

11
What, dost thou scorn me for my gentle counsel?
And soothe the devil that I warn thee from?
Richard III. Act i, sc. 3, l. 297. [Queen Margaret]

For then this land was famously enrich'd
With politic grave counsel.
Richard III. Act ii, sc. 3, l. 19. [Citizen] "Famously" is used only once again, in *Coriolanus,* i, 1, 37.

Full of wise care is this your counsel.
Richard III. Act iv, sc. 1, l. 48. [Stanley]

My counsel is my shield.—*Richard III,* iv, 3, 56.

12
What man art thou that thus bescreen'd in night
So stumblest on my counsel?
Romeo and Juliet. Act ii, sc. 2, l. 52. [Juliet] The only use of "bescreen'd."

He lent me counsel.—*Romeo and Juliet,* ii, 2, 81.

13 Out of thy long-experienced time,
Give me some present counsel.
Romeo and Juliet. Act iv, sc. 1, l. 60. [Juliet] "Long-experienced" is repeated in *The Rape of Lucrece,* l. 1820: "Long-experienced wit."

Counsel me, Tranio, for I know thou canst.
The Taming of the Shrew. Act i, sc. 1, l. 162. [Lucentio]

Thy counsel's sound.—*The Taming of the Shrew,* i, 1, 169.

Thy counsel, lad, smells of no cowardice.
Titus Andronicus. Act ii, 1, 132. [Chiron]

I like thy counsel; well hast thou advised.
The Two Gentlemen of Verona. Act i, sc. 3, l. 34. [Antonio]

1
He would embrace no counsel, take no warning.
Timon of Athens. Act iii, sc. 1, l. 28. [Lucullus]

I 'll take the gold thou givest me,
Not all thy counsel.
Timon of Athens. Act iv, sc. 3, l. 129. [Alcibiades]

Phrynia and Timandra: More counsel with more money, bounteous Timon.
Timon: More whore, more mischief first; I have given you earnest.
Timon of Athens. Act iv, sc. 3, l. 167.

2
His counsel now might do me golden service.
Twelfth Night. Act iv, sc. 3, l. 8. [Sebastian]

3
But wherefore waste I time to counsel thee?
The Two Gentlemen of Verona. Act i, sc. 1, l. 51. [Valentine]

Good Proteus, go with me to my chamber,
In these affairs to aid me with thy counsel.
The Two Gentlemen of Verona. Act ii, sc. 4, l. 184. [Valentine]

Counsel, Lucetta; gentle girl, assist me.
The Two Gentlemen of Verona. Act ii, sc. 7, l. 1. [Julia]

I 'll in to counsel them.—*The Taming of the Shrew,* Ind., 1, 136.

Counsel and aid them.—*The Winter's Tale,* iii, 2, 20.

4
Mark my counsel,
Which must be even as swiftly follow'd as
I mean to utter it, or both yourself and me
Cry lost, and so good night!
The Winter's Tale. Act i, sc. 2, l. 408. [Camillo]

'Tis your counsel
My lord should to the heavens be contrary,
Oppose against their wills.
The Winter's Tale. Act v, sc. 1, l. 44. [Paulina]

O, that ever I Had squared me to thy counsel!
The Winter's Tale. Act v, sc. 1, l. 51. [Leontes]

II—Keeping Counsel

5
I will lock his counsel in my breast.
I Henry VI. Act ii, sc. 5, l. 118. [Plantagenet]

Blest be
You bees that make these locks of counsel.
Cymbeline. Act iii, sc. 2, l. 35. [Imogen]

6
Tell me your counsels, I will not disclose 'em.
Julius Cæsar. Act ii, sc. 1, l. 298. [Portia]

7
I pray you, turn the key and keep our counsel.
Othello. Act iv, sc. 2, l. 94. [Othello]

I will at the least keep your counsel.
The Merry Wives of Windsor, iv, 6, 7. See also *Much Ado about Nothing,* iii, 3, 92; *Hamlet,* iv, 2, 11; *King Lear,* i, 4, 34. See also under Actors and Women.

Did ever keep your counsels.—*A Midsummer-Night's Dream,* iii, 2, 308.

8
Two may keep counsel when the third 's away.
Titus Andronicus. Act iv, sc. 2, l. 144. [Aaron]

Two may keep counsel, putting one away.
Romeo and Juliet. Act ii, sc. 4, l. 209. [Nurse]

III—Counsellor

9
These are counsellors
That feelingly persuade me what I am.
As You Like It. Act ii, sc. 1, l. 10. [Duke Senior]

10
Can he that speaks with the tongue of an enemy be a good counsellor, or no?
II Henry VI. Act iv, sc. 2, l. 181. [Cade]

11
Good counsellors lack no clients.
Measure for Measure. Act i, sc. 2, l. 109. [Pompey] "Clients" is repeated in *Richard III,* iv, 4, 127; and in *Pericles,* iv, 6, 6.

Noble counsellors.—*Henry V,* ii, 4, 33.

Sage counsellors.—*II Henry VI,* iv, 5, 121.

12
Is he not a most profane and liberal counsellor?
Othello. Act ii, sc. 1, l. 164. [Desdemona]

13
Fit counsellor and servant for a prince,
Who by thy wisdom makest a prince thy servant.
Pericles. Act i, sc. 2, l. 63. [Pericles]

Thou art a grave and noble counsellor,
Most wise in general.
Pericles. Act v, sc. 1, l. 184. [Pericles]

14
He, his own affections' counsellor,
Is to himself—I will not say how true.
Romeo and Juliet. Act i, sc. 1, l. 153. [Montague]

15
You are a counsellor; if you can command these elements to silence, and work the peace of the present, we will not hand a rope more; use your authority.
The Tempest. Act i, sc. 1, l. 23. [Boatswain]

You are a counsellor,
And, by that virtue, no man dare accuse you.
Henry VIII. Act v, sc. iii, l. 49. [Suffolk]

A counsellor, a traitress, and a dear.
All's Well that Ends Well, i, 1, 184. See under Love for full quotation.

An emperor's counsellor.—*The Two Gentlemen of Verona,* ii, 4, 77.

Your most obedient counsellor.—*The Winter's Tale,* ii, 3, 55.

COUNTENANCE

See also Face, Visage

16
That noble countenance,
Wherein the worship of the whole world lies.
Antony and Cleopatra. Act iv, sc. 14, l. 85. [Eros]

1
The something that nature gave me his countenance seems to take from me.
As You Like It. Act i, sc. 1, l. 19. [Orlando]
He waged me with his countenance, as if
I had been mercenary.
Coriolanus. Act v, sc. 6, l. 40. [Aufidius]
Keep that countenance still.—*Cymbeline,* iii, 4, 14.

2
A countenance more in sorrow than in anger.
Hamlet. Act i, sc. 2, l. 232. [Horatio]

3
How he holds his countenance!
I Henry IV. Act ii, sc. 4, l. 432. [Hostess]
Look how he looks! there 's a countenance!
Troilus and Cressida. Act i, sc. 2, l. 218. [Pandarus]
Dangerous countenance.—*I Henry IV,* v, 1, 69.

4
I will leer upon him as a' comes by; and do but mark the countenance that he will give me.
II Henry IV. Act v, sc. 5, l. 7. [Falstaff]

5
My grisly countenance made others fly;
None durst come near for fear of sudden death.
I Henry VI. Act i, sc. 4, l. 47. [Talbot] "Grisly" is repeated in *A Midsummer-Night's Dream,* v, 1, 140: "Grisly beast."

6
Can you not see? or will ye not observe
The strangeness of his alter'd countenance?
II Henry VI. Act iii, sc. 1, l. 4. [Queen]
Yea, subject to your countenance, glad or sorry
As I saw it inclined.
Henry VIII. Act ii, sc. 4, l. 26. [Queen Katharine] See under WIFE.
His countenance likes me not.
King Lear. Act ii, sc. 2, l. 96. [Kent]

7
This pert Biron was out of countenance quite.
Love's Labour 's Lost. Act v, sc. 2, l. 272. [Princess] "Pert" is used once again in *A Midsummer-Night's Dream,* i, 1, 14.
Holofernes: I will not be put out of countenance.
Biron: Because thou hast no face.
Love's Labour 's Lost. Act v, sc. 2, l. 611.
Biron: We have put thee in countenance.
Holofernes: You have put me out of countenance.
Biron: False; we have given thee faces.
Holofernes: But you have out-faced them all.
Love's Labour 's Lost. Act v, sc. 2, l. 623.

8
You should lay my countenance in pawn.
The Merry Wives of Windsor. Act ii, sc. 2, l. 5. [Falstaff]

9
With confirmed countenance.
Much Ado about Nothing. Act v, sc. 4, l. 17. [Antonio]
Such a confirmed countenance.
Coriolanus. Act i, sc. 3, l. 65. [Valeria]

10
But when your countenance fill'd up his line,
Then lack'd I matter; that enfeebled mine.
Sonnets. No. lxxxvi.

11
You must meet my master to countenance my mistress.
The Taming of the Shrew, iv, 1, 101.
Calls for company to countenance her.
The Taming of the Shrew, iv, 1, 104.
To countenance this horror!
Macbeth, ii, 8, 85. "Countenance" in the sense of approve is used twenty-four times.

12
Set your countenance, sir.
The Taming of the Shrew. Act iv, sc. 4, l. 18. [Tranio]
He did bear my countenance in the town.
The Taming of the Shrew. Act v, sc. 1, l. 129. [Lucentio]
Puts my . . . countenance on.—*The Taming of the Shrew,* i, 1, 234.

13
Clear up, fair queen, that cloudy countenance:
Though chance of war hath wrought this change of cheer.
Titus Andronicus. Act i, sc. 1, l. 263. [Saturninus]

14
But this thy countenance, still lock'd in steel,
I never saw till now.
Troilus and Cressida. Act iv, sc. 5, l. 195. [Nestor]
A countenance as clear
As friendship wears at feasts.
The Winter's Tale. Act i, sc. 2, l. 343. [Camillo]

15
The king hath on him such a countenance
As he had lost some province and a region
Loved as he loves himself.
The Winter's Tale. Act i, sc. 2, l. 368. [Polixenes]
Countenance of such distraction that they were to be known by garment, not by favour.
The Winter's Tale. Act v, sc. 2, l. 52. [Gentleman]

16
Lift up your countenance, as it were the day
Of celebration of that nuptial which
We two have sworn shall come.
The Winter's Tale. Act iv, sc. 4, l. 49. [Florizel]

COUNTERFEIT

17
Now counterfeit to swoon; why now fall down;
Or if thou canst not, O, for shame, for shame,
Lie not, to say mine eyes are murderers!
As You Like It. Act iii, sc. 5, l. 17. [Phebe]
Rosalind: This was well counterfeited!
I pray you, tell your brother how well I counterfeited. Heigh-ho!
Oliver: This was not counterfeit; there is too

great testimony in your complexion that it was a passion of earnest.
Rosalind: Counterfeit, I assure you.
Oliver: Well then, take a good heart and counterfeit to be a man.
Rosalind: So I do; but, i' faith, I should have been a woman by right.
As You Like It. Act iv, sc. 3, l. 167.

I pray you, commend my counterfeiting to him.
As You Like It. Act iv, sc. 3, l. 183. [Rosalind]

1 Never call a true piece of gold a counterfeit.
I Henry IV. Act ii, sc. 4, l. 539. [Falstaff]

I fear thou art another counterfeit.
I Henry IV. Act v, sc. 4, l. 35 [Douglas]

'Sblood, 'twas time to counterfeit, or that hot termagant Scot had paid me scot and lot too. Counterfeit? I lie, I am no counterfeit: to die, is to be a counterfeit; for he is but the counterfeit of a man who hath not the life of a man: but to counterfeit dying, when a man thereby liveth, is to be no counterfeit, but the true and perfect image of life indeed.
I Henry IV. Act v, sc. 4, l. 113. [Falstaff] "Termagant" is repeated in *Hamlet*, iii, 2, 15. The only use of "scot and lot."

2 'Tis but his policy to counterfeit.
III Henry VI. Act ii, sc. 6, l. 65. [Richard]

Counterfeit assurance.—*The Taming of the Shrew,* iv, 4, 92.

Counterfeit oppression.—*Richard II,* i, 4, 14.

Counterfeit sad looks.—*A Midsummer-Night's Dream,* iii, 2, 237.

3 Fie, fie! you counterfeit, you puppet, you!
A Midsummer-Night's Dream. Act iii, sc. 2, l. 288. [Helena]

4 Antonio: To tell you true, I counterfeit him.
Ursula: You could never do him so ill-well, unless you were the very man.
Much Ado about Nothing. Act ii, sc. 1, l. 122. The only use of "ill-well."

Thou counterfeit to thy true friend!
The Two Gentlemen of Verona. Act v, sc. 4, l. 53. [Proteus]

5 Don Pedro: May be she doth but counterfeit.
Claudio: Faith, like enough.
Leonato: O God, counterfeit! There was never counterfeit of passion came so near the life of passion as she discovers it.
Much Ado about Nothing. Act ii, sc. 3, l. 107.

These may be counterfeits.
Othello. Act v, sc. 1, l. 43. [Lodovico]

6 Mercutio: You gave us the counterfeit fairly last night.
Romeo: . . . What counterfeit did I give you?
Mercutio: The slip, sir, the slip.
Romeo and Juliet. Act ii, sc. 4, l. 48.

7 Timon: Good honest men! Thou draw'st a counterfeit
Best in all Athens: thou 'rt, indeed, the best;
Thou counterfeit'st most lively.
Painter: So, so, my lord.
Timon of Athens. Act v, sc. 1, l. 83.

What art thou
That counterfeit'st the person of a king?
I Henry IV. Act v, sc. 4, l. 28. [Douglas]

In one little body
Thou counterfeit'st a bark, a sea, a wind.
Romeo and Juilet, iii, 5, 131. [Capulet]

The knave counterfeits well.—*Twelfth Night,* iv, 2, 22.

Do you but counterfeit?—*Twelfth Night,* iv, 2, 122.

8 If I could have remembered a gilt counterfeit, thou wouldst not have slipped out of my contemplation.
Troilus and Cressida. Act ii, sc. 3, l. 28. [Thersites]

'Tis no counterfeit.
Henry VIII. Act v, sc. 3, l. 102. [Surrey]

Painted counterfeit.—*Sonnets,* xvi.

Poor counterfeit.—*Rape of Lucrece,* l. 1269.

COUNTRY

"My Country," see under Patriotism

9 When he did love his country,
It honour'd him.
Coriolanus. Act iii, sc. 1, l. 305. [Brutus]

Alas, how can we for our country pray?
Coriolanus. Act v, sc. 3, l. 107. [Volumnia]

Whereto are we bound? alack, or we must lose
The country, our dear nurse, or else thy person,
Our comfort in the country.
Coriolanus. Act v, sc. 3, l. 109. [Volumnia]

10 Triumphantly tread on thy country's ruin.
Coriolanus. Act v, sc. 3, l. 116. [Volumnia]

Thou shalt no sooner
March to assault thy country than to tread—
Trust to 't, thou shalt not—on thy mother's womb,
That brought thee to this world.
Coriolanus. Act v, sc. 3, l. 122. [Volumnia]

My canker'd country.—*Coriolanus,* iv, 5, 97.

11 The undiscover'd country from whose bourn
No traveller returns.
Hamlet, iii, 1, 79. See under SUICIDE for full quotation.

12 The rest of thy low countries have made a shift to eat up thy holland.
II Henry IV. Act ii, sc. 2, l. 25. [Prince]

13 All the country is laid for me.
II Henry VI. Act iv, sc. 10, l. 4. [Cade]

In mine own country.—*Henry VIII,* iii, 1, 91.

14 This our suffering country!
Macbeth. Act iii, sc. 6, l. 48. [Lennox]

Bleed, bleed, poor country!
Macbeth. Act iv, sc. 3, l. 31. [Macduff]

Our country sinks beneath the yoke:
It weeps, it bleeds; and each new day a gash
Is added to her wounds.
Macbeth. Act iv, sc. 3, l. 39. [Malcolm]

When I shall tread upon the tyrant's head,
Or wear it on my sword, yet my poor country
Shall have more vices than it had before.
Macbeth. Act iv, sc. 3, l. 45. [Malcolm]
Alas, poor country!—*Macbeth,* iv, 3, 164.
Skirr the country round.—*Macbeth,* v, 3, 35. "Skirr" is repeated in *Henry V,* iv, 7, 64: "Skirr away."

1
Escalus: Of whence are you?
Duke: Not of this country, though my chance is now
To use it for my time.
Measure for Measure. Act iii, sc. 2, l. 229.

2
Imp out our drooping country's broken wing.
Richard II. Act ii, sc. 1, l. 292. [Northumberland] The only use of "imp" in this sense: a term of falconry, meaning to ingraft feathers in the wing of a bird to make it stronger.
Their o'er-cloyed country.—*Richard III,* v, 3, 318. The only use of "o'er-cloyed."

3
Viola: What country, friends, is this?
Captain: This is Illyria, lady.
Viola: And what should I do in Illyria?
Twelfth Night. Act i, sc. 2, l. 1.
Of that fatal country, Sicilia, prithee speak no more.
The Winter's Tale. Act iv, sc. 2, l. 23. [Polixenes]
Some heavenly power guide us
Out of this fearful country!
Tempest. Act v, sc. 1, l. 106. [Gonzalo]

II—Countryman

4
Here you shall see a countryman of yours
That has done worthy service.
All's Well that Ends Well. Act iii, sc. 5, l. 50. [Widow]
A countryman of ours.—*I Henry VI,* i, 2, 29.
Your countrywoman.—*Troilus and Cressida,* iv, 1, 67.
What countrywoman?—*Pericles,* v, 1, 103. The only uses of "countrywoman."

5
See, then, thou fight'st against thy countrymen
And join'st with them will be thy slaughter-men.
I Henry VI. Act iii, sc. 3, l. 74. [La Pucelle] "Slaughter-men" is used five times in as many different plays.

6
Farewell: our countrymen are gone and fled,
As well assured Richard their king is dead.
Richard II. Act ii, sc. 4, l. 16. [Captain]
Our well-dealing countrymen.—*The Comedy of Errors,* i, 1, 7. The only use of "well-dealing."
Dear countryman.—*Henry V,* ii, 2, 189; *Timon of Athens,* v, 4, 38; *Othello,* v, 1, 89.
Loving countrymen.—*I Henry VI,* iii, 1, 137; *Timon of Athens,* v, 1, 197.
Petitionary countrymen.—*Coriolanus,* v, 2, 82. "Petitionary" is repeated in *As You Like It,* iii, 2, 199: "Petitionary vehemence."
Seditious countrymen.—*The Comedy of Errors,* i, 1, 12. "Seditious" is repeated in *II Henry VI,* v, 1, 37.
A simple countryman.—*Antony and Cleopatra,* v, 2, 342.
Thrice valiant countrymen.—*Henry V,* iv, 6, 1.

COURAGE

See also Mettle, Valour

7
I, that with my sword
Quarter'd the world, and o'er green Neptune's back
With ships made cities, condemn myself to lack
The courage of a woman.
Antony and Cleopatra. Act iv, sc. 14, l. 57. [Antony]
Weak of courage.—*III Henry VI,* iv, 1, 12.

8
That 's my brave lord!
Antony and Cleopatra. Act iii, sc. 13, l. 177. [Cleopatra] "Brave lords" is repeated in *Titus Andronicus,* iv, 2, 136.
Doughty-handed are you.—*Antony and Cleopatra,* iv, 8, 5. The only use of "doughty-handed."

9
O, that 's a brave man! he writes brave verses, speaks brave words, swears brave oaths and breaks them bravely.
As You Like It. Act iii, sc. 4, l. 43. [Celia]
Is not that a brave man?—*Troilus and Cressida,* i, 2, 202.
Is 't not a brave man?—*Troilus and Cressida,* i, 2, 219.
There 's a brave man.—*Troilus and Cressida,* i, 2, 217.
This is a brave fellow.—*The Winter's Tale,* iv, 4, 202.
This is most brave.—*Hamlet,* ii, 2, 611.
Why, this is brave now.—*Troilus and Cressida,* i, 2, 232.
Be brave, then.—*II Henry VI,* iv, 2, 69.
Are you so brave?—*Coriolanus,* iv, 5, 18.
Grow ye so brave?—*Titus Andronicus,* ii, 1, 45.

10
When he might act the woman in the scene,
He proved best man i' the field, and for his meed
Was brow-bound with the oak.
Coriolanus. Act ii, sc. 2, l. 100. [Cominius] The only use of "brow-bound." "Best man" occurs six times.
Many there could behold the sun with as firm eyes as he.
Cymbeline. Act i, sc. 4, l. 12. [Frenchman]

11
Hold, hold, my heart;
And you, my sinews, grow not instant old,
But bear me stiffly up.
Hamlet. Act i, sc. 5, l. 93. [Hamlet] The only use of "stiffly."

12
You were advised his flesh was capable
Of wounds and scars and that his forward spirit

Would lift him where most trade of danger ranged.
II Henry IV. Act i, sc. 1, l. 172. [Morton]
Full of haughty courage.—*I Henry VI,* iv, 1, 35.
Best-temper'd courage.—*II Henry IV,* i, 1, 115. The only use of "best-temper'd."
Desperate courage.—*Venus and Adonis,* l. 556.
Hot courage.—*Venus and Adonis,* l. 276.
New courage.—*I Henry VI,* iii, 3, 87.
Outward courage.—*Henry V,* iv, 1, 118.
Superfluous courage.—*Henry V,* iv, 2, 11.
Unmatchable courage.—*Henry V,* iii, 7, 152.
Valiant courage.—*I Henry VI,* v, 5, 70.
Waggish courage.—*Cymbeline,* iii, 4, 160. "Waggish" is repeated in *A Midsummer-Night's Dream,* i, 1, 240.
Strut with courage.—*Cymbeline,* iii, 1, 33.

1
Bardolph, be blithe: Nym, rouse thy vaunting veins:
Boy, bristle thy courage up.
Henry V. Act ii, sc. 3, l. 4. [Pistol]
Therefore courage, good Aliena!—*As You Like It,* ii, 4, 8.
Courage and comfort!—*King John,* iii, 4, 4.
O courage, courage, princes!—*Troilus and Cressida,* v, 5, 30.

2 'Tis true that we are in great danger;
The greater therefore should our courage be.
Henry V. Act iv, sc. 1, l. 1. [King Henry]
There 's not a piece of feather in our host—
Good argument, I hope, we will not fly.
Henry V. Act iv, sc. 3, l. 112. [King Henry]

3
She takes upon her bravely at first dash.
I Henry VI. Act i, sc. 2, l. 71. [Reignier]
Pucelle hath bravely play'd her part.
I Henry VI, iii, 3, 88. See under PART.
O, bravely came we off!
King John. Act v, sc. 5, l. 4. [Lewis]
Came off bravely.—*Henry V,* iii, 6, 77.
See you do it bravely.
Titus Andronicus. Act iv, sc. 3, l. 113. [Titus]
Do bravely.—*Antony and Cleopatra,* i, 5, 22.
'Twas bravely done.—*Much Ado about Nothing,* v, 1, 280.
So bravely done.—*Cymbeline,* ii, 4, 73.
Full bravely.—*I Henry IV,* v, 4, 133.

4
My courage try by combat, if thou darest.
I Henry VI. Act i, sc. 2, l. 89. [La Pucelle]
My breast I 'll burst with straining of my courage.
I Henry VI. Act i, sc. 5, l. 10. [Talbot]

5
Three times did Richard make a lane to me,
And thrice cried 'Courage, father! fight it out!'
III Henry VI. Act i, sc. 4, l. 9. [York]
Strike up the drum; cry 'Courage!' and away.
III Henry VI. Act iv, sc. 3, l. 24. [King Edward.]
Cry 'Courage! to the field.'
I Henry IV. Act ii, sc. 3, l. 53. [Lady Percy]

6
I saw him in the battle range about;
And watch'd him how he singled Clifford forth.
Methought he bore him in the thickest troop
As doth a lion in a herd of neat;
Or as a bear, encompass'd round with dogs,
Who having pinch'd a few and made them cry,
The rest stand all aloof, and bark at him.
III Henry VI. Act ii, sc. 1, l. 11. [Richard]
The steer, the heifer and the calf
Are all call'd neat.
Winter's Tale, i, 2, 125. See under Ox. The only uses of "neat" in this sense.

7
This may plant courage in their quailing breasts;
For yet is hope of life and victory.
III Henry VI. Act ii, sc. 3, l. 54. [George]
There is no quailing now.
I Henry IV, iv, 1, 39. The only uses of "quailing."

8 Yield not thy neck
To fortune's yoke, but let thy dauntless mind
Still ride in triumph over all mischance.
III Henry VI, iii, 3, 16. [King Lewis]

9 Two braver men
Ne'er spurr'd their coursers at the trumpet's sound.
III Henry VI, v, 7, 8. [King Edward]
A braver choice of dauntless spirits
Than now the English bottoms have waft o'er
Did never float upon the swelling tide.
King John. Act ii, sc. 1, l. 72. [Chatillon]

10 Come down
With fearful bravery, thinking by this face
To fasten in our thoughts that they have courage;
But 'tis not so.
Julius Cæsar. Act v, sc. 1, l. 9. [Antony]
Malicious bravery.—*Othello,* i, 1, 100.
Natural bravery.—*Cymbeline,* iii, 1, 18.
Witless bravery.—*Measure for Measure,* i, 3, 10.

11
Courage mounteth with occasion.
King John. Act ii, sc. 1, l. 82. [Austria]
I will not stir, nor wince, nor speak a word.
King John. Act iv, sc. 1, l. 81. [Arthur]
Lift up thy brow, renowned Salisbury,
And with a great heart heave away this storm.
King John. Act v, sc. 2, l. 54. [Dauphin]

12
But screw your courage to the sticking-place,
And we 'll not fail.
Macbeth. Act i, sc. 7, l. 60. [Lady Macbeth] The only use of "sticking-place." Often misquoted "sticking-point." "Screw" is used once again in *Twelfth Night,* v, 1, 120
Approach thou like the rugged Russian bear,
The arm'd rhinoceros, or the Hyrcan tiger;
Take any shape but that, and my firm nerves
Shall never tremble.
Macbeth. Act iii, sc. 4, l. 100. [Macbeth] The only mention of the rhinoceros and the Hyrcan tiger.

1
Good cheer, Antonio! What, man, courage yet!
The Merchant of Venice. Act iv, sc. 1, l. 111. [Bassanio]
Cheer thy heart, and be thou not dismay'd.
Richard III. Act v, sc. 3, l. 174. [Ghost of Buckingham] See under CHEERFULNESS.
He is very courageous.—*The Merry Wives of Windsor,* iv, 1, 4.
2
The fortitude of the place is best known to you.
Othello. Act i, sc. 3, l. 222. [Duke]
Infused with a fortitude from heaven.
The Tempest. Act i, sc. 2, l. 154. [Prospero]
Fortitude of soul.—*Henry VIII,* iii, 2, 388.
His own arm's fortitude.—*I Henry VI,* ii, 1, 17.
Courage, fortitude.—*Macbeth,* iv, 3, 94. The only uses of "fortitude."
3
I 'd such a courage to do him good.
Timon of Athens. Act iii, sc. 3, l. 24. [Sempronius]
Nothing so full of heart.
Troilus and Cressida. Act i, sc. 3, l. 239. [Æneas] The only use of the phrase "full of heart" in the plays.
Courage and hope both teaching him.
Twelfth Night. Act i, sc. 2, l. 13. [Captain]

COURSE

See also Path, Plan, Way

4
Therefore homeward did they bend their course.
The Comedy of Errors. Act i, sc. 1, l. 118. [Ægeon]
Bend their course.—*Richard III,* iv, 5, 14.
5
Whose course Will on the way it takes.
Coriolanus. Act i, sc. 1, l. 71. [Menenius]
Take thou what course thou wilt!
Julius Cæsar. Act iii, sc. 2, l. 266. [Antony] See under MISCHIEF.
We must take another course with you.
Pericles. Act iv, sc. 6, l. 130. [Boult]
Give me leave
To take that course by your consent and voice
Which you do here forbid me.
Troilus and Cressida. Act v, sc. 3, l. 73. [Hector]
Take the course that you have done.
The Winter's Tale. Act ii, sc. 3, l. 48. [Paulina]
Take their course.—*King John,* v, 7, 38; *II Henry IV,* iv, 2, 103.
Take this course.—*Cymbeline,* v, 1, 3.
6
It is the humane way: the other course
Will prove too bloody.
Coriolanus. Act iii, sc. 1, l. 327. [Senator]
Our course will seem too bloody, Caius Cassius,
To cut the head off and then hack the limbs,
Like wrath in death and envy afterwards.
Julius Cæsar. Act ii, sc. 1, l. 162. [Brutus]
Bloody courses.—*II Henry IV,* i, 1, 159.
7 Determine on some course,
More than a wild exposture to each chance
That starts i' the way before thee.
Coriolanus. Act iv, sc. 1, l. 35. [Volumnia] The only use of "exposture" (exposure).
8 You should tread a course
Pretty and full of view.
Cymbeline, iii, 4, 149. See under MIND.
Stick to your journal course.
Cymbeline. Act iv, sc. 2, l. 10. [Imogen]
I know my course.—*Hamlet,* ii, 2, 627.
This course I fittest choose.—*The Comedy of Errors,* iv, 3, 96.
9 All the courses of my life do show
I am not in the roll of common men.
I Henry IV, iii, 1, 42. See under GREATNESS.
In the course And process of this time.
Henry VIII. Act ii, sc. 4, l. 36. [Queen Katharine]
Course of altering things.—*Sonnets,* cxv.
Course of breath.—*II Henry IV,* iv, 5, 151.
Course of death.—*King Lear,* iii, 7, 101.
Course of direct session.—*Othello,* i, 2, 86.
Course of fight.—*Coriolanus,* i, 5, 17.
Course of fortune.—*Much Ado about Nothing* iv, 1, 159.
Course of gratitude.—*Cymbeline,* iii, 5, 121.
Course of growth.—*Troilus and Cressida,* i, 3, 9.
Course of honour.—*All's Well that Ends Well,* v, 3, 98.
Course of impious stubbornness.—*Hamlet,* i, 2, 93.
Course of justice.—*Richard III,* iv, 4, 105; *The Merchant of Venice,* iv, 1, 199; *Measure for Measure,* v, 1, 35.
Course of law.—*II Henry VI,* iii, 1, 237; *Richard III,* i, 4, 192; *II Henry IV,* v, 2, 87; *The Merchant of Venice,* iii, 3, 26.
Course of learning.—*The Taming of the Shrew,* i, 1, 9.
Course of love.—*Romeo and Juliet,* v, 3, 287; *Othello,* i, 3, 91.
Course of true love.—*A Midsummer-Night's Dream,* i, 1, 134.
Course of loyalty.—*King Lear,* iii, 5, 23.
Course of mischief.—*Henry V,* iv, 3, 106.
Course of this revenge.—*Titus Andronicus,* iv, 4, 67.
Course of things.—*Henry V,* Prol., 4.
Course of thought.—*King John,* iv, 2, 24; *Hamlet,* iii, 3, 83.
Course of time.—*The Two Gentlemen of Verona,* i, 3, 23; *King John,* i, 1, 113; *The Rape of Lucrece,* l. 774.
Course of true delight.—*Pericles,* iii, 2, 39.
Course of war.—*All's Well that Ends Well,* iii, 4, 8.
Course of wooing.—*Othello,* iii, 3, 112.
Courses of his youth.—*Henry V,* i, 1, 24.
10
Mark how he bears his course, and runs me up
With like advantage on the other side.
I Henry IV. Act iii, sc. 1, l. 108. [Mortimer]
Steering with due course towards the isle of Rhodes.
Othello. Act i, sc. 3, l. 34. [Messenger] The only use of "steering." Rhodes is mentioned six times in this play, and in no other.
Due course.—*Henry V,* iii, Prol., 17; *The Winter's Tale,* iii, 2, 6.

Now they do re-stem Their backward course.
Othello. Act i, sc. 3, l. 37. [Messenger] The only use of "re-stem."

Gentle mariner, Alter thy course for Tyre.
Pericles. Act iii, sc. 1, l. 76. [Pericles] Tyre is mentioned twenty-three times in this play, and in no other.

Holding their course to Paphos.
Venus and Adonis, l. 1193. Paphos is mentioned again in *The Tempest,* iv, 1, 93, and in *Pericles,* iv, Gower, 32.

Set her two courses off to sea again.
The Tempest. Act i, sc. 1, l. 52. [Boatswain]

1
Be it thy course to busy giddy minds
With foreign quarrels.
II Henry IV. Act iv, sc. 5, l. 214. [King Henry]

2
His addiction was to courses vain.
Henry V. Act i, sc. 1, l. 54. [Canterbury] "Addiction" is repeated in *Othello,* ii, 2, 7.

3
Let me persuade you take a better course.
I Henry VI, iv, 1, 132. See under REFORMATION.

Best courses.—*Pericles,* iv, 1, 39.

4
We are advertised by our loving friends
That they do hold their course toward Tewksbury.
III Henry VI. Act v, sc. 3, l. 18. [King Edward] Tewksbury is mentioned seven times.

I 'll write straight to my sister
To hold my very course.
King Lear. Act i, sc. 3, l. 25. [Goneril]

What course I mean to hold
Shall nothing befit your knowledge, nor
Concern me the reporting.
The Winter's Tale. Act iv, sc. 4, l. 512. [Florizel]

Hold their course.—*Hamlet,* iv, 6, 29.

5
Keep our course, though the rough wind say no.
III Henry VI, v, 4, 22. See under SHIP.

Keeps his course.—*Henry V,* v, 2, 173.

Kept on his course.—*Richard II,* v, 2, 10.

Kept their course.—*Antony and Cleopatra,* v, 2, 80.

6 The emperor thus desired
That he would please to alter the king's course.
Henry VIII. Act i, sc. 1, l. 188. [Buckingham]

Change the course.—*King Lear,* v, 1, 3.

7
Is not this course pious?
Henry VIII. Act ii, sc. 2, l. 37. [Norfolk]

Follow your envious courses, men of malice.
Henry VIII. Act iii, sc. 2, l. 243. [Wolsey]

8
I . . . did entreat your highness to this course
Which you are running here.
Henry VIII. Act ii, sc. 2, l. 216. [Bishop of Lincoln]

He has run his course.
Henry VIII, iii, 2, 398. See under BONES.

Stand you directly in Antonius' way
When he doth run his course.
Julius Cæsar. Act i, sc. 2, l. 3. [Cæsar]

You shall run a certain course.
King Lear. Act i, sc. 2, l. 89. [Edmund]

9
Will you go see the order of the course?
Julius Cæsar. Act i, sc. 2, l. 25. [Cassius]

10
He 'll shape his old course in a country new.
King Lear. Act i, sc. 1, l. 190. [Kent]

Protect this course.—*King Lear,* i, 4, 227.

11 To 's seemeth it a needful course,
Before we enter his forbidden gates,
To know his pleasure.
Love's Labour 's Lost. Act ii, sc. 1, l. 25. [Princess of France]

12
Great nature's second course.
Macbeth, ii, 2, 39. See under SLEEP.

Nature's course.—*Richard II,* i, 2, 14.

Nature's changing course.—*Sonnets,* xviii.

Affection's course.—*Rape of Lucrece,* l. 500.

Fancy's course.—*All's Well that Ends Well,* v, 3, 214.

13
I must fight the course.
Macbeth, v, 7, 2. See under DESTINY.

I must stand the course.—*King Lear,* iii, 7, 54.

We have done our course.—*Othello,* iv, 2, 93.

14
You know the course is common.
Measure for Measure. Act iv, sc. 2, l. 190. [Duke]

Common course.—*All's Well that Ends Well,* iv, 3, 26.

15
Your grace hath ta'en great pains to qualify
His rigorous course.
The Merchant of Venice. Act iv, sc. 1, l. 7. [Antonio]

16
Not for that dream I on this strange course.
Much Ado about Nothing. Act iv, sc. 1, l. 214. [Friar]

17
You call my course unnatural.
Pericles. Act iv, sc. 3, l. 36. [Dionyza]

18
He needs no indirect nor lawless course
To cut off those that have offended him.
Richard III. Act i, sc. 4, l. 224. [Clarence]

Fie, what an indirect and peevish course
Is this of hers!
Richard III. Act iii, sc. 1, l. 31. [Buckingham]

Indirect and forced courses.—*Othello,* i, 3, 111.

Bad courses.—*Richard II,* ii, 1, 213.

Compulsive course.—*Othello,* iii, 3, 454. "Compulsive" is repeated in *Hamlet,* iii, 4, 86: "Compulsive ardour."

Freer course.—*King Lear,* iv, 2, 95.

Full course.—*Henry V,* Epil., 4.

General course.—*I Henry IV,* ii, 3, 23.

Irregular course.—*King John,* v, 4, 54. "Irregular" is repeated in *I Henry IV,* i, 1, 40 and iii, 2, 27.

Monthly course.—*King Lear,* i, 1, 134.

Yearly course.—*King John,* iii, 1, 81.

Noblest course.—*Antony and Cleopatra,* iii, 13, 78.
Obscured course.—*King Lear,* ii, 2, 175.
Parallel course.—*Othello,* ii, 3, 355.
Quiet course.—*Othello,* iv, 1, 54.
Secret course.—*King John,* iii, 1, 178.
Strong course.—*Henry VIII,* v, 3, 35; *Venus and Adonis,* l. 960.
True course.—*Much Ado about Nothing,* v, 4, 6.
Upward course.—*III Henry VI,* v, 3, 1.
Wisest course.—*III Henry VI,* iii, 1, 25.

1 Draw forth your noble ancestry . . .
Unto a lineal true-derived course.
Richard III. Act iii, sc. 7, l. 198. [Buckingham] The only use of "true-derived."

2
Direct his course as please himself.
Richard III. Act ii, sc. 2, l. 129. [Buckingham]

Direct your course.—*I Henry IV,* i, 3, 293.

3
Uneven is the course, I like it not.
Romeo and Juliet. Act iv, sc. 1, l. 5. [Friar Laurence]

Upon thy life, I charge thee,
Whate'er thou hear'st or seest, stand all aloof,
And do not interrupt me in my course.
Romeo and Juliet. Act v, sc. 3, l. 25. [Romeo]

4
Say thou wilt course.
The Taming of the Shrew, Ind., 2, 49. See under HOUND: GREYHOUND.

5
You must consider that a prodigal course
Is like the sun's; but not, like his, recoverable.
Timon of Athens. Act iii, sc. 4, l. 12. [Servant] The only use of "recoverable."

Liberal course.—*Timon of Athens,* iii, 3, 41.

6
Confound them by some course.
Timon of Athens. Act v, sc. 1, l. 106. [Timon]

7
A speedier course than lingering languishment
Must we pursue, and I have found the path.
Titus Andronicus. Act ii, sc. 1, l. 110. [Aaron] The only use of "languishment."

I 'll teach thee another course.
Titus Andronicus. Act iv, sc. 1, l. 119. [Titus]

8
A thousand complete courses of the sun.
Troilus and Cressida, iv, 1, 27. See under LIFE AND DEATH.

So many courses of the sun.
Henry VIII. Act ii, sc. 3, l. 6. [Anne]

Courses of the sun.—*Sonnets,* lix.

9 When his fair course is not hindered,
He makes sweet music with the enamell'd stones. . . .
Then let me go and hinder not my course:
I 'll be as patient as a gentle stream.
The Two Gentlemen of Verona. Act ii, sc. 7, l. 27. [Julia]

10 A course more promising
Than a wild dedication of yourselves
To unpath'd waters, undream'd shores.
Winter's Tale. Act iv, sc. 4, l. 575. [Camillo]

COURT AND COURTIER

See also Courtship

I—Court

11
The court 's a learning place.
All 's Well that Ends Well. Act i, sc. 1, l. 191. [Helena]

Clown: I know my business is but to the court.
Countess: To the court! why, what place make you special, when you put off that with such contempt? But to the court!
Clown: Truly, madam, if God have lent a man any manners, he may easily put it off at court: he that cannot make a leg, put off 's cap, kiss his hand and say nothing, has neither leg, hands, lip, nor cap; and indeed such a fellow, to say precisely, were not for the court.
All 's Well that Ends Well. Act ii, sc. 2, l. 4.

Touchstone: If thou never wast at court, thou never sawest good manners; if thou never sawest good manners, then thy manners must be wicked. . . .
Corin: . . . Those that are good manners at the court are as ridiculous in the country as the behavior of the country is most mockable at the court. You told me you salute not at the court, but you kiss your hands: that courtesy would be uncleanly, if courtiers were shepherds.
As You Like It. Act iii, sc. 2, l. 41. The only use of "mockable."

12
I have no mind to Isbel since I was at court: our old ling and our Isbels o' the country are nothing like your old ling and your Isbels o' the court.
All 's Well that Ends Well. Act iii, sc. 2, l. 13. [Clown] The only use of "old ling" (salted cod).

The sportive court, where thou
Wast shot at with fair eyes.
All 's Well that Ends Well. Act iii, sc. 2, l. 109. [Helena] "Sportive" is repeated in *Richard III,* i, 1, 14: "Sportive tricks"; and in *The Comedy of Errors,* i, 2, 58: "Sportive humour."

13 The art o' the court,
As hard to leave as keep; whose top to climb
Is certain falling, or so slippery that
The fear 's as bad as falling.
Cymbeline. Act iii, sc. 3, l. 46. [Belarius]

Our courtiers say all 's savage but at court.
Cymbeline. Act iv, sc. 2, l. 33. [Imogen]

14
It jumps with my humour as well as waiting in the court, I can tell you.
I Henry IV. Act i, sc. 2, l. 77. [Falstaff]

You must to the court in the morning.
I Henry IV. Act ii, sc. 4, l. 368. [Falstaff]

I 'll to the court in the morning.
I Henry IV. Act ii, sc. 4, l. 598. [Prince]

You must away to court, sir, presently;
A dozen captains stay at door for you.
II Henry IV. Act ii, sc. 4, l. 401. [Bardolph]

A' must, then, to the inns o' court shortly. I

was once of Clement's Inn, where I think they will talk of mad Shallow yet.
II Henry IV. Act iii, sc. 2, l. 14. [Shallow] "Inns o' court" is repeated in iii, 2, 25; and in *II Henry VI*, iv, 7, 2. Clement's Inn is mentioned four times in this scene, and nowhere else.

1
This is the English, not the Turkish court;
Not Amurath an Amurath succeeds,
But Harry Harry.
II Henry IV. Act v, sc. 2, l. 47. [King Henry] The only mention of Amurath, who, in 1596, succeeded his father of the same name, and thereupon invited his brothers to a feast, where he had them all strangled—an allusion which helps to fix the date of the play. "English court" is repeated in *I Henry IV*, iii, 1, 122; *II Henry IV*, iv, 5, 122; *Richard II*, iv, 1, 12; *Macbeth*, iii, 6, 26.

Court of England.—*II Henry VI*, i, 3, 46; *Macbeth*, iii, 6, 46.
The court of Britain.—*Cymbeline*, v, 5, 25.
Britain court.—*Cymbeline*, ii, 4, 37.
Court of France.—*Henry V*, i, 2, 265; *All 's Well that Ends Well*, v, 1, 10; *The Merry Wives of Windsor*, iii, 3, 57.
Court of Rome.—*Titus Andronicus*, ii, 1, 52; *Henry VIII*, ii, 2, 105.
Court of heaven.—*King John*, iii, 4, 87.
The mistress-court of mighty Europe.
Henry V. Act ii, sc. 4, l. 133. [Exeter] The only use of "mistress-court."

2
Lord, who would live turmoiled in the court,
And may enjoy such quiet walks as these?
II Henry VI. Act iv, sc. 10, l. 18. [Iden] See under CONTENT for full quotation.

Envious court.—*As You Like It*, ii, 1, 4.
Great court.—*Cymbeline*, iii, 5, 50.
New court.—*As You Like It*, i, 1, 102.
Perturb'd court.—*Cymbeline*, iii, 4, 108. "Perturbed" is repeated in *Hamlet*, i, 5, 183: "Perturbed spirit."
Pompous court.—*As You Like It*, v, 4, 188.
Silent court.—*Love's Labour 's Lost*, ii, 1, 24.

3
'Tis a needful fitness
That we adjourn this court till further day.
Henry VIII. Act ii, sc. 4, l. 232. [Campeius]

Break up the court.—*Henry VIII*, ii, 4, 240.
Do you take the court for Paris-garden? ye rude slaves, leave your gaping.
Henry VIII. Act v, sc. 4, l. 2. [Porter] The only mention of "Paris-garden," a bear-garden in Southwark.

This strict court of Venice,
Must needs give sentence 'gainst the merchant there.
The Merchant of Venice. Act iv, sc. 1, l. 204. [Portia]

Open court.—*Merchant of Venice*, iv, 1, 338.
Public court.—*As You Like It*, i, 3, 46.

4
Our court shall be a little Academe,
Still and contemplative in living art.
Love's Labour 's Lost. Act i, sc. 1, l. 13. [King] "Academe" occurs three times in this play, and in no other.

You shall be welcome, madam, to my court.
Love's Labour 's Lost. Act ii, sc. 1, l. 95. [King]

5
Northumberland: My lord, in the base court he doth attend
To speak with you; may it please you to come down. . . .
King Richard: In the base court? Base court, where kings grow base,
To come at traitors' calls and do them grace.
Richard II. Act iii, sc. 3, l. 176.

6
This cell 's my court: here have I few attendants
And subjects none abroad: pray you, look in.
Tempest. Act v, sc. 1, l. 166. [Prospero]

7
The emperor's court is like the house of Fame,
The palace full of tongues, of eyes, and ears.
Titus Andronicus. Act ii, sc. 1, l. 126. [Aaron]

Emperor's court.—*The Two Gentlemen of Verona*, i, 3, 38; i, 3, 67; *Titus Andronicus*, i, 1, 489; v, 2, 104.
Imperial's court.—*The Two Gentlemen of Verona*, ii, 3, 5.
Princes' courts.—*II Henry VI*, iii, 2, 69.
Royal court.—*II Henry VI*, iv, 4, 53; *The Two Gentlemen of Verona*, i, 3, 27; iii, 1, 165.

8
Lucius and I 'll go brave it at the court;
Ay, marry, will we, sir; and we 'll be waited on.
Titus Andronicus. Act iv, sc. 1, l. 121. [Titus]

9
I must Forsake the court.
The Winter's Tale. Act i, sc. 2, l. 361. [Camillo]

Whipped out of the court.—*The Winter's Tale*, iv, 3, 95; 14, 3, 97.
For court in the sense of woo, see COURTSHIP.

II—Courtier

10
'Tis an unseason'd courtier.
All's Well that Ends Well. Act i, sc. 1, l. 80. [Countess]

I will return perfect courtier; in the which, my instruction shall serve to naturalize thee, so thou wilt be capable of a courtier's counsel.
All 's Well that Ends Well. Act i, sc. 1, l. 221. [Parolles] The only use of "naturalize."

Ask me if I am a courtier: it shall do you no harm to learn.
All 's Well that Ends Well. Act ii, sc. 2, l. 38. [Clown]

Courtiers of beauteous freedom.—*Antony and Cleopatra*, ii, 6, 17.

11
The courtier's hands are perfumed with civet.
As You Like It. Act iii, sc. 2, l. 65. [Corin]

He hath been a courtier, he swears.
As You Like It. Act v, sc. 4, l. 42. [Jaques]

One that hath been a courtier.—*As You Like It*, ii, 7, 36.

1
But not a courtier,
Although they wear their faces to the bent
Of the king's looks, hath a heart that is not
Glad at the thing they scowl at.
Cymbeline. Act i, sc. 1, l. 12. [Gentleman]

Or a that way accomplished courtier.
Cymbeline. Act i, sc. 4, l. 101. [Iachimo]

Your Italy contains none so accomplished a courtier.
Cymbeline. Act i, sc. 4, l. 103. [Posthumus]

2
Our chiefest courtier.
Hamlet. Act i, sc. 2, l. 117. [King]

A courtier; which could say 'Good morrow, sweet lord!
How dost thou, good lord?'
Hamlet. Act v, sc. 1, l. 90. [Hamlet]

Silken-coated slaves.—*II Henry VI*, iv, 2, 136. The only use of "silken-coated."

3
An English courtier may be wise,
And never see the Louvre.
Henry VIII, i, 3, 22. See under TRAVEL.

French courtier.—*Love's Labour 's Lost*, i, 2, 65.

4
I have been begging sixteen years in court,
Am yet a courtier beggarly.
Henry VIII. Act ii, sc. 3, l. 82. [Old Lady]

Thou 'ldst courtier be again,
Wert thou not beggar.
Timon of Athens. Act iv, sc. 3, l. 241. [Apemantus] See under HABIT.

5
O, you are a flattering boy: now I see you 'll be a courtier.
The Merry Wives of Windsor. Act iii, sc. 2, l. 7. [Mrs. Page]

Thou wouldst make an absolute courtier.
The Merry Wives of Windsor. Act iii, sc. 3, l. 66. [Falstaff]

The best courtier of them all.
The Merry Wives of Windsor. Act ii, sc. 2, l. 62. [Mistress Quickly]

6
Sometime she gallops o'er a courtier's nose,
And then dreams he of smelling out a suit.
Romeo and Juliet. Act i, sc. 4, l. 77. [Mercutio]

Courtiers . . . that dream on court'sies straight.
Romeo and Juliet. Act i, sc. 4, l. 72. [Mercutio]

7
How to grant suits,
How to deny them, who to advance and who
To trash for over-topping.
The Tempest. Act i, sc. 2, l. 79. [Prospero] The only use of "trash" in this sense. It is a hunting term, meaning to check a dog that is too fast by attaching a weight to its neck. "O'ertopping" occurs in *Henry VIII*, ii, 4, 83.

8
Agamemnon: The men of Troy
Are ceremonious courtiers.
Æneas: Courtiers as free, as debonair, unarm'd,
As bending angels.
Troilus and Cressida. Act i, sc. 3, l. 233. The only use of "debonair."

That youth 's a rare courtier.
Twelfth Night. Act iii, sc. 1, l. 97. [Sir Andrew]

9
Shepherd: Are you a courtier, an 't like you, sir?
Autolycus: Whether it like me or no, I am a courtier. Seest thou not the air of the court in these enfoldings? hath not my gait in it the measure of the court? receives not thy nose court-odour from me? reflect I not thy baseness court-contempt? . . . I am a courtier cap-a-pe.
The Winter's Tale. Act iv, sc. 4, l. 752. The only use of "enfoldings," "court-odour," and "court-contempt." "Cap-a-pe" is repeated in *Hamlet*, i, 2, 200.

COURTESY

See also Politeness

10
Let thy courtesies alone, they are scurvy ones.
All's Well that Ends Well. Act v, sc. 3, l. 324. [Lafeu]

For he hath laid strange courtesies and great
Of late upon me.
Antony and Cleopatra. Act ii, sc. 2, l. 157. [Antony]

11
The courtesy of nations allows you my better, in that you are the first-born.
As You Like It. Act i, sc. 1, l. 49. [Orlando]

12
Look sweet, speak fair.
The Comedy of Errors. Act iii, sc. 2, l. 11. [Luciana]

Courteous to the people.—*Coriolanus*, ii, 2, 30.

13
I have been debtor to you for courtesies, which I will be ever to pay and yet pay still.
Cymbeline. Act i, sc. 4, l. 38. [Posthumus]

14
This courtesy is not of the right breed.
Hamlet. Act iii, sc. 2, l. 326. [Guildenstern]

15
Why, what a candy deal of courtesy
This fawning greyhound then did proffer me!
I Henry IV. Act i, sc. 3, l. 251. [Hotspur] The only use of "candy" except as a proper noun in *Twelfth Night*, v, 1, 64.

Apish courtesy.—*Richard III*, i, 3, 49.

Breathing courtesy.—*The Merchant of Venice*, v, 1, 141.

Dissembling courtesy!—*Cymbeline*, i, 1, 84.

16
Though I be but Prince of Wales, yet I am king of courtesy.
I Henry IV. Act ii, sc. 4, l. 10. [Prince of Wales]

Mercutio: I am the very pink of courtesy.
Romeo: Pink for flower.
Mercutio: Right.
Romeo and Juliet. Act ii, sc. 4, l. 61. "Pink" is repeated in *Antony and Cleopatra*, ii, 7, 121: "Pink eyne."

The mirror of all courtesy.—*Henry VIII*, ii, 1, 53.

1
He shall shrink under my courtesy.
I Henry IV. Act v, sc. 2, l. 75. [Hotspur]

For, heaven to earth, some of us never shall
A second time do such a courtesy.
I Henry IV. Act v, sc. 2, l. 100. [Hotspur]

If thou wert sensible of courtesy,
I should not make so dear a show of zeal.
I Henry IV. Act v, sc. 4, l. 94. [Prince of Wales]

I thank your grace for this high courtesy.
I Henry IV. Act v, sc. 5, l. 32. [Lancaster]

Christian courtesy.—*The Merchant of Venice*, iii, 1, 52.
Excellent courtesy.—*Othello*, ii, 1, 177.
Fair courtesy.—*Pericles*, ii, 3, 107.
Graceful courtesy.—*Pericles*, ii, 2, 41.
Princely courtesy.—*Titus Andronicus*, i, 1, 272.
Smiling courtesy.—*Love's Labour 's Lost*, v, 2, 755.

2
You do not use me with that affability as in discretion you ought to use me.
Henry V. Act iii, sc. 2, l. 138. [Fluellen]

Affability and bashful modesty.
The Taming of the Shrew, ii, 1, 49. See under CHARACTER.

Hide it in . . . affability.—*Julius Cæsar*, ii, 1, 82. The only uses of "affability."
Affable and courteous.—*The Taming of the Shrew*, i, 2, 98.
Mild and affable.—*II Henry VI*, iii, 1, 9.
Soft and affable.—*The Taming of the Shrew*, ii, 1, 253.
Wondrous affable.—*I Henry IV*, iii, 1, 168.
Affable ghost.—*Sonnets*, lxxxvi.
Affable wolves.—*Timon of Athens*, iii, 6, 105. The only uses of "affable."

3
I need not crave this courtesy.
I Henry VI. Act v, sc. 3, l. 105. [Margaret]

4
I thank you for your pains and courtesy.
Julius Cæsar. Act ii, sc. 2, l. 115. [Cæsar]

For your many courtesies I thank you.
Much Ado about Nothing. Act v, sc. 1, l. 191. [Benedick]

Low-crooked court'sies.—*Julius Cæsar*, iii, 1, 43. The only use of "low-crooked."

5
Brutus: A word, Lucilius;
How he received you, let me be resolved.
Lucilius: With courtesy and with respect enough;
But not with such familiar instances,
Nor with such free and friendly conference,
As he hath used of old.
Julius Cæsar. Act iv, sc. 2, l. 13.

6
Return, and force Their scanted courtesy.
King Lear. Act iii, sc. 2, l. 67. [Kent]

7
I do beseech thee, remember thy courtesy.
Love's Labour 's Lost. Act v, sc. 1, l. 102. [Armado]

A new-devised courtesy.—*Love's Labour 's Lost*, i, 2, 66. The only use of "new-devised."

This is he
That kiss'd his hand away in courtesy.
Love's Labour 's Lost. Act v, sc. 2, l. 323. [Biron]

My lady, to the manner of the days,
In courtesy gives undeserving praise.
Love's Labour 's Lost. Act v, sc. 2, l. 365. [Rosaline]

8
You are to do me both a present and a dangerous courtesy.
Measure for Measure. Act iv, sc. 2, l. 171. [Duke]

9
Outward courtesies would fain proclaim
Favours that keep within.
Measure for Measure. Act v, sc. 1, l. 15. [Duke]

Do him courtesies.—*A Midsummer-Night's Dream*, iii, 1, 177.

10
Stubborn Turks and Tartars, never train'd
To offices of tender courtesy.
The Merchant of Venice. Act iv, sc. 1, l. 32. [Duke]

This lack-love, this kill-courtesy.
Midsummer-Night's Dream. Act ii, sc. 2, l. 77. [Puck] The only use of either phrase.

11
Be kind and courteous to this gentleman.
A Midsummer-Night's Dream. Act iii, sc. 1, l. 169. [Titania]

Go give him courteous conduct to this place.
The Merchant of Venice. Act iv, sc. 1, l. 148. [Duke]

12
If you were civil and knew courtesy,
You would not do me thus much injury.
A Midsummer-Night's Dream. Act iii, sc. 2, l. 147. [Helena]

Pray you, leave your courtesy, good mounsieur.
A Midsummer-Night's Dream. Act iv, sc. 1, l. 21. [Bottom]

In courtesy, in all reason, we must stay the time.
A Midsummer-Night's Dream. Act v, sc. 1, l. 258. [Theseus]

13
They do discharge their shot of courtesy.
Othello. Act ii, sc. 1, l. 56. [Gentleman]

14
How courtesy would seem to cover sin.
Pericles. Act i, sc. 1, l. 121. [Pericles]

A courtesy
Which if we should deny, the most just gods
For every graff would send a caterpillar,
And so afflict our province.
Pericles. Act v, sc. 1, l. 58. [Lysander]

15
How he did seem to dive into their hearts
With humble and familiar courtesy.
Richard II, i, 4, 24. See under POPULARITY.

Me rather had my heart might feel your love
Than my unpleased eye see your courtesy.
Richard II. Act iii, sc. 3, l. 192. [King Richard] The only use of "unpleased."

16
Romeo: My business was great; and in such a case as mine a man may strain courtesy.
Mercutio: That 's as much as to say, such a

case as yours constrains a man to bow in the hams.
Romeo: Meaning to court'sy.
Mercutio: Thou hast most kindly hit it.
Romeo and Juliet. Act ii, sc. 4, l. 53.
Let them curtsy with their left legs.
The Taming of the Shrew, iv, 1, 95. See under MANNERS.
Curtsy, sweet hearts.—*Love's Labour 's Lost,* v, 2, 221.
Curtsy at his frowns.—*I Henry IV,* iii, 2, 127.
Curtsy to them.—*Merchant of Venice,* i, 1, 13.
Curtsy to great kings.—*Henry V,* v, 2, 293.
Make curtsy.—*As You Like It,* Epil., 23; *Much Ado about Nothing,* ii, 1, 56.
Make another curtsy.—*Much Ado about Nothing,* ii, 1, 58.
Seals it with a curtsy.—*III Henry VI,* iii, 2, 57.
What is that curtsy worth?—*Coriolanus,* v, 3, 27. The only uses of "curtsy."

1
With soft low tongue and lowly courtesy.
The Taming of the Shrew. Induction. Sc. 1, l. 114. [Lord]
If this be courtesy, sir, accept of it.
The Taming of the Shrew. Act iv, sc. 2, l. 111. [Tranio]

2
That there should be small love 'mongst these sweet knaves,
And all this courtesy.
Timon of Athens. Act i, sc. 1, l. 258. [Apemantus]

3
Friend, we understand not one another. I am too courtly and thou art too cunning.
Troilus and Cressida. Act iii, sc. 1, l. 29. [Pandarus] "Too courtly" is repeated in *As You Like It,* iii, 2, 72.
She hath all courtly parts more exquisite
Than lady, ladies, woman.
Cymbeline. Act iii, sc. 5, l. 71. [Cloten]
Most courtly and fashionable.—*Timon of Athens,* v, 1, 29.
Courtly company.—*II Henry VI,* i, 1, 27.
Courtly counsel.—*Troilus and Cressida,* iv, 5, 22.
Courtly friends.—*All's Well that Ends Well,* iii, 4, 14. The only uses of "courtly."

4
Thou dost not use me courteously.
Troilus and Cressida. Act iv, sc. 4, l. 123. [Troilus] The only use of "courteously."
Weigh him well,
And that which looks like pride is courtesy.
Troilus and Cressida. Act iv, sc. 5, l. 81. [Æneas]
I do disdain thy courtesy, proud Trojan.
Troilus and Cressida. Act v, sc. 6, l. 15. [Achilles]

COURTSHIP

See also Wooing

5
One that knew courtship too well, for there he fell in love.
As You Like It. Act iii, sc. 2, l. 364. [Rosalind] A play upon the two meanings in which Shakespeare uses "courtship": (1) wooing; (2) state or behaviour befitting a courtier.
I thought King Henry had resembled thee
In courage, courtship, and proportion.
II Henry VI. Act i, sc. 3, l. 56. [Queen]
Trim gallants, full of courtship and of state.
Love's Labour 's Lost. Act v, sc. 2, l. 363. [Princess of France]
More courtship lives in carrion flies than Romeo.
Romeo and Juliet. Act iii, sc. 3, l. 34. [Romeo]
Rated them at courtship.—*Love's Labour 's Lost,* v, 2, 790. The only uses of "courtship" in this sense.

6
Their purpose is to parle, to court and dance;
And every one his love-feat will advance
Unto his several mistress.
Love's Labour 's Lost. Act v, sc. 2, l. 122. [Boyet] The only use of "love feat."
Hold, Rosaline, this favour thou shalt wear,
And then the king will court thee for his dear.
Love's Labour 's Lost. Act v, sc. 2, l. 130. [Princess of France]

7
Courtship and such fair ostents of love.
The Merchant of Venice. Act ii, sc. 8, l. 44. [Salarino]
I will gyve thee in thine own courtship.
Othello. Act ii, sc. 1, l. 171. [Iago]

8
If I court moe women, you 'll couch with moe men.
Othello. Act iv, sc. 3, l. 57. [Desdemona]

9
If either of you both love Katharina,
Because I know you well and love you well,
Leave shall you have to court her at your pleasure.
The Taming of the Shrew. Act i, sc. 1, l. 52. [Baptista]
Court Margaret.—*Much Ado about Nothing,* v, 1, 244.

10 I may, by this device, at least
Have leave and leisure to make love to her
And unsuspected court her by herself.
The Taming of the Shrew. Act i, sc. 2, l. 135. [Hortensio]
Now, for my life, the knave doth court my love.
The Taming of the Shrew. Act iii, sc. 1, l. 49. [Hortensio]
See, how they kiss and court! . . . here I firmly vow
Never to woo her more.
The Taming of the Shrew. Act iv, sc. 2, l. 27. [Hortensio]
See, how beastly she doth court him!
The Taming of the Shrew. Act iv, sc. 2, l. 34. [Tranio]

11
Then why should he despair that knows to court it
With words, fair looks and liberality.
Titus Andronicus. Act ii, sc. 1, l. 91. [Demetrius]
Long agone I have forgot to court.
The Two Gentlemen of Verona. Act iii, sc. 1, l. 85. [Duke] "Agone" is used only once more, in *Twelfth Night,* v, 1, 204: "An hour agone."

COVETOUSNESS

See also Usury

1
Why, that were covetousness.
As You Like It. Act iii, sc. 5, l. 91. [Phebe]
You must in no way say he is covetous.
Coriolanus. Act i, sc. 1, l. 43. [Citizen]
Coveting for more.—*I Henry VI*, v, 4, 145.
Covetings, change of prides.—*Cymbeline,* ii, 5, 25. Only use of "coveting" and "covetings."

2
When Marcus Brutus grows so covetous,
To lock such rascal counters from his friends,
Be ready, gods, with all your thunderbolts;
Dash him to pieces!
Julius Cæsar. Act iv, sc. 3, l. 79. [Brutus]

3
There grows
In my most ill-composed affection such
A stanchless avarice that, were I king,
I should cut off the nobles for their lands,
Desire his jewels and this other's house:
And my more-having would be as a sauce
To make me hunger more.
Macbeth. Act iv, sc. 3, l. 76. [Malcolm] The only use of "ill-composed," "stanchless" and "more-having."

This avarice
Sticks deeper, grows with more pernicious root
Than summer-seeming lust, and it hath been
The sword of our slain kings.
Macbeth. Act iv, sc. 3, l. 84. [Macduff] The only use of "summer-seeming."
Scarcely have coveted what was mine own.
Macbeth. Act iv, sc. 3, l. 127. [Malcolm]

4
Those that much covet are with gain so fond,
For what they have not, that which they possess
They scatter and unloose it from their bond,
And so, by hoping more, they have but less;
Or, gaining more, the profit of excess
Is but to surfeit, and such griefs sustain,
That they prove bankrupt in this poor-rich gain.
The Rape of Lucrece, l. 134. The only use of "poor-rich."
The aged man that coffers-up his gold
Is plagued with cramps and gouts and painful fits;
And scarce hath eyes his treasure to behold,
But like still-pining Tantalus he sits,
And useless barns the harvest of his wits;
Having no other pleasure of his gain
But torment that it cannot cure his pain.
The Rape of Lucrece, l. 855. The only use of "coffers-up," "still-pining," and "barns" as a verb. Tantalus is mentioned again in *Venus and Adonis,* l. 599.
Makest waste in niggarding.—*Sonnets,* i. The only use of "niggarding."
Covetously reserve it.—*Timon of Athens,* iv, 3, 408. The only use of "covetously."

5
Thou art covetous and he is kind.
Sonnets. No. cxxxiv.
Covetous of praise.—*Troilus and Cressida,* ii, 3, 248.
Covetous of wisdom.—*Henry VIII,* v, 5, 25.

6
I would not have you to think that my desire of having is the sin of covetousness: but, as you say, sir, let your bounty take a nap, I will awake it anon.
Twelfth Night. Act v, sc. 1, l. 49. [Clown]

COWARDICE

7
I think him . . . solely a coward.
All's Well that Ends Well. Act i, sc. 1, l. 112. [Helena]
He's a most notable coward.
All's Well that Ends Well. Act iii, sc. 6, l. 11. [Lord]
He excels his brother for a coward, yet his brother is reputed one of the best that is: in a retreat he outruns any lackey; marry, in coming on he has the cramp.
All's Well that Ends Well. Act iv, sc. 3, l. 321. [Parolles] The only instance of the use of the phrase, "One of the best that is."
'Tis sport to maul a runner.
Antony and Cleopatra. Act iv, sc. 7, l. 14. [Scarus] "Maul" is repeated in *King John,* iv, 3, 99.

8
For though abundantly they lack discretion,
Yet are they passing cowardly.
Coriolanus. Act i, sc. 1, l. 206. [Menenius] The only use of "abundantly."
Come on, you cowards! you were got in fear,
Though you were born in Rome.
Coriolanus. Act i, sc. 3, l. 36. [Volumnia]
Being press'd to the war,
Even when the navel of the state was touch'd,
They would not thread the gates.
Coriolanus. Act iii, sc. 1, l. 122. [Coriolanus] The only use of "navel."
He whined and roar'd away your victory,
That pages blush'd at him and men of heart
Look'd wondering each at other.
Coriolanus. Act v, sc. 6, l. 98. [Aufidius]

9
Cowards living
To die with lengthen'd shame.
Cymbeline. Act v, sc. 3, l. 12. [Posthumus]
Some, turn'd coward But by example.
Cymbeline. Act v, sc. 3, l. 35. [Posthumus]

10
You souls of geese,
That bear the shapes of men, how have you run
From slaves that apes would beat! Pluto and hell!
All hurt behind; backs red, and faces pale
With flight and agued fear!
Coriolanus. Act i, sc. 4, l. 34. [Caius Marcius] The only use of "agued."
The mouse ne'er shunn'd the cat as they did budge
From rascals worse than they.
Coriolanus. Act i, sc. 6, l. 44. [Marcius]
Let the first budger die the other's slave,
And the gods doom him after!
Coriolanus. Act i, sc. 8, l. 5. [Marcius] The only use of "budger."

11
Thou mayst be valiant in a better cause;
But now thou seem'st a coward.
Cymbeline. Act iii, sc. 4, l. 74. [Imogen]

Our cowards,
Like fragments in hard voyages, became
The life o' the need.

Cymbeline. Act v, sc. 3, l. 43. [Posthumus]

To-day how many would have given their honours
To have saved their carcases! took heel to do 't,
And yet died too!

Cymbeline. Act v, sc. 3, l. 66. [Posthumus]

1
Am I a coward?
Who calls me villain? breaks my pate across?
Plucks off my beard, and blows it in my face,
Tweaks me by the nose? gives me the lie i' the throat,
As deep as to the lungs? who does me this? . . .
'Swounds, I should take it: for it cannot be
But I am pigeon-liver'd and lack gall.

Hamlet. Act ii, sc. 2, l. 598. [Hamlet] The only use of "tweaks," "'swounds," and "pigeon-liver'd."

Three parts coward.—*Hamlet,* iv, 4, 43.

2
I know them to be as true-bred cowards as ever turned back.

I Henry IV. Act i, sc. 2, l. 205. [Poins] "True-bred" is used four times.

Prince of Wales: What, a coward, Sir John Paunch?
Falstaff: Indeed, I am not John of Gaunt, your grandfather; but yet no coward, Hal.

I Henry IV. Act ii, sc. 2, l. 69.

No coward nor no flatterer.—*I Henry VI,* ii, 4, 31.

3
An' the Prince and Poins be not two arrant cowards, there 's no equity stirring: there 's no more valour in that Poins than in a wild-duck.

I Henry IV. Act ii, sc. 2, l. 105. [Falstaff]

Such a commodity of warm slaves, as had as lieve hear the devil as a drum; such as fear the report of a caliver worse than a struck fowl or a hurt wild-duck.

I Henry IV. Act iv, sc. 2, l. 19. [Falstaff] "Caliver" (musket) occurs twice in *II Henry IV,* iii, 2, 289; 292. The only uses of "wild-duck," which occurs in no other play.

4
Darest thou be so valiant as to play the coward with thy indenture and show it a fair pair of heels and run from it?

I Henry IV. Act ii, sc. 4, l. 51. [Prince of Wales] The only use of the phrase, "fair pair of heels."

A plague of all cowards, I say, and a vengeance too! marry, and amen!

I Henry IV. Act ii, sc. 4, l. 127. [Falstaff]

A coward is worse than a cup of sack with lime in it. A villanous coward!

I Henry IV. Act ii, sc. 4, l. 139. [Falstaff]

Falstaff: Are not you a coward? answer me to that; and Poins there?
Poins: 'Zounds, ye fat paunch, an ye call me coward, by the Lord, I 'll stab thee.
Falstaff: I call thee coward! I 'll see thee damned ere I call thee coward.

I Henry IV. Act ii, sc. 4, l. 157.

5
You carried your guts away as nimbly, with as quick dexterity, and roared for mercy and still run and roared, as ever I heard bull-calf.

I Henry IV. Act ii, sc. 4, l. 285. [Prince of Wales] The only use of "bull-calf," except as a man's name in *II Henry IV*.

I was now a coward on instinct.

I Henry IV, ii, 4, 301. See under INSTINCT for full quotation.

A natural coward, without instinct.

I Henry IV. Act ii, sc. 4, l. 542. [Falstaff]

Toasts-and-butter, with hearts in their bellies no bigger than pins' heads.

I Henry IV. Act iv, sc. 2, l. 23. [Falstaff] The only use of "toasts-and-butter."

6
I was not born a yielder, thou proud Scot.

I Henry IV. Act v, sc. 3, l. 11. [Blunt] "Yielder" is repeated in *II Henry IV,* iv, 2, 123; and in *A Midsummer-Night's Dream,* iii, 2, 30.

7
A rascal bragging slave! the rogue fled from me like quicksilver.

II Henry IV. Act ii, sc. 4, l. 247. [Falstaff]

Swift as quicksilver.

Hamlet, i, 5, 66. The only uses of "quicksilver."

8
Puff in thy teeth, most recreant coward base!

II Henry IV. Act v, sc. 3, l. 96. [Pistol]

O faithless coward! O dishonest wretch!

Measure for Measure. Act iii, sc. 1, l. 137. [Isabella]

False murderous coward.—*II Henry VI,* iii, 2, 220.

Murderous coward.—*King Lear,* ii, 1, 64.

Traitor coward.—*Richard II,* i, 1, 102.

9
He is white-livered and red-faced; by the means whereof a' faces it out, but fights not.

Henry V. Act iii, sc. 2, l. 33. [Boy] The only use of "red-faced."

White-liver'd runagate.

Richard III. Act iv, sc. 4, l. 465. [King Richard] The only uses of "white-liver'd." "Runagate" occurs four times.

Milk-liver'd man!
That bear'st a cheek for blows.

King Lear. Act iv, sc. 2, l. 50. [Goneril] The only use of "milk-liver'd."

How many cowards, whose hearts are all as false
As stairs of sand, wear yet upon their chins
The beards of Hercules and frowning Mars,
Who, inward search'd, have livers white as milk.

The Merchant of Venice. Act iii, sc. 2, l. 83. [Bassanio]

Go, prick thy face, and over-red thy fear,
Thou lily-liver'd boy.

Macbeth. Act v, sc. 3, l. 14. [Macbeth] The only use of "over-red."

A lily-liver'd, action-taking knave.
King Lear, ii, 2, 18. The only uses of "lily-liver'd" and "action-taking."

No more man's blood in 's belly than will sup a flea.
Love's Labour 's Lost. Act v, sc. 2, l. 697. [Biron]

1 He which hath no stomach to this fight,
Let him depart; his passport shall be made
And crowns for convoy put into his purse.
Henry V. Act iv, sc. 3, l. 35. [King Henry] "Passport" is repeated in *All 's Well that Ends Well,* iii, 2, 58: "Here 's my passport"; and in *Pericles,* iii, 2, 66: "A passport too!"

For did I but suspect a fearful man,
He should have leave to go away betimes,
Lest in our need he might infect another
And make him of like spirit to himself.
III Henry VI. Act v, sc. 4, l. 44. [Prince of Wales]

2
Here had the conquest fully been seal'd up,
If Sir John Fastolfe had not play'd the coward:
He, being in the vaward, placed behind
With purpose to relieve and follow them,
Cowardly fled, not having struck one stroke.
I Henry VI. Act i, sc. 1, l. 130. [Messenger] "Vaward" is used five times in the plays.

Sheep run not half so treacherous from the wolf,
Or horse or oxen from the leopard,
As you fly from your oft-subdued slaves.
I Henry VI. Act i, sc. 5, l. 30. [Talbot] The only use of "oft-subdued."

3
O monstrous coward! what, to come behind folks?
II Henry VI. Act iv, sc. 7, l. 89. [Bevis]

You are all recreants and dastards, and delight to live in slavery to the nobility.
II Henry VI. Act iv, sc. 8, l. 28. [Cade]

A dastard and a treacherous coward.
III Henry VI. Act ii, sc. 2, l. 114. [Richard]

4
Exhort all the world to be cowards; for I, that never feared any, am vanquished by famine, not by valour.
II Henry VI. Act iv, sc. 10, l. 79. [Cade]

Proclaim'd a coward.—*II Henry VI,* iv, 1, 43.

5 Cowardice
Hath made us by-words to our enemies.
III Henry VI. Act i, sc. 1, l. 41. [Warwick] The only use of "by-words."

I hold it cowardice
To rest mistrustful where a noble heart
Hath pawn'd an open hand in sign of love.
III Henry VI. Act iv, sc. 2, l. 7. [Warwick] The only use of "mistrustful."

The gods do this in shame of cowardice.
Julius Cæsar. Act ii, sc. 2, l. 41. [Cæsar]

Nor did he soil the fact with cowardice.
Timon of Athens. Act iii, sc. 5, l. 16. [Alcibiades]

Entire cowardice.—*II Henry IV,* ii, 4, 353.

6
So cowards fight when they can fly no further;
So doves do peck the falcon's piercing talons;
So desperate thieves, all hopeless of their lives,
Breathe out invectives 'gainst the officers.
III Henry VI. Act i, sc. 4, l. 40. [Clifford] The only use of "invectives." "Invectively" occurs in *As You Like It,* ii, 1, 58.

This soft courage makes your followers faint.
III Henry VI. Act ii, sc. 2, l. 57. [Queen Margaret]

7
But, woe the while! our fathers' minds are dead,
And we are govern'd with our mothers' spirits;
Our yoke and sufferance show us womanish.
Julius Cæsar. Act i, sc. 3, l. 82. [Cassius]

O coward that I am.—*Julius Cæsar,* v, 3, 34.

8
Cowards die many times before their deaths;
The valiant never taste of death but once.
Julius Cæsar. Act ii, sc. 2, l. 32. [Cæsar]

9
Out, dunghill! darest thou brave a nobleman?
King John. Act iv, sc. 3, l. 87. [Lord Bigot] "Out, dunghill!" is repeated in *King Lear,* iv, 6, 249. "Dunghill" occurs twelve times.

Dunghill curs.—*II Henry IV,* v, 3, 108.
Dunghill grooms.—*I Henry VI,* i, 3, 14.
Dunghill villain.—*II Henry VI,* i, 3, 196.
Thou coward!—*King John,* iii, 1, 115.

10
And hang a calf-skin on his recreant limbs.
King John. Act iii, sc. 1, l. 199. [Bastard]

Hang nothing but a calf-skin, my sweet lout.
King John. Act iii, sc. 1, l. 220. [Bastard]

It is the cowish terror of his spirit,
That dares not undertake.
King Lear. Act iv, sc. 2, l. 12. [Goneril] The only use of "cowish."

11 Wouldst thou have that
Which thou esteem'st the ornament of life,
And live a coward in thine own esteem,
Letting 'I dare not' wait upon 'I would,'
Like the poor cat i' the adage?
Macbeth. Act i, sc. 7, l. 41. [Lady Macbeth] The adage is, "The cat would eat fish but would not wet her feet," which appeared first in a manuscript by an unknown author, dating from about 1250, and now in Trinity College, Cambridge. Chaucer included it in his *Hous of Fame* (bk. iii, ll. 693–5), written about 1384: "For ye by lyk the sweynte cat, That wolde have fish; but wostow what? He wolde no-thing wete his clowes."

O, these flaws and starts,
Impostors to true fear, would well become
A woman's story at a winter's fire,
Authorized by her grandam.
Macbeth. Act iii, sc. 4, l. 63. [Lady Macbeth] The only use of "authorized."

Protest me The baby of a girl.
Macbeth. Act iii, sc. 4, l. 105. [Macbeth]

1
By gar, you are de coward, de Jack dog, John ape.
The Merry Wives of Windsor. Act iii, sc. 1, l. 85. [Caius]
Coward, why comest thou not?—*A Midsummer-Night's Dream,* iii, 2, 241.
Thou runaway, thou coward, art thou fled?
A Midsummer-Night's Dream. Act iii, sc. 2, l. 405. [Demetrius]
You are a tame man.
A Midummer-Night's Dream. Act iii, sc. 2, l. 259. [Demetrius]
2
I will protest your cowardice.
Much Ado about Nothing. Act v, sc. 1, l. 149. [Benedick]
Twit with cowardice.—*I Henry VI,* iii, 2, 55.
Either I must shortly hear from him, or I will subscribe him a coward.
Much Ado about Nothing. Act v, sc. 2, l. 58. [Benedick]
3
I do shame
To think of what a noble strain you are,
And of how coward a spirit.
Pericles. Act iv, sc. 3, l. 23. [Dionyza]
4
Pale cowards, marching on with trembling paces.
The Rape of Lucrece, l. 1391.
Pale trembling coward.—*Richard II,* i, 1, 69.
5
That which in mean men we intitle patience
Is pale cold cowardice in noble breasts.
Richard II. Act i, sc. 2, l. 33. [Duchess of Gloucester] The only use of "intitle." "Intitled" occurs in *Love's Labour 's Lost,* v, 2, 822.
6
Go, coward as thou art.
Richard III. Act i, sc. 4, l. 286. [Murderer]
A milk-sop, one that never in his life
Felt so much cold as over shoes in snow.
Richard III. Act v, sc. 3, l. 325. [King Richard] "Milk-sop" is repeated in *Much Ado about Nothing,* v, 1, 91.
Have at thee, coward!—*Romeo and Juliet,* i, 1, 79.
7
A cripple soon can find a halt.
The Passionate Pilgrim, l. 308.
8
I . . . say thou art a caitiff.
Timon of Athens. Act iv, sc. 3, l. 235. [Apemantus]
A caitiff recreant to my cousin Hereford!
Richard II. Act i, sc. 2, l. 53. [Duchess]
A very caitiff.—*Richard III,* iv, 4, 100.
Caitiff, to pieces shake.
King Lear. Act iii, sc. 2, l. 55. [King Lear]
Caitiff wretch.—*Romeo and Juliet,* v, 1, 52.
Pernicious caitiff.—*Measure for Measure,* v, 1, 88; *Othello,* v, 2, 318.
Poor caitiff.—*Othello,* iv, 1, 109.
Wicked caitiff.—*Measure for Measure,* ii, 1, 193; *Timon of Athens,* v, 4, 71.
Wicked'st caitiff.—*Measure for Measure,* v, 1, 53.
O thou caitiff!—*Measure for Measure,* ii, 1, 182.
I am the caitiff.—*All 's Well that Ends Well,* iii, 2, 117. The only uses of "caitiff."
9
Faint-hearted boy, arise.
Titus Andronicus. Act iii, sc. 1, l. 65. [Titus]
Faint-hearted king.—*III Henry VI,* i, 1, 183.
Faint-hearted Woodville.—*I Henry VI,* i, 3, 22. The only uses of "faint-hearted."
Sir Toby: A very dishonest paltry boy, and more a coward than a hare: his dishonesty appears in leaving his friend here in necessity and denying him; and for his cowardship ask Fabian.
Fabian: A coward, a most devout coward, religious in it.
Twelfth Night. Act iii, sc. 4, l. 420. The only use of "cowardship."
10
Less valiant than the virgin in the night.
Troilus and Cressida. Act i, sc. 1, l. 11. [Troilus]
They tax our policy, and call it cowardice.
Troilus and Cressida. Act i, sc. 3, l. 197. [Ulysses]
Can it be
That so degenerate a strain as this
Should once set footing in your generous bosoms?
Troilus and Cressida. Act ii, sc. 2, l. 153. [Paris]
Come, come, thou boy-queller, show thy face.
Troilus and Cressida. Act v, sc. 5, l. 45. [Achilles] The only use of "boy-queller."
Thou great-sized coward.—*Troilus and Cressida,* v, 10, 26. "Great-sized" is repeated in iii, 3, 147: "Great-sized monster"; and appears in no other play.
11
Like soldiers, when their captain once doth yield,
They basely fly and dare not stay the field.
Venus and Adonis, l. 893.
Not a more cowardly rogue in all Bohemia: if you had but looked big and spit at him, he 'ld have run.
Winter's Tale. Act iv, sc. 3, l. 112. [Clown]
Thou art a coward.—*Winter's Tale,* i, 2, 243.

COXCOMB

See also Fop

12
As many coxcombs
As you threw hats up will he tumble down.
Coriolanus. Act iv, sc. 6, l. 134. [Menenius]
13
Let me hire him too: here 's my coxcomb. . . . Sirrah, you were best take my coxcomb. . . . There, take my coxcomb. . . . Thou must needs wear my coxcomb. How now, nuncle! Would I had two coxcombs and two daughters! . . . If I gave them all my living, I 'ld keep my coxcombs myself.
King Lear. Act i, sc. 4, l. 105. [Fool] The fool is referring to his cap.
14
She knapped 'em o' the coxcombs with a stick.
King Lear, ii, 4, 125. See under EEL. "Knapped" is repeated in *The Merchant of Venice,* iii, 1, 10.
Bloody coxcomb.—*Henry V,* v, 1, 45; *Twelfth Night,* v, 1, 179; 193; 195.

Broken coxcomb.—*Henry V,* v, 1, 57.
Knave's cogscomb.—*The Merry Wives of Windsor,* iii, 1, 91.

1 Shall I have a coxcomb of frize?
The Merry Wives of Windsor. Act v, sc. 5, l. 146. [Falstaff] "Frize" (coarse woollen cloth) is repeated in *Othello,* ii, 1, 127.

2 Conrade: Off, coxcomb!
Dogberry: God 's my life, where 's the sexton? let him write down the prince's officer coxcomb.
Much Ado about Nothing. Act iv, sc. 2, l. 71.

Coxcomb, idiot, patch!—*The Comedy of Errors,* iii, 1, 32.
A coxcomb and a knave.—*Twelfth Night,* v, 1, 213.
O murderous coxcomb!—*Othello,* v, 2, 233.
Prating coxcomb.—*Henry V,* iv, 1, 79; 81.
O most profane coxcomb!—*Love's Labour 's Lost,* iv, 3, 84.

3 Katharina: What is your crest? a coxcomb?
Petruchio: A combless cock.
The Taming of the Shrew, ii, 1, 226. See under COCK.

COZENAGE, see Cheating

CRAFT, see Cunning

CREATURE

4 My lord, this is a fond and desperate creature,
Whom sometime I have laugh'd with.
All's Well that Ends Well. Act v, sc. 3, l. 178. [Bertram]

It is a creature That dotes on Cassio.
Othello. Act iv, sc. 1, l. 96. [Iago]

5 No, not a creature enters in my house.
The Comedy of Errors. Act v, sc. 1, l. 92. [Lady Abbess]

Let no creature enter.—*The Comedy of Errors,* ii, 2, 212.

6 Such creatures as
We count not worth the hanging.
Cymbeline. Act i, sc. 5, l. 19. [Queen]

Creatures vile, as cats and dogs,
Of no esteem.
Cymbeline. Act v, sc. 5, l. 252. [Cornelius]

Creatures may be alike.—*Cymbeline,* v, 5, 125.
God's creatures.—*Hamlet,* iii, 1, 151.
Feather'd creatures.—*Sonnets,* cxliii.

7 Ingrateful, savage and inhuman creature!
Henry V. Act ii, sc. 2, l. 95. [King Henry]

Beastly creature.—*The Comedy of Errors,* iii, 2, 88; *Titus Andronicus,* ii, 3, 182.
Common'st creature.—*Richard II,* v, 3, 17.
Deformed'st creature.—*Sonnets,* cxiii. The only use of "deformed'st."
Fearful creatures.—*Venus and Adonis,* l. 677.
Foul creature.—*Venus and Adonis,* l. 1005.
Guilty creatures.—*Hamlet,* ii, 2, 618.
Idle creatures.—*Julius Cæsar,* i, 1, 1.
Jealous creatures.—*Othello,* iii, 4, 28.
Needless creatures.—*Timon of Athens,* i, 2, 101.
Poor creature.—*II Henry IV,* ii, 2, 13; *King Lear,* iii, 4, 124; *Titus Andronicus,* iii, 2, 5.
Slippery creatures.—*Timon of Athens,* i, 1, 53.
Unreasonable creatures.—*III Henry VI,* ii, 2, 26.
Wicked creature.—*All's Well that Ends Well,* i, 3, 37; *King Lear,* ii, 4, 259.
Wretched creature.—*Julius Cæsar,* i, 2, 117.

8 She is a gallant creature, and complete
In mind and feature.
Henry VIII. Act iii, sc. 2, l. 49. [Suffolk]

She 's a good creature, and, sweet lady, does
Deserve our better wishes.
Henry VIII. Act v, sc. 1, l. 25. [Lovell]

She 's a good creature.—*The Merry Wives of Windsor,* ii, 2, 56.
Good creature.—*All's Well that Ends Well,* iii, 5, 69.

O wonder!
How many goodly creatures are there here!
The Tempest. Act v, sc. 1, l. 181. [Miranda]

Leonine: She is a goodly creature.
Dionyza: The fitter, then, the gods should have her.
Pericles. Act iv, sc. 1, l. 9.

Capable creature.—*Troilus and Cressida,* iii, 3, 310.
Dear creature.—*Comedy of Errors,* iii, 2, 33.
Dearest creatures.—*Cymbeline,* iii, 2, 43.
Delicate creatures.—*Othello,* iii, 3, 269.
Divinest creature.—*I Henry VI,* i, 6, 4.
Gracious creature.—*King John,* iii, 4, 81.
Kind creatures.—*Cymbeline,* iv, 2, 32.
Kindly creatures.—*Antony and Cleopatra,* ii, 5, 78.
Most sovereign creature.—*Antony and Cleopatra,* v, 2, 81.
Noble creature.—*The Tempest,* i, 2, 7.
Precious creature.—*The Tempest,* iii, 1, 25; *The Winter's Tale,* i, 2, 452.
Pretty creatures.—*The Rape of Lucrece,* l. 1233.
Primest creature.—*Henry VIII,* ii, 4, 229.
Sweet creature.—*All's Well that Ends Well,* v, 3, 78; *I Henry IV,* ii, 4, 359; *Othello,* iii, 3, 422.
The sweet'st, dear'st creature.—*The Winter's Tale,* iii, 2, 202.
Valiant creatures.—*Henry V,* iii, 7, 151.
Virtuous creature.—*The Merry Wives of Windsor,* iv, 2, 137.

9 A creature unprepared, unmeet for death.
Measure for Measure. Act iv, sc. 3, l. 71. [Duke]

I am not such a sickly creature, I give heaven praise.
Merry Wives of Windsor, iii, 4, 61. [Slender]

Thou art as foolish Christian creatures as I would desires.
Merry Wives of Windsor, iv, 1, 73. [Evans]

10 Never did I know
A creature, that did bear the shape of man,
So keen and greedy to confound a man.
The Merchant of Venice. Act iii, sc. 2, l. 277. [Salerio]

A reasonable creature.—*Much Ado about Nothing,* i, 1, 71.

1 This honest creature doubtless
Sees and knows more, much more, than he unfolds.
Othello. Act iii, sc. 3, l. 242. [Othello]
Honest creatures.—*Cymbeline,* iv, 2, 299.

2 Hundreds call themselves
Your creatures, who by you have been restored.
Pericles. Act iii, sc. 2, l. 44. [Gentleman]
Creature of sale.—*Pericles,* iv, 6, 84. See under WHORE.

3
With shining falchion in my chamber came
A creeping creature, with a flaming light
And softly cried "Awake, thou Roman dame,
And entertain my love."
The Rape of Lucrece, l. 1626.

4
I took him for the plainest harmless creature
That breathed upon this earth a Christian.
Richard III. Act iii, sc. 5, l. 25. [Gloucester]
Harmless creatures.—*The Rape of Lucrece,* l. 1347.

5
From fairest creatures we desire increase,
That thereby beauty's rose might never die.
Sonnets. No. i.
She was the fairest creature in the world;
And yet she is inferior to none.
The Taming of the Shrew. Ind., sc. 2, l. 68. [Servant]
Fairest creature.—*The Merchant of Venice,* ii, 1, 4.
Fair creature.—*Richard III,* i, 2, 132, and six times in later plays.

6 New created
The creatures that were mine, I say, or changed 'em,
Or else new form'd 'em.
The Tempest. Act i, sc. 2, l. 81. [Prospero]
Created Of every creature's best.
The Tempest, iii, 1, 47. See WOMAN: HER VIRTUES, 1700:6, for full quotation.

7 Call the creatures
Whose naked natures live in all the spite
Of wreakful heaven, whose bare unhoused trunks,
To the conflicting elements exposed,
Answer mere nature; bid them flatter thee.
Timon of Athens. Act iv, sc. 3, l. 227. [Apemantus] "Wreakful" is repeated in *Titus Andronicus,* v, 2, 32: "Wreakful vengeance"; and "unhoused" in *Othello,* i, 2, 26.
Creatures Of prey.—*The Winter's Tale,* iii, 3, 12.

8 To me comes a creature,
Sometimes her head on one side, some another.
The Winter's Tale. Act iii, sc. 3, l. 19. [Antigonus]
Familiar creature.—*Othello,* ii, 3, 314.
Live creature.—*A Midsummer-Night's Dream,* ii, 1, 172.
Two-legged creature.—*I Henry IV,* ii, 4, 208. The only use of "two-legged."

CREDIT

See also Reputation

9
You must hold the credit of your father.
All's Well that Ends Well. Act i, sc. 1, l. 89. [Lafeu]

10
You wrong me more, sir, in denying it:
Consider how it stands upon my credit.
The Comedy of Errors. Act iv, sc. 1, l. 67. [Angelo]
Got me credit.—*The Comedy of Errors,* iii, 1, 45; *Henry VIII,* i, 1, 37.
Being compact of credit.—*The Comedy of Errors,* iii, 2, 22.

11
So far as my coin would stretch; and where it would not, I have used my credit.
I Henry IV. Act i, sc. 2, l. 61. [Prince of Wales]
I have but a very little credit with your worship.
II Henry IV. Act v, sc. 1, l. 54. [Davy]

12
My credit now stands on such slippery ground,
That one of two bad ways you must conceit me,
Either a coward or a flatterer.
Julius Cæsar. Act iii, sc. 1, l. 191. [Antony]

13
Thus will I save my credit.
Love's Labour's Lost. Act iv, sc. 1, l. 26. [Princess]

14
Try what my credit can in Venice do.
The Merchant of Venice. Act i, sc. 1, l. 180. [Antonio]
'Tis a goodly credit for you.
The Merry Wives of Windsor. Act iv, sc. 2, l. 200. [Mrs. Ford]
Of great credit.—*Othello,* ii, 1, 296.
Of credit infinite.—*The Comedy of Errors,* v, 1, 6.
Undo her credit.—*Othello,* ii, 3, 365.

15
Letters of good credit.
Pericles. Act v, sc. 3, l. 77. [Thaisa]
Almost beyond credit.—*The Tempest,* ii, 1, 59.
Want credit.—*The Tempest,* iii, 3, 25.

16
Kept his credit with his purse.
Timon of Athens. Act iii, sc. 2, l. 75. [First Stranger]

17
This is much credit to you.
Twelfth Night. Act ii, sc. 3, l. 117. [Malvolio]
What! lack I credit?—*The Winter's Tale,* ii, 1, 157.
Give us better credit.—*The Winter's Tale,* ii, 3, 146. "Credit" as a verb is used eight times in the plays and poems.

CREDITOR

See also Debt

18
Bear me forthwith unto his creditor.
The Comedy of Errors. Act iv, sc. 4, l. 123. [Adriana]

1
You have no true debitor and creditor but it.
Cymbeline, v, 4, 172. See under HANGING.
Debitor and creditor.—*Othello,* i, 1, 31. The only uses of "debitor."
2
I break, and you, my creditors, lose.
II Henry IV. Epil., l. 14. See also under BANKRUPTCY.
3
If I could speak so wisely under an arrest,
I would send for certain of my creditors.
Measure for Measure. Act i, sc. 2, l. 135. [Lucio]
4
My creditors grow cruel, my estate is very low, my bond to the Jew is forfeit.
The Merchant of Venice. Act iii, sc. 2, l. 319. [Bassanio, reading]
His creditors most strait.—*Timon of Athens,* i, 1, 96.
Creditors? devils!—*Timon of Athens,* iii, 4, 105.
Bloody creditor.—*Merchant of Venice,* iii, 3, 34.

CRIME

5
Our crimes would despair, if they were not cherished by our virtues.
All's Well that Ends Well. Act iv, sc. 3, l. 86. [First Lord]
6
He took my father grossly, full of bread;
With all his crimes broad blown, as flush as May;
And how his audit stands who knows save heaven?
Hamlet. Act iii, sc. 3, l. 80. [Hamlet]
7
If little faults, proceeding on distemper,
Shall not be wink'd at, how shall we stretch our eye
When capital crimes, chew'd, swallow'd and digested,
Appear before us?
Henry V. Act ii, sc. 2, l. 54. [King Henry]
My lord, these faults are easy, quickly answer'd:
But mightier crimes are laid unto your charge.
II Henry VI. Act iii, sc. 1, l. 133. [Suffolk]
8
In writing I preferr'd
The manner of thy vile outrageous crimes.
I Henry VI. Act iii, sc. 1, l. 10. [Gloucester]
Detested crimes.—*Love's Labour's Lost,* iv, 1, 31.
Foul crimes.—*Hamlet,* i, 5, 12.
9
Every hour
He flashes into one gross crime or other,
That sets us all at odds.
King Lear. Act i, sc. 3, l. 3. [Goneril]
That hast within thee undivulged crimes,
Unwhipp'd of justice.
King Lear. Act iii, sc. 2, l. 52. [King Lear] The only use of "unwhipp'd." "Undivulged" occurs again in *Macbeth,* ii, 3, 137.
Nether crimes.—*King Lear,* iv, 2, 79.
10
Do me the common right
To let me see them and to make me know
The nature of their crimes, that I may minister
To them accordingly.
Measure for Measure. Act ii, sc. 3, l. 5. [Duke]
11
Being criminal, in double violation
Of sacred chastity and of promise-breech.
Measure for Measure. Act v, sc. 1, l. 409. [Duke] The only use of "promise-breech."
More criminal.—*The Winter's Tale,* iii, 2, 90.
So criminal.—*Coriolanus,* iii, 3, 81. The only uses of "criminal."
12
If you bethink yourself of any crime
Unreconciled as yet to heaven and grace,
Solicit for it straight.
Othello. Act v, sc. 2, l. 26. [Othello] The only use of "unreconciled."
13
Whose crime will bear an ever-during blame.
The Rape of Lucrece, l. 224. The only use of "ever-during."
And ever let his unrecalling crime
Have time to wail th' abusing of his time.
The Rape of Lucrece, l. 993. The only use of "unrecalling."
Cureless crime.—*The Rape of Lucrece,* l. 772.
Prenominate crimes.—*Hamlet,* ii, 1, 43. "Prenominate" (named beforehand) is repeated in *Troilus and Cressida,* iv, 5, 250.
14
These grievous crimes
Committed by your person and your followers
Against the state and profit of this land.
Richard II. Act iv, sc. 1, l. 223. [Northumberland]
But I forbid thee one most heinous crime.
Sonnets. No. xix.
Self-doing crime.—*Sonnets,* lviii. The only use of "self-doing."
15
Crimes, like lands, Are not inherited.
Timon of Athens. Act v, sc. 4, l. 37. [Senator]
Weigh but the crime.—*Timon of Athens,* iii, 5, 58.
16
Such like petty crimes as these.
The Two Gentlemen of Verona. Act iv, sc. 1, l. 52. [First Outlaw]

CRITICISM

See also Censure

17
My taxing like a wild-goose flies,
Unclaim'd of any man.
As You Like It. Act ii, sc. 7, l. 86. [Jaques] The only use of "unclaim'd." "Taxing" is repeated in *Troilus and Cressida,* v, 1, 46.
Their writers do them wrong, to make them exclaim against their own succession.
Hamlet. Act ii, sc. 2, l. 367. [Hamlet]
In faith, my lord, you are too wilful-blame.
I Henry IV. Act iii, sc. 1, l. 177. [Worcester] The only use of "wilful-blame."
18
Happy are they that hear their detractions and can put them to mending.
Much Ado about Nothing. Act ii, sc. 3, l. 237. [Benedick]

Detraction at your heels.—*Twelfth Night,* ii, 5, 149. See under EYE.
Detraction will not suffer it.—*I Henry IV,* v, 1, 141.
Unspeak mine own detraction.—*Macbeth,* iv, 3, 123. The only uses of "detraction."

1
These paper bullets of the brain.
Much Ado about Nothing. Act ii, sc. 3, l. 249. [Benedick]
Sure, sure, such carping is not commendable.
Much Ado about Nothing. Act iii, sc. 1, l. 71. [Ursula]
Envious carping.—*I Henry VI,* iv, 1, 90.
Carping censures.—*Richard III,* iii, 5, 68. The only uses of "carping."
Carp and quarrel.—*King Lear,* i, 4, 222. The only use of "carp" in this sense.
Cunning of a carper.—*Timon of Athens,* iv, 3, 209. The only use of "carper."
You forget yourself, To hedge me in.
Julius Cæsar. Act iv, sc. 3, l. 29. [Cassius]
We'll not be nice.—*Love's Labour's Lost,* v, 2, 219.

2
I am nothing, if not critical.
Othello. Act ii, sc. 1, l. 120. [Iago]
Keen and critical.—*A Midsummer-Night's Dream,* v, 1, 54. The only uses of "critical." "Criticism" does not occur in the plays.

3
None are for me
That look into me with considerate eyes.
Richard III. Act iv, sc. 2, l. 29. [King Richard] "Considerate" is repeated in *Antony and Cleopatra,* ii, 2, 112.

4
Stubborn critics, apt, without a theme.
Troilus and Cressida, v, 2, 131. See WOMAN: HER FAULTS, 1703:2, for full quotation.
In so profound abysm I throw all care
Of others' voices, that my adder's sense
To critic and to flatterer stopped are.
Sonnets. No. cxii.
A critic, nay, a night-watch constable.
Love's Labour's Lost, iii, 1, 178. See under LOVE. The only use of "night-watch."
Critic Timon.—*Love's Labour's Lost,* iv, 3, 170. The only uses of "critic" and "critics."

CROSSES, see Misfortune

CROW

5
Antipholus of Ephesus: Go borrow me a crow.
Dromio of Ephesus: A crow without a feather? Master, mean you so?
For a fish without a fin, there's a fowl without a feather:
If a crow help us in, sirrah, we'll pluck a crow together.
Antipholus of Ephesus: Go get thee gone; fetch me an iron crow.
The Comedy of Errors. Act iii, sc. 1, l. 80.
Get me an iron crow, and bring it straight
Unto my cell.
Romeo and Juliet. Act v, sc. 2, l. 21. [Friar]

6
Bring in the crows to peck the eagles.
Coriolanus. Act iii, sc. 1, l. 138. [Coriolanus]

7
If you fall in the adventure, our crows shall fare the better for you; and there's an end.
Cymbeline. Act iii, sc. 1, l. 83. [Cloten]
He'll yield the crow a pudding one of these days.
Henry V. Act ii, sc. 1, l. 91. [Hostess]
Their executors, the knavish crows,
Fly o'er them, all impatient for their hour.
Henry V. Act iv, sc. 2, l. 51. [Grandpré]
Leaving thy trunk for crows to feed upon.
II Henry VI. Act iv, sc. 10, l. 90. [Iden]

8
The crows and choughs that wing the midway air
Show scarce so gross as beetles.
King Lear. Act iv, sc. 6, l. 13. [Edgar]

9
The crow doth sing as sweetly as the lark
When neither is attended.
The Merchant of Venice. Act v, sc. 1, l. 102. [Portia]
The crow Makes wing to the rooky wood.
Macbeth. Act iii, sc. 2, l. 50. [Macbeth]

10
And crows are fatted with the murrion flock.
A Midsummer-Night's Dream. Act ii, sc. 1, l. 97. [Titania] The only use of "murrion" (diseased).
Carrion . . . crows.—*II Henry VI,* v, 2, 11.
Ribald crows.—*Troilus and Cressida,* iv, 2, 9.
A crow o' the same nest.—*All's Well that Ends Well,* iv, 3, 319.

11
With the dove of Paphos might the crow
Vie feathers white.
Pericles. Act iv, Gower, l. 32.
And thou treble-dated crow,
That thy sable gender makest
With the breath thou givest and takest,
'Mongst our mourners shalt thou go.
The Phœnix and the Turtle, l. 17. The only use of "treble-dated" (living three times as long as man).

12
The crow may bathe his coal-black wings in mire,
And unperceived fly with the filth away;
But if the like the snow-white swan desire,
The stain upon his silver down will stay.
The Rape of Lucrece, l. 1009. The only use of "unperceived." "Coal-black" occurs eight times in the plays and poems, and "snow-white" six times.

13
Like a crow-keeper.—*Romeo and Juliet,* i, 4, 6; *King Lear,* iv, 6, 88. The only uses of "crow-keeper."

CROWD, see People

CROWN

See also King

14
Your crown's awry;
I'll mend it, and then play.
Antony and Cleopatra. Act v, sc. 2, l. 321. [Charmian]

1
His crown bequeathing to his banish'd brother.
As You Like It. Act v, sc. 4, l. 169. [Jaques]

2
Now, the gods crown thee!
Coriolanus. Act ii, sc. 1, l. 196. [Menenius]

3 She being down
I have the placing of the British crown.
Cymbeline. Act iii, sc. 5, l. 64. [Queen]

Crown of England.—*King John,* ii, 1, 273.
England's crown.—*II Henry VI,* ii, 2, 5.
English crown.—*II Henry VI,* i, 1, 152; i, 3, 187; *III Henry VI,* i, 1, 49; iii, 2, 179; iv, 3, 49; iv, 4, 24.
Crown of France.—*Henry V,* i, 2, 68; i, 2, 80; i, 2, 85.
French crown.—*Measure for Measure,* i, 2, 52; *Love's Labour's Lost,* iii, 1, 142; *All's Well that Ends Well,* ii, 2, 23.

4
Why doth the crown lie there upon his pillow,
Being so troublesome a bedfellow?
O polish'd perturbation! golden care!
That keep'st the ports of slumber open wide
To many a watchful night! sleep with it now!
Yet not so sound and half so deeply sweet
As he whose brow with homely biggen bound
Snores out the watch of night.
II Henry IV. Act iv, sc. 5, l. 21. [Prince of Wales] The only use of "biggen" (nightcap). "Polish'd" is repeated in *Sonnets,* lxxxv.

There is your crown;
And He that wears the crown immortally
Long guard it yours!
II Henry IV. Act iv, sc. 5, l. 143. [Prince of Wales] The only use of "immortally."

God knows, my son,
By what by-paths and indirect crook'd ways
I met this crown; and I myself know well
How troublesome it sat upon my head.
II Henry IV. Act iv, sc. 5, l. 184. [King Henry] The only use of "by-paths."

King: How I came by the crown, O God forgive;
And grant it may with thee in true peace live! . . .
Prince Henry: You won it, wore it, kept it, gave it me;
Then plain and right must my possession be:
Which I with more than with a common pain
'Gainst all the world will rightfully maintain.
II Henry IV. Act iv, sc. 5, l. 219. The only use of "rightfully."

5
My due from thee is this imperial crown,
Which, as immediate from thy place and blood,
Derives itself to me.
II Henry IV. Act iv, sc. 5, l. 41. [Prince]

The crown imperial.—*Henry V,* iv, 1, 278; *The Winter's Tale,* iv, 4, 126.
Crowns imperial.—*Henry V,* ii, Prol., 10.

6 If you hide the crown
Even in your hearts, there will he rake for it.
Henry V. Act ii, sc. 4, l. 97. [Exeter]

Deliver up the crown.—*Henry V,* ii, 4, 103; *King John,* iv, 2, 152.
Yield up my crown.—*King John,* iv, 2, 157.

His crown shall be the ransom of my friend.
I Henry VI. Act i, sc. 1, l. 150. [Bedford]

7
Gloucester: Lord bishop, set the crown upon his head.
Winchester: God save King Henry, of that name the sixth!
I Henry VI. Act iv, sc. 1, l. 1.

Set a precious crown upon thy head.
I Henry VI. Act v, sc. 3, l. 119. [Suffolk]

Precious crown.—*Richard II,* iii, 3, 90.
Precious rich crown.—*I Henry IV,* ii, 4, 420.

Set the triple crown upon his head.
II Henry VI. Act i, sc. 3, l. 66. [Queen]

He comes towards London,
To set the crown once more on Henry's head.
III Henry VI. Act iv, sc. 4, l. 26. [Queen Elizabeth]

You, that set the crown
Upon the head of this forgetful man
And for his sake wear the detested blot
Of murderous subornation.
I Henry IV. Act i, sc. 3, l. 160. [Hotspur] "Subornation" occurs twice in *II Henry VI,* iii, 1, 45, and iii, 1, 145.

8
Adorn his temples with a coronet.
I Henry VI, v, 4, 134. See under PRIVILEGE.

A coronet of gold.—*I Henry VI,* iii, 3, 89.
Coronet of fresh and fragrant flowers.—*A Midsummer-Night's Dream,* iv, 1, 57.
Crowns and coronets.—*Henry V,* ii, Prol., 10.

'Twas not a crown neither, 'twas one of these coronets.
Julius Cæsar. Act i, sc. 2, l. 238. [Casca]

This coronet part betwixt you.
King Lear. Act i, sc. 1, l. 141. [King Lear]

Subject his coronet to the crown and bend
The dukedom yet unbow'd.
The Tempest. Act i, sc. 2, l. 114. [Prospero]

Coronet weeds.—*Hamlet,* iv, 7, 173. The only uses of "coronet."

9 With all speed provide
To see her coronation be perform'd.
II Henry VI. Act i, sc. 1, l. 74. [King Henry]

First will I see the coronation.
III Henry VI. Act ii, sc. 6, l. 96. [Warwick]

Haste unto your coronation.—*I Henry VI,* iv, 1, 10.
Show my duty in your coronation.—*Hamlet,* i, 2, 53.
Sit about the coronation.—*Richard III,* iii, 1, 173.
Determine of the coronation.—*Richard III,* iii, 4, 2.
Double coronation.—*King John,* iv, 2, 40.

On Wednesday next we solemnly set down
Our coronation.
Richard II. Act iv, sc. 1, l. 320. [Bolingbroke]

Coronation-day.—*II Henry IV,* iii, 2, 195; *Richard II,* v, 5, 77. The only uses of "coronation-day."

1 And, when I spy advantage, claim the crown,
For that 's the golden mark I seek to hit.
II Henry VI. Act i, sc. 1, l. 242. [York]

Force perforce, I 'll make him yield the crown,
Whose bookish rule hath pull'd fair England down.
II Henry VI. Act i, sc. 1, l. 258. [York]

Pluck the crown from feeble Henry's head.
II Henry VI. Act v, sc. 1, l. 2. [York]

Then, nobly, York; 'tis for a crown thou fight'st.
II Henry VI. Act v, sc. 2, l. 16. [Warwick]

2 Confirm the crown to me and to mine heirs,
And thou shalt reign in quiet while thou livest.
III Henry VI. Act i, sc. 1, l. 172. [York]

I here entail
The crown to thee and to thine heirs for ever;
Conditionally, that here thou take an oath
To cease this civil war, and, whilst I live,
To honour me as thy king and sovereign.
III Henry VI. Act i, sc. 1, l. 196. [King Henry] The only use of "conditionally."

3 How sweet a thing it is to wear a crown;
Within whose circuit is Elysium
And all that poets feign of bliss and joy.
III Henry VI. Act i, sc. 2, l. 29. [Richard]

'A crown, or else a glorious tomb!
A sceptre, or an earthly sepulchre!'
III Henry VI. Act i, sc. 4, l. 16. [York]

4 Off with the crown; and, with the crown, his head;
And, whilst we breathe, take time to do him dead.
III Henry VI. Act i, sc. 4, l. 107. [Queen Margaret] The only instance of the use of the phrase, "do him dead."

Can I do this, and cannot get a crown?
Tut, were it farther off, I 'll pluck it down.
III Henry VI. Act iii, sc. 2, l. 194. [Gloucester]

I was the chief that raised him to the crown,
And I 'll be chief to bring him down again.
III Henry VI. Act iii, sc. 3, l. 262. [Warwick]

5 I 'll make my heaven to dream upon the crown,
And, whiles I live, to account this world but hell,
Until my mis-shaped trunk that bears this head
Be round impaled with a glorious crown.
III Henry VI. Act iii, sc. 2, l. 170. [Gloucester] The only use of "mis-shaped" and "impaled."

Did I impale him with the regal crown?
III Henry VI. Act iii, sc. 3, l. 189. [Warwick] The only use of "impale."

Fearless minds climb soonest unto crowns.
III Henry VI. Act iv, sc. 7, l. 62. [Gloucester]

6 Young Ned, for thee, thine uncles and myself
Have in our armours watch'd the winter's night,
Went all afoot in summer's scalding heat
That thou mightst repossess the crown in peace.
III Henry VI. Act v, sc. 7, l. 16. [King Edward]

Pray that I may repossess the crown.
III Henry VI. Act iv, sc. 5, l. 29. [King Edward]

7 Casca: Why, there was a crown offered him: and being offered him, he put it by with the back of his hand, thus; and then the people fell a-shouting.
Brutus: What was the second noise for?
Casca: Why, for that too.
Cassius: They shouted thrice: what was the last cry for?
Casca: Why, for that too.
Brutus: Was the crown offered him thrice?
Casca: Ay, marry, was 't, and he put it by thrice, every time gentler than other, and at every putting-by mine honest neighbours shouted.
Julius Cæsar. Act i, sc. 2, l. 220. The only use of "putting-by."

I thrice presented him a kingly crown,
Which he did thrice refuse.
Julius Cæsar. Act iii, sc. 2, l. 101. [Antony]

He would not take the crown;
Therefore 'tis certain he was not ambitious.
Julius Cæsar. Act iii, sc. 2, l. 117. [Citizen]

8 Thou hast . . .
Out-faced infant state and done a rape
Upon the maiden virtue of the crown.
King John. Act ii, sc. 1, l. 95. [King Philip]

The circle of my glory.
King John. Act v, sc. 1, l. 2. [King John]

9 The golden round,
Which fate and metaphysical aid doth seem
To have thee crown'd withal.
Macbeth. Act i, sc. 5, l. 29. [Lady Macbeth] The only use of "metaphysical."

And wears upon his baby-brow the round
And top of sovereignty.
Macbeth. Act iv, sc. 1, l. 88. [Macbeth] The only use of "baby-brow."

10 Upon my head they placed a fruitless crown.
Macbeth. Act iii, sc. 1, l. 61. [Macbeth]

Thy crown does sear mine eye-balls.
Macbeth. Act iv, sc. 1, l. 113. [Macbeth]

11 Some of your French crowns have no hair at all.
A Midsummer-Night's Dream. Act i, sc. 2, l. 99. [Quince] See also under HEAD.

Pitiful bald crown!—*I Henry IV*, ii, 4, 420.

Crack'd crowns.—*I Henry IV*, ii, 3, 96.

12 Redeem from broking pawn the blemish'd crown.
Richard II. Act ii, sc. 1, l. 293. [Northumberland] The only use of "broking."

To lift shrewd steel against our golden crown.
Richard II. Act iii, sc. 2, l. 59. [King Richard]

Now is this golden crown like a deep well
That owes two buckets, filling one another,
The emptier ever dancing in the air,
The other down, unseen and full of water:
The bucket down and full of tears am I,
Drinking my griefs, whilst you mount up on high.

Richard II. Act iv, sc. 1, l. 185. [King Richard] "Emptier" is repeated in *II Henry IV*, ii, 4, 66: "Emptier vessel."

Hidest thou that forehead with a golden crown?

Richard III. Act iv, sc. 4, l. 140. [Queen]

1
Thou didst crown his warlike brows with paper.

Richard III. Act i, sc. 3, l. 175. [Gloucester]

Crowning of the King.—*Richard III*, iii, 4, 29. The only use of "crowning."

2
Hastings: How! wear the garland! dost thou mean the crown?
Catesby: Ay, my good lord.
Hastings: I 'll have this crown of mine cut from my shoulders
Ere I will see the crown so foul misplaced.

Richard III. Act iii, sc. 2, l. 41.

I would to God that the inclusive verge
Of golden metal that must round my brow
Were red-hot steel, to sear me to the brain!

Richard III. Act iv, sc. 1, l. 59. [Anne] "Inclusive" is repeated in *All's Well that Ends Well*, i, 3, 232.

The imperial metal, circling now thy brow.

Richard III, iv, 4, 381. See under OATH.

3
Lord Stanley: He makes for England, there to claim the crown.
King Richard: Is the chair empty? is the sword unsway'd?
Is the king dead? the empire unpossess'd?

Richard III. Act iv, sc. 4, l. 469. The only use of "unsway'd" and "unpossess'd."

The first was I that help'd thee to the crown.

Richard III. Act v, sc. 3, l. 167. [Ghost]

Lo, here, this long-usurped royalty
From the dead temples of this bloody wretch
Have I pluck'd off, to grace thy brows withal.

Richard III. Act v, sc. 5, l. 4. [Derby] The only use of "long-usurped."

4
My strong imagination sees a crown
Dropping upon thy head.

The Tempest. Act ii, sc. 1, l. 208. [Antonio]

Blessed crown!—*The Tempest*, v, 1, 202.
Chaste crowns.—*The Tempest*, iv, 1, 66.
Sedged crowns.—*The Tempest*, iv, 1, 129.
Icy crown.—*A Midsummer-Night's Dream*, ii, 1, 109.

5
The crown will find an heir.

The Winter's Tale, v, 1, 47. See under ALEXANDER.

II—Crowns

6
I will . . . give no thousand crowns neither.

As You Like It. Act i, sc. 1, l. 91. [Oliver]

Owy, cuppele gorge, permafoy,
Peasant, unless thou give me crowns, brave crowns.

Henry V. Act iv, sc. 4, l. 39. [Pistol] Pistol is trying to tell his French prisoner that he will cut his throat unless he gets a ransom.

Give crowns like pins!—*II Henry IV*, ii, 4, 188.

7
I have five hundred crowns.

As You Like It. Act ii, sc. 3, l. 38. [Adam]

A thousand crowns.—*As You Like It*, i, 1, 3.
Twenty thousand crowns.—*The Taming of the Shrew*, v, 2, 113.
A hundred thousand crowns.—*Love's Labour's Lost*, ii, 1, 130; ii, 1, 144; ii, 1, 145.

8
I will stuff your purses full of crowns.

I Henry IV. Act i, sc. 2, l. 147. [Poins]

Here 's four Harry ten shillings in French crowns for you.

II Henry IV. Act iii, sc. 2, l. 236. [Bullcalf]

Fill this glove with crowns,
And give it to this fellow

Henry V. Act iv, sc. 8, l. 61. [King Henry]

9
Fool: Give me an egg, uncle, and I 'll give thee two crowns.
King Lear: What two crowns shall they be?
Fool: Why, after I have cut the egg i' the middle, and eat up the meat, the two crowns of the egg.

King Lear. Act i, sc. 4, l. 170.

10
Crowns in my purse I have.

The Taming of the Shrew. Act i, sc. 2, l. 57. [Petruchio]

In ivory coffers I have stuff'd my crowns.

The Taming of the Shrew, iii, 1, 352. See under POSSESSIONS.

CRUELTY

11
Be not so holy-cruel.

All's Well that Ends Well. Act iv, sc. 2, l. 32. [Bertram] The only use of "holy-cruel."

Justice, and your father's wrath, should he take me in his dominion, could not be so cruel to me, as you.

Cymbeline. Act iii, sc. 2, l. 40. [Imogen, reading]

12
Let me be cruel, not unnatural.

Hamlet. Act iii, sc. 2, l. 413. [Hamlet]

I must be cruel, only to be kind.

Hamlet. Act iii, sc. 4, l. 178. [Hamlet]

13
He will spare neither man, woman, nor child.

II Henry IV, ii, 1, 18. See under LIFE.

Thunders to his captives blood and death.

III Henry VI. Act ii, sc. 1, l. 127. [Warwick]

14
In cruelty will I seek out my fame.

II Henry VI. Act v, sc. 2, l. 60. [Clifford]

Fell cruelty, Which is too nigh your person.

Macbeth. Act iv, sc. 2, l. 71. [Messenger] The only use of the phrase "fell cruelty."

Household cruelty.—*II Henry IV*, iv, 1, 95.

1
But you are more inhuman, more inexorable,
O, ten times more, than tigers of Hyrcania.
III Henry VI. Act i, sc. 4, l. 154. [York] "Inexorable" is used once again in *Romeo and Juliet,* v, 3, 38. The only use of "Hyrcania." "Hyrcan tigers" occurs in *Macbeth,* 3, 4, 101, and "Hyrcanian" in the *Merchant of Venice,* ii, 7, 41, and *Hamlet,* ii, 2, 472. Hyrcania was the ancient name of a country south of the Caspian Sea.

A stony adversary, an inhuman wretch
Uncapable of pity, void and empty
From any dram of mercy.
The Merchant of Venice. Act iv, sc. 1, l. 4. [Duke] "Uncapable" is used once again in *Othello,* iv, 2, 235.

2
'Tis a cruelty To load a falling man.
Henry VIII. Act v, sc. 3, l. 76. [Cromwell]

Thou hast a cruel nature and a bloody.
Henry VIII. Act v, sc. 3, l. 129. [King Henry]

Now we must appear bloody and cruel.
Julius Cæsar. Act iii, sc. 1, l. 165. [Brutus]

3
O you hard hearts, you cruel men of Rome!
Julius Cæsar. Act i, sc. 1, l. 41. [Marullus]

Alas, what need you be so boisterous-rough?
King John. Act iv, sc. 1, l. 76. [Arthur] The only use of "boisterous-rough."

4
Most savage and unnatural!
King Lear. Act iii, sc. 3, l. 7. [Edmund]

O cruel! O you gods!
King Lear. Act iii, sc. 7, l. 70. [Cornwall]

Most barbarous, most degenerate!
King Lear. Act iv, sc. 2, l. 43. [Albany]

5
Come, you spirits
That tend on mortal thoughts, unsex me here,
And fill me from the crown to the toe top-full
Of direst cruelty!
Macbeth. Act i, sc. 5, l. 41. [Lady Macbeth] The only use of "unsex." "Topfull" (unhyphenated) is repeated in *King John,* iii, 4, 180: "Topfull of offence."

The current of thy cruelty.
The Merchant of Venice. Act iv, sc. 1, l. 64. [Bassanio]

Pierced through the heart with your stern cruelty.
A Midsummer-Night's Dream. Act iii, sc. 2, l. 59. [Demetrius]

6
Farewell, fair cruelty.
Twelfth Night. Act i, sc. 5, l. 307. [Viola]

The youth, bears in his visage no great presage of cruelty.
Twelfth Night. Act iii, sc. 2, l. 68. [Fabian]

CRY AND CRYING

7
When Antony found Julius Cæsar dead,
He cried almost to roaring.
Antony and Cleopatra. Act iii, sc. 2, l. 54. [Agrippa]

I could find in my heart to disgrace my man's apparel and to cry like a woman.
As You Like It. Act ii, sc. 4, l. 4. [Rosalind]

Mercy on me! I have a great dispositions to cry.
The Merry Wives of Windsor. Act iii, sc. 1, l. 22. [Evans]

Cry myself awake.—*Cymbeline,* iii, 4, 46.

8
You 'll cry for this.
The Comedy of Errors. Act iii, sc. 1, l. 59. [Antipholus of Ephesus]

Cry for blessings.—*Henry VIII,* ii, 1, 90.
Cry for food.—*Titus Andronicus,* v, 3, 180.
Cry for vengeance.—*I Henry VI,* v, 4, 53.
Crying confusion.—*Coriolanus,* iv, 6, 29.
Crying for a surgeon.—*Henry V,* iv, 1, 145.
Crying out for help.—*Othello,* ii, 3, 226.
Crying with loud voice.—*II Henry VI,* i, 1, 160.
Leave crying.—*Romeo and Juliet,* i, 3, 51.

9
Cry to be heard, as 'twere from heaven to earth.
Hamlet. Act iv, sc. 5, l. 216. [Laertes]

Cry a match.—*Romeo and Juliet,* ii, 4, 74.
Cry a mutiny.—*Othello,* ii, 3, 157.
Cry out.—*II Henry VI,* iii, 2, 395, and fifteen times in later plays.
Cry you (thee) mercy.—*II Henry VI,* i, 3, 142, and fifteen times in later plays.

10
Methinks I could Cry the amen.
Henry VIII. Act v, sc. 1, l. 24. [Lovell]

Cry amen.—*Henry V,* v, 2, 21, and seven times in later plays. "Amen" occurs forty times.

11
A cry more tuneable
Was never holla'd to, nor cheer'd with horn.
A Midsummer-Night's Dream, iv, 1, 129. See HOUND, 725:7.

12
What are you here that cry so grievously?
Othello. Act v, sc. 1, l. 53. [Iago]

Alas, what cry is that?—*Othello,* v, 2, 117.
The cry is very direful.—*Othello,* v, 1, 38.
Did not you hear a cry?—*Othello,* v, 1, 49.

13
O, the cry did knock Against my very heart.
The Tempest. Act i, sc. 2, l. 8. [Miranda]

I, not remembering how I cried out then,
Will cry it o'er again: it is a hint
That wrings mine eyes to 't.
The Tempest. Act i, sc. 2, l. 133. [Miranda]

Cry to the sea.—*The Tempest,* i, 2, 149.
Cry you all amain.—*Troilus and Cressida,* v, 8, 13.

14
Weke, weke! so cries a pig prepared to the spit.
Titus Andronicus. Act iv, sc. 2, l. 146. [Aaron] The only use of "weke, weke."

15
Julia: Alas!
Proteus: Why dost thou cry 'alas'? . . .
Julia: 'Twas pity love should be so contrary;
And thinking on it makes me cry 'alas!'
The Two Gentlemen of Verona. Act iv, sc. 4, l. 81.

Alas, the day!—*As You Like It,* iii, 2, 231, and six times in later plays.
Alas the while!—*The Merchant of Venice,* ii, 1, 31.
Alas, 'tis true.—*Sonnets,* cx.
Alas, poor Milan!—*The Tempest,* i, 2, 115.
Alas, poor world!—*Venus and Adonis,* l. 1075.

1
This dismal cry rings sadly in her ear,
Through which it enters to surprise her heart.
Venus and Adonis, l. 889.

2
O, the most piteous cry of the poor souls!
The Winter's Tale, iii, 3, 91. See under SHIPWRECK.
Bootless cries.—*Sonnets,* xxix.
Death-boding cries.—*The Rape of Lucrece,* l. 2165. The only use of "death-boding."

CUCKOLD

3
He that ears my land spares my team and gives me leave to in the crop; if I be his cuckold, he 's my drudge.
All's Well that Ends Well. Act i, sc. 3, l. 47. [Clown]
Young Charbon the puritan and old Poysam the papist, howsome'er their hearts are severed in religion, their heads are both one; they may joul horns together, like any deer i' the herd.
All's Well that Ends Well. Act i, sc. 3, l. 56. [Clown] The only use of "papist" and "joul." "Puritan" occurs five times.

4
As the nail to his hole, the cuckold to his horn.
All's Well that Ends Well. Act ii, sc. 2, l. 26. [Clown]
As horns are odious, they are necessary.
As You Like It. Act iii, sc. 3, l. 52. [Touchstone]
Many a man has good horns, and knows no end of them. Well, that is the dowry of his wife; 'tis none of his own getting. Horns? Even so. Poor men alone? No, no; the noblest deer hath them as huge as the rascal.
As You Like It. Act iii, sc. 3, l. 54. [Touchstone]
Horns, which such as you are fain to be beholding to your wives for.
As You Like It. Act iv, sc. 1, l. 59. [Rosalind]
What shall he have that kill'd the deer?
His leather skin and horns to wear.
Then sing him home;
Take thou no scorn to wear the horn;
It was a crest ere thou wast born:
Thy father's father wore it,
And thy father bore it:
The horn, the horn, the lusty horn
Is not a thing to laugh to scorn.
As You Like It. Act iv, sc. 2, l. 11. [Forester]
He may sleep in security; for he hath the horn of abundance, and the lightness of his wife shines through it.
II Henry IV. Act i, sc. 2, l. 51. [Falstaff]
Pistol: O, odious is the name!
Ford: What name, sir?
Pistol: The horn, I say.
The Merry Wives of Windsor. Act ii, sc. 1, l. 123.

5
Your highness said even now, I made you a duke: good my lord, do not recompense me in making me a cuckold.
Measure for Measure. Act v, sc. 1, l. 522. [Lucio]
Fifty-fold a cuckold!
Antony and Cleopatra. Act i, sc. 2, l. 69. [Charmian] The only use of "fifty-fold."
Made Lucifer cuckold.—*I Henry IV,* ii, 4, 371.

6
What, are we cuckolds ere we have deserved it?
The Merchant of Venice. Act v, sc. 1, l. 265. [Gratiano]
Poor cuckoldly knave.
The Merry Wives of Windsor. Act ii, sc. 2, l. 281. [Falstaff]
A crooked-pated, old, cuckoldly ram.
As You Like It, iii, 2, 87. The only use of "crooked-pated."

7
I will awe him with my cudgel: it shall hang like a meteor o'er the cuckold's horns.
The Merry Wives of Windsor. Act ii, sc. 2, l. 291. [Falstaff]
Buck! I would I could wash myself of the buck! Buck, buck, buck! Ay, buck; I warrant you, buck; and of the season too, it shall appear.
The Merry Wives of Windsor. Act iii, sc. 3, l. 167. [Ford]
Fate, ordaining he should be a cuckold, held his hand.
The Merry Wives of Windsor. Act iii, sc. 5, l. 106. [Falstaff] The only use of "ordaining."
If I have horns to make one mad, let the proverb go with me: I 'll be horn-mad.
The Merry Wives of Windsor. Act iii, sc. 5, l. 153. [Ford] "Horn-mad" is used also in *The Comedy of Errors,* ii, 1, 57, and *Much Ado about Nothing,* i, 1, 272.

8
Pluck off the bull's horns and set them in my forehead.
Much Ado about Nothing. Act i, sc. 1, l. 265. [Benedick]
But when shall we set the savage bull's horns on the sensible Benedick's head?
Much Ado about Nothing. Act v, sc. 1, l. 183. [Don Pedro]
Prince, thou art sad; get thee a wife, get thee a wife: there is no staff more reverend than one tipped with horn.
Much Ado about Nothing. Act v, sc. 4, l. 124. [Benedick]

9
If thou canst cuckold him, thou dost thyself a pleasure, me a sport.
Othello. Act i, sc. 3, l. 375. [Iago]
Othello: A horned man 's a monster and a beast.
Iago: There 's many a beast then in a populous city,
And many a civil monster.
Othello. Act iv, sc. 1, l. 63.

Othello: I will chop her into messes; cuckold me!
Iago: O, 'tis foul in her.
Othello. Act iv, sc. 1, l. 211.

1
Under your patience, gentle empress,
'Tis thought you have a goodly gift in horning; . . .
Jove shield your husband from his hounds to-day!
'Tis pity they should take him for a stag.
Titus Andronicus. Act ii, sc. 3, l. 66. [Lavinia] The only use of "horning."

Thy temples should be planted presently
With horns, as was Actæon's.
Titus Andronicus. Act ii, sc. 3, l. 62. [Tamora]

2
Paris is gored with Menelaus' horn.
Troilus and Cressida. Act i, sc. 1, l. 115. [Troilus]

The primitive statue, and oblique memorial of cuckolds; a thrifty shoeing-horn in a chain, hanging at his brother's leg.
Troilus and Cressida. Act v, sc. 1, l. 60. [Thersites] The only use of "shoeing-horn." "Oblique" occurs again in *Timon of Athens,* iv, 3, 18.

The cuckold and the cuckold-maker are at it. Now, bull! now, dog! 'Loo, Paris, 'loo! now my double-henned sparrow!
Troilus and Cressida. Act v, sc. 7, l. 9. [Thersites, referring to the encounter between Menelaus and Paris] The only use of "double-henned." "'Loo" (for halloo) is repeated in *King Lear,* iii, 4, 79.

If I spared any
That had a head to hit, either young or old,
He or she, cuckold or cuckold-maker,
Let me ne'er hope to see a chine again.
Henry VIII. Act v, sc. 4, l. 23. [Man] The only uses of "cuckold-maker." "Chine" (backbone) is repeated in *II Henry VI,* iv, 10, 61: "Chines of beef"; and in *The Taming of the Shrew,* iii, 2, 51.

3
There have been,
Or I am much deceived, cuckolds ere now;
And many a man there is, even at this present,
Now while I speak this, holds his wife by the arm,
That little thinks she has been sluiced in 's absence
And his pond fish'd by his next neighbour, by
Sir Smile, his neighbour; nay, there 's comfort in 't
Whiles other men have gates and those gates open'd,
As mine, against their will.
The Winter's Tale. Act i, sc. 2, l. 190. [Leontes] "Sluiced" is repeated in Richard II, i, 1, 103.

CUCKOO

4
The cuckoo builds not for himself.
Antony and Cleopatra. Act ii, sc. 6, l. 28. [Pompey]

5
So when he had occasion to be seen,
He was but as the cuckoo is in June,
Heard, not regarded.
I Henry IV. Act iii, sc. 2, l. 74. [King Henry]

6
The hedge-sparrow fed the cuckoo so long,
That it had its head bit off by its young.
King Lear. Act i, sc. 4, l. 235. [Fool] The only use of "hedge-sparrow."

7
The cuckoo then, on every tree,
Mocks married men; for thus sings he,
Cuckoo, cuckoo: O word of fear,
Unpleasing to a married ear!
Love's Labour's Lost. Act v, sc. 2, l. 908. [Song]

The plain-song cuckoo gray,
Whose note full many a man doth mark,
And dares not answer nay;—
for, indeed, who would set his wit to so foolish a bird? who would give a bird the lie, though he cry 'cuckoo' never so?
A Midsummer-Night's Dream. Act iii, sc. 1, l. 134. [Bottom] "Plain-song" (a simple melody) is repeated in *Henry V*, iii, 2, 6, and in *Henry VIII*, i, 3, 45.

Your cuckoo sings by kind.—*All's Well that Ends Well,* i, 3, 67.

8
Hateful cuckoos hatch in sparrows' nests.
The Rape of Lucrece, l. 849.

CUDGELLING

See also Beating, Whipping

9
Cudgel thy brains no more about it.
Hamlet, v, 1, 63. See under BRAIN.

10
An he were here, I would cudgel him like a dog.
I Henry IV. Act iii, sc. 3, l. 100. [Falstaff]

I 'll cudgel him and make him cry O!
Twelfth Night. Act ii, sc. 5, l. 145. [Sir Toby]

Strucken him with a cudgel.—*Coriolanus,* iv, 5, 156.

11
Hostess: He . . . said he would cudgel you.
Prince: What! he did not?
Hostess: There 's neither faith, truth, nor womanhood in me else. . . . He called you Jack, and said he would cudgel you.
Falstaff: Did I, Bardolph?
Bardolph: Indeed, Sir John, you said so.
I Henry IV. Act iii, sc. 3, l. 123.

Pistol: Quiet thy cudgel; thou dost see I eat.
Fluellen: Much good do you, scauld knave, heartily. . . . If I owe you any thing, I will pay you in cudgels: you shall be a woodmonger, and buy nothing of me but cudgels.
Henry V. Act v, sc. 1, l. 54. "Scauld" is used three times in this scene, and occurs nowhere else. The only use of "woodmonger."

One sound cudgel of four foot.—*Henry VIII,* iv, 4, 19.

1
I will awe him with my cudgel.
The Merry Wives of Windsor, ii, 2, 292. See under CUCKOLD.

Heaven guide him to my husband's cudgel, and the devil guide his cudgel afterwards!
The Merry Wives of Windsor. Act iv, sc. 2, l. 87. [Mrs. Page]

I'll have the cudgel hallowed and hung o'er the alter; it hath done meritorious service.
The Merry Wives of Windsor. Act iv, sc. 2, l. 216.

Washed and cudgelled.—*The Merry Wives of Windsor,* iv, 5, 99.

2
I might have cudgelled thee out of thy single life, to make thee a double-dealer.
Much Ado about Nothing. Act v, sc. 4, l. 115. [Claudio] "Double-dealer" is repeated in *Twelfth Night,* v, 1, 38. See under DECEIT.

I have been to-night exceedingly well cudgelled.
Othello. Act ii, sc. 3, l. 371. [Roderigo]

Our ears are cudgell'd.—*King John,* ii, 1, 464.

Honour is cudgell'd.—*Henry V,* v, 1, 90.

3
Prophetically proud of an heroical cudgelling.
Troilus and Cressida. Act iii, sc. 3, l. 249. [Thersites] The only use of "cudgelling." "Prophetically" is repeated in *I Henry IV,* iii, 2, 38.

CUNNING

See also Deceit, Policy

4
She is cunning past man's thought.
Antony and Cleopatra. Act i, sc. 2, l. 150. [Antony]

This cannot be cunning in her.
Antony and Cleopatra. Act i, sc. 2, l. 155. [Enobarbus]

And in our sports my better cunning faints
Under his chance.
Antony and Cleopatra. Act ii, sc. 3, l. 34. [Antony]

Try thy cunning.—*Antony and Cleopatra,* iii, 12, 31.

A noble cunning.—*Coriolanus,* iv, 1, 9.

5
I'll potch at him some way
Or wrath or craft may get him.
Coriolanus. Act i, sc. 10, l. 15. [Aufidius] The only use of "potch" (to thrust at).

You have made fair hands,
You and your crafts! you have crafted fair!
Coriolanus. Act iv, sc. 6, l. 117. [Menenius] The only use of "crafted."

She had fitted you with her craft.
Cymbeline. Act v, sc. 5, l. 55. [Cornelius]

6
And thus do we of wisdom and of reach,
With windlasses and with assays of bias,
By indirections find directions out.
Hamlet. Act ii, sc. 1, l. 64. [Polonius] The only use of "windlasses" (devious ways).

I went round to work.
Hamlet. Act ii, sc. 2, l. 139. [Polonius]

7
I essentially am not in madness,
But mad in craft.
Hamlet. Act iii, sc. 4, l. 187. [Hamlet]

Crafty-sick.—*II Henry IV,* Ind., l. 37. The only use of the compound.

O, 'tis most sweet,
When in one line two crafts directly meet.
Hamlet. Act iii, sc. 4, l. 209. [Hamlet]

8
Rather choose to hide them in a net.
Henry V. Act i, sc. 2, l. 93. [Canterbury]

9
Is this thy cunning, thou deceitful dame?
I Henry VI. Act ii, sc. 1, l. 50. [Charles]

We have been guided by thee hitherto
And of thy cunning had no diffidence.
I Henry VI. Act iii, sc. 3, l. 9. [Charles]

10
Would ye not think his cunning to be great, that could restore this cripple to his legs again?
II Henry VI. Act ii, sc. 1, l. 132. [Gloucester]

11
I can add colours to the chameleon,
Change shapes with Proteus for advantages,
And set the murderous Machiavel to school.
III Henry VI. Act iii, sc. 2, l. 191. [Gloucester]

Notorious Machiavel!—*I Henry VI,* v, 4, 74.

Am I a Machiavel?—*Merry Wives of Windsor,* iii, 1, 104. The only references to Machiavel.

12
We shall find of him A shrewd contriver.
Julius Cæsar. Act ii, sc. 1, l. 157. [Cassius]

A secret and villanous contriver.
As You Like It, i, 1, 151.

Close contriver.—*Macbeth,* iii, 5, 7.

Dam'd contriver.—*Titus Andronicus,* iv, 1, 36. The only uses of "contriver."

13
There's the cunning of it.
King Lear. Act i, sc. 2, l. 64. [Edmund]

In cunning I must draw my sword upon you.
King Lear. Act ii, sc. 1, l. 31. [Edmund]

In the boldness of my cunning, I will lay my self in hazard.
Measure for Measure. Act iv, sc. 2, l. 165. [Duke]

14
Craft against vice I must apply.
Measure for Measure. Act iii, sc. 2, l. 291. [Duke]

False-creeping craft and perjury.
The Rape of Lucrece, l. 1517. The only use of "false-creeping."

15
With cunning hast thou filch'd my daughter's heart.
A Midsummer-Night's Dream. Act i, sc. 1, l. 36. [Egeus] The only use of "filch'd."

You do advance your cunning more and more.
A Midsummer-Night's Dream. Act iii, sc. 2, l. 128. [Helena]

Be cunning in the working this.
Much Ado about Nothing. Act ii, sc. 2, l. 53. [Don John]

As cunning as fast and loose.—*Love's Labour's Lost,* iii, 1, 104.

Cunning in dumbness.—*Troilus and Cressida,* iii, 2, 140.

Cunning in fence.—*Twelfth Night,* iii, 4, 312.

1
Sir, she can turn, and turn, and yet go on,
And turn again.
Othello. Act iv, sc. 1, l. 264. [Othello]

2
So cunning and so young is wonderful.
Richard III. Act iii, sc. 1, l. 135. [Buckingham]

What need'st thou wound with cunning when thy might
Is more than my o'er-press'd defence can bide?
Sonnets. No. cxxxix.

3
To cunning men
I will be very kind, and liberal.
The Taming of the Shrew. Act i, sc. 1, l. 97. [Baptista]

Cunning in music, . . . cunning in Greek.
The Taming of the Shrew, ii, 1, 56.

4
We 'll over-reach the greybeard.
The Taming of the Shrew. Act iii, sc. 2, l. 147. [Tranio]

And will o'erreach them in their own devices.
Titus Andronicus. Act v, sc. 2, l. 142. [Titus] "O'erreach" is used a third time in *Hamlet*, v, 1, 87.

Gross overreaching.—*The Merry Wives of Windsor*, v, 5, 145. The only use of "overreaching."

5
I 'll find some cunning practice out of hand.
Titus Andronicus. Act v, sc. 2, l. 77. [Tamora]

Hence, bashful cunning!
The Tempest. Act iii, sc. 1, l. 81. [Miranda]

6
The serpentine craft of thy caduceus.
Troilus and Cressida. Act ii, sc. 3, l. 13. [Thersites] The only use of "serpentine" and "caduceus."

I show more craft than love.
Troilus and Cressida. Act iii, sc. 2, l. 160. [Cressida]

7
Under your hard construction must I sit,
To force that on you, in a shameful cunning,
Which you knew none of yours.
Twelfth Night. Act iii, sc. 1, l. 126. [Olivia]

His false cunning,
Not meaning to partake with me in danger,
Taught him to face me out of his acquaintance,
And grew a twenty years removed thing
While one would wink.
Twelfth Night. Act v, sc. 1, l. 89. [Antonio]

I will so plead
That you shall say my cunning drift excels.
The Two Gentlemen of Verona. Act iv, sc. 2, l. 82. [Proteus]

8
Do it so cunningly
That my discovery be not aimed at.
The Two Gentlemen of Verona. Act iii, sc. 1, l. 44. [Proteus]

Cunningly effected.—*Titus Andronicus*, ii, 3, 6.

Most cunningly.—*Troilus and Cressida*, iv, 4, 93.

Ne'er so cunningly.—*I Henry VI*, iv, 1, 110. **The only uses of "cunningly."**

CUP

See also Drinking, Wine

9
Where 's this cup I call'd for?
Antony and Cleopatra. Act ii, sc. 7, l. 60. [Pompey]

Fill till the cup be hid.
Antony and Cleopatra. Act ii, sc. 7, l. 93. [Pompey]

Cup us, till the world go round,
Cup us, till the world go round!
Antony and Cleopatra, ii, 7, 124. See under WINE.

Scant not thy cups.—*Antony and Cleopatra*, iv, 2, 21.

10
I think you all have drunk of Circe's cup.
The Comedy of Errors, v, 1, 270. See under MYSTERY.

Plenty's cup.—*Pericles*, i, 4, 52.

It is the poison'd cup.
Hamlet. Act v, sc. 2, l. 203. [King]

Give him the cup.—*Hamlet*, v, 2, 294.

Give me the cups.—*Hamlet*, v, 2, 285; v, 2, 354.

11
Fill the cup, and let it come.
II Henry IV, v, 3, 56. See under DRINKING.

In . . . his cups.—*Henry V*, iv, 7, 48.

12
How often hast thou waited at my cup.
II Henry VI, iv, 1, 56. See under HUMILITY.

13
Taste . . . The cup of their deservings.
King Lear, v, 3, 304. See under FRIEND AND ENEMY.

Welcome the sour cup of prosperity!
Love's Labour 's Lost, i, 1, 315. See under PROSPERITY.

Cup of alteration.—*II Henry IV*, iii, 1, 52.

Cup of canary.—*Twelfth Night*, i, 3, 85.

Cup of charneco.—*II Henry VI*, ii, 3, 62. The only use of "charneco," a kind of wine.

Cup of Madeira.—*I Henry IV*, i, 2, 128.

Cup of sack.—*I Henry IV*, i, 2, 8; ii, 2, 49; ii, 4, 129; 139; 345; 423; *II Henry IV*, ii, 4, 121; *II Henry VI*, ii, 3, 60; *The Taming of the Shrew*, Ind., 2, 2.

Cup of wine.—*II Henry IV*, v, 3, 47; 48; *Richard III*, i, 4, 166; *Romeo and Juliet*, i, 2, 86.

Cup of hot wine.—*Coriolanus*, ii, 1, 52.

14
They could never get her so much as sip on a cup with the proudest of them all.
The Merry Wives of Windsor. Act ii, sc. 2, l. 76. [Mistress Quickly]

15
I have drunk but one cup to-night, and that was craftily qualified too.
Othello. Act ii, sc. 3, l. 40. [Cassio] "Craftily" is repeated in *Measure for Measure*, ii, 4, 75.

If I can fasten but one cup upon him,
With that which he has drunk to-night already,
He 'll be as full of quarrel and offence
As my young mistress' dog.
Othello. Act ii, sc. 3, l. 50. [Iago]

The very elements of this warlike isle,
Have I to-night fluster'd with flowing cups.
Othello. Act ii, sc. 3, l. 59. [Iago] The only use of "fluster'd."

Flowing cups.—*Henry V,* iv, 3, 55.
Fresh cups.—*Cymbeline,* v, 3, 71.
Golden cup.—*III Henry VI,* ii, 5, 52.

1 Every inordinate cup is unblessed.
Othello, ii, 3, 311. See under DRINKING.

Second cup.—*Romeo and Juliet,* iii, 1, 9.

2 Here, with a cup that 's stored unto the brim.
Pericles, ii, 3, 50. See under DRINKING HEALTHS.

3 What 's here? a cup, closed in my true love's hand?
Romeo and Juliet. Act v, sc. 3, l. 161. [Juliet]

4 And to his palate doth prepare the cup.
Sonnets. No. cxiv.

I am his cupbearer.—*Winter's Tale,* i, 2, 345.
Thou, his cupbearer.—*The Winter's Tale,* i, 2, 313. The only uses of "cupbearer."

CUPID

5 A world
Of pretty, fond, adoptious christendoms,
That blinking Cupid gossips.
All's Well that Ends Well. Act i, sc. 1, l. 187. [Helena] The only use of "adoptious."

6 It may be said of him that Cupid hath clapped him o' the shoulder, but I 'll warrant him heart-whole.
As You Like It. Act iv, sc. 1, l. 47. [Rosalind] The only use of "heart-whole."

That same wicked bastard of Venus that was begot of thought, conceived of spleen and born of madness, that blind rascally boy that abuses every one's eyes because his own are out, let him be judge how deep I am in love.
As You Like It. Act iv, sc. 1, l. 216. [Rosalind]

Methinks I should out-swear Cupid.
Love's Labour 's Lost. Act i, sc. 2, l. 67. [Armado]

We 'll outface them and outswear them too.
The Merchant of Venice. Act iv, sc. 2, l. 17. The only uses of "outswear."

7 Cupid's butt-shaft is too hard for Hercules' club; and therefore too much odds for a Spaniard's rapier. The first and second cause will not serve my turn; the passado he respects not, the duello he regards not: his disgrace is to be called boy; but his glory is to subdue men.
Love's Labour 's Lost. Act i, sc. 2, l. 181. [Armado] "Duello" is repeated in *Twelfth Night,* iii, 4, 337; "passado" in *Romeo and Juliet,* ii, 4, 26, and iii, 1, 88.

The very pin of his heart cleft with the blind bow-boy's butt-shaft.
Romeo and Juliet. Act ii, sc. 4, l. 15. [Mercutio] The only use of "bow-boy." "Butt-shaft" occurs only in this and the preceding quotation.

I swear to thee, by Cupid's strongest bow,
By his best arrow with the golden head.
A Midsummer-Night's Dream. Act i, sc. 1, l. 169. [Hermia]

8 This wimpled, whining, purblind, wayward boy;
This senior-junior, giant-dwarf, Dan Cupid;
Regent of love-rhymes, lord of folded arms,
The anointed sovereign of sighs and groans,
Liege of all loiterers and malcontents,
Dread prince of plackets, king of codpieces,
Sole imperator and great general
Of trotting 'paritors.
Love's Labour 's Lost. Act iii, sc. 1, l. 181. [Biron] The only use of "wimpled," "senior-junior," "giant-dwarf," "Dan Cupid," "love-rhymes," "imperator," "trotting" and "'paritors" (apparitors, summoning officers of an ecclesiastical court). "Plackets" (petticoats, or openings in petticoats) occurs five times.

It is a plague
That Cupid will impose for my neglect
Of his almighty dreadful little might.
Love's Labour 's Lost. Act iii, sc. 1, l. 203. [Biron]

Shot, by heaven! Proceed, sweet Cupid: thou hast thumped him with thy bird-bolt under the left pap.
Love's Labour 's Lost. Act iv, sc. 3, l. 22. [Biron] "Thumped" is repeated in *Richard III,* v, 3, 334; and "bird-bolt" in *Much Ado about Nothing,* i, 1, 42, and in *Twelfth Night,* i, 5, 100.

Saint Cupid, then! and soldiers, to the field!
Love's Labour 's Lost. Act iv, sc. 3, l. 366. [King Ferdinand]

9 Come, come, Nerissa; for I long to see
Quick Cupid's post that comes so mannerly.
The Merchant of Venice. Act ii, sc. 9, l. 99. [Portia]

Now is Cupid a child of conscience.
The Merry Wives of Windsor. Act v, sc. 5, l. 32. [Falstaff]

10 Love looks not with the eyes, but with the mind;
And therefore is wing'd Cupid painted blind.
A Midsummer-Night's Dream. Act i, sc. 1, l. 233. [Helena]

A naked blind boy.—*Henry V,* v, 2, 325.

No, do thy worst, blind Cupid; I 'll not love.
King Lear. Act iv, sc. 6, l. 140. [King Lear]

Smiling Cupids.—*Antony and Cleopatra,* ii, 2, 207.
Winking Cupids.—*Cymbeline,* ii, 4, 89.

11 As waggish boys in game themselves forswear
So the boy Love is perjured every where.
A Midsummer-Night's Dream. Act i, sc. 1, l. 240. [Helena]

Cupid is a knavish lad,
Thus to make poor females mad.
A Midsummer-Night's Dream. Act iii, sc. 2, l. 440. [Puck]

12 O god of love!
Much Ado about Nothing. Act iii, sc. 1, l. 47. [Hero]

The god of love, That sits above.
Much Ado about Nothing, v, 2, 26. The only uses of "god of love."

1 Of this matter
Is little Cupid's crafty arrow made,
That only wounds by hearsay.
Much Ado about Nothing. Act iii, sc. 1, l. 21. [Hero] The only use of "hearsay" in the plays. It occurs again in *Sonnets*, xxi.

Some Cupid kills with arrows, some with traps.
Much Ado about Nothing. Act iii, sc. 1, l. 106. [Hero]

He hath twice or thrice cut Cupid's bow-string and the little hangman dare not shoot at him.
Much Ado about Nothing. Act iii, sc. 2, l. 10. [Don Pedro] "Bow-string" is repeated in *A Midsummer-Night's Dream*, i, 2, 114.

2
Light-wing'd toys Of feather'd Cupid.
Othello. Act i, sc. 3, l. 269. [Othello] The only use of "light-wing'd."

3
She 'll not be hit With Cupid's arrow.
Romeo and Juliet. Act i, sc. 1, l. 214. [Romeo]

We 'll have no Cupid hoodwink'd with a scarf,
Bearing a Tartar's painted bow of lath,
Scaring the ladies with a crow-keeper.
Romeo and Juliet. Act i, sc. 4, l. 4. [Benvolio] The only use of "scaring." "Crow-keeper" is repeated in *King Lear*, iv, 6, 88.

Mercutio: You are a lover; borrow Cupid's wings,
And soar with them above a common bound.
Romeo: I am too sore enpierced with his shaft
To soar with his light feathers.
Romeo and Juliet. Act i, sc. 4, l. 17. The only use of "enpierced."

Therefore do nimble-pinion'd doves draw love,
And therefore hath the wind-swift Cupid wings.
Romeo and Juliet. Act ii, sc. 5, l. 7. [Juliet] The only use of "nimble-pinion'd" and "wind-swift."

4
Speak to my gossip Venus one fair word,
One nick-name for her purblind son and heir,
Young Adam Cupid, he that shot so trim,
When King Cophetua loved the beggar-maid!
Romeo and Juliet. Act ii, sc. 1, l. 11. [Mercutio] The only use of "beggar-maid." Mercutio is paraphrasing a line of the old ballad, *King Cophetua and the Beggar Maid* (Percy, *Reliques of Ancient English Poetry*. Ser. i, bk. ii, No. 6):

The blinded boy, that shootes so trim,
From heaven downe did hie;
He drew a dart and shot at him,
In place where he did lye.

5
The little Love-god lying once asleep
Laid by his side his heart-inflaming brand,
Whilst many nymphs that vow'd chaste life to keep
Came tripping by; but in her maiden hand
The fairest votary took up that fire
Which many legions of true hearts had warmed;
And so the general of hot desire
Was sleeping by a virgin hand disarm'd.
This brand she quenched in a cool well by,
Which from Love's fire took heat perpetual,
Growing a bath and healthful remedy
For men diseased; but I, my mistress' thrall,
Came there for cure, and this by that I prove,
Love's fire heats water, water cools not love.
Sonnets. No. cliv. The only use of "heart-inflaming" and "disarm'd."

Cupid is no longer an archer: his glory shall be ours, for we are the only love-gods.
Much Ado about Nothing. Act ii, sc. 1, l. 401. [Don Pedro] The only uses of "love-gods."

6
Her waspish-headed son has broke his arrows,
Swears he will shoot no more but play with sparrows
And be a boy right out.
The Tempest. Act iv, sc. 1, l. 99. [Iris] The only use of "waspish-headed."

7
Let thy song be love: this love will undo us all. O Cupid, Cupid, Cupid!
Troilus and Cressida. Act iii, sc. 1, l. 119. [Helen]

From Cupid's shoulder pluck his painted wings.
Troilus and Cressida. Act iii, sc. 2, l. 15. [Troilus]

In all Cupid's pageant there is presented no monster.
Troilus and Cressida. Act iii, sc. 2, l. 80. [Troilus]

And Cupid grant all tongue-tied maidens here
Bed, chamber, Pandar to provide this gear!
Troilus and Cressida. Act iii, sc. 2, l. 219. [Pandarus]

The weak wanton Cupid
Shall from your neck unloose his amorous fold,
And, like a dew-drop from the lion's mane,
Be shook to air.
Troilus and Cressida. Act iii, sc. 3, l. 222. [Patroclus]

CUR

See also Dog

8
Shall dunghill curs confront the Helicons?
II Henry IV. Act v, sc. 3, l. 108. [Pistol] The only use of "Helicons."

9
Small curs are not regarded when they grin;
But great men tremble when the lion roars.
II Henry VI. Act iii, sc. 1, l. 18. [Queen]

Oft have I seen a hot o'erweening cur
Run back and bite, because he was withheld;
Who, being suffer'd with the bear's fell paw,
Hath clapp'd his tail between his legs and cried.
II Henry VI. Act v, sc. 1, l. 151. [Richard]

Village-curs, Bark when their fellows do.—
Henry VIII, ii, 4, 159. See under Enemy. The only use of "village-curs."

10
This butcher's cur is venom-mouth'd, and I
Have not the power to muzzle him.
Henry VIII. Act i, sc. 1, l. 120. [Buckingham] The only use of "venom-mouth'd."

It is the most impenetrable cur
That ever kept with men.
The Merchant of Venice. Act iii, sc. 3, l. 18. [Salarino] The only use of "impenetrable."
Cruel-hearted cur.—*The Two Gentlemen of Verona,* ii, 3, 10. The only use of "cruel-hearted."
Damned cur!—*Troilus and Cressida,* ii, 1, 93.
Fell-lurking curs.—*II Henry VI,* v, 1, 146. The only use of "fell-lurking."
Foolish curs.—*Henry V,* iii, 7, 153.
French curs.—*I Henry VI,* iv, 2, 47.
Mongrel cur.—*Troilus and Cressida,* v, 4, 14.
Poor cur.—*Taming of the Shrew,* Ind., 1, 17.
Prick-ear'd cur.—*Henry V,* ii, 1, 44. The only use of "prick-ear'd."
Stranger cur.—*Merchant of Venice,* i, 3, 119.
Whoreson cur.—*Troilus and Cressida,* ii, 1, 44.
Whoreson indistinguishable cur.—*Troilus and Cressida,* v, 1, 33. The only use of "indistinguishable."
Common cry of curs!—*Coriolanus,* iii, 3, 120.

1
Like curs to tear us all to pieces.
Richard II. Act ii, sc. 2, l. 139. [Bushy]
This carnal cur
Preys on the issue of his mother's body.
Richard III. Act iv, sc. 4, l. 56. [Queen]

2
Two of thy whelps, fell curs of bloody kind,
Have here bereft my brother of his life.
Titus Andronicus. Act ii, sc. 3, l. 281. [Saturninus]
Freckled whelp.—*The Tempest,* i, 2, 283.
Young whelp.—*I Henry VI,* iv, 7, 35.
Lion's whelp.—*I Henry IV,* iii, 3, 167; *Henry V,* i, 2, 109; *Antony and Cleopatra,* iii, 13, 94; *Cymbeline,* v, 5, 138; 435; 443.
Like to whelps.—*I Henry VI,* i, 5, 26. The only uses of "whelp."

3
Two curs shall tame each other: pride alone
Must tarre the mastiffs on, as 'twere their bone.
Troilus and Cressida. Act i, sc. 3, l. 391. [Nestor]
Mastiffs of unmatchable courage.—*Henry V,* ii, 7, 151.

4
O, 'tis a foul thing when a cur cannot keep himself in all companies! I would have, as one should say, one that takes upon him to be a dog indeed, to be, as it were, a dog at all things.
The Two Gentlemen of Verona. Act iv, sc. 4, l. 11. [Launce]
Marry, she says your dog was a cur, and tells you currish thanks is good enough for such a present.
The Two Gentlemen of Verona. Act iv, sc. 4, l. 52. [Launce]
Currish Jew.—*Merchant of Venice,* iv, 1, 292.
Currish riddles.—*III Henry VI,* v, 5, 26.
Currish spirit.—*Merchant of Venice,* iv, 1, 133.
Something currish.—*The Taming of the Shrew,* v, 2, 54. The only uses of "currish."
Play the cur.—*The Two Gentlemen of Verona,* iv, 4, 2.
The cur is excellent at faults.
Twelfth Night. Act ii, sc. 5, l. 140. [Fabian]

CURE

See also Remedy

5
I 'ld venture
The well-lost life of mine on his grace's cure
By such a day and hour.
All's Well that Ends Well. Act i, sc. 3, l. 253. [Helena] The only use of "well-lost."
Will you be cured of your infirmity?
All's Well that Ends Well. Act ii, sc. 1, l. 71. [Lafeu]
But may not be so credulous of cure.
All's Well that Ends Well. Act ii, sc. 1, l. 118. [King]
Thou know'st she has raised me from my sickly bed.
All's Well that Ends Well. Act ii, sc. 3, l. 118. [King]

6
Rosalind: I profess curing it [love] by counsel.
Orlando: Did you ever cure any so?
Rosalind: Yes, one. . . . Thus I cured him; and this way will I take upon me to wash your liver as clean as a sound sheep's heart, that there shall not be one spot of love in 't.
Orlando: I would not be cured, youth.
As You Like It. Act iii, sc. 2, l. 426.
Thou must cure me.—*Hamlet,* iv, 3, 69.
Cure her of that.—*Macbeth,* v, 3, 39.
Must I take the cure upon me?—*Timon of Athens,* iii, 3, 12.
Bold cure.—*Othello,* ii, 1, 51.
Hard cure.—*King Lear,* iii, 6, 107.

7
Thou art a cure fit for a king.
Henry VIII. Act ii, sc. 2, l. 76. [King Henry]
Is there no way to cure this?
No new device to beat this from his brains?
Henry VIII. Act iii, sc. 2, l. 216. [Wolsey]
Cure thy brains!—*The Tempest,* v, 1, 59.
Cure deafness.—*The Tempest,* i, 2, 106.

8
In him
It lies to cure me: and the cure is, to
Remove these thoughts from you.
Henry VIII. Act ii, sc. 4, l. 100. [Wolsey]

9
'Past cure is still past care.'
Love's Labour's Lost. Act v, sc. 2, l. 28. [Rosaline] The line is quoted, for Rosaline is repeating an old proverb, referred to by Robert Greene (*Works,* ii, 154), "Remember the old proverb . . . past cure, past care, without remedie, without remembrance."
Such a one and such a one were past cure of the thing you wot of, unless they kept very good diet.
Measure for Measure. Act ii, sc. 1, l. 114. [Pompey]
Past cure I am, now reason is past care.
Sonnets. No. cxlvii.
But know I think and think I know most sure
My art is not past power nor you past cure.
All's Well that Ends Well. Act ii, sc. 1, l. 160. [Helena]
Past cure.—*The Taming of the Shrew,* iii, 2, 54; *Romeo and Juliet,* iv, 1, 45; *King John,* iv, 2, 86; *The Tempest,* v, 1, 141.

1
He is a curer of souls, and you a curer of bodies.
The Merry Wives of Windsor. Act ii, sc. 3, l. 40. [Shallow]
I 'll be a curer of madmen.
Troilus and Cressida. Act v, sc. 1, l. 55. [Thersites] The only uses of "curer."
2
To strange sores strangely they strain the cure.
Much Ado about Nothing. Act iv, sc. 1, l. 254. [Friar Francis]
First Senator: Leave us to cure this cause.
Menenius: For 'tis a sore upon us,
You cannot tent yourself.
Coriolanus. Act iii, sc. 1, l. 235.
3
A seething bath, which yet men prove
Against strange maladies a sovereign cure.
Sonnets. No. cliii.
I sick withal, the help of bath desired,
And thither hied, a sad distemper'd guest,
But found no cure; the bath for my help lies
Where Cupid got new fire—my mistress' eyes.
Sonnets. No. cliii.
A bath and healthful remedy For men diseased.
Sonnets. No. cliv.

CURIOSITY

4
My youngest boy, and yet my eldest care,
At eighteen years became inquisitive.
The Comedy of Errors. Act i, sc. 1, l. 126. [Ægeon] "Inquisitive" is repeated in *The Comedy of Errors,* i, 2, 38.
5
For your desire to know what is between us,
O'ermaster 't as you may.
Hamlet. Act i, sc. 5, l. 139. [Hamlet] The only use of "o'ermaster."
6
For curious I cannot be with you.
The Taming of the Shrew. Act iv, sc. 4, l. 36. [Pedant]
I am something curious.—*Cymbeline,* i, 6, 191.
7
Mock'd thee for too much curiosity.
Timon of Athens, iv, 3, 303. See under EXTREMITY.
Curiosity of nations.—*King Lear,* i, 2, 4.
Jealous curiosity.—*King Lear,* i, 4, 75.
Curiosity in neither.—*King Lear,* i, 1, 6. The only uses of "curiosity."

CURRENT

See also River, Stream

8
He 'll turn your current in a ditch,
And make your channel his?
Coriolanus. Act iii, sc. 1, l. 96. [Coriolanus]
Their currents turn awry.—*Hamlet,* iii, 1, 87.
9
O'er-walk a current roaring loud.
I Henry IV, i, 3, 192. See under BOOK.
10
It holds current that I told you yesternight.
I Henry IV. Act ii, sc. 1, l. 59. [Chamberlain]
Go so general current through the world.
I Henry IV. Act iv, sc. 1, l. 5. [Hotspur]
Go current.—*Richard III,* ii, 1, 94.
Come current.—*I Henry IV,* i, 3, 68.
Current in our land.—*Richard II,* v, 3, 123.
Current with him.—*Richard II,* i, 3, 231.
Pass them current.—*I Henry IV,* ii, 3, 97.
Scarce current.—*Richard III,* i, 3, 256.
Current gold.—*Richard III,* iv, 2, 9.
Current music.—*Henry VIII,* i, 3, 47.
Current repentance.—*II Henry IV,* ii, 1, 132.
11
I 'll have the current in this place damm'd up.
I Henry IV, iii, 1, 101. See under RIVER.
12
We Must take the current when it serves,
Or lose our ventures.
Julius Cæsar, iv, 3, 223. See under TIDE, and OPPORTUNITY.
13
Say, shall the current of our right run on?
King John. Act ii, sc. 1, l. 335. [King John]
Thus ebbs and flows the current of her sorrow.
The Rape of Lucrece, l. 1569.
Current of thy cruelty.—*The Merchant of Venice,* iv, 1, 64.
Currents of a heady fight.—*I Henry IV,* ii, 3, 58.
Corrupted currents of this world.—*Hamlet,* iii, 3, 57.
14
O, two such silver currents, when they join,
Do glorify the banks that bound them in.
King John. Act ii, sc. 1, l. 441. [Citizen]
Brinish current.—*A Lover's Complaint,* l. 284.
Icy current.—*Othello,* iii, 3, 454.
15
Currents that spring from one most gracious head.
Richard II, iii, 3, 108. See under ANCESTRY.
16
The current that with gentle murmur glides,
Thou know'st, being stopp'd, impatiently doth rage;
But when his fair course is not hindered,
He makes sweet music with the enamell'd stones,
Giving a gentle kiss to every sedge
He overtaketh in his pilgrimage,
And so by many winding nooks he strays
With willing sport to the wild ocean.
The Two Gentlemen of Verona. Act ii, sc. 7, l. 25. [Julia] "Enamell'd" is repeated in *The Comedy of Errors,* ii, 1, 109, and in *A Midsummer-Night's Dream,* ii, 1, 255.
Like an impediment in the current, made it more violent and unruly.
Measure for Measure, iii, 1, 251. See under UNKINDNESS.

CURSE

See also Denunciation, Swearing

I—Curses and Cursing

17
I would the gods had nothing else to do
But to confirm my curses!
Coriolanus. Act iv, sc. 2, l. 45. [Volumnia]
Curse them as enemies.—*Coriolanus,* i, 1, 80.
Cursing yourselves.—*Coriolanus,* iii, 3, 78.
Dogg'd with curses.—*Coriolanus,* v, 3, 144.

1 The primal eldest curse, . . .
A brother's murder.
Hamlet. Act iii, sc. 3, l. 37. [King] "Primal" is repeated in *Antony and Cleopatra,* i, 4, 41: "Primal state."

2 Shall it be,
That you a world of curses undergo,
Being the agents, or base second means,
The cords, the ladder, or the hangman rather?
I Henry IV. Act i, sc. 3, l. 163. [Hotspur]

And some are yet ungotten and unborn
That shall have cause to curse the Dauphin's scorn.
Henry V. Act i, sc. 2, l. 287. [King Henry] The only use of "ungotten."

3
What! shall we curse the planets of mishap
That plotted thus our glory's overthrow?
I Henry VI. Act i, sc. 1, l. 23. [Exeter]

La Pucelle: I prithee, give me leave to curse awhile.
York: Curse, miscreant, when thou comest to the stake.
I Henry VI. Act v, sc. 3, l. 43.

4
And these dread curses, like the sun 'gainst glass,
Or like an overcharged gun, recoil,
And turn the force of them upon thyself.
II Henry VI. Act iii, sc. 2, l. 330. [Queen]

Now, by the ground that I am banish'd from,
Well could I curse away a winter's night,
Though standing naked on a mountain top,
Where biting cold would never let grass grow,
And think it but a minute spent in sport.
II Henry VI. Act iii, sc. 2, l. 334. [Suffolk]

Fall a-cursing.—*Hamlet,* ii, 2, 615. The only use of "a-cursing."

Wrathful curse.—*II Henry VI,* iii, 2, 155.

5
Ere sunset I 'll make thee curse the deed.
III Henry VI. Act ii, sc. 2, l. 116. [Richard]

Curse the cause.—*I Henry VI,* iv, 3, 44.

6 Their curses now
Live where their prayers did.
Henry VIII. Act i, sc. 2, l. 62. [Queen]

It calls,
I fear, too many curses on their heads
That were the authors.
Henry VIII. Act ii, sc. 1, l. 137. [Gentleman]

His curses and his blessings
Touch me alike, they 're breath I not believe in.
Henry VIII. Act ii, sc. 2, l. 53. [Norfolk]

7
Forget not, in your speed, Antonius,
To touch Calpurnia; for our elders say,
The barren, touched in this holy chase,
Shake off their sterile curse.
Julius Cæsar. Act i, sc. 2, l. 6. [Cæsar]

A curse shall light upon the limbs of men.
Julius Cæsar. Act iii, sc. 1, l. 262. [Antony]

8 By the lawful power that I have,
Thou shalt stand cursed and excommunicate.
King John. Act iii, sc. 1, l. 172. [Pandulph] The only use of "excommunicate." "Excommunication" is also used only once, in *Much Ado about Nothing,* iii, 5, 69.

Constance: O, lawful let it be
That I have room with Rome to curse awhile!
Good father cardinal, cry thou amen
To my keen curses; for without my wrong
There is no tongue hath power to curse him right.
Cardinal Pandulph: There 's law and warrant, lady, for my curse.
King John. Act iii, sc. 1, l. 179.

Philip of France, on peril of a curse,
Let go the hand of that arch-heretic.
King John. Act iii, sc. 1, l. 191. [Pandulph] "Arch heretic" (unhyphenated) is repeated in *Henry VIII,* v, 1, 45.

The peril of our curses light on thee
So heavy as thou shalt not shake them off,
But in despair die under their black weight.
King John. Act iii, sc. 1, l. 295. [Pandulph]

I will denounce a curse upon his head.
King John. Act iii, sc. 1, l. 319. [Pandulph] The only use of "denounce."

That 's the curse of Rome.
King John. Act iii, sc. 1, l. 207. [Blanch]

Curse of kings.—*King John,* iv, 2, 208.
Curse of marriage.—*Othello,* iii, 3, 268
Curse of service.—*Othello,* i, 1, 35.

9
Dower'd with our curse, and stranger'd with our oath.
King Lear. Act i, sc. 1, l. 207. [King Lear] The only use of "dower'd" and "stranger'd."

10
Curses, not loud but deep.
Macbeth. Act v, sc. 3, l. 27. [Macbeth]

11
I give him curses, yet he gives me love.
A Midsummer-Night's Dream. Act i, sc. 1, l. 196. [Hermia]

For thou, I fear, hast given me cause to curse.
A Midsummer-Night's Dream. Act iii, sc. 2, l. 46. [Hermia]

My curses on her!
King Lear. Act ii, sc. 4, l. 148. [King Lear]

12
If any wretch have put this in your head,
Let heaven requite it with the serpent's curse!
Othello. Act iv, sc. 2, l. 15. [Emilia]

The curse of heaven and men succeed their evils!
Pericles. Act i, sc. 4, l. 104. [Cleon]

To make him curse this cursed crimeful night.
The Rape of Lucrece, l. 970. "Crimeful" is repeated in *Hamlet,* iv, 7, 7.

Curse my bones.—*The Rape of Lucrece,* l. 209.

13
I would my skill were subject to thy curse.
Richard II. Act iii, sc. 4, l. 103. [Gardener]

14
Sweet saint, for charity, be not so curst.
Richard III. Act i, sc. 2, l. 49. [Gloucester]

I was never curst.—*A Midsummer-Night's Dream,* iii, 2, 300.

15 Give me leave,
By circumstance, to curse thy cursed self.
Richard III. Act i, sc. 2, l. 79. [Lady Anne]

Curse not thyself, fair creature.
Richard III. Act i, sc. 2, l. 132. [Gloucester]

With curses in her mouth.—*Richard III,* i, 2, 233.

1
The curse my noble father laid on thee,
When thou didst crown his warlike brows with paper . . .
His curses, then from bitterness of soul
Denounced against thee, are all fall'n upon thee.
Richard III. Act i, sc. 3, l. 174. [Gloucester]
Did York's dread curse prevail so much with heaven?
Richard III. Act i, sc. 3, l. 191. [Queen Margaret]
Can curses pierce the clouds and enter heaven?
Why, then, give way, dull clouds, to my quick curses!
Richard III. Act i, sc. 3, l. 195. [Queen Margaret]
O, let me make the period to my curse!
Richard III. Act i, sc. 3, l. 238. [Queen Margaret]
Thus have you breathed your curse against yourself.
Richard III. Act i, sc. 3, l. 240. [Queen Elizabeth]
The time will come when thou shalt wish for me
To help thee curse that poisonous bunch-back'd toad.
Richard III. Act i, sc. 3, l. 245. [Queen Margaret] The only use of "bunch-back'd."
False-boding woman, end thy frantic curse,
Lest to thy harm thou move our patience.
Richard III. Act i, sc. 3, l. 247. [Hastings] The only use of "false-boding."

2
Duke of Buckingham: Curses never pass
The lips of those that breathe them in the air.
Queen Margaret: I 'll not believe but they ascend the sky,
And there awake God's gentle-sleeping peace.
Richard III. Act i, sc. 3, l. 285. The only use of "gentle-sleeping."
My hair doth stand on end to hear her curses.
Richard III. Act i, sc. 3, l. 304. [Hastings]
Had I cursed now, I had cursed myself.
Richard III. Act i, sc. 3, l. 319. [Gloucester]

3
Grey: Now Margaret's curse is fall'n upon our heads,
For standing by when Richard stabb'd her son.
Rivers: Then cursed she Hastings, then cursed she Buckingham,
Then cursed she Richard.
Richard III. Act iii, sc. 3, l. 15.
O Margaret, Margaret, now thy heavy curse
Is lighted on poor Hastings' wretched head!
Richard III. Act iii, sc. 4, l. 94. [Hastings]
Now Margaret's curse is fallen upon my head.
Richard III. Act v, sc. 1, l. 25. [Buckingham]
And make me die the thrall of Margaret's curse.
Richard III. Act iv, sc. 1, l. 46. [Queen Elizabeth]
My own soul's curse,
Which ever since have kept my eyes from rest.
Richard III. Act iv, sc. 1, l. 81. [Anne]

4
O thou well skill'd in curses, stay awhile,
And teach me how to curse mine enemies!
Richard III. Act iv, sc. 4, l. 116. [Queen Elizabeth]
Revolving this will teach thee how to curse.
Richard III. Act iv, sc. 4, l. 123. [Queen Margaret] "Revolving" is repeated in *The Rape of Lucrece,* l. 127.
Though far more cause, yet much less spirit to curse
Abides in me: I say amen to all.
Richard III. Act iv, sc. 4, l. 196. [Queen Elizabeth]
Curse my fate.—*Sonnets,* xxix.

5
Her elder sister is so curst and shrewd
That till the father rid his hands of her,
Master, your love must live a maid at home.
The Taming of the Shrew. Act i, sc. 1, l. 185. [Tranio] "Curst and shrewd" is repeated in i, 2, 70.
Curst and sad.—*A Midsummer-Night's Dream,* iii, 2, 439.

6
She is intolerable curst.
The Taming of the Shrew. Act i, sc. 2, l. 89. [Hortensio]
If she be curst, it is for policy.
The Taming of the Shrew. Act ii, sc. 1, l. 294. [Petruchio]
She shall be curst in company.
The Taming of the Shrew. Act ii, sc. 1, l. 307. [Petruchio]
Curster than she? why, 'tis impossible.
The Taming of the Shrew. Act iii, sc. 2, l. 156. [Tranio] The only use of "curster."
Be curst and brief.—*Twelfth Night,* iii, 2, 46.

7
How fain would I have hated all mankind!
And thou redeem'st thyself: but all, save thee,
I fell with curses.
Timon of Athens. Act iv, sc. 3, l. 506. [Timon]
Curse all.—*Timon of Athens,* iv, 3, 534.
If thou hatest curses,
Stay not; fly, whilst thou art blest, and free;
Ne'er see thou man, and let me ne'er see thee.
Timon of Athens. Act iv, sc. 3, l. 541. [Timon]

8
Few come within the compass of my curse.
Titus Andronicus. Act v, sc. 1, l. 126. [Aaron]
What meanest thou to curse thus?
Troilus and Cressida. Act v, sc. 1, l. 30. [Patroclus]
I curse myself.—*The Two Gentlemen of Verona,* iii, 1, 148.

9
How accursed In being so blest!
Winter's Tale. Act ii, sc. 1, l. 38. [Leontes]
For, as the case now stands, it is a curse
He cannot be compell'd to 't.
Winter's Tale. Act ii, sc. 3, l. 87. [Paulina]

II—Curses: Some Examples

10
Scurvy, old, filthy, scurvy lord!
All's Well that Ends Well. Act ii, sc. 3, l. 250. [Parolles]

1
All the contagion of the south light on you.
Coriolanus. Act i, sc. 4, l. 30. [Marcius]
Boils and plagues
Plaster you o'er, that you may be abhorr'd
Further than seen and one infect another
Against the wind a mile!
Coriolanus. Act i, sc. 4, l. 31. [Marcius]
See also under DISEASE.

2
Let her languish
A drop of blood a day; and, being aged,
Die of this folly!
Cymbeline. Act i, sc. 1, l. 156. [Cymbeline]

3
All the fiends of hell
Divide themselves between you!
Cymbeline. Act ii, sc. 4, l. 129. [Posthumus]
All curses madded Hecuba gave the Greeks,
And mine to boot, be darted on thee!
Cymbeline. Act iv, sc. 2, l. 313. [Imogen]

4
Let him be damned, like the glutton! pray God his tongue be hotter!
II Henry IV. Act i, sc. 2, l. 39. [Falstaff]

5
A plaguing mischief light on Charles and thee!
And may ye both be suddenly surprised
By bloody hands, in sleeping on your beds!
I Henry VI. Act v, sc. 3, l. 39. [La Pucelle]
The only use of "plaguing."
Then lead me hence; with whom I leave my curse:
May never glorious sun reflex his beams
Upon the country where you make abode;
But darkness and the gloomy shade of death
Environ you, till mischief and despair,
Drive you to break your necks or hang yourselves!
I Henry VI. Act v, sc. 4, l. 86. [La Pucelle]
"Reflex" is repeated in *Romeo and Juliet,* iii, 5, 20.

6
Mischance and sorrow go along with you!
Heart's discontent and sour affliction
Be playfellows to keep you company!
II Henry VI. Act iii, sc. 2, l. 300. [Queen Margaret]
A plague upon them! wherefore should I curse them?
Would curses kill, as doth the mandrake's groan,
I would invent as bitter-searching terms,
As curst, as harsh and horrible to hear,
Deliver'd strongly through my fixed teeth,
With full as many signs of deadly hate,
As lean-faced Envy in her loathsome cave:
My tongue should stumble in mine earnest words;
Mine eyes should sparkle like the beaten flint;
Mine hair be fix'd on end, as one distract;
Ay, every joint should seem to curse and ban:
And even now my burthen'd heart would break,
Should I not curse them. Poison be their drink!
Gall, worse than gall, the daintiest that they taste!
Their sweetest shade a grove of cypress trees!
Their chiefest prospects murdering basilisks!
Their softest touch as smart as lizards' stings!
Their music frightful as the serpent's hiss.
II Henry VI. Act iii, sc. 2, l. 309. [Suffolk]
The only use of "bitter-searching." "Lean-faced" is repeated in *The Comedy of Errors,* v, 1, 237: "Lean-faced villain."

7
Ay, kennel, puddle, sink; whose filth and dirt
Troubles the silver spring where England drinks.
II Henry VI. Act iv, sc. 1, l. 71. [Captain]
Thou didst drink
The stale of horses, and the gilded puddle
Which beasts would cough at.
Antony and Cleopatra. Act i, sc. 4, l. 61. [Cæsar] The only uses of "puddle."

8
Die, damned wretch, the curse of her that bare thee;
And as I thrust thy body in with my sword,
So wish I, I might thrust thy soul to hell.
II Henry VI. Act iv, sc. 10, l. 83. [Iden]
God's curse light upon you all!
II Henry VI. Act iv, sc. 8, l. 34. [Cade]
Heaven's curse upon thee!
Timon of Athens. Act iv, sc. 3, l. 131. [Timon]

9
In dreadful war mayst thou be overcome,
Or live in peace abandon'd and despised!
III Henry VI. Act i, sc. 1, l. 187. [Clifford]
There, take the crown, and, with the crown, my curse.
III Henry VI. Act i, sc. 4, l. 164. [York]
Would he were wasted, marrow, bones and all,
That from his loins no hopeful branch may spring,
To cross me from the golden time I look for!
III Henry VI. Act iii, sc. 2, l. 125. [Gloucester]

10
Darkness and devils!
King Lear. Act i, sc. 4, l. 273. [King Lear]
Hear, nature, hear; dear goddess, hear!
Suspend thy purpose, if thou didst intend
To make this creature fruitful!
Into her womb convey sterility!
Dry up in her the organs of increase;
And from her derogate body never spring
A babe to honour her! If she must teem,
Create her child of spleen; that it may live,
And be a thwart disnatured torment to her!
King Lear. Act i, sc. 4, l. 297. [King Lear]
The only use of "sterility" and "disnatured."
Blasts and fogs upon thee!
The untented woundings of a father's curse
Pierce every sense about thee!
King Lear. Act i, sc. 4, l. 321. [King Lear]
The only use of "untented."
All the stored vengeances of heaven fall
On her ingrateful top! Strike her young bones,
You taking airs, with lameness!
King Lear. Act ii, sc. 4, l. 164. [King Lear]
The only use of "lameness."
You nimble lightnings, dart your blinding flames
Into her scornful eyes! Infect her beauty,
You fen-suck'd fogs, drawn by the powerful sun,
To fall and blast her pride!
King Lear. Act ii, sc. 4, l. 167. [King Lear]
The only use of "fen-suck'd."

A plague upon you, murderers, traitors all!
King Lear. Act v, sc. 3, l. 269. [King Lear] See under PLAGUE.

1
Weary se'nnights nine times nine
Shall he dwindle, peak and pine.
Macbeth. Act i, sc. 3, l. 22. [First Witch] "Dwindle" is repeated in *I Henry IV*, iii, 3, 3; and "peak" in *Hamlet*, ii, 2, 594. "Se'en-night" occurs three times, and "seven-night" twice.

Infected be the air whereon they ride.
Macbeth. Act iv, sc. 1, l. 138. [Macbeth]

Deny me this, And an eternal curse fall on you!
Macbeth. Act iv, sc. 1, l. 104. [Macbeth]

Here let them lie
Till famine and the ague eat them up.
Macbeth. Act v, sc. 5, l. 3. [Macbeth]

2
A pox o' your throats!
Measure for Measure. Act iv, sc. 3, l. 26. [Barnardine] Repeated in *Tempest*, i, 1, 43.

A pox o' your bottle!—*The Tempest*, iii, 2, 87.

A pox of the devil!—*Henry V*, iii, 7, 130.

A pox of this gout!—*II Henry IV*, i, 2, 272.

A pox of that jest!—*Love's Labour's Lost*, v, 2, 46.

Pox of your love-letters!—*The Two Gentlemen of Verona*, iii, 1, 390.

A pox of wrinkles.—*Timon of Athens*, iv, 3, 148.

3
Cursed be my stones for thus deceiving me!
A Midsummer-Night's Dream. Act v, sc. 1, l. 182. [Pyramus]

Cursed be my tribe!—*The Merchant of Venice*, i, 3, 52.

Cursed be that heart!—*Titus Andronicus*, iv, 1, 72.

Cursed be the time of thy nativity!—*I Henry VI*, iii, 2, 88.

4
Ay, let her rot, and perish, and be damned to-night.
Othello. Act iv, sc. 1, l. 191. [Othello]

May his pernicious soul rot half a grain a day!
Othello. Act v, sc. 2, l. 155. [Emilia]

The south-fog rot him!
Cymbeline. Act ii, sc. 3, l. 136. [Cloten] The only use of "south-fog."

Thy lips rot off!
Timon of Athens. Act iv, sc. 3, l. 63. [Phrynia]

Go rot!—*The Winter's Tale*, i, 2, 324.

5
A curse upon him, die he like a thief!
Pericles. Act iv, sc. 6, l. 121. [Lysimachus]

6
Cursed be the hand that made these fatal holes!
Cursed be the heart that had the heart to do it!
Cursed the blood that let this blood from hence!
More direful hap betide that hated wretch,
That makes us wretched by the death of thee,
Than I can wish to adders, spiders, toads,
Or any creeping venom'd thing that lives!
Richard III. Act i, sc. 2, l. 14. [Lady Anne]

Lady Anne: Ill rest betide the chamber where thou liest!
Gloucester: So will it, madam, till I lie with you.
Richard III. Act i, sc. 2, l. 112.

Black night o'ershade thy day, and death thy life!
Richard III. Act i, sc. 2, l. 131. [Lady Anne]

Long mayst thou live to wail thy children's loss;
And see another, as I see thee now,
Deck'd in thy rights, as thou art stall'd in mine!
Richard III. Act i, sc. 3, l. 204. [Queen Margaret] The only use of "stall'd."

God, I pray him,
That none of you may live your natural age,
But by some unlook'd accident cut off!
Richard III. Act i, sc. 3, l. 212. [Queen Margaret] The only use of "unlook'd."

If heaven have any grievous plague in store
Exceeding those that I can wish upon thee,
O, let them keep it till thy sins be ripe,
And then hurl down their indignation
On thee.
Richard III. Act i, sc. 3, l. 217. [Queen Margaret]

Cancel his bond of life, dear God, I pray,
That I may live to say, The dog is dead!
Richard III. Act iv, sc. 4, l. 77. [Queen Margaret]

Take with thee my most heavy curse;
Which, in the day of battle, tire thee more
Than all the complete armour that thou wear'st!
Richard III. Act iv, sc. 4, l. 187. [Duchess of York]

7
As wicked dew as e'er my mother brush'd
With raven's feather from unwholesome fen
Drop on you both! a south-west blow on ye
And blister you all o'er!
The Tempest. Act i, sc. 2, l. 321. [Caliban] "South-west" is repeated in *Pericles*, iv, 1, 51.

All the charms
Of Sycorax, toads, beetles, bats, light on you!
The Tempest. Act i, sc. 2, l. 339. [Caliban]

All the infections that the sun sucks up
From bogs, fens, flats, on Prosper fall and make him
By inch-meal a disease! His spirits hear me
And yet I needs must curse.
The Tempest. Act ii, sc. 2, l. 1. [Caliban] The only use of "inch-meal."

A murrain on your monster, and the devil take your fingers!
The Tempest. Act iii, sc. 2, l. 88. [Trinculo]

Lingering perdition, worse than any death
Can be at once, shall step by step attend
You and your ways.
The Tempest. Act iii, sc. 3, l. 77. [Ariel]

The dropsy drown this fool!
The Tempest. Act iv, sc. 1, l. 230. [Caliban] The only use of "dropsy." "Dropsies" occurs in *I Henry IV*, ii, 4, 496.

8
Aches contract and starve your supple joints!
Timon of Athens. Act i, sc. 1, l. 257. [Apemantus]

O you gods,
I feel my master's passion! this slave,
Unto his honour, has my lord's meat in him:

Why should it thrive and turn to nutriment,
When he is turn'd to poison?
O, may diseases only work upon 't!
And, when he 's sick to death, let not that part of nature
Which my lord paid for, be of any power
To expel sickness, but prolong his hour!
Timon of Athens. Act iii, sc. 1, l. 58. [Flaminius] The only use of "nutriment."

Tear me, take me, and the gods fall upon you!
Timon of Athens. Act iii, sc. 4, l. 100. [Timon]

Thou cold sciatica,
Cripple our senators, that their limbs may halt
As lamely as their manners!
Timon of Athens. Act iv, sc. 1, l. 23. [Timon] "Sciatica" is repeated in *Measure for Measure,* i, 2, 59; and in *Troilus and Cressida,* v, 1, 25.

Itches, blains,
Sow all the Athenian bosoms; and their crop
Be general leprosy.
Timon of Athens. Act iv, sc. 1, l. 28. [Timon] The only use of "blains."

The canker gnaw thy heart
For showing me again the eyes of man!
Timon of Athens. Act iv, sc. 3, l. 49. [Timon]

Consumptions sow
In hollow bones of man; strike their sharp shins,
And mar men's spurring.
Timon of Athens. Act iv, sc. 3, l. 151. [Timon]

Do you damn others, and let this damn you,
And ditches grave you all!
Timon of Athens. Act iv, sc. 3, l. 165. [Timon]

Timon: Would thou wert clean enough to spit upon!
Apemantus: A plague on thee! thou art too bad to curse.
Timon: All villains that do stand by thee are pure.
Apemantus: There is no leprosy but what thou speak'st.
Timon of Athens. Act iv, sc. 3, l. 364.

Away, thou issue of a mangy dog!
Choler does kill me that thou art alive;
I swound to see thee.
Timon of Athens. Act iv, sc. 3, l. 371. [Timon] The only use of "mangy." See also under SWOONING.

1
The bone-ache! for that, methinks, is the curse dependant on those that war for a placket.
Troilus and Cressida. Act ii, sc. 3, l. 20. [Thersites] "Bone-ache" is repeated in v, 1, 26, and occurs in no other play.

The common curse of mankind, folly and ignorance, be thine in great revenue!
Troilus and Cressida. Act ii, sc. 3, l. 30. [Thersites]

Now, the dry serpigo on the subject! and war and lechery confound all!
Troilus and Cressida. Act ii, sc. 3, l. 81. [Thersites] "Serpigo" (skin eruption) is repeated in *Measure for Measure,* iii, 1, 31.

A pestilence on him!—*Troilus and Cressida,* iv, 2, 21.

A bugbear take him!—*Troilus and Cressida,* iv, 2, 34. The only use of "bugbear."

Would he were knock'd i' the head!
Troilus and Cressida. Act iv, sc. 2, l. 35. [Cressida]

A plague upon Antenor! I would they had broke 's neck!
Troilus and Cressida. Act iv, sc. 2, l. 78. [Pandarus]

CURTAIN

2
Their ragged curtains poorly are let loose.
Henry V, iv, 2, 41. See under ENGLISH.

3
Drew Priam's curtain in the dead of night.
II Henry IV, i, 1, 72. See under COMPARISON.

4
Close up his eyes and draw the curtain close.
II Henry VI, iii, 3, 32. See under MEDITATION.

Let 'em alone, and draw the curtain close.
Henry VIII. Act v, sc. 2, l. 34. [King Henry]

5
Go draw aside the curtains.
The Merchant of Venice, ii, 7, 1. See under CHOICE.

Draw the curtains.—*The Merchant of Venice,* ii, 7, 78; *King Lear,* iii, 6, 90.

Draw the curtain straight.—*The Merchant of Venice,* ii, 9, 1.

Come, draw the curtain.—*Merchant of Venice,* ii, 9, 84; *Troilus and Cressida,* iii, 2, 49.

Let me the curtains draw.—*Othello.* v, 2, 104.

We will draw the curtain.—*Twelfth Night,* i, 5, 251.

Do not draw the curtain.—*The Winter's Tale,* v, 3, 59.

I 'll draw the curtain.—*Winter's Tale,* v, 3, 68.

Shall I draw the curtain?—*The Winter's Tale,* v, 3, 83.

Draws a curtain.—*I Henry IV,* iv, 1, 73.

6
The curtains being close, about he walks,
Rolling his greedy eyeballs in his head.
The Rape of Lucrece, l. 367.

The curtain drawn, his eyes began To wink.
The Rape of Lucrece, l. 374.

7
Draw The shady curtains from Aurora's bed.
Romeo and Juliet, i, 1, 142. See under SUNRISE.

Spread thy close curtain.—*Romeo and Juliet,* iii, 2, 5.

8
The fringed curtains of thine eye advance
And say what thou seest yond.
The Tempest. Act i, sc. 2, l. 408. [Prospero]

9
Curtain'd with a counsel-keeping cave.
Titus Andronicus. Act ii, sc. 3, l. 24. [Tamora] The only use of "counsel-keeping."

Curtain'd sleep.—*Macbeth,* ii, 1, 51. The only uses of "curtain'd."

CUSTOM

See also Habit

10
Hath not old custom made this life more sweet
Than that of painted pomp?
As You Like It. Act ii, sc. 1, l. 2. [Duke]

1
Let me o'erleap that custom.
Coriolanus. Act ii, sc. 2, l. 140. [Coriolanus]
Pray you, go fit you to the custom and
Take to you, as your predecessors have,
Your honour with your form.
Coriolanus. Act ii, sc. 2, l. 146. [Menenius]
What custom wills, in all things should we do 't,
The dust on antique time would lie unswept,
And mountainous error be too highly heapt
For truth to o'er-peer.
Coriolanus. Act ii, sc. 3, l. 125. [Coriolanus] The only use of "mountainous" and "heapt."
2
The breach of custom Is breach of all.
Cymbeline. Act iv, sc. 2, l. 10. [Imogen]
I 'll break a custom.—*The Merchant of Venice,* i, 3, 65.
3
Horatio: Is it a custom?
Hamlet: Ay, marry, is 't:
But to my mind, though I am native here
And to the manner born, it is a custom
More honour'd in the breach than the observance.
Hamlet. Act i, sc. 4, l. 12.
As the manner of our country is.
Romeo and Juliet. Act iv, sc. 1, l. 109. [Friar Laurence]
4
My custom always of an afternoon.
Hamlet, i, 5, 60. See under SLEEP.
After my custom.—*Much Ado about Nothing,* i, 1, 169.
'Tis a custom with him.
The Tempest. Act iii, sc. 2, l. 95. [Caliban]
By custom.—*Henry VIII,* iv, 1, 16.
With a custom.—*The Winter's Tale,* iv, 4, 12.
Aged custom.—*Coriolanus,* ii, 3, 176.
Custom and condition.—*Troilus and Cressida,* iii, 3, 9.
Customs, and laws.—*Timon of Athens,* iv, 1, 19.
Custom of exercises.—*Hamlet,* ii, 2, 308.
Custom of fell deeds.—*Julius Cæsar,* iii, 1, 269.
Custom of entertainment.—*Othello,* ii, 3, 36.
Custom of request.—*Coriolanus,* ii, 3, 150.
Office and custom.—*Troilus and Cressida,* i, 3, 88.
Privilege and custom.—*Coriolanus,* i, 10, 23.
5
That monster, custom, who all sense doth eat,
Of habits devil, is angel yet in this,
That to the use of actions fair and good
He likewise gives a frock or livery,
That aptly is put on.
Hamlet. Act iii, sc. 4, l. 161. [Hamlet] The only use of "frock."
Antiquity forgot, custom not known,
The ratifiers and props of every word.
Hamlet. Act iv, sc. 5, l. 104. [Gentleman] The only use of "ratifiers."
Custom hath made it in him a property of easiness.
Hamlet. Act v, sc. 1, l. 75. [Horatio]
6
Nice customs curtsy to great kings.
Henry V. Act v, sc. 2, l. 293. [King Henry]
7 New customs,
Though they be never so ridiculous,
Nay, let 'em be unmanly, yet are follow'd.
Henry VIII. Act i, sc. 3, l. 2. [Sands]
Wherefore should I
Stand in the plague of custom?
King Lear. Act i, sc. 2, l. 2. [Edmund]
Think of this, good peers,
But as a thing of custom.
Macbeth. Act iii, sc. 4, l. 96. [Lady Macbeth]
8
The tyrant custom, most grave senators,
Hath made the flinty and steel couch of war
My thrice-driven bed of down.
Othello. Act i, sc. 3, l. 230. [Othello] The only use of "thrice-driven."
9
But custom what they did begin
Was with long use account no sin.
Pericles. Act i, Gower, l. 29.
You 'll lose nothing by custom.
Pericles. Act iv, sc. 2, l. 150. [Bawd]

CUSTOMER, see under Merchant

D

DAGGER

See also Weapon

10
I wear not My dagger in my mouth.
Cymbeline. Act iv, sc. 2, l. 79. [Guiderius] See under WORD.
I will speak daggers to her, but use none.
Hamlet. Act iii, sc. 2, l. 414. [Hamlet]
Thou hidest a thousand daggers in thy thoughts,
Which thou hast whetted on thy stony heart.
II Henry IV. Act iv, sc. 5, l. 107. [King Henry]
There 's daggers in men's smiles.
Macbeth. Act ii, sc. 3, l. 146. [Donalbain]
11
And now is this Vice's dagger become a squire.
II Henry IV. Act iii, sc. 2, l. 343. [Falstaff]
Dagger of lath.—*I Henry IV,* ii, 4, 151; *Twelfth Night,* iv, 2, 136.
Wooden dagger.—*Henry V,* iv, 4, 77.
12
Do not you wear your dagger in your cap that day.
Henry V. Act iv, sc. 1, l. 56. [King Henry]
I know where I will wear this dagger then.
Julius Cæsar. Act i, sc. 3, l. 89. [Cassius]
13 There is my dagger,
And here my naked breast.
Julius Cæsar. Act iv, sc. 3, l. 100. [Cassius]

Sheathe your dagger.—*Julius Cæsar,* iv, 3, 107.

Your vile daggers
Hack'd one another in the sides of Cæsar.
Julius Cæsar. Act v, sc. 1, l. 39. [Antony]

Used their very daggers.—*Macbeth,* i, 7, 76.

Stabb'd with bloody daggers.—*Richard III,* i, 3, 212.

1
Is this a dagger which I see before me,
The handle toward my hand? Come, let me clutch thee.
I have thee not, and yet I see thee still.
Art thou not, fatal vision, sensible
To feeling as to sight? or art thou but
A dagger of the mind, a false creation,
Proceeding from the heat-oppressed brain?
I see thee yet, in form as palpable
As this which now I draw.
Thou marshall'st me the way that I was going;
And such an instrument I was to use.
Mine eyes are made the fools o' the other senses,
Or else worth all the rest; I see thee still,
And on thy blade and dudgeon gouts of blood,
Which was not so before. There 's no such thing:
It is the bloody business which informs
Thus to mine eyes.
Macbeth. Act ii, sc. 1, l. 33. [Macbeth] The only use of "heat-oppressed," "marshall'st," and "dudgeon" (hilt).

This is the air-drawn dagger which, you said,
Led you to Duncan.
Macbeth. Act iii, sc. 4, l. 62. [Lady Macbeth] The only use of "air-drawn."

Their daggers, which unwiped we found
Upon their pillows.
Macbeth. Act ii, sc. 3, l. 108. [Lennox]

Their daggers Unmannerly breech'd with gore.
Macbeth. Act ii, sc. 3, l. 121. [Macbeth]

Thou stickest a dagger in me.
The Merchant of Venice. Act iii, sc. 1, l. 115. [Shylock]

His dagger drew, and died.
A Midsummer-Night's Dream. Act v, sc. 1, l. 150. [Quince]

Hath no man's dagger here a point for me?
Much Ado about Nothing. Act iv, sc. 1, l. 110. [Leonato]

2
Then will I lay the serving-creature's dagger on your pate.
Romeo and Juliet. Act iv, sc. 5, l. 119. [Peter] The only use of "serving-creature."

Pray you, put up your dagger.—*Romeo and Juliet,* iv, 5, 123.

I will . . . put up my iron dagger.—*Romeo and Juliet,* iv, 5, 127.

3
O happy dagger!
This is thy sheath [*Stabs herself*]; there rust, and let me die.
Romeo and Juliet. Act v, sc. 3, l. 169. [Juliet]

This dagger hath mista'en, . . .
And it mis-sheathed in my daughter's bosom!
Romeo and Juliet. Act v, sc. 3, l. 203. [Capulet] The only use of "mis-sheathed."

4
Hold, sir, or I 'll throw your dagger o'er the house.
Twelfth Night. Act iv, sc. 1, l. 30. [Sir Toby]

My dagger muzzled,
Lest it should bite its master.
The Winter's Tale, i, 2, 156. See under Boyhood for full quotation.

DAME

See also Lady, Woman

5
A holy parcel of the fairest dames.
Love's Labour 's Lost, v, 2, 160. See under Beauty.

The fairest dame
That lived, that loved, that liked, that look'd with cheer.
A Midsummer-Night's Dream. Act v, sc. 1, l. 298. [Pyramus]

Fair dame.—*The Comedy of Errors,* ii, 2, 149; *Macbeth,* iv, 2, 65.

Lovely dame.—*I Henry VI,* v, 5, 12.

Loyal dame.—*The Rape of Lucrece,* l. 1034.

Peerless dame.—*The Rape of Lucrece,* l. 21.

Worthy and chaste dames.—*Othello,* iv, 1, 47.

Grecian dames.—*Troilus and Cressida,* i, 3, 282.

Roman dame.—*Rape of Lucrece,* l. 51; 1628.

Gallantest dames of Rome.—*Titus Andronicus,* i, 1, 317. The only use of "gallantest."

6
Behold yond simpering dame,
Whose face between her forks presages snow.
King Lear. Act iv, sc. 6, l. 121. [King Lear] "Simpering" is used again in *As You Like It,* Epil., 16.

Deceitful dame.—*I Henry VI,* ii, 1, 50.

Dishonour'd dame.—*Titus Andronicus,* iv, 1, 90.

Fickle dame.—*The Passionate Pilgrim,* l. 259.

Presumptuous dame.—*II Henry VI,* i, 2, 42.

Proud dame.—*II Henry VI,* i, 3, 79.

Sinful dame.—*Pericles,* i, Gower, 31.

Veil'd dames.—*Coriolanus,* ii, 1, 231.

Willing dames.—*Macbeth,* iv, 3, 73.

DAMNATION

7
Truly, thou art damned, like an ill-roasted egg all on one side.
As You Like It. Act iii, sc. 2, l. 38. [Touchstone] The only use of "ill-roasted."

Wilt thou rest damned? God help thee, shallow man!
As You Like It. Act iii, sc. 2, l. 74. [Touchstone]

If thou beest not damned for this, the devil himself will have no shepherds.
As You Like It. Act iii, sc. 2, l. 88. [Touchstone]

God damn me.—*The Comedy of Errors,* iv, 3, 54. The only use of this phrase.

She is damned.—*Cymbeline,* i, 2, 30.

8
Is 't not to be damn'd,
To let this canker of our nature come
In further evil?
Hamlet. Act v, sc. 2, l. 68. [Hamlet]

Abuses me to damn me.—*Hamlet,* ii, 2, 632.

1
I 'll be damned for never a king's son in Christendom.
I Henry IV. Act i, sc. 2, l. 109. [Falstaff]
2
I 'll see her damned first: to Pluto's damned lake, by this hand, to the infernal deep, with Erebus and tortures vile also.
II Henry IV. Act ii, sc. 4, l. 169. [Pistol]
I 'll see thee damned.—*I Henry IV*, ii, 4, 161.
Let him be damned.—*II Henry IV*, i, 2, 39.
Nay, rather damn them with King Cerberus.
II Henry IV. Act ii, sc. 4, l. 181. [Pistol]
Look, with a spot I damn him.
Julius Cæsar. Act v, sc. 1, l. 6. [Antony]
3
Thou 'rt damn'd as black—nay, nothing is so black;
Thou art more deep damn'd than Prince Lucifer:
There is not yet so ugly a fiend of hell
As thou shalt be, if thou didst kill this child.
King John. Act iv, sc. 3, l. 121. [Bastard]
Damn'd as thou art.—*Othello*, i, 2, 63.
4
Damn her, lewd minx! O, damn her!
Othello. Act iii, sc. 3, l. 475. [Othello] "Minx" is repeated in iv, 1, 159, and in *Twelfth Night*, iii, 4, 133.
Let her . . . be damned.—*Othello*, iv, 1, 192.
Be double damn'd.—*Othello*, iv, 2, 37.
5
Lady Anne: Didst thou not kill this king?
Duke of Gloucester: I grant ye.
Lady Anne: Dost grant me, hedgehog? then, God grant me too
Thou mayst be damned for that wicked deed!
Richard III. Act i, sc. 2, l. 101. The only use of "hedgehog." "Hedgehogs" occurs in *A Midsummer-Night's Dream*, ii, 2, 10; and in *The Tempest*, ii, 2, 10.
First Murderer: What, art thou afraid?
Second Murderer: Not to kill him, having a warrant for it; but to be damned for killing him, from which no warrant can defend us.
Richard III. Act i, sc. 4, l. 111.
6
'Twere damnation
To think so base a thought.
The Merchant of Venice. Act ii, sc. 7, l. 49. [Prince of Morocco]
I dare damnation.—*Hamlet*, iv, 5, 133.
Deep damnation.—*Macbeth*, i, 7, 20.
Share damnation.—*The Merry Wives of Windsor*, iii, 2, 40.
For nothing canst thou to damnation add
Greater than that.
Othello. Act iii, sc. 3, l. 372. [Othello]
Ancient damnation! O most wicked fiend!
Romeo and Juliet, iii, 5, 235. [Juliet]
7
Shylock: She is damned for it.
Salarino: That 's certain, if the devil may be her judge.
The Merchant of Venice. Act iii, sc. 1, l. 34.
Be of good cheer, for truly I think you are damned.
The Merchant of Venice. Act iii, sc. 5, l. 5. [Launcelot]
8
I am damned in hell for swearing to gentlemen my friends.
The Merry Wives of Windsor. Act ii, sc. 2, l. 9. [Falstaff]
Thou art damn'd to hell for this.
Richard II. Act iv, sc. 1, l. 43. [Aumerle]
Mark'd with a blot, damn'd in the book of heaven.
Richard II. Act iv, sc. 1, l. 236. [King Richard]

DANCING

9
Though the devil lead the measure, such are to be followed.
All's Well that Ends Well. Act ii, sc. 1, l. 57. [Parolles]
I have trod a measure.
As You Like It. Act v, sc. 4, l. 45. [Touchstone]
So, to your pleasures:
I am for other than for dancing measures.
As You Like It. Act v, sc. 4, l. 198. [Jaques]
We have measured many miles
To tread a measure with her on this grass.
Love's Labour 's Lost. Act v, sc. 2, l. 184. [King] Repeated by Boyet in following lines.
Curtsy, sweet hearts; and so the measure ends.
Love's Labour 's Lost. Act v, sc. 2, l. 221. [Rosaline]
10
Shall we dance now the Egyptian Bacchanals,
And celebrate our drink?
Antony and Cleopatra. Act ii, sc. 7, l. 110. [Enobarbus] "Bacchanals" is repeated in *A Midsummer-Night's Dream*, v, 1, 48: "Tipsy Bacchanals."
Dance canary.—*All 's Well that Ends Well*, ii, 1, 77. A lively dance said to have been borrowed from the Canary Islands.
Busied with a Whitsun morris-dance.
Henry V. Act ii, sc. 4, l. 25. [Dauphin] The only mention of morris-dance.
11
That were but light payment, to dance out of your debt.
II Henry IV. Epilogue, l. 21.
12
They bid us to the English dancing-schools,
And teach lavoltas high and swift corantos.
Henry V. Act iii, sc. 5, l. 32. [Bourbon] The only use of "dancing-schools" and "lavoltas" (a lively dance for two persons). For "corantos" see under ABILITY.
Your grace,
I fear, with dancing is a little heated.
Henry VIII. Act i, sc. 4, l. 99. [Wolsey]
13
I will play
On the tabor to the Worthies, and let them dance the hay.
Love's Labour 's Lost. Act v, sc. 1, l. 160. [Dull]
Rosaline: But shall we dance, if they desire us to 't?
Princess of France: No, to the death, we will not move a foot.
Love's Labour 's Lost. Act v, sc. 2, l. 145.

King: The music plays; vouchsafe some motion to it.
Rosaline: Our ears vouchsafe it.
King: But your legs should do it.
Love's Labour 's Lost. Act v, sc. 2, l. 216.

I will wish thee never more to dance.
Love's Labour 's Lost. Act v, sc. 2, l. 400. [Biron]

1
I 'll charm the air to give a sound,
While you perform your antic round.
Macbeth. Act iv, sc. 1, l. 129. [First Witch]

2
Our dance of custom round about the oak
Of Herne the hunter, let us not forget.
The Merry Wives of Windsor. Act v, sc. 5, l. 79. [Mrs. Quickly]

I 'll make him dance.—*The Merry Wives of Windsor,* iii, 2, 91.

3
To dance our ringlets to the whistling wind.
A Midsummer-Night's Dream. Act ii, sc. 1, l. 86. [Titania] "Ringlets" is repeated in *The Tempest,* v, 1, 37. The only use of "whistling wind."

If you will patiently dance in our round
And see our moonlight revels, go with us.
A Midsummer-Night's Dream. Act ii, sc. 1, l. 140. [Titania]

Sound, music! Come, my queen, take hands with me,
And rock the ground whereon these sleepers be.
A Midsummer-Night's Dream. Act iv, sc. 1, l. 89. [Oberon]

What dances shall we have,
To wear away this long age of three hours?
A Midsummer-Night's Dream. Act v, sc. 1, l. 32. [Lysander]

4
God match me with a good dancer!
Much Ado about Nothing. Act ii, sc. 1, l. 111. [Margaret] "Dancer" is used only once again, in *Antony and Cleopatra,* iii, 11, 36.

Let 's have a dance ere we are married, that we may lighten our own hearts and our wives' heels.
Much Ado about Nothing. Act v, sc. 4, l. 119. [Benedick]

We 'll have dancing afterward.—*Much Ado about Nothing,* v, 4, 122.

Soldier's dance.—*Pericles,* ii, 3, 95.

5
And I have heard, you knights of Tyre
Are excellent in making ladies trip;
And that their measures are as excellent.
Pericles. Act ii, sc. 3, l. 102. [Simonides]

Like a fairy, trip upon the green.
Venus and Adonis, l. 146.

About him, fairies; sing a scornful rhyme;
And, as you trip, still pinch him to your time.
The Merry Wives of Windsor. Act v, sc. 5, l. 95. [Mistress Quickly]

Trip and go.—*Love's Labour 's Lost,* iv, 2, 144.

Trip away.—*A Midsummer-Night's Dream,* v, 1, 428.

Trip no further.—*Twelfth Night,* ii, 3, 43.

Trip we after.—*A Midsummer-Night's Dream,* iv, 1, 101. See also under DISSEMBLING.

6
Thy steps no more
Than a delightful measure or a dance.
Richard II. Act i, sc. 3, l. 290. [Gaunt]

My legs can keep no measure in delight,
When my poor heart no measure keeps in grief:
Therefore, no dancing, girl; some other sport.
Richard II. Act iii, sc. 4, l. 7. [Queen]

But let them measure us by what they will;
We 'll measure them a measure, and be gone.
Romeo and Juliet. Act i, sc. 4, l. 9. [Benvolio]

The triplex, sir, is a good tripping measure.
Twelfth Night. Act v, sc. 1, l. 40. [Clown] The only use of "triplex" (triple time).

All the Greekish girls shall tripping sing.
Troilus and Cressida. Act iii, sc. 3, l. 211. [Ulysses]

Many nymphs . . . Came tripping by.
Sonnets. No. cliv.

Tripping after drums.—*King John,* v, 2, 155.

Tripping on his toe.—*The Tempest,* iv, 1, 46. The only uses of "tripping."

7
He capers nimbly in a lady's chamber
To the lascivious pleasing of a lute.
Richard III. Act i, sc. 1, l. 12. [Gloucester]

I have seen
Him caper upright like a wild Morisco,
Shaking the bloody darts as he his bells.
II Henry VI. Act iii, sc. 1, l. 364. [York] The only use of "Morisco."

He capers, he dances.—*The Merry Wives of Windsor,* iii, 2, 68.

Sir Toby: Were we not born under Taurus?
Sir Andrew: Taurus! That 's sides and heart.
Sir Toby: No, sir; it is legs and thighs. Let me see thee caper: ha! higher: ha, ha! excellent!
Twelfth Night. Act i, sc. 3, l. 146.

Dance and leap.—*Richard II,* ii, 4, 12.

8
Mercutio: We must have you dance.
Romeo: Not I, believe me: you have dancing shoes
With nimble soles.
Romeo and Juliet. Act i, sc. 4, l. 13.

Let wantons light of heart
Tickle the senseless rushes with their heels.
Romeo and Juliet. Act i, sc. 4, l. 35. [Romeo]

9
You and I are past our dancing days.
Romeo and Juliet. Act i, sc. 5, l. 33. [Capulet]

Here 's my fiddlestick; here 's that shall make you dance.
Romeo and Juliet. Act iii, sc. 1, l. 52. [Mercutio] "Fiddlestick" is repeated in *I Henry IV,* ii, 4, 535. See under DEVIL.

You would never dance again after a tabor and pipe; no, the bagpipe could not move you.
The Winter's Tale. Act iv, sc. 4, l. 182. [Servant]

Lincolnshire bagpipe.—*I Henry IV,* i, 2, 86. "Bagpipe" is repeated twice in *The Merchant of Venice,* iv, 1, 49; 56.

10
Come unto these yellow sands,
And then take hands:
Courtsied when you have and kiss'd

The wild waves whist,
Foot it featly here and there;
And, sweet sprites, the burthen bear.
The Tempest. Act i, sc. 2, l. 376. [Ariel] The only use of "courtsied," "wild waves" and "whist" (silent). "Featly" is repeated in *The Winter's Tale,* iv, 4, 176. See No. 6 below.

Foot it, girls.—*Romeo and Juliet,* i, 5, 28.

1
I must dance bare-foot on her wedding day.
The Taming of the Shrew. Act ii, sc. 1, l. 33. [Katharina]

Wooing dance.—*Taming of the Shrew,* i, 2, 68.

Dancing up to the chins.—*Tempest,* iv, 1, 183.

2
Sir Toby: What is thy excellence in a galliard, knight?
Sir Andrew: Faith, I can cut a caper. . . . And I think I have the back-trick simply as strong as any man in Illyria.
Twelfth Night. Act i, sc. 3, l. 127. The only use of "back-trick."

He offered to cut a caper at the proclamation.
Pericles. Act iv, sc. 2, l. 116. [Boult] These are the only two uses of "cut a caper."

3
My very walk should be a jig; I would not so much as make water but in a sink-a-pace.
Twelfth Night. Act i, sc. 3, l. 137. [Sir Toby Belch] The only use of "sink-a-pace" (cinquepace).

To jig off a tune at the tongue's end.
Love's Labour's Lost. Act iii, sc. 1, l. 11. [Moth] See under TUNE.

Tune a jig.—*Love's Labour's Lost,* iv, 3, 168.

He 's for a jig.—*Hamlet,* ii, 2, 522.

You jig, you amble.—*Hamlet,* iii, 1, 150.

A Scotch jig.—*Much Ado about Nothing,* ii, 1, 77; ii, 1, 78.

Jigging fools.—*Julius Cæsar,* iv, 3, 137. The only use of "jigging."

O God, your only jig-maker.—*Hamlet,* iii, 2, 132. The only use of "jig-maker."

4
Or, like a nymph, with long dishevell'd hair,
Dance on the sands, and yet no footing seen.
Venus and Adonis, l. 147. "Dishevell'd hair" is repeated in *The Rape of Lucrece,* l. 1129.

Dance on sands.—*The Two Gentlemen of Verona,* iii, 2, 81.

Dance her turn.—*The Winter's Tale,* iv, 4, 58.

Danced before the king.—*The Winter's Tale,* iv, 4, 346.

Danced thee on his knee.—*Titus Andronicus,* v, 3, 162.

5 When you do dance, I wish you
A wave o' the sea, that you might ever do
Nothing but that.
The Winter's Tale. Act iv, sc. 4, l. 140. [Florizel]

But come; our dance, I pray:
Your hand, my Perdita: so turtles pair,
That never mean to part.
The Winter's Tale. Act iv, sc. 4, l. 153. [Florizel]

They have a dance which the wenches say is a gallimaufry of gambols.
The Winter's Tale. Act iv, sc. 4, l. 334. [Servant] "Gallimaufry" (a hodge-podge, a ridiculous medley) occurs again in *The Merry Wives of Windsor,* ii, 1, 119.

6
She dances featly.
The Winter's Tale. Act iv, sc. 4, l. 176. [Polixenes]

She dances
As goddess-like to her admired lays.
Pericles. Act v, Gower, l. 3.

Dances well.—*Othello,* iii, 3, 185.

DANGER

See also Hazard, Peril

7
Only to seem to deserve well, and to beguile the supposition of that lascivious young boy the count, have I run into this danger.
All's Well that Ends Well. Act iv, sc. 3, l. 332. [Parolles]

Main danger.—*All's Well that Ends Well,* iii, 6, 17.

8 These quick-sands, Lepidus,
Keep off them, for you sink.
Antony and Cleopatra. Act ii, sc. 7, l. 65. [Antony] "Quicksand" (unhyphenated) is repeated in *III Henry VI,* v, 4, 26: "Quicksand of deceit."

In negligent danger.—*Antony and Cleopatra,* iii, 6, 81.

9 There is
No danger in what show of death it makes,
More than the locking-up the spirits a time,
To be more fresh, reviving.
Cymbeline. Act i, sc. 5, l. 39. [Cornelius] The only use of "locking-up." "Reviving" occurs only once more, in *Julius Cæsar,* ii, 2, 88: "Reviving blood."

10
Send danger from the east unto the west,
So honour cross it from the north to south.
I Henry IV. Act i, sc. 3, l. 195. [Hotspur]

'The purpose you undertake is dangerous;'—why, that 's certain: 'tis dangerous to take a cold, to sleep, to drink: but I tell you, my lord fool, out of this nettle, danger, we pluck this flower, safety.
I Henry IV. Act ii, sc. 3, l. 7. [Hotspur]

11
There is not a dangerous action can peep out his head but I am thrust upon it.
II Henry IV. Act i, sc. 2, l. 238. [Falstaff]

Baying him at the heels.
II Henry IV. Act i, sc. 3, l. 80. [Hastings] The only use of "baying."

12
But I must go and meet with danger there,
Or it will seek me in another place
And find me worse provided.
II Henry IV. Act ii, sc. 3, l. 48. [Northumberland]

Seek danger.—*Coriolanus,* i, 3, 14; *Cymbeline,* iv, 2, 162.

13
The dangers of the days but newly gone,
Whose memory is written on the earth
With yet appearing blood.
II Henry IV. Act iv, sc. 1, l. 80. [Archbishop of York]

1
'Tis true that we are in great danger.
Henry V, iv, 1, 1. See under COURAGE.
We'll deliver you Of your great danger.
Coriolanus. Act v, sc. 6, l. 14. [Conspirator] "Great danger" is repeated in *Coriolanus,* v, 6, 138; in *Julius Cæsar,* i, 1, 28; and in *Venus and Adonis,* l. 206.
Extreme dangers.—*Coriolanus,* iv, 5, 75.
2
Thou art come unto a feast of death,
A terrible and unavoided danger.
I Henry VI. Act iv, sc. 5, l. 7. [Talbot]
Your danger 's ours.—*Cymbeline,* v, 5, 314.
Shared dangers with you.—*Othello,* iii, 4, 95.
3
Where danger was, still there I met him.
II Henry VI. Act v, sc. 3, l. 11. [Richard]
Be in danger.—*II Henry VI,* iv, 4, 45.
Danger of my life.—*II Henry VI,* ii, 1, 103.
4
Edward and Richard, like a brace of greyhounds
Having the fearful flying hare in sight,
With fiery eyes sparkling for very wrath,
And bloody steel grasp'd in their ireful hands,
Are at our backs.
III Henry VI. Act ii, sc. 5, l. 129. [Queen Margaret]
5
What danger or what sorrow can befall thee?
III Henry VI. Act iv, sc. 1, l. 76. [King Edward]
Yet am I arm'd against the worst can happen.
III Henry VI. Act iv, sc. 1, l. 128. [King Edward]
For many men that stumble at the threshold
Are well foretold that danger lurks within.
III Henry VI. Act iv, sc. 7, l. 11. [Gloucester]
6
Danger serves among them.
Henry VIII. Act i, sc. 2, l. 37. [Norfolk]
Dangers, doubts, wringing of the conscience,
Fears, and despairs.
Henry VIII. Act ii, sc. 2, l. 28. [Norfolk]
I weigh'd the danger.
Henry VIII. Act ii, sc. 4, l. 197. [King Henry]
7
Into what dangers would you lead me, Cassius,
That you would have me seek into myself
For that which is not in me?
Julius Cæsar. Act i, sc. 2, l. 63. [Brutus]
8
And he that stands upon a slippery place
Makes nice of no vile hold to stay him up.
King John. Act iii, sc. 4, l. 137. [Pandulph]
Danger deviseth shifts.—*Venus and Adonis,* l. 690.
9
Look to thyself, thou art in jeopardy.
King John. Act iii, sc. 1, l. 346. [King Philip] The only use of "jeopardy."
Much danger do I undergo for thee.
King John. Act iv, sc. 1, l. 134. [Hubert]
Apt, liable to be employ'd in danger.
King John. Act iv, sc. 2, l. 226. [King John]
Nor tempt the danger.—*King John,* iv, 3, 84.
10
I am amazed, methinks, and lose my way
Among the thorns and dangers of this world.
King John. Act iv, sc. 3, l. 140. [Bastard]
Even in the jaws of danger and of death.
King John. Act v, sc. 2, l. 116. [Dauphin]
11
Strike up your drums, to find this danger out.
King John. Act v, sc. 2, l. 179. [Lewis]
Tell us how near is danger,
That we may arm us to encounter it.
Richard II. Act v, sc. 3, l. 47. [Bolingbroke]
Now I spy a danger.
King Lear. Act ii, sc. 4, l. 250. [Regan]
12
Dangers are to me indifferent.
Julius Cæsar. Act i, sc. 3, l. 115. [Cassius]
Danger knows full well
That Cæsar is more dangerous than he.
Julius Cæsar. Act ii, sc. 2, l. 44. [Cæsar]
13
I doubt some danger does approach you nearly.
Macbeth. Act iv, sc. 2, l. 67. [Messenger]
If this which he avouches does appear,
There is nor flying hence nor tarrying here.
Macbeth. Act v, sc. 5, l. 47. [Macbeth]
14
Acquaint her with the danger of my state.
Measure for Measure. Act i, sc. 2, l. 184. [Claudio]
And how shall we continue Claudio,
To save me from the danger that might come?
Measure for Measure. Act iv, sc. 3, l. 89. [Provost]
15
Let the danger light
Upon your charter and your city's freedom.
The Merchant of Venice. Act iv, sc. 1, l. 38. [Shylock]
You stand within his danger, do you not?
The Merchant of Venice. Act iv, sc. 1, l. 180. [Portia]
16
Neglecting an attempt of ease and gain,
To wake and wage a danger profitless.
Othello. Act i, sc. 3, l. 29. [Senator] Profitless" is repeated in *Much Ado about Nothing,* v, 1, 4.
17
Danger, which I fear'd is at Antioch,
Whose arm seems far too short to hit me here.
Pericles. Act i, sc. 2, l. 7. [Pericles]
You have at large received
The danger of the task you undertake.
Pericles. Act i, sc. 1, l. 1. [Antiochus]
Revolving
The sundry dangers of his will 's obtaining.
The Rape of Lucrece, l. 127.
18
Some apparent danger seen in him
Aim'd at your highness.
Richard II. Act i, sc. 1, l. 13. [Gaunt]
You pluck a thousand dangers on your head.
Richard II. Act ii, sc. 1, l. 205. [York] "Thousand dangers" is repeated in *Titus Andronicus,* iii, 1, 196.
Full of danger.—*Richard III,* ii, 3, 27.

1
By a divine instinct men's minds mistrust
Ensuing dangers.
Richard III. Act ii, sc. 3, l. 42. [Citizen]
Shun the danger that his soul divines.
Richard III. Act iii, sc. 2, l. 18. [Messenger]
Shun the danger.—*Pericles,* i, 1, 142.
Run into no further danger.—*The Tempest,* iii, 2, 76.
Regard thy danger.—*The Two Gentlemen of Verona,* iii, 1, 256.

2
My master through his art foresees the danger.
The Tempest. Act ii, sc. 1, l. 297. [Ariel]
I do see Danger.—*I Henry IV,* i, 3, 16.

3
For now I stand as one upon a rock
Environ'd with a wilderness of sea,
Who marks the waxing tide grow wave by wave,
Expecting ever when some envious surge
Will in his brinish bowels swallow him.
Titus Andronicus. Act iii, sc. 1, l. 93. [Titus] The only use of "waxing." "Brinish" is repeated in *III Henry VI,* iii, 1, 41: "Brinish tears."

4
And danger, like an ague, subtly taints
Even then when we sit idly in the sun.
Troilus and Cressida. Act iii, sc. 3, l. 232. [Patroclus]
Cressida: You shall be exposed, my lord, to dangers
As infinite as imminent! but I 'll be true.
Troilus: And I 'll grow friend with danger.
Troilus and Cressida. Act iv, sc. 4, l. 70.

5
I do not without danger walk these streets.
Twelfth Night. Act iii, sc. 3, l. 25. [Antonio]
This place is dangerous;
The time right deadly.
Troilus and Cressida. Act v, sc. 2, l. 38. [Ulysses]

6
I conjure thee, . . . that thou declare
What incidency thou dost guess of harm
Is creeping toward me; how far off, how near;
Which way to be prevented, if to be;
If not, how best to bear it.
The Winter's Tale. Act i, sc. 2, l. 400. [Polixenes] The only use of "incidency."
Upon mine honour, I
Will stand betwixt you and danger.
The Winter's Tale. Act ii, sc. 2, l. 65. [Paulina]
What dangers, by his highness' fail of issue,
May drop upon his kingdom and devour
Incertain lookers on.
The Winter's Tale. Act v, sc. 1, l. 27. [Dion]

DARING, see Boldness

DARKNESS

7
To darkness fleet souls that fly backwards.
Cymbeline. Act v, sc. 3, l. 25. [Posthumus]

8
It was so dark, Hal, that thou couldst not see thy hand.
I Henry IV. Act ii, sc. 4, l. 247. [Falstaff]

9
Darkness be the burier of the dead!
II Henry IV, i, 1, 160. The only use of "burier." See under CHAOS.
Darkness . . . Environ you!—*I Henry VI,* v, 4, 89.
Descend to darkness.—*II Henry VI,* i, 4, 42. See under CURSE.
Foul contagious darkness.—*II Henry VI,* iv, 1, 7.
There 's darkness.—*King Lear,* iv, 6, 130. See under HELL.

10
Darkness does the face of earth entomb,
When living light should kiss it.
Macbeth. Act ii, sc. 4, l. 9. [Ross]
Flaky darkness.—*Richard III,* v, 3, 86. See under MORNING. The only use of "flaky."
Flecked darkness.—*Romeo and Juliet,* ii, 3, 3. See under MORNING.

11
I will encounter darkness as a bride.
Measure for Measure, iii, 1, 84. See under DEATH.
Following darkness like a dream.
A Midsummer-Night's Dream. Act v, sc. 1, l. 393. [Puck]

12
Clarence, whom I, indeed, have laid in darkness.
Richard III. Act i, sc. 3, l. 327. [Gloucester]
Eternal darkness.—*Richard III,* i, 3, 269.

13
I' the dead of darkness.
The Tempest. Act i, sc. 2, l. 130. [Prospero]
This thing of darkness I Acknowledge mine.
The Tempest. Act v, sc. 1, l. 275. [Prospero]

14
Clown: Sayest thou that house is dark?
Malvolio: As hell, Sir Topas.
Twelfth Night. Act iv, sc. 2, l. 38.
They have laid me here in hideous darkness.
Twelfth Night. Act iv, sc. 2, l. 33. [Malvolio]
Remain thou still in darkness.
Twelfth Night. Act iv, sc. 2, l. 61. [Clown]
You have put me into darkness.
Twelfth Night. Act v, sc. 1, l. 312. [Fabian]
Keep me in darkness.—*Twelfth Night,* iv, 2, 100; v, 1, 156.
No darkness but ignorance.—*Twelfth Night,* iv, 2, 47. See under IGNORANCE.

DAUGHTER

15
Helen: Can 't no other,
But, I your daughter, he must be my brother?
Countess: Yes, Helen, you might be my daughter-in-law:
God shield you mean it not! daughter and mother
So strive upon your pulse.
All's Well that Ends Well. Act i, sc. 3, l. 171. "Daughter-in-law" is repeated in iii, 2, 21 and iv, 5, 4, and occurs in no other play.

1
A poor physician's daughter, thou dislikest
Of virtue for the name.
All's Well that Ends Well. Act ii, sc. 3, l. 130. [King]
Would I were
A neat-herd's daughter, and my Leonatus
Our neighbour shepherd's son!
Cymbeline. Act i, sc. 1, l. 148. [Imogen]
"Neat-herd" is repeated in *The Winter's Tale,* iv, 4, 332.
A baker's daughter.—*Hamlet,* iv, 5, 42.
A pedler's daughter.—*II Henry VI,* iv, 2, 49.

2
If that thy father live, let him repent
Thou wast not made his daughter.
Antony and Cleopatra. Act iii, sc. 13, l. 134. [Antony]

3
Thou art thy father's daughter.
As You Like It. Act i, sc. 3, l. 60. [Duke]
If there be truth in sight, you are my daughter.
As You Like It. Act v, sc. 4, l. 124. [Duke Senior]
Neither his daughter, if we judge by manners.
As You Like It. Act i, sc. 2, l. 283. [Le Beau]

4
A daughter who He not respects at all.
Cymbeline. Act i, sc. 6, l. 154. [Imogen]
Your daughter, whom she bore in hand to love
With such integrity, she did confess
Was as a scorpion to her sight; whose life,
But that her flight prevented it, she had
Ta'en off by poison.
Cymbeline. Act v, sc. 5, l. 43. [Cornelius]
That paragon, thy daughter.
Cymbeline. Act v, sc. 5, l. 147. [Iachimo]
This piece of tender air, thy virtuous daughter.
Cymbeline. Act v, sc. 5, l. 446. [Soothsayer]

5
I have a daughter—have while she is mine—
Who, in her duty and obedience, mark,
Hath given me this.
Hamlet. Act ii, sc. 2, l. 106. [Polonius]
I 'll loose my daughter to him.
Hamet. Act ii, sc. 2, l. 162. [Polonius]
Hamlet: Have you a daughter?
Polonius: I have, my lord.
Hamlet: Let her not walk i' the sun: conception is a blessing: but not as your daughter may conceive.
Hamlet. Act ii, sc. 2, l. 182.
Still harping on my daughter.
Hamlet. Act ii, sc. 2, l. 188. [Polonius]
"Harping" is used only once again, in *Antony and Cleopatra,* iii, 13, 142: "Harping on what I am."

6
Hamlet: O Jephthah, judge of Israel, what a treasure hadst thou!
Polonius: What a treasure had he, my lord?
Hamlet: Why,
'One fair daughter, and no more,
The which he loved passing well.'
Polonius: [*Aside*] Still on my daughter.
Hamlet: Am I not i' the right, old Jephthah?
Polonius: If you call me Jephthah, my lord,
I have a daughter that I love passing well.
Hamlet. Act ii, sc. 2, l. 422. Jephthah is mentioned again in *III Henry VI,* v, 1, 91. The only mention of Israel.
Fair daughter.—*II Henry VI,* i, 1, 219, and nine times in later plays.
And how doth . . . your fairest daughter and mine, my god-daughter Ellen?
II Henry IV. Act iii, sc. 2, l. 8. [Shallow]
The only use of "god-daughter."
Fairest daughter.—*Henry V,* iv, 5, 16.

7
I am afraid my daughter will run mad,
So much she doteth on her Mortimer.
I Henry IV. Act iii, sc. 1, l. 145. [Glendower]
My daughter weeps: she will not part with you;
She 'll be a soldier too, she 'll to the wars.
I Henry IV. Act iii, sc. 1, l. 194. [Glendower]

8
Blithild, which was daughter to King Clothair.
Henry V. Act i, sc. 2, l. 67. [Canterbury]
Lady Lingare, Daughter to Charlemain.
Henry V. Act i, sc. 2, l. 75. [Canterbury]
Lady Ermengare, Daughter to Charles the foresaid duke of Lorraine.—*Henry V,* i, 2, 83.
Astræa's daughter.—*I Henry VI,* i, 6, 4.
Phillipe, Sole daughter unto Lionel Duke of Clarence.
II Henry VI. Act ii, sc. 2, l. 50. [Salisbury]
Sir Thomas Bullen's daughter.—*Henry VIII,* i, 4, 92.
Cato's daughter.—*Julius Cæsar,* ii, 1, 295.
Eve's daughters.—*The Merry Wives of Windsor,* iv, 2, 24.
Leonato's short daughter.—*Much Ado about Nothing,* i, 1, 216.
Saint Philip's daughters.—*I Henry VI,* i, 2, 143.

9
King Henry: Give me your daughter.
French King: Take her, fair son, and from her blood raise up
Issue to me.
Henry V. Act v, sc. 2, l. 375.
Take of me my daughter, and with her my fortunes.
Much Ado about Nothing. Act ii, sc. 1, l. 313. [Leonato]
My daughter shall be thine.—*III Henry VI,* iv, 2, 12.

10
Dauphin, I am by birth a shepherd's daughter,
My wit untrain'd in any kind of art.
Heaven and our Lady gracious hath it pleased
To shine on my contemptible estate.
I Henry VI. Act i, sc. 2, l. 72. [La Pucelle]
"Contemptible" is repeated in *Much Ado about Nothing,* ii, 3, 187: "Contemptible spirit."
A shepherd's daughter.—*The Winter's Tale,* iv, 1, 27; iv, 4, 794; v, 1, 185; v, 2, 127.
I did beget her, all the parish knows:
Her mother liveth yet, can testify
She was the first fruit of my bachelorship.
I Henry VI. Act v, sc. 4, l. 11. [Shepherd]
The only use of "bachelorship."

God knows thou art a collop of my flesh.
I Henry VI. Act v, sc. 4, l. 18. [Shepherd] "Collop" (slice) is repeated in *A Winter's Tale,* i, 2, 137: "My collop."

1
Thy daughter shall be wedded to my king.
I Henry VI. Act v, sc. 3, l. 137. [Suffolk]

And this her easy-held imprisonment
Hath gain'd thy daughter princely liberty.
I Henry VI. Act v, sc. 3, l. 139. [Suffolk] The only use of "easy-held."

My daughter shall be Henry's, if he please.
I Henry VI. Act v, sc. 3, l. 156. [Reignier]

A poor earl's daughter is unequal odds.
I Henry VI, v, 5, 34. See under ODDS.

A knight's daughter.—*Henry VIII,* iii, 2, 94.

2
Whom should we match with Henry, being a king,
But Margaret, that is daughter to a king?
Her peerless feature, joined with her birth,
Approves her fit for none but for a king.
I Henry VI. Act v, sc. 5, l. 67. [Suffolk]

I am the daughter to King Pericles.
Pericles. Act v, sc. 1, l. 180. [Marina]

Daughter to a king.—*I Henry VI,* v, 3, 51; *Henry VIII,* iv, 2, 172.

Leontes: Is this the daughter of a king?
Florizel: She is, When once she is my wife.
Leontes: That 'once,' I see by your good father's speed,
Will come on very slowly.
The Winter's Tale. Act v, sc. 1, l. 208.

The daughter of a king.—*The Winter's Tale,* iii, 2, 3; *Pericles,* iii, 2, 73; v, 1, 159.

Daughter of a worthless king.—*II Henry VI,* iv, 1, 81.

Many other evidences proclaim her with all certainty to be the king's daughter.
The Winter's Tale. Act v, sc. 2, l. 43. [Third Gentleman]

She was of Tyrus the king's daughter.
Pericles. Act iv, sc. 4, l. 36. [Gower]

King's daughter.—*Cymbeline,* i, 4, 15; *The Winter's Tale,* v, 2, 25; *Pericles,* v, 1, 151.

A great king's daughter.—*The Winter's Tale,* iii, 2, 40.

3
The model of our chaste loves, his young daughter:
The dews of heaven fall thick in blessings on her!
Beseeching him to give her virtuous breeding,—
She is young, and of a noble modest nature,
I hope she will deserve well,—and a little
To love her for her mother's sake, that loved him,
Heaven knows how dearly.
Henry VIII. Act iv, sc. 2, l. 132. [Katharine]

4
Or he that makes his generation messes
To gorge his appetite, shall to my bosom
Be as well neighbour'd, pitied, and relieved,
As thou my sometime daughter.
King Lear. Act i, sc. 1, l. 119. [King Lear] "Neighbour'd" is repeated in *Henry V,* i, 1, 62, and in *Hamlet,* ii, 2, 12.

Thy youngest daughter does not love thee least.
King Lear. Act i, sc. 1, l. 154. [Kent]

Youngest daughter.—*Richard III,* i, 1, 153; *The Taming of the Shrew,* i, 1, 50; 245; i, 2, 120; 260; *King Lear,* i, 1, 47.

5
Thy dowerless daughter, king, thrown to my chance,
Is queen of us, of ours, and our fair France.
King Lear. Act i, sc. 1, l. 259. [King of France]

The hot-blooded France, that dowerless took
Our youngest born.
King Lear, ii, 4, 215. The only uses of "dowerless."

6
We
Have no such daughter, nor shall ever see
That face of hers again.
King Lear. Act i, sc. 1, l. 265. [King Lear]

This fellow has banished two on 's daughters, and did the third a blessing against his will.
King Lear. Act i, sc. 4, l. 114. [Fool]

I marvel what kin thou and thy daughters are.
King Lear. Act i, sc. 4, l. 199. [Fool]

By the marks of sovereignty, knowledge, and reason, I should be false persuaded I had daughters.
King Lear. Act i, sc. 4, l. 252. [King Lear]

A fox, when one has caught her,
And such a daughter,
Should sure to the slaughter,
If my cap would buy a halter.
King Lear. Act i, sc. 4, l. 340. [Fool]

7
Yet have I left a daughter,
Who, I am sure, is kind and comfortable.
King Lear. Act i, sc. 4, l. 327. [King Lear]

Thy other daughter will use thee kindly.
King Lear. Act i, sc. 5, l. 14. [Fool]

Thou hast one daughter,
Who redeems nature from the general curse
Which twain have brought her to.
King Lear. Act iv, sc. 6, l. 209. [Gentleman]

8
But thou art yet my flesh, my blood, my daughter;
Or rather a disease that 's in my flesh,
Which I must needs call mine: thou art a boil,
A plague-sore, an embossed carbuncle,
In my corrupted blood.
King Lear. Act ii, sc. 4, l. 224. [King Lear] The only use of "plague-sore."

My own flesh and blood to rebel! . . . My daughter is my flesh and blood.
The Merchant of Venice. Act iii, sc. 1, l. 37. [Shylock]

9
If it be you that stir these daughters' hearts
Against their father, fool me not so much
To bear it tamely.
King Lear. Act ii, sc. 4, l. 277. [King Lear]

Hast thou given all to thy two daughters?
And art thou come to this?
King Lear. Act iii, sc. 4, l. 49. [King Lear]

Lear: What, have his daughters brought him to this pass?
Couldst thou save nothing? Didst thou give them all?

Fool: Nay, he reserved a blanket, else we had been all shamed.
Lear: Now, all the plagues that in the pendulous air
Hang fated o'er men's faults light on thy daughters!
Kent: He hath no daughters, sir.
Lear: Death, traitor! nothing could have subdued nature,
To such a lowness but his unkind daughters.
Is it the fashion, that discarded fathers
Should have thus little mercy on their flesh?
Judicious punishment! 'twas this flesh begot
Those pelican daughters.
King Lear. Act iii, sc. 4, l. 66. The only use of "pendulous." "Pelican" is repeated in *Richard II,* ii, 1, 126, and in *Hamlet,* iv, 5, 146.

Pernicious daughters.—*King Lear,* iii, 2, 22.

Shrill-shrieking daughters.—*Henry V,* iii, 3, 35. See WAR, 1627:5.

Stern daughter.—*Cymbeline,* ii, 3, 42.

Tigers, not daughters, what have you perform'd?
King Lear. Act iv, sc. 2, l. 40. [Albany]

His daughters seek his death.
King Lear. Act iii, sc. 4, l. 168. [Gloucester]

His dog-hearted daughters.
King Lear. Act iv, sc. 3, l. 47. [Kent] The only use of "dog-hearted."

Your eldest daughters have foredone themselves,
And desperately are dead.
King Lear. Act v, sc. 3, l. 291. [Kent] "Foredone" is repeated in *A Midsummer-Night's Dream,* v, 1, 381.

Eldest daughter.—*The Taming of the Shrew,* i, 1, 142.

1
My daughters Got 'tween the lawful sheets.
King Lear. Act iv, sc. 6, l. 117. [King Lear]

Whether our daughter were legitimate.
Henry VIII. Act ii, sc. 4, l. 179. [King Henry]

2
Longaville: Pray you, sir, whose daughter?
Boyet: Her mother's, I have heard.
Love's Labour's Lost. Act ii, sc. 1, l. 201.

Don Pedro: I think this is your daughter.
Leonato: Her mother hath many times told me so.
Much Ado about Nothing. Act i, sc. 1, l. 105.

3
Alack, what heinous sin is it in me
To be ashamed to be my father's child!
But though I am a daughter to his blood,
I am not to his manners.
The Merchant of Venice. Act ii, sc. 3, l. 16. [Jessica]

'My daughter! O my ducats! O my daughter!
Fled with a Christian! O my Christian ducats!
Justice! the law! my ducats, and my daughter!'
The Merchant of Venice. Act ii, sc. 8, l. 15. [Salanio, quoting Shylock]

I would my daughter were dead at my foot.
The Merchant of Venice. Act iii, sc. 1, l. 92. [Shylock]

Your daughter spent in Genoa, as I heard, in one night fourscore ducats.
The Merchant of Venice. Act iii, sc. 1, l. 113. [Tubal]

4
I told you, sir, my daughter is disposed of.
The Merry Wives of Windsor. Act iii, sc. 4, l. 74. [Page]

As she is mine, I may dispose of her.
A Midsummer-Night's Dream. Act i, sc. 1, l. 42. [Egeus]

5
My daughter will I question how she loves you,
And as I find her, so am I affected.
The Merry Wives of Windsor. Act iii, sc. 4, l. 97. [Mrs. Page]

My daughter tells us all.—*Much Ado about Nothing,* ii, 3, 138.

My daughter says so.—*Much Ado about Nothing,* ii, 3, 156.

The old man's daughter told us all.—*Much Ado about Nothing,* v, 1, 179.

6
My lord, they stay for you to give your daughter to her husband.
Much Ado about Nothing. Act iii, sc. 5, l. 60. [Messenger]

Will you with free and unconstrained soul,
Give me this maid, your daughter?
Much Ado about Nothing. Act iv, sc. 1, l. 25. [Claudio] "Unconstrained" is repeated in *III Henry VI,* i, 1, 143.

Your daughter here the princes left for dead.
Much Ado about Nothing. Act iv, sc. 1, l. 204. [Friar Francis]

I cannot bid you bid my daughter live;
That were impossible; but, I pray you both,
Possess the people in Messina here
How innocent she died.
Much Ado about Nothing. Act v, sc. 1, l. 288. [Leonato]

7
In honest plainness thou hast heard me say
My daughter is not for thee.
Othello. Act i, sc. 1, l. 97. [Brabantio]

Your daughter, if you have not given her leave,
I say again, hath made a gross revolt;
Tying her duty, beauty, wit and fortunes
In an extravagant and wheeling stranger
Of here and every where.
Othello. Act i, sc. 1, l. 134. [Roderigo] The only use of "wheeling" (wandering).

O treason of the blood!
Fathers, from hence trust not your daughters' minds
By what you see them act.
Othello. Act i, sc. 1, l. 170. [Brabantio]

8
O thou foul thief, where hast thou stow'd my daughter?
Damn'd as thou art, thou hast enchanted her.
Othello. Act i, sc. 2, l. 62. [Brabantio] "Stow'd" is repeated in *Hamlet,* iv, 2, 1: "Safely stowed"; and in *The Tempest,* i, 2, 320: "Under hatches stow'd."

Brabantio: My daughter! O, my daughter!
Duke and Senators: Dead?
Brabantio: Ay, to me;
She is abused, stol'n from me, and corrupted
By spells and medicines bought of mountebanks.
Othello. Act i, sc. 3, l. 59.

Beguiled your daughter of herself.
Othello. Act i, sc. 3, l. 66. [Duke]

That I have ta'en away this old man's daughter,
It is most true; true, I have married her.
Othello. Act i, sc. 3, l. 78. [Othello]

1
It was a lordling's daughter, the fairest one of three,
That liked of her master as well as well might be,
Till looking on an Englishman, the fair'st that eye could see,
Her fancy fell a-turning.
The Passionate Pilgrim, l. 211. Probably not by Shakespeare. The only use of "lordling."

2
Simonides: What do you think of my daughter, sir?
Pericles: A most virtuous princess.
Simonides: And she is fair too, is she not?
Pericles: As a fair day in summer, wondrous fair.
Simonides: Sir, my daughter thinks very well of you;
Ay, so well, that you must be her master.
Pericles. Act ii, sc. 5, l. 33.

What says he to your daughter? have you spoke?
All's Well that Ends Well. Act v, sc. 3, l. 28. [King]

Thou hast bewitch'd my daughter, and thou art
A villain.
Pericles. Act ii, sc. 5, l. 49. [Simonides]

3
Here 's all that is left living of your queen,
A little daughter; for the sake of it,
Be manly, and take comfort.
Pericles. Act iii, sc. 1, l. 20. [Lychorida]

Sole daughter.—*Pericles,* iv, 3, 39.

4
His daughter meanly have I match'd in marriage.
Richard III. Act iv, sc. 3, l. 37. [King Richard]

For my daughters, Richard,
They shall be praying nuns, not weeping queens.
Richard III. Act iv, sc. 4, l. 200. [Queen Elizabeth]

King Richard: You have a daughter call'd Elizabeth,
Virtuous and fair, royal and gracious.
Queen Elizabeth: And must she die for this? O, let her live,
And I 'll corrupt her manners, stain her beauty;
Slander myself as false to Edward's bed;
Throw over her the veil of infamy:
So she may live unscarr'd of bleeding slaughter,
I will confess she was not Edward's daughter.
Richard III. Act iv, sc. 4, l. 203. "Unscarr'd" is repeated in *Timon of Athens,* iv, 3, 161: "Unscarr'd braggarts."

Thou know'st my daughter 's of a pretty age.
Romeo and Juliet. Act i, sc. 3, l. 10. [Lady Capulet]

5
Baptista: What, will my daughter prove a good musician?
Hortensio: I think she 'll sooner prove a soldier:
Iron may hold with her, but never lutes.
The Taming of the Shrew. Act ii, sc. 1, l. 145.

6
Proceed in practice with my younger daughter;
She 's apt to learn.
The Taming of the Shrew. Act ii, sc. 1, l. 165. [Baptista] "Younger daughter" is repeated in l. 334, and occurs nowhere else.

Our second daughter.—*King Lear,* i, 1, 68.

7
Baptista: How speed you with my daughter?
Petruchio: How but well, sir? how but well?
The Taming of the Shrew. Act ii, sc. 1, l. 283.

Call you me daughter? now, I promise you,
You have show'd a tender fatherly regard,
To wish me wed to one half lunatic.
The Taming of the Shrew. Act ii, sc. 1, l. 287. [Katharina]

If I may have your daughter to my wife,
I 'll leave her houses three or four.
The Taming of the Shrew. Act ii, sc. 1, l. 367. [Tranio]

That have by marriage made thy daughter mine.
The Taming of the Shrew. Act v, sc. 1, l. 119. [Lucentio]

Have you married my daughter without asking my good will?
The Taming of the Shrew. Act v, sc. 1, l. 137. [Baptista]

8
I have done nothing but in care of thee,
Of thee, my dear one, thee, my daughter.
The Tempest. Act i, sc. 2, l. 16. [Prospero]

His daughter and I will be king and queen,—save our graces!
The Tempest. Act iii, sc. 2, l. 114. [Stephano]

Then, as my gift and thine own acquisition,
Worthily purchased, take my daughter.
The Tempest. Act iv, sc. 1, l. 13. [Prospero] The only use of "acquisition."

Give him thy daughter:
What you bestow, in him I 'll counterpoise,
And make him weigh with her.
Timon of Athens. Act i, sc. 1, l. 144. [Timon]

He shall buy my daughter.—*Troilus and Cressida,* iii, 3, 28.

9
One only daughter have I, no kin else,
On whom I may confer what I have got:
The maid is fair, o' the youngest for a bride,
And I have bred her at my dearest cost
In qualities of the best.
Timon of Athens. Act i, sc. 1, l. 121. [Old Athenian]

The cordial of mine age to glad my heart!
Titus Andronicus. Act i, sc. 1, l. 166. [Titus]

10
For worse than Philomel you used my daughter,
And worse than Progne I will be revenged;
And now prepare your thoats.
Titus Andronicus. Act v, sc. 2, l. 195. [Titus] The plot of Shakespeare's play resembles the

Greek legend of Tereus, King of Thrace, who brought Philomela to visit his wife Procne, her sister, but dishonoured her and cut out her tongue: whereupon Procne, in revenge, killed her son and served his flesh to Tereus.

Was it well done of rash Virginius
To slay his daughter with his own right hand,
Because she was enforced, stain'd, and deflower'd?
Titus Andronicus. Act v, sc. 3, l. 37. [Titus]

Why hast thou slain thine only daughter thus?
Titus Andronicus. Act v, sc. 3, l. 55. [Tamora]

Mangled daughter.—*Titus Andronicus,* iii, 1, 256.

1
His more braver daughter.
The Tempest. Act i, sc. 2, l. 439. [Prospero]

Admiring daughter.—*Winter's Tale,* v, 3, 41.
Beauteous daughter.—*Richard III,* iv, 4, 315.
Beauteous princely daughter!—*Richard III,* iv, 4, 405.
Beloved daughter.—*Pericles,* v, 1, 30.
Chaste daughter.—*Cymbeline,* v, 5, 194.
Dear daughter.—*King Lear,* ii, 4, 156.
Gentle daughter.—*The Two Gentlemen of Verona,* iii, 1, 14, and three times in later plays.
Gracious daughter.—*Measure for Measure,* iv, 3, 116.
Lady daughter.—*Cymbeline,* i, 1, 154.
Pensive daughter.—*Romeo and Juliet,* iv, 1, 39.

2
I am all the daughters of my father's house,
And all the brothers too.
Twelfth Night. Act ii, sc. 4, l. 123. [Viola]

3
I have three daughters; the eldest is eleven;
The second and the third, nine, and some five.
The Winter's Tale. Act ii, sc. 1, l. 144. [Antigonus]

Bear three daughters.—*III Henry VI,* ii, 1, 41.

4
A daughter, and a goodly babe,
Lusty and like to live.
Winter's Tale. Act ii, sc. 2, l. 26. [Paulina]

The good queen,
For she is good, hath brought you forth a daughter.
Winter's Tale. Act ii, sc. 3, l. 64. [Paulina]

A daughter of most rare note.
Winter's Tale. Act iv, sc. 2, l. 48. [Camillo]

'Tis none of your daughter.—*The Winter's Tale,* iv, 4, 850.

5
Worries his daughter with clipping her.
The Winter's Tale. Act v, sc. 2, l. 58. [Gentleman] The only use of "clipping" (embracing).

Him, whose daughter
His tears proclaim'd his, parting with her.
The Winter's Tale. Act v, sc. 1, l. 159. [Florizel]

DAWN

See also Morning, Sunrise

6
Swift, swift, you dragons of the night, that dawning
May bare the raven's eye!
Cymbeline. Act ii, sc. 2, l. 48 [Iachimo]

He longs not for the dawning.—*Henry V,* iii, 7, 141.
Near the dawning.—*Measure for Measure,* iv, 2, 97.
Good dawning.—*King Lear,* ii, 2, 1.
Dawning day.—*Titus Andronicus,* ii, 2, 10.
Bird of dawning.—*Hamlet,* i, 1, 60. The only uses of "dawning."

7
The day begins to break, and night is fled,
Whose pitchy mantle over-veil'd the earth.
I Henry VI. Act ii, sc. 2, l. 1. [Bedford] The only use of "over-veil'd."

When dying clouds contend with growing light,
What time the shepherd, blowing of his nails,
Can neither call it perfect day nor night.
III Henry VI. Act ii, sc. 5, l. 2. [King Henry]

8
At the first opening of the gorgeous east.
Love's Labour's Lost. Act iv, sc. 3, l. 223. [Biron]

9
My mistress will before the break of day
Be here at Belmont.
The Merchant of Venice. Act v, sc. 1, l. 29. [Stephano] "Break of day" occurs eight times in the plays and twice in the poems.

Nurse: The day is broke; be wary, look about.
Juliet: Then, window, let day in, and let life out.
Romeo and Juliet. Act iii, sc. 5, l. 40.

The day broke Before we parted.—*Othello,* iii, 1, 34.

10
For night's swift dragons cut the clouds full fast,
And yonder shines Aurora's harbinger.
A Midsummer-Night's Dream. Act iii, sc. 2, l. 379. [Puck]

The eastern gate, all fiery-red,
Opening on Neptune with fair blessed beams,
Turns into yellow gold his salt green streams.
A Midsummer-Night's Dream. Act iii, sc. 2, l. 391. [Oberon] "Fiery-red" is repeated in *Richard II,* ii, 3, 58.

Come, thou gentle day!
For if but once thou show me thy grey light,
I'll find Demetrius and revenge this spite.
A Midsummer-Night's Dream. Act iii, sc. 2, l. 418. [Lysander]

Shine comforts from the east,
That I may back to Athens by daylight,
From these that my poor company detest.
A Midsummer-Night's Dream. Act iii, sc. 2, l. 433. [Helena]

11
The wolves have prey'd; and look, the gentle day,
Before the wheels of Phœbus, round about
Dapples the drowsy east with spots of grey.
Much Ado about Nothing. Act v, sc. 3, l. 25. [Don Pedro] The only use of "dapples."

Lo, the blushing morrow
Lends light to all fair eyes that light will borrow.
The Rape of Lucrece, l. 1082.

DAY

See also To-day

1
This last day was A shrewd one to 's.
Antony and Cleopatra. Act iv, sc. 9, l. 4. [Soldier] "Last day" is repeated in *II Henry VI,* v, 2, 41.
Latter days.—*III Henry VI,* iv, 6, 43; *Henry V,* iv, 1, 143.
The general all-ending day.—*Richard III,* iii, 1, 78. See JUDGEMENT DAY.
2
You have look'd on better days.
As You Like It. Act ii, sc. 7, l. 113. [Orlando]
True is it that we have seen better days.
As You Like It. Act ii, sc. 7, l. 120. [Duke Senior]
We have seen better days.
Timon of Athens, iv, 2, 27. See under ADVERSITY.
3
How does your honour for this many a day?
Hamlet. Act iii, sc. 1, l. 91. [Ophelia]
4
Of all the days i' the year, I came to 't that day that our last king Hamlet overcame Fortinbras. . . . It was the very day that young Hamlet was born.
Hamlet. Act v, sc. 1, l. 155. [Clown]
Of all days in the year.—*Romeo and Juliet,* i, 3, 16; i, 3, 25.
5
And then to horse before day.
I Henry IV. Act ii, sc. 2, l. 105. [Falstaff]
Ere day.—*Julius Cæsar,* i, 3, 153; i, 3, 163.
Ere it be day.—*The Passionate Pilgrim,* l. 315.
6
Jesu, Jesu, the mad days that I have spent!
II Henry IV. Act iii, sc. 2, l. 36. [Shallow]
Jesus, the days that we have seen!
II Henry IV. Act iii, sc. 2, l. 233. [Shallow]
How he comes o'er us with our wilder days,
Not measuring what use we made of them.
Henry V. Act i, sc. 2, l. 267. [King Henry]
7
The day, my friends and all things stay for me.
Henry V. Act iv, sc. 1, l. 325. [King Henry]
It is my day.—*Richard III,* i, 2, 130.
8
The sun is high, and we outwear the day.
Henry V. Act iv, sc. 2, l. 63. [Constable]
Now, soldiers, march away:
And how thou pleasest, God, dispose the day!
Henry V. Act iv, sc. 3, l. 131. [King Henry]
9
King Henry: I know not if the day be ours or no;
For yet a many of your horsemen peer
And gallop o'er the field.
Montjoy: The day is yours.
Henry V. Act iv, sc. 7, l. 87.
This day is ours, as many more shall be.
I Henry VI. Act i, sc. 5, l. 18. [La Pucelle]
The day is ours.—*Richard III,* v, 5, 2; *I Henry IV,* v, 4, 163.
The day almost itself professes yours,
And little is to do.
Macbeth. Act v, sc. 7, l. 27. [Siward]
The day Was yours.—*Cymbeline,* v, 5, 75.
The day is lost.—*Richard III,* v, 4, 6.
Losing day.—*Julius Cæsar,* v, 5, 36.
Pandulph: What have you lost by losing of this day?
Dauphin: All days of glory, joy and happiness.
King John. Act iii, sc. 4, l. 116.
O day untowardly turned!
Much Ado about Nothing. Act iii, sc. 2, l. 134. [Don Pedro] The only use of "untowardly."
It is a day turn'd strangely.
Cymbeline. Act v, sc. 2, l. 17. [Lucius]
10
Expect Saint Martin's summer, halcyon days.
I Henry VI. Act i, sc. 2, l. 131. [La Pucelle] The only mention of Saint Martin, and the only use of "halcyon days." "Halcyon" is repeated in *King Lear,* ii, 2, 84: "Halcyon beaks."
A summer's day.—*Henry V,* iii, 6, 67; iv, 8, 24; *A Midsummer-Night's Dream,* i, 2, 89; *Sonnets,* xviii.
Summer-days.—*Pericles,* iv, 1, 18.
Winter's day.—*Sonnets,* xiii.
11
Exeter doth wish
His days may finish ere that hapless time.
I Henry VI. Act iii, sc. 1, l. 200. [Exeter]
Our day is gone;
Clouds, dews, and dangers come.
Julius Cæsar. Act v, sc. 3, l. 63. [Titinius]
Cassius' day is set.—*Julius Cæsar,* v, 3, 62.
His days are almost done.—*Twelfth Night,* ii, 3, 112.
My day is dim.—*II Henry IV,* iv, 5, 101.
My days are past the best.—*Sonnets,* cxxxviii.
12
Had York and Somerset brought rescue in,
We should have found a bloody day of this.
I Henry VI. Act iv, sc. 7, l. 33. [Charles]
He would make this a bloody day to somebody.
II Henry IV. Act v, sc. 4, l. 14. [Hostess]
These bloody days.—*Richard III,* v, 5, 36.
13
A day will come when York shall claim his own.
II Henry VI. Act i, sc. 1, l. 239. [York]
14
Do you as I do in these dangerous days.
II Henry VI. Act ii, sc. 2, l. 69. [York]
These days are dangerous.
II Henry VI. Act iii, sc. 1, l. 142. [Gloucester]
15
The day is almost spent.
II Henry VI. Act iii, sc. 1, l. 325. [Beaufort]
The day is spent.
Richard III. Act iii, sc. 2, l. 91. [Stanley]
Declining day.—*Antony and Cleopatra,* v, 1, 38.
16
All my days.—*III Henry VI,* i, 3, 43.
Busy days.—*Richard III,* i, 3, 145.
Day by day.—*Titus Andronicus,* v, 2, 58; *All's Well that Ends Well,* iii, 1, 18; *The Tempest,* v, 1, 163; *Sonnets,* lxxv, cxvii.
From day to day.—*Love's Labour's Lost,* v, 2, 860; *Macbeth,* v, 5, 20.
Of late days.—*Henry VIII,* v, 3, 29.

The live-long day.—*Julius Cæsar,* i, 1, 46; *Troilus and Cressida,* i, 3, 147.
Never 's my day.—*Troilus and Cressida,* iv, 5, 52.
One of these days.—*Henry V,* ii, 1, 92; *As You Like It,* i, 2, 91; *Troilus and Cressida,* v, 3, 104; *The Winter's Tale,* ii, 1, 18.
I have seen the day.—*Othello,* v, 2, 261; *King Lear,* v, 3, 276.
T' other day.—*II Henry VI,* i, 3, 87, and frequently in later plays. Sometimes printed "th' other day."
This many a day.—*Henry VIII,* v, 2, 21.
This present day.—*Richard III,* i, 1, 69.
These present days.—*Sonnets,* cvi.
This very day.—*The Comedy of Errors,* i, 2, 3; *All 's Well that Ends Well,* iii, 3, 8; *Measure for Measure,* iv, 2, 215.
Twice a-day.—*Henry V,* iv, 1, 316.
Twice or thrice a day.—*Winter's Tale,* v, 2, 114.

1
In former golden days.
III Henry VI. Act iii, sc. 3, l. 7. [Queen]
Former days.—*II Henry IV,* iv, 5, 216; *Sonnets,* lix; *Timon of Athens,* v, 1, 127.
Days foregone.—*All 's Well that Ends Well,* i, 3, 140.
Elder days.—*Richard II,* ii, 3, 43.
Long-vanish'd days.—*Henry V,* ii, 4, 86. The only use of "long-vanish'd."
Quondam day.—*Love's Labour 's Lost,* v, 1, 7. "Quondam" is used six times in the plays.
Riper days.—*Sonnets,* cii.

2
How many days will finish up the year.
III Henry VI, ii, 5, 27. See under TIME.

3
Each following day
Became the next day's master.
Henry VIII. Act i, sc. 1, l. 16. [Norfolk]
Many days shall see her,
And yet no day without a deed to crown it.
Henry VIII. Act v, sc. 5, l. 58. [Cranmer]

4
This hot malicious day.
King John. Act ii, sc. 1, l. 314. [Herald]
Now, by my life, this day grows wondrous hot.
King John. Act iii, sc. 2, l. 1. [Bastard]
The day is hot.—*Henry V,* iii, 2, 113; *Romeo and Juliet,* iii, 1, 2.
Hot day.—*II Henry IV,* i, 2, 234; *Romeo and Juliet,* iii, 1, 4.
If it be a hot day, and I brandish any thing but a bottle, I would I might never spit white again.
II Henry IV. Act i, sc. 2, l. 236. [Falstaff] "Brandish" is repeated in *I Henry VI,* i, 1, 3, and in *Richard II,* iv, 1, 50.
In the hottest day prognostication proclaims, shall he be set against a brick-wall.
The Winter's Tale. Act iv, sc. 4, l. 816. [Autolycus] "Brick wall" (unhyphenated) is used also in *II Henry VI,* iv, 10, 7. "Prognostication" is repeated in *Antony and Cleopatra,* i, 2, 54.
Hottest summer's day.—*Titus Andronicus,* v, 1, 14.
Warmer days.—*Cymbeline,* ii, 4, 6.

5
How goes the day with us?
King John. Act v, sc. 3, l. 1. [King John]

6
Dumain: As fair as day.
Biron: Ay, as some days; but then no sun must shine.
Love's Labour 's Lost. Act iv, sc. 3, l. 90.
Fair time of day!—*Love's Labour 's Lost,* v, 2, 339; *Henry V,* v, 2, 3.
Good time of day!—*Richard III,* i, 1; i, 3; *III Henry IV,* i, 2; *Timon of Athens,* iii, 6.

7
The posteriors of this day, which the rude multitude call the afternoon.
Love's Labour 's Lost. Act v, sc. 1, l. 94. [Armado] "Posterior of the day" is repeated in l. 96, and l. 126. "Afternoon" occurs twenty-six times.

8
So foul and fair a day I have not seen.
Macbeth. Act i, sc. 3, l. 38. [Macbeth]
When shalt thou see thy wholesome days again?
Macbeth. Act iv, sc. 3, l. 105. [Macduff]

9
Let good Antonio look he keep his day.
The Merchant of Venice. Act ii, sc. 8, l. 23. [Salanio]

10
Sat all day Playing on pipes of corn.
A Midsummer-Night's Dream. Act ii, sc. 1, l. 66. [Titania]
You shall seek all day ere you find them.
The Merchant of Venice. Act i, sc. 1, l. 116. [Bassanio]
I 'll fit you, And not be all day neither.
All's Well that Ends Well. Act ii, sc. 1, l. 93. [Lafeu]
I have sat here all day.
Measure for Measure. Act iv, sc. 1, l. 20. [Mariana]
Trot . . . all day long.
Titus Andronicus. Act v, sc. 2, l. 55. [Titus]

11
Tarry for the comfort of the day.
A Midsummer-Night's Dream. Act ii, sc. 2, l. 38. [Lysander]
The tell-tale Day.—*Rape of Lucrece,* l. 806.

12
As it fell upon a day
In the merry month of May.
The Passionate Pilgrim, l. 373.

13
O, but remember this another day!
Richard III. Act i, sc. 3, l. 299. [Queen Margaret] "Another day" occurs six times in later plays.

14
In the day of battle.
Richard III. Act iv, sc. 4, l. 188. [Duchess]
Day of combat.—*II Henry VI,* i, 3, 224.
Day of desolation.—*Love's Labour 's Lost,* i, 2, 164.
Day of doom.—*III Henry VI,* v, 6, 93; *Titus Andronicus,* ii, 3, 42; *Richard II,* iii, 2, 189.
Day of joy.—*Romeo and Juliet,* iii, 5, 110.
Day of judgement.—*The Merry Wives of Windsor,* iii, 3, 226.
Day of success.—*Macbeth,* i, 5, 1.
Day of trial.—*Richard II,* iv, 1, 106; iv, 1, 153.
Day of triumph.—*Richard III,* iii, 4, 44.
Day of victory.—*I Henry VI,* i, 6, 31. With the exception of "day of doom" and "day of trial," each of these phrases was used but once; and "day of trial" but twice, both times in the same scene.

1
It is not yet near day.
Richard III. Act v, sc. 3, l. 220. [King Richard] Also *Romeo and Juliet,* iii, 5, 1.
It is not day.—*Romeo and Juliet,* iii, 5, 25; *Julius Cæsar,* ii, 1, 39.
2
Now is the day we long have looked for.
The Taming of the Shrew. Act ii, sc. 1, l. 335. [Gremio]
This is the 'pointed day.
The Taming of the Shrew. Act iii, sc. 2, l. 1. [Baptista]
3
The days are wax'd shorter with him.
Timon of Athens. Act iii, sc. 4, l. 11. [Lucius' Servant]
4
In my young days.
Titus Andronicus. Act iv, sc. 3, l. 91. [Clown] "Young days" is repeated in *Love's Labour's Lost,* i, 2, 15, and in *Hamlet,* ii, 2, 11. See also under YOUTH.
Youngest days.—*II Henry VI,* ii, 3, 46.
Boyish days.—*Othello,* i, 3, 132.
Dancing days.—*Romeo and Juliet,* i, 5, 33.
Early days.—*Troilus and Cressida,* iv, 5, 12.
5
Were your days
As green as Ajax' and your brain so temper'd,
You should not have the eminence of him.
Troilus and Cressida. Act ii, sc. 3, l. 264. [Ulysses]
Greener days.—*Henry V,* ii, 4, 136.
Salad days.—*Antony and Cleopatra,* i, 5, 73.
Unfledged days.—*The Winter's Tale,* i, 2, 78.
6
Alas the day, how loath you are to offend daylight!
Troilus and Cressida. Act iii, sc. 2, l. 50. "Daylight" occurs twelve times in the plays.
On a day, alack the day!—*The Passionate Pilgrim,* l. 227.
Alack (alas) the day!
II Henry VI, ii, 1, 14, and thirteen times in later plays.
Alack (alas) the heavy day!
Richard II, iii, 3; iv, 1; *Othello,* iv, 2.
7
Deliberate a day or two.
The Two Gentlemen of Verona. Act i, sc. 3, l. 73. [Proteus]
Make pastime with us a day or two.
Cymbeline, iii, 1, 79.
Pause a day or two.
The Merchant of Venice, iii, 2, 1.
8
Trust me, I think 'tis almost day.
The Two Gentlemen of Verona. Act iv, sc. 2, l. 139. [Host]
Good faith, 'tis day.—*Romeo and Juliet,* iv, 4, 20.
It is almost day.—*Measure for Measure,* iv, 2, 109.
The vaward of the day.—*A Midsummer-Night's Dream,* iv, 1, 110. "Vaward" is used five times.
Will it never be day?—*Henry V,* iii, 7, 86.
Would it were day!—*Henry V,* iii, 7, 2. See also under DAWN.
9
He makes a July's day short as December.
The Winter's Tale. Act i, sc. 2, l. 169. [Polixenes]
'O, the twelfth day of December.'
Twelfth Night. Act ii, sc. 3, l. 90. [Sir Toby]

II—Happy Days

10
The gods make this a happy day to Antony!
Antony and Cleopatra. Act iv, sc. 5, l. 1. [Soldier]
This happy day Is not itself.
II Henry VI. Act v, sc. 3, l. 5. [York] "Happy day" occurs eleven times in later plays.
Beauteous day.—*Sonnets,* xxxiv.
Blessed day.—*King John,* iii, 1, 75.
Bright day.—*Julius Cæsar,* ii, 1, 14.
Bright-shining day.—*III Henry VI,* v, 3, 3. The only use of "bright-shining."
Clear day!—*Sonnets,* xliii.
Fair day.—*King John,* iii, 1, 326; *Richard II,* iii, 2, 218; *Troilus and Cressida,* iii, 3, 296; *Pericles,* ii, 5, 36.
Fair prosperous days.—*Richard III,* v, 5, 34.
Fair well-spoken days.—*Richard III,* i, 1, 29. "Well-spoken" is repeated in i, 3, 348, and in *The Two Gentlemen of Verona,* i, 2, 10.
Gentle day.—*A Midsummer-Night's Dream,* iii, 2, 418; *Much Ado about Nothing,* v, 3, 25.
Good day.—*Henry V,* v, 2, 13. See also under GREETING.
Joyful day!—*II Henry IV,* v, 3, 132; *As You Like It,* v, 3, 1.
Living day!—*Sonnets,* xliii.
Lusty days.—*Sonnets,* ii.
Pleasant days!—*II Henry IV,* v, 3, 148.
Quiet days.—*The Tempest,* iv, 1, 24.
Sunshine day.—*III Henry VI,* ii, 1, 187; *Richard II,* iv, 1, 221.
Tender days.—*The Two Gentlemen of Verona,* i, 1, 3.
Well-contented day.—*Sonnets,* xxxii. The only use of "well-contented."
11
A merrier day did never yet greet Rome.
Coriolanus. Act v, sc. 4, l. 46. [Messenger]
Merry day.—*Love's Labour's Lost,* i, 2, 164; *Richard II,* iv, 1, 334; *The Merry Wives of Windsor,* v, 5, 254.
12
O, such a day,
So fought, so follow'd and so fairly won.
II Henry IV. Act i, sc. 1, l. 20. [Bardolph]
So great a day.—*I Henry IV,* iv, 1, 132.
This day
Shall change all griefs and quarrels into love.
Henry V. Act v, sc. 2, l. 19. [Queen Isabel]
13
Now, by my faith, lords, 'twas a glorious day; . . .
And more such days as these to us befall!
II Henry VI. Act v, sc. 3, l. 29. [Warwick]
Glorious day.—*I Henry IV,* iii, 2, 133; *The Rape of Lucrece,* l. 1013.
So great a day as this is cheaply bought.
Macbeth. Act v, sc. 8, l. 37. [Malcolm] The only use of "cheaply."
14
The sun is in the heaven, and the proud day,

Attended with the pleasures of the world,
Is all too wanton and too full of gawds.
King John. Act iii, sc. 3, l. 34. [King John]

1
Four happy days bring in Another moon.
A Midsummer-Night's Dream. Act i, sc. 1, l. 2. [Theseus]

O most courageous day! O most happy hour!
A Midsummer-Night's Dream. Act iv, sc. 2, l. 27. [Quince]

2
Each day still better other's happiness;
Until the heavens, envying earth's good hap,
Add an immortal title to your crown!
Richard II. Act i, sc. 1, l. 22. [Bolingbroke]

3
A holy day shall this be kept hereafter.
Richard III. Act ii, sc. 1, l. 73. [Queen Elizabeth]

A wicked day, and not a holy day.
King John, iii, 1, 83. The only uses of "holy day."

4
What! we have many goodly days to see.
Richard III. Act iv, sc. 4, l. 320. [King Richard] "Goodly day" is repeated in *Cymbeline,* iii, 3, 1.

When is the royal day?—*Richard III,* iii, 4, 3.

Time-bettering days.—*Sonnets.* No. lxxxii. The only use of the phrase.

5
This day shall be a love-day.
Titus Andronicus. Act i, sc. 1, l. 491. [Saturninus] The only use of "love-day."

Nuptial day.—*A Midsummer-Night's Dream,* iii, 2, 12; *Coriolanus,* i, 6, 31.

6
'Tis a lucky day, boy, and we'll do good deeds on 't.
The Winter's Tale. Act iii, sc. 3, l. 142. [Shepherd] The only use of "lucky day."

III—Unhappy Days

7
And every day that comes comes to decay
A day's work in him.
Cymbeline. Act i, sc. 5, l. 56. [Queen]

8
Would I had met my dearest foe in heaven
Or ever I had seen that day, Horatio!
Hamlet. Act i, sc. 2, l. 182. [Hamlet]

9
The day looks pale At his distemperature.
I Henry IV. Act v, sc. 1, l. 2. [King Henry] "Distemperature" occurs six times.

Bates: We have no great cause to desire the approach of day.
Williams: We see yonder the beginning of the day, but I think we shall never see the end of it.
Henry V. Act iv, sc. 1, l. 89.

10
A raw and gusty day.
Julius Cæsar. Act i, sc. 2, l. 100. [Cassius] The only use of "gusty."

This raw rheumatic day!—*The Merry Wives of Windsor,* iii, 1, 47.

Blustering day.—*I Henry IV,* v, 1, 6.

Loud day.—*King John,* v, 4, 14.

Stormy day.—*Richard II,* iii, 2, 106; *Venus and Adonis,* l. 965.

11
What hath this day deserved? what hath it done,
That it in golden letters should be set
Among the high tides in the calendar?
Nay, rather turn this day out of the week,
This day of shame, oppression, perjury.
King John. Act iii, sc. 1, l. 84. [Constance] The only use of "high tides."

This day, all things begun come to ill end,
Yea, faith itself to hollow falsehood change!
King John. Act iii, sc. 1, l. 94. [Constance]

Let not the hours of this ungodly day
Wear out the day in peace; but, ere sunset,
Set armed discord 'twixt these perjured kings!
King John. Act iii, sc. 1, l. 109. [Constance]

Brooded watchful day.—*King John,* iii, 3, 52. The only use of "brooded."

12
She prays she never may behold the day.
'For day,' quoth she, 'night's scapes doth open lay.'
The Rape of Lucrece, l. 746.

Revealing day through every cranny spies,
And seems to point her out where she sits weeping;
To whom she sobbing speaks: 'O eye of eyes,
Why pry'st thou through my window? leave thy peeping.'
The Rape of Lucrece, l. 1086. The only use of "revealing." "Cranny" is repeated in *Midsummer-Night's Dream,* iii, 1, 73; v, 1, 164.

13
One day too late, I fear me, noble lord,
Hath clouded all thy happy days on earth.
Richard II. Act iii, sc. 2, l. 67. [Salisbury]

14
Alack the heavy day!
Richard II, iii, 3, 7; iv, 1, 257.

Alas the heavy day!—*Othello,* iv, 2, 42.

Most heavy day!—*Antony and Cleopatra,* iv, 14, 134.

O heavy day!—*Romeo and Juliet,* iv, 5, 18.

15
Accursed and unquiet wrangling days,
How many of you have mine eyes beheld!
Richard III. Act ii, sc. 4, l. 55. [Duchess of York]

A black day will it be to somebody.
Richard III. Act v, sc. 3, l. 280. [King Richard]

16
This day's black fate on more days doth depend;
This but begins the woe others must end.
Romeo and Juliet. Act iii, sc. 1, l. 124. [Romeo]

Accursed, unhappy, wretched, hateful day!
Romeo and Juliet. Act iv, sc. 5, l. 43. [Lady Capulet]

Unhappy day.—*Richard II,* iii, 2, 71.

O most unhappy days!—*The Comedy of Errors,* iv, 4, 126.

O woe! O woful, woful, woful day!
Most lamentable day, most woful day,
That ever, ever, I did yet behold!
O day! O day! O day! O hateful day!
Never was seen so black a day as this:
O woful day, O woful day!
Romeo and Juliet, iv, 5, 49. [Nurse]

O woful day!—*Julius Cæsar,* iii, 2, 204.
O, woe the day!—*The Tempest,* i, 2, 15.

1 The dismall'st day is this that e'er I saw.
Titus Andronicus. Act i, sc. 1, l. 384. [Titus] "Dismall'st" is repeated in ii, 3, 204, and occurs in no other play.

Dark days.—*Sonnets,* xcvii.
Distemper'd day.—*King John,* iii, 4, 154.
Doleful days.—*II Henry IV,* ii, 4, 211.
Hateful days.—*Titus Andronicus,* iii, 1, 132; *The Rape of Lucrece,* l. 161.
Ill day.—*The Comedy of Errors,* v, 1, 138.
Lamentable day!—*Romeo and Juliet,* iv, 5, 30.
Perilous day.—*I Henry IV,* v, 2, 96.
Pitchy day.—*III Henry VI,* v, 6, 85.
Roughest day.—*Macbeth,* i, 3, 147.
Sickly days.—*Hamlet,* iii, 3, 96.
Tedious days.—*Richard III,* iv, 4, 28; *Hamlet,* iii, 2, 237.
Worse days.—*Julius Cæsar,* i, 2, 326.

2 The day frowns more and more.
The Winter's Tale. Act iii, sc. 3, l. 54. [Antigonus]

This day is ominous.—*Troilus and Cressida,* v, 3, 66.

IV—Day and Night

3 You have made the days and nights as one.
All's Well that Ends Well. Act v, sc. 1, l. 3. [Helena]

Come, night; end, day!—*All's Well that Ends Well,* iii, 2, 131.

4 We did sleep day out of countenance, and made the night light with drinking.
Antony and Cleopatra. Act ii, sc. 2, l. 181. [Enobarbus]

One that converses more with the buttock of the night than with the forehead of the morning.
Coriolanus. Act ii, sc. 1, l. 56. [Menenius]

Endured shrewd days and nights with us.
As You Like It. Act v, sc. 4, l. 179. [Duke Senior]

5 May
This night forestall him of the coming day!
Cymbeline. Act iii, sc. 5, l. 68. [Queen]

6 Winding up days with toil and nights with sleep.
Henry V. Act iv, sc. 1, l. 296. [King Henry]

7 By day, by night, waking and in my dreams.
II Henry VI. Act i, sc. 1, l. 26. [Queen]

Let never day nor night unhallow'd pass.
II Henry VI. Act ii, sc. 1, l. 85. [King Henry]

Dark shall be my light and night my day.
II Henry VI. Act ii, sc. 4, l. 40. [Duchess of Gloucester]

8 The gaudy, blabbing and remorseful day
Is crept into the bosom of the sea.
II Henry VI. Act iv, sc. 1, l. 1. [Captain] The only use of "blabbing."

How still the evening is,
As hush'd on purpose to grace harmony!
Much Ado about Nothing. Act ii, sc. 3, l. 40. [Claudio]

Light thickens; and the crow
Makes wing to the rooky wood:
Good things of day begin to droop and drowse;
Whiles night's black agents to their preys do rouse.
Macbeth. Act iii, sc. 2, l. 50. [Macbeth] The only use of "rooky" and "drowse."

The bright day is done,
And we are for the dark.
Antony and Cleopatra. Act v, sc. 2, l. 193. [Iras]

See the brave day sunk in hideous night.
Sonnets. No. xii.

Yield day to night!—*I Henry VI,* i, 1, 1.
Neither . . . day nor night.—*III Henry VI,* ii, 5, 4.
Neither night nor day.—*Macbeth,* i, 3, 19.

9 Who dares not stir by day must walk by night.
King John. Act i, sc. 1, l. 172. [Bastard]

Day is day, night night.—*Hamlet,* ii, 2, 88.

10 And then, to sleep but three hours in the night,
And not be seen to wink of all the day—
When I was wont to think no harm all night
And make a dark night too of half the day.
Love's Labour's Lost. Act i, sc. 1, l. 43. [Biron]

O, but for my love, day would turn to night!
Love's Labour's Lost. Act iv, sc. 3, l. 233. [Biron]

11 By the clock, 'tis day,
And yet dark night strangles the travelling lamp:
Is 't night's predominance, or the day's shame,
That darkness does the face of earth entomb,
When living light should kiss it?
Macbeth. Act ii, sc. 4, l. 6. [Ross] "Entomb" is repeated in *Troilus and Cressida,* iii, 3, 186: "Entomb thyself alive."

This night methinks is but the daylight sick;
It looks a little paler: 'tis a day,
Such as the day is when the sun is hid.
The Merchant of Venice. Act v, sc. 1, l. 124. [Portia] "Paler" is repeated in *As You Like It,* iv, 3, 178: "You look paler and paler."

But were the day come, I should wish it dark,
That I were couching with the doctor's clerk.
The Merchant of Venice. Act v, sc. 1, l. 304. [Gratiano]

12 Four days will quickly steep themselves in night;
Four nights will quickly dream away the time.
A Midsummer-Night's Dream. Act i, sc. 1, l. 7. [Hyppolyta]

13 Pack night, peep day; good day, of night now borrow:
Short, night, to-night, and length thyself to-morrow.
The Passionate Pilgrim, l. 209.

14 Day hath nought to do what 's done by night.
The Rape of Lucrece, l. 1092.

1
Black night o'ershade thy day.
Richard III. Act i, sc. 2, l. 131. [Anne]
Day, yield me not thy light; nor, night, thy rest!
Richard III. Act iv, sc. 4, l. 401. [King Richard]
2
Go, girl, seek happy nights to happy days.
Romeo and Juliet. Act i, sc. 3, l. 106. [Nurse]
Come, thou day in night.—*Romeo and Juliet*, iii, 2, 17.
3
Night's candles are burnt out, and jocund day
Stands tiptoe on the misty mountain tops.
Romeo and Juliet. Act iii, sc. 5, l. 9. [Romeo] "Tiptoe" repeated in *Henry V*, iv, 3, 42.
4
When day's oppression is not eased by night,
But day by night, and night by day, oppress'd?
And each, though enemies to either's reign,
Do in consent shake hands to torture me.
Sonnets. No. xxviii.
All days are nights to see till I see thee,
And nights bright days when dreams do show thee me.
Sonnets. No. xliii.
As gentle day Doth follow night.
Sonnets. No. cxlv.
5
When the day serves, before black-corner'd night,
Find that thou want'st by free and offer'd light.
Timon of Athens. Act v, sc. 1, l. 47. [Painter] The only use of "black-corner'd."
6
Witness the tiring day and heavy night.
Titus Andronicus. Act v, sc. 2, l. 24. [Titus]
By day and [or] night.—*Titus Andronicus*, iv, 3, 28, and twelve times in later plays.
By night and day.—*The Comedy of Errors*, iv, 2, 60; *Troilus and Cressida*, iii, 2, 122.
Nor night nor day no rest.—*The Winter's Tale*, ii, 3, 1.
7
The busy day,
Waked by the lark, hath roused the ribald crows,
And dreaming night will hide our joys no longer.
Troilus and Cressida. Act iv, sc. 2, l. 8. [Troilus] The only use of "ribald."

V—Special Days

8
To-morrow is Saint Valentine's day,
All in the morning betime,
And I a maid at your window,
To be your Valentine.
Hamlet. Act iv, sc. 5, l. 48. [Ophelia] St. Valentine's day is February 14, the supposed day of his martyrdom.
Good morrow, friends. Saint Valentine is past:
Begin these wood-birds but to couple now?
A Midsummer-Night's Dream. Act iv, sc. 1, l. 143. [Theseus] The only use of "wood-birds."
There's not a hair on's head but 'tis a Valentine.
The Two Gentlemen of Verona. Act iii, sc. 1, l. 191. [Launce]
9
The day is call'd the feast of Crispian.
Henry V. Act iv, sc. 3, l. 40. [King Henry] St. Crispin's day is October 25.
Crispin's day.—*Henry V*, iv, 3, 48; iv, 3, 67.
The day of Crispin Crispianus.—*Henry V*, iv, 7, 94.
10
Upon Saint Davy's day.
Henry V. Act iv, sc. 1, l. 55. [Pistol] St. David's day is March 1.
Saint Davy's day is past.—*Henry V*, v, 1, 2.
11
Buckingham: This is All-Souls' day, fellows, is it not?
Sheriff: It is, my lord.
Buckingham: Why, then All-Souls' day is my body's doomsday.
This is the day that, in King Edward's time,
I wish'd might fall on me, when I was found
False to his children or his wife's allies;
This is the day wherein I wish'd to fall
By the false faith of him I trusted most.
Richard III. Act v, sc. 1, l. 12. All-Souls' day is November 2.
Holy-rood day.—*I Henry IV*, i, 1, 52. September 14.
Saint Lambert's day.—*Richard II*, i, 1, 199. September 17.
12
Capulet: But soft! what day is this?
Paris: Monday, my lord.
Capulet: Monday! ha, ha! Well, Wednesday is too soon,
O' Thursday let it be: o' Thursday, tell her,
She shall be married to this noble earl.
Romeo and Juliet. Act iii, sc. 4, l. 18. Monday is mentioned five times; Tuesday seven times; Wednesday fourteen times; Thursday fourteen times; Friday three times; Saturday twice; Sunday ten times, and Sabbath twice.

DEAFNESS

See also Ear

13
Therefore be deaf to my unpitied folly.
Antony and Cleopatra. Act i, sc. 3, l. 98. [Cleopatra]
I will be deaf to pleading and excuses.
Romeo and Juliet. Act iii, sc. 1, l. 197. [Prince]
Falstaff: Boy, tell him I am deaf.
Page: You must speak louder; my master is deaf.
Chief Justice: I am sure he is, to the hearing of any thing good.
II Henry IV. Act i, sc. 2, l. 77.
Come on my right hand, for this ear is deaf.
Julius Cæsar. Act i, sc. 2, l. 213. [Cæsar]
14
What! art thou, like the adder, waxen deaf?
II Henry VI. Act iii, sc. 2, l. 76. [Queen Margaret]
Why dost not speak? what, deaf? not a word?
Titus Andronicus, v, 1, 46. [Lucius]

DEATH

See also Life and Death; Man: Dead Men

I—Familiar Phrases

1
Let the white death sit on thy cheek for ever.
All's Well that Ends Well. Act ii, sc. 3, l. 77. [Helena]
Let me see my death!
All's Well that Ends Well. Act iv, sc. 3, l. 345. [Parolles]
Death 's the word.—*Antony and Cleopatra,* i, 2, 139.

2
Cleopatra: How now! is he dead?
Diomedes: His death 's upon him, but not dead.
Antony and Cleopatra. Act iv, sc. 15, l. 7.
I am dying, Egypt, dying.
Antony and Cleopatra. Act iv, sc. 15, l. 18. [Antony] Also Act iv, sc. 15, l. 41.
The hand of death hath raught him.
Antony and Cleopatra. Act iv, sc. 9, l. 30. [Soldier]
The sudden hand of death close up mine eye!
Love's Labour 's Lost. Act v, sc. 2, l. 825. [King] "Hand of death" is repeated in *Richard II,* iii, 1, 30; and a third time in *I Henry IV,* v, 4, 84.

3
Hold death awhile at the arm's end.
As You Like It. Act ii, sc. 6, l. 10. [Orlando]
With one hand beats Cold death aside.
Romeo and Juliet. Act iii, sc. 1, l. 166. [Benvolio]

4
Orlando: Then in mine own person I die.
Rosalind: No, faith, die by attorney.
As You Like It. Act iv, sc. 1, l. 94.

5
Thou art adjudged to the death.
The Comedy of Errors. Act i, sc. 1, l. 147. [Duke]
To the death.—*Richard III,* iii, 2, 55; *Love's Labour 's Lost,* v, 2, 146.
Unto the death.—*King John,* i, 1, 154.
We will behold his death.—*The Comedy of Errors,* v, 1, 128.

6
On my face he turn'd an eye of death.
I Henry IV. Act i, sc. 3, l. 143. [Hotspur]

7
It was the death of him.
I Henry IV. Act ii, sc. 1, l. 14. [Carrier]
'Twill be his death.—*Troilus and Cressida,* iv, 2, 98.
I 'll be thy death.—*III Henry VI,* v, 6, 88.
I knew thou wouldst be his death.
Troilus and Cressida. Act iv, sc. 2, l. 91. [Pandarus]

8
The end of life cancels all bands.
I Henry IV. Act iii, sc. 2, l. 157. [Prince of Wales]

9
Hotspur: Thou art dust, And food for—
Prince of Wales: For worms, brave Percy.
I Henry IV. Act v, sc. 4, l. 85. The only instance of the use of "food for worms" in the plays.

Death hath not struck so fat a deer to-day,
Though many dearer.
I Henry IV. Act v, sc. 4, l. 107. [Prince of Wales]

10
He doth sin that doth belie the dead.
II Henry IV. Act i, sc. 1, l. 98. [Morton]
Beat not the bones of the buried.
Love's Labour 's Lost. Act v, sc. 2, l. 667. [Armado]
Speak me fair in death.
The Merchant of Venice. Act iv, sc. 1, l. 275. [Antonio]

11
Die men like dogs! give crowns like pins!
Have we not Hiren here?
II Henry IV. Act ii, sc. 4, l. 188. [Pistol] Repeated in l. 174. Hiren is a corruption of Irene, and the line is probably a quotation from a lost play by George Peele, entitled *The Turkish Mahomet and Hyren the Fair Greek.* It occurs in the old comedy of *Law Tricks,* 1608. Pistol applies it to his sword, but Mistress Quickly supposes he is asking for some woman.
Do not speak like a death's-head; do not bid me remember mine end
II Henry IV. Act ii, sc. 4, l. 254. [Falstaff] "Death's-head" is repeated in *I Henry IV,* iii, 3, 34; *The Merchant of Venice,* i, 2, 55.

12
A man can die but once: we owe God a death.
II Henry IV. Act iii, sc. 2, l. 250. [Feeble]
Prince of Wales: Why, thou owest God a death.
Falstaff: 'Tis not due yet; I would be loath to pay him before his day.
I Henry IV. Act v, sc. 1, l. 127.
Let it go which way it will, he that dies this year is quit for the next.
II Henry IV. Act iii, sc. 2, l. 254. [Feeble]
Now my death Changes the mode.
II Henry IV. Act iv, sc. 5, l. 199. [Prince Henry] The only use of "mode."
Go to death.—*Henry V,* iii, 2, 124.
Espoused to death.—*Henry V,* iv, 6, 26.

13
Bedford: What say'st thou, man, before dead Henry's corse?
Speak softly, or the loss of those great towns
Will make him burst his lead and rise from death.
I Henry VI. Act i, sc. 1, l. 62. [Bedford]
The treacherous manner of his mournful death.
I Henry VI. Act ii, sc. 2, l. 16. [Talbot]
Run a tilt at death.—*I Henry VI,* iii, 2, 51.

14
Triumphant death, smear'd with captivity.
I Henry VI. Act iv, sc. 7, l. 3. [Talbot]
Antic death.—*I Henry VI,* iv, 7, 18.

15
Had death been French, then death had died to-day.
I Henry VI. Act iv, sc. 7, l. 28. [Talbot]
Death, lie thou there, by a dead man interr'd.
Romeo and Juliet. Act v, sc. 3, l. 87. [Romeo]
So shalt thou feed on Death, that feeds on men,

And Death once dead, there 's no more dying then.
Sonnets. No. cxlvi.

1 To beat assailing death from his weak legions.
I Henry VI. Act iv, sc. 4, l. 16. [Lucy]

Now thou art come unto a feast of death.
I Henry VI. Act iv, sc. 5, l. 7. [Talbot]

2 But him outlive, and die a violent death.
II Henry VI, i, 4, 34. "Violent death" is repeated in l. 64; in *I Henry VI,* v, 4, 64; and in *Titus Andronicus,* v, 2, 108.

Bloody death.—*The Rape of Lucrece,* l. 430.
Canker death.—*Romeo and Juliet,* ii, 3, 30.
A carrion Death.—*The Merchant of Venice,* ii, 7, 63.
Cruel death.—*Richard III,* ii, 1, 105; *A Midsummer-Night's Dream,* i, 2, 12.
Deserved death.—*Richard II,* v, 1, 68. See under DESERVING.
Dire death.—*Richard III,* iv, 4, 143.
Direful slaughtering death.—*Titus Andronicus,* v, 3, 144.
Double death.—*Titus Andronicus,* iii, 1, 246.
Dusty death.—*Macbeth,* v, 5, 23.
Engrossing death!—*Romeo and Juliet,* v, 3, 115. The only use of "engrossing."
Foul death.—*Pericles,* iv, 4, 37.
Grim death.—*The Taming of the Shrew,* Ind., 1, 35.
Hard-favour'd death.—*I Henry VI,* iv, 7, 23.
Hideous death.—*King John,* v, 4, 22.
Languishing death.—*Cymbeline,* i, 5, 9. "Desperate languishings" occurs in *All 's Well that Ends Well,* i, 3, 235.
Lingering death.—*II Henry VI,* iii, 2, 247.
A living death.—*Richard III,* i, 2, 153; *The Rape of Lucrece,* l. 726.
Threefold death.—*III Henry VI,* v, 4, 32.
Timeless death.—*I Henry VI,* v, 4, 5; *II Henry VI,* iii, 2, 187; *III Henry VI,* v, 6, 42; *Richard III,* i, 2, 117. A phrase used by Shakespeare once in each of his first four plays, and never thereafter.
Timeless end.—*Romeo and Juliet,* v, 3, 162; *Richard II,* iv, 1, 5.
Ungentle death!—*III Henry VI,* ii, 3, 6.
Death by the law.—*Timon of Athens,* i, 1, 195.
Bed of death!—*Richard III,* iv, 1, 54; *All 's Well that Ends Well,* ii, 1, 107. "Death-bed" is used ten times.
Stroke of death.—*Richard II,* iii, 1, 31.
At point of death.—*II Henry VI,* iii, 2, 369; *Romeo and Juliet,* v, 3, 88; *Twelfth Night,* v, 1, 121.
Till the point of death.—*I Henry VI,* iii, 1, 168.
Half dead.—*I Henry VI,* iii, 2, 55; *Coriolanus,* iv, 5, 132; *Pericles,* i, 4, 96.

3 That he should die is worthy policy;
But yet we want a colour for his death.
II Henry VI. Act iii, sc. 1, l. 235. [Cardinal]

So the poor chicken should be sure of death.
II Henry VI. Act iii, sc. 1, l. 251. [Queen]

Resign to death.—*II Henry VI,* iii, 1, 334.

4 Why, Warwick, who should do the duke to death?
II Henry VI. Act iii, sc. 2, l. 179. [Suffolk]

Done to death.—*II Henry VI,* iii, 2, 244; *III Henry VI,* ii, 1, 103; iii, 3, 103; *Much Ado about Nothing,* v, 3, 3.

5 To die by thee were but to die in jest;
From thee to die were torture more than death.
II Henry VI. Act iii, sc. 2, l. 400. [Suffolk]

This way fall I to death.
II Henry VI. Act iii, sc. 2, l. 412. [Suffolk]

6 Their thread of life is spun.
II Henry VI. Act iv, sc. 2, l. 31. [Bevis] "Spun" is repeated in *Coriolanus,* i, 3, 93.

He 's walk'd the way of nature.
II Henry IV. Act v, sc. 2, l. 4. [Warwick]

He quit being.
Cymbeline. Act i, sc. 1, l. 38. [Gentleman]

7 If I do not leave you all as dead as a door-nail, I pray God I may never eat grass more.
II Henry VI. Act iv, sc. 10, l. 43. [Cade] The only use of "door-nail."

Falstaff: What, is the old king dead?
Pistol: As nail in door.
II Henry IV. Act v, sc. 3, l. 126.

De herring is no dead so as I vill kill him.
The Merry Wives of Windsor. Act ii, sc. 3, l. 12. [Doctor Caius] This is Shakespeare's nearest approach to the proverb, "dead as a herring."

8 The noble gentleman gave up the ghost.
III Henry VI. Act ii, sc. 3, l. 22. [Richard]

Ready to give up the ghost.
Julius Cæsar. Act v, sc. 1, l. 89. [Cassius]

These news would cause him once more yield the ghost.
I Henry VI. Act i, sc. 1, l. 67. [Gloucester]

9 Nature brought him to the door of death.
III Henry VI. Act iii, sc. 3, l. 105. [Oxford]

Shook hands with death.—*III Henry VI,* i, 4, 102.
Breathed his last.—*III Henry VI,* v, 2, 40. The only use of this phrase. Nearest is "Where your brave father breathed his latest gasp," in the same play (Shakespeare's second play), *III Henry IV,* ii, 1, 108.
To the latest gasp.—*III Henry VI,* v, 2, 41.

10 Death's black veil.
III Henry VI. Act v, sc. 2, l. 16. [Warwick]

Death's dart.—*Cymbeline,* iv, 2, 211.
Death's face.—*Love's Labour 's Lost,* v, 2, 616.
Death's hand.—*I Henry IV,* iv, 1, 136.
Death's hour.—*Julius Cæsar,* iii, 1, 154.
Death's instrument.—*Richard II,* v, 5, 107. Instrument of death, *The Rape of Lucrece,* l. 1038.
Death's net.—*Pericles,* i, 1, 40.
Death's pale flag.—*Romeo and Juliet,* v, 3, 96.
Death's stamp.—*Coriolanus,* ii, 2, 111. Each of these phrases was used only once.

11 Nothing but death shall stay me.
Julius Cæsar. Act iv, sc. 3, l. 128. [Poet]

I would have that drum or another, or 'hic jacet.'
All's Well that Ends Well. Act iii, sc. 6, l. 65. [Parolles] The only use of "hic jacet."

1
Titinius: He lies not like the living. O my heart!
Messala: Is not that he?
Titinius: No, this was he.
Julius Cæsar. Act v, sc. 3, l. 59.

2
Go pronounce his present death.
Macbeth. Act i, sc. 2, l. 64. [Duncan]
A present death Had been more merciful.
The Winter's Tale. Act ii, sc. 3, l. 184. [Antigonus]
'Tis present death.—*I Henry VI,* iii, 4, 39. "Present death" occurs seven times in later plays.

3
I will not be afraid of death and bane,
Till Birnam forest come to Dunsinane.
Macbeth. Act v, sc. 3, l. 59. [Macbeth]
Strange images of death.—*Macbeth,* i, 3, 97.

4
He 's not prepared for death.
Measure for Measure. Act ii, sc. 2, l. 84. [Isabella]
Prepare yourself to death.
Measure for Measure. Act iii, sc. 1, l. 169. [Duke]
Unprepared, unmeet for death.
Measure for Measure. Act iv, sc. 3, l. 71. [Duke]
Away with him to death!
Measure for Measure. Act v, sc. 1, l. 434. [Duke]
He dies for Claudio's death.
Measure for Measure. Act v, sc. 1, l. 448. [Duke]

5
Death 's a great disguiser.
Measure for Measure. Act iv, sc. 2, l. 186. [Duke] The only use of "disguiser."

6
Deceased, or, as you would say in plain terms, gone to heaven.
The Merchant of Venice. Act ii, sc. 2, l. 67. [Launcelot] The only instance of the use of the phrase "gone to heaven" in the plays.
She 's dead, deceased, she 's dead; alack the day!
Romeo and Juliet. Act iv, sc. 5, l. 23. [Nurse]
Arthur is deceased to-night.—*King John,* iv, 2, 85.
Late deceased.—*I Henry VI,* iii, 2, 132.

7
I suffered the pangs of three several deaths; first, an intolerable fright, to be detected with a jealous rotten bell-wether; next, to be compassed, like a good bilbo, in the circumference of a peck, hilt to point, heel to head; and then, to be stopped in, like a strong distillation, with stinking clothes that fretted in their own grease.
The Merry Wives of Windsor. Act iii, sc. 5, l. 115. [Falstaff] "Distillation" is repeated in *Sonnet* v: "Summer's distillation"; and **"bell-wether"** in *As You Like It,* iii, 2, 85.

Pangs of death.—*III Henry VI,* ii, 3, 17; *Twelfth Night,* iii, 4, 262.
Pain of death.—*II Henry VI,* iii, 2, 257; iii, 2, 288; and six times in later plays.

8
He shall die a flea's death.
The Merry Wives of Windsor. Act iv, sc. 2, l. 158. [Mrs. Ford]
Die the death.—*A Midsummer-Night's Dream,* i, 1, 65; *Measure for Measure,* ii, 4, 165; *Antony and Cleopatra,* iv, 14, 26; *Cymbeline,* iv, 2, 96.

9
That death 's unnatural that kills for loving.
Othello. Act v, sc. 2, l. 43. [Desdemona]
A guiltless death I die.
Othello. Act v, sc. 2, l. 122. [Desdemona]

10
Think death no hazard in this enterprise.
Pericles. Act i, sc. 1, l. 5. [Pericles]
Against the face of death,
I sought the purchase of a glorious beauty,
From whence an issue I might propagate.
Pericles. Act i, sc. 2, l. 71. [Pericles]
Death may usurp on nature many hours,
And yet the fire of life kindle again
The o'erpress'd spirits.
Pericles. Act iii, sc. 2, l. 82. [Cerimon]

11
Death is now the phœnix' nest;
And the turtle's loyal breast
To eternity doth rest.
The Phœnix and the Turtle, l. 56.

12
Within the hollow crown
That rounds the mortal temples of a king
Keeps Death his court.
Richard II, iii, 2, 160. See under KING.
Poor key-cold figure of a holy king!
Pale ashes of the house of Lancaster!
Richard III. Act i, sc. 2, l. 5. [Lady Anne] The only use of "key-cold."
Death of kings.—*Richard II,* iii, 2, 156.

13
That grim ferryman which poets write of.
Richard III. Act i, sc. 4, l. 46. [Clarence] This is the only use of "ferryman" in the plays, and "ferry" is also used only once, in *The Merchant of Venice,* iii, 4, 53.

14
The kingdom of perpetual night.
Richard III. Act i, sc. 4, l. 47. [Clarence]
The blind cave of eternal night.
Richard III. Act v, sc. 3, l. 62. [King Richard]
Grim cave of death.—*Rape of Lucrece,* l. 769.

15
Let me die, to look on death no more!
Richard III. Act ii, sc. 4, l. 65. [Duchess of York]
If thou wilt outstrip death, go cross the seas.
Richard III. Act iv, sc. 1, l. 42. [Queen Elizabeth] "Outstrip" is repeated in *Henry V,* iv, 1, 177: "Outstrip men"; and in *The Tempest,* iv, 1, 10: "Outstrip all praise."

16
This day those enemies are put to death.
Richard III, iii, 2, 105. "Put to death" is repeated in iii, 5, 76, and in *Julius Cæsar,* iv, 3, 175.
Without debatement further, more or less,
He should the bearers put to sudden death,

Not shriving-time allow'd.
Hamlet. Act v, sc. 2, l. 45. [Hamlet] The only use of "shriving-time." "Sudden death" is repeated in *I Henry VI,* i, 4, 48; and *II Henry VI,* iii, 2, 133; and "debatement" in *Measure for Measure,* v, 1, 99: "After much debatement."
Immediate death.—*Comedy of Errors,* i, 1, 69.
Imminent death.—*II Henry VI,* v, 3, 19.
Instant death.—*Cymbeline,* v, 5, 278.

1
King Richard: But didst thou see them dead?
Tyrrel: I did, my lord.
King Richard: And buried, gentle Tyrrel?
Tyrrel: The chaplain of the Tower hath buried them;
But how or in what place I do not know.
King Richard: Come to me, Tyrrel, soon at after supper,
And thou shalt tell the process of their death.
Richard III. Act iv, sc. 3, l. 27.
Dead and buried.—*As You Like It,* i, 2, 123.
Dead and gone.—*II Henry VI,* ii, 3, 37; *I Henry VI,* i, 4, 93; *Hamlet,* iv, 5, 29.
Dead and rotten.—*Love's Labour 's Lost,* v, 2, 666; *King Lear,* v, 3, 285; *The Winter's Tale,* iii, 3, 82.

2
Death and destruction dog thee at the heels.
Richard III. Act iv, sc. 1, l. 40. [Queen Elizabeth]
Death and damnation!—*Othello,* iii, 3, 396.

3
Seeking for Richmond in the throat of death.
Richard III. Act v, sc. 4, l. 5. [Catesby]
Mouth of death.—*Richard III,* iv, 4, 2.

4
Beshrew your heart for sending me about,
To catch my death with jaunting up and down!
Romeo and Juliet. Act ii, sc. 5, l. 52. [Nurse] The only use of "catch my death" and "jaunting." For "catch cold" see under DISEASE.

5
Death 's the end of all.
Romeo and Juliet. Act iii, sc. 3, l. 92. [Nurse]
We were born to die.
Romeo and Juliet. Act iii, sc. 4, l. 4. [Capulet]

6
When that churl Death my bones with dust shall cover.
Sonnets. No. xxxii.
When I perhaps compounded am with clay.
Sonnets. No. lxxi.
When I in earth am rotten.
Sonnets. No. lxxxi.

7
Beat me to death.
The Taming of the Shrew, iv, 3, 137. See under BEATING.
Bite him to death.—*Antony and Cleopatra,* iii, 2, 38.
Bleed to death.—*The Merchant of Venice,* iv, 1, 258; *Troilus and Cressida,* ii, 3, 80; *Othello,* v, 1, 45.
Boiled to death.—*Twelfth Night,* ii, 5, 3.
Bowl'd to death.—*The Merry Wives of Windsor,* iii, 4, 91.
Bruise to death.—*Measure for Measure,* ii, 1, 6.
Eaten to death.—*II Henry IV,* i, 2, 245.
Frozen almost to death.—*Richard III,* ii, 1, 115.
Frozen to death.—*The Taming of the Shrew,* iv, 1, 40.
Hack'd to death.—*Richard III,* iii, 3, 12.
Hurt to the death.—*Othello,* ii, 3, 164.
Press'd to death.—*Richard II,* iii, 4, 72.
Press it to death.—*Troilus and Cressida,* iii, 2, 218.
Press me to death.—*Much Ado about Nothing,* iii, 1, 76.
Pressing to death.—*Measure for Measure,* v, 1, 529.
Sweats to death.—*I Henry IV,* ii, 2, 115.
Torture me to death!—*Much Ado about Nothing,* iv, 1, 186. See under TORTURE.

8
The wills above be done! but I would fain die a dry death.
The Tempest. Act i, sc. 1, l. 71. [Gonzalo]

9
The perpetual wink.
The Tempest. Act ii, sc. 1, l. 285. [Antonio]
To give mine enemy a lasting wink.
The Winter's Tale, i, 2, 317. [Leontes]

10
Aaron: I tell you, lords, you do but plot your deaths
By this device.
Chiron: Aaron, a thousand deaths
Would I propose to achieve her whom I love.
Titus Andronicus. Act ii, sc. 1, l. 78.
I, most jocund, apt and willingly,
To do you rest, a thousand deaths would die.
Twelfth Night. Act v, sc. 1, l. 135. [Viola] "Thousand deaths" is repeated in *Measure for Measure,* iii, 1, 40.
Die a hundred thousand deaths.—*I Henry IV,* iii, 2, 158.
Twenty thousand deaths.—*Coriolanus,* iii, 3, 70.

11
Sir Toby: 'But I will never die.'
Clown: Sir Toby, there you lie.
Twelfth Night. Act ii, sc. 3, l. 115.

12
Snatch'd . . . out of the jaws of death.
Twelfth Night. Act iii, sc. 4, l. 394. [Antonio]
Jaws of danger and of death.—*King John,* v, 2, 116.

13
Thurio, give back, or else embrace thy death.
The Two Gentlemen of Verona. Act v, sc. 4, l. 126. [Valentine]
Death's ebon dart.—*Venus and Adonis,* l. 948.

14
Look down And see what death is doing.
The Winter's Tale. Act iii, sc. 2, l. 149. [Paulina]

15
Some say he shall be stoned; but that death is too soft for him, say I.
The Winter's Tale. Act iv, sc. 4, l. 806. [Autolycus]
All deaths are too few, the sharpest too easy.
The Winter's Tale. Act iv, sc. 4, l. 809. [Autolycus]
Suffer'd death.—*The Winter's Tale,* iii, 3, 42.

II—Death the Comforter

1
We use To say the dead are well.
Antony and Cleopatra. Act ii, sc. 5, l. 32. [Cleopatra]
Till death enlarge his confine.
Antony and Cleopatra. Act iii, sc. 5, l. 13. [Eros]

2
I have seen her die twenty times upon far poorer moment: I do think there is mettle in death, which commits some loving act upon her, she hath such a celerity in dying.
Antony and Cleopatra. Act i, sc. 2, l. 146. [Enobarbus]
It was the swift celerity of his death,
Which I did think with slower foot came on,
That brain'd my purpose.
Measure for Measure. Act v, sc. 1. l. 399. [Duke]

3
The stroke of death is as a lover's pinch,
Which hurts, and is desired.
Antony and Cleopatra. Act v, sc. 2, l. 298. [Cleopatra]

4
And by the doom of death end woes and all.
The Comedy of Errors. Act i, sc. 1, l. 2. [Ægeon]
And happy were I in my timely death.
The Comedy of Errors. Act i, sc. 1, l. 139. [Ægeon]

5
For me, my ransom's death;
On either side I come to spend my breath.
Cymbeline. Act v, sc. 3, l. 80. [Posthumus]
Yet am I better
Than one that 's sick o' the gout; since he had rather
Groan so in perpetuity than be cured
By the sure physician, death, who is the key
To unbar these locks.
Cymbeline. Act v, sc. 4, l. 4. [Posthumus] The only use of "unbar."

6
Death rock me asleep, abridge my doleful days!
II Henry IV. Act ii, sc. 4, l. 211. [Pistol]
This sleep is sound indeed; this is a sleep
That from this golden rigol hath divorced
So many English kings.
II Henry IV. Act iv, sc. 5, l. 35. [Prince of Wales] "Rigol" (circle, crown) occurs again in *The Rape of Lucrece,* l. 1745.
Goodman death.—*II Henry IV,* v, 4, 32.
Craved death.—*I Henry VI,* i, 4, 32.

7
The arbitrator of despairs,
Just death, kind umpire of men's miseries.
I Henry VI. Act ii, sc. 5, l. 28. [Mortimer] "Arbitrator" is repeated in *Troilus and Cressida,* iv, 5, 225; and in *The Rape of Lucrece,* l. 1017.
My joy is death;
Death, at whose name I oft have been afear'd,
Because I wish'd this world's eternity.
II Henry VI. Act ii, sc. 4, l. 88. [Duchess of Gloucester]

8
Death, death; O amiable lovely death!
Thou odoriferous stench! sound rottenness!
Arise forth from the couch of lasting night,
Thou hate and terror to prosperity,
And I will kiss thy detestable bones
And put my eyeballs in thy vaulty brows
And ring these fingers with thy household worms
And stop this gap of breath with fulsome dust
And be a carrion monster like thyself:
Come, grin on me, and I will think thou smilest
And buss thee as thy wife. Misery's love,
O, come to me!
King John. Act iii, sc. 4, l. 25. [Constance] "Odoriferous" is repeated in *Love's Labour 's Lost,* iv, 2, 128; and "rottenness" in *Cymbeline,* i, 6, 125.
That fell anatomy
Which cannot hear a lady's feeble voice,
Which scorns a modern invocation.
King John. Act iii, sc. 4, l. 40. [Constance]

9
Vex not his ghost: O, let him pass! he hates him much
That would upon the rack of this tough world
Stretch him out longer.
King Lear. Act v, sc. 3, l. 313. [Kent]
Nor steel, nor poison,
Malice domestic, foreign levy, nothing,
Can touch him further.
Macbeth. Act iii, sc. 2, l. 24. [Macbeth]

10
Death is the fairest cover for her shame
That may be wish'd for.
Much Ado about Nothing. Act iv, sc. 1, l. 117. [Leonato]
Though death be poor, it ends a mortal woe.
Richard II. Act ii, sc. 1, l. 152. [York]
Those whom you curse
Have felt the worst of death's destroying wound
And lie full low, graved in the hollow ground.
Richard II. Act iii, sc. 2, l. 138. [Scroop] "Graved" is repeated in *The Merchant of Venice,* ii, 7, 36.

11
Witness my son, now in the shade of death;
Whose bright out-shining beams thy cloudy wrath
Hath in eternal darkness folded up.
Richard III. Act i, sc. 3, l. 267. [Queen Margaret] The only use of "out-shining."

12
Art thou so bare and full of wretchedness,
And fear'st to die?
Romeo and Juliet. Act v, sc. 1, l. 68. [Romeo]
Here will I remain
With worms that are thy chamber-maids; O, here
Will I set up my everlasting rest,
And shake the yoke of inauspicious stars
From this world-wearied flesh.
Romeo and Juliet. Act v, sc. 3, l. 108. [Romeo] The only use of "inauspicious" and "world-wearied." "Chamber-maids" is used twice more, in *King Lear,* iv, 1, 65, and *Twelfth Night,* i, 3, 54.
For restful death I cry.—*Sonnets,* lxvi. "Restful" is repeated in *Richard II,* iv, 1, 12.

1 Say, this were death
That now hath seized them; why, they were no worse
Than now they are.
Tempest. Act ii, sc. 1, l. 260. [Antonio]

And why not death rather than living torment?
The Two Gentlemen of Verona. Act iii, sc. 1, l. 170. [Valentine]

Death was lively joy.—*Venus and Adonis,* l. 497.

III—Death the Inevitable

2
Uncertain life, and sure death.
All's Well that Ends Well. Act ii, sc. 3, l. 20. [Lafeu]

Sure of death.—*Coriolanus,* iii, 1, 155.
Certain death.—*Coriolanus,* iii, 1, 289.
Death is certain.—*II Henry IV,* iii, 2, 45.

3
Fear no more the heat o' the sun,
Nor the furious winter's rages;
Thou thy worldly task hast done,
Home art gone, and ta'en thy wages:
Golden lads and girls all must,
As chimney-sweepers, come to dust.
Cymbeline. Act iv, sc. 2, l. 258. [Guiderius]
"Chimney-sweepers" is repeated in *Love's Labour's Lost,* iv, 3, 266.

Fear no more the frown o' the great;
Thou art past the tyrant's stroke;
Care no more to clothe and eat;
To thee the reed is as the oak:
The sceptre, learning, physic, must
All follow this, and come to dust.
Cymbeline. Act iv, sc. 2, l. 264. [Arviragus]

4
Thou knowest 'tis common; all that lives must die,
Passing through nature to eternity.
Hamlet. Act i, sc. 2, l. 72. [Queen]

Whose common theme
Is death of fathers, and who still hath cried,
From the first corse till he that died to-day,
'This must be so.'
Hamlet. Act i, sc. 2, l. 103. [King]

5
Get you to my lady's chamber, and tell her, let her paint an inch thick, to this favour she must come.
Hamlet. Act v, sc. 1, l. 213. [Hamlet]

This fell sergeant, death,
Is strict in his arrest.
Hamlet. Act v, sc. 2, l. 347. [Hamlet]

6
Certain, 'tis certain; very sure, very sure: death, as the Psalmist saith, is certain to all; all shall die.
II Henry IV. Act iii, sc. 2, l. 40. [Shallow]
The only use of "psalmist."

Doting death is near.—*Henry V,* ii, 1, 65.
The doom of death.—*Henry V,* iii, 6, 46.

7
But kings and mightiest potentates must die,
For that 's the end of human misery.
I Henry VI. Act iii, sc. 2, l. 136. [Talbot]

I must waft thee to thy death.
II Henry VI. Act iv, sc. 1, l. 115. [Whitmore]

8
Away! for death doth hold us in pursuit.
III Henry VI. Act ii, sc. 5, l. 127. [Prince of Wales]

Now death shall stop his dismal threatening sound,
And his ill-boding tongue no more shall speak.
III Henry VI. Act ii, sc. 6, l. 58. [Edward]
"Ill-boding" is repeated in *I Henry VI,* iv, 5, 6: "Ill-boding stars."

Live how we can, yet die we must.
III Henry VI. Act v, sc. 2, l. 28. [Warwick]

9
Of all the wonders that I yet have heard,
It seems to me most strange that men should fear;
Seeing that death, a necessary end,
Will come when it will come.
Julius Cæsar. Act ii, sc. 2, l. 34. [Cæsar]

Brutus: That we shall die, we know; 'tis but the time
And drawing days out, that men stand upon.
Cassius: Why, he that cuts off twenty years of life
Cuts off so many years of fearing death.
Brutus: Grant that, and then is death a benefit.
Julius Cæsar. Act iii, sc. 1, l. 99.

With meditating that she must die once,
I have the patience to endure it now.
Julius Cæsar. Act iv, sc. 3, l. 191. [Brutus]

10 Men must endure
Their going hence, even as their coming hither:
Ripeness is all.
King Lear. Act v, sc. 2, l. 9. [Edgar]

11 See that Claudio
Be executed by nine to-morrow morning:
Bring him his confessor, let him be prepared;
For that 's the utmost of his pilgrimage.
Measure for Measure. Act ii, sc. 1, l. 33. [Angelo]

Thou art death's fool;
For him thou labour'st by thy flight to shun
And yet runn'st toward him still.
Measure for Measure. Act iii, sc. 1, l. 11. [Duke]

12
For, ere the six years that he hath to spend
Can change their moons and bring their times about,
My oil-dried lamp and time-bewasted light
Shall be extinct with age and endless night;
My inch of taper will be burnt and done,
And blindfold death not let me see my son.
Richard II. Act i, sc. 3, l. 219. [Gaunt]
The only use of "oil-dried" and "time-bewasted."

Thy word is current with him for my death,
But dead, thy kingdom cannot buy my breath.
Richard II. Act i, sc. 3, l. 231. [Gaunt]

13
Cry woe, destruction, ruin and decay;
The worst is death, and death will have his day.
Richard II. Act iii, sc. 2, l. 102. [King Richard]

And nothing can we call our own but death
And that small model of the barren earth

Which serves as paste and cover to our bones.
Richard II. Act iii, sc. 2, l. 152. [King Richard]

1
Make haste; the hour of death is expiate.
Richard III. Act iii, sc. 3, l. 23. [Ratcliffe]
Then look I death my days should expiate.
Sonnets. No. xxii. These are the only uses of "expiate." "Expiation" does not occur at all.

2
Either thou wilt die, by God's just ordinance,
Ere from this war thou turn a conqueror,
Or I with grief and extreme age shall perish
And never look upon thy face again.
Richard III. Act iv, sc. 4, l. 183. [Duchess of York]
Turn thee, Benvolio, look upon thy death.
Romeo and Juliet. Act i, sc. 1, l. 74. [Tybalt]
Obey, and go with me; for thou must die.
Romeo and Juliet. Act v, sc. 3, l. 57. [Paris]
This sight of death is as a bell,
That warns my old age to a sepulchre.
Romeo and Juliet. Act v, sc. 3, l. 206. [Lady Capulet]

3
That fell arrest Without all bail.
Sonnets. No. lxxiv.
King of graves and grave for kings,
Imperious supreme of all mortal things.
Venus and Adonis, l. 995.
Invisible commander.
Venus and Adonis, l. 1004.

IV—Death: Its Terrors

4
Death, that dark spirit, in 's nervy arm doth lie.
Coriolanus. Act ii, sc. 1, l. 177. [Volumnia] The only use of "nervy."
Death on the wheel or at wild horses' heels.
Coriolanus. Act iii, sc. 2, l. 2. [Coriolanus]
Sicinius: What you have seen him do and heard him speak, . . .
So criminal and in such capital kind,
Deserves the extremest death. . . .
Coriolanus: Let them pronounce the steep Tarpeian death.
Coriolanus. Act iii, sc. 3, l. 77.
Death by inches.—*Coriolanus,* v, 4, 43.

5
I, in mine own woe charm'd,
Could not find death where I did hear him groan,
Nor feel him where he struck: being an ugly monster,
'Tis strange he hides him in fresh cups, soft beds,
Sweet words; or hath more ministers than we
That draw his knives i' the war.
Cymbeline. Act v, sc. 3, l. 68. [Posthumus]

6
To die: to sleep;
No more; and by a sleep to say we end
The heart-ache and the thousand natural shocks
That flesh is heir to, 'tis a consummation
Devoutly to be wish'd. To die, to sleep;
To sleep; perchance to dream: ay, there 's the rub;
For in that sleep of death what dreams may come
When we have shuffled off this mortal coil,
Must give us pause: there 's the respect
That makes calamity of so long life.
Hamlet. Act iii, sc. 1, l. 60. [Hamlet] The only use of "heart-ache." "Consummation" is repeated in *Cymbeline,* iv, 2, 280.
O proud death,
What feast is toward in thine eternal cell,
That thou so many princes at a shot
So bloodily hast struck?
Hamlet. Act v, sc. 2, l. 375. [Horatio]

7
Where hateful death put on his ugliest mask.
II Henry IV. Act i, sc. 1, l. 66. [Morton] The only use of "ugliest."
Darkness and the gloomy shade of death
Environ you.
I Henry VI. Act v, sc. 4, l. 89. [La Pucelle]
Whitmore: How now! why start'st thou? what, doth death affright?
Suffolk: Thy name affrights me, in whose sound is death.
II Henry VI. Act iv, sc. 1, l. 32.

8
O, now doth Death line his dead chaps with steel;
The swords of soldiers are his teeth, his fangs;
And now he feasts, mousing the flesh of men.
King John. Act ii, sc. 1, l. 352. [Bastard] "Mousing" is repeated in *Macbeth,* ii, 4, 13.
In his forehead sits A bare-ribb'd death.
King John. Act v, sc. 2, l. 176. [Bastard] The only use of "bare-ribbed."
For I do see the cruel pangs of death
Fight in thine eye.
King John. Act v, sc. 4, l. 59. [Salisbury]
Death, having prey'd upon the outward parts,
Leaves them invisible, and his siege is now
Against the mind, the which he pricks and wounds
With many legions of strange fantasies.
King John. Act v, sc. 7, l. 15. [Prince Henry]
All this thou seest is but a clod
And module of confounded royalty.
King John. Act v, sc. 7, l. 57. [King John] "Module" (counterfeit) is repeated in *All's Well that Ends Well,* iv, 3, 114.

9
Death is a fearful thing.
Measure for Measure. Act iii, sc. 1, l. 116. [Claudio]
Ay, but to die, and go we know not where;
To lie in cold obstruction and to rot;
This sensible warm motion to become
A kneaded clod; and the delighted spirit
To bathe in fiery floods, or to reside
In thrilling region of thick-ribbed ice;
To be imprison'd in the viewless winds,
And blown with restless violence about
The pendent world; or to be worse than worst
Of those that lawless and incertain thought
Imagine howling: 'tis too horrible!
The weariest and most loathed worldly life
That age, ache, penury and imprisonment
Can lay on nature is a paradise

To what we fear of death.
Measure for Measure. Act iii, sc. 1, l. 118. [Claudio] The only use of "kneaded," "thick-ribbed" "thrilling" "viewless" and "weariest."

1
A bare-boned death by time outworn.
The Rape of Lucrece, l. 1761. The only use of "bare-boned."

2
But now two mirrors of his princely semblance
Are crack'd in pieces by malignant death.
Richard III. Act ii, sc. 2, l. 51. [Duchess of York]

'Tis a vile thing to die, my gracious lord,
When men are unprepared and look not for it.
Richard III. Act iii, sc. 2, l. 64. [Catesby]

3
Most detestable death, by thee beguiled,
By cruel cruel thee quite overthrown!
Romeo and Juliet. Act iv, sc. 5, l. 56. [Paris]

A vengeful canker eat him up to death.
Sonnets. No. xcix.

4 They would bind me here
Unto the body of a dismal yew,
And leave me to this miserable death.
Titus Andronicus. Act ii, sc. 3, l. 106. [Tamora]

Look, how thou diest! look, how thy eye turns pale!
Look, how thy wounds do bleed at many vents!
Troilus and Cressida. Act v, sc. 3, l. 81. [Cassandra]

Fell as death.—*Troilus and Cressida,* iv, 5, 269.

5
'Hard-favour'd tyrant, ugly, meagre, lean,
Hateful divorce of love,'—thus chides she Death,—
'Grim-grinning ghost, earth's worm, what dost thou mean
To stifle beauty?'
Venus and Adonis, l. 931. The only use of "grim-grinning."

With Death she humbly doth insinuate;
Tells him of trophies, statues, tombs, and stories
His victories, his triumphs and his glories.
Venus and Adonis, l. 1012.

6
I will devise a death as cruel for thee
As thou art tender to 't.
The Winter's Tale. Act iv, sc. 4, l. 450. [Polixenes]

V—The Good Death

7 I . . . do . . . wish too,
Since I nor wax nor honey can bring home,
I quickly were dissolved from my hive,
To give some labourers room.
All 's Well that Ends Well. Act i, sc. 2, l. 64. [King]

Unpitied let me die,
And well deserved: not helping, death 's my fee.
All 's Well that Ends Well. Act ii, sc. 1, l. 191. [Helena]

8 The next time I do fight,
I 'll make death love me; for I will contend
Even with his pestilent scythe.
Antony and Cleopatra. Act iii, sc. 13, l. 192. [Antony]

I will be
A bridegroom in my death, and run into 't
As to a lover's bed.
Antony and Cleopatra. Act iv, sc. 14, l. 99. [Antony]

If I must die,
I will encounter darkness as a bride,
And hug it in mine arms.
Measure for Measure. Act iii, sc. 1, l. 83. [Claudio]

9 Where art thou, death?
Come hither, come! come, come, and take a queen
Worth many babes and beggars!
Antony and Cleopatra. Act v, sc. 2, l. 46. [Cleopatra]

Come, death, and welcome!
Romeo and Juliet. Act iii, sc. 5, l. 24. [Romeo]

10
I mock at death With as big heart as thou.
Coriolanus. Act iii, sc. 2, l. 127. [Volumnia]

He that hath a will to die by himself fears it not from another.
Coriolanus. Act v, sc. 2, l. 110. [Menenius]

11 To my shame, I see
The imminent death of twenty thousand men,
That, for a fantasy and trick of fame,
Go to their graves like beds, fight for a plot . . .
Which is not tomb enough and continent
To hide the slain.
Hamlet. Act iv, sc. 4, l. 59. [Hamlet]

12
They say he made a good end.
Hamlet. Act iv, sc. 5, l. 186. [Ophelia]

A' made a finer end and went away an it had been any christom child; a' parted even just between twelve and one, even at the turning o' the tide: for after I saw him fumble with the sheets and play with flowers and smile upon his fingers' ends, I knew there was but one way; for his nose was as sharp as a pen, and a' babbled of green fields.
Henry V. Act ii, sc. 3, l. 11. [Hostess] The only use of "christom" (in christening-robe, innocent), and of "babbled."

13
Well, I doubt not but to die a fair death for all this, if I 'scape hanging for killing that rogue.
I Henry IV. Act ii, sc. 2, l. 14. [Falstaff]

Hotspur: Doomsday is near; die all, die merrily.
Douglas: Talk not of dying: I am out of fear
Of death or death's hand for this one-half year.
I Henry IV. Act iv, sc. 1, l. 134. The only use of "one-half."

14 His death, whose spirit lent a fire
Even to the dullest peasant in his camp,
Being bruited once, took fire and heat away
From the best-temper'd courage in his troops.
II Henry IV. Act i, sc. 1, l. 112. [Morton] The only use of "best-temper'd."

1
We would not die in that man's company
That fears his fellowship to die with us.
Henry V. Act iv, sc. 3, l. 38. [King Henry]
Here was a royal fellowship of death!
Henry V. Act iv, sc. 8, l. 106. [King Henry]

2 Death's dishonourable victory
We with our stately presence glorify.
I Henry VI. Act i, sc. 1, l. 20. [Exeter]
Then follow thou thy desperate sire of Crete,
Thou Icarus; thy life to me is sweet:
If thou wilt fight, fight by thy father's side;
And, commendable proved, let 's die in pride.
I Henry VI. Act iv, sc. 6, l. 54. [Talbot]
Brave death.—*I Henry VI,* iv, 7, 25; *I Henry IV,* v, 2, 87; *Coriolanus,* i, 6, 71.

3
Here could I breathe my soul into the air,
As mild and gentle as the cradle-babe
Dying with mother's dug between its lips.
II Henry VI. Act iii, sc. 2, l. 391. [Suffolk]
The only use of "cradle-babe."
I am resolved for death or dignity.
II Henry VI. Act v, sc. 1, l. 194. [York]

4 Full of repentance,
Continual meditations, tears, and sorrows,
He gave his honours to the world again,
His blessed part to heaven, and slept in peace.
Henry VIII. Act iv, sc. 2, l. 27. [Griffith]
And there at Venice gave
His body to that pleasant country's earth
And his pure soul unto his captain Christ,
Under whose colours he had fought so long.
Richard II, iv, 1, 97. See under KNIGHTHOOD.
And, to add greater honours to his age
Than man could give him, he died fearing God.
Henry VIII. Act iv, sc. 2, l. 67. [Griffith]

5
The question of his death is enrolled in the Capitol: his glory not extenuated, wherein he was worthy, nor his offences enforced, for which he suffer'd death.
Julius Cæsar. Act iii, sc. 2, l. 41. [Brutus]
The only use of "extenuated." "Extenuate" occurs six times.

6 Bear me hence
From forth the noise and rumour of the field,
Where I may think the remnant of my thoughts
In peace, and part this body and my soul
With contemplation and devout desires.
King John. Act v, sc. 4, l. 44. [Melun]

7 Live a thousand years,
I shall not find myself so apt to die.
Julius Cæsar. Act iii, sc. 1, l. 159. [Antony]
O, if thou wert the noblest of thy strain,
Young man, thou couldst not die more honourable.
Julius Cæsar. Act v, sc. 1, l. 59. [Brutus]

8 Nothing in his life
Became him like the leaving it; he died
As one that had been studied in his death
To throw away the dearest thing he owed,
As 'twere a careless trifle.
Macbeth. Act i, sc. 4, l. 7. [Malcolm]
They say he parted well, and paid his score:
And so, God be with him!
Macbeth. Act v, sc. 8, l. 52. [Siward]
Blow, wind! come, wrack!
At least we 'll die with harness on our back.
Macbeth. Act v, sc. 5, l. 51. [Macbeth]
"Wrack" is repeated in *Pericles,* iv, Gower, 12.

9
Be absolute for death; either death or life
Shall thereby be the sweeter.
Measure for Measure. Act iii, sc. 1, l. 5. [Duke]
Darest thou die?
The sense of death is most in apprehension;
And the poor beetle, that we tread upon,
In corporal sufferance finds a pang as great
As when a giant dies.
Measure for Measure. Act iii, sc. 1, l. 77. [Isabella]
Immediate sentence then and sequent death
Is all the grace I beg.
Measure for Measure. Act v, sc. 1, l. 378. [Angelo]

10
I am a tainted wether of the flock,
Meetest for death: the weakest kind of fruit
Drops earliest to the ground; and so let me.
The Merchant of Venice. Act iv, sc. 1, l. 114. [Antonio]
The ripest fruit first falls, and so doth he.
Richard II. Act ii, sc. 1, l. 153. [King Richard]
Why, now let me die, for I have lived long enough.
The Merry Wives of Windsor. Act iii, sc. 3, l. 46. [Falstaff]

11 If it were now to die,
'Twere now to be most happy; for, I fear,
My soul hath her content so absolute
That not another comfort like to this
Succeeds in unknown fate.
Othello. Act ii, sc. 1, l. 191. [Othello]
If I might die within this hour, I have lived
To die when I desire.
The Winter's Tale. Act iv, sc. 4, l. 472. [Shepherd]

12
Choose out some secret place, some reverend room,
More than thou hast, and with it joy thy life;
So as thou livest in peace, die free from strife.
Richard II. Act v, sc. 6, l. 25. [Bolingbroke]

VI—The Bad Death

13 I will go seek
Some ditch wherein to die; the foul'st best fits
My latter part of life.
Antony and Cleopatra. Act iv, sc. 6, l. 37. [Enobarbus]

14
Die in many irreconciled iniquities.
Henry V. Act iv, sc. 1, l. 161. [King Henry]
The only use of "irreconciled."

'Tis certain, every man that dies ill, the ill upon his own head.

Henry V. Act iv, sc. 1, l. 197. [Williams]

A damned death!—*Henry V,* iii, 6, 43.

1

King: How fares my lord? speak, Beaufort, to thy sovereign.
Cardinal: If thou be'st death, I'll give thee England's treasure,
Enough to purchase such another island,
So thou wilt let me live, and feel no pain.
King: Ah, what a sign it is of evil life,
Where death's approach is seen so terrible! . . .
Cardinal: Died he not in his bed? where should he die? . . .
Alive again? then show me where he is:
I'll give a thousand pound to look upon him. . . .
Warwick: See how the pangs of death do make him grin!
Salisbury: Disturb him not; let him pass peaceably.
King: Peace to his soul, if God's good pleasure be!
Lord cardinal, if thou think'st on heaven's bliss,
Hold up thy hand, make signal of thy hope.
He dies, and makes no sign. O God, forgive him!
Warwick: So bad a death argues a monstrous life.
King: Forbear to judge, for we are sinners all.
Close up his eyes and draw the curtain close;
And let us all to meditation.

II Henry VI. Act iii, sc. 3, l. 2.

2

It is impossible that I should die
By such a lowly vassal as thyself.

II Henry VI. Act iv, sc. 1, l. 110. [Suffolk]

Great men oft die by vile besonians:
A Roman sworder and banditto slave
Murder'd sweet Tully; Brutus' bastard hand
Stabb'd Julius Cæsar; savage islanders
Pompey the Great; and Suffolk dies by pirates.

II Henry VI. Act iv, sc. 1, l. 134. [Suffolk] The only use of "banditto." "Sworder" is repeated in *Antony and Cleopatra,* iii, 13, 31.

Shallow: I am, sir, under the king, in some authority.
Pistol: Under which king, Besonian? speak, or die.

II Henry IV. Act v, sc. 3, l. 117. The only uses of "besonian." Recruits sent from Spain to Rome were called *besogni,* because they were in need of everything, from the Italian *bisogno,* need.

3

And never be forgot in mighty Rome
Th' adulterate death of Lucrece and her groom.

The Rape of Lucrece, l. 1644.

VII—Death and Youth

4

Let it die as it was born.

Cymbeline. Act i, sc. 4, l. 131. [Philario]

Shall rotten death make conquest of the stronger
And leave the faltering feeble souls alive?

The Rape of Lucrece, l. 1767. The only use of "faltering."

5

Fair creature, kill'd too soon by death's sharp sting!
Like a green plum that hangs upon a tree,
And falls, through wind, before the fall should be.

The Passionate Pilgrim, l. 134.

6

Die in his youth by like untimely violence.

Richard III. Act i, sc. 3, l. 201. [Queen Margaret]

The term
Of a despised life closed in my breast
By some vile forfeit of untimely death.

Romeo and Juliet. Act i, sc. 4, l. 109. [Romeo]

Alas! she's cold;
Her blood is settled, and her joints are stiff;
Life and these lips have long been separated:
Death lies on her like an untimely frost
Upon the sweetest flower of all the field.

Romeo and Juliet. Act iv, sc. 5, l. 25. [Capulet]

Untimely death.—*Romeo and Juliet,* v, 3, 234; *The Rape of Lucrece,* l. 1178; *King Lear,* iv, 6, 256.

7

May not young men die, as well as old?

The Taming of the Shrew. Act ii, sc. 1, l. 393. [Gremio]

As the most forward bud
Is eaten by the canker ere it blow.

Two Gentlemen of Verona. Act i, sc. 1, l. 45. [Valentine]

8

Thy mark is feeble age, but thy false dart
Mistakes that aim and cleaves an infant's heart.

Venus and Adonis, l. 941.

VIII—Death and Love

9 Though I kill him not, I am the cause
His death was so effected.

All's Well that Ends Well. Act iii, sc. 2, l. 118. [Helena]

The tenderness of her nature became as a prey to her grief; in fine, made a groan of her last breath, and now she sings in heaven.

All's Well that Ends Well. Act iv, sc. 3, l. 60. [First Lord]

10 Her clothes spread wide;
And, mermaid-like, awhile they bore her up: . . .
. . . but long it could not be
Till that her garments, heavy with their drink,
Pull'd the poor wretch from her melodious lay
To muddy death.

Hamlet. Act iv, sc. 7, l. 176. [Queen] The only use of "mermaid-like."

11 I will withdraw,
To furnish me with some swift means of death

For the fair devil.
Othello. Act iii, sc. 3, l. 476. [Othello]

1 Love-devouring death.
Romeo and Juliet. Act ii, sc. 6, l. 7. [Romeo] The only use of "love-devouring."

Who is living, if those two are gone?
Romeo and Juliet. Act iii, sc. 2, l. 68. [Juliet]

Death, that hath ta'en her hence to make me wail,
Ties up my tongue, and will not let me speak.
Romeo and Juliet. Act iv, sc. 5, l. 31. [Capulet]

2 O son! the night before thy wedding-day
Hath Death lain with thy wife. There she lies,
Flower as she was, deflowered by him.
Death is my son-in-law, Death is my heir;
My daughter he hath wedded: I will die,
And leave him all; life, living, all is Death's.
Romeo and Juliet. Act iv, sc. 5, l. 35. [Capulet]

Shall I believe
That unsubstantial death is amorous,
And that the lean abhorred monster keeps
Thee here in dark to be his paramour?
Romeo and Juliet. Act v, sc. 3, l. 102. [Romeo] "Unsubstantial" is repeated in *King Lear*, iv, 1, 7: "Unsubstantial air."

3 Come away, come away, death,
And in sad cypress let me be laid;
Fly away, fly away, breath;
I am slain by a fair cruel maid.
My shroud of white, stuck all with yew,
O, prepare it!
My part of death, no one so true
Did share it.
Twelfth Night. Act ii, sc. 4, l. 52. [Clown]

4 Thyself hast loved; and I have heard thee say
No grief did ever come so near thy heart
As when thy lady and thy true love died.
The Two Gentlemen of Verona. Act iv, sc. 3, l. 18. [Silvia]

IX—Death: Its Finality

5 Death of one person can be paid but once,
And that she has discharged.
Antony and Cleopatra. Act iv, sc. 14, l. 27. [Mardian]

Now boast thee, death, in thy possession lies
A lass unparallel'd.
Antony and Cleopatra. Act v, sc. 2, l. 318. [Charmian]

6 Death,
The undiscover'd country from whose bourn
No traveller returns.
Hamlet. Act iii, sc. 1, l. 78. [Hamlet]

Your death has eyes in 's head then; I have not seen him so pictured: you must either be directed by some that take upon them to know, or to take upon yourself that which I am sure you do not know, or jump the after inquiry on your own peril: and how you shall speed in your journey's end, I think you 'll never return to tell one.
Cymbeline. Act v, sc. 4, l. 184. [First Gaoler] The only use of "inquiry."

7 He is dead and gone, lady,
He is dead and gone;
At his head a grass-green turf,
At his heels a stone.
Hamlet. Act iv, sc. 5, l. 29. [Ophelia] The only use of "grass-green."

And will he not come again?
No, no, he is dead:
Go to thy death-bed:
He never will come again.
Hamlet. Act iv, sc. 5, l. 191. [Ophelia] "Death-bed" occurs nine times in the plays.

She 's gone for ever!
I know when one is dead, and when one lives;
She 's dead as earth. Lend me a looking-glass;
If that her breath will mist or stain the stone,
Why, then she lives.
King Lear. Act v, sc. 3, l. 259. [King Lear]

If you can bring
Tincture or lustre in her lip, her eye,
Heat outwardly or breath within, I 'll serve you
As I would do the gods.
The Winter's Tale. Act iii, sc. 2, l. 205. [Paulina] "Tincture" is repeated in *Julius Cæsar*, ii, 2, 89, and in *Sonnets*, liv.

DEBATE

See also Argument

8 In debating which was best, we shall part with neither.
The Comedy of Errors. Act iii, sc. 1, l. 67. [Balthazar]

I will debate this matter at more leisure.
The Comedy of Errors. Act iv, sc. 1, l. 100. [Antipholus of Ephesus]

She is not worth our debate.
Cymbeline. Act i, sc. 4, l. 174. [Posthumus]

9 Two thousand souls and twenty thousand ducats
Will not debate the question of this straw.
Hamlet. Act iv, sc. 4, l. 26. [Hamlet]

God doth give successful end
To this debate that bleedeth at our doors.
II Henry IV. Act iv, sc. 4, l. 1. [King]

10 Sat in the council-house
Early and late, debating to and fro.
II Henry VI. Act i, sc. 1, l. 90. [Gloucester] "Council-house" is repeated in *Richard III*, iii, 5, 38.

King Edward: Awhile, and we 'll debate. . . .
Montague: What talk you of debating?
III Henry VI. Act iv, sc. 7, l. 51.

Debate this business.—*Henry VIII*, ii, 4, 52.

I have debated, even in my soul.—*The Rape of Lucrece*, l. 498.

Quietly debated.—*Titus Andronicus*, v, 3, 20.

11 My state
Stands on me to defend, not to debate.
King Lear. Act v, sc. 1, l. 68. [Edmund]

Lost in the world's debate.—*Love's Labour 's Lost*, i, 1, 174.

1 After much debatement,
My sisterly remorse confutes mine honour.
Measure for Measure. Act v, sc. 1, l. 99. [Isabella] The only use of "sisterly."
Without debatement further.—*Hamlet,* v, 2, 45. The only uses of "debatement."

2
I am debating of my present store.
The Merchant of Venice. Act i, sc. 3, l. 54. [Shylock]
Debate where leisure serves with dull debaters.
The Rape of Lucrece, l. 1019. The only use of "debaters."
For thee against myself I 'll vow debate.
Sonnets. No. lxxxix.

DEBT

3
There is more owing her than is paid; and more shall be paid her than she 'll demand.
All's Well that Ends Well. Act i, sc. 3, l. 107. [Countess] The only use of "owing."

4
I stand debted to this gentleman.
The Comedy of Errors. Act iv, sc. 1, l. 31. [Angelo] The only use of "debted."
I shall remain your debtor.—*Antony and Cleopatra,* v, 2, 205.
I have been debtor to you.—*Cymbeline,* i, 4, 38.
I am yet thy debtor.—*The Merry Wives of Windsor,* ii, 2, 138.
Debtor for my sake.—*Sonnets,* cxxxiv.
Rest debtor.—*Merchant of Venice,* i, 1, 152.
Rest your debtor.—*Pericles,* ii, 1, 149.
I am your debtor.—*Troilus and Cressida,* iv, 5, 51.
Bad debtors.—*The Rape of Lucrece,* l. 964.
Reproach's debtor.—*Rape of Lucrece,* l. 1155.

5 This I wonder at,
That he, unknown to me, should be in debt.
The Comedy of Errors. Act iv, sc. 2, l. 47. [Adriana]
He is my prisoner: if I let him go,
The debt he owes will be required of me.
The Comedy of Errors. Act iv, sc. 4, l. 120. [Officer]
Knowing how the debt grows, I will pay it.
The Comedy of Errors. Act iv, sc. 4, l. 124. [Adriana]

6
I must die much your debtor.
Cymbeline. Act ii, sc. 4, l. 8. [Posthumus]
Let me not die your debtor.
Love's Labour 's Lost. Act v, sc. 2, l. 43. [Rosaline]
Die in debt.—*Love's Labour 's Lost,* v, 2, 333; *Romeo and Juliet,* i, 1, 244.

7
I know you are more clement than vile men,
Who of their broken debtors take a third,
A sixth, a tenth, letting them thrive again
On their abatement.
Cymbeline. Act v, sc. 4, l. 18. [Posthumus] The only use of "clement."
Due debt.—*Cymbeline,* iv, 2, 233.
Pious debts.—*Cymbeline,* iii, 3, 72.

8 Who studies day and night
To answer all the debt he owes to you.
I Henry IV. Act i, sc. 3, l. 184. [Hotspur]
For, bear ourselves as even as we can,
The king will always think him in our debt.
I Henry IV. Act i, sc. 3, l. 285. [Worcester]
I am undone by his going; I warrant you, he 's an infinitive thing upon my score.
II Henry IV. Act ii, sc. 1, l. 25. [Hostess] The only use of "infinitive."

9
As to speak . . . det, when he should pronounce debt,
—d, e, b, t, not d, e, t.
Love's Labour 's Lost. Act v, sc. 1, l. 23. [Holofernes]

10 The time approaches
That will with due decision make us know
What we shall say we have and what we owe.
Macbeth. Act v, sc. 4, l. 16. [Siward] "Decision" is used only three times in the plays, as above, and in *All's Well that Ends Well,* iii, 1, 3, and *Troilus and Cressida,* ii, 2, 173.

11 My chief care
Is to come fairly off from the great debts
Wherein my time something too prodigal
Hath left me gaged.
The Merchant of Venice. Act i, sc. 1, l. 127. [Bassanio] "Gaged" is repeated in *Hamlet,* i, 1, 91.
How to get clear of all the debts I owe.
The Merchant of Venice. Act i, sc. 1, l. 134. [Bassanio]
Petty debt.—*Merchant of Venice,* iii, 2, 309.

12
All debts are cleared between you and I.
The Merchant of Venice. Act iii, sc. 2, l. 322. [Bassanio, quoting a letter from Antonio] Shakespeare says elsewhere (*The Merry Wives of Windsor,* iii, 2, 25) "between my good man and he."

13 Pray God, Bassanio come
To see me pay his debt, and then I care not!
The Merchant of Venice. Act iii, sc. 3, l. 35. [Antonio]
He repents not that he pays your debt.
The Merchant of Venice. Act iv, sc. 1, l. 279. [Antonio]
You have paid . . . the very debt of your calling.
Measure for Measure. Act iii, sc. 2, l. 264. [Escalus]
Pay the debt.—*I Henry IV,* i, 2, 233; *Timon of Athens,* i, 1, 103.

14 My sovereign liege was in my debt
Upon remainder of a dear account.
Richard II. Act i, sc. 1, l. 129. [Mowbray]
In common worldly things, 'tis call'd ungrateful,
With dull unwillingness to repay a debt
Which with a bounteous hand was kindly lent.
Richard III. Act ii, sc. 2, l. 91. [Dorset]
Royal debt.—*Richard III,* ii, 2, 95.
I am in your debt.—*Richard III,* iii, 2, 113.

15
Having come . . . To gather in some debts.
The Taming of the Shrew. Act iv, sc. 4, l. 24.

16
He that dies pays all debts.
The Tempest. Act iii, sc. 2, l. 140. [Stephano]

1 Five talents is his debt,
His means most short, his creditors most strait.
Timon of Athens. Act i, sc. 1, l. 95. [Messenger]

2
How goes the world, that I am thus encounter'd
With clamorous demands of date-broke bonds,
And the detention of long-since-due debts.
Timon of Athens. Act ii, sc. 2, l. 38. [Timon] The only use of "date-broke," "detention" and "long-since-due."

I have
Prompted you in the ebb of your estate
And your great flow of debts.
Timon of Athens. Act ii, sc. 2, l. 149. [Flaminius]

Why then preferr'd you not your sums and bills,
When your false masters eat of my lord's meat?
Then they could smile and fawn upon his debts
And take down the interest into their gluttonous maws.
Timon of Athens. Act iii, sc. 4, l. 49. [Flaminius] The only use of "gluttonous."

Methinks he should the sooner pay his debts,
And make a clear way to the gods.
Timon of Athens. Act iii, sc. 4, l. 76. [Servant]

These debts may well be called desperate ones, for a madman owes 'em.
Timon of Athens. Act iii, sc. 4, l. 102. [Hortensius]

In like manner was I in debt to my importunate business.
Timon of Athens. Act iii, sc. 6, l. 15. [Second Lord]

3 We should, for perpetuity,
Go hence in debt.
The Winter's Tale. Act i, sc. 2, l. 5. [Polixenes]

DECEIT

See also Cheating, Cunning, Dissembling, Hypocrisy, Pretence, Seeming, Treachery

4
Come, bring forth this counterfeit module, has deceived me, like a double-meaning prophesier.
All's Well that Ends Well. Act iv, sc. 3, l. 113. [Bertram] The only use of "prophesier." "Module" occurs once again in *King John,* v, 7, 58.

There 's a double meaning in that.
Much Ado about Nothing. Act ii, sc. 3, l. 267. [Benedick] The only uses of "double meaning" in the plays.

This deceit so lawful.—*All's Well that Ends Well,* iii, 7, 38.

5
Did it from his teeth.
Antony and Cleopatra. Act iii, sc. 4, l. 10. [Antony]

I do not greatly care to be deceived,
That have no use for trusting.
Antony and Cleopatra. Act v, sc. 2, l. 14. [Cleopatra]

6
Be secret-false.
The Comedy of Errors. Act iii, sc. 1, l. 15. [Luciana] The only use of the phrase.

Here we wander in illusions.
The Comedy of Errors. Act iv, sc. 3, l. 43. [Antipholus of Syracuse]

By the devil's illusions
The monk might be deceived.
Henry VIII. Act i, sc. 2, l. 178. [Surveyor]

7 I 'll mountebank their loves,
Cog their hearts from them, and come home beloved
Of all the trades in Rome.
Coriolanus. Act iii, sc. 2, l. 132. [Coriolanus]

The fellow dares not deceive me.
Cymbeline. Act iv, sc. 1, l. 27. [Cloten]

8
My uncle-father and aunt-mother are deceived.
Hamlet. Act ii, sc. 2, l. 393. [Hamlet] The only use of either phrase.

9
They fool me to the top of my bent.
Hamlet. Act iii, sc. 2, l. 401. [Hamlet]

We will fool him black and blue.
Twelfth Night. Act ii, sc. 5, l. 12. [Sir Toby]

She is fool'd With a most false effect.
Cymbeline. Act i, sc. 5, l. 42. [Cornelius]

10
I 'll not be juggled with.
Hamlet. Act iv, sc. 5, l. 130. [Laertes] The only use of "juggled."

11
The tongues of men are full of deceits.
Henry V. Act v, sc. 2, l. 120. [King Henry]

You have, as it appears to me, practised upon the easy-yielding spirit of this woman, and made her serve your uses both in purse and in person.
II Henry IV. Act ii, sc. 1, l. 124. [Chief Justice] The only use of "easy-yielding."

12
I have deluded you.
I Henry VI, v, 4, 76. The only use of "deluded."

13 A man
Unsounded yet and full of deep deceit.
II Henry VI. Act iii, sc. 1, l. 56. [Suffolk]

That fraudful man.—*II Henry VI,* iii, 1, 81. "Fraudful," used in the first play, was never repeated.

14 That is good deceit
Which mates him first that first intends deceit.
II Henry VI. Act iii, sc. 1, l. 264.]Suffolk]

15
To soothe your forgery and his.
III Henry VI. Act iii, sc. 3, l. 175. [King Lewis]

Forgeries of jealousy.—*A Midsummer-Night's Dream,* ii, 1, 81.

Put on him what forgeries you please.—*Hamlet,* ii, 1, 20. See under SLANDER.

He so far topp'd my thought,
That I, in forgery of shapes and tricks,
Came short of what he did.
Hamlet. Act iv, sc. 7, l. 89. [King] "Topp'd is repeated in *Pericles,* i, 4, 9.

1
Deceive more slily than Ulysses could.
III Henry VI. Act iii, sc. 2, l. 189. [Gloucester]
Deceit bred by necessity.
III Henry VI. Act iii, sc. 3, l. 68. [Queen Margaret]
Thy sly conveyance and thy lord's false love.
III Henry VI. Act iii, sc. 3, l. 160. [Queen Margaret]
A quicksand of deceit.—*III Henry VI,* v, 4, 26. The only use of "quicksand." "Quick-sands" occurs in *Antony and Cleopatra,* ii, 7, 65.
Thou art deceived.—*III Henry VI,* i, 1, 155. A favourite phrase of Shakespeare, who uses it, or "you are deceived," eighteen times.
Deceive me not now.—*Love's Labour's Lost,* ii, 1, 230.

2
Have spoke the word, And will not palter.
Julius Cæsar. Act ii, sc. 1, l. 125. [Brutus]
Foh, foh! adieu; you palter.
Troilus and Cressida. Act v, sc. 2, l. 48. [Diomedes]
A whoreson dog, that shall palter thus with us!
Troilus and Cressida, ii, 3, 244. [Ajax]
Palter with us in a double sense.
Macbeth. Act v, sc. 8, l. 20. [Macbeth]
Palter in the shifts of lowness.
Antony and Cleopatra. Act iii, sc. 11, l. 63. [Antony] The only uses of "palter."

3
By heaven, I had rather coin my heart,
And drop my blood for drachmas, than to wring
From the hard hands of peasants their vile trash
By any indirection.
Julius Cæsar. Act iv, sc. 3, l. 72. [Brutus]
Though indirect,
Yet indirection thereby grows direct.
King John. Act iii, sc. 1, l. 275. [Pandulph]
By indirections find directions out.
Hamlet, ii, 1, 66. See under CUNNING. The only uses of "indirection."

4
Though I will not practise to deceive,
Yet, to avoid deceit, I mean to learn;
For it will strew the footsteps of my rising.
King John. Act i, sc. 1, l. 214. [Bastard] The only use of "footsteps."
What in the world should make me now deceive,
Since I must lose the use of all deceit?
Why should I then be false, since it is true
That I must die here and live hence by truth?
King John. Act v, sc. 4, l. 26. [Melun]

5
Saw how deceits were gilded in his smiling.
A Lover's Complaint, l. 172.
I will try confusions with him.
The Merchant of Venice. Act ii, sc. 2, l. 38. [Launcelot]

6
And this deceit loses the name of craft,
Of disobedience, or unduteous title,
Since therein she doth evitate and shun
A thousand irreligious cursed hours,
Which forced marriage would have brought upon her.
The Merry Wives of Windsor. Act v, sc. 5, l. 239. [Fenton] The only use of "unduteous" and "evitate." "Irreligious" is repeated in *Titus Andronicus,* i, 1, 130; v, 3, 121.
Boys of art, I have deceived you both.
The Merry Wives of Windsor. Act iii, sc. 1, l. 109. [Host]

7
To vow and swear, and superpraise my parts,
When I am sure you hate me with your hearts.
A Midsummer-Night's Dream. Act iii, sc. 2, l. 153. [Helena] The only use of "superpraise."
You speak not as you think.—*A Midsummer-Night's Dream,* iii, 2, 191.

8
Sing no more ditties, sing no moe,
Of dumps so dull and heavy;
The fraud of men was ever so,
Since summer first was leavy.
Much Ado about Nothing. Act ii, sc. 3, l. 72. [Balthazar] "Leavy" is repeated in *Macbeth,* v, 6, 1. "Leafy" occurs in *Pericles,* v, 1, 51.
Men were deceivers ever.—*Much Ado about Nothing,* ii, 3, 65. See under INCONSTANCY.
Pardon'd the deceiver.—*The Tempest,* Epil., 7. The only uses of "deceiver."

9
I should think this a gull.
Much Ado about Nothing. Act ii, sc. 3, l. 123. [Benedick]
'Tis a gull.—*Henry V,* iii, 6, 70.
Naked gull.—*Timon of Athens,* ii, 1, 31.
Simple gulls.—*Richard III,* i, 3, 328.
Notorious gull.—*Twelfth Night,* v, 1, 351. See under RIDICULE.

10
Then go we near her, that her ear lose nothing
Of the false sweet bait that we lay for it.
Much Ado about Nothing. Act iii, sc. 1, l. 32. [Hero]
Partly by his oaths, which first possessed them, partly by the dark night, which did deceive them, but chiefly by my villany, which did confirm any slander that Don John had made, away went Claudio enraged.
Much Ado about Nothing. Act iii, sc. 3, l. 165. [Borachio]

11
I might have cudgelled thee out of thy single life to make thee a double-dealer.
Much Ado about Nothing. Act v, sc. 4, l. 115. [Claudio]
Well, I will be so much a sinner, to be a double-dealer.
Twelfth Night. Act v, sc. 1, l. 37. [Duke] The only uses of "double-dealer."
It would be double-dealing, sir.
Twelfth Night. Act iv, sc. 1, l. 32. [Clown] The only use of "double-dealing."

12
O, she deceives me Past thought!
Othello. Act i, sc. 1, l. 166. [Brabantio]
Look at her, Moor, if thou hast eyes to see:
She has deceived her father, and may thee.
Othello. Act i, sc. 3, l. 293. [Brabantio]
She did deceive her father, marrying you.
Othello. Act iii, sc. 3, l. 206. [Iago]

She that, so young, could give out such a seeming,
To seel her father's eyes up close as oak.
Othello. Act iii, sc. 3, l. 209. [Iago] See also SEEMING.

1 Oh, that deceit should steal such gentle shapes,
And with a virtuous vizard hide foul guile!
Richard III. Act ii, sc. 2, l. 27. [Duchess of York]

O nature, what hadst thou to do in hell,
When thou didst bower the spirit of a fiend
In mortal paradise of such sweet flesh?
Was ever book containing such vile matter
So fairly bound? O, that deceit should dwell
In such a gorgeous palace!
Romeo and Juliet. Act iii, sc. 2, l. 80. [Juliet] See also under APPEARANCE.

Thou look'st not like deceit; do not deceive me.
The Rape of Lucrece, l. 585.

Thou speak'st like him 's untutor'd to repeat:
Who makes the fairest show means most deceit.
Pericles. Act i, sc. 4, l. 74. [Cleon]

2 From my dugs he drew not this deceit.
Richard III. Act ii, sc. 2, l. 30. [Duchess of York]

The untainted virtue of your years
Hath not yet dived into the world's deceit.
Richard III. Act iii, sc. 1, l. 7. [Gloucester]

3 Lucentia: Counterfeit supposes blear'd thine eyne.
Gremio: Here 's packing, with a witness, to deceive us all!
The Taming of the Shrew. Act v, sc. 1, l. 121.

Thou deceivest thyself.—*Richard III,* i, 4, 249. The only use of "deceivest."

4 Here 's a maze trod indeed
Through forth-rights and meanders!
The Tempest. Act iii, sc. 3, l. 2. [Gonzalo] "Forthright" is repeated in *Troilus and Cressida,* iii, 3, 158. The only use of "meanders."

This is as strange a maze as e'er man trod.
The Tempest, v, 1, 242.

I have thrust myself into this maze
Haply to wive and thrive.
The Taming of the Shrew. Act i, sc. 2, l. 55. [Petruchio]

Winding maze.—*The Rape of Lucrece,* l. 1152. The only uses of "maze."

Quaint mazes.—*A Midsummer-Night's Dream,* ii, 1, 99. The only use of "mazes."

5 If that be call'd deceit, I will be honest,
And never, whilst I live, deceive men so.
Titus Andronicus. Act iii, sc. 1, l. 189. [Aaron]

But I 'll deceive you in another sort,
And that you 'll say, ere half an hour pass.
Titus Andronicus. Act iii, sc. 1, l. 191. [Aaron]

6 Thus it shall become
High-witted Tamora to gloze with all.
Titus Andronicus. Act iv, sc. 4, l. 34. [Tamora] The only use of high-witted."

I will gloze with him.—*Pericles,* i, 1, 110.

Lay these glozes by.—*Love's Labour 's Lost,* iv, 3, 370.

Taught to gloze.—*Richard II,* ii, 1, 10.

Unjustly gloze.—*Henry V,* i, 2, 40. The only uses of "gloze."

Glozed, but superficially.—*Troilus and Cressida,* ii, 2, 165. The only use of "glozed."

7 Thou dost thyself and all our Troy deceive.
Troilus and Cressida. Act v, sc. 3, l. 90. [Cassandra]

8 I will drop in his way some obscure epistles of love; wherein, by the colour of his beard, the shape of his leg, the manner of his gait, the expressure of his eye, forehead, and complexion, he shall find himself most feelingly personated.
Twelfth Night. Act ii, sc. 3, l. 168. [Maria] The only use of "personated."

There 's something in 't That is deceiveable.
Twelfth Night. Act iv, sc. 3, l. 20. [Sebastian]

Deceiveable and false.—*Richard II,* ii, 3, 84. The only uses of "deceiveable."

9 We have been
Deceived in thy integrity, deceived
In that which seems so.
Winter's Tale. Act i, sc. 2, l. 239. [Leontes]

You are abused and by some putter-on
That will be damn'd for 't.
The Winter's Tale Act ii, sc. 1, l. 141. [Antigonus] "Putter-on" occurs again in *Henry VIII,* i, 2, 24.

DEED

See also Act; Thought and Act; Word and Deed

I—Familiar Phrases

10 What thou wouldst do
Is done unto thy hand.
Antony and Cleopatra. Act iv, sc. 14, l. 28. [Mardian]

See it done.—*Antony and Cleopatra,* iv, 1, 14.

11 The best is yet to do.
As You Like It. Act i, sc. 2, l. 121. [Le Beau]

This I must do, or know not what to do:
Yet this I will not do, do how I can.
As You Like It. Act ii, sc. 3, l. 34. [Orlando]

Do 't and thou hast the one half of my heart;
Do 't not, thou split'st thine own.
Winter's Tale. Act i, sc. 2, l. 348. [Leontes]

12 We 'll show 'em in deeds.
Coriolanus. Act i, sc. 1, l. 61. [Citizen]

Rewards His deeds with doing them.
Coriolanus. Act ii, sc. 2, l. 131. [Cominius] An echo, perhaps, of Seneca's "Recte facti fecisse merces est." (*Epistulæ ad Lucilium,* epis. 81, sec. 20).

13 Brutus: We do it not alone, sir.
Menenius: I know you can do very little alone; for your helps are many, or else your actions would grow wondrous single.
Coriolanus. Act ii, sc. 1, l. 37.

Alone I did it.—*Coriolanus,* v, 6, 117.

1 It takes
From our achievements, though perform'd at height.
The pith and marrow of our attribute.
Hamlet. Act i, sc. 4, l. 20. [Hamlet]
How my achievements mock me!
Troilus and Cressida, iv, 2, 71. [Troilus]
Achievements, plots, orders.—*Troilus and Cressida,* i, 3, 181.
Achievements of no less account.—*I Henry VI,* ii, 3, 8. The only uses of "achievements."
Achievement is command.
Troilus and Cressida, i, 2, 319. See under WOOING.
For all the soil of the achievement goes
With me into the earth.
II Henry IV. Act iv, sc. 5, l. 190. [King]
For achievement offer us his ransom.
Henry V. Act iii, sc. 5, l. 60. The only uses of "achievement."

2
There was much to do on both sides.
Hamlet, ii, 2, 369. See under ARGUMENT.
Little is to do.—*Macbeth,* v, 7, 28.

3
Queen: What shall I do?
Hamlet: Not this, by no means, that I bid you do.
Hamlet. Act iii, sc. 4, l. 180.
What shall I do? say what; what shall I do?
The Tempest. Act i, sc. 2, l. 300. [Ariel]
What should I do, I do not?—*Antony and Cleopatra,* i, 3, 8.
Man: What would you have me do?
Porter: What should you do, but knock 'em down by the dozens?
Henry VIII. Act v, sc. 4, l. 31.
Cressida: You bring me to do, and then you flout me too.
Pandarus: To do what? to do what? let her say what: what have I brought you to do?
Troilus and Cressida. Act iv, sc. 2, l. 27.
What 's to do?—*Measure for Measure,* i, 1, 64; *Twelfth Night,* iii, 3, 18.
What will this do?—*Much Ado about Nothing,* iv, 1, 211.
What hast thou to do?—*The Taming of the Shrew,* iii, 2, 218.
What have you to do?—*The Taming of the Shrew,* i, 2, 226.
What will you do now?—*Macbeth,* iv, 2, 31.

4 What we mean to do,
And what 's untimely done.
Hamlet. Act iv, sc. 1, l. 39. [King]
I do not know
Why yet I live to say 'This thing 's to do;'
Sith I have cause and will and strength and means
To do 't.
Hamlet. Act iv, sc. 4, l. 43. [Hamlet]
Is not this a strange fellow, my lord, that so confidently seems to undertake this business, which he knows is not to be done; damns himself to do and dares better be damned than to do 't?
All's Well that Ends Well, iii, 6, 93. [Lord]
That we would do,
We should do when we would.
Hamlet. Act iv, sc. 7, l. 119. [King]

5
Thou wo 't, wo 't thou? thou wo 't, wo 't ta? do, do, thou rogue! do, thou hemp-seed!
II Henry IV. Act ii, sc. 1, l. 63. [Hostess] The only use of "hemp-seed."
Woo 't weep? woo 't fight? woo 't fast? woo 't tear thyself?
Woo 't drink up eisel? eat a crocodile? I 'll do 't.
Hamlet. Act v, sc. 1, l. 298. [Hamlet] "Eisel" (vinegar) is repeated in *Sonnets,* cxi.
But in a sieve I 'll thither sail,
And, like a rat without a tail,
I 'll do, I 'll do, and I 'll do.
Macbeth. Act i, sc. 3, l. 8. [First Witch]

6
Let each man do his best.
I Henry IV. Act v, sc. 2, l. 93. [Hotspur]
I will do my good will: you can have no more.
II Henry IV. Act iii, sc. 2, l. 167. [Feeble]
We are but men; and what so many may do,
Not being torn a-pieces, we have done.
Henry VIII. Act v, sc. 4, l. 79. [Porter] The only use of "a-pieces."

7
Turning the accomplishment of many years
Into an hour-glass.
Henry V. Act i, Prologue, l. 30. [Chorus] "Hour-glass" is repeated in *The Merchant of Venice,* i, 1, 25.
So fares it with this faultful lord of Rome,
Who this accomplishment so hotly chased.
The Rape of Lucrece, l. 715. The only uses of "accomplishment" and of "faultful."

8
There is throats to be cut, and works to be done; and there ish nothing done.
Henry V. Act iii, sc. 2, l. 119. [Macmorris]
Timon: That 's a deed thou 'lt die for.
Apemantus: Right, if doing nothing be death by the law.
Timon of Athens. Act i, sc. 1, l. 194.
For three performers are the file when all
The rest do nothing.
Cymbeline. Act v, sc. 3, l. 30. [Posthumus]
In hand with all things, nought at all effecting.
Venus and Adonis, l. 912.

9
Doing is activity; and he will still be doing.
Henry V. Act ii, sc. 7, l. 107. [Constable]
A very little little let us do, And all is done.
Henry V. Act iv, sc. 2, l. 33. [Constable]
All 's done.—*I Henry IV,* v, 3, 16.
All 's not done.—*Henry V,* iv, 6, 1.
Now all is done.—*Sonnets,* cx.
When all is done.—*A Midsummer-Night's Dream,* iii, 1, 16; *Twelfth Night,* ii, 3, 31; *Macbeth,* iii, 4, 67.
Done all.—*Antony and Cleopatra,* iv, 12, 17.
Done enough.—*Antony and Cleopatra,* iii, 1, 12.

10 More will I do;
Though all that I can do is nothing worth.
Henry V. Act iv, sc. 1, l. 319. [King Henry]
I will do as I may.—*Henry V,* ii, 1, 17.

11
Do what you will, the like do I.
I Henry VI. Act iv, sc. 5, l. 50. [John Talbot]
Do with 'em what thou wilt.
I Henry VI. Act iv, sc. 7, l. 94. [Charles]
Do as thou wilt, for I have done with thee.
Romeo and Juliet. Act iii, sc. 5, l. 205. [Lady Capulet]

1
O that it were to do! what have we done?
II Henry VI. Act iii, sc. 2, l. 3. [Murderer]
2
Didst thou not hear me swear I would not do it?
III Henry VI, v, 5, 74. See under OATH.
I have sworn to do it.—*King John,* iv, 1, 58.
Now might I do it pat, now he is praying;
And now I 'll do 't.
Hamlet. Act iii, sc. 3, l. 73. [Hamlet]
Do it at once.—*Antony and Cleopatra,* iv, 14, 82.
They durst not do 't;
They could not, would not do 't.
King Lear. Act ii, sc. 4, l. 23. [King Lear]
I must do 't.—*Coriolanus,* iii, 2, 110.
I will not do 't.—*Coriolanus,* iii, 2, 120.
Let us do it.—*Henry V,* ii, 4, 23.
See thou do it.—*Comedy of Errors,* ii, 2, 141.
We will do it.—*The Merry Wives of Windsor,* ii, 3, 83.
How dearly they do 't!—*Cymbeline,* ii, 2, 18.
"Do it" is used forty-five times in the plays.
3
Work thou the way,—and thou shalt execute.
III Henry VI. Act v, sc. 7, l. 25. [Gloucester]
Execute all things.—*The Tempest,* ii, 1, 148.
What is written shall be executed.
Titus Andronicus. Act v, sc. 2, l. 15. [Titus]
Commands shall be executed.—*Twelfth Night,* iii, 4, 30.
4
No day without a deed to crown it.
Henry VIII. Act v, sc. 5, l. 59. [Cranmer]
5 Let no man abide this deed,
But we the doers.
Julius Cæsar. Act iii, sc. 1, l. 94. [Brutus]
Justice on the doers!—*All 's Well that Ends Well,* v, 3, 154.
Good doers.—*Richard III,* i, 3, 352.
Great doers.—*Measure for Measure,* iv, 3, 20.
"Doers" is used once again in *Cymbeline,* v, 1, 15: "Doers' thrift." "Doer" occurs twice, in *All 's Well that Ends Well,* ii, 3, 133: "Doer's deed"; and in *Twelfth Night,* iii, 4, 91: "The doer of this."
6
You know not what you do.
Julius Cæsar. Act iii, sc. 1, l. 232. [Cassius]
Why, friends, you go to do you know not what.
Julius Cæsar. Act iii, sc. 2, l. 240. [Antony]
Do I know not what.—*Julius Cæsar,* ii, 1, 333.
O, what men dare do! what men may do! what men daily do, not knowing what they do!
Much Ado about Nothing. Act iv, sc. 1, l. 9. [Claudio]
Look, what you do, you do it still i' the dark.
Love's Labour 's Lost, v, 2, 24. [Rosaline]
O heavens, what some men do,
While some men leave to do!
Troilus and Cressida, iii, 3, 132. [Ulysses]
7
I may do that I shall be sorry for.
Julius Cæsar, iv, 3, 64. See under WARNING.
8
For that which thou hast sworn to do amiss
Is not amiss when it is truly done,
And being not done, where doing tends to ill,
The truth is then most done not doing it.
King John. Act iii, sc. 1, l. 270. [Pandulph]

What 's sweet to do, to do will aptly find.
A Lover's Complaint, l. 88.
9
Thus thou must do, if thou have it;
And that which rather thou dost fear to do
Than wishest should be undone.
Macbeth, i, 5, 24. See under INDECISION.
10
If it were done when 'tis done, then 'twere well
It were done quickly.
Macbeth. Act i, sc. 7, l. 1. [Macbeth]
Twice done and then done double.
Macbeth, i, 6, 15. See under HONOUR.
This deed I 'll do before this purpose cool.
Macbeth. Act iv, sc. 1, l. 154. [Macbeth]
Come, to the forge with it then; shape it: I would not have things cool.
The Merry Wives of Windsor. Act iv, sc. 2, l. 239. [Mrs. Page]
Something to be done immediately.
Julius Cæsar. Act v, sc. 1, l. 15. [Messenger]
11
I have done the deed.
Macbeth. Act ii, sc. 2, l. 15. [Macbeth]
O, who hath done this deed?—*Othello,* v, 2, 123. "Hath done this deed" is repeated in *Julius Cæsar,* iii, 1, 172, and iii, 2, 216.
Thou hast done a deed.—*Othello,* v, 2, 164.
Tell who did the deed.—*Titus Andronicus,* v, 3, 53.
O heavens! what have I done?—*Troilus and Cressida,* iii, 2, 146.
What hast thou done?—*Cymbeline,* iv, 2, 117.
What shall be done?—*Timon of Athens,* ii, 2, 7.
12
I am afraid to think what I have done;
Look on 't again I dare not.
Macbeth. Act ii, sc. 2, l. 51. [Macbeth]
A little water clears us of this deed:
How easy is it, then!
Macbeth. Act ii, sc. 2, l. 67. [Lady Macbeth]
To know my deed, 'twere best not know myself.
Macbeth. Act ii, sc. 2, l. 73. [Macbeth]
13 'Tis unnatural,
Even like a deed that 's done.
Macbeth. Act ii, sc. 4, l. 10. [Old Man]
Unnatural deeds Do breed unnatural troubles.
Macbeth. Act v, sc. 1, l. 79. [Doctor]
We are yet but young in deed.
Macbeth. Act iii, sc. 4, l. 144. [Macbeth]
14
Was not that nobly done? Ay, and wisely too.
Macbeth. Act iii, sc. 6, l. 14. [Lennox]
Nobly done.—*Coriolanus,* ii, 2, 72.
He has done nobly.—*Coriolanus,* ii, 3, 139.
Noble deeds.—*Coriolanus,* ii, 3, 8.
15
If to do were as easy as to know what were good to do, chapels had been churches and poor men's cottages princes' palaces.
The Merchant of Venice. Act i, sc. 2, l. 13. [Portia]
Let them say 'tis grossly done; so it be fairly done, no matter.
The Merry Wives of Windsor. Act ii, sc. 2, l. 148. [Falstaff]
16
My deeds upon my head!
The Merchant of Venice, iv, 1, 206. [Shylock]

1
Give him this deed And let him sign it.
The Merchant of Venice. Act iv, sc. 2, l. 1. [Portia]
Send the deed after me, And I will sign it.
The Merchant of Venice. Act iv, sc. 1, l. 396. [Shylock]
2
Strange things in hand, Master Brook!
The Merry Wives of Windsor. Act v, sc. 1, l. 32. [Falstaff]
Come, shall we to this gear?
Richard III. Act i, sc. 4, l. 157. [Murderer]
3
Brother, we have done deeds of charity.
Richard III. Act ii, sc. 1, l. 49. [King Edward] "Deed of charity" is repeated in *Titus Andronicus,* v, 1, 89.
Deed of courage.—*II Henry IV,* iv, 3, 122.
Deed of darkness.—*Pericles,* iv, 6, 32. Act of darkness, *King Lear,* iii, 4, 90. See under Act.
Deed of kind.—*Merchant of Venice,* i, 3, 86.
Deed of love.—*King Lear,* i, 1, 73.
Deed of malice.—*King John,* ii, 1, 380.
Deeds of men.—*Julius Cæsar,* i, 2, 203.
Deed of mercy.—*The Merchant of Venice,* iv, 1, 202.
Deed of policy.—*Titus Andronicus,* iv, 2, 148.
Deed of rage.—*I Henry VI,* iv, 7, 8.
Deed of shame.—*King John,* iv, 2, 222.
Deed of war.—*II Henry VI,* i, 1, 97.
Deeds of youth.—*Sonnets,* xxxvii. Each of these phrases, except the first, was used only once.
Actual deed.—*Othello,* iv, 2, 153.
Faint deeds.—*Timon of Athens,* i, 2, 16.
Lawful deed.—*All 's Well that Ends Well,* iii, 7, 45.
Past deeds.—*All 's Well that Ends Well,* iv, 2, 63.
Unlucky deeds.—*Othello,* v, 2, 341.
4
What is done cannot be now amended.
Richard III. Act iv, sc. 4, l. 291. [King Richard]
Mar not the thing that cannot be amended.
The Rape of Lucrece, l. 578.
To wish Things done, undone.
Julius Cæsar. Act iv, sc. 2, l. 8. [Brutus]
What 's done is done.
Macbeth. Act iii, sc. 2, l. 12. [Lady Macbeth]
What 's done cannot be undone.
Macbeth. Act v, sc. 1, l. 75. [Lady Macbeth]
Can it be undone?—*Pericles,* iv, 3, 1.
Demetrius: Villain, what hast thou done?
Aaron: That which thou canst not undo.
Titus Andronicus. Act iv, sc. 2, l. 73.
They would do that
Which should undo more doing.
Winter's Tale. Act i, sc. 2, l. 311. [Leontes]
Undo the deed.—*Pericles,* iv, 3, 6.
Undo 't when I had done.—*Othello,* iv, 3, 71.
Do and undo.—*III Henry VI,* ii, 6, 105; *Cymbeline,* ii, 3, 78.
Do or undo.—*II Henry VI,* iii, 1, 196.
5
That my deeds shall prove.
The Taming of the Shrew. Act i, sc. 2, l. 177. [Gremio]
So said, so done.
The Taming of the Shrew. Act i, sc. 2, l. 186. [Gremio] See Word and Deed.
I would fain be doing.
The Taming of the Shrew. Act ii, sc. 1, l. 74. [Petruchio]
'Tis deeds must win the prize.
The Taming of the Shrew. Act ii, sc. 1, l. 344. [Baptista]
To talk in deeds, while others saucily
Promise more speed, but do it leisurely.
The Rape of Lucrece, l. 1348. See also Word and Deed.
6
There 's something else to do.
The Tempest. Act iv, sc. 1, l. 126. [Prospero]
7
What we can do, we 'll do, to do you service.
Timon of Athens, v, 1, 78.
8
[I] will with deeds requite thy gentleness.
Titus Andronicus. Act i, sc. 1, l. 237. [Saturninus]
My nephew Mutius' deeds do plead for him.
Titus Andronicus. Act i, sc. 1, l. 356. [Marcus]
To it, boy!—*Titus Andronicus,* iv, 3, 58.
9
Omission to do what is necessary
Seals a commission to a blank of danger.
Troilus and Cressida. Act iii, sc. 3, l. 230. [Patroclus] The only use of "omission," and consequently the only play upon omission and commission.
10
As much as I can do, I will effect.
Two Gentlemen of Verona. Act iii, sc. 2, l. 66. [Proteus]
I 'll see what I can do.
Measure for Measure. Act i, sc. 4, l. 84. [Isabella]
To do this is within the compass of man's wit; and therefore I will attempt the doing it.
Othello. Act iii, sc. 4, l. 21. [Clown]
What I can do I will; and more I will
Than for myself I dare.
Othello. Act iii, sc. 4, l. 130. [Desdemona]
I have done
As you have done; that 's what I can.
Coriolanus. Act i, sc. 9, l. 15. [Caius Marcius]
11
What you do Still betters what is done.
The Winter's Tale. Act iv, sc. 4, l. 135. [Florizel]
Each your doing,
So singular in each particular,
Crowns what you are doing in the present deed,
That all your acts are queens.
The Winter's Tale. Act iv, sc. 4, l. 143. [Florizel]

II—Great Deeds

12 The deeds of Coriolanus
Should not be utter'd feebly.
Coriolanus. Act ii, sc. 2, l. 86. [Cominius] The only use of "feebly."
I never saw
Such noble fury in so poor a thing;
Such precious deeds in one that promised nought

But beggary and poor looks.
Cymbeline. Act v, sc. 5, l. 7. [Belarius]

1
Engross up glorious deeds on my behalf.
I Henry IV. Act iii, sc. 2, l. 148. [Prince of Wales]

Whose glorious deeds, but in these fields of late,
Made emulous missions 'mongst the gods themselves.
Troilus and Cressida. Act iii, sc. 3, l. 188. [Ulysses] The only use of "missions."

Stopping my greedy ear with their bold deeds.
II Henry IV. Act i, sc. 1, l. 78. [Northumberland]

Great deeds.—*Timon of Athens,* iv, 3, 94. The only use of this phrase in the plays.

Valiant and magnanimous deeds.—*Troilus and Cressida,* ii, 2, 200.

2
Turk Gregory never did such deeds in arms as I have done this day.
I Henry IV. Act v, sc. 3, l. 46. [Falstaff] The only reference to "Turk Gregory," Pope Gregory VII, called Hildebrand.

Let it be booked with the rest of this day's deeds.
II Henry IV. Act iv, sc. 3, l. 50. [Falstaff] The only use of "booked."

3
Awake remembrance of these valiant dead
And with your puissant arm renew their feats.
Henry V. Act i, sc. 2, l. 115. [Bishop of Ely]

Old men forget; yet all shall be forgot,
But he 'll remember with advantages
What feats he did that day.
Henry V. Act iv, sc. 3, l. 49. [King Henry]

4
Fair maid, is 't thou wilt do these wondrous feats?
I Henry VI. Act i, sc. 2, l. 64. [Reignier]

Break the ice and do this feat.
The Taming of the Shrew. Act i, sc. 2, l. 267.

The feats he hath done.—*II Henry IV,* iii, 2, 328.

The feats of a lion.—*Much Ado about Nothing,* i, 1, 15.

Tell them your feats.—*Antony and Cleopatra,* iv, 8, 9.

High feats.—*Henry VIII,* i, 1, 61.

Noble feat.—*Much Ado about Nothing,* v, 4, 50.

Warlike feats.—*Cymbeline,* iii, 1, 7.

5
His deeds exceed all speech.
I Henry VI. Act i, sc. 1, l. 15. [Gloucester]

Thy deeds, thy plainness and thy housekeeping,
Hath won the greatest favour of the commons.
I Henry VI. Act i, sc. 1, l. 191. [Salisbury] "Housekeeping" is repeated in *Love's Labour's Lost,* ii, 1, 104; and in *The Taming of the Shrew,* ii, 1, 358.

Warlike and martial Talbot, Burgundy
Enshrines thee in his heart and there erects
Thy noble deeds as valour's monuments.
I Henry VI. Act iii, sc. 2, l. 118. [Burgundy] The only use of "enshrines."

6
Stay we no longer, dreaming of renown,
But sound the trumpets, and about our task.
III Henry VI. Act ii, sc. 1, l. 199. [Warwick]

Thou art fortunate in all thy deeds.
III Henry VI. Act iv, sc. 6, l. 25. [King Henry]

7 They did perform
Beyond thought's compass.
Henry VIII. Act i, sc. 1, l. 35. [Norfolk]

8 It is my father's music
To speak your deeds, not little of his care
To have them recompensed as thought on.
The Winter's Tale. Act iv, sc. 4, l. 528. [Florizel]

III—Good Deeds

9
From lowest place when virtuous things proceed,
The place is dignified by the doer's deed.
Where great additions swell 's, and virtue none,
It is a dropsied honour.
All's Well that Ends Well. Act ii, sc. 3, l. 132. [King] The only use of "dropsied."

10
I will hope Of better deeds to-morrow.
Antony and Cleopatra. Act i, sc. 1, l. 61. [Demetrius] "Better deeds" is repeated in *The Two Gentlemen of Verona,* ii, 1, 18.

T'is a worthy deed,
And shall become you well.
Antony and Cleopatra. Act ii, sc. 2, l. 1. [Lepidus]

His worthy deeds did claim no less
Than what he stood for.
Coriolanus. Act ii, sc. 3, l. 194. [Brutus]

11
I love thee brotherly, but envy much
Thou hast robb'd me of this deed.
Cymbeline. Act iv, sc. 2, l. 158. [Arviragus]

If there be any good thing to be done,
That may to thee do ease and grace to me.
Hamlet. Act i, sc. 1, l. 130. [Horatio]

12
Seeing the deed is meritorious.
II Henry VI. Act iii, sc. 1, l. 270. [Suffolk]

Here is my hand, the deed is worthy doing.
II Henry VI. Act iii, sc. 1, l. 278. [Suffolk]

13
I 'll leave my son my virtuous deeds behind;
And would my father had left me no more!
For all the rest is held at such a rate
As brings a thousand-fold more care to keep
Than in possession any jot of pleasure.
III Henry VI. Act ii, sc. 2, l. 49. [King Henry] "Thousand-fold" occurs four times in the plays.

To deck his fortune with his virtuous deeds.
The Taming of the Shrew. Act i, sc. 1, l. 16. [Lucentio] "Virtuous deed" is repeated in *The Rape of Lucrece,* l. 252.

Charitable deeds.—*The Rape of Lucrece,* l. 908.

14
Let my deeds be witness of my worth.
Titus Andronicus. Act v, sc. 1, l. 103. [Aaron]

15 Good deeds past; which are devour'd
As fast as they are made, forgot as soon
As done.
Troilus and Cressida. Act iii, sc. 3, l. 148. [Ulysses]

One good deed dying tongueless
Slaughters a thousand waiting upon that.
The Winter's Tale. Act i, sc. 2, l. 92. [Hermione]

My last good deed was to entreat his stay:
What was my first? it has an elder sister.
The Winter's Tale. Act i, sc. 2, l. 97. [Hermione]

That 's a good deed.—*The Winter's Tale,* iii, 3, 137. "Good deed" is used fourteen times in the plays.

IV—Doing Well

1
Guard: What work is here! Charmian, is this well done?
Charmian: It is well done, and fitting for a princess.
Antony and Cleopatra. Act v, sc. 2, l. 328.

You can do better yet.
Antony and Cleopatra. Act i, sc. 3, l. 81. [Cleopatra] "Do better" is repeated in *Macbeth,* v, 8, 3.

2
Fear not, neighbour, you shall do well enough.
II Henry VI. Act ii, sc. 3, l. 60. [Neighbour]

They shall do well enough.—*Titus Andronicus,* ii, 3, 305.
These fellows will do well.—*II Henry IV,* iii, 2, 307.
I shall do well.—*Antony and Cleopatra,* ii, 1, 8.
I 'll do well yet.—*Coriolanus,* iv, 1, 21.
We will yet do well.—*Antony and Cleopatra,* iii, 13, 188.
You do well.—*Henry VIII,* i, 4, 87. "Do well" is used sixteen times in the plays.
Do bravely.—*Macbeth,* v, 7, 26; *Antony and Cleopatra,* i, 5, 22.

3
Things done well,
And with a care, exempt themselves from fear;
Things done without example, in their issue
Are to be fear'd.
Henry VIII. Act i, sc. 2, l. 88. [King Henry]

4
May you see things well done there.
Macbeth. Act ii, sc. 4, l. 37. [Macduff]

He hath done well in people's eyes.
The Merchant of Venice, iii, 2, 143. See under PRIZE.

All have done well.—*Pericles,* ii, 3, 108.
Thou hast done well.—*The Tempest,* i, 2, 494.
You have done well.—*Othello,* v, 2, 169.

5
This was well done, my bird.
The Tempest. Act iv, sc. 1, l. 184. [Prospero]

Olivia: Is 't not well done?
Viola: Excellently done, if God did all.
Twelfth Night, i, 5, 253. See under BEAUTY.

Well done!—*Love's Labour 's Lost,* v, 1, 145; *Macbeth,* iv, 1, 39; *Cymbeline,* i, 5, 82.
'Tis very clerkly done.—*The Two Gentlemen of Verona,* ii, 1, 114.
Masterly done.—*The Winter's Tale,* v, 3, 65.
Done famously.—*Coriolanus,* i, 1, 36.

V—Evil Deeds

6
Being done unknown,
I should have found it afterwards well done;
But must condemn it now.
Antony and Cleopatra. Act ii, sc. 7, l. 84. [Pompey]

And strange it is,
That nature must compel us to lament
Our most persisted deeds.
Antony and Cleopatra. Act v, sc. 1, l. 28. [Agrippa] The only use of "persisted."

Thou hast done a deed whereat valour will weep.
Coriolanus. Act v, sc. 6, l. 134. [Lord]

7
Queen: O, what a rash and bloody deed is this!
Hamlet: A bloody deed! almost as bad, good mother,
As kill a king, and marry with his brother.
Hamlet. Act iii, sc. 4, l. 27.

O, such a deed
As from the body of contraction plucks
The very soul, and sweet religion makes
A rhapsody of words.
Hamlet. Act iii, sc. 4, l. 45. [Hamlet] The only use of "contraction" and "rhapsody."

This vile deed
We must, with all our majesty and skill,
Both countenance and excuse.
Hamlet. Act iv, sc. 1, l. 30. [King]

O heavy deed!—*Hamlet,* iv, 1, 12.
Accursed deed.—*Titus Andronicus,* v, 3, 64.
Cursed deed.—*Pericles,* v, 3, Gower, 96.
Dark deeds.—*Measure for Measure,* iii, 2, 187.
Deadly deed.—*Titus Andronicus,* v, 3, 66; *The Rape of Lucrece,* l. 1730.
Evil deeds.—*III Henry VI,* i, 4, 117; *Measure for Measure,* i, 3, 38.
Fell deeds.—*Julius Cæsar,* iii, 1, 269.
Filthy deeds.—*Othello,* v, 2, 149.
Grievous deeds.—*The Rape of Lucrece,* l. 1822.
Guilty deeds.—*Romeo and Juliet,* iii, 2, 111.
Harmful deeds.—*Sonnets,* cxi.
Murderous deed.—*II Henry VI,* v, 1, 185.

8
These feats,
So crimeful and so capital in nature.
Hamlet. Act iv, sc. 7, l. 6. [Laertes] "Crimeful" is repeated in *Rape of Lucrece,* l. 970.

Fell feats.—*Henry* V, iii, 3, 17. See under WAR.
Terrible feat.—*Macbeth,* i, 7, 80.

9
Whose bloody deeds shall make all Europe quake.
I Henry VI. Act i, sc. 1, l. 156. [Bedford]

God, not we, hath plagued thy bloody deed.
Richard III. Act i, sc. 3, l. 181. [Gloucester]

A bloody deed, and desperately dispatch'd!
Richard III. Act i, sc. 4, l. 278. [Murderer]

This is the man should do the bloody deed.
King John. Act iv, sc. 2, l. 69. [Pembroke]

Alas, how shall this bloody deed be answer'd?
Hamlet. Act iv, sc. 1, l. 16. [King]

Is 't known who did this more than bloody deed?
Macbeth. Act ii, sc. 4, l. 22. [Ross] "Bloody deed" is used ten times in the plays.

10
Like a hungry lion, did commence
Rough deeds of rage and stern impatience.
I Henry VI. Act iv, sc. 7, l. 7. [Talbot]

Die in bands for this unmanly deed.
III Henry VI. Act i, sc. 1, l. 186. [Northumberland]

O that my death should stay these ruthful deeds!
III Henry VI. Act ii, sc. 5, l. 95. [King Henry]

1
Quoted and sign'd to do a deed of shame.
King John. Act iv, sc. 2, l. 222. [King John]
I do fearfully believe 'tis done,
What we so fear'd he had a charge to do.
King John. Act iv, sc. 2, l. 74. [Pembroke]

2
How oft the sight of means to do ill deeds
Make deeds ill done!
King John. Act iv, sc. 2, l. 219. [King John]
Tish ill done: . . . O, tish ill done, tish ill done; by my hand, tish ill done!
Henry V. Act iii, sc. 2, l. 93. [Macmorris] The only uses of "ill done." "Ill-doing" occurs in *The Winter's Tale,* i, 2, 70.
By the kind gods, 'tis most ignobly done.
King Lear. Act iii, sc. 7, l. 35. [Gloucester]
'Tis most ignobly done.—*King Lear,* iii, 7, 35.
Alas! for whose sake did I that ill deed?
Richard III. Act i, sc. 4, l. 216. [Clarence]
If the deed were ill, Be you contented.
II Henry IV. Act v, sc. 2, l. 83. [Chief Justice]
Ransom all ill deeds.—*Sonnets,* xxxiv.

3
Yea, without stop, didst let thy heart consent,
And consequently thy rude hand to act
The deed, which both our tongues held vile to name.
King John. Act iv, sc. 2, l. 239. [King John]
Knew you of this fair work?
Beyond the infinite and boundless reach
Of mercy, if thou didst this deed of death,
Art thou damn'd, Hubert.
King John. Act iv, sc. 3, l. 116. [Bastard]

4
This foul deed shall smell above the earth
With carrion men, groaning for burial.
Julius Cæsar. Act iii, sc. 1, l. 274. [Antony]
Our deeds are done!
Mistrust of my success hath done this deed.
Julius Cæsar. Act v, sc. 3, l. 64. [Titinius]

5
These deeds must not be thought
After these ways; so, it will make us mad.
Macbeth. Act ii, sc. 2, l. 33. [Lady Macbeth]
Ere the bat hath flown
His cloister'd flight, ere to black Hecate's summons
The shard-borne beetle with his drowsy hums
Hath rung night's yawning peal, there shall be done
A deed of dreadful note.
Macbeth. Act iii, sc. 2, l. 40. [Macbeth] "Cloister'd" is repeated in *The Rape of Lucrece,* l. 1085. The only use of "shard-borne."
Macbeth: What is 't you do?
Witches: A deed without a name.
Macbeth. Act iv, sc. 1, l. 49.
This deed unshapes me quite.
Measure for Measure. Act iv, sc. 4, l. 23. [Angelo] The only use of "unshapes."

6
I thank you, princes, for my daughter's death:
Record it with your high and worthy deeds:
'Twas bravely done.
Much Ado about Nothing. Act v, sc. 1, l. 278. [Leonato]

7
Deeds to make heaven weep, all earth amazed.
Othello. Act iii, sc. 3, l. 371. [Othello]
I should make very forges of my cheeks,
That would to cinders burn up modesty,
Did I but speak thy deeds.
Othello. Act iv, sc. 2, l. 74. [Othello]
Desdemona: Wouldst thou do such a deed for all the world?
Emilia: Why, would not you?
Desdemona: No, by this heavenly light!
Emilia: Nor I neither by this heavenly light; I might do 't as well i' the dark.
Desdemona: Wouldst thou do such a deed for all the world?
Emilia: The world 's a huge thing: it is a great price For a small vice.
Desdemona: In troth, I think thou wouldst not.
Emilia: In troth, I think I should; and undo 't when I had done. Marry, I would not do such a thing for a joint-ring, nor for measures of lawn, nor for gowns, petticoats, nor caps, nor any petty exhibition; but, for the whole world,—why, who would not make her husband a cuckold to make him a monarch? I should venture purgatory for 't.
Othello. Act iv, sc. 3, l. 73. The only use of "joint-ring."
This deed of thine is no more worthy heaven
Than thou wast worthy her.
Othello. Act v, sc. 2, l. 160. [Emilia]

8
My life's foul deed, my life's fair end shall free it.
The Rape of Lucrece, l. 1208. "Foul deed" occurs four times in the plays.
Deeds degenerate.—*Rape of Lucrece,* l. 1003.

9 O forfend it, God,
That in a Christian climate souls refined
Should show so heinous, black, obscene a deed!
Richard II. Act iv, sc. 1, l. 129. [Bishop of Carlisle]
So black a deed.—*The Rape of Lucrece,* l. 226.
In nothing art thou black save in thy deeds.
Sonnets. No. cxxxi.

10 O would the deed were good!
For now the devil, that told me I did well,
Says that this deed is chronicled in hell.
Richard II. Act v, sc. 5, l. 115. [Exton]
Thou hast wrought
A deed of slander with thy fatal hand
Upon my head and all this famous land.
Richard II. Act v, sc. 6, l. 34. [Bolingbroke]

11
If thou delight to view thy heinous deeds,
Behold this pattern of thy butcheries.
Richard III. Act i, sc. 2, l. 53. [Lady Anne] "Butcheries" is repeated in l. 100, and occurs in no other scene.
Thy deed, inhuman and unnatural.
Richard III. Act i, sc. 2, l. 60. [Lady Anne]
Wicked deed.—*Richard III,* i, 2, 104. See under DAMNATION.

1
O, 'twas the foulest deed to slay that babe,
And the most merciless that e'er was heard of!
Richard III. Act i, sc. 3, l. 183. [Hastings]
How now, my hardy, stout resolved mates!
Are you now going to dispatch this deed?
Richard III. Act i, sc. 3, l. 340. [Gloucester]
I have done those things,
Which now bear evidence against my soul.
Richard III. Act i, sc. 4, l. 66. [Clarence]
The deed you undertake is damnable.
Richard III. Act i, sc. 4, l. 197. [Clarence]
O, no! alas, I rather hate myself
For hateful deeds committed by myself!
Richard III. Act v, sc. 3, l. 189. [King Richard]
2
You undergo too strict a paradox,
Striving to make an ugly deed look fair.
Timon of Athens. Act iii, sc. 5, l. 24. [Senator]
O monument
And wonder of good deeds evilly bestow'd!
Timon of Athens. Act iv, sc. 3, l. 466. [Flavius] "Evilly" is repeated in *King John,* iii, 4, 149. "Evilly born."
3 Leave to plead my deeds:
'Tis thou and those that have dishonour'd me.
Titus Andronicus. Act i, sc. 1, l. 424. [Titus]
Tut, I have done a thousand dreadful things
As willingly as one would kill a fly,
And nothing grieves me heartily indeed
But that I cannot do ten thousand more.
Titus Andronicus. Act v, sc. 1, l. 141. [Aaron]
4 Why do you now . . .
Do a deed that fortune never did,
Beggar the estimation which you prized
Richer than sea and land?
Troilus and Cressida. Act ii, sc. 2, l. 88. [Troilus]
To do this deed,
Promotion follows. If I could find example
Of thousands that had struck anointed kings
And flourish'd after, I 'ld not do 't; but since
Nor brass nor stone nor parchment bears not one,
Let villany itself forswear 't.
Winter's Tale. Act i, sc. 2, l. 356. [Camillo]

DEEP, THE, see Sea

DEER

5 Moody-mad and desperate stags,
Turn on the bloody hounds with heads of steel.
I Henry VI. Act iv, sc. 2, l. 50. [Talbot] The only use of "moody-mad."
A poor sequester'd stag,
That from the hunter's aim hath ta'en a hurt.
As You Like It. Act ii, sc. 1, l. 33. [First Lord] "Sequester'd" is repeated in *Titus Andronicus,* ii, 3, 75.
Like the stag.—*Antony and Cleopatra,* i, 4, 65.
Take him for a stag.—*Titus Andronicus,* ii, 3, 71.
Breathed stags.—*The Taming of the Shrew,* Ind., 2, 50.
Windsor stag.—*The Merry Wives of Windsor,* v, 5, 14. The only uses of "stag" and "stags."
6 Seek thou out some other chase,
For I myself must hunt this deer to death.
II Henry VI. Act v, sc. 2, l. 15. [York]
7
Under this thick-grown brake we 'll shroud ourselves;
For through this laund anon the deer will come;
And in this covert will we make our stand,
Culling the principal of all the deer.
III Henry VI. Act iii, sc. 1, l. 1. [Keeper] The only use of "thick-grown." "Laund" (an open space between woods) is repeated in *Venus and Adonis,* l. 813.
Ay, here 's a deer whose skin 's a keeper's fee:
This is the quondam king; let 's seize upon him.
III Henry VI. Act iii, sc. 1, l. 22. [Keeper]
How like a deer, strucken by many princes,
Dost thou here lie!
Julius Cæsar. Act iii, sc. 1, l. 209. [Antony]
Murder'd deer.—*Macbeth,* iv, 3, 206.
Small deer.—*King Lear,* iii, 4, 144.
The sobbing deer.—*As You Like It,* ii, 1, 66. The only use of "sobbing."
Unruly deer.—*The Comedy of Errors,* ii, 1, 100.
8
Holofernes: The deer was, as you know, sanguis, in blood. . . .
Sir Nathaniel: It was a buck of the first head.
Holofernes: Sir Nathaniel, haud credo.
Dull: 'Twas not a haud credo; 'twas a pricket.
Holofernes: Most barbarous intimation! . . . to insert again my haud credo for a deer.
Dull: I said the deer was not a haud credo; 'twas a pricket.
Love's Labour 's Lost. Act iv, sc. 2, l. 3. The only use of "sanguis," "haud credo," and "intimation."
9
Falstaff: Who comes here? My doe?
Mrs. Ford: Art thou there, my deer? my male deer?
Falstaff: My doe with the black scut!
The Merry Wives of Windsor. Act v, sc. 5, l. 17. The only use of "scut."
I will never take you for my love again; but I will always count you my deer.
The Merry Wives of Windsor. Act v, sc. 5, l. 123. [Mrs. Ford]
10
When night-dogs run, all sorts of deer are chased.
Merry Wives of Windsor. Act v, sc. 5, l. 252. [Falstaff] The only use of "night-dogs."
11
The poor frighted deer, that stands at gaze.
The Rape of Lucrece, l. 1149.
Stall'd the deer.—*The Passionate Pilgrim,* 300.
12
What, hast not thou full often struck a doe,
And borne her cleanly by the keeper's nose?
Titus Andronicus. Act ii, sc. 1, l. 93. [Demetrius]

Single you thither then this dainty doe,
And strike her home by force, if not by words.
Titus Andronicus. Act ii, sc. 1, l. 117. [Aaron]

We . . . hope to pluck a dainty doe to ground.
Titus Andronicus. Act ii, sc. 2, l. 26. [Demetrius]

Whiles, like a doe, I go to find my fawn
And give it food.
As You Like It. Act ii, sc. 7, l. 128. The only use of "fawn" in this meaning.

1
Within the circuit of this ivory pale,
I 'll be a park, and thou wilt be my deer.
Venus and Adonis, l. 230.

Then be my deer, since I am such a park;
No dog shall rouse thee, though a thousand bark.
Venus and Adonis, l. 239.

The fleet-foot roe that 's tired with chasing.
Venus and Adonis, l. 561. The only use of "fleet-foot." "Roe" occurs four times in the plays.

And sometime sorteth with a herd of deer.
Venus and Adonis, l. 689.

DEFEAT

See also Failure

2
Then is he the ground Of my defeatures.
The Comedy of Errors. Act ii, sc. 1, l. 98. [Adriana] "Defeature" is used again in Act v, sc. 1, l. 299, and in no other play.

3
Their defeat
Does by their own insinuation grow.
Hamlet. Act v, sc. 2, l. 58. [Hamlet]

Defeat thy favour.—*Othello,* i, 3, 346.
Defeat the law.—*Henry VIII,* ii, 1, 14.
Defeated the law.—*Henry V,* iv, 1, 175.
Defeat my life.—*Othello,* iv, 2, 160.
Defeated you and me.—*A Midsummer-Night's Dream,* iv, 1, 162.
'Tis Cæsar thou defeatest.—*Antony and Cleopatra,* iv, 14, 68. The only use of "defeatest."

4
Have I sent him
Bootless home and weather-beaten back.
I Henry IV. Act iii, sc. 1, l. 66. [Glendower] The only use of "weather-beaten."

Making defeat on the full power of France.
Henry V. Act i, sc. 2, l. 107. [Canterbury]

Clifford: Ay, ay, so strives the woodcock with the gin.
Northumberland: So doth the cony struggle in the net.
York: So triumph thieves upon their conquer'd booty;
So true men yield, with robbers so o'ermatch'd.
III Henry VI. Act i, sc. 4, l. 61.

5
Cardinal Pandulph: Courage and comfort! all shall yet go well.
King Philip: What can go well, when we have run so ill?
Are we not beaten?
King John. Act iii, sc. 4, l. 4.

He 's beat from his best ward.
Winter's Tale. Act i, sc. 2, l. 33. [Hermione]

6
When did I see thee so put down?
Twelfth Night. Act i, sc. 3, l. 86. [Sir Toby]

DEFECT

See also Fault, Infirmity

7
I saw her once
Hop forty paces through the public street;
And having lost her breath, she spoke, and panted,
That she did make defect perfection,
And, breathless, power breathe forth.
Antony and Cleopatra. Act ii, sc. 2, l. 233. [Enobarbus]

8
So, oft it chances in particular men,
That for some vicious mole of nature in them, . . .
Carrying . . . the stamp of one defect,
Being nature's livery, or fortune's star,—
Their virtues else—be they as pure as grace,
As infinite as man may undergo—
Shall in the general censure take corruption
From that particular fault.
Hamlet. Act i, sc. 4, l. 23. [Hamlet]

Full oft 'tis seen,
Our means secure us, and our mere defects
Prove our commodities.
King Lear. Act iv, sc. 1, l. 21. [Gloucester]

9
So mighty and so many my defects.
Richard III. Act iii, sc. 7, l. 160. [Gloucester] See under MODESTY for full quotation.

Those defects which I have before rehearsed.
The Taming of the Shrew. Act i, sc. 2, l. 124. [Hortensio]

Defect of spirit.—*The Rape of Lucrece,* l. 1345.

DEFENCE

10
By how much defence is better than no skill.
As You Like It. Act iii, sc. 3, l. 62. [Touchstone]

Second Servingman: For the defence of a town, our general is excellent.
First Servingman: Ay, and for an assault too.
Coriolanus. Act iv, sc. 5, l. 178.

11
Soft, soft! we 'll no defence.
Cymbeline. Act iii, sc. 4, l. 81. [Imogen]

12
Seeing thou fall'st on me so luckily,
I will assay thee: so, defend thyself.
I Henry IV. Act v, sc. 4, l. 33. [King Henry] The only use of "luckily."

Defend ourselves.—*III Henry VI,* iv, 1, 45; *Othello,* ii, 3, 203.
Defend yourself.—*Coriolanus,* iii, 2, 94.
Defending of myself.—*Richard II,* i, 3, 23.
O defend me!—*The Tempest,* ii, 2, 92.
O, defend me still!—*Richard III,* v, 3, 117.
O, yet defend me, friends.—*Hamlet,* v, 2, 335.

13
In cases of defence 'tis well to weigh
The enemy more mighty than he seems:
So the proportions of defence are fill'd.
Henry V. Act ii, sc. 4, l. 43. [Dauphin]

Empty of defence.—*Henry V,* i, 2, 153.

14
In defence of my lord's worthiness,
I crave the benefit of law of arms.
I Henry VI. Act iv, sc. 1, l. 99. [Basset]

In defence.—*Timon of Athens,* iii, 5, 55.
In her defence.—*Troilus and Cressida,* ii, 2, 198.

In her own defence.—*Hamlet,* v, 1, 7.
In our defences.—*Henry V,* ii, 4, 3.
In thy defence.—*III Henry VI,* i, 1, 160.
In your defence.—*III Henry VI,* ii, 2, 79; *Hamlet,* iv, 7, 98.

1 Ay, wherefore else guard we his royal tent,
But to defend his person from night-foes?
III Henry VI. Act iv, sc. 3, l. 21. [Second Watchman] The only use of "night-foes."

Alas, I am not coop'd here for defence!
III Henry VI. Act v, sc. 1, l. 109. [Warwick] The only use of "coop'd."

2 By how much unexpected, by so much
We must awake endeavour for defence.
King John. Act ii, sc. 1, l. 80. [Austria] "Unexpected" is repeated in v, 7, 64: "Unexpected flood"; and occurs in no other play.

Perchance the cardinal cannot make your peace;
Or if he do, let it at least be said
They saw we had a purpose of defence.
King John. Act v, sc. 1, l. 74. [Bastard]

Ourselves well sinewed to our defence.
King John. Act v, sc. 7, l. 88. [Bastard] The only use of "sinewed."

Honourable . . . defence
Cries out upon the name of Salisbury!
King John. Act v, sc. 2, l. 18. [Salisbury]

Great defence.—*Macbeth,* i, 3, 99.
Small defence.—*III Henry VI,* v, 1, 64.
Prepared defence.—*II Henry IV,* Ind., 12.

He is bold in his defence.
King Lear. Act v, sc. 3, l. 114. [Herald]

3 Why then, alas,
Do I put up that womanly defence,
To say I have done no harm?
Macbeth. Act iv, sc. 2, l. 78. [Lady Macduff]

Needs no defence.—*Passionate Pilgrim,* l. 110.
Make defence.—*Sonnets,* xxii.
Making no defence.—*Sonnets,* lxxxix.

4 As so defend thee heaven and thy valour!
Richard II. Act i, sc. 3, l. 15. [Marshal] Repeated in l. 34.

Defend me heaven!—*Richard II,* i, 3, 25.
Heavens defend me.—*The Merry Wives of Windsor,* v, 5, 85.
The gods defend me!—*Pericles,* iv, 2, 95. See under GODS.
Pray God defend me!—*Twelfth Night,* iii, 4, 331. See under GOD.

5 Thou great defender of this Capitol,
Stand gracious to the rites that we intend.
Titus Andronicus. Act i, sc. 1, l. 77. "Defender" is repeated in *Coriolanus,* iii, 3, 128, and v, 2, 42.

DEFIANCE

6 I dare, and do defy thee for a villain.
The Comedy of Errors. Act v, sc. 1, l. 32. [Second Merchant]

Thy registers and thee I both defy.
Sonnets. No. cxxiii.

I defy thee.—*III Henry VI,* ii, 2, 170; *I Henry IV,* iii, 3, 71; *III Henry VI,* v, 1, 98; *The Tempest,* iii, 2, 140.
I do defy thee.—*I Henry VI,* iii, 1, 27.
I for him defy you.—*Twelfth Night,* iii, 4, 345.
I 'ld defy them all.—*II Henry VI,* iv, 10, 67.
At heel of that, defy him.—*Antony and Cleopatra,* ii, 2, 160.

7 I do defy The tongues of soothers.
I Henry IV, iv, 1, 6. See under FLATTERY.

Is it even so? then I defy you, stars!
Romeo and Juliet. Act v, sc. 1, l. 24. [Romeo]

Defy augury.—*Hamlet,* v, 2, 230.
Defy thy conjurations.—*Romeo and Juliet,* v, 3, 68.
Defy all counsel.—*King John,* iii, 4, 23.
Defy the devil.—*Twelfth Night,* iii, 4, 108.
Defy the foul fiend.—*King Lear,* iii, 4, 101.
Defy lechery.—*Twelfth Night,* i, 5, 133.
Defy the matter.—*The Merchant of Venice,* iii, 5, 75.
Defy the surgeon.—*Pericles,* iv, 6, 29.
Solemnly defy.—*I Henry IV,* i, 3, 228.

8 To fill the mouth of deep defiance up.
I Henry IV. Act iii, sc. 2, l. 116. [King Henry]

No man so potent breathes upon the ground
But I will beard him.
I Henry IV. Act iv, sc. 1, l. 11. [Douglas]

I beard thee to thy face.—*I Henry VI,* i, 3, 44. See under BEARD.

9 Fear we broadsides? no, let the fiend give fire.
II Henry IV. Act ii, sc. 4, l. 196. [Pistol] The only use of "broadsides."

Defy us to our worst.—*Henry V,* iii, 3, 5.

10 Shall I be flouted thus by dunghill grooms?
I Henry VI. Act i, sc. 3, l. 14. [Gloucester]

Why, madam, have I offer'd love for this,
To be so flouted?
Richard III. Act ii, sc. 1, l. 77. [Gloucester]

What, wilt thou flout me thus unto my face?
The Comedy of Errors. Act i, sc. 2, l. 91. [Antipholus of Syracuse]

Yea, dost thou jeer and flout me in the teeth?
The Comedy of Errors. Act ii, sc. 2, l. 22. [Antipholus of Syracuse] The only use of "jeer." "Jeering" also is used only once, in *I Henry IV,* i, 3, 183: "Jeering and disdain'd contempt."

Why will you suffer her to flout me thus?
Let me come to her.
A Midsummer-Night's Dream. Act iii, sc. 2, l. 327. [Hermia]

Never flout at me for what I have said.
Much Ado about Nothing. Act v, sc. 4, l. 108. [Benedick]

You bring me to do, and then you flout me too.
Troilus and Cressida. Act iv, sc. 2, l. 26. [Cressida]

11 In despite of the devils and hell, have through the very middest of you!
II Henry VI. Act iv, sc. 8, l. 63. [Cade] The only use of "middest."

12 I dare your quenchless fury to more rage:
I am your butt, and I abide your shot.
III Henry VI. Act i, sc. 4, l. 28. [York] "Quenchless" is repeated in *The Rape of Lucrece,* l. 1554.

1
Then take my king's defiance from my mouth.
King John. Act i, sc. 1, l. 21. [Chatillon]
Defiance, traitors, hurl we in your teeth.
Julius Cæsar. Act v, sc. 1, l. 64. [Octavius]
Take my defiance!—*Measure for Measure,* iii, 1, 143.
He breathed defiance to my ears.
Romeo and Juliet. Act i, sc. 1, l. 117. [Benvolio]
There 's my gauntlet;
I 'll prove it on a giant.
King Lear. Act iv, sc. 6, l. 90. [King Lear]
2
As she spit in his face, so she defied him.
Measure for Measure. Act ii, sc. 1, l. 1. [Elbow]
I do defy him and I spit at him;
Call him a slanderous coward and a villain.
Richard II. Act i, sc. 1, l. 60. [Mowbray]
See also under SPITTING.
3
I 'll buckler thee against a million.
The Taming of the Shrew. Act iii, sc. 2, l. 241. [Petruchio]
The guilt of murder bucklers thee.
II Henry VI, iii, 2, 216. See under GUILT.
Buckler falsehood.—*III Henry VI,* iii, 3, 99.
The only uses of "buckler" as a verb. As a noun it occurs in *I Henry IV,* ii, 4, 186, and in *Much Ado about Nothing,* v, 2, 17.
4
Face not me: thou hast braved many men; brave not me;
I will neither be faced nor braved.
The Taming of the Shrew. Act iv, sc. 3, l. 125. [Grumio]
5
But when I meet you arm'd, as black defiance
As heart can think or courage execute.
Triolus and Cressida. Act iv, sc. 1, l. 12. [Æneas]

DEFORMITY

6
Thou art neither like thy sire nor dam;
But like a foul mis-shapen stigmatic,
Mark'd by the destinies to be avoided,
As venom toads, or lizards' dreadful stings.
III Henry VI. Act ii, sc. 2, l. 135. [Queen Margaret]
Foul stigmatic.—*II Henry VI,* v, 1, 215. The only uses of "stigmatic" (deformed by nature).
Stigmatical in making.—*The Comedy of Errors,* iv, 2, 22. The only use of "stigmatical."
7
To make an envious mountain on my back,
Where sits deformity to mock my body.
III Henry VI. Act iii, sc. 2, l. 157. [Gloucester]
I, that am curtail'd of this fair proportion,
Cheated of feature by dissembling nature,
Deform'd, unfinish'd, sent before my time
Into this breathing world, scarce half made up,
And that so lamely and unfashionable
That dogs bark at me as I halt by them.
Richard III. Act i, sc. 1, l. 18. [Gloucester]
The only use of "curtail'd" and "unfashionable."
I . . . Have no delight to pass away the time,
Unless to spy my shadow in the sun
And descant on mine own deformity.
Richard III. Act i, sc. 1, l. 25. [Gloucester]
8
Blush, blush, thou lump of foul deformity;
For 'tis thy presence that exhales this blood
From cold and empty veins.
Richard III. Act i, sc. 2, l. 57. [Lady Anne]
Me, that halt and am unshapen thus.
Richard III. Act i, sc. 2, l. 251. [Gloucester]
The only use of "unshapen."
9
What curious eye doth quote deformities?
Romeo and Juliet. Act i, sc. 4, l. 31. [Mercutio]
Her passing deformity.—*The Two Gentlemen of Verona,* ii, 1, 82.

DEGREE

See also Order, Quality

10
You called me yesterday mountain-squire; but I will make you to-day a squire of low degree.
Henry V. Act v, sc. 1, l. 36. [Fluellen] The only use of "mountain-squire."
Under the degree of a squire.—*The Merry Wives of Windsor,* iii, 4, 48.
He was a wight of high renown,
And thou art but of low degree.
Othello. Act ii, sc. 3, l. 96. [Iago]
Base degrees.—*Julius Cæsar,* ii, 1, 26.
Worst degree.—*Richard II,* ii, 3, 109.
Fair degree.—*Richard II,* i, 1, 80.
High degree.—*I Henry VI,* iv, 1, 17.
High'st degree.—*Richard III,* v, 3, 196; *Coriolanus,* v, 6, 85.
11
You know your own degrees; sit down.
Macbeth. Act iii, sc. 4, l. 1. [Macbeth]
What is thy degree?—*II Henry VI,* v, 1, 73.
Easy degrees.—*Coriolanus,* ii, 2, 29.
Successive degree.—*Measure for Measure,* ii, 2, 98.
12
In the third degree of drink.
The Taming of the Shrew, i, 5, 143. See under DRUNKENNESS.
13
The sweet degrees that this brief world affords.
Timon of Athens. Act iv, sc. 3, l. 253. [Timon]
Sequence of degree.—*Timon of Athens,* v, 1, 211.
14
Degree being vizarded,
The unworthiest shows as fairly in the mask.
The heavens themselves, the planets and this centre
Observe degree, priority and place.
Troilus and Cressida. Act i, sc. 3, l. 83. [Ulysses] "Vizarded" is repeated in *The Merry Wives of Windsor,* iv, 6, 40: "Masked and vizarded"; and "priority" in *Coriolanus,* i, 1, 251. See also under ORDER.
When degree is shaked,
Which is the ladder to all high designs,
The enterprise is sick!
Troilus and Cressida. Act i, sc. 3, l. 101. [Ulysses]

Take but degree away, untune that string,
And, hark, what discord follows!
Troilus and Cressida. Act i, sc. 3, l. 109. [Ulysses] The only use of "untune."

This chaos, when degree is suffocate,
Follows the choking.
And this neglection of degree it is
That by a pace goes backward, with a purpose
It hath to climb. The general 's disdain'd
By him one step below, he by the next,
That next to him beneath.
Troilus and Cressida. Act i, sc. 3, l. 125. [Ulysses] "Neglection" is repeated in *I Henry VI*, iv, 3, 49, and in *Pericles*, iii, 3, 20.

May he be suffocate.—*II Henry VI*, i, 1, 124.
His wind-pipe suffocate.—*Henry V*, iii, 6, 45. The only uses of "suffocate." "Suffocation" is used once, in *The Merry Wives of Windsor*, iii, 5, 119; and "suffocating" once, in *Othello*, iii, 3, 389. "Windpipe" occurs again in *Timon of Athens*, i, 2, 52.

DELAY

See also Pause, Tarry

1
One inch of delay more is a South-sea of discovery.
As You Like It. Act iii, sc. 2, l. 206. [Rosalind] The only use of "South-sea."

Delay me not.—*As You Like It*, iii, 2, 222.

2
To procrastinate his lifeless end.
The Comedy of Errors. Act i, sc. 1, l. 159. [Ægeon] The only use of "procrastinate." "Procrastination" does not occur.

Seek delays.—*The Comedy of Errors*, i, 1, 75.
Use delay.—*III Henry VI*, iv, 8, 60.
The more delay'd, delighted.—*Cymbeline*, v, 4, 102.

3
You loiter here too long.
II Henry IV. Act ii, sc. 2, l. 198. [Chief Justice] The only use of "loiter."

Where have you been these two days loitering?
Two Gentlemen of Verona. Act iv, sc. 4, l. 48. [Proteus] The only use of "loitering."

O illiterate loiterer!
The Two Gentlemen of Verona, iii, 1, 296. The only use of "loiterer." "Loiterers" occurs in *Love's Labour 's Lost*, iii, 1, 185: "Loiterers and malcontents."

4
Leave off delays.
I Henry VI. Act i, sc. 2, l. 146. [Alençon]

Delays have dangerous ends.
I Henry VI. Act iii, sc. 2, l. 33. [Reignier]

I cannot brook delay.
III Henry VI, iii, 2, 18. [Lady Grey]

I have not stopped mine ears to their demands,
Nor posted off their suits with slow delays.
III Henry VI. Act iv, sc 8, l. 39. [King]

A fine-baited delay.—*The Merry Wives of Windsor*, ii, 1, 99. Only use of "fine-baited."
The law's delay.—*Hamlet*, iii, 1, 72.

5
Delay not, Cæsar; read it instantly.
Julius Cæsar. Act iii, sc. 1, l. 9. [Artemidorus]

Delay not.—*III Henry VI*, iii, 3, 246.
Delay it not.—*Hamlet*, iv, 3, 57.
Without delay.—*Henry VIII*, i, 2, 59; ii, 4, 67.
Without any further delay.—*King Lear*, i, 2, 100.
I might well delay.—*King Lear*, v, 3, 144.

6
Dull not device by coldness and delay.
Othello. Act ii, sc. 3, l. 394. [Iago]

I would not be delay'd.—*Othello*, iii, 4, 114.

7
Take heed you dally not.
Richard III, ii, 1, 12. See under KING. "Dally not" is repeated in *I Henry VI*, iv, 5, 11; *The Comedy of Errors*, i, 2, 59; *The Taming of the Shrew*, iv, 4, 68.

Is it a time to . . . dally?
I Henry IV. Act v, sc. 3, l. 57. [Prince of Wales]

If thou shouldst dally half an hour, his life,
With thine, and all that offer to defend him,
Stand in assured loss.
King Lear. Act iii, sc. 6, l. 100. [Gloucester]

You but dally.—*Hamlet*, v, 2, 308.
Dally nicely.—*Twelfth Night*, iii, 1, 16.
Dally, smile and jest.—*Venus and Adonis*, l. 106.
Dally with my excrement.—*Love's Labour 's Lost*, v, 1, 109. The only uses of "dally."

8
We make woe wanton with this fond delay:
Once more, adieu; the rest let sorrow say.
Richard II. Act v, sc. 1, l. 101. [King Richard]

Be not ta'en tardy by unwise delay.
Richard III. Act iv, sc. 1, l. 52. [Stanley]

Tardied my swift command.—*The Winter's Tale*, iii, 2, 163. The only use of "tardied." For "tardy" see under LATENESS.

9
Come, I have heard that fearful commenting
Is leaden servitor to dull delay;
Delay leads impotent and snail-paced beggary.
Richard III. Act iv, sc. 3, l. 51. [King Richard] "Commenting" is repeated in *As You Like It*, ii, 1, 65; and "snail-paced" in *Troilus and Cressida*, v, 5, 18.

10
In delay
We waste our lights in vain, like lamps by day.
Romeo and Juliet. Act i, sc. 4, l. 44. [Mercutio]

Come, we burn daylight.
Romeo and Juliet. Act i, sc. 4, l. 43. [Mercutio]

We burn daylight.—*The Merry Wives of Windsor*, ii, 1, 54.

11
Nothing may prorogue it.
Romeo and Juliet. Act iv, sc. 1, l. 48. [Friar Laurence] "Prorogue" is repeated in *Antony and Cleopatra*, ii, 1, 26: "Prorogue his honour"; and in *Pericles*, v, 1, 26: "Prorogue his grief." "Prorogued" occurs in *Romeo and Juliet*, ii, 2, 78.

12
Who of my people hold him in delay?
Twelfth Night. Act i, sc. 5, l. 112. [Olivia]

In delay there lies no plenty.
Twelfth Night. Act ii, sc. 3, l. 51. [Clown]

13
No more of stay!
The Two Gentlemen of Verona. Act i, sc. 3, l. 75. [Antonio]

DELIGHT

1 His delights
Were dolphin like; they show'd his back above
The element they lived in.
Antony and Cleopatra. Act v, sc. 2, l. 88. [Cleopatra] The only use of "dolphin-like."

2
Hast thou delight to see a wretched man
Do outrage and displeasure to himself?
The Comedy of Errors. Act iv, sc. 4, l. 118. [Adriana]

3
Never to be infected with delight.
King John. Act iv, sc. 3, l. 69. [Salisbury]

Why, all delights are vain; but that most vain,
Which with pain purchased doth inherit pain.
Love's Labour 's Lost. Act i, sc. 1, l. 72. [Biron]

Take delight.—*I Henry VI,* iii, 1, 111; *Hamlet,* ii, 2, 341; *Twelfth Night,* i, 5, 89; *Sonnets,* xxxvii.

Take no delight.—*Love's Labour 's Lost,* i, 2, 134.

4
Speak, brave Hector: we are much delighted.
Love's Labour 's Lost. Act v, sc. 2, l. 671. [Princess] "Delighted" is used only five times in the plays and once in the poems.

5
I pray thee, let me go and find him out
And quicken his embraced heaviness
With some delight or other.
The Merchant of Venice. Act ii, sc. 8, l. 51. [Salanio]

Do you think . . . that ever the devil could have made you our delight?
The Merry Wives of Windsor. Act v, sc. 5, l. 154. [Mrs. Page]

6 How shall we beguile
The lazy time, if not with some delight?
A Midsummer-Night's Dream. Act v, sc. 1, l. 40. [Theseus]

7
Nor let no comforter delight mine ear.
Much Ado about Nothing. Act v, sc. 1, l. 6. [Antonio]

Delight his ear.—*The Passionate Pilgrim,* l. 47.

Delight the taste.—*Pericles,* i, 4, 40.

8
Make after him, poison his delight.
Othello. Act i, sc. 1, l. 68. [Iago]

And then too late she will repent
That thus dissembled her delight.
The Passionate Pilgrim, l. 313.

9
Her joy, her life, her world's delight.
The Rape of Lucrece, l. 385.

My earth's delight.—*Rape of Lucrece,* l. 487.

Life's delight.—*Pericles,* iv, 4, 12.

Loathed delight.—*The Rape of Lucrece,* l. 742.

False delight.—*The Rape of Lucrece,* l. 927.

10 Even such delight
Among fresh female buds shall you this night
Inherit at my house.
Romeo and Juliet. Act i, sc. 2, l. 28. [Capulet]

These violent delights have violent ends
And in their triumph die, like fire and powder,
Which as they kiss consume.
Romeo and Juliet. Act ii, sc. 6, l. 9. [Friar Laurence]

11
Possessing or pursuing no delight,
Save what is had or must from you be took.
Sonnets. No. lxxv.

Eye's delight.—*Sonnets,* lxvii.

Love's delight.—*Sonnets,* xxxvi.

12 She taketh most delight
In music, instruments and poetry.
The Taming of the Shrew. Act i, sc. 1, l. 92. [Baptista]

13 You speak
Like one besotted on your sweet delights.
Troilus and Cressida. Act ii, sc. 2, l. 141. [Priam] The only use of "besotted."

Dear delight.—*Sonnets,* cii.

Fair delight.—*Venus and Adonis,* l. 1030.

Sweet delight.—*The Rape of Lucrece,* l. 357.

True delight.—*A Midsummer-Night's Dream,* iii, 2, 455; *As You Like It,* v, 4, 204; *Pericles,* iii, 2, 39.

14
My day's delight is past.
Venus and Adonis, l. 380.

DEMAND

15
In true fear They gave us our demands.
Coriolanus. Act iii, sc. 1, l. 135. [Coriolanus]

Let him demand his fill.
Hamlet. Act iv, sc. 5, l. 129. [King]

That is her demand.—*All 's Well that Ends Well,* ii, 1, 89.

I Demand the like.—*Antony and Cleopatra,* iii, 6, 37.

Make demand.—*Antony and Cleopatra,* v, 2, 305.

16
She is our capital demand, comprised
Within the fore-rank of our articles.
Henry V. Act v, sc. 2, l. 96. [King Henry] The only use of "comprised," and "fore-rank."

Clamorous demands.—*Timon of Athens,* ii, 2, 38.

Fair demands.—*Antony and Cleopatra,* v, 2, 10.

Mannerly demand.—*Cymbeline,* iii, 6, 92.

Religiously demand.—*King John,* iii, 1, 140.

Particular demands.—*Hamlet,* ii, 1, 12.

17
The king hath yielded unto thy demand.
II Henry VI. Act v, sc. 1, l. 40. [York]

18 Why may not I demand
Of thine affairs, as well as thou of mine?
King John. Act v, sc. 6, l. 4. [Hubert]

This . . . I do demand of thee.
King John. Act iii, sc. 1, l. 146. [Pandulph]

19
You will demand of me why I do this?
Measure for Measure. Act i, sc. 3, l. 17. [Duke]

Why demand you this?—*Love's Labour 's Lost,* v, 2, 386.

Demand me nothing.—*Othello,* v, 2, 303.

20
Then speak at once what is it thou demand'st.
Richard III. Act ii, sc. 1, l. 98. [King Edward] The only use of "demand'st."

How now? moody? What is 't thou canst demand?
The Tempest. Act i, sc. 2, l. 245. [Prospero]

1
What says your highness to my just demand?
Richard III. Act iv, sc. 2, l. 97. [Buckingham] The only use of "just demand." "Just demands" occurs in *Henry V,* v, 2, 71, and in *King John,* ii, 1, 56.

Wherein
It shall appear that your demands are just,
You shall enjoy them.
II Henry IV. Act iv, sc. 1, l. 143. [Westmoreland]

2
What wouldst thou of us, Trojan? make demand.
Troilus and Cressida. Act iii, sc. 3, l. 17. [Agamemnon]

Make demands.—*Troilus and Cressida,* iii, 3, 272.

Make that demand.—*Troilus and Cressida,* ii, 3, 72.

No more Can I demand.—*Romeo and Juliet,* v, 3, 298.

DENIAL

See also Refusal

3
Our dearest friend
Prejudicates the business and would seem
To have us make denial.
All's Well that Ends Well. Act i, sc. 2, l. 7. [King] The only use of "prejudicates."

Can you deny it?—*Comedy of Errors,* v, 1, 22.

Canst thou deny it?—*II Henry IV,* ii, 1, 101.

Deny it, if thou canst.—*II Henry IV,* ii, 1, 112.

4
Yet dare I never Deny your asking.
Coriolanus. Act i, sc. 6, l. 65. [Cominius]

I will deny thee nothing.—*King Lear,* iii, 3, 76.

I would not deny you.—*Much Ado about Nothing,* v, 4, 94.

You must not deny me.—*The Merchant of Venice,* ii, 2, 187.

5
The thing I have forsworn to grant may never
Be held by you denials.
Coriolanus. Act v, sc. 3, l. 80. [Coriolanus]

Who heard me to deny it or forswear it?
The Comedy of Errors. Act v, sc. 1, l. 25. [Antipholus of Syracuse]

Deny him, forswear him, or else we are all undone.
The Taming of the Shrew. Act v, sc 1, l. 114. [Biondello]

As faithfully as I deny the devil.
King John. Act i, sc. 1, l. 252. [Bastard]

6
Princess: If this thou do deny, let our hands part,
Neither intitled in the other's heart.
King: If this, or more than this, I would deny,
To flatter up these powers of mine with rest,
The sudden hand of death close up mine eye!
Hence ever then my heart is in thy breast.
Love's Labour's Lost. Act v, sc. 2, l. 821. The only use of "intitled."

For 'twould have anger'd any heart alive
To hear the men deny 't.
Macbeth. Act iii, sc. 6, l. 15. [Lennox]

7
I could not for my heart deny it him.
The Merchant of Venice. Act v, sc. 1, l. 165. [Gratiano]

I 'll not deny him any thing I have,
No, not my body nor my husband's bed.
The Merchant of Venice. Act v, sc. 1, l. 227. [Portia]

Do not deny him.—*Troilus and Cressida,* iv, 2, 51.

8
I did deny him
And suffer'd him to go displeased away.
The Merchant of Venice. Act v, sc. 1, l. 212. [Bassanio]

They have all denied him.—*Timon of Athens,* iii, 3, 7.

Do all they deny her?—*All's Well that Ends Well,* ii, 3, 92.

9
You hear all these matters denied, gentlemen; you hear it.
The Merry Wives of Windsor. Act i, sc. 1, l. 193. [Falstaff]

That gracious denial which he is most glad to receive.
Measure for Measure, iii, 1, 166. [Duke]

10
Thou seest that all the grace that she hath left
Is that she will not add to her damnation
A sin of perjury; she not denies it.
Much Ado about Nothing. Act iv, sc. 1, l. 173. [Leonato]

This is more, masters, than you can deny.
Much Ado about Nothing. Act iv, sc. 2, l. 63. [Sexton]

I deny nothing.—*Much Ado about Nothing,* iv, 1, 274.

She cannot deny it.—*King Lear,* iii, 6, 53.

Not denied by himself.—*Measure for Measure,* iv, 2, 145.

You may not deny it.—*Love's Labour's Lost,* v, 2, 712.

It cannot be denied.—*Coriolanus,* iv, 5, 243; *Antony and Cleopatra,* ii, 6, 92.

It must not be denied.—*Much Ado about Nothing,* i, 3, 33.

That will not be denied.—*Antony and Cleopatra,* v, 2, 234.

11
Let him come when he will;
I will deny thee nothing.
Othello. Act iii, sc. 3, l. 75. [Othello]

He denies it faintly.—*Othello,* iv, 1, 113.

12
I 'll beg her love; but she is not her own:
The worst is but denial and reproving.
The Rape of Lucrece, l. 241.

13
Marry, God forbid his grace should say us nay!
Richard III. Act iii, sc. 7, l. 81. [Mayor]

If thou hadst said him nay.
King John, i, 1, 275. See under SIN.

Past all saying nay.—*The Merchant of Venice,* iii, 2, 232.
Dares not answer nay.—*A Midsummer-Night's Dream,* iii, 1, 136.
Still answer nay.—*Richard III,* iii, 7, 51.
I 'll . . . say thee nay.—*Romeo and Juliet,* ii, 2, 96.
No; I say nay to that.—*The Comedy of Errors,* v, 1, 371.

1
Never make denial.
The Taming of the Shrew. Act ii, sc. 1, l. 281. [Petruchio]

2
Be not ceased With slight denial.
Timon of Athens. Act i, sc. 2, l. 17. [Senator]
Be not denied.—*Twelfth Night,* i, 4, 16.
I will not be denied.—*Titus Andronicus,* i, 1, 481.
Will you deny me now?—*Twelfth Night,* iii, 4, 381.
'Twere needful I denied it.—*The Winter's Tale,* i, 2, 23.

3
He 's fortified against any denial.
Twelfth Night. Act i, sc. 5, l. 153. [Malvolio]
In your denial I would find no sense;
I would not understand it.
Twelfth Night. Act i, sc. 5, l. 285. [Viola]

4
'Tis a sickness denying thee any thing; a death to grant this.
Winter's Tale. Act iv, sc. 2, l. 2. [Polixenes]

DENUNCIATION

See also Curse, Dismissal

5
Thou drone, thou snail, thou slug, thou sot!
The Comedy of Errors. Act ii, sc. 2, l. 196. [Luciana] "Slug" is repeated in *Richard III,* iii, 1, 22.
Mome, malt-horse, capon, coxcomb, idiot!
The Comedy of Errors. Act iii, sc. 1, l. 32. The only use of "mome" (blockhead). "Malt-horse" (a heavy horse used by maltsters) is repeated in the quotation which follows.
You logger-headed and unpolish'd grooms! . . .
You peasant swain! you whoreson malthorse drudge!
The Taming of the Shrew. Act iv, sc. 1, l. 128. [Petruchio] The only use of "logger-headed."
Thou pale and common drudge.—*Merchant of Venice,* iii, 2, 103.
Paltry, servile abject drudges.—*II Henry VI,* iv, 1, 105.
Base drudge.—*II Henry VI,* iv, 2, 159.
Poor drudge.—*Sonnets,* cli.
Drudge of nature's.—*Cymbeline,* v, 2, 5.
He 's my drudge.—*All 's Well that Ends Well,* i, 3, 49.
This drudge.—*The Comedy of Errors,* iii, 2, 144. The only uses of "drudge."

6
'Tis pity that thou livest
To walk where any honest men resort.
The Comedy of Errors. Act v, sc. 1, l. 27. [Merchant]

7
A scullion! Fie upon 't! foh!
Hamlet. Act ii, sc. 2, l. 616. [Hamlet]
Away, you scullion!—*II Henry IV,* ii, 1, 65. The only uses of "scullion."

8
Prince of Wales: Thou clay-brained guts, thou knotty-pated fool, thou whoreson, obscene, greasy tallow-catch,— . . . this sanguine coward, this bed-presser, this horse-back-breaker, this huge hill of flesh,—
Falstaff: 'Sblood, you starveling, you elf-skin, you dried neat's tongue, you bull's pizzle, you stock-fish! O for breath to utter what is like thee! you tailor's yard, you sheath, you bow-case, you vile standing-tuck.
I Henry IV. Act ii, sc. 4, l. 251. A succession of unique epithets, which Shakespeare evidently loved to coin.
Distrustful recreants!
I Henry VI. Act i, sc. 2, l. 126. [La Pucelle] The only use of "distrustful."

9
You whoreson dog! you slave! you cur!
King Lear. Act i, sc. 4, l. 89. [King Lear] "Whoreson" was a favourite adjective with Shakespeare, who used it forty times in the plays in various combinations: "Whoreson ass," "Whoreson cur," "Whoreson knave," "Whoreson rabbit," "Whoreson rascal," "Whoreson villain," and so on.
O, be thou damn'd, inexecrable dog!
The Merchant of Venice. Act iv, sc. 1, l. 128. [Gratiano] The only use of "inexecrable."
Cut-throat dog.—*Merchant of Venice,* i, 3, 112.
Egregious dog.—*Henry V,* ii, 1, 49.
A pox o' your throat, you bawling, blasphemous, incharitable dog!
The Tempest. Act i, sc. 1, l. 43. [Sebastian] Shakespeare was fond of calling a man a dog and did so many times with various qualifying adjectives: "Thou common dog," "Unmanner'd dog," "Inhuman dog," "Mangy dog," and so on. This is the only use of "incharitable."

10
We do the denunciation lack
Of outward order.
Measure for Measure. Act i, sc. 2, l. 152. [Claudio] The only use of "denunciation."

11
With an outstretch'd throat I 'll tell the world aloud
What man thou art.
Measure for Measure. Act ii, sc. 4, l. 153. [Isabella]

12
You witch, you hag, you baggage, you polecat, you ronyon!
The Merry Wives of Windsor. Act iv, sc. 2, l. 194. [Ford] "You witch, you hag" is repeated in l. 187; and "ronyon" in *Macbeth,* i, 3, 6: "Rump-fed ronyon" (a scabby person fed on offal).
There are fairer things than polecats, sure.
The Merry Wives of Windsor, iv, 1, 29. "Polecat" is used in no other play.
Hang off, thou cat, thou burr! vile thing, let loose,

Or I will shake thee from me like a serpent!
A Midsummer-Night's Dream. Act iii, sc. 2, l. 260. [Lysander]

1
You ruinous butt, you whoreson indistinguishable cur.
Troilus and Cressida. Act v, sc. 1, l. 32. [Patroclus] The only use of "indistinguishable."

Thou idle immaterial skein of sleave-silk, thou green sarcenet flap for a sore eye, thou tassel of a prodigal's purse.
Troilus and Cressida. Act v, sc. 1, l. 35. [Thersites] "Immaterial," "sleave-silk," "sarcenet flap," and "tassel" are all unique.

Patroclus: Out, gall!
Thersites: Finch-egg.
Troilus and Cressida. Act v, sc. 1, l. 41. The only use of "finch-egg."

O thou thing!—*The Winter's Tale,* ii, 1, 82.

DEPARTURE

See also Parting, Separation

2
I have congied with the duke, done my adieu with his nearest.
All's Well that Ends Well. Act iv, sc. 3, l. 100. [Bertram] The only use of "congied" (take leave of).

3
If they suffer our departure, death 's the word.
Antony and Cleopatra. Act i, sc. 2, l. 138. [Enobarbus]

Else had she with her father ranged along.
As You Like It. Act i, sc. 3, l. 70. [Duke] The only use of "ranged along." "Range about" occurs in *III Henry VI,* ii, 1, 11, and "range abroad" in *Richard II,* iii, 2, 39.

4
I am glad of your departure.
As You Like It. Act iii, sc. 2, l. 311. [Orlando]

Therefore tremble, and depart.—*As You Like It,* v, 1, 63.

5
Say in brief the cause
Why thou departed'st from thy native home.
The Comedy of Errors. Act i, sc. 1, l. 29. [Duke] The only use of "departed'st."

'Tis strange that they should so depart from home.
King Lear. Act ii, sc. 4, l. 1. [King Lear]

Depart his house.—*King Lear,* iii, 5, 1.

6
Balthazar: Be ruled by me: depart in patience. . . .
Antipholus of Ephesus: You have prevail'd: I will depart in quiet.
The Comedy of Errors. Act iii, sc. 1, l. 94.

Be quiet and depart.—*The Comedy of Errors,* v, 1, 112.

7
If every one knows us and we know none,
'Tis time, I think, to trudge, pack and be gone.
The Comedy of Errors. Act iii, sc. 2, l. 157. [Antipholus of Syracuse] See also under Dismissal.

Trudge . . . in all haste.—*The Merry Wives of Windsor,* iii, 3, 13.

8
Break with your wives of your departure hence.
I Henry IV. Act iii, sc. 1, l. 144. [Glendower]

My people did expect my hence departure
Two days ago.
Winter's Tale. Act i, sc. 2, l. 450. [Polixenes]

Your departure hence.—*All 's Well that Ends Well,* iv, 3, 108; *The Two Gentlemen of Verona,* iii, 1, 160.

Depart'st hence safe.—*Antony and Cleopatra,* iv, 14, 36. The only use of "depart'st."

Departure thence.—*I Henry IV,* iv, 1, 23.

Depart from thence.—*The Comedy of Errors,* iv, 4, 79.

We license your departure.—*I Henry IV,* i, 3, 123.

Dire departure.—*I Henry VI,* iv, 2, 41.

9
See the coast clear'd, and then we will depart.
I Henry VI. Act i, sc. 3, l. 89. [Mayor] The only use of the idiom, "a clear coast," or "clear the coast."

10
If I depart from thee, I cannot live;
And in thy sight to die, what were it else
But like a pleasant slumber in thy lap?
II Henry VI. Act iii, sc. 2, l. 388. [Suffolk]

Depart the field.—*III Henry VI,* ii, 2, 73.

At my depart.—*III Henry VI,* iv, 1, 92; *The Two Gentlemen of Verona,* v, 4, 96.

Let him depart.—*III Henry VI,* v, 4, 49; *Henry V,* iv, 3, 36.

Depart away.—*Love's Labour 's Lost,* v, 2, 156.

Depart untouch'd.—*Julius Cæsar,* iii, 1, 142.

With this I depart.—*Julius Cæsar,* iii, 2, 49.

Let me depart alone.—*Julius Cæsar,* iii, 2, 60.

Depart in peace.—*King John,* i, 1, 23; *Much Ado about Nothing,* iii, 3, 73.

11
I pray God grant them a fair departure.
The Merchant of Venice. Act i, sc. 2, l. 121. [Portia]

You must be gone from hence immediately.
The Merchant of Venice. Act ii, sc. 9, l. 8. [Portia]

A gentle riddance.—*The Merchant of Venice,* ii, 7, 78.

A good riddance.—*Troilus and Cressida,* ii, 1, 132. The only uses of "riddance."

12
Brief, he must hence depart to Tyre.
Pericles. Act iii, Gower, l. 39.

Depart to Paris.—*I Henry VI,* iii, 2, 128.

Depart for France.—*II Henry VI,* i, 1, 2.

13
Lo, this is all:—nay, yet depart not so;
Though this be all, do not so quickly go.
Richard II. Act i, sc. 3, l. 63. [Duchess]

Looking awry upon your lord's departure.
Richard II. Act ii, sc. 2, l. 21. [Bushy]

Never . . . depart again.—*Romeo and Juliet,* v, 3, 108.

14
Fellows, let 's be gone.
Taming of the Shrew, i, 2, 280. [Grumio]

Wilt thou be gone? Sweet Valentine, adieu.
The Two Gentlemen of Verona. Act i, sc. 1, l. 11. [Proteus] "Be gone" occurs thirty-seven times.

Let us depart.—*Troilus and Cressida,* v, 2, 36.
Let us avoid.—*The Winter's Tale,* i, 2, 462.
In mine own accord I'll off.—*The Winter's Tale,* ii, 3, 63.

1 Let him that moved you hither
Remove you hence.
The Taming of the Shrew. Act ii, sc. 1, l. 196. [Katharina]
By and by depart.—*Twelfth Night,* iii, 4, 192.
Depart from me.—*Twelfth Night,* iv, 1, 19.

2
Ere we depart, we 'll share a bounteous time.
Timon of Athens. Act i, sc. i, l. 263. [Timon]
Ere you depart.—*Cymbeline,* iii, 6, 68.
Ere you shall depart.—*Pericles,* i, 3, 39.

3
Which is another spur to my departure.
Winter's Tale. Act iv, sc. 2, l. 9. [Camillo]
Let them depart.—*The Winter's Tale,* v, 3, 97.
Get you hence, for I must go
Where it fits not you to know.
The Winter's Tale. Act iv, sc. 4, l. 303. [Autolycus]

DEPUTY, see Substitute

DERISION, see Ridicule

DESCENT, see Ancestry

DESCRIPTION

4
It beggar'd all description.
Antony and Cleopatra. Act ii, sc. 2, l. 203. [Enobarbus]
A maid That paragons description.
Othello. Act ii, sc. 1, l. 61. [Cassio]

5
Will this description satisfy him?
Antony and Cleopatra. Act ii, sc. 7, l. 56. [Cæsar]
His description Proved us unspeaking sots.
Cymbeline. Act v, sc. 5, l. 177. [Iachimo]
Sir, his definement suffers no perdition in you.
Hamlet. Act v, sc. 2, l. 117. [Hamlet] The only use of "definement."

6
Description cannot suit itself in words.
Henry V. Act iv, sc. 2, l. 53. [Grandpré]

7
Your wondrous rare description, noble earl,
Of beauteous Margaret hath astonish'd me.
I Henry VI. Act v, sc. 5, l. 1. [King Henry]
He went to bed to her very description.
Pericles, iv, 2, 108. See under INCLINATION.

8
I will describe them; and, according to my description, level at my affection.
The Merchant of Venice. Act i, sc. 2, l. 41. [Portia]
Excellent description.—*Henry V,* iii, 6, 39.
A right description.—*Love's Labour 's Lost,* v, 2, 522.

9
First Bandit: Is not this he? . . .
Second Bandit: 'Tis his description.
Timon of Athens. Act iv, sc. 3, l. 410.

10
By all description this should be the place.
Timon of Athens. Act v, sc. 3, l. 1. [Soldier]
This is the very description of their meeting-place.
Cymbeline. Act iv, sc. 1, l. 26. [Cloten] The only use of "meeting-place."

DESERT

See also Solitude

11 This desert inaccessible,
Under the shade of melancholy boughs.
As You Like It. Act ii, sc. 7, l. 110. [Orlando] "Inaccessible" is used only once again, in the following quotation:
Desert . . . Uninhabitable and almost inaccessible.
The Tempest, ii, 1, 37. [Adrian] The only use of "uninhabitable."

12
Why should this a desert be?
For it is unpeopled?
As You Like It. Act iii, sc. 2, l. 133. [Celia]

13
O, thou wilt be a wilderness again,
Peopled with wolves, thy old inhabitants!
II Henry IV. Act iv, sc. 5, l. 137. [King Henry] "Inhabitants" is used only once again, in *Macbeth,* i, 3, 41: "Inhabitants o' the earth."
A wilderness where are no laws.
The Rape of Lucrece, l. 544.
Live, as we do, in this wilderness.
The Two Gentlemen of Verona, iv, 1, 63.
Wilderness of sea.—*Titus Andronicus,* iii, 1, 94.
Wilderness of monkeys.—*The Merchant of Venice,* iii, 1, 128.
Wilderness of tigers.—*Titus Andronicus,* iii, 1, 54.
Warped slip of wilderness.—*Measure for Measure,* iii, 1, 142.

14
The Hyrcanian deserts and the vasty wilds
Of wide Arabia.
The Merchant of Venice. Act ii, sc. 7, l. 41. [Prince of Morocco] "Hyrcanian" is repeated in *Hamlet,* ii, 2, 472: "Hyrcanian beast."
The deserts of Bohemia.—*The Winter's Tale,* iii, 3, 2.

15
Wherein of antres vast and deserts idle,
Rough quarries, rocks and hills whose heads touch heaven,
It was my hint to speak.
Othello. Act i, sc. 3, l. 140. [Othello] The only use of "antres" (caverns).

16
Some dark deep desert, seated from the way,
That knows not parching heat nor freezing cold,
Will we find out.
The Rape of Lucrece, l. 1144.
Here never shines the sun; here nothing breeds,
Unless the nightly owl or fatal raven.
Titus Andronicus. Act ii, sc. 3, l. 96. [Tamora]

17
This shadowy desert, unfrequented woods,
I better brook than flourishing peopled towns:
Here can I sit alone, unseen of any.
And to the nightingale's complaining notes

Tune my distresses and record my woes.
The Two Gentlemen of Verona. Act v, sc. 4, l. 2. [Valentine] "Shadowy" is repeated in *King Lear,* i, 1, 65: "Shadowy forests"; and "unfrequented" in *Titus Andronicus,* ii, 1, 115: "Unfrequented plots."

1
Bear it To some remote and desert place.
Winter's Tale. Act ii, sc. 3, l. 175. [Leontes]
Desert place.—*A Midsummer-Night's Dream,* ii, 1, 218; *As You Like It,* ii, 4, 72; iv, 3, 142.

DESERVING

See also Merit, Worth

2
Nor would I have him till I do deserve him;
Yet never know how that desert should be.
All's Well that Ends Well. Act i, sc. 3, l. 205. [Helena]
I deserve it.—*The Merry Wives of Windsor,* iii, 3, 161.
I 'll deserve it.—*The Merry Wives of Windsor,* iii, 3, 89.
How may I deserve it?—*Henry VIII,* v, 3, 165.

3
Vanish, or I shall give thee thy deserving.
Antony and Cleopatra. Act iv, sc. 12, l. 32. [Antony]
You shall not be
The grave of your deserving.
Coriolanus. Act i, sc. 9, l. 19. [Cominius]
Some of us love you well; and even those some
Envy your great deservings and good name.
I Henry IV. Act iv, sc. 3, l. 34. [Hotspur] The only use of "great deservings."
I shall study deserving.
King Lear. Act i, sc. 1, l. 32. [Edmund]
This seems a fair deserving.
King Lear. Act iii, sc. 3, l. 24. [Edmund]

4 You have deserved
High commendation, true applause and love.
As You Like It. Act i, sc. 2, l. 274. [Le Beau]
Your patience and your virtue well deserves it.
As You Like It. Act v, sc. 4, l. 193. [Jaques]

5 Ladies, you deserve
To have a temple built you.
Coriolanus. Act v, sc. 3, l. 206. [Coriolanus]
Deserve a coronet of gold.—*I Henry VI,* iii, 3, 89.
Deserve a crown.—*King John,* iii, 1, 50.
Deserves an heir.—*Timon of Athens,* i, 1, 119.
Deserves To have the heir.—*III Henry VI,* iv, 1, 47; *Richard II,* ii, 1, 193.
Deserves a help.—*Timon of Athens,* i, 1, 102.
Deserve love.—*Coriolanus,* ii, 3, 165.
Deserve pity.—*Cymbeline,* i, 6, 85.
Deserved praise.—*Henry V,* iii, 7, 35.
Deserve a sweet look.—*A Midsummer-Night's Dream,* ii, 2, 127.
Deserve his change.—*Antony and Cleopatra,* iii, 6, 34.
Deserves thanks.—*Richard III,* iii, 7, 154; *King Lear,* ii, 1, 63.
Deserves thy trust.—*Cymbeline,* i, 6, 158.

6
Let me deserve so ill as you.
Coriolanus. Act iii, sc. 1, l. 51. [Coriolanus]
Without desert.—*Richard III,* ii, 1, 67; *The Comedy of Errors,* iii, 1, 112.
Undeserving as I am.—*The Two Gentlemen of Verona,* iii, 1, 7. "Undeserving" is repeated in *Love's Labour 's Lost,* v, 2, 366.

7
Great nature, like his ancestry,
Moulded the stuff so fair,
That he deserved the praise o' the world.
Cymbeline. Act v, sc. 4, l. 48. [Sicilius]

8
Polonius: I will use them according to their desert.
Hamlet: God's bodykins, man, much better: use every man after his desert, and who should 'scape whipping? Use them after your own honour and dignity: the less they deserve, the more merit is in your bounty.
Hamlet. Act ii, sc. 2, l. 552. The only use of "God's bodykins."

9
We . . . shall forget the office of our hand,
Sooner than quittance of desert and merit
According to the weight and worthiness.
Henry V. Act ii, sc. 2, l. 32. [King Henry]
Dick: I desire no more.
Jack Cade: And, to speak truth, thou deservest no less.
II Henry VI. Act iv, sc. 3, l. 10.

10
Richard hath best deserved of all my sons.
III Henry VI. Act i, sc. 1, l. 17. [York]
To deserve well.—*III Henry VI,* v, 1, 93. A favourite expression with Shakespeare, and used many times in later plays.
She well deserves it.—*III Henry VI,* iii, 3, 249.
Deserve by doing well.—*Cymbeline,* iii, 3, 54.

11
There 's nothing I have done yet, o' my conscience,
Deserves a corner.
Henry VIII. Act iii, sc. 1, l. 30. [Queen]
What he deserves of you and me I know.
Henry VIII. Act iii, sc. 2, l. 14. [Chamberlain]
The duke by law Found his deserts.
Henry VIII. Act iii, sc. 2, l. 266. [Wolsey]
He will deserve more.—*Henry VIII,* iv, 1, 113; *Cymbeline,* i, 4, 129.

12
You less know how to value her desert
Than she to scant her duty.
King Lear. Act ii, sc. 4, l. 141. [Regan]

13 Would thou hadst less deserved,
That the proportion both of thanks and payment
Might have been mine! only I have left to say,
More is thy due than more than all can pay.
Macbeth. Act i, sc. 4, l. 18. [Duncan]
That hast no less deserved, nor must be known
No less to have done so.
Macbeth. Act i, sc. 4, l. 30. [Duncan]

14
O, your desert speaks loud; and I should wrong it,
To lock it in the wards of covert bosom,
When it deserves, with characters of brass,
A forted residence 'gainst the tooth of time
And razure of oblivion.
Measure for Measure. Act v, sc. 1, l. 9. [Duke] The only use of "forted" and "razure."

You, sirrah, that knew me for a fool, a coward,
One all of luxury, an ass, a madman;
Wherein have I so deserved of you,
That you extol me thus?
Measure for Measure, v, 1, 505. [Duke]

I crave death more willingly than mercy;
'Tis my deserving, and I do entreat it.
Measure for Measure, v, 1, 481. [Angelo]

1
He, of all men that ever my foolish eyes looked upon, was the best deserving a fair lady.
The Merchant of Venice. Act i, sc. 2, l. 129. [Nerissa]

And yet to be afeard of my deserving
Were but a weak disabling of myself.
The Merchant of Venice. Act ii, sc. 7, l. 29. [Morocco] The only use of "disabling."

How much unlike my hopes and my deservings! . . .
Did I deserve no more than a fool's head?
Is that my prize? are my deserts no better? . . .
With one fool's head I came to woo,
But I go away with two.
The Merchant of Venice. Act ii, sc. 9, l. 57. [Arragon]

You shall have An fool's head of your own.
Merry Wives of Windsor. Act i, sc. 4, l. 134.

Let his deservings and my love withal
Be valued 'gainst your wife's commandment.
The Merchant of Venice. Act iv, sc. 1, l. 450. [Antonio]

As much as he deserves.—*The Merchant of Venice,* ii, 7, 7; ii, 7, 24.

As much as I deserve!—*The Merchant of Venice,* ii, 7, 31.

2 I know he doth deserve
As much as may be yielded to a man.
Much Ado about Nothing. Act iii, sc. 1, l. 47. [Hero]

For others say thou dost deserve, and I
Believe it better than reportingly.
Much Ado about Nothing. Act iii, sc. 1, l. 115. [Beatrice] Only use of "reportingly."

Thy desert may merit praise,
By ringing in thy lady's ear.
The Passionate Pilgrim, l. 325. "Ringing" occurs once in the plays, in *II Henry IV,* iii, 2, 194, and in *The Rape of Lucrece,* l. 1495.

3
A dearer merit, not so deep a maim
As to be cast forth in the common air,
Have I deserved at your highness' hands.
Richard II. Act i, sc. 3, l. 156. [Mowbray]

4
Well you deserve: they well deserve to have,
That know the strong'st and surest way to get.
Richard II. Act iii, sc. 3, l. 200. [King] "Surest" is repeated in *Julius Cæsar,* iv, 1, 47.

5
'Tis more than you deserve.
Richard III. Act i, sc. 2, l. 223. [Lady Anne]

All may be well; but, if God sort it so,
'Tis more than we deserve, or I expect.
Richard III. Act ii, sc. 3, l. 36. [Citizen]

I, in my condition,
Shall better speak of you than you deserve.
II Henry IV. Act iv, sc. 3, l. 90. [Lancaster]

6
I pray you all, tell me what they deserve
That do conspire my death.
Richard III. Act iii, sc. 4, l. 61. [Gloucester]

Now, fair befall you! he deserved his death.
Richard III. Act iii, sc. 5, l. 47. [Mayor]

Deserved to lie in death.—*Julius Cæsar,* iii, 1, 132.

Deserved death.—*Richard II,* v, 1, 68.

This deserves death.—*Coriolanus,* iii, 1, 207.

Deserves the extremest death.—*Coriolanus,* iii, 3, 82.

Deserve to die.—*Love's Labour's Lost,* iv, 3, 209.

Deserved hate.—*III Henry VI,* v, 1, 104; *Coriolanus,* i, 1, 180.

Deserved no pity.—*III Henry VI,* ii, 6, 28.

Deserved vexation.—*Coriolanus,* iii, 3, 140.

Deserves to lose.—*Macbeth,* i, 3, 121.

7
Not my deserts, but what I will deserve.
Richard III, iv, 4, 415. See under Wooing.

8
Against the time do I ensconce me here
Within the knowledge of mine own desert.
Sonnets. No. xlix.

Behold desert a beggar born.
Sonnets. No. lxvi.

Mine own desert.—*Sonnets,* lxxii.

Accuse me thus: that I have scanted all
Wherein I should your great deserts repay.
Sonnets. No. cxvii.

9 Therefore wast thou
Deservedly confined into this rock,
Who hadst deserved more than a prison.
The Tempest. Act i, sc. 2, l. 360. [Prospero] The only use of "deservedly."

10
Let desert in pure election shine.
Titus Andronicus. Act i, sc. 1, l. 16. [Bassianus]

Plead your deserts.—*Titus Andronicus,* i, 1, 45.

O, none of both but are of high desert.
Titus Andronicus, iii, 1, 171. [Marcus]

High deserts.—*Sonnets,* xvii.

Approved . . . desert.—*Richard II,* ii, 3, 44.

Great deserts.—*Titus Andronicus,* i, 1, 24.

Unspeakable deserts.—*Titus Andronicus,* i, 1, 256.

11 Will you deny me now?
Is 't possible that my deserts to you
Can lack persuasion?
Twelfth Night. Act iii, sc. 4, l. 381. [Antonio]

12
Thou hast shown some sign of good desert.
The Two Gentlemen of Verona. Act iii, sc. 2, l. 18. [Duke]

Take thou thy Silvia, for thou hast deserved her.
The Two Gentlemen of Verona. Act v, sc. 4, l. 147. [Duke]

Good deserts.—*I Henry IV,* iv, 3, 46; *I Henry VI,* iii, 4, 25; *II Henry VI,* i, 4, 49.

13
Thou canst not speak too much; I have deserved
All tongues to talk their bitterest.
Winter's Tale. Act iii, sc. 2, l. 216. [Leontes]

Very nobly Have you deserved.
Winter's Tale. Act iv, sc. 4, l. 527. [Florizel]

DESIGN, see Intention, Plan, Purpose

DESIRE

I—Desire: Mental

See also Wish

1 Your desires are yours.
Antony and Cleopatra. Act iii, sc. 4, l. 28. [Antony]

Gave him away In all his own desires.
Coriolanus. Act v, sc. 6, l. 32. [Aufidius]

Trimm'd in thine own desires.
II Henry IV. Act i, sc. 3, l. 94. [Archbishop]

You shall have your desires with interest.
I Henry IV. Act iv, sc. 3, l. 49. [Blunt]

Now hast thou thy desire.
King John. Act i, sc. 1, l. 176. [King John]

Have thy desire.—*Richard II,* v, 3, 38.

2 Can one desire too much of a good thing?
As You Like It. Act iv, sc. 1, l. 123. [Rosalind]

3 Most miserable Is the desire that 's glorious.
Cymbeline. Act i, sc. 6, l. 6. [Imogen]

That 's not my desire.—*Cymbeline,* v, 4, 21.

It is most retrograde to our desire.
Hamlet. Act i, sc. 2, l. 114. [King] "Retrograde" is repeated in *All 's Well that Ends Well,* i, 1, 212.

I will tell him a little piece of my desires.
Henry V. Act v, sc. 1, l. 14. [Fluellen]

Devout desires.—*King John,* v, 4, 48.

Most just and right desires.—*II Henry IV,* iv, 2, 40.

Proud desire.—*I Henry VI,* iv, 6, 11.

4 I desire no more.
II Henry VI. Act iv, sc. 3, l. 10. [Dick]

I do desire no more.—*Julius Cæsar,* iii, 1, 252.

5 My soul's desire.
III Henry VI. Act iii, sc. 2, l. 128. [Gloucester]

God send every one their heart's desire!
Much Ado about Nothing. Act iii, sc. 4, l. 60. [Margaret]

Your heart's desires be with you!
As You Like It. Act i, sc. 2, l. 211. [Celia]

6 When was the hour
I ever contradicted your desire,
Or made it not mine too?
Henry VIII. Act ii, sc. 4, l. 27. [Queen Katharine] The only use of "contradicted."

7 At Christmas I no more desire a rose
Than wish a snow in May's new-fangled mirth;
But like of each thing that in season grows.
Love's Labour 's Lost. Act i, sc. 1, l. 105. [Biron] Christmas is mentioned again in v, 2, 462: "A Christmas comedy"; and in *The Taming of the Shrew,* Ind., 2, 140: "A Christmas gambold." "New-fangled" is repeated in *As You Like It,* iv, 1, 152: "More new-fangled than an ape."

Would you desire more?—*Love's Labour 's Lost,* iii, 1, 101.

8 Stars, hide your fires;
Let not light see my black and deep desires.
Macbeth. Act i, sc. 4, l. 50. [Macbeth]

Nought 's had, all 's spent,
Where our desire is got without content.
Macbeth. Act iii, sc. 2, l. 4. [Lady Macbeth]

9 Thy desires
Are wolvish, bloody, starved and ravenous.
The Merchant of Venice. Act iv, sc. 1, l. 137. [Gratiano] "Wolvish" is repeated in *King Lear,* i, 4, 330, and "wolvish-ravening" occurs in *Romeo and Juliet,* iii, 2, 76.

10 I desire you in friendship.
The Merry Wives of Windsor, iii, 1, 89.

I desire you that we may be friends.
The Merry Wives of Windsor, iii, 1, 121.

I desire your more acquaintance.
A Midsummer-Night's Dream, iii, 1, 200, and, with slight variations, in a number of later plays.

11 Welcomed and settled to his own desire.
Pericles. Act iv, Gower, l. 2.

12 Fair desires, in all fair measure, fairly guide them!
Troilus and Cressida. Act iii, sc. 1, l. 47. [Pandarus]

Fair desires.—*Love's Labour 's Lost,* ii, 1, 178.

13 Get you on and give him his desire.
Twelfth Night. Act iii, sc. 4, l. 271. [Sir Toby]

Desire to live.—*The Winter's Tale,* i, 1, 48; i, 1, 50.

II—Desire: Physical

See also Lust

14 Give thyself unto my sick desires.
All's Well that Ends Well. Act iv, sc. 2, l. 35. [Bertram]

As the ox hath his bow, sir, the horse his curb and the falcon her bells, so man hath his desires.
As You Like It. Act iii, sc. 3, l. 80. [Touchstone]

15 The cloyed will,
That satiate yet unsatisfied desire, that tub
Both fill'd and running, ravening first the lamb
Longs after for the garbage.
Cymbeline. Act i, sc. 6, l. 47. [Iachimo] The only use of "satiate" and "ravening." "Garbage" occurs again in *Hamlet,* i, 5, 57.

16 Is it not strange that desire should so many years outlive performance?
II Henry IV. Act ii, sc. 4, l. 286. [Poins]

Impatiently I burn with thy desire.
I Henry VI. Act i, sc. 2, l. 108. [Charles]

I confess that often ere this day,
When I have heard your king's desert recounted,
Mine ear hath tempted judgement to desire.
III Henry VI. Act iii, sc. 3, l. 131. [Bona]

17 If drawing my sword against the humour of affection would deliver me from the repro-

bate thought of it, I would take Desire prisoner.
Love's Labour's Lost. Act i, sc. 2, l. 62. [Armado]

Pensived and subdued desires.—*Lover's Complaint,* l. 219. The only use of "pensived."

1 My desire
All continent impediments would o'erbear
That did oppose my will.
Macbeth. Act iv, sc. 3, l. 63. [Malcolm]

Dost thou desire her foully for those things
That make her good?
Measure for Measure. Act ii, sc. 2, l. 174. [Angelo]

Why, that 's the lady; all the world desires her;
From the four corners of the earth they come,
To kiss this shrine, this mortal-breathing saint.
The Merchant of Venice. Act ii, sc. 7, l. 38. [Morocco] The only use of "mortal-breathing." The two words, unhyphenated, occur in *Richard II,* iv, 1, 48.

2
My desires had instance and argument to commend themselves.
The Merry Wives of Windsor. Act ii, sc. 2, l. 256. [Ford]

Methinks his flesh is punished, he shall have no desires.
The Merry Wives of Windsor. Act iv, sc. 4, l. 24. [Evans]

Leave your desires, and fairies will not pinse you.
The Merry Wives of Windsor. Act v, sc. 5, l. 137. [Evans] The only use of "pinse."

Tainted in desire!—*The Merry Wives of Windsor,* v, 5, 94.

3 Question your desires,
Know of your youth, examine well your blood.
A Midsummer-Night's Dream. Act i, sc. 1, l. 67. [Theseus]

Come thronging soft and delicate desires.
Much Ado about Nothing. Act i, sc. 1, l. 305. [Claudio]

And twice desire, ere it be day,
That which with scorn she put away.
The Passionate Pilgrim, l. 315.

4
You gods that made me man, and sway in love,
That have inflamed desire in my breast
To taste the fruit of yon celestial tree,
Or die in the adventure, be my helps.
Pericles. Act i, sc. 1, l. 19. [Pericles]

5
Borne by the trustless wings of false desire.
The Rape of Lucrece, l. 2. The only use of "trustless." "False desire" is repeated in l. 642.

But, poorly rich, so wanteth in his store,
That, cloy'd with much, he pineth still for more.
The Rape of Lucrece, l. 97.

Madly toss'd between desire and dread.
The Rape of Lucrece, l. 171.

Brain-sick rude desire.—*The Rape of Lucrece,* l. 175.

6
As from this cold flint I enforced this fire,
So Lucrece must I force to my desire.
The Rape of Lucrece, l. 181.

Desire my pilot is.—*The Rape of Lucrece,* l. 279.

By reprobate desire thus madly led,
The Roman lord marcheth to Lucrece' bed.
The Rape of Lucrece, l. 300.

Fond desire.—*The Rape of Lucrece,* l. 314.

7
Hot desire converts to cold disdain.
The Rape of Lucrece, l. 691. "Hot desire" is repeated in *Sonnets,* cliv; and in *Venus and Adonis,* l. 1074.

Drunken desire must vomit his receipt,
Ere he can see his own abomination.
The Rape of Lucrece, l. 703.

Rash desire.—*The Rape of Lucrece,* l. 706.

Feebly desire, all recreant, poor, and meek,
Like to a bankrupt beggar wails his case:
The flesh being proud, Desire doth fight with Grace,
For there it revels.
The Rape of Lucrece, l. 710.

8
The insatiate greediness of his desires,
And his enforcement of the city wives.
Richard III. Act iii, sc. 7, l. 7. [Buckingham]

9
Now old desire doth in his death-bed lie,
And young affection gapes to be his heir.
Romeo and Juliet. Act ii, Prologue, l. 1. [Chorus]

10
Then can no horse with my desire keep pace;
Therefore desire, of perfect'st love being made,
Shall neigh—no dull flesh—in his fiery race.
Sonnets. No. li.

I desperate now approve
Desire is death, which physic did except.
Sonnets. No. cxlvii.

11 Though Venus govern your desires,
Saturn is dominator over mine.
Titus Andronicus. Act ii, sc. 3, l. 30. [Aaron] "Dominator" is repeated in *Love's Labour's Lost,* i, 1, 222: "Sole dominator."

Why are you . . . wandered hither to an obscure plot,
Accompanied but with a barbarous Moor,
If foul desire had not conducted you?
Titus Andronicus. Act ii, sc. 3, l. 75. [Bassianus] "Foul desire" is repeated in *The Rape of Lucrece,* l. 574.

12
And my desires, like fell and cruel hounds,
E'er since pursue me.
Twelfth Night. Act i, sc. 1, l. 22. [Duke]

My desire,
More sharp than filed steel, did spur me forth.
Twelfth Night. Act iii, sc. 3, l. 4. [Antonio]

13
Nay, if the gentle spirit of moving words
Can no way change you to a milder form, . . .
I 'll force thee yield to my desire.
The Two Gentlemen of Verona. Act v, sc. 4, l. 55. [Proteus]

14
Being so enraged, desire doth lend her force
Courageously to pluck him from his horse.
Venus and Adonis, l. 29.

She red and hot as coals of glowing fire,
He red for shame, but frosty in desire.
Venus and Adonis, l. 35.
High desire.—*Venus and Adonis,* l. 276.
The warm approach of sweet desire.
Venus and Adonis, l. 386.
The sea hath bounds, but deep desire hath none.
Venus and Adonis, l. 389.
Now quick desire hath caught the yielding prey,
And glutton-like she feeds, yet never filleth.
Venus and Adonis, l. 547. The only use of "glutton-like."
'In night,' quoth she, 'desire sees best of all.'
Venus and Adonis, l. 720.

1 My desires
Run not before mine honour, nor my lusts
Burn hotter than my faith.
Winter's Tale. Act iv, sc. 4, l. 33. [Florizel]

DESOLATION

2 My desolation does begin to make
A better life.
Antony and Cleopatra. Act v, sc. 2, l. 1. [Cleopatra]

3 Every thing about you demonstrating a careless desolation.
As You Like It, iii, 2, 400. See under LOVE.
Unfenced desolation.—*King John,* ii, 1, 386. The only use of "unfenced."
Desolation, ruin and decay.—*Richard III,* iv, 4, 409.
Waste and desolation.—*Henry V,* iii, 3, 18.

4 O, there was desolation of gaolers and gallowses!
Cymbeline, v, 4, 213. See under HANGING.

5 Where thou art not, desolation.
II Henry VI, iii, 2, 364. See under LOVE.

6 O you have lived in desolation here,
Unseen, unvisited, much to our shame.
Love's Labour's Lost. Act v, sc. 2, l. 357. [King]
Merry days of desolation.—*Love's Labour's Lost,* i, 2, 164. See under SIGHT.

7 We have . . . seen the desolation of your streets.
Pericles. Act i, sc. 4, l. 89. [Pericles]

8 Desolate, desolate, will I hence and die.
Richard II. Act i, sc. 2, l. 73. [Duchess of Gloucester]
Leave me desolate.—*II Henry VI,* iv, 8, 60.
Desolate and left!—*The Two Gentlemen of Verona,* iv, 4, 179.
Makes them desolate.—*I Henry VI,* ii, 3, 66.
Desolate isle.—*The Tempest,* iii, 3, 80.
Desolate shade.—*Macbeth,* iv, 3, 1. The only uses of "desolate."

DESPAIR

See also Hope and Despair

9 Haply, despair hath seized her.
Cymbeline. Act iii, sc. 5, l. 60. [Queen]

10 Trow'st thou that e'er I'll look upon the world,
Or count them happy that enjoy the sun?
No; dark shall be my light and night my day.
II Henry VI. Act ii, sc. 4, l. 38. [Duchess of Gloucester]
From his bosom purge this black despair!
II Henry VI. Act iii, sc. 3, l. 23. [King Henry]
Why should he despair?—*Titus Andronicus,* ii, 1, 91.
Despair not.—*Taming of the Shrew,* iii, 1, 45.
Do but despair.—*King John,* iv, 3, 126.

11 Warwick: What hap? what hope of good?
George: Our hap is loss, our hope but sad despair.
III Henry VI. Act ii, sc. 3, l. 8.
Thou, poor soul,
Art then forsaken, as thou went'st forlorn!
III Henry VI. Act iii, sc. 1, l. 53. [King Henry]
Whence springs this deep despair?
III Henry VI. Act iii, sc. 3, l. 12. [King Lewis]
How shall poor Henry live,
Unless thou rescue him from foul despair?
III Henry VI. Act iii, sc. 3, l. 214. [Queen Margaret]
Comfortless despair.—*The Comedy of Errors,* v, 1, 80.
Damn'd despair.—*Venus and Adonis,* l. 743.
Rash-embraced despair.—*The Merchant of Venice,* iii, 2, 109. The only use of "rash-embraced."
White despair.—*Sonnets,* xcix.

12 Why I do trifle thus with his despair
Is done to cure it.
King Lear. Act iv, sc. 6, l. 33. [Edgar]

13 Call it not patience, Gaunt; it is despair.
Richard II. Act i, sc. 2, l. 29. [Duchess of Gloucester]
Beshrew thee, cousin, which didst lead me forth
Of that sweet way I was in to despair!
Richard II. Act iii, sc. 2, l. 204. [King Richard]
Driven into despair.—*Richard II,* ii, 2, 47.
Full of despair.—*Venus and Adonis,* l. 955.

14 Gloucester: By such despair, I should accuse myself.
Lady Anne: And, by despairing, shouldst thou stand excused.
Richard III. Act i, sc. 2, l. 85.
I'll join with black despair against my soul,
And to myself become an enemy.
Richard III. Act ii, sc. 2, l. 36. [Queen Elizabeth]

15 Despair, therefore, and die!
Richard III. Act v, sc. 3, l. 120. [Ghost of Prince Edward]
Fainting, despair; despairing, yield thy breath!
Richard III. Act v, sc. 3, l. 172. [Ghost of Buckingham]
Fearful and despairing!—*III Henry VI,* i, 1, 178.

1
Why should you fall into so deep an O?
Romeo and Juliet. Act iii, sc. 3, l. 90. [Nurse]
O that your face were not so full of O's!
Love's Labour's Lost. Act v, sc. 2, l. 45. [Rosaline]

2
Past hope, past cure, past help!
Romeo and Juliet. Act iv, sc. 1, l. 43. [Juliet]

3
Would I were as deep under the earth as I am above!
Troilus and Cressida. Act iv, sc. 2, l. 84. [Pandarus]
Tear my bright hair and scratch my praised cheeks,
Crack my clear voice with sobs and break my heart.
Troilus and Cressida. Act iv, sc. 2, l. 113. [Cressida]

4
O thou tyrant!
Do not repent these things, for they are heavier
Than all thy woes can stir: therefore betake thee
To nothing but despair.
Winter's Tale. Act iii, sc. 2, l. 208 [Paulina]

DESPERATION

5
Desperately he hurried through the street.
The Comedy of Errors, v, 1, 140. See under MADNESS.
Desperately are dead.—*King Lear,* v, 3, 292.
Desperately dispatch'd!—*Richard III,* i, 4, 278.
Toiling desperately.—*III Henry VI,* iii, 2, 178.
Desperately mortal.—*Measure for Measure,* iv, 2, 152. The only uses of "desperately."

6
Desperation
Is all the policy, strength and defence
That Rome can make against him.
Coriolanus. Act iv, sc. 6, l. 126. [Cominius]
The very place puts toys of desperation,
Without more motive, into every brain
That looks so many fathoms to the sea
And hears it roar beneath.
Hamlet. Act i, sc. 4, l. 75. [Horatio]

7
She, desperate, with her nails her flesh doth tear.
The Rape of Lucrece, l. 739.
She's desperate.—*King Lear,* v, 3, 161.
Monstrous desperate.—*All's Well that Ends Well,* ii, 1, 187.
Shameless-desperate.—*Cymbeline,* v, 5, 58. The only use of the phrase.
As dissolute as desperate.—*Richard II,* v, 3, 20.
This is desperate, sir.—*Winter's Tale,* iv, 4, 495.

8
Not a soul
But felt a fever of the mad and play'd
Some tricks of desperation.
The Tempest. Act i, sc. 2, l. 208. [Ariel]
All three of them are desperate.
The Tempest. Act iii, sc. 3, l. 104. [Gonzalo]

9
I am desperate of obtaining her.
The Two Gentlemen of Verona. Act iii, sc. 2, l. 5. [Thurio]
My state is desperate for my master's love.
Twelfth Night. Act ii, sc. 3, l. 38. [Viola]
Desperate in his suit.—*Venus and Adonis,* l. 336.

DESPISING, see Contempt

DESTINY

See also Fate, Fortune, Providence

10
But let determined things to destiny
Hold unbewail'd their way.
Antony and Cleopatra. Act iii, sc. 6, l. 84. [Cæsar] The only use of "unbewail'd."
'Tis fond to wail inevitable strokes,
As 'tis to laugh at 'em.
Coriolanus. Act iv, sc. 1, l. 26. [Coriolanus]

11
Let ordinance Come as the gods foresay it.
Cymbeline. Act iv, sc. 2, l. 145. [Arviragus] The only use of "foresay."
God's fair ordinance.—*Richard III,* v, 5, 31.
God's just ordinance.—*Richard III,* iv, 4, 183.

12
Let come what comes.
Hamlet. Act iv, sc. 5, l. 135. [Laertes]
If it be now, 'tis not to come; if it be not to come, it will be now; if it be not now, yet it will come: the readiness is all.
Hamlet. Act v, sc. 2, l. 232. [Hamlet]

13
An 't be my destiny, so; an 't be not, so.
II Henry IV. Act iii, sc. 2, l. 252. [Feeble]
Things must be as they may.
Henry V. Act ii, sc. 1, l. 22. [Nym]

14
What cannot be avoided
'Twere childish weakness to lament or fear.
III Henry VI. Act v, sc. 4, l. 37. [Queen Margaret]
For this, amongst the rest, was I ordain'd.
III Henry VI. Act v, sc. 6, l. 58. [Gloucester]
What can be avoided
Whose end is purposed by the mighty gods?
Julius Cæsar. Act ii, sc. 2, l. 26. [Cæsar]

15
Think you I bear the shears of destiny?
King John. Act iv, sc. 2, l. 91. [King John]
You are born
To set a form upon that indigest
Which he hath left so shapeless and so rude.
King John. Act v, sc. 7, l. 25. [Salisbury] "Indigest" (shapeless mass) is repeated in *Sonnets,* cxiv.

16
My father compounded with my mother under the dragon's tail; and my nativity was under Ursa major; so that it follows, I am rough and lecherous. Tut, I should have been that I am, had maidenliest star in the firmament twinkled on my bastardizing.
King Lear. Act i, sc. 2, l. 140. [Edmund] The only use of "dragon's tail" (the descending node of the moon's orbit with the ecliptic), "Ursa major," "maidenliest," "twinkled" and "bastardizing."
'Tis in his buttons; he will carry 't.
Merry Wives of Windsor. Act iii, sc. 2, l. 70. [Host]

17
I am tied to the stake, and I must stand the course.
King Lear. Act iii, sc. 7, l. 54. [Gloucester]

They have tied me to a stake; I cannot fly,
But, bear-like, I must fight the course.
Macbeth. Act v, sc. 7, l. 1. [Macbeth] The only use of "bear-like."

1
It stands as an edict in destiny.
A Midsummer-Night's Dream. Act i, sc. 1, l. 151. [Hermia] See under LOVE for full quotation.

'Tis destiny unshunnable, like death.
Othello. Act iii, sc. 3, l. 275. [Othello] The only use of "unshunnable."

Shunless destiny.—*Coriolanus,* ii, 2, 116. The only use of "shunless."

Cancell'd destiny.—*Rape of Lucrece,* l. 1729.

2
King Richard: All unavoided is the doom of destiny.
Queen Elizabeth: True, when avoided grace makes destiny.
Richard III. Act iv, sc. 4, l. 217.

3
Make the rope of his destiny our cable, for our own doth little advantage.
The Tempest. Act i, sc. 1, l. 34. [Gonzalo]

Destiny,
That hath to instrument this lower world.
The Tempest. Act iii, sc. 3, l. 53. [Ariel]

4
The bitter disposition of the time
Will have it so.
Troilus and Cressida. Act iv, sc. 1, l. 48. [Paris]

I would conspire against destiny.
Troilus and Cressida. Act v, sc. 1, l. 70. [Thersites]

5
And therefore hath she bribed the Destinies
To cross the curious workmanship of nature.
Venus and Adonis, l. 733.

The Destinies will curse thee for this stroke.
Venus and Adonis, l. 945.

As the Destinies decree.
As You Like It. Act i, sc. 2, l. 111. [Touchstone]

Till the Destinies do cut his thread of life.
Pericles. Act i, sc. 2, l. 108. [Helicanus]

Some of those branches by the Destinies cut.
Richard II. Act i, sc. 2, l. 15. [Duchess of Gloucester]

Marked by the Destinies.—*III Henry VI,* i, 2, 137.

Fates and Destinies.—*The Merchant of Venice,* ii, 2, 65. The only uses of "Destinies."

DESTRUCTION

See also Ruin

6
Winking leap'd into destruction.
II Henry IV. Act i, sc. 3, l. 33. [Bardolph]

You take a precipice for no leap of danger,
And woo your own destruction.
Henry VIII. Act v, sc. 1, l. 139. [King Henry] The only use of "precipice."

Into destruction cast him.—*Coriolanus,* iii, 1, 214.

7
Pale destruction meets thee in the face.
I Henry VI. Act iv, sc. 2, l. 27. [General]

Girdled with a waist of iron,
And hemm'd about with grim destruction.
I Henry VI. Act iv, sc. 3, l. 20. [Lucy]

8
We from the west will send destruction
Into this city's bosom.
King John. Act ii, sc. 1, l. 409. [King John] "Send destruction" is repeated in *Julius Cæsar,* i, 3, 13.

To push destruction and perpetual shame
Out of the weak door of our fainting land.
King John. Act v, sc. 5, l. 77. [Bastard]

9
'Tis safer to be that which we destroy
Than by destruction dwell in doubtful joy.
Macbeth. Act iii, sc. 2, l. 6. [Lady Macbeth]

10
Destruction straight shall dog them at the heels.
Richard II. Act v, sc. 3, l. 139. [Bolingbroke]

Fell destruction.—*Pericles,* v, 3, Gower, 89.

11
Welcome, destruction, death, and massacre!
Richard III. Act ii, sc. 4, l. 53. [Queen Elizabeth]

What is amiss in them, you gods, make suitable for destruction.
Timon of Athens. Act iii, sc. 6, l. 92. [Timon] The only use of "suitable."

Destruction fang mankind!
Timon of Athens. Act iv, sc. 3, l. 23. [Timon]

12
Linger not our sure destructions on!
Troilus and Cressida. Act v, sc. 10, l. 9. [Troilus]

It shall be to him . . . a sure destruction.
Coriolanus. Act ii, sc. 1, l. 258. [Sicinius]

DETERMINATION, see Resolution

DETESTATION, see Hate

DETRACTION, see Criticism

DEVICE

See also Plot, Stratagem, Trick

13
Entrap thee by some treacherous device.
As You Like It. Act i, sc. 1, l. 158. [Oliver]

Upon my life, by some device or other
The villain is o'er-raught of all my money.
The Comedy of Errors. Act i, sc. 2, l. 95. [Antipholus of Syracuse] "O'er-raught" is repeated in *Hamlet,* iii, 1, 17.

By this device.—*The Taming of the Shrew,* i, 2, 135.

Rare device.—*Cymbeline,* i, 6, 189.

14
I think, by some odd gimmors or device
Their arms are set like clocks, still to strike on.
I Henry VI. Act i, sc. 2, l. 41. [Reignier] The only use of "gimmors" (the connecting parts for transmitting motion in clockwork).

15 It was thy device
By this alliance to make void my suit.
III Henry VI. Act iii, sc. 3, l. 141. [Queen Margaret]

16 Is there . . .
No new device to beat this from his brains?
Henry VIII, iii, 2, 216. See under CURE.

The net has fall'n upon me! I shall perish
Under device and practice.
Henry VIII. Act i, sc. 1, l. 203. [Buckingham]
Deliver us from devices.—*Measure for Measure,* iv, 4, 15.

1 I 'll tell thee all my whole device
When I am in my coach.
The Merchant of Venice. Act iii, sc. 4, l. 81. [Portia]

2
There is also another device in my prain, which peradventure brings goot discretions with it.
The Merry Wives of Windsor. Act i, sc. 1, l. 43. [Evans]
I have a device to make all well.
A Midsummer-Night's Dream. Act iii, sc. 1, l. 17. [Bottom]
That is an old device.
A Midsummer-Night's Dream. Act v, sc. 1, l. 50. [Theseus]

3 Why who 's so gross,
That seeth not this palpable device?
Richard III. Act iii, sc. 6, l. 10. [Scrivener]

4
Whether by device or no, the heavens can tell.
Titus Andronicus. Act i, sc. 1, l. 395. [Titus]
Let us, that have our tongues,
Plot some device of further misery,
To make us wonder'd at in time to come.
Titus Andronicus. Act iii, sc. 1, l. 133. [Titus]
I know from whence this same device proceeds.
Titus Andronicus. Act iv, sc. 4, l. 52. [Saturninus]
What says Andronicus to this device?
Titus Andronicus. Act v, sc. 2, l. 120. [Tamora]

5
Sir Toby: I smell a device.
Sir Andrew: I have 't in my nose too.
Twelfth Night. Act ii, sc. 3, l. 176.
I could marry this wench for this device.
Twelfth Night, ii, 5, 200. See under MARRIAGE.
Sir Toby: His very genius hath taken the infection of the device, man.
Maria: Nay, pursue him now, lest the device take air and taint.
Twelfth Night. Act iii, sc. 4, l. 142.
Most freely I confess, myself and Toby
Set this device.
Twelfth Night. Act v, sc. 1, l. 368. [Fabian]

6
O excellent device! was there ever heard a better?
The Two Gentlemen of Verona. Act ii, sc. 1, l. 145. [Speed]
O excellent device!—*Richard III*, i, 4, 162.
An excellent device!
Love's Labour 's Lost. Act v, sc. 1, l. 144. [Moth]
For device in the sense of blazon, see under KNIGHTHOOD.

DEVIL

See also Fiend; God and Devil

7
He must needs go that the devil drives.
All 's Well that Ends Well. Act i, sc. 3, l. 31. [Clown]

8
But, sure, he is the prince of the world.
All's Well that Ends Well. Act iv, sc. 5, l. 51. [Clown]
Clown: Faith, sir, a' has an English name; but his fisnomy is more hotter in France than there.
Lafeu: What prince is that?
Clown: The black prince, sir; alias, the prince of darkness; alias, the devil.
All's Well that Ends Well. Act iv, sc. 5, l. 41. The only use of "fisnomy," an old form of physiognomy.
The prince of darkness is a gentleman:
Modo he 's call'd, and Mahu.
King Lear. Act iii, sc. 4, l. 148. [Edgar]

9
The devil himself will not eat a woman.
Antony and Cleopatra, v, 2, 274. [Clown]
The devil himself.—*Hamlet,* iii, 1, 49; *The Merry Wives of Windsor,* ii, 2, 314; *Macbeth,* v, 7, 8.

10
A devil in an everlasting garment hath him.
The Comedy of Errors. Act iv, sc. 2, l. 33. [Dromio of Syracuse]

11
Antipholus of Syracuse: Satan, avoid! I charge thee, tempt me not.
Dromio of Syracuse: Master, is this Mistress Satan?
Antipholus of Syracuse: It is the devil.
Dromio of Syracuse: Nay, she is worse, she is the devil's dam.
The Comedy of Errors. Act iv, sc. 3, l. 48.
I charge thee, Satan, housed within this man,
To yield possession to my holy prayers
And to thy state of darkness hie thee straight;
I conjure thee by all the saints in heaven!
The Comedy of Errors. Act iv, sc. 4, l. 57. [Doctor Pinch]
That old white-bearded Satan.
I Henry IV. Act ii, sc. 4, l. 509. [Prince of Wales] "White-bearded" is repeated in *Much Ado about Nothing*, ii, 3, 124.
Fie, thou dishonest Satan! I call thee by the most modest terms; for I am one of those gentle ones that will use the devil himself with courtesy.
Twelfth Night. Act iv, sc. 2, l. 35. [Clown]
Play at cherry-pit with Satan.—*Twelfth Night*, iii, 4, 130. See under GRAVITY.
Slanderous as Satan.—*The Merry Wives of Windsor*, v, 5, 163. See under SLANDER.
Talked of Satan.—*All 's Well that Ends Well*, v, 3, 261. The only references to Satan.

12
Courtesan: Will you go with me? We 'll mend our dinner here?
Dromio of Syracuse: Master, if you do, expect spoon-meat; or bespeak a long spoon.
Antipholus of Syracuse: Why, Dromio?
Dromio of Syracuse: Marry, he must have a long spoon that must eat with the devil.
The Comedy of Errors. Act iv, sc. 3, l. 59. Shakespeare is quoting a proverb which appeared first in Chaucer's *The Squieres Tale* (l. 594), about 1386: "Therfor bihoveth him a ful long spoon That shal ete with a feend." Chaucer puts it in quotation marks. The only use of "spoon-meat" (liquid food).

This is a devil, and no monster: I will leave him;
I have no long spoon.
The Tempest. Act ii, sc. 2, l. 102. [Stephano]

1
Some devils ask but the parings of one's nail,
A rush, a hair, a drop of blood, a pin,
A nut, a cherry-stone;
But she, more covetous, would have a chain.
The Comedy of Errors. Act iv, sc. 3, l. 72. [Dromio of Syracuse] The only use of "cherry-stone."

2
Soldier: He 's the devil
Aufidius: Bolder, though not so subtle.
Coriolanus. Act i, sc. 10, l. 16.

He is a devil.—*Twelfth Night,* iii, 4, 259.

He 's a very devil.—*Twelfth Night,* iii, 4, 301.

3 The spirit that I have seen
May be the devil: and the devil hath power
To assume a pleasing shape.
Hamlet. Act ii, sc. 2, l. 627. [Hamlet]

Let the devil wear black, for I'll have a suit of sables.
Hamlet. Act iii, sc. 2, l. 137. [Hamlet]

4 What devil was 't
That thus hath cozen'd you at hoodman-blind?
Hamlet. Act iii, sc. 4, l. 76. [Hamlet] The only use of "hoodman-blind" (blindman's buff).

5
Prince of Wales: Sir John stands to his word, the devil shall have his bargain; for he was never yet a breaker of proverbs: he will give the devil his due.
Poins: Then art thou damned for keeping thy word with the devil.
Prince of Wales: Else he had been damned for cozening the devil.
I Henry IV. Act i, sc. 2, l. 130. "Breaker" is used a second time in *I Henry VI,* i, 3, 80: "Breaker of the law."

Give the devil his due.
Henry V. Act iii, sc. 7, l. 126. [Orleans] Quoted as a proverb.

6
Heigh, heigh! the devil rides upon a fiddle-stick: what 's the matter?
I Henry IV. Act ii, sc. 4, l. 534. [Prince of Wales] The prince was probably quoting this as a proverb, but no instance has been found of its previous use in English literature. It means much ado about nothing. Beaumont and Fletcher used it later in *The Humorous Lieutenant,* iv, 4. "Fiddlestick" is used a second time in *Romeo and Juliet,* iii, 1, 51.

7
Glendower: Why, I can teach you, cousin, to command The devil.
Hotspur: And I can teach thee, coz, to shame the devil
By telling truth: tell truth and shame the devil.
If thou have power to raise him, bring him hither,
And I 'll be sworn I have power to shame him hence.
O, while you live, tell truth and shame the devil.
I Henry IV. Act iii, sc. 1, l. 56. An old proverb. In 1552, Hugh Latimer, in one of his sermons (*Sermons,* p. 506) had said: "There is a common saying amongst us, 'Say the truth and shame the devil.' "

Now shall the devil be shamed.
Merry Wives of Windsor, iv, 2, 124. [Ford]

8 I tell you what;
He held me last night at least nine hours
In reckoning up the several devils' names
That were his lackeys.
I Henry IV. Act iii, sc. 1, l. 155. [Hotspur]

Now I perceive the devil understands Welsh;
And 'tis no marvel he is so humorous.
By 'r lady, he is a good musician.
I Henry IV. Act iii, sc. 1, l. 233. [Hotspur]

9
That same demon that hath gull'd thee thus.
Henry V. Act ii, sc. 2, l. 121. [King Henry] "Demon" is repeated in *Antony and Cleopatra,* ii, 3, 19. The only use of "gull'd." "Gull" appears ten times and "gull-catcher" once, in *Twelfth Night,* ii, 5, 205.

10
A pox of the devil.
Henry V. Act iii, sc. 7, l. 130. [Constable] Quoted as a proverb.

Make a moral of the devil himself.
Henry V. Act iv, sc. 1, l. 12. [King Henry]

The devil was in arms.
I Henry VI. Act i, sc. 1, l. 125. [Messenger]

11
This devil here shall be my substitute.
II Henry VI. Act iii, sc. 1, l. 371. [York]

There 's two of you; the devil make a third!
II Henry VI. Act iii, sc. 2, l. 303. [Queen]

12 The devil is a niggard,
Or has given all before, and he begins
A new hell in himself.
Henry VIII. Act i, sc. 1, l. 70. [Abergavenny]

The devil speed him!—*Henry VIII,* i, 1, 52.

The devil fiddle 'em.—*Henry VIII,* i, 3, 42.

O, all the devils!—*Cymbeline,* ii, 5, 13.

13
Duke of Austria: What the devil art thou?
Bastard: One that will play the devil, sir, with you.
King John. Act ii, sc. 1, l. 134. "Play the devil" is repeated in *Richard III,* i, 3, 338.

What the devil?—*All 's Well that Ends Well,* iv, 1, 37; *II Henry IV,* ii, 4, 1; *Henry V,* iv, 5, 22; and other plays.

Where the devil?—*The Tempest,* ii, 2, 69; *Romeo and Juliet,* ii, 4, 1.

Why the devil?—*Henry VIII,* i, 1, 72; *Romeo and Juliet,* iii, 1, 107.

Cheat the devil.—*Love's Labour 's Lost,* iv, 3, 288.

14 The devil tempts thee here
In likeness of a new untrimmed bride.
King John. Act iii, sc. 1, l. 208. [Constance] The only use of "untrimmed."

Devils soonest tempt, resembling spirits of light.
Love's Labour 's Lost, iv, 3, 257. [Biron]

1 'Tis the eye of childhood
That fears a painted devil.
Macbeth. Act ii, sc. 2, l. 54. [Lady Macbeth]
Not in the legions
Of horrid hell can come a devil more damn'd
In evils.
Macbeth. Act iv, sc. 3, l. 55. [Macduff]
The devil damn thee black.—*Macbeth*, v, 3, 11.

2
Let 's write good angel on the devil's horn;
'Tis not the devil's crest.
Measure for Measure. Act ii, sc. 4, l. 16. [Angelo]
Let the devil
Be sometime honour'd for his burning throne!
Measure for Measure. Act v, sc. 1, l. 294. [Duke]

3
The devil can cite Scripture for his purpose.
The Merchant of Venice. Act i, sc. 3, l. 99. [Antonio]
But then I sigh; and, with a piece of scripture,
Tell them that God bids us do good for evil:
And thus I clothe my naked villany
With old odd ends stolen out of holy writ.
Richard III. Act i, sc. 3, l. 334. [Gloucester]

4
Why, then the devil give him good of it!
The Merchant of Venice. Act iv, sc. 1, l. 345. [Shylock]

5
Lucifer take all!
The Merry Wives of Windsor. Act i, sc. 3, l. 84. [Pistol]
Prince Lucifer.—*King John*, iv, 3, 122.
Falls like Lucifer.—*Henry VIII*, iii, 2, 371.
Made Lucifer cuckold.—*I Henry IV*, ii, 4, 371.
Lucifer and Belzebub.—*Henry V*, iv, 7, 145.
Lucifer's privy-kitchen.—*II Henry IV*, ii, 4, 360. The only references to Lucifer.
He holds Belzebub at the staves's end as well as a man in his case may do.
Twelfth Night. Act v, sc. 1, l. 291. [Clown] The only uses of "Belzebub."
The devil guide his cudgel!—*The Merry Wives of Windsor*, iv, 2, 91. See CUDGELLING.

6
If the devil have him not in fee-simple, with fine and recovery.
The Merry Wives of Windsor. Act iv, sc. 2, l. 224. [Mrs. Page]
Doth all the winter-time, at still midnight,
Walk round about an oak, with great ragg'd horns;
And there he blasts the tree and takes the cattle
And make milch-kine yield blood and shakes a chain
In a most hideous and dreadful manner.
The Merry Wives of Windsor. Act iv, sc. 4, l. 30. [Mrs. Page] The only use of "winter-time." "Milch-kine" is repeated in *The Taming of the Shrew*, ii, 1, 359.
Set spurs and away, like three German devils, three Doctor Faustuses.
The Merry Wives of Windsor. Act iv, sc. 5, l. 70. [Bardolph] The only mention of Doctor Faustus.
No man means evil but the devil, and we shall know him by his horns.
Merry Wives of Windsor, v, 2, 15. [Page]
The devil will not have me damned, lest the oil that 's in me should set hell on fire.
The Merry Wives of Windsor. Act v, sc. 5, l. 38. [Falstaff]

7
Is there no young squarer now that will make a voyage with him to the devil?
Much Ado about Nothing. Act i, sc. 1, l. 82. [Beatrice] The only use of "squarer" (quarreler).

8
Awake the snorting citizens with the bell,
Or else the devil will make a grandsire of you.
Othello. Act i, sc. 1, l. 90. [Iago] "Snorting" is repeated in *I Henry IV*, ii, 4, 578: "Snorting like a horse."

9
When devils will the blackest sins put on,
They do suggest at first with heavenly shows,
As I do now.
Othello. Act ii, sc. 3, l. 357. [Iago]

10
For here 's a young and sweating devil here,
That commonly rebels.
Othello, iii, 4, 42. See under HAND.
Thou art a devil.—*Othello*, v, 2, 133.
If that thou be'st a devil, I cannot kill thee.
Othello. Act v, sc. 2, l. 286. [Othello]

11
Will you, I pray, demand that demi-devil
Why he hath thus ensnared my soul and body?
Othello. Act v, sc. 2, l. 301. [Othello] The only use of "ensnared."
This demi-devil—
For he 's a bastard one—had plotted with them
To take my life.
The Tempest. Act v, sc. 1, l. 272. [Prospero] The only uses of "demi-devil."

12
She would make a puritan of the devil, if he should cheapen a kiss of her.
Pericles. Act iv, sc. 6, l. 9. [Bawd]
Sometimes he is a kind of puritan.
Twelfth Night. Act ii, sc. 3, l. 151. [Maria]
The devil a puritan that he is.—*Twelfth Night*, ii, 3, 159.
But one puritan amongst them.—*The Winter's Tale*, iv, 3, 46.
Young Charbon the puritan.—*All's Well that Ends Well*, i, 3, 56.
No puritan.—*All's Well that Ends Well*, i, 3, 98. The only uses of "puritan."

13 O unlook'd-for evil,
When virtue is profaned in such a devil!
The Rape of Lucrece, l. 846.
Such devils steal effects from lightless hell.
The Rape of Lucrece, l. 1555. "Lightless" is used also in l. 4: "Lightless fire." It occurs nowhere else.

14 You are mortal,
And mortal eyes cannot endure the devil.
Richard III. Act i, sc. 2, l. 44. [Lady Anne]
Foul devil, for God's sake, hence, and trouble us not.
Richard III. Act i, sc. 2, l. 50. [Lady Anne]
This ravenous tiger, this accursed devil.
Titus Andronicus. Act v, sc. 3, l. 5. [Lucius]

Blackest devil.—*Hamlet,* iv, 5, 131.
A constant and confirmed devil.—*The Rape of Lucrece,* l. 1513.
Crafty devil.—*Cymbeline,* ii, 1, 57.
Cruel devil.—*Merchant of Venice,* iv, 1, 217.
Fair devil.—*Othello,* iii, 3, 279.
Good man devil.—*Twelfth Night,* iv, 2, 141.
Hideous shapeless devil.—*The Rape of Lucrece,* l. 973.
Irregulous devil.—*Cymbeline,* iv, 2, 315. The only use of "irregulous" (lawless).
Mad devil.—*The Merry Wives of Windsor,* v, 1, 19.
Misbegotten devil.—*King John,* v, 4, 4.
Plain devil.—*Richard III,* i, 2, 237.
Roaring devil.—*Henry V,* iv, 4, 75.
Sly devil.—*King John,* ii, 1, 567.
Ugly devils.—*Richard III,* i, 3, 227.
Welsh devil.—*The Merry Wives of Windsor,* v, 3, 13.
Whoreson devils.—*Antony and Cleopatra,* v, 2, 277.

1
O wonderful, when devils tell the truth!
Richard III. Act i, sc. 2, l. 73. [Lady Anne]
What, can the devil speak true?
Macbeth. Act i, sc. 3, l. 107. [Banquo]

2
Second Murderer: Take the devil in thy mind, and believe him not: he would insinuate with thee but to make thee sigh.
First Murderer: Tut, I am strong-framed, he cannot prevail with me, I warrant thee.
Richard III. Act i, sc. 4, l. 151. The only use of "strong-framed."

3
What devil art thou, that dost torment me thus?
Romeo and Juliet. Act iii, sc. 2, l. 43. [Juliet]
From all such devils, good Lord deliver us!
The Taming of the Shrew. Act i, sc. 1, l. 66. [Hortensio]

4
Have we devils here?
The Tempest. Act ii, sc. 2, l. 59. [Stephano]
All the devils are here.—*The Tempest,* i, 2, 215.
All the devils of hell.—*Twelfth Night,* iii, 4, 94.

5
If thou beest a man, show thyself in thy likeness: if thou beest a devil, take 't as thou list.
The Tempest. Act iii, sc. 2, l. 137. [Stephano]
Some of you there present
Are worse than devils.
The Tempest. Act iii, sc. 3, l. 35. [Prospero]
A devil, a born devil, on whose nature
Nurture can never stick.
The Tempest. Act iv, sc. 1, l. 188. [Prospero] "Nurture" is repeated in *As You Like It,* ii, 7, 97.
The devil speaks in him.
The Tempest. Act v, sc. 1, l. 129. [Sebastian]

6
This is the incarnate devil.
Titus Andronicus. Act v, sc. 1, l. 40. [Lucius]
We took him for a coward, but he 's the very devil incardinate.
Twelfth Night. Act v, sc. 1, l. 184. [Sir Andrew] The only use of "incardinate."
Devils incarnate.
Henry V. Act ii, sc. 3, l. 34. [Boy]
The very devil incarnal.—*The Merchant of Venice,* ii, 2, 28. The only use of "incarnal."

7
If there be devils, would I were a devil,
To live and burn in everlasting fire,
So I might have your company in hell,
But to torment you with my bitter tongue!
Titus Andronicus. Act v, sc. 1, l. 147. [Aaron]
Could not all hell afford you such a devil?
Titus Andronicus. Act v, sc. 2, l. 86. [Titus]
It were convenient you had such a devil.
Titus Andronicus. Act v, sc. 2, l. 90. [Titus]
An the devil come to him, it 's all one.
Troilus and Cressida. Act i, sc. 2, l. 227. [Pandarus]

8
The devil take Antenor!
Troilus and Cressida. Act iv, sc. 2, l. 77. [Pandarus]
A burning devil take them!
Troilus and Cressida. Act v, sc. 2, l. 197. [Thersites]
The devil take thee.—*Troilus and Cressida,* v, 7, 24.
The devil take thy soul!—*Hamlet,* v, 1, 281.
The devil take your fingers!—*The Tempest,* iii, 2, 89. "The devil take" occurs in *Richard II,* v, 5, 103, and in *I Henry IV,* i, 3, 255.

9
In each grace of these
There lurks a still and dumb-discoursive devil
That tempts most cunningly.
Troilus and Cressida. Act iv, sc. 4, l. 91. [Troilus] The only use of "dumb-discoursive."

10
Sir Toby: What, man! defy the devil: consider, he 's an enemy to mankind.
Malvolio: Do you know what you say?
Maria: La you, an you speak ill of the devil, how he takes it at heart!
Twelfth Night. Act iii, sc. 4, l. 107.
A devil
Would have shed water out of fire ere done 't.
The Winter's Tale. Act iii, sc. 2, l. 193. [Paulina]

II—The Devil's Dam

11
She is the devil's dam.
The Comedy of Errors, iv, 3, 53. See preceding section for full quotation.

12
Devil or devil's dam, I 'll conjure thee.
I Henry VI. Act i, sc. 5, l. 5. [Talbot]
Let the devil and his dam haunt you!
Othello, iv, 1, 153. See under Ghost.

13
The tevil and his tam!
The Merry Wives of Windsor. Act i, sc. 1, l. 151. [Evans]
The devil take one party and his dam the other!
The Merry Wives of Windsor. Act iv, sc. 5, l. 108. [Falstaff]

14
You may go to the devil's dam.
The Taming of the Shrew. Act i, sc. 1, l. 106. [Gremio]
Gremio: Why, he 's a devil, a devil, a very fiend.

Tranio: Why, she 's a devil, a devil, the devil's dam.
Taming of the Shrew. Act iii, sc. 2, l. 157.

1
Got by the devil himself
Upon thy wicked dam!
The Tempest. Act i, sc. 2, l. 319. [Prospero]

2
Nurse: She is brought a-bed.
Aaron: Well, God give her good rest! What hath he sent her?
Nurse: A devil.
Aaron: Why, then she is the devil's dam; a joyful issue.
Titus Andronicus. Act iv, sc. 2, l. 62.

A pair of cursed hell-hounds and their dam!
Titus Andronicus. Act v, sc. 2, l. 144. [Titus] The only use of "hell-hounds." "Hell-hound" occurs in *Richard III,* iv, 4, 48, and in *Macbeth,* v, 8, 3.

DEVOTION

See also Love, Loyalty

3 I myself will lead a private life
And in devotion spend my latter days,
To sin's rebuke and my Creator's praise.
III Henry VI. Act iv, sc. 6, l. 42. [King Henry] Shakespeare used "Creator" in his second play, and never again.

Of devotion.—*II Henry VI,* ii, 1, 88.
Tell our devotion.—*III Henry VI,* ii, 1, 164.

4
For you
I would be trebled twenty times myself;
A thousand times more fair, ten thousand times
More rich.
The Merchant of Venice. Act iii, sc. 2, l. 153. [Portia] The only use of "trebled."

I know a lady in Venice would have walked barefoot to Palestine for a touch of his nether lip.
Othello. Act iv, sc. 3, l. 38. [Emilia]

In the devotion of a subject's love.
Richard II. Act i, sc. 1, l. 31. [Bolingbroke]

5
I have no great devotion to the deed.
Othello. Act v, sc. 1, l. 8. [Roderigo]

Greater devotion.—*Coriolanus,* ii, 2, 21.

6
And pardon us the interruption
Of thy devotion and right Christian zeal.
Richard III. Act iii, sc. 7, l. 102. [Buckingham]

Pure heart's love,
Immaculate devotion, holy thoughts.
Richard III. Act iv, sc. 4, l. 403. [King Richard]

God shield I should disturb devotion!
Romeo and Juliet. Act iv, sc. 1, l. 41. [Paris]

Mannerly devotion.—*Romeo and Juliet,* i, 5, 100.
Like devotion.—*Richard III,* iv, 1, 9.

7
His life I gave him and did thereto add
My love, without retention or restraint,
All his in dedication; for his sake
Did I expose myself, pure for his love,
Into the danger of this adverse town.
Twelfth Night. Act v, sc. 1, l. 83. [Antonio]

You uncivil lady,
To whose ingrate and unauspicious altars
My soul the faithfull'st offerings hath breathed out
That e'er devotion tender'd!
Twelfth Night. Act v, sc. 1, l. 115. [Duke] The only use of "unauspicious" and "faithfull'st."

DEW

8
Being three parts melted away with rotten dews.
Coriolanus. Act ii, sc. 3, l. 35. [Citizen]

Dissolve to dew.—*Richard II,* v, 1, 9.
Wash'd with dew.—*The Taming of the Shrew,* ii, 1, 174.

9
His dews fall every where.
Henry VIII. Act i, sc. 3, l. 57. [Chamberlain]

God's dew.—*Henry VIII,* ii, 4, 80.
Dews of heaven.—*Henry VIII,* iv, 2, 133.
Dews of blood.—*Hamlet,* i, 1, 117.
Dews of flattery.—*Coriolanus,* v, 6, 23.
Golden dew of sleep.—*Richard III,* iv, 1, 84.
Honey-heavy dew of slumber.—*Julius Cæsar,* ii, 1, 230. The only use of "honey-heavy."
Liquid dew of youth.—*Hamlet,* i, 3, 41.

10
Decking with liquid pearl the bladed grass.
A Midsummer-Night's Dream. Act i, sc. 1, l. 211. [Lysander] Only use of "decking."

I must go seek some dewdrops here
And hang a pearl in every cowslip's ear.
A Midsummer-Night's Dream. Act ii, sc. 1, l. 14. [Fairy] Only use of "dew-drops." "Dew-drop" occurs in *Troilus and Cressida,* iii, 3, 224.

Dew, which sometime on the buds
Was wont to swell like round and orient pearls,
Stood now within the pretty flowerets' eyes
Like tears that did their own disgrace bewail.
A Midsummer-Night's Dream. Act iv, sc. 1, l. 56. [Oberon] "Flowerets" is repeated in *I Henry IV,* i, 1, 8.

With this field-dew consecrate,
Every fairy take his gait.
A Midsummer-Night's Dream. Act v, sc. 1, l. 422. [Oberon] The only use of "field-dew."

Bedabbled with the dew.—*A Midsummer-Night's Dream,* iii, 2, 443. The only use of "bedabbled."
Morning dew.—*A Midsummer-Night's Dream,* iv, 1, 126.
Fresh morning's dew.—*Romeo and Juliet,* i, 1, 138.
Relenting dew.—*The Rape of Lucrece,* l. 1829.
Vain dew.—*The Winter's Tale,* ii, 1, 109.
O'ertrip the dew.—*Merchant of Venice,* v, 1, 7.

11
When the sun sets, the air doth drizzle dew.
Romeo and Juliet. Act iii, sc. 5, l. 127. [Capulet] The only use of "drizzle." "Drizzles" occurs in *Much Ado about Nothing,* iii, 3, 111: "Drizzles rain."

Cold dew o' the night.—*Cymbeline,* iv, 2, 284.
Dew of night.—*The Rape of Lucrece,* l. 396.
Night's dank dew.—*Romeo and Juliet,* ii, 3, 6.

1
Thou call'dst me up at midnight to fetch dew
From the still-vex'd Bermoothes.
The Tempest. Act i, sc. 2, l. 228. [Ariel] The only use of "still-vex'd" and "Bermoothes."

DIALOGUE

2
Shall we have this dialogue between the fool and the soldier?
All's Well that Ends Well. Act iv, sc. 3, l. 112. [Bertram]
Will you hear the dialogue that the two learned men have compiled in praise of the owl and the cuckoo?
Love's Labour's Lost. Act v, sc. 2, l. 894. [Armado]
Dialogue of compliment.—*King John,* i, 1, 201.
Wooden dialogue.—*Troilus and Cressida,* i, 3, 155.
3
Fear you not my part of the dialogue.
Much Ado about Nothing. Act iii, sc. 1, l. 31. [Ursula]
4
Dost dialogue with thy shadow?
Timon of Athens. Act ii, sc. 2, l. 52. [Apemantus]
5
'Tis not that time of the moon with me to make one in so skipping a dialogue.
Twelfth Night. Act i, sc. 5, l. 212. [Olivia]

DIAMOND

See also Gem, Jewel

6
This diamond was my mother's: take it, heart;
But keep it till you woo another wife,
When Imogen is dead.
Cymbeline. Act i, sc. 1, l. 112. [Imogen]
I shall but lend my diamond till your return.
Cymbeline. Act i, sc. 4, l. 154. [Posthumus]
I beg but leave to air this jewel; see! . . .
It must be married To that your diamond.
Cymbeline. Act ii, sc. 4, l. 96. [Iachimo]
That diamond upon your finger, say
How came it yours?
Cymbeline. Act v, sc. 5, l. 137. [Cymbeline]
Deck'd with diamonds.—*III Henry VI,* iii, 1, 63.
Precious diamond.—*Cymbeline,* i, 4, 81.
7
The diamond,—why, 'twas beautiful and hard.
A Lover's Complaint, l. 211. See under JEWEL.
This diamond he greets your wife withal.
Macbeth. Act ii, sc. 1, l. 15. [Banquo]
A diamond gone, cost me two thousand ducats!
The Merchant of Venice. Act iii, sc. 1, l. 87. [Shylock]
8
You shall like diamonds sit about his crown.
Pericles. Act ii, sc. 4, l. 53. [Helicanus]
The diamonds of a most praised water
Do appear, to make the world twice rich.
Pericles. Act iii, sc. 2, l. 102. [Cerimon]
9
One day he gives us diamonds, next day stones.
Timon of Athens. Act iii, sc. 6, l. 131. [Lord]

DIFFERENCE

See also Distinction

10
What 's amiss,
May it be gently heard: when we debate
Our trivial difference loud, we do commit
Murder in healing wounds.
Antony and Cleopatra. Act ii, sc. 2, l. 19. [Lepidus]
Petty difference.—*Antony and Cleopatra,* ii, 1, 49.
If we contend, Out of our question wipe him.
Antony and Cleopatra. Act ii, sc. 2, l. 80. [Antony] See CONTENTION.
11
Much different from the man he was.
The Comedy of Errors, v, 1, 46. See under SADNESS.
O, the difference of man and man!
King Lear, iv, 2, 26. See under MAN.
The difference of a year or two.
Titus Andronicus, ii, 1, 31. See under FORTUNE.
Seasons' difference.—*As You Like It,* ii, 1, 6.
12
There is differency between a grub and a butterfly; yet your butterfly was a grub. This Marcius is grown from man to dragon: he has wings; he is more than a creeping thing.
Coriolanus. Act v, sc. 4, l. 11. [Menenius] The only use of "differency."
'Twixt you there 's difference.—*Coriolanus,* v, 6, 18.
What was the difference?—*Cymbeline,* i, 4, 57.
Weighty difference.—*Henry VIII,* iii, 1, 58.
Wide difference.—*Cymbeline,* v, 5, 194.
Differences so mighty.—*All's Well that Ends Well,* ii, 3, 128.
Some difference.—*Julius Cæsar,* i, 2, 40.
Such difference.—*All's Well that Ends Well,* i, 3, 116; *Hamlet,* iii, 4, 76.
All the difference.—*The Two Gentlemen of Verona,* iv, 4, 195.
At difference.—*Coriolanus,* v, 3, 201.
Difference and decay.—*King Lear,* v, 3, 288.
13
O, you must wear your rue with a difference.
Hamlet. Act iv, sc. 5, l. 183. [Ophelia] For full quotation, see under FLOWER.
With difference.—*Othello,* i, 3, 7.
14
Making such difference 'twixt wake and sleep
As is the difference betwixt day and night.
I Henry IV. Act iii, sc. 1, l. 219. [Glendower]
Make difference.—*The Merry Wives of Windsor,* ii, 1, 57.
Know the difference.—*King Lear,* i, 4, 151.
15
Proclaim There 's difference in no persons.
Henry VIII. Act i, sc. 1, l. 138. [Buckingham]
Private difference.—*Henry VIII,* i, 1, 101.

1 Undetermined differences of kings.
King John. Act ii, sc. 1, l. 355. [Bastard] The only use of "undetermined."
The fearful difference of incensed kings.
King John. Act iii, sc. 1, l. 238. [King Philip]

The difference
Is purchase of a heavy curse from Rome,
Or the light loss of England for a friend.
King John. Act iii, sc. 1, l. 204. [Lewis]

2 What is your difference? speak.
King Lear. Act ii, sc. 2, l. 56. [Cornwall]

Our drops this difference bore,
His poison'd me, and mine did him restore.
A Lover's Complaint, l. 300.

3 Between the lists and the velvet.
Measure for Measure. Act i, sc. 2, l. 30. [Lucio] The list is the selvage of the cloth.

4 Thou shalt see the difference of our spirits.
The Merchant of Venice. Act iv, sc. 1, l. 368. [Duke]
The swelling difference of your settled hate.
Richard II. Act i, sc. 1, l. 201. [King Richard]
All different.—*Romeo and Juliet,* ii, 3, 14.
Different in blood.—*A Midsummer-Night's Dream,* i, 1, 135.

5 To me the difference forges dread.
Winter's Tale. Act iv, sc. 4, l. 17. [Perdita]

DIGESTION, see Appetite

DIGNITY

6 The great dignity that his valour hath here acquired for him shall at home be encountered with a shame as ample.
All's Well that Ends Well. Act iv, sc. 3, l. 80. [Second Lord]

7 Forget this new-fall'n dignity.
As You Like It. Act v, sc. 4, l. 182. [Duke Senior] "New-fall'n" is repeated in *I Henry IV,* v, 1, 44: "New-fall'n right."
Thou wert dignified enough.—*Cymbeline,* ii, 3, 132.

8 I . . . will fit you
With dignities becoming your estates.
Cymbeline. Act v, sc. 5, l. 22. [Cymbeline] See also Honours, Titles.
Pistol, I will double-charge thee with dignities.
II Henry IV. Act v, sc. 3, l. 130. [Falstaff] The only use of "double-charge."
Special dignities, which vacant lie
For thy best use and wearing.
Timon of Athens. Act v, sc. 1, l. 145. [First Senator]

Nothing but death
Shall e'er divorce my dignities.
Henry VIII. Act iii, sc. 1, l. 141. [Queen Katharine]
Dignities of church.—*I Henry VI,* i, 3, 50.
Earthly dignities.—*Henry VIII,* iii, 2, 379.
Mature dignities.—*The Winter's Tale,* i, 1, 27.
New dignities.—*Julius Cæsar,* iii, 1, 178.

9 My cloud of dignity
Is held from falling with so weak a wind.
That it will quickly drop.
II Henry IV. Act iv, sc. 5, l. 99. [King Henry]
Hear your own dignity so much profaned.
II Henry IV. Act v, sc. 2, l. 93. [Chief Justice]
Kingly dignity.—*Henry VIII,* ii, 4, 227.
Regal dignity.—*I Henry VI,* v, 4, 132.
Royal dignity.—*II Henry VI,* iii, 2, 209.
Dignity of your office.—*Henry VIII,* i, 2, 16.
Advantageable for our dignity.—*Henry V,* v, 2, 88. The only use of "advantageable."

10 Let none presume
To wear an undeserved dignity.
The Merchant of Venice. Act ii, sc. 9, l. 39. [Arragon]

11 What state, what dignity, what honour,
Canst thou demise to any child of mine?
Richard III. Act iv, sc. 4, l. 246. [Queen Elizabeth] The only use of "demise."
High promotions and great dignity.
Richard III. Act iv, sc. 4, l. 314. [King Richard]
Alike in dignity.—*Romeo and Juliet,* Prol., 1.

12 Why, this hath not a finger's dignity.
Troilus and Cressida. Act i, sc. 3, l. 204. [Ulysses]

13 My dignity would last But till 'twere known!
Winter's Tale. Act iv, sc. 4, l. 485. [Perdita]
His dignity and duty both cast off.
Winter's Tale. Act v, sc. 1, l. 183. [Lord]
The dignity of this act was worth the audience of kings and princes.
Winter's Tale. Act v, sc. 2, l. 86. [Gentleman]

DILEMMA

14 I will presently pen down my dilemmas.
All's Well that Ends Well. Act iii, sc. 6, l. 80. [Parolles]
Doubtful dilemma.—*The Merry Wives of Windsor,* iv, 5, 86. The only uses of "dilemma."

15 Thus must I from the smoke into the smother.
As You Like It. Act i, sc. 2, l. 299. [Orlando]

16 Thou 'ldst shun a bear;
But if thy flight lay toward the raging sea,
Thou 'ldst meet the bear i' the mouth.
King Lear. Act iii, sc. 4, l. 9. [Kent]

17 Then I shall pose you quickly.
Measure for Measure. Act ii, sc. 4, l. 51. [Angelo] The only use of "pose."

18 Thus when I shun Scylla, your father, I fall into Charybdis, your mother.
The Merchant of Venice. Act iii, sc. 5, l. 18. [Launcelot] The only mention of Scylla and Charybdis.

DILIGENCE

See also Industry

19 I will receive it, sir, with all diligence of spirit.
Hamlet. Act v, sc. 2, l. 94. [Hamlet]

1
This speedy and quick appearance argues proof
Of your accustom'd diligence to me.
I Henry VI. Act v, sc. 3, l. 8. [La Pucelle]

2
The best of me is diligence.
King Lear. Act i, sc. 4, l. 37. [Kent]

If your diligence be not speedy, I shall be there afore you.
King Lear. Act i, sc. 5, l. 4. [King Lear]

Go, hence with diligence!
The Tempest. Act i, sc. 2, l. 304. [Prospero]
See also under HASTE.

3
With whispering and most guilty diligence.
Measure for Measure. Act iv, sc. 1, l. 39. [Isabella]

With all due diligence.—*Pericles.* Act iii, Gower, l. 19. The only use of the phrase "due diligence."

True diligence.—*The Taming of the Shrew,* Ind., l. 70.

4
Tush, I will stir about.
Romeo and Juliet. Act iv, sc. 2, l. 39. [Capulet] "Tush" is repeated in *The Taming of the Shrew,* i, 2, 211, and in *Much Ado about Nothing,* iii, 3, 130.

5
Thou see'st how diligent I am.
The Taming of the Shrew. Act iv, sc. 3, l. 39. [Petruchio]

You are too diligent.
Timon of Athens. Act iii, sc. 4, l. 40. [Flaminius]

DIMPLE

6
Pandarus: She . . . puts me her white hand to his cloven chin—
Cressida: Juno have mercy! how came it cloven?
Pandarus: Why, you know, 'tis dimpled.
Troilus and Cressida. Act i, sc. 2, l. 131.

Dimpled chin.—*The Rape of Lucrece,* l. 420. See under CHIN.

Dimpled boys.—*Antony and Cleopatra,* ii, 2, 207.

Dimpled smiles.—*Timon of Athens,* iv, 3, 119. The only uses of "dimpled."

7 In each cheek appears a pretty dimple:
Love made those hollows, if himself were slain,
He might be buried in a tomb so simple;
Foreknowing well, if there he came to lie,
Why, there Love lived and there he could not die.
Venus and Adonis, l. 242.

These lovely caves, these round enchanting pits.
Venus and Adonis, l. 247.

8
The pretty dimples of his chin and cheek.
The Winter's Tale. Act ii, sc. 3, l. 101. [Paulina] "Dimple" is used only twice in the plays and once in the poems.

DIN, see Noise

DINING

See also Eating, Feast

9
Thou shalt not die for lack of a dinner.
As You Like It. Act ii, sc. 6, l. 18. [Orlando]

10
Within this hour it will be dinner-time.
The Comedy of Errors. Act i, sc. 2, l. 11. [Antipholus of Syracuse]

Julia: Is 't near dinner-time?
Lucetta: I would it were,
That you might kill your stomach on your meat.
The Two Gentlemen of Verona. Act i, sc. 2, l. 67. Shakespeare uses "dinner-time" ten times in the plays, twice as above, and eight times as follows:

Is it dinner-time?—*Comedy of Errors,* ii, 2, 56.
'Tis dinner-time.—*The Two Gentlemen of Verona,* ii, 1, 176; *Comedy of Errors,* ii, 1, 62.
At dinner-time.—*Merchant of Venice,* i, 1, 70.
By dinner-time.—*The Taming of the Shrew,* iv, 3, 190.
Ere dinner-time.—*I Henry IV,* iii, 3, 222.
Till dinner-time.—*Merchant of Venice,* i, 1, 105.
To-morrow dinner-time.—*I Henry IV,* ii, 4, 564.

11
She that doth fast till you come home to dinner.
The Comedy of Errors. Act i, sc. 2, l. 89. [Dromio of Ephesus]

And prays that you will hie you home to dinner.
The Comedy of Errors. Act i, sc. 2, l. 90. [Dromio of Ephesus]

Home to dinner.—*The Comedy of Errors,* ii, 1, 60; ii, 2, 10; ii, 2, 156.

What, have you dined at home?—*Romeo and Juliet,* ii, 5, 46.

12
Come, sir, to dinner. Dromio, keep the gate.
Husband, I 'll dine above with you to-day
And shrive you of a thousand idle pranks.
The Comedy of Errors. Act ii, sc. 2, l. 208. [Adriana]

Will you . . . dine with me?—*The Comedy of Errors,* i, 2, 23.

Let us dine and never fret.—*The Comedy of Errors,* ii, 1, 6.

We dine too late.—*Comedy of Errors,* ii, 2, 221.

13
I have not dined to-day.
The Comedy of Errors. Act iii, sc. 1, l. 40. [Antipholus of Ephesus]

Adriana: O husband, God doth know you dined at home. . . .
Antipholus of Ephesus: Dined at home! Thou villain, what sayest thou?
Dromio of Ephesus: Sir, sooth to say, you did not dine at home.
The Comedy of Errors. Act iv, sc. 4, l. 68.

Which of you two did dine with me to-day?
The Comedy of Errors, v, 1, 369. [Adriana]

14
Let us to the Tiger all to dinner.
The Comedy of Errors. Act iii, sc. 1, l. 95. [Balthazar]

There will we dine.—*The Comedy of Errors,* iii, 1, 111.

We 'll mend our dinner here?—*The Comedy of Errors,* iv, 3, 60.

Dine together.—*The Comedy of Errors,* v, 1, 208; v, 1, 223.

1 He had not dined:
The veins unfill'd, our blood is cold, and then
We pout upon the morning, are unapt
To give or to forgive; but when we have stuff'd
These pipes and these conveyances of our blood
With wine and feeding, we have suppler souls
Than in our priest-like fasts.

Coriolanus. Act v, sc. 1, l. 50. [Menenius] The only use of "pout." "Poutest" occurs in *Romeo and Juliet,* iii, 3, 144; "pouted" in *Venus and Adonis,* l. 33. "Suppler" is repeated in *The Tempest,* iii, 3, 107: "Suppler joints"; and "priest-like" in *The Winter's Tale,* i, 2, 237.

Has he dined, canst thou tell? for I would not speak with him till after dinner.

Coriolanus. Act v, sc. 2, l. 36. [Menenius]

What, hast thou dined?—*The Taming of the Shrew,* iv, 3, 59.

I have dined.—*The Two Gentlemen of Verona,* ii, 1, 177.

The duke hath dined.—*A Midsummer-Night's Dream,* iv, 2, 35.

Having fully dined.—*Coriolanus,* i, 9, 11.

2

He is indited to dinner.

II Henry IV. Act ii, sc. 1, l. 30. [Hostess] "Indited" is repeated in *Love's Labour's Lost,* iv, 1, 96.

3

Shall I entreat you with me to dinner?

II Henry IV. Act ii, sc. 1, l. 194. [Falstaff]

I entreat you home with me to dinner.

The Merchant of Venice. Act iv, sc. 1, l. 401. [Duke]

I pray you home to dinner with me.—*Measure for Measure,* ii, 1, 292.

Some of you go home with me to dinner.—*The Merry Wives of Windsor,* iii, 2, 81.

Shallow: I pray you, go in with me to dinner.
Falstaff: Come, I will go drink with you, but I cannot tarry dinner.

II Henry IV. Act iii, sc. 2, l. 202.

Cassius: Will you dine with me to-morrow?
Casca: Ay, if I be alive and your mind hold and your dinner worth the eating.

Julius Cæsar. Act i, sc. 2, l. 294.

Come, let 's to dinner.—*II Henry IV,* iii, 2, 233.

Go with me to dinner.—*II Henry IV,* v, 5, 94.

Come, let us four to dinner.—*I Henry VI,* ii, 4, 133.

4

A thousand men have broke their fasts to-day
That ne'er shall dine.

II Henry VI. Act ii, sc. 2, l. 127. [Edward]

5

Lorenzo: Go in, sirrah; bid them prepare for dinner.
Launcelot: That is done, sir; they have all stomachs.
Lorenzo: Then bid them prepare dinner.
Launcelot: That is done too, sir; only 'cover' is the word. . . .
Lorenzo: Go to thy fellows; bid them cover the table, serve in the meat, and we will come in to dinner.

The Merchant of Venice. Act iii, sc. 5, l. 52.

Prepare for dinner.—*King Lear,* i, 3, 26.

Let me not stay a jot for dinner; go get it ready.

King Lear. Act i, sc. 4, l. 8. [King Lear]

Go bid the servants spread for dinner.—*The Comedy of Errors,* ii, 2, 189.

6

I am fain to dine and sup with water and bran; I dare not for my head fill my belly; one fruitful meal would set me to 't.

Measure for Measure. Act iv, sc. 3, l. 159. [Lucio]

7

Bassanio: If it please you to dine with us.
Shylock: Yes, to smell pork; to eat of the habitation which your prophet the Nazarite conjured the devil into. I will buy with you, sell with you, talk with you, walk with you, and so following, but I will not eat with you, drink with you, nor pray with you.

The Merchant of Venice. Act i, sc. 3, l. 33. The only use of "Nazarite."

First, let us go to dinner.—*The Merchant of Venice,* iii, 5, 91.

8

The dinner is on the table.

The Merry Wives of Windsor. Act i, sc. 1, l. 270. [Anne Page]

The dinner attends you, sir.—*The Merry Wives of Windsor,* i, 1, 279.

Dinner is ready.—*The Two Gentlemen of Verona,* i, 2, 131; *Much Ado about Nothing,* ii, 3, 218.

9

You 'll come to dinner, George.

The Merry Wives of Windsor. Act ii, sc. 1, l. 162. [Mrs. Page]

I promised you a dinner.—*The Merry Wives of Windsor,* iii, 3, 239.

Call him in to dinner.—*Much Ado about Nothing,* ii, 3, 227.

Come in to dinner.—*Much Ado about Nothing,* ii, 3, 257.

10

I will make an end of my dinner; there 's pippins and cheese to come.

Merry Wives of Windsor. Act i, sc. 2, l. 12.

A last year's pippin.—*II Henry IV,* v, 3, 2. The only uses of "pippin" and "pippins."

11

Your dinner, and the generous islanders
By you invited, do attend your presence.

Othello. Act iii, sc. 3, l. 280. [Desdemona]

I shall not dine at home.—*Othello,* iii, 3, 58.

He dined not at home.—*The Two Gentlemen of Verona,* v, 1, 255.

Say he dines forth.—*The Comedy of Errors,* ii, 2, 212.

He 's somewhere gone to dinner.—*The Comedy of Errors,* ii, 1, 5.

He dines in London.—*II Henry IV,* iv, 4, 51.

12

I stay dinner there.

Richard III. Act iii, sc. 2, l. 122. [Hastings]

Stay dinner.—*Romeo and Juliet,* iv, 5, 150.

1
Where shall we dine?
Romeo and Juliet. Act i, sc. 1, l. 179. [Romeo]
We 'll to dinner.—*Romeo and Juliet,* ii, 4, 148.
I 'll to dinner.—*Romeo and Juliet,* ii, 5, 79; *I Henry IV,* iii, 1, 50.

2
I know you think to dine with me to-day.
The Taming of the Shrew. Act iii, sc. 2, l. 187. [Petruchio]
Dine with my father, drink a health to me.
The Taming of the Shrew. Act iii, sc. 2, l. 198. [Petruchio]
Gentlemen, forward to the bridal dinner.
The Taming of the Shrew. Act iii, sc. 2, l. 221. [Katharina]
A good dinner.—*The Taming of the Shrew,* i, 2, 218.

3
I must eat my dinner.
The Tempest. Act i, sc. 2, l. 330. [Caliban]

4
We must needs dine together.
Timon of Athens. Act i, sc. 1, l. 164. [Timon]
You must needs dine with me.
Timon of Athens. Act i, sc. 1, l. 253. [Timon]
Many a time and often I ha' dined with him.
Timon of Athens. Act iii, sc. 1, l. 25. [Lucullus]
Dinner 's done.—*Timon of Athens,* i, 1, 254; ii, 2, 14.
After dinner.—*The Merchant of Venice,* i, 1, 104; ii, 1, 44; *Timon of Athens,* ii, 2, 42.
Our dinner will not recompense this long stay.
Timon of Athens. Act iii, sc. 6, l. 35. [Timon]

5
But for your health and your digestion sake,
An after-dinner's breath.
Troilus and Cressida. Act ii, sc. 3, l. 120. [Patroclus] A reference to the proverb, "after dinner, walk a mile." "After-dinner's" as a hyphenated adjective is repeated in *Measure for Measure,* iii, 1, 33: "An after-dinner's sleep."

DIRECTION

6
By indirections find directions out.
Hamlet, ii, 1, 66. See under CUNNING.
Thou variest no more from picking of purses than giving direction doth from labouring.
I Henry IV. Act ii, sc. 1, l. 55. [Gadshill]

7
By Chesu, I think a' will plow up all, if there is not better directions.
Henry V. Act iii, sc. 2, l. 68. [Fluellen]
Altogether directed by an Irishman.
Henry V. Act iii, sc. 2, l. 70. [Gower]
Modestly directed.—*I Henry VI,* v, 3, 179.

8
Is all things well,
According as I gave directions?
II Henry VI. Act iii, sc. 2, l. 11. [Suffolk]
There is no English soul
More stronger to direct you than yourself.
Henry VIII. Act i, sc. 1, l. 146. [Norfolk]

9
I do commit his youth To your direction.
King John. Act iv, sc. 2, l. 67. [King John]
Even now I put myself to thy direction.
Macbeth. Act iv, sc. 3, l. 121. [Macduff]
I am directed by you.
Measure for Measure. Act iv, sc. 3, l. 141. [Isabella]
Direction just.—*Macbeth,* iii, 3, 4.
A good direction.—*Richard III,* v, 3, 302.
Nice direction.—*Merchant of Venice,* ii, 1, 14.

10
I ha' told them over and over; they lack no direction.
The Merry Wives of Windsor. Act iii, sc. 3, l. 18. [Mrs. Ford]
Iago hath directions what to do.
Othello. Act ii, sc. 3, l. 4. [Cassio]

11
I, like a child, will go by thy direction.
Richard III. Act ii, sc. 3, l. 153. [Gloucester]
I will stoop and humble my intents
To your well-practised wise directions.
II Henry IV. Act v, sc. 2, l. 120. [King Henry V] The only use of "well-practised."
Give direction.—*Richard III,* v, 3, 236; *Othello,* ii, 3, 128.
My direction-giver.
The Two Gentlemen of Verona. Act iii, sc. 2, l. 90. [Thurio] The only use of the phrase.
It standeth north-north-east and by east.
Love's Labour's Lost. Act i, sc. 1, l. 247. [King Ferdinand] The only "north-north-east." "North-north-west" occurs in *Hamlet,* ii, 2, 396.

12
Call for some men of sound direction.
Richard III. Act v, sc. 3, l. 16. [King Richard]
Embrace but my direction.
Winter's Tale. Act iv, sc. 4, l. 533. [Camillo]

DISASTER

See also Miscarriage, Misfortune

13
It was a disaster of war that Cæsar himself could not have prevented, if he had been there to command.
All's Well that Ends Well. Act iii, sc. 6, l. 55. [First Lord]
This very instant disaster of his setting i' the stocks.
All's Well that Ends Well. Act iv, sc. 3, l. 127.
Sent it us Upon her great disaster.
All's Well that Ends Well. Act v, sc. 3, l. 111. [King] Shakespeare used the word "disaster" only ten times in all his plays, and four of these were in *All's Well that Ends Well.*

14
To be called into a huge sphere, and not to be seen to move in 't, are the holes where eyes should be, which pitifully disaster the cheeks.
Antony and Cleopatra. Act ii, sc. 7, l. 16. [First Servant]

15
O, pardon me that I descend so low,
To show the line and the predicament.
I Henry IV. Act i, sc. 3, l. 167. [Hotspur]
Piteous predicament!—*Romeo and Juliet,* iii, 3, 86.
Predicament, Wherein you range.—*I Henry IV,* i, 3, 168. The only uses of "predicament."

1
Our people and our peers are both misled,
Our treasure seized, our soldiers put to flight,
And, as thou seest, ourselves in heavy plight.
III Henry VI. Act iii, sc. 3, l. 35. [Queen Margaret]
Distressed plight.—*Titus Andronicus,* iv, 4, 32. "Plight," in the sense of misfortune, occurs five times.
2
But if you be afeard to hear the worst,
Then let the worst unheard fall on your head.
King John. Act iv, sc. 2, l. 135. [Bastard]
And is 't not pity, O my grieved friends,
That we, the sons and children of this isle,
Were born to see so sad an hour as this;
Wherein we step after a stranger march
Upon her gentle bosom, and fill up
Her enemies' ranks?
King John. Act v, sc. 2, l. 24. [Salisbury]
O, they were all in lamentable cases!
Love's Labour's Lost. Act v, sc. 2, l. 273. [Rosaline]
3 This was a goodly person,
Till the disaster that, one mortal night,
Drove him to this.
Pericles. Act v, sc. 1, l. 36. [Helicanus]
4
Glad am I that your highness is so arm'd
To bear the tidings of calamity.
Richard II. Act iii, sc. 2, l. 104. [Scroop]
His wits
Are drown'd and lost in his calamities.
Timon of Athens. Act iv, sc. 3, l. 88. [Alcibiades] The only use of "calamities."
There is no true cuckold but calamity.
Twelfth Night. Act i, sc. 5, l. 56. [Clown]
You are transported by calamity
Thither where more attends you.
Coriolanus. Act i, sc. 1, l. 77. [Menenius]
Wedded to calamity.—*Romeo and Juliet,* iii, 3, 3.
Evident calamity.—*Richard III,* v, 3, 112. "Calamity" occurs ten times.
5 Checks and disasters
Grow in the veins of actions highest rear'd.
Troilus and Cressida. Act i, sc. 3, l. 5. [Agamemnon]
Private check.—*Othello,* iii, 3, 67.
Shameful check.—*Antony and Cleopatra,* iv, 4, 31.
Slight check.—*Timon of Athens,* ii, 2, 149.

DISCIPLINE

6
Has he disciplined Aufidius soundly?
Coriolanus. Act ii, sc. 1, l. 139. [Menenius]
Disciplined thy arms to fight.—*Troilus and Cressida,* ii, 3, 255.
Disciplined . . . in grace.—*A Lover's Complaint,* l. 261. The only uses of "disciplined."
7
Discipline ought to be used.
Henry V. Act iii, sc. 6, l. 58. [Fluellen]
8
O, negligent and heedless discipline!
I Henry VI. Act iv, sc. 2, l. 44. [Talbot]
Civil discipline.—*II Henry VI,* i, 1, 195.
Excellent discipline.—*Henry V,* iii, 6, 12.
Military discipline.—*Henry V,* iii, 2, 107.
O prudent discipline!—*King John,* ii, 1, 413.
Discipline in war.—*Richard III,* iii, 7, 16.
Disciplines of war.—*Henry V,* iii, 2, 63; 76, 86, 103, 141, 152.
Tainting his discipline.—*Othello,* ii, 1, 275.
9
Heaven bless thee from a tutor, and discipline come not near thee!
Troilus and Cressida. Act ii, sc. 3, l. 32. [Thersites]
This discipline shows thou hast been in love.
The Two Gentlemen of Verona. Act iii, sc. 2, l. 88. [Duke]

DISCOMFORT

10 What mean you, sir,
To give them this discomfort?
Antony and Cleopatra. Act iv, sc. 2, l. 34. [Enobarbus]
Yet, though I distrust,
Discomfort you, my lord, it nothing must.
Hamlet. Act iii, sc. 2, l. 175. [Player Queen]
11 Uncurable discomfit
Reigns in the hearts of all our present parts.
II Henry VI. Act v, sc. 2, l. 86. [Young Clifford] The only use of "discomfit." "Uncurable" is repeated in iii, 1, 286, and occurs in no other play.
Go with me and be not so discomfited.
The Taming of the Shrew. Act ii, sc. 1, l. 164. [Baptista]
Be discomfited.—*II Henry VI,* v, 1, 63.
The Earl of Douglas is discomfited.—*I Henry IV,* i, 1, 67.
Discomfited great Douglas.—*I Henry IV,* iii, 2, 114. The only uses of "discomfited."
12
As whence the sun 'gins his reflection
Shipwrecking storms and direful thunders break,
So from that spring whence comfort seem'd to come
Discomfort swells.
Macbeth. Act i, sc. 2, l. 25. [Sergeant] The only use of "shipwrecking."
Should I stay longer,
It would be . . . your discomfort.
Macbeth. Act iv, sc. 2, l. 29. [Ross]
Slaughter and discomforture.—*I Henry VI,* i, 1, 59. The only use of "discomforture."
13 Discomfort guides my tongue
And bids me speak of nothing but despair.
Richard II. Act iii, sc. 2, l. 65. [Salisbury]
My lord, you do discomfort all the host.
Troilus and Cressida. Act v, sc. 10, l. 10. [Æneas]
Discomfort us.—*Julius Cæsar,* v, 3, 106.

DISCONTENT

14 I leave you, sir,
To the worst of discontent.
Cymbeline. Act ii, sc. 3, l. 159. [Imogen]
15
My body round engirt with misery,
For what 's more miserable than discontent?
II Henry VI. Act iii, sc. 1, l. 200. [King Henry]

Full of sorrow and heart's discontent.
III Henry VI. Act iii, sc. 3, l. 173. [Warwick]
He's discontented.—*Henry VIII,* iii, 2, 91.

1 'Tis wonderful
What may be wrought out of their discontent,
Now that their souls are topfull of offence.
King John. Act iii, sc. 4, l. 178. [Pandulph] "Top-full" (hyphenated) is repeated in *Macbeth,* i, 5, 43: "Top-full of cruelty."
Discontents at home.—*King John,* iv, 3, 151.

2
Here comes a man of comfort, whose advice
Hath often still'd my brawling discontent.
Measure for Measure. Act iv, sc. 1, l. 8. [Mariana]

3
Thou art the Mars of malecontents.
Merry Wives of Windsor. Act i, sc. 3, l. 113. [Pistol] The only use of "malecontents."
Liege of all loiterers and malcontents.
Love's Labour's Lost, iii, 1, 185. See under CUPID. The only use of "malcontents."
Thou art malcontent?—*III Henry VI,* iv, 1, 60.
Half malcontent.—*III Henry VI,* iv, 1, 10.
Like a malcontent.—*Two Gentlemen of Verona,* ii, 1, 20. The only uses of "malcontent."

4
Can you make no use of your discontent?
Much Ado about Nothing. Act i, sc. 3, l. 40. [Conrade]
What is he for a fool that betroths himself to unquietness?
Much Ado about Nothing. Act i, sc. 3, l. 49. [Don John] The only use of "betroth" and "unquietness."

5
Thy discontent thou didst bequeath to me.
The Passionate Pilgrim, l. 142.
Why art thou thus attired in discontent?
The Rape of Lucrece, l. 1601.
I see your brows are full of discontent,
Your hearts of sorrow and your eyes of tears.
Richard II. Act iv, sc. 1, l. 331. [Abbot]

6
Now is the winter of our discontent
Made glorious summer by this sun of York.
Richard III. Act i, sc. 1, l. 1. [Gloucester]

7
Wishing me like to one more rich in hope,
Featured like him, like him with friends possess'd,
Desiring this man's art and that man's scope,
With what I most enjoy contented least.
Sonnets. No. xxix. "Featured" is repeated in *Much Ado about Nothing,* iii, 1, 60.
Happy thou art not;
For what thou hast not, still thou strivest to get,
And what thou hast, forget'st.
Measure for Measure. Act iii, sc. 1, l. 21. [Duke]
The blow of thralled discontent.
Sonnets. No. cxxiv.

8
Sister, content you in my discontent.
The Taming of the Shrew. Act i, sc. 1, l. 80. [Bianca]

9
My lord leans wondrously to discontent: his comfortable temper has forsook him.
Timon of Athens. Act iii, sc. 4, l. 70. [Servant] The only use of "wondrously."
His discontents are unremoveably
Coupled to nature.
Timon of Athens. Act v, sc. 1, l. 227. Senator] The only use of "unremoveably."
Best state, contentless,
Hath a distracted and most wretched being,
Worse than the worst, content.
Thou shouldst desire to die, being miserable.
Timon of Athens. Act iv, sc. 3, l. 245. [Apemantus] The only use of "contentless."

10
Let not discontent Daunt all your hopes.
Titus Andronicus. Act i, sc. 1, l. 267. [Saturninus]
Dissemble all your . . . discontents.—*Titus Andronicus,* i, 1, 443.

DISCORD

See also Dissension, Quarrel

11
His jarring concord, and his discord dulcet.
All's Well that Ends Well. Act i, sc. 1, l. 186. [Helena]
Jarring discord.—*I Henry VI,* iv, 1, 188.
Jarring notes.—*Taming of the Shrew,* v, 2, 1.
Jarring senses.—*King Lear,* iv, 7, 16. The only uses of "jarring."
If he, compact of jars, grow musical,
We shall have shortly discord in the spheres.
As You Like It. Act ii, sc. 7, l. 5. [Duke Senior] For "jar" see QUARREL.
How shall we find the concord of this discord?
A Midsummer-Night's Dream. Act v, sc. 1, l. 60. [Theseus]

12
You two never meet but you fall to some discord: you are both, i' good truth, as rheumatic as two dry toasts; you cannot one bear with another's infirmities.
II Henry IV. Act ii, sc. 4, l. 61. [Hostess]

13
O, how this discord doth afflict my soul!
I Henry VI. Act iii, sc. 1, l. 106. [King Henry]
My restless discord loves no stops nor rests.
The Rape of Lucrece, l. 1124.
Dismal discords.—*III Henry VI,* v, 6, 48.
Private discord.—*I Henry VI,* iv, 4, 22.
Sour-eyed . . . discord.—*The Tempest,* iv, 1, 20. The only use of "sour-eyed."

14
An thou make minstrels of us, look to hear nothing but discords.
Romeo and Juliet. Act iii, sc. 1, l. 51. [Mercutio]
Should the empress know
This discord's ground, the music would not please.
Titus Andronicus. Act ii, sc. 1, l. 69. [Aaron]
What discord follows!—*Troilus and Cressida,* i, 3, 110.

15 Nay, now you are too flat
And mar the concord with too harsh a descant:
There wanteth but a mean to fill your song.
The Two Gentlemen of Verona. Act i, sc. 2,

l. 93. [Lucetta] "Descant" is repeated in *Richard III,* i, 1, 27: "Descant on mine own deformity"; and iii, 7, 49: "Holy descant."

Melodious discord, heavenly tune harsh-sounding,
Ear's deep-sweet music, and heart's deep-sore wounding.
Venus and Adonis, l. 431. "Harsh-sounding" is repeated in *King John,* iv, 2, 150. The only use of "deep-sweet" and "deep-sore."

DISCOURSE

See also Speech

1
Hear at large discoursed all our fortunes.
The Comedy of Errors. Act v, sc. 1, l. 395. [Abbess]

The manner of their taking may appear
At large discoursed in this paper here.
Richard II. Act v, sc. 6, l. 9. [Northumberland] The only uses of "discoursed."

2
Discourse is heavy, fasting; when we have supp'd,
We 'll mannerly demand thee of thy story.
Cymbeline. Act iii, sc. 6, l. 91. [Belarius]

3
Put your discourse into some frame and start not so wildly from my affair.
Hamlet. Act iii, sc. 2, l. 320. [Guildenstern]

Alas, how is 't with you,
That you do bend your eye on vacancy
And with the incorporal air do hold discourse.
Hamlet. Act iii, sc. 4, l. 116. [Queen] The only use of "incorporal."

4
List his discourse of war, and you shall hear
A fearful battle render'd you in music.
Henry V. Act i, sc. 1, l. 43. [Canterbury]

It is no time to discourse, . . . the day is hot, and the weather, and the wars, and the king, and the dukes: it is no time to discourse.
Henry V. Act iii, sc. 2, l. 112. [Macmorris]

Brief discourse.—*Othello,* iii, 1, 55.

Large discourse.—*Midsummer-Night's Dream,* v, 1, 152.

5
Discourse, I prithee, on this turret's top.
I Henry VI. Act i, sc. 4, l. 26. [Salisbury] "Turret" is repeated in iii, 2, 30, and occurs in no other play.

6
Nephew, what means this passionate discourse,
This peroration with such circumstance?
II Henry VI. Act i, sc. 1, l. 104. [Beaufort] "Peroration" was used in the first scene of the first act of the first play, and never again.

His discourse peremptory.—*Love's Labour 's Lost,* v, 1, 11.

Hot discourse.—*Troilus and Cressida,* ii, 3, 183.

7
According to the which, thou shalt discourse
To young Octavius of the state of things.
Julius Cæsar. Act iii, sc. 1, l. 295. [Antony]

8
I think the best grace of wit will shortly turn into silence, and discourse grow commendable in none only but parrots.
The Merchant of Venice. Act iii, sc. 5, l. 49. [Lorenzo]

Of this discourse we more will hear anon.
A Midsummer-Night's Dream. Act iv, sc. 1, l. 182. [Theseus]

9
The body of your discourse is sometime guarded with fragments.
Much Ado about Nothing. Act i, sc. 1, l. 287. [Benedick]

Our whole discourse Is all of her.
Much Ado about Nothing. Act iii, sc. 1, l. 5. [Hero]

10
And yet your fair discourse hath been as sugar,
Making the hard way sweet and delectable.
Richard II. Act ii, sc. 3, l. 6. [Northumberland] "Delectable" is repeated in *II Henry IV,* iv, 3, 108.

Admirable discourse.—*The Merry Wives of Windsor,* ii, 2, 235.

Smooth discourse.—*III Henry VI,* iii, 3, 88.

Good discourser.—*Henry VIII,* i, 1, 41. The only use of "discourser."

11
Farewell: the leisure and the fearful time
Cuts off the ceremonious vows of love
And ample interchange of sweet discourse,
Which so long sunder'd friends should dwell upon.
Richard III. Act v, sc. 3, l. 97. [Derby]

Sweet discourses.—*Romeo and Juliet,* iii, 5, 53.

12
Such shapes, such gesture and such sound, expressing
Although they want the use of tongue, a kind
Of excellent dumb discourse.
The Tempest. Act iii, sc. 3, l. 37. [Alonso]

13
Speak, Rome's dear friend, as erst our ancestor
When with his solemn tongue he did discourse
To love-sick Dido's sad attending ear.
Titus Andronicus. Act v, sc. 3, l. 80. [Marcus] "Love-sick" is repeated in *Antony and Cleopatra,* ii, 2, 199.

O madness of discourse,
That cause sets up with and against itself!
Troilus and Cressida. Act v, sc. 2, l. 142. [Troilus]

14
Leave off discourse of disability.
The Two Gentlemen of Verona. Act ii, sc. 4, l. 109. [Valentine] The only use of "disability."

Discourse of reason.—*Troilus and Cressida,* ii, 2, 116; *Hamlet,* i, 2, 150.

Discourse of thought.—*Othello,* iv, 2, 153.

15
Now no discourse, except it be of love.
The Two Gentlemen of Verona, ii, 4, 140. See under LOVE.

Thurio: How likes she my discourse?
Proteus: Ill, when you talk of war.

Thurio: But well, when I discourse of love and peace?
Julia [aside]: But better, indeed, when you hold your peace.
Two Gentlemen of Verona. Act v, sc. 2, l. 15.

Stand not to discourse.—*The Two Gentlemen of Verona,* v, 2, 44.

1 Bid me discourse, I will enchant thine ear.
Venus and Adonis, l. 145.

Of enchanting . . . discourse.—*The Comedy of Errors,* iii, 2, 166.

Of excellent discourse.—*The Comedy of Errors,* iii, 1, 109.

Of good discourse.—*Much Ado about Nothing,* ii, 3, 35.

DISCOVERY

2 The heavens have thought well on thee, Lafeu,
To bring forth this discovery.
All's Well that Ends Well. Act v, sc. 3, l. 150. [King]

A South-sea of discovery.—*As You Like It,* iii, 2, 207. The only use of "South-sea."

3 Send discoverers forth
To know the numbers of our enemies.
II Henry IV. Act iv, sc. 1, l. 3. [Archbishop] The only use of "discoverers."

By your espials were discovered
Two mightier troops.
I Henry VI. Act iv, sc. 3, l. 6. [Messenger]

You have discovered thus.—*Much Ado about Nothing,* ii, 2, 40.

Thou hast painfully discover'd.—*Timon of Athens,* v, 2, 1.

Traitorously discovered.—*All's Well that Ends Well,* iv, 3, 339.

4 Make discovery Err in report of us.
Macbeth. Act v, sc. 4, l. 6. [Malcolm]

She dares not thereof make discovery.
The Rape of Lucrece, l. 1314.

5 I shall discover a thing to you.
The Merry Wives of Windsor. Act ii, sc. 2, l. 190. [Ford]

I think I can discover him.—*Othello,* i, 1, 179.

I can discover all.—*Romeo and Juliet,* iii, 1, 147.

I will discover nought to thee.—*Titus Andronicus,* v, 1, 85.

6 Some to discover islands far away.
The Two Gentlemen of Verona, i, 3, 9. See under HOME.

Discover how.—*Comedy of Errors,* v, 1, 203.

Diligent discovery.—*King Lear,* v, 1, 53.

Fair discovery.—*Venus and Adonis,* l. 828.

Preposterous discoveries!—*Troilus and Cressida,* v, 1, 28.

Discoveries of dishonour.—*Measure for Measure,* iii, 1, 236.

Deal of discoveries.—*All's Well that Ends Well,* iii, 6, 100. The only uses of "discoveries."

DISCRETION

See also Prudence

7 Helena: You go so much backward when you fight.
Parolles: That 's for advantage.
Helena: So is running away, when fear proposes the safety: but the composition that your valour and fear makes in you is a virtue of a good wing.
All's Well that Ends Well. Act i, sc. 1, l. 214.

Where they would be safe they perish.
Henry V. Act iv, sc. 1, l. 187. [King Henry]

She that her fame so to herself contrives,
The scars of battle 'scapeth by the flight,
And makes her absence valiant, not her might.
A Lover's Complaint, l. 243.

Who marvels then, when Helenus beholds
A Grecian and his sword, if he do set
The very wings of reason to his heels
And fly like chidden Mercury from Jove,
Or like a star disorb'd?
Troilus and Cressida. Act ii, sc. 2, l. 42. [Troilus] The only use of "disorb'd."

8 Use thy discretion.
As You Like It. Act i, sc. 1, l. 152. [Oliver]

Let your own discretion be your tutor.
Hamlet. Act iii, sc. 1, l. 19. [Hamlet]

9 The better part of valour is discretion.
I Henry IV. Act v, sc. 4, l. 121. [Falstaff]

10 Covering discretion with a coat of folly;
As gardeners do with ordure hide those roots
That shall first spring and be most delicate.
Henry V. Act ii, sc. 4, l. 38. [Constable] The only use of "ordure."

11 But your discretions better can persuade
Than I am able to instruct or teach.
I Henry VI. Act iv, sc. 1, l. 158. [King Henry]

Was it discretion, lords, to let this man,
This good man,—few of you deserve that title,—
This honest man, wait like a lousy footboy
At chamber-door? and one as great as you are?
Henry VIII. Act v, sc. 3, l. 137. [King Henry]

You should be ruled and led
By some discretion, that discerns your state
Better than yourself.
King Lear. Act ii, sc. 4, l. 150. [Regan]

12 Thou pigeon-egg of discretion.
Love's Labour 's Lost. Act v, sc. 1, l. 77. [Costard] The only use of "pigeon-egg," used as a type of smallness or triviality.

I have seen the day of wrong through the little hole of discretion.
Love's Labour 's Lost. Act v, sc. 2, l. 733. [Armado]

Best discretion.—*The Merry Wives of Windsor,* iv, 4, 1.

Good discretion.—*Henry VIII,* i, 1, 50; *Hamlet,* ii, 2, 489; *The Merry Wives of Windsor,* i, 1, 44; *Pericles,* i, 3, 5.

Great discretion.—*Much Ado about Nothing,* ii, 3, 198.

1
Old folks, you know, have discretion, as they say, and know the world.
The Merry Wives of Windsor. Act ii, sc. 2, l. 134. [Mistress Quickly]

2
Let us teach ourselves that honourable stop,
Not to outsport discretion.
Othello. Act ii, sc. 3, l. 2. [Othello] The only use of "outsport."

Do your discretion.—*Othello,* iii, 3, 34.

With some discretion.—*The Two Gentlemen of Verona,* iv, 4, 70.

3
I will not adventure my discretion so weakly.
The Tempest. Act ii, sc. 1, l. 187. [Gonzalo]

Why, have you any discretion?
Troilus and Cressida. Act i, sc. 2, l. 273. [Pandarus]

Lack discretion.—*Hamlet,* ii, 1, 117.

DISDAIN

See also Scorn

4
Believe not thy disdain.
All's Well that Ends Well. Act ii, sc. 3, l. 166. [King]

They do disdain us much beyond our thoughts,
Which makes me sweat with wrath.
Coriolanus. Act i, sc. 4, l. 26. [Marcius]

Disdain with cause.—*Coriolanus,* iii, 1, 143.

5
Once in contempt they would have barter'd me:
Which I disdaining scorn'd.
I Henry VI. Act i, sc. 4, l. 31. [Talbot] The only use of "barter'd."

Disdaining me and throwing favours on
The low Posthumus.
Cymbeline. Act iii, sc. 5, l. 75. [Cloten]

Disdaining duty.—*II Henry VI,* iii, 1, 17.

Disdaining fortune.—*Macbeth,* i, 2, 17. The only uses of "disdaining."

6
The false revolting Normans thorough thee
Disdain to call us lord.
II Henry VI. Act iv, sc. 1, l. 87. [Captain]

Disdains to shine.—*Richard III,* v, 3, 278.

7
What safe and nicely I might well delay
By rule of knighthood, I disdain and spurn.
King Lear. Act v, sc. 3, l. 144. [Edmund]

8
Benedick: What, my dear Lady Disdain! are you yet living?
Beatrice: Is it possible disdain should die while she hath such meet food to feed it as Signior Benedick? Courtesy itself must convert to disdain, if you come in her presence.
Benedick: Then is courtesy a turncoat.
Much Ado about Nothing. Act i, sc. 1, l. 119. "Turncoat" is repeated in *Timon of Athens,* iv, 3, 143.

No, truly, Ursula, she is too disdainful;
I know her spirits are as coy and wild
As haggerds of the rock.
Much Ado about Nothing. Act iii, sc. 1, l. 34. [Hero]

Disdain and scorn ride sparkling in her eyes,
Misprising what they look on.
Much Ado about Nothing. Act iii, sc. 1, l. 51. [Hero]

9
It better fits my blood to be disdained of all than to fashion a carriage to rob love from any.
Much Ado about Nothing, i, 3, 29. See under CANDOUR.

Disdain'd of fortune.—*Cymbeline,* iii, 4, 20.

By a son disdain'd.—*II Henry IV,* v, 2, 95.

10
For of the two the trusty knight was wounded with disdain:
Alas, she could not help it!
The Passionate Pilgrim, l. 221. Probably not by Shakespeare.

Cold disdain.—*The Rape of Lucrece,* l. 691.

Sour-eyed disdain.—*The Tempest,* iv, 1, 20. The only use of "sour-eyed."

11 Disdainfully did sting
His high-pitch'd thoughts.
The Rape of Lucrece, l. 40. See under ENVY. The only use of "high-pitch'd."

Greet him not,
Or else disdainfully, which shall shake him more
Than if not look'd on.
Troilus and Cressida. Act iii, sc. 3, l. 52. [Agamemnon] The only uses of "disdainfully."

12
Thy kinsmen hang their heads at this disdain.
The Rape of Lucrece, l. 521.

Such disdain.—*Venus and Adonis,* l. 501.

13 My heart disdained that my tongue
Should so profane the word.
Richard II, i, 4, 12. See under FAREWELL.

I disdain'd it.—*Richard III,* iii, 4, 85.

Let him have time . . . to see one that by alms doth live
Disdain to him disdained scraps to give.
The Rape of Lucrece, l. 986.

Disdain'd contempt.—*I Henry IV,* i, 3, 183.

Disdain'd the ground.—*Richard II,* v, 5, 83.

Lies disdain'd.—*Pericles,* v, 1, 120.

14 Do not press
My tongue-tied patience with too much disdain.
Sonnets. No. cxl.

That I disdain.—*The Taming of the Shrew,* ii, 1, 3.

15
His semblable, yea, himself, Timon disdains.
Timon of Athens. Act iv, sc. 3, l. 22. [Timon] "Semblable" is used five times.

16
Trampling contemptuously on thy disdain.
The Two Gentlemen of Verona. Act i, sc. 2, l. 112. [Julia] The only use of "contemptuously." "Trampling" is repeated in *Venus and Adonis,* l. 261.

Smiles as in disdain.—*Venus and Adonis,* l. 241.

The world will hold thee in disdain.—*Venus and Adonis,* l. 761.

Held in disdain.—*Venus and Adonis,* l. 394.

1
Yet nature might have made me as these are,
Therefore I will not disdain.
The Winter's Tale. Act iv, sc. 4, l. 773. [Autolycus]

DISEASE

See also Doctor, Illness, Infirmity, Pestilence, Sickness

2 My heart
Will not confess he owes the malady
That doth my life besiege.
All's Well that Ends Well. Act ii, sc. 1, l. 8. [King]

We must not
So stain our judgement, or corrupt our hope,
To prostitute our past-cure malady
To empirics, or to dissever so
Our great self and our credit, to esteem
A senseless help when help past sense we deem.
All's Well that Ends Well. Act ii, sc. 1, l. 122. [King] The only use of "past-cure" as a hyphenated adjective, and of "empirics." "Prostitute" is repeated in *Pericles,* iv, 6, 201.

But where the greater malady is fix'd,
The lesser is scarce felt.
King Lear. Act iii, sc. 4, l. 8. [King Lear]

A malady most incident to maids.
Winter's Tale, iv, 4, 124. See under FLOWER.

Not the least of all these maladies.
Venus and Adonis, l. 745. "Maladies" is used a second time in *Love's Labour's Lost,* iv, 3, 295: "Abstinence engenders maladies."

Former malady.—*The Taming of the Shrew,* Ind., 2, 124.

Infinite malady.—*Timon of Athens,* iii, 6, 108.

Pining malady.—*I Henry VI,* iii, 3, 49.

3
We do lance Diseases in our bodies.
Antony and Cleopatra. Act v, sc. 1, l. 36. [Cæsar]

4 Those cold ways,
That seem like prudent helps, are very poisonous
Where the disease is violent.
Coriolanus. Act iii, sc. 1, l. 220. [Brutus]

Sicinius: He 's a disease that must be cut away.
Menenius: O, he 's a limb that has but a disease;
Mortal, to cut it off; to cure it, easy.
Coriolanus. Act iii, sc. 1, l. 295.

5
But, like the owner of a foul disease,
To keep it from divulging, let it feed
Even on the pith of life.
Hamlet. Act iv, sc. 1, l. 21. [King] The only use of "divulging."

Kill thy physician, and the fee bestow
Upon thy foul disease.
King Lear. Act i, sc. 1, l. 166. [Kent] The only uses of "foul disease."

6 Diseases desperate grown
By desperate appliance are relieved.
Hamlet. Act iv, sc. 3, l. 9. [King]

7
I will turn diseases to commodity.
II Henry IV. Act i, sc. 2, l. 278. [Falstaff]

Diseases have been sold dearer than physic.
Pericles. Act iv, sc. 6, l. 105. [Marina]

8
You help to make the diseases, Doll: we catch of you,
Doll, we catch of you; grant that, my poor virtue, grant that.
II Henry IV. Act ii, sc. 4, l. 49. [Falstaff]

Rank diseases.—*II Henry IV,* iii, 1, 39.

Lucio: I have purchased as many diseases under her roof as come to—
Second Gentleman: To what, I pray?
Lucio: Judge.
Second Gentleman: To three thousand dolours a year.
Measure for Measure. Act i, sc. 2, l. 46.

Thou art always figuring diseases in me; but thou art full of error; I am sound.
Measure for Measure. Act i, sc. 2, l. 53. [First Gentleman]

How now! which of your hips has the most profound sciatica?
Measure for Measure. Act i, sc. 2, l. 58. [First Gentleman]

Cold sciatica.—*Timon of Athens,* iv, 1, 23. "Sciatica" is used a third time in *Troilus and Cressida,* v, 1, 25. See below.

9 We are all diseased,
And with our surfeiting and wanton hours
Have brought ourselves into a burning fever,
And we must bleed for it.
II Henry IV. Act iv, sc. 1, l. 54. [Archbishop of York]

This part of his conjoins with my disease,
And helps to end me.
II Henry IV. Act iv, sc. 5, l. 64. [King Henry] "Conjoin" is repeated in *Richard III,* v, 5, 31.

The disease is incurable.—*II Henry IV,* i, 2, 266.

I'll tell thee my disease.—*I Henry VI,* ii, 5, 44.

10
Long sitting to determine poor men's causes
Hath made me full of sickness and diseases.
II Henry VI. Act iv, sc. 7, l. 93. [Lord Say]

11
Before the curing of a strong disease,
Even in the instant of repair and health,
The fit is strongest.
King John. Act iii, sc. 4, l. 112. [Dauphin]

12 Strangely-visited people,
All swoln and ulcerous, pitiful to the eye,
The mere despair of surgery, he cures,
Hanging a golden stamp about their necks,
Put on with holy prayers.
Macbeth. Act iv, sc. 3, l. 150. [Malcolm] The only use of "strangely-visited."

Find her disease,
And purge it to a sound and pristine health.
Macbeth. Act v, sc. 3, l. 51. [Macbeth] "Pristine" occurs again in *Henry V,* iii, 2, 87.

This disease is beyond my practice.
Macbeth. Act v, sc. 1, l. 65. [Doctor]

His dissolute disease will scarce obey this medicine.
The Merry Wives of Windsor. Act iii, sc. 3, l. 203. [Mrs. Page]

13
He will hang upon him like a disease: he is sooner caught than the pestilence, and the

taker runs presently mad. God help the noble Claudio! if he have caught the Benedick, it will cost him a thousand pound ere a' be cured.

Much Ado about Nothing. Act i, sc. 1, l. 86. [Beatrice] "Taker" is repeated in *Romeo and Juliet,* v, 1, 62.

His lady mourns at his disease.

The Taming of the Shrew. Induction. Sc. 1, l. 62. [Lord]

1

Till then I 'll sweat and seek about for eases,
And at that time bequeathe you my diseases.

Troilus and Cressida. Act v, sc. 10, l. 56. [Pandarus]

Diseases of the world.—*King Lear,* i, 1, 177.

2

Many thousand on 's
Have the disease, and feel 't not.

The Winter's Tale. Act i, sc. 2, l. 206. [Leontes]

There is a sickness
Which puts some of us in distemper, but
I cannot name the disease.

Winter's Tale. Act i, sc. 2, l. 384. [Camillo]

II—Ague

3

He is so shaked of a burning quotidian tertian, that it is most lamentable to behold.

Henry V. Act ii, sc. 1, l. 123. [Hostess] The only use of "tertian." "Quotidian" occurs again in *As You Like It,* iii, 2, 383: "Quotidian of love."

4

Home without boots, and in foul weather, too!
How 'scapes he agues, in the devil's name?

I Henry VI. Act iii, sc. 1, l. 68. [Hotspur] There are fourteen references to the ague in the different plays.

5

An untimely ague
Stay'd me a prisoner in my chamber.

Henry VIII. Act i, sc. 1, l. 4. [Buckingham]

That same ague which has made you lean.

Julius Cæsar. Act ii, sc. 2, l. 113. [Cæsar]

Ague fit.—*Richard II,* iii, 2, 190.
I will help his ague.—*The Tempest,* ii, 2, 97.
How does thine ague?—*The Tempest,* ii, 2, 139.
Heavenly agues.—*Timon of Athens,* iv, 3, 137.

III—Apoplexy

6

His highness is fallen into this same whoreson apoplexy. . . . This apoplexy is, as I take it, a kind of lethargy, an 't please your lordship; a kind of sleeping in the blood, a whoreson tingling. . . . It hath its original from much grief, from study and perturbation of the brain: I have read the cause of his effects in Galen: it is a kind of deafness.

II Henry IV. Act i, sc. 2, l. 122. [Falstaff] The only use of "tingling." Galen is mentioned five times. "Original" is repeated in *A Midsummer-Night's Dream,* ii, 1, 117.

This apoplexy will certain be his end.

II Henry IV. Act iv, sc. 4, l. 130. [Humphrey]

IV—Cold

7

Bullcalf: O Lord, sir! I am a diseased man.
Falstaff: What disease hast thou?
Bullcalf: A whoreson cold, sir, a cough, sir, which I caught with ringing in the king's affairs upon his coronation-day, sir.

II Henry IV. Act iii, sc. 2, l. 191. "Coronation-day" is repeated in *Richard II,* v, 5, 77.

Falls into a cough.—*A Midsummer-Night's Dream,* ii, 1, 54.
Cough and spit.—*Troilus and Cressida,* i, 3, 173.

8

I have a salt and sorry rheum offends me.

Othello. Act iii, sc. 4, l. 51. [Othello]

That year, indeed, he was troubled with a rheum.

Antony and Cleopatra. Act iii, sc. 2, l. 57. [Enobarbus] See under RHEUM.

9

Fire; for I have caught extreme cold.

The Taming of the Shrew. Act iv, sc. 1, l. 47. [Grumio]

You will catch cold, and curse me.

Troilus and Cressida. Act iv, sc. 2, l. 15. [Troilus]

Catch cold.—*The Comedy of Errors,* iii, 1, 37; *King Lear,* i, 4, 113; *Cymbeline,* i, 4, 180.
Catching cold.—*The Two Gentlemen of Verona,* i, 2, 136.

10

A whoreson tisick, a whoreson rascally tisick so troubles me, . . . and I have a rheum in mine eyes too, and such an ache in my bones that, unless a man were cursed, I cannot tell what to think on 't.

Troilus and Cressida. Act v, sc. 3, l. 101. [Pandarus] The only use of "tisick."

V—Epilepsy

11

Casca: He fell down in the market-place, and foamed at mouth, and was speechless.
Brutus: 'Tis very like: he hath the falling sickness.
Cassius: No, Cæsar hath it not; but you and I
And honest Casca, we have the falling sickness.
Casca: I know not what you mean by that; but, I am sure, Cæsar fell down.

Julius Cæsar. Act i, sc. 2, l. 254. The only uses of "falling sickness."

These fits
Are with his highness very ordinary.
Stand from him, give him air; he 'll straight be well.

II Henry IV. Act iv, sc. 4, l. 114. [Warwick]

The fit is momentary; upon a thought
He will again be well.

Macbeth. Act iii, sc. 4, l. 55. [Lady Macbeth]

12

My lord is fall'n into an epilepsy:
This is his second fit; he had one yesterday.

Othello. Act iv, sc. 1, l. 51. [Iago] The only mention of epilepsy. "Epileptic visage" occurs in *King Lear,* ii, 2, 87.

The lethargy must have his quiet course:
If not, he foams at mouth and by and by
Breaks out to savage madness.

Othello. Act iv, sc. 1, l. 54. [Iago]

How have you come so early by this lethargy?
Twelfth Night. Act i, sc. 5, l. 131. [Olivia]
Time of lethargy.—*Winter's Tale,* iv, 4, 627.
Apoplexy, lethargy.—*Coriolanus,* iv, 5, 234. The only uses of "lethargy."
Gravel, . . . lethargies.—*Troilus and Cressida,* v, 1, 23. The only use of "lethargies."

1
Plagued with painful fits.
The Rape of Lucrece, l. 856.
He 's in his fit now and does not talk after the wisest.
The Tempest. Act ii, sc. 2, l. 76. [Stephano]
His fits, his frenzy.—*Titus Andronicus,* iv, 4, 12.
What fit is this?—*The Winter's Tale,* iii, 2, 175.
Jealous fits.—*The Comedy of Errors,* v, 1, 85.
Sickly fit.—*King Lear,* ii, 4, 112.
Sullen fits.—*As You Like It,* ii, 1, 67.

VI—Fever

2
And what 's a fever but a fit of madness?
The Comedy of Errors. Act v, sc. 1, l. 76. [Abbess]

3
The wretch, whose fever-weaken'd joints,
Like strengthless hinges, buckle under life.
II Henry IV. Act i, sc. 1, l. 140. [Northumberland] The only use of "fever-weaken'd." "Strengthless" is repeated in *I Henry VI,* ii, 5, 13.

4
He had a fever when he was in Spain,
And when the fit was on him, I did mark
How he did shake.
Julius Cæsar. Act i, sc. 2, l. 119. [Cassius]
This fever, that has troubled me so long,
Lies heavy on me.
King John. Act v, sc. 3, l. 3. [King John]
Ay me! This tyrant fever burns me up.
King John. Act v, sc. 3, l. 14. [King John]
There is so hot a summer in my bosom,
That all my bowels crumble up to dust.
King John. Act v, sc. 7, l. 30. [King John] The only use of "crumble."

5
A fever in your blood! why, then incision
Would let her out in saucers: sweet misprision!
Love's Labour 's Lost. Act iv, sc. 3, l. 97. [Biron] The only use of "saucers."
A fever, longing still
For that which longer nurseth the disease,
Feeding on that which doth preserve the ill,
The uncertain sickly appetite to please.
Sonnets. No. cxlvii.

6
The fever whereof all our power is sick.
Troilus and Cressida, i, 3, 139. [Nestor]

7
Burning fevers, agues pale and faint.
Venus and Adonis, l. 739.
The marrow-eating sickness, whose attaint
Disorder breeds by heating of the blood.
Venus and Adonis, l. 741. The only use of "marrow-eating."

VII—Green-Sickness

8
Thin drink doth so over-cool their blood, and making many fish-meals, that they fall into a kind of male green-sickness.
II Henry IV. Act iv, sc. 3, l. 98. [Falstaff] The only use of "over-cool" and "fish-meals."
Now, a pox upon her green-sickness for me!
Pericles. Act iv, sc. 6, l. 14. [Pandar] The green-sickness was a kind of anæmia, called chlorosis, affecting young women.
Since Pompey's feast, . . .
Troubled with the green sickness.
Antony and Cleopatra. Act iii, sc. 2, l. 6. [Enobarbus] A reference to the morbid appetite characterizing the disease.

VIII—Miscellaneous Diseases

9
Bertram: What is it, my good lord, the king languishes of?
Lafeu: A fistula, my lord.
All 's Well that Ends Well. Act i, sc. 1, l. 37. The only mention of fistula.

10 A most instant tetter bark'd about,
Most lazar-like, with vile and loathsome crust,
All my smooth body.
Hamlet. Act i, sc. 5, l. 71. [Ghost] The only use of "lazar-like."
As for my country I have shed my blood,
Not fearing outward force, so shall my lungs
Coin words till their decay against those measles,
Which we disdain should tetter us, yet sought
The very way to catch them.
Coriolanus. Act iii, sc. 1, l. 76. [Coriolanus] The only mention of measles. "Tetter" occurs a third time in *Troilus and Cressida,* v, 1, 27. See last quotation in this section.

11
Pinched with the colic.
I Henry IV, iii, 1, 129; *Coriolanus,* ii, 1, 83.
The colic of puff'd Aquilon.—*Troilus and Cressida,* iv, 5, 9. Only mention of Aquilon.

12
A pox of this gout! or, a gout of this pox! for the one or the other plays the rogue with my great toe.
II Henry IV. Act i, sc. 2, l. 273. [Falstaff] Gout is mentioned six times in the plays and once in *The Rape of Lucrece,* l. 856.
A gouty Briareus, many hands and no use.
Troilus and Cressida, i, 2, 30. The only mention of Briareus. "Gouty" occurs again in *Timon of Athens,* iv, 3, 46, and in *A Lover's Complaint,* l. 140.

13
Macduff: What 's the disease he means?
Malcolm: 'Tis call'd the evil.
Macbeth. Act iv, sc. 3, l. 146.

14
Rheumatic diseases do abound.
A Midsummer-Night's Dream. Act ii, sc. 1, l. 105. [Titania]
He was rheumatic.—*Henry V,* ii, 3, 4.
Rheumatic and cold.—*Venus and Adonis,* l. 135.
Rheumatic as two dry toasts.—*II Henry IV,* ii, 4, 62.
Rheumatic day.—*The Merry Wives of Windsor,* iii, 1, 47. The only uses of "rheumatic."

15
How if he had boils? full, all over, gener-

ally? . . . And those boils did run? say so: did not the general run then? were not that a botchy core? . . . Then would come some matter from him; I see none now.

Troilus and Cressida. Act ii, sc. 1, l. 2. [Thersites] The only use of "botchy."

Boils and plagues.—*Coriolanus,* i, 4, 31. The only uses of "boils" in this sense.

Thou art a boil.—*King Lear,* ii, 4, 226. The only use of "boil" in this sense.

The rotten diseases of the south, the guts-griping, ruptures, catarrhs, loads o' gravel i' the back, lethargies, cold palsies, raw eyes, dirt-rotten livers, wheezing lungs, bladders full of imposthume, sciaticas, limekilns i' the palm, incurable bone-ache, and the rivelled fee-simple of the tetter, take and take again such preposterous discoveries!

Troilus and Cressida. Act v, sc. 1, l. 21. [Thersites] The only use of "guts-griping," "catarrhs," "dirt-rotten," "wheezing," and "rivelled." "Ruptures," "palsies," "imposthume," "sciatica," and "bone-ache" are used only once again. A striking example of Shakespeare's use of unique words and phrases. "Limekiln" is repeated in *The Merry Wives of Windsor,* iii, 3, 86.

DISGRACE

See also Dishonour, Indignity, Infamy

1
Disgraces have of late knocked too often at my door.

All's Well that Ends Well. Act iv, sc. 1, l. 31. [Parolles]

2
The inevitable prosecution of
Disgrace and horror.

Antony and Cleopatra. Act iv, sc. 14, l. 65. [Antony] The only use of "prosecution."

3
Brook such disgrace well as he shall run into.

As You Like It. Act i, sc. 1, l. 140. [Charles]

4
You must not think to fob off our disgrace with a tale.

Coriolanus. Act i, sc. 1, l. 96. [Citizen] The only use of "fob."

5
Disgraced me in my happy victories.

I Henry IV. Act iv, sc. 3, l. 97. [Hotspur]

Disgrace my man's apparel.—*As You Like It,* ii, 4, 4.

My disgrace.—*Macbeth,* iv, 2, 29.

6
Disgrace we have digested.

Henry V. Act iii, sc. 6, l. 136. [Montjoy]

Let it not disgrace me.—*Henry V,* v, 2, 31.

Come, come, 'tis only I that must disgrace thee.

I Henry VI. Act i, sc. 5, l. 8. [La Pucelle]

7
To be disgraced by an inkhorn mate.

I Henry VI. Act iii, sc. 1, l. 99. [Servant]

Disgracing of these colours that I wear.

I Henry VI. Act iii, sc. 4, l. 29. [Vernon] The only use of "disgracing."

Disgrace not so your king.—*I Henry VI,* v, 5, 48.

8
Causeless have laid disgraces on my head.

II Henry VI. Act iii, sc. 1, l. 162. [Gloucester]

Brought . . . in disgrace.—*II Henry VI,* i, 3, 99.

9
When you disgraced me in my embassade,
Then I degraded you from being king.

III Henry VI. Act iv, sc. 3, l. 32. [Warwick] The only use of "embassade."

Quite degraded.—*I Henry VI,* iv, 1, 43. The only uses of "degraded."

10
I cannot promise
But that you shall sustain moe new disgraces,
With these you bear already.

Henry VIII. Act iii, sc. 2, l. 4. [Norfolk]

You'll part away disgraced.—*Henry VIII,* iii, 1, 97.

He hath disgraced me.—*The Merchant of Venice,* iii, 1, 56.

11
How earnestly he cast his eyes upon me!
Pray heaven, he sound not my disgrace!

Henry VIII. Act v, sc. 1, l. 12. [Cranmer]

Full disgrace.—*Coriolanus,* v, 3, 42.

High disgrace.—*Richard II,* i, 1, 194.

Disgrace of death.—*Love's Labour's Lost,* i, 1, 3.

Lives in disgrace.—*Macbeth,* iii, 6, 23.

12
Have I lived to be carried in a basket, like a barrow of butcher's offal, and to be thrown in the Thames?

The Merry Wives of Windsor. Act iii, sc. 5, l. 4. [Falstaff] The only use of "barrow."

Disgrace him for it.—*The Merry Wives of Windsor,* iv, 4, 16.

Unworthily disgrace the man.—*The Two Gentlemen of Verona,* iii, 1, 29.

13
I will join with thee to disgrace her.

Much Ado about Nothing. Act iii, sc. 2, l. 130. [Don Pedro]

You disgraced her, when you should marry her.

Much Ado about Nothing. Act v, sc. 1, l. 245. [Borachio]

14
Through the length of times he stands disgraced.

The Rape of Lucrece, l. 718. "Stand disgraced" is used in l. 1833.

Every eye can see
The same disgrace which they themselves behold.

The Rape of Lucrece, l. 750.

Sighs and groans and tears may grace the fashion
Of her disgrace.

The Rape of Lucrece, l. 1319.

Invisible disgrace.—*The Rape of Lucrece,* l. 827.

15
Nor my own disgrace,
Have ever made me sour my patient cheek,
Or bend one wrinkle on my sovereign's face.

Richard II. Act ii, sc. 1, l. 168. [York]

Their own disgrace.—*A Midsummer-Night's Dream,* iv, 1, 61.

Disgrace to them.—*Romeo and Juliet,* i, 1, 49.

Did them that disgrace.—*Troilus and Cressida,* ii, 2, 95.
Stately Rome's disgrace!—*Titus Andronicus,* iv, 2, 60.

1 In disgrace with fortune and men's eyes.
Sonnets. No. xxix.
Stealing unseen to west with this disgrace.
Sonnets. No. xxxiii.
Thou canst not, love, disgrace me half so ill,
To set a form upon desired change,
As I'll myself disgrace.
Sonnets. No. lxxxix.
Lives in disgrace.—*Sonnets,* cxxvii.

2 Ignomy and shame
Pursue thy life, and live aye with thy name!
Troilus and Cressida. Act v, sc. 10, l. 33. [Troilus]
I blush to think upon this ignomy.
Titus Andronicus, iv, 2, 115.
Ignomy in ransom.—*Measure for Measure,* ii, 4, 111. The only uses of "ignomy."
Thy ignominy sleep with thee in the grave!
I Henry IV, v, 4, 100. The only use of "ignominy."

DISGUISE

See also Mask

3 When his disguise and he parted, tell me what a sprat you shall find him.
All's Well that Ends Well. Act iii, sc. 6, l. 112. [First Lord] The only use of "sprat."

4 Known unto these, and to myself disguised!
The Comedy of Errors. Act ii, sc. 2, l. 216. [Antipholus of Syracuse]
Come in disguised.—*As You Like It,* i, 1, 131.

5 Jove sometime went disguised, and why not I?
II Henry VI. Act iv, sc. 1, l. 48. [Suffolk]
From a God to a bull? a heavy descension! it was Jove's case. From a prince to a prentice? a low transformation! that shall be mine.
II Henry IV. Act ii, sc. 2, l. 192. [Prince of Wales] The only use of "descension."
A botcher's 'prentice.—*All's Well that Ends Well,* iv, 3, 211. "'Prentice" occurs also in *II Henry VI,* i, 3, 201; ii, 3, 71.

6 O, now you look like Hubert! all this while
You were disguised.
King John. Act iv, sc. 1, l. 126. [Arthur]
There's few or none do know me: if they did,
This ship-boy's semblance hath disguised me quite.
King John. Act iv, sc. 3, l. 3. [Arthur]

7 Disguised like Muscovites, in shapeless gear.
Love's Labour's Lost. Act v, sc. 2, l. 303. [Rosaline] "Muscovites" is used also in l. 121 and l. 265, and occurs in no other scene.
Princess: Were not you here but even now disguised?
King: Madam, I was.
Love's Labour's Lost. Act v, sc. 2, l. 433.

8 So disguise shall, by the disguised,
Pay falsehood false exacting,
And perform an old contracting.
Measure for Measure. Act iii, sc. 2, l. 294. [Duke] The only use of "exacting" and "contracting."

9 I'll hold thee any wager,
When we are both accoutred like young men,
I'll prove the prettier fellow of the two,
And wear my dagger with a braver grace.
The Merchant of Venice. Act iii, sc. 4, l. 62. [Portia]

10 I have a disguise to sound Falstaff.
The Merry Wives of Windsor. Act ii, sc. 1, l. 246. [Ford]
Mrs. Ford: How might we disguise him?
Mrs. Page: Alas the day, I know not! There is no woman's gown big enough for him; otherwise he might put on a hat, a muffler and a kerchief.
Merry Wives of Windsor. Act iv, sc. 2, l. 70. "Muffler" is used twice more in this scene, in l. 81 and l. 205, and in *Henry V,* iii, 6, 33.
Go out disguised.—*The Merry Wives of Windsor,* iv, 2, 69.
Strange disguises.—*Much Ado about Nothing,* iii, 2, 33.

11 Do me grace,
And offer me disguised in sober robes.
The Taming of the Shrew. Act i, sc. 2, l. 131. [Hortensio]
Disguised thus to get your love.
The Taming of the Shrew. Act iii, sc. 1, l. 33. [Lucentio]
Disguise of love.—*The Two Gentlemen of Verona,* v, 4, 107.

12 Disguise the holy strength of their command.
Troilus and Cressida. Act ii, sc. 3, l. 136. [Patroclus]

13 Such disguise as haply shall become
The form of my intent.
Twelfth Night. Act i, sc. 2, l. 54. [Viola]
Disguise, I see, thou art a wickedness,
Wherein the pregnant enemy does much.
Twelfth Night. Act ii, sc. 2, l. 28. [Viola]

14 Take your sweetheart's hat
And pluck it o'er your brows, muffle your face,
Dismantle you, and, as you can, disliken
The truth of your own seeming.
The Winter's Tale. Act iv, sc. 4, l. 663. [Camillo] The only use of "disliken."

DISH

See also Cookery, Eating, Food

15 He will to his Egyptian dish again.
Antony and Cleopatra. Act ii, sc. 6, l. 134. [Enobarbus]
Dutch dish.—*The Merry Wives of Windsor,* iii, 5, 121.
Chameleon's dish.—*Hamlet,* iii, 2, 99.
Cold dishes.—*Cymbeline,* ii, 3, 119.
Covered dishes.—*Timon of Athens,* iii, 6, 55.
Dainty dish.—*The Comedy of Errors,* iii, 1, 23.
Full dish.—*Troilus and Cressida,* v, 1, 10.

Nourishing dishes.—*Othello,* iii, 3, 78.
Strange dishes.—*Much Ado about Nothing,* ii, 3, 23.
Unclean dish.—*As You Like It,* iii, 3, 37.
An unwholesome dish.—*Troilus and Cressida,* ii, 3, 129.
A velvet dish.—*The Taming of the Shrew,* iv, 3, 65.

1
If I prove a good repast to the spectators, the dish pays the shot
Cymbeline. Act v, sc. 4, l. 157. [Posthumus]

2
She had a good dish of prawns; whereby thou didst desire to eat some.
II Henry IV. Act ii, sc. 1, l. 104. [Hostess] The only mention of prawns.
The prince once set a dish of apple-johns before him.
II Henry IV. Act ii, sc. 4, l. 5. [Drawer] Apple-johns, a kind of apple supposed to keep three years, are mentioned again in l. 2, and in *I Henry IV,* iii, 3, 5.
A dish of butter.—*I Henry IV,* ii, 4, 134.
A dish of caraways.—*II Henry IV,* v, 3, 3. The only mention of caraways.
A dish of doves.—*The Merchant of Venice,* ii, 2, 144.
A dish o' poison.—*Twelfth Night,* ii, 5, 123.
A dish of skim milk.—*I Henry IV,* ii, 3, 35.
A dish of stewed prunes.—*The Merry Wives of Windsor,* i, 1, 296.

3
A dish fit for the gods.
Julius Cæsar. Act ii, sc. 1, l. 173. [Brutus]
A dish for the gods.—*Antony and Cleopatra,* v, 2, 275.
A dish for a king.—*The Winter's Tale,* iv, 3, 8.

4
Pompey: A fruit-dish, a dish of some three-pence; your honours have seen such dishes; they are not China dishes, but very good dishes.
Escalus: Go to, go to: no matter for the dish, sir.
Measure for Measure. Act ii, sc. 1, l. 95. The only use of "fruit-dish" and "China."

5
Here 's a dish I love not.
Much Ado about Nothing. Act ii, sc. 1, l. 283. [Benedick]
Here, take away this dish.
The Taming of the Shrew. Act iv, sc. 3, l. 44. [Petruchio]

6
Grumio: What say you to a piece of beef and mustard?
Katharina: A dish that I do love to feed upon.
The Taming of the Shrew. Act iv, sc. 3, l. 23.

DISHONESTY

7
Most dishonestly he doth deny it.
The Comedy of Errors. Act v, sc. 1, l. 3. [Angelo]
Dishonestly afflicted.—*Cymbeline,* iv, 2, 40. The only uses of "dishonestly."

8
Don John: How canst thou cross this marriage?
Borachio: Not honestly, my lord; but so covertly that no dishonesty shall appear in me.
Much Ado about Nothing. Act ii, sc. 2, l. 8. The only use of "covertly."

9
I 'll no more of you: besides you grow dishonest.
Twelfth Night. Act i, sc. 5, l. 45. [Olivia]
Bid the dishonest man mend himself; if he mend, he is no longer dishonest; if he cannot let the botcher mend him.
Twelfth Night. Act i, sc. 5, l. 49. [Clown]

10
Fie, thou dishonest Satan!
Twelfth Night. Act iv, sc. 2, l. 35. [Clown]
Hang him, dishonest rascal!
The Merry Wives of Windsor. Act iii, sc. 3, l. 196. [Mrs. Page]
Hang him, dishonest varlet!
The Merry Wives of Windsor. Act iv, sc. 2, l. 104. [Mrs. Page]
O dishonest Wretch!
Measure for Measure. Act iii, sc. 1, l. 137. [Isabella]

11
To bide upon 't, thou art not honest, or,
If thou inclinest that way, thou art a coward,
Which hoxes honesty behind.
The Winter's Tale. Act i, sc. 2, l. 242. [Leontes] The only use of "hoxes" (hamstring)

DISHONOUR

See also Disgrace, Shame, Stain

12
Dodge
And palter in the shifts of lowness; who
With half the bulk o' the world play'd as I pleased,
Making and marring fortunes.
Antony and Cleopatra. Act iii, sc. 11, l. 62. [Antony] The only use of "dodge."
I have lived in such dishonour, that the gods
Detest my baseness.
Antony and Cleopatra. Act iv, sc. 14, l. 56. [Antony]
Shall they hoist me up
And show me to the shouting varletry
Of censuring Rome? Rather a ditch in Egypt
Be gentle grave unto me! rather on Nilus' mud
Lay me stark naked, and let the water-flies
Blow me into abhorring!
Antony and Cleopatra. Act v, sc. 2, l. 55. [Cleopatra] The only use of "varletry."
'Stroy'd in dishonour.—*Antony and Cleopatra,* iii, 11, 54. The only use of "'stroy'd."

13
This so dishonour'd rub, laid falsely
I' the plain way of his merit.
Coriolanus. Act iii, sc. 1, l. 60. [Cominius]
Your dishonour
Mangles true judgement and bereaves the state
Of that integrity which should become 't,
Not having the power to do the good it would,
For the ill which doth control 't.
Coriolanus. Act iii, sc. 1, l. 157. [Coriolanus]
A brand to the end o' the world.
Coriolanus. Act iii, sc. 1, l. 304. [Menenius]
Why brand they us with base?
King Lear, i, 2, 9. See under **Baseness.**

1
Now, this no more dishonours you at all
Than to take in a town with gentle words.
Coriolanus. Act iii, sc. 2, l. 58. [Volumnia]
To beg of thee, it is my more dishonour.
Coriolanus. Act iii, sc. 2, l. 124. [Volumnia]
2
What is the matter I am so dishonour'd?
Coriolanus. Act iii, sc. 3, l. 60. [Coriolanus]
So dishonoured.—*The Rape of Lucrece,* l. 1185.
Dishonour'd to your noses.—*Coriolanus,* iv, 6, 83.
Dishonour'd by my sons!—*Titus Andronicus,* i, 1, 385.
Dishonoured by this new marriage.—*III Henry VI,* iv, 1, 33.
In this marriage . . . dishonour'd.—*Romeo and Juliet,* iv, 3, 26.
Dishonour'd in the court of Rome.—*Titus Andronicus,* ii, 1, 52.
Dshonour'd openly.—*Titus Andronicus,* i, 1, 432.
Profaned, dishonour'd.—*Richard III,* iv, 4, 367.
3
Cloten: Is it fit I went to look upon him? is there no derogation in 't?
Second Lord: You cannot derogate, my lord.
Cymbeline. Act ii, sc. 1, l. 46. The only use of "derogation."
Your issues . . . do not derogate.
Cymbeline. Act ii, sc. 1, l. 51. [Lord]
Derogate body.—*King Lear,* i, 4, 302. The only uses of "derogate." "Derogately" occurs once, in *Antony and Cleopatra,* ii, 2, 34.
4
Could you on this fair mountain leave to feed,
And batten on this moor?
Hamlet. Act iii, sc. 4, l. 66. [Hamlet] "Batten" is used again in *Coriolanus,* iv, 5, 35: "Batten on cold bits."
That would dishonour him.—*Hamlet,* ii, 1, 27.
I may dishonour him.—*Pericles,* i, 2, 21.
5
Whilst I, by looking on the praise of him,
See riot and dishonour stain the brow
Of my young Harry.
I Henry IV. Act i, sc. 1, l. 84. [King Henry]
O, who shall believe
But you misuse the reverence of your place,
Employ the countenance and grace of heaven,
As a false favourite doth his prince's name,
In deeds dishonourable?
II Henry IV. Act iv, sc. 2, l. 22. [Lancaster]
6
Do not so dishonour me.
I Henry VI. Act iii, sc. 2, l. 90. [Bedford]
My sons would never so dishonour me.
Titus Andronicus. Act i, sc. 1, l. 295.
Confederates all thus to dishonour me.
Titus Andronicus. Act i, sc. 1, l. 303. [Saturninus]
'Tis thou and those that have dishonour'd me.
Titus Andronicus. Act i, sc. 1, l. 425. [Titus]
Abused and dishonour'd me.—*The Comedy of Errors,* v, 1, 199.
Dishonour'd all our family.—*Titus Andronicus,* i, 1, 345.
Dishonoured my kinswoman.—*Much Ado about Nothing,* iv, 1, 304.
Dishonour'd Gloucester's honest name.—*II Henry VI,* ii, 1, 199.
7
This dishonour in thine age
Will bring thy head with sorrow to the ground!
II Henry VI. Act ii, sc. 3, l. 18. [Gloucester]
I rather would have lost my life betimes
Than bring a burthen of dishonour home.
II Henry VI. Act iii, sc. 1, l. 297. [York]
Never yet did base dishonour blur our name,
But with our sword we wiped away the blot.
II Henry VI. Act iv, sc. 1, l. 39. [Whitmore]
8
It were dishonour to deny it her.
III Henry VI. Act iii, sc. 2, l. 9. [King Edward]
Pronounce dishonour of her.—*Henry VIII,* ii, 3, 4.
Dark dishonour.—*Richard II,* i, 1, 169.
Dishonour, shame.—*Rape of Lucrece,* l. 654.
Danger and dishonour.—*III Henry VI,* iii, 3, 75.
Disgrace and dishonour.—*Tempest,* iv, 1, 209.
9
It is no vicious blot, murder, or foulness,
No unchaste action, or dishonour'd step,
That hath deprived me of your grace and favour.
King Lear. Act i, sc. 1, l. 230. [Cordelia]
10
Dishonour not your eye
By throwing it on any other object.
Measure for Measure, v, 1, 22. See under JUSTICE.
My lord, I am more amazed at his dishonour
Than at the strangeness of it.
Measure for Measure. Act v, sc. 1, l. 385. [Escalus]
11
O, she is fallen
Into a pit of ink, that the wide sea
Hath drops too few to wash her clean again
And salt too little which may season give
To her foul-tainted flesh!
Much Ado about Nothing. Act iv, sc. 1, l. 141. [Leonato] The only use of "foul-tainted."
For charitable prayers,
Shards, flints and pebbles should be thrown on her.
Hamlet. Act v, sc. 1, l. 253. [First Priest] "Shards" is repeated in *Antony and Cleopatra,* iii, 2, 19.
Not palating the taste of her dishonour.
Troilus and Cressida. Act iv, sc. 1, l. 59. [Diomedes] The only use of "palating."
Gone she is To death or to dishonour.
Cymbeline. Act iii, sc. 5, l. 62. [Queen]
Dishonour her.—*Much Ado about Nothing,* v, 1, 44.
12
Most heathenish and most gross!
Othello. Act v, sc. 2, l. 313. [Cassio] The only use of "heathenish."
13
O foul dishonour to my household's grave!
The Rape of Lucrece, l. 198.
It had been dishonour to disdain him.
The Rape of Lucrece, l. 844.
14
Shall I so much dishonour my fair stars,
On equal terms to give him chastisement?
Richard II. Act iv, sc. 1, l. 21. [Aumerle]

1
The George, profaned, hath lost his holy honour;
The garter, blemish'd, pawn'd his knightly virtue;
The crown, usurp'd, disgraced his kingly glory.
Richard III. Act iv, sc. 4, l. 369. [Queen Elizabeth]

Inglorious league!—*King John*, v, 1, 65. The only use of "inglorious."

2 No, precious creature;
I had rather crack my sinews, break my back,
Than you should such dishonour undergo,
While I sit lazy by.
The Tempest. Act iii, sc. 1, l. 25. [Ferdinand]

3 Suffer not dishonour to approach
The imperial seat, to virtue consecrate,
To justice, continence and nobility.
Titus Andronicus. Act i, sc. 1, l. 13. [Bassianus] The only use of "continence."

When wert thou wont to walk alone,
Dishonour'd thus, and challenged of wrongs?
Titus Andronicus. Act i, sc. 1, l. 339. [Titus]

The gods of Rome forfend
I should be author to dishonour you!
Titus Andronicus. Act i, sc. 1, l. 434. [Tamora]

DISLIKE

See also Hatred

4 Mere dislike
Of our proceedings kept the earl from hence.
I Henry IV. Act iv, sc. 1, l. 64. [Worcester]

I have not sought the day of this dislike.
I Henry IV. Act v, sc. 1, l. 26. [Worcester]

5
Your affections and your appetites and your disgestions doo 's not agree with it.
Henry V. Act v, sc. 1, l. 26. [Fluellen] The only use of "disgestions."

6
'Tis not my speeches that you do mislike,
But 'tis my presence that doth trouble ye.
II Henry VI. Act i, sc. 1, l. 140. [Gloucester]

Mislike my speech.—*Antony and Cleopatra*, iii, 13, 147.

Mislike me not.—*Merchant of Venice*, ii, 1, 1.

Setting your . . . mislike aside.—*III Henry VI*, iv, 1, 24. The only uses of "mislike."

7
So your dislike, to whom I would be pleasing,
Doth cloud my joys with danger and with sorrow.
III Henry VI. Act iv, sc. 1, l. 73. [Queen Elizabeth]

We like not this; thou dost forget thyself.
King John. Act iii, sc. 1, l. 134. [King John]

I 'll do 't; but it dislikes me.
Othello. Act ii, sc. 3, l. 49. [Cassio]

People dislike it.—*Twelfth Night*, i, 5, 119.

8
The ground of your ill-will.
Richard III. Act i, sc. 3, l. 69. [Queen Elizabeth]

Ill will never said well.
Henry V. Act iii, sc. 7, l. 123. [Orleans]

Rosalind: Why look you so upon me?
Phebe: For no ill will I bear you.
As You Like It. Act iii, sc. 5, l. 70.

Derive me ill will.—*All's Well that Ends Well*, v, 3, 265. The only uses of "ill will."

9
Ill-thought on of her and ill-thought on of you.
Troilus and Cressida. Act i, sc. 1, l. 70. [Pandarus] The only uses of "ill-thought."

What, in ill thoughts again?
King Lear, v, 2, 9. See under THOUGHT. The only use of "ill thoughts."

10
You feed too much on this dislike.
Troilus and Cressida. Act ii, sc. 3, l. 235. [Ulysses]

11
In my conscience, sir, I do not care for you: if that be to care for nothing, sir, I would it would make you invisible.
Twelfth Night. Act iii, sc. 1, l. 33. [Clown]

You are now sailed into the north of my lady's opinion; where you will hang like an icicle on a Dutchman's beard, unless you do redeem it by some laudable attempt either of valour or policy.
Twelfth Night. Act iii, sc. 2, l. 28. [Fabian] "Laudable" is repeated in *Macbeth*, iv, 2, 76.

I can hardly forbear hurling things at him.
Twelfth Night. Act iii, sc. 2, l. 87. [Maria] The only use of "hurling."

DISLOYALTY, see Falseness

DISMAY

12
Be not dismay'd, for succour is at hand.
I Henry VI. Act i, sc. 2, l. 50. [Bastard]

Be not dismay'd.—*I Henry VI*, ii, 3, 73; *The Merry Wives of Windsor*, iii, 4, 26; *Coriolanus*, iv, 6, 150.

Be thou not dismay'd.—*Richard III*, v, 3, 174.

Dismay not.—*I Henry VI*, iii, 3, 1.

13
In this there can be no dismay.
The Merchant of Venice. Act i, sc. 3, l. 182. [Antonio]

She shall not dismay me.—*The Merry Wives of Windsor*, iii, 4, 27.

14
Live thou, I live: with much much more dismay
I view the fight than thou that makest the fray.
The Merchant of Venice. Act iii, sc. 2, l. 61. [Portia]

Brimful of . . . dismay.—*Tempest*, v, 1, 14.

Full of . . . dismay.—*Hamlet*, iv, 1, 45.

15
Do you go back dismay'd? 'tis a lost fear;
Man but a rush against Othello's breast,
And he retires.
Othello. Act v, sc. 2, l. 269. [Othello]

Ran dismay'd away.—*The Merchant of Venice*, v, 1, 9.

16
You do look, my son, in a moved sort,
As if you were dismay'd.
The Tempest. Act iv, sc. 1, l. 146. [Prospero]

DISMISSAL

1
Will you dismiss the people?
Coriolanus. Act ii, sc. 3, l. 162. [Brutus]
Dimiss them home.—*Coriolanus,* iv, 2, 7.

2
In rage dismiss'd my father from the court.
I Henry IV. Act iv, sc. 3, l. 100. [Hotspur]
Show us the hand of God
That hath dismiss'd us from our stewardship.
Richard II. Act iii, sc. 3, l. 77. [King Richard] "Stewardship" is repeated in ii, 2, 59.
Dismiss'd me thus.—*Coriolanus,* v, 1, 66.
My best train
I have from your Sicilian shores dismiss'd.
Winter's Tale. Act v, sc. 1, l. 163. [Florizel] The only use of "Sicilian."
His army dismiss'd.—*II Henry VI,* iv, 9, 40.
Fifty men dismiss'd?—*King Lear,* ii, 4, 210.
Ere they be dismiss'd, let them march by.
II Henry IV. Act iv, sc. 2, l. 96. [Lancaster]
Dismissed bachelor.—*The Tempest,* iv, 1, 67.
Dismiss'd offence.—*Measure for Measure,* ii, 2, 102. The only uses of "dismiss'd."

3 With thanks and pardon to you all,
I do dismiss you to your several countries.
II Henry VI. Act iv, sc. 9, l. 20. [King]
I do dismiss my powers.
II Henry VI. Act v, sc. 1, l. 44. [York]
Dismiss his power.—*I Henry IV,* iv, 4, 37.
Dismiss the powers.—*King John,* v, 1, 64.
Dismiss your army.—*I Henry VI,* v, 4, 173.
Dismiss your attendant.—*Othello,* iv, 3, 8.
Dismiss your followers.—*Titus Andronicus,* i, 1, 44.
Dismiss my soldiers.—*Coriolanus,* v, 3, 82.

4
O, dismiss this audience, and I shall tell you more.
Love's Labour's Lost, iv, 3, 210. [Biron]
Bassianus: I will here dismiss my loving friends . . .
Saturninus: I thank you all and here dismiss you all.
Titus Andronicus. Act i, sc. 1, l. 53.
Dismiss the controversy.—*Coriolanus,* ii, 1, 85.
Dismiss this court.—*The Merchant of Venice,* iv, 1, 104.
Dismiss your vows.—*Venus and Adonis,* l. 425.

5
Desdemona: He hath . . . bade me to dismiss you.
Emilia: Dismiss me!
Desdemona: It was his bidding; therefore, good Emilia,
Give me my nightly wearing, and adieu.
Othello. Act iv, sc. 3, l. 13.
Dismiss me.—*Macbeth,* iv, 1, 72.
Dismiss me hence.—*I Henry VI,* ii, 5, 30.
Please you dismiss me.—*III Henry VI,* iii, 2, 78.
Dismiss him.—*Measure for Measure,* iv, 2, 27.
Dismiss it.—*Twelfth Night,* i, 5, 117.
Dismiss itself.—*Julius Cæsar,* i, 3, 97.

II—Some Variations

6
Go thy ways, I begin to be aweary of thee.
All's Well that Ends Well. Act iv, sc. 5, l. 59. [Lafeu] "Go thy ways" occurs sixteen times.
Go to; away!—*The Tempest,* v, 1, 297. "Go to" is used as a terminal throughout the plays.

7
Your dismission Is come from Cæsar.
Antony and Cleopatra. Act i, sc. 1, l. 26. [Cleopatra] "Dismission" is repeated in *Cymbeline,* ii, 3, 57.

8
Mistress, dispatch you with your safest haste
And get you from our court.
As You Like It. Act i, sc. 3, l. 43. [Duke]

9
Thou basest thing, avoid! hence, from my sight!
If after this command thou fraught the court
With thy unworthiness, thou diest: away!
Cymbeline. Act i, sc. 1, l. 125. [Cymbeline]
O, get thee from my sight.
Cymbeline. Act v, sc. 5, l. 236. [Imogen]

10
Get thee to a nunnery. . . . Go thy ways to a nunnery. . . . Get thee to a nunnery, go: farewell. . . . To a nunnery, go, and quickly too.
Hamlet. Act iii, sc. 1, l. 122. [Hamlet] "Nunnery" is used these four times in this scene, and nowhere else.
Bestow this place on us a little while.
Hamlet. Act iv, sc. 1, l. 4. [Queen]
Give us the place alone.
Twelfth Night. Act i, sc. 5, l. 235. [Olivia]

11
You have good leave to leave us: when we need
Your use and counsel, we shall send for you.
I Henry IV. Act i, sc. 3, l. 20. [King Henry]

12
You hunt counter; hence! avaunt!
II Henry IV. Act i, sc. 2, l. 102. [Falstaff]
Rogues, hence, avaunt! vanish like hailstones, go.
The Merry Wives of Windsor. Act i, sc. 3, l. 90. [Falstaff] The only use of "hailstones." "Hailstone" occurs in *Coriolanus,* i, 1, 178.
Peasant, avaunt!—*I Henry VI,* v, 4, 21.
Avaunt, thou dreadful minister of hell!—*Richard III,* i, 2, 46.
Avaunt, thou witch!—*Comedy of Errors,* iv, 3, 80.
Traitors, avaunt!—*Titus Andronicus,* i, 1, 283.
Avaunt, thou hateful villain!—*King John,* iv, 3, 77.
Avaunt, you cullions!—*Henry V,* iii, 2, 21.
Avaunt, be gone! . . . Hence, avaunt!—*Othello,* iii, 3, 335; iv, 1, 271.
Avaunt, you curs!—*King Lear,* iii, 6, 68.
Avaunt! and quit my sight!—*Macbeth,* iii, 4, 93.

13
No more, Pistol; I would not have you go off here: discharge yourself of our company, Pistol.
I Henry IV. Act ii, sc. 4, l. 146. [Falstaff]

14
No; to the spital go.
Henry V. Act ii, sc. 1, l. 78. [Pistol] "Spital" (hospital) is repeated in v, 1, 86: "Dead i' the spital," and occurs in no other play. "Spital-house" is used in *Timon of Athens,* iv, 3, 39.

1
Away, base cullions!
II Henry VI. Act i, sc. 3, l. 43. [Queen Margaret] "Cullion" (base fellow) is repeated in *The Taming of the Shrew,* iv, 2, 20, and in *Henry V,* iii, 2, 22.

Away, and talk not; trouble us no more.
Titus Andronicus. Act i, sc. 1, l. 478. [Saturninus]

I will not hear her speak; away with her!
Titus Andronicus. Act ii, sc. 3, l. 137. [Tamora]

Away, thou rag, thou quantity, thou remnant.
The Taming of the Shrew. Act iv, sc. 3, l. 112. [Petruchio]

Thou rag of honour.—*Richard III,* i, 3, 233.
Poor rag.—*Timon of Athens,* iv, 3, 271.

Away, I say! stay'st thou to vex me here?
The Two Gentlemen of Verona. Act iv, sc. 4, l. 66. [Proteus]

Away, you Ethiope!
A Midsummer-Night's Dream. Act iii, sc. 2, l. 257. [Lysander]

Away, you scullion! you rampallian! you fustilarian!
II Henry IV. Act ii, sc. 1, l. 65. [Falstaff] "Scullion" (kitchen servant) is used again in *Hamlet,* ii, 2, 616. "Rampallian" (ruffian) and "fustilarian" (frowzy woman) are unique.

Away, you whoreson upright rabbit, away!
II Henry IV. Act ii, sc. 2, l. 91. [Bardolph]

What! you poor base, rascally, cheating, lack-linen mate! Away, you mouldy rogue, away! . . . Away, you cut-purse rascal! you filthy bung, away! . . . Away, you bottle-ale rascal! you basket-hilt stale juggler, you!
II Henry IV. Act ii, sc. 4, l. 133. [Doll Tearsheet] The only use of "lack-linen," "bung," "bottle-ale rascal," and "basket-hilt juggler."

Away, away, be gone!—*Julius Cæsar,* iv, 3, 138.
Away, slight man!—*Julius Cæsar,* iv, 3, 37.

2
To send me packing.
II Henry VI. Act iii, sc. 1, l. 342. [York]

Be packing, therefore, thou that wast a knight.
I Henry VI. Act iv, sc. 1, l. 46. [King]

Ere a fortnight make me elder,
I'll send some packing that yet think not on it.
Richard III. Act iii, sc. 2, l. 62. [Hastings]

'Faith, and I'll send him packing.
I Henry IV. Act ii, sc. 4, l. 328. [Falstaff]

Trudge, plod away o' the hoof; seek shelter, pack!
The Merry Wives of Windsor. Act i, sc. 3, l. 91. [Falstaff]

Pack and be gone.—*The Comedy of Errors,* iii, 2, 158.
Hence, pack!—Timon of Athens, v, 1, 115.
Bid me pack.—*The Taming of the Shrew,* ii, 1, 178; *The Merchant of Venice,* ii, 2, 11.
Pack up.—*Coriolanus,* i, 5, 9.

3
But, with an angry wafture of your hand,
Gave sign for me to leave you.
Julius Cæsar. Act ii, sc. 1, l. 246. [Portia] The only use of "wafture."

4
Hie hence.
Julius Cæsar. Act iii, sc. 1, l. 290. [Antony]

Get you hence, sirrah; saucy fellow, hence!
Julius Cæsar. Act iv, sc. 3, l. 134. [Brutus]

Hence, and avoid my sight!
King Lear. Act i, sc. 1, l. 126. [King Lear]

As for thee, boy, go get thee from my sight.
Titus Andronicus. Act iii, sc. 1, l. 284. [Titus]

5
Stand not upon the order of your going,
But go at once.
Macbeth. Act iii, sc. 4, l. 119. [Lady Macbeth]

6
Leave procreants alone and shut the door.
Othello. Act iv, sc. 2, l. 28. [Othello] "Procreant" (bringing forth young) is repeated in *Macbeth,* i, 6, 8.

7
If thou love me, 'tis time thou wert away.
Richard II. Act v, sc. 5, l. 96. [King Richard]

8
Out of my sight! thou dost infect my eyes.
Richard III. Act i, sc. 2, l. 149. [Lady Anne]

Out, you green-sickness carrion! out, you baggage!
You tallow-face!
Romeo and Juliet. Act iii, sc. 5, l. 157. [Capulet] The only use of "tallow-face." For "green-sickness" see under DISEASE.

Out, tawny Tartar, out!
Out, loathed medicine! hated potion, hence!
A Midsummer-Night's Dream. Act iii, sc. 2, l. 263. [Lysander]

9
Away with the joint-stools, remove the court-cupboard, look to the plate.
Romeo and Juliet. Act i, sc. 5, l. 7. [Servant] The only use of "court-cupboard" (a movable cabinet to display plate).

I took you for a joint-stool.
King Lear, iii, 6, 54. The only uses of "joint-stool" (a stool finely made by a joiner as distinguished from one of rough make).

10
An you be mine, I'll give you to my friend;
An you be not, hang, beg, starve, die in the streets.
Romeo and Juliet. Act iii, sc. 5, l. 193. [Capulet]

Go, you cot-quean, go.
Romeo and Juliet. Act iv, sc. 4, l. 6. [Nurse] The only use of "cot-quean" (a man who busies himself unduly in the housewife's affairs).

Go, get thee hence, for I will not away.
Romeo and Juliet. Act v, sc. 3, l. 160. [Juliet]

Go, hop me over every kennel home.
The Taming of the Shrew. Act iv, sc. 3, l. 98. [Petruchio]

11
Second Lord: Away, unpeaceable dog, or I'll spurn thee hence!
Apemantus: I will fly, like a dog, the heels o' the ass.
Timon of Athens. Act i, sc. 1, l. 281. The only use of "unpeaceable."

I prithee, beat thy drum, and get thee gone.
Timon of Athens. Act iv, sc. 3, l. 96. [Timon]

Thy back, I prithee.—*Timon of Athens,* iv, 3, 395.

1
Trouble me no more, but get you gone.
Titus Andronicus. Act i, sc. 1, l. 367. [Titus]
Go, get you gone.
Titus Andronicus. Act iv, sc. 3, l. 21. [Titus]
Hence, get thee gone, and follow me no more.
A Midsummer-Night's Dream. Act ii, sc. 1, l. 194. [Demetrius]

Get you gone, you dwarf;
You minimus, of hindering knot-grass made;
You bead, you acorn.
A Midsummer-Night's Dream. Act iii, sc. 2, l. 328. [Lysander] The only use of "minimus" (dwarf) and "knot-grass" (a weed supposed to stunt the growth).
Get thee gone, but do it.
The Merchant of Venice. Act iv, sc. 1, l. 397. [Duke]

2
If you be not mad, be gone.
Twelfth Night. Act i, sc. 5, l. 211. [Olivia]

Therefore be gone
Without our grace, our love, our benison.
King Lear. Act i, sc. 1, l. 267. [King Lear]
Hence with thy stripes, be gone!
Antony and Cleopatra. Act iii, sc. 13, l. 152. [Antony] Shakespeare uses "be gone" thirty-seven times.

3
Maria: Will you hoist sail, sir? here lies your way.
Viola: No, good swabber; I am to hull here a little longer.
Twelfth Night. Act i, sc. 5, l. 215. "Swabber" is repeated in *The Tempest,* ii, 2, 48; and "hull" in *Richard III,* iv, 4, 438.
Sir Toby: 'Shall I bid him go, and spare not?'
Clown: 'O no, no, no, no, you dare not.'
Twelfth Night. Act ii, sc. 3, l. 120.
Go, sir, rub your chain with crums.
Twelfth Night. Act ii, sc. 3, l. 128. [Sir Toby] "Crums" is repeated in *King Lear,* i, 4, 217.
Out, scab!—*Twelfth Night,* ii, 5, 82.
Go off; I discard you: let me enjoy my private: go off.
Twelfth Night. Act iii, sc. 4, l. 99. [Malvolio]

4
We 'll thwack him hence with distaffs.
The Winter's Tale. Act i, sc. 2, l. 37. [Hermione] "Thwack" is used three times in *Coriolanus,* iv, 5, 189 *et seq.*

DISOBEDIENCE

5
They nourish'd disobedience, fed
The ruin of the state.
Coriolanus. Act iii, sc. 1, l. 117. [Coriolanus]

6
Thou that didst set up
My disobedience 'gainst the king my father.
Cymbeline. Act iii, sc. 4, l. 90. [Imogen]

Prepare to die
For disobedience to your father's will.
A Midsummer-Night's Dream. Act i, sc. 1, l. 86. [Theseus]

7
I do see
Danger and disobedience in thine eye.
I Henry IV. Act i, sc. 3, l. 15. [King Henry]
Both disobedience and ingratitude.—*The Winter's Tale,* iii, 2, 69.
Most infallible disobedience.—*All's Well that Ends Well,* i, 1, 150.
Wilful disobedience!—*I Henry VI,* iv, 1, 142.

8
Swear . . . never to disobey.
I Henry VI. Act v, sc. 4, l. 170. [York]
Disobey the wife of Jupiter.—*The Tempest,* iv, 1, 77.

9
The sin Of disobedient opposition.
Romeo and Juliet. Act iv, sc. 2, l. 17. [Juliet]

She is peevish, sullen, froward,
Proud, disobedient, stubborn, lacking duty.
The Two Gentlemen of Verona. Act iii, sc. 1, l. 68. [Duke]
Most disobedient.—*Troilus and Cressida,* ii, 2, 182.
Disobedient wretch!—*Romeo and Juliet,* iii, 5, 161. The only uses of "disobedient."

DISORDER, see Confusion

DISPLEASURE

10
Parolles: I know not how I have deserved to run into my lord's displeasure.
Lafeu: You have made shift to run into 't, boots and spurs and all, like him, that leaped into the custard; and out of it you 'll run again, rather than suffer question for your residence.
All's Well that Ends Well. Act ii, sc. 5, l. 37. The only use of "custard."
He hath incurred the everlasting displeasure of the king.
All's Well that Ends Well. Act iv, sc. 3, l. 10. [Lord]
Stop up the displeasure he hath conceived against your son.
All's Well that Ends Well. Act iv, sc. 5, l. 80. [Lafeu]
Fallen into the unclean fishpond of her displeasure.
All's Well that Ends Well, v, 2, 22. See under KNAVE. The only use of "fishpond."
Not fearing the displeasure of your master,
Which on your just proceeding I 'll keep off.
All's Well that Ends Well. Act v, sc. 3, l. 235. [King]
Strong displeasure.—*All's Well that Ends Well,* v, 2, 6.
Fortune's displeasure.—*All's Well that Ends Well,* v, 2, 7.

11
Oft our displeasures, to ourselves unjust,
Destroy our friends and after weep their dust.
All's Well that Ends Well. Act v, sc. 3, l. 63. [King]
Do displeasure to himself.—*The Comedy of Errors,* iv, 4, 119.
Doing displeasure.—*The Comedy of Errors,* v, 1, 142.

12
When it appears to you where this begins,
Turn your displeasure that way.
Antony and Cleopatra. Act iii, sc. 4, l. 33. [Antony]
Displeasure of the people.—*Coriolanus,* ii, 2, 24.
Malice and displeasure.—*Coriolanus,* iv, 5, 78.

1
Villain, thou didst deny the gold's receipt
And told'st me of a mistress and a dinner;
For which, I hope, thou felt'st I was displeased.
The Comedy of Errors. Act ii, sc. 2, l. 17. [Antipholus of Syracuse] The only use of "felt'st."

There's reason he should be displeased at it.
II Henry VI. Act i, sc. 1, l. 155. [Beaufort]

No matter who's displeased when you are gone.
The Two Gentlemen of Verona. Act ii, sc. 7, l. 66. [Lucetta]

Go displeased away.—*The Merchant of Venice,* v, 1, 213.

You are not displeased?—*Titus Andronicus,* i, 1, 270.

Much displeased.—*Richard III,* ii, 2, 89; *Measure for Measure,* iv, 1, 13.

According as he pleased and displeased.—*Julius Cæsar,* i, 2, 262.

Having displeased my father.—*Romeo and Juliet,* iii, 5, 232. The only uses of "displeased."

2
I shall incur I know not
How much of his displeasure.
Cymbeline. Act i, sc. 1, l. 102. [Queen]

My fear is, your displeasure.—*II Henry IV,* Epil., 2.

3
That's a perilous shot out of an elder-gun, that a poor and a private displeasure can do against a monarch!
Henry V. Act iv, sc. 1, l. 210. [Williams] The only use of "elder-gun" (pop-gun made of a hollowed shoot of elder).

His moods, and his displeasures.—*Henry V,* iv, 7, 38. See under MOOD.

4
Wolsey: What news abroad?
Cromwell: The heaviest and the worst
Is your displeasure with the king.
Henry VIII, iii, 2, 391. See under NEWS.

He's settled . . . in his displeasure.
Henry VIII. Act iii, sc. 2, l. 23. [Norfolk]

5
Run To meet displeasure.
King John. Act v, sc. 1, l. 60. [Bastard]

Run in your displeasure.—*Henry VIII,* i, 2, 110.

6
Parted you in good terms? Found you no displeasure in him by word or countenance?
King Lear. Act i, sc. 2, l. 171. [Edmund]

Forbear his presence till some little time hath qualified the heat of his displeasure.
King Lear. Act i, sc. 2, l. 175. [Edmund]

He, conjunct, and flattering his displeasure,
Tripp'd me behind.
King Lear. Act ii, sc. 2, l. 125. [Oswald] "Conjunct" is repeated in v, 1, 12, and occurs in no other play.

On pain of their perpetual displeasure.
King Lear. Act iii, sc. 3, l. 4. [Gloucester]

7
Leave him to my displeasure.
King Lear. Act iii, sc. 7, l. 6. [Cornwall]

With our displeasure pieced.—*King Lear,* i, 1, 202.

8
This may prove food to my displeasure.
Much Ado about Nothing. Act i, sc. 3, l. 67. [Don John]

I am sick in displeasure to him.
Much Ado about Nothing. Act ii, sc. 2, l. 5. [Don John]

9
I am sorry
For your displeasure; but all will sure be well.
Othello. Act iii, sc. 1, l. 44. [Emilia]

I have been talking with a suitor here,
A man that languishes in your displeasure.
Othello. Act iii, sc. 3, l. 42. [Desdemona]

Stood within the blank of his displeasure.
Othello. Act iii, sc. 4, l. 128. [Desdemona]

10
Urged withal Your high displeasure.
Romeo and Juliet. Act iii, sc. 1, l. 160. [Benvolio]

On height of our displeasure.—*Timon of Athens,* iii, 5, 87.

11
Let it not displease thee.
The Taming of the Shrew. Act i, sc. 1, l. 76. [Baptista]

We must not now displease him.—*Othello,* iv, 3, 17.

12
If I should take a displeasure against you.
The Tempest. Act iv, sc. 1, l. 201. [Stephano]

Took some displeasure at him.
Pericles. Act i, sc. 3, l. 21. [Helicanus]

Ta'en displeasure.—*As You Like It,* i, 2, 290.

13
Let us depart, I pray you,
Lest your displeasure should enlarge itself
To wrathful terms.
Troilus and Cressida. Act v, sc. 2, l. 36. [Ulysses]

14
On your displeasure's peril and on mine,
She should not visit you.
The Winter's Tale. Act ii, sc. 3, l. 45. [Antigonus]

Though full of our displeasure, yet we free thee
From the dead blow of it.
The Winter's Tale. Act iv, sc. 4, l. 443. [Polixenes]

DISPOSITION

See also Character, Temperament

15
Cleopatra: What, was he sad or merry?
Alexas: Like to the time o' the year between the extremes
Of hot and cold, he was nor sad nor merry.
Cleopatra: O well-divided disposition! note him,
Note him, good Charmian, 'tis the man; but note him:
He was not sad, for he would shine on those
That make their looks by his; he was not merry,
Which seemed to tell them his remembrance lay
In Egypt with his joy; but between both:
O heavenly mingle! Be'st thou sad or merry,
The violence of either thee becomes,

So does it no man else.
Antony and Cleopatra. Act i, sc. 5, l. 50. The only use of "well-divided," and of "mingle" as a noun.

1
My father's rough and envious disposition
Sticks me at heart.
As You Like It. Act i, sc. 2, l. 253. [Celia]

Coming-on disposition.—*As You Like It,* iv, 1, 112. The only use of "coming-on" as a hyphenated phrase.

Evil disposition.—*Measure for Measure,* i, 2, 122; *King Lear,* iii, 5, 7.

Goatish disposition.—*King Lear,* i, 2, 138. The only use of "goatish."

Man's disposition.—*The Merry Wives of Windsor,* iv, 5, 111.

2
Away, my disposition, and possess me
Some harlot's spirit!
Coriolanus. Act iii, sc. 2, l. 111. [Coriolanus]

3
Put an antic disposition on.
Hamlet. Act i, sc. 5, l. 172. [Hamlet]

A truant disposition.—*Hamlet,* i, 2, 169.

4
Put away
These dispositions that of late transform you
From what you rightly are.
King Lear. Act i, sc. 4, l. 241. [Goneril]

Never afflict yourself to know the cause;
But let this disposition have that scope
That dotage gives it.
King Lear. Act i, sc. 4, l. 313. [Goneril]

I fear your disposition:
That nature, which contemns its origin,
Cannot be border'd certain in itself;
She that herself will sliver and disbranch
From her material sap, perforce must wither,
And come to deadly use.
King Lear. Act iv, sc. 2, l. 31. [Albany] The only use of "border'd" and "disbranch," and of "sliver" as a verb. As a noun, it occurs in *Hamlet,* iv, 7, 174: "Envious sliver."

5
Of what disposition was the duke?
Measure for Measure. Act iii, sc. 2, l. 244. [Duke]

'Tis the duke's pleasure,
Whose disposition, all the world well knows,
Will not be rubb'd nor stopp'd.
King Lear. Act ii, sc. 2, l. 159. [Gloucester]

6
He is of a very melancholy disposition.
Much Ado about Nothing, ii, 1, 6. [Hero]

Her disposition, being addicted to a melancholy.
Twelfth Night. Act ii, sc. 5, l. 222. [Maria]

7
Entertain a cheerful disposition.
Richard II. Act ii, sc. 2, l. 4. [Bushy]

Of disposition gentle.—*Henry VIII,* ii, 4, 87.

Of free disposition.—*Twelfth Night,* i, 5, 99.

Good disposition.—*Twelfth Night,* iii, 1, 146.

Better disposition.—*Winter's Tale,* iii, 3, 28.

Royal disposition.—*Richard III,* i, 3, 63; *As You Like It,* iv, 3, 118.

So blessed a disposition.—*Othello,* ii, 3, 326.

8
It is the base, though bitter, disposition of Beatrice.
Much Ado about Nothing. Act ii, sc. 1, l. 215. [Benedick] "Bitter disposition" is repeated in *Troilus and Cressida,* iv, 1, 48.

9
I know our country disposition well.
Othello. Act iii, sc. 3, l. 201. [Iago]

I thought thy disposition better temper'd.
Romeo and Juliet. Act iii, sc. 3, l. 115. [Friar Laurence]

DISPUTE

See also Argument, Debate

10
He is too disputable for my company.
As You Like It. Act ii, sc. 5, l. 36. [Jaques] The only use of "disputable."

11
Vouchsafe me, look you, a few disputations with you . . . in way of argument, look you, and friendly communication.
Henry V. Act iii, sc. 2, l. 101. [Fluellen]

12
Thou disputest like an infant: go, whip thy gig.
Love's Labour's Lost. Act v, sc. 1, l. 69. [Holofernes] The only use of "disputest."

Whipping a gig.—*Love's Labour's Lost,* iv, 3, 167.

I will whip . . . a gig of cuckold's horn.—*Love's Labour's Lost,* v, 1, 73. The only uses of "gig."

13
I 'll have 't disputed on.
Othello, i, 2, 75. The only use of "disputed."

14
Thus, graceless, holds he disputation
'Tween frozen conscience and hot-burning will.
The Rape of Lucrece, l. 246. "Hot-burning" is repeated in l. 1557: "Hot-burning fire."

Holds disputation with each thing she views.
The Rape of Lucrece, l. 1101.

A theme for disputation.—*The Rape of Lucrece,* l. 822.

A feeling disputation.—*I Henry IV,* iii, 1, 206. The only uses of "disputation." "Disputations" occurs in *Henry V,* iii, 2, 101. See above.

15
Let me dispute with thee of thy estate.
Romeo and Juliet. Act iii, sc. 3, l. 63. [Friar Laurence]

Dispute it like a man.—*Macbeth,* iv, 3, 220.

Dispute not that.—*II Henry VI,* i, 3, 111.

Dispute not with her.—*Richard III,* i, 3, 254.

Disputes well.—*Twelfth Night,* iv, 3, 9.

Dispute his own estate.—*The Winter's Tale,* iv, 4, 411.

Disputing of your generals.—*I Henry VI,* i, 1, 73. The only use of "disputing."

DISSEMBLING

See also Deceit, Pretence, Seeming

16
I prithee, turn aside and weep for her;
Then bid adieu to me, and say the tears
Belong to Egypt: good now, play one scene

Of excellent dissembling; and let it look
Like perfect honour.
Antony and Cleopatra. Act i, sc. 3, l. 76. [Cleopatra]

1
I would dissemble with my nature where
My fortunes and my friends at stake required
I should do so in honour.
Coriolanus. Act iii, sc. 2, l. 62. [Volumnia]

2
So help me God, as I dissemble not!
I Henry VI. Act iii, sc. 1, l. 140. [Gloucester]

I must dissemble.—*II Henry VI,* v, 1, 13; *Pericles,* ii, 5, 23.
I will dissemble.—*Twelfth Night,* iv, 2, 5.
See thou dissemble not.—*The Taming of the Shrew,* ii, 1, 9.
Dissemble not your hatred.—*Richard III,* ii, 1, 8.
See him dissemble.—*Timon of Athens,* v, 1, 98.
All dissembling set aside.—*III Henry VI,* iii, 3, 119.

3
O, hardness to dissemble!
Othello. Act iii, sc. 4, l. 34. [Othello]

4
Arise, dissembler.
Richard III. Act i, sc. 2, l. 185. [Anne]

Thou dissembler, thou.—*Much Ado about Nothing,* v, 1, 53. The only uses of "dissembler."
All dissemblers.—*Romeo and Juliet,* iii, 2, 87. The only use of "dissemblers."

5
Think you my uncle did dissemble, grandam?
Richard III. Act ii, sc. 2, l. 31. [Boy]

Dissemble deeply.—*The Taming of the Shrew,* iv, 4, 42.
Dissemble all your griefs and discontents.
Titus Andronicus, i, 1, 443. [Tamora]

6
I will dissemble myself in it; and I would I were the first that ever dissembled in such a gown.
Twelfth Night. Act iv, sc. 2, l. 5. [Clown]

Dissembled her delight.—*The Passionate Pilgrim,* l. 314.
Dissembled with an outward show.—*The Passionate Pilgrim,* l. 336.
Fury not dissembled.—*Titus Andronicus,* i, 1, 438. The only uses of "dissembled."

7
O thou dissembling cub! what wilt thou be
When time hath sow'd a grizzle on thy case?
Or will not else thy craft so quickly grow,
That thine own trip shall be thine overthrow?
Twelfth Night. Act v, sc. 1, l. 167. [Duke] The only use of "grizzle."

Dissembling colour.—*As You Like It,* iii, 4, 7.
Dissembling courtesy.—*Cymbeline,* i, 1, 84.
Dissembling luxurious drab.—*Troilus and Cressida,* v, 4, 8.
Dissembling glass.—*A Midsummer-Night's Dream,* ii, 2, 98.
Dissembling guile.—*I Henry VI,* iv, 1, 63.
Dissembling harlot.—*The Comedy of Errors,* iv, 4, 103.
Dissembling knight.—*The Merry Wives of Windsor,* iii, 3, 152.
Dissembling looks.—*Richard III,* i, 2, 237.
Dissembling nature.—*Richard III,* i, 1, 19.

DISSENSION

See also Discord, Quarrel

8
And for dissension, who preferreth peace
More than I do?—except I be provoked.
I Henry VI. Act iii, sc. 1, l. 33. [Gloucester]

Civil dissension is a viperous worm
That gnaws the bowels of the commonwealth.
I Henry VI. Act iii, sc. 1, l. 72. [King Henry]

9
This late dissension grown betwixt the peers
Burns under feigned ashes of forged love
And will at last break out into a flame.
I Henry VI. Act iii, sc. 1, l. 189. [Exeter]

Let this dissension first be tried by fight,
And then your highness shall command a peace.
I Henry VI. Act iv, sc. 1, l. 116. [York]

If they perceive dissension in our looks
And that within ourselves we disagree,
How will their grudging stomachs be provoked
To wilful disobedience!
I Henry VI. Act iv, sc. 1, l. 139. [King] The only use of "disagree."

I feel such sharp dissension in my breast,
Such fierce alarums both of hope and fear,
As I am sick with working of my thoughts.
I Henry VI. Act v, sc. 5, l. 84. [King Henry] Though Shakespeare uses the word "dissension" only ten times in all the plays, he repeats it six times in *I Henry VI.*

10
Now join your hands, and with your hands your hearts,
That no dissension hinder government.
III Henry VI. Act iv, sc. 6, l. 39. [King Henry]

This same progeny of evils comes
From our debate, from our dissension.
A Midsummer-Night's Dream. Act ii, sc. 1, l. 115. [Titania]

DISTANCE

See also Space

11
If there be breadth enough in the world, I will hold a long distance.
All's Well that Ends Well. Act iii, sc. 2, l. 26. [Countess]

Just distance.—*II Henry IV,* iv, 1, 226.
Safest distance.—*A Lover's Complaint,* l. 151.

12
Pray, how far thither?
'Ods pittikins! can it be six mile yet?
Cymbeline. Act iv, sc. 2, l. 293. [Imogen] The only use of "'Ods pittikins."

13
We 'll digest The abuse of distance.
Henry V. Act ii, Prologue, l. 31. [Chorus]

14
How fearful
And dizzy 'tis, to cast one's eyes so low!
The crows and choughs that wing the midway air
Show scarce so gross as beetles: half way down

Hangs one that gathers samphire, dreadful trade!
Methinks he seems no bigger than his head:
The fishermen, that walk upon the beach,
Appear like mice; and yond tall anchoring bark,
Diminish'd to her cock; her cock, a buoy
Almost too small for sight: the murmuring surge,
That on the unnumber'd idle pebbles chafes,
Cannot be heard so high. I 'll look no more;
Lest my brain turn, and the deficient sight
Topple down headlong.
King Lear. Act iv, sc. 6, l. 11. [Edgar] The only use of "samphire" and "buoy."

1 He shall in strangeness stand no further off
Than in a politic distance.
Othello. Act iii, sc. 3, l. 12. [Desdemona]
Fell off a distance.—*Henry VIII,* iv, 1, 65.
Keeps distance.—*Romeo and Juliet,* ii, 4, 22.

2 She that dwells
Ten leagues beyond man's life.
The Tempest. Act ii, sc. 1, l. 246. [Antonio]
In strands afar remote.
I Henry IV. Act i, sc. 1, l. 4. [King Henry]

DISTINCTION

See also Difference

3 I have no skill in sense To make distinction.
All's Well that Ends Well. Act iii, sc. 4, l. 40. [Countess]
We can hardly make distinction.—*Twelfth Night,* ii, 3, 175.
Make distinction.—*Cymbeline,* iv, 2, 248.
Confound distinction.—*All's Well that Ends Well,* ii, 3, 127. See under Blood.
Your distinction?—*All's Well that Ends Well,* iv, 5, 27.
Scarce distinction.—*Antony and Cleopatra,* iii, 1, 29.
Without distinction.—*Coriolanus,* iii, 1, 323.

4 In the wind and tempest of her frown,
Distinction, with a broad and powerful fan,
Puffing at all, winnows the light away;
And what hath mass or matter, by itself
Lies rich in virtue and unmingled.
Troilus and Cressida. Act i, sc. 3, l. 26. [Agamemnon] The only use of "winnows." "Winnow" occurs in *Cymbeline,* v, 5, 134: "Winnow the truth from falsehood"; and "unmingled" in *The Comedy of Errors,* ii, 2, 129.
I do fear besides
That I shall lose distinction in my joys.
Troilus and Cressida, iii, 2, 27. See under Joy.

DISTRACTION

See also Madness

5 Give him no breath, but now
Make boot of his distraction.
Antony and Cleopatra. Act iv, sc. 1, l. 9. [Mecænas]

6 The fellow is distract, and so am I.
The Comedy of Errors. Act iv, sc. 3, l. 42. [Antipholus of Syracuse]
Is not this a heavy case,
To see thy noble uncle thus distract?
Titus Andronicus. Act iv, sc. 3, l. 25. [Marcus]
They say, poor gentleman, he 's much distract.
Twelfth Night. Act v, sc. 1, l. 287. [Viola]
As one distract.—*II Henry VI,* iii, 2, 318.
She fell distract.—*Julius Cæsar,* iv, 3, 155.
She is . . . distract.—*Hamlet,* iv, 5, 2.
Better I were distract.—*King Lear,* iv, 6, 288.

7 He does confess he feels himself distracted;
But from what cause he will by no means speak.
Hamlet. Act iii, sc. 1, l. 5. [Rosencrantz]
They stared, and were distracted.
Macbeth. Act ii, sc. 3, l. 110. [Lennox]
All three distracted.—*The Tempest,* v, 1, 12.

8 I am punish'd With sore distraction.
Hamlet. Act v, sc. 2, l. 240. [Hamlet]
This is a mere distraction.
Henry VIII. Act iii, sc. 1, l. 112. [Wolsey]

9 Stop again, As if thou wert distraught.
Richard III, iii, 5, 4. See under Terror.
Shall I not be distraught,
Environed with all these hideous fears?
Romeo and Juliet. Act iv, sc. 3, l. 49. [Juliet] The only uses of "distraught."

10 And these mine enemies are all knit up
In their distractions.
The Tempest. Act iii, sc. 3, l. 89. [Prospero]
In the distraction of this madding fever!
Sonnets. No. cxix. See under Eye.

11 You flow to great distraction.
Troilus and Cressida. Act v, sc. 2, l. 41. [Ulysses]
Behold, distraction, frenzy and amazement,
Like witless antics, one another meet.
Troilus and Cressida. Act v, sc. 3, l. 85. [Cassandra]

12 You look
As if you held a brow of much distraction.
The Winter's Tale. Act i, sc. 2, l. 148. [Hermione]

DISTRESS

See also Misery, Suffering

13 I do pity his distress in my similes of comfort.
All's Well that Ends Well. Act v, sc. 2, l. 26. [Clown]

14 Art thou thus bolden'd, man, by thy distress?
As You Like It. Act ii, sc. 7, l. 91. [Duke Senior] "Bolden'd" is repeated in *Henry VIII,* i, 2, 55.
The thorny point
Of bare distress hath ta'en from me the show
Of smooth civility.
As You Like It. Act ii, sc. 7, l. 94. [Orlando]
Hard distress.—*I Henry VI,* ii, 5, 87.

1
Poor distressed soul!
The Comedy of Errors. Act iv, sc. 4, l. 62. [Adriana]
Distressed queen.—*III Henry VI,* iii, 3, 213; *Titus Andronicus,* i, 1, 103.
Distressed lord.—*I Henry VI,* iv, 3, 30; *Pericles,* i, 4, 7.
Distressed plight.—*Titus Andronicus,* iv, 4, 32.
Distressed gentleman.—*Pericles,* i, 4, 7.
Distressed widow.—*Richard III,* iii, 7, 185; iv, 4, 98.
Poor distressed Lear.—*King Lear,* v, 3, 40.
Do not Upbraid 's with our distress.
Coriolanus, v, 1, 35. See under AID.
In my distress.—*Richard III,* i, 4, 273.
Answer my distress.—*Titus Andronicus,* iii, 1, 38.

2
Belarius: He wrings at some distress.
Arviragus: Would I could free 't!
Cymbeline. Act iii, sc. 6, l. 79.

3
Distress likes dumps when time is kept with tears.
The Rape of Lucrece, l. 1127. See under MELANCHOLY.
Where all distress and dolour dwell'd.
The Rape of Lucrece, l. 1446. For "dolour" see under SORROW.

4
Our fatherless distress was left unmoan'd.
Richard III. Act ii, sc. 2, l. 64. [Girl] The only use of "unmoan'd." "Fatherless" is repeated in *Macbeth,* iv, 2, 27.
Despised, distressed, hated, martyr'd, kill'd!
Romeo and Juliet. Act iv, sc. 5, l. 59. [Capulet]
Deeply distress'd.—*Venus and Adonis,* l. 814.
Threefold distress'd.—*Richard III,* ii, 2, 86.

5
She is much out of quiet.
Twelfth Night. Act ii, sc. 3, l. 144. [Maria] See also QUIET.

DISTRUST

See also Mistrust; Suspicion; Trust: Lack of Trust

6
Make me not offended In your distrust.
Antony and Cleopatra. Act iii, sc. 2, l. 33. [Antony]
It had been vicious To have mistrusted her.
Cymbeline. Act v, sc. 5, l. 65. [Cymbeline]

7
You are so sick of late,
So far from cheer and from your former state,
That I distrust you. Yet, though I distrust,
Discomfort you, my lord, it nothing must.
Hamlet. Act iii, sc. 2, l. 173. [Player Queen]

8
One sudden foil shall never breed distrust.
I Henry VI. Act iii, sc. 3, l. 11. [Charles]

9
Too hot, too hot!
To mingle friendship far is mingling bloods.
I have tremor cordis on me: my heart dances;
But not for joy; not joy.
The Winter's Tale. Act i, sc. 2, l. 108. [Leontes] The only use of "tremor cordis."
The infection of my brains
And hardening of my brows.
Winter's Tale. Act i, sc. 2, l. 145. [Leontes]

DIVISION

10
Cement their divisions and bind up
The petty difference.
Antony and Cleopatra. Act ii, sc. 1, l. 48. [Pompey]

11
You shall Divide in all with us.
Coriolanus. Act i, sc. 6, l. 86. [Cominius]
My having is not much;
I 'll make division of my present with you:
Hold, there 's half my coffer.
Twelfth Night. Act iii, sc. 4, l. 379. [Viola]

12
His divisions, as the times do brawl,
Are in three heads: one power against the French,
And one against Glendower; perforce a third
Must take up us.
II Henry IV. Act i, sc. 3, l. 70. [Hastings] The only use of "divisions" in the sense of battalions or squadrons.

13
Into a thousand parts divide one man,
And make imaginary puissance.
Henry V. Prologue, l. 24.
Divide him inventorially.—*Hamlet,* v, 2, 118. The only use of "inventorially."
Divide me from your bosom.—*Antony and Cleopatra,* ii, 3, 2.
Divide themselves between you.—*Cymbeline,* ii, 4, 130.
Divides one thing entire to many objects.
Richard II, ii, 2, 17. See under EYE.
Divide the conquest of thy sight.
Sonnets. No. xlvi.
Divide in two slow rivers.
The Rape of Lucrece, l. 1737.
Divide my crown.—*I Henry VI,* i, 6, 18.
Divide our equalness.—*Antony and Cleopatra,* v, 1, 47. The only use of "equalness."
Divide eternity in twain.—*Troilus and Cressida,* ii, 3, 256.
Divide thy lips.—*Troilus and Cressida,* i, 3, 72.
Divide our power.—*I Henry IV,* v, 5, 34.
Divide the realm.—*Richard II,* v, 1, 60.
Divide the Sunday from the week.—*Hamlet,* i, 2, 76.
Divide the times.—*III Henry VI,* ii, 5, 30.
The three-fold world divided.—*Julius Cæsar,* iv, 1, 14.

14
Never come such division 'tween our souls!
Julius Cæsar. Act iv, sc. 3, l. 235. [Cassius]

15
Know that we have divided
In three our kingdom.
King Lear. Act i, sc. 1, l. 38. [King Lear]
Division of the kingdom.—*King Lear,* i, 1, 4.

16
Beshrew your eyes,
They have o'erlook'd me and divided me;
One half of me is yours, the other half yours,
Mine own, I would say; but if mine, then yours,
And so all yours.
The Merchant of Venice. Act iii, sc. 2, l. 14. [Portia]

1
Lodovico: Is there division 'twixt my lord and Cassio?
Desdemona: A most unhappy one.
Othello. Act iv, sc. 1, l. 242.
There 's a division betwixt the dukes.
King Lear. Act iii, sc. 3, l. 9. [Gloucester]
There is division,
Although as yet the face of it be cover'd
With mutual cunning.
King Lear. Act iii, sc. 1, l. 19. [Kent]
Ravishing division.—*I Henry IV,* iii, 1, 211.
Sweet division.—*Romeo and Juliet,* iii, 5, 29.
Unkind division.—*I Henry VI,* iv, 1, 193.
Division of our amity.—*II Henry IV,* iii, 1, 79.
The division of the twentieth part
Of one poor scruple.
The Merchant of Venice. Act iv, sc. 1, l. 329. [Portia]

2
Reason, in itself confounded,
Saw division grow together,
To themselves yet either neither,
Simple was so well compounded.
The Phœnix and the Turtle, l. 41.
Division none.—*Phœnix and the Turtle,* l. 27.

3
O, if you raise this house against this house,
It will the woefullest division prove
That ever fell upon this cursed earth.
Richard II. Act iv, sc. 1, l. 145. [Bishop of Carlisle] "Woefullest" is repeated in *II Henry VI,* iii, 2, 409: "Woefull'st cask"; and in *Titus Andronicus,* iii, 1, 290: "Woefull'st man."

4
Must we be divided? must we part?
Richard II, v, 1, 81. See under Parting.
Divided in their dire division.
Richard III. Act v, sc. 5, l. 28. [Richmond]

5
We to-morrow hold divided councils.
Richard III, iii, 1, 179. See under Council.
Divided duty.—*Othello,* i, 3, 181.
Divided friendship.—*Richard III,* i, 4, 244.

6
Even for this let us divided live.
Sonnets, xxxix.
Divided . . . Into two.—*I Henry VI,* v, 2, 11.
Divided it Into three.—*I Henry IV,* iii, 1, 72.
In three divided.—*II Henry IV,* i, 3, 74.
Divided Between her heart and lips.—*Antony and Cleopatra,* iv, 14, 32.
Divided from herself.—*Hamlet,* iv, 5, 85.
She divideth us.—*Romeo and Juliet,* iii, 5, 30. The only use of "divideth."

7
Even in a dream, were we divided from them.
The Tempest. Act v, sc. 1, l. 238. [Boatswain]

8
And yet the spacious breadth of this division
Admits no orifex for a point as subtle
As Ariachne's broken woof to enter.
Troilus and Cressida. Act v, sc. 2, l. 150. [Troilus] The only mention of Ariachne, and the only use of "orifex" and "woof."

9
How have you made division of yourself?
Twelfth Night, v, 1, 229. See under Likeness.
In his own division.—*Much Ado about Nothing,* v, 1, 230.

DIVORCE

10
Deadly divorce step between me and you!
All's Well that Ends Well. Act v, sc. 3, l. 319. [Helena]
And from my false hand cut the wedding-ring
And break it with a deep-divorcing vow?
The Comedy of Errors. Act ii, sc. 2, l. 139. [Adriana] The only use of "wedding-ring" and "deep-divorcing."

11
That horrid act Of the divorce he 'ld make!
Cymbeline. Act ii, sc. 1, l. 67. [Lord]
Make divorce.—*Henry V,* v, 2, 394.

12
I here divorce myself
Both from thy table, Henry, and thy bed.
III Henry VI. Act i, sc. 1, l. 247. [Queen Margaret]

13
The long divorce of steel falls on me.
Henry VIII, ii, 1, 76. See under Prayer.

14
In the divorce his contrary proceedings
Are all unfolded.
Henry VIII. Act iii, sc. 2, l. 26. [Norfolk]
He counsels a divorce; a loss of her
That, like a jewel, has hung twenty years
About his neck yet never lost her lustre.
Henry VIII. Act ii, sc. 2, l. 31. [Norfolk]
He will divorce you.
Othello. Act i, sc. 2, l. 14. [Iago]

15
By the main assent
Of all these learned men she was divorced,
And the late marriage made of none effect.
Henry VIII. Act iv, sc. 1, l. 32. [Gentleman]
Divorced, wronged, spited!—*Romeo and Juliet,* iv, 5, 55.

16
I would divorce me from my mother's tomb.
King Lear, ii, 4, 133. See under Tomb.
Quite divorce his memory from his part.
Love's Labour's Lost, v, 2, 150. See under Contempt.
Divorce this terror from my heart.
Richard II, v, 4, 9. See under Terror.
Divorce not wisdom from your honour.
II Henry IV, i, 1, 162. See under Wisdom.
Divorce my dignities.—*Henry VIII,* iii, 1, 142.

17
You have in manner with your sinful hours
Made a divorce betwixt his queen and him.
Richard II. Act iii, sc. 1, l. 11. [Bolingbroke]
Doubly divorced! Bad men, you violate
A twofold marriage, 'twixt my crown and me,
And then betwixt me and my married wife.
Richard II. Act v, sc. 1, l. 71. [King Richard]
Lamentable divorce.—*Cymbeline,* i, 4, 20.
Ugly, meagre, lean, Hateful divorce.—*Venus and Adonis,* l. 932.
Unjust divorce.—*The Comedy of Errors,* i, 1, 105.
Beggarly divorcement.—*Othello,* iv, 2, 158. The only use of "divorcement."

1
Dear divorce 'Twixt natural son and sire!
Timon of Athens, iv, 3, 382. See under GOLD.

2
Florizel: Mark our contract.
Polixenes: Mark your divorce, young sir.
The Winter's Tale. Act iv, sc. 4, l. 427.

DOCTOR

See also Disease, Medicine

3
A father . . . whose skill was almost as great as his honesty; had it stretched so far, would have made nature immortal, and death should have play for lack of work. Would, for the king's sake, he were living! I think it would be the death of the king's disease.
All's Well that Ends Well. Act i, sc. 1, l. 21. [Countess]

King: How long is 't, count,
Since the physician at your father's died?
He was much famed.
Bertram: Some six months since, my lord.
King: If he were living, I would try him yet.
All's Well that Ends Well. Act i, sc. 2, l. 70.

He and his physicians
Are of a mind; he, that they cannot help him,
They, that they cannot help.
All's Well that Ends Well. Act i, sc. 3, l. 243. [Countess]

Doctor She.
All's Well that Ends Well. Act ii, sc. 1, l. 82. [Lafeu]

Sit, my preserver, by thy patient's side.
All's Well that Ends Well. Act ii, sc. 3, l. 53. [King]

4
Good Doctor Pinch, you are a conjurer;
Establish him in his true sense again.
The Comedy of Errors. Act iv, sc. 4, l. 50. [Adriana]

Give me your hand and let me feel your pulse.
The Comedy of Errors. Act iv, sc. 4, l. 55. [Pinch]

5 Who worse than a physician
Would this report become? But I consider,
By medicine life may be prolong'd, yet death
Will seize the doctor too.
Cymbeline. Act v, sc. 5, l. 27. [Cymbeline]

The sure physician, death.
Cymbeline, v, 4, 7. See under DEATH.

Death is our physician.—*Othello,* i, 3, 311.

6
He was much fear'd by his physicians.
I Henry IV. Act iv, sc. 1, l. 24. [Messenger] See under SICKNESS.

His physicians fear him mightily.
Richard III, i, 1, 137. See under KING.

7
I care not if I do become your physician.
II Henry IV, i, 2, 143. See under ATTENTION.

I take not on me here as a physician.
II Henry IV. Act iv, sc. 1, l. 60. [Archbishop of York]

Profess myself your . . . physician.—*The Winter's Tale,* ii, 3, 54.

Poor physician.—*All's Well that Ends Well,* ii, 3, 122.

Renowned French physician.—*The Merry Wives of Windsor,* iii, 1, 61.

King's physician.—*Henry VIII,* v, 2, 11.

8
I 'll to the surgeon's.
I Henry VI. Act iii, sc. 1, l. 146. [Servant]

Go, villain, fetch a surgeon.
Romeo and Juliet. Act iii, sc. 1, l. 97. [Mercutio]

For the love of God, a surgeon!
Twelfth Night. Act v, sc. 1, l. 175. [Sir Andrew]

O, help, ho! light! a surgeon!
Othello. Act v, sc. 1, l. 30. [Cassio]

Go get him surgeons.
Macbeth. Act i, sc. 2, l. 44. [Duncan]

Let me have surgeons; I am cut to the brains.
King Lear. Act iv, sc. 6, l. 196. [King Lear]

For your hurts, myself will be your surgeon.
Othello. Act ii, sc. 3, l. 253. [Othello]

9
Kill thy physician, and the fee bestow
Upon thy foul disease.
King Lear, i, 1, 166. See under DISEASE.

10
More needs she the divine than the physician.
Macbeth. Act v, sc. 1, l. 82. [Doctor]

11
Now, by mine honour, which is yet mine own,
I 'll have that doctor for my bedfellow.
The Merchant of Venice. Act v, sc. 1, l. 232. [Portia]

By this ring, the doctor lay with me.
The Merchant of Venice. Act v, sc. 1, l. 259. [Portia]

Sweet doctor, you shall be my bed-fellow:
When I am absent, then lie with my wife.
The Merchant of Venice. Act v, sc. 1, l. 284. [Bassanio]

A learned doctor.—*The Merchant of Venice,* iv, 1, 105.

Doctors learn'd.—*Henry VIII,* ii, 4, 206.

A young and learned doctor.—*The Merchant of Venice,* iv, 1, 144.

Young doctor.—*Merchant of Venice,* iv, 1, 153.

Most reverend doctor.—*The Merchant of Venice,* iv, 1, 226.

A civil doctor.—*Merchant of Venice,* v, 1, 210.

Worthy doctor.—*The Merchant of Venice,* v, 1, 222.

French doctor.—*The Merry Wives of Windsor,* i, 4, 99; ii, 1, 210.

Bully doctor!—*The Merry Wives of Windsor,* ii, 3, 18.

12
What says my Æsculapius? my Galen? my heart of elder?
The Merry Wives of Windsor. Act ii, sc. 3, l. 29. [Host]

Æsculapius guide us!—*Pericles,* iii, 2, 111.
These are the only references to Æsculapius.

He has no more knowledge in Hibocrates and Galen.
The Merry Wives of Windsor. Act iii, sc. 1, l. 66. [Evans] Shakespeare mentions Hippocrates once, and Galen five times.

1
You have showed yourself a wise physician.
The Merry Wives of Windsor. Act ii, sc. 3, l. 55. [Shallow]

That calls himself doctor of physic.
The Merry Wives of Windsor. Act iii, sc. 1, l. 4. [Evans]

Shall I lose my doctor? no; he gives me the potions and the motions.
The Merry Wives of Windsor. Act iii, sc. 1, l. 104. [Host]

Will you cast away your child on a fool, and a physician?
The Merry Wives of Windsor. Act iii, sc. 4, l. 100. [Mistress Quickly]

2
Thou speak'st like a physician.
Pericles. Act i, sc. 2, l. 67. [Pericles]

This we prescribe, though no physician.
Richard II. Act i, sc. 1, l. 154. [King]

Prescribe to other as each other's leech.
Timon of Athens, v, 4, 84. See under MEDICINE. The only use of "leech."

The patient dies while the physician sleeps.
The Rape of Lucrece, l. 904.

3
Now put it, God, in the physician's mind
To help him to his grave immediately!
Richard II. Act i, sc. 4, l. 59. [King Richard]

And thou, too careless patient as thou art,
Commit'st thy anointed body to the cure
Of those physicians that first wounded thee.
Richard II. Act ii, sc. 1, l. 97. [Gaunt]

4
I do remember an apothecary,—
And hereabouts he dwells,—which late I noted
In tatter'd weeds, with overwhelming brows,
Culling of simples; meagre were his looks,
Sharp misery had worn him to the bones:
And in his needy shop a tortoise hung,
An alligator stuff'd, and other skins
Of ill-shaped fishes; and about his shelves
A beggarly account of empty boxes,
Green earthen pots, bladders and musty seeds,
Remnants of packthread and old cakes of roses,
Were thinly scatter'd, to make up a show.
Romeo and Juliet. Act v, sc. 1, l. 37. [Romeo] The only use of "overwhelming," "alligator" and "ill-shaped." "Tortoise" occurs again in *The Tempest,* i, 2, 316; and "thinly" in *Othello,* iii, 3, 431.

A poor 'pothecary.—*Romeo and Juliet,* v, 3, 289. "'Pothecary" is repeated in *Pericles,* iii, 2, 9.

5 Trust not the physician;
His antidotes are poison, and he slays
Moe than you rob.
Timon of Athens. Act iv, sc. 3, l. 434. [Timon]

6
He will be the physician that should be the patient.
Troilus and Cressida. Act ii, sc. 3, l. 223. [Agamemnon]

The surgeon's box, or the patient's wound.
Troilus and Cressida. Act v, sc. 1, l. 12. [Thersites]

DOG

See also Cur, Hound

For dog as a term of opprobrium see under Curse, Denunciation

7
He 's a very dog to the commonalty.
Coriolanus. Act i, sc. 1, l. 28. [Citizens] "Commonalty" is repeated in *Henry VIII,* i, 2, 170.

Dogs that are as often beat for barking
As therefore kept to do so.
Coriolanus. Act ii, sc. 3, l. 224. [Brutus] "Barking" is used again in *I Henry VI,* iii, 4, 33: "Envious barking."

8
The dog will have his day.
Hamlet. Act v, sc. 1, l. 315. [Hamlet] A proverb included in John Heywood's *Proverbs* (Pt. i, ch. 11), published in 1546.

9
'Tis our setter: I know his voice.
I Henry IV, ii, 2, 53. The only use of "setter" in this sense.

10
Hold-fast is the only dog.
Henry V. Act ii, sc. 3, l. 54. [Pistol] The only use of "hold-fast" as a hyphenated phrase. So far as known, the first appearance of this proverb in English literature.

Turn head, and stop pursuit; for coward dogs
Most spend their mouths when what they seem to threaten
Runs far before them.
Henry V. Act ii, sc. 4, l. 69. [Dauphin]

English dogs.—*I Henry VI,* i, 5, 25.

11
Le chien est retourné à son propre vomissement.
Henry V. Act iii, sc. 7, l. 68. [Dauphin] The only use of this French adage, and of "chien."

So, so, thou common dog, didst thou disgorge
Thy glutton bosom of the royal Richard;
And now thou wouldst eat thy dead vomit up,
And howl'st to find it.
II Henry IV. Act i, sc. 3, l. 97. [Archbishop of York] "Vomit," as a noun, is repeated in *Othello,* ii, 3, 86. As a verb, it is used four times.

12
The ancient proverb will be well effected:
'A staff is quickly found to beat a dog.'
II Henry VI. Act iii, sc. 1, l. 170. [Gloucester] A proverb which first appeared in Thomas Becon's *Early Works* (*Preface,* 28), in 1563: "How easy a thing it is to find a staff if a man be minded to beat a dog."

Dogs howl'd.—*III Henry VI,* v, 6, 46.

The dogs did yell.—*Love's Labour 's Lost,* iv, 2, 60.

Play the dog.—*III Henry VI,* v, 6, 77.

13
I had rather be a dog, and bay the moon,
Than such a Roman.
Julius Cæsar. Act iv, sc. 3, l. 27. [Brutus]

'Tis like the howling of Irish wolves against the moon.
As You Like It, v, 2, 118. [Rosalind]

1
And like a dog that is compell'd to fight,
Snatch at his master that doth tarre him on.
King John. Act iv, sc. 1, l. 116. [Arthur]
Tarre the mastiffs on.—*Troilus and Cressida,* i, 3, 392.
Tarre them to controversy.—*Hamlet,* ii, 2, 370.
The only uses of "tarre" (incite).

2 The little dogs and all,
Tray, Blanch, and Sweet-heart, see, they bark at me.
King Lear. Act iii, sc. 6, l. 65. [King Lear]
The only use of "Tray."
Be thy mouth or black or white,
Tooth that poisons if it bite;
Mastiff, greyhound, mongrel grim,
Hound or spaniel, brach or lym,
Or bobtail tike or trundle-tail,
Tom will make them weep and wail:
For, with throwing thus my head,
Dogs leap the hatch, and all are fled.
King Lear. Act iii, sc. 6, l. 69. [Edgar]
The only use of "lym" (bloodhound), "bobtail," and "trundle-tail" (curly-tailed). "Tike" (a small dog, a cur) is repeated in *Henry V,* ii, 1, 31: "Base tike." "Mastiff" occurs four times.

3
A dog's obeyed in office.
King Lear. Act iv, sc. 6, l. 160. [King Lear]
For full quotation, see under AUTHORITY.

4
Great Hercules is presented by this imp,
Whose club kill'd Cerberus, that three-headed canis.
Love's Labour 's Lost. Act v, sc. 2, l. 593. [Holofernes] The only use of "three-headed" and "canis." Cerberus is mentioned also in *Troilus and Cressida,* ii, 1, 51, and in *Titus Andronicus,* ii, 4, 51.

5
Hath a dog money? is it possible
A cur can lend three thousand ducats?
The Merchant of Venice. Act i, sc. 3, l. 122. [Shylock]
Thou call'dst me dog before thou hadst a cause;
But, since I am a dog, beware my fangs.
The Merchant of Venice. Act iii, sc. 3, l. 6. [Shylock]

6
I am your spaniel; and, Demetrius,
The more you beat me, I will fawn on you . . .
What worser place can I beg in your love,—
And yet a place of high respect with me,—
Than to be used as you use your dog?
A Midsummer-Night's Dream. Act ii, sc. 1, l. 203. [Helena]
Where 's my spaniel?—*The Taming of the Shrew,* iv, 1, 153.
You play the spaniel.—*Henry VIII,* v, 3, 126.
Gelded like a spaniel.—*Pericles,* iv, 6, 133.
Spaniel'd me at heels.—*Antony and Cleopatra,* iv, 12, 21. The only use of "spaniel'd."

7
Dogs, easily won to fawn on any man!
Richard II. Act iii, sc. 2, l. 130. [King Richard]
Sad dog.—*Richard II,* v, 5, 70.
A curtal dog.—*The Comedy of Errors,* iii, 2, 151; *The Merry Wives of Windsor,* ii, 1, 114.
The only uses of "curtal dog" (having the tail docked).

8
Dogs bark at me as I halt by them.
Richard III, i, 1, 23. See under DEFORMITY.
Take heed of yonder dog!
Look, when he fawns, he bites; and when he bites,
His venom tooth will rankle to the death.
Richard III. Act i, sc. 3, l. 289. [Queen Margaret] "Rankle" is repeated in *Richard II,* i, 3, 302.
That dog, that had his teeth before his eyes,
To worry lambs and lap their gentle blood.
Richard III. Act iv, sc. 4, l. 49. [Queen Margaret]
Bloody dogs.—*Richard III,* iv, 3, 6; v, 5, 2.
The phrase is used in no other play.

9
I would not lose the dog for twenty pound.
The Taming of the Shrew. Induction, sc. 1, l. 21. [Lord]
Trust me, I take him for the better dog.
The Taming of the Shrew. Induction, sc. 1, l. 25. [First Huntsman]
What dogs are these!—*The Taming of the Shrew,* iv, 1, 165.

10
The watch-dogs bark: Bow-wow.
The Tempest. Act i, sc. 2, l. 383. [Ariel]
The only use of "watch-dogs."

11
Thou hast whelped a dog, and thou shalt famish a dog's death.
Timon of Athens. Act ii, sc. 2, l. 90. [Page]
For thy part, I do wish thou wert a dog,
That I might love thee something.
Timon of Athens. Act iv, sc. 3, l. 53. [Timon]

12
Thou dost not keep a dog.
Timon of Athens. Act iv, sc. 3, l. 200. [Timon]
Thou hadst some means to keep a dog.
Timon of Athens. Act iv, sc. 3, l. 317. [Timon]

13 I have dogs, my lord,
Will rouse the proudest panther in the chase,
And climb the highest promontory top.
Titus Andronicus. Act ii, sc. 2, l. 20. [Marcus] The panther is mentioned again in i, 1, 493, and ii, 3, 194, and in no other play.
As true a dog as ever fought at head.
Titus Andronicus. Act v, sc. 1, l. 102. [Aaron]

14
Sir Andrew: I am dog at a catch.
Clown: By 'r lady, sir, and some dogs will catch well.
Twelfth Night. Act ii, sc. 3, l. 64.
This is, to give a dog, and in recompense desire my dog again.
Twelfth Night. Act v, sc. 1, l. 7. [Fabian]

15
I think Crab my dog be the sourest-natured dog that lives.
The Two Gentlemen of Verona. Act ii, sc. 3, l. 5. [Launce] The only use of "sourest-natured."

This hat is Nan, our maid: I am the dog: no, the dog is himself, and I am the dog—Oh! the dog is me, and I am myself; ay, so, so.
The Two Gentlemen of Verona. Act ii, sc. 3, l. 24. [Launce]

Now the dog all this while sheds not a tear nor speaks a word.
The Two Gentlemen of Verona. Act ii, sc. 3, l. 34. [Launce]

When a man's servant shall play the cur with him, look you, it goes hard: one that I brought up of a puppy; one that I saved from drowning, when three or four of his blind brothers and sisters went to it. . . . He thrusts me himself into the company of three or four gentlemanlike dogs, under the duke's table: he had not been there—bless the mark!—a pissing while, but all the chamber smelt him. 'Out with the dog!' says one: 'What cur is that?' says another: 'Whip him out' says the third: 'Hang him up' says the duke. I, having been acquainted with the smell before, knew it was Crab, and goes to the fellow that whips the dogs: 'Friend,' quoth I, 'you mean to whip the dog?' 'Ay, marry, do I,' quoth he. 'You do him the more wrong,' quoth I; ''twas I did the thing you wot of.' He makes me no more ado, but whips me out of the chamber. How many masters would do that for his servant?
The Two Gentlemen of Verona. Act iv, sc. 4, l. 1. [Launce]

Drowned a blind bitch's puppies.—*The Merry Wives of Windsor,* iii, 5, 11.
Drown . . . blind puppies.—*Othello,* i, 3, 341.
A kind of puppy.—*Henry VIII,* i, 1, 175.
Puppy greyhound.—*II Henry IV,* ii, 4, 107.
Master puppy.—*Henry VIII,* v, 4, 30.
Puppy-dog.—*Henry V,* iii, 2, 78; *King John,* ii, 1, 460.

1
Another flap-mouth'd mourner, black and grim,
Against the welkin volleys out his voice.
Venus and Adonis, l. 920. The only use of "flap-mouth'd."

DOLOUR, see Grief

DOOM

See also Judgement

2
Tell him, from his all-obeying breath I hear
The doom of Egypt.
Antony and Cleopatra. Act iii, sc. 13, l. 77. [Cleopatra] The only use of "all-obeying."

3
Firm and irrevocable is my doom.
As You Like It. Act i, sc. 3, l. 85. [Duke]

Thou hear'st thy doom.—*I Henry VI,* iv, 1, 45.
This is your doom.—*Richard II,* v, 6, 24.
Confined doom.—*Sonnets,* cvii.
Ending doom.—*Sonnets,* lv.
Everlasting doom.—*Titus Andronicus,* iii, 1, 51.
Gentle doom.—*Sonnets,* cxlv.
Great doom.—*Macbeth,* ii, 3, 83.
Injurious doom.—*III Henry VI,* iii, 3, 101.
Perpetual doom.—*The Merry Wives of Windsor,* v, 5, 62.
Doom perpetual.—*Richard III,* iv, 4, 12.
Secret doom.—*I Henry IV,* iii, 2, 6.
Doom of death.—*The Comedy of Errors,* i, 1, 2; *Titus Andronicus,* iii, 1, 24; *Henry V,* iii, 6, 46.
Doom her death.—*Titus Andronicus,* iv, 2, 114.
Doom my brother's death.—*Richard III,* ii, 1, 102.
Doom men to death.—*Titus Andronicus,* iii, 1, 47.
Doom thee death.—*Romeo and Juliet,* iii, 1, 139.
Doom of destiny.—*Richard III,* iv, 4, 217.
Doom of mercy.—*III Henry VI,* ii, 6, 46.
Doomed to die.—*Comedy of Errors,* i, 1, 155.

4
It skills not greatly who impugns our doom.
II Henry VI. Act iii, sc. 1, l. 281. [York] The only use of "impugns." "Impugn" occurs in *The Merchant of Venice,* iv, 1, 179: "Cannot impugn you."

And humbly thus, with halters on their necks,
Expect your highness' doom, of life or death.
II Henry VI. Act iv, sc. 9, l. 11. [Clifford]

5
Alter not the doom Forethought by heaven!
King John. Act iii, sc. 1, l. 311. [Constance] The only use of "forethought."

Reverse thy doom.—*King Lear,* i, 1, 151; i, 1, 167.
Reverse a prince's doom.—*Romeo and Juliet,* iii, 3, 59.
Revoke that doom.—*III Henry VI,* ii, 6, 46.
Revoke thy doom.—*King Lear,* i, 1, 167.

The doom—
Which, unreversed, stands in effectual force.
The Two Gentlemen of Verona. Act iii, sc. 1, l. 222. [Proteus] The only use of "unreversed."

6
Now against himself he sounds this doom.
The Rape of Lucrece, l. 717.

7
For thee remains a heavier doom,
Which I with some unwillingness pronounce.
Richard II. Act i, sc. 3, l. 148. [King Richard]

Abide Thy kingly doom.
Richard II. Act v, sc. 6, l. 22. [Percy]

8
Then, dreadful trumpet, sound the general doom!
Romeo and Juliet. Act iii, sc. 2, l. 67. [Juliet] See under JUDGEMENT DAY.

Friar Laurence: I'll bring thee tidings of the prince's doom.
Romeo: What less than dooms-day is the prince's doom?
Romeo and Juliet. Act iii, sc. 3, l. 8. For "doomsday" see JUDGEMENT-DAY.

9
If any one relieves or pities him,
For the offence he dies. This is our doom.
Titus Andronicus. Act v, sc. 3, l. 181. [Lucius]

DOOR

10
He is here at the door and importunes access to you.
As You Like It. Act i, sc. 1, l. 96. [Dennis]

He is ready at the door.
The Merchant of Venice, iv, 1, 15. "At the door" occurs ten times in the plays.

They stay at door.—*Winter's Tale,* iv, 4, 352.
Hard at door.—*The Merry Wives of Windsor,* iv, 2, 111.
Near the door.—*Henry VIII,* v, 4, 41.

1
Come not within these doors.
As You Like It. Act ii, sc. 3, l. 17. [Adam]

2
Either get thee from the door or sit down at the hatch. . . .
Go get thee from the door.
The Comedy of Errors. Act iii, sc. 1, l. 33. [Dromio of Syracuse]

Who is at the door that keeps all this noise? . . .
Go get you from the door.
The Comedy of Errors. Act iii, sc. 1, l. 61. [Adriana]

The doors are made against you.
The Comedy of Errors. Act iii, sc. 1, l. 93. [Balthazar]

Since mine own doors refuse to entertain me,
I 'll knock elsewhere, to see if they 'll disdain me.
The Comedy of Errors. Act iii, sc. 1, l. 120. [Antipholus of Ephesus]

From door to door.—*The Comedy of Errors,* iv, 4, 41.

3
Locking me out of my doors by day.
The Comedy of Errors. Act iv, sc. 1, l. 18. [Antipholus of Ephesus] The only use of "locking."

Are your doors lock'd?—*Othello,* i, 1, 85.
Her doors lock'd?—*Cymbeline,* iii, 5, 51.
My door is lock'd.—*The Comedy of Errors,* iii, 1, 30.
Let the door be lock'd.—*Hamlet,* v, 2, 322.
Lock up my doors.—*The Merchant of Venice,* ii, 5, 29.
Double-lock the door.—*Venus and Adonis,* l. 448. The only use of "double-lock."
Bar the door.—*Hamlet,* iii, 2, 351; *King Lear,* iii, 4, 155.
Clap to the doors.—*I Henry IV,* ii, 4, 305.
Guard the door.—*Hamlet,* iv, 5, 97; *Julius Cæsar,* iv, 2, 52; *Othello,* v, 2, 241.
Keep the door.—*Hamlet,* iv, 5, 115.
Make fast the doors.—*The Merchant of Venice,* ii, 6, 49.
Make the doors.—*As You Like It,* iv, 1, 162.
Seal'd up the doors.—*Romeo and Juliet,* v, 2, 11.
Watch the door.—*The Merry Wives of Windsor,* iv, 2, 53.

4
His own doors being shut against his entrance.
The Comedy of Errors. Act iv, sc. 3, l. 90. [Courtezan]

Upon me the guilty doors were shut.
The Comedy of Errors. Act iv, sc. 4, l. 66. [Antipholus of Ephesus]

Antipholus of Ephesus: Were not my doors lock'd up and I shut out?
Dromio of Ephesus: Perdie, your doors were lock'd and you shut out.
The Comedy of Errors. Act iv, sc. 4, l. 73.

She shut the doors upon me.
The Comedy of Errors. Act v, sc. 1, l. 204. [Antipholus of Ephesus]

Let the doors be shut upon him.
Hamlet. Act iii, sc. 1, l. 135. [Hamlet]

Shut door upon me.—*Henry VIII,* ii, 4, 43.
Shut doors after you.—*The Merchant of Venice,* ii, 5, 53.
Shut up your doors.—*King Lear,* ii, 4, 307; 311.
O, shut the door!—*Romeo and Juliet,* iv, 1, 44; *II Henry IV,* ii, 4, 82; 85; *Macbeth,* i, 7, 15; *Othello,* iv, 2, 28.

5
Virgilia: I will not out of doors.
Valeria: Not out of doors!
Volumnia: She shall, she shall.
Virgilia: Indeed, no, by your patience; I 'll not over the threshold till my lord return from the wars.
Coriolanus. Act i, sc. 3, l. 78. "Out of doors" occurs fifteen times in the plays.

Without doors.—*Antony and Cleopatra,* ii, 1, 13.

6
Attend you here the door of our stern daughter.
Cymbeline. Act ii, sc. 3, l. 42. [Cymbeline]

Doors of breath.—*Romeo and Juliet,* v, 3, 114.
Door of death.—*III Henry VI,* iii, 3, 105.
Door of truth.—*Othello,* iii, 3, 407.

7
Falstaff: Have you turned him out o' doors?
Bardolph: Yea, sir. The rascal 's drunk.
II Henry IV. Act ii, sc. 4, l. 229.

Bid him turn you out of doors.
Twelfth Night. Act ii, sc. 3, l. 78. [Maria] Also *The Merry Wives of Windsor,* i, 4, 132; *The Tempest,* iii, 2, 78.

8
Now go to the door, and stay there till we call.
Macbeth. Act iii, sc. 1, l. 73. [Macbeth]

Go to the door.—*Coriolanus,* iv, 5, 9.

9
Keep in-a-door.
King Lear. Act i, sc. 4, l. 137. [Fool] The only use of the phrase.

10
A little door
Which from the vineyard to the garden leads.
Measure for Measure. Act iv, sc. 1, l. 32. [Isabella]

Garden door.—*Twelfth Night,* iii, 1, 103.

11
'Twere not amiss to keep our door hatched.
Pericles. Act iv, sc. 2, l. 37. [Pandarus]

Keep the door close.—*Henry VIII,* v, 4, 30.

12
Avaunt, thou damned door-keeper!
Pericles. Act iv, sc. 6, l. 126. [Lysimachus]

Thou art the damned doorkeeper to every
Coistrel that comes inquiring for his Tib.
Pericles. Act iv, sc. 6, l. 175. [Marina] The only uses of "doorkeeper" and sole use of "coistrel" (knave). "Tib," a generic name for a woman of the lower class, is used again in *All's Well that Ends Well,* ii, 2, 24.

13
Now he is come unto the chamber door.
The Rape of Lucrece, l. 337.

Dupp'd the chamber-door.—*Hamlet,* iv, 5, 53. The only use of "dupp'd" (opened).
Hold the chamber-door.—*Henry V,* iv, 5, 14.
At our chamber-doors.—*I Henry VI,* ii, 1, 42; *King Lear,* ii, 4, 119; *Henry VIII,* v, 3, 140. The only uses of "chamber-door."

1 This said, his guilty hand pluck'd up the latch,
And with his knee the door he opens wide.
The Rape of Lucrece, l. 358.

2 Open the door, or I will break it open.
Richard II. Act v, sc. 3, l. 45. [York] "Open the door" occurs five times in the plays.

The door is open, sir; there lies your way.
The Taming of the Shrew. Act iii, sc. 2, l. 212. [Katharina]

What, 's all the doors open here?
Troilus and Cressida. Act iv, sc. 2, l. 19. [Pandarus]

The doors are open.—*Macbeth,* ii, 2, 5.

This door is open.—*II Henry IV,* iv, 5, 56.

3 Men shut their doors against a setting sun.
Timon of Athens. Act i, sc. 2, l. 150. [Apemantus]

4 What, are the doors opposed against my passage?
Timon of Athens. Act ii, sc. 4, l. 80. [Timon]

Now his friends are dead,
Doors, that were ne'er acquainted with their wards
Many a bounteous year must be employ'd
Now to guard sure their master.
Timon of Athens. Act iii, sc. 3, l. 37. [Servant]

5 I stalk about her door.
Troilus and Cressida. Act iii, sc. 2, l. 9. [Troilus]

I have charged thee not to haunt about my doors.
Othello. Act i, sc. 1, l. 96. [Brabantio]

6 Who 's that at door? good uncle, go and see.
Troilus and Cressida. Act iv, sc. 2, l. 36. [Cressida]

Will you beat down the door?
Troilus and Cressida. Act iv, sc. 2, l. 44. [Pandarus]

Beat the door down.—*The Comedy of Errors,* iii, 1, 59.

The doors are broke.—*Hamlet,* iv, 5, 111.

DOUBT

7 I will be even with thee, doubt it not.
Antony and Cleopatra. Act iii, sc. 7, l. 1. [Cleopatra] "Doubt it not" occurs eight times in the plays.

Doubt not.—*II Henry VI,* iv, 8, 54, and thirty-four times in later plays.

Do not doubt.—*King John,* v, 2, 180; *Othello,* iii, 3, 5; 19.

Doubt you not.—*Richard III,* iii, 5, 64; *Troilus and Cressida,* v, 3, 35.

We doubt it nothing.—*Hamlet,* i, 2, 41; *Macbeth,* v, 4, 2.

No doubt.—*III Henry VI,* v, 1, 62, and twenty-five times in later plays, ten times in *Richard III* alone.

Past all doubt.—*The Winter's Tale,* ii, 3, 80.

Past doubt.—*Coriolanus,* ii, 3, 265; *The Winter's Tale,* i, 2, 268; ii, 3, 80.

Without . . . doubt.—*Romeo and Juliet,* iv, 1, 88; *Henry VIII,* iv, 1, 113.

8 From hence I go,
To make these doubts all even.
As You Like It. Act v, sc. 4, l. 24. [Rosalind]

9 It were sin to doubt.
Coriolanus. Act i, sc. 6, l. 68. [Marcius]

Hang no more in doubt.
King John. Act iii, sc. 1, l. 219. [Austria]

10 Doubting things go ill often hurts more
Than to be sure they do.
Cymbeline. Act i, sc. 6, l. 95. [Imogen]

All other doubts, by time let them be clear'd.
Cymbeline. Act iv, sc. 3, l. 45. [Pisanio]

This is, sir, a doubt
In such a time nothing becoming you,
Nor satisfying us.
Cymbeline. Act iv, sc. 4, l. 14. [Guiderius]

11 He cannot so precisely weed this land
As his misdoubts present occasion.
II Henry IV. Act iv, sc. 1, l. 205. [Archbishop of York]

12 Out of doubt and out of question too, and ambiguities.
Henry V. Act v, sc. 1, l. 47. [Fluellen] "Out of doubt" occurs six times in the plays.

Clear these ambiguities.—*Romeo and Juliet,* v, 3, 217. The only uses of "ambiguities."

13 Answer me one doubt.
III Henry VI. Act iii, sc. 3, l. 238. [King Lewis]

Resolve my doubt.—*III Henry VI,* iv, 1, 135.

Why stand you in a doubt?—*III Henry VI,* iv, 7, 27.

Were you in doubt?—*Much Ado about Nothing,* i, 1, 106.

Do you doubt that?—*Hamlet,* i, 3, 4.

Ay, who doubts that?—*King John,* ii, 1, 193.

14 I speak not this as doubting any here.
III Henry VI. Act v, sc. 4, l. 43. [Prince Edward]

I do not doubt.—*II Henry IV,* iv, 2, 77; *A Midsummer-Night's Dream,* iv, 2, 44; *The Merchant of Venice,* i, 1, 149.

I do nothing doubt.—*Cymbeline,* i, 4, 106.

They nothing doubt.—*Coriolanus,* i, 3, 111.

I make no doubt.—*Love's Labour 's Lost,* v, 2, 151.

15 A noble spirit . . . ever casts
Such doubts, as false coin, from it.
Henry VIII. Act iii, sc. 1, l. 169. [Campeius] The only use of the phrase "false coin" in the plays.

16 Of that I doubt, as all men's children may.
King John. Act i, sc. 1, l. 63. [Bastard]

I doubt me.—*Timon of Athens,* i, 2, 159.

Ere long I doubt.—*King John,* iv, 2, 102.

I must ever doubt.—*Timon of Athens,* iv, 3, 514.

Driven to doubt.—*Venus and Adonis,* l. 692.

Live in doubt.—*Sonnets,* cxliv.

Overcome by doubt.—*Venus and Adonis,* l. 891.

Stood in doubt.—*A Lover's Complaint,* l. 97.

1
But now I am cabin'd, cribb'd, confined, bound in
To saucy doubts and fears.
Macbeth. Act iii, sc. 4, l. 24. [Macbeth] The only use of "cabin'd" and "cribb'd."
The mind I sway by and the heart I bear
Shall never sag with doubt nor shake with fear.
Macbeth. Act v, sc. 3, l. 9. [Macbeth] The only use of "sag."
I pull in resolution, and begin
To doubt the equivocation of the fiend
That lies like truth.
Macbeth. Act v, sc. 5, l. 42. [Macbeth] "Equivocation" occurs again in *Hamlet,* v, 1, 149: "Equivocation will undo us."
2 Our doubts are traitors
And make us lose the good we oft might win
By fearing to attempt.
Measure for Measure. Act i, sc. 4, l. 77 [Lucio]
3
'Tis a shrewd doubt, though it be but a dream.
Othello. Act iii, sc. 3, l. 429. [Othello]
With thousand doubts.—*Pericles,* i, 2, 97.
Yet he seems to doubt.—*Pericles,* v, 1, 227.
4
Urge doubts to them that fear.
Richard II. Act ii, sc. 1, l. 299. [Ross]
Overcome by doubt and bloodless fear.
Venus and Adonis, l. 891.
5 Modest doubt is call'd
The beacon of the wise, the tent that searches
To the bottom of the worst.
Troilus and Cressida. Act ii, sc. 2, l. 15. [Hector]
What wicked deem is this?
Troilus and Cressida. Act iv, sc. 4, l. 61. [Cressida] The only use of "deem" as a noun.
Clear that doubt.—*Winter's Tale,* iv, 4, 633.

DOVE

6 Loving turtle-doves
That could not live asunder day or night.
I Henry VI. Act ii, sc. 2, l. 30. [Bedford] The only use of "turtle-doves."
I, an old turtle,
Will wing me to some wither'd bough and there
My mate, that 's never to be found again,
Lament till I am lost.
Winter's Tale. Act v, sc. 3, l. 132. [Paulina]
O slow-wing'd turtle!—*Taming of the Shrew,* ii, 1, 208. The only use of "slow-wing'd."
We 'll teach him to know turtles from jays.
The Merry Wives of Windsor. Act iii, sc. 3, l. 44. [Mrs. Ford] Shakespeare uses "turtle" twelve times, always with reference to the bird.
7
Doves will peck in safeguard of their brood.
III Henry VI. Act ii, sc. 2, l. 18. [Clifford]
So doves do peck the falcon's piercing talons.
III Henry VI. Act i, sc. 4, l. 41. [Clifford] For full quotation, see under COWARDICE.
The dove will peck the estridge.
Antony and Cleopatra. Act iii, sc. 13, l. 197. [Enobarbus] For full quotation, see under FURY.
The dove pursues the griffin.
A Midsummer-Night's Dream. Act ii, sc. 1, l. 232. [Helena] The griffin is mentioned again in *I Henry IV,* iii, 1, 152: "Clip-wing'd griffin," which is also the only use of "clip-wing'd."
Wrathful dove.—*II Henry IV,* iii, 2, 171.
8
Who will not change a raven for a dove?
A Midsummer-Night's Dream. Act ii, sc. 2, l. 114. [Lysander]
9
The dove sleeps fast that this night-owl will catch.
The Rape of Lucrece, l. 360.
10
So shows a snowy dove trooping with crows.
Romeo and Juliet. Act i, sc. 5, l. 50. [Romeo] The only use of "snowy" and "trooping."
Milk-white dove.—*The Passionate Pilgrim,* l. 119.
11
Therefore do nimble-pinion'd doves draw love.
Romeo and Juliet, ii, 5, 7. See under CUPID. The only use of "nimble-pinion'd."
Dove-drawn.—*The Tempest,* iv, 1, 94. The only use of the phrase.
Dove of Paphos.—*Pericles,* iv, Gower, 32.
Venus' doves.—*A Midsummer-Night's Dream,* i, 1, 171; *The Rape of Lucrece,* l. 58.
12
Two strengthless doves will draw me through the sky,
From morn till night.
Venus and Adonis, l. 153.
Female dove.—*Hamlet,* v, 1, 309.
Harmless dove.—*II Henry VI,* iii, 1, 71.
Silver doves.—*Venus and Adonis,* l. 366; l. 1190.
Sucking dove.—*A Midsummer-Night's Dream,* i, 2, 85.
Dove . . . of peace.—*II Henry IV,* iv, 1, 46.
Dove-cote.—*Coriolanus,* v, 6, 115. The only use of the word.
Dove-house.—*Romeo and Juliet,* i, 3, 27; 33. The only uses of the word.

DOWRY

See also Marriage and Money

13
To marry her, I 'll add three thousand crowns
To what is past already.
All's Well that Ends Well. Act iii, sc. 7, l. 35. [Helena]
Doubt not but heaven
Hath brought me up to be your daughter's dower.
All's Well that Ends Well. Act iv, sc. 4, l. 18. [Helena]
14
A large and sumptuous dowry.
I Henry VI. Act v, sc. 1, l. 20. [Gloucester]
His wealth doth warrant a liberal dower.
I Henry VI. Act v, sc. 5, l. 46. [Exeter]
15
I never read but England's kings have had

Large sums of gold and dowries with their wives.
II Henry VI. Act i, sc. 1, l. 128. [York] The only use of "dowries."
Without having any dowry.—*II Henry VI,* i, 1, 62.
Dowerless took our youngest born.
King Lear. Act ii, sc. 4, l. 215. [King Lear]
Dowerless daughter.—*King Lear,* i, 1, 259. The only uses of "dowerless."
Dower'd with our curse.—*King Lear,* i, 1, 207. The only use of "dower'd."

1
Mine honesty shall be my dower.
III Henry VI. Act iii, sc. 2, l. 72. [Lady Grey]
Virtue and she is her own dower.
All's Well that Ends Well. Act ii, sc. 3, l. 150. [King]
Thy truth, then, be thy dower.
King Lear. Act i, sc. 1, l. 110. [King Lear]
She is herself a dowry.
King Lear. Act i, sc. 1, l. 244. [King of France]
Then let her beauty be her wedding-dower.
The Two Gentlemen of Verona. Act iii, sc. 1, l. 78. [Duke] The only use of "wedding-dower."

2
The jointure that your king must make,
Which with her dowry shall be counterpoised.
III Henry VI. Act iii, sc. 3, l. 136. [King Lewis]
Besides two thousand ducats by the year
Of fruitful land, all which shall be her jointure.
The Taming of the Shrew. Act ii, sc. 1, l. 371. [Tranio]
This is my daughter's jointure.
Romeo and Juliet. Act v, sc. 3, l. 297. [Capulet]
He will make you a hundred and fifty pounds jointure.
The Merry Wives of Windsor. Act iii, sc. 4, l. 50. [Shallow]
Better jointure.—*As You Like It,* iv, 1, 56. The only uses of "jointure."

3
Give with our niece a dowry large enough.
King John. Act ii, sc. 1, l. 469. [Queen Elinor]
Her dowry shall weigh equal with a queen: . . .
Shall gild her bridal bed and make her rich
In titles, honours and promotions.
King John. Act ii, sc. 1, l. 486. [King John]
A dowry for a queen.
Love's Labour's Lost. Act ii, sc. 1, l. 8. [Boyet]

4
What, in the least,
Will you require in present dower with her,
Or cease your quest of love?
King Lear. Act i, sc. 1, l. 194. [King Lear]

5
For propagation of a dower
Remaining in the coffer of her friends.
Measure for Measure. Act i, sc. 2, l. 154. [Claudio] The only use of "propagation."
Dowry of a second head.—*The Merchant of Venice,* iii, 2, 95.

6
Will you, upon good dowry, marry her?
The Merry Wives of Windsor. Act i, sc. 1, l. 246. [Shallow]
Not spend the dowry of a lawful bed.
The Rape of Lucrece, l. 938.

7
I cannot tell; but I had as lief take her dowry with this condition, to be whipped at the high cross every morning.
The Taming of the Shrew. Act i, sc. 1, l. 135. [Gremio]
Petruchio: Then tell me, if I get your daughter's love,
What dowry shall I have with her to wife?
Baptista: After my death the one half of my lands,
And in possession twenty thousand crowns.
Petruchio: And, for that dowry, I'll assure her of
Her widowhood, be it that she survives me.
The Taming of the Shrew. Act ii, sc. 1, l. 120.
He of both
That can assure my daughter's greatest dower
Shall have my Bianca's love.
The Taming of the Shrew. Act ii, sc. 1, l. 344. [Baptista]
If you should die before him, where's her dower?
The Taming of the Shrew. Act ii, sc. 1, l. 391. [Baptista]
Assurance of a dower.—*The Taming of the Shrew,* iv, 2, 117.
And therefore, if you say no more than this,
That like a father you will deal with him
And pass my daughter a sufficient dower,
The match is made, and all is done:
Your son shall have my daughter with consent.
The Taming of the Shrew. Act iv, sc. 4, l. 43. [Baptista]
She is of good esteem,
Her dowry wealthy, and of worthy birth.
The Taming of the Shrew. Act iv, sc. 5, l. 64. [Petruchio]
Another dowry to another daughter.
The Taming of the Shrew. Act v, sc. 2, l. 114. [Baptista]

DRAGON

8
Like to a lonely dragon, that his fen
Makes fear'd and talk'd of more than seen.
Coriolanus. Act iv, sc. 1, l. 30. [Coriolanus] "Lonely" is used only once again in the plays, in *The Winter's Tale,* v, 3, 18: "Therefore I keep lonely, apart."
Dragons of the night.—*Cymbeline,* ii, 2, 48.
Night's swift dragons.—*A Midsummer-Night's Dream,* iii, 2, 379.

9
Come not between the dragon and his wrath.
King Lear. Act i, sc. 1, l. 124. [King Lear]

10
Death-like dragons here affright thee hard.
Pericles. Act i, sc. 1, l. 29. [Antiochus] The only use of "death-like."
Fierce dragons.—*King John,* ii, 1, 68.
Fiery dragons.—*Richard III,* v, 3, 350.
Dragons, wolves, and bears.—*Timon of Athens,* iv, 3, 189.
Dragonish.—*Antony and Cleopatra,* iv, 14, 2. The only use of the word.

Dragon-like.—*Coriolanus,* iv, 7, 23. The only use of the phrase.

1
Did ever dragon keep so fair a cave?
Romeo and Juliet. Act iii, sc. 2, l. 74. [Juliet]

DREAD, see Fear

DREAM

I—Familiar Sayings

2
Let her lie still and dream.
Cymbeline. Act ii, sc. 3, l. 70. [Cloten]
What have you dream'd of late?
Cymbeline. Act iv, sc. 2, l. 345. [Lucius]
Dream often so, And never false.
Cymbeline. Act iv, sc. 2, l. 352. [Lucius]

3
What it should be . . .
I cannot dream of.
Hamlet. Act ii, sc. 2, l. 7. [King]
I did dream to-night.—*II Henry VI,* iii, 2, 31.
What is 't I dream on?—*Measure for Measure,* ii, 2, 179.
Dream on court'sies.—*Romeo and Juliet,* i, 4, 72.
Dream on evil.—*II Henry VI,* iii, 1, 73; *The Rape of Lucrece,* l. 87.
Dream on fees.—*Romeo and Juliet,* 1, 4, 73.
Dream upon the crown.—*III Henry VI,* iii, 2, 168.
Straight on kisses dream.—*Romeo and Juliet,* i, 4, 74.

4
If dreams prove true.
II Henry VI. Act v, sc. 1, l. 195. [Clifford]
We . . . long have dream'd so.—*Henry VIII,* ii, 4, 71.

5
Brutus: Didst thou dream, Lucius, that thou so criedest out?
Lucius: My lord, I do not know that I did cry.
Brutus: Yes, that thou didst: didst thou see any thing?
Lucius: Nothing, my lord.
Julius Cæsar. Act iv, sc. 3, l. 296.

6
Full of idle dreams.
King John. Act iv, sc. 2, l. 145. [Bastard] "Idle dreams" is repeated in *Measure for Measure,* iv, 1, 64.
Thou idle dreamer.
King John. Act iv, sc. 2, l. 153. [King John]
He is a dreamer; let us leave him.
Julius Cæsar. Act i, sc. 2, l. 24. [Cæsar]

7
It seems to me
That yet we sleep, we dream.
A Midsummer-Night's Dream. Act iv, sc. 1, l. 197. [Demetrius]
Dream away the time.—*A Midsummer-Night's Dream,* i, 1, 9.

8
We will hold it as a dream till it appear itself.
Much Ado about Nothing. Act i, sc. 2, l. 21. [Leonato]

9
If ever I did dream of such a matter,
Abhor me.
Othello. Act i, sc. 1, l. 5. [Iago]
Nay, this was but his dream.
Othello. Act iii, sc. 3, l. 427. [Iago]

10
Who dream'd . . . of such a thing?
Pericles. Act iii, Gower, l. 38.
Did you ever dream of such a thing?
Pericles. Act iv, sc. 5, l. 5.
Dream of friendship.—*Timon of Athens,* iv, 2, 34.
Dream of impediment!—*Antony and Cleopatra,* ii, 2, 148.
Dream of love.—*Romeo and Juliet,* i, 4, 71.
Dream of passion.—*Hamlet,* ii, 2, 578.

11
A dream, a breath, a froth of fleeting joy.
The Rape of Lucrece, l. 212.
Starts . . . as from a dream.
The Rape of Lucrece, l. 1772.
Sits as one new-risen from a dream.
The Taming of the Shrew. Act iv, sc. 1, l. 189. [Curtis]
As in a dream.—*The Tempest,* i, 2, 486.

12
Look, how thou dream'st!
Richard III. Act iv, sc. 2, l. 57. [King Richard]
Soft! I did but dream.
Richard III. Act v, sc. 3, l. 178. [King Richard]

13
I talk of dreams,
Which are the children of an idle brain,
Begot of nothing but vain fantasy,
Which is as thin of substance as the air.
Romeo and Juliet. Act i, sc. 4, l. 96. [Mercutio]
Said he not so? or did I dream it so?
Romeo and Juliet. Act v, sc. 3, l. 79. [Romeo]

14
Even as a flattering dream or worthless fancy.
The Taming of the Shrew. Induction, sc. 1, l. 44. [Lord]
When he says he is, say that he dreams.
The Taming of the Shrew. Induction, sc. 1, l. 64. [Lord]

15
Do I dream? or have I dream'd till now?
The Taming of the Shrew. Induction, sc. 2, l. 71. [Sly]
Hum! ha! is this a vision? is this a dream? do I sleep?
The Merry Wives of Windsor. Act iii, sc. 5, l. 141. [Ford]
Thy wife hath dream'd; thy mother hath had visions.
Troilus and Cressida. Act v, sc. 3, l. 63. [Priam] See also VISION.

16
These fifteen years you have been in a dream;
Or when you waked, so waked as if you slept.
The Taming of the Shrew. Induction, sc. 2, l. 81. [Second Servant]
They say that I have dream'd
And slept above some fifteen year or more.
The Taming of the Shrew. Induction, sc. 2, l. 114. [Sly]
Nay, then, 'tis time to stir him from his trance.
The Taming of the Shrew. Act i, sc. 1, l. 182.

[Tranio] The only use of "trance" in the plays. The nearest is in *King Lear,* v, 3, 218: "There I left him tranced." *The Rape of Lucrece* (l. 974) has, "Disturb his hours of rest with restless trances," and (l. 1595) "Like old acquaintance in a trance."

1
Rather like a dream than an assurance.
The Tempest. Act i, sc. 2, l. 45. [Miranda]
We are such stuff As dreams are made on.
The Tempest, iv, 1, 156. See under LIFE.

2
You are for dreams and slumbers, brother priest.
Troilus and Cressida. Act ii, sc. 2, l. 37. [Troilus]

3
Poor lady, she were better love a dream.
Twelfth Night. Act ii, sc. 2, l. 27. [Viola]
What relish is in this? how runs the stream?
Or I am mad, or else this is a dream:
Let fancy still my sense in Lethe steep;
If it be thus to dream, still let me sleep!
Twelfth Night. Act iv, sc. 1, l. 63. [Sebastian]

4
Forgive me that I do not dream on thee,
Because thou see'st me dote upon my love.
The Two Gentlemen of Verona. Act ii, sc. 4, l. 172. [Valentine]
She dreams on him that has forgot her love.
The Two Gentlemen of Verona. Act iv, sc. 4, l. 86. [Julia]

5
How like a dream is this I see and hear!
The Two Gentlemen of Verona. Act v, sc. 4, l. 26. [Valentine]
I but dream'd it.—*The Winter's Tale,* iii, 2, 85.

6
Your actions are my dreams.
The Winter's Tale. Act iii, sc. 2, l. 83. [Leontes]
Ne'er was dream So like a waking.
The Winter's Tale. Act iii, sc. 3, l. 18. [Antigonus]
I did in time collect myself and thought
This was so and no slumber. Dreams are toys.
The Winter's Tale. Act iii, sc. 3, l. 38. [Antigonus]

7
She shall bring him that
Which he not dreams of.
The Winter's Tale. Act iv, sc. 4, l. 179. [Shepherd]
I shall have more than you can dream of yet.
The Winter's Tale. Act iv, sc. 4, l. 399. [Florizel]

II—Pleasant Dreams

8
I hope I dream;
For so I thought I was a cave-keeper,
And cook to honest creatures.
Cymbeline. Act iv, sc. 2, l. 297. [Imogen] The only use of "cave-keeper."
The dream 's here still: even when I wake.
Cymbeline. Act iv, sc. 2, l. 306. [Imogen]

9
Why, then, I do but dream on sovereignty;
Like one that stands upon a promontory,
And spies a far-off shore where he would tread,
Wishing his foot were equal with his eye,
And chides the sea that sunders him from thence,
Saying, he 'll lade it dry to have his way.
III Henry VI. Act iii, sc. 2, l. 134. [Gloucester] The only use of "lade."

10
I am most joyful, madam, such good dreams
Possess your fancy.
Henry VIII. Act iv, sc. 2, l. 93. [Griffith] The only use of "good dreams."

11
This dream is all amiss interpreted;
It was a vision fair and fortunate.
Julius Cæsar. Act ii, sc. 2, l. 83. [Brutus]

12
I did dream of money-bags to-night.
The Merchant of Venice. Act ii, sc. 5, l. 18. [Shylock] "Money-bags" is repeated in *The Winter's Tale,* iv, 4, 267.
In dreaming,
The clouds methought would open and show riches
Ready to drop upon me, that, when I waked,
I cried to dream again.
The Tempest. Act iii, sc. 2, l. 149. [Caliban]

13
Learn, good soul,
To think our former state a happy dream.
Richard II. Act v, sc. 1, l. 17. [King Richard] The only use of "happy dream."

14
Dream of success and happy victory!
Richard III. Act v, sc. 3, l. 165. [Ghost of Lady Anne]
The sweetest sleep, and fairest-boding dreams
That ever enter'd in a drowsy head, . . .
I promise you, my soul is very jocund
In the remembrance of so fair a dream.
Richard III. Act v, sc. 3, l. 227. [Richmond] The only use of "fairest-boding."

15
O blessed, blessed night! I am afeared,
Being in night, all this is but a dream,
Too flattering-sweet to be substantial.
Romeo and Juliet. Act ii, sc. 2, l. 139. [Romeo] The only use of "flattering-sweet."
If I may trust the flattering truth of sleep,
My dreams presage some joyful news at hand.
Romeo and Juliet. Act v, sc. 1, l. 1. [Romeo]

16
Sir Toby: Thou hast put him in such a dream, that when the image of it leaves him he must run mad.
Maria: Nay, but say true; does it work upon him?
Sir Toby: Like aqua-vitæ with a midwife.
Twelfth Night. Act ii, sc. 5, l. 211.

III—Bad Dreams

17
'Tis still a dream, or else such stuff as madmen
Tongue and brain not; either both or nothing;
Or senseless speaking or a speaking such
As sense cannot untie.
Cymbeline. Act v, sc. 4, l. 146. [Posthumus]

18
Hamlet: O God, I could be bounded in a nutshell and count myself a king of infinite

space, were it not that I have bad dreams.
Guildenstern: Which dreams indeed are ambition, for the very substance of the ambitious is merely the shadow of a dream.
Hamlet: A dream itself is but a shadow.
Hamlet. Act ii, sc. 2, l. 260. The only use of "bad dreams." "Nutshell" is repeated in *The Tempest,* i, 1, 50.

For in that sleep of death what dreams may come
When we have shuffled off this mortal coil,
Must give us pause.
Hamlet. Act iii, sc. 1, l. 66. [Hamlet] The only use of "mortal coil."

1
Page: Away, you rascally Althæa's dream, away!
Prince: Instruct us, boy; what dream, boy?
Page: Marry, my lord, Althæa dreamed she was delivered of a fire-brand; and therefore I call him her dream.
II Henry IV. Act ii, sc. 2, l. 93. Althea and her fire-brand are referred to once again in *II Henry VI,* i, 1, 234.

I have long dream'd of such a kind of man,
So surfeit-swell'd, so old and so profane;
But, being awaked, I do despise my dream.
II Henry IV. Act v, sc. 5, l. 53. [King Henry V] The only use of "surfeit-swelled."

2
Gloucester: My troublous dream this night doth make me sad.
Duchess: What dream'd my lord? tell me, and I'll requite it
With sweet rehearsal of my morning's dream.
Gloucester: Methough this staff, mine office-badge in court,
Was broke in twain; by whom I have forgot; . . .
This was my dream: what it doth bode, God knows.
II Henry VI. Act i, sc. 2, l. 22. "Rehearsal" is repeated in *A Midsummer-Night's Dream,* iii, 1, 3. The only use of "office-badge."

3
Merciful powers,
Restrain in me the cursed thoughts that nature
Gives way to in repose!
Macbeth. Act ii, sc. 1, l. 7. [Banquo]

Now o'er the one half-world
Nature seems dead, and wicked dreams abuse
The curtain'd sleep.
Macbeth. Act ii, sc. 1, l. 49. [Macbeth] The only use of "half-world."

4
Ay me, for pity! what a dream was here!
A Midsummer-Night's Dream. Act ii, sc. 2, l. 147. [Hermia]

The fierce vexation of a dream.—*Midsummer-Night's Dream,* iv, 1, 72.

5
This is the rarest dream that e'er dull sleep
Did mock sad fools withal.
Pericles. Act v, sc. 1, l. 163. [Pericles]

And for his dreams, I wonder he is so fond
To trust the mockery of unquiet slumbers.
Richard III. Act iii, sc. 2, l. 26. [Hastings]

6
For never yet one hour in his bed
Have I enjoy'd the golden dew of sleep,
But have been waked by his timorous dreams.
Richard III. Act iv, sc. 1, l. 83. [Anne]

Dream on, dream on, of bloody deeds and death.
Richard III. Act v, sc. 3, l. 171. [Ghost of Buckingham]

Let not our babbling dreams affright our souls.
Richard III. Act v, sc. 3, l. 308. [King Richard]

Banish hence these abject lowly dreams.
The Taming of the Shrew. Induction, sc. 2, l. 34. [Lord]

7
If I do dream, would all my wealth would wake me!
If I do wake, some planet strike me down,
That I may slumber in eternal sleep!
Titus Andronicus. Act ii, sc. 4, l. 13. [Marcus]

8
My dreams will, sure, prove ominous to the day.
Troilus and Cressida. Act v, sc. 3, l. 6. [Andromache]

IV—Telling One's Dreams

9
You laugh when boys or women tell their dreams.
Antony and Cleopatra. Act v, sc. 2, l. 74. [Cleopatra]

What I told you then,
I hope I shall have leisure to make good;
If this be not a dream I see and hear.
The Comedy of Errors. Act v, sc. 1, l. 374. [Antipholus of Syracuse]

I have dreamed to-night; I'll tell you my dream.
The Merry Wives of Windsor. Act iii, sc. 3, l. 172. [Ford]

And by the way let us recount our dreams.
A Midsummer-Night's Dream. Act iv, sc. 1, l. 204. [Demetrius]

What was your dream? I long to hear you tell it.
Richard III. Act i, sc. 4, l. 8. [Brakenbury]

10
Next time, I'll keep my dreams unto myself,
And not be check'd.
II Henry VI. Act i, sc. 2, l. 53. [Duchess of Gloucester]

11
She dreamt to-night she saw my statua,
Which, like a fountain with an hundred spouts,
Did run pure blood.
Julius Cæsar. Act ii, sc. 2, l. 76. [Cæsar] "Statua" occurs four times in the plays.

I dreamt to-night that I did feast with Cæsar.
Julius Cæsar. Act iii, sc. 3, l. 1. [Cinna, the poet]

I dreamt last night of the three weird sisters.
Macbeth. Act ii, sc. 1, l. 20. [Banquo]

12
I have had a dream, past the wit of man to say what dream it was: man is but an ass,

if he go about to expound this dream. . . . The eye of man hath not heard, the ear of man hath not seen, man's hand is not able to taste, his tongue to conceive, nor his heart to report, what my dream was. I will get Peter Quince to write a ballad of this dream: it shall be called Bottom's Dream, because it hath no bottom.

A Midsummer-Night's Dream. Act iv, sc. 1, l. 209. [Bottom]

1
My dream was lengthen'd after life.

Richard III. Act i, sc. 4, l. 43. [Clarence]

With that, methoughts, a legion of foul fiends
Environ'd me about, and howled in mine ears
Such hideous cries, that with the very noise
I trembling waked, and for a season after
Could not believe but that I was in hell,
Such terrible impression made the dream.

Richard III. Act i, sc. 4, l. 58. [Clarence]

He dreamt to-night the boar had razed his helm.

Richard III. Act iii, sc. 2, l. 11. [Messenger]

I have dream'd a fearful dream!

Richard III. Act v, sc. 3, l. 212. [King Richard]

2
Romeo: I dream'd a dream to-night.
Mercutio: And so did I.
Romeo: Well, what was yours?
Mercutio: That dreamers often lie.
Romeo: In bed asleep, while they do dream things true.

Romeo and Juliet. Act i, sc. 4, l. 50.

I dreamt my lady came and found me dead—
Strange dream, that gives a dead man leave to think!

Romeo and Juliet. Act v, sc. 1, l. 6. [Romeo]

As I did sleep under this yew-tree here,
I dreamt my master and another fought,
And that my master slew him.

Romeo and Juliet. Act v, sc. 3, l. 137. [Balthasar] "Yew-tree" is repeated in l. 3 of the same scene, and occurs nowhere else.

I dreamt of a silver basin and ewer to-night.

Timon of Athens. Act ii, sc. 1, l. 5. [Lucullus]

3
I have dream'd
Of bloody turbulence, and this whole night
Hath nothing been but shapes and forms of slaughter.

Troilus and Cressida. Act v, sc. 3, l. 10. [Andromache] The only use of "turbulence."

DRESS

See also Cap, Cloak, Coat, Fashion, Garment, Gown, Hat, Robe, Shirt, Weeds

I—Dress: Its Varieties

4
The soul of this man is his clothes.

All's Well that Ends Well. Act ii, sc. 5, l. 48. [Lafeu]

Donn'd his clothes.—*Hamlet,* iv, 5, 52.
Wrapped in sweet clothes.—*The Taming of the Shrew,* Ind., 1, 38.
Swathling clothes.—*I Henry IV,* iii, 2, 112.
Tatter'd clothes.—*King Lear,* iv, 6, 168.

Let me make men know
More valour in me than my habits show.

Cymbeline. Act v, sc. 1, l. 29. [Posthumus]

5
Your old smock brings forth a new petticoat.

Antony and Cleopatra. Act i, sc. 2, l. 175. [Enobarbus] "Petticoat" occurs nine times.

A smock shall be your shroud.

Love's Labour's Lost, v, 2, 479. [Biron]

You would think a smock were a she-angel.

The Winter's Tale, iv, 4, 210. See under POSSESSIONS. The only use of "she-angel."

Sit in her smock.—*Much Ado about Nothing,* ii, 3, 137. "Smock" is used ten times.
Foul . . . smocks.—*The Merry Wives of Windsor,* iii, 5, 91.
Summer smocks.—*Love's Labour's Lost,* v, 2, 916. The only uses of "smocks."

6
You are rather point-device in your accoutrements.

As You Like It. Act iii, sc. 2, l. 401. [Rosalind] "Point-devise" (with an s) is used in *Love's Labour's Lost,* v, 1, 21: "Point-devise companions"; and in *Twelfth Night,* ii, 5, 177: "Point-devise the very man."

Poor accoutrements.—*Taming of the Shrew,* iii, 2, 121. The only uses of "accoutrements."
Outward accoutrement.—*King John,* i, 1, 211. "Accoutrement" is used again in *The Merry Wives of Windsor,* iv, 2, 5.

7
Costly thy habit as thy purse can buy,
But not express'd in fancy; rich, not gaudy;
For the apparel oft proclaims the man.

Hamlet. Act i, sc. 3, l. 70. [Polonius]

8
Prince: Is not a buff jerkin a most sweet robe of Durance?
Falstaff: How now, how now, mad wag! what, in thy quips and thy quiddities? what a plague have I to do with a buff jerkin?

I Henry IV. Act i, sc. 2, l. 48.

An old cloak makes a new jerkin.

The Merry Wives of Windsor. Act i, sc. 3, l. 18. [Falstaff]

My jerkin is a doublet.

The Two Gentlemen of Verona. Act ii, sc. 4, l. 19. [Thurio]

Mistress line, is not this my jerkin? Now is the jerkin under the line: now, jerkin, you are like to lose your hair and prove a bald jerkin.

Tempest. Act iv, sc. 1, l. 235. [Stephano]

Leather jerkin.—*Troilus and Cressida,* iii, 3, 266. The only uses of "jerkin."
Leathern jerkins.—*II Henry IV,* ii, 2, 189.
Jerkins and aprons.—*II Henry IV,* ii, 4, 18. The only uses of "jerkins."

9
What stuff wilt have a kirtle of?

II Henry IV. Act ii, sc. 4, l. 297. [Falstaff]

A kirtle
Embroider'd all with leaves of myrtle.

The Passionate Pilgrim, l. 363. The only uses of "kirtle."

10
Prove that I ever dress myself handsome till thy return.

II Henry IV. Act ii, sc. 4, l. 302. [Doll]

Help to dress me, good coz.
Much Ado about Nothing. Act iii, sc. 4, l. 98. [Hero]
Help to dress.—*The Taming of the Shrew,* iii, 1, 83.
Dress us fairly.—*Henry V,* iv, 1, 10.
So carefully have dressed.—*Richard II,* v, 5, 80.
What, dress'd! and in your clothes! and down again!
Romeo and Juliet. Act iv, sc. 5, l. 12. [Nurse]

1
O, what a time have you chose out, brave Caius,
To wear a kerchief!
Julius Cæsar. Act ii, sc. 1, l. 314. [Brutus]
A plain kerchief, Sir John: my brows become nothing else; nor that well neither.
The Merry Wives of Windsor. Act iii, sc. 3, l. 62. [Mrs. Ford]
He might put on a kerchief.—*The Merry Wives of Windsor,* iv, 2, 74. The only uses of "kerchief."

2
Behold our Cæsar's vesture wounded.
Julius Cæsar, iii, 2, 200. See under WEEPING.
Essential vesture of creation.—*Othello,* ii, 1, 64.
Muddy vesture of decay.—*The Merchant of Venice,* v, 1, 64.
Napless vesture of humility.—*Coriolanus,* ii, 1, 250. The only use of "napless."
From her vesture chance to steal a kiss.—*The Two Gentlemen of Verona,* ii, 4, 160. The only uses of "vesture."

3
Off, off, you lendings! come, unbutton here.
King Lear. Act iii, sc. 4, l. 114. [Lear] The only use of "unbutton." "Lendings" is repeated in *Richard II,* i, 1, 89. "Lending" is used four times.
Unbuckle, unbuckle.—*The Winter's Tale,* iv, 4, 660. "Unbuckle" is repeated in *Antony and Cleopatra,* iv, 4, 12.
Unbuckling helms.—*Coriolanus,* iv, 5, 131. The only use of "unbuckling."

4
Disfigure not his slop.
Love's Labour's Lost. Act iv, sc. 3, l. 59. [Biron] See under RHYME.
Satin for my slops.—*II Henry IV,* i, 2, 34.
All slops.—*Much Ado about Nothing,* iii, 2, 36.
French slop.—*Romeo and Juliet,* ii, 4, 47. The only use of "slop" or "slops" (loose breeches).

5
Ford: Behold what honest clothes you send forth to bleaching! . . .
Evans: Will you take up your wife's clothes? Come away!
The Merry Wives of Windsor. Act iv, sc. 2, l. 126.
What should I do with him? dress him in my apparel and make him my waiting-gentlewoman?
Much Ado about Nothing. Act ii, sc. 1, l. 36. [Beatrice] "Waiting-gentlewoman" occurs four times in the plays.

6
My gay apparel for an almsman's gown.
Richard II, iii, 3, 149. See under GRAVE. "Gay apparel" is repeated in v, 2, 66, and occurs in no other play.
Do their gay vestments his affections bait?
The Comedy of Errors. Act ii, sc. 1, l. 94. [Adriana] "Vestments" is repeated in *Timon of Athens,* iv, 3, 125.
Deck my body in gay ornaments.
III Henry VI, iii, 2, 149. See under WOOING.
Gay new coats.—*Henry V,* iv, 3, 118.

7
Didst thou not fall out with a tailor for wearing his new doublet before Easter?
Romeo and Juliet. Act iii, sc. 1, l. 29. [Mercutio] The only mention of Easter.
Doublets that hangmen would
Bury with those that wore them
Coriolanus. Act i, sc. 5, l. 7. [Marcius]
The fashion of a doublet is nothing to a man.
Much Ado about Nothing, iii, 3, 125. See under FASHION.
Fashion of a new doublet.—*Much Ado about Nothing,* ii, 3, 19.
Is not, sir, my doublet as fresh as the first day I wore it?
The Tempest. Act ii, sc. 1, l. 102. [Gonzalo]
He plucked me ope his doublet.
Julius Cæsar. Act i, sc. 2, l. 267. [Casca]
Give me your doublet.—*II Henry IV,* v, 5, 87.
Off with your doublet.—*II Henry VI,* ii, 1, 151.
Doublet of changeable taffeta.—*Twelfth Night,* ii, 4, 76.
Silken doublet.—*The Taming of the Shrew,* v, 1, 68.
Thin-belly doublet.—*Love's Labour's Lost,* iii, 1, 19. The only use of "thin-belly."
White canvas doublet.—*I Henry IV,* ii, 4, 84. "Doublet" is used twenty-one times.
Doublet and hose ought to show itself courageous.
As You Like It, ii, 4, 6. See under WOMAN. "Doublet and hose" is used seven times in the plays, four times in *As You Like It.*

8
Go, waken Juliet, go and trim her up.
Romeo and Juliet, iv, 4, 24. [Capulet]
Dainty trims.—*Cymbeline,* iii, 4, 167.
Trimly dress'd.—*I Henry IV,* i, 3, 33.
We'll dress him up.—*Troilus and Cressida,* i, 3, 382.
We'll be dressed together.—*Twelfth Night,* v, 1, 211.

9
Servant: What raiment will your honour wear to-day? . . .
Sly: Ne'er ask me what raiment I'll wear; for I have no more doublets than backs, . . . nor no more shoes than feet; nay, sometime more feet than shoes.
Taming of the Shrew. Induction, sc. 2, l. 4.
I'll pull them off myself,
Yea, all my raiment, to my petticoat.
Taming of the Shrew, ii, 1, 4. [Bianca]
Be thou ashamed that I have took upon me
Such an immodest raiment.
The Two Gentlemen of Verona, v, 4, 105. See SHAME, 1348:11.
Our raiment . . . would bewray what life
We have led.
Coriolanus. Act v, sc. 3, l. 94. [Volumnia]
Like his raiment.—*Timon of Athens,* iii, 5, 33.
Vouchsafe me raiment.—*King Lear,* ii, 4, 158.
Seemly raiment.—*Sonnets,* xxii. The only uses of "raiment."

1
I have no more . . . stockings than legs.
The Taming of the Shrew. Induction, sc. 2, l. 9. [Sly]
To take note how many pair of silk stockings thou hast, viz. these, and those that were thy peach-coloured ones!
II Henry IV. Act ii, sc. 2, l. 17. [Prince] The only use of "viz." "Peach-coloured" is repeated in *Measure for Measure,* iv, 3, 12: "Peach-coloured satin." "Peach," referring to the fruit, does not occur at all.
His stockings foul'd.—*Hamlet,* ii, 1, 79.
Foul stockings.—*The Merry Wives of Windsor,* iii, 5, 92.
Tall stockings.—*Henry VIII,* i, 3, 30.
Yellow stockings.—*Twelfth Night,* ii, 5, 166; ii, 5, 186; ii, 5, 219; iii, 2, 78; iii, 4, 53; v, 1, 346.
White stockings.—*The Taming of the Shrew,* iv, 1, 50. The only uses of "stockings."

2
These honest mean habiliments.
The Taming of the Shrew. Act iv, sc. 3, l. 172. [Petruchio]
Poor habiliments.—*The Two Gentlemen of Verona,* iv, 1, 13.
Habiliments of the goddess Isis.—*Antony and Cleopatra,* iii, 6, 17.
Habiliments of war.—*Richard II,* i, 3, 28.
Strange and sad habiliment.—*Titus Andronicus,* v, 2, 1. The only uses of "habiliment" and "habiliments."

3
Caparisoned like the horse; with a linen stock on one leg and a kersey boot-hose on the other gartered with a red and blue list.
Taming of the Shrew. Act iii, sc. 2, l. 68. [Biondello] The only use of "boot-hose."
Caparisoned like a man.—*As You Like It,* iii, 2, 205.
Rich caparisons or trapping gay.
Venus and Adonis, l. 286.
With die and drab I purchased this caparison.
The Winter's Tale. Act iv, sc. 3, l. 27. [Autolycus] "Caparison" is repeated in *Richard III,* v, 3, 289, and in *Coriolanus,* i, 9, 12.

4
What is the jay more precious than the lark,
Because his feathers are more beautiful?
Or is the adder better than the eel,
Because his painted skin contents the eye?
The Taming of the Shrew. Act iv, sc. 3, l. 177. [Petruchio]

5
Hold up, you sluts, Your aprons mountant.
Timon of Athens. Act iv, sc. 3, l. 135. [Timon] The only use of "mountant" (rising).
I give thee my apron.—*II Henry VI,* ii, 3, 75.
Line your apron.—*Pericles,* iv, 6, 64.
Put on two of our . . . aprons.—*II Henry IV,* ii, 4, 18.
Greasy aprons.—*Antony and Cleopatra,* v, 2, 210.
Leather aprons.—*II Henry VI,* iv, 2, 14; *Julius Cæsar,* i, 1, 7; *II Henry IV,* ii, 1, 90. The only uses of "apron" and "aprons."
Apron-men.—*Coriolanus,* iv, 6, 96. The only use of the phrase.

6
These clothes are good enough to drink in; and so be these boots too: an they be not, let them hang themselves in their own straps.
Twelfth Night. Act i, sc. 3, l. 11. [Sir Toby] The only use of "straps."

7
What need a man care for a stock with a wench, when she can knit him a stock?
The Two Gentlemen of Verona. Act iii, sc. 1, l. 311. [Launce]
Flame-coloured stock.—*Twelfth Night,* i, 3, 144. "Flame-coloured" is repeated in *I Henry IV,* i, 2, 11.
Linen stock.—*Taming of the Shrew,* iii, 2, 67.
I 'll sew nether stocks.—*I Henry IV,* ii, 4, 130.
Only uses of "stock" and "stocks" in this sense.

II—Becoming and Lovely Dress

8 So well apparell'd,
So clear, so shining and so evident
That it will glimmer through a blind man's eye.
I Henry VI. Act ii, sc. 4, l. 22. [Somerset]
Not so well apparell'd As I wish you were.
The Taming of the Shrew. Act iii, sc. 2, l. 91. [Tranio]
Apparell'd like the spring.
Pericles. Act i, sc. 1, l. 12. [Pericles]
Is my apparel sumptuous to behold?
II Henry VI. Act iv, sc. 7, l. 106. [Lord Say]
You shall find her the infernal Ate in good apparel.
Much Ado about Nothing. Act ii, sc. 1, l. 263. [Benedick] The only use of "good apparel."
I 'll bring him the best 'parel that I have.
King Lear. Act iv, sc. 1, l. 51. [Old Man] The only use of "'parel."
What dost thou with thy best apparel on?
Julius Cæsar. Act i, sc. 1, l. 8. [Marullus]
Put you in your best array.
As You Like It. Act v, sc. 2, l. 79. [Rosalind]
In her best array.—*Romeo and Juliet,* iii, 3, 142; iv, 5, 81.
And do you now put on your best attire?
Julius Cæsar. Act i, sc. 1, l. 53. [Marullus]
Go fetch my best attires.
Antony and Cleopatra. Act v, sc. 2, l. 228. [Cleopatra]

9 Thou art a lady;
If only to go warm were gorgeous,
Why, nature needs not what thou gorgeous wear'st,
Which scarcely keeps thee warm.
King Lear. Act ii, sc. 4, l. 270. [King Lear]
Thou owest the worm no silk, the beast no hide, the sheep no wool, the cat no perfume.
King Lear. Act iii, sc. 4, l. 108. [King Lear]

10
With ribands pendent, flaring 'bout her head.
The Merry Wives of Windsor. Act iv, sc. 6, l. 42. [Fenton] "Riband" is used again in *Romeo and Juliet,* iii, 1, 32, and in *Hamlet,* iv, 7, 78. The only use of "flaring."

Ribbons of all the colours i' the rainbow.
The Winter's Tale, iv, 4, 205. See under POSSESSIONS.
New ribbons to your pumps.
A Midsummer-Night's Dream, iv, 2, 37. See under SHOE.
Carnation ribbon.—*Love's Labour's Lost,* iii, 1, 146.
Certain ribbons.—*The Winter's Tale,* iv, 4, 236.
Not a ribbon.—*The Winter's Tale,* iv, 4, 609.
The only uses of "ribbon" and "ribbons."

1
I will be bright, and shine in pearl and gold,
To wait upon this new-made empress.
Titus Andronicus. Act ii, sc. 1, l. 19. [Aaron]

2
She shall be habited as it becomes
The partner of your bed.
Winter's Tale. Act iv, sc. 4, l. 556. [Camillo]
Or is it Dian, habited like her?
Titus Andronicus. Act ii, sc. 3, l. 57. [Bassianus] The only uses of "habited."
Most goddess-like prank'd up.
The Winter's Tale. Act iv, sc. 4, l. 10. [Florizel] The only use of "prank'd up."

III—Unbecoming and Ugly Dress

3
Why dost thou garter up thy arms o' this fashion? dost make hose of thy sleeves? do other servants so?
All's Well that Ends Well. Act ii, sc. 3, l. 264. [Lafeu]

4
I have ere now, sir, been better known to you, when I have held familiarity with fresher clothes.
All's Well that Ends Well. Act v, sc. 2, l. 2. [Parolles]

5
I 'll put myself in poor and mean attire.
As You Like It. Act i, sc. 3, l. 113. [Celia]

6
His doublet all unbraced;
No hat upon his head; his stockings foul'd,
Ungarter'd, and down-gyved to his ancle.
Hamlet. Act ii, sc. 1, l. 78. [Ophelia] The only use of "foul'd," "down-gyved," and "ancle."
A clout upon that head
Where late the diadem stood, and for a robe,
About her lank and all o'er-teemed loins,
A blanket, in the alarm of fear caught up.
Hamlet. Act ii, sc. 2, l. 529. [First Player] The only use of "o'er-teemed." "Lank" is used once again in *II Henry VI,* i, 3, 132. "Lank-lean" occurs in *Henry V,* iv, Prol., 26. "Clout" is used six times.

7
No eye hath seen such scarecrows.
I Henry IV. Act iv, sc. 2, l. 42. [Falstaff] The only use of "scarecrows."
The scarecrow that affrights our children so.
I Henry VI. Act i, sc. 4, l. 43. [Talbot]
Scarecrow of the law.—*Measure for Measure,* ii, 1, 1. The only uses of "scarecrow."

8
I will inset you neither in gold nor silver, but in vile apparel.
II Henry IV. Act i, sc. 2, l. 19. [Falstaff] The only use of "inset."
Yet oftentimes he goes but mean-apparell'd.
The Taming of the Shrew. Act iii, sc. 2, l. 75. [Tranio] The only use of "mean-apparell'd."

9
Their clothes are after such a pagan cut too,
That, sure, they 've worn out Christendom.
Henry VIII. Act i, sc. 3, l. 14. [Lord Chamberlain]

10
How oddly he is suited! I think he bought his doublet in Italy, his round hose in France, his bonnet in Germany and his behaviour every where.
The Merchant of Venice. Act i, sc. 2, l. 79. [Portia]

11
Stinking clothes that fretted in their own grease.
The Merry Wives of Windsor. Act iii, sc. 5, l. 115. [Falstaff]
Foul clothes.—*The Merry Wives of Windsor,* iii, 5, 101; 108.

12
Her vestal livery is but sick and green
And none but fools do wear it; cast it off.
Romeo and Juliet. Act ii, sc. 2, l. 8. [Romeo]

13
Petruchio is coming in a new hat and an old jerkin, a pair of old breeches thrice turned, a pair of boots that have been candle-cases, one buckled, another laced, an old rusty sword ta'en out of the town-armoury, with a broken hilt, and chapeless.
The Taming of the Shrew. Act iii, sc. 2, l. 43. [Biondello] The only use of "candle-cases," "town-armoury," and "chapeless" (lacking the metal tip which covers the point of a scabbard).
What fashion, madam, shall I make your breeches?
The Two Gentlemen of Verona, ii, 7, 49. See under COD-PIECE.
Put'st down thine own breeches.
King Lear, i, 4, 190. See under WHIPPING.
His breeches cost him but a crown.
Othello, ii, 3, 93. See under TAILOR.
Short blister'd breeches.—*Henry VIII,* i, 3, 31.
Wear no breeches.—*II Henry VI,* i, 3, 149.
Your breeches.—*King John,* iii, 1, 201. The only references to breeches.
What, Patch-breech, I say!
Pericles. Act ii, sc. 1, l. 14. [First Fisherman] The only use of "Patch-breech."

14
O immortal gods! O fine villain! A silken doublet! a velvet hose! a scarlet cloak! and a copatain hat!
The Taming of the Shrew. Act v, sc. 1, l. 68. [Vincentio] The only use of "copatain" (high-crowned, pointed).
A monster, a very monster in apparel.
The Taming of the Shrew. Act iii, sc. 2, l. 71. [Biondello]
He hath some meaning in his mad attire.
Taming of the Shrew, iii, 2, 126. [Tranio]

15
Remember who commended thy yellow

stockings, and wished to see thee ever cross-gartered.

Twelfth Night. Act ii, sc. 5, l. 166. [Malvolio]

I will be strange, stout, in yellow stockings, and cross-gartered, even with the swiftness of putting on.

Twelfth Night. Act ii, sc. 5, l. 185. [Malvolio]

This does make some obstruction in the blood, this cross-gartering; but what of that? if it please the eye of one, it is with me as the very true sonnet is, 'Please one, and please all.'

Twelfth Night. Act iii, sc. 4, l. 21. [Maria] Cross-gartering (wearing garters above and below the knee so as to cross behind it) is referred to six times in this scene, and nowhere else.

1 I should blush
To see you so attired, sworn, I think,
To show myself a glass.

Winter's Tale. Act iv, sc. 4, l. 12. [Perdita]

2
Clown: Alack, poor soul! thou hast need of more rags to lay on thee, rather than have these off.

Autolycus: O sir, the loathsomeness of them offends.

The Winter's Tale. Act iv, sc. 3, l. 56. The only use of "loathsomeness."

O, the Fates!
How would he look, to see his work so noble
Vilely bound up?

Winter's Tale. Act iv, sc. 4, l. 20. [Perdita]

DRIFT, see Meaning

DRINKING

See also Cup; Eating and Drinking

3
I had rather heat my liver with drinking.

Antony and Cleopatra. Act i, sc. 2, l. 23. [Charmian]

4
Pompey: Hast thou drunk well?
Menas: No, Pompey, I have kept me from the cup.

Antony and Cleopatra. Act ii, sc. 7, l. 71.

I had rather fast from all four days
Than drink so much in one.

Antony and Cleopatra. Act ii, sc. 7, l. 108. [Cæsar]

5
We will drink together.

Coriolanus. Act v, sc. 3, l. 203. [Coriolanus]

Let 's drink together friendly and embrace.

II Henry IV. Act iv, sc. 2, l. 63. [Lancaster]

He calls for drink.—*Hamlet,* iv, 7, 160.

6
A long lease for the clinking of pewter.

I Henry IV. Act ii, sc. 4, l. 50. [Prince of Wales] The only use of "clinking." Pewter is mentioned again in *The Taming of the Shrew,* ii, 1, 357.

Such as will strike sooner than speak, and speak sooner than drink, and drink sooner than pray.

I Henry IV. Act ii, sc. 1, l. 85. [Gadshill]

They call drinking deep, dyeing scarlet.

I Henry IV. Act ii, sc. 4, l. 17. [Prince of Wales]

I am so good a proficient in one quarter of an hour, that I can drink with any tinker in his own language during my life.

I Henry IV. Act ii, sc. 4, l. 20. [Prince of Wales] The only use of "proficient."

7
Glasses, glasses, is the only drinking.

II Henry IV. Act ii, sc. 1, l. 155. [Falstaff]

I 'll drink no more than will do me good, for no man's pleasure, I.

II Henry IV. Act ii, sc. 4, l. 128. [Hostess]

Come, I will go drink with you.

II Henry IV. Act iii, sc. 2, l. 203. [Falstaff]

Drink freely.—*II Henry IV,* iv, 2, 75.

8
Proface! What you want in meat, we 'll have in drink.

II Henry IV. Act v, sc. 3, l. 29. [Davy] For "meat and drink" see under FOOD. The only use of "proface" (welcome).

By the mass, you 'll crack a quart together.

II Henry IV. Act v, sc. 3, l. 66. [Shallow] The only use of "crack a quart."

9
Archbishop of Canterbury: A thousand pounds by the year: thus runs the bill.
Bishop of Ely: This would drink deep.
Archbishop of Canterbury: 'Twould drink the cup and all.

Henry V. Act i, sc. 1, l. 19.

We 'll teach you to drink deep ere you depart.

Hamlet. Act i, sc. 2, l. 175. [Hamlet] The only two instances in the plays of the use of the phrase "drink deep."

10
Give me some drink.

II Henry VI. Act iii, sc. 3, l. 17. [Cardinal]

Give me drink.—*Hamlet,* v, 2, 293.

11 Anon we 'll drink a measure
The table round.

Macbeth. Act iii, sc. 4, l. 11. [Macbeth]

We shall have all the world drink brown and white bastard.

Measure for Measure. Act iii, sc. 2, l. 3. [Elbow]

When we drink we die.—*Measure for Measure,* i, 2, 134.

12
I will do any thing, Nerissa, ere I 'll be married to a sponge.

The Merchant of Venice. Act i, sc. 2, l. 107. [Portia]

Hamlet: Besides, to be demanded of a sponge! . . .
Rosencrantz: Take you me for a sponge, my lord?
Hamlet: Ay, sir, that soaks up the King's countenance, his rewards, his authorities. . . . When he needs what you have gleaned, it is but squeezing you, and, sponge, you shall be dry again.

Hamlet. Act iv, sc. 2, l. 12. The only uses of "sponge." "Spongy" occurs four times.

13
I hope we shall drink down all unkindness.

The Merry Wives of Windsor. Act i, sc. 1, l. 203. [Mistress Page]

We 'll have a posset for 't soon at night, in faith, at the end of a sea-coal fire.

The Merry Wives of Windsor. Act i, sc. 4,

l. 8. [Mistress Quickly] "Sea-coal fire" occurs again in *II Henry IV*, ii, 1, 95.

Thou shalt eat a posset to-night at my house.
The Merry Wives of Windsor. Act v, sc. 5, l. 180. [Page]

I have drugg'd their possets.
Macbeth. Act ii, sc. 2, l. 6. [Lady Macbeth]

Posset And curd.—*Hamlet*, i, 5, 68. The only uses of "posset," a drink of hot milk curdled with wine.

1
Host: Farewell, my hearts: I will to my honest knight Falstaff, and drink canary with him.
Ford: I think I shall drink in pipe-wine first with him; I 'll make him dance.
The Merry Wives of Windsor. Act iii, sc. 2, l. 88. The only use of "pipe-wine," i.e., wine from the wood.

Drink blood.—*I Henry VI*, ii, 4, 134.
Drink hot blood.—*Hamlet*, iii, 2, 408.
Drink off this potion.—*Hamlet*, v, 2, 337.
Drink potions.—*II Henry IV*, i, 1, 197.
Drink Potions of eisel.—*Sonnets*, cxi.
Woo 't drink up eisel?—*Hamlet*, v, 1, 299.
I have drunk medicines.—*I Henry IV*, ii, 2, 21.

2
Potations pottle-deep.
Othello. Act ii, sc. 3, l. 56. [Iago] The only appearance of "pottle-deep." "Potations" is used one other time in *II Henry IV*, iv, 3, 135: "To forswear thin potations."

'Tis evermore the prologue to his sleep:
He 'll watch the horologue a double set,
If drink rock not his cradle.
Othello. Act ii, sc. 3, l. 134. [Iago] The only use of "horologue" (clock).

3
Gramercy, fellow: there, drink that for me.
Richard III. Act iii, sc. 2, l. 108. [Hastings]

Thou 'rt a tall fellow: hold thee that to drink.
The Taming of the Shrew. Act iv, sc. 4, l. 17. [Tranio]

You shall not choose but drink before you go.
The Taming of the Shrew. Act v, sc. 1, l. 12. [Vincentio]

4
Open your mouth; here is that which will give language to you, cat: open your mouth; this will shake your shaking, I can tell you.
The Tempest. Act ii, sc. 2, l. 85. [Stephano]

He shall drink nought but brine; for I 'll not show him
Where the quick freshes are.
The Tempest. Act iii, sc. 2, l. 74. [Caliban] The only use of "freshes."

I drink the air before me.—*The Tempest*, v, 1, 102; *Venus and Adonis*, l. 273.
Drink the free air.—*Timon of Athens*, i, 1, 83.
Drink tears.—*Venus and Adonis*, l. 949.

5
He ne'er drinks,
But Timon's silver treads upon his lips.
Timon of Athens. Act iii, sc. 2, l. 77. [Stranger]

6
Alas, sir, I know not Jupiter, I never drank with him in all my life.
Titus Andronicus. Act iv, sc. 3, l. 84. [Clown] Shakespeare used "drank" in only one other place, *The Taming of the Shrew*, Induction, sc. 2, l. 6: "I ne'er drank sack in my life."

7
That quaffing and drinking will undo you.
Twelfth Night. Act i, sc. 3, l. 14. [Maria] The only use of "quaffing."

Toss-pots still had drunken heads.
Twelfth Night. Act v, sc. 1, l. 412. [Clown] The only use of "toss-pots."

8
Speed: She will often praise her liquor.
Launce: If her liquor be good, she shall.
The Two Gentlemen of Verona. Act iii, sc. 1, l. 350.

Liquor likewise will I give to thee.
Henry V, ii, 1, 113. See under BROTHERHOOD.

Fetch me a stoup of liquor.
Hamlet, v, 1, 68. See under WINE.

Horatio: Here 's yet some liquor left.
Hamlet: As thou 'rt a man, Give me the cup.
Hamlet. Act v, sc. 2, l. 353.

There is . . . liquor in his pate.
The Merry Wives of Windsor. Act ii, sc. 1, l. 197. [Page]

The liquor is not earthly.
The Tempest. Act ii, sc. 2, l. 130. [Caliban]

Celestial liquor.—*The Tempest*, ii, 2, 122.
Distilled liquor.—*Romeo and Juliet*, iv, 1, 94.
Divers liquors.—*II Henry IV*, iii, 1, 53.
Hateful liquor.—*Titus Andronicus*, v, 2, 200.
Hot and rebellious liquors.—*As You Like It*, ii, 3, 49. See under AGE: ITS COMPENSATIONS.
Precious liquor.—*Richard II*, i, 2, 19.

9
We will give you sleepy drinks.
The Winter's Tale. Act i, sc. 1, l. 14. [Archidamus]

II—Drinking Healths

10
Menas: I have a health for you.
Enobarbus: I shall take it, sir: we have used our throats in Egypt.
Antony and Cleopatra. Act ii, sc. 6, l. 142.

11
No jocund health that Denmark drinks today,
But the great cannon to the clouds shall tell.
Hamlet, i, 2, 125. See under CANNON.

Here 's to thy health.
Hamlet. Act v, sc. 2, l. 294. [King]

12
Fill the cup, and let it come;
I 'll pledge you a mile to the bottom.
II Henry IV. Act v, sc. 3, l. 56. [Silence]

I 'll pledge you all.—*II Henry VI*, ii, 3, 66.

13
I 'll drink to Master Bardolph, and to all the cavaleros about London.
II Henry IV. Act v, sc. 3, l. 61. [Shallow] The only use of "cavaleros."

I drink unto your grace.—*II Henry IV*, iv, 2, 68.

14
I drink to you in a cup of sack.
II Henry VI. Act ii, sc. 3, l. 59. [Neighbour]

I drink to thee: and be not afraid.
II Henry VI. Act ii, sc. 3, l. 68. ['Prentice]

15
A health, gentlemen! Let it go round.
Henry VIII. Act i, sc. 4, l. 96. [King]

I have half a dozen healths
To drink to these fair ladies.
Henry VIII. Act i, sc. 4, l. 105. [King Henry]

1 Come, love and health to all; . . .
Give me some wine; fill full.
I drink to the general joy o' the whole table.
Macbeth. Act iii, sc. 4, l. 87. [Macbeth]

To the health of our general!
Othello. Act ii, sc. 3, l. 88. [Cassio]

2
Here, with a cup that 's stored unto the brim,—
As you do love, fill to your mistress' lips,—
We drink this health to you.
Pericles. Act ii, sc. 3, l. 50. [Simonides]

Here, say we drink this standing-bowl of wine to him.
Pericles. Act ii, sc. 3, l. 65. [Simonides] The only use of "standing-bowl" (a bowl standing on a foot), except in the stage directions for *Henry VIII,* v, 5.

3
Quaff carouses to our mistress' health.
The Taming of the Shrew. Act i, sc. 2, l. 277. [Tranio]

He calls for wine: 'A health!' quoth he, as if
He had been aboard, carousing to his mates
After a storm; quaff'd off the muscadel.
Taming of the Shrew. Act iii, sc. 2, l. 172. [Gremio] The only mention of muscadel.

Drink carouses.—*Antony and Cleopatra,* iv, 8, 34.
Carouses to thy fortune.—*Hamlet,* v, 2, 300.
Carouse full measure.—*The Taming of the Shrew,* iii, 2, 227.
Carouse together.—*Antony and Cleopatra,* iv, 12, 12. The only uses of "carouse" and "carouses."

4
Therefore a health to all that shot and miss'd.
The Taming of the Shrew. Act v, sc. 2, l. 51. [Petruchio]

Well, here 's my comfort.
The Tempest. Act ii, sc. 2, l. 47. [Stephano]

Health to you, valiant sir.
Troilus and Cressida. Act iv, sc. 1, l. 10. [Æneas]

5
Apemantus: Great men should drink with harness on their throats.
Timon: My lord, in heart; and let the health go round.
Second Lord: Let it flow this way, my good lord.
Apemantus: Flow this way! A brave fellow! He keeps his tides well. Those healths will make thee and thy state look ill, Timon.
Timon of Athens. Act i, sc. 2, l. 53.

III—Drunkenness

6
Drunkenness is his best virtue, for he will be swine-drunk; and in his sleep he does little harm, save to his bed-clothes about him; but they know his conditions and lay him in straw.
All's Well that Ends Well. Act iv, sc. 3, l. 285. [Parolles] The only use of "swine-drunk" and "bed-clothes."

7
Ere the ninth hour, I drunk him to his bed.
Antony and Cleopatra. Act ii, sc. 5, l. 21. [Cleopatra]

Drunk to bed.—*Antony and Cleopatra,* i, 2, 45.

To . . . keep the turn of tippling with a slave;
To reel the streets at noon, and stand the buffet
With knaves that smell of sweat.
Antony and Cleopatra. Act i, sc. 4, l. 19. [Cæsar] The only use of "tippling."

You see we have burnt our cheeks: strong Enobarb
Is weaker than the wine; and mine own tongue
Splits what it speaks: the wild disguise hath almost
Antick'd us all.
Antony and Cleopatra. Act ii, sc. 7, l. 129. [Cæsar] The only use of "antick'd."

8
They clepe us drunkards.
Hamlet. Act i, sc. 4, l. 19. [Hamlet] The only use of "clepe."

One drunkard loves another of the name.
Love's Labour's Lost, iv, 3, 50. [Biron]

I will, like a true drunkard, utter all to thee.
Much Ado about Nothing. Act iii, sc. 3, l. 111. [Borachio]

Flemish drunkard.—*The Merry Wives of Windsor,* ii, 1, 24.
Poor drunkard!—*The Tempest,* ii, 2, 170.

9
There 's a whole merchant's venture of Bourdeaux stuff in him; you have not seen a hulk better stuffed in the hold.
II Henry IV. Act ii, sc. 4, l. 69. [Doll Tearsheet] Bourdeaux, as Shakespeare always spelled it, is mentioned seven times.

The rascal 's drunk.—*II Henry IV,* ii, 4, 230.

10
Drunk many times a day, if not many days entirely drunk.
Measure for Measure. Act iv, sc. 2, l. 157. [Provost]

Barnardine: I have been drinking all night; I am not fitted for 't.
Pompey: O, the better, sir; for he that drinks all night, and is hanged betimes in the morning, may sleep the sounder all the next day.
Measure for Measure. Act iv, sc. 3, l. 46.

He would be drunk too.—*Measure for Measure,* iii, 2, 136.
He was drunk then.—*Measure for Measure,* v, 1, 188.

11
I cannot remember what I did when you made me drunk.
The Merry Wives of Windsor. Act i, sc. 1, l. 175. [Slender]

The gentleman had drunk himself out of his five sentences.
The Merry Wives of Windsor. Act i, sc. 1, l. 178. [Bardolph]

Being fap, sir, was, as they say, cashiered.
Merry Wives of Windsor. Act i, sc. 1, l. 183. [Bardolph] The only use of "fap" (drunk).

I 'll ne'er be drunk whilst I live again, but in honest, civil, godly company, for this trick: if I be drunk, I 'll be drunk with those that have the fear of God, and not with drunken knaves.
The Merry Wives of Windsor. Act i, sc. 1, l. 186. [Slender]

1
Have you make-a de sot of us?
The Merry Wives of Windsor. Act iii, sc. 1, l. 118. [Caius]

He 's but a sot.
The Tempest. Act iii, sc. 2, l. 101. [Caliban]

Unspeaking sots.—*Cymbeline,* v, 5, 178. The only use of "unspeaking."

How now, sot?—*Twelfth Night,* i, 5, 129.

Thou sot!—*The Comedy of Errors,* ii, 2, 196.

He call'd me sot.—*King Lear,* iv, 2, 8. "Sot" is used once again in *Twelfth Night,* v, 1, 202. See 387 : 3.

2
Now, in madness,
Being full of supper and distempering draughts,
Upon malicious bravery, dost thou come
To start my quiet.
Othello. Act i, sc. 1, l. 98. [Brabantio] "Distempering" is repeated in *Venus and Adonis,* l. 653.

Fluster'd with flowing cups.
Othello. Act ii, sc. 3, l. 60. [Iago] The only use of "fluster'd." See under CUP.

3
Do not think, gentlemen, I am drunk: this is my ancient; this is my right hand, and this is my left: I am not drunk now; I can stand well enough, and speak well enough.
Othello. Act ii, sc. 3, l. 117. [Cassio]

4
I have very poor and unhappy brains for drinking: I could well wish courtesy would invent some other custom of entertainment.
Othello. Act ii, sc. 3, l. 34. [Cassio]

Drunk? and speak parrot? and squabble? swagger? swear? and discourse fustian with one's own shadow?
Othello. Act ii, sc. 3, l. 280. [Cassio] The only use of "squabble."

5
O God, that men should put an enemy in their mouths to steal away their brains! that we should, with joy, pleasance, revel and applause, transform ourselves into beasts!
Othello. Act ii, sc. 3, l. 291. [Cassio] "Pleasance" is repeated in *The Passionate Pilgrim,* l. 158.

To be now a sensible man, by and by a fool, and presently a beast! O strange! Every inordinate cup is unblessed and the ingredient is a devil.
Othello. Act ii, sc. 3, l. 309. [Cassio]

Cassio: I drunk!
Iago: You or any man living may be drunk at a time, man.
Othello. Act ii, sc. 3, l. 317.

Unlawfully made drunk.—*Richard III,* iv, 4, 30.

6
Drunkenly caroused.
Richard II. Act ii, sc. 1, l. 127. [Gaunt] The only use of "drunkenly."

To-night caroused.—*Othello,* ii, 3, 55.

Caroused and banqueted.—*I Henry VI,* ii, 1, 12. The only uses of "caroused."

Porter: We were carousing till the second cock: and drink, sir, is a great provoker of three things.
Macduff: What three things does drink especially provoke?
Porter: Marry, sir, nose-painting, sleep, and urine. Lechery, sir, it provokes, and unprovokes; it provokes the desire, but it takes away the performance: therefore, much drink may be said to be an equivocator with lechery: it makes him, and it mars him; it sets him on, and it takes him off; it persuades him, and disheartens him; makes him stand to, and not stand to; in conclusion, equivocates him in a sleep, and, giving him the lie, leaves him.
Macduff: I believe drink gave thee the lie last night.
Porter: That it did, sir, i' the very throat on me: but I requited him for his lie; and, I think, being too strong for him, though he took up my legs sometime, yet I made a shift to cast him.
Macbeth. Act ii, sc. 3, l. 26. The only use of "provoker," "nose-painting" and "unprovokes." "Carousing" is repeated in *Taming of the Shrew,* iii, 2, 173: "Carousing to his mates"; and "urine" in *Measure for Measure,* iii, 2, 118, and in *Merchant of Venice,* iv, 1, 50.

7
Lord: What 's here? one dead, or drunk? See, doth he breathe?
Huntsman: He breathes, my lord. Were he not warm'd with ale,
This were a bed but cold to sleep so soundly.
The Taming of the Shrew. Induction, sc. 1, l. 31.

He drinks . . . your Dane dead drunk.
Othello. Act ii, sc. 3, l. 84. [Iago] The only use of "dead drunk."

By mine honour, half drunk.
Twelfth Night. Act i, sc. 5, l. 124. [Olivia] The only use of "half drunk."

8
'Scape being drunk for want of wine.
The Tempest. Act ii, sc. 1, l. 146. [Sebastian]

I told you, sir, they were red-hot with drinking.
The Tempest. Act iv, sc. 1, l. 171. [Ariel]

Sebastian: He is drunk now: where had he wine?
Alonzo: And Trinculo is reeling ripe: where should they
Find this grand liquor that hath gilded 'em?
The Tempest. Act v, sc. 1, l. 278. The only use of "reeling ripe."

What a thrice-double ass
Was I, to take this drunkard for a god.
The Tempest. Act v, sc. 1, l. 295. [Caliban] The only use of "thrice-double."

9
Maria: They that add, moreover, he 's drunk nightly in your company.
Sir Toby: With drinking healths to my niece: I 'll drink to her as long as there is a passage in my throat and drink in Illyria: he 's a coward and a coystrill that will not drink to my niece till his brains turn o' the toe like a parish-top.
Twelfth Night. Act i, sc. 3, l. 38. The only use of "coystrill" (paltry fellow), and of "parish-top" (whipping-top).

10
Oliver: What 's a drunken man like, fool?
Clown: Like a drowned man, a fool and a mad man: one draught above heat makes

him a fool; the second mads him; and a third drowns him.
Twelfth Night. Act i, sc. 5, l. 138.
He's in the third degree of drink, he's drowned.
Twelfth Night. Act i, sc. 5, l. 143. [Olivia]
1
Who is but drunken when she seemeth drown'd.
Venus and Adonis, l. 984.
2
If he had not been in drink, he would have tickled you othergates than he did.
Twelfth Night. Act v, sc. 1, l. 197. [Sir Andrew] The only use of "othergates" (in another way).
The poor monster's in drink.—*The Tempest,* ii, 2, 162.
Gotten in drink.—*The Merry Wives of Windsor,* i, 3, 25.
I do not speak to thee in drink.—*I Henry IV,* ii, 4, 458. The only uses of "in drink" in this sense.
3
Sir Toby: Sot, didst see Dick surgeon, sot?
Clown: O, he's drunk, Sir Toby, an hour agone; his eyes were set at eight i' the morning.
Twelfth Night. Act v, sc. 1, l. 202.
Thy eyes are almost set in thy head.
The Tempest. Act iii, sc. 2, l. 10. [Stephano]

DRONE, see Idleness

DROWNING

4
Drown my clothes, and say I was stripped.
All's Well that Ends Well. Act iv, sc. 1, l. 57. [Parolles]
Drown my book.—*The Tempest,* v, 1, 57.
Drown my manly spirit.—*The Merchant of Venice,* ii, 3, 14.
Drown my oratory.—*Titus Andronicus,* v, 3, 90.
Drown me with their sweetness.—*Pericles,* v, 1, 196.
Drown consideration.—*Antony and Cleopatra,* iv, 2, 45.
Drown desperate sorrow.—*Richard III,* ii, 2, 99.
Drown King Edward's fruit.—*III Henry VI,* iv, 4, 23.
Drown or hang themselves.—*Hamlet,* v, 1, 31.
Drown their proper selves.—*The Tempest,* iii, 3, 59.
Drown her remembrance.—*Twelfth Night,* ii, 1, 31.
Drown the sad remembrance.—*Richard III,* iv, 4, 251.
Drown our gain in tears!—*All's Well that Ends Well,* iv, 3, 79.
Drown the fragrant meads.—*Titus Andronicus,* ii, 4, 54.
Drown the weeds.—*Timon of Athens,* v, 2, 30.
Drown the wind.—*Macbeth,* i, 7, 25.
Drown the world!—*Richard III,* ii, 2, 70.
Drown their eyes.—*Rape of Lucrece,* l. 1239.
Drown an eye.—*Sonnets,* xxx.
Drown their shores.—*Richard II,* iii, 2, 107.
Drown this fool.—*The Tempest,* iv, 1, 230.
Drown thy cries!—*Richard III,* ii, 2, 61.
Drown'd the cocks!—*King Lear,* iii, 2, 3.
Drown'd their enmity.—*Titus Andronicus,* v, 3, 107.
5
He went but forth to wash him in the Hellespont and being taken with the cramp was drowned.
As You Like It. Act iv, sc. 1, l. 103. [Rosalind] The Hellespont is mentioned four times.
6
Second Clown: The crowner hath sat on her, and finds it Christian burial.
First Clown: How can that be, unless she drowned herself in her own defence?
Second Clown: Why, 'tis found so.
First Clown: It must be 'se offendendo;' it cannot be else. For here lies the point: if I drown myself wittingly, it argues an act: and an act hath three branches; it is to act, to do, and to perform: argal, she drowned herself wittingly.
Second Clown: Nay, but hear you, goodman delver,—
First Clown: Give me leave. Here lies the water; good: here stands the man; good: if the man go to this water, and drown himself, it is, will he, nill he, he goes,—mark you that; but if the water comes to him and drowns him, he drowns not himself: argal, he that is not guilty of his own death shortens not his own life.
Hamlet. Act v, sc. 1, l. 4. "Crowner" (coroner) is repeated in l. 24, and in *Twelfth Night,* i, 5, 142. The only use of "se offendendo" (in self-offence), a comic blunder for "se defendendo," in self-defence. "Wittingly" is used a third time in *III Henry VI,* ii, 2, 8. "Argal" (for ergo) is repeated in l. 55, and occurs in no other scene. The only use of "delver," and of "will he, nill he."
Wouldst thou drown thyself,
Put but a little water in a spoon,
And it shall be as all the ocean,
Enough to stifle such a villain up.
King John. Act iv, sc. 3, l. 130. [Bastard]
Roderigo: I will incontinently drown myself. . . .
Iago: Ere I would say, I would drown myself for the love of a guinea-hen, I would change my humanity with a baboon. . . . Come, be a man. Drown thyself! drown cats and blind puppies. . . . If thou wilt needs damn thyself, do it a more delicate way than drowning. . . . A pox of drowning thyself! it is clean out of the way: seek thou rather to be hanged in compassing thy joy than to be drowned and go without her.
Othello. Act i, sc. 3, l. 305. The only mention of guinea-hen.
Drown themselves.—*Timon of Athens,* iv, 1, 28.
7
You may know by my size that I have a kind of alacrity in sinking; if the bottom were as deep as hell, I should down. I had been drowned, but that the shore was shelvy and shallow,—a death that I abhor; for the water swells a man; and what a thing I should have been when I had been swelled!

I should have been a mountain of mummy.
The Merry Wives of Windsor. Act iii, sc. 5, l. 12. [Falstaff] The only use of "shelvy."
'Scape drowning thrice.—*The Merchant of Venice,* ii, 2, 172.

1 Is 't not drowned in the last rain?
Measure for Measure. Act iii, sc. 2, l. 51. [Lucio]
Drown'd him in the flood.—*The Rape of Lucrece,* l. 266.
Drown'd in cares.—*III Henry VI,* iii, 3, 14.
Drown'd with grief.—*II Henry VI,* iii, 1, 198.
I am drown'd.—*The Two Gentlemen of Verona,* i, 3, 79.
He 's drowned.—*Twelfth Night,* i, 5, 144; *The Tempest,* ii, 2, 91.
Perchance he is not drown'd.—*Twelfth Night,* i, 2, 5.
Lie drown'd.—*Henry V,* iv, 7, 79; *Troilus and Cressida,* i, 1, 49.

2 If that the Turkish fleet
Be not enshelter'd and embay'd, they are drown'd.
Othello. Act ii, sc. 1, l. 17. [Montano] The only use of "enshelter'd" and "embay'd."
The Turks are drown'd.—*Othello,* ii, 1, 204.
Dead and drown'd.—*Pericles,* v, 3, 36.
Often drown'd.—*Romeo and Juliet,* i, 2, 95.

3 'Tis double death to drown in ken of shore.
The Rape of Lucrece, l. 1114.
Drown'd on shore.—*II Henry VI,* iii, 2, 95.
Drowns for want of skill.—*The Rape of Lucrece,* l. 1099. See under SWIMMING.

4 Lord, Lord! methought, what pain it was to drown!
What dreadful noise of waters in mine ears!
What ugly sights of death within mine eyes!
Richard III. Act i, sc. 4, l. 21. [Clarence]
I 'll drown you in the malmsey-butt within.
Richard III. Act i, sc. 4, l. 277. [Murderer] "Malmsey-butt" is repeated in l. 161, and occurs in no other scene.
Drown them in a draught.—*Timon of Athens,* v, 1, 105.

5 Shall we give o'er and drown? Have you a mind to sink?
The Tempest. Act i, sc. 1, l. 41. [Boatswain]
Antonio: We are less afraid to be drowned than thou art.
Gonzalo: I 'll warrant him for drowning; though the ship were no stronger than a nutshell and as leaky as an unstanched wench.
The Tempest. Act i, sc. 1, l. 47. "Nutshell" is used again in *Hamlet,* ii, 2, 260, and "unstanched" in *III Henry VI,* ii, 6, 83.
Would thou mightest lie drowning
The washing of ten tides!
The Tempest. Act i, sc. 1, l. 60. [Antonio]
'Tis as impossible that he 's undrown'd
As he that sleeps here swims.
The Tempest. Act ii, sc. 1, l. 237. [Antonio] The only use of "undrown'd."
I have not 'scaped drowning to be afeard now of your four legs.
The Tempest. Act ii, sc. 2, l. 61. [Stephano]
But art thou not drowned, Stephano? I hope now thou art not drowned.
The Tempest. Act ii, sc. 2, l. 113. [Trinculo]
He is drown'd Whom thus we stray to find.
The Tempest. Act iii, sc. 3, l. 8. [Alonso]

6 One that I saved from drowning.
The Two Gentlemen of Verona. Act iv, sc. 4, l. 3. [Launce]

DRUM

7 I 'll no more drumming; a plague of all drums!
All's Well that Ends Well. Act iv, sc. 3, l. 331. [Parolles] The only use of "drumming."
Hear the drum.—*All 's Well that Ends Well,* ii, 5, 96.

8 Hark! the drums
Demurely wake the sleepers.
Antony and Cleopatra. Act iv, sc. 9, l. 31. [Soldier]

9 Beat thou the drum, that it speak mournfully.
Coriolanus. Act v, sc. 6, l. 151. [Aufidius] The only use of "mournfully."

10 The kettle-drum and trumpet thus bray out.
Hamlet. Act i, sc. 4, l. 11. The only use of "kettle-drum."
Let the kettle to the trumpet speak.
Hamlet. Act v, sc. 2, l. 286. The only use of "kettle."

11 Hark! by the sound of drum you may perceive
Their powers are marching unto Paris-ward.
I Henry VI. Act iii, sc. 3, l. 30. [La Pucelle] The only use of "Paris-ward."

12 Then strike up drums; God and Saint George for us!
III Henry VI. Act ii, sc. 1, l. 204. [Edward] See also *III Henry VI,* v, 3, 24; *Richard III,* iv, 4, 179; *King John,* v, 2, 164; *II Henry IV,* iv, 2, 120.
Strike up the drum towards Athens!
Timon of Athens. Act iv, sc. 3, l. 169. [Alcibiades]
Drummer, strike up, and let us march away.
III Henry VI. Act iv, sc. 7, l. 50. The only use of "drummer."
Let the drum strike.—*King Lear,* v, 3, 81.
Strike alarum, drums!—*Richard III,* iv, 4, 148.
Sound drums and trumpets!—*II Henry VI,* v, 3, 32; *III Henry VI,* i, 1, 118; v, 7, 45; *Richard III,* v, 3, 269.

13 The interruption of their churlish drums
Cuts off more circumstance.
King John. Act ii, sc. 1, l. 76. [Chatillon]
His churlish drum.—*Venus and Adonis,* l. 107.
Boisterous untuned drums.—*Richard II,* i, 3, 134.
The spirit-stirring drum.—*Othello,* iii, 3, 352. See FAREWELL, 502:9, for full quotation. The only use of "spirit-stirring."

1
Indeed, your drums, being beaten, will cry out;
And so shall you, being beaten: do but start
An echo with the clamour of thy drum,
And even at hand a drum is ready braced
That shall reverberate all as loud as thine;
Sound but another, and another shall
As loud as thine rattle the welkin's ear
And mock the deep-mouth'd thunder.

King John. Act v, sc. 2, l. 166. [Bastard] "Deep-mouth'd" is used three times: *The Taming of the Shrew,* Ind., 1, 18, "Deep-mouth'd brach"; *Henry V,* Prol., 11, "Deep-mouth'd sea."

Far off, methinks, I hear the beaten drum.
King Lear. Act iv, sc. 6, l. 292. [Edgar]

2 Bid them come forth and hear me,
Or at their chamber-door I 'll beat the drum
Till it cry sleep to death.
King Lear. Act ii, sc. 4, l. 118. [King Lear]

Beat thy drum.—*Timon of Athens,* iv, 3, 96.

3
Let 's march without the noise of threatening drum.
Richard II. Act iii, sc. 3, l. 51. [Bolingbroke]

Let your drums be still.—*I Henry VI,* v, 4, 174.
Be still, drum!—*Love's Labour 's Lost,* i, 2, 188.

DUELLING

See also Challenge

4
Sword against sword, Ourselves alone.
Antony and Cleopatra. Act iii, sc. 13, l. 27. [Antony]

So we measured swords and parted.
As You Like It. Act v, sc. 4, l. 91. [Touchstone]

5
He . . . gave you such a masterly report
For art and exercise in your defence
And for your rapier most especial,
That he cried out, 'twould be a sight indeed,
If one could match you: the scrimers of their nation,
He swore, had neither motion, guard, nor eye,
If you opposed them.

Hamlet. Act iv, sc. 7, l. 96. [King] The only use of "scrimers" (swordsmen).

6
I am content that he shall take the odds
Of his great name and estimation,
And will, to save the blood on either side,
Try fortune with him in a single fight.
I Henry IV. Act v, sc. 1, l. 97. [Prince of Wales]

7
He will foin like any devil.
II Henry IV. Act ii, sc. 1, l. 17. [Hostess]

No matter for your foins.
King Lear. Act iv, sc. 6, l. 251. [Edgar] "Foin" (thrust in fencing) is used a third time in *The Merry Wives of Windsor,* ii, 3, 24. See fourth quotation under 389: 11.

Sir boy, I 'll whip you from your foining fence.
Much Ado about Nothing. Act v, sc. 1, l. 84. [Antonio] "Foining" is used again in a figurative sense in *II Henry IV,* ii, 4, 252, when the Prince of Wales accuses Falstaff of "foining o' nights."

8
This is the right fencing grace, my lord; tap for tap, and so part fair.
II Henry IV. Act ii, sc. 1, l. 205. [Falstaff]

Fencing, dancing.—*Twelfth Night,* i, 3, 98.
Fencing, swearing.—*Hamlet,* ii, 1, 25.
Virginal fencing.—*Pericles,* iv, 6, 63. The only uses of "fencing."

9
What! shall we have incision? shall we imbrue?
II Henry IV. Act ii, sc. 4, l. 210. [Pistol] "Imbrue" is repeated in *A Midsummer-Night's Dream,* v, 1, 351: "My breast imbrue."

As manhood shall compound: push home.
Henry V. Act ii, sc. 1, l. 103. [Pistol]

10
He will fence with his own shadow.
The Merchant of Venice. Act i, sc. 2, l. 66. [Portia]

Alas, sir, I cannot fence.—*The Merry Wives of Windsor,* ii, 3, 15.
Teach us some fence!—*King John,* ii, 1, 290.
He hath learnt so much fence.—*II Henry VI,* ii, 3, 79.
My fence shall fail.—*II Henry VI,* ii, 1, 52.
Master of fence.—*The Merry Wives of Windsor,* i, 1, 295. The only use of the phrase.

11
If I were young again, the sword should end it.
The Merry Wives of Windsor. Act i, sc. 1, l. 40. [Shallow]

Slice, I say! pauca, pauca: slice! that 's my humour.
The Merry Wives of Windsor. Act i, sc. 1, l. 134. [Nym] The only use of "slice." "Pauca" occurs six times.

In these times you stand on distance, your passes, stoccadoes, and I know not what: 'tis the heart, Master Page; 'tis here, 'tis here. I have seen the time, with my long sword I would have made you four tall fellows skip like rats.
The Merry Wives of Windsor. Act ii, sc. 1, l. 233. [Shallow] The only use of "stoccadoes" (thrusts).

To see thee fight, to see thee foin, to see thee traverse; to see thee here, to see thee there; to see thee pass thy punto, thy stock, thy reverse, thy distance, thy montant.
The Merry Wives of Windsor. Act ii, sc. 3, l. 24. [Host] The only use of "montant" (an upright thrust).

If you should fight, you go against the hair of your professions.
The Merry Wives of Windsor. Act ii, sc. 3, l. 41. [Shallow]

12
I 'll prove it on his body, if he dare,
Despite his nice fence and his active practice.
Much Ado about Nothing. Act v, sc. 1, l. 74. [Leonato]

I will bid thee draw, as we do the minstrels; draw, to pleasure us.

Much Ado about Nothing. Act v, sc. 1, l. 128. [Claudio]

Draw, if you be men. Gregory, remember thy swashing blow.

Romeo and Juliet. Act i, sc. 1, l. 69. [Sampson] "Swashing" is repeated in *As You Like It,* i, 3, 122: "A swashing and a martial outside."

1
He fights as you sing prick-song, keeps time, distance, and proportion; rests me his minim rest, one, two, and the third in your bosom: the very butcher of a silk button, a duellist, a duellist; a gentleman of the very first house, of the first and second cause: ah, the immortal passado! the punto reverso! the hai!

Romeo and Juliet. Act ii, sc. 4, l. 21. [Mercutio] The only use of "prick-song" (written music, as distinguished from extemporaneous), "minim," "duellist," "punto reverso" and "hai." "Punto" occurs in *Merry Wives of Windsor,* ii, 3, 26. See 389: 11.

Come, sir, your passado.—*Romeo and Juliet,* iii, 1, 88.

The passado he respects not.—*Love's Labour 's Lost,* i, 2, 184. The only uses of "passado" (thrust).

2
That defence thou hast, betake thee to 't: of what nature the wrongs are thou hast done him, I know not; but thy intercepter, full of despite, bloody as the hunter, attends thee at the orchard-end: dismount thy tuck, be yare in thy preparation, for thy assailant is quick, skilful and deadly.

Twelfth Night. Act iii, sc. 4, l. 240. [Sir Toby] The only use of "intercepter," "orchard-end," and "tuck."

If you hold your life at any price, betake you to your guard; for your opposite hath in him what youth, strength, skill and wrath can furnish man withal.

Twelfth Night. Act iii, sc. 4, l. 252. [Sir Toby]

He is a devil in private brawl: souls and bodies hath he divorced three; and his incensement at this moment is so implacable, that satisfaction can be none but by pangs of death and sepulchre.

Twelfth Night. Act iii, sc. 4, l. 258. [Sir Toby] The only use of "incensement" and "implacable."

Strip your sword stark naked; for meddle you must, that 's certain, or forswear to wear iron about you.

Twelfth Night. Act iii, sc. 4, l. 274. [Sir Toby]

Why, man, he 's a very devil; I have not seen such a firago. I had a pass with him, rapier, scabbard and all, and he gives me the stuck in with such a mortal motion, that it is inevitable; and on the answer, he pays you as surely as your feet hit the ground they step on. They say he has been fencer to the Sophy.

Twelfth Night. Act iii, sc. 4, l. 301. [Sir Toby] The only use of "firago" (meant for virago, which does not otherwise occur). The Sophy (the Shah of Persia) is mentioned again in ii, 5, 198; and in *The Merchant of Venice,* ii, 1, 25. "Fencer" is repeated in *Much Ado about Nothing,* v, 2, 13.

Plague on 't, an I thought he had been valiant and so cunning in fence, I 'ld have seen him damned ere I 'ld have challenged him. Let him let the matter slip, and I 'll give him my horse, grey Capilet.

Twelfth Night, iii, 4, 311. [Sir Andrew]

3
He will fight with you for 's oath sake: marry, he hath better bethought him of his quarrel, and he finds that now scarce to be worth talking of: therefore draw, for the supportance of his vow.

Twelfth Night. Act iii, sc. 4, l. 326. [Sir Toby] "Supportance" is repeated in *Richard II,* iii, 4, 32.

The gentleman will, for his honour's sake, have one bout with you; he cannot by the duello avoid it.

Twelfth Night. Act iii, sc. 4, l. 336. [Sir Toby] "Duello" is used a second time in *Love's Labour 's Lost,* i, 2, 185: "The duello he regards not." See under CUPID.

Sebastian: If thou darest tempt me further, draw thy sword.
Sir Toby: What, what? Nay, then I must have an ounce or two of this malapert blood from you.

Twelfth Night. Act iv, sc. 1, l. 46. "Malapert" is repeated in *III Henry VI,* v, 5, 32: "Thou art too malapert"; and in *Richard III,* i, 3, 255: "You are malapert."

Primo, secundo, tertio, is a good play; and the old saying is, the third pays for all.

Twelfth Night. Act v, sc. 1, l. 39. [Clown] The only use of "primo," "secundo" and "tertio."

DULNESS

See also Stupidity

4
The dulness of the fool is the whetstone of the wits.

As You Like It. Act i, sc. 2, l. 58. [Celia] "Whetstone" is repeated in *Troilus and Cressida,* v, 2, 75, and *Macbeth,* iv, 3, 228.

My better parts
Are all thrown down, and that which here stands up
Is but a quintain, a mere lifeless block.

As You Like It. Act i, sc. 2, l. 261. [Orlando] The only use of "quintain" (a figure to be tilted at).

God make incision in thee! thou art raw.

As You Like It, iii, 2, 75. [Touchstone]

Raw as he is.—*The Winter's Tale,* iv, 8, 816.

Raw in her entertainment.—*Pericles,* iv, 2, 60.

Why then, 'tis good to be a post.

As You Like It. Act iv, sc. 1, l. 9. [Rosalind] The only use of "post" in this sense.

5
What, makest thou me a dullard in this act?

Cymbeline. Act v, sc. 5, l. 265. [Cymbeline] "Dullard" is used only twice in the plays, as above, and in *King Lear,* ii, 1, 76: "Thou must make a dullard of the world."

1
You blocks, you stones, you worse than senseless things!
Julius Cæsar. Act i, sc. 1, l. 40. [Marullus]
What a block art thou.
The Two Gentlemen of Verona. Act ii, sc. 5, l. 27. [Launce]
What tongueless blocks were they!
Richard III, iii, 7, 42. See under TONGUE for full quotation.
Thou block!—*Pericles,* iii, 2, 90.
2
You are dull, Casca, and those sparks of life
That should be in a Roman you do want,
Or else you use not.
Julius Cæsar. Act i, sc. 3, l. 57. [Cassius]
Dull as night.—*Merchant of Venice,* v, 1, 86.
Dull with care.—*Comedy of Errors,* i, 2, 20.
Dull to all proceedings.—*Measure for Measure,* iv, 4, 24.
3
Most dull, honest Dull!
Love's Labour's Lost. Act v, sc. 1, l. 162. [Holofernes]
Duller than a great thaw.
Much Ado about Nothing. Act ii, sc. 1, l. 251. [Benedick]
Duller shouldst thou be.—*Hamlet,* i, 5, 32.
Dull and blunt.—*Richard III,* iv, 4, 226.
Dull and dead.—*Venus and Adonis,* l. 212.
Dull and heavy.—*Much Ado about Nothing,* ii, 3, 73; *II Henry IV,* i, 1, 118. *Timon of Athens,* ii, 2, 228.
Dull and muddy-mettled.—*Hamlet,* ii, 2, 594. The only use of "muddy-mettled."
Dull and slow.—*Love's Labour's Lost,* iii, 1, 60; *The Rape of Lucrece,* l. 1336.
Flat and dull.—*Hamlet,* iv, 7, 31.
Tame and dull.—*I Henry IV,* iv, 3, 23.
Dull brainless.—*Troilus and Cressida,* i, 3, 381.
Dull of tongue.—*Antony and Cleopatra,* iii, 3, 19.
4
Cousin, thou wert not wont to be so dull.
Richard III. Act iv, sc. 2, l. 17. [King Richard]
She is not bred so dull but she can learn.
The Merchant of Venice, iii, 2, 164. See under GIRL. "So dull" is repeated in *II Henry IV,* i, 1, 71.
Too dull.—*Cymbeline,* ii, 4, 41.
Very dull.—*Titus Andronicus,* ii, 3, 195.
5
Do not kill
The spirit of love with a perpetual dullness.
Sonnets. No. lvi. The only use of this spelling of "dullness."
'Tis a good dulness.—*The Tempest,* i, 2, 185.
Thy dulness would torment thee.—*Timon of Athens,* iv, 3, 335.
Lethe'd dulness.—*Antony and Cleopatra,* ii, 1, 27. The only use of "Lethe'd."
Wanton dulness.—*Othello,* i. 3, 270. "Dulness" is used a fifth time in *As You Like It,* i, 2, 58. See 390: 4.
6
What a pied ninny's this!
Thou scurvy patch!
The Tempest. Act iii, sc. 2, l. 71. [Caliban] The only use of "ninny."
Dull thing.—*The Tempest,* i, 2, 285.

DUMPS, see under Melancholy

DUST

7
She whom all men praised and whom myself,
Since I have lost, have loved, was in mine eye
The dust that did offend it.
All's Well that Ends Well. Act v, sc. 3, l. 53. [Bertram]
Blows dust in others' eyes.—*Pericles,* i, 1, 97.
8
The dust
Should have ascended to the roof of heaven,
Raised by your populous troops.
Antony and Cleopatra, iii, 6, 48. [Cæsar]
Fearful scouring
Doth choke the air with dust.
Timon of Athens. Act v, sc. 2, l. 15. [Senator]
9
Rosencrantz: What have you done, my lord, with the dead body?
Hamlet: Compounded it with dust, whereto 'tis kin.
Hamlet. Act iv, sc. 2, l. 5. See under DEATH.
Noble dust.—*Hamlet,* v, 1, 225.
Crumble up to dust.—*King John,* v, 7, 31.
Returneth into dust.—*Hamlet,* v, 1, 232.
Dust . . . of age.—*Sonnets,* cviii.
Dust of old oblivion.—*Henry V,* ii, 4, 87.
10
No worthier than the dust!
Julius Cæsar. Act iii, sc. 1, l. 116. [Brutus]
11
Sweep the dust behind the door.
A Midsummer-Night's Dream. Act v, sc. 1, l. 397. [Puck]
Smear with dust.—*The Rape of Lucrece,* l. 945.
Smeared all with dust.—*Rape of Lucrece,* 1381.
12
Would it not grieve a woman to be overmastered with a piece of valiant dust? to make an account of her life to a clod of wayward marl?
Much Ado about Nothing. Act ii, sc. 1, l. 63. [Beatrice] The only use of "marl."
13
Wipe off the dust that hides our sceptre's gilt.
Richard II. Act ii, sc. 1, l. 294. [Northumberland]
Dust of England's ground.—*Richard II,* ii, 3, 91.
14
Dust was thrown upon his sacred head;
Which with such gentle sorrow he shook off, . . .
That . . . barbarism itself have pitied him.
Richard II. Act v, sc. 2, l. 30. [York]
Thou, that threw'st dust upon his goodly head.
II Henry IV. Act i, sc. 3, l. 103. [Archbishop]
Threw dust and rubbish.—*Richard II,* v, 2, 6.
Are they like to take dust?—*Twelfth Night,* i, 3, 135.
In the dust.—*Coriolanus,* iii, 1, 171; *Hamlet,* i, 2, 71; *I Henry IV,* i, 3, 134; *Pericles,* ii, 2, 55.
To the dust.—*I Henry VI,* v, 3, 29.
15
See how I lay the dust with my tears.
The Two Gentlemen of Verona. Act ii, sc. 3, l. 35. [Launce]
Laying Autumn's dust.—*King Lear,* iv, 6, 201.
Summer's dust.—*Richard II,* iii, 3, 43.

DUTY

1
My duty then shall pay me for my pains.
All's Well that Ends Well. Act ii, sc. 1, l. 128. [Helena]
My mother did but duty; such, my lord,
As you owe to your wife.
All's Well that Ends Well. Act iv, sc. 2, l. 12. [Diana]
2
I have done my duty.
Antony and Cleopatra. Act ii, sc. 5, l. 88. [Messenger]
Do my duties.—*Othello,* iii, 2, 2.
3
A charitable duty of my order.
The Comedy of Errors. Act v, sc. 1, l. 107. [Abbess]
Ceremonious duty.—*Richard II,* iii, 2, 173.
Child-like duty.—*The Two Gentlemen of Verona,* iii, 1, 75. "Child-like" is repeated in *King Lear,* ii, 1, 108: "Child-like office."
Free duty.—*Othello,* i, 3, 41.
Humble duty.—*II Henry IV,* ii, 1, 137.
Mourning duties.—*Hamlet,* i, 2, 88.
Particular duties.—*Much Ado about Nothing,* iv, 1, 3.
Peculiar duties.—*The Rape of Lucrece,* l. 14.
Personal duty.—*A Lover's Complaint,* l. 130.
4
Coriolanus: Sink, my knee, i' the earth;
Of thy deep duty more impression show
Than that of common sons.
Volumnia: O, stand up blest!
Whilst, with no softer cushion than the flint,
I kneel before thee; and unproperly
Show duty, as mistaken all this while
Between the child and parent.
Coriolanus: What is this?
Your knees to me? to your corrected son?
Then let the pebbles on the hungry beach
Fillip the stars.
Coriolanus. Act v, sc. 3, l. 50. The only use of "unproperly" and "corrected."
5
Always reserved my holy duty.
Cymbeline. Act i, sc. 1, l. 87. [Imogen]
She hath not appear'd
Before the Roman, nor to us hath tender'd
The duty of the day.
Cymbeline. Act iii, sc. 5, l. 30. [Cymbeline]
She should that duty leave unpaid to you,
Which daily she was bound to proffer.
Cymbeline. Act iii, sc. 5, l. 48. [Queen]
Be duteous, and true preferment will tender itself to thee.
Cymbeline. Act iii, sc. 5, l. 159. [Cloten]
We will discharge our duty.
Cymbeline. Act iii, sc. 7, l. 16. [Tribune]
6
In that and all things will we show our duty.
Hamlet. Act i, sc. 2, l. 40. [Cornelius and Voltimand]
I hold my duty, as I hold my soul.
Hamlet. Act ii, sc. 2, l. 44. [Polonius]
If my duty be too bold, my love is too unmannerly.
Hamlet. Act iii, sc. 2, l. 363. [Guildenstern]
We shall express our duty in his eye.
Hamlet. Act iv, sc. 4, l. 6. [Fortinbras]
7
Osric: I commend my duty to your lordship.
Hamlet: Yours, yours. [*Exit Osric*] He does well to commend it himself; there are no tongues else for 's turn.
Hamlet. Act v, sc. 2, l. 189.
My duty to you.—*All's Well that Ends Well,* iii, 2, 27; *Henry V,* v, 2, 23.
Our duty this way lies.
I Henry IV. Act v, sc. 4, l. 16. [Lancaster]
They know their duties.—*II Henry IV,* iv, 2, 101.
8
My lord, it were your duty to forbear.
I Henry VI. Act iii, sc. 1, l. 52. [Somerset]
I owe him little duty, and less love.
I Henry VI. Act iv, sc. 4, l. 34. [Somerset]
9
I know my duty; you are all undutiful.
III Henry VI. Act v, sc. 5, l. 33. [Prince of Wales] The only use of "undutiful."
The duty that I owe unto your majesty
I seal upon the lips of this sweet babe.
III Henry VI. Act v, sc. 7, l. 28. [Clarence]
10
Though all the world should crack their duty to you,
And throw it from their soul; . . . yet my duty
As doth a rock against the chiding flood,
Should the approach of this wild river break,
And stand unshaken yours.
Henry VIII. Act iii, sc. 2, l. 193. [Wolsey] "Unshaken" is used only once again, in *Hamlet,* iii, 2, 201.
It is my duty.—*Henry VIII,* v, 1, 90.
'Twas my duty.—*King Lear,* ii, 1, 108.
11
I should not urge thy duty past thy might.
Julius Cæsar. Act iv, sc. 3, l. 261. [Brutus]
12
Be pleased then
To pay that duty which you truly owe
To him that owes it.
King John. Act ii, sc. 1, l. 246. [King Philip]
With all true duty.—*King John,* iii, 3, 73.
True duty.—*Richard III,* ii, 2, 108; *Titus Andronicus,* v, 3, 155.
13
Think'st thou that duty shall have dread to speak,
When power to flattery bows?
King Lear. Act i, sc. 1, l. 149. [Kent]
My duty cannot be silent when I think your highness wronged.
King Lear. Act i, sc. 4, l. 70. [Knight]
My duty cannot suffer
To obey in all your daughters' hard commands.
King Lear. Act iii, sc. 4, l. 153. [Gloucester]
14
Devoted and heart-burning heat of duty.
Love's Labour's Lost. Act i, sc. 1, l. 280. [King Ferdinand] The only use of "heart-burning." "Heart-burned" occurs in *I Henry IV,* iii, 3, 59, and in *Much Ado about Nothing,* ii, 1, 4.
Our duty is so rich, so infinite,
That we may do it still without accompt.
Love's Labour's Lost. Act v, sc. 2, l. 199 [Biron]

Cast accompt.—*II Henry VI*, iv, 2, 93.
For accompt.—*Measure for Measure*, ii, 4, 58.
Great accompt.—*Henry V*, Prol., 17. The only uses of "accompt."

1
What poor duty cannot do, noble respect
Takes it in might, not merit.
A Midsummer-Night's Dream. Act v, sc. 1, l. 91. [Theseus]

You know me dutiful; therefore, dear sir,
Let me not shame respect.
Troilus and Cressida. Act v, sc. 3, l. 72. [Hector] "Dutiful" is used only once more in the plays, in *Henry V*, ii, 2, 127: "Show men dutiful?"

2 My noble father,
I do perceive here a divided duty.
Othello. Act i, sc. 3, l. 180. [Desdemona]

Have you forgot all sense of place and duty?
Othello. Act ii, sc. 3, l. 167. [Iago]

3
Fleet-wing'd duty with thought's feathers flies.
The Rape of Lucrece, l. 1216. The only use of "fleet-wing'd."

His kindled duty kindled her mistrust.
The Rape of Lucrece, l. 1352.

4 To my own disgrace
Neglected my sworn duty in that case.
Richard II. Act i, sc. 1, l. 133. [Mowbray]

How long shall I be patient? ah, how long
Shall tender duty make me suffer wrong?
Richard II. Act ii, sc. 1, l. 163. [York]

My stooping duty.
Richard II. Act iii, sc. 3, l. 48. [Bolingbroke]

Stand all apart,
And show fair duty to his majesty.
Richard II. Act iii, sc. 3, l. 187. [Bolingbroke]

5
I will with all expedient duty see you.
Richard III. Act i, sc. 2, l. 217. [Gloucester]

Lord Rivers: Were you well served, you would be taught your duty.
Queen Margaret: To serve me well, you all should do me duty,
Teach me to be your queen, and you my subjects:
O, serve me well, and teach yourselves that duty!
Richard III. Act i, sc. 3, l. 250.

6
Lord of my love, to whom in vassalage
Thy merit hath my duty strongly knit,
To thee I send this written embassage,
To witness duty, not to show my wit:
Duty so great, with wit so poor as mine
May make seem bare, in wanting words to show it,
But that I hope some good conceit of thine
In my soul's thought, all naked, will bestow it.
Sonnets. No. xxvi. "Vassalage" is repeated in *Troilus and Cressida*, iii, 2, 40.

7
So shall I no whit be behind in duty.
The Taming of the Shrew. Act i, sc. 2, l. 175. [Hortensio]

Accept our duty.—*The Taming of the Shrew*, Ind., 1, 82.
Show her duty.—*The Taming of the Shrew*, Ind., 1, 117.

8
My duty hushes me.
Twelfth Night. Act v, sc. 1, l. 110. [Viola]

9
Made me neglect my duties, lose my time.
The Two Gentlemen of Verona. Act i, sc. 1, l. 67. [Valentine]

Lacking duty.—*The Two Gentlemen of Verona*, iii, 1, 69.
Scant her duty.—*King Lear*, ii, 4, 142.
Slack their duties.—*Othello*, iv, 3, 88.

10
Proteus: My duty will I boast of; nothing else.
Silvia: And duty never yet did want his meed.
The Two Gentlemen of Verona. Act ii, sc. 4, l. 111.

My duty pricks me on to utter that
Which else no worldly goods should draw from me.
The Two Gentlemen of Verona. Act iii, sc. 1, l. 8. [Proteus]

My ever-esteemed duty pricks me on.
Love's Labour's Lost. Act i, sc. 1, l. 268. [King] The only use of "ever-esteemed."

What pricks you on?—*Richard II*, ii, 3, 78.
Honour pricks me on.—*I Henry IV*, v, 1, 131. The only uses of "pricks on."

E

EAGLE

11
If you have writ your annals true, 'tis there,
That, like an eagle in a dove-cote, I
Flutter'd your Volscians in Corioli.
Coriolanus. Act v, sc. 6, l. 114. [Coriolanus] The only use of "annals," "dove-cote" and "flutter'd."

12
I chose an eagle, And did avoid a puttock.
Cymbeline. Act i, sc. 1, l. 139. [Imogen] "Puttock" (kite) occurs three times.

Full-wing'd eagle.—*Cymbeline*, iii, 3, 21. The only use of "full-winged."
Mighty eagles.—*Julius Cæsar*, v, 1, 81.
Princely eagle.—*III Henry VI*, v, 2, 12; *Cymbeline*, v, 5, 473.
Princely eagle's bird.—*III Henry VI*, ii, 1, 91.

13
I saw Jove's bird, the Roman eagle, wing'd
From the spongy south to this part of the west,

There vanish'd in the sunbeams.
Cymbeline. Act iv, sc. 2, l. 348. [Soothsayer] The only use of "sunbeams."
The Roman eagle,
From south to west on wing soaring aloft,
Lessen'd herself, and in the beams o' the sun
So vanish'd.
Cymbeline. Act v, sc. 5, l. 470. [Soothsayer]
Mount, eagle, to my palace crystalline.
Cymbeline. Act v, sc. 4, l. 113. [Jupiter] The only use of "crystalline."
The holy eagle Stoop'd, as to foot us.
Cymbeline. Act v, sc. 4, l. 115. [Sicilius]
Stoop'd eagles.—*Cymbeline,* v, 3, 42.

1
Were 't not all one, an empty eagle were set
To guard the chicken from a hungry kite.
II Henry VI. Act iii, sc. 1, l. 248. [York]
Like an empty eagle
Tire on the flesh of me and of my son!
III Henry VI. Act i, sc. 1, l. 268. [King Henry]
Even as an empty eagle, sharp by fast,
Tires with her beak on feathers, flesh and bone,
Shaking her wings, devouring all in haste,
Till either gorge be stuff'd or prey be gone.
Venus and Adonis, l. 55. The only uses of "tire" in the sense of prey or feed ravenously.

2
And like an eagle o'er his aery towers,
To souse annoyance that comes near his nest.
King John. Act v, sc. 2, l. 149. [Bastard] The only use of "souse" (sweep down upon).
The eagle, feather'd king.
The Phœnix and the Turtle, l. 11.

3
More pity that the eagle should be mew'd,
While kites and buzzards prey at liberty.
Richard III. Act i, sc. 1, l. 132. [Hastings]
But flies an eagle flight, bold and forth on,
Leaving no tract behind.
Timon of Athens. Act i, sc. 1, l. 49. [Poet] "Tract" is repeated in *Henry VIII,* i, 1, 40.

4
The eagle suffers little birds to sing,
And is not careful what they mean thereby,
Knowing that with the shadow of his wings
He can at pleasure stint their melody.
Titus Andronicus. Act iv, sc. 4, l. 83. [Tamora]
The eagles are gone: crows and daws, crows and daws!
Troilus and Cressida. Act i, sc. 2, l. 265. [Pandarus]

EAR

See also Eye and Ear; Hearing

5
The Florentines and Senoys are by the ears.
All's Well that Ends Well. Act i, sc. 2, l. 1. [King] The only use of "Senoys" (Sienese). "Florentine" occurs eleven times. "By the ears" is repeated in iii, 5, 53; and in *Romeo and Juliet,* iii, 1, 84.

6
She does abuse our ears.
All's Well that Ends Well. Act v, sc. 3, l. 295. [King]
Being apt To have his ear abused.
King Lear. Act ii, sc. 4, l. 309. [Regan]
I have heard Your royal ear abused.
Measure for Measure. Act v, sc. 1, l. 139. [Friar Peter]

7
I could have given less matter A better ear.
Antony and Cleopatra. Act ii, sc. 1, l. 31. [Pompey]
Say in mine ear: what is 't?
Antony and Cleopatra. Act ii, sc. 7, l. 42. [Pompey]
Hark, in thine ear.—*King Lear,* iv, 6, 156.
Breathe it in mine ear.—*The Two Gentlemen of Verona,* iii, 1, 239.

8
That my two ears can witness.
The Comedy of Errors. Act ii, sc. 1, l. 46. [Dromio of Ephesus]
Teach your ears to list me with more heed.
The Comedy of Errors. Act iv, sc. 1, l. 101. [Antipholus of Ephesus]
I tell you, 'twill sound harshly in her ears.
The Comedy of Errors. Act iv, sc. 4, l. 7. [Antipholus of Ephesus]

9
These ears of mine, thou know'st, did hear thee.
The Comedy of Errors. Act v, sc. 1, l. 26. [Second Merchant]
These ears of mine Heard you.
The Comedy of Errors. Act v, sc. 1, l. 259. [Second Merchant]

10
We do request your kindest ears.
Coriolanus. Act ii, sc. 2, l. 56. [Senator]
Mine ears against your suits are stronger than
Your gates against my force.
Coriolanus. Act v, sc. 2, l. 94. [Coriolanus]
Away! I do condemn mine ears that have
So long attended thee.
Cymbeline. Act i, sc. 6, l. 141. [Imogen]

11
Love's counsellor should fill the bores of hearing,
To the smothering of the sense.
Cymbeline. Act iii, sc. 2, l. 59. [Imogen] The only use of "bores of hearing" and "smothering."

12
And let us once again assail your ears,
That are so fortified against our story.
Hamlet. Act i, sc. 1, l. 31. [Barnardo]
Nor shall you do mine ear that violence,
To make it truster of your own report
Against yourself.
Hamlet, i, 2, 171. [Hamlet] "Truster" is repeated in *Timon of Athens,* iv, 1, 10.

13
Give every man thy ear, but few thy voice.
Hamlet. Act i, sc. 3, l. 68. [Polonius]
But this eternal blazon must not be
To ears of flesh and blood.
Hamlet. Act i, sc. 5, l. 21. [Ghost]
The porches of my ears.
Hamlet, i, 5, 63. See under POISON.

14
At each ear a hearer.
Hamlet. Act ii, sc. 2, l. 400. [Hamlet]
Split the ears of the groundlings.
Hamlet, iii, 2, 12. See ACTING, 10:11. The only use of "groundlings."

You have heard, and with a knowing ear.
Hamlet. Act iv, sc. 7, l. 3. [King]
The ears are senseless that should give us hearing.
Hamlet. Act v, sc. 2, l. 380. [Ambassador]
1
God give thee . . . the ears of profiting.
I Henry IV. Act i, sc. 2, l. 170. [Falstaff]
Ear of greatness.—*I Henry IV,* iii, 2, 24.
Ears of death.—*Pericles,* iii, 1, 9.
Ear of grief.—*Love's Labour 's Lost,* v, 2, 763.
2
Tying thine ear to no tongue but thine own!
I Henry IV. Act i, sc. 3, l. 238. [Northumberland]
Nor are mine ears with thy tongue's tune delighted.
Sonnets. No. cxli.
Let not your ears despise my tongue for ever,
Which shall possess them with the heaviest sound
That ever yet they heard.
Macbeth. Act iv, sc. 3, l. 201. [Ross]
3
Prince of Wales: Lie down; lay thine ear close to the ground and list if thou can'st hear the tread of travellers.
Falstaff: Have you any levers to lift me up again, being down?
I Henry IV. Act ii, sc. 2, l. 36. The only use of "levers."
Under yond yew-trees lay thee all along,
Holding thine ear close to the hollow ground.
Romeo and Juliet. Act v, sc. 3, l. 3. [Paris] "Yew-tree" is repeated in l. 137, and occurs in no other scene.
4
Up to the ears in blood.
I Henry IV. Act iv, sc. 1, l. 117. [Hotspur]
Up to the ears.—*Romeo and Juliet,* i, 4, 43.
O'er head and ears.—*Winter's Tale,* i, 2, 186.
5
I can hear it with mine own ears.
II Henry IV. Act ii, sc. 2, l. 70. [Poins]
Would not this nave of a wheel have his ears cut off?
II Henry IV. Act ii, sc. 4, l. 281. [Prince of Wales] "Nave" is repeated in *Macbeth,* i, 2, 22, and in *Hamlet,* ii, 2, 518.
I come to draw you out by the ears.
II Henry IV. Act ii, sc. 4, l. 313. [Prince]
6
Give him a box o' the ear and that will make 'em red again.
II Henry VI. Act iv, sc. 7, l. 91. [Cade] "Box o' the ear" is repeated in *II Henry IV,* i, 2, 218; *Henry V,* iv, 7, 133; 181; *Measure for Measure,* ii, 1, 189; *The Merchant of Venice,* i, 2, 86.
I will take thee a box on the ear.
Henry V. Act iv, sc. 1, l. 231. [Williams]
She will not stick to round me i' the ear.
The Passionate Pilgrim, l. 349.
This cuff was but to knock at your ear.—*Taming of the Shrew,* iv, 1, 67. See under BEATING.
7
Whose warlike ears could never brook retreat.
III Henry VI. Act i, sc. 1, l. 5. [York]
Had you a healthful ear to hear of it.
Julius Cæsar, ii, 1, 319. See under EXPLOIT.
8
I think your grace . . . gave no ear to 't.
Henry VIII. Act iv, sc. 2, l. 7. [Griffith]
9
Hear me without thine ears.
King John. Act iii, sc. 3, l. 49. [King John]
Deafs our ears.—*King John,* ii, 1, 147.
Our ears are cudgell'd.—*King John,* ii, 1, 464.
Light of ear.—*King Lear,* iii, 4, 96.
10
Break the neck of the wax, and every one give ear.
Love's Labour 's Lost. Act iv, sc. 1, l. 59. [Princess] See also v, 2, 286.
Perpend, my princess, and give ear.
Twelfth Night. Act v, sc. 1, l. 307. [Clown]
Listen, ear.—*Love's Labour 's Lost,* iv, 3, 45.
If sickly ears,
Deaf'd with the clamours of their own dear groans,
Will hear your idle scorns, continue then.
Love's Labour 's Lost. Act v, sc. 2, l. 873. [Rosaline] The only use of "deaf'd."
Had I three ears, I 'ld hear thee.
Macbeth. Act iv, sc. 1, l. 78. [Macbeth]
11
Lord Angelo hath to the public ear
Profess'd the contrary.
Measure for Measure. Act iv, sc. 2, l. 102.
Public ear.—*Antony and Cleopatra,* iii, 4, 5.
12
Falstaff: Pistol!
Pistol: He hears with ears.
Evans: The tevil and his tam! what phrase is this, 'He hears with ear'? why, it is affectations.
The Merry Wives of Windsor. Act i, sc. 1, l. 149.
Give ear to his motions.
The Merry Wives of Windsor. Act i, sc. 1, l. 221. [Evans]
If it should come to the ear of the court.
The Merry Wives of Windsor. Act iv, sc. 5, l. 97. [Falstaff]
13
Mine ear, I thank it, brought me to thy sound.
A Midsummer-Night's Dream. Act iii, sc. 2, l. 182. [Hermia]
Fair large ears.—*A Midsummer-Night's Dream,* iv, 1, 4.
14
My cousin tells him in his ear that he is in her heart.
Much Ado about Nothing. Act ii, sc. 1, l. 327. [Beatrice]
To tell you in your ear.
The Merry Wives of Windsor. Act i, sc. 4, l. 109. [Mistress Quickly]
Let me tell you in your ear.
The Merry Wives of Windsor. Act ii, sc. 2, l. 100. [Mistress Quickly]
I must tell you friendly in your ear.
As You Like It. Act iii, sc. 5, l. 59. [Rosalind]
I 'll tell you in your ear.
Antony and Cleopatra. Act iii, sc. 2, l. 46 [Octavia]
15
A greedy ear.
Othello. Act i, sc. 3, l. 149. [Othello]

Aged ear.—*Titus Andronicus,* iv, 4, 96.
Ancient ears.—*Romeo and Juliet,* ii, 3, 74.
Attending ears.—*Romeo and Juliet,* ii, 2, 167.
Attent ear.—*Hamlet,* i, 2, 193. "Attent" is re-repeated in *Pericles,* iii, Gower, 11 (probably not by Shakespeare): "Be attent."
Christian ear.—*II Henry VI,* iv, 7, 44.
Credent ear.—*Hamlet,* i, 3, 30.
Diligent ear.—*The Tempest,* iii, 1, 42.
Dull ear.—*Henry V,* iv, Prol., 11; *King John,* iii, 4, 109.
Foolish ear.—*Hamlet,* iv, 2, 26.
Grave ears.—*Othello,* i, 3, 124.
Grieved ear.—*Antony and Cleopatra,* iii, 6, 59.
Heedful ears.—*III Henry VI,* iii, 3, 63.
Kingly ears.—*Troilus and Cressida,* i, 3, 219.
Listening ear.—*Venus and Adonis,* l. 698.
Mad ears.—*Sonnets,* cxl.
Married ear.—*Love's Labour's Lost,* v, 2, 912.
Mortal ears.—*Taming of the Shrew,* i, 1, 178.
Patient ears.—*Romeo and Juliet,* Prol., 13.
Pleasing ears.—*The Rape of Lucrece,* l. 1126.
Pretty ear.—*Venus and Adonis,* l. 24.
Ruin'd ears.—*Richard II,* iii, 3, 34.
Sad attending ear.—*Titus Andronicus,* v, 3, 82.
Savage ears.—*Love's Labour's Lost,* iv, 3, 348.
Short ears.—*Venus and Adonis,* l. 297.
Thievish ears.—*The Rape of Lucrece,* l. 35.
Treacherous ear.—*Richard II,* iv, 1, 54.

1 I never yet did hear
That the bruised heart was pierced through the ear.
Othello. Act i, sc. 3, l. 218. [Brabantio]

By our ears our hearts oft tainted be.
The Rape of Lucrece, l. 38.

In thy piteous heart plant thou thine ear.
Richard II. Act v, sc. 3, l. 126. [Duchess of York]

2
Away he steals with open listening ear.
The Rape of Lucrece, l. 283.

Mine ear is open.—*Richard II,* iii, 2, 93.
The open ear of youth.—*Richard II,* ii, 1, 20.
Not an ear open.—*The Winter's Tale,* v, 2, 68.

3
His ear her prayers admits.
The Rape of Lucrece, l. 558.

4
Bid his ears a little while be deaf.
Richard II. Act i, sc. 1, l. 112. [Mowbray]

Old ears deaf.—*Titus Andronicus,* iv, 4, 97.
Undeaf his ear.—*Richard II,* ii, 1, 16.

5
Quick is mine ear to hear of good towards him.
Richard II. Act ii, sc. 1, l. 234. [Willoughby]

Quick of ear.—*Pericles,* iv, 1, 70.
You have a quick ear.—*The Two Gentlemen of Verona,* iv, 2, 63.
Your ear is good.—*Julius Cæsar,* i, 3, 42.

6
Pitchers have ears.
Richard III. Act ii, sc. 4, l. 37. [Queen Elizabeth] An echo of the proverb included in John Heywood's *Proverbs* (Pt. ii, ch. 5), in 1546: "Small pitchers have wide ears."

Pitchers have ears, and I have many servants.
The Taming of the Shrew. Act iv, sc. 4, l. 52. [Baptista]

7
Lend favourable ears to our request.
Richard III. Act iii, sc. 7, l. 101. [Buckingham]

Rise, and lend thine ear.
Richard III. Act iv, sc. 2, l. 80. [Tyrrel]

Lend thine ear.
The Taming of the Shrew. Act iv, sc. 1, l. 62. [Grumio]

Friends, Romans, countrymen, lend me your ears.
Julius Cæsar. Act iii, sc. 2, l. 78. [Antony]

To my unfolding lend your prosperous ear.
Othello. Act i, sc. 3, l. 245. [Desdemona]

If you 'll a willing ear incline.
Measure for Measure. Act v, sc. 1, l. 542. [Duke]

8
Shot through the ear with a love-song.
Romeo and Juliet. Act ii, sc. 4, l. 14. [Mercutio]

9
It struck mine ear most terribly.
Tempest. Act ii, sc. 1, l. 313. [Sebastian]

They prick'd their ears.
The Tempest. Act iv, sc. 1, l. 176. [Ariel]

Ears up-prick'd.—*Venus and Adonis,* l. 271. The only use of "up-prick'd."

10
Thou gavest thine ears like tapsters that bid welcome
To knaves and all approachers.
Timon of Athens. Act iv, sc. 3, l. 215. [Apemantus] The only use of "approachers."

11
Tell us what Sinon hath bewitch'd our ears.
Titus Andronicus. Act v, sc. 3, l. 85. [Marcus] Sinon, who persuaded Priam to admit the wooden horse into Troy, is mentioned again in *III Henry VI,* iii, 2, 190: "Like a Sinon, take another Troy"; and in *Cymbeline,* iii, 4, 61: "Sinon's weeping."

I charm'd their ears.
The Tempest. Act iv, sc. 1, l. 178. [Ariel]

I will enchant thine ear.
Venus and Adonis, l. 145.

Delight his ear.—*Passionate Pilgrim,* l. 47.

12
Go shake your ears.
Twelfth Night. Act ii, sc. 3, l. 134. [Maria]

Crop the ears.—*Cymbeline,* ii, 1, 15.

13
Valentine: My ears are stopt and cannot hear good news,
So much of bad already hath possess'd them.
Proteus: Then in dumb silence will I bury mine,
For they are harsh, untuneable and bad.
The Two Gentlemen of Verona. Act iii, sc. 1, l. 205. The only use of "stopt." "Untuneable" is repeated in *As You Like It,* v, 3, 37.

Her ear Is stopp'd with dust.
King John. Act iv, sc. 2, l. 119. [Messenger]

You have . . . stopp'd your ears.
Coriolanus. Act v, sc. 3, l. 5. [Aufidius]

What! do you stop your ears?
Pericles. Act iv, sc. 2, l. 86. [Bawd]

Stop your ears.—*The Taming of the Shrew,* iv, 3, 76.
Stops his ears.—*The Winter's Tale,* v, 1, 201.

1
Mine ears, that to your wanton talk attended,
Do burn themselves for having so offended.
Venus and Adonis, l. 809. An echo of the proverb which originated with Pliny the Elder (*Historia Naturalis*, xxviii, 2), "Quin et absentes [tinnitu] aurium præsentire sermones de te?"
What fire is in mine ears?
Much Ado about Nothing. Act iii, sc. 1, l. 107. [Beatrice]
2
Shaking their scratch'd ears, bleeding as they go.
Venus and Adonis, l. 924.
Scratch mine ear.—*Antony and Cleopatra*, i, 2, 54.
3
Mamillius: I will tell it softly;
Yond crickets shall not hear it.
Hermione: Come on, then,
And give 't me in mine ear.
The Winter's Tale. Act ii, sc. 1, l. 31.
It alone concerns your ear.—*Twelfth Night*, i, 5, 224.
4
All men's ears grew to his tunes.
The Winter's Tale. Act iv, sc. 4, l. 186. [Servant]
All their senses stuck in ears.
The Winter's Tale. Act iv, sc. 4, l. 621. [Autolycus]

EARNESTNESS, see Sincerity

EARTH

See also Heaven and Earth; World

5
Our dungy earth alike Feeds beast as man.
Antony and Cleopatra, i, 1, 35. See under LOVE. "Dungy earth" is repeated in *The Winter's Tale*, ii, 1, 157.
The crown o' the earth doth melt.
Antony and Cleopatra. Act iv, sc. 15, l. 63. [Cleopatra]
6
The little O, the earth.
Antony and Cleopatra. Act v, sc. 2, l. 81. [Cleopatra]
This orb o' the earth.—*Coriolanus*, v, 6, 127.
The orbed earth.—*A Lover's Complaint*, l. 25.
This ball of earth.—*II Henry IV*, Ind., 5.
This mortal round.—*Venus and Adonis*, l. 368.
7
Where is this young gallant that is so desirous to lie with his mother earth?
As You Like It. Act i, sc. 2, l. 212. [Charles] The only use of "mother earth."
8
There 's nothing situate under heaven's eye
But hath his bound, in earth, in sea, in sky.
The Comedy of Errors. Act ii, sc. 1, l. 16. [Luciana]
9
I . . . am not
Of stronger earth than others.
Coriolanus. Act v, sc. 3, l. 28. [Coriolanus]
10
This goodly frame, the earth, seems to me a sterile promontory.
Hamlet. Act ii, sc. 2, l. 310. [Hamlet]

Face of the earth.—*I Henry IV*, ii, 4, 143.
Our grandam earth.—*I Henry IV*, iii, 1, 34.
11
O, that that earth, which kept the world in awe,
Should patch a wall to expel the winter's flaw!
Hamlet, v, 1, 238. See under CÆSAR.
Thou bleeding piece of earth.—*Julius Cæsar*, iii, 1, 254.
12
Hold off the earth awhile,
Till I have caught her once more in mine arms.
Hamlet. Act v, sc. 1, l. 272. [Laertes]
Earth of France.—*I Henry VI*, iv, 3, 18.
13
Then let the earth be drunken with our blood.
III Henry VI. Act ii, sc. 3, l. 23. [Warwick]
O earth, which this blood drink'st, revenge his death!
Either heaven with lightning strike the murderer dead,
Or earth, gape open wide and eat him quick.
Richard III. Act i, sc. 2, l. 63. [Lady Anne]
O earth, what else?—*Hamlet*, i, 5, 92.
14
This naughty earth.
Henry VIII. Act v, sc. 1, l. 138. [King Henry]
Terra, the soil, the land, the earth.
Love's Labour 's Lost. Act iv, sc. 2, l. 7. [Holofernes] "Terra" is repeated in *II Henry VI*, iv, 7, 61: "Bona terra."
Thou sure and firm-set earth.
Macbeth. Act ii, sc. 1, l. 56. [Macbeth] The only use of "firm-set."
Barren earth.—*Richard II*, iii, 2, 153.
Base earth.—*Richard II*, ii, 4, 20; iii, 3, 191; *The Two Gentlemen of Verona*, ii, 4, 159.
The bearing earth.—*Venus and Adonis*, l. 267.
Cursed earth.—*Richard II*, iv, 1, 147.
Discolour'd earth.—*King John*, ii, 1, 306.
Farthest earth.—*Sonnets*, xliv.
The fat earth.—*The Rape of Lucrece*, l. 1837.
Harmless earth.—*I Henry IV*, i, 3, 61.
Huge firm earth.—*King John*, iii, 1, 72.
Lean earth.—*I Henry IV*, ii, 2, 116.
Meagre cloddy earth.—*King John*, iii, 1, 80.
Proud earth.—*The Tempest*, iv, 1, 82.
Rebellious earth.—*Richard II*, v, 1, 5.
Receiving earth.—*Henry V*, Prol., 27.
Sandy earth.—*Troilus and Cressida*, iii, 2, 199.
Sinful earth.—*Sonnets*, cxlvi.
Sullen earth.—*II Henry VI*, i, 2, 5; *Sonnets*, xxix.
Thirsty earth.—*III Henry VI*, ii, 3, 15.
Universal earth.—*Romeo and Juliet*, iii, 2, 94.
15
I'll put a girdle round about the earth
In forty minutes.
A Midsummer-Night's Dream. Act ii, sc. 1, l. 175. [Puck]
We the globe can compass soon,
Swifter than the wandering moon.
A Midsummer-Night's Dream. Act iv, sc. 1, l. 101. [Oberon]
Whirl along with thee about the globe
Titus Andronicus. Act v, sc. 2, l. 49. [Titus]

Behind the globe.—*Richard II,* iii, 2, 38.
The great globe itself.—*The Tempest,* iv, 1, 153. The only use of "great globe."
This solid globe.—*Troilus and Cressida,* i, 3, 113.
This under globe.—*King Lear,* ii, 2, 170.
Affrighted globe.—*Othello,* v, 2, 100.
Distracted globe.—*Hamlet,* i, 5, 97.
Ivory globes.—*The Rape of Lucrece,* l. 407.
Globe of sinful continents.—*II Henry IV,* ii, 4, 309.
The world's globe.—*II Henry VI,* iii, 2, 406.

1
The dank earth weeps at thy languishment.
The Rape of Lucrece, l. 1130. "Languishment" is repeated in l. 1141, and in *Titus Andronicus,* ii, 1, 110.
The earth doth weep, the sun being set.
The Rape of Lucrece, l. 1226.

2
For thou hast made the happy earth thy hell,
Fill'd it with cursing cries and deep exclaims.
Richard III. Act i, sc. 2, l. 51. [Lady Anne]
Thou camest on earth to make the earth my hell.
Richard III. Act iv, sc. 4, l. 166. [Duchess of York]
Let the earth hide thee!—*Macbeth,* iii, 4, 93.

3
Turn back, dull earth, and find thy centre out.
Romeo and Juliet. Act ii, sc. 1, l. 2. [Romeo]
Dull earth.—*The Two Gentlemen of Verona,* iv, 2, 52; *Venus and Adonis,* l. 340.
The earth that 's nature's mother is her tomb;
What is her burying grave that is her womb,
And from her womb children of divers kind
We sucking on her natural bosom find,
Many for many virtues excellent,
None but for some and yet all different.
Romeo and Juliet. Act ii, sc. 3, l. 9. [Friar Laurence]
Vile earth, to earth resign; end motion here.
Romeo and Juliet. Act iii, sc. 2, l. 59. [Juliet]
Vilest earth.—*I Henry IV,* v, 4, 91.

4
Make the earth devour her own sweet brood.
Sonnets. No. xix.
The earth can yield me but a common grave,
Though you entombed in men's eyes shall lie.
Sonnets. No. lxxxi.

5
Earth, yield me roots!
Who seeks for better of thee, sauce his palate
With thy most operant poison!
Timon of Athens. Act v, sc. 3, l. 23. [Timon] "Operant" is repeated in *Hamlet,* iii, 2, 184: "Operant powers."

6
Say, who art thou that lately didst descend
Into this gaping hollow of the earth?
Titus Andronicus. Act ii, sc. 3, l. 248. [Saturninus]
Earth gapes.—*Richard III,* iv, 4, 75.
Hollow earth.—*The Taming of the Shrew,* Ind., 2, 48.

7
Then must my earth with her continual tears
Become a deluge, overflow'd and drown'd.
Titus Andronicus. Act iii, sc. 1, l. 229. [Titus] "Deluge" is repeated in *Richard III,* i, 2, 61.
The earth, fearing to be o'erflow'd.—*Pericles,* iv, 4, 40. The only uses of "over-flow'd."

8
'Tis you must dig with mattock and with spade,
And pierce the inmost centre of the earth.
Titus Andronicus. Act iv, sc. 3, l. 11. [Titus] "Mattock" is repeated in *Romeo and Juliet,* v, 3, 22, and v, 3, 185.
Like to the earth swallow her own increase.
Titus Andronicus. Act v, sc. 2, l. 192. [Titus]

9
The earth, in love with thee, thy footing trips.
Venus and Adonis, l. 733. See under FALL.

EARTHQUAKE

10
Diseased nature oftentimes breaks forth
In strange eruptions; oft the teeming earth
Is with a kind of colic pinch'd and vex'd
By the imprisoning of unruly wind
Within her womb; which, for enlargement striving,
Shakes the old beldam earth and topples down
Steeples and moss-grown towers.
I Henry IV. Act iii, sc. 1, l. 27. [Hotspur] The only use of "imprisoning" and "moss-grown."

11
Are not you moved, when all the sway of earth
Shakes like a thing unfirm?
Julius Cæsar. Act i, sc. 3, l. 3. [Casca]

12
Though bladed corn be lodged and trees blown down;
Though castles topple on their warders' heads;
Though palaces and pyramids do slope
Their heads to their foundations; though the treasure
Of nature's germens tumble all together,
Even till destruction sicken.
Macbeth. Act iv, sc. 1, l. 55. [Macbeth] The only use of "slope." "Germens" (germs) is repeated in *King Lear,* iii, 2, 8.

13
I look for an earthquake too, then.
Much Ado about Nothing. Act i, sc. 1, l. 275. [Benedick]
'Tis since the earthquake now eleven years.
Romeo and Juliet. Act i, sc. 3, l. 23. [Nurse]
At an earthquake.—*All 's Well that Ends Well,* i, 3, 92.
Coming . . . in earthquake.—*Henry V,* ii, 4, 100.
Like an earthquake.—*Venus and Adonis,* l. 648.
Make an earthquake.—*King John,* v, 2, 42; *The Tempest,* ii, 1, 315. The only uses of "earthquake."
Removed with earthquakes.—*As You Like It,* iii, 2, 196. The only use of "earthquakes."

EASE

See also Leisure

1
Shall I not take mine ease in mine inn but I shall have my pocket picked?
I Henry IV. Act iii, sc. 3, l. 92. [Falstaff]
For mine ease.—*Hamlet*, v, 2, 109.
A kind of easiness.—*Hamlet*, iii, 4, 166.
A property of easiness.—*Hamlet*, v, 1, 76.
Easiness and childish pity.—*Henry VIII*, v, 3, 25. The only uses of "easiness."

2
It could not . . . ease my heart.
III Henry VI, i, 3, 29. See HATE, 677:5. "Ease my heart" is repeated in *I Henry IV*, i, 3, 127.
Ease the heart.—*Richard III*, iv, 4, 131.
Ease thy angry heart.—*Titus Andronicus*, v, 2, 119.
Heart's ease.—*Julius Cæsar*, i, 2, 208.
Ease his breast.—*Coriolanus*, ii, 2, 126.
Ease our legs.—*I Henry IV*, ii, 2, 84.
Ease my mind.—*Titus Andronicus*, ii, 4, 35.
Ease the gnawing vulture of thy mind.—*Titus Andronicus*, v, 2, 31.
Ease thy misery.—*Titus Andronicus*, ii, 4, 57.
Ease thy smart.—*Troilus and Cressida*, iv, 4, 20.
Ease their stomachs.—*Titus Andronicus*, iii, 1, 234.
Ease them of their griefs.—*Timon of Athens*, v, 1, 201.
Ease ourselves.—*Julius Cæsar*, iv, 1, 20.

3
While he enjoys the honour and his ease.
III Henry VI. Act iv, sc. 6, l. 52. [Warwick]
By heaven, I will not do thee so much ease.
III Henry VI. Act v, sc. 5, l. 72. [Clarence]
To thee do ease.—*Hamlet*, i, 1, 131.
Do him ease.—*Taming of the Shrew*, v, 2, 179.
Got with much ease.—*I Henry IV*, ii, 2, 111.
With such ease.—*I Henry IV*, iv, 1, 107.
With ease.—*King John*, ii, 1, 513; *Measure for Measure*, iv, 2, 205; *Hamlet*, iv, 7, 137; *Cymbeline*, v, 5, 363.
At his ease.—*III Henry VI*, iii, 3, 151.

4
Reach a chair:
So; now, methinks, I feel a little ease.
Henry VIII. Act iv, sc. 2, l. 3. [Katharine]
I shall be eased.—*III Henry VI*, iii, 3, 20.
Till he be eased.—*Richard II*, v, 5, 40.
Eased by night.—*Sonnets*, xxviii. The only uses of "eased."

5
Forego the easier.
King John. Act iii, sc. 1, l. 207. [Lewis] "Easier" is used nine times.
Easiest passage.—*The Winter's Tale*, iii, 2, 91. The only use of "easiest."
Easiliest harbour in.—*Cymbeline*, iv, 2, 206. The only use of "easiliest."

6
Nor conversant with ease and idleness.
King John. Act iv, sc. 3, l. 70. [Salisbury]

7
Seek thine own ease.
King Lear. Act iii, sc. 4, l. 23. [King Lear]
Seek about for eases.—*Troilus and Cressida*, v, 10, 56.
Give . . . ease to the pain'd.—*The Rape of Lucrece*, l. 901.
There 's seldom ease.—*Pericles*, ii, Gower, 28.
A minute's ease.—*Pericles*, ii, 4, 44.
Easing me of the carriage.—*The Merry Wives of Windsor*, ii, 2, 179.
Hurts by easing.—*Hamlet*, iv, 7, 124. The only uses of "easing."

EATING

See also Dining, Feast, Feeding, Food, Meat, Supper

8
Please it this matron and this gentle maid
To eat with us to-night, the charge and thanking
Shall be for me.
All's Well that Ends Well. Act iii, sc. 5, l. 100. [Helena]
Eat together.—*As You Like It*, i, 3, 76.
I will go eat with thee.—*Troilus and Cressida*, iv, 5, 158.
Eat with the devil.—*Comedy of Errors*, iv, 3, 65.

9
He is a very epicure.
Antony and Cleopatra. Act ii, sc. 7, l. 58. [Antony]
English epicures.—*Macbeth*, v, 3, 8. The only uses of "epicure."
Epicurean rascal.—*The Merry Wives of Windsor*, ii, 2, 300.
Epicurean cooks.—*Antony and Cleopatra*, ii, 1, 24. The only uses of "epicurean." Epicurus is mentioned only once, in *Julius Cæsar*, v, 1, 77; and "epicurism" occurs once, in *King Lear*, i, 4, 265.

10
Let 's to-night be bounteous at our meal.
Antony and Cleopatra. Act iv, sc. 2, l. 9. [Antony]
Give them great meals of beef and iron and steel, they will eat like wolves and fight like devils.
Henry V. Act iii, sc. 7, l. 161. [Constable]
Give me but the ten meals I have lost, and I 'ld defy them all.
II Henry VI. Act iv, sc. 10, l. 66. [Cade]
Eat our meal.—*Macbeth*, iii, 2, 17.
Made his meal.—*The Tempest*, ii, 1, 113.
Made my meal.—*Cymbeline*, iii, 6, 52.
Keep with you at meals.—*Julius Cæsar*, ii, 1, 284.
But one meal on every day.—*Love's Labour 's Lost*, i, 1, 40.
So many meals.—*Troilus and Cressida*, ii, 3, 45.
Fruitful meal.—*Measure for Measure*, iv, 3, 161.
Unquiet meals.—*Comedy of Errors*, v, 1, 74.
Meal and bran together
He throws without distinction.
Coriolanus, iii, 1, 322. See under CANDOUR. "Meal and bran" is repeated in *Cymbeline*, iv, 2, 27. See under ANCESTRY.

11
If I bring thee not something to eat, I will give thee leave to die.
As You Like It. Act ii, sc. 6, l. 12. [Orlando]
Orlando: Forbear, and eat no more.
Jaques: Why, I have eat none yet.

Orlando: Nor shalt not, till necessity be served.
As You Like It. Act ii, sc. 7, l. 88.

Look you eat no more
Than will preserve just so much strength in us
As will revenge these bitter woes of ours.
Titus Andronicus. Act iii, sc. 2, l. 1. [Titus]

Eat no fish.—*King Lear,* i, 4, 18.

Eat no grapes.—*All's Well that Ends Well,* ii, 1, 73.

Eat no meat.—*II Henry VI,* iv, 10, 41; *The Taming of the Shrew,* iv, 1, 200; *Antony and Cleopatra,* v, 2, 49.

Eat none of it.—*The Comedy of Errors,* ii, 2, 61.

1
Pray God our cheer
May answer my good will and your good welcome here.
The Comedy of Errors. Act iii, sc. 1, l. 19. [Antipholus of Ephesus]

Much thanks for my good cheer.
The Comedy of Errors. Act v, sc. 1, l. 392. [Antipholus of Ephesus] See also *The Taming of the Shrew,* v, 2, 10; *Much Ado about Nothing,* v, 1, 153; *Julius Cæsar,* iii, 2, 89; *Antony and Cleopatra,* iv, 15, 83.

Welcome! one mess is like to be your cheer.
The Taming of the Shrew. Act iv, sc. 4, l. 70. [Tranio]

And welcome, all: although the cheer be poor,
'Twill fill your stomachs; please you eat of it.
Titus Andronicus. Act v, sc. 3, l. 28. [Titus]

Ah, sirrah! quoth-a, we shall
Do nothing but eat, and make good cheer,
And praise God for the merry year.
II Henry IV. Act v, sc. 3, l. 17. [Silence] "Good cheer" occurs thirteen times.

2
They are up already, and call for eggs and butter.
I Henry IV. Act ii, sc. 1, l. 66. [Chamberlain]

Hostess, my breakfast, come!
O, I could wish this tavern were my drum!
I Henry IV. Act iii, sc. 3, l. 229. [Falstaff]

Go, make ready breakfast.
I Henry IV. Act iii, sc. 3, l. 193. [Falstaff]

I will bestow a breakfast to make you friends.
Henry V. Act ii, sc. 1, l. 12. [Bardolph]

Eat his breakfast.—*Henry V,* iii, 7, 156.

I do invite you to-morrow morning to my house for breakfast.
The Merry Wives of Windsor. Act iii, sc. 3, l. 245. [Page]

Then to breakfast.—*Henry VIII,* iii, 2, 202.

Call'd . . . to breakfast.—*Richard III,* iv, 4, 176.

A sorry breakfast for my lord protector.
II Henry VI. Act i, sc. 4, l. 79. [York]

3
He hath eaten me out of house and home; he hath put all my substance into that fat belly of his: but I will have some of it out again, or I will ride thee o' nights like the mare.
II Henry IV. Act ii, sc. 1, l. 80. [Hostess] The only use of "eaten out of house and home," a phrase which dates from about 1400 (*Towneley Plays,* xiii, 124).

Eating draff and husks.—*I Henry IV,* iv, 2, 38. "Draff" (hog-wash) is repeated in *The Merry Wives of Windsor,* iv, 2, 109.

Eating toasted cheese.—*II Henry VI,* iv, 7, 13.

4
Pistol: Hence! I am qualmish at the smell of leek.
Fluellen: I peseech you heartily, scurvy, lousy knave, at my desires, and my requests, and my petitions, to eat, look you, this leek. . . . I would desire you to eat it.
Pistol: Not for Cadwallader and all his goats.
Fluellen: There is one goat for you. [Strikes him.] Will you be so good, scauld knave, as eat it? . . . I pray you, fall to: if you can mock a leek, you can eat a leek. . . . Bite, I pray you; it is good for your green wound and your ploody coxcomb.
Pistol: Must I bite?
Fluellen: Yes, certainly, and out of doubt and out of question too, and ambiguities.
Pistol: By this leek, I will most horribly revenge: I eat and eat, I swear—
Fluellen: Eat, I pray you: you will have some more sauce to your leek? there is not enough leek to swear by.
Pistol: Quiet thy cudgel; thou dost see I eat.
Henry V. Act v, sc. 1, l. 22. The only use of "qualmish," and mention of Cadwallader, the last king of the Britons, who reigned in the seventh century. "Ambiguities" is used a second time in *Romeo and Juliet,* v, 3, 217.

I have another leek in my pocket which you shall eat.
Henry V. Act v, sc. 1, l. 66. [Fluellen]

5
We 'll fall to it with our teeth.
I Henry VI. Act iii, sc. 1, l. 90. [Servant]

So fall to 't.
Timon of Athens, i, 2, 71; *The Tempest,* i, 1, 3. The only uses of "fall to it."

My lord, will 't please you to fall to?
Richard II. Act v, sc. 5, l. 98. [Keeper] See also *The Taming of the Shrew,* i, 1, 38; *Henry V,* v, 1, 38; *As You Like It,* ii, 7, 171; *Titus Andronicus,* iii, 2, 34. The only uses of "fall to."

6
Poor Tom; that eats the swimming frog, the toad, the tadpole, the wall-newt and the water; that in the fury of his heart, when the foul fiend rages, eats cow-dung for sallets; swallows the old rat and the ditch-dog.
King Lear. Act iii, sc. 4, l. 134. [Edgar] The only use of "wall-newt," "cow-dung" and "ditch-dog." "Frog" is used only once more, in *Macbeth,* v, 1, 14; and "tadpole" in *Titus Andronicus,* iv, 2, 85. "Sallet" is an obsolete form of salad.

Eat the air.—*Hamlet,* iii, 2, 99.

Eating the air.—*II Henry IV,* i, 3, 28.

Eat blackberries.—*I Henry IV,* ii, 4, 450.

Eat bread.—*Richard II,* v, 5, 85.

Eat chickens i' the shell.—*Troilus and Cressida,* i, 2, 147.

Eats conger and fennel.—*II Henry IV,* ii, 4, 266. "Conger" is repeated in l. 58, and occurs in no other scene.

Eat a crocodile.—*Hamlet,* v, 1, 299.

Eat strange flesh.—*Antony and Cleopatra,* i, 4, 67.

Eat a grape.—*As You Like It,* v, 1, 37.

Eat grass.—*II Henry VI,* iv, 10, 9.
Eat my heart.—*A Midsummer-Night's Dream,* ii, 2, 149.
Eat honey.—*Pericles,* ii, Gower, 18.
Eat husks.—*As You Like It,* i, 1, 40.
Eat of my lord's meat.—*Timon of Athens,* iii, 4, 50. See under MEAT.
Eat men.—*Timon of Athens,* iv, 3, 428.
Eat dried oats.—*King Lear,* v, 3, 38.
Eat rocks.—*Troilus and Cressida,* iii, 2, 84.
Eat roots.—*Timon of Athens,* i, 2, 72; v, 1, 77.
Eat swords.—*Troilus and Cressida,* ii, 3, 227.
Eats the sword.—*Antony and Cleopatra,* iii, 13, 200.
Eat a piece of my sword.—*I Henry IV,* v, 4, 157.
Eat your victuals.—*Henry V,* v, 1, 35.
Eats our victuals.—*Cymbeline,* iii, 6, 41.
Eat thy dead vomit up.—*II Henry IV,* i, 3, 99.
Eat twenty of his words.—*II Henry IV,* ii, 2, 149.
Eat up her own!—*Coriolanus,* iii, 1, 294.
Eater of youth.—*The Rape of Lucrece,* l. 927.
A great eater of beef.—*Twelfth Night,* i, 3, 90.
An eater of broken meats.—*King Lear,* ii, 2, 15.
An eater of her mother's flesh.—*Pericles,* i, 1, 130. The only uses of "eater."
He eats nothing but doves.—*Troilus and Cressida,* iii, 1, 140. See under LOVE.

1 Thou shalt not gormandize,
As thou hast done with me.
The Merchant of Venice. Act ii, sc. 5, l. 3. [Shylock] The only use of "gormandize."

Leave gormandizing.—*II Henry IV,* v, 5, 57. The only use of "gormandizing."
Gorging and feeding from our soldiers' hands.
Julius Cæsar. Act v, sc. 1, l. 82. [Cassius] The only use of "gorging."
He is a very valiant trencherman.
Much Ado about Nothing. Act i, sc. 1, l. 51. [Beatrice] The only use of "trencherman."
They eat us hungerly.—*Othello,* iii, 4, 105.
Eat him quick!—*Richard III,* i, 2, 65.
Eat it up all.—*Taming of the Shrew,* iv, 3, 50.
Eat apace.—*Taming of the Shrew,* iv, 3, 52.
Eat up himself.—*Troilus and Cressida,* i, 3, 124; ii, 3, 164.

2
Nothing but sit and sit, and eat and eat!
The Taming of the Shrew. Act v, sc. 2, l. 12. [Petruchio]

Eat and drink as friends.
The Taming of the Shrew, i, 2, 279. [Tranio]
I will eat and drink.
All's Well that Ends Well, iv, 3, 368.
Let us therefore eat and drink.
Twelfth Night, ii, 3, 13.
All shall eat and drink on my score.
II Henry VI, iv, 2, 79.

ECHO

3
The replication of your sounds.
Julius Cæsar. Act i, sc. 1, l. 51. [Marullus] "Replication" is repeated in *Love's Labour 's Lost,* iv, 2, 15, and *Hamlet,* iv, 2, 13.

To the very echo.—*Macbeth,* v, 3, 53.

4 By heaven, he echoes me,
As if there were some monster in his thought
Too hideous to be shown.
Othello. Act iii, sc. 3, l. 106. [Othello]

5
Bondage is hoarse, and may not speak aloud;
Else would I tear the cave where Echo lies,
And make her airy tongue more hoarse than mine.
Romeo and Juliet. Act ii, sc. 2, l. 161. [Juliet]

6 Ring a hunter's peal,
That all the court may echo with the noise.
Titus Andronicus, ii, 2, 5. See under HUNTING.

All the church did echo.—*The Taming of the Shrew,* iii, 2, 181.

7 The babbling echo mocks the hounds,
Replying shrilly to the well-tuned horns,
As if a double hunt were heard at once.
Titus Andronicus. Act ii, sc. 3, l. 17. [Tamora] "Well tuned" is repeated in *Othello,* ii, 1, 202.

A very echo.—*Twelfth Night,* ii, 4, 21.

8
Then do they spend their mouths: Echo replies,
As if another chase were in the skies.
Venus and Adonis, l. 695.

'Ay me'! she cries, and twenty times 'Woe, woe!'
And twenty echoes twenty times cry so.
Venus and Adonis, l. 833.
Still the choir of echoes answer so.
Venus and Adonis, l. 840.

9 Like an arch, reverberates
The voice again.
Troilus and Cressida. Act iii, sc. 3, l. 120. [Ulysses] The only use of "reverberates." "Reverberate" occurs twice.

ECSTASY

10
Mark how he trembles in his ecstasy!
The Comedy of Errors. Act iv, sc. 4, l. 54. [Courtezan]

Thus stands she in a trembling ecstasy.
Venus and Adonis, l. 895.

11
That unmatch'd form and feature of blown youth
Blasted with ecstasy.
Hamlet. Act iii, sc. 1, l. 167. [Ophelia]

Queen: This bodiless creation ecstasy
Is very cunning in.
Hamlet: Ecstasy!
My pulse, as yours, doth temperately keep time.
Hamlet. Act iii, sc. 4, l. 138.

Suffering ecstasy.—*A Lover's Complaint,* l. 69.
A modern ecstasy.—*Macbeth,* iv, 3, 170.
Allay thy ecstasy.—*The Merchant of Venice,* iii, 2, 112.

12
The ecstasy hath so much overborne her that my daughter is sometime afeared she will do a desperate outrage to herself.
Much Ado about Nothing. Act ii, sc. 3, l. 157. [Leonato]

13 Follow them swiftly
And hinder them from what this ecstasy
May now provoke them to.
Tempest. Act iii, sc. 3, l. 107. [Gonzalo]

1 If I live, his feigned ecstasies
Shall be no shelter to these outrages.
Titus Andronicus. Act iv, sc. 4, l. 21. [Saturninus]

EDICT, see Law

EDUCATION

See also Teaching

2
I have those hopes of her good that her education promises.
All's Well that Ends Well. Act i, sc. 1, l. 45. [Rousillon]

3
Mines my gentility with my education.
As You Like It. Act i, sc. 1, l. 22. [Orlando] "Gentility" is repeated in *Love's Labour's Lost,* i, 1, 129.

4
Smith: The clerk of Chatham: he can write and read and cast accompt.
Cade: O monstrous!
Smith: We took him setting of boys' copies.
Cade: Here's a villain!
Smith: Has a book in his pocket with red letters in 't.
Cade: Nay, then, he is a conjurer.
II Henry VI. Act iv, sc. 2, l. 92.

Cade: Dost thou use to write thy name? or hast thou a mark to thyself, like an honest plain-dealing man?
Clerk: Sir, I thank God, I have been so well brought up that I can write my name.
All: He hath confessed: away with him! he's a villain and a traitor.
Cade: Away with him, I say! hang him with his pen and ink-horn about his neck.
II Henry VI. Act iv, sc. 2, l. 109.

Thou hast most traitorously corrupted the youth of the realm in erecting a grammar school: and whereas, before, our forefathers had no other books but the score and the tally, thou hast caused printing to be used, and, contrary to the king, his crown and dignity, thou hast built a paper-mill. It will be proved to thy face that thou hast men about thee that usually talk of a noun and a verb, and such abominable words as no Christian ear can endure to hear.
II Henry VI. Act iv, sc. 7, l. 35. [Cade] The only use of "erecting," "tally," "paper-mill" and "verb." "Usually" is repeated in *Macbeth,* iii, 3, 12, and "noun" in *The Merry Wives of Windsor,* iv, 1, 22.

5
Armado: Arts-man, preambulate, we will be singuled from the barbarous. Do you not educate youth at the charge-house on the top of the mountain?
Holofernes: Or mons, the hill. . . . I do, sans question.
Love's Labour's Lost. Act v, sc. 1, l. 85. [Armado] The only use of "arts-man," "preambulate," "singuled," "charge-house" (boarding-school), and "mons."

Well-educated infant.—*Love's Labour's Lost,* i, 2, 99. The only use of "well-educated."

6
To be a well-favoured man is the gift of fortune; but to write and read comes by nature.
Much Ado about Nothing. Act iii, sc. 3, l. 14. [Dogberry]

For your writing and reading, let that appear when there is no need of such vanity.
Much Ado about Nothing. Act iii, sc. 3, l. 20. [Dogberry]

7
My education been in arts and arms.
Pericles. Act ii, sc. 3, l. 182. [Pericles]

By Cleon train'd
In music, letters; who hath gain'd
Of education all the grace,
Which makes her both the heart and place
Of general wonder.
Pericles. Act iv, Gower, l. 7.

EEL

8
Cry to it, nuncle, as the cockney did to the eels when she put 'em i' the paste alive; she knapped 'em o' the coxcombs with a stick, and cried 'Down, wantons, down!'
King Lear. Act ii, sc. 4, l. 123. [Fool] "Knapped" (to give a sharp blow) is used again in *Merchant of Venice,* iii, 1, 10, in the sense of to bite noisily: "Knapped ginger."

9
Moth: I will praise an eel with the same praise.
Armado: What, that an eel is ingenious?
Moth: That an eel is quick.
Love's Labour's Lost. Act i, sc. 2, l. 28.

Beds of eels.—*Pericles,* iv, 2, 155.
Better than the eel.—*The Taming of the Shrew,* iv, 3, 179. The only uses of "eel."
Eel-skins stuff'd.—*King John,* i, 1, 141. "Eel-skin" is used again in *II Henry IV,* iii, 2, 351.

EFFECT

See also Result

10
Alack, in me what strange effect
Would they work in mild aspect!
As You Like It, iv, 3, 52. See under EYE.

Strange effects.—*Measure for Measure,* iii, 1, 24.

The seeing these effects will be
Both noisome and infectious.
Cymbeline. Act i, sc. 5, l. 25. [Cornelius]

Accursed effect.—*Richard III,* i, 2, 20.
Base effect.—*The Two Gentlemen of Verona,* ii, 7, 73.
Cleft effect.—*A Lover's Complaint,* l. 293.
False effect.—*Cymbeline,* i, 5, 43.
Foul effect.—*King John,* iv, 1, 38.
Large effects.—*King Lear,* i, 1, 133.
Manifested effect.—*Measure for Measure,* iv, 2, 169.
Particular effects.—*Henry V,* v, 2, 72.
Proved effects.—*All's Well that Ends Well,* i, 3, 228.
Sequent effects.—*King Lear,* i, 2, 115.
Stern effects.—*Hamlet,* iii, 4, 129.
Untempering effect.—*Henry V,* v, 2, 241. The only use of "untempering."
Warm effects.—*Venus and Adonis,* l. 605.
Took effect.—*Romeo and Juliet,* v, 3, 244.

1 The effect of judgement
Is oft the cause of fear.
Cymbeline. Act iv, sc. 2, l. 111. [Belarius] See also under CAUSE.

Effects of courtesy.—*King Lear,* ii, 4, 181.
Effect of fire.—*The Comedy of Errors,* iv, 3, 57.
Effect of gravity.—*II Henry IV,* i, 2, 183.
Effect of humour.—*Julius Cæsar,* ii, 1, 250.
Effect of love.—*Measure for Measure,* v, 1, 199.
Effect of your reputation.—*II Henry IV,* ii, 1, 142.
Effects of sorrow.—*Titus Andronicus,* iv, 4, 30.
Effects of terror and dear modesty.—*A Lover's Complaint,* l. 202.
Effects of watching.—*Macbeth,* v, 1, 12.
Effect of wine.—*Comedy of Errors,* v, 1, 215.

2 Let thy effects
So follow, to be most unlike our courtiers,
As good as promise.
Cymbeline. Act v, sc. 4, l. 135. [Posthumus]

3
I shall the effect of this good lesson keep,
As watchman to my heart.
Hamlet. Act i, sc. 3, l. 45. [Ophelia]

I am still possess'd
Of these effects for which I did the murder.
Hamlet. Act iii, sc. 3, l. 54. [King]

Wilt thou know The effect of what I wrote?
Hamlet. Act v, sc. 2, l. 37. [Hamlet]

4
Good effects may spring from words of love.
King Lear, i, 1, 188. See WORD AND DEED.

Heavenly effect.—*All's Well that Ends Well,* ii, 3, 27.
Pure effects.—*The Rape of Lucrece,* l. 251.

5
The effects he writes of succeed unhappily.
King Lear, i, 2, 156. See under OMEN.

6
Don Pedro: What effects of passion shows she? . . .
Leonato: What effects, my lord? She will sit you, you heard my daughter tell you how.
Much Ado about Nothing. Act ii, sc. 3, l. 112.

But see, while idly I stood looking on,
I found the effect of love in idleness.
The Taming of the Shrew. Act i, sc. 1, l. 155. [Lucentio] "Love-in-idleness" (hyphenated) is used once again in *A Midsummer-Night's Dream,* ii, 1, 168.

7
Beauty's effect with beauty were bereft.
Sonnets. No. v.

Gold's effect.—*Taming of the Shrew,* i, 2, 93.
Love's sole effect.—*Sonnets,* xxxvi.
Lust's effect.—*Venus and Adonis,* l. 800.
Prayer's effect.—*Romeo and Juliet,* i, 5, 108.

8
All my study be to no effect?
Titus Andronicus, v, 2, 12. See under TRICK.

To such effect.—*Titus Andronicus,* ii, 3, 111.
To that effect.—*Richard III,* ii, 2, 15; *Hamlet,* iv, 3, 66.
To this effect.—*I Henry VI,* v, 4, 102; *King John,* iv, 2, 35; *Hamlet,* v, 2, 187; *Othello,* i, 3, 105; *Troilus and Cressida,* iii, 3, 216.
To what effect?—*Julius Cæsar,* i, 2, 283.

9
The effect doth operate another way.
Troilus and Cressida. Act v, sc. 3, l. 109. [Troilus]

10
All the fair effects of future hopes.
The Two Gentlemen of Verona. Act i, sc. 1, l. 50. [Valentine]

The effects of his fond jealousies so grieving
That he shuts up himself.
The Winter's Tale. Act iv, sc. 1, l. 18. [Time]

ELECTION

See also Choice

11 Thy frank election make;
Thou hast power to choose, and they none to forsake.
All's Well that Ends Well. Act ii, sc. 3, l. 61. [King]

12
On a safer judgement all revoke
Your ignorant election.
Coriolanus. Act ii, sc. 3, l. 226. [Sicinius]

You must Cast your election on him.
Coriolanus. Act ii, sc. 3, l. 236. [Brutus]

Almost all Repent in their election.
Coriolanus. Act ii, sc. 3, l. 262. [Citizens]

13
By her election may be truly read
What kind of man he is.
Cymbeline. Act i, sc. 1, l. 53. [Gentleman]

If it be a sin to make a true election, she is damned.
Cymbeline. Act i, sc. 2, l. 29. [Lord]

The election of a sir so rare.—*Cymbeline,* i, 6, 175.

14
Her election Hath seal'd thee for herself.
Hamlet. Act iii, sc. 2, l. 69. [Hamlet]

I cannot live to hear the news from England;
But I do prophesy the election lights
On Fortinbras: he has my dying voice.
Hamlet. Act v, sc. 2, l. 366. [Hamlet] See also under VOICE.

15
Before we make election, give me leave
To show some reason, of no little force,
That York is most unmeet of any man.
II Henry VI. Act i, sc. 3, l. 165. [Suffolk]

Election makes not up on such conditions.
King Lear. Act i, sc. 1, l. 209. [Burgundy]

16 We have with special soul
Elected him our absence to supply,
Lent him our terror, dress'd him with our love,
And given his deputation all the organs
Of our own power.
Measure for Measure. Act i, sc. 1, l. 18. [Duke]

17
The Prince of Arragon hath ta'en his oath,
And comes to his election presently.
The Merchant of Venice. Act ii, sc. 9, l. 2. [Nerissa]

He, sir, had the election.—*Othello,* i, 1, 27.

18
Titus Andronicus, the people of Rome . . .
Send thee by me, their tribune and their trust,

This palliament of white and spotless hue;
And name thee in election for the empire.
Titus Andronicus. Act i, sc. 1, l. 179. [Marcus] The only use of "palliament," the white gown of a candidate for the Roman consulship.

Be chosen with proclamations to-day,
To-morrow yield up rule.
Titus Andronicus. Act i, sc. 1, l. 190. [Titus]

If you will elect by my advice,
Crown him, and say 'Long live our emperor!'
Titus Andronicus. Act i, sc. 1, l. 228. [Titus]

Pure election.—*Titus Andronicus,* i, 1, 16.

ELEMENT

1
The elements be kind to thee!
Antony and Cleopatra, iii, 2, 40. See under Farewell.

Give him defence against the elements.
Othello, ii, 1, 45. See under Sea.

The unfriendly elements Forgot thee utterly.
Pericles. Act iii, sc. 1, l. 58. [Pericles]

2
I am fire and air; my other elements
I give to baser life.
Antony and Cleopatra. Act v, sc. 2, l. 292. [Cleopatra]

He is pure air and fire; and the dull elements of earth and water never appear in him.
Henry V. Act iii, sc. 7, l. 22. [Dauphin]

Dauphin: Via! les eaux et la terre.
Orleans: Rien puis? l'air et le feu.
Henry V. Act iv, sc. 2, l. 4.

But that so much of earth and water wrought
I must attend time's leisure with my moan,
Receiving nought by elements so slow
But heavy tears, badges of either's woe.
The other two, slight air and purging fire,
Are both with thee, wherever I abide;
The first my thought, the other my desire,
These present-absent with quick motion slide.
For when these quicker elements are gone
In tender embassy of love to thee,
My life, being made of four, with two alone
Sinks down to death, oppress'd with melancholy.
Sonnets. Nos. xliv, xlv. The only use of "present-absent."

Elements of air and earth.—*Twelfth Night,* i, 5, 294.

Elements of fire and water.—*Richard II,* iii, 3, 55.

Does not our life consist of the four elements?
Twelfth Night. Act ii, sc. 3, l. 10. [Sir Toby]

3
The element shows to him as it doth to me.
Henry V, iv, 1, 107. See under King.

4
The elements So mix'd in him.
Julius Cæsar, v, 5, 73. See under Man.

5
I tax not you, you elements, with unkindness,
I never gave you kingdom, call'd you children,
You owe me no subscription.
King Lear. Act iii, sc. 2, l. 16. [King Lear] The only use of "subscription."

6
The very elements of this warlike isle,
Have I to-night fluster'd with flowing cups.
Othello. Act ii, sc. 3, l. 59. [Iago] The only use of "fluster'd."

You elements that clip us round about.
Othello. Act iii, sc. 3, l. 464. [Iago]

Conflicting elements.—*Timon of Athens,* iv, 3, 230.

Dim element.—*The Rape of Lucrece,* l. 1588.

Free elements.—*Othello,* ii, 3, 348.

Fretful element.—*King Lear,* iii, 1, 4.

Melancholy element.—*Much Ado about Nothing,* ii, 1, 357.

7
Command these elements to silence.
The Tempest. Act i, sc. 1, l. 24. [Boatswain]

8
Bounding between the two moist elements,
Like Perseus' horse.
Troilus and Cressida, i, 3, 41. See under Ship.

9
The element itself, till seven years' heat,
Shall not behold her face at ample view.
Twelfth Night. Act i, sc. 1, l. 26. [Valentine]

I might say 'element,' but the word is overworn.
Twelfth Night, iii, 1, 65. See under Word.

I am not of your element.—*Twelfth Night,* iii, 4, 137.

Thy element 's below.—*King Lear,* ii, 4, 58.

Beyond our element.—*The Merry Wives of Windsor,* iv, 2, 186. See under Magic.

ELOQUENCE

See also Oratory

10
To try thy eloquence, now 'tis time: dispatch.
Antony and Cleopatra. Act iii, sc. 12, l. 26. [Cæsar]

His eloquence the parcel of a reckoning.
I Henry IV. Act ii, sc. 4, l. 113. [Prince of Wales]

11
For I have neither wit, nor words, nor worth,
Action, nor utterance, nor the power of speech,
To stir men's blood: I only speak right on.
Julius Cæsar. Act iii, sc. 2, l. 225. [Antony]

12
Aged ears play truant at his tales
And younger hearings are quite ravished,
So sweet and voluble is his discourse.
Love's Labour 's Lost, ii, 1, 74. See under Wit.

He had the dialect and different skill,
Catching all passions in his craft of will.
A Lover's Complaint, l. 125.

13
Her modest eloquence with sighs is mixed,
Which to her oratory adds more grace.
The Rape of Lucrece, l. 563.

Heavenly eloquence.—*Romeo and Juliet,* iii, 2, 33.

1
Be eloquent in my behalf to her.
Richard III. Act iv, sc. 4, l. 357. [King Richard]
It is no matter how witty, so it be eloquent and full of invention.
Twelfth Night. Act iii, sc. 2, l. 46. [Sir Toby]
Eloquent music.—*Hamlet,* iii, 2, 375.
Eloquent tongues.—*Henry V,* iii, 7, 37.
2
When rank Thersites opes his mastic jaws,
We shall hear music, wit and oracle.
Troilus and Cressida. Act i, sc. 3, l. 73. [Agamemnon] The only use of "mastic" (massive).
3 She is nice and coy
And nought esteems my aged eloquence.
The Two Gentlemen of Verona. Act iii, sc. 1, l. 82. [Duke]

EMBRACE

4
He knows that you embrace not Antony
As you did love, but as you fear'd him.
Antony and Cleopatra. Act iii, sc. 13, l. 56. [Thyreus]
5
Drew me from kind embracements of my spouse.
The Comedy of Errors. Act i, sc. 1, l. 44. [Ægeon] "Kind embracements" is repeated in *The Taming of the Shrew,* Ind., 1, 118; and in *Venus and Adonis,* l. 312.
Embracements of his bed.—*Coriolanus,* i, 3, 4.
6 They clung
In their embracement, as they grew together.
Henry VIII. Act i, sc. 1, l. 9. [Norfolk]
Lends embracements unto every stranger.
Venus and Adonis, l. 790.
Bring them to our embracement.
Winter's Tale. Act v, sc. 1, l. 114. [Leontes]
7
With joy he will embrace you, for he 's honourable.
Cymbeline. Act iii, sc. 4, l. 179. [Pisanio]
Last embrace.—*Romeo and Juliet,* v, 3, 113.
8
I will embrace him with a soldier's arm.
I Henry IV. Act v, sc. 2, l. 74. [Hotspur]
Let us all embrace.—*I Henry IV,* v, 2, 99.
9
Direct mine arms I may embrace his neck,
And in his bosom spend my latest gasp.
I Henry VI. Act ii, sc. 5, l. 37. [Mortimer]
And, lords, accept this hearty kind embrace.
I Henry VI. Act iii, sc. 3, l. 82. [Burgundy]
I do embrace thee, as I would embrace
The Christian prince, King Henry, were he here.
I Henry VI. Act v, sc. 3, l. 171. [Reignier]
I embrace you.—*Pericles,* v, 1, 223.
I embrace it freely.—*Hamlet,* v, 2, 263.
10
Let me embrace thee in my weary arms.
III Henry VI. Act ii, sc. 3, l. 45. [Richard]
Let me embrace thee.—*III Henry VI,* iii, 1, 24; *Troilus and Cressida,* iv, 5, 135; 202.
Let an old man embrace thee.—*Troilus and Cressida,* iv, 5, 199.
I must embrace thee.—*King Lear,* v, 3, 176.
Embrace me as a friend.—*Titus Andronicus,* v, 3, 108.
Embrace him, dear Thaisa.—*Pericles,* v, 3, 55.
Dorset, embrace him.—*Richard III,* ii, 1, 25.
11
Where 's the body that I should embrace?
II Henry VI. Act iv, sc. 4, l. 6. [Queen]
I embrace thy body.
The Tempest. Act v, sc. 1, l. 109. [Prospero]
12
And as he fell to her, so fell she to him.
'Even thus,' quoth she, 'the warlike god embraced me,'
And then she clipp'd Adonis in her arms.
The Passionate Pilgrim, l. 146.
13
We will descend and fold him in our arms.
Richard II. Act i, sc. 3, l. 54. [King Richard]
14 When I parted with him,
He hugg'd me in his arms.
Richard III. Act i, sc. 4, l. 251. [Clarence] See also *Measure for Measure,* iii, 1, 85.
Hugs his kicky-wicky.—*All 's Well that Ends Well,* ii, 3, 297. The only use of "kicky-wicky."
Hug him in their melting bosoms.—*Titus Andronicus,* iii, 1, 214.
Hug them hard.—*Julius Cæsar,* 1, 2, 75.
Embrace and hug.—*Timon of Athens,* i, 1, 44.
Hugg'd and embraced.—*The Merchant of Venice,* ii, 6, 16.
Embraced, kissed, protested.—*The Merry Wives of Windsor,* iii, 5, 74.
15
Let me embrace with old Vincentio.
The Taming of the Shrew. Act iv, sc. 5, l. 68. [Petruchio]
16
Let me embrace thine age.
The Tempest. Act v, sc. 1, l. 121. [Prospero]
Embrace my bosom.—*Troilus and Cressida,* iii, 2, 37.
Embrace thy brother.—*The Comedy of Errors,* v, 1, 413.
Embrace your charge.—*Much Ado about Nothing,* i, 1, 103.
Embrace these conditions.—*Cymbeline,* i, 4, 168.
Embrace no counsel.—*Timon of Athens,* iii, 1, 27.
Embrace thy death.—*The Two Gentlemen of Verona,* v, 4, 126.
Embrace but my direction.—*The Winter's Tale,* iv, 4, 534.
Embrace this fortune.—*I Henry IV,* v, 5, 12; *Hamlet,* v, 2, 399.
Embrace mine infamy.—*The Rape of Lucrece,* l. 504.
Embrace the occasion.—*The Merchant of Venice,* i, 1, 64.
Embrace your offer.—*King John,* iv, 3, 12; *All's Well that Ends Well,* v, 1, 328; *Much Ado about Nothing,* v, 1, 303; *Pericles,* iii, 3, 37.
Embrace we this opportunity.—*I Henry VI,* ii, 1, 13.
Embrace his pardon.—*II Henry VI,* iv, 8, 14.
Embrace your own safety.—*As You Like It,* i, 2, 189.

1
The one and other Diomed embraces.
Troilus and Cressida. Act iv, sc. 1, l. 14. [Diomedes]

2
Sometimes her arms infold him like a band:
She would, he will not in her arms be bound.
Venus and Adonis, l. 225.

Her arms do lend his neck a sweet embrace.
Venus and Adonis, l. 539.

Hot, faint, and weary with her hard embracing.
Venus and Adonis, l. 559.

With this, he breaketh from the sweet embrace
Of those fair arms which bound him to her breast,
And homeward through the dark laund runs apace;
Leaves Love upon her back deeply distress'd.
Venus and Adonis, l. 811. "Laund" (glade) is used a second time in *III Henry VI*, iii, 1, 2.

She wildly breaketh from their strict embrace,
Like a milch doe, whose swelling dugs do ache,
Hasting to feed her fawn hid in some brake.
Venus and Adonis, l. 874. "Hasting" is repeated in *The Winter's Tale*, ii, 3, 197, and "hastening" occurs in the same play, v, 1, 189, and nowhere else. "Milch" occurs again in *Hamlet*, ii, 2, 540; "milch-kine" in *The Taming of the Shrew*, ii, 1, 359, and in *The Merry Wives of Windsor*, iv, 4, 33.

3
Hoop his body more with thy embraces.
The Winter's Tale. Act iv, sc. 4, l. 449. [Polixenes] The only use of "hoop" in this sense as a verb.

So locks her heart in embracing, as if she would pin her to her heart that she might no more be in danger of losing.
The Winter's Tale. Act v, sc. 2, l. 84. [Gentleman]

Polixenes: She embraces him.
Camillo: She hangs about his neck.
The Winter's Tale. Act v, sc. 3, l. 111.

EMPEROR AND EMPRESS

I—Emperor

4
Your emperor Continues still a Jove.
Antony and Cleopatra. Act iv, sc. 6, l. 28. [Soldier]

5
The emperor 's coming in behalf of France.
Henry V. Act v, Prologue, l. 38. [Chorus]

I am sure the emperor Paid ere he promised.
Henry VIII. Act i, sc. 1, l. 185. [Buckingham]

6
Thou 'rt an emperor, Cæsar, Keisar, and Pheezar.
The Merry Wives of Windsor. Act i, sc. 3, l. 9. [Host] The only use of "Keisar" and "Pheezar."

Brave emperor.—*Antony and Cleopatra*, ii, 7, 109; iv, 7, 4.
Gracious emperor.—*Titus Andronicus*, iii, 1, 157.
High emperor.—*Titus Andronicus*, ii, 3, 288.
Late-deceased emperor.—*Titus Andronicus*, i, 1, 184. "Late deceased" (unhyphenated) is repeated in *I Henry VI*, iii, 2, 132, and in *A Midsummer-Night's Dream*, v, 1, 53.
Noble emperor.—*Titus Andronicus*, i, 1, 334; *Antony and Cleopatra*, iii, 7, 62.
Sweet emperor.—*Titus Andronicus*, i, 1, 456; 479; iv, 4, 111.
Wicked emperor.—*Titus Andronicus*, iv, 3, 23.

7
We create
Lord Saturninus Rome's great emperor.
Titus Andronicus. Act i, sc. 1, l. 232. [Marcus]

Long live our emperor!—*Titus Andronicus*, i, 1, 229.
My lord the emperor.—*Titus Andronicus*, iii, 1, 150; v, 3, 35.

8
The emperor, in his rage, will doom her death.
Titus Andronicus. Act iv, sc. 2, l. 114. [Nurse]

Let the emperor dandle him for his own.
Titus Andronicus. Act iv, sc. 2, l. 161. [Aaron]

We will afflict the emperor in his pride.
Titus Andronicus. Act iv, sc. 3, l. 62. [Marcus]

I fear the emperor means no good to us.
Titus Andronicus. Act v, sc. 3, l. 10. [Lucius]

9
Was ever seen
An emperor in Rome thus overborne,
Troubled, confronted thus?
Titus Andronicus. Act iv, sc. 4, l. 1. [Saturninus]

10
The Roman emperor greets you all by me.
Titus Andronicus. Act v, sc. 1, l. 157. [Æmilius]

Roman emperor.—*Cymbeline*, iv, 2, 384.
Rome's emperor.—*Titus Andronicus*, i, 1, 205; v, 3, 19.
Rome's royal emperor.—*Titus Andronicus*, v, 3, 141.
Emperor of Russia.—*Measure for Measure*, iii, 2, 93; *The Winter's Tale*, iii, 2, 120.
The wide world's emperor.—*Titus Andronicus*, i, 1, 248.

II—Empress

11
She sweeps it through the court with troops of ladies,
More like an empress than Duke Humphrey's wife.
II Henry VI. Act i, sc. 3, l. 80. [Queen]

Empress of my love!—*Love's Labour 's Lost*, iv, 3, 56.
Empress of my soul.—*Titus Andronicus*, ii, 3, 40.

12
Lavinia will I make my empress,
Rome's royal mistress.
Titus Andronicus. Act i, sc. 1, l. 240. [Saturninus]

Empress of Rome.—*Titus Andronicus*, i, 1, 320.
Rome's royal empress.—*Titus Andronicus*, ii, 3, 55.

13
Were our witty empress well afoot,
She would applaud Andronicus' conceit.
Titus Andronicus. Act iv, sc. 2, l. 29. [Aaron]

Gentle empress.—*Titus Andronicus*, ii, 3, 66.
Gracious empress.—*Henry V*, v, Prol., 30.
Great empress.—*Titus Andronicus*, ii, 3, 52.

Most noble empress.—*Antony and Cleopatra,* v, 2, 71.
New-made empress.—*Titus Andronicus,* ii, 1, 20.
Proud empress.—*Titus Andronicus,* v, 2, 26.
Royal Egypt! Empress!—*Antony and Cleopatra,* iv, 15, 71.

1
For well I wot the empress never wags
But in her company there is a Moor.
Titus Andronicus. Act v, sc. 2, l. 87. [Titus]

2
Tamora: How now, good fellow! wouldst thou speak with us?
Clown: Yea, forsooth, an your mistership be emperial.
Tamora: Empress I am, but yonder sits the emperor.
Titus Andronicus. Act iv, sc. 4, l. 39. The only use of "mistership." "Emperial" is repeated in iv, 3, 94, and occurs in no other play.
Tamora: I will bring the empress and her sons,
The emperor himself. . . .
Titus: The emperor and the empress too
Feast at my house.
Titus Andronicus. Act v, sc. 2, l. 116.

EMPLOYMENT

3 Let him alone, for I remember now
How he 's employ'd.
Antony and Cleopatra. Act v, sc. 1, l. 71. [Cæsar]
Be better employed, and be naught awhile.
As You Like It. Act i, sc. 1, l. 38. [Oliver]

4 But to win time
To lose so bad employment.
Cymbeline. Act iii, sc. 4, l. 113. [Pisanio]
Ill employment.—*The Merry Wives of Windsor,* v, 5, 135.
Lewd employments.—*Richard II,* i, 1, 90.

5
They did make love to this employment.
Hamlet. Act v, sc. 2, l. 57. [Hamlet]
Dear employment.—*Romeo and Juliet,* v, 3, 32.
Desired employment.—*Love's Labour 's Lost,* iv, 2, 140.

6
Being upon hasty employment in the king's affairs.
II Henry IV. Act ii, sc. 1, l. 139. [Falstaff]
At your employment.—*King John,* i, 1, 198.

7
I was employ'd in passing to and fro,
About relieving of the sentinels.
I Henry VI. Act ii, sc. 1, l. 69. [Charles] The only use of "relieving."
But that I am prevented,
I should have begg'd I might have been employ'd.
I Henry VI. Act iv, sc. 1, l. 71. [Talbot]
I . . . have employ'd him.—*I Henry IV,* ii, 4, 562.

8
'Tis meet that lucky ruler be employ'd;
Witness the fortune he hath had in France.
II Henry VI. Act iii, sc. 1, l. 291. [York]
While you are thus employ'd.
III Henry VI. Act i, sc. 2, l. 44. [York]
Thus employ'd.—*Richard II,* iii, 4, 37; *I Henry IV,* i, 3, 265.
Employ'd in danger.—*King John,* iv, 2, 226.
Glad to be employ'd.—*II Henry VI,* iii, 2, 273.
You cannot better be employ'd.—*The Merchant of Venice,* iv, 1, 117.

9
Employ thee then, sweet virgin, for our good.
I Henry VI. Act iii, sc. 3, l. 16. [Alençon]
We shall employ thee in a worthier place.
Measure for Measure. Act v, sc. 1, l. 537. [Duke]
I must employ you in some business.
A Midsummer-Night's Dream. Act i, sc. 1, l. 124. [Lysander] See also *The Two Gentlemen of Verona,* iv, 4, 45; *Love's Labour 's Lost,* iii, 1, 6; iii, 1, 52; v, 1, 159; *As You Like It,* iii, 5, 96; *Othello,* i, 3, 48; *Antony and Cleopatra,* iii, 3, 39.
If you 'll employ me.—*Antony and Cleopatra,* v, 2, 70.
When 't pleased you to employ me.
Cymbeline, i, 1, 173.
Employ my father.—*King John,* i, 1, 96.
Employ a friend.—*Richard III,* ii, 1, 36.
He employ'd my mother.—*King John,* i, 1, 98.
Employ those soldiers.—*Hamlet,* ii, 2, 74.
Employ them all.—*Winter's Tale,* iv, 4, 387.

10 Whoever the king favours,
The cardinal instantly will find employment,
And far enough from court too.
Henry VIII. Act ii, sc. 1, l. 47. [Gentleman]
Thy great employment Will not bear question.
King Lear. Act v, sc. 3, l. 32. [Edmund]
Proud of employment, willingly I go.
Love's Labour 's Lost. Act ii, sc. 1, l. 35. [Boyet]

11
And whatsoever you will employ me in, . . .
I will perform it.
Richard III. Act i, sc. 1, l. 108. [Gloucester]
You shall be employ'd.—*The Two Gentlemen of Verona,* Ind. 1, 3, 76.
Thou shalt be employ'd.—*Titus Andronicus,* iii, 1, 282.
Thyself shalt highly be employ'd.—*Richard III,* iii, 1, 180.

12
Chiron: Tell us, old man, how shall we be employ'd?
Titus: Tut, I have work enough for you to do.
Titus Andronicus. Act v, sc. 2, l. 149.
She is so employ'd.—*Titus Andronicus,* iv, 3, 39.

13
What employment have we here?
Twelfth Night, ii, 5, 91.
Not much employment for you, you understand me?
All's Well that Ends Well, ii, 2, 71.
You have no employment for me?
Much Ado about Nothing, ii, 1, 280.
Is there not employment?—*II Henry IV,* i, 2, 85.

EMULATION

See also Rivalry

14
An envious emulator of every man's good parts.
As You Like It, i, 1, 150. See under CHARACTER. The only use of "emulator."

1
Mine emulation Hath not that honour in 't it had.
Coriolanus. Act i, sc. 10, l. 12. [Aufidius]

2
Keep off aloof with worthless emulation.
I Henry VI. Act iv, sc. 4, l. 21. [Lucy]

Factious emulations.—*I Henry VI,* iv, 1, 114.

Gory emulation.—*Troilus and Cressida,* iv, 5, 123.

Emulation in the army crept.—*Troilus and Cressida,* ii, 2, 212.

Emulation in their woe.—*The Rape of Lucrece,* l. 1808.

3
Emulation now, who shall be nearest,
Will touch us all too near.
Richard III. Act ii, sc. 3, l. 25. [Citizen]

4
An envious fever
Of pale and bloodless emulation.
Troilus and Cressida. Act i, sc. 3, l. 133. [Ulysses]

For emulation hath a thousand sons
That one by one pursue: if you give way,
Or hedge aside from the direct forthright,
Like to an enter'd tide, they all rush by
And leave you hindmost.
Troilus and Cressida. Act iii, sc. 3, l. 156. [Ulysses] "Hindmost" is repeated in *II Henry VI,* iii, 1, 2: "Hindmost man."

5
He is not emulous, as Achilles is.
Troilus and Cressida. Act ii, sc. 3, l. 242. [Nestor]

Emulous factions.—*Troilus and Cressida,* ii, 3, 79.

Emulous honour.—*Troilus and Cressida,* iv, 1, 28.

Emulous missions.—*Troilus and Cressida,* iii, 3, 189. The only uses of "emulous," which, it will be noted, are all in a single play.

ENCOUNTER

See also Meeting

6
You are well encounter'd here.
II Henry IV. Act iv, sc. 2, l. 1. [Lancaster]

Well encountered.—*Love's Labour's Lost,* v, 1, 37; *Cymbeline,* iii, 6, 66.

7
Encounters mounted are
Against your peace.
Love's Labour's Lost. Act v, sc. 2, l. 82. [Boyet]

Appoints him an encounter.—*All's Well that Ends Well,* iii, 7, 32.

Mark the encounter.—*Hamlet,* ii, 2, 164.

8
If the encounter acknowledge itself hereafter, it may compel him to her recompense.
Measure for Measure. Act iii, sc. 1, l. 261. [Duke]

In the instant of our encounter.—*The Merry Wives of Windsor,* iii, 5, 74.

9
Confess'd the vile encounters they have had
A thousand times in secret.
Much Ado about Nothing. Act iv, sc. 1, l. 94. [Don Pedro]

Loose encounters.—*The Two Gentlemen of Verona,* ii, 7, 41.

10
Give you over at this first encounter.
The Taming of the Shrew. Act i, sc. 2, l. 105. [Petruchio]

First encounter.—*Antony and Cleopatra,* i, 2, 98.

Last encounter.—*Henry VIII,* iv, 1, 4.

Next encounter.—*Julius Cæsar,* i, 3, 156.

11
Fair encounter Of two most rare affections!
The Tempest. Act iii, sc. 1, l. 74. [Prospero]

Amiable encounter.—*Much Ado about Nothing,* iii, 3, 161.

Dear encounter.—*Romeo and Juliet,* ii, 6, 29.

Hot encounter.—*Venus and Adonis,* l. 596.

Keen encounter.—*Richard III,* i, 2, 115.

Pretty encounters.—*Troilus and Cressida,* iii, 2, 217.

Strange encounter.—*The Taming of the Shrew,* iv, 5, 54.

Strong encounter.—*Much Ado about Nothing,* i, 1, 327.

12
O these encounterers, so glib of tongue!
Troilus and Cressida. Act iv, sc. 5, l. 58. See under COQUETRY. The only use of "encounterers."

13
Their encounters, though not personal, have been royally attorneyed with interchange of gifts.
The Winter's Tale. Act i, sc. 1, l. 29. [Camillo] "Attorney'd" is used a second time in *Measure for Measure,* v, 1, 390: "Attorney'd at your service."

I never heard of such another encounter, which lames report to follow it and undoes description to do it.
The Winter's Tale. Act v, sc. 2, l. 62. [Gentleman]

ENCOURAGEMENT

14
Let us go thank him and encourage him.
As You Like It. Act i, sc. 2, l. 252. [Celia]

Encourage him.—*Richard III,* iii, 1, 175; *The Winter's Tale,* iii, 2, 165.

Encourage myself.—*As You Like It,* i, 2, 252.

15
Cheer thyself a little.
As You Like It. Act ii, sc. 6, l. 5. [Orlando]

Upon these words I came and cheer'd him up.
Henry V. Act iv, sc. 6, l. 20. [Exeter] See also *III Henry VI,* i, 1, 6; ii, 1, 133; *Richard III,* i, 2, 129; *King John,* iv, 1, 47.

16
Whet not on these furious peers.
II Henry VI. Act ii, sc. 1, l. 34. [King Henry]

Whet on Warwick to this enterprise.
III Henry VI. Act i, sc. 2, l. 37. [York]

They . . . whet me to be revenged.
Richard III. Act i, sc. 3, l. 332. [Gloucester]

To whet thy almost blunted purpose.
Hamlet. Act iii, sc. 4, l. 111. [Ghost]

I will whet on the king.
King John. Act iii, sc. 4, l. 181. [Pandulph]

17
Hearten those that fight in your defence:
Unsheathe your sword, good father; cry 'Saint George!'
III Henry VI. Act ii, sc. 2, l. 79. [Prince of Wales] The only use of "hearten."

Encoding the Greeks to fight.

The Rape of Lucrece, l. 1402. The only use of "encouraging."

1
Refresh'd, new-added, and encouraged.

Julius Cæsar. Act iv, sc. 3, l. 209. [Brutus] The only use of "refresh'd," "new-added" and "encouraged."

2
Lines of fair comfort and encouragement.

Richard III. Act v, sc. 2, l. 6. [Richmond] "Encouragement" is used only once again, in *Measure for Measure,* i, 2, 192.

END

See also Beginning and End; Purpose

3
We still see them reveal themselves, till they attain to their abhorred ends.

All's Well that Ends Well. Act iv, sc. 3, l. 26. [Second Lord]

With colours fairer painted their foul ends.

The Tempest. Act i, sc. 2, l. 143. [Prospero]

Basest ends.—*Timon of Athens,* iv, 3, 471.

Corrupter ends.—*King Lear,* ii, 2, 108.

Ill end.—*King John,* iii, 1, 94.

Violent ends.—*Romeo and Juliet,* ii, 6, 9.

4
All 's well that ends well: still the fine 's the crown:
Whate'er the course, the end is the renown.

All's Well that Ends Well. Act iv, sc. 4, l. 35. [Helena]

All 's well that ends well yet,
Though time seems so adverse and means unfit.

All's Well that Ends Well. Act v, sc. 1, l. 25. [Helena]

All is well ended.—*All's Well that Ends Well,* Epil., 336.

Well ended.—*Hamlet,* ii, 2, 85.

5
I hope I shall see an end of him.

As You Like It. Act i, sc. 1, l. 170.

You may see the end.—*As You Like It,* i, 2, 120.

6
First, in this forest, let us do those ends
That here were well begun and well begot.

As You Like It. Act v, sc. 4, l. 176. [Duke Senior]

7
Antipholus of Ephesus: To what end did I bid thee hie thee home?
Dromio of Ephesus: To a rope's-end, sir; and to that end am I returned.
Antipholus: And to that end, sir, will I welcome you.

The Comedy of Errors. Act iv, sc. 4, l. 15. "Rope's-end" is used three times in this scene, and nowhere else.

8
'Respice finem,' respect your end.

The Comedy of Errors. Act iv, sc. 4, l. 44. [Dromio of Ephesus] The only use of the phrase.

9
I see into thy end, and am almost
A man already.

Cymbeline. Act iii, sc. 4, l. 169. [Imogen]

How ended she?—*Cymbeline,* v, 5, 30.

Is it ended then?—*Coriolanus,* iv, 3, 16.

10
'Tis a consummation Devoutly to be wish'd.

Hamlet. Act iii, sc. 1, l. 63. [Hamlet] "Consummation" is repeated in *Cymbeline,* iv, 2, 280: "Quiet consummation."

11
Indeed, la, without an oath, I 'll make an end on 't.

Hamlet. Act iv, sc. 5, l. 57. [Ophelia]

They say he made a good end.—*Hamlet,* iv, 5, 186.

That 's the end.—*Hamlet,* iv, 3, 26.

And there an end.—*The Taming of the Shrew,* v, 2, 98, and twelve times in later plays.

12
Meet me at town's end.

I Henry IV, iv, 2, 10; v, 3, 39.

Hard by; at street end.—*The Merry Wives of Windsor,* iv, 2, 40.

At arms' end.—*The Two Gentlemen of Verona,* v, 4, 57; *As You Like It,* ii, 6, 10.

At the fingers' end.—*Love's Labour 's Lost,* v, 1, 81; *Henry V,* ii, 3, 16; *Twelfth Night,* i, 3, 83.

Bloody fingers' ends.—*King John,* iii, 4, 168.

At the staves's end.—*Twelfth Night,* v, 1, 292.

At the twelvemonth's end.—*Love's Labour 's Lost,* v, 2, 843.

At the tongue's end.—*Love's Labour 's Lost,* iii, 1, 12.

13
Let the end try the man.

II Henry IV. Act ii, sc. 2, l. 50. [Prince of Wales]

End in peace.—*II Henry IV,* iv, 1, 180.

Every thing is ended.—*II Henry IV,* iv, 3, 30.

14
From this day to the ending of the world.

Henry V, iv, 3, 58. See under Glory.

To the world's end.—*The Comedy of Errors,* ii, 2, 108. *Much Ado about Nothing,* ii, 1, 272; *Troilus and Cressida,* iii, 2, 209.

15
Here let them end it.

II Henry VI. Act ii, sc. 3, l. 55. [King Henry]

End it between them.—*The Merry Wives of Windsor,* i, 1, 144.

16
La fin couronne les œuvres.

II Henry VI. Act v, sc. 2, l. 28. [Clifford]

The end crowns all.

Troilus and Cressida. Act iv, sc. 5, l. 224. [Hector]

17
Mine own ends Have been mine.

Henry VIII. Act iii, sc. 2, l. 171. [Wolsey] "Mine own ends" is repeated in l. 212.

Let all the ends thou aim'st at be thy country's,
Thy God's and truth's.

Henry VIII. Act iii, sc. 2, l. 447. [Wolsey]

Our ends are honest.—*Henry VIII,* iii, 1, 154.

18
But on, my liege; for very little pains
Will bring this labour to an happy end.

King John. Act iii, sc. 2, l. 9. [Bastard]

Fair end.—*Titus Andronicus,* iv, 4, 49.

Honourable end.—*Titus Andronicus,* v, 3, 22.

Sweet end.—*Measure for Measure,* iv, 6, 8.

Wholesome end.—*King Lear,* ii, 4, 146.

Worthy end.—*Titus Andronicus,* iii, 1, 174.

1
Is this the promised end?
King Lear. Act v, sc. 3, l. 263. [Kent]
Wished end.—*I Henry VI,* iii, 3, 28.

2 This night I 'll spend
Unto a dismal and a fatal end.
Macbeth. Act iii, sc. 5, l. 20. [Hecate]
A swan-like end.—*The Merchant of Venice,* iii, 2, 44. The only use of "swan-like."

3 Not I for love and duty,
But seeming so, for my peculiar end.
Othello. Act i, sc. 1, l. 59. [Iago]
Particular endings.—*Henry V,* iv, 1, 164.
Ominous endings.—*Much Ado about Nothing,* v, 2, 40.

4
Here is my journey's end, here is my butt,
And very sea-mark of my utmost sail.
Othello. Act v, sc. 2, l. 267. [Othello] See also under DEATH. "Sea-mark" is repeated in *Coriolanus,* v, 3, 74.

5 Could I rage and roar
As doth the sea she lies in, yet the end
Must be as 'tis.
Pericles. Act iii, sc. 3, l. 10. [Pericles]
I will end here.—*Pericles,* v, 1, 154.
The end of all.—*Pericles,* i, 1, 98.

6
A little harm done to a great good end
For lawful policy remains enacted.
The Rape of Lucrece, l. 528.
All with me 's meet that I can fashion fit.
King Lear. Act i, sc. 2, l. 200. [Edmund]

7
Lo, as at English feasts, so I regreet
The daintiest last, to make the end most sweet.
Richard II. Act i, sc. 3, l. 67. [Bolingbroke] "Daintiest" is repeated in *II Henry VI,* iii, 2, 322. "Regreet" occurs five times.
More are men's ends mark'd than their lives before.
Richard II. Act ii, sc. 1, l. 11. [Gaunt]
Join not with grief, fair woman, do not so,
To make my end too sudden.
Richard II. Act v, sc. 1, l. 16. [King Richard]

8
At the lower end of the hall.
Richard III. Act iii, sc. 7, l. 35. [Buckingham]
Upper end.—*Coriolanus,* iv, 5, 205; *The Winter's Tale,* iv, 4, 59.

9 At hand, at hand,
Ensues his piteous and unpitied end.
Richard III. Act iv, sc. 4, l. 73. [Queen Margaret]
End thy days.—*Richard III,* v, 3, 147.
And there an end.—*Romeo and Juliet,* iii, 4, 28; *Macbeth,* iii, 4, 80.

10 Of thee this I prognosticate:
Thy end is truth's and beauty's doom and date.
Sonnets. No. xiv. The only use of "prognosticate." "Prognostication" is used twice: *The Winter's Tale,* iv, 4, 817; *Antony and Cleopatra,* i, 2, 54.

11
I see, as in a map, the end of all.
Richard III. Act ii, sc. 4, l. 54. [Queen Elizabeth]
To what end?—*The Taming of the Shrew,* i, 2, 250, and five times in later plays.

12
Neglecting worldly ends.
The Tempest. Act i, sc. 2, l. 89. [Prospero]
Most poor matters Point to rich ends.
The Tempest. Act iii, sc. 1, l. 3. [Ferdinand]
Work mine end.—*The Tempest,* v, 1, 53.
Chief end.—*Antony and Cleopatra,* iv, 12, 27.
Extremest ends.—*Troilus and Cressida,* i, 3, 167.
Latter end.—*All 's Well that Ends Well,* ii, 5, 31; *Henry V,* v, 2, 341; *Love's Labour 's Lost,* v, 2, 630; *A Midsummer-Night's Dream,* iv, 1, 223.
Main end.—*Henry VIII,* ii, 2, 41.
Necessary end.—*Julius Cæsar,* ii, 2, 36.
Odd ends.—*Richard III,* i, 3, 337.
Timeless end.—*Richard II,* iv, 1, 5; *Romeo and Juliet,* v, 3, 162.

13
Believe 't, my lord and I have made an end;
I have no more to reckon, he to spend.
Timon of Athens. Act iii, sc. 4, l. 55. [Flavius]

14
For, by my soul, Were there worse end than death,
That end upon them should be executed.
Titus Andronicus. Act ii, sc. 3, l. 302. [Saturninus]
Would we had so ended!—*Twelfth Night,* ii, 1, 22.

ENDEAVOUR

15
Their endeavour keeps in the wonted pace.
Hamlet. Act ii, sc. 2, l. 353. [Rosencrantz]
Setting endeavour in continual motion.
Henry V, i, 2, 185. See under OBEDIENCE.

16 My endeavours
Have ever come too short of my desires,
Yet filed with my abilities.
Henry VIII. Act iii, sc. 2, l. 169. [Wolsey]

17
The endeavour of this present breath may buy
That honour which shall bate his scythe's keen edge.
Love's Labour 's Lost. Act i, sc. 1, l. 5. [King]
I thank you, gracious lords,
For all your fair endeavours.
Love's Labour 's Lost. Act v, sc. 2, l. 739. [Princess]

18
My best endeavours shall be done herein.
The Merchant of Venice. Act ii, sc. 2, l. 182. [Leonardo]
With your best endeavour.—*II Henry VI,* iii, 1, 163.
With my best endeavours.—*The Winter's Tale,* iv, 4, 542.
Excellent endeavour.—*II Henry IV,* iv, 3, 130.
Fierce endeavour.—*Love's Labour 's Lost,* v, 2, 863; *King Lear,* ii, 1, 36.

Past endeavours.—*All's Well that Ends Well,* i, 3, 5.
Strong endeavours.—*Henry V,* v, 2, 25.

1
Use thou all the endeavour of a man.
The Merchant of Venice. Act iii, sc. 4, l. 48. [Portia]
Man's endeavours.—*Henry VIII,* iii, 2, 169.
Only to despite them, I will endeavour any thing.
Much Ado about Nothing. Act ii, sc. 2, l. 31. [Don John]

ENDURANCE

2
I could endure any thing.
All's Well that Ends Well. Act iv, sc. 3, l. 266. [Bertram]
I will endure.—*As You Like It,* iii, 5, 96.
Pour on; I will endure.—*King Lear,* iii, 4, 18.
It will endure.—*Henry V,* ii, 1, 10.

3
Alas, poor princess,
Thou divine Imogen, what thou endurest!
Cymbeline. Act ii, sc. 1, l. 62. [Second Lord] The only use of "endurest."
But you must bear; the heart 's all.
II Henry IV. Act v, sc. 3, l. 31. [Davy]

4
Have done, for more I hardly can endure.
II Henry VI. Act i, sc. 4, l. 41. [Spirit]
You can endure.—*A Midsummer-Night's Dream,* i, 1, 70.

5
Shall I endure the sight of Somerset?
II Henry VI. Act v, sc. 1, l. 90. [York]
As hardly
Will he endure your sight as yet, I fear.
Winter's Tale. Act iv, sc. 4, l. 479. [Camillo]
Endure the sight of day.—*Richard II,* iii, 2, 52.

6
What man of good temper would endure this tempest of exclamation?
II Henry IV. Act ii, sc. 1, l. 86. [Chief Justice]
Can ye endure to hear this arrogance?
Henry VIII. Act iii, sc. 2, l. 278. [Surrey]
We can both
Endure the winter's cold as well as he.
Julius Cæsar, i, 2, 99. See under COMPARISON.
She cannot endure to hear tell of a husband.
Much Ado about Nothing, ii, 1, 362. See under HUSBAND.
Endure a husband.—*Much Ado about Nothing,* ii, 1, 32.
Shall I endure this monstrous villany?
Titus Andronicus, iv, 4, 51. See under WRONG.
Endure the like.—*I Henry VI,* ii, 3, 38; *Much Ado about Nothing,* v, 1, 30.
Endured the like.—*Richard II,* v, 5, 30.
Endure my absence.—*Antony and Cleopatra,* i, 2, 179.
Endure her loud alarums.—*The Taming of the Shrew,* i, 1, 131.
Endure your heaviest censure.—*Coriolanus,* v, 6, 142.
Endured shrewd days and nights.—*As You Like It,* v, 4, 179.
Endure the devil.—*Richard III,* i, 2, 45.
Endure the din.—*The Taming of the Shrew,* i, 1, 178.
Endure friends.—*Coriolanus,* i, 6, 58.
Endure handling.—*Henry V,* v, 2, 337.
Endure our law.—*Cymbeline,* v, 5, 299.
Endure the load.—*Richard III,* iii, 7, 230.
Endure this wooden slavery.—*The Tempest,* iii, 1, 61.
Endure the flinty streets.—*II Henry VI,* ii, 4, 8.
Endure my Lady Tongue.—*Much Ado about Nothing,* ii, 1, 284.
Endure the toothache.—*Much Ado about Nothing,* v, 1, 36.
Endure a further view.—*Antony and Cleopatra,* iii, 10, 18.
Endure wind and weather.—*Twelfth Night,* i, 5, 255.
Endured all weathers.—*The Winter's Tale,* v, 1, 195.
Endure your wrath.—*Macbeth,* v, 5, 36.
Endure sweet beauty's wreck.—*Richard III,* i, 2, 127.
Endure his yoke.—*Cymbeline,* iii, 5, 5.
Have patience and endure.—*Much Ado about Nothing,* iv, 1, 256. See under PATIENCE.

7
O ye gods, ye gods! must I endure all this?
Julius Cæsar. Act iv, sc. 3, l. 41. [Cassius]
Men must endure.—*King Lear,* v, 2, 9.

8
The wonder is, he hath endured so long.
King Lear, v, 3, 316. See under DEATH.
He shall endure.—*Love's Labour 's Lost,* i, 1, 132.

9
What cannot be eschew'd must be embraced.
The Merry Wives of Windsor. Act v, sc. 5, l. 251. [Page] The only use of "eschew'd."

10
I will not endure it.
Richard III. Act i, sc. 3, l. 42. [Gloucester]
I 'll not endure it.—*Othello,* iii, 3, 390; *King Lear,* i, 3, 5.
I will no longer endure it.—*As You Like It,* i, 1, 25; i, 1, 74; *Othello,* iv, 2, 180.
I never shall endure her.—*King Lear,* v, 1, 15.
I 'll not endure him.—*Romeo and Juliet,* i, 5, 78.
I endure him not.—*Othello,* ii, 1, 297.
You 'll not endure him!—*Romeo and Juliet,* i, 5, 81.
Your betters have endured me say my mind.
The Taming of the Shrew, iv, 3, 75. See under CANDOUR.

11
O vile,
Intolerable, and not to be endured!
The Taming of the Shrew. Act v, sc. 2, l. 93. [Petruchio]
Not to be endured.—*Much Ado about Nothing,* iii, 3, 37; *As You Like It,* iv, 3, 69.
Past endurance.—*Much Ado about Nothing,* ii, 1, 246. "Endurance" occurs only once again in the plays, in *Pericles,* v, 1, 137.

12
I did endure
Not seldom, nor no slight checks.
Timon of Athens. Act ii, sc. 2, l. 148. [Flavius]
Why do fond men expose themselves to battle,
And not endure all threats? sleep upon 't,
And let the foes quietly cut their throats,
Without repugnancy? If there be
Such valour in the bearing, what make we
Abroad? why, then, women are more valiant

That stay at home, if bearing carry it.
Timon of Athens. Act iii, sc. 5, l. 42. [Alcibiades] The only use of "repugnancy."

1
O Valentine, this I endure for thee!
The Two Gentlemen of Verona. Act v, sc. 3, l. 15. [Silvia]

ENEMY

See also Foe; Friends and Enemies

2
The world esteem'd thy father honourable,
But I did find him still mine enemy.
As You Like It. Act i, sc. 2, l. 237. [Duke]
Sir, you have wrestled well and overthrown
More than your enemies.
As You Like It. Act i, sc. 2, l. 266. [Rosalind]
Within this roof
The enemy of all your graces lives.
As You Like It. Act ii, sc. 3, l. 17. [Adam]

3
Here shall he see No enemy
But winter and rough weather.
As You Like It. Act ii, sc. 5, l. 6. [Amiens]

4
You have found,
Scaling his present bearing with his past,
That he's your fixed enemy.
Coriolanus. Act ii, sc. 3, l. 256. [Sicinius] The only use of "scaling."
As enemy to the people and his country.
Coriolanus. Act iii, sc. 3, l. 117. [Brutus]
Ædile: The people's enemy is gone, is gone!
Citizens: Our enemy is banish'd! he is gone!
Coriolanus. Act iii, sc. 3, l. 136.
Say their great enemy is gone, and they
Stand in their ancient strength.
Coriolanus. Act iv, sc. 1, l. 6. [Sicinius]

5
Your enemies, with nodding of their plumes,
Fan you into despair!
Coriolanus. Act iii, sc. 3, l. 126. [Coriolanus]
Your old enemy.—*Coriolanus,* i, 2, 12.
Where is the enemy?—*Coriolanus,* i, 6, 47.
He was your enemy.—*Coriolanus,* ii, 3, 187.
Chief enemy.—*Coriolanus,* i, 1, 8.
Chiefest enemy.—*Macbeth,* iii, 5, 33.
The common enemy.—*Macbeth,* iii, 1, 69.
Cunning enemy.—*Measure for Measure,* ii, 2, 180.
Great enemy.—*Romeo and Juliet,* i, 5, 139.
Loathed enemy.—*Romeo and Juliet,* i, 5, 143.
Pregnant enemy.—*Twelfth Night,* ii, 2, 29.
Rancorous enemy.—*Richard III,* i, 3, 50.
Repining enemy.—*Troilus and Cressida,* i, 3, 243.
Retentive enemy.—*Timon of Athens,* iii, 4, 82.

6
If you make your voyage upon her and give me directly to understand you have prevailed, I am no further your enemy.
Cymbeline. Act i, sc. 4, l. 171. [Posthumus]
I . . . am right sorry that I must report ye
My master's enemy.
Cymbeline. Act iii, sc. 5, l. 2. [Lucius]

7
Thus mine enemy fell,
And thus I set my foot on 's neck.
Cymbeline. Act iii, sc. 3, l. 91. [Belarius]
And though he came our enemy, remember
He was paid for that.
Cymbeline. Act iv, sc. 2, l. 245. [Belarius]
The enemy full-hearted,
Lolling the tongue with slaughtering, having work
More plentiful than tools to do 't.
Cymbeline. Act v, sc. 3. l. 7. [Posthumus] The only use of "full-hearted."

8
Malevolent to you in all aspects.
I Henry IV. Act i, sc. 1, l. 97. [Westmoreland] The only use of "malevolent."
My near'st and dearest enemy.
I Henry IV. Act iii, sc. 2, l. 123. [King Henry] The only use of "dearest enemy" in the plays. "Dearest foe" occurs in *Hamlet,* i, 2, 182.

9
Could the world pick thee out three such enemies?
I Henry IV. Act ii, sc. 4, l. 404. [Falstaff]
Baleful enemies.—*I Henry VI,* v, 4, 122.
Deadly enemies.—*The Rape of Lucrece,* l. 674.
Foreign enemies.—*Richard III,* iv, 4, 531.
Rival enemies.—*Midsummer-Night's Dream,* iv, 1, 147.
Vaunting enemies.—*I Henry IV,* v, 3, 43.
Weak-hearted enemies.—*Henry VIII,* iii, 2, 390. The only use of "weak-hearted."

10
West of this forest, scarcely off a mile,
In goodly form comes on the enemy;
And, by the ground they hide, I judge their number
Upon or near the rate of thirty thousand.
II Henry IV. Act iv, sc. 1, l. 19. [Messenger]
A most furious knight and valorous enemy.
II Henry IV. Act iv, sc. 3, l. 43. [Falstaff]
From enemies heaven keep your majesty;
And, when they stand against you, may they fall.
II Henry IV. Act iv, sc. 4, l. 94. [Harcourt]

11
True: those that were your father's enemies
Have steep'd their gall in honey and do serve you
With hearts create of duty and of zeal.
Henry V. Act ii, sc. 2, l. 29. [Grey]
'Tis best to weigh
The enemy more mighty than he seems.
Henry V. Act ii, sc. 4, l. 43. [Dauphin]
An enemy of craft and vantage.
Henry V. Act iii, sc. 6, l. 153. [King Henry]
Gower: The enemy is loud; you hear him all night.
Fluellen: If the enemy is an ass and a fool and a prating coxcomb, is it meet, think you, that we should also, look you, be an ass and a fool and a prating coxcomb? in your own conscience, now?
Henry V. Act iv, sc. 1, l. 76.
It may be his enemy is a gentleman of great sort.
Henry V. Act iv, sc. 7, l. 141. [King Henry]

12
Enclosed were they with their enemies:
A base Walloon, to win the Dauphin's grace,
Thrust Talbot with a spear into the back,

Whom all France with their chief assembled strength
Durst not presume to look once in the face.
I Henry VI. Act i, sc. 1, l. 136. [Messenger] The only use of "Walloon."

What men have I!
Dogs! cowards! dastards! I would ne'er have fled,
But that they left me 'midst my enemies.
I Henry VI. Act i, sc. 2, l. 22. [Charles]

Arm! arm! the enemy doth make assault!
I Henry VI. Act ii, sc. 1, l. 38. [Sentinel]

The enemy 's in view; draw up your powers.
King Lear. Act v, sc. 1, l. 51. [Edmund]

1
But gather we our forces out of hand
And set upon our boasting enemy.
I Henry VI. Act iii, sc. 2, l. 102. [Talbot]

I hear the enemy:
Out, some light horsemen, and peruse their wings.
I Henry VI. Act iv, sc. 2, l. 42. [Talbot]

2
'Tis known to you he is mine enemy,
Nay, more, an enemy unto you all.
II Henry VI. Act i, sc. 1, l. 148. [Beaufort]

O God, have I overcome mine enemy in this presence? O Peter, thou hast prevailed in right!
II Henry VI. Act ii, sc. 3, l. 100. [Peter]

Ban thine enemies, both mine and thine!
II Henry VI. Act ii, sc. 4, l. 25. [Duchess of Gloucester]

And with your best endeavour have stirr'd up
My liefest liege to be mine enemy.
II Henry VI. Act iii, sc. 1, l. 163. [Gloucester] The only use of "liefest" (dearest).

So mighty are his vowed enemies.
II Henry VI. Act iii, sc. 1, l. 220. [King Henry]

With thy brave bearing should I be in love,
But that thou art so fast mine enemy.
II Henry VI. Act v, sc. 2, l. 20. [York]

Our enemies shall fall before us.
II Henry VI. Act iv, sc. 2, l. 37. [Cade]

Priests pray for enemies, but princes kill.
II Henry VI. Act v, sc. 2, l. 71. [Richard]

Give the enemy way.—*II Henry VI*, v, 2, 76.

3
And who shines now but Henry's enemies?
III Henry VI. Act ii, sc. 6, l. 10. [Clifford]

Hamlet's enemy.—*Hamlet*, v, 2, 250.
Orsino's enemy.—*Twelfth Night*, v, 1, 79.
Honour's enemy.—*Pericles*, ii, 5, 64.
Enemy to faith.—*King John*, iii, 1, 263.
Enemy to life.—*Twelfth Night*, i, 3, 3.
Enemy to mankind.—*Twelfth Night*, iii, 4, 108.
Enemy to peace.—*I Henry VI*, iii, 1, 18; *II Henry IV*, iv, 1, 61; *Romeo and Juliet*, i, 1, 88.
Enemy to our person.—*Henry V*, iv, 7, 164.
Enemy to virginity.—*All's Well that Ends Well*, i, 1, 123.

4
Becomes your enemy, for mocking him.
III Henry VI. Act iv, sc. 1, l. 30. [Clarence]

Shroud yourself from enemies.
III Henry VI. Act iv, sc. 3, l. 40. [Warwick]

All these the enemies to our poor bark.
III Henry VI. Act v, sc. 4, l. 28. [Queen Margaret]

5 You have many enemies, that know not
Why they are so, but, like to village-curs,
Bark when their fellows do.
Henry VIII. Act ii, sc. 4, l. 158. [King Henry] The only use of "village-curs."

Your enemies are many, and not small.
Henry VIII. Act v, sc. 1, l. 128. [King Henry]

You are mine enemy.—*Henry VIII*, ii, 4, 77.

6
Had I as many eyes as thou hast wounds,
Weeping as fast as they stream forth thy blood,
It would become me better than to close
In terms of friendship with thine enemies.
Julius Cæsar. Act iii, sc. 1, l. 200. [Antony]

We are at the stake,
And bay'd about with many enemies.
Julius Cæsar. Act iv, sc. 1, l. 48. [Octavius]

'Tis better that the enemy seek us:
So shall he waste his means, weary his soldiers,
Doing himself offence; whilst we, lying still,
Are full of rest, defence, and nimbleness.
Julius Cæsar. Act iv, sc. 3, l. 199. [Cassius] The only use of "nimbleness."

The enemy increaseth every day;
We, at the height, are ready to decline.
Julius Cæsar. Act iv, sc. 3, l. 216. [Brutus]

The enemy comes on in gallant show.
Julius Cæsar. Act v, sc. 1, l. 13. [Messenger]

I dare assure thee that no enemy
Shall ever take alive the noble Brutus.
Julius Cæsar. Act v, sc. 4, l. 21. [Lucilius]

Our enemies have beat us to the pit.
Julius Cæsar. Act v, sc. 5, l. 23. [Brutus]

7
Being no further enemy to you
Than the constraint of hospitable zeal
In the relief of this oppressed child
Religiously provokes.
King John. Act ii, sc. 1, l. 243. [King Philip]

O, let me have no subject enemies,
When adverse foreigners affright my towns
With dreadful pomp of stout invasion!
King John. Act iv, sc. 2, l. 171. [King John] The only use of "foreigners." "Invasion" is repeated in *The Rape of Lucrece*, l. 287.

8
To know our enemies' minds, we 'ld rip their hearts.
King Lear. Act iv, sc. 6, l. 265. [Edgar] "Rip" is repeated in *Cymbeline*, iii, 5, 86.

9
His master and he, saving your worship's reverence, are scarce cater-cousins.
The Merchant of Venice. Act ii, sc. 2, l. 138. [Gobbo] The only use of "cater-cousins" (good friends).

10
She would not hold out enemy for ever.
The Merchant of Venice. Act iv, sc. 1, l. 447. [Portia]

11
We must straight employ you
Against the general enemy, Ottoman.
Othello. Act i, sc. 3, l. 48. [Duke] The only use of "Ottoman."

O God, that men should put an enemy in their mouths to steal away their brains!
Othello, ii, 3, 291. See under Drinking.

1
Yield stinging nettles to mine enemies.
Richard II. Act iii, sc. 2, l. 18. [King]
They have let the dangerous enemy
Measure our confines with such peaceful steps.
Richard II. Act iii, sc. 2, l. 124. [King]
Herein all breathless lies
The mightiest of thy greatest enemies.
Richard II. Act v, sc. 6, l. 31. [Exton]

2
For they that were your enemies are his.
Richard III. Act i, sc. 1, l. 130. [Gloucester]
They have been still mine enemies.
Richard III. Act iii, sc. 2, l. 52. [Hastings]
Prove us enemies.—*Richard III,* i, 3, 146.

3
This day those enemies are put to death,
And I in better state than e'er I was.
Richard III. Act iii, sc. 2, l. 105. [Hastings]
Triumphing at mine enemies.
Richard III. Act iii, sc. 4, l. 91. [Hastings]

4
His ancient knot of dangerous adversaries.
Richard III. Act iii, sc. 1, l. 182. [Gloucester]
Here in these confines slily have I lurk'd,
To watch the waning of mine adversaries.
Richard III. Act iv, sc. 4, l. 3. [Queen Margaret]
Our adversaries.—*Richard III,* v, 3, 112; *I Henry IV,* v, 5, 31.
Their adversaries.—*I Henry IV,* iii, 2, 83; *Coriolanus,* iv, 3, 45.
Carried into the leaguer of the adversaries.
All's Well that Ends Well, iii, 6, 28. The only use of "leaguer" (camp).
Do as adversaries do.—*The Taming of the Shrew,* i, 2, 278.
Fearful adversaries.—*Richard III,* i, 1, 11.
Proud adversaries.—*Richard III,* i, 3, 123.
Soon-believing adversaries.—*Richard II,* i, 1, 101. The only uses of "adversaries," and sole use of "soon-believing."
I will be thy adversary.—*The Merry Wives of Windsor,* ii, 3, 98.
A stony adversary.—*The Merchant of Venice,* iv, 1, 4. "Adversary" is used eight times.

5
'Tis death to me to be at enmity;
I hate it, and desire all good men's love.
Richard III. Act ii, sc. 1, l. 60. [Gloucester] "Be at enmity" is repeated in *Richard II,* ii, 2, 68.
I am proof against their enmity.
Romeo and Juliet. Act ii, sc. 2, l. 73. [Romeo]
Lesser enmities may give way to greater.
Antony and Cleopatra. Act ii, sc. 1, l. 43. [Pompey] The only use of "enmities."
To poor we Thine enmity's most capital.
Coriolanus. Act v, sc. 3, l. 103. [Volumnia]
All-oblivious enmity.—*Sonnets,* lv. The only use of "all oblivious."
Bitterest enmity.—*Coriolanus,* iv, 4, 18.
Civil enmity.—*III Henry VI,* iv, 6, 98.
Covert enmity.—*II Henry IV,* Ind., 9.
Deadly enmity.—*Titus Andronicus,* v, 1, 131; *The Rape of Lucrece,* l. 503.
Enmity and discord.—*The Comedy of Errors,* i, 1, 5.
Enmity o' the air.—*King Lear,* ii, 4, 212.
Fear no enmity.—*A Midsummer-Night's Dream,* iv, 1, 150.
Enmity he flung aside.—*The Tempest,* ii, 1, 116.

6
Look back, defend thee, here are enemies.
Richard III. Act iii, sc. 5, l. 19. [Gloucester]
King Richard: Darest thou resolve to kill a friend of mine?
Sir James Tyrrel: Ay, my lord;
But I had rather kill two enemies.
King Richard: Why, there thou hast it: two deep enemies,
Foes to my rest and my sweet sleep's disturbers.
Richard III. Act iv, sc. 2, l. 70. "Disturber" is repeated in *Titus Andronicus,* iv, 4, 6.
My lord, the enemy is past the marsh.
Richard III, v, 3, 345. The only use of "marsh."

7
He fears you mean no good to him.
Richard III. Act iii, sc. 7, l. 87. [Catesby]
You know an enemy intends you harm.
Troilus and Cressida. Act ii, sc. 2, l. 39. [Troilus]

8
A thing devised by the enemy.
Richard III. Act v, sc. 3, l. 306. [King]

9
I have been feasting with my enemy.
Romeo and Juliet. Act ii, sc. 3, l. 49. [Romeo]
Where be these enemies?—*Romeo and Juliet,* v, 3, 291.

10
An enemy To me inveterate.
The Tempest. Act i, sc. 1, l. 121. [Prospero]
At this hour
Lie at my mercy all mine enemies.
The Tempest. Act iv, sc. 1, l. 263. [Prospero]

11
How rarely does it meet with this time's guise,
When man was wish'd to love his enemies!
Grant I may ever love, and rather woo
Those that would mischief me than those that do!
Timon of Athens. Act iv, sc. 3, l. 472. [Flavius]
Those enemies of Timon's and mine own
Whom you yourselves shall set out for reproof
Fall and no more.
Timon of Athens. Act v, sc. 4, l. 56. [Alcibiades]
Enemies of Cæsar.—*Julius Cæsar,* iii, 1, 212.
Enemies of his kin.—*Richard II,* ii, 1, 183.
Enemies of Rome.—*Titus Andronicus,* i, 1, 69.
Rome's enemies.—*Titus Andronicus,* v, 3, 106.
Enemy of France.—*Henry V,* v, 2, 177; 178.

12
Chastised with arms Our enemies' pride.
Titus Andronicus. Act i, sc. 1, l. 32. [Marcus]
I have many enemies.—*Twelfth Night,* ii, 1, 46.

13
Finding their enemy to be so curst,
They all strain courtesy who shall cope him first.
Venus and Adonis, l. 887.

ENGLAND

I—Familiar Phrases

1 Britain is
A world by itself; and we will nothing pay
For wearing our own noses.
Cymbeline. Act iii, sc. 1, l. 12. [Cloten]
"Britain" is used twenty-seven times in *Cymbeline,* and only three times in other plays.

You, the liver, heart and brain of Britain,
By whom I grant she lives.
Cymbeline. Act v, sc. 5, l. 14. [Cymbeline]

2
Everything is bent For England.
Hamlet. Act iv, sc. 3, l. 48. [King]
Bound for England.—*Hamlet,* iv, 6, 10.
Away for England!—*King John,* iii, 3, 6.
For England go.—*King John,* iii, 4, 181.
I 'll to England.—*Macbeth,* ii, 3, 143.
To England, if you will.—*King John,* iii, 4, 68.
I must to England.—*Macbeth,* iii, 4, 200.
Hold their course for England.—*Macbeth,* iv, 6, 29.
He makes for England.—*Richard III,* iv, 4, 469.

3
No king of England, if not king of France.
Henry V. Act ii, sc. 2, l. 193. [King Henry]

4
When they were in health, I tell thee, herald,
I thought upon one pair of English legs
Did march three Frenchmen.
Henry V. Act iii, sc. 6, l. 157. [King Henry]
The only use of the phrase "English legs."

5
God and Saint George, Talbot and England's right,
Prosper our colours in this dangerous fight!
I Henry VI. Act iv, sc. 2, l. 55. [Talbot]
Saint George, a legendary hero who is supposed to have suffered martyrdom under Diocletian in A. D. 303, has been recognized as the patron saint of England from the time of Edward III (c. 1350). Why he was chosen is unknown—perhaps because he had been regarded as the patron of the Order of the Garter.

God and Saint George!—*III Henry VI,* iv, 2, 29.
Saint George and victory! fight, soldiers, fight.
I Henry VI. Act iv, sc. 6, l. 1. [Talbot]
Saint George and victory!—*III Henry VI,* v, 1, 113.

Saint George, that swinged the dragon, and e'er since
Sits on his horse back at mine hostess' door,
Teach us some fence!
King John. Act ii, sc. 1, l. 288. [Bastard]

Sound drums and trumpets boldly and cheerfully;
God and Saint George! Richmond and victory!
Richard III. Act v, sc. 3. l. 269. [Richmond]

Our ancient word of courage, fair Saint George,
Inspire us with the spleen of fiery dragons!
Richard III. Act v, sc. 3. l. 349. [King Richard]

Follow your spirit, and upon this charge
Cry 'God for Harry, England, and Saint George!'
***Henry V.* Act iii, sc. 1, l. 33. [King Henry]**

6
Spare England, for it is your native coast.
II Henry VI. Act iv, sc. 8, l. 52. [Clifford]

7
England is safe, if true within itself.
III Henry VI. Act iv, sc. 1, l. 40. [Lord Hastings]

In faith, for little England
You 'ld venture an emballing.
Henry VIII. Act ii, sc. 3, l. 46. [Old Lady]
The only use of "emballing."

8
God and our right!
King John. Act ii, sc. 1, l. 299. [King Philip]
"Dieu et mon droit" is said to have been the password given by Richard I at the battle of Gisors in 1198, and has been the motto of the sovereigns of England since about 1450, when it was adopted by Henry VI.

I bid them that did love their country's good
Cry 'God save England, England's royal king!'
Richard III. Act iii, sc. 7, l. 21. [Buckingham]

9
Child Rowland to the dark tower came,
His word was still,—Fie, foh, and fum,
I smell the blood of a British man.
King Lear. Act iii, sc. 4, l. 187. [Edgar]
The only use of "fum." An adaptation of an old Scottish ballad. See Jamison, *Illustrations of Northern Antiquities.* The only use of "Child Rowland," but "Rowlands" occurs in *I Henry VI,* i, 2, 30. See 418: 4.

British crown.—*Cymbeline,* iii, 5, 65.
British ensign.—*Cymbeline,* v, 5, 480.
British party.—*King Lear,* iv, 6, 256.
British powers.—*King Lear,* iv, 4, 21. The only uses of "British."

10 To the furthest verge
That ever was survey'd by English eye.
Richard II. Act i, sc. 1, l. 93. [Bolingbroke]
The only use of "survey'd."

11
The seat royal of this famous isle.
Richard III. Act iii, sc. 1, l. 164. [Buckingham]

12
Woe, woe for England! not a whit for me.
Richard III. Act iii, sc. 4, l. 82. [Hastings]

Happy were England, would this gracious prince
Take on himself the sovereignty thereof.
Richard III. Act iii, sc. 7, l. 78. [Buckingham]

13
Make poor England weep in streams of blood!
Richard III. Act v, sc. 5, l. 37. [Richmond]

Bloody England.—*King John,* iii, 4, 8. The only use of the phrase.

II—This Scepter'd Isle

14
The natural bravery of your isle, which stands
As Neptune's park, ribbed and paled in
With rocks unscaleable and roaring waters,
With sands that will not bear your enemies' boats,

But suck them up to the topmast.
Cymbeline. Act iii, sc. 1, l. 18. [Queen] The only use of "ribbed," "paled" and "unscaleable." "Topmast" occurs four times.

You shall find us in our salt-water girdle.
Cymbeline. Act iii, sc. 1, l. 80. [Cloten]

Clipp'd in with the sea.
I Henry IV. Act iii, sc. 1, l. 44. [Owen Glendower]

Like to his island girt in with the ocean.
III Henry VI. Act iv, sc. 8, l. 20. [Warwick] The only use of "girt."

Britain's isle.—*II Henry VI,* i, 3, 47.

1
That nook-shotten isle of Albion.
Henry V. Act iii, sc. 5, l. 14. [Bourbon] The only use of "nook-shotten."

The realm of Albion.—*King Lear,* iii, 2, 91.
Albion's wished coast.—*II Henry VI,* iii, 2, 113.
Albion's king.—*II Henry VI,* i, 3, 48.
King of Albion.—*III Henry VI,* iii, 3, 49.
Albion's queen.—*III Henry VI,* iii, 3, 7. The only uses of "Albion."

2
That pale, that white-faced shore,
Whose foot spurns back the ocean's roaring tides
And coops from other lands her islanders, . . .
That England, hedged in with the main,
That water-walled bulwark, still secure
And confident from foreign purposes, . . .
That utmost corner of the west.
King John. Act ii, sc. 1, l. 23. [Austria] The only use of "coops," "white-faced," and "water-walled."

O nation, that thou couldst remove!
That Neptune's arms, who clippeth thee about,
Would bear thee from the knowledge of thyself,
And grapple thee unto a pagan shore.
King John. Act v, sc. 2, l. 33. [Salisbury] The only use of "clippeth."

3
This royal throne of kings, this scepter'd isle,
This earth of majesty, this seat of Mars,
This other Eden, demi-paradise,
This fortress built by Nature for herself
Against infection and the hand of war,
This happy breed of men, this little world,
This precious stone set in the silver sea,
Which serves it in the office of a wall
Or as a moat defensive to a house,
Against the envy of less happier lands,
This blessed plot, this earth, this realm, this England.
Richard II. Act ii, sc. 1, l. 40. [John of Gaunt] The only use of "Eden" and of "demi-paradise," and "moat." "Moated" occurs in *Measure for Measure,* iii, 1, 277.

This land of such dear souls, this dear dear land,
Dear for her reputation through the world. . . .
England, bound in with the triumphant sea,
Whose rocky shore beats back the envious siege
Of watery Neptune.
Richard II. Act ii, sc. 1, l. 57. [Gaunt]

Our sea-walled garden.—*Richard II,* iii, 4, 43. The only use of "sea-walled."

III—England: Her Virtues

4
Our not-fearing Britain.
Cymbeline. Act ii, sc. 4, l. 19. [Posthumus] The only use of "not-fearing."

5
O England! model to thy inward greatness,
Like little body with a mighty heart!
Henry V. Act ii, Prologue, l. 16. [Chorus]

6
There shall be in England seven halfpenny loaves sold for a penny: the three-hooped pot shall have ten hoops; and I will make it felony to drink small beer; all the realm shall be in common; and in Cheapside shall my palfry go to grass.
II Henry VI. Act iv, sc. 2, l. 71. [Cade] The only use of "loaves" and "three-hooped." "Felony" is repeated in *Tempest,* ii, 1, 160.

Then shall . . . Britain be fortunate and flourish in peace and plenty.
Cymbeline. Act v, sc. 4, l. 144. [Posthumus, reading] Also v, 4, 441.

7
Kent, in the Commentaries Cæsar writ,
Is term'd the civil'st place of all this isle:
Sweet is the country, because full of riches;
The people liberal, valiant, active, wealthy.
II Henry VI. Act iv, sc. 7, l. 64. [Say] The only mention of the *Commentaries,* and the only use of "civil'st."

Fair England.—*II Henry VI,* i, 1, 259; iii, 2, 110; 245; *Richard III,* iv, 4, 343; v, 3, 150.
Fertile England.—*II Henry VI,* i, 1, 238; iii, 1, 88.
Great England.—*II Henry VI,* v, 1, 4.
Happy England.—*I Henry VI,* v, 3, 115; *II Henry IV,* i, 2, 214.
Sweet England.—*Othello,* ii, 3, 91.

8
England we love; and for that England's sake
With burden of our armour here we sweat.
King John. Act ii, sc. 1, l. 91. [King Philip]

This England never did, nor never shall,
Lie at the proud foot of a conqueror, . . .
Come the three corners of the world in arms,
And we shall shock them. Nought shall make us rue,
If England to itself do rest but true.
King John. Act v, sc. 7, l. 112. [Prince Henry]

Dear mother England.—*King John,* v, 2, 153.

9
Now no way can I stray;
Save back to England, all the world's my way.
Richard II. Act i, sc. 3, l. 206. [Mowbray]

IV—England: Her Faults

10
A lordly nation
That will not trust thee but for profit's sake.
I Henry VI. Act iii, sc. 3, l. 62. [La Pucelle]

It was always yet the trick of our English

nation, if they have a good thing, to make it too common.
II Henry IV. Act i, sc. 2, l. 241. [Falstaff] The only use of the phrase "English nation."

1
Is not their climate foggy, raw and dull,
On whom, as in despite, the sun looks pale,
Killing their fruit with frowns?
Henry V. Act iii, sc. 5, l. 16. [Constable]

Hath Britain all the sun that shines? Day, night,
Are they not but in Britain? I' the world's volume
Our Britain seems as of it, but not in 't;
In a great pool a swan's nest: prithee, think
There 's livers out of Britain.
Cymbeline. Act iii, sc. 4, l. 139. [Imogen]

2
Is this the fashion in the court of England?
Is this the government of Britain's isle,
And this the royalty of Albion's king?
II Henry VI. Act i, sc. 3, l. 46. [Queen Margaret]

Thereby is England maimed, and fain to go with a staff.
II Henry VI. Act iv, sc. 2, l. 171. [Cade]

3
Would I had never trod this English earth,
Or felt the flatteries that grow upon it!
Henry VIII. Act iii, sc. 1, l. 143. [Queen Katharine] The only use of the phrase "English earth."

4
How easy dost thou take all England up!
From forth this morsel of dead royalty,
The life, the right and truth of all this realm
Is fled to heaven; and England now is left
To tug and scamble and to part by the teeth
The unowed interest of proud-swelling state.
King John. Act iv, sc. 3, l. 142. [Bastard] The only use of "scamble" (scramble), "unowed" and "proud-swelling."

That England that was wont to conquer others,
Hath made a shameful conquest of itself.
Richard II. Act ii, sc. 1, l. 65. [Gaunt]

5 Miserable England!
I prophesy the fearfull'st time to thee
That ever wretched age hath look'd upon.
Richard III. Act iii, sc. 4, l. 105. [Hastings] The only use of "fearfull'st."

England hath long been mad, and scarr'd herself;
The brother blindly shed the brother's blood,
The father rashly slaughter'd his own son,
The son, compell'd, been butcher to the sire.
Richard III. Act v, sc. 5, l. 23. [Richmond]

V—The English

6 Our countrymen
Are men more order'd than when Julius Cæsar
Smiled at their lack of skill, but found their courage
Worthy his frowning at: their discipline,
Now mingled with their courages, will make known
To their approvers they are people such
That mend upon the world.
Cymbeline. Act ii, sc. 4, l. 20. [Posthumus] The only use of "approvers."

Mulmutius made our laws,
Who was the first of Britain which did put
His brows within a golden crown and call'd
Himself a king.
Cymbeline. Act iii, sc. 1, l. 59. [Cymbeline] The only mention of Mulmutius.

7
Your valiant Britons.
Cymbeline. Act iii, sc. 5, l. 20. [Cloten]

A very valiant Briton and a good.
Cymbeline. Act iv, sc. 2, l. 369. [Imogen]

Britons strut with courage.—*Cymbeline*, iii, 1, 33.

Jolly Briton.—*Cymbeline*, i, 6, 67.

Briton reveller.—*Cymbeline*, i, 6, 61.

The fall'n-off Britons.—*Cymbeline*, iii, 7, 6. The only use of "fall'n-off."

A Briton born.—*Cymbeline*, v, 5, 84. Briton is used seventeen times in *Cymbeline*, and occurs in no other play.

Our Britain's harts die flying, not our men.
Cymbeline. Act v, sc. 3, l. 24. [Posthumus]

8
First Clown: He that is mad, and sent into England.
Hamlet: Ay, marry, why was he sent into England?
First Clown: Why, because he was mad: he shall recover his wits there; or, if he do not, it 's no great matter there. . . . 'Twill not be seen in him there; there the men are as mad as he.
Hamlet. Act v, sc. 1, l. 161.

9
O noble English, that could entertain
With half their forces the full pride of France
And let another half stand laughing by,
All out of work and cold for action!
Henry V. Act i, sc. 2, l. 111. [Archbishop of Canterbury]

Never king of England
Had nobles richer and more loyal subjects,
Whose hearts have left their bodies here in England
And lie pavilion'd in the fields of France.
Henry V. Act i, sc. 2, l. 126. [Westmoreland] The only use of "pavilion'd."

10
See you, my princes and my noble peers,
These English monsters?
Henry V. Act ii, sc. 2, l. 84. [King Henry] The only use of the phrase "English monsters."

Thus comes the English with full power upon us;
And more than carefully it us concerns
To answer royally in our defences.
Henry V. Act ii, sc. 4, l. 1. [French King]

Take up the English short, and let them know
Of what a monarchy you are the head.
Henry V. Act ii, sc. 4, l. 72. [Dauphin]

I would fain be about the ears of the English.
Henry V. Act iii, sc. 7, l. 91. [Constable]

Lord Rambures: He longs to eat the English.

Constable of France: I think he will eat all he kills.
Henry V. Act iii, sc. 7, l. 99.

1
Constable of France: If the English had any apprehension, they would run away.
Duke of Orleans: That they lack; for if their heads had any intellectual armour, they could never wear such heavy head-pieces.
Henry V. Act iii, sc. 7, l. 145. "Intellectual" is repeated in *The Comedy of Errors,* ii, 1, 22: "Intellectual sense."
Rambures: That island of England breeds very valiant creatures; their mastiffs are of unmatchable courage.
Orleans: Foolish curs, that run winking into the mouth of a Russian bear and have their heads crushed like rotten apples! You may as well say, that 's a valiant flea that dare eat his breakfast on the lip of a lion.
Constable: Just, just; and the men do sympathize with the mastiffs in robustious and rough coming on, leaving their wits with their wives: and then give them great meals of beef and iron and steel, they will eat like wolves and fight like devils.
Orleans: Ay, but these English are shrewdly out of beef.
Henry V. Act iii, sc. 7, l. 150. "Robustious" is repeated in *Hamlet,* iii, 2, 10: "Robustious fellow."

2
The low-rated English play at dice.
Henry V. Act iv, Prologue, l. 22. [Chorus] The only use of "low-rated."

The poor condemned English,
Like sacrifices, by their watchful fires
Sit patiently and inly ruminate
The morning's danger.
Henry V. Act iv, Prologue, l. 22. [Chorus]

Yon island carrions, desperate of their bones,
Ill-favouredly become the morning field:
Their ragged curtains poorly are let loose,
And our air shakes them passing scornfully:
Big Mars seems bankrupt in their beggar'd host
And faintly through a rusty beaver peeps.
Henry V. Act iv, sc. 2, l. 39. [Grandpré] "Scornfully" is repeated in *Coriolanus,* ii, 3, 171. "Ill-favouredly" is used four times.

3
Mark then abounding valour in our English,
That being dead, like to the bullet's grazing,
Break out into a second course of mischief,
Killing in relapse of mortality.
Henry V. Act iv, sc. 3, l. 104. [King Henry] The only use of "abounding." "Grazing" occurs again in *The Winter's Tale,* iv, 4, 109.

4
Charles: The famish'd English, like pale ghosts,
Faintly besiege us one hour in a month.
Alençon: They want their porridge and their fat bull-beeves:
Either they must be dieted like mules
And have their provender tied to their mouths
Or piteous they will look, like drowned mice.
I Henry VI. Act i, sc. 2, l. 7. The only use of "bull-beeves."

Froissart, a countryman of ours, records;
England all Olivers and Rowlands bred
During the time Edward the Third did reign.
More truly now may this be verified;
For none but Samsons and Goliases
It sendeth forth to skirmish. One to ten!
Lean raw-boned rascals! Who would e'er suppose
They had such courage and audacity?
I Henry VI. Act i, sc. 2, l. 29. [Alençon] The only mention of Froissart. The only use of "Goliases" and "raw-boned." Goliath occurs in *The Merry Wives of Windsor,* v, 1, 23. Samson is referred to seven times.

5
They call'd us for our fierceness English dogs;
Now, like to whelps, we crying run away.
I Henry VI. Act i, sc. 5, l. 25. [Talbot] The only use of the phrase "English dogs."

How are we park'd and bounded in a pale,
A little herd of England's timorous deer,
Mazed with a yelping kennel of French curs!
I Henry VI. Act iv, sc. 2, l. 45. [Talbot] The only use of "park'd."

If we be English deer, be then in blood;
Not rascal-like, to fall down with a pinch,
But rather, moody-mad and desperate stags,
Turn on the bloody hounds with heads of steel
And make the cowards stand aloof at bay.
I Henry VI. Act iv, sc. 2, l. 48. [Talbot] Only use of "rascal-like" and "moody-mad."

Submission, Dauphin! 'tis a mere French word;
We English warriors wot not what it means.
I Henry VI. Act iv, sc. 7, l. 54. [Lucy]

6
Yet not so wealthy as an English yeoman.
III Henry VI. Act i, sc. 4, l. 123. [York] The only use of the phrase "English yeoman."

7
In brief, we are the king of England's subjects:
For him, and in his right, we hold this town.
King John. Act ii, sc. 1, l. 267. [Citizen]

Doth not the crown of England prove the king?
And if not that, I bring you witnesses,
Twice fifteen thousand hearts of England's breed.
King John. Act ii, sc. 1, l. 273. [King John]

Our lusty English, all with purpled hands,
Dyed in the dying slaughter of their foes.
King John. Act ii, sc. 1, l. 322. [Herald] "Purpled hands" is repeated in *Julius Cæsar,* iii, 1, 158; the only uses of "purpled."

Fly, noble English, you are bought and sold.
King John. Act v, sc. 4, l. 10. [Melun]

8
Iago: England, where, indeed, they are most potent in potting: your Dane, your German, and your swag-bellied Hollander —Drink, ho!—are nothing to your English.
Cassio: Is your Englishman so expert in his drinking?
Iago: Why he drinks you, with facility.
Othello. Act ii, sc. 3, l. 78. The only use of "potting" and "swag-bellied."

1
Then, England's ground, farewell; sweet soil, adieu;
My mother, and my nurse, that bears me yet!
Where'er I wander, boast of this I can,
Though banish'd, yet a trueborn Englishman.
Richard II. Act i, sc. 3, l. 306. [Bolingbroke] "Trueborn" is repeated in *I Henry VI*, ii, 4, 27: "Trueborn gentleman."
For that my grandsire was an Englishman.
King John. Act v, sc. 4, l. 42. [Melun]
King Henry: An Englishman?
Williams: An 't please your majesty, a rascal.
Henry V. Act iv, sc. 7, l. 129.
Arm'd Englishman.—*King John*, v, 2, 145.
Slaughter'd Englishmen.—*Richard II*, iii, 3, 44. "Englishman" is used sixteen times.
The princess is the better Englishwoman.
Henry V. Act v, sc. 2, l. 124. [King Henry] The only use of "Englishwoman."

2
But ere the crown he looks for live in peace,
Ten thousand bloody crowns of mothers' sons
Shall ill become the flower of England's face,
Change the complexion of her maid-pale peace
To scarlet indignation and bedew
Her pastures' grass with faithful English blood.
Richard II. Act iii, sc. 3, l. 96. [King Richard] The only use of "maid-pale" and "English blood."
Quiet untroubled soul, awake, awake!
Arm, fight, and conquer, for fair England's sake!
Richard III. Act v, sc. 3, l. 149. [Ghost of Hastings]

3
Were I in England now, as once I was, and had but this fish painted, not a holiday fool there but would give a piece of silver. . . . Any strange beast there makes a man: when they will not give a doit to relieve a lame beggar, they will lay out ten to see a dead Indian.
The Tempest. Act ii, sc. 2, l. 29. [Trinculo]

VI—The English Language

4
An under-skinker, one that never spake other English in his life than 'Eight shillings and sixpence,' and 'You are welcome,' with this shrill addition, 'Anon, anon, sir!'
I Henry IV. Act ii, sc. 4, l. 27. [Prince Henry] The only use of "under-skinker" (tapster).
I can speak English, lord, as well as you.
I Henry IV. Act iii, sc. 1, l. 121. [Glendower]
They speak English.—*The Merry Wives of Windsor*, iv, 3, 8.

5
This is the deadly spite that angers me;
My wife can speak no English, I no Welsh.
I Henry IV. Act iii, sc. 1, l. 192. [Mortimer]

6
You thought, because he could not speak English in the native garb, he could not therefore handle an English cudgel: you find it otherwise.
Henry V. Act v, sc. 1, l. 79. [Gower]
I am glad thou canst speak no better English; for, if thou couldst, thou wouldst find me such a plain king that thou wouldst think I had sold my farm to buy my crown.
Henry V. Act v, sc. 2, l. 127. [King Henry]
But, Kate, dost thou understand thus much English, canst thou love me?
Henry V. Act v, sc. 2, l. 205. [King Henry]
Thy voice is music and thy English broken; therefore, queen of all, Katharine, break thy mind to me in broken English.
Henry V. Act v, sc. 2, l. 263. [King Henry]
Burgundy: My royal cousin, teach you our princess English?
King Henry: I would have her learn, my fair cousin, how perfectly I love her, and that is good English.
Henry V. Act v, sc. 2, l. 308.
In true English.—*Henry V*, v, 2, 237.

7 O, good my lord, no Latin;
I am not such a truant since my coming,
As not to know the language I have lived in:
A strange tongue makes my cause more strange, suspicious;
Pray, speak in English.
Henry VIII. Act iii, sc. 1, l. 42. [Queen]
Absolved in English.—*Henry VIII*, iii, 1, 50.

8
The king's English.
The Merry Wives of Windsor. Act i, sc. 4, l. 6. [Mistress Quickly] The only use of this phrase in the plays.
Our English tongue.—*The Merry Wives of Windsor*, ii, 3, 62; *Henry V*, v, 2, 107.

9
Here 's a fellow frights English out of his wits.
The Merry Wives of Windsor. Act ii, sc. 1, l. 142. [Page]
Let them keep their limbs whole and hack our English.
The Merry Wives of Windsor. Act iii, sc. 1, l. 79. [Host]
Have I lived to stand at the taunt of one that makes fritters of English?
The Merry Wives of Windsor. Act v, sc. 5, l. 150. [Falstaff] The only use of "fritters."

10
The language I have learn'd these forty years,
My native English, now I must forego:
And now my tongue's use is to me no more
Than an unstringed viol or a harp.
Richard II. Act i, sc. 3, l. 159. [Mowbray] The only use of "unstringed."

ENTERPRISE

See also Exploit

11
Be magnanimous in the enterprise and go on; I will grace the attempt for a worthy exploit.
All's Well that Ends Well. Act iii, sc. 6, l. 70. [Bertram]

1
Shark'd up a list of lawless resolutes,
For food and diet, to some enterprise
That hath a stomach in 't.
Hamlet. Act i, sc. 1, l. 98. [Horatio] The only use of "shark'd" and "resolutes."
Enterprises of great pitch and moment.
Hamlet. Act iii, sc. 1, l. 86. See under INDECISION for full quotation.
Equal enterprise.—*As You Like It,* i, 2, 188.
Great enterprise.—*I Henry IV,* iv, 1, 78.
Younger enterprise.—*I Henry IV,* v, 1, 71.
Enterprise of kindness.—*Pericles,* iv, 3, 38.
Another's enterprise.—*Troilus and Cressida,* i, 2, 309.

2
What hath this bold enterprise brought forth,
More than that being which was like to be?
II Henry IV. Act i, sc. 1, l. 178. [Morton]

3 An enterprise
Of honourable-dangerous consequence.
Julius Cæsar. Act i, sc. 3, l. 123. [Cassius] The only use of "honourable-dangerous."

4
The heavens speed thee in thine enterprise!
Juliue Cæsar. Act ii, sc. 4, l. 41. [Portia]
I wish your enterprise to-day may thrive.
Julius Cæsar. Act iii, sc. 1, l. 13. [Popilius]

5
She 'll take the enterprise upon her, father,
If you advise it.
Measure for Measure. Act iv, sc. 1, l. 66. [Isabella]
And so far blameless proves my enterprise.
A Midsummer-Night's Dream. Act iii, sc. 2, l. 350. [Puck]

6 He doth premeditate
The dangers of his loathsome enterprise.
The Rape of Lucrece, l. 183. The only use of "premeditate."

ENTERTAINMENT

7 Get thee back to Cæsar,
Tell him thy entertainment.
Antony and Cleopatra. Act iii, sc. 13, l. 139. [Antony]

8
I prithee, shepherd, if that love or gold
Can in this desert place buy entertainment,
Bring us where we may rest ourselves and feed.
As You Like It. Act ii, sc. 4, l. 71. [Rosalind]
In brief, he led me to the gentle duke,
Who gave me fresh array and entertainment,
As You Like It. Act iv, sc. 3, l. 143. [Oliver]

9
Here comes the Briton: let him be so entertained amongst you as suits, with gentlemen of your knowing, to a stranger of his quality.
Cymbeline. Act i, sc. 4, l. 27. [Philario]
Royally entertained.—*Much Ado about Nothing,* i, 3, 45.
Well entertain'd.—*Timon of Athens,* ii, 2, 45.
Worthily entertain'd.—*Timon of Athens,* i, 2, 191.

10
So please you entertain me.
Cymbeline. Act iv, sc. 2, l. 394. [Imogen]
Then entertain him.—*As You Like It,* iii, 2, 436.
Entertain him with hope.—*The Merry Wives of Windsor,* ii, 1, 68.
Entertain them sprightly.—*The Winter's Tale,* iv, 4, 53.

11
Do not dull thy palm with entertainment.
Hamlet, i, 3, 64. See under FRIEND.
Lenten entertainment.—*Hamlet,* ii, 2, 329.
Free entertainment.—*Cymbeline,* i, 4, 167.
Mutual entertainment.—*Measure for Measure,* i, 2, 158.

12
Salisbury: Yet tell'st thou not how thou wert entertain'd.
Talbot: With scoffs and scorns and contumelious taunts.
In open market-place produced they me,
To be a public spectacle to all.
I Henry VI. Act i, sc. 4, l. 38. "Contumelious" is repeated in *II Henry VI,* iii, 2, 204: "Contumelious spirit."

13
All that served Brutus, I will entertain them.
Julius Cæsar. Act v, sc. 5, l. 60. [Octavius]
Therefore know thou, for this I entertain thee.
The Two Gentlemen of Verona. Act iv, sc. 4. l. 75. [Proteus]

14
I am now from home, and out of that provision
Which shall be needful for your entertainment.
King Lear. Act ii, sc. 4, l. 208. [Regan]

15
Let us devise Some entertainment for them.
Love's Labour 's Lost. Act iv, sc. 3, l. 372. [King]
Some entertainment of time, some show in the posterior of this day.
Love's Labour 's Lost. Act v, sc. 1, l. 124. [Holofernes] The only use of "posterior." "Posteriors of the day" occurs in l. 94 of the same scene, and nowhere else.
I 'll entertain myself.—*The Merry Wives of Windsor,* ii, 1, 89.

16
Note, if your lady strain his entertainment
With any strong or vehement importunity.
Othello. Act iii, sc. 3, l. 250. [Iago]

17 Your entertain shall be
As doth befit our honour and your worth.
Pericles. Act i, sc. 1, l. 119. [Antiochus] The only use of "entertain" as a noun. "Entertainer" also occurs only once, in *The Tempest,* ii, 1, 17.

18
Have you so soon forgot the entertainment?
The Taming of the Shrew. Act iii, sc. 1, l. 2. [Lucentio]
I will resist such entertainment till
Mine enemy has more power.
Tempest. Act i, sc. 2, l. 465. [Ferdinand]

19
Entertain'd me with mine own device.
Timon of Athens. Act i, sc. 2, l. 155. [Timon]

I prithee, let 's be provided to show them entertainment.
Timon of Athens. Act i, sc. 2, l. 185. [Timon]
Amplest entertainment.—*Timon of Athens*, i, 1, 45.

1 I would be sure to have all well,
To entertain your highness.
Titus Andronicus. Act v, sc. 3, l. 31. [Titus]

2
Pardon me, sir, your bad entertainment.
Twelfth Night. Act ii, sc. 1, l. 34. [Antonio]

3
Witness the entertainment that he gave.
Venus and Adonis, l. 1108.
I have deserved no better entertainment.
Coriolanus. Act iv, sc. 5, l. 10. [Coriolanus]

4 This entertainment
May a free face put on, derive a liberty
From heartiness, from bounty, fertile bosom,
And well become the agent; 't may, I grant;
But to be paddling palms and pinching fingers,
As now they are, and making practised smiles,
As in a looking-glass, and then to sigh, as 'twere
The mort o' the deer.
The Winter's Tale. Act i, sc. 2, l. 111. [Leontes] The only use of "heartiness." "Paddling" is repeated in *Hamlet*, iii, 4, 185: "Paddling in your neck." "Mort" is used four times in French phrases ("Mort Dieu!" *II Henry VI*, i, 1, 23; "Mort du vinaigre!" *All's Well that Ends Well*, ii, 3, 50; "Mort de ma vie!" *Henry V*, iii, 5, 11; iv, 5, 3), but this is its only use as English.

5 O, that is entertainment
My bosom likes not, nor my brows!
Winter's Tale. Act i, sc. 2, l. 118. [Leontes]

ENTRAILS

See also Bowels, Guts

6
Plucking the entrails of the offering forth,
They could not find a heart within the beast.
Julius Cæsar. Act ii, sc. 2, l. 39. [Servant]
See, lord and father, how we have perform'd
Our Roman rites: Alarbus' limbs are lopp'd,
And entrails feed the sacrificing fire.
Titus Andronicus. Act i, sc. 1, l. 142. [Lucius]
Alarbus goes to rest; and we survive.
Titus Andronicus, i, 1, 133. Alarbus is mentioned only in this scene.

7
Round about the cauldon go;
In the poisoned entrails throw.
Macbeth. Act iv, sc. 1, l. 4. [Witch]
Knotty entrails.—*The Tempest*, i, 2, 295.
Ragged entrails.—*Titus Andronicus*, ii, 3, 230.

8
Old, cold, withered and of intolerable entrails?
The Merry Wives of Windsor. Act v, sc. 5, l. 161. [Page]
Entrails of my lambs.—*Richard III*, iv, 4, 228.
Entrails of the wolf.—*Richard III*, iv, 4, 23.
Our own proper entrails.—*Julius Cæsar*, v, 3, 96.

ENTREATY

9
I did not then entreat to have her stay.
As You Like It. Act i, sc. 3, l. 71. [Celia]
He will not be entreated.—*As You Like It*, i, 2, 171.
You shall not entreat him.—*As You Like It*, i, 2, 218.

10
She puts you to entreaty, and there begins new matter.
As You Like It. Act iv, sc. 1, l. 80. [Rosalind]
Use no entreaty, for it is in vain.
I Henry VI. Act v, sc. 4, l. 85. [York]

11
O, let me entreat thee cease.
II Henry VI. Act iii, sc. 2, l. 339. [Queen]
Let me entreat you.—*I Henry IV*, ii, 4, 567; iii, 1, 176; *Measure for Measure*, ii, 4, 140; *Pericles*, ii, 4, 45; v, 1, 62.
Let me entreat of you.—*The Taming of the Shrew*, Ind., 2, 120.

12
Entreat him, speak him fair.
II Henry VI. Act iv, sc. 1, l. 120. [Gentleman]
I 'll write unto them and entreat them fair.
III Henry VI, i, 1, 271. See also *Troilus and Cressida*, iv, 4, 115.
Entreat me fair.—*Richard III*, iv, 4, 151.
Fair entreaties.—*Coriolanus*, v, 1, 74.

13
Let me entreat, for I command no more.
III Henry VI. Act iv, sc. 6, l. 59. [King Henry]
I will entreat you.—*All's Well that Ends Well*, iii, 2, 95.

14
Shall I entreat a word?
Julius Cæsar. Act ii, sc. 1, l. 100. [Cassius]
I 'll entreat for thee.—*King Lear*, ii, 2, 161.
Entreat for him.—*King Lear*, iii, 3, 6.

15
Entreat, Out of a new-sad soul.
Love's Labour 's Lost. Act v, sc. 2, l. 740. [Princess] The only use of "new-sad."

16 To him again, entreat him;
Kneel down before him, hang upon his gown.
Measure for Measure. Act ii, sc. 2, l. 43. [Lucio]
It is not my consent, But my entreaty too.
Measure for Measure. Act iv, sc. 1, l. 67. [Duke]
I do entreat it.—*Measure for Measure*, v, 1, 482.
I would entreat you.—*The Merchant of Venice*, ii, 2, 210.
We shall entreat you.—*Measure for Measure*, v, 1, 266.

17
Sir, I entreat you home with me to dinner.
The Merchant of Venice. Act iv, sc. 1, l. 401. [Duke]
Let me entreat you stay till after dinner.
The Taming of the Shrew. Act iii, sc. 2, l. 199. [Tranio]
Entreat Your company at dinner.—*The Merchant of Venice*, iv, 2, 7.
Entreat you with me to dinner.—*II Henry IV*, ii, 1, 194.

1
He did intreat me, past all saying nay.
The Merchant of Venice. Act iii, sc. 2, l. 232. [Lorenzo] The only use of "intreat."

They did entreat me.—*Much Ado about Nothing,* iii, 1, 40.

2
For God's sake, fairly let her be entreated.
Richard II. Act iii, sc. 1, l. 37. [Bolingbroke]

3
Obdurate to mild entreaties.
Richard III, iii, 1, 91. See also *III Henry VI,* iii, 1, 91.

Kind entreats.—*Richard III,* iii, 7, 225.

4
'Zounds! I'll entreat no more!
Richard III. Act iii, sc. 7, l. 219. [Buckingham]

5
Hortensio: Go and entreat my wife
To come to me forthwith.
Petruchio: O, ho! entreat her!
Nay, then she must needs come.
Hortensio: I am afraid, sir,
Do what you can, yours will not be entreated.
The Taming of the Shrew. Act v, sc. 2, l. 86.

6
Yield at entreats.
Titus Andronicus. Act i, sc. 1, l. 449. [Saturninus]

I will entreat the king.—*Titus Andronicus,* ii, 3, 304.

7
If I might in entreaties find success—
As seld I have the chance—I would desire
My famous cousin to our Grecian tents.
Troilus and Cressida. Act iv, sc. 5, l. 149. [Ajax] The only use of "seld" in the plays; it is used again in *Passionate Pilgrim,* l. 175. "Seld-shown" occurs in *Coriolanus,* ii, 1, 229.

Dost thou entreat me?—*Troilus and Cressida,* iv, 5, 268.

I could hardly entreat him back.
Twelfth Night. Act iii, sc. 4, l. 63. [Servant]

8
Still she entreats, and prettily entreats,
For to a pretty ear she tunes her tale.
Venus and Adonis, l. 73.

ENVY

See also Jealousy

9
I never hated thee: I have seen thee fight,
When I have envied thy behaviour.
Antony and Cleopatra. Act ii, sc. 6, l. 76. [Pompey]

10
Envenom with his envy.
Hamlet. Act iv, sc. 7, l. 104. [King]

11
Yea, there thou makest me sad and makest me sin
In envy.
I Henry IV. Act i, sc. 1, l. 78. [King Henry]

12 When envy breeds unkind division;
There comes the ruin, there begins confusion.
I Henry VI. Act iv, sc. 1, l. 193. [Exeter]

13
No black envy Shall mark my grave.
Henry VIII. Act ii, sc. 1, l. 85. [Buckingham]

Now I feel
Of what coarse metal ye are moulded, envy:
How eagerly you follow my disgraces,
As if it fed ye! and how sleek and wanton
Ye appear in everything may bring my ruin!
Henry VIII. Act iii, sc. 2, l. 238. [Wolsey] The only use of "coarse."

14
Such men as he be never at heart's ease
Whiles they behold a greater than themselves,
And therefore are they very dangerous.
Julius Cæsar. Act i, sc. 2, l. 208. [Cæsar]

15
Either this is envy in you, folly, or mistaking.
Measure for Measure. Act iii, sc. 2, l. 149. [Duke]

16 No lawful means can carry me
Out of his envy's reach.
The Merchant of Venice. Act iv, sc. 1, l. 9. [Antonio]

No metal can,
No, not the hangman's axe, bear half the keenness
Of thy sharp envy.
The Merchant of Venice. Act iv, sc. 1, l. 124. [Gratiano] The only use of "keenness."

Hack'd down, and his summer leaves all faded,
By envy's hand and murder's bloody axe.
Richard II. Act i, sc. 2, l. 20. [Duchess of Gloucester]

17 Envy of so rich a thing
Braving compare, disdainfully did sting
His high-pitch'd thoughts.
The Rape of Lucrece, l. 39. "Disdainfully" is repeated in *Troilus and Cressida,* iii, 3, 53. The only use of "high-pitch'd."

18
You envy my advancement and my friends'.
Richard III. Act i, sc. 3, l. 75. [Queen Elizabeth]

19
Advanced above pale envy's threatening reach.
Titus Andronicus. Act ii, sc. 1, l. 4. [Aaron]

Ancient envy.—*Coriolanus,* iv, 5, 109.

Rival-hating envy.—*Richard II,* i, 3, 131. The only use of the phrase.

20
Thou art as full of envy at his greatness as Cerberus is at Proserpina's beauty, ay, that thou barkest at him.
Troilus and Cressida. Act ii, sc. 1, l. 36. [Thersites]

What envy can say worst shall be a mock for his truth.
Troilus and Cressida. Act iii, sc. 2, l. 104. [Troilus]

Thou core of envy!—*Troilus and Cressida,* v, 1, 4.

Thou damnable box of envy.—*Troilus and Cressida,* v, 1, 29.
Devil Envy.—*Troilus and Cressida,* ii, 3, 23.

EPILOGUE

See also Prologue

1
If it be true that good wine needs no bush, 'tis true that a good play needs no epilogue; yet to good wine they do use good bushes, and good plays prove the better by the help of good epilogues.
As You Like It. Epilogue, l. 3. [Rosalind] "Good epilogue" is used a second time in l. 8.

2
Armado: Come, thy l'envoy; begin. . . .
Moth: Is not l'envoy a salve?
Armado: No, page: it is an epilogue or discourse, to make plain
Some obscure precedence that hath tofore been sain.
Love's Labour's Lost. Act iii, sc. 1, l. 73. "Tofore" is used once again in *Titus Andronicus,* iii, 1, 294. The only use of "sain." "L'envoy" is used five times in this scene, and occurs nowhere else.

3
Bottom: Will it please you to see the epilogue? . . .
Theseus: No epilogue, I pray you; for your play needs no excuse. . . . Let your epilogue alone.
A Midsummer-Night's Dream. Act v, sc. 1, l. 359.

EPITAPH

4
So in approof lives not his epitaph
As in your royal speech.
All's Well that Ends Well, i, 2, 50. See under REMEMBRANCE.
Let's talk of . . . epitaphs.—*Richard II,* iii, 2, 145.

5
And hath as oft a slanderous epitaph
As record of fair act.
Cymbeline. Act iii, sc. 3, l. 52. [Belarius]
Bad epitaph.—*Hamlet,* ii, 2, 550.
Extemporal epitaph.—*Love's Labour's Lost,* iv, 2, 51.
Waxen epitaph.—*Henry V,* i, 21, 233.

6
Adieu, and take thy praise with thee to heaven!
Thy ignominy sleep with thee in the grave,
But not remember'd in thy epitaph!
I Henry IV. Act v, sc. 4, l. 99. [Prince of Wales] The only use of "ignominy." "Ignomy" occurs three times.

7
You cannot better be employ'd, Bassanio,
Than to live still and write mine epitaph.
The Merchant of Venice. Act iv, sc. 1, l. 117. [Antonio]

8
On your family's old monument
Hang mournful epitaphs.
Much Ado about Nothing. Act iv, sc. 1, l. 208. [Leonato]

If your love
Can labour aught in sad invention,
Hang her an epitaph upon her tomb
And sing it to her bones, sing it to-night.
Much Ado about Nothing. Act v, sc. 1, l. 292. [Leonato]

9
Her monument
Is almost finish'd, and her epitaphs
In glittering golden characters express
A general praise to her.
Pericles. Act iv, sc. 3, l. 42. [Dionyza]

Now please you wit
The epitaph is for Marina writ
By wicked Dionyza. [*Reads*]
'The fairest, sweet'st, and best lies here,
Who wither'd in her spring of year.
She was of Tyrus the king's daughter,
On whom foul death hath made this slaughter;
Marina was she call'd; and at her birth,
Thetis, being proud, swallowed some part o' the earth:
Therefore the earth, fearing to be o'erflow'd,
Hath Thetis' birth-child on the heavens bestow'd:
Wherefore she does, and swears she'll never stint,
Make raging battery upon shores of flint.'
Pericles. Act iv, sc. 4, l. 31. [Gower] The only use of "birth-child."

Beauty, truth, and rarity,
Grace in all simplicity,
Here enclosed in cinders lie.
The Phœnix and the Turtle, l. 53.

10
I shall live your epitaph to make.
Sonnets. No. lxxxi.

11
Make thine epitaph,
That death in me at others' lives may laugh.
Timon of Athens. Act iv, sc. 3, l. 380. [Timon]

Why, I was writing of my epitaph;
It will be seen to-morrow.
Timon of Athens. Act v, sc. 1, l. 188. [Timon]

Soldier: My noble general, Timon is dead;
Entomb'd upon the very hem o' the sea;
And on his grave-stone this insculpture, which
With wax I brought away, whose soft impression
Interprets for my poor ignorance.
Alcibiades [reading]: 'Here lies a wretched corse, of wretched soul bereft:
Seek not my name: a plague consume you wicked caitiffs left!
Here lie I, Timon; whom alive, all living men did hate:
Pass by and curse thy fill, but pass and stay not here thy gait.'
Timon of Athens. Act v, sc. 4, l. 67. The only use of "insculpture."

EQUALITY

12
Equality of two domestic powers
Breed scrupulous faction.
Antony and Cleopatra. Act i, sc. 3, l. 47. [Antony]

Your armies; whose equality
By our best eyes cannot be censured.
King John. Act ii, sc. 1, l. 327. [Citizen] The only uses of "equality."

Divide Our equalness.—*Antony and Cleopatra,* v, 1, 48. The only use of "equalness."

1
Two equal men.
Henry VIII. Act ii, sc. 2, l. 108. [King Henry]

Equal in lustre.—*Henry VIII,* i, 1, 29.
Equal with the king.—*II Henry IV,* i, 3, 67.
Equal with a queen.—*King John,* ii, 1, 486.

2
Equalities are so weighed, that curiosity in neither can make choice of either's moiety.
King Lear. Act i, sc. 1, l. 5. [Gloucester] The only use of "equalities." "Curiosity" occurs only four times in the plays, and three of these are in the first act of *King Lear.* The fourth is in *Timon of Athens,* iv, 3, 303.

You weigh equally.—*Measure for Measure,* iv, 2, 31.
Very equally.—*I Henry IV,* iii, 1, 73.

3
In my rights,
By me invested, he compeers the best.
King Lear. Act v, sc. 3, l. 68. [Regan] "Compeers" is repeated in *Sonnets,* lxxxvi.

She had not been, Nor was not to be equall'd.
Winter's Tale. Act v, sc. 1, l. 100. [Paulina] "Equall'd" is used a second time in *Timon of Athens,* iii, 4, 32.

EQUITY, see Right

ERRAND

4
This Jack of Cæsar's shall
Bear us an errand to him.
Antony and Cleopatra. Act 3, sc. 13, l. 103. [Antony]

Sent on errands.—*Julius Cæsar,* iv, 1, 13.

5
My errand is to you, fair youth.
As You Like It. Act iv, sc. 3, l. 6. [Silvius]

6
My errand, due unto my tongue,
I thank him, I bare home upon my shoulders.
The Comedy of Errors. Act ii, sc. 1, l. 72. [Dromio of Ephesus]

I'll say an errand for you.—*Coriolanus,* v, 2, 65.
First I'll do my errand.—*The Winter's Tale,* ii, 3, 64.
Hast thou done thy errand?—*The Taming of the Shrew,* iv, 4, 14.

7
I know thy errand, I will go with thee.
Henry V. Act iv, sc. 1, l. 324. [King Henry]

Great errand.—*The Winter's Tale,* ii, 2, 46.
Holy errand.—*King John,* iii, 1, 147.

8
Hear the truth of it: he came of an errand to me from Parson Hugh.
The Merry Wives of Windsor. Act i, sc. 4, l. 80. [Mistress Quickly]

I must of another errand.—*The Merry Wives of Windsor,* iii, 4, 144.
She comes of errands, does she?—*The Merry Wives of Windsor,* iv, 2, 182.

9
Let me come in, and you shall know my errand.
Romeo and Juliet. Act iii, sc. 3, l. 79. [Nurse]

Know my errand.—*Julius Cæsar,* ii, 4, 3.

10
That dissembling abominable varlet, Diomed, has got that same scurvy doting foolish young knave's sleeve of Troy there in his helm: I would fain see them meet; that that same young Trojan ass, that loves the whore there, might send that Greekish whoremasterly villain, with the sleeve, back to the dissembling luxurious drab, of a sleeveless errand.
Troilus and Cressida. Act v, sc. 4, l. 2. [Thersites] The only use of "whoremasterly" and "sleeveless." The origin of "sleeveless errand" is explained in the following extract from Lady Charlotte Guest's translation of the *Mabinogion* (*Dream of Mayen Wledig*): "Now this is the guise in which the messengers journeyed: one sleeve was on the cap of each of them in front, as a sign that they were messengers, in order that through what hostile land soever they might pass, no harm might be done them." Without the sleeve, they would be unable to perform their errand, thus sleeveless, bootless, or futile errand.

ERROR

See also Mistake

11
My dial goes not true: I took this lark for a bunting.
All's Well that Ends Well. Act ii, sc. 5, l. 6. [Lafeu] The only use of "bunting."

12
What error drives our eyes and ears amiss?
The Comedy of Errors. Act ii, sc. 2, l. 186. [Antipholus of Syracuse]

I was ta'en for him, and he for me,
And thereupon these ERRORS are arose.
The Comedy of Errors. Act v, sc. 1, l. 387. [Antipholus of Syracuse]

Smother'd in errors.—*The Comedy of Errors,* iii, 2, 35.
One day's error.—*The Comedy of Errors,* v, 1, 397.

13
Mountainous error be too highly heapt
For truth to o'er-peer.
Coriolanus, ii, 3, 127. See under CUSTOM. The only use of "mountainous." "Over-peer is repeated in *I Henry VI,* i, 4, 11, and in *The Merchant of Venice,* i, 1, 12.

14
And yet thy tongue will not confess thy error.
I Henry VI. Act ii, sc. 4, l. 67. [Somerset]

15
Thou aimest all awry.
II Henry VI. Act ii, sc. 4, l. 58. [Gloucester]

Pardon, sir; error.—*Love's Labour's Lost,* v, 1, 137.
There was our error.—*Cymbeline,* v, 5, 260.

16
Erroneous, mutinous and unnatural!
III Henry VI, ii, 5, 90. See under QUARREL.

Erroneous vassal!—*Richard III,* i, 4, 200. The only uses of "erroneous."

17
O hateful error, melancholy's child,
Why dost thou show to the apt thoughts of men

The things that are not? O error, soon conceived,
Thou never comest unto a happy birth,
But kill'st the mother that engender'd thee!
Julius Cæsar. Act v, sc. 3, l. 67. [Messala]

1 Errors of the blood, none of the mind.
A Lover's Complaint, l. 184.

2 Leave no rubs nor botches in the work.
Macbeth. Act iii, sc. 1, l. 134. [Macbeth]

It is but botch'd.—*Timon of Athens*, iv, 3, 285.
Botch'd up.—*Twelfth Night*, iv, 1, 60. The only uses of "botch'd."

3 Thou art full of error; I am sound.
Measure for Measure. Act i, sc. 2, l. 54. [Gentleman]

This is the greatest error of all the rest.
A Midsummer-Night's Dream. Act v, sc. 1, l. 250. [Theseus]

4 Call me a fool;
Trust not my reading nor my observations,
Which with experimental seal doth warrant
The tenour of my book; trust not my age,
My reverence, calling, nor divinity,
If this sweet lady lie not guiltless here
Under some biting error.
Much Ado about Nothing. Act iv, sc. 1, l. 166. [Friar Francis] The only use of "experimental."

Damned error.—*The Merchant of Venice*, iii, 2, 78.
Faithless error.—*King John*, ii, 1, 230.

5 I do not so secure me in the error.
Othello. Act i, sc. 3, l. 10. [Duke]

6 It is the very error of the moon.
Othello, v, 2, 109. See under MOON.

Error of her choice.—*Othello*, i, 3, 357.

7 By false intelligence, or wrong surmise.
Richard III. Act ii, sc. 1, l. 54. [Gloucester]

8 So are those errors that in thee are seen
To truths translated and for true things deem'd.
Sonnets. No. xcvi.

If this be error and upon me proved,
I never writ, nor no man ever loved.
Sonnets. No. cxvi. See under LOVE for full quotation.

Book both my wilfulness and errors down.
Sonnets. No. cxvii.

What wretched errors hath my heart committed!
Sonnets. No. cxix.

9 To say they err I dare not be so bold,
Although I swear it to myself alone.
Sonnets. No. cxxxi.

I cannot err.—*The Comedy of Errors*, v, 1, 317.
You cannot . . . Err.—*All's Well that Ends Well*, iii, 7, 12; *Cymbeline*, i, 6, 176.
They may err.—*Pericles*, i, 2, 43.
Thou errest.—*Twelfth Night*, iv, 2, 46. The only use of "errest."
Errs in ignorance.—*Othello*, iii, 3, 49.
Err in report of us.—*Macbeth*, v, 4, 7.
Err like others.—*Measure for Measure*, ii, 2, 134.
Preposterously to err.—*Othello*, i, 3, 62.

10 Error i' the bill, sir; error i' the bill.
The Taming of the Shrew. Act iv, sc. 3, l. 146. [Grumio]

11 The error of our eye directs our mind:
What error leads must err.
Troilus and Cressida, v, 2, 110. See under EYE.

Errors by opinion bred.
The Rape of Lucrece, l. 937.

12 My soul disputes well with my sense,
That this may be some error, but no madness.
Twelfth Night. Act iv, sc. 3, l. 9. [Sebastian]

13 That one error fills him with faults.
The Two Gentlemen of Verona. Act v, sc. 4, l. 111. [Proteus]

'Tis a causeless fantasy, And childish error.
Venus and Adonis, l. 897.

ESCAPE

14 For a week escape a great deal of discoveries.
All's Well that Ends Well. Act iii, sc. 6, l. 99. [Lord]

Escape calumny.—*Hamlet*, iii, 1, 141.

15 He that escapes me without some broken limb shall acquit him well.
As You Like It. Act i, sc. 1, l. 133. [Charles]

16 I cannot see how else thou shouldst 'scape.
As You Like It. Act iii, sc. 2, l. 89. [Touchstone]

He cannot 'scape.—*Two Gentlemen of Verona*, v, 3, 11; *Merry Wives of Windsor*, iii, 5, 147.
How didst thou 'scape?—*Tempest*, ii, 2, 124.
In sooth you 'scape not so.—*The Taming of the Shrew*, ii, 1, 241.
The villain shall not 'scape.—*King Lear*, ii, 1, 82.

17 Anon, I wot not by what strong escape
He broke from those that had the guard of him.
The Comedy of Errors. Act v, sc. 1, l. 148. [Adriana]

Foul escape.—*Titus Andronicus*, iv, 2, 113.
Late escape.—*The Winter's Tale*, ii, 1, 95.

18 I have 'scaped by miracle.
I Henry IV. Act ii, sc. 4, l. 184. [Falstaff]

19 Hardly we escaped the pride of France.
I Henry VI. Act iii, sc. 2, l. 40. [Talbot]

These Lincoln Washes have devoured them;
Myself, well mounted, hardly have escaped.
King John. Act v, sc. 6, l. 41. [Bastard]

20 I 'll direct thee how thou shalt escape
By sudden flight.
I Henry VI. Act iv, sc. 5, l. 10. [Talbot]

21 Ah, whither shall I fly to 'scape their hands?
III Henry VI. Act i, sc. 3, l. 1. [Rutland]

Escaped our hands.—*III Henry VI*, i, 1, 1.

1
No, 'tis impossible he should escape.
III Henry VI. Act ii, sc. 6, l. 38. [Warwick]

Had he 'scaped, methinks we should have heard
The happy tidings of his good escape.
III Henry VI. Act ii, sc. 1, l. 6. [Edward] See under NEWS.

How made he escape?—*III Henry VI,* iv, 6, 80.

2
I 'll find a thousand shifts to get away:
As good to die and go, as die and stay.
King John. Act iv, sc. 3, l. 7. [Arthur] The only use of "get away."

Whiles I may 'scape, I will preserve myself.
King Lear. Act ii, sc. 3, l. 5. [Edgar]

3
Give him leave to escape hence, he would not.
Measure for Measure. Act iv, sc. 2, l. 156. [Provost]

Thousand escapes of wit.—*Measure for Measure,* iv, 1, 63.

4
To 'scape drowning thrice, and to be in peril of my life with the edge of a feather-bed; here are simple 'scapes.
The Merchant of Venice. Act ii, sc. 2, l. 172. [Launcelot] The only mention of feather-bed.

Escaped the hunt.—*King Lear,* ii, 3, 3.

Escaped the wreck.—*The Merchant of Venice,* iii, 1, 110.

He aught escapen but himself.—*Pericles,* ii, Gower, 36. The only use of "escapen."

5
Put on a hat, a muffler and a kerchief, and so escape.
The Merry Wives of Windsor, iv, 2, 73. See under DISGUISE.

Tranio . . . puts my apparel . . . on,
And I for my escape have put on his.
The Taming of the Shrew, i, 1, 233. See under LIFE.

6
Hair-breadth 'scapes.
Othello, i, 3, 136. For full quotation see under ADVENTURE. The only use of "hair-breadth" in the plays. *The Merry Wives of Windsor,* iv, 2, 3, has: "I profess requital to a hair's breadth." "'Scape" or "'scapes" is used forty-five times.

7
Our escape Is much beyond our loss.
The Tempest. Act ii, sc. 1, l. 2. [Gonzalo]

Stephano: How didst thou 'scape? . . . I escaped upon a butt of sack . . . swear then how thou escapedst.
Trinculo: Swum ashore, man, like a duck.
The Tempest. Act ii, sc. 2, l. 123. The only use of "escapedst." "Swum" is used a second time in *The Two Gentlemen of Verona,* i, 1, 26: "Swum the Hellespont."

8
Mine own escape unfoldeth to my hope.
Twelfth Night. Act i, sc. 2, l. 19. [Viola]

Thus I do escape.—*Antony and Cleopatra,* iv, 14, 94.

ETERNITY

See also Immortality

9
Eternity was in our lips and eyes.
Antony and Cleopatra. Act i, sc. 3, l. 35. [Cleopatra]

10
For ever and a day.
As You Like It. Act iv, sc. 1, l. 145. [Orlando] Repeated in *The Taming of the Shrew,* iv, 4, 97.

Eternized in all age to come.
II Henry VI, v, 3, 118. "Eternized" was used in the first play, and never again.

Heirs of all eternity.
Love's Labour's Lost. Act i, sc. 1, l. 7. [King Ferdinand]

11
Sells eternity to get a toy.
The Rape of Lucrece, l. 214.

12
Beyond all date, even to eternity.
Sonnets. No. cxxii.

13
Let Mars divide eternity in twain.
Troilus and Cressida. Act ii, sc. 3, l. 256. [Ulysses]

ETHIOPIAN

14
And Ethiopes of their sweet complexion crack.
Love's Labour's Lost. Act iv, sc. 3, l. 268. [King]

Thou for whom Jove would swear
Juno but an Ethiope were.
Love's Labour's Lost, iv, 3, 118. See under BEAUTY.

15
Is he dead, my Ethiopian?
The Merry Wives of Windsor. Act ii, sc. 3, l. 27. [Host] "Ethiopian is used a second time in *The Winter's Tale,* iv, 4, 375: "Ethiopian's tooth."

16
I 'll hold my mind, were she an Ethiope.
Much Ado about Nothing, v, 4, 38.

A black Ethiope.—*Pericles,* ii, 2, 20.

A swarthy Ethiope.—*The Two Gentlemen of Verona,* ii, 6, 26.

Away, you Ethiope!—*A Midsummer-Night's Dream,* iii, 2, 257.

EUNUCH

17
Send them to the Turk, to be made eunuchs of.
All's Well that Ends Well. Act ii, sc. 3, l. 94. [Lafeu]

18
Cleopatra: Thou, eunuch Mardian!
Mardian: What 's your highness' pleasure? . . .
Cleopatra: I take no pleasure
In aught an eunuch has. . . . Hast thou affections?
Mardian: Yes, gracious madam.
Cleopatra: Indeed!
Mardian: Not in deed, madam; for I can do nothing
But what indeed is honest to be done:

Yet have I fierce affections, and think
What Venus did with Mars.
Antony and Cleopatra. Act i, sc. 5, l. 8.
Saucy eunuch.—*Antony and Cleopatra,* iv, 14, 25.
Unpaved eunuch.—*Cymbeline,* ii, 3, 34. The only use of "unpaved" (without stones).
Athenian eunuch.—*A Midsummer-Night's Dream,* v, 1, 45.
Small as an eunuch.—*Coriolanus,* iii, 2, 114.

1
Does your worship mean to geld and splay all the youth of the city?
Measure for Measure. Act ii, sc. 1, l. 242. [Pompey] The only use of "splay."
Would he were gelt that had it.
The Merchant of Venice. Act v, sc. 1, l. 144. [Gratiano] The only use of "gelt."
By gar, I will cut all his two stones; by gar, he shall not have a stone to throw at his dog.
The Merry Wives of Windsor. Act i, sc. 4, l. 117. [Caius]
By mine honour,
I 'll geld them all; fourteen they shall not see,
To bring false generations.
The Winter's Tale. Act ii, sc. 1, l. 146. [Antigonus]
Geld a codpiece.—*The Winter's Tale,* iv, 4, 623. The only uses of "geld."
Let me be gelded like a spaniel.
Pericles. Act iv, sc. 6, l. 133. [Boult] "Gelded" is used four times. For "gelding" see under HORSE.

2
Thou shalt present me as an eunuch to him.
Twelfth Night. Act i, sc. 2, l. 56. [Viola]
Be you his eunuch, and your mute I 'll be.
Twelfth Night. Act i, sc. 2, l. 62. [Captain]
I would I were an eunuch.—*Titus Andronicus,* ii, 3, 128.

EVASION

3
I do not like 'But yet,' it does allay
The good precedence; fie upon 'But yet'!
'But yet' is as a gaoler to bring forth
Some monstrous malefactor.
Antony and Cleopatra. Act ii, sc. 5, l. 50. [Cleopatra]
And yet another 'yet.'
The Two Gentlemen of Verona. Act ii, sc. 1, l. 126. [Speed]

4 If he evade us there,
Enforce him with his envy to the people.
Coriolanus. Act iii, sc. 2, l. 2. [Brutus] The only use of "evade."
But he . . .
Evades them, with a bombast circumstance.
Othello. Act i, sc. 1, l. 12. [Iago] The only use of "evades."

5
All 's well; and might have been much better, if
He could have temporised.
Coriolanus. Act iv, sc. 6, l. 16. [Menenius] The only use of "temporized."

6
This paltering Becomes not Rome.
Coriolanus. Act iii, sc. 1, l. 58. [Cominius] The only use of "paltering."

7
A' would about and about.
II Henry IV. Act iii, sc. 2, l. 302. [Shallow]
Go not about.—*All 's Well that Ends Well,* i, 3, 194.

8
I . . . am fain to shuffle, to hedge and to lurch.
The Merry Wives of Windsor, ii, 2, 26. See under HONOUR. The only use of "lurch."
How he coasts And hedges his own way.
Henry VIII, iii, 2, 38. [Chamberlain]
Nay, this shall not hedge us out.
Troilus and Cressida, iii, 1, 65. [Helen]
Hedge aside.—*Troilus and Cressida,* iii, 3, 158.

9
His evasions have ears thus long.
Troilus and Cressida. Act ii, sc. 1, l. 75. [Thersites] The only use of "evasions."
His evasion . . .
Cannot outfly our apprehension.
Troilus and Cressida, ii, 3, 123. See under APPREHENSION.
There can be no evasion.—*Troilus and Cressida,* ii, 2, 67.
No more evasion.—*Measure for Measure,* i, 1, 51. The only uses of "evasion."

10
If! thou protector of this damned strumpet,
Tellest thou me of 'ifs'?
Richard III. Act iii, sc. 4, l. 76. [Gloucester]
All these you may avoid but the Lie Direct; and you may avoid that too with an If. I knew when seven justices could not take up a quarrel, but when the parties were met themselves, one of them thought but of an If, as, 'If you said so, then I said so'; and they shook hands and swore brothers. Your If is the only peacemaker; much virtue in If.
As You Like It. Act v, sc. 4, l. 111. [Touchstone]
Some doubtful phrase,
As 'Well, well, we know,' or 'We could, an if we would,'
Or 'If we list to speak,' or 'There be, an if they might,'
Or such ambiguous giving out.
Hamlet. Act i, sc. 5, l. 175. [Hamlet] The only use of "ambiguous." "Ambiguities" occurs twice, in *Henry V,* v, 1, 48, and in *Romeo and Juliet,* v, 3, 217. See under DOUBT.

EVENING

11
I 'll about it this evening.
All 's Well that Ends Well. Act iii, sc. 6, l. 79. [Parolles]
This evening must I leave you.
I Henry IV. Act ii, sc. 3, l. 109. [Hotspur]
Eglamour: When will you go?
Silvia: This evening coming.
Two Gentlemen of Verona. Act iv, sc. 3, l. 42.
This evening.—*II Henry VI,* ii, 1, 43; *A Midsummer-Night's Dream,* v, 1, 39.
This present evening.—*King Lear,* ii, 1, 103.
This very evening.—*King Lear,* i, 2, 101.

12
About evening come yourself alone.
The Comedy of Errors. Act iii, sc. 1, l. 96. [Balthazar]
In the evening.—*Henry VIII,* iii, 2, 226.
Made an evening.—*III Henry VI,* i, 4, 34.

Morning and evening.—*Much Ado about Nothing,* ii, 1, 31.

1
'Twas on a summer's evening.
Julius Cæsar. Act iii, sc. 2, l. 176. [Antony]

2 How still the evening is,
As hush'd on purpose to grace harmony!
Much Ado about Nothing. Act ii, sc. 3, l. 40. [Claudio]

Lady, a happy evening!—*The Two Gentlemen of Verona,* v, 1, 7.
Evening mass.—*Romeo and Juliet,* iv, 1, 38.
Evening music.—*The Two Gentlemen of Verona,* iv, 2, 17.
Evening prayer.—*The Merry Wives of Windsor,* ii, 2, 102.
Evening sport.—*The Passionate Pilgrim,* l. 291.
Evening sun.—*The Comedy of Errors,* i, 1, 28.
Dew of evening.—*King John,* ii, 1, 285. The only uses of "evening."

EVENT

See also Result

3
All strange and terrible events are welcome.
Antony and Cleopatra, iv, 15, 3. See under COMFORT.

I'll show you how to observe a strange event.
Timon of Athens. Act iii, sc. 4, l. 17. [Titus]

These are not natural events; they strengthen
From strange to stranger.
The Tempest. Act v, sc. 1, l. 227. [Alonso]

Strange events.—*As You Like It,* v, 4, 133.
Confused events.—*Macbeth,* ii, 3, 63.

4 High events as these
Strike those that make them: and their story is
No less in pity than his glory which
Brought them to be lamented.
Antony and Cleopatra, v, 2, 363. [Cæsar]

5
It doth presage some ill event.
I Henry VI. Act iv, sc. 1, l. 191. [Exeter]

What uncouth ill event
Hath thee befall'n, that thou dost trembling stand?
The Rape of Lucrece, l. 1598.

Dire events.—*Titus Andronicus,* v, 3, 178; *Venus and Adonis,* l. 1159.
Fierce events.—*Hamlet,* i, 1, 121.

6
The event Is yet to name the winner.
Cymbeline. Act iii, sc. 5, l. 14. [Lucius]

7 Some craven scruple
Of thinking too precisely on the event.
Hamlet. Act iv, sc. 4, l. 40. [Hamlet]

Customed event.—*King John,* iii, 4, 155.
Invisible event.—*Hamlet,* iv, 4, 50.
Like event.—*I Henry VI,* v, 5, 105; *Titus Andronicus,* v, 3, 204.
True event.—*Macbeth,* v, 4, 15.

8
You cast the event of war, my noble lord.
II Henry IV, i, 1, 166. See under WAR.

Event Of the none-sparing war.—*All's Well that Ends Well,* iii, 2, 107. The only use of "none-sparing."
Event o' the journey.—*Winter's Tale,* iii, 1, 11.

9
That obscene and most preposterous event,
that draweth from my snow-white pen the ebon-coloured ink.
Love's Labour's Lost. Act i, sc. 1, l. 244. [King Ferdinand] The only use of "ebon-coloured." "Snow-white" is repeated in iv, 2, 136, and in *Titus Andronicus,* ii, 3, 76.

10
Leave we him to his events, with a prayer they may prove prosperous.
Measure for Measure. Act iii, sc. 2, l. 252. [Escalus]

Crown what I profess with kind event.
Tempest. Act iii, sc. 1, l. 69. [Ferdinand]

Good event.—*II Henry IV,* iv, 2, 82.

11 The unborn event
I do commend to your intent.
Pericles. Act iv, Gower, l. 45.

12
There are many events in the womb of time which will be delivered.
Othello. Act i, sc. 3, l. 377. [Iago]

13
What will ensue hereof, there's none can tell;
But by bad courses may be understood
That their events can never fall out good.
Richard II. Act ii, sc. 1, l. 212. [York]

As the event stamps them.—*Much Ado about Nothing,* i, 2, 7.

14
I'll after him, and see the event of this.
The Taming of the Shrew, iii, 2, 129. See also *Twelfth Night,* iii, 4, 431.

Let's see the event.—*Twelfth Night,* iii, 4, 431.
Mark . . . the event.—*The Tempest,* i, 2, 117.
Well, well; the event.—*King Lear,* i, 4, 371.

EVIDENCE

See also Proof

15
You have wound a goodly clew.
All's Well that Ends Well. Act i, sc. 3, l. 188. [Countess] The only use of "clew."

16
Thou art too fine in thy evidence.
All's Well that Ends Well. Act v, sc. 3, l. 268. [King]

It was wise nature's end in the donation,
To be his evidence now.
Cymbeline. Act v, sc. 5, l. 367. [Belarius]

17
True evidence of good esteem.
II Henry VI. Act iii, sc. 2, l. 21. [King Henry]

Give true evidence to his love, which stands
An honourable trial.
Antony and Cleopatra. Act i, sc. 3, l. 74. [Antony]

Give in evidence.—*Hamlet,* iii, 3, 64.
Bear evidence.—*Richard III,* i, 4, 67.
Evidence to swear.—*The Rape of Lucrece,* l. 1650.
Modest evidence.—*Much Ado about Nothing,* iv, 1, 38.

18
Who finds the heifer dead and bleeding fresh
And sees fast by a butcher with an axe,
But will suspect 'twas he that made the slaughter?

Who finds the partridge in the puttock's nest,
But may imagine how the bird was dead,
Although the kite soar with unbloodied beak?

II Henry VI. Act iii, sc. 2, l. 188. [Warwick] "Partridge" is repeated in *Much Ado about Nothing,* ii, 1, 155. "Puttock" is used in *Troilus and Cressida,* v, 1, 68, and in *Cymbeline,* i, 1, 140. "Kite" is mentioned fifteen times. The only use of "unbloodied."

Sir, he made a chimney in my father's house, and the bricks are alive at this day to testify it; therefore deny it not.

II Henry VI. Act iv, sc. 2, l. 156. [Smith]

1 His peers, upon this evidence,
Have found him guilty.

Henry VIII. Act ii, sc. 1, l. 26. [Gentleman]

2
Bring in the evidence.

King Lear. Act iii, sc. 6, l. 37. [King Lear]

Where are the evidence that do accuse me?
What lawful quest have given their verdict up
Unto the frowning judge? or who pronounced
The bitter sentence?

Richard III. Act i, sc. 4, l. 188. [Clarence]

EVIL

See also Good and Evil; Man: Bad Men; Wrong

3
All the embossed sores and headed evils,
That thou with license of free foot hast caught,
Wouldst thou disgorge into the general world.

As You Like It. Act ii, sc. 7, l. 67. [Duke Senior] The only use of "headed."

Orlando: Can you remember any of the principal evils that he laid to the charge of women?
Rosalind: There were none principal; they were all like one another as half-pence are.

As You Like It, iii, 2, 370. See under Woman. "Half-pence" is repeated in *Henry V,* iii, 2, 47, and in *Much Ado about Nothing,* ii, 3, 147.

4
No evil lost is wail'd when it is gone.

The Comedy of Errors. Act iv, sc. 2, l. 24. [Luciana]

5
The evils she hatch'd were not effected.

Cymbeline. Act v, sc. 5, l. 60. [Cornelius]

6 Now could I drink hot blood,
And do such bitter business as the day
Would quake to look on.

Hamlet. Act iii, sc. 2, l. 408. [Hamlet]

7
Turning past evils to advantages.

II Henry IV. Act iv, sc. 4, l. 78. [Warwick]

Future evils.—*Measure for Measure,* ii, 2, 95.

8
May it be possible, that foreign hire
Could out of thee extract one spark of evil
That might annoy my finger?

Henry V. Act ii, sc. 2, l. 100. [King Henry] The only use of "extract."

9 I can give you inkling
Of an ensuing evil, if it fall,
Greater than this.

Henry VIII. Act ii, sc. 1, l. 140. [Second Gentleman] "Inkling" occurs only once again in the plays, in *Coriolanus,* i, 1, 59.

10 Evils that take leave,
On their departure most of all show evil.

King John. Act iii, sc. 4, l. 114. [Pandulph]

11
Or, whilst I can vent clamour from my throat,
I 'll tell thee thou dost evil.

King Lear. Act i, sc. 1, l. 168. [Kent]

Thou worse than any name, read thine own evil.

King Lear. Act v, sc. 3, l. 156. [Albany]

12
These evils thou repeat'st upon thyself
Have banish'd me from Scotland.

Macbeth. Act iv, sc. 3, l. 112. [Macduff]

13 Our natures do pursue,
Like rats that ravin down their proper bane,
A thirsty evil, and when we drink we die.

Measure for Measure. Act i, sc. 2, l. 132. [Claudio]

Shall we desire to raze the sanctuary
And pitch our evils there?

Measure for Measure. Act ii, sc. 2, l. 171. [Angelo]

In my heart the strong and swelling evil
Of my conception.

Measure for Measure, ii, 4, 5. See under Hypocrisy.

The evil that thou causest to be done,
That is thy means to live.

Measure for Measure. Act iii, sc. 2, l. 21. [Duke]

Keep me in patience, and with ripen'd time
Unfold the evil which is here wrapt up
In countenance!

Measure for Measure. Act v, sc. 1, l. 116. [Isabella]

Well, Angelo, your evil quits you well.

Measure for Measure. Act v, sc. 1, l. 501. [Duke]

14
And 'Honi soit qui mal y pense' write.

The Merry Wives of Windsor. Act v, sc. 5, l. 73. [Mistress Quickly] The only time Shakespeare quotes this phrase, which is the motto of the Order of the Garter.

15
It is too true an evil.

Othello. Act i, sc. 1, l. 161. [Brabantio]

16
Cave-keeping evils that obscurely sleep.

The Rape of Lucrece, l. 1250. The only use of "cave-keeping." "Cave-keeper" occurs in *Cymbeline,* iv, 2, 298.

Accidental evils.—*Julius Cæsar,* iv, 3, 146.
Beauteous evil.—*Twelfth Night,* iii, 4, 403.
Committed evil.—*The Rape of Lucrece,* l. 972.
Female evil.—*Sonnets,* cxliv; *Passionate Pilgrim,* l. 19.
Fix'd evils.—*All's Well that Ends Well,* i, 1, 113.
Further evil.—*Hamlet,* v, 2, 70.
General evil.—*Sonnets,* cxxi.
Known evils.—*Richard III,* i, 2, 79.
Purposed evil.—*Hamlet,* v, 2, 252.
Secret evil.—*The Rape of Lucrece,* l. 1515.
Supposed evils.—*Richard III,* i, 2, 76.
Unlook'd-for evil.—*The Rape of Lucrece,* l. 846.

Weak evils.—*As You Like It,* ii, 7, 132.
Evils imminent.—*Julius Cæsar,* ii, 2, 81.
Progeny of evils.—*A Midsummer-Night's Dream,* ii, 1, 115.

1
O, he hath kept an evil diet long.
Richard III. Act i, sc. 1, l. 139. [Gloucester]

2
Then be your eyes the witness of this ill.
Richard III. Act iii, sc. 4, l. 69. [Gloucester]
I have done ill;
Of which I do accuse myself so sorely,
That I will joy no more.
Antony and Cleopatra. Act iv, sc. 6, l. 18. [Enobarbus] The only use of "done ill."
Do ill.—*The Merry Wives of Windsor,* iv, 1, 67; *Hamlet,* v, 1, 53.

3
Who lives that 's not depraved or depraves?
Timon of Athens. Act i, sc. 2, l. 145. [Apemantus] "Depraved" is repeated in *King Lear,* ii, iv, 139.

4 Breed a nursery of like evil,
To overbulk us all.
Troilus and Cressida. Act i, sc. 3, l. 319. The only use of "overbulk."

5
I shall crave of you your leave that I may bear my evils alone: it were a bad recompense for your love, to lay any of them on you.
Twelfth Night. Act ii, sc. 1, l. 5. [Sebastian]

EXAMPLE

See also Instance, Precedent

6
O, he has given example for our flight,
Most grossly, by his own!
Antony and Cleopatra. Act iii, sc. 10, l. 28. [Canidius]

7
And by his rare example made the coward
Turn terror into sport.
Coriolanus. Act ii, sc. 2, l. 108. [Cominius]
Three examples of the like hath been
Within my age.
Coriolanus. Act iv, sc. 6, l. 50. [Menenius]

8
A sample to the youngest, to the more mature
A glass that feated them, and to the graver
A child that guided dotards.
Cymbeline. Act i, sc. 1, l. 48. [First Gentleman] The only use of "sample" and "feated."

9
Examples gross as earth exhort me.
Hamlet. Act iv, sc. 4, l. 46. [Hamlet]

10
The examples Of every minute's instance.
II Henry IV. Act iv, sc. 1, l. 82. [Archbishop of York]

11 In speech, in gait,
In diet, in affections of delight,
In military rules, humours of blood,
He was the mark and glass, copy and book,
That fashion'd others.
II Henry IV. Act ii, sc. 3, l. 28. [Lady Percy]
Be copy now to men of grosser blood,
And teach them how to war.
Henry V. Act iii, sc. 1, l. 24. [King Henry]
Such a man
Might be a copy to these younger times;
Which, follow'd well, would demonstrate them now
But goers backward.
All's Well that Ends Well. Act i, sc. 2, l. 45. [King] The only use of "goers backward."
Prick the goer-back.—*Cymbeline,* i, 1, 169. The only use of "goer-back."

12
For hear her but exampled by herself.
Henry V. Act i, sc. 2, l. 156. [Canterbury]
Exampled by this heinous spectacle.
King John. Act iv, sc. 3, l. 56. [Pembroke]
So every step,
Exampled by the first pace that is sick
. . . grows to an envious fever.
Troilus and Cressida. Act i, sc. 3, l. 131. [Ulysses] The only uses of "exampled."

13
Let him be punish'd, sovereign, lest example
Breed, by his sufferance, more of such a kind.
Henry V. Act ii, sc. 2, l. 45. [Scroop]

14
Proclaim them traitors that are up with Cade;
That those which fly before the battle ends
May, even in their wives' and children's sight,
Be hang'd up for example at their doors.
II Henry VI. Act iv, sc. 2, l. 187. [Stafford]
Hang him, he 'll be made an example.
The Winter's Tale. Act iv, sc. 4, l. 847. [Autolycus]
To make him an example.
Measure for Measure, i, 4, 68. [Lucio]
I 'll make thee an example.
Othello. Act ii, sc. 3, l. 251. [Othello]
Make examples.—*Othello,* iii, 3, 65.
Find example.—*The Winter's Tale,* i, 2, 357.
By example.—*Cymbeline,* v, 3, 36.
By the same example.—*The Merchant of Venice,* iv, 1, 221.
By your example.—*King John,* v, 1, 52.
Upon example.—*Henry V,* iv, 1, 19.

15
Men of his way should be most liberal;
They are set here for examples.
Henry VIII. Act i, sc. 3, l. 61. [Sands]
For example.—*II Henry VI,* iv, 7, 58; *Measure for Measure,* i, 2, 26.
For my example.—*Henry VIII,* iv, 2, 11.

16
Of his own body he was ill, and gave
The clergy ill example.
Henry VIII. Act iv, sc. 2, l. 43. [Katharine]

17
So hot a speed with such advice disposed,
Such temperate order in so fierce a cause,
Doth want example.
King John. Act iii, sc. 4, l. 11. [Dauphin]
Without example.—*Henry VIII,* i, 2, 90.

17 Ill, to example ill,
Would from my forehead wipe a perjured note;

For none offend where all alike do dote.
Love's Labour 's Lost. Act iv, sc. 3, l. 124. [Dumain]

1 What are precepts worth Of stale example?
A Lover's Complaint, l. 267.

Forced examples.—*A Lover's Complaint,* l. 157.
Late examples.—*Henry V,* ii, 4, 12.
No such example have we.
Measure for Measure. Act iv, sc. 2, l. 100. [Provost]

2 It is a good divine that follows his own instructions: I can easier teach twenty what were good to be done, than be one of the twenty to follow mine own teaching.
The Merchant of Venice. Act i, sc. 2, l. 15. [Portia]

Christian example.—*The Merchant of Venice,* iii, 1, 74.
Example of others.—*Much Ado about Nothing,* v, 1, 332.

3 If thou dost seek to have what thou dost hide,
By self-example mayst thou be denied!
Sonnets. No. cxlii. The only use of "self-example."

4 There 's much example for 't.
Timon of Athens. Act i, sc. 2, l. 47. [Apemantus]

There is example for 't.
Twelfth Night. Act ii, sc. 5, l. 44. [Malvolio]
I 'll example you.—*Timon of Athens,* iv, 3, 438.
I will example it.—*Love's Labour 's Lost,* iii, 1, 84.

EXCELLENCE

5 We 'll put on those shall praise your excellence.
Hamlet. Act iv, sc. 7, l. 132. [King]

Osric: You are not ignorant of what excellence Lærtes is—
Hamlet: I dare not confess that, lest I should compare with him in excellence.
Hamlet. Act v, sc. 2, l. 143.

Breathless excellence.—*King John,* iv, 3, 66.
Divided excellence.—*King John,* ii, 1, 439.
Neat excellence.—*Cymbeline,* i, 6, 44.
Wondrous excellence.—*Sonnets,* cv.

6 Excellent Pucelle, if thy name be so.
I Henry VI, iii, 1, 230. "Excellent" was a favourite adjective with Shakespeare, who used it no less than 121 times.

7 Dat is very good; excellent.
The Merry Wives of Windsor. Act iii, sc. 1, l. 101. [Caius]

That will be excellent.
The Merry Wives of Windsor. Act iv, sc. 4, l. 69. [Ford]
This comes off well and excellent.
Timon of Athens. Act i, sc. 1, l. 29. [Poet]
Excellently done.—*Twelfth Night,* i, 5, 254; *All's Well that Ends Well,* iv, 3, 237.

8 It is the witness still of excellency
To put a strange face on his own perfection.
Much Ado about Nothing. Act ii, sc. 3, l. 48. [Don Pedro]

Is there not a double excellency in this?
The Merry Wives of Windsor. Act iii, sc. 3, l. 187. [Mrs. Page]
The excellency of her honour.
The Merry Wives of Windsor, ii, 2, 252. The only uses of "excellency."
So crammed, as he thinks, with excellencies.
Twelfth Night, ii, 3, 163. See under CONCEIT. The only use of "excellencies."

9 Then to Silvia let us sing,
That Silvia is excelling;
She excels each mortal thing
Upon the dull earth dwelling.
The Two Gentlemen of Verona. Act iv, sc. 2, l. 49. "Excelling is used only once again, in *Othello,* v, 2, 11: "Excelling nature."

10 So much the more our carver's excellence.
The Winter's Tale. Act v, sc. 3, l. 30. Paulina] "Carver" is repeated in *Richard II,* ii, 3, 144: "Be his own carver."

Study's excellence.—*Love's Labour 's Lost,* iv, 3, 300.

EXCEPTION

11 With proviso and exception.
I Henry IV. Act i, sc. 3, l. 78. [King Henry] The only use of "proviso."

12 'Tis positive 'gainst all exceptions.
Henry V. Act iv, sc. 2, l. 25. [Constable]

How modest in exception.
Henry V. Act iv, sc. 4, l. 34. [Constable]

13 Maria: By my troth, Sir Toby, you must come in earlier o' nights: your cousin, my lady, takes great exceptions to your ill hours.
Sir Toby Belch: Why, let her except, before excepted.
Twelfth Night. Act i, sc. 3, l. 4. The only use of "earlier."

Thou hast taken against me a most just exception.
Othello. Act iv, sc. 2, l. 211. [Iago]
Take exceptions.—*III Henry VI,* iii, 2, 46; *I Henry VI,* iv, 1, 105; *The Two Gentlemen of Verona,* i, 3, 81; v, 2, 3. Always in the plural.

14 Proteus: Except my mistress.
Valentine: Sweet, except not any;
Except thou will except against my love.
Two Gentlemen of Verona. Act ii, sc. 4, l. 154.

Only you excepted.—*Much Ado about Nothing,* i, 1, 126.
Always excepted.—*Much Ado about Nothing,* iii, 1, 93.
Excepting none.—*II Henry VI,* i, 1, 193.
Excepting one.—*Richard III.* i, 1, 99; *Richard II,* iv, 1, 31.

EXCESS

15 If the living be enemy to the grief, the excess makes it soon mortal.
All's Well that Ends Well, i, 1, 66. [Count]

1
To gild refined gold, to paint the lily,
To throw a perfume on the violet,
To smooth the ice, or add another hue
Unto the rainbow, or with taper-light
To seek the beauteous eye of heaven to garnish,
Is wasteful and ridiculous excess.
King John. Act iv, sc. 2, l. 11. [Salisbury] "Taper-light" is repeated in *Pericles,* i, Gower, 16; and "garnish" in *The Merchant of Venice,* ii, 6, 45.

2
Where want cries some, but where excess begs all.
A Lover's Complaint, l. 42.

3
Excess will make me surfeit.
The Two Gentlemen of Verona, iii, 1, 220.
Scant this excess . . . For fear I surfeit.
The Merchant of Venice, iii, 2, 113.
Give me excess of it, that, surfeiting,
The appetite may sicken.
Twelfth Night, i, 1, 2. See under MUSIC for full quotation.
Excess of laughter.—*Othello,* iv, 1, 100.
Excess of wine.—*Henry V,* ii, 2, 42.

EXCLAMATION

4
Say, gentlemen, what makes you thus exclaim?
I Henry VI, iv, 1, 83. See under COMBAT.

5
I trust we shall,
If not fill up the measure of her will,
Yet in some measure satisfy her so
That we shall stop her exclamation.
King John. Act ii, sc. 1, l. 555. [King John]

6
I hear as good exclamation on your worship as of any man in the city.
Much Ado about Nothing. Act iii, sc. 5, l. 28. [Dogberry]
You suffer Too hard an exclamation.
Henry VIII. Act i, sc. 2, l. 51. [Queen Katharine]

7
Be copious in exclaims.
Richard III. Act iv, sc. 4, l. 135. [Duchess of York] The only use of "copious."
Deep exclaims.—*Richard III,* i, 2, 52.
Exclaim no more against it.—*Othello,* ii, 3, 314.
'Tis bootless to exclaim.—*Richard III,* iii, 4, 104.

EXCUSE

See also Forgiveness, Pardon

8
You patch'd up your excuses.
Antony and Cleopatra. Act ii, sc. 2, l. 56. [Cæsar]
That was excusable.
Antony and Cleopatra. Act iii, sc. 4, l. 2. [Antony] The only use of "excusable."

9
I 'll make you amends next, to give you nothing for something.
The Comedy of Errors. Act ii, sc. 2, l. 54. [Antipholus of Syracuse]
We will make amends ere long;
Else the Puck a liar call.
A Midsummer-Night's Dream. Act v, sc. 1, l. 441. [Puck]
He will make thee amends.
The Merry Wives of Windsor. Act ii, sc. 3, l. 70. [Host]
I will one way or other make you amends.
The Merry Wives of Windsor. Act iii, sc. 1, l. 90. [Evans]
Make her amends; she weeps.
Othello. Act iv, sc. 1, l. 255. [Lodovico]
Make amends now.—*Macbeth,* iii, 5, 14. "Make amends" is used fifteen times in the plays.

10
Give me excuse, good madam.
Coriolanus. Act i, sc. 3, l. 114. [Virgilia]
I must excuse What cannot be amended.
Coriolanus. Act iv, sc. 7, l. 11. [Aufidius]

11
This admits no excuse.
Coriolanus. Act v, sc. 6, l. 71. [First Lord]
I will not excuse you; you shall not be excused; excuses shall not be admitted; there is no excuse shall serve; you shall not be excused.
II Henry IV. Act v, sc. 1, l. 5. [Shallow]
He would not hear my excuse.
Timon of Athens. Act iii, sc. 6, l. 17. [Lord]
I will not have excuse.—*Pericles,* ii, 3, 96.

12
Such extenuation let me beg.
I Henry IV. Act iii, sc. 2, l. 22. [Prince of Wales] The only use of "extenuation." "Extenuate" is used seven times, and "extenuated" once.

13
I have borne, and borne, and borne, and have been fubbed off, and fubbed off, and fubbed off, from this day to that day, that it is a shame to be thought on.
II Henry IV. Act ii, sc. 1, l. 36. [Hostess] The only use of "fubbed off."
Why should excuse be born or e'er begot?
Cymbeline. Act iii, sc. 2, l. 67. [Imogen]

14
You must excuse us all.
The Comedy of Errors. Act iii, sc. 1, l. 1. [Antipholus of Ephesus]
Hear my excuse.—*A Midsummer-Night's Dream,* iii, 2, 245.
I must excuse myself.—*The Merry Wives of Windsor,* iii, 2, 54.
Excuse myself.—*Richard III,* i, 2, 82.
Excuse himself.—*II Henry VI,* i, 3, 181.
Excuse yourself.—*Timon of Athens,* ii, 2, 141.
Let me excuse me.—*Measure for Measure,* iv, 1, 12.
Let me excuse thee.—*Sonnets,* cxxxix.
Excuse me.—*III Henry VI,* v, 5, 46; *Love's Labour 's Lost,* i, 1, 176; v, 2, 78; *Troilus and Cressida,* i, 2, 87; *Henry VIII,* ii, 2, 59.
Excusez-moi.—*Henry V,* iii, 4, 30; v, 2, 276.
I do excuse you.—*Henry VIII,* ii, 4, 156.
You 're excused.—*Henry VIII,* ii, 4, 161.
Well excused.—*All's Well that Ends Well,* v, 3, 55.

15
Devise excuses for thy faults.
III Henry VI. Act ii, sc. 6, l. 71. [Warwick]
Make your excuse wisely, you were best.
Twelfth Night. Act i, sc. 5, l. 33. [Maria]

He makes excuses for his being there.
The Rape of Lucrece, l. 114.
O, teach me how to make mine own excuse!
The Rape of Lucrece, l. 1653.
You will make his excuse.—*Troilus and Cressida,* iii, 1, 85.
Well, I 'll make excuse.—*Troilus and Cressida,* iii, 1, 99.

1
I something do excuse the thing I hate,
For his advantage that I dearly love.
Measure for Measure. Act ii, sc. 4, l. 119. [Isabella]

2
That 'scuse serves many men to save their gifts.
The Merchant of Venice. Act iv, sc. 1, l. 144. [Portia]
Good 'scuse.—*Othello,* iv, 1, 80. The only uses of " 'scuse."
Good excuse.—*As You Like It,* iii, 3, 94. The only uses of the phrase.

3
Be not as extreme in submission
As in offence.
The Merry Wives of Windsor. Act iv, sc. 4, l. 11. [Page]
Never excuse.
A Midsummer-Night's Dream. Act v, sc. 1, l. 363. [Theseus]

4
Why seek'st thou then to cover with excuse
That which appears in proper nakedness?
Much Ado about Nothing. Act iv, sc. 1, l. 176. [Leonato]

5
O, what excuse can my invention make,
When thou shalt charge me with so black a deed?
The Rape of Lucrece, l. 225.
Why hunt I then for colour or excuses?
The Rape of Lucrece, l. 267. See under Colour.
Fold my fault in cleanly-coin'd excuses.
The Rape of Lucrece, l. 1073. The only use of "cleanly-coin'd."
'Few words,' quoth she, 'shall fit the trespass best,
Where no excuse can give the fault amending.'
The Rape of Lucrece, l. 1613. The only use of "amending."
No dame, hereafter living,
By my excuse shall claim excuse's giving.
The Rape of Lucrece, l. 1714.

6
Let me have
Some patient leisure to excuse myself.
Richard III. Act i, sc. 2, l. 81. [Gloucester]
Stand excused.—*Richard III,* i, 2, 86; *King John,* iv, 3, 51.

7
There needs no such apology.
Richard III. Act iii, sc. 7, l. 104. [Gloucester]
What needeth then apologies be made,
To set forth that which is so singular?
The Rape of Lucrece, l. 31.
Strengthen'd with what apology you think
May make it probable need.
All's Well That Ends Well. Act ii, sc. 4, l. 51. [Parolles]
I will have an apology.
Love's Labour 's Lost. Act v, sc. 1, l. 142. [Holofernes]
I come with this apology.
Love's Labour 's Lost. Act v, sc. 2, l. 597. [Holofernes]
What, shall this speech be spoke for our excuse?
Or shall we on without apology?
Romeo and Juliet. Act i, sc. 4, l. 1. [Romeo] The only uses of "apology."

8
The excuse that thou dost make in this delay
Is longer than the tale thou dost excuse.
Romeo and Juliet. Act ii, sc. 5, l. 33. [Juliet]
I will be deaf to pleading and excuses;
Nor tears nor prayers shall purchase out abuses.
Romeo and Juliet. Act iii, sc. 1, l. 197. [Prince]

9
Thus can my love excuse the slow offence
Of my dull bearer when from thee I speed.
Sonnets. No. li.
O, what excuse will my poor beast then find,
When swift extremity can seem but slow?
Sonnets. No. li.

10
I hope this reason stands for my excuse.
The Taming of the Shrew. Induction, sc. 2, l. 126. [Page]
At more leisure, I will so excuse
That you shall well be satisfied withal.
The Taming of the Shrew. Act iii, sc. 2, l. 110. [Petruchio]
Excuse it not, for I am peremptory.
The Two Gentlemen of Verona. Act i, sc. 3, l. 71. [Antonio]

11
You shall not bob us out of our melody.
Troilus and Cressida. Act iii, sc. 1, l. 75. [Helen] "Bob" is repeated in *As You Like It,* ii, 7, 55, and in *A Midsummer-Night's Dream,* ii, 1, 49.

12
What 's his excuse?
Troilus and Cressida. Act ii, sc. 3, l. 173. [Agamemnon]
Excuse of youth.—*I Henry IV,* v, 2, 17.
Excuse of time.—*Henry V,* v, Prologue, 3.

13
I will not open my lips so wide as a bristle may enter in way of thy excuse.
Twelfth Night. Act i, sc. 5, l. 2. [Maria]

14
And yet I will not name it; and yet I care not;
And yet take this again; and yet I thank you,
Meaning henceforth to trouble you no more.
The Two Gentlemen of Verona. Act ii, sc. 1, l. 123. [Silvia]
Be gone! I will not hear thy vain excuse.
The Two Gentlemen of Verona. Act iii, sc. 1, l. 168. [Duke]
What bare excuses makest thou to be gone!
Venus and Adonis, l. 188.
You do it for increase: O strange excuse,
When reason is the bawd to lust's abuse.
Venus and Adonis, l. 791.
Clear excuse.—*I Henry IV,* iii, 2, 19.
Old excuse.—*Sonnets,* ii.

EXECUTION

1
By . . . present execution of our wills.
II Henry IV. Act iv, sc. 1, l. 174. [York]
Enforce the present execution.—*Coriolanus,* iii, 3, 21.
Present execution.—*II Henry IV,* iv, 3, 80.
Sudden execution.—*I Henry VI,* v, 5, 99.
Be sudden in the execution.—*Richard III,* i, 3, 346.
Put it in execution.—*Coriolanus,* ii, 1, 257.

2 My father's execution
Was nothing less than bloody tyranny.
I Henry VI. Act ii, sc. 5, l. 99. [Richard]
Away with her to execution!
I Henry VI. Act v, sc. 4, l. 54. [York]
From thence unto the place of execution.
II Henry VI. Act ii, sc. 3, l. 6. [King Henry]
Deliver'd over
To execution and the hand of death.
Richard II. Act iii, sc. 1, l. 30. [Bolingbroke]
His execution sworn.—*Winter's Tale,* i, 2, 446.
Prepare for your execution.—*Coriolanus,* v, 2, 52.
Stay upon execution.—*Coriolanus,* v, 4, 8.
Wait for execution in the morn.—*The Two Gentlemen of Verona,* iv, 2, 134.

3 Scarce I can refrain
The execution of my big-swoln heart
Upon that Clifford, that cruel child-killer.
III Henry VI. Act ii, sc. 2, l. 110. [Richard] "Big-swoln" is repeated in *Titus Andronicus,* iii, 1, 224: "Big-swoln face." The only use of "child-killer."
[Quick] . . . in execution
Of any bold or noble enterprise.
Julius Cæsar. Act i, sc. 2, l. 301. [Cassius]

4 The . . . execution of the rest,
Beloved sons, be yours.
King Lear. Act i, sc. 1, l. 139. [King Lear]
Hopeful execution.—*Measure for Measure,* i, 1, 60.

5
Is execution done on Cawdor?
Macbeth. Act i, sc. 4, l. 1. [Duncan]
The provost hath A warrant for his execution.
Measure for Measure. Act i, sc. 4, l. 74. [Lucio]
Carry him to execution.—*Measure for Measure,* iv, 2, 159.
Put him to execution.—*Henry V,* iii, 6, 58.
After execution.—*Measure for Measure,* ii, 2, 11.

6 Let no man but I
Do execution on my flesh and blood.
Titus Andronicus. Act iv, sc. 2, l. 83. [Aaron]
Do shameful execution on herself.
Titus Andronicus, v, 3, 76. See under Suicide.
Do execution on the watch.—*I Henry VI,* iii, 2, 35.

7 Troilus, who hath done to-day
Mad and fantastic execution.
Troilus and Cressida. Act v, sc. 5, l. 37. [Ulysses]
Bloody execution.—*Macbeth,* i, 2, 18.
Fatal execution.—*Titus Andronicus,* ii, 3, 36.
Sorry execution.—*Comedy of Errors,* v, 1, 121.

EXECUTIONER

8 The common executioner,
Whose heart the accustom'd sight of death makes hard,
Falls not the axe upon the humbled neck
But first begs pardon.
As You Like It. Act iii, sc. 5, l. 3. [Silvius]
A common executioner, who in his office lacks a helper.
Measure for Measure. Act iv, sc. 2, l. 9. [Provost]

9
Say you consent and censure well the deed,
And I 'll provide his executioner.
II Henry VI. Act iii, sc. 1, l. 275. [Cardinal]

10
Duke of Gloucester: Think'st thou I am an executioner?
King Henry: A persecutor, I am sure, thou art:
If murdering innocents be executing,
Why, then thou art an executioner.
III Henry VI. Act v, sc. 6, l. 30. The only use of "persecutor."

11
Go thou, and like an executioner,
Cut off the heads of too fast-growing sprays.
Richard II. Act iii, sc. 4, l. 33. [Gardener] "Fast-growing" is repeated in *Pericles,* iv, Gower, 6.

12 Though I wish thy death,
I will not be the executioner.
Richard III. Act i, sc. 2, l. 185. [Lady Anne]
I would not be thy executioner.
As You Like It. Act iii, sc. 5, l. 8. [Phebe]

13
But soft! here come my executioners.
Richard III. Act i, sc. 3, l. 399. [Gloucester]

14
Let 's choose executors and talk of wills.
Richard II, iii, 2, 148. See under Will.
Lives th' executor to be.—*Sonnets,* iv.
Their executors, the knavish crows.—*Henry V,* iv, 2, 51.
Like executor.—*The Tempest,* iii, 1, 13.
Executors pale.—*Henry V,* i, 2, 203. The only uses of "executor" and "executors."

EXERCISE

15
Thy exercise hath been too violent
For a second course of fight.
Coriolanus. Act i, sc. 5, l. 16. [Titus]
Arts and exercises.—*II Henry IV,* iv, 5, 74; *Troilus and Cressida,* iv, 4, 80; *Hamlet,* iv, 7, 98.

16
The rich advantage of good exercise.
King John. Act iv, sc. 2, l. 60. [Pembroke]
Gentle exercise.—*I Henry IV,* v, 2, 55.
Main exercise.—*Othello,* ii, 1, 269.

17
I am in your debt for your last exercise.
Richard III. Act iii, sc. 2, l. 112. [Hastings]
Holy exercise.—*Richard III,* iii, 7, 64.
Exercise devout.—*Othello,* iii, 4, 41.

1
They are now starved for want of exercise.
Pericles. Act i, sc. 4, l. 38. [Cleon]
2
Fettle your fine joints.
Romeo and Juliet. Act iii, sc. 5, l. 154. [Capulet] The only use of "fettle."
3
Urchins Shall . . . All exercise on thee.
The Tempest. Act i, sc. 2, l. 326. [Prospero]
4 Every exercise
Worthy his youth and nobleness of birth.
The Two Gentlemen of Verona. Act i, sc. 3, l. 32. [Panthino]
Such exercises as may become a gentleman.
As You Like It. Act i, sc. 1, l. 75. [Orlando]
5 So long as nature
Will bear up this exercise, so long
I daily vow to use it.
Winter's Tale. Act iii, sc. 2, l. 241. [Leontes]
Daily exercise.—*III Henry VI,* iv, 6, 85.
6
He is . . . less frequent in his princely exercises than formerly he hath appeared.
Winter's Tale. Act iv, sc. 1, l. 37. [Camillo]
Forgone all . . . exercises.—*Hamlet,* ii, 2, 308.
He's all my exercise.—*Winter's Tale,* i, 2, 166.

EXILE

See also Banishment

7
Condemning . . . some to exile.
Coriolanus. Act i, sc. 6, l. 35. [Marcius]
Vagabond exile.—*Coriolanus,* iii, 3, 89.
8
And suffer'd me by the voice of slaves to be
Whoop'd out of Rome.
Coriolanus. Act iv, sc. 5, l. 83. [Coriolanus] The only use of "whoop'd."
9
To draw upon an exile! O brave sir!
Cymbeline. Act i, sc. 1, l. 166. [Imogen]
The exile of her minion is too new;
She hath not yet forgot him.
Cymbeline. Act ii, sc. 3, l. 46. [Cymbeline]
10
They wilfully themselves exile from light.
A Midsummer-Night's Dream, iii, 2, 386. See under GHOST.
11
She joy'd to jest at my exile.
The Passionate Pilgrim, l. 189.
Voluntary exile.—*As You Like It,* i, 1, 107.
12
The sly slow hours shall not determinate
The dateless limit of thy dear exile.
Richard II. Act i, sc. 3, l. 150. [King Richard]
13 With a fearful soul
Leads discontented steps in foreign soil.
Richard III. Act iv, sc. 4, l. 311. [King Richard]
14
Immediately we do exile him hence.
Romeo and Juliet. Act iii, sc. 1, l. 192. [Prince]
Exile hath more terror in his look,
Much more than death.
Romeo and Juliet. Act iii, sc. 3, l. 13. [Romeo]
And say'st thou yet that exile is not death?
Romeo and Juliet. Act iii, sc. 3, l. 43. [Romeo]
15
The law that threaten'd death becomes thy friend
And turns it to exile.
Romeo and Juliet. Act iii, sc. 3, l. 139. [Friar Laurence]
Thou art an exile, and thou must not stay.
Titus Andronicus. Act iii, sc. 1, l. 285. [Titus]
16
Let them be recalled from their exile.
The Two Gentlemen of Verona. Act v, sc. 4, l. 155. [Valentine]
Recall'd to life again.—*I Henry VI,* i, 1, 66.
Recall'd in rage.—*The Rape of Lucrece,* l. 1671.
Passed sentence may not be recall'd.—*The Comedy of Errors,* i, 1, 148. The only uses of "recall'd."

EXPECTATION

17
Oft expectation fails and most oft there
Where most it promises, and oft it hits
Where hope is coldest and despair most fits.
All's Well that Ends Well. Act ii, sc. 1, l. 145. [Helena]
Expectation fainted,
Longing for what it had not.
Antony and Cleopatra. Act iii, sc. 6, l. 47. [Cæsar]
18
Our expectation . . . Hath made us forward.
Cymbeline. Act iii, sc. 5, l. 28. [Cymbeline]
19
The expectancy and rose of the fair state.
Hamlet, iii, 1, 160. See under MIND.
Expectancy of more arrivance.
Othello, ii, 1, 41. The only uses of "expectancy" and "arrivance."
20 We now possess'd
The utmost man of expectation.
II Henry IV. Act i, sc. 3, l. 64. [Hastings]
You stand in coldest expectation.
II Henry IV. Act v, sc. 2, l. 31. [Lancaster]
Sadly I survive
To mock the expectation of the world,
To frustrate prophecies and to raze out
Rotten opinion, who hath writ me down
After my seeming.
II Henry IV. Act v, sc. 2, l. 125. [King Henry V]
21
For now sits Expectation in the air.
Henry V. Act ii, Prologue, l. 8. [Chorus]
Full of expectation.—*I Henry IV,* ii, 3, 20.
Our expectation hath this day an end.
Henry V. Act iii, sc. 3, l. 44. [Governor]
22
Fresh expectation troubled not the land
With any long'd-for change or better state.
King John. Act iv, sc. 2, l. 7. [Pembroke] The only use of "long'd-for."
Patient expectation.—*Julius Cæsar,* i, 1, 46.
Expectation and surmise.—*II Henry IV,* i, 3, 23.
23 The rest
That are within the note of expectation

Already are i' the court.
Macbeth. Act iii, sc. 3, l. 9. [Murderer]

1
When it is least expected.
Measure for Measure. Act iv, sc. 3, l. 115. [Duke] The only use of the phrase.
When it was less expected.—*Coriolanus,* v, 1, 19.

2
He hath indeed better bettered expectation.
Much Ado about Nothing. Act i, sc. 1, l. 15. [Messenger]

3
Expectations and comforts of sudden respect and acquaintance, but I find none.
Othello. Act iv, sc. 2, l. 191. [Roderigo]
Expectation of our prosperity.—*Othello,* ii, 1, 287.

4
Expecting in return twenty for one.
Timon of Athens, iv, 3, 517. See under GIFT.
Expecting ever.—*Titus Andronicus,* iii, 1, 96.
Expecting absent friends.—*All's Well that Ends Well,* ii, 3, 189.
Expecting overthrow.—*Pericles,* i, 4, 94.
Expecting thy reply.—*Love's Labour's Lost,* iv, 1, 85.
The onset still expecting.—*The Rape of Lucrece,* l. 432.
Expecting but the aid of Buckingham.—*Richard III,* iv, 4, 438. The only uses of "expecting."

5
Now expectation, tickling skittish spirits, . . .
Sets all on hazard.
Troilus and Cressida. Prologue, l. 20.

Expectation whirls me round.
The imaginary relish is so sweet
That it enchants my sense.
Troilus and Cressida. Act iii, sc. 2, l. 19. [Troilus]

There is expectance here from both the sides,
What further you will do.
Troilus and Cressida. Act iv, sc. 5, l. 146. [Æneas] The only use of "expectance."

And signify this loving interview
To the expecters of our Trojan part.
Troilus and Cressida. Act iv, sc. 5, l. 155. [Hector] The only use of "expecters."

EXPEDITION

See also Haste

6
Do this expediently and turn him going.
As You Like It. Act iii, sc. 1, l. 18. [Duke Frederick] The only use of "expediently."

7
Have I, in my poor old motion, the expedition of thought?
II Henry IV, iv, 3, 37. See under SPEED.

The expedition of my violent love
Outrun the pauser, reason.
Macbeth. Act ii, sc. 3, l. 116. [Macbeth] The only use of "pauser."

8
Omit no happy hour
That may give furtherance to our expedition.
Henry V. Act i, sc. 2, l. 300. [King Henry]

Hasten on this expedition.—*The Two Gentlemen of Verona,* i, 3, 77.
God bless your expedition!—*II Henry IV,* i, 2, 249.
This expedition was . . . Too rashly plotted.
I Henry VI. Act iv, sc. 4, l. 2. [Somerset]
Who intercepts my expedition?
Richard III, iv, 4, 136. See under MOTHER.
His expedition promises Present approach.
Timon of Athens. Act v, sc. 2, l. 3. [Messenger]
Boisterous expedition.—*Othello,* i, 3, 229.
Great expedition.—*Henry V,* iii, 2, 82.
Irish expedition.—*I Henry IV,* i, 3, 150.
Last expedition.—*Coriolanus,* ii, 1, 169.

9
Then forth, dear countrymen: let us deliver
Our puissance into the hand of God,
Putting it straight in expedition.
Henry V. Act ii, sc. 1, l. 189. [King Henry]

How much unlook'd for is this expedition!
King John. Act ii, sc. 1, l. 79. [King Philip]

10
A breach that craves a quick expedient stop!
II Henry VI. Act iii, sc. 1, l. 288. [Beaufort]
Expedient manage must be made.—*Richard II,* i, 4, 39.
His marches are expedient to this town.—*King John,* ii, 1, 60.
Painfully with much expedient march.—*King John,* ii, 1, 223.
With all expedient haste.—*King John,* iv, 2, 268.
Seem expedient.—*All's Well that Ends Well,* ii, 3, 186.
Expedient for the wise.—*Much Ado about Nothing,* v, 2, 85.
Expedient duty.—*Richard III,* i, 2, 217. The only uses of "expedient."

11
With all due expedience.
Richard II. Act ii, sc. 1, l. 287.
With all expedience.—*Henry V,* iv, 3, 70.
Dear expedience.—*I Henry IV,* i, 1, 33.
Expedience to the queen.—*Antony and Cleopatra,* i, 2, 185. The only uses of "expedience."

12
Then fiery expedition be my wing,
Jove's Mercury, and herald for a king!
Richard III. Act iv, sc. 3, l. 54. [King Richard]

Calm seas, auspicious gales
And sail so expeditious.
The Tempest. Act v, sc. 1, l. 314. [Prospero] The only use of "expeditious."

13
Even with the speediest expedition
I will dispatch him.
The Two Gentlemen of Verona. Act i, sc. 3, l. 37. [Antonio]

Longer than swiftest expedition
Will give thee time to leave.
The Two Gentlemen of Verona. Act iii, sc. 1, l. 164. [Duke]

Good expedition be my friend, and comfort.
The Winter's Tale. Act i, sc. 2, l. 458. [Polixenes]

EXPENSE

1 What expense by the hour
Seems to flow from him!
Henry VIII. Act iii, sc. 2, l. 108. [King Henry]
More hath he spent in peace than they in wars.
Richard II. Act ii, sc. 1, l. 255. [Northumberland]

2
To have the expense and waste of his revenues.
King Lear. Act ii, sc. 1, l. 102. [Regan]

3
We shall not spend a large expense of time.
Macbeth, v, 8, 60. See under TIME.
Expense of . . . breath.—*Love's Labour 's Lost,* v, 2, 523.
Expense of so much money.—*The Merry Wives of Windsor,* ii, 2, 147.
Expense of spirit.—*Sonnets,* cxxix.

4 My state being gall'd with my expense,
I seek to heal it only by his wealth.
The Merry Wives of Windsor. Act iii, sc. 4, l. 5. [Fenton]

5 For this intelligence
If I have thanks, it is a dear expense.
A Midsummer-Night's Dream. Act i, sc. 1, l. 248. [Helena]
High expense.—*Pericles,* iii, Gower, 20.
Rich expense.—*Pericles,* v, Gower, 19.
Cost me some expense.—*The Comedy of Errors,* iii, 1, 123.
At what expense.—*Hamlet,* ii, 1, 9.
At whose expense.—*Pericles,* iv, 3, 46.
Without expense at all.—*I Henry VI,* i, 1, 76.

6
Moan the expense of many a vanish'd sight.
Sonnets. No. xxx.
Husband nature's riches from expense.
Sonnets. No. xciv.

7
No care, no stop! so senseless of expense,
That he will neither know how to maintain it,
Nor cease his flow of riot.
Timon of Athens. Act ii, sc. 2, l. 1. [Flavius]
I might so have rated my expense,
As I had leave of means.
Timon of Athens. Act ii, sc. 2, l. 135. [Timon]

8
Hold, there 's expenses for thee.
Twelfth Night. Act iii, sc. 1, l. 49. [Viola]
For your expenses.—*I Henry VI,* v, 5, 92. The only uses of "expenses."

EXPERIENCE

9
Pawn their experience to their present pleasure.
Antony and Cleopatra, i, 4, 32. See under BOY.
Experience . . . ne'er before
Did violate so itself.
Antony and Cleopatra, iii, 10, 23. See under SHAME.

10
Jaques: I have gained my experience.
Rosalind: And your experience makes you sad: I had rather have a fool to make me merry than experience to make me sad.
As You Like It. Act iv, sc. 1, l. 26.

11
In my every action to be guided by others' experiences.
Cymbeline. Act i, sc. 4, l. 49. [Posthumus]
Nor gives it satisfaction to our blood,
That we must curb it upon others' proof.
A Lover's Complaint, l. 162.

12
Experience, O, thou disprovest report!
Cymbeline. Act iv, sc. 2, l. 34. [Imogen]

13
Ha! here 's three on 's are sophisticated!
King Lear. Act iii, sc. 4, l. 110. [King Lear] The only use of "sophisticated."

14
Armado: How hast thou purchased this experience?
Moth: By my penny of observation.
Love's Labour 's Lost. Act iii, sc. 1, l. 27.
Experience be a jewel that I have purchased at an infinite rate.
The Merry Wives of Windsor. Act ii, sc. 2, l. 213. [Ford]
Thou art experienced.—*Coriolanus,* iv, 5, 145.
Clerk-like experienced.—*The Winter's Tale,* i, 2, 392. The only use of "clerk-like."
Experienced tongue.—*Troilus and Cressida,* i, 3, 68. The only uses of "experienced."

15
Experience for me many bulwarks builded
Of proofs new-bleeding, which remain'd the foil
Of this false jewel, and his amorous spoil.
A Lover's Complaint, l. 152. The only use of "new-bleeding."

16
I shall have so much experience for my pains.
Othello. Act ii, sc. 3, l. 373. [Roderigo]

17 An arrow shot
From a well-experienced archer hits the mark
His eye doth level at.
Pericles. Act i, sc. 1, l. 163. [Messenger] The only use of "well-experienced."

18
Peace, peace, and give experience tongue.
Pericles. Act i, sc. 2, l. 37. [Helicanus]

19
Make bold her bashful years with your experience.
Richard III. Act iv, sc. 4, l. 326. [King Richard]

20 My frosty signs and chaps of age,
Grave witnesses of true experience.
Titus Andronicus. Act v, sc. 3, l. 77. [Marcus]
Long experience.—*Comedy of Errors,* iii, 1, 89.
Manifest experience.—*All 's Well that Ends Well,* i, 3, 229.
Old experience.—*All 's Well that Ends Well,* ii, 1, 110.
Small experience.—*The Taming of the Shrew,* i, 2, 52.
Thou . . . want'st experience.—*II Henry VI,* v, 1, 171.

1
Experience is by industry achieved
And perfected by the swift course of time.
The Two Gentlemen of Verona. Act i, sc. 3, l. 22. [Antonio]
His years but young, but his experience old.
The Two Gentlemen of Verona. Act ii, sc. 4, l. 69. [Valentine]

EXPERIMENT

2
Dear sir, to my endeavours give consent;
Of heaven, not me, make an experiment.
All's Well that Ends Well. Act ii, sc. 1, l. 156. [Helena]
3
And bring him out that is but woman's son
Can trace me in the tedious ways of art
And hold me pace in deep experiments.
I Henry IV. Act iii, sc. 1, l. 47. [Glendower]
Make another experiment.—*The Merry Wives of Windsor,* iv, 2, 36.
4
Singled forth to try experiments.
Titus Andronicus. Act ii, sc. 3, l. 69. [Lavinia] The only uses of "experiment." "Experimental" occurs in *Much Ado about Nothing,* iv, 1, 168.

EXPLOIT

See also Enterprise

5
Do more exploits with his mace than a morris-pike.
The Comedy of Errors. Act iv, sc. 3, l. 28. [Dromio of Syracuse] The only use of "morris-pike" (Moorish-pike).
I will work him
To an exploit, now ripe in my device,
Under the which he shall not choose but fall.
Hamlet. Act iv, sc. 7, l. 64. [King]
6
Of all exploits since I first follow'd arms,
Ne'er heard I of a warlike enterprise
More venturous or desperate than this.
I Henry VI. Act ii, sc. 1, l. 43. [Alençon]
A trim exploit, a manly enterprise.
A Midsummer-Night's Dream, iii, 2, 157. See under Ridicule.
Close exploit.—*Richard III,* iv, 2, 35.
Dread exploit.—*King Lear,* ii, 2, 130; *Macbeth,* iv, 1, 144.
Fell exploits.—*The Rape of Lucrece,* l. 429.
Fond exploit.—*Richard III,* v, 3, 330.
Great exploit.—*I Henry IV,* i, 3, 199.
High exploits.—*Titus Andronicus,* v, 1, 11.
Late exploits.—*II Henry VI,* i, 1, 196.
Night's exploit.—*II Henry IV,* i, 2, 169.
Worthy exploit.—*All's Well that Ends Well,* iii, 6, 72.
7
Brutus: Would you were not sick!
Ligarius: I am not sick, if Brutus have in hand
Any exploit worthy the name of honour.
Brutus: Such an exploit have I in hand, Ligarius,
Had you a healthful ear to hear of it.
Julius Cæsar. Act ii, sc. 1, l. 315.
What exploit 's in hand?
Troilus and Cressida. Act iii, sc. 1, l. 89. [Paris]
Ripe for exploits.—*Henry V,* i, 2, 121.
Sick for . . . exploit.—*All's Well that Ends Well,* i, 2, 17.

EXTREMES

8
Between the extremes Of hot and cold.
Antony and Cleopatra, i, 5, 51. See under Year.
No midway 'Twixt these extremes at all.
Antony and Cleopatra. Act iii, sc. 4, l. 19. [Octavia]
'Twixt two extremes.—*King Lear,* v, 3, 198.
Fierce extremes.—*King John,* v, 7, 13.
Undeserved extremes.—*King John,* iv, 1, 108.
9
Devise extremes beyond eternity.
The Rape of Lucrece, l. 969.
10 Haply my presence
May well abate the over-merry spleen
Which otherwise would grow into extremes.
Taming of the Shrew. Induction, sc. 1, l. 136. [Lord] The only use of "over-merry."
11 Speak with possibilities,
And do not break into these deep extremes.
Titus Andronicus. Act iii, sc. 1, l. 215. [Marcus] "Possibilities" is repeated in *The Merry Wives of Windsor,* i, 1, 65.
To chide at your extremes it not becomes me.
Winter's Tale. Act iv, sc. 4, l. 6. [Perdita]

EXTREMITY

See also Adversity

12 You were used
To say extremity was the trier of spirits;
That common chances common men could bear;
That when the sea was calm all boats alike
Show'd mastership in floating; fortune's blows,
When most struck home, being gentle wounded, craves
A noble cunning.
Coriolanus. Act iv, sc. 1, l. 3. [Coriolanus] The only use of "trier."
This extremity Hath brought me to thy hearth.
Coriolanus. Act iv, sc. 5, l. 84. [Coriolanus]
13
What blows, what extremities he endured.
I Henry VI. Act i, sc. 2, l. 213. [Poins]
Any extremity rather than a mischief.
The Merry Wives of Windsor. Act iv, sc. 2, l. 75. [Falstaff]
14
What it was that next came in her eye,
Which she must dote on in extremity.
A Midsummer-Night's Dream. Act iii, sc. 2, l. 2. [Oberon]
15
Extremity still urgeth such extremes.
The Rape of Lucrece, l. 1337.
Tempering extremities with extreme sweet.
Romeo and Juliet. Act ii, Prologue, l. 14.
16 'Tis she
That tempers him to this extremity.
Richard III. Act i, sc. 1, l. 64. [Clarence]

1
Every thing in extremity.
Romeo and Juliet. Act i, sc. 3, l. 102. [Servant]

In extremity.—*As You Like It,* iv, 1, 5; *Richard II,* ii, 2, 72; *Winter's Tale,* v, 2, 20; *Hamlet,* iii, 2, 178; *Troilus and Cressida,* iv, 5, 78.

In great extremity.—*Henry VIII,* v, 1, 19.

In this extremity.—*The Taming of the Shrew,* iv, 2, 102.

2
The middle of humanity thou never knewest, but the extremity of both ends: when thou wast in thy gilt and thy perfume, they mocked thee for too much curiosity; in thy rags thou knowest none, but art despised for the contrary.
Timon of Athens. Act iv, sc. 3, l. 300. [Apemantus]

Extremity of griefs.—*Titus Andronicus,* iv, 1, 19.

Extremity of love.—*As You Like It,* iv, 3, 23.

Extremity of dire mishap.—*The Comedy of Errors,* i, 1, 142.

Extremity of rage.—*The Comedy of Errors,* v, 1, 48.

Extremity of the skies.—*King Lear,* iii, 4, 106.

Extremity of weather.—*The Winter's Tale,* v, 2, 129.

Time's extremity.—*Comedy of Errors,* v, 1, 307.

3
The edge of all extremity.
Troilus and Cressida. Act iv, sc. 5, l. 68. [Æneas]

EYE

See also Blindness, Sight

I—Familiar Phrases

4
Her eye is sick on 't: I observe her now.
All's Well that Ends Well. Act i, sc. 3, l. 142. [Countess]

Mine eyes did sicken at the sight, and could not
Endure a further view.
Antony and Cleopatra. Act iii, sc. 10, l. 17. [Enobarbus]

To see 't mine eyes are blasted.
Antony and Cleopatra. Act iii, sc. 10, l. 4. [Enobarbus]

5
In such a business give me leave to use
The help of mine own eyes.
All's Well that Ends Well. Act ii, sc. 3, l. 114. [Bertram]

Now, when thou wakest, with thine own fool eyes peep.
A Midsummer-Night's Dream. Act iv, sc. 1, l. 87. [Puck]

6
Mecænas: This in the public eye?
Cæsar: I' the common show-place, where they exercise.
Antony and Cleopatra. Act iii, sc. 6, l. 11. The only use of "show-place."

The vulgar eye.—*Coriolanus,* iv, 7, 21. The only use of the phrase.

The world's eye.—*Sonnets,* lxix.

7
I have eyes upon him,
And his affairs come to me on the wind.
Antony and Cleopatra. Act iii, sc. 6, l. 62. [Cæsar]

I have an eye of you.
Hamlet. Act ii, sc. 2, l. 301. [Hamlet]

Still keep eyes upon her.—*Macbeth,* v, 1, 85.

Turn your eyes upon me.—*Pericles,* v, 1, 102.

8
The wise gods seel our eyes.
Antony and Cleopatra, iii, 13, 112. "Seel" is used twice more, both times in *Othello,* i, 3, 270; iii, 3, 210.

To flatter Cæsar, would you mingle eyes
With one that ties his points?
Antony and Cleopatra. Act iii, sc. 13, l. 156. [Antony]

I will not . . . be chastised with the sober eye
Of dull Octavia.
Antony and Cleopatra. Act v, sc. 2, l. 54. [Cleopatra]

9
He threw his eye aside,
And mark what object did present itself.
As You Like It. Act iv, sc. 3, l. 103. [Oliver]

Throw thine eye On yon young boy.
King John, iii, 3, 59. See under Serpent.

10
Fixing our eyes on whom our care was fix'd.
The Comedy of Errors. Act i, sc. 1, l. 85. [Ægeon]

Gazing in mine eyes, feeling my pulse.
The Comedy of Errors. Act v, sc. 1, l. 243. [Antipholus of Ephesus]

Gazed for tidings in my eager eyes.
The Rape of Lucrece, l. 254.

11
Whither do you follow your eyes so fast?
Coriolanus. Act ii, sc. 1, l. 108. [Menenius]

What a haste looks through his eyes! So should he look
That seems to speak things strange.
Macbeth. Act i, sc. 2, l. 46. [Lennox]

12
Turns up the white o' the eye to his discourse.
Coriolanus. Act iv, sc. 5, l. 209. [Third Servant] The only use of the phrase "white of the eye."

These eyes are not the same I wore in Rome.
Coriolanus. Act v, sc. 3, l. 38. [Coriolanus]

13
This object, which
Takes prisoner the wild motion of mine eye,
Fixing it only here.
Cymbeline. Act i, sc. 6, l. 102. [Iachimo]

He eyes us not.—*Cymbeline,* v, 5, 124.

14
Their oppress'd and fear-surprised eyes.
Hamlet. Act i, sc. 2, l. 203. [Horatio] The only use of "fear-surprised."

Fearful eyes.—*Venus and Adonis,* l. 927.

15
I mine eyes will rivet to his face.
Hamlet. Act iii, sc. 2, l. 90. [Hamlet]

Bear a wary eye.—*Hamlet,* v, 2, 290.

16
Hast thou never an eye in thy head?
I Henry IV. Act ii, sc. 1, l. 31. [Carrier]

Have you eyes?—*Hamlet,* iii, 4, 65.

Where are his eyes?—*King Lear,* i, 4, 247. See under Identity.

1 Not an eye
But is a-weary of thy common sight.
I Henry IV. Act iii, sc. 2, l. 87. [King Henry]

Nothing confutes me but eyes, and nobody sees me.
I Henry IV. Act v, sc. 4, l. 129. [Falstaff]

2
These mine eyes saw him in bloody state,
Rendering faint quittance, wearied and out-breathed,
To Harry Monmouth; whose swift wrath beat down
The never-daunted Percy to the earth.
II Henry IV. Act i, sc. 1, l. 107. [Morton] The only use of "out-breathed" and "never-daunted."

His eye is hollow.
II Henry IV. Act iv, sc. 5, l. 6. [Clarence]

Hollow eye.—*The Merchant of Venice,* iv, 1, 270; *Pericles,* i, 4, 51.

3
For there is none of you so mean and base,
That hath not noble lustre in your eyes.
Henry V. Act iii, sc. 1, l. 29. [King Henry]

And that same eye whose bend doth awe the world
Did lose his lustre.
Julius Cæsar. Act i, sc. 2, l. 123. [Cassius]

Out, vile jelly! Where is thy lustre now?
King Lear. Act iii, sc. 7, l. 83. [Cornwall]

An eye
Base and unlustrous as the smoky light
That 's fed with stinking tallow.
Cymbeline. Act i, sc. 6, l. 108. [Iachimo] The only use of "unlustrous."

Lack-lustre eye.—*As You Like It,* ii, 7, 21. The only use of this phrase in the plays. See under TIME for full quotation.

4
His eyes are humbler than they used to be.
Henry V. Act iv, sc. 7, l. 70. [Gloucester]

5
I have but with a cursorary eye
O'erglanced the articles.
Henry V. Act v, sc. 2, l. 77. [French King] The only use of "cursorary" and "o'erglanced." "Overglance" occurs in *Love's Labour 's Lost,* iv, 2, 135: "I will overglance the superscript," which is the only use of "superscript."

6
Gloucester: Let me see thine eyes: wink now: now open them:
In my opinion yet thou see'st not well.
Simpcox: Yes, master, clear as day, I thank God and Saint Alban.
II Henry VI. Act ii, sc. 1, l. 105.

O thou eternal Mover of the heavens,
Look with a gentle eye upon this wretch!
II Henry VI. Act iii, sc. 3, l. 19. [King Henry]

O Thou, whose captain I account myself,
Look on my forces with a gracious eye.
Richard III, v, 3, 108. See under PRAYER.

7
Oppose thy steadfast-gazing eyes to mine,
See if thou canst outface me with thy looks.
II Henry VI. Act iv, sc. 10, l. 48. [Iden] The only use of "steadfast-gazing."

They seemed almost, with staring on one another, to tear the cases of their eyes.
The Winter's Tale. Act v, sc. 2, l. 13. [Gentleman]

Eye to eye.—*Henry V,* v, 2, 30; *Troilus and Cressida,* iii, 3, 107.

8
Let thine eye be thy cook.
Henry V. Act v, sc. 2, l. 156. [King Henry]

9
These eyes, like lamps whose wasting oil is spent,
Wax dim, as drawing to their exigent.
I Henry VI. Act ii, sc. 5, l. 8. [Mortimer] "Exigent," in the sense of end, is repeated in *Antony and Cleopatra,* iv, 14, 63. In the sense of emergency, it is used in *Julius Cæsar,* v, 1, 19.

Were never four such lamps together mix'd.
Venus and Adonis, l. 489.

Two lamps, burnt out.—*Venus and Adonis,* l. 1128.

Wasting lamps.—*The Comedy of Errors,* v, 1, 315. The only uses of "lamps" with reference to the eyes.

10
Let some graver eye pierce into that.
Henry VIII. Act i, sc. 1, l. 67. [Abergavenny]

Every eye saw 'em.—*Henry VIII,* iii, 1, 35.

11
The eye sees not itself, But by reflection.
Julius Cæsar. Act i, sc. 2, l. 52. [Brutus]

If that thou couldst see me without eyes.
King John. Act iii, sc. 3, l. 48. [King John]

12
Turn'd an eye of doubt upon my face.
King John. Act iv, sc. 2, l. 233. [King John]

On my face he turn'd an eye of death.
I Henry IV. Act i, sc. 3, l. 143. [Hotspur]

The eye of anguish.—*King Lear,* iv, 4, 15.

A still-soliciting eye.—*King Lear,* i, 1, 234. The only use of "still-soliciting."

False eyes.—*Measure for Measure,* iv, 1, 60.

Foolish eyes.—*Merchant of Venice,* i, 2, 130.

Foul imaginary eyes.—*King John,* iv, 2, 269.

Glutton eye.—*Venus and Adonis,* l. 399.

Hawking eye.—*All 's Well that Ends Well,* i, 1, 105.

Sovereign eye.—*Sonnets,* xxxiii.

Traitor eye.—*The Rape of Lucrece,* l. 73.

Unattainted eye.—*Romeo and Juliet,* i, 2, 90. The only use of "unattainted."

Wilful eye.—*The Rape of Lucrece,* l. 426.

Wounded eye.—*Taming of the Shrew,* i, 1, 225.

13
I remember thine eyes well enough. Dost thou squiny at me?
King Lear. Act iv, sc. 6, l. 139. [King Lear] The only use of "squiny" in the plays. "Squints the eye" also occurs but once, in *King Lear,* iii, 4, 122.

That eye that told you so look'd but a-squint.
King Lear. Act v, sc. 3, l. 72. [Goneril] The only use of "a-squint."

14
By heaven, the wonder in a mortal eye!
Love's Labour 's Lost. Act iv, sc. 3, l. 85. [Dumain]

Mortal eyes.—*Richard III,* i, 2, 45; *The Rape of Lucrece,* l. 163.

Admiring eyes.—*I Henry IV,* iii, 2, 80.

Charmed eye.—*A Midsummer-Night's Dream,* iii, 2, 376.
Enthralled eyes.—*The Two Gentlemen of Verona,* ii, 4, 134.
Up-turned wondering eyes.—*Romeo and Juliet,* ii, 2, 29. The only use of "up-turned."

1
Your eyes do make no coaches.
Love's Labour 's Lost. Act iv, sc. 3, l. 155. [Biron]

My eyes are then no eyes.
Love's Labour 's Lost. Act iv, sc. 3, l. 232. [Biron]

His eye ambitious.—*Love's Labour 's Lost,* v, 1, 12.

2
Under the cool shade of a sycamore
I thought to close mine eyes some half an hour.
Love's Labour 's Lost. Act v, sc. 2, l. 89. [Boyet]

Sleeping eyes.—*A Midsummer-Night's Dream,* iii, 1, 176.

3
And laugh upon the apple of her eye.
Love's Labour 's Lost. Act v, sc. 2, l. 475. [Biron] "Apple of his eye" is used in *A Midsummer-Night's Dream,* iii, 2, 104.

4
Mine eyes are made the fools o' the other senses,
Or else worth all the rest.
Macbeth. Act ii, sc. 1, l. 44. [Macbeth]

Doctor: You see, her eyes are open.
Gentlewoman: Ay, but their sense is shut.
Macbeth. Act v, sc. 1, l. 29.

Do not ope thine eyes.—*Much Ado about Nothing,* iv, 1, 125.
Take heed, have open eye.—*The Merry Wives of Windsor,* ii, 1, 126.
Eyes wide open.—*The Tempest,* ii, 1, 214.

5
You that have worn your eyes almost out in the service.
Measure for Measure. Act i, sc. 2, l. 113. [Pompey]

6
Methinks I see a quickening in his eye.
Measure for Measure. Act v, sc. 1, l. 500. [Duke] "Quickening" is repeated in *Timon of Athens,* iv, 3, 184.

A quick eye.—*The Winter's Tale,* iv, 4, 685.

7
In the twinkling of an eye.
Merchant of Venice, ii, 2, 177. The only use of this phrase in the plays. The nearest to it is "Every wink of an eye some new grace will be born," *The Winter's Tale,* v, 2, 119.

8
Well, thou shalt see, thy eyes shall be thy judge.
The Merchant of Venice. Act ii, sc. 5, l. 1, [Shylock]

My eyes, my lord, can look as swift as yours.
The Merchant of Venice. Act iii, sc. 2, l. 199. [Gratiano]

9
Whether had you rather lead mine eyes, or eye your master's heels?
The Merry Wives of Windsor. Act iii, sc. 2, l. 3. [Mistress Page]

10
Of force she must be eyed.
A Midsummer-Night's Dream. Act iii, sc. 2, l. 40. [Puck]

I eyed them Even to their ships.
The Winter's Tale. Act ii, sc. 1, l. 35. [First Lord]

Full many a lady I have eyed with best regard.
Tempest. Act iii, sc. 1, l. 40. [Ferdinand]

You throw a strange regard upon me.
Twelfth Night. Act v, sc. 1, l. 219. [Sebastian]

11
O, how mine eyes do loathe his visage now!
A Midsummer-Night's Dream. Act iv, sc. 1, l. 82. [Titania]

Methinks I see these things with parted eye,
When every thing seems double.
A Midsummer-Night's Dream. Act iv, sc. 1, l. 193. [Hermia]

12
I have a good eye, uncle; I can see a church by daylight.
Much Ado about Nothing. Act ii, sc. 1, l. 85. [Beatrice]

May I be so converted and see with these eyes? I cannot tell; I think not.
Much Ado about Nothing. Act ii, sc. 3, l. 123. [Benedick]

How you may be converted I know not, but methinks you look with your eyes as other women do.
Much Ado about Nothing. Act iii, sc. 4, l. 91. [Margaret]

13
Are our eyes our own?
Much Ado about Nothing. Act iv, sc. 1, l. 72. [Claudio]

I have deceived even your very eyes.
Much Ado about Nothing. Act v, sc. 1, l. 238. [Borachio]

Mine eye may be deceived.—*Sonnets,* civ.

14
With my personal eye Will I look to 't.
Othello. Act ii, sc. 3, l. 5. [Cassio]

Wear your eye thus, not jealous nor secure.
Othello. Act iii, sc. 3, l. 198. [Iago]

Let me see your eyes; Look in my face.
Othello. Act iv, sc. 2, l. 25. [Othello]

Do you perceive the gastness of her eye?
Othello. Act v, sc. 1, l. 106. [Iago] The only use of "gastness."

15
Make it a darling like your precious eye.
Othello. Act iii, sc. 4, l. 66. [Othello]

Precious eye.—*King John,* iii, 1, 79.

16
Not daring trust the office of mine eyes.
The Passionate Pilgrim, l. 196.

I am ready to distrust mine eyes.
Twelfth Night. Act iv, sc. 3, l. 13. [Sebastian]

Is there no exorcist
Beguiles the truer office of mine eyes?
All's Well that Ends Well. Act v, sc. 3, l. 305. [King] "Exorcist" is repeated in *Julius Cæsar,* ii, 1, 323.

17
The sore eyes see clear.
Pericles. Act i, sc. 1, l. 99. [Pericles]

Sore eye.—*Troilus and Cressida,* v 1, 36.

1
The eye of heaven is out.
The Rape of Lucrece, l. 356.
Sometimes too hot the eye of heaven shines.
Sonnets, xviii. See under SUN.
Eye of heaven.—*Richard II,* i, 3, 275.
Heaven's eye.—*Titus Andronicus,* ii, 1, 130; iv, 2, 59.
2
She, much amazed, breaks ope her lock'd-up eyes.
The Rape of Lucrece, l. 446. The only use of "lock'd-up."
Her pity-pleading eyes are sadly fixed
In the remorseless wrinkles of his face.
The Rape of Lucrece, l. 561. The only use of "pity-pleading."
An eye of pity.—*Merchant of Venice,* iv, 1, 27.
Eyes of pity.—*The Winter's Tale,* iii, 2, 123.
3
Men's eyes were made to look, and let them gaze.
Romeo and Juliet. Act iii, sc. 1, l. 57. [Mercutio]
To prison, eyes, ne'er look on liberty!
Romeo and Juliet. Act iii, sc. 2, l. 58. [Juliet]
Eyes, look your last.—*Romeo and Juliet,* v, 3, 112.
They look'd but with divining eyes.
Sonnets. No. cvi.
4
Against that time when thou shalt strangely pass
And scarcely greet me with that sun, thine eye.
Sonnets. No. xlix.
All askance he holds her in his eye.
Venus and Adonis, l. 342.
Askance their eyes.—*Rape of Lucrece,* l. 637.
Look askance.—*Taming of the Shrew,* ii, 1, 249.
Look'd . . . Askance and strangely.—*Sonnets,* cx. The only uses of "askance."
Wafting his eyes to the contrary.
The Winter's Tale. Act i, sc. 2, l. 372. [Polixenes]
5
To make mine eye the witness
Of that report which I so oft have heard.
The Taming of the Shrew. Act ii, sc. 1, l. 52. [Petruchio]
His eyes had seen the proof.
Othello. Act i, sc. 1, l. 28. [Iago]
If these be true spies which I wear in my head, here's a goodly sight.
The Tempest. Act v, sc. 1, l. 259. [Trinculo]
6
An eye-sore to our solemn festival!
The Taming of the Shrew. Act iii, sc. 2, l. 103. [Baptista]
Be an eye-sore in my golden coat.
The Rape of Lucrece, l. 205. The only uses of "eye-sore."
7
Mine eyes, never since at ebb.
Tempest. Act i, sc. 2, l. 435. [Ferdinand]
They only now come but to feast thine eyes.
Timon of Athens. Act i, sc. 2, l. 133. [Cupid]
8
We worldly men
Have miserable, mad, mistaking eyes.
Titus Andronicus. Act v, sc. 2, l. 65. [Titus]
Deep-sunken eyes.—*Sonnets,* ii. The only use of "deep-sunken."

Wretched eyes.—*Titus Andronicus,* iii, 1, 263.
9
Unplausive eyes are bent on him.
Troilus and Cressida. Act iii, sc. 3, l. 43. [Ulysses] The only use of "unplausive."
Assailing eyes.—*Romeo and Juliet,* i, 1, 219.
10
The present eye praises the present object.
Troilus and Cressida. Act iii, sc. 3, l. 180. [Ulysses]
Mine own searching eyes
Shall find him by his large and portly size.
Troilus and Cressida. Act iv, sc. 5, l. 161. [Hector]
I have fed mine eyes on thee;
I have with exact view perused thee, Hector,
And quoted joint by joint.
Troilus and Cressida. Act iv, sc. 5, l. 231. [Achilles]
Why dost thou so oppress me with thine eye?
Troilus and Cressida. Act iv, sc. 5, l. 241. [Hector]
Catch the eye.—*Troilus and Cressida,* iii, 3, 183.
11
O, for a stone-bow, to hit him in the eye!
Twelfth Night. Act ii, sc. 5, l. 51. [Sir Toby] The only use of "stone-bow."
12
Ay, an you had any eye behind you, you might see more detraction at your heels than fortunes before you.
Twelfth Night. Act ii, sc. 5, l. 148. [Fabian]
13
Not an eye that sees you but is a physician, to comment on your malady.
The Two Gentlemen of Verona. Act ii, sc. 1, l. 41. [Speed]
O, that you had mine eyes.
The Two Gentlemen of Verona. Act ii, sc. 1, l. 76. [Speed]
Having no eyes.—*The Two Gentlemen of Verona,* ii, 3, 14.
Nought but mine eye Could have persuaded me.
The Two Gentlemen of Verona. Act v, sc. 4, l. 64. [Valentine]
14
She had one eye declined for the loss of her husband, another elevated that the oracle was fulfilled.
The Winter's Tale. Act v, sc. 2, l. 81. [Third Gentleman] The only use of "elevated."
One of the prettiest touches of all and that which angled for mine eyes, caught the water though not the fish.
The Winter's Tale. Act v, sc. 2, l. 88. [Third Gentleman]

II—The Angry Eye

15
His eyes full of anger.
As You Like It. Act i, sc. 3, l. 42. [Celia]
I shall here abide the hourly shot
Of angry eyes.
Cymbeline. Act i, sc. 1, l. 89. [Imogen]
Angry eyes.—*The Rape of Lucrece,* l. 1469.
16
Thou tell'st me there is murder in mine eye:
'Tis pretty, sure, and very probable,
That eyes, that are the frail'st and softest things,
Who shut their coward gates on atomies,

Should be call'd tyrants, butchers, murderers!
Now I do frown on thee with all my heart;
And if mine eyes can wound, now let them kill thee. . . .
Lie not to say mine eyes are murderers!
Now show the wound mine eye hath made in thee:
Scratch thee but with a pin, and there remains
Some scar of it; lean but upon a rush,
The cicatrice and capable impressure
Thy palm some moment keeps; but now mine eyes
Which I have darted at thee, hurt thee not,
Nor, I am sure, there is no force in eyes
That can do hurt.
As You Like It. Act iii, sc. 5, l. 10. [Phebe] The only use of "frail'st." "Atomies" is repeated in *As You Like It,* iii, 2, 245, and in *Romeo and Juliet,* i, 4, 57. "Atomy" occurs once, in *II Henry IV,* v, 4, 33. "Impressure" is repeated in *Troilus and Cressida,* iv, 5, 131, and in *Twelfth Night,* ii, 5, 103.

I have look'd on thousands, who have sped the better
By my regard, but kill'd none so.
The Winter's Tale. Act i, sc. 2, l. 389. [Polixenes]

Dangerous eyes may well be charm'd asleep
With grant of our most just and right desires.
II Henry IV. Act iv, sc. 2, l. 39. [Archbishop]

1
His sparkling eyes, replete with wrathful fire,
More dazzled and drove back his enemies
Than mid-day sun fierce bent against their faces.
I Henry VI. Act i, sc. 1, l. 12. [Gloucester]

2
His eye reviled Me, as his abject object.
Henry VIII. Act i, sc. 1, l. 126. [Buckingham]

3
I have not from your eyes that gentleness
And show of love as I was wont to have.
Julius Cæsar. Act i, sc. 2, l. 32. [Cassius]

4
Such ferret and such fiery eyes.
Julius Cæsar. Act i, sc. 2, l. 186. [Brutus]

With fiery eyes sparkling for very wrath.
III Henry VI, ii, 5, 131. See under DANGER for full quotation.

His eye drops fire, no water thence proceeds;
Those round clear pearls of his, that move thy pity,
Are balls of quenchless fire to burn thy city.
The Rape of Lucrece, l. 1552.

Fiery eyes.—*Venus and Adonis,* l. 219.
Rolling eyes.—*King John,* iv, 2, 192.
Threatening eye.—*King John,* iii, 4, 120.
Unpleased eye.—*Richard II,* iii, 3, 193.

5
A fearful eye thou hast.
King John. Act iv, sc. 2, l. 106. [King John]

Look, where he sits and glares!
Wantest thou eyes at trial, madam?
King Lear. Act iii, sc. 6, l. 25. [Edgar]

6
Thy eye Jove's lightning bears.
Love's Labour's Lost. Act iv, sc. 2, l. 119. [Sir Nathaniel]

Thine eye Jove's lightning seems.
The Passionate Pilgrim, l. 67.

7
Their savage eyes turn'd to a modest gaze
By the sweet power of music.
The Merchant of Venice, v, 1, 78. See under MUSIC.

8
In her eye there hath appear'd a fire,
To burn the errors that these princes hold
Against her maiden truth.
Much Ado about Nothing. Act iv, sc. 1, l. 164. [Friar Francis]

9
Eyne of burning coal.
Pericles. Act iii, Gower, l. 5.

Burning eye.—*Romeo and Juliet,* ii, 3, 5; *Hamlet,* ii, 2, 540; *Venus and Adonis,* l. 178.

10
With much more contempt, men's eyes
Did scowl on gentle Richard; no man cried 'God save him!'
Richard II. Act v, sc. 2, l. 28. [York] "Scowl" is repeated in *Cymbeline,* i, 1, 15.

11
Your eyes do menace me.
Richard III. Act i, sc. 4, l. 176. [Clarence]

Me from myself thy cruel eye hath taken.
Sonnets. No. cxxxiii.

12
And we were better parch in Afric sun
Than in the pride and salt scorn of his eyes.
Troilus and Cressida. Act i, sc. 3, l. 370. [Ulysses] The only use of "parch."

Scornful eyes.—*King Lear,* ii, 4, 168.

13
A heavy, dark, disliking eye.
Venus and Adonis, l. 182. The only use of "disliking."

Thine eye darts forth the fire that burneth me.
Venus and Adonis, l. 196.

His eye, which scornfully glisters like fire,
Shows his hot courage and his high desire.
Venus and Adonis, l. 275.

III—The Gentle Eye

14
His goodly eyes, . . . now bend, now turn,
The office and devotion of their view
Upon a tawny front.
Antony and Cleopatra. Act i, sc. 1, l. 2. [Philo]

Beauteous eye.—*King John,* iv, 2, 15.
Bonny eye.—*Richard III,* i, 1, 94.
Chaste eye.—*As You Like It,* iii, 2, 3.
Cheerful eyes.—*King John,* iv, 2, 2.
Considerate eyes.—*Richard III,* iv, 2, 30.
Constant eye.—*The Two Gentlemen of Verona,* v, 4, 115.
Dainty eye.—*I Henry VI,* v, 3, 38.
Gentle eye.—*II Henry VI,* iii, 3, 20; *King John,* iv, 3, 150.
Graceful eyes.—*Antony and Cleopatra,* ii, 2, 60.
Gracious eye.—*Richard III,* v, 3, 108.
Modest eyes.—*Antony and Cleopatra,* iv, 15, 27.
Pleasing eye.—*I Henry IV,* ii, 4, 465.
Pretty eyes.—*Troilus and Cressida,* iv, 2, 4.

Richest eyes.—*All's Well that Ends Well,* v, 3, 17.
Steadfast eye.—*The Rape of Lucrece,* l. 1339.
Tender eye.—*Macbeth,* iii, 2, 47.
Tender dying eyes.—*I Henry VI,* iii, 3, 48.

1
And she, like harmless lightning, throws her eye
On him, her brothers, me, her master, hitting
Each object with a joy.
Cymbeline. Act v, sc. 5, l. 394. [Cymbeline]

2
With an auspicious and a dropping eye.
Hamlet. Act i, sc. 2, l. 11. [King]

Downward eye.—*Venus and Adonis,* l. 1106.

3 Cast thy nighted colour off,
And let thine eye look like a friend on Denmark.
Hamlet. Act i, sc. 2, l. 68. [Queen]

Here, in the cheer and comfort of our eye.
Hamlet. Act i, sc. 2, l. 116. [King]

To-morrow shall I beg leave to see your kingly eyes.
Hamlet. Act iv, sc. 7, l. 44. [King]

Kingly eye.—*King John,* v, 1, 47.
Princely eyes.—*Titus Andronicus,* i, 1, 429.

4
A largess universal like the sun
His liberal eye doth give to every one,
Thawing cold fear.
Henry V. Act iv, Prologue, l. 43. [Chorus] The only use of "thawing."

5 Her eyes are fierce; but thine
Do comfort and not burn.
King Lear. Act ii, sc. 4, l. 175. [King Lear]

Bless thy sweet eyes.—*King Lear,* iv, 1, 56.
Thy sweet eyes.—*Midsummer-Night's Dream,* v, 1, 336.
Those sweet eyes.—*A Midsummer-Night's Dream,* v, 1, 329.

6
And my true eyes have never practised how
To cloak offences with a cunning brow.
The Rape of Lucrece, l. 748.

When the devout religion of mine eye
Maintains such falsehood, then turn tears to fires.
Romeo and Juliet. Act i, sc. 2, l. 93. [Romeo]

7 Securely I espy
Virtue with valour couched in thine eye.
Richard II. Act i, sc. 3, l. 97. [King Richard]

8
There lives more life in one of your fair eyes
Than both your poets can in praise devise.
Sonnets. No. lxxxiii.

Fair eyes.—*All's Well that Ends Well,* ii, 3, 86; iii, 2, 110; *As You Like It,* i, 2, 198; *The Merchant of Venice,* v, 1, 242; *Henry VIII,* iv, 1, 84.

9
There can live no hatred in thine eye.
Sonnets. No. xciii.

Look on me with your welkin eye: sweet villain!
Winter's Tale. Act i, sc. 2, l. 136. [Leontes]

IV—The Mind's Eye

10
A mote it is to trouble the mind's eye.
Hamlet. Act i, sc. 1, l. 112. [Horatio]

You found his mote; the king your mote did see;
But I a beam do find in each of three.
Love's Labour's Lost. Act iv, sc. 3, l. 161. [Biron] See under BEAM.

O heaven, that there were but a mote in yours,
A grain, a dust, a gnat, a wandering hair,
Any annoyance in that precious sense!
King John. Act iv, sc. 1, l. 92. [Arthur]

11
Hamlet: Methinks I see my father.
Horatio: Where, my lord?
Hamlet: In my mind's eye, Horatio.
Hamlet. Act i, sc. 2, l. 184.

12
Each eye that saw him did enchant the mind.
A Lover's Complaint, l. 89.

13
Unseen, save to the eye of mind.
The Rape of Lucrece, l. 1426.

Eye of reason.—*I Henry IV,* iv, 1, 72.

With the eyes of heavy mind I see.
Richard II. Act ii, sc. 4, l. 18. [Salisbury]

14
Since I left you, mine eye is in my mind;
And that which governs me to go about
Doth part his function and is partly blind,
Seems seeing, but effectually is out; . . .
For if it see the rudest or gentlest sight,
The most sweet favour or deformed'st creature,
The mountain or the sea, the day or night,
The crow or dove, it shapes them to your feature:
Incapable of more, replete with you,
My most true mind thus makes mine eye untrue.
Sonnets. No. cxiii. "Effectually" is repeated in *Titus Andronicus,* iv, 4, 107. The only use of "deformed'st."

Ah, poor our sex! this fault in us I find,
The error of our eye directs our mind:
What error leads must err; O, then conclude
Minds sway'd by eyes are full of turpitude.
Troilus and Cressida. Act v, sc. 2, l. 109. [Cressida] "Turpitude" is repeated in *Antony and Cleopatra,* iv, 6, 33.

15
I do I know not what, and fear to find
Mine eye too great a flatterer for my mind.
Twelfth Night. Act i, sc. 5, l. 327. [Olivia]

Oft the eye mistakes, the brain being troubled.
Venus and Adonis, l. 1068.

V—The Speaking Eye

16
Let not my sister read it in your eye.
The Comedy of Errors. Act iii, sc. 2, l. 9. [Luciana]

17
The heart's still rhetoric disclosed with eyes.
Love's Labour's Lost. Act ii, sc. 1, l. 229. [Boyet]

Did not the heavenly rhetoric of thine eye,
'Gainst whom the world cannot hold argument,
Persuade my heart to this false perjury?
Love's Labour's Lost. Act iv, sc. 3, l. 60. [Longaville] Also *Passionate Pilgrim,* l. 29.

Methought all his senses were lock'd in his eye,
As jewels in crystal for some prince to buy.
Love's Labour's Lost. Act ii, sc. 1, l. 242. [Boyet]

1 Sometimes from her eyes
I did receive fair speechless messages.
The Merchant of Venice. Act i, sc. 1, l. 163. [Bassanio]

2
She speaks, yet she says nothing: what of that?
Her eye discourses; I will answer it.
Romeo and Juliet. Act ii, sc. 2, l. 12. [Romeo]

There's language in her eye.
Troilus and Cressida. Act iv, sc. 5, l. 55. [Ulysses]

3 I wish mine eyes
Would, with themselves, shut up my thoughts.
The Tempest. Act ii, sc. 1, l. 191. [Alonso]

VI—The Starry Eye

4 Those opposed eyes, . . .
Like the meteors of a troubled heaven.
I Henry IV. Act i, sc. 1, l. 9. [King Henry]

As I stood here below, methought his eyes
Were two full moons.
King Lear. Act iv, sc. 6, l. 69. [Edgar]

But hers, which through the crystal tears gave light,
Shone like the moon in water seen by night.
Venus and Adonis, l. 491.

5
Moth: Once to behold with your sun-beamed eyes,—with your sun-beamed eyes—
Boyet: They will not answer to that epithet;
You were best call it 'daughter-beamed eyes.'
Love's Labour's Lost. Act v, sc. 2, l. 168. The only use of "sun-beamed" and "daughter-beamed."

Her sun-bright eye.—*The Two Gentlemen of Verona,* iii, 1, 88. The only use of the phrase.

My mistress' eyes are nothing like the sun.
Sonnets. No. cxxx.

6
And those eyes, the break of day,
Lights that do mislead the morn.
Measure for Measure. Act iv, sc. 1, l. 3. [Song]

Her eyes in heaven
Would through the airy region stream so bright
That birds would sing and think it were not night.
Romeo and Juliet. Act ii, sc. 2, l. 20. [Romeo]

7
Thine eye would emulate the diamond.
The Merry Wives of Windsor. Act iii, sc. 3, l. 58. [Falstaff]

Your eyes are lode-stars.
A Midsummer-Night's Dream. Act i, sc. 1, l. 183. [Helena] "Lode-stars" is repeated in *The Rape of Lucrece,* l. 179.

Her eyes are jewel-like And cased as richly.
Pericles. Act v, sc. 1, l. 111. [Pericles] The only use of "jewel-like." "Cased" is repeated in *Richard II,* i, 3, 163, and in *Cymbeline,* v, 3, 22.

8
How came her eyes so bright? Not with salt tears:
If so, my eyes are oftener wash'd than hers.
A Midsummer-Night's Dream. Act ii, sc. 2, l. 92. [Helena]

Mortal stars, as bright as heaven's beauties.
The Rape of Lucrece, l. 13.

Bright eyes.—*Romeo and Juliet,* ii, 1, 17.

9
To what, my love, shall I compare thine eye?
Crystal is muddy.
A Midsummer-Night's Dream. Act iii, sc. 2, l. 138. [Demetrius]

Go, clear thy crystals.
Henry V. Act ii, sc. 3, l. 56. [Pistol]

Both crystals.—*Venus and Adonis,* l. 961.

Crystal the other's eyes.—*Love's Labour's Lost,* iv, 3, 142.

Thy crystal window ope.—*Cymbeline,* v, 4, 81.

Crystal eyne.—*Venus and Adonis,* l. 633.

Crystal eyes.—*Sonnets,* xlvi.

Crystal looks.—*The Two Gentlemen of Verona,* ii, 4, 89. The only uses of "crystal" and "crystals" as relating to the eye.

10
But from thine eyes my knowledge I derive,
And, constant stars, in them I read such art
As truth and beauty shall together thrive.
Sonnets. No. xiv.

What stars do spangle heaven with such beauty,
As those two eyes become that heavenly face?
The Taming of the Shrew. Act iv, sc. 5, l. 31. [Petruchio] The only use of "spangle."

Paulina: Were I the ghost that walk'd, I 'ld bid you mark
Her eye, and tell me for what dull part in 't
You chose her; then I 'ld shriek, that even your ears
Should rift to hear me; and the words that follow'd
Should be 'Remember mine.'
Leontes: Stars, stars,
And all eyes else dead coals!
The Winter's Tale. Act v, sc. 1, l. 63.

11
His eyes, like glow-worms, shine when he doth fret.
Venus and Adonis, l. 621.

Her eyes, as murder'd with the view,
Like stars ashamed of day, themselves withdrew.
Venus and Adonis, l. 1031.

VII—The Unseeing Eye

12 Our very eyes
Are sometimes like our judgements, blind.
Cymbeline. Act iv, sc. 2, l. 301. [Imogen]

There are none that want eyes to direct them the way I am going, but such as wink and will not use them.
Cymbeline. Act v, sc. 4, l. 192. [Posthumus]

What an infinite mock is this, that a man should have the best use of eyes to see the way of blindness!
Cymbeline. Act v, sc. 4, l. 195. [First Gaoler]

Mine eyes are weak.—*Cymbeline,* ii, 2, 3.

13 Seen, but with such eyes
As, sick and blunted with community,
Afford no extraordinary gaze,

Such as is bent on sun-like majesty
When it shines seldom in admiring eyes.
I Henry IV. Act iii, sc. 2, l. 76. [King Henry] The only use of "community" and "sun-like." "Blunted" occurs again in *Hamlet*, iii, 4, 111: "Blunted purpose."

See better, Lear; and let me still remain
The true blank of thine eye.
King Lear. Act i, sc. 1, l. 160. [Kent]

1
Here she exclaims against repose and rest,
And bids her eyes hereafter still be blind.
The Rape of Lucrece, l. 757.

2
When most I wink, then do mine eyes best see,
For all the day they view things unrespected;
But when I sleep, in dreams they look on thee,
And darkly bright are bright in dark directed.
Sonnets. No. xliii. "Unrespected" is repeated in *Sonnets*, liv, and occurs nowhere else.

Gave eyes to blindness,
Or made them swear against the thing they see.
Sonnets. No. clii.

3
She shall have no more eyes to see withal than a cat.
The Taming of the Shrew. Act i, sc. 2, l. 115. [Grumio]

4
Pardon, old father, my mistaking eyes,
That have been so bedazzled with the sun
That every thing I look on seemeth green.
The Taming of the Shrew. Act iv, sc. 5, l. 45. [Katharina] The only use of "bedazzled."

Empty eye.—*The Merchant of Venice*, ii, 7, 63.
Purblind eye.—*I Henry VI*, ii, 4, 21.
Sightless eyes.—*Sonnets*, xliii.
Unseeing eyes.—*Sonnets*, xliii.

5
At his bloody view, her eyes are fled
Into the deep dark cabins of her head.
Venus and Adonis, l. 1037.

VIII—The Wanton Eye

6
I know his eye doth homage otherwhere.
The Comedy of Errors. Act ii, sc. 1, l. 104. [Adriana]

Hath not else his eye
Stray'd his affection in unlawful love?
A sin prevailing much in youthful men,
Who give their eyes the liberty of gazing.
The Comedy of Errors. Act v, sc. 1, l. 50. [Abbess]

To cast thy wandering eyes on every stale.
The Taming of the Shrew. Act iii, sc. 1, l. 90. [Hortensio]

7
At last I spied his eyes, and methought he had made two holes in the ale-wife's new petticoat and so peeped through.
II Henry IV. Act ii, sc. 2, l. 87. [Page] "Ale-wife" is repeated in *The Taming of the Shrew*, Ind., 2, 23.

False adulterate eyes.—*Sonnets*. No. cxxi.
Lewd eyes.—*The Rape of Lucrece*, l. 371, l. 392.
Lustful eye.—*III Henry VI*, iii, 5, 83; iii, 7, 187; *The Rape of Lucrece*, l. 179.

8
Her eye must be fed; and what delight shall she have to look on the devil?
Othello. Act ii, sc. 1, l. 228. [Iago]

Iago: What an eye she has! methinks it sounds a parley of provocation.
Cassio: An inviting eye; and yet methinks right modest.
Othello. Act ii, sc. 3, l. 22.

9
Nothing in him seem'd inordinate,
Save sometime too much wonder of his eye.
The Rape of Lucrece, l. 94.

She, that never coped with stranger eyes,
Could pick no meaning from their parling looks.
The Rape of Lucrece, l. 99. The only use of "parling."

Nor could she moralize his wanton sight,
More than his eyes were open'd to the light.
The Rape of Lucrece, l. 104.

That eye which looks on her confounds his wits.
The Rape of Lucrece, l. 290.

His eye, which late his mutiny restrains,
Unto a greater uproar tempts his veins.
The Rape of Lucrece, l. 426.

10
Tell me thou lovest elsewhere, but in my sight,
Dear heart, forbear to glance thine eye aside.
Sonnets. No. cxxxix.

Those
Whom thine eyes woo as mine importune thee.
Sonnets. No. cxlii.

Love's eye is not so true as all men's 'No.'
How can it? O, how can Love's eye be true,
That is so vex'd with watching and with tears?
Sonnets. No. cxlviii.

11
All eyes
Blind with the pin and web but theirs, theirs only,
That would unseen be wicked.
Winter's Tale. Act i, sc. 2, l. 290. [Leontes]

Your eye hath too much youth in 't.
Winter's Tale. Act v, sc. 1, l. 225. [Paulina]

IX—The Weeping Eye

See also Tears

12
The April 's in her eyes: it is love's spring,
And these the showers to bring it on.
Antony and Cleopatra. Act iii, sc. 2, l. 43. [Antony]

13
No longer will I be a fool,
To put the finger in the eye and weep,
Whilst man and master laugh my woes to scorn.
The Comedy of Errors. Act ii, sc. 2, l. 205. [Adriana]

Turn'd mine eye and wept.
Cymbeline. Act i, sc. 3, l. 22. [Imogen]

14
Such eyes the widows in Corioli wear,

And mothers that lack sons.
Coriolanus. Act ii, sc. 1, l. 195. [Coriolanus]

1
Have you not a moist eye?
II Henry IV, i, 2, 204. See under AGE AND YOUTH.
His eye brimful of tears.—*II Henry IV,* iii, 1, 67.

2
For, hearing this, I must perforce compound
With mistful eyes, or they will issue too.
Henry V. Act iv, sc. 6, l. 33. [King Henry] The only use of "mistful."
Rainy eyes.—*Richard II,* iii, 2, 146.
Wash'd eyes.—*King Lear,* i, 1, 271.
Weeping eyes.—*The Rape of Lucrece,* l. 1680; *Richard II,* i, 2, 74.

3
Why are thine eyes fix'd to the sullen earth,
Gazing on that which seems to dim thy sight?
II Henry VI. Act i, sc. 2, l. 5. [Duchess of Gloucester]
Mine eyes are full of tears, my heart of grief.
II Henry VI. Act ii, sc. 3, l. 17. [Gloucester]
I 'll prepare
My tear-stain'd eyes to see her miseries.
II Henry VI. Act iv, sc. 1, l. 15. [Gloucester] The only use of "tear-stain'd."

4
And if thine eyes can water for his death,
I give thee this to dry thy cheeks withal.
III Henry VI. Act i, sc. 4, l. 82. [Queen Margaret]
Beshrew me, but his passion moves me so
That hardly can I check my eyes from tears.
III Henry VI. Act i, sc. 4. l. 150. [Northumberland]
With tearful eyes add water to the sea.
III Henry VI. Act v, sc. 4, l. 8. [Queen Margaret] The only use of "tearful."

5
Many an orphan's water-standing eye.
III Henry VI, v, 6, 40. See under PROPHECY for full quotation. The only use of "water-standing."
Commend these waters to those baby eyes
That never saw the giant world enraged.
King John. Act v, sc. 2, l. 56. [Dauphin]
Shine . . . upon our watery eyne.
Love's Labour 's Lost, v, 2, 206. Shakespeare uses "eyne" thirteen times.
His watery eyes he did dismount,
Whose sights till then were levell'd on my face;
Each cheek a river running from a fount
With brinish current downward flow'd apace.
A Lover's Complaint, l. 281.
Mine eyes cannot hold out water, methinks.
Timon of Athens. Act i, sc. 2, l. 112. [Timon]

6
Things now,
That bear a weighty and a serious brow,
Sad, high, and working, full of state and woe,
Such noble scenes as draw the eye to flow.
Henry VIII. Prologue, l. 1.

7
If thou wilt weep my fortunes, take my eyes.
King Lear. Act iv, sc. 6, l. 180. [King Lear]

8
Oft did she heave her napkin to her eyne.
A Lover's Complaint, l. 15.
Fluxive eyes.—*A Lover's Complaint,* l. 50. The only use of "fluxive."

9
His eye being big with tears.
The Merchant of Venice. Act ii, sc. 8, l. 46. [Salarino]
My eye shall be the stream
And watery death-bed for him.
The Merchant of Venice. Act iii, sc. 2, l. 46. [Portia]

10
Rain, which I could well
Beteem them from the tempest of my eyes.
A Midsummer-Night's Dream. Act i, sc. 1, l. 130. [Hermia] "Beteem" is used again in *Hamlet,* i, 2, 146.
Made mine eyes water; but more merry tears
The passion of loud laughter never shed.
A Midsummer-Night's Dream. Act v, sc. 1, l. 69. [Philostrate]

11
Mine eyes do itch; Doth that bode weeping?
Othello. Act iv, sc. 3, l. 58. [Desdemona]
One whose subdued eyes,
Albeit unused to the melting mood,
Drop tears as fast as the Arabian trees
Their medicinal gum.
Othello. Act v, sc. 2, l. 348. [Othello]

12
And wipe the dim mist from thy doting eyne,
That thou shalt see thy state and pity mine.
The Rape of Lucrece, l. 642.
Wipe thine eyes;
The good-years shall devour them, flesh and fell,
Ere they shall make us weep: we 'll see 'em starve first.
King Lear. Act v, sc. 3, l. 23. [King Lear] "Good-year" as a hyphenated phrase is repeated in *II Henry IV,* ii, 4, 64; 191; and in *Much Ado about Nothing,* i, 3, 1.
Wipe thine eyes.—*Cymbeline,* iv, 2, 402; *The Tempest,* i, 2, 25.
Bid her dry her weeping eyes.
Richard III. Act iv, sc. 4, l. 278. [Queen]
Dry thine eyes.—*Titus Andronicus,* iii, 1, 138.
Dry your eyes.—*Richard II,* iii, 3, 202; *Measure for Measure,* iv, 3, 132.
Let 's dry our eyes.—*Henry VIII,* iii, 2, 431.
Dry thy cheeks.—*III Henry VI,* i, 4, 83; *III Henry VI,* ii, 1, 61.

13
Mine eyes, like sluices,
As from a mountain-spring that feeds a dale,
Shall gush pure streams to purge my impure tale.
The Rape of Lucrece, l. 1076. The only use of "mountain-spring" and "gush."
But durst now ask of her audaciously
Why her two suns were cloud-eclipsed so.
The Rape of Lucrece, l. 1223. The only use of "cloud-eclipsed." "Audaciously" is used only once again, in *Love's Labour 's Lost,* v, 2, 104.
And round about her tear-distained eye
Blue circles stream'd, like rainbows in the sky.
The Rape of Lucrece, l. 1586. The only use of "tear-distained."
Heavy eye.—*The Rape of Lucrece,* l. 709.

1
O, let no noble eye profane a tear
For me, if I be gored with Mowbray's spear.
Richard II. Act i, sc. 3, l. 59. [Bolingbroke]

For sorrow's eye, glazed with blinding tears,
Divides one thing entire to many objects.
Richard II. Act ii, sc. 2, l. 16. [Bushy] The only use of "glazed."

False sorrow's eye,
Which for things true weeps things imaginary.
Richard II. Act ii, sc. 2, l. 26. [Bushy]

2
Mine eyes are full of tears, I cannot see;
And yet salt water blinds them not so much
But they can see a sort of traitors here.
Richard II. Act iv, sc. 1, l. 244. [King Richard]

His eyes do drop no tears.
Richard II. Act v, sc. 3, l. 101. [Duchess of York]

3
Those eyes of thine from mine have drawn salt tears,
Shamed their aspect with store of childish drops.
These eyes, which never shed remorseful tear.
Richard III. Act i, sc. 2, l. 154. [Gloucester]

My manly eyes did scorn an humble tear.
Richard III. Act i, sc. 2, l. 165. [Gloucester]

All springs reduce their currents to mine eyes,
That I, being govern'd by the watery moon,
May send forth plenteous tears to drown the world!
Richard III. Act ii, sc. 2, l. 68. [Queen Elizabeth]

4
Bid him shed tears, as being overjoy'd
To see her noble lord restored to health. . . .
And if the boy have not a woman's gift
To rain a shower of commanded tears,
An onion will do well for such a shift,
Which in a napkin being close convey'd
Shall in despite enforce a watery eye.
The Taming of the Shrew. Induction, sc. 1, l. 120. [Lord]

Good Master Mustardseed, I know your patience well: . . . I promise you your kindred hath made my eyes water ere now.
A Midsummer-Night's Dream. Act iii, sc. 1, l. 196. [Bottom]

Mine eyes smell onions; I shall weep anon:
Good Tom Drum, lend me a handkercher.
All's Well that Ends Well. Act v, sc. 3, l. 321. [Lafeu]

5
Mine eyes, even sociable to the show of thine,
Fall fellowly drops.
The Tempest. Act v, sc. 1, l. 63. [Prospero] The only use of "fellowly."

I have retired me to a wasteful cock,
And set mine eyes at flow.
Timon of Athens. Act ii, sc. 2, l. 171. [Flavius]

6
One hour's storm will drown the fragrant meads;
What will whole months of tears thy father's eyes?
Titus Andronicus. Act ii, sc. 4, l. 54. [Marcus]

7
Practise your eyes with tears!
Troilus and Cressida. Act ii, sc. 2, l. 8. [Cassandra]

Lend me ten thousand eyes,
And I will fill them with prophetic tears.
Troilus and Cressida. Act ii, sc. 2, l. 101. [Cassandra]

Their eyes o'ergalled with recourse of tears.
Troilus and Cressida. Act v, sc. 3, l. 55. [Troilus] The only use of "o'ergalled."

8
O, how her eyes and tears did lend and borrow!
Her eyes seen in the tears, tears in her eye;
Both crystals, where they view'd each other's sorrow.
Venus and Adonis, l. 961.

9
Her eyes Became two spouts.
The Winter's Tale. Act iii, sc. 3, l. 25. [Antigonus]

X—Women's Eyes

10
In her eye I find
A wonder, or a wondrous miracle,
The shadow of myself form'd in her eye.
King John. Act ii, sc. 1, l. 496. [Dauphin]

I do protest I never loved myself
Till now infixed I beheld myself
Drawn in the flattering table of her eye.
King John. Act ii, sc. 1, l. 501. [Dauphin] The only use of "infixed."

11
Study his bias leaves, and makes his book thine eyes,
Where all those pleasures live that art would comprehend.
Love's Labour's Lost. Act iv, sc. 2, l. 113. [Sir Nathaniel] Repeated in *The Passionate Pilgrim,* l. 61.

From women's eyes this doctrine I derive;
They are the ground, the books, the academes
From whence doth spring the true Promethean fire . . .
Now, for not looking on a woman's face,
You have in that forsworn the use of eyes.
Love's Labour's Lost. Act iv, sc. 3, l. 302. [Biron]

From women's eyes this doctrine I derive:
They sparkle still the right Promethean fire;
They are the books, the arts, the academes,
That show, contain and nourish all the world.
Love's Labour's Lost. Act iv, sc. 3, l. 350. [Biron] "Promethean" is repeated in *Othello,* v, 2, 12: "Promethean heat."

Our court shall be a little Academe.
Love's Labour's Lost, i, 1, 13. "Academe" is used in no other play.

12
For where is any author in the world
Teaches such beauty as a woman's eye?
Love's Labour's Lost. Act iv, sc. 3, l. 312. [Biron]

1
So sweet a kiss the golden sun gives not
To those fresh morning drops upon the rose,
As thy eye-beams, when their fresh rays have smote
The night of dew that on my cheeks down flows.
Love's Labour's Lost. Act iv, sc. 3, l. 26. [King] The only use of "eye-beams."

What peremptory eagle-sighted eye
Dares look upon the heaven of her brow,
That is not blinded by her majesty?
Love's Labour's Lost. Act iv, sc. 3, l. 226. [Biron] The only use of "eagle-sighted."

A wither'd hermit, five-score winters worn,
Might shake off fifty, looking in her eye.
Love's Labour's Lost. Act iv, sc. 3, l. 242. [Biron] "Five-score" is used again in *Love's Labour's Lost,* iv, 2, 41.

The prompting eyes Of beauty's tutors.
Love's Labour's Lost. Act iv, sc. 3, l. 322. [Biron] "Prompting" is repeated in *Much Ado about Nothing,* i, 1, 306.

2
Sometimes her levell'd eyes their carriage ride,
As they did battery to the spheres intend;
Sometime diverted their poor balls are tied
To the orbed earth; sometimes they do extend
Their view right on; anon their gazes lend
To every place at once, and, nowhere fix'd,
The mind and sight distractedly commix'd.
A Lover's Complaint, l. 22. The only use of "distractedly" and "commix'd." "Commix" occurs in *Cymbeline,* iv, 2, 55.

3
When thou wakest, Thou takest
True delight In the sight
Of thy former lady's eye.
A Midsummer-Night's Dream. Act iii, sc. 2, l. 453. [Puck]

She hath spied him already with those sweet eyes.
A Midsummer-Night's Dream. Act v, sc. 1, l. 329. [Lysander] "Sweet eyes" is repeated in l. 336.

4
Her eyes, like marigolds, had sheathed their light,
And canopied in darkness sweetly lay,
Till they might open to adorn the day.
The Rape of Lucrece, l. 397.

Her earnest eye did make him more amazed.
The Rape of Lucrece, l. 1356.

5
And then she reprehends her mangling eye,
That makes more gashes where no breach should be.
Venus and Adonis, l. 1065. "Mangling" is repeated in *Henry V,* Epil., 4.

6
I might have looked upon my queen's full eyes.
Winter's Tale. Act v, sc. 1, l. 53. [Leontes]

A full eye will wax hollow.
Henry V, v, 2, 170. See under HEART.

XI—Eyes and Love

7
Great Pompey
Would stand and make his eyes grow in my brow;
There would he anchor his aspect and die
With looking on his life.
Antony and Cleopatra. Act i, sc. 5, l. 31. [Cleopatra]

8
If the scorn of your bright eyne
Have power to raise such love in mine,
Alack, in me what strange effect
Would they work in mild aspect!
As You Like It. Act iv, sc. 3, l. 50. [Rosalind]

9
And, with his head over his shoulder turn'd,
He seem'd to find his way without his eyes;
For out o' doors he went without their helps,
And, to the last, bended their light on me.
Hamlet. Act ii, sc. 1, l. 97. [Ophelia]

10
O, but her eye,—by this light, but for her eye,
I would not love her; yes, for her two eyes.
Love's Labour's Lost. Act iv, sc. 3, l. 10. [Biron]

Love . . . adds a precious seeing to the eye;
A lover's eyes will gaze an eagle blind.
Love's Labour's Lost. Act iv, sc. 3, l. 333. [Biron] See under LOVE for full quotation.

11
What, do I love her,
That I desire to hear her speak again,
And feast upon her eyes?
Measure for Measure. Act ii, sc. 2, l. 177. [Angelo]

Fond eye.—*The Merchant of Venice,* ii, 9, 27.
Melting eye.—*The Rape of Lucrece,* l. 1227.

12
Your eyes, where I o'erlook
Love's stories written in love's richest book.
A Midsummer-Night's Dream. Act ii, sc. 2, l. 121. [Lysander]

13
I look'd upon her with a soldier's eye,
That liked, but had a rougher task in hand
Than to drive liking to the name of love.
Much Ado about Nothing. Act i, sc. 1, l. 300. [Claudio] "Rougher" is repeated in *Coriolanus,* iii, 3, 55.

Your niece regards me with an eye of favour . . .
And I do with an eye of love requite her.
Much Ado about Nothing. Act v, sc. 4, l. 22. [Benedick]

14
He hath an eye to gaze on beauty,
And dotes on what he looks, 'gainst law or duty.
The Rape of Lucrece, l. 496.

Mine eyes
Were not in fault, for she was beautiful.
Cymbeline. Act v, sc. 5, l. 62. [Cymbeline]

15
Thou blind fool, Love, what dost thou to mine eyes,
That they behold, and see not what they see?
Sonnets. No. cxxxvii.

How have mine eyes out of their spheres been fitted

In the distraction of this madding fever!
Sonnets. No. cxix.

O me, what eyes hath Love put in my head,
Which have no correspondence with true sight!
Sonnets. No. cxlviii. The only use of "correspondence."

What merit do I in myself respect,
That is so proud my service to despise,
When all my best doth worship thy defect,
Commanded by the motion of thine eyes?
Sonnets. No. cxlix.

1 At the first sight
They have changed eyes.
The Tempest. Act i, sc. 2, l. 440. [Prospero]

Whose eyes are on this sovereign lady fix'd.
Timon of Athens. Act i, sc. 1, l. 68. [Poet]

2
And faster bound to Aaron's charming eyes
Than is Prometheus tied to Caucasus.
Titus Andronicus. Act iii, sc. 1, l. 16. [Aaron] The only mention of Prometheus. Caucasus is repeated in *Richard II,* i, 3, 295: "Frosty Caucasus."

His mistress
Did hold his eyes lock'd in her crystal looks.
The Two Gentlemen of Verona. Act ii, sc. 4, l. 88. [Valentine]

All eyes saw his eyes enchanted with gazes.
Love's Labour's Lost. Act ii, sc. 1, l. 247. [Boyet]

I think she means to tangle my eyes too!
As You Like It. Act iii, sc. 5, l. 44. [Rosalind]

3
Love doth to her eyes repair,
To help him of his blindness,
And, being help'd, inhabits there.
The Two Gentlemen of Verona. Act iv, sc. 2, l. 46. [Song]

4
O, what a war of looks was then between them!
Her eyes petitioners to his eyes suing;
His eyes saw her eyes as they had not seen them;
Her eyes woo'd still, his eyes disdain'd the wooing.
Venus and Adonis, l. 355.

XII—Eyes: Their Power

5
What is that curt'sy worth? or those doves' eyes,
Which can make gods forsworn? I melt, and am not
Of stronger earth than others.
Coriolanus. Act v, sc. 3, l. 27. [Coriolanus]

6
An eye like Mars, to threaten and command.
Hamlet. Act iii, sc. 4, l. 55. [Hamlet] See under APPEARANCE for full quotation.

7
Then lend the eye a terrible aspect;
Let it pry through the portage of the head
Like the brass cannon.
Henry V. Act iii, sc. 1, l. 9. [King Henry] "Portage" is repeated in *Pericles,* iii, 1, 35.

So shall inferior eyes,
That borrow their behaviours from the great,
Grow great by your example and put on
The dauntless spirit of resolution.
King John. Act v, sc. 1, l. 50. [Bastard]

8
How far your eyes may pierce I cannot tell.
King Lear. Act i, sc. 4, l. 368. [Albany]

He is able to pierce a corslet with his eye.
Coriolanus. Act v, sc. 4, l. 21. [Menenius] The only use of "corslet."

9
Study me how to please the eye indeed
By fixing it upon a fairer eye,
Who dazzling so, that eye shall be his heed
And give him light that it was blinded by.
Love's Labour's Lost. Act i, sc. 1, l. 80. [Biron] "Dazzling" is repeated in *Venus and Adonis,* l. 1064.

The virtue of your eye must break my oath.
Love's Labour's Lost. Act v, sc. 2, l. 348. [King]

10 There's an eye
Wounds like a leaden sword.
Love's Labour's Lost. Act v, sc. 2, l. 480. [Biron]

Alack, there lies more peril in thine eye
Than twenty of their swords.
Romeo and Juliet. Act ii, sc. 2, l. 71. [Romeo]

But no more deep will I endart mine eye
Than your consent gives strength to make it fly.
Romeo and Juliet. Act i, sc. 3, l. 98. [Juliet] The only use of "endart."

He is already dead; stabbed with a white wench's black eye.
Romeo and Juliet. Act ii, sc. 4, l. 13. [Mercutio]

11
Thine eyes that taught the dumb on high to sing
And heavy ignorance aloft to fly
Have added feathers to the learned's wings
And given grace a double majesty.
Sonnets. No. lxxviii.

XIII—Eyes: Their Colour

12
He said mine eyes were black and my hair black;
And, now I am remember'd, scorned at me.
As You Like It. Act iii, sc. 5, l. 130. [Phebe]

My mistress' brows are raven black,
Her eyes so suited, and they mourners seem. . . .
Yet so they mourn, becoming of their woe,
That every tongue says beauty should look so.
Sonnets. No. cxxvii.

Thine eyes I love, and they, as pitying me,
Knowing thy heart torments me with disdain,
Have put on black and loving mourners be,
Looking with pretty ruth upon my pain.
Sonnets. No. cxxxii.

Those two mourning eyes become thy face.
Sonnets. No. cxxxii.

With two pitch-balls stuck in her face for eyes.
Love's Labour's Lost. Act iii, sc. 1, l. 199. [Biron] The only use of "pitch-balls."

13
Her two blue windows faintly she upheaveth,

Like the fair sun, when in his fresh array
He cheers the morn and all the earth relieveth;
And as the bright sun glorifies the sky,
So is her face illumined with her eye.
Venus and Adonis, l. 482. The only use of "up-heaveth."

A blue eye and sunken.
As You Like It, iii, 2, 393. See under LOVE for full quotation.

The flame o' the taper
Bows toward her, and would under-peep her lids,
To see the enclosed lights, now canopied
Under these windows, white and azure laced
With blue of heaven's own tinct.
Cymbeline. Act ii, sc. 2, l. 19. [Iachimo] The only use of "under-peep." "Azure" does not occur again in the plays, but is repeated in *The Rape of Lucrece,* l. 419: "He admired her azure veins."

1 An eagle, madam,
Hath not so green, so quick, so fair an eye.
Romeo and Juliet. Act iii, sc. 5, l. 221. [Nurse]

His eyes were green as leeks.
A Midsummer-Night's Dream. Act v, sc. 1, l. 342. [Thisbe]

2
Mine eyes are gray and bright and quick in turning.
Venus and Adonis, l. 140. "Gray" is used three times in *King Lear,* always with an "a," and this form occurs also in *Julius Cæsar,* ii, 1, 103, and in *A Midsummer-Night's Dream,* iii, 1, 134. Elsewhere it is always "grey."

Her eyes are grey as glass.
The Two Gentlemen of Verona. Act iv, sc. 4, l. 197. [Julia]

Two grey eyes, with lids to them.
Twelfth Night, i, 5, 266. See under BEAUTY for full quotation.

3
Thou hast hazel eyes.
Romeo and Juliet, iii, 1, 22. See under QUARREL for full quotation. The only use of "hazel."

4
Plumpy Bacchus with pink eyne!
Antony and Cleopatra, ii, 7, 121. The only use of "plumpy."

XIV—Eyes Red with Tears or Anger

5
His eye Red as 'twould burn Rome.
Coriolanus. Act v, sc. 1, l. 64. [Cominius]

6
With eyes like carbuncles.
Hamlet. Act ii, sc. 2, l. 485. [Hamlet]

7
Give me a cup of sack to make my eyes look red, that it may be thought I have wept.
I Henry IV. Act ii, sc. 4, l. 422. [Falstaff]

8
Poor soul! his eyes are red as fire with weeping.
Julius Cæsar. Act iii, sc. 2, l. 120. [Citizen] "As red as fire" is repeated in *III Henry VI,* iii, 2, 51.

Eyes as red as new-enkindled fire.
King John. Act iv, sc. 2, l. 163. [Bastard] The only use of "new-enkindled."

9
Beaufort's red sparkling eyes blab his heart's malice.
II Henry VI. Act iii, sc. 1, l. 154. [Gloucester]

10
I am pale at mine heart to see thine eyes so red.
Measure for Measure. Act iv, sc. 3, l. 157. [Lucio]

11
Her eyes, though sod in tears, look'd red and raw.
The Rape of Lucrece, l. 1592. The only use of "sod."

Raw eyes.—*Troilus and Cressida,* v, 1, 23.

12
Mine eyes are turn'd to fire, my heart to lead:
Heavy heart's lead, melt at mine eyes' red fire!
Venus and Adonis, l. 1072.

XV—Eye and Ear

13
And carry with us ears and eyes for the time,
But hearts for the event.
Coriolanus. Act ii, sc. 1, l. 285. [Brutus]

In such business
Action is eloquence, and the eyes of the ignorant
More learned than the ears.
Coriolanus. Act iii, sc. 2, l. 75. [Volumnia]

'Fore your own eyes and ears.
Coriolanus. Act v, sc. 6, l. 120. [Aufidius]

Have both their eyes
And ears so cloy'd importantly as now.
Cymbeline. Act iv, sc. 3, l. 18. [Arviragus] The only use of "importantly."

14 We will not trust our eyes
Without our ears.
I Henry IV. Act v, sc. 4, l. 139. [Prince of Wales]

Not working with the eye without the ear.
Henry V, ii, 2, 135. For full quotation see under CHARACTER.

Fain would mine eyes be witness with mine ears.
I Henry VI. Act ii, sc. 3, l. 9. [Countess of Auvergne]

15
A man may see how this world goes with no eyes. Look with thine ears.
King Lear. Act iv, sc. 6, l. 153. [King Lear]

16
My ear should catch your voice, my eye your eye.
A Midsummer-Night's Dream. Act i, sc. 1, l. 188. [Helena]

Mine ear is much enamour'd of thy note;
So is mine eye enthralled to thy shape.
A Midsummer-Night's Dream. Act iii, sc. 1, l. 141. [Titania]

17
To glad your ear, and please your eyes.
Pericles. Act i, Gower, l. 4.

Your ears unto your eyes I 'll reconcile.
Pericles. Act iv, sc. 4, l. 22. [Gower]

1
To see sad sights moves more than hear them told:
For then the eye interprets to the ear.
The Rape of Lucrece, l. 1324.

2
Impartial are our eyes and ears.
Richard II. Act i, sc. 1, l. 115. [King Richard]

3
Friar Laurence: O, then I see that madmen have no ears.
Romeo: How should they, when that wise men have no eyes?
Romeo and Juliet. Act iii, sc. 3, l. 61.

4
My will enkindled by mine eyes and ears,
Two traded pilots 'twixt the dangerous shores
Of will and judgement.
Troilus and Cressida. Act ii, sc. 2, l. 63. [Troilus]

5
Had I no eyes but ears, my ears would love
That inward beauty and invisible.
Venus and Adonis, l. 433.

XVI—Eye and Heart

6
I . . . bid mine eyes be packing with my heart
And call'd them blind and dusty spectacles.
II Henry VI. Act iii, sc. 2, l. 111. [Queen Margaret]

7
They are infected; in their hearts it lies;
They have the plague, and caught it of your eyes.
Love's Labour 's Lost. Act v, sc. 2, l. 420. [Biron]

Behold the window of my heart, mine eye.
Love's Labour 's Lost. Act v, sc. 2, l. 848. [Biron]

8
Mine eye hath play'd the painter and hath stell'd
Thy beauty's form in table of my heart.
Sonnets. No. xxiv.

Now see what good turns eyes for eyes have done:
Mine eyes have drawn thy shape, and thine for me
Are windows to my breast, where-through the sun
Delights to peep, to gaze therein on thee:
Yet eyes this cunning want to grace their art;
They draw but what they see. know not the heart.
Sonnets. No. xxiv. The only use of "where-through."

9
Mine eye and heart are at a mortal war
How to divide the conquest of thy sight;
Mine eye my heart thy picture's sight would bar,
My heart mine eye the freedom of that right. . . .
As thus; mine eye's due is thy outward part,
And my heart's right thy inward love of heart.
Sonnets. No. xlvi.

Betwixt mine eye and heart a league is took,
And each doth good turns now unto the other.
Sonnets. No. xlvii.

If eyes corrupt by over-partial looks
Be anchor'd in the bay where all men ride,
Why of eyes' falsehood hast thou forged hooks,
Whereto the judgement of my heart is tied?
Why should my heart think that a several plot
Which my heart knows the wide world 's common place?
Or mine eyes seeing this, say this is not,
To put fair truth upon so foul a face?
In things right true my heart and eyes have err'd,
And to this false plague are they now transferr'd.
Sonnets. No. cxxxvii. The only use of "over-partial" and "transferr'd."

In faith, I do not love thee with mine eyes,
For they in thee a thousand errors note;
But 'tis my heart that loves what they despise,
Who in despite of view is pleased to dote.
Sonnets. No. cxli.

Bear thine eyes straight, though thy proud heart go wide.
Sonnets. No. cxl.

10
My eye 's too quick, my heart o'erweens too much,
Unless my hand and strength could equal them.
III Henry VI. Act iii, sc. 2, l. 144. [Gloucester]

11
Thy heart is big, get thee apart and weep.
Passion, I see, is catching; for mine eyes,
Seeing those beads of sorrow stand in thine,
Began to water.
Julius Cæsar. Act iii, sc. 1, l. 282. [Antony]

12 Young men's love then lies
Not truly in their hearts, but in their eyes.
Romeo and Juliet. Act ii, sc. 3, l. 67. [Friar Laurence]

13
His drumming heart cheers up his burning eye
His eye commends the leading to his hand.
The Rape of Lucrece, l. 435.

Heart hath his hope, and eyes their wished sight.
The Passionate Pilgrim, l. 202.

Lord, how mine eyes throw gazes to the east!
My heart doth charge the watch.
The Passionate Pilgrim, l. 193.

XVII—Eye and Tongue

14 Faster than his tongue
Did make offence his eye did heal it up.
As You Like It. Act iii, sc. 5, l. 116. [Phebe]

If that an eye may profit by a tongue,
Then should I know you by description.
As You Like It. Act iv, sc. 3, l. 84. [Oliver]

15
Hubert, the utterance of a brace of tongues
Must needs want pleading for a pair of eyes:

Let me not hold my tongue, let me not, Hubert;
Or, Hubert, if you will, cut out my tongue,
So I may keep mine eyes: O, spare mine eyes,
Though to no use but still to look on you!
King John. Act iv, sc. 1, l. 98. [Arthur]

1 To speak that in words which his eye hath disclosed,
I only have made a mouth of his eye,
By adding a tongue which I know will not lie.
Love's Labour's Lost. Act ii, sc. 1, l. 251. [Boyet]

2 O, could I play the woman with mine eyes
And braggart with my tongue!
Macbeth. Act iv, sc. 3, l. 230. [Macduff]

Thine eye begins to speak; set thy tongue there.
Richard II. Act v, sc. 3, l. 125. [Duchess of York]

3 For we, which now behold these present days,
Have eyes to wonder, but lack tongues to praise.
Sonnets. No. cvi.

4 She made good view of me; indeed, so much,
That sure methought her eyes had lost her tongue.
Twelfth Night. Act ii, sc. 2, l. 20. [Viola]

XVIII—The Eyes and Death

5 These eyes, that now are dimm'd with death's black veil,
Have been as piercing as the mid-day sun,
To search the secret treasons of the world.
III Henry VI. Act v, sc. 2, l. 16. [Warwick]

Dimm'd eyes.—*II Henry VI,* iii, 1, 218.

6 And dying eyes gleam'd forth their ashy lights,
Like dying coals burnt out in tedious nights.
The Rape of Lucrece, l. 1378. "Ashy" is repeated in *II Henry VI,* iii, 2, 162.

7 Lo, in these windows that let forth thy life,
I pour the helpless balm of my poor eyes.
Richard III. Act i, sc. 2, l. 12. [Lady Anne]

8 Thy eyes' windows fall,
Like death, when he shuts up the day of life.
Romeo and Juliet. Act iv, sc. 1, l. 100. [Friar Laurence]

Downy windows, close;
And golden Phœbus never be beheld
Of eyes again so royal!
Antony and Cleopatra. Act v, sc. 2, l. 319. [Charmian]

9 Why hast thou cast into eternal sleeping
Those eyes that taught all other eyes to see?
Venus and Adonis, l. 951.

She lifts the coffer-lids that close his eyes,
Where, lo, two lamps, burnt out, in darkness lies;
Two glasses, where herself herself beheld
A thousand times, and now no more reflect;
Their virtue lost, wherein they late excell'd.
Venus and Adonis, l. 1127. The only use of "coffer-lids."

10 His eyes do show his days are almost done.
Twelfth Night. Act ii, sc. 3, l. 112. [Clown]

XIX—The Eyes: Their Destruction

11 With these nails I'll pluck out these false eyes.
The Comedy of Errors. Act iv, sc. 4, l. 107. [Antipholus of Ephesus] See also under NAIL.

By Jove, I vow,
I should have scratch'd out your unseeing eyes,
To make my master out of love with thee!
The Two Gentlemen of Verona. Act iv, sc. 4, l. 208. [Julia]

O, I will to him and pluck out his eyes!
Measure for Measure. Act iv, sc. 3, l. 124. [Isabella]

Pluck out his eyes.—*King Lear,* iii, 7, 5.

I would not see thy cruel nails
Pluck out his poor old eyes; nor thy fierce sister
In his anointed flesh stick boarish fangs.
King Lear. Act iii, sc. 7, l. 56. [Gloucester] The only use of "boarish."

I'll never see 't; for, I am sure, my nails
Are stronger than mine eyes.
Antony and Cleopatra. Act v, sc. 2, l. 223. [Iras]

12 And stop all sight-holes, every loop from whence
The eye of reason may pry in upon us.
I Henry IV. Act iv, sc 1, l. 71. [Worcester] The only use of "sight-holes."

13 He hath no eyes, the dust hath blinded them.
II Henry VI. Act iii, sc. 3, l. 14. [Cardinal]

I lost mine eye in laying the prize aboard,
And therefore to revenge it, shalt thou die.
II Henry VI. Act iv, sc. 1, l. 25. [Whitmore]

14 Must you with hot irons burn out both mine eyes?
King John. Act iv, sc. 1, l. 39. [Arthur]

Will you put out mine eyes?
These eyes that never did nor never shall
So much as frown on you.
King John. Act iv, sc. 1, l. 56. [Arthur]

The iron of itself, though heat red-hot,
Approaching near these eyes, would drink my tears
And quench his fiery indignation.
King John. Act iv, sc. 1, l. 61. [Arthur]

O, save me, Hubert, save me! my eyes are out
Even with the fierce looks of these bloody men.
King John. Act iv, sc. 1, l. 73. [Arthur]

Well, see to live; I will not touch thine eye
For all the treasure that thine uncle owes.
King John. Act iv, sc. 1, l. 122. [Hubert]

He is forsworn, if e'er those eyes of yours
Behold another day break in the east.
King John. Act v, sc. 4, l. 31. [Melun]

15 Beweep this cause again, I'll pluck ye out,

And cast you, with the waters that you lose,
To temper clay.
King Lear. Act i, sc. 4, l. 324. [King Lear]
Upon these eyes of thine I 'll set my foot.
King Lear. Act iii, sc. 7, l. 65. [Cornwall]
Alack, I have no eyes.—*King Lear,* iv, 6, 60.

1 Either my eyesight fails, or thou look'st pale.
Romeo and Juliet. Act iii, sc. 5, l. 57. [Juliet]
Blind the eyesight.—*Love's Labour 's Lost,* i, 1, 76.
Eyesight lost.—*Romeo and Juliet,* i, 1, 239.
Dearer that eyesight.—*King Lear,* i, 1, 57.
In his eyesight.—*Love's Labour 's Lost,* ii, 1, 239.
Plays upon our eyesight.—*I Henry IV,* v, 4, 138.
Precious eyesight.—*Love's Labour 's Lost,* v, 2, 445. The only uses of "eyesight."

2 Him will I tear out of that cruel eye,
Where he sits crowned in his master's spite.
Twelfth Night. Act v, sc. 1, l. 130. [Duke]

3 Thou hast no eyes to see,
But hatefully at random dost thou hit.
Venus and Adonis, l. 939. The only use of "hatefully."

XX—Eyeballs

4 I 'll wake mine eye-balls blind first.
Cymbeline. Act iii, sc. 4, l. 104. [Pisanio]

5 Upon thy eye-balls murderous tyranny
Sits in grim majesty, to fright the world.
Look not upon me, for thine eyes are wounding.
II Henry VI. Act iii, sc. 2, l. 49. [King Henry]
O, were mine eye-balls into bullets turn'd,
That I in rage might shoot them at your faces!
I Henry VI. Act iv, sc. 7, l. 79. [Lucy]

6 His eye-balls further out than when he lived,
Staring full ghastly like a strangled man.
II Henry VI. Act iii, sc. 2, l. 169. [Warwick]

7 Put my eyeballs in thy vaulty brows.
King John, iii, 4, 30. See under DEATH for full quotation.
Make his eyeballs roll with wonted sight.
A Midsummer-Night's Dream. Act iii, sc. 2, l. 369. [Oberon]
Rolling his greedy eyeballs in his head:
By their high treason is his heart misled.
The Rape of Lucrece, l. 368.

8 Move these eyes?
Or whether, riding on the balls of mine,
Seem they in motion?
The Merchant of Venice. Act iii, sc. 2, l. 117. [Bassanio]
Fatal balls.—*Henry V,* v, 2, 17.
Poor balls.—*A Lover's Complaint,* l. 24.
Balls of quenchless fire.—*The Rape of Lucrece,* l. 1554. The only uses of "balls" for eyeballs.

9 Look in mine eye-balls, there thy beauty lies;
Then why not lips on lips, since eyes in eyes?
Venus and Adonis, l. 119.

XXI—Eyelids

10 My eyelids will no longer wag.
Hamlet, v, 1, 290. See under FIGHTING.
Hung their eyelids down.—*I Henry IV,* iii, 2, 81.
Weigh my eyelids down.—*II Henry IV,* iii, 1, 7.
Drooping eyelids.—*Sonnets,* xxvi.
Heavy eyelids.—*Sonnets,* lxi.
Sleeping eyelids.—*A Midsummer-Night's Dream,* ii, 1, 170.

11 And on my eyelids shall conjecture hang.
Much Ado about Nothing. Act iv, sc. 1, l. 107. [Claudio]

12 Her eyelids, cases to those heavenly jewels, . . .
Begin to part their fringes of bright gold.
Pericles. Act iii, sc. 2, l. 99.
The fringed curtains of thine eye advance
And say what thou seest yond.
The Tempest. Act i, sc. 2, l. 408. [Prospero] The only use of "fringed."
Why Doth not then our eyelids sink?
The Tempest. Act ii, sc. 1, l. 200. [Sebastian]

XXII—Basilisk and Cockatrice

13 It is a basilisk unto mine eye,
Kills me to look on 't.
Cymbeline. Act ii, sc. 4, l. 107. [Posthumus]
Come, basilisk,
And kill the innocent gazer with thy sight.
II Henry VI. Act iii, sc. 2, l. 52. [King Henry]
I 'll slay more gazers than the basilisk.
III Henry VI. Act iii, sc. 2, l. 187. [Gloucester]
Make me not sighted like the basilisk.
The Winter's Tale. Act i, sc. 2, l. 388. [Polixenes]

14 We are now glad to behold your eyes;
Your eyes, which hitherto have borne in them
Against the French, that met them in their bent,
The fatal balls of murdering basilisks:
The venom of such looks, we fairly hope,
Have lost their quality.
Henry V. Act v, sc. 2, l. 14. [Queen Isabel]
Gloucester: Thine eyes, sweet lady, have infected mine.
Lady Anne: Would they were basilisks, to strike thee dead!
Gloucester: I would they were, that I might die at once;
For now they kill me with a living death.
Richard III. Act i, sc. 2, l. 150.

15 A cockatrice hast thou hatch'd to the world,
Whose unavoided eye is murderous.
Richard III. Act iv, sc. 1, l. 55. [Duchess of York]

A cockatrice' dead-killing eye.
The Rape of Lucrece, l. 540. "Dead-killing" is repeated in *Richard III*, iv, 1, 36.
Death-darting eye of cockatrice.
Romeo and Juliet. Act iii, sc. 2, l. 47. [Juliet] The only use of "death-darting."
They will kill one another by the look, like cockatrices.
Twelfth Night. Act iii, sc. 4, l. 214. [Sir Toby]

EYEBROW, see Brow

F

FABLE

1
He fables not.
I Henry VI. Act iv, sc. 2, l. 42. [Talbot]
By the world, I recount no fable.
Love's Labour 's Lost. Act v, sc. 1, l. 111. [Armado]
Sans fable.—*The Comedy of Errors*, iv, 4, 76.
2
Let Æsop fable in a winter's night.
II Henry VI. Act v, sc. 5, l. 25. [Prince Edward] The only mention of Æsop.
I never may believe
3
These antique fables, nor these fairy toys.
A Midsummer-Night's Dream. Act v, sc. 1, l. 2. [Theseus]
4
But that 's a fable.
Othello. Act v, sc. 2, l. 286. [Othello] The only uses of "fable."

FACE

See also Cheek, Countenance, Feature, Forehead, Visage

I—Familiar Phrases

5
His face I know not.
All's Well that Ends Well. Act iii, sc. 5, l. 54. [Helena]
Know we this face or no?—*Othello*, v, 1, 88.
6
His face subdued to penetrative shame.
Antony and Cleopatra. Act iv, sc. 14, l. 74. [Antony] The only use of "penetrative."
7
I . . . would gladly Look him i' the face.
Antony and Cleopatra. Act v, sc. 2, l. 31. [Cleopatra]
I look'd her in the face.—*Antony and Cleopatra*, iii, 3, 12.
Look in my face.—*Othello*, iv, 2, 26.
Look . . . in the face.—*I Henry VI*, i, 1, 140.
Look me in the face.—*A Midsummer-Night's Dream*, iii, 2, 424.
I 'll ne'er look you i' the face again.
Julius Cæsar. Act i, sc. 2, l. 285. [Casca]
Never after look me in the face.
Romeo and Juliet. Act iii, sc. 5, l. 163. [Capulet]
8
Here 's a villain that would face me down.
The Comedy of Errors. Act iii, sc. 1, l. 6. [Antipholus of Ephesus]
And with no face, as 'twere, outfacing me.
The Comedy of Errors. Act v, sc. 1, l. 244. [Antipholus of Ephesus] "Outfacing" is repeated in *Much Ado about Nothing*, v, 1, 94.
Thou hast faced many things. . . . Face not me.
The Taming of the Shrew. Act iv, sc. 3, l. 123. [Grumio]
Face me out of my wits.—*Twelfth Night*, iv, 2, 101.
Face me out of his acquaintance.—*Twelfth Night*, v, 1, 91.
Give me them that will face me.—*I Henry IV*, ii, 4, 167.
Let us sway on and face them in the field.—*II Henry IV*, iv, 1, 24.
Front him to his face.—*II Henry VI*, v, 1, 86.
Face the matter out.—*The Taming of the Shrew*, ii, 1, 291.
Faces it out.—*Henry V*, iii, 2, 35.
I have not the face
To say 'Beseech you, cease.'
Coriolanus. Act iv, sc. 6, l. 116. [Menenius]
9
They wear their faces to the bent
Of the king's looks.
Cymbeline. Act i, sc. 1, l. 13. [Gentleman]
10
Hamlet: Then saw you not his face?
Horatio: O, yes, my lord; he wore his beaver up.
Hamlet. Act i, sc. 2, l. 229.
Tell me, good Brutus, can you see your face?
Julius Cæsar. Act i, sc. 2, l. 51. [Cassius]
Let me see his face.—*Julius Cæsar*, i, 2, 20.
Let me behold thy face.—*Timon of Athens*, iv, 3, 500.
Let me see your face.—*Twelfth Night*, i, 5, 248.
Let 's see thy face.—*Measure for Measure*, v, 1, 205.
11
Do thou amend thy face, and I 'll amend my life.
I Henry IV. Act iii, sc. 3, l. 27. [Falstaff]
'Sblood, I would my face were in your belly!
I Henry IV. Act iii, sc. 3, l. 56. [Bardolph]
12
I know this face full well.
I Henry IV. Act v, sc. 3, l. 19. [Hotspur]
That face of his I do remember well.
Twelfth Night. Act v, sc. 1, l. 54. [Duke]
13
Go, wash thy face.
II Henry IV. Act ii, sc. 1, l. 162. [Falstaff] See under WASHING.
14
Till now we never saw your face.
I Henry VI. Act iii, sc. 4, l. 24. [King Henry]
15
What, dost thou turn away and hide thy face?
I am no loathsome leper; look on me.
II Henry VI. Act iii, sc. 2, l. 74. [Queen

Margaret] The only use of "leper." "Leperous" occurs in *Hamlet*, i, 5, 64, and leprosy is mentioned four times.

In his mantle muffling up his face.
Julius Cæsar. Act iii, sc. 2, l. 191. [Antony] The only use of "muffling."

Hide her face.—*Romeo and Juliet*, ii, 4, 113.

Hide my face.—*A Midsummer-Night's Dream*, i, 2, 53.

1
Before his face I speak the words.
III Henry VI. Act ii, sc. 6, l. 39. [Warwick]

Before his face.—*Henry V*, v, 2, 260.

Before my face.—*II Henry IV*, iv, 5, 168.

2
Frame my face to all occasions.
III Henry VI. Act iii, sc. 2, l. 185. [Gloucester]

3
Had their faces
Been loose, this day they had been lost.
Henry VIII. Act v, sc. 1, l. 74. [Gentleman]

4
That smooth-faced gentleman.
King John. Act ii, sc. 1, l. 573. [Bastard]

Smooth-faced peace.—*Richard III*, v, 5, 33.

Smooth-faced wooers.—*Love's Labour's Lost*, v, 2, 838. The only uses of "smooth-faced."

5
Was this a face
To be opposed against the warring winds?
King Lear. Act iv, sc. 7, l. 31. [Cordelia] The only use of "warring."

6
O that your face were not so full of O's!
Love's Labour's Lost. Act v, sc. 2, l. 45. [Rosaline]

Can any face of brass hold longer out?
Love's Labour's Lost. Act v, sc. 2, l. 395. [Biron]

7
He makes faces.
Love's Labour's Lost. Act v, sc. 2, l. 649. [Dumain]

Why do you make such faces?
Macbeth. Act iii, sc. 4, l. 67. [Lady Macbeth]

Make faces like mummers.—*Coriolanus*, ii, 1, 83.

Make a crooked face.—*Coriolanus*, ii, 1, 62.

What are these faces?—*Macbeth*, iv, 2, 79.

8
Take thy face hence.
Macbeth. Act v, sc. 3, l. 19. [Macbeth]

9
You must not show your face.
Measure for Measure, i, 4, 10. See under SPEECH.

Show his face.
Love's Labour's Lost, iv, 3, 216. Repeated in *The Merry Wives of Windsor*, ii, 3, 33.

Show their faces.—*Love's Labour's Lost*, v, 2, 271.

Show thy face!—*Macbeth*, v, 7, 14; *Troilus and Cressida*, v, 5, 45.

10
Gaze on Christian fools with varnish'd faces.
The Merchant of Venice. Act ii, sc. 6, l. 32. [Shylock]

Varnish'd friends.—*Timon of Athens*, iv, 2, 36. The only uses of "varnish'd."

11
He no more shall see my face.
A Midsummer-Night's Dream. Act i, sc. 1, l. 202. [Hermia]

Thou shalt buy this dear,
If ever I thy face by daylight see.
A Midsummer-Night's Dream. Act iii, sc. 2, l. 426. [Demetrius]

12
Against the face of death.
Pericles. Act i, sc. 2, l. 71. [Pericles]

Face of the earth.—*I Henry IV*, ii, 4, 142.

Face of terra.—*Love's Labour's Lost*, iv, 2, 7.

Earth's cold face.—*II Henry VI*, ii, 3, 35; *Richard III*, v, 3, 266.

Face of the gods.—*Pericles*, iv, 6, 145.

Face of heaven.—*Richard III*, iv, 4, 239; *Romeo and Juliet*, iii, 2, 23; *The Merchant of Venice*, ii, 7, 45; *King Lear*, iii, 4, 91.

Heaven's face.—*Hamlet*, iii, 4, 48.

Face of peril.—*Cymbeline*, v, 1, 28.

Face of right.—*King John*, v, 2, 88.

Face of war.—*Antony and Cleopatra*, iii, 13, 5.

Outward face.—*The Tempest*, i, 2, 104.

Upward face.—*Timon of Athens*, iv, 3, 190.

A little wee face.—*The Merry Wives of Windsor*, i, 4, 23.

Strange face.—*Much Ado about Nothing*, ii, 3, 49.

Well noted face.—*King John*, iv, 2, 21.

13
A press of gaping faces.
The Rape of Lucrece, l. 1408.

14
Face to face, And frowning brow to brow.
Richard II. Act i, sc. 1, l. 15. [King Richard]

Face to face and bloody point to point.
King John. Act ii, sc. 1, l. 390. [Bastard]

Face to face and royal eye to eye.
Henry V. Act v, sc. 2, l. 30. [Burgundy]

Face to face.—*Much Ado about Nothing*, v, 1, 307.

15
O, let my sovereign turn away his face.
Richard II. Act i, sc. 1, l. 111. [Mowbray]

Ah, now thou turn'st away thy face.
Titus Andronicus. Act ii, sc. 4, l. 28. [Marcus]

Turn away thy face.—*Julius Cæsar*, v, 5, 47.

Turn away her face.—*Love's Labour's Lost*, v, 2, 148.

Turn thy face in peace.—*King John*, v, 2, 159.

16
I shall . . . never look upon thy face again.
Richard III. Act iv, sc. 4, l. 186. [Duchess of York]

Look upon his face.—*Richard II*, v, 3, 100.

17
Juliet: What I spake, I spake it to my face.
Paris: Thy face is mine, and thou hast slander'd it.
Juliet: It may be so, for it is not mine own.
Romeo and Juliet. Act iv, sc. 1, l. 34.

It shall be read to his face.—*All's Well that Ends Well*, iv, 3, 131.

18
His face thou hast, for even so look'd he,
Accomplish'd with the number of thy hours.
Richard II. Act ii, sc. 1, l. 176. [York]

Look here upon thy brother Geffrey's face;
These eyes, these brows, were moulded out of his.
King John. Act ii, sc. 1, l. 99. [King Philip]

1 What dares the slave
Come hither, cover'd with an antic face.
Romeo and Juliet. Act i, sc. 5, l. 57. [Tybalt]
2
Fairing the foul with art's false borrow'd face.
Sonnets. No. cxxvii. The only use of "fairing."
3
Is thine own heart to thine own face affected?
Venus and Adonis, l. 157.
Incorporate then they seem; face grows to face.
Venus and Adonis, l. 540.
Her face doth reek and smoke.
Venus and Adonis, l. 555.
Alas, he nought esteems that face of thine.
Venus and Adonis, 631.
Didst thou not mark my face? was it not white?
Venus and Adonis, l. 643.
His face seems twain.—*Venus and Adonis,* l. 1067.
What face remains alive that 's worth the viewing?
Venus and Adonis, l. 1076.

II—The Pleasing Face

4
His face was as the heavens.
Antony and Cleopatra. Act v, sc. 2, l. 79. [Cleopatra]
Her face, like heaven.
Pericles. Act i, sc. 1, l. 30. [Antiochus]
'Twas thy heavenly face that set me on.
Richard III. Act i, sc. 2, l. 183. [Gloucester]
Heavenly face.—*The Taming of the Shrew,* iv, 5, 32.
Celestial face.—*Sonnets,* xxxiii.
5
Shining morning face.
As You Like It, ii, 7, 146. For full quotation see under MAN.
Thy most mervailous face.
Henry V. Act ii, sc. 1, l. 50. [Pistol] The only use of "mervailous."
Flowering face!—*Romeo and Juliet,* iii, 2, 73.
Golden face.—*Sonnets,* xxxiii.
Good faces.—*As You Like It,* Epil., 22; *Coriolanus,* ii, 1, 67; *Pericles,* iv, 2, 51.
Honest face.—*Othello,* iii, 3, 50.
Manly face.—*II Henry VI,* ii, 2, 40.
6
His foot Mercurial; his Martial thigh;
The brawns of Hercules: but his Jovial face—
Murder in heaven?—How!—'Tis gone.
Cymbeline. Act iv, sc. 2, l. 310. [Imogen] The only use of "Mercurial," and of "Martial" and "Jovial" capitalized.
7
He will not stick to say his face is a face-royal: God may finish it when he will, 'tis not a hair amiss yet: he may keep it still at a face-royal, for a barber shall never earn sixpence out of it.
II Henry IV. Act i, sc. 2, l. 26. [Falstaff] The only use of "face-royal."
Royal face.—*Henry V,* iv, Prol., 35.
8
For thou hast given me in this beauteous face
A world of earthly blessings to my soul,
If sympathy of love unite our thoughts.
II Henry VI. Act i, sc. 1, l. 21. [King Henry]
In thy face I see
The map of honour, truth and loyalty.
II Henry VI. Act iii, sc. 1, l. 202. [King Henry]
True face.—*I Henry IV,* ii, 4, 550; *Antony and Cleopatra,* ii, 6, 105.
9 Hath this lovely face
Ruled, like a wandering planet, over me.
II Henry VI. Act iv, sc. 4, l. 15. [Queen Margaret]
Lovely face.—*The Taming of the Shrew,* Ind., 2, 67.
10
That face of his the hungry cannibals
Would not have touch'd, would not have stain'd with blood.
III Henry VI. Act i, sc. 4, l. 152. [York]
11
Ye have angels' faces, but heaven knows your hearts.
Henry VIII. Act iii, sc. 1, l. 145. [Queen Katharine]
Thou hast the sweetest face I ever look'd on.
Sir, as I have a soul, she is an angel.
Henry VIII. Act iv, sc. 1, l. 43. [Gentleman]
Angels' faces.—*The Two Gentlemen of Verona,* iii, 1, 103; *Pericles,* iv, 3, 47.
12 Was this the face
That every day under his household roof
Did keep ten thousand men? was this the face
That, like the sun, did make beholders wink?
Was this the face that faced so many follies? . . .
A brittle glory shineth in this face:
As brittle as the glory is the face.
Richard II. Act iv, sc. 1, l. 281. [King Richard]
13
Read o'er the volume of young Paris' face
And find delight writ there with beauty's pen;
Examine every married lineament
And see how one another lends content,
And what obscured in this fair volume lies
Find written in the margent of his eyes.
Romeo and Juliet. Act i, sc. 3, l. 81. [Lady Capulet]
14
Look in your glass, and there appears a face
That over-goes my blunt invention quite,
Dulling my lines and doing me disgrace.
Sonnets. No. ciii. The only use of "over-goes." "Dulling" is repeated in *The Tempest,* iii, 3, 6.
Look in thy glass, and tell the face thou viewest
Now is the time that face should form another.
Sonnets. No. iii.
15 Thy face and thy behaviour,
Which, if augury deceive me not,

Witness good bringing up, fortune and truth.

The Two Gentlemen of Verona. Act iv, sc. 4, l. 72. [Proteus]

That face of thine,
To which Love's eyes pay tributary gazes.

Venus and Adonis, l. 631.

III—The Repellent Face

1
Your carbonadoed face.

All's Well that Ends Well. Act iv, sc. 5, l. 107. [Clown] "Carbonadoed" is used also in *The Winter's Tale,* iv, 4, 268.

Big-swoln face.—*Titus Andronicus,* iii, 1, 224. "Big-swoln" is repeated in *III Henry VI,* ii, 2, 111: "Big-swoln heart."

Carved-bone face.—*Love's Labour's Lost,* v, 2, 619. The only use of "carved-bone."

Congealed face.—*The Rape of Lucrece,* l. 1744.

Fiend-like face.—*Titus Andronicus,* v, 1, 45. "Fiend-like" is repeated in *Macbeth,* v, 8, 69: "Fiend-like queen."

Foul face.—*Venus and Adonis,* l. 983.

Foul-faced.—*Richard III,* iii, 7, 231. The only use of the phrase.

Plain face.—*Othello,* ii, 1, 321; *The Rape of Lucrece,* l. 1532.

Purple-colour'd face.—*Venus and Adonis,* l. 1. The only use of the phrase.

Red face.—*Merry Wives of Windsor,* i, 1, 173.

Storm-beaten face.—*Sonnets,* xxxiv. The only use of "storm-beaten."

2
So tart a favour
To trumpet such good tidings!

Antony and Cleopatra. Act ii, sc. 5, l. 38. [Cleopatra]

The tartness of his face sours ripe grapes.

Coriolanus. Act v, sc. 4, l. 18. [Menenius]

So sour a face.—*Romeo and Juliet,* ii, 5, 24.

Sour-faced.—*The Rape of Lucrece,* l. 1334. The only use of the phrase.

3
They lie deadly that tell you you have good faces.

Coriolanus. Act ii, sc. 1, l. 67. [Menenius]

Faces fit for masks, or rather fairer
Than those for preservation cased, or shame.

Cymbeline. Act v, sc. 3, l. 21. [Posthumus]

4
How! poor? look upon his face; what call you rich? let them coin his nose, let them coin his cheeks.

I Henry IV. Act iii, sc. 3, l. 89. [Falstaff]

Bardolph: Why, Sir John, my face does you no harm.

Falstaff: No, I'll be sworn; I make as good use of it as many a man doth of a Death's-head or a memento mori: I never see thy face but I think upon hell-fire and Dives that lived in purple; for there he is in his robes, burning, burning. If thou wert any way given to virtue, I would swear by thy face; my oath should be 'By this fire, that's God's angel:' but thou art altogether given over; and wert indeed, but for the light in thy face, the son of utter darkness. When thou rannest up Gadshill in the night to catch my horse, if I did not think thou hadst been an ignis fatuus or a ball of wildfire, there's no purchase in money. O, thou art a perpetual triumph, an everlasting bonfire-light!

I Henry IV. Act iii, sc. 3, l. 31. The only reference to Dives in the plays, and the only use of "memento mori," "ignis fatuus," and "bonfire-light." "Hell-fire" is repeated in *Henry V,* ii, 3, 44; and "wildfire" in *The Rape of Lucrece,* l. 1523. "Death's-head" is used three times.

The fiend hath pricked down Bardolph irrecoverable; and his face is Lucifer's privy-kitchen.

II Henry IV. Act ii, sc. 4, l. 360. [Falstaff] The only use of "irrecoverable" and "privy-kitchen."

5
Put thy face between his sheets, and do the office of a warming-pan.

Henry V. Act ii, sc. 1, l. 87. [Boy] The only use of "warming-pan."

His face is all bubukles, and whelks, and knobs, and flames o' fire.

Henry V. Act iii, sc. 6, l. 108. [Fluellen] The only use of "bubukles" (pimples: a word found only in this passage of Shakespeare, where it is put into the mouth of a Welshman), "whelks" (pustules), and "knobs." In *King Lear,* iv, 6, 71, there is the phrase, "Horns whelk'd and waved," that is, formed like a whelk, which has a spiral gibbous shell.

He should be a brazier by his face, for, o' my conscience, twenty of the dog-days now reign in's nose.

Henry VIII. Act v, sc. 4, l. 41. [Man] The only use of "brazier" and "dog-days."

6
But see, his face is black and full of blood.

II Henry VI. Act iii, sc. 2, l. 168. [Warwick]

Hath now this dread and black complexion smear'd
With heraldry more dismal.

Hamlet. Act ii, sc. 2, l. 477. [Hamlet]

Bleeding face.—*King Lear,* iii, 7, 107.

Blood-stain'd face!—*Titus Andronicus,* v, 3, 154.

Mangled face.—*I Henry IV,* v, 4, 96.

7
Whose face is not worth sun-burning.

Henry V. Act v, sc. 2, l. 154. [King Henry] The only use of "sun-burning."

8
Thy face is, visard-like, unchanging,
Made impudent with use of evil deeds.

III Henry VI. Act i, sc. 4, l. 116. [York] Only use of "visard-like" and "unchanging."

He hath a half-face, like my father.
With half that face would he have all my land:
A half-faced groat five hundred pound a year!

King John. Act i, sc. 1, l. 92. [Bastard] The only use of "half-face."

Half-faced fellow.—*II Henry IV,* iii, 2, 283.

Half-faced fellowship.—*I Henry IV,* i, 3, 208.

Half-faced sun.—*II Henry VI,* iv, 1, 98. The only uses of "half-faced."

9
Your face hath got five hundred pound a year,
Yet sell your face for five pence and 'tis dear.

King John. Act i, sc. 1, l. 152. [Bastard]

10
I have seen better faces in my time
Than stands on any shoulder that I see

Before me at this instant.
King Lear. Act ii, sc. 2, l. 99. [Kent]
Show'd the better face.—*Love's Labour 's Lost,* v, 2, 388.
With better face.—*The Merchant of Venice,* i, 3, 137.

1
Pompey: Doth your honour see any harm in his face?
Escalus: Why, no.
Pompey: I 'll be supposed upon a book, his face is the worst thing about him.
Measure for Measure. Act ii, sc. 1, l. 161.

Why, you bald-pated, lying rascal, you must be hooded, must you? Show your knave's visage, with a pox to you! show your sheep-biting face, and be hanged an hour!
Measure for Measure. Act v, sc. 1, l. 356. [Lucio] The only use of "bald-pated" and "sheep-biting." "Baldpate" occurs in the same scene, l. 329, and nowhere else, and "sheep-biter" in *Twelfth Night,* ii, 5, 6.

2
Benedick: Some gentleman or other shall 'scape a predestinate scratched face.
Beatrice: Scratching could not make it worse, an 'twere such a face as yours were.
Much Ado about Nothing. Act i, sc. 1, l. 135. The only use of "predestinate."

3
Thurio: What says she to my face?
Proteus: She says it is a fair one.
Thurio: Nay then, the wanton lies; my face is black.
Proteus: But pearls are fair; and the old saying is,
Black men are pearls in beauteous ladies' eyes.
The Two Gentlemen of Verona. Act v, sc. 2, l. 8. George Chapman, in *An Humourous Day's Mirth,* sc. 8 (1599), quoted the proverb: "Black is a pearl in a woman's eye."

I tell thee, lady, this aspect of mine
Hath fear'd the valiant: by my love, I swear
The best-regarded virgins of our clime
Have loved it too: I would not change this hue.
The Merchant of Venice. Act ii, sc. 1, l. 8. [Prince of Morocco] The only use of "best-regarded."

The air hath starved the roses in her cheeks
And pinch'd the lily-tincture of her face,
That now she is become as black as I.
The Two Gentlemen of Verona. Act iv, sc. 4, l. 159. [Julia] The only use of "lily-tincture."

IV—The Sorrowful Face

4
How long her face is drawn.
Henry VIII. Act v, sc. 2, l. 97. [Patience]

5
Why, what 's the matter
That you have such a February face,
So full of frost, of storm and cloudiness?
Much Ado about Nothing. Act v, sc. 4, l. 40. [Don Pedro] The only use of February and "cloudiness."

6
That face
Which underneath thy black all-hiding cloak
Immodestly lies martyr'd with disgrace!
The Rape of Lucrece, l. 800. The only use of "all-hiding" and "immodestly."

Her face wore sorrow's livery.
The Rape of Lucrece, l. 1222.

A face where all distress is stell'd.
The Rape of Lucrece, l. 1444.

His face, though full of cares, yet show'd content.
The Rape of Lucrece, l. 1503.

The face, that map which deep impression bears
Of hard misfortune, carved in it with tears.
The Rape of Lucrece, l. 1712.

Sad face.—*The Rape of Lucrece,* l. 1591; *Twelfth Night,* iii, 4, 80.
Sad-faced.—*Titus Andronicus,* v, 3, 67. The only use of the phrase.

7
King Richard: Mark, silent king, the moral of this sport,
How soon my sorrow hath destroy'd my face.
Bolingbroke: The shadow of your sorrow hath destroy'd
The shadow of your face.
Richard II. Act iv, sc. 1, l. 290.

8
His face still combating with tears and smiles,
The badges of his grief and patience.
Richard II. Act v, sc. 2, l. 32. [York]

Poor soul, thy face is much abused with tears.
Romeo and Juliet. Act iv, sc. 1, l. 29. [Paris]

9
Unknit that sorrow-wreathen knot.
Titus Andronicus. Act iii, sc. 2, l. 4. [Titus] The only use of "sorrow-wreathen."

V—The Revealing Face

10
Nay, I knew by his face that there was something in him: he had, sir, a kind of face, methought,—I cannot tell how to term it.
Coriolanus. Act iv, sc. 5, l. 162. [Servant]

11
And in thy face strange motions have appear'd,
Such as we see when men restrain their breath
On some great sudden hest.
I Henry IV. Act ii, sc. 3, l. 63. [Lady Percy]

12
There 's no art
To find the mind's construction in the face.
Macbeth. Act i, sc. 4, l. 11. [Duncan]

Your face, my thane, is as a book where men
May read strange matters.
Macbeth. Act i, sc. 5, l. 63. [Lady Macbeth]

Away, and mock the time with fairest show:
False face must hide what the false heart doth know.
Macbeth. Act i, sc. 7, l. 81. [Macbeth]

False face.—*Troilus and Cressida,* v, 6, 6; *Macbeth,* i, 7, 82.
False-faced.—*Coriolanus,* i, 9, 44. The only use of the phrase.
False borrow'd face.—*Sonnets,* cxxvii.

13
In Ajax and Ulysses, O, what art
Of physiognomy might one behold!
The face of either cipher'd either's heart;

Their face their manners most expressly told.

The Rape of Lucrece, l. 1395. The only use of "physiognomy," and "cipher'd."

It cannot be, I find,
But such a face should bear a wicked mind.

The Rape of Lucrece, l. 1539.

1
By his face straight shall you know his heart.

Richard III. Act iii, sc. 4, l. 55. [Hastings]

Methinks I see it in thy face
What thou shouldst be.

The Tempest. Act ii, sc. 1, l. 206. [Antonio]

VI—The Painted Face

2
Iras: You shall paint when you are old.
Charmian: Wrinkles forbid!

Antony and Cleopatra. Act i, sc. 2, l. 18.

With a kind of umber smirch my face.

As You Like It. Act i, sc. 3, l. 114. [Celia] The only use of "umber." "Umber'd face" occurs in *Henry V*, iv, Prol., 9.

3
I have heard of your paintings too, well enough; God has given you one face, and you make yourselves another.

Hamlet. Act iii, sc. 1, l. 148. [Hamlet]

Let her paint an inch thick.—*Hamlet*, v, 1, 213.

4
A woman's face with Nature's own hand painted
Hast thou, the master-mistress of my passion.

Sonnets. No. xx. The only use of "master-mistress."

5
Paint till a horse may mire upon your face:
A pox of wrinkles!

Timon of Athens. Act iv, sc. 3, l. 147. [Timon]

Paint your face.—*The Taming of the Shrew*, i, 1, 65.

6
No more than were I painted I would wish
This youth should say 'twere well and only therefore
Desire to breed by me.

The Winter's Tale. Act iv, sc. 4, l. 101. [Perdita]

VII—Women's Faces

7
Was this fair face the cause, quoth she,
Why the Grecians sacked Troy?
Fond done, done fond,
Was this King Priam's joy?

All's Well that Ends Well. Act i, sc. 3, l. 74. [Clown] The only use of "sacked."

An if my face were but as fair as yours,
My favour were as great.

Love's Labour's Lost. Act v, sc. 2, l. 32. [Rosaline]

A fair face will wither.—*Henry V*, v, 2, 169.

Her fair face's field.—*Rape of Lucrece*, l. 72.

8
Menas: All men's faces are true, whatsome'er their hands are.
Enobarbus: But there is never a fair woman has a true face.
Menas: No slander; they steal hearts.

Antony and Cleopatra. Act ii, sc. 6, l. 102.

Cleopatra: Bear'st thou her face in mind? is 't long or round?
Messenger: Round even to faultiness.
Cleopatra: For the most part, too, they are foolish that are so.

Antony and Cleopatra. Act iii, sc. 3, l. 32. The only use of "faultiness."

9
He falls to such perusal of my face
As he would draw it.

Hamlet. Act ii, sc. 1, l. 90. [Ophelia] "Perusal" is repeated in *Sonnets*, xxxviii.

Let me peruse this face.

Romeo and Juliet. Act v, sc. 3, l. 74. [Romeo]

10
Nor shines the silver moon one half so bright
Through the transparent bosom of the deep,
As doth thy face through tears of mine give light.

Love's Labour's Lost. Act iv, sc. 3, l. 30. [King Ferdinand]

For when would you, my lord, or you, or you,
Have found the ground of study's excellence
Without the beauty of a woman's face?

Love's Labour's Lost. Act iv, sc. 3, l. 299. [Biron]

Biron: Vouchsafe to show the sunshine of your face,
That we, like savages, may worship it.
Rosaline: My face is but a moon, and clouded too.
King Ferdinand: Blessed are clouds, to do as such clouds do!

Love's Labour's Lost. Act v, sc. 2, l. 201.

11
This is that face, thou cruel Angelo,
Which once thou sworest was worth the looking on.

Measure for Measure. Act v, sc. 1, l. 207. [Mariana]

Her face was to mine eye beyond all wonder.

Pericles. Act i, sc. 2, l. 75. [Pericles]

12
The Roman dame,
Within whose face beauty and virtue strived
Which of them both should underprop her fame:
When virtue bragg'd, beauty would blush for shame;
When beauty boasted blushes, in despite
Virtue would stain that o'er with silver white.

The Rape of Lucrece, l. 51.

Her face defaced with scars of infamy.

Richard III. Act iii, sc. 7, l. 126. [Buckingham]

13
With unattainted eye,
Compare her face with some that I shall show,
And I will make thee think thy swan a crow.

Romeo and Juliet. Act i, sc. 2, l. 90. [Benvolio] The only use of "unattainted."

14
If I could write the beauty of your eyes

And in fresh numbers number all your graces,
The age to come would say 'This poet lies;
Such heavenly touches ne'er touch'd earthly faces.'
Sonnets. No. xvii.
In many's looks the false heart's history
Is writ in moods and frowns and wrinkles strange,
But heaven in thy creation did decree
That in thy face sweet love should ever dwell.
Sonnets. No. xciii.
My love's sweet face survey,
If Time have any wrinkle graven there.
Sonnets. No. c. The only use of "graven."
Thy face hath not the power to make love groan.
Sonnets. No. cxxxi.

1
Why, she hath a face of her own.
The Taming of the Shrew. Act iv, sc. 1, l. 102. [Grumio]
No woman's face remember,
Save, from my glass, mine own.
The Tempest. Act iii, sc. 1, l. 49. [Miranda]
Thou bear'st a woman's face.
Titus Andronicus. Act ii, sc. 3, l. 136. [Lavinia]

2
If I had such a tire, this face of mine
Were full as lovely as is this of hers.
The Two Gentlemen of Verona. Act iv, sc. 4, l. 190. [Julia]
What is in Silvia's face, but I may spy
More fresh in Julia's with a constant eye?
The Two Gentlemen of Verona. Act v, sc. 4, l. 114. [Proteus]

3
Her face o' fire
With labour and the thing she took to quench it,
She would to each one sip.
The Winter's Tale. Act iv, sc. 4, l. 60. [Shepherd]

FACT

4
To say the truth, this fact was infamous
And ill beseeming any common man.
I Henry VI. Act iv, sc. 1, l. 30. [Gloucester]
"Infamous" is used only once again, in *Antony and Cleopatra,* iv, 9, 19.
A fouler fact
Did never traitor in the land commit.
II Henry VI. Act i, sc. 3, l. 176. [Warwick]
Damned fact!—*Macbeth,* iii, 6, 10.
Sinful fact.—*All's Well that Ends Well,* iii, 7, 47.

5
Whom we have apprehended in the fact.
II Henry VI. Act ii, sc. 1, l. 173. [Buckingham]
Ay, if the fact be known.
The Rape of Lucrece, l. 239.

FAIL

6
I'll not fail, if I live.
As You Like It. Act v, sc. 2, l. 132. [Silvius]
I will not fail.—*The Two Gentlemen of Verona,* iv, 3, 45, and five times in later plays.
She will not fail.—*The Two Gentlemen of Verona,* v, 1, 4.
We will not fail.—*Much Ado about Nothing,* v, 1, 339.
It cannot fail.—*The Winter's Tale,* iv, 4, 487.
I pray you, fail me not.—*A Midsummer-Night's Dream,* i, 2, 109.
Fail not.—*All's Well that Ends Well,* iv, 2, 64; *Julius Cæsar,* ii, 1, 214; *Macbeth,* iii, 1, 28.
This fail you not to do.—*Othello,* iv, 1, 240.

7
Goodly and gallant shall be false and perjured
From thy great fail.
Cymbeline. Act iii, sc. 4, l. 65. [Imogen]
"Failure" does not occur in Shakespeare.

8
If he chance to fail, he hath sentenced himself.
Measure for Measure. Act iii, sc. 2, l. 271. [Duke]
And so may I, blind fortune leading me,
Miss that which one unworthier may attain,
And die with grieving.
The Merchant of Venice. Act ii, sc. 1, l. 36. [Prince of Morocco] The only use of "unworthier."

FAINTING

See also Swooning

9
He fainted
And cried in fainting upon Rosalind.
As You Like It. Act iv, sc. 3, l. 149. [Oliver]
He had fainted.—*The Rape of Lucrece,* l. 1543.
Expectation fainted.—*Antony and Cleopatra,* iii, 6, 47. The only uses of "fainted."
Almost at fainting.—*The Comedy of Errors,* i, 1, 46.
Fainting, despair!—*Richard III,* v, 3, 172.
Fainting hand.—*Titus Andronicus,* ii, 3, 233.
Fainting kiss.—*I Henry VI,* ii, 5, 40.
Fainting land.—*King John,* v, 7, 78.
Fainting words.—*I Henry VI,* ii, 5, 95. The only uses of "fainting."

10
Give me leave; I faint.
Cymbeline. Act v, sc. 5, l. 149. [Iachimo]
Lead me from hence; I faint.
Antony and Cleopatra. Act ii, sc. 5, l. 110. [Cleopatra]
I grow faint.—*Julius Cæsar,* ii, 4, 43.
I shall faint.—*Romeo and Juliet,* iii, 1, 111.
My wits faint.—*Romeo and Juliet,* ii, 4, 72.
Alas, he faints!—*Othello,* v, 1, 84; *King Lear,* v, 3, 311.
Why faint you, lords?—*III Henry VI,* i, 1, 129.

11
Ah, hark! the fatal followers do pursue;
And I am faint and cannot fly their fury.
III Henry VI. Act i, sc. 4, l. 22. [York]
I am faint.—*Macbeth,* i, 2, 42.
Faint with dearth.—*Venus and Adonis,* l. 545.
Most faint.—*The Tempest,* Epil., 3.

12
Would I had no being,
If this salute my blood a jot; it faints me,
To think what follows.
Henry VIII. Act ii, sc. 3, l. 102. [Anne]

1
Fair love, you faint with wandering in the wood.
A Midsummer-Night's Dream. Act ii, sc. 2, l. 35. [Lysander]

Faintness constraineth me
To measure out my length on this cold bed.
A Midsummer-Night's Dream. Act iii, sc. 2, l. 428. [Demetrius] "Faintness" is repeated in *I Henry VI,* iv, 1, 107: "Faintness of heart."

2
O, how I faint when I of you do write.
Sonnets. No. lxxx.

Grew I not faint? and fell I not downright?
Venus and Adonis, l. 645.

3
Paris should ne'er retract what he hath done,
Nor faint in the pursuit.
Troilus and Cressida. Act ii, sc. 2, l. 141. [Paris] The only use of "retract."

FAIRNESS, see Beauty

FAIRY

4
To this great fairy I'll commend thy acts.
Antony and Cleopatra. Act iv, sc. 8, l. 12. [Antony]

Night-tripping fairy.—*I Henry IV,* i, 1, 87. The only use of "night-tripping."

5
This is the fairy land: O spite of spites!
We talk with goblins, owls and sprites:
If we obey them not, this will ensue,
They'll suck our breath or pinch us black and blue.
The Comedy of Errors. Act ii, sc. 2, l. 191. [Dromio of Syracuse] "Fairy land," always in two words, is mentioned four times in the plays, three times in *A Midsummer-Night's Dream,* ii, 1, 65; ii, 1, 122; iv, 1, 66. "Fairy Kingdom" is used once, in *A Midsummer-Night's Dream,* ii, 1, 144.

Sweet sprites.—*The Tempest,* i, 2, 381. See also SPIRITS.

6
Urchins, ouphes and fairies, green and white.
The Merry Wives of Windsor. Act iv, sc. 4, l. 49. [Mrs. Page] "Ouphes" (elves) is repeated in v, 5, 61, and occurs in no other play. "Urchins" (goblins) is used again in *The Tempest,* i, 2, 326, and in *Titus Andronicus,* ii, 3, 101.

Fairies, black, grey, green, and white,
You moonshine revellers, and shades of night,
You orphan heirs of fixed destiny,
Attend your office and your quality.
The Merry Wives of Windsor. Act v, sc. 5, l. 41. [Mistress Quickly]

7
Go get us properties
And tricking for our fairies.
Merry Wives of Windsor. Act iv, sc. 5, l. 78. [Mrs. Page] The only use of "tricking."

They are fairies; he that speaks to them shall die:
I'll wink and couch: no man their works must eye.
The Merry Wives of Windsor. Act v, sc. 5, l. 51. [Falstaff]

And nightly, meadow-fairies, look you sing,
Like to the Garter's compass, in a ring.
The Merry Wives of Windsor. Act v, sc. 5, l. 69. [Mistress Quickly] The only use of "meadow-fairies."

8
Over hill, over dale,
Thorough bush, thorough brier,
Over park, over pale,
Thorough flood, thorough fire,
I do wander every where,
Swifter than the moon's sphere;
And I serve the fairy queen,
To dew her orbs upon the green.
A Midsummer-Night's Dream. Act ii, sc. 1, l. 2. [Fairy] "Fairy queen" occurs five times in the plays, once in *Merry Wives of Windsor,* iv, 6, 20, and four times in *A Midsummer-Night's Dream.* "Fairy king" is used only once, in *Midsummer-Night's Dream,* iv, 1, 98.

Fairy: Either I mistake your shape and making quite,
Or else you are that shrewd and knavish sprite
Call'd Robin Goodfellow: are not you he
That frights the maidens of the villagery;
Skim milk, and sometimes labour in the quern
And bootless make the breathless housewife churn;
And sometime make the drink to bear no barm;
Mislead night-wanderers, laughing at their harm?
Those that Hobgoblin call you and sweet Puck,
You do their work, and they shall have good luck:
Are you not he?
Puck: Thou speak'st aright;
I am that merry wanderer of the night.
I jest with Oberon and make him smile
When I a fat and bean-fed horse beguile,
Neighing in likeness of a filly foal:
And sometime lurk I in a gossip's bowl,
In very likeness of a roasted crab,
And when she drinks, against her lips I bob
And on her wither'd dewlap pour the ale.
The wisest aunt, telling the saddest tale,
Sometime for three-foot stool mistakest me;
Then slip I from her bum, down topples she,
And 'tailor' cries, and falls into a cough;
And then the whole quire hold their hips and laugh,
And waxen in their mirth and neeze and swear
A merrier hour was never wasted there.
A Midsummer-Night's Dream. Act ii, sc. 1, l. 32. Robin Goodfellow is mentioned five times in this play, and in no other. The only use of "villagery," "quern" (hand-mill), "churn," "barm," "night-wanderers," "bean-fed," "filly foal," "dewlap," and "neeze" (sneeze). "Hobgoblin" is repeated in *The Merry Wives of Windsor,* v, 5, 45. Puck is mentioned five times in this play, and in no other. "Three-foot stool" occurs again in *Cymbeline,* iii, 3, 89. Nobody knows why she should cry "tailor." "Skim milk" is used again in *I Henry IV,* 2, 3, 36, and it should be noted that "skim" is used in no other connection.

1
I 'll give thee fairies to attend on thee.
A Midsummer-Night's Dream, iii, 1, 160. [Titania]
Peaseblossom! Cobweb! Moth! and Mustard-seed!
A Midsummer-Night's Dream. Act iii, sc. 1, l. 165. [Titania]
I have a venturous fairy that shall seek
The squirrel's hoard.
A Midsummer-Night's Dream. Act iv, sc. 1, l. 39. [Titania]
'Tis almost fairy time.
A Midsummer-Night's Dream. Act v, sc. 1, l. 371. [Theseus]

2
Every elf and fairy sprite
Hop as light as bird from brier.
A Midsummer-Night's Dream. Act v, sc. 1, l. 400. [Oberon] "Elf" is repeated in *King Lear,* ii, 3, 10: "Elf all my hair in knots."
Farewell, thou lob of spirits, I 'll be gone:
Our queen and all her elves come here anon.
A Midsummer-Night's Dream. Act ii, sc. 1, l. 16. [Fairy] "Lob" is repeated in *Henry V,* iv, 2, 47: "Lob down their heads."
All their elves for fear
Creep into acorn-cups and hide them there.
A Midsummer-Night's Dream. Act ii, sc. 1, l. 31. [Puck] The only use of "acorn-cup."
Elves and fairies in a ring.
Macbeth, iv, 1, 42. See under SINGING.
Ye elves of hills, brooks, standing lakes and groves,
And ye that on the sands with printless foot
Do chase the ebbing Neptune and do fly him
When he comes back; you demi-puppets that
By moonshine do the green sour ringlets make,
Whereof the ewe not bites, and you whose pastime
Is to make midnight mushrooms, that rejoice
To hear the solemn curfew.
The Tempest. Act v, sc. 1, l. 33. [Prospero] The only mention of mushrooms, and the only use of "printless" and "demi-puppets."
Small elves.—*A Midsummer-Night's Dream,* ii, 2, 5.

3 But are you flesh and blood?
Have you a working pulse? and are no fairy?
Pericles. Act v, sc. 1, l. 154. [Pericles]

4
O, then, I see Queen Mab hath been with you,
She is the fairies' midwife, and she comes
In shape no bigger than an agate-stone
On the fore-finger of an alderman,
Drawn with a team of little atomies
Athwart men's noses as they lie asleep;
Her waggon-spokes made of long spinners' legs,
The cover of the wings of grasshoppers,
The traces of the smallest spider's web,
The collars of the moonshine's watery beams,
Her whip of cricket's bone, the lash of film,
Her waggoner a small grey-coated gnat,
Not half so big as a round little worm
Prick'd from the lazy finger of a maid;
Her chariot is an empty hazel-nut
Made by the joiner squirrel or old grub,
Time out o' mind the fairies' coachmakers.
And in this state she gallops night by night
Through lovers' brains, and then they dream of love.
Romeo and Juliet. Act i, sc. 4, l. 53. [Mercutio] The only use of "agate-stone," "waggon-spokes," "grasshoppers," "grey-coated," and "coach-makers." "Collar" occurs in i, 1, 6, and in no other play. "Fore-finger" (unhyphenated) is repeated in *All 's Well that Ends Well,* ii, 2, 24; "film" in *Hamlet,* iii, 4, 147; and "hazel nut" (unhyphenated) in *The Taming of the Shrew,* ii, 1, 257.
This is that very Mab
That plats the manes of horses in the night,
And bakes the elf-locks in foul sluttish hairs,
Which once untangled much misfortune bodes.
Romeo and Juliet. Act i, sc. 4, l. 88. [Mercutio] The only use of "elf-locks," though *King Lear,* ii, 3, 10, has, "Elf all my hair in knots." Mab is mentioned a third time in i, 4, 75, and in no other play. "Plats" is repeated in *A Lover's Complaint,* l. 29.

5
Go charge my goblins that they grind their joints.
The Tempest, iv, 1, 259. See under PUNISHMENT.
With ho! such bugs and goblins in my life.
Hamlet. Act v, sc. 2, l. 22. [Hamlet]
Goblin, lead them up and down.—*A Midsummer-Night's Dream,* iii, 2, 399.
Goblins swift as frenzy's thoughts.—*Troilus and Cressida,* v, 10, 29.
Goblin damn'd.—*Hamlet,* i, 4, 40.
Goblins, owls and sprites.—*The Comedy of Errors,* ii, 2, 192.
Sprites and goblins.—*The Winter's Tale,* ii, 1, 26. The only references to goblins.

6 Where the bee sucks, there suck I:
In a cowslip's bell I lie;
There I couch when owls do cry.
On the bat's back I do fly
After summer merrily.
Merrily, merrily shall I live now
Under the blossom that hangs on the bough.
The Tempest. Act v, sc. 1, l. 88. [Ariel]

FAITH

7
Betake thee to thy faith, for seventeen poniards are at thy bosom.
All 's Well that Ends Well. Act iv, sc. 1, l. 83. [Soldier] "Seventeen" is used six times in the plays.

8
Hast no faith in thee?
I Henry IV. Act ii, sc. 1, l. 34. [Carrier]
There 's no more faith in thee than in a stewed prune.
I Henry IV. Act iii, sc. 3, l. 127. [Falstaff]
I have a saving faith within me.
Henry V. Act v, sc. 2, l. 217. [King Henry]

9
Ay, by my faith.
II Henry VI, iv, 2, 55. "By my faith" is repeated fourteen times in later plays.

By my two faiths.—*Much Ado about Nothing,* i, 1, 228.
By the faith of men.—*Coriolanus,* ii, 1, 204; *Othello,* i, 1, 10.
Faith of valour.—*Troilus and Cressida,* v, 3, 69.
On my faith.—*Romeo and Juliet,* iv, 5, 115.
Upon my faith.—*Measure for Measure,* v, 1, 224.
Faith (as a prefix).—*II Henry VI,* ii, 1, 38, and sixteen times in later plays.
In faith.—*The Taming of the Shrew,* Induction, l. 1, and thirty-six times in later plays.
In good faith.—*Love's Labour's Lost,* v, 2, 279, and seven times in later plays.
Good faith.—*III Henry VI,* iii, 2, 23, and thirteen times in later plays.
Fair faith.—*Troilus and Cressida,* iii, 2, 103.
True faith.—*Richard II,* iii, 3, 37; *Julius Cæsar,* iii, 1, 137; *As You Like It,* v, 4, 194.
Faith irrevocable.—*III Henry VI,* iii, 3, 247.

1
There are no tricks in plain and simple faith.
Julius Cæsar. Act iv, sc. 2, l. 22. [Brutus]

2
Blanch: The Lady Constance speaks not from her faith,
But from her need.
Constance: O, if thou grant my need,
Which only lives but by the death of faith,
That need must needs infer this principle,
That faith would live again by death of need.
O then, tread down my need, and faith mounts up;
Keep my need up, and faith is trodden down!
King John. Act iii, sc. 1, l. 210.

King Philip: I may disjoin my hand, but not my faith.
Pandulph: So makest thou faith an enemy to faith.
King John. Act iii, sc. 1, l. 262.

Welcome home again discarded faith.
King John. Act v, sc. 4, l. 12. [Melun]

3 A faith that reason without miracle
Could never plant in me.
King Lear. Act i, sc. 1, l. 225. [France]

4
Ah, never faith could hold, if not to beauty vow'd!
Love's Labour's Lost. Act iv, sc. 2, l. 110. [Sir Nathaniel] Repeated in *The Passionate Pilgrim,* l. 58.

O beauty! where is thy faith?
Troilus and Cressida. Act v, sc. 2, l. 67. [Troilus]

5
Quick Biron hath plighted faith to me.
Love's Labour's Lost. Act v, sc. 2, l. 283. [Princess]

Plight me the full assurance of your faith;
That my most jealous and too doubtful soul
May live at peace.
Twelfth Night. Act iv, sc. 3, l. 26. [Olivia]

Plighted faith.—*I Henry VI,* v, 3, 162.
Faith and troth.—*Troilus and Cressida,* iv, 5, 168.

6
Disparage not the faith thou dost not know.
A Midsummer-Night's Dream. Act iii, sc. 2, l. 174. [Demetrius]

I will disparage her no farther.
Much Ado about Nothing, iii, 2, 131. The only uses of "disparage." "Disparagement" occurs three times.

My life upon her faith!
Othello. Act i, sc. 3, l. 295. [Othello]

7 Here is my bond of faith,
To tie thee to my strong correction.
Richard II. Act iv, sc. 1, l. 76. [Fitzwater]

8
Look your faith be firm.
Richard III. Act iv, sc. 4, l. 497. [King Richard]

Keep our faiths firm and inviolable.
King John. Act v, sc. 2, l. 7. [Dauphin] "Inviolable" is repeated in *III Henry VI,* i, 1, 30.

Firm faith.—*Troilus and Cressida,* iii, 2, 116.

9
They pray, grant thou, lest faith turn to despair.
Romeo and Juliet. Act i, sc. 5, l. 106. [Romeo]

My husband is on earth, my faith in heaven;
How shall that faith return again to earth,
Unless that husband send it me from heaven
By leaving earth?
Romeo and Juliet. Act iii, sc. 5, l. 207. [Juliet]

10
You to non-regardance cast my faith.
Twelfth Night. Act v, sc. 1, l. 124. [Duke] The only use of "non-regardance."

O, do not swear!
Hold little faith, though thou hast too much fear.
Twelfth Night. Act v, sc. 1, l. 173. [Olivia]

It is required You do awake your faith.
Winter's Tale. Act v, sc. 3, l. 94. [Paulina]

Give me faith, I say.—*Twelfth Night,* i, 5, 137.

II—Faithlessness

11
Men's faiths are wafer-cakes.
Henry V. Act ii, sc. 3, l. 53. [Pistol] The only use of "wafer-cakes."

12 Why hast thou broken faith with me,
Knowing how hardly I can brook abuse?
II Henry VI. Act v, sc. 1, l. 91. [York]

Trust him not that hath once broken faith.
III Henry VI. Act iv, sc. 4, l. 30. [Queen Elizabeth]

At no time broke my faith.
Macbeth. Act iv, sc. 3, l. 128. [Malcolm]

13
Play fast and loose with faith.
King John. Act iii, sc. 1, l. 242. [King Philip] "Fast and loose" is repeated in *Love's Labour's Lost,* i, 2, 162; iii, 1, 104; and in *Antony and Cleopatra,* iv, 12, 28.

Waver in my faith.—*The Merchant of Venice,* iv, 1, 130.

14
O faithless coward!
Measure for Measure, iii, 1, 137. See under COWARDICE.

Faithless error.—*King John,* ii, 1, 20.
Faithless Jew.—*Merchant of Venice,* ii, 4, 38.
Faithless service.—*Henry VIII,* ii, 1, 123. The only uses of "faithless."

1 Your lord
Will never more break faith advisedly.
The Merchant of Venice. Act v, sc. 5, l. 252. [Antonio]
I must not break my faith.
Troilus and Cressida. Act v, sc. 3, l. 71. [Hector]
Break faith.—*Love's Labour's Lost,* i, 1, 154; iv, 3, 143; *The Merchant of Venice,* v, 1, 253; *King John,* ii, 1, 597.
Break his faith.—*A Midsummer-Night's Dream,* ii, 1, 79.
Breaking faith.—*The Two Gentlemen of Verona,* iv, 2, 11.

2
He wears his faith but as the fashion of his hat; it ever changes with the next block.
Much Ado about Nothing. Act i, sc. 1, l. 75. [Beatrice]
False faith.—*Richard III,* v, 1, 17.

3
Purest faith unhappily forsworn.
Sonnets. No. lxvi.
All my honest faith in thee is lost.
Sonnets. No. clii.

4
Thou hast no faith left now, unless thou 'dst two;
And that 's far worse than none; better have none
Than plural faith which is too much by one.
The Two Gentlemen of Verona. Act v, sc. 4, l. 50. [Silvia] "Plural" is repeated in *The Merry Wives of Windsor,* iv, 1, 59.
Without faith.—*The Two Gentlemen of Verona,* v, 4, 62.

5 It cannot fail but by
The violation of my faith; and then
Let nature crush the sides o' the earth together
And mar the seeds within!
The Winter's Tale. Act iv, sc. 4, l. 486. [Florizel]

FALCON

6
King: But what a point, my lord, your falcon made,
And what a pitch she flew above the rest! . . .
Suffolk: No marvel, an it like your majesty,
My lord protector's hawks do tower so well;
They know their master loves to be aloft
And bears his thoughts above his falcon's pitch.
II Henry VI. Act ii, sc. 1, l. 5.

7 On Tuesday last,
A falcon, towering in her pride of place,
Was by a mousing owl hawk'd at and kill'd.
Macbeth. Act ii, sc. 4, l. 11. [Old Man] "Mousing" is repeated in *King John,* ii, 1, 354. The only use of "hawk'd."

8
Like a falcon towering in the skies,
Coucheth the fowl below with his wings' shade.
The Rape of Lucrece, l. 506.
With trembling fear, as fowl hears falcon's bells.
The Rape of Lucrece, l. 511.

9
Dost thou love hawking? thou hast hawks will soar
Above the morning lark.
The Taming of the Shrew. Induction, sc. 2, l. 45. [Lord]
I have a fine hawk for the bush.
The Merry Wives of Windsor. Act iii, sc. 3, l. 247. [Page]

10
My falcon now is sharp and passing empty;
And till she stoop she must not be full-gorged,
For then she never looks upon her lure.
The Taming of the Shrew. Act iv, sc. 1, l. 193. [Petruchio] The only use of "full-gorged." "Lure" is repeated in *Romeo and Juliet,* ii, 2, 160.
As falcon to the lure, away she flies.
Venus and Adonis, l. 1027.
The falcon as the tercel, for all the ducks i' the river.
Troilus and Cressida. Act iii, sc. 2, l. 56. [Pandarus] The only use of "tercel."

11 I bless the time
When my good falcon made her flight across
Thy father's ground.
The Winter's Tale. Act iv, sc. 4, l. 14. [Florizel]

12
We 'll e'en to 't like French falconers, fly at any thing we see.
Hamlet. Act ii, sc. 2, l. 450. [Hamlet]
O, for a falconer's voice.—*Romeo and Juliet,* ii, 2, 159. The only uses of "falconer."

FALL

13
When better fall, for your avails they fell.
All's Well that Ends Well. Act iii, sc. 1, l. 22. [Duke]
But we have almost embossed him; you shall see his fall to-night.
All's Well that Ends Well. Act iii, sc. 6, l. 107. [Second Lord]

14 Tremblingly she stood
And on a sudden dropp'd.
Antony and Cleopatra. Act v, sc. 2, l. 346. [Guard] The only use of "tremblingly."
Dropp'd, as by a thunder-stroke.—*The Tempest,* ii, 1, 204.
Dropp'd down.—*I Henry IV,* iv, 1, 108; *The Winter's Tale,* iii, 2, 203.
Dropp'd from heaven.—*The Tempest,* ii, 2, 140.

15
Duke: You shall try but one fall.
Charles: No, I warrant your grace, you shall not entreat him to a second.
As You Like It. Act i, sc. 2, l. 216. "Try a fall" is repeated in i, 1, 132, and occurs nowhere else.
You will try in time, in despite of a fall.
As You Like It. Act i, sc. 3, l. 24. [Celia]

16 Be cheerful; wipe thine eyes:
Some falls are means the happier to arise.
Cymbeline. Act iv, sc. 2, l. 402. [Caius]

1
What a falling-off was there!
Hamlet. Act i, sc. 5, l. 47. [Ghost] The only use of "falling-off."

2
The hope and expectation of thy time
Is ruin'd, and the soul of every man
Prophetically doth forethink thy fall.
I Henry IV. Act iii, sc. 2, l. 36. [King Henry] The only use of "forethink." "Prophetically" is repeated in *Troilus and Cressida,* iii, 3, 248.
And thus thy fall hath left a kind of blot,
To mark the full-fraught man and best indued
With some suspicion. I will weep for thee;
For this revolt of thine, methinks, is like
Another fall of man.
Henry V. Act ii, sc. 2, l. 138. [King Henry] "Full-fraught" is repeated in *The Two Gentlemen of Verona,* iii, 2, 70.
Fall of cursed man.—*Richard II,* iii, 4, 76.
Fall of an ass.—*Cymbeline,* i, 2, 39.
Fall of blood.—*Henry V,* i, 2, 25.
Fall of kings.—*Richard II,* ii, 4, 15.
Fall of many kings.—*Macbeth,* iv, 3, 69.
A true king's fall.—*Richard II,* iv, 1, 318.
Sovereign's fall.—*II Henry VI,* iii, 1, 52.
Fall of leaf.—*Richard II,* iii, 4, 49.
Fall of vanity.—*Richard III,* iii, 7, 97.
Fall of waters.—*Richard III,* iv, 4, 512.
England's fall.—*Henry V,* iii, 5, 68.

3
Cardinal: What, art thou lame?
Simpcox: Ay, God Almighty help me!
Suffolk: How camest thou so?
Simpcox: A fall off of a tree.
Wife: A plum-tree, master.
II Henry VI. Act ii, sc. 1, l. 95. "Off of" used in the first play and never again. "Plum-tree" is repeated in *Hamlet,* ii, 2, 201.

4
This way fall I to death.
II Henry VI, iii, 2, 412. See under DEATH.
Fall, and bruise to death.—*Measure for Measure,* ii, 1, 6.
Fall and die.—*I Henry VI,* iv, 6, 47; *King John,* iii, 1, 33; *The Rape of Lucrece,* l. 1139.
Fall dead.—*Romeo and Juliet,* v, 1, 62.
Dying fall.—*Twelfth Night,* i, 1, 4.

5
I shall fall
Like a bright exhalation in the evening,
And no man see me more.
Henry VIII. Act iii, sc. 2, l. 225. [Wolsey]
I have ventured,
Like little wanton boys that swim on bladders,
This many summers in a sea of glory,
But far beyond my depth: my high-blown pride
At length broke under me and now has left me,
Weary and old with service, to the mercy
Of a rude stream, that must for ever hide me.
Henry VIII. Act iii, sc. 2, l. 358. [Wolsey] The only use of "high-blown."
And when he falls, he falls like Lucifer,
Never to hope again.
Henry VIII. Act iii, sc. 2, l. 371. [Wolsey]
What, amazed
At my misfortunes? can thy spirit wonder
A great man should decline? Nay, an you weep,
I am fall'n indeed.
Henry VIII. Act iii, sc. 2, l. 373. [Wolsey]
I am a poor fall'n man, unworthy now
To be thy lord and master.
Henry VIII. Act iii, sc. 2, l. 413. [Wolsey]
Fall'n from favour.—*Henry VIII,* iii, 1, 20.
Mark but my fall, and that that ruin'd me.
Henry VIII, iii, 2, 439. See under AMBITION.
If thou fall'st, O Cromwell,
Thou fall'st a blessed martyr!
Henry VIII. Act iii, sc. 2, l. 448. [Wolsey]

6
Press not a falling man too far!
Henry VIII. Act iii, sc. 2, l. 333. [Lord Chamberlain] "Falling man" is repeated in v, 3, 77.
Falling from a hill.—*I Henry IV,* v, 5, 21.
Falling Merely through fear.—*Cymbeline,* v, 3, 10.
Certain falling.—*Cymbeline,* iii, 3, 48.

7
He swounded and fell down at it.
Julius Cæsar. Act i, sc. 2, l. 250. [Casca]
He fell down in the market-place.
Julius Cæsar. Act i, sc. 2, l. 254. [Casca] "Fell down" is repeated in i, 2, 260; and iii, 2, 195. It occurs in no other play.
Fell gently down.—*III Henry VI,* ii, 1, 132.
I Costard, running out, that was safely within,
Fell over the threshold, and broke my shin.
Love's Labour's Lost. Act iii, sc. 1, l. 117. [Costard]
The fourth turn'd on the toe, and down he fell.
Love's Labour's Lost. Act v, sc. 2, l. 114. [Boyet]
Fell I not downright?—*Venus and Adonis,* l. 645.
And without trial fell.—*Henry VIII,* ii, 1, 111.

8
As low as to thy foot doth Cassius fall.
Julius Cæsar. Act iii, sc. 1, l. 56. [Cassius]
O, what a fall was there, my countrymen!
Then I, and you, and all of us fell down,
Whilst bloody treason flourish'd over us.
Julius Cæsar. Act iii, sc. 2, l. 194. [Antony]

9
I know not what may fall.
Julius Cæsar. Act iii, sc. 1, l. 243. [Cassius]
What might fall.—*Julius Cæsar,* v, 1, 105.

10
Hadst thou been aught but gossamer, feathers, air,
So many fathom down precipitating,
Thou 'dst shiver'd like an egg: but thou dost breathe;
Hast heavy substance; bleed'st not; speak'st; art sound.
Ten masts at each make not the altitude
Which thou hast perpendicularly fell.
King Lear. Act iv, sc. 6, l. 50. [Edgar] The only use of "precipitating" and "perpendicularly." "Perpendicular" occurs in *I Henry IV,* ii, 4, 378. "Gossamer" is repeated in *Romeo and Juliet,* ii, 6, 18.
An the worst fall that ever fell, I hope I shall make shift to go without him.
The Merchant of Venice. Act i, sc. 2, l. 96. [Portia]
Heavy fall.—*Richard III,* v, 3, 111.
Fall heavy.—*Much Ado about Nothing,* v, 1, 150.
Present fall.—*The Rape of Lucrece,* l. 551.
Untimely fall.—*Richard III,* i, 2, 4.

1
Submissive fall his princely feet before.
Love's Labour's Lost. Act iv, sc. 1, l. 92. [Boyet]
Fall before his feet.—*King John*, v, 4, 13.
Fall by thy side.—*Sonnets*, cli.
Fall from the faith.—*Much Ado about Nothing*, i, 1, 257.
Fall in twenty pieces.—*Romeo and Juliet*, ii, 5, 50.
Fall into Charybdis.—*The Merchant of Venice*, iii, 5, 19.
Fall into the fire.—*As You Like It*, i, 2, 47.
Fall into the trap.—*Henry VIII*, v, 1, 141.
Fall together.—*Julius Cæsar*, ii, 1, 161.
Fall all together.—*Troilus and Cressida*, v, 3, 62.
Fall upon the ground.—*Romeo and Juliet*, iii, 3, 69.
Rise and fall.—*Titus Andronicus*, ii, 4, 24; *Sonnets*, cli.
Rise up and fall.—*The Rape of Lucrece*, l. 466.

2
Then down upon her knees she falls.
Much Ado about Nothing. Act ii, sc. 3, l. 152. [Claudio]
Fall upon your knees.—*Julius Cæsar*, i, 1, 58. See under KNEE.
Fall on your head.—*King John*, iv, 2, 136.
Falls Upon your heads.—*The Tempest*, iii, 3, 80.

3
He falls, and bathes the pale fear in his face.
The Rape of Lucrece, l. 1775.

4
And Richard falls in height of all his pride.
Richard III. Act v, sc. 3, l. 176. [Ghost]

5
'Yea,' quoth he, 'dost thou fall upon thy face?
Thou wilt fall backward when thou hast more wit.'
Romeo and Juliet. Act i, sc. 3, l. 41. [Nurse] The only use of "fall backward."
Fall back.—*Romeo and Juliet*, ii, 2, 30.
Fall away.—*I Henry VI*, iii, 1, 193; *Henry VIII*, ii, 1, 129.
Fall down.—*I Henry VI*, iv, 2, 49, and seven times in later plays.
Fall flat.—*The Tempest*, ii, 2, 16.
Fallen flat-long.—*The Tempest*, ii, 1, 181. The only use of "flat-long."
Fall foul.—*II Henry IV*, ii, 4, 183.
Fall in.—*II Henry VI*, ii, 4, 183; *I Henry IV*, i, 3, 194; *II Henry IV*, i, 1, 171.
Fall in love.—*The Two Gentlemen of Verona*, i, 2, 2, and eight times in later plays.
Fallen in love.—*As You Like It*, iii, 5, 66.
Fall off.—*The Two Gentlemen of Verona*, v, 4, 113; *I Henry IV*, i, 3, 94; *King Lear*, i, 2, 116.
Fall out.—*I Henry VI*, ii, 3, 4, and seventeen times in later plays.
Fall over.—*King John*, iii, 1, 127.
Fall prostrate.—*The Comedy of Errors*, v, 1, 114; *Romeo and Juliet*, iv, 2, 20.
Fall to.—*Henry V*, v, 1, 38, and four times in later plays.
Fall to 't.—*I Henry VI*, iii, 1, 90; *Timon of Athens*, i, 2, 71; *The Tempest*, i, 1, 3.
Fall to blows.—*II Henry VI*, ii, 3, 80.
Fall to decay.—*Sonnets*, xv.
Fall to the earth.—*Venus and Adonis*, l. 546.
Fall to play.—*Hamlet*, v, 2, 216.
Fall to quarrel.—*King Lear*, iv, 6, 37.
Fall to reprobation.—*Othello*, v, 2, 209.
Fall to ruin.—*Pericles*, ii, 4, 37.
Fall To cureless ruin.—*The Merchant of Venice*, iv, 1, 141.

6
Now falls on her bed; and then starts up,
. . . And then down falls again.
Romeo and Juliet. Act iii, sc. 3, l. 100. [Nurse]
You will fall again.—*Venus and Adonis*, l. 769.

7
Down fell priest and book and book and priest.
The Taming of the Shrew. Act iii, sc. 2, l. 166. [Gremio]
They fell together.—*The Tempest*, ii, 1, 203.

8
Such a house broke!
So noble a master fall'n!
Timon of Athens. Act iv, sc. 2, l. 5. [Servant]
Ours is the fall, I fear; our foes the snare.
Timon of Athens. Act v, sc. 2, l. 17. [Senator]

9
If you say we shall,
Lo, hand in hand, Lucius and I will fall.
Titus Andronicus. Act v, sc. 3, l. 135. [Marcus]
When they fall, as being slippery standers,
The love that lean'd on them as slippery too,
Do one pluck down another and together
Die in the fall.
Troilus and Cressida. Act iii, sc. 3, l. 84. [Achilles] The only use of "standers."

10
If one break, the other will hold; or, if both break, your gaskins fall.
Twelfth Night. Act i, sc. 5, l. 26. [Maria] The only use of "gaskins" (hose).

11
And at his look she flatly falleth down.
Venus and Adonis, l. 463.
With this, she falleth in the place she stood.
Venus and Adonis, l. 1121.
Falleth like a crab.—*Love's Labour's Lost*, iv, 2, 6. The only uses of "falleth."

12
He on her belly falls, she on her back.
Venus and Adonis, l. 594.
And now 'tis dark, and going I shall fall.
Venus and Adonis, l. 719.
She must fall.—*Henry VIII*, ii, 1, 167.
But if thou fall, O, then imagine this,
The earth, in love with thee, thy footing trips.
Venus and Adonis, l. 721.

FALSEHOOD

See also Lie; Truth and Falsehood

13
Thou speak'st it falsely, as I love mine honour;
And make conjectural fears to come into me,
Which I would fain shut out.
All's Well that Ends Well. Act v, sc. 3, l. 113. [King] "Conjectural" is repeated in *Coriolanus*, i, 1, 198: "Conjectural marriages."

1
Falsehood Is worse in kings than beggars.
Cymbeline, iii, 6, 13. See under Lie.

2
Can Oxford, that did ever fence the right,
Now buckler falsehood with a pedigree?
III Henry VI. Act iii, sc. 3, l. 98. [Warwick]

3
Falsehood falsehood cures, as fire cools coal.
King John. Act iii, sc. 1, l. 277. [Pandulph]

4
O, what a goodly outside falsehood hath!
The Merchant of Venice. Act i, sc. 3, l. 103. [Antonio]

5
I will turn thy falsehood to thy heart,
Where it was forged.
Richard II, iv, 1, 39. See under Lie.

6
When I protest true loyalty to her,
She twits me with my falsehood to my friend.
The Two Gentlemen of Verona. Act iv, sc. 2, l. 8. [Proteus] "Twits" is used twice more in the plays, *II Henry VI,* iii, 1, 178; *I Henry VI,* iii, 2, 55. "Twitting" is used once, *III Henry VI,* iii, 1, 178. These are the first three plays.

Your falsehood shall become you well.
The Two Gentlemen of Verona. Act iv, sc. 2, l. 130. [Silvia]

This is mere falsehood.—*The Winter's Tale,* iii, 2, 142.

Excellent falsehood!—*Antony and Cleopatra,* i, 1, 40.

Hidden falsehood.—*Richard III,* ii, 1, 14.

Hollow falsehood.—*King John,* iii, 1, 95.

Hourly falsehood.—*Cymbeline,* i, 6, 107.

Eyes' falsehood.—*Sonnets,* cxxxvii.

FALSENESS

See also Inconstancy, Infidelity

7
The story then goes false.
All's Well that Ends Well. Act v, sc. 2, l. 229. [King]

8
Thou art
The armourer of my heart: false, false.
Antony and Cleopatra. Act iv, sc. 4, l. 4. [Antony]

I am falser than vows made in wine.
As You Like It. Act iii, sc. 5, l. 73. [Rosalind] "Falser" is repeated in *Julius Cæsar,* ii, 2, 63.

A thing falsing.—*The Comedy of Errors,* ii, 2, 95. The only use of "falsing."

9
For if we two be one and thou play false,
I do digest the poison of thy flesh,
Being strumpeted by thy contagion.
The Comedy of Errors. Act ii, sc. 2, l. 144. [Adriana] The only use of "strumpeted."

Adriana: Dissembling villain, thou speak'st false in both.
Antipholus of Ephesus: Dissembling harlot, thou art false in all.
The Comedy of Errors. Act iv, sc. 4, l. 103.

That is false thou dost report to us.
The Comedy of Errors. Act v, sc. 1, l. 179. [Adriana]

This is false he burdens me withal!
The Comedy of Errors. Act v, sc. 1, l. 209. [Adriana]

This is false you burden me withal.
The Comedy of Errors. Act v, sc. 1, l. 268. [Antipholus of Ephesus]

10
False to his bed! What is it to be false?
To lie in watch there and to think on him?
To weep 'twixt clock and clock? if sleep charge nature,
To break it with a fearful dream of him
And cry myself awake? that's false to's bed, is it?
Cymbeline. Act iii, sc. 4, l. 42. [Imogen]

O, above measure false!—*Cymbeline,* ii, 4, 113.

11
Great Northumberland, then false to him,
Would of that seed grow to a greater falseness.
II Henry IV. Act iii, sc. 1, l. 89. [Warwick]

Livery falseness in a pride of truth.
A Lover's Complaint, l. 105.

Falseness cannot come from thee.
Pericles. Act v, sc. 1, l. 121. [Pericles] The only uses of "falseness."

12
We to ourselves prove false,
By being once false for ever to be true
To those that make us both,—fair ladies, you:
And even that falsehood, in itself a sin,
Thus purifies itself and turns to grace.
Love's Labour's Lost. Act v, sc. 2, l. 786. [Biron] The only use of "purifies."

13
Don John: The lady is disloyal. . . .
Claudio: Disloyal?
Don John: The word is too good to paint out her wickedness. I could say she were worse: think of a worse title, and I will fit her to it.
Much Ado about Nothing. Act iii, sc. 2, l. 107.

Our most disloyal lady.—*The Winter's Tale,* ii, 3, 202.

She's disloyal.—*Othello,* iii, 3, 409.

Disloyal to thy bed.—*Richard II,* v, 2, 105.

Disloyal! No: She's punish'd for her truth.
Cymbeline, iii, 2, 6. See under Punishment.

To God, his sovereign and to him disloyal.
Richard II. Act i, sc. 3, l. 114. [Herald]

To me disloyal.—*Cymbeline,* iii, 4, 33.

O disloyal thing.—*Cymbeline,* i, 1, 131.

Disloyal knave.—*Othello,* iii, 3, 121.

Disloyal man.—*The Two Gentlemen of Verona,* iv, 2, 95.

Disloyal traitor.—*Macbeth,* i, 2, 52. The only uses of "disloyal."

Become disloyalty.—*The Comedy of Errors,* iii, 2, 11.

Hero's disloyalty.—*Much Ado about Nothing,* ii, 2, 49. The only uses of "disloyalty."

14
If she be false, O, then heaven mocks itself!
Othello. Act iii, sc. 3, l. 278. [Othello]

For every inch of woman in the world,
Ay, every dram of woman's flesh is false,
If she be.
The Winter's Tale. Act ii, sc. 1, l. 137. [Antigonus]

1
On pain to be found false and recreant.
Richard II. Act i, sc. 3, l. 111. [Herald]
You are all recreants.—*II Henry VI,* iv, 8, 28.
All recreant.—*The Rape of Lucrece,* l. 710.
A mere recreant.—*Troilus and Cressida,* i, 3, 287.
A caitiff recreant!—*Richard II,* i, 2, 53.
Distrustful recreants.—*I Henry VI,* i, 2, 126.
Foreign recreant.—*Coriolanus,* v, 3, 114.
Recreant coward.—*II Henry IV,* v, 3, 96.
Recreant limbs.—*King John,* iii, 1, 129.
Recreant . . . traitor.—*Richard II,* i, 1, 144.
Come, recreant.—*Midsummer-Night's Dream,* iii, 2, 409.
Hear me, recreant!—*King Lear,* i, 1, 169. The only uses of "recreant" and "recreants."

2
Lady Anne: I fear me both are false.
Gloucester: Then never man was true.
Richard III. Act i, sc. 2, l. 195.
As false by heaven, as heaven itself is true.
Richard II. Act iv, sc. 1, l. 64. [Surrey]
You'll be so true to him, to be false to him.
Troilus and Cressida. Act iv, sc. 2, l. 57. [Æneas]
Say what you can, my false o'erweighs your true.
Measure for Measure. Act ii, sc. 4, l. 170. [Angelo]

3
But what so blessed-fair that fears no blot?
Thou mayst be false, and yet I know it not.
Sonnets. No. xcii. The only use of "blessed-fair."
O, never say that I was false of heart,
Though absence seem'd my flame to qualify.
Sonnets. No. cix.
False of heart.—*King Lear,* iii, 4, 95.

4
If I be false, or swerve a hair from truth,
When time is old and hath forgot itself,
When waterdrops have worn the stones of Troy,
And blind oblivion swallow'd cities up,
And mighty states characterless are grated
To dusty nothing, yet let memory,
From false to false, among false maids in love,
Upbraid my falsehood! when they've said 'as false
As air, as water, wind, or sandy earth,
As fox to lamb, as wolf to heifer's calf,
Pard to the hind, or stepdame to her son,'
'Yea,' let them say, to stick the heart of falsehood,
'As false as Cressid.'
Troilus and Cressida. Act iii, sc. 2, l. 191. [Cressida] The only use of "characterless." "Waterdrops" is repeated in *Richard II,* iv, 1, 262, and in *King Lear,* ii, 4, 280; and "grated" in *Merry Wives of Windsor,* ii, 2, 6.
Heaven truly knows that thou art false as hell.
Othello. Act iv, sc. 2, l. 39. [Othello]
Othello: She was false as water.
Emilia: Thou art rash as fire, to say
That she was false: O, she was heavenly true!
Othello. Act v, sc. 2, l. 134.

5
He plays false, father.
The Two Gentlemen of Verona. Act iv, sc. 2, l. 59. [Julia]
Sweet lord, you play me false.
The Tempest. Act v, sc. 1, l. 172. [Miranda]

FAME

See also Renown, Reputation

6
He was famous, sir, in his profession.
All's Well that Ends Well. Act i, sc. 1, l. 29. [Countess]
He was much famed.—*All's Well that Ends Well,* i, 2, 71.
Most famed.—*Henry V,* ii, 4, 92.
Famed for mildness.—*III Henry VI,* ii, 1, 156.
Famed for virtuous.—*III Henry VI,* iv, 6, 26.
High in fame.—*All's Well that Ends Well,* v, 3, 31.

7
When
The bravest questant shrinks, find what you seek,
That fame may cry you loud.
All's Well that Ends Well. Act ii, sc. 1, l. 15. [King] The only use of "questant."

8
Cæsar: By sea he is absolute master.
Antony: So is the fame.
Antony and Cleopatra. Act ii, sc. 2, l. 166. See also Report, Rumour.
Fame answering the most strange inquire.
Pericles. Act iii, Gower, l. 22.
When fame Had spread their cursed deed.
Pericles. Act v, sc. 3, l. 95. [Gower]

9
Better to leave undone, than by our deed
Acquire too high a fame when him we serve 's away.
Antony and Cleopatra. Act iii, sc. 1, l. 14. [Ventidius]
Fame, at which he aims, . . . can not
Better be held nor more attain'd than by
A place below the first.
Coriolanus. Act i, sc. 1, l. 267. [Brutus]

10
Help to reap the fame
Which he did end all his.
Coriolanus. Act v, sc. 6, l. 36. [Aufidius]
Fame unparallel'd.—*Coriolanus,* v, 2, 16.

11
Set a double varnish on the fame
The Frenchman gave you.
Hamlet. Act iv, sc. 7, l. 133. [King] "Varnish" is also used twice in *Love's Labour's Lost,* i, 2, 46; iv, 3, 244.

12
I in the clear sky of fame o'ershine you as much as the full moon doth the cinders of the element.
II Henry IV. Act iv, sc. 3, l. 56. [Falstaff]
Imp of fame!—*II Henry IV,* v, 5, 46; *Henry V,* iv, 1, 45.

13
Knocks go and come; God's vassals drop and die;
And sword and shield,
In bloody field,
Doth win immortal fame.
Henry V. Act iii, sc. 2, l. 8. [Pistol]

Those that leave their valiant bones in France,
Dying like men, though buried in your dunghills,
They shall be famed; for there the sun shall greet them,
And draw their honours reeking up to heaven.
Henry V. Act iv, sc. 3, l. 98. [King Henry]

1
Too famous to live long!
I Henry VI. Act i, sc. 1, l. 6. [Bedford]

I shall as famous be by this exploit
As Scythian Tomyris by Cyrus' death.
I Henry VI. Act ii, sc. 3, l. 5. [Countess of Auvergne] The only mention in the plays of either Tomyris or Cyrus.

2
So famous,
So excellent in art, and still so rising.
Henry VIII. Act iv, sc. 2, l. 61. [Griffith]

3
I find thou art no less than fame hath bruited.
I Henry VI. Act ii, sc. 3, l. 68. [Countess of Auvergne]

We will make thee famous through the world.
I Henry VI. Act iii, sc. 3, l. 13. [Bastard]

4
His fame lives in the world.
I Henry VI. Act iv, sc. 4, l. 46. [Lucy]

The man is noble and his fame folds-in
This orb o' the earth.
Coriolanus. Act v, sc. 6, l. 126. [Second Lord] The only use of "folds-in."

5
To save a paltry life and slay bright fame.
I Henry VI. Act iv, sc. 6, l. 45. [John Talbot]

Bright with fame.—*Rape of Lucrece*, l. 1491.
All-telling fame.—*Love's Labour's Lost*, ii, 1, 21. The only use of "all-telling."
Bastard fame.—*Comedy of Errors*, iii, 2, 19.
Greatest fame.—*I Henry VI*, iii, 2, 76.
Vulgar fame.—*Antony and Cleopatra*, iii, 13, 119.
Wild fame.—*Othello*, ii, 1, 62.

6
My meed hath got me fame.
III Henry VI. Act iv, sc. 8, l. 38. [King Henry]

7
Let fame, that all hunt after in their lives,
Live register'd upon our brazen tombs
And then grace us in the disgrace of death.
Love's Labour's Lost. Act i, sc. 1, l. 1. [King]

Either our history shall with full mouth
Speak freely of our acts, or else our grave,
Like Turkish mute, shall have a tongueless mouth,
Not worshipp'd with a waxen epitaph.
Henry V. Act i, sc. 2, l. 230. [King Henry]

Fame in time to come canonize us.
Troilus and Cressida. Act ii, sc. 2, l. 202. [Troilus] The only use of "canonize."

8
I have played the part of Lady Fame.
Much Ado about Nothing. Act ii, sc. 1, l. 220. [Benedick]

Death, in guerdon of her wrongs,
Gives her fame which never dies.
So the life that died with shame
Lives in death with glorious fame.
Much Ado about Nothing. Act v, sc. 3, l. 5. [Claudio] "Guerdon" is repeated in *Love's Labour's Lost*, iii, 1, 170.

9
He you hurt is of great fame in Cyprus
And great affinity.
Othello. Act iii, sc. 1, l. 48. [Emilia] The only use of "affinity."

10
He stories to her ears her husband's fame,
Won in the fields of fruitful Italy.
The Rape of Lucrece, l. 106.

11
Without characters, fame lives long.
Richard III. Act iii, sc. 1, l. 81. [Gloucester]

Death makes no conquest of this conqueror;
For now he lives in fame, though not in life.
Richard III. Act iii, sc. 1, l. 87. [Prince of Wales]

Many moe of noble fame and worth.
Richard III. Act iv, sc. 5, l. 13. [Urswick]

12
My noble lord and father, live in fame!
Titus Andronicus. Act i, sc. 1, l. 158. [Lavinia]

You that survive, and you that sleep in fame!
Titus Andronicus. Act i, sc. 1, l. 173. [Marcus]

13
Having his ear full of his airy fame.
Troilus and Cressida. Act i, sc. 3, l. 144. [Ulysses]

Famed be thy tutor, and thy parts of nature
Thrice famed, beyond all erudition.
Troilus and Cressida. Act ii, sc. 3, l. 253. [Ulysses] The only use of "erudition." "Thrice-famed" (hyphenated) is repeated in *II Henry VI*, iii, 2, 157.

When fame shall in our islands sound her trump.
Troilus and Cressida. Act iii, sc. 3, l. 210. [Ulysses]

My fame is shrewdly gored.
Troilus and Cressida. Act iii, sc. 3, l. 228. [Achilles]

Not Neoptolemus so mirable,
On whose bright crest Fame with her loud'st Oyes
Cries 'This is he.'
Troilus and Cressida. Act iv, sc. 5, l. 142. [Hector] The only use of "Neoptolemus" and "mirable" (marvellous). "Oyes" is used once again in *Merry Wives of Windsor*, v, 5, 45.

14
A bawbling vessel was he captain of,
For shallow draught and bulk unprizable;
With which such scathful grapple did he make
With the most noble bottom of our fleet,
That very envy and the tongue of loss
Cried fame and honour on him.
Twelfth Night. Act v, sc. 1, l. 57. [Duke] The only use of "bawbling" and "scathful." "Unprizable" is repeated in *Cymbeline*, i, 4, 99.

FAMILIAR PHRASES *

See also Slang

A

1
I will tell you what I am about.
The Merry Wives of Windsor. Act i, sc. 3, l. 42. [Falstaff]
How these things came about.—*Hamlet,* v, 2, 391.
Come about.—*The Merchant of Venice,* ii, 6, 64; *Romeo and Juliet,* i, 3, 45; *King Lear,* iv, 3, 42.
Go about it.—*Coriolanus,* iii, 2, 98; iii, 3, 24. "Go about" is used sixteen times.
I am about it.—*Othello,* ii, 1, 126.
I will about it.—*The Merry Wives of Windsor,* ii, 2, 327.
He is about it.—*Macbeth,* ii, 2, 4.
Do not turn me about.—*The Tempest,* ii, 2, 118.
What is about to be?—*Coriolanus,* iii, 1, 189.

2
This above all.
Hamlet. Act i, sc. 3, l. 78. [Polonius]
Above compare.—*Romeo and Juliet,* ii, 3, 238.
Keep him above deck.—*The Merry Wives of Windsor,* ii, 1, 94. For full quotation, see under WOOING.
Not above once.—*Hamlet,* ii, 2, 455. For full quotation, see under SPEECH.

3
I leave him to your gracious acceptance.
The Merchant of Venice. Act iv, sc. 1, l. 165. [Clerk]
Good acceptance.—*Henry V,* i, 1, 83.
Noble acceptance.—*Coriolanus,* ii, 3, 9.

4
We are denied access unto his person.
II Henry IV. Act iv, sc. 1, l. 78. [Archbishop of York] Shakespeare was fond of this phrase, and used it, with slight variations, over twenty times.

5
Let 's ha' no more ado.
III Henry VI. Act iv, sc. 5, l. 27. [Gloucester]
Then should not we be tired with this ado.
Titus Andronicus. Act ii, sc. 1, l. 99. [Aaron]
Make no more ado.—*Titus Andronicus,* iv, 3, 102; *Henry VIII,* v, 3, 159.
I made no more ado.—*I Henry IV,* ii, 4, 223.
We 'll keep no great ado.—*Romeo and Juliet,* iii, 4, 23.
Here 's ado.—*The Winter's Tale,* ii, 2, 9.
Here 's much ado.—*The Winter's Tale,* ii, 2, 19.
Much Ado about Nothing.—The title of Shakespeare's seventeenth play, written in 1598.

6
Do as I advise.
Pericles. Act iv, sc. 3, l. 51. [Dionyza]

7
But where 's the great Alcides of the field?
I Henry VI. Act iv, sc. 7, l. 60. [Lucy] Alcides (Hercules) is mentioned seven times.

*These phrases are grouped alphabetically by the key word. Other phrases will be found under their appropriate headings: "lack-lustre eye," for example, under EYE. The index at the end of the volume should be consulted whenever any phrase is not found where expected. All phrases cited but once are unique.

8
All at once.
As You Like It, iii, 5, 37; *Henry V,* i, 1, 36.

9
He that can do all in all.
II Henry VI. Act ii, sc. 4, l. 51. [Duchess of Gloucester]
He will do all in all as Hastings doth.
Richard III. Act iii, sc. 1, l. 168. [Catesby]
That is all in all.
The Taming of the Shrew. Act ii, sc. 1, l. 130. [Baptista]
All in all his study.
Henry V. Act i, sc. 1, l. 42. [Canterbury]
Take him for all in all.
I shall not look upon his like again.
Hamlet. Act i, sc. 2, l. 187. [Hamlet]
All in all in spleen.—*Othello,* iv, 1, 89.
All in all sufficient.—*Othello,* iv, 1, 276.
The very all of all.—*Love's Labour 's Lost,* v, 1, 115.

10
I hope all 's for the best.
III Henry VI. Act iii, sc. 3, l. 170. [Prince of Wales]
I thought all for the best.
Romeo and Juliet. Act iii, sc. 1, l. 109. [Romeo]

11
All is done.
The Taming of the Shrew, iv, 4, 46, and three times in later plays.
All is said.—*Richard II,* ii, 1, 148.
All the better.—*As You Like It,* i, 2, 102.

12
All 's one to me.
II Henry VI. Act i, sc. 3, l. 105. [King] Although Shakespeare used this expression in his first play, written in 1590, he did not use it again until eleven years later:
'Tis all one to me.
Troilus and Cressida. Act i, sc. 1, l. 80. [Pandarus] And then again in 1610:
But 'tis all one to me.
The Winter's Tale. Act v, sc. 2, l. 131. [Autolycus]
All 's one for that.—*Richard III,* v, 3, 8; *I Henry IV,* ii, 4, 172.
It 's ('tis) all one.—*Romeo and Juliet,* i, 1, 25, and five times in later plays.
That 's all one.—*The Two Gentlemen of Verona,* iii, 1, 263, and seven times in later plays.
'Twere all one.—*All 's Well that Ends Well,* i, 1, 96.
Ten to one.—*II Henry VI,* ii, 1, 4, and eight times in later plays.

13
Break it all to pieces.
Henry V. Act i, sc. 2, l. 225. [King Henry]
I 'll tear her all to pieces.
Othello. Act iii, sc. 3, l. 433. [Othello]
Dash'd all to pieces.
The Tempest. Act i, sc. 2, l. 8. [Miranda]

14
Cymbeline: I stand on fire: Come to the matter.
Iachimo: All too soon I shall.
Cymbeline. Act v, sc. 5, l. 168.

1
All unknown to me.
Richard III. Act ii, sc. 4, l. 48. [Messenger]

2
The good old man would fain that all were well.
III Henry VI. Act iv, sc. 7, l. 31. [Hastings]
All goes well.—*III Henry VI*, iv, 2, 1; *Love's Labour's Lost*, v, 2, 113; *I Henry IV*, iv, 1, 83.
All's well.—*Macbeth*, ii, 1, 19.
All's well that ends well.—*All's Well that Ends Well*, v, 1, 25.

3
Alone I did it.—*Coriolanus*, v, 6, 117.

4
Come amain.
II Henry VI, iii, 1, 282; v, 1, 114.
Here she comes amain.—*Love's Labour's Lost*, v, 2, 549.
March amain.—*III Henry VI*, ii, 1, 182; iv, 8, 4; iv, 8, 64; *Titus Andronicus*, iv, 4, 65.
Towards Berwick post amain.—*III Henry VI*, ii, 5, 128.
Make we hence amain.—*III Henry VI*, ii, 3, 56; ii, 5, 133. It is curious to note that Shakespeare used "amain" in one of these combinations no less than six times in *III Henry VI*, and only eight times in all the other plays.

5
Where America, the Indies?
The Comedy of Errors. Act iii, sc. 2, l. 136. [Antipholus of Syracuse] The only mention of America in Shakespeare's plays.

6
What, all amort?—*I Henry VI*, iii, 2, 124; *The Taming of the Shrew*, iv, 3, 36.

7
I'll be with you anon.—*Twelfth Night*, iii, 4. 353; *II Henry IV*, v, 3, 28.
He will be here anon.—*The Merry Wives of Windsor*, iv, 2, 41.
I shall find you anon.—*The Merry Wives of Windsor*, iv, 2, 146.
Our friends Will greet us here anon.—*Measure for Measure*, iv, 5, 13.
More of him anon.—*Measure for Measure*, iv, 2, 162.
Ever and anon.—*Love's Labour's Lost*, v, 2, 101; *I Henry IV*, i, 3, 38. Shakespeare used "anon," in various phrases, eighty-five times.

8
One time or another.
Twelfth Night. Act ii, sc. 4, l. 73. [Clown]
Some one way, some another.
Othello. Act i, sc. 1, l. 177. [Brabantio] See under WAY.
What one thing, what another.
Troilus and Cressida. Act v, sc. 3, l. 103. [Pandarus]

9
Quick-shifting antics, ugly in her eyes.
The Rape of Lucrece, l. 459. The only use of "quick-shifting."
Witless antics.—*Troilus and Cressida*, v, 3, 86.

10
Apace, Eros, apace.
Antony and Cleopatra. Act iv, sc. 14, l. 41. [Antony]
Come apace, good Audrey.
As You Like It. Act iii, sc. 3, l. 1. [Touchstone] Shakespeare used the phrase eleven times.

11
Is she not apt?
Henry V. Act v, sc. 1, l. 312. [Burgundy]
She is young and apt.—*Timon of Athens*, i, 1, 132.
Apt, in good faith, very apt.—*Twelfth Night*, i, 5, 28.
Apt to learn.—*The Taming of the Shrew*, ii, 1, 166; *Much Ado about Nothing*, i, 1, 294.

12
As aforesaid.
The Merchant of Venice. Act ii, sc. 2, l. 8. [Launcelot] Also, *Troilus and Cressida*, ii, 3, 64.

13
As I am a Christian.
Richard III. Act i, sc. 4, l. 4. [Clarence] Also *The Comedy of Errors*, i, 2, 77; *The Merry Wives of Windsor*, iii, 1, 96; *Othello*, iv, 2, 82.
As I am a gentleman.—*Richard II*, iii, 3, 120, and six times in later plays.
As I am an honest man.—*Much Ado about Nothing*, v, 1, 130; *Othello*, ii, 3, 266.
As I am a soldier.—*Henry V*, ii, 1, 69; iii, 3, 5; *Othello*, ii, 3, 69.
As I live.—*Henry V*, iv, 7, 153; *Henry VIII*, iii, 2, 221; v, 4, 81; *Coriolanus*, iii, 1, 64.
As I take it.—*Henry V*, iv, 7, 22; *Othello*, v, 1, 51.

14
This is as 't should be.
Romeo and Juliet. Act iv, sc. 2, l. 29. [Capulet]
Thereafter as they be.
II Henry IV. Act iii, sc. 2, l. 56. [Silence] The only use of "thereafter."
As 'tis.—*The Tempest*, i, 2, 310.
As it were.—*II Henry VI*, ii, 3, 86, and eleven times in later plays.
As much as to say.—*The Comedy of Errors*, iv, 3, 54, and five times in later plays.
As one would say.—*Measure for Measure*, i, 2, 55; *The Merchant of Venice*, ii, 2, 134.

15
I do assure you.
I Henry IV, ii, 4, 561; *Henry VIII*, iii, 2, 60, and many other plays. The phrase in various forms was a favorite of Shakespeare.

16
O, they are at it!
Coriolanus. Act i, sc. iv, l. 21. [Marcius]
They are at it, hark!
Troilus and Cressida. Act v, sc. 3, l. 95. [Troilus]
Arm'd and at it.—*Troilus and Cressida*, v, 5, 36.

17
Good cousin, give me audience for a while.
I Henry IV. Act i, sc. 3, l. 211. [Worcester]
Give me audience, good madam.
As You Like It. Act iii, sc. 2, l. 251. [Celia] A phrase used by Shakespeare many times.

B

18
To-morrow toward London back again.
II Henry VI. Act ii, sc. 1, l. 201. [King Henry] "Back again" was used three times in the first play, and frequently thereafter.

1
Having found the back-door open.
Cymbeline. Act v, sc. 3, l. 45. [Posthumus]
My master, Sir John, is come in at your back-door.
The Merry Wives of Windsor. Act iii, sc. 3, l. 25. [Robin] The only instances of the use of "back-door."

2
A back-friend, a shoulder-clapper.
The Comedy of Errors. Act iv, sc. 2, l. 37. [Dromio of Syracuse] The only use of either phrase.

3
Shallow: They . . . will backbite.
Davy: No worse than they are backbitten.
II Henry VI. Act v, sc. 1, l. 36. The only use of "backbite" and "backbitten."

4
I have a gammon of bacon.
I Henry IV. Act ii, sc. 1, l. 26. [Second Carrier] The only use of "gammon."
On, bacons, on!
I Henry VI. Act ii, sc. 2, l. 95. [Falstaff]
'Hang-hog' is Latin for bacon, I warrant you.
The Merry Wives of Windsor. Act iv, sc. 1, l. 50. [Mistress Quickly] Derived from the famous story of the thief named Hogg, who, when condemned to death by Sir Francis Bacon, prayed for mercy on the score of kinship. "Ay, but," replied the judge, "you and I cannot be of kindred unless you are hanged; for hog is not bacon till it be well hanged." (Sir Francis Bacon, *Apothegms.*) The only use of "hang-hog" in the plays.

5
Ye are a baggage.
The Taming of the Shrew. Induction, sc. 1, l. 3. [Sly] "Baggage," as a term of opprobrium, is used six times in the plays.

6
Nay, but I bar to-night: you shall not gauge me
By what we do to-night.
The Merchant of Venice. Act ii, sc. 2, l. 208. [Gratiano] The only use of "gauge."
I bar confusion.—*As You Like It,* v, 4, 131.

7
Be it as it may.
III Henry VI. Act i, sc. 1, l. 194. [King Henry] Also *As You Like It,* iii, 3, 41.
Be it possible.—*The Taming of the Shrew,* iii, 2, 127.
Be it so.—*A Midsummer-Night's Dream,* i, 1, 39; *Coriolanus,* v, 2, 12; *Antony and Cleopatra,* iii, 12, 10; *Pericles,* iv, 3, 28.

8
Be not afraid.
II Henry VI. Act ii, sc. 3, l. 69. [First 'Prentice] Also six times in later plays.

9
Can such things be?
Macbeth. Act iii, sc. 4, l. 110. [Macbeth]
How can this be?—*The Winter's Tale,* i, 2, 140.

10
That but this blow
Might be the be-all and the end-all here,
But here, upon this bank and shoal of time,
We 'ld jump the life to come.
Macbeth. Act i, sc. 7, l. 4. [Macbeth] The only use of the phrase "be-all and end-all."

11
He 's a bear.
Coriolanus. Act ii, sc. 1, l. 13. [Menenius]
Bear with me.—*Richard III,* iii, 1, 127, and twelve times in later plays.

12
Beat him like a dog.
Twelfth Night. Act ii, sc. 3, l. 153. [Sir Andrew]

13
Con tutto il cruore, ben trovato.
The Taming of the Shrew. Act i, sc. 2, l. 24. [Petruchio] Hortensio repeats the phrase, an echo of the Italian epigram made famous by Giordano Bruno in 1585: "Se non è vero, è ben trovato," (If it is not true, it is certainly well invented). Antonio Doni had said the same thing, in slightly different form, in 1552.

14
The still-vex'd Bermoothes.
The Tempest. Act i, sc. 2, l. 229. [Ariel] The only use of "still-vex'd" and "Bermoothes."

15
Beshrew me.
III Henry VI. Act i, sc. 4, l. 150. [Northumberland] Repeated six times in later plays.
Beshrew thy (your) heart.—*II Henry IV,* ii, 3, 45; v, 3, 59; *Romeo and Juliet,* ii, 5, 52; *Troilus and Cressida,* iv, 2, 30.

16
Beside themselves with fear.
Julius Cæsar. Act iii, sc. 1, l. 180. [Brutus]
Besides myself.—*Comedy of Errors,* iii, 2, 78.

17
I am the besom that must sweep the court clean.
II Henry VI. Act iv, sc. 7, l. 34. [Jack Cade] It is interesting to note that Shakespeare used the word "besom" in his first play, and never after that.

18
To be merry best becomes you.
Much Ado about Nothing. Act ii, sc. 1, l. 346. [Don Pedro] "Best becomes" is repeated in *The Taming of the Shrew,* i, 2, 87, and in *The Winter's Tale,* iv, 4, 406.
It would become me as well as it does you.
The Tempest. Act iii, sc. 1, l. 28. [Miranda]

19
With your best endeavour.
II Henry VI. Act iii, sc. 1, l. 163. [Gloucester]
My best endeavours.—*Merchant of Venice,* ii, 2, 182; *The Winter's Tale,* iv, 4, 542.

20
Live to be the best of all.
II Henry VI, i, 3, 115. "Best of all" is also used in *III Henry VI,* ii, 5, 18; *The Merry Wives of Windsor,* iv, 4, 87; and *Cymbeline,* v, 5, 159.
The best of them.—*Love's Labour 's Lost,* i, 2, 88; *II Henry IV,* iii, 2, 27; *Coriolanus,* ii, 1, 102; iii, 1, 244; *The Tempest,* i, 2, 429.

21
Let 's make the best of it.
Coriolanus. Act v, sc. 6, l. 148. [Second Lord]
Make your best of it.
The Taming of the Shrew. Act iv, sc. 3, l. 100. [Petruchio]

1
All these I better in one general best.
Sonnets. No. xci.
What you do Still betters what is done.
The Winter's Tale. Act iv, sc. 4, l. 136.

2
This falls out better than I could devise.
A Midsummer-Night's Dream. Act iii, sc. 2, l. 35.
All the better.—*Romeo and Juliet,* iv, 5, 68; *Troilus and Cressida,* ii, 3, 107.
'Tis all the better.—*Cymbeline,* iii, 5, 19; 68.
'Tis better as it is.—*Othello,* i, 2, 6.
Better and better.
Henry V. Act v, sc. 2, l. 251. [King Henry] The only instance of the use of this phrase.
Better far.—*I Henry VI,* ii, 1, 29; *III Henry VI,* i, 1, 130.
Better far off than near.—*Richard II,* v, 1, 88.
The sooner the better.—*II Henry VI,* i, 4, 17. This phrase was used in the first act of the first play and never afterwards.
For fault of a better.—*The Merry Wives of Windsor,* i, 4, 17.

3
It shall be the better for you.
Measure for Measure. Act ii, sc. 1, l. 233.
'Twere better for you.—*The Merry Wives of Windsor,* i, 1, 121.
The better for him.—*The Taming of the Shrew,* Ind., 1, 123.
The better for our purpose.—*Richard III,* v, 3, 274.
You can do better yet.—*Antony and Cleopatra,* i, 3, 81.
Be better at thy leisure.—*King Lear,* ii, 4, 232.

4
His better doth not breathe upon the earth.
Richard III. Act i, sc. 2, l. 140.
I took thee for thy better.
Hamlet. Act iii, sc. 4, l. 32. [Hamlet]
I am better than thou art.—*King Lear,* i, 4, 212.
A better than thou.—*II Henry IV,* ii, 4, 311.
I am your better.—*III Henry VI,* v, 5, 36.

5
Corin: Who calls?
Touchstone: Your betters, sir.
As You Like It. Act ii, sc. 4, l. 67. "Your betters" is repeated in *The Taming of the Shrew,* iv, 3, 75.
Under the degree of my betters.—*Twelfth Night,* i, 3, 125. "My betters" repeated in *I Henry IV,* iv, 3, 71.
Our betters.—*King John,* i, 1, 156; *Timon of Athens,* i, 2, 12; *King Lear,* iii, 6, 109.

6
Leave thy vain bibble babble.
Twelfth Night, iv, 2, 105. The only use of "bibble babble."

7
Mistress Ford, good heart, is beaten black-and-blue.
Merry Wives of Windsor. Act iv, sc. 5, l. 115. [Mistress Quickly]
Pinch us black and blue.—*The Comedy of Errors,* ii, 2, 194.
Fool him black and blue.—*Twelfth Night,* ii, 5, 12.

8
As plentiful as black berries.
I Henry IV, ii, 4, 265. See under Reason.

9
You boggle shrewdly, every feather starts you.
All's Well that Ends Well. Act v, sc. 3, l. 232. [King] The only use of "boggle."
You have been a boggler ever.
Antony and Cleopatra. Act iii, sc. 13, l. 110. [Antony] The only use of "boggler."

10
I 'll give you boot, I 'll give you three for one.
Troilus and Cressida. Act iv, sc. 5, l. 40. [Menelaus]
What an exchange had this been without boot!
What a boot is here with this exchange!
The Winter's Tale. Act iv, sc. 4, l. 688. [Autolycus]
My sceptre and my soul to boot.
I Henry IV, iii, 2, 97. See also *The Winter's Tale,* i, 2, 80; *II Henry IV,* iii, 1, 29; *Richard III,* v, 3, 301; *Macbeth,* iv, 3, 37; *King Lear,* iv, 6, 229.
There is no boot.—*Richard II,* i, 1, 164.
It boots thee not.—*The Two Gentlemen of Verona,* i, 1, 28.

11
Leave this idle theme, this bootless chat.
Venus and Adonis, l. 422.
Bootless cries.—*Sonnets,* xxix.
Bootless grief.—*Othello,* i, 3, 209.
Bootless inquisition.—*The Tempest,* i, 2, 35.
Bootless labour.—*III Henry VI,* i, 4, 20.
Bootless penitence.—*III Henry VI,* ii, 6, 70.
Bootless prayers.—*The Merchant of Venice,* iii, 3, 20; *Titus Andronicus,* iii, 1, 75.
Bootless rhymes.—*Love's Labour 's Lost,* v, 2, 64.
Bootless speed.—*A Midsummer-Night's Dream,* ii, 1, 233.

12
Botch and bungle.
Henry V. Act ii, sc. 2, l. 115. [King Henry]
Botch the words.—*Hamlet,* iv, 5, 10.

13
Both here and hence.
II Henry IV. Act iv, sc. 1, l. 171. [Archbishop of York] See also *Hamlet,* iii, 2, 232.
Both in one, or one in both.—*Love's Labour 's Lost,* iv, 1, 79.
Either both or none.—*As You Like It,* v, 3, 175.
Either both or nothing.—*Cymbeline,* v, 4, 147.
Both together.—*II Henry VI,* i, 2, 13; *Richard III,* iii, 2, 32; *Cymbeline,* i, 1, 167 .
Two of both kinds makes up four.—*A Midsummer-Night's Dream,* iii, 2, 438.

14
You are gone both ways.
The Merchant of Venice. Act iii, sc. 5, l. 20. [Launcelot]
Better both ways.—*Hamlet,* ii, 2, 345.

15
Give him a box o' the ear.
II Henry VI, iv, 7, 91. Repeated six times in later plays.

16
Tush, tush! fear boys with bugs.
The Taming of the Shrew. Act i, sc. 2, l. 211. [Petruchio]

17
You shall find no boy's play here.
I Henry IV. Act v, sc. 4, l. 76. [Falstaff] The only use of "boy's play."

1 I was bred and born
Not three hours' travel from this very place.
Twelfth Night. Act i, sc. 2, l. 22. [Captain] The only use of "bred and born."
Bred out.—*Henry V,* iii, 5, 29.
Well bred.—*II Henry IV,* i, 1, 26.
Where were you bred?—*Pericles,* v, 1, 116; v, 1, 165.

2
What need the bridge much broader than the flood?
Much Ado about Nothing. Act i, sc. 1, l. 318. [Don Pedro]

3
Which time will bring to light.
II Henry VI. Act iii, sc. 1, l. 65. [Buckingham] Only once, in his first play, did Shakespeare use the phrase, "bring to light." "Bring them to light" occurs in *Measure for Measure,* iii, 2, 189, and "Bring truth to light" in *The Rape of Lucrece,* l. 940.
Bring to pass.—*The Taming of the Shrew,* iii, 2, 131; *The Merchant of Venice,* i, 3, 93.

4 The twelve celestial signs
Have brought about the annual reckoning.
Love's Labour's Lost. Act v, sc. 2, l. 808. [Princess of France] The only use of "brought about."
Brought away.—*Timon of Athens,* v, 4, 68.
Brought forth.—*III Henry VI,* v, 6, 50, and seven times in later plays.
Brought home.—*Troilus and Cressida,* ii, 2, 86; *Coriolanus,* v, 6, 77.
Brought in.—*Twelfth Night,* i, 3, 16; *Timon of Athens,* ii, 2, 142.
Brought low.—*I Henry IV,* iv, 3, 26; *Timon of Athens,* iv, 2, 37.
Brought to bed.—*Titus Andronicus,* iv, 2, 62; 153; *The Winter's Tale,* iv, 4, 266.
Brought to know.—*Henry VIII,* iii, 1, 154.
Brought to light.—*Richard III,* i, 2, 22; *Henry V,* ii, 2, 185; *Much Ado about Nothing,* v, 1, 240.
Brought to pass.—*The Merry Wives of Windsor,* iv, 2, 183.

5
I 'll not budge an inch.
The Taming of the Shrew. Induction, sc. 1, l. 14. [Sly]
I will not budge a foot.—*I Henry VI,* i, 3, 38; *I Henry IV,* ii, 4, 388.
I will not budge for no man's pleasure.—*Romeo and Juliet,* iii, 1, 58.
Hence we will not budge.—*III Henry VI,* v, 4, 66.
Let the first budger die!—*Coriolanus,* i, 8, 5. The only use of "budger."

6
They burn in indignation.
King John. Act iv, sc. 2, l. 103. [King John]

7
Master, let me take you a button-hole lower.
Love's Labour's Lost. Act v, sc. 2, l. 706. [Moth] The only use of "button-hole."

8
By all means.
The Merry Wives of Windsor, iv, 2, 230; *Twelfth Night,* iii, 2, 62.
By no means.—*A Midsummer Night's Dream,* i, 1, 120, and also twelve times in later plays.
By day and night.—*Henry VIII,* i, 2, 213.

9
By and by is easily said.
Hamlet. Act iii, sc. 2, l. 404. [Hamlet]
By and by.—*II Henry VI,* i, 3, 2; ii, 1, 42. Shakespeare used this phrase forty-three times.

C

10
Our cake is dough on both sides.
The Taming of the Shrew. Act i, sc. 1, l. 110.
My cake is dough.—*Taming of the Shrew,* v, 1, 145. It will be noted that this phrase is used only in this play. These are also the only uses of "dough." "Doughy" occurs in *All's Well that Ends Well,* iv, 5, 3: "Doughy youth."
Cakes and ale.—*Twelfth Night,* ii, 3, 124. See under ALE.

11
Call it what you will.
II Henry IV. Act iv, sc. 3, l. 66. [Falstaff] Repeated in *Cymbeline,* iii, 3, 62.
An there be any matter of weight chances, call up me.
Much Ado about Nothing. Act iii, sc. 3, l. 91. [Dogberry]

12
How these things came about.
Hamlet. Act v, sc. 2, l. 391. [Horatio]
Then I came away.—*Coriolanus,* i, 6, 13.
How I came by it.—*The Merchant of Venice,* i, 1, 3; *Cymbeline,* ii, 4, 118.
When he came to himself.—*Julius Cæsar,* i, 2, 271.

13
Can such things be?
Macbeth. Act iii, sc. 4, l. 111. [Macbeth]
Can this be true?—*Much Ado about Nothing,* iii, 1, 107.

14
Be candidatus then.
Titus Andronicus. Act i, sc. 1, l. 185. [Marcus] The only use of "candidatus."

15
Faith, I can cut a caper.
Twelfth Night, i, 3, 150. See under DANCING.
He offered to cut a caper.—*Pericles,* iv, 2, 116.

16
Upon my soul two reverend cardinal virtues;
But cardinal sins and hollow hearts I fear ye.
Henry VIII. Act iii, sc. 1, l. 103. [Queen Katharine.] The only use of "cardinal virtues" and "cardinal sins." The queen is referring to the two cardinals, Wolsey and Campeius, who are urging her to consent to a divorce. "Hollow hearts" is also unique.

17
Have a care.
A Midsummer-Night's Dream, iv, i, 16; and six times in later plays.

18
A rotten case abides no handling.
II Henry IV, iv, 1, 161. [Westmoreland]

19
Cast aside so soon.
Macbeth, i, 7, 35. Only use of "cast aside."
Cast away.—*II Henry VI,* i, 3, 205, and sixteen times in later plays.
Cast by.—*Romeo and Juliet,* i, 1, 100. Unique.
Cast down.—*King Lear,* v, 3, 5. Unique.
Cast forth.—*Richard II,* i, 3, 157. Unique.

Cast off.—*II Henry IV,* iv, 4, 75, and six times in later plays.

Cast up.—*The Two Gentlemen of Verona,* iii, 1, 118; *Pericles,* i, 4, 6.

1
Here is the cate-log of her condition.
The Two Gentlemen of Verona, iii, 1, 273. The only use of "cate-logue." "Catalogue" occurs four times.

2
Why, what a caterwauling dost thou keep!
Titus Andronicus. Act iv, sc. 2, l. 57. [Aaron]

What a caterwauling do you keep here!
Twelfth Night. Act ii, sc. 3, l. 76. [Maria] The only uses of "caterwauling."

3
Cattle of this colour.
As You Like It. Act iii, sc. 2, l. 435. [Rosalind]

A horse of that colour.
Twelfth Night. Act ii, sc. 3, l. 182. [Maria]

This is a fellow of the self-same colour.
King Lear. Act ii, sc. 2, l. 145. [Cornwall]

A crow of the same nest.—*All's Well that Ends Well,* iv, 3, 319.

4
You cavil, widow.
III Henry VI. Act iii, sc. 2, l. 99. [King Edward]

That 's but a cavil.—*The Taming of the Shrew,* ii, 1, 392. "Cavil" is used in four other plays.

5
'Twere the cheaper way.
Measure for Measure. Act ii, sc. 4, l. 105. [Isabella]

6
I 'll go with thee, cheek by jole.
A Midsummer-Night's Dream. Act iii, sc. 2, l. 338. [Demetrius] The only use of "cheek by jole," and of "jole."

7
Some tricks, some quillets, how to cheat the devil.
Love's Labour 's Lost. Act iv, sc. 3, l. 288. [Longaville]

Be of good cheer.—*Richard III,* iv, 1, 38, and twelve times in later plays.

Chew upon this.—*Julius Cæsar,* i, 2, 171.

8
Let 's have the first choice.
The Winter's Tale. Act iv, sc. 4, l. 319. [Clown] The only use of "first choice."

Take his choice.—*Troilus and Cressida,* i, 2, 257.

Take your choice.—*Coriolanus,* i, 6, 65.

There 's small choice in rotten apples.—*The Taming of the Shrew,* i, 1, 138.

9
You are as good as a chorus, my lord.
Hamlet. Act iii, sc. 2, l. 155. [Ophelia] "Chorus" is repeated in *Henry V,* Prol., 32.

10
Clear as day.
II Henry VI, ii, 1, 107. Shakespeare used this phrase in his first play, and never again.

11
This is close dealing.
II Henry VI. Act ii, sc. 4, l. 73. [Gloucester] A phrase used by Shakespeare in his first play and never repeated.

12
See the coast clear'd, and then we will depart.
I Henry VI. Act i, sc. 3, l. 89. [Mayor] The only use of "coast clear'd."

13
You will set cock-a-hoop! you 'll be the man!
Romeo and Juliet. Act i, sc. 5, l. 83. [Capulet] The only use of "cock-a-hoop" (by the ears).

By cock and pie!—*II Henry IV,* v, 1, 1; *The Merry Wives of Windsor,* i, 1, 316.

Cock-sure.—*I Henry IV,* ii, 1, 95. The only use of the word.

14
Throw cold water.
The Merry Wives of Windsor, ii, 3, 89. The only use of the phrase.

All the colours of the rainbow.—*The Merry Wives of Windsor,* iv, 5, 118; *The Winter's Tale,* iv, 4, 205.

15
Before you can say "come" and "go."
The Tempest, iv, 1, 44.

16
That he should come about.
II Henry VI, iii, 1, 26. "Come about" occurs five times in later plays.

Come again.—*Richard III,* iv, 4, 322, and twenty-five times in later plays.

Come along.—*II Henry VI,* iv, 9, 28, and five times in later plays.

Come apace.—*The Taming of the Shrew,* iii, 3, 1, and five times in later plays.

Come at once.—*Merchant of Venice,* ii, 6, 46.

Come away.—*As You Like It,* i, 2, 60, and eight times in later plays.

Come behind.—*II Henry VI,* iv, 7, 89.

Come between.—*Romeo and Juliet,* ii, 4, 71, and five times in later plays.

Come down.—*III Henry VI,* i, 1, 77, and fourteen times in later plays.

Come first.—*Antony and Cleopatra,* ii, 2, 12.

Come foremost.—*Coriolanus,* v, 3, 22.

Come forth.—*II Henry VI,* v, 2, 5, and eleven times in later plays.

Come hither.—*II Henry VI,* ii, 3, 87, and twenty-two times in later plays.

Come home.—*The Taming of the Shrew,* iv, 1, 90, and eighteen times in later plays.

Come safe home.—*Henry V,* iv, 3, 41.

Come last.—*Troilus and Cressida,* iii, 3, 42.

This comes off well.—*Measure for Measure,* ii, 1, 57; *Timon of Athens,* i, 1, 29.

Come safe off.—*Troilus and Cressida,* i, 3, 381.

Come straight.—*Measure for Measure,* ii, 2, 1; *Troilus and Cressida,* iii, 2, 31; *Hamlet,* iii, 4, 1.

Marry, come up.—*Romeo and Juliet,* ii, 5, 64; *Pericles,* iv, 6, 159.

17
Come to dust.
Cymbeline, iv, 2, 263; 269; 275. The phrase occurs only in this scene.

Come to good.—*Hamlet,* i, 2, 158, *King Lear,* iii, 7, 100.

Come to harbour.—*The Merchant of Venice,* v, 1, 277.

Come to harvest.—*Twelfth Night,* iii, 1, 143; *Antony and Cleopatra,* ii, 7, 26.

Come to it.—*Measure for Measure,* ii, 1, 125;

v, 1, 194; *Troilus and Cressida,* i, 2, 90; *Hamlet,* iv, 5, 61.
Come to judgement.—*The Merchant of Venice,* iv, 1, 223.
Come to life.—*II Henry IV,* iii, 1, 84.
Come to light.—*Henry V,* iv, 8, 22; *The Merchant of Venice,* ii, 2, 83.
Come to nought.—*Richard III,* iii, 6, 13.
Come to pass.—*All's Well that Ends Well,* iv, 3, 371, and five times in later plays.
Come to town.—*II Henry IV,* ii, 2, 177; *The Merry Wives of Windsor,* iv, 5, 78.

1
Your honour cannot come to that yet.
Measure for Measure. Act ii, sc. 1, l. 123. [Pompey]
Is 't come to that?—*II Henry IV,* ii, 2, 2.
Would 'twere come to that!—*II Henry VI,* ii, 1, 38.
Is it come to this?—*Much Ado about Nothing,* i, 1, 200, and five times in later plays.
That it should come to this!—*Hamlet,* i, 2, 137.

2
He comes too late.
The Comedy of Errors, iii, 1, 49. Repeated seven times in later plays.
Come too near.—*Merchant of Venice,* iii, 4, 22.
Come too short.—*Much Ado about Nothing,* iii, 5, 45, and six times in later plays.
Come too soon.—*II Henry VI,* iii, 1, 95. Used only in the first play.

3
Come what may.
Twelfth Night, ii, 1, 48. The only use of the phrase.
Come what come may.—*Macbeth,* i, 3, 146.
Let come what comes.—*Hamlet,* iv, 5, 135.
Come what will.—*Love's Labour's Lost,* v, 2, 112; *I Henry IV,* i, 2, 162.
Chance it as it may.—*Timon of Athens,* v, 1, 129.

4
I beg cold comfort.
King John, v, 7, 42. "Cold comfort" is repeated in *The Taming of the Shrew,* iv, 1, 33.

5
Cast forth in the common air.
Richard II. Act i, sc. 3, l. 157. [Mowbray]
Common arbitrator.—*Troilus and Cressida,* iv, 5, 225.
Common course.—*All's Well that Ends Well,* iv, 3, 26.
Common curse.—*Troilus and Cressida,* ii, 3, 30.
Common dog.—*II Henry IV,* i, 3, 97.
Common drudge.—*The Merchant of Venice,* iii, 2, 103.
Common enemy.—*Macbeth,* iii, 1, 69.
Common liar.—*Antony and Cleopatra,* i, 1, 60.
Common mother.—*Timon of Athens,* iv, 3, 177.
Common sense.—*Love's Labour's Lost,* i, 1, 57; 64; *II Henry IV,* iv, 2, 33; *All's Well that Ends Well,* ii, 1, 181.
Common sight.—*I Henry IV,* iii, 2, 88.
Common talk.—*Taming of the Shrew,* i, 1, 35.
Common tongue.—*Timon of Athens,* i, 1, 174. With the exception of "common sense" all these phrases are unique.

6
But this denoted a foregone conclusion.
Othello. Act iii, sc. 3, l. 428. [Othello] The only use of the phrase.

7
Thy god confound thee!
Timon of Athens, i, 1, 247. "Confound thee" is repeated four times in *Timon,* and in *Antony and Cleopatra,* ii, 5, 92.
Confound you!—*Timon of Athens,* iv, 3, 452.
Confound you both!—*Titus Andronicus,* iv, 2, 6.
Confound them all!—*Timon of Athens,* iv, 3, 103; v, 1, 106.
Myself myself confound!—*Richard III,* iv, 4, 399.
O, confound the rest!—*Hamlet,* iii, 2, 187.

8
Under correction.
Love's Labour's Lost, v, 2, 489; 493.
Under your correction.—*Henry V,* iii, 2, 130.
Under your good correction.—*Measure for Measure,* ii, 1, 10.

9
Crack your cheeks!
King Lear. Act iii, sc. 2, l. 1. [Lear]
Crack thy lungs.—*Troilus and Cressida,* iv, 5, 7.
Now cracks a noble heart.
Hamlet. Act v, sc. 2, l. 370. [Horatio]
Crack my clear voice with sobs.
Troilus and Cressida. Act iv, sc. 2, l. 114. [Cressida]
Crack a quart together.—*II Henry IV,* v, 3, 66.
Crack of doom.—*Macbeth,* iv, 1, 117. See JUDGEMENT DAY.

D

10
The primrose path of dalliance.
Hamlet, i, 3, 50. See under PREACHER.
And silken dalliance in the wardrobe lies.
Henry V. Act ii. Prologue, l. 2. [Chorus]
Wanton dalliance.—*I Henry VI,* v, 1, 23.

11
You but dally.
Hamlet. Act v, sc. 2, l. 308. [Hamlet]
Dally not.—*I Henry VI,* iv, 5, 11; *The Comedy of Errors,* i, 2, 59; *The Taming of the Shrew,* iv, 4, 68.

12
I dance attendance here.
Richard III. Act iii, sc. 7, l. 56. [Buckingham] See also *II Henry VI,* i, 3, 174; *Henry VIII,* v, 2, 31.

13
And not be all day neither.
All's Well that Ends Well. Act ii, sc. 1, l. 94. [Lafeu]
All day long.—*Titus Andronicus,* v, 2, 55.
How 's the day?—*The Tempest,* v, 1, 3.

14
Give the devil his due.
I Henry IV, i, 2, 132. See under DEVIL.
Play the devil.—*Richard III,* i, 3, 338; *King John,* ii, 1, 134.
What, i' devil's name?—*The Taming of the Shrew,* iv, 3, 92.

15
All difficulties are but easy when they are known.
Measure for Measure. Act iv, sc. 2, l. 221. [Duke]
It were a tedious difficulty.
Othello. Act iii, sc. 3, l. 397. [Iago]

1

But this is mere digression.
II Henry IV, iv, 1, 140. [Westmoreland]

She knew her distance.
All's Well that Ends Well. Act v, sc. 3, l. 212. [Bertram]

2

Divided friendship.
Richard III, i, 4, 244. See under FRIENDSHIP.

Divided councils.—*Richard III*, iii, 1, 179.

Divided duty.—*Othello*, i, 3, 181.

3

The dog will have his day.
Hamlet. Act v, sc. 1, l. 315. [Hamlet]

The dog is dead.—*Richard III*, iv, 4, 78.

Die like dogs.—*II Henry IV*, ii, 4, 188.

Dog-days.—*Henry VIII*, v, 4, 44. The only use of the phrase. See under FACE.

4

Happy man be his dole!
The Taming of the Shrew, i, 1, 144; *I Henry IV*, ii, 2, 81; *The Merry Wives of Windsor*, iii, 4, 68; *The Winter's Tale*, i, 2, 162.

5

He has done nobly.
Coriolanus, ii, 3, 139. The only use of "done nobly."

6

How I dote on thee!
A Midsummer-Night's Dream. Act iv, sc. 1, l. 48. [Titania]

Dote on her.—*The Two Gentlemen of Verona*, iv, 4, 87; *Much Ado about Nothing*, ii, 3, 219.

Dote on me.—*Twelfth Night*, ii, 2, 36.

Dote on you!—*A Midsummer-Night's Dream*, i, 1, 225.

Make me dote.—*Comedy of Errors*, v, 1, 195.

Make thee dote.—*Comedy of Errors*, v, 1, 329.

Fell a-doting.—*Sonnets*, xx.

7

It would be double-dealing.
Twelfth Night, v, 1, 32. See under DECEIT. The only use of "double-dealing."

A double-dealer.—*Much Ado about Nothing*, v, 4, 116; *Twelfth Night*, v, 1, 38.

8

Did you ever dream of such a thing?
Pericles. Act iv, sc. 5, l. 5. [Gentleman]

9

Shed my dear blood drop by drop.
I Henry IV, i, 3, 134. "Drop by drop" is repeated in *The Merry Wives of Windsor*, iv, 5, 100.

10

I will drain him dry as hay.
Macbeth. Act i, sc. 3, l. 18. [Witch]

11

I must be one of these same dumb wise men.
The Merchant of Venice, i, 1, 106. See MAN, 944:1.

I am dumb.—*The Merchant of Venice*, v, 1, 279; *Much Ado about Nothing*, v, 3, 10.

A dumb innocent.—*All's Well that Ends Well*, iv, 3, 213.

Strike dumb.—*The Two Gentlemen of Verona*, ii, 2, 21.

Struck dumb.—*King John*, iv, 2, 235.

Deep clerks she dumbs.—*Pericles*, iii, Gower, 5.

12

How now, . . . in your dumps?
The Taming of the Shrew. Act ii, sc. 1, l. 286. [Baptista]

Distress likes dumps.—*Rape of Lucrece*, l. 1127.

Step out of these dreary dumps.—*Titus Andronicus*, i, 1, 391.

Deploring dump.—*The Two Gentlemen of Verona*, iii, 2, 85.

Doleful dumps.—*Romeo and Juliet*, iv, 5, 129.

Dumps so dull and heavy.—*Much Ado about Nothing*, ii, 3, 73.

Merry dump.—*Romeo and Juliet*, iv, 5, 108.

Not a dump.—*Romeo and Juliet*, iv, 5, 109. The only uses of "dump" and "dumps."

E

13

I come to draw you out by the ears.
II Henry IV. Act ii, sc. 4, l. 314. [Prince of Wales] "By the ears" is repeated in four later plays.

14

That 's as easy As to set dogs on sheep.
Coriolanus. Act ii, sc. 1, l. 272. [Sicinius]

'Tis as easy as lying.—*Hamlet*, iii, 2, 372.

As easy as thanks.—*Much Ado about Nothing*, ii, 3, 271.

15

He hath eaten me out of house and home.
II Henry IV, ii, 1, 80. The only use of the phrase, which dates from about 1400 (*Towneley Plays*, xiii, 124).

16

The sea will ebb and flow.
Love's Labour 's Lost. Act iv, sc. 3, l. 216. [Biron]

Ebb and flow.—*I Henry IV*, i, 2, 36; *Romeo and Juliet*, iii, 5, 134; *King Lear*, v, 3, 19.

His ebbs, his flows.—*Troilus and Cressida*, ii, 3, 139.

Make flows and ebbs.—*The Tempest*, v, 1, 270.

17

In as low an ebb as the foot of the ladder.
I Henry IV, i, 2, 42. [Prince]

It is a low ebb.—*II Henry IV*, ii, 2, 22.

18

As addle as an egg.
Romeo and Juliet. Act iii, sc. 1, l. 26. [Mercutio]

Addle egg.—*Troilus and Cressida*, i, 2, 145; 146. The only uses of "addle."

As an egg is full of meat.—*Romeo and Juliet*, iii, 1, 24. See under QUARREL.

19

Thou shalt have egress and regress.
The Merry Wives of Windsor. Act ii, sc. 1, l. 226. [Host] The only use of "egress" and "regress."

20

I 'll be at thy elbow.
Othello. Act v, sc. 1, l. 3. [Iago]

At your elbow.—*II Henry IV*, ii, 1, 22.

Elbows him.—*King Lear*, iv, 3, 44.

Elbow-room.—*King John*, v, 7, 28. The only use of the phrase.

21

He 's out at elbow.
Measure for Measure. Act ii, sc. 1, l. 61. [Pompey] The only use of "out at elbow."

Pluck him by the elbow.—*II Henry IV*, i, 2, 81.

Up to the elbows.—*Julius Cæsar*, iii, 1, 107.

22

I am not of your element.
Twelfth Night. Act iii, sc. 4, l. 137. [Malvolio]

Beyond our element.—*The Merry Wives of Windsor*, iv, 2, 186.

1
Stir no embers up.
Antony and Cleopatra. Act ii, sc. 2, l. 13. [Lepidus] The only use of "embers."

2
There 's the end on 't.
Twelfth Night, v, 1, 202. See under END.

3
A rare enginer!
Troilus and Cressida. Act ii, sc. 3, l. 8. [Thersites] "Enginer" is used also in *Hamlet,* iii, 4, 206. "Engineer" does not occur.

4
I intend to have it ere long.
I Henry VI, i, 3, 88. "Ere long" is repeated sixteen times in later plays.
Ere now.—*I Henry VI,* v, 3, 107, and ten times in later plays.
Ere this.—*III Henry VI,* i, 4, 48, and five times in later plays.

5
I pray you, ergo, old man, ergo, I beseech you.
The Merchant of Venice. Act ii, sc. 2, l. 58. [Launcelot] "Ergo" is used in three other plays, *The Comedy of Errors,* iv, 3, 57, *The Taming of the Shrew,* iv, 3, 129, and *All's Well that Ends Well,* i, 3, 53.

6
I will be even with thee.
Antony and Cleopatra, iii, 7, 1, [Cleopatra]
Even so.—*III Henry VI,* v, 1, 47, and forty-nine times in later plays. One of Shakespeare's favourite phrases, as was also "Even now," which he uses forty-six times.
Ever and anon.—*Love's Labour 's Lost,* v, 2, 101; *I Henry IV,* i, 3, 38.

7
In faith, it is exceedingly well aim'd.
I Henry IV. Act i, sc. 3, l. 282. [Hotspur]
Exceedingly well read.—*I Henry IV,* iii, 1, 166.

8
Be more expressive to them.
All 's Well that Ends Well. Act ii, sc. 1, l. 54. [Parolles] The only use of "expressive."

9
In the twinkling of an eye.
The Merchant of Venice, ii, 2, 177. See under HASTE.
Made my eyes water.—*A Midsummer-Night's Dream,* iii, 1, 200. See under EYE: THE WEEPING EYE.

10
An eye-sore to our solemn festival!
The Taming of the Shrew. Act iii, sc. 2, l. 103. [Baptista]
An eye-sore in my golden coat.
The Rape of Lucrece, l. 205. The only uses of "eye-sore."

F

11
Fair enough.
The Merchant of Venice, v, 1, 264. The only use of the phrase.

12
It will fall pat as I told you.
A Midsummer-Night's Dream. Act v, sc. 1, l. 188. [Pyramus] The only use of "fall pat."
It falls right.
Hamlet. Act iv, sc. 7, l. 71. [King]
This falls out better than I could devise.
A Midsummer-Night's Dream, iii, 2, 35. "Fall out," in the sense of happen, is used eight times in later plays.

13
Sought . . . far and near.
I Henry VI, v, 4, 3. "Far and near" is repeated in *King Lear,* ii, 1, 84.
Far and wide.—*Romeo and Juliet,* ii, 4, 90. The only use of the phrase.
Far away.—*The Two Gentlemen of Verona,* i, 3, 9. The only use of the phrase.
Far before.—*III Henry VI,* i, 1, 237; *Henry V,* ii, 4, 71; *Macbeth,* i, 4, 16.
Far behind.—*Troilus and Cressida,* i, 2, 59; *The Two Gentlemen of Verona,* ii, 4, 71.
Far beneath.—*Twelfth Night,* v, 1, 331. The only use of the phrase.
Far beyond.—*III Henry VI,* ii, 5, 51; *Timon of Athens,* iii, 4, 78; *Henry VIII,* iii, 2, 361.
Far enough.—*II Henry VI,* i, 3, 154; *Julius Cæsar,* v, 3, 12; *Henry VIII,* ii, 1, 49.
Far gone.—*Richard II,* ii, 1, 184; *Hamlet,* ii, 2, 190; *The Winter's Tale,* i, 2, 218; iv, 4, 354.
Far hence.—*III Henry VI,* v, 1, 2; *Henry VIII,* iii, 1, 90.
Far off.—*II Henry VI,* iii, 1, 10, and twenty-one times in later plays.

14
A little out of fashion.
Henry V, iv, 1, 85. See under FASHION.

15
That were fast and loose.
Love's Labour 's Lost. Act i, sc. 2, l. 162. [Moth]
As cunning as fast and loose. *Love's Labour 's Lost.* Act iii, sc. 1, l. 104. [Costard]
Fast and loose.—*King John,* iii, 1, 242; *Antony and Cleopatra,* iv, 12, 28.
Fast enough.—*The Merry Wives of Windsor,* iv, 1, 69.
Not too fast: soft, soft!—*Twelfth Night,* i, 5, 312.

16
Fat-brained.
Henry V, iii, 7, 143.
Fat-witted.
I Henry IV, i, 2, 2. The only use of either phrase.

17
For fault of a better.
II Henry IV, ii, 2, 45; *The Merry Wives of Windsor,* i, 4, 17.
For fault of a worse.—*Romeo and Juliet,* ii, 4, 129.
'Tis not my fault.—*III Henry VI,* ii, 2, 7. See under FAULT.

18
Stops the mouth of all find-faults.
Henry V, v, 1, 298.
Like or find fault.—*Troilus and Cressida,* Prol., 30.

19
His feathers are but borrow'd.
II Henry VI. Act iii, sc. 1, l. 75. [Queen]
A feather will turn the scale.
Measure for Measure. Act iv, sc. 2, l. 31. [Provost]
Anon he starts at stirring of a feather.
Venus and Adonis, l. 302.
I am a feather for each wind that blows.
Winter's Tale. Act ii, sc. 3, l. 154. [Leontes]

1
He fell in with Mistress Shore.
Richard III. Act iii, sc. 5, l. 51. [Mayor]
Fell in love.—*As You Like It,* iii, 2, 364.
Fell off.—*Henry VIII,* iv, 1, 64; v, 4, 50.
Fell on.—*Henry VIII,* v, 4, 56.
Fell out.—*A Midsummer-Night's Dream,* iv, 2, 32, and four times in later plays.
Fell sick.—*The Merchant of Venice,* iii, 4, 71; *Henry VIII,* iv, 2, 15.
At one fell swoop.—*Macbeth,* iv, 3, 219.

2
Fie on myself!
II Henry VI, iv, 10, 1. "Fie" as a term of reproach is used twenty-seven times.

3
Come and fight it out.
I Henry VI. Act iii, sc. 2, l. 66. [Talbot]
Let 's fight it out.—*III Henry VI,* i, 1, 117.
We 'll fight it out.—*I Henry VI,* i, 2, 128.

4
Finely put off!
Love's Labour 's Lost. Act iv, sc. 1, l. 112. [Rosaline]
Finely put on, indeed!—*Love's Labour 's Lost,* iv, 1, 118.
We will turn it finely off, sir.—*Love's Labour 's Lost,* v, 2, 511.

5
I have him between my finger and my thumb.
II Henry IV. Act iv, sc. 3, l. 141. [Falstaff]

6
At first and last.
I Henry VI, v, 5, 102. "First and last" is repeated in *Macbeth,* iii, 4, 1, and in *Cymbeline,* i, 4, 102.
From first to last.—*King John,* ii, 1, 326; *As You Like It,* iv, 3, 140; *Othello,* iii, 3, 96; *King Lear,* v, 3, 195; *Pericles,* v, 3, 61.
First or last.—*Antony and Cleopatra,* ii, 6, 63.
First of all.—*Cymbeline,* iii, 2, 63.
First place.—*Timon of Athens,* iii, 6, 77.
First remembrance.—*Othello,* iii, 3, 291. The only use of any of the last four phrases.

7
The first thing we do.
II Henry VI. Act iv, sc. 2, l. 83. [Dick]
That's the first thing that we have to do.—*III Henry VI,* iv, 3, 62.
The first thing thou doest.—*I Henry IV,* iii, 3, 205. The only use of any of these phrases.

8
He 's flint.
II Henry IV. Act iv, sc. 4, l. 33. [King Henry]

9
You must not think to fob off our disgrace with a tale.
Coriolanus. Act i, sc. 1, l. 96. [First Citizen] The only use of "fob off."

10
It follow'd hard upon.
Hamlet. Act i, sc. 2, l. 179. [Horatio] The only use of the phrase.

11
Food for powder.
I Henry IV, iv, 2, 70. The only use of the phrase.
Grind to powder.—*Titus Andronicus,* v, 2, 199.

12
Call me a fool.
Much Ado about Nothing, iv, 1, 166, and four later plays.
After all this fooling.—*Measure for Measure,* i, 2, 71.

13
The better foot before.
King John, iv, 2, 170. Repeated in *Titus Andronicus,* ii, 3, 192.

14
For all that.
The Merchant of Venice, iii, 4, 73; *Much Ado about Nothing,* ii, 1, 57; v, 1, 177.
For all this.—*Romeo and Juliet,* v, 3, 43; *Merchant of Venice,* ii, 5, 41; *King Lear,* ii, 4, 54.
For any thing I know.—*II Henry IV,* Epilogue, 31.
For aught I know.—*Richard II,* v, 2, 53, and five later plays.
For aught I see.—*I Henry VI,* i, 4, 68, and two later plays.
For aught that I can tell.—*A Midsummer-Night's Dream,* iii, 2, 76.

15
Most forcible Feeble.
II Henry IV. Act iii, sc. 2, l. 179. [Falstaff]

16
Forget, forgive; conclude and be agreed.
Richard II. Act i, sc. 1, l. 156. [King Richard]
Forget and forgive.—*King Lear,* iv, 7, 84.

17
Did on my own free will.
Antony and Cleopatra. Act iii, sc. 6, l. 57. [Cæsar] The only use of "free will."

18
We know what belongs to a frippery.
The Tempest. Act iv, sc. 1, l. 224. [Trinculo] The only use of "frippery."

19
My profession 's sacred from above.
I Henry VI. Act i, sc. 2, l. 114. [La Pucelle] The only use of "from above."
From among.—*Titus Andronicus,* iv, 1, 44.
From behind.—*I Henry VI,* i, 2, 66; *The Merry Wives of Windsor,* iv, 5, 69.
From below.—*All 's Well that Ends Well,* ii, 2, 32; *Timon of Athens,* iv, 3, 32.
From under.—*II Henry VI,* ii, 1, 174; *Richard II,* iii, 2, 41.

20
You fustilarian! I 'll tickle your catastrophe.
II Henry IV. Act ii, sc. 1, l. 66. [Falstaff] The only use of "fustilarian" (a comic formation on "fustilugs," a fat, frowsy woman).

G

21
In that I 'll no gainsaying.
The Winter's Tale, i, 2, 19. The only use of "gainsaying." "Gainsay" appears in five of the plays.

22
The game is up.
Cymbeline, iii, 3, 107. See under GAME.

23
Gave up the ghost.
III Henry VI, ii, 3, 22. See under DEATH.

24
Gaze your fill.
The Taming of the Shrew, i, 1, 73. The only use of the phrase.

1
As gentle as a lamb.
Romeo and Juliet, ii, 5, 45. See under GENTLENESS.

2
Get on thy boots!
II Henry IV. Act v, sc. 3, l. 137. [Falstaff]
Get on your cloak.—*Timon of Athens,* ii, 1, 15.
Get on your nightgown.—*Macbeth,* ii, 2, 70.
Get the better of them.—*Julius Cæsar,* ii, 1, 326.
Get the start.—*Julius Cæsar,* i, 2, 130. All these phrases are used only once.

3
Get thee away.
The Comedy of Errors, i, 2, 16. Repeated in *Timon of Athens,* iv, 3, 174.
Get you away.—*Coriolanus,* iv, 5, 16; *Othello,* iv, 1, 269.
Get thee gone.—*II Henry VI,* iii, 2, 346, and seventeen times in later plays.
Get you gone.—*The Two Gentlemen of Verona,* i, 2, 100, and eleven times in later plays.
Get thee hence.—*Richard III,* iv, 1, 39; *The Two Gentlemen of Verona,* iv, 4, 64; *Romeo and Juliet,* v, 3, 160; *Antony and Cleopatra,* ii, 5, 95.
Get you hence.—*II Henry VI,* iii, 2, 86, and six times in later plays. See under DISMISSAL.
Get thee in.—*The Taming of the Shrew,* ii, 1, 30; *Troilus and Cressida,* iv, 2, 89; *King Lear,* iii, 4, 27.
Get you in.—*The Comedy of Errors,* iii, 2, 25; *As You Like It,* i, 1, 80; *The Taming of the Shrew,* i, 1, 75; *Troilus and Cressida,* v, 3, 78.
Get thee to bed.—*Romeo and Juliet,* iv, 3, 13; *Macbeth,* ii, 1, 32; *Hamlet,* i, 1, 7.
Get you to bed.—*Romeo and Juliet,* iv, 4, 7; *Julius Cæsar,* ii, 1, 39; *Othello,* v, 3, 7; *Pericles,* ii, 5, 93.
Get up.—*II Henry IV,* ii, 1, 85; *Henry VIII,* v, 4, 93.
Get your living.—*Love's Labour's Lost,* v, 2, 497; *As You Like It,* iii, 2, 84.

4
What is 't that you took up so gingerly?
The Two Gentlemen of Verona. Act i, sc. 2, l. 70. [Julia] The only use of "gingerly."

5
Every one give ear.
Love's Labour's Lost, iv, 1, 59. "Give ear" is repeated four times in later plays.
Give ground.—*Twelfth Night,* iii, 4, 334; *The Tempest,* ii, 2, 64.
Give notice.—*I Henry VI,* iii, 2, 8; *Richard III,* iii, 5, 108; *Measure for Measure,* iv, 4, 19.
Give over.—*I Henry VI,* i, 2, 125, and fourteen times in later plays.
Give place.—*II Henry VI,* and seven times in later plays.
Give thanks.—*The Taming of the Shrew,* iv, 1, 162; *Timon of Athens,* i, 2, 62; *The Tempest,* i, 1, 26; *Henry VIII,* i, 2, 3.
Give up.—*II Henry VI,* ii, 3, 23, and twelve times in later plays.
Give way.—*Richard III,* i, 3, 196, and seventeen times in later plays.
Given over.—*I Henry IV,* iii, 3, 40; *II Henry IV,* ii, 3, 5; *Henry V,* iii, 2, 92.
Given to understand.—*The Merchant of Venice,* ii, 8, 7; *I Henry IV,* iv, 4, 11.
Given way.—*Much Ado about Nothing,* iv, 1, 158; *King Lear,* iii, 6, 4.
Giving out.—*Hamlet,* i, 5, 178; *Measure for Measure,* i, 4, 54; *Othello,* iv, 1, 131; *Pericles,* iv, 2, 155.
Giving over.—*Pericles,* iv, 2, 39.

6
Broken glass no cement can redress.
The Passionate Pilgrim, l. 178.

7
Go about my preparation.
I Henry VI, i, 1, 166. "Go about" is repeated seventeen times in later plays.
Go after.—*King John,* iv, 2, 178; *King Lear,* v, 3, 161; *Othello,* iv, 1, 291.
Go alone.—*Romeo and Juliet,* v, 3, 135. Unique.
Go along.—*Richard III,* ii, 4, 67, and four times in later plays.
Go away.—*II Henry VI,* iii, 2, 52, and seven times in later plays.
Go back.—*Troilus and Cressida,* v, 3, 62; *Antony and Cleopatra,* v, 2, 156.
Go before.—*II Henry VI,* i, 2, 61, and thirteen times in later plays.
Go between.—*The Merry Wives of Windsor,* ii, 2, 130; *All's Well that Ends Well,* v, 3, 258; *Antony and Cleopatra,* iii, 4, 25.
Go by.—*Richard III,* ii, 1, 94, and eight times in later plays.
Go down.—*Henry V,* iii, 5, 53. Unique.
Go even.—*Cymbeline,* i, 4, 47. Unique.
Go far.—*Hamlet,* iv, 5, 139. Unique.
Go first.—*The Merry Wives of Windsor,* i, 1, 320; *King Lear,* iii, 4, 26.
Go forth.—*II Henry VI,* v, 3, 26, and three times in later plays.
Go forward.—*Romeo and Juliet,* ii, 1, 1; *The Merry Wives of Windsor,* iv, 4, 13.
Go free.—*Henry V,* iii, 6, 44. Unique.
Go great.—*Timon of Athens,* iv, 3, 189. Unique.
Go hard.—*II Henry VI,* iv, 2, 108, and four times in later plays.
Go hence.—*Romeo and Juliet,* v, 3, 307, and four times in later plays.
Go home.—*III Henry VI,* iv, 6, 152, and five times in later plays.
Go in peace.—*II Henry VI,* ii, 3, 26; *Love's Labour's Lost,* iv, 3, 192.
Go in person.—*The Comedy of Errors,* v, 1, 234. Unique.
Go in quest.—*King John,* ii, 1, 426. Unique.
Go in search.—*King John,* ii, 1, 428. Unique.
Go like lightning.—*Romeo and Juliet,* iii, 1, 177. Unique.
Go loose.—*The Merry Wives of Windsor,* iv, 2, 128. Unique.
Go mad.—*Troilus and Cressida,* iv, 2, 78; *King Lear,* ii, 4, 289.
Go near.—*II Henry VI,* i, 2, 102, and three times in later plays.
Go no farther.—*Much Ado about Nothing,* v, 1, 236. Unique.
Go no further.—Three times in *As You Like It,* and four times in later plays.
Go on wheels.—*Antony and Cleopatra,* ii, 7, 99. Unique.
Go right.—*Love's Labour's Lost,* iii, 1. 195; *The Winter's Tale,* iv, 3, 18.
Go round.—*Antony and Cleopatra,* ii, 7, 124, and three times in later plays.
Go see.—*Julius Cæsar,* i, 2, 25; *Twelfth Night,* iii, 3, 19; 20.

Go slip-shod.—*King Lear,* i, 5, 12. Unique.
Go through.—*Julius Cæsar,* i, 3, 10; *Measure for Measure,* ii, 1, 285; *Henry VIII,* i, 2, 76.
Go thy ways.—*The Taming of the Shrew,* iv, 5, 23, and fifteen times in later plays.
Go to dinner.—*The Merchant of Venice,* iii, 5, 91. Unique.
Go to grass.—*II Henry VI,* iv, 2, 75. Unique.
Go to hell.—*The Merchant of Venice,* iii, 2, 21; *Julius Cæsar,* i, 2, 270; *The Merry Wives of Windsor,* ii, 1, 49.
Go to it.—*The Taming of the Shrew,* ii, 1, 45; *Hamlet,* v, 2, 56; *Pericles,* iv, 6, 80.
Go to prison.—*The Taming of the Shrew,* v, 1, 98. Unique.
Go to supper.—*King Lear,* iii, 6, 90. Unique.
Go to the door.—*Macbeth,* iii, 1, 73; *Coriolanus,* iv, 5, 9.
Go together.—*Much Ado about Nothing,* i, 1, 161, and three times in later plays.
Go under.—*Much Ado about Nothing,* ii, 1, 212; *All's Well that Ends Well,* iii, 5, 22.
Go well.—*King John,* iii, 4, 4; *Othello,* ii, 3, 380; *Coriolanus,* i, 1, 274.
Go without.—*King John,* iii, 1, 66; *The Merchant of Venice,* i, 2, 97; *Othello,* i, 3, 368; *Coriolanus,* ii, 3, 139.
Go wrong.—*King John,* i, 1, 41; *Troilus and Cressida,* v, 1, 74.
Go your gait.—*King Lear,* iv, 6, 242. Unique.
Go your way.—*As You Like It,* iv, 3, 69. Unique.
Go your ways.—*As You Like It,* iv, 1, 186; *The Merry Wives of Windsor,* i, 2, 1; iv, 1, 81.

1
Her assistant or go-between.
The Merry Wives of Windsor, ii, 2, 273. The only use of "go-between."

2
I hope your lordship goes abroad by advice.
II Henry IV, i, 2, 109.
Goes along.—*Pericles,* iv, 4, 16.
Goes away.—*Timon of Athens,* iii, 4, 42.
Goes down.—*Macbeth,* ii, 1, 3.
Goes even.—*Twelfth Night,* v, 1, 246.
Goes forth.—*Antony and Cleopatra,* iv, 4, 36.
Goes hard.—*III Henry VI,* ii, 6, 77; *The Taming of the Shrew,* iv, 2, 80; *The Two Gentlemen of Verona,* iv, 4, 2.
Goes off and on.—*All's Well that Ends Well,* v, 3, 279.
Goes right.—*Measure for Measure,* iv, 4, 37.
How it goes with us.—*Measure for Measure,* i, 1, 58.
How goes all in France?—*King John,* iv, 2, 109.
How goes the day with us?—*King John,* v, 3, 1.
How goes the field?—*I Henry IV,* v, 5, 16.
How goes her business?—*Henry VIII,* iv, 1, 23.
How goes the night?—*Macbeth,* ii, 1, 1.
Thus it goes.—*As You Like It,* 2, 5, 51. All these phrases are used only once, with the exception of "goes hard."

3
With him Gratiano is gone along.
The Merchant of Venice, ii, 8, 2. The only use of "gone along."
Gone back.—*King Lear,* iv, 3, 2. Unique.
Gone before.—*The Merry Wives of Windsor,* i, 1, 14; *Troilus and Cressida,* i, 3, 13; *Othello,* ii, 3, 126; *Macbeth,* i, 4, 57.
Gone between.—*Troilus and Cressida,* i, 1, 71. Unique.
Gone by.—*Hamlet,* i, 1, 66, and four times in later plays.
Gone forth.—*As You Like It,* iv, 3, 5; *Coriolanus,* iv, 6, 35; *The Tempest,* i, 2, 448.
Gone off.—*Henry V,* iii, 6, 96; *Henry VIII,* i, 2, 186.
Gone round.—*Hamlet,* iii, 2, 165; *Measure for Measure,* i, 2, 172.
Gone well.—*Antony and Cleopatra,* iii, 10, 27. Unique.

4
He 's as good at any thing.
As You Like It. Act v, sc. 4, l. 110. [Jaques] The only use of the phrase.

5
The soul of sound good-fellowship.
Troilus and Cressida. Act iv, sc. 1, l. 52. [Paris] See also *I Henry IV,* i, 2, 156; ii, 4, 307.

6
For goodness' sake.
Henry VIII. Prologue, l. 23; iii, 1, 159.

7
On the instant they got clear.
Hamlet, iv, 6, 19. The only use of "got clear."
Got leave.—*Romeo and Juliet,* ii, 5, 68. Unique.
Got off.—*Coriolanus,* ii, 1, 141. Unique.

8
Your soldiers use him as the grace 'fore meat.
Coriolanus. Act iv, sc. 7, l. 4. [Lieutenant]
Grace of God.—*II Henry VI,* i, 2, 72, and four times in later plays.

9
Against the grain.
Coriolanus, ii, 3, 241. The only use of the phrase.
'Tis in grain.—*The Comedy of Errors,* iii, 2, 108; *Twelfth Night,* i, 5, 255.

10
Given them gratis.
Coriolanus. Act iii, sc. 1, l. 43. [Brutus]
Gavest thyself away gratis.—*II Henry IV,* iv, 3, 76. "Gratis" is used nine times in the plays.

11
How green you are and fresh in this old world!
King John. Act iii, sc. 4, l. 145. [Pandulph]
Green indeed is the colour of lovers.
Love's Labour's Lost. Act i, sc. 2, l. 90. [Armado]

H

12
All hail!
III Henry VI, v, 7, 34, and nine times in later plays.

13
My hair doth stand on end.
Richard III. Act i, sc. 3, l. 304. [Hastings] The only use of "stand on end."
Not a hair amiss.—*II Henry IV,* i, 2, 27.

14
Pandarus: You 'll remember your brother's excuse?
Paris: To a hair.
Troilus and Cressida. Act iii, sc. 1, l. 155.

1
Hair-breadth scapes.
Othello, i, 3, 136. The only use of "hair-breadth."
To hair's breadth.—*Merry Wives of Windsor,* iv, 2, 3. The only use of "hair's breadth."
2
I 'll hammer it out.
Richard II. Act v, sc. 5, l. 5. [King Richard]
3
I cannot rid my hands of him.
II Henry IV. Act i, sc. 2, l. 226. [Falstaff]
Hand in hand.—*Richard III,* v, 3, 313, and twelve times in later plays.
Hard at hand.—*Othello,* ii, 1, 268. Unique.
Hard by.—*II Henry VI,* and ten times in later plays.
4
They are hare-brain'd.
I Henry VI, i, 2, 37. "Hare-brain'd" is repeated in *I Henry IV,* v, 2, 19.
5
Hap what hap may.
The Taming of the Shrew. Act iv, sc. 4, l. 108. [Lucentio] The only use of the phrase.
6
That were hard to compass.
Twelfth Night. Act i, sc. 2, l. 44. [Captain] The only use of "hard to compass."
7
King Richard: Harp not on that string, madam; that is past.
Queen Elizabeth: Harp on it still shall I till heart-strings break.
Richard III. Act iv, sc. 4, l. 364. "Heart-strings" is used four times.
Harp not on that.—*Measure for Measure,* v, 1, 64.
Harp on that still.—*Coriolanus,* ii, 3, 260.
Still harping on my daughter.—*Hamlet,* ii, 2, 189.
Harping on what I am.—*Antony and Cleopatra,* iii, 13, 142.
8
And so, have at thee!
III Henry VI. Act ii, sc. 4, l. 11. [Clifford] Also *II Henry VI,* ii, 3, 92; *Romeo and Juliet,* v, 3, 70.
Have at him!—*II Henry IV,* i, 2, 217.
I 'll venture one have-at-him.—*Henry VIII,* ii, 2, 85.
Have at it.—*Cymbeline,* v, 5, 315; *The Winter's Tale,* iv, 4, 302.
Have at ye!—*Henry VIII,* v, 3, 118.
Have at you!—*The Comedy of Errors,* iii, 1, 51, and five times in later plays.
Have with thee.—*I Henry VI,* ii, 4, 114; *Love's Labour 's Lost,* iv, 2, 151.
Have with you.—*Richard III,* iii, 2, 92, and seven times in later plays.
9
From the crown of his head to the sole of his foot.
Much Ado about Nothing, iii, 2, 9.
From toe to crown.—*The Tempest,* iv, 1, 233.
From head to heel.—*Winter's Tale,* iv, 4, 229.
O'er head and ears.—*Winter's Tale,* i, 2, 186.
10
Sir, give him head: I know he 'll prove a jade.
The Taming of the Shrew. Act i, sc. 2, l. 249. [Lucentio] The only use of "give him head."
11
Whatsoever you may hear to the contrary.
Measure for Measure. Act iv, sc. 2, l. 123. [Provost, reading]
So I heard you say.—*Love's Labour 's Lost,* i, 2, 147.
12
A heart of gold.
Henry V. Act iv, sc. 1, l. 44. [Pistol]
Hearts of gold.—*I Henry IV,* ii, 4, 307.
13
For heaven sake, Hubert, let me not be bound!
King John. Act iv, sc. 1, l. 78. [Arthur]
For heaven's sake, help me!—*Othello,* v, 1, 50.
For heaven's sake, take heed!—*Henry VIII,* iii, 1, 110.
I would to heaven.—*Measure for Measure,* ii, 2, 67.
14
I will but look upon the hedge and follow you.
The Winter's Tale. Act iv, sc. 4, l. 855. [Autolycus] A famous euphemism.
15
To dog his heels and curtsy at his frowns.
I Henry IV, iii, 2, 127.
I 'll lay ye all By the heels.—*Henry VIII,* v, 4, 83.
Out at heels.—*The Merry Wives of Windsor,* i, 3, 34; *King Lear,* ii, 2, 164. See under HEEL for other familiar phrases.
16
Why dost not . . . help me out?
Titus Andronicus. Act ii, sc. 3, l. 209. [Martius]
17
Here, there, and every where.
I Henry VI. Act i, sc. 1, l. 124. [Messenger]
18
Hereabouts he dwells.
Romeo and Juliet, v, 1, 38. The only use of "hereabouts."
I 'll hide me hereabout.
Romeo and Juliet, v, 3, 43. "Hereabout" is used also in *Othello,* iii, 4, 165; v, 1, 57; and *The Tempest,* ii, 2, 41.
19
It out-herods Herod.
Hamlet. Act iii, sc. 2, l. 16. [Hamlet] Herod is mentioned eight times in the plays. The only use of "out-herods."
20
She shall be a high and mighty queen.
Richard III. Act iv, sc. 4, l. 347. [King Richard] "High and mighty" is repeated in *Hamlet,* iv, 7, 43; *Troilus and Cressida,* i, 3, 232; *Henry VIII,* v, 5, 3.
'Tis high time that I were hence.
The Comedy of Errors, iii, 2, 162. The only use of "high time."
21
Now, infidel, I have you on the hip.
The Merchant of Venice. Act iv, sc. 1, l. 334. [Gratiano]
Catch him on the hip.—*The Merchant of Venice,* i, 3, 47.
22
A hit, a very palpable hit.
Hamlet. Act v, sc. 2, l. 292. [Osric]
Thou hast hit it.—*II Henry VI,* iv, 2, 21; *Titus*

Andronicus, ii, 1, 97; *The Taming of the Shrew,* ii, 1, 199.
You have hit it.—*I Henry IV,* ii, 4, 381.
Then here I hit it right.—*Romeo and Juliet,* ii, 3, 41.
Why, this hits right.—*Timon of Athens,* iii, 1, 5.
Thou mightst have hit upon it.—*Timon of Athens,* iv, 3, 351.
He 'll never hit the clout.—*Love's Labour's Lost,* iv, 1, 136.
I can never hit on 's name.—*The Merry Wives of Windsor,* iii, 2, 24.
Thou canst not hit it.—*Love's Labour's Lost,* iv, 1, 127.
'Twill be a hard way to hit.—*The Merchant of Venice,* ii, 2, 48.
What, not one hit?—*The Merchant of Venice,* iii, 2, 270.
Touching the hit it.—*Love's Labour's Lost,* iv, 1, 123.

1
Hit or miss.
Troilus and Cressida. Act i, sc. 3, l. 384. [Ulysses] The only use of the phrase.
In that hit you miss.
Romeo and Juliet. Act i, sc. 1, l. 214. [Romeo]
I missed the meteor once, and hit the woman; who cried out 'Clubs!'
Henry VIII. Act v, sc. 4, l. 52. [Man] See also *Hamlet,* iv, 1, 44.

2
Hold-fast is the only dog.
Henry V, ii, 3, 54. The only use of "hold-fast," hyphenated. As two words it occurs in *Timon of Athens,* iv, i, 8, and in *Macbeth* iv, 3, 3.
Hold off.—*Hamlet,* i, 4, 80; v, 1, 272; 286. Used only in this play.
Hold out.—*I Henry VI,* i, 2, 43, and ten times in later plays.
Hold firm.—*Cymbeline,* ii, 1, 67.
Hold hard.—*Henry V,* iii, 1, 16.
Hold her own.—*II Henry IV,* iii, 2, 218.
Hold thine own.—*III Henry III,* ii, 2, 42; *Troilus and Cressida,* iv, 5, 114.
Hold your own.—*The Taming of the Shrew,* iv, 4, 6.
Hold in.—*I Henry IV,* ii, 1, 85.
Hold together.—*The Winter's Tale,* ii, 2, 23.
Hold my (your) peace.—*II Henry VI,* i, 3, 179, and seven times in later plays.
Hold my (your) tongue.—*King John,* iv, 1, 100, and ten times in later plays. See under TONGUE.
Hold your hand.—*The Comedy of Errors,* i, 2, 93, and four times in later plays.
Hold your word.—*The Merry Wives of Windsor,* v, 5, 258. All phrases cited but once are unique.

3
By all that 's holy.
Henry VIII, v, 3, 132. The only use of the phrase.
I' the name of something holy.
The Two Gentlemen of Verona, iii, 3, 94. The only use of the phrase.

4
Honey, you shall be well desired in Cyprus.
Othello. Act ii, sc. 1, l. 206. [Othello]
My honey love.—*The Taming of the Shrew,* iv, 3, 52.
O honey nurse, what news?—*Romeo and Juliet,* ii, 5, 18.
My good sweet honey lord.—*I Henry IV,* i, 2, 179.
Sweet honey Greek, tempt me no more.—*Troilus and Cressida,* v, 2, 18.

5
We will hoodwink him.
All's Well that Ends Well. Act iii, sc. 6, l. 26. [Second Lord] "Hoodwink" is repeated in *Macbeth,* iv, 3, 72, and in *The Tempest,* iv, 1, 206.

6
Hoot him out o' the city.
Coriolanus. Act iv, sc. 6, l. 123. [Menenius]
Hooted at.—*The Winter's Tale,* v, 3, 116.
Fell a-hooting.—*Love's Labour's Lost,* iv, 2, 61.

7
A team of horse shall not pluck that from me.
The Two Gentlemen of Verona. Act iii, sc. 1, l. 265. [Launce]

8
Touch'd with choler, hot as gunpowder.
Henry V. Act iv, sc. 7, l. 188. [King Henry]
Red-hot.—*Richard III,* iv, 1, 61; *King John,* iv, 1, 61; *The Tempest,* iv, 1, 171. See under HEAT.

9
He hath eaten me out of house and home.
II Henry IV. Act ii, sc. 1, l. 80. [Hostess] The only use of "house and home."

10
How and which way you will.
All's Well that Ends Well, iv, 3, 156.
How or which way.—*I Henry VI,* ii, 1, 71; *Richard II,* ii, 2, 109.

I

11
Break the ice.
The Taming of the Shrew, i, 2, 267. See under ICE.

12
Being the right idea of your father.
Richard III. Act iii, sc. 7, l. 13. [Buckingham] The only use of "right idea."
Idea of her life.—*Much Ado about Nothing,* iv, 1, 226.
Full of . . . ideas.—*Love's Labour's Lost,* iv, 2, 69. The only uses of "idea" and "ideas."

13
Blinking idiot.
The Merchant of Venice, ii, 9, 54. See under IDIOT.

14
Your If is the only peace-maker; much virtue in If.
As You Like It. Act v, sc. 4, l. 104. [Touchstone]

15
I am very ill at ease.
Othello. Act iii, sc. 3, l. 32. [Cassio] The only use of "ill at ease."
I never did . . . ill turn to any.
Pericles, iv, 1, 76. The only use of "ill turn."

16
In this I 'll be impartial.
Measure for Measure. Act v, sc. 1, l. 166. [Duke]

1
Great importance.
Twelfth Night, v, 1, 371. The only use of the phrase.

2
An inkhorn mate.
I Henry VI. Act iii, sc. 1, l. 99. [Servant]

3
I can give you inkling.
Henry VIII. Act ii, sc. 1, l. 140. [Gentleman]
They have had inkling.
Coriolanus, i, 1, 59. The only uses of "inkling."

J

4
He speak for a jack-an-ape.
The Merry Wives of Windsor. Act ii, sc. 3, l. 86. [Caius] See also under JACK.
I will be like a jack-an-apes also.
The Merry Wives of Windsor. Act iv, sc. 4, l. 67. [Evans]
That jack-an-apes with scarfs.
All's Well that Ends Well. Act iii, sc. 5, l. 88. [Diana]
Whoreson jackanapes.—*Cymbeline*, ii, 1, 4. The only use of the word unhyphenated.

5
The jaws of darkness do devour it up.
A Midsummer-Night's Dream. Act i, sc. 1, l. 148. [Lysander]
The jaws of death.—*Twelfth Night*, iii, 4, 393.
Jaws of danger and of death.—*King John*, v, 2, 116.

6
Fie on him, Jezebel!
Twelfth Night, ii, 5, 46. The only mention of Jezebel.

7
You may be jogging.
The Taming of the Shrew, iii, 2, 213. The only use of "jogging."

8
John-a-dreams.
Hamlet, ii, 2, 595. The only use of the word.

K

9
Keep aloof from strict arbitrament.
I Henry IV. Act iv, sc. 1, l. 70. [Worcester] "Keep aloof" is repeated in *Hamlet*, iii, 1, 8.
Keep away.—*I Henry VI*, iv, 4, 22.
Keep back.—*A Midsummer-Night's Dream*, ii, 2, 5.
Keep below.—*Much Ado about Nothing*, v, 2, 10; *The Tempest*, i, 1, 12.
Keep close.—*I Henry IV*, ii, 4, 593; *Henry V*, ii, 3, 65; *Hamlet*, iv, 7, 130.
Keep fresh.—*Twelfth Night*, i, 1, 31.
Keep house.—*The Taming of the Shrew*, i, 1, 201; i, 1, 208; *Cymbeline*, iii, 3, 1.
Keep lodgers.—*Henry V*, ii, 1, 33.
Keep peace.—*Much Ado about Nothing*, ii, 3, 202; *King Lear*, ii, 2, 52; *Macbeth*, i, 5, 47.
Keep the peace.—*I Henry VI*, and five times in later plays.
Keep safe.—*Titus Andronicus*, iv, 2, 110.
Keep shut.—*The Two Gentlemen of Verona*, iii, 1, 358.
Keep time.—*Romeo and Juliet*, and four times in later plays.
Keep tune.—*The Two Gentlemen of Verona*, i, 2, 89.
Keep whole.—*Antony and Cleopatra*, iii, 7, 75; iii, 8, 3.
Keep warm.—*The Taming of the Shrew*, ii, 1, 268; *Othello*, iii, 3, 78.
Keep your place.—*Coriolanus*, ii, 2, 70.
Keep your promise.—*As You Like It*, i, 2, 255; iv, 1, 200.

10
'Twill out at the key-hole.
As You Like It, iv, 1, 164. The only use of "key-hole." See WIT, 1687:10.

11
Any pretty little kickshaws.
II Henry IV, v, 1, 29. See under FOOD.
Art thou good at these kickshawses?
Twelfth Night, i, 3, 122. The only use of "kickshawses." See REVELRY, 1275:11.

12
Hugs his kicky-wicky.
All's Well that Ends Well, ii, 3, 297. The only use of "kicky-wicky." See under HONOUR.

13
Never Yields us kind answer.
The Tempest. Act i, sc. 2, l. 309. [Prospero]
Kind father.—*King Lear*, iii, 4, 20.
Kind friends.—*Pericles*, ii, 1, 142.
Kind gentleman.—*Henry V*, iv, 1, 98; *Othello*, v, 1, 124; *Macbeth*, i, 3, 50.
Kind gods.—*King Lear*, iii, 7, 35; iii, 7, 92; iv, 7, 14.
Kind heart.—*I Henry IV*, iv, 3, 64; *The Merry Wives of Windsor*, iii, 4, 106.
Kind-hearted.—*Sonnets*, x.
Kind nature.—*Titus Andronicus*, v, 3, 168.
Kind service.—*Measure for Measure*, i, 2, 181.

14
Kill with kindness.
The Taming of the Shrew, iv, 1, 211. See under WIFE.

15
I know him as myself.
The Two Gentlemen of Verona, ii, 4, 62.
I know you of old.
Much Ado about Nothing, i, 1, 146.

L

16
Thy godhead laid apart.
All's Well that Ends Well. Act iv, sc. 3, l. 44. [Rosaline]
Laid aside.—*III Henry VI*, ii, 4, 10; iii, 3, 229.
Laid by.—*Henry V*, i, 2, 276; iv, 1, 109.
Laid low.—*Romeo and Juliet*, v, 1, 20.
Laid on.—*As You Like It*, i, 2, 112; *Twelfth Night*, i, 5, 258; *The Winter's Tale*, v, 3, 49.
Laid open.—*Richard III*, iii, 7, 15; *The Winter's Tale*, iii, 2, 19.
Laid up.—*The Comedy of Errors*, ii, 2, 1; *II Henry IV*, v, 1, 95; *As You Like It*, i, 3, 7; *Henry VIII*, v, 5, 8.

17
That was laid on with a trowel.
As You Like It, i, 2, 112. See under FLATTERY.

18
Although the last, not least.
King Lear. Act i, sc. 1, l. 85. [King Lear]
Last account.—*King John*, iv, 2, 216.
Last attempt.—*Coriolanus*, v, 3, 146.
Last breath.—*All's Well that Ends Well*, iv, 3, 62.

Last day.—*II Henry VI*, v, 2, 41; *Antony and Cleopatra*, iv, 9, 4.
Last embrace.—*Romeo and Juliet*, v, 3, 113.
Last farewell.—*Romeo and Juliet*, iii, 2, 143.
Last gasp.—*I Henry VI*, i, 2, 127; *As You Like It*, ii, 3, 70; *Cymbeline*, i, 5, 53.
Last man.—*The Merchant of Venice*, i, 3, 61; *II Henry IV*, iv, 2, 44.
Last penny.—*Henry VIII*, iii, 2, 452.
Last refuge.—*Timon of Athens*, iii, 3, 11.
Last step.—*The Two Gentlemen of Verona*, ii, 7, 36.
Last trumpet.—*Hamlet*, v, 1, 253.

1
Lastly and finally.
Merry Wives of Windsor, i, 1, 142. The only use of "finally" in the plays. "Lastly" is used only twice more: "Sixth and lastly," in *Much Ado about Nothing*, v, 1, 221; v, 1, 227.

2
He 'll lay about him to-day, I can tell them that.
Troilus and Cressida. Act i, sc. 2, l. 58.
Lay along.—*As You Like It*, ii, 1, 30.
Lay apart.—*Henry V*, ii, 4, 78; iii, 7, 41.
Lay aside.—*Richard II*, i, 1, 71, and six times in later plays.
Lay bare.—*The Merchant of Venice*, iv, 1, 252.
Lay by.—*Richard II*, i, 3, 119, and four times in later plays.
Lay claim.—*The Comedy of Errors*, iii, 2, 89; *King John*, i, 1, 72; *As You Like It*, v, 1, 7.
Lay down.—*II Henry VI*, iv, 1, 16, and thirteen times in later plays.
Lay flat.—*Cymbeline*, i, 4, 23.
Lay odds.—*II Henry IV*, v, 5, 111.
Lay open.—*The Comedy of Errors*, iii, 2, 34; *The Merry Wives of Windsor*, ii, 2, 191.
Lay out.—*I Henry IV*, iv, 2, 5; *Timon of Athens*, i, 2, 241; *Cymbeline*, ii, 3, 92; *The Tempest*, ii, 2, 34.
Lay the dust.—*The Two Gentlemen of Verona*, ii, 3, 35.
Lay their heads together.—*II Henry VI*, iv, 8, 60; *The Taming of the Shrew*, i, 2, 139.

3
Learn her by heart.
Love's Labour 's Lost, iii, 1, 36. [Moth]

4
Let it not be said.
King John. Act v, sc. 1, l. 59. [Bastard]

5
The let-alone lies not in your good-will.
King Lear. Act v, sc. 3, l. 79. [Albany] The only use of "let-alone."
Let it alone.—*Titus Andronicus*, iv, 1, 101, and five times in later plays.
Let me alone.—*Romeo and Juliet*, iv, 2, 42.
Let them alone.—*I Henry VI*, i, 2, 44, and frequently thereafter.
Let me know.—*Othello*, iv, 1, 73.
Let that pass.—*Love's Labour 's Lost*, v, 1, 106; *Merry Wives of Windsor*, i, 4, 14; *Richard III*, iv, 2, 88.
Let the matter slip.—*Twelfth Night*, iii, 4, 314.

6
Ah, let be, let be!
Antony and Cleopatra. Act iv, sc. 4, l. 6. [Antony] "Let be" is repeated in *Winter's Tale*, v, 3, 61, and in *Henry VIII*, i, 1, 171.
Let it be.—*Antony and Cleopatra*, iii, 3, 24.
Let it be so.—*King Lear*, i, 1, 110; i, 4, 327.
Let blood.—*Richard III*, iii, 1, 183; *Julius Cæsar*, iii, 1, 152.
Let drive.—*I Henry IV*, ii, 4, 217; ii, 4, 247.
Let go.—*King Lear*, ii, 4, 72.
Let it go.—*Richard III*, iii, 3, 146.
Let her go hang.—*The Tempest*, ii, 2, 56.
Let loose.—*Richard III*, iv, 4, 54, and four times in later plays.
Let out.—*II Henry VI*, iv, 3, 18; *Timon of Athens*, iii, 5, 107.
Let us hence.—*III Henry VI*, iv, 1, 148; iv, 6, 87; *Much Ado about Nothing*, v, 3, 30.
Let us in.—*II Henry VI*, i, 1, 73, and five times in later plays.
Let us on.—*III Henry VI*, iv, 2, 28; *I Henry VI*, iii, 3, 90; *II Henry IV*, i, 3, 85.

7
I had as lief.
The Taming of the Shrew, i, 1, 135, and seventeen times in later plays.

8
In lieu thereof, dispatch me hence.
The Two Gentlemen of Verona. Act ii, sc. 7, l. 88. [Julia] "In lieu thereof" is repeated in *Love's Labour 's Lost*, iii, 1, 130.
In lieu whereof.—*The Merchant of Venice*, iv, 1, 410; *King John*, v, 4, 44.

9
Bring to light.
II Henry VI, iii, 1, 65. [Buckingham]
Bring them to light.—*Measure for Measure*, iii, 2, 189.
Bring truth to light.—*Rape of Lucrece*, l. 940.
Brought to light.—*Richard III*, i, 2, 22.
Come to light.—*Henry V*, iv, 8, 23; *The Merchant of Venice*, ii, 2, 28; *Titus Andronicus*, iv, 2, 125; *Henry VIII*, iii, 2, 29.

10
No more light answers.
Antony and Cleopatra, i, 2, 183. [Antony]
Light behaviour.—*Othello*, iv, 1, 103.
Light heart.—*Love's Labour 's Lost*, v, 2, 18; *Measure for Measure*, iv, 3, 152.
Light of heart.—*Romeo and Juliet*, i, 4, 35.
Light love.—*Romeo and Juliet*, ii, 2, 105.
Light of love.—*Much Ado about Nothing*, iii, 4, 44; 47; *Two Gentlemen of Verona*, i, 2, 83.
Light word.—*Love's Labour 's Lost*, v, 2, 19.

11
'Tis like enough.
Richard III, iii, 2, 122. Repeated seven times in later plays.
Good morrow.—The like to you!—*Timon of Athens*, iii, 4, 2.
Good repose the while!—Thanks, sir, the like to you!—*Macbeth*, ii, 1, 30.
Was ever heard the like?—*Titus Andronicus*, ii, 3, 276.
Who ever saw the like?—*I Henry VI*, i, 2, 22.
I never saw the like.—*Coriolanus*, ii, 1, 284.
Did you ever hear the like?—*The Merry Wives of Windsor*, ii, 1, 70; *Pericles*, iv, 5, 1.
Endure the like.—*I Henry VI*, ii, 3, 38.
Do what you will, the like do I.—*I Henry VI*, iv, 5, 50, and frequently in later plays.

12
There 's little can be said.
All's Well that Ends Well, i, 1, 147. [Parolles]
Little longer.—*Twelfth Night*, i, 5, 218.
Little nearer.—*The Merry Wives of Windsor*, ii, 2, 46; 50.

Little off.—*Much Ado about Nothing*, iii, 5, 10.
Little or nothing.—*The Merry Wives of Windsor*, iii, 4, 65.
Little while.—*III Henry VI*, ii, 3, 2, and nine times in later plays.

1
And live alone as secret as I may.
II Henry VI. Act iv, sc. 4, l. 48. [Say]
Live at jar.—*II Henry VI*, iv, 8, 43.
Live at peace.—*Twelfth Night*, iv, 3, 28.
Live in bliss.—*Othello*, iii, 3, 167.
Live in hope.—*Richard III*, i, 2, 200.
Live in peace.—*III Henry VI*, i, 1, 188; *Richard II*, iii, 3, 95; *King John*, ii, 1, 90.

2
There have sat The live-long day.
Julius Cæsar, i, 1, 46. "Live-long day" is repeated in *Troilus and Cressida*, i, 3, 147.
The livelong night.—*Macbeth*, ii, 3, 65.

3
So long as I live.
The Taming of the Shrew, v, 1, 25.
Long lost.—*Antony and Cleopatra*, iv, 12, 13.
Long past.—*Richard II*, ii, 1, 14.
Long-since-due.—*Timon of Athens*, ii, 2, 39.

4
One poor penny-worth of sugar-candy to make thee long-winded.
I Henry IV. Act iii, sc. 3, l. 180. [Prince of Wales] The only use of "sugar-candy" and "long-winded."

5
Look, who comes here.
As You Like It. Act iv, sc. 3, l. 5. [Celia]
Look here.—*III Henry VI*, v, 1, 82, and six times in later plays.
Look out.—*The Taming of the Shrew*, v, 1, 57, and ten times in later plays.
Look there.—*King Lear*, v, 3, 311; *Henry VIII*, v, 3, 98.

6
What have we to lose?
Cymbeline. Act iv, sc. 2, l. 124. [Guiderius]

7
A notable lubber, as thou reportest him to be.
The Two Gentlemen of Verona. Act ii, sc. 5, l. 47. [Launce]
Great lubber.—*Twelfth Night*, iv, 1, 14.
The lubber Ajax.—*Troilus and Cressida*, iii, 3, 139. The only uses of "lubber."
Lubber's-head.—*II Henry IV*, ii, 1, 30.
Lubber's length.—*King Lear*, i, 4, 101.
Lubberly boy.—*The Merry Wives of Windsor*, v, 5, 195. The only use of "lubberly."

M

8
Main chance, father, you meant.
II Henry VI, i, 1, 212. "Main chance" is repeated in *II Henry IV*, iii, 1, 83.
Main force.—*II Henry VI*, i, 1, 210.
Main hope.—*Macbeth*, v, 4, 10.

9
A man of my kidney.
The Merry Wives of Windsor, iii, 5, 116. The only use of "kidney."
Be a man.—*Othello*, i, 3, 340.
He knew his man.—*Troilus and Cressida*, ii, 1, 141. See under KNOWLEDGE.
To the last man.—*II Henry IV*, iv, 2, 44.

10
This many a day.
Hamlet, iii, 1, 91. "Many a day" is repeated in *Henry VIII*, v, 2, 21.
Many a time.—*Richard II*, iv, 1, 92; *Titus Andronicus*, v, 3, 162.
Many a time and oft.—*I Henry IV*, i, 2, 56; *The Merchant of Venice*, i, 3, 107; *Julius Cæsar*, i, 1, 42.

11
Striving to better, oft we mar what 's well.
King Lear. Act i, sc. 4, l. 369. [Albany]

12
Oliver: Now, sir! what make you here?
Orlando: Nothing; I am not taught to make any thing.
Oliver: What mar you then, sir?
Orlando: Marry, sir, I am helping you to mar that which God made.
As You Like It. Act i, sc. 1, l. 34.
Make and mar.—*A Midsummer-Night's Dream*, i, 2, 39.
It [drink] makes him, and it mars him.—*Macbeth*, ii, 3, 36. See under DRUNKENNESS.
It makes us, or it mars us.—*Othello*, v, 1, 4.

13
Bless the mark!
The Two Gentlemen of Verona, iv, 4, 21.
God bless the mark!—*The Merchant of Venice*, ii, 2, 25; *Othello*, i, 1, 33.
God save the mark!—*Romeo and Juliet*, iii, 2, 53; *I Henry IV*, i, 3, 56.

14
Do you mark me, sir?
The Two Gentlemen of Verona, ii, 1, 169. [Gonzalo]
Mark what I say.—*Measure for Measure*, iv, 3, 130.
Mark you this.—*The Merchant of Venice*, i, 3, 98. A phrase, in various forms, used over a hundred times in the plays.

15
A right fair mark, fair coz, is soonest hit.
Romeo and Juliet. Act i, sc. 1, l. 213. [Benvolio]
You have hit the mark.—*Henry VIII*, ii, 1, 165. See also *Pericles*, i, 1, 164.

16
A right good mark-man!
Romeo and Juliet. Act i, sc. 1, l. 212. [Romeo] The only use of "mark-man." "Marksman" does not appear in the plays.

17
There may be matter in it.
The Winter's Tale, iv, 4, 874. [Autolycus]
Matter of weight.—*Much Ado about Nothing*, iii, 3, 190.
Matters of great moment.—*Richard III*, iii, 7, 67.
That 's no matter.—*Much Ado about Nothing*, v, 1, 81; *As You Like It*, iii, 2, 176; iv, 3, 27; *Coriolanus*, ii, 3, 41.
What 's the matter?—*II Henry VI*, iii, 2, 28, and fifty times in later plays.

18
May be so we shall.
I Henry IV. Act iv, sc. 3, l. 113. [Hotspur] "May be" occurs fourteen times in the plays.
That may be.—*Romeo and Juliet*, iv, 1, 19.
As best I may.—*Taming of the Shrew*, i, 2, 56.
Be as it may.—*Henry V*, ii, 1, 7; 25.
Be it as it may.—*III Henry VI*, i, 1, 194.

It may not be.—*The Taming of the Shrew,* iii, 2, 200; *Richard II,* ii, 3, 145.

1
By fair or foul means.
III Henry VI. Act iv, sc. 7, l. 14. [King Edward]

By all means.—*Twelfth Night,* iii, 2, 62; *The Merry Wives of Windsor,* iv, 2, 230.

By no means.—*As You Like It,* iii, 2, 326, and twelve times in later plays.

What do you mean?—*Julius Cæsar,* iv, 3, 130, and four times in later plays.

What means this?—*I Henry VI,* i, 3, 29, and six times in later plays.

What mean you?—*The Comedy of Errors,* i, 2, 93, and seven times in later plays.

2
I meant well.
The Winter's Tale, v, 3, 3. See MEANING, 970:15.

3
Are you good men and true?
Much Ado about Nothing, iii, 3, 1. The only use of the phrase.

4
As merry as the day is long.
Much Ado about Nothing, ii, 1, 51; *King John,* iv, 1, 18. See under MERRIMENT.

5
The milk of human kindness.
Macbeth, i, 5, 18. See under KINDNESS. The only use of the phrase.

Thy honesty and love doth mince this matter.
Othello. Act ii, sc. 3, l. 247. [Othello] The only use of "mince this matter."

6
There, at the moated grange, resides this dejected Mariana.
Measure for Measure. Act iii, sc. 1, l. 277. [Duke]

7
Give me the moiety.
The Winter's Tale. Act iv, sc. 4, l. 841. [Autolycus] "Moiety" occurs fifteen times.

8
Brought moping hither.
The Tempest. Act v, sc. 1, l. 240. [Boatswain] The only use of "moping."

9
But more of this hereafter.
All's Well that Ends Well. Act iv, sc. 4, l. 26. [Helena]

10
Mort du vinaigre.
All's Well that Ends Well, ii, 3, 50. Used only once.

11
He . . . foam'd at mouth.
Julius Cæsar, i, 2, 255. The only use of "foam'd at mouth." "Foam'd at the mouth" occurs in *Cymbeline,* v, 5, 276.

Foams at mouth.—*Troilus and Cressida,* v, 5, 36; *Othello,* iv, 1, 55.

Mouth so watered.—*Pericles,* iv, 2, 108.

Dumb mouths.—*Julius Cæsar,* iii, 1, 260; iii, 2, 229. See under WOUND.

Make mouths.—*A Midsummer-Night's Dream,* iii, 2, 38.

12
Too much of a good thing.
As You Like It. Act iv, sc. 1, l. 123. [Rosalind]

N

13
Nay, I have ta'en you napping, gentle love.
The Taming of the Shrew. Act iv, sc. 2, l. 46. [Tranio]

You may look pale, but I should blush, I know,
To be o'erheard and taken napping so.
Love's Labour's Lost. Act iv, sc. 3, l. 129. [Longaville] The only uses of "taken napping."

14
That 's neither here nor there.
The Merry Wives of Windsor. Act i, sc. 4, l. 112. [Mistress Quickly]

'Tis neither here nor there.
Othello. Act iv, sc. 3, l. 59. [Emilia]

15
Be it known to you I do remain as neuter.
Richard II. Act ii, sc. 3, l. 158. [York] The only use of "neuter."

16
Here 's snip and nip and cut and slish and slash.
The Taming of the Shrew. Act iv, sc. 3, l. 90. [Petruchio] See GOWN, 631:6.

Nips his root.—*Henry VIII,* iii, 2, 357.

Nips youth i' the head.—*Measure for Measure,* iii, 1, 91.

These tidings nip me.—*Titus Andronicus,* iv, 4, 70.

It nips me.—*Pericles,* v, 1, 235.

17
It is a most pathetical nit.
Love's Labour's Lost. Act iv, sc. 1, l. 150. [Costard]

Thou flea, thou nit!—*The Taming of the Shrew,* iv, 3, 110. The only uses of "nit."

18
Will he give you the nod?
Troilus and Cressida. Act i, sc. 2, l. 212. [Cressida]

I will practise the insinuating nod.
Coriolanus. Act ii, sc. 3, l. 107. [Coriolanus]

19
Comb your noddle with a three-legg'd stool.
The Taming of the Shrew. Act i, sc. 1, l. 64. [Katharina] The only use of "three-legg'd."

I will smite his noddles.—*The Merry Wives of Windsor,* iii, 1, 128.

20
My office is to noise abroad.
II Henry IV. Induction, l. 29. [Rumour] "Noise abroad" is repeated in *Love's Labour's Lost,* ii, 1, 22.

21
This is a riddling merchant for the nonce.
I Henry VI. Act ii, sc. 3, l. 57. [Countess] "For the nonce" is repeated in *I Henry IV,* i, 2, 201, and in *Hamlet,* iv, 7, 161.

22
Take note of him.
Julius Cæsar, v, 3, 50. See under NOTE.

23
He gets nothing by that.
Much Ado about Nothing. Act i, sc. 1, l. 65. [Beatrice]

Little or nothing.—*The Merry Wives of Windsor,* iii, 4, 66.

Nothing at all.—*The Two Gentlemen of Verona,* i, 1, 144, and four times in later plays.

Nothing but this.—*II Henry VI,* iv, 7, 61, and three times in later plays.

Nothing else.—*II Henry VI,* ii, 1, 50, and twenty-six times in later plays.
Nothing in the world.—*Love's Labour's Lost,* iv, 3, 12, and six times in later plays.
Nothing less.—*I Henry VI,* ii, 5, 100.
Nothing like.—*The Comedy of Errors,* iii, 2, 105, and three times in later plays.
Nothing more.—*Timon of Athens,* iii, 5, 85; *Hamlet,* v, 2, 125; *King Lear,* i, 1, 203.

1
Uncle, how now!
II Henry VI. Act i, sc. 1, l. 54. [King Henry] "How now" is repeated twenty-one times in later plays.
What now?—*The Comedy of Errors,* i, 2, 42; *Troilus and Cressida,* v, 3, 98.
Now-a-days.—*Midsummer-Night's Dream,* iii, 1, 148; *Hamlet,* v, 1, 181; *Pericles,* ii, 1, 73.
Now and then.—*The Merchant of Venice,* ii, 2, 200; *Henry V,* iii, 6, 71; *As You Like It,* iii, 4, 103; *King Lear,* iv, 3, 14.

O

2
I have o'ershot myself.
Julius Cæsar. Act iii, sc. 2, l. 155. [Antony]

3
Off and on.
II Henry IV, iii, 2, 281. "Off and on" is repeated in *All's Well that Ends Well,* v, 3, 279, and in *The Tempest,* iii, 2, 17.

4
Omittance is no quittance.
As You Like It. Act iii, sc. 5, l. 133. [Phebe] The only use of "omittance."

5
On business to my brother.
Julius Cæsar. Act iv, sc. 3, l. 248. [Brutus]
On purpose.—*The Comedy of Errors,* iv, 3, 92, and six times in later plays.
On sale.—*As You Like It,* ii, 4, 84. Unique.

6
Once again proclaim it publicly.
The Comedy of Errors, v, 1, 130. "Once again" is repeated four times in later plays.
Once before.—*Much Ado about Nothing,* ii, 1, 289.
Once more.—*Henry V,* iii, 1, 1.
Once or twice.—*The Merry Wives of Windsor,* iii, 5, 103.

7
One is one too many.
The Comedy of Errors. Act iii, sc. 1, l. 35. [Dromio of Syracuse]
One at a time.—*The Tempest,* iii, 3, 102.
One of these days.—*Henry V,* ii, 1, 92, and three times in later plays.
One or the other.—*II Henry IV,* i, 2, 273.

8
This only child.
Romeo and Juliet. Act iii, sc. 5, l. 166. [Capulet]
Only choice.—*Coriolanus,* i, 9, 36.
Only hate.—*Romeo and Juliet,* i, 5, 140.
Only heir.—*The Tempest,* i, 2, 58.
Only love.—*Romeo and Juliet,* i, 5, 140.
Only son.—*II Henry VI,* ii, 2, 19, and four times in later plays. All these phrases except the last are unique.

9
I, an ass, am onion-eyed.
Antony and Cleopatra. Act iv, sc. 2, l. 35. [Enobarbus] The only use of "onion-eyed."

10
Not knowing how to find the open air.
III Henry VI, iii, 2, 177. "Open air" is repeated four times in later plays.
Open ear.—*Richard II,* ii, 1, 20; *The Winter's Tale,* iv, 4, 685.
Open hand.—*III Henry VI,* iv, 2, 9; *Twelfth Night,* iv, 1, 22.
Open mouth.—*King John,* iv, 2, 195. Unique.
Open nature.—*Othello,* i, 3, 405. Unique.

11
Launcelot and I are out.
The Merchant of Venice, iii, 5, 34. [Jessica]
Nay, I beseech you, sir, be not out with me.
Julius Cæsar. Act i, sc. 1, l. 18. [Commoner]
This will out.—*Richard III,* i, 4, 290.
Out at elbow.—*Measure for Measure,* ii, 1, 61. Unique.
Out at heels.—*The Merry Wives of Windsor,* i, 3, 34; *King Lear,* ii, 2, 164.
Out of breath.—*The Comedy of Errors,* iv, 1, 57, and five times in later plays.
Out of doors.—*The Comedy of Errors,* ii, 1, 11, and eighteen times in later plays.
Out of fashion.—*All's Well that Ends Well,* i, 1, 170; *Troilus and Cressida,* iii, 3, 152; *Othello,* ii, 1, 208; *Cymbeline,* iii, 4, 53.
Out of hand.—*I Henry VI,* iii, 2, 102, and three times in later plays.
Out of health.—*Timon of Athens,* iii, 4, 72. Unique.
Out of hearing.—*Midsummer-Night's Dream,* ii, 2, 152. Unique.
Out of heart.—*I Henry IV,* iii, 3, 6; *Love's Labour's Lost,* iii, 1, 45.
Out of hope.—*A Midsummer-Night's Dream,* iii, 2, 279, and three times in later plays.
Out of love.—*The Two Gentlemen of Verona,* iv, 4, 210; *Measure for Measure,* iii, 1, 174.
Out of season.—*The Comedy of Errors,* i, 2, 68; ii, 2, 48; *King Lear,* ii, 1, 121.
Out of town.—*Troilus and Cressida,* i, 1, 116. Unique.
Out of tune.—*The Two Gentlemen of Verona,* iv, 2, 60, and five times in later plays.
Out of use.—*Timon of Athens,* v, 1, 28, and three times in later plays.

12
And stand indebted, over and above.
The Merchant of Venice, iv, 1, 413. "Over and above" is repeated in *The Merry Wives of Windsor,* v, 5, 177.
Over and beside.—*The Taming of the Shrew,* i, 2, 149.
Over and over.—*The Two Gentlemen of Verona,* i, 1, 115, and seven times in later plays.

13
Over-careful fathers.
II Henry IV, iv, 5, 68. This and the following phrases occur only once.
Over-careful.—*II Henry IV,* iv, 5, 68.
Over-credulous.—*Macbeth,* iv, 3, 120.
Over-daring.—*I Henry VI,* iv, 4, 5.
Over-earnest.—*Julius Cæsar,* iv, 3, 122.
Over-fed.—*Pericles,* iii, Gower, 3.
Over-full.—*A Midsummer-Night's Dream,* i, 1, 113.
Over-greedy.—*II Henry IV,* i, 3, 88.

Over-hasty.—*Hamlet*, ii, 2, 57.
Over-kind.—*The Winter's Tale*, i, 1, 23. Shakespeare was fond of "over" as an adverb, and used it more than 300 times, usually in unique phrases.

P

1
To have an itching palm.
Julius Cæsar, iv, 3, 10. See under BRIBERY.

2
Pardon me, princely Henry and the rest.
I Henry VI, iv, 1, 18. "Pardon me" is repeated 56 times in later plays.

3
Thou art in a parlous state.
As You Like It. Act iii, sc. 2, l. 45. [Touchstone]

A parlous boy.—*Richard III*, ii, 4, 35; iii, 1, 154.
A parlous knock.—*Romeo and Juliet*, i, 3, 54.
A parlous fear.—*Midsummer-Night's Dream*, iii, 1, 14. The only uses of "parlous."

4
Give me particulars.
Antony and Cleopatra. Act i, sc. 2, l. 57. [Iras]

Give us particulars.—*The Tempest*, v, 1, 135.

5
You may not pass, you must return.
Coriolanus. Act v, sc. 2, l. 5. [Senator]

6
He 's not past it yet.
Measure for Measure, iii, 2, 193.

Past enduring.—*The Winter's Tale*, ii, 1, 2.
Past fearing.—*Measure for Measure*, v, 1, 402.
Past help.—*Romeo and Juliet*, iv, 1, 45; *The Winter's Tale*, iii, 2, 223.
Past hope.—*Romeo and Juliet*, iv, 1, 45; *Twelfth Night*, v, 1, 82; *Cymbeline*, i, 1, 137.
Past patience.—*Titus Andronicus*, v, 3, 126.
Past praying for.—*I Henry IV*, ii, 4, 211. All except "past help" and "past hope" are unique.

7
It will fall pat as I told you.
A Midsummer-Night's Dream. Act v, sc. 1, l. 188. [Pyramus]

Pat, pat.—*Midsummer-Night's Dream*, iii, 1, 2.
Now might I do it pat.
Hamlet. Act iii, sc. 3, l. 73. [Hamlet]
Come pat betwixt too early and too late.
Henry VIII. Act ii, sc. 3, l. 84. [Lady]
Pat he comes like the catastrophe of the old comedy.
King Lear. Act i, sc. 2, l. 147. [Edmund] The only uses of "pat."
The catastrophe is a nuptial.—*Love's Labour 's Lost*, iv, 1, 77.
I 'll tickle your catastrophe.—*II Henry IV*, ii, 1, 66.
Catastrophe . . . of pastime.—*All 's Well that Ends Well*, i, 2, 57. The only uses of "catastrophe."

8
Most pretty and pathetical!
Love's Labour 's Lost. Act i, sc. 2, l. 102. [Armado]

It is most pathetical.—*Love's Labour 's Lost*, iv, 1, 150.

9
They 'll pay for it.
The Winter's Tale, ii, 1, 146. See under PAYMENT.

10
Let us to 't pell-mell.
Richard III, v, 3, 312. Repeated in *King Lear*, iv, 6, 119.

Pell-mell, down with them!—*Love's Labour 's Lost*, iv, 3, 368.
Pell-mell havoc and confusion.—*I Henry IV*, v, 1, 82.
Pell-mell Make work upon themselves.—*King John*, ii, 1, 406.

11
How camest thou in this pickle?
The Tempest. Act v, sc. 1, l. 281. [Alonso] The only use of the phrase.

12
I would not care a pin.
Love's Labour 's Lost. Act iv, sc. 3, l. 19. [Biron]

Not worth a pin.—*The Two Gentlemen of Verona*, ii, 7, 56. Both phrases unique.

13
All which we pine for now.
Macbeth. Act iii, sc. 6, l. 37. [Lord]

Dwindle, peak and pine.—*Macbeth*, i, 3, 23.
Pine and die.—*Love's Labour 's Lost*, i, 1, 31.
Pine away.—*Richard II*, iii, 2, 209.

14
She is pistol-proof.
II Henry IV. Act ii, sc. 4, l. 125. [Falstaff] The only use of "pistol-proof."

15
I am toiling in a pitch,—pitch that defiles.
Love's Labour 's Lost. Act iv, sc. 3, l. 3. [Biron]

They that touch pitch will be defiled.
Much Ado about Nothing. Act iii, sc. 3, l. 60. [Dogberry]
Pitch doth defile.—*I Henry IV*, ii, 4, 456. See under COMPANY.

16
Pitchers have ears.
Richard III, ii, 4, 37. Repeated in *The Taming of the Shrew*, iv, 4, 52.

17
I know my place.
Twelfth Night. Act ii, sc. 5, l. 59. [Malvolio]

18
As plain as the plain bald pate of father Time.
The Comedy of Errors. Act ii, sc. 2, l. 70. [Dromio of Syracuse]

As plain as I see you now.—*Twelfth Night*, iii, 2, 11.

19
Be plain, good son, and homely in thy drift.
Romeo and Juliet. Act ii, sc. 3, l. 55. [Friar Laurence]

I was always plain with you.
The Merchant of Venice. Act iii, sc. 5, l. 4. [Launcelot]
I must be plain with you.
The Merchant of Venice. Act v, sc. 1, l. 166. [Portia]
Shall I be plain?—*Richard III*, iv, 2, 18.
Make all things plain.—*A Midsummer-Night's Dream*, v, 1, 129.
Plain and bluntly.—*I Henry VI*, iv, 1, 51.

Plain and to the purpose.—*Much Ado about Nothing,* ii, 3, 19.
To be plain.—*II Henry VI,* i, 2, 96; *The Winter's Tale,* iv, 4, 174.
I 'll tell her plain.—*The Taming of the Shrew,* ii, 1, 171.
Tell thee plain.—*III Henry VI,* iii, 2, 69.
To tell you plain.—*Love's Labour's Lost,* iv, 3, 272.

1
Fair play.
King John, v, 1, 67; v, 2, 118; *Troilus and Cressida,* v, 3, 43; *The Tempest,* v, 1, 175; *Henry VIII,* iv, 2, 36.
Foul play.
Love's Labour's Lost, v, 2, 766; *King John,* iv, 2, 93; *I Henry IV,* iii, 2, 169; *Hamlet,* i, 2, 256; *King Lear,* iii, 7, 31; *The Tempest,* i, 2, 60; *Pericles,* iv, 3, 19.

2
Well, then, here 's the point.
Cymbeline. Act iii, sc. 4, l. 156. [Pisanio] For additional phrases, see under POINT.

3
My friends were poor, but honest.
All's Well that Ends Well, i, 3, 201. Unique.
As poor as Job.—*II Henry IV,* i, 2, 44; *The Merry Wives of Windsor,* v, 5, 164.

4
It is not possible, it cannot be.
I Henry IV. Act v, sc. 2, l. 4. [Worcester]
It is not possible.—*Midsummer-Night's Dream,* iv, 2, 7.
It 's not possible?—*Hamlet,* v, 2, 131.
'Tis not possible.—*Measure for Measure,* iii, 2, 132; *Othello,* ii, 1, 222.
It were not possible.—*All's Well that Ends Well,* iv, 3, 203.
Not possible.—*The Taming of the Shrew,* i, 1, 199; *Coriolanus,* iv, 6, 56.
I never thought it possible.—*The Taming of the Shrew,* i, 1, 154.

5
Messenger: Is it possible?
Beatrice: Very easily possible.
Much Ado about Nothing. Act i, sc. 1, l. 74. "Is it possible?" is used thirty times.
Can it be possible?—*As You Like It,* ii, 2, 1.
May it be possible?—*Henry V,* ii, 2, 100.
May this be possible?—*King John,* v, 4, 21.
'Tis very possible.—*Much Ado about Nothing,* ii, 3, 186.
It is possible enough.—*Othello,* i, 3, 9.
Possible enough.—*Henry VIII,* i, 1, 37.

6
If without peril it be possible.
Richard III. Act v, sc. 3, l. 39. [Richmond]
If it be possible.—*Coriolanus,* v, 4, 4.
Antigonus: Any thing, my lord, . . . any thing possible.
Leontes: It shall be possible.
The Winter's Tale. Act ii, sc. 3, l. 163.

7
'Tis good to be a post.
As You Like It. Act iv, sc. 1, l. 9. [Rosalind] See under DULNESS.

8
Such a pother.
Coriolanus. Act ii, sc. 1, l. 234. [Brutus]
Dreadful pother.—*King Lear,* iii, 2, 50. The only uses of "pother."

9
Do not presume too much.
Julius Cæsar. Act iv, sc. 3, l. 63. [Cassius]

10
To pry into the secrets of the state.
II Henry VI, i, 1, 250. "Pry into" is repeated in *The Taming of the Shrew,* iii, 1, 87, and in *I Henry IV,* iv, 3, 103.
Pry on every side.—*Richard III,* iii, 5, 6.

11
Belike you mean to make a puppet of me.
The Taming of the Shrew. Act iv, sc. 3, l. 103. [Katharina]

12
As pure as snow.
Macbeth, iv, 3, 53; *Hamlet,* iii, 1, 41. See under PURITY.

Q

13
Call in question.
As You Like It, v, 2, 6; *Julius Cæsar,* iv, 3, 165; *Troilus and Cressida,* iii, 2, 60; *Twelfth Night,* i, 4, 6.
Call 't in question.—*Hamlet,* iv, 5, 217.
There 's the question.—*II Henry VI,* iv, 2, 149; *Julius Cæsar,* ii, 1, 13.

14
'Tis for the dead, not for the quick.
Hamlet, v, 1, 137. "The quick and dead" is repeated in l. 274. The phrase occurs in no other scene.

15
I am struck to the quick.
The Tempest. Act v, sc. 1, l. 25. [Prospero]
I 'll tent him to the quick.
Hamlet. Act ii, sc. 2, l. 626. [Hamlet]
Touch thee to the quick.
The Comedy of Errors, ii, 2, 132; *Titus Andronicus,* iv, 4, 36.
To the quick o' the ulcer.
Hamlet. Act iv, sc. 7, l. 124. [King]

16
'Tis but Quid for Quo.
I Henry VI, v, 3, 109. Only use of the phrase.

17
As quiet as a lamb.
King John. Act iv, sc. 1, l. 80. [Arthur] The only use of the phrase.

R

18
Red, master; red as blood.
II Henry VI, ii, 1, 110. Shakespeare used "red as blood" in his first play and never in any other, but repeated it in *A Lover's Complaint,* l. 198.
As red as fire.—*III Henry VI,* iii, 2, 51; *Julius Cæsar,* iii, 2, 120.
Red as any rose.—*II Henry IV,* ii, 4, 423.
Fiery red.—*Richard II,* ii, 3, 58; *A Midsummer-Night's Dream,* iii, 2, 391.

19
Rest assured.
Julius Cæsar. Act v, sc. 3, l. 17. [Cassius]
Let it rest.—*Taming of the Shrew,* iii, 1, 56.
Here it rests.—*The Merry Wives of Windsor,* iv, 6, 48.
Thus it rests.—*The Merry Wives of Windsor,* iv, 6, 34. All these phrases are unique.

20
Neither rhyme nor reason.
The Comedy of Errors, ii, 4, 49; *As You*

 FAMILIAR PHRASES

Like It, iii, 2, 418; *The Merry Wives of Windsor*, v, 5, 133. See under RHYME.

1
I think there be six Richmonds in the field.
Richard III. Act v, sc. 4, l. 11. [King]

2
A gentle riddance. Draw the curtains, go.
The Merchant of Venice. Act ii, sc. 7, l. 78. [Portia]

A good riddance.—*Troilus and Cressida*, ii, 1, 132. The only uses of "riddance."

3
I am right glad.
Timon of Athens, iii, 1, 13. "Right glad" is repeated in *The Tempest*, iii, 3, 11; *Cymbeline*, v, 5, 296; *Henry VIII*, v, 1, 109.

Right glad I am.—*Romeo and Juliet*, i, 1, 124.

Right good.—*Romeo and Juliet*, i, 1, 212; *Henry VIII*, iv, 2, 146.

The right idea.—*Richard III*, iii, 7, 13.

Right in thine eye.—*King John*, v, 4, 60.

Right now.—*II Henry VI*, iii, 2, 40.

Right out.—*The Tempest*, iv, 1, 101.

Right well.—*Richard III*, iv, 1, 15, and six times in later plays.

4
Kiss the rod.
The Two Gentlemen of Verona, i, 2, 59; *Richard II*, v, 1, 32.

5
Something is rotten in the state of Denmark.
Hamlet, i, 4, 90. See under ROTTENNESS for other quotations.

6
Let her be round with him.
Hamlet. Act iii, sc. 1, l. 191. [Polonius]

Am I so round with you as you with me?
The Comedy of Errors. Act ii, sc. 1, l. 82. [Dromio of Ephesus]

7
There 's the rub.
Hamlet. Act iii, sc. 1, l. 65. [Hamlet]

The world is full of rubs.—*Richard II*, iii, 4, 4.

Every rub is smoothed.—*Henry V*, ii, 2, 188.

8
Against all rules of nature.
Othello. Act i, sc. 3, l. 101. [Brabantio]

The new-made duke that rules the roast.
II Henry VI. Act i, sc. 1, l. 109. [Gloucester] The only use of "rules the roast," a phrase dating from about 1400, when it was used in *Carpenter's Tools*, by an unknown author. (Halliwell, *Nugæ Poeticæ*, 17.)

9
I cannot find those runagates.
Cymbeline. Act iv, sc. 2, l. 62. [Cloten] The only use of "runagates." "Runagate" occurs three times in the plays: *Richard III*, iv, 4, 465; *Romeo and Juliet*, iii, 6, 90; *Cymbeline*, i, 6, 137.

10
Do they grow rusty?
Hamlet. Act ii, sc. 2, l. 352. [Hamlet] The only use of "grow rusty."

S

11
More sacks to the mill!
Love's Labour's Lost. Act iv, sc. 3, l. 81. [Biron]

12
'Tis better said than done.
III Henry VI. Act iii, sc. 2, l. 90. [Lady Grey]

There is no more to be said.—*Coriolanus*, iii, 3, 117.

As I have said.—*Romeo and Juliet*, i, 3, 200, and seven times in later plays.

As I said before.—*Antony and Cleopatra*, ii, 6, 136.

I have heard it said.—*I Henry VI*, ii, 2, 55; *Coriolanus*, iv, 3, 33; *Winter's Tale*, iv, 4, 86.

So 'tis said.—*Timon of Athens*, v, 1, 81; *The Winter's Tale*, iv, 4, 793.

That 's well said.—*II Henry VI*, ii, 1, 111, and frequently throughout the plays.

13
For God's sake!
II Henry VI, i, 3, 217, and twenty times in later plays. It occurs ten times in the first five plays, and in no play after the fourteenth, *The Merchant of Venice*.

For goodness' sake.—*Henry VIII*, Prologue, l. 23; iii, 1, 159. It will be noted that this phrase occurs only in the last play.

For heaven's sake.—*King John*, iv, 1, 78; *Othello*, v, 1, 50; *Henry VIII*, iii, 1, 110.

For the Lord's sake.—*Measure for Measure*, iv, 3, 21. Unique.

14
There is some sap in this.
The Winter's Tale. Act iv, sc. 4, l. 575. [Florizel]

There 's sap in 't yet.—*Antony and Cleopatra*, iii, 13, 192.

15
Say that I said so.
Measure for Measure. Act iii, sc. 2, l. 195. [Lucio] The only use of the phrase.

16
But, as I say.
Hamlet, v, 2, 89. Used five times, only in the later plays.

As much as to say.—*The Two Gentlemen of Verona*, iii, 1, 324 and five times in later plays.

I dare say.—*I Henry VI*, ii, 4, 134, and three times in later plays.

Say on.—*Richard III*, iv, 2, 11, and four times in later plays.

Say you so?—*III Henry VI*, iv, 7, 29, and five times in later plays.

So I say (say I).—*III Henry VI*, iii, 2, 142, and seven times in later plays.

To say the truth.—*I Henry VI*, iv, 1, 30, and seven times in later plays.

Say what I think.—*All's Well that Ends Well*, iii, 1, 14.

How say you?—*I Henry VI*, ii, 3, 61, and fifteen times in later plays.

What say you?—*II Henry VI*, iv, 7, 60, and frequently thereafter.

Sooth to say.—*The Comedy of Errors*, iv, 4, 72; *The Taming of the Shrew*, iv, 2, 99.

17
Methinks, I see him now.
Cymbeline. Act v, sc. 5, l. 209. [Iachimo]

Methinks I hear him now.—*All's Well that Ends Well.* Act i, sc. 2, l. 53. [King]

1
At thy service.
The Two Gentlemen of Verona, ii, 5, 63. Used only once.
At your service.—*All's Well that Ends Well,* iv, 5, 36; *Antony and Cleopatra,* i, 2, 90; *King John,* i, 1, 198; *Twelfth Night,* i, 5, 218.

2
Hic et ubique? then we'll shift our ground.
Hamlet. Act i, sc. 5, l. 156. [Hamlet]

3
There's the short and the long.
The Merry Wives of Windsor. Act ii, sc. 1, l. 137. [Nym]
This is the short and the long of it.
The Merry Wives of Windsor, ii, 1, 137; ii, 2, 60; *A Midsummer-Night's Dream,* iv, 2, 39; *The Merchant of Venice,* ii, 2, 135.
That is the breff and the long.
Henry V. Act iii, sc. 2, l. 126. [Captain Jamy]
That is the brief and the tedious of it.
All's Well that Ends Well. Act ii, sc. 3, l. 33. [Parolles]

4
Come, side by side together live and die.
I Henry VI, iv, 5, 54. The only use of "side by side."

5
We'll sift this matter further.
All's Well that Ends Well. Act v, sc. 3, l. 124. [King] "Sift" occurs again in *Richard II,* i, 1, 12, and in Hamlet, ii, 2, 58.

6
'Tis my familiar sin.
Measure for Measure. Act i, sc. 4, l. 31. [Lucio] The only use of "familiar sin."
Familiar spirits.—*I Henry VI,* v, 3, 10.
Familiar style.—*The Merry Wives of Windsor,* i, 3, 51. All these phrases used but once.

7
Help me, Cassius, or I sink!
Julius Cæsar, i, 2, 111. [Cassius is quoting Cæsar]
Or sink or swim.—*I Henry IV,* i, 3, 194. The only use of the phrase.

8
Will you sit down?
I Henry IV. Act iii, sc. 1, l. 4. [Hotspur]
Sit fast.—*III Henry VI,* v, 2, 3.
Sit you fast.—*III Henry VI,* iv, 1, 119.

9
And every thing is left at six and seven.
Richard II. Act ii, sc. 2, l. 122. [York] The only use of "six and seven."

10
Your skins are whole.
Merry Wives of Windsor, iii, 1, 111. Unique.

11
I will not be slack.
II Henry VI, i, 2, 66, and, in various combinations, in nine later plays.
What a beast am I to slack it.
The Merry Wives of Windsor, iii, 4, 115.
My behind-hand slackness.
The Winter's Tale. Act v, sc. 1, l. 151. [Leontes] The only use of "behind-hand." "Slackness" is repeated in *Antony and Cleopatra,* iii, 7, 28.

12
Let him let the matter slip.
Twelfth Night, iii, 4, 314. [Sir Andrew]
Let slip.—*Measure for Measure,* i, 3, 21.
Let the world slip.—*The Taming of the Shrew,* Ind., 2, 146.
Slip down.—*Timon of Athens,* i, 1, 87.
Slip so grossly.—*Measure for Measure,* v, 1, 477.
'Tis a venial slip.—*Othello,* iv, 1, 9. The only use of "venial." All these phrases used but once.

13
You gave us . . . the slip.
Romeo and Juliet, ii, 4, 48. Used only once.
Slip away.—*The Merry Wives of Windsor,* iv, 2, 54; iv, 6, 23; *As You Like It,* iv, 3, 113.

14
There I smelt 'em out.
King Lear. Act iv, sc. 6, l. 105. [King Lear]
Smell a fox.—*II Henry IV,* i, 2, 175. Both unique.

15
And so forth.
Love's Labour's Lost, iv, 2, 96; *Twelfth Night,* i, 5, 267; iii, 4, 82; *The Winter's Tale,* i, 2, 218; *II Henry IV,* v, 3, 4.

16
So much for him.
Hamlet. Act i, sc. 2, l. 25. [King]

17
His leg is but so so.
As You Like It, iii, 5, 119.
Touchstone: Art rich?
William: Faith, sir, so so.
Touchstone: 'So so' is good, very good, very excellent good; and yet it is not; it is but so so.
As You Like It. Act v, sc. 1, l. 27.
Well of his wealth; but of himself, so so.
The Two Gentlemen of Verona. Act i, sc. 2, l. 13. [Lucetta]
Before you can . . . breathe twice and cry 'so so.'
The Tempest, iv, 1, 45. "So so" is used eleven times in the plays.

18
So be it.
King John, iii, 4, 140. Unique.
So help me.—*Othello,* iii, 4, 126.
So help me Heaven!—*The Comedy of Errors,* v, 1, 267.
So long as.—*II Henry VI,* ii, 4, 63, and six times in later plays.
May this be so?—*Much Ado about Nothing,* iii, 2, 120.
So say I.—*Much Ado about Nothing,* iii, 2, 16; *The Merry Wives of Windsor,* iv, 2, 134.

19
Can he not be sociable?
Troilus and Cressida. Act ii, sc. 3, l. 220. [Ajax]
Now art thou sociable.
Romeo and Juliet. Act ii, sc. 4, l. 93. [Mercutio]

20
But, soft!
II Henry VI, ii, 4, 15. A phrase used forty-nine times throughout the plays.
Soft and fair, friar.
Much Ado about Nothing. Act v, sc. 4, l. 72. [Benedick]
Softly, my masters!
The Taming of the Shrew, i, 2, 238, and in four later plays.

1
There 's something in 't.
All 's Well that Ends Well, i, 3, 248; iv, 3, 4; *Twelfth Night,* iv, 3, 20; *Hamlet,* ii, 2, 384.
There is something in the wind.—*The Comedy of Errors,* iii, 1, 69.
Something tells me.—*The Merchant of Venice,* iii, 2, 4.
Something too much of this.—*Hamlet,* iii, 2, 79.
I was about to say something.—*Hamlet,* ii, 1, 51. All but the first phrase used but once.

2
Every mother's son.
Midsummer-Night's Dream, i, 2, 80; iii, 1, 75.

3
The sooner, the better.
II Henry VI, i, 4, 17. Used only once.

4
Tawny Spain.
Love's Labour 's Lost. Act i, sc. 1, l. 174. [King Ferdinand]

5
'Tis not his fault, the spark.
All 's Well that Ends Well. Act ii, sc. 1, l. 25. [Parolles]
Good sparks and lustrous, a word, good metals.
All 's Well that Ends Well. Act ii, sc. 1, l. 41. [Parolles]
Spark of honour.—*III Henry VI,* i, 1, 184; *Richard II,* v, 6, 29.
Spark of life.—*III Henry VI,* v, 6, 66; *Julius Cæsar,* i, 3, 57.
Sparks of fire.—*Troilus and Cressida,* i, 3, 294; *Henry VIII,* ii, 4, 73.
Sparks of nature.—*King Lear,* iii, 7, 86; *Cymbeline,* iii, 3, 79.

6
What a pair of spectacles is here!
Troilus and Cressida. Act iv, sc. 4, l. 14. [Pandarus]

7
O spite!
III Henry VI, v, 1, 18; *A Midsummer-Night's Dream,* i, 1, 138; iii, 2, 145; v, 1, 281.
O cursed spite!—*Hamlet,* i, 5, 189.
Spite of spite.—*III Henry VI,* ii, 3, 5; *King John,* v, 4, 5.
O spite of spites!—*Comedy of Errors,* ii, 2, 191.
In spite of all.—*Richard II,* iii, 2, 28.
In spite of us.—*I Henry VI,* i, 5, 37.

8
Out, damned spot! out, I say!
Macbeth. Act v, sc. 1, l. 39. [Lady Macbeth]

9
How stands the matter with them?
The Two Gentlemen of Verona. Act ii, sc. 5, l. 21. [Speed]
I will stand for 't a little.
All 's Well that Ends Well. Act i, sc. 1, l. 145. [Helena] "Stand for" is used twenty times in the plays.
Stand aloof.—*III Henry VI,* ii, 1, 17, and three times in later plays.
Stand apart.—*II Henry VI,* iii, 2, 242; *The Comedy of Errors,* v, 1, 364.
Stand aside.—*III Henry VI,* iii, 3, 110, and eleven times in later plays.
Stand away.—*All 's Well that Ends Well,* v, 2, 17; *Henry V,* iv, 8, 14.
Stand back.—*I Henry VI,* i, 2, 70; i, 3, 33; i, 3, 38; four times in later plays.
Stand by.—*II Henry VI,* ii, 1, 72, and ten times in later plays.
Stander-by.—*Richard III,* i, 2, 163; i, 3, 210; *Troilus and Cressida,* iv, 5, 190; *The Winter's Tale,* i, 2, 279; *Cymbeline,* ii, 1, 12.
Stand close.—*II Henry VI,* i, 3, 1, and ten times in later plays.
Stand fast.—*The Two Gentlemen of Verona,* iv, 1, 1, and nine times in later plays.
Stand firm.—*Troilus and Cressida,* ii, 2, 68.
Stand fix'd.—*Henry VIII,* v, 5, 48.
Stand forth.—*II Henry VI,* ii, 3, 1, and seven times in later plays.
Stand high.—*Richard III,* i, 3, 259; *The Merchant of Venice,* iii, 2, 157.
Stand indebted.—*The Merchant of Venice,* iv, 1, 413.
Stand in need.—*The Two Gentlemen of Verona,* ii, 7, 84.
Stand in fear.—*II Henry VI,* iv, 2, 66; *Measure for Measure,* ii, 3, 34.
Stand on end.—*Richard III,* 1, 3, 304.
Stand opposed.—*I Henry IV,* v, 1, 67.
Stand possessed.—*Richard II,* ii, 1, 162.
Stand resolved.—*Titus Andronicus,* i, 1, 135.
Stand sentinel.—*A Midsummer-Night's Dream,* ii, 2, 26.
Stand still.—*III Henry VI,* ii, 3, 30, and seven times in later plays.
Stand stone-still.—*King John,* iv, 1, 77. The only use of "stone-still."
Stand the push.—*I Henry IV,* iii, 2, 66; *II Henry IV,* ii, 2, 40; *King John,* iv, 1, 77; *Troilus and Cressida,* ii, 2, 137.
Stand tiptoe.—*Henry V,* iv, 3, 42; *Romeo and Juliet,* iii, 5, 10.
Stand to.—*III Henry VI,* ii, 3, 51, and nine times in later plays.
Stand to it.—*I Henry IV,* iii, 3, 183, and four times in later plays.
Stand under.—*The Two Gentlemen of Verona,* ii, 5, 33, and five times in later plays.
Stand up.—*I Henry VI,* iii, 4, 25, and twenty-nine times in later plays.
Stand upon.—*I Henry VI,* ii, 4, 28, and thirteen times in later plays.
Stand upright.—*II Henry VI,* iii, 3, 15; *Richard III,* iii, 2, 39; *Timon of Athens,* iv, 3, 14.

10
Many a nobleman lies stark and stiff.
I Henry IV. Act v, sc. 3, l. 42. [Prince of Wales]
Stiff and stark.—*Romeo and Juliet,* iv, 1, 103.

11
As hard as steel.
The Two Gentlemen of Verona. Act i, sc. 1, l. 148. [Speed]
As true as steel.—*Romeo and Juliet,* ii, 4, 210; *A Midsummer-Night's Dream,* ii, 1, 197; *Troilus and Cressida,* iii, 2, 184.

12
From stem to stern.
Pericles, iv, 1, 64. Used but once.

13
Do it on a full stomach.
Love's Labour 's Lost. Act i, sc. 2, l. 154. [Costard]
It goes much against my stomach.
As You Like It. Act iii, sc. 2, l. 22. [Touchstone]

1
Turned to stone.
II Henry VI, v, 2, 50. Used in the first play and never again.

2
I will be with thee straight.
A Midsummer-Night's Dream. Act iii, sc. 2, l. 403. [Lysander]
I 'll be with you straight.—*II Henry IV,* v, 3, 46; *Hamlet,* iv, 4, 31.
I will answer it straight.—*The Merry Wives of Windsor,* i, 1, 118. "Straight" is used throughout the plays in the sense of promptly.

3
Nay, 'tis strange, 'tis very strange.
All 's Well that Ends Well. Act ii, sc. 3, l. 33. [Parolles]
Wondrous strange.—*Hamlet,* i, 5, 165.
Strange beginning.—*King John,* i, 1, 5.
Strange capers.—*As You Like It,* ii, 4, 55.
Strange course.—*Much Ado about Nothing,* iv, 1, 214.
Strange encounter.—*The Taming of the Shrew,* iv, 5, 54.
Strange fellow.—*The Merchant of Venice,* i, 1, 51, and four times in later plays.
Strange fish.—*The Tempest,* ii, 1, 112; ii, 2, 28.
Strange men.—*All 's Well that Ends Well,* iv, 4, 21.
Strange shapes.—*Love's Labour 's Lost,* v, 2, 773.
Strange sight.—*Julius Cæsar,* i, 3, 138; *The Winter's Tale,* iv, 4, 849.
Strange stuff.—*The Tempest,* iv, 1, 234.
Strange tongue.—*II Henry IV,* iv, 4, 69; *Henry VIII,* iii, 1, 45.

4
Strike now, or else the iron cools.
III Henry VI. Act v, sc. 1, l. 49. [Gloucester]
Strike home.—*Measure for Measure,* i, 3, 41. Used only once.

5
Here 's goodly stuff toward!
II Henry IV. Act ii, sc. 4, l. 214. [Hostess]
This is the silliest stuff that ever I heard.
A Midsummer-Night's Dream, v, 1, 212. The only use of "silliest."
Make us strange stuff.—*The Tempest,* iv, 1, 234.
What stuff is here?—*Measure for Measure,* iii, 2, 5.
What stuff is this?—*The Tempest,* ii, 1, 254.

6
Of stuff'd sufficiency.
Winter's Tale. Act ii, sc. 1, l. 185. [Leontes]

7
Tell you of such and such.
Henry V, iii, 6, 75. "Such and such" is repeated in *Cymbeline,* ii, 2, 25.
Such-like.—*Richard III,* i, 1, 60, and eight times in later plays.

8
That is the sum of all.
Much Ado about Nothing. Act i, sc. 1, l. 147. [Don Pedro]

9
I am sunburnt.
Much Ado about Nothing. Act ii, sc. 1, l. 331. [Beatrice]
The Grecian dames are sunburnt.
Troilus and Cressida, i, 3, 282.
Sunburnt sicklemen.—*The Tempest,* iv, 1, 134.

10
Sure, the boy heard me.
Julius Cæsar. Act ii, sc. 3, l. 42. [Portia]
Sure he 'll come.—*The Merry Wives of Windsor,* iv, 4, 77.
Sure, it is no sin.—*Measure for Measure,* iii, 1, 110.
As sure as day.—*I Henry IV,* iii, 1, 255.
Sure as I live.—*The Two Gentlemen of Verona,* iv, 4, 17.

11
Swim like a duck.
The Tempest, ii, 2, 238. See under SWIMMING. Unique.

12
At one fell swoop.
Macbeth, iv, 3, 219. The only use of "swoop."

T

13
Take her, or leave her.
King Lear. Act i, sc. 1, l. 208. [King Lear]
Take advantage.—*Richard II,* ii, 3, 79; *King John,* ii, 1, 297.
Take alive.—*Julius Cæsar,* v, 4, 22.
Take and give.—*Twelfth Night,* iv, 3, 18; *Troilus and Cressida,* iv, 5, 37.
Take care.—*The Winter's Tale,* iv, 4, 459; *The Tempest,* v, 1, 257.
Take cold.—*The Taming of the Shrew,* iv, 1, 11.
Take comfort.—*A Midsummer-Night's Dream,* i, 1, 202; *Pericles,* iii, 1, 22.
Take delight.—*I Henry VI,* iii, 1, 111; *Twelfth Night,* i, 5, 89; *Hamlet,* ii, 2, 342.
Take exceptions.—*III Henry VI,* iii, 2, 46; *Two Gentlemen of Verona,* i, 3, 81; v, 2, 3.
Take heart.—*Antony and Cleopatra,* iv, 15, 85.
Take heed.—*II Henry VI,* iii, 1, 80, and thirty-two times in later plays.
Take hold.—*Richard III,* ii, 1, 131; *Hamlet,* i, 1, 24; *King Lear,* iii, 4, 156; *Othello,* i, 3, 55.
Take horse.—*II Henry VI,* iv, 5, 54; *Richard III,* iii, 2, 16; *I Henry IV,* i, 1, 60.
Take it at heart.—*Twelfth Night,* iii, 4, 112.
Take it to heart.—*Hamlet,* i, 2, 101.
Take my death.—*II Henry VI,* ii, 3, 90; *III Henry VI,* i, 3, 35.
Take offence.—*III Henry VI,* iv, 1, 14; *Pericles,* ii, 5, 72.
Take pity.—*The Comedy of Errors,* iv, 3, 25; *Much Ado about Nothing,* ii, 3, 271; *Henry V,* iii, 3, 28.
Take root.—*Henry VIII,* i, 2, 87.
Take ship.—*Henry V,* ii, Prol., 30.
Take that.—*III Henry VI,* v, 5, 38, and four times in later plays.
Take the hint.—*Antony and Cleopatra,* iii, 11, 18.
Take thought.—*Julius Cæsar,* ii, 1, 187.
Take time.—*III Henry VI,* i, 4, 108; *A Midsummer-Night's Dream,* i, 1, 83.
Take your time.—*Antony and Cleopatra,* ii, 6, 23.
Take vengeance.—*Titus Andronicus,* v, 2, 63.
Taken napping.—*Love's Labour 's Lost,* iv, 3, 130.
Taken prisoner.—*I Henry VI,* iv, 1, 26; *III Henry VI,* iv, 4, 7; *King John,* iii, 4, 7; *II Henry IV,* i, 1, 126.
Taking-off.—*King Lear,* v, 1, 65; *Macbeth,* i, 7, 20.

1
Loves to hear herself talk.
Romeo and Juliet, ii, 4, 155. See under TALK: LOQUACITY.

2
Tarry a little.
The Merchant of Venice, iv, 1, 305. Repeated in *Merry Wives of Windsor,* i, 4, 93.
I cannot tarry.—*The Taming of the Shrew,* iv, 4, 99; *II Henry IV,* iii, 2, 204.
I will not tarry.—*Henry VIII,* ii, 4, 131.
I tarry too long.—*The Merry Wives of Windsor,* i, 4, 64.
I 'll tarry no longer.—*As You Like It,* iii, 2, 309.
I 'll tarry at home.—*I Henry IV,* i, 2, 162.
Tarry and be hanged!—*III Henry VI,* iv, 5, 26.

3
We are no tell-tales, madam.
The Merchant of Venice. Act v, sc. 1, l. 123. [Lorenzo] "Tell-tale" is used six times in the plays.
Tell me that.—*The Two Gentlemen of Verona,* iii, 1, 123; *The Merchant of Venice,* iv, 1, 183; *Hamlet,* v, 1, 59.
Tell me this.—*The Comedy of Errors,* i, 2, 53, and four times in later plays.
Tell me true.—*The Two Gentlemen of Verona,* ii, 5, 35, and nine times in later plays.
I 'll tell you what.—*Richard III,* i, 1, 78, and sixteen times in later plays.

4
As you think fit.
Romeo and Juliet, iv, 2, 35. "Think fit" is repeated in *Othello,* iii, 1, 54.
Think it fit.—*Cymbeline,* i, 6, 150; *The Winter's Tale,* iv, 4, 869.
Think it best.—*Romeo and Juliet,* iii, 5, 219.
Think it good.—*A Midsummer-Night's Dream,* ii, 2, 37; *Julius Cæsar,* iv, 3, 198.
Think it meet.—*I Henry IV,* iv, 1, 33; *Measure for Measure,* iv, 2, 24.
Think it strange.—*III Henry VI,* iii, 2, 111; *Measure for Measure,* iv, 6, 7.
Think it well.—*Twelfth Night,* ii, 4, 36; *Measure for Measure,* iv, 6, 7; *Henry VIII,* Prol., 6.

5
I thought as much.
II Henry VI, ii, 1, 15; *Pericles,* 1, 4, 62.
Thought fit.—*A Midsummer-Night's Dream,* i, 2, 5.
Thought it fit.—*King Lear,* ii, 1, 125; v, 3, 45.
Thought good.—*Macbeth,* i, 5, 11.
Thought it good.—*The Taming of the Shrew,* Ind., 2, 135; *The Winter's Tale,* ii, 1, 193.
Thought meet.—*Troilus and Cressida,* ii, 2, 72.
Thought it meet.—*Measure for Measure,* i, 2, 156.

6
Cut through and through.
I Henry IV, ii, 4, 186. "Through and through" is repeated five times in later plays.

7
Thus far fortune maketh us amends.
II Henry VI, iv, 7, 2. "Thus far" is repeated nineteen times in later plays.
Thus high.—*Richard III,* iv, 2, 3; *II Henry IV,* iii, 2, 34; *Richard II,* iii, 3, 195.
Thus long.—*Richard II,* iii, 3, 72; *Troilus and Cressida,* ii, 1, 75; *Henry VIII,* iii, 1, 125.
Thus much.—*The Taming of the Shrew,* iv, 1, 115, and seventeen times in later plays.

8
I 'll warrant you, that there is no tiddle taddle nor pibble pabble in Pompey's camp.
Henry V, iv, 1, 70. The only use of either "tiddle taddle" or "pibble pabble."
Tittle-tattling.—*The Winter's Tale,* iv, 4, 248. Used only once.

9
Glad tidings.
II Henry VI, iv, 9, 7. Used in the first play and never repeated.

10
There is a time for all things.
The Comedy of Errors. Act ii, sc. 2, l. 65. [Antipholus of Syracuse]
'Tis time to look about.
King Lear. Act iv, sc. 7, l. 92. [Kent]
One, two, three: time, time!
Cymbeline. Act ii, sc. 2, l. 51. [Iachimo]
From time to time.—*Romeo and Juliet,* iii, 3, 170, and three times in later plays.
In good time.—*Richard III,* ii, 1, 45, and thirteen times in later plays.
In very good times.—*Measure for Measure,* v, 1, 286.
Time out of mind.—*Romeo and Juliet,* i, 4, 69; *Measure for Measure,* iv, 2, 17.
'Tis high time.—*The Comedy of Errors,* iii, 2, 162. The only use of "high time."
Another time I 'll hear thee.—*Timon of Athens,* i, 2, 184.
The tooth of time.—*Measure for Measure,* v, 1, 12.

11
To and fro.
I Henry VI, ii, 1, 69; *II Henry VI,* i, 1, 91; iv, 8, 57. A phrase used only in these two plays—the earliest ones.
To wit.—*III Henry VI,* v, 6, 51; *Henry V,* i, 2, 50; *The Merchant of Venice,* ii, 9, 90; *As You Like It,* v, 1, 57.

12
To-night, or never.
The Merry Wives of Windsor. Act v, sc. 1, l. 9. [Falstaff]

13
From toe to crown.
The Tempest, iv, 1, 233. "From the crown to the toe" occurs in *Macbeth,* i, 5, 43.
From top to toe.—*Richard III,* iii, 1, 156; *Hamlet,* i, 2, 228.

14
As I told you.
The Taming of the Shrew, iii, 1, 31, and five times in later plays.
Told me of.—*III Henry VI,* v, 6, 69; *Much Ado about Nothing,* ii, 3, 92.

15
I have been told so.
As You Like It, iii, 2, 361. See also *Troilus and Cressida,* ii, 3, 88; *Twelfth Night,* i, 5, 156.
Who told you so?—*Much Ado about Nothing,* ii, 1, 130; *Measure for Measure,* ii, 1, 256; *King Lear,* v, 3, 72.
You told me so.—*The Merchant of Venice,* i, 3, 68. "Told me so" is repeated five times in the plays.

16
Hold my tongue.
Hamlet, i, 2, 159. See under TONGUE.

Wag thy tongue.—*Hamlet,* iii, 4, 39; *Henry VIII,* i, 1, 33.

1
Overturn it topsy-turvy.
I Henry IV, iv, 1, 82. The only use of "topsy-turvy."

2
Touch me not.
Othello. Act ii, sc. 3, l. 220. [Iago] See also *The Tempest,* v, 1, 286. See also under TOUCH.

3 We are tougher, brother,
Than you can put us to 't.
The Winter's Tale. Act i, sc. 2, l. 15. [Leontes] The only use of "tougher."

4
It is but trash.
The Tempest. Act iv, sc. 1, l. 223. [Caliban]
'Tis trash.
Troilus and Cressida. Act ii, sc. 1, l. 138. [Achilles] "Trash" is used ten times in the plays.

5
Trifles light as air.
Othello, iii, 3, 322. See under TRIFLE.
Light as chaff.—*II Henry IV,* iv, 1, 195.

6
True as I live.
I Henry IV, iii, 1, 254. Used only once.
True enough.—*The Winter's Tale,* iii, 2, 58. Used only once.
'Tis true indeed.—*Love's Labour 's Lost,* iv, 2, 43; *Much Ado about Nothing,* ii, 3, 131; *Coriolanus,* i, 1, 81; *Othello,* v, 2, 188.

7 Art thou there, truepenny?
Come on—you hear this fellow in the cellarage.
Hamlet. Act i, sc. 5, l. 150. [Hamlet] The only use of "truepenny" and "cellarage."

8
Tell truth and shame the devil!
I Henry IV, iii, 1, 57; 62.

9
Be no turncoats.
Timon of Athens, iv, 3, 142. The only use of "turncoats." "Turncoat" occurs in *Much Ado about Nothing,* i, 1, 125.

10
Aaron: Why, then, it seems, some certain snatch or so
Would serve your turns.
Chiron: Ay, so the turn were served.
Titus Andronicus. Act ii, sc. 1, l. 95.
She is not for your turn.
The Taming of the Shrew. Act ii, sc. 1, l. 63. [Baptista]
I 'll look you out a good turn.
Timon of Athens. Act iii, sc. 2, l. 67. [Lucius] "Good turn" is used nine times. See under TURN.

11
Tut, tut.
I Henry VI, iv, 2, 71, and five times in later plays.

12
Twice-told tale.
King John, iii, 4, 108. See under TALE.

U

13
I will unbolt to you.
Timon of Athens. Act i, sc. 1, l. 51. [Poet]

14
Why, stand-under and under-stand is all one.
Two Gentlemen of Verona, ii, 5, 33. [Launce] The only use of "stand-under" and "understand" as hyphenated phrases.

15
Leaves nothing undone.
Coriolanus, ii, 2, 22. Only use of the phrase.
Now we are undone and brought to nothing.
The Taming of the Shrew. Act v, sc. 1, l. 44. [Biondello]
Undone, and forfeited to cares for ever!
All's Well that Ends Well. Act ii, sc. 3, l. 284. [Bertram]
The man 's undone for ever.
Troilus and Cressida, iii, 3, 259. [Thersites]
You have undone a man of fourscore three.
The Winter's Tale. Act iv, sc. 4, l. 464. [Shepherd]
I am undone!—*The Taming of the Shrew,* v, 1, 70; *Merry Wives of Windsor,* iv, 2, 42; iv, 5, 93; *All's Well that Ends Well,* i, 1, 95.
She is undone.—*Much Ado about Nothing,* iv, 1, 315.
You are undone.—*The Merry Wives of Windsor,* iii, 3, 117; *All's Well that Ends Well,* iv, 3, 358.
We are all undone.—*The Taming of the Shrew,* v, 1, 114.
We are undone.—*The Taming of the Shrew,* v, 1, 44.
Even here undone.—*Winter's Tale,* iv, 4, 452.

16
Unhand me, gentlemen.
Hamlet. Act i, sc. 4, l. 84. [Hamlet] The only use of "unhand."

17
To be up early and down late.
The Merry Wives of Windsor. Act i, sc. 4, l. 108. The only use of "up early."
Up higher.—*King John,* ii, 1, 295; *Julius Cæsar,* ii, 1, 109; *Cymbeline,* i, 5, 39.
Up late.—*Twelfth Night,* ii, 3, 5.
Up to the chins.—*The Tempest,* iv, 1, 183.
Up to the ears.—*I Henry IV,* iv, 1, 117.
Up to the elbows.—*Julius Cæsar,* iii, 1, 107.
Up to the neck.—*Henry V,* iv, 1, 120. The last five phrases occur but once.

18
Upon my faith and honour.
Measure for Measure, v, 1, 224. Used only once.
Upon mine honour.—*II Henry VI,* v, 1, 43; *The Two Gentlemen of Verona,* iii, 1, 48; *Measure for Measure,* v, 1, 524; *The Tempest,* ii, 1, 314.
Upon my life.—*The Comedy of Errors,* i, 2, 195; v, 1, 180; *The Taming of the Shrew,* iii, 2, 22; *Hamlet,* i, 1, 170; *The Merry Wives of Windsor,* v, 5, 200.
Upon my soul.—*King John,* iv, 3, 125; *II Henry IV,* iv, 2, 60; *Othello,* v, 2, 181; *Henry VIII,* v, 2, 181.

19
Turned upside down.
I Henry IV, ii, 1, 11; *Pericles,* ii, 2, 32.

V

20
In the vacation.
As You Like It, iii, 2, 349. The only use of "vacation."

1
Our valuation shall be such.
II Henry IV, iv, 1, 189.
Set so slight a valuation.
Cymbeline, iv, 4, 49. The only uses of "valuation."

2
There 's the vein.
Measure for Measure. Act ii, sc. 2, l. 70. [Lucio]

3
Thou art good velvet.
Measure for Measure. Act i, sc. 1, l. 32.

4
Verbatim to rehearse.
I Henry VI, iii, 1, 13. The only use of "verbatim."

W

5
There 's one thing wanting.
Coriolanus, ii, 1, 217. Used only once.

6
Thou art a very ragged wart.
II Henry IV. Act iii, sc. 2, l. 152. [Falstaff]

7
Throw cold water.
The Merry Wives of Windsor, ii, 3, 89. Used only once.

8
A kind of insinuation, as it were, in via, in way, of explication.
Love's Labour 's Lost. Act iv, sc. 2, l. 13. [Holofernes] The only use of "explication" in the plays. "Explanation" is not used at all, and "explain" only once, in *Pericles,* ii, 2, 14, probably not written by Shakespeare.

9
By eleven o'clock it will go one way or other.
Troilus and Cressida. Act iii, sc. 3, l. 297. [Thersites]
One way or other.
III Henry VI, iii, 2, 87; *The Merry Wives of Windsor,* iii, 1, 89.
Some one way, some another.
Othello, i, 1, 177.

10
The weakest goes to the wall.
Romeo and Juliet, i, 1, 18. See under WEAKNESS.

11
Let the welkin roar.
II Henry IV. Act ii, sc. 4, l. 182. [Pistol] "Welkin" is used seventeen times in the plays.

12
My well-famed lord of Troy.
Troilus and Cressida, iv, 5, 173. The only use of "well-famed."
Well said.—*II Henry VI,* i, 4, 16, and twenty-eight times in later plays.

13
Olivia: There lies your way, due west.
Viola: Then westward-ho!
Twelfth Night. Act iii, sc. 1, l. 145. The only use of either "due west" or "westward-ho" in the plays. *Eastward Hoe* and *Westward Hoe* were the titles of two popular comedies of the day, the one by Chapman and the other by Webster.

14
What 's mine is yours and what is yours is mine.
Measure for Measure. Act v, sc. 1, l. 543. [Duke]
Be what thou wilt.—*I Henry VI,* v, 3, 45.
What is that to him?—*Richard II,* v, 2, 100.
What now?—*The Comedy of Errors,* i, 2, 42; *King John,* i, 1, 31.
What of him?—*Merchant of Venice,* i, 3, 76.
What of that?—*III Henry VI,* iv, 1, 49; *A Midsummer-Night's Dream,* i, 1, 228; *Romeo and Juliet,* ii, 2, 12; *Twelfth Night,* iii, 4, 23.
What of this?—*Much Ado about Nothing,* iv, 1, 73.
What one thing, what another.—*Troilus and Cressida,* v, 3, 107.
What say you?—*Titus Andronicus,* v, 2, 137.
What then?—*Coriolanus,* iv, 2, 25.
What you will.—*As You Like It,* ii, 5, 20.
I know what.—*Romeo and Juliet,* i, 5, 86.
What in the world?—*King Lear,* v, 3, 97.
What 's to do?—*Julius Cæsar,* ii, 1, 326.

15
Good even, good Master What-ye-call 't: how do you, sir?
As You Like It. Act iii, sc. 3, l. 74. [Touchstone] The only use of "what-ye-call 't."

16
He . . . has wherewithal.
Henry VIII, i, 3, 59. The only use of "wherewithal."

17
White as snow.
Hamlet, iii, 3, 46. See under WHITENESS.

18
Whither away?
I Henry VI, iii, 2, 104, and seven times in later plays.
Whither bound?—*Cymbeline,* iii, 6, 58. Used but once.
Whither were you a-going?—*Henry VIII,* i, 3, 50. The only use of "a-going."

19
Who goes there?
III Henry VI, iv, 3, 26; *The Taming of the Shrew,* i, 2, 141; *Henry V,* iv, 1, 93.
Who have we here?—*Titus Andronicus,* ii, 3, 55. Used but once.

20
A whoo-bub against his daughter.
The Winter's Tale. Act iv, sc. 4, l. 629. [Autolycus] The only use of "whoo-bub" (clamour).

21
Every why hath a wherefore.
The Comedy of Errors, ii, 2, 43.
The why and the wherefore.—*The Comedy of Errors,* ii, 2, 49; *Henry V,* v, 1, 3.
For why?—*Titus Andronicus,* iii, 1, 251; *The Two Gentlemen of Verona,* iii, 1, 99; *The Taming of the Shrew,* iii, 2, 169; *Richard II,* v, 1, 46.

22
Will he, nill he.
Hamlet. Act v, sc. 1, l. 19. [First Clown]
Will you, nill you.
The Taming of the Shrew, ii, 1, 273. Both phrases unique.

23
Will this work?
Henry VIII, iii, 2, 37. Used but once.

1
Let the galled jade wince, our withers are unwrung.
Hamlet. Act iii, sc. 2, l. 253. [Hamlet]
I will not wince.—*King John,* iv, 1, 81. The only uses of "wince."
Wrung in the withers.—*I Henry IV,* ii, 1, 8. The only uses of "withers."

2
So woe-begone.
II Henry IV, ii, 1, 71. The only use of "woe-begone."

3
I 'll tell the world.
Measure for Measure, ii, 4, 153. See under WORLD for other quotations.

4
By word of mouth.
Julius Cæsar, iii, 1, 280; *Twelfth Night,* ii, 3, 141; iii, 4, 209.

5
So much the worse.
II Henry IV, iv, 2, 86. Used only once.
Worse and worse.—*The Taming of the Shrew,* v, 2, 93, and four times in later plays.

6
Not worth a gooseberry.
II Henry IV. Act i, sc. 2, l. 196. [Falstaff] The only use of "gooseberry."
Not worth the feeding.—*Antony and Cleopatra,* v, 2, 271. See under WORTH.

7
I would to God.
Richard III, i, 3, 140; *Much Ado about Nothing,* ii, 1, 264; *II Henry IV,* i, 2, 243; *Richard II,* ii, 2, 100.

8
Wrong side out.
Much Ado about Nothing, iii, 1, 68; *Othello,* ii, 3, 54; *King Lear,* iv, 2, 9.
How quickly the wrong side may be turned outward!
Twelfth Night. Act iii, sc. 1, l. 14. [Clown]

Y

9
By yea and nay.
Love's Labour 's Lost, i, 1, 54; *II Henry IV,* iii, 2, 10.
By yea and no.
II Henry IV, ii, 2, 142; *The Merry Wives of Windsor,* i, 1, 88; iv, 2, 202.
The very yea and no is.
The Merry Wives of Windsor, i, 4, 98.

10
Yet a while.
II Henry IV, v, 1, 30. Used only once.
Yet again!—*Julius Cæsar,* i, 2, 14; *Othello,* ii, 1, 177; *The Tempest,* i, 1, 41.
Yet once again.—*The Comedy of Errors,* v, 1, 130; *The Merry Wives of Windsor,* iv, 4, 14.
Yet once more.—*Henry VIII,* ii, 4, 82.

FAMILIARITY

11
Because that I familiarly sometimes
Do use you for my fool and chat with you,
Your sauciness will jest upon my love
And make a common of my serious hours.
The Comedy of Errors. Act ii, sc. 2, l. 26. [Antipholus of Syracuse]
Familiarly shall call.—*Richard III,* iv, 4, 316.
Talks as familiarly.—*II Henry IV,* iii, 2, 344; *King John,* ii, 1, 459. The only uses of "familiarly."

12
We are familiar at first.
Cymbeline. Act i, sc. 4, l. 112. [Posthumus]
I have surely seen him:
His favour is familiar to me.
Cymbeline. Act v, sc. 5, l. 92. [Cymbeline]

13
That we have been familiar,
Ingrate forgetfulness shall poison, rather
Than pity note how much.
Coriolanus. Act v, sc. 2, l. 91. [Coriolanus]

14
Be thou familiar, but by no means vulgar.
Hamlet. Act i, sc. 3, l. 61. [Polonius]
I do not allow this wen to be as familiar with me as my dog.
II Henry IV. Act ii, sc. 2, l. 115. [Prince of Wales] The only use of "wen."

15
Familiar in his mouth as household words.
Henry V, iv, 3, 52. See under NAME.
Familiar as his garter.—*Henry V,* i, 1, 47.
Familiar to my slaughterous thoughts.—*Macbeth,* v, 5, 14.
Familiar to us, and unknown.—*Henry V,* iii, 7, 40.
Familiar with men's pockets.—*Henry V,* iii, 2, 51.
Familiar with My playfellow.—*Antony and Cleopatra,* iii, 13, 124.
Most familiar.—*Troilus and Cressida,* iii, 2, 10.
So familiar.—*Julius Cæsar,* iii, 1, 266; *Troilus and Cressida,* v, 2, 8.
Too familiar.—*Romeo and Juliet,* iii, 3, 6.
Made familiar.—*Pericles,* iii, 2, 34.

16
Away with him! he has a familiar under his tongue.
II Henry VI, iv, 7, 114. See under SPEECH.
The King is . . . my familiar.
Love's Labour 's Lost. Act v, sc. 1, l. 100. [Armado]
Love is a familiar.—*Love's Labour 's Lost,* i, 2, 177.
Old familiar.—*I Henry VI,* iii, 2, 122.
Jack Falstaff with my familiars.—*II Henry IV,* ii, 2, 144.
So his familiars to his buried fortunes
Slink all away.
Timon of Athens, iv, 2, 10. See under FRIEND.

17
Upon familiarity will grow more contempt.
The Merry Wives of Windsor. Act i, sc. 1, l. 258. [Slender]
Their familiarity,
Which was as gross as ever touch'd conjecture.
Winter's Tale. Act ii, sc. 1, l. 175. [Leontes]
Desire me to be no more so familiarity with such poor people.
II Henry IV. Act ii, sc. 1, l. 108. [Hostess]
Familiarity with fresher clothes.—*All's Well that Ends Well,* v, 2, 3. The only uses of "familiarity."

18
He is too familiar with his wife.
Othello. Act i, sc. 3, l. 402. [Iago]
Be not familiar with her.
King Lear. Act v, sc. 1, l. 16. [Regan]

FAMILY, see Kin

FAMINE

See also Hunger, Starvation

1
At thy heel did famine follow.
Antony and Cleopatra. Act i, sc. 4, l. 58. [Cæsar]

Presageth famine.—*Antony and Cleopatra,* i, 2, 50.

2
Famine,
Ere clean it o'erthrow nature, makes it valiant.
Cymbeline. Act iii, sc. 6, l. 19. [Imogen]

3
A' was the very genius of famine.
II Henry IV, iii, 2, 337. See under CHARACTER.

Famine, sword and fire Crouch for employment.
Henry V. Act i, Prologue, l. 7. [Chorus]

Lean famine.—*I Henry VI,* iv, 2, 11.

4
O, I am slain! famine and no other hath slain me: let ten thousand devils come against me, and give me but the ten meals I have lost, and I 'ld defy them all.
II Henry VI. Act iv, sc. 10, l. 64. [Cade]

I . . . am vanquished by famine.
II Henry VI. Act iv, sc. 10, l. 81. [Cade]

5
Here let them lie
Till famine and the ague eat them up.
Macbeth. Act v, sc. 5, l. 3. [Macbeth]

Upon the next tree shalt thou hang alive
Till famine cling thee.
Macbeth, v, 5, 40. See under SPEECH.

6
And make a dearth in this revolting land.
Richard II, iii, 3, 163. See under TEAR.

For the dearth,
The gods, not the patricians, make it.
Coriolanus. Act i, sc. 1, l. 74. [Menenius]

The dearth is great.—*Coriolanus,* i, 2, 10. "Dearth" occurs nine times in the plays.

7
Famine is in thy cheeks,
Need and oppression starveth in thine eyes.
Romeo and Juliet. Act v, sc. 1, l. 69. [Romeo]

8
Making a famine where abundance lies.
Sonnets. No. i.

Suffer us to famish.—*Coriolanus,* i, 1, 82. See under HUNGER.

FAN

9
Divers-colour'd fans, whose wind did seem
To glow the delicate cheeks which they did cool.
Antony and Cleopatra. Act ii, sc. 2, l. 208. [Enobarbus] The only use of "divers-colour'd."

The fan To cool a gipsy's lust.—*Antony and Cleopatra,* i, 1, 9.

10
'Zounds, an I were now by this rascal, I could brain him with his lady's fan.
I Henry IV. Act ii, sc. 3, l. 25. [Hotspur]

11
O, a most dainty man!
To see him walk before a lady and to bear her fan!
Love's Labour 's Lost, iv, 1, 146. [Costard]

12
Nurse: My fan, Peter.
Mercutio: Good Peter, to hide her face; for her fan 's the fairer face.
Romeo and Juliet. Act ii, sc. 4, l. 112.

Fetch her fan.—*Othello,* iv, 2, 9.
Give me my fan.—*II Henry VI,* i, 3, 141.
Take my fan.—*Romeo and Juliet,* ii, 4, 232.
Powerful fan.—*Troilus and Cressida,* i, 3, 27.

FANCY

13
My idolatrous fancy
Must sanctify his reliques.
All's Well that Ends Well. Act i, sc. 1, l. 108. [Helena] "Reliques" is used a second time in *Twelfth Night,* iii, 3, 19.

Afflicted fancy.—*A Lover's Complaint,* l. 61.
Dreadful fancy.—*The Rape of Lucrece,* l. 450.
Excellent fancy.—*Hamlet,* v, 1, 204.
Fine fancies.—*Pericles,* iii, Gower, 13.
Particular fancy.—*Henry VIII,* ii, 3, 101.
Present fancies.—*The Tempest,* iv, 1, 122.
Soft fancy.—*The Rape of Lucrece,* l. 200.
Sorriest fancies.—*Macbeth,* iii, 2, 9. The only use of "sorriest."
Weak-hinged fancy.—*The Winter's Tale,* ii, 3, 119. The only use of "weak-hinged."
Worthless fancy.—*The Taming of the Shrew,* Ind., l. 44.

14
I submit My fancy to your eyes.
All's Well that Ends Well. Act ii, sc. 3, l. 175. [Bertram]

15
We must every one be a man of his own fancy.
All's Well that Ends Well. Act iv, sc. 1, l. 19. [Lord] See under LANGUAGE.

16
Pacing through the forest,
Chewing the food of sweet and bitter fancy.
As You Like It. Act iv, sc. 3, l. 101. [Oliver] The only use of "pacing" and "chewing."

If I could meet that fancy-monger, I would give him some good counsel.
As You Like It. Act iii, sc. 2, l. 381. [Rosalind] The only use of "fancy-monger."

17
I have lived
To see . . . the buildings of my fancy.
Coriolanus. Act ii, sc. 1, l. 214. [Coriolanus]

18
Play with your fancies.
Henry V. Act iii, Prologue, l. 7. [Chorus]

His spirits should hunt After new fancies.
Othello. Act iii, sc. 4, l. 62. [Othello]

19
Tush, that was but his fancy, blame him not.
I Henry VI. Act iv, sc. 1, l. 178. [Warwick]

Yet so my fancy may be satisfied.
I Henry VI. Act v, sc. 3, l. 91. [Suffolk]

20
We fancy not the cardinal.
II Henry VI. Act i, sc. 3, l. 97. [Suffolk]

Believe me, sister, of all the men alive
I never yet beheld that special face
Which I could fancy more than any other.
The Taming of the Shrew. Act ii, sc. 1, l. 10. [Bianca]

O then, belike, you fancy riches more.
The Taming of the Shrew. Act ii, sc. 1, l. 16. [Katharina]

Is 't possible, friend Licio, that Mistress Bianca
Doth fancy any other?
The Taming of the Shrew. Act iv, sc. 2, l. 1. [Tranio]

Never did young man fancy
With so eternal and so fix'd a soul.
Troilus and Cressida, v, 2, 165. See under CONSTANCY.

Cannot your grace win her to fancy him?
The Two Gentlemen of Verona. Act iii, sc. 1, l. 67. [Valentine]

1
This child of fancy.
Love's Labour's Lost. Act i, sc. 1, l. 171. [King Ferdinand]

She is troubled with thick-coming fancies,
That keep her from her rest.
Macbeth. Act v, sc. 3, l. 38. [Doctor] The only use of "thick-coming."

Fancies too weak for boys, too green and idle
For girls of nine.
Winter's Tale. Act iii, sc. 2, l. 182. [Paulina]

Wounded fancies.—*A Lover's Complaint,* l. 197.

2
Tell me where is fancy bred,
Or in the heart or in the head?
How begot, how nourished?
Reply, reply.
It is engender'd in the eyes,
With gazing fed; and fancy dies
In the cradle where it lies.
Let us all ring fancy's knell:
I 'll begin it,—Ding, dong, bell.
The Merchant of Venice. Act iii, sc. 2, l. 63. [Song]

3 Thoughts and dreams and sighs,
Wishes and tears, poor fancy's followers.
A Midsummer-Night's Dream. Act i, sc. 1, l. 154. [Hermia]

For you, fair Hermia, look you arm yourself
To fit your fancies to your father's will.
A Midsummer-Night's Dream. Act i, sc. 1, l. 117. [Theseus]

4
All fancy-sick she is and pale of cheer.
A Midsummer-Night's Dream, iii, 2, 96. See under LOVE. The only use of "fancy-sick."

Fancy-free.—*A Midsummer-Night's Dream.* Act ii, sc. 1, l. 164. [Oberon] The only use of this phrase.

5
There is no appearance of fancy in him.
Much Ado about Nothing. Act iii, sc. 2, l. 31. [Don Pedro]

Speaking my fancy.—*Much Ado about Nothing,* iii, 1, 95.

Have a fancy to this foolery.—*Much Ado about Nothing,* iii, 2, 37.

Be as your fancies teach you.—*Othello,* iii, 3, 88.

6
What horrible fancy 's this?
Othello. Act v, sc. 2, l. 26. [Desdemona]

An unsettled fancy.
The Tempest. Act v, sc. 1, l. 59. [Prospero]

Her fancy fell a-turning.—*The Passionate Pilgrim,* l. 214.

7 So full of shapes is fancy
That it alone is high fantastical.
Twelfth Night. Act i, sc. 1, l. 14. [Duke]

Our fancies are more giddy and unfirm,
More longing, wavering, sooner lost and worn,
Than women's are.
Twelfth Night, ii, 4, 34. See under MAN AND WOMAN.

Let fancy still my sense in Lethe steep.
Twelfth Night, iv, 1, 66. See under DREAM.

8
Camillo: Be advised.
Florizel: I am, and by my fancy.
The Winter's Tale. Act iv, sc. 4, l. 491.

FANTASY

9
Horatio says 'tis but our fantasy,
And will not let belief take hold of him.
Hamlet. Act i, sc. 1, l. 23. [Marcellus]

Is not this something more than fantasy?
Hamlet. Act i, sc. 1, l. 54. [Bernardo]

Things unluckily charge my fantasy.
Julius Cæsar. Act iii, sc. 3, l. 2. [Cinna]

10
I find the people strangely fantasied;
Possess'd with rumours, full of idle dreams,
Not knowing what they fear, but full of fear.
King John. Act iv, sc. 2, l. 144. [Bastard] The only use of "fantasied."

11
Fie on sinful fantasy!
The Merry Wives of Windsor. Act v, sc. 5, l. 97. [Song]

Full of hateful fantasies.
A Midsummer-Night's Dream. Act ii, sc. 1, l. 258. [Oberon]

Strange fantasies.—*King John,* v, 7, 18.

Vain fantasy.—*Romeo and Juliet,* i, 4, 98.

12
I nothing but to please his fantasy.
Othello. Act iii, sc. 3, l. 299. [Emilia]

FARDEL, see Burden

FAREWELL *

See also Absence, Parting

13
You have restrained yourself within the list of too cold an adieu . . . take a more dilated farewell.
All 's Well that Ends Well. Act ii, sc. 1, l. 52. [Parolles]

Farewell; hie home.—*All 's Well that Ends Well,* ii, 5, 82.

14
Let Neptune hear we bid a loud farewell
To these great fellows.
Antony and Cleopatra. Act ii, sc. 7, l. 139. [Menenius]

A brief farewell.—*Coriolanus,* iv, 1, 1.

Happy farewell.—*III Henry VI,* iv, 8, 31.

Latest farewell.—*Titus Andronicus,* i, 1, 149.

* No attempt is made here to list all the quotations in which the word "farewell" appears. There are 165 of them in the plays and five in the poems; there are 87 instances in which "farewell" is used alone, and 29 instances of "and (so) farewell." "Fare thee well" is repeated often. "Adieu" is used 23 times; "good day," 13 times; "good night," 41 times; "good-bye," not at all.

Loving farewell.—*Richard II*, i, 3, 51.
Short farewell.—*Cymbeline*, iii, 4, 188.

1 Farewell, my dearest sister, fare thee well:
The elements be kind to thee, and make
Thy spirits all of comfort! fare thee well.
Antony and Cleopatra. Act iii, sc. 2, l. 39. [Cæsar]

Fare thee well, great heart!—*I Henry IV*, v, 4, 87. "Fare thee (you) well" is repeated frequently throughout the plays.
Fare thou well.—*The Tempest*, v, 1, 318.
Fare ye well.—*Twelfth Night*, ii, 1, 40.

2 When I make curtsy, bid me farewell.
As You Like It. Epilogue, l. 24. [Rosalind]

Farewell till then.—*The Comedy of Errors*, i, 2, 30.
Heartily farewell.—*Hamlet*, i, 2, 41.

3 Farewell! a long farewell, to all my greatness!
Henry VIII. Act iii, sc. 2, l. 351. [Wolsey] See under GREATNESS.

Long farewell.—*Antony and Cleopatra*, v, 2, 295.

4 Farewell, and stand fast.
I Henry IV. Act ii, sc. 2, l. 75. [Poins]

Farewell, and sit you fast.—*III Henry VI*, iv, 1, 119.
Farewell to you; and you; and you.—*Julius Cæsar*, v, 5, 31.
Farewell to you all.—*The Taming of the Shrew*, iii, 2, 199.
Farewell, master; farewell, farewell!—*The Tempest*, ii, 2, 182.
Farewell, fair cruelty.—*Twelfth Night*, i, 5, 307.

5 Now, for a while farewell.
III Henry VI. Act iv, sc. 3, l. 57. [Warwick]

And now farewell Till half an hour hence.
The Tempest. Act iii, sc. 1, l. 90. [Miranda]

Farewell till soon.—*Richard III*, iv, 3, 35.
Till then farewell.—*The Merry Wives of Windsor*, iii, 4, 96.

6 Warwick bids you all farewell, to meet in heaven.
III Henry VI. Act v, sc. 2, l. 49. [Warwick]

Adieu, and take thy praise with thee to heaven!
I Henry IV. Act v, sc. 4, l. 99. [Prince Henry] "Adieu" is used twenty-three times in the plays.

And so adieu, sweet Jude! nay, why dost thou stay?
Love's Labour's Lost. Act v, sc. 2, l. 629. [Boyet]

Adieu! tears exhibit my tongue.
The Merchant of Venice. Act ii, sc. 3, l. 10. [Launcelot]

7 Brutus: This same day
Must end that work the ides of March begun;
And whether we shall meet again I know not.
Therefore our everlasting farewell take:
For ever, and for ever, farewell, Cassius!
If we do meet again, why, we shall smile;
If not, why then, this parting was well made.
Cassius: For ever, and for ever, farewell, Brutus!
Julius Cæsar. Act v, sc. 1, l. 113.

So fare you well at once; for Brutus' tongue
Hath almost ended his life's history.
Julius Cæsar. Act v, sc. 5, l. 39. [Brutus]

Give me your hand, Bassanio: fare you well!
The Merchant of Venice. Act iv, sc. 1, l. 265. [Antonio]

But fare thee well, most foul, most fair! farewell.
Much Ado about Nothing. Act iv, sc. 1, l. 104. [Claudio]

8 Good night unto you all.
A Midsummer-Night's Dream. Act v, sc. 1, l. 443. [Oberon]

A kind good night to all!
Macbeth. Act iii, sc. 4, l. 120. [Lady Macbeth]

Good night, good rest. Ah, neither be my share:
She bade good night that kept my rest away;
And daff'd me to a cabin hang'd with care,
To descant on the doubts of my decay.
'Farewell,' quoth she, 'and come again tomorrow:'
Fare well I could not, for I supp'd with sorrow.
The Passionate Pilgrim, l. 181.

Good night, ladies; good night, sweet ladies;
good night, good night.
Hamlet. Act iv, sc. 5, l. 72. [Ophelia] "Good night" occurs forty-one times.

9 O, now, for ever
Farewell the tranquil mind! farewell content!
Farewell the plumed troop, and the big wars,
That make ambition virtue! O, farewell!
Farewell the neighing steed, and the shrill trump,
The spirit-stirring drum, the ear-piercing fife,
The royal banner, and all quality,
Pride, pomp and circumstance of glorious war!
Othello. Act iii, sc. 3, l. 347. [Othello] The only use of "spirit-stirring" and "ear-piercing."

Farewell; for I must leave you.
Othello. Act i, sc. 1, l. 145. [Iago]

Loath to bid farewell, we take our leaves.
Pericles. Act ii, sc. 5, l. 13. [Knight]

Hie thee, whiles I say
A priestly farewell to her.
Pericles. Act iii, sc. 1, l. 70. [Pericles] The only use of "priestly."

10 King Richard: What said our cousin when you parted with him?
Duke of Aumerle: 'Farewell:'
And, for my heart disdained that my tongue
Should so profane the word, that taught me craft
To counterfeit oppression of such grief
That words seem'd buried in my sorrow's grave.

Marry, would the word 'farewell' have lengthen'd hours
And added years to his short banishment,
He should have had a volume of farewells;
But since it would not, he had none of me.
Richard II. Act i, sc. 4, l. 10.

1
Green: Farewell at once, for once, for all, and ever.
Bushy: Well, we may meet again.
Bagot: I fear me, never.
Richard II. Act ii, sc. 2, l. 148.
And so farewell, till we shall meet again.
The Merchant of Venice, iii, 4, 40. [Portia]

2
Gloucester: Bid me farewell.
Anne: 'Tis more than you deserve;
But since you teach me how to flatter you,
Imagine I have said farewell already.
Richard III. Act i, sc. 2, l. 223.
Bid farewell to your sisters.—*King Lear,* i, 1, 270.
Bid him farewell.—*Titus Andronicus,* v, 3, 170.
Bid them farewell.—*King Lear,* i, 1, 263.
Bade farewell.—*Macbeth,* i, 2, 21.
Bidding farewell.—*Richard II,* ii, 2, 8.
We bid farewell.—*Richard III,* iii, 5, 71.

3
O, find him! give this ring to my true knight,
And bid him come to take his last farewell.
Romeo and Juliet. Act iii, sc. 2, l. 142. [Juliet]
Farewell! God knows when we shall meet again.
Romeo and Juliet. Act iv, sc. 3, l. 14. [Juliet]
Farewell for ever and a day.
The Taming of the Shrew. Act iv, sc. 4, l. 97. [Biondello]

4
Farewell! thou art too dear for my possessing,
And like enough thou know'st thy estimate:
The charter of thy worth gives thee releasing;
My bonds in thee are all determinate.
Sonnets. No. lxxxvii.

5
Second Lord: Fare thee well, fare thee well.
Apemantus: Thou art a fool to bid me farewell twice.
Timon of Athens. Act i, sc. 1, l. 272.

6
As many farewells as be stars in heaven,
With distinct breath and consign'd kisses to them,
He fumbles up into a loose adieu.
Troilus and Cressida. Act iv, sc. 4, l. 46. [Troilus] The only use of "consign'd." The only use of "fumbles." "Fumble" occurs in *Henry V,* ii, 3, 14, and in *Titus Andronicus,* iv, 2, 58.
Troilus, farewell! one eye yet looks on thee;
But with my heart the other eye doth see.
Troilus and Cressida. Act v, sc. 2, l. 107. [Cressida]

7
Malvolio: My lady bade me tell you, that, though she harbours you as her kinsman, she 's nothing allied to your disorders. If you can separate yourself and your misdemeanours, you are welcome to the house; if not, an it would please you to take leave of her, she is very willing to bid you farewell.
Sir Toby: 'Farewell, dear heart, since I must needs be gone.'
Twelfth Night. Act ii, sc. 3, l. 103. The only use of "misdemeanours."

FARMING

8
Let me be no assistant for a state,
But keep a farm and carters.
Hamlet. Act ii, sc. 2, l. 166. [Polonius]
A slobbery and dirty farm.—*Henry V,* iii, 5, 13. The only use of "slobbery."
Low farms.—*King Lear,* ii, 3, 17.
Pelting farm.—*Richard II,* ii, 1, 60.

9
Davy: Shall we sow the headland with wheat?
Shallow: With red wheat, Davy.
II Henry IV. Act v, sc. 1, l. 15. The only use of "headland."
White wheat.—*King Lear,* iii, 4, 123.
When wheat is green.—*A Midsummer-Night's Dream,* i, 1, 185.
Measures of wheat.—*Antony and Cleopatra,* ii, 6, 37.
Two grains of wheat.—*The Merchant of Venice,* i, 1, 115.
A cake out of the wheat.—*Troilus and Cressida,* i, 1, 15.
Wheat, rye, barley.—*The Tempest,* iv, 1, 61. See below. The only references to wheat.
Wheaten garland.—*Hamlet,* v, 2, 41. The only use of "wheaten."

10
Here 's a farmer, that hanged himself on the expectation of plenty.
Macbeth. Act ii, sc. 3, l. 5. [Porter] A reference to the proverb that "Farmers fatten most when famine reigns."

11
Let them go
To ear the land that hath some hope to grow.
Richard II. Act iii, sc. 2, l. 211. [King Richard]

12
And, for our coffers, with too great a court
And liberal largess, are grown somewhat light,
We are inforced to farm our royal realm;
The revenue whereof shall furnish us
For our affairs in hand.
Richard II. Act i, sc. 4, l. 43. [King Richard] The only use of "inforced."
The Earl of Wiltshire hath the realm in farm.
Richard II. Act ii, sc. 1, l. 256. [Ross]

13
Gonzalo: Had I plantation of this isle, my lord,—
Antonio: He 'ld sow 't with nettle-seed.
Sebastian: Or docks, or mallows.
The Tempest. Act ii, sc. 1, l. 144. The only use of "nettle-seed."

14
Ceres, most bounteous lady, thy rich leas
Of wheat, rye, barley, vetches, oats and pease;

Thy turfy mountains, where live nibbling sheep,
And flat meads thatch'd with stover, them to keep.

The Tempest. Act iv, sc. 1, l. 60. [Iris] The only use of "barley" ("barley-broth" occurs in *Henry V,* iii, 5, 19), "vetches," "turfy," and "stover" (fodder). "Rye" is used only once more, in *As You Like It,* v, 3, 23.

Earth's increase, foison plenty,
Barns and garners never empty,
Vines with clustering bunches growing,
Plants with goodly burthen bowing.

The Tempest. Act iv, sc. 1, l. 110. [Ceres] "Foison" (plentiful crop) occurs in three other plays: *Measure for Measure,* i, 4, 43; *Macbeth,* iv, 3, 88; *Antony and Cleopatra,* ii, 7, 23.

FASHION

See also Dress

1
Let 's do it after the high Roman fashion.

Antony and Cleopatra, iv, 15, 87. See under NOBILITY.

False women's fashion.—*Sonnets,* xx.

Newgate fashion.—*I Henry IV,* iii, 3, 104. The only mention of Newgate.

2
'Tis just the fashion.

As You Like It. Act ii, sc. 1, l. 56. [Lord]

These are now the fashion.—*Hamlet,* ii, 2, 357.

In the fashion.—*Merchant of Venice,* i, 2, 23.

3
It is not the fashion.

As You Like It. Epilogue, l. 1.

It is not a fashion.—*Henry V,* v, 2, 289.

'Tis no the fashion.—*The Merry Wives of Windsor,* iii, 3, 183.

A little out of fashion.—*Henry V,* iv, 1, 85.

Quite out of fashion.—*Troilus and Cressida,* iii, 3, 152.

A garment out of fashion.—*Cymbeline,* iii, 4, 53. "Out of fashion" is repeated in *All's Well that Ends Well,* i, 1, 170, in *Troilus and Cressida,* ii, 3, 226, and in *Othello,* ii, 1, 208.

4
Thou art not for the fashion of these times,
Where none will sweat but for promotion.

As You Like It. Act ii, sc. 3, l. 59. [Orlando]

To shame the guise o' the world, I will begin
The fashion, less without and more within.

Cymbeline. Act v, sc. 1, l. 32. [Posthumus]

In what fashion?—*Coriolanus,* i, 1, 281.

In their own fashion.—*Love's Labour 's Lost,* v, 2, 794.

Much upon my fashion.—*As You Like It,* ii, 4, 62.

Put the fashion on.—*II Henry IV,* v, 2, 52.

5
Ophelia: He hath importuned me with love
In honourable fashion.
Polonius: Ay, fashion you may call it; go to, go to.

Hamlet. Act i, sc. 3, l. 110.

6
The glass of fashion and the mould of form.

Hamlet. Act iii, sc. 1, l. 161. [Ophelia]

Fashion's own knight.—*Love's Labour 's Lost,* i, 1, 179.

Courtly and fashionable.—*Timon of Athens,* v, 1, 29.

Fashionable host.—*Troilus and Cressida,* iii, 3, 165. The only uses of "fashionable."

7
A' came ever in the rearward of the fashion.

II Henry IV, iii, 2, 340. See under CHARACTER.

8
Dat is not be de fashion pour les ladies of France.

Henry V. Act v, sc. 2, l. 284. [Alice]

The nice fashion of your country.

Henry V. Act v, sc. 2, l. 299. [King Henry]

Is this the fashion in the court of England?

II Henry VI, i, 3, 46. See under ENGLAND.

Fashion of the days.—*Love's Labour 's Lost,* iv, 3, 262.

Fashion of your garments.—*King Lear,* iii, 6, 84.

Fashion of thy malice.—*The Merchant of Venice,* iv, 1, 18.

Fashion of a man.—*Henry VIII,* iv, 2, 159.

Fashion of the world.—*Much Ado about Nothing,* i, 1, 97.

9
Men may construe things after their fashion.

Julius Cæsar. Act i, sc. 3, l. 34. [Cicero]

Fashion it thus.—*Julius Cæsar,* ii, 1, 30.

I 'll fashion him.—*Julius Cæsar,* ii, 1, 220.

It was upon this fashion.—*As You Like It,* i, 1, 2.

10
Bear with him, Brutus; 'tis his fashion.

Julius Cæsar. Act iv, sc. 3, l. 135. [Cassius]

It is my fashion.—*The Taming of the Shrew,* ii, 1, 230.

Is it the fashion?—*King Lear,* iii, 4, 74.

I . . . observed your fashion.—*Love's Labour 's Lost,* iv, 3, 139.

11
Borachio: Thou knowest that the fashion of a doublet, or a hat, or a cloak, is nothing to a man.
Conrade: Yes, it is apparel.
Borachio: I mean, the fashion.
Conrade: Yes, the fashion is the fashion.
Borachio: Tush! I may as well say the fool 's the fool. But seest thou not what a deformed thief this fashion is?

Much Ado about Nothing. Act iii, sc. 3, l. 125.

Fashion of a new doublet.—*Much Ado about Nothing,* ii, 3, 18.

Borachio: Seest thou not, I say, what a deformed thief this fashion is? how giddily a' turns about all the hot bloods between fourteen and five-and-thirty? sometimes fashioning them like Pharaoh's soldiers in the reechy painting, sometime like god Bel's priests in the old church-window, sometime like the shaven Hercules in the smirched worm-eaten tapestry, where his codpiece seems as massy as his club?
Conrade: All this I see; and I see that the fashion wears out more apparel than the man.

Much Ado about Nothing. Act iii, sc. 3, l. 139. "Giddily" is repeated in *Twelfth Night,* ii, 4, 87, "five-and-thirty" in *The Tempest,* iii, 2, 16, and "fashioning" in *Love's Labour 's Lost,* v, 2, 767. Pharaoh is mentioned again in *I Henry IV,* ii, 4, 520. The only use of "Bel," "church-window," and "shaven."

1
A fine, quaint, graceful and excellent fashion.
Much Ado about Nothing, iii, 4, 23. See under GOWN.

Chargeful fashion.—*The Comedy of Errors,* iv, 1, 29. The only use of "chargeful."
Ill fashion.—*The Two Gentlemen of Verona,* v, 4, 61.
New fashion.—*Love's Labour 's Lost,* i, 1, 165.
Rare fashion.—*Much Ado about Nothing,* iii, 4, 15.
Righteous fashion.—*The Merry Wives of Windsor,* iii, 4, 83.
The same fashion.—*The Tempest,* v, 1, 8.
Sour fashion.—*Julius Cæsar,* i, 2, 180.
Unconfirmed fashion.—*Love's Labour 's Lost,* iv, 2, 19.

2
Report of fashions in proud Italy,
Whose manners still our tardy apish nation
Limps after in base imitation.
Richard II. Act ii, sc. 1, l. 21. [York]

3
Study fashions to adorn my body.
Richard III. Act i, sc. 2, l. 258. [Gloucester]

Fashion-monger.—*Romeo and Juliet,* ii, 4, 34. The only use of the phrase.
Fashion-monging.—*Much Ado about Nothing,* v, 1, 94. The only use of the phrase.

4
Old fashions please me best; I am not so nice,
To change true rules for old inventions.
The Taming of the Shrew. Act iii, sc. 1, l. 80. [Bianca]

By my troth, this is the old fashion.
II Henry IV. Act ii, sc. 4, l. 60. [Hostess]

5
I 'll have no bigger: this doth fit the time,
And gentlewomen wear such caps as these.
The Taming of the Shrew. Act iv, sc. 3, l. 69. [Katharina] See also CAP.

You bid me make it orderly and well,
According to the fashion and the time.
The Taming of the Shrew. Act iv, sc. 3, l. 94. [Tailor]

The fashion of the time is changed.
The Two Gentlemen of Verona. Act iii, sc. 1, l. 86. [Duke]

6
You have done our pleasures much grace, fair ladies,
Set a fair fashion on our entertainment.
Timon of Athens. Act i, sc. 2, l. 151. [Timon]

Nothing else holds fashion.—*Troilus and Cressida,* v, 2, 196.

7
He will come to her in yellow stockings, and 'tis a colour she abhors, and cross-gartered, a fashion she detests.
Twelfth Night. Act ii, sc. 5, l. 219. [Maria]

8
Lucetta: What fashion, madam, shall I make your breeches? . . .
Julia: Why even what fashion thou best likest.
The Two Gentlemen of Verona. Act ii, sc. 7, l. 49. See under CODPIECE.

What fashion will you wear the garland of?
Much Ado about Nothing. Act ii, sc. 1, l. 195. [Benedick] See under GARLAND.

FASTING

See also Famine, Hunger

9
Make less thy body hence, and more thy grace;
Leave gormandizing; know the grave doth gape
For thee thrice wider than for other men.
II Henry IV. Act v, sc. 5, l. 56. [King Henry V] The only use of "gormandizing."

10
A thousand men have broke their fasts today.
III Henry VI, ii, 2, 127.

Broke his fast.—*King John,* i, 1, 235.
Broke your fast.—*Comedy of Errors,* i, 2, 50.
Now can I break my fast.—*The Two Gentlemen of Verona,* ii, 4, 141.
Fell into a . . . fast.—*Hamlet,* ii, 2, 147.

11
'Tis but a three years' fast.
Love's Labour 's Lost. Act i, sc. 1, l. 24. [Longaville]

And one day in a week to touch no food
And but one meal on every day beside.
Love's Labour 's Lost. Act i, sc. 1, l. 39. [Biron]

You shall fast a week with bran and water.
Love's Labour 's Lost. Act i, sc. 1, l. 303. [King]

A' must fast three days a week.
Love's Labour 's Lost. Act i, sc. 2, l. 134. [Dull]

Study, fast, not sleep.—*Love's Labour 's Lost,* i, 1, 48.
To fast, to study.—*Love's Labour 's Lost,* iv, 3, 292.
Fast and pray.—*The Comedy of Errors,* i, 2, 51.
I fast and pray'd.—*Cymbeline,* iv, 2, 347.
Fasting and prayer.—*Othello,* iii, 4, 40.
Fasts, hard lodging and thin weeds.—*Love's Labour 's Lost,* v, 2, 811.

12
Armado: Villain, thou shalt fast for thy offences ere thou be pardoned.
Costard: Well, sir, I hope, when I do it, I shall do it on a full stomach.
Love's Labour 's Lost. Act i, sc. 2, l. 151.

Costard: Let me not be pent up, sir: I will fast, being loose.
Moth: No, sir; that were fast and loose: thou shalt to prison.
Love's Labour 's Lost. Act i, sc. 2, l. 160. "Fast and loose" is used four times.

Say, can you fast? your stomachs are too young.
Love's Labour 's Lost. Act iv, sc. 3, l. 294. [Biron]

Woo 't fast?—*Hamlet,* v, 1, 298.

13
One who never feels
The wanton stings and motions of the sense,
But doth rebate and blunt his natural edge

With profits of the mind, study and fast.
Measure for Measure. Act i, sc. 4, l. 58. [Lucio] The only use of "rebate."

1
Therein fasting, hast thou made me gaunt.
Richard II. Act ii, sc. 1, l. 81. [Gaunt]

Fasting and waking.—*Troilus and Cressida,* i, 2, 37.

Bitter fasts.—*The Two Gentlemen of Verona,* ii, 4, 131.

Priest-like fasts.—*Coriolanus,* v, 1, 56. "Priest-like" is repeated in *Winter's Tale,* i, 2, 237.

Public fast.—*The Rape of Lucrece,* l. 891.

Strict fast.—*Richard II,* ii, 1, 80.

Tedious fast.—*Richard II,* ii, 1, 75.

2
Forbear to sleep the nights, and fast the days.
Richard III. Act iv, sc. 4, l. 118. [Queen Margaret]

3
Better 'twere that both of us did fast,
Since, of ourselves, ourselves are choleric.
The Taming of the Shrew, iv, 1, 176. See under MEAT.

For this night, we 'll fast for company.
The Taming of the Shrew. Act iv, sc. 1, l. 180. [Petruchio]

Fast it fairly out.—*The Taming of the Shrew,* i, 1, 109.

FATE

See also Destiny, Fortune, Occasion

4
The fated sky
Gives us free scope, only doth backward pull
Our slow designs when we ourselves are dull.
All's Well that Ends Well. Act i, sc. 1, l. 232. [Helena]

Fated to the purpose.—*The Tempest,* i, 2, 129.

5
We all would sup together;
And drink carouses to the next day's fate,
Which promises royal peril.
Antony and Cleopatra. Act iv, sc. 8, l. 33. [Antony]

Nay, good my fellows, do not please sharp fate
To grace it with your sorrows.
Antony and Cleopatra. Act iv, sc. 14, l. 135. [Antony]

6
If thou art privy to thy country's fate,
Which, happily, foreknowing may avoid.
Hamlet. Act i, sc. 1, l. 133. [Horatio] "Foreknowing" is repeated in *King John,* iv, 2, 154.

For what we know must be and is as common
As any the most vulgar thing to sense,
Why should we in our peevish opposition
Take it to heart?
Hamlet. Act i, sc. 2, l. 98. [King]

My fate cries out,
And makes each petty artery in this body
As hardy as the Nemean lion's nerve.
Hamlet. Act i, sc. 4, l. 81. [Hamlet] The only use of "artery." "Arteries" occurs in *Love's Labour's Lost,* iv, 3, 306. "Nemean lion" is repeated in *Love's Labour's Lost,* iv, 1, 90.

7
O God! that one might read the book of fate,
And see the revolution of the times
Make mountains level, and the continent,
Weary of solid firmness, melt itself
Into the sea!
II Henry IV. Act iii, sc. 1, l. 45. [King Henry]

8
What fates impose, that men must needs abide;
It boots not to resist both wind and tide.
III Henry VI. Act iv, sc. 3, l. 58. [King Edward]

It must be as it may.
Henry V. Act ii, sc. 1, l. 25. [Nym]

'Tis but the fate of place.
Henry VIII. Act i, sc. 2, l. 75. [Wolsey]

9
Men at some time are masters of their fates.
Julius Cæsar. Act i, sc. 2, l. 139. [Cassius]

I am the mistress of my fate.
The Rape of Lucrece, l. 1069.

Fates, we will know your pleasures.
Julius Cæsar. Act iii, sc. 1, l. 98. [Brutus]

10
That he should be my fool and I his fate.
Love's Labour's Lost. Act v, sc. 2, l. 68. [Rosaline]

11
Our fate,
Hid in an auger-hole, may rush, and seize us.
Macbeth. Act ii, sc. 3, l. 127. [Donalbain] The only use of "auger-hole."

Come fate into the list,
And champion me to the utterance!
Macbeth. Act iii, sc. 1, l. 71. [Macbeth]

Must embrace the fate Of that dark hour.
Macbeth. Act iii, sc. 1, l. 137. [Macbeth]

12
Then fate o'er-rules, that, one man holding troth,
A million fail, confounding oath on oath.
A Midsummer-Night's Dream. Act iii, sc. 2, l. 92. [Puck]

13
O Fates, come, come, Cut thread and thrum;
Quail, crush, conclude and quell!
A Midsummer-Night's Dream. Act v, sc. 1, l. 290. [Pyramus] The only use of "thrum."

O fate!—*Henry VIII,* ii, 3, 85.

O, the Fates!—*The Winter's Tale,* iv, 4, 20.

O Sisters Three, Come, come to me,
With hands as pale as milk.
A Midsummer-Night's Dream. Act v, sc. 1, l. 343. [Thisbe]

Fates and Destinies and such odd sayings, the Sisters
Three and such branches of learning.
The Merchant of Venice. Act ii, sc. 2, l. 65. [Launcelot]

The Fates with traitors do contrive.
Julius Cæsar. Act ii, sc. 3, l. 16. [Artemidorus]

Thy Fates open their hands; let thy blood and spirit embrace them.
Twelfth Night. Act ii, sc. 5, l. 159. [Malvolio]

Foolish Fates.—*A Midsummer-Night's Dream,* i, 2, 40.
Strict fates.—*Pericles,* iii, 3, 8.

1
O Fate! take not away thy heavy hand.
Much Ado about Nothing. Act iv, sc. 1, l. 116. [Leonato]
Fate . . . held his hand.—*The Merry Wives of Windsor,* iii, 5, 106.
But, O vain boast! Who can control his fate?
Othello. Act v, sc. 2, l. 264. [Othello]

2
Look upon myself and curse my fate.
Sonnets. No. xxix.
Cursed fate.—*Othello,* iii, 3, 426.
Black fate.—*Romeo and Juliet,* iii, 1, 124.
Cruel fate.—*Henry V,* iii, 6, 28.
Good fate.—*The Tempest,* i, 1, 33.
Hard fate!—*Timon of Athens,* iii, 5, 75.
Unblest fate.—*Othello,* v, 1, 34.
Unknown fate.—*Othello,* ii, 1, 195.

3
I and my fellows Are ministers of Fate.
The Tempest. Act iii, sc. 3, l. 60. [Ariel]

4 Fate, hear me what I say!
I reck not though I end my life to-day.
Troilus and Cressida. Act v, sc. 6, l. 25. [Troilus]
Fate, show thy force: ourselves we do not owe;
What is decreed must be, and be this so.
Twelfth Night. Act i, sc. 5, l. 329. [Olivia]
The malignancy of my fate might perhaps distemper yours.
Twelfth Night. Act ii, sc. 1, l. 4. [Sebastian] The only use of "malignancy."

5
As the old hermit of Prague, that never saw pen and ink, very wittily said to a niece of King Gorboduc, 'That that is is.'
Twelfth Night. Act iv, sc. 2, l. 14. [Clown] The "hermit of Prague" was perhaps Jerome, the hermit of Camaldoli, but more probably an invention of Shakespeare. The only mention of Prague and of Gorboduc, a legendary king of Britain.

6
Fate, against thy better disposition,
Hath made thy person for the thrower-out
Of my poor babe.
The Winter's Tale. Act iii, sc. 3, l. 28. [Antigonus. The only use of "thrower-out."

FATHER

See also Sire

7
This young gentlewoman had a father,—O, that 'had'! how sad a passage 'tis!
All's Well that Ends Well. Act i, sc. 1, l. 19. [Countess]
Be thou blest, Bertram, and succeed thy father
In manners, as in shape!
All's Well that Ends Well. Act i, sc. 1, l. 70. [Countess]
Youth, thou bear'st thy father's face. . . .
Thy father's moral parts Mayst thou inherit too!
All's Well that Ends Well. Act i, sc. 2, l. 19. [King]
Your father's image is so hit in you,
His very air, that I should call you brother.
The Winter's Tale. Act v, sc. 1, l. 127. [Leontes] See also under LIKENESS.

8 I think not on my father;
And these great tears grace his remembrance more
Than those I shed for him.
All's Well that Ends Well. Act i, sc. 1, l. 90. [Helena]

9
I have as much of my father in me as you.
As You Like It. Act i, sc. 1, l. 52. [Orlando]
The spirit of my father grows strong in me.
As You Like It. Act i, sc. 1, l. 73. [Orlando]

10
My father's love is enough to honour him.
As You Like It. Act i, sc. 2, l. 89. [Celia]
Rosalind: My father loved his father dearly . . .
Celia: My father hated his father dearly.
As You Like It. Act i, sc. 3, l. 30.
Wilt thou change fathers? I will give thee mine.
As You Like It. Act i, sc. 3, l. 93. [Celia]
But what talk we of fathers?
As You Like It. Act iii, sc. 4, l. 41. [Rosalind]

11
I never saw my father in my life.
The Comedy of Errors. Act v, sc. 1, l. 319. [Antipholus of Ephesus]
Was not a man my father?
Coriolanus. Act iv, sc. 2, l. 18. [Volumnia]
O boy, thou hadst a father!
The Merry Wives of Windsor. Act iii, sc. 4, l. 36. [Shallow]
His father was called Sicilius.—*Cymbeline,* i, 1, 28.

12 Their father,
Then old and fond of issue, took such sorrow
That he quit being.
Cymbeline. Act i, sc. 1, l. 36. [Gentleman]
Whose father then, as men report
Thou orphans' father art,
Thou shouldst have been, and shielded him
From this earth-vexing smart.
Cymbeline. Act v, sc. 4, l. 39. [Sicilius] The only use of "shielded" and "earth-vexing."

13
You are my father too, and did relieve me
To see this gracious season.
Cymbeline. Act v, sc. 5, l. 400. [Imogen]
I 'm not their father.—*Cymbeline,* iv, 2, 28.

14
Do not for ever with thy vailed lids
Seek for thy noble father in the dust.
Hamlet. Act i, sc. 2, l. 70. [Queen] The only use of "vailed."
Your father lost a father;
That father lost, lost his.
Hamlet. Act i, sc. 2, l. 89. [King]
So have I a noble father lost.
Hamlet. Act iv, sc. 7, l. 25. [Laertes]

15
Queen: Hamlet, thou hast thy father much offended.
Hamlet: Mother, you have my father much offended.
Hamlet. Act iii, sc. 4, l. 9.

My father, in his habit as he lived!
Hamlet. Act iii, sc. 4, l. 135. [Hamlet]

1
Fie, cousin Percy! how you cross my father!
I Henry IV. Act iii, sc. 1, l. 147. [Mortimer]

2
For this the foolish over-careful fathers
Have broke their sleep with thoughts, their brains with care,
Their bones with industry.
II Henry IV. Act iv, sc. 5, l. 68. [King Henry] The only use of "over-careful."

I 'll be your father and your brother too;
Let me but bear your love, I 'll bear your cares.
II Henry IV. Act v, sc. 2, l. 57. [King Henry V]

My father is gone wild into his grave,
For in his tomb lie my affections.
II Henry IV. Act v, sc. 2, l. 123. [King Henry V]

3
Beshrew my father's ambition! he was thinking of civil wars when he got me: therefore was I created with a stubborn outside, with an aspect of iron, that, when I come to woo ladies, I fright them.
Henry V. Act v, sc. 2, l. 242. [King Henry]

4
Decrepit miser! base ignoble wretch!
I am descended of a gentler blood:
Thou art no father nor no friend of mine.
I Henry VI. Act v, sc. 4, l. 7. [La Pucelle]

Dost thou deny thy father, cursed drab?
I Henry VI. Act v, sc. 4, l. 32. [Shepherd]

5
Gloucester: Her father is no better than an earl,
Although in glorious titles he excel.
Suffolk: Yes, my lord, her father is a king.
I Henry VI. Act v, sc. 5, l. 37.

Thy royal father Was a most sainted king.
Macbeth. Act iv, sc. 3, l. 108. [Macduff] "Royal father" occurs eight times in the plays.

6
Wast thou ordain'd, dear father,
To lose thy youth in peace, and to achieve
The silver livery of advised age,
And, in thy reverence and thy chair-days, thus
To die in ruffian battle?
II Henry VI. Act v, sc. 2, l. 45. [Young Clifford] The only use of "chair-days." "Dear father" is repeated eight times in later plays.

Dearest father.—*The Tempest,* i, 2, 1.

7
Cade: My father was a Mortimer,—
Dick [Aside]: He was an honest man, and a good bricklayer.
II Henry VI. Act iv, sc. 2, l. 41. "Bricklayer" is repeated in l. 153, and occurs in no other scene.

Thy father was a plasterer.—*II Henry VI,* iv, 2, 140. The only use of "plasterer."

Thy father! O villain! he is a sail-maker in Bergamo.
The Taming of the Shrew. Act v, sc. 1, l. 80. [Vincentio] The only use of "sail-maker."

8
My noble father,
Three times to-day I holp him to his horse,
Three times bestrid him; thrice I led him off,
Persuaded him from any further act:
But still, where danger was, still there I met him:
And like rich hangings in a homely house,
So was his will in his old feeble body.
II Henry VI. Act v, sc. 3, l. 7. [Richard]

This gentleman . . . had a most noble father.
Measure for Measure. Act ii, sc. 1, l. 7. [Escalus]

Not one of those but had a noble father.
All's Well that Ends Well. Act ii, sc. 3, l. 68. [King] "Noble father" occurs fifteen times in the plays.

9
May that ground gape and swallow me alive,
Where I shall kneel to him that slew my father!
III Henry VI. Act i, sc. 1, l. 161. [Clifford]

Ah, wretched man! would I had died a maid,
And never seen thee, never borne thee son,
Seeing thou hast proved so unnatural a father!
III Henry VI. Act i, sc. 1, l. 216. [Queen Margaret]

10
Wont to cheer his dad.
III Henry VI, i, 4, 77. "Dad" is used also in *King John,* ii, 1, 467, and in *Twelfth Night,* iv, 2, 140.

So fared our father with his enemies;
So fled his enemies my warlike father.
III Henry VI. Act ii, sc. 1, l. 18. [Richard] "Warlike father" is repeated in *Richard III,* i, 2, 160.

Victorious father.—*II Henry VI,* v, 1, 211.

11
By many hands your father was subdued;
But only slaughter'd by the ireful arm
Of unrelenting Clifford and the queen.
III Henry VI. Act ii, sc. 1, l. 56. [Messenger]

Your brave father breathed his latest gasp.
III Henry VI. Act ii, sc. 1, l. 108. [Warwick] "Brave father" is repeated in *The Winter's Tale,* v, 1, 136.

Who 's this? O God! it is my father's face,
Who in this conflict I unwares have kill'd.
III Henry VI. Act ii, sc. 5, l. 61. [Son] The only use of "unwares."

And I, who at his hands received my life,
Have by my hands of life bereaved him.
III Henry VI. Act ii, sc. 5, l. 67. [Son]

12
The ghostly father now hath done his shrift.
III Henry VI. Act iii, sc. 2, l. 107. [Gloucester]

Here comes your ghostly father.
Measure for Measure. Act iv, sc. 3, l. 51. [Abhorson] "Ghostly father" is repeated in v, 1, 126, and in *Romeo and Juliet,* ii, 2, 189; ii, 3, 45.

13
Did I forget that by the house of York
My father came untimely to his death?
III Henry VI, iii, 3, 187. [Warwick]

1 Outgo
His father by as much as a performance
Does an irresolute purpose.
Henry VIII. Act i, sc. 2, l. 207. [Surveyor] The only use of "irresolute."

Out-go my thinking on you.—*Antony and Cleopatra,* iii, 2, 61. The only uses of "out-go."

He outgoes the very heart of kindness.—*Timon of Athens,* i, 1, 285. The only use of "outgoes."

2
Here will be father, godfather, and all together.
Henry VIII. Act v, sc. 4, l. 38. [Porter]

You must be godfather.—*Henry VIII,* v, 3, 163.

Thou shalt have two godfathers.—*The Merchant of Venice,* iv, 1, 398.

Every godfather can give a name.—*Love's Labour's Lost,* i, 1, 93.

Earthly godfathers.—*Love's Labour's Lost,* i, 1, 88.

Commit your godfathers.—*Richard III,* i, 1, 48. The only uses of "godfather."

3
O old sir Robert, father, on my knee
I give heaven thanks I was not like to thee!
King John. Act i, sc. 1, l. 82. [Bastard]

My father gave me honour, yours gave land,
Now blessed be the hour, by night or day,
When I was got, sir Robert was away!
King John. Act i, sc. 1, l. 164. [Bastard]

Then, good my mother, let me know my father;
Some proper man, I hope: who was it, mother?
King John. Act i, sc. 1, l. 249. [Bastard]

Now, by this light, were I to get again,
Madam, I would not wish a better father.
King John. Act i, sc. 1, l. 259. [Bastard]

Ay, my mother,
With all my heart I thank thee for my father!
King John. Act i, sc. 1, l. 269. [Bastard]

You may partly hope that your father got you not.
The Merchant of Venice. Act iii, sc. 5, l. 11. [Launcelot]

4
You have begot me, bred me, loved me: I
Return those duties back as are right fit,
Obey you, love you, and most honour you.
King Lear. Act i, sc. 1, l. 98. [Cordelia]

The dear father
Would with his daughter speak, commands her service.
King Lear. Act ii, sc. 4, l. 102. [King Lear]

Your old kind father, whose frank heart gave all.
King Lear. Act iii, sc. 4, l. 20. [King Lear] The only use of "kind father."

So kind a father!—*King Lear,* i, 5, 36.

5
Is it the fashion, that discarded fathers
Should have thus little mercy on their flesh?
King Lear. Act iii, sc. 4, l. 74. [King Lear]

Thou shalt find a dearer father in my love.
King Lear. Act iii, sc. 5, l. 25. [Cornwall]

'Faith, once or twice she heaved the name of 'father'
Pantingly forth, as if it press'd her heart.
King Lear. Act iv, sc. 3, l. 27. [Gentleman]

6
Father'd he is, and yet he 's fatherless.
Macbeth. Act iv, sc. 2, l. 26. [Lady Macduff] "Fatherless" is repeated in *Richard III,* ii, 2, 64: "Fatherless distress."

He childed as I father'd!—*King Lear,* iii, 6, 117. The only use of "childed."

Being so father'd.—*Julius Cæsar,* ii, 1, 297. The only uses of "father'd."

7
Your father was ever virtuous.
The Merchant of Venice. Act i, sc. 2, l. 30. [Nerissa]

My father did something smack, something grow to, he had a kind of taste.
The Merchant of Venice. Act ii, sc. 2, l. 18. [Launcelot]

This is my true-begotten father!
The Merchant of Venice. Act ii, sc. 2, l. 36. [Launcelot] The only use of "true-begotten."

His father, though I say it, is an honest exceeding poor man and, God be thanked, well to live.
The Merchant of Venice. Act ii, sc. 2, l. 54. [Gobbo]

Though old man, yet poor man, my father.
The Merchant of Venice. Act ii, sc. 2, l. 148. [Launcelot]

8
To you your father should be as a god;
One who composed your beauties, yea, and one
To whom you are but as a form in wax
By him imprinted and within his power
To leave the figure or disfigure it.
A Midsummer-Night's Dream. Act i, sc. 1, l. 47. [Theseus] The only use of "imprinted."

Hermia: I would my father look'd but with my eyes.
Theseus: Rather your eyes must with his judgement look.
A Midsummer-Night's Dream. Act i, sc. 1, l. 56.

You have her father's love, Demetrius;
Let me have Hermia's: do you marry him.
A Midsummer-Night's Dream. Act i, sc. 1, l. 93. [Lysander]

Antonio: I trust you will be ruled by your father.
Beatrice: Yes, faith; it is my cousin's duty to make curtsy and say 'Father, as it please you.'
Much Ado about Nothing. Act ii, sc. 1, l. 54.

9
Who would be a father!
Othello. Act i, sc. 1, l. 165. [Brabantio]

To you I am bound for life and education;
My life and education both do learn me
How to respect you; you are the lord of duty.
Othello. Act i, sc. 3, l. 182. [Desdemona]

I would not there reside,
To put my father in impatient thoughts
By being in his eye.
Othello. Act i, sc. 3, l. 242. [Desdemona]

Poor Desdemona! I am glad thy father 's dead:
Thy match was mortal to him.
Othello. Act v, sc. 2, l. 204. [Gratiano]

10
O thou, the earthly author of my blood,
Whose youthful spirit, in me regenerate,

Doth with a twofold vigour lift me up.
Richard II. Act i, sc. 3, l. 69. [Bolingbroke]
The only use of "regenerate."
You urged me as a judge; but I had rather
You would have bid me argue like a father.
Richard II. Act i, sc. 3, l. 237. [Gaunt]
O loyal father of a treacherous son!
Thou sheer, immaculate and silver fountain,
From whence this stream through muddy passages
Hath held his current and defiled himself!
Richard II. Act v, sc. 3, l. 60. [Bolingbroke]

1 The first that there did greet my stranger soul,
Was my great father-in-law, renowned Warwick.
Richard III. Act i, sc. 4, l. 48. [Clarence]
I am joyful
To meet the least occasion that may give me,
Remembrance of my father-in-law.
Henry VIII. Act iii, sc. 2, l. 6. [Surrey]
Noble Buckingham, my father-in-law.—*Henry VIII,* iii, 2, 256.
Noble father-in-law!—*Richard III,* v, 3, 81.
The only uses of "father-in-law."

2 Well, well, thou hast a careful father, child;
One who, to put thee from thy heaviness,
Hath sorted out a sudden day of joy.
Romeo and Juliet. Act iii, sc. 5, l. 108. [Lady Capulet]

3 Ah, Tranio, what a cruel father 's he!
The Taming of the Shrew. Act i, sc. 1, l. 190. [Lucentio]
A father cruel.—*Cymbeline,* i, 6, 1.

4 Your father were a fool
To give thee all, and in his waning age
Set foot under thy table.
The Taming of the Shrew. Act ii, sc. 1, l. 402. [Gremio]
Fathers commonly
Do get their children; but in this case of wooing,
A child shall get a sire.
The Taming of the Shrew. Act ii, sc. 1, l. 411. [Tranio]
In gait and countenance surely like a father.
The Taming of the Shrew. Act iv, sc. 2, l. 65. [Biondello]
'Tis well; and hold your own, in any case,
With such austerity as 'longeth to a father.
The Taming of the Shrew. Act iv, sc. 4, l. 6. [Tranio]

5 I pray you, stand good father to me now.
The Taming of the Shrew. Act iv, sc. 4, l. 21. [Tranio]
Now I perceive thou art a reverend father.
The Taming of the Shrew. Act iv, sc. 5, l. 48. [Katharina]
Reverend father.—*King John,* iii, 1, 224; iii, 1, 249; *Henry VIII,* ii, 4, 58; ii, 4, 205; iii, 1, 181; iv, 1, 26.

6 And now by law, as well as reverend age,
I may entitle thee my loving father.
The Taming of the Shrew. Act iv, sc. 5, l. 60. [Petruchio]

My fair Bianca, bid my father welcome,
While I with self-same kindness welcome thine.
The Taming of the Shrew. Act v, sc. 2, l. 4. [Lucentio]

7 Vincentio: Art thou his father?
Pedant: Ay, sir; so his mother says, if I may believe her.
The Taming of the Shrew. Act v, sc. 1, l. 33.
Miranda: Sir, are you not my father?
Prospero: Thy mother was a piece of virtue, and
She said thou wast my daughter.
The Tempest. Act i, sc. 2, l. 55.

8 Full fathom five thy father lies;
Of his bones are coral made;
Those are pearls that were his eyes:
Nothing of him that doth fade
But doth suffer a sea-change
Into something rich and strange.
The Tempest. Act i, sc. 2, l. 396. [Ariel]
The only use of "sea-change."
The ditty does remember my drown'd father.
The Tempest. Act i, sc. 2, l. 404. [Ferdinand]

9 My father 's of a better nature, sir,
Than he appears by speech.
The Tempest. Act i, sc. 2, l. 496. [Miranda]
So rare a wonder'd father.
Tempest. Act iv, sc. 1, l. 123. [Ferdinand]
And second father This lady makes to me.
The Tempest. Act v, sc. 1, l. 195. [Ferdinand]

10 It hath pleased the gods to remember my father's age,
And call him to long peace.
He is gone happy, and has left me rich.
Timon of Athens. Act i, sc. 2, l. 2. [Ventidius]
My father is deceased.—*The Taming of the Shrew,* i, 2, 54.

11 If thou wilt curse, thy father, that poor rag,
Must be thy subject, who in spite put stuff
To some she beggar and compounded thee
Poor rogue hereditary.
Timon of Athens. Act iv, sc. 3, l. 271. [Timon]

12 Father, and in that name doth nature speak.
Titus Andronicus. Act i, sc. 1, l. 371. [Quintus]
Dear father, soul and substance of us all.
Titus Andronicus. Act i, sc. 1, l. 374. [Lucius]
For thy father's sake, That gave thee life.
Titus Andronicus. Act ii, sc. 3, l. 158. [Lavinia]

13 Come, let us go, and make thy father blind;
For such a sight will blind a father's eye.
Titus Andronicus. Act ii, sc. 4, l. 52. [Marcus]
Look, how the black slave smiles upon the father,
As who should say 'Old lad, I am thine own.'
Titus Andronicus. Act iv, sc. 2, l. 120. [Aaron]

1
Viola: My father had a mole upon his brow.
Sebastian: And so had mine.
Twelfth Night. Act v, sc. 1, l. 249.
My father was that Sebastian of Messaline, whom I know you have heard of.
Twelfth Night. Act ii, sc. 1, l. 18. [Sebastian]
Sebastian was my father.—*Twelfth Night,* v, 1, 239.
Priam is his father.—*Troilus and Cressida,* i, 3, 261.
The Emperor of Russia was my father;
O that he were alive.
The Winter's Tale. Act iii, sc. 2, l. 120. [Hermione]
2
O, that our fathers would applaud our loves,
To seal our happiness with their consents!
The Two Gentlemen of Verona. Act i, sc. 3, l. 48. [Proteus]
3 You have a holy father,
A graceful gentleman.
The Winter's Tale. Act v, sc. 1, l. 170. [Leontes] "Holy father" occurs four times in the plays.
Angry father.—*Pericles,* ii, 5, 68.
Child-changed father.—*King Lear,* iv, 7, 17. The only use of "child-changed."
Credulous father!—*King Lear,* i, 2, 195.
Decrepit father.—*Sonnets,* xxxvii.
Dread father.—*Troilus and Cressida,* ii, 2, 27.
Good father.—*III Henry VI,* ii, 2, 80, and eleven times in later plays.
Gracious father.—*III Henry VI,* ii, 2, 63; *Macbeth,* iii, 6, 10.
Grave fathers!—*Titus Andronicus,* iii, 1, 1.
Hapless father.—*III Henry VI,* i, 4, 156.
Happy father.—*King Lear,* iv, 6, 72.
Honourable father.—*Much Ado about Nothing,* i, 1, 113; *Richard II,* i, 1, 136.
Narrow-prying father.—*The Taming of the Shrew,* iii, 2, 148. The only use of "narrow-prying."
Natural father.—*Cymbeline,* iii, 3, 107.
Poor father.—*Hamlet,* i, 2, 148; *King Lear,* iv, 7, 38; *The Winter's Tale,* v, 1, 202.
Princely father.—*III Henry VI,* ii, 1, 1; ii, 1, 47; ii, 6, 51; *Richard III,* iii, 5, 88.
Sweet father.—*III Henry VI,* i, 1, 115; *Titus Andronicus,* iii, 1, 136; iii, 1, 180; *The Taming of the Shrew,* v, 1, 115; v, 1, 133.
Temporal fathers.—*Cymbeline,* v, 4, 12.

II—Father and Child

4
You know my father hath no child but I, nor none is like to have.
As You Like It. Act i, sc. 2, l. 18. [Celia]
I will not call him son
Of him I was about to call his father.
As You Like It. Act ii, sc. 3, l. 20. [Adam]
5
This is a poor epitome of yours,
Which by the interpretation of full time
May show like all yourself.
Coriolanus. Act v, sc. 3, l. 68. [Volumnia] The only use of "epitome."
6
These two young gentlemen, that call me father
And think they are my sons, are none of mine.
Cymbeline. Act v, sc. 5, l. 328. [Belarius]
7 With no less nobility of love
Than that which dearest father bears his son.
Hamlet. Act i, sc. 2, l. 110. [King]
8
I, the son of a dear father murder'd,
Prompted to my revenge by heaven and hell.
Hamlet. Act ii, sc. 2, l. 612. [Hamlet]
I do not know
Wherefore my father should revengers want,
Having a son and friends.
Antony and Cleopatra. Act ii, sc. 6, l. 10. [Pompey] "Revenger" is repeated in iii, 1, 3, and occurs in no other play.
9 The father to so blest a son,
A son who is the theme of honour's tongue;
Amongst a grove, the very straightest plant;
Who is sweet Fortune's minion and her pride.
I Henry IV. Act i, sc. 1, l. 80. [King Henry] The only use of "straightest."
A son that well deserves
The honour and regard of such a father.
The Two Gentlemen of Verona. Act ii, sc. 4, l. 59. [Valentine]
10
Thy mother's son! like enough, and thy father's shadow: so the son of the female is the shadow of the male.
II Henry IV. Act iii, sc. 2, l. 139. [Falstaff]
Be now the father and propose a son.
II Henry IV. Act v, sc. 2, l. 92. [Chief Justice]
11 His most mighty father on a hill
Stood smiling to behold his lion's whelp
Forage in blood of French nobility.
Henry V. Act i, sc. 2, l. 108. [Archbishop of Canterbury]
12
O, twice my father, twice am I thy son!
I Henry VI. Act iv, sc. 6, l. 6. [John Talbot]
O thou, whose wounds become hard-favour'd death,
Speak to thy father ere thou yield thy breath! . . .
Come, come and lay him in his father's arms.
I Henry VI. Act iv, sc. 7, l. 23. [Talbot]
13
Thou, being a king, blest with a goodly son,
Didst yield consent to disinherit him,
Which argued thee a most unloving father.
III Henry VI. Act ii, sc. 2, l. 23. [Clifford] The only use of "unloving."
And happy always was it for that son
Whose father for his hoarding went to hell.
III Henry VI. Act ii, sc. 2, l. 47. [King Henry]
Who should succeed the father but the son?
III Henry VI. Act ii, sc. 2, l. 94. [Clifford]
Son: Was ever son so rued a father's death?
Father: Was ever father so bemoan'd his son?
III Henry VI. Act ii, sc. 5, l. 109. The only use of "bemoan'd."
Why, 'tis a happy thing
To be the father unto many sons.
III Henry VI. Act iii, sc. 2, l. 104. [King]

1 How if my brother,
Who, as you say, took pains to get this son,
Had of your father claim'd this son for his?
In sooth, good friend, your father might have kept
This calf bred from his cow from all the world.
King John. Act i, sc. 1, l. 120. [King John]

2
Sons at perfect age, and fathers declining, the father should be as ward to the son, and the son manage his revenue.
King Lear. Act i, sc. 2, l. 76. [Edmund]

There 's son against father: the king falls from bias of nature; there 's father against child.
King Lear. Act i, sc. 2, l. 120. [Gloucester]

3
With how manifold and strong a bond
The child was bound to the father.
King Lear. Act ii, sc. 1, l. 49. [Edmund]

Fathers that wear rags
Do make their children blind;
But fathers that bear bags
Shall see their children kind.
King Lear. Act ii, sc. 4, l. 48. [Fool]

4 I had a son,
Now outlaw'd from my blood; he sought my life,
But lately, very late: I love him, friend:
No father his son dearer.
King Lear. Act iii, sc. 4, l. 171. [Gloucester]

5
It is a wise father that knows his own child.
The Merchant of Venice. Act ii, sc. 2, l. 80. [Launcelot]

Let the emperor dandle him for his own.
Titus Andronicus. Act iv, sc. 2, l. 161. [Aaron]

Duchess of York: Art thou my son?
King Richard: Ay, I thank God, my father, and yourself.
Richard III. Act iv, sc. 4, l. 154.

You had a father: let your son say so.
Sonnets. No. xiii.

6
The deceiving father of a deceitful son.
The Taming of the Shrew. Act iv, sc. 4, l. 83. [Biondello]

7
Can a son's eyes behold his father bleed?
Titus Andronicus. Act v, sc. 3, l. 65. [Lucius]

The rude son should strike his father dead.
Troilus and Cressida. Act i, sc. 3, l. 115. [Ulysses]

8 Methinks a father
Is at the nuptial of his son a guest
That best becomes the table.
The Winter's Tale. Act iv, sc. 4, l. 405. [Polixenes]

Reason my son
Should choose himself a wife, but as good reason
The father, all whose joy is nothing else
But fair posterity, should hold some counsel
In such a business.
The Winter's Tale. Act iv, sc. 4, l. 416. [Polixenes]

Your discontenting father strive to qualify.
And bring him up to liking.
The Winter's Tale. Act iv, sc. 4, l. 543. [Camillo] The only use of "discontenting."

Should I now meet my father
He would not call me son.
The Winter's Tale. Act iv, sc. 4, l. 670. [Florizel]

FATNESS

See also Flesh

9
Dromio of Syracuse: An ell and three quarters, will not measure her from hip to hip.
Antipholus of Syracuse: Then she bears some breadth?
Dromio of Syracuse: No longer from head to foot than from hip to hip; she is spherical like a globe; I could find out countries in her. . . .
Antipholus of Syracuse: Where stood Belgia, the Netherlands?
Dromio of Syracuse: Oh, sir, I did not look so low.
The Comedy of Errors. Act iii, sc. 2, l. 112. Belgia is mentioned again in *III Henry VI*, iv, 8, 1. The only mention of the Netherlands.

10
The fatness of these pursy times.
Hamlet, iii, 4, 153. See under VICE AND VIRTUE. The only use of "fatness."

We fat all creatures else to fat us, and we fat ourselves for maggots.
Hamlet, iv, 3, 21. See under WORM.

11
He 's fat, and scant of breath.
Hamlet. Act v, sc. 2, l. 298. [Queen]

12
Thou knowest he is no starveling.
I Henry IV. Act ii, sc. 1, l. 77. [Gadshill] The only use of "starveling," except as a proper noun.

'Rivo!' says the drunkard. Call in ribs, call in tallow.
I Henry IV. Act ii, sc. 4, l. 125. The only use of 'rivo,' a Spanish exclamation.

Peace, ye fat-guts!—*I Henry IV*, ii, 2, 33. The only use of "fat-guts."

Ye fat chuffs.—*I Henry IV*, ii, 2, 94. The only use of "chuffs."

You whoreson round man.—*I Henry IV*, ii, 4, 155.

13
If to be fat be to be hated, then Pharaoh's lean kine are to be loved.
I Henry IV. Act ii, sc. 4, l. 519. [Falstaff] The only use of "kine." Pharaoh is mentioned only once again, in *Much Ado about Nothing*, iii, 3, 142.

14
Sheriff: A gross fat man.
Carrier: As fat as butter.
I Henry IV. Act ii, sc. 4, l. 560.

Why, you are so fat, Sir John, that you must needs be out of all compass, out of all reasonable compass, Sir John.
I Henry IV. Act iii, sc. 3, l. 24. [Bardolph]

Thou seest I have more flesh than another man, and therefore more frailty.
I Henry IV. Act iii, sc. 3, l. 188. [Falstaff]

Could not all this flesh Keep in a little life?
I Henry IV. Act v, sc. 4, l. 102. [Prince of Wales]

Three fingers on the ribs.—*I Henry IV,* iv, 2, 80.

1
Feed, and be fat.
II Henry IV, ii, 4, 193. See under FEEDING.

Grew fat with feasting.—*Antony and Cleopatra,* ii, 6, 66.

Fat and fulsome.—*Twelfth Night,* v, 1, 112.

Fat as tame things.—*Winter's Tale,* i, 2, 92.

2
Let me have men about me that are fat;
Sleek-headed men and such as sleep o' nights:
Yond Cassius has a lean and hungry look;
He thinks too much: such men are dangerous. . . .
Would he were fatter!
Julius Cæsar. Act i, sc. 2, l. 192. [Cæsar] The only use of "sleek-headed" and "fatter."

3
Fat paunches have lean pates, and dainty bits
Make rich the ribs, but bankrupt quite the wits.
Love's Labour's Lost. Act i, sc. 1, l. 26. [Longaville]

Ye fat paunch.—*I Henry IV,* ii, 4, 159.

Sir John Paunch.—*I Henry IV,* ii, 2, 69. The only uses of "paunch" as a noun. It is used as a verb in *The Tempest,* iii, 2, 98: "Paunch him with a stake."

4
I shall think the worse of fat men, as long as I have an eye to make difference of men's liking.
The Merry Wives of Windsor. Act ii, sc. 1, l. 55. [Mrs. Ford]

This unwholesome humidity, this gross watery pumpion.
The Merry Wives of Windsor. Act iii, sc. 3, l. 42. [Mrs. Ford] The only use of "pumpion" (pumpkin). "Humidity" is used a second time in *Timon of Athens,* iv, 3, 2.

A man of continual dissolution and thaw.
The Merry Wives of Windsor. Act iii, sc. 5, l. 118. [Falstaff]

What, a hodge-pudding? a bag of flax?
The Merry Wives of Windsor. Act v, sc. 5, l. 159. [Ford] The only use of "hodge-pudding" (a pudding made of a medley of ingredients).

5
They would melt me out of my fat drop by drop and liquor fishermen's boots with me.
Merry Wives of Windsor. Act iv, sc. 5, l. 99. [Falstaff] "Drop by drop" is repeated in *I Henry IV,* i, 3, 134.

I am here a Windsor stag; and the fattest, I think, i' the forest. Send me a cool rut-time, Jove, or who can blame me to piss my tallow?
The Merry Wives of Windsor. Act v, sc. 5, l. 14. [Falstaff] The only use of "rut-time" and of "piss." "Pissing" occurs in *Two Gentlemen of Verona,* iv, 4, 21, and "pissing-conduit" in *II Henry VI,* iv, 6, 4. "Fattest" is used only once again, in *II Henry IV,* iv, 4, 54.

Frank'd up to fatting.—*Richard III,* i, 3, 314. The only use of "fatting."

6
It is the pasture lards the rother's sides,
The want that makes him lean.
Timon of Athens. Act iv, sc. 3, l. 12. [Timon] The only use of "rother" (steer or cow). For "lards" see under SWEAT.

FAULT

See also Defect, Imperfection, Trespass

I—Familiar Phrases

7
A man who is the abstract of all faults.
Antony and Cleopatra. Act i, sc. 4, l. 9. [Cæsar]

His faults in him seem as the spots of heaven,
More fiery by night's blackness; hereditary,
Rather than purchased.
Antony and Cleopatra. Act i, sc. 4, l. 12. [Lepidus]

8
What mean you, madam? I have made no fault.
Antony and Cleopatra. Act ii, sc. 5, l. 74. [Messenger]

O, that his fault should make a knave of thee.
Antony and Cleopatra. Act ii, sc. 5, l. 102. [Cleopatra]

9
Let me the knowledge of my fault bear with me.
As You Like It. Act i, sc. 3, l. 48. [Rosalind]

Every one fault seeming monstrous till his fellow-fault came to match it.
As You Like It. Act iii, sc. 2, l. 372. [Rosalind] The only use of "fellow-fault,"

10
She will score your fault upon my pate.
The Comedy of Errors. Act i, sc. 2, l. 65. [Dromio of Ephesus]

11
That 's not my fault.
The Comedy of Errors. Act ii, sc. 1, l. 228. [Adriana]

'Tis not my fault.—*Venus and Adonis,* l. 1003.

It is no fault of mine.
Love's Labour's Lost. Act iv, sc. 3, l. 71. [Longaville] Repeated in *The Passionate Pilgrim,* l. 40.

Hermia: His folly, Helena, is no fault of mine.
Helena: None, but your beauty: would that fault were mine!
A Midsummer-Night's Dream. Act i, sc. 1, l. 200.

Your fault was not your folly.
King John. Act i, sc. 1, l. 262. [Bastard]

Take it for your own fault and not mine.
Henry V. Act iv, sc. 8, l. 57. [Williams]

Alas the day! good heart, that was not her fault.
The Merry Wives of Windsor. Act iii, sc. 5, l. 39. [Mistress Quickly]

That 's no fault of his.
Cymbeline. Act ii, sc. 3, l. 62. [Cymbeline]

'Tis not his fault, the spark.
All's Well that Ends Well. Act ii, sc. 1, l. 25. [Parolles]

1
It is a fault that springeth from your eye.
The Comedy of Errors. Act iii, sc. 2, l. 55. [Luciana]
A grievous fault!—*The Comedy of Errors,* v, 1, 206.
2
He hath faults, with surplus, to tire in repetition.
Coriolanus. Act i, sc. 1, l. 46. [Citizen] "Surplus" is repeated in *The Winter's Tale,* v, 3, 7.
Menenius: In what enormity is Marcius poor in, that you two have not in abundance?
Brutus: He 's poor in no one fault, but stored with all.
Sicinius: Especially in pride.
Brutus: And topping all others in boasting.
Coriolanus. Act ii, sc. 1, l. 18. The only use of "enormity."
3
My fault being nothing—as I have told you oft.
Cymbeline. Act iii, sc. 3, l. 65. [Belarius]
4 Fie! 'tis a fault to heaven,
A fault against the dead, a fault to nature,
To reason most absurd.
Hamlet. Act i, sc. 2, l. 101. [King]
Breathe his faults so quaintly
That they may seem the taints of liberty,
The flash and outbreak of a fiery mind,
A savageness in unreclaimed blood.
Hamlet. Act i, sc. 5, l. 31. [Polonius] The only use of "unreclaimed."
Then I 'll look up; My fault is past.
Hamlet. Act iii, sc. 3, l. 51. [King]
5
Either envy, therefore, or misprision
Is guilty of this fault.
I Henry IV. Act i, sc. 3, l. 27. [Northumberland]
Their faults are open.—*Henry V,* ii, 2, 142.
6 See here the tainture of thy nest,
And look thyself be faultless, thou wert best.
II Henry VI. Act ii, sc. 1, l. 188. [Queen Margaret] The only use of "tainture." "Faultless" is used only twice more in the plays: again in the first play, *II Henry VI,* iii, 2, 24, and in the fourth play, *Richard III,* i, 3, 178.
Will you blame and lay the fault on me?
I Henry VI. Act ii, sc. 1, l. 57. [La Pucelle]
He were not privy to those faults.
II Henry VI. Act iii, sc. 1, l. 47. [Suffolk]
Tut, these are petty faults to faults unknown,
Which time will bring to light.
II Henry VI. Act iii, sc. 1, l. 64. [Buckingham]
7
I am faulty.
II Henry VI, iii, 2, 202. "Faulty" is used twice more in the plays: *I Henry IV,* iii, 2, 27, and *Henry VIII,* v, 3, 75.
8
O, 'tis a fault too too unpardonable!
III Henry VI. Act i, sc. 4, l. 106. [Queen Margaret] The only use of "unpardonable."
Ah, what a shame! ah, what a fault were this!
III Henry VI. Act v, sc. 4, l. 12. [Queen Margaret]
Whose fault is this?—*Henry VIII,* i, 4, 43.
Is this her fault or mine?—*Measure for Measure,* ii, 2, 162.
I dare make faults.—*Henry VIII,* ii, 1, 71.
I made a little fault.—*Love's Labour 's Lost,* v, 2, 562.
9
His faults lie gently on him!
Henry VIII. Act iv, sc. 2, l. 31. [Katharine]
10
The fault, dear Brutus, is not in our stars,
But in ourselves, that we are underlings.
Julius Cæsar. Act i, sc. 2, l. 140. [Cassius] The only use of "underlings."
11
Brutus: I do not like your faults.
Cassius: A friendly eye could never see such faults.
Brutus: A flatterer's would not, though they do appear
As huge as high Olympus.
Julius Cæsar. Act iv, sc. 3, l. 89.
All his faults observed,
Set in a note-book, learn'd, and conn'd by rote,
To cast into my teeth.
Julius Cæsar. Act iv, sc. 3, l. 97. [Cassius] "Note-book" is repeated in *II Henry IV,* ii, 4, 290, and in *The Merry Wives of Windsor,* i, 1, 147.
Full of faults.—*Julius Cæsar,* i, 3, 45.
12
And oftentimes excusing of a fault
Doth make the fault the worse by the excuse,
As patches set upon a little breach
Discredit more in hiding of the fault
Than did the fault before it was so patch'd.
King John. Act iv, sc. 2, l. 30. [Pembroke]
Who cover faults, at last shame them derides.
King Lear. Act i, sc. 1, l. 284. [Cordelia] The only use of "derides."
13
The image of a wicked heinous fault
Lives in his eye.
King John. Act iv, sc. 2, l. 71. [Pembroke]
Vile fault.—*Titus Andronicus,* v, 2, 173.
14
Do you smell a fault?
King Lear. Act i, sc. 1, l. 16. [Gloucester]
O most small fault,
How ugly didst thou in Cordelia show!
That, like an engine, wrench'd thy frame of nature
From the fix'd place.
King Lear. Act i, sc. 4, l. 288. [King Lear]
15 We are made to be no stronger
Than faults may shake our frames.
Measure for Measure. Act ii, sc. 4, l. 132. [Angelo]
That we were all, as some would seem to be,
From our faults, as faults from seeming, free!
Measure for Measure. Act iii, sc. 2, l. 40. [Duke]
16
They say, best men are moulded out of faults;
And, for the most, become much more the better
For being a little bad.
Measure for Measure. Act v, sc. 1, l. 444. [Mariana]

Give us Some faults to make us men.
Antony and Cleopatra. Act v, sc. 1, l. 32. [Agrippa]

1
O, what a world of vile ill-favour'd faults
Looks handsome in three hundred pounds a-year!
The Merry Wives of Windsor. Act iii, sc. 4, l. 32. [Anne]

Take her with all faults, and money enough.
The Taming of the Shrew. Act i, sc. 1, l. 133. [Hortensio]

Speed: 'She hath more hair than wit, and more faults than hairs, and more wealth than faults.'
Launce: More hair than wit? It may be: I 'll prove it. . . .
Speed: 'And more faults than hairs,'—
Launce: That 's monstrous: Oh, that that were out!
Speed: 'And more wealth than faults.'
Launce: Why, that word makes the faults gracious.
The Two Gentlemen of Verona. Act iii, sc. 1, l. 361.

Faults that are rich are fair.
Timon of Athens. Act i, sc. 2, l. 13. [Timon]

2
A fault done first in the form of a beast. O Jove, a beastly fault! And then another fault in the semblance of a fowl; think on 't, Jove; a foul fault!
The Merry Wives of Windsor. Act v, sc. 5, l. 9. [Falstaff]

That 's a foul fault.—*Henry V*, iii, 2, 148.

Of all the faults beneath the heavens, the gods
Do like this worst.
Pericles. Act iv, sc. 3, l. 20. [Cleon]

3
The fault unknown is as a thought unacted.
The Rape of Lucrece, l. 527. The only use of "unacted."

For marks descried in men's nativity
Are nature's faults, not their own infamy.
The Rape of Lucrece, l. 538.

4
Men's faults do seldom to themselves appear;
Their own transgressions partially they smother.
The Rape of Lucrece, l. 633. For "transgression" see under TRESPASS.

5
This is my fault.
Richard II. Act i, sc. 1, l. 142. [Mowbray]

'Tis my fault, Master Page; I suffer for it.
The Merry Wives of Windsor. Act iii, sc. 3, l. 233. [Ford]

'Tis partly my own fault.
A Midsummer-Night's Dream. Act iii, sc. 2, l. 243. [Helena]

'Tis your fault, 'tis your fault.
The Merry Wives of Windsor. Act i, sc. 1, l. 95. [Shallow] *Venus and Adonis,* l. 381.

The fault is thine.—*Rape of Lucrece,* l. 482.

The fault 's your own.—*The Tempest,* ii, 1, 135.

Let it be his fault.—*Measure for Measure,* ii, 2, 35.

That is a fault.—*Othello,* iii, 4, 54.

I take the fault on me.—*Twelfth Night,* iii, 4, 344.

6
His fault concludes but what the law should end.
Romeo and Juliet. Act iii, sc. 1, l. 190. [Montague]

His faults lie open to the laws; let them,
Not you, correct him.
Henry VIII. Act iii, sc. 2, l. 334. [Lord Chamberlain]

7
All men make faults.
Sonnets. No. xxxv.

Nobody but has his fault.
The Merry Wives of Windsor. Act i, sc. 4, l. 15. [Mistress Quickly]

Every man has his fault.
Timon of Athens. Act iii, sc. 1, l. 29. [Lucullus]

All the kind of the Launces have this very fault.
The Two Gentlemen of Verona. Act ii, sc. 3, l. 2. [Launce]

8
Upon my part I can set down a story
Of faults conceal'd.
Sonnets. No. lxxxviii.

Say that thou didst forsake me for some fault,
An I will comment upon that offence.
Sonnets. No. lxxxix.

Some say thy fault is youth, some wantonness;
Some say thy grace is youth and gentle sport;
Both grace and faults are loved of more and less;
Thou makest faults graces that to thee resort.
Sonnets. No. xcvi.

9
Hortensio, have you told him all her faults?
The Taming of the Shrew. Act i, sc. 2, l. 187. [Gremio]

Her only fault, and that is faults enough,
Is that she is intolerable curst
And shrewd and froward.
The Taming of the Shrew. Act i, sc. 2, l. 88. [Hortensio]

Patience, I pray you; 'tis a fault unwilling.
The Taming of the Shrew. Act iv, sc. 1, l. 159. [Katharina]

10 My honest-natured friends,
I must needs say you have a little fault.
Timon of Athens. Act v, sc. 1, l. 89. [Timon] The only use of "honest-natured."

11 We cite our faults,
That they may hold excused our lawless lives.
The Two Gentlemen of Verona. Act iv, sc. 1, l. 53. [First Outlaw]

12
You have tripp'd since.
The Winter's Tale. Act i, sc. 2, l. 76. [Hermione]

13 I cannot
Believe this crack to be in my dread mistress.
The Winter's Tale. Act i, sc. 2, l. 321. [Camillo]

Sans crack or flaw.
Love's Labour 's Lost, v, 2, 415. See under LOVE. The only use of "flaw" in the sense of fault or blemish, but the word is remarkable for the fact that, while it occurs only eleven

times in the plays and poems, it is used in no less than six meanings. See under WIND.

Howe'er the business goes, you have made fault
I' the boldness of your speech.
The Winter's Tale. Act iii, sc. 2, l. 218. [Lord]

1
Whilst I remember
Her and her virtues, I cannot forget
My blemishes in them.
Winter's Tale. Act v, sc. 1, l. 6. [Leontes]

Read not my blemishes in the world's report.
Antony and Cleopatra. Act ii, sc. 3, l. 5. [Antony]

The blemish that will never be forgot.
Rape of Lucrece, l. 536. See under SHAME.

She thought he spied in her some blemish.
Rape of Lucrece, l. 1358. See BLUSHING, 115:9.

No blemish.—*Twelfth Night,* iii, 4, 401; *The Winter's Tale,* i, 2, 341.

Not a blemish.—*The Tempest,* i, 2, 218.

Without blemish.—*Measure for Measure,* v, 1, 108.

Constrain'd blemishes.—*Antony and Cleopatra,* iii, 13, 59.

II—Faults: Their Forgiveness

2
No way excuse his soils, when we do bear
So great weight in his lightness.
Antony and Cleopatra. Act i, sc. 4, l. 24. [Cæsar]

Free from soil.—*Measure for Measure,* v, 1, 141.

Shield from soil.—*Henry VIII,* i, 2, 26.

Our faults
Can never be so equal, that your love
Can equally move with them.
Antony and Cleopatra. Act iii, sc. 4, l. 34. [Antony]

3
Orlando: I will chide no breather in the world but myself, against whom I know most faults.
Jaques: The worst fault you have is to be in love.
Orlando: 'Tis a fault I will not change for your best virtue.
As You Like It. Act iii, sc. 2, l. 297.

4
What faults he made before the last, I think
Might have found easy fines.
Coriolanus. Act v, sc. 6, l. 64. [First Lord]

5
I forgive and quite forget old faults.
III Henry VI. Act iii, sc. 3, l. 200. [Queen Margaret]

I do remit these young men heinous faults.
Titus Andronicus. Act i, sc. 1, l. 484. [Saturninus]

For these earthly faults, I quit thee all.
Measure for Measure. Act v, sc. 1, l. 488. [Duke]

I do forgive The rankest fault.
The Tempest. Act v, sc. 1, l. 131. [Prospero]

6
Rich conceit
Taught thee to make vast Neptune weep for aye
On thy low grave, on faults forgiven.
Timon of Athens. Act v, sc. 4, l. 77. [Alcibiades]

That shall be the ransom for their fault.
Titus Andronicus. Act iii, sc. 1, l. 156. [Aaron]

III—Faults: Their Punishment

7
Taunt my faults
With such full licence as both truth and malice
Have power to utter. O, then we bring forth weeds,
When our quick minds lie still; and our ills told us
Is as our earing.
Antony and Cleopatra. Act i, sc. 2, l. 111. [Antony] The only use of "earing"

To suffer lawful censure for such faults
As shall be proved upon you.
Coriolanus. Act iii, sc. 3, l. 46. [Sicinius]

The fault Would not 'scape censure.
King Lear. Act i, sc. 4, l. 228. [Goneril]

8
Know, if you kill me for my fault, I should
Have died had I not made it.
Cymbeline. Act iii, sc. 6, l. 57. [Imogen]

Gods! if you
Should have ta'en vengeance on my faults, I never
Had lived to put on this.
Cymbeline. Act v, sc. 1, l. 7. [Posthumus]

You snatch some hence for little faults; that 's love,
To have them fall no more: you some permit
To second ills with ills, each elder worse,
And make them dread it, to the doers' thrift.
Cymbeline. Act v, sc. 1, l. 12. [Posthumus]

9
I did correct him for his fault.
II Henry VI. Act i, sc. 3, l. 202. [Horner]

10
And he that throws not up his cap for joy
Shall for the fault make forfeit of his head.
III Henry VI. Act ii, sc. 1, l. 196. [Warwick]

His fault is much, and the good king his master
Will check him for 't.
King Lear. Act ii, sc. 2, l. 148. [Gloucester]

11
Condemn the fault, and not the actor of it?
Why, every fault 's condemned ere it be done:
Mine were the very cipher of a function,
To find the faults whose fine stands in record,
And let go by the actor.
Measure for Measure. Act ii, sc. 2, l. 37. [Angelo]

Thy fault 's thus manifested;
Which, though thou wouldst deny, denies thee vantage.
Measure for Measure. Act v, sc. 1, l. 417. [Duke]

12
Shame to him whose cruel striking
Kills for faults of his own liking!
Measure for Measure. Act iii, sc. 2, l. 281. [Duke]

It imports no reason
That with such vehemency he should pursue
Faults proper to himself.
Measure for Measure. Act v, sc. 1, l. 110. [Duke] "Vehemency" is repeated in *The Merry Wives of Windsor,* ii, 2, 247, and in *Henry VIII,* v, 1, 148.

Wilt thou whip thine own faults in other men?
Timon of Athens. Act v, sc. 1, l. 40. [Timon]

1
O, had it been a stranger, not my child,
To smooth his fault I should have been more mild.
Richard II. Act i, sc. 3, l. 239. [Gaunt]

2 The fault 's
Bloody; 'tis necessary he should die.
Timon of Athens. Act iii, sc. 5, l. 1. [Senator]

This fell fault of my accursed sons,
Accursed, if the fault be proved in them.
Titus Andronicus. Act ii, sc. 3, l. 290. [Titus]

For their fell faults their brothers were beheaded.
Titus Andronicus. Act v, sc. 3, l. 100. [Lucius] The only uses of "fell fault."

3
But were you banish'd for so small a fault?
The Two Gentlemen of Verona. Act iv, sc. 1, l. 31. [First Outlaw]

Poor wretch,
That for thy mother's fault art thus exposed
To loss and what may follow.
The Winter's Tale. Act iii, sc. 3, l. 49. [Antigonus]

IV—Faults: Their Repentance

4
By our remembrances of days foregone,
Such were our faults, or then we thought them none.
All's Well that Ends Well. Act i, sc. 3, l. 140. [Countess]

Our rash faults
Make trivial price of serious things we have,
Not knowing them until we know their grave.
All's Well that Ends Well. Act v, sc. 3, l. 60. [King]

5
And I repent my fault more than my death;
Which I beseech your highness to forgive,
Although my body pay the price of it.
Henry V. Act ii, sc. 2, l. 152. [Scroop]

My fault, but not my body, pardon, sovereign.
Henry V. Act ii, sc. 2, l. 165. [Grey]

6 Do not frown upon my faults,
For I will henceforth be no more unconstant.
III Henry VI. Act v, sc. 1, l. 101. [Clarence]

I thought it was a fault, but knew it not;
Yet did repent me, after more advice.
Measure for Measure. Act v, sc. 1, l. 468. [Provost]

7
It hath pleased the devil drunkenness to give place to the devil wrath: one unperfectness shows me another, to make me frankly despise myself.
Othello. Act ii, sc. 3, l. 297. [Cassio] The only use of "unperfectness."

8 Would it might please your grace,
At our entreaties, to amend that fault!
Richard III. Act iii, sc. 7, l. 114. [Buckingham]

Antipholus of Syracuse: That 's a fault that water will mend.
Dromio of Syracuse: No, sir, 'tis in grain; Noah's flood could not do it.
The Comedy of Errors. Act iii, sc. 2, l. 107. Noah is mentioned again in *Twelfth Night,* iii, 2, 18.

You must needs learn, lord, to amend this fault:
Though sometimes it show greatness, courage, blood,—
And that 's the dearest grace it renders you,—
Yet oftentimes it doth present harsh rage,
Defect of manners, want of government,
Pride, haughtiness, opinion and disdain.
I Henry IV. Act iii, sc. 1, l. 180. [Worcester] The only use of "haughtiness."

Two faults, madonna, that drink and good counsel will amend.
Twelfth Night. Act i, sc. 5, l. 47. [Clown]

9
There 's something in me that reproves my fault;
But such a headstrong potent fault it is,
That it but mocks reproof.
Twelfth Night. Act iii, sc. 4, l. 223. [Olivia]

10
Pardon the fault, I pray.
The Two Gentlemen of Verona. Act i, sc. 2, l. 40. [Lucetta]

Pardon this fault, and by my soul I swear
I never more will break an oath with thee.
The Merchant of Venice. Act v, sc. 1, l. 247. [Bassanio]

Pardon me all the faults I have committed to your worship.
The Winter's Tale, v, 2, 160. [Autolycus]

11
All faults I make, when I shall come to know them,
I do repent.
The Winter's Tale. Act iii, sc. 2, l. 220. [Paulina]

No fault could you make,
Which you have not redeem'd.
The Winter's Tale. Act v, sc. 1, l. 2. [Cleomemes]

FAVOUR

See also Benefit, Gift, Kindness

12
Certain it is, that he will steal himself into a man's favour.
All's Well that Ends Well. Act iii, sc. 6, l. 98. [First Lord]

Give a favour from you
To sparkle in the spirits of my daughter,
That she may quickly come.
All's Well that Ends Well. Act v, sc. 3, l. 74. [Lafeu]

By thy favour.—*Love's Labour 's Lost,* iii, 1, 68.
By your favour.—*All's Well that Ends Well,* iv, 3, 245; *King Lear,* iv, 6, 215; *Twelfth Night,* ii, 4, 25.
By your good favour.—*Henry VIII,* v, 3, 74.
For your favour.—*Much Ado about Nothing,* iii, 3, 19.

1
Favours, by Jove that thunders!
Antony and Cleopatra. Act iii, sc. 13, l. 85. [Antony]
He did ask favour.—*Antony and Cleopatra,* iii, 13, 133.
2
I will favour thee in what I can.
The Comedy of Errors. Act i, sc. 1, l. 150. [Duke]
3
Uncertain favour!
Cymbeline. Act iii, sc. 3, l. 64. [Guiderius]
Fairy favours.—*A Midsummer-Night's Dream,* ii, 1, 12.
Gracious favours.—*Henry V,* ii, 2, 9.
Sweet favour.—*All's Well that Ends Well,* i, 1, 107; *A Midsummer-Night's Dream,* iv, 1, 54; *Sonnets,* cxiii.
4
Many dream not to find, neither deserve,
And yet are steep'd in favours.
Cymbeline. Act v, sc. 4, l. 130. [Posthumus]
His favour is familiar to me.—*Cymbeline,* v, 5, 93. For favour in the sense of appearance, see under APPEARANCE.
5
For Hamlet and the trifling of his favour,
Hold it a fashion and a toy in blood.
Hamlet. Act i, sc. 3, l. 5. [Laertes]
I'll court his favours.—*Hamlet,* v, 2, 78.
I beg no favour.—*II Henry VI,* ii, 4, 92.
6
Let my favours hide thy mangled face.
I Henry IV. Act v, sc. 4, l. 96. [Prince of Wales]
Wear thou this favour for me and stick it in thy cap.
Henry V. Act iv, sc. 7, l. 160. [King Henry]
That a' wears next his heart for a favour.—*Love's Labour's Lost,* v, 2, 721. See under SHIRT.
This favour thou shalt wear.—*Love's Labour's Lost,* v, 2, 130.
Wear the favours most in sight.—*Love's Labour's Lost,* v, 2, 136.
Wear it as a favour.—*Richard II,* v, 3, 18.
7
Captain, I thee beseech to do me favours!
Henry V. Act iii, sc. 6, l. 22. [Pistol]
Do me the favour.—*Comedy of Errors,* i, 1, 123.
Do thee favours.—*Richard II,* iii, 2, 11.
Pray, give me favour.—*Henry VIII,* i, 1, 168.
Show favour.—*Twelfth Night,* iii, 2, 19.
Throwing favours.—*Cymbeline,* iii, 5, 75.
8
Your royal graces,
Shower'd on me daily, have been more than could
My studied purposes requite.
Henry VIII. Act iii, sc. 2, l. 166. [Wolsey] The only use of "shower'd."
Secure in grace and favour.—*Richard III,* iii, 4, 93.
Grace and favour.—*King Lear,* i, 1, 232; *Othello,* iv, 3, 21.
9
Do I not know you for a favourer
Of this new sect?
Henry VIII. Act v, sc. 3, l. 80. [Gardiner]
Favourers of my right.—*Titus Andronicus,* i, 1, 9.
Favourer to the Briton.—*Cymbeline,* v, 3, 74.
Come to us as favourers.—*Pericles,* i, 4, 73.
The only uses of "favourer" and "favourers."
10
As thou wilt win my favour, good my knave,
Do one thing for me that I shall entreat.
Love's Labour's Lost. Act iii, sc. 1, l. 153. [Biron]
If you my favour mean to get,
A twelvemonth shall you spend, and never rest,
But seek the weary beds of people sick.
Love's Labour's Lost. Act v, sc. 2, l. 830. [Rosaline]
11
A thousand favours from a maund she drew
Of amber, crystal, and of beaded jet.
A Lover's Complaint, l. 36. The only use of "maund," a word, now obsolete, meaning basket or hamper.
12
To alter favour ever is to fear.
Macbeth. Act i, sc. 5, l. 73. [Lady Macbeth]
13
To buy his favour, I extend this friendship.
The Merchant of Venice. Act i, sc. 3, l. 169. [Shylock]
14
I am in the favour of Margaret, the waiting gentlewoman.
Much Ado about Nothing. Act ii, sc. 2, l. 13. [Borachio]
Let those who are in favour . . . boast.
Sonnets. No. xxv. See under STAR.
In favour.—*King John,* ii, 1, 393; *Othello,* iii, 4, 125; *Twelfth Night,* iii, 4, 416.
In your favour.—*Twelfth Night,* v, 1, 126.
15
She show'd him favours to allure his eye.
The Passionate Pilgrim, l. 48.
16
Neither my good word nor princely favour.
Richard II. Act v, sc. 6, l. 42. [Bolingbroke]
Princes' favours.—*Henry VIII,* iii, 2, 367.
Ladies' favours.—*Henry V,* ii, 1, 47.
People's favour.—*Titus Andronicus,* i, 1, 54.
Favour of the king.—*All's Well that Ends Well,* ii, 3, 184; *Henry VIII,* iii, 2, 103.
Favours of so good a king.—*All's Well that Ends Well,* iii, 2, 31.
Favour of the climate.—*Winter's Tale,* ii, 3, 179.
Favour of my country.—*Titus Andronicus,* i, 1, 58.
Favour of speech.—*Othello,* iii, 1, 28.
Favours of the world.—*II Henry VI,* i, 2, 4.
17
Since I am crept in favour with myself,
I will maintain it with some little cost.
Richard III. Act i, sc. 2, l. 259. [Gloucester]
Keep in favour.—*Richard III,* i, 1, 79.
18
O, what more favour can I do to thee,
Than with that hand that cut thy youth in twain
To sunder his that was thine enemy?
Romeo and Juliet. Act v, sc. 3, l. 98. [Romeo]
19
Good my lord, give me thy favour still.
The Tempest. Act iv, sc. 1, l. 204. [Caliban]
Give me your favour.—*Macbeth,* i, 3, 149.
Deign this favour.—*Venus and Adonis,* l. 15.

1
Confirm his welcome with some special favour.
The Two Gentlemen of Verona. Act ii, sc. 4, l. 101. [Valentine]
Hospitable favours.—*King Lear,* iii, 7, 40.
2
Thank me for this more than for all the favours
Which all too much I have bestow'd on thee.
The Two Gentlemen of Verona. Act iii, sc. 1, l. 161. [Duke]
3
If you prized my lady's favour at any thing more than contempt, you would not give means for this uncivil rule.
Twelfth Night. Act ii, sc. 3, l. 130. [Malvolio]
Take 't for a great favour.—*Twelfth Night,* iii, 2, 89. "Great favour" is repeated in *II Henry VI,* i, 1, 71.
So great a favour.—*The Two Gentlemen of Verona,* ii, 4, 161.
Greatest favour.—*II Henry VI,* i, 1, 192.
Favour infinite.—*The Two Gentlemen of Verona,* ii, 1, 60.
4 Tell me, in the modesty of honour,
Why you have given me such clear lights of favour.
Twelfth Night. Act v, sc. 1, l. 343. [Malvolio]
5
Methinks My favour here begins to warp.
The Winter's Tale. Act i, sc. 2, l. 364. [Polixenes]
The crown and comfort of my life, your favour,
I do give lost.
The Winter's Tale. Act iii, sc. 2, l. 95. [Hermione]
Fall'n from favour.—*Henry VIII,* iii, 1, 20.
Lost his favour.—*Antony and Cleopatra,* iii, 1, 20.
Out of favour.—*King Lear,* i, 4, 112; *Twelfth Night,* ii, 5, 9.
Out of her favour.—*Romeo and Juliet,* i, 1, 174.
Out of your favours.—*Love's Labour 's Lost,* v, 2, 166.

FAWNING

See also Servility

6
No, let the candied tongue lick absurd pomp,
And crook the pregnant hinges of the knee
Where thrift may follow fawning.
Hamlet. Act iii, sc. 2, l. 65. [Hamlet] "Pregnant" is used fourteen times in the plays, but never in the sense of enceinte.
Fawning greyhound.—*I Henry IV,* i, 3, 252; *Coriolanus,* i, 6, 38.
Fawning publican.—*The Merchant of Venice,* i, 3, 42.
Fawning smiles.—*The Two Gentlemen of Verona,* iii, 1, 158. The only uses of "fawning."
7
Forbear to fawn upon their frowns.
III Henry VI. Act iv, sc. 1, l. 75. [King Edward]
8
If thou dost bend and pray and fawn for him,
I spurn thee like a cur out of my way.
Julius Cæsar. Act iii, sc. 1, l. 45. [Cæsar]
You show'd your teeth like apes, and fawn'd like hounds,
And bow'd like bondmen.
Julius Cæsar. Act v, sc. 1, l. 41. [Antony]
They that fawn'd on him before
Use his company no more.
The Passionate Pilgrim, l. 421. The only uses of "fawn'd."
9
How would I make him fawn and beg and seek.
Love's Labour 's Lost. Act v, sc. 2, l. 62. [Rosaline]
10
The more you beat me, I will fawn on you.
A Midsummer-Night's Dream, ii, 1, 204. See under Dog.
I am too old to fawn upon a nurse.
Richard II, i, 3, 170. See under Age.
Easily won to fawn on any man.
Richard II, iii, 2, 130. See under Dog.
Fawn on men.—*Julius Cæsar,* i, 2, 75.
Fawn on rage.—*Richard II,* v, 1, 33.
Fawn upon his debts.—*Timon of Athens,* iii, 4, 51.

FEAR

See also Hope and Fear; Terror

I—Familiar Phrases

11 I lodge in fear;
Though this a heavenly angel, hell is here.
Cymbeline. Act ii, sc. 2, l. 49. [Iachimo]
On good ground we fear.
Cymbeline. Act iv, sc. 2, l. 143. [Belarius]
The fear 's as bad as falling.—*Cymbeline,* iii, 3, 49.
12
It harrows me with fear and wonder.
Hamlet. Act i, sc. 1, l. 44. [Horatio]
Harrow up thy soul.—*Hamlet,* i, 5, 16.
Plough Rome, harrow Italy.—*Coriolanus,* v, 3, 34. The only uses of "harrow" and "harrows."
13
What, frighted with false fire!
Hamlet. Act iii, sc. 2, l. 277. [Hamlet]
How have I frighted thee?—*II Henry IV,* iii, 1, 6.
Shall I be frighted?—*Julius Cæsar,* iv, 3, 40.
Frighted out of fear.—*Antony and Cleopatra,* iii, 13, 196.
Frighted from my country.—*Pericles,* v, 3, 3.
14
I fear thee as I fear the roaring of the lion's whelp.
I Henry IV. Act iii, sc. 3, l. 166. [Falstaff]
A kind of fear Before not dreamt of.
I Henry IV. Act iv, sc. 1, l. 74. [Worcester]
You speak it out of fear and cold heart.
I Henry IV. Act iv, sc. 3, l. 7. [Douglas]
Possess'd with fear.—*I Henry IV,* ii, 2, 112.
Full of fear.—*Venus and Adonis,* l. 320.
15
Here 's a goodly tumult! I 'll forswear keeping house, afore I 'll be in these tirrits and frights.
II Henry IV. Act ii, sc. 4, l. 219. [Hostess] The only use of "tirrits" (terrors).

Pure fear and entire cowardice.
II Henry IV. Act ii, sc. 4, l. 352. [Prince Henry]
Absolute fear.—*Macbeth,* iv, 3, 38.
Cold fear.—*Henry V,* iv, Prol., 45.
Common fear.—*III Henry VI,* ii, 1, 126.
Conjectural fears.—*All's Well that Ends Well,* v, 3, 114. "Conjectural" is repeated in *Coriolanus,* i, 1, 198: "Conjectural marriages."
Distracted fear.—*Midsummer-Night's Dream,* iii, 2, 31.
Filial fears.—*A Lover's Complaint,* l. 270.
Great fear.—*I Henry VI,* i, 4, 50; *Antony and Cleopatra,* ii, 2, 135.
Guilty fear.—*Richard III,* v, 3, 142.
Living fear.—*Richard II,* v, 4, 2.
Pale fear.—*The Rape of Lucrece,* l. 1775.
Recanting fear.—*Richard II,* i, 1, 193. "Recanting" is repeated in *Timon of Athens,* i, 2, 17: "Recanting goodness."
Religious fear.—*Hamlet,* iii, 3, 8.
Shuddering fear.—*The Merchant of Venice,* iii, 2, 110. The only use of "shuddering." "Shudder" occurs in *Timon of Athens,* iv, 3, 137, and in *Venus and Adonis,* l. 880.
Trembling fear.—*The Rape of Lucrece,* l. 511.
True fear.—*Coriolanus,* iii, 1, 134; *Macbeth,* iii, 4, 64.
Vassal fear.—*I Henry IV,* iii, 2, 124.

1
Brothers, you mix your sadness with some fear.
II Henry IV. Act v, sc. 2, l. 46. [King Henry V] The only use of "mix."

2
She hath been then more fear'd than harm'd.
Henry V. Act i, sc. 2, l. 155. [Canterbury]

3
Of all base passions, fear is most accursed.
I Henry VI. Act v, sc. 2, l. 18. [La Pucelle]
Alas, it is the baseness of thy fear
That makes thee strangle thy propriety.
Twelfth Night. Act v, sc. 1, l. 149. [Olivia]
Base fear.—*All's Well that Ends Well,* iii, 6, 31.

4
Nor durst come near for fear of sudden death.
I Henry VI. Act i, sc. 4, l. 48. [Talbot]
Fear of death.—*The Comedy of Errors,* v, 1, 195; *Measure for Measure,* iii, 1, 132.
Fear death.—*Julius Cæsar,* i, 2, 89; *Henry VIII,* ii, 1, 37.
Fear to die.—*The Winter's Tale,* iii, 2, 109.
Fearing death.—*Julius Cæsar,* iii, 1, 105.
Not fearing death.—*I Henry VI,* iv, 1, 37.
Past fearing death.—*Measure for Measure,* v, 1, 402.
Fear of burning.—*The Two Gentlemen of Verona,* i, 3, 78.
Fear of God.—*Love's Labour's Lost,* iv, 2, 152; *The Merry Wives of Windsor,* i, 1, 37; 38, 189; i, 2, 24.
Fear God.—*Much Ado about Nothing,* ii, 3, 201; ii, 3, 205.
Fear of harms.—*A Lover's Complaint,* l. 165.
Fear of my name.—*I Henry VI,* i, 4, 50.
For fear of slips.—*Venus and Adonis,* l. 515.

5
Ah, that my fear were false! ah, that it were!
II Henry VI. Act iii, sc. 1, l. 193. [Gloucester]
I fear me.—*II Henry VI,* i, 1, 150, and sixteen times in later plays.

6
Why come you not? what! multitudes, and fear?
III Henry VI. Act i, sc. 4, l. 39. [York]
By doubtful fear
My joy of liberty is half eclipsed.
III Henry VI. Act iv, sc. 6, l. 62. [King Henry]
So doth my heart misgive me, in these conflicts
What may befall him, to his harm and ours.
III Henry VI. Act iv, sc. 6, l. 94. [Somerset]

7
Die thou, and die our fear;
For Warwick was a bug that fear'd us all.
III Henry VI. Act v, sc. 2, l. 1. [King Edward]
Tush, tush! fear boys with bugs.
The Taming of the Shrew. Act i, sc. 2, l. 211. [Petruchio]
With, ho! such bugs and goblins in my life.
Hamlet. Act v, sc. 2, l. 22. [Hamlet]
Those that would die or ere resist are grown
The mortal bugs o' the field.
Cymbeline. Act v, sc. 3, l. 50. [Posthumus]
Sir, spare your threats:
The bug which you would fright me with I seek.
The Winter's Tale. Act iii, sc. 2, l. 92. [Hermione] The only uses of "bug" and "bugs," always in the sense of bogey.

8
The thief doth fear each bush an officer.
III Henry VI. Act v, sc. 6, l. 12. [Gloucester]
Or in the night, imagining some fear,
How easy is a bush supposed a bear!
A Midsummer-Night's Dream. Act v, sc. 1, l. 21. [Theseus]
And the dire thought of his committed evil
Shape every bush a hideous shapeless devil.
The Rape of Lucrece, l. 972.

9
I rather tell thee what is to be fear'd
Than what I fear.
Julius Cæsar. Act i, sc. 2, l. 211. [Cæsar]
Yet have I a mind
That fears him much; and my misgiving still
Falls shrewdly to the purpose.
Julius Cæsar. Act iii, sc. 1, l. 144. [Cassius] The only use of "misgiving."

10
For I am sick and capable of fears,
Oppress'd with wrongs and therefore full of fears.
King John. Act iii, sc. 1, l. 12. [Constance]
And more, more strong, then lesser is my fear.
King John. Act iv, sc. 2, l. 42. [King John]
Fears, which, as they say, attend
The steps of wrong.
King John. Act iv, sc. 2, l. 56. [Pembroke]
Subject to fears.—*King John,* iii, 1, 14.

11
Why seek'st thou to possess me with these fears?
King John. Act iv, sc. 2, l. 203. [King John]

Those thy fears might have wrought fears in me.
King John. Act iv, sc. 2, l. 236. [King John]
Inform her full of my particular fear;
And thereto add such reasons of your own
As may compact it more.
King Lear. Act i, sc. 4, l. 360. [Goneril]
That 's my fear.—*King Lear,* i, 2, 181.

1
Poor Tom hath been scared out of his good wits.
King Lear. Act iv, sc. 1, l. 59. [Edgar]
Scared from the use of wits.—*The Comedy of Errors,* v, 1, 86.
Fright the ladies out of their wits.—*A Midsummer-Night's Dream,* i, 2, 82.
Scared my choughs from the chaff.—*The Winter's Tale,* iv, 4, 630.

2
Duncan: Dismay'd not this Our captains?
Sergeant: As sparrows eagles, or the hare the lion.
Macbeth. Act i, sc. 2, l. 35.
She shall not dismay me: I care not for that, but that I am afeard.
The Merry Wives of Windsor. Act iii, sc. 4, l. 27. [Slender] See under DISMAY.

3
Present fears
Are less than horrible imaginings.
Macbeth. Act i, sc. 3, l. 137. [Macbeth]
Yet I do fear thy nature.
Macbeth. Act i, sc. 5, l. 17. [Lady Macbeth]
Fears and scruples shake us.
Macbeth. Act ii, sc. 3, l. 135. [Banquo]
This is the very painting of your fear.
Macbeth. Act iii, sc. 4, l. 61. [Lady Macbeth]
My strange and self-abuse
Is the initiate fear that wants hard use.
Macbeth. Act iii, sc. 4, l. 142. [Macbeth] The only use of "self-abuse" and "initiate."
Thou hast harp'd my fear aright.
Macbeth. Act iv, sc. 1, l. 74. [Macbeth]

4
His flight was madness: when our actions do not,
Our fears do make us traitors.
Macbeth. Act iv, sc. 2, l. 3. [Lady Macduff]
All is the fear and nothing is the love.
Macbeth. Act iv, sc. 2, l. 12. [Lady Macduff]
I cannot taint with fear.
Macbeth. Act v, sc. 3, l. 3. [Macbeth]

5
To fright you thus, methinks, I am too savage.
Macbeth. Act iv, sc. 2, l. 70. [Messenger]
Fall in fright.—*Othello,* ii, 3, 232.
Intolerable fright.—*The Merry Wives of Windsor,* iii, 5, 110.

6
By 'r lakin, a parlous fear.
A Midsummer-Night's Dream. Act iii, sc. 1, l. 14. [Snout] "By 'r lakin" occurs only once more in the plays, in *The Tempest,* iii, 3, 1.
A most Christian-like fear.—*Much Ado about Nothing,* ii, 3, 200.

7
Let me be thought too busy in my fears.
Othello. Act iii, sc. 3, l. 253. [Iago]
O! my fear interprets.—*Othello,* v, 2, 73.

8
Which fear so grew in me, I hither fled,
Under the covering of a careful night.
Pericles. Act i, sc. 2, l. 80. [Pericles]
They fright him, yet he still pursues his fear.
The Rape of Lucrece, l. 308.

9
This ague fit of fear is over-blown.
Richard II. Act iii, sc. 2, l. 190. [King Richard]
Agued fear!—*Coriolanus,* i, 4, 38.

10
Yet am I sick with fear.
Richard II. Act v, sc. 3, l. 133. [Duchess of York]
I was not sick of any fear from thence.
Sonnets. No. lxxxvi.

11
I promise you, I am afraid to hear you tell it.
Richard III. Act i, sc. 4, l. 65. [Brakenbury]
I am afraid; and yet I 'll venture it.
King John. Act iv, sc. 3, l. 5. [Arthur]
I am afraid.—*I Henry IV,* iii, 1, 145; v, 4, 123; v, 4, 126; *The Taming of the Shrew,* v, 2, 88; *Twelfth Night,* iv, 1, 14; *Macbeth,* ii, 2, 10; ii, 2, 51; *The Tempest,* v, 1, 262; *Henry VIII,* iii, 2, 133.
I am almost afraid.—*Romeo and Juliet,* v, 3, 10.
Almost afraid.—*Macbeth,* iv, 3, 165.
I am half afraid.—*The Merry Wives of Windsor,* iii, 3, 193. The only use of the phrase.
He is afraid of me and I of him.
King John. Act iv, sc. 1, l. 21. [Arthur]
They are afraid.—*Venus and Adonis,* l. 898.
You are afraid, and therein the wiser.
Cymbeline. Act i, sc. 4, l. 146. [Iachimo]
You are afraid.—*The Merry Wives of Windsor,* i, 1, 304.
Are you all afraid?—*Richard III,* i, 2, 43.
Art thou afraid?—*Richard III,* i, 4, 111.
Seems afraid.—*The Passionate Pilgrim,* l. 274.
Afraid to fight.—*II Henry VI,* ii, 3, 57.

12
Come, come, we fear the worst.
Richard III. Act ii, sc. 3, l. 31. [Citizen]
For fear of the worst.—*The Merchant of Venice,* i, 2, 103.

13
Truly, the souls of men are full of dread.
Richard III. Act ii, sc. 3, l. 38. [Second Citizen] "Dread," as a noun, occurs only twice in the plays, as above and in *The Merchant of Venice,* iv, 1, 192: "The dread and fear of kings." But as an adjective it occurs frequently; four times in the first play, *II Henry VI,* alone: "dread King," iii, 2, 154; "dread lord," iii, 2, 243; "dread curses," iii, 2, 330; "dread liege," v, 1, 17.

14
Ye cannot reason almost with a man
That looks not heavily and full of fear.
Richard III. Act ii, sc. 3, l. 39. [Citizen]
Tell him his fears are shallow, wanting instance.
Richard III. Act iii, sc. 2, l. 25. [Hastings]
Intend some fear.—*Richard III,* iii, 7, 45.

15
For one being fear'd of all, now fearing one.
Richard III. Act iv, sc. 4, l. 103. [Queen Margaret]

Thou art less happy being fear'd
Than they in fearing.
Henry V. Act iv, sc. 1, l. 265. [King Henry]

1
O, much I fear some ill unlucky thing.
Romeo and Juliet. Act v, sc. 3, l. 136. [Friar Laurence]

What fear is this which startles in our ears?
Romeo and Juliet. Act v, sc. 3, l. 194. [Prince]

Ay, so I fear.—*Romeo and Juliet,* i, 5, 122.

We had cause of fear.—*Timon of Athens,* v, 4, 15.

I felt a kind of fear.—*Venus and Adonis,* l. 998.

2
Ne'er till now
Was I a child to fear I know not what.
Titus Andronicus. Act ii, sc. 3, l. 220. [Quintus]

3
Troilus: Fears make devils of cherubins; they never see truly.
Cressida: Blind fear, that seeing reason leads, finds safer footing than blind reason stumbling without fear: to fear the worst oft cures the worse.
Troilus and Cressida. Act iii, sc. 2, l. 74.

4
A plague break thy neck for frighting me!
Troilus and Cressida. Act v, sc. 4, l. 34. [Thersites]

Thou shalt be punish'd for thus frighting me.
King John. Act iii, sc. 1, l. 11. [Constance]

Frighting her pale-faced villages with war.
Richard II. Act ii, sc. 3, l. 94. [York] The only uses of "frighting" in the plays.

5
I am question'd by my fears.
Winter's Tale. Act i, sc. 2, l. 11. [Polixenes]

If ever fearful
To do a thing, where I the issue doubted,
Whereof the execution did cry out
Against the non-performance, 'twas a fear
Which oft infects the wisest.
The Winter's Tale. Act i, sc. 2, l. 258. [Camillo] The only use of "non-performance."

Fear o'ershades me.—*Winter's Tale,* i, 2, 457.

II—Fear: Its Effects

6
What 's the matter,
That this distemper'd messenger of wet,
The many-colour'd Iris, rounds thine eye?
All's Well that Ends Well. Act i, sc. 3, l. 156. [Countess] "Many-colour'd" is repeated in *The Tempest,* iv, 1, 76.

What, pale again?
My fear hath catch'd your fondness.
All's Well that Ends Well. Act i, sc. 3, l. 175. [Countess]

7
Put thyself
Into a haviour of less fear, ere wildness
Vanquish my staider senses.
Cymbeline. Act iii, sc. 4, l. 8. [Imogen] The only use of "staider." "Staid" does not appear in the plays.

Good faith, I tremble still with fear.
Cymbeline. Act iv, sc. 2, l. 302. [Imogen]

8
You tremble and look pale.
Hamlet. Act i, sc. 1, l. 53. [Bernardo]

Shiver and look pale,
Make periods in the midst of sentences.
A Midsummer-Night's Dream, v, 1, 95.

9
Distill'd Almost to jelly with the act of fear.
Hamlet. Act i, sc. 2, l. 204. [Horatio]

Pale as his shirt; his knees knocking each other.
Hamlet. Act ii, sc. 1, l. 81. [Ophelia]

10
But tell me, Hal, art not thou horrible afeard? . . . Art thou not horribly afraid? doth not thy blood thrill at it?
I Henry IV. Act ii, sc. 4, l. 401. [Falstaff] Shakespeare used "afeard" almost as often as "afraid"—thirty times for "afeard" to thirty-nine for "afraid."

11
The whiteness in thy cheek
Is apter than thy tongue to tell thy errand.
II Henry IV. Act i, sc. 1, l. 68. [Northumberland]

Feel, masters, how I shake; . . . in very truth, do I, an 'twere an aspen leaf.
II Henry IV. Act ii, sc. 4, l. 113. [Hostess]

Tremble, like aspen-leaves.—*Titus Andronicus,* ii, 4, 45. The only references to the aspen.

The fear whereof doth make him shake and shudder.
Venus and Adonis, l. 880.

How now, good fellow! why shakest thou so? Fear not, man; here 's no harm intended to thee.
Winter's Tale. Act iv, sc. 4, l. 640. [Camillo]

Shake and fear.—*Othello,* iii, 3, 207.

Shake with fear.—*Coriolanus,* v, 3, 100; *Macbeth,* v, 3, 10. See under DOUBT.

12
What see you in those papers that you lose
So much complexion? Look ye, how they change!
Their cheeks are paper.
Henry V. Act ii, sc. 2, l. 72. [King Henry]

He 'll drop his heart into the sink of fear.
Henry V. Act iii, sc. 5, l. 59. [Constable]

13
Dick: Why dost thou quiver, man?
Lord Say: The palsy, and not fear, provokes me.
II Henry VI. Act iv, sc. 7, l. 97. "Palsy" is repeated in *Richard II,* ii, 3, 104.

14
You look pale and gaze
And put on fear and cast yourself in wonder.
Julius Cæsar. Act i, sc. 3, l. 59. [Cassius]

That makest my blood cold and my hair to stare.
Julius Cæsar. Act iv, sc. 3, l. 280. [Brutus]

15
Good sir, why do you start; and seem to fear
Things that do sound so fair?
Macbeth. Act i, sc. 3, l. 51. [Banquo]

Death of thy soul! those linen cheeks of thine
Are counsellors to fear. . . . Whey-face!
Macbeth. Act v, sc. 3, l. 16. [Macbeth] The only use of "whey-face."

16
I quaked for fear.
The Merry Wives of Windsor. Act iii, sc. 5, l. 104. [Falstaff] "Quaked" is used only once again, in *Coriolanus,* i, 9, 5.

I do quake with fear.
A Midsummer-Night's Dream. Act ii, sc. 2, l. 148. [Hermia]

I swoon almost with fear.
A Midsummer-Night's Dream. Act ii, sc. 2, l. 154. [Hermia]

1
I fear you; for you are fatal then
When your eyes roll so: why I should fear I know not,
Since guiltiness I know not; but yet I feel I fear.
Othello. Act v, sc. 2, l. 37. [Desdemona]

2
Here pale with fear he doth premeditate
The dangers of this loathsome enterprise.
The Rape of Lucrece, l. 183.

And extreme fear can neither fight nor fly,
But coward-like with trembling terror die.
The Rape of Lucrece, l. 230. The only use of "coward-like."

O, how her fear did make her colour rise!
First red as roses that on lawn we lay,
Then white as lawn, the roses took away.
The Rape of Lucrece, l. 257.

Wrapp'd and confounded in a thousand fears,
Like to a new-kill'd bird she trembling lies.
The Rape of Lucrece, l. 456. "New-kill'd" is repeated in *Romeo and Juliet,* v, 3, 197.

Sweating with guilty fear.
The Rape of Lucrece, l. 740.

Such danger to resistance did belong,
That dying fear through all her body spread.
The Rape of Lucrece, l. 1265.

3
What, do you tremble? are you all afraid?
Richard III. Act i, sc. 2, l. 43. [Lady Anne]

Which of you trembles not that looks on me?
Richard III. Act i, sc. 3, l. 160. [Queen Margaret]

Cold fearful drops stand on my trembling flesh.
What do I fear? myself? there 's none else by.
Richard III. Act v, sc. 3, l. 181. [King Richard]

One would swear he saw them quake and tremble.
The Rape of Lucrece, l. 1393.

I fear'd thy fortune, and my joints did tremble.
Venus and Adonis, l. 642.

4
My hair doth stand on end.
Richard III, i, 3, 304. See under HAIR.

5
I have a faint cold fear thrills through my veins,
That almost freezes up the heat of life.
Romeo and Juliet. Act iv, sc. 3, l. 15. [Juliet]

6
Baptista: How now, my friend! why dost thou look so pale?
Hortensio: For fear, I promise you, if I look pale.
The Taming of the Shrew. Act ii, sc. 1, l. 143.

7
I am surprised with an uncouth fear:
A chilling sweat o'er-runs my trembling joints.
Titus Andronicus. Act ii, sc. 3, l. 211. [Quintus]

Fear hath made thee faint, as me it hath.
Titus Andronicus. Act ii, sc. 3, l. 234. [Martius]

8
He . . . pants and looks pale, as if a bear were at his heels.
Twelfth Night. Act iii, sc. 4, l. 323. [Fabian]

9
A sudden pale,
Like lawn being spread upon the blushing rose,
Usurps her cheek.
Venus and Adonis, l. 589.

Saw'st thou not signs of fear lurk in mine eye?
Venus and Adonis, l. 644.

A second fear through all her sinews spread,
Which madly hurries her she knows not whither.
Venus and Adonis, l. 903.

III—Woman's Fears

10
In my heart
Lie there what hidden woman's fear there will.
As You Like It. Act i, sc. 3, l. 120. [Rosalind]

If it be fond, call it a woman's fear.
II Henry VI. Act iii, sc. 1, l. 36. [Queen Margaret]

11
You wrong your virtues
With these weak women's fears.
Henry VIII. Act iii, sc. 1, l. 168. [Campeius]

A woman, naturally born to fears.
King John. Act iii, sc. 1, l. 15. [Constance]

Womanish fear.—*Romeo and Juliet.* Act iv, sc. 1, l. 119. [Friar Laurence]

IV—Absence of Fear

12
You shall not need to fear me.
All's Well that Ends Well. Act iii, sc. 5, l. 31. [Diana]

Fear me not, man.—*The Comedy of Errors,* iv, 4, 1; *Measure for Measure,* iv, 1, 70.

Tut, fear not me.—*The Taming of the Shrew,* iv, 4, 13.

Fear nothing.—*The Comedy of Errors,* v, 1, 185; *Othello,* v, 1, 3; *Antony and Cleopatra,* v, 2, 22; *Henry VIII,* v, 1, 125.

13
Thou canst not fear us, Pompey, with thy sails.
Antony and Cleopatra. Act ii, sc. 6, l. 24. [Antony]

14
Go home, And show no sign of fear.
Coriolanus. Act iv, sc. 6, l. 152. [Sicinius]

Fear no more.—*Cymbeline,* iv, 2, 258; iv, 2, 264; iv, 2, 270; *Venus and Adonis,* l. 899.

15
For we will fetters put upon this fear,
Which now goes too free-footed.
Hamlet. Act iii, sc. 3, l. 25. [King] The only use of "free-footed."

Why, what should be the fear?—*Hamlet,* i, 4, 64.

16
Dost thou think I 'll fear thee as I fear thy father?
I Henry IV. Act iii, sc. 3, l. 171. [Falstaff]

1
All these bold fears
Thou see'st with peril I have answered.
II Henry IV. Act iv, sc. 5, l. 196. [King]

2
Let us do it with no show of fear.
Henry V. Act ii, sc. 4, l. 23. [Dauphin]

Fear attends her not.—*Henry V*, ii, 4, 29.

Possess them not with fear.—*Henry V*, iv, 1, 307.

You need not fear.—*I Henry VI*, v, 2, 17; *I Henry IV*, iv, 4, 13; *Measure for Measure*, ii, 1, 248; *The Merchant of Venice*, i, 2, 109; *The Tempest*, iii, 3, 43.

Nay, you need not fear us.—*The Merchant of Venice*, iii, 5, 33.

Do not fear.—*I Henry VI*, v, 3, 46.

Nay, fear not, man.—*II Henry VI*, i, 2, 68. "Fear not" is repeated frequently in later plays.

Fear you not.—*II Henry VI*, i, 4, 6; *The Merchant of Venice*, v, 1, 123.

Fear not thou.—*II Henry VI*, ii, 4, 56; *Love's Labour's Lost*, v, 2, 104.

Fear not you.—*Measure for Measure*, i, 2, 109; *The Two Gentlemen of Verona*, iv, 2, 82.

3
Let pale-faced fear keep with the mean-born man,
And find no harbour in a royal heart.
II Henry VI. Act iii, sc. 1, l. 335. [York] "Pale-faced" is repeated three times in later plays; "mean-born" is used again in *Richard III*, iv, 2, 54: "Mean-born gentleman."

4
Cade: I fear neither sword nor fire.
Smith: [Aside] He need not fear the sword; for his coat is of proof.
Dick: [Aside] But methinks he should stand in fear of fire, being burnt i' the hand for stealing of sheep.
II Henry VI. Act iv, sc. 2, l. 63.

What should we fear?—*III Henry VI*, i, 2, 69.

5
I fear him not:
Yet if my name were liable to fear,
I do not know the man I should avoid
So soon as that spare Cassius.
Julius Cæsar. Act i, sc. 2, l. 198. [Cæsar]

I fear not him.—*Richard III*, iv, 2, 56.

I fear thee not.—*Much Ado about Nothing*, v, 1, 55; *The Taming of the Shrew*, ii, 1, 401.

I fear you not.—*Measure for Measure*, iii, 2, 173.

6
There is no fear in him; let him not die.
Julius Cæsar. Act ii, sc. 1, l. 190. [Trebonius]

7
But I do find it cowardly and vile,
For fear of what might fall, so to prevent
The time of life.
Julius Cæsar. Act v, sc. 1, l. 104. [Brutus]

8
King'd of our fears, until our fears, resolved,
Be by some certain king purged and deposed.
King John. Act ii, sc. 1, l. 371. [Citizen]

Let not the world see fear and sad distrust
Govern the motion of a kingly eye.
King John. Act v, sc. 1, l. 46. [Bastard]

9
Duke of Albany: You may fear too far.
Goneril: Safer than trust too far:
Let me still take away the harms I fear,
Not fear still to be taken.
King Lear. Act i, sc. 4, l. 351.

10
Shook off my sober guards and civil fears.
A Lover's Complaint, l. 298.

11
But let the frame of things disjoint, both the worlds suffer,
Ere we will eat our meal in fear and sleep
In the affliction of these terrible dreams
That shake us nightly.
Macbeth. Act iii, sc. 2, l. 16. [Macbeth] "Disjoint" is used only once again, in *Hamlet*, i, 2, 20.

What need I fear of thee?—*Macbeth*, iv, 1, 82.

You need not fear it.—*Winter's Tale*, ii, 2, 58.

12
That I may tell pale-hearted fear it lies,
And sleep in spite of thunder.
Macbeth. Act iv, sc. 1, l. 85. [Macbeth] The only use of "pale-hearted."

I have almost forgot the taste of fears:
The time has been, my senses would have cool'd
To hear a night-shriek; and my fell of hair
Would at a dismal treatise rouse and stir
As life were in 't.
Macbeth. Act v, sc. 5, l. 9. [Macbeth] The only use of "night-shriek." "Treatise" is repeated in *Much Ado about Nothing*, i, 1, 317, and in *Venus and Adonis*, l. 774.

'Tis a lost fear.—*Othello*, v, 2, 269.

That 's the least fear.—*Pericles*, i, 2, 102.

What need we fear?—*Pericles*, i, 4, 77.

13
Be not afraid, though you do see me weapon'd.
Othello. Act v, sc. 2, l. 266. [Othello] The only use of "weapon'd."

Be not afraid.—*II Henry VI*, ii, 3, 69; *Richard III*, v, 3, 215; *All's Well that Ends Well*, ii, 3, 95; *The Merry Wives of Windsor*, iv, 1, 20; *A Midsummer-Night's Dream*, iii, 2, 321; *Twelfth Night*, ii, 5, 156; iii, 1, 142; iii, 4, 42; *A Lover's Complaint*, l. 179.

I am not afraid.—*Midsummer-Night's Dream*, iii, 1, 127.

I will not be afraid.—*Macbeth*, v, 3, 59.

14
In black mourn I, All fears scorn I.
The Passionate Pilgrim, l. 264.

15
Then, childish fear, avaunt!
The Rape of Lucrece, l. 274.

16
Shall I seem crest-fall'n in my father's sight?
Or with pale beggar-fear impeach my height
Before this out-dared dastard?
Richard II. Act i, sc. 1, l. 188. [Bolingbroke] The only use of "beggar-fear" and "out-dared." "Crest-fall'n" is repeated in *II Henry VI*, iv, 1, 59, and *The Merry Wives of Windsor*, iv, 5, 102.

To fear the foe, since fear oppresseth strength,
Gives in your weakness strength unto your foe,
And so your follies fight against yourself.
Fear, and be slain; no worse can come to fight:

And fight and die is death destroying death;
Where fearing dying pays death servile breath.
Richard II. Act iii, sc. 2, l. 180. [Carlisle]

Thy buried fear.—*Richard II,* v, 6, 31.

1
Soon I 'll rid you from the fear of them.
Richard III. Act iv, sc. 2, l. 78. [Tyrrel]

2
O, tell not me of fear!
Romeo and Juliet. Act iv, sc. 1, l. 121. [Juliet]

Without fear.—*Romeo and Juliet,* iv, 1, 87.

3
I' faith, sir, you shall never need to fear.
The Taming of the Shrew. Act i, sc. 1, l. 61. [Katharina]

4
Be blithe again,
And bury all thy fear in my devices.
Titus Andronicus. Act iv, sc. 4, l. 111. [Tamora]

Why should you fear?—*Titus Andronicus,* iv, 4, 112.

Fear no colours.—*Twelfth Night,* i, 5, 6; *II Henry IV,* v, 5, 92.

I fear no colours.—*Twelfth Night,* i, 5, 10.

5
O, let my lady apprehend no fear.
Troilus and Cressida. Act iii, sc. 2, l. 79. [Troilus]

6
I think you have
As little skill to fear as I have purpose
To put you to 't.
Winter's Tale. Act iv, sc. 4, l. 151. [Florizel]

Fear not thou, man, thou shalt lose nothing here.
Winter's Tale. Act iv, sc. 4, l. 258. [Clown]

Tush, fear not, man.—*Much Ado about Nothing,* v, 4, 44.

Fear you not.—*Much Ado about Nothing,* iii, 1, 31.

Fear not that.—*II Henry VI,* iv, 3, 19; *III Henry VI,* iv, 2, 5.

Fear you not him.—*The Taming of the Shrew,* iv, 4, 10.

Fear not you that.—*The Merry Wives of Windsor,* iv, 4, 78.

Fear you not that.—*II Henry IV,* iv, 1, 185.

Never fear that.—*Julius Cæsar,* ii, 1, 202.

Fear none of this.—*Winter's Tale,* iv, 4, 601.

FEAST

7
We had much more monstrous matter of feast, which worthily deserved noting.
Antony and Cleopatra. Act ii, sc. 2, l. 186. [Enobarbus]

We 'll feast each other ere we part.
Antony and Cleopatra. Act ii, sc. 6, l. 61. [Pompey]

Four feasts are toward.
Antony and Cleopatra. Act ii, sc. 6, l. 75. [Enobarbus]

Pompey: This is not yet an Alexandrian feast.
Antony: It ripens towards it.
Antony and Cleopatra. Act ii, sc. 7, l. 102. Alexandrian is repeated in v, 2, 218, "Alexandrian revels," and occurs in no other play.

8
But though my cates be mean, take them in good part;
Better cheer may you have, but not with better heart.
The Comedy of Errors. Act iii, sc. 1, l. 28. [Antipholus of Ephesus] "Cates" appears also in *I Henry VI,* ii, 3, 79; *I Henry IV,* iii, 1, 157; *Pericles,* ii, 3, 29.

Go to a gossips' feast, and go with me;
After so long grief, such festivity!
The Comedy of Errors. Act v, sc. 1, l. 405. [Abbess] The only use of "festivity."

9
Yet camest thou to a morsel of this feast,
Having fully dined before.
Coriolanus. Act i, sc. 9, l. 10. [Cominius]

The feast smells well; but I
Appear not like a guest.
Coriolanus. Act iv, sc. 5, l. 5. [Coriolanus]

10
He that strikes
The venison first shall be lord o' the feast.
Cymbeline. Act iii, sc. 3, l. 74. [Belarius]

Master of the feast.—*Cymbeline,* iii, 6, 29.

Mistress o' the feast.—*The Winter's Tale,* iv, 3, 43; iv, 4, 68.

Queen o' the feast.—*Pericles,* ii, 3, 17.

11
'Twas at a feast,—O, would
Our viands had been poison'd, or at least
Those which I heaved to head!
Cymbeline. Act v, sc. 5, l. 155. [Iachimo]

12
Come in, and let us banquet royally,
After this golden day of victory.
I Henry VI. Act i, sc. 6, l. 30. [Charles]

O, what banquet wert thou to the taste!
Venus and Adonis, l. 445.

A most delicious banquet.
The Taming of the Shrew. Induction, sc. 1, l. 39. [Lord] Shakespeare uses "delicious" only twice more in the plays, "Rotted with delicious feed," *Titus Andronicus,* iv, 4, 93; and "Now I feed myself With most delicious poison," *Antony and Cleopatra,* i, 5, 27. In *The Rape of Lucrece,* l. 699, he speaks of "His taste delicious, in digestion souring."

We have a trifling foolish banquet towards.
Romeo and Juliet. Act i, sc. 5, l. 124. [Capulet]

An idle banquet attends you.—*Timon of Athens,* i, 2, 160.

Is the banquet ready I' the privy chamber?
Henry VIII. Act i, sc. 4, l. 98. [Wolsey]

His banquet is prepared.—*As You Like It,* ii, 5, 64.

Come, let us to the banquet.
Much Ado about Nothing. Act ii, sc. 1, l. 178. [Don John]

Bring in the banquet quickly.
Antony and Cleopatra. Act i, sc. 2, l. 11. [Enobarbus]

This night in banqueting must all be spent.
Troilus and Cressida. Act v, sc. 1, l. 51. [Achilles] "Banqueting" is repeated in *Julius Cæsar,* i, 2, 77.

Caroused and banqueted.—*I Henry VI,* ii, 1, 12. The only use of "banqueted."

13
You have now a broken banquet; but we 'll mend it.
Henry VIII, i, 4, 61. See under MENDING.

Fantastical banquet.—*Much Ado about Nothing,* ii, 3, 22.

Painted banquet.—*Sonnets,* xlvii.
Running banquet.—*Henry VIII,* i, 4, 12; v, 4, 69.

1
What, shall our feast be kept with slaughter'd men?
King John. Act iii, sc. 1, l. 302. [Blanch]

Feasts,
Full of warm blood, of mirth, of gossiping.
King John. Act v, sc. 2, l. 58. [Dauphin]

2
Feast upon her eyes.
Measure for Measure. Act ii, sc. 2, l. 179. [Angelo]
My eye doth feast.—*Sonnets,* xlvii.
Feast thine eyes.—*Timon of Athens,* i, 2, 133.
Feast your ears.—*Timon of Athens,* iii, 6, 36.

3
I have no mind of feasting forth to-night.
The Merchant of Venice. Act ii, sc. 5, l. 37. [Shylock]
Private feasting.—*The Rape of Lucrece,* l. 891.

4
Don Pedro: What, a feast, a feast?
Claudio: I' faith, I thank him; he hath bid me to a calf's head and a capon; the which if I do not carve most curiously, say my knife 's naught. Shall I not find a woodcock too?
Much Ado about Nothing. Act v, sc. 1, l. 154.

5
This we desire,
As friends to Antioch, we may feast in Tyre.
Pericles. Act i, sc. 3, l. 39. [Helicanus]

6
Celebrate this feast of battle.
Richard II, i, 3, 92. The only use of "feast of battle."
Feast of death.—*I Henry VI,* iv, 5, 7. The only use of the phrase.

7
This night I hold an old accustom'd feast,
Whereto I have invited many a guest,
Such as I love; and you, among the store,
One more, most welcome, makes my number more.
Romeo and Juliet. Act i, sc. 2, l. 20. [Capulet]
Ancient feast.—*Romeo and Juliet,* i, 2, 87.
I do feast to-night.—*The Merchant of Venice,* ii, 2, 180.

8
We 'll hold a feast in great solemnity.
A Midsummer-Night's Dream. Act iv, sc. 1, l. 189. [Theseus]
Therefore are feasts so solemn and so rare,
Since, seldom coming, in the long year set,
Like stones of worth they thinly placed are,
Or captain jewels in the carcanet.
Sonnets. No. lii. The only use of "carcanet" (collar of gold).

9
Provide the feast, father, and bid the guests.
The Taming of the Shrew. Act ii, sc. 1, l. 318. [Petruchio]
Go to the feast, revel and domineer.
Taming of the Shrew. Act iii, sc. 2, l. 226. [Petruchio] The only use of "domineer."
You know there wants no junkets at the feast.
The Taming of the Shrew, iii, 2, 250. The only use of "junkets."

We will hence forthwith,
To feast and sport us at thy father's house.
The Taming of the Shrew. Act iv, sc. 3, l. 184. [Petruchio]
Feast with the best, and welcome to my house:
My banquet is to close our stomachs up,
After our great good cheer.
The Taming of the Shrew. Act v, sc. 2, l. 8. [Lucentio] For "good cheer" see under EATING.
At night we 'll feast together.
Hamlet. Act ii, sc. 2, l. 84. [King]

10
Second Lord: Thou art going to Lord Timon's feast?
Apemantus: Ay, to see meat fill knaves and wine heat fools.
Timon of Athens. Act i, sc. 1, l. 270.
Feasts are too proud to give thanks to the gods.
Timon of Athens. Act i, sc. 2, l. 62. [Apemantus]
What need these feasts, pomps and vainglories?
Timon of Athens. Act i, sc. 2, l. 248. [Apemantus]
Make not a city feast of it, to let the meat cool ere we can agree upon the first place.
Timon of Athens. Act iii, sc. 6, l. 75. [Timon]
Here 's a noble feast toward.
Timon of Athens. Act iii, sc. 6, l. 67. [Lord]
May you a better feast never behold.
Timon of Athens. Act iii, sc. 6, l. 98. [Timon]

Henceforth be no feast,
Whereat a villain 's not a welcome guest.
Timon of Athens. Act iii, sc. 6, l. 112. [Timon]

11
This is the feast that I have bid her to,
And this the banquet she shall surfeit on.
Titus Andronicus. Act v, sc. 2, l. 193. [Titus]
Come, come, be every one officious
To make this banquet; which I wish may prove
More stern and bloody than the Centaurs' feast.
Titus Andronicus. Act v, sc. 2, l. 202. [Titus]
The feast is ready.—*Titus Andronicus,* v, 3, 21.

12
I beseech you next
To feast with me and see me in my tent.
Troilus and Cressida. Act iv, sc. 5, l. 228. [Ulysses]
Let us feast him to the height.
Troilus and Cressida. Act v, sc. 1, l. 3. [Achilles]
Factious feasts.—*Troilus and Cressida,* i, 3, 191.
Great feast.—*Love's Labour 's Lost,* v, 1, 40. *Macbeth,* iii, 1, 12; *Hamlet,* ii, 2, 52.

13
Would they not wish the feast might ever last?
Venus and Adonis, l. 447.

14
Our feasts
In every mess have folly and the feeders
Digest it with a custom.
Winter's Tale. Act iv, sc. 4, l. 10. [Perdita]

FEAT, see Deed

FEATHER

1 Most courteous feathers, which . . . nod at every man.
All's Well that Ends Well. .Act iv, sc. 5, l. 111. [Clown]
Downy feather.—*II Henry IV*, iv, 5, 32.
Growing feathers.—*Julius Cæsar*, i, 1, 77.
Light feathers.—*Romeo and Juliet*, i, 4, 20.
Peacock's feather.—*Henry V*, iv, 1, 213.
Raven's feather.—*The Tempest*, i, 2, 322.
Feather of lead.—*Romeo and Juliet*, i, 1, 186.
A forest of feathers.—*Hamlet*, iii, 2, 286.

2 The best feather of our wing.
Cymbeline. Act i, sc. 6, l. 186. [Iachimo]
Add More feathers to our wings.
Henry V. Act i, sc. 2, l. 307. [King Henry]
Have added feathers to the learned's wing.
Sonnets. No. lxxviii.
Moult no feather.—*Hamlet*, ii, 2, 306.

3 And of their feather many moe proud birds.
III Henry VI. Act ii, sc. 1, l. 170. [Warwick]
I am not of that feather.—*Timon of Athens*, i, 1, 100.

4 Be Mercury, set feathers to thy heels.
King John. Act iv, sc. 2, l. 174. [King John]

5 I do fear,
When every feather sticks in his own wing,
Lord Timon will be left a naked gull,
Which flashes now a phœnix.
Timon of Athens. Act ii, sc. 1, l. 29. [Senator]

FEATURE

See also Face

6 Bid him
Report the feature of Octavia, her years,
Her inclination.
Antony and Cleopatra. Act ii, sc. 5, l. 111. [Cleopatra]

7 Doth my simple feature content you?
As You Like It. Act iii, sc. 3, l. 3. [Touchstone]

8 For feature, laming
The shrine of Venus, or straight-pight Minerva.
Cymbeline. Act v, sc. 5, l. 163. [Iachimo] The only use of "laming" and "straight-pight" (erect).
Feature of blown youth.—*Hamlet*, iii, 1, 167.

9 Her peerless feature, joined with her birth,
Approves her fit for none but for a king.
I Henry VI. Act v, sc. 5, l. 68. [Suffolk]

10 Forgive the comment that my passion made
Upon thy feature; for my rage was blind,
And foul imaginary eyes of blood
Presented thee more hideous than thou art.
King John. Act iv, sc. 2, l. 263. [King John]
Be-monster not thy feature.—*King Lear*, iv, 2, 63. The only use of "be-monster."

11 Cheated of feature by dissembling nature.
Richard III, i, 1, 19. See under DEFORMITY.
Featured like him.—*Sonnets*, xxix.
Rarely featured.—*Much Ado about Nothing*, iii, 1, 60. The only uses of "featured."

12 How features are abroad, I am skilless of.
The Tempest. Act iii, sc. 1, l. 52. [Miranda]

13 Thou hast, Sebastian, done good feature shame.
Twelfth Night. Act iii, sc. 4, l. 400. [Officer]

14 He is complete in feature and in mind
With all good grace to grace a gentleman.
The Two Gentlemen of Verona. Act ii, sc. 4, l. 73. [Valentine]
Complete In mind and feature.—*Henry VIII*, iii, 2, 50.

FEEDING

See also Eating

15 Bring us where we may rest ourselves and feed.
As You Like It, ii, 4, 73. See under ENTERTAINMENT.
Sit down and feed, and welcome to our table.
As You Like It, ii, 7, 105. See under FOOD.
Let him feed.—*As You Like It*, ii, 7, 168.
Feed yourselves.—*As You Like It*, v, 4, 144.
Feed myself.—*Antony and Cleopatra*, i, 5, 26.

16 At board he fed not for my urging it.
The Comedy of Errors. Act v, sc. 1, l. 64. [Adriana]
Fed from my trencher.—*II Henry VI*, iv, 1, 57.
Fed with the same food.—*The Merchant of Venice*, iii, 1, 63.
Better fed.—*Pericles*, ii, 5, 27.
Highly fed.—*All's Well that Ends Well*, ii, 2, 3.
Well fed.—*All's Well that Ends Well*, ii, 4, 39.
Fed as well.—*Julius Cæsar*, i, 2, 98.
Fed Upon fresh beauty.—*Venus and Adonis*, l. 795.

17 [You] Grew by our feeding to so great a bulk
That even our love durst not come near your sight
For fear of swallowing.
I Henry IV. Act v, sc. 1, l. 62. [Worcester]
High feeding.—*II Henry IV*, i, 1, 10.
Worthy feeding.—*The Winter's Tale*, iv, 4, 169.
Gorging and feeding.—*Julius Cæsar*, v, 1, 82.
Feeding his own stomach.—*All's Well that Ends Well*, i, 1, 155.
Feeding life.—*Titus Andronicus*, iii, 1, 74.
Sleep and feeding.—*Antony and Cleopatra*, ii, 1, 26.
Feed, and sleep.—*Antony and Cleopatra*, v, 2, 187.
Sleep and feed.—*Hamlet*, iv, 4, 35.

18 We shall feed like oxen at a stall.
I Henry IV, v, 2, 14. See under OX.

19 Then feed, and be fat, my fair Calipolis.
II Henry IV. Act ii, sc. 4, l. 193. [Pistol] The only mention of Calipolis, a character in *The Battle of Alcazar* (1594), wife of Muley Mahomet, who comes to her with lion's flesh

on his sword and says, "Feed then, and faint not, my fair Calypolis."
Feed fat.—*The Merchant of Venice,* i, 3, 48.
Feeds him fat.—*I Henry IV,* iii, 2, 180.
Feeds well.—*Othello,* iii, 3, 184.
Those that feed grow full.—*Measure for Measure,* i, 4, 41.
So full hath fed.—*Venus and Adonis,* l. 339.

1
Nor care I who doth feed upon my cost.
Henry V, iv, 3, 25. See under HONOUR.

2
Feeds On abjects, orts and imitations.
Julius Cæsar, iv, 1, 36. See under CHARACTER.
Feed on one another.—*Coriolanus,* i, 1, 192.
Feed on the air.—*The Two Gentlemen of Verona,* ii, 1, 179.
Feed on your blood.—*The Two Gentlemen of Verona,* ii, 4, 27.
Feed on your lips.—*Love's Labour's Lost,* ii, 1, 220.
Feed upon the shadow of perfection.—*The Two Gentlemen of Verona,* iii, 1, 177.
Feed on her damask cheek.—*Twelfth Night,* ii, 4, 115.
Feed on nourishing dishes.—*Othello,* iii, 3, 78.
Feed On mother's flesh.—*Pericles,* i, 1, 64.
Feed On sweetest flowers.—*Pericles,* i, 1, 132.
Feed on life.—*Cymbeline,* v, 5, 51.
Feed Even on the pith of life.—*Hamlet,* iv, 1, 22.
Feeds on his wonder.—*Macbeth,* iv, 5, 89.

3 To feed were best at home;
From thence the sauce to meat is ceremony;
Meeting were bare without it.
Macbeth. Act iii, sc. 4, l. 35. [Lady Macbeth]
Feeds from home.—*Comedy of Errors,* ii, 1, 101.

4
Feed, and regard him not.
Macbeth. Act iii, sc. 4, l. 58. [Lady Macbeth]

5 I'll go in hate, to feed upon
The prodigal Christian.
Merchant of Venice, ii, 5, 14. See HATE, 677:9.
On what I hate I feed not.—*Timon of Athens,* iv, 3, 306.

6
Feed upon such nice and waterish diet.
Othello, iii, 3, 15. See under POLICY.
Feeding on that which doth preserve the ill.
Sonnets. No. cxlvii.

7
I will stand to and feed.
The Tempest. Act iii, sc. 3, l. 49. [Alonso]
Will't please you eat? will't please your highness feed?
Titus Andronicus. Act v, sc. 3, l. 54. [Titus]
I feed Most hungerly.—*Timon of Athens,* i, 1, 261.
Delicious feed.—*Titus Andronicus,* iv, 4, 93.

8
Timon: Where feed'st thou o' days, Apemantus?
Apemantus: Where my stomach finds meat.
Timon of Athens. Act iv, sc. 3, l. 293.
Feed'st me with the very name of meat.
The Taming of the Shrew, iv, 3, 32.
Feed's thy light's flame.—*Sonnets,* i. The only uses of "feed'st."

9
I'll make you feed on berries and on roots,
And feed on curds and whey.
Titus Andronicus, iv, 2, 177. See under WARRIOR.

10
You feed too much on this dislike.
Troilus and Cressida, ii, 3, 235. See under DISLIKE.

11
Upon the earth's increase why shouldst thou feed,
Unless the earth with thy increase be fed?
Venus and Adonis, l. 169. See under CHILD.
Within be fed.—*Sonnets,* cxlvi.

12
Feed where thou wilt, on mountain or in dale:
Graze on my lips; and if those hills be dry,
Stray lower, where the pleasant fountains lie.
Venus and Adonis, l. 232.
Glutton-like she feeds, yet never filleth.
Venus and Adonis, l. 548. See under DESIRE.
He fed them with his sight, they him with berries.
Venus and Adonis, l. 1104.
Feed me with delays.—*Titus Andronicus,* iv, 3, 42.
Feed and clothe thee.—*Hamlet,* iii, 2, 64.
Feed capons.—*Hamlet,* iii, 2, 100.
Feed her fawn.—*Venus and Adonis,* l. 876.
Feed this fire.—*King John,* v, 2, 85.
Feed his brain-sick fits.—*Titus Andronicus,* v, 2, 71.
Feed their flocks.—*Passionate Pilgrim,* l. 358.
Feed his humour.—*Titus Andronicus,* iv, 3, 29.
Feed my humour.—*Richard III,* iv, 1, 65.
Feed your knowledge.—*Twelfth Night,* iii, 3, 41.
Feed my means.—*The Merchant of Venice,* iii, 2, 266.
Feed my revenge.—*The Merchant of Venice,* iii, 1, 55.
Feed her sight.—*Venus and Adonis,* l. 822.
Feed their young.—*III Henry VI,* ii, 2, 26; *As You Like It,* i, 2, 99.

II—The Feeder

13
I will your very faithful feeder be.
As You Like It. Act ii, sc. 4, l. 99. [Corin]
The patch is kind enough, but a huge feeder.
The Merchant of Venice. Act ii, sc. 5, l. 46. [Shylock]

14
With eager feeding food doth choke the feeder.
Richard II. Act ii, sc. 1, l. 37. [Gaunt]
Beastly feeder.—*II Henry IV,* i, 3, 95.
Riotous feeders.—*Timon of Athens,* ii, 2, 168.
Feeder of my riots.—*II Henry IV,* v, 5, 66.
Nurse and feeder.—*Venus and Adonis,* l. 448.

FEELING

15
Has this fellow no feeling of his business, that he sings at grave-making?
Hamlet. Act v, sc. 1, l. 73. [Hamlet] The only use of "grave-making."
Thou hast no feeling of it.
Love's Labour's Lost. Act iii, sc. 1, l. 115. [Costard]

1
With my fingers feel thy hand unfeeling.
II Henry VI. Act iii, sc. 2, l. 145. [King Henry]
Unfeeling fools.—*Comedy of Errors,* ii, 1, 103.
Unfeeling . . . ignorance.—*Richard II,* i, 3, 168.
Unfeeling man.—*The Merchant of Venice,* iv, 1, 63. The only uses of "unfeeling."
I will not swear these are my hands: let 's see;
I feel this pin prick.
King Lear. Act iv, sc. 7, l. 56. [King Lear]
2
We cannot feel too little, hear too much.
Henry VIII. Act i, sc. 2, l. 128. [King Henry]
3
How dost thou feel thyself now?
Richard III. Act i, sc. 4, l. 123. [Murderer]
4
Not by our feeling but by others' seeing.
Sonnets. No. cxxi.
That will not see Because he doth not feel.
King Lear. Act iv, sc. 1, l. 71. [Gloucester]
5
Nor tender feeling, to base touches prone,
Nor taste, nor smell, desire to be invited
To any sensual feast with thee alone.
Sonnets. No. cxli.
Greater feeling.—*Richard II,* i, 3, 301.
Ingenious feeling.—*King Lear,* iv, 6, 287.
Painful feeling.—*Measure for Measure,* i, 2, 38.
6
Hast thou, which art but air, a touch, a feeling
Of their afflictions, and shall not myself,
One of their kind, that relish all as sharply,
Passion as they, be kindlier moved than thou art?
The Tempest. Act v, sc. 1, l. 24. [Prospero] The only use of "kindlier."
7
Say, that the sense of feeling were bereft me,
And that I could not see, nor hear, nor touch,
And nothing but the very smell were left me,
Yet would my love to thee be still as much.
Venus and Adonis, l. 439.
8
I do feel 't and see 't.
Twelfth Night. Act iv, sc. 3, l. 2. [Sebastian]
I do see 't and feel 't, As you feel doing thus.
Winter's Tale. Act ii, sc. 1, l. 152. [Leontes]

FELLOW

9
All the learned and authentic fellows.
All's Well that Ends Well. Act ii, sc. 3, l. 14. [Lafeu]
10
I did think thee, for two ordinaries, to be a pretty wise fellow.
All's Well that Ends Well. Act ii, sc. 3, l. 211. [Lafeu] The only use of "ordinaries."
I am a wise fellow, and, which is more, an officer, and, which is more, a householder.
Much Ado about Nothing. Act iv, sc. 2, l. 81. [Dogberry] "Householder" is repeated in *I Henry IV,* iv, 2, 16.
I perceive he was a wise fellow.—*Pericles,* i, 3, 4.

11
A very tainted fellow, and full of wickedness.
All's Well that Ends Well. Act iii, sc. 2, l. 89. [Countess]
Abominable fellows.—*As You Like It,* iv, 1, 6.
A barren-spirited fellow.—*Julius Cæsar,* iv, 1, 36. See under CHARACTER. The only use of "barren-spirited."
Crying fellow.—*Othello,* ii, 3, 230.
Damnable fellow!—*Measure for Measure,* v, 1, 342.
Dangerous fellow.—*Cymbeline,* v, 5, 237.
Half-blooded fellow.—*King Lear,* v, 3, 80. The only use of "half-blooded."
Half-faced fellow.—*II Henry IV,* iii, 2, 283. "Half-faced" occurs four times.
Hook-nosed fellow.—*II Henry IV,* iv, 3, 45. The only use of "hook-nosed," referring to Julius Cæsar.
A little quiver fellow.—*II Henry IV,* iii, 2, 301.
Melancholy fellow.—*As You Like It,* iv, 1, 3.
Monstrous fellow.—*King Lear,* ii, 2, 27.
A paltry fellow.—*Richard III,* v, 3, 323.
A paltry insolent fellow.—*Troilus and Cressida,* ii, 3, 218.
Particular fellow.—*II Henry VI,* iv, 2, 119.
Peevish fellow. *Henry V,* iii, 7, 142.
Profane fellow!—*Cymbeline,* ii, 3, 129.
A snipt-taffeta fellow.—*All's Well that Ends Well,* iv, 5, 2. The only use of "snipt-taffeta" (wearing slashed garments of taffeta).
Top-proud fellow.—*Henry VIII,* i, 1, 151. The only use of "top-proud."
12
'Tis a most gallant fellow.
All's Well that Ends Well. Act iii, sc. 5, l. 81. [Diana]
Blessed fellow.—*II Henry IV,* ii, 2, 61.
A fit fellow.—*Henry VIII,* ii, 2, 117.
Great fellow.—*Antony and Cleopatra,* ii, 7, 140; *Henry VIII,* v, 4, 91.
A handsome fellow.—*Much Ado about Nothing,* ii, 1, 58; *Pericles,* ii, 1, 84.
A likely fellow.—*II Henry IV,* iii, 2, 186.
A notable fellow.—*Measure for Measure,* v, 1, 268.
A pretty fellow.—*King Lear,* i, 4, 210.
The prettier fellow.—*The Merchant of Venice,* iii, 4, 64.
Princely fellows.—*Cymbeline,* iii, 4, 93.
Proper fellow.—*II Henry IV,* ii, 2, 72.
Respected fellow.—*Measure for Measure,* ii, 1, 170.
Sweet fellow.—*The Winter's Tale,* v, 1, 34.
A very valiant fellow.—*Othello,* v, 1, 52.
13
There 's a strong fellow, Menas.
Antony and Cleopatra. Act ii, sc. 7, l. 94. [Enobarbus] "Strong fellow" is repeated in *As You Like It,* i, 2, 224.
Here is a rural fellow
That will not be denied your highness' presence;
He brings you figs.
Antony and Cleopatra. Act v, sc. 2, l. 233. [Guard] "Rural" is repeated in *The Winter's Tale,* iv, 4, 448: "Rural latches."
A woodland fellow.—*All's Well that Ends Well,* iv, 5, 49. The only use of "woodland."

1
Is not this a rare fellow, my lord?
As You Like It. Act v, sc. 4, l. 109. [Jaques] The only use of "rare fellow."

2
Third Servant: What fellow 's that?
First Servant: A strange one as ever I looked on.
Coriolanus. Act iv, sc. 5, l. 20.

A strange fellow.—*All 's Well that Ends Well,* iii, 6, 93, and four times in later plays.

This is the strangest fellow.—*I Henry IV,* v, 4, 159.

3
First Servant: A noble fellow, I warrant him.
Second Servant: The worthy fellow is our general.
Coriolanus. Act v, sc. 2, l. 115.

Noble fellows.—*All 's Well that Ends Well,* ii, 3, 308; *The Winter's Tale,* ii, 3, 142; *Coriolanus,* i, 4, 52.

4
This fellow might be in 's time a great buyer of land, with his statutes, his recognizances, his fines, his double vouchers, his recoveries.
Hamlet. Act v, sc. 1, l. 112. [Hamlet] The only use of "recognizances." "Recognizance" occurs in *Othello,* v, 2, 214.

A fellow of infinite jest, of most excellent fancy.
Hamlet. Act v, sc. 1, l. 203. [Hamlet]

Fellows of infinite tongue.—*Henry V.* v, 2, 163.

A robustious periwig-pated fellow.—*Hamlet,* iii, 2, 11. "Robustious" is repeated in *Henry V,* iii, 7, 159. Only use of "periwig-pated."

5
That same mad fellow of the north.
I Henry IV. Act ii, sc. 4, l. 369. [Falstaff]

What, is the fellow mad?—*Julius Cæsar,* iii, 1, 10.

Mad fellow.—*I Henry IV,* ii, 4, 369; iv, 2, 39; *Hamlet,* v, 1, 193.

6
A fellow of no mark nor likelihood.
I Henry IV. Act iii, sc. 2, l. 45. [King Henry] See under Opinion.

7
He was some hilding fellow that had stolen
The horse he rode on.
II Henry IV. Act i, sc. 1, l. 57. [Bardolph]

I am the fellow with the great belly, and he my dog.
II Henry IV. Act i, sc. 2, l. 165. [Falstaff]

8
A good shallow young fellow.
II Henry IV. Act ii, sc. 4, l. 257. [Falstaff]

Young fellow.—*As You Like It,* i, 1, 149; *Twelfth Night,* i, 5, 147.

9
I am a proper fellow of my hands.
II Henry IV. Act ii, sc. 2, l. 72. [Poins]

I shall ne'er see such a fellow.
II Henry IV. Act iii, sc. 2, l. 306. [Shallow]

The most active fellow in Europe.
II Henry IV. Act iv, sc. 3, l. 24. [Falstaff]

A fellow that never had the ache in his shoulders!
II Henry IV. Act v, sc. 1, l. 93. [Falstaff]

10
A fellow
In a long motley coat guarded with yellow.
Henry VIII. Prol., l. 15.

A fellow all in buff.—*The Comedy of Errors,* iv, 2, 36.

11
You are a saucy fellow.
Henry VIII. Act iv, sc. 2, l. 100. [Katharine] See also *Julius Cæsar,* i, 1, 21; iv, 3, 134.

12
Thou art a fellow of a good respect.
Julius Cæsar. Act v, sc. 5, l. 45. [Brutus]

A good blunt fellow.—*King John,* i, 1, 71. See under Candour.

13
A fellow by the hand of nature mark'd.
King John. Act iv, sc. 2, l. 221. [King John]

14
Lear: What art thou?
Kent: A very honest-hearted fellow, and as poor as the king.
King Lear. Act i, sc. 4, l. 20. The only use of "honest-hearted."

This is some fellow,
Who, having been praised for bluntness, doth affect
A saucy roughness.
King Lear. Act ii, sc. 2, l. 101. [Cornwall] The only use of "roughness."

This is the fellow of the self-same colour
Our sister speaks of.
King Lear. Act ii, sc. 2, l. 145. [Cornwall]

Being the very fellow that of late
Display'd so saucily against your highness.
King Lear. Act ii, sc. 4, l. 40. [Kent] "Saucily" is repeated in i, 1, 22, and occurs in no other play.

Is that the naked fellow?—*King Lear,* iv, 1, 42. "Naked fellow" is repeated in l. 53, and occurs only in this scene.

Old fellow.—*King Lear,* ii, 2, 91; *Timon of Athens,* ii, 2, 223.

This old fat fellow.—*The Two Gentlemen of Verona,* iv, 4, 15.

Bearded fellow.—*Othello,* iv, 1, 67.

White-bearded fellow.—*Much Ado about Nothing,* ii, 3, 124. The only use of "white-bearded."

15
Truly, sir, I am a poor fellow that would live.
Measure for Measure. Act ii, sc. 1, l. 234. [Pompey]

Poor fellow.—*II Henry VI,* ii, 3, 106, and five times in later plays.

Shy fellow.—*Measure for Measure,* iii, 2, 139.

16
That fellow is a fellow of much licence.
Measure for Measure. Act iii, sc. 2, l. 216. [Escalus]

What muffled fellow 's that?—*Measure for Measure,* v, 1, 491.

Lewd fellow.—*Measure for Measure,* v, 1, 515.

17
An honest, willing, kind fellow.
The Merry Wives of Windsor. Act i, sc. 4, l. 10. [Mistress Quickly]

Like a kind fellow.—*II Henry IV,* iv, 3, 75.

An honest fellow enough, and one that loves quails.
Troilus and Cressida. Act v, sc. 1, l. 57. [Thersites] "Honest fellow" occurs also in *III Henry VI,* v, 1, 2, and *Othello,* iii, 3, 5. The only use of "quails" in this meaning.

I will swear to the prince thou art as honest a true fellow as any is in Bohemia.
Winter's Tale. Act v, sc. 2, l. 168. [Clown]

Honest fellow.—*III Henry VI,* v, 1, 2; *Othello,* iii, 3, 5.

Honest good fellows.—*Romeo and Juliet,* iv, 5, 98.

1
A marvellous witty fellow, I assure you.
Much Ado about Nothing. Act iv, sc. 2, l. 27. [Dogberry]

A fellow that hath had losses.
Much Ado about Nothing. Act iv, sc. 2, l. 87. [Dogberry]

A rich fellow enough.—*Much Ado about Nothing,* iv, 2, 86.

2
Mercutio: Thou art like one of those fellows that when he enters the confines of a tavern claps me his sword upon the table and says 'God send me no need of thee!' and by the operation of the second cup draws it on the drawer, when indeed there is no need.
Benvolio: Am I like such a fellow?
Mercutio: Come, come, thou art as hot a Jack in thy mood as any in Italy, and as soon moved to be moody, and as soon moody to be moved.
Romeo and Juliet. Act iii, sc. 1, l. 5.

3
There be good fellows in the world, an a man could light on them.
Taming of the Shrew, i, 1, 132. [Hortensio]

If he be not fellow with the best King, thou shalt find the best king of good fellows.
Henry V. Act v, sc. 2, l. 261. [King Henry]

He 's a good fellow, I can tell you that;
He 'll strike, and quickly too.
King Lear. Act v, sc. 3, l. 284. [King Lear]

Good fellow.—*Richard III,* iii, 2, 97, and eight times in later plays.

A good-limbed fellow.—*II Henry IV,* iii, 2, 114. The only use of "good-limbed."

A good sharp fellow.—*Much Ado about Nothing,* i, 2, 17.

4 He hath lost his fellows
And strays about to find 'em.
The Tempest. Act i, sc. 2, l. 416. [Prospero]

All those which were his fellows but of late,
Some better than his value, on the moment
Follow his strides, his lobbies fill with tendance,
Rain sacrificial whisperings in his ear,
Make sacred even his stirrup, and through him
Drink the free air.
Timon of Athens. Act i, sc. 1, l. 78. [Poet] The only use of "lobbies." "Lobby" occurs three times.

Fellows in arms.—*Richard III,* v, 2, 1. See also under COMPANION and COMRADESHIP.

5 Two of these fellows you
Must know and own.
The Tempest. Act v, sc. 1, l. 274. [Prospero]

6
Apemantus: Thou hast feigned him a worthy fellow.
Poet: That 's not feigned; he is so.
Timon of Athens. Act i, sc. 1, l. 229.

A worthy fellow.—*Henry VIII,* iii, 2, 72; *Macbeth,* iv, 3, 183; *Cymbeline,* ii, 3, 60.

Worthy fellows.—*All 's Well that Ends Well,* ii, 1, 61.

7
Second Servant: More of our fellows.
Flavius: All broken implements of a ruin'd house.
Third Servant: Yet do our hearts wear Timon's livery:
That see I by our faces: we are fellows still,
Serving alike in sorrow.
Timon of Athens. Act iv, sc. 2, l. 15.

Let 's yet be fellows.—*Timon of Athens,* iv, 2, 25.

The fellow of servants.—*Twelfth Night,* ii, 5, 170.

8
What sneaking fellow comes yonder?
Troilus and Cressida. Act i, sc. 2, l. 246. [Cressida]

Ajax: A paltry, insolent fellow!
Nestor: How he describes himself!
Troilus and Cressida. Act ii, sc. 3, l. 218.

There 's a fellow!—*Troilus and Cressida,* i, 2, 216.

9
I am a fellow o' the strangest mind i' the world.
Twelfth Night. Act i, sc. 3, l. 119. [Sir Andrew]

I warrant thou art a merry fellow and carest for nothing.
Twelfth Night. Act iii, sc. 1, l. 30. [Viola]

10
Thou art but a scurvy fellow.
Twelfth Night. Act iii, sc. 4, l. 162. [Sir Toby]

A very scurvy fellow.—*Measure for Measure,* v, 1, 136; *Othello,* iv, 2, 140.

11
Go to, go to, thou art a foolish fellow.
Twelfth Night. Act iv, sc. 1, l. 3. [Sebastian]

Foolish fellow.—*Comedy of Errors,* iv, 1, 75.

A good sensible fellow.—*The Two Gentlemen of Verona,* ii, 1, 151.

12
Behold me A fellow of the royal bed.
The Winter's Tale. Act iii, sc. 2, l. 38. [Hermione]

Clown: What manner of fellow was he that robbed you?
Autolycus: A fellow, sir, that I have known to go about with troll-my-dames.
The Winter's Tale. Act iv, sc. 3, l. 89. The only use of "troll-my-dames" (a sort of bagatelle).

13
Polixenes: This a brave fellow.
Clown: Believe me, thou talkest of an admirable conceited fellow.
The Winter's Tale. Act iv, sc. 4, l. 202.

Brave fellow.—*Coriolanus,* ii, 2, 5; v, 1, 30; *Timon of Athens,* i, 2, 56.

We are but plain fellows.—*The Winter's Tale,* iv, 4, 743.

1
Clown: I 'll swear to the prince thou art a tall fellow of thy hands and that thou wilt not be drunk; but I know thou art no tall fellow of thy hands and that thou wilt be drunk: but I 'll swear it, and I would thou wouldst be a tall fellow of thy hands.
Autolycus: I will prove so, sir, to my power.
Clown: Ay, by any means prove a tall fellow; if I do not wonder how thou darest venture to be drunk, not being a tall fellow, trust me not.
The Winter's Tale. Act v, sc. 2, l. 177. "Tall fellow" occurs eleven times.

FELLOWSHIP

See also Brotherhood

2
Kneels and holds up hands for fellowship.
Coriolanus. Act v, sc. 3, l. 175. [Volumnia]

3
Hamlet: Would not this . . . get me a fellowship in a cry of players, sir?
Horatio: Half a share.
Hamlet. Act iii, sc. 2, l. 286.

Fellowship i' the cause.—*Timon of Athens,* v, 2, 12.

Great men's fellowship.—*Antony and Cleopatra,* ii, 7, 13.

Fellowship of death.—*Henry V,* iv, 8, 106.

4
There 's neither honesty, manhood, nor good fellowship in thee.
I Henry IV. Act i, sc. 2, l. 155. [Falstaff]

Gallants, lads, boys, hearts of gold, all the titles of good fellowship come to you!
I Henry IV. Act ii, sc. 4, l. 307. [Falstaff]

Sound good-fellowship.—*Troilus and Cressida,* iv, 1, 52.

Good fellowship come to you!—*I Henry IV,* ii, 4, 307. The only uses of "good fellowship."

5
But out upon this half-faced fellowship!
I Henry IV. Act i, sc. 3, l. 208. [Hotspur]

6
All the fellowship I hold now with him
Is only my obedience.
Henry VIII. Act iii, sc. 1, l. 121. [Queen Katharine]

Disjoin'd from fellowship.—*King John,* iii, 4, 3.

7
Everlasting bond of fellowship.
A Midsummer-Night's Dream. Act i, sc. 1, l. 85. [Theseus]

Sweet fellowship.—*Love's Labour 's Lost,* iv, 3, 49.

8
The great contention of the sea and skies
Parted our fellowship.
Othello. Act ii, sc. 1, l. 92. [Cassio]

FIDELITY

See also Constancy, Loyalty, Service

9 Let death and honesty
Go with your impositions, I am yours
Upon your will to suffer.
All's Well that Ends Well. Act iv, sc. 4, l. 28. [Diana]

I go from hence
Thy soldier, servant; making peace or war
As thou affect'st.
Antony and Cleopatra. Act i, sc. 3, l. 69. [Antony]

If I knew
What hoop should hold us stanch, from edge to edge
O' the world I would pursue it.
Antony and Cleopatra. Act ii, sc. 2, l. 116. [Cæsar]

Thou hast served me with much faith.
Antony and Cleopatra. Act ii, sc. 7, l. 64. [Pompey]

Whose he is we are.
Antony and Cleopatra. Act iii, sc. 13, l. 52. [Enobarbus]

10 There is an old poor man,
Who after me hath many a weary step
Limp'd in pure love.
As You Like It. Act ii, sc. 7, l. 129. [Orlando]

11
But when to my good lord I prove untrue,
I 'll choke myself: there 's all I 'll do for you.
Cymbeline. Act i, sc. 5, l. 86. [Pisanio]

Your means abroad,
You have me, rich; and I will never fail
Beginning nor supplyment.
Cymbeline. Act iii, sc. 4, l. 180. [Pisanio]
The only use of "supplyment."

12 To thine own self be true,
And it must follow, as the night the day,
Thou canst not then be false to any man.
Hamlet. Act i, sc. 3, l. 78. [Polonius]

13
Yea, on his part I 'll empty all these veins,
And shed my dear blood drop by drop in the dust.
I Henry IV. Act i, sc. 3, l. 133. [Hotspur]

For you my staff of office did I break
In Richard's time; and posted day and night
To meet you on the way, and kiss your hand,
When yet you were in place and in account
Nothing so strong and fortunate as I.
I Henry IV. Act v, sc. 1, l. 34. [Worcester]

14
I will never be a truant, love.
I Henry IV. Act iii, sc. 1, l. 207. [Mortimer]

I know you are no truant.
Hamlet. Act i, sc. 2, l. 173. [Hamlet]

I am not such a truant.—*Henry VIII,* iii, 1, 43.

I have a truant been.—*I Henry IV,* v, 1, 94.

I have been a truant.—*I Henry VI,* ii, 4, 7.

Play truant.—*Love's Labour 's Lost,* ii, 1, 74.

Played truant.—*The Merry Wives of Windsor,* v, 1, 27.

Truant with your bed.—*The Comedy of Errors,* iii, 2, 17.

Idle truant.—*The Two Gentlemen of Verona,* ii, 4, 64.

15
Call you that backing of your friends? A plague upon such backing! give me them that will face me.
I Henry IV. Act ii, sc. 4, l. 165. [Falstaff]

Backing of the duke.—*III Henry VI,* ii, 2, 69. The only uses of "backing."

1
He 's followed both with body and with mind.
II Henry IV. Act i, sc. 1, l. 203. [Morton]
Who like a brother toil'd in my affairs
And laid his love and life under my foot.
II Henry IV. Act iii, sc. 1, l. 62. [King Henry]
To stand stained with travel, and sweating with desire to see him; thinking of nothing else, putting all affairs else in oblivion, as if there were nothing else to be done but to see him.
II Henry IV. Act v, sc. 5, l. 25. [Falstaff]

2
The knave will stick by thee, I can assure thee that. A' will not out; he is true bred.
II Henry IV. Act v, sc. 3, l. 69. [Shallow]
I am a kind of burr: I shall stick.
Measure for Measure. Act iv, sc. 3, l. 190. [Lucio]
They 'll stick.—*Troilus and Cressida,* iii, 2, 120.

3
I kiss his dirty shoe, and from heart-string
I love the lovely bully.
Henry V. Act iv, sc. 1, l. 47. [Pistol]
My hand, bully.—*The Merry Wives of Windsor,* ii, 1, 225. "Bully" is used eight times in this play as a term of endearment, and twice in *A Midsummer-Night's Dream,* both times as "Bully Bottom."

4
No more can I be sever'd from your side,
Than can yourself yourself in twain divide.
I Henry VI. Act iv, sc. 5, l. 48. [John Talbot]

5
Let former grudges pass,
And henceforth I am thy true servitor.
III Henry VI. Act iii, sc. 3, l. 195. [Warwick]
Heaven bear witness,
And if I have a conscience, let it sink me,
Even as the axe falls, if I be not faithful!
Henry VIII. Act ii, sc. 1, l. 59. [Buckingham]

6
Set on your foot,
And with a heart new-fired I follow you,
To do I know not what: but it sufficeth
That Brutus leads me on.
Julius Cæsar. Act ii, sc. 1, l. 331. [Ligarius] "New-fired" is repeated in *Sonnets,* cliii.
Mark Antony shall not love Cæsar dead
So well as Brutus living; but will follow
The fortunes and affairs of noble Brutus
Thorough the hazards of this untrod state
With all true faith.
Julius Cæsar. Act iii, sc. 1, l. 133. [Servant] The only use of "untrod."
We 'll hear him, we 'll follow him, we 'll die with him.
Julius Cæsar. Act iii, sc. 2, l. 212. [Citizen]
My heart doth joy that yet in all my life
I found no man but he was true to me.
Julius Cæsar. Act v, sc. 5, l. 34. [Brutus]

7
Madam, I 'll follow you unto the death.
King John. Act i, sc. 1, l. 154. [Bastard]
To the death, my lord.—*Much Ado about Nothing,* i, 3, 72.
Yours in the ranks of death.—*King Lear,* iv, 2, 25.

8
What you bid me undertake,
Though that my death were adjunct to my act,
By heaven, I would do it.
King John. Act iii, sc. 3, l. 56. [Hubert]
I honour'd him, I loved him, and will weep
My date of life out for his sweet life's loss.
King John. Act iv, sc. 3, l. 105. [Hubert]
To whom, with all submission, on my knee
I do bequeath my faithful services
And true subjection everlastingly.
King John. Act v, sc. 7, l. 103. [Bastard]

9
Though to myself forsworn, to thee I 'll faithful prove.
Love's Labour 's Lost. Act iv, sc. 2, l. 111. [Sir Nathaniel, reading]
Sweet lords, sweet lovers, O, let us embrace!
As true we are as flesh and blood can be.
Love's Labour 's Lost. Act iv, sc. 3, l. 214. [Biron]
I 'll serve thee true and faithfully.
Love's Labour 's Lost. Act v, sc. 2, l. 841. [Dumain]

10
Still keep
My bosom franchised and allegiance clear.
Macbeth. Act ii, sc. 1, l. 27. [Banquo] The only use of "franchised."
To the which my duties
Are with a most indissoluble tie
For ever knit.
Macbeth. Act iii, sc. 1, l. 16. [Macbeth] The only use of "indissoluble."

11
As I have ever found thee honest-true,
So let me find thee still.
The Merchant of Venice. Act iii, sc. 4, l. 46. [Portia] The only use of "honest-true."

12
By my fidelity, this is not well.
Merry Wives of Windsor. Act iv, sc. 2, l. 160. [Shallow] Shakespeare used "fidelity" only once, either in the plays or the poems.

13
My heart Is true as steel.
A Midsummer-Night's Dream. Act ii, sc. 1, l. 196. [Helena]
As true as steel.—*Romeo and Juliet,* ii, 4, 210; *Troilus and Cressida,* iii, 2, 184.

14
The sun was not so true unto the day
As he to me.
A Midsummer-Night's Dream. Act iii, sc. 2, l. 50. [Hermia]

15
Thou art sure of me.
Othello. Act i, sc. 3, l. 371. [Iago]
I am bound to thee for ever.
Othello. Act iii, sc. 3, l. 213. [Othello]
I am your own for ever.
Othello. Act iii, sc. 3, l. 479. [Iago]

16
A man that all his time
Hath founded his good fortunes on your love,
Shared dangers with you.
Othello. Act iii, sc. 4, l. 93. [Desdemona]

Be a member of his love
Whom I with all the office of my heart
Entirely honour.
Othello. Act iii, sc. 4, l. 112. [Cassio]
If e'er my will did trespass 'gainst his love,
Either in discourse of thought or actual deed,
Or that mine eyes, mine ears, or any sense,
Delighted them in any form;
Or that I do not yet, and ever did,
And ever will—though he do shake me off
To beggarly divorcement—love him dearly,
Comfort forswear me!
Othello. Act iv, sc. 2, l. 152. [Desdemona] The only use of "divorcement."

1
Like a bold champion, I assume the lists,
Nor ask advice of any other thought
But faithfulness and courage.
Pericles. Act i, sc. 1, l. 61. [Pericles]
For your faithfulness we will advance you.
Pericles. Act i, sc. 1, l. 154. [Antiochus] "Faithfulness" occurs only in this scene, which is probably not by Shakespeare.
Day serves not light more faithful than I 'll be.
Pericles. Act i, sc. 2, l. 110. [Helicanus]

2 I'll kiss thy hand,
In sign of league and amity with thee.
Richard III. Act i, sc. 3, l. 280. [Queen Margaret]
His lordship knows me well, and loves me well.
Richard III. Act iii, sc. 4, l. 31. [Gloucester]
You have no cause to hold my friendship doubtful:
I never was nor never will be false.
Richard III. Act iv, sc. 4, l. 493. [Stanley]
Upon my life, my lord, I 'll undertake it.
Richard III. Act v, sc. 3, l. 42. [Blount]

3 I 'll prove more true
Than those that have more cunning to be strange.
Romeo and Juliet. Act ii, sc. 2, l. 100. [Juliet]
And all my fortunes at thy foot I 'll lay
And follow thee my lord throughout the world.
Romeo and Juliet. Act ii, sc. 2, l. 147. [Juliet]
He 'll go along o'er the wide world with me.
As You Like It. Act i, sc. 3, l. 134. [Celia]
In following him, I follow but myself.
Othello. Act i, sc. 1, l. 58. [Iago]

4
All hail, great master! grave sir, hail! I come
To answer thy best pleasure; be 't to fly,
To swim, to dive into the fire, to ride
On the curl'd clouds.
The Tempest. Act i, sc. 2, l. 189. [Ariel]
Lord of my life, commander of my thoughts.
Titus Andronicus. Act iv, sc. 4, l. 28. [Tamora]

5
I . . . have preserved her welfare in my blood;
And from her bosom took the enemy's point.
Titus Andronicus. Act v, sc. 3, l. 109. [Lucius]

6
But, come what may, I do adore thee so,
That danger shall seem sport, and I will go.
Twelfth Night. Act ii, sc. 1, l. 48. [Antonio]
My willing love,
The rather by these arguments of fear,
Set forth in your pursuit.
Twelfth Night. Act iii, sc. 3, l. 11. [Antonio]
Let me speak a little. This youth that you see here
I snatch'd one half out of the jaws of death,
Relieved him with such sanctity of love,
And to his image, which methought did promise
Most venerable worth, did I devotion.
Twelfth Night. Act iii, sc. 4, l. 393. [Antonio]
I 'll follow this good man, and go with you;
And, having sworn truth, ever will be true.
Twelfth Night. Act iv, sc. 3, l. 32. [Sebastian]

FIELD

7
Where is the enemy? are you lords o' the field?
If not, why cease you till you are so?
Coriolanus. Act i, sc. 6, l. 47. [Marcius]
If we lose the field, We cannot keep the town.
Coriolanus. Act i, sc. 7, l. 4. [Lartius]
How goes the field?—*I Henry IV*, i, 1, 18.

8
A' babbled of green fields.
Henry V. Act ii, sc. 3, l. 18. [Hostess] See under DEATH for full quotation.

9
This glorious and well-foughten field.
Henry V. Act iv, sc. 6, l. 18. [Exeter] The only use of "well-foughten." For full quotation see under SOUL, 1411:8.
Then call we this the field of Agincourt,
Fought on the day of Crispin Crispianus.
Henry V. Act iv, sc. 7, l. 93. [King Henry] Agincourt is also mentioned in the prologue, l. 14.
Here pitch our tents, even here is Bosworth field.
Richard III. Act v, sc. 3, l. 1. [King Richard] The only mention of Bosworth.
Barnet field.—*III Henry VI*, v, 3, 20. Barnet is mentioned again in v, 1, 110.
Philippi fields.—*Julius Cæsar*, v, 5, 19.
Saint Alban's field.—*III Henry VI*, iii, 2, 1.
Saint George's field.—*II Henry IV*, iii, 2, 207; *II Henry VI*, v, 1, 46.
The field of Golgotha.—*Richard II*, iv, 1, 144. Golgotha is mentioned again in *Macbeth*, i, 2, 40.

10
Dare ye come forth and meet us in the field?
I Henry VI. Act iii, sc. 2, l. 61. [Talbot]
I pray you, let us see you in the field.
Troilus and Cressida, iv, 5, 266.
Already in the field.—*I Henry IV*, iv, 2, 81.
Face them in the field.—*II Henry IV*, iv, 1, 24.

11
Did he so often lodge in open field?
II Henry VI. Act i, sc. 1, l. 80. [Gloucester]
Bloody field.—*II Henry IV*, Ind., 24; *Henry V*, iii, 2, 10; iv, 7, 75.
Christian field.—*Richard II*, iv, 1, 93.
Drowned field.—*A Midsummer-Night's Dream*, ii, 1, 96.
Even field.—*Julius Cæsar*, v, 1, 17.
Fair field.—*The Rape of Lucrece*, l. 58.

Frighted fields.—*I Henry IV*, iii, 1, 40.
High-grown field.—*King Lear*, v, 4, 7. The only use of "high-grown."
Holy fields.—*I Henry IV*, i, 1, 24.
Painful field.—*Henry V*, iv, 3, 111.
Pitch'd field.—*Timon of Athens*, i, 2, 231.
Rich fields.—*Henry V*, iii, 5, 25.
Shameful field.—*Troilus and Cressida*, v, 10, 5.
Stained field.—*King John*, ii, 1, 357.
Summer fields.—*Richard III*, v, 2, 8.
Unknown field.—*Comedy of Errors*, iii, 2, 38.

1
I think it cites us, brother, to the field.
III Henry VI. Act ii, sc. 1, l. 34. [Edward] "To the field" is repeated in *III Henry VI*, v, 1, 113; *Henry V*, iii, 5, 39; iv, 2, 60; *Julius Cæsar*, v, 3, 107; *All's Well that Ends Well*, iii, 1, 23; *Cymbeline*, iv, 2, 42.

2
He himself keeps in the cold field.
III Henry VI. Act iv, sc. 3, l. 14. [Watchman]

3
Speed then, to take advantage of the field.
King John. Act ii, sc. 1, l. 297. [Bastard]
Let us survey the vantage of the field.
Richard III. Act v, sc. 3, l. 15. [King Richard]
The tented field.—*Othello*, i, 3, 85.

4
Last in the field, and almost lords of it!
King John. Act v, sc. 5, l. 8. [Lewis]
Go thy ways; the field is won.
The Taming of the Shrew. Act iv, sc. 5, l. 23. [Hortensio]

5
He rather means to lodge you in the field.
Love's Labour's Lost. Act ii, sc. 1, l. 85. [Boyet]
Welcome to the wide fields too base to be mine.
Love's Labour's Lost. Act ii, sc. 1, l. 93. [King]
I will bring the doctor about by the fields.
The Merry Wives of Windsor. Act ii, sc. 3, l. 81. [Host]

6
The fields are near, and you are gallant grooms.
Titus Andronicus. Act iv, sc. 2, l. 164. [Aaron]
Go about the fields.—*The Merry Wives of Windsor*, ii, 3, 90.
The fields of fruitful Italy.—*The Rape of Lucrece*, l. 107.

FIEND

See also Devil

7
A fiend, a fury, pitiless and rough;
A wolf, nay, worse, a fellow all in buff;
A back-friend, a shoulder-clapper, one that countermands
The passages of alleys, creeks and narrow lands;
A hound that runs counter and yet draws dry-foot well;
One that before the judgement carries poor souls to hell.
The Comedy of Errors. Act iv, sc. 2, l. 35. [Dromio of Syracuse] The only use of "back-friend," "shoulder-clapper," and "dry-foot." Dromio is referring to a constable.
The fiend is strong within him.
The Comedy of Errors. Act iv, sc. 4, l. 110. [Pinch]

8
The fiend hath pricked down Bardolph irrecoverable.
II Henry IV, ii, 4, 359. See under FACE. The only use of "irrecoverable."

9
Let . . . fiends for food howl on!
Henry V, ii, 1, 97. See under FLOOD.
Let the fiend give fire.—*II Henry IV*, ii, 4, 196.

10
Whatsoever cunning fiend it was
That wrought upon thee so preposterously
Hath got the voice in hell for excellence.
Henry V. Act ii, sc. 2, l. 111. [King Henry] "Preposterously" is used in three later plays.

11
Foul fiend of France, and hag of all despite!
I Henry VI. Act iii, sc. 2, l. 52. [Talbot] Talbot is addressing La Pucelle.

12
Descend to darkness and the burning lake!
False, fiend, avoid!
II Henry VI. Act i, sc. 4, l. 42. [Bolingbroke]
Avoid then, fiend!—*The Comedy of Errors*, iv, 3, 66.

13
O, beat away the busy meddling fiend
That lays strong siege unto this wretch's soul!
II Henry VI. Act iii, sc. 3, l. 21. [King Henry]

14
There is not yet so ugly a fiend of hell
As thou shalt be.
King John, iv, 3, 123. See under DAMNATION.
Fiend of hell.—*I Henry VI*, ii, 1, 46; *The Taming of the Shrew*, i, 1, 88.
Fiends of hell.—*Cymbeline*, ii, 4, 129.
Pained'st fiend of hell.—*Pericles*, iv, 6, 173.
Fiend of Scotland.—*Macbeth*, iv, 3, 233.

15
Take heed o' the foul fiend.
King Lear. Act iii, sc. 4, l. 82. [Edgar]
Pray, innocent, and beware the foul fiend.
King Lear. Act iii, sc. 6, l. 8. [Edgar]
The foul fiend bites my back.
King Lear. Act iii, sc. 6, l. 18. [Edgar]
The foul fiend haunts poor Tom in the voice of a nightingale.
King Lear. Act iii, sc. 6, l. 31. [Edgar]
Defy the foul fiend.—*King Lear*, iii, 4, 101. "Foul fiend" is used eleven times in this act.
Foul fiends.—*Richard III*, i, 4, 58; *Venus and Adonis*, l. 638.
So foul a fiend!—*Titus Andronicus*, iv, 2, 79.

16
Five fiends have been in poor Tom at once; of lust as Obidicut; Hobbididance, prince of dumbness; Mahu, of stealing; Modo, of murder; Flibbertigibbet, of mopping and mowing, who since possesses chambermaids and waiting-women.
King Lear. Act iv, sc. 1, l. 61. [Edgar] The only mention of Obidicut and Hobbididance. Mahu and Modo occur in iii, 4, 149.

The foul fiend Flibbertigibbet.—*King Lear,* iii, 4, 120.

Edgar: He had a thousand noses,
Horns whelk'd and waved like the enridged sea;
It was some fiend. . . .
Gloucester: That thing you speak of,
I took it for a man; often 'twould say
'The fiend, the fiend.'

King Lear. Act iv, sc. 6, l. 70. The only use of "whelk'd" (twisted), and "enridged."

1
The fiend is at my elbow and tempts me. . . . The most courageous fiend bids me pack: 'Via!' says the fiend; 'away!' says the fiend; 'for the heavens, rouse up a brave mind,' says the fiend, 'and run.' . . . 'Budge,' says the fiend. . . . To run away from the Jew, I should be ruled by the fiend, who, saving your reverence, is the devil himself. . . . The fiend gives the more friendly counsel: I will run, fiend; my heels are at your command.

The Merchant of Venice. Act ii, sc. 2, l. 2. [Launcelot]

2
What black magician conjures up this fiend?

Richard III. Act i, sc. 2, l. 34. [Lady Anne]

One fiend at a time.—*The Tempest,* iii, 1, 102.

Fiend-like.—*Titus Andronicus,* v, 1, 45; *Macbeth,* v, 8, 69. The only uses of the phrase.

3
Lo, how hollow the fiend speaks within him!

Twelfth Night. Act iii, sc. 4, l. 101. [Maria]

4
A fiend like thee might bear my soul to hell.

Twelfth Night. Act iii, sc. 4, l. 237. [Olivia]

Out, hyperbolical fiend!

Twelfth Night. Act iv, sc. 2, l. 28. [Clown] "Hyperbolical" occurs again in *Coriolanus,* i, 9, 51: "Acclamations hyperbolical."

Fiend angelical!—*Romeo and Juliet,* iii, 2, 75.

Italian fiend!—*Cymbeline,* v, 5, 210.

Juggling fiends.—*Macbeth,* v, 8, 19.

Marble-hearted fiend!—*King Lear,* i, 4, 281. The only use of "marble-hearted."

Naked and concealed fiend.—*A Lover's Complaint,* l. 317.

Under fiends.—*Coriolanus,* iv, 5, 98.

A very fiend.—*The Taming of the Shrew,* iii, 2, 157.

Vile fiend.—*I Henry VI,* iii, 2, 45.

O most wicked fiend!—*Romeo and Juliet,* iii, 5, 235.

FIGHTING

See also Battle, Combat, Duelling, Fray, War

5
We came hither to fight with you.

Antony and Cleopatra. Act ii, sc. 6, l. 107. [Enobarbus]

Enobarbus: So hath my lord dared him to single fight.
Canidius: Ay, and to wage this battle at Pharsalia,
Where Cæsar fought with Pompey.

Antony and Cleopatra. Act iii, sc. 7, l. 32. The only mention of Pharsalia.

Antony: I 'll fight at sea.
Cleopatra: I have sixty sails, Cæsar none better.

Antony and Cleopatra. Act iii, sc. 7, l. 49.

O noble emperor, do not fight by sea.

Antony and Cleopatra. Act iii, sc. 7, l. 62. [Soldier]

To-morrow, soldier, By sea and land I 'll fight.

Antony and Cleopatra. Act iv, sc. 2, l. 4. [Antony]

Would thou and those thy scars had once prevail'd
To make me fight at land!

Antony and Cleopatra. Act iv, sc. 5, l. 2. [Antony]

The next day Was our sea-fight.

Hamlet. Act v, sc. 2, l. 54. [Hamlet] "Sea-fight" is repeated in *Twelfth Night,* iii, 3, 26.

6
I will be treble-sinew'd, hearted, breathed,
And fight maliciously.

Antony and Cleopatra. Act iii, sc. 13, l. 178. [Antony] The only use of "treble-sinew'd."

Fight cheerfully.—*Henry V,* iv, 1, 204.

Fight lustily.—*Henry V,* iv, 1, 201.

Fight singly.—*Troilus and Cressida,* iii, 3, 247.

Single fight.—*I Henry IV,* v, 2, 47; *Antony and Cleopatra,* iii, 7, 31; iv, 4, 37.

7
Antony: Woo 't thou fight well?
Enobarbus: I 'll strike, and cry 'Take all.'

Antony and Cleopatra. Act iv, sc. 2, l. 7.

You that will fight,
Follow me close; I 'll bring you to 't.

Antony and Cleopatra. Act iv, sc. 4, l. 33. [Antony]

I would they 'ld fight i' the fire or i' the air;
We 'ld fight there too.

Antony and Cleopatra. Act iv, sc. 10, l. 3. [Antony]

Fighting foot to foot.—*Antony and Cleopatra,* iii, 7, 67.

8
He hath fought to-day
As if a god, in hate of mankind, had
Destroy'd in such a shape.

Antony and Cleopatra. Act iv, sc. 8, l. 24. [Antony]

He fought Beyond the mark of others.

Coriolanus. Act ii, sc. 2, l. 92. [Cominius]

O, well fought!—*Troilus and Cressida,* v, 6, 12; *Coriolanus,* i, 6, 1.

9
I 'll lean upon one crutch and fight with t' other,
Ere stay behind this business.

Coriolanus. Act i, sc. 1, l. 246. [Titus]

Now put your shields before your hearts, and fight
With hearts more proof than shields.

Coriolanus. Act i, sc. 4, l. 24. [Caius]

We have at disadvantage fought and did
Retire to win our purpose.

Coriolanus. Act i, sc. 6, l. 49. [Cominius]

10
I 'll fight with none but thee.

Coriolanus. Act i, sc. 8, l. 1. [Marcius]

There 's some among you have beheld me fighting;

Come, try upon yourselves what you have seen me.
Coriolanus. Act iii, sc. 1, l. 224. [Coriolanus]
I will fight
Against my canker'd country with the spleen
Of all the under fiends.
Coriolanus. Act iv, sc. 5, l. 96. [Coriolanus]
I'll run away till I am bigger, but then I'll fight.
Coriolanus, v, 3, 128. [Young Marcius]
Fights dragon-like.—*Coriolanus,* iv, 7, 23. The only use of "dragon-like."

1
Every Jack-slave hath his bellyful of fighting.
Cymbeline. Act ii, sc. 1, l. 22. [Cloten] The only use of "Jack-slave." "Bellyful" occurs once again in *King Lear,* iii, 2, 14: "Rumble thy bellyful."
Fight I will no more,
But yield me to the veriest hind that shall
Once touch my shoulder.
Cymbeline. Act v, sc. 3, l. 76. [Posthumus]
Stand, stand, and fight!—*Cymbeline,* v, 2, 13.

2
Why, I will fight with him upon this theme
Until my eyelids will no longer wag.
Hamlet. Act v, sc. 1, l. 289. [Hamlet]
Sir, in my heart there was a kind of fighting,
That would not let me sleep: methought I lay
Worse than the mutines in the bilboes.
Hamlet. Act v, sc. 2, l. 4. [Hamlet] The only use of "bilboes" (shackles sliding on an iron bar locked to the floor; used for mutinous sailors). "Mutines" is repeated in *King John,* ii, 1, 378: "Mutines of Jerusalem."

3
In single opposition, hand to hand,
He did confound the best part of an hour
In changing hardiment with great Glendower.
I Henry IV. Act i, sc. 3, l. 99. [Hotspur] "Hardiment" is used twice more in the plays: *Troilus and Cressida,* iv, 5, 28; *Cymbeline,* v, 4, 75.
If I fought not with fifty of them, I am a bunch of radish: if there were not two or three and fifty upon poor old Jack, then am I no two-legged creature.
I Henry IV. Act ii, sc. 4, l. 205. [Falstaff] The only use of the phrase "bunch of radish," and of "two-legged."
You had not four such swinge-bucklers in all the inns o' court.
II Henry IV. Act iii, sc. 2, l. 24. [Shallow] The only use of "swinge-bucklers."
We rose both at one instant and fought a long hour by Shrewsbury clock.
I Henry IV. Act v, sc. 4, l. 150. [Falstaff]
We'll fight with him to-night.—*I Henry IV,* iv, 3, 1.

4
I have led my ragamuffins where they are peppered.
I Henry IV. Act v, sc. 3, l. 36. [Falstaff] The only use of "ragamuffins."
I have peppered two of them.—*I Henry IV,* ii, 4, 212.
I am peppered.—*Romeo and Juliet,* iii, 1, 102. The only uses of "peppered."

5
They did fight with queasiness, constrain'd,
As men drink potions.
II Henry IV. Act i, sc. 1, l. 196. [Morton] The only use of "queasiness."
Strike up our drums, pursue the scatter'd stray:
God, and not we, hath safely fought to-day.
II Henry IV. Act iv, sc. 2, l. 120. [Lancaster]

6
The knocks are too hot; and, for my part, I have not a case of lives.
Henry V. Act iii, sc. 2, l. 3. [Nym]
King Richard: Norfolk, we must have knocks; ha! must we not?
Norfolk: We must both give and take, my gracious lord.
Richard III. Act v, sc. 3, l. 5. See also under KNOCKING.

7
Farewell, kind lord; fight valiantly to-day:
And yet I do thee wrong to mind thee of it.
Henry V. Act iv, sc. 3, l. 12. [Exeter]
Thrice within this hour
I saw him down: thrice up again, and fighting.
Henry V. Act iv, sc. 6, l. 4. [King Henry]
Renew the fight.—*I Henry VI,* i, 5, 27.

8
Salisbury is a desperate homicide;
He fighteth as one weary of his life.
I Henry VI. Act i, sc. 2, l. 25. [Reignier] The only use of "fighteth." For "homicide" see under MURDERER.

9
Fight till the last gasp.
I Henry VI. Act i, sc. 2, l. 127. [La Pucelle]
Fight and die.—*I Henry VI,* iv, 5, 45.
Fight like devils.—*Henry V,* iii, 7, 162.
Fight for France.—*I Henry VI,* i, 1, 85.
Fight for freedom.—*Titus Andronicus,* i, 1, 17.
Fight for bitten apples.—*Henry VIII,* v, 4, 64.

10
Talbot: Will ye, like soldiers, come and fight it out?
Alençon: Signior, no.
Talbot: Signior, hang! base muleters of France!
Like peasant foot-boys do they keep the walls
And dare not take up arms like gentlemen.
I Henry VI. Act iii, sc. 2, l. 68. "Muleters" is repeated in *Antony and Cleopatra,* iii, 7, 36.
Christian footboy.—*The Taming of the Shrew,* iii, 2, 72.
Lousy footboy.—*Henry VIII,* v, 3, 139.
Pages, and footboys.—*Henry VIII,* v, 2, 25. The only uses of "footboy" and "footboys."

11
Talbot: Upon my blessing, I command thee go.
John Talbot: To fight I will, but not to fly the foe.
I Henry VI. Act iv, sc. 5, l. 36.
Had the maidenhood Of thy first fight.
I Henry VI. Act iv, sc. 6, l. 17. [Talbot]
Bloody fight!—*The Passionate Pilgrim,* l. 280.
Dangerous fight.—*I Henry VI,* iv, 2, 56.
Dismal fight.—*I Henry VI,* i, 1, 105.
Great fights.—*Antony and Cleopatra,* i, 1, 7.

Unworthy fight.—*I Henry VI,* iv, 7, 43.

1
Sirrah, or you must fight, or else be hang'd.
II Henry VI. Act i, sc. 3, l. 222. [Gloucester]

2
I cannot fight; for God's sake, pity my case. . . .
I shall never be able to fight a blow.
II Henry VI. Act i, sc. 3, l. 217. [Peter]

I never saw a fellow worse bested,
Or more afraid to fight.
II Henry VI. Act ii, sc. 3, l. 56. [York] The only use of "bested."

I myself fight not once in forty year.
I Henry VI. Act i, sc. 3, l. 91. [Mayor]

3
Fight for your king, your country and your lives.
II Henry VI. Act iv, sc. 5, l. 12. [Lord Scales]

Let 's go fight with them.—*II Henry VI,* iv, 6, 15.
Fight with flint.—*II Henry VI,* v, 1, 24.
Fight in thy defence.—*III Henry VI,* i, 1, 160.
Fight in your defence.—*III Henry VI,* ii, 2, 79.

4
Clifford, I say, come forth and fight with me.
II Henry VI. Act v, sc. 2, l. 5. [Warwick]

Now, by my sword, well hast thou fought to-day.
II Henry VI. Act v, sc. 3, l. 15. [Salisbury]

5
Let 's fight it out and not stand cavilling thus.
III Henry VI. Act i, sc. 1, l. 117. [Montague] The only use of "cavilling."

Fight it out!—*III Henry VI,* i, 4, 10.
We 'll fight it out.—*I Henry VI,* i, 2, 128; iii, 2, 66.
I 'll fight it out.—*I Henry VI,* i, 1, 99.

6
We at Saint Alban's met,
Our battles join'd, and both sides fiercely fought.
III Henry VI. Act ii, sc. 1, l. 120. [Edward] The only use of "fiercely."

They had no heart to fight,
And we in them no hope to win the day.
III Henry VI. Act ii, sc. 1, l. 135. [Warwick]

Making another head to fight again.
III Henry VI. Act ii, sc. 1, l. 141. [Warwick]

With resolution then to fight.
III Henry VI. Act ii, sc. 2, l. 77. [Northumberland]

Let them fight that will,
For I have murdered where I should not kill.
III Henry VI. Act ii, sc. 5, l. 121. [Father]

Wilt thou leave the town and fight?
Or shall we beat the stones about thine ears?
III Henry VI. Act v, sc. 1, l. 107. [King Edward]

He that will not fight for such a hope,
Go home to bed, and like the owl by day,
If he arise, be mock'd and wonder'd at.
III Henry VI. Act v, sc. 4, l. 55. [Somerset]

Ready to fight.—*III Henry VI,* v, 4, 61.
Give signal to the fight.—*III Henry VI,* v, 4, 72; v, 4, 81.

7
Now here a period of tumultuous broils.
III Henry VI. Act v, sc. 5, l. 1. [King Edward]

More rancorous spite, more furious raging broils,
Than yet can be imagined or supposed.
I Henry VI. Act iv, sc. 1, l. 185. [Exeter]

Civil broils.—*I Henry VI,* i, 1, 53; *II Henry VI,* iv, 8, 46.
Domestic broils.—*Richard III,* ii, 4, 60; *King Lear,* v, 1, 30.
New broils.—*I Henry IV,* i, 1, 3.
Outrageous broils.—*I Henry VI,* v, 4, 97.
Peevish broil.—*I Henry VI,* iii, 1, 92.

8
If you dare fight to-day, come to the field;
If not, when you have stomachs.
Julius Cæsar. Act v, sc. 1, l. 65. [Octavius]

9
They are at hand, To parley or to fight.
King John. Act ii, sc. 1, l. 77. [Chatillon]

Compell'd to fight.—*King John,* iv, 1, 116.
To fight when I cannot choose.—*King Lear,* i, 4, 18.

10
A man so breathed, that certain he would fight; yea
From morn till night, out of his pavilion.
Love's Labour's Lost. Act v, sc. 2, l. 659. [Armado]

Dares not fight.—*Love's Labour's Lost,* i, 1, 230.

11
I 'll fight till from my bones my flesh be hack'd.
Macbeth. Act v, sc. 3, l. 32. [Macbeth]

Do we but find the tyrant's power to-night,
Let us be beaten, if we cannot fight.
Macbeth. Act v, sc. 6, l. 7. [Siward]

I 'll not fight with thee.—*Macbeth,* v, 8, 22.
I must fight the course.—*Macbeth,* v, 7, 2.

12
Lay on, Macduff,
And damn'd be him that first cries 'Hold, enough!'
Macbeth. Act v, sc. 8, l. 33. [Macbeth] "Lay on" is used only once again in the plays, in *Henry V,* v, 2, 147.

13
You have yourself been a great fighter, though now a man of peace.
The Merry Wives of Windsor. Act ii, sc. 3, l. 44. [Page]

I am no fighter.—*Twelfth Night,* iii, 4, 265; *The Winter's Tale,* iv, 3, 116.
Dull fighter.—*I Henry IV,* iv, 2, 86. The only uses of "fighter."

14
He 's the man should fight with him.
The Merry Wives of Windsor. Act iii, sc. 1, l. 71. [Mistress Page]

Thou see 'st these lovers seek a place to fight.
A Midsummer-Night's Dream. Act iii, sc. 2, l. 354. [Oberon]

Counsel him to fight.—*Much Ado about Nothing,* iii, 1, 83.

15
Were it my cue to fight, I should have known it
Without a prompter.
Othello. Act i, sc. 2, l. 83. [Othello]

"Prompter" is repeated in *Romeo and Juliet,* i, 4, 8.

1
For Christian shame, put by this barbarous brawl.
Othello. Act ii, sc. 3, l. 172. [Othello] "Brawl" is used twenty-one times in the plays, and "brawling" seven times.
With thy brawls thou hast disturb'd our sport.
A Midsummer-Night's Dream, ii, 1, 87.
Right ill-disposed in brawl ridiculous.
Henry V, iv, Prol., 51. "Ill-disposed" is repeated in *Troilus and Cressida,* ii, 3, 84.
Keep you out of prawls, and prabbles, and quarrels, and dissensions.
Henry V. Act iv, sc. 8, l. 69. [Fluellen]
This will grow to a brawl anon.
II Henry IV. Act ii, sc. 4, l. 186. [Bardolph]
Three civil brawls, bred of an airy word.
Romeo and Juliet. Act i, sc. 1, l. 96. [Prince]
How now, Sir John! what are you brawling here?
Doth this become your place, your time and business?
II Henry IV. Act ii, sc. 1, l. 71. [Chief Justice]
I am going with my pigeons to the tribunal plebs, to take up a matter of brawl betwixt my uncle and one of the emperial's men.
Titus Andronicus. Act iv, sc. 3, l. 92. [Clown] The only use of "plebs"; "emperial" is repeated in iv, 4, 40, and occurs in no other play; "tribunal" is repeated in *Antony and Cleopatra,* iii, 6, 3.

2
As I truly fight, defend me heaven!
Richard II. Act i, sc. 3, l. 25. [Mowbray]
Never did captive with a freer heart
Cast off his chains of bondage and embrace
His golden uncontroll'd enfranchisement,
More than my dancing soul doth celebrate
This feast of battle with mine adversary.
Richard II. Act i, sc. 3, l. 88. [Mowbray]
As gentle and as jocund as to jest
Go I to fight.
Richard II. Act i, sc. 3, l. 95. [Mowbray]
Dares him to set forward to the fight.
Richard II. Act i, sc. 3, l. 109. [Herald]
Unjustly fight!—*Richard II,* i, 1, 83.
Fighting-men.—*Richard II,* iii, 2, 70; *Henry V,* iv, 3, 3.

3
Fight, gentlemen of England! fight, bold yeomen!
Richard III. Act v, sc. 3, l. 338. [King Richard]
His horse is slain, and all on foot he fights.
Richard III. Act v, sc. 4, l. 4. [Catesby]
Fight in thy behalf.—*Richard III,* v, 3, 122.

4
I 'll fight their legions o'er.
The Tempest. Act iii, sc. 3, l. 103. [Sebastian]

5
To ruffle in the commonwealth of Rome.
Titus Andronicus, i, 1, 313. [Saturninus]
You should not ruffle thus.—*King Lear,* iii, 7, 41.
Ruffle up your spirits.—*Julius Cæsar,* iii, 2, 232.
Ruffle knew of court.—*Lover's Complaint,* l. 58.
Sorely ruffle.—*King Lear,* ii, 4, 304. The only uses of "ruffle."

6
He 'll fight indifferent well.
Troilus and Cressida. Act i, sc. 2, l. 242. [Pandarus]
Ay, you shall fight your hearts out ere I part you.
Troilus and Cressida. Act iii, sc. 2, l. 55. [Pandarus]
I am not warm yet; let us fight again.
Troilus and Cressida. Act iv, sc. 5, l. 118. [Ajax]
You must prepare to fight.—*Troilus and Cressida,* ii, 3, 238.
I 'll fight no more.—*Troilus and Cressida,* iii, 3, 56.

7
Within my soul there doth conduce a fight
Of this strange nature that a thing inseparate
Divides more wider than the sky and earth.
Troilus and Cressida. Act v, sc. 2, l. 147. [Troilus] The only use of "inseparate."
Unarm, unarm, and do not fight to-day.
Troilus and Cressida. Act v, sc. 3, l. 3. [Andromache]
How now, young man! mean'st thou to fight to-day?
Troilus and Cressida. Act v, sc. 3, l. 29. [Hector]
Troilus, I would not have you fight to-day.
Troilus and Cressida. Act v, sc. 3, l. 50. [Hector]
We 'll forth and fight,
Do deeds worth praise and tell you them at night.
Troilus and Cressida. Act v, sc. 3, l. 92. [Hector]
I 'll fight with him alone.—*Troilus and Cressida,* v, 6, 9.
Turn, slave, and fight.—*Troilus and Cressida,* v, 7, 13.

8
Now they are clapper-clawing one another.
Troilus and Cressida. Act v, sc. 4, l. 1. [Thersites] The only use of "clapper-clawing." "Clapper-de-claw" is used twice in *The Merry Wives of Windsor,* ii, 3, 69; ii, 3, 71, and "clapper-claw" once in the same play, ii, 3, 67.
Close fighting.—*Romeo and Juliet,* i, 1, 114.

FIGURE

See also Number

9
Never saw I figures
So likely to report themselves.
Cymbeline. Act ii, sc. 4, l. 82. [Iachimo]
As like a figure.—*Cymbeline,* iii, 3, 96.

10
What would your gracious figure?
Hamlet. Act iii, sc. 4, l. 104. [Hamlet]
A figure like your father.—*Hamlet,* i, 2, 199.

11
A crooked figure may
Attest in little place a million.
Henry V. Act i, Prologue, l. 15. [Chorus]
There is figures in all things.
Henry V. Act iv, sc. 7, l. 35. [Fluellen]

12
Armado: A most fine figure!
Moth: To prove you a cipher.
Love's Labour 's Lost. Act i, sc. 2, l. 49.

Baby figure.—*Troilus and Cressida,* i, 3, 345.
Fixed figure.—*Othello,* iv, 2, 54.
Foolish figure.—*Hamlet,* ii, 2, 98.
Great figure.—*All 's Well that Ends Well,* iii, 1, 12.
So great a figure.—*Measure for Measure,* i, 1, 50.
Pencill'd figures.—*Timon of Athens,* i, 1, 159.
Portentous figure.—*Hamlet,* i, 1, 109.
Silken figures.—*A Lover's Complaint,* l. 17.
Unbodied figure.—*Troilus and Cressida,* i, 3, 16.
Figures pedantical.—*Love's Labour 's Lost,* v, 2, 408. The only use of "pedantical."
Figure in rhetoric.—*As You Like It,* v, 1, 45.

1
What figure of us think you he will bear?
Measure for Measure. Act i, sc. 1, l. 17. [Duke]

2
Poor key-cold figure of a holy king!
Richard III. Act i, sc. 2, l. 5. [Anne] The only use of "key-cold."

The figure of God's Majesty.
Richard II, iv, 1, 125. See under JUDGEMENT.

A figure of truth, of faith, of loyalty.
Pericles. Act v, sc. 3, Gower, l. 92. [Gower]

What is the figure?—*Love's Labour 's Lost,* v, 1, 67.
Figure of an angel.—*The Merchant of Venice,* ii, 7, 56.
Figure of this harpy.—*The Tempest,* iii, 3, 83.
Figure of my heart.—*Othello,* i, 1, 62.
Figure of the house.—*II Henry IV,* i, 3, 43.
Figure of a lamb.—*Much Ado about Nothing,* i, 1, 15.
Figures of delight.—*Sonnets,* xcviii.

3
He will throw a figure in her face and so disfigure her.
The Taming of the Shrew. Act i, sc. 2, l. 114. [Grumio]

4
Write in thee the figures of their love,
Ever to read them thine.
Timon of Athens. Act v, sc. 1, l. 157. [Senator]

FINENESS

5
Spirits are not finely touch'd
But to fine issues.
Measure for Measure. Act i, sc. 1, l. 36. [Duke]

6
I will be sure my Katharine shall be fine.
The Taming of the Shrew. Act ii, sc. 1, l. 319. [Petruchio]

There shall be none fine but Adam, Ralph and Gregory.
The Taming of the Shrew. Act iv, sc. 1, l. 139. [Grumio]

Fine array.—*Taming of the Shrew,* ii, 1, 325.
Fine fancies.—*Pericles,* iii, Gower, 13.
Fine foot.—*Romeo and Juliet,* ii, 1, 19.
Fine forehead.—*Troilus and Cressida,* iii, 1, 117.
Fine hand.—*Henry VIII,* v, 4, 74.
Fine hats.—*All 's Well that Ends Well,* iv, 5, 111.
Fine linen.—*Taming of the Shrew,* ii, 1, 355.
Fine spirit.—*The Tempest,* i, 2, 420.
Fine things.—*The Tempest,* ii, 2, 121.
A fine woman.—*Othello,* iv, 1, 189.
A fine workman.—*Julius Cæsar,* i, 1, 10. It will be noted that none of these phrases is used more than once.

7
How fine my master is!
The Tempest. Act v, sc. 1, l. 262. [Caliban]

8
Those that will the fineness of their souls
By reason guide.
Troilus and Cressida. Act i, sc. 3, l. 209. [Ulysses] "Fineness" appears only twice more in the plays: *The Comedy of Errors,* iv, 1, 29, and *Troilus and Cressida,* i, 3, 22.

FINGER

9
Put the finger in the eye and weep.
The Comedy of Errors. Act ii, sc. 2, l. 206. [Adriana]

Put finger in the eye.—*The Taming of the Shrew,* i, 1, 79.

10
The fingers of the powers above do tune
The harmony of this peace.
Cymbeline. Act v, sc. 5, l. 466. [Soothsayer]

11
Still your fingers on your lips, I pray.
Hamlet. Act i, sc. 5, l. 188. [Hamlet]

Her choppy finger laying
Upon her skinny lips.
Macbeth, i, 3, 44. See under UNDERSTANDING. The only use of "choppy" (chapped), and "skinny."

Yet again your fingers to your lips? would they were clyster-pipes for your sake!
Othello. Act ii, sc. 1, l. 177. [Iago] The only use of "clyster-pipes" in the plays, meaning the anal tube of an enema syringe.

Lay thy finger on thy lips!—*Troilus and Cressida,* i, 3, 240.
Lays his finger on his temple.—*Henry VIII,* iii, 2, 115.
Lay his fingers off it.—*Julius Cæsar,* i, 2, 243.

12
I prithee, take thy fingers from my throat.
Hamlet, v, 1, 283. See under CHARACTER.

13
'Twixt his finger and his thumb.
I Henry IV. Act i, sc. 3, l. 37. [Hotspur]

Between my finger and my thumb.—*II Henry IV,* iv, 3, 141.

He turned me about with his finger and his thumb, as one would set up a top.
Coriolanus, iv, 5, 160. See under ARM.

With his finger and his thumb.—*Love's Labour 's Lost,* v, 2, 111.
With your fingers and thumb.—*Hamlet,* iii, 2, 373.

Here I have a pilot's thumb,
Wreck'd as homeward he did come.
Macbeth. Act i, sc. 3, l. 28. [Witch]

By the pricking of my thumbs,
Something wicked this way comes.
Macbeth, iv, 1, 44. See under OMEN.

Do you bite your thumb at us, sir?
Romeo and Juliet, i, 1, 49. See under QUARREL.

14
Prick not your finger as you pluck it off.
I Henry VI, ii, 4, 49. See under ROSE.

His finger pricks.—*The Rape of Lucrece,* l. 319.

Prick thy finger.—*III Henry VI,* i, 4, 55.
Prick their finger.—*II Henry IV,* ii, 2, 121.
Pinching fingers.—*The Winter's Tale,* i, 2, 115.

1
I kiss these fingers for eternal peace,
And lay them gently on thy tender side.
I Henry VI. Act v, sc. 3, l. 48. [Suffolk]
I will kiss thy royal finger and take leave.
Love's Labour's Lost. Act v, sc. 2, l. 891. [Armado] "Royal finger" is repeated in l. 109.
Give them thy fingers . . . to kiss.—*Sonnets,* cxxviii.

2 Do you think, my lords,
The king will suffer but the little finger
Of this man to be vex'd?
Henry VIII. Act v, sc. 3, l. 105. [Norfolk]
I 'll break thy little finger.—*I Henry IV,* ii, 3, 90.
Thy little finger.—*The Taming of the Shrew,* iv, 3, 149.
Your little finger.—*Coriolanus,* v, 4, 5. The only uses of "little finger."

3 Now let me see the proudest
He, that dares most, but wag his finger at thee.
Henry VIII. Act v, sc. 3, l. 130. [King Henry]
Ambitious finger.—*Henry VIII,* i, 1, 53.
Barky fingers.—*A Midsummer-Night's Dream,* iv, 1, 49. The only use of "barky."
Bloody fingers.—*Julius Cæsar,* iii, 1, 198; *Titus Andronicus,* ii, 3, 226.
Damn'd fingers.—*Hamlet,* iii, 4, 185.
Dead finger.—*Romeo and Juliet,* v, 3, 30.
Dead men's fingers.—*Hamlet,* iv, 7, 172.
False finger.—*The Two Gentlemen of Verona,* iv, 4, 141.
Honour'd finger.—*Cymbeline,* v, 5, 184.
Icy fingers.—*King John,* v, 7, 37.
Lazy finger.—*Romeo and Juliet,* i, 4, 66.
Slow unmoving finger.—*Othello,* iv, 2, 55.
Sweet fingers.—*Sonnets,* cxxviii.
Fortune's fingers.—*Twelfth Night,* ii, 5, 171; *Hamlet,* iii, 2, 75.
Lawyers' fingers.—*Romeo and Juliet,* i, 4, 73.
Finger of birth-strangled babe.—*Macbeth,* iv, 1, 30. The only use of "birth-strangled."
Finger of a throned queen.—*Sonnets,* xcvi.

4
Go to; thou hast it ad dunghill, at the fingers' ends, as they say.
Love's Labour's Lost. Act v, sc. 1, l. 81. [Costard]
I have them at my fingers' ends.
Twelfth Night. Act i, sc. 3, l. 83. [Maria]
Smile upon his fingers' ends.—*Henry V,* ii, 3, 16.
Touch me his finger-end.—*The Merry Wives of Windsor,* v, 5, 88.
Bloody fingers' ends.—*King John,* iii, 4, 168. The only uses of "fingers' ends."

5 The duke
Dare no more stretch this finger of mine than he
Dare rack his own.
Measure for Measure. Act v, sc. 1, l. 316. [Duke]

6
You may tell every finger I have with my ribs.
The Merchant of Venice, ii, 2, 114. See under HUNGER.
Three fingers on the ribs.—*I Henry IV,* iv, 2, 80.
Three fingers.—*Othello,* ii, 1, 174.

7
I 'll ne'er put my finger in the fire.
The Merry Wives of Windsor. Act i, sc. 4, l. 90. [Mistress Quickly]

8
Good Master Cobweb: if I cut my finger, I shall make bold with you.
A Midsummer-Night's Dream. Act iii, sc. 1, l. 186. [Bottom]

9
Lay thy finger thus, and let thy soul be instructed.
Othello. Act ii, sc. 1, l. 223. [Iago]
Let him hold his fingers thus.—*A Midsummer-Night's Dream,* iii, 1, 72.
Lay to your fingers.
The Tempest. Act iv, sc. 1, l. 251. [Stephano] The only use of "lay to."

10 She weaved the sleided silk
With fingers long, small, and white as milk.
Pericles. Act iv, Gower, l. 21. [Gower] The only use of "sleided" (sleeve silk).

11
My fingers itch.
Romeo and Juliet, iii, 5, 165; *The Merry Wives of Windsor,* ii, 3, 48; *Troilus and Cressida,* ii, 1, 27.

12
He that cannot lick his fingers goes not with me.
Romeo and Juliet, iv, 2, 9. See under COOK.
Lick his own fingers.—*Romeo and Juliet,* iv, 2, 7.
Lick their fingers.—*Romeo and Juliet,* iv, 2, 4.

13
The devil take your fingers!
The Tempest, iii, 2, 89. See under CURSE.
Put some lime upon your fingers.
The Tempest. Act iv, sc. 1, l. 247. [Trinculo]

14
I . . . must not break my back to heal his finger.
Timon of Athens. Act ii, sc. 1, l. 24. [Senator]
I had as lief thou didst break his neck as his finger.
As You Like It, i, 1, 153. See under NECK.

15
And he hath cut those pretty fingers off,
That could have better sew'd than Philomel.
Titus Andronicus. Act ii, sc. 4, l. 42. [Marcus]
These your white enchanting fingers.
Troilus and Cressida. Act iii, sc. 1, l. 164. [Paris]
She locks her lily fingers one in one.
Venus and Adonis, l. 228.
He bends her fingers.—*Venus and Adonis,* l. 476.

FIRE

16
I am a woodland fellow, sir, that always loved a great fire.
All's Well that Ends Well. Act iv, sc. 5, l. 49. [Clown] The only use of "woodland." "Great fire" is repeated in l. 58, and occurs in no other scene.
Flashing fire.—*Henry V,* ii, 1, 56.

Glowing fire.—*Venus and Adonis,* l. 35.
Golden fire.—*Hamlet,* ii, 2, 313.
Hot-burning fire.—*The Rape of Lucrece,* l. 1556. "Hot-burning" is repeated in l. 247, and occurs only in this poem.
Spritely fire.—*All's Well that Ends Well,* ii, 1, 78.
Sweet fire.—*Love's Labour's Lost,* iv, 2, 120.
Unbated fire.—*Merchant of Venice,* ii, 6, 11.

1
By the fire That quickens Nilus' slime.
Antony and Cleopatra. Act i, sc. 3, l. 68. [Antony]

I am fire and air; my other elements
I give to baser life.
Antony and Cleopatra. Act v, sc. 2, l. 292. [Cleopatra] See under ELEMENT.

2
By Fortune fall into the fire.
As You Like It, i, 2, 47. See under FORTUNE.
Embraced with fire.—*Coriolanus,* v, 2, 7.
On fire.—*I Henry IV,* iii, 1, 24; iv, 1, 117. *Henry V,* ii, Prol., 1.
On fire to go.—*I Henry IV,* iii, 1, 269.

3
I stand on fire: Come to the matter.
Cymbeline. Act v, sc. 5, l. 168. [Cymbeline]

4
An the fire of grace be not quite out of thee.
I Henry IV, ii, 4, 421. See under GRACE.
Fire of life.—*Pericles,* iii, 2, 83.
Fire of love.—*The Two Gentlemen of Verona,* ii, 7, 20; *Pericles,* i, 1, 53.
Fire of lust.—*The Merry Wives of Windsor,* ii, 1, 68.
Fire of passion.—*Henry VIII,* i, 1, 149.
Fire of rage.—*Cymbeline,* i, 1, 77.
Fire of youth.—*All's Well that Ends Well,* iv, 2, 5. It will be noted that only one of these phrases was used more than once, and even that one was probably used only once by Shakespeare, the first act of *Pericles* being usually attributed to another hand.

5
Nay, then, this spark will prove a raging fire,
If wind and fuel be brought to feed it with.
II Henry VI. Act iii, sc. 1, l. 302. [Queen Margaret]

And where two raging fires meet together
They do consume the thing that feeds their fury.
The Taming of the Shrew. Act ii, sc. 1, l. 133. [Petruchio]
Raging fire.—*The Comedy of Errors,* v, 1, 75.
Climbing fire.—*I Henry VI,* iv, 2, 11.
Fierce fire.—*King John,* iv, 1, 120.
Living fire.—*Richard II,* i, 2, 10.
Never-quenching fire.—*Richard II,* v, 5, 109. The only use of "never-quenching."
Quenchless fire.—*III Henry VI,* i, 4, 28; *The Rape of Lucrece,* l. 1554.
Wrathful fire.—*I Henry VI,* i, 1, 12.

6
Set London bridge on fire; and, if you can, burn down the Tower too.
II Henry VI. Act iv, sc. 6, l. 16. [Cade]

Set fire on barns and hay-stacks in the night,
And bid the owners quench them with their tears.
Titus Andronicus. Act v, sc. 1, l. 133. [Aaron] The only use of "hay-stacks."
Set hell on fire.—*The Merry Wives of Windsor,* v, 5, 39.
Set whole realms on fire.—*Timon of Athens,* iii, 3, 34.
Set on fire.—*II Henry VI,* i, 4, 20; *King John,* ii, 1, 351.

7
A little fire is quickly trodden out;
Which, being suffer'd, rivers cannot quench.
III Henry VI. Act iv, sc. 8, l. 7. [Clarence]

Though little fire grows great with little wind,
Yet extreme gusts will blow out fire and all.
The Taming of the Shrew. Act ii, sc. 1, l. 135. [Petruchio]

Small lights are soon blown out, huge fires abide,
And with the wind in greater fury fret.
The Rape of Lucrece, l. 647.

Can you think to blow out the intended fire your city is ready to flame in, with such weak breath as this?
Coriolanus. Act v, sc. 2, l. 48. [Sentinel]

That were to blow at fire in hope to quench it.
Pericles. Act i, sc. 4, l. 4. [Dionyza]

8
I need not add more fuel to your fire,
For well I wot ye blaze to burn them out.
III Henry VI. Act v, sc. 4, l. 70. [King Edward]

The fuel is gone that maintained that fire.
Henry V. Act ii, sc. 3, l. 45. [Bardolph]
Fetch us in fuel.—*The Tempest,* i, 2, 366.
Self-substantial fuel.—*Sonnets,* i. The only use of "self-substantial." "Fuel" is used a fifth time in *II Henry VI,* iii, 1, 302. See above.

9
The fire that mounts the liquor till 't run o'er,
In seeming to augment it wastes it.
Henry VIII. Act i, sc. 1, l. 144. [Norfolk]

10
Those that with haste will make a mighty fire
Begin it with weak straws.
Julius Cæsar. Act i, sc. 3, l. 107. [Cassius]

I am sent before to make a fire, and they are coming after to warm them.
The Taming of the Shrew. Act iv, sc. 1, l. 4. [Grumio]
Make a fire.—*Julius Cæsar,* v, 5, 55.
Make a fire within.—*Pericles,* iii, 2, 80.
New-enkindled fire.—*King John,* iv, 2, 163. The only use of "new-enkindled."

11 The fire is dead with grief,
Being create for comfort, to be used
In undeserved extremes: see else yourself;
There is no malice in this burning coal;
The breath of heaven hath blown his spirit out
And strew'd repentant ashes on his head.
King John. Act iv, sc. 1, l. 106. [Arthur] See also under COAL.

12
Quench'd the stelled fires.
King Lear, iii, 7, 61. See under SEA. "Stelled" (fixed) is repeated in *The Rape of Lucrece,* l. 1444, and in *Sonnets,* xxiv.

13
Fire enough for a flint.
Love's Labour's Lost. Act iv, sc. 2, l. 89. [Holofernes]

The fire i' the flint Shows not till it be struck.
Timon of Athens. Act i, sc. 1, l. 22. [Poet]
Fire in a flint.—*Troilus and Cressida,* iii, 3, 257.

1
The true Promethean fire.
Love's Labour's Lost, iv, 3, 304. See under Eye. "Promethean fire" is repeated in l. 351, and occurs in no other scene.

2
Some delightful ostentation, . . . or firework.
Love's Labour's Lost, v, 1, 119.
Fights and fireworks.—*Henry VIII,* i, 3, 27. The only uses of "firework" or "fireworks."

3
The fire seven times tried this.
The Merchant of Venice. Act ii, sc. 9, l. 63. [Prince of Arragon, reading]

4
Where fires you find'st unraked and hearths
unswept.
The Merry Wives of Windsor. Act v, sc. 5, l. 48. [Pistol] The only use of "unraked." "Unswept" is repeated in *Coriolanus,* ii, 3, 126.

5
That fire which burn'd the Carthage queen,
When the false Troyan under sail was seen.
A Midsummer-Night's Dream. Act i, sc. 1, l. 173. [Hermia]
Love-kindling fire.—*Sonnets,* cliii. The only use of "love-kindling."

6
And run through fire I will for thy sweet
sake.
A Midsummer-Night's Dream. Act ii, sc. 2, l. 103. [Lysander]

7
Do, with like timorous accent and dire yell
As when, by night and negligence, the fire
Is spied in populous cities.
Othello. Act i, sc. 1, l. 75. [Iago]
Give renew'd fire to our extincted spirits.
Othello. Act ii, sc. 1, l. 81. [Cassio] The only use of "extincted."
Put fire in your heart.—*Twelfth Night,* iii, 2, 21.

8
A fire from heaven came and shrivell'd up
Their bodies, even to loathing; for they so
stunk,
That all those eyes adored them ere their fall
Scorn now their hand should give them
burial.
Pericles. Act ii, sc. 4, l. 9. [Helicanus] The only use of "shrivell'd" and "stunk."

9
O, who can hold a fire in his hand
By thinking on the frosty Caucasus?
Richard II. Act i, sc. 3, l. 294. [Bolingbroke] The Caucasus are mentioned again in *Titus Andronicus,* ii, 1, 17.

10
His rash fierce blaze of riot cannot last,
For violent fires soon burn out themselves.
Richard II. Act ii, sc. 1, l. 33. [Gaunt]

11
One fire burns out another's burning.
Romeo and Juliet. Act i, sc. 2, l. 46. [Benvolio]
Fire drives out fire.—*Julius Cæsar,* iii, 1, 171.
One fire drives out one fire.—*Coriolanus,* iv, 7, 54.

12
Slight air and purging fire,
Are both with thee wherever I abide;
The first my thought, the other my desire.
Sonnets. No. xlv.

13
Were not I a little pot and soon hot, my very lips might freeze to my teeth, my tongue to the roof of my mouth, my heart in my belly, ere I should come by a fire to thaw me.
The Taming of the Shrew. Act iv, sc. 1, l. 6. [Grumio] "A little pot is soon hot" appeared first in Heywood's *Proverbs* (pt. i, ch. 11) in 1546.
I, with blowing the fire, shall warm myself.
The Taming of the Shrew. Act iv, sc. 1, l. 9. [Grumio]
Fire: do thy duty, and have thy duty; for my master and mistress are almost frozen to death.
The Taming of the Shrew. Act iv, sc. 1, l. 38. [Grumio]
Frozen almost to death.—*Richard III,* ii, 1, 115. The only uses of the phrase.

14
They sit conferring by the parlour fire.
The Taming of the Shrew. Act v, sc. 2, l. 102. [Katharina]
A country fire.—*The Merry Wives of Windsor,* v, 5, 256.
A farmer's fire.—*The Taming of the Shrew,* i, 2, 210.
A winter's fire.—*Macbeth,* iii, 4, 65.

15
Like a firebrand, in the dark.
The Tempest, ii, 2, 6. See also *II Henry IV,* ii, 2, 97; *Troilus and Cressida,* ii, 2, 110; *Julius Cæsar,* iii, 3, 41. The only uses of "firebrand."

16
But there was more temperate fire under the pot of her eyes.
Troilus and Cressida. Act i, sc. 2, l. 160. [Cressida]
Cold fire.—*Romeo and Juliet,* i, 1, 186.
Cover'd fire.—*Much Ado about Nothing,* iii, 1, 77.
Dead and drowsy fire.—*A Midsummer-Night's Dream,* v, 1, 399.
Lightless fire.—*The Rape of Lucrece,* l. 4.
Pale fire.—*Timon of Athens,* iv, 3, 441.
Uneffectual fire.—*Hamlet,* i, 5, 90. The only use of "uneffectual."

17
Fire and brimstone!
Twelfth Night, ii, 5, 56; *Othello,* iv, 1, 245. "Brimstone" occurs a third time in *Twelfth Night,* iii, 2, 22: "Put fire in your heart, and brimstone in your liver."
Everlasting fire.—*Titus Andronicus,* v, 1, 148.

18
Fire that 's closest kept burns most of all.
The Two Gentlemen of Verona. Act i, sc. 2, l. 30. [Lucetta] The only use of "closest."

II—Fire and Water

19
The property of rain is to wet and fire to burn.
As You Like It. Act iii, sc. 2, l. 27. [Corin]

O my son, my son! thou art preparing fire for us; look thee, here 's water to quench it.
Coriolanus. Act v, sc. 2, l. 77. [Menenius]

Fire, fire; cast on no water.
The Taming of the Shrew. Act iv, sc. 1, l. 20. [Grumio]

1
The elements Of fire and water.
Richard II, iii, 3, 56. See under ELEMENT and MEETING.

Through fire and water.
The Merry Wives of Windsor, iii, 4, 107.

2
Be he the fire, I 'll be the yielding water.
Richard II, iii, 3, 58. See under MEETING.

3
Thus have I shunn'd the fire for fear of burning,
And drench'd me in the sea, where I am drown'd.
The Two Gentlemen of Verona. Act i, sc. 3, l. 78. [Proteus]

She bathes in water, yet her fire must burn.
Venus and Adonis, l. 94.

FIRMAMENT, see Sky

FISH AND FISHING

I—Fish

4
No more than a fish loves water.
All's Well that Ends Well. Act iii, sc. 6, l. 92. [Second Lord]

Unclean fishpond.—*All's Well that Ends Well,* v, 2, 22. The only use of "fishpond."

5
I will henceforth eat no fish of fortune's buttering.
All's Well that Ends Well, v, 2, 9. See under FORTUNE. The only use of "buttering."

Eat no fish.—*King Lear,* i, 4, 18.

6
When fowls have no feathers and fish have no fin.
The Comedy of Errors. Act iii, sc. 1, l. 79. [Dromio of Syracuse]

For a fish without a fin, there 's a fowl without a feather.
The Comedy of Errors. Act iii, sc. 1, l. 82. [Dromio of Ephesus]

Finless fish.—*I Henry IV,* iii, 1, 151. The only use of "finless."

Fish and fowls.—*The Comedy of Errors,* ii, 1, 23.

Fishes and the winged fowls.—*The Comedy of Errors,* ii, 1, 18.

Birds and fishes.—*Timon of Athens,* iv, 3, 426; 428.

7
The imperious seas breed monsters, for the dish
Poor tributary rivers as sweet fish.
Cymbeline. Act iv, sc. 2, l. 35. [Imogen]

Half a fish and half a monster.—*The Tempest,* iii, 2, 32.

8
A very fresh fish here.
Henry VIII. Act ii, sc. 3, l. 86. [Old Lady]

The luce is the fresh fish; the salt fish is an old coat.
The Merry Wives of Windsor. Act i, sc. 1, l. 22. [Shallow] The only use of "luce," as referring to a pike, in the plays. Shallow is punning upon Slender's reference "the dozen white luces in their coat," (l. 16). In heraldry, the luce occurs in the arms of the Lucy family as far back as Henry II.

9
The ravin'd salt-sea shark.
Macbeth. Act iv, sc. 1, l. 24. [Third Witch] The only use of "ravin'd" and "shark." "Sharked" is used in *Hamlet,* i, 1, 98: "Sharked up a list of lawless resolutes."

10
Here 's a fish hangs in the net, like a poor man's right in the law; 'twill hardly come out.
Pericles. Act ii, sc. 1, l. 122. [Fisherman]

11
The fish lives in the sea.
Romeo and Juliet. Act i, sc. 3, l. 89. [Lady Capulet]

Third Fisherman: Master, I marvel how the fishes live in the sea.
First Fisherman: Why, as men do a-land; the great ones eat up the little ones: I can compare our rich misers to nothing so fitly as to a whale: a' plays and tumbles, driving the poor fry before him, and at last devours them all at a mouthful: such whales have I heard on o' the land, who never leave gaping till they 've swallowed the whole parish, church, steeple, bells, and all.
Pericles. Act ii, sc. 1, l. 29. The only use of "mouthful."

What tempest, I trow, threw this whale, with so many tuns of oil in his belly, ashore at Windsor?
The Merry Wives of Windsor. Act ii, sc. 1, l. 64. [Mrs. Ford]

The belching whale.—*Troilus and Cressida,* v, 5, 23; *Pericles,* iii, 1, 63. The only use of "belching."

A whale to virginity.—*All's Well that Ends Well,* iv, 3, 249.

Like a whale on ground.—*II Henry IV,* iv, 4, 40.

Very like a whale.—*Hamlet,* iii, 2, 398.

White as whale's bone.—*Love's Labour's Lost,* v, 2, 332. The only references to the whale.

12
What strange fish
Hath made his meal on thee?
The Tempest. Act ii, sc. 1, l. 112. [Alonso]

A strange fish!—*The Tempest,* ii, 2, 29.

Thou deboshed fish.—*The Tempest,* iii, 2, 29.

Ill-shaped fishes.—*Romeo and Juliet,* v, 1, 44. The only use of "ill-shaped."

Ravenous fishes.—*Henry VIII,* i, 2, 79.

13
One of them
Is a plain fish, and no doubt, marketable.
The Tempest. Act v, sc. 1, l. 265. [Antonio] "Marketable" is repeated in *As You Like It,* i, 2, 103.

14
A plague o' these pickle-herring!
Twelfth Night. Act i, sc. 5, l. 128. [Sir Toby] The only use of "pickle-herring."

Like . . . as pilchards are to herrings.
Twelfth Night, iii, 1, 40. See under FOOL. The only mention of pilchards.

Benvolio: Here comes Romeo, here comes Romeo.

Mercutio: Without his roe, like a dried herring.
Romeo and Juliet. Act ii, sc. 4, l. 38.

A herring without a roe.—*Troilus and Cressida,* v, 1, 68.

Shotten herring.—*I Henry IV,* ii, 4, 143. The only use of "shotten" (a herring which has shot or shed its roe and so is worthless).

White herring.—*King Lear,* iii, 6, 33.

Stealing a cade of herrings.—*II Henry VI,* iv, 2, 36. The only use of "cade" in this sense, a barrel of 500 herrings.

De herring is no dead.—*The Merry Wives of Windsor,* ii, 3, 12. The only references to the herring.

1 Here comes the trout that must be caught with tickling.
Twelfth Night. Act ii, sc. 5, l. 25. [Maria]

Groping for trouts in a peculiar river.
Measure for Measure, i, 2, 92. The only uses of "trout" and "trouts."

2 They are both as whole as a fish.
The Two Gentlemen of Verona. Act ii, sc. 5, l. 20. [Launce]

II—Fishing

3 Give me mine angle; we'll to the river: there,
My music playing far off, I will betray
Tawny-finn'd fishes; my bended hook shall pierce
Their slimy jaws.
Antony and Cleopatra. Act ii, sc. 5, l. 10. [Cleopatra] The only use of "tawny-finn'd." "Slimy" occurs only once more, in *Richard III,* i, 4, 32: "Slimy bottom of the deep."

4 Nero is an angler in the lake of darkness.
King Lear. Act iii, sc. 6, l. 7. [Edgar] The only use of "angler."

5 The pleasant'st angling is to see the fish
Cut with her golden oars the silver stream,
And greedily devour the treacherous bait.
Much Ado about Nothing. Act iii, sc. 1, l. 26. [Ursula] The only use of "pleasant'st" and "greedily."

'Twas merry when
You wager'd on your angling; when your diver
Did hang a salt-fish on his hook, which he
With fervency drew up.
Antony and Cleopatra. Act ii, sc. 5, l. 15. [Charmian] The only use of "diver" and "fervency." "Salt fish" (unhyphenated) is repeated in *The Merry Wives of Windsor,* i, 1, 22.

I am angling now,
Though you perceive me not how I give line.
The Winter's Tale. Act i, sc. 2, l. 180. [Leontes] The only uses of "angling."

6 How from the finny subject of the sea
These fishers tell the infirmities of men;
And from their watery empire recollect
All that may men approve or men detect!
Peace be at your labour, honest fishermen.
Pericles. Act ii, sc. 1, l. 52. [Pericles] The only use of "finny" and "recollect." "Fishers" occurs also in *The Comedy of Errors,* i, 1, 116, and in *Romeo and Juliet,* i, 2, 41.

No fisher but the ungrown fry forbears.
Venus and Adonis, l. 526.

Rude fishermen of Corinth.—*The Comedy of Errors,* v, 1, 351. "Fishermen" occurs also in *The Merry Wives of Windsor,* iv, 5, 100, and in *King Lear,* iv, 6, 17.

7 Second Fisherman: Canst thou catch any fishes, then?
Pericles: I never practised it.
Second Fisherman: Nay, then thou wilt starve, sure, for here's nothing to be got now-a-days, unless thou canst fish for't.
Pericles. Act ii, sc. 1, l. 70.

8 She touch'd no unknown baits, nor fear'd no hooks.
The Rape of Lucrece, l. 103.

If the young dace be a bait for the old pike, I see no reason in the law of nature but I may snap at him.
II Henry IV. Act iii, sc. 2, l. 355. [Falstaff] The only mention of dace and pike.

Bait the hook well; this fish will bite.
Much Ado about Nothing. Act ii, sc. 3, l. 114. [Claudio]

A man may fish with the worm that hath eat of a king.
Hamlet, iv, 3, 28. See under WORM.

Fish not, with this melancholy bait.—*The Merchant of Venice,* i, 1, 101. See under OPINION.

Bait fish.—*The Merchant of Venice,* iii, 1, 55.

The tender nibbler would not touch the bait.
The Passionate Pilgrim, l. 53. [Authorship uncertain] The only use of "nibbler." "Nibbling" is used in *As You Like It,* iii, 3, 83, and *The Tempest,* iv, 1, 62.

9 I'll fish for thee and get thee wood enough.
The Tempest. Act ii, sc. 2, l. 165. [Caliban]

10 His pond fish'd by his next neighbour.
Winter's Tale, i, 2, 195. See under CUCKOLD.

Well fished for.—*The Tempest,* ii, 1, 104. The only uses of "fished."

Caught the water though not the fish.—*The Winter's Tale,* v, 2, 91.

11 Polonius: Do you know me, my lord?
Hamlet: Excellent well; you are a fishmonger.
Hamlet. Act ii, sc. 2, l. 173.

He said I was a fishmonger.
Hamlet. Act ii, sc. 2, l. 190. The only uses of "fishmonger."

III—Fish and Flesh

See also Flesh

12 She's neither fish nor flesh.
I Henry IV. Act iii, sc. 3, l. 144. [Falstaff] The first appearance of the proverb, "neither fish nor flesh nor good red herring" in English literature is in the anonymous *Rede Me and Be not Wrothe* (i, 3), published in 1528. John Heywood's *Proverbs* (Pt. i, ch. 10), published in 1546, gave it in its familiar form.

Either at flesh or fish.—*The Comedy of Errors,* iii, 1, 22.

1
I saw the porpus how he bounced and tumbled; they say they're half fish, half flesh.
Pericles. Act ii, sc. 1, l. 26. [Third Fisherman] The only use of "porpus." "Porpoise" does not occur.
We'll have flesh for holidays, fish for fasting-days.
Pericles, ii, 1, 86. See under FOOD. The only use of "fasting-days."

2
Sampson: 'Tis known I am a pretty piece of flesh.
Gregory: 'Tis well thou art not fish.
Romeo and Juliet. Act i, sc. 1, l. 34.
O, flesh, flesh, how art thou fishified!
Romeo and Juliet. Act ii, sc. 4, l. 40. [Mercutio] The only use of "fishified."

3
She . . . was turned into a cold fish for she would not exchange flesh with one that loved her.
Winter's Tale. Act iv, sc. 4, l. 284. [Autolycus] For full quotation see under BALLAD.

FIST

See also Hand

4
Fisting each other's throats.
Coriolanus. Act iv, sc. 5, l. 131. [Aufidius]
To the choleric fisting of every rogue
Thy ear is liable.
Pericles. Act iv, sc. 6, l. 177. [Marina] The only uses of "fisting."

5
Give me thy fist, thy fore-foot to me give.
Henry V. Act ii, sc. 1, l. 71. [Pistol] The only use of "fore-foot."

6
But, O! the treacherous Falstolfe wounds my heart,
Whom with my bare fists I would execute,
If I now had him brought into my power.
I Henry VI. Act i, sc. 4, l. 35. [Talbot]
An I but fist him once.
II Henry IV, Act ii, sc. 1, l. 24. [Fang]
Of fist most valiant.—*Henry V,* iv, 1, 46.

7
Hold the sceptre in his childish fist.
II Henry VI. Act i, sc. 1, l. 245. [York]

8
He would pun thee into shivers with his fist, as a sailor breaks a biscuit.
Troilus and Cressida. Act ii, sc. 1, l. 42. [Thersites] "Pun," i.e., pound. Its only appearance in the plays.
With my armed fist I'll pash him o'er the face.
Troilus and Cressida. Act ii, sc. 3, l. 212. [Ajax] "Pash" is repeated in *The Winter's Tale,* i, 2, 128.

FITNESS

9
It is not fit.
Antony and Cleopatra, iii, 7, 4; *Cymbeline,* ii, 1, 28.
Indeed he is not fit.—*Julius Cæsar,* ii, 1, 153.
You are not fit.—*Hamlet,* v, 2, 229.
Not fit for your beholding.—*King Lear,* iii, 7, 9.
Not fit to govern.—*II Henry VI,* v, 1, 94.

10
We are fit to bid her welcome.
Coriolanus. Act i, sc. 3, l. 47. [Volumnia]
Fit to instruct her youth.—*The Taming of the Shrew,* i, 1, 95.
Fit to do 't.—*The Tempest,* i, 2, 440.
Most fit.—*Hamlet,* iv, 1, 20; *Antony and Cleopatra,* iii, 3, 39.
This is meetly.—*Antony and Cleopatra,* i, 3, 81. The only use of "meetly."

11
'Tis said a woman's fitness comes by fits.
Cymbeline. Act iv, sc. 1, l. 6. [Cloten]
If his fitness speaks, mine is ready; now or whensoever, provided I am so able as now.
Hamlet. Act v, sc. 2, l. 210. [Hamlet]
My fitness.—*King Lear,* iv, 2, 63.
Their fitness now Does unmake you.—*Macbeth,* i, 7, 53.
Fitness calls them on.—*Troilus and Cressida,* i, 3, 202.
Fitness for the world.—*Coriolanus,* ii, 1, 266.
Necessary fitness.—*Measure for Measure,* ii, 4, 23.
Needful fitness.—*Henry VIII,* ii, 4, 231. The only uses of "fitness."

12
Fit for the gods.
Julius Cæsar, ii, 1, 173. The only use of this phrase in Shakespeare.
Fit for great employment.—*The Two Gentlemen of Verona,* v, 4, 157.
Fit for his attempt.—*Measure for Measure,* iii, 1, 266.
Fit for the place.—*The Two Gentlemen of Verona,* i, 2, 45.
Fit for thee to use.—*Coriolanus,* iii, 2, 83.

13
That which ordinary men are fit for, I am qualified in.
King Lear. Act i, sc. 4, l. 37. [Kent]
Fit in his place and time.
Love's Labour's Lost, i, 1, 98. [Biron]
Fit time.—*Measure for Measure,* iv, 5, 1; *Othello,* i, 2, 85.
Fit occasion.—*Twelfth Night,* iii, 4, 190.

14
What will serve is fit.
Much Ado about Nothing. Act i, sc. 1, l. 320. [Don Pedro]

15
If you think fit.
Othello, iii, 1, 54. The only use of this phrase in the plays.
Thought it fit.—*King Lear,* v, 3, 45.
It's fit it should be so.—*Pericles,* ii, 2, 10.

16
We'll fit him to our turn.
The Taming of the Shrew. Act iii, sc. 2, l. 134. [Tranio]

17
Get you hence, for I must go
Where it fits not you to know.
The Winter's Tale, iv, 4, 304. [Autolycus]
'Tis not fit you know.—*The Winter's Tale,* iv, 4, 423.

FLAG

1
Stand for your own; unwind your bloody flag.
Henry V. Act i, sc. 2, l. 101. [Archbishop of Canterbury] "Bloody flag" is repeated in *Coriolanus,* ii, 1, 84.
Pennons painted in the blood of Harfleur.
Henry V. Act iii, sc. 5, l. 49. [French King] The only use of "pennons."
I stay but for my guidon; to the field!
I will the banner from a trumpet take,
And use it for my haste.
Henry V. Act iv, sc. 2, l. 60. [Constable] The only use of "guidon."

2
Flag of truce.
I Henry VI, iii, 1, 138. The only use of this phrase in the plays.
Their white flags display'd, they bring us peace.
Pericles. Act i, sc. 4, l. 72. [Lord] The only use of "white flags."
Flying flags.—*Antony and Cleopatra,* iii, 13, 11.
Garish flag.—*Richard III,* iv, 4, 89.
Vagabond flag.—*Antony and Cleopatra,* i, 4, 45.
Death's pale flag.—*Romeo and Juliet,* v, 3, 96.

3
Advance our waving colours on the walls.
I Henry VI. Act i, sc. 6, l. 1. [La Pucelle]
And know us by these colours for thy foes.
I Henry VI. Act ii, sc. 4, l. 105. [Somerset]

4 Their colours, often borne in France,
And now in England to our heart's great sorrow,
Shall be my winding-sheet.
III Henry VI. Act i, sc. 1, l. 127. [King Henry]
These arms of mine shall be thy winding-sheet.
III Henry VI, ii, 5, 114. The only uses of "winding-sheet."

5
Sound trumpets! let our bloody colours wave!
III Henry VI. Act ii, sc. 2, l. 173. [Edward]
O cheerful colours! see where Oxford comes!
III Henry VI. Act v, sc. 1, l. 58. [Warwick]
Hopeful colours.—*II Henry VI,* iv, 1, 97.

6
Our colours do return in those same hands
That did display them when we first march'd forth.
King John. Act ii, sc. 1, l. 319. [English Herald]
Mocking the air with colours idly spread.
King John. Act v, sc. 1, l. 72. [Bastard]
And follow unacquainted colours here.
King John. Act v, sc. 2, l. 32. [Salisbury]

7
These flags of France, that are advanced here
Before the eye and prospect of your town,
Have hither march'd to your endamagement.
King John. Act ii, sc. 1, l. 209. [King John] The only use of "endamagement."

8
France spreads his banners in our noiseless land.
King Lear. Act iv, sc. 2, l. 56. [Goneril]
The Norweyan banners flout the sky
And fan our people cold.
Macbeth. Act i, sc. 2, l. 49. [Ross] "Norweyan" is repeated in i, 2, 31 and i, 3, 95, and occurs in no other play.

9
Hang out our banners on the outward walls.
Macbeth. Act v, sc. 5, l. 1. [Macbeth]
March, noble lord,
Into our city with thy banners spread.
Timon of Athens. Act v, sc. 4, l. 29. [Second Senator]
His conquering banner shook.
Antony and Cleopatra. Act i, sc. 2, l. 106. [Messenger]

FLATTERY

10
That was laid on with a trowel.
As You Like It. Act i, sc. 2, l. 112. [Celia] The only use of this phrase in the plays, and the only use of "trowel."

11
'Tis not her glass, but you, that flatters her.
As You Like It. Act iii, sc. 5, l. 54. [Rosalind]
I have flattered a lady.
As You Like It. Act v, sc. 4, l. 45. [Touchstone]

12
'Tis holy sport to be a little vain,
When the sweet breath of flattery conquers strife.
The Comedy of Errors. Act iii, sc. 2, l. 27. [Luciana]

13
He that will give good words to thee will flatter
Beneath abhorring.
Coriolanus. Act i, sc. 1, l. 171. [Marcius]
When drums and trumpets shall
I' the field prove flatterers, let courts and cities be
Made of false-faced soothing!
When steel grows soft as the parasite's silk,
Let him be made a coverture for the wars!
Coriolanus. Act i, sc. 9, l. 42. [Marcius] The only use of "false-faced." "Soothing" is used once again in iii, 1, 69, and in no other play. "Coverture" is repeated in *III Henry VI,* iv, 2, 13, and *Much Ado about Nothing,* iii, 1, 30.
He water'd his new plants with dews of flattery.
Coriolanus. Act v, sc. 6, l. 23. [Aufidius] "Water'd" is repeated in *Pericles,* iv, 2, 108.

14
What drink'st thou oft, instead of homage sweet,
But poison'd flattery?
Henry V. Act iv, sc. 1, l. 267. [King Henry]
Think'st thou the fiery fever will go out
With titles blown from adulation?
Will it give place to flexure and low bending?
Henry V. Act iv, sc. 1, l. 270. [King Henry] The only use of "adulation." "Flexure" is repeated in *Troilus and Cressida,* ii, 3, 115.

15
This flattering gloss.
II Henry VI. Act i, sc. 1, l. 163. [Beaufort]
By flattery he won the commons' hearts.
II Henry VI. Act iii, sc. 1, l. 28. [Queen]

1
'Tis sin to flatter.
III Henry VI. Act v, sc. 6, l. 3. [King Henry]

2
I come not To hear such flattery now; . . .
They are too thin and bare to hide offences.
Henry VIII. Act v, sc. 3, l. 123. [King Henry]

3 He loves to hear
That unicorns may be betray'd with trees,
And bears with glasses, elephants with holes,
Lions with toils and men with flatterers;
But when I tell him he hates flatterers,
He says he does, being then most flattered.
Julius Cæsar. Act ii, sc. 1, l. 203. [Decius]
O you flatterers!—*Julius Cæsar,* v, 1, 44.

4
They flattered me like a dog.
King Lear. Act iv, sc. 6, l. 98. [King Lear]
They flatter me.—*Merchant of Venice,* ii, 5, 13.

5
Ay, marry, there; some flattery for this evil.
Love's Labour's Lost. Act iv, sc. 3, l. 286. [Dumain]

6 Mouth-honour, breath,
Which the poor heart would fain deny, and dare not.
Macbeth. Act v, sc. 3, l. 27. [Macbeth] The only use of "mouth-honour."

7
Flattery is the bellows blows up sin.
Pericles. Act i, sc. 2, l. 39. [Helicanus] "Bellows" is repeated in *Antony and Cleopatra,* i, 1, 9.
No visor doth become black villany
So well as soft and tender flattery.
Pericles. Act iv, sc. 4, l. 44. [Gower]
Sweet flattery!—*Sonnets,* xlii.
Sweetly flatters.—*The Rape of Lucrece,* l. 172.

8
One but flatters us.
Richard II. Act i, sc. 1, l. 25. [King Richard]
King Richard: Should dying men flatter with those that live?
John of Gaunt: No, no, men living flatter those that die.
King Richard: Thou, now a-dying, say'st thou flatterest me.
John of Gaunt: O, no! thou diest, though I the sicker be.
Richard II. Act ii, sc. 1, l. 88.
A thousand flatterers sit within thy crown,
Whose compass is no bigger than thy head.
Richard II. Act ii, sc. 1, l. 100. [John of Gaunt]
Basely led By flatterers.
Richard II. Act ii, sc. 1, l. 241. [Northumberland]

9 He does me double wrong
That wounds me with the flatteries of his tongue.
Richard II. Act iii, sc. 2, l. 215. [King Richard]
That flattering tongue of yours won me.
As You Like It. Act iv, sc. 1, l. 187. [Rosalind]
Never trust to what my tongue can do
I' the way of flattery.
Coriolanus. Act iii, sc. 2, l. 136. [Coriolanus]

10
You teach me how to flatter you.
Richard III. Act i, sc. 2, l. 224. [Lady Anne]

11
The monarch's plague, this flattery.
Sonnets. No. cxiv.
'Tis flattery in my seeing,
And my great mind most kingly drinks it up.
Sonnets. No. cxiv.

12
The glass-faced flatterer.
Timon of Athens. Act i, sc. 1, l. 58. [Poet] The only use of "glass-faced."
He that loves to be flattered is worthy o' the flatterer.
Timon of Athens. Act i, sc. 1, l. 232. [Apemantus]
Would all those flatterers were thine enemies then, that then thou mightst kill 'em and bid me to 'em!
Timon of Athens. Act i, sc. 2, l. 83. [Apemantus]
We . . . spend our flatteries, to drink those men
Upon whose age we void it up again,
With poisonous spite and envy.
Timon of Athens. Act i, sc. 2, l. 142. [Apemantus]

13
O, that men's ears should be
To counsel deaf, but not to flattery!
Timon of Athens. Act i, sc. 2, l. 256. [Apemantus]

14
Who, stuck and spangled with your flatteries,
Washes it off, and sprinkles in your faces
Your reeking villany.
Timon of Athens. Act iii, sc. 6, l. 101. [Timon]
Live loathed and long,
Most smiling, smooth, detested parasites,
Courteous destroyers, affable wolves, meek bears,
You fools of fortune, trencher-friends, time's flies,
Cap and knee slaves, vapours, and minute-jacks!
Timon of Athens. Act iii, sc. 6, l. 103. [Timon] A succession of unique phrases.
Who dares,
In purity of manhood stand upright,
And say 'This man's a flatterer'? if one be,
So are they all; for every grise of fortune
Is smooth'd by that below.
Timon of Athens. Act iv, sc. 3, l. 13. [Timon] "Grise" (step) is used again in *Othello,* i, 3, 200, and "grize" in *Twelfth Night,* iii, 1, 135.
Thy flatterers yet wear silk, drink wine, lie soft;
Hug their diseased perfumes.
Timon of Athens. Act iv, sc. 3, l. 206. [Apemantus]

15 Shame not these woods,
By putting on the cunning of a carper.
Be thou a flatterer now, and seek to thrive
By that which has undone thee.
Timon of Athens. Act iv, sc. 3, l. 208. [Apemantus] This is the only use of "carper."

Why shouldst thou hate men?
They never flatter'd thee.
Timon of Athens. Act iv, sc. 3, l. 269. [Timon]

If thou hadst not been born the worst of men,
Thou hadst been a knave and flatterer.
Timon of Athens. Act iv, sc. 3, l. 275. [Timon]

Apemantus: What things in the world canst thou nearest compare to thy flatterers?
Timon: Women nearest; but men, men are the things themselves.
Timon of Athens. Act iv, sc. 3, l. 318.

A discovery of the infinite flatteries that follow youth and opulency.
Timon of Athens. Act v, sc. 1, l. 38. [Poet] The only use of "opulency."

1
Flatter and praise, commend, extol their graces;
Though ne'er so black, say they have angels' faces.
The Two Gentlemen of Verona. Act iii, sc. 1, l. 102. [Valentine]

Thou subtle, perjured, false, disloyal man!
Think'st thou I am so shallow, so conceitless,
To be seduced by thy flattery.
The Two Gentlemen of Verona. Act iv, sc. 2, l. 95. [Silvia] The only use of "conceitless."

Seducing to my friends.—*Coriolanus,* v, 6, 24. "Seducing" is repeated in *The Rape of Lucrece,* l. 639.

2
Dismiss your vows, your feigned tears, your flattery;
For where a heart is hard they make no battery.
Venus and Adonis, l. 425.

II—"I Cannot Flatter"

3
He would not flatter Neptune for his trident,
Or Jove for 's power to thunder.
Coriolanus. Act iii, sc. 1, l. 256. [Menenius]

Thou hadst rather
Follow thine enemy in a fiery gulf
Than flatter him in a bower.
Coriolanus. Act iii, sc. 2, l. 90. [Volumnia]

4
Do not think I flatter;
For what advancement may I hope from thee
That no revenue hast but thy good spirits,
To feed and clothe thee? Why should the poor be flatter'd?
Hamlet. Act iii, sc. 2, l. 61. [Hamlet]

The words I utter
Let none think flattery, for they 'll find 'em truth.
Henry VIII. Act v, sc. 5, l. 17. [Cranmer]

5
By God, I cannot flatter; I do defy
The tongues of soothers; but a braver place
In my heart's love hath no man than yourself.
I Henry IV. Act iv, sc. 1, l. 6. [Hotspur] The only use of "soothers."

Having neither the voice nor the heart of flattery about me.
Henry V. Act v, sc. 2, l. 314. [King Henry]

6
Suffolk doth not flatter, face or feign.
I Henry VI. Act v, sc. 3, l. 142. [Suffolk]

7
I cannot flatter thee in pride.
II Henry VI. Act i, sc. 3, l. 169. [York]

I kiss thy hand, but not in flattery.
Julius Cæsar. Act iii, sc. 1, l. 52. [Brutus]

Further I will not flatter you, my lord.
King John. Act ii, sc. 1, l. 516. [Blanch]

8
He cannot flatter, he,
An honest mind and plain, he must speak truth!
King Lear. Act ii, sc. 2, l. 104. [Cornwall]

I know, sir, I am no flatterer.
King Lear. Act ii, sc. 2, l. 116. [Kent]

Thou art no flatterer.—*Pericles,* i, 2, 60.

9
I hardly yet have learn'd
To insinuate, flatter, bow, and bend my limbs.
Richard II. Act iv, sc. 1, l. 164. [King Richard]

I cannot flatter and speak fair,
Smile in men's faces, smooth, deceive and cog,
Duck with French nods and apish courtesy.
Richard III. Act i, sc. 3, l. 47. [Gloucester]

Fool, of thyself speak well: fool, do not flatter.
Richard III. Act v, sc. 3, l. 192. [King Richard]

10
Timon: Thou flatter'st misery.
Apemantus: I flatter not; but say thou art a caitiff.
Timon of Athens. Act iv, sc. 3, l. 234.

11
Now, farewell, flattery.
Titus Andronicus. Act iii, sc. 1, l. 254. [Marcus]

FLEA

12
Second Carrier: I think this be the most villanous house in all London road for fleas: I am stung like a tench.
First Carrier: Like a tench! by the mass, there is ne'er a king christen could be better bit than I have been since the first cock.
I Henry IV. Act ii, sc. 1, l. 15. The only use of "tench."

Your chamber-lie breeds fleas like a loach.
I Henry IV. Act ii, sc. 1, l. 23. [Second Carrier] The only use of "chamber-lie" and "loach."

13
A' saw a flea stick upon Bardolph's nose, and a' said it was a black soul burning in hell-fire.
Henry V. Act ii, sc. 3, l. 42. [Boy] "Hell-fire" is repeated in *I Henry IV,* iii, 3, 36.

14
That 's a valiant flea that dare eat his breakfast on the lip of a lion.
Henry V. Act iii, sc. 7, l. 156. [Orleans]

15
He shall die a flea's death.
The Merry Wives of Windsor. Act iv, sc. 2, l. 157. [Mrs. Ford]

Thou flea, thou nit!—*The Taming of the Shrew,* iv, 3, 110. "Nit" is repeated in *Love's Labour 's Lost,* iv, 1, 150: "Pathetical nit!"

FLEET, see Ship

FLESH

See also Fatness; Fish and Flesh; Meat

1
Thou worms-meat, in respect of a good piece of flesh indeed!
As You Like It. Act iii, sc. 2, l. 67. [Touchstone]
They have made worms' meat of me.
Romeo and Juliet, iii, 1, 112. The only uses of "worms' meat."

2
The mountain of mad flesh that claims marriage of me.
The Comedy of Errors. Act iv, sc. 4, l. 159. [Dromio of Syracuse]

3
An arrogant piece of flesh.
Cymbeline. Act iv, sc. 2, l. 127. [Guiderius]

4
O, that this too too solid flesh would melt,
Thaw and resolve itself into a dew!
Hamlet. Act i, sc. 2, l. 129. [Hamlet]
Lay her i' the earth:
And from her fair and unpolluted flesh
May violets spring!
Hamlet. Act v, sc. 1, l. 261. [Laertes] The only use of "unpolluted."

5
Marry, there is another indictment upon thee, for suffering flesh to be eaten in thy house, contrary to the law.
II Henry IV. Act ii, sc. 4, l. 371. [Falstaff]

6
When flesh is cheap and females dear.
II Henry IV. Act v, sc. 3, l. 20. [Silence]
If you buy ladies' flesh at a million a dram, you cannot preserve it from tainting.
Cymbeline. Act i, sc. 4, l. 147. [Iachimo]

7
Such is the simplicity of man to hearken after the flesh.
Love's Labour's Lost. Act i, sc. 1, l. 219. [Costard]
My sweet ounce of man's flesh.
Love's Labour's Lost. Act iii, sc. 1, l. 136. [Costard]

8
Let the forfeit
Be nominated for an equal pound
Of your fair flesh, to be cut off and taken
In what part of your body pleaseth me.
The Merchant of Venice. Act i, sc. 3, l. 149. [Shylock]
A pound of man's flesh taken from a man
Is not so estimable, profitable neither,
As flesh of muttons, beefs, or goats.
The Merchant of Venice. Act i, sc. 3, l. 166. [Shylock] "Estimable" is repeated in *Twelfth Night,* ii, 1, 28.
Salarino: Why, I am sure, if he forfeit, thou wilt not take his flesh: what 's that good for?
Shylock: To bait fish withal.
The Merchant of Venice. Act iii, sc. 1, l. 54.
A weight of carrion flesh.
The Merchant of Venice. Act iv, sc. 1, l. 41. [Shylock]
The pound of flesh, which I demand of him,
Is dearly bought; 'tis mine and I will have it.
The Merchant of Venice. Act iv, sc. 1, l. 99. [Shylock]
The Jew shall have my flesh, blood, bones and all,
Ere thou shalt loose for me one drop of blood.
The Merchant of Venice. Act iv, sc. 1, l. 112. [Bassanio]
The words expressly are 'a pound of flesh:'
Take then thy bond, take thou thy pound of flesh;
But, in the cutting it, if thou dost shed
One drop of Christian blood, thy lands and goods
Are, by the laws of Venice, confiscate.
The Merchant of Venice. Act iv, sc. 1, l. 307. [Portia]
There is more difference between thy flesh and hers than between jet and ivory.
The Merchant of Venice. Act iii, sc. 1, l. 41. [Salarino]

9
Flesh of thy flesh.
Pericles. Act v, sc. 3, l. 46. [Pericles]

10
This frail sepulchre of our flesh.
Richard II. Act i, sc. 3, l. 196. [Bolingbroke]
This flesh which walls about our life.
Richard II. Act iii, sc. 2, l. 167. [King Richard] See under KING for full quotation.
This wall of flesh.
King John. Act iii, sc. 3, l. 20. [King John]

11
'Tis known I am a pretty piece of flesh.
Romeo and Juliet. Act i, sc. 1, l. 34. [Sampson]
As pretty a piece of flesh as any is in Messina.
Much Ado about Nothing. Act iv, sc. 2, l. 85. [Dogberry]
As witty a piece of Eve's flesh as any in Illyria.
Twelfth Night. Act i, sc. 5, l. 30. [Clown]

12
This world-wearied flesh.
Romeo and Juliet. Act v, sc. 3, l. 112. [Romeo] See under DEATH for full quotation.
Dull flesh.—*Sonnets,* li.
Sweet flesh.—*Romeo and Juliet,* iii, 2, 82.
Trembling flesh.—*Richard III,* v, 3, 181.
Makes my flesh tremble.—*Romeo and Juliet,* i, 5, 92.

13
Why, there they are both, baked in that pie;
Whereof their mother daintily hath fed,
Eating the flesh that she herself hath bred.
Titus Andronicus. Act v, sc. 3, l. 60. [Titus] The only use of "daintily."

14
Good traders in the flesh.
Troilus and Cressida. Act v, sc. 10, l. 46. [Pandar] See also under PANDAR.
Was the duke a fleshmonger?
Measure for Measure. Act v, sc. 1, l. 337. [Lucio] The only use of "fleshmonger."

15
My flesh is soft and plump, my marrow burning.
Venus and Adonis, l. 142.

II—Flesh and Blood

16
My flesh and blood.
II Henry VI, i, 1, 233; *All's Well that Ends Well,* i, 3, 38; 50; *Titus Andronicus,* iv, 2, 84.

I would see his own person in flesh and blood.
Love's Labour's Lost. Act i, sc. 1, l. 185. [Dull]

I will be flesh and blood.
Much Ado about Nothing. Act v, sc. 1, l. 34. [Leonato]

1
Our flesh and blood is grown so vile, my lord,
That it doth hate what gets it.
King Lear. Act iii, sc. 4, l. 150. [Gloucester]

She being none of your flesh and blood, your flesh and blood has not offended the king; and so your flesh and blood is not to be punished by him.
Winter's Tale. Act iv, sc. 4, l. 709. [Clown]

In despite of the flesh and the blood.
The Taming of the Shrew, Ind., 2, 130.

Thou art mine own flesh and blood.
The Merchant of Venice, ii, 2, 98; iii, 1, 37.

Your flesh and blood.—*Twelfth Night,* v, 1, 36.

Ears of flesh and blood.—*Hamlet,* i, 5, 22.

Wicked . . . as all flesh and blood are.
All's Well that Ends Well, i, 3, 38. See under WICKEDNESS.

2
Flesh and blood, You, brother mine.
The Tempest, v, 1, 74.

But are you flesh and blood?
Pericles, v, 1, 154. "Flesh and blood" is used twenty times in the plays. See CHILD, DAUGHTER, SON.

Dislocate and tear Thy flesh and bones.
King Lear, iv, 2, 65. The only use of "dislocate" and of "flesh and bones."

FLIGHT

3
Bertram: Away, and for our flight.
Parolles: Bravely, coragio!
All's Well that Ends Well. Act ii, sc. 5, l. 97. "Coragio" (courage) is used a second time in *The Tempest,* v, 1, 258.

Come, night; end, day!
For with the dark, poor thief, I 'll steal away.
All's Well that Ends Well. Act iii, sc. 2, l. 131. [Helena] "Steal away" is used nine times in the plays.

Steal forth.—*A Midsummer-Night's Dream,* i, 1, 164.

Steal out.—*Julius Cæsar,* ii, 1, 264.

4
Fly and turn the rudder.
Antony and Cleopatra. Act iii, sc. 10, l. 3. [Enobarbus] "Rudder" is repeated in iii, 11, 57, and occurs in no other play.

Yon ribaudred nag of Egypt,—
Whom leprosy o'ertake!—i' the midst o' the fight,
When vantage like a pair of twins appear'd,
Both as the same, or rather ours the elder,
The breeze upon her, like a cow in June,
Hoists sails and flies.
Antony and Cleopatra. Act iii, sc. 10, l. 10. [Scarus] The only use of "ribaudred" (wanton). Ribaud is an old form of ribald.

She once being loof'd.
Antony and Cleopatra. Act iii, sc. 10, l. 18. [Scarus] The only use of "loof'd" (luffed).

I have fled myself; and have instructed cowards
To run and show their shoulders.
Antony and Cleopatra. Act iii, sc. 11, l. 7. [Antony]

5
Sir, if you 'ld save your life, fly to your house.
Coriolanus. Act v, sc. 4, l. 38. [Messenger]

6
Or, like the Parthian, I shall flying fight;
Rather, directly fly.
Cymbeline. Act i, sc. 6, l. 20. [Iachimo] "Parthian" is used four times.

And but the backs of Britons seen, all flying
Through a strait lane.
Cymbeline. Act v, sc. 3, l. 6. [Posthumus]

7
And as the thing that 's heavy in itself,
Upon enforcement flies with greatest speed,
So did our men, heavy in Hotspur's loss,
Lend to their weight such lightness with their fear
That arrows fled not swifter toward their aim
Than did our soldiers, aiming at their safety.
II Henry IV. Act i, sc. 1, l. 119. [Mortimer]

With nimble wing
We were enforced, for safety sake, to fly.
I Henry IV. Act v, sc. 1, l. 64. [Worcester]

Upon the foot of fear, fled with the rest.
I Henry IV. Act v, sc. 5, l. 20. [Prince]

8
We will not fly, but to our enemies' throats.
I Henry VI. Act i, sc. 1, l. 98. [Gloucester]

Him I forgive my death that killeth me
When he sees me go back one foot or fly.
I Henry VI. Act i, sc. 2, l. 20. [Charles]

They that of late were daring with their scoffs
Are glad and fain by flight to save themselves.
I Henry VI. Act iii, sc. 2, l. 113. [Bedford]

On either hand thee there are squadrons pitch'd,
To wall thee from the liberty of flight.
I Henry VI. Act iv, sc. 2, l. 23. [General]

9
Talbot: Fly, to revenge my death, if I be slain.
John Talbot: He that flies so will ne'er return again.
I Henry VI. Act iv, sc. 5, l. 18.

Flight cannot stain the honour you have won;
But mine it will, that no exploit have done:
You fled for vantage, every one will swear;
But, if I bow, they 'll say it was for fear.
I Henry VI. Act iv, sc. 5, l. 26. [John Talbot]

Then talk no more of flight, it is no boot;
If son to Talbot, die at Talbot's foot.
I Henry VI. Act iv, sc. 6, l. 52. [John Talbot]

10
He that flies shall die.
III Henry VI. Act i, sc. 1, l. 30. [Norfolk]

What counsel give you? whither shall we fly?
III Henry VI. Act ii, sc. 3, l. 11. [George]

Whither should I fly?—*Macbeth,* iv, 2, 73.

Fly this place.—*King Lear,* ii, 1, 22.

Fly abreast.—*Henry V,* iv, 6, 17.

Fly amain.—*The Tempest,* iv, 1, 74.

11
Bootless is flight, they follow us with wings;

And weak we are and cannot shun pursuit.
III Henry VI. Act ii, sc. 3, l. 12. [Edward]
No way to fly, nor strength to hold out flight.
III Henry VI. Act ii, sc. 6, l. 24. [Clifford]
Let us fly while we may fly.
III Henry VI. Act iv, sc. 4, l. 34. [Queen Elizabeth]
Ah, couldst thou fly!—*III Henry VI,* v, 2, 32.

1
Duke of Gloucester: Why, what a peevish fool was that of Crete,
That taught his son the office of a fowl!
And yet, for all his wings, the fool was drown'd.
King Henry: I, Dædalus; my poor boy, Icarus;
Thy father, Minos, that denied our course;
The sun that sear'd the wings of my sweet boy
Thy brother Edward, and thyself the sea
Whose envious gulf did swallow up his life.
III Henry VI. Act v, sc. 6, l. 18. The only mention of Dædalus and Minos. Icarus is mentioned again in iv, 7, 16, and in *III Henry VI,* v, 6, 21.

2
This morning are they fled away and gone.
Julius Cæsar. Act v, sc. 1, l. 84. [Cassius]
Fled and gone.—*Much Ado about Nothing,* v, 2, 101.
Gone and fled.—*Richard II,* ii, 4, 16.
She 's gone, she 's fled.—*Titus Andronicus,* iv, 3, 5.
Stol'n away and fled.—*Macbeth,* ii, 4, 26.
Now all are fled.—*Timon of Athens,* iii, 3, 36.

3 Gasted by the noise I made,
Full suddenly he fled.
King Lear. Act ii, sc. 1, l. 57. [Edmund] The only use of "gasted" (terrified).

4
The bat hath flown His cloister'd flight.
Macbeth. Act iii, sc. 2, l. 40. [Macbeth] The only use of "cloister'd."

5
Little is the wisdom, where the flight
So runs against all reason.
Macbeth. Act iv, sc. 2, l. 13. [Lady Macduff]
Do not say they be fled.—*The Merry Wives of Windsor,* iv, 5, 73.

6
The villain is much lighter-heeled than I:
I follow'd fast, but faster he did fly.
A Midsummer-Night's Dream. Act iii, sc. 2, l. 415. [Lysander] The only use of "lighter-heeled."
Take thy flight.—*A Midsummer-Night's Dream,* v, 1, 310.
Ta'en in flight.—*Much Ado about Nothing,* v, 4, 127.

7
By flight I 'll shun the danger which I fear.
Pericles. Act i, sc. 1, l. 142. [Pericles]

8
To fly the boar before the boar pursues,
Were to incense the boar to follow us
And make pursuit where he did mean no chase.
Richard III. Act iii, sc. 2, l. 28. [Hastings]

9
Fly not; for shouldst thou take the river Styx,
I would swim after.
Troilus and Cressida. Act v, sc. 4, l. 20. [Troilus] The Styx is mentioned again in *Titus Andronicus,* i, 1, 88.

10
All the cunning manner of our flight.
The Two Gentlemen of Verona. Act ii, sc. 4, l. 180. [Valentine]
These likelihoods confirm her flight from hence.
The Two Gentlemen of Verona. Act v, sc. 2, l. 43. [Duke]
Fearful flight.—*III Henry VI,* ii, 2, 30.
Horrid flight.—*Timon of Athens,* v, 4, 13.
Lazy flight.—*III Henry VI,* ii, 1, 130.
Pretended flight.—*The Two Gentlemen of Verona,* ii, 6, 37.
Unjust flight.—*The Two Gentlemen of Verona,* iv, 4, 173.
Falcon's flight.—*Richard II,* i, 3, 61.
Soul's flight.—*Macbeth,* iii, 1, 141.

FLINT

11
Being incensed, he 's flint.
II Henry IV, iv, 4, 33. See under CHARACTER.
Flinty, rough, remorseless.
III Henry VI, i, 4, 142. See WOMAN, 1701:9.
Art thou obdurate, flinty, hard as steel,
Nay, more than flint, for stone at rain relenteth?
Venus and Adonis, l. 199. "Flinty" is used ten times in the plays, and once in the poems.

12
The ruthless flint doth cut my tender feet.
II Henry VI. Act ii, sc. 4, l. 34. [Duchess of Gloucester]
Beaten flint.—*II Henry VI,* iii, 2, 317.
Cold flint.—*The Rape of Lucrece,* l. 181.
Everlasting flint.—*Romeo and Juliet,* ii, 6, 17.
Unrelenting flint.—*Titus Andronicus,* ii, 3, 141.
Flint and hardness.—*Antony and Cleopatra,* iv, 9, 16.
Flints and pebbles.—*Hamlet,* v, 1, 254.
Flint nor steel.—*Titus Andronicus,* v, 3, 88.
Flint bosom.—*Richard II,* v, 1, 3.
Heart of flint.—*Twelfth Night,* i, 5, 305.
Rough hearts of flint.—*The Merchant of Venice,* iv, 1, 31. See under HEART.
Shores of flint.—*Pericles,* iv, 4, 43.
Snore upon the flint.—*Cymbeline,* iii, 6, 34.
Fight with flint.—*II Henry VI,* v, 1, 24.

13
The flint bears fire.
Julius Cæsar, iv, 3, 111. See under ANGER.
For "fire in the flint" see under FIRE.

FLOOD

14
There is, sure, another flood toward, and these couples are coming to the ark.
As You Like It. Act v, sc. 4, l. 35. [Jaques] The only use of "ark."

15
The flood-gates of her eyes.
I Henry IV, ii, 4, 435. "Flood-gates" is repeated in *Othello,* i, 3, 56, and in *Venus and Adonis,* l. 959.

1
Noah's flood could not do it.
The Comedy of Errors, iii, 2, 108. Noah is mentioned again in *Twelfth Night,* iii, 2, 18.
Severn's flood.—*I Henry IV,* i, 3, 103.
2
Let floods o'erswell, and fiends for food
howl on!
Henry V. Act ii, sc. 1, l. 97. [Pistol]
3
All unwarily
Devoured by the unexpected flood.
King John. Act v, sc. 7, l. 63. [Bastard] The only use of "unwarily."
4
Montano: What from the cape can you discern at sea?
Gentleman: Nothing at all; it is a high-wrought flood.
Othello. Act ii, sc. 1, l. 1. The only use of "high-wrought."
I never did like molestation view
On the enchafed flood.
Othello. Act ii, sc. 1, l. 16. [Gentleman] The only use of "molestation." "Enchafed" is repeated in *Cymbeline,* iv, 2, 174.
5
Between our Ilium and where she resides,
Let it be call'd the wild and wandering flood.
Troilus and Cressida, i, 1, 104. [Troilus]
Angry flood.—*Julius Cæsar,* i, 2, 103.
Boundless flood.—*The Rape of Lucrece,* l. 653.
Chiding flood.—*Henry VIII,* iii, 2, 197.
Envious flood.—*Richard III,* i, 4, 37; *The Taming of the Shrew,* Ind., 2, 67.
Fearful flood.—*The Rape of Lucrece,* l. 1741.
Gentle flood.—*The Rape of Lucrece,* l. 1118.
Imperious flood.—*II Henry IV,* i, 1, 62.
Melancholy flood.—*Richard III,* i, 4, 45.
Wild flood.—*II Henry IV,* i, 1, 154.
6
Flood of fortune.
Twelfth Night, iv, 3, 11. See under FORTUNE.
Flood of greatness.—*I Henry IV,* v, 1, 48.
Flood of mutiny.—*Julius Cæsar,* iii, 2, 215.
Flood of tears.—*I Henry VI,* iii, 3, 56; *Titus Andronicus,* v, 3, 90.
Flood of visitors.—*Timon of Athens,* i, 1, 42.

FLOUTING, see Defiance

FLOWER

7
Whiles yet the dew's on ground, gather those flowers.
Cymbeline. Act i, sc. 5, l. 1. [Queen]
With fairest flowers
Whilst summer lasts and I live here, Fidele,
I'll sweeten thy sad grave: thou shalt not lack
The flower that's like thy face, pale primrose, nor
The azured harebell, like thy veins, no, nor
The leaf of eglantine, whom not to slander,
Out-sweeten'd not thy breath.
Cymbeline. Act iv, sc. 2, l. 218. [Arviragus] The only use of "harebell" and "out-sweetened." Eglantine occurs again in *A Midsummer-Night's Dream,* ii, 1, 252.
Fair flower.—*Twelfth Night,* ii, 4, 39; *The Passionate Pilgrim,* l. 131; *Sonnets,* lxix.
Fairest flowers.—*Richard II,* iii, 4, 44; *The Winter's Tale,* iv, 4, 80.
Beauteous flower.—*Romeo and Juliet,* ii, 2, 122.
Chaliced flowers.—*Cymbeline,* ii, 3, 25. The only use of "chaliced."
Fresh flowers.—*Venus and Adonis,* l. 665.
Fresh and fragrant flowers.—*A Midsummer-Night's Dream,* iv, 1, 55.
Fresh uncropped flower.—*All's Well that Ends Well,* v, 3, 327.
Innocent flower.—*Macbeth,* i, 5, 66.
Living flowers.—*Sonnets,* xvi.
Maiden flowers.—*Henry VIII,* iv, 2, 169.
Precious flower.—*The Merry Wives of Windsor,* v, 5, 66.
Unblown flowers.—*Richard III,* iv, 4, 10.
8
These flowers are like the pleasures of the world;
This bloody man, the care on 't.
Cymbeline. Act iv, sc. 2, l. 296. [Imogen]
Never-withering banks of flowers.—*Cymbeline,* v, 4, 98. The only use of "never-withering."
Wither'd flower.—*The Rape of Lucrece,* l. 1254; *Richard II,* ii, 1, 134.
9
Sweet flowers;
Which bewept to the grave did go
With true-love showers.
Hamlet. Act iv, sc. 5, l. 37. [Ophelia] "Bewept" is repeated in *Richard III,* ii, 2, 49.
Sweet flowers.—*Richard III,* ii, 4, 15; *Romeo and Juliet,* v, 3, 12, *Hamlet,* iv, 5, 37.
Sweetest flower.—*Romeo and Juliet,* iv, 5, 29; *Pericles,* i, 1, 133.
10
There's rosemary, that's for remembrance; pray, love, remember: and there is pansies, that's for thoughts. . . . There's fennel for you, and columbines: there's rue for you; and here's some for me: we may call it herb-grace o' Sundays: O, you must wear your rue with a difference. There's a daisy: I would give you some violets.
Hamlet. Act iv, sc. 5, l. 175. [Ophelia] Rosemary is mentioned nine times; pansies but once; fennel and columbine twice; rue four times; and daisies four times. The only use of "herb-grace."
For you there's rosemary and rue; these keep
Seeming and savour all the winter long.
Winter's Tale. Act iv, sc. 4, l. 74. [Perdita]
11
There with fantastic garlands did she come
Of crow-flowers, nettles, daisies, and long purples
That liberal shepherds give a grosser name,
But our cold maids do dead men's fingers call them.
Hamlet. Act iv, sc. 7, l. 169. [Queen] The only mention of crow-flowers (buttercups) and long purples (the early purple orchis). "The rampant widow" was one of the "grosser names."
12
The freckled cowslip, burnet and green clover.
Henry V. Act v, sc. 2, l. 49. [Burgundy] The only mention of burnet and clover.
The cowslips tall her pensioners be:
In their gold coats spots you see;

Those be rubies, fairy favours,
In those freckles live their savours.
A Midsummer-Night's Dream. Act ii, sc. 1, l. 10. [Fairy] The only use of "freckles." "Freckled" occurs twice: "the freckled cowslip," *Henry V,* v, 2, 49; "a freckled whelp," *The Tempest,* i, 2, 283.
Yellow cowslip.—*A Midsummer-Night's Dream,* v, 1, 339.

1
I pluck this pale and maiden blossom here.
I Henry VI, ii, 4, 47. See under Rose.

A blossom passing fair
Playing in the wanton air.
Love's Labour 's Lost. Act iv, sc. 3, l. 103. [Dumain, reading]
Beauteous blossom.—*Titus Andronicus,* iv, 2, 72.
Gaudy blossoms.—*Love's Labour 's Lost,* v, 2, 812.
Good blossom.—*II Henry IV,* ii, 2, 101.
Blossoms of their fortune.—*The Winter's Tale,* v, 2, 135.
Blossoms of my sin.—*Hamlet,* i, 5, 76.
Blossoming Cæsar.—*Antony and Cleopatra,* iv, 12, 23.
Blossoming time.—*Measure for Measure,* i, 4, 41.
Thus are my blossoms blasted in the bud
And caterpillars eat my leaves away.
II Henry VI. Act iii, sc. 1, l. 89. [York]
My blossom.—*I Henry VI,* iv, 7, 16.
The blossom that hangs on the bough.
The Tempest, v, 1, 94. See under Fairy.
Blossom, speed thee well!—*The Winter's Tale,* iii, 3, 46.

2
I am bound to you,
That you on my behalf would pluck a flower.
I Henry VI. Act ii, sc. 4, l. 129. [Plantagenet]
Cull their flower.—*Troilus and Cressida,* ii, 3, 275.

3
This is the flower that smiles on every one.
Love's Labour 's Lost. Act v, sc. 2, l. 331. [Biron]
Armado: I am that flower,—
Dumain: That mint.
Longaville: That columbine.
Love's Labour 's Lost. Act v, sc. 2, l. 661.

4
I might as yet have been a spreading flower,
Fresh to myself, if I had self-applied
Love to myself and to no love beside.
A Lover's Complaint, l. 76. The only use of "self-applied."

5
Flowers purple, blue, and white.
The Merry Wives of Windsor. Act v, sc. 5, l. 74. [Mistress Quickly]

6
Yet mark'd I where the bolt of Cupid fell:
It fell upon a little western flower,
Before milk-white, now purple with love's wound,
And maidens call it love-in-idleness.
A Midsummer-Night's Dream. Act ii, sc. 1, l. 165. [Oberon] "Love in idleness" (unhyphenated) occurs also in *The Taming of the Shrew,* i, 1, 156.

Flower of this purple dye,
Hit with Cupid's archery.
A Midsummer-Night's Dream. Act iii, sc. 2, l. 102. [Oberon]
By this, the boy that by her side lay kill'd
Was melted like a vapour from her sight,
And in his blood that on the ground lay spill'd,
A purple flower sprung up, chequer'd with white,
Resembling well his pale cheeks and the blood
Which in round drops upon their whiteness stood.
Venus and Adonis, l. 1164. The only use of "chequer'd." "Checkered" occurs in *II Henry VI,* iii, 1, 229.

7
I know a bank where the wild thyme blows,
Where oxlips and the nodding violet grows,
Quite over-canopied with luscious woodbine,
With sweet musk-roses and with eglantine.
A Midsummer-Night's Dream. Act ii, sc. 1, l. 249. [Oberon] Thyme is mentioned again in *Othello,* i, 3, 326, oxlips in *The Winter's Tale,* iv, 4, 125, and eglantine in *Cymbeline,* iv, 2, 223. "Nodding" is repeated in *Coriolanus,* iii, 3, 126. The only use of "over-canopied." "Luscious" occurs again in *Othello,* i, 3, 354.

The pleached bower,
Where honeysuckles, ripen'd by the sun,
Forbid the sun to enter, like favourites,
Made proud by princes, that advance their pride
Against that power that bred it.
Much Ado about Nothing. Act iii, sc. 1, l. 7. [Hero] The only use of "pleached" in this sense, formed of intertwining boughs. "Pleach'd (folded) arms" occurs in *Antony and Cleopatra,* iv, 14, 73.
Sweet honeysuckle.—*A Midsummer-Night's Dream,* iv, 1, 47.
Honeysuckle villain!—*II Henry IV,* ii, 1, 56.

8
The flowers fair ladies.
Richard II. Act i, sc. 3, l. 290. [Gaunt]

9
Lady Capulet: Verona's summer hath not such a flower.
Nurse: Nay, he 's a flower; in faith, a very flower.
Romeo and Juliet. Act i, sc. 3, l. 77.
He came with flowers to strew his lady's grave.
Romeo and Juliet. Act v, sc. 1, l. 281. [Page]
Sweet flower, with flowers thy bridal bed I strew.
Romeo and Juliet. Act v, sc. 3, l. 12. [Paris]
Bridal flowers.—*Romeo and Juliet,* iv, 5, 89.

10
But flowers distill'd, though they with winter meet,
Leese but their show; their substance still lives sweet.
Sonnets. No. v. The only use of "leese" (lose).
Nor did I wonder at the lily's white,
Nor praise the deep vermillion in the rose.
Sonnets. No. xcviii. The only use of "vermillion."
More flowers I noted, yet I none could see
But sweet or colour it had stol'n from thee.
Sonnets. No. xcix.

1
Away before me to sweet beds of flowers:
Love-thoughts lie rich when canopied with
bowers.
Twelfth Night. Act i, sc. 1, l. 40. [Duke]
The only use of "love-thoughts."

Not a flower, not a flower sweet,
On my black coffin let there be strown.
Twelfth Night. Act ii, sc. 4, l. 60. [Clown]
The only use of "strown."

2
The field's chief flower, sweet above compare.
Venus and Adonis, l. 8.

Fair flowers that are not gather'd in their prime
Rot and consume themselves in little time.
Venus and Adonis, l. 131.

Who plucks the bud before one leaf put forth?
Venus and Adonis, l. 416.

3
She bows her head, the new-sprung flower
to smell,
Comparing it to her Adonis' breath,
And says, within her bosom it shall dwell,
Since he himself is reft from her by death:
She crops the stalk, and in the breach appears
Green dropping sap, which she compares
to tears.
Venus and Adonis, l. 1171. The only use of "new-sprung."

There shall not be one minute in an hour
Wherein I will not kiss my sweet love's flower.
Venus and Adonis, l. 1187.

4
She hath made me four and twenty nosegays.
The Winter's Tale. Act iv, sc. 3, l. 44. [Clown] "Nosegays" is used also in *A Midsummer-Night's Dream,* i, 1, 34.

5
The year growing ancient,
Not yet on summer's death, nor on the birth
Of trembling winter, the fairest flowers o'
the season
Are our carnations and streak'd gillyvors,
Which some call nature's bastards.
Winter's Tale. Act iv, sc. 4, l. 79. [Perdita]

Polixenes: Then make your garden rich in
gillyvors,
And do not call them bastards.
Perdita: I 'll not put
The dibble in earth to set one slip of them.
The Winter's Tale. Act iv, sc. 4, l. 98. The only uses of "gillyvors" and "dibble."

O Proserpina,
For the flowers now, that frighted thou let'st
fall
From Dis's waggon! daffodils,
That come before the swallow dares, and take
The winds of March with beauty; violets dim,
But sweeter than the lids of Juno's eyes
Or Cytherea's breath; pale primroses,
That die unmarried, ere they can behold
Bright Phœbus in his strength—a malady
Most incident to maids; bold oxlips and
The crown imperial; lilies of all kinds,
The flower-de-luce being one! O, these I lack,
To make you garlands of, and my sweet friend,
To strew him o'er and o'er!
Winter's Tale. Act iv, sc. 4, l. 116. [Perdita] Proserpina is mentioned again in *Troilus and Cressida,* ii, 1, 37, and Dis in *The Tempest,* iv, 1, 89. Juno was more popular with Shakespeare, and is mentioned twenty times. Cytherea is mentioned three times, and Phœbus eighteen. Daffodils are mentioned again in *Winter's Tale,* iv, 3, 1, and in no other play, while primroses are referred to seven times. Oxlips are mentioned again in *Midsummer-Night's Dream,* ii, 1, 250, and the flower-de-luce five times. The only use of "unmarried."

6
Here 's flowers for you;
Hot lavender, mints, savory, marjoram;
The marigold, that goes to bed wi' the sun
And with him rises weeping: these are
flowers
Of middle summer, and I think they are
given
To men of middle age.
The Winter's Tale. Act iv, sc. 4, l. 103. [Perdita] The only mention of lavender, savory. Mint is mentioned again in *Love's Labour 's Lost,* v, 2, 661; marjoram in *King Lear,* iv, 6, 94 and *Sonnet* xcix; and marigold in *Pericles,* iv, 1, 16, *The Rape of Lucrece,* l. 397, and *Sonnet* xxv.

Flowers o' the spring.—*The Winter's Tale,* iv, 4, 113.

Spring-time flowers.—*The Taming of the Shrew,* ii, 1, 248.

Summer-swelling flower.—*The Two Gentlemen of Verona,* ii, 4, 162. The only use of "summer-swelling."

Flowers of winter.—*Winter's Tale,* iv, 4, 79.

II—Flower and Weed

7
To dew the sovereign flower and drown the
weeds.
Macbeth. Act v, sc. 2, l. 30. [Lennox]

Unwholesome weeds take root with precious
flowers.
The Rape of Lucrece, l. 870.

8
Sweet flowers are slow and weeds make
haste.
Richard III. Act ii, sc. 4, l. 15. [York]

The noisome weeds, which without profit suck
The soil's fertility from wholesome flowers.
Richard II. Act iii, sc. 4, l. 38. [Gardener]

Baleful weeds and precious-juiced flowers.
Romeo and Juliet. Act ii, sc. 3, l. 8. [Friar Laurence] The only use of "precious-juiced."

9
To thy fair flower add the rank smell of
weeds.
Sonnets. No. lxix.

The summer's flower is to the summer sweet,
Though to itself it only live and die,
But if that flower with base infection meet
The basest weed outbraves his dignity:
For sweetest things turn sourest by their
deeds;
Lillies that fester smell far worse than weeds.
Sonnets. No. xciv.

Weeds among weeds, or flowers with flowers
gather'd.
Sonnets. No. cxxiv.

1
They bid thee crop a weed, thou pluck'st a flower.
Venus and Adonis, l. 946.

FLY

2
This was but as a fly by an eagle.
Antony and Cleopatra, ii, 2, 186. See under COMPARISON.
Flies and gnats.—*Antony and Cleopatra,* iii, 13, 166.

3
Swarm like summer flies.
III Henry VI, ii, 6, 8. See under PEOPLE.
Sprung like summer flies.—*III Henry VI,* ii, 6, 17.
As summer flies are in the shambles.—*Othello,* iv, 2, 66.
Flies at Bartholomew-tide.—*Henry V,* v, 2, 336.
Mortal flies.—*Cymbeline,* v, 4, 31.
Poor flies.—*Venus and Adonis,* l. 316.
Small gilded fly.—*King Lear,* iv, 6, 114.
Time's flies.—*Timon of Athens,* iii, 6, 106.

4
As flies to wanton boys, are we to the gods,
They kill us for their sport.
King Lear. Act iv, sc. 1, l. 38. [Gloucester]

5
And, though he in a fertile climate dwell,
Plague him with flies.
Othello. Act i, sc. 1, l. 70. [Iago]

6
That we should be thus afflicted with these strange flies.
Romeo and Juliet, ii, 4, 34. See under FOP.
Flies may do this, but I from this must fly.
Romeo and Juliet, iii, 3, 41.

7
I shall not fear fly-blowing.
The Tempest. Act v, sc. 1, l. 284. [Trinculo] The only use of "fly-blowing." "Fly-blown" occurs in *I Henry VI,* iv, 7, 76; and "fly-bitten" in *II Henry IV,* ii, 1, 159.
With flies blown to death.
The Winter's Tale. Act iv, sc. 4, l. 821. [Autolycus]

8
One cloud of winter showers,
These flies are couch'd.
Timon of Athens. Act ii, sc. 2, l. 180. [Flavius] See PRAISE, 1185:11.

9
Titus Andronicus: What dost thou strike at, Marcus, with thy knife?
Marcus Andronicus: At that that I have kill'd, my lord; a fly.
Titus: Out on thee, murderer! thou kill'st my heart;
Mine eyes are cloy'd with view of tyranny:
A deed of death done on the innocent
Becomes not Titus' brother: get thee gone;
I see thou art not for my company.
Marcus: Alas, my lord, I have but kill'd a fly.
Titus: But how, if that fly had a father and a mother?
How would he hang his slender gilded wings,
And buzz lamenting doings in the air!
Poor harmless fly,
That, with his pretty buzzing melody,
Came here to make us merry! and thou hast kill'd him.
Marcus: Pardon me, sir; it was a black ill-favour'd fly,
Like to the empress' Moor; therefore I kill'd him. . . .
Titus: Yet, I think, we are not brought so low,
But that between us we can kill a fly
That comes in likeness of a coal-black Moor.
Titus Andronicus. Act iv, sc. 1, l. 52.
It will not kill a fly.
As You Like It. Act iv, sc. 1, l. 111. [Rosalind]
Killing flies.—*Coriolanus,* iv, 6, 95.
Kills the flies.—*Pericles,* iv, 3, 50.
I never . . . hurt a fly.—*Pericles,* iv, 1, 78.
Catch the fly.—*Henry V,* v, 2, 340.

FOE

See also Enemy; Friend and Foe

10
A foe to the public weal.
Coriolanus. Act iii, sc. 1, l. 176. [Sicinius]
A foe to citizens.—*I Henry VI,* i, 3, 62.
Foes to life.—*The Comedy of Errors,* v, 1, 82.
Foes to nobleness.—*Coriolanus,* iii, 1, 45.
Foe to tyrants.—*Julius Cæsar,* v, 4, 5.
Bounty's foe.—*Timon of Athens,* ii, 2, 241.
Country's foes.—*Richard III,* v, 3, 257.
Sovereign's foes.—*Richard II,* iii, 2, 12.

11
Our foe was princely;
And though you took his life, as being our foe,
Yet bury him as a prince.
Cymbeline. Act iv, sc. 2, l. 249. [Belarius]
Noble foe.—*Troilus and Cressida,* i, 3, 309.
Such a foe, good heavens!—*Cymbeline,* iii, 6, 27.

12
It is most meet we arm us 'gainst the foe.
Henry V. Act ii, sc. 4, l. 15. [Dauphin]
To purge this field of such a hilding foe.
Henry V. Act iv, sc. 2, l. 29. [Constable of France] Shakespeare uses "hilding" (mean, worthless, cowardly) seven times.

13
Once I read
That stout Pendragon in his litter sick
Came to the field and vanquished his foes.
I Henry VI. Act iii, sc. 2, l. 94. [Bedford] The only mention of Pendragon.
Was not the Duke of Orleans thy foe?
And was he not in England prisoner?
But when they heard he was thine enemy,
They set him free without his ransom paid.
I Henry VI. Act iii, sc. 3, l. 69. [La Pucelle]

14
But fear not thou, until thy foot be snared,
Nor never seek prevention of thy foes.
II Henry VI. Act ii, sc. 4, l. 56. [Duchess of Gloucester]
Salisbury: 'Tis not enough our foes are this time fled,
Being opposites of such repairing nature.
York: I know our safety is to follow them. . . .
What says Lord Warwick? shall we after them?

Warwick: After them! nay, before them, if we can.
II Henry VI. Act v, sc. 3, l. 21.

1 Foe as he was to me,
Might liquid tears or heart-offending groans
Or blood-consuming sighs recall his life,
I would be blind with weeping, sick with groans,
Look pale as primrose with blood-drinking sighs,
And all to have the noble duke alive.
II Henry VI. Act iii, sc. 2, l. 59. [Queen] The only use of "heart-offending" and "blood-consuming." "Blood-drinking" is repeated in *I Henry VI,* ii, 4, 108: "Blood-drinking hate"; and in *Titus Andronicus,* ii, 3, 224: "Blood-drinking pit."

2
Environed he was with many foes.
III Henry VI. Act ii, sc. 1, l. 50. [Messenger]

Our foes are nigh.—*III Henry VI,* ii, 2, 56.

The foe is merciless, and will not pity.
III Henry VI. Act ii, sc. 6, l. 25. [Clifford]

3 Thou shalt not dread
The scatter'd foe that hopes to rise again;
For though they cannot greatly sting to hurt,
Yet look to have them buzz to offend thine ears.
III Henry VI. Act ii, sc. 6, l. 92. [Warwick]

4
His sworn and mortal foe.
III Henry V. Act iii, sc. 3, l. 257. [Warwick]

I here proclaim myself thy mortal foe.
III Henry VI. Act v, sc. 1, l. 94. [Clarence] The only uses of "mortal foe."

My most malicious foe.
Henry VIII. Act ii, sc. 4, l. 83. [Queen Katharine]

5
By his foe surprised at unawares.
III Henry VI. Act iv, sc. 4, l. 9. [Queen Elizabeth]

So other foes may set upon our backs.
III Henry VI. Act v, sc. 1, l. 61. [King Edward]

6
What valiant foemen like to autumn's corn,
Have we mow'd down in tops of all their pride!
III Henry VI. Act v, sc. 7, l. 3. [King Edward]

Unto his dastard foemen is betray'd.
I Henry VI. Act i, sc. 1, l. 144. [Bedford] "Foemen" is used a third time in *Titus Andronicus,* iv, 1, 127: "Foemen's marks." "Foeman" occurs in *III Henry VI,* ii, 5, 82, and in *II Henry IV,* iii, 2, 285.

7
Her foes shake like a field of beaten corn,
And hang their heads with sorrow.
Henry VIII. Act v, sc. 5, l. 32. [Cranmer] See under PROPHECY.

8
Shaking the bloody fingers of thy foes,
Most noble! in the presence of thy corse.
Julius Cæsar. Act iii, sc. 1, l. 198. [Antony]

9
Away, then, with good courage! yet, I know,
Our party may well meet a prouder foe.
King John. Act v, sc. 1, l. 78. [Bastard]

That oft in field, with targe and shield, did make my foes to sweat.
Love's Labour's Lost. Act v, sc. 2, l. 555. [Costard]

Bitter foe.—*A Midsummer-Night's Dream,* iii, 2, 44.

Camping foes.—*All's Well that Ends Well,* iii, 4, 14. The only use of "camping."

Cruel foe.—*I Henry VI,* iii, 3, 46; *The Rape of Lucrece,* l. 1460.

Dearest foe.—*Hamlet,* i, 2, 182.

Eager foe.—*III Henry VI,* i, 4, 3.

So false a foe.—*The Rape of Lucrece,* l. 77.

Fast foe.—*Coriolanus,* ii, 3, 192.

Fellest foes.—*Coriolanus,* iv, 4, 18.

Flattering foe.—*The Passionate Pilgrim,* l. 430.

Hateful foe.—*The Rape of Lucrece,* l. 1698.

Heartless foe.—*The Rape of Lucrece,* l. 471.

Insolent foe.—*Othello,* i, 3, 137.

Wicked foe.—*The Rape of Lucrece,* l. 1035.

10
The foe vaunts in the field.
Richard III. Act v, sc. 3, l. 288. [Norfolk]

Thou shalt not stir a foot to seek a foe.
Romeo and Juliet. Act i, sc. 1, l. 87. [Lady Montague]

This is . . . our foe.—*Romeo and Juliet,* i, 5, 63.

Held a foe.—*Romeo and Juliet,* ii, Prol., 9.

11
Thyself thy foe, to thy sweet self too cruel.
Sonnets. No. i.

We must not be foes.—*Sonnets,* xl.

12 I have kept back their foes,
While they have told their money and let out
Their coin upon large interest, I myself
Rich only in large hurts.
Timon of Athens. Act iii, sc. 5, l. 106. [Alcibiades]

13
A terror to our foes.
Titus Andronicus. Act i, sc. 1, l. 29. [Marcus]

My foes I do repute you every one.
Titus Andronicus. Act i, sc. 1, l. 366. [Titus]

Look, thy foes are bound.—*Titus Andronicus,* v, 2, 167.

FOG

14
Lose itself in a fog.
Coriolanus. Act ii, sc. 3, l. 34. [Citizen]

15 Nor here, nor here,
Nor what ensues, but have a fog in them,
That I cannot look through.
Cymbeline. Act iii, sc. 2, l. 80. [Imogen]

16
Is not their climate foggy?
Henry V, iii, 5, 16. See under ENGLAND.

Foggy cloud.—*Macbeth,* iii, 5, 35.

Foggy Night!—*The Rape of Lucrece,* l. 771.

Foggy south.—*As You Like It,* iii, 5, 50. The only uses of "foggy."

17
Therefore the winds, piping to us in vain,
As in revenge, have suck'd up from the sea
Contagious fogs.
A Midsummer-Night's Dream. Act ii, sc. 1, l. 88. [Titania]

Fen-suck'd fogs.—*King Lear,* ii, 4, 169. The only use of "fen-suck'd."

The starry welkin cover thou anon
With drooping fog as black as Acheron.
A Midsummer-Night's Dream. Act iii, sc. 2, l. 356. [Oberon] The only use of "starry." Acheron is mentioned again in *Timon of Athens,* iv, 3, 44, and in *Macbeth,* iii, 5, 15.

Stain the sun with fog.—*Titus Andronicus,* iii, 1, 213.

FOLLY

See also Foolery; Wisdom and Folly.

1
Your son,
As mad in folly, lack'd sense to know
Her estimation home.
All's Well that Ends Well. Act v, sc. 3, l. 2. [King]

2
And they that are most galled with my folly,
They most must laugh.
As You Like It. Act ii, sc. 7, l. 50. [Jaques]

Or what is he of basest function
That says his bravery is not on my cost,
Thinking that I mean him, but therein suits
His folly to the mettle of my speech?
As You Like It. Act ii, sc. 7, l. 79. [Jaques]

3
Either you must
Confess yourselves wondrous malicious,
Or be accused of folly.
Coriolanus. Act i, sc. 1, l. 90. [Menenius]

You confine yourself most unreasonably.
Coriolanus. Act i, sc. 3, l. 84. [Valeria] The only use of "unreasonably."

'Twas folly.—*Coriolanus,* v, 1, 26.

Too much folly.—*I Henry VI,* iv, 6, 32.

What folly!—*Timon of Athens,* iii, 5, 37.

4
Dost thou think in time
She will not quench and let instructions enter
Where folly now possesses?
Cymbeline. Act i, sc. 5, l. 46. [Queen]

That it was folly in me, thou mayst say,
And prove it in thy feeling.
Cymbeline. Act v, sc. 5, l. 67. [Cymbeline]

5
I think thou art enamoured On his follies.
I Henry IV. Act v, sc. 2, l. 70. [Vernon]

Love his follies.—*Henry VIII,* iii, 2, 275.

6
Beat at this gate, that let thy folly in,
And thy dear judgement out!
King Lear. Act i, sc. 4, l. 293. [King Lear]

Folly, in wisdom hatch'd.—*Love's Labour's Lost,* v, 2, 70. See under FOOL, 566:6.

What, quite unmann'd in folly?
Macbeth. Act iii, sc. 4, l. 73. [Macbeth] "Unmann'd" is repeated in *Romeo and Juliet,* iii, 2, 14: "Unmann'd blood."

7
As you have one eye upon my follies, as you hear them unfolded, turn another into the register of your own; that I may pass with a reproof the easier.
The Merry Wives of Windsor. Act ii, sc. 2, l. 192. [Ford]

The folly of my soul dares not present itself.
The Merry Wives of Windsor, ii, 2, 253. See under HONOUR.

He gives her folly motion and advantage.
The Merry Wives of Windsor. Act iii, sc. 2, l. 35. [Ford]

Why, this is your own folly.
The Merry Wives of Windsor. Act v, sc. 5, l. 206. [Page]

8
And now, so you will let me quiet go,
To Athens will I bear my folly back.
A Midsummer-Night's Dream. Act iii, sc. 2, l. 314. [Helena]

9
Even her folly help'd her to an heir.
Othello, ii, 1, 138. See under CHILD.

She turn'd to folly.—*Othello,* v, 2, 132.

10
Why should . . . tyrant folly lurk in gentle breasts?
The Rape of Lucrece, l. 851.

Dangerous folly.—*Macbeth,* iv, 2, 77.

Daring folly.—*The Two Gentlemen of Verona,* iii, 1, 155.

Mere folly.—*As You Like It,* ii, 7, 181; *Antony and Cleopatra,* iii, 13, 43.

Present folly.—*The Two Gentlemen of Verona,* ii, 1, 81.

Pretty follies.—*Merchant of Venice,* ii, 6, 37.

Shallow follies.—*Much Ado about Nothing,* ii, 3, 11.

Slightest folly.—*As You Like It,* ii, 4, 34.

Superfluous folly.—*All's Well that Ends Well,* i, 1, 116.

Unpitied folly.—*Antony and Cleopatra,* i, 3, 98.

Vulture folly.—*The Rape of Lucrece,* l. 556.

Wise man's folly.—*As You Like It,* ii, 7, 56.

Folly past.—*Two Gentlemen of Verona,* i, 2, 65.

11
Your follies fight against yourself.
Richard II, iii, 2, 182. See under FEAR.

O my follies!—*King Lear,* iii, 7, 91.

12
Must I ravel out My weaved-up folly?
Richard II. Act iv, sc. 1, l. 228. [King Richard] The only use of "weaved-up."

13
Folly doctor-like controlling skill.
Sonnets. No. lxvi. The only use of "doctor-like."

Methinks you prescribe to yourself very preposterously.
The Merry Wives of Windsor. Act ii, sc. 2, l. 249. [Falstaff]

Befal preposterously.—*A Midsummer-Night's Dream,* iii, 2, 121.

So preposterously.—*Henry V,* ii, 2, 112; *Othello,* i, 3, 62. The only uses of "preposterously."

14
The folly of this island! They say there's but five men upon this isle: we are three of them; if the other two be brained like us, the state totters.
The Tempest. Act iii, sc. 2, l. 5. [Trinculo] The only use of "totters."

15
His folly sauced with discretion.
Troilus and Cressida, i, 2, 24. See under CHARACTER.

Covering discretion with a coat of folly.
Henry V, ii, 4, 38. See under DISCRETION.

1
What folly I commit, I dedicate to you.
Troilus and Cressida. Act iii, sc. 2, l. 110. [Cressida]
Sweet honey Greek, tempt me no more to folly.
Troilus and Cressida. Act v, sc. 2, l. 18. [Cressida]
2
Sebastian: I prithee, vent thy folly somewhere else:
Thou know'st not me.
Clown: Vent my folly! . . . Vent my folly!
Twelfth Night, iv, 1, 10. See under WORD.
3 A folly bought with wit,
Or else a wit by folly vanquished.
The Two Gentlemen of Verona, i, 1, 34. See under LOVE.
Wit Is turn'd to folly.—*The Two Gentlemen of Verona,* i, 1, 48.
4
What folly reigns in us!
The Two Gentlemen of Verona. Act i, sc. 2, l. 15. [Lucetta]
You are so without these follies, that these follies are within you and shine through you like the water in an urinal.
The Two Gentlemen of Verona. Act ii, sc. 1, l. 39. [Speed] The only use of "urinal." "Urinals" occurs twice in *The Merry Wives of Windsor,* iii, 1, 14; 91.
I 'll double your folly.—*The Two Gentlemen of Verona,* ii, 4, 21.
You, that are thus so tender o'er his follies,
Will never do him good, not one of you.
Winter's Tale. Act ii, sc. 3, l. 128. [Paulina]
5 Swear his thought over
By each particular star in heaven and
By all their influences, you may as well
Forbid the sea for to obey the moon
As or by oath remove or counsel shake
The fabric of his folly.
Winter's Tale. Act i, sc. 2, l. 424. [Camillo]
It was my folly.—*The Winter's Tale,* i, 2, 256.
All mine own folly.—*Winter's Tale,* v, 1, 135.

FOOD

See also Eating, Feeding, Meat

6
Eight wild-boars roasted whole at a breakfast, and but twelve persons there; is this true?
Antony and Cleopatra. Act ii, sc. 2, l. 183. [Mecænas] The only mention of "wild-boars."
7
They were good pancakes.
As You Like It, i, 2, 67. Pancakes are mentioned three times in this play and once in *All's Well that Ends Well,* ii, 2, 25.
8
Seeking the food he eats
And pleased with what he gets.
As You Like It, ii, 5, 42. See under AMBITION.
9
Orlando: I almost die for food; and let me have it.
Duke Senior: Sit down and feed; and welcome to our table.
As You Like It. Act ii, sc. 7, l. 104.
O, I die for food!—*As You Like It,* ii, 6, 2.
Give it food.—*As You Like It,* ii, 7, 127.
Brings me food.—*Richard II,* v, 5, 71.
Touch no food.—*Love's Labour 's Lost,* i, 1, 39.
10
In food, in sport and life-preserving rest
To be disturb'd would mad or man or beast.
The Comedy of Errors. Act v, sc. 1, l. 84. [Abbess] The only use of "life-preserving."
Food and diet.—*Hamlet,* i, 1, 99.
Food and living.—*Timon of Athens,* iv, 3, 524.
Eternal food.—*The Merry Wives of Windsor,* ii, 1, 104.
Hard food.—*The Merchant of Venice,* iii, 2, 102.
Meet food.—*Much Ado about Nothing,* i, 1, 122.
Moody food.—*Antony and Cleopatra,* ii, 5, 1.
Unwholesome food.—*Henry V,* ii, 3, 59.
Soul's food.—*The Two Gentlemen of Verona,* ii, 7, 15.
11 I receive the general food at first
Which you do live upon.
Coriolanus, i, 1, 135. See under BELLY.
I do live by food.—*As You Like It,* ii, 7, 14.
Fed with the same food.—*The Merchant of Venice,* iii, 1, 63.
12
Food for powder, food for powder.
I Henry IV. Act iv, sc. 2, l. 71. [Falstaff]
Food for worms.—*I Henry IV,* v, 4, 86.
13
He lives upon mouldy stewed prunes and dried cakes.
II Henry IV. Act ii, sc. 4, l. 158. [Doll]
Sir, she came in great with child; and longing, saving your honour's reverence, for stewed prunes.
Measure for Measure. Act ii, sc. 1, l. 91. [Pompey]
Longing, as I said, for prunes.
Measure for Measure. Act ii, sc. 1, l. 103. [Pompey]
Three veneys for a dish of stewed prunes.
Merry Wives of Windsor. Act i, sc. 1, l. 295. [Slender] The only use of "veney" (venue).
Stewed prune.—*I Henry IV,* iii, 3, 128.
Four pound of prunes.—*Winter's Tale,* iv, 3, 51.
The foresaid prunes.—*Measure for Measure,* ii, 1, 111. The only references to prunes.
14
Some pigeons, Davy, a couple of short-legged hens, a joint of mutton, and any pretty little tiny kickshaws, tell William cook.
II Henry IV. Act v, sc. 1, l. 27. [Shallow] The only use of "short-legged" and "kickshaws." *Twelfth Night,* i, 3, 122, has "kickshawses."
15
His viands sparkling in a golden cup.
III Henry VI, ii, 5, 52. See under KING.
Let their palates Be season'd with such viands.
The Merchant of Venice. Act iv, sc. 1, l. 96. [Shylock]
They have left their viands behind.
The Tempest, iii, 3, 41.
All viands that I eat do seem unsavoury.
Pericles. Act ii, sc. 3, l. 31. [Thaisa]
The remainder viands
We do not throw in unrespective sieve,
Because we now are full.
Troilus and Cressida. Act ii, sc. 2, l. 70.

[Troilus] "Unrespective" is used a second time in *Richard III,* iv, 2, 29: "Unrespective boys."

Still cupboarding the viand.—*Coriolanus,* i, 1, 103. The only use of "cupboarding."

Our viands!—*Antony and Cleopatra,* iii, 11, 73; *Cymbeline,* v, 5, 156. The only uses of "viand" and "viands."

1
Boyet, you can carve; Break up this capon.
Love's Labour's Lost. Act iv, sc. 1, l. 55. [Princess of France]

Carve a capon and eat it.
I Henry IV, ii, 4, 502. See under CHARACTER.

He hath bid me to a calf's head and a capon.
Much Ado about Nothing. Act v, sc. 1, l. 156. [Claudio] See under FEAST.

The capon burns.—*Comedy of Errors,* i, 2, 44.

Steals her capon's leg.—*The Two Gentlemen of Verona,* iv, 4, 10.

Cold capon's leg.—*I Henry IV,* i, 2, 129.

Good capon.—*As You Like It,* ii, 7, 154.

Cock and capon.—*Cymbeline,* ii, 1, 25.

2
Make the gruel thick and slab.
Macbeth. Act iv, sc. 1, l. 32. [Third Witch] The only mention of gruel in the plays, and the only use of "slab" (viscous, semi-solid).

3
Fair ladies, you drop manna in the way
Of starved people.
The Merchant of Venice. Act v, sc. 1, l. 294. [Lorenzo] The only use of "manna."

4
Come, we have a hot venison pasty to dinner.
The Merry Wives of Windsor. Act i, sc. 1, l. 202. [Mistress Page] "Venison" occurs three times in this play; once in *As You Like It,* and twice in *Cymbeline.*

5
I had as lief you would tell me of a mess of porridge.
The Merry Wives of Windsor. Act iii, sc. 1, l. 63. [Evans]

They want their porridge.—*I Henry VI,* i, 2, 9.

Porridge after meat!—*Troilus and Cressida,* i, 2, 263.

Cold porridge.—*The Tempest,* ii, 1, 10.

6
Feed him with apricocks and dewberries,
With purple grapes, green figs, and mulberries.
A Midsummer-Night's Dream. Act iii, sc. 1, l. 169. [Titania] *Richard II,* iii, 4, 29, has "dangling apricocks." This is the only use of "dewberries." "Mulberry" occurs again in *A Midsummer-Night's Dream,* v, 1, 149, and in *Coriolanus,* iii, 2, 79.

7
Titania: Say, sweet love, what thou desirest to eat.
Bottom: Truly, a peck of provender: I could munch your good dry oats. Methinks I have a great desire to a bottle of hay: good hay, sweet hay, hath no fellow.
A Midsummer-Night's Dream. Act iv, sc. 1, l. 33. [Bottom] The only use of "munch." "Munch'd" occurs in *Macbeth,* i, 3, 5.

Give their fasting horses provender.
Henry V. Act iv, sc. 2, l. 58. [Dauphin]

Like mules . . . their provender tied to their mouths.
I Henry VI. Act i, sc. 2, l. 11. [Alençon]

I do appoint him store of provender.
Julius Cæsar. Act iv, sc. 1, l. 30. [Antony]

Wears out his time . . . for nought but provender.
Othello, i, 1, 48. The only uses of "provender."

8
This may prove food to my displeasure.
Much Ado about Nothing, i, 3, 68. See under DISPLEASURE.

Food to the suck'd and hungry lioness.—*As You Like It,* iv, 3, 127.

Food for his rage.—*Love's Labour's Lost,* iv, 1, 95.

Food of sweet and bitter fancy.—*As You Like It,* iv, 3, 102.

9
The food that to him now is as luscious as locusts, shall be to him shortly as bitter as coloquintida.
Othello. Act i, sc. 3, l. 354. [Iago] The only use of "locusts" and "coloquintida."

10
We'll have flesh for holidays, fish for fasting-days, and moreover puddings and flap-jacks.
Pericles. Act ii, sc. 1, l. 85. [First Fisherman] The only use of "fasting-days" and "flap-jacks" in the plays, and this scene is probably not by Shakespeare. See FISH AND FLESH.

Thy food is such
As hath been belch'd on by infected lungs.
Pericles. Act iv, sc. 6, l. 178. [Marina]

11
Save me a piece of marchpane.
Romeo and Juliet. Act i, sc. 5, l. 9. [First Servant] The only use of "marchpane" (almond paste).

12
Buy food, and get thyself in flesh.
Romeo and Juliet. Act v, sc. 1, l. 84. [Romeo]

I'll cram thee with more food.—*Romeo and Juliet,* v, 3, 48.

13
Second Servant: Will 't please your honour taste of these conserves? . . .
Sly: If you give me any conserves, give me conserves of beef.
The Taming of the Shrew. Induction, sc. 2, l. 4. The only use of "conserves."

I prithee go and get me some repast;
I care not what, so it be wholesome food.
The Taming of the Shrew. Act iv, sc. 3, l. 15. [Katharina]

How say you to a fat tripe finely broil'd?
The Taming of the Shrew. Act iv, sc. 3, l. 20. [Grumio] The only mention of tripe.

14
First Bandit: We cannot live on grass, on berries, water,
As beasts and birds and fishes.
Timon: Nor on the beasts themselves, the birds and fishes;
You must eat men.
Timon of Athens. Act iv, sc. 3, l. 425.

Thy food shall be
The fresh-brook muscles, wither'd roots and husks

Wherein the acorn cradled.
The Tempest, i, 2, 462. See under PUNISHMENT. The only use of "fresh-brook" and "muscles." "Acorn" is used twice more, in *As You Like It*, iii, 2, 248, and in *A Midsummer-Night's Dream*, iii, 2, 330.

Cry for food.—*Titus Andronicus*, v, 3, 180.

1
Let him receive no sustenance.
Titus Andronicus. Act v, sc. 3, l. 6. [Lucius]

Nor taken sustenance.—*Pericles*, v, 1, 25. The only uses of "sustenance."

Kept without my food.—*Romeo and Juliet*, i, 2, 56.

I have no food for thee.—*King Lear*, iii, 6, 34.

2
Though the chameleon Love can feed on the air, I am one that am nourished by my victuals and would fain have meat.
The Two Gentlemen of Verona. Act ii, sc. 1, l. 178. [Speed] "Food of love" occurs in *Twelfth Night*, i, 1, 1, and "lovers' food" in *A Midsummer-Night's Dream*, i, 1, 223. For NOURISHMENT, *see* SUPPER.

You had musty victual, and he hath holp to eat it.
Much Ado about Nothing. Act i, sc. 1, l. 50. [Beatrice]

I will desire you to live in the mean time, and eat your victuals.
Henry V. Act v, sc. 1, l. 34. [Fluellen]

But that it eats our victuals, I should think
Here was a fairy.
Cymbeline. Act iii, sc. 6, l. 41. [Belarius] The only uses of "victuals."

I must go victual Orleans forthwith.
I Henry VI. Act i, sc. 5, l. 14. [La Pucelle] The only use of "victual."

All victuallers do so.
II Henry IV. Act ii, sc. 4, l. 375. [Hostess] The only use of "victuallers."

3
Let me see; what am I to buy for our sheep-shearing feast? Three pound of sugar, five pound of currants, rice,—what will this sister of mine do with rice?
Winter's Tale. Act iv, sc. 3, l. 40. [Clown] The only use of "currants" and "rice."

I must have saffron to colour the warden pies; mace; dates?—none, that 's out of my note; nutmegs, seven; a race or two of ginger, but that I may beg; four pound of prunes, and as many of raisins o' the sun.
The Winter's Tale. Act iv, sc. 3, l. 48. [Clown] The only use of "warden pies" (pies made of pears) and "raisins."

FOOL

See also Idiot

4
I will be a fool in question, hoping to be the wiser by your answer.
All's Well that Ends Well. Act ii, sc. 2, l. 41. [Countess]

I play the noble housewife with the time,
To entertain 't so merrily with a fool.
All's Well that Ends Well. Act ii, sc. 2, l. 62. [Countess]

The count 's a fool, and full of gold.
All's Well that Ends Well. Act iv, sc. 3, l. 238. [Soldier]

5
But, cousin, what if we assay'd to steal
The clownish fool out of your father's court?
Would he not be a comfort to our travel?
As You Like It. Act i, sc. 3, l. 131. [Rosalind] The only use of "clownish."

An ordinary fool that has no more brain than a stone.
Twelfth Night. Act i, sc. 5, l. 91. [Malvolio]

All-licensed fool.—*King Lear*, i, 4, 220. The only use of "all-licensed."

Blind fool.—*Sonnets*, cxxxvii.

Christian fools.—*The Merchant of Venice*, ii, 5, 33.

Death's fool.—*Measure for Measure*, iii, 1, 11.

Good fool.—*Twelfth Night*, iv, 2, 86; iv, 2, 113; *King Lear*, i, 5, 41.

A great way fool.—*All's Well that Ends Well*, i, 1, 112.

Hairy fool.—*As You Like It*, ii, 1, 40.

Hateful fool.—*A Midsummer-Night's Dream*, iv, 1, 54.

Honest fool.—*Othello*, ii, 3, 359.

Lamenting fool.—*Titus Andronicus*, iii, 2, 20.

A lunatic lean-witted fool.—*Richard II*, ii, 1, 115. The only use of "lean-witted." "Lunatic" appears fourteen times.

A material fool!—*As You Like It*, iii, 3, 32.

Moral fool.—*King Lear*, iv, 2, 58.

Mumbling fool!—*Romeo and Juliet*, iii, 5, 174. "Mumbling" is repeated in *King Lear*, ii, 1, 41.

Poor fool.—*The Two Gentlemen of Verona*, iv, 4, 98, and six times in later plays.

Pretty fool.—*Romeo and Juliet*, i, 3, 31; i, 3, 48.

Relenting fool.—*Richard III*, iv, 4, 431.

Roman fool.—*Macbeth*, v, 8, 1.

Secure fool.—*The Merry Wives of Windsor*, ii, 1, 241.

Shallow fools!—*The Rape of Lucrece*, l. 1016.

Time's fool.—*Sonnets*, cxvi.

Vain fool.—*King Lear*, iv, 2, 61.

Venomous fool.—*Antony and Cleopatra*, v, 2, 308.

Witty fool.—*All's Well that Ends Well*, ii, 4, 32.

Wretched fools!—*Measure for Measure*, v, 1, 161; *Othello*, iii, 3, 375.

6
Much fool may you find in you, even to the world's pleasure and the increase of laughter.
All's Well that Ends Well. Act ii, sc. 4, l. 36. [Clown]

7
I 'll seem the fool I am not.
Antony and Cleopatra. Act i, sc. 1, l. 42. [Cleopatra]

Thou teachest like a fool.
Antony and Cleopatra. Act i, sc. 3, l. 10. [Cleopatra]

8
Jaques: If it do come to pass
That any man turn ass,
Leaving his wealth and ease,
A stubborn will to please,
Ducdame, ducdame, ducdame:
Here shall he see
Gross fools as he,

An if he will come to me.
Amiëns: What 's that ducdame?
Jaques: 'Tis a Greek invocation, to call fools into a circle.
As You Like It. Act ii, sc. 5, l. 52. The only use of "ducdame," perhaps a corruption of the Latin *duc ad me* (come hither).

1
A fool, a fool! I met a fool i' the forest,
A motley fool; a miserable world!
As I do live by food, I met a fool;
Who laid him down and bask'd him in the sun.
As You Like It. Act ii, sc. 7, l. 12. [Jaques] "Motley fool" is repeated in ll. 17 and 29. The only use of "bask'd."

The motley-minded gentleman.
As You Like It, v, 4, 41. The only use of the phrase.

Jaques: O noble fool!
A worthy fool! Motley's the only wear.
Duke Senior: What fool is this?
Jaques: O worthy fool! One that hath been a courtier.
As You Like It. Act ii, sc. 7, l. 33.

O that I were a fool!
I am ambitious for a motley coat.
As You Like It. Act ii, sc. 7, l. 42. [Jaques]

A long motley coat guarded with yellow.
Henry VIII. Prologue, l. 16.

Invest me in my motley.—*As You Like It,* ii, 7, 58.

Will you be married motley?—*As You Like It,* iii, 3, 79.

I wear not motley in my brain.—*Twelfth Night,* i, 5, 63. "Motley" is used once again in *King Lear,* i, 4, 160. See 563: 3.

2
He that a fool doth very wisely hit
Doth very foolishly, although he smart,
Not to seem senseless of the bob.
As You Like It. Act ii, sc. 7, l. 53. [Jaques]

3
Jaques: By my troth, I was seeking for a fool when I found you.
Orlando: He is drowned in the brook: look but in, and you shall see him.
Jaques: There I shall see mine own figure.
Orlando: Which I take to be either a fool or a cipher.
As You Like It. Act iii, sc. 2, l. 303.

Here comes a pair of very strange beasts, which in all tongues are called fools.
As You Like It. Act v, sc. 4, l. 36. [Jaques]

He 's as good at any thing and yet a fool.
As You Like It. Act v, sc. 4, l. 109. [Jaques]

4
Come, come, no longer will I be a fool.
The Comedy of Errors. Act ii, sc. 2, l. 205. [Adriana]

You are no fool.—*Twelfth Night,* i, 5, 87.

5
Patient fools,
Whose children he hath slain, their base throats tear
With giving him glory.
Coriolanus. Act v, sc. 6, l. 52. [Conspirator]

6
You had measured how long a fool you were upon the ground.
Cymbeline. Act i, sc. 2, l. 24. [Lord]

Imogen: Fools are not mad folks.
Cloten: Do you call me fool?
Imogen: As I am mad, I do.
Cymbeline. Act ii, sc. 3, l. 106.

I am sprited with a fool,
Frighted, and anger'd worse.
Cymbeline. Act ii, sc. 3, l. 144. [Imogen] The only use of "sprited."

Thou art some fool; I am loath to beat thee.
Cymbeline. Act iv, sc. 2, l. 85. [Guiderius]

7
These tedious old fools!
Hamlet. Act ii, sc. 2, l. 223. [Hamlet]

You are a tedious fool.
Measure for Measure. Act ii, sc. 1, l. 119. [Escalus]

8
Thou wretched, rash, intruding fool, farewell!
Hamlet. Act iii, sc. 4, l. 31. [Hamlet]

Thou art the cap of all the fools alive.
Timon of Athens. Act iv, sc. 3, l. 363. [Apemantus]

What a fool art thou, A ramping fool.
King John. Act iii, sc. 1, l. 121. [Constance]

Thou art a fool.—*The Taming of the Shrew,* Ind., i, 26; *Richard II,* v, 2, 68; *As You Like It,* i, 3, 82.

Thou art a great fool.—*II Henry IV,* ii, 1, 209.

You are a fool.—*As You Like It,* i, 3, 89; iv, 3, 22.

You 'll be a fool still.—*II Henry IV,* ii, 1, 170.

So, by your circumstance, you call me fool.
The Two Gentlemen of Verona. Act i, sc. 1, l. 36. [Proteus]

9
Cannot you tell that? every fool can tell that.
Hamlet. Act v, sc. 1, l. 159. [First Clown]

10
Why, what a wasp-stung and impatient fool
Art thou to break into this woman's mood.
I Henry IV. Act i, sc. 3, l. 236. [Northumberland] The only use of "wasp-stung."

What a lack-brain is this!
I Henry IV. Act ii, sc. 3, l. 18. [Hotspur] The only use of "lack-brain."

Poins: Where hast thou been, Hal?
Prince of Wales: With three or four loggerheads amongst three or four score hogsheads.
I Henry IV. Act ii, sc. 4, l. 3. "Loggerhead" occurs also in *Love's Labour 's Lost,* iv, 3, 204, and *Romeo and Juliet,* iv, 4, 20. "Logger-headed" in *Taming of the Shrew,* iv, 1, 128. "Hogshead" is used four times.

11
The nimble-footed madcap.
I Henry IV. Act iv, sc. 1, l. 95. [Hotspur] See also under MERRIMENT.

12
They are generally fools and cowards; which some of us should be too, but for inflammation.
II Henry IV. Act iv, sc. 3, l. 101. [Falstaff] The only use of "inflammation."

13
A fool's bolt is soon shot.
Henry V. Act iii, sc. 7, l. 132. [Duke of

Orleans] Quoted as a proverb. It dates from the *Proverbs of Alfred,* c. 1275.

According to the fool's bolt, sir, and such dulcet diseases.
As You Like It. Act v, sc. 4, l. 67. [Touchstone]

1 He was a fool;
For he would needs be virtuous.
Henry VIII. Act ii, sc. 2, l. 132. [Wolsey]

2
What should the wars do with these jigging fools?
Julius Cæsar. Act iv, sc. 3, l. 137. [Brutus] The only use of "jigging."

3
Dost thou know the difference, my boy, between a bitter fool and a sweet fool?
King Lear. Act i, sc. 4, l. 151. [Fool]

The sweet and bitter fool
Will presently appear;
The one in motley here,
The other found out there.
King Lear. Act i, sc. 4, l. 158. [Fool]

Fools by heavenly compulsion.—*King Lear,* i, 2, 132.

4
King Lear: Dost thou call me fool, boy?
Fool: All thy other titles thou hast given away; that thou wast born with.
King Lear. Act i, sc. 4, l. 162.

If I had a monopoly out, . . . they will not let me have all fool to myself; they will be snatching.
King Lear. Act i, sc. 4, l. 167. [Fool] The only use of "monopoly" and "snatching."

I had rather any kind o' thing than a fool: and yet I would not be thee, nuncle; thou hast pared thy wit o' both sides, and left nothing i' the middle.
King Lear. Act i, sc. 4, l. 203. [Fool]

I am better than thou art now; I am a fool, thou art nothing.
King Lear. Act i, sc. 4, l. 212. [Fool]

This is not altogether fool.—*King Lear,* i, 4, 165.

5 None of these rogues and cowards
But Ajax is their fool.
King Lear. Act ii, sc. 2, l. 131. [Kent]

The fool; who labours to out-jest
His heart-struck injuries.
King Lear. Act iii, sc. 1, l. 16. [Gentleman] The only use of "out-jest" and "heart-struck."

Fools do those villains pity who are punish'd
Ere they have done their mischief.
King Lear. Act iv, sc. 2, l. 54. [Goneril]

And my poor fool is hang'd! No, no, no life!
Why should a dog, a horse, a rat, have life,
And thou no breath at all? Thou'lt come no more,
Never, never, never, never, never!
King Lear. Act v, sc. 3, l. 305. [King Lear]

6
So they say the fool said, and so say I, and I the fool.
Love's Labour's Lost. Act iv, sc. 3, l. 5. [Biron]

The clown bore it, the fool sent it, and the lady hath it: sweet clown, sweeter fool, sweetest lady!
Love's Labour's Lost. Act iv, sc. 3, l. 17. [Biron]

Then fools you were these women to forswear,
Or keeping what is sworn, you will prove fools.
Love's Labour's Lost. Act iv, sc. 3, l. 355. [Biron]

I dare not call them fools; but this I think,
When they are thirsty, fools would fain have drink.
Love's Labour's Lost. Act v, sc. 2, l. 371. [Rosaline]

7
I am a fool, and full of poverty.
Love's Labour's Lost. Act v, sc. 2, l. 380. [Biron]

How much a fool was I
To be of such a weak and silly mind.
Venus and Adonis, l. 1015.

I am a fool.—*King Lear,* i, 4, 313.

But what a fool am I.—*The Taming of the Shrew,* iii, 2, 123.

The more fool I.—*As You Like It,* ii, 4, 17.

The more fool you.—*The Taming of the Shrew,* v, 2, 129.

8 Let me play the fool:
With mirth and laughter let old wrinkles come.
The Merchant of Venice. Act i, sc. 1, l. 79. [Gratiano]

Let the doors be shut upon him, that he may play the fool no where but in's own house.
Hamlet. Act iii, sc. 1, l. 135. [Hamlet]

Play fool.—*King Lear,* iv, 1, 40.

9
That fool of Hagar's offspring.
The Merchant of Venice. Act ii, sc. 5, l. 44. [Shylock] The only mention of Hagar.

There be fools alive, I wis, Silver'd o'er.
The Merchant of Venice. Act ii, sc. 9, l. 68. [Arragon] "Silver'd" is repeated in *Hamlet,* i, 2, 242, and in *Antony and Cleopatra,* iii, 6, 3.

O, these deliberate fools! when they do choose,
They have the wisdom by their wit to lose.
The Merchant of Venice. Act ii, sc. 9, l. 80. [Portia]

This is the fool that lent out money gratis.
The Merchant of Venice. Act iii, sc. 3, l. 2. [Shylock] "Gratis" occurs nine times.

I'll not be made a soft and dull-eyed fool,
To shake the head, relent, and sigh, and yield
To Christian intercessors.
The Merchant of Venice. Act iii, sc. 3, l. 16. [Shylock] The only use of "intercessors." "Dull-eyed" is repeated in *Pericles,* i, 2, 2.

Make a fool of him.—*Twelfth Night,* ii, 3, 138.
See under PROMISE, 1213:11.

10 I do know
A many fools, that stand in better place,
Garnish'd like him, that for a tricksy word
Defy the matter.
The Merchant of Venice. Act iii, sc. 5, l. 72. [Lorenzo] "Tricksy" is repeated in *The Tempest,* v, 1, 226: "Tricksy spirit."

11 You shall have
An fool's-head of your own.
The Merry Wives of Windsor. Act i, sc. 4, l. 133. [Mistress Quickly] See also under DESERVING. "Fool's head" (unhyphenated) is

used twice in *The Merchant of Venice,* ii, 9, 59; 75.

1
What fools these mortals be!
A Midsummer-Night's Dream. Act iii, sc. 2, l. 115. [Puck]

2
Why, he is the prince's jester: a very dull fool.
Much Ado about Nothing. Act ii, sc. 1, l. 142. [Beatrice] "Dull fool" is repeated in *As You Like It,* iii, 2, 121, and in *The Tempest,* v, 1, 297.

The prince's fool! Ha? It may be I go under that title because I am merry.
Much Ado about Nothing. Act ii, sc. 1, l. 211. [Benedick]

My cousin 's a fool, and thou art another.
Much Ado about Nothing. Act iii, sc. 4, l. 11. [Hero]

3
Thus do I ever make my fool my purse;
For I mine own gain'd knowledge should profane,
If I would time expend with such a snipe,
But for my sport and profit.
Othello. Act i, sc. 3, l. 391. [Iago] The only use of "snipe."

These are old fond paradoxes to make fools laugh i' the alehouse.
Othello. Act ii, sc. 1, l. 139. [Desdemona] For "paradox" see under RHETORIC.

Fools as gross As ignorance made drunk.
Othello. Act iii, sc. 3, l. 404. [Iago]

Credulous fools are caught.
Othello. Act iv, sc. 1, l. 46. [Iago] "Credulous fool" occurs in *Cymbeline,* v, 5, 210.

O murderous coxcomb! what should such a fool
Do with so good a woman?
Othello. Act v, sc. 2, l. 233. [Emilia]

4
Then fell she on her back, fair queen, and toward:
He rose and ran away; ah, fool too froward!
The Passionate Pilgrim, l. 55.

And merry fools to mock at him resort.
The Rape of Lucrece, l. 989.

5
If ye should lead her into a fool's paradise, as they say, it were a very gross kind of behaviour.
Romeo and Juliet. Act ii, sc. 4, l. 175. [Nurse] The only use of the phrase "fool's paradise."

6
A wretched puling fool, A whining mammet.
Romeo and Juliet. Act iii, sc. 5, l. 185. [Capulet]

This is no world to play with mammets.
I Henry IV, ii, 3, 95. The only uses of "mammet" (or maumet, meaning an idol or puppet), a corruption of Mahomet, in the belief that Mohammedans were idolaters.

7
Thou art proclaimed a fool, I think.
Troilus and Cressida. Act ii, sc. 1, l. 26. [Thersites]

Thou full dish of fool.
Troilus and Cressida. Act v, sc. 1, l. 10. [Thersites]

8
O, I am fortune's fool!
Romeo and Juliet. Act iii, sc. 1, l. 141. [Romeo]

I am even The natural fool of fortune.
King Lear. Act iv, sc. 6, l. 194. [King Lear]

Call me not fool till heaven hath sent me fortune.
As You Like It. Act ii, sc. 7, l. 19. [Jaques]

9
The fools of time,
Which die for goodness, who have lived for crime.
Sonnets. No. cxxiv.

10
The veriest antic in the world.
The Taming of the Shrew. Induction, sc. 1, l. 101. [A Player]

Three such antics do not amount to a man.
Henry V. Act iii, sc. 2, l. 32. [Boy]

There the antic sits,
Scoffing his state and grinning at his pomp.
Richard II, iii, 2, 162. See under KING.

She dares not look; yet, winking, there appears
Quick-shifting antics, ugly in her eyes.
The Rape of Lucrece, l. 458. The only use of "quick-shifting."

Witless antics.—*Troilus and Cressida,* v, 3, 86.

Father antic.—*I Henry IV,* i, 2, 69.

Antic death.—*I Henry VI,* iv, 7, 18.

Antic disposition.—*Hamlet,* i, 5, 172.

Antic face.—*Romeo and Juliet,* i, 5, 58.

Antic . . . fantasticoes!—*Romeo and Juliet,* ii, 4, 29. The only use of "fantasticoes."

Antic round.—*Macbeth,* iv, 1, 130. The only uses of "antic."

I told you, I, he was a frantic fool,
Hiding his bitter jests in blunt behaviour.
The Taming of the Shrew. Act iii, sc. 2, l. 12. [Katharina]

Away, you three-inch fool!
The Taming of the Shrew. Act iv, sc. 1, l. 27. [Curtis] The only use of "three-inch."

11
You heedless joltheads.
The Taming of the Shrew. Act iv, sc. 1, l. 169. [Petruchio] "Heedless" is used only once again, in *I Henry VI,* iv, 2, 44: "Heedless discipline." The only use of "joltheads."

Fie on thee, jolt-head!—*The Two Gentlemen of Verona,* iii, 1, 290. The only use of "jolthead."

12
Baptista: How likes Gremio these quick-witted folks?
Gremio: Believe me, sir, they butt together well.
The Taming of the Shrew. Act v, sc. 2, l. 38. The only use of "quick-witted."

13
We make ourselves fools, to disport ourselves.
Timon of Athens. Act i, sc. 2, l. 141. [Apemantus]

Honest fools lay out their wealth on court'sies.
Timon of Athens. Act i, sc. 2, l. 241. [Apemantus]

I see thou art a fool, and fit for thy master.
Timon of Athens. Act iii, sc. 1, l. 52. [Lucullus]

It may prove an argument of laughter
To the rest, and 'mongst lords I be thought a fool.
Timon of Athens. Act iii, sc. 3, l. 20. [Sempronius]

A madman so long, now a fool.
Timon of Athens. Act iv, sc. 3, l. 221. [Apemantus]

1
What fool hath added water to the sea,
Or brought a faggot to bright-burning Troy?
Titus Andronicus. Act iii, sc. 1, l. 68. [Titus] The only use of "bright-burning."

2
The fool will not: he there: that he.
Troilus and Cressida. Act ii, sc. 1, l. 91. [Thersites]

Thersites: Agamemnon is a fool; Achilles is a fool; Thersites is a fool, and, as aforesaid, Patroclus is a fool.
Achilles: Derive this; come.
Thersites: Agamemnon is a fool to offer to command Achilles; Achilles is a fool to be commanded of Agamemnon; Thersites is a fool to serve such a fool, and Patroclus is a fool positive.
Patroclus: Why am I a fool?
Thersites: Make that demand of the prover. It suffices me thou art.
Troilus and Cressida. Act ii, sc. 3, l. 62. The only use of "prover."

Nestor: What moves Ajax thus to bay at him?
Ulysses: Achilles hath inveigled his fool from him.
Troilus and Cressida. Act ii, sc. 3, l. 99. The only use of "inveigled."

The fool slides o'er the ice that you should break.
Troilus and Cressida. Act iii, sc. 3, l. 215. [Ulysses]

I'll be your fool no more.
Troilus and Cressida, v, 2, 32. [Diomedes]

3
Fair lady, do you think you have fools in hand?
Twelfth Night, i, 3, 68. [Sir Andrew]

4
Go to, you're a dry fool.
Twelfth Night. Act i, sc. 5, l. 45. [Olivia]

Give the dry fool drink, then is the fool not dry.
Twelfth Night. Act i, sc. 5, l. 48. [Clown]

Clown: Good madonna, give me leave to prove you a fool.
Olivia: Can you do it?
Clown: Dexteriously, good madonna. . . . Why mournest thou?
Olivia: Good fool, for my brother's death.
Clown: I think his soul is in hell, madonna.
Olivia: I know his soul is in heaven, fool.
Clown: The more fool, madonna, to mourn for your brother's soul being in heaven. Take away the fool, gentlemen.
Twelfth Night. Act i, sc. 5, l. 63. The only use of "dexteriously."

Now Mercury endue thee with leasing, for thou speakest well of fools!
Twelfth Night. Act i, sc. 5, l. 105. [Clown] "Leasing" (lying) occurs again in *Coriolanus,* v, 2, 22.

5
Many do call me fool.
Twelfth Night. Act ii, sc. 5, l. 89. [Sir Andrew]

Viola: Art thou not the Lady Olivia's fool?
Clown: No, indeed, sir; the Lady Olivia has no fool; she will keep no fool, sir, till she be married; and fools are as like husbands as pilchards are to herrings; the husband's the bigger. I am indeed not her fool, but her corrupter of words.
Twelfth Night. Act iii, sc. 1, l. 36. The only mention of "pilchards," and only use of "corrupter" as a noun. As an adjective it occurs in *King Lear,* ii, 2, 108: "Corrupter ends." "Corrupters" is used in *Cymbeline,* iii, 4, 85: "Corrupters of my faith."

6
A fool
That seest a game play'd home, the rich stake drawn,
And takest it all for jest.
Winter's Tale. Act i, sc. 2, l. 247. [Leontes]

Either thou art most ignorant by age,
Or thou wert born a fool.
Winter's Tale. Act ii, sc. 1, l. 173. [Leontes]

II—Fool and Knave

7
Lafeu: Whether dost thou profess thyself, a knave or a fool?
Clown: A fool, sir, at a woman's service, and a knave at a man's.
All's Well that Ends Well. Act iv, sc. 5, l. 23.

I will subscribe for thee, thou art both knave and fool.
All's Well that Ends Well. Act iv, sc. 5, l. 35. [Lafeu]

Though you are a fool and a knave, you shall eat.
All's Well that Ends Well, v, 2, 57. [Lafeu]

8
More knave than fool.
King Lear. Act i, sc. 4, l. 337. [Goneril]

But I will tarry; the fool will stay,
And let the wise man fly:
The knave turns fool that runs away;
The fool no knave, perdy.
King Lear. Act ii, sc. 4, l. 83. [Fool]

Poor fool and knave, I have one part in my heart
That's sorry yet for thee.
King Lear. Act iii, sc. 2, l. 72. [King Lear]

Where's my knave? my fool? Go you, and call my fool hither. . . . Call the clotpoll back. Where's my fool, ho?
King Lear. Act iii, sc. 4, l. 45. [King Lear] "Clotpoll" is used also in *Troilus and Cressida,* ii, 1, 128, and *Cymbeline,* iv, 2, 184.

9
I am but a fool, look you; and yet I have the wit to think my master is a kind of knave.
The Two Gentlemen of Verona. Act iii, sc. 1, l. 261. [Launce]

III—Fool and Wise Man

See also Wisdom and Folly

10
Touchstone: The more pity, that fools may not speak wisely what wise men do foolishly.
Celia: By my troth, thou sayest true; for

since the little wit that fools have was silenced, the little foolery that wise men have makes a great show.

As You Like It. Act i, sc. 2, l. 92.

The wise man's folly is anatomized
Even by the squandering glances of the fool.

As You Like It. Act ii, sc. 7, l. 56. [Jaques] The only use of "squandering."

I would gladly see his company anatomized.

All's Well that Ends Well. Act iv, sc. 3, l. 37. [First Lord] The only uses of "anatomized." "Anatomize" occurs three times.

1
The fool doth think he is wise, but the wise man knows himself to be a fool.

As You Like It. Act v, sc. 1, l. 34. [Touchstone]

2
If you are learn'd, Be not as common fools.

Coriolanus. Act iii, sc. 1, l. 99. [Coriolanus]

3
Those that I reverence those I fear, the wise:
At fools I laugh, not fear them.

Cymbeline. Act iv, sc. 2, l. 95. [Guiderius]

4
Well, thus we play the fools with the time, and the spirits of the wise sit in the clouds and mock us.

II Henry IV. Act ii, sc. 2, l. 154. [Prince]

5
Fools had ne'er less wit in a year;
For wise men are grown foppish,
They know not how their wits to wear,
Their manners are so apish.

King Lear. Act i, sc. 4, l. 181. [Fool] The only use of "foppish."

6
Folly, in wisdom hatch'd,
Hath wisdom's warrant and the help of school
And wit's own grace to grace a learned fool.

Love's Labour 's Lost. Act v, sc. 2, l. 70. [Princess]

Folly in fools bears not so strong a note
As foolery in the wise, when wit doth dote.

Love's Labour 's Lost. Act v, sc. 2, l. 75. [Maria]

7
What your wisdoms could not discover these shallow fools have brought to light.

Much Ado about Nothing. Act v, sc. 1, l. 239. [Borachio]

8
There 's none so foul and foolish thereunto,
But does foul pranks which fair and wise ones do.

Othello. Act ii, sc. 1, l. 142. [Iago]

9
Let my unsounded self, supposed a fool,
Now set thy long-experienced wit to school.

The Rape of Lucrece, l. 1819. "Long-experienced" is repeated in *Romeo and Juliet,* iv, 1, 60: "Long-experienced time."

10
Servant: Thou art not altogether a fool.
Fool: Nor thou altogether a wise man: as much foolery as I have, so much wit thou lackest.

Timon of Athens. Act ii, sc. 2, l. 122.

11
Nestor: It was a strong composure a fool could disunite.
Ulysses: The amity that wisdom knits not, folly may easily untie.

Troilus and Cressida. Act ii, sc. 3, l. 108.

12
I protest, I take these wise men, that crow so at these set kind of fools, no better than the fools' zanies.

Twelfth Night. Act i, sc. 5, l. 94. [Malvolio] The only use of "zanies." "Zany" occurs in *Love's Labour 's Lost,* v, 2, 463.

These wise men that give fools money get themselves a good report.

Twelfth Night. Act iv, sc. 1, l. 23. [Clown]

13
He that is so yoked by a fool,
Methinks, should not be chronicled for wise.

The Two Gentlemen of Verona. Act i, sc. 1, l. 40. [Valentine]

FOOLERY

14
Being fool'd, by foolery thrive!

All's Well that Ends Well. Act iv, sc. 3, l. 374. [Parolles]

But this is foolery.—*Cymbeline,* iii, 2, 75.

It is but foolery.—*Hamlet,* v, 2, 225.

15
Have done your foolishness.

The Comedy of Errors, i, 2, 72. The only use of "foolishness."

16
It was mere foolery; I did not mark it.

Julius Cæsar. Act i, sc. 2, l. 236. [Casca]

There was more foolery yet, if I could remember it.

Julius Cæsar. Act i, sc. 2, l. 290. [Casca]

17
O, what a scene of foolery have I seen,
Of sighs, of groans, of sorrow and of teen!

Love's Labour 's Lost. Act iv, sc. 3, l. 163. [Biron]

Now he shall see his own foolery.

The Merry Wives of Windsor. Act iv, sc. 2, l. 37. [Mrs. Page]

18
Unless he have a fancy to this foolery, as it appears he hath, he is no fool for fancy.

Much Ado about Nothing. Act iii, sc. 2, l. 37. [Don Pedro]

19
Let 's have no more fooling about it.

The Merchant of Venice. Act ii, sc. 2, l. 88. [Launcelot]

I do not like this fooling.

Troilus and Cressida. Act v, sc. 2, l. 101. [Diomedes]

Your fooling grows old, and people dislike it.

Twelfth Night. Act i, sc. 5, l. 119. [Olivia]

After all this fooling.—*Measure for Measure,* i, 2, 71.

While I stand fooling here.—*Richard II,* v, 5, 60.

Excellent! why, this is the best fooling, when all is done.

Twelfth Night. Act ii, sc. 2, l. 30. [Sir Andrew]

In sooth, thou wast in very gracious fooling last night, when thou spokest of Pigrogromitus,

of the Vapians passing the equinoctial of Queubus: 'twas very good, i' faith.
Twelfth Night. Act ii, sc. 3, l. 22. [Sir Andrew] The proper nouns invented for the occasion, and never repeated. The only use of "equinoctial."
Beshrew me, the knight's in admirable fooling.
Twelfth Night. Act ii, sc. 3, l. 85. [Clown]
Good fooling.—*Twelfth Night,* i, 5, 36.
Merry fooling.—*The Tempest,* ii, 1, 177. The only uses of "fooling."

1
Foolery, sir, does walk about the orb like the sun, it shines every where.
Twelfth Night. Act iii, sc. 1, l. 43. [Clown]

2
Thy by-gone fooleries were but spices of it.
The Winter's Tale. Act iii, sc. 2, l. 185. [Paulina]
Here has been too much homely foolery already.
The Winter's Tale, iv, 4, 340. [Shepherd]

FOOT

3
Service of the foot
Being once gangrened, is not then respected
For what before it was.
Coriolanus. Act iii, sc. 1, l. 306. [Menenius] The only reference to gangrene in the plays.

4
Be on foot at an hour's warning.
Coriolanus. Act iv, sc. 3, l. 49. [Volsce]
On foot.—*The Winter's Tale,* i, 1, 1; *II Henry IV,* i, 3, 37; *Henry V,* i, 2, 310; *Richard III,* v, 4, 4; *Troilus and Cressida,* i, 3, 135; *Coriolanus,* iv, 5, 125.

5
Thus I set my foot on 's neck.
Cymbeline. Act iii, sc. 3, l. 92. [Belarius]
Under my foot.—*II Henry IV,* iii, 1, 63.

6
I will not budge a foot.
I Henry VI, i, 3, 38; *I Henry IV,* ii, 4, 388.
We will not move a foot.
Love's Labour's Lost, v, 2, 146.
Thou shalt not stir a foot.
Romeo and Juliet, i, 1, 87.
No foot shall stir.—*The Winter's Tale,* v, 3, 98.
Stir thy foot.—*King John,* iv, 3, 96.
Set my foot.—*King Lear,* iii, 7, 68.
Set his foot.—*Richard II,* i, 1, 66.
Set foot.—*I Henry IV,* iii, 2, 95; *III Henry VI,* ii, 2, 16.

7
Yet are these feet, whose strengthless stay is numb,
Unable to support this lump of clay,
Swift-winged with desire to get a grave,
As witting I no other comfort have.
I Henry VI. Act ii, sc. 5, l. 13. [Mortimer] The only use of "witting." "Strengthless" is repeated in *II Henry IV,* i, 1, 141, and in *The Rape of Lucrece,* l. 709; and "swift-winged" in *Richard III,* ii, 2, 44.

8
Uneath may she endure the flinty streets,
To tread them with her tender-feeling feet.
II Henry VI. Act ii, sc. 4, l. 8. [Gloucester] The only use of "tender-feeling." "Uneath" (difficult) is also unique.
The ruthless flint doth cut my tender feet.
II Henry VI, ii, 4, 34. See under FLINT.
Blessed feet.—*I Henry IV,* i, 1, 25.
Princely feet.—*Love's Labour's Lost,* iv, 1, 92.

9
And when the hardiest warriors did retire,
Richard cried 'Charge! and give no foot of ground!'
III Henry VI. Act i, sc. 4, l. 15. [York] The only use of "hardiest" and "foot of ground."

10
We will not line his thin bestained cloak
With our pure honours, nor attend the foot
That leaves the print of blood where'er it walks.
King John. Act iv, sc. 3, l. 24. [Salisbury] The only use of "bestained."
Printless foot.—*The Comedy of Errors,* v, 1, 34.

11
How oft to-night
Have my old feet stumbled at graves!
Romeo and Juliet. Act v, sc. 3, l. 121. [Friar Laurence]
Declining foot.—*Timon of Athens,* i, 1, 88.

12
Keep thy foot out of brothels.
King Lear, iii, 4, 99. See under BEHAVIOUR.

13
I profane my lips on thy foot.
Love's Labour's Lost. Act iv, sc. 1, l. 86. [Boyet]

14
And I, thy Caliban, For aye thy foot-licker.
The Tempest. Act iv, sc. 1, l. 218. [Caliban] The only use of "foot-licker."
I will kiss thy foot.
The Tempest, ii, 2, 153; ii, 2, 157.

15
O, if the streets were paved with thine eyes,
Her feet were much too dainty for such tread!
Love's Labour's Lost. Act iv, sc. 3, l. 278. [Biron]
Do not you know my lady's foot by the squier.
Love's Labour's Lost. Act v, sc. 2, l. 474. [Biron] "Squier" (square, foot-rule) is used also in *I Henry IV,* ii, 2, 13, and *The Winter's Tale,* iv, 4, 348.
Armado: I do adore thy sweet grace's slipper.
Boyet: Loves her by the foot.
Love's Labour's Lost. Act v, sc. 2, l. 672.

16
And foot me as you spurn a stranger cur
Over your threshold.
The Merchant of Venice. Act i, sc. 3, l. 119. [Shylock]

17
But, hark, I hear the footing of a man.
The Merchant of Venice. Act v, sc. 1, l. 24. [Jessica]
Set no footing on an unkind shore.
II Henry VI, iii, 2, 87. "Set footing" is used in five later plays.

18
The firm fixture of thy foot would give an excellent motion to thy gait in a semi-circled farthingale.
The Merry Wives of Windsor. Act iii, sc. 3, l. 67. [Falstaff] The only use of "semi-circled." "Farthingale" is mentioned twice more in the plays, both times in *The Two Gentlemen of Verona,* ii, 7, 51, and iv, 4, 42.

Foot it, girls.—*Romeo and Juliet,* i, 5, 28.

1
Who even but now did spurn me with his foot.
A Midsummer-Night's Dream. Act iii, sc. 2, l. 225. [Helena]

2
The treacherous feet
Which with usurping steps do trample thee.
King Richard II. Act iii, sc. 2, l. 16. [King Richard]

Churlish feet.—*The Two Gentlemen of Verona,* iii, 1, 225.

Contrary feet.—*King John,* iv, 2, 198.

3
So light a foot
Will ne'er wear out the everlasting flint.
Romeo and Juliet. Act ii, sc. 6, l. 16. [Friar Laurence]

Light of foot.—*Richard II,* iii, 4, 92.

4
What cursed foot wanders this way to-night,
To cross my obsequies and true love's rite?
Romeo and Juliet. Act v, sc. 3, l. 19. [Paris]

Lazy foot.—*As You Like It,* iii, 2, 322.

Noiseless foot.—*All's Well that Ends Well,* v, 3, 41.

Proud foot.—*King John,* v, 7, 113; *The Rape of Lucrece,* l. 1449.

Foot of fear.—*I Henry IV,* v, 5, 20.

Foot of majesty.—*II Henry IV,* iv, 2, 42.

5
Out, you rogue! you pluck my foot awry.
The Taming of the Shrew. Act iv, sc. 1, l. 150. [Petruchio]

6
What? I say, My foot my tutor?
The Tempest. Act i, sc. 2, l. 468. [Prospero]

7
The foot above the head.
Timon of Athens. Act i, sc. 1, l. 94. [Painter]

8
It requires swift foot.
Timon of Athens. Act v, sc. 1, l. 231. [First Senator] "Swift foot" is repeated in *Sonnets,* lxv.

Speedy foot.—*King Lear,* iv, 6, 217.

Swift of foot.—*Othello,* ii, 3, 232.

Sure of foot.—*Macbeth,* iii, 1, 38.

His foot Mercurial.—*Cymbeline,* iv, 2, 310. The only use of "Mercurial." See under FACE.

9
Set but thy foot
Against our rampired gates, and they shall ope.
Timon of Athens. Act v, sc. 4, l. 46. [First Senator] The only use of "rampired."

Fix thy foot.—*Coriolanus,* i, 8, 4.

Fixed foot.—*Twelfth Night,* i, 4, 17.

Hold-fast foot.—*The Rape of Lucrece,* l. 555.

10
The better foot before.
Titus Andronicus. Act ii, sc. 3, l. 192. [Aaron] Repeated in *King John,* iv, 2, 170.

11
Nay, her foot speaks.
Troilus and Cressida. Act iv, sc. 5, l. 56. [Ulysses]

12
Horsing foot on foot.
The Winter's Tale. Act i, sc. 2, l. 288. [Leontes] The only use of "horsing."

FOP

See also Coxcomb

13
To be so pester'd with a popinjay.
I Henry IV. Act i, sc. 3, l. 50. [Hotspur] The only use of "popinjay."

14
A whole tribe of fops.
King Lear, i, 2, 14. See under BASTARD. The only use of "fops."

Wise men are grown foppish.—*King Lear,* i, 4, 182. The only use of "foppish."

15
This is the excellent foppery of the world, that, when we are sick in fortune,—often the surfeit of our own behaviour,—we make guilty of our disasters the sun, the moon, and the stars.
King Lear. Act i, sc. 2, l. 129. [Edmund]

Foppery of freedom.—*Measure for Measure,* i, 2, 138.

Let not the sound of shallow foppery enter
My sober house.
The Merchant of Venice. Act ii, sc. 5, l. 35. [Shylock]

Grossness of the foppery.—*The Merry Wives of Windsor,* v, 5, 132. The only uses of "foppery."

16
These lisping hawthorn-buds, that come like women in men's apparel, and smell like Bucklersbury in simple time.
The Merry Wives of Windsor. Act iii, sc. 3, l. 77. [Falstaff] The only mention of Bucklersbury.

17
The most exquisite Claudio?
Much Ado about Nothing. Act i, sc. 3, l. 52. [Don John]

My most exquisite Sir Topas!—*Twelfth Night,* iv, 2, 67.

My very exquisite friend.—*Timon of Athens,* iii, 2, 32.

18
The wealthy curled darlings of our nation.
Othello. Act i, sc. 2, l. 68. [Brabantio] The only use of the phrase "curled darlings."

19
The pox of such antic, lisping affecting fantasticoes; these new tuners of accents! 'By Jesu, a very good blade! a very tall man! a very good whore!' Why, is not this a lamentable thing, grandsire, that we should be thus afflicted with these strange flies, these fashion-mongers, these perdona-mi's, who stand so much on the new form, that they cannot sit at ease on the old bench? O, their bones, their bones!
Romeo and Juliet. Act ii, sc. 4, l. 29. [Mercutio] The only use of "fantasticoes," "tuners," "fashion-mongers," and "perdona-mi's."

FORBEARANCE

20
Forbear me till anon.
Antony and Cleopatra. Act ii, sc. 7, l. 44. [Pompey]

Better forbear.—*The Two Gentlemen of Verona,* ii, 7, 14.

Forbear awhile.—*The Two Gentlemen of Verona,* v, 4, 27; *The Merchant of Venice,* iii, 2, 3; *I Henry VI,* iii, 1, 105; *III Henry VI,* iii, 1, 27.

1
I could well forbear 't.
Antony and Cleopatra. Act ii, sc. 7, l. 104. [Cæsar]

I would forbear.—*Comedy of Errors,* ii, 1, 31.
I 'll forbear.—*King Lear,* ii, 4, 110.

2 One of your great knowing
Should learn, being taught, forbearance.
Cymbeline. Act ii, sc. 3, l. 102. [Imogen]

Forbear sharp speeches.—*Cymbeline,* iii, 5, 39.
Forbear this talk.—*III Henry VI,* iv, 1, 6.

3
What! canst thou not forbear me half an hour?
II Henry IV. Act iv, sc. 5, l. 110. [King Henry]

Forbear to judge.—*II Henry VI,* iii, 3, 31.
Forbear to murder.—*II Henry VI,* iv, 7, 81.
Forbear to fawn.—*III Henry VI,* iv, 1, 75.
Forbear to sleep.—*Richard III,* iv, 4, 118.
Forbear his presence.—*King Lear,* i, 2, 175.
Forbear your suffrages!—*Pericles,* ii, 4, 41.
Forbear this outrage!—*Romeo and Juliet,* iii, 1, 90.

4
Here is a mannerly forbearance.
I Henry VI. Act ii, sc. 4, l. 19. [Plantagenet]

Have a continent forbearance till the speed of his rage goes slower.
King Lear. Act i, sc. 2, l. 181. [Edmund]

5
I shall crave your forbearance a little.
Measure for Measure. Act iv, sc. 1, l. 22. [Duke]

FORCE

See also Might, Power, Strength

6
By strong hand And terms compulsatory.
Hamlet. Act i, sc. 1, l. 102. [Horatio] The only use of "compulsatory."

7
Force perforce.
II Henry VI, i, 1, 258; *King John,* iii, 1, 142; *II Henry IV,* iv, 1, 116; iv, 4, 46.

8
Hither we have broken in by force.
III Henry VI. Act i, sc. 1, l. 29. [York]

By force.—*Comedy of Errors,* v, 1, 352; *I Henry VI,* ii, 2, 30; *Titus Andronicus,* ii, 1, 118.

9
Enforce these rights so forcibly withheld.
King John. Act i, sc. 1, l. 18. [Chatillon]

Forcibly prevents Our lock'd embrasures.
Troilus and Cressida. Act iv, sc. 4, l. 38. [Troilus] The only instances of the use of "forcibly," and of "embrasures."

10
Engaging and redeeming of himself
With such a careless force and forceless care.
Troilus and Cressida. Act v, sc. 5, l. 39. [Ulysses] The only use of "engaging." "Forceless" is repeated in *Venus and Adonis,* l. 152.

Effectual force.—*The Two Gentlemen of Verona,* iii, 1, 223.
Equal force.—*Coriolanus,* i, 10, 14.
Imaginary forces.—*Henry V,* Prol., 18.
Outward force.—*Coriolanus,* iii, 1, 77.
Main force.—*II Henry VI,* i, 1, 210.
Mighty force.—*III Henry VI,* ii, 2, 44.
Two-fold force.—*Hamlet,* iii, 3, 48.
Utmost force.—*King John,* iii, 3, 11.
Of no force.—*King John,* i, 1, 130.
Renew thy force.—*Sonnets,* lvi.
Force her hence.—*The Winter's Tale,* ii, 3, 61.

11
Force should be right.
Troilus and Cressida. Act i, sc. 3, l. 116. [Ulysses] See also under RIGHT.

FOREHEAD

See also Face

12
So is the forehead of a married man more honourable than the bare brow of a bachelor.
As You Like It, iii, 3, 60. [Touchstone]

Forehead of this action.—*Troilus and Cressida,* ii, 2, 205.
Forehead of the morning.—*Coriolanus,* ii, 1, 57.
Forehead of our faults.—*Hamlet,* iii, 3, 63.
Hector's forehead.—*Coriolanus,* i, 3, 45.

13
The front of Jove himself.
Hamlet, iii, 4, 56. See under APPEARANCE.

Why stand these royal fronts amazed thus?
King John. Act ii, sc. 1, l. 356. [Bastard]

14
Look with forehead bold and big enough.
II Henry IV. Act i, sc. 3, l. 8. [Archbishop]

15
Thou hast a fine forehead.
Troilus and Cressida, iii, 1, 117. [Helen]

Fair forehead.—*Hamlet,* iii, 4, 43.
High forehead.—*Romeo and Juliet,* ii, 1, 18.
Unbashful forehead.—*As You Like It,* ii, 3, 50. The only use of "unbashful."

16
In his forehead sits a bare-ribb'd death.
King John, v, 2, 176. See under DEATH. The only use of "bare-ribb'd."

In 's forehead.—*All 's Well that Ends Well,* iv, 3, 263.
In her forehead.—*Comedy of Errors,* iii, 2, 126.
In my forehead.—*Much Ado about Nothing,* i, 1, 243; 266.
From my forehead.—*Love's Labour 's Lost,* iv, 3, 125.
Buffets himself on the forehead.—*The Merry Wives of Windsor,* iv, 2, 26.
Upon my forehead.—*Othello,* iii, 3, 284.

17
Brand not my forehead with thy piercing light.
The Rape of Lucrece, l. 1091.

Hidest thou that forehead?—*Richard III,* iv, 4, 140.

18
Her forehead 's low, and mine 's as high.
Two Gentlemen of Verona, iv, 4, 198. [Julia]

Her forehead As low as she would wish it.
Antony and Cleopatra. Act iii, sc. 3, l. 36. [Messenger]

Foreheads villanous low.
The Tempest. Act iv, sc. 1, l. 250. [Caliban]

FOREST

See also Wood

1
He is already in the forest of Arden, and a many merry men with him; and there they live like the old Robin Hood of England: . . . and fleet the time carelessly, as they did in the golden world.
As You Like It. Act i, sc. 1, l. 120. [Charles]
Well, this is the forest of Arden.
As You Like It. Act ii, sc. 4, l. 15. [Rosalind] See under TRAVEL. "Forest of Arden" is used a third time in i, 3, 109.
Uncouth forest.—*As You Like It,* ii, 6, 6. "Uncouth" is repeated in *Titus Andronicus,* ii, 3, 211: "Uncouth fear."
Let the forest judge.—*As You Like It,* iii, 2, 130.
2
In the skirts of the forest, like fringe upon a petticoat.
As You Like It. Act iii, sc. 2, l. 354. [Rosalind] The only use of "fringe." "Fringes" occurs in *Pericles,* iii, 2, 101: "Fringes of bright gold"; and "fringed" is also used once, in *The Tempest,* i, 2, 408: "The fringed curtains of thine eye advance."
The purlieus of this forest.
As You Like It. Act iv, sc. 3, l. 77. [Oliver] The only use of "purlieus."
3
Archbishop: What is this forest call'd?
Hastings: 'Tis Gaultree Forest, an 't shall please your grace.
II Henry IV. Act iv, sc. 1, l. 1.
Till Birnam forest come to Dunsinane.—*Macbeth,* v, 3, 60.
Windsor forest.—*The Merry Wives of Windsor,* iv, 4, 29.
4
With shadowy forests and with champains rich'd.
King Lear. Act i, sc. 1, l. 65. [King Lear] "Champain" is repeated in *Twelfth Night,* ii, 5, 174.
5
To trace the forests wild.
A Midsummer-Night's Dream. Act ii, sc. 1, l. 25. [Puck]
Forest woods.—*Richard II,* iii, 1, 23.
Forest of beasts.—*Timon of Athens,* iv, 3, 352.
Forest of feathers.—*Hamlet,* iii, 2, 286.

FORGETFULNESS

See also Forgive and Forget

6
Teach me to forget.
As You Like It. Act i, sc. 2, l. 5. [Rosalind]
I do forget.—*Macbeth,* iii, 4, 84.
I will forget.—*As You Like It,* i, 2, 16; *King Lear,* i, 5, 35.
Forget them quite.—*Antony and Cleopatra,* ii, 2, 100.
7
You must forget to be a woman.
Cymbeline, iii, 4, 157. See under WOMAN. "You must forget" is repeated in l. 163, and in *Othello,* iv, 1, 190.
I would they would forget me.—*Coriolanus,* ii, 3, 63.
8
O heavens! die two months ago, and not forgotten yet? Then there 's hope a great man's memory may outlive his life half a year; but by 'r lady, he must build churches, then.
Hamlet. Act iii, sc. 2, l. 138. [Hamlet]
Most necessary 'tis that we forget
To pay ourselves what to ourselves is debt.
Hamlet. Act iii, sc. 2, l. 202. [Player King]
Do not forget.—*Hamlet,* iii, 4, 110.
Let 's not forget.—*I Henry VI,* iii, 2, 131.
9
Steep my senses in forgetfulness.
II Henry IV, iii, 1, 8. See under SLEEP.
Blind forgetfulness.—*Richard III,* iii, 7, 129.
Ingrate forgetfulness.—*Coriolanus,* v, 2, 92.
10
Was this easy?
May this be wash'd in Lethe, and forgotten?
II Henry IV. Act v, sc. 2, l. 71. [King Henry V]
Still my sense in Lethe steep.
Twelfth Night. Act iv, sc. 1, l. 66. [Sebastian]
Steep'd our sense In soft and delicate Lethe.
Antony and Cleopatra. Act ii, sc. 7, l. 114. [Antony] See under WINE.
Crimson'd in thy lethe.—*Julius Cæsar,* iii, 1, 206.
The Lethe of thy angry soul.—*Richard III,* iv, 4, 250.
Lethe wharf.—*Hamlet,* i, 5, 33. The only references to Lethe. "Lethe'd" is used once, in *Antony and Cleopatra,* ii, 1, 27: "Lethe'd dulness."
11
Henceforth I charge you, as you love our favour,
Quite to forget this quarrel and the cause.
I Henry VI. Act iv, sc. 1, l. 135. [King Henry]
Forget this grief.—*II Henry VI,* ii, 4, 26.
Forget to pity him.—*Richard II,* v, 3, 57.
Forget their faults.—*Timon of Athens,* i, 2, 112.
12
Ah, Gloucester, teach me to forget myself!
II Henry VI. Act ii, sc. 4, l. 26. [Duchess]
Queen Elizabeth: Shall I forget myself to be myself?
King Richard: Ay, if yourself's remembrance wrong yourself.
Richard III. Act iv, sc. 4, l. 420.
I do forget myself.—*Hamlet,* i, 2, 161.
I had forgot myself.—*Richard II,* iii, 2, 83.
I shall forget myself.—*Julius Cæsar,* iv, 3, 35.
'Tis like I should forget myself.—*King John,* iii, 4, 49.
Hast thou forgot thyself?—*Twelfth Night,* v, 1, 144.
Thou dost forget thyself.—*King John,* iii, 1, 134.
I would not have you forget yourself.—*King John,* iv, 3, 85.
You forget yourself.—*Julius Cæsar,* iv, 3, 29.
13
Did my commission
Bid ye so far forget yourselves?
Henry VIII. Act v, sc. 3, l. 141. [King Henry]
14
The queen is comfortless, and we forgetful
In our long absence.
Henry VIII. Act ii, sc. 3, l. 105. [Anne Bullen]

Bear with me, good boy, I am much forgetful.
Julius Cæsar. Act iv, sc. 3, l. 255. [Brutus]

1 I would forget her; but a fever she
Reigns in my blood and will remember'd be.
Love's Labour's Lost. Act iv, sc. 3, l. 95. [Dumain]

Benvolio: Be ruled by me, forget to think of her.
Romeo: O, teach me how I should forget to think.
Romeo and Juliet. Act i, sc. 1, l. 231.

2 Let us not forget.
The Merry Wives of Windsor, v, 5, 80.

Do not forget.—*Much Ado about Nothing,* v, 1, 263.

Forget not.—*Much Ado about Nothing,* iv, 2, 80; *Coriolanus,* ii, 3, 228; *Julius Cæsar,* i, 2, 6.

3 Men are men; the best sometimes forget.
Othello. Act ii, sc. 3, l. 241. [Iago]

This forgetful man.—*I Henry IV,* i, 3, 161.

4 Or that I could forget what I have been,
Or not remember what I must be now!
Richard II. Act iii, sc. 3, l. 138. [King Richard]

5 Farewell: thou canst not teach me to forget.
Romeo and Juliet. Act i, sc. 1, l. 243. [Romeo]

I warrant, an I should live a thousand years,
I never should forget it.
Romeo and Juliet. Act i, sc. 3, l. 46. [Nurse]

And I'll still stay, to have thee still forget,
Forgetting any other home but this.
Romeo and Juliet. Act ii, sc. 2, l. 175. [Romeo]

I would forget it fain.—*Romeo and Juliet,* iii, 2, 109.

6 After my death, dear love, forget me quite,
For you in me can nothing worthy prove.
Sonnets. No. lxxii.

To keep an adjunct to remember thee
Were to import forgetfulness in me.
Sonnets. No. cxxii.

7 Vincentio: Come hither, you rogue. What, have you forgot me?
Biondello: Forgot you! no, sir: I could not forget you, for I never saw you before in all my life.
The Taming of the Shrew. Act v, sc. 1, l. 49.

That is not forgot
Which ne'er I did remember.
Richard II. Act ii, sc. 3, l. 37. [Percy]

8 O, forget
What we are sorry for ourselves in thee.
Timon of Athens. Act v, sc. 1, l. 141. [Senator]

They confess
Toward thee forgetfulness too general, gross.
Timon of Athens. Act v, sc. 1, l. 146. [Senator]

They quite forget.—*III Henry VI,* iv, 6, 15.

9 When I do forget
The least of these unspeakable deserts,
Romans, forget your fealty to me.
Titus Andronicus. Act i, sc. 1, l. 255. [Saturninus]

10 What, are my deeds forgot?
Troilus and Cressida. Act iii, sc. 3, l. 144. [Achilles]

11 I will forget that Julia is alive.
The Two Gentlemen of Verona. Act ii, sc. 6, l. 27. [Proteus]

I cannot forget.—*The Winter's Tale,* v, 1, 7.

FORGIVENESS

See also Faults: Their Forgiveness; Pardon

12 All is whole.
All's Well that Ends Well. Act v, sc. 3, l. 37. [King]

13 Forgive my fearful sails!
Antony and Cleopatra. Act iii, sc. 11, l. 55.

Forgive me this my virtue.—*Hamlet,* iii, 4, 152.

Forgive a foolish woman.—*The Winter's Tale,* iii, 2, 228.

14 We are unapt To give or to forgive.
Coriolanus. Act v, sc. 1, l. 52. [Menenius]

15 Exchange forgiveness with me.
Hamlet. Act v, sc. 2, l. 340. [Laertes]

I as free forgive you As I would be forgiven.
Henry VIII. Act ii, sc. 1, l. 82. [Buckingham]

16 Pray, forgive me,
If I have used myself unmannerly.
Henry VIII. Act iii, sc. 1, l. 175. [Queen Katharine]

Forgive me, country.—*I Henry VI,* iii, 3, 81.

17 God shall forgive you Cœur-de-lion's death
The rather that you give his offspring life.
King John. Act ii, sc. 1, l. 12. [Arthur]

Kind gods, forgive me that, and prosper him!
King Lear. Act iii, sc. 7, l. 92. [Gloucester]

Forgive me, God.—*Henry V,* iii, 6, 159; *II Henry VI,* iii, 2, 139.

God forgive me!—*Much Ado about Nothing,* iv, 1, 283; *I Henry IV,* i, 3, 255; *Henry VIII,* ii, 1, 136; *Romeo and Juliet,* iv, 5, 7.

God forgive thee for it!—*I Henry IV,* i, 2, 103.

God forgive them.—*I Henry IV,* iii, 2, 130.

God, God forgive us all!—*Macbeth,* v, i, 83.

O God forgive!—*II Henry IV,* iv, 5, 219; *III Henry VI,* v, 6, 60.

18 I'll forgive you,
Whatever torment you put me to.
King John. Act iv, sc. 1, l. 83. [Arthur]

If he would despise me, I would forgive him.
The Merchant of Venice. Act i, sc. 2, l. 68. [Portia]

I do forgive thee.—*King Lear,* v, 3, 166.

Hostess, I forgive thee.—*I Henry IV,* iii, 3, 192.

I heartily forgive 'em.—*Henry VIII,* ii, 1, 65.

19 When thou dost ask me blessing, I'll kneel down,
And ask of thee forgiveness.
King Lear. Act v, sc. 3, l. 10. [King Lear]

Ask forgiveness.—*Measure for Measure,* iv, 2, 54; *The Winter's Tale,* v, 2, 57.

Ask her forgiveness.—*King Lear,* ii, 4, 154.

Asks thee the son forgiveness.—*The Winter's Tale,* iv, 4, 560.

1 Cursed be my tribe, If I forgive him!
The Merchant of Venice. Act i, sc. 3, l. 52. [Shylock]

2 Heaven forgive him! and forgive us all!
Measure for Measure. Act ii, sc. 1, l. 37. [Escalus]

Well, heaven forgive you and all of us, I pray!
The Merry Wives of Windsor. Act ii, sc. 2, l. 57. [Mistress Quickly]

Heaven forgive him too!—*Macbeth,* iv, 3, 235.

Heaven forgive me!—*The Merry Wives of Windsor,* ii, 1, 28; *Othello,* iii, 3, 373; *Henry VIII,* iii, 2, 135.

O, heaven forgive us!—*Othello,* iv, 2, 88.

Heavens forgive it!—*Pericles,* iv, 3, 39.

3 If thy revengeful heart cannot forgive,
Lo, here I lend thee this sharp-pointed sword;
Which if thou please to hide in this true bosom,
And let the soul forth that adoreth thee,
I lay it naked to the deadly stroke,
And humbly beg the death upon my knee.
Richard III. Act i, sc. 2, l. 174. [Gloucester] The only use of "sharp-pointed."

4 I do forgive thy robbery, gentle thief,
Although thou steal thee all my poverty.
Sonnets. No. xl.

5 The rarer action is
In virtue than in vengeance: they being penitent,
The sole drift of my purpose doth extend
Not a frown further.
The Tempest. Act v, sc. 1, l. 27. [Prospero]

I do forgive thee, Unnatural though thou art.
The Tempest. Act v, sc. 1, l. 78. [Prospero]

But, O; how oddly will it sound that I
Must ask my child forgiveness!
The Tempest. Act v, sc. 1, l. 197. [Alonso]

6 And rather comfort his distressed plight
Than prosecute the meanest or the best
For these contempts.
Titus Andronicus. Act iv, sc. 4, l. 32. [Tamora]

II—Forgive and Forget

7 I have forgiven and forgotten all.
All's Well that Ends Well. Act v, sc. 3, l. 9. [King]

8 Pray you now, forget and forgive.
King Lear. Act iv, sc. 7, l. 84. [King Lear]

Forget, forgive; conclude and be agreed.
Richard II. Act i, sc. 1, l. 156. [King Richard]

9 Do as the heavens have done, forget your evil;
With them forgive yourself.
The Winter's Tale. Act v, sc. 1, l. 5. [Cleomenes]

FORM

See also Body, Shape

10 Thou hast thine own form.
The Comedy of Errors. Act ii, sc. 2, l. 200. [Antipholus of Syracuse]

Lose his form.—*The Two Gentlemen of Verona,* iii, 2, 8.

11 That fair and warlike form
In which the majesty of buried Denmark
Did sometimes march.
Hamlet. Act i, sc. 1, l. 47. [Horatio]

So fair a form lodged not a mind so ill.
The Rape of Lucrece, l. 1530.

Exquisite form.—*Cymbeline,* i, 6, 190.

Goodly form.—*II Henry IV,* iv, 1, 20.

Unmatch'd form.—*Hamlet,* iii, 1, 167.

Well-balanced form.—*Measure for Measure,* iv, 3, 104. The only use of "well-balanced."

Well-seeming forms!—*Romeo and Juliet,* i, 1, 185. "Well-seeming" is repeated in *Measure for Measure,* iii, 1, 232.

Proud was his form.—*Love's Labour's Lost,* ii, 1, 237.

12 And there assume some other horrible form.
Hamlet. Act i, sc. 4, l. 72. [Horatio]

Mangled forms.—*As You Like It,* ii, 7, 42.

Meaner form.—*The Winter's Tale,* i, 2, 313.

Monstrous form.—*II Henry IV,* iv, 2, 34.

Saint-like forms.—*Rape of Lucrece,* l. 1519.

Strange forms.—*Antony and Cleopatra,* v, 2, 98; *A Lover's Complaint,* l. 303.

Ugly form.—*II Henry IV,* iv, 1, 39.

Vicious forms.—*Henry VIII,* i, 2, 117.

Forms imaginary.—*II Henry IV,* iv, 4, 59.

13 Pluck down forms, windows, anything.
Julius Cæsar. Act iii, sc. 2, l. 264. [Citizen]

New form.—*Romeo and Juliet,* ii, 4, 36.

14 Brutus, this sober form of yours hides wrongs.
Julius Cæsar. Act iv, sc. 2, l. 40. [Cassius]

15 All form is formless, order orderless,
Save what is opposite to England's love.
King John. Act iii, sc. 1, l. 253. [Pandulph] "Formless" is repeated in *Troilus and Cressida,* iv, 5, 167: "Formless ruin of oblivion." The only use of "orderless."

16 You have slander'd nature in my form,
Which, however rude exteriorly,
Is yet the cover of a fairer mind
Than to be butcher of an innocent child.
King John. Act iv, sc. 2, l. 257. [Hubert] The only use of "exteriorly."

Exterior form.—*King John,* i, 1, 211.

Plain old forms.—*King John,* iv, 2, 22.

17 I am a scribbled form, drawn with a pen
Upon a parchment, and against this fire
Do I shrink up.
King John. Act v, sc. 7, l. 32. [King John] "Scribbled" occurs again in *II Henry VI,* iv, 2, 88.

18 Full of forms, figures, shapes.
Love's Labour's Lost, iv, 2, 68. See under SPIRIT.

Full of strange . . . forms.—*Love's Labour's Lost,* v, 2, 773.
Shape, and form.—*Much Ado about Nothing,* v, 1, 24.
Form a shape.—*The Tempest,* iii, 1, 56. See under SHAPE.
Country forms.—*Othello,* iii, 3, 237.
Milder form.—*The Two Gentlemen of Verona,* v, 4, 56.
Necessary form.—*II Henry IV,* iii, 1, 87.

1
Their form confounded makes most form in mirth,
When great things labouring perish in their birth.
Love's Labour's Lost. Act v, sc. 2, l. 520. [Princess of France]

2
If my form lie there, Then I am yours.
The Merchant of Venice. Act ii, sc. 7, l. 61. [Portia]

3
Putting on the mere form of civil and humane seeming.
Othello, ii, 1, 243. See SEEMING, 1330:9.
Form of a beast.—*The Merry Wives of Windsor,* v, 5, 10.
Form of death.—*Romeo and Juliet,* v, 3, 246.
Forms . . . of duty.—*Othello,* i, 1, 50.
Forms . . . of grief.—*Hamlet,* i, 2, 82.
Form of justice.—*King Lear,* iii, 7, 25.
Form of law.—*II Henry VI,* iii, 1, 58; *Richard III,* iii, 5, 42.
Form of plausive manners.—*Hamlet,* i, 4, 30.
Plain form of marriage.—*Much Ado about Nothing,* iv, 1, 2.
Form of prayer.—*Hamlet,* iii, 3, 51.
Forms of slaughter.—*Troilus and Cressida,* v, 3, 12.
Form of a soldier.—*Henry V,* iii, 6, 72.
Form of strangeness.—*Troilus and Cressida,* iii, 3, 51.
Forms of things unknown.—*A Midsummer-Night's Dream,* v, 1, 15.
Form of the thing.—*Hamlet,* i, 2, 210.
Form of wax.—*King John,* v, 4, 24; *Romeo and Juliet,* iii, 3, 126.
Form in wax.—*A Midsummer-Night's Dream,* i, 1, 49.
Beauty's form.—*Sonnets,* xxiv.
Shadow's form.—*Sonnets,* xliii.

4
Fain would I dwell on form.
Romeo and Juliet. Act ii, sc. 2, l. 88. [Juliet]

5
They were but sweet, but figures of delight,
Drawn after you, you pattern of all those.
Sonnets. No. xcviii.

6
Merchant: 'Tis a good form.
Jeweller: And rich; here is a water, look ye.
Timon of Athens. Act i, sc. 1, l. 17.
It carries a brave form.—*The Tempest,* i, 2, 411.

7
O thou senseless form,
That shalt be worshipp'd.
The Two Gentlemen of Verona. Act iv, sc. 4, l. 203. [Julia]
Lawful form.—*Coriolanus,* iii, 1, 325.
Outward form.—*Sonnets,* cviii.
Polish'd form.—*Sonnets,* lxxxv.
Substantial form.—*II Henry IV,* iv, 1, 173.
Tardy form.—*Julius Cæsar,* 1, 2, 303.
Without-door form.—*The Winter's Tale,* ii, 1, 69. The only use of "without-door."
Forms of hope.—*II Henry IV,* i, 3, 35.
Form of war.—*Julius Cæsar,* ii, 2, 20.

FORNICATION, see Wantonness

FORSWORN, see Oath: Broken Oaths

FORTITUDE, see Courage

FORTUNE

See also Chance, Destiny, Hap, Luck, Providence

8
And fortune play upon thy prosperous helm,
As thy auspicious mistress!
All's Well that Ends Well. Act iii, sc. 3, l. 7. [Duke]
Fortune love you!—*King Lear,* v, 1, 46.
Fortune pursue thee!—*Antony and Cleopatra,* iii, 12, 25.

9
Alexas: We'll know all our fortunes.
Enobarbus: Mine, and most of our fortunes, to-night, shall be—drunk to bed.
Antony and Cleopatra. Act i, sc. 2, l. 44.
Antony: Say to me,
Whose fortune shall rise higher, Cæsar's or mine?
Soothsayer: Cæsar's.
Antony and Cleopatra. Act ii, sc. 3, l. 15.
Our fortune lies Upon this jump.
Antony and Cleopatra. Act iii, sc. 8, l. 5. [Cæsar]

10
Fortune knows
We scorn her most when most she offers blows.
Antony and Cleopatra. Act iii, sc. 11, l. 73. [Antony]
If fortune be not ours to-day, it is
Because we brave her.
Antony and Cleopatra, iv, 4, 4. [Antony]

11
Happy is your grace,
That can translate the stubbornness of fortune
Into so quiet and so sweet a style.
As You Like It. Act ii, sc. 1, l. 18. [Amiens]
Yet fortune cannot recompense me better
Than to die well and not my master's debtor.
As You Like It. Act ii, sc. 3, l. 75. [Adam]

12
And rail'd on Lady Fortune in good terms,
In good set terms.
As You Like It. Act ii, sc. 7, l. 16. [Jaques]
And bear his courses to be ordered
By Lady Fortune.
Pericles. Act iv, sc. 4, l. 48. [Gower]
O lady Fortune, Stand you auspicious!
Winter's Tale. Act iv, sc. 4, l. 51. [Perdita]
Her humourous ladyship.—*King John,* iii, 1, 119.

13
The residue of your fortune,
Go to my cave and tell me.
As You Like It. Act ii, sc. 7, l. 196. [Duke]
The only use of "residue."

Give me your hand,
And let me all your fortunes understand.
As You Like It. Act ii, sc. 7, l. 199. [Duke Senior]

Inform us of thy fortunes, for it seems
They crave to be demanded.
Cymbeline. Act iv, sc. 2, l. 361. [Lucius]

He comes armed in his fortune.
As You Like It. Act iv, sc. 1, l. 60. [Rosalind]

1 Out of that I 'll work
Myself a former fortune.
Coriolanus. Act v, sc. 3, l. 201. [Aufidius]

2 Fortune brings in some boats that are not steer'd.
Cymbeline. Act iv, sc. 3, l. 46. [Pisanio] The only use of "steer'd."

3 To bear our fortunes in our own strong arms,
Which now we hold at much uncertainty.
I Henry IV. Act i, sc. 3, l. 298. [Worcester]

The very list, the very utmost bound
Of all our fortunes.
I Henry IV. Act iv, sc. 1, l. 51. [Hotspur]

But in short space
It rain'd down fortune showering on your head.
I Henry IV. Act v, sc. 1, l. 46. [Worcester]

4 He is retired, to ripe his growing fortunes.
II Henry IV. Act iv, sc. 1, l. 13. [Archbishop of York]

Repair his fortunes.—*Othello,* ii, 3, 360.

5 Who knows on whom fortune would then have smiled?
II Henry IV. Act iv, sc. 1, l. 133. [Westmoreland]

We ready are to try our fortunes
To the last man.
II Henry IV. Act iv, sc. 2, l. 43. [Mowbray]

Yet ere night
We shall try fortune in a second fight.
Julius Cæsar. Act v, sc. 3, l. 109. [Brutus]

To try a larger fortune.
Antony and Cleopatra. Act ii, sc. 6, l. 34. [Cæsar]

To try my fortune.—*The Merchant of Venice,* ii, 1, 24.

Try their fortune.—*The Two Gentlemen of Verona,* i, 3, 8.

6 I am fortune's steward.
II Henry IV. Act v, sc. 3, l. 137. [Falstaff]

7 Doth Fortune play the huswife with me now?
Henry V. Act v, sc. 1, l. 85. [Pistol]

Fortune made his sword:
By which the world's best garden he achieved.
Henry V. Epilogue, l. 6. [Chorus]

8 Bide the mortal fortune of the field.
III Henry VI. Act ii, sc. 2, l. 83. [Edward]

Lord Clifford: I would your highness would depart the field:
The queen hath best success when you are absent.
Queen Margaret: Ay, good my lord, and leave us to our fortune.
King Henry: Why, that 's my fortune too; therefore I 'll stay.
III Henry VI. Act ii, sc. 2, l. 73.

9 On thy fortune I repose myself.
III Henry VI. Act iv, sc. 6, l. 47. [Clarence]

I 'll leave you to your fortune and be gone.
III Henry VI. Act iv, sc. 7, l. 55. [Montague]

Be thou fortunate!—*III Henry VI,* iv, 8, 27.

10 A hazard of new fortunes.
King John. Act ii, sc. 1, l. 71. [Chatillon]

I like thee well: wilt thou forsake thy fortune,
Bequeath thy land to him and follow me?
King John. Act i, sc. 1, l. 148. [Queen Elinor]

Dauphin: Lady, with me, with me thy fortune lies.
Blanch: There where my fortune lives, there my life dies.
King John. Act iii, sc. 1, l. 337.

11 No, no; when Fortune means to men most good,
She looks upon them with a threatening eye.
King John. Act iii, sc. 4, l. 119. [Pandulph]

12 A good man's fortune may grow out at heels.
King Lear. Act ii, sc. 2, l. 164. [Kent]

Briefness and fortune, work!
King Lear. Act ii, sc. 1, l. 20. [Edmund]

13 It was he in the times past which held you
So under fortune.
Macbeth. Act iii, sc. 1, l. 76. [Macbeth]

14 Fortune now To my heart's hope!
The Merchant of Venice. Act ii, sc. 9, l. 19. [Arragon]

Let me to my fortune.—*The Merchant of Venice,* iii, 2, 39.

Your fortune stood upon the casket there,
And so did mine too, as the matter falls.
The Merchant of Venice. Act iii, sc. 2, l. 203. [Gratiano]

15 What a full fortune does the thick-lips owe,
If he can carry 't thus!
Othello. Act i, sc. 1, l. 66. [Roderigo] The only use of "thick-lips."

Would you would bear your fortune like a man!
Othello. Act iv, sc. 1, l. 62. [Iago]

16 Till fortune, tired with doing bad,
Threw him ashore, to give him glad.
Pericles. Act ii, Gower, l. 37.

'Tis more by fortune, lady, than by merit.
Pericles. Act ii, sc. 3, l. 12. [Pericles]

Your shafts of fortune, though they hurt you mortally,
Yet glance full wanderingly on us.
Pericles. Act iii, sc. 3, l. 6. [Cleon] The only use of "wanderingly."

You have fortunes coming upon you.
Pericles. Act iv, sc. 2, l. 126. [Bawd]

17 Reckoning his fortune at such high-proud rate.
The Rape of Lucrece, l. 19. The only use of "high-proud."

Hie to high fortune!—*Romeo and Juliet,* ii, 5, 80.

1
Thou let'st thy fortune sleep—die, rather; wink'st
Whiles thou are waking.
The Tempest. Act ii, sc. 1, l. 216. [Antonio]

2
Every man shift for all the rest, and let no man take care for himself; for all is but fortune.
The Tempest. Act v, sc. 1, l. 256. [Stephano]

3
Fortune with her ivory hand.
Timon of Athens. Act i, sc. 1, l. 70. [Poet]

4 Every grise of fortune
Is smooth'd by that below.
Timon of Athens. Act iii, sc. 3, l. 16. [Timon] "Grise" (step) is repeated in *Twelfth Night,* iii, 1, 135, and in *Othello,* i, 3, 200.

5
Fair lords, your fortunes are alike in all,
That in your country's service drew your swords.
Titus Andronicus. Act i, sc. 1, l. 174. [Marcus]

'Tis not the difference of a year or two
Makes me less gracious or thee more fortunate.
Titus Andronicus. Act ii, sc. 1, l. 31. [Chiron]

Safe out of fortune's shot.—*Titus Andronicus,* ii, 1, 2.

Befall what fortune will.—*Titus Andronicus,* v, 3, 3.

6
'Tis but fortune; all is fortune.
Twelfth Night. Act ii, sc. 5, l. 27. [Malvolio]

7 Take thy fortunes up;
Be that thou know'st thou art, and then thou art
As great as that thou fear'st.
Twelfth Night. Act v, sc. 1, l. 151. [Olivia]

8
Partner of his fortune.
The Two Gentlemen of Verona. Act i, sc. 3, l. 59. [Proteus]

Call his fortunes thine.—*Twelfth Night,* i, 4, 40.

9
Enough; I read your fortune in your eye.
The Two Gentlemen of Verona. Act ii, sc. 4, l. 143. [Proteus]

10 I think you know my fortunes
Do all lie there.
Winter's Tale. Act iv, sc. 4, l. 600. [Camillo]

If fortune please.—*The Winter's Tale,* iii, 3, 48.

Fortune speed us!—*Winter's Tale,* iv, 4, 681.

Fortune forbid.—*Twelfth Night,* ii, 2, 19.

II—Good Fortune

11
Parolles: Bless you, my fortunate lady!
Helena: I hope, sir, I have your good will to have mine own good fortunes.
All's Well that Ends Well. Act ii, sc. 4, l. 14.

12
Good, sir, give me good fortune.
Antony and Cleopatra. Act i, sc. 2, l. 13. [Charmian]

Good now, some excellent fortune!
Antony and Cleopatra. Act i, sc. 2, l. 25. [Charmian]

Charmian: Prithee, tell her but a worky-day fortune.
Soothsayer: Your fortunes are alike. . . .
Iras: Am I not an inch of fortune better than she?
Antony and Cleopatra. Act i, sc. 2, l. 55. The only use of "worky-day."

13 Every of this happy number
That have endured shrewd days and nights with us
Shall share the good of our returned fortune.
As You Like It. Act v, sc. 4, l. 178. [Duke Senior]

14 Now the fair goddess, Fortune,
Fall deep in love with thee; and her great charms
Misguide thy opposers' swords!
Coriolanus. Act i, sc. 5, l. 21. [Titus] The only use of "misguide."

15 O joyful day!
I would not take a knighthood for my fortune.
II Henry IV. Act v, sc. 3, l. 132. [Bardolph]

16
Good fortune bids us pause.
III Henry VI. Act ii, sc. 6, l. 31. [Edward] "Good fortune" is repeated fourteen times in later plays.

Good fortune come to thee!—*King John,* i, 1, 180.

Good fortune guide thee!—*Richard III,* iv, 1, 92.

Good fortune, worthy soldier.—*Antony and Cleopatra,* iii, 2, 22.

Good fortune then!—*The Merchant of Venice,* ii, 1, 45.

Now heaven send thee good fortune!—*The Merry Wives of Windsor,* iii, 4, 105.

17
Thus far fortune maketh us amends.
III Henry VI. Act iv, sc. 7, l. 2. [King Edward]

Thus far our fortune keeps an upward course.
III Henry VI. Act v, sc. 3, l. 1. [King Edward]

18
You have, by fortune and his highness' favours,
Gone slightly o'er low steps.
Henry VIII. Act ii, sc. 4, l. 111. [Queen Katharine]

19 Fortune is merry,
And in this mood will give us any thing.
Julius Cæsar. Act iii, sc. 2, l. 271. [Antony]

20
Turn face to face and bloody point to point;
Then, in a moment, Fortune shall cull forth
Out of one side her happy minion,
To whom in favour she shall give the day,
And kiss him with a glorious victory.
King John. Act ii, sc. 1, l. 390. [Bastard]

Fortune led you well.—*King Lear,* v, 3, 41.

21
If any man in Italy have a fairer table which doth offer to swear upon a book, I shall have good fortune.
The Merchant of Venice. Act ii, sc. 2, l. 167. [Launcelot]

Well, if Fortune be a woman, she's a good wench for this gear.
The Merchant of Venice. Act ii, sc. 2, l. 175. [Launcelot]

Since this fortune falls to you,
Be content and seek no new.
The Merchant of Venice. Act iii, sc. 2, l. 134. [Bassanio, reading]

For herein Fortune shows herself more kind
Than is her custom.
The Merchant of Venice. Act iv, sc. 1, l. 267. [Antonio]

1
Bountiful Fortune, Now my dear lady.
The Tempest. Act i, sc. 2, l. 178. [Prospero]

Fire-new fortune.—*King Lear,* v, 3, 132.
Gracious fortune.—*Measure for Measure,* v, 1, 76.
Great fortune.—*All's Well that Ends Well,* ii, 5, 81; *Timon of Athens,* iv, 2, 43; iv, 3, 7.
Honourable fortune.—*Othello,* iv, 2, 241.
Promising fortune.—*All's Well that Ends Well,* iii, 3, 3.
O rare fortune!—*Merchant of Venice,* ii, 2, 118.
Successful fortune.—*III Henry VI,* ii, 2, 41.
Wondrous fortune.—*Titus Andronicus,* ii, 3, 112.

2
Sir, I have upon a high and pleasant hill
Feign'd Fortune to be throned: the base o' the mount
Is rank'd with all deserts, all kind of natures,
That labour on the bosom of this sphere
To propagate their states.
Timon of Athens. Act i, sc. 1, l. 63. [Poet]

This throne, this Fortune, and this hill, methinks,
With one man beckon'd from the rest below,
Bowing his head against the steepy mount
To climb his happiness, would be well express'd
In our condition.
Timon of Athens. Act i, sc. 1, l. 73. [Painter] The only use of "steepy."

3
Fortune and I are friends.
Troilus and Cressida. Act iii, sc. 3, l. 88. [Achilles]

4
Yet doth this accident and flood of fortune
So far exceed all instance, all discourse.
Twelfth Night. Act iv, sc. 3, l. 11. [Sebastian]

In the blossoms of their fortune.
The Winter's Tale. Act v, sc. 2, l. 136. [Autolycus]

III—Ill Fortune

5
Parolles: I am now, sir, muddied in fortune's mood, and smell somewhat strong of her strong displeasure.
Clown: Truly, fortune's displeasure is but sluttish, if it smell so strongly as thou speakest of: I will henceforth eat no fish of fortune's buttering.
All's Well that Ends Well. Act v, sc. 2, l. 4. The only use of "buttering." "Muddied" is repeated in l. 23, and in *Hamlet,* iv, 5, 81. "Mudded" occurs twice.

Parolles: My lord, I am a man whom fortune hath cruelly scratched.
Lafeu: And what would you have me to do? 'Tis too late to pare her nails now. Wherein have you played the knave with fortune, that she should scratch you, who of herself is a good lady and would not have knaves thrive long under her? There's a quart d'écu for you: let the justices make you and fortune friends: I am for other business.
All's Well that Ends Well. Act v, sc. 2, l. 28. "Quart d'écu" is repeated in iv, 3, 311, and occurs in no other play.

6
I know not
What counts harsh fortune casts upon my face;
But in my bosom shall she never come,
To make my heart her vassal.
Antony and Cleopatra. Act ii, sc. 6, l. 55. [Pompey]

Menas: Pompey doth this day laugh away his fortune.
Enobarbus: If he do, sure, he cannot weep 't back again.
Antony and Cleopatra. Act ii, sc. 6, l. 109.

I 'll never follow thy pall'd fortunes more.
Antony and Cleopatra. Act ii, sc. 7, l. 88. [Menas] The only use of "pall'd."

Our fortune on the sea is out of breath,
And sinks most lamentably.
Antony and Cleopatra. Act iii, sc. 10, l. 25. [Canidius] "Lamentably" is repeated in *The Winter's Tale,* iv, 4, 190.

By starts,
His fretted fortunes give him hope, and fear,
Of what he has, and has not.
Antony and Cleopatra. Act iv, sc. 12, l. 7. [Scarus]

Fortune and Antony part here; even here
Do we shake hands.
Antony and Cleopatra. Act iv, sc. 12, l. 19. [Antony]

7
One out of suits with fortune.
As You Like It. Act i, sc. 2, l. 258. [Rosalind]

I know into what straits of fortune she is driven.
As You Like It. Act v, sc. 2, l. 70. [Rosalind]

8
This man has marr'd his fortune.
Coriolanus. Act iii, sc. 1, l. 254. [A Patrician]

His fortunes all lie speechless and his name
Is at last gasp.
Cymbeline. Act i, sc. 5, l. 52. [Queen]

And you shall find me, wretched man, a thing
The most disdain'd of fortune.
Cymbeline. Act iii, sc. 4, l. 19. [Pisanio]

9
The slings and arrows of outrageous fortune.
Hamlet, iii, 1, 58. See under INDECISION.

I took thee for thy better: take thy fortune.
Hamlet. Act iii, sc. 4, l. 32. [Hamlet]

With sorrow I embrace my fortune.
Hamlet. Act v, sc. 2, l. 399. [Fortinbras]

10
I embrace this fortune patiently,
Since not to be avoided it falls on me.
I Henry IV. Act v, sc. 5, l. 12. [Worcester]

1
Will Fortune never come with both hands full,
But write her fair words still in foulest letters?
She either gives a stomach and no food;
Such are the poor, in health; or else a feast
And takes away the stomach.
II Henry IV. Act iv, sc. 4, l. 103. [King Henry]

2
Fortune is Bardolph's foe, and frowns on him.
Henry V. Act iii, sc. 6, l. 41. [Pistol]
O méchante fortune!—*Henry V*, iv, 5, 5. [Dauphin] The only use of "méchante."

3
Ill fortune follow thee!
I Henry VI, iii, 2, 109. The only use of "ill fortune."

4
The bottom Of all our fortunes.
II Henry VI. Act v, sc. 2, l. 78. [Queen Margaret]
This breach now in our fortunes made
May readily be stopp'd.
II Henry VI. Act v, sc. 2, l. 82. [Queen] "Readily" is repeated in *The Rape of Lucrece*, l. 1152.
Thy fortune, York, hadst thou been regent there,
Might happily have proved far worse than his.
II Henry VI. Act iii, sc. 1, l. 305. [Queen]

5
Meaner than myself have had like fortune.
III Henry VI. Act iv, sc. 1, l. 71. [Queen Elizabeth]
I may conquer fortune's spite
By living low, where fortune cannot hurt me.
III Henry VI. Act iv, sc. 6, l. 19. [King Henry]
Spying and avoiding fortune's malice.
III Henry VI. Act iv, sc. 6, l. 28. [Warwick]
I . . . stoop with patience to my fortune.
III Henry VI. Act v, sc. 5, l. 6. [Somerset]

6
Fie, fie, fie upon This compell'd fortune!
Henry VIII. Act ii, sc. 3, l. 86. [Old Lady]
Alas, poor wenches, where are now your fortunes!
Shipwreck'd upon a kingdom, where no pity,
No friends, no hope; no kindred weep for me.
Henry VIII. Act iii, sc. 1, l. 148. [Queen Katharine]

7
But Fortune, O,
She is corrupted, changed and won from thee;
She adulterates hourly with thine uncle John,
And with her golden hand hath pluck'd on France
To tread down fair respect of sovereignty,
And made his majesty the bawd to theirs.
King John. Act iii, sc. 1, l. 54. [Constance] The only use of "adulterates."

8
That strumpet Fortune.
King John. Act iii, sc. 1, l. 61. [Constance]
Guildenstern: On fortune's cap we are not the very button.
Hamlet: Nor the soles of her shoe? . . . Then you live about her waist, or in the middle of her favours?
Guildenstern: 'Faith, her privates we.
Hamlet: In the secret parts of fortune? O, most true; she is a strumpet.
Hamlet. Act ii, sc. 2, l. 233.
Out, out, thou strumpet, Fortune! All you gods,
In general synod, take away her power;
Break all the spokes and fellies from her wheel,
And bowl the round nave down the hill of heaven.
Hamlet. Act ii, sc. 2, l. 515. [First Player] The only use of "fellies."
And fortune, on his damned quarrel smiling,
Show'd like a rebel's whore.
Macbeth. Act i, sc. 2, l. 14. [Sergeant]

9
How malicious is my fortune!
King Lear. Act iii, sc. 5, l. 10. [Edmund]
Hence;
Lest that the infection of his fortune take
Like hold on thee.
King Lear. Act iv, sc. 6, l. 236. [Oswald]
If fortune brag of two she loved and hated,
One of them we behold.
King Lear. Act v, sc. 3, l. 280. [Kent]

10
The malevolence of fortune nothing
Takes from his high respect.
Macbeth. Act iii, sc. 6, l. 28. [Lord] The only use of "malevolence."

11
Let fortune go to hell for it.
The Merchant of Venice. Act iii, sc. 2, l. 21. [Portia]

12
If Fortune thy foe were not,
Nature thy friend.
The Merry Wives of Windsor. Act iii, sc. 3, l. 69. [Falstaff]

13
What though I be not so in grace as you,
So hung upon with love, so fortunate.
A Midsummer-Night's Dream. Act iii, sc. 2, l. 232. [Helena] "Fortunate" is used seventeen times in the plays.

14
I am desperate of my fortunes if they check me here.
Othello. Act ii, sc. 3, l. 337. [Cassio]
It is my wretched fortune.
Othello. Act iv, sc. 2, l. 128. [Desdemona]

15
Their father was too weak, and they too strong,
To hold their cursed-blessed fortune long.
The Rape of Lucrece, l. 865. The only use of "cursed-blessed."

16
My fortune runs against the bias.
Richard II. Act iii, sc. 4, l. 5. [Queen] "Against the bias" is repeated in *The Taming of the Shrew*, iv, 5, 25.

17
Since you will buckle fortune on my back,
To bear her burthen, whether I will or no,
I must have patience to endure the load.
Richard III. Act iii, sc. 7, l. 228. [Gloucester]

I call'd thee then vain flourish of my fortune.
Richard III. Act iv, sc. 4, l. 82. [Queen Margaret]

Heaven and fortune bar me happy hours!
Richard III. Act iv, sc. 4, l. 400. [King Richard]

Unhappy fortune!—*Romeo and Juliet,* v, 2, 17.
Crooked fortune.—*The Two Gentlemen of Verona,* iv, 1, 22.

1
Join with the spite of fortune, make me bow.
Sonnets. No. xc.

So shall I taste
At first the very worst of fortune's might.
Sonnets. No. xc.

O, for my sake do you with Fortune chide,
The guilty goddess of my harmful deeds.
Sonnets. No. cxi.

2
The fouler fortune mine, and there an end.
The Taming of the Shrew. Act v, sc. 2, l. 98. [Petruchio]

3
Exposed myself . . .
To doubtful fortune; sequestering from me all
That time, acquaintance, custom and condition
Made tame and most familiar to my nature.
Troilus and Cressida. Act iii, sc. 3, l. 6. [Calchas] The only use of "sequestering."

4
Let myself and fortune
Tug for the time to come.
Winter's Tale. Act iv, sc. 4, l. 506. [Florizel]

Though Fortune, visible an enemy,
Should chase us with my father, power no jot
Hath she to change our loves.
Winter's Tale. Act v, sc. 1, l. 216. [Florizel]

IV—Fickle Fortune

5
Rosalind: What shall be our sport, then?
Celia: Let us sit and mock the good housewife Fortune from her wheel, that her gifts may henceforth be bestowed equally.
As You Like It. Act i, sc. 2, l. 34.

Fortune, good night: smile once more; turn thy wheel!
King Lear. Act ii, sc. 2, l. 180. [Kent]

Now in as low an ebb as the foot of the ladder and by and by in as high a flow as the ridge of the gallows.
I Henry IV. Act i, sc. 2, l. 42. [Prince of Wales]

6
Rosalind: Fortune reigns in gifts of the world, not in the lineaments of Nature.
Celia: No? when Nature hath made a fair creature, may she not by Fortune fall into the fire? Though Nature hath given us wit to flout at Fortune, hath not Fortune sent in this fool to cut off the argument?
Rosalind: Indeed, there is Fortune too hard for Nature when Fortune makes Nature's natural the cutter-off of Nature's wits.
As You Like It. Act i, sc. 2, l. 44. The only use of "cutter-off."

Blind fortune.—*The Merchant of Venice,* ii, 1, 36; *Coriolanus,* v, 6, 118.

O giglot fortune!
Cymbeline. Act iii, sc. 1, l. 31. [Queen] Giglot wench.—*I Henry VI,* iv, 7, 41. Away with those giglots.—*Measure for Measure,* v, 1, 352. The only uses of "giglot" (wanton).

Strange fortune.—*Winter's Tale,* ii, 3, 179.

7
The giddy round of Fortune's wheel.
The Rape of Lucrece, l. 952.

Pistol: Giddy Fortune's furious fickle wheel,
That goddess blind,
That stands upon the rolling restless stone—
Fluellen: By your patience, Aunchient Pistol. Fortune is painted blind, with a muffler afore her eyes, to signify to you that Fortune is blind; and she is painted also with a wheel, to signify to you, which is the moral of it, that she is turning, and inconstant, and mutability, and variation: and her foot, look you, is fixed upon a spherical stone, which rolls, and rolls, and rolls: in good truth, the poet makes a most excellent description of it: Fortune is an excellent moral.
Henry V. Act iii, sc. 6, l. 29. "Mutability" is repeated in *Cymbeline,* ii, 5, 26; "variation" in *I Henry IV,* i, 1, 64, and in *Sonnets,* lxxvi; and "spherical" in *The Comedy of Errors,* iii, 2, 116, and *King Lear,* i, 2, 134.

8
Whilst as fickle Fortune smiled,
Thou and I were both beguiled.
The Passionate Pilgrim, l. 401.

Wayward fortune.—*Pericles,* v, 1, 90.

9
O fortune, fortune! all men call thee fickle:
If thou art fickle, what dost thou with him
That is renown'd for faith? Be fickle, fortune;
For then, I hope, thou wilt not keep him long.
Romeo and Juliet. Act iii, sc. 5, l. 60. [Juliet]

Fortune's fickleness.—*I Henry VI,* v, 3, 134.

V—Fortune: Wealth

10
For you have show'd me that which well approves
You 're great in fortune.
All's Well that Ends Well. Act iii, sc. 7, l. 13. [Widow]

11
A province I will give thee,
And make thy fortunes proud.
Antony and Cleopatra. Act ii, sc. 5, l. 68. [Cleopatra]

It much would please him,
That of his fortunes you should make a staff
To lean upon.
Antony and Cleopatra. Act iii, sc. 13, l. 67. [Thyreus]

O, my fortunes have Corrupted honest men!
Antony and Cleopatra, iv, 5, 16. [Antony]

12
Fair sir, I pity her
And wish, for her sake more than for mine own,
My fortunes were more able to relieve her.
As You Like It. Act ii, sc. 4, l. 75. [Corin]

13
Not beneath him in fortunes, beyond him in the advantage of the time.
Cymbeline. Act iv, sc. 1, l. 12. [Cloten]

My fortunes every way as fairly rank'd,
If not with vantage, as Demetrius'.
A Midsummer-Night's Dream. Act i, sc. 1, l. 101. [Lysander]

1 He shall not knit a knot in his fortunes with the finger of my substance.
The Merry Wives of Windsor. Act iii, sc. 2, l. 75. [Page]

2 Were my fortunes equal to my desires, I could wish to make one there.
Pericles. Act ii, sc. 1, l. 117. [Pericles]

3 His large fortune
Upon his good and gracious nature hanging
Subdues and properties to his love and tendance
All sorts of hearts.
Timon of Athens. Act i, sc. 1, l. 55. [Poet]

Long may he live in fortunes!
Timon of Athens. Act i, sc. 1, l. 293. [Lord]

To build his fortune I will strain a little,
For 'tis a bond in men.
Timon of Athens. Act i, sc. 1, l. 143. [Old Athenian]

More welcome are ye to my fortunes
Than my fortunes to me.
Timon of Athens. Act i, sc. 2, l. 19. [Timon]

Buried fortunes.—*Timon of Athens,* iv, 2, 10.

4 I 'll put My fortunes to your service.
Winter's Tale. Act i, sc. 2, l. 439. [Camillo]

FOULNESS

5 He 's fallen in love with your foulness.
As You Like It. Act iii, sc. 5, l. 66. [Rosalind]

6 Touchstone: To cast away honesty upon a foul slut were to put good meat into an unclean dish.
Audrey: I am not a slut, though I thank the gods I am foul.
Touchstone: Well, praised be the gods for thy foulness! sluttishness may come hereafter.
As You Like It. Act iii, sc. 3, l. 35. The only use of "sluttishness."

Our radiant queen hates sluts and sluttery.
The Merry Wives of Windsor. Act v, sc. 5, l. 50. [Pistol]

Sluttery to such neat excellence opposed
Should make desire vomit emptiness,
Not so allured to feed.
Cymbeline. Act i, sc. 6, l. 44. [Iachimo] The only uses of "sluttery."

Hold up, you sluts.—*Timon of Athens,* iv, 3, 134. The only uses of "slut" and "sluts."

7 Shall we fall foul for toys?
II Henry IV, ii, 4, 183. See under QUARREL.

8 If you grow foul with me, Pistol, I will scour you with my rapier.
Henry V. Act ii, sc. 1, l. 59. [Nym]

Grow foul.—*Love's Labour 's Lost,* iv, 1, 139.

9 Who loves her so, that, speaking of her foulness,
Wash'd it with tears.
Much Ado about Nothing. Act iv, sc. 1, l. 155. [Leonato]

Foulness is the punishment.—*Henry VIII,* iii, 2, 183.

It is no . . . foulness.—*King Lear,* i, 1, 230.

10 'Tis foul in her.
Othello. Act iv, sc. 1, l. 213. [Othello]

O, she was foul!—*Othello,* v, 2, 200.

Hard-favour'd foul.—*Venus and Adonis,* l. 133.

Foul as slander.—*Othello,* iv, 2, 19.

How foul it is.—*II Henry IV.* iii, 1, 39.

Foul is most foul.—*As You Like It,* iii, 5, 62.

Most foul.—*Hamlet,* i, 5, 27; 28; *Much Ado about Nothing,* iv, 1, 104.

Foul and dangerous.—*Richard II,* i, 3, 39.

Foul and fair.—*Macbeth,* i, 3, 38.

Foul is fair.—*Macbeth,* i, 1, 11.

Fair and foul.—*Cymbeline,* i, 6, 38.

Foul and foolish.—*Othello,* ii, 1, 141; 142.

Foul and loathsome.—*The Taming of the Shrew,* Ind., 1, 35.

Foul and muddy.—*The Tempest,* v, 1, 82.

Foul and pestilent.—*Hamlet,* ii, 2, 314.

Foul and ugly.—*I Henry IV,* i, 2, 226; *Henry V,* iv, Prol., 21.

Foul and violent.—*Othello,* ii, 1, 34. "Foul" was a favourite adjective with Shakespeare, and was used 206 times in the plays and 42 times in the poems.

11 Fouler than heart can think thee.
Richard III. Act i, sc. 2, l. 83. [Lady Anne]

Grows fouler.—*Antony and Cleopatra,* ii, 7, 106.

That 's fouler.—*Othello,* iv, 1, 215. "Fouler" is used eight times.

The foul'st best fits.—*Antony and Cleopatra,* iv, 6, 38. "Foul'st" is used five times.

Thou play'dst most foully.—*Macbeth,* iii, 1, 3. "Foully" occurs four times.

12 Be she as foul as was Florentius' love,
. . . She moves me not.
The Taming of the Shrew. Act i, sc. 2, l. 69. [Petruchio] The only reference to Florentius, the knight in Gower's *Confessio Amantis* (bk. i), who agreed to marry an old hag if she would solve the riddle, "What do women most desire?"

FOUNTAIN

See also Spring

13 You are the fount that makes small brooks to flow:
Now stops thy spring; my sea shall suck them dry.
III Henry VI. Act iv, sc. 8, l. 54. [King Edward]

Consecrated fount.—*Measure for Measure,* iv, 3, 102.

Fair founts.—*The Rape of Lucrece,* l. 850. "Fount" is used twice more, in *A Lover's Complaint,* l. 283, and in *Henry VIII,* i, 1, 154.

14 By fountain clear.
A Midsummer-Night's Dream. Act ii, sc. 1, l. 29. [Puck]

By paved fountain.
A Midsummer-Night's Dream. Act ii, sc. 1, l. 84. [Titania]
Bubbling fountain.—*Titus Andronicus,* ii, 4, 23. "Bubbling" is repeated in *The Rape of Lucrece,* l. 1737.
Cold valley-fountain.—*Sonnets,* cliii. The only use of "valley-fountain."
Pleasant fountains.—*Venus and Adonis,* l. 234.
Purple fountain.—*The Rape of Lucrece,* l. 1734; *Romeo and Juliet,* i, 1, 92.
Silver fountain.—*Sonnets,* xxxv.
A fountain stirr'd.—*Troilus and Cressida,* iii, 3, 331.
A fountain troubled.—*The Taming of the Shrew,* v, 2, 142.

1 But there, where I have garner'd up my heart,
Where either I must live, or bear no life;
The fountain from the which my current runs,
Or else dries up; to be discarded thence!
Or keep it as a cistern for foul toads
To knot and gender in!
Othello. Act iv, sc. 2, l. 57. [Othello] The only use of "garner'd," and of "knot" as a verb. "Cistern" is repeated in *Macbeth,* iv, 3, 63, and in *Antony and Cleopatra,* ii, 5, 95.

2 Mud not the fountain that gave drink to thee.
The Rape of Lucrece, l. 577. The only use of "mud" as a verb. As a noun it occurs eight times.
The poison'd fountain clears itself again;
And why not I from this compelled stain?
The Rape of Lucrece, l. 1707.

3 Thou sheer, immaculate and silver fountain.
Richard II, v, 3, 61. See under FATHER.

4 Sit round about some fountain,
Looking all downwards, to behold our cheeks; .
And in the fountain shall we gaze so long
Till the fresh taste be taken from that clearness,
And made a brine-pit with our bitter tears?
Titus Andronicus. Act iii, sc. 1, l. 123. [Titania] "Brine-pit" is repeated in *The Tempest,* i, 2, 338.

5 Would the fountain of your mind were clear again.
Troilus and Cressida, iii, 3, 314. See under MIND.
Fountain of your blood.—*Macbeth,* ii, 3, 103.

FOWL

6 Strange fowl light upon neighbouring ponds.
Cymbeline. Act i, sc. 4, l. 96. [Iachimo]
Lagging fowls.—*The Rape of Lucrece,* l. 1335.
Struck fowl.—*I Henry IV,* iv, 2, 21.
Wild fowl.—*Twelfth Night,* iv, 2, 55.
Winged fowls.—*Comedy of Errors,* ii, 1, 18.
Flight of fowl.—*Titus Andronicus,* v, 3, 68.
Fowl without a feather.—*The Comedy of Errors,* iii, 1, 82. See under FISH.
Creeping fowler.—*Midsummer-Night's Dream,* iii, 2, 20. The only use of "fowler."

7 From this session interdict
Every fowl of tyrant wing.
A Lover's Complaint, l. 9. The only use of "interdict." "Interdiction" occurs in *Macbeth,* iv, 3, 107.

8 Even for our kitchens
We kill the fowl of season.
Measure for Measure. Act ii, sc. 2, l. 84. [Isabella]

9 Alas, poor hurt fowl! now will he creep into sedges.
Much Ado about Nothing. Act ii, sc. 1, l. 209. [Benedick]

10 Stalk on, stalk on; the fowl sits.
Much Ado about Nothing. Act ii, sc. 3, l. 95. [Claudio]

FOX

11 O, will you eat no grapes, my royal fox?
Yes, but you will my noble grapes, an if
My royal fox could reach them.
All's Well that Ends Well. Act ii, sc. 1, l. 73. [Lafeu]
Drawn fox.—*I Henry IV,* iii, 3, 129.
Ingrateful fox!—*King Lear,* iii, 7, 28.

12 Hide fox, and after all.
Hamlet. Act iv, sc. 2, l. 32. [Hamlet]

13 The fox barks not when he would steal the lamb.
II Henry VI. Act iii, sc. 1, l. 55. [Suffolk]
Were 't not madness then,
To make the fox surveyor of the fold?
II Henry VI. Act iii, sc. 1, l. 252. [Suffolk]
No; let him die, in that he is a fox,
By nature proved an enemy to the flock,
Before his chaps be stain'd with crimson blood.
II Henry VI. Act iii, sc. 1, l. 257. [Suffolk]
Alas, poor Proteus! thou hast entertain'd
A fox to be the shepherd of thy lambs.
The Two Gentlemen of Verona. Act iv, sc. 4, l. 96. [Julia]
O, poor souls,
Come you to seek the lamb here of the fox?
Measure for Measure. Act v, sc. 1, l. 299. [Duke]

14 But when the fox hath once got in his nose,
He 'll soon find means to make the body follow.
III Henry VI. Act iv, sc. 7, l. 25. [Gloucester]

15 Fox in stealth.—*King Lear,* iii, 4, 97.
A very fox for his valour.—*A Midsummer-Night's Dream,* v, 1, 234.

16 I 'll warrant we 'll unkennel the fox.
The Merry Wives of Windsor. Act iii, sc. 3, l. 173. [Ford] "Unkennel" is repeated in *Hamlet,* iii, 2, 86.
The fox carries the goose.—*A Midsummer-Night's Dream,* v, 1, 237. See under LION.

1
An old Italian fox is not so kind, my boy.
The Taming of the Shrew. Act ii, sc. 1, l. 405. [Gremio]
The fox which lives by subtlety.
Venus and Adonis, l. 675. "Subtlety" is repeated in *II Henry VI,* iii, 1, 262, and in *Sonnets,* cxxxviii.

FRAILTY

2
Frailty, thy name is woman!
Hamlet. Act i, sc. 2, l. 146. [Hamlet]
Angelo: We are all frail. . . . Nay, women are frail too.
Isabella: Ay, as the glasses where they view themselves;
Which are as easy broke as they make forms.
. . . Nay, call us ten times frail;
For we are soft as our complexions are.
Measure for Measure. Act ii, sc. 4, l. 121.
The frail'st and softest things.—*As You Like It,* iii, 5, 12. The only use of "frail'st."
Frailties which before
Have often shamed our sex.
Antony and Cleopatra. Act v, sc. 2, l. 123. [Cleopatra]
The one is but frail, the other casual.
Cymbeline. Act i, sc. 4, l. 100. [Iachimo] "Casual" is repeated in *Hamlet,* v, 2, 393.
You term her frail.—*Cymbeline,* i, 4, 106.
3
Frailty hath examples for his falling.
Measure for Measure. Act iii, sc. 1, l. 191. [Duke]
4
Bid her think what a man is; let her consider his frailty.
The Merry Wives of Windsor. Act iii, sc. 5, l. 51. [Falstaff]
We are all men,
In our own natures frail, and capable
Of our flesh; few are angels: out of which frailty
And want of wisdom, you, that best should teach us,
Have misdemean'd yourself.
Henry VIII. Act v, sc. 3, l. 10. [Chancellor] The only use of "misdemean'd."
Is 't frailty that thus errs? . . .
Have not we . . . frailty, as men have?
Othello, iv, 3, 100. See under Wife.
Wife's frailty.—*The Merry Wives of Windsor,* ii, 1, 242.
Frailty of our powers.—*Troilus and Cressida,* iv, 4, 98.
Naked frailties.—*Macbeth,* ii, 3, 132.
5
In my nature reign'd
All frailties that besiege all kinds of blood.
Sonnets. No. cix.
Or on my frailties why are frailer spies,
Which in their wills count bad what I think good?
Sonnets. No. cxxi.
6
Alas, our frailty is the cause, not we!
For such as we are made of, such we be.
Twelfth Night. Act ii, sc. 2, l. 32. [Viola]

FRANCE AND THE FRENCH

I—France

7
France is a dog-hole, and it no more merits
The tread of a man's foot.
All's Well that Ends Well. Act ii, sc. 3, l. 291. [Parolles] The only use of "dog-hole."
France is a stable; we that dwell in 't jades.
All's Well that Ends Well. Act ii, sc. 3, l. 301. [Parolles]
8
France being ours, we 'll bend it to our awe,
Or break it all to pieces: or there we 'll sit,
Ruling in large and ample empery
O'er France and all her almost kingly dukedoms.
Henry V. Act i, sc. 2, l. 224. [King Henry] The only use of "ruling."
Katharine: Is it possible dat I sould love de enemy of France?
King Henry: No; it is not possible you should love an enemy of France, Kate: but in loving me, you should love the friend of France; for I love France so well that I will not part with a village of it; I will have it all mine: and, Kate, when France is mine and I am yours, then yours is France and you are mine.
Henry V. Act v, sc. 2, l. 178.
9
This best garden of the world
Our fertile France.
Henry V. Act v, sc. 2, l. 36. [Burgundy]
Look on thy country, look on fertile France.
I Henry VI. Act iii, sc. 3, l. 44. [La Pucelle]
Fair France.—*Henry V,* v, 2, 383; *King Lear,* i, 1, 260.
10
France and England, whose very shores look pale
With envy of each other's happiness.
Henry V. Act v, sc. 2, l. 378. [French King]
11
Whom all France . . .
Durst not presume to look once in the face.
I Henry VI. Act i, sc. 1, l. 139. [Messenger]
All France will be replete with mirth and joy.
I Henry VI. Act i, sc. 6, l. 15. [Alençon]
12
Charles: France were no place for Henry's warriors;
Nor should that nation boast it so with us,
But be extirped from our provinces.
Alençon: For ever should they be expulsed from France
And not have title of an earldom here.
I Henry VI. Act iii, sc. 3, l. 25. The only use of "extirped" and "expulsed."
We mourn, France smiles.
I Henry VI. Act iv, sc. 3, l. 32. [York]
Now the time is come
That France must vail her lofty-plumed crest
And let her head fall into England's lap.
I Henry VI. Act v, sc. 3, l. 25. [Fiends] The only use of "lofty-plumed."
Now, France, thy glory droopeth to the dust.
I Henry VI. Act v, sc. 3, l. 29. [La Pucelle]
13
His father revell'd in the heart of France,

And tamed the king, and made the dauphin stoop.
III Henry VI. Act ii, sc. 2, l. 150. [Edward]
Who by his prowess conquered all France.
III Henry VI. Act iii, sc. 3, l. 86. [Oxford]
'Tis far from hence to France.
III Henry VI. Act iv, sc. 1, l. 4. [Clarence]
'Tis better using France than trusting France.
III Henry VI. Act iv, sc. 1, l. 42. [Hastings]

1
The coward hand of France.
King John. Act ii, sc. 1, l. 158. [King John]
France, hast thou yet more blood to cast away?
King John. Act ii, sc. 1, l. 334. [King John]
And France, whose armour conscience buckled on,
Whom zeal and charity brought to the field
As God's own soldier.
King John. Act ii, sc. 1, l. 564. [Bastard]
The hot-blooded France.—*King Lear,* ii, 4, 215.

2
And go well satisfied to France again.
Love's Labour's Lost. Act ii, sc. 1, l. 153. [King]
We have now no thought in us but France.
Henry V. Act i, sc. 2, l. 302. [King Henry]
My thoughts and wishes bend again toward France.
Hamlet. Act i, sc. 2, l. 55. [Laertes]
I am for France too.—*All's Well that Ends Well,* iv, 3, 364.

3
France is a bawd to Fortune.
King John. Act iii, sc. 1, l. 60. [Constance]
Tell me, thou fellow, is not France forsworn?
King John. Act iii, sc. 1, l. 62. [Constable]

4
By gar, 'tis no the fashion of France; it is not jealous in France.
The Merry Wives of Windsor. Act iii, sc. 3, l. 183. [Caius]

II—The French People

5
There is a Frenchman his companion, one
An eminent monsieur.
Cymbeline. Act i, sc. 6, l. 64. [Iachimo]
Monsieur the nice.—*Love's Labour's Lost,* v, 2, 325.
Monsieur the challenger.—*As You Like It,* i, 2, 175.
Monsieur Remorse.—*I Henry IV,* i, 2, 125.
Petit monsieur.—*Henry V,* iv, 4, 52. "Monsieur" is used eighteen times.
Worthy Frenchman.—*All's Well that Ends Well,* ii, 1, 12.

6
Mazed with a yelping kennel of French curs.
I Henry VI. Act iv, sc. 2, l. 47. [Talbot] "Yelping" is repeated in *Titus Andronicus,* ii, 3, 20: "Yelping noise."
French gallants.—*Henry V,* iv, 2, 22.
French heart.—*Henry V,* v, 2, 105.
French maid.—*Henry V,* v, 2, 345.
French nobility.—*Henry V,* i, 2, 110.
French nods.—*Richard III,* i, 3, 49.
French thrift.—*The Merry Wives of Windsor,* i, 3, 93.
French word.—*I Henry VI,* iv, 7, 54. It will be noted that none of these phrases is used twice.

7
My people are with sickness much enfeebled, . . .
Almost no better than so many French.
Henry V. Act iii, sc. 6, l. 154. [King Henry] "Enfeebled" is repeated in *I Henry VI,* i, 4, 69.

Indeed, the French may lay twenty French crowns to one, they will beat us; for they bear them on their shoulders: but it is no English treason to cut French crowns, and to-morrow the king himself will be a clipper.
Henry V. Act iv, sc. 1, l. 242. [King Henry] The only use of "clipper."

The French are bravely in their battles set.
Henry V. Act iv, sc. 3, l. 69. [Salisbury]

8
The subtle-witted French.
I Henry VI, i, 1, 25. The only use of "subtle-witted."
The aspiring French.—*I Henry VI,* v, 4, 99.
The confident and over-lusty French.—*Henry V,* iv, Prol., 18. "Over-lusty" is repeated in *King Lear,* ii, 4, 10.

9 The terror of the French,
The scarecrow that affrights our children so.
I Henry VI. Act i, sc. 4, l. 42. [Talbot]
And what a terror he had been to France.
I Henry VI. Act ii, sc. 2, l. 17. [Talbot] Referring to the Earl of Salisbury.
Our nation's terror and their bloody scourge!
I Henry VI. Act iv, sc. 2, l. 16. [French General] Referring to Lord Talbot, the English leader.

10
Done like a Frenchman: turn, and turn again!
I Henry VI. Act iii, sc. 3, l. 85. [La Pucelle]
A fickle wavering nation.—*I Henry VI,* iv, 1, 138.
Fickle France.—*King John,* ii, 1, 583.
False Frenchwoman.—*III Henry VI,* i, 4, 149.
Proud Frenchwoman.—*II Henry VI,* i, 3, 143. The only uses of "Frenchwoman."

11
Were 't not a shame, that whilst you live at jar,
The fearful French, whom you late vanquished,
Should make a start o'er seas and vanquish you?
I Henry VI. Act iv, sc. 8, l. 43. [Clifford]

12 The French,
All clinquant, all in gold, like heathen gods.
Henry VIII. Act i, sc. 1, l. 18. [Norfolk] The only use of "clinquant."
Men fear'd the French would prove perfidious.
Henry VIII. Act i, sc. 2, l. 156. [Surveyor]

13
O foul revolt of French inconstancy!
King John. Act iii, sc. 1, l. 322. [Queen Elinor]

To thrill and shake
Even at the crying of your nation's crow,
Thinking his voice an armed Englishman.
King John. Act v, sc. 2, l. 143. [Bastard]

1
The Frenchman hath good skill in his rapier.
The Merry Wives of Windsor. Act ii, sc. 1, l. 230. [Page]

2
Let 's whip these stragglers o'er the seas again;
Lash hence these overweening rags of France.
Richard III. Act v, sc. 3, l. 327. [King Richard] The only use of "stragglers."

III—The French Language

3
Pistol: Ask me this slave in French
What is his name.
Boy: Écoutez: comment êtes-vous appelé?
French Soldier: Monsieur le Fer.
Boy: He says his name is Master Fer.
Pistol: Master Fer! I 'll fer him, and firk him, and ferret him: discuss the same in French unto him.
Boy: I do not know the French for fer and ferret and firk.
Henry V. Act iv, sc. 4, l. 23. The only use of "firk" (beat). "Ferret" is used only once more, in *Julius Cæsar,* i, 2, 86.

King Henry: I will tell thee in French; which I am sure will hang upon my tongue like a new-married wife about her husband's neck, hardly to be shook off. . . . It is as easy for me, Kate, to conquer the kingdom as to speak so much more French: I shall never move thee in French, unless it be to laugh at me. . . .
Katharine: Your majestee ave fausse French enough to deceive de most sage demoiselle dat is en France.
Henry V. Act v, sc. 2, l. 187.

Now, fie upon my false French!
Henry V. Act v, sc. 2, l. 236. [King Henry]

4
Cade: He can speak French; and therefore he is a traitor.
Stafford: O gross and miserable ignorance!
Cade: Nay, answer, if you can: the Frenchmen are our enemies; go to, then, I ask but this: can he that speaks with the tongue of an enemy be a good counsellor or no?
II Henry VI. Act iv, sc. 2, l. 177.

You can speak the French tongue.
Henry VIII. Act i, sc. 4, l. 57. [Wolsey]

5
The chopping French we do not understand.
Richard II. Act v, sc. 3, l. 124. [Duchess of York] The only use of "chopping."

6
Bon jour! there 's a French salutation to your French slop.
Romeo and Juliet. Act ii, sc. 4, l. 46. [Mercutio] The only use of "French salutation" and "French slop."

FRANKNESS, see Candour

FRAUD, see Deceit

FRAY

See also Combat, Fighting

7
Speak of frays Like a fine bragging youth.
The Merchant of Venice. Act iii, sc. 4, l. 68. [Portia]

8
Sir, there is a fray to be fought between Sir Hugh the Welsh priest and Caius the French doctor.
The Merry Wives of Windsor. Act ii, sc. 1, l. 208. [Shallow]

9
Heavens shield Lysander, if they mean a fray!
A Midsummer-Night's Dream. Act iii, sc. 2, l. 447. [Hermia]

Devilish-holy fray.—*A Midsummer-Night's Dream,* iii, 2, 129. The only use of "devilish-holy."

Bloody fray.—*III Henry VI,* ii, 1, 107; *I Henry IV,* v, 4, 108; *Romeo and Juliet,* iii, 1, 156.

10
Right glad I am he was not at this fray.
Romeo and Juliet. Act i, sc. 1, l. 124. [Lady Montague]

O me! What fray was here?—*Romeo and Juliet,* i, 1, 179.

11
Signior Hortensio, come you to part the fray?
'Con tutto il cuore, ben trovato,' may I say.
The Taming of the Shrew. Act i, sc. 2, l. 23. [Petruchio] The only use of the Italian phrase, meaning, "With all my heart, well thought of."

You are almost come to part almost a fray.
Much Ado about Nothing. Act v, sc. 1, l. 113. [Don Pedro]

Thou partest a fair fray.—*Love's Labour's Lost,* v, 2, 484.

FREEDOM

See also Liberty

12
Courtiers of beauteous freedom.
Antony and Cleopatra. Act ii, sc. 6, l. 17. [Pompey]

Ancient freedom.—*II Henry VI,* iv, 8, 28.
Immediate freedom.—*Julius Cæsar,* iii, 1, 54.
Freedom and liberty!—*Julius Cæsar,* iii, 1, 110.
Freedom of my knowledge.—*The Winter's Tale,* i, 1, 12.
Freedom of the state.—*The Merchant of Venice,* iii, 2, 280.
City's freedom.—*Merchant of Venice,* iv, 1, 39.

13
Gnawing with my teeth my bonds in sunder,
I gain'd my freedom.
The Comedy of Errors. Act v, sc. 1, l. 249. [Antipholus of Ephesus]

14
I request you To give my poor host freedom.
Coriolanus. Act i, sc. 9, l. 86. [Coriolanus]

Give me freedom.—*Antony and Cleopatra,* i, 3, 57.

15
I have lived at honest freedom.
Cymbeline, iii, 3, 71. See under World.

Live in freedom.—*Henry VIII,* i, 2, 200.

Live free.—*All's Well that Ends Well,* ii, 1, 171.
Freedom lives hence.—*King Lear,* i, 1, 184.

1
I am called to be made free.
Cymbeline. Act v, sc. 4, l. 201. [Posthumus]
Make thee free.—*Antony and Cleopatra,* iv, 14, 81.
More free.—*As You Like It,* ii, 1, 4; *King John,* ii, 1, 453; *Othello,* iii, 1, 41; *The Winter's Tale,* ii, 3, 30.
Most free.—*Julius Cæsar,* ii, 1, 79; *Hamlet,* iii, 1, 14.
Very free.—*Twelfth Night,* iii, 4, 249.
Free for ever.—*Cymbeline,* v, 4, 11.

2
We 'll learn our freeness of a son-in-law.
Cymbeline. Act v, sc. 5, l. 421. [Cymbeline] The only use of "freeness."

3
Deliver him . . . ransomless and free.
I Henry IV. Act v, sc. 5, l. 27. [Prince] "Ransomless" is repeated in *Titus Andronicus,* i, 1, 274.
Blest and free.—*Timon of Athens,* iv, 3, 542.
Most generous and free.—*Hamlet,* iv, 7, 136.
Unswayable and free.—*Coriolanus,* v, 6, 26. The only use of "unswayable."
Well and free.—*Antony and Cleopatra,* ii, 5, 27.
Free and bounteous.—*Hamlet,* i, 3, 93; *Othello,* i, 3, 266.
Free and healthful.—*Antony and Cleopatra,* ii, 5, 38.
Free and merry.—*Othello,* iii, 3, 340.
Free and noble.—*Othello,* iii, 3, 199.
Free and open.—*Othello,* i, 3, 405.

4
What concerns his freedom unto me?
I Henry VI. Act v, sc. 3, l. 116. [Margaret]

5
Free from a stubborn opposite intent.
II Henry VI, iii, 2, 251. See under INTENTION.
Free from . . . blood-shedding.—*II Henry VI,* iv, 7, 108.
Free from . . . bondage.—*Julius Cæsar,* v, 5, 54.
Free from . . . hate.—*Richard II,* i, 1, 33.
Free from oppression.—*I Henry VI,* v, 3, 155.
Free from gross passion.—*Henry V,* ii, 2, 132.
Free from strife.—*Richard II,* v, 6, 27.
Free from vainness.—*Henry V,* v, Prol., 20.

6
As free as heart can wish or tongue can tell.
II Henry VI, iv, 7, 132. See under WIFE.
Go and be free again.—*I Henry VI,* v, 3, 59.
Free us from his slavery.—*Henry VIII,* ii, 2, 44.
I free you from 't.—*Henry VIII,* ii, 4, 157.
I 'll . . . free him.—*Timon of Athens,* i, 1, 103.
I will free myself.—*III Henry VI,* iii, 2, 180.

7
Come now, keep thine oath;
Now be a freeman.
Julius Cæsar. Act v, sc. 3, l. 40. [Cassius] The only use of "freeman."
So, I am free; yet would not so have been,
Durst I have done my will.
Julius Cæsar. Act v, sc. 3, l. 47. [Pindarus]
I was born free.—*Julius Cæsar,* i, 2, 97.

8
Biron: You are not free,
For the Lord's tokens on you do I see.
Princess of France: No, they are free that gave these tokens to us.
Love's Labour 's Lost. Act v, sc. 2, l. 422.

Yet am I not free.—*Sonnets,* cxxxiv.
Have I been ever free?—*Timon of Athens,* iii, 4, 81.
No man is free.—*The Winter's Tale,* i, 2, 251.
Let man go free.—*Henry V,* iii, 6, 44.

9
I had as lief have the foppery of freedom as the morality of imprisonment.
Measure for Measure. Act i, sc. 2, l. 137. [Lucio] The only use of "morality."

10
And now, dear maid, be you as free to us.
Measure for Measure. Act v, sc. 1, l. 393. [Duke]
Hold her free, I do beseech your honour.
Othello. Act iii, sc. 3, l. 255. [Iago]
Let them be free.—*Merchant of Venice,* iv, 1, 94.

11
Untainted, unexamined, free, at liberty.
Richard III. Act iii, sc. 6, l. 9. [Scrivener] The only use of "unexamined."
Free as is the wind.
Coriolanus. Act i, sc. 9, l. 89. [Cominius]
Thou shalt be as free As mountain winds.
The Tempest. Act i, sc. 2, l. 498. [Prospero]

12
Why, sir, I pray, are not the streets as free
For me as for you?
The Taming of the Shrew. Act i, sc. 2, l. 233. [Tranio]

13
I will be free, Even to the uttermost.
The Taming of the Shrew, iv, 3, 79. See under WORD.
I will be free.—*Twelfth Night,* iv, 1, 44.

14
I 'll free thee within two days for this.
The Tempest. Act i, sc. 2, l. 420. [Prospero]
I 'll set thee free for this.
The Tempest. Act i, sc. 2, l. 420. [Prospero]
Set Caliban and his companions free.
The Tempest. Act v, sc. 1, l. 252. [Prospero]
Set him free.—*I Henry VI,* iii, 3, 72; *III Henry VI,* iv, 5, 13; *All's Well that Ends Well,* iii, 4, 17.
Set me free.—*III Henry VI,* iv, 6, 16; *The Tempest,* Epil., 20; *Pericles,* iv, 6, 107.
Set the younger free.—*The Taming of the Shrew,* i, 2, 268.

15
Freedom, hey-day! hey-day, freedom! freedom, hey-day, freedom!
The Tempest. Act ii, sc. 2, l. 190. [Caliban]
Thou shalt have freedom.—*Tempest,* v, 1, 96.
Thou shalt have the air at freedom.—*The Tempest,* iv, 1, 266.
Thou shalt ere long be free.
The Tempest. Act v, sc. 1, l. 87. [Prospero]
Thou shalt be free.—*The Tempest,* v, 1, 241.
Be free, and fare thou well!
The Tempest. Act v, sc. 1, l. 318. [Prospero]

16
Shall I play my freedom at tray-trip?
Twelfth Night, ii, 5, 208. See under SERVILITY. The only use of "tray-trip" (a game at dice).

17
Steal thine own freedom and complain on theft.
Venus and Adonis, l. 160.

FRETTING

See also Annoyance, Vexation, Worry

1
Though you can fret me, yet you cannot play upon me.
Hamlet, iii, 2, 388. See PLAY, 1161:8.
I did but tell her she mistook her frets. . .
'Frets, call you these?' quoth she; 'I 'll fume with them.'
The Taming of the Shrew. Act ii, sc. 1, l. 150. [Hortensio]
Her fume needs no spurs.—*II Henry VI,* i, 3, 153. The only uses of "fume" in this sense.
Frets upon an instrument.—*The Rape of Lucrece,* l. 1140.
2
He frets like a gummed velvet.
I Henry IV. Act ii, sc. 2, l. 2. [Poins] The only use of "gummed."
3
He frets
That Lepidus . . . Should be deposed.
Antony and Cleopatra. Act iii, sc. 6, l. 27. [Cæsar]
4
You are so fretful, you cannot live long.
I Henry IV. Act iii, sc. 3, l. 13. [Bardolph]
Fretful corrosive.—*II Henry VI,* iii, 2, 404.
Fretful element.—*King Lear,* iii, 1, 4.
Fretful porpentine.—*Hamlet,* i, 5, 20. The only uses of "fretful."
5
He may well in fretting spend his gall.
I Henry VI. Act i, sc. 2, l. 16. [Reignier]
Lay fretting.—*Taming of the Shrew,* ii, 1, 330.
Fretting gust.—*III Henry VI,* ii, 6, 35.
Fretting waters.—*Measure for Measure,* iv, 3, 151. The only uses of "fretting."
6
Fret and bite his tongue.
II Henry VI. Act i, sc. 1, l. 230. [York]
Fret till your proud heart break.
Julius Cæsar. Act iv, sc. 3, l. 42. [Brutus]
Do not fret yourself too much in the action.
A Midsummer-Night's Dream. Act iv, sc. 1, l. 14. [Bottom]
Still he lours and frets.
Venus and Adonis, l. 75.
Let Henry fret.—*I Henry VI,* v, 2, 20.
Fret fetlock deep.—*Henry V,* iv, 7, 82.
Fret the clouds.—*Julius Cæsar,* ii, 1, 104.
Fret the string.—*Henry VIII,* iii, 2, 106.
7
You sleeping safe, they bring to you unrest.
Richard III. Act v, sc. 3, l. 320. [King Richard]
The more is my unrest.—*Romeo and Juliet,* i, 5, 122.
Rest in her unrest.—*Titus Andronicus,* iv, 2, 31.
Rest thy unrest.—*Richard III,* iv, 4, 29.
Repose . . . for their unrest.—*Titus Andronicus,* ii, 3, 8.
Woe, and unrest.—*Richard II,* ii, 4, 22.
Evermore unrest.—*Sonnets,* cxlvii.
Deep unrest.—*The Rape of Lucrece,* l. 1725. The only uses of "unrest."
8
Nay, look not big, nor stamp, nor stare, nor fret.
The Taming of the Shrew. Act iii, sc. 2, l. 230. [Petruchio]
Never fret.—*The Comedy of Errors,* ii, 1, 6.
Stamp, rave, and fret.—*III Henry VI,* i, 4, 91.
Struts and frets.—*Macbeth,* v, 5, 25.
Who chafes, who frets.—*Macbeth,* iv, 1, 91.
Resistance made him fret.—*Venus and Adonis,* l. 69.

FRIEND

9
My friends were poor, but honest.
All's Well that Ends Well. Act i, sc. 3, l. 201. [Helena]
Poor friend.—*A Midsummer-Night's Dream,* iii, 2, 216; *As You Like It,* ii, 7, 10; *All's Well that Ends Well,* ii, 2, 45.
All-disgraced friend.—*Antony and Cleopatra,* iii, 12, 22. The only use of "all-disgraced."
10
Though thou the waters warp,
Thy sting is not so sharp
As friend remember'd not.
As You Like It. Act ii, sc. 7, l. 187. [Amiens]
11
He that wants money, means and content is without three good friends.
As You Like It. Act iii, sc. 2, l. 25. [Corin]
12
There 's not a man I meet but doth salute me
As if I were their well-acquainted friend.
The Comedy of Errors. Act iv, sc. 3, l. 1. [Antipholus of Syracuse] The only use of "well-acquainted."
There is a fat friend at your master's house,
That kitchen'd me for you to-day at dinner.
The Comedy of Errors. Act v, sc. 1, l. 414. [Dromio of Syracuse] The only use of "kitchen'd."
13
Be sprightly, for you fall 'mongst friends.
Cymbeline. Act iii, sc. 6, l. 75. [Arviragus]
14
Those friends thou hast, and their adoption tried,
Grapple them to thy soul with hoops of steel;
But do not dull thy palm with entertainment
Of each new-hatch'd, unfledged comrade.
Hamlet. Act i, sc. 3, l. 62. [Polonius] The only use of "hoops of steel." "New-hatch'd" appears again in *Macbeth,* ii, 3, 64. "Unfledged" is used in *Cymbeline,* iii, 3, 27, and *The Winter's Tale,* i, 2, 78.
Keep thy friend Under thy own life's key.
All's Well that Ends Well. Act i, sc. 1, l. 75. [Countess]
Held thee dearly as his soul's redemption.
III Henry VI. Act ii, sc. 1, l. 102. [Edward]
15 Make friends with speed:
Never so few, and never yet more need.
II Henry IV. Act i, sc. 1, l. 214. [Northumberland] "Make friends" is repeated in *Measure for Measure,* i, 2, 185.
Come, I 'll be friends with thee, Jack.
II Henry IV. Act ii, sc. 4, l. 71. [Doll]
Reconcile your friends.—*Romeo and Juliet,* iii, 3, 151.
16
A friend i' the court is better than a penny in purse.
II Henry IV. Act v, sc. 1, l. 33. [Shallow] A quotation from *The Romaunt of the Rose*

(ll. 5541–2), translated from the French by Chaucer about 1365: "For friend in court aye better is Than peny in [his] purs, certis."

Blessed are they that have been my friends.
II Henry IV. Act v, sc. 3, l. 144. [Falstaff]

1
Thou art no friend to God or to the king.
I Henry VI. Act i, sc. 3, l. 25. [Gloucester]

Thou art . . . no friend of mine.—*I Henry VI*, v, 4, 9.

2
I'll find friends to wear my bleeding roses.
I Henry VI. Act ii, sc. 4, l. 72. [Somerset]

Esteem none friends but such as are his friends.
I Henry VI. Act iv, sc. 1, l. 5. [Gloucester]

3
Speak suddenly, my lords, are we all friends?
III Henry VI. Act iv, sc. 2, l. 4. [Warwick]

The bruit thereof will bring you many friends.
III Henry VI. Act iv, sc. 7, l. 64. [Gloucester] "Bruit" is used four times in the plays, as above, and in *Hamlet*, i, 2, 127; *Troilus and Cressida*, v, 9, 4; *Timon of Athens*, v, 1, 96.

4
We are advertised by our loving friends.
III Henry VI. Act v, sc. 3, l. 18. [King Edward]

Your very worshipful and loving friends.
Richard III. Act iii, sc. 7, l. 138. [Buckingham]

Loving friends.—*Richard II*, i, 4, 34; *Much Ado about Nothing*, i, 1, 285; *Titus Andronicus*, i, 1, 53; v, 3, 191.

Most loving friends.—*Richard III*, v, 2, 1.

5
Be to yourself As you would to your friend.
Henry VIII. Act i, sc. 1, l. 135. [Norfolk]

Make me no more ado, but all embrace him:
Be friends, for shame, my lords!
Henry VIII. Act i, sc. 3, l. 99. [King Henry]

Your . . . friends are infinite.—*Henry VIII*, iii, 1, 82.

6
You bear too stubborn and too strange a hand
Over your friend that loves you.
Julius Cæsar. Act i, sc. 2, l. 34. [Cassius]

A friend should bear a friend's infirmities.
Julius Cæsar. Act iv, sc. 3, l. 86. [Cassius]

Love, and be friends, as two such men should be.
Julius Cæsar. Act iv, sc. 3, l. 131. [Poet]

7
I shall beseech him to befriend himself.
Julius Cæsar. Act ii, sc. 4, l. 30. [Soothsayer]

Thou mayst befriend me.—*King John*, v, 6, 10.

Will you befriend me?—*Timon of Athens*, iii, 2, 64.

I will befriend thee.—*Titus Andronicus*, iii, 1, 16.

God befriend us.—*I Henry IV*, v, 1, 120.

8
We shall be blest
To do your pleasure and continue friends.
King John. Act iii, sc. 1, l. 251. [King Philip]

I did not think the king so stored with friends.
King John. Act v, sc. 4, l. 1. [Salisbury]

9
Nor never come in vizard to my friend.
Love's Labour's Lost. Act v, sc. 2, l. 404. [Biron]

10
At the twelvemonth's end
I'll change my black gown for a faithful friend.
Love's Labour's Lost. Act v, sc. 2, l. 843. [Maria]

Companion friends.—*Pericles*, v, 1, 238.
Courageous friends.—*Richard III*, v, 2, 14.
Powerful friends.—*Richard II*, ii, 2, 55.
Private friends.—*Coriolanus*, v, 3, 18; *Richard II*, iii, 3, 4.
Victorious friends.—*Richard III*, v, 5, 1.
Well-advised friend.—*Richard III*, iv, 4, 517.
Well-armed friends.—*King Lear*, iii, 7, 20. "Well arm'd" (unhyphenated) is repeated in *Romeo and Juliet*, i, 1, 216.

11
Certain friends that are both his and mine,
Whose loves I may not drop.
Macbeth. Act iii, sc. 1, l. 121. [Macbeth]

12
A friend! what friend? your name, I pray you, friend?
The Merchant of Venice. Act v, sc. 1, l. 27. [Lorenzo]

A friend of mine.—*Measure for Measure*, iii, 2, 44.

The friend of men.—*Measure for Measure*, iv, 2, 90.

Friend to truth.—*Henry VIII*, ii, 4, 84.

Friends of France.—*III Henry VI*, v, 4, 18.

13
I beseech you, be ruled by your well-willers.
The Merry Wives of Windsor, i, 1, 72. [Evans] The only use of "well-willers."

14
He speaks but for his friend.
The Merry Wives of Windsor. Act i, sc. 4, l. 120. [Mistress Quickly]

15
It stood upon the choice of friends.
A Midsummer-Night's Dream. Act i, sc. 1, l. 139. [Lysander]

Choice of friends.—*Much Ado about Nothing*, iv, 1, 201. See under Ability for full quotation.

To seek new friends and stranger companies.
A Midsummer-Night's Dream. Act i, sc. 1, l. 219. [Hermia]

Newer friend.—*Othello*, iii, 4, 181.

16
Give not this rotten orange to your friend.
Much Ado about Nothing. Act iv, sc. 1, l. 33. [Claudio]

I will never love that which my friend hates.
Much Ado about Nothing. Act v, sc. 2, l. 71. [Beatrice]

17
When wilt thou be the humble supplicant's friend,
And bring him where his suit may be obtain'd?
The Rape of Lucrece, l. 897. The only use of "supplicant." "Suppliant" occurs eight times.

18
My friend and I are one.
Sonnets. No. xlii.

Mine appetite I never more will grind
On newer proof, to try an older friend.
Sonnets. No. cx.

With friends possess'd.—*Sonnets,* xxix.

1
Thou 'rt too much my friend.
The Taming of the Shrew. Act i, sc. 2, l. 63. [Hortensio]

'Twixt such friends as we Few words suffice.
The Taming of the Shrew. Act i, sc. 2, l. 65. [Petruchio]

2
You cannot tell who 's your friend.
The Tempest. Act ii, sc. 2, l. 88. [Stephano]

3
I am wealthy in my friends.
Timon of Athens. Act ii, sc. 2, l. 193. [Timon]

4
Lose not so noble a friend on vain suppose.
Titus Andronicus. Act i, sc. 1, l. 440. [Tamora]

5
We must all be friends.
Titus Andronicus. Act i, sc. 1, l. 479. [Tamora]

6
For shame, be friends, and join for that you jar.
Titus Andronicus. Act ii, sc. 1, l. 103. [Aaron]

I must needs be friends with thee.
Love's Labour's Lost. Act v, sc. 2, l. 552. [Biron]

I would be friends with you and have your love.
The Merchant of Venice. Act i, sc. 3, l. 139. [Shylock]

You must put me in your heart for friend.
Hamlet. Act iv, sc. 7, l. 2. [King]

You must needs be friends with him.
Henry V. Act iv, sc. 8, l. 66. [King Henry]

I desire you that we may be friends.
The Merry Wives of Windsor. Act iii, sc. 1, l. 121. [Evans]

I pray you, make us friends; I will pursue the amity.
All's Well that Ends Well. Act ii, sc. 5, l. 14. [Lafeu] See also AMITY.

7
Purchase us thy lasting friends.
Titus Andronicus. Act ii, sc. 3, l. 275. [Saturninus]

Friends should associate friends in grief and woe.
Titus Andronicus. Act v, sc. 3, l. 169. [Lucius]

8
He leaves his friends to dignify them more.
The Two Gentlemen of Verona. Act i, sc. 1, l. 64. [Proteus]

Proteus: Your friends are well and have them much commended.
Valentine: And how do yours?
Proteus: I left them all in health.
The Two Gentlemen of Verona. Act ii, sc. 4, l. 123.

9
To wrong my friend, I shall be much forsworn.
The Two Gentlemen of Verona. Act ii, sc. 6, l. 3. [Proteus]

I to myself am dearer than a friend.
The Two Gentlemen of Verona. Act ii, sc. 6, l. 23. [Proteus]

In love Who respects friend?
The Two Gentlemen of Verona. Act v, sc. 4, l. 53. [Proteus]

10
'I am,' quoth he, 'expected of my friends.'
Venus and Adonis, l. 718.

After him she darts, as one on shore
Gazing upon a late-embarked friend.
Venus and Adonis, l. 818. The only use of "late-embarked."

Departing friend.—*II Henry IV,* i, 1, 103.

11
If it be ne'er so false, a true gentleman may swear it in behalf of his friend.
Winter's Tale. Act v, sc. 2, l. 175. [Clown]

II—True Friends

12
I am a poor friend of yours, that loves you.
All's Well that Ends Well. Act ii, sc. 2, l. 45. [Countess]

Ever a friend whose thoughts more truly labour
To recompense your love.
All's Well that Ends Well. Act iv, sc. 4, l. 17. [Helena]

13
Some friends that will
Sweep your way for you.
Antony and Cleopatra. Act iii, sc. 11, l. 16. [Antony]

14
March from hence,
To help our fielded friends!
Coriolanus. Act i, sc. 4, l. 11. [Marcius] The only use of "fielded."

My friends of noble touch.
Coriolanus. Act iv, sc. 1, l. 49. [Coriolanus]

A noble friend of mine.
Cymbeline. Act i, sc. 4, l. 32. [Philario]

Noble friend.—*II Henry IV,* i, 3, 2, and nine times in later plays.

15
Thy general is my lover: I have been
The book of his good acts, whence men have read
His fame unparallel'd, haply amplified;
For I have ever verified my friends,
Of whom he 's chief.
Coriolanus. Act v, sc. 2, l. 14. [Menenius] The only use of "amplified."

Chiefest friend.—*III Henry VI,* iv, 3, 11.

16
My excellent good friends! . . . Good lads, how do ye both?
Hamlet. Act ii, sc. 2, l. 228. [Hamlet]

Since my dear soul was mistress of her choice
And could of men distinguish, her election
Hath seal'd thee for herself.
Hamlet. Act iii, sc. 2, l. 68. [Hamlet]

To his good friends thus wide I'll ope my arms;
And like the kind life-rendering pelican,
Repast them with my blood.
Hamlet. Act iv, sc. 5, l. 145. [Laertes] The only use of "life-rendering."

You are always my good friend.
Henry VIII. Act v, sc. 3, l. 59. [Cranmer]

I count myself in nothing else so happy
As in a soul remembering my good friends.
Richard II. Act ii, sc. 3, l. 46. [Bolingbroke]
He 's a good friend of mine.
Love's Labour 's Lost. Act iv, sc. 1, l. 54. [Princess of France]
My familiar, I do assure ye, very good friend.
Love's Labour 's Lost. Act v, sc. 1, l. 101. [Armado] "Good friend" is repeated seventeen times in later plays.

1
Here is a dear, a true industrious friend.
I Henry IV. Act i, sc. 1, l. 62. [King Henry]
But if the while I think on thee, dear friend,
All losses are restored and sorrows end.
Sonnets. No. xxx.
Dear friend.—*The Comedy of Errors,* v, 1, 50, and nineteen times in later plays.

2
Our friends true and constant.
I Henry IV. Act ii, sc. 3, l. 13. [Hotspur]
True friend.—*The Two Gentlemen of Verona,* v, 4, 53; *The Merchant of Venice,* iii, 2, 310.
Well-deserving friend.—*I Henry IV.* Act iii, sc. 1, l. 138. [Hotspur] "Well-deserving" is used twice more in the plays: *Richard II,* ii, 1, 194; *The Merchant of Venice,* iv, 1, 239. "Well-deserved" is used once: *As You Like It,* v, 4, 196.

3
We were the first and dearest of your friends.
I Henry IV. Act v, sc. 1, l. 33. [Worcester]
Both he and they and you, yea, every man
Shall be my friend again and I 'll be his.
I Henry IV. Act v, sc. 1, l. 107. [King Henry]

4
I have done the part of a careful friend and a true subject.
II Henry IV. Act ii, sc. 4, l. 348. [Falstaff]
Thou shalt prove a shelter to thy friends.
II Henry IV. Act iv, sc. 4, l. 42. [King Henry]

5
Gather'd flocks of friends.
III Henry VI. Act ii, sc. 1, l. 112. [Warwick]
Best friend.—*III Henry VI,* ii, 2, 54, and six times in later plays.
Our trusty friend, unless I be deceived.
III Henry VI. Act iv, sc. 7, l. 41. [Gloucester]
Unfeigned friend.—*III Henry VI,* iii, 3, 202.

6 I have true-hearted friends,
Not mutinous in peace, yet bold in war.
III Henry VI. Act iv, sc. 8, l. 9. [Warwick]
I swear he is true-hearted.—*Henry VIII,* v, 1, 154.
Noble and true-hearted.—*King Lear,* i, 2, 126. The only uses of "true-hearted."

7
By that you love the dearest in this world,
As you wish Christian peace to souls departed,
Stand these poor people's friend.
Henry VIII. Act iv, sc. 2, l. 155. [Katharine]
There 's a trim rabble let in: are all these
Your faithful friends o' the suburbs?
Henry VIII. Act v, sc. 4, l. 75. [Lord Chamberlain]

Our old and faithful friend, we are glad to see you.
Measure for Measure. Act v, sc. 1, l. 2. [Duke]
Faithful friends.—*Titus Andronicus,* v, 1, 1; *Love's Labour 's Lost.* v, 2, 843.

8
Friends am I with you all and love you all.
Julius Cæsar. Act iii, sc. 1, l. 220. [Antony]
He was my friend, faithful and just to me.
Julius Cæsar. Act iii, sc. 2, l. 90. [Antony]
O, coward that I am, to live so long,
To see my best friend ta'en before my face!
Julius Cæsar. Act v, sc. 3, l. 34. [Cassius]

9
Remember him hereafter as my honourable friend.
King Lear. Act i, sc. 1, l. 28. [Gloucester]
Friends of my soul.—*King Lear,* v, 3, 319.

10
She is pretty, and honest, and gentle; and one that is your friend.
The Merry Wives of Windsor. Act i, sc. 4, l. 148. [Mistress Quickly]
Gentle friend.—*Richard III,* iii, 7, 247, and eight times in later plays.

11
I have professed me thy friend and I confess me knit to thy deserving with cables of perdurable toughness.
Othello. Act i, sc. 3, l. 341. [Iago] The only use of "toughness."
Perdurable shame.—*Henry V,* iv, 5, 7. The only uses of "perdurable." "Perdurably" occurs once, in *Measure for Measure,* iii, 1, 115.

12
I rather do beseech you pardon me,
Who, earnest in the service of my God,
Neglect the visitation of my friends.
Richard III. Act iii, sc. 7, l. 105. [Gloucester]
Your very worshipful and loving friends.
Richard III. Act iii, sc. 7, l. 138. [Buckingham] "Loving friends" is repeated in *Richard II,* i, 4, 34.
I 'll muster up my friends, and meet your grace
Where and what time your majesty shall please.
Richard III. Act iv, sc. 4, l. 489. [Stanley]
Your friends are up and buckle on their armour.
Richard III. Act v, sc. 3, l. 211. [Ratcliff]

13
This gentleman, the prince's near ally,
My very friend, hath got his mortal hurt
In my behalf.
Romeo and Juliet. Act iii, sc. 1, l. 114. [Romeo] The only use of "ally."
My friend profess'd.—*Romeo and Juliet,* iii, 3, 50.

14
My best beloved and approved friend.
The Taming of the Shrew. Act i, sc. 2, l. 3. [Petruchio] The only use of "best beloved."
The best friend I had!—*Romeo and Juliet,* iii, 2, 61. "Best friend" is used seven times.
Brave friend!—*Macbeth,* i, 2, 5.
Great friends.—*II Henry VI,* i, 1, 150; *II Henry IV,* iii, 1, 58; *All 's Well that Ends Well,* i, 3, 45.
Greatest friend.—*III Henry VI,* iii, 3, 45.

Honest friend.—*The Comedy of Errors,* v, 1, 19, and six times in later plays.
Honour'd friend.—*The Winter's Tale,* iv, 4, 504; v, 1, 113.
Known friend.—*Henry VIII,* iii, 1, 85.
Sweet friend.—*The Taming of the Shrew,* i, 2, 48, and six times in later plays.
Sweet'st friend.—*Sonnets,* cxxxiii.
True-telling friend.—*Sonnets,* lxxxiii. The only use of "true-telling."
Vowed friend.—*III Henry VI,* iii, 3, 50.
Worthy friends.—*Macbeth,* iii, 4, 53; *Timon of Athens,* iii, 6, 66.

1
I am not of that feather to shake off
My friend when he must need me.
Timon of Athens. Act i, sc. 1, l. 100. [Timon]

What better or properer can we call our own than the riches of our friends?
Timon of Athens. Act i, sc. 2, l. 107. [Timon] "Properer" is repeated in *As You Like It,* iii, 5, 51, and in *Romeo and Juliet,* ii, 4, 217, both times as "properer man."

Methinks, I could deal kingdoms to my friends,
And ne'er be weary.
Timon of Athens. Act i, sc. 2, l. 226. [Timon]

My very exquisite friend.—*Timon of Athens,* iii, 2, 32.

2
Friends, that have been thus forward in my right.
Titus Andronicus. Act i, sc. 1, l. 56. [Saturninus]

3
Pray you, bid
These unknown friends to 's welcome; for it is
A way to make us better friends, more known.
Winter's Tale. Act iv, sc. 4, l. 64. [Shepherd]

Nameless friend.—*The Two Gentlemen of Verona,* ii, 1, 111.
Friends unknown.—*Winter's Tale,* iv, 4, 395.

4
Your honour not o'erthrown by your desires,
I am friend to them and you.
Winter's Tale. Act v, sc. 1, l. 230. [Leontes]

III—False Friends

5
Left and abandon'd of his velvet friends.
As You Like It. Act ii, sc. 1, l. 50. [First Lord]

6
I hope you know that we
Must not continue friends.
Cymbeline. Act ii, sc. 4, l. 48. [Posthumus]

7
And all my friends, which thou must make thy friends,
Have but their stings and teeth newly ta'en out.
II Henry IV. Act iv, sc. 5, l. 205. [King Henry]

8
It is known we were but hollow friends.
II Henry VI. Act iii, sc. 2, l. 66. [Queen Margaret]

I rather wish you foes than hollow friends.
III Henry VI. Act iv, sc. 1, l. 139. [King Edward]

Doubtful hollow-hearted friends.
Richard III. Act iv, sc. 4, l. 435. [Ratcliff] The only use of "hollow-hearted."

9
But a feigned friend to our proceedings.
III Henry VI. Act iv, sc. 2, l. 11. [Warwick]

10
Will you be prick'd in number of our friends;
Or shall we on, and not depend on you?
Julius Cæsar. Act iii, sc. 1, l. 216. [Cassius]

Thou hast described A hot friend cooling.
Julius Cæsar. Act iv, sc. 2, l. 18. [Brutus]

11
The little number of our doubtful friends.
King John. Act v, sc. 1, l. 36. [Bastard]

12
Or were he not my dear friend, this desire
Might have excuse to work upon his wife.
The Rape of Lucrece, l. 234.

13
When I have most need to employ a friend,
And most assured that he is a friend,
Deep, hollow, treacherous, and full of guile,
Be he unto me! this do I beg of God.
Richard III. Act ii, sc. 1, l. 36. [Buckingham]

Gloucester: God keep you from them, and from such false friends!
Prince of Wales: God keep me from false friends! but they were none.
Richard III. Act iii, sc. 1, l. 15. The only uses of "false friends."

To their lives bad friends were contrary.
Richard III. Act iv, sc. 4, l. 216. [Queen Elizabeth]

Some light-foot friend.—*Richard III,* iv, 4, 440. The only use of "light-foot."

14
Stanley: No, my good lord, my friends are in the north.
King Richard: Cold friends to Richard: what do they in the north,
When they should serve their sovereign in the west?
Richard III. Act iv, sc. 4, l. 484.

What thinkest thou, will our friends prove all true?
Richard III. Act v, sc. 3, l. 213. [King Richard]

15
For these my present friends, as they are to me nothing, so in nothing bless them, and to nothing are they welcome.
Timon of Athens. Act iii, sc. 6, l. 93. [Timon]

You knot of mouth-friends! smoke and lukewarm water
Is your perfection.
Timon of Athens. Act iii, sc. 6, l. 99. [Timon] The only use of "mouth-friends." "Luke-warm" appears again in *III Henry VI,* i, 2, 34.

Who would be so mock'd with glory? or to live
But in a dream of friendship?
To have his pomp and all what state compounds
But only painted, like his varnish'd friends?
Timon of Athens. Act iv, sc. 2, l. 33. [Flavius]

What viler thing upon the earth than friends

Who can bring noblest minds to basest ends!

Timon of Athens. Act iv, sc. 3, l. 470. [Flavius]

1
Thou friend of an ill fashion! . . .
Thou common friend, that 's without faith or love,
For such is a friend now.

The Two Gentlemen of Verona. Act v, sc. 4, l. 61. [Valentine]

IV—Friends and Adversity

2
My love and fear glued many friends to thee;
And, now I fall, thy tough commixture melts.

III Henry VI. Act ii, sc. 6, l. 5. [Clifford] "Glued" is used once again in *Titus Andronicus,* ii, 1, 41. "Glue" appears twice: *III Henry VI,* v, 2, 38; *King John,* iii, 4, 65. "Commixture" is repeated in *Love's Labour's Lost,* v, 2, 296.

3
Those you make friends
And give your hearts to, when they once perceive
The least rub in your fortunes, fall away
Like water from ye, never found again
But where they mean to sink ye.

Henry VIII. Act ii, sc. 1, l. 127. [Buckingham]

4
Every one that flatters thee
Is no friend in misery.
Words are easy, like the wind;
Faithful friends are hard to find:
Every man will be thy friend
While thou hast wherewith to spend;
But if store of crowns be scant,
No man will supply thy want.

The Passionate Pilgrim, l. 403.

5
Now shall he try his friends that flatter'd him.

Richard II. Act ii, sc. 2, l. 85. [York]

6
When Fortune in her shift and change of mood
Spurns down her late beloved, all his dependants
Which labour'd after him to the mountain's top
Even on their knees and hands, let him slip down,
Not one accompanying his declining foot.

Timon of Athens. Act i, sc. 1, l. 84. [Poet] The only use of "accompanying."

O, no doubt, my good friends, but the gods themselves have provided that I shall have much help from you: how had you been my friends else?

Timon of Athens. Act i, sc. 2, l. 91. [Timon]

What need we have any friends, if we should ne'er have need of 'em? they were the most needless creatures living, should we ne'er have use for 'em, and would most resemble sweet instruments hung up in cases that keep their sounds to themselves.

Timon of Athens. Act i, sc. 2, l. 99. [Timon]

7
In some sort, these wants of mine are crown'd,
That I account them blessings; for by these
Shall I try friends.

Timon of Athens. Act ii, sc. 2, l. 190. [Timon]

First Servant: Such a house broke!
So noble a master fall'n! All gone! and not
One friend to take his fortune by the arm
And go along with him!
Second Servant: As we do turn our backs
From our companion thrown into his grave,
So his familiars to his buried fortunes
Slink all away, leave their false vows with him,
Like empty purses pick'd; and his poor self,
A dedicated beggar to the air,
With his disease of all-shunn'd poverty,
Walks, like contempt, alone.

Timon of Athens. Act iv, sc. 2, l. 5. The only use of "all-shunn'd."

Your friends fall'n off,
Whose thankless natures—O abhorred spirits!—
Not all the whips of heaven are large enough.

Timon of Athens. Act v, sc. 1, l. 62. [Poet]

V—Friends and Enemies

8
Clown: I am out o' friends, madam; and I hope to have friends for my wife's sake.
Countess: Such friends are thine enemies.
Clown: You 're shallow, madam, in great friends; for the knaves come to do that for me which I am aweary of. He that ears my land spares my team and gives me leave to in the crop; if I be his cuckold, he 's my drudge: he that comforts my wife is the cherisher of my flesh and blood; he that cherisheth my flesh and blood loves my flesh and blood; he that loves my flesh and blood is my friend: ergo, he that kisses my wife is my friend.

All's Well that Ends Well. Act i, sc. 3, l. 42. The only use of "cherisher."

9
You have been a scourge to her enemies, you have been a rod to her friends.

Coriolanus. Act ii, sc. 3, l. 98. [Citizen]

We have as many friends as enemies.

Coriolanus. Act iii, sc. 1, l. 232. [Cominius]

Third Servant: He has as many friends as enemies; which friends, sir, as it were, durst not . . . show themselves, as we term it, his friends whilst he 's in directitude.
First Servant: Directitude! what 's that?
Third Servant: But when they shall see, sir, his crest up again, and the man in blood, they will out of their burrows, like conies after rain, and revel all with him.

Coriolanus. Act iv, sc. 5, l. 220. The only use of "directitude."

More a friend than e'er an enemy.

Coriolanus. Act iv, sc. 5, l. 152. [Aufidius]

10
Who dares not stand his foe, I 'll be his friend,
For if he 'll do as he is made to do,
I know he 'll quickly fly my friendship too.

Cymbeline. Act v, sc. 3, l. 60. [Posthumus]

For who not needs shall never lack a friend,
And who in want a hollow friend doth try,
Directly seasons him his enemy.
Hamlet. Act iii, sc. 2, l. 217. [Player King]

1
'Tis like you would not feast him like a friend;
And 'tis well seen he found an enemy.
II Henry VI. Act iii, sc. 2, l. 184. [Warwick]

His foes are so enrooted with his friends
That, plucking to unfix an enemy,
He doth unfasten so and shake a friend.
II Henry IV. Act iv, sc. 1, l. 207. [Archbishop of York] The only use of "enrooted" and "unfasten."

2
An thou wilt be friends, be friends: an thou wilt not, why, then, be enemies.
Henry V. Act ii, sc. 1, l. 107. [Bardolph]

3
Now the battle 's ended,
If friend or foe, let him be gently used.
III Henry VI. Act ii, sc. 6, l. 44. [Edward]

Come to me, friend or foe.
III Henry VI. Act v, sc. 2, l. 5. [Warwick]

4
Which of your friends
Have I not strove to love, although I knew
He were mine enemy? what friend of mine
That had to him derived your anger, did I
Continue in my liking?
Henry VIII. Act ii, sc. 4, l. 29. [Queen Katharine]

5
Give him all kindness: I had rather have
Such men my friends than enemies.
Julius Cæsar. Act v, sc. 4, l. 28. [Antony]

All friends shall taste
The wages of their virtue, and all foes
The cup of their deservings.
King Lear. Act v, sc. 3, l. 302. [Kent]

6
Those
That would make good of bad, and friends of foes!
Macbeth. Act ii, sc. 4, l. 40. [Old Man]

7
I have engaged myself to a dear friend,
Engaged my friend to his mere enemy,
To feed my means.
The Merchant of Venice. Act iii, sc. 2, l. 264. [Bassanio]

I will not be your friend nor enemy.
The Merry Wives of Windsor. Act iii, sc. 4, l. 93. [Mrs. Page]

Benedick: We 'll be friends first.
Beatrice: You dare easier be friends with me than fight with mine enemy.
Much Ado about Nothing. Act iv, sc. 1, l. 299.

8
Friends all but now, even now,
In quarter, and in terms like bride and groom
Devesting them for bed; and then, but now—
As if some planet had unwitted men—
Swords out, and tilting one at other's breast,
In opposition bloody.
Othello. Act ii, sc. 3, l. 179. [Iago]. The only use of "devesting" and "unwitted."

Friends now fast sworn,
Whose double bosoms seem to wear one heart,
Whose hours, whose bed, whose meal, and exercise,
Are still together, who twin, as 'twere, in love
Unseparable, shall within this hour,
On a dissension of a doit, break out
To bitterest enmity: so, fellest foes,
Whose passions and whose plots have broke their sleep
To take the one the other, by some chance,
Some trick not worth an egg, shall grow dear friends
And interjoin their issues.
Coriolanus. Act iv, sc. 4, l. 12. [Coriolanus] The only use of "interjoin."

9
He that is thy friend indeed,
He will help thee in thy need:
If thou sorrow, he will weep;
If thou wake, he cannot sleep;
Thus of every grief in heart
He with thee doth bear a part.
These are certain signs to know
Faithful friend from flattering foe.
The Passionate Pilgrim, l. 423.

10
Let him have time to see his friends his foes.
The Rape of Lucrece, l. 988.

Myself, thy friend, will kill myself, thy foe.
The Rape of Lucrece, l. 1196.

11
Nor friends nor foes, to me welcome you are.
Richard II. Act ii, sc. 3, l. 170. [York]

Thy friends are fled to wait upon thy foes.
Richard II, ii, 4, 23. See under GLORY.

12
A weeder-out of his proud adversaries,
A liberal rewarder of his friends.
Richard III. Act i, sc. 3, l. 123. [Gloucester] The only use of "weeder-out."

Thy friends suspect for traitors while thou livest,
And take deep traitors for thy dearest friends!
Richard III. Act i, sc. 3, l. 223. [Queen Margaret]

13
Timon: You had rather be at a breakfast of enemies than a dinner of friends.
Alcibiades: So they were bleeding-new, my lord, there 's no meat like 'em.
Timon of Athens. Act i, sc. 2, l. 78. The only use of "bleeding-new."

Happier is he that has no friend to feed
Than such that do e'en enemies exceed.
Timon of Athens. Act i, sc. 2, l. 209. [Flavius]

14
Set deadly enmity between two friends.
Titus Andronicus. Act v, sc. 1, l. 131. [Aaron]

Who drown'd their enmity in my true tears,
And oped their arms to embrace me as a friend.
Titus Andronicus. Act v, sc. 3, l. 107. [Lucius]

15
To-morrow do I meet thee, fell as death;
To-night all friends.
Troilus and Cressida. Act iv, sc. 5, l. 269. [Achilles]

1
Thy friend, as thou usest him, and thy sworn enemy.
Twelfth Night. Act iii, sc. 4, l. 186. [Sir Toby]
Now my sworn friend, and then mine enemy.
The Winter's Tale, i, 2, 167. See under SON.
2
Duke: How dost thou, my good fellow?
Clown: Truly, sir, the better for my foes and the worse for my friends.
Duke: Just the contrary; the better for thy friends.
Clown: No, sir, the worse.
Duke: How can that be?
Clown: Marry, sir, they praise me and make an ass of me; now my foes tell me plainly I am an ass: so that by my foes, sir, I profit in the knowledge of myself and by my friends I am abused: so that, conclusions to be as kisses, if your four negatives make your two affirmatives, why then, the worst for my friends and the better for my foes.
Twelfth Night. Act v, sc. 1, l. 11. The only use of "affirmatives." "Negative" is repeated in *The Winter's Tale,* i, 2, 274.
3
Valentine: My friends,—
First Outlaw: That 's not so, sir: we are your enemies.
Two Gentlemen of Verona. Act iv, sc. 1, l. 7.
O time most accurst,
'Mongst all foes that a friend should be the worst!
The Two Gentlemen of Verona. Act v, sc. 4, l. 71. [Valentine]

VI—Friends: Their Loss

4
O, good my lord, you have lost a friend indeed.
II Henry IV. Act v, sc. 2, l. 27. [Humphrey]
Will leave us never an understanding friend.
Henry VIII. Prologue, l. 22.
5
Alas, I then have chid away my friend!
He hath a stern look, but a gentle heart.
King John. Act iv, sc. 1, l. 87. [Arthur]
To wail friends lost
Is not by much so wholesome-profitable
As to rejoice at friends but newly found.
Love's Labour 's Lost. Act v, sc. 2, l. 759. [King Ferdinand] The only use of "wholesome-profitable."
6
Repent but you that you shall lose your friend.
The Merchant of Venice. Act iv, sc. 1, l. 278. [Antonio]
7
All thy friends are lapp'd in lead.
The Passionate Pilgrim, l. 396.
My friend is dead.—*Othello,* iii, 3, 474.
Now his friends are dead.—*Timon of Athens,* iii, 3, 37.
8
Here friend by friend in bloody channel lies,
And friend to friend gives unadvised wounds.
The Rape of Lucrece, l. 1487.
Slaughter'd friends.—*III Henry VI,* v, 4, 15.
9
Feeling so the loss,
I cannot choose but ever weep the friend.
Romeo and Juliet. Act iii, sc. 5, l. 77. [Juliet]
Then can I drown an eye, unused to flow,
For precious friends hid in death's dateless night.
Sonnets. No. xxx.
10
I have heard you say
That we shall see and know our friends in heaven.
King John. Act iii, sc. 4, l. 76. [Constance]

VII—Friendlessness

11
I am out o' friends.
All's Well that Ends Well. Act i, sc. 3, l. 42. [Clown]
I shall do my friends no wrong, for I have none to lament me.
As You Like It. Act i, sc. 2, l. 201. [Orlando]
12
What shalt thou expect,
To be depender on a thing that leans,
Who cannot be new built, nor has no friends,
So much as but to prop him?
Cymbeline. Act i, sc. 5, l. 57. [Queen] The only use of "depender."
13
Friend hast thou none.
Measure for Measure. Act iii, sc. 1, l. 28. [Duke]
14
We are barren and bereft of friends.
Richard II. Act iii, sc. 3, l. 84. [King Richard]
Have I no friend will rid me of this living fear?
Richard II. Act v, sc. 4, l. 2. [Exton]
He hath no friends but who are friends for fear.
Richard III. Act v, sc. 2, l. 20. [Blount]
15
Canst thou the conscience lack
To think I shall lack friends?
Timon of Athens. Act ii, sc. 2, l. 184. [Timon]
16
Not a friend, not a friend greet
My poor corpse, where my bones shall be thrown.
Twelfth Night. Act ii, sc. 4, l. 62. [Clown]
17
Now I dare not say I have one friend alive.
The Two Gentlemen of Verona. Act v, sc. 4, l. 65. [Valentine]

FRIENDSHIP

See also Amity

18
The band that seems to tie their friendship together will be the very strangler of their amity.
Antony and Cleopatra. Act ii, sc. 6, l. 129. [Enobarbus] The only use of "strangler."
19
Most friendship is feigning, most loving mere folly.
As You Like It. Act ii, sc. 7, l. 181. [Amiens]

Such childish friendliness.—*Coriolanus,* ii, 3, 183. The only use of "friendliness," in a scene probably not by Shakespeare.

1
And what so poor a man as Hamlet is
May do, to express his love and friending to you,
God willing, shall not lack.
Hamlet. Act i, sc. 5, l. 185. [Hamlet] The only use of "friending."

2
Falstaff: Hal, if thou see me down in the battle and bestride me, so; 'tis a point of friendship.
Prince Henry: Nothing but a colossus can do thee that friendship.
I Henry IV. Act v, sc. 1, l. 121. "Colossus" is repeated in *Julius Cæsar,* i, 2, 136. "Colossus-wise" occurs in *Troilus and Cressida,* v, 5, 9.

3
Friendship shall combine, and brotherhood.
Henry V. Act ii, sc. 1, l. 114. [Pistol]
There is flattery in friendship.
Henry V. Act iii, sc. 7, l. 124. [Constable of France] Quoted as a proverb.

4
Die and be damn'd! and figo for thy friendship!
Henry V. Act iii, sc. 6, l. 59. [Pistol]
Figo for thee then.—*Henry V,* iv, 1, 60. The only play in which this expression appears.

5
Join in friendship, as your lords have done.
I Henry VI. Act iii, sc. 1, l. 145. [King Henry]
In friendship.—*All's Well that Ends Well,* i, 2, 25; *As You Like It,* i, 2, 273; *Antony and Cleopatra,* ii, 2, 115.
In the beaten way of friendship.—*Hamlet,* ii, 2, 277.
In terms of friendship.—*Julius Cæsar,* iii, 1, 203.

6
Thy friendship makes us fresh.
I Henry VI. Act iii, sc. 3, l. 86. [Charles]
They are so link'd in friendship.
III Henry VI. Act iv, sc. 1, l. 116. [Post]

7
Gracious my lord, hard by here is a hovel;
Some friendship will it lend you 'gainst the tempest.
King Lear. Act iii, sc. 2, l. 61. [Kent]

8 When did friendship take
A breed for barren metal of his friend?
The Merchant of Venice. Act i, sc. 3, l. 134. [Antonio]

9
I desire you in friendship.
The Merry Wives of Windsor. Act iii, sc. 1, l. 89. [Evans]
I extend this friendship.—*The Merchant of Venice,* i, 3, 169.
Equal friendship.—*Henry VIII,* ii, 4, 18.
Fair friendship.—*Love's Labour's Lost,* ii, 1, 141.
Sweet friendship.—*The Rape of Lucrece,* l. 569.
School-days' friendship.—*Midsummer-Night's Dream,* iii, 2, 202.

10
Friendship is constant in all other things
Save in the office and affairs of love.
Much Ado about Nothing. Act ii, sc. 1, l. 182. [Claudio]
Benedick: Is there any way to show such friendship?
Beatrice: A very even way, but no such friend.
Much Ado about Nothing. Act iv, sc. 1, l. 265.
Show me friendship.—*Romeo and Juliet,* v, 3, 41.

11
If I do vow a friendship, I 'll perform it
To the last article.
Othello. Act iii, sc. 3, l. 21. [Desdemona]

12
He little thought of this divided friendship.
Richard III. Act i, sc. 4, l. 244. [Clarence]
You have no cause to hold my friendship doubtful.
Richard III, iv, 4, 493. See FIDELITY, 534:2.

13
What friendship may I do thee?
Timon of Athens, iv, 3, 70. See under OPINION.
Promise me friendship.—*Timon of Athens,* iv, 3, 72.

14
Friendship 's full of dregs.
Timon of Athens. Act i, sc. 2, l. 239. [Apemantus]
Friendship falls off.—*King Lear,* i, 2, 116.
Let molten coin be thy damnation,
Thou disease of a friend, and not himself!
Has friendship such a faint and milky heart,
It turns in less than two nights?
Timon of Athens. Act iii, sc. 1, l. 56. [Flaminius] "Molten" is repeated in *I Henry IV,* v, 3, 34, and in *King Lear,* iv, 7, 48, both times as "Molten lead."
Bare friendship.—*Timon of Athens,* iii, 1, 45.

15
Nothing but himself which looks like man
Is friendly with him.
Timon of Athens. Act v, sc. 1, l. 122. [Flavius]
It is not friendly.
A Midsummer-Night's Dream. Act iii, sc. 2, l. 217. [Helena]
I will seem friendly.—*Winter's Tale,* i, 2, 350.
Very friendly.—*Titus Andronicus,* iv, 2, 40.

16
My gracious lord, that which I would discover
The law of friendship bids me to conceal.
The Two Gentlemen of Verona. Act iii, sc. 1, l. 4. [Proteus]

17
Nay, I 'll be sworn, I have sat in the stocks for puddings he hath stolen, otherwise he had been executed; I have stood on the pillory for geese he hath killed, otherwise he had suffer'd for 't.
The Two Gentlemen of Verona. Act iv, sc. 4, l. 33. [Launce]
When your head did but ache,
I knit my handkercher about your brows, . . .
And with my hand at midnight held your head,
And like the watchful minutes to the hour,
Still and anon cheer'd up the heavy time.
King John. Act iv, sc. 1, l. 41. [Arthur]

1
To mingle friendship far is mingling bloods.
Winter's Tale, i, 2, 109. See under DISTRUST.
My profit therein the heaping friendships.
Winter's Tale. Act iv, sc. 2, l. 21. [Polixenes]

FRIGHT, see Fear

FROST

2
Frosty, but kindly.
As You Like It, ii, 3, 53. See under AGE.
Frosty in desire.—*Venus and Adonis,* l. 36.
Seem frosty.—*Henry V,* iii, 5, 22. "Frosty" is used nine times.
Frosty-spirited.—*I Henry IV,* ii, 3, 21. The only use of the phrase.
3
Frost itself as actively doth burn.
Hamlet. Act iii, sc. 4, l. 87. [Hamlet]
4
The third day comes a frost, a killing frost.
Henry VIII, iii, 2, 355. See under GREATNESS.
5 An envious sneaping frost
That bites the first-born infants of the spring.
Love's Labour's Lost. Act i, sc. 1, l. 100. [King Ferdinand] "Sneaping" (nipping) is repeated in *Winter's Tale,* i, 2, 13: "Sneaping winds." "Sneap" occurs in *II Henry IV,* ii, 1, 133.
Frosts do bite the meads.—*The Taming of the Shrew,* v, 2, 139.
Frosts will bite them.—*II Henry IV,* i, 3, 41.
6 Hoary-headed frosts
Fall in the fresh lap of the crimson rose.
A Midsummer-Night's Dream. Act ii, sc. 1, l. 107. [Titania] The only use of "hoary-headed."
Frosts and fasts.—*Love's Labour's Lost,* v, 2, 811.
Full of frost.—*Much Ado about Nothing,* v, 4, 42.
7
Like little frosts that sometimes threat the spring.
The Rape of Lucrece, l. 331.
Untimely frost.—*Romeo and Juliet,* iv, 5, 28.
Fear's frost.—*The Rape of Lucrece,* l. 355.

FROWN

See also Brow

8
I do frown on thee with all my heart.
As You Like It, iii, 5, 15. See under EYE.
Frowns on you.—*The Two Gentlemen of Verona,* ii, 4, 3.
9
Her frown might kill me.
As You Like It. Act iv, sc. 1, l. 110. [Orlando]
10
Look strange and frown.
The Comedy of Errors. Act ii, sc. 2, l. 112. [Adriana]
How you can frown.—*Coriolanus,* iii, 2, 67.
Look back in frown.—*Cymbeline,* v, 3, 28.
11
Fear no more the frown o' the great.
Cymbeline, iv, 2, 264. See under DEATH.
Princes' frowns.—*Pericles,* i, 2, 53.

12
What, look'd he frowningly?
Hamlet. Act i, sc. 2, l. 231. [Hamlet] The only use of "frowningly."
So frown'd he once, when, in an angry parle,
He smote the sledded Polacks on the ice.
Hamlet. Act i, sc. 1, l. 62. [Horatio] The only use of "sledded."
When he frown'd, it was against the French
And not against his friends.
Richard II. Act ii, sc. 1, l. 178. [York]
Frown'd in Greece.—*Coriolanus,* iii, 1, 107.
Frown'd upon their enmity.—*Richard III,* v, 5, 21.
13
Frowning at the favours of the world.
II Henry VI, i, 2, 4. See under BROW.
He goes hence frowning.
Cymbeline. Act iii, sc. 5, l. 18. [Queen]
He parted frowning from me, as if ruin
Leap'd from his eyes.
Henry VIII, iii, 2, 205. See under ANGER.
Pass away frowning.—*Henry VIII,* i, 4, 33.
A better bad habit of frowning.
The Merchant of Venice. Act i, sc. 2, l. 64. [Portia]
Frowning brow to brow.—*Richard II,* i, 1, 16.
14
Shield thee from Warwick's frown.
III Henry VI. Act iv, sc. 5, l. 28. [King Edward]
Wherefore frowns he thus?
'Tis his aspect of terror.
Henry VIII. Act v, sc. 1, l. 87. [Cranmer]
Frowns of war.—*III Henry VI,* ii, 6, 32.
Rough frown of war.—*King John,* iii, 1, 104.
15
What makes that frontlet on? Methinks you are too much of late i' the frown.
King Lear. Act i, sc. 4, l. 207. [King Lear] The only use of "frontlet."
Myself could else out-frown false fortune's frown.
King Lear. Act v, sc. 3, l. 6. [Cordelia] The only use of "out-frown."
16
He doth nothing but frown, as who should say 'If you will not have me, choose.'
The Merchant of Venice. Act i, sc. 2, l. 50. [Portia]
17
Hermia: I frown upon him, yet he loves me still.
Helena: O that your frowns would teach my smiles such skill.
A Midsummer-Night's Dream. Act i, sc. 1, l. 194.
Frowns on him.—*Henry V,* iii, 6, 41.
Frown upon this.—*I Henry VI,* iv, 2, 9.
18
All without desert have frown'd on me.
Richard III. Act ii, sc. 1, l. 67. [Gloucester]
Frowns on me.—*Richard III,* v, 3, 287; *King John,* iv, 3, 96.
Frown on my defects.—*Sonnets,* xlix.
Frown upon my faults.—*III Henry VI,* v, 1, 101.
Frown and lour.—*Richard III,* v, 3, 283.

1
I will frown as I pass by, and let them take it as they list.
Romeo and Juliet. Act i, sc. 1, l. 46. [Gregory]
I 'll frown and be perverse.—*Romeo and Juliet,* ii, 2, 96.
Show a fair presence and put off these frowns,
An ill-beseeming semblance for a feast.
Romeo and Juliet, i, 5, 75. [Capulet]

2
Bring me within the level of your frown.
Sonnets. No. cxvii.
On whom frown'st thou that I do fawn upon?
Nay, if thou lour'st on me, do I not spend
Revenge upon myself with present moan?
Sonnets. No. cxlix.

3
Say that she frown; I 'll say she looks as clear
As morning roses newly wash'd with dew.
The Taming of the Shrew, ii, 1, 173. See under WOOING.

4
Thou canst not frown, thou canst not look askance.
The Taming of the Shrew, ii, 1, 249. See under CHARACTER.
Gentles, methinks you frown.—*The Taming of the Shrew,* iii, 2, 95.
To bandy . . . frown for frown.—*The Taming of the Shrew,* v, 2, 172.

5
Were I so minded,
I here could pluck his highness' frown upon you.
The Tempest. Act v, sc. 1, l. 26. [Prospero]
Not a frown further.—*The Tempest,* v, 1, 30.

6
Cheer the heart
That dies in tempest of thy angry frown.
Titus Andronicus. Act i, sc. 1, l. 457. [Tamora]
The wind and tempest of her frown—*Troilus and Cressida,* i, 3, 26.

7
I frown the while; and perchance wind up my watch, or play with my—some rich jewel.
Twelfth Night. Act ii, sc. 5, l. 65. [Malvolio]
Bade me . . . to frown.—*Twelfth Night,* v, 1, 346.
Frown on.—*Troilus and Cressida,* v, 10, 6.

8
If she do frown, 'tis not in hate of you.
The Two Gentlemen of Verona, iii, 1, 96. See under COQUETRY.

9
Now doth he frown, And 'gins to chide.
Venus and Adonis, l. 45.
When he did frown, O, had she then gave over,
Such nectar from his lips she had not suck'd.
Venus and Adonis, l. 571. "Nectar" is repeated in *The Two Gentlemen of Verona,* ii, 4, 171, and in *Troilus and Cressida,* iii, 2, 23.

FRUIT

See also Tree

10
Nay, you shall see my orchard, where, in an arbour, we will eat a last year's pippin of my own graffing.
II Henry IV. Act v, sc. 3, l. 1. [Shallow] The only use of "pippin." "Pippins" occurs in *The Merry Wives of Windsor,* i, 2, 13: "There 's pippins and cheese to come." The only use of "graffing."
There 's a dish of leather-coats for you.
II Henry IV. Act v, sc. 3, l. 44. [Davy] The only use of "leather-coats," referring to the "last year's pippins" which Shallow has promised his guests.
A goodly apple rotten at the heart.
The Merchant of Venice, i, 3, 102. See HYPOCRISY, 745:1.
Rotten apples.—*The Taming of the Shrew,* i, 1, 139; *Henry V,* iii, 7, 155.
Bitten apples.—*Henry VIII,* v, 4, 64. Apples are mentioned nine times in the plays; peaches not at all, though "peach-coloured" occurs twice.

11
Gloucester: Thou lovedst plums well. . . .
Simpcox: My wife desired some damsons.
II Henry VI. Act ii, sc. 1, l. 101. The only mention of damsons.
Give it a plum, a cherry and a fig.
King John, ii, 1, 162.
Green plum.—*The Passionate Pilgrim,* l. 135.
Mellow plum.—*Venus and Adonis,* l. 527. The only references to plums.

12
As crestfallen as a dried pear.
The Merry Wives of Windsor, iv, 5, 103. See under WIT.
Poperin pear.—*Romeo and Juliet,* ii, 1, 38. The only use of "poperin," from Poperinghe, a town in West Flanders.
Withered pears.—*All's Well that Ends Well,* i, 1, 175; 176. The only references to pears.

13
Though other things grow fair against the sun,
Yet fruits that blossom first will first be ripe.
Othello. Act ii, sc. 3, l. 382. [Iago]

14
The ripest fruit falls first.
Richard II, ii, 1, 153. [King Richard]
The weakest kind of fruit
Drops earliest to the ground.
The Merchant of Venice. Act iv, sc. 1, l. 115. [Antonio]
Like fruit unripe, sticks on the tree;
But fall, unshaken, when they mellow be.
Hamlet. Act iii, sc. 2, l. 200. [Player King] The only use of "unripe."
The mellow plum doth fall, the green sticks fast,
Or being early pluck'd is sour to taste.
Venus and Adonis, l. 527.

15
Go, bind thou up yon dangling apricocks,
Which like unruly children, make their sire
Stoop with oppression of their prodigal weight.
Richard II. Act iii, sc. 4, l. 29. [Gardener] The only use of "dangling."
Feed him with apricocks.—*A Midsummer-Night's Dream,* iii, 1, 169. The only uses of "apricocks." "Apricot" does not occur in the plays.

16
Now will he sit under a medlar tree,

And wish his mistress were that kind of fruit
As maids call medlars, when they laugh alone.
Romeo and Juliet. Act ii, sc. 1, l. 34. [Mercutio] Nobody has been able to penetrate this obscenity, but some editors have nevertheless considered the lines too gross to be used!

Apemantus: There 's a medlar for thee, eat it.
Timon: On what I hate I feed not.
Apemantus: Dost hate a medlar?
Timon: Ay, though it look like thee.
Timon of Athens. Act iv, sc. 3, l. 305.

Rotten medlar.—*Measure for Measure,* iv, 3, 184. The medlar, a fruit like a small brown-skinned apple, is referred to a fourth time in *As You Like It,* iii, 2, 125.

1 Yea, like fair fruit in an unwholesome dish,
Are like to rot untasted.
Troilus and Cressida. Act ii, sc. 3, l. 129. [Agamemnon] The only use of "untasted."

Bad fruit.—*As You Like It,* iii, 2, 123.
Base fruit.—*Titus Andronicus,* v, 1, 43.
Earliest fruit.—*As You Like It,* iii, 2, 126.
Golden fruit.—*Pericles,* i, 1, 28.
First fruit.—*I Henry VI,* v, 4, 13.
Mellow fruit.—*Coriolanus,* iv, 6, 100.
Mighty fruit.—*King John,* ii, 1, 473.
Fruit of baser quality.—*Henry V,* i, 1, 62.
One Sampson Stockfish, a fruiterer.—*II Henry IV,* iii, 2, 36. The only use of "fruiterer."

2 This is the fruit of rashness!
Richard III, ii, 1, 134. See under RASHNESS.

If you will then see the fruits of the sport, mark his first approach before my lady.
Twelfth Night. Act ii, sc. 5, l. 217. [Maria]

Fruit of such a goodly tree.—*III Henry VI,* v, 6, 52.
Fruit of yon celestial tree.—*Pericles,* i, 1, 21.
Fruits of my advice.—*Hamlet,* ii, 2, 145.
Fruits of duty.—*Richard II,* iii, 4, 63.
The fruits are to ensue.—*Othello,* ii, 3, 9.

3 Bring him mulberries and ripe-red cherries.
Venus and Adonis, l. 1103. The only use of "ripe-red." Cherries are mentioned nine times.

Purple grapes, green figs, and mulberries.
A Midsummer-Night's Dream, iii, 1, 170. Figs are mentioned nine times, mulberries five times.

4 The fruit she goes with
I pray for heartily, that it may find
Good time, and live; but for the stock, Sir Thomas,
I wish it grubb'd up now.
Henry VIII. Act v, sc. 1, l. 20. [Gardiner] The only use of "grubb'd."

Fruit of bastardy.—*Titus Andronicus,* v, 1, 48.
Fruits of love.—*III Henry VI,* iii, 2, 58; 59.
Fruit of whoring.—*Othello,* v, 1, 116.
Fruit of the womb.—*I Henry VI,* 5, 4, 63; *II Henry IV,* v, 4, 15.
Royal fruit.—*Richard III,* iii, 7, 167.
Unfather'd fruit.—*Sonnets,* xlvii.
King Edward's fruit.—*III Henry VI,* iv, 4, 24.

FUNERAL

5 We have done our obsequies: come, lay him down.
Cymbeline. Act iv, sc. 2, l. 282. [Guiderius]

Her obsequies have been as far enlarged
As we have warranty: her death was doubtful.
Hamlet. Act v, sc. 1, l. 249. [First Priest]

But all in vain are these mean obsequies;
And to survey his dead and earthly image,
What were it but to make my sorrow greater?
II Henry VI. Act iii, sc. 2, l. 146. [King Henry]

The obsequies that I for thee will keep
Nightly shall be to strew thy grave and weep.
Romeo and Juliet. Act v, sc. 3, l. 16. [Paris]

My brethren's obsequies.—*Titus Andronicus,* i, 1, 160.
Rutland's obsequies.—*III Henry VI,* i, 4, 147. The only uses of "obsequies."

6 His obscure funeral—
No trophy, sword, nor hatchment o'er his bones,
No noble rite nor formal ostentation.
Hamlet. Act iv, sc. 5, l. 213. [Laertes] The only use of "hatchment."

Funeral baked meats.—*Hamlet,* i, 2, 180.
Funeral bell.—*III Henry VI,* ii, 5, 117.
Funeral rite.—*Titus Andronicus,* v, 3, 196.

7 Mourn not, except thou sorrow for my good;
Only give order for my funeral.
I Henry VI. Act ii, sc. 5, l. 111. [Mortimer]

8 All things that we ordained festival,
Turn from their office to black funeral.
Romeo and Juliet. Act iv, sc. 5, l. 84. [Capulet]

9 But safer triumph is this funeral pomp,
That hath aspired to Solon's happiness
And triumphs over chance in honour's bed.
Titus Andronicus. Act i, sc. 1, l. 176. [Marcus] The only mention of Solon.

I have given her physic,
And you must needs bestow her funeral.
Titus Andronicus. Act iv, sc. 2, l. 162. [Aaron]

FURY

See also Anger, Rage, Wrath

10 Thou shouldst come like a Fury crown'd with snakes,
Not like a formal man.
Antony and Cleopatra. Act ii, sc. 5, l. 40. [Cleopatra]

Welcome, dread Fury, to my woful house.
Titus Andronicus. Act v, sc. 2, l. 82. [Titus]

A fury, pitiless and rough.—*The Comedy of Errors,* iv, 2, 35.

Seize on him, Furies!
Richard III, i, 4, 57. See under TORMENT.

Approach, ye Furies fell!—*A Midsummer-Night's Dream,* v, 1, 289.
Talked of . . . Furies.—*All's Well that Ends Well,* v, 3, 261.
Furies' lap.—*II Henry IV,* v, 3, 110. The only references to the Furies.

1 To be furious,
Is to be frighted out of fear; and in that mood
The dove will peck the estridge.
Antony and Cleopatra. Act iii, sc. 13, l. 195. [Enobarbus] The estridge is mentioned again in *I Henry IV,* iv, 1, 98.
Give ground, if you see him furious.
Twelfth Night, iii, 4, 334. See under GROUND.
Furious and impatient.—*Titus Andronicus,* ii, 1, 76.
Hot and furious.—*Cymbeline,* ii, 3, 7.
Temperate and furious.—*Macbeth,* ii, 3, 114.
Wild, and furious.—*Richard III,* iv, 4, 169.

2
But better 'twere Thou fell'st into my fury.
Antony and Cleopatra. Act iv, sc. 12, l. 41. [Antony]

3
Look For fury not to be resisted.
Cymbeline. Act iii, sc. 1, l. 78. [Lucius]
I never saw such noble fury in so poor a thing.
Cymbeline, v, 5, 8. See under DEED.

4
Tell him my fury shall abate.
Henry V. Act iv, sc. 4, l. 50. [Pistol] Repeated in ii, 1, 70.

5
You tempt the fury of my three attendants.
I Henry VI, iv, 2, 10. See under WAR.
Fury of his heart.—*King Lear,* iii, 4, 136.
Fury of two desperate men.—*King John,* iii, 1, 32.
Fury of the wind.—*III Henry VI,* ii, 5, 8.
Fury of ungovern'd youth.—*The Two Gentlemen of Verona,* iv, 1, 45.

6
Proud prelate, in thy face I see thy fury.
II Henry VI. Act i, sc. 1, l. 142. [Gloucester]
Dizzy-eyed fury and great rage of heart.
I Henry VI. Act iv, sc. 7, l. 11. [Talbot] The only use of "dizzy-eyed."
Fury to torment my soul!—*III Henry VI,* i, 3, 31.
Fly their fury.—*III Henry VI,* i, 4, 23.

7
What fury hath inspired thee now?
Love's Labour's Lost. Act iv, sc. 3, l. 229. [King]
Possessed with a fury.—*Much Ado about Nothing,* i, 1, 193.

8
O, yet I do repent me of my fury.
Macbeth. Act ii, sc. 3, l. 112. [Macbeth]
I understand a fury in your words.
Othello, iv, 2, 32. See under WORDS.

9
Make pale our cheek, chasing the royal blood
With fury from his native residence.
Richard II. Act ii, sc. 1, l. 118. [King Richard]

10
Away to heaven, respective lenity,
And fire-eyed fury be my conduct now!
Romeo and Juliet. Act iii, sc. 1, l. 128. [Romeo]
Fire-eyed maid of smoky war.
I Henry IV, iv, 1, 114. The only uses of "fire-eyed."

11
Spend'st thou thy fury on some worthless song,
Darkening thy power to lend base subjects light?
Sonnets. No. c. "Darkening" is repeated in *Henry VIII,* i, 1, 226.
Spend my fury.—*II Henry VI,* v, 1, 27.
Spend his fury.—*Antony and Cleopatra,* iv, 6, 10.
Spend their fury.—*III Henry VI,* v, 5, 57.
Thy fury spent.—*Timon of Athens,* iv, 3, 127.

12
With a noble fury and fair spirit, . . .
He did oppose his foe.
Timon of Athens. Act iii, sc. 5, l. 18. [Alcibiades]
Beastly fury.—*Timon of Athens,* iii, 5, 71.
Discontented fury.—*I Henry VI,* iii, 1, 123.
Domestic fury.—*Julius Cæsar,* iii, 1, 263.
Greater fury.—*The Rape of Lucrece,* l. 648.
Headlong fury.—*The Rape of Lucrece,* l. 501.
Mortal fury.—*King John,* ii, 1, 454.
Prophetic fury.—*Othello,* iii, 4, 72.
Quenchless fury.—*III Henry VI,* i, 4, 28.
Unreasonable fury.—*Romeo and Juliet,* iii, 3, 111.
Valiant fury.—*Macbeth,* v, 2, 14.
Wrathful fury.—*I Henry VI,* iv, 3, 28.
Fury and impetuosity.—*Twelfth Night,* iii, 4, 213.
Spleen and fury.—*Timon of Athens,* iii, 5, 113.

13
Whose fury not dissembled speaks his griefs.
Titus Andronicus. Act i, sc. 1, l. 438. [Tamora]

14
Now is a time to storm; why art thou still?
Titus Andronicus. Act iii, sc. 1, l. 264. [Marcus]
Why, look you, how you storm!
The Merchant of Venice. Act i, sc. 3, l. 138. [Shylock] See also under STORM.

15
Lost in the labyrinth of thy fury!
Troilus and Cressida. Act ii, sc. 3, l. 1. [Thersites] "Labyrinth" is repeated in *I Henry VI,* v, 3, 188, and in *Venus and Adonis,* l. 684.

16
And having felt the sweetness of the spoil,
With blindfold fury she begins to forage.
Venus and Adonis, l. 553.

17 Till the fury of his highness settle,
Come not before him.
Winter's Tale. Act iv, sc. 4, l. 481. [Camillo]

FUTILITY

18 You may as well
Strike at the heaven with your staves as lift them
Against the Roman state.
Coriolanus. Act i, sc. 1, l. 69. [Menenius]
To as much end As give a crutch to the dead.
Henry VIII. Act i, sc. 1, l. 171. [Buckingham]

1 This nor hurts him nor profits you a jot.
Measure for Measure. Act iv, sc. 3, l. 128. [Duke]

2 Why, this is like the mending of highways
In summer, where the ways are fair enough.
The Merchant of Venice. Act v, sc. 1, l. 263. [Gratiano]

3 Come, come, dispatch; 'tis bootless to exclaim.
Richard III. Act iii, sc. 4, l. 104. [Lovel]

4 All in vain you strive against the stream.
Venus and Adonis, l. 772.

FUTURE

See also Present and Future

5 He 'ld lay the future open.
Cymbeline. Act iii, sc. 2, l. 29. [Imogen]

6 The blood weeps from my heart when I do shape
In forms imaginary the unguided days
And rotten times that you shall look upon
When I am sleeping with my ancestors.
II Henry IV. Act iv, sc. 4, l. 58. [King Henry]

7 In time to come, I hope to reign.
II Henry VI. Act iv, sc. 2, l. 138. [Cade] "Time to come" is repeated eleven times in later plays.

8 O, that a man might know
The end of this day's business ere it come!
But it sufficeth that the day will end,
And then the end is known.
Julius Cæsar. Act v, sc. 1, l. 123. [Brutus]

Look, what thy soul holds dear, imagine it
To lie that way thou go'st, not whence thou comest.
Richard II. Act i, sc. 3, l. 286. [Gaunt]

9 I feel now The future in the instant.
Macbeth, i, 5, 58. See under PRESENT.

10 The future comes apace:
What shall defend the interim?
Timon of Athens. Act ii, sc. 2, l. 157. [Flavius] Shakespeare used "interim" thirteen times. "Future" is used as an adjective eight times in the plays. It does not occur at all in the poems.

G

GAIN

See also Loss and Gain; Profit

11 How mightily some other times we drown our gain in tears!
All's Well that Ends Well. Act iv, sc. 3, l. 78. [Lord]

12 That call'd me timelier than my purpose hither;
For I have gain'd by 't.
Antony and Cleopatra. Act ii, sc. 6, l. 52. [Antony] The only use of "timelier."

13 If we give you any thing, we hope to gain by you.
Coriolanus. Act ii, sc. 3, l. 77. [Citizen]

It is such a kind of gain-giving, as would perhaps trouble a woman.
Hamlet. Act v, sc. 2, l. 216. [Hamlet] The only use of "gain-giving."

14 The gain proposed
Choked the respect of likely peril fear'd.
II Henry IV, i, 1, 183. See under VENTURE.

15 By me they nothing gain an if I stay.
I Henry VI, iv, 6, 36. See under LIFE.

I will gain nothing.—*Hamlet,* v, 2, 184.

Little gain.—*I Henry VI,* ii, 1, 52.

16 Of our labours thou shalt reap the gain.
III Henry VI. Act v, sc. 7, l. 20. [King Edward]

17 Gain, be my lord, for I will worship thee.
King John. **Act ii, sc. 1, l. 598. [Bastard]**

18 What should I gain
By the exaction of the forfeiture?
The Merchant of Venice. Act i, sc. 3, l. 65. [Shylock]

What win I, if I gain the thing I seek?
A dream, a breath, a froth of fleeting joy.
The Rape of Lucrece, l. 211.

19 Who chooseth me shall gain what many men desire.
The Merchant of Venice. Act ii, sc. 7, l. 37. [Morocco, reading]

20 Wilt thou, after the expense of so much money, be now a gainer?
The Merry Wives of Windsor. Act ii, sc. 2, l. 147. [Falstaff]

And I by this will be a gainer too.
Sonnets. No. lxxxviii. The only uses of "gainer."

21 Every way makes my gain.
Othello. Act v, sc. 1, l. 14. [Iago]

Despair to gain doth traffic oft for gaining.
The Rape of Lucrece, l. 131.

Gaining more.—*The Rape of Lucrece,* l. 138. The only uses of "gaining," which does not occur at all in the plays.

Most gain.—*Pericles,* iv, 2, 129.

22 When they are gone, then must I count my gains.
Richard III. Act i, sc. 1, l. 162. [Gloucester]

Not as protector, steward, substitute,

Or lowly factor for another's gain.
Richard III. Act iii, sc. 7, l. 133. [Buckingham]
Uncertain way of gain!—*Richard III,* iv, 2, 64.

1 But if I thrive, the gain of my attempt
The least of you shall share his part thereof.
Richard III. Act v, sc. 3, l. 267. [Richmond]
Every one shall share i' the gains.
Macbeth. Act iv, sc. 1, l. 40. [Hecate]

2 'Twill bring you gain, or perish on the seas.
The Taming of the Shrew. Act ii, sc. 1, l. 331. [Tranio]
Double gain.—*Richard III,* iv, 4, 324.
Hapless gain.—*The Two Gentlemen of Verona,* i, 1, 32.
Happy gain.—*III Henry VI,* v, 1, 71.
Poor-rich gain.—*The Rape of Lucrece,* l. 140. The only use of "poor-rich."
Worthy gains.—*Richard II,* v, 6, 12.
Love's gain.—*Sonnets,* xlii.
Study's gain.—*Love's Labour 's Lost,* i, 1, 67.

GAIT, see Walking

GALL

See also Bitterness

3 I have seen you gleeking and galling at this gentleman once or twice.
Henry V. Act v, sc. 1, l. 78. [Gower] The only use of "gleeking" (jibing).
Galling His kingly hands.—*Pericles,* iv, 1, 54.
Galling the gleaned land.—*Henry V,* i, 2, 151. The only uses of "galling."

4 Salisbury: Stand by, or I shall gall you, Faulconbridge.
Faulconbridge: Thou wert better gall the devil, Salisbury.
King John. Act iv, sc. 3, l. 94.
I am loath to gall a new-healed wound.
II Henry IV, i, 2, 166. See under Wound.
Let it not gall your patience.
Othello, ii, 1, 98. See under Manners.
Gall him slightly.—*Hamlet,* iv, 7, 148.
Gall him with some check.—*Othello,* i, 1, 149.
Galls his kibe.—*Hamlet,* v, 1, 153. "Kibe" (chilblain) occurs four times.
Gall and pinch.—*I Henry IV,* i, 3, 229.
Strike and gall them.—*Measure for Measure,* i, 3, 36.

5 A pestilent gall to me!
King Lear. Act i, sc. 4, l. 127. [King Lear]
Choking gall.—*Romeo and Juliet,* i, 1, 200.
Deadly gall.—*Troilus and Cressida,* iv, 5, 30.

6 Biron: Thou grievest my gall.
Princess: Gall! bitter.
Love's Labour 's Lost. Act v, sc. 2, l. 237. The only use of "grievest."
Fraughted with gall.—*The Passionate Pilgrim,* l. 270. The only use of "fraughted."
Bitter gall.—*Romeo and Juliet,* i, 5, 94.
Bitterness of your galls.—*II Henry IV,* i, 2, 199.

7 A' has a little gall'd me, I confess.
The Taming of the Shrew. Act v, sc. 2, l. 60. [Petruchio] See under Ridicule.
It would have gall'd his surly nature.
Coriolanus, ii, 3, 203. See under Nature.
How I am gall'd.—*The Winter's Tale,* i, 2, 316.
Galled by the king.—*II Henry IV,* iv, 1, 89.
Gall'd with my expense.—*The Merry Wives of Windsor,* iii, 4, 5.
Galled with my folly.—*As You Like It,* ii, 7, 50.

8 Whose gall coins slanders like a mint.
Troilus and Cressida, i, 3, 193. See under Slander.
Flow of gall.—*Henry VIII,* i, 1, 152.
Spend his gall.—*I Henry VI,* i, 2, 16.

9 But when they would seem soldiers, they have galls.
Troilus and Cressida, i, 3, 237. See under Soldier.
We have galls.—*Othello,* iv, 3, 93.
Lack gall.—*Hamlet,* ii, 2, 605.
Out, gall!—*Troilus and Cressida,* v, 1, 40.
Gall of goat.—*Macbeth,* iv, 1, 27.

10 You have the honey still, but these the gall.
Troilus and Cressida, ii, 2, 144. See under Sweet and Sour.
Steep'd their galls in honey.—*Henry V,* ii, 2, 30.

11 Let there be gall enough in thy ink.
Twelfth Night, iii, 2, 52. See under Writing.
Made of gall.—*Cymbeline,* i, 1, 101.

GALLANTRY

12 He goes forth gallantly.
Antony and Cleopatra. Act iv, sc. 4, l. 36. [Cleopatra] "Gallantly" is repeated in *I Henry IV,* iv, 1, 105, and in *Henry V,* iii, 6, 95.

13 This gallant pins the wenches on his sleeve.
Love's Labour 's Lost. Act v, sc. 2, l. 321. [Biron]
Count Comfect; a sweet gallant, surely!
Much Ado about Nothing. Act iv, sc. 1, l. 318. [Beatrice]
This gallant which thou seest
Was in the wreck; and, but he 's something stain'd
With grief that 's beauty's canker, thou mightst call him
A goodly person.
The Tempest. Act i, sc. 2, l. 413. [Prospero]
Little gallant.—*The Merry Wives of Windsor,* iii, 2, 1.
Young gallant.—*As You Like It,* i, 2, 212; *The Merry Wives of Windsor,* ii, 1, 22.

14 Gallants, lads, boys, hearts of gold.
I Henry IV, ii, 4, 306. See under Fellowship.
Trim gallants, full of courtship and of state.
Love's Labour 's Lost. Act v, sc. 2, l. 363. [Princess of France] "Courtship" in the sense of behaviour befitting a courtier is repeated in l. 790, *II Henry VI,* i, 3, 57; and in *Romeo and Juliet,* iii, 3, 34.
All the gallants of the town.—*Much Ado about Nothing,* iii, 4, 96.
Without are a brace of Cyprus gallants.
Othello. Act ii, sc. 3, l. 31. [Iago]
French gallants.—*Henry V,* iv, 2, 22.

Travell'd gallants.—*Henry VIII,* i, 3, 19.

1
Like a gallant in the brow of youth.
II Henry VI, v, 3, 4. See under OCCASION.

2
He hath borne himself beyond the promise of his age, doing, in the figure of a lamb, the feats of a lion.
Much Ado about Nothing. Act i, sc. 1, l. 13. [Messenger]

3
Cressida: Hector 's a gallant man.
Alexander: As may be in the world, lady.
Troilus and Cressida. Act i, sc. 2, l. 40.
Is 't not a gallant man too, is 't not?
Troilus and Cressida. Act i, sc. 2, l. 231. [Pandarus]
A gallant gentleman.—*Love's Labour 's Lost,* v, 1, 133; *Romeo and Juliet,* iii, 5, 114; *Henry V,* iv, 8, 89; *Pericles,* ii, 3, 32.
A gallant lady.—*Love's Labour 's Lost,* ii, 1, 196; *Pericles,* v, 1, 66.
Gallant child.—*The Winter's Tale,* i, 1, 42.
Gallant creature.—*Henry VIII,* iii, 2, 49.
Gallant fellow.—*All 's Well that Ends Well,* iii, 5, 81.
Gallant king.—*Henry V,* iv, 7, 11.
Gallant knave.—*All 's Well that Ends Well,* iv, 3, 117.
Gallant knight.—*I Henry IV,* v, 3, 20; *The Passionate Pilgrim,* l. 216.
Gallant leader.—*II Henry IV,* iii, 2, 68.
Gallant militarist.—*All 's Well that Ends Well,* iv, 3, 161. The only use of "militarist."
Gallant prince.—*Henry V,* iii, 7, 102; iv, 2, 15.
Gallant warriors.—*I Henry IV,* iv, 2, 26.
Gallant youth.—*As You Like It,* i, 2, 242; *Henry V,* iii, 5, 25.
Gallant'st dames of Rome.—*Titus Andronicus,* i, 1, 317. The only use of "gallant'st."

4
All the gallantry of Troy.
Troilus and Cressida, iii, 1, 149. The only use of "gallantry."

GALLOWS, see Hanging

GAME

See also Gaming

5
If thou dost play with him at any game,
Thou art sure to lose; and, of that natural luck,
He beats thee 'gainst the odds.
Antony and Cleopatra. Act ii, sc. 3, l. 25. [Soothsayer]
Play at subtle games.—*Troilus and Cressida,* iv, 4, 89.
Play at that game.—*Timon of Athens,* i, 2, 12.
A game play'd home.—*Winter's Tale,* i, 2, 248.
Let 's to billiards.
Antony and Cleopatra. Act ii, sc. 5, l. 3. [Cleopatra] The only mention of billiards.

6
The game is up.
Cymbeline. Act iii, sc. 3, l. 107. [Belarius]
Before the game is afoot, thou still let'st slip.
I Henry IV. Act i, sc. 3, l. 278. [Northumberland]
The game 's afoot.—*Henry V,* iii, 1, 32.
The game is roused!—*Cymbeline,* iii, 3, 98.
This way lies the game.—*III Henry VI,* iv, 5, 14.

7
First Ambassador: He therefore sends you, meeter for your spirit,
This tun of treasure; and, in lieu of this,
Desires you let the dukedoms that you claim
Hear no more of you. This the Dauphin speaks.
King Henry: What treasure, uncle?
Exeter: Tennis-balls, my liege.
King Henry: We are glad the Dauphin is so pleasant with us;
His present and your pains we thank you for:
When we have match'd our rackets to these balls,
We will, in France, by God's grace, play a set
Shall strike his father's crown into the hazard.
Henry V. Act i, sc. 2, l. 254. "Meeter" is repeated in *Antony and Cleopatra,* v, 1, 49, and "rackets" in *II Henry IV,* ii, 2, 23. Tennis is referred to in *Henry VIII,* i, 3, 30, and in *Hamlet,* ii, 1, 59. "Tennis-balls" occurs again in *Much Ado about Nothing,* iii, 2, 47; "tennis-court" in *Pericles,* ii, 1, 64; and "tennis-court-keeper" in *II Henry IV,* ii, 2, 21.

8
He knows the game: how true he keeps the wind!
III Henry VI. Act iii, sc. 2, l. 14. [Clarence]
Under the colour of his usual game.
III Henry VI. Act iv, sc. 5, l. 11. [Gloucester]

9
So thrive it in your game!
King John. Act iv, sc. 2, l. 95. [Salisbury]

10
Like a football you do spurn me.
The Comedy of Errors. Act ii, sc. 1, l. 83. [Dromio of Ephesus]
You base foot-ball player.—*King Lear,* i, 4, 95. The only mention of foot-ball in the plays.

11
Foolishly lost at a game of tick-tack.
Measure for Measure. Act i, sc. 2, l. 196. [Lucio] The only mention of tick-tack.

12
Ay, that way goes the game.
A Midsummer-Night's Dream. Act iii, sc. 2, l. 289. [Hermia]

13
I 'll warrant her full of game.
Othello, ii, 3, 19. See under WANTONNESS.

14
The game was ne'er so fair, and I am done.
Romeo and Juliet. Act i, sc. 4, l. 39. [Romeo]
Intended game.—*Love's Labour 's Lost,* v, 2, 155.
Pleasant game.—*Love's Labour 's Lost,* v, 2, 360.
Sugar'd game.—*Timon of Athens,* iv, 3, 250.
The games are done.—*Julius Cæsar,* i, 2, 178.
Olympian games.—*III Henry VI,* ii, 3, 53.

GAMING

See also Game, Hazard, Odds, Wager

1
We 'll draw cuts for the senior.
The Comedy of Errors. Act v, sc. 1, l. 422. [Dromio of Syracuse]

Draw lots.—*Antony and Cleopatra*, ii, 3, 35; ii, 6, 62; *Pericles*, i, 4, 46.

2
There was a' gaming; there o'ertook in 's rouse.
Hamlet. Act ii, sc. 1, l. 58. [Polonius] "O'ertook" is repeated in *II Henry IV*, ii, 4, 387, and in *Macbeth*, iv, 1, 145.

Gaming, swearing.—*Hamlet*, iii, 3, 91. "Gaming" is used a third time in ii, 1, 24, and occurs in no other play.

3
That 's the French bet against the Danish.
Hamlet. Act v, sc. 2, l. 170. [Hamlet] The only use of "bet."

I shall have my eight shillings I won of you at betting?
Henry V. Act ii, sc. 1, l. 110. [Nym] The only use of "betting."

Betted much money.—*II Henry IV*, iii, 2, 50. The only use of "betted."

4
Moth: You are a gentleman and a gamester, sir.
Armado: I confess both: they are both the varnish of a complete man.
Love's Labour's Lost. Act i, sc. 2, l. 44. "Varnish" is repeated in iv, 3, 244, and in *Hamlet*, iv, 7, 133.

Anne Bullen: You are a merry gamester,
My Lord Sands.
Sands: Yes, if I make my play.
Henry VIII. Act i, sc. 4, l. 45.

The gentler gamester is the soonest winner.
Henry V. Act iii, sc. 6, l. 120. [King Henry]

Now will I stir this gamester.
As You Like It. Act i, sc. 1, l. 170. [Oliver]

Common gamester.—*All's Well that Ends Well*, v, 3, 188. See also WHORE.

Young gamester.—*The Taming of the Shrew*, ii, 1, 402.

5
This is the ape of form, monsieur the nice,
That, when he plays at tables, chides the dice
In honourable terms.
Love's Labour's Lost. Act v, sc. 2, l. 325. [Biron]

If Hercules and Lichas play at dice
Which is the better man, the greater throw
May turn by fortune from the weaker hand.
The Merchant of Venice. Act ii, sc. 1, l. 32. [Morocco] Lichas is mentioned again in *Antony and Cleopatra*, iv, 12, 45. Hercules is mentioned thirty-six times.

Keep a gamester from the dice, and a good student from his book, and it is wonderful.
The Merry Wives of Windsor. Act iii, sc. 1, l. 37. [Shallow]

Diced not above seven times a week.
I Henry IV, iii, 3, 18. See under VIRTUE.

He won it of me with false dice.
Much Ado about Nothing. Act ii, sc. 1, l. 290. [Beatrice]

Dice [loved I] dearly.—*King Lear*, iii, 4, 93.

The very dice obey him.—*Antony and Cleopatra*, ii, 3, 33.

Well run, dice!—*Love's Labour's Lost*, v, 2, 233. For "dicers' oaths" see under VOW.

6
One for all, or all for one we gage;
As life for honour in full battle's rage;
Honour for wealth; and oft that wealth doth cost
The death of all, and all together lost.
So that in venturing ill we leave to be
The things we are for that which we expect;
And this ambitious foul infirmity,
In having much, torments us with defect
Of that we have: so that we do neglect
The thing we have; and, all for want of wit,
Make something nothing by augmenting it.
The Rape of Lucrece, l. 144.

7
Make a lottery;
And, by device, let blockish Ajax draw
The sort to fight with Hector.
Troilus and Cressida. Act i, sc. 3, l. 374. [Ulysses] The only use of "blockish."

'Tis put to lottery.—*Troilus and Cressida*, ii, 1, 140.

The lottery, that he hath devised.—*The Merchant of Venice*, 1, 2, 32.

The lottery of my destiny.—*The Merchant of Venice*, ii, 1, 15.

Till each man drop by lottery.—*Julius Cæsar*, ii, 1, 119.

'Twould mend the lottery well.—*All's Well that Ends Well*, i, 3, 92.

A blessed lottery to him.—*Antony and Cleopatra*, ii, 2, 248. The only uses of "lottery."

GARDEN

8
This best garden of the world.
Henry V, v, 2, 36. See under FRANCE.

Best garden.—*Henry V*, Epil., 7.

Thy curious-knotted garden.—*Love's Labour's Lost*, i, 1, 248. The only use of "curious-knotted."

Sea-walled garden.—*Richard II*, iii, 4, 43. The only use of "sea-walled."

Pleasant garden.—*Taming of the Shrew*, i, 1, 4.

Rustic garden.—*The Winter's Tale*, iv, 4, 84.

Unweeded garden.—*Hamlet*, i, 2, 135.

Adonis' gardens.—*I Henry VI*, i, 6, 6.

Gardens full of flowers.—*Venus and Adonis*, l. 65.

9
Wither, garden; and be henceforth a burying-place to all that do dwell in this house.
II Henry VI. Act iv, sc. 10, l. 67. [Cade] The only use of "burying-place."

10
He hath a garden circummured with brick,
Whose western side is with a vineyard back'd.
Measure for Measure. Act iv, sc. 1, l. 28. [Isabella] The only use of "circummured."

1
God saw him when he was hid in the garden.
Much Ado about Nothing. Act v, sc. 1, l. 181. [Claudio]
2
And many maiden gardens yet unset
With virtuous wish would bear your living flowers.
Sonnets. No. xvi. The only use of "unset."
3
There is no ancient gentlemen but gardeners.
Hamlet, v, 1, 34. See under ADAM. There are six references to gardeners in the plays.

GARLAND

4
O, wither'd is the garland of the war.
Antony and Cleopatra, iv, 15, 64. See under SOLDIER.
5
Therefore, be it known, . . . that Caius Marcius
Wears this war's garland.
Coriolanus. Act i, sc. 9, l. 58. [Cominius]
On 's brows: Menenius, he comes the third time home with the oaken garland.
Coriolanus. Act ii, sc. 1, l. 137. [Volumnia] The only use of "oaken garland."
6
There with fantastic garlands did she come.
Hamlet. Act iv, sc. 7, l. 169. [Queen]
7
So thou the garland wear'st successively.
II Henry IV. Act iv, sc. 5, l. 202. [King Henry]
And brought me garlands, Griffith, which I feel
I am not worthy yet to wear.
Henry VIII. Act iv, sc. 2, l. 91. [Katharine]
Wearing now the garland.—*II Henry IV,* v, 2, 84.
8
I 'll wear the willow garland for his sake.
III Henry VI. Act iii, sc. 3, l. 228. [Bona] Repeated in iv, 1, 100.
Sing all a green willow must be my garland.
Othello. Act iv, sc. 3, l. 51. [Desdemona]
Wheaten garland.—*Hamlet,* v, 2, 41.
9
But, hold thee, take this garland on thy brow.
Julius Cæsar. Act v, sc. 3, l. 85. [Titinius]
Make a garland for thy head.—*I Henry IV,* v, 4, 73.
Put garlands on thy head.—*Antony and Cleopatra,* iii, 1, 11.
Charge his horns with garlands!—*Antony and Cleopatra,* i, 2, 5.
10
What fashion will you wear the garland of? about your neck, like an usurer's chain? or under your arm, like a lieutenant's scarf?
Much Ado about Nothing. Act ii, sc. 1, l. 195. [Benedick]
The garland he might have worn himself.
Much Ado about Nothing. Act ii, sc. 1, l. 235. [Benedick]
11
Catesby: It is a reeling world, indeed, my lord;
And I believe 'twill never stand upright
Till Richard wear the garland of the realm.
Hastings: How! wear the garland! dost thou mean the crown?
Richard III, iii, 2, 38. See under CROWN.
Bound with triumphant garlands will I come.
Richard III, iv, 4, 333. See MARRIAGE, 961:5.
To her let us garlands being.—*The Two Gentlemen of Verona,* iv, 2, 53.

GARMENT

See also Dress

12
Winter garments must be lined,
So must slender Rosalind.
As You Like It. Act iii, sc. 2, l. 111. [Touchstone]
13
May I change these garments?
Coriolanus. Act ii, sc. 3, l. 154. [Coriolanus]
I do not like the fashion of your garments: you will say they are Persian attire; but let them be changed.
King Lear. Act iii, sc. 6, l. 84. [King Lear]
In nothing am I changed But in my garments.
King Lear. Act iv, sc. 6, l. 9. [Edgar]
Bawd: Come, young one, I like the manner of your garments well.
Boult: Ay, by my faith, they shall not be changed yet.
Pericles. Act iv, sc. 2, l. 144.
Change garments.—*Winter's Tale,* iv, 4, 649.
14
Imogen: His meanest garment,
That ever hath but clipp'd his body, is dearer
In my respect than all the hairs above thee,
Were they all made such men. . . .
Cloten: You have abused me: 'His meanest garment!'
Imogen: Ay, I said so, sir.
Cymbeline. Act ii, sc. 3, l. 138.
She held the very garment of Posthumus in more respect than my noble and natural person.
Cymbeline. Act iii, sc. 5, l. 138. [Cloten]
A garment out of fashion.
Cymbeline, iii, 4, 53. See BETRAYAL, 95:13.
15
How fit the garments serve me!
Cymbeline. Act iv, sc. 1, l. 2. [Cloten]
Look how well my garments sit upon me
Much feater than before.
The Tempest. Act ii, sc. 1, l. 272. [Antonio] The only use of "feater."
16
I have cases of buckram for the nonce, to immask our noted outward garments.
I Henry IV. Act i, sc. 2, l. 201. [Poins] The only use of "immask."
Buckram suits.—*I Henry IV,* ii, 4, 227. "Buckram" is used five times in this scene.
17 I will wear a garment all of blood
And stain my favours in a bloody mask,
Which, wash'd away, shall scour my shame with it.
I Henry IV. Act iii, sc. 2, l. 135. [Prince of Wales]
Beslubber our garments.—*I Henry IV,* ii, 4, 342. The only use of "beslubber."

1
It yearns me not if men my garments wear;
Such outward things dwell not in my desires.
Henry V. Act iv, sc. 3, l. 26. [King Henry]

2
Cordelia: Is he array'd?
Gentleman: Ay, madam; in the heaviness of his sleep
We put fresh garments on him.
King Lear. Act iv, sc. 7, l. 20.

Give me fresh garments.—*Pericles*, v, 1, 216.

3 Thou shalt know the man
By the Athenian garments he hath on.
A Midsummer-Night's Dream, ii, 1, 264; iii, 2, 349.

Rich garments, linens, stuffs and necessaries,
Which since have steaded much.
The Tempest. Act i, sc. 2, l. 164. [Prospero] The only use of "steaded."

Everlasting garment.—*The Comedy of Errors*, iv, 2, 33.
Gorgeous garment.—*II Henry IV*, v, 2, 44.
Magic garment.—*The Tempest*, i, 2, 24.
Maid's garments.—*Twelfth Night*, v, 1, 282.
Strange garments.—*Macbeth*, i, 3, 145.
Vacant garments.—*King John*, iii, 4, 97.
Our garments poor.—*The Taming of the Shrew*, iv, 3, 173.
If your garments were thin.—*The Comedy of Errors*, iii, 1, 70.
Garment of a Grace.—*A Lover's Complaint*, l. 316.
Garment of this peace.—*Henry VIII*, i, 1, 93.
Garment of rebellion.—*King John*, v, 1, 74.

4
Thy garments are not spotted with our blood.
Richard III, i, 3, 283. See under Blood.

5
On their sustaining garments not a blemish,
But fresher than before.
The Tempest. Act i, sc. 2, l. 219. [Ariel]

Methinks our garments are now as fresh as when we put them on first in Afric.
The Tempest. Act ii, sc. 1, l. 68. [Gonzalo] "Afric" is used four times, and "Africa" once.

Our garments now seem as fresh as when we were at Tunis.
The Tempest. Act ii, sc. 1, l. 96. [Gonzalo] Tunis is mentioned eight times in this play, and in no other.

Here's a garment for 't.—*Tempest*, iv, 1, 241.
There's another garment for 't.—*The Tempest*, iv, 1, 244.

6
Who wears a garment shapeless and unfinish'd?
Venus and Adonis, l. 415.

His garments are rich, but he wears them not handsomely.
The Winter's Tale. Act iv, sc. 4, l. 776. [Shepherd] "Handsomely" is repeated in *Titus Andronicus*, ii, 3, 268, and in *The Tempest*, v, 1, 293.

GASH, see Wound

GATE

7
Go fetch me something; I'll break ope the gate.
The Comedy of Errors. Act iii, sc. 1, l. 73. [Antipholus of Ephesus]

So, now the gates are ope: now prove good seconds.
Coriolanus. Act i, sc. 4, l. 43. [Marcius]

Ope your gates.—*King John*, ii, 1, 536.

8
Alone he enter'd The mortal gate of the city.
Coriolanus. Act ii, sc. 2, l. 114. [Cominius]

They would not thread the gates.
Coriolanus, iii, 1, 124. See under Cowardice.

9
Sicinius: Go, see him out at gates, and follow him,
As he hath follow'd you, with all despite. . . .
Citizens: Come, come; let's see him out at gates.
Coriolanus. Act iii, sc. 3, l. 138.

Go thrust him out at gates, and let him smell
His way to Dover.
King Lear. Act iii, sc. 7, l. 93. [Regan]

Bring me out at gate.—*Coriolanus*, iv, 1, 47.

You have pushed out your gates the very defender of them.
Coriolanus. Act v, sc. 2, l. 41. [Menenius]

10
Never more To enter our Rome gates.
Coriolanus. Act iii, sc. 3, l. 103. [Coriolanus] "Rome gates" is repeated in iv, 5, 214.

Whether to knock against the gates of Rome,
Or rudely visit them in parts remote,
To fright them, ere destroy.
Coriolanus. Act iv, sc. 5, l. 147. [Aufidius]

The gates of Rome.—*Coriolanus*, v, 6, 77; *Julius Cæsar*, iii, 2, 274.
Gates of Bourdeaux.—*I Henry VI*, iv, 2, 1.
Corioli gates.—*Coriolanus*, ii, 1, 180.
London gates.—*II Henry VI*, iv, 8, 24.
Gates of Lud's-town.—*Cymbeline*, iv, 2, 99.
Gates of York.—*III Henry VI*, ii, 1, 65; ii, 6, 52; iv, 7, 8.
York gates.—*III Henry VI*, i, 4, 179.

11 Stoop, boys; this gate
Instructs you how to adore the heavens and bows you
To a morning's holy office; the gates of monarchs
Are arch'd so high that giants may jet through
And keep their impious turbans on, without
Good morrow to the sun.
Cymbeline. Act iii, sc. 3, l. 2. [Belarius] The only use of "turbans." "Turban'd" occurs in *Othello*, v, 2, 353: "Turban'd Turk."

12
Who keeps the gate here, ho?
II Henry IV. Act i, sc. 1, l. 1. [Bardolph]

Keep the gate.—*Comedy of Errors*, ii, 2, 208.
Hent the gates.—*Measure for Measure*, iv, 6, 34. "Hent" (seize) is repeated in *The Winter's Tale*, iv, 3, 133.
Stay at the gate.—*Romeo and Juliet*, ii, 5, 20.

13 By his gates of breath
There lies a downy feather which stirs not.
II Henry IV. Act v, sc. 5, l. 31. [Prince]

Gates of heaven.—*I Henry VI,* v, 4, 53.
Gate of hell!—*Othello,* iv, 2, 92.
Gates of love.—*Much Ado about Nothing,* iv, 1, 106.
Gate of mercy.—*III Henry VI,* i, 4, 177; *Henry V,* iii, 3, 10.

1
Break up the gates, I 'll be your warrantize.
I Henry VI. Act i, sc. 3, l. 13. [Gloucester] The only use of "warrantize."

These are the city gates, the gates of Rouen
Through which our policy must make a breach.
I Henry VI. Act iii, sc. 2, l. 1. [La Pucelle]

Now, Warwick, wilt thou ope the city gates?
III Henry VI, v, 1, 21. [King Edward]

Open your city gates.—*I Henry VI,* iv, 2, 5.

2
The gates made fast! Brother, I like not this.
III Henry VI. Act iv, sc. 7, l. 10. [Gloucester]

Clapp'd to their gates.—*Coriolanus,* i, 4, 51.

3
We . . . shut the gates for safety of ourselves.
III Henry VI. Act iv, sc. 7, l. 18. [Mayor]

These gates must not be shut
But in the night or in the time of war.
III Henry VI. Act iv, sc. 7, l. 35. [King Edward]

Our gates,
Which yet seem shut, we have but pinn'd with rushes;
They 'll open of themselves.
Coriolanus. Act i, sc. 4, l. 17. [Senator]

Hence, and shut your gates upon 's.
Coriolanus. Act i, sc. 7, l. 6. [Lartius]

The gates shut on me.—*Titus Andronicus,* v, 3, 105.

Let 's shut our gates and sleep.
Troilus and Cressida. Act ii, sc. 2, l. 47. [Troilus]

Fast-closed gates.—*King John,* ii, 1, 447. The only use of "fast-closed."

Strong-barr'd gates.—*King John,* ii, 1, 370. The only use of "strong-barr'd."

4
Hastings: Open the gates; we are King Henry's friends.
Mayor: Ay, say you so? the gates shall then be open'd.
III Henry VI. Act iv, sc. 7, l. 28.

The gates are open, let us enter too.
III Henry VI. Act v, sc. 1, l. 60. [Gloucester]

Open the gates.—*I Henry VI,* i, 3, 4; *Henry V,* iii, 3, 51; *Titus Andronicus,* i, 1, 62.
Open wide your gates.—*King John,* ii, 1, 300.

Open your gates and give the victors way.
King John. Act ii, sc. 1, l. 334. [Herald]

Unbolt the gates.—*Troilus and Cressida,* iv, 2, 3.
I will unbolt to you.—*Timon of Athens,* i, 1, 51. The only uses of "unbolt."

5
So you, to study now it is too late,
Climb o'er the house to unlock the little gate.
Love's Labour 's Lost. Act i, sc. 1, l. 108. [Biron]

6
And to that vineyard is a planched gate,
That makes his opening with this bigger key.
Measure for Measure. Act iv, sc. 1, l. 30. [Isabella] The only use of "planched" (boarded).

7
Like a gate of steel
Fronting the sun, receives and renders back
His figure and his heat.
Troilus and Cressida. Act iii, sc. 3, l. 121. [Ulysses]

Brazen gates.—*III Henry VI,* ii, 3, 40.
Broad gate.—*All 's Well that Ends Well,* iv, 5, 57.
Coward gates.—*As You Like It,* iii, 5, 13.
Eastern gate.—*A Midsummer-Night's Dream,* iii, 2, 391.
Everlasting gates.—*II Henry VI,* iv, 9, 13.
Forbidden gates.—*Love's Labour 's Lost,* ii, 1, 26.
Golden gates.—*III Henry VI,* ii, 1, 21.
Heaven's gate.—*Cymbeline,* ii, 3, 22.
Narrow gate.—*All 's Well that Ends Well,* iv, 5, 53: *Henry V,* i, 2, 201.
Palace gates.—*III Henry VI,* i, 1, 92; iii, 2, 119; *Titus Andronicus,* iv, 2, 35; *Macbeth,* iii, 1, 47; iii, 3, 13.
Prison gates.—*A Midsummer-Night's Dream,* i, 2, 36.
Winking gates.—*King John,* ii, 1, 215.

GEM

See also Jewel

8
Of six preceding ancestors, that gem
Conferr'd by testament to the sequent issue,
Hath it been owned and worn.
All's Well that Ends Well. Act v, sc. 3, l. 196. [Count] "Preceding" is repeated in *Hamlet,* i, 1, 122.

9
With the annexions of fair gems enrich'd.
A Lover's Complaint, l. 208.

10
Never so rich a gem
Was set in worse than gold.
The Merchant of Venice. Act ii, sc. 7, l. 54. [Prince of Morocco]

Queen of gems.—*Twelfth Night,* ii, 4, 88.
Earth and sea's rich gems.—*Sonnets,* xxi.
Reflecting gems.—*Richard III,* i, 4, 29.
Gem of all the nation.—*Hamlet,* iv, 7, 95.
Gem of women.—*Antony and Cleopatra,* iii, 13, 108.

GENERAL, see Soldier: Officer

GENEROSITY

See also Bounty, Liberality

11
My house, mine honour, yea, my life, be thine.
All's Well that Ends Well. Act iv, sc. 2, l. 52. [Bertram]

Ask me what you will, I will grant it.
As You Like It. Act iv, sc. 1, l. 113. [Rosalind]

It is an earnest of a further good
That I mean to thee.
Cymbeline. Act i, sc. 5, l. 65. [Queen]

1
Break the heart of generosity.
Coriolanus, i, 1, 215. The only use of "generosity."

2
And though he were unsatisfied in getting,
Which was a sin, yet in bestowing, madam,
He was most princely.
Henry VIII. Act iv, sc. 2, l. 55. [Griffith]

3
An I had but one penny in the world, thou shouldst have it to buy gingerbread.
Love's Labour's Lost. Act v, sc. 1, l. 74. [Costard] The only use of "gingerbread."

4
This is not generous, not gentle, not humble.
Love's Labour's Lost. Act v, sc. 2, l. 632. [Holofernes]

Generous . . . and of free disposition.—*Twelfth Night,* i, 5, 98.
Generous and free.—*Hamlet,* iv, 7, 136.

5
My purse, my person, my extremest means,
Lie all unlock'd to your occasions.
The Merchant of Venice. Act i, sc. 1, l. 138. [Antonio]

6
I 'll mend it with a largess.
The Taming of the Shrew. Act i, sc. 2, l. 151. [Gremio]

He hath . . .
Sent forth great largess to your offices.
Macbeth. Act ii, sc. 1, l. 13. [Banquo]

Why dost thou abuse
The bounteous largess given thee to give?
Sonnets. No. iv.

A largess universal like the sun.
Henry V, iv, Prol., 43. See under Eye.

Liberal largess.—*Richard II,* i, 4, 44. The only uses of "largess."

7
What if a man bring him a hundred pound or two, to make merry withal?
The Taming of the Shrew. Act v, sc. 1, l. 22. [Vincentio]

8
'Tis not enough to help the feeble up,
But to support him after.
Timon of Athens. Act i, sc. 1, l. 107. [Timon]

No meed, but he repays
Sevenfold above itself; no gift to him,
But breeds the giver a return exceeding
All use of quittance.
Timon of Athens. Act i, sc. 1, l. 288. [Second Lord] "Seven-fold" (hyphenated) is repeated in *Antony and Cleopatra,* iv, 14, 38. See also under Meed.

9
By my troth, thou hast an open hand.
Twelfth Night. Act iv, sc. 1, l. 22. [Clown] See under Hand.

GENIUS, see Angel: Guardian Angel

GENTLEMAN

10
Is 't not a handsome gentleman?
All's Well that Ends Well. Act iii, sc. 5, l. 83. [Diana]

So please your majesty, my master hath been an honourable gentleman: tricks he hath had in him, which gentlemen have.
All's Well that Ends Well. Act v, sc. 3, l. 238. [Parolles]

How does that honourable, complete, free-hearted gentleman?
Timon of Athens. Act iii, sc. 1, l. 9. [Lucullus] The only use of "free-hearted."

Honourable gentleman.—*Timon of Athens,* i, 2, 193; iii, 2, 2; iii, 2, 63.

11
Call you that keeping for a gentleman of my birth, that differs not from the stalling of an ox?
As You Like It. Act i, sc. 1, l. 9. [Orlando] The only use of "stalling."

I know you are a gentleman of good conceit.
As You Like It. Act v, sc. 2, l. 58. [Rosalind]

12
The motley-minded gentleman that I have so often met in the forest.
As You Like It. Act v, sc. 4, l. 41. [Jaques] The only use of "motley-minded." See under Fool.

13
Servingman: What are you?
Coriolanus: A gentleman.
Servingman: A marvellous poor one.
Coriolanus: True, so I am.
Servingman: Pray you, poor gentleman, take up some other station; here 's no place for you; pray you, avoid: come.
Coriolanus. Act iv, sc. 5, l. 28.

A poor but worthy gentleman.
Cymbeline. Act i, sc. 1, l. 7. [Gentleman]

I live like a poor gentleman born.
The Merry Wives of Windsor. Act i, sc. 1, l. 286. [Slender]

Poor gentlemen.—*I Henry VI,* ii, 5, 22, and seven times in later plays.
Distressed gentleman.—*Pericles,* ii, 5, 46.

14
A gentleman . . .
Yes, and a gentlewoman's son.
Cymbeline. Act ii, sc. 3, l. 82. [Cloten] See also Gentlewoman.

15
Queen: Did he receive you well?
Rosencrantz: Most like a gentleman.
Hamlet. Act iii, sc. 1, l. 10.

16
Now you speak
Like a good child and a true gentleman.
Hamlet. Act iv, sc. 5, l. 147. [King] "True gentleman" is repeated in *The Winter's Tale,* v, 2, 175.

An absolute gentleman, full of most excellent differences, of very soft society and great showing: indeed, to speak feelingly of him, he is the card or calendar of gentry, for you shall find in him the continent of what part a gentleman would see.
Hamlet. Act v, sc. 2, l. 111. [Osric]

Fair gentleman.—*As You Like It,* i, 2, 260.
Graceful gentleman.—*Winter's Tale,* v, 1, 171.
Princely gentleman.—*Richard II,* ii, 1, 175.
Prosperous gentleman.—*Macbeth,* i, 3, 73.
Renowned noble gentleman.—*I Henry VI,* iv, 4, 24.
Wise gentleman.—*Much Ado about Nothing,* v, 1, 166.

1
In faith, he is a worthy gentleman,
Exceedingly well read.
I Henry IV. Act iii, sc. 1, l. 165. [Mortimer]
O valiant cousin! worthy gentleman!
Macbeth. Act i, sc. 2, l. 24. [Duncan]
Worthy gentleman.—*The Merchant of Venice,* iv, 1, 408; *III Henry VI,* iii, 2, 7.
Thrice-worthy gentleman.—*Love's Labour 's Lost,* v, 1, 151.

2
I do not think a braver gentleman,
More active-valiant or more valiant-young,
More daring or more bold, is now alive
To grace this latter age with noble deeds.
I Henry IV. Act v, sc. 1, l. 89. [Prince of Wales] The only use of "active-valiant" and "valiant-young."
A valiant and most expert gentleman.
Henry V. Act iii, sc. 7, l. 138. [Constable]
A marvellous falorous gentleman, that is certain.
Henry V. Act iii, sc. 2, l. 81. [Fluellen]
Valiant gentleman.—*I Henry IV,* iv, 1, 132; *Henry V,* iii, 2, 71.

3
This earth that bears thee dead
Bears not alive so stout a gentleman.
I Henry IV. Act v, sc. 4, l. 92. [Prince of Wales]
Bold gentleman.—*Coriolanus,* i, 5, 23.
Bold brave gentleman.—*Henry VIII,* iv, 1, 40.
Lusty gentleman.—*King John,* i, 1, 108; *Romeo and Juliet,* i, 4, 113.

4
As good a gentleman as the emperor.
Henry V. Act iv, sc. 1, l. 42. [Pistol]
Good gentleman.—*Othello,* v, 1, 115; *The Winter's Tale,* v, 1, 148.

5
He is a gentleman of a good house.
Henry V. Act iv, sc. 4, l. 48. [Boy]
A gentleman of the very first house.
Romeo and Juliet. Act ii, sc. 4, l. 25. [Mercutio]
Gentlemen of blood and quality.
Henry V. Act iv, sc. 8, l. 95. [King Henry]
A gentleman of blood and breeding.
King Lear. Act iii, sc. 1, l. 40. [Kent]
A gentleman well bred and of good name.
II Henry IV. Act i, sc. 1, l. 26. [Bardolph]
A true-born gentleman.—*I Henry VI,* ii, 4, 27.

6
So should we save a valiant gentleman
By forfeiting a traitor and a coward.
I Henry VI. Act iv, sc. 3, l. 26. [York]
The name and port of gentlemen.
II Henry VI. Act iv, sc. 1, l. 19. [Captain]
Well, I say it was never merry world in England since gentlemen came up.
II Henry VI. Act iv, sc. 2, l. 9. [Holland]

7
You 're a gentleman Of mine own way.
Henry VIII. Act v, sc. 1, l. 27. [Gardiner]
A tall gentleman.—*I Henry IV,* iii, 2, 67.
Gentlemen all.—*Julius Cæsar,* iii, 1, 190.
Gentlemen both.—*Much Ado about Nothing,* v, 1, 102.

8
That smooth-faced gentleman, tickling Commodity.
King John. Act ii, sc. 1, l. 573. [Bastard]
Smooth-faced peace.—*Richard III,* v, 5, 33.
Smooth-faced wooers.—*Love's Labour 's Lost,* v, 2, 838. The only uses of "smooth-faced."

9
Spoke like a sprightful noble gentleman.
King John. Act iv, sc. 2, l. 177. [King John] The only use of "sprightful."
Noble gentleman.—*II Henry VI,* i, 1, 184, and fourteen times in later plays.

10
He 's a mad yeoman that sees his son a gentleman before him.
King Lear. Act iii, sc. 6, l. 14. [Fool]
Young gentleman.—*King John,* iv, 1, 15, and eight times in later plays.

11
As I am a gentleman.
Love's Labour 's Lost, i, 1, 236, and six times in later plays.
As you are a gentleman.—*Hamlet,* v, 2, 238.

12
This most gallant, illustrate, and learned gentleman.
Love's Labour 's Lost, v, 1, 128. See under GALLANTRY for "gallant gentleman."
This gallant gentleman, Judas Maccabæus.
Love's Labour 's Lost, v, 1, 134. Judas Maccabæus is mentioned twice again in the same play (v, 2, 602; v, 2, 634) and in no other.
Gallant gentlemen.—*Henry V,* iv, 8, 89; *Love's Labour 's Lost,* v, 1, 134.

13
He was a gentleman on whom I built
An absolute trust.
Macbeth. Act i, sc. 4, l. 13. [Duncan]

14
Here 's a gentleman and a friend of mine.
Measure for Measure. Act iii, sc. 2, l. 43. [Pompey]

15
A kinder gentleman treads not the earth.
The Merchant of Venice. Act ii, sc. 8, l. 35. [Salarino]
Kind gentleman.—*Henry V,* iv, 1, 98; *Macbeth,* i, 3, 150.

16
But if you knew to whom you show this honour,
How true a gentleman you send relief,
How dear a lover of my lord your husband,
I know you would be prouder of the work
Than customary bounty can enforce you.
The Merchant of Venice. Act iii, sc. 4, l. 5. [Lorenzo]
So rare a gentleman.—*Much Ado about Nothing,* iii, 1, 91.

17
All the wealth I had
Ran in my veins, I was a gentleman.
The Merchant of Venice. Act iii, sc. 2, l. 257. [Bassanio]

18
How now, bully-rook! thou 'rt a gentleman.
Cavaleiro-justice, I say!
The Merry Wives of Windsor. Act ii, sc. 1, l. 201. [Host]

Tell him, cavaleiro-justice; tell him, bully-rook.
The Merry Wives of Windsor. Act ii, sc. 1, l. 206. [Host] The only uses of "cavaleiro-justice." "Bully-rook" is repeated in i, 3, 2, and in ii, 1, 213. It occurs in no other play.

1
I am a gentleman that have spent much.
The Merry Wives of Windsor. Act ii, sc. 2, l. 166. [Ford]

The gentleman is of no having.
The Merry Wives of Windsor. Act iii, sc. 2, l. 73. [Page]

2
You are a gentleman of excellent breeding, admirable discourse, of great admittance, authentic in your place and person, generally allowed for your many war-like, court-like, and learned preparations.
The Merry Wives of Windsor. Act ii, sc. 2, l. 234. [Ford] The only use of "court-like."

Yonder is a most reverend gentleman.
The Merry Wives of Windsor. Act iii, sc. 1, l. 52. [Page]

You seem a sober ancient gentleman.
The Taming of the Shrew, v, 1, 75. See under WORD.

Old gentleman.—*As You Like It,* v, 1, 4.

3
A most lovely gentleman-like man.
A Midsummer-Night's Dream. Act i, sc. 2, l. 90. [Quince]

Gentlemanlike dogs.—*The Two Gentlemen of Verona,* iv, 4, 19.

Gentlemanlike offer.—*Romeo and Juliet,* ii, 4, 189.

Gentleman-like qualities.—*As You Like It,* i, 1, 72.

Gentleman-like tears.—*The Winter's Tale,* v, 2, 156. All the uses of "gentlemanlike."

4
I see, lady, the gentleman is not in your books.
Much Ado about Nothing. Act i, sc. 1, l. 78. [Messenger]

5 We are gentlemen
That neither in our hearts nor outward eyes
Envy the great nor do the low despise.
Pericles. Act ii, sc. 3, l. 24. [First Knight]

Thaisa: Sure, he 's a gallant gentleman.
Simonides: He 's but a country gentleman;
Has done no more than other knights have done;
Has broken a staff or so; so let it pass.
Thaisa: To me he seems like diamond to glass.
Pericles. Act ii, sc. 3, l. 32.

6
A loyal, just and upright gentleman.
Richard II. Act i, sc. 3, l. 87. [Mowbray]

Loyal gentleman.—*Richard II,* i, 1, 148.

7
A happy gentleman in blood and lineaments,
By you unhappied and disfigured clean.
Richard II. Act iii, sc. 1, l. 9. [Bolingbroke] The only use of "unhappied."

Razed out my imprese, leaving me no sign,
Save men's opinions and my living blood,
To show the world I am a gentleman.
Richard II. Act iii, sc. 1, l. 25. [Bolingbroke] The only use of "imprese" (emblem).

8
A sweeter and a lovelier gentleman,
Framed in the prodigality of nature,
Young, valiant, wise, and, no doubt, right royal,
The spacious world cannot again afford.
Richard III. Act i, sc. 2, l. 243. [Gloucester] The only use of "prodigality." "Lovelier" is repeated in *Coriolanus,* i, 3, 44.

9 A discontented gentleman,
Whose humble means match not his haughty mind.
Richard III. Act iv, sc. 2, l. 36. [Page]

Inquire me out some mean-born gentleman,
Whom I will marry straight to Clarence' daughter.
Richard III. Act iv, sc. 2, l. 54. [King Richard] "Mean-born" is repeated in *II Henry VI,* iii, 1, 335: "Mean-born man."

Riotous gentleman.—*Richard III,* ii, 1, 100.

Silly gentleman.—*Othello,* i, 3, 308.

Testy gentleman.—*Richard III,* iii, 4, 39.

10
He bears him like a portly gentleman.
Romeo and Juliet. Act i, sc. 5, l. 68. [Capulet]

11
An honest gentleman, and a courteous, and a kind, and a handsome, and, I warrant, a virtuous.
Romeo and Juliet. Act ii, sc. 5, l. 56. [Nurse]

Honest gentleman.—*Romeo and Juliet,* i, 5, 126, and seven times in later plays.

12
A gentleman of noble parentage,
Of fair demesnes, youthful, and nobly train'd,
Stuff'd, as they say, with honourable parts,
Proportion'd as one's thought would wish a man.
Romeo and Juliet. Act iii, sc. 5, l. 181. [Capulet] "Demesnes" is used twice more in the plays, in *Romeo and Juliet,* ii, 1, 20, and in *Cymbeline,* iii, 3, 70.

O, he 's a lovely gentleman!
Romeo 's a dishclout to him.
Romeo and Juliet. Act iii, sc. 5, l. 220. [Nurse] "Dishclout" is used again in *Love's Labour 's Lost,* v, 2, 720.

Lovely gentlemen.—*The Two Gentlemen of Verona,* i, 2, 19.

13
An affable and courteous gentleman.
The Taming of the Shrew. Act i, sc. 2, l. 98. [Hortensio]

14
If you strike me, you are no gentleman;
And if no gentleman, why then no arms.
The Taming of the Shrew. Act ii, sc. 1, l. 223. [Katharina]

15
You are gentlemen of brave mettle.
The Tempest. Act ii, sc. 1, l. 182. [Gonzalo]

I do know him
A gentleman that well deserves a help.
Timon of Athens. Act i, sc. 1, l. 102. [Timon]

Thy lord 's a bountiful gentleman.
Timon of Athens. Act iii, sc. 1, l. 42. [Lucullus]

1
Olivia: What is he at the gate, cousin?
Sir Toby: A gentleman.
Olivia: A gentleman! what gentleman?
Sir Toby: 'Tis a gentleman here—a plague o' these pickle-herring!
Twelfth Night. Act i, sc. 5, l. 124. The only use of "pickle-herring."
Olivia: What is your parentage?
Viola: Above my fortunes, yet my state is well: I am a gentleman.
Twelfth Night. Act i, sc. 5, l. 296.
Art thou a gentleman?—*Henry V*, iv, 4, 5.
I am a gentleman.—*II Henry VI*, iv, 1, 29, and five times in later plays.
A gentleman and a soldier.—*Twelfth Night*, iii, 4, 338.

2
Of all the fair resort of gentlemen
That every day with parle encounter me,
In thy opinion which is worthiest love?
The Two Gentlemen of Verona. Act i, sc. 2, l. 4. [Julia] For "parle" see TALK.
Thou art a gentleman—
Think not I flatter, for I swear I do not—
Valiant, wise, remorseful, well accomplish'd.
The Two Gentlemen of Verona. Act iv, sc. 3, l. 11. [Silvia]
Thou art a gentleman and well derived.
The Two Gentlemen of Verona. Act v, sc. 4, l. 146. [Duke]
Thou 'rt a gentleman.—*The Merry Wives of Windsor*, ii, 1, 200.
Gentlemen of good esteem.—*The Two Gentlemen of Verona*, i, 3, 40.

3
'Tis an ill office for a gentleman.
The Two Gentlemen of Verona. Act iii, sc. 2, l. 40. [Proteus]
Know, then, that some of us are gentlemen,
Such as the fury of ungovern'd youth
Thrust from the company of awful men.
The Two Gentlemen of Verona. Act iv, sc. 1, l. 44. [Third Outlaw]

4
It is a gentleman of the greatest promise that ever came into my note.
The Winter's Tale. Act i, sc. 1, l. 39. [Archidamus]
You are certainly a gentleman, thereto
Clerk-like experienced, which no less adorns
Our gentry than our parents' noble names,
In whose success we are gentle.
The Winter's Tale. Act i, sc. 2, l. 392. [Polixenes] The only use of "clerk-like."
A very simple gentleman!—*The Winter's Tale*, iv, 4, 607.

5
Clown: You denied to fight with me this other day, because I was no gentleman born. See you these clothes? say you see them not and think me still no gentleman born: you were best say these robes are not gentleman born: give me the lie, do, and try whether I am not now a gentleman born.
Autolycus: I know you are now, sir, a gentleman born.
Clown: Ay, and have been so any time these four hours.
Shepherd: And so have I, boy.
Clown: So have you: but I was a gentleman born before my father.
The Winter's Tale. Act v, sc. 2, l. 141.
We must be gentle, now we are gentlemen.
The Winter's Tale. Act v, sc. 2, l. 164. [Shepherd]

GENTLENESS

See also Mildness

6
Your gentleness shall force
More than your force move us to gentleness.
As You Like It. Act ii, sc. 7, l. 102. [Duke Senior]
If ever from your eyelids wiped a tear
And know what 'tis to pity and be pitied,
Let gentleness my strong enforcement be.
As You Like It. Act ii, sc. 7, l. 116. [Orlando]
Therefore sit you down in gentleness.
As You Like It. Act ii, sc. 7, l. 124. [Duke Senior]

7
When lenity and cruelty play for a kingdom, the gentler gamester is the soonest winner.
Henry V. Act iii, sc. 6, l. 119. [King Henry] For "lenity" see MERCY.

8
Let him be gently used.
III Henry VI. Act ii, sc. 6, l. 45. [Edward]
Use all gently.—*Hamlet*, iii, 2, 6.
We must deal gently with him.—*Twelfth Night*, iii, 4, 106.
Speak you so gently?—*As You Like It*, ii, 7, 106.
Full gently.—*III Henry VI*, ii, 1, 123; *Venus and Adonis*, l. 361.

9
You bear a gentle mind, and heavenly blessings
Follow such creatures.
Henry VIII. Act ii, sc. 3, l. 57. [Lord Chamberlain] The only use of "gentle mind."
Who . . .
Have stood to charity, and display'd the effects
Of disposition gentle, and of wisdom
O'ertopping woman's power.
Henry VIII. Act ii, sc. 4, l. 85. [Wolsey] "O'ertopping" is repeated in *Tempest*, i, 2, 81.
Your gentleness was guilty.
Love's Labour's Lost. Act v, sc. 2, l. 745. [Princess]
This milky gentleness.—*King Lear*, i, 4, 364. "Milky" is repeated in *Hamlet*, ii, 2, 500: "Milky head"; and in *Timon of Athens*, iii, 1, 57: "Milky heart."
Humane gentleness.—*Troilus and Cressida*, iv, 1, 20.
Sweet gentleness.—*Henry VIII*, ii, 4, 137.
Gentleness and show of love.—*Julius Cæsar*, i, 2, 33.
Gentleness, virtue, youth.—*Troilus and Cressida*, i, 2, 276.

10
Touch'd with human gentleness and love.
The Merchant of Venice. Act iv, sc. 1, l. 25. [Duke]
I thought you lord of more true gentleness.
A Midsummer-Night's Dream. Act ii, sc. 2, l. 132. [Helena]

Thrice-gentle Cassio.—*Othello,* iii, 4, 122. The only use of "thrice-gentle."

1
He is not the flower of courtesy, but, I'll warrant him, as gentle as a lamb.
Romeo and Juliet. Act ii, sc. 5, l. 44. [Nurse] The only use of "gentle as a lamb." "Gentle lamb" occurs in *Richard III,* iv, 2, 22, and *Richard II,* ii, 1, 174.

I find you passing gentle.
The Taming of the Shrew. Act ii, sc. 1, l. 244. [Petruchio]

2
He's gentle and not fearful.
The Tempest. Act i, sc. 2, l. 468. [Miranda]

He's gentle.—*As You Like It,* i, 1, 172.

O, she is
Ten times more gentle than her father's crabbed.
The Tempest. Act iii, sc. 1, l. 7. [Ferdinand]

3
Till I be gentle, stay thou for thy good morrow;
When thou art Timon's dog, and these knaves honest.
Timon of Athens. Act i, sc. 1, l. 179. [Apemantus] "Be gentle" is repeated in *Antony and Cleopatra,* v, 2, 68.

Thou art too gentle and too free a man.
Troilus and Cressida. Act iv, sc. 5, l. 139. [Ajax]

Gentle thou art.—*Sonnets,* xli.

Gentle and fair.—*Measure for Measure,* i, 4, 24.

Gentle, mild, and virtuous!—*Richard III,* i, 2, 104.

Most gentle.—*Troilus and Cressida,* iv, 5, 227; *Antony and Cleopatra,* v, 2, 127.

Wherefore are you gentle?—*As You Like It,* ii, 3, 6.

4
The gentleness of all the gods go with thee!
Twelfth Night, ii, 1, 45. See under BLESSING.

5
No way but gentleness; gently, gently: the fiend is rough, and will not be roughly used.
Twelfth Night. Act iii, sc. 4, l. 123. [Fabian]

GENTLEWOMAN

See also Lady

6
The most virtuous gentlewoman that ever nature had praise for creating.
All's Well that Ends Well. Act iv, sc. 5, l. 9. [Countess]

This honest, virtuous, civil gentlewoman!
II Henry IV. Act ii, sc. 4, l. 328. [Prince of Wales] "Virtuous gentlewoman" is repeated in l. 354.

A virtuous gentlewoman, mild and beautiful!
The Two Gentlemen of Verona. Act iv, sc. 4, l. 185. [Julia]

7
A proper gentlewoman, sir, and a kinswoman of my master's.
II Henry IV. Act ii, sc. 2, l. 169. [Page]

Dear gentlewoman.—*Winter's Tale,* ii, 2, 20.

Fair gentlewoman.—*The Comedy of Errors,* v, 1, 373; *Romeo and Juliet,* ii. 4, 116; *King Lear,* i, 4, 257.

Poor gentlewoman.—*The Two Gentlemen of Verona,* iv, 4, 146; *Measure for Measure,* iii, 1, 227.

8
Gentlewomen that live honestly by the prick of their needles.
Henry V. Act ii, sc. 1, l. 36. [Hostess]

Honest gentlewoman.—*The Merry Wives of Windsor,* i, 4, 87.

9
He will maintain you like a gentlewoman.
The Merry Wives of Windsor. Act iii, sc. 4, l. 45. [Shallow]

Young gentlewoman.—*The Merry Wives of Windsor,* i, 1, 63; *All's Well that Ends Well,* i, 1, 19; iv, 3, 17.

10
Brought up as best becomes a gentlewoman.
The Taming of the Shrew. Act i, sc. 2, l. 87. [Hortensio]

Tell me, sweet Kate, and tell me truly too,
Hast thou beheld a fresher gentlewoman?
The Taming of the Shrew. Act iv, sc. 5, l. 28. [Petruchio]

GEORGE, SAINT, see under England

GERMANY

11
Yet with their own authors ſaithfully affirm
That the land Salique is in Germany,
Between the floods of Sala and of Elbe. . . .
Which Salique, as I said, 'twixt Elbe and Sala,
Is at this day in Germany call'd Meisen.
Henry V. Act i, sc. 2, l. 43. [Canterbury] The only mention of Elbe and Meisen. Sala is repeated in l. 63.

Upper Germany.—*Henry VIII,* v, 3, 30. Germany is mentioned six times.

12
Holding in disdain the German women
For some dishonest manners of their life.
Henry V. Act i, sc. 2, l. 48. [Canterbury]

13
Hasty Germans and blunt Hollanders.
III Henry VI. Act iv, sc. 8, l. 2. [Warwick] "Hollander" is repeated in *Coriolanus,* i, 8, 7, and in *Othello,* ii, 3, 8: "Your swag-bellied Hollander," which is also the only use of "swag-bellied."

Young German.—*Merchant of Venice,* i, 2, 90.

14
Germans are honest men.
The Merry Wives of Windsor. Act iv, sc. 5, l. 73. [Host]

15
A German from the waist downward, all slops.
Much Ado about Nothing. Act iii, sc. 2, l. 35. [Don Pedro]

GHOST

See also Shadow, Spirits

16
Ægeon art thou not? or else his ghost?
The Comedy of Errors. Act v, sc. 1, l. 337. [Antipholus of Syracuse]

17
What art thou that usurp'st this time of night?
Hamlet. Act i, sc. 1, l. 46. [Horatio]

This portentous figure
Comes armed through our watch.
Hamlet. Act i, sc. 1, l. 109. [Bernardo] "Portentous" is repeated in *Romeo and Juliet,* i, 1, 147, and in *Julius Cæsar,* i, 3, 31.

Stay, illusion!
If thou hast any sound, or use of voice,
Speak to me.
Hamlet. Act i, sc. 1, l. 127. [Horatio] "Illusion" is used five times, the other four times in the sense of deception.

It is, as the air, invulnerable,
And our vain blows malicious mockery.
Hamlet. Act i, sc. 1, l. 145. [Marcellus] "Invulnerable" occurs also in *King John,* ii, 1, 252, and *The Tempest,* iii, 3, 66.

1 It shrunk in haste away,
And vanish'd from our sight.
Hamlet. Act i, sc. 2, l. 219. [Horatio]

Banquo: Whither are they vanish'd?
Macbeth: Into the air; and what seem'd corporal melted
As breath into the wind.
Macbeth. Act i, sc. 3, l. 80.

And so, with shrieks, She melted into air.
The Winter's Tale. Act iii, sc. 3, l. 36. [Antigonus]

Melted into air, into thin air.
The Tempest, iv, 1, 150. See under Air.

2
By heaven, I'll make a ghost of him that lets me!
Hamlet. Act i, sc. 4, l. 86. [Hamlet]

There needs no ghost, my lord, come from the grave
To tell us this.
Hamlet, i, 5, 125. See under Villain.

3 Touching this vision here,
It is an honest ghost, that let me tell you.
Hamlet. Act i, sc. 5, l. 137. [Hamlet] See also Vision.

It is a damned ghost that we have seen.
Hamlet, iii, 2, 87. See under Guilt.

4 Art thou alive?
Or is it fantasy that plays upon our eyesight?
I prithee, speak; we will not trust our eyes
Without our ears: thou art not what thou seem'st.
I Henry IV. Act v, sc. 4, l. 137. [Prince of Wales]

5
Presenteth them unto the gazing moon
So many horrid ghosts.
Henry V. Act iv, Prologue, l. 27. [Chorus]

6
Thy ghost I invocate.
I Henry VI. Act i, sc. 1, l. 52. [Bedford]

Be it lawful that I invocate thy ghost!
Richard III. Act i, sc. 2, l. 8. [Lady Anne] The only uses of "invocate."

7
Oft have I seen a timely-parted ghost,
Of ashy semblance, meagre, pale and bloodless.
II Henry VI. Act iii, sc. 2, l. 161. [Warwick] The only use of "timely-parted."

8
And ghosts did shriek and squeal about the streets.
Julius Cæsar, ii, 2, 24. See under Omen.

Make the ghosts gaze.—*Antony and Cleopatra,* iv, 14, 52.

9
I think it is the weakness of mine eyes
That shapes this monstrous apparition.
Julius Cæsar. Act iv, sc. 3, l. 276. [Brutus]

If again this apparition come,
He may approve our eyes.
Hamlet. Act i, sc. 1, l. 28. [Marcellus]

The apparition comes.—*Hamlet,* i, 2, 211.
Fine apparition!—*The Tempest,* i, 2, 317.
Blushing apparitions.—*Much Ado about Nothing,* iv, 1, 161.
Amazed At apparitions.—*Venus and Adonis,* l. 926. The only uses of "apparition."

10
The ghost of Cæsar hath appear'd to me
Two several times by night: at Sardis once,
And, this last night, here in Philippi fields.
Julius Cæsar. Act v, sc. 5, l. 17. [Brutus]

11
Ready to give up the ghost.
Julius Cæsar. Act v, sc. 1, l. 89. [Cassius]

Gave up the ghost.—*III Henry VI,* ii, 3, 22.
Yield the ghost.—*I Henry VI,* i, 1, 67; *Richard III,* i, 4, 37. See under Death.

12
And he will look as hollow as a ghost,
As dim and meagre as an ague's fit,
And so he'll die.
King John. Act iii, sc. 4, l. 84. [Constance]

13 The time has been,
That, when the brains were out, the man would die,
And there an end; but now they rise again,
With twenty mortal murders on their crowns,
And push us from our stools: this is more strange
Than such a murder is.
Macbeth. Act iii, sc. 4, l. 78. [Macbeth]

Avaunt! and quit my sight! let the earth hide thee!
Thy bones are marrowless, thy blood is cold;
Thou hast no speculation in those eyes
Which thou dost glare with!
Macbeth. Act iii, sc. 4, l. 93. [Macbeth] The only use of "marrowless."

14
If thou be'st slain and with no stroke of mine,
My wife and children's ghosts will haunt me still.
Macbeth. Act v, sc. 7, l. 15. [Macduff]

I charge thee, hence, and do not haunt me thus.
A Midsummer-Night's Dream. Act ii, sc. 2, l. 85. [Demetrius]

Cassio: What do you mean by this haunting of me?
Bianca: Let the devil and his dam haunt you!
Othello. Act iv, sc. 1, l. 152. "Haunting" is used a second time in *I Henry IV,* iii, 1, 186.

One that haunts me.—*The Comedy of Errors,* iii, 2, 82.
She haunts me in every place.—*Othello,* iv, 1, 136.
Haunt me in my sleep.—*Richard III,* i, 2, 122.
Haunt about my doors.—*Othello,* i, 1, 96.
Haunt my house.—*The Merry Wives of Windsor,* iii, 4, 73.

I 'll haunt thee like a wicked conscience still.
Troilus and Cressida, v, 10, 28. See under CONSCIENCE.
Haunt thee in the battle.—*I Henry IV,* v, 3, 4.
Haunt you in the field.—*Troilus and Cressida,* iv, 1, 10.
Haunt thy bed.—*Richard III,* iv, 1, 74.

1
Should she kneel down in mercy of this fact,
Her brother's ghost his paved bed would break,
And take her hence in horror.
Measure for Measure. Act v, sc. 1, l. 439. [Duke]

2
Quince: O monstrous! O strange! we are haunted. Pray, masters! fly, masters! Help!
Puck: I 'll follow you, I 'll lead you about a round,
Through bog, through bush, through brake, through brier:
Sometimes a horse I 'll be, sometime a hound,
A hog, a headless bear, sometime a fire;
And neigh, and bark, and grunt, and roar, and burn,
Like horse, hound, hog, bear, fire, at every turn.
A Midsummer-Night's Dream. Act iii, sc. 1, l. 107. "Grunt" is repeated in *Hamlet,* iii, 1, 77.
Haunted us in our familiar paths.
Henry V, ii, 4, 52. See under ANCESTRY.
Haunted by the ghosts they have deposed.
Richard II, iii, 2, 158. See under KING.
Haunted with a refined traveller.—*Love's Labour's Lost,* i, 1, 163.
Following where he haunted.—*A Lover's Complaint,* l. 130.
Be haunted.—*Cymbeline,* iv, 2, 217. The only uses of "haunted."

3 Ghosts, wandering here and there,
Troop home to churchyards: damned spirits all,
That in crossways and floods have burial,
Already to their wormy beds are gone;
For fear lest day should look their shames upon,
They wilfully themselves exile from light
And must for aye consort with black-brow'd night.
A Midsummer-Night's Dream. Act iii, sc. 2, l. 381. [Puck] The only use of "crossways" and "wormy."

4
Blind sight, dead life, poor mortal living ghost,
Woe's scene, world's shame, grave's due by life usurp'd.
Richard III. Act iv, sc. 4, l. 26. [Duchess of York]

5
O, look! methinks I see my cousin's ghost
Seeking out Romeo, that did spit his body
Upon a rapier's point.
Romeo and Juliet. Act iv, sc. 3, l. 55. [Juliet]
Duke Humphrey's ghost.—*II Henry VI,* iii, 2, 231; iii, 2, 373.
Ghost of Talbot.—*I Henry VI,* v, 2, 16.
Talbot's ghost.—*I Henry VI,* iv, 7, 87.
Your first queen's ghost.—*The Winter's Tale,* v, 1, 80.

6 That affable familiar ghost,
Which nightly gulls him.
Sonnets. No. lxxxvi.
Angry ghost.—*Richard III,* iii, 1, 144.
Gliding ghosts.—*Julius Cæsar,* i, 3, 63.
Grim-grinning ghost.—*Venus and Adonis,* l. 933. The only use of "grim-grinning."
Pale ghosts.—*I Henry VI,* i, 2, 7.
Poor ghost.—*Hamlet.* i, 5, 4; 96; *Cymbeline,* v, 4, 88. "Ghosted" is used only once, in *Antony and Cleopatra,* ii, 6, 13. "Ghostly" occurs seven times, five times in "ghostly father," and twice in "ghostly confessor."

GIANT

7
Colbrand the giant, that same mighty man?
King John. Act i, sc. 1, l. 225. [Bastard] Colbrand, a famous Danish giant, is mentioned again in *Henry VIII,* v, 4, 22.

8
I had rather be a giantess, and lie under Mount Pelion.
The Merry Wives of Windsor. Act ii, sc. 1, l. 81. [Mrs. Page] The only use of "giantess." Mount Pelion is mentioned again in *Hamlet,* v, 1, 276.

9
A stirring dwarf we do allowance give
Before a sleeping giant.
Troilus and Cressida. Act ii, sc. 3, l. 146. [Agamemnon]

10
Some mollification for your giant, sweet lady.
Twelfth Night. Act i, sc. 5, l. 218. [Viola] The only use of "mollification."

GIFT

See also Boon, Bounty, Presents

11
The gift doth stretch itself as 'tis received.
All's Well that Ends Well. Act ii, sc. 1, l. 4. [King]
His present gift
Shall furnish me to those Italian fields
Where noble fellows strike.
All's Well that Ends Well. Act ii, sc. 3, l. 306. [Bertram]
My dear father's gift.—*All's Well that Ends Well,* ii, 1, 115.
My father's gift.—*Pericles,* ii, 1, 140.
Your wife's first gift.—*The Merchant of Venice,* v, 1, 167.
'Twas my first gift.—*Othello,* iii, 3, 436.

12
And I will boot thee with what gift beside
Thy modesty can beg.
Antony and Cleopatra. Act ii, sc. 5, l. 71. [Cleopatra]
He partly begs To be desired to give.
Antony and Cleopatra. Act iii, sc. 13, l. 66. [Thyreus]

13
This nothing that he so plentifully gives me.
As You Like It. Act i, sc. 1, l. 18. [Orlando]

Heaven would that she these gifts should have.
As You Like It. Act iii, sc. 2, l. 161. [Celia]

1
I see a man here needs not live by shifts,
When in the streets he meets such golden gifts.
The Comedy of Errors. Act iii, sc. 2, l. 187. [Antipholus of Syracuse] The only use of the phrase "live by shifts."

2
To the noble mind
Rich gifts wax poor when givers prove unkind.
Hamlet. Act iii, sc. 1, l. 100. [Ophelia]

3
Laid gifts before him.
I Henry IV. Act iv, sc. 3, l. 71. [Hotspur]
External gifts.—*I Henry VI,* v, 5, 3.
Fair gift.—*Sonnets,* lxxxvii.
Gift after gift.—*The Merry Wives of Windsor,* ii, 2, 67.
Good gift.—*All's Well that Ends Well,* ii, 3, 158; *The Merry Wives of Windsor,* i, 1, 64; *Twelfth Night,* i, 3, 29.
A goodly gift.—*III Henry VI,* v, 1, 31; *Titus Andronicus,* ii, 3, 67.
Heavenly gift.—*Macbeth,* iv, 3, 157.
New-year's gift.—*The Merry Wives of Windsor,* iii, 5, 9. The only use of "New-year's."
Promised gift.—*All's Well that Ends Well,* ii, 3, 56.
Virtuous gifts.—*I Henry VI,* v, 1, 43.

4
I know not how they sold themselves: but thou, like a kind fellow, gavest thyself away gratis; and I thank thee for thee.
II Henry IV. Act iv, sc. 3, l. 74. [Falstaff]
For competence of life I will allow you,
That lack of means enforce you not to evil.
II Henry IV. Act v, sc. 5, l. 70. [Henry V]
I will bestow a breakfast to make you friends.
Henry V. Act ii, sc. 1, l. 12. [Bardolph]

5
The happiest gift that ever marquess gave.
II Henry VI. Act i, sc. 1, l. 15. [Suffolk]
Prayers and tears have moved me, gifts could never.
II Henry VI. Act iv, sc. 7, l. 73. [Lord Say]
Large gifts have I bestow'd on learned clerks.
II Henry VI. Act iv, sc. 7, l. 76. [Lord Say]
I 'll do thee service for so good a gift.
III Henry VI. Act v, sc. 1, l. 33. [Gloucester]

6
If aught within that little seeming substance,
Or all of it, with our displeasure pieced,
And nothing more, may fitly like your grace,
She 's there, and she is yours.
King Lear. Act i, sc. 1, l. 201. [King Lear]

7
Dost thou not wish in heart
The chain were longer and the letter short?
Love's Labour's Lost. Act v, sc. 2, l. 55. [Princess of France]
Armado: The armipotent Mars, of lances the almighty,
Gave Hector a gift,—
Dumain: A gilt nutmeg.
Biron: A lemon.
Longaville: Stuck with cloves.
Love's Labour's Lost. Act v, sc. 2, l. 650. The only mention of lemon and cloves. Nutmeg occurs three times.
Armipotent soldier.—*All's Well that Ends Well,* iv, 3, 265. The only uses of "armipotent" (mighty in arms).

8
Clerk, draw a deed of gift.
The Merchant of Venice. Act iv, sc. 1, l. 394. [Portia] "Deed of gift" is repeated in v, 1, 292, and occurs in no other play.

9
And what have I to give you back, whose worth
May counterpoise this rich and precious gift?
Much Ado about Nothing. Act iv, sc. 1, l. 28. [Claudio]
I here do give thee that with all my heart
Which, but thou hast already, with all my heart
I would keep from thee.
Othello. Act i, sc. 3, l. 193. [Brabantio]

10
Men take women's gifts for impudence.
Pericles. Act ii, sc. 3, l. 69. [Thaisa]
A woman's gift.—*The Taming of the Shrew,* Ind., 1, 124.

11
Though he divide the realm and give thee half,
It is too little, helping him to all.
Richard II. Act v, sc. 1, l. 60. [King Richard]

12
To take is not to give.
Richard III. Act i, sc. 2, l. 203. [Lady Anne]
You mistake my love:
I gave it freely ever; and there 's none
Can truly say he gives, if he receives.
Timon of Athens. Act i, sc. 2, l. 9. [Timon]
As rich men deal with gifts,
Expecting in return twenty for one.
Timon of Athens. Act iv, sc. 3, l. 516. [Timon]
O, then, I see, you will part but with light gifts;
In weightier things you 'll say a beggar nay.
Richard III. Act iii, sc. 1, l. 118. [York]
I claim your gift, my due by promise,
For which your honour and your faith is pawn'd.
Richard III. Act iv, sc. 2, l. 91. [Buckingham]

13
First Musician: What will you give us?
Peter: No money, on my faith, but the gleek.
Romeo and Juliet. Act iv, sc. 5, l. 114. "Gleek" (ridicule) occurs also in *A Midsummer-Night's Dream,* iii, 1, 150: "Nay, I can gleek upon occasion," with the meaning of get the better of.

14
Neighbour, this is a gift very grateful.
The Taming of the Shrew. Act ii, sc. 1, l. 76. [Gremio]
Here, afore Heaven, I ratify this my rich gift.
The Tempest. Act iv, sc. 1, l. 7. [Prospero]

15
He commands us to provide, and give great gifts,

And all out of an empty coffer.
Timon of Athens. Act i, sc. 2, l. 98. [Flavius]

A gift, I warrant. Why, this hits right; I dreamt of a silver basin and ewer to-night.
Timon of Athens. Act iii, sc. 1, l. 5. [Lucullus]

1
How proud I am of thee and of thy gifts.
Titus Andronicus. Act i, sc. 1, l. 254. [Saturninus]

Highly moved to wrath
To be controll'd in that he frankly gave.
Titus Andronicus. Act i, sc. 1, l. 419. [Bassianus]

For your own gifts, make yourselves praised: but reserve still to give, lest your deities be despised.
Timon of Athens. Act iii, sc. 6, l. 80. [Timon]

2
Sir Andrew: I sent thee sixpence for thy leman: hadst it?
Clown: I did impeticos thy gratility.
Twelfth Night. Act ii, sc. 3, l. 26. The only use of "impeticos" (a nonsense word), and "gratility" (gratuity).

And drink unto the leman mine.
II Henry IV, v, 3, 49. "Leman" is used a third time in *The Merry Wives of Windsor*, iv, 2, 172.

There 's a testril of me too.
Twelfth Night. Act ii, sc. 3, l. 34. [Sir Andrew] The only use of "testril" (tester, shilling).

3
Well, sir, here is for your pains.
The Two Gentlemen of Verona. Act i, sc. 1, l. 139. [Proteus]

Leonato: There 's for thy pains.
Dogberry: God save the foundation!
Much Ado about Nothing. Act v, sc. 1, l. 327.

4
Win her with gifts, if she respect not words:
Dumb jewels often in their silent kind
More than quick words do move a woman's mind.
The Two Gentlemen of Verona. Act iii, sc. 1, l. 89. [Valentine]

But Silvia is too fair, too true, too holy,
To be corrupted with my worthless gifts.
The Two Gentlemen of Verona. Act iv, sc. 2, l. 5. [Proteus]

She prizes not such trifles as these are:
The gifts she looks from me are pack'd and lock'd
Up in my heart; which I have given already,
But not deliver'd.
The Winter's Tale. Act iv, sc. 4, l. 367. [Florizel]

5
The gift hath made me happy.
The Two Gentlemen of Verona. Act v, sc. 4, l. 148. [Valentine]

6 Sooth, when I was young
And handed love as you do, I was wont
To load my she with knacks: I would have ransack'd
The pedlar's silken treasury and have pour'd it
To her acceptance.
The Winter's Tale. Act iv, sc. 4, l. 357. [Polixenes]

Knacks, trifles, nosegays.—*A Midsummer-Night's Dream,* i, 1, 34.
A knack, a toy, a trick.—*The Taming of the Shrew,* iv, 3, 67.
See this knack.—*The Winter's Tale,* iv, 4, 439.
The only uses of "knack" and "knacks."

II—Gifts of the Gods

7
Leonato: Indeed, neighbour, he comes too short of you.
Dogberry: Gifts that God gives.
Much Ado about Nothing. Act iii, sc. 5, l. 46.

Gift of the gods.—*Cymbeline,* i, 4, 91.
Gift of heaven.—*Henry V,* ii, 4, 79.
A gift that heaven gives.—*Henry VIII,* i, 1, 65.

8 O you gods!
Why do you make us love your goodly gifts,
And snatch them straight away?
Pericles. Act iii, sc. 1, l. 23. [Pericles]

III—Gifts of Nature

9
The other gifts appertinent to man.
II Henry IV. Act i, sc. 2, l. 194. [Falstaff] "Appertinent" is repeated in *Love's Labour 's Lost,* i, 2, 17, and in *Henry V,* ii, 2, 87.

He hath not the gift.—*Henry V,* v, 2, 162.
Gift of learning.—*Passionate Pilgrim,* l. 224.
Gift of tongue.—*I Henry IV,* v, 2, 78.

10
Of Nature's gifts thou mayst with lilies boast
And with the half-blown rose.
King John. Act iii, sc. 1, l. 53. [Constable] The only use of "half-blown."

11
This is a gift that I have, simple, simple.
Love's Labour 's Lost. Act iv, sc. 2, l. 67. [Holofernes]

The gift is good in those in whom it is acute, and I am thankful for it.
Love's Labour 's Lost. Act iv, sc. 2, l. 73. [Holofernes]

12 The valued file
Distinguishes the swift, the slow, the subtle,
The housekeeper, the hunter, every one
According to the gift which bounteous nature
Hath in him closed.
Macbeth. Act iii, sc. 1, l. 95. [Macbeth]

Well composed with gifts of nature.
Troilus and Cressida. Act iv, sc. 4, l. 79. [Troilus]

He . . . hath all the good gifts of nature.
Twelfth Night. Act i, sc. 3, l. 29. [Sir Toby]

Natural gifts.—*Hamlet,* i, 5, 51.

13
Slender: I know the young gentlewoman; she has good gifts.
Evans: Seven hundred pounds and possibilities is good gifts.
Merry Wives of Windsor. Act i, sc. 1, l. 63.

1
Your gifts are so good, here 's none will hold you.
The Taming of the Shrew. Act i, sc. 1, l. 106. [Gremio]

2
Wherefore are these things hid? wherefore have these gifts a curtain before 'em?
Twelfth Night. Act i, sc. 3, l. 133. [Sir Toby]

GIRL

See also Maid

3
Why, here 's a girl!
I Henry VI. Act v, sc. 4, l. 80. [York]
Country girl.—*Love's Labour 's Lost,* i, 2, 122.
Gentle girl.—*The Two Gentlemen of Verona,* ii, 7, 1; *Titus Andronicus,* iii, 2, 34.
Golden . . . girls.—*Cymbeline,* iv, 2, 262.
Green girl.—*Hamlet,* i, 3, 101.
Modest girl.—*Taming of the Shrew,* i, 1, 161.
Noble girls!—*Antony and Cleopatra,* iv, 15, 84.
Poor girl!—*The Taming of the Shrew,* ii, 1, 24; *Troilus and Cressida,* v, 3, 99.
Sick girl.—*Julius Cæsar,* i, 2, 128.
Sweet girl.—*As You Like It,* i, 3, 100; *Titus Andronicus,* iv, 1, 51; iv, 1, 61.
Unhappy girl!—*Othello,* i, 1, 164.
Wayward girl.—*Romeo and Juliet,* iv, 2, 47.
Wise girls.—*Love's Labour 's Lost,* v, 2, 58.
Gallian girl.—*Cymbeline,* i, 6, 66. "Gallian" is repeated in *I Henry VI,* v, 4, 139: "Gallian territories."
Greekish girls.—*Troilus and Cressida,* iii, 3, 211.
Girls of France.—*Love's Labour 's Lost,* iv, 3, 371.
Girls of Italy.—*All 's Well that Ends Well,* ii, 1, 19.
Girls of nine.—*The Winter's Tale,* iii, 2, 183.
Girls and boys.—*Cymbeline,* v, 5, 107.

4
'Tis a girl, Promises boys hereafter.
Henry VIII. Act v, sc. 1, l. 165. [Old Lady]
The girl was like to him.—*Henry VIII,* v, 1, 174.

5
The full sum of me . . .
Is an unlesson'd girl, unschool'd, unpractised;
Happy in this, she is not yet so old
But she may learn; happier than this,
She is not bred so dull but she can learn;
Happiest of all is that her gentle spirit
Commits itself to yours to be directed,
As from her lord, her governor, her king.
The Merchant of Venice. Act iii, sc. 2, l. 159. [Portia] The only use of "unlesson'd." "Unschool'd" is repeated in *Hamlet,* i, 2, 97; and "unpractised" in *Troilus and Cressida,* i, 1, 12.

6
O heavens bless my girl!
Pericles. Act v, sc. 1, l. 225. [Pericles]
Anne is a good girl.—*The Merry Wives of Windsor,* i, 4, 53.
Jaquenetta is a true girl.—*Love's Labour 's Lost,* i, 1, 315.

7
This foolish, dreaming, superstitious girl
Makes all these bodements.
Troilus and Cressida. Act v, sc. 3, l. 79. [Troilus]
Sweet bodements!—*Macbeth,* iv, 1, 96. The only uses of "bodements."

8
Why, this it is to be a peevish girl,
That flies her fortune when it follows her.
The Two Gentlemen of Verona. Act v, sc. 2, l. 49. [Thurio] Shakespeare was fond of "peevish" and used it twenty-eight times.

9
This is the prettiest low-born lass that ever
Ran on the green-sward: nothing she does or seems
But smacks of something greater than herself,
Too noble for this place.
The Winter's Tale. Act iv, sc. 4, l. 156. [Polixenes] The only use of "low-born" and "green-sward."
Is it so brave a lass?
The Tempest. Act iii, sc. 2, l. 111. [Stephano]
Sweet lass.—*The Passionate Pilgrim,* l. 293.
Sweet lass of France.—*Love's Labour 's Lost,* v, 2, 558.
The lass I spoke of.—*All 's Well that Ends Well,* iii, 6, 119.
A lass unparallel'd.—*Antony and Cleopatra,* v, 2, 319.
A lover and his lass.—*As You Like It,* v, 3, 17.
Your lass.—*The Winter's Tale,* iv, 4, 231; 363. The only uses of "lass."

10
Thou no more shalt see this knack.
The Winter's Tale. Act iv, sc. 4, l. 438. [Polixenes] For "knack" see under GIFT.

GLADNESS

See also Happiness

11
I am very glad to see you.
As You Like It. Act iii, sc. 3, l. 76. [Touchstone] Repeated in *Hamlet,* i, 2, 167, and in *Othello,* iv, 1, 133.
I am glad to see you.—*The Comedy of Errors,* ii, 2, 20; *The Merry Wives of Windsor,* i, 1, 89; *Othello,* v, 1, 95.
I am glad to see you well.—*II Henry IV,* iii, 2, 94; *Hamlet,* i, 2, 160; ii, 2, 440.
Regan: I am glad to see your highness.
King Lear: Regan, I think you are; I know what reason I have to think so: if thou shouldst not be glad, I would divorce me from thy mother's tomb.
King Lear. Act ii, sc. 4, l. 130.
I am glad to see your honour.
Richard III. Act iii, sc. 2, l. 110. [Priest]
I am glad to see your ladyship.
Coriolanus. Act i, sc. 3, l. 53. [Virgilia]
I would be glad to see it.—*Love's Labour 's Lost,* ii, 1, 182.
We are glad to see you.—*Measure for Measure,* v, 1, 2.

12
I am most glad You think of other place.
Cymbeline. Act iii, sc. 4, l. 143. [Pisanio]
Most glad.—*Coriolanus,* iv, 3, 54; *Measure for Measure,* iii, 1, 167.

1
I am glad of it with all my heart.
I Henry IV. Act iii, sc. 1, l. 128. [Hotspur]
I am glad of it.—*II Henry IV*, iv, 2, 77; *The Merchant of Venice*, iii, 1, 122; *The Merry Wives of Windsor*, iii, 3, 124; *Hamlet*, iv, 2, 25; *Othello*, iii, 3, 193.
I am very glad of it.—*The Merchant of Venice*, iii, 1, 121.
Very much glad of it.—*Much Ado about Nothing*, i, 1, 19.
I am glad on 't with all my heart.
Pericles. Act ii, sc. 5, l. 74. [Simonides]
I am glad on 't.—*The Merchant of Venice*, ii, 6, 67; *Coriolanus*, i, 1, 229; *Julius Cæsar*, i, 3, 137; *Romeo and Juliet*, iv, 2, 28; *Othello*, ii, 1, 30; iv, 1, 249.
I am very glad on 't.—*Cymbeline*, i, 1, 164.
2
We are glad the Dauphin is so pleasant with us.
Henry V, i, 2, 259. See under GAME.
We are now glad.—*Henry V*, v, 2, 14.
3
I am glad Your grace has grown so pleasant.
Henry VIII. Act i, sc. 4, l. 89. [Wolsey]
Glad am I.—*Richard II*, iii, 2, 104.
I am glad.—*Richard III*, iii, 2, 110, and fifty-nine times in later plays.
I am glad at heart.—*Winter's Tale*, iii, 3, 14.
I am glad at soul.—*Othello*, i, 3, 196.
I am heartily glad.—*As You Like It*, i, 1, 165.
I am right glad.—*Timon of Athens*, iii, 1, 13; *Cymbeline*, v, 5, 296; *The Tempest*, iii, 3, 11; *Henry VIII*, v, 1, 109.
Right glad I am.—*Romeo and Juliet*, i, 1, 124.
I am so glad.—*The Merry Wives of Windsor*, iv, 2, 18.
I shall be glad.—*The Merry Wives of Windsor*, ii, 2, 185; iii, 1, 12.
I will be glad.—*Henry V*, v, 2, 106.
You 'll be glad.—*Measure for Measure*, ii, 1, 253.
4
I should be glad of his approach.
The Merchant of Venice. Act i, sc. 2, l. 142. [Portia]
I should be glad.—*Henry VIII*, iii, 2, 24.
5
I know he will be glad of our success.
The Merchant of Venice. Act iii, sc. 2, l. 243. [Gratiano]
I am glad he is come.—*The Taming of the Shrew*, iii, 2, 76.
Glad you are come.—*The Merchant of Venice*, ii, 2, 115.
Glad to be employ'd.—*II Henry VI*, iii, 2, 273.
Glad to hear it.—*Much Ado about Nothing*, iii, 5, 30.
Glads our days.—*Pericles*, ii, 3, 21.
Glad your ear.—*Pericles*, i, Gower, 4.
Glad my heart.—*III Henry VI*, iv, 6, 93; *Titus Andronicus*, i, 1, 166.
Glad her presence.—*Pericles*, i, 1, 9.
Glad the sight.—*Pericles*, i, 4, 28.
6
I 'll make him glad.
The Taming of the Shrew. Act iv, sc. 2, l. 68. [Tranio]
Make me glad.—*Pericles*, ii, 5, 72.
Make glad.—*Sonnets*, xix.
7
So glad of this as they I cannot be,
Who are surprised withal.
The Tempest. Act iii, sc. 1, l. 92. [Prospero]
He 'll be glad of this.—*All 's Well that Ends Well*, iv, 3, 75.
They are glad.—*Measure for Measure*, ii, 1, 283.
8
Couch'd in seeming gladness.
Troilus and Cressida, i, 1, 39. See JOY AND SORROW, 790:19.
Thine own gladness.—*As You Like It*, iii, 5, 98.
With most gladness.—*Antony and Cleopatra*, ii, 2, 169. The only uses of "gladness."
9
I would most gladly know the issue of it.
Winter's Tale, v, 2, 9. See ISSUE, 778:2.
Most gladly.—*Othello*, iv, 1, 19.
Very gladly.—*Macbeth*, i, 2, 155. "Gladly" is used fourteen times in the plays and once in the poems.
Be gladded.—*Henry VIII*, ii, 4, 196. The only use of "gladded."
Gladding of Your highness.—*Henry VIII*, v, 1, 71. The only use of "gladding."

GLANCE

10
In company I often glanced it.
The Comedy of Errors, v, 1, 66. See under QUARREL.
Glanced at.—*Julius Cæsar*, i, 2, 324.
Your arrow hath glanced.—*The Merry Wives of Windsor*, v, 5, 249. The only uses of "glanced."
11
Vouchsafe one glance unto the ground.
II Henry VI, i, 2, 16. See under HEAD.
If we did but glance a far-off look,
Immediately he was upon his knee.
II Henry VI, iii, 1, 10. See under CHARACTER.
12
Glance from him To the duke himself?
Measure for Measure. Act v, sc. 1, l. 311. [Escalus]
Glance at my credit.—*A Midsummer-Night's Dream*, ii, 1, 75.
Glance from heaven to earth.—*A Midsummer-Night's Dream*, v, 1, 13.
Glance full wanderingly.—*Pericles*, iii, 3, 7.
13
Glancing an eye of pity on his losses.
The Merchant of Venice, iv, 1, 27. The only use of "glancing." See under LOSS.
14 The mild glance that sly Ulysses lent
Show'd deep regard and smiling government.
The Rape of Lucrece, l. 1399.
First glance.—*Troilus and Cressida*, iii, 2, 126.
Squandering glances.—*As You Like It*, ii, 7, 57.
Sweet glances.—*The Two Gentlemen of Verona*, i, 1, 4.
15
Why with the time do I not glance aside?
Sonnets. No. lxxvi. See under NOVELTY.
Forbear to glance thine eye aside.
Sonnets. No. cxxxix. See under EYE.
Glance away.—*Taming of the Shrew*, v, 2, 61.
Glance by.—*King Lear*, v, 3, 148.

1
Dart not scornful glances from those eyes.
The Taming of the Shrew. Act v, sc. 2, l. 136. [Katharina]

GLASS, see Mirror

GLOBE, see Earth

GLORY

2
Let him partake in the glory of the action.
Antony and Cleopatra. Act iii, sc. v, l. 9. [Eros]

3
Patient fools,
Whose children he hath slain, their base throats tear
With giving him glory.
Coriolanus. Act v, sc. 6, l. 52. [Conspirator]

He served with glory and admired success,
So gain'd the sur-addition Leonatus.
Cymbeline. Act i, sc. 1, l. 32. [First Gentleman] The only use of "sur-addition."

4
And I will call him to so strict account,
That he shall render every glory up.
I Henry IV. Act iii, sc. 2, l. 149. [Prince of Wales]

5
Think not, Percy,
To share with me in glory any more.
I Henry IV, v, 4, 64. See under Rivalry.

What glory our Achilles shares from Hector,
Were he not proud, we all should share with him.
Troilus and Cressida. Act i, sc. 3, l. 367. [Ulysses]

Share the glory.—*Romeo and Juliet,* i, 3, 91.

6
Divest yourself, and lay apart
The borrow'd glories.
Henry V. Act ii, sc. 4, l. 78. [Exeter]

7
I will rise there with so full a glory
That I will dazzle all the eyes of France.
Henry V. Act i, sc. 2, l. 278. [King Henry]

Glory on his head!—*Henry V*, iv, Prol., 31.

This day is call'd the feast of Crispian:
He that outlives this day, and comes safe home,
Will stand a tip-toe when this day is named,
And rouse him at the name of Crispian.
He that shall live this day, and see old age,
Will yearly on the vigil feast his neighbours,
And say 'To-morrow is Saint Crispian:'
Then will he strip his sleeve and show his scars,
And say 'These wounds I had on Crispin's day.'
Old men forget; yet all shall be forgot,
But he'll remember with advantages
What feats he did that day: then shall our names,
Familiar in his mouth as household words,
Harry the king, Bedford and Exeter,
Warwick and Talbot, Salisbury and Gloucester,
Be in their flowing cups freshly remember'd.
This story shall the good man teach his son;
And Crispin Crispian shall ne'er go by,
From this day to the ending of the world,
But we in it shall be remembered;
We few, we happy few, we band of brothers;
For he to-day that sheds his blood with me
Shall be my brother; be he ne'er so vile,
This day shall gentle his condition;
And gentlemen in England now a-bed
Shall think themselves accursed they were not here,
And hold their manhoods cheap whiles any speaks
That fought with us upon Saint Crispin's day.
Henry V. Act iv, sc. 3, l. 40. [King Henry] The only use of "vigil." "Tiptoe" is repeated in *Romeo and Juliet,* iii, 5, 10; and "flowing cups" in *Othello,* ii, 3, 60. The only references to Saint Crispian are in this passage.

In complete glory she reveal'd herself.
I Henry VI. Act i, sc. 2, l. 83. [La Pucelle]

8
Glory is like a circle in the water,
Which never ceaseth to enlarge itself
Till by broad spreading it disperse to nought.
I Henry VI. Act i, sc. 2, l. 133. [La Pucelle] "Spreading" is repeated in *III Henry VI,* 5, 2, 14.

The man
Whose glory fills the world with loud report.
I Henry VI. Act ii, sc. 2, l. 42. [Messenger]

9
Before whose glory I was great in arms.
I Henry VI. Act ii, sc. 5, l. 24. [Mortimer]

Glorious in arms.—*Love's Labour's Lost,* i, 1, 84.

10
Yet heavens have glory for this victory!
I Henry VI. Act iii, sc. 2, l. 117. [Talbot]

Who hath obtain'd the glory of the day.
I Henry VI. Act iv, sc. 7, l. 52. [Lucy]

By all the glory you have won.—*I Henry VI,* iv, 6, 50.

God's glory.—*I Henry VI,* v, 1, 27.

11
Thy glory droopeth to the dust.
I Henry VI. Act v, sc. 3, l. 29. [Fiends]

12
Lo, now my glory smear'd in dust and blood!
III Henry VI. Act v, sc. 2, l. 23. [Warwick]

13
His glory not extenuated, wherein he was worthy.
Julius Cæsar. Act iii, sc. 2, l. 42. [Brutus] The only use of "extenuated."

I shall have glory by this losing day.
Julius Cæsar. Act v, sc. 5, l. 36. [Brutus]

Let's away
To part the glories of this happy day.
Julius Cæsar. Act v, sc. 5, l. 80. [Octavius]

How high thy glory towers.—*King John,* ii, 1, 350.

14
And out of question so it is sometimes,
Glory grows guilty of detested crimes,
When, for fame's sake, for praise, an outward part,
We bend to that the working of the heart.
Love's Labour's Lost. Act iv, sc. 1, l. 30. [Princess of France]

15
So doth the greater glory dim the less.
The Merchant of Venice. Act v, sc. 1, l. 93. [Portia]

That young start-up hath all the glory of my overthrow.
Much Ado about Nothing. Act i, sc. 3, l. 68. [Don John] The only use of "start-up."

"Upstart" occurs twice, in *I Henry VI,* iv, 7, 87, and in *Richard II,* ii, 3, 122.
His glory shall be ours.—*Much Ado about Nothing,* ii, 1, 401.

1 Time's glory is to calm contending kings.
The Rape of Lucrece, l. 939. See under TIME.

2 I see thy glory like a shooting star
Fall to the base earth from the firmament.
Thy sun sets weeping in the lowly west,
Witnessing storms to come, woe and unrest:
Thy friends are fled to wait upon thy foes,
And crossly to thy good all fortune goes.
Richard II. Act ii, sc. 4, l. 19. [Salisbury]
The only use of "crossly."

A puny subject strikes at thy great glory.
Richard II, iii, 2, 87. The only use of the phrase "great glory."
A brittle glory shineth in this face.
Richard II, iv, 1, 287. See under FACE.
Countless glory.—*Pericles,* i, 1, 31.
Kingly glory.—*Richard III,* iv, 4, 371.
Latest glory.—*I Henry VI,* iv, 2, 33.
Shining glory.—*The Rape of Lucrece,* l. 1523.
Uncertain glory.—*The Two Gentlemen of Verona,* i, 3, 85.

3 Made glory base and sovereignty a slave,
Proud majesty a subject, state a peasant.
Richard II. Act iv, sc. 1, l. 251. [King Richard]

4 Go, go, poor soul, I envy not thy glory.
Richard III. Act iv, sc. 1, l. 64. [Queen Elizabeth]
Queen Elizabeth: Farewell, thou woful welcomer of glory!
Duchess of Gloucester: Adieu, poor soul, that takest thy leave of it!
Richard III. Act iv, sc. 1, l. 90. The only use of "welcomer."

5 The high imperial type of this earth's glory.
Richard III. Act iv, sc. 4, l. 244. [King Richard]
Then you lost The view of earthly glory.
Henry VIII. Act i, sc. 1, l. 14. [Norfolk]

6 Thou in losing me shalt win much glory.
Sonnets. No. lxxxviii.
Small glory.—*Sonnets,* lxxxiv.
Some glory in their birth.—*Sonnets,* xci.
Lineal glory.—*Richard III,* iii, 7, 121.

7 Like madness is the glory of this life.
Timon of Athens. Act i, sc. 2, l. 139. [Apemantus]
O, the fierce wretchedness that glory brings us!
Timon of Athens. Act iv, sc. 2, l. 30. [Flavius]

8 Were it not glory that we more affected
Than the performance of our heaving spleens,
I would not wish a drop of Trojan blood
Spent more in her defence.
Troilus and Cressida. Act ii, sc. 2, l. 195. [Troilus]

9 For, I presume, brave Hector would not lose
So rich advantage of a promised glory
As smiles upon the forehead of this action
For the wide world's revenue.
Troilus and Cressida. Act ii, sc. 2, l. 203. [Troilus]
The glory of our Troy does this day lie
On his fair worth and single chivalry.
Troilus and Cressida, iv, 4, 149. See under TROY.
Glory of our art.—*Macbeth,* iii, 5, 9.
Glory of his conquest.—*I Henry VI,* iii, 4, 11.
Glory of a creditor.—*Measure for Measure,* i, 1, 40.
Glory of her praise.—*Pericles,* i, 1, 4.
Glory of this world.—*Henry VIII,* iii, 2, 365.

GLOVE

10 The glove which I have given him for a favour
May hapless purchase him a box o' th' ear.
Henry V. Act iv, sc. 7, l. 180. [King Henry]

11 Williams: Sir, know you this glove?
Fluellen: Know the glove? I know the glove is a glove.
Henry V. Act iv, sc. 8, l. 6.
Williams: This was my glove; here is the fellow of it. . . .
King Henry: Give me thy glove, soldier: look, here is the fellow of it.
Henry V. Act iv, sc. 8, l. 29.

12 By this white glove.
Love's Labour's Lost. Act v, sc. 2, l. 411. [Biron]
By these gloves.
Merry Wives of Windsor, i, 1, 156; 161; 168.

13 Give me your gloves, I'll wear them for your sake.
The Merchant of Venice. Act iv, sc. 1, l. 425. [Portia]
Wore gloves in my cap.—*King Lear,* iii, 4, 88.

14 These gloves the count sent me; they are an excellent perfume.
Much Ado about Nothing. Act iii, sc. 4, l. 62. [Hero]
Gloves as sweet as damask roses.
The Winter's Tale, iv, 4, 222. See under POSSESSIONS for full quotation.

15 By the light he spies
Lucretia's glove, wherein her needle sticks:
He takes it from the rushes where it lies,
And griping it, the needle his finger pricks;
As who would say 'This glove to wanton tricks
Is not inured; return again in haste;
Thou see'st our mistress' ornaments are chaste.
The Rape of Lucrece, l. 316. "Griping" is repeated in *Romeo and Juliet,* iv, 5, 128. The only use of "inured." "Inure" occurs in *Twelfth Night,* ii, 5, 160.

1
No milliner can so fit his customers with gloves.
Winter's Tale, iv, 4, 193. See under SONG. "Milliner" is repeated in *I Henry IV,* i, 3, 36.
Come, you promised me a tawdry-lace and a pair of sweet gloves.
The Winter's Tale. Act iv, sc. 4, l. 252. [Mopsa] The only use of "tawdry-lace," a sort of neckerchief, said to be so called from St. Audrey, who thought herself punished by a goiter for wearing rich necklaces.
Cheveril glove.—*Twelfth Night,* iii, 1, 13.
Easy glove.—*All's Well that Ends Well,* v, 3, 278.
Old gloves.—*As You Like It,* iv, 3, 26.

GLOW-WORM

2
The glow-worm shows the matin to be near,
And 'gins to pale his uneffectual fire.
Hamlet. Act i, sc. 5, l. 89. [Ghost] The only use of "matin" and "uneffectual."
3
And twenty glow-worms shall our lanterns be,
To guide our measure round about the tree.
The Merry Wives of Windsor. Act v, sc. 5, l. 82. [Evans]
4 Like a glow-worm in the night,
The which hath fire in darkness, none in light.
Pericles. Act ii, sc. 3, l. 43. [Pericles]

GNAT

5
When the sun shines let foolish gnats make sport,
But creep in crannies when he hides his beams.
The Comedy of Errors. Act ii, sc. 2, l. 30. [Antipholus of Syracuse] The only use of "crannies." "Cranny" is used twice: in *A Midsummer-Night's Dream,* iii, 1, 73, and v, 1, 164.
Gnats of Nile.—*Antony and Cleopatra,* iii, 13, 166.
6
Melted from The smallness of a gnat to air.
Cymbeline. Act i, sc. 3, l. 20. [Imogen] The only use of "smallness."
7
Whither fly the gnats but to the sun?
III Henry VI. Act ii, sc. 6, l. 9. [Clifford]
Is the sun dimm'd, that gnats do fly in it?
Titus Andronicus. Act iv, sc. 4, l. 82. [Tamora]
8 Like to gnats,
Which make a sound, but kill'd are wonder'd at.
Pericles. Act ii, sc. 3, l. 62. [Simonides]
9
Gnats are unnoted wheresoe'er they fly,
But eagles gazed upon with every eye.
The Rape of Lucrece, l. 1014.
10
Her waggoner a small grey-coated gnat,
Not half so big as a round little worm.
Romeo and Juliet. Act i, sc. 4, l. 64. [Mercutio] The only use of "grey-coated." See under FAIRY for full quotation.

GOAT

11
Hence, old goat!
Coriolanus. Act iii, sc. 1, l. 177. [Coriolanus]
12
The goats ran from the mountains.
I Henry IV, iii, 1, 39. See under BIRTH.
13
Wanton as youthful goats, wild as young bulls.
I Henry IV, iv, 1, 103. See under WANTONNESS.
Prime as goats.—*Othello,* iii, 3, 403.
Hot goats.—*Cymbeline,* iv, 4, 37.
14
Thou damned and luxurious mountain goat.
Henry V. Act iv, sc. 4, l. 20. [Pistol]
Goatish disposition.—*King Lear,* i, 2, 138. The only use of "goatish."
15
Am I ridden with a Welsh goat too? shall I have a coxcomb of frize?
The Merry Wives of Windsor. Act v, sc. 5, l. 146. [Falstaff] "Frize" (curl) occurs again in *Othello,* ii, 1, 127.
Exchange me for a goat.—*Othello,* iii, 3, 180.
Suck the goat.—*Titus Andronicus,* iv, 2, 178.
Goats and monkeys!—*Othello,* iv, 1, 274.

GOD

16
Would God would serve the world so all the year.
All's Well that Ends Well. Act i, sc. 3, l. 87. [Clown]
Dost thou put upon me at once both the office of God and the devil?
All's Well that Ends Well. Act v, sc. 2, l. 51. [Lafeu]
You are one of those that will not serve God, if the devil bid you.
Othello. Act i, sc. 1, l. 108. [Iago]
17
God quit you!
Antony and Cleopatra. Act iii, sc. 13, l. 124. [Antony]
God keep your worship!—*As You Like It,* i, 1, 168; *Much Ado about Nothing,* v, 1, 332.
God protect thee!—*Henry V,* v, 5, 11.
God reward him!—*I Henry IV,* v, 4, 167.
18
Is he of God's making?
As You Like It. Act iii, sc. 2, l. 216. [Rosalind]
God made him.—*Merchant of Venice,* i, 2, 60.
19
God 'ild you for your last company.
As You Like It. Act iii, sc. 3, l. 76. [Touchstone]
God 'ild you!—*As You Like It,* v, 4, 56; *Hamlet,* iv, 5, 41.
God 'ild us.—*Macbeth,* i, 6, 13. The only uses of "'ild" (yield).
20
Nay, before God, Hal.
I Henry IV, v, 3, 51. "Before God" is repeated ten times in later plays.
Good, an God will!—*II Henry IV,* i, 1, 13.
God willing.—*Hamlet,* i, 5, 187.
God wot.—*Richard III,* ii, 3, 18; *Hamlet,* ii, 2, 435.

1
Let God for ever keep it from my head.
II Henry IV. Act iv, sc. 5, l. 175. [Prince Henry]

2
But all this lies within the will of God,
To whom I do appeal.
Henry V. Act i, sc. 2, l. 289. [King Henry]

So a' cried out 'God, God, God!' three or four times. Now I, to comfort him, bid him a' should not think of God; I hoped there was no need to trouble himself with any such thoughts yet.
Henry V. Act ii, sc. 3, l. 20. [Hostess]

3
O God of battles! steel my soldiers' hearts.
Henry V. Act iv, sc. 1, l. 152. [King Henry]

God of day.—*Hamlet,* i, 1, 152.
God of fight.—*Venus and Adonis,* l. 114.
God of heaven.—*II Henry VI,* iv, 1, 126, and four times in later plays.
God of love.—*Much Ado about Nothing,* iii, 1, 47; v, 2, 26. Used only in this play.
God of war.—*Titus Andronicus,* iv, 2, 95; iv, 4, 15; *King John,* v, 1, 54; *II Henry IV,* ii, 3, 35; *Venus and Adonis,* l. 98.

4
If these men have defeated the law and outrun native punishment, though they can outstrip men, they have no wings to fly from God: war is his beadle, war is his vengeance.
Henry V. Act iv, sc. 1, l. 178. [King Henry]

5
French Soldier: O Seigneur Dieu!
Pistol: O, Signieur Dew should be a gentleman;
Perpend my words, O Signieur Dew, and mark:
O Signieur Dew, thou diest on point of fox.
Henry V. Act iv, sc. 4, l. 6. "Seigneur Dieu" is repeated in iii, 4, 43, and iii, 4, 55.

6
O God, thy arm was here;
And not to us, but to thy arm alone,
Ascribe we all!
Henry V. Act iv, sc. 8, l. 111. [King Henry]

Take it, God, For it is none but thine!
Henry V. Act iv, sc. 8, l. 116. [King Henry]

God fought for us.—*Henry V,* iv, 8, 125.
God speak this Amen!—*Henry V,* v, 2, 396.

7
God is our fortress.
I Henry VI. Act ii, sc. 1, l. 26. [Talbot]

God speed!—*I Henry VI,* iii, 2, 60, and three times in later plays.
God be at your table!—*Hamlet,* iv, 5, 44.
God be with him!—*Macbeth,* v, 8, 53.
God be with you.—*I Henry VI,* iii, 2, 73, and seventeen times in later plays.
God be with my old master!—*As You Like It,* i, 1, 87.
God knows.—*II Henry VI,* i, 2, 31, and twenty times in later plays.

8
The eternal God, whose name and power
Thou tremblest at.
II Henry VI. Act i, sc. 4, l. 28. [Margery] The only use of "eternal God."

God Almighty.—*II Henry VI,* ii, 1, 95; *Henry V,* ii, 4, 77; iv, 1, 3.

9
Now, God be praised, that to believing souls
Gives light in darkness, comfort in despair!
II Henry VI. Act ii, sc. 1, l. 66. [King Henry]

God defend the right!—*II Henry VI,* ii, 3, 55; *Love's Labour's Lost,* i, 1, 217; *Richard II,* i, 3, 101.
God defend me.—*The Merchant of Venice,* i, 2, 57; *Much Ado about Nothing,* iv, 1, 78; *Twelfth Night,* iii, 4, 331.
God almighty help me!—*II Henry VI,* ii, 1, 95.
God help me!—*Richard III,* iii, 7, 24; *Love's Labour's Lost,* v, 2, 414; *Much Ado about Nothing,* iii, 4, 67.
So help me God!—*II Henry VI,* iii, 1, 110; iii, 1, 120; *I Henry VI,* iii, 1, 140. It will be noted that this phrase appears only in the first and third plays.
God help us!—*Much Ado about Nothing,* iii, 5, 38.
So help you righteous God!—*I Henry VI,* iv, 1, 8.
God save you!—*The Taming of the Shrew,* iv, 2, 72, and six times in later plays.
God save the foundation!—*Much Ado about Nothing,* v, 1, 327.
God shield us!—*Midsummer-Night's Dream,* iii, 1, 31.
God forbid!—*II Henry VI,* iii, 2, 23, and seventeen times in later plays.
God prohibit it!—*Much Ado about Nothing,* v, 1, 335.

10
O God, seest Thou this, and bearest so long?
II Henry VI. Act ii, sc. 1, l. 153. [King Henry]

O God, that seest it, do not suffer it!
Richard III. Act i, sc. 3, l. 271. [Queen Margaret]

11
God shall be my hope,
My stay, my guide and lantern to my feet.
II Henry VI. Act ii, sc. 3, l. 24. [King Henry]

Great God, how just art Thou!—*II Henry VI,* v, 1, 68.
Gracious God!—*III Henry VI,* i, 4, 177.

12
What God will, that let your king perform.
III Henry VI. Act iii, sc. 1, l. 100. [King Henry]

God's will!—*Henry V,* iv, 3, 23; 74; iv, 8, 2; *Henry VIII,* ii, 3, 12; *Romeo and Juliet,* iii, 3, 76; *Othello,* ii, 3, 162.
God's good will.—*III Henry VI,* ii, 5, 19.
By God's will.—*I Henry VI,* ii, 4, 82.
God's will be done!—*II Henry VI,* iii, 1, 86. The only use of the phrase.

13
And chiefly therefore I thank God and thee;
He was the author, thou the instrument.
III Henry VI. Act iv, sc. 6, l. 17. [King Henry]

14
God turn their hearts!
Henry VIII. Act v, sc. 2, l. 15. [Cranmer]

God shall be truly known.
Henry VIII. Act v. sc. 5, l. 37. [Cranmer]

1
God grant us patience!
Love's Labour's Lost. Act i, sc. 1, l. 195. [Longaville]
God give me patience!—*Much Ado about Nothing,* ii, 3, 154.
God give thee joy!—*Much Ado about Nothing,* ii, 1, 312.
2
Sir, you have done this in the fear of God, very religiously.
Love's Labour's Lost. Act iv, sc. 2, l. 152. [Sir Nathaniel]
3
God save thy life!
Love's Labour's Lost. Act ii, sc. 1, l. 191. [Biron]
God comfort thy capacity!—*Love's Labour's Lost,* iv, 2, 44.
God give him grace.—*Love's Labour's Lost,* iv, 3, 20.
God give thee joy of him!—*Love's Labour's Lost,* v, 2, 526.
4
God, God forgive us all!
Macbeth. Act v, sc. 1, l. 83. [Doctor]
God forgive me!—*Romeo and Juliet,* iv, 5, 7, and three times in later plays.
God sort all!—*Merchant of Venice,* v, 1, 132.
God-a-mercy!—*The Taming of the Shrew,* iv, 3, 154, and five times in later plays.
God damn me.—*The Comedy of Errors,* iv, 3, 54. The only use of "God damn."
God-den.—*Romeo and Juliet,* i, 2, 57, and four times in later plays.
5
God's my judge.
The Merchant of Venice. Act v, sc. 1, l. 157. [Gratiano]
God warrant us.—*A Midsummer-Night's Dream,* v, 1, 326.
6
Benedick: And so I commit you—
Claudio: To the tuition of God.
Much Ado about Nothing. Act i, sc. 1, l. 282. The only use of "tuition."
Please God.—*Much Ado about Nothing,* ii, 3, 37.
7
God is to be worshipped.
Much Ado about Nothing. Act iii, sc. 5, l. 42. [Dogberry]
God's above all.
Othello. Act ii, sc. 3, l. 105. [Cassio]
8
The god of this great vast, rebuke these surges,
Which wash both heaven and hell; and thou, that hast
Upon the winds command, bind them in brass,
Having call'd them from the deep!
Pericles. Act iii, sc. 1, l. 1. [Pericles]
9
God, the widow's champion and defence.
Richard II. Act i, sc. 2, l. 43. [Gaunt]
However God or fortune cast my lot.
Richard II. Act i, sc. 3, l. 85. [Mowbray]
If he serve God,
We'll serve Him too and be His fellow so.
Richard II, iii 2, 98. [King Richard]
My master, God omnipotent,
Is mustering in His clouds on our behalf
Armies of pestilence; and they shall strike
Your children yet unborn and unbegot.
Richard II. Act iii, sc. 3, l. 85. [King Richard] The only use of the phrase "God omnipotent," and of "mustering," and "unbegot."
God save King Harry!—*Richard II,* iv, 1, 220.
God save King Richard!—*Richard III,* iii, 7, 36.
No man cried 'God save him.'—*Richard II,* v, 2, 28.
10
If God will be revenged for this deed,
O, know you yet, he doth it publicly.
Richard III. Act i, sc. 4, l. 220. [Clarence]
Leave it all to God.—*Richard III,* ii, 3, 45.
God be thanked.—*Richard III,* iii, 7, 165.
God witness with me.—*Richard III,* iv, 4, 60.
God in heaven.—*Richard III,* iii, 1, 40, and three times in later plays.
I would to God.—*Rich rd III,* i, 3, 140, and frequently in later plays.
11
God bless your grace with health and happy days!
Richard III. Act iii, sc. 1, l. 18. [Mayor] Also iii, 7, 237.
First Sailor: God bless you, sir.
Horatio: Let him bless thee too.
Hamlet. Act iv, sc. 6, l. 6.
God bless thee (or you).—*All's Well that Ends Well,* iv, 3, 350; *Hamlet,* iii, 2, 390; *Richard III,* ii, 2, 107; *Twelfth Night,* i, 5, 41.
God bless thy lungs, good knight.
II Henry IV. Act v, sc. 5, l. 5. [Pistol]
God bless my ladies!—*Love's Labour's Lost,* ii, 1, 77.
God bless them and make them his servants!
The Merry Wives of Windsor. Act ii, sc. 2, l. 53. [Mistress Quickly]
God bless the mark!—*The Merchant of Venice,* ii, 2, 25; *Othello,* i, 1, 33; *Two Gentlemen of Verona,* iv, 4, 20.
God save the mark!—*Romeo and Juliet,* iii, 2, 53; *I Henry IV,* i, 3, 56.
12
One that hath ever been God's enemy:
Then, if you fight against God's enemy,
God will in justice ward you as his soldiers.
Richard III. Act v, sc. 3, l. 252. [Richmond] The only use of the phrase "God's enemy."
13
Well, Susan is with God;
She was too good for me.
Romeo and Juliet. Act i, sc. 3, l. 19. [Nurse] Susan is referred to again in i, 5, 110, and in no other play.
God rest all Christian souls!—*Romeo and Juliet,* i, 3, 18.
God give her good rest!—*Titus Andronicus,* iv, 2, 63.
God pardon him!—*Romeo and Juliet,* iii, 5, 83.
God be bless'd.—*Taming of the Shrew,* iv, 5, 18.
For the love of God!—*Twelfth Night,* v, 1, 175; 180.
14
God send 'em good shipping!
The Taming of the Shrew. Act v, sc. 1, l. 43. [Biondello]
God send him well!—*All's Well that Ends Well,* i, 1, 190.

1
No, I warrant you, he will not hear of godliness.
Twelfth Night. Act iii, sc. 4, l. 134. [Maria]
With the little godliness I have,
I did full hard forbear him.
Othello, i, 2, 9. The only uses of "godliness."
God-like.—*Love's Labour's Lost,* i, 1, 58, and four times in later plays.
Godly.—*I Henry VI,* v, 1, 5, and three times in later plays.
2
O thou clear god, and patron of all light.
Venus and Adonis, l. 860.
Angry god.—*Macbeth,* iv, 3, 17.
Dear God.—*III Henry VI,* ii, 2, 7; *Richard III,* iii, 3, 21; iv, 4, 77.
Incensed god.—*Pericles,* v, 1, 144.
Visible god.—*Timon of Athens,* iv, 3, 387.
Warlike god.—*Passionate Pilgrim,* l. 147; 149.
God and our right!—See under England.

GODS

3
Be 't as our gods will have 't!
Antony and Cleopatra. Act ii, sc. 1, l. 50. [Pompey]
Pompey: If the great gods be just, they shall assist
The deeds of justest men.
Menecrates: Know, worthy Pompey,
That what they do delay, they not deny.
Pompey: Whiles we are suitors to their throne, decays
The thing we sue for.
Antony and Cleopatra. Act ii, sc. 1, l. 1. The only use of "justest."
4
Gods and goddesses,
All the whole synod of them!
Antony and Cleopatra. Act iii, sc. 10, l. 4. [Scarus]
O gods and goddesses!—*Cymbeline,* iv, 2, 295.
5
He is a god, and knows What is most right.
Antony and Cleopatra. Act iii, sc. 13, l. 60. [Cleopatra]
The gods rebuke me.—*Antony and Cleopatra,* v, 1, 27.
The gods preserve thee!—*Antony and Cleopatra,* v, 1, 60.
The gods themselves do weep!—*Antony and Cleopatra,* v, 2, 303.
6
Art thou god to shepherd turn'd,
That a maiden's heart hath burn'd? . . .
Why, thy godhead laid apart,
Warr'st thou with a woman's heart?
As You Like It. Act iv, sc. 3, l. 40. [Rosalind] "Godhead" is repeated in *Love's Labour's Lost,* v, 2, 10; *Timon of Athens,* iii, 6, 84; and *Cymbeline,* v, 4, 103.
Are you a god? would you create me new?
Transform me then, and to your power I'll yield.
The Comedy of Errors. Act iii, sc. 2, l. 39. [Antipholus of Syracuse]
I pray God make thee new.—*Richard II,* v, 3, 146.

7
He wants nothing of a god but eternity and a heaven to throne in.
Coriolanus. Act v, sc. 4, l. 25. [Menenius]
He's a god or a painter; for he makes faces.
Love's Labour's Lost. Act v, sc. 2, l. 649. [Dumain]
This man Is now become a god.
Julius Cæsar. Act i, sc. 2, l. 115. [Cassius]
The gods can have no mortal officer
More like a god than you.
Pericles. Act v, sc. 3, l. 62. [Pericles]
A god on earth thou art.
Richard II. Act v, sc. 3, l. 136. [Duchess of York]
I prithee, be my god.
The Tempest. Act ii, sc. 2, l. 153. [Caliban]
Play the god.—*Othello,* ii, 3, 353.
8
The gods be good to us!
Coriolanus. Act iv, sc. 6, l. 153. [Citizen]
The gods give thee good on 't!—*Pericles,* ii, 1, 152.
9 Behold, the heavens do ope,
The gods look down, and this unnatural scene
They laugh at.
Coriolanus. Act v, sc. 3, l. 183. [Coriolanus]
10
To your protection I commend me, gods.
From fairies and the tempters of the night
Guard me, beseech ye.
Cymbeline. Act ii, sc. 2, l. 8. [Imogen]
The gods protect you!—*Cymbeline,* i, 1, 128.
The gods protect thee.—*Pericles,* ii, 1, 135.
The gods of Greece protect you!—*Pericles,* i, 4, 97.
Roman gods.—*The Rape of Lucrece,* l. 1831.
11
An 't please the gods.
Cymbeline. Act iv, sc. 2, l. 387. [Imogen]
The odds
Is that we scarce are men and you are gods.
Cymbeline. Act v, sc. 2, l. 9. [Iachimo]
Laud we the gods;
And let our crooked smokes climb to their nostrils
From our blest altars.
Cymbeline. Act v, sc. 5, l. 476. [Cymbeline]
Worship dirty gods.—*Cymbeline,* iii, 6, 56. See under Gold.
Marry, the gods forfend!—*Cymbeline,* v, 5, 287.
The gods forbid!—*Midsummer-Night's Dream,* iii, 2, 276, and four times in later plays.
12
It is the part of men to fear and tremble,
When the most mighty gods by tokens send
Such dreadful heralds to astonish us.
Julius Cæsar. Act i, sc. 3, l. 54. [Casca]
13
The mighty gods defend thee!
Julius Cæsar. Act ii, sc. 3, l. 9. [Artemidorus]
Marina: The gods defend me!
Bawd: If it please the gods to defend you by men, then men must comfort you, men must feed you, men must stir you up.
Pericles. Act iv, sc. 2, l. 95.
The gods defend her!—*King Lear,* v, 3, 256.
The gods defend him.—*Julius Cæsar,* v, 4, 23.

1
As flies to wanton boys, are we to the gods,
They kill us for their sport.
King Lear. Act iv, sc. 1, l. 38. [Gloucester]
The clearest gods, who make them honours
Of men's impossibilities, have preserved thee.
King Lear. Act iv, sc. 6, l. 73. [Edgar] The only use of "clearest."

2
Now, the hot-blooded gods assist me!
Merry Wives of Windsor. Act v, sc. 5, l. 2. [Falstaff] "Hot-blooded" is repeated in *King Lear,* ii, 4, 215: "Hot-blooded France."

When gods have hot backs, what shall poor men do?
The Merry Wives of Windsor, Act v, sc. 5, l. 12. [Falstaff]

3
The gods revenge it upon me and mine,
To the end of generation!
Pericles. Act iii, sc. 3, l. 24. [Cleon]

The gods make her prosperous!—*Pericles,* v, 1, 80.
The gods preserve you!—*Pericles,* iv, 6, 115; v, 1, 14; v, 1, 39.
The gods requite his charity!—*Pericles,* iii, 2, 75.
The gods strengthen thee!—*Pericles,* iv, 6, 114.
By the gods.—*Pericles,* ii, 3, 72; 90; ii, 5, 51; 58.

4
Bawd: Come, the gods have done their part in you.
Marina: I accuse them not.
Pericles. Act iv, sc. 2, l. 74.

5
Be thou the tenth Muse, ten times more in worth
Than those old nine which rhymers invocate.
Sonnets. No. xxxviii. "Rhymers" is repeated in *Antony and Cleopatra,* v, 2, 215.

The thrice three Muses.—*A Midsummer-Night's Dream,* v, 1, 52.

6
Makes a god of such a cullion.
The Taming of the Shrew. Act iv, sc. 2, l. 20. [Hortensio]

Away, base cullions!—*II Henry VI,* i, 3, 42.
Avaunt, you cullions!—*Henry V,* iii, 2, 22. The only uses of "cullion" (rascal).

7
Dally not with the gods.
The Taming of the Shrew. Act iv, sc. 4, l. 68. [Tranio]

Before the gods.—*Timon of Athens,* iii, 2, 19; 54.
The gods confound them.—*Timon of Athens,* iv, 3, 103.

8
The self-same gods that arm'd the Queen of Troy
With opportunity of sharp revenge . . .
May favour Tamora, the Queen of Goths— . . .
To quit the bloody wrongs upon her foes.
Titus Andronicus. Act i, sc. 1, l. 136. [Demetrius]

The gods delight in tragedies.
Titus Andronicus. Act iv, sc. 1, l. 60. [Marcus]

9
Pray to the devils; the gods have given us over.
Titus Andronicus. Act iv, sc. 2, l. 48. [Aaron]

There 's not a god left unsolicited.
Titus Andronicus. Act iv, sc. 3, l. 60. [Titus] "Unsolicited" is repeated in *Henry VIII,* ii, 4, 219.

Vow By that same god, what god soe'er it be,
That thou adorest and hast in reverence.
Titus Andronicus. Act v, sc. 1, l. 82. [Aaron]

10
Well, the gods are above.
Troilus and Cressida. Act i, sc. 2, l. 83. [Pandarus]

Blessed gods.—*The Winter's Tale,* v, 1, 168.
O the blest gods!—*King Lear,* ii, 4, 171.
O immortal gods!—*The Taming of the Shrew,* v, 1, 68; *Troilus and Cressida,* iv, 2, 100; *Julius Cæsar,* iv, 3, 157; *Timon of Athens,* i, 2, 63; iv, 3, 138.
O you gods divine!—*Troilus and Cressida,* iv, 2, 105.
The everlasting gods.—*Troilus and Cressida,* v, 3, 5.
Gentle gods.—*Cymbeline,* i, 1, 115.
Good gods.—*Antony and Cleopatra,* iii, 4, 15, and four times in later plays.
Great gods.—*II Henry VI,* v, 1, 68; *Richard III,* v, 5, 8; *King Lear,* iii, 2, 49; *Antony and Cleopatra,* ii, 1, 1.
Holy gods.—*Pericles,* iii, 4, 7; v, 1, 200.
Kind gods.—*King Lear,* iii, 7, 35; iii, 7, 92; iv, 7, 14.
Mightful gods.—*Titus Andronicus,* iv, 4, 5. The only use of "mightful."
Mighty gods.—*Julius Cæsar,* i, 3, 55; ii, 2, 27.
The most high gods.—*Pericles,* ii, 4, 3.
Prosperous gods.—*Timon of Athens,* v, 1, 186.
Righteous gods.—*Timon of Athens,* iv, 2, 4.
Throned gods.—*Antony and Cleopatra,* i, 3, 28.
Wise gods.—*Antony and Cleopatra,* iii, 13, 112.

11
Have the gods envy?
Troilus and Cressida. Act iv, sc. 4, l. 30. [Cressida]

12
Sure the gods do this year connive at us, and we may do any thing extempore.
The Winter's Tale. Act iv, sc. 4, l. 690. [Autolycus] The only use of "connive." "Extempore" is used five times.

The gods
Will have fulfill'd their secret purposes.
Winter's Tale. Act v, sc. 1, l. 35. [Paulina]

II—Goddess

13
A woman I forswore; but I will prove,
Thou being a goddess, I forswore not thee.
Love's Labour's Lost. Act iv, sc. 3, l. 64. [Longaville] Repeated in *The Passionate Pilgrim,* l. 33.

I were the fairest goddess on the ground.
Love's Labour's Lost. Act v, sc. 2, l. 36. [Rosaline]

Dear goddess.—*King Lear,* i, 4, 297; *Antony and Cleopatra,* i, 2, 73.
Fair goddess.—*Coriolanus,* i, 5, 21.
Good goddess.—*The Winter's Tale,* ii, 3, 104.

Guilty goddess.—*Sonnets,* cxi.
Thrifty goddess.—*Measure for Measure,* i, 1, 39.
That goddess blind.—*Henry V,* iii, 6, 30.
This goddess, this Semiramis.—*Titus Andronicus,* ii, 1, 22. Semiramis is mentioned again in ii, 3, 118, and in *The Taming of the Shrew,* Ind., 2, 41.
Goddess, nymph.—*Midsummer-Night's Dream,* iii, 2, 137; 226.
A goddess, and a sovereign.—*All's Well that Ends Well,* i, 1, 183.
Goddess of the night.—*Much Ado about Nothing,* v, 3, 12.
O goddess!—*Pericles,* v, 3, 6.
O thou goddess!—*Cymbeline,* iv, 2, 169.
Goddess-like.—*Cymbeline,* iii, 2, 8; *The Winter's Tale,* iv, 4, 10; *Pericles,* v, 1, 251.

1
I grant I never saw a goddess go.
Sonnets. No. cxxx.

2
The goddess On whom these airs attend!
Tempest. Act i, sc. 2, l. 421. [Ferdinand]
Is she the goddess that hath sever'd us,
And brought us thus together?
The Tempest. Act v, sc. 1, l. 187. [Alonso]

III—Individual Gods and Goddesses

3
Adonis painted by a running brook,
And Cytherea all in sedges hid.
The Taming of the Shrew. Induction, sc. 2, l. 52. [Second Servant] "Adonis" occurs again in *I Henry VI,* i, 6, 6, and twenty-two times in the poems. "Cytherea" is used in *The Winter's Tale,* iv, 4, 122; *Cymbeline,* ii, 4, 14; and twice in *The Passionate Pilgrim.*

4
Daphne roaming through a thorny wood,
Scratching her legs that one shall swear she bleeds,
And at that sight shall sad Apollo weep,
So workmanly the blood and tears are drawn.
The Taming of the Shrew. Induction, sc. 2, l. 59. [Third Servant] The only use of "workmanly." Daphne is mentioned also in *A Midsummer-Night's Dream,* ii, 1, 231, and *Troilus and Cressida,* i, 1, 101. Apollo appears twenty-three times.

5
Diana: Diana.
Bertram: Titled goddess.
All's Well that Ends Well. Act iv, sc. 2, l. 2. "Titled" is repeated in *Troilus and Cressida,* ii, 3, 203.
Celestial Dian, goddess argentine.
Pericles, v, 1, 251. Dian, or Diana, is mentioned no less than forty-seven times in the plays and twice in the poems. The only use of "argentine."

6
Two-headed Janus.
Merchant of Venice. Act i, sc. 1, l. 50. [Salarino] "Janus" occurs once again in *Othello,* i, 2, 33. The only use of "two-headed."

7
Great Jove, Othello guard,
And swell his sail with thine own powerful breath,
That he may bless this bay with his tall ship.
Othello. Act ii, sc. 1, l. 77. [Cassio] Jove is mentioned eighty times in the plays and six times in the poems.
O thou great thunder-darter of Olympus, forget that thou art Jove, the king of gods.
Troilus and Cressida. Act ii, sc. 3, l. 10. [Thersites] The only use of "thunder-darter." See also under THUNDER.
Jove multipotent.—*Troilus and Cressida,* iv, 5, 129. The only use of "multipotent."

8
Juno, that is queen of marriage.
Pericles. Act ii, sc. 3, l. 30. [Thaisa] Juno is mentioned seventeen times.
Great Juno.—*As You Like It,* v, 4, 147; *Antony and Cleopatra,* iv, 15, 34; *Cymbeline,* iii, 4, 168; *The Tempest,* iv, 1, 102.
Juno-like.—*Coriolanus,* iv, 2, 53.

9
The gods themselves,
Humbling their deities to love, have taken
The shapes of beasts upon them: Jupiter
Became a bull, and bellow'd; the green Neptune
A ram, and bleated; and the fire-robed god,
Golden Apollo, a poor humble swain,
As I seem now.
The Winter's Tale. Act iv, sc. 4, l. 25. [Florizel] Jupiter is mentioned thirty times in the plays. The only use of "humbling" and "fire-robed."
God Bel.—*Much Ado about Nothing,* iii, 3, 143. The only mention of Bel.
'Tis the god Hercules.—*Antony and Cleopatra,* iv, 3, 16. Hercules is mentioned thirty-six times in the plays.
The goddess Isis.—*Antony and Cleopatra,* iii, 6, 17. Isis is mentioned eight times in this play, and in no other.
God Neptune.—*Pericles,* v, Gower, 17. Neptune is mentioned twenty-three times.
Plutus, the god of gold.—*Timon of Athens,* i, 1, 287. Plutus is mentioned four times.
God Priapus.—*Pericles,* iv, 6, 4. The only mention of Priapus.

GOLD

See also Money

10
The gold I give thee will I melt and pour
Down thy ill-uttering throat.
Antony and Cleopatra. Act ii, sc. 5, l. 34. [Cleopatra] The only use of "ill-uttering."
I'll set thee in a shower of gold, and hail
Rich pearls upon thee.
Antony and Cleopatra. Act ii, sc. 5, l. 45. [Cleopatra]

11
The gold bides still,
That others touch, and often touching will
Wear gold.
The Comedy of Errors. Act ii, sc. 1, l. 110. [Adriana]
Dromio of Syracuse: Here's the gold you sent me for. . . .
Antipholus of Syracuse: What gold is this?
The Comedy of Errors. Act iv, sc. 3, l. 12.

12
I will wage against your gold, gold to it.
Cymbeline. Act i, sc. 4, l. 144. [Posthumus]
'Tis gold
Which buys admittance; oft it doth; yea, and makes

Diana's rangers false themselves, yield up
Their deer to the stand o' the stealer; and 'tis gold
Which makes the true man kill'd and saves the thief;
Nay, sometime hangs both thief and true man: what Can it not do and undo?
Cymbeline. Act ii, sc. 3, l. 72. [Cloten] The only use of "rangers." "Stealer" is repeated in *Much Ado about Nothing*, ii, 1, 233, and in *Hamlet*, iii, 2, 349.

All gold and silver rather turn to dirt!
As 'tis no better reckon'd, but of those
Who worship dirty gods.
Cymbeline. Act iii, sc. 6, l. 54. [Arviragus]

Gold and silver.—*The Merchant of Venice*, i, 3, 96; ii, 9, 20; *King John*, iii, 3, 13; *II Henry IV*, i, 2, 20; *Merry Wives of Windsor*, i, 1, 52.

Gold and jewels.—*The Merchant of Venice*, ii, 4, 32; *Othello*, v, 1, 16.

Gold and pearl.—*The Taming of the Shrew*, Ind., 2, 44; v, 1, 78; *Henry V*, iv, 1, 279; *Titus Andronicus*, ii, 1, 19.

Plate and gold.—*Taming of the Shrew*, ii, 1, 349.

1
How quickly nature falls into revolt
When gold becomes her object!
II Henry IV. Act iv, sc. 5, l. 66. [King Henry]

Canker'd heaps of strange-achieved gold.
II Henry IV. Act iv, sc. 5, l. 72. [King Henry] The only use of "strange-achieved."

Therefore, thou best of gold art worst of gold;
Other, less fine in carat, is more precious.
II Henry IV. Act iv, sc. 5, l. 161. [Prince]

How much your chain weighs to the utmost carat.
The Comedy of Errors, iv, 1, 28. The only uses of "carat."

2
For me, the gold of France did not seduce;
Although I did admit it as a motive
The sooner to effect what I intended.
Henry V. Act ii, sc. 2, l. 155. [Cambridge]

3
Put forth thy hand, reach at the glorious gold.
II Henry VI. Act i, sc. 2, l. 11. [Duchess of Gloucester]

Dame Eleanor gives gold to bring the witch:
Gold cannot come amiss, were she a devil,
Yet have I gold flies from another coast.
II Henry VI. Act i, sc. 2, l. 91. [Hume]

I shall have gold for all.—*II Henry VI*, i, 2, 107.

4
Are my chests fill'd up with extorted gold?
II Henry VI. Act iv, sc. 7, l. 105. [Say]

Gold must round engirt these brows of mine.
II Henry VI, v, 1, 99. See under KING.

5
Give me thy gold, if thou hast any gold;
For I have bought it with an hundred blows.
III Henry VI. Act ii, sc. 5, l. 80. [Father]

6
I did send to you
For certain sums of gold, which you denied me. . . . I did send
To you for gold to pay my legions,
Which you denied me: was that done like Cassius?
Julius Cæsar. Act iv, sc. 3, l. 69. [Brutus]

7
To gild refined gold.
King John, iv, 2, 11. See under EXCESS.

8
All that glisters is not gold.
The Merchant of Venice. Act ii, sc. 7, l. 65. [Prince of Morocco] See under APPEARANCE.

9
I shall never see my gold again.
The Merchant of Venice. Act iii, sc. 1, l. 115. [Shylock]

Thou gaudy gold,
Hard food for Midas, I will none of thee.
The Merchant of Venice. Act iii, sc. 2, l. 101. [Bassanio] The only mention of Midas.

10
Gold that 's by the touchstone tried.
Pericles. Act ii, sc. 2, l. 37. [Thaisa] The only use of "touchstone," except as the name of the clown in *As You Like It*.

11
Never lack'd gold and yet went never gay.
Othello, ii, 1, 151. See under CHARACTER.

12
Gold were as good as twenty orators.
Richard III. Act iv, sc. 2, l. 38. [Page]

13
There is thy gold, worse poison to men's souls,
Doing more murders in this loathsome world,
Than these poor compounds that thou mayst not sell.
I sell thee poison; thou hast sold me none.
Romeo and Juliet. Act v, sc. 1, l. 80. [Romeo]

14
The strongest castle, tower, and town,
The golden bullet beats it down.
The Passionate Pilgrim, l. 327. "Golden" is used 103 times in the plays and poems, always preceding a noun.

Thou know'st not gold's effect.
The Taming of the Shrew. Act i, sc. 2, l. 93. [Petruchio]

15
He pours it out; Plutus, the god of gold,
Is but his steward.
Timon of Athens. Act i, sc. 1, l. 287. [Second Lord]

Plutus' gold.—*Troilus and Cressida*, iii, 3, 197.

Plutus' mine.—*Julius Cæsar*, iv, 3, 102. Plutus is mentioned a fourth time in *All's Well that Ends Well*, v, 3, 101.

16
If I want gold, steal but a beggar's dog,
And give it Timon, why, the dog coins gold.
Timon of Athens. Act ii, sc. 1, l. 5. [Senator]

17
Gold? yellow, glittering, precious gold? . . .
Thus much of this will make black white, foul fair,
Wrong right, base noble, old young, coward valiant. . . .
This yellow slave
Will knit and break religions, bless the accursed,
Make the hoar leprosy adored, place thieves
And give them title, knee and approbation

With senators on the bench: this is it
That makes the wappen'd widow wed again;
She, whom the spital-house and ulcerous sores
Would cast the gorge at, this embalms and spices
To the April day again. Come, damned earth,
Thou common whore of mankind.
Timon of Athens. Act iv, sc. 3, l. 26. [Timon] The only use of "wappen'd" (meaning unknown, apparently coined by Shakespeare, possibly obscene, or perhaps a misprint), and of "spital-house" (hospital).

I have but little gold of late, brave Timon,
The want whereof doth daily make revolt
In my penurious band.
Timon of Athens. Act iv, sc. 3, l. 90. [Alcibiades] The only use of "penurious."

1
O thou sweet king-killer, and dear divorce
'Twixt natural son and sire! thou bright defiler
Of Hymen's purest bed! thou valiant Mars!
Thou ever young, fresh, loved and delicate wooer,
Whose blush doth thaw the consecrated snow
That lies on Dian's lap! thou visible god,
That solder'st close impossibilities,
And makest them kiss! that speak'st with every tongue
To every purpose! O thou touch of hearts!
Think, thy slave man rebels, and by thy virtue
Set them into confounding odds, that beasts
May have the world in empire!
Timon of Athens. Act iv, sc. 3, l. 382. [Timon] The only use of "king-killer," "defiler" and "solder'st."

What a god 's gold,
That he is worshipp'd in a baser temple
Than where swine feed!
Timon of Athens. Act v, sc. 1, l. 50. [Timon]

2
Alcibiades: Here is some gold for thee.
Timon: Keep it, I cannot eat it.
Timon of Athens. Act iv, sc. 3, l. 100.

Rascal thieves, Here 's gold.—*Timon of Athens,* iv, 3, 432; *As You Like It,* ii, 3, 45; *Pericles,* i, 1, 155; iv, 6, 112.

Here is that gold I have.—*The Winter's Tale,* iv, 4, 837.

I 'll give you gold.—*Timon of Athens,* v, 1, 103; 107; *Pericles,* v, 1, 258.

Give him gold.—*The Winter's Tale,* iv, 4, 831.

I have gold for thee.—*Timon of Athens,* v, 1, 41.

You shall have gold.—*The Merchant of Venice,* iii, 2, 308.

Put up thy gold.—*Timon of Athens,* iv, 3, 107.

3
Timon: There 's gold to pay thy soldiers. . . .
Alcibiades: Hast thou gold yet? I'll take the gold thou givest. . . .
Phrynia and Timandra: Give us some gold, good Timon: hast thou more?
Timon: Enough to make a whore forswear her trade,
And to make whores, a bawd. . . .
Phrynia and Timandra: Well more gold: what then?
Believe 't, we 'll do any thing for gold.
Timon: . . . There 's more gold:
Do you damn others, and let this damn you.
Timon of Athens. Act iv, sc. 3, l. 126.

Timon: Tell them there I have gold; look, so I have.
Apemantus: Here is no use for gold.
Timon: The best and truest;
For here it sleeps, and does no hired harm.
Timon of Athens. Act iv, sc. 3, l. 289.

I 'll say thou 'st gold;
Thou wilt be throng'd to shortly.
Timon of Athens. Act iv, sc. 3, l. 394. [Apemantus]

Where should he have this gold? It is some poor fragment, some slender ort of his remainder; the mere want of gold, and the falling-from of his friends, drove him into this melancholy.
Timon of Athens. Act iv, sc. 3, l. 399. [First Bandit] The only use of "falling-from."

Gold confound you whosoe'er!—*Timon of Athens,* iv, 3, 452.

4
Poet: Does the rumour hold for true, that he 's so full of gold?
Painter: Certain: Alcibiades reports it; Phrynia and Timandra had gold of him; he likewise enriched poor straggling soldiers with great quantity; 'tis said he gave unto his steward a mighty sum.
Timon of Athens. Act v, sc. 1, l. 3.

5
Hence, pack! there 's gold; you came for gold, ye slaves;
[To Painter] You have work'd for me; there 's payment for you; hence!
[To Poet] You are an alchemist; make gold of that.
Timon of Athens. Act v, sc. 1, l. 115. [Timon] "Alchemist" is used a second time in *King John,* iii, 1, 78: "Plays the alchemist."

There 's a poor piece of gold for thee.
Othello. Act iii, sc. 1, l. 25. [Cassio]

There 's gold for thee.—*Antony and Cleopatra,* iii, 3, 37; *Twelfth Night,* i, 2, 18; v, 1, 31; *Cymbeline,* ii, 3, 87.

There 's more gold.—*Timon of Athens,* iv, 3, 448; *Antony and Cleopatra,* ii, 5, 31.

6
He that had wit would think that I had none,
To bury so much gold under a tree,
And never after to inherit it.
Let him that thinks of me so abjectly
Know that this gold must coin a stratagem,
Which, cunningly effected, will beget
A very excellent piece of villany:
And so repose, sweet gold, for their unrest.
Titus Andronicus. Act ii, sc. 3, l. 1. [Aaron] The only use of "abjectly."

1
Foul-cankering rust the hidden treasure frets;
But gold that 's put to use more gold begets.
Venus and Adonis, l. 767. The only use of "foul-cankering."

2
Clown: You 're a made old man: if the sins of your youth are forgiven you, you 're well to live. Gold! all gold!
Shepherd: This is fairy gold, boy, and 'twill prove so.
The Winter's Tale. Act iii, sc. 3, l. 124.

Beaten gold.—*Antony and Cleopatra,* ii, 2, 197.
Bright gold.—*The Merchant of Venice,* iv, 1, 59; *Pericles,* iii, 2, 101.
Burnish'd gold.—*Venus and Adonis,* l. 858. "Burnish'd" is repeated in *Merchant of Venice,* ii, 1, 2: "Burnish'd sun"; and in *Antony and Cleopatra,* ii, 2, 196: "Burnish'd throne."
Corrupting gold.—*Richard III,* iv, 2, 34.
Current gold.—*Richard III,* iv, 2, 9.
Glittering gold.—*King John,* iii, 1, 80.
Pure gold.—*The Two Gentlemen of Verona,* ii, 4, 171; *Romeo and Juliet,* v, 3, 299.
Saint-seducing gold.—*Romeo and Juliet,* i, 1, 220. The only use of "saint-seducing."
Tried gold.—*The Merchant of Venice,* ii, 7, 53.
Uncurrent gold.—*Hamlet,* ii, 2, 448.
Venice gold.—*Taming of the Shrew,* ii, 1, 356.
Vile gold, dross, dust.—*King John,* iii, 1, 165.
Yellow gold.—*A Midsummer-Night's Dream,* iii, 2, 393.

GOODNESS

See also Man: Good Men; Virtue

I—Goodness

3
Good alone Is good without a name.
All's Well that Ends Well. Act ii, sc. 3, l. 135. [King]

He is too good and fair for death and me.
All's Well that Ends Well. Act iii, sc. 4, l. 16. [Steward]

I do presume, sir, that you are not fallen
From the report that goes upon your goodness.
All's Well that Ends Well. Act v, sc. 1, l. 13. [Helena]

4
And towards himself, his goodness forespent on us,
We must extend our notice.
Cymbeline. Act ii, sc. 3, l. 64. [Cymbeline] "Forespent" is repeated in *Henry V,* ii, 4, 36.

Your very goodness . . . O'erpays all I can do.
Cymbeline. Act ii, sc. 4, l. 9. [Philario]

5
Goodness, growing to a plurisy,
Dies in his own too much.
Hamlet. Act iv, sc. 7, l. 118. [King] The only mention of plurisy.

There is so great a fever on goodness, that the dissolution of it must cure it.
Measure for Measure. Act iii, sc. 2, l. 235. [Duke]

6
Talbot means no goodness by his looks.
I Henry VI. Act iii, sc. 2, l. 72. [La Pucelle]

There 's no goodness in thy face.
Antony and Cleopatra. Act ii, sc. 5, l. 37. [Cleopatra]

7
God's goodness hath been great to thee.
II Henry VI. Act ii, sc. 1, l. 84. [King Henry]

And when old time shall lead him to his end,
Goodness and he fill up one monument!
Henry VIII. Act ii, sc. 1, l. 93. [Buckingham]

8
For goodness' sake, consider what you do.
Henry VIII, iii, 1, 159. See under Consideration. "For goodness' sake" is repeated in the Prologue, l. 23, and occurs in no other play.

9
Wolsey: All goodness
Is poison to thy stomach.
Surrey: Yes, that goodness
Of gleaning all the land's wealth into one,
Into your own hands, cardinal, by extortion;
The goodness of your intercepted packets
You writ to the pope against the king; your goodness,
Since you provoke me, shall be most notorious.
Henry VIII. Act iii, sc. 2, l. 282. The only use of "gleaning."

Confirm his goodness.—*Henry VIII,* iii, 2, 249.
Abundant goodness.—*Richard II,* v, 3, 65.
Endless goodness.—*Henry VIII,* v, 5, 1.
Great goodness.—*Henry VIII,* iii, 2, 263.
Perfect goodness.—*Cymbeline,* i, 6, 158.

10
Common good to all.
Julius Cæsar. Act v, sc. 5, l. 72. [Antony]

As you respect the common good.
Henry VIII, iii, 2, 290. The only uses of "common good."

11
O thou good Kent, how shall I live and work,
To match thy goodness? My life will be too short,
And every measure fail me.
King Lear. Act iv, sc. 7, l. 1. [Cordelia]

You know the goodness I intend upon you.
King Lear. Act v, sc. 1, l. 7. [Regan]

Some good I mean to do,
Despite of mine own nature.
King Lear. Act v, sc. 3, l. 243. [Edmund]

12
Now we 'll together; and the chance of goodness
Be like our warranted quarrel!
Macbeth. Act iv, sc. 4, l. 136. [Malcolm]

13
The hand that hath made you fair hath made you good: the goodness that is cheap in beauty makes beauty brief in goodness; but grace, being the soul of your complexion, shall keep the body of it ever fair.
Measure for Measure. Act iii, sc. 1, l. 184. [Duke]

Thanks, good friend Escalus, for thy much goodness.
Measure for Measure. Act v, sc. 1, l. 534. [Duke] The only use of "much goodness."

1
Shylock: Antonio is a good man.
Bassanio: Have you heard any imputation to the contrary?
Shylock: Oh, no, no, no, no: my meaning in saying he is a good man is to have you understand me that he is sufficient.
The Merchant of Venice. Act i, sc. 3, l. 12. The phrase "good man" occurs thirty-seven times in the plays.

Are you good men and true?
Much Ado about Nothing. Act iii, sc. 3, l. 1. [Dogberry]

2
I never did repent for doing good,
Nor shall not now.
The Merchant of Venice. Act iii, sc. 4, l. 10. [Portia]

He did us great good.
Henry V. Act iv, sc. 8, l. 126. [Fluellen] The only use of the phrase "great good."

Much good do it your good heart.
The Merry Wives of Windsor. Act i, sc. 1, l. 83. [Shallow]

Let 't not be doubted I shall do good.
Winter's Tale. Act ii, sc. 2, l. 54. [Paulina]

Thrive and do good.—*II Henry VI*, iv, 3, 17.

Who can do good?—*Measure for Measure,* iv, 2, 71.

3
The goodness of the night upon you, friends!
Othello. Act i, sc. 2, l. 35. [Othello]

Bliss and goodness on you!—*Measure for Measure,* iii, 2, 228.

4
Fair one, all goodness that consists in bounty
Expect even here.
Pericles. Act v, sc. 1, l. 70. [Lysimachus]

5
What good is cover'd with the face of heaven,
To be discover'd, that can do me good?
Richard III. Act iv, sc. 4, l. 239. [Queen Elizabeth]

6
A most incomparable man, breathes, as it were,
To an untirable and continuate goodness.
Timon of Athens. Act i, sc. 1, l. 10. [Merchant] The only use of "untirable." "Continuate" occurs again in *Othello,* iii, 4, 178.

Recanting goodness, sorry ere 'tis shown.
Timon of Athens, i, 2, 17. See under CEREMONY.

Poor honest lord, brought low by his own heart,
Undone by goodness! Strange, unusual blood,
When man's worst sin is, he does too much good!
Timon of Athens. Act iv, sc. 2, l. 37. [Flavius]

7
O heavens, can you hear a good man groan,
And not relent, or not compassion him?
Titus Andronicus. Act iv, sc. 1, l. 123. [Marcus]

8
You 'll ne'er be good, Nor suffer others.
Troilus and Cressida. Act iv, sc. 2, l. 30. [Cressida]

9
Of many good I think him best.
The Two Gentlemen of Verona. Act i, sc. 2, l. 21. [Lucetta]

10 'Good' should be pertinent;
But, so it is, it is not.
The Winter's Tale. Act i, sc. 2, l. 221. [Leontes] "Pertinent" is repeated in *Coriolanus,* ii, 2, 67.

Our natural goodness imparts this.
Winter's Tale. Act ii, sc. 1, l. 164. [Leontes]

The need I have of thee thine own goodness hath made; better not to have had thee than thus to want thee.
The Winter's Tale, iv, 2, 13. [Polixenes]

II—Good and Evil

11
Yet these fix'd evils sit so fit in him,
That they take place, when virtue's steeley bones
Look bleak i' the cold wind.
All's Well that Ends Well. Act i, sc. 1, l. 113. [Helena] "Steely" is used a second time in *III Henry VI,* ii, 3, 16: "Steely point."

Among nine bad if one be good,
There 's yet one good in ten.
All's Well that Ends Well. Act i, sc. 3, l. 82. [Clown]

Not altogether so great as the first in goodness, but greater a great deal in evil.
All's Well that Ends Well. Act iv, sc. 3, l. 319. [Parolles]

12 I must not think there are
Evils enow to darken all his goodness.
Antony and Cleopatra. Act i, sc. 4, l. 10. [Lepidus]

His taints and honours Waged equal with him.
Antony and Cleopatra. Act v, sc. 1, l. 30. [Mecænas]

13
Many times, Doth ill deserve by doing well.
Cymbeline. Act iii, sc. 3, l. 53. [Belarius]

He was too good to be
Where ill men were; and was the best of all
Amongst the rarest of good ones.
Cymbeline. Act v, sc. 5, l. 158. [Iachimo]

14
There is some soul of goodness in things evil,
Would men observingly distil it out.
Henry V. Act iv, sc. 1, l. 4. [King Henry] The only use of "observingly."

15
Make my ill the advantage of my good.
I Henry VI. Act ii, sc. 5, l. 129. [Plantagenet]

16 What we oft do best,
By sick interpreters, once weak ones, is
Not ours, or not allow'd; what worst, as oft,
Hitting a grosser quality, is cried up
For our best act.
Henry VIII. Act i, sc. 2, l. 81. [Wolsey]

17
The evil that men do lives after them;
The good is oft interred with their bones.
Julius Cæsar. Act iii, sc. 2, l. 80. [Antony]

Men's evil manners live in brass; their virtues
We write in water.
Henry VIII. Act iv, sc. 2, l. 45. [Griffith]

1
Wisdom and goodness to the vile seem vile:
Filths savour but themselves.
King Lear. Act iv, sc. 2, l. 38. [Albany]

2
This supernatural soliciting
Cannot be ill, cannot be good.
Macbeth. Act i, sc. 3, l. 130. [Macbeth]

I am in this earthly world; where to do harm
Is often laudable, to do good sometime
Accounted dangerous folly.
Macbeth. Act iv, sc. 2, l. 75. [Lady Macduff]

Such welcome and unwelcome things at once
'Tis hard to reconcile.
Macbeth. Act iv, sc. 3, l. 138. [Macduff]

3
Maintained so politic a state of evil that they will not admit any good part to intermingle with them.
Much Ado about Nothing. Act v, sc. 2, l. 63. [Beatrice] "Intermingle" is repeated in *Othello,* iii, 3, 25.

What may you be? are you of good or evil?
Othello. Act v, sc. 1, l. 65. [Iago]

4
What is vile shows like a virtuous deed.
The Rape of Lucrece, l. 252.

5
Would not this ill do well?
Richard II. Act iii, sc. 3, l. 170. [King Richard]

Thy overflow of good converts to bad.
Richard II. Act v, sc. 3, l. 64. [Bolingbroke]

6
Tell them that God bids us do good for evil.
Richard III. Act i, sc. 3, l. 335. [Richard]

We must do good against evil.
All's Well that Ends Well. Act ii, sc. 5, l. 53. [Lafeu]

7
For nought so vile that on the earth doth live
But to the earth some special good doth give,
Nor aught so good but strain'd from that fair use
Revolts from true birth, stumbling on abuse.
Romeo and Juliet. Act ii, sc. 3, l. 17. [Friar Laurence]

Two such opposed kings encamp them still
In man as well as herbs, grace and rude will;
And where the worser is predominant,
Full soon the canker death eats up that plant.
Romeo and Juliet. Act ii, sc. 3, l. 27. [Friar Laurence] The only use of the phrase "full soon."

8
Captive good attending captain ill.
Sonnets. No. lxvi.

Creating every bad a perfect best.
Sonnets. No. cxiv.

O benefit of ill! now I find true
That better is by evil still made better.
Sonnets. No. cxix.

Thy worst all best exceeds.
Sonnets. No. cl.

9
Abhorred slave,
Which any print of goodness wilt not take,
Being capable of all ill!
The Tempest. Act i, sc. 2, l. 351. [Prospero]

10
When we for recompense have praised the vile,
It stains the glory in that happy verse
Which aptly sings the good.
Timon of Athens. Act i, sc. 1, l. 15. [Poet]

11
The bold and coward,
The wise and fool, the artist and unread,
The hard and soft, seem all affined and kin.
Troilus and Cressida. Act i, sc. 3, l. 23. [Agamemnon] The only use of "unread." "Affined" occurs twice in *Othello,* i, 1, 39, and ii, 3, 218.

GOOSE

12
Breaks his staff like a noble goose.
As You Like It. Act iii, sc. 4, l. 47. [Celia]

Broad goose.—*Romeo and Juliet,* ii, 4, 90.
Giddy goose.—*I Henry IV,* iii, 1, 232.
Good goose.—*Romeo and Juliet,* ii, 4, 82.
Green goose.—*Love's Labour's Lost,* iv, 3, 75.
Sweet goose.—*Romeo and Juliet,* ii, 4, 86.

13
I'll never Be such a gosling.
Coriolanus, v, 3, 35. "Gosling" is used once again, in *Pericles,* iv, 2, 91: "Whip thee, gosling."

14
Goose, if I had you upon Sarum plain,
I'ld drive ye cackling home to Camelot.
King Lear. Act ii, sc. 2, l. 89. [Kent] The only mention of Sarum plain and Camelot.

When every goose is cackling.—*The Merchant of Venice,* v, 1, 105. The only uses of "cackling."

15
Moth: Until the goose came out of door. . . .
Armado: Until the goose came out of door,
And stayed the odds by adding four.
Moth: A good l'envoy, ending in the goose: would you desire more?
Costard: The boy hath sold him a bargain, a goose, that's flat.
Sir, your pennyworth is good, and your goose be fat.
To sell a bargain well is as cunning as fast and loose;
Let me see; a fat l'envoy; ay, that's a fat goose.
. . . The goose that you bought.
Love's Labour's Lost. Act iii, sc. 1, l. 92.

I smell . . . some goose, in this.—*Love's Labour's Lost,* iii, 1, 123.

Roast your goose.—*Macbeth,* ii, 3, 17.

16
The devil damn thee black, thou cream-faced loon!
Where got'st thou that goose look?
Macbeth. Act v, sc. 3, l. 11. [Macbeth] The only use of "cream-faced," "loon," and "goose look."

1
As wild geese that the creeping fowler eye.
A Midsummer-Night's Dream. Act iii, sc. 2, l. 20. [Oberon] The only use of "fowler."
Geese he hath killed.—*The Two Gentlemen of Verona,* iv, 4, 35.
Plucked geese.—*The Merry Wives of Windsor,* v, 1, 27.
Stole two geese.—*The Merry Wives of Windsor,* iii, 4, 41.
Souls of geese.—*Coriolanus,* i, 4, 34.
Green geese.—*Love's Labour 's Lost,* i, 1, 97.

2
A goose for his discretion.
A Midsummer-Night's Dream, v, 1, 235. See under LION.
The goose carries not the fox.
A Midsummer-Night's Dream. Act v, sc. 1, l. 239. [Theseus]

3
Mercutio: Was I with you there for the goose?
Romeo: Thou wast never with me for any thing when thou wast not there for the goose.
Romeo and Juliet. Act ii, sc. 4, l. 78.

4
My fear is this,
Some galled goose of Winchester would hiss.
Troilus and Cressida. Act v, sc. 10, l. 54. [Pandarus]
Winchester goose.—*I Henry VI,* i, 3, 53. The only references to "Winchester goose," a swelling in the groin caused by venereal disease.

GORE, see Blood

GOSSIP

See also Prattle, Report, Rumour, Scandal

5
I 'll gossip at this feast.
The Comedy of Errors. Act v, sc. 1, l. 407. [Duke]
Will you walk in to see their gossiping?
The Comedy of Errors. Act v, sc. 1, l. 419. [Dromio of Ephesus] "Gossiping" occurs again in *King John,* v, 2, 59. See under FEAST.

6
Wants not buzzers to infect his ear.
Hamlet. Act iv, sc. 5, l. 90. [King] The only use of "buzzers."

7
Buz these conjurations in her brain.
II Henry VI, i, 2, 99. See under AMBITION.
Buz in the people's ears.—*Titus Andronicus,* iv, 4, 7.
Buzz'd into his ears.—*Richard II,* ii, 1, 26. The only use of "buzz'd."
Buzz to offend thine ears.—*III Henry VI,* ii, 6, 95.
Buzz lamenting doings.—*Titus Andronicus,* iii, 2, 62.
Buzz about.—*Henry VIII,* iii, 2, 55.
Buz abroad.—*III Henry VI,* v, 6, 86.
Each buzz, each fancy.—*King Lear,* i, 4, 348.
Should be! should—buzz!—*The Taming of the Shrew,* ii, 1, 207. The only uses of "buzz."

8
Did you not of late days hear
A buzzing of a separation?
Henry VIII. Act ii, sc. 2, l. 147. [Gentleman]
You have stol'n their buzzing.—*Julius Cæsar,* v, 1, 37. See under WORD.
Buzzing melody.—*Titus Andronicus,* iii, 2, 64.
Buzzing multitude.—*The Merchant of Venice,* iii, 2, 182.
Buzzing night-flies.—*II Henry IV,* iii, 1, 11. The only uses of "buzzing."

9
Salarino: If my gossip Report be a woman of her word.
Salanio: I would she were as lying a gossip in that as ever knapped ginger.
The Merchant of Venice. Act iii, sc. 1, l. 7. The only use of "knapped" in the sense of biting noisily. It occurs in *King Lear,* ii, 4, 125, in the sense of striking a sharp blow: "Knapped 'em o' the coxcombs."
Noble gossips.—*Henry VIII,* v, 5, 13.

10
Full often hath she gossip'd by my side.
A Midsummer-Night's Dream. Act ii, sc. 1, l. 125. [Titania] The only use of "gossip'd."

11
The one is too like an image and says nothing, and the other too like my lady's eldest son, evermore tattling.
Much Ado about Nothing. Act ii, sc. 1, l. 9. [Beatrice]
Let the ladies tattle what they please.
Titus Andronicus. Act iv, sc. 2, l. 168. [Aaron] The only use of "tattle."
She 's a very tattling woman.
The Merry Wives of Windsor. Act iii, sc. 3, l. 98. [Mrs. Ford]
Peace your tattlings.
The Merry Wives of Windsor, iv, 1, 26. The only uses of "tattling" and "tattlings."

12
The jealous o'erworn widow and herself, . . .
Are mighty gossips in this monarchy.
Richard III. Act i, sc. 1, l. 81. [Gloucester] The only use of "o'erworn."
She hath had gossips.—*The Two Gentlemen of Verona,* iii, 1, 269.

13
Smatter with your gossips, go.
Romeo and Juliet. Act iii, sc. 5, l. 172. [Capulet] The only use of "smatter."

14
A long-tongued babbling gossip.
Titus Andronicus. Act iv, sc. 2, l. 150. [Aaron] "Long-tongued" is repeated in *III Henry VI,* ii, 2, 102: "Long-tongued Warwick." "Babbling gossip" occurs again in *Twelfth Night,* i, 5, 292.
To babble and to talk is most tolerable and not to be endured.
Much Ado about Nothing. Act iii, sc. 3, l. 36. [Dogberry]
This babble shall not henceforth trouble me.
The Two Gentlemen of Verona. Act i, sc. 2, l. 98. [Julia]
Vain bibble babble.—*Twelfth Night,* iv, 2, 105. The only uses of "babble."
Babbled of green fields.—*Henry V,* ii, 3, 17. The only use of "babbled."

GOVERNMENT

See also Commonwealth, State

1
For government, though high and low and lower,
Put into parts, doth keep in one consent,
Congreeing in a full and natural close,
Like music.
Henry V. Act i, sc. 2, l. 180. [Exeter] The only use of "congreeing." "Congreeted" occurs in *Henry V,* v, 2, 31.
There 's not, I think, a subject
That sits in heart-grief and uneasiness
Under the sweet shade of your government.
Henry V. Act ii, sc. 2, l. 26. [Cambridge] The only use of "heart-grief" and "uneasiness."
2
Is this the government of Britain's isle?
II Henry VI, i, 3, 47. See under ENGLAND.
'Tis government that makes them seem divine.
III Henry VI, i, 4, 132. See under WOMAN.
I here resign my government to thee.
III Henry VI. Act iv, sc. 6, l. 24. [King Henry]
3
He being of age to govern himself.
II Henry VI. Act i, sc. 1, l. 166. [Buckingham]
Govern her.—*King Lear,* v, 3, 161.
Govern your desires.—*Titus Andronicus,* ii, 3, 30.
4
Come, wife, let 's in and learn to govern better;
For yet may England curse my wretched reign.
II Henry VI. Act iv, sc. 9, l. 48. [King Henry]
I am sorry for thy much misgovernment.
Much Ado about Nothing. Act iv, sc. 1, l. 100. [Don John] The only use of "misgovernment."
Want of government.—*I Henry IV,* iii, 1, 184.
Weight of government.—*III Henry VI,* iv, 6, 51.
Yoke of government.—*II Henry IV,* iv, 4, 10.
5
Malcolm: If such a one be fit to govern, speak:
I am as I have spoken.
Macduff: Fit to govern! No, not to live.
Macbeth. Act iv, sc. 3, l. 101.
Left to govern.—*Pericles,* iv, 4, 15.
6
Of government the properties to unfold,
Would seem in me to affect speech and discourse.
Measure for Measure. Act i, sc. 1, l. 3. [Duke]
7
Fear not my government.
Othello. Act iii, sc. 3, l. 256. [Othello]
Be resolved he lives to govern us.
Pericles. Act ii, sc. 4, l. 31. [First Lord]
8
Deep regard and smiling government.
The Rape of Lucrece, l. 1400.
Good government.—*I Henry IV,* i, 2, 31; *Pericles,* ii, 1, 108.
Supple government.—*Romeo and Juliet,* iv, 1, 102.
9
All must be even in our government.
Richard II. Act iii, sc. 4, l. 36. [Gardener]
10
Woe to the land that 's govern'd by a child!
Richard III. Act ii, sc. 3, l. 11. [Citizen]
Governed by humours.—*I Henry IV,* iii, 1, 237.
Govern'd by your knowledge.—*King Lear,* iv, 7, 19.
Govern'd by the watery moon.—*Richard III,* ii, 2, 69.
Govern'd by a spleen.—*I Henry IV,* v, 2, 19.
Govern'd with our mothers' spirits.—*Julius Cæsar,* i, 3, 83.
11
In him there is a hope of government,
That in his nonage council under him,
And in his full and ripened years himself,
No doubt, shall then and till then govern well.
Richard III. Act ii, sc. 3, l. 12. [Second Citizen] The only use of "nonage."
We heartily solicit
Your gracious self to take on you the charge
And kingly government of this your land.
Richard III. Act iii, sc. 7, l. 130. [Buckingham]
Govern the country.—*Pericles,* iv, 6, 59.
Govern Rome.—*Titus Andronicus,* iv, 4, 60.
12
The government I cast upon my brother
And to my state grew stranger.
The Tempest. Act i, sc. 2, l. 75. [Prospero]
13
May I govern so,
To heal Rome's harms, and wipe away her woe!
Titus Andronicus. Act v, sc. 3, l. 147. [Lucius]
I would with such perfection govern, sir,
To excel the golden age.
The Tempest. Act ii, sc. 1, l. 167. [Gonzalo]

GOVERNOR

See also Ruler

14
Being ordain'd his special governor.
I Henry VI. Act i, sc. 1, l. 171. [Exeter]
New governor.—*Measure for Measure,* i, 2, 169.
Worthy governor.—*Othello,* ii, 1, 30.
15
My hopes do shape him for the governor.
Othello. Act ii, sc. 1, l. 55. [Cassio]
Governor of this country.—*Pericles,* iv, 6, 57.
Governor of Paris.—*I Henry VI,* iv, 1, 3.
Governor of this place.—*Pericles,* iv, 6, 87; v, 1, 21.
Governor of the town.—*Henry V,* iii, 3, 1.
Her lord, her governor.—*The Merchant of Venice,* iii, 2, 167.
Thy king, thy governor.—*The Taming of the Shrew,* v, 2, 138.
Lord governor.—*Richard II,* ii, 1, 220; *Othello,* v, 2, 367.
16
Where their dear governess and lady lies.
The Rape of Lucrece, l. 443.
Governess of floods.—*A Midsummer-Night's Dream,* ii, 1, 103. The only uses of "governess."

GOWN

See also Dress, Garment

1
Come, thou shalt go to the wars in a gown.
II Henry IV. Act iii, sc. 2, l. 197. [Falstaff]
Hang upon his gown.—*Measure for Measure,* ii, 2, 44.

2
Allowed by order of law a furred gown to keep him warm; and furred with fox and lambskins too.
Measure for Measure. Act iii, sc. 2, l. 8. [Pompey] The only use of "lambskins."
Furr'd gowns.—*King Lear,* iv, 6, 169.
Almsman's gown.—*Richard II,* iii, 3, 149.
Black gown.—*Love's Labour 's Lost.* v, 2, 844; *All's Well that Ends Well,* i, 3, 99.
Black mourning gowns.—*III Henry VI,* ii, 1, 161.
Branched velvet gown.—*Twelfth Night,* ii, 5, 53. The only use of "branched."
Customary gown.—*Coriolanus,* ii, 3, 93.
Loose gown.—*I Henry IV,* iii, 3, 4.
Woman's gown.—*The Merry Wives of Windsor,* iv, 2, 72.
Worst wearing gown.—*II Henry VI,* i, 3, 88.
Gown of humility.—*Coriolanus,* ii, 3, 44.

3
Quick, quick! we 'll come dress you straight: put on the gown the while.
The Merry Wives of Windsor. Act iv, sc. 2, l. 80. [Mistress Page] "Put on the gown" is repeated in l. 85, and also in *Coriolanus,* ii, 2, 141.
Put on your gown.—*Othello,* i, 1, 86.

4
Margaret: Your gown 's a most rare fashion, i' faith. I saw the Duchess of Milan's gown that they praise so.
Hero: O, that exceeds, they say.
Margaret: By my troth, 's but a night-gown in respect of yours; cloth o' gold, and cuts, and laced with silver, set with pearls, down sleeves, side sleeves, and skirts, round underborne with a bluish tinsel; but for a fine, quaint, graceful and excellent fashion, yours is worth ten on 't.
Much Ado about Nothing. Act iii, sc. 4, l. 15. The only use of "underborne," "bluish," and "tinsel." "Night-gown" occurs five times.
One that hath two gowns and every thing handsome about him.
Much Ado about Nothing. Act iv, sc. 2, l. 88. [Dogberry]

5
I have a gown here; come, put it on: keep thee warm.
Pericles. Act ii, sc. 1, l. 83. [Fisherman]
Thou shalt have my best gown.
Pericles. Act ii, sc. 1, l. 169. [Fisherman]

6
Thy gown? why, ay: come, tailor, let us see 't.
O mercy, God! what masquing stuff is here?
What 's this? a sleeve? 'tis like a demi-cannon:
What, up and down, carved like an apple-tart?
Here 's snip and nip and cut and slish and slash,
Like to a censer in a barber's shop:
Why, what, i' devil's name, tailor, call'st thou this?
Taming of the Shrew. Act iv, sc. 3, l. 86. [Petruchio] The only use of "demi-cannon," "apple-tart," and "slish." "Snip" occurs again in *Love's Labour 's Lost,* iii, 1, 22, and v, 1, 63; and "censer" in *II Henry IV,* v, 4, 21.
I never saw a better-fashion'd gown,
More quaint, more pleasing, nor more commendable.
The Taming of the Shrew. Act iv, sc. 3, l. 101. [Petruchio] The only use of "better-fashion'd."

Petruchio: I tell thee, I, that thou hast marr'd her gown.
Tailor: Your worship is deceived; the gown is made
Just as my master had direction:
Grumio gave order how it should be done.
Grumio: I gave him no order. I gave him the stuff.
Tailor: But how did you desire it should be made?
Grumio: Marry, sir, with needle and thread.
Tailor: But did you not request to have it cut?
Grumio: Thou hast faced many things.
Tailor: I have.
Grumio: Face not me: thou hast braved many men; brave not me: I will neither be faced nor braved. I say unto thee, I bid thy master cut out the gown; but I did not bid him cut it to pieces: ergo, thou liest.
Tailor: Why, here is the note of the fashion to testify.
Petruchio: Read it.
Grumio: The note lies in 's throat, if he say I said so.
Tailor: [Reads] 'Imprimis, a loose-bodied gown:'
Grumio: Master, if ever I said loose-bodied gown, sew me in the skirts of it, and beat me to death with a bottom of brown thread: I said a gown.
The Taming of the Shrew. Act iv, sc. 3, l. 115. The only use of "loose-bodied."

Petruchio: Well, sir, in brief, the gown is not for me.
Grumio: You are i' the right, sir: 'tis for my mistress.
Petruchio: Go, take it up unto thy master's use.
Grumio: Villain, not for thy life; take up my mistress' gown for thy master's use. . . .
Oh, fie, fie, fie!
The Taming of the Shrew. Act iv, sc. 3, l. 156.

7
Put off that gown, Trinculo; by this hand, I 'll have that gown.
Tempest. Act iv, sc. 1, l. 227. [Stephano]

8
I was trimm'd in Madame Julia's gown,
Which served me as fit, by all men's judgements,
As if the garment had been made for me.
The Two Gentlemen of Verona. Act iv, sc. 4, l. 166. [Julia]

GRACE

1
The great'st grace lending grace.
All's Well that Ends Well. Act ii, sc. 1, l. 163. [Helena]
Great grace.—*Henry VIII*, iii, 2, 174; v, 1, 48.
I hope your own grace will keep you where you are.
All's Well that Ends Well. Act iii, sc. 5, l. 27. [Mariana]
2 So full of grace, that it flows over
On all that need.
Antony and Cleopatra. Act v, sc. 2, l. 24. [Proculeis]
3
Know you not, master, to some kind of men
Their graces serve them but as enemies?
As You Like It. Act ii, sc. 3, l. 10. [Adam]
4
Possess'd with such a gentle sovereign grace,
Of such enchanting presence and discourse.
The Comedy of Errors. Act iii, sc. 2, l. 165. [Antipholus of Syracuse]
Sovereign grace.—*The Tempest*, iv, 1, 72.
Ample grace.—*Measure for Measure*, i, 1, 24.
Best grace.—*The Merchant of Venice*, iii, 5, 49; *Hamlet*, i, 2, 63; *Henry VIII*, iii, 2, 138.
Braver grace.—*Merchant of Venice*, iii, 4, 65.
Celestial grace.—*I Henry VI*, v, 4, 40.
Common grace.—*Timon of Athens*, iii, 5, 95.
Devil's grace.—*I Henry VI*, v, 3, 33.
Double grace.—*Hamlet*, i, 3, 53.
Fair grace.—*All's Well that Ends Well*, v, 3, 133.
Fairy grace.—*A Midsummer-Night's Dream*, v, 1, 406.
Fickle grace.—*King Lear*, ii, 4, 189.
Gentle grace.—*Sonnets*, lxxix.
Good grace.—*Richard III*, ii, 3, 10, and six times in later plays.
Loose grace.—*Love's Labour's Lost*, v, 2, 869.
Modern grace.—*All's Well that Ends Well*, v, 3, 216.
Noble grace.—*Coriolanus*, v, 3, 121.
Noblest grace.—*The Tempest*, iii, 1, 45.
Present grace.—*Timon of Athens*, i, 1, 71; *Macbeth*, i, 3, 55.
Soft grace.—*The Tempest*, v, 1, 142.
Grace in speech.—*II Henry VI*, i, 1, 32.
5 'Tis your graces
That from my mutest conscience to my tongue
Charms this report out.
Cymbeline. Act i, sc. 6, l. 115. [Iachimo]
The only use of "mutest."
6
Thou hast look'd thyself into my grace,
And art mine own.
Cymbeline. Act v, sc. 5, l. 94. [Cymbeline]
He may keep his own grace, but he's almost out of mine,
I can assure him.
II Henry IV. Act i, sc. 2, l. 32. [Falstaff]
Gain my grace.—*A Lover's Complaint*, l. 79.
7
Thyself do grace to them, and bring them in.
Hamlet. Act ii, sc. 2, l. 53. [King]
I will make the king do you grace.
II Henry IV. Act v, sc. 5, l. 6. [Falstaff]
Do grace.—*Julius Cæsar*, iii, 2, 62.
Do me grace.—*Taming of the Shrew*, i, 2, 131.
Do thee grace.—*I Henry IV*, v, 4, 161.
Do them grace.—*Richard II*, iii, 3, 181.
8
See, what a grace was seated on this brow.
Hamlet, iii, 4, 55. See under APPEARANCE.
9
Falstaff: God save thy grace,—majesty I should say, for grace thou wilt have none,—
Prince of Wales: What, none?
Falstaff: No, by my troth, not so much as will serve to be prologue to an egg and butter.
I Henry IV. Act i, sc. 2, l. 18.
It shall please you to gratify the table with a grace.
Love's Labour's Lost. Act iv, sc. 2, l. 161. [Holofernes]
Lucio: I think thou never wast where grace was said.
Second Gent.: No? a dozen times at least.
First Gent.: What, in meter?
Lucio: In any proportion or in any language.
First Gent.: I think, or in any religion.
Measure for Measure. Act i, sc. 2, l. 19.
I will not be absence at the grace.
The Merry Wives of Windsor. Act i, sc. 1, l. 273. [Evans]
Titus Andronicus: Tell me, can you deliver an oration to the emperor with a grace?
Clown: Nay, truly, sir, I could never say grace in all my life.
Titus Andronicus. Act iv, sc. 3, l. 98.
Grace 'fore meat.—*Coriolanus*, iv, 7, 3.
Thanksgiving before meat.—*Measure for Measure*, i, 2, 15.
I cannot stay thanksgiving.—*Love's Labour's Lost*, ii, 1, 193. The only uses of "thanksgiving."
10
Well, an the fire of grace be not quite out of thee, now shalt thou be moved.
I Henry IV. Act ii, sc. 4, l. 421. [Falstaff]
Thou art violently carried away from grace.
I Henry IV. Act ii, sc. 4, l. 491. [Prince]
11
This is the right fencing grace, my lord.
II Henry IV, ii, 1, 206. See under DUELLING.
12
The cool and temperate wind of grace.
Henry V. Act iii, sc. 3, l. 30. [King Henry]
Our grace is only in our heels,
And that we are most lofty runaways.
Henry V. Act iii, sc. 5, l. 34. [Bourbon]
13
Natural graces that extinguish art.
I Henry VI. Act v, sc. 3, l. 192. [Suffolk]
The only use of "extinguish."
Heaven give thee moving graces!
Measure for Measure. Act ii, sc. 2, l. 36. [Provost]
Graces will appear, and there's an end.
Much Ado about Nothing. Act ii, sc. 1, l. 128. [Ursula]
Heaven's graces.—*Sonnets*, xciv.
Grace of heaven.—*II Henry IV*, iv, 2, 21; 24.
King's grace.—*Henry VIII*, i, 2, 104.
Grace of kings.—*Henry V*, ii, Prol., 28.
Princely graces.—*Henry VIII*, v, 5, 26.
Sweet graces.—*Sonnets*, lxxviii.
Save our graces!—*The Tempest*, iii, 2, 115.

1
Ask mercy and obtain no grace.
III Henry VI. Act ii, sc. 6, l. 69. [Richard]
These graces challenge grace.
III Henry VI. Act iv, sc. 8, l. 48. [King Henry]
2
In his own grace he doth exalt himself.
King Lear. Act v, sc. 3, l. 67. [Goneril] The only use of "exalt."
3
For every man with his affects is born,
Not by might master'd but by special grace.
Love's Labour's Lost. Act i, sc. 1, l. 152. [Biron]
Be now as prodigal of all dear grace
As Nature was in making graces dear
When she did starve the general world beside
And prodigally gave them all to you.
Love's Labour's Lost. Act ii, sc. 1, l. 9. [Boyet] The only use of "prodigally."
Dearest grace.—*I Henry IV,* iii, 1, 182.
Free of grace!—*Love's Labour's Lost,* iii, 1, 67.
4
Thy grace being gain'd cures all disgrace in me.
Love's Labour's Lost. Act iv, sc. 3, l. 67. [Longaville] Repeated in *The Passionate Pilgrim,* l. 36.
That is the way to make an offence gracious, though few have the grace to do it.
Love's Labour's Lost. Act v, sc. 1, l. 146. [Moth] "Gracious" was a favourite adjective with Shakespeare, who used it 189 times.
5
We that sell by gross, the Lord doth know,
Have not the grace to grace it with such show.
Love's Labour's Lost. Act v, sc. 2, l. 319. [Biron]
Come to him by the gross.—*The Winter's Tale,* iv, 4, 208. The only uses of "gross" in this sense.
6
His real habitude gave life and grace
To appertainings and to ornament,
Accomplish'd in himself, not in his case.
A Lover's Complaint, l. 114. The only use of "habitude" and "appertainings." "Appertaining" occurs three times.
'Twas merely with the garment of a Grace
The naked and concealed fiend he cover'd.
A Lover's Complaint, l. 316.
7
Though all things foul would wear the brows of grace,
Yet grace must still look so.
Macbeth. Act iv, sc. 3, l. 23. [Malcolm]
The king-becoming graces,
As justice, verity, temperance, stableness.
Macbeth, iv, 3, 91. See under CHARACTER.
Sundry blessings hang about his throne,
That speak him full of grace.
Macbeth. Act iv, sc. 3, l. 158. [Malcolm]
8
Grace is grace, despite of all controversy: as, for example, thou thyself art a wicked villain, despite of all grace.
Measure for Measure. Act i, sc. 2, l. 25. [Lucio]
Grace, being the soul of your complexion, shall keep the body of it ever fair.
Measure for Measure, iii, 1, 187. See under GOODNESS.
Alack, when once our grace we have forgot,
Nothing goes right: we would, and we would not.
Measure for Measure. Act iv, sc. 4, l. 36. [Angelo]
9
The old proverb is very well parted between my master Shylock and you, sir: you have the grace of God, sir, and he hath enough.
The Merchant of Venice. Act ii, sc. 2, l. 157. [Launcelot]
By the grace of God.—*II Henry VI,* i, 2, 72; *III Henry VI,* iv, 7, 71; *Richard III,* iii, 4, 99; *Richard II,* i, 3, 22.
Grace de Dieu.—*Henry V,* iii, 4, 44.
God's grace.—*Richard II,* i, 3, 37; *Henry V,* i, 2, 262.
God's good grace.—*Richard III,* ii, 3, 10.
Graces of the gods.—*Coriolanus,* v, 3, 150.
10
They have not so little grace, I hope.
The Merry Wives of Windsor. Act ii, sc. 2, l. 116. [Mistress Quickly]
11
Conrade: He hath ta'en you newly into his grace. . . .
Don John: I had rather be a canker in a hedge than a rose in his grace.
Much Ado about Nothing. Act i, sc. 3, l. 23.
12
He hath devoted and given up himself to the contemplation, mark, and denotement of her parts and graces.
Othello. Act ii, sc. 3, l. 321. [Iago] The only use of "denotement."
13
Grace me no grace, nor uncle me no uncle;
I am no traitor's uncle; and that word 'grace'
In an ungracious mouth is but profane.
Richard II. Act ii, sc. 3, l. 87. [York]
Ungracious boy.—*I Henry IV,* ii, 4, 490.
Ungracious clamours!—*Troilus and Cressida,* i, 1, 92.
Ungracious head.—*II Henry VI,* iv, 10, 88.
Ungracious paper.—*King Lear,* iv, 6, 283.
Ungracious pastors.—*Hamlet,* i, 3, 47.
Ungracious wretch.—*Twelfth Night,* iv, 1, 51.
I, ungracious.—*Richard III,* ii, 3, 89. The only uses of "ungracious."
Ill mayst thou thrive, if thou grant any grace!
Richard II. Act v, sc. 3, l. 99. [York]
14
Thee, that hast nor honesty nor grace.
Richard III. Act i, sc. 3, l. 55. [Gloucester]
O momentary grace of mortal men,
Which we more hunt for than the grace of God!
Who builds his hopes in air of your good looks,
Lives like a drunken sailor on a mast,
Ready, with every nod, to tumble down
Into the fatal bowels of the deep.
Richard III. Act iii, sc. 4, l. 98. [Hastings]
15
God mark thee to his grace!
Romeo and Juliet. Act i, sc. 3, l. 59. [Nurse]
16
O, mickle is the powerful grace that lies

In herbs, plants, stones, and their true qualities.
Romeo and Juliet. Act ii, sc. 3, l. 15. [Friar Laurence]

She whom I love now
Doth grace for grace, and love for love allow.
Romeo and Juliet. Act ii, sc. 3, l. 85. [Romeo]

1
Lascivious grace, in whom all ill well shows,
Kill me with spites; yet we must not be foes.
Sonnets. No. xl.

In external grace you have some part.
Sonnets. No. liii.

Some say thy grace is youth and gentle sport.
Sonnets. No. xcvi.

2
Mistress Bianca, bless you with such grace
As 'longeth to a lover's blessed case.
The Taming of the Shrew. Act iv, sc. 2, l. 44. [Tranio]

3
I 'll be wise hereafter And seek for grace.
The Tempest. Act v, sc. 1, l. 294. [Caliban]

4
Villains, for shame you could not beg for grace.
Titus Andronicus. Act v, sc. 2, l. 180. [Titus]

5
He does it with a better grace, but I do it more natural.
Twelfth Night. Act ii, sc. 3, l. 88. [Sir Andrew]

6 Grace and good disposition
Attend your ladyship!
Twelfth Night. Act iii, sc. 1, l. 146. [Viola]

Grace go with you, Benedicite!
Measure for Measure, ii, 3, 39. See under BLESSING.

7
Put your grace in your pocket, sir, for this once, and let your flesh and blood obey it.
Twelfth Night. Act v, sc. 1, l. 35. [Clown]

Your grace is welcome to a man disgraced.
The Two Gentlemen of Verona. Act v, sc. 4, l. 123.

8
Grace to boot!
Winter's Tale. Act i, sc. 2, l. 80. [Hermione]

Grace to groan.—*Love's Labour 's Lost,* iv, 3, 20.

Grace to stand.—*Measure for Measure,* iii, 2, 278.

9 This action I now go on
Is for my better grace.
The Winter's Tale. Act ii, sc. 1, l. 121. [Hermione]

Grace Equal with wondering.
Winter's Tale. Act iv, sc. 1, l. 24. [Time]

Grace and remembrance be to you both.
Winter's Tale. Act iv, sc. 4, l. 76. [Perdita]

Every wink of an eye some new grace will be born.
The Winter's Tale. Act v, sc. 2, l. 119. [First Gentleman]

It is a surplus of your grace, which never
My life may last to answer.
Winter's Tale. Act v, sc. 3, l. 7. [Paulina] "Surplus" is repeated in *Coriolanus,* i, 1, 46.

GRANDFATHER

10
O brave young prince! thy famous grandfather
Doth live again in thee: long mayst thou live
To bear his image and renew his glories!
III Henry VI. Act v, sc. 4, l. 52. [Oxford]

Your grandfather of famous memory.
Henry V. Act iv, sc. 7, l. 95. [Fluellen]

Grandfather to this king.—*I Henry VI,* ii, 5, 63.

Cupid's grandfather.—*Love's Labour 's Lost,* ii, 1, 254.

11
What my great-grandfather and grandsire got
My careless father fondly gave away.
III Henry VI. Act ii, sc. 2, l. 37. [Clifford]

My great-grandfather.—*Henry V,* i, 2, 146.

His great-grandfather.—*Henry V,* i, 1, 89. The only uses of "great-grandfather."

12
My grandsire was an Englishman.
King John, v, 4, 42. See under ENGLAND.

O, had thy grandsire with a prophet's eye
Seen how his son's son should destroy his sons,
From forth thy reach he would have laid thy shame.
Richard II. Act ii, sc. 1, l. 104. [Gaunt]

Good grandsire.—*Titus Andronicus,* iii, 2, 46.

Good old grandsire.—*The Taming of the Shrew,* iv, 5, 50.

Royal grandsire.—*Richard II,* iii, 3, 106.

13 Thy grandsire loved thee well:
Many a time he danced thee on his knee,
Sung thee asleep, his loving breast thy pillow.
Titus Andronicus. Act v, sc. 3, l. 161. [Lucius]

I knew thy grandsire,
And once fought with him.
Troilus and Cressida. Act iv, sc. 5, l. 196. [Nestor]

Our great-grandsire, Edward.—*II Henry IV,* iv, 4, 128.

Great-grandsire's tomb.—*Henry V,* i, 2, 103. The only uses of "great-grandsire."

14
Launce: Tell me this: who begot thee?
Speed: Marry, the son of my grandfather.
Launce: O illiterate loiterer! it was the son of thy grandmother.
The Two Gentlemen of Verona. Act iii, sc. 1, l. 293. The only use of "illiterate" in the plays. It occurs in *Rape of Lucrece,* l. 810.

GRANDMOTHER

15
I am thy grandam, Richard; call me so.
King John. Act i, sc. 1, l. 168. [Queen Elinor]

Queen Elinor: Come to thy grandam, child.
Constance: Do, child, go to it grandam, child;
Give grandam kingdom, and it grandam will
Give it a plum, a cherry and a fig:
There 's a good grandam.
King John. Act ii, sc. 1, l. 159.

Good grandam.—*Richard III,* ii, 2, 1; *King John,* ii, 1, 133.

Canker'd grandam.—*King John,* ii, 1, 194.

1
His grandam's wrongs, and not his mother's shames,
Draws those heaven-moving pearls from his poor eyes.
King John. Act ii, sc. 1, l. 168. [Constance] The only use of "heaven-moving."

2 Had she been light, like you
Of such a merry, nimble, stirring spirit,
She might ha' been a grandam ere she died.
Love's Labour's Lost. Act v, sc. 2, l. 15. [Katharine]

3
A grandam's name is little less in love
Than is the doting title of a mother.
Richard III. Act iv, sc. 4, l. 299. [King Richard]

I should sin
To think but nobly of my grandmother.
The Tempest. Act i, sc. 2, l. 118. [Miranda]
Our grandmother Eve.—*Love's Labour's Lost,* i, 1, 266.

4
My grandam, having no eyes, look you, wept herself blind at my parting.
The Two Gentlemen of Verona. Act ii, sc. 3, l. 13. [Launce]

GRAPE

5
O, will you eat not grapes, my royal fox?
All's Well that Ends Well, ii, 1, 73. See under Fox.

6
With thy grapes our hairs be crown'd.
Antony and Cleopatra, ii, 7, 123. See under Wine.

7
The heathen philosopher, when he had a desire to eat a grape, would open his lips when he put it into his mouth; meaning thereby that grapes were made to eat and lips to open.
As You Like It. Act v, sc. 1, l. 37. [Touchstone]

8
For one sweet grape who will the vine destroy?
The Rape of Lucrece, l. 215.

9
Poor birds, deceived with painted grapes,
Do surfeit by the eye and pine the maw.
Venus and Adonis, l. 601.
Bunch of Grapes.—*Measure for Measure,* ii, 1, 133.
Egypt's grape.—*Antony and Cleopatra,* v, 2, 285.
Noble grapes.—*All's Well that Ends Well,* ii, 1, 74.
Purple grapes.—*Midsummer-Night's Dream,* iii, 1, 170.
Ripe grapes.—*Coriolanus,* v, 4, 18.

GRASS

10
I am no great Nebuchadnezzar, sir; I have not much skill in grass.
All's Well that Ends Well. Act iv, sc. 5, l. 21. [Clown] The only mention of Nebuchadnezzar.

I long for grass.—*Comedy of Errors,* ii, 2, 202.

11
'While the grass grows,'—the proverb is something musty.
Hamlet. Act iii, sc. 2, l. 358. [Hamlet] "While the grass grows the steed starves" is the proverb, which first appeared about 1440 in John Capgrave's *Life of Saint Katharine,* and was included in John Heywood's *Proverbs* in 1546.

12
Grew like the summer grass, fastest by night,
Unseen, yet crescive in his faculty.
Henry V. Act i, sc. 1, l. 65. [Bishop of Ely] Shakespeare seems to have coined "crescive" for this occasion, and never used it again. The only use of "fastest."

13
I climbed into this garden to see if I can eat grass.
II Henry VI. Act iv, sc. 10, l. 8. [Cade]
Never eat grass more.—*II Henry VI,* iv, 10, 44.
We cannot live on grass.—*Timon of Athens,* iv, 3, 425.
Go to grass.—*II Henry VI,* iv, 2, 75.

14
Upon the grassy carpet of this plain.
Richard II. Act iii, sc. 3, l. 50. [Bolingbroke] The only use of "grassy."

15
Gonzalo: How lush and lusty the grass looks! how green!
Antonio: The ground indeed is tawny.
Sebastian: With an eye of green in it.
Antonio: He misses not much.
The Tempest. Act ii, sc. 1, l. 52. The only use of "lush."
Here on this grass-plot, in this very place.
The Tempest. Act iv, sc. 1, l. 73. [Iris] The only use of "grass-plot."

16
Grass beat down with storms.
Titus Andronicus. Act iv, sc. 4, l. 71. [Saturninus]
Bladed grass.—*A Midsummer-Night's Dream,* i, 1, 211.
Chew'd grass.—*Henry V,* iv, 2, 50.

17
The grass stoops not, she treads on it so light.
Venus and Adonis, l. 1028.
The grass whereon thou tread'st.—*Richard II,* i, 3, 289.

GRATITUDE

See also Thankfulness

18 Gratitude
Through flinty Tartar's bosom would peep forth,
And answer, thanks.
All's Well that Ends Well. Act iv, sc. 4, l. 6. [Helena]

19
Thou canst not, in the course of gratitude, but be a diligent follower of mine.
Cymbeline. Act iii, sc. 5, l. 121. [Cloten]

20 Thou better know'st
The offices of nature, bond of childhood,

Effects of courtesy, dues of gratitude.
King Lear. Act ii, sc. 4, l. 180. [King Lear]
Whose gratitude . . . is enroll'd.
Coriolanus, iii, 1, 291. See under ROME. These four quotations give the only uses of "gratitude."

1 God's goodness hath been great to thee:
Let never day nor night unhallow'd pass,
But still remember what the Lord hath done.
II Henry VI. Act ii, sc. 1, l. 84. [King Henry]
I take it kindly.
II Henry VI. Act iii, sc. 1, l. 346. [York]

2 Your hand and heart,
Your brain, and every function of your power,
Should, notwithstanding that your bond of duty,
As 'twere in love's particular, be more
To me, your friend, than any.
Henry VIII. Act iii, sc. 2, l. 186. [King Henry]

GRAVE

See also Burial

3 Lie graveless, 'till the flies and gnats of Nile
Have buried them for prey!
Antony and Cleopatra. Act iii, sc. 13, l. 166. [Cleopatra] The only use of "graveless."
No grave allow'd me.—*Henry VIII,* iii, 1, 151.

4 No grave upon the earth shall clip in it
A pair so famous.
Antony and Cleopatra. Act v, sc. 2, l. 362. [Cæsar]

5 Here lie I down, and measure out my grave.
As You Like It. Act ii, sc. 6, l. 2. [Adam]

6 Graves i' the holy churchyard.
Coriolanus, iii, 3, 51. See under WOUND.
Hungry churchyard.—*Romeo and Juliet,* v, 3, 36.
Churchyards yawn.—*Hamlet,* iii, 2, 407. "Churchyard" is used twelve times. "Graveyard" does not occur.

7 I 'll hide my master from the flies, as deep
As these poor pickaxes can dig; and when
With wild wood-leaves and weeds I ha' strew'd his grave,
And on it said a century of prayers,
Such as I can, twice o'er, I 'll weep and sigh;
And leaving so his service, follow you.
Cymbeline. Act iv, sc. 2, l. 388. [Imogen] The only use of "wood-leaves" and "pickaxes." "Pick-axe" hyphenated) occurs in *Hamlet,* v, 1, 102. See 636: 10.
Find out the prettiest daisied plot we can,
And make him with our pikes and partisans
A grave.
Cymbeline. Act iv, sc. 2, l. 398. [Caius Lucius] The only use of "daisied."

8 Polonius: Will you walk out of the air, my lord?
Hamlet: Into my grave.
Hamlet. Act ii, sc. 2, l. 208.
We must be patient: but I cannot choose but weep, to think they should lay him i' the cold ground.
Hamlet. Act iv, sc. 5, l. 68. [Ophelia]

9 Second Clown: 'Who builds stronger than a mason, a shipwright, or a carpenter?' . . .
First Clown: . . . 'A grave-maker:' the houses that he makes last till doomsday.
Hamlet. Act v, sc. 1, l. 57. "Grave-maker" is used three times in this scene, and nowhere else in the plays.
Goodman delver.—*Hamlet,* v, 1, 15. The only use of "delver."

10 A pick-axe, and a spade, a spade,
For and a shrouding sheet:
O, a pit of clay for to be made
For such a guest is meet.
Hamlet. Act v, sc. 1, l. 102. [First Clown]

11 Get thee gone and dig my grave thyself.
II Henry IV. Act iv, sc. 5, l. 111. [King Henry]
Dig his grave.—*III Henry VI,* v, 2, 21.
The grave is digg'd.—*II Henry VI,* iv, 10, 55.
Make his grave.—*I Henry VI,* ii, 1, 34.
Make her grave straight.—*Hamlet,* v, 1, 4. See under BURIAL.

12 O braggart vile and damned furious wight!
The grave doth gape, and doting death is near:
Therefore exhale.
Henry V. Act ii, sc. 1, l. 64. [Pistol]
The dead with charity enclosed in clay.
Henry V. Act iv, sc. 8, l. 129. [King Henry]

13 But I will remedy this gear ere long,
Or sell my title for a glorious grave.
II Henry VI. Act iii, sc. 1, l. 91. [York]
Hence will I drag thee headlong by the heels
Unto a dunghill that shall be thy grave.
II Henry VI. Act iv, sc. 10, l. 86. [Iden]

14 To make thy sepulchre
And creep into it far before thy time.
III Henry VI. Act i, sc. 1, l. 236. [Queen Margaret]
The sepulchre
Wherein we saw thee quietly inurn'd,
Hath oped his ponderous and marble jaws,
To cast thee up again.
Hamlet. Act i, sc. 4, l. 48. [Hamlet] The only use of "inurn'd."
The sepulchre in stubborn Jewry
Of the world's ransom.
Richard II, ii, 1, 55. See under CHRIST.
The sepulchre of Christ.—*I Henry IV,* i, 1, 19.
Frail sepulchre of our flesh.—*Richard II,* i, 3, 196.
Earthly sepulchre.—*III Henry VI,* i, 4, 17.
Kingly sepulchres.—*III Henry VI,* v, 2, 20.

15 I 'll go with thee,
And find the inheritance of this poor child,
His little kingdom of a forced grave.
That blood which owed the breadth of all this isle,

Three foot of it doth hold.
King John. Act iv, sc. 2, l. 96. [Pembroke]
When he doom'd this beauty to a grave,
Found it too precious-princely for a grave.
King John. Act iv, sc. 3, l. 39. [Lord Bigot] The only use of "precious-princely."

1
Why, thou wert better in thy grave than to answer with thy uncovered body this extremity of the skies.
King Lear. Act iii, sc. 4, l. 105. [King Lear]

2
The sacred storehouse of his predecessors,
And guardian of their bones.
Macbeth. Act ii, sc. 4, l. 34. [Macduff]
There my father's grave Did utter forth a voice.
Measure for Measure. Act iii, sc. 1, l. 86. [Isabella]

3
Banquo's buried; he cannot come out on 's grave.
Macbeth. Act v, sc. 1, l. 70. [Lady Macbeth]
To break his grave And come again to me.
Winter's Tale. Act v, sc. 1, l. 42. [Paulina]

4
Graves, yawn and yield your dead,
Till death be uttered,
Heavily, heavily.
Much Ado about Nothing. Act v, sc. 3, l. 19. [Song]
Graves have yawn'd, and yielded up their dead.
Julius Cæsar. Act ii, sc. 2, l. 18. [Calpurnia]
Graves at my command
Have waked their sleepers, oped, and let 'em forth.
The Tempest. Act v, sc. 1, l. 48. [Prospero]
Graves all gaping wide.—*A Midsummer-Night's Dream,* v, 1, 387.
The graves stood tenantless.—*Hamlet,* i, 1, 115. "Tenantless" is repeated in *The Two Gentlemen of Verona,* v, 4, 8.

5
Still as the grave.
Othello. Act v, sc. 2, l. 94. [Othello]
Sleep in their graves.—*Henry VIII,* v, 1, 32.

6
The yellows, blues,
The purple violets, and marigolds,
Shall as a carpet hang upon thy grave.
Pericles. Act iv, sc. 1, l. 15. [Marina] The marigold is mentioned again in *The Winter's Tale,* iv, 4, 105.
The herbs that have on them cold dew o' the night
Are strewings fitt'st for graves.
Cymbeline. Act iv, sc. 2, l. 284. [Belarius] The only use of "strewings." "Strewing" occurs in *Love's Labour 's Lost,* iv, 3, 380.

7
Gaunt am I for the grave, gaunt as a grave,
Whose hollow womb inherits nought but bones.
Richard II. Act ii, sc. 1, l. 82. [Gaunt]
John of Gaunt: Convey me to my bed, then to my grave:
Love they to live that love and honour have.
King Richard: And let them die that age and sullens have;
For both hast thou, and both become the grave.
Richard II. Act ii, sc. 1, l. 137. The only use of "sullens."
With clog of conscience and sour melancholy
Hath yielded up his body to the grave.
Richard II. Act v, sc. 6, l. 20. [Percy]

8
Let 's talk of graves, of worms and epitaphs.
Richard II. Act iii, sc. 2, l. 145. [King Richard]
I 'll give my jewels for a set of beads,
My gorgeous palace for a hermitage,
My gay apparel for an almsman's gown,
My figured goblets for a dish of wood,
My sceptre for a palmer's walking-staff,
My subjects for a pair of carved saints
And my large kingdom for a little grave;
A little, little grave, an obscure grave;
Or I 'll be buried in the king's highway,
Some way of common trade, where subjects' feet
May hourly trample on their sovereign's head;
For on my heart they tread now whilst I live.
Richard II. Act iii, sc. 3, l. 147. [King Richard] The only use of "almsman," "walking-staff," and "king's highway." "Hermitage" is repeated in *Love's Labour 's Lost,* v, 2, 805.

9
Wet his grave with my repentant tears.
Richard III. Act i, sc. 2, l. 216. [Gloucester]
But first I 'll turn yon fellow in his grave.
Richard III. Act i, sc. 2, l. 261. [Gloucester]

10
I to my grave, where peace and rest lie with me!
Richard III. Act iv, sc. 1, l. 95. [Duchess of York]
So be my grave my peace.
King Lear. Act i, sc. 1, l. 127. [King Lear]

11
O, that thou wouldst as well afford a grave
As thou canst yield a melancholy seat!
Then would I hide my bones, not rest them here.
Richard III. Act iv, sc. 4, l. 31. [Queen Elizabeth]
The beholders of this tragic play, . . .
Untimely smother'd in their dusky graves.
Richard III. Act iv, sc. 4, l. 68. [Queen Margaret]

12
Go, ask his name: if he be married,
My grave is like to be my wedding bed.
Romeo and Juliet. Act i, sc. 5, l. 136. [Juliet] "Wedding-bed" (hyphenated) is repeated in iii, 2, 136, and occurs nowhere else in the plays.
And fall upon the ground, as I do now,
Taking the measure of an unmade grave.
Romeo and Juliet. Act iii, sc. 3, l. 69. [Romeo] The only use of "unmade."
I would the fool were married to her grave!
Romeo and Juliet. Act iii, sc. 5, l. 141. [Lady Capulet]

13 Bid me go into a new-made grave
And hide me with a dead man in his shroud.
Romeo and Juliet. Act iv, sc. 1, l. 84. [Juliet]
I 'll bury thee in a triumphant grave;
A grave? O, no! a lantern, slaughter'd youth,
For here lies Juliet, and her beauty makes
This vault a feasting presence full of light.
Romeo and Juliet. Act v, sc. 3, l. 83. [Romeo]

O thou untaught! what manners is in this,
To press before thy father to a grave?
Romeo and Juliet. Act v, sc. 3, l. 214. [Montague]

1
Thou art the grave where buried love doth live,
Hung with the trophies of my lovers gone.
Sonnets. No. xxxi.

2
Every third thought shall be my grave.
The Tempest. Act v, sc. 1, l. 311. [Prospero]

3
Prepare thy grave;
Lie where the light foam of the sea may beat
Thy grave-stone daily.
Timon of Athens. Act iv, sc. 3, l. 378. [Timon]

Timon hath made his everlasting mansion
Upon the beached verge of the salt flood;
Who once a day with his embossed froth
The turbulent surge shall cover: thither come,
And let my grave-stone be your oracle. . . .
Graves only be men's works and death their gain!
Timon of Athens. Act v, sc. 1, l. 218. [Timon] "Grave-stone" is used once more in v, 4, 67, and occurs in no other play. "Beached" is repeated in *A Midsummer-Night's Dream,* ii, 1, 85: "Beached margent of the sea."

4
Their latest home.
Titus Andronicus. Act i, sc. 1, l. 83. [Titus]
His earthly prison of their bones.
Titus Andronicus. Act i, sc. 1, l. 99. [Lucius]

5
There greet in silence, as the dead are wont,
And sleep in peace, slain in your country's wars!
O sacred receptacle of my joys,
Sweet cell of virtue and nobility,
How many sons of mine hast thou in store,
That thou wilt never render to me more!
Titus Andronicus. Act i, sc. 1, l. 90. [Titus]
In peace and honour rest you here, my sons;
Rome's readiest champions, repose you here in rest,
Secure from worldly chances and mishaps!
Here lurks no treason, here no envy swells,
Here grow no damned grudges; here are no storms,
No noise, but silence and eternal sleep.
Titus Andronicus. Act i, sc. 1, l. 150. [Titus]

6
Suffer thy brother Marcus to inter
His noble nephew here in virtue's nest.
Titus Andronicus. Act i, sc. 1, l. 375. [Marcus]
Do thou so much as dig the grave for him.
Titus Andronicus. Act ii, sc. 3, l. 270. [Saturninus]
Bid him farewell: commit him to the grave;
Do him that kindness, and take leave of him.
Titus Andronicus. Act v, sc. 3, l. 170. [Lucius]

7
'Tis thought among the prudent he would quickly have the gift of a grave.
Twelfth Night, i, 3, 34. See under QUARREL.

8
Silvia: In his grave
Assure thyself my love is buried.
Proteus: Sweet lady, let me rake it from the earth.
Silvia: Go to thy lady's grave and call hers hence,
Or, at the least, in hers sepulchre thine.
The Two Gentlemen of Verona. Act iv, sc. 2, l. 114.

9
His snout digs sepulchres where'er he goes.
Venus and Adonis, l. 622. The only use of "snout" except as a proper name.

10
One grave shall be for both.
Winter's Tale. Act iii, sc. 2, l. 237. [Leontes]
Come, I 'll fill your grave up.
Winter's Tale. Act v, sc. 3, l. 100. [Paulina]
Burying grave.—*Romeo and Juliet,* ii, 3, 10.
Common grave.—*Sonnets,* lxxxi.
Dishonourable graves.—*Julius Cæsar,* i, 2, 138.
Drowsy grave.—*Henry V,* iv, 1, 22.
Low grave.—*Timon of Athens,* v, 4, 79.
Mouthed graves.—*Sonnets,* lxxvii.
Native graves.—*Henry V,* iv, 3, 96.
Obscure grave.—*Merchant of Venice,* ii, 7, 51.
Quiet grave.—*III Henry VI,* ii, 5, 40.
Sad grave.—*Cymbeline,* iv, 2, 220.
Swallowing grave.—*Venus and Adonis,* l. 757.
Timeless grave.—*The Two Gentlemen of Verona,* iii, 1, 21.
Dead men's graves.—*II Henry VI,* iv, 1, 6.
Graves of great men.—*Henry VIII,* ii, 1, 67.

GRAVITY

11
How ill agrees it with your gravity
To counterfeit thus grossly with your slave.
The Comedy of Errors. Act ii, sc. 2, l. 170. [Adriana]

12
What doth gravity out of his bed at midnight?
I Henry IV. Act ii, sc. 4, l. 325. [Falstaff]

13
Chief Justice: There is not a white hair on your face but should have his effect of gravity.
Falstaff: His effect of gravy, gravy, gravy.
II Henry IV. Act i, sc. 2, l. 182. The only use of "gravy" in the plays.

14
Our youths and wildness shall no whit appear,
But all be buried in his gravity.
Julius Cæsar. Act ii, sc. 1, l. 148. [Metellus]
Yea, my gravity,
Wherein—let no man hear me—I take pride,
Could I with boot change for an idle plume,
Which the air beats for vain.
Measure for Measure. Act ii, sc. 4, l. 9. [Angelo]

15
Utter your gravity o'er a gossip's bowl;
For here we need it not.
Romeo and Juliet. Act iii, sc. 5, l. 175. [Capulet]
Settled gravity.—*Sonnets,* xlix.
Gravity and learning.—*The Merry Wives of Windsor,* iii, 1, 57; *Henry VIII,* iii, 1, 73.

1
What, man! 'tis not for gravity to play at cherry-pit with Satan: hang him, foul collier!
Twelfth Night. Act iii, sc. 4, l. 128. [Sir Toby] The only use of "cherry-pit."

2
O grave and good!
Winter's Tale. Act v, sc. 3, l. 1. [Leontes]
Grave and learned?—*Henry V*, ii, 2, 128.
Grave and prosperous.—*Macbeth*, iii, 1, 22.
Grave but reckless.—*Coriolanus*, iii, 1, 92.

GREATNESS

See also Man: Great Men

3
One of the greatest in the Christian world.
All's Well that Ends Well, iv, 4, 2. See under SURETY.
I am the greatest, able to do least.
Romeo and Juliet, v, 3, 223. See MURDER, 1037:7.
The greatest of his profession.—*All's Well that Ends Well*, i, 3, 249.
Greatest commander.—*All's Well that Ends Well*, iii, 5, 6.
Great'st king.—*Cymbeline*, i, 6, 121.
Greatest lady.—*Love's Labour's Lost*, iv, 1, 46.
Sweet knight, thou art now one of the greatest men in this realm.
II Henry IV. Act v, sc. 3, l. 91. [Pistol] The only use of "greatest men." "Greatest man" occurs in *II Henry VI*, ii, 2, 82.
Greatest monarch.—*Henry VIII*, v, 3, 164.
Greatest prince.—*Antony and Cleopatra*, iv, 15, 54.
Greatest soldier.—*Antony and Cleopatra*, i, 3, 39.
One must prove greatest.—*King John*, ii, 1, 332.

4
It hath been taught us from the primal state,
That he which is was wish'd until he were;
And the ebb'd man, ne'er loved till ne'er worth love,
Comes dear'd by being lack'd.
Antony and Cleopatra. Act i, sc. 4, l. 41. [Cæsar] "Primal" is repeated in *Hamlet*, iii, 3, 37: "Primal eldest curse."
The soul and body rive not more in parting
Than greatness going off.
Antony and Cleopatra. Act iv, sc. 13, l. 5. [Charmian]
There is nothing left remarkable
Beneath the visiting moon.
Antony and Cleopatra. Act iv, sc. 15, l. 67. [Cleopatra] "Remarkable" occurs only once again in the plays, in *Cymbeline*, iv, 1, 14.

5 O noble strain!
O worthiness of nature! breed of greatness!
Cymbeline. Act iv, sc. 1, l. 24. [Belarius]

6 Poor wretches that depend
On greatness' favour dream as I have done,
Wake and find nothing.
Cymbeline. Act v, sc. 4, l. 127. [Posthumus]

7 Rightly to be great
Is not to stir without great argument,
But greatly to find quarrel in a straw
When honour 's at the stake.
Hamlet. Act iv, sc. 4, l. 53. [Hamlet] "Greatly" is used twelve times.

The more pity that great folk should have countenance in this world to drown or hang themselves, more than their even Christian.
Hamlet. Act v, sc. 1, l. 29. [First Clown] The only use of the phrase "great folk."

8
Our house, my sovereign liege, little deserves
The scourge of greatness to be used on it;
And that same greatness too which our own hands
Have holp to make so portly.
I Henry IV. Act i, sc. 3, l. 10. [Worcester] "Portly" is used seven times.

9
Accompany the greatness of thy blood.
I Henry IV, iii, 2, 16. See under BEHAVIOUR.
Greatness of his name.—*Henry VIII*, v, 5, 52.
Greatness of his person.—*Henry VIII*, ii, 1, 100.
Greatness of his place.—*II Henry VI*, i, 1, 173.
Greatness of your powers.—*Pericles*, ii, 1, 8.
Greatness of my word.—*As You Like It*, i, 3, 91.

10
These signs have mark'd me extraordinary;
And all the courses of my life do show
I am not in the roll of common men.
I Henry IV. Act iii, sc. 1, l. 41. [Glendower]
There 's something extraordinary in thee.
The Merry Wives of Windsor. Act iii, sc. 3, l. 75. [Falstaff]
Extraordinary gaze.—*I Henry IV*, iii, 2, 78.
Extraordinary pleasure.—*As You Like It*, i, 2, 7.
Head-piece extraordinary.—*The Winter's Tale*, i, 2, 227. The only uses of "extraordinary."

11
He presently, as greatness knows itself,
Steps me a little higher than his vow.
I Henry IV. Act iv, sc. 3, l. 74. [Hotspur]
A flood of greatness fell on you.
I Henry IV. Act v, sc. 1, l. 48. [Worcester]

12
You are too great to be by me gainsaid.
II Henry IV. Act i, sc. 1, l. 91. [Morton] The only use of "gainsaid."
Fear not your advancements; I will be the man yet that shall make you great.
II Henry IV. Act v, sc. 5, l. 84. [Falstaff]

13
Show my sail of greatness.
Henry V. Act i, sc. 2, l. 274. [King Henry]
This is a stem
Of that victorious stock; and let us fear
The native mightiness and fate of him.
Henry V. Act ii, sc. 4, l. 62. [French King]
Twin-born with greatness.—*Henry V*, iv, 1, 251. The only use of "twin-born."
Co-rivall'd greatness.—*Troilus and Cressida*, i, 3, 44. The only use of "co-rivall'd."
Inward greatness.—*Henry V*, ii, Prol., 16.
Sovereign greatness.—*King John*, v, 1, 4.
Wonted greatness.—*Henry VIII*, iv, 2, 102.

14 Eminence, wealth, sovereignty;
Which, to say sooth, are blessings.
Henry VIII. Act ii, sc. 3, l. 29. [Old Lady]

15
I have touch'd the highest point of all my greatness;
And, from that full meridian of my glory,

I haste now to my setting.
Henry VIII. Act iii, sc. 2, l. 223. [Wolsey] The only use of "meridian."

Farewell! a long farewell, to all my greatness!
This is the state of man: to-day he puts forth
The tender leaves of hopes; to-morrow blossoms,
And bears his blushing honours thick upon him;
The third day comes a frost, a killing frost,
And, when he thinks, good easy man, full surely
His greatness is a-ripening, nips his root,
And then he falls, as I do.
Henry VIII. Act iii, sc. 2, l. 351. [Cardinal Wolsey] The only use of "blushing honours" and "a-ripening."

You speak of two
The most remark'd i' the kingdom.
Henry VIII. Act v, sc. 1, l. 32. [Lovell] The only use of "remark'd."

1
Why, man, he doth bestride the narrow world
Like a Colossus, and we petty men
Walk under his huge legs and peep about
To find ourselves dishonourable graves.
Julius Cæsar. Act i, sc. 2, l. 135. [Cassius] "Colossus" appears once again in *I Henry IV*, v, 1, 123, where Prince Henry remarks that only a colossus could bestride Falstaff.

Now, in the name of all the gods at once,
Upon what meat doth this our Cæsar feed,
That he is grown so great?
Julius Cæsar. Act i, sc. 2, l. 148. [Cassius]

The abuse of greatness is, when it disjoins
Remorse from power.
Julius Cæsar. Act ii, sc. 1, l. 18. [Brutus] The only use of "disjoins." "Disjoin" occurs in *King John*, iii, 1, 262.

2
Let go thy hold when a great wheel runs down a hill, lest it break thy neck with following it; but the great one that goes up the hill, let him draw thee after.
King Lear. Act ii, sc. 4, l. 71. [Fool]

3
Costard: I Pompey am, Pompey surnamed the Big,—
Dumain: The Great.
Costard: It is, 'Great,' sir:—Pompey surnamed the Great.
Love's Labour 's Lost. Act v, sc. 2, l. 554.

4
Greater than both, by the all-hail hereafter!
Macbeth. Act i, sc. 5, l. 56. [Lady Macbeth] The only use of the hyphenated phrase "all-hail" as an adjective.

A good and virtuous nature may recoil
In an imperial charge.
Macbeth. Act iv, sc. 3, l. 19. [Malcolm]

5
O place and greatness! millions of false eyes
Are stuck upon thee; volumes of report
Run with these false and most contrarious quests
Upon thy doings: thousand escapes of wit
Make thee the father of their idle dreams
And rack thee in their fancies.
Measure for Measure. Act iv, sc. 1, l. 60. [Duke] "Contrarious" is repeated in *I Henry IV*, v, 1, 52: "Contrarious winds."

6
He is of too high a region.
The Merry Wives of Windsor. Act iii, sc. 2, l. 74. [Page]

7
O that I were as great
As is my grief, or lesser than my name!
Richard II. Act iii, sc. 3, l. 136. [King Richard]

8
If I were a huge man, I should fear to drink at meals;
Lest they should spy my windpipe's dangerous notes:
Great men should drink with harness on their throats.
Timon of Athens. Act i, sc. 2, l. 50. [Apemantus] "Wind-pipe" (hyphenated) is repeated in *Henry V*, iii, 6, 45: "Let not hemp his wind-pipe suffocate."

As you are great, be pitifully good.
Timon of Athens. Act iii, sc. 5, l. 52. [Alcibiades]

9
Possess'd he is with greatness.
Troilus and Cressida. Act ii, sc. 3, l. 180. [Ulysses]

What, am I poor of late?
'Tis certain, greatness, once fall'n out with fortune,
Must fall out with men too: what the declined is
He shall as soon read in the eyes of others
As feel in his own fall; for men, like butterflies,
Show not their mealy wings but to the summer.
Troilus and Cressida. Act iii, sc. 3, l. 74. [Achilles] The only use of "mealy."

10
In my stars I am above thee; but be not afraid of greatness: some are born great, some achieve greatness and some have greatness thrust upon 'em.
Twelfth Night. Act ii, sc. 5, l. 155. [Malvolio, reading] Repeated in iii, 4, 45, and v, 1, 378.

11
Your greatness Hath not been used to fear.
Winter's Tale. Act iv, sc. 4, l. 17. [Perdita]

A great man, I 'll warrant; I know by the picking on 's teeth.
Winter's Tale. Act iv, sc. 4, l. 779. [Clown]

II—Greatness: Its Penalties

12
Be it known, that we, the greatest, are misthought
For things that others do; and, when we fall,
We answer others' merits in our name.
Antony and Cleopatra. Act v, sc. 2, l. 176. [Cleopatra] The only use of "misthought."

13
Who deserves greatness Deserves your hate.
Coriolanus. Act i, sc. 1, l. 180. [Marcius]

14
His greatness weigh'd, his will is not his own.
Hamlet. Act i, sc. 3, l. 17. [Laertes]

1
Thou seek'st the greatness that will overwhelm thee.
II Henry IV. Act iv, sc. 5, l. 98. [King Henry]

2
Think you see them great,
And follow'd with the general throng and sweat
Of thousand friends; then in a moment, see
How soon this mightiness meets misery.
Henry VIII. Prologue, l. 27.

3
'Tis the plague of great ones;
Prerogatived are they less than the base.
Othello. Act iii, sc. 3, l. 273. [Othello] The only use of "prerogatived."

4
The mightier man, the mightier is the thing
That makes him honour'd, or begets him hate;
For greatest scandal waits on greatest state.
The Rape of Lucrece, l. 1004.

5
This careful height.
Richard III. Act i, sc. 3, l. 83. [Queen Elizabeth]
They that stand high have many blasts to shake them;
And if they fall, they dash themselves to pieces.
Richard III. Act i, sc. 3, l. 259. [Queen Margaret]
One heaved a-high, to be hurl'd down below.
Richard III. Act iv, sc. 4, l. 86. [Queen Margaret] The only use of "a-high."

6
These humble considerations make me out of love with my greatness.
II Henry IV. Act ii, sc. 2, l. 14. [Prince of Wales]

III—Great and Small

7
Small to greater matters must give way.
Antony and Cleopatra. Act ii, sc. 2, l. 11. [Lepidus]

8
The great man down, you mark his favourite flies;
The poor advanced makes friends of enemies
Hamlet. Act iii, sc. 2, l. 214. [Player King]
'Tis dangerous when the baser nature comes
Between the pass and fell incensed points
Of mighty opposites.
Hamlet. Act v, sc. 2, l. 60. [Hamlet]

9
I swear, 'tis better to be lowly born,
And range with humble livers in content,
Than to be perk'd up in a glistering grief,
And wear a golden sorrow.
Henry VIII. Act ii, sc. 3, l. 19. [Anne] The only use of "perk'd."

10
Great men may jest with saints; 'tis wit in them,
But in the less foul profanation.
Measure for Measure. Act ii, sc. 2, l. 127. [Isabella]

11
Men's natures wrangle with inferior things,
Though great ones are their object.
Othello. Act iii, sc. 4, l. 144. [Desdemona]

12
I am too little to contend,
Since he 's so great can make his will his act.
Pericles. Act i, sc. 2, l. 17. [Pericles]

13
The lesser thing should not the greater hide.
The Rape of Lucrece, l. 663.
The greater scorns the lesser.
Timon of Athens. Act iv, sc. 3, l. 6. [Timon]
The greater hides the less.
The Two Gentlemen of Verona. Act iii, sc. 1, l. 372. [Launce]

14
Things small as nothing, for request's sake only,
He makes important.
Troilus and Cressida. Act ii, sc. 3, l. 179. [Ulysses]
Light boats sail swift, though greater hulks draw deep.
Troilus and Cressida. Act ii, sc. 3, l. 277. [Agamemnon]

GREECE AND THE GREEKS

15
Cassius: Did Cicero say any thing?
Casca: Ay, he spoke Greek.
Cassius: To what effect?
Casca: Nay, an I tell you that, I 'll ne'er look you i' the face again: but those that understood him smiled at one another and shook their heads; but, for mine own part, it was Greek to me.
Julius Cæsar. Act i, sc. 2, l. 281.

16
Hail, all you state of Greece!
Troilus and Cressida. Act iv, sc. 5, l. 65. [Æneas]
All Greece.—*Troilus and Cressida*, i, 2, 267.
Furthest Greece.—*Comedy of Errors*, i, 1, 133.
Isles of Greece.—*Troilus and Cressida*, Prol., 1.
Our country of Greece.—*Pericles*, ii, 1, 68.

17
Now on Dardan plains
The fresh and yet unbruised Greeks do pitch
Their brave pavilions.
Troilus and Cressida Prologue, l. 14. "Dardan" is used two lines later, and not again in the plays.
The Greeks are strong and skilful to their strength,
Fierce to their skill and to their fierceness valiant.
Troilus and Cressida. Act i, sc. 1, l. 7. [Troilus]

Agamemnon,
Thou great commander, nerve and bone of Greece.
Troilus and Cressida. Act i, sc. 3, l. 54. [Ulysses]

18
She 's a merry Greek indeed.
Troilus and Cressida. Act i, sc. 2, l. 119. [Cressida] "Merry Greeks" is repeated in iv, 4, 58.
Fair Greek.—*Troilus and Cressida*, iv, 4, 115.
Foolish Greek—*Twelfth Night*, iv, 1, 19.
Sweet Greek.—*Troilus and Cressida*, v, 2, 27.

Sweet honey Greek.—*Troilus and Cressida,* v, 2, 18.

Valiant Greek.—*Troilus and Cressida,* iv, 3, 2.

1

A Grecian that is true in love.
Troilus and Cressida. Act i, sc. 3, l. 279. [Æneas]

2

No man lesser fears the Greeks than I.
Troilus and Cressida. Act ii, sc. 2, l. 8. [Hector]

3

The Grecian dames are sunburnt and not worth
The splinter of a lance.
Troilus and Cressida. Act i, sc. 3, l. 282. [Æneas]

I am sunburnt.—*Much Ado about Nothing,* ii, 1, 331.

Sunburnt sicklemen.—*The Tempest,* iv, 1, 134. The only uses of "sunburnt."

This broken joint . . . entreat her to splinter. —*Othello,* ii, 3, 329. The only uses of "splinter."

Scarr'd the moon with splinters.—*Coriolanus,* iv, 5, 115. The only use of "splinters."

4

The Grecian youths are full of quality;
They 're loving, well composed with gifts of nature,
Flowing and swelling o'er with arts and exercise.
Troilus and Cressida. Act iv, sc. 4, l. 78. [Troilus]

You cogging Greeks.
Troilus and Cressida. Act v, sc. 6, l. 11. [Troilus] "Cogging" is used twice more in the plays, "cogging companion" in *The Merry Wives of Windsor,* iii, 1, 123, and "cogging slave" in *Othello,* iv, 2, 132.

The strawy Greeks.—*Troilus and Cressida,* v, 5, 24. The only use of "strawy."

Subtle Greeks.—*Titus Andronicus,* v, 3, 84.

GREETING

5

Captain, what greeting will you to my Lord Lafeu?
All 's Well that Ends Well. Act iv, sc. 3, l. 352. [Lord]

6

He shall have every day a several greeting,
Or I 'll unpeople Egypt.
Antony and Cleopatra. Act i, sc. 5, l. 77. [Cleopatra]

Unpeople the province.—*Measure for Measure,* iii, 2, 184.

Unpeople this my realm.—*III Henry VI,* i, 1, 126.

Quite unpeople her.—*Cymbeline,* i, 5, 79. The only uses of "unpeople." "Unpeopled" occurs four times.

7

We should have met you
By sea and land; supplying every stage
With an augmented greeting.
Antony and Cleopatra. Act iii, sc. 6, l. 53. [Cæsar] The only use of "supplying."

8

Cæsar sends greeting to the Queen of Egypt.
Antony and Cleopatra. Act v, sc. 2, l. 9. [Proculeius]

Greeting to old Norway.—*Hamlet,* i, 2, 35.

Bear my greeting to the senators.
Julius Cæsar. Act ii, sc. 2, l. 61. [Cæsar]

They shall give their greeting to the citadel.
Othello. Act ii, sc. 1, l. 94. [Gentleman]

9

William: Good even, Audrey.
Audrey: God ye good even, William.
William: And good even to you, sir.
Touchstone: Good even, gentle friend.
As You Like It. Act v, sc. 1, l. 15.

Give ye good even.—*The Two Gentlemen of Verona,* ii, 1, 104.

Good even and twenty.—*The Merry Wives of Windsor,* ii, 1, 202.

Good even to your ladyship.—*The Two Gentlemen of Verona,* iv, 2, 85. "Good even" is used thirteen times.

10

Salutation and greeting to you all!
As You Like It. Act v, sc. 4, l. 39. [Touchstone]

Most military sir, salutation.
Love's Labour 's Lost. Act v, sc. 1, l. 38. [Holofernes]

Panting forth . . . his mistress salutations.
King Lear. Act ii, sc. 4, l. 32. [Kent]

Do you salutation.—*Julius Cæsar,* iv, 2, 5.

Speak my salutation.—*Macbeth,* v, 8, 57.

French salutation.—*Romeo and Juliet,* ii, 4, 47.

11

I have received not only greetings,
But with them change of honours.
Coriolanus. Act ii, sc. 1, l. 213. [Coriolanus]

12

Most fair return of greetings.
Hamlet. Act ii, sc. 2, l. 60. [Voltimand]

Health and fair greeting.—*II Henry IV,* iv, 1, 27.

13

Now we are well prepared to know the pleasure
Of our fair cousin Dauphin; for we hear
Your greeting is from him, not from the king.
Henry V. Act i, sc. 2, l. 234. [King Henry]

Unless the Dauphin be in presence here,
To whom expressly I bring greeting too.
Henry V. Act ii, sc. 4, l. 111. [Exeter]

14

If thou meanest well, I greet thee well.
I Henry VI. Act v, sc. 1, l. 14. [Buckingham]

I accept thy greeting.—*II Henry VI,* v, 1, 15.

15

First, to do greetings to thy royal people.
III Henry VI. Act iii, sc. 3, l. 52. [Warwick]

Give you all greetings.—*The Winter's Tale,* v, 1, 140.

Different greeting.—*Romeo and Juliet,* i, 5, 92.

Gentle adieus and greetings.—*Antony and Cleopatra,* iv, 5, 14.

Journal greeting.—*Measure for Measure,* iv, 3, 92.

Loving greetings.—*All 's Well that Ends Well,* i, 3, 258.

Prophetic greeting.—*Macbeth,* i, 3, 78.

16

Gentle and fair, your brother kindly greets you.
Measure for Measure, i, 4, 24. [Lucio]

My mother greets me kindly.—*All's Well that Ends Well,* ii, 4, 1.

1
Mark my greeting well.
Richard II. Act i, sc. 1, l. 36. [Bolingbroke]
I send to her my kind commends;
Take special care my greetings be deliver'd.
Richard II. Act iii, sc. 1, l. 38.

2
A happy time of day!
Richard III. Act ii, sc. 1, l. 47. [Gloucester]
God give your graces both
A happy and a joyful time of day!
Richard III. Act iv, sc. 1, l. 5. [Anne] See also under BLESSING.

King Ferdinand: All hail, sweet madam, and fair time of day!
Princess of France: 'Fair' in 'all hail' is foul.
Love's Labour 's Lost. Act v, sc. 2, l. 339.

God give your lordship good time of day.
II Henry IV. Act i, sc. 2, l. 106. [Falstaff]

Health and fair time of day; joy and good wishes.
Henry V. Act v, sc. 2, l. 3. [King Henry]

Jamy: I say gud-day, Captain Fluellen.
Fluellen: God-den to your worship.
Henry V. Act iii, sc. 2, l. 88.

Good day and happiness!—*As You Like It,* iv, 1, 30.

Once more good day to thee.—*The Taming of the Shrew,* iv, 5, 33.

Good day at once.—*Timon of Athens,* iii, 4, 7. "Good day" is used thirteen times.

3
Many good morrows to my noble lord!
Richard III. Act iii, sc. 2, l. 35. [Catesby]

Warwick: Many good morrows to your majesty!
King: Is it good morrow, lords?
Warwick: 'Tis one o'clock, and past.
King: Why, then, good morrow to you all.
II Henry IV. Act iii, sc. 1, l. 32.

Many good morrows to your majesty.
Titus Andronicus. Act ii, sc. 2, l. 11. [Titus]

Vouchsafe good morrow from a feeble tongue.
Julius Cæsar. Act ii, sc. 1, l. 313. [Ligarius]

Achilles: Good morrow.
Ajax: Ay, and good next day too.
Troilus and Cressida. Act iii, sc. 3, l. 68.

A thousand times good morrow.
The Two Gentlemen of Verona. Act iv, sc. 3, l. 6. [Silvia]

A thousand good-morrows.—*The Two Gentlemen of Verona,* ii, 1, 102.

Bids them good-morrow.—*Henry V,* iv, Prol., 33.

Do my good morrow to them.—*Henry V,* iv, 1, 26.

Give you good morrow.—*Richard III,* ii, 3, 6; and four times in later plays.

It is good morrow, is it not?—*I Henry IV,* ii, 4, 573. See under TO-MORROW.

God give you good morrow.—*Love's Labour 's Lost,* iv, 2, 84.

4
I will omit no opportunity
That may convey my greetings, love, to thee.
Romeo and Juliet. Act iii, sc. 5, l. 49. [Romeo]

Thus much for greeting.—*The Taming of the Shrew,* iv, 1, 115.

I pray you, do my greeting.—*Timon of Athens,* v, 1, 215.

5
God and Saint Stephen give you good den.
Titus Andronicus. Act iv, sc. 4, l. 42. [Clown]

God dig-you-den all!
Love's Labour 's Lost. Act iv, sc. 1, l. 42. [Costard] The only use of the phrase.

God gi' god-den.
Romeo and Juliet. Act i, sc. 2, l. 59. [Servant]

Nurse: God ye good morrow, gentlemen.
Merchant: God ye good den, fair gentlewoman.
Romeo and Juliet. Act ii, sc. 4, l. 115.

Don John: My lord and brother, God save you!
Don Pedro: Good den, brother.
Much Ado about Nothing. Act iii, sc. 2, l. 82.

Good den, good den.—*Much Ado about Nothing,* v, 1, 46.

6
This is the most despiteful gentle greeting.
Troilus and Cressida. Act iv, sc. 1, l. 32. [Paris]

Let me confirm my princely brother's greeting.
Troilus and Cressida. Act iv, sc. 5, l. 174. [Menelaus]

GRIEF

See also Joy and Sorrow; Sorrow; Woe

7
If thou engrossest all the griefs are thine,
Thou robb'st me of a moiety.
All's Well that Ends Well. Act iii, sc. 2, l. 68. [Countess] The only use of "engrossest" and "robb'st." "Moiety" is used fifteen times.

My greatest grief,
Though little he do feel it, set down sharply.
All's Well that Ends Well. Act iii, sc. 4, l. 32. [Countess]

Grief would have tears, and sorrow bids me speak.
All's Well that Ends Well. Act iii, sc. 4, l. 42. [Countess]

8
This grief is crowned with consolation.
Antony and Cleopatra. Act i, sc. 2, l. 174. [Enobarbus] "Consolation" is repeated in *The Taming of the Shrew,* ii, 1, 191.

A grief that smites My very heart at root.
Antony and Cleopatra. Act v, sc. 2, l. 104. [Dolabella]

9
Celia: I charge thee, be not thou more grieved than I am.
Rosalind: I have more cause.
As You Like It. Act i, sc. 3, l. 94.

And do not seek to take your change upon you,
To bear your griefs yourself and leave me out.
As You Like It. Act i, sc. 3, l. 104. [Celia]

Do not you grieve at this.—*II Henry IV,* v, 5, 82.

How it grieves me.—*As You Like It,* v, 2, 22.

Grieves my heart.—*III Henry VI,* iii, 2, 183; *Romeo and Juliet,* iii, 5, 84; *Macbeth,* iv, 1, 110; *Pericles,* ii, 1, 21.

It grieves my soul.—*II Henry VI,* v, 2, 18; *King John,* v, 2, 15.

It grieves many.—*Henry VIII,* i, 2, 110.

Grieve to hear 't.—*Coriolanus,* v, 6, 63.
It may grieve him.—*The Merchant of Venice,* ii, 8, 34.
Doth that grieve thee?—*Troilus and Cressida,* v, 2, 45.
Nothing grieves me.—*Titus Andronicus,* v, 1, 143.
You shall not grieve.—*King Lear,* iv, 3, 55.

1 A heavier task could not have been imposed
Than I to speak my griefs unspeakable.
Comedy of Errors. Act i, sc. 1, l. 32. [Ægeon]

O grief hath changed me since you saw me last,
And careful hours with time's deformed hand
Have written strange defeatures in my face.
The Comedy of Errors. Act v, sc. 1, l. 297. [Ægeon] "Defeatures" is used earlier in the same play (ii, 1, 98) and nowhere else.

2 Some griefs are med'cinable.
Cymbeline. Act iii, sc. 2, l. 33. [Imogen] The only use of "med'cinable." "Medicinable" occurs three times: *Much Ado about Nothing,* ii, 2, 5; *Troilus and Cressida,* i, 3, 91; iii, 3, 44.

Guiderius: Grief and patience, rooted in him both,
Mingle their spurs together.
Arviragus: Grow, patience!
And let the stinking elder, grief, untwine
His perishing root with the increasing vine!
Cymbeline. Act iv, sc. 2, l. 57.

Great griefs, I see, medicine the less.
Cymbeline. Act iv, sc. 2, l. 243. [Belarius]

3 'Tis unmanly grief;
It shows a will most incorrect to heaven,
A heart unfortified, a mind impatient,
An understanding simple and unschool'd.
Hamlet. Act i, sc. 2, l. 94. [King] The only use of "incorrect" and "unfortified."

You do, surely, bar the door upon your own liberty, if you deny your griefs to your friend.
Hamlet. Act iii, sc. 2, l. 351. [Rosencrantz]

4 We dearly grieve
For that which thou hast done.
Hamlet. Act iv, sc. 3, l. 43. [King]

Make the judicious grieve.—*Hamlet,* ii, 2, 30.

5 O, this is the poison of deep grief.
Hamlet. Act iv, sc. 5, l. 76. [King]

I must commune with your grief.
Hamlet. Act iv, sc. 5, l. 202. [King]

What is he whose grief
Bears such an emphasis? whose phrase of sorrow
Conjures the wandering stars, and makes them stand
Like wonder-wounded hearers?
Hamlet. Act v, sc. 1, l. 278. [Hamlet] The only use of "wonder-wounded."

The bravery of his grief did put me
Into a towering passion.
Hamlet. Act v, sc. 2, l. 79. [Hamlet] "Towering" is used only once again, in *Macbeth,* ii, 4, 12.

Show his grief.—*Hamlet,* iii, 1, 191.
Sensibly in grief.—*Hamlet,* iv, 5, 150.

6 Yet for your part, it not appears to me
Either from the king or in the present time,
That you should have an inch of any ground
To build a grief on.
II Henry IV. Act iv, sc. 1, l. 107. [Westmoreland]

Here come I from our princely general
To know your griefs.
II Henry IV. Act iv, sc. 1, l. 141. [Westmoreland]

My lord, these griefs shall be with speed redress'd;
Upon my soul, they shall.
II Henry IV. Act iv, sc. 2, l. 59. [Lancaster] "Redressed" is repeated in *II Henry IV,* iv, 1, 170, and in *The Merry Wives of Windsor,* i, 1, 107.

My grief
Stretches itself beyond the hour of death.
II Henry IV. Act iv, sc. 4, l. 56. [King Henry]

Griefs are green.—*II Henry IV,* iv, 5, 204.

7 Conduct me where, from company,
I may revolve and ruminate my grief.
I Henry VI. Act v, sc. 5, l. 100. [King Henry]

8 His grief
Your grief, the common grief of all the land.
II Henry VI. Act i, sc. 1, l. 76. [Gloucester]

My heart is drown'd with grief,
Whose flood begins to flow within mine eyes.
II Henry VI. Act iii, sc. 1, l. 198. [King Henry]

My grief was at the height before thou camest,
And now, like Nilus, it disdaineth bounds.
Titus Andronicus. Act iii, sc. 1, l. 70. [Titus]

9 Oft have I heard that grief softens the mind
And makes it fearful and degenerate.
II Henry VI. Act iv, sc. 4, l. 1. [Queen Margaret]

Grief has so wrought on him,
He takes false shadows for true substances.
Titus Andronicus. Act iii, sc. 2, l. 79. [Titus]

10 I prithee, grieve, to make me merry, York.
III Henry VI. Act i, sc. 4, l. 86. [Queen Margaret]

She, poor wretch, for grief can speak no more.
III Henry VI. Act iii, sc. 1, l. 47. [King Henry]

Full of grief.—*III Henry VI,* iv, 4, 13.
Grief of heart.—*Henry VIII,* iii, 1, 13.

11 But let not therefore my good friends be grieved.
Julius Cæsar. Act i, sc. 2, l. 43. [Brutus]

O grief, Where hast thou led me?
Julius Cæsar. Act i, sc. 3, l. 111. [Cassius]

Make me acquainted with your cause of grief.
Julius Cæsar. Act ii, sc. 1, l. 256. [Portia]

What private griefs they have, alas, I know not.
Julius Cæsar. Act iii, sc. 2, l. 216. [Antony]

Speak your griefs softly.
Julius Cæsar. Act iv, sc. 2, l. 42. [Brutus]

In my tent, Cassius, enlarge your griefs,
And I will give you audience.
Julius Cæsar. Act iv, sc. 2, l. 46. [Brutus]

Now is that noble vessel full of grief,
That it runs over even at his eyes.
Julius Cæsar. Act v, sc. 5, l. 13. [Clitus]

1
I am sick of many griefs.
Julius Cæsar. Act iv, sc. 3, l. 144. [Brutus]
I am sick of that grief too.
Timon of Athens. Act iii, sc. 6, l. 19. [Lord]
2 My grief 's so great
That no supporter but the huge firm earth
Can hold it up: here I and sorrows sit.
King John. Act iii, sc. 1, l. 71. [Constance]
Pandulph: You hold too heinous a respect of grief. . . .
King Philip: You are as fond of grief as of your child.
Constance: Grief fills the room up of my absent child,
Lies in his bed, walks up and down with me.
Puts on his pretty looks, repeats his words,
Remembers me of all his gracious parts,
Stuffs out his vacant garments with his form;
Then, have I reason to be fond of grief?
King John. Act iii, sc. 4, l. 90.
Salisbury: Our griefs, and not our manners, reason now.
Bastard: But there is little reason in your grief;
Therefore 'twere reason you had manners now.
King John. Act iv, sc. 3, l. 29.
O, let us pay the time but needful woe,
Since it hath been beforehand with our griefs.
King John. Act v, sc. 7, l. 110. [Bastard]
Grief is proud.—*King John,* iii, 1, 69.
Sensible of grief.—*King John,* iii, 4, 53.
Where lies your grief?—*King John,* iv, 1, 48.
3
The grief hath crazed my wits.
King Lear. Act iii, sc. 4, l. 175. [Gloucester]
Better I were distract:
So should my thoughts be sever'd from my griefs,
And woes by wrong imaginations lose
The knowledge of themselves.
King Lear. Act iv, sc. 6, l. 288. [Gloucester]
4 She shook
The holy water from her heavenly eyes,
And clamour moisten'd: then away she started
To deal with grief alone.
King Lear. Act iv, sc. 3, l. 31. [Gentleman]
The only use of "moisten'd."
His grief grew puissant, and the strings of life
Began to crack.
King Lear. Act v, sc. 3, l. 216. [Edgar]
5
Where lies thy grief, O, tell me?
Love's Labour's Lost. Act iv, sc. 3, l. 171. [Biron]
My griefs are double.—*Love's Labour's Lost,* v, 2, 762.
6
Malcolm: What 's the newest grief?
Ross: That of an hour's age doth hiss the speaker:
Each minute teems a new one.
Macbeth. Act iv, sc. 3, l. 174.
Is it a fee-grief Due to some single breast?
Macbeth. Act iv, sc. 3, l. 196. [Macduff]
The only use of "fee-grief."
What, man! ne'er pull your hat upon your brows;
Give sorrow words: the grief that does not speak
Whispers the o'er-fraught heart and bids it break.
Macbeth. Act iv, sc. 3, l. 208. [Malcolm]
The only use of "o'er-fraught."
Let grief
Convert to anger; blunt not the heart, enrage it.
Macbeth. Act iv, sc. 3, l. 229. [Malcolm]
7
It grieves me for the death of Claudio:
But there 's no remedy.
Measure for Measure. Act ii, sc. 1, l. 294. [Escalus]
8
Grieve not that I am fallen to this for you.
The Merchant of Venice. Act iv, sc. 1, l. 266. [Antonio]
Grieve not you.—*Merchant of Venice,* v, 1, 239.
9
Every one can master a grief but he that has it.
Much Ado about Nothing. Act iii, sc. 2, l. 28. [Benedick]
'Tis not wisdom thus to second grief
Against yourself.
Much Ado about Nothing. Act v, sc. 1, l. 2. [Antonio]
Patch grief with proverbs.
Much Ado about Nothing. Act v, sc. 1, l. 17. [Leonato]
My griefs cry louder than advertisement.
Much Ado about Nothing. Act v, sc. 1, l. 32. [Leonato]
10 My particular grief
Is of so flood-gate and o'erbearing nature
That it engluts and swallows other sorrows.
Othello. Act i, sc. 3, l. 55. [Brabantio] The only use of "engluts." "Flood-gates" is repeated in *I Henry IV,* ii, 4, 435.
He robs himself that spends a bootless grief.
Othello. Act i, sc. 3, l. 209. [Duke]
O'erwhelmed with your grief—
A passion most unsuiting such a man.
Othello. Act iv, sc. 1, l. 77. [Iago] The only use of "unsuiting."
Pure grief Shore his old thread in twain.
Othello. Act v, sc. 2, l. 205. [Gratiano]
Dead with grieving.—*Othello,* ii, 3, 177.
I'll kill myself for grief.—*Othello,* v, 2, 192.
11
It shall no longer grieve without reproof.
Pericles. Act ii, sc. 4, l. 19. [Second Lord]
12
True grief is fond and testy as a child.
The Rape of Lucrece, l. 1094.
Grief best is pleased with grief's society.
The Rape of Lucrece, l. 1111.
Great grief grieves most at that would do it good.
The Rape of Lucrece, l. 1117.
Grief dallied with nor law nor limit knows.
The Rape of Lucrece, l. 1120.
13 Grief boundeth where it falls,
Not with the empty hollowness, but weight.
Richard II. Act i, sc. 2, l. 58. [Duchess of Gloucester]
Must I not serve a long apprenticehood
To foreign passages, and in the end,
Having my freedom, boast of nothing else

But that I was a journeyman to grief?
Richard II. Act i, sc. 3, l. 271. [Bolingbroke] The only use of "apprenticehood" and "journeyman."

Within me grief hath kept a tedious fast.
Richard II. Act ii, sc. 1, l. 75. [Gaunt]

I know no cause
Why I should welcome such a guest as grief.
Richard II. Act ii, sc. 2, l. 6. [Queen]

1
Each substance of a grief hath twenty shadows,
Which shows like grief itself, but is not so.
Richard II. Act ii, sc. 2, l. 14. [Bushy]

Taste grief.—*Richard II,* iii, 2, 176.

2
Still my griefs are mine:
You may my glories and my state depose,
But not my griefs; still I am king of those.
Richard II. Act iv, sc. 1, l. 191. [King Richard]

Make me, that nothing have, with nothing grieved,
And thou with all pleased, that hast all achieved!
Richard II. Act iv, sc. 1, l. 216. [King Richard]

'Tis very true, my grief lies all within;
And these external manners of laments
Are merely shadows to the unseen grief
That swells with silence in the tortured soul.
Richard II. Act iv, sc. 1, l. 295. [King Richard]

3
'Tis very grievous to be thought upon.
Richard III. Act i, sc. 1, l. 141. [Gloucester] "Grievous" is used twenty-two times in the plays, but in every other instance as an adjective directly modifying a noun.

4
Long die thy happy days before thy death;
And, after many lengthen'd hours of grief.
Richard III. Act i, sc. 3, l. 207. [Queen Margaret]

5
Griefs of mine own lie heavy in my breast.
Romeo and Juliet. Act i, sc. 1, l. 192. [Romeo]

One desperate grief cures with another's languish.
Romeo and Juliet. Act i, sc. 2, l. 49. [Benvolio]

These griefs, these woes, these sorrows make me old.
Romeo and Juliet. Act iii, sc. 2, l. 89. [Nurse]

Some grief shows much of love;
But much of grief shows still some want of wit.
Romeo and Juliet. Act iii, sc. 5, l. 73. [Lady Capulet]

Thy grief . . . strains me past the compass of my wits.
Romeo and Juliet. Act iv, sc. 1, l. 46. [Friar Laurence]

Pale with grief.—*Romeo and Juliet,* ii, 2, 15.

6
No more be grieved at that which thou hast done.
Sonnets. No. xxxv.

That thou hast her, it is not all my grief,
And yet it may be said I loved her dearly;
That she hath thee, is of my wailing chief,
A loss in love that touches me more nearly.
Sonnets. No. xlii.

7
Was ever gentleman thus grieved as I?
The Taming of the Shrew. Act ii, sc. 1, l. 37. [Baptista]

Be not grieved.—*The Taming of the Shrew,* iv, 5, 64.

8
Grief that 's beauty's canker.
The Tempest. Act i, sc. 2, l. 415. [Prospero]

9
I will present My honest grief unto him.
Timon of Athens. Act iv, sc. 3, l. 477. [Flavius]

Accept my grief.—*Timon of Athens,* iv, 3, 495.

Ease them of their griefs.—*Timon of Athens,* v, 1, 201. See under KINDNESS.

10
Thou abhorr'dst in us our human griefs.
Timon of Athens. Act v, sc. 4, l. 75. [Alcibiades]

Grieved with killing grief.
Titus Andronicus. Act ii, sc. 3, l. 260. [Saturninus]

Bitter grief.—*Titus Andronicus,* v, 3, 89.
Burthening grief.—*I Henry VI,* ii, 5, 10.
Deep grief.—*Hamlet,* iv, 5, 76.
Excessive grief.—*All's Well that Ends Well,* i, 1, 65.
Great grief.—*King John,* iii, 1, 70; *Cymbeline,* iv, 2, 243; *The Winter's Tale,* iii, 2, 1.
Greatest grief.—*Sonnets,* xlviii.
Griping grief.—*Romeo and Juliet,* iv, 5, 128.
Hateful griefs.—*Titus Andronicus,* iii, 1, 296.
Love's grief.—*Love's Labour's Lost,* iv, 3, 128; *Much Ado about Nothing,* i, 1, 315.
Mortal griefs.—*Henry V,* iv, 1, 259.
Petty griefs.—*Sonnets,* xc.
Present grief.—*II Henry IV,* i, 1, 211.
Sociable grief.—*King John,* iii, 4, 65.
Swelling griefs.—*III Henry VI,* iv, 8, 42.
Tenfold grief.—*Titus Andronicus,* iii, 2, 6. "Ten-fold" (hyphenated) is repeated in *Antony and Cleopatra,* iv, 7, 14.

11
What grief hath set the jaundice on your cheeks?
Troilus and Cressida. Act i, sc. 3, l. 2. [Agamemnon] Jaundice is mentioned once again in *The Merchant of Venice,* i, 1, 85.

The grief is fine, full, perfect, that I taste,
And violenteth in a sense as strong
As that which causeth it: . . .
If I could temporise with my affection,
Or brew it to a weak and colder palate,
The like allayment could I give my grief:
My love admits no qualifying dross;
No more my grief, in such a precious loss.
Troilus and Cressida. Act iv, sc. 4, l. 3. [Cressida] The only use of "violenteth" and "qualifying." "Temporise" is repeated in *King John,* v, 2, 125, and in *Much Ado about Nothing,* i, 1, 276. Only use of "allayment." "Allayments" occurs in *Cymbeline,* i, 5, 22.

12
As ending anthem of my endless dolour.
The Two Gentlemen of Verona. Act iii, sc. 1, l. 240. [Valentine] "Anthem" occurs only once again, in *II Henry IV,* i, 2, 213.

Gonzalo: When every grief is entertain'd that 's offer'd,

Comes to the entertainer—
Sebastian: A dollar.
Gonzalo: Dolour comes to him, indeed.
The Tempest. Act ii, sc. 1, l. 16. The only use of "entertainer." "Dollar" is mentioned once again in *Macbeth,* i, 2, 62, an English corruption of the German thaler, or perhaps a reference to the so-called "Spanish dollar," or "piece of eight."

Thou shalt have as many dolours for thy daughters as thou canst tell in a year.
King Lear. Act ii, sc. 4, l. 54. [Fool]

Abundant dolour.—*Richard II,* i, 3, 257.

All to dolours turn'd.—*Cymbeline,* v, 4, 80.

Three thousand dolours a day.—*Measure for Measure,* i, 2, 50.

1
Think upon my grief, a lady's grief.
The Two Gentlemen of Verona. Act iv, sc. 3, l. 28. [Silvia]

2
And now his grief may be compared well
To one sore sick that hears the passing-bell.
Venus and Adonis, l. 701. The only use of "passing-bell."

3
Grief hath two tongues, and never woman yet
Could rule them both without ten women's wit.
Venus and Adonis, l. 1007.

My tongue cannot express my grief.
Venus and Adonis, l. 1069.

4 How will this grieve you,
When you shall come to clearer knowledge, that
You thus have publish'd me!
Winter's Tale. Act ii, sc. 1, l. 96. [Hermione]

Her . . . griefs,
Which never tender lady hath borne greater.
Winter's Tale. Act ii, sc. 2, l. 23. [Emilia]

5 What 's gone and what 's past help
Should be past grief.
Winter's Tale. Act iii, sc. 2, l. 223. [Paulina]

GRIEVANCE

6
I told him gently of our grievances.
I Henry IV. Act v, sc. 2, l. 37. [Worcester]

General grievances.—*II Henry IV,* iv, 1, 169.

The king is weary
Of dainty and such picking grievances.
II Henry IV. Act iv, sc. 1, l. 197. [Archbishop of York]

7
I 'll know his grievance, or be much denied.
Romeo and Juliet. Act i, sc. 1, l. 163. [Benvolio]

Withdraw unto some private place,
And reason coldly of your grievances.
Romeo and Juliet. Act iii, sc. 1, l. 54. [Benvolio]

8
Then can I grieve at grievances foregone.
Sonnets. No. xxx. See under MOAN.

9
Commend thy grievance to my holy prayers.
The Two Gentlemen of Verona. Act i, sc. 1, l. 17. [Proteus]

Great grievance.—*Henry VIII,* i, 2, 20.

Sweet-complaining grievance.—*The Two Gentlemen of Verona,* iii, 2, 86. The only use of "sweet-complaining."

10
I pity much your grievances.
The Two Gentlemen of Verona. Act iv, sc. 4, l. 37. [Eglamour]

GROAN

11
You ne'er oppress'd me with a mother's groan.
All's Well that Ends Well. Act i, sc. 3, l. 153. [Countess]

Mothers' groans.—*The Rape of Lucrece,* l. 431.

Dearest groans of a mother.—*All's Well that Ends Well,* iv, 5, 12.

12
Made a groan of her last breath.
All's Well that Ends Well. Act iv, sc. 3, l. 62. [First Lord]

Groaning every hour.—*As You Like It,* iii, 2, 321.

Groan and drop.—*Coriolanus,* iv, 4, 4.

Groan and sweat.—*Julius Cæsar,* iv, 1, 22.

13
I have not art to reckon my groans.
Hamlet. Act ii, sc. 2, l. 120. [Polonius]

14
Hear, hear how dying Salisbury doth groan!
I Henry VI. Act i, sc. 4, l. 104. [Talbot]

A deadly groan, like life and death's departing.
III Henry VI. Act ii, sc. 6, l. 43. [Richard] "Deadly groan" is repeated in *Venus and Adonis,* l. 1044.

Bleeding groans.—*A Lover's Complaint,* l. 275.

Easy groans.—*Coriolanus,* v, 2, 45.

General groan.—*Hamlet,* iii, 3, 23.

Heart-offending groans.—*II Henry VI,* iii, 2, 60. The only use of "heart-offending."

Heart-sick groans.—*Romeo and Juliet,* iii, 3, 72. "Heart-sick" is repeated in *Cymbeline,* iv, 2, 37.

Mortifying groans.—*The Merchant of Venice,* i, 1, 82. "Mortifying" is repeated in *Much Ado about Nothing,* i, 3, 13: "Mortifying mischief."

Penitential groans.—*Two Gentlemen of Verona,* ii, 4, 131. The only use of "penitential."

Pining maidens' groans.—*Henry V,* ii, 4, 107.

Tearing groan.—*Antony and Cleopatra,* iv, 14, 31.

The mandrake's groan.—*II Henry VI,* iii, 2, 310.

15
Groaning underneath this age's yoke.
Julius Cæsar. Act i, sc. 2, l. 61. [Cassius]

Groaning for burial.—*Julius Cæsar,* iii, 1, 275.

16
I would you heard it groan.
Love's Labour 's Lost. Act ii, sc. 1, l. 183. [Rosaline]

God give him grace to groan!
Love's Labour 's Lost. Act iv, sc. 3, l. 21. [Biron]

He made a groan at it.—*Pericles,* iv, 2, 117.

17
Afflict him in his bed with bedrid groans.
The Rape of Lucrece, l. 975.

With deep groans the diapason bear.
Rape of Lucrece, l. 1132. The only use of "diapason." "Deep groan" is repeated in l. 1276.
Deep-fet groans.—*II Henry VI,* ii, 4, 33. The only use of "deep-fet" (deep-fetched).

1
What hear there for welcome but my groans?
Richard II. Act i, sc. 2, l. 70. [Duchess]
Hadst thou groan'd for him
As I have done, thou wouldst be more pitiful.
Richard II. Act v, sc. 2, l. 102. [Duchess]
Now sir, the sound that tells what hour it is
Are clamorous groans, which strike upon my heart,
Which is the bell: so sighs and tears and groans
Show minutes, times, and hours.
Richard II. Act v, sc. 5, l. 55. [King Richard]
Groans and shrieks.—*Macbeth,* iv, 3, 168.

2
Benvolio: Tell me in sadness, who is that you love.
Romeo: What, shall I groan and tell thee?
Benvolio: Groan! why, no;
But sadly tell me who.
Romeo and Juliet. Act i, sc. 1, l. 205.
Heavily he answers with a groan.
Sonnets. No. l.

3
A thousand groans, but thinking on thy face,
One on another's neck, do witness bear.
Sonnets. No. cxxxi.

4 Thou didst vent thy groans
As fast as mill-wheels strike.
The Tempest. Act i, sc. 2, l. 280. [Prospero] The only use of "mill-wheels."
Thy groans
Did make wolves howl and penetrate the breasts
Of ever angry bears.
The Tempest. Act i, sc. 2, l. 287. [Prospero]

5
Oh! oh! groans out for ha! ha! ha!
Troilus and Cressida. Act iii, sc. 1, l. 136. [Pandarus]
If you cannot weep, yet give some groans.
Troilus and Cressida. Act v, sc. 10, l. 50. [Pandarus]

6
Love's deep groans I never shall regard.
Venus and Adonis, l. 377.
Groan for love.—*Love's Labour's Lost,* iv, 3, 182.
Groaning for love.—*Romeo and Juliet,* ii, 4, 92.

7
What may a heavy groan advantage thee?
Venus and Adonis, l. 950.

GROOM

See also Bridegroom

8 The surfeited grooms
Do mock their charge with snores.
Macbeth. Act ii, sc. 2, l. 5. [Lady Macbeth]
Smear The sleepy grooms with blood.
Macbeth. Act ii, sc. 2, l. 49. [Lady Macbeth]

9
'Some hard-favour'd groom of thine,' quoth he,
. . . I 'll murder straight.'
The Rape of Lucrece, l. 1632.
Basest groom.—*Pericles,* iv, 6, 201.
Detested groom.—*King Lear,* ii, 4, 220.
Dunghill grooms.—*I Henry VI,* i, 3, 14.
Gallant grooms.—*Titus Andronicus,* iv, 2, 164.
Jaded groom.—*II Henry VI,* iv, 1, 52. "Jaded" is repeated in *Antony and Cleopatra,* iii, 1, 34, and in *Henry VIII,* iii, 2, 280.
Meanest groom.—*II Henry VI,* ii, 1, 185.
Ordinary groom.—*Henry VIII,* v, 1, 172.
Rascal groom.—*The Rape of Lucrece,* l. 671.
Silly groom.—*The Rape of Lucrece,* l. 1345.
Sour-faced groom.—*The Rape of Lucrece,* l. 1334. The only use of "sour-faced."
Vulgar groom.—*II Henry VI,* iv, 1, 128.

10
I was a poor groom of thy stable, king,
When thou wert king.
Richard II. Act v, sc. 5, l. 72. [Groom]
Poor grooms.—*The Rape of Lucrece,* l. 1013.
Grooms, and lackeys.—*Henry VIII,* v, 2, 18.

11 'Tis a groom indeed,
A grumbling groom, and that the girl shall find.
The Taming of the Shrew, iii, 2, 154. See under BRIDEGROOM.
'Tis like you 'll prove a jolly surly groom.
The Taming of the Shrew. Act iii, sc. 2, l. 215. [Katharina]
You logger-headed and unpolish'd grooms!
The Taming of the Shrew. Act iv, sc. 1, l. 128. [Petruchio] The only use of "logger-headed." "Logger-head" occurs three times.
Forsake this groom.—*II Henry VI,* iv, 2, 132.

GROSSNESS

12
The grosser manner of these world's delights
He throws upon the gross world's baser slaves.
Love's Labour's Lost. Act i, sc. 1, l. 29. [Dumain]
Grosser blood.—*Henry V,* iii, 1, 24.
Grosser issues.—*Othello,* iii, 3, 219.
Grosser name.—*Hamlet,* iv, 7, 171.
Grosser quality.—*Henry VIII,* i, 2, 84. The only uses of "grosser."

13
As gross As black and white.
Henry V. Act ii, sc. 2, l. 103. [King Henry]
Gross as earth.—*Hamlet,* iv, 4, 46.
Gross as a mountain.—*I Henry IV,* ii, 4, 250.
Gross in sense.—*Othello,* i, 2, 72.
Gross in taste.—*Love's Labour's Lost,* iv, 3, 339.
Our gross selves.—*Measure for Measure,* ii, 2, 87.

14
To be received plain, I 'll speak more gross.
Measure for Measure. Act ii, sc. 4, l. 82. [Angelo]
Speak not so grossly.
The Merchant of Venice. Act v, sc. 1, l. 266. [Portia]
So grossly.—*Henry V,* ii, 2, 107; *King John,* iv, 2, 94; *Measure for Measure,* v, 1, 477.

Most grossly.—*I Henry IV,* iii, 2, 150; *Antony and Cleopatra,* iii, 10, 39.
Too grossly.—*King Lear,* i, 1, 295.
It were too gross.—*The Merchant of Venice,* ii, 7, 50.

1 Hiding the grossness with fair ornament.
The Merchant of Venice, iii, 2, 80. See under RELIGION.

I will purge thy mortal grossness so
That thou shalt like an airy spirit go.
A Midsummer-Night's Dream. Act iii, sc. 1, l. 163. [Titania]

Grossness of this age.—*Richard III,* iii, 1, 46.
Grossness of the foppery.—*The Merry Wives of Windsor,* v, 5, 131.
Impossible passages of grossness.—*Twelfth Night,* iii, 2, 77.
Whose grossness little characters sum up.—*Troilus and Cressida,* i, 3, 325. The only uses of "grossness."

2 This gross watery pumpion.
The Merry Wives of Windsor, iii, 3, 43. See under FATNESS.

Gross, gross; fat, fat.—*Love's Labour's Lost,* v, 2, 268. See also under FATNESS.
A great gross one.—*Much Ado about Nothing,* v, 1, 164.

3 It wants matter to prevent so gross o'er-reaching as this.
The Merry Wives of Windsor. Act v, sc. 5, l. 144. [Falstaff]

I never saw him so gross.—*The Merry Wives of Windsor,* iii, 3, 201.

4 Most heathenish and most gross!
Othello. Act v, sc. 2, l. 313. [Cassio] The only use of "heathenish."

5 It were a very gross kind of behaviour, as they say.
Romeo and Juliet. Act ii, sc. 4, l. 176. [Nurse]

Grossly shown in thy behaviours.—*All's Well that Ends Well,* i, 3, 184.
Grossly gape on.—*Othello,* iii, 3, 395.
'Tis grossly done.—*The Merry Wives of Windsor,* ii, 2, 149.

GROUND

6 The ground shrinks before his treading.
Coriolanus. Act v, sc. 4, l. 20. [Menenius]

Rock the ground.—*A Midsummer-Night's Dream,* iv, 1, 91.
Sweep the ground.—*II Henry VI,* iv, 1, 75.

7 I have tired myself, and for two nights together
Have made the ground my bed.
Cymbeline. Act iii, sc. 6, l. 2. [Imogen]

8 Hic et ubique? then we'll shift our ground.
Hamlet. Act i, sc. 5, l. 156. [Hamlet] The only use of "hic et ubique."

9 We go to gain a little patch of ground
That hath in it no profit but the name.
To pay five ducats, five, I would not farm it.
Hamlet. Act iv, sc. 4, l. 18. [Captain]

Plot of ground.—*I Henry VI,* ii, 4, 89.

10 Lay him i' the cold ground.
Hamlet. Act iv, sc. 5, l. 70. [Ophelia] "Cold ground" is repeated in *All's Well that Ends Well,* iii, 4, 6.

Ground unsanctified.—*Hamlet,* v, 1, 252.
You shall help to put him i' the ground.
Winter's Tale. Act iii, sc. 3, l. 141. [Clown]
Under ground.—*II Henry VI,* ii, 1, 174.
The ground that gave them first has them again.
Cymbeline. Act iv, sc. 2, l. 289. [Belarius]

11 Eight yards of uneven ground is threescore and ten miles afoot with me.
I Henry IV. Act ii, sc. 2, l. 27. [Falstaff]

Gloucester: Methinks the ground is even.
Edgar: Horrible step.
King Lear. Act iv, sc. 6, l. 3.

Even ground.—*King John,* ii, 1, 576.

12 By this heavenly ground I tread on.
II Henry IV. Act ii, sc. 1, l. 152. [Hostess]

Get ground.—*II Henry IV,* ii, 3, 53.
Ground to root upon.—*II Henry IV,* iii, 1, 91.

13 Who hath measured the ground?
Henry V. Act iii, sc. 7, l. 137. [Constable]

14 May that ground gape and swallow me alive.
III Henry VI. Act i, sc. 1, l. 161. [Clifford]

Sink in the ground.—*III Henry VI,* v, 6, 62.

15 Give no foot of ground!
III Henry VI. Act i, sc. 3, l. 15. [York]

Giving no ground.—*III Henry VI,* ii, 6, 16.
Began to give me ground.—*I Henry IV,* ii, 4, 240.
Give ground, if you see him furious.
Twelfth Night. Act iii, sc. 4, l. 334. [Fabian]
Give ground.—*The Tempest,* ii, 2, 64.

16 Good ground, be pitiful and hurt me not!
King John. Act iv, sc. 3, l. 2. [Arthur]

17 Now for the ground which: which, I mean, I walked upon; it is ycleped thy park.
Love's Labour's Lost. Act i, sc. 1, l. 241. [King] "Ycleped" is repeated in v, 2, 602, and occurs in no other play.

18 Mrs. Overdone: But shall all our houses of resort in the suburbs be pulled down?
Pompey: To the ground, mistress.
Measure for Measure. Act i, sc. 2, l. 104.

To the ground.—*I Henry VI,* iii, 2, 17.
Come to ground.—*Macbeth,* iii, 5, 25.
Hit the ground.—*Twelfth Night,* iii, 4, 306.

19 Follow me, then, To plainer ground.
A Midsummer-Night's Dream. Act iii, sc. 2, l. 404. [Puck]

20 Look not to the ground,
Ye favourites of a king; are we not high?
Richard II. Act iii, sc. 2, l. 87. [King Richard]

21 The ground is bloody.
Romeo and Juliet. Act v, sc. 3, l. 172. [Watchman]

Barren ground.—*The Tempest,* i, 1, 69.

Base ground.—*Love's Labour's Lost,* iv, 3, 225.
Bleeding ground.—*King John,* ii, 1, 304.
Dank and dirty ground.—*A Midsummer-Night's Dream,* ii, 2, 75.
Fair ground.—*Coriolanus,* iii, 1, 242.
French ground.—*Henry V,* i, 2, 106.
God's ground.—*Henry V,* iv, 7, 149.
Hollow ground.—*Richard II,* iii, 2, 140; *Romeo and Juliet,* v, 3, 4.
Orbed ground.—*Hamlet,* iii, 2, 166.
Sable ground.—*The Rape of Lucrece,* l. 1074.
Slippery ground.—*Julius Cæsar,* iii, 1, 191.
Sluttish ground.—*Venus and Adonis,* l. 983.
Subtle ground.—*Coriolanus,* v, 2, 20.
Sullen ground.—*I Henry IV,* i, 2, 236.
Tawny ground.—*Henry V,* iii, 6, 170.
The ground indeed is tawny.—*The Tempest,* ii, 1, 54.
Virtue's ground.—*III Henry VI,* iii, 3, 125.
Waste ground.—*Measure for Measure,* ii, 2, 170.

GROVE, see Wood

GROWTH

1
I, his brother, gain nothing under him but growth.
As You Like It. Act i, sc. 1, l. 15. [Orlando]

2 His pupil age
Man-enter'd thus, he waxed like a sea,
And in the brunt of seventeen battles since
He lurch'd all swords of the garland.
Coriolanus. Act ii, sc. 2, l. 104. [Cominius] "Pupil age" is repeated in *I Henry IV,* ii, 4, 106. The only use of "man-enter'd," "brunt," and "lurch'd." "Lurch" occurs in *The Merry Wives of Windsor,* ii, 2, 26.

This Marcius is grown from man to dragon: he has wings; he 's more than a creeping thing.
Coriolanus. Act v, sc. 4, l. 13. [Menenius]

3
By 'r lady, your ladyship is nearer to heaven than when I saw you last, by the altitude of a chopine.
Hamlet. Act ii, sc. 2, l. 445. [Hamlet] The only use of "chopine" (clog or patten).

4
That was the way to make his godhead wax,
For he hath been five thousand years a boy.
Love's Labour's Lost. Act v, sc. 2, l. 10. [Rosaline]

5
I have begun to plant thee, and will labour
To make thee full of growing.
Macbeth. Act i, sc. 4, l. 28. [Duncan]

6 My son of York
Hath almost overta'en him in his growth.
Richard III, ii, 4, 7. [Queen Elizabeth]

You said that idle weeds are fast in growth;
The prince my brother hath outgrown me far.
Richard III. Act iii, sc. 1, l. 103. [York] The only use of "outgrown."

Of excellent growth.—*As You Like It,* i, 2, 130.
Vital growth.—*Othello,* v, 2, 14.
Come to growth.—*The Rape of Lucrece,* l. 1062.

7
Give full growth to that which still doth grow.
Sonnets. No. cxv.

Growth of riper days.—*Sonnets,* cii.

8
Things growing to themselves are growth's abuse.
Venus and Adonis, l. 166.

9
A man, they say, that from very nothing, and beyond the imagination of his neighbours, is grown into an unspeakable estate.
The Winter's Tale. Act iv, sc. 2, l. 44. [Polixenes]

Leave the growth untried.—*The Winter's Tale,* iv, 1, 6.

GRUDGE

10
Your private grudge . . . will out,
Though ne'er so cunningly you smother it.
I Henry VI. Act iv, sc. 1, l. 109. [Somerset]

11
There is some grudge between 'em.
Julius Cæsar. Act iv, sc. 3, l. 125. [Poet]

Grudge my pleasures.—*King Lear,* ii, 4, 177.

12
They have grudged us contribution.
Julius Cæsar. Act iv, sc. 3, l. 206. [Brutus] The only use of "grudged."

13
If I can catch him once upon the hip,
I will feed fat the ancient grudge I bear him.
The Merchant of Venice. Act i, sc. 3, l. 47. [Shylock] The phrase "on the hip" is used three times in the plays, once again in *The Merchant of Venice,* iv, 1, 334, and in *Othello,* ii, 1, 314.

Ancient grudge.—*Romeo and Juliet,* Prol., 3.

14
If ever any grudge was lodged between us.
Richard III. Act ii, sc. 1, l. 65. [Gloucester]

15
Without or grudge or grumblings.
The Tempest. Act i, sc. 2, l. 249. [Ariel]

Without grudging.—*Much Ado about Nothing,* iii, 4, 90.
Grudging hate.—*Richard III,* ii, 1, 9.
Grudging stomachs.—*I Henry VI,* iv, 1, 141. The only uses of "grudging."

16
Here grow no damned grudges.
Titus Andronicus, i, 1, 154. See under GRAVE.

Full well I wot the ground of all this grudge.
Titus Andronicus. Act ii, sc. 1, l. 48. [Aaron]

I here . . . Cancel all grudge.—*The Two Gentlemen of Verona,* v, 4, 143.

GRUMBLING, see Complaint

GUARD

17 She . . . keeps her guard
In honestest defence.
All's Well that Ends Well, iii, 5, 76. See under SEDUCTION.

18
Have you had quiet guard?
Hamlet. Act i, sc. 1, l. 10. [Bernardo]

Appointed guard.—*King Lear,* v, 3, 47.
Defensive guard.—*I Henry VI,* ii, 1, 49.

Fearful guard.—*The Merchant of Venice,* i, 3, 176.
Good guard.—*King Lear,* v, 3, 1; *Othello,* i, 1, 180; *Antony and Cleopatra,* iv, 1, 10.
Heavenly guards!—*Hamlet,* iii, 4, 104.
Sickly guard.—*Henry V,* iii, 6, 164.
Simple guard.—*III Henry VI,* iv, 2, 16.
Weak guard.—*III Henry VI,* iv, 5, 7.

1 Hence, thou sickly quoif!
Thou art a guard too wanton for the head
Which princes, flesh'd with conquest, aim to hit.
II Henry IV. Act i, sc. 1, l. 147. [Northumberland] "Quoif" is used a second time in *Winter's Tale,* iv, 4, 226: "Golden quoifs."

I will be your guard.—*I Henry VI,* i, 2, 127.

2 A guard of chosen shot I had
That walk'd about me every minute while.
I Henry VI. Act i, sc. 4, l. 53. [Talbot]

My angry guardant stood alone,
Tendering my ruin and assail'd of none.
I Henry VI. Act iv, sc. 7, l. 9. [Talbot] "Guardant" is used once again in *Coriolanus,* v, 2, 67.

3
They will guard you, whether you will or no.
II Henry VI. Act iii, sc. 2, l. 265. [Salisbury]

Guard thee well.—*Troilus and Cressida,* iv, 5, 253.
Guard him sure.—*II Henry IV,* iv, 3, 81; *II Henry VI,* iii, 1, 188.
Guard with halberds!—*The Comedy of Errors,* v, 1, 185.

4
At unawares may beat down Edward's guard.
III Henry VI. Act iv, sc. 2, l. 23. [Warwick]

5
He may enguard his dotage with their powers.
King Lear. Act i, sc. 4, l. 349. [Goneril] The only use of "enguard."

6
Made you my guardians, my depositaries.
King Lear. Act ii, sc. 4, l. 254. [King Lear] The only use of "depositaries."

Guardian of their bones.—*Macbeth,* ii, 4, 35.
Guardian to this boy.—*King John,* ii, 1, 115.
Her uncle and her guardian.—*Much Ado about Nothing,* ii, 3, 174.
Sweet guardian!—*Troilus and Cressida,* v, 2, 7.
Guardian!—*Troilus and Cressida,* v, 2, 47. The only uses of "guardian."
Run from her guardage.—*Othello,* i, 2, 70. The only use of "guardage." See under MAID.

7
Guarded with fragments, and the guards are but slightly basted on neither.
Much Ado about Nothing. Act i, sc. 1, l. 289. [Benedick] See under DISCOURSE. The only use of "basted." "Bastes" occurs in *Troilus and Cressida,* ii, 3, 195.

Guarded with grandsires.—*Henry V,* iii, Prol., 20.
Guarded with rags.—*II Henry IV,* iv, 1, 34.
Guarded with a sting.—*The Rape of Lucrece,* l. 493.
Guarded with yellow.—*Henry VIII,* Prol., 16.
Strongly guarded.—*King John,* iii, 3, 2.
So slackly guarded.—*Cymbeline,* i, 1, 64. "Slackly" is repeated in *A Lover's Complaint,* l. 35.
Weakly guarded.—*I Henry VI,* ii, 1, 74.

8 With no worse nor better guard
But with a knave of common hire, a gondolier.
Othello. Act i, sc. 1, l. 125. [Roderigo] The only mention of gondolier.

9
'Tis best we stand upon our guard.
The Tempest. Act ii, sc. 1, l. 321. [Gonzalo]

Stands at a guard.—*Measure for Measure,* i, 3, 51.

10
Look you now, he's out of his guard already.
Twelfth Night. Act i, sc. 5, l. 92. [Malvolio]

Betake you to your guard.
Twelfth Night, iii, 4, 253. See under DUELLING.

11
Your ladyship were best to have some guard about you.
Twelfth Night. Act iii, sc. 4, l. 12. [Maria]

GUESS

See also Surmise

12
Square our guess by shows.
All's Well that Ends Well. Act ii, sc. 1, l. 153. [Helena]

13
Corin: I partly guess. . . .
Silvius: No, Corin, being old, thou canst not guess.
As You Like It. Act ii, sc. 4, l. 24.

14
My good lord, I guess their tenour.
I Henry IV. Act iv, sc. 4, l. 7. [Michael]

Guess thy message.—*Henry VIII,* v, 1, 162.
Guess the sequel.—*The Two Gentlemen of Verona,* ii, 1, 122.
Guess at her years, I prithee.—*Antony and Cleopatra,* iii, 3, 29.

15
King Richard might create a perfect guess.
II Henry IV. Act iii, sc. 1, l. 88. [Warwick]

Ready guess.—*Henry V,* i, 1, 96.

16
I am ignorant and cannot guess.
I Henry VI, ii, 5, 60. See under IGNORANCE.

I cannot guess.—*Richard III,* iv, 4, 475.
I guess not.—*Measure for Measure,* iv, 4, 8.

17
Well guessed, believe me.
III Henry VI. Act iv, sc. 5, l. 22. [Gloucester]

As often as I guess'd.—*All's Well that Ends Well,* iii, 1, 16.
Guess'd that it was she.—*Two Gentlemen of Verona,* v, 2, 39. The only uses of "guess'd."

18
Guess thou the rest.
III Henry VI. Act iv, sc. 4, l. 28. [Queen Elizabeth]

By thy guess.—*III Henry VI,* v, 1, 8.
As I guess.—*III Henry VI,* v, 5, 84; *Richard III,* iv, 1, 8; *Love's Labour's Lost,* v, 2, 121;

Richard II, ii, 3, 68; *As You Like It,* iv, 3, 8; *Coriolanus,* i, 6, 52.

1
Second Gentleman: Pray, speak what has happen'd.
First Gentleman: You may guess quickly what.
Henry VIII. Act ii, sc. 1, l. 7.

2
Here is the guess of their true strength and forces.
King Lear. Act v, sc. 1, l. 52. [Edmund]
Guessingly set down.—*King Lear,* iii, 7, 47. The only use of "guessingly."

3
We may guess by this what you are.
Much Ado about Nothing, i, 1, 111. See under CHARACTER.
Hum! I guess at it.
Macbeth. Act iv, sc. 3, l. 203. [Macduff]
By the near guess of my memory.
The Merchant of Venice. Act i, sc. 3, l. 55. [Shylock]

4
I perchance am vicious in my guess.
Othello. Act iii, sc. 3, l. 145. [Iago]
Throw your vile guesses in the devil's teeth,
From whence you have them.
Othello. Act iii, sc. 4, l. 184. [Cassio]
Giving themselves to guess.
The Rape of Lucrece, l. 1238.

5
You cannot guess who caused your father's death.
Richard III. Act ii, sc. 2, l. 19. [Duchess]
Canst thou guess?—*Richard III,* iii, 2, 45.

6
Stanley: I know not . . . but by guess.
King Richard: Well, sir, as you guess, as you guess?
Richard III. Act iv, sc. 4, l. 466.
As you guess.—*Henry VIII,* i, 1, 47; *Othello,* i, 3, 36.

7
He thereby may give a likely guess.
Titus Andronicus. Act ii, sc. 3, l. 207. [Aaron]
Marcus: Canst thou not guess wherefore she plies thee thus?
Young Lucius: My lord, I know not, I, nor can I guess.
Titus Andronicus. Act iv, sc. 1, l. 15.

GUEST

See also Hospitality

8
Agrippa: Good Enobarbus, make yourself my guest
Whilst you abide here.
Enobarbus: Humbly, sir, I thank you.
Antony and Cleopatra. Act ii, sc. 2, l. 249.
I Appear not like a guest.—*Coriolanus,* iv, 5, 6.
Prithee, tell my master what a strange guest he has here.
Coriolanus. Act iv, sc. 5, l. 38. [Servant]

9
Look to the guests within.
I Henry IV. Act ii, sc. 4, l. 91. [Vintner]
Cherish thy guests.—*I Henry IV,* iii, 3, 194.
Take heed what guests you receive.
II Henry IV. Act ii, sc. 4, l. 101. [Hostess]

10
To-night in Harfleur will we be your guest;
To-morrow for the march are we addrest.
Henry V. Act iii, sc. 3, l. 57. [King Henry]

11
And I have heard it said, unbidden guests
Are often welcomest when they are gone.
I Henry VI. Act ii, sc. 2, l. 55. [Bedford] The only use of "unbidden."

12
Come, gentlemen, ye shall go my way, which
Is to the court, and there ye shall be my guests:
Something I can command.
Henry VIII. Act iv, sc. 1, l. 115. [Gentleman]
You are my guests: do me no foul play, friends.
King Lear. Act iii, sc. 7, l. 31. [Gloucester]
You are . . . my guests.—*Pericles,* ii, 3, 8.

13
A world of torments though I should endure,
I would not yield to be your house's guest.
Love's Labour's Lost. Act v, sc. 2, l. 353. [Princess of France]

14
Fair and noble hostess,
We are your guest to-night.
Macbeth. Act i, sc. 6, l. 24. [Duncan]
Macbeth: Here's our chief guest.
Lady Macbeth: If he had been forgotten,
It had been as a gap in our great feast,
And all-thing unbecoming.
Macbeth. Act iii, sc. 1, l. 11. The only use of "all-thing" and "unbecoming."

15
Hast thou no suit against my knight, my guest-cavaleire?
The Merry Wives of Windsor. Act ii, sc. 1, l. 220. [Hostess] The only use of the phrase.
I shall procure-a you de good guest, de earl, de knight, de lords, de gentlemen, my patients.
The Merry Wives of Windsor. Act ii, sc. 3, l. 96. [Caius]
I have turned away my other guests; they must come off: I'll sauce them.
The Merry Wives of Windsor. Act iv, sc. 3, l. 12. [Host]

16
Report what a sojourner we have.
Pericles. Act iv, sc. 2, l. 149. [Bawd] The only use of "sojourner."

17
So many guests invite as here are writ.
Romeo and Juliet. Act iv, sc. 2, l. 1. [Capulet]
I have invited many a guest.—*Romeo and Juliet,* i, 2, 21.
Bid the guests.—*The Taming of the Shrew,* ii, 1, 318.
The guests are come.—*Romeo and Juliet,* i, 3, 100.
Your guests are coming.—*The Winter's Tale,* iv, 4, 48.
Your guests approach.—*Winter's Tale,* iv, 4, 52.

18
A forward guest Within your house.
The Taming of the Shrew. Act ii, sc. 1, l. 51. [Petruchio]
Alehouse guest.—*Richard II,* v, 1, 15.

Fair guests.—*Henry VIII,* i, 4, 35.
Keen guest.—*I Henry IV,* iv, 2, 86.
Kingly guest.—*The Winter's Tale,* iii, 2, 167.
Master guest.—*The Merry Wives of Windsor,* ii, 3, 77.
Merry guests.—*The Rape of Lucrece,* l. 1125.
Parting guest.—*Troilus and Cressida,* iii, 3, 166.
Princely guest.—*The Rape of Lucrece,* l. 90.
Sad distemper'd guest.—*Sonnets,* cliii.
Shipwreck'd guests.—*The Comedy of Errors,* i, 1, 115.
Sour unwelcome guest.—*Venus and Adonis,* l. 449.
Sparing guest.—*Comedy of Errors,* iii, 1, 27.
Welcome guest.—*Timon of Athens,* iii, 6, 113.
Young guest.—*The Two Gentlemen of Verona,* iv, 2, 26.
Guest of summer.—*Macbeth,* i, 6, 3.
Heart's guest.—*Sonnets,* xlvii.

1
You are my guest, Lavinia, and your friends.
Titus Andronicus. Act i, sc. 1, l. 490. [Saturninus]

2
Hermione: How say you?
My prisoner? or my guest? by your dread 'Verily,'
One of them you shall be.
Polixenes: Your guest, then, madam.
The Winter's Tale. Act i, sc. 2, l. 54.

GUILT

3
He 's guilty, and he is not guilty.
All's Well that Ends Well. Act v, sc. 3, l. 290. [Diana]
Guilty to self-wrong.—*The Comedy of Errors,* iii, 2, 168.
Guilty in defence.—*Henry V,* iii, 3, 43.
Guilty of high treason.—*Henry VIII,* ii, 1, 27.
Guilty of detested crimes.—*Love's Labour 's Lost,* iv, 1, 31.

4
The heaviness of guilt within my bosom
Takes off my manhood.
Cymbeline. Act v, sc. 2, l. 1. [Iachimo]

5
It started like a guilty thing
Upon a fearful summons.
Hamlet. Act i, sc. 1, l. 148. [Horatio]
If his occulted guilt
Do not itself unkennel in one speech,
It is a damned ghost that we have seen.
Hamlet. Act iii, sc. 2, l. 85. [Hamlet] The only use of "occulted." "Unkennel" occurs again in *The Merry Wives of Windsor,* iii, 3, 174.
My stronger guilt defeats my strong intent.
Hamlet. Act iii, sc. 3, l. 40. [King]
So full of artless jealousy is guilt,
It spills itself in fearing to be spilt.
Hamlet. Act iv, sc. 5, l. 19. [Queen] The only use of "artless."

6
England shall double gild his treble guilt.
II Henry IV. Act iv, sc. 5, l. 129. [King Henry]
The gilt of France,—O guilt indeed!
Henry V. Act ii, Prologue, l. 26. [Chorus]
I 'll gild the faces of the grooms withal;
For it must seem their guilt.
Macbeth. Act ii, sc. 2, l. 57. [Lady Macbeth]

7
In sight of God and us, your guilt is great.
II Henry VI. Act ii, sc. 3, l. 2. [King Henry]
Thy guilt is great.—*The Rape of Lucrece,* l. 876.

8
Who can accuse me? wherein am I guilty?
II Henry VI. Act iii, sc. 1, l. 103. [Gloucester]
His guilt should be but idly posted over,
Because his purpose is not executed.
II Henry VI. Act iii, sc. 1, l. 255. [Suffolk]

9
Approved in practice culpable.
II Henry VI. Act iii, sc. 2, l. 22. [King Henry] The only use of "culpable."

10
The guilt of murder bucklers thee.
II Henry VI. Act iii, sc. 2, l. 216. [Warwick]
Guilt of . . . murder.—*Henry V,* iv, 1, 170.
Murderous guilt.—*Twelfth Night,* iii, 1, 159.
Guilty thou art of murder and of theft,
Guilty of perjury and subornation,
Guilty of treason, forgery, and shift,
Guilty of incest, that abomination.
The Rape of Lucrece, l. 918.

11
Second Gentleman: Is he found guilty?
First Gentleman: Yes, truly is he, and condemn'd upon 't
Henry VIII. Act ii, sc. 1, l. 9.
He pleaded still not guilty and alleged
Many sharp reasons to defeat the law.
Henry VIII. Act ii, sc. 1, l. 13. [Gentleman]

12
They vanish tongue-tied in their guiltiness.
Julius Cæsar. Act i, sc. 1, l. 67. [Flavius] "Tongue-tied" is used eight times.
Guiltiness will speak,
Though tongues were out of use.
Othello. Act v, sc. 1, l. 109. [Iago]
Die in terror of thy guiltiness!
Richard III. Act v, sc. 3, l. 170. [Ghost of Buckingham]
Guiltiness I know not.—*Othello,* v, 2, 39.
Full of dear guiltiness.—*Love's Labour 's Lost,* v, 2, 801.
Natural guiltiness.—*The Merry Wives of Windsor,* ii, 2, 139.
Guiltiness of my mind.—*The Merry Wives of Windsor,* v, 5, 130.

13
If I in act, consent, or sin of thought,
Be guilty of the stealing that sweet breath
Which was embounded in this beauteous clay,
Let hell want pains enough to torture me.
King John. Act iv, sc. 3, l. 135. [Hubert] The only use of "embounded."

14
Close pent-up guilts,
Rive your concealing continents, and cry
These dreadful summoners grace.
King Lear. Act iii, sc. 2, l. 57. [King Lear] The only use of "summoners." "Pent-up" occurs again in *III Henry VI,* i, 3, 12.

15
Guilty, my lord, guilty! I confess, I confess.
Love's Labour 's Lost. Act iv, sc. 3, l. 205. [Biron]

I confess me much guilty.
As You Like It. Act i, sc. 2, l. 196. [Orlando]

1
His spongy officers, who shall bear the guilt
Of our great quell.
Macbeth. Act i, sc. 7, l. 71. [Lady Macbeth] "Spongy" is used four times. The only use of "quell" as a noun.

2
I should be guiltier than my guiltiness.
Measure for Measure. Act v, sc. 1, l. 372. [Angelo]

Guiltier than him they try.—*Measure for Measure,* ii, 1, 21. The only uses of "guiltier."

3
I cannot think it,
That he would steal away so guilty-like,
Seeing you coming.
Othello. Act iii, sc. 3, l. 38. [Iago] The only use of "guilty-like."

4
The guilt being great, the fear doth still exceed.
The Rape of Lucrece, l. 229.

This guilt would seem death-worthy in thy brother.
The Rape of Lucrece, l. 635. The only use of "death-worthy."

5
The burthen of a guilty mind.
The Rape of Lucrece, l. 735.

The clogging burthen of a guilty soul.
Richard II. Act i, sc. 3, l. 200. [Bolingbroke] The only use of "clogging."

6
Not that devour'd, but that which doth devour,
Is worthy blame.
The Rape of Lucrece, l. 1256. See under BLAME.

But they whose guilt within their bosoms lie
Imagine every eye beholds their blame.
The Rape of Lucrece, l. 1342.

Let guiltless souls be freed from guilty woe.
The Rape of Lucrece, l. 1482.

7
My guilt be on my head, and there an end.
Richard II. Act v, sc. 1, l. 69. [Northumberland]

Laid their guilt upon my guiltless shoulders.
Richard III. Act i, sc. 2, l. 98. [Gloucester] For "guiltless" see INNOCENCE.

Apparent guilt.—*Richard II,* iv, 1, 124.
Bewailed guilt.—*Sonnets,* xxxvi.
Open guilt.—*Richard III,* iii, 5, 30.
Guilt of conscience.—*Richard II,* v, 6, 41.

8
Bloody and guilty, guiltily awake,
And in a bloody battle end thy days!
Richard III. Act v, sc. 3, l. 146. [Ghost of Hastings] The only use of "guiltily."

9
Their great guilt,
Like poison given to work a great time after,
Now 'gins to bite the spirits.
The Tempest. Act iii, sc. 3, l. 104. [Gonzalo]

10
Let them not speak a word; the guilt is plain.
Titus Andronicus. Act ii, sc. 3, l. 301. [Saturninus]

The old man hath found their guilt.
Titus Andronicus. Act iv, sc. 2, l. 26. [Aaron]

Shall she live to betray this guilt of ours?
Titus Andronicus. Act iv, sc. 2, l. 149. [Aaron]

11
He is not guilty of her coming hither.
The Winter's Tale. Act ii, sc. 3, l. 144. [Lords]

It shall scarce boot me To say 'not guilty.'
The Winter's Tale. Act iii, sc. 2, l. 26. [Hermione]

I am not guilty.—*A Midsummer-Night's Dream,* iii, 2, 75.
Not guilty.—*Winter's Tale,* i, 2, 74; ii, 2, 62.

GUTS

See also Bowels, Entrails

12
I'll lug the guts into the neighbour room.
Hamlet. Act iii, sc. 4, l. 212. [Hamlet] "Lug" repeated in *Timon of Athens,* iv, 3, 31.

13
How would thy guts fall about thy knees! But, sirrah, there's no room for faith, truth nor honesty in this bosom of thine; it is all filled up with guts and midriff.
I Henry IV. Act iii, sc. 3, l. 172. [Prince of Wales] The only use of "midriff."

14
If you would walk off, I would prick your guts a little, in good terms.
Henry V. Act ii, sc. 1, l. 61. [Nym]

15
Let vultures gripe thy guts! for gourd and fullam holds.
The Merry Wives of Windsor. Act i, sc. 3, l. 94. [Pistol] The only use of "gourd" and "fullam." Both words denote a kind of false dice.

As sure as his guts are made of puddings.
The Merry Wives of Windsor. Act ii, sc. 1, l. 32. [Mrs. Page]

Clay-brained guts.—*I Henry IV,* ii, 4, 251. The only use of "clay-brained."
Cloak-bag of guts.—*I Henry IV,* ii, 4, 498. The only use of "cloak-bag."
Sheeps' guts.—*Much Ado about Nothing,* ii, 3, 61.
Guts of a beggar.—*Hamlet,* iv, 3, 33.
Guts-griping.—*Troilus and Cressida,* v, 1, 21. The only use of the phrase.

H

HABIT

See also Use

1 Some habit that too much o'er-leavens
The form of plausive manners.

Hamlet. Act i, sc. 4, l. 30. [Hamlet] The only use of "o'er-leavens." "Plausive" is repeated twice in *All's Well that Ends Well,* i, 2, 53; iv, 1, 29.

2
If thou didst put this sour-cold habit on
To castigate thy pride, 'twere well: but thou
Dost it enforcedly; thou'ldst courtier be again,
Wert thou not beggar.

Timon of Athens. Act iv, sc. 3, l. 239. [Apemantus] The only use of "sour-cold," "castigate," and "enforcedly."

Bad habit.—*The Merchant of Venice,* i, 2, 63.
Monstrous habits.—*Henry VIII,* i, 2, 122.
Outward habit.—*Hamlet,* v, 2, 198. For "habit" in the sense of garment, see under DRESS.
Shallow habit.—*The Rape of Lucrece,* l. 1814.

HAG, see under Woman

HAIR

3
My very hairs do mutiny; for the white
Reprove the brown for rashness, and they them
For fear and doting.

Antony and Cleopatra. Act iii, sc. 11, l. 13. [Antony]

4
I 'll cavil on the ninth part of a hair.

I Henry IV. Act iii, sc. 1, l. 140. [Hotspur]

The tithe of a hair was never lost in my house before.

I Henry IV. Act iii, sc. 3, l. 66. [Hostess]

'Tis not a hair amiss.—*II Henry IV,* i, 2, 27.
Swerve a hair.—*Troilus and Cressida,* iii, 2, 191.

5
My mistress wears her own hair.

Henry V. Act iii, sc. 7, l. 64. [Dauphin]

6
Comb down his hair; look, look! it stands upright,
Like lime-twigs set to catch my winged soul.

II Henry VI. Act iii, sc. 3, l. 15. [Beaufort] The only use of "lime-twigs."

My hair doth stand on end.
Richard III. Act i, sc. 3, l. 304. [Hastings]
Mine hair be fix'd on end, as one distract.
II Henry VI, iii, 2, 318. See under CURSE.
And each particular hair to stand on end,
Like quills upon the fretful porpentine.
Hamlet, i, 5, 19. See under TALE.
Your bedded hair, like life in excrements,
Start up, and stand an end.
Hamlet. Act iii, sc. 4, l. 121. [Queen]
With hair up-staring,—then like reeds, not hair.
The Tempest. Act i, sc. 2, l. 213. [Ariel] The only use of "up-staring."
His hair uprear'd.—*II Henry VI,* iii, 2, 171.
Makest . . . my hair to stare.—*Julius Cæsar,* iv, 3, 280.
Bristled hair.—*A Midsummer-Night's Dream,* ii, 2, 31. "Bristled" is repeated in *Coriolanus,* ii, 2, 96: "Bristled lips."

7
Yea, beg a hair of him for memory,
And, dying, mention it within their wills,
Bequeathing it as a rich legacy
Unto their issue.

Julius Cæsar. Act iii, sc. 2, l. 139. [Antony]

8
Bind up those tresses. O, what love I note
In the fair multitude of those her hairs!
Where now by chance a silver drop hath fallen,
Even to that drop ten thousand wiry friends
Do glue themselves in sociable grief,
Like true, inseparable, faithful loves,
Sticking together in calamity.

King John. Act iii, sc. 4, l. 61. [King Philip] "Tresses" is used only once more in the plays, in *I Henry VI,* i, 1, 3; "wiry" is repeated in *Sonnets* cxxviii; and "glue" in *III Henry VI,* v, 2, 38. See under TEAR.

King Philip: Bind up your hairs.
Constance: Yes, that I will; and wherefore will I do it?
I tore them from their bonds and cried aloud
'O that these hands could so redeem my son,
As they have given these hairs their liberty!'
King John. Act iii, sc. 4, l. 68.
This hair I tear is mine.—*King John,* iii, 4, 45.

9
Elf all my hair in knots.

King Lear, ii, 3, 10. [Edgar] The only use of "elf" as a verb. As a noun it is repeated in *A Midsummer-Night's Dream,* v, 1, 400.

Bakes the elf-locks in foul sluttish hairs.
Romeo and Juliet, i, 4, 90. The only use of "elf-locks." See under FAIRY.

10
These hairs, which thou dost ravish from my chin,
Will quicken, and accuse thee.

King Lear. Act iii, sc. 7, l. 38. [Gloucester]

11
Her hair, nor loose nor tied in formal plat,
Proclaim'd in her a careless hand of pride
For some, untuck'd, descended her sheaved hat,
Hanging her pale and pined cheek beside,
Some in her threaden fillet still did bide,
And true to bondage would not break from thence,
Though slackly braided in loose negligence.

A Lover's Complaint, l. 29. The only use of "untuck'd," "sheaved." "Plats," as a verb, is repeated in *Romeo and Juliet,* i, 4, 89: "Plats the manes of horses." "Slackly" is used a second time in *Cymbeline,* i, 1, 64: "Slackly guarded"; and "braided" in *Venus and Adonis,* l. 271: "Braided mane."

1
Thou canst not say I did it: never shake
Thy gory locks at me.
Macbeth. Act iii, sc. 4, l. 50. [Macbeth]

2 If the scale do turn
But in the estimation of a hair.
The Merchant of Venice. Act iv, sc. 1, l. 330. [Portia]

The weight of a hair will turn the scales.
II Henry IV. Act ii, sc. 4, l. 279. [Falstaff]

3
Fetch you a hair off the great Cham's beard.
Much Ado about Nothing, ii, 1, 277. See SERVICE, 1340:21. The only reference to the great Cham.

4
Let him have time to tear his curled hair.
The Rape of Lucrece, l. 981.

Curled my hair.—*King Lear*, iii, 4, 88.
Tears her hair.—*Much Ado about Nothing*, ii, 3, 153.
Tear thy hair.—*Romeo and Juliet*, iii, 3, 68.
Dishevell'd hair.—*Rape of Lucrece*, l. 1129.
Wandering hair.—*King John*, iv, 1, 93.

5
If hairs be wires, black wires grow on her head.
Sonnets. No. cxxx.

6
Unscissar'd shall this hair of mine remain.
Pericles. Act iii, sc. 3, l. 29. [Pericles] The only use of "unscissar'd."

7
No, not so much perdition as an hair
Betid to any creature.
The Tempest. Act i, sc. 2, l. 30. [Prospero]

Not a hair perish'd.—*The Tempest*, i, 2, 217.

8
My fleece of woolly hair that now uncurls.
Titus Andronicus. Act ii, sc. 3, l. 34. [Aaron] "Woolly" is used a second time in *The Merchant of Venice*: "Woolly breeders."

Unfix my hair.—*Macbeth*, i, 3, 135.
O'ergrown with hair.—*As You Like It*, iv, 3, 107; *Henry V*, v, 2, 43.

9
You go against the hair.
The Merry Wives of Windsor. Act ii, sc. 3, l. 41. [Shallow]

Against the hair.—*Troilus and Cressida*, i, 2, 28; *Romeo and Juliet*, ii, 4, 100.

10
Sir Toby: Then hadst thou had an excellent head of hair.
Sir Andrew: Why, would that have mended my hair?
Sir Toby: Past question; for thou seest it will not curl by nature.
Sir Andrew: But it becomes me well enough, does 't not?
Sir Toby: Excellent; it hangs like flax on a distaff; and I hope to see a housewife take thee between her legs and spin it off.
Twelfth Night. Act i, sc. 3, l. 100. The only use of the phrase "head of hair."

11
Lucetta: Why, then, your ladyship must cut your hair.
Julia: No, girl; I'll knit it up in silken strings
With twenty odd-conceited true-love knots.
The Two Gentlemen of Verona. Act ii, sc. 7, l. 44. The only use of "odd-conceited."

Cut his hairs.—*Pericles*, iv, 4, 28.

12
I 'll make a shadow for thee of my hairs.
Venus and Adonis, l. 191.

II—Hair: Its Colour

13 Let him not leave out
The colour of her hair.
Antony and Cleopatra. Act ii, sc. 5, l. 113. [Cleopatra]

Black silk hair.—*As You Like It*, iii, 5, 46.
Coal-black hair.—*III Henry VI*, v, 1, 54. "Coal-black" is used five times.

14
Cleopatra: Her hair, what colour?
Messenger: Brown, madam.
Antony and Cleopatra. Act iii, sc. 3, l. 35.

Rosalind: His very hair is of the dissembling colour.
Celia: Something browner than Judas's. . . .
Rosalind: I' faith, his hair is of a good colour.
Celia: An excellent colour: your chestnut was ever the only colour.
As You Like It. Act iii, sc. 4, l. 7.

His browny locks did hang in crooked curls.
A Lover's Complaint, l. 85. The only use of "browny."

15
Spread o'er the silver waves thy golden hairs.
The Comedy of Errors. Act iii, sc. 2, l. 48. [Antipholus of Syracuse]

Golden hairs.—*Venus and Adonis*, l. 51.
Her hairs were gold.—*Love's Labour's Lost*, iv, 3, 142.

Thy hair,
Thou other gold-bound brow, is like the first.
Macbeth. Act iv, sc. 1, l. 113. [Macbeth] The only use of "gold-bound."

Her hair, like golden threads, play'd with her breath.
The Rape of Lucrece, l. 400.

Her sunny locks
Hang on her temples like a golden fleece; . . .
And many Jasons come in quest of her.
The Merchant of Venice. Act i, sc. 1, l. 169. [Bassanio]

So are those crisped snaky golden locks
Which make such wanton gambols with the wind,
Upon supposed fairness, often known
To be the dowry of a second head,
The skull that bred them in the sepulchre.
The Merchant of Venice. Act iii, sc. 2, l. 92. [Bassanio] The only use of "crisped" and "snaky." "Locks" in this sense is used seven times.

Here in her hairs
The painter plays the spider and hath woven
A golden mesh to entrap the hearts of men
Faster than gnats in cobwebs.
The Merchant of Venice. Act iii, sc. 2, l. 121. [Bassanio]

The golden tresses of the dead,
The right of sepulchres, were shorn away,
To live a second life on second head.
Sonnets. No. lxviii.

Bright hair.—*Richard III,* i, 4, 53; *Troilus and Cressida,* iv, 2, 113.

1
All flaxen was his poll.
Hamlet. Act iv, sc. 5, l. 196. [Ophelia] The only use of "flaxen." For "poll" see HEAD.

Her amber hair for foul hath amber quoted.
Love's Labour's Lost. Act iv, sc. 3, l. 87. [Dumain] "Amber" occurs only twice more, in *The Taming of the Shrew,* iv, 3, 58, and *Hamlet,* ii, 2, 201.

2
Grey locks, the pursuivants of death,
Nestor-like aged in an age of care.
I Henry VI. Act ii, sc. 5 l. 6. [Mortimer] The only use of "Nestor-like."

With grey hairs and bruise of many days.
Much Ado about Nothing. Act v, sc. 1, l. 65. [Leonato]

Grey locks.—*I Henry VI,* ii, 5, 5.

3
Rend off thy silver hair.
Titus Andronicus. Act iii, sc. 1, l. 261. [Marcus]

His silver hairs
Will purchase us a good opinion
And buy men's voices to commend our deeds.
Julius Cæsar. Act ii, sc. 1, l. 144. [Metellus]

Sable curls all silver'd o'er with white.
Sonnets. No. xii.

Silver hair.—*II Henry VI,* v, 1, 162.

Hatch'd in silver.—*Troilus and Cressida,* i, 3, 65. See also AGE: ITS SILVER LIVERY.

4
Bring white hairs unto a quiet grave.
III Henry VI. Act ii, sc. 5, l. 40. [King Henry] "White hairs," or "white hair" is repeated eleven times in the plays.

Tears his white hair,
Which the impetuous blasts, with eyeless rage,
Catch in their fury, and make nothing of.
King Lear. Act iii, sc. 1, l. 7. [Gentleman]

5
Her hair is auburn, mine is perfect yellow.
The Two Gentlemen of Verona. Act iv, sc. 4, l. 194. [Julia]

III—Hairlessness

6
And high top bald with dry antiquity.
As You Like It, iv, 3, 106. See under OAK.

Grow bald.—*Henry V,* v, 2, 169.

Stand bald before him.—*Coriolanus,* iv, 5, 206.

Bald crown.—*I Henry IV,* ii, 4, 420; *King Lear,* i, 4, 178.

Bald pate.—*The Comedy of Errors,* ii, 2, 71.

Goodman baldpate.—*Measure for Measure,* v, 1, 329. The only use of "baldpate."

Bald-pated rascal.—*Measure for Measure,* v, 1, 357. The only use of "bald-pated."

Whoreson smooth-pates.—*II Henry IV,* i, 2, 43. The only use of "smooth-pates." See SURETY, 1471:13.

7
Dromio: of Syracuse: There 's no time for a man to recover his hair that grows bald by nature.
Antipholus of Syracuse: May he not do it by fine and recovery?
Dromio of Syracuse: Yes, to pay a fine for a periwig and recover the lost hair of another man.
The Comedy of Errors. Act ii, sc. 2, l. 76. "Periwig" is repeated in *The Two Gentlemen of Verona,* iv, 4, 196.

Antipholus of Syracuse: You would all this time have proved there is no time for all things.
Dromio of Syracuse: Marry, and did, sir; namely, no time to recover hair lost by nature.
Antipholus of Syracuse: But your reason was not substantial, why there is no time to recover.
Dromio of Syracuse: Thus I mend it: Time himself is bald and therefore to the world's end will have bald followers.
Antipholus of Syracuse: I knew 'twould be a bald conclusion.
The Comedy of Errors. Act ii, sc. 2, l. 101.

You are like to lose your hair and prove a bald jerkin.
Tempest. Act iv, sc. 1, l. 238. [Stephano]

Lose a hair.—*Merchant of Venice,* iii, 2, 304.

Lost many a hair.—*I Henry IV,* iii, 3, 69.

8
Antipholus of Syracuse: Why is Time such a niggard of hair, being, as it is, so plentiful an excrement?
Dromio of Syracuse: Because it is a blessing that he bestows on beasts; and what he hath scanted men in hair he hath given them in wit.
Antipholus of Syracuse: Why, but there 's many a man hath more hair than wit.
Dromio of Syracuse: Not a man of those but he hath the wit to lose his hair.
Antipholus of Syracuse: Why, thou didst conclude hairy men plain dealers without wit.
Dromio of Syracuse: The plainer dealer, the sooner lost; yet he loseth it in a kind of jollity.
The Comedy of Errors. Act ii, sc. 2, l. 78. The only use of "dealer" and "dealers."

Speed: She hath more hair than wit—
Launce: More hair than wit? It may be: I 'll prove it. . . . The hair that covers the wit is more than the wit for the greater hides the less.
The Two Gentlemen of Verona, iii, 1, 366.

9
Thatch your poor thin roofs
With burthens of the dead;—some that were hanged,
No matter:—wear them.
Timon of Athens. Act iv, sc. 3, l. 144. [Timon]

10
He has not past three or four hairs on his chin.
Troilus and Cressida, i, 2, 122. See under BEARD.

Have no hair.—*A Midsummer-Night's Dream,* i, 2, 100.

Not a hair.—*Coriolanus,* iv, 6, 133.

Hairless face.—*Venus and Adonis,* l. 487.

Thin and hairless scalps.—*Richard II,* iii, 2, 112. The only uses of "hairless."

Bare scalp.—*The Two Gentlemen of Verona,* iv, 1, 36.

HAND

See also Fist; Heart and Hand; Palm

I—Familiar Phrases

1
By the hand of a soldier, I will undertake it.
All's Well that Ends Well. Act iii, sc. 6, l. 76. [Parolles] "By this hand" is used frequently throughout the plays.

2
Had a hand in it.
Much Ado about Nothing, v, 1, 277.

3
Hand and seal.
King John, iv, 2, 215; *Measure for Measure,* iv, 2, 207; *Henry VIII,* ii, 4, 222.

Hand in hand.—*Richard III,* v, 3, 313, and eleven times in later plays.

Hand to hand.
III Henry VI, ii, 1, 73; ii, 5, 56; *I Henry IV,* i, 3, 99.

Have in hand.—*II Henry VI,* i, 3, 162, and frequently thereafter.

4
Hand of death.—*Love's Labour Lost,* v, 2, 825; *Richard II,* iii, 1, 30; *I Henry IV,* v, 4, 84; *Antony and Cleopatra,* iv, 9, 30.

Hand of fortune.—*Hamlet,* ii, 2, 246.

Hand of God.—*Richard II,* iii, 3, 77; *Henry V,* ii, 2, 190; *Macbeth,* ii, 3, 136.

Hand of heaven.—*King John,* v, 2, 66; *Merchant of Venice,* i, 3, 94; *All's Well that Ends Well,* ii, 3, 37.

Hand of justice.—*II Henry IV,* v, 2, 112.

Hand of man.—*The Winter's Tale,* v, 3, 17.

Hand of peace.—*II Henry IV,* iv, 1, 43.

Hand of time.—*King John,* ii, 1, 102.

5
I 'll be at hand.
Titus Andronicus, iv, 3, 113.

Here at hand.—*II Henry VI,* iii, 2, 10, and frequently in later plays.

6
Nay, by your leave, hold your hands.
All's Well that Ends Well. Act iv, sc. 3, l. 215.

Hold your slaughtering hands and keep the peace.
I Henry VI. Act iii, sc. 1, l. 87. [King Henry]

Hold thy desperate hand.—*Romeo and Juliet,* iii, 3, 108.

Hold your hand.—*King Lear,* iii, 7, 72.

Hold off thy hand.—*Hamlet,* v, 1, 286.

Hold off your hands.—*Hamlet,* i, 4, 80.

Hold his hands.—*Comedy of Errors,* iv, 4, 24.

Hold you his hands.—*III Henry VI,* i, 4, 95.

Hands off.—*Coriolanus,* iii, 1, 178.

Stay, stay thy hands!—*I Henry VI,* i, 2, 104.

7
Hold up thy hand.
II Henry VI. Act iii, sc. 3, l. 28. [King]

Hold up your hands.—*Measure for Measure,* v, 1, 443.

8
I cannot rid my hands of him.
II Henry IV. Act i, sc. 2, l. 226. [Falstaff]

I leave him to your hand.—*Measure for Measure,* v, 1, 491.

In the palm of the hand.—*The Comedy of Errors,* iii, 2, 124.

9
Lay not thy hands on me; forbear, I say;
Their touch affrights me as a serpent's sting.
II Henry VI. Act iii, sc. 2, l. 46. [King Henry]

Lay no hands on me.—*Richard III,* i, 4, 196.

Why linger we? let us lay hands upon him.
III Henry VI. Act iii, sc. 1, l. 26. [Second Keeper]

Shall we not lay hands on him?
Much Ado about Nothing. Act iii, sc. 3, l. 57. [Watch]

Lay hands upon him.—*Coriolanus,* iii, 1, 222; 227; *King Lear,* iv, 6, 192; *Cymbeline,* v, 3, 91.

Lay hands on them.—*Titus Andronicus,* v, 2, 159.

Lay hands on the villain.—*The Taming of the Shrew,* v, 1, 39.

10
Lend me thy hand, I 'll help thee: come, lend me thy hand.
Winter's Tale. Act iv, sc. 3, l. 72. [Clown]

Lend thy hand.—*The Tempest,* i, 2, 23.

Lend me your hand.—*Julius Cæsar,* iii, 1, 297.

O brother, help me with thy fainting hand.
Titus Andronicus. Act ii, sc. 3, l. 233. [Martius]

11
Let go my hand.
King Lear. Act iv, sc. 6, l. 27. [Gloucester] Repeated in *Twelfth Night,* iv, 1, 40.

Let our hands part.—*Love's Labour's Lost,* v, 2, 821.

12
On either hand.
I Henry VI, iv, 2, 23. [Falstaff]

Out of hand.—*III Henry VI,* iv, 7, 63; *II Henry IV,* iii, 1, 107.

Takes in hand.—*The Rape of Lucrece,* l. 1235.

13
Unbind my hands.
The Taming of the Shrew, ii, 1, 4. [Bianca]

Untie my hands.—*The Taming of the Shrew,* ii, 1, 21.

14
The upper hand.
Richard III. Act iv, sc. 4, l. 37. [Queen]

15
With his own hand.
All's Well that Ends Well, iii, 5, 6. [Widow]

By this bottle! which I made of the bark of a tree with mine own hands.
Tempest. Act ii, sc. 2, l. 126. [Stephano]

II—Shaking Hands

16
Let me shake thy hand.
Antony and Cleopatra, ii, 6, 75. [Pompey]

Shake hands and part.—*Hamlet,* i, 5, 128.

Shook hands.—*III Henry VI,* i, 4, 102; *As You Like It,* v, 4, 107; *The Winter's Tale,* i, 1, 33.

17
Cox my passion! give me your hand.
All's Well that Ends Well, v, 2, 43. The only use of "Cox."

Give me with thy kingly hand.—*All's Well that Ends Well,* ii, 1, 196.

1
Let me have thy hand.
Antony and Cleopatra, ii, 2, 148; ii, 6, 49.
Give 's your hand.—*Antony and Cleopatra,* ii, 7, 134.
Give me thy hand.—*II Henry VI,* iii, 2, 339, and frequently thereafter.
Here is my hand.—*II Henry VI,* iii, 1, 278, and frequently thereafter.
I offer thee my hand.—*I Henry VI,* iii, 1, 126.
Raught me his hand.—*Henry V,* iv 6, 21.

2 Give me both your hands:
Now join your hands, and with your hands your hearts.
III Henry VI. Act iv, sc. 6, l. 38. [King Henry]

3
First, Marcus Brutus, will I shake with you.
Julius Cæsar. Act iii, sc. 1, l. 184. [Antony]

4
This royal hand and mine are newly knit.
King John, iii, 1, 226. See LEAGUE, 847:11.
Join hands.—*King John,* ii, 1, 532.
We 'll clasp hands.—*Pericles,* ii, 4, 57.

5
My hand, bully.
The Merry Wives of Windsor. Act ii, sc. 1, l. 225. [Host]
Your hand, Leonato.—*Much Ado about Nothing,* i, l. 161.

6
Give me thy hand, terrestrial; so. Give me thy hand, celestial; so.
The Merry Wives of Windsor. Act iii, sc. 1, l. 108. [Host]
Let me touch your hand.—*Troilus and Cressida,* i, 3, 304.
Dear queen, that ended when I but began,
Give me that hand of yours to kiss.
Winter's Tale. Act iv, sc. 3, l. 46. [Perdita]

7
Take hands, a bargain!
The Winter's Tale, iv, 4, 394. [Shepherd]
Take hands.—*The Tempest,* i, 2, 377.
Take hands with me.—*A Midsummer-Night's Dream,* iv, 1, 90.

8
At last he takes her by the bloodless hand.
The Rape of Lucrece, l. 1597.
She took me kindly by the hand.
The Rape of Lucrece, l. 253.
Take her by the hand, And tell her she is thine.
All's Well that Ends Well. Act ii, sc. 3, l. 180. [King]
Take her by the hand.—*The Merry Wives of Windsor,* iv, 6, 37; v, 3, 3.
Pinch her by the hand.—*The Merry Wives of Windsor,* iv, 6, 44.

9
Come, come, a hand from either:
Let me be blest to make this happy close.
The Two Gentlemen of Verona. Act v, sc. 4, l. 116. [Valentine]

III—The Hand

10
And with this healthful hand, whose banish'd sense
Thou hast repeal'd, a second time receive
The confirmation of my promised gift,
Which but attends thy naming.
All's Well that Ends Well. Act ii, sc. 3, l. 54. [King]

11
The hand could pluck her back that shoved her on.
Antony and Cleopatra. Act i, sc. 2, l. 131. [Antony]

12 The silken tackle
Swell with the touches of those flower-soft hands,
That yarely frame the office.
Antony and Cleopatra. Act ii, sc. 2, l. 214. [Enobarbus] The only use of "flower-soft." "Yarely" occurs again in *The Tempest,* i, 1, 4. "Soft hand" is repeated in *Venus and Adonis,* ll. 353, 633.
A hand that kings
Have lipp'd, and trembled kissing.
Antony and Cleopatra. Act ii, sc. 5, l. 29. [Cleopatra] The only use of "lipp'd."
Commend unto his lips thy favouring hand.
Antony and Cleopatra. Act iv, sc. 8, l. 23. [Antony]

13
These hands do lack nobility, that they strike
A meaner than myself.
Antony and Cleopatra. Act ii, sc. 5, l. 82. [Cleopatra]

14
My playfellow, your hand.
Antony and Cleopatra. Act iii, sc. 13, l. 125. [Antony] See under PLAYFELLOW.

15
You 're fall'n into a princely hand.
Antony and Cleopatra. Act v, sc. 2, l. 22. [Proculeis]

16
I saw her hand: she has a leathern hand,
A freestone-colour'd hand; I verily did think
That her old gloves were on, but 'twas her hands:
She has a huswife's hand.
As You Like It. Act iv, sc. 3, l. 24. [Rosalind] The only use of "freestone-colour'd."
Dirty hand.—*II Henry IV,* v, 5, 38.
Foul hand.—*Henry V,* iii, 3, 34.
Wither'd hands.—*Henry V,* iv, 1, 316.

17
Adriana: Say, is your tardy master now at hand?
Dromio of Ephesus: Nay, he 's at two hands with me, and that my two ears can witness. . . .
Ay, ay, he told his mind upon mine ear:
Beshrew his hand, I scarce could understand it.
The Comedy of Errors. Act ii, sc. 1, l. 44.
Pinch: Give me your hand and let me feel your pulse.
Antipholus of Ephesus: There is my hand, and let it feel your ear.
The Comedy of Errors. Act iv, sc. 4, l. 55.

18 Dismiss'd me
Thus, with his speechless hand.
Coriolanus. Act v, sc. 1, l. 67. [Cominius]
He beckons with his hand and smiles on me.
I Henry VI. Act i, sc. 4, l. 92. [Talbot]
There pleading might you see grave Nestor stand,

As 'twere encouraging the Greeks to fight;
Making such sober action with his hand,
That it beguiled attention, charm'd the sight.
The Rape of Lucrece, l. 1401.

1 This hand, whose touch,
Whose every touch, would force the feeler's soul
To the oath of loyalty.
Cymbeline. Act i, sc. 6, l. 100. [Iachimo] The only use of "feeler."

2 What if this cursed hand
Were thicker than itself with brother's blood,
Is there not rain enough in the sweet heavens
To wash it white as snow?
Hamlet. Act iii, sc. 3, l. 43. [King]

What accursed hand
Hath made thee handless in thy father's sight?
Titus Andronicus. Act iii, sc. 1, l. 66. [Titus] "Handless" is repeated in *Troilus and Cressida,* v, 5, 34.

Accursed fatal hand.—*I Henry VI,* i, 4, 76.
Damn'd hand.—*King John,* v, 1, 41.
Fatal hand.—*Richard II,* v, 6, 35.
Fell hand.—*Sonnets,* lxiv.
Guilty hands.—*Richard II,* v, 6, 50.
Injurious hand.—*Sonnets,* lxiii.
Insulting hand.—*I Henry IV,* v, 4, 54.
Mortal hand.—*King John,* iii, 1, 158.

3
The hand of little employment hath the daintier sense.
Hamlet. Act v, sc. 1, l. 77. [Hamlet] The only use of "daintier."

4
While that the armed hand doth fight abroad,
The advised head defends itself at home.
Henry V. Act i, sc. 2, l. 178. [Exeter] "Armed hand" is repeated in *The Rape of Lucrece,* l. 1425.

To put forth
My rightful hand is a well-hallow'd cause.
Henry V. Act i, sc. 2, l. 293. [King Henry] The only use of "well-hallow'd."

5
Some violent hands were laid on Humphrey's life!
II Henry VI. Act iii, sc. 2, l. 138. [King Henry] "Violent hands" is repeated in *Macbeth,* v, 8, 70.

I do believe that violent hands were laid
Upon the life of this thrice-famed duke.
II Henry VI. Act iii, sc. 2, l. 156. [Warwick] "Thrice famed" (unhyphenated) is repeated in *Troilus and Cressida,* ii, 3, 254.

Boisterous hand.—*II Henry IV,* iv, 5, 192.
Careless hand.—*A Lover's Complaint,* l. 30.
Cruel hand!—*III Henry VI,* i, 4, 166; *Sonnets,* lx.
Cunning hand.—*Twelfth Night,* i, 5, 258.
Disjoining hands.—*King John,* iii, 1, 197.
Heavy hand.—*II Henry IV,* iv, 1, 102; *King John,* iv, 3, 58; *Much Ado about Nothing,* iv, 1, 116.
Ireful hands.—*III Henry VI,* ii, 5, 132.
Nimble hand.—*The Winter's Tale,* iv, 4, 686.
Reaching hands.—*II Henry VI,* iv, 7, 86.
Rigorous hands.—*Coriolanus,* iii, 1, 267.
Rude hand.—*I Henry IV,* i, 1, 41; *King John,* iv, 2, 240.
Unruly hand.—*King John,* iii, 4, 135.
Warlike hand.—*Titus Andronicus,* iii, 1, 256.

6
This hand of mine hath writ in thy behalf
And therefore shall it charm thy riotous tongue.
II Henry VI. Act iv, sc. 1, l. 63. [Suffolk]

7
There 's no better sign of a brave mind than a hard hand.
II Henry VI. Act iv, sc. 2, l. 21. [Bevis]

Hard as the palm of ploughman.
Troilus and Cressida. Act i, sc. 1, l. 59. [Troilus] See under PALM.

Join gripes with hands
Made hard with hourly falsehood—falsehood, as
With labour.
Cymbeline. Act i, sc. 6, l. 106. [Iachimo]

Our hands are hard.—*As You Like It,* iii, 2, 60.

8
This hand was made to handle nought but gold.
II Henry VI. Act v, sc. 1, l. 7. [York]

Thy hand is made to grasp a palmer's staff,
And not to grace an awful princely sceptre.
II Henry VI, v, 1, 97. See under KING.

9 This strong right hand of mine
Can pluck the diadem from faint Henry's head,
And wring the awful sceptre from his fist,
Were he as famous and as bold in war
As he is famed for mildness, peace and prayer.
III Henry VI. Act ii, sc. 1, l. 152. [Warwick] The only use of "strong right hand."

This poor right hand of mine
Is left to tyrannize upon my breast.
Titus Andronicus. Act iii, sc. 2, l. 7. [Titus]

Strong hand.—*The Comedy of Errors,* iii, 1, 98; *King John,* ii, 1, 33; iv, 2, 82; *Hamlet,* i, 1, 102; *Sonnets,* lxv.
Right hand.—*III Henry VI,* ii, 1, 15, and fifteen times in later plays.

10
This is the hand that stabb'd thy father York;
And this the hand that slew thy brother Rutland;
And here 's the heart that triumphs in their death
And cheers these hands that slew thy sire and brother
To execute the like upon thyself.
III Henry VI. Act ii, sc. 4, l. 6. [Richmond]

11
If this right hand would buy two hours' life,
That I in all despite might rail at him,
This hand should chop it off.
III Henry VI. Act ii, sc. 6, l. 80. [Richard]

Warwick: I had rather chop this hand off at a blow,
And with the other fling it at thy face,
Than bear so low a sail, to strike to thee.

King Edward: Sail how thou canst, have wind and tide thy friend,
This hand, fast wound about thy coal-black hair,
Shall, whiles thy head is warm and new cut off,
Write in the dust this sentence with thy blood,
'Wind-changing Warwick now can change no more.'
III Henry VI. Act v, sc. 1, l. 50. The only use of "wind-changing."

1
With one hand on his dagger,
Another spread on 's breast.
Henry VIII. Act i, sc. 2, l. 204. [Surveyor]
Lay hand on heart.—*Romeo and Juliet,* iii, 5, 192.
A hand as fruitful as the land that feeds us.
Henry VIII. Act i, sc. 3, l. 56. [Lovell]
Ye have made a fine hand, fellows.
Henry VIII. Act v, sc. 4, l. 74. [Chamberlain]

2
The fairest hand I ever touch'd! O beauty!
Till now I never knew thee!
Henry VIII. Act i, sc. 4, l. 75. [King Henry]
Fair immortal hand.—*Venus and Adonis,* l. 80.
Clean hands.—*The Two Gentlemen of Verona,* iii, 1, 278.
Gentle hands.—*All's Well that Ends Well,* Epil., 340.
Gilded hand.—*Hamlet,* iii, 3, 58.
Golden hand.—*King John,* iii, 1, 57.
Gracious hands.—*II Henry VI,* i, 1, 13; *Richard III,* i, 2, 208; *All's Well that Ends Well,* v, 1, 31.
Loving hand.—*Much Ado about Nothing,* iii, 1, 112.
Pure hands.—*The Two Gentlemen of Verona,* iii, 1, 229.
Reverent hands.—*I Henry VI,* v, 3, 47.

3
A common slave—you know him well by sight—
Held up his left hand, which did flame and burn
Like twenty torches join'd, and yet his hand,
Not sensible of fire, remain'd unscorch'd.
Julius Cæsar. Act i, sc. 3, l. 15. [Casca] The only use of "unscorch'd."
Left hand.—*The Merchant of Venice,* v, 1, 177; *Julius Cæsar,* v, 1, 17; *The Merry Wives of Windsor,* ii, 2, 24; *Othello,* ii, 3, 119.

4
Now, whilst your purple hands do reek and smoke.
Julius Cæsar. Act iii, sc. 1, l. 158. [Antony] "Purpled hands" occurs in *King John,* ii, 1, 322.
Yet see you but our hands
And this the bleeding business they have done:
Our hearts you see not; they are pitiful.
Julius Cæsar. Act iii, sc. 1, l. 167. [Brutus]
Woe to the hand that shed this costly blood!
Julius Cæsar. Act iii, sc. 1, l. 258. [Antony]

5
Let each man render me his bloody hand:
First, Marcus Brutus, will I shake with you.
Julius Cæsar. Act iii, sc. 1, l. 184. [Antony]
Bloody hand.—*I Henry VI,* iv, 3, 41; *Romeo and Juliet,* i, 1, 93; *Henry V,* iii, 3, 12; *King Lear,* iii, 2, 53; iv, 6, 164; *Cymbeline,* v, 5, 485.
Bloody of hand.—*King Lear,* iii, 4, 96.

6
And meritorious shall that hand be call'd,
Canonized and worshipp'd as a saint,
That takes away by any secret course
Thy hateful life.
King John. Act iii, sc. 1, l. 176. [Pandulph]
Thy hand hath murdered him.—*King John,* iv, 2, 205.

7
And shall these hands, so lately purged of blood,
So newly join'd in love, so strong in both,
Unyoke this seizure and this kind regreet?
King John. Act iii, sc. 1, l. 239. [King Philip] "Unyoke" is repeated in *Hamlet,* v, 1, 59. "Regreet" occurs five times.
This hand of mine
Is yet a maiden and an innocent hand,
Not painted with the crimson spots of blood.
King John. Act iv, sc. 2, l. 251. [Hubert]
Maiden hand.—*Sonnets,* cliv.

8
Till I have set a glory to this hand,
By giving it the worship of revenge.
King John. Act iv, sc. 3, l. 71. [Salisbury]
Shall that victorious hand be feebled here,
That in your chambers gave you chastisement?
King John. Act v, sc. 2, l. 146. [Bastard] The only use of "feebled."
Powerless hand.—*King John,* ii, 1, 15.
Weak hand.—*Cymbeline,* iii, 4, 80.

9
Your hands in your pocket like a man after the old painting.
Love's Labour's Lost. Act iii, sc. 1, l. 20. [Moth]
Putting the hand in the pocket and extracting it clutched.
Measure for Measure. Act iii, sc. 2, l. 48. [Lucio]
Keep . . . thy hand out of plackets.—*King Lear,* iii, 4, 100. See under BEHAVIOUR.

10
A giving hand, though foul, shall have fair praise.
Love's Labour's Lost. Act iv, sc. 1, l. 23. [Princess of France]
Thou hast an open hand.
Twelfth Night, iv, 1, 22. See under GENEROSITY.
An open hand.—*III Henry VI,* iv, 2, 9.
A hand Open as day.—*II Henry IV,* iv, 4, 31.
Aiding hand.—*Richard III,* i, 3, 96.
Bounteous hand.—*Richard III,* ii, 3, 93.
Charitable hand.—*Much Ado about Nothing,* iv, 1, 133.
Helping hands.—*Richard II,* iv, 1, 161.

11
Maria: Wide o' the bow hand! i' faith, your hand is out. . . .
Boyet: An if my hand be out, then belike your hand is in.
Love's Labour's Lost. Act iv, sc. 1, l. 135.

12
I would these hands might never part.
Love's Labour's Lost. Act v, sc. 2, l. 57. [Maria]
Virgin hand.—*Sonnets,* cliv.

1
Wash your hands, put on your nightgown.
Macbeth. Act v, sc. 1, l. 68. [Lady Macbeth]

Doctor: What is it she does now? Look, how she rubs her hands.
Gentleman: It is an accustomed action with her, to seem thus washing her hands: I have known her continue in this a quarter of an hour. . . .
Lady Macbeth: What, will these hands ne'er be clean? . . . Here's the smell of blood still: all the perfumes of Arabia will not sweeten this little hand.
Macbeth. Act v, sc. 1, l. 30.

Chiron: Go home, call for sweet water, wash thy hands.
Demetrius: She hath no tongue to call, nor hands to wash.
Titus Andronicus. Act ii, sc. 4, l. 6. See also under WASHING.

2
What hands are here? ha! they pluck out mine eyes.
Macbeth. Act ii, sc. 2, l. 59. [Macbeth]

3
This is the hand which, with a vow'd contract,
Was fast belock'd in thine.
Measure for Measure. Act v, sc. 1, l. 209. [Mariana] The only use of "belock'd."

4
He is as tall a man of his hands as any is between this and his head; he hath fought with a warrener.
The Merry Wives of Windsor. Act i, sc. 4, l. 27. [Simple] See under FELLOW. The only use of "warrener" (keeper of a warren).

5
Here 's his dry hand up and down.
Much Ado about Nothing. Act ii, sc. 1, l. 124. [Ursula]

I am not such an ass but I can keep my hand dry.
Twelfth Night. Act i, sc. 3, l. 79. [Sir Andrew]

Dry hand.—*II Henry IV,* i, 2, 204.

6 If they speak but truth of her,
These hands shall tear her.
Much Ado about Nothing. Act iv, sc. 1, l. 192. [Leonato]

7
Men do their broken weapons rather use
Than their bare hands.
Othello. Act i, sc. 3, l. 174. [Duke] The only use of "bare hands."

8
How her hand, in my hand being lock'd,
Forced it to tremble with her loyal fear!
The Rape of Lucrece, l. 260.

His guilty hand pluck'd up the latch.
The Rape of Lucrece, l. 358.

His hand, as proud of such a dignity,
Smoking with pride, march'd on to make his stand
On her bare breast, the heart of all her land.
The Rape of Lucrece, l. 458.

Such wretched hands such wretched blood should spill.
The Rape of Lucrece, l. 999.

Poor hand, why quiver'st thou at this decree?
Honour thyself to rid me of this shame;
For if I die, my honour lives in thee;
But if I live, thou livest in my defame;
Since thou couldst not defend thy loyal dame,
And wast afeard to scratch her wicked foe,
Kill both thyself and her for yielding so.
The Rape of Lucrece, l. 1030.

Yield to my hand; my hand shall conquer thee.
The Rape of Lucrece, l. 1210.

This said, he struck his hand upon his breast,
And kiss'd the fatal knife, to end his vow.
The Rape of Lucrece, l. 1842.

Till after many accents and delays,
Untimely breathings, sick and short assays,
She utters this, 'He, he, fair lords, 'tis he,
That guides this hand to give this wound to me.'
The Rape of Lucrece, l. 1719.

9
Lay on our royal sword your banish'd hands.
Richard II. Act i, sc. 3, l. 179. [King Richard]

Lift your vassal hands against my head.
Richard II. Act iii, sc. 3, l. 89. [King Richard]

10 His noble hand
Did win what he did spend and spent not that
Which his triumphant father's hand had won;
His hands were guilty of no kindred blood,
But bloody with the enemies of his kin.
Richard II. Act ii, sc. 1, l. 179. [York]

That noble hand of thine,
That hath thrown down so many enemies,
Shall not be sent: my hand will serve the turn.
Titus Andronicus. Act iii, sc. 1, l. 163. [Lucius]

11 No hand of blood and bone
Can gripe the sacred handle of our sceptre,
Unless he do profane, steal, or usurp.
Richard II. Act iii, sc. 3, l. 79. [King Richard]

May my hands rot off
And never brandish more revengeful steel
Over the glittering helmet of my foe!
Richard II. Act iv, sc. 1, l. 49. [Aumerle]

12 Here, cousin;
On this side my hand, and on that side yours.
Richard II. Act iv, sc. 1, l. 182. [King Richard]

With mine own hands I give away my crown.
Richard II, iv, 1, 208. See under POMP for full quotation.

13
Rude misgovern'd hands from windows' tops
Threw dust and rubbish on King Richard's head.
Richard II. Act v, sc. 2, l. 5. [Duchess] The only use of "misgovern'd."

Stay thy revengeful hand.
Richard II. Act v, sc. 3, l. 42. [Aumerle]

14
That jade hath eat bread from my royal hand;

This hand hath made him proud with clapping him.
Richard II. Act v, sc. 5, l. 85. [King Richard] "Clapping" is repeated in *II Henry VI,* i, 1, 160: "Clapping their hands." See under APPLAUSE.

Royal hands.—*Love's Labour's Lost,* iv, 2, 146; *Richard II,* iii, 2, 11; iv, i, 110; *King John,* iii, 1, 226.

1
Villain, thy own hand yields thy death's instrument.
Richard II. Act v, sc. 5, l. 107. [King Richard]

That hand shall burn in never-quenching fire
That staggers thus my person. Exton, thy fierce hand
Hath with the king's blood stain'd the king's own land.
Richard II. Act v, sc. 5, l. 109. [King Richard] The only use of "never-quenching."

2
Stabb'd by the selfsame hand that made these wounds!
Richard III. Act i, sc. 2, l. 11. [Anne]

The very hand.—*The Merry Wives of Windsor,* ii, 1, 85.

3
Cursed be the hand that made these fatal holes!
Richard III, i, 2, 14. See under CURSE.

That hand, which, for thy love, did kill thy love,
Shall, for thy love, kill a far truer love.
Richard III. Act i, sc. 2, l. 190. [Gloucester]

4
We come to use our hands and not our tongues.
Richard III. Act i, sc. 3, l. 353. [First Murderer] See also WORD AND DEED.

5 I'll watch her place of stand,
And, touching hers, make blessed my rude hand.
Romeo and Juliet. Act i, sc. 5, l. 52. [Romeo]

6
Good pilgrim, you do wrong your hand too much,
Which mannerly devotion shows in this;
For saints have hands that pilgrims' hands do touch,
And palm to palm is holy palmers' kiss.
Romeo and Juliet. Act i, sc. 5, l. 99. [Juliet]

7
Will 't please your lordship cool your hands?
The Taming of the Shrew. Induction, sc. 1, l. 58. [Lord]

Basins and ewers to lave her dainty hands.
The Taming of the Shrew. Act ii, sc. 1, l. 350. [Gremio]

I dreamt of a silver basin and ewer.
Timon of Athens, iii, 1, 6.

Bear the ewer.—*The Taming of the Shrew,* Ind., 1, 57. The only uses of "ewer." "Basin" occurs also in *The Taming of the Shrew,* Ind., 1, 55: "Silver basin"; and in *Titus Andronicus,* v, 2, 184: "Bear the basin."

8
Our mistress, whose hand, she being now at hand, thou shalt soon feel.
The Taming of the Shrew, iv, 1, 32. [Grumio]

I tell you, sir, she bears me fair in hand.
The Taming of the Shrew. Act iv, sc. 2, l. 3. [Tranio]

9
And place your hands below your husband's foot;
In token of which duty, if he please,
My hand is ready; may it do him ease.
The Taming of the Shrew, v, 2, 177. See under WOMAN.

10
O, bless me here with thy victorious hand,
Whose fortunes, Rome's best citizens applaud!
Titus Andronicus. Act i, sc. 1, l. 163. [Lavinia]

11 What stern ungentle hands
Have lopp'd and hew'd and made thy body bare
Of her two branches, those sweet ornaments,
Whose circling shadows kings have sought to sleep in,
And might not gain so great a happiness?
Titus Andronicus. Act ii, sc. 4, l. 16. [Marcus] "Circling" is repeated in *Richard III,* iv, 4, 382.

Give me a sword, I'll chop off my hands too;
For they have fought for Rome, and all, in vain; . . .
Now all the service I require of them
Is that the one will help to cut the other.
Titus Andronicus. Act iii, sc. 1, l. 72. [Titus]

Thou hast no hands, to wipe away thy tears.
Titus Andronicus. Act iii, sc. 1, l. 106. [Titus]

12
Which of your hands hath not defended Rome,
And rear'd aloft the bloody battle-axe,
Writing destruction on the enemy's castle?
Titus Andronicus. Act iii, sc. 1, l. 168. [Marcus] The only use of "battle-axe."

My hand hath been but idle; let it serve
To ransom my two nephews from their death.
Titus Andronicus. Act iii, sc. 1, l. 172. [Marcus]

It was a hand that warded him
From thousand dangers; bid him bury it.
Titus Andronicus. Act iii, sc. 1, l. 195. [Titus] The only use of "warded."

O, here I lift this one hand up to heaven,
And bow this feeble ruin to the earth.
Titus Andronicus. Act iii, sc. 1, l. 207. [Titus]

Heaved-up hand.—*The Rape of Lucrece,* ll. 111, 638. The only uses of "heaved-up."

Thy other hand Gnawing with thy teeth.
Titus Andronicus. Act iii, sc. 1, l. 261. [Marcus]

13
What violent hands can she lay on her life?
Ah, wherefore dost thou urge the name of hands? . . .
O, handle not the theme, to talk of hands,
Lest we remember still that we have none.
Titus Andronicus, iii, 2, 25. [Titus] See under SUICIDE.

How can I grace my talk,
Wanting a hand to give it action?
Titus Andronicus. Act v, sc. 2, l. 17. [Titus]

My hand cut off and made a merry jest.
Titus Andronicus. Act v, sc. 2, l. 175. [Titus]

This one hand yet is left to cut your throats.
Titus Andronicus. Act v, sc. 2, l. 182. [Titus]

That true hand that fought Rome's quarrel out,
And sent her enemies unto the grave.
Titus Andronicus. Act v, sc. 3, l. 102. [Lucius]

1
Bring your hand to the buttery-bar and let it drink.
Twelfth Night. Act i, sc. 3, l. 74. [Maria] The only use of "buttery-bar."

2
I think we do know the sweet Roman hand.
Twelfth Night, iii, 4, 31. See under WRITING: HANDWRITING.

3
O hateful hands, to tear such loving words!
The Two Gentlemen of Verona. Act i, sc. 2, l. 105. [Julia]

4
Wringing her hands, whose whiteness so became them
As if but now they waxed pale for woe.
The Two Gentlemen of Verona. Act iii, sc. 1, l. 227. [Proteus]

Wringing her hands.—*The Two Gentlemen of Verona,* ii, 3, 9.

Why dost thou wring thy hands?—*Romeo and Juliet,* iii, 2, 36.

Leave wringing of your hands.—*Hamlet,* iii, 4, 34.

5
My smooth moist hand, were it with thy hand felt,
Would in thy palm dissolve, or seem to melt.
Venus and Adonis, l. 143.

With one fair hand she heaveth up his hat,
Her other tender hand his fair cheek feels.
Venus and Adonis, l. 351.

You hurt my hand with wringing; let us part.
Venus and Adonis, l. 421.

She takes him by the hand, and that is cold.
Venus and Adonis, l. 1124.

6
There was casting up of eyes, holding up of hands.
The Winter's Tale. Act v, sc. 2, l. 51. [Third Gentleman]

For ever Unvenerable be thy hands.
The Winter's Tale, ii, 3, 77. The only use of "unvenerable."

IV—White Hands

7
Henceforth
The white hand of a lady fever thee,
Shake thou to look on 't.
Antony and Cleopatra. Act iii, sc. 13, l. 137. [Antony]

By the white hand of my lady.
Henry V, iii, 7, 101.

8
The snow-white hand of the most beauteous Lady Rosaline.
Love's Labour's Lost. Act iv, sc. 2, l. 136. [Holofernes, reading]

9
That phraseless hand,
Whose white weighs down the airy scale of praise.
A Lover's Complaint, l. 225. The only use of "phraseless."

10
I know the hand: in faith, 'tis a fair hand;
And whiter than the paper it writ on
Is the fair hand that writ.
The Merchant of Venice. Act ii, sc. 4, l. 12. [Lorenzo] See also under WRITING: HANDWRITING.

11
That pure congealed white high Taurus' snow,
Fann'd with the eastern wind, turns to a crow
When thou hold'st up thy hand: O let me kiss
This princess of pure white, this seal of bliss!
A Midsummer-Night's Dream. Act iii, sc. 2, l. 141. [Demetrius] "Kiss thy hand," see under KISS.

Hands as pale as milk.—*A Midsummer-Night's Dream,* v, 1, 345.

12
Her lily hand her rosy cheek lies under,
Cozening the pillow of a lawful kiss.
The Rape of Lucrece, l. 386.

The lily I condemned for thy hand.
Sonnets. No. xcix.

O, had the monster seen those lily hands
Tremble, like aspen leaves, upon a lute,
And make the silken strings delight to kiss them,
He would not then have touch'd them for his life!
Titus Andronicus. Act ii, sc. 4, l. 44. [Marcus]

13
Without the bed her other fair hand was,
On the green coverlet; whose perfect white
Show'd like an April daisy on the grass.
The Rape of Lucrece, l. 393. "Coverlet" is repeated in *The Taming of the Shrew,* iv, 4, 205.

14
The white wonder of dear Juliet's hand.
Romeo and Juliet. Act iii, sc. 3, l. 36. [Romeo]

Her hand,
In whose comparison all whites are ink.
Troilus and Cressida. Act i, sc. 1, l. 55. [Troilus]

She has a marvellous white hand.
Troilus and Cressida. Act i, sc. 2, l. 150. [Pandarus]

My lady has a white hand.
Twelfth Night. Act ii, sc. 3, l. 28. [Clown]

15
Full gently now she takes him by the hand,
A lily prison'd in a gaol of snow,
Or ivory in an alabaster band;

So white a friend engirts so white a foe.
Venus and Adonis, l. 361.
I take thy hand, this hand,
As soft as dove's down and as white as it,
Or Ethiopian's tooth, or the fann'd snow that's bolted
By the northern blasts twice o'er.
Winter's Tale. Act iv, sc. 4, l. 372. [Florizel]

HANDKERCHIEF

1
Good Tom Drum, lend me a handkercher.
All's Well that Ends Well, v, 3, 322. "Handkercher" is used five times.

Lend me thy handkerchief.
Othello, iii, 4, 52. "Handkerchief" occurs twenty-eight times, twenty-three times in *Othello* alone, referring to the loss of Desdemona's handkerchief.

2
Well I wot
Thy napkin cannot drink a tear of mine.
For thou, poor man, hast drown'd it with thine own.
Titus Andronicus. Act iii, sc. 1, l. 139. [Titus]

His napkin, with his true tears all bewet,
Can do no service on her sorrowful cheeks.
Titus Andronicus. Act iii, sc. 1, l. 146. [Titus] The only use of "bewet."

Take my napkin; rub thy brows.
Hamlet. Act v, sc. 2, l. 299. [Queen]

Have napkins enow about you; here you'll sweat for 't.
Macbeth. Act ii, sc. 3, l. 6. [Porter] "Napkin" occurs sixteen times in the plays.

HANDWRITING, see Writing

HANGING

3
I perceive, sir, by the general's looks, we shall be fain to hang you.
All's Well that Ends Well. Act iv, sc. 3, l. 268. [First Soldier]

4
A halter'd neck which does the hangman thank
For being yare about him.
Antony and Cleopatra. Act iii, sc. 13, l. 130. [Antony] The only use of "halter'd."

5
The melancholy vale,
The place of death and sorry execution.
The Comedy of Errors. Act v, sc. 1, l. 120. [Second Merchant]

6
Guess, . . . if thou standest not i' the state of hanging, or of some death more long in spectatorship, and crueller in suffering.
Coriolanus. Act v, sc. 2, l. 71. [Menenius] The only use of "spectatorship" and "crueller."

7
First Gaoler: Come, sir, are you ready for death?
Posthumus: Over-roasted rather; ready long ago.
First Gaoler: Hanging is the word, sir: if you be ready for that, you are well cooked.
Cymbeline. Act v, sc. 4, l. 152. "Over-roasted" is repeated in *The Taming of the Shrew,* iv, 1, 178.

O, the charity of a penny cord! it sums up thousands in a trice: you have no true debitor and creditor but it; of what's past, is, and to come, the discharge: your neck, sir, is pen, book and counters; so the acquittance follows.
Cymbeline. Act v, sc. 4, l. 170. [First Gaoler] "Trice" occurs three more times in the plays, *Twelfth Night,* iv, 2, 133; *King Lear,* i, 1, 219; *The Tempest,* v, 1, 238. "Debitor and creditor" is used once again in *Othello,* i, 1, 31.

Hanging's the way of winking.
Cymbeline. Act v, sc. 4, l. 197. [Gaoler]

8
Gadshill: There's enough to make us all.
Falstaff: To be hanged.
I Henry IV. Act ii, sc. 2, l. 60.

All: That would hang us, every mother's son.
Bottom: I grant you, friends, if that you should fright the ladies out of their wits, they would have no more discretion but to hang us.
A Midsummer-Night's Dream. Act i, sc. 2, l. 80.

9
There live not three good men unhanged in England; and one of them is fat and grows old.
I Henry IV. Act ii, sc. 4, l. 144. [Falstaff] The only use of "unhanged."

If I become not a cart as well as another man, a plague on my bringing up! I hope I shall as soon be strangled with a halter as another.
I Henry IV. Act ii, sc. 4, l. 545. [Falstaff]

10
If thou gettest any leave of me, hang me; if thou takest leave, thou wert better be hanged.
II Henry IV. Act i, sc. 2, l. 100. [Falstaff]

I would to God that I might die, that I might have thee hanged.
II Henry IV. Act v, sc. 4, l. 1. [Hostess]

11
He hath stolen a pax, and hanged must a' be:
A damned death!
Let gallows gape for dog; let man go free
And let not hemp his wind-pipe suffocate; . . .
And let not Bardolph's vital thread be cut
With edge of penny cord and vile reproach.
Henry V. Act iii, sc. 6, l. 42. [Pistol] "Pax" occurs again five lines later, and nowhere else in the plays. The only use of "hemp." "Crack-hemp" occurs in *The Taming of the Shrew,* v, 1, 46.

They are both hanged; and so would this be, if he durst steal any thing adventurously.
Henry V. Act iv, sc. 4, l. 77. [Boy] The only use of "adventurously."

12
O, burn her, burn her! hanging is too good.
I Henry VI. Act v, sc. 4, l. 33. [Shepherd]

Bring down the devil; for he must not die
So sweet a death as hanging presently.
Titus Andronicus. Act v, sc. 1, l. 145. [Lucius]

Not worth the hanging.—*Cymbeline,* i, 5, 20.
Thou art worthy to be hang'd.—*The Winter's Tale,* ii, 3, 109.

1
Hang him with his pen and ink-horn about his neck.
II Henry VI. Act iv, sc. 2, l. 116. [Cade] "Hang him (her, them)" is used frequently throughout the plays, beginning with the first one.

2
Ye shall have a hempen caudle then and the help of hatchet.
II Henry VI. Act iv, sc. 7, l. 95. [Cade] "Hempen" is repeated in *Henry V,* iii, Prol., 8: "Hempen tackle"; and in *A Midsummer-Night's Dream,* iii, 1, 79: "Hempen home-spuns." "Caudle" (gruel) occurs again in *Love's Labour's Lost,* iv, 3, 174, and in *Timon of Athens,* iv, 3, 226. "Hatchet" is used in this, the first play, and never again.

Will you needs be hanged with your pardons about your necks?
II Henry VI. Act iv, sc. 8, l. 22. [Cade]

3
With halters on their necks.
II Henry VI. Act iv, sc. 9, l. 11. [Clifford]

Give him a halter.—*The Merchant of Venice,* ii, 2, 113.

A halter gratis.—*The Merchant of Venice,* iv, 1, 379.

A halter pardon him!—*Othello,* iv, 2, 136.

Hath . . . halters in his pew.—*King Lear,* iii, 4, 55.

4
Tarry and be hang'd.
III Henry VI. Act iv, sc. 5, l. 26. [Huntsman]

Tarry at home and be hanged.
I Henry IV. Act i, sc. 2, l. 147. [Poins]

Come, and be hanged!—*I Henry IV,* ii, 1, 34.

I 'll be hanged.—*I Henry IV,* ii, 1, 2; ii, 2, 20; *Romeo and Juliet,* iii, 1, 60; *A Midsummer-Night's Dream,* iv, 2, 23; *Othello,* iv, 2, 130; *Cymbeline,* v, 4, 203. "Be hanged" is of frequent occurrence.

I 'll be hanged first.
Measure for Measure. Act iii, sc. 2, l. 178. [Lucio]

Be hang'd up for example.—*II Henry VI,* iv, 2, 190.

5
And on that day at noon, whereon he says
I shall yield up my crown, let him be hang'd.
King John. Act iv, sc. 2, l. 156. [King John]

And if thou want'st a cord, the smallest thread
That ever spider twisted from her womb
Will serve to strangle thee; a rush will be a beam
To hang thee on.
King John. Act iv, sc. 3, l. 127. [Bastard]

6
I kill'd the slave that was a-hanging thee.
King Lear. Act v, sc. 3, l. 274. [King Lear] The only use of "a-hanging."

7
Son: And must they all be hanged that swear and lie?
Lady Macduff: Every one.
Son: Who must hang them?
Lady Macduff: Why, the honest men.
Son: Then the liars and swearers are fools, for there are liars and swearers enow to beat the honest men and hang up them.
Macbeth. Act iv, sc. 2, l. 51.

8
Hang those that talk of fear.
Macbeth. Act v, sc. 3, l. 36. [Macbeth]

Let them hang.—*Coriolanus,* iii, 2, 23.

Hang them on this line.—*Tempest,* iv, 1, 193.

9
It is but heading and hanging.
Measure for Measure. Act ii, sc. 1, l. 250. [Escalus] The only use of "heading."

Hang'd and drawn and quarter'd.
King John, ii, 1, 508. [Bastard]

10
This may prove worse than hanging.
Measure for Measure. Act v, sc. 1, l. 365. [Lucio]

Lucio: If you will hang me for it, you may; but I had rather it would please you I might be whipt.
Duke: Whipt first, sir, and hanged after.
Measure for Measure. Act v, sc. 1, l. 510.

11
The ancient saying is no heresy,
Hanging and wiving goes by destiny.
The Merchant of Venice. Act ii, sc. 9, l. 82. [Nerissa] Horman's *Vulgaria,* fo. 19 (1519), has "It is my destenye to be hanged." Heywood's *Proverbs,* pt. i, ch. 3 (1546), has "Wedding is destiny, And hanging likewise, saith the proverb." Shakespeare's version dates from 1595.

Many a good hanging prevents a bad marriage.
Twelfth Night. Act i, sc. 5, l. 20. [Clown]

12
Thou must be hang'd at the state's charge.
The Merchant of Venice. Act iv, sc. 1, l. 367. [Gratiano]

Would I were hanged!—*The Merry Wives of Windsor,* v, 5, 191.

I would I might be hanged.—*The Merry Wives of Windsor,* i, 1, 266.

Hang me up in chains!—*Antony and Cleopatra,* v, 2, 62.

Hang me by the neck.—*Love's Labour 's Lost,* iv, 1, 114.

13
It were an alms to hang him.
Much Ado about Nothing. Act ii, sc. 3, l. 164. [Don Pedro]

Hang him instantly.—*King Lear,* iii, 7, 4.

Hang him up.—*The Two Gentlemen of Verona,* iv, 4, 24.

Hang up thy mistress.—*The Comedy of Errors,* ii, 1, 67.

Hang her up for ever!—*Pericles,* iv, 6, 146.

Hang all the husbands.—*The Winter's Tale,* ii, 3, 110.

14
Truly, I would not hang a dog by my will, much more a man who hath any honesty in him.
Much Ado about Nothing. Act iii, sc. 3, l. 66. [Dogberry]

15
Petruchio: Upon Sunday is the wedding-day.
Katharina: I 'll see thee hang'd on Sunday first.

Gremio: Hark, Petruchio; she says she 'll see thee hang'd first.
Taming of the Shrew. Act ii, sc. 1, l. 300.
I 'll see thee hanged first.
I Henry IV. Act ii, sc. 1, l. 44. [Carrier]
I will see you hanged, like clotpoles.
Troilus and Cressida. Act ii, sc. 1, l. 128. [Thersites] The only use of "clotpoles." "Clot-poll" occurs in *King Lear,* i, 4, 51, and in *Cymbeline,* iv, 2, 184.

1
Come hither, crack-hemp.
The Taming of the Shrew. Act v, sc. 1, l. 48. [Vincentio] The only use of "crack-hemp."

2
Hang, cur! hang, you whoreson, insolent noisemaker!
The Tempest. Act i, sc. 1, l. 46. [Antonio] The only use of "noisemaker."

3
Would cry to a sailor, Go hang!
The Tempest. Act ii, sc. 2, l. 53. [Stephano]
Let her go hang!
The Tempest. Act ii, sc. 2, l. 56. [Stephano] "Go hang" occurs four times in the plays.

4
Saturninus: Take him away, and hang him presently. . . .
Clown: Hanged! by 'r lady, then I have brought up a neck to a fair end.
Titus Andronicus. Act iv, sc. 4, l. 45.
A halter, soldiers! hang him on this tree,
And by his side his fruit of bastardy.
Titus Andronicus. Act v, sc. 1, l. 47. [Lucius]
Upon the next tree shalt thou hang alive.
Macbeth, v, 5, 39. See under SPEECH.
The trees by the way should have borne men.
Antony and Cleopatra, iii, 6, 36. [Cæsar]
If you prove a mutineer—the next tree!—*The Tempest,* iii, 2, 41.

5
Maria: My lady will hang thee for thy absence.
Clown: Let her hang me: he that is well hanged in this world needs to fear no colours.
Twelfth Night. Act i, sc. 5, l. 3.
Marry, hang thee, brock!
Twelfth Night. Act ii, sc. 5, l. 114. [Sir Toby] The only use of "brock" (badger).

6
Go, go, be gone, to save your ship from wreck,
Which cannot perish having thee aboard,
Being destined to a drier death on shore.
The Two Gentlemen of Verona. Act i, sc. 1, l. 156. [Proteus]
Methinks he hath no drowning mark upon him; his complexion is perfect gallows. Stand fast, good Fate, to his hanging.
The Tempest. Act i, sc. 1, l. 32. [Gonzalo]
If he be not born to be hanged, our case is miserable.
The Tempest. Act i, sc. 1, l. 35. [Gonzalo]
He 'll be hang'd yet,
Though every drop of water swear against it
And gape at widest to glut him.
The Tempest. Act i, sc. 2, l. 61. [Gonzalo] The only use of "glut."
I prophesied, if a gallows were on land,
This fellow could not drown.
The Tempest. Act v, sc. 1, l. 217. [Gonzalo]

7
Yet you will be hanged for being so long absent; or to be turned away, is not that as good as a hanging to you?
Twelfth Night. Act i, sc. 5, l. 17. [Maria]

8
A man is never undone till he be hanged.
The Two Gentlemen of Verona. Act ii, sc. 5, l. 5. [Launce]

9
Thou old traitor,
I am sorry that by hanging thee I can
But shorten thy life one week.
The Winter's Tale. Act iv, sc. 4, l. 430. [Polixenes]
If they have overheard me now, why, hanging.
The Winter's Tale. Act iv, sc. 4, l. 639. [Autolycus]

II—Hanging Oneself

10
He that hangs himself is a virgin.
All's Well that Ends Well, i, 1, 150. See under VIRGINITY.

11
Go hang thyself in thine own heir-apparent garters!
I Henry IV. Act ii, sc. 2, l. 46. [Falstaff]
Hanged himself in Thisbe's garter.—*A Midsummer-Night's Dream,* v, 1, 366.

12
Hang yourself, you muddy conger, hang yourself!
II Henry IV. Act ii, sc. 4, l. 58. [Doll Tearsheet] "Conger" is repeated in the same scene, l. 266, and occurs nowhere else.
Go hang yourself, you naughty mocking uncle!
Troilus and Cressida. Act iv, sc. 2, l. 25. [Cressida]

13
Holofernes: What mean you, sir?
Boyet: To make Judas hang himself.
Holofernes: Begin, sir; you are my elder.
Biron: Well followed: Judas was hanged on an elder.
Love's Labour 's Lost. Act v, sc. 2, l. 607.

14
Thou canst make
No excuse current, but to hang thyself.
Richard III. Act i, sc. 2, l. 83. [Lady Anne]
Beg that thou mayst have leave to hang thyself.
The Merchant of Venice. Act iv, sc. 1, l. 364. [Gratiano]
Hang thyself!—*Timon of Athens,* i, 1, 277.

15
For want of means, poor rats, had hang'd themselves.
Richard III. Act v, sc. 3, l. 331. [King Richard]
Will they not, think you, hang themselves tonight?
Love's Labour 's Lost. Act v, sc. 2, l. 270. [Princess of France]

16
Be mad and merry, or go hang yourselves.
The Taming of the Shrew. Act iii, sc. 2, l. 228. [Katharina]

Go, hang yourselves all! you are idle shallow things.
Twelfth Night. Act iii, sc. 4, l. 136. [Malvolio]

1 Whoso please
To stop affliction, let him take his haste,
Come hither, . . . and hang himself.
Timon of Athens. Act v, sc. 1, l. 212. [Timon]

2
An 'twere my case, I should go hang myself.
Titus Andronicus. Act ii, sc. 4, l. 9. [Chiron]

III—The Hangman

3
The under-hangman of his kingdom.
Cymbeline. Act ii, sc. 3, l. 135. [Imogen] The only use of "under-hangman."

4
Thou shalt have the hanging of the thieves and so become a rare hangman.
I Henry IV. Act i, sc. 2, l. 75. [Prince of Wales]

The hangman hath no lean wardrobe.
I Henry IV. Act i, sc. 2, l. 82. [Falstaff]

Gadshill: Sirrah, if they meet not with Saint Nicholas' clerks, I 'll give thee this neck.
Chamberlain: No, I 'll none of it: I pray thee, keep that for the hangman.
I Henry IV. Act ii, sc. 1, l. 68.

What talkest thou to me of the hangman? if I hang, I 'll make a fat pair of gallows.
I Henry IV. Act ii, sc. 1, l. 74. [Gadshill]

5
I will be content to be a lawful hangman.
Measure for Measure. Act iv, sc. 2, l. 17. [Pompey]

Abhorson: He will discredit our mystery. . . .
Pompey: Do you call, sir, your occupation a mystery? . . .
Abhorson: Ay, sir; a mystery.
Pompey: Painting, sir, I have heard say, is a mystery; and your whores, sir, being members of my occupation, using painting, do prove my occupation a mystery: but what mystery there should be in hanging, if I should be hanged, I cannot imagine.
Measure for Measure. Act iv, sc. 2, l. 29.

6
I do find your hangman is a more penitent trade than your bawd; he doth oftener ask forgiveness.
Measure for Measure. Act iv, sc. 2, l. 52. [Pompey]

7
I rather would have been his hangman.
Othello. Act i, sc. 1, l. 34. [Roderigo]

8
Some hangman must put on my shroud and lay me
Where no priest shovels in dust.
The Winter's Tale. Act iv, sc. 4, l. 469. [Shepherd]

Those that are germane to him, though removed fifty times, shall all come under the hangman.
The Winter's Tale. Act iv, sc. 4, l. 801. [Autolycus]

IV—The Gallows

9
Unless a man would marry a gallows and beget young gibbets, I never saw one so prone.
Cymbeline. Act v, sc. 4, l. 206. [Gaoler]

O, there were desolation of gaolers and gallowses! I speak against my present profit, but my wish hath a preferment in 't.
Cymbeline. Act v, sc. 4, l. 213. [Gaoler] The only use of "gallowses."

10
First Clown: What is he that builds stronger than either the mason, the shipwright, or the carpenter?
Second Clown: The gallows-maker; for that frame outlives a thousand tenants.
Hamlet. Act v, sc. 1, l. 46. The only use of "gallows-maker." "Shipwright" is repeated in i, 1, 75 and v, 1, 58, and occurs in no other play.

O, the gibbet-maker! he says that he hath taken them down again, for the man must not be hanged till the next week.
Titus Andronicus. Act iv, sc. 3, l. 80. [Clown] The only use of "gibbet-maker."

11
The gallows does well; but how does it well? it does well to those that do ill.
Hamlet. Act v, sc. 1, l. 52. [First Clown]

12
Shall there be gallows standing in England when thou art king?
I Henry IV. Act i, sc. 2, l. 66. [Falstaff]

13
An you do not make him hanged among you, the gallows shall have wrong.
II Henry IV. Act ii, sc. 2, l. 104. [Bardolph]

Rebellious hinds, the filth and scum of Kent, Mark'd for the gallows.
II Henry VI. Act iv, sc. 2, l. 130. [Stafford]

When every thing is ended, then you come:
These tardy tricks of yours will, on my life,
One time or other break some gallows' back.
II Henry IV. Act iv, sc. 3, l. 30. [Lancaster]

14
Belong to the gallows, and be hanged, ye rogue!
Henry VIII. Act v, sc. 4, l. 6. [Porter]

15
Hang no more about me, I am no gibbet for you.
The Merry Wives of Windsor. Act ii, sc. 2, l. 17. [Falstaff] "Gibbet" occurs six times.

16
Gallows and knock are too powerful on the highway: beating and hanging are terrors to me.
The Winter's Tale. Act iv, sc. 3, l. 28. [Autolycus]

HAP

See also Chance, Fortune

17 A woman, happy but for me,
And by me, had not our hap been bad.
The Comedy of Errors. Act i, sc. 1, l. 38. [Ægeon]

Heavy haps.—*Titus Andronicus*, v, 3, 202.
Ill hap.—*Henry VIII*, Epil., 13.

18
More blessed hap did ne'er befall our state.
I Henry VI. Act i, sc. 6, l. 10. [Charles]

Meaner men should vaunt
That golden hap which their superiors want.
The Rape of Lucrece, l. 41.
Contented hap.—*Richard III,* i, 3, 84.

1 Warwick: What hap? what hope of good?
George: Our hap is loss.
III Henry VI, ii, 3, 8. See under DESPAIR.
Be it art or hap.—*Antony and Cleopatra,* ii, 3, 32.
Hap what hap may.—*The Taming of the Shrew,* iv, 4, 108.
How haps it?—*III Henry VI,* iii, 3, 88.
Howe'er my haps.—*Hamlet,* iv, 3, 70.
Try your hap.—*II Henry VI,* iii, 1, 314.

2 More direful hap betide that hated wretch!
Richard III, i, 2, 17. See under CURSE.

3 And he shall signify from time to time
Every good hap to you that chances here.
Romeo and Juliet. Act iii, sc. 3, l. 170. [Friar Laurence]
By good hap.—*The Two Gentlemen of Verona,* i, 1, 15; *Love's Labour's Lost,* ii, 1, 210; *Romeo and Juliet,* iii, 3, 171; *Richard II,* i, 1, 23; *Timon of Athens,* iii, 2, 27.
Dear hap.—*Romeo and Juliet,* ii, 2, 190.

HAPPINESS

See also Cheerfulness, Gladness, Joy

4 O, how bitter a thing it is to look into happiness through another man's eyes!
As You Like It. Act v, sc. 2, l. 47. [Orlando]

5 Happy were I in my timely death.
The Comedy of Errors, i, 1, 139. [Ægeon]
'Tis happiness to die.—*Othello,* v, 2, 290.

6 A happiness that often madness hits on.
Hamlet, ii, 2, 113. See under MADNESS.

7 Happy, in that we are not over-happy.
Hamlet. Act ii, sc. 2, l. 232. [Guildenstern]
The only use of "over-happy."
Not so happy, yet much happier.
Macbeth. Act i, sc. 3, l. 66. [Second Witch]

8 Be happy, he will trouble you no more.
II Henry IV. Act iv, sc. 5, l. 128. [King Henry]
Be happy.—*Troilus and Cressida,* v, 6, 16; *Antony and Cleopatra,* iii, 2, 64.
Happy am I.—*II Henry IV,* v, 2, 108.
Ever happy!—*Henry VIII,* v, 5, 2.
Most happy!—*King Lear,* iv, 6, 230; *Othello,* ii, 1, 192.
So happy.—*Measure for Measure,* v, 1, 404.
Truly happy.—*Henry VIII,* iii, 2, 377.

9 All happiness unto my lord the king!
II Henry VI, iii, 1, 93; v, 1, 124.
All happiness bechance to thee.
The Two Gentlemen of Verona. Act i, sc. 1, l. 61. [Proteus]
All happiness to your honour!—*Timon of Athens,* i, 1, 109.
He wishes you all happiness.—*Cymbeline,* iii, 2, 46.
All happiness.—*Richard II,* v, 6, 6.
Lancaster: Health, peace and happiness to my royal father!
King: Thou bring'st me happiness and peace, son John.
II Henry IV. Act iv, sc. 5, l. 227.
Health and happiness!—*Richard II,* iii, 2, 91.
Good day and happiness!—*As You Like It,* iv, 1, 30.
Happiness to him.—*All's Well that Ends Well,* iv, 3, 12.
Happiness to his accomplices!—*I Henry VI,* v, 2, 9.
Happiness to their sheets!
Othello. Act ii, sc. 3, l. 29. [Iago]
The best of happiness,
Honour and fortunes, keep with you.
Timon of Athens. Act i, sc. 2, l. 234. [First Lord]
I wish thee happiness!—*Pericles,* i, 1, 60.
Rest you happy.—*Antony and Cleopatra,* i, 1, 62.
Happy be you!—*Cymbeline,* v, 5, 404; *The Winter's Tale,* iv, 4, 635.
May you be happy.—*Henry VIII,* iii, 2, 43.
Be happy, lady.—*Much Ado about Nothing,* i, 1, 112.
I have made you happy.—*The Two Gentlemen of Verona,* v, 4, 30.
Made me happy.—*Henry VIII,* ii, 1, 117.
Make me happy.—*Richard III,* ii, 1, 31.

10 They promised me eternal happiness.
Henry VIII, iv, 2, 90. See under VISION.

11 Lead forth and bring you back in happiness.
Measure for Measure. Act i, sc. 1, l. 75. [Escalus]

12 Fair thoughts and happy hours attend on you!
The Merchant of Venice. Act iii, sc. 4, l. 41. [Lorenzo]

13 You are the happier woman.
The Merry Wives of Windsor. Act ii, sc. 1, l. 110. [Mrs. Ford]

14 How happy some o'er other some can be!
A Midsummer-Night's Dream. Act i, sc. 1, l. 226. [Helena]

15 I were but little happy, if I could say how much.
Much Ado about Nothing. Act ii, sc. 1, l. 318. [Claudio]
He hath indeed a good outward happiness.
Much Ado about Nothing. Act ii, sc. 3, l. 190. [Don Pedro]
And, lo, the happiness!—*Othello,* iii, 4, 108.
Boundless happiness!—*Pericles,* i, 1, 24.
Dear happiness.—*Much Ado about Nothing,* i, 1, 129.
Great happiness!—*Macbeth,* i, 2, 58.
So great a happiness.—*Titus Andronicus,* ii, 4, 20.
Imagined happiness.—*Romeo and Juliet,* ii, 6, 28.
Mean happiness.—*Merchant of Venice,* i, 2, 7.
Mutual happiness.—*The Two Gentlemen of Verona,* v, 4, 173.
New happiness.—*II Henry IV,* iv, 4, 81.

Happiness of life.—*Love's Labour 's Lost,* iv, 2, 168.
Happiness of England.—*Henry VIII,* v, 5, 57.
England's happiness!—*II Henry VI,* i, 1, 37.
Solon's happiness.—*Titus Andronicus,* i, 1, 177. The only mention of Solon.

1
O happiness enjoy'd but of a few!
And, if possess'd, as soon decay'd and done
As is the morning's silver-melting dew
Against the golden splendour of the sun!
The Rape of Lucrece, l. 22. The only use of "silver-melting."
There 's no man happy.
Othello. Act iv, sc. 2, l. 18. [Emilia]
Sick of happiness.—*II Henry IV,* iv, 1, 64.
To sour your happiness.—*Cymbeline,* v, 5, 26.
Happiness takes his leave.—*Much Ado about Nothing,* i, 1, 102.
Dead happiness.—*Richard III,* iv, 4, 119.

2
She is all happy as the fairest of all.
Pericles. Act v, sc. 1, l. 49. [Lysimachus]
Happy what follows!—*Pericles,* iii, 1, 31.

3
I fear our happiness is at the highest.
Richard III. Act i, sc. 3, l. 41. [Queen Elizabeth]
If to have done the thing you gave in charge
Beget your happiness, be happy then,
For it is done, my lord.
Richard III. Act iv, sc. 3, l. 25. [Tyrrel]
In her consists my happiness and thine.
Richard III. Act iv, sc. 4, l. 406. [King Richard]

4
There art thou happy.
Romeo and Juliet. Act iii, sc. 3, l. 137. [Friar Laurence]
Happiness courts thee in her best array.
Romeo and Juliet. Act iii, sc. 3, l. 142. [Friar Laurence]
Tell him Wherein you 're happy.—*Cymbeline,* iii, 4, 177.

5
Then happy I, that love and am beloved.
Sonnets. No. xxv.
Then ten times happy me!—*Sonnets,* xxxvii.
O, what a happy title do I find,
Happy to have thy love, happy to die!
Sonnets. No. xcii.

6
Happy be thy speed!
The Taming of the Shrew. Act ii, sc. 1, l. 139. [Baptista]
He is gone happy.—*Timon of Athens,* i, 2, 4.

7
Might we but have that happiness, my lord, that you would once use our hearts, whereby we might express some part of our zeals, we should think ourselves for ever perfect.
Timon of Athens. Act i, sc. 2, l. 86. [Lord]
Wish me partaker in thy happiness.—*The Two Gentlemen of Verona,* i, 1, 14.
Seal our happiness.—*The Two Gentlemen of Verona,* i, 3, 49.

8
What his happier affairs may be, are to me unknown.
Winter's Tale. Act iv, sc. 2, l. 34. [Camillo]

HARE

See also under Lion

9
You are the hare of whom the proverb goes,
Whose valour plucks dead lions by the beard.
King John. Act ii, sc. 1, l. 137. [Bastard]
Coward hares.—*Cymbeline,* iv, 4, 37.
Poulter's hare.—*I Henry IV,* ii, 4, 481. The only use of "poulter."

10
Romeo: What hast thou found?
Mercutio: No hare, sir; unless a hare, sir, in a lenten pie, that is something stale and hoar ere it be spent.
An old hare hoar,
And an old hare hoar,
Is very good meat in lent:
But a hare that is hoar
Is too much for a score,
When it hoars ere it be spent.
Romeo and Juliet. Act ii, sc. 4, l. 137.

11
The timorous flying hare.
Venus and Adonis, l. 674.
Fearful flying hare.—*III Henry VI,* ii, 5, 130.
When thou hast on foot the purblind hare,
Mark the poor wretch, to overshoot his troubles
How he outruns the wind and with what care
He cranks and crosses with a thousand doubles:
The many musets through the which he goes
Are like a labyrinth to amaze his foes.
Venus and Adonis, l. 679. The only use of "musets" (gaps in hedges).
Sometime he runs among a flock of sheep,
To make the cunning hounds mistake their smell.
Venus and Adonis, l. 685.
Poor Wat, far off upon a hill,
Stands on his hinder legs with listening ear,
To hearken if his foes pursue him still.
Venus and Adonis, l. 697. The only use of "Wat."
Holloa me like a hare.—*Coriolanus,* i, 8, 7.
What sayest thou to a hare?—*I Henry IV,* i, 2, 87.

HARLOT, see Whore

HARM

See also Injury, Mischief, Wrong

12
Though yet he never harm'd me, here I quit him.
All's Well that Ends Well. Act v, sc. 3, l. 300. [Diana]

13
Ten thousand harms, more than the ills I know,
My idleness doth hatch.
Antony and Cleopatra. Act i, sc. 2, l. 133. [Antony]
Thousand harms.—*The Taming of the Shrew,* Ind., 2, 138.
Confineless harms.—*Macbeth,* iv, 3, 55.
Foul harms!—*The Rape of Lucrece,* l. 199.
Outward harm.—*The Rape of Lucrece,* l. 91.
Violent harms.—*King Lear,* iv, 7, 28.

1
They will surely do us no harm.
The Comedy of Errors. Act iv, sc. 4, l. 156. [Dromio of Syracuse]

I do suspect you, madam;
But you shall do no harm.
Cymbeline. Act i, sc. 5, l. 31. [Cornelius]

2
Pisanio: My lord your son drew on my master.
Queen: Ha! No harm, I trust, is done?
Pisanio: There might have been,
But that my master rather play'd than fought
And had no help of anger.
Cymbeline. Act i, sc. 1, l. 159.

That I suffer'd Was all the harm I did.
Cymbeline. Act v, sc. 5, l. 335. [Belarius]

Harm not yourself.—*Cymbeline,* i, 1, 134.

3
Thou hast done much harm upon me, Hal; God forgive thee for it! Before I knew thee, Hal, I knew nothing; and now am I, if a man should speak truly, little better than one of the wicked.
I Henry IV. Act i, sc. 2, l. 102. [Falstaff]

To say I know more harm in him than in myself, were to say more than I know.
I Henry IV. Act ii, sc. 4, l. 512. [Falstaff]

4
She hath been then more fear'd than harm'd.
Henry V. Act i, sc. 2, l. 155. [Canterbury]

Orleans: He never did harm, that I heard of.
Constable: Nor will do none to-morrow: he will keep that good name still.
Henry V. Act iii, sc. 7, l. 109.

Follow, and see there be no harm between them.
Henry V. Act iv, sc. 7, l. 190. [King Henry]

5
He thought no harm.
I Henry VI. Act iv, sc. 1, l. 179. [Warwick]

Think no harm.—*Richard III,* i, 3, 51; *Love's Labour's Lost,* i, 1, 44.

'Twere best he speak no harm of Brutus here.
Julius Cæsar. Act iii, sc. 2, l. 73. [Citizen]

Hear no harm.—*The Taming of the Shrew,* i, 2, 189.

Saw no harm.—*Othello,* iv, 2, 4.

Take no harm.—*King Lear,* iii, 6, 46.

6
I never did thee harm.
III Henry VI. Act i, sc. 3, l. 38. [Rutland]

Alcibiades: I never did thee harm.
Timon: Yes, thou spokest well of me.
Alcibiades: Call'st thou that harm?
Timon: Men daily find it. Get thee away, and take
Thy beagles with thee.
Timon of Athens. Act iv, sc. 3, l. 172. "Beagle" is repeated in *Twelfth Night,* ii, 3, 195.

But indeed I can do you little harm.
Measure for Measure. Act iii, sc. 2, l. 176. [Duke]

I have done no harm.—*Macbeth,* iv, 2, 75; 79.

We will do no harm.—*A Midsummer-Night's Dream,* iii, 1, 19.

It shall do you no harm.—*All's Well that Ends Well,* ii, 2, 39.

7
To do them good, I would sustain some harm.
III Henry VI. Act iii, sc. 2, l. 39. [Lady Grey]

8
From this league
Peep'd harms that menaced him.
Henry VIII. Act i, sc. 1, l. 182. [Buckingham]

Tush, It can do me no damage.
Henry VIII. Act i, sc. 2, l. 182. [Surveyor] "Damage" is repeated in *Richard III,* iv, 2, 60, and in *Troilus and Cressida,* ii, 2, 3.

9
Portia: Why, know'st thou any harm 's intended towards him?
Soothsayer: None that I know will be, much that I fear may chance.
Julius Cæsar. Act ii, sc. 4, l. 31.

There is no harm intended to your person
Nor to no Roman else.
Julius Cæsar. Act iii, sc. 1, l. 90. [Brutus]

10
Salisbury: What other harm have I, good lady, done,
But spoke the harm that is by others done?
Constance: Which harm within itself so heinous is
As it makes harmful all that speak of it.
King John. Act iii, sc. 1, l. 38.

Be no further harmful.—*King John,* v, 2, 77.

But yet more harmful.—*Richard III,* iv, 4, 172.

I doubt
My uncle practises more harm to me.
King John. Act iv, sc. 1, l. 19. [Arthur]

If heaven be pleased that you must use me ill,
Why then you must.
King John. Act iv, sc. 1, l. 55. [Arthur]

Lo, by my troth, the instrument is cold
And would not harm me.
King John. Act iv, sc. 1, l. 105. [Arthur]

11
Most power to do most harm, least knowing ill.
Love's Labour's Lost. Act ii, sc. 1, l. 58. [Katharina]

12
Harm have I done to them, but ne'er was harm'd.
A Lover's Complaint, l. 194.

13
None of woman born Shall harm Macbeth.
Macbeth. Act iv, sc. 1, l. 81. [Apparition]

14
How could Master Froth do the constable's wife any harm?
Measure for Measure. Act ii, sc. 1, l. 165. [Pompey]

15
Lysander: Be not afraid; she shall not harm thee, Helena.
Demetrius: No, sir, she shall not, though you take her part.
A Midsummer-Night's Dream. Act iii, sc. 2, l. 321.

I'll not harm her.—*A Midsummer-Night's Dream,* iii, 2, 270.

16
Yet bend not all the harm upon yourself;

Make those that do offend you suffer, too.
Much Ado about Nothing. Act v, sc. 1, l. 39. [Antonio]

1
Iago: To be naked with her friend in bed
An hour or more, not meaning any harm?
Othello: Naked in bed, Iago, and not mean harm!
It is hypocrisy against the devil:
They that mean virtuously, and yet do so,
The devil their virtue tempts, and they tempt heaven.
Othello. Act iv, sc. 1, l. 3.

Thou hast not half that power to do me harm
As I have to be hurt.
Othello. Act v, sc. 2, l. 162. [Emilia]

2
A little harm done to a great good end
For lawful policy remains enacted.
The Rape of Lucrece, l. 528.

3 Alack, alack, for woe,
That any harm should stain so fair a show!
Richard II. Act iii, sc. 3, l. 70. [York]

4
Queen Elizabeth: If he were dead, what would betide of me?
Rivers: No other harm but loss of such a lord.
Queen Elizabeth: The loss of such a lord includes all harm.
Richard III. Act i, sc. 3, l. 6.

5
None can cure their harms by wailing them.
Richard III. Act ii, sc. 2, l. 103. [Gloucester]

Where every horse bears his commanding rein,
And may direct his course as please himself,
As well the fear of harm, as harm apparent,
In my opinion, ought to be prevented.
Richard III. Act ii, sc. 2, l. 128. [Buckingham]

Wish thyself no harm.—*Richard III,* iv, 1, 65.

6 Tell your piteous heart
There 's no harm done.
The Tempest. Act i, sc. 2, l. 14. [Prospero]

She loves thee, boy, too well to do thee harm.
Titus Andronicus. Act iv, sc. 1, l. 6. [Titus]

Do thee harm!—*Richard II,* ii, 1, 231.

7
You know a sword employ'd is perilous,
And reason flies the object of all harm.
Troilus and Cressida. Act ii, sc. 2, l. 40. [Troilus]

Why, 'tis this naming of him does him harm.
Troilus and Cressida. Act ii, sc. 3, l. 239. [Ulysses]

8
Whoop, do me no harm, good man.
Winter's Tale, iv, 4, 201. See under Song.

Good masters, harm me not.—*Cymbeline,* iii, 6, 46.

Here 's no harm intended to thee.—*The Winter's Tale,* iv, 4, 642.

HARMONY

See also Music

9
These cannot I command to any utterance of harmony.
Hamlet. Act iii, sc. 2, l. 377. [Guildenstern]

10
How irksome is this music to my heart!
When such strings jar, what hope of harmony?
II Henry VI. Act ii, sc. 1, l. 56. [King Henry] "Irksome" is repeated in *The Taming of the Shrew,* i, 2, 188: "Irksome brawling scold"; and in *As You Like It,* iii, 5, 95: "Irksome to me."

11 Soft stillness and the night
Become the touches of sweet harmony.
The Merchant of Venice. Act v, sc. 1, l. 56. [Lorenzo]

Such harmony is in immortal souls;
But whilst this muddy vesture of decay
Doth grossly close it in, we cannot hear it.
The Merchant of Venice. Act v, sc. 1, l. 63. [Lorenzo]

12
I do Protest my ears were never better fed
With such delightful pleasing harmony.
Pericles. Act ii, sc. 5, l. 27. [Simonides]

Celestial harmony.—*Henry VIII,* iv, 2, 80.
Deceiving harmony.—*Venus and Adonis,* l. 781.
Deep harmony.—*Richard II,* ii, 1, 6.
Enchanting harmony.—*Love's Labour's Lost,* i, 1, 168.
Household harmony.—*III Henry VI,* iv, 6, 14.
Sweet harmony.—*Pericles,* v, 1, 45.
Harmony of this peace.—*Cymbeline,* v, 5, 467.
Harmony of their tongues.—*Tempest,* iii, 1, 41.
Tune the harmony.—*Richard II,* i, 3, 165.

13
What harmony is this? My good friends, hark!
The Tempest. Act iii, sc. 3, l. 18. [Alonso]

Harmonious charmingly.
The Tempest. Act iv, sc. 1, l. 119. [Ferdinand] "Harmonious" is repeated in *A Midsummer-Night's Dream,* ii, 1, 151. The only use of "charmingly."

14
Or, had he heard the heavenly harmony
Which that sweet tongue hath made,
He would have dropp'd his knife, and fell asleep
As Cerberus at the Thracian poet's feet.
Titus Andronicus. Act ii, sc. 4, l. 48. [Marcus] Cerberus is mentioned again in *Love's Labour's Lost,* v, 2, 593; *II Henry IV,* ii, 4, 182; and *Troilus and Cressida,* ii, 1, 37. "Thracian" is used five times.

Heavenly harmony.—*Taming of the Shrew,* iii, 1, 5.

15
He is full of harmony.
Troilus and Cressida. Act iii, sc. 1, l. 56. [Paris]

HARSHNESS

16 Why, trow'st thou, Warwick,
That Clarence is so harsh?
III Henry VI. Act v, sc. 1, l. 85. [Clarence]

17
Turn'd her obedience . . . To stubborn harshness.
A Midsummer-Night's Dream. Act i, sc. 1, l. 37. [Egeus]

He 's composed of harshness.
The Tempest. Act iii, sc. 1, l. 9. [Ferdinand] The only uses of "harshness."

1 Harsh to hear.
The Taming of the Shrew, iii, 2, 107. [Petruchio]

Harsh hearing.—*The Taming of the Shrew,* v, 2, 183.

Harsh in sound.—*Coriolanus,* iv, 5, 65.

Harsh and heavy.—*Henry VIII,* iv, 2, 95.

Too harsh a descant.—*The Two Gentlemen of Verona,* i, 2, 94. See under DISCORD.

Harsh, untuneable and bad.—*The Two Gentlemen of Verona,* iii, 1, 208. "Untuneable" is repeated in *As You Like It,* v, 3, 37.

HARVEST

2 The seedsman
Upon the slime and ooze scatters his grain,
And shortly comes to harvest.
Antony and Cleopatra, ii, 7, 24. See under RIVER. The only use of "seedsman."

Come to harvest.—*Twelfth Night,* iii, 1, 143.

Became a harvest.—*Cymbeline,* i, 1, 46.

3 They that reap must sheaf and bind.
As You Like It. Act iii, sc. 2, l. 113. [Touchstone] "Sheaf" is repeated in *Titus Andronicus,* v, 3, 71.

Like to a harvest-man that 's task'd to mow
Or all or lose his hire.
Coriolanus. Act i, sc. 3, l. 39. [Volumnia] The only use of "harvest-man."

Mow down thorns.—*II Henry VI,* iii, 1, 67.

Mow all down.—*Coriolanus,* iv, 5, 214.

Mow 'em down.—*Henry VIII,* v, 4, 23.

4 Reap the harvest which that rascal sow'd.
II Henry VI. Act iii, sc. 1, l. 381. [York]

That harvest reap.—*Sonnets,* cxxviii.

I 'll blast his harvest, if your head were laid.
III Henry VI. Act v, sc. 7, l. 21. [Gloucester]

5 Scarce show a harvest of their heavy toil.
Love's Labour 's Lost. Act iv, sc. 3, l. 326. [Biron]

Harvest of perpetual peace.—*Richard III,* v, 2, 15.

Harvest of his wits.—*Rape of Lucrece,* l. 859.

Main harvest.—*As You Like It,* iii, 5, 103.

6 Our corn 's to reap, for yet our tithe 's to sow.
Measure for Measure. Act iv, sc. 1, l. 76. [Duke]

Harvest of that corn.—*I Henry VI,* iii, 2, 47.

7 There 's my harvest-home.
The Merry Wives of Windsor, ii, 2, 287. "Harvest-home" is used again in *I Henry IV,* i, 3, 35.

8 It is needful that you frame the season for your own harvest.
Much Ado about Nothing. Act i, sc. 3, l. 26. [Conrade]

The harvest is your own.—*Macbeth,* i, 4, 33.

9 Thou hast the harvest out of thine own report.
Pericles. Act iv, sc. 2, l. 152. [Bawd]

10 Though we have spent our harvest of this king,
We are to reap the harvest of his son.
Richard III. Act ii, sc. 2, l. 115. [Buckingham]

11 You sunburnt sicklemen, of August weary,
Come hither from the furrow and be merry:
Make holiday; your rye-straw hats put on
And these fresh nymphs encounter every one
In country footing.
The Tempest. Act iv, sc. 1, l. 134. [Iris] The only use of "sicklemen" and "rye-straw."

The very end of harvest!—*Tempest,* iv, 1, 115.

HASTE

See also Expedition, Speed, Swiftness

12 This haste hath wings indeed.
All's Well that Ends Well. Act ii, sc. 1, l. 96. [King]

I am there before my legs.
All's Well that Ends Well. Act ii, sc. 2, l. 73. [Clown]

My haste is very great.
All's Well that Ends Well. Act ii, sc. 5, l. 82. [Bertram]

I am in great haste.—*The Merry Wives of Windsor,* i, 4, 174; *Much Ado about Nothing,* iii, 5, 54.

Make great haste.—*Henry VIII,* v, 2, 3.

13 I must with haste from hence.
Antony and Cleopatra. Act i, sc. 2, l. 136. [Antony]

Our pleasure . . . requires
Our quick remove from hence.
Antony and Cleopatra. Act i, sc. 2, l. 201. [Antony]

Make your soonest haste.
Antony and Cleopatra. Act iii, sc. 4, l. 27. [Antony]

Go put it to the haste.
Antony and Cleopatra. Act v, sc. 2, l. 196. [Cleopatra]

14 What might be toward, that this sweaty haste
Doth make the night joint-labourer with the day.
Hamlet. Act i, sc. 1, l. 77. [Marcellus] The only use of "joint-labourer." "Sweaty" is repeated in *Julius Cæsar,* i, 2, 247: "Sweaty night-caps."

Farewell, and let your haste commend your duty.
Hamlet. Act i, sc. 2, l. 39. [Horatio]

We will haste us.—*Hamlet,* iii, 3, 26.

I pray you, haste in this.—*Hamlet,* iv, 1, 37.

The ocean, overpeering of his list,
Eats not the flats with more impetuous haste.
Hamlet. Act iv, sc. 5, l. 99. [Gentleman] The only use of "overpeering."

1
This haste was hot in question.
I Henry IV. Act i, sc. 1, l. 34. [Westmoreland]

2
Whither away, Sir John Fastolfe, in such haste?
I Henry VI. Act iii, sc. 2, l. 104. [Captain]

How now! what news? why comest thou in such haste?
II Henry VI. Act iv, sc. 4, l. 26. [King Henry]

Let's make haste away.—*II Henry VI*, i, 1, 208.

3
In haste, post-haste, are come to join with you.
III Henry VI. Act ii, sc. 1, l. 139. [Warwick]

Hath sent post haste.
Richard II. Act i, sc. 4, l. 55. [Bushy]

This post-haste and romage in the land.
Hamlet. Act i, sc. 1, l. 107. [Horatio] The only use of "romage" (commotion).

The duke . . . requires your haste-post-haste appearance.
Othello. Act i, sc. 2, l. 36. [Cassio] The only use of "haste-post-haste."

Post-post-haste dispatch.—*Othello*, i, 3, 46. The only use of the phrase.

4
Forslow no longer, make we hence amain.
III Henry VI. Act ii, sc. 3, l. 56. [George] The only use of "forslow."

Haste is needful in this desperate case.
III Henry VI. Act iv, sc. 1, l. 129. [King Edward]

The time and case requireth haste.
III Henry VI. Act iv, sc. 5, l. 18. [Gloucester]

It seems you are in haste.—*Henry VIII*, v, 1, 11.

5
He's sudden, if a thing comes in his head.
III Henry VI. Act v, sc. 5, l. 86. [King Edward]

But, sirs, be sudden in the execution.
Richard III. Act i, sc. 3, l. 346. [Gloucester]

I will be sudden and dispatch.
King John. Act iv, sc. 1, l. 27. [Hubert]

Do this suddenly.
As You Like It. Act ii, sc. 2, l. 19. [Duke]

There was never anything so sudden but the fight of two rams.
As You Like It. Act v, sc. 2, l. 33. [Rosalind]

That's somewhat sudden.—*Henry VIII*, iii, 2, 394.

6
Here comes one in haste.
Julius Cæsar. Act i, sc. 3, l. 131. [Casca]

Where haste you so?—*Julius Cæsar*, i, 3, 133.

Leave me with haste.—*Julius Cæsar*, ii, 1, 309.

But who comes in such haste?—*King John*, i, 1, 217.

7
We must do something, and i' the heat.
King Lear. Act i, sc. 1, l. 312. [Goneril]

Not so hot.—*King Lear*, v, 3, 66.

Hot with haste.—*King John*, iv, 3, 74.

Stew'd in his haste.—*King Lear*, ii, 4, 31.

8
All this done Upon the gad!
King Lear. Act i, sc. 2, l. 25. [Gloucester] "Gad" occurs once again in *Titus Andronicus*, iv, 1, 103: "Gad of steel."

9
Edmund: Your haste Is now urged on you.
Albany: We will greet the time.
King Lear. Act iii, sc. 1, l. 53.

Haste thee, for thy life.—*King Lear*, v, 3, 251.

Haste you speedily.—*Measure for Measure*, iii, 1, 273.

Hasten on.—*The Two Gentlemen of Verona*, i, 3, 77.

Hasten . . . to bed.—*Romeo and Juliet*, iii, 3, 156.

Hasten your return.—*King Lear*, i, 4, 363.

10
You must not be so quick.
Love's Labour's Lost. Act ii, sc. 1, l. 118. [Biron]

Quick proceeders, marry!
Taming of the Shrew. Act iv, sc. 2, l. 11. [Hortensio] The only use of "proceeders."

Quick, quick!—*The Merchant of Venice*, ii, 9, 1; *I Henry IV*, iii, 1, 230; *The Merry Wives of Windsor*, iv, 2, 84; *Othello*, v, 1, 3; *Antony and Cleopatra*, v, 2, 39.

11 Modest wisdom plucks me
From over-credulous haste.
Macbeth. Act iv, sc. 3, l. 119. [Malcolm] The only use of "over-credulous."

Continual haste.—*Sonnets*, cxxiii.

Expedient haste.—*King John*, iv, 2, 268.

Moderate haste.—*Hamlet*, i, 2, 238.

Modest haste.—*King Lear*, ii, 4, 25.

Nimble haste.—*King John*, iv, 2, 197.

Rash haste.—*King John*, ii, 1, 49.

Winged haste.—*I Henry IV*, iv, 4, 2.

12
Our haste from hence is of so quick condition
That it prefers itself and leaves unquestion'd
Matters of needful value.
Measure for Measure. Act i, sc. 1, l. 54. [Duke]

I will about it straight.
Measure for Measure. Act i, sc. 4, l. 85. [Isabella]

How now! what noise? That spirit's possessed with haste
That wounds the unsisting postern with these strokes.
Measure for Measure. Act iv, sc. 2, l. 91. [Duke] The only use of "unsisting" (unassisting).

13
I'll take my leave of the Jew in the twinkling of an eye.
The Merchant of Venice. Act ii, sc. 2, l. 177. [Launcelot] The only use of "twinkling of an eye."

Ay, with a twink.
The Tempest. Act iv, sc. 1, l. 43. [Prospero]

In a twink she won me.
The Taming of the Shrew, ii, 1, 312. The only uses of "twink."

1 Therefore haste away,
For we must measure twenty miles to-day.
The Merchant of Venice. Act iii, sc. 4, l. 83. [Portia]

Away! make haste: thou know'st where I will tarry.
The Merchant of Venice. Act iv, sc. 2, l. 18. [Portia]

Soft! no haste.—*The Merchant of Venice,* iv, 1, 321.

2
Trudge with it in all haste, and carry it among the whitsters in Datchet-mead.
The Merry Wives of Windsor. Act iii, sc. 3, l. 14. [Mrs. Ford] The only use of "whitsters" (bleachers of linen).

Speak, breathe, discuss; brief, short, quick, snap.
The Merry Wives of Windsor. Act iv, sc. 5, l. 2. [Host]

3 Be thou here again
Ere the leviathan can swim a league.
A Midsummer-Night's Dream. Act ii, sc. 1, l. 173. [Oberon] Leviathan is mentioned again in *Henry V,* iii, 3, 26, and *The Two Gentlemen of Verona,* iii, 2, 80.

But, notwithstanding, haste; make no delay;
We may effect this business yet ere day.
A Midsummer-Night's Dream. Act iii, sc. 2, l. 394. [Oberon]

4
His unhallow'd haste her words delays.
The Rape of Lucrece, l. 552.

Return again in haste.—*The Rape of Lucrece,* l. 321.

5
The cause craves haste.
The Rape of Lucrece, l. 1295.

His designs crave haste, his haste good hope.
Richard II. Act ii, sc. 2, l. 44. [Queen]

The affair cries haste,
And speed must answer it.
Othello. Act i, sc. 3, l. 277. [Duke]

6 To hie as fast
As lagging fowls before the northern blast.
The Rape of Lucrece, l. 1334. "Lagging" is repeated in *Richard II,* i, 3, 214: "Lagging winters."

Hie you, make haste, for it grows very late.
Romeo and Juliet. Act iii, sc. 3, l. 164. [Nurse]

Hie hence.—*Romeo and Juliet,* iii, 5, 26; *Julius Cæsar,* iii, 1, 290.

Hie thee (you) home.—*The Taming of the Shrew,* iv, 4, 62, and seven times in later plays.

Hie thee to hell.—*Richard III,* i, 3, 143.

Hie thee to thy charge.—*Richard III,* v, 3, 53.

Hie to the Goths.—*Titus Andronicus,* iii, 1, 286.

Hie to the field.—*Henry V,* iii, 5, 39.

Hie to your chamber.—*Romeo and Juliet,* iii, 2, 138.

Hie you to church.—*Romeo and Juliet,* ii, 5, 74.

Hie you to horse.—*Macbeth,* iii, 1, 35.

Well, I will hie.—*Julius Cæsar,* i, 3, 150.

7
Pray God we may make haste, and come too late!
Richard II. Act i, sc. 4, l. 64. [King Richard]

Make haste.—*Richard III,* iii, 3, 23; and sixteen times in later plays.

8
He tires betimes that spurs too fast betimes.
Richard II. Act ii, sc. 1, l. 36. [Gaunt]

Bloody with spurring, fiery-red with haste.
Richard II. Act ii, sc. 3, l. 58. [Northumberland]

9
Make all the speedy haste you may.
Richard III. Act iii, sc. 1, l. 60. [Prince]

The loving haste of these our friends.
Richard III. Act iii, sc. 5, l. 54. [Gloucester]

In all haste.—*Richard III,* iv, 1, 57.

10
Art thou so hasty? I have stay'd for thee,
God knows, in anguish, pain and agony.
Richard III. Act iv, sc. 4, l. 162. [Duchess of York]

Are you so hasty now?
Much Ado about Nothing. Act v, sc. 1, l. 49. [Leonato]

Is he so hasty?—*II Henry IV,* iv, 5, 61.

Be not so hasty.—*Richard III,* iv, 4, 261.

11
Come, bustle, bustle.
Richard III. Act v, sc. 3, l. 289. [King Richard]

And leave the world for me to bustle in.
Richard III, i, 1, 152. The only uses of "bustle."

12
Romeo: O, let us hence; I stand on sudden haste.
Friar Laurence: Wisely and slow; they stumble that run fast.
Romeo and Juliet. Act ii, sc. 3, l. 93.

Stumble with haste.—*Love's Labour's Lost,* ii, 1, 239.

13
Jesu, what haste? can you not stay awhile?
Do you not see that I am out of breath?
Romeo and Juliet. Act ii, sc. 5, l. 29. [Nurse]

I am nothing slow to slack his haste.
Romeo and Juliet. Act iv, sc. 1, l. 3. [Paris]

Paris: Now do you know the reason of this haste.
Friar Laurence: I would I knew not why it should be slow'd.
Romeo and Juliet. Act iv, sc. 1, l. 15. The only use of "slow'd."

Do you like this haste?—*Romeo and Juliet,* iii, 4, 22.

I wonder at this haste.—*Romeo and Juliet,* iii, 5, 119.

14
Before you can say 'come' and 'go,'
And breathe twice and cry 'so, so,'
Each one, tripping on his toe,
Will be here with mop and mow.
The Tempest. Act iv, sc. 1, l. 44. [Ariel] The only use of "mop."

I drink the air before me, and return
Or ere your pulse twice beat.
The Tempest. Act v, sc. 1, l. 102. [Ariel]

Bestir, bestir.—*The Tempest,* i, 1, 4. The only use of "bestir."

15
In all swift haste.
Troilus and Cressida. Act i, sc. 1, l. 119. [Æneas]

Posts, like the commandment of a king,
Sans check to good and bad.
Troilus and Cressida. Act i, sc. 3, l. 93. [Ulysses]

1
I scarce have leisure to salute you,
My matter is so rash.
Troilus and Cressida. Act iv, sc. 2, l. 61. [Æneas]

My haste made me unmannerly.
Henry VIII. Act iv, sc. 2, l. 105. [Messenger]

2
Blame not this haste of mine.
Twelfth Night. Act iv, sc. 3, l. 22. [Olivia]

Will you make haste?—*The Two Gentlemen of Verona,* ii, 4, 190.

3
Her more than haste is mated with delays.
Venus and Adonis, l. 909.

And in her haste unfortunately spies
The foul boar's conquest on her fair delight.
Venus and Adonis, l. 1029. The only use of "unfortunately."

4
Take the urgent hour.
The Winter's Tale. Act i, sc. 2, l. 465. [Camillo] "Urgent" is repeated in *Antony and Cleopatra,* i, 2, 187: "Urgent touches."

Make your best haste.
Winter's Tale. Act iii, sc. 3, l. 10. [Mariner]

HAT

See also Cap

5
Delicate fine hats and most courteous feathers.
All's Well that Ends Well. Act iv, sc. 5, l. 110. [Clown]

6
You have caused
Your holy hat to be stamped on the king's coin.
Henry VIII, iii, 2, 325. See under AMBITION.

Cardinal's hat.—*I Henry VI,* i, 3, 49.

Broad cardinal's hat.—*I Henry VI,* i, 3, 36.

7
Their hats are pluck'd about their ears.
Julius Cæsar. Act ii, sc. 1, l. 73. [Lucius]

Your hat penthouse-like o'er the shop of your eyes.
Love's Labour's Lost. Act iii, sc. 1, l. 18. [Moth] "Pent-house" occurs again in *Merchant of Venice,* ii, 6, 1; *Much Ado about Nothing,* iii, 3, 110; and *Macbeth,* i, 3, 20.

Ne'er pull your hat upon your brows.
Macbeth, iv, 3, 208. See under GRIEF.

Take your sweetheart's hat
And pluck it o'er your brows.
The Winter's Tale, iv, 4, 664. See under DISGUISE.

8
My hat to a halfpenny.
Love's Labour's Lost, v, 2, 563. See under WAGER.

By this hat.—*The Merry Wives of Windsor,* i, 1, 173.

9
Upon her head a platted hive of straw,
Which fortified her visage from the sun.
A Lover's Complaint, l. 8. The only use of "platted."

There's her thrummed hat.—*The Merry Wives of Windsor,* iv, 2, 80. The only use of "thrummed" (made of thrums, or waste yarn).

Cockle hat.—*Hamlet,* iv, 5, 25.

Colour'd hat.—*Taming of the Shrew,* i, 1, 212.

Copatain hat.—*The Taming of the Shrew,* v, 1, 70. The only use of "copatain" (sugar-loaf).

Rye-straw hats.—*The Tempest,* iv, 1, 136. The only use of "rye-straw."

Sheaved hat.—*A Lover's Complaint,* l. 31. The only use of "sheaved" (made of straw).

10
A' brushes his hat o' mornings: what should that bode?
Much Ado about Nothing, iii, 2, 42. See LOVE: ITS MANIFESTATIONS, 900:8.

11
An old hat and 'the humour of forty fancies' pricked in 't for a feather.
The Taming of the Shrew. Act iii, sc. 2, l. 69. [Biondello]

New hat.—*The Taming of the Shrew,* iii, 2, 43.

12
With one fair hand she heaveth up his hat.
Venus and Adonis, l. 351.

No hat upon his head.—*Hamlet,* ii, 1, 79.

Nay, you shall have no hat.—*The Winter's Tale,* iv, 4, 672.

Putting off his hat.—*II Henry IV,* ii, 4, 7.

Put on a hat.—*The Merry Wives of Windsor,* iv, 2, 73.

Wear their hats.—*Richard III,* iii, 2, 95.

13
And with his bonnet hides his angry brow.
Venus and Adonis, l. 339.

Bonnet nor veil henceforth no creature wear.
Venus and Adonis, l. 1081.

He put his bonnet on,
Under whose brim the gaudy sun would peep.
Venus and Adonis, l. 1087.

Put your bonnet to his right use; 'tis for the head.
Hamlet. Act v, sc. 2, l. 95. [Hamlet]

Go to them, with this bonnet in thy hand.
Coriolanus. Act iii, sc. 2, l. 73. [Volumnia]

He bought . . . his bonnet in Germany.
The Merchant of Venice. Act i, sc. 2, l. 81. [Portia]

Off goes his bonnet to an oyster-wench.
Richard II. Act i, sc. 4, l. 31. [King Richard] The only use of "oyster-wench."

Your bonnet unbanded.—*As You Like It,* iii, 2, 398.

Wear it in thy bonnet.—*Henry V,* iv, 1, 224. The only uses of "bonnet." "Bonneted" occurs in *Coriolanus,* ii, 2, 30.

HATE

See also Love and Hate; Rancour

14
Thou didst hate her deadly, And she is dead.
All's Well that Ends Well. Act v, sc. 3, l. 117. [King]

15
I cannot hate thee worser than I do.
Antony and Cleopatra. Act ii, sc. 5, l. 90. [Cleopatra]

I never hated thee.—*Antony and Cleopatra,* ii, 6, 76.

Hate of mankind.—*Antony and Cleopatra,* iv, 8, 25.

1
My soul, yet I know not why, hates nothing more than he.
As You Like It. Act i, sc. 1, l. 174. [Oliver]
I should hate him, for my father hated his father dearly.
As You Like It. Act i, sc. 3, l. 34. [Celia]
I . . . owe no man hate.
As You Like It, iii, 2, 78. See under LABOUR.
Silvius, the time was that I hated thee.
As You Like It. Act iii, sc. 5, l. 92. [Phebe]
2
There is the man of my soul's hate.
Coriolanus. Act i, sc. 5, l. 16. [Marcius]
Marcius: I do hate thee
Worse than a promise-breaker.
Aufidius: We hate alike:
Not Afric owns a serpent I abhor
More than thy fame and envy.
Coriolanus. Act i, sc. 8, l. 1. "Promise-breaker" is repeated in *All's Well that Ends Well,* iii, 6, 12: "An hourly promise-breaker." "Afric" is used four times.
The prayers of priests nor times of sacrifice,
Embarquements all of fury, shall lift up
Their rotten privilege and custom 'gainst
My hate to Marcius.
Coriolanus. Act i, sc. 10, l. 21. [Aufidius] The only use of "embarquements."
He seeks their hate with greater devotion than they can render it him.
Coriolanus. Act ii, sc. 2, l. 21. [Officer]
I have ever followed thee with hate.
Coriolanus. Act iv, sc. 5, l. 104. [Coriolanus]
3 Learn now, for all,
That I, which know my heart, do here pronounce,
By the very truth of it, I care not for you,
And am so near the lack of charity—
To accuse myself—I hate you.
Cymbeline. Act ii, sc. 3, l. 111. [Imogen]
4
All the country in a general voice
Cried hate upon him.
II Henry IV. Act iv, sc. 1, l. 136. [Westmoreland]
5
No, if I digg'd up thy forefathers' graves
And hung their rotten coffins up in chains,
It could not slake mine ire, nor ease my heart.
III Henry VI. Act i, sc. 3, l. 27. [Clifford]
But that I hate thee deadly,
I should lament thy miserable state.
III Henry VI. Act i, sc. 4, l. 84. [Queen Margaret]
They seek for hatred at my hands.
III Henry VI. Act iv, sc. 1, l. 80. [King Edward]
6
What his high hatred would effect wants not
A minister in his power.
Henry VIII. Act i, sc. 1, l. 107. [Norfolk]
All the commons
Hate him perniciously, and, o' my conscience,
Wish him ten fathom deep.
Henry VIII. Act ii, sc. 1, l. 49. [Gentleman] The only use of "perniciously."
Hated by one he loves.—*Julius Cæsar,* iv, 3, 96.
7 Nothing do I see in you,
Though churlish thoughts themselves should be your judge,
That I can find should merit any hate.
King John. Act ii, sc. 1, l. 518. [Blanch]
8
No contraries hold more antipathy
Than I and such a knave.
King Lear. Act ii, sc. 2, l. 93. [Kent] The only use of "antipathy."
Thou call'st on him that hates thee.
King Lear. Act iii, sc. 7, l. 88. [Regan]
Let sorrow split my heart, if ever I
Did hate thee or thy father!
King Lear. Act v, sc. 3, l. 177. [Albany]
9
But yet I'll go in hate, to feed upon
The prodigal Christian.
The Merchant of Venice. Act ii, sc. 5, l. 14. [Shylock]
A lodged hate and a certain loathing.
The Merchant of Venice. Act iv, sc. 1, l. 60. [Shylock]
Deepest loathing.—*A Midsummer-Night's Dream,* ii, 2, 138.
Even to loathing.—*Pericles,* ii, 4, 10. The only uses of "loathing."
10
Why seek'st thou me? could not this make thee know,
The hate I bear thee made me leave thee so?
A Midsummer-Night's Dream. Act iii, sc. 2, l. 189. [Lysander]
'Tis no jest That I do hate thee.
A Midsummer-Night's Dream. Act iii, sc. 2, l. 280. [Lysander]
Tempt not too much the hatred of my spirit.
A Midsummer-Night's Dream. Act ii, sc. 1, l. 211. [Demetrius]
I am sure you hate me with your hearts.
A Midsummer-Night's Dream. Act iii, sc. 2, l. 154. [Helena]
Lysander: Although I hate her, I'll not harm her so.
Hermia: What, can you do me greater harm than hate?
A Midsummer-Night's Dream. Act iii, sc. 2, l. 270.
How comes this gentle concord in the world,
That hatred is so far from jealousy?
A Midsummer-Night's Dream. Act iv, sc. 1, l. 147. [Theseus]
11
Thou told'st me thou didst hold him in thy hate.
Othello. Act i, sc. 1, l. 7. [Roderigo]
Nought I did in hate.
Othello. Act v, sc. 2, l. 295. [Othello]
12 I am abused: and my relief
Must be to loathe her.
Othello. Act iii, sc. 3, l. 267. [Othello]
Loathe him.—*As You Like It,* iii, 2, 436.
Loathe his visage.—*A Midsummer-Night's Dream,* iv, 1, 84.
13
Free from other misbegotten hate.
Richard II. Act i, sc. 1, l. 33. [Bolingbroke]
Nor never write, regreet, nor reconcile

This louring tempest of your home-bred hate.
Richard II. Act i, sc. 3, l. 186. [King Richard] "Home-bred" occurs again in *III Henry VI*, iv, 1, 38. "Regreet" is used four times.

I 'll hate him everlastingly.—*Richard II*, iii, 2, 207.

1
The love of wicked men converts to fear;
That fear to hate, and hate turns one or both
To worthy danger and deserved death.
Richard II. Act v, sc. 1, l. 66. [King Richard]

In time we hate that which we often fear.
Antony and Cleopatra. Act i, sc. 3, l. 12. [Charmian]

2
What! I, that kill'd her husband and his father,
To take her in her heart's extremest hate,
With curses in her mouth, tears in her eyes,
The bleeding witness of her hatred by.
Richard III. Act i, sc. 2, l. 231. [Gloucester]

Your interior hatred,
Which in your outward actions shows itself.
Richard III. Act i, sc. 3, l. 65. [Queen Elizabeth]

What! were you snarling all before I came,
Ready to catch each other by the throat,
And turn you all your hatred now on me?
Richard III. Act i, sc. 3, l. 188. [Queen Margaret] The only use of "snarling."

Live each of you the subjects to his hate,
And he to yours, and all of you to God's!
Richard III. Act i, sc. 3, l. 302. [Queen Margaret]

He that set you on
To do this deed will hate you for the deed.
Richard III. Act i, sc. 4, l. 261. [Clarence]

3
By heaven, my heart is purged from grudging hate.
Richard III. Act ii, sc. 1, l. 9. [Rivers]

I will never more remember
Our former hatred, so I thrive I and mine!
Richard III. Act ii, sc. 1, l. 23. [Queen Elizabeth]

Cease their hatred.—*Henry V*, v, 2, 380.

Dissemble not your hatred.—*Richard III*, ii, 1, 8.

Kind in hatred.—*Richard III*, iv, 4, 172.

Seek for hatred.—*III Henry VI*, iv, 1, 80.

Urge his hatred.—*Richard III*, i, 1, 147.

High hatred.—*Henry VIII*, i, 1, 107.

Immodest hatred.—*Winter's Tale*, iii, 2, 103.

4
I bear no hatred, blessed man, for, lo,
My intercession likewise steads my foe.
Romeo and Juliet. Act ii, sc. 3, l. 53. [Romeo]

The hate I bear thee can afford
No better term than this,—thou art a villain.
Romeo and Juliet. Act iii, sc. 1, l. 63. [Tybalt]

5
For thou art so possess'd with murderous hate
That 'gainst thyself thou stick'st not to conspire,
Seeking that beauteous roof to ruinate
Which to repair should be thy chief desire.
Sonnets. No. x. "Ruinate" occurs again in *III Henry VI*, v, 1, 83; *Titus Andronicus*, v, 3, 204; and *The Rape of Lucrece*, l. 944.

Then hate me when thou wilt; if ever, now.
Sonnets. No. xc.

Shoot not at me in your waken'd hate.
Sonnets. No. cxvii.

Past reason hated.—*Sonnets*, cxxix.

6
'I hate' she alter'd with an end,
That follow'd it as gentle day
Doth follow night, who like a fiend
From heaven to hell is flown away;
'I hate' from hate away she threw,
And saved my life, saying 'not you.'
Sonnets. No. cxlv.

Hate on, for now I know thy mind.
Sonnets. No. cxlix.

7
They all do hate him As rootedly as I.
The Tempest. Act iii, sc. 2, l. 102. [Caliban] The only use of "rootedly."

8
Burn, house! sink, Athens! henceforth hated be
Of Timon man and all humanity!
Timon of Athens. Act iii, sc. 6, l. 114. [Timon]

Grant, as Timon grows, his hate may grow
To the whole race of mankind, high and low!
Timon of Athens. Act iv, sc. 1, l. 39. [Timon]

How fain would I have hated all mankind!
Timon of Athens. Act iv, sc. 3, l. 506. [Timon]

Hate all.—*Timon of Athens*, iv, 3, 534.

9
No space of earth shall sunder our two hates.
Troilus and Cressida. Act v, sc. 10, l. 27. [Troilus]

Barren hate.—*The Tempest*, iv, 1, 19.

Blood-drinking hate.—*I Henry VI*, ii, 4, 108. "Blood-drinking" occurs again in *II Henry VI*, iii, 2, 63: "Blood-drinking sighs"; and in *Titus Andronicus*, ii, 3, 224: "Blood-drinking pit."

Canker'd hate.—*Romeo and Juliet*, i, 1, 102.

Deadly hate.—*II Henry VI*, iii, 2, 314; *Richard III*, i, 1, 35; *Richard II*, ii, 2, 131; iii, 2, 136.

Enforced hate.—*The Rape of Lucrece*, l. 668.

Inveterate hate.—*Coriolanus*, ii, 3, 234.

Settled hate.—*Richard II*, i, 1, 201.

Stormy hate.—*II Henry VI*, iii, 1, 155.

Waken'd hate.—*Sonnets*, cxvii.

10
Thurio, whom my very soul abhors.
The Two Gentlemen of Verona. Act iv, sc. 3, l. 17. [Silvia]

Few things loves better Than to abhor himself.
Timon of Athens. Act i, sc. 1, l. 59. [Poet]

Utterly abhor.—*Henry VIII*, ii, 4, 81.

11
I hate thee,
Pronounce thee a gross lout, a mindless slave,
Or else a hovering temporizer, that

Canst with thine eyes at once see good and evil.
The Winter's Tale. Act i, sc. 2, l. 300. [Leontes] The only use of "hovering" and "temporizer." "Mindless" occurs again in *Timon of Athens,* iv, 3, 93.

HAVOC

1
Cry, 'havoc!' kings; back to the stained field, ...
Then let confusion of one part confirm
The other's peace; till then, blows, blood and death!
King John. Act ii, sc. 1, l. 357. [Bastard] To cry "havoc," i. e., to give no quarter.

Cry 'Havoc,' and let slip the dogs of war.
Julius Cæsar. Act iii, sc. 1, l. 273. [Antony]

This quarry cries on havoc.
Hamlet. Act v, sc. 2, l. 375. [Horatio] "Quarry" is repeated in *Coriolanus,* i, 1, 202, and in *Macbeth,* iv, 3, 206.

Do not cry havoc, where you should but hunt
With modest warrant.
Coriolanus. Act iii, sc. 1, l. 275. [Menenius]

2 Wide havoc made
For bloody power to rush upon your peace.
King John. Act ii, sc. 1, l. 220. [King John]

Pell-mell havoc.—*I Henry IV,* v, 1, 82.

3
Who hath made this havoc with them?
Twelfth Night. Act v, sc. 1, l. 208. [Olivia]

Made such havoc.—*Much Ado about Nothing,* iv, 1, 197.

Tear and havoc.—*Henry V,* i, 2, 173. The only uses of "havoc."

HAWK, see Falcon

HAZARD

See also Chance, Uncertainty

4
To the extreme edge of hazard.
All's Well that Ends Well. Act iii, sc. 3, l. 6. [Bertram]

5
I hazarded the loss of whom I loved.
The Comedy of Errors. Act i, sc. 1, l. 132. [Ægeon]

Hazarded to thy grace.—*Antony and Cleopatra,* iii, 12, 19. The only uses of "hazarded."

6 You wot well
My hazards still have been your solace.
Coriolanus. Act iv, sc. 1, l. 27. [Coriolanus]

Yet he hath left undone
That which shall break his neck or hazard mine.
Coriolanus. Act iv, sc. 7, l. 24. [Aufidius]

Put in hazard.—*Coriolanus,* ii, 3, 264.

Hazard the winning.—*Cymbeline,* i, 4, 101.

7 Were it good
To set the exact wealth of all our states
All at one cast? to set so rich a main
On the nice hazard of one doubtful hour?
I Henry IV. Act iv, sc. 1, l. 45. [Hotspur]

O, too much folly is it, well I wot,
To hazard all our lives in one small boat!
I Henry VI. Act iv, sc. 6, l. 32. [Talbot]

8
Rambures: Who will go to hazard with me for twenty prisoners?
Constable: You must first go yourself to hazard, ere you have them.
Henry V. Act iii, sc. 7, l. 93.

9
Why, now, blow wind, swell billow and swim bark!
The storm is up, and all is on the hazard.
Julius Cæsar. Act v, sc. 1, l. 67. [Cassius]

10
A hazard of new fortunes.
King John. Act ii, sc. 1, l. 71. [Chatillon] See under ADVENTURE for full quotation.

The hazards of this untrod state.—*Julius Cæsar,* iii, 1, 136.

Upon all hazards.—*King John,* v, 6, 7.

11
Bring your latter hazard back again.
The Merchant of Venice. Act i, sc. 1, l. 151. [Bassanio]

Portia: After dinner Your hazard shall be made.
Morocco: Good fortune then!
To make me blest or cursed'st among men.
The Merchant of Venice. Act ii, sc. 1, l. 44. The only use of "cursed'st."

Men that hazard all
Do it in hope of fair advantages.
The Merchant of Venice. Act ii, sc. 7, l. 18. [Morocco]

'Who chooseth me must give and hazard all he hath,'
You shall look fairer, ere I give or hazard.
The Merchant of Venice. Act ii, sc. 9, l. 21. [Arragon] The first line is repeated in ii, 7, 9.

I pray you, tarry: pause a day or two
Before you hazard.
The Merchant of Venice. Act iii, sc. 2, l. 1. [Portia]

Comes to hazard.—*The Merchant of Venice,* ii, 9, 18.

12
Slave, I have set my life upon a cast,
And I will stand the hazard of the die.
Richard III. Act v, sc. 4, l. 9. [King Richard]

13 By the hazard of the spotted die
Let die the spotted.
Timon of Athens. Act v, sc. 4, l. 34. [Second Senator]

14
What folly 'tis to hazard life for ill!
Timon of Athens, iii, 5, 37. See under WRONG.

Oft thou shouldst hazard thy life for thy dinner.
Timon of Athens, iv, 3, 338. See under BEAST.

Hazard life.—*The Two Gentlemen of Verona,* v, 4, 21.

Hazard of his life.—*The Two Gentlemen of Verona,* iii, 1, 116.

Hazard of much blood.—*Coriolanus,* iii, 2, 61.

Hazard of my head.—*I Henry IV,* i, 3, 128.

All these and more we hazard.—*I Henry VI,* iv, 6, 40.

We stand much hazard.—*Timon of Athens,* v, 2, 5.

Endure hazard.—*Hamlet,* iii, 3, 6.

Lay myself in hazard.—*Measure for Measure,* iv, 2, 166.

1
[He] Unclasp'd my practice, quit his fortunes here,
Which you knew great, and to the hazard
Of all incertainties himself commended,
No richer than his honour.
The Winter's Tale. Act iii, sc. 2, l. 168. [Leontes] The only use of "incertainties."

HEAD

See also Pate

I—Familiar Phrases

2
Bow the head and nod at every man.
All's Well that Ends Well. Act iv, sc. 5, l. 112. [Clown]
She bows her head.—*Venus and Adonis,* l. 1171.
Bowing his head.—*Timon of Athens,* i. 1, 75.
Nod their heads!—*II Henry VI,* ii, 4 22.

3
I 'll unhair thy head.
Antony and Cleopatra, ii, 5, 64. [Cleopatra] The only use of "unhair." "Unhaired" occurs in *King John,* v, 2, 133.

4
Her head 's declined, and death will seize her.
Antony and Cleopatra, iii, 11, 47. [Eros]
Decline your head.—*King Lear,* iv, 2, 22.
With head declined.—*Rape of Lucrece,* l. 1661.

5
Is his head worth a hat?
As You Like It, iii, 2, 217.
Cover thy head, cover thy head; nay, prithee, be covered.
As You Like It. Act v, sc. 1, l. 18. [Touchstone]

6
I shall break that merry sconce of yours.
The Comedy of Errors. Act i, sc. 2, l. 79. [Antipholus of Syracuse]
Sconce call you it? So you would leave battering, I had rather have it a head: an you use these blows long, I must get a sconce for my head and insconce it too; or else I shall seek my wit in my shoulders.
Comedy of Errors. Act ii, sc. 2, l. 35. [Dromio of Syracuse] The only use of "insconce."
Why does he suffer this rude knave now to knock him about the sconce with a dirty shovel?
Hamlet. Act v, sc. 1, l. 109. [Hamlet]
Must I go show them my unbarbed sconce?
Coriolanus. Act iii, sc. 2, l. 99. [Coriolanus] The only use of "unbarbed."

7
In our own house I do shade my head.
Coriolanus. Act ii, sc. 1, l. 211. [Coriolanus]

8
His head over his shoulder turn'd.
Hamlet, ii, 1, 97. See under EYE.
Turn your head.—*The Merry Wives of Windsor,* i, 4, 132.
Turn head, and stop pursuit.—*Henry V,* ii, 4, 69.

9
Wouldst thou have thy head broken?
I Henry IV, iii, 1, 242. [Lady Percy]
A' never broke any man's head but his own, and that was against a post when he was drunk.
Henry V. Act iii, sc. 2, l. 42. [Boy]
I broke your head.—*The Merry Wives of Windsor,* i, 1, 125.
He has broke my head across and has given Sir Toby a bloody coxcomb too. . . . You broke my head for nothing.
Twelfth Night, v, 1, 178. [Sir Andrew]
I think you set nothing by a bloody coxcomb.
Twelfth Night. Act v, sc. 1, l. 194. [Sir Andrew] See also COXCOMB.
The prince broke thy head.—*II Henry IV,* ii, 1, 97.

10
No bigger than pins' heads.
I Henry IV, iv, 2, 24. See under COWARDICE.
Like pins' heads.—*II Henry IV,* iv, 3, 59.

11
Look, whether the withered elder hath not his poll clawed like a parrot.
II Henry IV. Act ii, sc. 4, l. 284. [Prince] "Clawed" is repeated in *Hamlet,* v, 1, 80.
All flaxen was his poll.—*Hamlet,* iv, 5, 196. The only use of "flaxen."
Set down by the poll.—*Coriolanus,* iii, 3, 10.
We are the greater poll.—*Coriolanus,* iii, 1, 134.
Fifteen thousand poll.—*All's Well that Ends Well,* iv, 3, 190. The only uses of "poll."

12
Shakes his head and trembling stands aloof.
II Henry VI. Act i, sc. 1, l. 227. [York]
What dost thou mean by shaking of thy head?
King John. Act iii, sc. 1, l. 19. [Constance]
Thou shakest thy head.—*II Henry IV,* i, 1, 95.
You shake the head.—*Much Ado about Nothing,* ii, 1, 377; *The Merchant of Venice,* iii, 3, 15; *King Lear,* iv, 6, 122.
Sometimes she shakes her head.—*Venus and Adonis,* l. 223.
Those that understood him smiled at one another and shook their heads.
Julius Cæsar. Act i, sc. 2, l. 285. [Casca]
They do shake their heads.—*Timon of Athens,* ii, 2, 210.
Let 's shake our heads.—*Timon of Athens,* iv, 2, 25.
Why do you look on us, and shake your head,
And call us wretches, orphans, castaways?
Richard III. Act ii, sc. 2, l. 5. [Girl] The only use of "castaways." "Castaway" occurs in *Antony and Cleopatra,* iii, 6, 40: "That ever I should call thee castaway"; in *Titus Andronicus,* v, 3, 75: "Desperate castaway"; and in *The Rape of Lucrece,* l. 744: "Hopeless castaway."

13
Rouen hangs her head for grief.
I Henry VI. Act iii, sc. 2, l. 124. [Talbot]
Over one shoulder doth she hang her head.
Venus and Adonis, l. 1058.
Thy kinsmen hang their heads at this disdain.
The Rape of Lucrece, l. 521. "Hang their heads" is repeated in *Lucrece,* l. 793, and *Henry VIII,* v, 5, 33.
Hung their heads.—*Henry VIII,* iii, 1, 11.
Hang my head all at one side.—*Othello,* iv, 3, 32.

1
Ay, all of you have laid your heads together.
II Henry VI. Act iii, sc. 1, l. 165. [Gloucester]

I see them lay their heads together to surprise me.
II Henry VI. Act iv, sc. 8, l. 60. [Cade]

How the young folks lay their heads together!
Taming of the Shrew, i, 2, 139. [Grumio]

2
Hold up thy head, vile Scot, or thou art like
Never to hold it up again!
I Henry IV. Act v, sc. 4, l. 39. [Prince Henry]

Hold up thy head.—*Venus and Adonis,* l. 118.

Yet, countrymen, O, yet hold up your heads!
Julius Cæsar. Act v, sc. 4, l. 1. [Brutus]

Hold up your head.—*The Merry Wives of Windsor,* iv, 1, 20.

Hold up his head.—*The Merry Wives of Windsor,* i, 4, 30.

Hold up head.—*II Henry IV,* i, 3, 17.

3 Then happy low, lie down!
Uneasy lies the head that wears a crown.
II Henry IV. Act iii, sc. 1, l. 30. [King Henry]

4
A head fantastically carved.
II Henry IV, iii, 2, 334. See under CHARACTER.

5
Heads of steel.—*I Henry VI,* iv, 2, 51.

6
Hide thy head, Achilles; here comes Hector in arms.
Love's Labour's Lost. Act v, sc. 2, l. 635. [Biron]

Speak! In some bush? Where dost thou hide thy head?
A Midsummer-Night's Dream. Act iii, sc. 2, l. 406. [Demetrius]

Richard not far from hence hath hid his head.
Richard II. Act iii, sc. 3, l. 6. [Northumberland]

I know not where to hide my head.
The Tempest. Act ii, sc. 2, l. 23. [Trinculo]

This brave shall oft make thee to hide thy head.
Troilus and Cressida. Act iv, sc. 4, l. 139. [Troilus]

Make me hide my head.—*I Henry VI,* i, 5, 39.

Hide his head.—*II Henry VI,* v, 1, 85; *Julius Cæsar,* iv, 3, 16; *Richard II,* iii, 3, 8.

Hide your heads.—*Love's Labour's Lost,* v, 2, 86.

Hid his crisp head.—*I Henry IV,* i, 3, 106.

7
Nor thrust your head into the public street.
The Merchant of Venice. Act ii, sc. 6, l. 32. [Shylock]

8
Scratch my head, Peaseblossom.
A Midsummer-Night's Dream. Act iv, sc. 1, l. 7. [Bottom]

I 'll scratch your heads.
Henry VIII. Act v, sc. 4, l. 9. [Porter]

I had rather have one scratch my head i' the sun
When the alarum were struck than idly sit
To hear my nothings monster'd.
Coriolanus. Act ii, sc. 2, l. 79. [Coriolanus] The only use of "monster'd."

9
She would not have his head on her shoulders for all Messina, as like him as she is.
Much Ado about Nothing. Act i, sc. 1, l. 114. [Benedick]

By the head and shoulders.—*The Merry Wives of Windsor,* v, 5, 156. The only use of the phrase. See under VIRTUE for full quotation.

By my head.—*Troilus and Cressida,* ii, 3, 95; *Romeo and Juliet,* iii, 1, 38.

10
I know by the waggling of your head.
Much Ado about Nothing. Act ii, sc. 1, l. 119. [Ursula] The only use of "waggling."

Not wagging his sweet head.—*Cymbeline,* iv, 2, 173.

11
From the crown of his head to the sole of his foot.
Much Ado about Nothing. Act iii, sc. 2, l. 9. [Don Pedro]

From the extremest upward of thy head
To the descent and dust below thy foot.
King Lear. Act v, sc. 3, l. 136. [Edgar] See TREASON, 1562:1, for full quotation.

From head to foot.—*Hamlet,* i, 2, 228; ii, 2, 478; *Troilus and Cressida,* ii, 1, 29; *Antony and Cleopatra,* v, 2, 239; *Cymbeline,* i, 6, 19.

12
Put this in your head.
Othello. Act iv, sc. 2, l. 15. [Emilia]

Heaven, that I had thy head!
Pericles. Act i, sc. 1, l. 109. [Antiochus]

13
Lord, how my head aches! what a head have I!
It beats as it would fall in twenty pieces.
Romeo and Juliet. Act ii, sc. 5, l. 49. [Nurse]

Stand close up, or I 'll make your head ache.
Henry VIII. Act v, sc. 4, l. 92. [Man]

14
I have a head, sir, that will find out logs.
Romeo and Juliet. Act iv, sc. 4, l. 17. [Second Servant]

Thou shalt be logger-head.
Romeo and Juliet. Act iv, sc. 4, l. 20. [Capulet] "Loggerhead" (unhyphenated) is repeated in *Love's Labour's Lost,* iv, 3, 204: "Whoreson loggerhead." "Logger-headed" is used in *Taming of the Shrew,* iv, 1, 128.

15 Doubt not her care should be
To comb your noddle with a three-legg'd stool
And paint your face and use you like a fool.
The Taming of the Shrew. Act i, sc. 1, l. 63. [Katharina] The only use of "three-legged."

I will smite his noddles.—*The Merry Wives of Windsor,* iii, 1, 128. The only uses of "noddle" and "noddles."

16
Let their heads be sleekly combed.
The Taming of the Shrew. Act iv, sc. 1, l. 93. [Grumio] The only use of "sleekly" and "combed." "Comb" appears four times.

17
Now does the project gather to a head.
The Tempest. Act v, sc. 1, l. 1. [Prospero]

1
Troilus, thou coward Troilus, show thy head!
Troilus and Cressida. Act v, sc. 6, l. 1. [Ajax]
Never show thy head.—*Richard II,* v, 6, 44.
Show his head.—*Romeo and Juliet,* v, 3, 306.
2
Inch-thick, knee-deep, o'er head and ears a fork'd one!
The Winter's Tale. Act i, sc. 2, l. 186. [Leontes] The only use of "knee-deep" and "o'er head and ears." "Inch-thick" occurs again in *Hamlet,* v, 1, 214.

II—Head

3
Our heads are some brown, some black, some auburn, some bald.
Coriolanus, ii, 3, 20. See under MULTITUDE.
Golden head.—*A Midsummer-Night's Dream,* i, 1, 170; *The Rape of Lucrece,* l. 777.
Bare unarmed heads.—*II Henry IV,* ii, 4, 394.
4
She bids you on the wanton rushes lay you down
And rest your gentle head upon her lap.
I Henry IV. Act iii, sc. 1, l. 214. [Glendower]
Come, Kate, thou art perfect in lying down; come, quick, quick, that I may lay my head in thy lap.
I Henry IV. Act iii, sc. 1, l. 229. [Hotspur]
Here may his head lie on my throbbing breast.
II Henry VI. Act iv, sc. 4, l. 5. [Queen]
Lay thy head in Furies' lap.—*II Henry IV,* v, 3, 110.
My head upon your lap.—*Hamlet,* iii, 2, 121.
Her head on her knee.—*Othello,* iv, 3, 43.
With libbard's head on knee.—*Love's Labour's Lost,* v, 2, 551. The only use of "libbard" (old form of leopard).
5
Stoop'd his anointed head as low as death.
II Henry IV. Induction, l. 32. [Rumour]
Gallant head.—*King John,* v, 2, 113.
Goodly head.—*II Henry IV,* i, 3, 103.
Gracious head.—*Richard II,* iii, 3, 108.
Kingly-crowned head.—*Coriolanus,* i, 1, 119. The only use of "kingly-crowned."
Proud head.—*Venus and Adonis,* l. 14.
Reverend heads.—*Henry V,* iii, 3, 37.
Royal head.—*Henry VIII,* v, 1, 160.
Supreme head.—*King John,* iii, 1, 155.
6
A good soft pillow for that good white head.
Henry V, iv, 1, 14. See under PILLOW.
Frosty head.—*II Henry VI,* v, 1, 167.
Grizzled head.—*Antony and Cleopatra,* iii, 13, 17.
Milky head.—*Hamlet,* ii, 2, 500.
White head.—*II Henry IV,* i, 2, 211; *Henry V,* iv, 1, 14; *King Lear,* iii, 2, 6.
7
Why droops my lord, like over-ripen'd corn,
Hanging the head at Ceres' plenteous load?
II Henry VI. Act i, sc. 2, l. 1. [Duchess of Gloucester] "Over-ripen'd" used in the first act of the first play and never afterward.
We'll both together lift our heads to heaven,
And never more abase our sight so low
As to vouchsafe one glance unto the ground.
II Henry VI. Act i, sc. 2, l. 14. [Duchess Eleanor]
Lifted up its head.—*Hamlet,* i, 2, 216.
8
Nor wear the diadem upon his head,
Whose church-like humours fits not for a crown.
II Henry VI. Act i, sc. 1, l. 246. [York] The only use of "church-like."
That head of thine doth not become a crown.
II Henry VI, v, 1, 96. See under KING.
His head by nature framed to wear a crown.
III Henry VI, iv, 6, 72. See under CHARACTER.
9 Rather let my head
Stoop to the block than these knees bow to any
Save to the God of heaven and to my king;
And sooner dance upon a bloody pole
Than stand uncover'd to the vulgar groom.
II Henry VI. Act iv, sc. 1, l. 124. [Suffolk]
10
This word 'sallet' was born to do me good: for many a time, but for a sallet, my brain-pan had been cleft with a brown bill; . . . and now the word 'sallet' must serve me to feed on.
II Henry VI. Act iv, sc. 10, l. 11. [Cade] "Brain-pan" was used in the first play and never again. Cade is punning upon "sallet," which was the usual Elizabethan word for salad and also for a light armoured head-piece.
11
The heads of all thy brother cardinals,
With thee and all thy best parts bound together,
Weigh'd not a hair of his.
Henry VIII. Act iii, sc. 2, l. 257. [Surrey]
12
That eyeless head of thine was first framed flesh
To raise my fortunes.
King Lear. Act iv, sc. 6, l. 231. [Oswald]
13 Men whose heads
Do grow beneath their shoulders.
Othello, i, 3, 144. See under MONSTER.
Men Whose heads stood in their breasts.
The Tempest, iii, 3, 46. See under MONSTER.
Monstrous heads.—*II Henry IV,* iii, 1, 23.
Forked heads.—*As You Like It,* ii, 1, 24.
14
The scalps of many, almost hid behind,
To jump up higher seem'd, to mock the mind.
The Rape of Lucrece, l. 1413.
Bare scalp.—*The Two Gentlemen of Verona,* iv, 1, 36.
Hairless scalps.—*Richard II,* iii, 2, 112.
Transformed scalp.—*A Midsummer-Night's Dream,* iv, 1, 69. The only uses of "scalp."
15
They, for their truth, might better wear their heads

Than some that have accused them wear their hats.
Richard III. Act iii, sc. 2, l. 94. [Stanley]
1
Marcus Andronicus: Help to set a head on headless Rome.
Titus Andronicus: A better head her glorious body fits
Than his that shakes for age and feebleness.
Titus Andronicus. Act i, sc. 1, l. 186.
2
Ajax is grown self-will'd, and bears his head
In such a rein, in full as proud a place
As broad Achilles.
Troilus and Cressida. Act i, sc. 3, l. 188. [Nestor]
Bold head.—*The Tempest,* ii, 1, 117.
Burning head.—*Sonnets,* vii.
Calf's head.—*Much Ado about Nothing,* v, 1, 156.
Cursed head!—*Hamlet,* v, 1, 270.
Drowsy head.—*Richard III,* v, 3, 228.
Drunken heads.—*Twelfth Night,* v, 1, 412.
Fool's head.—*The Merchant of Venice,* ii, 9, 59; ii, 9, 75.
Houseless heads.—*King Lear,* iii, 4, 30.
Idle head.—*Troilus and Cressida,* i, 2, 147.
Riotous head.—*Hamlet,* iv, 5, 101.
Shameful heads.—*Titus Andronicus,* v, 2, 190.
Sleek smooth head.—*A Midsummer-Night's Dream,* iv, 1, 3.
Small head.—*Venus and Adonis,* l. 296.
Suspicious head.—*Love's Labour's Lost,* iv, 3, 336.
Weary head.—*The Rape of Lucrece,* l. 1621.
His head unmellow'd.—*The Two Gentlemen of Verona,* ii, 4, 70.

III—Off With His Head!

3
Thy head, which now is growing upon thy shoulders, shall within this hour be off.
Cymbeline. Act iv, sc. 1, l. 18. [Cloten]
4 I have ta'en
His head from him: I 'll throw 't into the creek.
Cymbeline. Act iv, sc. 2, l. 150. [Guiderius]
Damn'd Pisanio Hath with his forged letters, . . .
From this most bravest vessel of the world
Struck the main-top! O Posthumus! alas,
Where is thy head? where 's that? Ay me! where 's that?
Pisanio might have kill'd thee at the heart,
And left this head on.
Cymbeline. Act iv, sc. 2, l. 318. [Imogen] The only use of "main-top."
I cut off 's head.—*Cymbeline,* v, 5, 295.
Cut the head off.—*Julius Cæsar,* ii, 1, 163.
5 An exact command,
Larded with many several sorts of reasons . . .
That, on the supervise, no leisure bated,
No, not to stay the grinding of the axe,
My head should be struck off.
Hamlet. Act v, sc. 2, l. 19. [Hamlet] "Supervise" occurs again in *Love's Labour's Lost,* iv, 2, 124.
6
Cut this head off from my shoulders.
I Henry IV. Act i, sc. 2, l. 185. [Poins]
Cut me off the heads Of all the favourites.
I Henry IV. Act iv, sc. 3, l. 85. [Hotspur]
Cut me off the villain's head.
II Henry IV. Act ii, sc. 1, l. 50. [Falstaff]
So Chrish save me, I will cut off your head.
Henry V. Act iii, sc. 2, l. 145. [Macmorris]
7
Abominable Gloucester, guard thy head;
For I intend to have it ere long.
I Henry VI. Act i, sc. 3, l. 87. [Winchester]
Base dunghill villain and mechanical,
I 'll have thy head for this thy traitor's speech.
II Henry VI. Act i, sc. 3, l. 196. [York]
We 'll have his head.—*II Henry VI,* iv, 2, 183.
8
He who breaks a stick of Gloucester's grove
Shall lose his head for his presumption.
II Henry VI. Act i, sc. 2, l. 34. [Duchess]
He will lose his head ere give consent.
Richard III. Act iii, sc. 4, l. 40. [Gloucester]
Ay, all of them at Bristol lost their heads.
Richard II. Act iii, sc. 2, l. 142. [Scroop]
Lost his head.—*I Henry VI,* ii, 5, 54; *Measure for Measure,* v, 1, 493.
9
I 'll see if his head will stand steadier on a pole, or no. Take him away and behead him.
II Henry VI. Act iv, sc. 7, l. 100. [Cade] The only use of "behead."
10
Convey him hence and on our long-boat's side
Strike off his head.
II Henry VI. Act iv, sc. 1, l. 69. [Captain] The only use of "long-boat."
Go, take him away, I say, and strike off his head presently; . . . strike off his head.
II Henry VI. Act iv, sc. 7, l. 116. [Cade]
And there cut off thy most ungracious head,
Which I will bear in triumph to the king.
II Henry VI. Act iv, sc. 10, l. 88. [Iden]
11
Chop away that factious pate.
II Henry VI, v, 1, 135. See under PATE.
Chop off his head, man.
Richard III. Act iii, sc. 1, l. 193. [Gloucester]
Within these three days his head to be chopped off.
Measure for Measure. Act i, sc. 2, l. 69. [Mistress Overdone]
12
Off with his head, and set it on York gates.
III Henry VI. Act i, sc. 4, l. 179. [Queen Margaret]
Off with the traitor's head.
III Henry VI. Act ii, sc. 6, l. 85. [Warwick]
Off with his guilty head.
III Henry VI. Act v, sc. 5, l. 3. [King Edward]
Thou art a traitor: Off with his head!
Richard III. Act iii, sc. 4, l. 77. [Gloucester]
Come, headsman, off with his head.
All's Well that Ends Well. Act iv, sc. 3, l. 342. [Soldier] The only use of "headsman."

1
And after many scorns, many foul taunts,
They took his head, and on the gates of York
They set the same; and there it doth remain,
The saddest spectacle that e'er I view'd.
III Henry VI. Act ii, sc. 1, l. 64. [Messenger]

Queen Margaret: Yonder 's the head of that arch-enemy
That sought to be encompass'd with your crown:
Doth not the object cheer your heart, my lord?
King Henry: Ay, as the rocks cheer them that fear their wreck.
III Henry VI. Act ii, sc. 2, l. 2. The only use of "arch-enemy."

Ah, cousin York! would thy best friends did know
How it doth grieve me that thy head is here!
III Henry VI. Act ii, sc. 2, l. 54. [King Henry]

2
He unseam'd him from the nave to the chaps,
And fix'd his head upon our battlements.
Macbeth. Act i, sc. 2, l. 22. [Sergeant] The only use of "unseam'd."

3
Thy head stands so tickle on thy shoulders that a milkmaid, if she be in love, may sigh it off.
Measure for Measure. Act i, sc. 2, l. 176. [Lucio] "Tickle," in the sense of unstable, is repeated in *II Henry VI*, i, 1, 216.

Call your executioner, and off with Barnadine's head.
Measure for Measure. Act iv, sc. 2, l. 222. [Duke]

His head is off.—*Measure for Measure,* iv, 3, 120.

4
Their heads shall pay for it.
Richard II. Act iii, sc. 2, l. 126. [King Richard]

5
To shorten you,
For taking so the head, your whole head's length.
Richard II. Act iii, sc. 3, l. 13. [York]

6
Make a short shrift; he longs to see your head.
Richard III. Act iii, sc. 4, l. 97. [Ratcliff] The only use of "short shrift."

Here is the head of that ignoble traitor.
Richard III. Act iii, sc. 5, l. 22. [Lovel]

7
O, let me think on Hastings, and be gone
To Brecknock, while my fearful head is on.
Richard III. Act iv, sc. 2, l. 124. [Buckingham]

8
King Richard: The advancement of your children, gentle lady.
Queen Elizabeth: Up to some scaffold, there to lose their heads?
Richard III. Act iv, sc. 4, l. 241. "Scaffold" is repeated in *Henry V,* Prol., 10.

9
If I revolt, off goes young George's head.
Richard III. Act iv, sc. 5, l. 4. [Derby]

Off with his son George's head!
Richard III. Act v, sc. 3, l. 344. [King Richard]

HEALTH

See also Drinking: Drinking Healths

10
What is infirm from your sound parts shall fly,
Health shall live free and sickness freely die.
All's Well that Ends Well. Act ii, sc. 1, l. 170. [Helena]

Heaven hath through me restored the king to health.
All's Well that Ends Well. Act ii, sc. 3, l. 70. [Helena]

Free and healthful.—*Antony and Cleopatra,* ii, 5, 38. "Healthful" occurs eight times.

11
Imogen: Continues well my lord? His health, beseech you?
Iachimo: Well, madam.
Cymbeline. Act i, sc. 6, l. 56.

His health was never better worth than now.
I Henry IV. Act iv, sc. 1, l. 27. [Worcester]

12
I most humbly beseech your lordship to have a reverent care of your health.
II Henry IV. Act i, sc. 2, l. 113. [Falstaff]

13
All health unto my gracious sovereign!
II Henry VI. Act iii, sc. 1, l. 82. [Somerset] See under GREETING.

Health and glad tidings to your majesty!
II Henry VI. Act iv, sc. 9, l. 7. [Buckingham]

Health and all happiness to my lord the king!
II Henry VI. Act v, sc. 1, l. 124. [Clifford] A form of salutation used many times in the plays, these three examples being from the first one.

Better health Attend his majesty!—*Macbeth,* iii, 4, 120.

God grant him health!—*Richard III,* i, 3, 35.

God restore you to health!—*Much Ado about Nothing,* v, 1, 334.

Restored to health.—*The Taming of the Shrew,* Ind., 1, 121.

14
Health, alack, with youthful wings is flown
From this bare wither'd trunk.
II Henry IV. Act iv, sc. 5, l. 229. [King Henry]

15
It is not for your health thus to commit
Your weak condition to the raw cold morning.
Julius Cæsar. Act ii, sc. 1, l. 235. [Brutus]

Brutus: I am not well in health, and that is all.
Portia: Brutus is wise, and, were he not in health,
He would embrace the means to come by it.
Julius Cæsar. Act ii, sc. 1, l. 257.

Have mind upon your health, tempt me no farther.
Julius Cæsar. Act iv, sc. 3, l. 36. [Cassius]

1
Nay, not as one would say, healthy; but so sound as things that are hollow: thy bones are hollow: impiety has made a feast of thee.
Measure for Measure. Act i, sc. 2, l. 55. [Lucio] "Healthy" is used again in *II Henry IV*, i, 2, 4: "Healthy water."

2
He hath no power to ask her how she fares.
The Rape of Lucrece, l. 1594.

3
Queen Elizabeth: How fares the prince?
Messenger: Well, madam, and in health.
Richard III. Act ii, sc. 4, l. 39. "How fares the king?" (*The Tempest*, v, 1, 7), "How fares your majesty?" (*Love's Labour's Lost*, v, 2, 736), and similar forms are used throughout the plays.
Northumberland: How fares your uncle?
Percy: I had thought, my lord, to have learn'd his health of you.
Richard II. Act ii, sc. 3, l. 23.

4
Helena: My mother greets me kindly: is she well?
Clown: She is not well; but yet she has her health: she 's very merry; but yet she is not well: but thanks be given, she 's very well and wants nothing i' the world; but she is not well.
Helena: If she be very well, what does she ail that she 's not very well?
Clown: Truly, she 's very well indeed, but for two things.
Helena: What two things?
Clown: One, that she 's not in heaven, whither God send her quickly! the other, that she 's in earth, from whence God send her quickly!
All's Well that Ends Well. Act ii, sc. 4, l. 1. The only use of "ail."
Lucullus: How does . . . thy good lord and master?
Flaminius: His health is well, sir.
Lucullus: I am right glad that his health is well, sir.
Timon of Athens. Act iii, sc. 1, l. 10.
I am not so well as I should be, but I 'll ne'er out.
Antony and Cleopatra. Act ii, sc. 7, l. 35. [Lepidus]
Nothing can be ill, if she be well.
Romeo and Juliet. Act v, sc. 1, l. 16. [Romeo]

5
Most fit For your best health and recreation.
Richard III. Act iii, sc. 1, l. 66. [Gloucester]

6
He 's much out of health, and keeps his chamber.
Timon of Athens. Act iii, sc. 4, l. 71. [Servilius]

7
Why, how now, my bawcock! how dost thou, chuck?
Twelfth Night. Act iii, sc. 4, l. 125. [Sir Toby] For "bawcock" (beau coq) see KING: THE GOOD KING.
Dearest chuck.—*Macbeth*, iii, 2, 45.
Sweet chuck.—*Henry V*, iii, 2, 26; *Love's Labour's Lost*, v, 1, 117; v, 2, 667. "Chuck" is used eight times.

8
Your father 's in good health.
The Two Gentlemen of Verona. Act ii, sc. 4, l. 50. [Duke]
Good health.—*Henry VIII*, i, 4, 38; iv, 2, 124; *Pericles*, iv, 6, 24. The only uses of the phrase.
Accustom'd health.—*Richard III*, i, 3, 2.
Best health.—*Timon of Athens*, ii, 2, 206.
Bodily health.—*II Henry IV*, ii, 2, 111.
Fair health.—*Love's Labour's Lost*, v, 2, 834; *Sonnets*, xlv.
Pristine health.—*Macbeth*, v, 3, 52. "Pristine" is repeated in *Henry V*, iii, 2, 87: "Pristine wars."
Sweet health.—*Love's Labour's Lost*, ii, 1, 178.
Corporal soundness.—*All's Well that Ends Well*, i, 2, 24. The only use of "soundness."

9
I left them all in health.
The Two Gentlemen of Verona. Act ii, sc. 4, l. 124. [Proteus]
In health.—*A Midsummer-Night's Dream*, iv, 1, 179; *All's Well that Ends Well*, ii, 1, 7; *II Henry IV*, iv, 4, 106; *Henry V*, i, 2, 18; iii, 6, 157; *Richard III*, ii, 1, 92; ii, 4, 40.
In state of health.—*Antony and Cleopatra*, ii, 5, 56.

10
He has his health and ampler strength indeed
Than most have of his age.
The Winter's Tale. Act iv, sc. 4, l. 413. [Florizel] The only use of "ampler."

HEARING

See also Ear

11
No more . . . offend our hearing.
Cymbeline. Act v, sc. 4, l. 93. [Jupiter]
Bores of hearing.—*Cymbeline*, iii, 2, 59.
Vent of hearing.—*II Henry IV*, Ind., 2.

12
We beg your hearing patiently.
Hamlet. Act iii, sc. 2, l. 161. [Prologue]
Gentle hearing.—*Richard II*, iii, 3, 126.
Good hearing.—*The Taming of the Shrew*, v, 2, 182. The only use of the phrase.
Judicious hearing.—*Coriolanus*, v, 6, 128.
Serious hearing.—*Hamlet*, i, 5, 5.

13
Sweet madam, give me hearing in a cause.
I Henry VI. Act v, sc. 3, l. 106. [Suffolk]
I will tell you, sir, if you will give me the hearing.
The Merry Wives of Windsor. Act ii, sc. 2, l. 183. [Ford]
Give me hearing.—*I Henry VI*, iii, 1, 28; *Cymbeline*, v, 5, 116.
Give him hearing.—*Henry V*, i, 1, 93.
Vouchsafe me hearing.—*I Henry IV*, iv, 3, 31.
I 'll vouchsafe thee the hearing.—*The Merry Wives of Windsor*, ii, 2, 44.
Hear me.—*II Henry VI*, iv, 7, 64, and sixty-nine times in later plays.
Hear me speak.—*III Henry VI*, i, 1, 257, and twenty-two times in later plays.

Hear you.—*Richard III,* iv, 4, 496, and thirteen times in later plays.
Hear say.—*Romeo and Juliet,* ii, 4, 208; *Coriolanus,* ii, 2, 74; *Pericles,* iv, 6, 86.
Hear tell.—*Much Ado about Nothing,* ii, 1, 362.
Did you ever hear the like?—*The Merry Wives of Windsor,* ii, 1, 70; *Pericles,* iv, 5, 1.
Was ever heard the like?—*Titus Andronicus,* ii, 3, 276.

1
I did not think thou wast within hearing.
II Henry IV. Act ii, sc. 4, l. 334. [Falstaff]
She is not within hearing, sir.
The Two Gentlemen of Verona. Act ii, sc. 1, l. 8. [Speed]
Out of hearing.—*A Midsummer-Night's Dream,* ii, 2, 152.

2
I do confess much of the hearing it, but little of the marking of it.
Love's Labour 's Lost. Act i, sc. 1, l. 287. [Costard]
And overheard what you shall overhear.
Love's Labour 's Lost. Act v, sc. 2, l. 95. [Boyet] "Overheard" is used ten times; "overhear" three times.

3
Make passionate my sense of hearing.
Love's Labour 's Lost. Act iii, sc. 1, l. 1. [Armado] See under Song.
Bestow on me the sense of hearing.
Love's Labour 's Lost. Act v, sc. 2, l. 670. [Armado]
Younger hearings are quite ravished.—*Love's Labour 's Lost,* ii, 1, 75. See Wit, 1688:7.

4
He 's hearing of a cause.
Measure for Measure. Act ii, sc. 2, l. 1. [Servant]
Hearing a cause.—*Coriolanus,* ii, 1, 78.
Hearing of the cause.—*Measure for Measure,* ii, 1, 141.
Hearing of this business.—*Measure for Measure,* iii, 1, 210.

5
We will hear further of it.
Much Ado about Nothing. Act ii, sc. 3, l. 211. [Don Pedro]
Look to hear further from me.—*All's Well that Ends Well,* iii, 6, 82.
Till you hear further.—*Timon of Athens,* i, 1, 162; *Henry VIII,* iii, 2, 232.

6
Cassio: Dost thou hear, my honest friend?
Clown: No, I hear not your honest friend; I hear you.
Othello. Act iii, sc. 1, l. 22.

7
Well have you heard, but something hard of hearing.
The Taming of the Shrew. Act ii, sc. 1, l. 184. [Katharina] The only use of the phrase "hard of hearing."
Human hearing.—*The Tempest,* i, 2, 265.

8
I have Deserved this hearing.
Timon of Athens. Act ii, sc. 2, l. 206. [Timon]
Let the garden door be shut, and leave me to my hearing.
Twelfth Night. Act iii, sc. 1, l. 103. [Olivia]

HEART

I—Familiar Phrases

9 For his ordinary pays his heart
For what his eyes eat only.
Antony and Cleopatra. Act ii, sc. 2, l. 230. [Enobarbus] The only use of "ordinary" in the sense of table-d'hôte. "Ordinaries," in the same sense, occurs in *All's Well that Ends Well,* ii, 3, 211.

10
Plighter of high hearts!
Antony and Cleopatra, iii, 13, 126. The only use of "plighter" and "high hearts."
High-swoln hearts.—*Richard III,* ii, 2, 117. The only use of "high-swoln."

11
From my cold heart let heaven engender hail.
Antony and Cleopatra. Act iii, sc. 13, l. 159. [Cleopatra]
Cold heart.—*I Henry IV,* ii, 3, 33; *Henry VIII,* i, 2, 61.

12
Good sirs, take heart.
Antony and Cleopatra, iv, 15, 85. [Cleopatra]
Bid her have good heart.—*Antony and Cleopatra,* v, 1, 56. See also under Courage.
Now I have taken heart.—*Julius Cæsar,* iv, 3, 288.

13
These burs are in my heart.
As You Like It. Act i, sc. 3, l. 17. [Rosalind]
Why, how now, Adam! no greater heart in thee?
As You Like It. Act ii, sc. 6, l. 4. [Orlando]
You a man! you lack a man's heart.
As You Like It. Act iv, sc. 3, l. 164. [Oliver]
Fearful heart.—*As You Like It,* iii, 3, 49.

14
I 'll warrant him heart-whole.
As You Like It, iv, 1, 49. The only use of "heart-whole." See Love, 923:1.

15
We . . . have hearts Inclinable to honour.
Coriolanus. Act ii, sc. 2, l. 59. [First Senator] The only use of "inclinable."
I have such a heart that both mine ears
Must not in haste abuse.
Cymbeline. Act i, sc. 6, l. 130. [Imogen]

16 Correcting thy stout heart,
Now humble as the ripest mulberry
That will not hold the handling.
Coriolanus. Act iii, sc. 2, l. 78. [Volumnia]
Thou hast A heart of wreak in thee.
Coriolanus. Act iv, sc. 5, l. 90. [Coriolanus]

17
Their hearts were yours.
Coriolanus, iii, 2, 87. [Menenius]
He has my heart yet.—*Henry VIII,* iii, 1, 180.

18
It shows . . . A heart unfortified.
Hamlet. Act i, sc. 2, l. 96. [King] The only use of "unfortified."
Unguarded hearts.—*Cymbeline,* v, 3, 46. "Un-

guarded" is repeated in *Henry V,* i, 2, 170: "Unguarded nest"; and in *Macbeth,* i, 7, 70: "Unguarded Duncan."

1

O heart, lose not thy nature; let not ever
The soul of Nero enter this firm bosom.
Hamlet. Act iii, sc. 2, l. 411. [Hamlet]

2

I shall be out of heart shortly.
I Henry IV. Act iii, sc. 3, l. 6. [Falstaff]

This has put me in heart.
The Taming of the Shrew. Act iv, sc. 5, l. 77. [Hortensio]

3

It would have done a man's heart good to see.
II Henry IV. Act iii, sc. 2, l. 54. [Shallow]

It does a man's heart good.
Troilus and Cressida. Act i, sc. 2, l. 221. [Pandarus]

Do a man's heart good.—*Midsummer-Night's Dream,* i, 2, 73; *II Henry IV,* iii, 2, 54.

Manly heart.—*Henry V,* ii, 3, 3.

By God's lid, it does one's heart good.
Troilus and Cressida. Act i, sc. 2, l. 228. [Pandarus]

4

With all my heart, and think me honoured.
I Henry VI, ii, 3, 81. "With all my heart" is repeated thirty-two times in later plays, five times in *Richard III* alone.

With all our hearts.—*Richard III,* ii, 2, 145.

With all their hearts.—*Julius Cæsar,* i, 2, 276.

5

It warmed thy father's heart.
I Henry VI. Act iv, sc. 6, l. 11. [Talbot]

Even the very middle of my heart Is warm'd.
Cymbeline. Act i, sc. 6, l. 27. [Imogen]

6 O Lord, that lends me life,
Lend me a heart replete with thankfulness!
II Henry VI. Act i, sc. 1, l. 19. [King Henry]

7

Such is the fulness of my heart's content.
II Henry VI. Act i, sc. 1, l. 35. [King Henry] "Heart's content" is repeated in *The Merchant of Venice,* iii, 4, 42; and *Troilus and Cressida,* i, 2, 320.

Heart's core.—*Hamlet,* iii, 2, 78.

Heart's desire.—*Much Ado about Nothing,* iii, 4, 61; *As You Like It,* i, 2, 211.

Heart's discontent.—*II Henry VI,* iii, 2, 301; *III Henry VI,* iii, 3, 173.

Heart's ease.—*Romeo and Juliet,* iv, 5, 102; *Henry V,* iv, 1, 253; *Julius Cæsar,* i, 2, 208.

Heart's hope.—*Merchant of Venice,* ii, 9, 20.

Heart's love.—*Richard III,* ii, 1, 10; iv, 1, 4; iv, 4, 260; iv, 4, 403; *I Henry IV,* iv, 1, 8.

Heart's malice.—*II Henry VI,* iii, 1, 154.

8

Heart, be wrathful still.
II Henry VI. Act v, sc. 2, l. 70. [Richard]

My heart for anger burns.—*III Henry VI,* i, 1, 60.

Angry heart.—*Titus Andronicus,* v, 2, 119.

9

What, hath thy fiery heart so parch'd thine entrails
That not a tear can fall?
III Henry VI. Act i, sc. 4, l. 87. [Queen Margaret]

Set the heart on fire.—*Venus and Adonis,* l. 388.

10

O tiger's heart wrapt in a woman's hide!
III Henry VI. Act i, sc. 4, l. 137. [York]

O serpent heart, hid with a flowering face!
Romeo and Juliet. Act iii, sc. 2, l. 73. [Juliet]

11

My heart, sweet boy, shall be thy sepulchre.
III Henry VI. Act ii, sc. 5, l. 115. [Father]

Let me infold thee And hold thee to my heart.
Macbeth. Act i, sc. 4, l. 31. [Duncan]

Grapples you to the heart and love of us.
Macbeth. Act iii, sc. 1, l. 106. [Macbeth]

I have kept you next my heart.
Henry VIII. Act iii, sc. 2, l. 157. [King]

12

I speak it with a single heart.
Henry VIII. Act v, sc. 3, l. 38. [Cranmer]

Constant heart.—*II Henry IV,* ii, 4, 293; *Sonnets,* liii.

Frank heart.—*King Lear,* iii, 4, 20.

Free heart.—*Macbeth,* i, 3, 155; *Timon of Athens,* i, 2, 6.

13

I feel my heart new open'd.
Henry VIII. Act iii, sc. 2, l. 366. [Wolsey]

14

Be a beast without a heart.
Julius Cæsar. Act ii, sc. 2, l. 42. [Cæsar] "Without a heart" is repeated in *Troilus and Cressida,* ii, 2, 157.

I come not, friends, to steal away your hearts.
Julius Cæsar. Act iii, sc. 2, l. 220. [Antony]

15

Unhappy that I am, I cannot heave
My heart into my mouth.
King Lear. Act i, sc. 1, l. 93. [Cordelia]

Goes thy heart with this?
King Lear. Act i, sc. 1, l. 107. [King Lear]

16

Moth: Learn her by heart.
Armado: By heart and in heart, boy.
Love's Labour's Lost. Act iii, sc. 1, l. 36.

Their herald is a pretty knavish page,
That well by heart hath conn'd his embassage.
Love's Labour's Lost. Act v, sc. 2, l. 97. [Boyet]

17

O my little heart!
Love's Labour's Lost. Act iii, sc. 1, l. 188. [Biron]

O, my heart!—*The Winter's Tale,* iv, 4, 434.

18

The very firstlings of my heart shall be
The firstlings of my hand.
Macbeth. Act iv, sc. 1, l. 147. [Macbeth] "Firstlings" is repeated in *Troilus and Cressida,* Prol., 27.

Blunt not the heart, enrage it.
Macbeth. Act iv, sc. 3, l. 229. [Malcolm]

The heart is sorely charged.—*Macbeth,* v, 1, 59.

19

I will have the heart of him.
The Merchant of Venice. Act iii, sc. 1, l. 132. [Shylock]

20

Since you do take it, love, so much to heart.
The Merchant of Venice. Act v, sc. 1, l. 145. [Gratiano]

Why . . . Take it to heart?
Hamlet, i, 2, 101. See under FATE.

How he takes it at heart!—*Twelfth Night,* iii, 4, 112.

1
Lay it to thy heart.
Macbeth. Act i, sc. 5, l. 15. [Lady Macbeth]

Lay it to your heart.—*Much Ado about Nothing,* iii, 4, 74.

2
Here is the heart of my purpose.
The Merry Wives of Windsor, ii, 2, 233. [Ford]

3
My heart misgives me.
The Merry Wives of Windsor. Act v, sc. 5, l. 226. [Page]

Set your heart at rest.
A Midsummer-Night's Dream. Act ii, sc. 1, l. 121. [Titania]

Beshrew my heart.—*A Midsummer-Night's Dream,* v, 1, 295; *Winter's Tale,* i, 2, 281.

Beshrew thy (your) heart.—*II Henry IV,* ii, 3, 45; v, 3, 59; *Romeo and Juliet,* ii, 5, 52; *Troilus and Cressida,* iv, 2, 29.

Foolish heart.—*A Midsummer-Night's Dream,* iii, 2, 219.

4
My heart is true as steel.
A Midsummer-Night's Dream. Act ii, sc. 1, l. 96. [Helena] See INFLUENCE, 761:5.

True heart.—*Richard III,* ii, 1, 10, and six times in later plays.

True-hearted.—*III Henry VI,* iv, 8, 9; *King Lear,* i, 2, 126; *Henry VIII,* v, 1, 154.

True of heart.—*Twelfth Night,* ii, 4, 109; *Troilus and Cressida,* iv, 4, 60.

5
Ay, that left pap, Where heart doth hop.
A Midsummer-Night's Dream. Act v, sc. 1, l. 303. [Pyramus]

Thumped him . . . under the left pap.
Love's Labour's Lost, iv, 3, 24. The only uses of "pap."

6
She may wear her heart out first.
Much Ado about Nothing. Act ii, sc. 3, l. 209. [Leonato]

7
I would eat his heart in the market-place.
Much Ado about Nothing. Act iv, sc. 1, l. 309. [Beatrice]

Eat my heart away.—*A Midsummer-Night's Dream,* ii, 2, 149.

Gnaw thy heart.—*Timon of Athens,* iv, 3, 49.

8
But I will wear my heart upon my sleeve
For daws to peck at.
Othello. Act i, sc. 1, l. 64. [Iago]

9
My heart
Leaps to be gone into my mother's bosom.
Pericles. Act v, sc. 3, l. 44. [Marina]

10
My heart shall never countermand mine eye.
The Rape of Lucrece, l. 276.

Faint not, faint heart, but stoutly say "So be it."
The Rape of Lucrece, l. 1209.

11
[He hath] quite lost their hearts.
Richard II. Act ii, sc. 1, l. 247. Repeated in l. 248, and in no other scene.

12
Show me thy humble heart, and not thy knee,
Whose duty is deceivable and false.
Richard II. Act ii, sc. 3, l. 83. [York]

Penitent heart.—*Measure for Measure,* v, 1, 480.

Up, cousin, up; your heart is up, I know,
Thus high at least, although your knee be low.
Richard II. Act iii, sc. 3, l. 194. [King Richard]

13
Lady Anne: I would I knew thy heart.
Gloucester: 'Tis figured in my tongue.
Richard III. Act i, sc. 2, l. 193.

We know each other's faces,
But for our hearts, he knows no more of mine,
Than I of yours.
Richard III. Act iii, sc. 4, l. 10. [Buckingham]

O, that I knew thy heart!—*Titus Andronicus,* ii, 4, 34.

14
You scarcely have the hearts to tell me so,
And therefore cannot have the hearts to do it.
Richard III. Act i, sc. 4, l. 180. [Clarence]

Have you the heart?—*King John,* iv, 1, 41.

15
A thousand hearts are great within my bosom.
Richard III. Act v, sc. 3, l. 347. [King Richard]

Twice fifteen thousand hearts.—*King John,* ii, 1, 275.

Pierce a hundred thousand hearts.—*A Midsummer-Night's Dream,* ii, 1, 160.

16
O, how my heart abhors
To hear him named, and cannot come to him.
Romeo and Juliet. Act iii, sc. 5, l. 100. [Juliet]

17
With a heart as willing
As bondage e'er of freedom.
Tempest. Act iii, sc. 1, l. 88. [Ferdinand]

18
Timon: Captain Alcibiades, your heart 's in the field now.
Alcibiades: My heart is ever at your service, my lord.
Timon of Athens. Act i, sc. 2, l. 74.

What a beggar his heart is,
Being of no power to make his wishes good.
Timon of Athens. Act i, sc. 2, l. 201. [Flavius]

19
Arm thy heart.
Titus Andronicus. Act ii, sc. 1, l. 12. [Aaron]

My heart stands armed in mine ear,
And will not let a false sound enter there.
Venus and Adonis, l. 779.

20
Thou hast a true-divining heart.
Titus Andronicus. Act ii, sc. 3, l. 214. [Martius] The only use of "true-divining."

1 Liver, brain and heart,
These sovereign thrones.
Twelfth Night. Act i, sc. 1, l. 37. [Duke]

2 My heart accords thereto,
And yet a thousand times it answers 'no.'
The Two Gentlemen of Verona. Act i, sc. 3, l. 90. [Proteus]

3
He grieves my very heart-strings.
The Two Gentlemen of Verona. Act iv, sc. 2, l. 61. [Julia]
Till heart-strings break.—*Richard III,* iv, 4, 365.
From heart-string I love.—*Henry V,* iv, 1, 47.
My dear heart-strings.—*Othello,* iii, 3, 261.
Tune our heart-strings.—*The Rape of Lucrece,* l. 1141. The only uses of "heart-strings."

4
I saw his heart in 's face.
The Winter's Tale. Act i, sc. 2, l. 447. [Polixenes]
He is touch'd To the noble heart.
Winter's Tale. Act iii, sc. 2, l. 222. [Paulina]

II—The Good Heart

5
A good heart 's worth gold.
II Henry IV. Act ii, sc. 4, l. 34. [Hostess]
Good heart!—*Love's Labour 's Lost,* iv, 3, 153, and eight times in later plays.

6
A good leg will fall; a straight back will stoop; a black beard will turn white; a curled pate will grow bald; a fair face will wither; a full eye will wax hollow: but a good heart, Kate, is the sun and the moon; or rather the sun and not the moon; for it shines bright and never changes, but keeps his course truly.
Henry V. Act v, sc. 2, l. 168. [King Henry]

7
A gentler heart did never sway in court.
I Henry VI. Act iii, sc. 2, l. 135. [Talbot]
Gentle heart!—*Richard III,* iii, 7, 247, and nine times in later plays.

8 A pure unspotted heart,
Never yet taint with love.
I Henry VI, Act v, sc. 3, l. 182. [Margaret]
A heart unspotted is not easily daunted.
II Henry VI. Act iii, sc. 1, l. 100. [Gloucester]
Unspotted fire.—*Pericles,* i, 1, 53.
Unspotted lily.—*Henry VIII,* v, 5, 62.
Unspotted soldiers.—*Henry V,* iv, 1, 169.
Kept unspotted.—*The Rape of Lucrece,* l. 821. The only uses of "unspotted."

9 A heart that wishes towards you
Honour and plenteous safety.
Henry VIII. Act i, sc. 1, l. 103. [Norfolk]
King: Embrace and love this man.
Gardiner: With a true heart
And brother love I do it. . . .
King: These joyful tears show thy good heart.
Henry VIII. Act v, sc. 3, l. 172.

10 We will grace his heels
With the most boldest and best hearts of
Rome.
Julius Cæsar. Act iii, sc. 1, l. 20. [Cassius]
Our hearts
Of brothers' temper, do receive you in
With all kind love, good thoughts, and reverence.
Julius Cæsar. Act iii, sc. 1, l. 174. [Brutus]

11 A heart
Dearer than Plutus' mine, richer than gold.
Julius Cæsar. Act iv, sc. 3, l. 101. [Cassius]
I, that denied thee gold, will give my heart.
Julius Cæsar. Act iv, sc. 3, l. 104. [Cassius]
Hearts of gold.—*I Henry IV,* ii, 4, 307; *Henry V,* iv, 1, 44.

12
A kind heart he hath: a woman would run through fire and water for such a kind heart.
The Merry Wives of Windsor. Act iii, sc. 4, l. 106. [Mistress Quickly]
Kind heart.—*I Henry IV,* iv, 3, 64.
Heart of kindness.—*Timon of Athens,* i, 1, 286.
Tender heart.—*Richard III,* iv, 4, 224; 328. The phrase occurs nowhere else.

13
He was great of heart.
Othello. Act v, sc. 2, l. 361. [Cassio]
Great heart!—*King John,* v, 2, 55; *I Henry IV,* v, 4, 87.
Big heart.—*All's Well that Ends Well,* i, 3, 100; *Coriolanus,* iii, 2, 128.
Discreet heart.—*Othello,* ii, 1, 227.
Liberal heart.—*Othello,* iii, 4, 38.
Noble heart.—*III Henry VI,* iv, 2, 8, and six times in later plays.
Nobler hearts.—*Cymbeline,* v, 4, 65.
Princely heart.—*I Henry IV,* iii, 2, 17.
Profound heart.—*Twelfth Night,* i, 5, 195.
Well-disposed hearts.—*Richard II,* ii, 1, 206. The only use of the phrase.

14 My compassionate heart
Will not permit mine eyes once to behold
The thing whereat it trembles by surmise.
Titus Andronicus. Act ii, sc. 3, l. 217. [Quintus]

15
His heart as far from fraud as heaven from earth.
The Two Gentlemen of Verona. Act ii, sc. 7, l. 78. [Julia]

III—The Evil Heart

16 His captain's heart,
Which in the scuffles of great fights hath burst
The buckles on his breast, reneges all temper,
And is become the bellows and the fan
To cool a gipsy's lust.
Antony and Cleopatra. Act i, sc. 1, l. 6. [Philo] The only use of "scuffles." "Reneges" is used again in *King Lear,* ii, 2, 84.

17 Let our hearts, as subtle masters do,
Stir up their servants to an act of rage,
And after seem to chide 'em.
Julius Cæsar. Act ii, sc. 1, l. 175. [Brutus]

18
And here 's another, whose warp'd looks proclaim
What store her heart is made on.
King Lear. Act iii, sc. 6, l. 56. [King Lear]

19
My hands are of your colour; but I shame

To wear a heart so white.
Macbeth. Act ii, sc. 2, l. 64. [Lady Macbeth]

I would not have such a heart in my bosom for the dignity of the whole body.
Macbeth. Act v, sc. 1, l. 61. [Gentlewoman]

1 Go to your bosom;
Knock there, and ask your heart what it doth know
That 's like my brother's fault.
Measure for Measure. Act ii, sc. 2, l. 136. [Isabella]

2 The heart,
Which once corrupted takes the worser part.
The Rape of Lucrece, l. 293.

Anon his beating heart, alarum striking,
Gives the hot charge and bids them do their liking.
The Rape of Lucrece, l. 433.

Thy rocky and wreck-threatening heart.
The Rape of Lucrece, l. 590. The only use of "wreck-threatening."

3 Beshrew that heart that makes my heart to groan
For that deep wound it gives my friend and me!
Sonnets. No. cxxxiii.

4 Methinks, false hearts should never have sound legs.
Timon of Athens. Act i, sc. 2, l. 240. [Apemantus]

False heart.—*II Henry VI,* v, 1, 143; *The Merchant of Venice,* v, 1, 189; *Macbeth,* i, 7, 82; *Cymbeline,* ii, 4, 34; *The Rape of Lucrece,* ll. 228, 1512.

False of heart.—*King Lear,* iii, 4, 95; *The Winter's Tale,* iv, 3, 116.

Heart of falsehood.—*Troilus and Cressida,* iii, 2, 202.

5 Now let hot Ætna cool in Sicily,
And be my heart an ever-burning hell.
Titus Andronicus. Act iii, sc. 1, l. 242. [Marcus] Ætna is mentioned again in *The Rape of Lucrece,* l. 1042. "Ever-burning" is repeated in *Othello,* iii, 3, 463: "Ever-burning lights."

Base-born heart.—*III Henry VI,* ii, 2, 143.

Craven heart.—*I Henry VI,* ii, 4, 87.

Faint and milky heart.—*Timon of Athens,* iii, 1, 57.

Hollow heart.—*I Henry VI,* iii, 1, 136; *Henry VIII,* iii, 1, 104.

Revengeful heart.—*Richard III,* i, 2, 174.

Savage heart.—*Richard III,* iii, 5, 83.

Tyrannous heart.—*Twelfth Night,* iii, 1, 131.

Vulgar heart.—*II Henry IV,* i, 3, 90.

Wild heart.—*Much Ado about Nothing,* iii, 1, 112.

IV—The Light Heart

6 That I see thee here,
Thou noble thing! more dances my rapt heart
Than when I first my wedded mistress saw
Bestride my threshold.
Coriolanus. Act iv, sc. 5, l. 121. [Aufidius]

Make our . . . hearts dance.—*Coriolanus,* v, 3, 99.

7 But, by the mass, our hearts are in the trim.
Henry V. Act iv, sc. 3, l. 115. [King Henry]

My heart doth joy.—*Julius Cæsar,* v, 5, 34.

8 A light heart lives long.
Love's Labour 's Lost. Act v, sc. 2, l. 18. [Katharine]

My heart is wondrous light.
Romeo and Juliet. Act iv, sc. 2, l. 46. [Capulet]

My bosom's lord sits lightly in his throne.
Romeo and Juliet. Act v, sc. 1, l. 3. [Romeo]

Light of heart.—*Romeo and Juliet,* i, 4, 35.

9 Kept hearts in liveries, but mine own was free,
And reign'd, commanding in his monarchy.
A Lover's Complaint, l. 195.

V—The Heavy Heart

10 My heart is heavy and mine age is weak.
All's Well that Ends Well. Act iii, sc. 4, l. 41. [Steward]

Her heart weighs sadly.
All's Well that Ends Well. Act iii, sc. 5, l. 70. [Widow]

Heart-heaviness.—*As You Like It,* v, 2, 50. The only use of the phrase.

11 Unclog my heart Of what lies heavy to 't.
Coriolanus. Act iv, sc. 2, l. 47. [Volumnia] The only use of "unclog."

12 A heavy heart bears not a nimble tongue.
Love's Labour 's Lost. Act v, sc. 2, l. 747. [Princess of France]

Heavy heart.—*Richard III,* iii, 1, 149; *Richard II,* v, 1, 92; *Love's Labour 's Lost,* v, 2, 247; *Troilus and Cressida,* iv, 4, 17.

13 Hero: My heart is exceeding heavy.
Margaret: 'Twill be heavier soon by the weight of a man.
Much Ado about Nothing. Act iii, sc. 4, l. 24.

14 O heart, heavy heart,
Why sigh'st thou without breaking?
Troilus and Cressida. Act iv, sc. 4, l. 17. [Pandarus]

VI—The Merry Heart

15 There 's a merry heart!
II Henry IV. Act v, sc. 3, l. 24. [Falstaff]

And a merry heart lives long-a.
II Henry IV. Act v, sc. 3, l. 50. [Silence]

16 Don Pedro: In faith, lady, you have a merry heart.
Beatrice: Yea, my lord; I thank it, poor fool, it keeps on the windy side of care.
Much Ado about Nothing. Act ii, sc. 1, l. 324.

1
Jog on, jog on, the foot-path way,
And merrily hent the stile-a:
A merry heart goes all the day,
Your sad tires in a mile-a.
Winter's Tale. Act iv, sc. 3, l. 132. [Autolycus] The only use of "jog" or "jog on." "Jogging" occurs in *Taming of the Shrew,* iii, 2, 213. "Stile" is repeated in *Merry Wives of Windsor,* iii, 1, 33: "Over the stile"; and in *King Lear,* iv, 1, 58: "Both stile and gate."

VII—The Sad Heart

2
Measureless liar, thou hast made my heart
Too great for what contains it.
Coriolanus. Act v, sc. 6, l. 103. [Coriolanus] "Measureless" is repeated in *Macbeth,* ii, 1, 17: "Measureless content."

3
I draw the sword myself: take it, and hit
The innocent mansion of my love, my heart:
Fear not; 'tis empty of all things but grief.
Cymbeline. Act iii, sc. 4, l. 69. [Imogen]
Come, here 's my heart.
Something afore 't. Soft, soft! we 'll no defence;
Obedient as the scabbard.
Cymbeline. Act iii, sc. 4, l. 80. [Imogen]

4
My heart bleeds inwardly.
II Henry IV, ii, 2, 51. [Prince of Wales]
Heart is bleeding, All help needing.
The Passionate Pilgrim, l. 267.
The thought of it doth make my faint heart bleed,
And fear doth teach it divination.
Venus and Adonis, l. 669.
O, my heart bleeds.
The Tempest. Act i, sc. 2, l. 63. [Miranda]
Weep I cannot, But my heart bleeds.
The Winter's Tale. Act iii, sc. 3, l. 51. [Antigonus]
Send to her . . . A pair of bleeding hearts.
Richard III. Act iv, sc. 4, l. 271. [Queen Elizabeth]
Bleeding heart.—*II Henry VI,* iv, 1, 85.
My heart drops blood.—*Cymbeline,* v, 5, 148.
My heart wept blood.—*The Winter's Tale,* v, 2, 97.

5
Scarce I can refrain
The execution of my big-swoln heart
Upon that Clifford, that cruel child-killer.
III Henry VI. Act ii, sc. 2, l. 110. [Richmond] "Big-swoln" is used again in *Titus Andronicus,* iii, 1, 224. The only use of "child-killer."
O'er-fraught heart.—*Macbeth,* iv, 3, 210. The only use of "o'er-fraught."
Swelling heart.—*I Henry VI,* iii, 1, 26; *Titus Andronicus,* v, 3, 13.

6
My heart is drown'd with grief.
II Henry VI. Act iii, sc. 1, l. 198. [King Henry]
Heart-grief.—*Henry V,* ii, 2, 27. The only use of the phrase.

7
Hearts of most hard temper
Melt and lament for her.
Henry VIII. Act ii, sc. 3, l. 11. [Old Lady]

8
Thy heart is big, get thee apart and weep.
Julius Cæsar, iii, 1, 282. See Eye, 452:11.
My heart weeps to see him
So little of his great self.
Henry VIII. Act iii, sc. 2, l. 335. [Chamberlain]

9
My heart is in the coffin there with Cæsar.
Julius Cæsar. Act iii, sc. 2, l. 111. [Antony]

10
O, my heart is sick!
King John. Act v, sc. 3, l. 4. [King John]
Rosaline: Is the fool sick?
Biron: Sick at the heart.
Love's Labour 's Lost. Act ii, sc. 1, l. 184.
'Tis bitter cold, And I am sick at heart.
Hamlet. Act i, sc. 1, l. 8. [Francisco]
I am sick at heart.—*Macbeth,* v, 3, 19.
I am sick still; heart-sick.
Cymbeline. Act iv, sc. 2, l. 37. [Imogen]
Heart sick with thought.—*The Two Gentlemen of Verona,* i, 1, 69. "Heart-sick" is used a third time in *Romeo and Juliet,* iii, 3, 72: "Heart-sick groans."
Sick heart.—*III Henry VI,* v, 2, 8; *Venus and Adonis,* l. 584.
Sickly heart.—*Richard III,* ii, 1, 42.

11
O me, my heart, my rising heart! but, down!
King Lear. Act ii, sc. 4, l. 122. [King Lear]
Pluck up, my heart, and be sad.
Much Ado about Nothing. Act v, sc. 1, l. 207. [Don Pedro]

12
Even in the glasses of thine eyes I see thy grieved heart.
Richard II. Act i, sc. 3, l. 208. [King Richard]
Swell'st thou, proud heart? I 'll give thee scope to beat,
Since foes have scope to beat both thee and me.
Richard II. Act iii, sc. 3, l. 140. [King Richard]
Proud heart.—*I Henry VI,* iv, 3, 24, and five times in later plays.

13
Your hearts will throb and weep to hear him speak.
Titus Andronicus. Act v, sc. 3, l. 95. [Marcus]
Yet my heart Throbs to know one thing.
Macbeth. Act iv, sc. 1, l. 100. [Macbeth] The only uses of "throb" and "throbs."
My throbbing heart shall rock thee day and night.
Venus and Adonis, l. 1186.
Throbbing breast.—*II Henry VI,* iv, 4, 5. The only uses of "throbbing."

14
My heart, all mad with misery,
Beats in this hollow prison of my flesh.
Titus Andronicus. Act iii, sc. 2, l. 9. [Titus]
When thy poor heart beats with outrageous beating,
Thou canst not strike it thus to make it still.
Titus Andronicus. Act iii, sc. 2, l. 13. [Titus]
Poor heart.—*Richard III,* i, 2, 205, and ten times in later plays.

Poor old heart.—*King Lear*, iii, 7, 62.
Old hearts.—*The Winter's Tale*, i, 1, 43.

1
Out on thee, murderer! thou kill'st my heart.
Titus Andronicus. Act iii, sc. 2, l. 54. [Titus]

He comes to kill my heart.
As You Like It. Act iii, sc. 2, l. 260. [Rosalind]

The king has killed his heart.
Henry V. Act ii, sc. 1, l. 93. [Hostess]

Wounded heart.—*Titus Andronicus*, i, 1, 314.

2
My heart beats thicker than a feverous pulse.
Troilus and Cressida. Act iii, sc. 2, l. 38. [Troilus]

Feverous life.—*Measure for Measure*, iii, 1, 75.
The earth Was feverous.—*Macbeth*, ii, 3, 66.
The world Were feverous.—*Coriolanus*, i, 4, 61. The only uses of "feverous."

3
A heart
As full of sorrows as the sea of sands.
The Two Gentlemen of Verona. Act iv, sc. 3, l. 32. [Silvia]

Sad heart.—*Julius Cæsar*, ii, 1, 290.

4
And now she beats her heart, whereat it groans.
Venus and Adonis, l. 829.

5
Her heart is but o'ercharged.
Winter's Tale. Act iii, sc. 2, l. 151. [Leontes]

6
Your heart is full of something that does take
Your mind from feasting.
The Winter's Tale. Act iv, sc. 4, l. 356. [Polixenes]

VIII—The Hard Heart

7
Your highness
Shall from this practice but make hard your heart.
Cymbeline. Act i, sc. 5, l. 23. [Cornelius]

8
Will nothing turn your unrelenting hearts?
I Henry VI. Act v, sc. 4, l. 59. [La Pucelle]

Be your heart to them
As unrelenting flint to drops of rain.
Titus Andronicus. Act ii, sc. 3, l. 140. [Demetrius] "Unrelenting" is used a third time in *III Henry VI*, ii, 1, 58: "Unrelenting Clifford."

9
I would to God my heart were flint, like Edward's;
Or Edward's soft and pitiful, like mine.
Richard III. Act i, sc. 3, l. 140. [Gloucester]

Brassy bosoms and rough hearts of flint.
The Merchant of Venice, iv, 1, 31. See under Pity for full quotation.

My heart is not compact of flint nor steel.
Titus Andronicus. Act v, sc. 3, l. 88. [Marcus]

Throw my heart
Against the flint and hardness of my fault;
Which, being dried with grief, will break to powder.
Antony and Cleopatra. Act iv, sc. 9, l. 15. [Enobarbus]

Heart of flint.—*Twelfth Night*, i, 5, 305.
Thy flinty heart.—*II Henry VI*, iii, 2, 99.

10
My heart is turn'd to stone: and while 'tis mine,
It shall be stony.
II Henry VI. Act v, sc. 2, l. 50. [Clifford]

My heart is turned to stone; I strike it, and it hurts my hand.
Othello. Act iv, sc. 1, l. 193. [Othello]

O perjured woman! thou dost stone my heart,
And makest me call what I intend to do
A murder, which I thought a sacrifice.
Othello. Act v, sc. 2, l. 63. [Othello]

Stone him with harden'd hearts, harder than stones.
The Rape of Lucrece, l. 978.

Heart of stone.—*Twelfth Night*, iii, 4, 221.
Stone-hard heart.—*Richard III*, iv, 4, 227. The only use of "stone-hard." See under Knife.
Stony-hearted.—*I Henry IV*, ii, 2, 28. The only use of the phrase.
Marble heart.—*III Henry VI*, iii, 1, 38.
O gravel heart!—*Measure for Measure*, iv, 3, 68.

11
Were thy heart as hard as steel,
As thou hast shown it flinty by thy deeds,
I come to pierce it, or to give thee mine.
III Henry VI. Act ii, sc. 1, l. 201. [Richard]

One whose heart is button'd up with steel.
The Comedy of Errors. Act iv, sc. 2, l. 34. [Dromio of Syracuse] The only use of "button'd."

Covering your fearful land
With hard bright steel and hearts harder than steel.
Richard II. Act iii, sc. 2, l. 110. [Scroop]

Had not God, for some strong purpose, steel'd
The hearts of men, they must perforce have melted.
Richard II. Act v, sc. 2, l. 34. [York]

Steel thy melting heart.—*III Henry VI*, ii, 2, 41.
Heart of steel.—*Comedy of Errors*, iii, 2, 150.
Heart with strings of steel.—*Hamlet*, iii, 3, 70. See Knee, 818:12.

12
You may as well go stand upon the beach
And bid the main flood bate his usual height;
You may as well use question with the wolf
Why he hath made the ewe bleat for the lamb;
You may as well forbid the mountain pines
To wag their high tops and to make no noise,
When they are fretten with the gusts of heaven;
You may as well do any thing most hard,
As seek to soften that—than which what 's harder?—

His Jewish heart.
The Merchant of Venice. Act iv, sc. 1, l. 71. [Antonio] The only use of "fretten."

1
I would I could find in my heart that I had not a hard heart.
Much Ado about Nothing. Act i, sc. 1, l. 127. [Benedick]

Is there any cause in nature that makes these hard hearts?
King Lear. Act iii, sc. 6, l. 81. [King Lear]

Hard heart.—*The Comedy of Errors,* iv, 2, 34, and five times in later plays.

Hard of heart.—*Henry V,* iii, 3, 11.

Men grow hard-hearted.—*Much Ado about Nothing,* v, 1, 321.

I will not be so hard-hearted.—*Twelfth Night,* i, 5, 262.

Hard-hearted lord.—*Richard II,* v, 3, 121.

Hard-hearted man!—*Richard II,* v, 3, 87.

Hard-hearted wench.—*Romeo and Juliet,* ii, 4, 4.

Hard-hearted adamant.—*Midsummer-Night's Dream,* ii, 1, 195. "Adamant" is used also in *I Henry VI,* i, 4, 52, and in *Troilus and Cressida,* iii, 2, 186.

Hard-hearted Clifford. *III Henry VI,* i, 4, 167. The only uses of "hard-hearted."

2
The place where I have feasted, does it now,
Like all mankind, show me an iron heart?
Timon of Athens. Act iii, sc. 4, l. 83. [Timon]

All that have not hearts of iron.
Henry VIII. Act iii, sc. 2, l. 424. [Cromwell]

3
Obdurate, flinty, hard as steel,
Nay, more than flint, for stone at rain relenteth.
Venus and Adonis, l. 199.

Your heart be so obdurate.—*The Two Gentlemen of Verona,* iv, 2, 120.

4
Remove your siege from my unyielding heart;
To love's alarms it will not ope the gate.
Venus and Adonis, l. 423. The only use of "unyielding."

Thy eyes' shrewd tutor, that hard heart of thine,
Hath taught them scornful tricks and such disdain
That they have murder'd this poor heart of mine.
Venus and Adonis, l. 500.

IX—The Loving Heart

5
My full heart Remains in use with you.
Antony and Cleopatra. Act i, sc. 3, l. 43. [Antony]

To knit your hearts With an unslipping knot.
Antony and Cleopatra. Act ii, sc. 2, l. 128. [Agrippa] The only use of "unslipping."

6
When she first met Mark Antony, she pursed up his heart, upon the river of Cydnus.
Antony and Cleopatra. Act ii, sc. 2, l. 192. [Enobarbus] The only use of "pursed." The Cydnus is mentioned again in v, 2, 228, and in *Cymbeline,* ii, 4, 71.

My heart was to thy rudder tied by the strings,
And thou shouldst tow me after.
Antony and Cleopatra. Act iii, sc. 11, l. 57. [Antony] The only use of "tow."

Turn the rudder.—*Antony and Cleopatra,* iii, 10, 3. The only uses of "rudder."

7
Whose heart I thought I had, for she had mine;
Which whilst it was mine had annex'd unto 't
A million more, now lost.
Antony and Cleopatra. Act iv, sc. 14, l. 16. [Antony] The only use of "annex'd."

8
It is young Orlando, that tripped up the wrestler's heels and your heart both in an instant.
As You Like It. Act iii, sc. 2, l. 224. [Celia]

Rosalind: O, my dear Orlando, how it grieves me to see thee wear thy heart in a scarf!
Orlando: It is my arm.
Rosalind: I thought thy heart had been wounded with the claws of a lion.
Orlando: Wounded it is, but with the eyes of a lady.
As You Like It. Act v, sc. 2, l. 22.

9
My dear heart's dearer heart.
The Comedy of Errors. Act iii, sc. 2, l. 62. [Antipholus of Syracuse]

Dear heart.—*Titus Andronicus,* iii, 1, 211; *Twelfth Night,* ii, 3, 109; *Tempest,* i, 2, 305.

Sweet hearts.—*Love's Labour's Lost,* v, 1, 110, and sixteen times in later plays.

Lose your heart.—*Hamlet,* i, 3, 31.

10
Queen Margaret: And take my heart with thee.
Suffolk: A jewel, lock'd into the wofull'st cask
That ever did contain a thing of worth.
II Henry VI. Act iii, sc. 2, l. 408. The only use of "cask."

11
His heart, like an agate, with your print impress'd.
Love's Labour's Lost. Act ii, sc. 1, l. 236. [Boyet]

By heart you love her, because your heart cannot come by her; in heart you love her, because your heart is in love with her; and out of heart you love her, being out of heart that you cannot enjoy her.
Love's Labour's Lost. Act iii, sc. 1, l. 42. [Moth]

Hence ever then my heart is in thy breast.
Love's Labour's Lost. Act v, sc. 2, l. 826. [Princess]

12
Who could refrain,
That had a heart to love, and in that heart
Courage to make 's love known?
Macbeth. Act ii, sc. 3, l. 122. [Macbeth]

1 My heart unto yours is knit
So that but one heart we can make of it.
A Midsummer-Night's Dream. Act ii, sc. 2, l. 47. [Lysander]

A double heart for his single one.
Much Ado about Nothing. Act ii, sc. 1, l. 288. [Beatrice]

The very instant that I saw you, did
My heart fly to your service; there resides,
To make me slave to it; and for your sake
Am I this patient log-man.
The Tempest. Act iii, sc. 1, l. 67. [Ferdinand] The only use of "log-man."

Beshrew his soul for me,
He started one poor heart of mine in thee.
Twelfth Night. Act iv, sc. 1, l. 62. [Olivia]

I would my heart were in her body.
Troilus and Cressida. Act i, sc. 2, l. 85. [Pandarus]

2
Transparent Helena! Nature shows art,
That through thy bosom makes me see thy heart.
A Midsummer-Night's Dream. Act ii, sc. 2, l. 104. [Lysander]

My heart to her but as guest-wise sojourn'd.
A Midsummer-Night's Dream. Act iii, sc. 2, l. 171. [Demetrius] The only use of "guest-wise."

3
My heart is with your liking.
Much Ado about Nothing. Act v, sc. 4, l. 32. [Leonato]

My heart 's subdued
Even to the very quality of my lord.
Othello. Act i, sc. 3, l. 251. [Desdemona]

4
But his hot heart, which fond desire doth scorch,
Puffs forth another wind that fires the torch.
The Rape of Lucrece, l. 314.

5
Can I go forward when my heart is here?
Romeo and Juliet. Act ii, sc. 1, l. 1. [Romeo]

6
Bearing thy heart, which I will keep so chary
As tender nurse her babe from faring ill.
Presume not on thy heart when mine is slain;
Thou gavest me thine, not to give back again.
Sonnets. No. xxii. The only use of "chary."

No, let me be obsequious in my heart,
And take thou my oblation, poor but free.
Sonnets. No. cxxv. "Oblation" is repeated in *A Lover's Complaint,* l. 223.

Prison my heart in thy steel bosom's ward.
Sonnets. No. cxxxiii.

7
Mistress of my heart.
Titus Andronicus. Act i, sc. 1, l. 241. [Saturninus]

By innocence I swear, and by my youth,
I have one heart, one bosom and one truth,
And that no woman has; nor never none
Shall mistress be of it, save I alone.
Twelfth Night. Act iii, sc. 1, l. 169. [Viola]

8
My heart all whole as thine, thy heart my wound.
Venus and Adonis, l. 370.

'Give me my heart,' saith she, 'and thou shalt have it;
O, give it me, lest thy hard heart do steel it.'
Venus and Adonis, l. 374.

Bids him farewell, and look well to her heart,
The which, by Cupid's bow she doth protest,
He carries thence incaged in his breast.
Venus and Adonis, l. 580. "Incaged" is repeated in *III Henry VI,* iv, 6, 12, and *Richard II,* ii, 1, 102.

My boding heart pants, beats, and takes no rest,
But, like an earthquake, shakes thee on my breast.
Venus and Adonis, l. 647.

9 My little heart were quite undone,
In his bedchamber to be barr'd of rest.
Venus and Adonis, l. 783.

No, lady, no; my heart longs not to groan,
But soundly sleeps, while now it sleeps alone.
Venus and Adonis, l. 785.

10
Next to thyself and my young rover, he 's
Apparent to my heart.
The Winter's Tale. Act i, sc. 2, l. 176. [Leontes] The only use of "rover."

X—The Broken Heart

11 This blows my heart:
If swift thought break it not, a swifter mean
Shall outstrike thought: but thought will do 't, I feel.
Antony and Cleopatra. Act iv, sc. 6, l. 34. [Enobarbus] The only use of "outstrike."

Heart, once be stronger than thy continent,
Crack thy frail case!
Antony and Cleopatra. Act iv, sc. 14, l. 40. [Antony]

Now cracks a noble heart.
Hamlet. Act v, sc. 2, l. 370. [Horatio]

My old heart is crack'd, is crack'd!
King Lear. Act ii, sc. 1, l. 92. [Gloucester]

Thou hast a heart That even cracks for woe!
Pericles. Act iii, sc. 2, l. 76. [Cerimon]

Crack'd heart.—*Coriolanus,* v, 3, 9.

12
Leave wringing of your hands: peace! sit you down,
And let me wring your heart; for so I shall,
If it be made of penetrable stuff,
If damned custom have not brass'd it so
That it be proof and bulwark against sense.
Hamlet. Act iii, sc. 4, l. 34. [Hamlet] The only use of "brass'd." "Penetrable" is repeated in *Richard III,* iii, 7, 225.

Queen: O Hamlet, thou hast cleft my heart in twain.
Hamlet: O, throw away the worser part of it,
And live the purer with the other half.
Hamlet. Act iii, sc. 4, l. 156.

Break, my heart.—*Hamlet,* i, 2, 159.

13
His heart is fracted and corroborate.
Henry V. Act ii, sc. 1, l. 130. [Pistol] The only use of "corroborate." "Fracted" occurs again in *Timon of Athens,* ii, 1, 22.

1
And even now my burthen'd heart would break,
Should I not curse them.
II Henry VI. Act iii, sc. 2, l. 320. [Suffolk] See under CURSE.

2
No, no, my heart will burst, an if I speak:
And I will speak, that so my heart may burst.
III Henry VI. Act v, sc. 5, l. 59. [Queen Margaret]

If my heart were great, 'twould burst at this.
All's Well that Ends Well. Act iv, sc. 3, l. 366. [Parolles]

I cannot speak; if my heart be not ready to burst.
II Henry IV. Act ii, sc. 4, l. 409. [Doll Tearsheet]

Then burst his mighty heart.
Julius Cæsar. Act iii, sc. 2, l. 190. [Antony]

Your heart is burst, you have lost half your soul.
Othello. Act i, sc. 1, l. 87. [Iago]

O, that my heart would burst!
King Lear. Act v, sc. 3, l. 182. [Edgar]

His flaw'd heart,
Alack, too weak the conflict to support!
'Twixt two extremes of passion, joy and grief,
Burst smilingly.
King Lear. Act v, sc. 3, l. 196. [Edgar]

Flaw'd the heart.—*Henry VIII,* i, 2, 21. "Flaw'd" is used for a third time in *Henry VIII,* i, 1, 95.

3
Brutus hath rived my heart.
Julius Cæsar. Act iv, sc. 3, l. 85. [Cassius] "Rived" is repeated in i, 3, 6, "Rived the knotty oaks," and occurs in no other play.

My heart,
As wedged with a sigh, would rive in twain.
Troilus and Cressida. Act i, sc. 1, l. 34. [Troilus]

Cleave a heart in twain.—*Measure for Measure,* iii, 1, 63.

4
The tackle of my heart is crack'd and burn'd,
And all the shrouds wherewith my life should sail
Are turned to one thread, one little hair:
My heart hath one poor string to stay it by.
King John. Act v, sc. 7, l. 52. [King John]

5
King Lear: Wilt break my heart?
Kent: I had rather break mine own.
King Lear. Act iii, sc. 4, l. 4.

My heart breaks at it.
King Lear. Act iv, sc. 6, l. 145. [Edgar]

Break, heart; I prithee, break!
King Lear. Act v, sc. 3, l. 312. [Kent]

O break, my heart! poor bankrupt, break at once!
Romeo and Juliet. Act iii, sc. 2, l. 57. [Juliet]

6
Grieving themselves to guess at others' smarts,
And then they drown their eyes or break their hearts.
The Rape of Lucrece, l. 1238.

Break my heart.—*Troilus and Cressida,* iv, 2, 114.

Broke my heart.—*Titus Andronicus,* v, 1, 113.

7
O, cut my lace in sunder, that my pent heart
May have some scope to beat.
Richard III. Act iv, sc. 1, l. 34. [Queen Elizabeth]

O, cut my lace, lest my heart, cracking it,
Break too!
The Winter's Tale. Act iii, sc. 2, l. 174. [Paulina]

Cut my lace, Charmian, come.
Antony and Cleopatra. Act i, sc. 3, l. 71. [Cleopatra]

XI—Heart and Brain

8
A diminution in our captain's brain
Restores his heart.
Antony and Cleopatra. Act iii, sc. 13, l. 198. [Enobarbus] "Diminution" is repeated in *Cymbeline,* i, 3, 18.

9
The matter 's in my head and in my heart.
As You Like It. Act iii, sc. 5, l. 137. [Phebe]

10
I have a heart as little apt as yours,
But yet a brain that leads my use of anger
To better vantage.
Coriolanus. Act iii, sc. 2, l. 29. [Volumnia]

11
I will ease my heart,
Albeit I make a hazard of my head.
I Henry IV. Act i, sc. 3, l. 127. [Hotspur]

12
My mind hath been as big as one of yours,
My heart as great, my reason haply more.
The Taming of the Shrew. Act v, sc. 2, l. 170. [Katharina]

XII—Heart and Hand

13
My hand would free her, but my heart says no.
I Henry VI. Act v, sc. 3, l. 61. [Suffolk]

14
Cassius: Give me your hand.
Brutus: And my heart too.
Julius Cæsar. Act iv, sc. 3, l. 117.

Ferdinand: Here 's my hand.
Miranda: And mine, with my heart in 't.
The Tempest. Act iii, sc. 1, l. 89.

15
It is his hand, my lord; but I hope his heart is not in the contents.
King Lear. Act i, sc. 2, l. 72. [Edmund]

16
So many have, that never touch'd his hand,
Sweetly supposed them mistress of his heart.
A Lover's Complaint, l. 141.

17
Othello: Give me your hand: this hand is moist, my lady.
Desdemona: It yet hath felt no age nor known no sorrow.

Othello: This argues fruitfulness and liberal heart;
Hot, hot, and moist: this hand of yours requires
A sequester from liberty, fasting and prayer,
Much castigation, exercise devout;
For here 's a young and sweating devil here,
That commonly rebels. 'Tis a good hand,
A frank one.
Desdemona: You may, indeed, say so;
For 'twas that hand that gave away my heart.
Othello: A liberal hand: the hearts of old gave hands;
But our new heraldry is hands, not hearts.

Othello. Act iii, sc. 4, l. 36. The only use of "fruitfulness," "sequester," and "castigation."

1
His hand, that yet remains upon her breast,—
Rude ram, to batter such an ivory wall!—
May feel her heart—poor citizen!—distress'd,
Wounding itself to death, rise up and fall.

The Rape of Lucrece, l. 463.

She wakes her heart by beating on her breast,
And bids it leap from thence, where it may find
Some purer chest to close so pure a mind

The Rape of Lucrece, l. 759.

2
My heart this covenant makes, my hand thus seals it.

Richard II. Act ii, sc. 3, l. 50. [Bolingbroke]

My heart is not confederate with my hand.

Richard II. Act v, sc. 3, l. 53. [Aumerle]

3
Whose hand soever lanced their tender hearts,
Thy head, all indirectly, gave direction.

Richard III. Act iv, sc. 4, l. 224. [Queen Elizabeth] "Lanced" is repeated in *King Lear,* ii, 1, 54: "Lanced mine arm."

Here is her hand, the agent of her heart.

The Two Gentlemen of Verona. Act i, sc. 3, l. 46. [Proteus]

XIII—Heart and Tongue

4
Her tongue will not obey her heart, nor can
Her heart inform her tongue,—the swan's down-feather,
That stands upon the swell at full of tide,
And neither way inclines.

Antony and Cleopatra. Act iii, sc. 2, l. 47. [Antony] The only use of "down-feather."

5
My tongue, though not my heart, shall have his will.

The Comedy of Errors. Act iv, sc. 2, l. 18. [Adriana]

My heart prays for him, though my tongue do curse.

The Comedy of Errors. Act iv, sc. 2, l. 28. [Adriana]

But, break, my heart; for I must hold my tongue.

Hamlet. Act i, sc. 2, l. 159. [Hamlet]

6
My heart accordeth with my tongue.

II Henry VI. Act iii, sc. 1, l. 269. [Suffolk]

7
Nor can my tongue unload my heart's great burthen;
For selfsame wind that I should speak withal
Is kindling coals that fires all my breast,
And burns me up with flames that tears would quench.

III Henry VI. Act ii, sc. 1, l. 81. [Richard]

8
One that am the tongue of these
To sound the purposes of all their hearts.

King John. Act iv, sc. 2, l. 47. [Pembroke]

9
He hath a heart as sound as a bell and his tongue is the clapper, for what his heart thinks his tongue speaks.

Much Ado about Nothing. Act iii, sc. 2, l. 12. [Don Pedro] The only use of "clapper."

10
My heart is great; but it must break with silence,
Ere 't be disburden'd with a liberal tongue.

Richard II. Act ii, sc. 1, l. 228. [Ross] The only use of "disburden'd."

What my tongue dares not, that my heart shall say.

Richard II. Act v, sc. 5, l. 97. [Groom]

11
Were his heart
Almost impregnable, his old ears deaf,
Yet should both ear and heart obey my tongue.

Titus Andronicus. Act iv, sc. 4, l. 97. [Tamora]

12
For lovers say, the heart hath treble wrong
When it is barr'd the aidance of the tongue.

Venus and Adonis, l. 329. "Aidance" is repeated in *II Henry VI,* iii, 2, 165.

But when the heart's attorney once is mute,
The client breaks, as desperate in his suit.

Venus and Adonis, l. 335.

XIV—The Pulse

13
Let me feel your pulse.

The Comedy of Errors. Act iv, sc. 4, l. 55. [Pinch]

Gazing in mine eyes, feeling my pulse.

The Comedy of Errors. Act v, sc. 1, l. 243. [Antipholus of Ephesus]

14
My pulse, as yours, doth temperately keep time,
And makes as healthful music.

Hamlet. Act iii, sc. 4, l. 140. [Hamlet]

Your pulsidge beats as extraordinarily as heart would desire.

II Henry IV. Act ii, sc. 4, l. 25. [Hostess] The only use of "pulsidge." "Extraordinarily" is repeated in i, 2, 235, and occurs in no other play.

Thy pulse Beats as of flesh and blood.

The Tempest. Act v, sc. 1, l. 113. [Alonso]

1
Have you a working pulse?
Pericles. Act v, sc. 1, l. 155. [Pericles]
2
No pulse
Shall keep his native progress, but surcease.
Romeo and Juliet. Act iv, sc. 1, l. 96. [Friar Laurence] "Surcease" is repeated in *Coriolanus,* iii, 2, 121, and in *Macbeth,* i, 7, 4.

HEAT

See also Anger

3
Osric: It is very hot.
Hamlet: No, believe me, 'tis very cold; the wind is northerly.
Osric: It is indifferent cold, my lord, indeed.
Hamlet: But yet methinks it is very sultry and hot for my complexion.
Osric: Exceedingly, my lord; it is very sultry.
Hamlet. Act v, sc. 2, l. 97. The only uses of "northerly" and "sultry."
Very hot.—*II Henry IV,* ii, 4, 15.
'Tis hot, 'tis hot.—*I Henry IV,* v, 3, 55.
Too hot, too hot!—*The Winter's Tale,* i, 2, 108.
Too hot.—*II Henry VI,* i, 1, 137, seven times in later plays, and once in *Sonnets,* xviii.
4
I am as hot as molten lead, and as heavy too.
I Henry IV. Act v, sc. 3, l. 34. [Falstaff] "Molten lead" is repeated in *King Lear,* iv, 7, 48; and "molten coin" is used in *Timon of Athens,* iii, 1, 35. These are the only uses of "molten."
Hot as monkeys.—*Othello,* iii, 3, 403.
Hot as Perseus.—*Troilus and Cressida,* iv, 5, 186. Perseus is mentioned again in i, 3, 42, and in *Henry V,* iii, 7, 22.
5
I am hot with haste in seeking you.
King John. Act iv, sc. 3, l. 74. [Hubert] See under HASTE.
Hot and hasty.—*Much Ado about Nothing,* ii, 1, 78.
Hot and cold.—*Antony and Cleopatra,* i, 5, 52.
Hot and dry.—*Hamlet,* iv, 7, 158.
Hot and furious.—*Cymbeline,* ii, 3, 7.
Hot, faint, and weary.—*Venus and Adonis,* l. 559.
Wondrous hot.—*King John,* iii, 2, 1.
6
Thrown into the Thames, and cooled, glowing hot, in that surge, like a horse-shoe.
The Merry Wives of Windsor. Act iii, sc. 5, l. 121. [Falstaff] The only use of "horse-shoe."
Hissing hot.—*The Merry Wives of Windsor,* iii, 5, 122.
7
Heat me these irons hot.
King John. Act iv, sc. 1, l. 1. [Hubert]
Heat red-hot.—*King John,* iv, 1, 61.
8
The heat of his displeasure; which at this time so rageth in him, that with the mischief of your person it would scarcely allay.
King Lear. Act i, sc. 2, l. 177. [Edmund]
She knows the heat of a luxurious bed.
Much Ado about Nothing, iv, 1, 42. See under BED.
Heat of action.—*Troilus and Cressida,* iv, 5, 106.
Heat of blood.—*Love's Labour's Lost,* v, 2, 810; *I Henry IV,* v, 2, 17; *Measure for Measure,* v, 1, 477.
Heat of day.—*II Henry IV,* iv, 5, 30.
Heat of deeds.—*Macbeth,* ii, 1, 61.
Heart-burning heat of duty.—*Love's Labour's Lost,* i, 1, 280. Only use of "heart-burning."
Heat of the ginger.—*Henry V,* iii, 7, 21.
Heat of life.—*Romeo and Juliet,* iv, 3, 16.
Heat of lust.—*The Rape of Lucrece,* l. 1473.
Heat o' the sun.—*Cymbeline,* iv, 2, 258.
Heat of this descending sun.—*Venus and Adonis,* l. 190.
Thou heatest my blood.—*Love's Labour's Lost,* i, 2, 32. The only use of "heatest."
You'll heat my blood.—*Antony and Cleopatra,* i, 3, 80.
Heat his blood.—*Troilus and Cressida,* v, 1, 1.
Heat your blood.—*Pericles,* iv, 1, 49.
Heat my liver.—*Antony and Cleopatra,* i, 2, 23.
Heat of our livers.—*II Henry IV,* i, 2, 198.
Heat with wine.—*Merchant of Venice,* i, 1, 81.
9
As subject to heat as butter.
The Merry Wives of Windsor. Act iii, sc. 5, l. 117. [Falstaff]
10
Hot was the day; she hotter.
The Passionate Pilgrim, l. 77.
She red and hot as coals of glowing fire.
Venus and Adonis, l. 35.
She is not hot, but temperate as the morn.
The Taming of the Shrew. Act ii, sc. 1, l. 296. [Petruchio]
Is she so hot?—*Taming of the Shrew,* iv, 1, 22.
She is so hot.—*The Comedy of Errors,* i, 2, 47.
11
O rash false heat, wrapp'd in repentant cold!
The Rape of Lucrece, l. 48.
That knows not parching heat or freezing cold.
The Rape of Lucrece, l. 1145.
Parching heat.—*II Henry VI,* i, 1, 81; *I Henry VI,* i, 2, 77.
Lively heat.—*Sonnets,* cliii.
Mid-day heat.—*Venus and Adonis,* l. 177.
Scalding heat.—*III Henry VI,* v, 7, 18.
Summer's heat.—*Richard II,* i, 3, 299; *Venus and Adonis,* l. 91.
Valiant heat.—*Henry V,* iii, 5, 20.
Heat perpetual.—*Sonnets,* cliv.
12
The heat I have from thence doth little harm.
Venus and Adonis, l. 195.

HEAVEN

I—Familiar Phrases

13
Heavens bless him!
All's Well that Ends Well. Act i, sc. 1, l. 83. [Countess]
O heavens bless my girl!—*Pericles,* v, 1, 225.
Heavens bless my lord.—*Coriolanus,* i, 3, 48.
Heaven bless thee!—*Henry VIII,* iv, 1, 42.
Heaven bless us!—*Othello,* iii, 4, 81.
Heaven still move about her!—*Henry VIII,* v, 5, 18.

1
By my hopes of heaven.
All's Well that End Well, ii, 1, 195. [King]
By Heaven!—*The Two Gentlemen of Verona,* iii, 1, 166.
By yond marble heaven.—*Othello,* iii, 3, 460.
Afore Heaven.—*The Tempest,* iv, 1, 7.
Before heaven.—*Measure for Measure,* ii, 1, 69.
An 't please heaven.—*Macbeth,* iii, 6, 19.

2
Bertram: A heaven on earth I have won by wooing thee.
Diana: For which live long to thank both heaven and me!
All's Well that Ends Well. Act iv, sc. 2, l. 66. The only use of "heaven on earth."

Heaven is here
Where Juliet lives; and every cat and dog
And little mouse, every unworthy thing,
Live here in heaven and may look on her.
Romeo and Juliet. Act iii, sc. 3, l. 29 [Romeo]
Heaven in your cheek.—*Troilus and Cressida,* iv, 4, 120.
The heaven of his thought.—*The Rape of Lucrece,* l. 338.

3
The heavens have thought well on thee.
All's Well that Ends Well. Act v, sc. 3, l. 150. [King]

4 Heaven would in little show.
Therefore Heaven Nature charged
That one body should be fill'd
With all graces wide-enlarged.
As You Like It. Act iii, sc. 2, l. 148. [Celia] The only use of "wide-enlarged."

5
I never saw the chain, so help me Heaven!
The Comedy of Errors. Act v, sc. 1, l. 267. [Antipholus of Ephesus]
Now, heaven help him!—*King Lear,* iii, 7, 107.
Help Heaven!—*Measure for Measure,* ii, 4, 127.
Heaven aiding.—*All's Well that Ends Well,* iv, 4, 12.

6
I am in heaven for him.
Cymbeline, i, 3, 33. [Imogen]
The heavens still must work.—*Cymbeline,* iv, 3, 41.
Heaven mend all!—*Cymbeline,* v, 5, 68.

7
Even in that was heaven ordinant.
Hamlet. Act v, sc. 2, l. 48. [Hamlet] The only use of "ordinant."
Heaven hath pleased it so.—*Hamlet,* iii, 4, 174.
Heaven will direct it.—*Hamlet,* i, 4, 91.

8
Derives from heaven his quarrel and his cause.
II Henry IV. Act i, sc. 1, l. 206. [Morton]

9
The treasury of everlasting joy.
II Henry VI. Act ii, sc. 1, l. 18. [King Henry]

10
For myself, to heaven I do appeal.
II Henry VI. Act ii, sc. 1, l. 190. [Gloucester]
Heaven be my judge.—*II Henry VI,* iv, 10, 82.
Heaven is my judge.—*Othello,* i, 1, 59.

11
Smile, gentle heaven! or strike, ungentle death!
III Henry VI. Act ii, sc. 3, l. 6. [Edward]
I stood not in the smile of heaven.
Henry VIII. Act ii, sc. 4, l. 187. [King]

12 The will of heaven
Be done in this and all things!
Henry VIII. Act i, sc. 1, l. 209. [Buckingham] Repeated in l. 215.
It's heaven's will.—*Henry VIII,* iii, 2, 128.
Heaven has an end in all.—*Henry VIII,* ii, 1, 124.

13
Heaven knows your hearts.
Henry VIII, iii, 1, 145. [Queen Katharine]
Heaven knows.—*King John,* iii, 1, 236; *Macbeth,* v, 1, 54.
Heaven it knows.—*The Two Gentlemen of Verona,* iv, 4, 112.
Nay, heaven doth know.—*Othello,* iv, 2, 129.

14
Heaven is above all yet.
Henry VIII, iii, 1, 100. [Queen Katharine]
Heavens are just.—*III Henry VI,* iii, 3, 77.
Show the heavens more just.—*King Lear,* iii, 4, 36.
Heaven still guards the right.—*Richard II,* iii, 2, 62.

15 How much are we bound to heaven
In daily thanks.
Henry VIII. Act v, sc. 3, l. 114. [Gardiner]

16
But wherefore did you so much tempt the heavens?
Julius Cæsar. Act i, sc. 3, l. 53. [Cassius]
They tempt heaven.—*Othello,* iv, 1, 8.

17 You shall find
That heaven hath infused them with these spirits.
Julius Cæsar. Act i, sc. 3, l. 68. [Cassius]

18
Arm, arm, you heavens, against these perjured kings!
A widow cries; be husband to me, heavens!
King John. Act iii, sc. 1, l. 107. [Constance]
Heaven itself doth frown upon the land.
King John. Act iv, sc. 3, l. 159. [Bastard]
Withhold thine indignation, mighty heaven,
And tempt us not to bear above our power!
King John. Act v, sc. 6, l. 37. [Bastard]

19 Did heaven look on,
And would not take their part?
Macbeth. Act iv, sc. 3, l. 223. [Macduff]

20
Heaven doth with us as we with torches do,
Not light them for themselves.
Measure for Measure. Act i, sc. 1, l. 33. [Duke]
O heavens!—*Measure for Measure,* iii, 1, 99; iii, 2, 5. An exclamation frequently repeated.
O the heavens!—*Tempest,* i, 2, 59; i, 2, 116.

21
Heaven forgive him! and forgive us all!
Measure for Measure. Act ii, sc. 1, l. 37. [Escalus]
Heaven forgive you and all of us, I pray!
The Merry Wives of Windsor. Act ii, sc. 2, l. 57. [Mistress Quickly]

Heaven forgive me!—*The Merry Wives of Windsor,* ii, 1, 28; *Othello,* iii, 3, 373; *Henry VIII,* iii, 2, 135.
Heaven forgive him too!—*Macbeth,* iv, 3, 235.
Heavens forgive it!—*Pericles,* iv, 3, 39.
O, heaven forgive us!—*Othello,* iv, 2, 88.
Heaven forgive my sins!—*The Merry Wives of Windsor,* iii, 3, 226.
Heaven forgive our sins!—*The Merry Wives of Windsor,* v, 5, 35. A phrase frequently repeated. See also under SIN.

1 Shall we serve heaven
With less respect than we do minister
To our gross selves?
Measure for Measure. Act ii, sc. 2, l. 85. [Isabella]

2
Heaven give your spirits comfort!
Measure for Measure, iv, 2, 73. [Provost]
Heaven comfort her!—*Henry VIII,* iv, 2, 99.

3
Heaven so speed me in my time to come!
The Merry Wives of Windsor. Act iii, sc. 4, l. 12. [Fenton]
Sure, one of you does not serve heaven well, that you are so crossed.
The Merry Wives of Windsor. Act iv, sc. 5, l. 129. [Mistress Quickly]

4
Heavens defend me from that Welsh fairy.
The Merry Wives of Windsor. Act v, sc. 5, l. 85. [Falstaff]
Heaven defend your good souls.—*Othello,* i, 3, 267.
Defend me heaven!—*Richard II,* i, 3, 25; 41.
Defend thee heaven!—*Richard II,* i, 3, 34.
Heaven Have mercy on me!—*Othello,* v, 2, 33.
Heaven make thee free of it!—*Hamlet,* v, 2, 343.
Heaven pardon him!—*Othello,* iv, 2, 135.
Heaven preserve you!—*Macbeth,* iv, 2, 72.
Heavens rain grace.—*The Tempest,* iii, 1, 75.
Heaven rest them now!—*Macbeth,* iv, 3, 227.
Heaven restore me!—*Cymbeline,* i, 1, 148.
Heaven restore thee!—*Twelfth Night,* iii, 4, 51.
Heavens secure him!—*Hamlet,* i, 5, 113.
Heaven shield your grace.—*Measure for Measure,* v, 1, 118.

5
Heaven stops the nose at it and the moon winks.
Othello. Act iv, sc. 2, l. 77. [Othello]
Marry, heaven forbid!—*Othello,* v, 1, 72; *The Winter's Tale,* iv, 4, 541; *Pericles,* i, 2, 61.
Heaven forfend!—*Othello,* v, 2, 32; v, 2, 186.

6 The heavens,
Through you, increase our wonder.
Pericles. Act iii, sc. 2, l. 96. [Gentleman]
But see what heaven can do!—*Pericles,* i, 4, 33.
Heavens make a star of him!—*Pericles,* v, 3, 79.

7
Heaven, it seem'd, to kiss the turrets bow'd.
The Rape of Lucrece, l. 1372.

8
Heaven be the record to my speech!
Richard II. Act i, sc. 1, l. 30. [Bolingbroke]
Bear witness, Heaven.—*The Two Gentlemen of Verona,* v, 4, 119.
Heaven be my witness.—*The Merry Wives of Windsor,* iv, 2, 139.
Heaven bear witness.—*Henry VIII,* ii, 1, 59.
Heaven witness.—*Henry VIII,* ii, 4, 22.
Vouch with me, heaven.—*Othello,* i, 3, 262.

9
Let heaven revenge; for I may never lift
An angry arm against His minister.
Richard II. Act i, sc. 2, l. 40. [Gaunt]

10
All places that the eye of heaven visits
Are to a wise man ports and happy havens.
Richard II. Act i, sc. 3, l. 275. [Gaunt]
The means that heaven yields must be embraced,
And not neglected.
Richard II. Act iii, sc. 2, l. 29. [Carlisle]
But heaven hath a hand in these events,
To whose high will we bound our calm contents.
Richard II. Act v, sc. 2, l. 37. [York]

11
Alack, alack, that heaven should practise stratagems
Upon so soft a subject as myself!
Romeo and Juliet. Act iii, sc. 5, l. 211. [Juliet]
Can heaven be so envious?—*Romeo and Juliet,* iii, 2, 40.

12
Heavens keep him from these beasts!
The Tempest. Act ii, sc. 1, l. 324. [Gonzalo]
Heaven keep your honour!—*Measure for Measure,* ii, 2, 42; 157.

13
Heavens thank you for 't!
The Tempest. Act i, sc. 2, l. 175. [Miranda]

14
Hast thou not dropp'd from heaven?
The Tempest. Act ii, sc. 2, l. 140. [Caliban]
Titus Andronicus: Why, didst thou not come from heaven?
Clown: From heaven! alas, sir, I never came there: God forbid I should be so bold to press to heaven in my young days.
Titus Andronicus. Act iv, sc. 3, l. 88.

15
I 'll lock thy heaven from thee.
Timon of Athens. Act i, sc. 2, l. 255. [Apemantus]

16
Heaven shall hear our prayers.
Titus Andronicus. Act iii, sc. 1, l. 211. [Titus]
The heavens hear me!—*Troilus and Cressida,* ii, 3, 40.

17
Heaven guide thy pen to print thy sorrows plain.
Titus Andronicus. Act iv, sc. 1, l. 75. [Marcus]
The heavens continue their loves!—*The Winter's Tale,* i, 1, 34.
All-seeing heaven.—*Richard III,* ii, 1, 82. "All-seeing" is repeated in *Romeo and Juliet,* i, 2, 97: "All-seeing sun."
Blessed heavens!—*Coriolanus,* iv, 2, 20.
Crisp heaven.—*Timon of Athens,* iv, 3, 183.
Gentle heaven.—*III Henry VI,* ii, 5, 96.
Glorious heaven.—*Troilus and Cressida,* v, 6, 23.

High heaven.—*Measure for Measure,* i, 3, 198; ii, 2, 121; *Venus and Adonis,* l. 731.
Merciful heaven!—*Macbeth,* iv, 3, 207.
Righteous heavens.—*Titus Andronicus,* i, 1, 426.
Troubled heaven.—*I Henry IV,* i, 1, 10.
Wreakful heaven.—*Timon of Athens,* iv, 3, 229.

II—Going to Heaven

1
She 's not in heaven, whither God send her quickly!
All's Well that Ends Well. Act ii, sc. 4, l. 11. [Clown]

2
Then, heaven, set ope thy everlasting gates,
To entertain my vows of thanks and praise!
II Henry VI. Act iv, sc. 9, l. 13. [King Henry]

Ascend to heaven.—*King John,* ii, 1, 86.
Come to heaven.—*The Merchant of Venice,* ii, 4, 34.
Fled to heaven.—*King John,* iv, 3, 145.
Fly to heaven.—*II Henry VI,* iv, 7, 79.
Gone to heaven.—*The Merchant of Venice,* ii, 2, 68.

3
When I shall meet him in the court of heaven
I shall not know him.
King John. Act iii, sc. 4, l. 87. [Constance]

Heaven take my soul.—*King John,* iv, 3, 10.

4
Pack'd with post-horse up to heaven.
Richard III. Act i, sc. 1, l. 146. [Gloucester]

Lady Anne: He is in heaven, where thou shalt never come.
Gloucester: Let him thank me, that holp to send him thither;
For he was fitter for that place than earth.
Richard III. Act i, sc. 2, l. 106.

He delivers thee
From this world's thraldom to the joys of heaven.
Richard III. Act i, sc. 4, l. 254. [Second Murderer] The only use of "thraldom."

5
Heaven and yourself
Had part in this fair maid; now heaven hath all,
And all the better is it for the maid:
Your part in her you could not keep from death,
But heaven keeps his part in eternal life.
The most you sought was her promotion;
For 'twas your heaven she should be advanced:
And weep ye now, seeing she is advanced
Above the clouds, as high as heaven itself?
Romeo and Juliet. Act iv, sc. 5, l. 66. [Friar Laurence]

6
My brother he is in Elysium.
Twelfth Night. Act i, sc. 5, l. 1. [Viola]

A blessed soul . . . in Elysium.—*The Two Gentlemen of Verona,* ii, 7, 38.
Sleeps in Elysium.—*Henry V,* iv, 1, 291.
Sweet Elysium.—*II Henry VI,* iii, 2, 399.
To clip Elysium.—*Venus and Adonis,* l. 600.
Whose circuit is Elysium.—*III Henry VI,* i, 2, 30.
Poor shadows of Elysium.—*Cymbeline,* v, 4, 97.
The only references to Elysium.

III—Heaven and Earth

7
That heaven and earth may strike their sounds together.
Antony and Cleopatra, iv, 8, 38. [Antony]
"Heaven and earth" is repeated in *Hamlet,* i, 1, 124; i, 2, 142; *King John,* ii, 1, 173; 174; *King Lear,* i, 2, 105.

By heaven and earth.—*The Rape of Lucrece,* l. 572.
Between earth and heaven.—*Hamlet,* iii, 1, 131.
'Twixt heaven and earth.—*The Winter's Tale,* v, 1, 132; *King John,* iv, 2, 216.
From heaven to earth.—*Hamlet,* iv, 5, 216.
Heaven to earth.—*I Henry IV,* v, 2, 100.

8
Let heaven kiss earth!
II Henry IV. Act i, sc. 1, l. 153. [Northumberland]

Knit earth and heaven together!—*II Henry VI,* v, 2, 42.
In heaven or in earth.—*III Henry VI,* ii, 3, 43.
'Tis so set down in heaven, but not in earth.
Measure for Measure. Act ii, sc. 4, l. 50. [Isabella]

9
When heaven doth weep, doth not the earth o'erflow?
Titus Andronicus. Act iii, sc. 1, l. 222. [Titus]

10
There Diomed doth feast with him to-night;
Who neither looks upon the heaven nor earth,
But gives all gaze and bent of amorous view
On the fair Cressid.
Troilus and Cressida. Act iv, sc. 5, l. 280. [Ulysses]

11
Here comes the countess: now heaven walks on earth.
Twelfth Night. Act v, sc. 1, l. 100. [Duke]
"Countess" is used only once again, in *Henry VIII,* iv, 1, 53.

Nor of heaven nor earth.—*The Two Gentlemen of Verona,* v, 4, 80.

12
'O, where am I?' quoth she, 'in earth or heaven,
Or in the ocean?'
Venus and Adonis, l. 493.

IV—Heaven and Hell

13
Glendower: His cheek looks pale and with
A rising sigh he wisheth you in heaven.
Hotspur: And you in hell.
I Henry IV. Act iii, sc. 1, l. 9.

Either in heaven or in hell.—*Henry V,* ii, 3, 8.

14
Heavens, can you suffer hell so to prevail?
I Henry VI. Act i, sc. 5, l. 9. [Talbot]

Bastard: I think this Talbot is a fiend of hell.
Reignier: If not of hell, the heavens, sure, favour him.
I Henry VI. Act ii, sc. 1, l. 46.

Heaven or hell.—*II Henry VI,* iii, 1, 350.

1
I 'll make my heaven to dream upon the crown,
And, whiles I live, to account this world but hell.
III Henry VI. Act iii, sc. 2, l. 168. [Gloucester]

For heaven and hell.—*King John,* ii, 1, 407.
Both heaven and hell!—*Pericles,* iii, 1, 2.

2
My comfort is that heaven will take our souls
And plague injustice with the pains of hell.
Richard II. Act iii, sc. 1, l. 33. [Green]

3
March on, join bravely, let us to 't pell-mell;
If not to heaven, then hand in hand to hell.
Richard III. Act v, sc. 3, l. 312. [King Richard] For other uses of "pell-mell" see under FAMILIAR PHRASES.

V—The Heavens

See also Sky

4
Hail, thou fair heaven!
We house i' the rock, yet use thee not so hardly
As prouder livers do.
Cymbeline. Act iii, sc. 3, l. 7. [Belarius]

Hail, heaven!—Hail, heaven!—*Cymbeline,* iii, 3, 9.
Clear heavens!—*Timon of Athens,* iv, 3, 27.
Sweet heavens!—*Hamlet,* iii, 1, 138; iii, 3, 45; *King Lear,* i, 5, 50.

5
The heavens were all on fire.
I Henry IV. Act iii, sc. 1, l. 24. [Glendower]

Swelling heavens.—*I Henry IV,* iii, 1, 202.

6
Who ever knew the heavens menace so?
Julius Cæsar. Act i, sc. 3, l. 44. [Casca]

Angry heavens.—*II Henry VI,* v, 2, 34.

7
The vaulty top of heaven
Figured quite o'er with burning meteors.
King John. Act v, sc. 2, l. 52. [Dauphin]

Vaulty heaven.—*Romeo and Juliet,* iii, 5, 22. "Vaulty" is used a third time in *King John,* iii, 4, 30: "Vaulty brows."

8
The heavens, as troubled with man's act,
Threaten his bloody stage.
Macbeth. Act ii, sc. 4, l. 5. [Ross]

9
The self-same heaven
That frowns on me looks sadly upon him.
Richard III. Act v, sc. 3, l. 286. [King Richard]

The heavens do lour upon you for some ill;
Move them no more by crossing their high will.
Romeo and Juliet. Act iv, sc. 5, l. 94. [Friar Laurence]

10
In my conscience,
The heavens with that we have in hand are angry
And frown upon 's.
Winter's Tale. Act iii, sc. 3, l. 4. [Mariner]

I never saw The heavens so dim by day.
The Winter's Tale. Act iii, sc. 3, l. 55. [Antigonus]

HEEL

11
Keep from my heels and beware of an ass.
The Comedy of Errors. Act iii, sc. 1, l. 18. [Dromio of Ephesus]

I will fly, like a dog, the heels o' the ass.
Timon of Athens. Act i, sc. 1, l. 282. [Apemantus]

Armed heels.—*II Henry IV,* i, 1, 44; *Henry V,* iv, 7, 83.

12
Trip him, that his heels may kick at heaven.
Hamlet. Act iii, sc. 3, l. 93. [Hamlet]

Is it two days ago since I tripped up thy heels?
King Lear. Act ii, sc. 2, l. 31. [Kent]

Tripp'd up the wrestler's heels.—*As You Like It,* iii, 2, 225.

13
Show it a fair pair of heels.
I Henry IV, ii, 4, 53. See under COWARDICE.

14
Heavens and honour be witness that no want of resolution in me, but only my followers' base and ignominious treasons, makes me betake me to my heels.
II Henry VI. Act iv, sc. 8, l. 64. [Cade]

I 'll take my heels.—*The Comedy of Errors,* i, 2, 94.
Took heel.—*Cymbeline,* v, 3, 67.
To trust their heels.—*Macbeth,* i, 2, 30.

15
I 'll lay ye all By the heels, and suddenly.
Henry VIII. Act v, sc. 4, l. 82. [Lord Chamberlain]

By the heels.—*II Henry VI,* iv, 10, 86; *Titus Andronicus,* iv, 3, 44.

16
Many hundreds treading on his heels.
King John. Act iv, sc. 2, l. 149. [Bastard]

Baying him at the heels.—*II Henry IV,* i, 3, 80.
Come after my heel.—*The Merry Wives of Windsor,* i, 4, 62.
Follow my heels.—*The Merry Wives of Windsor,* i, 4, 132.
Follow . . . closely at the heels.—*Henry V,* iv, 7, 179.
Follow'd thy heels.—*Antony and Cleopatra,* iv, 5, 6.
Page thy heels.—*Timon of Athens,* iv, 3, 224.
Spaniel'd me at heels.—*Antony and Cleopatra,* iv, 12, 21.

17
Be Mercury, set feathers to thy heels.
King John. Act iv, sc. 2, l. 174. [King John]

Set . . . wings . . . to his heels.—*Troilus and Cressida,* ii, 2, 44.
Winged heels.—*Henry V,* ii, Prol., 7.
Atalanta's heels.—*As You Like It,* iii, 2, 294. Atalanta is referred to again in l. 155, and in no other scene.

18
My heels are at your command.
The Merchant of Venice. Act ii, sc. 2, l. 33. [Launcelot]

1
Well, sirs, I am almost out at heels.
The Merry Wives of Windsor. Act i, sc. 3, l. 34. [Falstaff]
Out at heels.—*King Lear,* ii, 2, 164.
2
Death and destruction dog thee at the heels.
Richard III. Act iv, sc. 1, l. 40. [Queen Elizabeth]
Dogs the heels.—*All's Well that Ends Well,* iii, 4, 15.
Dog his heels.—*I Henry IV,* iii, 2, 127. See under SERVILITY.
Dog them at the heels.—*Richard II,* v, 3, 139.
At my (thy, his) heels.—*II Henry VI,* iv, 3, 14, and frequently in later plays.
At one another's heels.—*Othello,* i, 2, 42.
Heel the high lavolt.—*Troilus and Cressida,* iv, 4, 88. See VIRTUE, 1608:16.
From head to heel.—*The Winter's Tale,* iv, 4, 229. See under HEAD.
Heel to head.—*The Merry Wives of Windsor,* iii, 5, 113.

HEIR

See also Inheritance

3
When he dies, thou shalt be his heir.
As You Like It. Act i, sc. 2, l. 20. [Celia]
Let my father seek another heir.
As You Like It. Act i, sc. 3, l. 101. [Celia]
4
The fall of either
Makes the survivor heir of all.
Coriolanus. Act v, sc. 6, l. 18. [Conspirator]
Rich-left heirs.—*Cymbeline,* iv, 2, 226. [Guiderius] The only use of "rich-left."
5
The first-begotten and the lawful heir.
I Henry VI. Act ii, sc. 5, l. 65. [Mortimer] The only use of "first-begotten."
Leaving no heir begotten of his body.
I Henry VI. Act ii, sc. 5, l. 72. [Mortimer]
6
They laboured to plant the rightful heir.
I Henry VI. Act ii, sc. 5, l. 80. [Mortimer]
Rightful heir to the crown.—*II Henry VI,* i, 3, 32.
I am the rightful heir.—*II Henry VI,* iv, 2, 139.
The rightful heir.—*II Henry VI,* v, 1, 178.
Thou art my heir.—*I Henry VI,* ii, 5, 96.
You are their heir.—*Henry V,* i, 2, 117.
Beauteous heir.—*Love's Labour's Lost,* ii, 1, 41.
Female heir.—*Pericles,* i, Gower, 22.
Immediate heir.—*All's Well that Ends Well,* ii, 3, 139; *II Henry IV,* v, 2, 71.
Next heir.—*III Henry VI,* i, 1, 146.
Successive heir.—*II Henry VI,* iii, 1, 49.
7
Heir apparent to the English crown.
II Henry VI, i, 1, 152. "Heir-apparent" occurs four times in *I Henry IV,* and once in *Pericles.*
Heir to the crown.—*Richard III,* iii, 5, 78; *I Henry IV,* i, 3, 157.
Heir unto the crown.—*II Henry VI,* ii, 2, 44.
True heir to the English crown.—*III Henry VI,* iv, 4, 24.
Heir of 's kingdom.—*Cymbeline,* i, 1, 4.
My kingdom's heir.—*Richard II,* i, 1, 116.
8
I was adopted heir by his consent.
III Henry VI. Act ii, sc. 2, l. 88. [Edward]
Adopted heir.—*As You Like It,* i, 2, 246.
Adopts thee heir.—*Richard II,* iv, 1, 109.
9
'Tis good you know not that you are his heirs.
Julius Cæsar. Act iii, sc. 2, l. 150. [Antony]
10
My mother's son did get your father's heir;
Your father's heir must have your father's land.
King John. Act i, sc. 1, l. 128. [King John] For "son and heir" see under SON.
Heir to all this land.—*King John,* i, 1, 144.
Heir to the lands of me.—*The Taming of the Shrew,* v, 1, 88.
Heirs of all eternity.—*Love's Labour's Lost,* i, 1, 7.
11
She alone is heir to both of us.
Much Ado about Nothing. Act v, sc. 1, l. 300. [Leonato]
12
Did not the one deserve to have an heir?
Is not his heir a well-deserving son?
Richard II. Act ii, sc. 1, l. 193. [York]
13
Heir to his unhappiness.
Richard III. Act i, sc. 2, l. 25. [Lady Anne]
Heirs of shame.—*Richard III,* v, 3, 335.
14
His tender heir might bear his memory.
Sonnets. No. i.
15
I am my father's heir and only son.
The Taming of the Shrew. Act ii, sc. 1, l. 366. [Tranio]
Left solely heir to all his lands and goods.
The Taming of the Shrew. Act ii, sc. 1, l. 118. [Petruchio]
Only heir.—*The Tempest,* i, 2, 58; *Much Ado about Nothing,* i, 1, 297.
Sole heir.—*Henry V,* i, 2, 78.
Sole heir male.—*Henry V,* i, 2, 70.
16
I will choose
Mine heir from forth the beggars of the world,
And dispossess her all.
Timon of Athens. Act i, sc. 1, l. 137. [Old Athenian]
17
The king shall live without an heir, if that which is lost be not found.
Winter's Tale. Act iii, sc. 2, l. 136. [Officer]
King Leontes shall not have an heir
Till his lost child be found.
Winter's Tale. Act v, sc. 1, l. 39. [Paulina]
Heirless it hath made my kingdom.
The Winter's Tale. Act v, sc. 1, l. 10. [Leontes] The only use of "heirless."
18
From my succession wipe me, father; I
Am heir to my affection.
Winter's Tale. Act iv, sc. 4, l. 490. [Florizel]
They are co-heirs.—*The Winter's Tale,* ii, 1, 148. The only use of "co-heirs."
Careless heirs.—*Pericles,* iii, 2, 28.
Contracted Heirs.—*Winter's Tale,* v, 3, 6.

Dismal heir.—*Richard II,* ii, 2, 63.
Orphan heirs.—*The Merry Wives of Windsor,* v, 5, 43.
Unfather'd heirs.—*II Henry IV,* iv, 4, 122.
Wronged heirs.—*Richard III,* v, 3, 137.

HELEN OF TROY

1
Helen of Greece was fairer far than thou,
Although thy husband may be Menelaus.
And ne'er was Agamemnon's brother wronged
By that false woman, as this king by thee.
III Henry VI. Act ii, sc. 2, l. 146. [Edward]

2
Thy eye kindled the fire that burneth here;
And here in Troy, for trespass of thine eye,
The sire, the son, the dame, and daughter die.
The Rape of Lucrece, l. 1475.

3
Helen and Hero hildings and harlots.
Romeo and Juliet. Act ii, sc. 4, l. 44. [Mercutio] "Hilding" (wretch) occurs seven times.

4
On Helen's cheek all art of beauty set.
Sonnets. No. liii.
Fair Leda's daughter.—*The Taming of the Shrew,* i, 2, 244.

5
The ravish'd Helen, Menelaus' queen,
With wanton Paris sleeps.
Troilus and Cressida. Prologue, l. 9.

6
Fools on both sides! Helen must needs be fair,
When with your blood you daily paint her thus.
Troilus and Cressida. Act i, sc. 1, l. 93. [Troilus]
Is she worth keeping? why, she is a pearl,
Whose price hath launch'd above a thousand ships,
And turn'd crown'd kings to merchants.
Troilus and Cressida. Act ii, sc. 2, l. 81. [Troilus]
There 's not the meanest spirit on our party
Without a heart to dare or sword to draw
When Helen is defended, nor none so noble
Whose life were ill bestow'd or death unfamed
Where Helen is the subject.
Troilus and Cressida. Act ii, sc. 2, l. 156. [Paris] The only use of "unfamed."
Cry, Trojans, cry! a Helen and a woe:
Cry, cry! Troy burns, or else let Helen go.
Troilus and Cressida. Act ii, sc. 2, l. 111. [Cassandra]
The mortal Venus, the heart-blood of beauty, love's invisible soul.
Troilus and Cressida. Act iii, sc. 1, l. 34. [Servant]
Hear me, Paris:
For every false drop in her bawdy veins
A Grecian's life has sunk: for every scruple
Of her contaminated carrion weight,
A Trojan hath been slain: since she could speak,
She hath not given so many good words breath
As for her Greeks and Trojans suffer'd death.
Troilus and Cressida. Act iv, sc. 1, l. 72. [Diomedes]

HELL

See also Heaven and Hell

7
If she lives till doomsday, she 'll burn a week longer than the whole world.
The Comedy of Errors. Act iii, sc. 2, l. 101. [Dromio of Syracuse]
He 's in Tartar limbo, worse than hell.
The Comedy of Errors. Act iv, sc. 2, l. 32. [Dromio of Syracuse] "Limbo" is used also in *Titus Andronicus,* iii, 1, 149; *All 's Well that Ends Well,* v, 3, 261; and *Henry VIII,* v, 4, 67.

8
Shall I couple hell?
Hamlet. Act i, sc. 5, l. 93. [Hamlet]
When he is drunk asleep, or in his rage,
Or in the incestuous pleasure of his bed;
At gaming, swearing, or about some act
That has no relish of salvation in 't;
Then trip him, that his heels may kick at heaven,
And that his soul may be as damn'd and black
As hell, whereto it goes.
Hamlet. Act iii, sc. 3, l. 89. [Hamlet]
Trip me, if I err.—*Cymbeline,* v, 5, 35.

9
She is in hell already, and burns poor souls.
II Henry IV. Act iii, sc. 4, l. 365. [Falstaff]
She 's, like a liar, gone to burning hell.
Othello. Act v, sc. 2, l. 129. [Othello]
Nay, sure, he 's not in hell.—*Henry V,* ii, 3, 9.

10
All hell shall stir for this.
Henry V. Act v, sc. 1, l. 72. [Pistol]
Cunning hell.—*Othello,* i, 3, 102.
Dark-seated hell.—*II Henry VI,* iii, 2, 328. The only use of the phrase.
Dismal hell.—*Romeo and Juliet,* iii, 2, 44.
Ever-burning hell.—*Titus Andronicus,* iii, 1, 243. "Ever-burning" is repeated in *Othello,* iii, 3, 463: "Ever-burning lights above."
Horrid hell.—*Macbeth,* iv, 3, 56.
Lightless hell.—*The Rape of Lucrece,* l. 1555.
Lowest hell.—*Coriolanus,* iii, 3, 68.
Rebellious hell.—*Hamlet,* iii, 4, 82.
Ugly hell.—*The Rape of Lucrece,* l. 1082.
Vast hell.—*Midsummer-Night's Dream,* v, 1, 9.
As big as hell.—*Cymbeline,* ii, 4, 140.
Wide as hell.—*Henry V,* iii, 3, 13.
Everlasting bonfire.—*Macbeth,* ii, 3, 23.
Everlasting fire.—*Titus Andronicus,* v, 1, 149.

11
My ancient incantations are too weak,
And hell too strong for me to buckle with.
I Henry VI. Act v, sc. 3, l. 27. [La Pucelle] The only use of "incantations."

12 Consume to ashes,
Thou foul accursed minister of hell!
I Henry VI. Act v, sc. 4, l. 92. [York]
Avaunt, thou dreadful minister of hell!
Richard III, i, 2, 46. See under DISMISSAL.
Hell's black intelligencer.—*Richard III,* iv, 4, 71. "Intelligencer" occurs again in *II Henry IV,* iv, 2, 20.

13
And till I root out their accursed line
And leave not one alive, I live in hell.
III Henry VI. Act i, sc. 3, l. 32. [Clifford]

Down, down to hell; and say I sent thee thither.
III Henry VI. Act v, sc. 6, l. 67. [Gloucester]
To hell!—*Hamlet,* iv, 5, 131.
Go to hell.—*The Merchant of Venice,* iii, 2, 21; *The Merry Wives of Windsor,* ii, 1, 49; *Julius Cæsar,* i, 2, 270.
Go you into hell?—*Much Ado about Nothing,* ii, 1, 44.
Went to hell.—*III Henry VI,* ii, 2, 48.
Come hot from hell.—*Julius Cæsar,* iii, 1, 271.
Loosed out of hell.—*Hamlet,* ii, 1, 83.
O hell!—*The Merchant of Venice,* ii, 7, 62; *A Midsummer-Night's Dream,* i, 1, 140; iii, 2, 145.

1
Let hell want pains enough to torture me.
King John, iv, 3, 138. See under GUILT.

2
Within me is a hell.
King John. Act v. sc. 7, l. 46. [King John] See also under REMORSE.
He begins a new hell in himself.
Henry VIII, i, 1, 72. See under DEVIL.
Hell our prison is.—*I Henry VI,* iv, 7, 58.
Hell is here.—*Cymbeline,* ii, 2, 50.

3
There 's hell, there 's darkness, there 's the sulphurous pit.
King Lear, iv, 6, 130. See under WOMAN.

4
Like a hell-broth boil and bubble.
Macbeth. Act iv, sc. 1, l. 19. [Witch] The only use of "hell-broth."
Hell-fire.—*I Henry IV,* iii, 3, 36; *Henry V,* ii, 3, 44.
Hell-gate.—*Macbeth,* ii, 3, 2.
Hell-hound.—*Richard III,* iv, 4, 48; *Titus Andronicus,* v, 2, 144; *Macbeth,* v, 8, 3.
Hell-kite.—*Macbeth,* iv, 3, 217.
Hell-pains.—*All's Well that Ends Well,* ii, 3, 245; *Othello,* i, 1, 155.

5
Hell is murky!
Macbeth. Act v, sc. 1, l. 40. [Lady Macbeth] The only use of "murky."
Dark as hell.—*Twelfth Night,* iv, 2, 38.
As deep as hell.—*The Merry Wives of Windsor,* iii, 5, 14; *Measure for Measure,* iii, 1, 94.

6
See the hell of having a false woman!
The Merry Wives of Windsor, ii, 2, 305. See under WIFE.
False as hell.—*Othello,* iv, 2, 39.
Foul as hell.—*Sonnets,* cxix.
Grim as hell.—*Othello,* iv, 2, 64.

7
You . . . have the office opposite to Saint Peter,
And keep the gate of hell!
Othello. Act iv, sc. 2, l. 90. [Othello]
Hell gnaw his bones!—*Othello,* iv, 2, 136.

8
I should venture purgatory for it.
Othello. Act iv, sc. 3, l. 77. [Emilia]
Purgatory, torture, hell itself.—*Romeo and Juliet,* iii, 3, 18. The only references to purgatory.

9
Hell only danceth at so harsh a chime.
Pericles. Act i, sc. 1, l. 85. [Pericles]

10
Terrible hell make war
Upon their spotted souls for this offence!
Richard II. Act iii, sc. 2, l. 133. [King Richard]

11
Go thou, and fill another room in hell.
Richard II. Act v, sc. 5, l. 108. [King Richard]

12
And thou unfit for any place but hell.
Richard III. Act i, sc. 2, l. 109. [Lady Anne]
Hie thee to hell for shame, and leave the world,
Thou cacodemon! there thy kingdom is.
Richard III. Act i, sc. 3, l. 143. [Queen Margaret] The only use of "cacodemon" (evil spirit). It must have startled Gloucester.
Thou that wast seal'd in thy nativity
The slave of nature and the son of hell!
Richard III. Act i, sc. 3, l. 229. [Queen Margaret]
Hell burns.—*Richard III,* iv, 4, 75.
Set hell on fire.—*The Merry Wives of Windsor,* v, 5, 39.

13
Thinkest thou, Hortensio, though her father be very rich, any man is so very a fool to be married to hell?
The Taming of the Shrew. Act i, sc. 1, l. 127. [Gremio]

14
Hell is empty, And all the devils are here.
The Tempest. Act i, sc. 2, l. 214. [Ariel]
Would thou wert shipp'd to hell!—*Titus Andronicus,* i, 1, 206.
By hell and all hell's torments.—*Troilus and Cressida,* v, 2, 43.

HELP

See also Aid

15
Give me some help here, ho!
All's Well that Ends Well. Act ii, sc. 1, l. 212. [King]
I am maim'd for ever. Help, ho! murder! murder!
Othello. Act v, sc. 1, l. 27. [Cassio]
Help, ho!—*Othello,* ii, 3, 159; v, 2, 120; 166; *Hamlet,* iii, 4, 22.
Help, help, O, help!—*King Lear* v, 3, 222.
Help me, help me!—*King Lear,* iii, 4, 40; *The Winter's Tale,* iv, 3, 55.
Help, masters, help!—*The Taming of the Shrew,* i, 2, 18.
Help, help, help!—*II Henry VI,* iii, 2, 33; *The Taming of the Shrew,* v, 1, 60; *Richard II,* v, 5, 105.
For the love of God, your help!—*Twelfth Night,* v, 1, 180.
Friendly help.—*All's Well that Ends Well,* iii, 7, 15.
Gentle help.—*Twelfth Night,* v, 1, 262.
Present help.—*Comedy of Errors,* v, 1, 176.
Prudent helps.—*Coriolanus,* iii, 1, 221.

16
We cannot help it.
All's Well that Ends Well. Act v, sc. 1, l. 2. [Helena]
I cannot help it now.—*Coriolanus,* iv, 7, 6.
I cannot help.—*II Henry IV,* ii, 2, 73.
I cannot help you.—*Henry VIII,* v, 2, 5.

She . . . cannot help herself.—*II Henry IV,* iii, 2, 247.
That cannot I help.—*The Two Gentlemen of Verona,* iii, 1, 359.
I will help you, if I can.—*As You Like It,* v, 2, 120.

1
Let 's call more help.
The Comedy of Errors. Act iv, sc. 4, l. 149. [Adriana]
So, come, help.—*The Comedy of Errors,* iii, 1, 56.
Your helps are many.—*Coriolanus,* ii, 1, 39.
A little help will serve.—*Coriolanus,* ii, 3, 16.
Sided in his behalf.—*Coriolanus,* iv, 2, 2. The only use of "sided."

2
Help, Jupiter; or we appeal,
And from thy justice fly.
Cymbeline. Act v, sc. 4, l. 91. [Brothers]
By God's help.—*Henry V,* i, 2, 222.
So help you righteous God!—*I Henry VI,* iv, 1, 8.
So help you mercy.—*Hamlet,* i, 5, 169.
So help you truth and God!—*Richard II,* i, 3, 183.

3
O, send some succour to the distress'd lord!
I Henry VI. Act iv, sc. 3, l. 30. [Lucy]
Be not dismay'd, for succour is at hand.
I Henry VI. Act i, sc. 2, l. 50. [Bastard]
I 'll succour thee.—*III Henry VI,* iii, 3, 41.
Flying for succour.—*Henry VIII,* ii, 1, 109.
Far from his succour.—*Henry VIII,* iii, 2, 261.

4
Fly, to revenge my death when I am dead;
The help of one stands me in little stead.
I Henry VI. Act iv, sc. 6, l. 30. [Talbot]
Help me this once.—*I Henry VI,* v, 3, 12.

5
So you do condescend to help me now.
I Henry VI. Act v, sc. 3, l. 17. [La Pucelle]
If thou wilt condescend.—*I Henry VI.* Act v, sc. 3, l. 120. The only uses of "condescend," which appears in no other play.

6
Thy greatest help is quiet, gentle Nell.
II Henry VI. Act ii, sc. 4, l. 67. [Gloucester]

7
Our prop to lean upon,
Now thou art gone, we have no staff, no stay.
III Henry VI. Act ii, sc. 1, l. 68. [Edward]

8
How can I help them, and not myself?
III Henry VI. Act iii, sc. 1, l. 21. [King Henry]
Make much of him, my lords, for this is he
Must help you more than you are hurt by me.
III Henry VI. Act iv, sc. 6, l. 75. [King Henry]
O, welcome, Oxford! for we want thy help.
III Henry VI. Act v, sc. 1, l. 66. [Warwick]

9
He that will think to live till he be old
Give me some help.
King Lear. Act iii, sc. 7, l. 69. [Gloucester]
He that helps him take all my outward worth.
King Lear. Act iv, sc. 4, l. 10. [Cordelia]
Now is the time of help.—*Macbeth,* iv, 3, 186.

10
Who in his office lacks a helper.
Measure for Measure. Act iv, sc. 2, l. 10. [Provost]
Helper to a husband.—*All 's Well that Ends Well,* iv, 4, 21.
Speedy helpers.—*I Henry VI,* v, 3, 5. The only uses of "helper."

11
Well then, it appears you need my help.
The Merchant of Venice, i, 3, 115.
Need you my help?—*Romeo and Juliet,* iv, 3, 6.
I do not need your help.—*I Henry IV,* v, 4, 10.
I shall desire your help.—*Much Ado about Nothing,* v, 4, 31.
Help me away.—*The Merry Wives of Windsor,* iii, 3, 149.

12
Poor helpless help, the treasure stol'n away,
To burn the guiltless casket where it lay!
The Rape of Lucrece, l. 1056.
The help that thou shalt lend me
Comes all too late.
The Rape of Lucrece, l. 1685.
Past help!—*Romeo and Juliet,* iv, 1, 45.

13
Assist me, Tranio, for I know thou wilt.
The Taming of the Shrew. Act i, sc. 1, l. 163. [Lucentio]
Don John: You will assist me?
Conrade: To the death.
Much Ado about Nothing, i, 3, 71. "Assist me" is used eleven times.
Let 's assist them.—*The Tempest,* i, 1, 57.
We 'll all assist you.—*III Henry VI,* i, 1, 28.
Minister such assistance as I shall give you direction.
Much Ado about Nothing. Act ii, sc. 1, l. 385. [Don Pedro]
I to your assistance do make love.
Macbeth. Act iii, sc. 1, l. 124. [Macbeth]
By the heavens' assistance.—*III Henry VI,* v, 4, 68.
By their assistance.—*II Henry IV,* iv, 5, 194.
By your assistance.—*King John,* v, 4, 39.
Crave your assistance.—*Love's Labour 's Lost,* v, 1, 123.
Swore him assistance.—*I Henry IV,* iv, 3, 65.
Present assistance.—*Timon of Athens,* iii, 1, 21.
Without assistance.—*Coriolanus,* iv, 6, 33; *King John,* iii, 1, 158.

14
Make some sign how I may do thee ease.
Titus Andronicus. Act iii, sc. 1, l. 121. [Titus]
There is no help.—*Troilus and Cressida,* iv, 1, 47.
I will help you to 't.—*Twelfth Night,* iv, 2, 121.

15
Haste we, Diomed,
To reinforcement, or we perish all.
Troilus and Cressida. Act v, sc. 5, l. 16. [Agamemnon] "Reinforcement" is repeated in *Coriolanus,* ii, 2, 117.

16
Cease to lament for that thou canst not help,

And study help for that which thou lament'st.
The Two Gentlemen of Verona. Act iii, sc. 1, l. 241. [Proteus]
What 's past help Should be past grief.
The Winter's Tale, iii, 2, 223. [Paulina]

1
Her help she sees, but help she cannot get.
Venus and Adonis, l. 93.
For one sweet look thy help I would assure thee,
Though nothing but my body's bane would cure thee.
Venus and Adonis, l. 371.

HERCULES

2
He is stronger than Hercules.
All's Well that Ends Well. Act iv, sc. 3, l. 283. [Parolles]
Valiant as Hercules.—*I Henry IV,* ii, 4, 299.

3
'Tis the god Hercules, whom Antony loved,
Now leaves him.
Antony and Cleopatra. Act iv, sc. 3, l. 16. [Soldier]
By Hercules!—*Antony and Cleopatra,* iii, 7, 68.
Hercules be thy speed!—*As You Like It,* i, 2, 222.

4
You were wont to say,
If you had been the wife of Hercules,
Six of his labours you 'ld have done, and saved
Your husband so much sweat.
Coriolanus. Act iv, sc. 1, l. 16. [Coriolanus]
I will in the interim undertake one of Hercules' labours.
Much Ado about Nothing. Act ii, sc. 1, l. 379. [Don Pedro]
Leave that labour to great Hercules.
The Taming of the Shrew. Act i, sc. 2, l. 257. [Gremio]

5
Let Hercules himself do what he may,
The cat will mew and dog will have his day.
Hamlet. Act v, sc. 1, l. 314. [Hamlet]

6
I thought I should have seen some Hercules,
A second Hector, for his grim aspect,
And large proportion of his strong-knit limbs.
I Henry VI. Act ii, sc. 3, l. 19. [Countess]
Strong-knit sinews.—*III Henry VI,* ii, 3, 4. The only uses of "strong-knit."
The brawns of Hercules.—*Cymbeline,* iv, 2, 311. The only use of "brawns." "Brawn" occurs five times; and "brawny" in *Venus and Adonis,* l. 625.

7
Hercules himself must yield to odds.
III Henry VI. Act ii, sc. 1, l. 53. [Messenger]

8
Armado: Comfort me, boy: what great men have been in love?
Moth: Hercules, master.
Armado: Most sweet Hercules!
Love's Labour 's Lost. Act i, sc. 2, l. 67.

9
To see great Hercules whipping a gig.
Love's Labour's Lost. Act iv, sc. 3, l. 167. [Biron]
Go, whip thy gig.—*Love's Labour 's Lost,* v, 1, 70.
I will whip about your . . . gig.—*Love's Labour's Lost,* v, 1, 73. "Gig" occurs in no other play.

10
Holofernes: Sir, you shall present before her the Nine Worthies. . . .
Nathaniel: Where will you find men worthy enough to present them?
Holofernes: Joshua, yourself; . . . the page, Hercules,—
Armado: Pardon, sir; error; he is not quantity enough for that Worthy's thumb: he is not so big as the end of his club.
Holofernes: Shall I have audience? he shall present Hercules in minority: his enter and exit shall be strangling a snake; and I will have an apology for that purpose.
Moth: An excellent device! so, if any of the audience hiss, you may cry 'Well done, Hercules! now thou crushest the snake!'
Love's Labour's Lost. Act v, sc. 1, l. 123.
Great Hercules is presented by this imp,
Whose club kill'd Cerberus, that three-headed canis;
And when he was a babe, a child, a shrimp,
Thus did he strangle serpents in his manus.
Love's Labour's Lost. Act v, sc. 2, l. 592. [Holofernes] The only use of "three-headed," "canis," and "manus."

11
Go, Hercules! Live thou, I live.
The Merchant of Venice. Act iii, sc. 2, l. 60. [Portia]
Bully Hercules.—*The Merry Wives of Windsor,* i, 3, 6.

12
I was with Hercules and Cadmus once,
When in a wood of Crete they bay'd the bear.
A Midsummer-Night's Dream. Act iv, sc. 1, l. 116. [Hippolyte]

13
She would have made Hercules have turned spit, yea, and have cleft his club to make the fire too.
Much Ado about Nothing. Act ii, sc. 1, l. 260. [Benedick]
The shaven Hercules in the smirched worm-eaten tapestry, where his codpiece seems as massy as his club.
Much Ado about Nothing, iii, 3, 145. The only use of "shaven." "Worm-eaten" is repeated in *As You Like It,* iii, 4, 27: "Worm-eaten nut"; and in *II Henry IV,* Ind., 35: "Worm-eaten hold." See under FASHION.

HERESY

14
The scriptures of the loyal Leonatus,
All turn'd to heresy?
Cymbeline. Act iii, sc. 4, l. 83. [Imogen] Leonatus is mentioned fourteen times in *Cymbeline,* the reference being to Lenantius,

who, so Holinshed says, was made King of Britain in 45 B. C.

1
An heretic, an arch one.
Henry VIII. Act iii, sc. 2, l. 102. [Wolsey]
A most arch heretic, a pestilence
That does infect the land.
Henry VIII. Act v, sc. 1, l. 45. [Gardiner]

2
Blessed shall he be that doth revolt
From his allegiance to an heretic.
King John. Act iii, sc. 1, l. 174. [Pandulph]
Of late an heretic.—*The Merry Wives of Windsor,* iv, 4, 9.

3
No heretics burn'd, but wenches' suitors.
King Lear, iii, 2, 84. See under PROPHECY.

4
O heresy is fair, fit for these days!
Love's Labour's Lost. Act iv, sc. 1, l. 22. [Princess]
It is heresy.—*Twelfth Night,* i, 5, 246.

5
The heresies that men do leave
Are hated most of those they did deceive.
A Midsummer-Night's Dream. Act ii, sc. 2, l. 139. [Lysander] "Heresies" is repeated in *Henry VIII,* v, 3, 18.

6
Thou wast ever an obstinate heretic in the despite of beauty.
Much Ado about Nothing. Act i, sc. 1, l. 236. [Don Pedro]

7
Transparent heretics, be burnt for liars!
Romeo and Juliet. Act i, sc. 2, l. 96. [Romeo]
It is an heretic that makes the fire,
Not she which burns in 't.
Winter's Tale. Act ii, sc. 3, l. 115. [Paulina]

HERITAGE, see Inheritance

HILL

See also Mountain

8
The dreadful summit of the cliff
That beetles o'er his base into the sea.
Hamlet. Act i, sc. 4, l. 70. [Hamlet] The only use of "beetles" as a verb.
There is a cliff, whose high and bending head
Looks fearfully in the confined deep.
King Lear. Act iv, sc. 1, l. 76. [Gloucester]

9
As far as I could ken thy chalky cliffs.
II Henry VI. Act iii, sc. 2, l. 101. [Queen]
I looked for the chalky cliffs, but I could find no whiteness in them.
The Comedy of Errors. Act iii, sc. 2, l. 129. [Dromio of Syracuse]
He can take her cliff.—*Troilus and Cressida,* v, 2, 11.
Crown o' the cliff.—*King Lear,* iv, 6, 67. The only uses of "cliff" and "cliffs."

10
Runs o' horseback up a hill perpendicular.
I Henry IV. Act ii, sc. 4, l. 377. [Falstaff] The only use of "perpendicular." "Perpendicularly" occurs in *King Lear,* iv, 6, 54.
The steep uprising of the hill.
Love's Labour's Lost, iv, 1, 2. The only use of "uprising."

Her stand she takes upon a steep-up hill.
The Passionate Pilgrim, l. 121.
Steep-up heavenly hill.—*Sonnets,* vii.
Heaven-kissing hill.—*Hamlet,* iii, 4, 59. The only use of "heaven-kissing."
Hill of heaven.—*Hamlet,* ii, 2, 518.

11
To sit upon a hill, as I do now.
III Henry VI, ii, 5, 23. See under LIFE.
Above the hill.—*III Henry VI,* iii, 1, 5.
Coming down the hill.—*The Taming of the Shrew,* iv, 2, 61; *I Henry IV,* ii, 2, 57.
Down the hill.—*I Henry IV,* ii, 2, 83; *Henry V,* iii, 3, 23; *King Lear,* ii, 4, 73.
Goes up the hill.—*King Lear,* ii, 4, 75.
Up to yond hill.—*Cymbeline,* iii, 3, 10.
Keep the hills.—*Julius Cæsar,* v, 1, 3.
Get higher on that hill.—*Julius Cæsar,* v, 3, 20.
On this hill.—*Julius Cæsar,* v, 3, 56.

12
To climb steep hills
Requires slow pace at first.
Henry VIII. Act i, sc. 1, l. 131. [Norfolk]

13
Who digs hills because they do aspire
Throws down one mountain to cast up a higher.
Pericles. Act i, sc. 4, l. 5. [Dionyza]

14
These high wild hills and rough uneven ways
Draws out our miles, and makes them wearisome.
Richard II. Act ii, sc. 3, l. 4. [Northumberland]
High and pleasant hill.—*Timon of Athens,* i, 1, 63.
High Dunsinane hill.—*Macbeth,* iv, 1, 93.
High eastward hill.—*Hamlet,* i, 1, 167.
Highest-peering hills.—*Titus Andronicus,* ii, 1, 8. The only use of "highest-peering."
Highmost hill.—*Romeo and Juliet,* ii, 5, 9. The only use of "highmost."
Hill of Basan.—*Antony and Cleopatra,* iii, 13, 127. The only mention of Basan.

15
We came down a foul hill.
The Taming of the Shrew. Act iv, sc. 1, l. 69. [Grumio]
Busky hill!—*I Henry IV,* v, 1, 2. The only use of "busky."
Copp'd hills.—*Pericles,* i, 1, 101. The only use of "copp'd" (peaked).
Louring hills.—*Romeo and Juliet,* ii, 5, 6.
Reverberate hills.—*Twelfth Night,* i, 5, 291.
Hills and valleys.—*Passionate Pilgrim,* l. 355.

HINT, see Suggestion

HISTORY

16
There is a history in all men's lives,
Figuring the nature of the times deceased.
II Henry IV. Act iii, sc. 1, l. 80. [Warwick]
The false heart's history.—*Sonnets,* xciii.
History his loss.—*II Henry IV,* iv, 1, 203. The only use of "history" as a verb.

17
My breast can better brook thy dagger's point
Than can my ears that tragic history.
III Henry VI. Act v, sc. 6, l. 27. [King Henry]

Life's history.—*Julius Cæsar,* v, 5, 40.
Strange eventful history.—*As You Like It,* ii, 7, 164.
History of lust.—*Othello,* ii, 1, 264.

1
If I should tell my history, it would seem
Like lies disdain'd in the reporting.
Pericles. Act v, sc. 1, l. 119. [Marina]

2
Duke: And what 's her history?
Viola: A blank, my lord.
Twelfth Night. Act ii, sc. 4, l. 112.

3
More
Than history can pattern, though devised
And play'd to take spectators.
The Winter's Tale. Act iii, sc. 2, l. 36. [Hermione]

HOBBY-HORSE

4
Armado: But O,—but O,—
Moth: 'The hobby-horse is forgot.'
Armado: Callest thou my love 'hobby-horse'?
Moth: No, master; the hobby-horse is but a colt, and your love perhaps a hackney.
Love's Labour's Lost. Act iii, sc. 1, l. 29. The reference is said to be to a ballad on the omission of the hobby-horse in May-games. The only use of "hackney."
Hobby-horse, whose epitaph is 'For, O, for, O, the hobby-horse is forgot.'
Hamlet. Act iii, sc. 2, l. 144. [Hamlet]

5
These hobby-horses must not hear.
Much Ado about Nothing, iii, 2, 75.

6
Give it to your hobby-horse.
Othello. Act iv, sc. 1, l. 159. [Bianca]
My wife 's a hobby-horse.
Winter's Tale. Act i, sc. 2, l. 276. [Leontes] The only uses of "hobby-horse."

HOG, see Swine

HOLIDAY

7
I am in a holiday humour.
As You Like It. Act iv, sc. 1, l. 69. [Rosalind]
Holiday fool.—*The Tempest,* ii, 2, 30.
Holiday foolery.—*As You Like It,* i, 3, 14.
Holiday . . . terms.—*I Henry IV,* i, 3, 46.

8
If all the year were playing holidays,
To sport would be as tedious as to work.
I Henry IV. Act i, sc. 2, l. 227. [Prince of Wales]
Awhile to work, and after holiday.
Richard II. Act iii, sc. 2, l. 44. [Bolingbroke]
Make holiday.—*The Tempest,* iv, 1, 136.
Speaks holiday.—*The Merry Wives of Windsor,* iii, 2, 69.

9
This day, no man think
Has business at his house; for all shall stay:
This little one shall make it holiday.
Henry VIII. Act v, sc. 5, l. 75. [King]

10
We make holiday, to see Cæsar and to rejoice in his triumph.
Julius Cæsar. Act i, sc. 1, l. 35. [Second Commoner]
And do you now cull out a holiday?
Julius Cæsar. Act i, sc. 1, l. 54. [Marullus]
Is this a holiday?—*Julius Cæsar,* i, 1, 2.

11
King Philip: The yearly course that brings this day about
Shall never see it but a holiday.
Constance: A wicked day, and not a holy day!
King John. Act iii, sc. 1, l. 81.

12
'Tis a playing-day, I see.
Merry Wives of Windsor. Act iv, sc. 1, l. 9. [Mrs. Page] The only use of the phrase.
Holiday-time.—*The Merry Wives of Windsor,* ii, 1, 2. The only use of the phrase.

13
Being holiday, the beggar's shop is shut.
Romeo and Juliet. Act v, sc. 1, l. 56. [Romeo]

HOLINESS

See also Goodness, Purity

14
What is not holy, that we swear not by,
But take the High'st to witness.
All's Well that Ends Well. Act iv, sc. 2, l. 23. [Diana]

15
I know him for a man divine and holy.
Measure for Measure. Act v, sc. 1, l. 144. [Friar Peter]
He 's honourable And doubting that, most holy.
Cymbeline. Act iii, sc. 4, l. 179. [Pisanio]

16
Virtuous and holy; chosen from above,
By inspiration of celestial grace,
To work exceeding miracles on earth.
I Henry VI. Act v, sc. 4, l. 39. [La Pucelle]
All his mind is bent to holiness,
To number Ave-Maries on his beads;
His champions are the prophets and apostles,
His weapons holy saws of sacred writ,
His study is his tilt-yard, and his loves
Are brazen images of canonized saints.
II Henry VI. Act i, sc. 3, l. 58. [Queen Margaret] "Tilt-yard" is repeated in *II Henry IV,* iii, 2, 347.
Rail thee into . . . holiness.—*Troilus and Cressida,* ii, 1, 18.
A holiness, a purity.—*King John,* iv, 3, 53. The only uses of "holiness," except in the titles, "His holiness," "Your holiness."
Numbering our Ave-Maries.—*III Henry VI,* ii, 1, 162. The only uses of "Ave-Maries."

17
You are full of heavenly stuff, and bear the inventory
Of your best graces in your mind; the which
You were now running o'er: you have scarce time
To steal from spiritual leisure a brief span
To keep your earthly audit.
Henry VIII. Act iii, sc. 2, l. 137. [King]

1
And in no worldly suit would he be moved,
To draw him from his holy exercise.
Richard III. Act iii, sc. 7, l. 63. [Catesby]
And, see, a book of prayer in his hand,
True ornaments to know a holy man.
Richard III, iii, 7, 98. [Buckingham]
He hath still been tried a holy man.
Romeo and Juliet, iv, 3, 29. [Juliet]

2
My sanctity
Will to my sense bend no licentious ear.
Pericles. Act v, sc. 3, l. 29. [Thaisa]
Such sanctity hath heaven given his hand.
Macbeth. Act iv, sc. 3, l. 144. [Doctor]
In pure white robes, Like very sanctity.
The Winter's Tale. Act iii, sc. 3, l. 22. [Antigonus]
Full of sanctity.—*As You Like It*, iii, 4, 14.
In the name of sanctity.—*Twelfth Night*, iii, 4, 94.
Sanctities of heaven.—*II Henry IV*, iv, 2, 21.
Sanctity of love.—*Twelfth Night*, iii, 4, 395.
The only uses of "sanctity."

3
The celestial habits,
Methinks I so should term them, and the reverence
Of the grave wearers.
The Winter's Tale. Act iii, sc. 1, l. 4. [Cleomenes]
Start not; her actions shall be holy as
You hear my spell is lawful.
Winter's Tale. Act v, sc. 3, l. 104. [Paulina]

HOME

4
I 'll stay at home.
All 's Well that Ends Well, i, 3, 259. [Countess] "Stay at home" is repeated in *Julius Cæsar*, ii, 2, 56, and in *The Two Gentlemen of Verona*, ii, 7, 62.
I 'll keep at home.—*Coriolanus*, v, 1, 7.
I 'll tarry at home.—*I Henry IV*, i, 2, 162.

5
Come thou home, Rousillon,
Whence honour but of danger wins a scar,
As oft loses all.
All 's Well that Ends Well. Act iii, sc. 2, l. 123. [Helena]
Go thou toward home, where I will never come
Whilst I can shake my sword or hear the drum.
All 's Well that Ends Well. Act ii, sc. 5, l. 95. [Bertram]

6
He keeps me rustically at home, or, to speak more properly, stays me here at home unkept.
As You Like It. Act i, sc. 1, l. 7. [Orlando]
The only use of "rustically" and "unkept."

7
I would I were at home.
As You Like It. Act iv, sc. 3, l. 162. [Rosalind]
When I was at home, I was in a better place.
As You Like It, ii, 4, 17. See under TRAVEL.
I had rather than forty pound I were at home.
Twelfth Night. Act v, sc. 1, l. 181. [Sir Andrew]
Native home.—*The Comedy of Errors*, i, 1, 30; *King John*, ii, 1, 69.

8
Come home to dinner.
The Comedy of Errors, ii, 1, 60. [Dromio of Ephesus]
Will you come home?—*The Comedy of Errors*, ii, 1, 64.

9
I prithee, noble friend, home to thy house.
Coriolanus. Act iii, sc. 1, l. 234. [Senator]
Home to my house.—*The Comedy of Errors*, iv, 4, 126.

10
We, poor unfledged,
Have never wing'd from view o' the nest, nor know not
What air 's from home.
Cymbeline. Act iii, sc. 3, l. 27. [Guiderius]

11
Men are merriest when they are from home.
Henry V. Act i, sc. 2, l. 272. [King Henry]

12
Alas, he hath no home, no place to fly to.
II Henry VI. Act iv, sc. 8, l. 40. [Clifford]
Earl of Douglas: A comfort of retirement lives in this.
Hotspur: A rendezvous, a home to fly unto.
I Henry IV. Act iv, sc. 1, l. 56. For RENDEZVOUS, see under MEETING.

13
Many lives stand between me and home.
III Henry VI. Act iii, sc. 2, l. 173. [Gloucester]

14
Hence! home, you idle creatures, get you home.
Julius Cæsar. Act i, sc. 1, l. 1. [Flavius]
Go, get you home, you fragments!
Coriolanus. Act i, sc. 1, l. 226. [Marcus]
I charge you, get you home.—*Othello*, v, 2, 194.
Get you home.—*Comedy of Errors*, iii, 1, 114.
Hie home.—*All 's Well that Ends Well*, ii, 5, 82; *The Comedy of Errors*, iv, 3, 93; *The Taming of the Shrew*, iv, 4, 62.
Hence to your homes; be gone!—*Coriolanus*, i, 1, 252.
Home to bed.—*III Henry VI*, v, 4, 56.
Home to your cottages.—*II Henry VI*, iv, 2, 132.
Home to your house.—*The Comedy of Errors*, i, 2, 75.

15
To my home I will no more return.
King John. Act ii, sc. 1, l. 21. [Austria]
Never go home.—*Troilus and Cressida*, v, 10, 2.
Is he come home yet?—*A Midsummer-Night's Dream*, iv, 2, 2.

16
What make you from home?
Othello. Act iii, sc. 4, l. 169. [Cassio]
I will ne'er go home.—*Othello*, v, 2, 197.
Far from home.—*The Rape of Lucrece*, l. 1596; *Sonnets*, lxi.
Welcome home.—*Richard III*, v, 3, 260, and ten times in later plays.
Who 's at home?—*The Taming of the Shrew*, iii, 2, 89.
Let 's home again.—*The Taming of the Shrew*, v, 1, 152.

1
Better at home, if 'would I might' were 'may.'
Troilus and Cressida. Act i, sc. 1, l. 117. [Troilus]
I 'll ride home to-morrow.—*Twelfth Night,* i, 3, 94.
I 'll home to-morrow.—*Twelfth Night,* i, 3, 111.

2
Home-keeping youth have ever homely wits.
Two Gentlemen of Verona. Act i, sc. 1, l. 2. [Valentine] The only use of "home-keeping."

He wondered that your lordship
Would suffer him to spend his youth at home,
While other men, of slender reputation,
Put forth their sons to seek preferment out:
Some to the wars, to try their fortune there;
Some to discover islands far away;
Some to the studious universities.

The Two Gentlemen of Verona. Act i, sc. 3, l. 4. [Panthino]

Let him spend his time no more at home,
Which would be great impeachment to his age,
In having known no travel in his youth.

The Two Gentlemen of Verona. Act i, sc. 3, l. 14. [Panthino] "Impeachment" is repeated in *Henry V,* iii, 6, 151, and in *Richard III,* ii, 2, 22.

3
I 'll leave you to confer of home affairs.
The Two Gentlemen of Verona. Act ii, sc. 4, l. 119. [Silvia]

4
O, let him keep his loathsome cabin still.
Venus and Adonis, l. 637.
Keep your cabins.—*The Tempest,* i, 1, 15.
Cabin in a cave.—*Titus Andronicus,* iv, 2, 179.
Willow cabin.—*Twelfth Night,* i, 5, 287.

5
Home, home, the next way; . . . come, good boy, the next way home.
The Winter's Tale. Act iii, sc. 3, l. 129. [Shepherd]
Paid home.—*The Winter's Tale,* v, 3, 4.
Pay . . . home.—*The Tempest,* v, 1, 71.
Push home.—*Henry V,* ii, 1, 103.
Strike home.—*Measure for Measure,* i, 3, 41.

HONESTY

See also Chastity; Integrity; Man: Honest Men

6
Though honesty be no puritan, yet it will do no hurt; it will wear the surplice of humility over the black gown of a big heart.
All's Well that Ends Well. Act i, sc. 3, l. 97. [Clown] "Surplice" occurs again in *The Phœnix and the Turtle,* l. 13.
No legacy is so rich as honesty.
All's Well that Ends Well. Act iii, sc. 5, l. 13. [Mariana]
All her deserving Is a reserved honesty.
All's Well that Ends Well. Act iii, sc. 5, l. 64. [Helena]

7
If he were honester He were much goodlier.
All's Well that Ends Well. Act iii, sc. 5, l. 82. [Diana] "Goodlier" is repeated in *The Tempest,* i, 2, 483. "Honester" occurs five times.
'Tis pity he is not honest.—*All's Well that Ends Well,* iii, 5, 85.
But you say she 's honest.—*All's Well that Ends Well,* iii, 6, 119. See under CHASTITY.

8
First Soldier: What is his honesty?
Parolles: He will steal, sir, an egg out of a cloister.
All's Well that Ends Well. Act iv, sc. 3, l. 280.
I have but little more to say, sir, of his honesty: he has every thing that an honest man should not have: what an honest man should have, he has nothing.
All's Well that Ends Well. Act iv, sc. 3, l. 289. [Parolles] "Honest man" or "honest men" is used 52 times. See MAN: HONEST MEN.

9
Mine honesty
Shall not make poor my greatness, nor my power
Work without it.

Antony and Cleopatra. Act ii, sc. 2, l. 92. [Antony]
Mine honesty and I begin to square.
Antony and Cleopatra. Act iii, sc. 13, l. 41. [Enobarbus]
And thou art honest too.
Antony and Cleopatra. Act iv, sc. 2, l. 15. [Antony]

10
Is it honest in deed and word? is it a true thing?
As You Like It. Act iii, sc. 3, l. 18. [Audrey]
I should think my honesty ranker than my wit.
As You Like It. Act iv, sc. 1, l. 85. [Rosalind]

11
Honesty coupled to beauty is to have honey a sauce to sugar.
As You Like It. Act iii, sc. 3, l. 30. [Touchstone]
Rich honesty dwells like a miser, sir, in a poor house; as your pearl in your foul oyster.
As You Like It. Act v, sc. 4, l. 62. [Touchstone]

12
I 'll prove mine honour and mine honesty.
The Comedy of Errors. Act v, sc. 1, l. 30. [Antipholus of Syracuse]
Thou art not honest; and the gods will plague thee.
Coriolanus. Act v, sc. 3, l. 166. [Volumnia]

Further to boast were neither true nor modest,
Unless I add, we are honest.

Cymbeline. Act v, sc. 5, l. 18. [Belarius]

13
To be honest, as this world goes, is to be one man picked out of ten thousand.
Hamlet. Act ii, sc. 2, l. 178. [Hamlet]
I am myself indifferent honest; but yet I could accuse me of such things that it were better my mother had not borne me.
Hamlet. Act iii, sc. 1, l. 123. [Hamlet]

14
Hamlet: What 's the news?
Rosencrantz: None, my lord, but that the world 's grown honest.

Hamlet.: Then is doomsday near.
Hamlet. Act ii, sc. 2, l. 240.

1 There is no honesty in such dealing.
II Henry IV. Act ii, sc. 1, l. 40. [Hostess]

2 He 's honest, on mine honour. God's blest mother!
I swear he is true-hearted.
Henry VIII. Act v, sc. 1, l. 153. [King]

Would you were half so honest!—*Henry VIII,* v, 3, 82.

3 There is written in your brow, provost, honesty and constancy.
Measure for Measure. Act iv, sc. 2, l. 162. [Duke]

4 'Cucullus non facit monachum:' honest in nothing but in his clothes.
Measure for Measure. Act v, sc. 1, l. 263. [Lucio] Cucullus, &c.: The hood doesn't make the monk. A medieval proverb.

It makes me almost ready to wrangle with mine own honesty.
The Merry Wives of Windsor. Act ii, sc. 1, l. 87. [Mrs. Page]

5 Dogberry: An old man, sir, and his wits are not so blunt as, God help, I would desire they were; but in faith, honest as the skin between his brows.
Verges: Yes, I thank God I am as honest as any man living that is an old man and no honester than I.
Much Ado about Nothing. Act iii, sc. 5, l. 11.

An honest soul, i' faith, sir; by my troth he is, as ever broke bread.
Much Ado about Nothing. Act iii, sc. 5, l. 41. [Dogberry] The only use of "honest soul."

An honest maid as ever broke bread.—*The Merry Wives of Windsor,* i, 4, 161.

Confirmed honesty.—*Much Ado about Nothing,* ii, 1, 395.

6 A man he is of honesty and trust.
Othello. Act i, sc. 3, l. 285. [Othello]

Othello: Is he not honest?
Iago: Honest, my lord!
Othello: Honest! ay, honest.
Iago: My lord, for aught I know.
Othello. Act iii, sc. 3, l. 103.

I dare be sworn I think that he is honest.
Othello. Act iii, sc. 3, l. 125. [Iago]

This fellow 's of exceeding honesty,
And knows all qualities, with a learned spirit,
Of human dealings.
Othello. Act iii, sc. 3, l. 258. [Othello]

An honest man he is, and hates the slime
That sticks on filthy deeds.
Othello. Act v, sc. 2, l. 148. [Othello]

7 O wretched fool,
That livest to make thine honesty a vice!
Othello. Act iii, sc. 3, l. 375. [Iago]

Take note, take note, O world,
To be direct and honest is not safe.
Othello. Act iii, sc. 3, l. 377. [Iago]

Honesty 's a fool And loses that it works for.
Othello. Act iii, sc. 3, l. 382. [Iago]

Foolish honesty.—*King Lear,* i, 2, 197; *Othello,* iii, 3, 412.

Outward honesty.—*The Rape of Lucrece,* l. 1545.

8 Though he be merry, yet withal he 's honest.
The Taming of the Shrew. Act iii, sc. 2, l. 25. [Tranio]

9 His honesty rewards him in itself.
Timon of Athens. Act i, sc. 1, l. 130. [Old Athenian]

Thou art true and honest.—*Timon of Athens,* ii, 2, 230.

10 Every man has his fault, and honesty is his.
Timon of Athens. Act iii, sc. 1, l. 29. [Lucullus]

Methinks thou art more honest now than wise.
Timon of Athens. Act iv, sc. 3, l. 509. [Timon]

11 Once again I do receive thee honest.
The Two Gentlemen of Verona. Act v, sc. 4, l. 78. [Valentine]

By mine honesty.—*The Two Gentlemen of Verona,* ii, 5, 1; *Measure for Measure,* v, 1, 59.

12 My honesty,
That lies enclosed in this trunk which you
Shall bear along impawn'd, away to-night!
The Winter's Tale. Act i, sc. 2, l. 434. [Camillo] "Impawned" occurs again *I Henry IV,* iv, 3, 108. "Impawn" is used in *Henry V,* i, 2, 21.

We need no grave to bury honesty:
There 's not a grain of it the face to sweeten
Of the whole dungy earth.
The Winter's Tale. Act ii, sc. 1, l. 155. [Antigonus] "Dungy earth" is used again in *Antony and Cleopatra,* i, 1, 35.

No less honest
Than you are mad; which is enough, I 'll warrant,
As this world goes, to pass for honest.
Winter's Tale. Act ii, sc. 3, l. 70. [Paulina]

I needs must think it honesty.
Winter's Tale. Act iv, sc. 4, l. 497. [Florizel]

Thou art not honest.—*Winter's Tale,* i, 2, 242.

'Tis pity she 's not honest.—*The Winter's Tale,* ii, 1, 68.

13 What a fool Honesty is!
The Winter's Tale. Act iv, sc. 4, l. 605. [Autolycus]

Breaking honesty.—*The Winter's Tale,* i, 2, 288.

Though I am not naturally honest, I am so sometimes by chance.
The Winter's Tale. Act iv, sc. 4, l. 731. [Autolycus]

If I had a mind to be honest, I see Fortune would not suffer me: she drops booties in my mouth. I am courted now with a double occasion, gold and a means to do the prince my master good; which who knows how that may turn back to my advancement?
The Winter's Tale. Act iv, sc. 4, l. 862. [Autolycus] The only use of "booties."

HONEY

See also Bee

1
Thus may we gather honey from the weed.
Henry V. Act iv, sc. 1, l. 11. [King Henry]
Honey of Hybla.—*I Henry IV*, i, 2, 47. See under Hostess for full quotation. "Hybla" is repeated in *Julius Cæsar,* v, 1, 34: "Hybla bees."
Honey-bag.—*A Midsummer-Night's Dream,* iii, 1, 171; iv, 1, 13; iv, 1, 16.
Honey-bee.—*Henry V*, i, 2, 187.
Honeycomb.—*The Tempest,* i, 2, 329.
Honey-dew.—*Titus Andronicus,* iii, 1, 112.
Honey-drop.—*The Tempest,* iv, 1, 79.
Honey-heavy.—*Julius Cæsar,* ii, 1, 230.
Honey-mouthed.—*The Winter's Tale,* ii, 2, 33.
Honey breath.—*Titus Andronicus,* ii, 4, 25; *Sonnets,* lxv.
Honey of thy breath.—*Romeo and Juliet,* v, 3, 92.
Honey words.—*Richard III,* iv, 1, 80.
Honey of his language.—*Henry VIII,* iii, 2, 22.
2 The sweetest honey
Is loathsome in his own deliciousness
And in the taste confounds the appetite.
Romeo and Juliet. Act ii, sc. 6, l. 11. [Friar Laurence] The only use of "deliciousness."
Surfeited with honey.—*I Henry IV*, iii, 2, 71.
Sweet honey.—*The Two Gentlemen of Verona,* i, 2, 106; *Troilus and Cressida,* v, 2, 18; v, 10, 43; *I Henry IV,* i, 2, 179.
3
I think the honey guarded with a sting.
The Rape of Lucrece, l. 493.

HONOUR

4 His honour,
Clock to itself, knew the true minute when
Exception bid him speak, and at this time
His tongue obey'd his hand.
All's Well that Ends Well. Act i, sc. 2, l. 38. [King]
Whose aged honour cites a virtuous youth.
All's Well that Ends Well. Act i, sc. 3, l. 216. [Helena]
See that you come
Not to woo honour, but to wed it.
All's Well that Ends Well. Act ii, sc. 1, l. 14. [King]
The honour, sir, that flames in your fair eyes,
Before I speak, too threateningly replies.
All's Well that Ends Well. Act ii, sc. 3, l. 86. [Helena] The only use of "threateningly."
5 She is young, wise, fair;
In these to nature she 's immediate heir,
And these breed honour: that is honour's scorn,
Which challenges itself as honour 's born
And is not like the sire: honours thrive,
When rather from our acts we them derive
Than our foregoers: the mere word 's a slave
Debosh'd on every tomb, on every grave
A lying trophy, and as oft is dumb
Where dust and damn'd oblivion is the tomb
Of honour'd bones indeed.
All's Well that Ends Well. Act ii, sc. 3, l. 138. [King] The only use of "foregoers."
6
My honour 's at the stake; which to defeat,
I must produce my power.
All's Well that Ends Well. Act ii, sc. 3, l. 156. [King]
It is in us to plant thine honour where
We please to have it grow.
All's Well that Ends Well. Act ii, sc. 3, l. 163. [King]
7
He wears his honour in a box unseen,
That hugs his kicky-wicky here at home,
Spending his manly marrow in her arms,
Which should sustain the bound and high curvet
Of Mars's fiery steed.
All's Well that Ends Well. Act ii, sc. 3, l. 296. [Parolles] The only use of "kicky-wicky." "Curvet" is repeated in *As You Like It,* iii, 2, 258.
8
The duke will lay upon him all the honour
That good convenience claims.
All's Well that Ends Well. Act iii, sc. 2, l. 74. [Second Gentleman]
His sword can never win
The honour that he loses.
All's Well that Ends Well. Act iii, sc. 2, l. 96. [Countess]
Hinder not the honour of his design.
All's Well that Ends Well. Act iii, sc. 6, l. 44. [Second Lord]
Thus your own proper wisdom
Brings in the champion Honour on my part,
Against your vain assault.
All's Well that Ends Well. Act iv, sc. 2, l. 49. [Diana]
Let your highness
Lay a more noble thought upon mine honour
Than for to think that I would sink it here.
All's Well that Ends Well. Act v, sc. 3, l. 179. [Bertram]
Fairer prove your honour
Than in my thought it lies.
All's Well that Ends Well. Act v, sc. 3, l. 183. [King]
9 Your honour calls you hence;
Therefore be deaf to my unpitied folly,
And all the gods go with you!
Antony and Cleopatra. Act i, sc. 3, l. 97. [Cleopatra]
The honour is sacred which he talks on now.
Antony and Cleopatra. Act ii, sc. 2, l. 85. [Antony]
'Tis not my profit that does lead mine honour;
Mine honour, it.
Antony and Cleopatra. Act ii, sc. 7, l. 82. [Pompey]
If I lose mine honour,
I lose myself: better I were not yours
Than yours so branchless.
Antony and Cleopatra. Act iii, sc. 4, l. 22. [Antony] The only use of "branchless."
I will . . . bathe my dying honour in the blood

Shall make it live again.
Antony and Cleopatra. Act iv, sc. 2, l. 5. [Antony]

1

If my son were my husband, I should freelier rejoice in that absence wherein he won honour than in the embracements of his bed where he would show most love.
Coriolanus. Act i, sc. 3, l. 2. [Volumnia] The only use of "freelier."

2

He had rather venture all his limbs for honour
Than one on 's ears to hear it.
Coriolanus. Act ii, sc. 2, l. 84. [Menenius]

Thou hast affected the fine strains of honour,
To imitate the graces of the gods.
Coriolanus. Act v, sc. 3, l. 149. [Volumnia]

Thou hast set thy mercy and thy honour
At difference in thee.
Coriolanus. Act v, sc. 3, l. 200. [Aufidius]

3 The heavens hold firm
The walls of thy dear honour, keep unshak'd
That temple, thy fair mind!
Cymbeline. Act ii, sc. 1, l. 67. [Lord]

Of him I gather'd honour;
Which he to seek of me again, perforce,
Behoves me to keep at utterance.
Cymbeline. Act iii, sc. 1, l. 71. [Cymbeline]

You do not understand yourself so clearly
As it behoves my daughter and your honour.
Hamlet. Act i, sc. 3, l. 96. [Polonius]

4

By heaven, methinks it were an easy leap,
To pluck bright honour from the pale-faced moon,
Or dive into the bottom of the deep,
Where fathom-line could never touch the ground,
And pluck up drowned honour by the locks.
I Henry IV. Act i, sc. 3, l. 201. [Hotspur] The only use of "fathom-line."

If well-respected honour bid me on,
I hold as little counsel with weak fear
As you, my lord, or any Scot that this day lives.
I Henry IV. Act iv, sc. 3, l. 10. [Vernon] The only use of "well-respected."

5

Thou hast lost much honour, that thou wert not with me in this action.
I Henry IV. Act ii, sc. 4, l. 23. [Prince of Wales] An echo of the letter of Henri IV of France to Crillon, after the battle of Amiens, 20 Sept., 1597, the same year in which this play was written: "Pend-toi, brave Crillon, nous avons vaincu, et tu n'y étais pas."

What never-dying honour hath he got.
I Henry IV. Act iii, sc. 2, l. 106. [King Henry] The only use of "never-dying."

6

Thou art the king of honour.
I Henry IV. Act iv, sc. 1, l. 10. [Douglas]

The very bent of honour.—*Much Ado about Nothing,* iv, 1, 188.

Thou map of honour.—*Richard II,* v, 1, 12.

Thou rag of honour!—*Richard III,* i, 3, 233.

The modesty of honour.—*Twelfth Night,* v, 1, 343.

Perfect honour.—*Cymbeline,* iii, 3, 67.

Sacred honour.—*The Winter's Tale,* ii, 3, 84.

7

Honour pricks me on. Yea, but how if honour prick me off when I come on? how then? Can honour set to a leg? no: or an arm? no: or take away the grief of a wound? no. Honour hath no skill in surgery, then? no. What is honour? a word. What is in that word honour? what is that honour? air. A trim reckoning! Who hath it? he that died o' Wednesday. Doth he feel it? no. Doth he hear it? no. 'Tis insensible, then? Yea, to the dead. But will it not live with the living? no. Why? detraction will not suffer it. Therefore I'll none of it. Honour is a mere scutcheon: and so ends my catechism.
I Henry IV. Act v, sc. 1, l. 131. [Falstaff] "Catechism" is repeated in *As You Like It,* iii, 2, 241; and "scutcheon" in *Love's Labour's Lost,* v, 2, 135, and in *Antony and Cleopatra,* v, 2, 135.

I like not such grinning honour as Sir Walter hath: give me life: which if I can save, so: if not, honour comes unlooked for, and there's an end.
I Henry IV. Act v, sc. 3, l. 62. [Falstaff]

There's honour for you!—*I Henry IV,* v, 3, 33.

8

There were two honours lost, yours and your son's.
For yours, the God of heaven brighten it!
For his, it stuck upon him as the sun
In the grey vault of heaven.
II Henry IV. Act ii, sc. 3, l. 16. [Lady Percy] The only use of "brighten."

Never, O never, do his ghost the wrong
To hold your honour more precise and nice
With others than with him!
II Henry IV. Act ii, sc. 3, l. 39. [Lady Percy]

And suffer the condition of these times
To lay a heavy and unequal hand
Upon our honours?
II Henry IV. Act iv, sc. 1, l. 101. [Mowbray]

What I did I did in honour,
Led by the impartial conduct of my soul.
II Henry IV. Act v, sc. 2, l. 35. [Chief Justice]

9 Honour's thought
Reigns solely in the breast of every man.
Henry V. Act ii, Prologue, l. 3. [Chorus]

With spirit of honour edged
More sharper than your swords, hie to the field.
Henry V. Act iii, sc. 5, l. 38. [French King]

10

The fewer men, the greater share of honour.
Henry V. Act iv, sc. 3, l. 22. [King Henry]

Second Watch: 'Tis the more honour, because more dangerous.
Third Watch: Ay, but give me worship and quietness;

I like it better than a dangerous honour.
III Henry VI. Act iv, sc. 3, l. 15.

1 By Jove, I am not covetous for gold, . . .
But if it be a sin to covet honour,
I am the most offending soul alive.
Henry V. Act iv, sc. 3, l. 24. [King Henry]

Let us die in honour.
Henry V. Act iv, sc. 5, l. 11. [Bourbon]

From my weary limbs Honour is cudgelled.
Henry V. Act v. sc. 1, l. 89. [Pistol]

2 Thou preferr'st thy life before thine honour.
III Henry VI. Act i, sc. 1, l. 246. [Queen Margaret]

3 Thereon I pawn my credit and mine honour.
III Henry VI. Act iii, sc. 3, l. 116. [Warwick]

My honour is at pawn.
II Henry IV. Act ii, sc. 3, l. 7. [Northumberland]

I pawn'd Mine honour for his truth.
Coriolanus. Act v, sc. 6, l. 21. [Aufidius]

Old Athenian: Pawn me to this your honour . . .
Timon: My hand to thee; mine honour on my promise.
Timon of Athens. Act i, sc. 1, l. 147.

Pawning his honour to obtain his lust.
The Rape of Lucrece, l. 156.

4 My desert is honour:
And to repair my honour lost for him,
I here renounce him.
III Henry VI. Act iii, sc. 3, l. 192. [Warwick]

Courage, my masters! honour now or never!
III Henry VI. Act iv, sc. 3, l. 24. [Warwick]

5 Whose honour heaven shield from soil!
Henry VIII. Act i, sc. 2, l. 26. [Queen Katharine]

6 Honour's train Is longer than his foreskirt.
Henry VIII. Act ii, sc. 3, l. 97. [Old Lady] The only use of "foreskirt."

7 You tender more your person's honour than
Your high profession spiritual.
Henry VIII. Act ii, sc. 4, l. 116. [Queen Katharine]

After my death I wish no other herald,
No other speaker of my living actions,
To keep mine honour from corruption,
But such an honest chronicler as Griffith.
Henry VIII. Act iv, sc. 2, l. 69. [Queen Katharine] The only use of "chronicler."

Whom I most hated living, thou hast made me,
With thy religious truth and modesty,
Now in his ashes honour.
Henry VIII. Act iv, sc. 2, l. 73. [Queen Katharine]

8 Set honour in one eye and death i' the other,
And I will look on both indifferently:
For let the gods so speed me as I love
The name of honour more than I fear death.
Julius Cæsar. Act i, sc. 2, l. 86. [Brutus]

Honour is the subject of my story.
Julius Cæsar. Act i, sc. 2, l. 92. [Cassius]

Believe me for mine honour, and have respect to mine honour, that you may believe.
Julius Cæsar. Act iii, sc. 2, l. 15. [Brutus]

9 For Brutus is an honourable man;
So are they all, all honourable men.
Julius Cæsar. Act iii, sc. 2, l. 87. [Antony] "Honourable man (men)" occurs eight times in the plays.

Honourable gentleman.—*All's Well that Ends Well,* v, 3, 239, and four times in later plays. The adjective, modifying various nouns, is used 115 times.

10 Such as he is, full of regard and honour.
Julius Cæsar. Act iv, sc. 2, l. 12. [Pindarus]

Thy life hath had some smatch of honour in it.
Julius Cæsar. Act v, sc. 5, l. 46. [Brutus] The only use of "smatch."

11 A foot of honour better than I was;
But many a many foot of land the worse.
King John. Act i, sc. 1, l. 182. [Bastard]

Where is that slave, thy brother? where is he,
That holds in chase mine honour up and down?
King John. Act i, sc. 1, l. 222. [Lady Faulconbridge]

12 Bound in honour.
King John. Act ii, sc. 1, l. 522. [Blanch]

That which upholdeth him that thee upholds,
His honour.
King John. Act iii, sc. 1, l. 315. [Constance]

13 Who hast not in thy brows an eye discerning
Thine honour from thy suffering.
King Lear. Act iv, sc. 2, l. 52. [Goneril] "Discerning" is repeated in i, 4, 248, and occurs in no other play.

The eye of honour.—*The Merchant of Venice,* i, 1, 137.

The ancient Roman honour.—*The Merchant of Venice,* iii, 2, 297. See under CHARACTER for full quotation.

14 How much low peasantry would then be glean'd
From the true seed of honour! and how much honour
Pick'd from the chaff and ruin of the times
To be new-varnish'd.
The Merchant of Venice. Act ii, sc. 9, l. 46. [Arragon] The only use of "peasantry" and "new-varnish'd."

My honour would not let ingratitude
So much besmear it.
The Merchant of Venice. Act v, sc. 1, l. 218. [Bassanio] "Besmear" is repeated in *Julius Cæsar,* iii, 1, 107.

15 You stand upon your honour! Why, thou unconfinable baseness, it is as much as I can do to keep the terms of my honour precise: I, I, I myself sometimes, leaving the fear of God on the left hand and hiding mine honour in my necessity, am fain to shuffle, to hedge and to lurch; and yet you rogue, will en-

sconce your rags, your cat-a-mountain looks, your red-lattice phrases, and your bold-beating oaths, under the shelter of your honour!
The Merry Wives of Windsor. Act ii, sc. 2, l. 20. [Falstaff] The only use of "unconfinable," "lurch," "cat-a-mountain," and "bold-beating." "Red lattice" occurs again in *II Henry IV*, ii, 2, 86.

Now doth thy honour stand,
In him that was of late an heretic,
As firm as faith.
The Merry Wives of Windsor. Act iv, sc. 4, l. 8. [Ford]

1 Honour we love;
For who hates honour hates the gods above.
Pericles. Act ii, sc. 3, l. 21. [Simonides]

If you were born to honour, show it now;
If put upon you, make the judgement good
That thought you worthy of it.
Pericles. Act iv, sc. 6, l. 99. [Marina]

2 Kill thine honour with thy life's decay.
The Rape of Lucrece, l. 516.

Stoop to honour, not to foul desire.
The Rape of Lucrece, l. 574.

Low-declined honour. *The Rape of Lucrece,* l. 1705. The only use of "low-declined."

3 Old John of Gaunt, time-honour'd Lancaster.
Richard II. Act i, sc. 1, l. 1. [King Richard] The only use of "time-honour'd."

4 Mine honour is my life; both grew in one;
Take honour from me, and my life is done.
Richard II. Act i, sc. 1, l. 182. [Mowbray]

Mine honour lives when his dishonour dies,
Or my shamed life in his dishonour lies.
Richard II. Act v, sc. 3, l. 70. [York]

Point of honour.—*Richard II,* v, 3, 11.

5 Say I sent thee forth to purchase honour.
Richard II. Act i, sc. 3, l. 282. [Gaunt]

Mine honour soil'd
With the attainder of his slanderous lips.
Richard II. Act iv, sc. 1, l. 23. [Aumerle]

He shall spend mine honour with his shame,
As thriftless sons their scraping father's gold.
Richard II. Act v, sc. 3, l. 68. [York] The only use of "scraping."

6 His honour is as true
In this appeal as thou art all unjust.
Richard II. Act iv, sc. 1, l. 44. [Henry Percy]

For though mine enemy thou hast ever been,
High sparks of honour in thee have I seen.
Richard II. Act v, sc. 6, l. 28. [Bolingbroke]

7 Honour may be shrouded in a hearse.
Richard III. Act i, sc. 2, l. 1. [Lady Anne]

Your fire-new stamp of honour is scarce current.
Richard III. Act i, sc. 3, l. 256. [Queen Margaret]

The dignity and height of honour.
Richard III. Act iv, sc. 4, l. 243. [King Richard]

8 More validity,
More honourable state, more courtship lives
In carrion-flies than Romeo.
Romeo and Juliet. Act iii, sc. 3, l. 35. [Romeo] The only use of "carrion-flies."

Gilded honour shamefully misplaced.
Sonnets. No. lxvi.

9 And as the sun breaks through the darkest clouds,
So honour peereth in the meanest habit.
The Taming of the Shrew. Act iv, sc. 3, l. 175. [Petruchio] "Darkest" occurs only once more, in *Hamlet,* v, 2, 267: "Darkest night." "Meanest" is used ten times.

10 What a wicked beast was I to disfurnish myself against such a good time, when I might ha' shown myself honourable!
Timon of Athens. Act iii, sc. 2, l. 49. [Lucullus] "Disfurnish" is repeated in *The Two Gentlemen of Verona,* iv, 1, 14, and in *Pericles,* iv, 6, 12.

Who bates mine honour shall not know my coin.
Timon of Athens. Act iii, sc. 3, l. 26. [Sempronius]

11 Laden with honour's spoils.
Titus Andronicus. Act i, sc. 1, l. 36. [Marcus]

So I love and honour thee and thine.
Titus Andronicus. Act i, sc. 1, l. 49. [Bassianus]

Give me a staff of honour for mine age,
But not a sceptre to control the world.
Titus Andronicus. Act i, sc. 1, l. 198. [Titus]

I do not flatter thee,
But honour thee, and will do till I die.
Titus Andronicus. Act i, sc. 1, l. 212. [Bassianus]

Even thou hast struck upon my crest,
And, with these boys, mine honour thou hast wounded.
Titus Andronicus. Act i, sc. 1, l. 364. [Titus]

12 Holds his honour higher than his ease.
Troilus and Cressida. Act i, sc. 3, l. 266. [Æneas]

There can be no evasion
To blench from this and to stand firm by honour.
Troilus and Cressida. Act ii, sc. 2, l. 67. [Troilus]

For honour travels in a strait so narrow,
Where one but goes abreast: keep then the path.
Troilus and Cressida. Act iii, sc. 3, l. 154. [Ulysses]

Life every man holds dear; but the brave man
Holds honour far more precious-dear than life.
Troilus and Cressida. Act v, sc. 3, l. 27. [Hector] The only use of "precious-dear."

13 He after honour hunts, I after love.
The Two Gentlemen of Verona. Act i, sc. 1, l. 63. [Proteus]

1
So sovereignly being honourable.
The Winter's Tale. Act i, sc. 2, l. 323. [Camillo] The only use of "sovereignly."
I am charged in honour and by him
That I think honourable.
Winter's Tale. Act i, sc. 2. l. 407. [Camillo]

2
Your honour and your goodness is so evident.
Winter's Tale. Act ii, sc. 2, l. 43. [Emilia]
For honour,
'Tis a derivative from me to mine,
And only that I stand for.
The Winter's Tale. Act iii, sc. 2, l. 44. [Hermione] The only use of "derivative."
He, most humane And fill'd with honour.
Winter's Tale. Act iii, sc. 2, l. 166. [Leontes]

3
Thou wouldst have poison'd good Camillo's honour,
To have him kill a king.
Winter's Tale. Act iii, sc. 2, l. 189. [Paulina]
Whose honour and whose honesty till now
Endured all weathers.
Winter's Tale. Act v, sc. 1, l. 194. [Florizel]

II—Woman's Honour

See also Chastity

4
The honour of a maid is her name.
All's Well that Ends Well. Act iii, sc. 5, l. 12. [Mariana]

5
Thyreus: He knows that you embrace not Antony
As you did love, but as you fear'd him. . . .
The scars upon your honour, therefore, he
Does pity, as constrained blemishes,
Not as deserved.
Cleopatra: He is a god, and knows
What is most right: mine honour was not yielded,
But conquer'd merely.
Enobarbus [aside]: To be sure of that,
I will ask Antony. Sir, sir, thou art so leaky,
That we must leave thee to thy sinking, for
Thy dearest quit thee.
Antony and Cleopatra. Act iii, sc. 13, l. 56.
Leaky as an unstanched wench.—*The Tempest,* i, 1, 51. The only uses of "leaky."

6 I have pick'd the lock and ta'en
The treasure of her honour.
Cymbeline. Act ii, sc. 2, l. 41. [Iachimo]
I now
Profess myself the winner of her honour.
Cymbeline. Act ii, sc. 4, l. 52. [Iachimo]

7 I would I were so sure
To win the king as I am bold her honour
Will remain hers.
Cymbeline. Act ii, sc. 4, l. 1. [Posthumus]
The foul opinion
You had of her pure honour gains or loses
Your sword or mine.
Cymbeline. Act ii, sc. 4, l. 58. [Posthumus]

8 Let there be no honour
Where there is beauty; truth, where semblance; love,
Where there 's another man.
Cymbeline. Act ii, sc. 4, l. 108. [Posthumus]
With unchaste purpose and with oath to violate
My lady's honour.
Cymbeline. Act v, sc. 5, l. 284. [Pisanio]

9 My maiden honour, yet as pure
As the unsullied lily.
Love's Labour 's Lost. Act v, sc. 2, l. 351. [Princess of France] The only use of "unsullied."

10
She dwells so securely on the excellency of her honour, that the folly of my soul dares not present itself.
The Merry Wives of Windsor. Act ii, sc. 2, l. 252. [Ford]
She 's but the sign and semblance of her honour.
Much Ado about Nothing. Act iv, sc. 1, l. 34. [Claudio]
If they wrong her honour,
The proudest of them shall well hear of it.
Much Ado about Nothing. Act iv, sc. 1, l. 193. [Leonato]

11
Othello: She is protectress of her honour too:
May she give that?
Iago: Her honour is an essence that 's not seen;
They have it very oft that have it not.
Othello. Act iv, sc. 1, l. 14. The only use of "protectress."
Why should honour outlive honesty?
Othello. Act v, sc. 2, l. 245. [Othello]

12
My honour I 'll bequeath unto the knife
That wounds my body so dishonoured.
The Rape of Lucrece, l. 1184.
'Tis honour to deprive dishonour'd life;
The one will live, the other being dead.
The Rape of Lucrece, l. 1186.
Mine honour be the knife's that makes my wound.
The Rape of Lucrece, l. 1201.

13 Thou didst seek to violate
The honour of my child.
Tempest. Act i, sc. 2, l. 347. [Prospero]
Him That would have forced your honour.
The Two Gentlemen of Verona. Act v, sc. 4, l. 21. [Proteus]

14
What we did was mildly as we might,
Tendering our sister's honour and our own.
Titus Andronicus. Act i, sc. 1, l. 475. [Lucius]
Believe me, queen, your swarth Cimmerian
Doth make your honour of his body's hue.
Titus Andronicus. Act ii, sc. 3, l. 72. The only use of "swarth" and "Cimmerian."

15
Have you not set mine honour at the stake
And baited it with all the unmuzzled thoughts
That tyrannous heart can think?
Twelfth Night. Act iii, sc. 1, l. 129. [Olivia] The only use of "unmuzzled."

I have said too much unto a heart of stone
And laid mine honour too unchary out.
Twelfth Night. Act iii, sc. 4, l. 221. [Olivia] The only use of "unchary."

1
I 'll give no blemish to her honour, none.
Winter's Tale. Act i, sc. 2, l. 341. [Leontes]
Be she honour-flaw'd, I have three daughters.
Winter's Tale. Act ii, sc. 1, l. 143. [Antigonus] The only use of "honour-flaw'd."

HONOURS

See also Dignities, Preferment, Titles

2
All the honours that can fly from us
Shall on them settle.
All's Well that Ends Well. Act iii, sc. 1, l. 20. [Duke]
I would do the man what honour I can.
All's Well that Ends Well. Act iv, sc. 3, l. 303. [Parolles]

3
By deed-achieving honour newly named.
Coriolanus. Act ii, sc. 1, l. 190. [Volumnia] The only use of "deed-achieving."

4
Yet time serves wherein you may redeem
Your banish'd honours.
I Henry IV. Act i, sc. 3, l. 180. [Hotspur]
All the budding honours on thy crest
I 'll crop, to make a garland for my head.
I Henry IV. Act v, sc. 4, l. 72. [Prince of Wales]

5
And I do wish your honours may increase.
II Henry IV. Act v, sc. 2, l. 104. [King Henry V]
Enchased with all the honours of the world.
II Henry VI. Act i, sc. 2, l. 8. [Duchess of Gloucester] The only use of "enchased."
Bears his blushing honours thick upon him.
Henry VIII, iii, 2, 354. See under GREATNESS for full quotation.
Wide-stretched honours.—*Henry V,* ii, 4, 82. The only use of the phrase.

6
Do not honour him so much
To prick thy finger, though to wound his heart.
III Henry VI. Act i, sc. 4, l. 54. [Northumberland]

7
Too much honour:
O, 'tis a burden, Cromwell, 'tis a burden
Too heavy for a man that hopes for heaven!
Henry VIII. Act iii, sc. 2, l. 383. [Wolsey]
Trod the ways of glory,
And sounded all the depths and shoals of honour.
Henry VIII. Act iii, sc. 2, l. 435. [Wolsey] The only use of "shoals." "Shoal" occurs in *Macbeth,* i, 7, 6: "Shoal of time."

8
Though we lay these honours on this man,
To ease ourselves of divers slanderous loads,
He shall but bear them as the ass bears gold.
Julius Cæsar. Act iv, sc. 1, l. 19. [Antony]

9
New honours come upon him,
Like our strange garments, cleave not to their mould
But with the aid of use.
Macbeth. Act i, sc. 3, l. 144. [Banquo]

All our service
In every point twice done and then done double
Were poor and single business to contend
Against those honours deep and broad wherewith
Your majesty loads our house: for those of old,
And the late dignities heap'd up to them,
We rest your hermits.
Macbeth. Act i, sc. 6, l. 14. [Lady Macbeth]

10
But shall we wear these honours for a day?
Or shall they last, and we rejoice in them?
Richard III. Act iv, sc. 2, l. 5. [King Richard]

11
Proclaim our honours, lords, with trump and drum.
Titus Andronicus. Act i, sc. 1, l. 275. [Saturninus]

12
And not a man, for being simply man,
Hath any honour, but honour for those honours
That are without him, as place, riches, favour,
Prizes of accident as oft as merit.
Troilus and Cressida. Act iii, sc. 3, l. 80. [Achilles]

13
She shall be dignified with this high honour—
To bear my lady's train, lest the base earth
Should from her vesture chance to steal a kiss
And, of so great a favour growing proud,
Disdain to root the summer-swelling flower
And make rough winter everlastingly.
The Two Gentlemen of Verona. Act ii, sc. 4, l. 158. [Valentine] The only use of "summer-swelling." "Everlastingly" is repeated in *King John,* v, 7, 105; *Richard II,* iii, 2, 207; *Richard III,* iv, 4, 309.

HOPE

14
He hath persecuted time with hope.
All's Well that Ends Well. Act i, sc. 1, l. 16. [Lafeu] The only use of "persecuted."
There 's hope in 't yet.—*Antony and Cleopatra,* iii, 13, 176.

15
There is little hope of life in him.
As You Like It. Act i, sc. 2, l. 136. [Le Beau]
Hope not after it.—*As You Like It,* iii, 5, 45.

16
But longer we did not retain much hope.
The Comedy of Errors. Act i, sc. 1, l. 66. [Ægeon]
All hope is vain.—*Coriolanus,* v, 1, 70.
There is no hope in 't.—*Coriolanus,* v, 4, 7.

17
Past hope, and in despair; that way, past grace.
Cymbeline. Act i, sc. 1, l. 137. [Imogen]
This forwardness Makes our hopes fair.
Cymbeline. Act iv, sc. 2, l. 342. [Lucius]

1
O esperance!
I Henry IV. Act ii, sc. 3, l. 74. [Hotspur]
Now, Esperance! Percy! and set on.
I Henry IV. Act v, sc. 2, l. 97. [Hotspur]
Sith yet there is a credence in my heart,
An esperance so obstinately strong,
That doth invert the attest of eyes and ears,
As if those organs had deceptious functions,
Created only to calumniate.
Troilus and Cressida. Act v, sc. 2, l. 120. [Troilus] The only use of "obstinately," "deceptious," and "calumniate." "Invert" occurs a second time in *The Tempest,* iii, 1, 70.
Stands still in esperance.—*King Lear*. Act iv, sc. 1, l. 4. The only uses of "esperance."

2
Full of prosperous hope.
I Henry IV. Act iii, sc. 1, l. 2. [Mortimer]
Brave hope.—*The Rape of Lucrece,* l. 1430.
Great hopes.—*II Henry VI,* iii, 1, 287; *II Henry IV,* v, 2, 68; *Measure for Measure,* i, 2, 187; *The Tempest,* ii, 1, 240.

3
The very bottom and the soul of hope.
I Henry IV. Act iv, sc. 1, l. 50. [Hotspur]
If he outlive the envy of this day,
England did never owe so sweet a hope,
So much misconstrued in his wantonness.
I Henry IV. Act v, sc. 2, l. 67. [Vernon] "Misconstrued" is repeated in *Julius Cæsar,* v, 3, 84, and in *The Merchant of Venice,* ii, 2, 197.

4 [He] lined himself with hope,
Eating the air on promise of supply.
II Henry IV. Act i, sc. 3, l. 27. [Bardolph]
It never yet did hurt
To lay down likelihoods and forms of hope.
II Henry IV. Act i, sc. 3, l. 34. [Hastings]
A cause on foot
Lives so in hope as in an early spring
We see the appearing buds; which to prove fruit,
Hope gives not so much warrant as despair
That frosts will bite them.
II Henry IV. Act i, sc. 3, l. 37. [Bardolph]
Grant that our hopes, yet likely of fair birth,
Should be still-born.
II Henry IV. Act i, sc. 3, l. 63. [Hastings] The only use of "still-born."
Si fortune me tormente, sperato me contento.
II Henry IV. Act ii, sc. 4, l. 195. [Pistol] Quoting an Italian proverb. Repeated in v, 5, 102.

5
Thus do the hopes we have in him touch ground
And dash themselves to pieces.
II Henry IV. Act iv, sc. 1, l. 17. [Mowbray]

6
The best hope I have.
Henry V. Act iv, sc. 3, l. 33. [King Henry]
This was my lord's best hope.
Timon of Athens. Act iii, sc. 3, l. 36. [Servant] The only uses of "best hope."

7 Fair be all thy hopes
And prosperous be thy life in peace and war!
I Henry VI. Act ii, sc. 5, l. 113. [Mortimer]
Fair hope must hinder life's decay.
III Henry VI. Act iv, sc. 4, l. 16. [Queen Elizabeth] The only use of "fair hope."

8
In you all hopes are lost.
I Henry VI. Act iv, sc. 5, l. 25. [John Talbot]
And if thou fail us, all our hope is done.
III Henry VI. Act iii, sc. 3, l. 33. [Queen Margaret]
Macduff: I have lost my hopes.
Malcolm: Perchance even there where I did find my doubts.
Macbeth. Act iv, sc. 3, l. 24.
Lose my hopes.—*The Merchant of Venice,* ii, 2, 198.

9
King Henry: God, our hope, will succour us.
Queen Margaret: My hope is gone.
II Henry VI. Act iv, sc. 4, l. 55.
Hope of help.—*II Henry VI,* iii, 2, 287.
Hope of good.—*III Henry VI,* ii, 3, 8.
Hope of life.—*III Henry VI,* ii, 3, 55.
Hoped-for hay.—*III Henry VI,* iv, 8, 61.
Hoped-for mercy.—*III Henry VI,* v, 4, 35. The phrase "hoped-for" is used only in this play.

10
And in that hope I throw mine eyes to heaven,
Scorning whate'er you can afflict me with.
III Henry VI. Act i, sc. 4, l. 37. [York]

11
There is hope All will be well.
Henry VIII. Act ii, sc. 3, l. 55. [Lord Chamberlain]

12 Farewell
The hopes of court! my hopes in heaven do dwell.
Henry VIII. Act iii, sc. 2, l. 458. [Wolsey]
A high hope for a low heaven.
Love's Labour 's Lost. Act i, sc. 1, l. 196. [Longaville] The only use of "high hope."

13
Our hopes are answered.
Julius Cæsar. Act v, sc. 1, l. 1. [Octavius]

14 Was the hope drunk
Wherein you dress'd yourself? hath it slept since?
And wakes it now, to look so green and pale
At what it did so freely?
Macbeth. Act i, sc. 7, l. 35. [Lady Macbeth]
'Tis his main hope.—*Macbeth,* v, 4, 10. The only use of this phrase.

15
O my breast, Thy hope ends here.
Macbeth. Act iv, sc. 3, l. 113. [Macduff]
All hope is gone.—*Measure for Measure,* i, 4, 68.
There 's no hope.—*Pericles,* iv, 1, 99.
Past hope.—*Twelfth Night,* v, 1, 82.

1
The miserable have no other medicine
But only hope.
Measure for Measure. Act iii, sc. 1, l. 2. [Claudio]

Do not satisfy your resolution with hopes that are fallible.
Measure for Measure. Act iii, sc. 1, l. 169. [Duke] "Fallible" is repeated in *Antony and Cleopatra,* v, 2, 258.

Provost: What comfort is for Claudio?
Duke Vincentio: There 's some in hope.
Provost: It is a bitter deputy.
Measure for Measure. Act iv, sc. 2, l. 80.

2
Launcelot: There is but one hope in it that can do you any good: and that is but a kind of bastard hope neither.
Jessica: And what hope is that, I pray thee?
Launcelot: Marry, you may partly hope that your father got you not, that you are not the Jew's daughter.
Jessica: That were a kind of bastard hope indeed.
The Merchant of Venice. Act iii, sc. 5, l. 7.

3
The best way were to entertain him with hope.
The Merry Wives of Windsor. Act ii, sc. 1, l. 68. [Mrs. Ford]

Give him another hope, to betray him to another punishment.
The Merry Wives of Windsor. Act iii, sc. 3, l. 207. [Mrs. Ford]

Hope is a curtal dog in some affairs.
The Merry Wives of Windsor. Act ii, sc. 1, l. 114. [Pistol] A curtal dog was a dog whose tail had been cut off, according to the old English forest laws, to show that its owner was hindered from coursing, and so, in later usage, a dog that had missed its game. Shakespeare uses the word again in *The Comedy of Errors,* iii, 2, 151; and it occurs a third time in *The Passionate Pilgrim,* l. 273, of uncertain authorship.

4
Therefore be out of hope.
A Midsummer-Night's Dream. Act iii, sc. 2, l. 279. [Lysander]

I am right glad that he 's so out of hope.
The Tempest. Act iii, sc. 3, l. 11. [Antonio]

5
Full of foul hope and full of fond mistrust.
The Rape of Lucrece, l. 284.

Weak-built hopes.—*The Rape of Lucrece,* l. 130. The only use of "weak-built."

6
Strong as a tower in hope, I cry amen.
Richard II. Act i, sc. 3, l. 102. [Bolingbroke]

7
I will despair, and be at enmity
With cozening hope: he is a flatterer,
A parasite, a keeper back of death,
Who gently would dissolve the bands of life,
Which false hope lingers in extremity.
Richard II. Act ii, sc. 2, l. 68. [Queen]

False hopes.—*I Henry VI,* iv, 4, 20.

8
Hope to joy is little less in joy
Than hope enjoy'd.
Richard II. Act ii, sc. 3, l. 15. [Northumberland]

I see some sparks of better hope, which elder years
May happily bring forth.
Richard II. Act v, sc. 3, l. 21. [Bolingbroke] The only use of "better hope."

9
Duke of Gloucester: But shall I live in hope?
Lady Anne: All men, I hope, live so.
Richard III. Act i, sc. 2, l. 200. The only use of "live in hope."

It stands me much upon,
To stop all hopes whose growth may damage me.
Richard III. Act iv, sc. 2, l. 59. [King Richard]

10
True hope is swift, and flies with swallow's wings;
Kings it makes gods, and meaner creatures kings.
Richard III. Act v, sc. 2, l. 23. [Richmond] "True hope" is used a second time in *III Henry VI,* iv, 8, 25: "My Troy's true hope."

11
The earth hath swallow'd all my hopes but she,
She is the hopeful lady of my earth.
Romeo and Juliet. Act i, sc. 2, l. 14. [Capulet]

Hopeful mother.—*Richard III,* i, 2, 24.
Hopeful prince.—*The Winter's Tale,* iii, 2, 41.
Hopeful son.—*The Winter's Tale,* ii, 3, 85.

12
I do spy a kind of hope,
Which craves as desperate an execution
As that is desperate which we would prevent.
Romeo and Juliet. Act iv, sc. 1, l. 68. [Friar Laurence]

13
So shall you quietly enjoy your hope.
The Taming of the Shrew. Act iii, sc. 2, l. 138. [Tranio]

Rich in hope.—*Sonnets,* xxix.

14
O, out of that 'no hope'
What great hope have you! no hope that way is
Another way so high a hope that even
Ambition cannot pierce a wink beyond,
But doubt discovery there.
The Tempest. Act ii, sc. 1, l. 239. [Antonio]

Sit down and rest.
Even here will I put off my hope and keep it
No longer for my flatterer.
The Tempest. Act iii, sc. 3, l. 6. [Alonso]

15
When I do tell thee, there my hopes lie drown'd,
Reply not in how many fathoms deep
They lie indrench'd.
Troilus and Cressida. Act i, sc. 1, l. 49. [Troilus] The only use of "indrench'd."

Our doubtful hope, our convoy and our bark.
Troilus and Cressida. Act i, sc. 1, l. 107. [Troilus]

The ample proposition that hope makes
In all designs begun on earth below
Fails in the promised largeness.

Troilus and Cressida. Act i, sc. 3, l. 3. [Agamemnon] The only use of "proposition" and "largeness."

1
Desire him not to flatter with his lord,
Nor hold him up with hopes.

Twelfth Night. Act i, sc. 5, l. 322. [Olivia]

Nothing that can be can come between me and the full prospect of my hopes.

Twelfth Night. Act iii, sc. 4, l. 90. [Malvolio]

2
Hope is a lover's staff; walk hence with that
And manage it against despairing thoughts.

The Two Gentlemen of Verona. Act iii, sc. 1, l. 246. [Proteus]

3
The dire imagination she did follow
This sound of hope doth labour to expel.

Venus and Adonis, l. 975.

Despair and hope make thee ridiculous:
The one doth flatter thee in thoughts unlikely,
In likely thoughts the other kills thee quickly.

Venus and Adonis, l. 988.

4
No hope to help you,
But as you shake off one to take another.

Winter's Tale. Act iv, sc. 4, l. 578. [Camillo]

II—Hope and Fear

5
As those that fear they hope, and know they fear.

As You Like It. Act v, sc. 4, l. 4. [Orlando]

6
Sir Michael: Doubt not, my lord, they shall be well opposed.
Archbishop: I hope no less, yet needful 'tis to fear.

I Henry IV. Act iv, sc. 4, l. 33.

Turn'd . . . My fear to hope.—*III Henry VI,* iv, 6, 4.

7
Applying fears to hopes and hopes to fears.

Sonnets. No. cxix.

III—Hopelessness

8
Hopeless to find, yet loathe to leave unsought.

The Comedy of Errors. Act i, sc. 1, l. 136. [Ægeon]

Hopeless and helpless does Ægeon wend,
But to procrastinate his lifeless end.

The Comedy of Errors. Act i, sc. 1, l. 158. [Ægeon] The only use of "procrastinate."

Friendless, hopeless.—*Henry VIII,* iii, 1, 80.
All hopeless of their lives.—*III Henry VI,* i, 4, 42.
Aye hopeless.—*Cymbeline,* iv, 4, 27.

9
She there remains a hopeless castaway.

The Rape of Lucrece, l. 744.

Hopeless merchant.—*Rape of Lucrece,* l. 1660

10
The hopeless word of 'never to return.'

Richard II, i, 3, 152. See SENTENCE, 1335:15.

Hopeless restitution.—*Coriolanus,* iii, 1, 16.
The only uses of "hopeless." "Hopelessness" does not occur.

HORN

See also Cuckold

11
'Tis Aufidius,
Who, hearing of our Marcius' banishment,
Thrusts forth his horns again into the world;
Which were inshell'd when Marcius stood for Rome,
And durst not once peep out.

Coriolanus. Act iv, sc. 6, l. 45. [Menenius] The only use of "inshell'd."

The horns o' the moon.

Coriolanus, i, 1, 217; *Antony and Cleopatra,* iv, 12, 45.

12
Boyet: My lady goes to kill horns; but, if thou marry,
Hang me by the neck, if horns that year miscarry.
Finely put on!
Rosaline: Well, then, I am the shooter.
Boyet: And who is your deer?
Rosaline: If we choose by the horns, yourself come not near.
Finely put on, indeed!

Love's Labour's Lost. Act iv, sc. 1, l. 116. The only use of "shooter."

13
Go, bid the huntsmen wake them with their horns.

A Midsummer-Night's Dream. Act iv, sc. 1, l. 142. [Theseus]

Merry horn.—*Venus and Adonis,* l. 1025.

14
It is said, 'God sends a curst cow short horns;' but to a cow too curst he sends none.

Much Ado about Nothing. Act ii, sc. 1, l. 25. [Beatrice] Quoting a proverb which made its first appearance in English literature in Barclay's *Ship of Fools* (i, 182) in 1509.

15
Well, a horn for my money, when all 's done.

Much Ado about Nothing. Act ii, sc. 3, l. 62. [Benedick]

Horn-beasts.—*As You Like It,* iii, 3, 51.
Horn-book.—*Love's Labour 's Lost,* v, 1, 49.
Horn-maker.—*As You Like It,* iv, 1, 63.
Hornpipe.—*The Winter's Tale,* iv, 3, 47.
Horn-ring.—*The Winter's Tale,* iv, 4, 611.

HORROR

16
Cymbeline: How ended she?
Cornelius: With horror, madly dying.

Cymbeline. Act v, sc. 5, l. 30.

Dying horror!—*Measure for Measure,* ii, 3, 42.
Bragging horror.—*King John,* v, 1, 50.
Present horror.—*Macbeth,* ii, 1, 59.
The . . . horror of it.—*King Lear,* i, 2, 192.
Horror and perturbation.—*Much Ado about Nothing,* ii, 1, 268.
Disgrace and horror.—*Antony and Cleopatra,* iv, 14, 66.
Disorder, horror, fear.—*Richard II,* iv, 1, 142.
Frights, changes, horrors.—*Troilus and Cressida,* i, 3, 98.

17
O, horrible! O, horrible! most horrible!

Hamlet. Act i, sc. 5, l. 80. [Ghost]

All horrible.—*The Tempest,* v, 1, 234.
So horrible.—*The Winter's Tale,* ii, 3, 152.
'Tis too horrible.—*Measure for Measure,* iii, 1, 128.
Comfortless and horrible.—*King John,* v, 6, 20.
Harsh and horrible.—*II Henry VI,* iii, 2, 312.
Horrible and grim.—*Othello,* v, 2, 203.

1
O horror, horror, horror! Tongue nor heart
Cannot conceive nor name thee!
Macbeth. Act ii, sc. 3, l. 69. [Macduff]

2
As from your graves rise up, and walk like sprites,
To countenance this horror!
Macbeth. Act ii, sc. 3, l. 84. [Macduff]
I have supp'd full with horrors.
Macbeth. Act v, sc. 5, l. 13. [Macbeth]

3
On horror's head horrors accumulate.
Othello. Act iii, sc. 3, l. 370. [Othello]

4 Here, at dead time of night,
A thousand fiends, a thousand hissing snakes,
Ten thousand swelling toads, as many urchins,
Would make such fearful and confused cries
As any mortal body hearing it
Should straight fall mad, or else die suddenly.
Titus Andronicus. Act ii, sc. 3, l. 99. [Tamora] "Urchins" (goblins) is repeated in *The Merry Wives of Windsor,* iv, 4, 49, and in *The Tempest,* i, 2, 326.
With this dear sight
Struck pale and bloodless; . . .
Even like a stony image, cold and numb.
Titus Andronicus. Act iii, sc. 1, l. 257. [Marcus]

HORSE

See also Jade, Steed

5
Or does he walk? or is he on his horse?
O happy horse, to bear the weight of Antony!
Do bravely, horse!
Antony and Cleopatra. Act i, sc. 5, l. 20. [Cleopatra]

6
If we should serve with horse and mares together,
The horse were merely lost; the mares would bear
A soldier and his horse.
Antony and Cleopatra. Act iii, sc. 7, l. 8. [Enobarbus]
How now! whose mare's dead?
II Henry IV. Act ii, sc. 1, l. 46. [Falstaff]
Hostess: I will ride thee o' nights like the mare.
Falstaff: I think I am as like to ride the mare, if I have any vantage of ground to get up.
II Henry IV. Act ii, sc. 1, l. 84.
The man shall have his mare again, and all shall be well.
A Midsummer-Night's Dream. Act iii, sc. 2, l. 463. [Puck]
Tired mare.—*Henry V,* ii, 1, 26. See under PATIENCE. The only uses of "mare" and "mares."

7
His horses are bred better; for besides that they are fair with their feeding, they are taught their manage, and to that end riders dearly hired.
As You Like It. Act i, sc. 1, l. 12. [Orlando]

8
Of no better report than a horse-drench.
Coriolanus. Act ii, sc. 1, l. 129. [Menenius]
Horse-hairs.—*Cymbeline,* ii, 3, 33.
Horse-leeches.—*Henry V,* ii, 3, 57.
Horse-piss.—*The Tempest,* iv, 1, 199.
Horse-shoe.—*The Merry Wives of Windsor,* iii, 5, 123.
Horse-stealer.—*As You Like It,* iii, 4, 25.
Horse-tail.—*Taming of the Shrew,* iv, 1, 96.
Horse-way.—*King Lear,* iv, 1, 58. None of these phrases is used more than once.

9
O, for a horse with wings!
Cymbeline. Act iii, sc. 2, l. 50. [Imogen]
I have heard of riding wagers,
Where horses have been nimbler than the sands
That run i' the clock's behalf.
Cymbeline. Act iii, sc. 2, l. 73. [Imogen] The only use of "nimbler."

10
Lend me thy lantern, to see my gelding in the stable.
I Henry IV. Act ii, sc. 1, l. 39. [Gadshill]
Bid the ostler bring my gelding out of the stable.
I Henry IV. Act ii, sc. 1, l. 105. [Gadshill] "Ostler" is used five times in *I Henry IV,* and once in *Coriolanus,* iii, 3, 32.
My ambling gelding.—*The Merry Wives of Windsor,* ii, 2, 319. The only uses of "gelding" except as a verb in *I Henry IV,* iii, 1, 110. "Stallion" does not occur in the plays.

11
Hotspur: Hath Butler brought those horses from the sheriff?
Servant: One horse, my lord, he brought even now.
Hotspur: What horse? a roan, a crop-ear, is it not?
Servant: It is, my lord.
Hotspur: That roan shall be my throne,
When I will back him straight; O esperance! . . .
Lady Percy: What is it carries you away?
Hotspur: Why, my horse, my love, my horse.
I Henry IV. Act ii, sc. 3, l. 70. The only use of "crop-ear."
Give my roan horse a drench.
I Henry IV, ii, 4, 120. See under BOASTING.
Roan Barbary,
That horse that thou so often hast bestrid,
That horse that I so carefully have dress'd!
Richard II. Act v, sc. 5, l. 78. [Groom] The only uses of "roan."

12 Come, let me taste my horse,
Who is to bear me like a thunderbolt.
I Henry IV. Act iv, sc. 1, l. 119. [Hotspur]

13
Being better horsed, Out-rode me.
II Henry IV. Act i, sc. 1, l. 35. [Travers] "Horsed" is used also in *II Henry IV,* i, 2, 60; *Macbeth,* i, 7, 22; *Coriolanus,* ii, 1, 227. The only use of "out-rode."

He gave his able horse the head.
II Henry IV. Act i, sc. 1, l. 43. [Travers]

1 Think, when we talk of horses, that you see them
Printing their proud hoofs i' the receiving earth.
Henry V. Act i, Prologue, l. 26. [Chorus]

They sell the pasture now to buy the horse.
Henry V. Act ii, Prologue, l. 5. [Chorus]

2 Orleans: Let my horse have his due.
Constable: It is the best horse of Europe.
Henry V. Act iii, sc. 7, l. 3.

Dauphin: I will not change my horse with any that treads but on four pasterns. Ça, ha! he bounds from the earth, as if his entrails were hairs; le cheval volant, the Pegasus, chez les narines de feu! When I bestride him, I soar, I am a hawk: he trots the air; the earth sings when he touches it; the basest horn of his hoof is more musical than the pipe of Hermes.
Duke of Orleans: He's of the colour of the nutmeg.
Dauphin: And of the heat of the ginger. It is a beast for Perseus: he is pure air and fire; . . . It is the prince of palfreys; his neigh is like the bidding of a monarch and his countenance enforces homage. . . . It is a theme as fluent as the sea: turn the sands into eloquent tongues, and my horse is argument for them all.
Henry V. Act iii, sc. 7, l. 11. The only use of "pasterns" and "fluent," and the only mention of Hermes. The French phrases are, of course, unique.

He doth nothing but talk of his horse; and he makes it a great appropriation to his own good parts, that he can shoe him himself. I am much afeard my lady his mother played false with a smith.
The Merchant of Venice. Act i, sc. 2, l. 44. [Portia] The only use of "appropriation."

3 Linger not, my lord; away, take horse.
II Henry VI. Act iv, sc. 4, l. 54. [Buckingham] "Take horse" is repeated in *Richard III,* iii, 2, 16, and in *I Henry IV,* i, 1, 60.

They summon'd up their meiny, straight took horse.
King Lear. Act ii, sc. 4, l. 35. [Kent] The only use of "meiny" (retainers), and "took horse."

Mount thou my horse, and hide thy spurs in him.
Julius Cæsar. Act v, sc. 3, l. 15. [Cassius]

Give me my boots, I say; saddle my horse.
Richard II. Act v, sc. 2, l. 77. [York]

To horse!—*Henry V,* iv, 2, 15, and frequently in later plays.

4 Your horse stands ready at the park-corner.
III Henry VI. Act iv, sc. 5, l. 19. [Gloucester] The only use of "park-corner."

5 'Twas her brother that, in pure kindness to his horse, buttered his hay.
King Lear. Act ii, sc. 4, l. 126. [Fool] "Buttered" is repeated in *The Merry Wives of Windsor,* iii, 5, 8. Hay is mentioned five times.

6 Ross: Duncan's horses—a thing most strange and certain—
Beauteous and swift, the minions of their race,
Turn'd wild in nature, broke their stalls, flung out,
Contending 'gainst obedience, as they would make
War with mankind.
Old Man: 'Tis said they eat each other.
Ross: They did so, to the amazement of mine eyes
That look'd upon 't.
Macbeth. Act ii, sc. 4, l. 14.

I wish your horses swift and sure of foot;
And so I do commend you to their backs.
Macbeth. Act iii, sc. 1, l. 38. [Macbeth]

I did hear
The galloping of horse: who was 't came by?
Macbeth. Act iv, sc. 1, l. 140. [Macbeth] The only use of "galloping."

7 Where is the horse that doth untread again
His tedious measures with the unbated fire
That he did pace them first?
Merchant of Venice. Act ii, sc. 6, l. 10. [Gratiano] "Untread" is repeated in *King John,* v, 4, 52: "Untread the steps of damned flight."

8 When I a fat and bean-fed horse beguile,
Neighing in likeness of a filly foal.
A Midsummer-Night's Dream. Act ii, sc. 1, l. 45. [Puck] The only use of "bean-fed," "filly," and "foal" as a noun.

If I would sell my horse, and buy twenty more
Better than he, why, give my horse to Timon,
Ask nothing, give it him, it foals me, straight,
And able horses.
Timon of Athens. Act ii, sc. 1, l. 7. [Senator] The only use of "foals" as a verb.

As true as truest horse that yet would never tire.
A Midsummer-Night's Dream. Act iii, sc. 1, l. 98. [Fluellen]

9 How fondly dost thou spur a forward horse!
Richard II. Act iv, sc. 1, l. 72. [Fitzwater]

Forgiveness, horse! why do I rail on thee,
Since thou, created to be awed by man,
Wast born to bear? I was not made a horse.
Richard II. Act v, sc. 5, l. 90. [King Richard]

10 A horse! a horse! my kingdom for a horse!
Richard III. Act v, sc. 4, l. 7. [King Richard]

11 The beast that bears me, tired with my woe,
Plods dully on, to bear that weight in me,
As if by some instinct the wretch did know
His rider loved not speed, being made from thee:
The bloody spur cannot provoke him on
That sometimes anger thrusts into his hide;
Which heavily he answers with a groan,
More sharp to me than spurring to his side;

For that same groan doth put this in my mind:
My grief lies onward and my joy behind.
Sonnets. No. l.

1
His horse hipped with an old mothy saddle and stirrups of no kindred; besides, possessed with the glanders and like to mose in the chine; troubled with the lampass, infected with the fashions, full of windgalls, sped with spavins, rayed with the yellows, past cure of the fives, stark spoiled with the staggers, begnawn with the bots, swayed in the back and shoulder-shotten; near-legged before and with a half-checked bit and a head-stall of sheep's leather which, being restrained to keep him from stumbling, hath been often burst and now repaired with knots; one girth six times pieced and a woman's crupper of velure, which hath two letters for her name fairly set down in studs, and here and there pieced with pack-thread.
The Taming of the Shrew. Act iii, sc. 2, l. 49. [Biondello] The only use of "hipped," "mothy," "glanders," "mose" (exact meaning unknown), "lampass" (a swelling of the mouth), "windgalls," "yellows," "begnawn," "shoulder-shotten," "near-legged," "half-cheeked," "head-stall," "girth," "velure," and "studs"—an extraordinary procession of unique words. "Bots" appears in *I Henry IV,* ii, 1, 11; "crupper" again in *The Taming of the Shrew,* iv, 1, 84, and in *The Comedy of Errors,* i, 2, 56; "packthread" in *Romeo and Juliet,* v, 1, 47; and "spavin" in *Henry VIII,* i, 3, 12.

2
Or wilt thou ride? thy horses shall be trapp'd,
Their harness studded all with gold and pearl.
The Taming of the Shrew. Induction, sc. 2, l. 43. [Lord] The only use of "studded."

Four milk-white horses, trapp'd in silver.
Timon of Athens, i, 2, 189. The only uses of "trapp'd."

3
Nay, by Saint Jamy,
I hold you a penny,
A horse and a man
Is more than one,
And yet not many.
The Taming of the Shrew. Act iii, sc. 2, l. 83. [Biondello]

4
Her horse fell, and she under her horse.
The Taming of the Shrew. Act iv, sc. 1, l. 76. [Grumio]

Or, like a gallant horse fall'n in first rank,
Lie there for pavement to the abject rear,
O'er-run and trampled on.
Troilus and Cressida. Act iii, sc. 3, l. 161. [Ulysses] "Pavement" is repeated in *Cymbeline,* v, 4, 120.

5
And I have horse will follow where the game
Makes way, and run like swallows o'er the plain.
Titus Andronicus. Act ii, sc. 2, l. 23. [Titus]

Two proper palfreys, black as jet.
Titus Andronicus. Act v, sc. 2, l. 50. [Titus] "Palfrey" is repeated in *Henry V,* iii, 7, 29 (see above); *Henry V,* iii, 7, 35; and *II Henry VI,* iv, 2, 75.

6
Achilles: Come, thou shalt bear a letter to him straight.
Thersites: Let me bear another to his horse; for that 's the more capable creature.
Troilus and Cressida. Act iii, sc. 3, l. 307.

7
'Imprimis: She can fetch and carry.' Why, a horse can do no more: nay, a horse cannot fetch, but only carry; therefore is she better than a jade.
The Two Gentlemen of Verona. Act iii, sc. 1, l. 274. [Launce] "Imprimis" is used again in this scene, l. 302; once in *II Henry VI,* i, 1, 43; and twice in *The Taming of the Shrew,* iv, 1, 68, and iv, 3, 135.

8
The bearing earth with his hard hoof he wounds,
Whose hollow womb resounds like heaven's thunder.
Venus and Adonis, l. 267.

Sometime he trots, as if he told the steps,
With gentle majesty and modest pride;
Anon he rears upright, curvets and leaps,
As who should say 'Lo, thus my strength is tried,
And this I do to captivate the eye
Of the fair breeder that is standing by.'
Venus and Adonis, l. 277.

So did this horse excel a common one
In shape, in courage, colour, pace and bone.
Venus and Adonis, l. 293.

Round-hoof'd, short-jointed, fetlocks shag and long,
Broad breast, full eye, small head and nostril wide,
High crest, short ears, straight legs and passing strong,
Thin mane, thick tail, broad buttock, tender hide:
Look, what a horse should have he did not lack,
Save a proud rider on so proud a back.
Venus and Adonis, l. 295. The only use of "round-hoof'd," "short-jointed," and "shag." "Fetlocks" is repeated in *Henry V,* iv, 7, 82, and in *III Henry VI,* ii, 3, 21.

9
The colt that 's back'd and burden'd being young
Loseth his pride and never waxeth strong.
Venus and Adonis, l. 419.

Rough colt.—*A Midsummer-Night's Dream,* v, 1, 120.

Unback'd colts.—*The Tempest,* iv, 1, 176.

Young hot colts.—*Richard II,* ii, 1, 70.

Youthful and unhandled colts.—*The Merchant of Venice,* v, 1, 72.

HORSEMANSHIP

1
Never bestrid a horse, save one that had
A rider like myself, who ne'er wore rowel
Nor iron on his heel!
Cymbeline. Act iv, sc. 4, l. 38. [Arviragus] The only use of "rowel." "Rowel-head" occurs in *II Henry IV,* i, 1, 46.

2
I 've seen myself, and served against, the French,
And they can well on horseback: but this gallant
Had witchcraft in 't; he grew unto his seat;
And to such wondrous doing brought his horse,
As had he been incorpsed and demi-natured
With the brave beast.
Hamlet. Act iv, sc. 7, l. 84. [King] The only use of "incorpsed" and "demi-natured."

When I am o' horseback.—*I Henry IV,* ii, 3, 104. "Horseback" is used also in *I Henry IV,* ii, 4, 378; 387; *King John,* ii, 1, 289; *Hamlet,* iv, 7, 85; *Henry VIII,* i, 1, 8.

Horse-back-breaker.—*I Henry IV,* ii, 4, 268. The only use of the phrase.

3
I saw young Harry, with his beaver on,
His cuisses on his thighs, gallantly arm'd,
Rise from the ground like feather'd Mercury,
And vaulted with such ease into his seat,
As if an angel dropp'd down from the clouds,
To turn and wind a fiery Pegasus
And witch the world with noble horsemanship.
I Henry IV. Act iv, sc. 1, l. 104. [Vernon] The only use of "cuisses."

Constable: You have good judgement in horsemanship.
Dauphin: Be warned by me, then: they that ride so and ride not warily, fall into foul bogs.
Henry V. Act iii, sc. 7, l. 58. "Warily" is repeated in *Love's Labour 's Lost,* v, 2, 93.

4
The horsemen sat like fixed candlesticks,
With torch-staves in their hand.
Henry V. Act iv, sc. 2, l. 45. [Grandpré] The only use of "candlesticks" and "torch-staves."

I could . . . sit like a jack-an-apes, never off.
Henry V. Act v, sc. 2, l. 147. [King Henry] "Jack-an-apes" occurs seven times. See under JACK.

5
Those that tame wild horses
Pace 'em not in their hands to make 'em gentle,
But stop their mouths with stubborn bits, and spur 'em
Till they obey the manage.
Henry VIII. Act v, sc. 3, l. 21. [Gardiner]

6
It is a creature that I teach to fight,
To wind, to stop, to run directly on,
His corporal motion govern'd by my spirit.
Julius Cæsar. Act iv, sc. 1, l. 31. [Antony]

7
Well could he ride, and often men would say
"That horse his mettle from his rider takes."
A Lover's Complaint, l. 106.

He rides well;
And his great love, sharp as his spur, hath holp him
To his home before us.
Macbeth. Act i, sc. 6, l. 22. [Duncan]

HOSPITALITY, see Welcome

HOST AND HOSTESS

I—Host

8
I will bring you Where you shall host.
All's Well that Ends Well. Act iii, sc. 5, l. 97. [Widow]

Your goods that lay at host, sir, in the Centaur.
The Comedy of Errors. Act v, sc. 1, l. 410. [Dromio of Syracuse]

9
Base tike, call'st thou me host?
Now, by this hand, I swear, I scorn the term.
Henry V. Act ii, sc. 1, l. 31. [Pistol] "Tike" is repeated in *King Lear,* iii, 6, 73.

10
Conduct me to mine host: we love him highly.
Macbeth. Act i, sc. 6, l. 29. [Duncan]

Mine host.—*The Two Gentlemen of Verona,* iv, 2, 28; once in *Comedy of Errors,* ii, 2, 4, and eight times in *Merry Wives of Windsor.*

11
His host,
Who should against his murderer shut the door,
Not bear the knife myself.
Macbeth. Act i, sc. 7, l. 14. [Macbeth]

Ourself will mingle with society,
And play the humble host.
Macbeth. Act iii, sc. 4, l. 4. [Macbeth]

12
Trust me, a mad host.
The Merry Wives of Windsor. Act iii, sc. 1, l. 115. [Shallow]

Fashionable host.—*Troilus and Cressida,* iii, 3, 165.

Good host.—*The Merry Wives of Windsor,* iv, 6, 47; *King Lear,* v, 2, 2.

Kind host.—*King John,* v, 1, 32.

Merry host.—*The Merry Wives of Windsor,* ii, 1, 215.

Niggardly host.—*The Comedy of Errors,* iii, 1, 27.

Old host.—*I Henry IV,* ii, 4, 518.

Poor host.—*Coriolanus,* i, 9, 87.

13
Mine host of the Garter.
The Merry Wives of Windsor, i, 1, 143. Repeated seven times in later acts.

My Host at Saint Alban's.—*I Henry IV,* iv, 2, 50.

14
It is thine host, thine Ephesian, calls.
The Merry Wives of Windsor. Act iv, sc. 5, l. 19. [Host] The only use of "Ephesian."

What company? Ephesians, my lord.
II Henry IV, ii, 2, 164. The only use of "Ephesians" (boon companions).

II—Hostess

1 I think I know your hostess
As ample as myself.
All's Well that Ends Well. Act iii, sc. 5, l. 45. [Widow]

2
Falstaff: Is not my hostess of the tavern a most sweet wench?
Prince of Wales: As the honey of Hybla, my old lad of the castle.
I Henry IV. Act i, sc. 2, l. 45. "Hybla" is repeated in *Julius Cæsar,* v, 1, 34: "Hybla bees."
Prince of Wales: Why, what a pox have I to do with my hostess of the tavern?
Falstaff: Well, thou hast called her to a reckoning many a time and oft.
I Henry IV. Act i, sc. 2, l. 53. "Many a time and oft" is repeated in *The Merchant of Venice,* i, 3, 107, and in *Julius Cæsar,* i, 1, 42.
My lady the hostess.—*I Henry IV,* ii, 4, 315.

3
Falstaff: Here, Pistol, I charge you with a cup of sack: do you discharge upon mine hostess.
Pistol: I will discharge upon her, Sir John, with two bullets.
Falstaff: She is pistol-proof, sir; you shall hardly offend her.
II Henry IV. Act ii, sc. 4, l. 120. "Mine hostess" is repeated in *The Comedy of Errors,* iii, 1, 119, and in *King John,* ii, 1, 289. The only use of "pistol-proof."
Is thine hostess here of the wicked?
II Henry IV, ii, 4, 355. See under WICKEDNESS.

4
Our hostess keeps her state, but in best time
We will require her welcome.
Macbeth. Act iii, sc. 4, l. 5. [Macbeth]

5
A woeful hostess brooks not merry guests.
The Rape of Lucrece, l. 1125.
Fair and noble hostess.—*Macbeth,* i, 6, 24.
Honour'd hostess.—*Macbeth,* i, 6, 10.
Kind hostess.—*The Winter's Tale,* i, 2, 60.
Most kind hostess.—*Macbeth,* ii, 1, 16.

6
It is my father's will I should take on me
The hostess-ship o' the day.
The Winter's Tale. Act iv, sc. 4, l. 72. [Perdita] The only use of "hostess-ship."

HOUND

See also Dog

7
A hound that runs counter and yet draws dry-foot well.
The Comedy of Errors. Act iv, sc. 2, l. 39. [Dromio of Syracuse] The only use of "dry-foot" (to track game by the scent of the foot).
Theseus: My love shall hear the music of my hounds.
Uncouple in the western valley; let them go: . . .
We will, fair queen, up to the mountain's top
And mark the musical confusion
Of hounds and echo in conjunction.
Hippolyta: I was with Hercules and Cadmus once
When in a wood of Crete they bay'd the bear
With hounds of Sparta: never did I hear
Such gallant chiding; for, besides the groves,
The skies, the fountains, every region near
Seem'd all one mutual cry: I never heard
So musical a discord, such sweet thunder.
Theseus: My hounds are bred out of the Spartan kind,
So flew'd, so sanded, and their heads are hung
With ears that sweep away the morning dew;
Crook-knee'd and dew-lapp'd like Thessalian bulls;
Slow in pursuit, but match'd in mouth like bells,
Each under each. A cry more tuneable
Was never holla'd to, nor cheer'd with horn,
In Crete, in Sparta, nor in Thessaly.
A Midsummer-Night's Dream. Act iv, sc. 1, l. 110. "Uncouple" is repeated in *Titus Andronicus,* ii, 2, 3. The only mention of Cadmus, and the only use of "flew'd" (having large chops), "sanded" (sandy coloured), "crook-knee'd," and "Thessalian." "Thessaly" is repeated in *Antony and Cleopatra,* iv, 13, 2, and "dew-lapp'd" in *The Tempest,* iii, 3, 45.

8
Huntsman, I charge thee, tender well my hounds.
The Taming of the Shrew. Induction, l. 16. [Lord]
Thy hounds shall make the welkin answer them
And fetch shrill echoes from the hollow earth.
The Taming of the Shrew. Induction, sc. 2, l. 47. [Lord]

9 The hounds
Should drive upon thy new-transformed limbs.
Titus Andronicus. Act ii, sc. 3, l. 64. [Lavinia] The only use of "new-transformed."
Bloody hounds.—*I Henry VI,* iv, 2, 51.
Cruel hounds.—*Twelfth Night,* i, 1, 22.
Cunning hounds.—*Venus and Adonis,* l. 678.
False hound.—*Coriolanus,* v, 6, 113.
Full-fed hound.—*The Rape of Lucrece,* l. 694. The only use of "full-fed."
Hound of Crete.—*Henry V,* ii, 1, 77.

10
The hot scent-snuffing hounds are driven to doubt,
Ceasing their clamorous cry till they have singled
With much ado the cold fault cleanly out;
Then do they spend their mouths: Echo replies,
As if another chase were in the skies.
Venus and Adonis, l. 692. The only use of "scent-snuffing."
She hearkens for his hounds and for his horn:
Anon she hears them chant it lustily,
And all in haste she coasteth to the cry.
Venus and Adonis, l. 868. The only use of "coasteth."
By this, she hears the hounds are at a bay.
Venus and Adonis, l. 877.

Even so the timorous yelping of the hounds
Appals her senses and her spirit confounds.
Venus and Adonis, l. 881.
Here kennell'd in a brake she finds a hound.
Venus and Adonis, l. 913. The only use of "kennell'd."

II—Greyhound

1
Like greyhounds in the slips.
Henry V, iii, 1, 31. See under IMPATIENCE.
Like a brace of greyhounds.
III Henry VI, ii, 5, 129. See under DANGER.
Two brace of greyhounds.—*Timon of Athens,* i, 2, 195.
2
Slender: How does your fallow greyhound, sir? I heard say he was outrun on Cotsall. . . .
Page: A cur, sir.
Shallow: Sir, he 's a good dog, and a fair dog; can there be more said? he is good and fair.
Merry Wives of Windsor. Act i, sc. 1, l. 91.
Fawning greyhound.—*I Henry IV,* i, 3, 252; *Coriolanus,* i, 6, 38.
Puppy greyhound.—*II Henry IV,* ii, 4, 107.
3
Say thou wilt course; thy greyhounds are as swift
As breathed stags, ay, fleeter than the roe.
The Taming of the Shrew. Induction, sc. 2, l. 49. [Servant] The only use of "fleeter."
O, sir, Lucentio slipp'd me like his greyhound,
Which runs himself and catches for his master.
The Taming of the Shrew. Act v, sc. 2, l. 52. [Tranio]

HOUR

See also Noon, Time

4 Poison'd hours had bound me up
From mine own knowledge.
Antony and Cleopatra. Act ii, sc. 2, l. 90. [Antony]
5 What hotter hours,
Unregister'd in vulgar fame, you have
Luxuriously pick'd out.
Antony and Cleopatra. Act iii, sc. 13, l. 118. [Antony] The only use of "unregister'd" and "luxuriously."
Hours of lust.—*Othello,* iii, 3, 338.
Profane hours.—*Richard II,* v, 1, 25.
Sinful hours.—*Richard II,* iii, 1, 11.
Soft hours.—*Antony and Cleopatra,* i, 1, 44.
Surfeiting and wanton hours.—*II Henry IV,* iv, 1, 55.
Sweet hours.—*Sonnets.* No. xxxvi.
6
Mine hours Were nice and lucky.
Antony and Cleopatra. Act iii, sc. 13, l. 179. [Antony]
Our hour Is fully out.—*Antony and Cleopatra,* iv, 9, 32.
7
Even now, even here, not half an hour since.
The Comedy of Errors. Act ii, sc. 2, l. 14. [Antipholus of Syracuse]
Not half an hour before.—*Twelfth Night,* v, 1, 95.
Half an hour since.—*Comedy of Errors,* iv, 1, 65; *King John,* v, 7, 83; *Coriolanus,* i, 6, 21.
Half an hour together.—*Coriolanus,* i, 3, 64.
Some half an hour or so.—*Henry VIII,* iv, 1, 66.
Ere half an hour pass.—*Titus Andronicus,* iii, 1, 192. "Half an hour" is repeated in *II Henry IV,* iv, 5, 110; *Love's Labour 's Lost,* v, 2, 90; *King Lear,* iii, 6, 100; *Othello,* v, 2, 82.
This half hour.—*Twelfth Night,* ii, 5, 21.
Quarter of an hour.—*I Henry IV,* ii, 4, 20; *The Merry Wives of Windsor,* iv, 4, 5; *Macbeth,* v, 1, 34.
8
The hour steals on.
The Comedy of Errors. Act iv, sc. 1, l. 52. [Second Merchant]
The silent hours steal on.
Richard III. Act v, sc. 3, l. 85. [Derby]
Our nuptial hour Draws on apace.
A Midsummer-Night's Dream. Act i, sc. 1, l. 1. [Theseus]
The hour draws on.—*Merry Wives of Windsor,* v, 3, 25; *Measure for Measure,* iv, 3, 83.
9
Hath he not reason to turn back an hour in a day?
The Comedy of Errors. Act iv, sc. 2, l. 62. [Dromio of Syracuse]
Adriana: Tell me, was he arrested on a band?
Dromio of Syracuse: Not on a band, but on a stronger thing;
A chain, a chain! Do you hear it ring?
Adriana: What, the chain?
Dromio of Syracuse: No, no, the bell: 'tis time that I were gone:
It was two ere I left him, and now the clock strikes one.
Adriana: The hours come back! that did I never hear.
Dromio of Syracuse: O, yes; if any hour meet a sergeant, a' turns back for very fear.
The Comedy of Errors. Act iv, sc. 2, l. 49.
An hour ago.—*I Henry IV,* ii, 3, 69.
An hour agone.—*Twelfth Night,* v, 1, 204.
An hour since.—*The Comedy of Errors,* iv, 3, 38; *The Winter's Tale,* ii, 3, 195.
One hour hence.—*Richard III,* iv, 1, 29.
Some hour hence.—*The Merchant of Venice,* ii, 4, 27.
In an hour.—*Cymbeline,* ii, 5, 14.
An hour together.—*Much Ado about Nothing,* v, 1, 171.
Within this hour.—*Richard III,* iii, 5, 105, and frequently in later plays, four times in *The Winter's Tale* alone.
An hour or more.—*Othello,* iv, 1, 4.
An hour and a quarter.—*Romeo and Juliet,* iii, 1, 36.
In two short hours.—*Henry VIII,* Prol., 13.
Some two hours hence.—*III Henry VI,* v, 1, 10.
Within these two hours.—*I Henry IV,* iii, 1, 266.
Two hours together.—*King Lear,* i, 2, 170.
Within these three hours.—*Coriolanus,* i, 8, 7.
Above five hours.—*Pericles,* iii, 2, 95.
10
See here these movers that do prize their hours

At a crack'd drachma!
Coriolanus. Act i, sc. 5, l. 5. [Marcius] "Drachma" is repeated in *Julius Cæsar*, iii, 2, 247; iv, 3, 73; and "movers" in *Cymbeline,* i, 5, 9. "Mover" occurs in *II Henry VI,* iii, 3, 19: "Eternal Mover of the heavens!"
In a better hour.—*Coriolanus,* iii, 1, 169.
To this hour.—*Coriolanus,* v, 6, 154.
At certain hours.—*Cymbeline,* i, 3, 27.
Once every hour.—*Henry VIII,* iii, 2, 24.
Free hours.—*Cymbeline,* i, 6, 72.

1
Take thy fair hour, Laertes; time be thine.
Hamlet. Act i, sc. 2, l. 62. [King]
Choice hour.—*Henry VIII,* i, 2, 162.
Secure hour.—*Hamlet,* i, 5, 61.

2
Jump at this dead hour.
Hamlet. Act i, sc. 1, l. 65. [Marcellus]
You come most carefully upon your hour.
Hamlet. Act i, sc. 1, l. 6. [Francisco]
Careful hours.—*Comedy of Errors,* v, 1, 298.

3 They did spend a sad and bloody hour;
As by discharge of their artillery,
And shape of likelihood, the news was told.
I Henry IV. Act i, sc. 1, l. 56. [Westmoreland]
The best part of an hour.—*I Henry IV,* i, 3, 100.

4 O, let the hours be short
Till fields and blows and groans applaud our sport!
I Henry IV. Act i, sc. 3, l. 301. [Hotspur]
Brief hours.—*Sonnets,* cxvi.
Short-number'd hours.—*Sonnets,* cxxiv. The only use of "short-number'd."

5
The ragged'st hour that time and spite dare bring.
II Henry IV. Act i, sc. 1, l. 151. [Northumberland] The only use of "ragged'st."
Let this pernicious hour
Stand aye accursed in the calendar!
Macbeth. Act iv, sc. 1, l. 133. [Macbeth]
Blasting hour.—*A Lover's Complaint,* l. 72.
Cursed hours.—*The Merry Wives of Windsor,* v, 5, 242.
Dark hour.—*Macbeth,* iii, 1, 28; 138.
Doubtful hour.—*I Henry IV,* iv, 1, 48.
Heinous hours.—*The Rape of Lucrece,* l. 910.
Ill hours.—*Twelfth Night,* i, 3, 6.
Sad hour.—*The Rape of Lucrece,* l. 1179.
So sad an hour.—*King John,* v, 2, 26.
Serious hours.—*Comedy of Errors,* ii, 2, 29.
Torturing hour.—*Midsummer-Night's Dream,* v, 1, 37.
Worser hours.—*King Lear,* iv, 7, 7.

6
Talbot, farewell; thy hour is not yet come.
I Henry VI. Act i, sc. 5, l. 13. [La Pucelle]
The hour is come To end the one of us.
I Henry IV. Act v, sc. 4, l. 68. [Hotspur]
I know my hour is come.
Julius Cæsar. Act v, sc. 5, l. 20. [Brutus]
My hour is almost come.
Hamlet. Act i, sc. 5, l. 2. [Ghost]
The last hour
Of my long weary life is come upon me.
Henry VIII. Act ii, sc. 1, l. 132. [Buckingham]
The hour 's now come.
The Tempest. Act i, sc. 2, l. 36. [Prospero]
Salarino: His hour is almost past.
Gratiano: And it is marvel he out-dwells his hour.
The Merchant of Venice. Act ii, sc. 6, l. 2. The only use of "out-dwells."

7
Finish the process of this sandy hour.
I Henry VI. Act iv, sc. 2, l. 36. [General]
Hour-glass.—*The Merchant of Venice,* i, 1, 25; *Henry V,* Prologue, l. 31.

8
'Tis like, my lord, you will not keep your hour.
II Henry VI. Act ii, sc. 1, l. 181. [Cardinal]

9
Now therefore let us hence; and lose no hour.
III Henry VI. Act iv, sc. 1, l. 148. [King Edward]
But wherefore grieve I at an hour's poor loss?
II Henry VI. Act iii, sc. 2, l. 381. [Queen]

10
These should be hours for necessities,
Not for delights; times to repair our nature
With comforting repose.
Henry VIII. Act v, sc. 1, l. 2. [Gardiner]

11 There is no hour so fit
As Cæsar's death's hour.
Julius Cæsar. Act iii, sc. 1, l. 153. [Antony]

12 Let go by
The swiftest hours, observed as they flew.
A Lover's Complaint, l. 59.
I have almost slipp'd the hour.
Macbeth. Act ii, sc. 3, l. 52. [Macduff]

13
The hour is fixed; the match is made.
The Merry Wives of Windsor. Act ii, sc. 2, l. 303. [Ford]
The hour draws on Prefix'd by Angelo.
Measure for Measure. Act iv, sc. 3, l. 83. [Duke]
It is great morning, and the hour prefix'd
Of her delivery to this valiant Greek
Comes fast upon.
Troilus and Cressida. Act iv, sc. 3, l. 1. [Paris]
Prefixed hour.—*Romeo and Juliet,* v, 3, 253.

14
Better three hours too soon than a minute too late.
The Merry Wives of Windsor. Act ii, sc. 2, l. 327. [Ford]
'Tis past the hour.—*The Merry Wives of Windsor,* ii, 3, 4.
O this blessed hour!—*The Merry Wives of Windsor,* iii, 3, 48.
Having the hour limited.—*The Merry Wives of Windsor,* iv, 2, 176.

15
A merrier hour was never wasted there.
A Midsummer-Night's Dream. Act ii, sc. 1, l. 57. [Puck]
Merrier hour.—*Comedy of Errors,* i, 2, 69.
Merry hours.—*Love's Labour 's Lost,* iv, 3, 379; *Much Ado about Nothing,* ii, 1, 347.

16
Well, you will temporize with the hours.
Much Ado about Nothing. Act i, sc. 1, l. 276. [Don Pedro] "Temporize" is repeated

in *King John,* v, 2, 125: "Temporize with my entreaties"; and in *Troilus and Cressida,* iv, 4, 6: "Temporize with my affection."

1
Go, then; find me a meet hour.
Much Ado about Nothing. Act ii, sc. 2, l. 33. [Borachio]
Hours unmeet!—*Much Ado about Nothing,* iv, 1, 184.

2
You have stayed me in a happy hour.
Much Ado about Nothing. Act iv, sc. 1, l. 285. [Beatrice]
Now stand you on the top of happy hours.
Sonnets. No. xvi.
Happy hour.—*III Henry VI,* i, 2, 63, and six times in later plays.
O most happy hour!—*A Midsummer-Night's Dream,* iv, 2, 28.
Hours of happiness.—*II Henry IV,* v, 2, 61.

3
Come, Desdemona; I have but an hour
Of love, of worldly matters and direction,
To spend with thee: we must obey the time.
Othello. Act i, sc. 3, l. 299. [Othello]
A pliant hour.—*Othello,* i, 3, 151. The only use of "pliant."

4
Pleasure and action make the hours seem short.
Othello. Act ii, sc. 3, l. 385. [Iago]

5
O, insupportable! O heavy hour!
Methinks it should be now a huge eclipse
Of sun and moon, and that the affrighted globe
Should yawn at alteration.
Othello. Act v, sc. 2, l. 98. [Othello] "Insupportable" is repeated in *All's Well that Ends Well,* ii, 3, 243: "Insupportable vexation"; and in *Julius Cæsar,* iv, 3, 151: "Insupportable loss."

6 At these early hours
Shake off the golden slumber of repose.
Pericles. Act iii, sc. 2, l. 22. [Gentleman]
Freezing hours.—*Cymbeline,* iii, 3, 39.
Unseason'd hours.—*II Henry IV,* iii, 1, 105.
Unusual hour.—*The Merry Wives of Windsor,* v, 1, 463.
Good hour of night.—*Henry VIII,* v, 1, 5.

7
Disturb his hours of rest.
The Rape of Lucrece, l. 974.
Peaceful hour.—*Venus and Adonis,* l. 652.
Quiet hour.—*Richard III,* v, 3, 160; *I Henry IV,* v, 1, 25.
Reposing hours.—*Richard III,* i, 4, 76.
Sleeping hour.—*Troilus and Cressida,* i, 3, 254.

8
Now comes the sick hour that his surfeit made.
Richard II. Act ii, sc. 2, l. 84. [York]

9
Duchess of York: What comfortable hour canst thou name,
That ever graced me in thy company?
King Richard: Faith, none, but Humphrey Hour, that call'd your grace
To breakfast once forth of my company.
Richard III. Act iv, sc. 4, l. 173.

10
After many lengthen'd hours of grief.
Richard III. Act i, sc. 3, l. 208. [Queen Margaret]
Sad hours seem long.
Romeo and Juliet. Act i, sc. 1, l. 167. [Romeo]
Hours with sorrow.—*Romeo and Juliet,* ii, 6, 2.
The world-without-end hour.—*Sonnets,* lvii.
World-without-end bargain.—*Love's Labour 's Lost,* v, 2, 799. The only uses of the phrase.

11 Acquaint the princess
With the sweet silent hours of marriage joys.
Richard III. Act iv, sc. 4, l. 329. [King Richard]
Nuptial hour.—*A Midsummer-Night's Dream,* i, 1, 1.
Happy wedlock hours.—*The Merchant of Venice,* v, 1, 32.

12 Behold this present hour,
Even for revenge mock my destruction!
Richard III. Act v, sc. 1, l. 8. [Buckingham] "Present hour" is repeated four times in later plays.
Stealing hours of time.—*Richard III,* iii, 7, 168.
Sly slow hours.—*Richard II,* i, 3, 150.
Creeping hours.—*As You Like It,* ii, 7, 112.

13
Most miserable hour that e'er time saw
In lasting labour of his pilgrimage!
Romeo and Juliet. Act iv, sc. 5, l. 44. [Lady Capulet]

14 Let Romeo hence in haste,
Else, when he 's found, that hour is his last.
Romeo and Juliet. Act iii, sc. 1, l. 199. [Prince]
Ah, what an unkind hour
Is guilty of this lamentable chance!
Romeo and Juliet. Act v, sc. 3, l. 145. [Friar Laurence]

15
Those hours, that with gentle work did frame
The lovely gaze where every eye doth dwell,
Will play the tyrants to the very same
And that unfair which fairly doth excel.
Sonnets. No. v.
But out, alack! he was but one hour mine.
Sonnets. No. xxxiii.

16
To find out . . . idle hours in me.
Sonnets. No. lxi.
Idle hours.—*Richard II,* iii, 4, 66.

17
Time's fickle glass, his sickle, hour.
Sonnets. No. cxxvi.
Hours of dross.—*Sonnets,* cxlvi.
Those holy antique hours.—*Sonnets,* lxviii.

18
What, shall I be appointed hours; as though, belike,
I knew not what to take, and what to leave, ha?
The Taming of the Shrew. Act i, sc. 1, l. 103. [Katharina]
I 'll not be tied to hours nor 'pointed times.
The Taming of the Shrew. Act iii, sc. 1, l. 19. [Bianca]
At all hours.—*Taming of the Shrew,* iv, 4, 89.

1
Lord Timon's happy hours are done and past
Timon of Athens. Act iii, sc. 2, l. 6. [Stranger]
Prolong his hour.—*Timon of Athens,* iii, 1, 66.
Some other hour.—*Timon of Athens,* iii, 4, 69.

2
Make use of thy salt hours.
Timon of Athens, iv, 3, 85. See under WHORE.

3
Brought hither in a most unlucky hour.
Titus Andronicus. Act ii, sc. 3, l. 251. [Martius]
'Tis not an hour since I left him there.
Titus Andronicus. Act ii, sc. 3, l. 256. [Saturninus]
Oft have you heard me wish for such an hour,
And now I find it.
Titus Andronicus. Act v, sc. 2, l. 160. [Titus]

4
Since when, my watch hath told me, toward my grave
I have travell'd but two hours.
Twelfth Night. Act v, sc. 1, l. 165. [Priest]
How have the hours rack'd and tortured me.
Twelfth Night. Act v, sc. 1, l. 226. [Sebastian]

5
Now it is about the very hour.
The Two Gentlemen of Verona. Act v, sc. 1, l. 2. [Eglamour] "The very hour" is repeated in *Coriolanus,* iii, 3, 60.
That very hour.—*The Comedy of Errors,* i, 1, 54; *Twelfth Night,* ii, 4, 40.
This very hour.—*Coriolanus,* i, 6, 62.
Hour of act.—*Merchant of Venice,* iv, 1, 19.
Hour of death.—*I Henry VI,* iv, 3, 42; *Richard III,* iii, 3, 23; *The Merchant of Venice,* v, 1, 153; *II Henry IV,* iv, 4, 57.

6
Wishing clocks more swift?
Hours, minutes? noon, midnight?
The Winter's Tale. Act i, sc. 2, l. 289. [Leontes]

II—Hour of Day

7
'Tis but an hour ago since it was nine,
And after one hour more 'twill be eleven;
And so, from hour to hour, we ripe and ripe,
And then, from hour to hour, we rot and rot;
And thereby hangs a tale.
As You Like It. Act ii, sc. 7, l. 24. [Jaques]
Eleven o'clock the hour.—*The Merry Wives of Windsor,* ii, 2, 325.

8
The bell then beating one.
Hamlet. Act i, sc. 1, l. 39. [Bernardo]
Hamlet: What hour now?
Horatio: I think it lacks of twelve.
Hamlet. Act i, sc. 4, l. 3.
Imogen: What hour is it?
Lady: Almost midnight, madam.
Cymbeline. Act ii, sc. 2, l. 3.

9
Falstaff: Now, Hal, what time of day is it, lad? . . .
Prince: What a devil hast thou to do with the time of day? Unless hours were cups of sack and minutes capons and clocks the tongues of bawds and dials the signs of leaping-houses and the blessed sun himself a fair hot wench in flame-coloured taffeta, I see no reason why thou shouldst be so superfluous to demand the time of the day.
I Henry IV. Act i, sc. 2, l. 1. The only use of "leaping-houses." "Flame-coloured" occurs again in *Twelfth Night,* i, 3, 144. "Taffeta" is used five times in the plays. "Superfluous" was a favourite adjective with Shakespeare, who used it seventeen times.
Heigh-ho! an it be not four by the day, I 'll be hanged: Charles' wain is over the new chimney.
I Henry IV. Act ii, sc. 1, l. 1. [First Carrier] The only mention of Charles' wain.
Sheriff: Good night, my noble lord.
Prince of Wales: I think it is good morrow, is it not?
Sheriff: Indeed, my lord, I think it be two o'clock.
I Henry IV. Act ii, sc. 4, l. 572.
Two o'clock is your hour?—*As You Like It,* iv, 1, 190.

10
Gloucester: Sirs, what 's o'clock?
Servant: Ten, my lord.
Gloucester: Ten is the hour that was appointed me
To watch the coming of my punish'd duchess.
II Henry VI. Act ii, sc. 4, l. 5.
Portia: What is 't o'clock?
Soothsayer: About the ninth hour, lady.
Julius Cæsar. Act ii, sc. 4, l. 23.
Servant: What do you think the hour?
Philotus: Labouring for nine.
Timon of Athens. Act iii, sc. 4, l. 8.
Ere the ninth hour.—*Antony and Cleopatra,* ii, 5, 21.
'Tis the ninth hour o' the morn.—*Cymbeline,* iv, 2, 30.

11
About the hour of eight, which he himself
Foretold should be his last.
Henry VIII. Act iv, sc. 2, l. 26. [Griffith]
Brutus: By the eighth hour: is that the uttermost?
Cinna: Be that the uttermost, and fail not then.
Julius Cæsar. Act ii, sc. 1, l. 213.

12
Isabella: At what hour to-morrow
Shall I attend your lordship?
Angelo: At any time 'fore noon.
Measure for Measure. Act ii, sc. 2, l. 159.
I have received from her another embassy of meeting; 'twixt eight and nine is the hour, Master Brook.
The Merry Wives of Windsor. Act iii, sc. 5, l. 130. [Falstaff]

13
And by the second hour in the morning
Desire the earl to see me in my tent.
Richard III. Act v, sc. 3, l. 31. [Richmond]
We shall embattle
By the second hour i' the morn.
Antony and Cleopatra. Act iv, sc. 9, l. 4. [First Soldier] The only use of "embattle."

1
From nine till twelve Is three long hours.
Romeo and Juliet. Act ii, sc. 5, l. 10. [Juliet]

2
What is the time o' the day?
The Tempest. Act i, sc. 2, l. 239. [Prospero]
Prospero: How 's the day?
Ariel: On the sixth hour.
The Tempest. Act v, sc. 1, l. 3.
About the sixth hour.—*Love's Labour 's Lost,* i, 1, 238.
At the sixth hour of the morn.—*Cymbeline,* i, 3, 27.
The fifth hour of the sun.—*Troilus and Cressida,* ii, 1, 134.

3
What hour is this? or morn or weary even?
Venus and Adonis, l. 495.

HOUSE

See also Home, Mansion, Roof

4
I am for the house with the narrow gate, which I take to be too little for pomp to enter.
All's Well that Ends Well. Act iv, sc. 5, l. 53. [Clown]

5
Look well to my husband's house.
Antony and Cleopatra. Act iii, sc. 2, l. 45. [Octavia]
Jessica, my girl, Look to my house.
The Merchant of Venice. Act ii, sc. 5, l. 14. [Shylock]
Lorenzo, I commit into your hands
The husbandry and manage of my house.
The Merchant of Venice. Act iii, sc. 4, l. 24. [Portia]
Look to my house.—*Titus Andronicus,* iv, 1, 120.
Look to your house.—*Othello,* i, 1, 80.

6
Rush into the secret house of death.
Antony and Cleopatra, iv, 15, 81. See under SUICIDE.
House of life.—*King John,* iv, 2, 210.
House of tears.—*Romeo and Juliet,* iv, 1, 8.
Sorrowful house.—*Titus Andronicus,* v, 3, 142.
Unquiet house.—*The Merchant of Venice,* iv, 1, 294.
Woful house.—*Titus Andronicus,* v, 2, 82.

7
This mortal house I 'll ruin.
Antony and Cleopatra, v, 2, 51. See under SUICIDE.
I will not ruinate my father's house,
Who gave his blood to lime the stones together.
III Henry VI. Act v, sc. 1, l. 83. [Clarence] "Ruinate" is repeated in *Titus Andronicus,* v, 3, 204, and in *The Rape of Lucrece,* l. 944. The only use of "lime" as a verb.
Ruin'd house.—*Timon of Athens,* iv, 2, 16.
Such a house broke!—*Timon of Athens,* iv, 2, 5.

8
This house is but a butchery.
As You Like It. Act ii, sc. 3, l. 27. [Adam] "Butchery" is repeated in *Richard III,* iv, 3, 5, and in *I Henry IV,* i, 1, 13.
If you will know my house,
'Tis at the tuft of olives here hard by.
As You Like It. Act iii, sc. 5, l. 73. [Rosalind]
But at this hour the house doth keep itself;
There 's none within.
As You Like It. Act iv, sc. 3, l. 82. [Celia]

9
My charge was but to fetch you from the mart
Home to your house.
The Comedy of Errors. Act i, sc. 2, l. 74. [Dromio of Ephesus]
My house was at the Phœnix.
The Comedy of Errors. Act ii, sc. 2, l. 11. [Antipholus of Syracuse]
Antipholus of Ephesus: What art thou that keepest me out from the house I owe?
Dromio of Syracuse: The porter for this time, sir, and my name is Dromio.
The Comedy of Errors. Act iii, sc. 1, l. 42.
I cannot get him out o' the house.
Coriolanus. Act iv, sc. 5, l. 22. [Servant]

10
This house is turned upside down since Robin Ostler died.
I Henry IV. Act ii, sc. 1, l. 11. [Carrier]
This house is turned bawdy-house; they pick pockets.
I Henry IV. Act iii, sc. 3, l. 113. [Falstaff] "Bawdy-house" is used six times. See under WHORE.
Now she professes a hot-house, which, I think, is a very ill house too.
Measure for Measure. Act ii, sc. 1, l. 67. [Elbow] The only use of "hot-house."
This house, if it be not a bawd's house, it is pity of her life, for it is a naughty house.
Measure for Measure. Act ii, sc. 1, l. 76. [Elbow]
Bottle-ale houses.—*Twelfth Night,* ii, 3, 29. "Bottle-ale" is repeated in *II Henry IV,* ii, 4, 140: "Bottle-ale rascal."
Common houses.—*Measure for Measure,* ii, 1, 43.
Infected house.—*Othello,* iv, 1, 21.

11
Worse than a smoky house.
I Henry IV, iii, 1, 161. See TEDIOUSNESS.

12
I 'll forswear keeping house.
II Henry IV, ii, 4, 220. See under FEAR.
A goodly day not to keep house, with such
Whose roof 's as low as ours!
Cymbeline. Act iii, sc. 3, l. 1. [Belarius] "Keep house" is repeated in four other plays.

13
'Fore God, you have here a goodly dwelling and a rich.
II Henry IV. Act v, sc. 3, l. 6. [Falstaff]
The place of your dwelling.—*The Winter's Tale,* iv, 4, 740.
So removed a dwelling.—*As You Like It,* iii, 2, 360.
The soul's frail dwelling-house.—*King John,* v, 7, 2. The only use of "dwelling-house."
Dwelling-place.—*I Henry VI,* i, 3, 77; *As You Like It,* ii, 1, 63.

14
Go, get you to my house.
II Henry VI. Act iii, sc. 2, l. 8. [Suffolk]
Go, get you to your house.
Coriolanus, iii, 1, 230. See under DISMISSAL.
Home to thy house.—*Coriolanus,* iii, 1, 234.

1
Cade: Therefore am I of an honourable house.
Dick: Ay, by my faith, the field is honourable; and there was he born, under a hedge, for his father had never a house but the cage.
II Henry VI. Act iv, sc. 2, l. 53.
Good house.—*Henry V,* iv, 4, 48.
Goodly house.—*Coriolanus,* iv, 5, 5.
Honest house.—*Pericles,* v, Gower, 2.
Noble house.—*Richard III,* i, 3, 282; *Coriolanus,* ii, 3, 246.
Royal house.—*Richard III,* iii, 7, 121; v, 5, 30. Used only in this play.

2
Home to your cottages.
II Henry VI. Act iv, sc. 2, l. 132. [Stafford]
Poor men's cottages.—*The Merchant of Venice,* i, 2, 15. "Cottage" is used six times in the plays.
Poor man's house.—*Coriolanus,* i, 9, 83.
Homely house.—*II Henry VI,* v, 3, 12.
Meanest house.—*Coriolanus,* iv, 2, 40.
Poor house.—*Romeo and Juliet,* i, 2, 24, and four times in later plays.
Thatched house.—*As You Like It,* iii, 3, 11.

3
The citizens fly and forsake their houses.
II Henry VI. Act iv, sc. 4, l. 50. [Messenger]
Fled from his house.—*All's Well that Ends Well,* iv, 3, 57.
Leave the house.—*I Henry IV,* ii, 4, 567.
Quit the house.—*Pericles,* iii, 2, 18.
Rid the house of her!—*The Taming of the Shrew,* i, 1, 150.

4
Break into his son-in-law's house.
II Henry VI. Act iv, sc. 7, l. 117. [Cade]
Take your houses over your heads.
II Henry VI, iv, 8, 31. See under SERVILITY.
Dry house.—*King Lear,* iii, 2, 11.
Religious house.—*Richard II,* v, 1, 23.
Removed house.—*The Winter's Tale,* v, 2, 116.
Unpeopled house.—*Love's Labour's Lost,* ii, 1, 88.

5
Let 's stay within this house.
III Henry VI. Act i, sc. 1, l. 38. [Richard]
You shall not stir out of your house to-day.
Julius Cæsar. Act ii, sc. 2, l. 9. [Calpurnia]
Be well contented
To make your house our Tower.
Henry VIII. Act v, sc. 1, l. 106. [King Henry]

6
We 'll burn the house of Brutus.
Julius Cæsar. Act iii, sc. 2, l. 236. [Citizen]
Burn, house!—*Timon of Athens,* iii, 6, 114.
He raised the house with loud and coward cries.
King Lear. Act ii, sc. 4, l. 43. [Kent]
This house is little: the old man and his people
Cannot be well bestow'd.
King Lear. Act ii, sc. 4, l. 291. [Regan]

7
He that has a house to put 's head in has a good head-piece.
King Lear. Act iii, sc. 2, l. 25. [Fool]
"Head-piece" is repeated in *Henry V,* iii, 7, 149, and in *The Winter's Tale,* i, 2, 227.
No house to put his head in.—*Timon of Athens,* iii, 4, 64.

8
This hard house—
More harder than the stones whereof 'tis raised;
Which even but now, demanding after you,
Denied me to come in.
King Lear. Act iii, sc. 2, l. 63. [Kent]

9
Pompey: All houses in the suburbs of Vienna must be plucked down.
Mrs. Overdone: And what shall become of those in the city?
Pompey: They shall stand for seed: they had gone down too, but that a wise burgher put in for them.
Mrs. Overdone: But shall all our houses of resort in the suburbs be pulled down?
Pompey: To the ground, mistress.
Measure for Measure. Act i, sc. 2, l. 98.
The house is a respected house.
Measure for Measure. Act ii, sc. 1, l. 169. [Elbow]

10
Like a fair house built on another man's ground; so that I have lost my edifice by mistaking the place where I erected it.
The Merry Wives of Windsor. Act ii, sc. 2, l. 224. [Ford]
Holy edifice.—*Merchant of Venice,* i, 1, 30.
Fair edifices.—*Coriolanus,* iv, 4, 3. The only uses of "edifice" and "edifices."

11
You wrong me, sir, thus still to haunt my house.
The Merry Wives of Windsor. Act iii, sc. 4, l. 73. [Page]
Out of the house.—*The Merry Wives of Windsor,* iii, 3, 132.
Forbade her my house.—*The Merry Wives of Windsor,* iv, 2, 89; 181.

12
There 's his chamber, his house, his castle, his standing-bed and truckle-bed.
The Merry Wives of Windsor. Act iv, sc. 5, l. 6. [Host] The only use of "standing-bed" (a bed with legs). "Truckle-bed" occurs again in *Romeo and Juliet,* ii, 1, 39.

13
Our house is hell, and thou, a merry devil,
Didst rob it of some taste of tediousness.
The Merchant of Venice. Act ii, sc. 3, l. 2. [Jessica]

14
My house is not a grange.
Othello. Act i, sc. 1, l. 106. [Brabantio]
Moated grange.—*Measure for Measure,* iii, 1, 277.
Goest to the grange.—*The Winter's Tale,* iv, 4, 309. The only uses of "grange."

15
Houses are defiled for want of use.
Pericles. Act i, sc. 4, l. 37. [Cleon]
Lysimachus: Why, the house you dwell in proclaims you to be a creature of sale.
Marina: Do you know this house to be a place of such resort, and will come into 't?
Pericles. Act iv, sc. 6, l. 83.

Your house, but for this virgin that doth prop it,
Would sink and overwhelm you.
Pericles. Act iv, sc. 6, l. 127. [Lysimachus]

1
Graze where you will, you shall not house with me.
Romeo and Juliet. Act iii, sc. 5, l. 190. [Capulet]

We house i' the rock.—*Cymbeline,* iii, 3, 8.
House him safe.—*Pericles,* ii, Gower, 32.

2
As I remember, this should be the house.
Romeo and Juliet. Act v, sc. 1, l. 55. [Romeo]

I trow this is the house.—*The Taming of the Shrew,* i, 2, 4.
This is the house.—*The Taming of the Shrew,* iv, 4, 51.
Here is her father's house.—*Othello,* i, 1, 74.
There 's the house.—*The Comedy of Errors,* iii, 1, 117.

3 For, lo, his house
Is empty on the back of Montague.
Romeo and Juliet. Act v, sc. 3, l. 202. [Capulet]

4
Who lets so fair a house fall to decay,
Which husbandry in honour might uphold
Against the stormy gusts of winter's day
And barren rage of death's eternal cold?
O, none but unthrifts!
Sonnets. No. xiii.

Upstart unthrifts.—*Richard II,* ii, 3, 122. The only uses of "unthrifts." "Unthrift" occurs in *The Merchant of Venice,* v, 1, 16: "Unthrift love"; and in *Timon of Athens,* iv, 3, 311: "Know unthrift."

5 My house within the city
Is richly furnished with plate and gold.
The Taming of the Shrew. Act ii, sc. 1, l. 348. [Gremio]

6 Now, my honey love,
Will we return unto thy father's house.
The Taming of the Shrew. Act iv, sc. 3, l. 52. [Petruchio]

My father's house . . . will I estate upon you.
As You Like It. Act v, sc. 2, l. 12. [Oliver]

7
Braved in mine own house with a skein of thread?
The Taming of the Shrew. Act iv, sc. 3, l. 111. [Petruchio] "Skein" is used once again in *Troilus and Cressida,* v, 1, 35.

Mine own house.—*Julius Cæsar,* ii, 4, 22; *King Lear,* iii, 3, 4.
Your own house.—*Troilus and Cressida,* i, 2, 300.
In 's own house.—*Hamlet,* iii, 1, 137.

8
Have I been ever free, and must my house
Be my retentive enemy, my gaol?
Timon of Athens. Act iii, sc. 4, l. 81. [Timon] "Retentive" is repeated in *Julius Cæsar,* i, 3, 95.

Frequents my house.—*Timon of Athens,* i, 1, 117.
He is about the house.—*Twelfth Night,* ii, 4, 13.

9
Clown: Sayest thou that house is dark?
Malvolio: As hell, Sir Topas.
Clown: Why, it hath bay windows transparent as barricadoes, and the clearstores toward the south north are as lustrous as ebony; and yet complainest thou of obstruction?
Malvolio: I am not mad, Sir Topas; I say to you this house is dark.
Clown: Madman, thou errest: I say, there is no darkness but ignorance, in which thou art more puzzled than the Egyptians in their fog.
Malvolio: I say, this house is as dark as ignorance, though ignorance were as dark as hell.
Twelfth Night. Act iv, sc. 2, l. 38. The only use of "bay windows" and "clearstores." "Barricado" is repeated in *All 's Well that Ends Well,* i, 1, 124, and in *The Winter's Tale,* i, 2, 204. "Lustrous" occurs again in *All 's Well that Ends Well,* ii, 1, 41.

Dark house.—*All 's Well that Ends Well,* ii, 3, 309; *As You Like It,* iii, 2, 421.
Kept in a dark house?—*Twelfth Night,* v, 1, 350.

HOUSEWIFE

10
You are manifest house-keepers. What are you sewing here?
Coriolanus. Act i, sc. 3, l. 55. [Valeria] "Sewing" occurs again in *Hamlet,* ii, 1, 77. "Housekeeper" (unhyphenated) is used twice more in the plays, in *Twelfth Night,* iv, 2, 10, and in *Macbeth,* iii, 1, 97, but in both instances with reference to men.

11
Come, lay aside your stitchery; I must have you play the idle huswife with me this afternoon.
Coriolanus. Act i, sc. 3, l. 75. [Valeria] The only use of "stitchery." "Play the huswife" is repeated in *Henry V,* v, 1, 85.

Overscutched huswives.—*II Henry IV,* iii, 2, 341. The only use of "overscutched" (overbeaten). "Huswife" is used a fourth time in *As You Like It,* iv, 3, 27: "She has a huswife's hand."

You would be another Penelope: yet, they say, all the yarn she spun in Ulysses' absence did but fill Ithaca full of moths.
Coriolanus. Act i, sc. 3, l. 92. [Valeria] The only mention of Penelope. Ithaca is referred to a second time in *Troilus and Cressida,* i, 3, 70.

12 Pray, be not sick,
For you must be our housewife.
Cymbeline. Act iv, sc. 2, l. 44. [Belarius]

13
Let housewifery appear: keep close, I thee command.
Henry V. Act ii, sc. 3, l. 65. [Pistol]

Players in your housewifery, and housewives in your beds.
Othello, ii, 1, 113. The only uses of "housewifery." See under WOMAN.

1
Your graces find me here part of a housewife,
I would be all, against the worst may happen.
Henry VIII. Act iii, sc. 1, l. 24. [Queen Katharine]

2
Let housewives make a skillet of my helm!
Othello, i, 3, 273. The only use of "skillet." See under ADVERSITY.

3
I 'll play the housewife for this once.
Romeo and Juliet. Act iv, sc. 2, l. 43. [Capulet]

Bounteous housewife.—*Timon of Athens,* iv, 3, 423.
Breathless housewife.—*A Midsummer-Night's Dream,* ii, 1, 37.
Careful housewife.—*Sonnets,* cxliii.
False housewife.—*Antony and Cleopatra,* iv, 15, 44.
A franklin's housewife.—*Cymbeline,* iii, 2, 79.
Good housewife.—*As You Like It,* i, 2, 34.
Noble housewife.—*All 's Well that Ends Well,* ii, 2, 62.

HUG, see Embrace

HUMANITY, see Man

HUMILITY

See also Meekness

4
He . . . bow'd his eminent top to their low ranks,
Making them proud of his humility.
All 's Well that Ends Well. Act i, sc. 2, l. 42. [King]

Proud humility.—*All 's Well that Ends Well,* i, 1, 185.
Mild humility.—*Love's Labour 's Lost,* iv, 3, 349.

5
I am prompt
To lay my crown at 's feet, and there to kneel.
Antony and Cleopatra. Act iii, sc. 13, l. 75. [Cleopatra]

Her humble self.—*The Two Gentlemen of Verona,* iii, 1, 226.
Humble and familiar.—*Richard II,* i, 4, 26.
Low and humble.—*All 's Well that Ends Well,* ii, 1, 200.

6
The napless vesture of humility.
Coriolanus. Act ii, sc. 1, l. 250. [Brutus] The only use of "napless."

The gown of humility.—*Coriolanus,* ii, 3, 44.
The surplice of humility.—*All 's Well that Ends Well,* i, 3, 99. The only use of "surplice."

7
Humble as the ripest mulberry
That will not hold the handling.
Coriolanus. Act iii, sc. 2, l. 79. [Volumnia] "Mulberry" is used twice in *A Midsummer-Night's Dream,* iii, 1, 170, and v, 1, 149. "Ripest" is repeated in *Richard II,* ii, 1, 153: "The ripest fruit falls first."

A mile before his tent fall down, and knee
The way into his mercy; nay, if he coy'd
To hear Cominius speak, I 'll keep at home.
Coriolanus. Act v, sc. 1, l. 5. [Menenius Agrippa] The only use of "coy'd."

He bow'd his nature, never known before
But to be rough, unswayable and free.
Coriolanus. Act v, sc. 6, l. 25. [Aufidius] The only use of "unswayable."

8
I have sounded the very base-string of humility.
I Henry IV. Act ii, sc. 4, l. 5. [Prince of Wales] The only use of "base-string."

I could have crept into any alderman's thumb-ring.
I Henry IV. Act ii, sc. 4, l. 364. [Falstaff] The only use of "thumb-ring."

I stole all courtesy from heaven,
And dress'd myself in such humility
That I did pluck allegiance from men's hearts,
Loud shouts and salutations from their mouths.
I Henry IV. Act iii, sc. 2, l. 50. [King Henry]

9
And humbly now upon my bended knee, . . .
Deliver up my title in the queen.
II Henry VI. Act i, sc. 1, l. 10. [Suffolk]

Speak gentle words and humbly bend thy knee.
III Henry VI. Act v, sc. 1, l. 22. [King Edward]

Humbly on thy knee.—*Henry V,* iv, 3, 129; *Richard III,* ii, 2, 105. See also under KNEE.
Most humbly.—*III Henry VI,* i, 2, 61; *Hamlet,* i, 3, 82; *Othello,* i, 3, 236.

10
Hast thou not kiss'd thy hand and held my stirrup?
Bare-headed plodded by my foot-cloth mule
And thought thee happy when I shook my head?
How often hast thou waited at my cup,
Fed from my trencher, kneel'd down at the board?
II Henry VI. Act iv, sc. 1, l. 53. [Suffolk] "Plodded" occurs again in *Henry V,* i, 2, 227. "Foot-cloth" is repeated in *II Henry VI,* iv, 7, 51: "Ride in a foot-cloth"; and in *Richard III,* iii, 4, 86: "Foot-cloth horse." A foot-cloth was a large ornamented cloth laid over the back of a horse or mule, and hanging down almost to the ground on either side.

Bareheaded, lower than his proud steed's neck.
Richard II. Act v, sc. 2, l. 19. [York]

Bare-headed, sweating.—*II Henry IV,* ii, 4, 388. "Bare-headed" occurs a fourth time in *King Lear,* iii, 2, 60.

11
He . . . most willingly humbles himself to the determination of justice.
Measure for Measure. Act iii, sc. 2, l. 257. [Duke]

12
So humbled
That he hath left part of his grief with me,
To suffer with him.
Othello. Act iii, sc. 3, l. 52. [Desdemona]

All humbled.—*The Two Gentlemen of Verona,* i, 2, 59.
All humbled on your knees.—*Titus Andronicus,* i, 1, 472.
Humbled at thy feet.—*Titus Andronicus,* i, 1, 252.
Humble-mouthed.—*Henry VIII,* ii, 4, 107.

Humble-visaged.—*Love's Labour 's Lost,* ii, 1, 34.

1 Kiss the rod,
And fawn on rage with base humility.
Richard II. Act v, sc. 1, l. 32. [Queen]

2
I thank my God for my humility.
Richard III. Act ii, sc. 1, l. 72. [Gloucester]
Fair humility.—*Richard III,* iii, 7, 17.
In all humility.—*Henry VIII,* iv, 2, 161.
In all submission and humility.—*II Henry VI,* v, 1, 58.

3
That made great Jove humble him to her hand,
When with his knees he kiss'd the Cretan strand.
The Taming of the Shrew. Act i, sc. 1, l. 174. [Lucentio] The only use of "Cretan."
Most humble.—*The Tempest,* i, 2, 482.

4
Dismiss your followers and, as suitors should,
Plead your deserts in peace and humbleness.
Titus Andronicus. Act i, sc. 1, l. 44. [Marcus]
With all the humbleness I may,
I greet your honours.
Titus Andronicus. Act iv, sc. 2, l. 4. [Young Lucius]
With all bound humbleness.—*All's Well that Ends Well,* ii, 1, 117.
All humbleness.—*As You Like It,* v, 2, 103.
Great'st humbleness.—*Henry VIII,* v, 1, 65.
Whispering humbleness.—*The Merchant of Venice,* i, 3, 125. The only uses of "humbleness."

5
To come as humbly as they used to creep
To holy altars.
Troilus and Cressida. Act iii, sc. 3, l. 73. [Patroclus]
I humbly beseech you.—*Othello,* i, 3, 114; *The Winter's Tale,* v, 2, 160; *Henry VIII,* ii, 4, 53.
Humbly take my leave.—*Hamlet,* ii, 2, 218; *Macbeth,* i, 4, 47; *Cymbeline,* i, 5, 45.
I humbly thank you.—*Hamlet,* iii, 1, 92, and eight times in later plays.
I humbly thank your highness.—*Henry VIII,* v, 1, 108; *Cymbeline,* i, 1, 175; *Cymbeline,* v, 5, 100.

HUMOUR

See also Foolery, Jesting

6
The duke is humorous: what he is indeed,
More suits you to conceive than I to speak of.
As You Like It. Act i, sc. 2, l. 278.
The humorous duke.—*As You Like It,* ii, 3, 8.
I am known to be a humorous patrician.
Coriolanus. Act ii, sc. 1, l. 51. [Menenius]
Her humorous ladyship.—*King John,* iii, 1, 119.
Humorous man.—*Hamlet,* ii, 2, 335.
A . . . humorous youth.—*Henry V,* ii, 4, 28.
As humorous as winter.—*II Henry IV,* iv, 4, 34.

7
It fits my humour well.
As You Like It. Act iii, sc. 2, l. 20. [Touchstone]
A poor humour of mine, sir.—*As You Like It,* v, 4, 61.
Aspiring humour.—*II Henry VI,* i, 2, 97.
Black-oppressing humour.—*Love's Labour 's Lost,* i, 1, 235. The only use of "black-oppressing."
Idle humour.—*The Taming of the Shrew,* Ind., 2, 14.
Impatient humour.—*The Taming of the Shrew,* iii, 2, 29.
Mistemper'd humour.—*King John,* v, 1, 12. "Mistemper'd" is repeated in *Romeo and Juliet,* i, 1, 94: "Mistemper'd weapons."
Unyoked humour.—*I Henry IV,* i, 2, 220. "Unyoked" is repeated in *II Henry IV,* iv, 2, 103: "Steers unyoked."

8
I am not in a sportive humour now.
The Comedy of Errors. Act i, sc. 2, l. 58. [Antipholus of Syracuse]
How now, sir! is your merry humour alter'd?
As you love strokes, so jest with me again.
The Comedy of Errors. Act ii, sc. 2, l. 7. [Antipholus of Syracuse]
Fie, now you run this humour out of breath.
The Comedy of Errors. Act iv, sc. 1, l. 57. [Antipholus of Ephesus]

9
I am now of all humours that have showed themselves humours since the old days of goodman Adam to the pupil age of this present twelve o'clock at midnight.
I Henry IV. Act ii, sc. 4, l. 104. [Prince of Wales]
You are altogether governed by humours.
II Henry IV. Act iii, sc. 1, l. 236. [Lady Percy]
It jumps with my humour.—*I Henry IV,* i, 2, 78.

10
Come, thou must not be in this humour with me.
II Henry IV. Act ii, sc. 1, l. 163. [Falstaff]
What humour 's the prince of?
II Henry IV. Act ii, sc. 4, l. 256. [Doll Tearsheet]
A bedlam and ambitious humour
Makes him oppose himself against his king.
II Henry VI. Act v, sc. 1, l. 132. [King Henry]

11
The humour of it is too hot, that is the very plain-song of it.
Henry V. Act iii, sc. 2, l. 5. [Nym] "Plain-song" (a simple melody or theme) is repeated in *A Midsummer-Night's Dream,* iii, 1, 134, and in *Henry VIII,* i, 3, 45.
That is the humour of it.—*Henry V,* ii, 1, 74; 101; 121; ii, 3, 63.
There 's the humour of it.—*The Merry Wives of Windsor,* ii, 1, 141.

12
These be good humours! your honour wins bad humours.
Henry V. Act iii, sc. 2, l. 27. [Nym] "Bad humours" is repeated in ii, 1, 127, and occurs in no other play.

Be advised, sir, and pass good humours: I will say 'marry trap' with you, if you run the nuthook's humour on me; that is the very note of it.
The Merry Wives of Windsor. Act i, sc. 1, l. 169. [Nym] The only use of "marry trap" (be off with you). "Nuthook" (constable) occurs again in *II Henry IV,* v, 4, 8.

Good humour.—*II Henry IV,* ii, 4, 177; *The Merry Wives of Windsor,* i, 3, 30.

1
If I were Brutus now and he were Cassius,
He should not humour me.
Julius Cæsar. Act i, sc. 2, l. 318. [Cassius]

I can give his humour the true bent.
Julius Cæsar. Act ii, sc. 1, l. 210. [Decius]

Hoping it was but an effect of humour,
Which sometime hath his hour with every man.
It will not let you eat, nor talk, nor sleep.
Julius Cæsar. Act ii, sc. 1, l. 250. [Portia]

I 'll know his humour.—*Julius Cæsar,* iv, 3, 136.

2 Fashioning our humours
Even to the opposed end of our intents.
Love's Labour 's Lost. Act v, sc. 2, l. 767. [Biron]

These are humours.—*Love's Labour 's Lost,* iii, 1, 23.

3
His humour is lofty.
Love's Labour 's Lost. Act v, sc. 1, l. 10. [Holofernes]

The humour rises; it is good.
The Merry Wives of Windsor. Act i, sc. 3, l. 63. [Nym]

4
Let it be as humours and conceits shall govern.
The Merchant of Venice. Act iii, sc. 5, l. 68. [Launcelot]

It is my humour.—*The Merchant of Venice,* iv, 1, 43.

That 's my humour.—*The Merry Wives of Windsor,* i, 1, 135.

5
Is not the humour conceited?
The Merry Wives of Windsor. Act i, sc. 3, l. 24. [Nym]

The anchor is deep: will that humour pass?
The Merry Wives of Windsor. Act i, sc. 3, l. 56. [Nym]

I thank thee for that humour.
The Merry Wives of Windsor. Act i, sc. 3, l. 71. [Nym]

I will run no base humour.
The Merry Wives of Windsor. Act i, sc. 3, l. 85. [Nym]

Falstaff will learn the humour of the age.
The Merry Wives of Windsor. Act i, sc. 3, l. 92. [Falstaff]

My humour shall not cool.—*The Merry Wives of Windsor,* i, 3, 109.

That is my true humour.—*The Merry Wives of Windsor,* i, 3, 112.

The humour of it.—*The Merry Wives of Windsor,* ii, 1, 142.

Let 's obey his humour a little further.
The Merry Wives of Windsor. Act iv, sc. 2, l. 210. [Page] "Humour" is used twenty-one times in this play.

6
My chief humour is for a tyrant.
A Midsummer-Night's Dream. Act i, sc. 2, l. 30. [Bottom]

7
I thank God and my cold blood, I am of your humour.
Much Ado about Nothing. Act i, sc. 1, l. 131. [Beatrice]

I will teach you how to humour your cousin.
Much Ado about Nothing. Act ii, sc. 1, l. 394. [Don Pedro]

I will leave you now to your gossip-like humour.
Much Ado about Nothing. Act v, sc. 1, l. 188. [Benedick] The only use of "gossip-like."

A college of wit-crackers cannot flout me out of my humour.
Much Ado about Nothing. Act v, sc. 4, l. 101. [Benedick] The only use of "wit-crackers."

8
I pray you, be content; 'tis but his humour.
Othello. Act iv, sc. 2, l. 165. [Iago]

Such childish humour from weak minds proceeds.
The Rape of Lucrece, l. 1825.

9
I hope my holy humour will change; 'twas wont to hold me but while one would tell twenty.
Richard III. Act i, sc. 4, l. 120. [Murderer]

Church-like humours.—*II Henry VI,* i, 1, 247. The only use of "church-like."

10
Pursued my humour not pursuing his,
And gladly shunn'd who glady fled from me.
Romeo and Juliet. Act i, sc. 1, l. 135. [Benedick]

Black and portentous that this humour prove,
Unless good counsel may the cause remove.
Romeo and Juliet. Act i, sc. 1, l. 147. [Montague]

Presently through all thy veins shall run
A cold and drowsy humour.
Romeo and Juliet. Act iv, sc. 1, l. 95. [Friar Laurence]

11
Every humour hath his adjunct pleasure,
Wherein it finds a joy above the rest.
Sonnets. No. xci.

12
Let him go while the humour lasts.
The Taming of the Shrew. Act i, sc. 2, l. 107. [Grumio]

'Tis some old humour pricks him to this fashion.
The Taming of the Shrew. Act iii, sc. 2, l. 74. [Tranio]

Thus I 'll curb her mad and headstrong humour.
The Taming of the Shrew. Act iv, sc. 1, l. 212. [Petruchio]

13
Fie, thou 'rt a churl; ye 've got a humour there
Does not become a man.
Timon of Athens. Act i, sc. 2, l. 26. [Timon]

There is no crossing him in 's humour.
Timon of Athens. Act i, sc. 2, l. 166. [Flavius]

He 's but a mad lord, and nought but humour sways him.
Timon of Athens. Act iii, sc. 6, l. 121. [First Lord]

1
A goodly humour, is it not, my lords?
Titus Andronicus. Act iv, sc. 4, l. 19. Saturninus]

Feed his humour kindly.—*Titus Andronicus,* iv, 3, 29.

2
I 'll let his humours blood.
Troilus and Cressida. Act ii, sc. 3, l. 222. [Ajax]

Achilles: Why, but he is not in this tune, is he?
Thersites: No, but he 's out o' tune thus.
Troilus and Cressida. Act iii, sc. 3, l. 301.

HUNGER

See also Famine, Starvation

3
Thy palate then did deign
The roughest berry on the rudest hedge;
Yea, like the stag, when snow the pasture sheets,
The barks of trees thou browsed'st; on the Alps
It is reported thou didst eat strange flesh,
Which some did die to look on.
Antony and Cleopatra. Act i, sc. 4, l. 63. [Cæsar] "Rudest" is repeated in *Cymbeline,* iv, 2, 174: "Rudest wind." The only use of "browsed'st" and of "sheets" as a verb.

4
I pray you, one of you question yond man
If he for gold will give us any food:
I faint almost to death.
As You Like It. Act ii, sc. 4, l. 64. [Celia]

Now I think on thee,
My hunger 's gone; but even before, I was
At point to sink for food.
Cymbeline. Act iii, sc. 6, l. 15. [Imogen]

Almost spent with hunger.—*Cymbeline,* iii, 6, 63.
Compell'd by hunger.—*Henry VIII,* i, 2, 34.
Hunger for bread.—*Coriolanus,* i, 1, 25.
Hunger for that food.—*Timon of Athens,* v, 4, 32.
Present hunger.—*Cymbeline,* ii, 4, 137.

5
Dost thou so hunger for mine empty chair
That thou wilt needs invest thee with my honours
Before thy hour be ripe?
II Henry IV. Act iv, sc. 5, l. 95. [King Henry]

6
Hunger will enforce them to be more eager.
I Henry VI. Act i, sc. 2, l. 38. [Charles]

7
Fie on myself, that have a sword, and yet am ready to famish!
II Henry VI. Act iv, sc. 10, l. 1. [Cade]

Or else you famish; that 's a threefold death.
III Henry VI. Act v, sc. 4, l. 32. [Queen Margaret]

Resolved rather to die than to famish.
Coriolanus. Act i, sc. 1, l, 5. [First Citizen]

8
Now am I so hungry that if I might have a lease of my life for a thousand years I could stay no longer.
II Henry VI. Act iv, sc. 10, l. 5. [Cade]

Lean and hungry.—*Julius Cæsar,* i, 2, 194.
Hungry for revenge.—*Richard III,* iv, 4, 61.
Makes hungry.—*Antony and Cleopatra,* ii, 2, 242.
Makes them hungry.—*Pericles,* v, 1, 113.

9
I am famished in his service; you may tell every finger I have with my ribs.
The Merchant of Venice. Act ii, sc. 2, l. 113. [Launcelot]

Sick and famished.—*Henry V,* iii, 5, 57.
Famished correctioner.—*II Henry IV,* v, 4, 22.
Famish'd beggars.—*Richard III,* v, 3, 329.
Famish'd English.—*I Henry VI,* i, 2, 7.
Famished flesh.—*Timon of Athens,* iv, 3, 535.
A poor famish'd man.—*II Henry VI,* iv, 10, 47.

10
Who wanteth food, and will not say he wants it,
Or can conceal his hunger till he famish?
Pericles. Act i, sc. 4, l. 11. [Cleon]

So sharp are hunger's teeth, that man and wife
Draw lots who first shall die to lengthen life.
Pericles. Act i, sc. 4, l. 45. [Cleon]

Sharp hunger.—*The Rape of Lucrece,* l. 422.

11
He ten times pines that pines beholding food.
The Rape of Lucrece, l. 1115.

12
What, did he marry me to famish me? . . .
I . . .
Am starved for meat, giddy for lack of sleep.
The Taming of the Shrew. Act iv, sc. 3, l. 3. [Katharina]

Famish him.—*Titus Andronicus,* v, 3, 179.
Suffer us to famish.—*Coriolanus,* i, 1, 82.
Famish in their nests.—*Titus Andronicus,* ii, 3, 154.
Famish a dog's death.—*Timon of Athens,* ii, 2, 91.
As hungry as the sea.—*Twelfth Night,* ii, 4, 103.
Hunger starved half dead.—*Pericles,* i, 4, 96.
Hunger-starved.—*III Henry VI,* i, 4, 5.
Hungry-starved.—*I Henry VI,* i, 5, 16.

13
They are never curst but when they are hungry.
The Winter's Tale. Act iii, sc. 3, l. 134. [Clown]

HUNTING

14
Come, shall we go and kill us venison?
And yet it irks me the poor dappled fools,
Being native burghers of this desert city,
Should in their own confines with forked heads
Have their round haunches gored.
As You Like It. Act ii, sc. 1, l. 21. [Duke

Senior] The only use of "dappled." "Venison" is mentioned six times. "Haunch" is repeated in *II Henry IV,* iv, 4, 92, and in *The Merry Wives of Windsor,* v, 5, 28.

This is not hunters' language: he that strikes
The venison first shall be the lord o' the feast.
Cymbeline. Act iii, sc. 3, l. 74. [Belarius]

1
Go you to hunting.
Cymbeline. Act iv, sc. 2, l. 6. [Guiderius]

Comes hunting this way.—*III Henry VI,* iv, 5, 8.

Comes from hunting.—*Timon of Athens,* ii, 2, 8.

Returns from hunting.—*King Lear,* i, 3, 7.

2
I had no mind To hunt this day.
Cymbeline. Act iv, sc. 2, l. 148. [Belarius]

We'll hunt no more to-day.
Cymbeline. Act iv, sc. 2, l. 162. [Belarius]

3
How cheerfully on the false trail they cry!
Hamlet. Act iv, sc. 5, l. 109. [Queen]

Sir Toby: He is now at a cold scent.
Fabian: Sowter will cry upon 't for all this, though it be as rank as a fox.
Twelfth Night. Act ii, sc. 5, l. 134.

4 Seek thee out some other chase,
For I myself must hunt this deer to death.
II Henry VI. Act v, sc. 2, l. 14. [York]

Single out some other chase;
For I myself will hunt this wolf to death.
III Henry VI. Act ii, sc. 4, l. 12. [Richard]

Hunt us all to death.—*Richard III,* iv, 4, 48.

I do follow here in the chase, not like a hound that hunts, but one that fills up the cry.
Othello. Act ii, sc. 3, l. 369. [Roderigo]

This chase is hotly follow'd.—*Henry V,* ii, 4, 68.

Apollo flies and Daphne holds the chase.
A Midsummer-Night's Dream. Act ii, sc. 1, l. 231. [Helena]

Holds in chase.—*King John,* i, 1, 223.

Held me in chase.—*Coriolanus,* i, 6, 19.

Gave us chase.—*Hamlet,* iv, 6, 16.

This is the chase.—*The Winter's Tale,* iii, 3, 57.

Fond chase.—*A Midsummer-Night's Dream,* ii, 2, 88.

Holy chase.—*Julius Cæsar,* i, 2, 8.

Piteous chase.—*As You Like It,* ii, 1, 40.

Pleasant chase.—*Titus Andronicus,* ii, 3, 225.

Wild-goose chase.—*Romeo and Juliet,* ii, 4, 75. See under WIT.

Hastening, in the chase.—*The Winter's Tale,* v, 1, 189.

5
Hunting was his daily exercise.
III Henry VI. Act iv, sc. 6, l. 85. [Post]

The king he is hunting the deer; I am coursing myself.
Love's Labour's Lost. Act iv, sc. 3, l. 1. [Biron] "Coursing" is used a second time in *Henry V,* i, 2, 143.

Our purposed hunting shall be set aside.
A Midsummer-Night's Dream. Act iv, sc. 1, l. 187. [Theseus]

Quick hunting.—*Othello,* ii, 1, 313.

6
To-morrow I intend to hunt again.
The Taming of the Shrew. Induction, sc. 1, l. 29. [Lord]

7
'Tis well, sir, that you hunted for yourself:
'Tis thought your deer does hold you at a bay.
The Taming of the Shrew. Act v, sc. 2, l. 55. [Tranio]

I hunted with his honour to-day.—*Timon of Athens,* ii, 2, 197.

O, had we never never hunted there!—*Titus Andronicus,* iv, 1, 56.

Let them be hunted soundly.
Tempest. Act iv, sc. 1, l. 263. [Prospero]

Hunted Even to falling.—*Antony and Cleopatra,* iv, 1, 7.

Past reason hunted.—*Sonnets,* cxxix.

Hunted boar.—*Venus and Adonis,* l. 900. The only uses of "hunted."

8 Instruct thee how
To snare the nimble marmoset.
The Tempest. Act ii, sc. 1, l. 173. [Caliban] The only mention of marmoset.

9
To-morrow, an it please your majesty
To hunt the panther and the hart with me,
With horn and hound we'll give your grace bonjour.
Titus Andronicus. Act i, sc. 1, l. 492. [Titus] The panther is mentioned again in ii, 2, 21, and ii, 3, 194, and in no other play. "Hart" occurs ten times. "Bonjour" (as two words) is repeated in *As You Like It,* i, 2, 104, and in *Romeo and Juliet,* ii, 4, 46.

Curio: Will you go hunt, my lord?
Duke: What, Curio?
Curio: The hart.
Duke: Why, so I do, the noblest that I have.
Twelfth Night. Act i, sc. 1, l. 16.

Wilt thou hunt?—*The Taming of the Shrew,* Ind., 2, 46.

Hunt these bear-whelps.—*Titus Andronicus,* iv, 1, 96. "Bear-whelp" is repeated in *III Henry VI,* iii, 2, 161.

Hunt a lion.—*Troilus and Cressida,* iv, 1, 19.

10
My lords, a solemn hunting is in hand.
Titus Andronicus. Act ii, sc. 1, l. 112. [Aaron]

The hunt is up, the morn is bright and grey,
The fields are fragrant and the woods are green:
Uncouple here and let us make a bay
And wake the emperor and his lovely bride
And rouse the prince and ring a hunter's peal,
That all the court may echo with a noise.
Titus Andronicus. Act ii, sc. 2, l. 1. [Titus]

Hunting thee hence with hunt's-up to the day.
Romeo and Juliet, iii, 5, 34. The only use of "hunt's-up."

11
Titus: I promised your grace a hunter's peal.
Saturninus: And you have rung it lustily, my lord.
Titus Andronicus. Act ii, sc. 2, l. 13.

Come on, then; horse and chariots let us have,
And to our sport. Madam, now shall ye see
Our Roman hunting.
Titus Andronicus. Act ii, sc. 2, l. 18. [Saturninus]

German hunting.—*II Henry IV,* ii, 1, 157.

1
We hunt not, we, with horse nor hound,
But hope to pluck a dainty doe to ground.
Titus Andronicus. Act ii, sc. 2, l. 25. [Demetrius]
Or is it Dian, habited like her,
Who hath abandoned her holy groves
To see the general hunting in this forest?
Titus Andronicus. Act ii, sc. 3, l. 57. [Bassianus] "Habited" is repeated in *The Winter's Tale,* iv, 4, 557.
2
Even as the sun with purple-colour'd face
Had ta'en his last leave of the weeping morn,
Rose-cheek'd Adonis hied him to the chase;
Hunting he loved, but love he laugh'd to scorn.
Venus and Adonis, l. 1. The only use of "purple-colour'd." "Purple-hued" occurs in *I Henry IV,* ii, 1, 83. "Rose-cheek'd" is repeated in *Timon of Athens,* iv, 3, 86: "Rose-cheek'd youth."
To-morrow he intends
To hunt the boar with certain of his friends.
Venus and Adonis, l. 587. "Hunt the boar" is repeated in l. 614; "hunting of the boar" in l. 711.
Pursue these fearful creatures o'er the downs,
And on thy well-breath'd horse keep with thy hounds.
Venus and Adonis, l. 677. The only use of "well-breath'd."
For now she knows it is no gentle chase,
But the blunt boar, rough bear, or lion proud.
Venus and Adonis, l. 883.
3
Would any but these boiled brains of nineteen and two-and-twenty hunt this weather?
Winter's Tale. Act iii, sc. 3, l. 64. [Shepherd] "Two-and-twenty" is used six times.

II—The Hunter

4
Huntsman: This way, my lord; for this way lies the game.
King Edward: Nay, this way, man: see where the huntsmen stand.
III Henry VI. Act iv, sc. 5, l. 14.
Here thy hunters stand.—*Julius Cæsar,* iii, 1, 205.
5
Go, bid the huntsmen wake them with their horns.
A Midsummer-Night's Dream, iv, 1, 143. See under HORN.
A jolly troop of huntsmen.—*King John,* ii, 1, 321.
6
You are a young huntsman, Marcus.
Titus Andronicus. Act iv, sc. 1, l. 101. [Titus]
Daring huntsman.—*Henry VIII,* iii, 2, 307.
Sweet huntsman.—*Titus Andronicus,* ii, 3, 269.
Find the huntsman out.—*Titus Andronicus,* ii, 3, 278.
7
By Jove, I 'll play the hunter for thy life.
Troilus and Cressida. Act iv, sc. 1, l. 17. [Diomedes]
He was furnished like a hunter.—*As You Like It,* iii, 2, 259.
Herne the hunter.—*The Merry Wives of Windsor,* iv, 4, 28, and four times in later scenes. "Huntress" is used only once, in *As You Like It,* iii, 2, 4.
8
Far off she hears some huntsman hollo.
Venus and Adonis, l. 973.

HURT

See also Injury, Wound

9
I must give myself some hurts, and say I got them in exploit: yet slight ones will not carry it; they will say, 'Came you off with so little?' and great ones I dare not give.
All's Well that Ends Well. Act iv, sc. 1, l. 40. [Parolles]
No hurt done!—*All's Well that Ends Well,* i, 3, 97.
10
Hold, hurt him not, for God's sake! he is mad.
The Comedy of Errors. Act v, sc. 1, l. 33. [Adriana]
I will not hurt him.—*Antony and Cleopatra,* ii, 5, 81.
He will not hurt you.—*Twelfth Night,* iii, 4, 339.
11
All hurt behind; backs red, and faces pale.
Coriolanus, i, 4, 37. See under COWARDICE.
Hurt behind.—*Cymbeline,* v, 3, 12.
12
Volumnia: He received in the repulse of Tarquin seven hurts i' the body.
Menenius: One i' the neck, and two i' the thigh—there 's nine that I know.
Coriolanus. Act ii, sc. 1, l. 165.
You soothed not, therefore hurt not.
Coriolanus. Act ii, sc. 2, l. 77. [Coriolanus]
Great hurt.—*Coriolanus,* iv, 5, 73.
Large hurts.—*Timon of Athens,* iii, 5, 109.
13
Cloten: Have I hurt him?
Second Lord: No, faith; not so much as his patience.
First Lord: Hurt him! his body 's a passable carcass, if he be not hurt: it is a throughfare for steel, if it be not hurt. . . .
Cloten: Would there had been some hurt done.
Second Lord: I wish not so; unless it had been the fall of an ass, which is no great hurt.
Cymbeline. Act i, sc. 2, l. 7. "Passable" is repeated in *Coriolanus,* v, 2, 13, and "throughfare" in *The Merchant of Venice,* ii, 7, 42.
14
Are you not hurt i' the groin? methought a' made a shrewd thrust at your belly.
II Henry IV. Act ii, sc. 4, l. 227. [Hostess] The only use of "groin."
You have hurt him, sir, in the shoulder.
II Henry IV. Act ii, sc. 4, l. 231. [Bardolph]
15
Strike those that hurt, and hurt not those that help.
I Henry VI. Act iii, sc. 3, l. 53. [La Pucelle]

You may hurt yourself.—*Henry VIII,* iii, 1, 160.

1
Regan: How is 't, my lord, how look you?
Cornwall: I have received a hurt: . . . I bleed apace:
Untimely comes this hurt.
King Lear. Act iii, sc. 7, l. 94.

I am but hurt.—*Hamlet,* v, 2, 335.

2
Siward: Had he his hurts before?
Ross: Ay, on the front.
Siward: Why then, God's soldier be he!
Macbeth. Act v, sc. 8, l. 46.

3
What, should I strike her, strike her, kill her dead?
A Midsummer-Night's Dream. Act iii, sc. 2, l. 269. [Lysander]

I pray you, . . . Let her not hurt me.
A Midsummer-Night's Dream. Act iii, sc. 2, l. 300. [Helena]

It hurts nobody.—*Much Ado about Nothing,* v, 1, 165.

4
I am hurt to the death.
Othello. Act ii, sc. 3, l. 164. [Montano]

I am hurt to danger.
Othello. Act ii, sc. 3, l. 197. [Montano]

Iago: What, are you hurt, lieutenant?
Cassio: Ay, past all surgery.
Othello. Act ii, sc. 3, l. 259.

5
I never did her hurt in all my life. . . .
I never . . . hurt a fly.
Pericles. Act iv, sc. 1, l. 75. [Marina]

I saw you lately,
When you caught hurt in parting two that fought.
Pericles. Act iv, sc. 1, l. 87. [Marina]

6
Mercutio: I am hurt.
A plague o' both your houses! I am sped. . . .
Benvolio: What, art thou hurt?
Mercutio: Ay, ay, a scratch, a scratch; marry, 'tis enough.
Where is my page? Go, villain, fetch a surgeon.
Romeo: Courage, man; the hurt cannot be much.
Mercutio: No, 'tis not so deep as a well, nor so wide as a church-door; but 'tis enough, 'twill serve: ask for me to-morrow, and you shall find me a grave man. I am peppered, I warrant, for this world. A plague o' both your houses. . . . Why the devil came you between us? I was hurt under your arm.
Romeo: I thought all for the best. . . .
This gentleman, the prince's near ally,
My very friend, hath got his mortal hurt
In my behalf.
Romeo and Juliet. Act iii, sc. 1, l. 93. The only use of "church-door."

I have peppered two of them.—*I Henry IV,* ii, 4, 212.

They are peppered.—*I Henry IV,* v, 3, 37. The only uses of "peppered."

7
Thou dost me yet but little hurt; thou wilt anon,
I know it by thy trembling.
The Tempest. Act ii, sc. 2, l. 81. [Caliban]

Small hurt.—*Othello,* ii, 3, 381.

8
Quintus: Speak, brother, hast thou hurt thee with the fall?
Martius: O brother, with the dismall'st object hurt
That ever eye with sight made heart lament.
Titus Andronicus. Act ii, sc. 3, l. 203. "Dismall'st" is repeated in i, 1, 384: "Dismall'st day." It occurs in no other play.

9
Troilus: What news, Æneas, from the field to-day?
Æneas: That Paris returned home and hurt.
Troilus and Cressida. Act i, sc. 1, l. 112.

Who said he came home hurt to-day? he 's not hurt.
Troilus and Cressida. Act i, sc. 2, l. 232.

I doubt he be hurt.—*Troilus and Cressida,* i, 2, 302.

Sore hurt and bruised.—*Troilus and Cressida,* v, 5, 12.

Hurt him in eleven places.—*Twelfth Night,* iii, 2, 37. See CHALLENGE, 167:11.

10
Viola: Why do you speak to me? I never hurt you:
You drew your sword upon me without cause,
But I bespake you fair, and hurt you not.
Sir Andrew: If a bloody coxcomb be a hurt, you have hurt me: I think you set nothing by a bloody coxcomb.
Twelfth Night. Act v, sc. 1, l. 190. See also COXCOMB.

Get him to bed, and let his hurt be look'd to.
Twelfth Night. Act v, sc. 1, l. 215. [Olivia]

11
He seeks
To mend the hurt that his unkindness marr'd.
Venus and Adonis, l. 477.

Upon his hurt she looks so steadfastly,
That her sight dazzling makes the wound seem three.
Venus and Adonis, l. 1063. The only use of "steadfastly."

HUSBAND

See also Lord; Wife: Man and Wife

12
Get thee a good husband, and use him as he uses thee.
All's Well that Ends Well. Act i, sc. 1, l. 229. [Parolles]

I will do any modest office, my lord, to help my cousin to a good husband.
Much Ado about Nothing. Act ii, sc. 1, l. 391. [Hero]

My wretched women . . .
Of which there is not one . . . but will deserve
For virtue and true beauty of the soul,
For honesty and decent carriage,
A right good husband, let him be a noble:

And, sure, those men are happy that shall have 'em.
Henry VIII. Act iv, sc. 2, l. 140. [Katharine] The only use of "decent."

You will turn good husband now, Pompey; you will keep the house.
Measure for Measure. Act iii, sc. 2, l. 73. [Lucio]

Play the good husband.—*The Taming of the Shrew,* v, 1, 71.
Allowing husband!—*Winter's Tale,* i, 2, 185.
Angel husband.—*Richard III,* iv, 1, 69.
Gentle husband.—*The Comedy of Errors,* iv, 4, 100.
Honey-sweet husband.—*Henry V,* ii, 3, 1.
Sweet husband.—*The Merry Wives of Windsor,* iv, 2, 189; *Richard II,* v, 2, 107; *Sonnets,* viii.
Virtuous husband.—*King Lear,* iv, 6, 279.

1

Then shalt thou give me with thy kingly hand
What husband in thy power I will command.
All's Well that Ends Well. Act ii, sc. 1, l. 196. [Helena]

When thou canst get the ring upon my finger which never shall come off, and show me a child begotten of thy body that I am father to, then call me husband: but in such a 'then' I write a 'never.'
All's Well that Ends Well. Act iii, sc. 2, l. 59. [Helena, reading]

Your reputation comes too short for my daughter; you are no husband for her.
All's Well that Ends Well. Act v, sc. 3, l. 176. [Lafeu]

If thou be'st yet a fresh uncropped flower,
Choose thou thy husband, and I'll pay thy dower;
For I can guess that by thy honest aid
Thou kep'st a wife herself, thyself a maid.
All's Well that Ends Well. Act v, sc. 3, l. 327. [King] The only use of "uncropped."

2

O, that I knew this husband, which, you say, must charge his horns with garlands!
Antony and Cleopatra. Act i, sc. 2, l. 4. [Charmian] See also Cuckold.

Whose beauty claims
No worse a husband than the best of men.
Antony and Cleopatra. Act ii, sc. 2, l. 130. [Agrippa]

Husband, I come:
Now to that name my courage prove my title!
Antony and Cleopatra. Act v, sc. 2, l. 290. [Cleopatra]

3

I do take thee, Orlando, for my husband.
As You Like It. Act iv, sc. 1, l. 139. [Rosalind] See also Marriage.

I'll have no husband, if you be not he:
Nor ne'er wed woman, if you be not she.
As You Like It. Act v, sc. 4, l. 129. [Rosalind]

4

Hurl the name of husband in my face.
The Comedy of Errors. Act ii, sc. 2, l. 137. [Adriana]

And may it be that you have quite forgot
A husband's office?
The Comedy of Errors. Act iii, sc. 2, l. 1. [Luciana]

Dowsabel did claim me for her husband.
The Comedy of Errors. Act iv, sc. 1, l. 110. [Dromio of Syracuse] The only mention of Dowsabel.

5

Courtezan: How say you now? is not your husband mad?
Adriana: His incivility confirms no less.
The Comedy of Errors. Act iv, sc. 4, l. 48. The only use of "incivility."

Abbess: Be quiet, people. Wherefore throng you hither?
Adriana: To fetch my poor distracted husband hence.
The Comedy of Errors. Act v, sc. 1, l. 38.

I will attend my husband, be his nurse,
Diet his sickness, for it is my office.
The Comedy of Errors. Act v, sc. 1, l. 98. [Adriana]

6

Ay me, it is my husband! Witness you,
That he is borne about invisible:
Even now we housed him in the abbey here;
And now he's there past thought of human reason.
The Comedy of Errors. Act v, sc. 1, l. 186. [Adriana]

I see two husbands, or mine eyes deceive me.
The Comedy of Errors. Act v, sc. 1, l. 331. [Adriana]

I will loose his bonds And gain a husband.
The Comedy of Errors. Act v, sc. 1, l. 340. [Abbess]

7

I will remain
The loyal'st husband that did e'er plight troth.
Cymbeline. Act i, sc. 1, l. 95. [Posthumus] The only use of "loyal'st."

O, that husband! My supreme crown of grief!
Cymbeline. Act i, sc. 6, l. 3. [Imogen]

In my life what comfort, when I am
Dead to my husband?
Cymbeline. Act iii, sc. 4, l. 132. [Imogen]

8

Make malicious sport
In mincing with his sword her husband's limbs.
Hamlet. Act ii, sc. 2, l. 536. [First Player] The only use of "mincing" in this sense.

Slaughter'd husband.—*The Rape of Lucrece,* l. 1376.

9

In second husband let me be accurst!
None wed the second but who kill'd the first.
Hamlet. Act iii, sc. 2, l. 189. [Player Queen]

A second time I kill my husband dead,
When second husband kisses me in bed.
Hamlet. Act iii, sc. 2, l. 194. [Player Queen]

Player King: So think thou wilt no second husband wed;
But die thy thoughts when thy first lord is dead.
Player Queen: Nor earth to me give food, nor heaven light!
Sport and repose lock from me day and night!
To desperation turn my trust and hope!
An anchor's cheer in prison be my scope!
Each opposite that blanks the face of joy
Meet what I would have well and it destroy!

Both here and hence pursue me lasting strife,
If, once a widow, ever I be wife!
Hamlet. Act iii, sc. 2, l. 224. The only use of "anchor" in the sense of anchorite.

I bury a second husband.—*All's Well that Ends Well,* i, 1, 2.

Third husband.—*The Merchant of Venice,* iii, 1, 12.

Escalus: Hath she had any more than one husband?
Pompey: Nine, sir; Overdone by the last.
Measure for Measure. Act ii, sc. 1, l. 210.

1
Here is your husband; like a mildew'd ear,
Blasting his wholesome brother.
Hamlet. Act iii, sc. 4, l. 64. [Hamlet] The only use of "mildew'd."

2
How doth thy husband? I love him well; he is an honest man.
I Henry IV. Act iii, sc. 3, l. 107. [Prince of Wales]

3
I . . . never shall have strength of life enough
To rain upon remembrance with mine eyes,
That it may grow and sprout as high as heaven,
For recordation to my noble husband.
II Henry IV. Act ii, sc. 3, l. 58. [Lady Percy] The only use of "sprout." "Recordation" is used again in *Troilus and Cressida,* v, 2, 116.

Your husband, He is noble, wise, judicious.
Macbeth. Act iv, sc. 2, l. 15. [Ross]

Noble husband!—*Richard III,* ii, 2, 48.

Royal husband.—*The Winter's Tale,* i, 2, 107; iii, 2, 17.

4
I deem you an ill husband, and am glad
To have you therein my companion.
Henry VIII. Act iii, sc. 2, l. 142. [King Henry]

Unworthy husband.—*All's Well that Ends Well,* iii, 4, 26; 30.

5
What woman-post is this? hath she no husband
That will take pains to blow a horn before her?
King John. Act i, sc. 1, l. 218. [Bastard] The only use of "woman-post."

Many a widow's husband grovelling lies,
Coldly embracing the discolour'd earth.
King John. Act ii, sc. 1, l. 305. [French Herald] The only use of "grovelling."

6 Ay, alack, how new
Is husband in my mouth! even for that name,
Which still this time my tongue did ne'er pronounce.
King John. Act iii, sc. 1, l. 306. [Blanch]

7
Why have my sisters husbands, if they say
They love you all?
King Lear. Act i, sc. 1, l. 101. [Cordelia]

I know your lady does not love her husband.
King Lear. Act iv, sc. 5, l. 23. [Regan]

Love thy husband.—*I Henry IV,* iii, 3, 193.

8 I marvel our mild husband
Not met us on the way.
King Lear. Act iv, sc. 2, l. 1. [Goneril]

You have so lost a father
That you must lose a husband.
King Lear. Act i, sc. 1, l. 249. [Burgundy]

9
Son: Nay, how will you do for a husband?
Lady Macduff: Why, I can buy me twenty at any market.
Macbeth. Act iv, sc. 2, l. 39.

For his possessions,
Although by confiscation they are ours,
We do instate and widow you withal,
To buy you a better husband.
Measure for Measure. Act v, sc. 1, l. 427. [Duke] The only use of "confiscation" and "instate."

Gloucester: He that bereft thee, lady, of thy husband,
Did it to help thee to a better husband.
Lady Anne: His better doth not breathe upon the earth.
Richard III. Act i, sc. 2, l. 138.

I seek you a better husband.
The Merry Wives of Windsor. Act iii, sc. 4, l. 88. [Mrs. Page] The only uses of "better husband."

Combinate husband.—*Measure for Measure,* iii, 1, 231. The only use of "combinate."

10
He is your husband on a pre-contract:
To bring you thus together, 'tis no sin,
Sith that the justice of your title to him
Doth flourish the deceit.
Measure for Measure. Act iv, sc. 1, l. 72. [Duke] The only use of "pre-contract."

11
Mariana: I have known my husband; yet my husband
Knows not that ever he knew me.
Lucio: He was drunk then, my lord: it can be no better.
Measure for Measure. Act v, sc. 1, l. 186.

She that accuses him of fornication,
In self-same manner doth accuse my husband.
Measure for Measure. Act v, sc. 1, l. 195. [Mariana]

Mariana: I hope you will not mock me with a husband.
Duke: It is your husband mock'd you with a husband.
Measure for Measure. Act v, sc. 1, l. 422.

12
This reasoning is not in the fashion to choose me a husband. O me, the word 'choose!' I may neither choose whom I would nor refuse whom I dislike.
The Merchant of Venice. Act i, sc. 2, l. 23. [Portia]

These be Christian husbands. I have a daughter;
Would any of the stock of Barrabas
Had been her husband rather than a Christian.
The Merchant of Venice. Act iv, sc. 1, l. 295. [Shylock] The only mention of Barrabas.

13
She gives you to notify that her husband

will be absence from his house between ten and eleven.
The Merry Wives of Windsor. Act ii, sc. 2, l. 85. [Mistress Quickly] "Notify" is repeated in *Othello,* iii, 1, 31.

Her husband will be from home.—*The Merry Wives of Windsor,* ii, 2, 91.

Her husband is seldom from home.—*The Merry Wives of Windsor,* ii, 2, 104.

1
The jealous rascally knave her husband.
The Merry Wives of Windsor. Act ii, sc. 2, l. 275. [Falstaff]

The peaking Cornuto her husband.
The Merry Wives of Windsor. Act iii, sc. 5, l. 71. [Falstaff] The only use of "peaking" and "Cornuto" (cuckold).

2
Ford: I think, if your husbands were dead, you two would marry.
Mrs. Page: Be sure of that,—two other husbands.
Merry Wives of Windsor. Act iii, sc. 2, l. 14.

I would thy husband were dead.
The Merry Wives of Windsor. Act iii, sc. 3, l. 52. [Falstaff]

3
Her husband goes this morning a-birding.
The Merry Wives of Windsor. Act iii, sc. 5, l. 45. [Mistress Quickly] Repeated in l. 130. The only use of "a-birding."

Your husband is in his old lunes again.
The Merry Wives of Windsor. Act iv, sc. 2, l. 21. [Mrs. Page] "Lunes" is used again in *Troilus and Cressida,* ii, 3, 139, and *The Winter's Tale,* ii, 2, 30.

Mrs. Ford: But is my husband coming?
Mrs. Page: Ay, in good sadness, is he.
The Merry Wives of Windsor. Act iv, sc. 2, l. 92.

Your husband 's coming.—*The Merry Wives of Windsor,* iii, 3, 121.

Your husband 's here at hand.—*The Merry Wives of Windsor,* iii, 3, 134.

4
I hope you have no intent to turn husband, have you?
Much Ado about Nothing. Act i, sc. 1, l. 195. [Benedick]

Let me be vilely painted, and in such great letters as they write 'Here is good horse to hire,' let them signify under my sign 'Here you may see Benedick the married man.'
Much Ado about Nothing. Act i, sc. 1, l. 266. [Benedick]

Benedick is not the unhopefullest husband that I know.
Much Ado about Nothing. Act ii, sc. 1, l. 392. [Don Pedro] The only use of "unhopefullest."

5
By my troth, niece, thou wilt never get thee a husband, if thou be so shrewd of thy tongue.
Much Ado about Nothing. Act ii, sc. 1, l. 19. [Leonato]

He that is more than a youth is not for me, and he that is less than a man, I am not for him.
Much Ado about Nothing. Act ii, sc. 1, l. 40. [Beatrice]

Leonato: I hope to see you one day fitted with a husband.
Beatrice: Not till God make men of some other metal than earth.
Much Ado about Nothing. Act ii, sc. 1, l. 60.

Your father got excellent husbands, if a maid could come by them.
Much Ado about Nothing. Act ii, sc. 1, l. 337. [Beatrice]

She cannot endure to hear tell of a husband.
Much Ado about Nothing. Act ii, sc. 1, l. 362. [Don Pedro]

I think you would have me say, 'saving your reverence, a husband.'
Much Ado about Nothing. Act iii, sc. 4, l. 32. [Margaret]

6
Is there any harm in 'the heavier for a husband'? None, I think, an it be the right husband and the right wife; otherwise 'tis light, and not heavy.
Much Ado about Nothing. Act iii, sc. 4, l. 34. [Margaret]

Beatrice: By my troth, I am exceeding ill: heigh-ho!
Margaret: For a hawk, a horse, or a husband?
Much Ado about Nothing. Act iii, sc. 4, l. 53.

I may sit in a corner and cry heigh-ho for a husband!
Much Ado about Nothing. Act ii, sc. 1, l. 332. [Beatrice] "Heigh-ho" is repeated in *As You Like It,* ii, 7, 180; 182. It occurs only in these two plays.

7 Here 's my husband,
And so much duty as my mother show'd
To you, preferring you before her father,
So much I challenge that I may profess
Due to the Moor my lord.
Othello. Act i, sc. 3, l. 185. [Desdemona] The only use of "preferring."

I dare think he 'll prove to Desdemona
A most dear husband.
Othello. Act ii, sc. 1, l. 299. [Iago] "Dear husband" is repeated in *Henry V,* i, 2, 285, and in *Cymbeline,* ii, 1, 66.

8
Desdemona: Dost thou in conscience think, —tell me, Emilia,—
That there be women do abuse their husbands
In such gross kind?
Emilia: There be some such, no question.
Desdemona: Wouldst thou do such a deed for all the world? . . .
Emilia: The world 's a huge thing: it is a great price
For a small vice. . . . Who would not make her husband a cuckold to make him a monarch?
Othello. Act iv, sc. 3, l. 61.

I say thy husband: dost understand the word?
My friend, thy husband.
Othello. Act v, sc. 2, l. 153. [Othello]

9
I sought a husband, in which labour
I found that kindness in a father:
He 's father, son, and husband mild;

I mother, wife, and yet his child.
Pericles. Act i, sc. 1, l. 66. [Pericles, reading]

So thy surviving husband shall remain
The scornful mark of every open eye.
The Rape of Lucrece, l. 519. "Surviving" is repeated in l. 223, and occurs nowhere else.

My husband is thy friend; for his sake spare me.
The Rape of Lucrece, l. 582.

1
Ah, my sour husband, my hard-hearted lord.
Richard II. Act v, sc. 3, l. 121. [Duchess of York]

My wayward husband.—*Othello,* iii, 3, 292.

2
What though I kill'd her husband and her father?
The readiest way to make the wench amends
Is to become her husband and her father.
Richard III. Act i, sc. 1, l. 154. [Gloucester]

I have bewept a worthy husband's death,
And lived by looking on his images.
Richard III. Act ii, sc. 2, l. 49. [Duchess of York]

Bewept to the grave did go.
Hamlet, iv, 5, 38. The only uses of "bewept."

Death hath snatch'd my husband from mine arms,
And pluck'd two crutches from my feeble limbs.
Richard III. Act ii, sc. 2, l. 57. [Duchess of York]

3 My husband—God be with his soul!
A' was a merry man.
Romeo and Juliet. Act i, sc. 3, l. 39. [Nurse]

Thy husband in thy bosom there lies dead.
Romeo and Juliet. Act v, sc. 3, l. 155. [Friar Laurence]

4
So shall I live, supposing thou art true,
Like a deceived husband; so love's face
May still seem love to me, though alter'd new;
Thy looks with me, thy heart in other place.
Sonnets. No. xciii.

My husband is deceived.—*The Merry Wives of Windsor,* iii, 3, 190.

5
Hortensio: Marry, sir, to get a husband for her sister.
Gremio: A husband! a devil.
Hortensio: I say, a husband.
Gremio: I say, a devil.
Taming of the Shrew. Act i, sc. 1, l. 123.

She is your treasure, she must have a husband.
The Taming of the Shrew. Act ii, sc. 1, l. 32. [Katharina]

I am a husband for your turn.
The Taming of the Shrew. Act ii, sc. 1, l. 274. [Petruchio]

6
Petruchio: Katharine, I charge thee, tell these headstrong women
What duty they do owe their lords and husbands. . . .
Katharina: Thy husband is thy lord, thy life, thy keeper,
Thy head, thy sovereign; one that cares for thee,
And for thy maintenance commits his body
To painful labour both by sea and land,
To watch the night in storms, the day in cold,
Whilst thou liest warm at home, secure and safe;
And craves no other tribute at thy hands
But love, fair looks and true obedience;
Too little payment for so great a debt.
Such duty as the subject owes the prince
Even such a woman oweth to her husband;
And when she is froward, peevish, sullen, sour,
And not obedient to his honest will,
What is she but a foul contending rebel
And graceless traitor to her loving lord?
Taming of the Shrew. Act v, sc. 2, l. 130.

7
Drag hence her husband to some secret hole,
And make his dead trunk pillow to our lust.
Titus Andronicus. Act ii, sc. 3, l. 129. [Chiron]

8
Olivia: Whither, my lord? Cesario, husband, stay.
Duke: Husband!
Olivia: Ay, husband: can he that deny?
Duke: Her husband, sirrah!
Viola: No, my lord, not I.
Twelfth Night. Act v, sc. 1, l. 146.

9
Thou dotard! thou art woman-tired, unroosted
By thy dame Partlet here.
The Winter's Tale. Act ii, sc. 3, l. 74. [Leontes] The only use of "woman-tired" and "unroosted."

How now, Dame Partlet the hen!—*I Henry IV,* iii, 3, 60. The only references to Dame Partlet.

10 I 'll not seek far— . . . to find thee
An honourable husband.
Winter's Tale. Act v, sc. 3, l. 141. [Leontes]

HYMN

11
Come, ho! and wake Diana with a hymn.
The Merchant of Venice. Act v, sc. 1, l. 66. [Lorenzo]

12
Chanting faint hymns to the cold fruitless moon.
A Midsummer-Night's Dream, i, 1, 73. See under Nun.

13
Now, music, sound, and sing your solemn hymn.
Much Ado about Nothing. Act v, sc. 3, l. 11. [Claudio]

Our solemn hymns to sullen dirges change.
Romeo and Juliet. Act iv, sc. 5, l. 88. [Capulet]

When her mournful hymns did hush the night.
Sonnets. No. cii.

Sings hymns at heaven's gate.
Sonnets. No. xxix.

Cry 'Amen' To every hymn.
Sonnets. No. lxxxv.

Doleful hymn.—*King John,* v, 7, 22.

Hymn or carol.—*Midsummer-Night's Dream,* ii, 1, 102. The only uses of "hymn" and "hymns."

HYPOCRISY

1 With devotion's visage
And pious action we do sugar o'er
The devil himself.
Hamlet. Act iii, sc. 1, l. 47. [Polonius] The only use of "sugar" as a verb.

2 Was your father dear to you?
Or are you like the painting of a sorrow,
A face without a heart?
Hamlet. Act iv, sc. 7, l. 108. [King]

By this face,
This seeming brow of justice, did he win
The hearts of all that he did angle for.
I Henry IV. Act iv, sc. 3, l. 82. [Hotspur]

3
Prince of Wales: What wouldst thou think of me, if I should weep?
Poins: I would think thee a most princely hypocrite.
II Henry IV. Act ii, sc. 2, l. 56.

My tongue and soul in this be hypocrites.
Hamlet. Act iii, sc. 2, l. 415. [Hamlet]

Calls virtue hypocrite.—*Hamlet,* iii, 4, 42.

I dare swear he is no hypocrite, but prays from his heart.
Much Ado about Nothing. Act i, sc. 1, l. 152. [Don Pedro]

An you be a cursing hypocrite once, you must be looked to.
Much Ado about Nothing. Act v, sc. 1, l. 216. [Dogberry]

Like an hypocrite.—*Pericles,* i, 1, 122.

An hypocrite, a virgin-violator.—*Measure for Measure,* v, 1, 41. The only use of "virgin-violator."

An hypocrite indeed.—*II Henry IV,* ii, 2, 64.

Scarlet hypocrite!—*I Henry VI,* i, 3, 56. The only uses of "hypocrite."

4
How smooth and even they do bear themselves!
As if allegiance in their bosoms sat,
Crowned with faith and constant loyalty.
Henry V. Act ii, sc. 2, l. 3. [Westmoreland]

5
Beguiles him as the mournful crocodile
With sorrow snares relenting passengers.
II Henry VI. Act iii, sc. 1, l. 226. [Queen Margaret]

Each drop she falls would prove a crocodile.
Othello. Act iv, sc. 1, l. 257. See under TEAR.

6
Cry 'Content' to that which grieves my heart.
III Henry VI. Act iii, sc. 2, l. 183. [Gloucester]

7 I want that glib and oily art,
To speak and purpose not; since what I well intend,
I 'll do 't before I speak.
King Lear. Act i, sc. 1, l. 227. [Cordelia]

This is some fellow,
Who, having been praised for bluntness, doth affect
A saucy roughness, and constrains the garb
Quite from his nature: he cannot flatter, he,
An honest mind and plain, he must speak truth!
An they will take it, so; if not, he 's plain.
These kind of knaves I know, which in this plainness
Harbour more craft and more corrupter ends
Than twenty silly ducking observants
That stretch their duties nicely.
King Lear. Act ii, sc. 2, l. 101. [Cornwall] The only use of "observants" as a noun.

8 Thou simular man of virtue
That art incestuous.
King Lear. Act iii, sc. 2, l. 54. [King Lear] "Simular" is repeated in *Cymbeline,* v, 5, 200.

Behold yon simpering dame, . . .
That minces virtue, and does shake the head
To hear of pleasure's name;
The fitchew, nor the soiled horse, goes to 't
With a more riotous appetite.
King Lear. Act iv, sc. 6, l. 120. [King Lear] "Simpering" is repeated in *As You Like It,* Epil., 16; and "fitchew" (polecat) in *Troilus and Cressida,* v, 1, 67, and in *Othello,* iv, 1, 150.

Thou rascal beadle, hold thy bloody hand!
Why dost thou lash that whore? Strip thine own back;
Thou hotly lust'st to use her in that kind
For which thou whipp'st her.
King Lear. Act iv, sc. 6, l. 164. [King Lear]

When he most burn'd in heart-wish'd luxury,
He preach'd pure maid, and praised cold chastity.
A Lover's Complaint, l. 314. The only use of "heart-wish'd."

9
Now step I forth to whip hypocrisy.
Love's Labour 's Lost. Act iv, sc. 3, l. 151. [Biron]

A huge translation of hypocrisy.
Love's Labour 's Lost. Act v, sc. 1, l. 51. [Katharine] The only use of "translation."

This spice of your hypocrisy.—*Henry VIII,* ii, 3, 26.

Hypocrisy against the devil.—*Othello,* iv, 1, 6.

False hypocrisy.—*Richard II,* v, 3, 107. The only uses of "hypocrisy."

10 We
Must lave our honours in these flattering streams,
And make our faces vizards to our hearts,
Disguising what they are.
Macbeth. Act iii, sc. 2, l. 32. [Macbeth]

11 Heaven in my mouth,
As if I did but only chew his name;
And in my heart the strong and swelling evil
Of my conception.
Measure for Measure. Act ii, sc. 4, l. 4. [Angelo]

This outward-sainted deputy,
Whose settled visage and deliberate word
Nips youth i' the head and follies doth emmew
As falcon doth the fowl, is yet a devil;

His filth within being cast, he would appear
A pond as deep as hell.
Measure for Measure. Act iii, sc. 1, l. 89. [Isabella] The only use of "outward-sainted" and "emmew."

1
An evil soul producing holy witness
Is like a villain with a smiling cheek,
A goodly apple rotten at the heart.
The Merchant of Venice. Act i, sc. 3, l. 100. [Antonio]

I like not fair terms and a villain's mind.
The Merchant of Venice. Act i, sc. 3, l. 181. [Bassanio]

2
O, what authority and show of truth
Can cunning sin cover itself withal!
Much Ado about Nothing. Act iv, sc. 1, l. 36. [Claudio]

Hiding base sin in plaits of majesty.
The Rape of Lucrece, l. 93.

3 Like a constant and confirmed devil,
He entertain'd a show so seeming just,
And therein so ensconced his secret evil,
That jealousy itself could not mistrust.
The Rape of Lucrece, l. 1513. The only use of "ensconced."

Beguiled
With outward honesty, but yet defiled
With inward vice.
The Rape of Lucrece, l. 1544.

4
Whate'er thy thoughts or thy heart's workings be,
Thy looks should nothing thence but sweetness tell.
How like Eve's apple doth thy beauty grow,
If thy sweet virtue answer not thy show!
Sonnets. No. xciii.

5
And wonder greatly that man's face can fold
In pleasing smiles such murderous tyranny.
Titus Andronicus. Act ii, sc. 3, l. 266. [Tamora]

I

ICE

6
Hot ice and wondrous strange snow.
A Midsummer-Night's Dream. Act v, sc. 1, l. 59. [Theseus]

Congealed ice.—*Measure for Measure,* iii, 2, 118.

Thick-ribbed ice.—*Measure for Measure,* iii, 1, 123. The only use of "thick-ribbed."

Ice of chastity.—*As You Like It,* iii, 4, 18. See under CHASTITY.

7
Tut, tut, thou art all ice, thy kindness freezeth.
Richard III. Act iv, sc. 2, l. 22. [King Richard] "Tut, tut" is used again in l. 121, and three times in other plays.

8
If you break the ice and do this feat.
The Taming of the Shrew. Act i, sc. 2, l. 267. [Tranio] The only use of "break the ice."

Smooth the ice.—*King John,* iv, 2, 13.

9
Curtis: Who is that calls so coldly?
Grumio: A piece of ice: if thou doubt it, thou mayst slide from my shoulder to my heel with no greater a run but my head and my neck.
The Taming of the Shrew. Act iv, sc. 1, l. 13.

Candied with ice.—*Timon of Athens,* iv, 3, 226.

10
Let us not hang like roping icicles
Upon our houses' thatch.
Henry V, iii, 5, 23. See under BLOOD.

When icicles hang by the wall.
Love's Labour's Lost, v, 2, 922. See under WINTER.

Hang like an icicle on a Dutchman's beard.
Twelfth Night, iii, 2, 29. See under DISLIKE.

Thaws the icicles.—*The Merchant of Venice,* ii, 1, 5. The only uses of "icicle" and "icicles."

IDENTITY

See also Personality

11
Ipse is he: now, you are not ipse, for I am he.
As You Like It. Act v, sc. 1, l. 48. [Touchstone] The only use of "ipse."

I am myself alone.—*III Henry VI,* v, 6, 83.

12 Thou art not thyself;
For thou exist'st on many a thousand grains
That issue out of dust.
Measure for Measure. Act iii, sc. 1, l. 19. [Duke]

13
Doth any here know me? This is not Lear:
Doth Lear walk thus? speak thus? Where are his eyes?
Either his notion weakens, his discernings
Are lethargied—Ha! waking? 'tis not so,
Who is it that can tell me who I am?
King Lear. Act i, sc. 4, l. 246. [King Lear] The only use of "lethargied."

14
Am not I Christopher Sly, old Sly's son-of-Burton-heath, by birth a pedlar, by education a card-maker, by transmutation a bear-herd, and now by present profession a tinker?
The Taming of the Shrew. Induction, sc. 2, l. 18. [Sly] The only use of "card-maker" and "transmutation." "Bear-herd" is repeated in *II Henry IV,* i, 2, 192: "True valour is turned bear-herd." The only mention of Burton-heath.

15
They shall be themselves.
The Tempest. Act v, sc. 1, l. 32. [Prospero]

1
My lady's a Cataian, we are politicians, Malvolio's a Peg-a-Ramsey, and 'Three merry men be we.'

Twelfth Night. Act ii, sc. 3, l. 80. [Sir Toby] "Cataian" is repeated in *The Merry Wives of Windsor,* ii, 1, 148. A Cataian was a man or woman of Cathay, hence a scoundrel. The only mention of Peg-a-Ramsey, the heroine of an old song of that name.

What kin are you to me?
What countryman? what name? what parentage?

Twelfth Night. Act v, sc. 1, l. 237. [Sebastian] The word "identity" does not occur in Shakespeare.

IDIOT

See also Fool

2 Idiots in this case of favour would
Be wisely definite.

Cymbeline. Act i, sc. 6, l. 42. [Iachimo] The only use of "definite."

3 What's here?
The portrait of a blinking idiot.

The Merchant of Venice. Act ii, sc. 9, l. 54. [Prince of Arragon] The only use of "portrait." "Portraiture" occurs in *Hamlet,* v, 2, 78. "Blinking" is repeated in *All's Well that Ends Well,* i, 1, 189: "Blinking Cupid."

Silly-jeering idiots.—*The Rape of Lucrece,* l. 1812. The only use of "silly-jeering."

Coxcomb, idiot, patch!—*The Comedy of Errors,* iii, 1, 32.

That idiot, laughter.—*King John,* iii, 3, 45.

Told by an idiot.—*Macbeth,* v, 5, 27.

4
That Slender, though well landed, is an idiot.

The Merry Wives of Windsor. Act iv, sc. 4, l. 86. [Mrs. Page] The only use of "well landed."

5
What hempen home-spuns have we swaggering here?

A Midsummer-Night's Dream. Act iii, sc. 1, l. 79. [Puck] The only use of "home-spuns." "Hempen" is repeated in *II Henry VI,* iv, 7, 95: "Hempen caudle"; and in *Henry V,* iii, Prol., 8: "Hempen tackle."

6
As addle as an egg.

Romeo and Juliet. Act iii, sc. 1, l. 26. [Mercutio]

Addle egg.—*Troilus and Cressida,* i, 2, 145; 146. The only uses of "addle." "Addled" does not occur.

7
An idiot holds his bauble for a god
And keeps the oath which by that god he swears.

Titus Andronicus. Act v, sc. 1, l. 79. [Aaron]

8
Mars his idiot! do, rudeness; do, camel; do, do.

Troilus and Cressida. Act ii, sc. 1, l. 58. [Thersites]

Play the idiots.—*Troilus and Cressida,* iii, 3, 135.

9
I know this letter will make a contemplative idiot of him.

Twelfth Night. Act ii, sc. 5, l. 22. [Maria] "Contemplative" is repeated in *Love's Labour's Lost,* i, 1, 14.

IDLENESS

See also Ease

10
Antony: But that your royalty
Holds idleness your subject, I should take you
For idleness itself.
Cleopatra: 'Tis sweating labour
To bear such idleness so near the heart.

Antony and Cleopatra. Act i, sc. 3, l. 91.

11
I am helping you to mar that which God made, a poor unworthy brother of yours, with idleness.

As You Like It. Act i, sc. 1, l. 35. [Orlando]

12
I know you all, and will awhile uphold
The unyoked humour of your idleness.

I Henry IV. Act i, sc. 2, l. 218. [Prince of Wales] "Unyoked" is repeated in *II Henry IV,* iv, 2, 103: "Like youthful steers unyoked, they take their courses."

Apes of idleness!—*II Henry IV,* iv, 5, 123.

Shapeless idleness.—*The Two Gentlemen of Verona,* i, 1, 8.

13
Living idly here in pomp and ease.

I Henry VI. Act i, sc. 1, l. 142. [Duke of Bedford]

Why live we idly here?—*I Henry VI,* i, 2, 13.

Idly I stood looking on.—*The Taming of the Shrew,* i, 1, 155.

Sit idly in the sun.—*Troilus and Cressida,* iii, 3, 233.

Idly sit.—*Coriolanus,* ii, 2, 80.

14
Drones suck not eagles' blood but rob bee-hives.

II Henry VI. Act iv, sc. 1, l. 109. [Suffolk] The only use of "bee-hives."

Drones hive not with me.

The Merchant of Venice. Act ii, sc. 5, l. 48. [Shylock]

15
Eat honey like a drone From other's labours.

Pericles. Act ii, Gower, l. 18.

We would purge the land of these drones, that rob the bee of her honey.

Pericles. Act ii, sc. 1, l. 50. [Fisherman]

Lazy-yawning drone.—*Henry V,* i, 2, 204. The only use of "lazy-yawning."

Thou drone, thou snail!—*The Comedy of Errors,* ii, 2, 196. The only uses of "drone."

I, a drone-like bee.—*The Rape of Lucrece,* l. 836. The only use of "drone-like."

16
As idle as she may hang together, for want of company.

The Merry Wives of Windsor. Act iii, sc. 2, l. 13. [Ford]

Sterile with idleness.—*Othello,* i, 3, 328.

1
No occupation; all men idle, all;
And women too, but innocent and pure.
The Tempest. Act ii, sc. 1, l. 154. [Gonzalo]
All idle: whores and knaves.
The Tempest. Act ii, sc. 1, l. 166. [Antonio]
2
No, gods, I am no idle votarist.
Timon of Athens. Act iv, sc. 3, l. 26. [Timon]
I must be idle.—*Hamlet,* iii, 2, 95.
Idle and unactive.—*Coriolanus,* i, 1, 102. See under BELLY.

IDOLATRY

See also Image

3
Pure, pure idolatry.
Love's Labour 's Lost. Act iv, sc. 3, l. 75. [Biron]
4 Thy gracious self,
Which is the god of my idolatry.
Romeo and Juliet. Act ii, sc. 2, l. 113. [Juliet]
Dotes in idolatry.—*A Midsummer-Night's Dream,* i, 1, 109.
Let not my love be call'd idolatry.
Sonnets. No. cv.
5
But O how vile an idol proves this god!
Twelfth Night. Act iii, sc. 4, l. 399. [Antonio]
6 'Tis mad idolatry
To make the service greater than the god.
Troilus and Cressida. Act ii, sc. 2, l. 56. [Hector]
Thou picture of what thou seemest, and idol of idiot-worshippers.
Troilus and Cressida. Act v, sc. 1, l. 6. [Thersites] The only use of "idiot-worshippers."
7
Was this the idol that you worship so?
The Two Gentlemen of Verona. Act ii, sc. 4, l. 144. [Proteus]
I am very loath to be your idol, sir.
The Two Gentlemen of Verona. Act iv, sc. 2, l. 129. [Silvia]
Soul's idol.—*Hamlet,* ii, 2, 109.
8
And, were there sense in his idolatry,
My substance should be statue in thy stead.
The Two Gentlemen of Verona. Act iv, sc. 4, l. 205. [Julia]
9
Fie, lifeless picture, cold and senseless stone,
Well-painted idol, image dull and dead,
Statue contenting but the eye alone,
Thing like a man, but of no woman bred!
Venus and Adonis, l. 211. "Well-painted" is repeated in *Othello,* iv, 1, 268: "Well-painted passion"; and in *The Rape of Lucrece,* l. 1443: "Well-painted piece."

IGNORANCE

10 We, ignorant of ourselves,
Beg often our own harms.
Antony and Cleopatra. Act ii, sc. 1, l. 5. [Menas] See under PRAYER.
The greater cantle of the world is lost
With very ignorance.
Antony and Cleopatra. Act iii, sc. 10, l. 6. [Scarus] "Cantle" (portion, fragment) is used only once again in the plays, in *I Henry IV,* iii, 1, 100.
Thine ignorance makes thee away.
All 's Well that Ends Well. Act i, sc. 1, l. 226. [Parolles]
Vail your ignorance.—*Coriolanus,* iii, 1, 98.
11
The yea and no Of general ignorance.
Coriolanus. Act iii, sc. 1, l. 145. [Coriolanus]
Your ignorance, which finds not till it feels.
Coriolanus. Act iii, sc. 3, l. 129. [Coriolanus]
The regions
Do smilingly revolt; and who resist
Are mock'd for valiant ignorance,
And perish constant fools.
Coriolanus. Act iv, sc. 6, l. 102. [Cominius] "Smilingly" is repeated in *King Lear,* v, 3, 199.
A violent popular ignorance.—*Coriolanus,* v, 2, 43.
12
I am ignorant in what I am commanded.
Cymbeline, iii, 2, 23. See under COMMAND.
O, I am ignorance itself in this!
I Henry IV. Act iii, sc. 1, l. 213. [Mortimer]
I am ignorant and cannot guess.
I Henry VI. Act ii, sc. 5, l. 60. [Plantagenet]
I am mainly ignorant What place this is.
King Lear. Act iv, sc. 7, l. 65. [King Lear]
13 O, answer me!
Let me not burst in ignorance.
Hamlet. Act i, sc. 4, l. 46. [Hamlet]
14
Ignorant of his birth.
II Henry VI, iv, 2, 152. See under BIRTH.
Ignorant of her good.—*Measure for Measure,* iv, 3, 114.
Ignorant of her worth.—*The Merchant of Venice,* i, 1, 167.
Ignorant to see 't.—*Coriolanus,* ii, 3, 182.
15
O gross and miserable ignorance!
II Henry VI. Act iv, sc. 2, l. 178. [Stafford]
Barbarous ignorance.—*King John,* iv, 2, 58.
Great ignorance.—*King Lear,* iv, 5, 9.
Poor ignorance.—*Timon of Athens,* v, 4, 69.
Short-armed ignorance.—*Troilus and Cressida,* ii, 3, 16. The only use of "short-armed."
Ignorance made drunk.—*Othello,* iii, 3, 405.
Honourable points of ignorance.—*Henry VIII,* i, 3, 26.
16
O graceless men! they know not what they do.
II Henry VI. Act iv, sc. 4, l. 38. [King Henry]
17 Ignorance is the curse of God,
Knowledge the wing wherewith we fly to heaven.
II Henry VI. Act iv, sc. 7, l. 78. [Lord Say]
The common curse of mankind, . . . ignorance.
Troilus and Cressida, ii, 3, 31. See under CURSE.
There is no darkness but ignorance.
Twelfth Night, iv, 2, 46. See under HOUSE.
18
That unlettered small-knowing soul.
Love's Labour 's Lost. Act i, sc. 1, l. 253. [King Ferdinand] The only use of "small-knowing."

His undressed, unpolished, uneducated, unpruned, untrained, or rather, unlettered, or ratherest, unconfirmed fashion.

Love's Labour 's Lost. Act iv, sc. 2, l. 17. [Holofernes] The only use of "undressed," "uneducated," and "ratherest."

His companies unletter'd.—*Henry V,* i, 1, 55. The only uses of "unlettered."

1 His ignorance were wise,
Where now his knowledge must prove ignorance.

Love's Labour 's Lost. Act ii, sc. 1, l. 102. [Princess of France]

2
Holofernes: O thou monster Ignorance, how deformed dost thou look!
Sir Nathaniel: Sir, he hath never fed of the dainties that are bred in a book; he hath not eat paper, as it were; he hath not drunk ink: his intellect is not replenished.

Love's Labour 's Lost. Act iv, sc. 2, l. 23.

3
All ignorant that soul that sees thee without wonder.

Love's Labour 's Lost. Act iv, sc. 2, l. 117. [Sir Nathaniel, reading] Repeated in *The Passionate Pilgrim,* l. 65.

4
Most ignorant of what he 's most assured.

Measure for Measure, ii, 2, 119. See under MAN.

Thou art most ignorant.—*The Winter's Tale,* ii, 1, 173.

So ignorant.—*Cymbeline,* iv, 3, 11.

Being ignorant.—*Macbeth,* i, 5, 13.

5
Angelo: Either you are ignorant,
Or seem so craftily; and that 's not good.
Isabella: Let me be ignorant, and in nothing good,
But graciously to know I am no better.

Measure for Measure. Act ii, sc. 4, l. 74. "Craftily" is repeated in *Othello,* ii, 3, 41.

6
Fie, what the ignorance is!

The Merry Wives of Windsor. Act i, sc. 1, l. 181. [Evans]

Ignorance itself is a plummet o'er me.

The Merry Wives of Windsor. Act v, sc. 5, l. 172. [Falstaff] "Plummet" is repeated twice in *The Tempest,* iii, 3, 101; v, 1, 56.

7
O heavy ignorance! thou praisest the worst best.

Othello. Act ii, sc. 1, l. 144. [Desdemona]

O gull! O dolt! As ignorant as dirt!

Othello. Act v, sc. 2, l. 163. [Emilia]

Asses, fools, dolts!—*Troilus and Cressida,* i, 2, 262. The only uses of "dolt" and "dolts."

8
And dull unfeeling barren ignorance
Is made my gaoler to attend on me.

Richard II. Act i, sc. 3, l. 168. [Mowbray]

You come to reprehend my ignorance.

Richard III. Act iii, sc. 7, l. 113. [Gloucester] "Reprehend" is repeated in *Love's Labour 's Lost,* i, 1, 184, and in *A Midsummer-Night's Dream,* v, 1, 436.

9
Ignorant of what thou art.

The Tempest. Act i, sc. 2, l. 18. [Prospero]

Ignorant what it is.—*Love's Labour 's Lost,* ii, 1, 101.

Ignorant what to fear.—*The Comedy of Errors,* i, 1, 74.

10
Fonder than ignorance.

Troilus and Cressida. Act i, sc. 1, l. 10. [Troilus] The only use of "fonder."

I had rather be a tick in a sheep than such a valiant ignorance.

Troilus and Cressida. Act iii, sc. 3, l. 315. [Thersites] The only use of "tick."

11
I think your lordship is not ignorant.

The Two Gentlemen of Verona. Act i, sc. 3, l. 25. [Panthino]

Thou art not Ignorant.—*The Two Gentlemen of Verona,* iii, 2, 25; iv, 3, 14; *Love's Labour 's Lost,* ii, 1, 21.

Osric: I know you are not ignorant—
Hamlet: I would you did, sir; yet, in faith, if you did, it would not much approve me.

Hamlet. Act v, sc. 2, l. 139.

You are not ignorant of what excellence Laertes is.

Hamlet. Act v, sc. 2, l. 143. [Osric]

I know she is not ignorant.—*The Taming of the Shrew,* ii, 1, 58.

Not ignorant.—*All's Well that Ends Well,* iv, 1, 38.

12
I am as ignorant in that as you
In so entitling me.

The Winter's Tale. Act ii, sc. 3, l. 69. [Paulina] The only use of "entitling."

The gods themselves,
Wotting no more than I, are ignorant.

The Winter's Tale. Act iii, sc. 2, l. 76. [Hermione] The only use of "wotting."

Excellently ignorant.—*Twelfth Night,* iii, 4, 207.

ILIUM, see Troy

ILLNESS

See also Disease, Sickness

13
I am quickly ill, and well.

Antony and Cleopatra. Act i, sc. 3, l. 72. [Cleopatra]

I am ill, but your being by me
Cannot amend me.

Cymbeline. Act iv, sc. 2, l. 11. [Imogen]

I am ill, and gone to bed.—*King Lear,* iii, 3, 18.

14
You wish me health in very happy season;
For I am, on the sudden, something ill.

II Henry IV. Act iv, sc. 2, l. 79. [Mowbray]

And now my sight fails, and my brain is giddy:
O me! come near me; now I am much ill.

II Henry IV. Act iv, sc. 4, l. 110. [King Henry]

This fortnight ill.—*II Henry IV,* iii, 1, 104.

Exceeding ill.—*II Henry IV,* iv, 5, 11; *Much Ado about Nothing,* iii, 4, 54.

15
Of his own body he was ill.

Henry VIII. Act iv, sc. 2, l. 43. [Katharine]

He 's very ill.—*Henry V,* ii, 1, 89.

You look very ill.—*The Merry Wives of Windsor,* ii, 1, 36.

So ill!—*Romeo and Juliet,* i, 1, 209. "Ill" was a favourite adjective with Shakespeare, and is used nearly two hundred times.

1
Without The illness should attend it.
Macbeth, i, 5, 20. See under AMBITION. The only use of "illness."

IMAGE

See also Statue

2 Our last king,
Whose image even now appear'd to us.
Hamlet. Act i, sc. 1, l. 80. [Horatio]

Image of the king.—*II Henry IV,* v, 2, 79.

Most royal image.—*II Henry IV,* v, 2, 89.

3 By the image of my cause, I see
The portraiture of his.
Hamlet. Act v, sc. 2, l. 77. [Hamlet] The only use of "portraiture."

The true and perfect image of life indeed.
I Henry IV, v, 4, 120. See under COUNTERFEIT.

4
The image of a wicked heinous fault
Lives in his eye.
King John, iv, 2, 71. See under FAULT.

5 His loves
Are brazen images of canonized saints.
II Henry VI, i, 3, 63. See under HOLINESS.

Make my image but an alehouse sign.
II Henry VI, iii, 2, 81. See under STATUE.

6
From my heart thine image ne'er shall go.
III Henry VI. Act ii, sc. 5, l. 116. [Father]

Within his thought her heavenly image sits.
The Rape of Lucrece, l. 288.

Heaven's image.—*Measure for Measure,* ii, 4, 45.

7
Long mayst thou live To bear his image.
III Henry VI, v, 4, 54. See GRANDFATHER.

Your father's image.—*The Winter's Tale,* v, 1, 127; *The Rape of Lucrece,* l. 1753.

8 Disrobe the images
If you do find them deck'd with ceremonies. . . .
Let no images Be hung with Cæsar's trophies.
Julius Cæsar. Act i, sc. 1, l. 69. [Flavius]

Cæsar's images.—*Julius Cæsar,* i, 2, 289.

Achilles' image.—*The Rape of Lucrece,* l. 1424.

9
Behold the great image of authority.
King Lear, iv, 6, 162. See under AUTHORITY.

Image of hell!—*The Rape of Lucrece,* l. 764.

Image of that horror.—*King Lear,* v, 3, 264.

Image of the jest.—*The Merry Wives of Windsor,* iv, 6, 17.

Image of a murder.—*Hamlet,* iii, 2, 248.

Image of offence.—*Twelfth Night,* iii, 4, 249.

Image of his power.—*II Henry IV,* v, 2, 74.

Image of pride.—*II Henry VI,* i, 3, 179.

Images of revolt.—*King Lear,* ii, 4, 91.

Noble image of my youth.—*II Henry IV,* iv, 4, 55.

Beauty's image.—*III Henry VI,* iii, 3, 64.

Great doom's image.—*Macbeth,* ii, 3, 83.

Fancy's images.—*Midsummer-Night's Dream,* v, 1, 25.

10
Nothing afeard of what thyself did make,
Strange images of death.
Macbeth. Act i, sc. 3, l. 86. [Ross]

11
What, is there none of Pygmalion's images, newly made woman, to be had now.
Measure for Measure. Act iii, sc. 2, l. 47. [Lucio] The only mention of Pygmalion.

12
It is too like an image and said nothing.
Much Ado about Nothing, ii, 1, 9. See under SPEECH.

Now thy image doth appear
In the rare semblance that I loved it first.
Much Ado about Nothing. Act v, sc. 1, l. 259. [Claudio]

13
The well-skill'd workman this mild image drew
For perjured Sinon, whose enchanting story
The credulous old Priam after slew.
The Rape of Lucrece, l. 1520. The only use of "well-skill'd."

14
O, from thy cheeks my image hast thou torn,
And shiver'd all the beauty of my glass,
That I no more can see what once I was!
The Rape of Lucrece, l. 1762.

15 Defaced
The precious image of our dear Redeemer.
Richard III. Act ii, sc. 1, l. 122. [King Edward] "Redeemer" is repeated in l. 4 of the same scene, and occurs nowhere else.

Image of his Maker.—*Henry VIII,* iii, 2, 442.

16
If thou live, remember'd not to be,
Die single, and thine image dies with thee.
Sonnets. No. iii.

Their images I loved I view in thee,
And thou, all they, hast all the all of me.
Sonnets. No. xxxi.

Show me your image in some antique book,
Since mind at first in character was done!
Sonnets. No. lix.

Is it thy will thy image should keep open
My heavy eyelids to the weary night?
Sonnets. No. lxi.

17
Even like a stony image, cold and numb.
Titus Andronicus, iii, 1, 259. See under HORROR.

Constant image.—*Twelfth Night,* ii, 4, 19.

Dead and earthy image.—*II Henry VI,* iii, 2, 147.

Image dull and dead.—*Venus and Adonis,* l. 212.

Horrid image.—*Macbeth,* i, 3, 135.

Painted images.—*The Rape of Lucrece,* l. 1577.

True image.—*Sonnets,* xxiv.

Waxen image.—*The Two Gentlemen of Verona,* ii, 4, 201.

Wretched image.—*Rape of Lucrece,* l. 1501.

18
Say, wall-eyed slave, whither wouldst thou convey
This growing image of thy fiend-like face?
Titus Andronicus. Act v, sc. 1, l. 44. [Lucius] "Wall-eyed" is repeated in *King John,*

iv, 3, 49: "Wall-eyed wrath"; and "fiend-like" in *Macbeth,* v, 8, 69: "Fiend-like queen." "Wall-eyed" is to have the iris of the eye discoloured, giving a look of fierceness.

1
To his image, which methought did promise
Most venerable worth, did I devotion.
Twelfth Night, iii, 4, 396. See under FIDELITY.

2
An image like thyself, all stain'd with gore.
Venus and Adonis, l. 664.

3
If I had thought the sight of my poor image
Would thus have wrought you,—for the stone is mine—
I 'ld not have shown it.
Winter's Tale. Act v, sc. 3, l. 57. [Paulina]

IMAGINATION

See also Fantasy, Invention

4
My imagination
Carries no favour in 't but Bertram's.
All's Well that Ends Well. Act i, sc. 1, l. 93. [Helena]

Nor can imagination form a shape,
Besides yourself, to like of.
The Tempest. Act iii, sc. 1, l. 56. [Miranda]

5
He was to imagine me his love, his mistress.
As You Like It. Act iii, sc. 2, l. 428. [Rosalind]

Imagine me taking your part.
II Henry IV. Act v, sc. 2, l. 96. [Chief Justice]

Imagine me . . . in fair Bohemia.
The Winter's Tale. Act iv, sc. 1, l. 19. [Time]

6
In my mind's eye.
Hamlet. Act i, sc. 2, l. 185. [Hamlet] The only use of this phrase.

7
He waxes desperate with imagination.
Hamlet. Act i, sc. 4, l. 87. [Horatio]

My imaginations are as foul
As Vulcan's stithy.
Hamlet. Act iii, sc. 1, l. 88. [Hamlet] The only use of "stithy."

How abhorred in my imagination it is! my gorge rises at it.
Hamlet. Act v, sc. 1, l. 206. [Hamlet]

8
This is the very coinage of your brain:
This bodiless creation ecstasy
Is very cunning in.
Hamlet. Act iii, sc. 4, l. 137. [Queen] The only use of "bodiless."

I 'll answer the coinage.—*I Henry IV,* iv, 2, 9. The only uses of "coinage."

9
She may strew
Dangerous conjectures in ill-breeding minds.
Hamlet. Act iv, sc. 5, l. 14. [Horatio] The only use of "ill-breeding."

On my eyelids shall conjecture hang.
Much Ado about Nothing. Act iv, sc. 1, l. 107. [Claudio]

Nice conjecture.—*Troilus and Cressida,* iv, 5, 250.

Simple conjectures.—*The Merry Wives of Windsor,* i, 1, 30.

Conjecture, expectation.—*II Henry IV,* i, 3, 23.

Jealousies, conjectures.—*II Henry IV,* Ind., 16.

By all conjectures.—*Henry VIII,* ii, 1, 41.

Entertain conjecture.—*Henry V,* Prol., 1.

Touch'd conjecture.—*Winter's Tale,* ii, 1, 176. The only uses of "conjecture" and "conjectures."

10
Imagination of some great exploit
Drives him beyond the bounds of patience.
I Henry IV, i, 3, 199. [Northumberland]

Great imagination Proper to madmen.
II Henry IV. Act i, sc. 3, l. 31. [Bardolph]

11
Shape
In forms imaginary the unguided days.
II Henry IV, iv, 4, 59. See under FUTURE.

Things imaginary.—*Richard II,* ii, 2, 27.

12
Work, work your thoughts, . . . Still be kind,
And eke out our performance with your mind.
Henry V. Act iii, Prologue, l. 25. [Chorus]

13
What I do imagine let that rest.
I Henry VI. Act ii, sc. 5, l. 119. [Plantagenet]

I can imagine.—*Coriolanus,* iv, 5, 217.

I cannot imagine.—*Measure for Measure,* iv, 2, 43.

Imagine howling.—*Measure for Measure,* iii, 1, 128.

Imagine it.—*Richard II,* i, 3, 286.

O, then imagine this.—*Venus and Adonis,* l. 721.

14
Give me an ounce of civet, good apothecary, to sweeten my imagination.
King Lear. Act iv, sc. 6, l. 132. [King Lear]

15
Like fools that in th' imagination set
The goodly objects which abroad they find
Of lands and mansions, theirs in thought assign'd;
And labouring in moe pleasures to bestow them
Than the true gouty landlord which doth owe them.
A Lover's Complaint, l. 136. "Gouty" is repeated in *Timon of Athens,* iv, 3, 46, and in *Troilus and Cressida,* i, 2, 30.

16
Whose salt imagination yet hath wrong'd
Your well defended honour.
Measure for Measure, v, 1, 406. [Duke]

Bare imagination.—*Richard II,* i, 3, 297.

Still imagination.—*The Rape of Lucrece,* l. 702.

Strong imagination.—*The Tempest,* ii, 1, 208.

Unfelt imagination.—*Richard III,* i, 4, 80.

Wrong imaginations.—*King Lear,* iv, 6, 290.

Horrible imaginings.—*Macbeth,* i, 3, 38. The only use of "imaginings."

17
What spirit, what devil suggests this imagination?
The Merry Wives of Windsor. Act iii, sc. 3, l. 230. [Page]

You must . . . not follow the imaginations of your own heart.
The Merry Wives of Windsor. Act iv, sc. 2, l. 162. [Evans]

1
The lunatic, the lover and the poet
Are of imagination all compact.
A Midsummer-Night's Dream. Act v, sc. 1, l. 7. [Theseus]
Imagination bodies forth
The forms of things unknown.
A Midsummer-Night's Dream, v, 1, 14. See under POET.
Such tricks hath strong imagination,
That, if it would but apprehend some joy,
It comprehends some bringer of that joy.
A Midsummer-Night's Dream. Act v, sc. 1, l. 18. [Theseus]
The best in this kind are but shadows; and the worst are no worse, if imagination amend them.
A Midsummer-Night's Dream. Act v, sc. 1, l. 213. [Theseus]

2
The idea of her life shall sweetly creep
Into his study of imagination,
And every lovely organ of her life
Shall come apparell'd in more precious habit,
More moving-delicate and full of life,
Into the eye and prospect of his soul,
Than when she lived indeed.
Much Ado about Nothing. Act iv, sc. 1, l. 226. [Friar Francis] The only use of "moving-delicate."

3
In your imagination hold This stage a ship.
Pericles. Act iii, Gower, l. 58.
Take your imagination
From bourn to bourn, region to region.
Pericles. Act iv, sc. 4, l. 3. [Gower]

4
A hand, a foot, a face, a leg, a head,
Stood for the whole to be imagined.
The Rape of Lucrece, l. 1427.

5
How big imagination Moves in this lip!
Timon of Athens, i, 1, 32. See under PAINTING.

6
O, peace! now he 's deeply in: look how imagination blows him.
Twelfth Night. Act ii, sc. 5, l. 47. [Fabian]
I do not now fool myself, to let imagination jade me.
Twelfth Night. Act ii, sc. 5, l. 178. [Malvolio]
Prove true, imagination, O, prove true.
Twelfth Night. Act iii, sc. 4, l. 409. [Viola]

7
Tremble at the imagination.
Venus and Adonis, l. 668.
Beyond imagination.—*The Comedy of Errors,* v, 1, 201; *The Winter's Tale,* iv, 2, 45.

IMITATION

See also Counterfeit, Substitute

8
With what imitation you can borrow.
Cymbeline. Act iii, sc. 4, l. 174. [Pisanio]

9
They imitated humanity so abominably.
Hamlet, iii, 2, 39. See under ACTING.
Poorly imitated.—*Sonnets,* liii. The only uses of "imitated."
Base imitation.—*Richard II,* ii, 1, 23.

10
Imitari is nothing: so doth the hound his master, the ape his keeper, the tired horse his rider.
Love's Labour 's Lost. Act iv, sc. 2, l. 130. [Holofernes] The only use of "imitari."

11
Forth my mimic comes.
A Midsummer-Night's Dream. Act iii, sc. 2, l. 19. [Puck] The only use of "mimic."

12
Stand to and do as we.
The Tempest. Act iii, sc. 3, l. 52. [Alonso]

13
If our betters play at that game, we must not dare
To imitate them.
Timon of Athens. Act i, sc. 2, l. 12. [Timon]
Him I imitate.—*Twelfth Night,* iii, 4, 418. See under BROTHER.

IMMORTALITY

See also Mortality

14
Woman, do what thou canst to save our honours;
Drive them from Orleans and be immortalized.
I Henry VI. Act i, sc. 2, l. 147. [Reignier] The only use of "immortalized."

15
If thou beest not immortal, look about you.
Julius Cæsar. Act ii, sc. 3, l. 7. [Artemidorus]
By eight to-morrow
Thou must be made immortal.
Measure for Measure. Act iv, sc. 2, l. 67. [Provost]
Made nature immortal.—*All 's Well that Ends Well,* i, 1, 23.
Like one immortal.—*Pericles,* v, Gower, 3.
A thing immortal.—*Hamlet,* i, 4, 67.
Wears the crown immortally.—*II Henry IV,* iv, 5, 144. The only use of "immortally."

16
Got deliver to a joyful resurrections!
Merry Wives of Windsor. Act i, sc. 1, l. 53. [Evans] The only use of "resurrections."

17
By their mortal fault brought in subjection
Her immortality, and made her thrall
To living death and pain perpetual.
The Rape of Lucrece, l. 724.
Immortality attends the former,
Making a man a god.
Pericles, iii, 2, 30. See under VIRTUE. The only uses of "immortality."

18
Her immortal part with angels lives.
Romeo and Juliet. Act v, sc. 1, l. 19. [Balthasar]
Immortal part.—*II Henry IV,* ii, 2, 112; *Othello,* ii, 3, 263.

19
For the life to come, I sleep out the thought of it.
The Winter's Tale. Act iv, sc. 3, l. 30. [Autolycus]

Jump the life to come.—*Macbeth,* i, 7, 7. The only uses of "life to come" in this sense. In *Measure for Measure,* v, 1, 437, is the phrase, "All my life to come."

IMPATIENCE

See also Patience

1 Her garboils, Cæsar,
Made out of her impatience, which not wanted
Shrewdness of policy too.
Antony and Cleopatra. Act ii, sc. 2, l. 67. [Antony]

The garboils she awaked.—*Antony and Cleopatra,* i, 3, 61. The only uses of "garboils" (tumults).

2
Mark Antony Put me to some impatience.
Antony and Cleopatra. Act ii, sc. 6, l. 42. [Pompey]

Impatience does Become a dog that 's mad.
Antony and Cleopatra, iv, 14, 79. See under PATIENCE.

All patience and impatience.—*As You Like It,* v, 2, 103.

3
Fie, how impatience loureth in your face!
The Comedy of Errors. Act ii, sc. 1, l. 86. [Luciana]

Stern impatience.—*I Henry VI,* iv, 7, 8.

Strange impatience.—*Julius Cæsar,* i, 3, 61.

4 His own impatience
Takes from Aufidius a great part of blame.
Coriolanus. Act v, sc. 6, l. 146. [Lord]

5 No further with your din
Express impatience, lest you stir up mine.
Cymbeline. Act v, sc. 4, l. 111. [Jupiter]

I stand on fire: Come to the matter.
Cymbeline. Act v, sc. 5, l. 168. [Cymbeline]

6
You are too impatient to bear crosses.
II Henry IV. Act i, sc. 2, l. 252. [Chief Justice]

I see you stand like greyhounds in the slips,
Straining upon the start.
Henry V. Act iii, sc. 1, l. 31. [King Henry]

7
O, but impatience waiteth on true sorrow.
III Henry VI. Act iii, sc. 3, l. 42. [Queen Margaret]

8 You scratch'd your head,
And too impatiently stamp'd with your foot.
Julius Cæsar. Act ii, sc. 1, l. 243. [Portia]

Impatiently I burn.—*I Henry VI,* i, 2, 108.

Impatiently doth rage.—*The Two Gentlemen of Verona,* ii, 7, 26. The only uses of "impatiently."

9 Impatience
Which seem'd too much enkindled.
Julius Cæsar. Act ii, sc. 1, l. 248. [Portia]

Impatient of my absence.—*Julius Cæsar,* iv, 3 152.

Impatient of your wrongs.—*Titus Andronicus,* v, 1, 6.

10
Impatience hath his privilege.
King John. Act iv, sc. 3, l. 32. [Pembroke]

All the power of his wits have given way to his impatience.
King Lear. Act iii, sc. 6, l. 5. [Kent]

11
Sheathe thy impatience.
The Merry Wives of Windsor. Act ii, sc. 2, l. 88. [Host]

My heart is ready to crack with impatience.
The Merry Wives of Windsor. Act ii, sc. 2, l. 301. [Ford]

12
I was too hot to do somebody good,
That is too cold in thinking of it now.
Richard III. Act i, sc. 3, l. 311. [Gloucester]

What means this scene of rude impatience?
Richard III. Act ii, sc. 2, l. 38. [Duchess of York]

What 's that to us? The time goes by: away!
Twelfth Night. Act iii, sc. 4, l. 398. [Officer]

13
Impatience chokes her pleading tongue.
Venus and Adonis, l. 217.

IMPEDIMENT

See also Cross, Difficulty

14 May I never
To this good purpose, that so fairly shows,
Dream of impediment!
Antony and Cleopatra. Act ii, sc. 2, l. 146. [Antony]

No impediment between.—*Coriolanus,* ii, 3, 236.

15 I wonder much,
Being men of such great leading as you are,
That you foresee not what impediments
Drag back our expedition.
I Henry IV. Act iv, sc. 3, l. 16. [Vernon]

Continent impediments.—*Macbeth,* iv, 3, 64.

Moist impediments.—*II Henry IV,* iv, 5, 140.

16
What was the impediment that broke this off?
Henry V. Act i, sc. 1, l. 90. [Ely]

I demand before this royal view,
What rub or what impediment there is.
Henry V. Act v, sc. 2, l. 32. [Burgundy]

17 When thou wilt inflame,
How coldly those impediments stand forth
Of wealth, of filial fear, law, kindred, fame!
A Lover's Complaint, l. 268.

18
Let his lack of years be no impediment.
The Merchant of Venice. Act iv, sc. 1, l. 250. [Clerk, reading]

19
Any bar, any cross, any impediment will be medicinable to me.
Much Ado about Nothing. Act ii, sc. 2, l. 4. [Don John]

Other bars he lays before me.
The Merry Wives of Windsor. Act iii, sc. 4, l. 7. [Fenton]

Those bars which stop the hourly dial.
The Rape of Lucrece, l. 327.

Female bar.—*Henry V,* i, 2, 42.

Iron bars.—*I Henry VI,* i, 4, 10.

Bars of steel.—*I Henry VI,* i, 4, 51.

Bar in law.—*Taming of the Shrew,* i, 1, 139.
So sweet a bar.—*Merchant of Venice,* iii, 2, 120.
Truest bars.—*Sonnets,* xlviii.
Worldly bars.—*Julius Cæsar,* i, 3, 96.
There is no bar.—*Henry V,* i, 2, 35.

1
If there be any impediment, I pray you discover it.
Much Ado about Nothing. Act iii, sc. 2, l. 96. [Claudio]
If either of you know any inward impediment why you should not be conjoined, I charge you, on your souls, to utter it.
Much Ado about Nothing. Act iv, sc. 1, l. 12. [Friar Francis]

2
The impediment most profitably removed, without the which there were no expectation of our prosperity.
Othello. Act ii, sc. 1, l. 286. [Iago]
I have seen the day,
That, with this little arm and this good sword,
I have made my way through more impediments
Than twenty times your stop.
Othello. Act v, sc. 2, l. 261. [Othello]

3
All obstacles were cut away.
Richard III. Act iii, sc. 7, l. 156. [Richard]
Fuel of obstacles.—*Richard III,* i, 4, 143.
No obstacle.—*Twelfth Night,* iii, 4, 88.
Fie, Joan, that thou wilt be so obstacle!
I Henry VI, v, 4, 17. See under Obstinacy. The only uses of "obstacle" and "obstacles."

4
Let me not to the marriage of true minds
Admit impediments.
Sonnets. No. cxvi.

5
I know not what impediment this complaint may be.
The Winter's Tale. Act iv, sc. 4, l. 728. [Autolycus]

IMPERFECTION

6
With all my imperfections on my head.
Hamlet, i, 5, 79. See under Murder.

7
Piece out our imperfections with your thoughts.
Henry V. Act i, Prologue, l. 23. [Chorus]
Imperfections Which you have cited.—*Henry V,* v, 2, 69.

8
The imperfections of long-engraffed condition.
King Lear, i, 1, 300. See under Age. The only use of "long-engraffed."

9
Something he left imperfect in the state.
King Lear. Act iv, sc. 3, l. 3. [Gentleman]
Grow imperfect.—*King Lear,* iv, 6, 5.
Most imperfect.—*Othello,* i, 3, 100.
Something imperfect.—*Coriolanus,* ii, 1, 54.
Imperfect shade.—*Sonnets,* xi.
Imperfect speakers.—*Macbeth,* i, 3, 70. The only uses of "imperfect."

10
I shall discover a thing to you, wherein I must very much lay open mine own imperfection.
The Merry Wives of Windsor. Act ii, sc. 2, l. 190. [Ford]

11
I will undo
This hateful imperfection of her eyes.
A Midsummer-Night's Dream. Act iv, sc. 1, l. 65. [Oberon]

12
One that so imperfectly conceits.
Othello. Act iii, sc. 3, l. 149. [Iago] The only use of "imperfectly."

13
Roses have thorns, and silver fountains mud;
Clouds and eclipses stain both moon and sun,
And loathsome canker lives in sweetest bud.
Sonnets. No. xxxv.

IMPOSSIBILITY

14
Impossible be strange attempts to those
That weigh their pains in sense and do suppose
What hath been cannot be.
All's Well that Ends Well. Act i, sc. 1, l. 239. [Helena]

15
What impossibility would slay
In common sense, sense saves another way.
All's Well that Ends Well, ii, 1, 80. See under Sense.
Not ignorant of the impossibility.—*All's Well that Ends Well,* iv, 1, 39.

16
It is not impossible to me, if it appear not inconvenient to you.
As You Like It. Act v, sc. 2, l. 72. [Rosalind] The only use of "inconvenient."
Not impossible.—*Measure for Measure,* v, 1, 52.

17
Murdering impossibility, to make
What cannot be, slight work.
Coriolanus. Act v, sc. 3, l. 61. [Coriolanus]
We cannot be here and there too.
Romeo and Juliet. Act i, sc. 5, l. 15. [Servant]

18
It is ('tis) impossible.
II Henry VI, ii, 1, 130. A phrase used in the first play and frequently repeated.
Nay, that's impossible.—*Much Ado about Nothing,* ii, 3, 209.
That were impossible.—*Much Ado about Nothing,* v, 1, 289.
A thing impossible.—*I Henry VI,* v, 4, 47; *The Taming of the Shrew,* i, 2, 123; *The Merry Wives of Windsor,* iii, 4, 9.
'Tis hard; almost impossible.—*King Lear,* ii, 4, 245.

19
I'll cut the causes off,
Flattering me with impossibilities.
III Henry VI. Act iii, sc. 2, l. 142. [Gloucester]
Close impossibilities!—*Timon of Athens,* iv, 3, 338.
Men's impossibilities.—*King Lear,* iv, 6, 74.

1 I will strive with things impossible,
Yes, get the better of them.
Julius Cæsar. Act ii, sc. 1, l. 325. [Ligarius]

2 Make not impossible
That which but seems unlike.
Measure for Measure. Act v, sc. 1, l. 51. [Isabella]

Seem impossible.—*Pericles,* v, 1, 125.

3
It were impossible I should speed amiss.
The Taming of the Shrew. Act ii, sc. 1, l. 285. [Petruchio]

4
Nothing is impossible.
The Two Gentlemen of Verona. Act iii, sc. 1, l. 379. [Launce]

5
Antonio: What impossible matter will he make easy next?
Sebastian: I think he will carry this island home in his pocket and give it his son for an apple.
Antonio: And, sowing the kernels of it in the sea, bring forth more islands.
The Tempest. Act ii, sc. 1, l. 92. The only use of "sowing."

You may as well go about to turn the sun to ice with fanning in his face with a peacock's feather.
Henry V. Act iv, sc. 1, l. 212. [Williams]

Hence! wilt thou lift up Olympus?
Julius Cæsar. Act iii, sc. 1, l. 74. [Cæsar]

I cannot draw a cart, nor eat dried oats.
King Lear. Act v, sc. 3, l. 38. [Captain]

Who can be wise, amazed, temperate and furious,
Loyal and neutral, in a moment? No man.
Macbeth. Act ii, sc. 3, l. 114. [Macbeth]

Alas, poor duke! the task he undertakes
Is numbering sands and drinking oceans dry.
Richard II. Act ii, sc. 2, l. 145. [Green]

IMPRISONMENT, see Prison

IMPUDENCE

See also Insolence, Presumption, Sauciness

6
She 's impudent, my lord.
All's Well that Ends Well. Act v, sc. 3, l. 187. [Bertram]

Impudent and mannish.—*Troilus and Cressida,* iii, 3, 217.

Impudent and shameless.—*III Henry VI,* iii, 3, 156.

Made impudent.—*III Henry VI,* i, 4, 117.

Impudently negative.—*The Winter's Tale,* i, 2, 274. The only use of "impudently."

Without impudency.—*Love's Labour 's Lost,* v, 1, 5. The only use of "impudency."

7
Untutor'd lad, thou art too malapert.
III Henry VI. Act v, sc. 5, l. 32. [Clarence]

Peace, master marquess, you are malapert.
Richard III. Act i, sc. 3, l. 255. [Queen Margaret]

Malapert blood.—*Twelfth Night,* iv, 1, 47. The only uses of "malapert."

8
Men take women's gifts for impudence.
Pericles, ii, 3, 69. See under Gift.

Hast thou . . . impudence?—*Measure for Measure,* v, 1, 368. See under Word.

Tax of impudence.—*All 's Well that Ends Well,* ii, 1, 173.

Less impudence.—*The Winter's Tale,* iii, 2, 57. The only uses of "impudence."

9
You are a princox.
Romeo and Juliet. Act i, sc. 5, l. 88. [Capulet] The only use of "princox" (an impudent boy).

Young start-up.—*Much Ado about Nothing,* i, 3, 68. The only use of "start-up."

INCERTAINTY, see Uncertainty

INCH

10
I would I had thy inches.
Antony and Cleopatra. Act i, sc. 3, l. 40. [Cleopatra]

Curtis: Away, you three-inch fool! . . .
Grumio: Am I but three inches? why, thy horn is a foot; and so long am I at the least.
The Taming of the Shrew. Act iv, sc. 1, l. 27. The only use of "three-inch."

Three inches of it.—*The Tempest,* ii, 1, 283.

Inches so diminutive.—*Troilus and Cressida,* ii, 2, 31.

11
As many inches as you have oceans.
Cymbeline, i, 2, 21. See under Land.

12
Ask them how many inches Is in one mile.
Love's Labour 's Lost. Act v, sc. 2, l. 188. [Rosalind]

How many inches doth fill up one mile.
Love's Labour 's Lost. Act v, sc. 2, l. 193. [Boyet]

13
My inch of taper will be burnt and done.
Richard II, i, 3, 223. See under Death.

Inch of delay.—*As You Like It,* iii, 2, 206.

Inch of fortune.—*Antony and Cleopatra,* 1, 2, 59.

Inch of ground.—*II Henry IV,* iv, 1, 109.

Extremest inch of possibility—*II Henry IV,* iv, 3, 39.

The furthest inch of Asia.—*Much Ado about Nothing,* ii, 1, 275. See under Errand.

Every inch a king.—*King Lear,* iv, 6, 109.

An inch narrow.—*Romeo and Juliet,* ii, 4, 88.

Saint Colme's inch.—*Macbeth,* i, 2, 61. The only mention of Saint Colme.

14
I 'll not budge an inch.
Taming of the Shrew. Ind., sc. 1, l. 14. [Sly]

Not an inch further.—*I Henry IV,* ii, 3, 117.

No inch farther.—*Winter's Tale,* iv, 4, 460.

15
I 'll show thee every fertile inch o' the island.
The Tempest. Act ii, sc. 2, l. 152. [Caliban]

16
I will begin at thy heel, and tell thee what thou art by inches.
Troilus and Cressida. Act ii, sc. 1, l. 53. [Thersites] See under Candour.

Lingering by inches.—*Cymbeline,* v, 5, 52. For "death by inches" see under Death.

INCLINATION

See also Desire

1
Your inclining cannot be removed.
All's Well that Ends Well. Act iii, sc. 6, l. 41. [First Lord]
Is it your own inclining?
Is it a free visitation?
Hamlet. Act ii, sc. 2, l. 283. [Hamlet]
Inclining to them both.—*The Winter's Tale,* i, 2, 304.
That way inclining.—*Winter's Tale,* iii, 2, 53.
Of my inclining.—*Othello,* i, 2, 82.
2
Observe his inclination in yourself.
Hamlet. Act ii, sc. 1, l. 71. [Polonius]
Report . . . her inclination.—*Antony and Cleopatra,* ii, 5, 113.
Tried his inclination.—*Coriolanus,* ii, 3, 200.
3
Base inclination and the start of spleen.
I Henry IV. Act iii, sc. 2, l. 125. [King Henry]
This merry inclination
Accords not with the sadness of my suit.
III Henry VI. Act iii, sc. 2, l. 76. [Lady Grey]
Bloody inclination.—*King John,* v, 2, 158.
Inclination of the day.—*Richard II,* iii, 2, 195.
4
Doth his majesty incline to it, or no?
Henry V. Act i, sc. 1, l. 72. [Ely]
More incline.—*I Henry VI,* iv, 1, 154.
Seriously incline.—*Othello,* i, 3, 146.
Neither way inclines.—*Antony and Cleopatra,* iii, 2, 50.
5
He 's inclined as is the ravenous wolf.
II Henry VI, iii, 1, 78. See SEEMING, 1330:4.
Never was inclined To accessary yieldings.
The Rape of Lucrece, l. 1657.
They are inclined to do so.
The Tempest. Act ii, sc. 1, l. 193. [Alonso]
Inclined to blood.—*II Henry VI,* iv, 2, 134.
Inclined to mirth.—*II Henry IV,* iv, 4, 38.
Inclined to sleep.—*As You Like It,* iv, 1, 157; *The Tempest,* i, 2, 185.
Inclined to thrift.—*Timon of Athens,* i, 1, 118.
6
Facere, as it were, replication, or rather, ostentare, to show, as it were, his inclination.
Love's Labour 's Lost. Act iv, sc. 2, l. 15. [Holofernes] The only use of "facere" and "ostentare." "Replication" occurs twice more, in *Julius Cæsar,* i, 1, 51, and *Hamlet,* iv, 2, 13.
7
I have never heard the absent duke much detected for women; he was not inclined that way.
Measure for Measure. Act iii, sc. 2, l. 129. [Duke]
Inclined my way!—*The Tempest,* i, 2, 447.
Inclinest that way.—*The Winter's Tale,* i, 2, 243. The only use of "inclinest."
What if we do omit
This reprobate till he were well inclined?
Measure for Measure. Act iv, sc. 3, l. 77. [Provost]
Well inclined.—*III Henry VI,* iv, 8, 16.
Best inclined.—*Coriolanus,* i, 6, 85.
So inclined.—*Hamlet,* iii, 1, 25.
8
He pieces out his wife's inclination.
The Merry Wives of Windsor. Act iii, sc. 2, l. 34. [Ford]
9
Bawd: How dost thou find the inclination of the people, especially of the younger sort? Boult: 'Faith, they listened to me as they would have hearkened to their father's testament. There was a Spaniard's mouth so watered, that he went to bed to her very description.
Pericles. Act iv, sc. 2, l. 103.
10
Break off your talk,
And give us notice of his inclination.
Richard III. Act iii, sc. 1, l. 177. [Buckingham]

INCONSTANCY

See also Constancy

11
But, too unruly deer, he breaks the pale
And feeds from home; poor I am but his stale.
The Comedy of Errors. Act ii, sc. 1, l. 100. [Adriana] For "stale" see under WHORE.
12
Look, as I blow this feather from my face,
And as the air blows it to me again,
Obeying with my wind when I do blow,
And yielding to another when it blows,
Commanded always by the greater gust;
Such is the lightness of you common men.
III Henry VI. Act iii, sc. 1, l. 84. [King Henry]
Mine eyes are witness of her lightness.
The Taming of the Shrew. Act iv, sc. 2, l. 24. [Tranio]
Woman's lightness.—*Measure for Measure,* ii, 2, 170.
Lightness of his wife.—*II Henry IV,* i, 2, 53.
Thence to a lightness.—*Hamlet,* ii, 2, 149.
O heavy lightness!—*Romeo and Juliet,* i, 1, 184.
Such lightness.—*II Henry IV,* i, 1, 122. The only uses of "lightness."
13
The villanous inconstancy of man's disposition.
The Merry Wives of Windsor. Act iv, sc. 5, l. 111. [Falstaff]
Men of inconstancy.—*Love's Labour 's Lost,* iv, 3, 180.
For now I see Inconstancy
More in women than in men remain.
The Passionate Pilgrim, l. 261.
Inconstancy falls off ere it begins.
The Two Gentlemen of Verona. Act v, sc. 4, l. 113. [Proteus]
Foul inconstancy.—*II Henry VI,* iii, 2, 115.
French inconstancy.—*King John,* iii, 1, 322. The only uses of "inconstancy."
14
I will henceforth be no more unconstant.
III Henry VI. Act v, sc. 1, l. 102. [Clarence]

Make such unconstant children of ourselves,
As now again to snatch our palm from palm,
Unswear faith sworn, and on the marriage-bed
Of smiling peace to march a bloody host,
And make a riot on the gentle brow
Of true sincerity?

King John. Act iii, sc. 1, l. 243. [King Philip] "Unswear" is repeated in *Othello,* iv, 1, 31.

Such unconstant starts are we like to have from him.

King Lear. Act i, sc. 1, l. 304. [Regan]

Unconstant womankind.—*The Taming of the Shrew,* iv, 2, 14. The only uses of "unconstant."

1

Sigh no more, ladies, sigh no more,
Men were deceivers ever,
One foot in sea and one on shore,
To one thing constant never.

Much Ado about Nothing. Act ii, sc. 3, l. 64. [Balthazar]

2

And more inconstant than the wind, who wooes
Even now the frozen bosom of the north.

Romeo and Juliet. Act i, sc. 4, l. 100. [Mercutio]

3

Alas, 'tis true I have gone here and there
And made myself a motley to the view,
Gored mine own thoughts, sold cheap what is most dear,
Made old offences of affections new.

Sonnets. No. cx.

Thou canst not vex me with inconstant mind,
Since that my life on thy revolt doth lie.

Sonnets. No. xcii.

4

The bonds of heaven are slipp'd, dissolved, and loosed;
And with another knot, five-finger-tied,
The fractions of her faith, orts of her love,
The fragments, scraps, the bits and greasy relics
Of her o'er-eaten faith, are bound to Diomed.

Troilus and Cressida. Act v, sc. 2, l. 156. [Troilus] The only use of the phrase "five-finger-tied" and "o'er-eaten."

O Cressid! O false Cressid! false, false, false!
Let all untruths stand by thy stained name,
And they'll seem glorious.

Troilus and Cressida. Act v, sc. 2, l. 178. [Troilus]

5

You either fear his humour or my negligence, that you call in question the continuance of his love: is he inconstant, sir, in his favours?

Twelfth Night. Act i, sc. 4, l. 5. [Viola]

Inconstant, full of tears.—*As You Like It,* iii, 2, 432.

Inconstant and damnable ingrateful.—*The Winter's Tale,* iii, 2, 187.

INCONTINENCE, see Wantonness

INDECISION

See also Timidity, Uncertainty

6 Why hast thou gone so far,
To be unbent when thou hast ta'en thy stand,
The elected deer before thee?

Cymbeline. Act iii, sc. 4, l. 110. [Imogen]

7

A dull and muddy-mettled rascal, peak,
Like John-a-dreams, unpregnant of my cause,
And can say nothing.

Hamlet. Act ii, sc. 2, l. 594. [Hamlet] The only use of "muddy-mettled" and "John-a-dreams." "Peak" occurs once again in *Macbeth,* i, 3, 23: "Peak and pine."

8

To be, or not to be: that is the question;
Whether 'tis nobler in the mind to suffer
The slings and arrows of outrageous fortune,
Or to take arms against a sea of troubles,
And by opposing end them?

Hamlet. Act iii, sc. 1, l. 56. [Hamlet] "Slings" is repeated in *Henry V,* iv, 7, 65: "Old Assyrian slings."

And thus the native hue of resolution
Is sicklied o'er with the pale cast of thought,
And enterprises of great pitch and moment
With this regard their currents turn awry,
And lose the name of action.

Hamlet. Act iii, sc. 1, l. 84. [Hamlet] The only use of "sicklied."

And, like a man to double business bound,
I stand in pause where I shall first begin.

Hamlet. Act iii, sc. 3, l. 41. [King]

9 'Tis with my mind
As with the tide swell'd up unto his height,
That makes a still-stand, running neither way.

II Henry IV. Act ii, sc. 3, l. 62. [Northumberland] The only use of "still-stand."

You'll nor fight nor fly.

II Henry VI. Act v, sc. 2, l. 74. [Queen Margaret]

10

Wherefore stand you on nice points?

III Henry VI. Act iv, sc. 7, l. 58. [Gloucester]

11

The colour of the king doth come and go
Between his purpose and his conscience,
Like heralds 'twixt two dreadful battles set.

King John. Act iv, sc. 2, l. 76. [Salisbury]

12 What thou wouldst highly,
That wouldst thou holily; wouldst not play false,
And yet wouldst wrongly win: thou 'ldst have, great Glamis,
That which cries 'Thus thou must do, if thou have it;
And that which rather thou dost fear to do
Than wishest should be undone.'

Macbeth. Act i, sc. 5, l. 21. [Lady Macbeth] "Holily" occurs twice more in the plays, in *Macbeth,* v, 1, 67, and *Henry VIII,* ii, 2, 24. The only use of "wrongly."

1
I am At war 'twixt will and will not.
Measure for Measure. Act ii, sc. 2, l. 32. [Isabella]
We would, and we would not.
Measure for Measure, iv, 4, 37. See under GRACE.
Now he vows a league, and now invasion.
The Rape of Lucrece, l. 287.
2
I pray thee, stay a while.
Richard III. Act i, sc. 4, l. 120. [Murderer]
3
Come, young waverer.
Romeo and Juliet. Act ii, sc. 3, l. 89. [Friar Laurence] The only use of "waverer."
Thou almost makest me waver.—*The Merchant of Venice,* iv, 1, 130. The only use of "waver."
Wavering, stood in doubt.—*A Lover's Complaint,* l. 97.
Longing, wavering.—*Twelfth Night,* ii, 4, 35.
Wavering commons.—*Richard II,* ii, 2, 129.
Wavering multitude.—*II Henry IV,* Ind., 19.
Wavering nation.—*I Henry VI,* iv, 1, 138. The only uses of "wavering."
4
Come your ways, come your ways; an you draw backward, we'll put you i' the fills.
Troilus and Cressida. Act iii, sc. 2, l. 46. [Pandarus] The only use of "fills" in the sense of shafts of a cart.
What makes this pretty abruption?
Troilus and Cressida. Act iii, sc. 2, l. 69. [Troilus] The only use of "abruption." "Indecision" does not occur in the plays.

INDENTURE, see Bond

INDEX

5
Thunders in the index.
Hamlet, iii, 4, 52. See under ACT.
6
Index to the story we late talk'd of.
Richard III. Act ii, sc. 3, l. 149. [Buckingham]
The flattering index of a direful pageant.
Richard III. Act iv, sc. 4, l. 85. [Queen Margaret]
An index . . . to the history of lust.
Othello, ii, 1, 263. The only uses of "index."
7
And in such indexes, although small pricks
To their subsequent volumes, there is seen
The baby figure of the giant mass
Of things to come at large.
Troilus and Cressida. Act i, sc. 3, l. 343. [Nestor] The only use of "indexes" and "subsequent."

INDIA

8
To-morrow, they Made Britain India.
Henry VIII. Act i, sc. 1, l. 20. [Buckingham]
Come from the farthest steppe of India?
A Midsummer-Night's Dream. Act ii, sc. 1, l. 69. [Titania] The only use of "steppe."
Her bed is India.—*Troilus and Cressida,* i, 1, 103.
Metal of India.—*Twelfth Night,* ii, 5, 17.
Mines of India.—*I Henry IV,* iii, 1, 169.
From Barbary and India.—*The Merchant of Venice,* iii, 2, 272.
Gone barefoot to India.—*Troilus and Cressida,* i, 2, 80. The only references to India.
9
A rude and savage man of Ind.
Love's Labour's Lost. Act iv, sc. 3, l. 222. [Biron]
Savages and men of Ind.—*Tempest,* ii, 2, 61.
Western Ind.—*As You Like It,* iii, 2, 93. The only uses of "Ind."
10
Have we some strange Indian with the great tool come to court, the women so besiege us?
Henry VIII. Act v, sc. 4, l. 34. [Porter]
Base Indian.—*Othello,* v, 2, 347.
Dead Indian.—*The Tempest,* ii, 2, 34.
11
They shall be my East and West Indies, and I will trade to them both.
The Merry Wives of Windsor. Act i, sc. 3, l. 79. [Falstaff]
All the Indies in his arms.—*Henry VIII,* iv, 1, 45.
Augmentation of the Indies.—*Twelfth Night,* iii, 2, 86.
Bound . . . to the Indies.—*The Merchant of Venice,* i, 3, 19.
Where . . . the Indies?—*The Comedy of Errors,* iii, 2, 136. The only references to the Indies.

INDIFFERENCE

12
He waved indifferently 'twixt doing them neither good nor harm.
Coriolanus. Act ii, sc. 2, l. 19. [Officer]
I will look on both indifferently.
Julius Cæsar. Act i, sc. 2, l. 87. [Brutus] See under HONOUR.
Hear me speak indifferently for all.
Titus Andronicus. Act 1, sc. 1, l. 430. [Tamora]
Reformed that indifferently.—*Hamlet,* iii, 2, 41.
Indifferently well.—*Henry V,* ii, 1, 58. The only uses of "indifferently."
13
He seems indifferent.
Henry V. Act i, sc. 1, l. 72. [Canterbury]
14
Take head from all indifferency.
King John. Act ii, sc. 1, l. 579. [Bastard] "Indifferency" is repeated in *II Henry IV,* iv, 3, 23.
15
It does indifferent well.
Twelfth Night. Act i, sc. 3, l. 143. [Sir Andrew] "Indifferent well" is repeated in *Henry V,* iv, 7, 34; and in *Troilus and Cressida,* i, 2, 242.
Indifferent good.—*The Taming of the Shrew,* i, 2, 181.

INDIGNATION

16 Quench his fiery indignation
Even in the matter of mine innocence.
King John. Act iv, sc. 1, l. 63. [Arthur]
Great indignation.—*The Tempest,* iv, 1, 200.
Iron indignation.—*King John,* ii, 1, 212.
Scarlet indignation.—*Richard II,* iii, 3, 99.

They burn in indignation.—*King John,* iv, 2, 103.

1
Suspend your indignation against my brother.
King Lear. Act i, sc. 2, l. 86. [Edmund] "Suspend" is used again in i, 4, 289, "Suspend thy purpose," and occurs in no other play.

Withhold thine indignation!—*King John,* v, 6, 37.

2
Hurl down their indignation On thee!
Richard III, i, 3, 220. See under CURSE.

Pluck his indignation on thy head.
All's Well that Ends Well, iii, 2, 32. See under RASHNESS.

3
I 'll deliver thy indignation to him by word of mouth.
Twelfth Night, ii, 3, 140. See under CHALLENGE.

His indignation derives itself out of a very competent injury.
Twelfth Night. Act iii, sc. 4, l. 269. [Sir Toby]

INDIGNITY

See also Insult

4
Parolles: My lord, you give me most egregious indignity.
Lafeu: Ay, with all my heart; and thou art worthy of it.
Parolles: I have not, my lord, deserved it.
Lafeu: Yes, good faith, every dram of it; and I will not bate thee a scruple.
All's Well that Ends Well. Act ii, sc. 3, l. 228.

5
Luciana: Complain unto the duke of this indignity.
Adriana: Come, go: I will fall prostrate at his feet.
The Comedy of Errors. Act v, sc. 1, l. 113.

Ran hither to your grace, whom I beseech
To give me ample satisfaction
For these deep shames and great indignities.
The Comedy of Errors. Act v, sc. 1, l. 251. [Antipholus of Ephesus]

6
How might a prince of my great hopes forget
So great indignities you laid upon me?
II Henry IV. Act v, sc. 2, l. 68. [King Henry V]

For it can never be
They will digest this harsh indignity.
Love's Labour 's Lost. Act v, sc. 2, l. 288. [Boyet]

Some strange indignity
Which patience could not pass.
Othello. Act ii, sc. 3, l. 244. [Othello]

7
The poor monster 's my subject and he shall not suffer indignity.
The Tempest. Act iii, sc. 2, l. 42. [Stephano]

8
Then let my father's honours live in me,
Nor wrong mine age with this indignity.
Titus Andronicus. Act i, sc. 1, l. 7. [Saturninus]

INDUSTRY

See also Diligence

9
The sweat of industry would dry and die,
But for the end it works to.
Cymbeline. Act iii, sc. 6, l. 31. [Belarius]

Serious industry.—*Cymbeline,* iii, 5, 112.

10
His industry is up-stairs and down-stairs.
I Henry IV. Act ii, sc. 4, l. 112. [Prince of Wales] The only instance of either "up-stairs" or "down-stairs" in the plays

11
Thine, in the dearest design of industry.
Love's Labour 's Lost. Act iv, sc. 1, l. 88. [Boyet, reading]

Manured with industry.—*Othello,* i, 3, 328.
Industry and courage.—*III Henry VI,* v, 4, 11.

12
With a dropping industry
They skip from stem to stern.
Pericles. Act iv, sc. 1, l. 63. [Marina]

Industrious friend.—*I Henry IV,* i, 1, 62.
Industrious scenes.—*King John,* ii, 1, 376.
Industrious servant.—*The Tempest,* iv, 1, 33.
Industrious soldiership.—*Macbeth,* v, 4, 16.
The four instances of the use of "industrious."

INFAMY

See also Disgrace

13
Chief Justice: Well, the truth is, Sir John, you live in great infamy.
Falstaff: He that buckles him in my belt cannot live in less.
II Henry IV. Act i, sc. 2, l. 155.

14
The powdering-tub of infamy.
Henry V. Act ii, sc. 1, l. 79. [Pistol] The only use of "powdering-tub," a name humorously applied to the sweating-tub used in the treatment of venereal disease.

15
This fact was infamous.
I Henry VI, iv, 1, 30. See under FACT.

My revolt is infamous.—*Antony and Cleopatra,* iv, 9, 19. The only uses of "infamous."

16
What infamy will there arise.
I Henry VI. Act iv, sc. 1, l. 143. [King Henry]

17
Look here, I throw my infamy at thee.
III Henry VI. Act v, sc. 1, l. 82. [Clarence]

I will whip about your infamy circum circa.
Love's Labour 's Lost. Act v, sc. 1, l. 72. [Moth] The only use of "circum circa."

18
Smirched thus and mired with infamy.
Much Ado about Nothing. Act iv, sc. 1, l. 135. [Leonato] The only use of "mired." "Smirched" occurs three times.

19
He must not live to trumpet forth my infamy.
Pericles. Act i, sc. 1, l. 145. [Antiochus]

1
Yet strive I to embrace mine infamy.
The Rape of Lucrece, l. 504.
O, how are they wrapp'd in with infamies
That from their own misdeeds askance their eyes!
The Rape of Lucrece, l. 636.
To mask their brows and hide their infamy.
The Rape of Lucrece, l. 794.
In vain I cavil with mine infamy,
In vain I spurn at my confirm'd despite.
The Rape of Lucrece, l. 1025.
Daring infamy.—*The Rape of Lucrece,* l. 1173.
Living infamy.—*The Rape of Lucrece,* l. 1055.
Perpetual infamy.—*Rape of Lucrece,* l. 1638.
2
Throw over her the veil of infamy.
Richard III, iv, 4, 208. See under DAUGHTER.
Scars of infamy.—*Richard III,* iii, 7, 126.
3
Never dream on infamy.
The Two Gentlemen of Verona. Act iii, sc. 1, l. 64. [Lucetta]

INFANCY

See also Baby, Childhood

4 At first the infant,
Mewling and puking in its nurse's arms.
As You Like It. Act ii, sc. 7, l. 143. [Jaques] See MAN, 940:12, for full quotation. The only use of "mewling" and "puking."
Chosen infant.—*Henry VIII,* v, 5, 49.
First-born infants.—*Love's Labour's Lost,* i, 1, 101.
Flowering infants.—*Henry V,* iii, 3, 14.
Froward infant.—*Venus and Adonis,* l. 562.
Poor infants.—*Richard III,* iv, 4, 363; *Pericles,* iii, 1, 41; *Sonnets,* cxliii.
Royal infant.—*Henry VIII,* v, 5, 18. See under PROPHECY.
Very infants.—*I Henry VI,* iii, 1, 16.
Well-educated infant.—*Love's Labour's Lost,* i, 2, 99. The only use of "well-educated."
Infants of the spring.—*Hamlet,* i, 3, 39.
5
Your naked infants spitted upon pikes,
Whiles the mad mothers with their howls confused
Do break the clouds, as did the wives of Jewry
At Herod's bloody-hunting slaughtermen.
Henry V. Act iii, sc. 3, l. 38. [King Henry] The only use of "bloody-hunting."
6
Meet I an infant of the house of York,
Into as many gobbets will I cut it
As wild Medea young Absyrtus did.
II Henry VI. Act v, sc. 2, l. 57. [Young Clifford] "Gobbets" is repeated in iv, 1, 85, and occurs in no other play. Medea is referred to again in *The Merchant of Venice,* v, 1, 13. The only mention of Absyrtus.
7
Your infants in your arms.
Julius Cæsar, i, 1, 45. See under PATIENCE.
8 My gentle babe, Marina, whom,
For she was born at sea, I have named so, here
I charge your charity withal, leaving her
The infant of your care; beseeching you
To give her princely training, that she may be
Manner'd as she is born.
Pericles. Act iii, sc. 3, l. 12. [Pericles]
This poor infant, this fresh-new sea-farer.
Pericles. Act iii, sc. 1, l. 41. [Pericles] The only use of "fresh-new" and "sea-farer."
9
Tetchy and wayward was thy infancy.
Richard III. Act iv, sc. 4, l. 168. [Duchess of York] "Tetchy" is repeated in *Romeo and Juliet,* i, 3, 22, and in *Troilus and Cressida,* i, 1, 99.
Soft infancy, that nothing canst but cry.
Troilus and Cressida. Act ii, sc. 2, l. 105. [Cassandra]
Careless infancy.—*The Merry Wives of Windsor,* v, 5, 56.
Tender infancy.—*I Henry VI,* v, 4, 50.
Unpractised infancy.—*Troilus and Cressida,* i, 1, 12.
10
Many a matter hath he told to thee,
Meet and agreeing with thine infancy.
Titus Andronicus. Act v, sc. 3, l. 164. [Lucius]

INFECTION

See also Disease, Pestilence, Plague

11
All the contagion of the south light on you.
Coriolanus, i, 4, 30. See under CURSE.
Vile contagion of the night.—*Julius Cæsar,* ii, 1, 265.
I'll touch my point With this contagion.
Hamlet, iv, 7, 148. See under POISON.
Breathes out contagion.—*Hamlet,* iii, 2, 408.
Dulcet in contagion.—*Twelfth Night,* ii, 3, 59.
Strumpeted by thy contagion.—*The Comedy of Errors,* ii, 2, 146.
Contagion, death.—*Romeo and Juliet,* v, 3, 152. The only uses of "contagion."
Contagious sickness.—*Henry VIII,* 4, 3, 26. "Contagious" occurs ten times.
12 One infect another
Against the wind a mile!
Coriolanus, i, 4, 33. See under CURSE.
Infect to the north star.—*Much Ado about Nothing,* ii, 1, 257. The only reference to the north star.
Why do you infect yourself?—*As You Like It,* iii, 2, 120.
Who does infect her?—*Winter's Tale,* i, 2, 306.
Many are infect.—*Troilus and Cressida,* i, 3, 187.
Infecting one another.—*Henry VIII,* i, 1, 162. The only use of "infecting."
13
Pursue him to his house, and pluck him thence;
Lest his infection, being of catching nature,
Spread further.
Coriolanus. Act iii, sc. 1, l. 309. [Brutus]
O master! what a strange infection
Is fall'n into thy ear!
Cymbeline. Act iii, sc. 2, l. 3. [Pisanio]
Base infection.—*Sonnets,* xciv.

1
He shall not breathe infection in this air
But three days longer, on the pain of death.
II Henry VI. Act iii, sc. 2, l. 287. [King Henry]

The blessed gods
Purge all infection from our air whilst you
Do climate here!
Winter's Tale. Act v, sc. 1, l. 168 [Leontes]

2
Such is the infection of the time.
King John, v, 2, 20. See under INJUSTICE.
Infection of his fortune.—*King Lear,* iv, 6, 237.

3
He hath a great infection, sir, as one would say, to serve.
The Merchant of Venice. Act ii, sc. 2, l. 133. [Gobbo]
Her husband has a marvellous infection to the little page.
The Merry Wives of Windsor. Act ii, sc. 2, l. 119. [Mistress Quickly]
Great'st infection.—*The Winter's Tale,* i, 2, 423.

4
He hath ta'en the infection.
Much Ado about Nothing. Act ii, sc. 3, l. 125. [Claudio]

5
Defused infection of a man.
Richard III. Act i, sc. 2, l. 78. [Lady Anne]

6
Take thou some new infection to thy eye,
And the rank poison of the old will die.
Romeo and Juliet. Act i, sc. 2, l. 50. [Benvolio]
Fearful . . . of infection.—*Romeo and Juliet,* v, 2, 16.
Infection breeds.—*The Rape of Lucrece,* l. 907.

7
Ah! wherefore with infection should he live,
And with his presence grave impiety.
Sonnets. No. lxvii.

I will drink
Potions of eisel 'gainst my strong infection.
Sonnets. No. cxi. "Eisel" (vinegar) is used once again in *Hamlet,* v, 1, 299.

8
All the infections that the sun sucks up.
The Tempest, ii, 2, 1. See under CURSE.

9
Thou art infected! This visitation shows it.
The Tempest. Act iii, sc. 1, l. 31. [Prospero]
Navarre is infected.—*Love's Labour's Lost,* ii, 1, 230.
They are infected.—*Love's Labour's Lost,* v, 2, 420.
Thrice infected.—*Hamlet,* iii, 2, 269.

10
Like a shepherd,
Approach the fold and cull the infected forth,
But kill not all together.
Timon of Athens. Act v, sc. 4, l. 42. [Senator]

11
Drive infection from the dangerous year.
Venus and Adonis, l. 508.

12
From his presence
I am barr'd, like one infectious.
Winter's Tale, iii, 2, 99. See under PRESENCE.

Infectious fevers.—*Timon of Athens,* iv, 1, 22.
Infectious pestilence.—*Romeo and Juliet,* v, 2, 10; *Antony and Cleopatra,* ii, 5, 61.
Infectious troop.—*Comedy of Errors,* v, 1, 81.
Noisome and infectious.—*Cymbeline,* i, 5, 26. The only uses of "infectious." "Infectiously" occurs once, in *Troilus and Cressida,* ii, 2, 59.

INFIRMITY

See also Defect, Disease, Fault

13
He said, If he had done or said any thing amiss, he desired their worships to think it was his infirmity.
Julius Cæsar. Act i, sc. 2, l. 272. [Casca]

14
Infirmity doth still neglect all office
Whereto our health is bound.
King Lear. Act ii, sc. 4, l. 107. [King Lear]

15
I have a strange infirmity, which is nothing
To those that know me.
Macbeth. Act iii, sc. 4, l. 86. [Macbeth]
I am unfortunate in the infirmity, and dare not task my weakness with any more.
Othello. Act ii, sc. 3, l. 42. [Cassio]
An ingraft infirmity.—*Othello,* ii, 3, 145. The only use of "ingraft." "Ingrafted" occurs in *Julius Cæsar,* ii, 1, 184.

16
This ambitious foul infirmity,
In having much, torments us with defect
Of that we have.
The Rape of Lucrece, l. 150.

17
Be not disturbed with my infirmity.
Tempest. Act iv, sc. 1, l. 160. [Prospero]
Discover thine infirmity.—*I Henry VI,* v, 4, 60.
Infirmity of sense.—*Measure for Measure,* v, 1, 47.

18
Malvolio: Infirmity, that decays the wise, doth ever make the better fool.
Clown: God send you, sir, a speedy infirmity, for the better increasing your folly.
Twelfth Night. Act i, sc. 5, l. 82.

These, my lord,
Are such allow'd infirmities that honesty
Is never free of.
Winter's Tale. Act i, sc. 2, l. 262. [Camillo]
Man's infirmities.—*Pericles,* i, Gower, 3.
The infirmities of men!—*Pericles,* ii, 1, 53.

19
Infirmity
Which waits upon worn times hath something seized
His wish'd ability.
Winter's Tale. Act v, sc. 1, l. 141. [Florizel]

INFLUENCE

See also Star

20
Pompey's name strikes more
Than could his war resisted.
Antony and Cleopatra. Act i, sc. 4, l. 54. [Messenger]

Your eye in Scotland
Would create soldiers, make our women fight,
To doff their dire distresses.
Macbeth. Act iv, sc. 3, l. 186. [Ross]

1 O'er my spirit
Thy full supremacy thou knew'st, and that
Thy beck might from the bidding of the gods
Command me.
Antony and Cleopatra. Act iii, sc. 11, l. 58. [Antony]

Things outward
Do draw the inward quality after them,
To suffer all alike.
Antony and Cleopatra. Act iii, sc. 13, l. 32. [Enobarbus]

2
For from his metal was his party steel'd.
II Henry IV. Act i, sc. 1, l. 116. [Morton]

I know thou wast set on to this.
II Henry IV. Act ii, sc. 1, l. 164. [Falstaff]

3
Have wrought the easy-melting king like wax.
III Henry VI. Act ii, sc. 1, l. 171. [Warwick] The only use of "easy-melting."

The bloody-minded queen,
That led calm Henry, though he were a king,
As doth a sail, fill'd with a fretting gust,
Command an argosy to stem the waves.
III Henry VI. Act ii, sc. 6, l. 33. [Edward] "Bloody-minded" is repeated in *II Henry VI,* iv, 1, 36.

4
Whose influence, like the wreath of radiant fire
On flickering Phœbus' front.
King Lear. Act ii, sc. 2, l. 113. [Kent] The only use of "flickering."

Yet be most proud of that which I compile,
Whose influence is thine and born of thee.
Sonnets. No. lxxviii.

Beauteous influence.—*Venus and Adonis,* l. 862.

Fair influence.—*The Two Gentlemen of Verona,* iii, 1, 183.

Planetary influence.—*King Lear,* i, 2, 136. "Planetary" is used a second time in *Timon of Athens,* iv, 3, 108: "Planetary plague."

Secret influence.—*Sonnets,* xv.

Skyey influences.—*Measure for Measure,* iii, 1, 9. The only use of "skyey."

5
You draw me, you hard-hearted adamant;
But yet you draw not iron, for my heart
Is true as steel; leave you your power to draw,
And I shall have no power to follow you.
A Midsummer-Night's Dream. Act ii, sc. 1, l. 195. [Helena] Adamant is mentioned again in *I Henry VI,* i, 4, 52, and in *Troilus and Cressida,* iii, 2, 186.

6
His soul is so enfetter'd to her love,
That she may make, unmake, do what she list,
Even as her appetite shall play the god
With his weak function.
Othello. Act ii, sc. 3, l. 351. [Iago] The only use of "enfetter'd." "Unmake" is repeated in *Macbeth,* i, 7, 54.

My advocation is not now in tune.
Othello. Act iii, sc. 4, l. 123. [Desdemona] The only use of "advocation."

7 Let our finger ache, and it indues
Our other healthful members even to that sense
Of pain.
Othello, Act iii, sc. 4, l. 146. [Desdemona]

8 Man, how dearly ever parted,
How much in having, or without or in,
Cannot make boast to have that which he hath,
Nor feels not what he owes, but by reflection;
As when his virtues shining upon others
Heat them and they retort that heat again
To the first giver.
Troilus and Cressida. Act iii, sc. 3, l. 96. [Ulysses]

INGRATITUDE

See also Treachery

9
Scourge the ingratitude that despiteful Rome
Cast on my noble father.
Antony and Cleopatra. Act ii, sc. 6, l. 22. [Pompey]

The ingratitude of this Seleucus does
Even make me wild.
Antony and Cleopatra. Act v, sc. 2, l. 153. [Cleopatra]

10
Blow, blow, thou winter wind,
Thou art not so unkind
As man's ingratitude;
Thy tooth is not so keen,
Because thou art not seen,
Although thy breath be rude.
As You Like It. Act ii, sc. 7, l. 174. [Amiens]

11
Well might they fester 'gainst ingratitude,
And tent themselves with death.
Coriolanus. Act i, sc. 9, l. 30. [Cominius]

Ingratitude is monstrous.
Coriolanus, ii, 3, 10. See under MULTITUDE.

Monster of ingratitudes.—*Troilus and Cressida,* iii, 3, 147.

12
And shall it in more shame be further spoken,
That you are fool'd, discarded and shook off
By him for whom these shames ye underwent?
I Henry IV. Act i, sc. 3, l. 177. [Hotspur] The only use of "underwent."

O Dieu vivant! shall a few sprays of us,
The emptying of our father's luxury,
Our scions, put in wild and savage stock,
Spirt up so suddenly into the clouds,
And overlook their grafters?
Henry V. Act iii, sc. 5, l. 5. [Dauphin] The only use of "vivant," "spirt," and "grafters."

13
This was the most unkindest cut of all;
For when the noble Cæsar saw him stab,
Ingratitude, more strong than traitors' arms,

Quite vanquish'd him.
Julius Cæsar. Act iii, sc. 2, l. 187. [Antony] The only use of "most unkindest."

1
Ingratitude, thou marble-hearted fiend,
More hideous when thou show'st thee in a child
Than the sea-monster!
King Lear. Act i, sc. 4, l. 281. [King Lear] The only use of "marble-hearted." "Sea-monster" occurs again in *The Merchant of Venice,* iii, 2, 57.

Filial ingratitude!
Is it not as this mouth should tear this hand
For lifting food to 't?
King Lear. Act iii, sc. 4, l. 14. [King Lear]
Monster ingratitude!—*King Lear,* i, 5, 43.

2
The sin of my ingratitude even now
Was heavy on me.
Macbeth. Act i, sc. 4, l. 15. [Duncan]

3 God is much displeased
That you take with unthankfulness his doing.
Richard III. Act ii, sc. 2, l. 89. [Dorset]
Thou diest in thine unthankfulness, and thine ignorance makes thee away.
All's Well that Ends Well. Act i, sc. 1, l. 226. [Parolles]
O rude unthankfulness!—*Romeo and Juliet,* iii, 3, 24.
Pay you with unthankfulness.—*Pericles,* i, 4, 102. The only uses of "unthankfulness."

4
Will not so graceless be to be ingrate.
The Taming of the Shrew. Act ii, sc. 1, l. 270. [Tranio] "Ingrate" is repeated four more times, always modifying a noun.

5 O, see the monstrousness of man
When he looks out in an ungrateful shape!
Timon of Athens. Act iii, sc. 2, l. 79. [First Stranger] The only use of "monstrousness."
'Tis call'd ungrateful.—*Richard III,* ii, 2, 91. "Ungrateful," always modifying a noun, is repeated four more times.

6
I know my lord hath spent of Timon's wealth,
And now ingratitude makes it worse than stealth.
Timon of Athens. Act iii, sc. 4, l. 27. [Hortensius]

Poet: I am rapt and cannot cover
The monstrous bulk of this ingratitude
With any size of words.
Timon: Let it go naked, men may see 't the better.
Timon of Athens. Act v, sc. 1, l. 67.

To wipe out our ingratitude with loves
Above their quantity.
Timon of Athens. Act v, sc. 4, l. 17. [Senator]

7 Ingratitude,
Which Rome reputes to be a heinous sin.
Titus Andronicus. Act i, sc. 1, l. 447. [Tamora]

Whose high exploits and honourable deeds
Ingrateful Rome requites with foul contempt.
Titus Andronicus. Act v, sc. 1, l. 11. [First Goth]

8
O traitors and bawds, how earnestly are you set a-work, and how ill requited!
Troilus and Cressida. Act v, sc. 10, l. 37. [Pandarus] The only use of "ill requited."

9
I hate ingratitude more in a man
Than lying, vainness, babbling, drunkenness,
Or any taint of vice whose strong corruption
Inhabits our frail blood.
Twelfth Night. Act iii, sc. 4, l. 388. [Viola]

10
Ingratitude To you and toward your friend.
The Winter's Tale. Act iii, sc. 2, l. 69. [Hermione]

11
That did but show thee, of a fool, inconstant
And damnable ingrateful.
Winter's Tale. Act iii, sc. 2, l. 187. [Paulina] "Ingrateful" is used twelve times.

INHERITANCE

See also Heir

12
Bequeathed me by will but poor a thousand crowns.
As You Like It. Act i, sc. 1, l. 2. [Orlando]
Give me the poor allotery my father left me by testament; with that I will go buy my fortunes.
As You Like It. Act i, sc. 1, l. 76. [Orlando] The only use of "allotery."

13
Tell me how Wales was made so happy as
To inherit such a haven.
Cymbeline. Act iii, sc. 2, l. 62. [Imogen]
God knows, whether those that bawl out the ruins of thy linen shall inherit his kingdom.
II Henry IV. Act ii, sc. 2, l. 26. [Prince of Wales]
Nothing but fair is that which you inherit.
Love's Labour's Lost. Act iv, sc. 1, l. 20. [Forester]
This, or else nothing, will inherit her.
The Two Gentlemen of Verona. Act iii, sc. 2, l. 87. [Proteus]
Let thine inherit first.—*The Merry Wives of Windsor,* ii, 1, 74.
Mayst thou inherit too!—*All's Well that Ends Well,* i, 2, 22.
We will inherit here.—*The Tempest,* ii, 2, 179.
Inherit heaven's graces.—*Sonnets,* xciv.
Inherits nought.—*Richard II,* ii, 1, 83.
Inherit pain.—*Love's Labour's Lost,* i, 1, 73.

14
The very conveyances of his lands will hardly lie in this box; and must the inheritor have no more?
Hamlet. Act v, sc. 1, l. 118. [Hamlet]
Inheritor of thy desire.—*Richard III,* iv, 3, 34.
Inheritors of this excess.—*Sonnets,* cxlvi.

15 The sole inheritor
Of all perfections that a man may owe.
Love's Labour's Lost. Act ii, sc. 1, l. 5. [Boyet]
Breed out your inheritors.—*Troilus and Cressida,* iv, 1, 64.
Succeed as his inheritor.—*Pericles,* i, 4, 64.
True inheritor.—*II Henry IV,* iv, 5, 169. The only uses of "inheritor."

1 No female
Should be inheritrix in Salique land.
Henry V. Act i, sc. 2, l. 50. [Canterbury] The only use of "inheritrix." There are six references to the Salique law in this play, and in no other.

2
For in the book of Numbers is it writ,
When the man dies, let the inheritance
Descend unto the daughter.
Henry V. Act i, sc. 2, l. 98. [Archbishop of Canterbury] The reference is to *Numbers,* xxvii, 8: "If a man die, and have no sons, then ye shall cause his inheritance to pass unto his daughter." The only mention of *Numbers.*

3
Deprived of honour and inheritance.
I Henry VI. Act ii, sc. 5, l. 27. [Mortimer]
True inheritance.—*II Henry VI,* i, 1, 82.
Whole inheritance.—*I Henry VI,* iii, 1, 164.

4
This small inheritance my father left me
Contenteth me.
II Henry VI, iv, 10, 20. See under CONTENT.
'Twas my inheritance.—*III Henry VI,* i, 1, 78.

5
To reave the orphan of his patrimony.
II Henry VI, v, i, 187. See under OATH. "Reave" is repeated in *All's Well that Ends Well,* v, 3, 86.
Bereft and gelded of his patrimony.
Richard II. Act ii, sc. 1, l. 237. [Lord Ross]
Give me Bianca for my patrimony.
The Taming of the Shrew. Act iv, sc. 4, l. 22. [Tranio]
Take thou my . . . patrimony.
King Lear. Act v, sc. 3, l. 75. [Regan] The only uses of "patrimony."

6 Why, being younger born,
Doth he lay claim to thine inheritance?
King John. Act i, sc. 1, l. 71. [King John]
I 'll go with thee,
And find the inheritance of this poor child.
King John, iv, 2, 97. See under GRAVE.

7 A' pops me out
At least from fair five hundred pound a year.
King John. Act i, sc. 1, l. 68. [Bastard] The only use of "pops."
I, by the honour of my marriage-bed,
After young Arthur, claim this land for mine.
King John. Act v, sc. 2, l. 93. [Dauphin]

8
Divide me like a bribe buck, each a haunch: I will keep my sides to myself, my shoulders for the fellow of this walk, and my horns I bequeath your husbands.
The Merry Wives of Windsor. Act v, sc. 5, l. 27. [Falstaff] The only use of "bribe buck" (stolen buck).

9
Thou left'st me nothing in thy will.
The Passionate Pilgrim, l. 138.
Fetch the will hither, and we shall determine
How to cut off some charge in legacies.
Julius Cæsar. Act iv, sc. 1, l. 8. [Antony]
What legacy shall I bequeathe to thee?
The Rape of Lucrece, l. 1192.
Eve's legacy.—*The Two Gentlemen of Verona,* iii, 1, 343.
Rich legacy.—*Julius Cæsar,* iii, 2, 141.
Beauty's legacy.—*Sonnets,* iv. "Legacy" is repeated in *All's Well that Ends Well,* i, 3, 251, and iii, 5, 13.

10
It was mine own, part of my heritage.
Pericles. Act ii, sc. 1, l. 129. [Pericles] "Heritage" appears only once more in the plays, in *All's Well that Ends Well,* i, 3, 26: "Service is no heritage."

11
What would you have me do? I am a subject,
And I challenge law: attorneys are denied me;
And therefore personally I lay my claim
To my inheritance of free descent.
Richard II. Act ii, sc. 3, l. 133. [Bolingbroke]
Inheritance of their loves.—*Coriolanus,* iii, 2, 68.
Inheritance of Fortinbras.—*Hamlet,* i, 1, 92.

12
All that is mine I leave at thy dispose,
My goods, my lands, my reputation.
The Two Gentlemen of Verona. Act ii, sc. 7, l. 86. [Julia]

INHUMANITY, see Cruelty

INIQUITY

See also Sin, Vice

13
I lack iniquity Sometimes to do me service.
Othello. Act i, sc. 1, l. 3. [Iago]
If you are so fond over her iniquity, give her patent to offend; for, if it touch not you, it comes near nobody.
Othello. Act iv, sc. 1, l. 208. [Iago]

14
Wholesome iniquity have you that a man may deal withal, and defy the surgeon?
Pericles. Act iv, sc. 6, l. 28. [Lysimachus]
The formal vice, Iniquity.—*Richard III,* iii, 1, 82.
Grey iniquity.—*I Henry IV,* ii, 4, 500.
Irreconciled iniquities.—*Henry V,* iv, 1, 160.

15
The prince himself is about a piece of iniquity.
The Winter's Tale. Act iv, sc. 4, l. 692. [Autolycus]

INJURY

See also Hurt, Mischief, Wound, Wrong

16
The record of what injuries you did us,
Though written in our flesh, we shall remember
As things but done by chance.
Antony and Cleopatra. Act v, sc. 2, l. 118. [Cæsar]
I fly thee, for I would not injure thee.
As You Like It. Act iii, sc. 5, l. 9. [Phebe] The only use of "injure."

17 That woman there . . .
That hath abused and dishonour'd me

Even in the strength and height of injury!
The Comedy of Errors. Act v, sc. 1, l. 197. [Antipholus of Ephesus]

1
He hath so planted his honours in their eyes, and his actions in their hearts, that for their tongues to be silent, and not confess so much, were a kind of ingrateful injury.
Coriolanus. Act ii, sc. 2, l. 32. [Officer]

His injury The gaoler to his pity.
Coriolanus. Act v, sc. 1, l. 64. [Cominius]

2
Thy crystal window ope; look out;
No longer exercise
Upon a valiant race thy harsh
And potent injuries.
Cymbeline. Act v, sc. 4, l. 81. [Sicilius]

Cursed injury.—*Cymbeline,* iii, 4, 125.

3
O God! they did me too much injury
That ever said I hearken'd for your death.
I Henry IV. Act v, sc. 4, l. 51. [Prince Henry]

4
The injuries of a wanton time.
I Henry IV. Act v, sc. 1, l. 50. [Worcester]

The service that I truly did his life
Hath left me open to all injuries.
II Henry IV. Act v, sc. 2, l. 7. [Chief Justice]

Bitter injuries.—*I Henry VI,* ii, 5, 124.

5
We thought not good to bruise an injury till it were full ripe.
Henry V. Act iii, sc. 6, l. 129. [Montjoy]

And quickly will return an injury.
Henry V. Act iv, sc. 7, l. 189. [King Henry]

6 Had I twenty times so many foes,
And each of them had twenty times their power,
All these could not procure me any scathe,
So long as I am loyal, true, and crimeless.
II Henry VI. Act ii, sc. 4, l. 60. [Gloucester]

Do offence and scathe.—*King John,* ii, 1, 75.

Done scathe to us.—*Richard III,* i, 3, 317.

Done you any scathe.—*Titus Andronicus,* v, 1, 7.

Chance to scathe you.—*Romeo and Juliet,* i, 5, 86. The only uses of "scathe."

Scatheful grapple.—*Twelfth Night,* v, 1, 59. The only use of "scatheful."

7
Whom have I injured, that ye seek my death?
II Henry VI. Act iv, sc. 7, l. 107. [Lord Say]

How hast thou injured both thyself and us!
III Henry VI. Act i, sc. 1, l. 179. [Clifford]

I do protest, I never injured thee,
But love thee better than thou canst devise.
Romeo and Juliet. Act iii, sc. 1, l. 71. [Romeo]

8
Thou monstrous injurer of heaven and earth!
King John, ii, 1, 174. The only use of Injurer. See SLANDER, 1376:7.

9 To wilful men,
The injuries that they themselves procure
Must be their schoolmasters.
King Lear. Act ii, sc. 4, l. 305. [Regan]

Labours to out-jest His heart-struck injuries.
King Lear. Act iii, sc. 1, l. 17. [Gentleman] The only use of "out-jest" and "heart-struck."

These injuries the king now bears will be revenged home.
King Lear. Act iii, sc. 3, l. 12. [Gloucester]

10 In me you behold
The injury of many a blasting hour.
A Lover's Complaint, l. 71.

Injury of age.—*Sonnets,* cviii.

Injury of chance.—*Troilus and Cressida,* iv, 4, 35.

Injury of tongues.—*The Winter's Tale,* i, 2, 338.

Hate's known injury.—*Sonnets,* xl.

11
Do with your injuries as seem you best.
Measure for Measure. Act v, sc. 1, l. 256. [Friar Peter]

12
Our sex, as well as I, may chide you for it,
Though I alone do feel the injury.
A Midsummer-Night's Dream. Act iii, sc. 2, l. 218. [Helena]

13
Gentlemen all, I do suspect this trash
To be a party in this injury.
Othello. Act v, sc. 1, l. 85. [Iago]

14
Toss'd from wrong to injury.
Pericles. Act v, sc. 1, l. 131. [Pericles]

15
Myself a prince by fortune of my birth . . .
Have stoop'd my neck under your injuries.
Richard II. Act iii, sc. 1, l. 16. [Bolingbroke]

16
When have I injured thee? when done thee wrong?
Richard III. Act i, sc. 3, l. 56. [Gloucester]

You do me shameful injury,
Falsely to draw me in these vile suspects.
Richard III. Act i, sc. 3, l. 88. [Queen Elizabeth]

Who knows not that the noble duke is dead?
You do him injury to scorn his corse.
Richard III. Act ii, sc. 1, l. 79. [Gloucester]

17
The injuries that to myself I do,
Doing thee vantage, double-vantage me.
Sonnets. No. lxxxviii. The only use of "double-vantage."

18
For such an injury would vex a very saint,
Much more a shrew of thy impatient humour.
The Taming of the Shrew. Act iii, sc. 2, l. 28. [Baptista]

Competent injury.—*Twelfth Night,* iii, 4, 269.

INJUSTICE

See also Justice

19
But such is the infection of the time,
That, for the health and physic of our right,
We cannot deal but with the very hand
Of stern injustice and confused wrong.
King John. Act v, sc. 2, l. 20. [Salisbury]

1
Some run from brakes of ice, and answer none:
And some condemned for a fault alone.
Measure for Measure. Act ii, sc. 1, l. 39. [Escalus]

Tax him with injustice.—*Measure for Measure,* iv, 4, 11.

2 The duke 's unjust,
Thus to retort your manifest appeal.
Measure for Measure. Act v, sc. 1, l. 302. [Duke]

Wherefore says she not she is unjust?
Sonnets. No. cxxxviii.

I see this is the time that the unjust man doth thrive.
The Winter's Tale. Act iv, sc. 4, l. 687. [Autolycus]

Thou art an unjust man.—*I Henry IV,* iii, 3, 146.

You are unjust.—*Titus Andronicus,* i, 1, 292.

Thou art all unjust.—*Richard II,* iv, 1, 45.

Now I must be as unjust.—*The Two Gentlemen of Verona,* iv, 2, 2.

Prove unjust.—*The Passionate Pilgrim,* l. 331.

What, 'unjust!'—*Measure for Measure,* v, 1, 315.

You charge me most unjustly.
Othello. Act iv, sc. 2, l. 186. [Iago] "Unjustly" is used eight times.

3
Ho! now you strike like the blind man: 'twas the boy that stole your meat, and you 'll beat the post.
Much Ado about Nothing. Act ii, sc. 1, l. 205. [Benedick]

They jump not on a just account.
Othello. Act i, sc. 3, l. 5. [Second Senator]

4
For 'tis a meritorious fair design
To chase injustice with revengeful arms.
The Rape of Lucrece, l. 1692.

5 All that have miscarried
By underhand corrupted foul injustice.
Richard III. Act v, sc. 1, l. 5. [Buckingham]

All have not offended:
For those that were, it is not square to take
On those that are, revenges.
Timon of Athens. Act v, sc. 4, l. 35. [Senator]

6
What 's this but libelling against the senate,
And blazoning our injustice every where?
Titus Andronicus. Act iv, sc. 4, l. 17. [Saturninus] The only use of "libelling." "Libels" occurs in *Richard III,* i, 1, 33. "Blazoning" is repeated in *Othello,* ii, 1, 63: "Blazoning pens."

7 If I shall be condemn'd
Upon surmises, all proofs sleeping else
But what your jealousies awake, I tell you
'Tis rigour and not law.
The Winter's Tale. Act iii, sc. 2, l. 112. [Hermione]

Apollo 's angry; and the heavens themselves
Do strike at my injustice.
The Winter's Tale. Act iii, sc. 2, l. 147. [Leontes]

INK

See also Pen, Writing

8 Get me ink and paper:
He shall have every day a several greeting.
Antony and Cleopatra. Act i, sc. 5, l. 76. [Cleopatra]

Ink and paper, Charmian.—*Antony and Cleopatra,* i, 5, 65.

Ebon-coloured ink.—*Love's Labour 's Lost,* i, 1, 246. See also BLACKNESS.

9
Give me some ink and paper in my tent.
Richard III. Act v, sc. 3, l. 23. [Richmond]

I will not sup to-night.
Give me some ink and paper.
Richard III. Act v, sc. 3, l. 48. [King Richard]

Is ink and paper ready?—*Richard III,* v, 3, 75.

Get me ink and paper.—*Romeo and Juliet,* v, 1, 25.

Ink and paper.—*Pericles,* iii, 1, 66.

10
Taunt him with the license of ink.
Twelfth Night. Act iii, sc. 2, l. 47. [Sir Toby]

Let there be gall enough in thy ink, though thou write with a goose-pen, no matter.
Twelfth Night. Act iii, sc. 2, l. 52. [Sir Toby] The only use of "goose-pen." "Goose-quill" occurs once, in *Hamlet,* ii, 2, 359.

11
Good fool, help me to some light and paper. . . .
Good fool, some ink, paper and light.
Twelfth Night. Act iv, sc. 2, l. 113. [Malvolio]

12
Write till your ink be dry, and with your tears
Moist it again.
The Two Gentlemen of Verona. Act iii, sc. 2, l. 75. [Proteus]

INN

13
Third Servant: Where dwellest thou?
Coriolanus: Under the canopy. . . .
Third Servant: Where 's that?
Coriolanus: I' the city of kites and crows.
Coriolanus. Act iv, sc. 5, l. 40.

14
Shall I not take mine ease in mine inn?
I Henry IV. Act iii, sc. 3, l. 92. [Falstaff]

Sleep within mine inn.—*The Comedy of Errors,* i, 2, 14.

15
O, I could wish this tavern were my drum!
I Henry IV. Act iii, sc. 3, l. 230. [Falstaff]

Given to . . . taverns.—*The Merry Wives of Windsor,* v, 5, 167.

Knocking at the taverns.—*II Henry IV,* ii, 4, 388. "Tavern" is used eleven times; "tavern-bills" once, in *Cymbeline,* v, 4, 161; and "tavern-reckonings" once, in *I Henry IV,* iii, 3, 178.

The King's tavern.—*I Henry IV,* ii, 2, 59.

16
The red-nose innkeeper of Daventry.
I Henry IV. Act iv, sc. 2, l. 51. [Falstaff]

The only use of "red-nose" and "innkeeper." See under SHIRT.

How like a fawning publican he looks!
The Merchant of Venice. Act i, sc. 3, l. 42. [Shylock] The only use of "publican."

1
A' must, then, to the inns o' court shortly.
I was once of Clement's Inn.
II Henry IV. Act iii, sc. 2, l. 15. Clement's Inn is mentioned again in l. 332.

Gray's Inn.—*II Henry IV,* iii, 2, 36.

2
An alehouse' paltry sign.
II Henry VI. Act v, sc. 2, l. 67. [Richard] "Alehouse sign" is repeated in iii, 2, 81, and in *Titus Andronicus,* iv, 2, 98.

Would I were in an alehouse in London.
Henry V. Act iii, sc. 2, l. 12. [Boy]

You are to call at all the ale-houses, and bid those that are drunk get them to bed.
Much Ado about Nothing. Act iii, sc. 3, l. 45. [Dogberry]

Do ye make an alehouse of my lady's house?
Twelfth Night. Act ii, sc. 3, l. 96. [Malvolio]

I 'll to the alehouse with you presently.
The Two Gentlemen of Verona. Act ii, sc. 5, l. 8. [Speed]

Go with me to the alehouse.—*The Two Gentlemen of Verona,* ii, 5, 57.

The Myrmidons are no bottle-ale houses.
Twelfth Night. Act ii, sc. 3, l. 29. [Clown]

Away you bottle-ale rascal!
II Henry IV, ii, 4, 140. The only uses of "bottle-ale."

3
For we cannot lodge and board a dozen or fourteen gentlewomen that live honestly by the prick of their needles, but it will be thought we keep a bawdy house straight.
Henry V. Act ii, sc. 1, l. 34. [Hostess]

4
The west yet glimmers with some streaks of day:
Now spurs the lated traveller apace
To gain the timely inn.
Macbeth. Act iii, sc. 3, l. 6. [Murderer]

So lated in the world.—*Antony and Cleopatra,* iii, 11, 3. The only uses of "lated."

Riotous inn.—*King Lear,* i, 4, 265.

Self-same inn.—*The Comedy of Errors,* i, 1, 54.

5
'Twas in the Bunch of Grapes, where indeed you have a delight to sit.
Measure for Measure. Act ii, sc. 1, l. 133. [Pompey]

We were lodgers at the Pegasus.
The Taming of the Shrew. Act iv, sc. 4, l. 5. [Pedant] "Lodgers" is repeated in *Henry V,* ii, 1, 33.

In the south suburbs, at the Elephant,
Is best to lodge: I will bespeak our diet.
Twelfth Night. Act iii, sc. 3, l. 39. [Antonio]

Bring it, I pray you, to the Porpentine.
The Comedy of Errors. Act iii, sc. 1, l. 116. [Antipholus of Ephesus] The Porpentine is mentioned five times in this play.

6
For my own part, I never come into any room in a tap-house, but I am drawn in.
Measure for Measure. Act ii, sc. 1, l. 218. [Froth] The only use of "tap-house."

7
To your manor of Pickt-hatch!
The Merry Wives of Windsor. Act ii, sc. 2, l. 18. [Falstaff] The only use of "Pickt-hatch," a quarter of London famous for its brothels, the houses having hatches or half-doors guarded with spikes.

Goodly manor.—*All's Well that Ends Well,* iii, 2, 10.

My manors.—*III Henry VI,* v, 2, 24; *Richard II,* iv, 1, 212. "Manors" is used for a fifth time in *Henry VIII,* i, 1, 84. "Manor-house" occurs once, in *Love's Labour 's Lost,* i, 1, 208.

8
Thou most beauteous inn,
Why should hard-favour'd grief be lodged in thee,
When triumph is become an alehouse guest?
Richard II. Act v, sc. 1, l. 13. [Queen] The original meaning of inn was a private habitation or abode, as opposed to a public one.

9
We 'll call thee at the cubiculo.
Twelfth Night. Act iii, sc. 2, l. 56. [Sir Toby] The only use of "cubiculo" (lodging, from the Latin cubiculum, one of Sir Toby's "affectioned words").

INNOCENCE

10
A dumb innocent, that could not say him nay.
All's Well that Ends Well, iv, 3, 213. See under SEDUCTION.

Incapable and shallow innocents.—*Richard III,* ii, 2, 18.

Sweetest innocent.—*Othello,* v, 2, 199.

11
Charmian: The man is innocent.
Cleopatra: Some innocents 'scape not the thunderbolt.
Antony and Cleopatra. Act ii, sc. 5, l. 76.

12
Innocence,
The dove and very blessed spirit of peace.
II Henry IV. Act iv, sc. 1, l. 45. [Westmoreland]

13
As innocent . . .
As is the sucking lamb or harmless dove.
II Henry VI. Act iii, sc. 1, l. 69. [King Henry]

They are as innocent as grace itself.
As You Like It, i, 3, 56. See TREASON, 1560:5.

I am as innocent as you.—*The Winter's Tale,* ii, 2, 29.

14
The purest spring is not so free from mud
As I am clear from treason to my sovereign.
II Henry VI. Act iii, sc. 1, l. 101. [Gloucester]

The trust I have is in mine innocence,
And therefore am I bold and resolute.
II Henry VI. Act iv, sc. 4, l. 59. [Lord Say]

These hands are free from guiltless blood-shedding,
This breast from harbouring foul deceitful thoughts.
II Henry VI. Act iv, sc. 7, l. 108. [Lord Say] The only use of "blood-shedding."

I am guiltless of your father's death,
And am most sensibly in grief for it.
Hamlet. Act iv, sc. 5, l. 149. [King]

I am guiltless.—*King Lear,* i, 4, 295.
All guiltless.—*Othello,* iv, 1, 48.
I will be guiltless.—*Richard III,* i, 4, 95.
Guiltless and of free disposition.—*Twelfth Night,* i, 5, 99.

We should have answer'd heaven
Boldly 'not guilty.'
Winter's Tale. Act i, sc. 2, l. 73. [Polixenes]

1 I here protest, in sight of heaven,
And by the hope I have of heavenly bliss,
That I am clear from this misdeed.
III Henry VI. Act iii, sc. 3, l. 181. [Warwick] "Misdeed" is repeated in *Richard III,* i, 4, 70.

2 It will help me nothing
To plead mine innocence; for that dye is on me
Which makes my whitest part black.
Henry VIII. Act i, sc. 1, l. 207. [Buckingham] "Whitest" is used only once again, in *Measure for Measure,* iii, 2, 198: "Whitest virtue."

How innocent I was
From any private malice in his end,
His noble jury and foul cause can witness.
Henry VIII. Act iii, sc. 2, l. 267. [Wolsey] "Jury" is used only once more, in *Measure for Measure,* ii, 1, 19.

So much fairer
And spotless shall mine innocence arise.
Henry VIII. Act iii, sc. 2, l. 300. [Wolsey]
Protect mine innocence.—*Henry VIII,* v, 1, 141.

3
What follows is pure innocence.
The Merchant of Venice. Act i, sc. 1, l. 145. [Bassanio]
Pure innocence.—*The Winter's Tale,* ii, 2, 41.
Bashful innocence.—*The Rape of Lucrece,* l. 1341.
Childhood innocence.—*A Midsummer-Night's Dream,* iii, 2, 202.

4
O, take the sense, sweet, of my innocence!
A Midsummer-Night's Dream. Act ii, sc. 2, l. 45. [Lysander]

5
Did I not tell you she was innocent?
Much Ado about Nothing. Act v, sc. 4, l. 1. [Friar]
Innocent and pure.—*The Tempest,* ii, 1, 155.
Innocent of the knowledge.—*Macbeth,* iii, 2, 45.

6
Unless you play the pious innocent.
Pericles. Act iv, sc. 3, l. 17. [Dionyza]

7 Give me leave,
By circumstance, but to acquit myself.
Richard III. Act i, sc. 2, l. 76. [Gloucester]
I will acquit you.—*Twelfth Night,* iii, 4, 235.
God acquit them!—*Henry V,* ii, 2, 144.
Well hast thou acquit thee.—*Richard III,* v, 5, 3.
Acquit him well.—*As You Like It,* i, 1, 134.
So the acquittance follows.—*Cymbeline,* v, 4, 174.
My acquittance seal.—*Hamlet,* iv, 7, 1.
Acquittance me.—*Richard III,* iii, 7, 233. The only uses of "acquittance."
Produce acquittances.—*Love's Labour 's Lost,* ii, 1, 161. The only use of "acquittances."

I and my friend
Have by your wisdom been this day acquitted.
The Merchant of Venice. Act iv, sc. 1, l. 408. [Bassanio]
Acquitted by a true substantial form.
II Henry IV. Act iv, sc. 1, l. 173. [Archbishop of York]
Well acquitted.—*The Merchant of Venice,* v, 1, 138. The only uses of "acquitted."

8
So just is God, to right the innocent.
Richard III. Act i, sc. 3, l. 182. [Queen]
Are you call'd forth from out a world of men
To slay the innocent?
Richard III. Act i, sc. 4, l. 186. [Clarence]
God and our innocency defend and guard us!
Richard III. Act iii, sc. 5, l. 20. [Buckingham]
Mine innocency and Saint George to thrive!
Richard II. Act i, sc. 3, l. 84. [Bolingbroke]
State of innocency.—*I Henry IV,* iii, 3, 186.
Upright innocency.—*II Henry IV,* v, 2, 39.

9 Hence, bashful cunning!
And prompt me, plain and holy innocence!
The Tempest. Act iii, sc. 1, l. 81. [Miranda]
Innocence of love.—*Twelfth Night,* ii, 4, 48.
By innocence I swear.—*Twelfth Night,* iii, 1, 169.

10 If powers divine
Behold our human actions, as they do,
I doubt not then but innocence shall make
False accusation blush and tyranny
Tremble at patience.
The Winter's Tale. Act iii, sc. 2, l. 29. [Hermione]
His innocence, which seems much.
The Winter's Tale. Act v, sc. 2, l. 70. [Third Gentleman]

INSOLENCE

See also Impudence

11
Queasy with his insolence.
Antony and Cleopatra. Act iii, sc. 6, l. 20. [Agrippa]
Queasy question.—*King Lear,* ii, 1, 19.
Queasy stomach.—*Much Ado about Nothing,* ii, 1, 399. The only uses of "queasy."

12 I do wonder
His insolence can brook to be commanded.
Coriolanus. Act i, sc. 1, l. 265. [Sicinius]
His soaring insolence.—*Coriolanus,* ii, 1, 270.

13
I 'll canvass thee in thy broad cardinal's hat,
If thou proceed in this thy insolence.
I Henry VI. Act i, sc. 3, l. 36. [Gloucester]

14
His insolence is more intolerable
Than all the princes in the land beside.
II Henry VI. Act i, sc. 1, l. 175. [Somerset]
Leave thine insolence.—*II Henry VI,* i, 3, 125.
England knows thine insolence.—*II Henry VI,* ii, 1, 31.
Insolence of office.—*Hamlet,* iii, 1, 273.

15
How insolent of late he is become.
II Henry VI, iii, 1, 7. See under CHARACTER.

Insolent, Overcome with pride.—*Coriolanus,* iv, 6, 30.
Out, insolent!—*King John,* ii, 1, 122.

1 I 'll to the king;
And from a mouth of honour quite cry down
This Ipswich fellow's insolence.
Henry VIII. Act i, sc. 1, l. 136. [Buckingham] Ipswich is mentioned again in iv, 2, 59, and in no other play.

2
Do you bandy looks with me, you rascal?
King Lear. Act i, sc. 4, l. 92. [King Lear]
Bandy hasty words.—*King Lear,* ii, 4, 178. See under WORD.

3
Why, how now, dame! whence grows this insolence?
The Taming of the Shrew. Act ii, sc. 1, l. 23. [Baptista]
And pursy insolence shall break his wind
With fear and horrid flight.
Timon of Athens. Act v, sc. 4, l. 12. [Alcibiades] "Pursy" is repeated in *Hamlet,* iii, 4, 153: "Pursy times."

4
He already is too insolent.
Troilus and Cressida. Act i, sc. 3, l. 369. [Ulysses]
His insolence draws folly from my lips.
Troilus and Cressida. Act iv, sc. 5, l. 258. [Hector]

INSPIRATION

5
Unless it be by inspiration.
The Comedy of Errors. Act ii, sc. 2, l. 169. [Antipholus of Syracuse]
Chosen from above
By inspiration of celestial grace.
I Henry VI, v, 4, 40. The only uses of "inspiration." See under HOLINESS.

6 So seem as if
You were inspired to do those duties which
You tender to her.
Cymbeline. Act ii, sc. 3, l. 54. [Queen]

7
Was Mahomet inspired with a dove?
Thou with an eagle art inspired then.
I Henry VI. Act i, sc. 2, l. 140. [Charles] The only mention of Mahomet.
Inspired with the spirit of putting down kings and princes.
II Henry VI. Act iv, sc. 2, l. 38. [Cade]
New inspired.—*Richard II,* ii, 1, 31.

8 Every man,
After the hideous storm that follow'd, was
A thing inspired.
Henry VIII. Act i, sc. 1, l. 89. [Buckingham]

9
Holy men at their death have good inspirations.
The Merchant of Venice. Act i, sc. 2, l. 31. [Nerissa] The only use of "inspirations."

10
Inspire us with the spleen of fiery dragons!
Richard III. Act v, sc. 3, l. 350. [King Richard]
Apollo, Pallas, Jove, or Mercury,
Inspire me, that I may this treason find!
Titus Andronicus. Act iv, sc. 1, l. 66. [Marcus] The only uses of "inspire."

11 By spirits taught to write
Above a mortal pitch.
Sonnets. No. lxxxvi.

INSTANCE

See also Example, Precedent

12
Wherefore, what 's the instance?
All's Well that Ends Well. Act iv, sc. 1, l. 44. [Parolles]

13
Instance, briefly; come, instance.
As You Like It. Act iii, sc. 2, l. 53. [Touchstone]
A more sounder instance, come.
As You Like It. Act iii, sc. 2, l. 62. [Touchstone]
Mend the instance, shepherd.
As You Like It. Act iii, sc. 2, l. 71. [Touchstone]

14
To comfort you the more, I have received
A certain instance that Glendower is dead.
II Henry IV. Act iii, sc. 1, l. 102. [Warwick]
What instance gives Lord Warwick for his vow?
II Henry VI. Act iii, sc. 2, l. 159. [Suffolk]

15
Not with such familiar instances.
Julius Cæsar. Act iv, sc. 2, l. 16. [Lucilius]
Guilty instance.—*The Rape of Lucrece,* l. 1511.
Modern instances.—*As You Like It,* ii, 7, 156.
Precious instance.—*Hamlet,* iv, 5, 162.
Present instance.—*The Comedy of Errors,* iv, 3, 88.
Tragic instance.—*Comedy of Errors,* i, 1, 65.
For instance.—*The Winter's Tale,* iv, 4, 604.

16 One of our convent . . .
Gives me this instance.
Measure for Measure. Act iv, sc. 3, l. 133. [Duke]

17
Offer them instances.
Much Ado about Nothing. Act ii, sc. 2, l. 42. [Borachio]
An old, an old instance, Beatrice, that lived in the time of good neighbours.
Much Ado about Nothing. Act. v, sc. 2, l. 78. [Benedick]

18
Instance, O instance! strong as Pluto's gates.
Troilus and Cressida. Act v, sc. 2, l. 153. [Troilus]
Instance, O instance! strong as heaven itself.
Troilus and Cressida. Act v, sc. 2, l. 155. [Troilus]
What verse for it? what instance for it?
Troilus and Cressida. Act v, sc. 10, l. 41. [Pandarus]

19
What instance of the contrary?
The Two Gentlemen of Verona. Act ii, sc. 4, l. 16. [Thurio]

Instances of infinite of love.—*The Two Gentlemen of Verona,* ii, 7, 70.
Instances of loss.—*II Henry IV,* i, 1, 56.

INSTINCT

1 I 'll never
Be such a gosling to obey instinct, but stand,
As if a man were author of himself
And knew no other kin.
Coriolanus. Act v, sc. 3, l. 34. [Coriolanus] "Gosling" occurs again in *Pericles,* iv, 2, 91.

2 'Tis wonder
That an invisible instinct should frame them
To royalty unlearn'd, honour untaught,
Civility not seen from other.
Cymbeline. Act iv, sc. 2, l. 176. [Belarius]

O rare instinct!—*Cymbeline,* v, 5, 381.

3
Falstaff: Beware instinct; the lion will not touch the true prince. Instinct is a great matter; I was now a coward on instinct. . . .
Prince: By 'r lady, you fought fair; so did you, Peto; so did you, Bardolph: you are lions too, you ran away upon instinct, you will not touch the true prince; no, fie!
Bardolph: 'Faith, I ran when I saw others run.
Prince: Thou rannest away: what instinct hadst thou for it? . . .
Falstaff: Afoot he will not budge a foot.
Prince: Yes, Jack, upon instinct.
Falstaff: I grant ye, upon instinct.
I Henry IV. Act ii, sc. 4, l. 299.

I lack some of thy instinct.
I Henry IV. Act ii, sc. 4, l. 409. [Prince]

4
By a divine instinct men's minds mistrust
Ensuing dangers.
Richard III. Act ii, sc. 3, l. 42. [Citizen]

By instinct.—*II Henry IV,* i, 1, 86.
Without instinct.—*I Henry IV,* ii, 4, 543.
Instinct of love.—*II Henry VI,* iii, 2, 250.

INSTRUCTION

See also Teaching

5
My instruction shall serve to naturalize thee.
All 's Well that Ends Well. Act i, sc. 1, l. 222. [Parolles] The only use of "naturalize."

Brave instruction.—*Antony and Cleopatra,* iv, 14, 98.
Poor instructions.—*All 's Well that Ends Well,* iv, 4, 27.
Your own instruction.—*Coriolanus,* iii, 2, 53.
They shall want no instruction.—*Love's Labour 's Lost,* iv, 2, 81.

6
We but teach Bloody instructions.
Macbeth, i, 7, 8. See under Retribution.

7 Instruct me
How I may formally in person bear me
Like a true friar.
Measure for Measure. Act i, sc. 3, l. 46. [Duke] "Formally" is used only once again, in *Richard II,* i, 3, 29.

She well instructs me.—*Hamlet,* v, 2, 218.
Instructs me.—*The Winter's Tale,* i, 1, 21; *The Tempest,* ii, 1, 223.
Instruct her what she has to do, that she may not be raw in her entertainment.
Pericles. Act iv, sc. 1, l. 59. [Pandar]

Instruct her.—*The Taming of the Shrew,* i, 1, 95; 192; ii, 1, 57.
I will instruct thee.—*Measure for Measure,* iv, 2, 57.
Instructs thee.—*King Lear,* v, 3, 29; *The Tempest,* ii, 2, 173.
Instruct them.—*Titus Andronicus,* v, 1, 98.
Instruct us.—*II Henry IV,* ii, 2, 95; *Timon of Athens,* i, 1, 133; *Othello,* iv, 3, 104; *Cymbeline,* iv, 2, 361.
I 'll instruct you.—*The Taming of the Shrew,* iv, 2, 119.
Instruct you.—*I Henry VI,* iii, 1, 133; *Henry VIII,* v, 1, 149; *The Winter's Tale,* ii, 1, 114; *Cymbeline,* iii, 3, 3.
Instruct great teachers.—*Henry VIII,* i, 2, 113.
Instruct our mistress.—*The Taming of the Shrew,* i, 2, 174.

8
I am going with instruction to him.
Measure for Measure. Act ii, sc. 3, l. 38. [Duke]

Instruction of his frailty.—*Measure for Measure,* iii, 2, 259.

9
I would be glad to receive some instruction.
Measure for Measure. Act iv, sc. 2, l. 19. [Pompey]

Let instructions enter.—*Cymbeline,* i, 5, 47.

10
If my instructions may be your guide.
Measure for Measure. Act iv, sc. 2, l. 181. [Duke]

Keep your instruction.—*Measure for Measure,* iv, 5, 3.

11
It is a good divine that follows his own instructions.
The Merchant of Venice, i, 2, 15. See under Example.

I will better the instruction.—*The Merchant of Venice,* iii, 1, 76.

12
Anon I 'll give thee more instructions.
The Taming of the Shrew. Induction, sc. 1, l. 130. [Lord]

Some good instruction give.—*The Tempest,* i, 2, 424.

13
Of my instruction hast thou nothing bated.
The Tempest. Act iii, sc. 3, l. 85. [Prospero]

She lacks instructions.—*The Winter's Tale,* iv, 4, 593.

14
Instructed by the antiquary times.
Troilus and Cressida, ii, 3, 262. See under Wisdom.

I am not yet instructed.—*Measure for Measure,* i, 1, 81.
Let thy soul be instructed.—*Othello,* ii, 1, 224.

INSTRUMENT

15 What poor an instrument
May do a noble deed!
Antony and Cleopatra. Act v, sc. 2, l. 236. [Cleopatra]

1
May these same instruments, which you profane,
Never sound more!
Coriolanus. Act i, sc. 9, l. 41. [Marcius]
My ingenious instrument!
Hark, Polydore, it sounds!
Cymbeline. Act iv, sc. 2, l. 186. [Belarius]

2
The treacherous instrument is in thy hand,
Unbated and envenom'd.
Hamlet. Act v, sc. 2, l. 327. [Laertes] "Unbated" is repeated in iv, 7, 139: "A sword unbated"; and in *The Merchant of Venice,* ii, 6, 11: "unbated fire."
Cursed instrument.—*I Henry VI,* ii, 5, 58.
Mortal instruments.—*Julius Cæsar,* ii, 1, 66.
Stringless instrument.—*Richard II,* ii, 1, 149. See under TONGUE.
Useful . . . instrument.—*King John,* v, 2, 81.

3
Sound all the lofty instruments of war.
I Henry IV. Act v, sc. 2, l. 98. [Hotspur] See also under TRUMPET.
The fatal instruments of war.
III Henry VI. Act v, sc. 1, l. 87. [Clarence]
Fraught with the . . . instruments
Of cruel war.
Troilus and Cressida. Prologue, l. 4.
Instruments of fear and warning
Unto some monstrous state.
Julius Cæsar. Act i, sc. 3, l. 70. [Cassius]
Instruments of chastisement.—*II Henry IV,* iv, 1, 216.
Instruments of darkness.—*Macbeth,* i, 3, 124.
Instrument of honour.—*All's Well that Ends Well,* iii, 6, 69.
Instrument of ill.—*I Henry VI,* iii, 3, 65.
Instruments to plague us.—*King Lear,* v, 3, 171.
Instrument To vice.—*Winter's Tale,* i, 2, 415.
Instruments that feel.—*The Winter's Tale,* ii, 1, 154.

4
No instrument
Of half that worth as those your swords.
Julius Cæsar. Act iii, sc. 1, l. 154. [Antony]

5
Canst thou hold up thy heavy eyes awhile,
And touch thy instrument a strain or two?
Julius Cæsar. Act iv, sc. 3, l. 256. [Brutus]
If thou dost nod, thou break'st thy instrument;
I'll take it from thee.
Julius Cæsar. Act iv, sc. 3, l. 271. [Brutus]
Lucius: The strings, my lord, are false.
Brutus: He thinks he still is at his instrument.
Julius Cæsar. Act iv, sc. 3, l. 292.

6
Such an instrument I was to use.
Macbeth. Act ii, sc. 1, l. 43. [Macbeth]
The instruments, Who wrought with them.
Macbeth. Act iii, sc. 1, l. 81. [Macbeth]

7
Clown: Why, masters, have your instruments been in Naples, that they speak i' the nose thus? . . . Are these, I pray you, wind-instruments?
Musician: Ay, marry, are they, sir.
Clown: O, thereby hangs a tail.
Musician: Whereby hangs a tail, sir?
Clown: Marry, sir, by many a wind-instrument that I know.
Othello. Act iii, sc. 1, l. 3. The only use of "wind-instrument."

8
I kiss the instrument of their pleasures.
Othello. Act iv, sc. 1, l. 231. [Othello]

9
The cursed Dionyza hath
The pregnant instrument of wrath
Prest for this blow.
Pericles. Act iv, Gower, l. 43.

10
This said, from her be-tumbled couch she starteth,
To find some desperate instrument of death:
But this no slaughterhouse no tool imparteth
To make more vent for passage of her breath.
The Rape of Lucrece, l. 1037. The only use of "be-tumbled."
Death's instrument.—*Richard II,* v, 5, 107.
Draw thy tool.—*Romeo and Juliet,* i, 1, 37.
Great tool.—*Henry VIII,* v, 4, 35. The only uses of "tool."
Sirs, take you to your tools.
Titus Andronicus. Act iv, sc. 3, l. 6. [Titus]
Some coiner with his tools.—*Cymbeline,* ii, 5, 5.
Tools to do 't.—*Cymbeline,* v, 3, 9. The only uses of "tools."

11
'Poor instrument,' quoth she, 'without a sound,
I'll tune thy woes with my lamenting tongue.'
The Rape of Lucrece, l. 1464.

12
Like a cunning instrument cased up,
Or, being open, put into his hands
That knows no touch to tune the harmony.
Richard II. Act i, sc. 3, l. 163. [Mowbray]
Sweet instruments hung up in cases that keep their sounds to themselves.
Timon of Athens, i, 2, 102. See under FRIEND.

13
Here is a friar, and slaughter'd Romeo's man;
With instruments upon them, fit to open
These dead men's tombs.
Romeo and Juliet. Act v, sc. 3, l. 199. [Watchman]

14
My . . . instruments shall be my company.
The Taming of the Shrew. Act i, sc. 1, l. 82. [Bianca]
Toward the education of your daughters,
I here bestow a simple instrument.
The Taming of the Shrew. Act ii, sc. 1, l. 99. [Tranio]
Take you your instrument, play you the whiles.
The Taming of the Shrew. Act iii, sc. 1, l. 22. [Bianca]
Hortensio: Madam, my instrument 's in tune.
Bianca: Let's hear. O fie! the treble jars.
Lucentio: Spit in the hole, man, and tune again.
The Taming of the Shrew. Act iii, sc. 1, l. 38.
Madam, before you touch the instrument,
To learn the order of my fingering,

I must begin with rudiments of art.
The Taming of the Shrew. Act iii, sc. 1, l. 64. [Hortensio] "Rudiments" is repeated in *As You Like It,* v, 4, 31: "Rudiments Of many desperate studies."

1
Come, give me an instrument.
Troilus and Cressida. Act iii, sc. 1, l. 104. [Pandarus]

2 I partly know the instrument
That screws me from my true place in your favour.
Twelfth Night. Act v, sc. 1, l. 125. [Duke]

3
We 'll make an instrument of this, omit
Nothing may give us aid.
Winter's Tale. Act iv, sc. 4, l. 636. [Camillo]

4
Sometimes a thousand twangling instruments
Will hum about mine ears.
The Tempest. Act iii, sc. 2, l. 146. [Caliban]

5
Here 's an engine fit for my proceeding.
The Two Gentlemen of Verona. Act iii, sc. 1, l. 138. [Duke]

Fatal engine.—*Titus Andronicus,* v, 3, 86.
Mortal engines.—*Othello,* iii, 3, 355. See under CANNON.
Devise engines for my life.—*Othello,* iv, 2, 221.
Engine of her thoughts.—*Titus Andronicus,* iii, 1, 82.
Engines of lust.—*All 's Well that Ends Well,* iii, 5, 21.
Like an engine not portable.—*Troilus and Cressida,* ii, 3, 143.
Like an engine.—*Coriolanus,* v, 4, 19; *King Lear,* i, 4, 290.

6
All the instruments which aided to expose the child were even then lost when it was found.
The Winter's Tale. Act v, sc. 2, l. 77. [Third Gentleman]

INSULT

See also Indignity

7 Who might be your mother,
That you insult, exult, and all at once,
Over the wretched?
As You Like It. Act iii, sc. 5, l. 35. [Rosalind]

Insult without all reason.—*Coriolanus,* iii, 1, 144.

8
My speech of insultment ended on his dead body.
Cymbeline. Act iii, sc. 5, l. 145. [Cloten] The only use of "insultment."

Insulted, rail'd.—*King Lear,* ii, 2, 126. The only use of "insulted." "Insulter" also is used only once, in *Venus and Adonis,* l. 550.

9
Thou haught insulting man.
Richard II. Act iv, sc. 1, l. 253. [King Richard] "Haught," for haughty, is used twice more in the plays, in *III Henry VI,* ii, 1, 169, and *Richard III,* ii, 3, 28.

Proud insulting boy!—*III Henry VI,* ii, 2, 84.
Proud insulting queen.—*III Henry VI,* ii, 1, 168.

10
I will bite my thumb at them; which is a disgrace to them, if they bear it.
Romeo and Juliet. Act i, sc. 1, l. 48. [Sampson]

Give me thy knife, I will insult on him.
Titus Andronicus. Act iii, sc. 2, l. 71. [Titus]

INTEGRITY

See also Honesty

11
My integrity ne'er knew the crafts
That you do charge men with.
All 's Well that Ends Well. Act iv, sc. 2, l. 33. [Bertram]

I am sorry my integrity should breed . . .
So deep suspicion.
Henry VIII. Act iii, sc. 1, l. 51. [Wolsey]

My integrity to heaven, is all
I dare now call mine own.
Henry VIII. Act iii, sc. 2, l. 453. [Wolsey]

12
His integrity Stands without blemish.
Measure for Measure. Act v, sc. 1, l. 107. [Duke Vincentio]

Deep integrity.—*Richard II,* v, 3, 108.
Divine integrity.—*Troilus and Cressida,* iv, 5, 170.

13 I do affy
In thy uprightness and integrity.
Titus Andronicus. Act i, sc. 1, l. 47. [Bassianus] "Affy" is repeated in *II Henry VI,* iv, 1, 80. The only use of "uprightness."

Integrity and learning.—*Henry VIII,* ii, 4, 59.
Integrity and truth.—*Troilus and Cressida,* iii, 2, 172.

14 Frame some feeling line
That may discover such integrity.
The Two Gentlemen of Verona. Act iii, sc. 2, l. 76.

15
Mine integrity Being counted falsehood.
The Winter's Tale. Act iii, sc. 2, l. 27. [Hermione]

INTELLIGENCE

I—Understanding

16 Thou hast, Ventidius, that
Without the which a soldier, and his sword,
Grants scarce distinction.
Antony and Cleopatra. Act iii, sc. 1, l. 27. [Silius]

He 's very knowing.
Antony and Cleopatra. Act iii, sc. 3, l. 26. [Cleopatra] The only use of this idiom. "Knowing ear" occurs in *Hamlet,* iv, 7, 3.

17 I find thee apt;
And duller shouldst thou be than the fat weed
That roots itself in ease on Lethe wharf,
Wouldst thou not stir in this.
Hamlet. Act i, sc. 5, l. 31. [Ghost]

Is she not apt?—*Henry V,* v, 2, 312.
Apt to learn.—*Taming of the Shrew,* ii, 1, 166.
Apt, because quick.—*Love's Labour 's Lost,* i, 2, 24.

Apt, in good faith; very apt.—*Twelfth Night,* i, 5, 28.
How apt.—*Henry V,* ii, 2, 86; *Twelfth Night,* iii, 1, 138.
Most apt.—*Othello,* ii, 1, 175; *Twelfth Night,* v, 1, 328.
Right apt.—*Twelfth Night,* i, 4, 35.
So apt.—*Romeo and Juliet,* iii, 1, 34; *Julius Cæsar,* iii, 1, 160; *Othello,* ii, 3, 326.
Apt enough.—*Romeo and Juliet,* iii, 1, 44.
Apt and true.—*Othello,* v, 2, 177.
Pretty and apt.—*Love's Labour 's Lost,* i, 2, 19.
Young and apt.—*Timon of Athens,* i, 1, 132.
She is apter.—*As You Like It,* iii, 2, 408. "Apter" is used only once again, in *II Henry IV,* i, 1, 69. "Aptest" occurs only once, in *II Henry IV,* i, 1, 213: "Aptest way." "Aptly" is used eight times.
Be friended with aptness of the season.
Cymbeline. Act ii, sc. 3, l. 52. [Queen]
Ripe aptness.—*Coriolanus,* iv, 3, 23.
In either's aptness.—*A Lover's Complaint,* l. 306. The only uses of "aptness."

1
O, where hath our intelligence been drunk?
Where hath it slept?
King John. Act iv, sc. 2, l. 116. [King John]
Be intelligent.—*The Winter's Tale,* i, 2, 378.
An intelligent party.—*King Lear,* iii, 5, 12.

2
Things hid and barr'd, you mean, from common sense?
Love's Labour 's Lost. Act i, sc. 1, l. 57. [Biron] "Common sense" is repeated in i, 1, 64; *II Henry IV,* iv, ?, 33; *All's Well that Ends Well,* ii, 1, 181.

3
He hath the joints of every thing, but every thing so out of joint that he is a gouty Briareus, many hands and no use.
Troilus and Cressida. Act i, sc. 2, l. 27. [Alexander] The only mention of Briareus.

II—Information

4
Hath the count all this intelligence?
All 's Well that Ends Well. Act iv, sc. 3, l. 69. [Lord]
He will be here to-morrow, or I am deceived by him that in such intelligence hath seldom failed.
All 's Well that Ends Well. Act iv, sc. 5, l. 87. [Lafeu]
You will be welcome with this intelligence.
Coriolanus. Act iv, sc. 3, l. 30. [Volsce]

5
With myself I hold intelligence.
As You Like It. Act i, sc. 3, l. 49. [Rosalind]

6
Sought to entrap me by intelligence.
I Henry IV. Act iv, sc. 3, l. 98. [Hotspur]
By intelligence.—*Henry VIII,* i, 1, 153.

7
O sir, fly this place;
Intelligence is given where you are hid.
King Lear. Act ii, sc. 1, l. 22. [Edmund]

8
Say from whence
You owe this strange intelligence? or why
Upon this blasted heath you stop our way
With such prophetic greeting?
Macbeth. Act i, sc. 3, l. 75. [Macbeth]
False intelligence.—*Richard III,* ii, 1, 54.
Good intelligence.—*Henry V,* ii, Prol., 12.
True intelligence.—*I Henry IV,* v, 5, 10.
My intelligence.is true.—*The Merry Wives of Windsor,* iv, 2, 154.

9
Nothing can proceed that toucheth us
Whereof I shall not have intelligence.
Richard III. Act iii, sc. 2, l. 23. [Hastings]
I have . . . received intelligence.—*Richard II,* ii, 1, 278.
He hath had intelligence.—*The Merry Wives of Windsor,* iv, 2, 95.

10
Patroclus will give me any thing for the intelligence of this whore.
Troilus and Cressida. Act v, sc. 2, l. 192. [Thersites]

11
That 's likewise part of my intelligence.
The Winter's Tale. Act iv, sc. 2, l. 51. [Polixenes]
Gives intelligence.—*The Merry Wives of Windsor,* iii, 5, 85; *Much Ado about Nothing,* i, 3, 46.

INTEMPERANCE

See also Drunkenness

12
I do beseech your majesty may salve
The long-grown wounds of my intemperance.
I Henry IV. Act iii, sc. 2, l. 155. [Prince of Wales] The only use of "long-grown."

13
Boundless intemperance
In nature is a tyranny.
Macbeth. Act iv, sc. 3, l. 66. [Macduff] The only uses of "intemperance."

14
You are more intemperate in your blood
Than Venus.
Much Ado about Nothing, iv, 1, 60. See under SEEMING.
Intemperate lust.—*Measure for Measure,* v, 1, 98. The only uses of "intemperate."

INTENTION

See also Meaning, Purpose

15
My intents are fix'd and will not leave me.
All 's Well that Ends Well. Act i, sc. 1, l. 244. [Helena]
Is it not meant damnable in us, to be trumpeters of our unlawful intents?
All 's Well that Ends Well. Act iv, sc. 3, l. 31. [First Lord]

16
Antony: How intend you, practised?
Cæsar: You may be pleased to catch at mine intent
By what did here befal me.
Antony and Cleopatra. Act ii, sc. 2, l. 40.
Apply yourself to our intents,
Which towards you are most gentle.
Antony and Cle^batra. Act v, sc. 2, l. 126. [Cæsar]
Absurd intents.—*Antony and Cleopatra,* v, 2, 226.

17
You might stay him from his intendment.
As You Like It, i, 1, 140. "Intendment" is

repeated in *Henry V,* i, 2, 144, and *Othello,* iv, 2, 206.

1
And I will stoop and humble my intents
To your well-practised wise directions.
II Henry IV. Act v, sc. 2, l. 120. [King Henry V] The only use of "well-practised."
Cold intent.—*II Henry IV,* iv, 1, 9.

2
So help me God, as I intend it not!
I Henry VI. Act iii, sc. 1, l. 141. [Winchester]
Their intent is this.—*I Henry VI,* v, 1, 3.
Bold intent.—*I Henry VI,* iv, 1, 103.
Virtuous chaste intents.—*I Henry VI,* v, 5, 20.

3
Free from a stubborn opposite intent.
II Henry VI. Act iii, sc. 2, l. 251. [Salisbury]

4
She was coming with a full intent
To dash our late decree in parliament.
III Henry VI. Act ii, sc. 1, l. 117. [Warwick]
To-morrow shall you bear our full intent
Back to our brother England.
Henry V. Act ii, sc. 4, l. 114. [French King]
And now be it known to you my full intent.
Titus Andronicus. Act iv, sc. 2, l. 151. [Aaron]

5
Well-minded Clarence.
III Henry VI. Act iv, sc. 8, l. 27. [King Henry] The only use of "well-minded."

6
I know not, gentlemen, what you intend,
Who else must be let blood, who else is rank.
Julius Cæsar. Act iii, sc. 1, l. 151. [Antony]
Well, I 'll not say what I intend for thee.
King John. Act iii, sc. 3, l. 68. [King John]

7
My good intent
May carry through itself to that full issue
For which I razed my likeness.
King Lear. Act i, sc. 4, l. 2. [Kent] The only use of "good intent." "Good intents" occurs in *II Henry IV,* v, 2, 143.
I dissuaded him from his intent,
And found him pight to do it.
King Lear. Act ii, sc. 1, l. 66. [Edmund] "Pight" (pitched) occurs again in *Troilus and Cressida,* v, 10, 24: "Tents proudly pight."
Fast intent.—*King Lear,* i, 1, 39.
Strong intent.—*Hamlet,* iii, 3, 40.
Swift intent.—*The Rape of Lucrece,* l. 46.
True intent.—*A Midsummer-Night's Dream,* v, 1, 114.

8
Katharine: What is your intent?
Princess: The effect of my intent is to cross theirs.
Love's Labour's Lost. Act v, sc. 2, l. 137.

9
Who knew of your intent and coming hither?
Measure for Measure. Act v, sc. 1, l. 124. [Duke]

10
She did so course o'er my exteriors with such a greedy intention.
The Merry Wives of Windsor, i, 3, 73. See under COQUETRY.
Thy intention stabs the centre.—*The Winter's Tale,* i, 2, 138. The only uses of "intention."

11
He comes to bad intent.
Othello. Act i, sc. 2, l. 56. [Iago]
Bad intent.—*Measure for Measure,* v, 1, 456. See under ACT.

12
For me, be you thoughten
That I came with no ill intent.
Pericles. Act iv, sc. 6, l. 115. [Lysimachus] The only use of "thoughten" and of "ill intent."
Intent to murder.—*Pericles,* ii, Gower, 24.

13
I intend more good to you and yours
Than ever you and yours were by me wrong'd!
Richard III. Act iv, sc. 4, l. 237. [King Richard] "I intend," "he intends," "we intend," etc., are used frequently throughout the plays.
Deep intent.—*Richard III,* i, 1, 149.
Secret close intent.—*Richard III,* i, 1, 158.

14
The time and my intents are savage-wild,
More fierce and more inexorable far
Than empty tigers or the roaring sea.
Romeo and Juliet. Act v, sc. 3, l. 37. [Romeo] The only use of "savage-wild."
More inexorable . . . than tigers.—*III Henry VI,* i, 4, 154. The only uses of "inexorable."
His looks I fear, and his intents I doubt.
Romeo and Juliet. Act v, sc. 3, l. 44. [Balthasar]
Sharp'st intents.—*Sonnets,* cxv.

15
Poet: I must tell him of an intent that 's coming toward him.
Painter: Good as the best.
Timon of Athens. Act v, sc. 1, l. 22.

16
Arm'd, and bloody in intent.
Troilus and Cressida. Act v, sc. 3, l. 8. [Andromache]

17
And all amazed brake off his late intent.
Venus and Adonis, l. 469.

INTEREST

18
He hath no interest in me in the world.
As You Like It. Act v, sc. 1, l. 8. [Audrey]
My lord hath interest in them.—*Cymbeline,* i, 3, 30.

19
What 's thy interest In this sad wreck?
Cymbeline. Act iv, sc. 2, l. 365. [Lucius]
He hath more worthy interest to the state
Than thou the shadow of succession.
I Henry IV. Act iii, sc. 2, l. 98. [King Henry]

20
All your interest in those territories
Is utterly bereft you.
II Henry VI. Act iii, sc. 1, l. 84. [Somerset]
You claim no interest In any of our towns.
I Henry VI. Act v, sc. 3, l. 167. [Charles]

Interest of territory.—*King Lear,* i, 1, 51.
Interest to this land.—*King John,* v, 2, 89.

1
My well-won thrift, Which he calls interest.
The Merchant of Venice. Act i, sc. 3, l. 51. [Shylock] The only use of "well-won."
Antonio: Did he take interest?
Shylock: No, not take interest, not, as you would say,
Directly interest.
The Merchant of Venice. Act i, sc. 3, l. 76.
Antonio: Was this inserted to make interest good?
Or is your gold and silver ewes and rams?
Shylock: I cannot tell; I make it breed as fast.
The Merchant of Venice. Act i, sc. 3, l. 95.
New interest.—*The Merchant of Venice,* iii, 2, 224.

2 Thy interest was not bought
Basely with gold, but stol'n from forth my gate.
The Rape of Lucrece, l. 1067.

3
Ah, so much interest have I in thy sorrow
As I had title in thy noble husband!
Richard III. Act ii, sc. 2, l. 47. [Duchess of York]
I have an interest in your hate's proceeding,
My blood for your rude brawls doth lie a-bleeding.
Romeo and Juliet. Act iii, sc. 1, l. 193. [Prince]

4
Advantaging their loan with interest.
Richard III, iv, 4, 323. The only use of "advantaging." See under TEAR.
With interest.—*I Henry IV,* iv, 3, 49.
Bosom interest.—*Macbeth,* i, 2, 64.
Unowed interest.—*King John,* iv, 3, 147. The only use of "unowed."

5 He is so kind that he now
Pays interest for 't.
Timon of Athens. Act i, sc. 2, l. 205. [Flavius]
Take down the interest into their gluttonous maws.
Timon of Athens, iii, 4, 52. See under DEBT.
Let out Their coin upon large interest.
Timon of Athens, iii, 5, 107. See under FOE.

6
He should give her interest, and she gives it him.
The Two Gentlemen of Verona. Act ii, sc. 1, l. 109. [Speed]
One for interest.—*Venus and Adonis,* l. 210. See under KISS.

INTERPRETATION

7 One, but painted thus,
Would be interpreted a thing perplex'd
Beyond self-explication.
Cymbeline. Act iii, sc. 4, l. 6. [Imogen] The only use of "self-explication."
All amiss interpreted.—*Julius Cæsar,* ii, 2, 83. The only uses of "interpreted."

8
I could interpret between you and your love, if I could see the puppets dallying.
Hamlet. Act iii, sc. 2, l. 256. [Hamlet]

9
Look how we can, or sad or merrily,
Interpretation will misquote our looks.
I Henry IV. Act v, sc. 2, l. 12. [Worcester] The only use of "misquote."
You did make him misinterpret me.
Richard II. Act iii, sc. 1, l. 18. [Bolingbroke] The only use of "misinterpret."
Your exposition misinterpreting.—*Pericles,* i, 1, 112. The only use of "misinterpreting."
Interpret false.—*Pericles,* i, 1, 124.
Interpret further.—*Macbeth,* iii, 6, 2.

10
A crown's worth of good interpretation.
II Henry IV. Act ii, sc. 2, l. 99. [Prince of Wales]
Interpretation of the time.—*Coriolanus,* iv, 7, 50.
Interpretation of full time.—*Coriolanus,* v, 3, 69.

11
I can interpret all her martyr'd signs.
Titus Andronicus. Act iii, sc. 2, l. 36. [Titus]

12 It will not lie where it concerns,
Unless it have a false interpreter.
The Two Gentlemen of Verona. Act i, sc. 2, l. 77. [Lucetta]
Some one among us whom we must produce for an interpreter.
All's Well that Ends Well. Act iv, sc. 1, l. 5. [Lord]
Let me be the interpreter.—*All's Well that Ends Well,* iv, 1, 8.
Our interpreter does it well.—*All's Well that Ends Well,* iv, 3, 236.
Aged interpreter.—*Timon of Athens,* v, 3, 8.
Lewd interpreter.—*The Merchant of Venice,* iii, 4, 80.
Madam my interpreter.—*Henry V,* v, 2, 282.
Sick interpreters.—*Henry VIII,* i, 2, 82.
Interpreters Of my behind-hand slackness.
The Winter's Tale. Act v, sc. 1, l. 150. [Leontes] The only use of "behind-hand." "Slackness" is repeated in *Antony and Cleopatra,* iii, 7, 28.

13
O exceeding puppet! Now will he interpret to her.
The Two Gentlemen of Verona. Act ii, sc. 1, l. 100. [Speed]
If your lass Interpretation should abuse.
The Winter's Tale. Act iv, sc. 4, l. 362. [Polixenes]

INTERRUPTION

14
He that interrupts him shall not live.
III Henry VI. Act i, sc. 1, l. 123. [Warwick]
Interrupt the monster one word further, and, by this hand, I 'll turn my mercy out o' doors and make a stock-fish of thee.
Tempest. Act iii, sc. 2, l. 76. [Stephano]

15
The interruption of their churlish drums
Cuts off more circumstance.
King John, ii, 1, 76. See under DRUM.
Interruption of thy devotion.—*Richard III,* iii, 7, 102.
O'erbearing interruption.—*King John,* iii, 4, 9. "O'erbearing" is repeated in *Othello,* i,

3, 56: "O'erbearing nature." The only uses of "interruption."

1
When lo! to interrupt my purposed rest . . .
The king and his companions.
Love's Labour's Lost. Act v, sc. 2, l. 91. [Boyet]
Thou interrupt'st our merriment.
Love's Labour's Lost. Act v, sc. 2, l. 725. [Princess] The only use of "interrupt'st."
I'll interrupt his reading.
Troilus and Cressida. Act iii, sc. 3, l. 93. [Achilles]

2
Do not interrupt me in my course.
Romeo and Juliet. Act v, sc. 3, l. 27. [Romeo]
I'll . . . never interrupt you.—*Pericles,* v, 1, 167.

3
And happily we might be interrupted.
The Taming of the Shrew. Act iv, sc. 4, l. 54. [Baptista]
Her quiet interrupted.—*The Rape of Lucrece,* l. 1170.
Interrupted much.—*King John,* ii, 1, 542.
Interrupted waters.—*Coriolanus,* iii, 1, 249. The only uses of "interrupted."

4 Interrupter of the good
That noble-minded Titus means to thee!
Titus Andronicus. Act i, sc. 1, l. 208. [Lucius] The only use of "interrupter." "Noble-minded" is repeated in *I Henry VI,* iv, 4, 37: "Noble-minded Talbot."

5
I have put you out.
The Winter's Tale. Act iv, sc. 4, l. 377. [Polixenes]

INVENTION

6 Invention is ashamed,
Against the proclamation of thy passion.
All's Well that Ends Well. Act i, sc. 3, l. 179. [Countess]
Return with an invention and clap upon you two or three probable lies.
All's Well that Ends Well. Act iii, sc. 6, l. 105. [Second Lord]
It must be a very plausive invention that carries it.
All's Well that Ends Well. Act iv, sc. 1, l. 29. [Parolles] "Plausive" is repeated in *All's Well that Ends Well,* i, 2, 53: "Plausive words"; and in *Hamlet,* i, 4, 30: "Plausive manners."
Add more, From thine invention.—*Antony and Cleopatra,* iii, 12, 29.

7
I say she never did invent this letter;
This is a man's invention and his hand.
. . . Women's gentle brain
Could not drop forth such giant-rude invention.
As You Like It. Act iv, sc. 3, l. 28. [Rosalind] The only use of "giant-rude."

8
The brain of this foolish-compounded clay, man, is not able to invent any thing that tends to laughter, more than I invent or is invented on me.
II Henry IV. Act i, sc. 2, l. 8. [Falstaff] The only use of "foolish-compounded."
I invented it myself.
II Henry VI. Act iv, sc. 2, l. 163. [Cade] The only uses of "invented."

9
The brightest heaven of invention.
Henry V. Act i, Prologue, l. 2. [Chorus]
Do it without invention, suddenly.
I Henry VI. Act iii, sc. 1, l. 5. [Winchester]
Such invention as I can devise.
III Henry VI. Act iv, sc. 1, l. 35. [King Edward]
If . . . my invention thrive.—*King Lear,* i, 2, 20.

10
Ovidius Naso was the man: and why, indeed, Naso, but for smelling out the odoriferous flowers of fancy, the jerks of invention?
Love's Labour's Lost. Act iv, sc. 2, l. 127. [Holofernes] The only use of "jerks." "Odoriferous" occurs again in *King John,* iii, 4, 26. The only mention of Ovid.

11
Return To plague the inventor.
Macbeth, i, 7, 9. See under RETRIBUTION.
Inventors' heads.—*Hamlet,* v, 2, 306. The only uses of "inventor."

12 Filling their hearers
With strange invention.
Macbeth. Act iii, sc. 1, l. 32. [Macbeth]
Blunt invention.—*Sonnets,* ciii.
Old inventions.—*The Taming of the Shrew,* iii, 1, 81. See under FASHION.
Sad invention.—*Much Ado about Nothing.* v, 1, 292.
In her invention, . . . they conveyed me into a buck-basket.
The Merry Wives of Windsor. Act iii, sc. 5, l. 86. [Falstaff] "Buck-basket" (dirty-linen basket) is used three times in this scene, and in v, 5, 117, and occurs in no other play.

13 My invention
Comes from my pate as birdlime does from frize;
It plucks out brains and all: but my Muse labours,
And thus she is deliver'd.
Othello. Act ii, sc. 1, l. 126. [Iago] The only use of "birdlime." "Frize" (coarse woollen cloth with a nap) is repeated in *The Merry Wives of Windsor,* v, 5, 146.
Of so high . . . invention.—*Othello,* iv, 1, 201.
Inventions to delight the taste.—*Pericles,* i, 4, 40. See under BREAD.

14
Much like a press of people at a door,
Throng her inventions, which shall go before.
The Rape of Lucrece, l. 1301.

15
In this change is my invention spent.
Sonnets. No. cv.
Labouring for invention.—*Sonnets,* lix.

1
Both our inventions meet and jump in one.
The Taming of the Shrew. Act i, sc. 1, l. 195. [Tranio]
2
Say 'tis not . . . your invention.
Twelfth Night. Act v, sc. 1, l. 341. [Malvolio]
Full of invention.—*Twelfth Night,* iii, 2, 47.

INVENTORY

3
The leanness that afflicts us, the object of our misery, is as an inventory to particularize their abundance.
Coriolanus. Act i, sc. 1, l. 20. [Citizen] The only use of "particularize." "Leanness" is repeated in *II Henry VI,* i, 1, 112, and in *Richard II,* ii, 1, 78.
4
I will write all down:
Such and such pictures; there the window; such
The adornment of her bed; the arms, figures,
Why, such and such; and the contents o' the story.
Ah, but some natural notes about her body,
Above ten thousand meaner moveables
Would testify, to enrich mine inventory.
Cymbeline. Act ii, sc. 2, l. 24. [Iachimo]
Divide him inventorially.—*Hamlet,* v, 2, 118. The only use of "inventorially."
5
The inventory of thy shirts, as, one for superfluity, and another for use!
II Henry IV. Act ii, sc. 2, l. 20. [Prince of Wales]
6
Bear the inventory
Of your best graces in your mind.
Henry VIII, iii, 2, 137. See under HOLINESS.
Take an inventory of all I have,
To the last penny.
Henry VIII. Act iii, sc. 2, l. 451. [Wolsey]
An inventory, thus importing.—*Henry VIII,* iii, 2, 124.
7
It shall be inventoried, and every particle and utensil labelled to thy will.
Twelfth Night, 263. See under BEAUTY. The only use of "inventoried" and "labelled."

INVISIBILITY

8
I would I were invisible.
As You Like It. Act i, sc. 2, l. 223. [Celia]
I would it would make you invisible.
Twelfth Night. Act iii, sc. 1, l. 35. [Clown]
9
Witness you,
That he is borne about invisible.
The Comedy of Errors. Act v, sc. 1, l. 186. [Adriana]
10
Gadshill: We have the receipt of fern-seed, we walk invisible.
Chamberlain: Nay, by my faith, I think you are more beholding to the night than to fern-seed for your walking invisible.
I Henry IV. Act ii, sc. 1, l. 96. The only use of "fern-seed."
I am invisible.—*Midsummer-Night's Dream,* ii, 1, 186.
11
Be subject
To no sight but thine and mine, invisible
To every eyeball else.
The Tempest. Act i, sc. 2, l. 301. [Prospero]
Thy shape invisible retain thou still.
The Tempest. Act iv, sc. 1, l. 185. [Prospero]
Invisible as thou art.—*The Tempest,* v, 1, 97.
12
Invisible, As a nose on a man's face.
The Two Gentlemen of Verona. Act ii, sc. 1, l. 141. [Speed]

IRELAND

13
An Irishman, a very gallant gentleman.
Henry V. Act iii, sc. 2, l. 71. [Gower]
I will rather trust . . . an Irishman.
The Merry Wives of Windsor. Act ii, sc. 2, l. 318. [Ford] The only uses of "Irishman."
14
Great lords, from Ireland am I come amain,
To signify that rebels there are up
And put the Englishmen unto the sword.
II Henry VI. Act iii, sc. 1, l. 282. [Post]
The uncivil kerns of Ireland are in arms
And temper clay with blood of Englishmen;
To Ireland will you lead a band of men, . . .
And try your hap against the Irishmen?
II Henry VI. Act iii, sc. 1, l. 310. [Beaufort] "Temper clay" is used again in *King Lear,* i, 4, 326. The only use of "Irishmen."
I cannot strike at wretched kerns, whose arms
Are hired to bear their staves.
Macbeth. Act v, sc. 7, l. 17. [Macduff]
Kern of Ireland.—*Henry V,* iii, 7, 56.
Shag-haired crafty kern.—*III Henry VI,* iii, 1, 367. "Shag-haired" is repeated in *Macbeth,* iv, 2, 83: "Shag-haired villain."
Skipping kerns.—*Macbeth,* i, 2, 30. A kern was a light-armed Irish foot-soldier.
15
Why, then from Ireland come I with my strength.
II Henry VI. Act iii, sc. 1, l. 380. [York]
Newly come from Ireland.—*II Henry VI,* iv, 9, 24.
From Ireland coming.—*Henry V,* v, Prol., 31.
16
In Ireland have I seen this stubborn Cade
Oppose himself against a troop of kerns,
And fought so long, till that his thighs with darts
Were almost like a sharp-quilled porpentine.
II Henry VI. Act iii, sc. 1, l. 360. [York] The only use of "sharp-quilled."
17
The western isles
Of kerns and gallowglasses.
Macbeth. Act i, sc. 2, l. 12. [Sergeant]
A mighty power
Of gallowglasses and stout kerns
Is marching hitherward.
II Henry VI. Act iv, sc. 9, l. 26. [Messenger] The only uses of "gallowglasses" (retainers maintained by Irish chiefs).
18
We will make for Ireland presently.
Richard II. Act i, sc. 4, l. 52. [King Richard]

Now for our Irish wars:
We must supplant those rough rug-headed kerns,
Which live like venom where no venom else
But only they have privilege to live.
Richard II. Act ii, sc. 1, l. 155. [King Richard] The only use of "rug-headed." "Irish wars" occurs five times.

To-morrow next
We will for Ireland; and 'tis time, I trow.
Richard II. Act ii, sc. 1, l. 217. [King Richard]

I will to Ireland.—*Richard II*, ii, 2, 141.

To Ireland, I.—*Macbeth*, ii, 3, 144.

Shipp'd for Ireland.—*Richard II*, ii, 2, 42.

IRON

1
Come, good fellow, put mine iron on.
Antony and Cleopatra, iv, 4, 3. See under ARMOUR.

Irons of a doit.—*Coriolanus*, i, 5, 7.

2
Ne'er wore . . . iron on his heel.
Cymbeline, iv, 4, 40. See under HORSEMANSHIP.

3
I dare not fight; but I will wink and hold out mine iron: it is a simple one; but what though? it will toast cheese, and it will endure cold as another man's sword will: and there 's an end.
Henry V. Act ii, sc. 1, l. 7. [Nym]

Come, my young soldier, put up your iron: you are well fleshed.
Twelfth Night. Act iv, sc. 1, l. 42. [Sir Toby]

Forswear to wear iron about you.—*Twelfth Night*, ii, 4, 276.

4
Now bind my brows with iron.
II Henry IV. Act i, sc. 1, l. 150. [Northumberland]

Strong links of iron.—*Julius Cæsar*, i, 3, 94.

Iron and steel.—*Henry V*, iii, 7, 161.

Old iron.—*I Henry VI*, i, 2, 101.

5
I 'll make thee eat iron like an ostrich.
II Henry VI, iv, 10, 30. See under THREAT.

6
Strike now, or else the iron cools.
III Henry VI. Act v, sc. 1, l. 49. [Gloucester]

His iron did on the anvil cool.
King John, iv, 2, 194. See TAILOR, 1486:2.

7
The iron of itself, though heat red-hot,
Approaching near these eyes, would drink my tears
And quench his fiery indignation.
King John. Act iv, sc. 1, l. 61. [Arthur] See under EYES. "Red-hot" is repeated in *Richard III*, iv, 1, 61: "Red-hot steel"; and in *The Tempest*, iv, 1, 171: "Red-hot with drinking."

Hot irons.—*King John*, iv, 1, 39; 59.

Hammer'd iron.—*King John*, iv, 1, 67.

Toasting-iron.—*King John*, iv, 3, 99. The only use of the phrase.

8
Put in their hands thy bruising irons of wrath!
Richard III, v, 3, 110. See under PRAYER.

9
Give me . . . that . . . wrenching iron.
Romeo and Juliet. Act v, sc. 3, l. 22. [Romeo]

Fetch me an iron crow.—*The Comedy of Errors*, iii, 1, 84.

Get me an iron crow.—*Romeo and Juliet*, v, 2, 21.

Give me the iron.—*King John*, iv, 1, 75.

10
Iron may hold with her, but never lutes.
The Taming of the Shrew, ii, 1, 147. See under DAUGHTER.

Loaden with irons.—*Timon of Athens*, iii, 5, 50.

Massy irons.—*Troilus and Cressida*, ii, 3, 18.

As iron to adamant.—*Troilus and Cressida*, iii, 2, 186. See under CONSTANCY.

ISSUE

I—Issue: Result

11
To what issue will this come?
Hamlet. Act i, sc. 4, l. 89. [Horatio]

It must shortly be known to him from England
What is the issue of the business there.
Hamlet. Act v, sc. 2, l. 71. [Horatio]

12
Uncertain of the issue any way.
I Henry IV. Act i, sc. 1, l. 61. [Westmoreland]

Come, what 's the issue?
I Henry IV. Act ii, sc. 4, l. 102. [Poins]

13
While it is hot, I 'll put it to the issue.
Henry VIII. Act v, sc. 1, l. 176. [Old Lady]

14
Lo, now! now see the issue of your peace.
King John. Act iii, sc. 4, l. 21. [Constance]

Issue of the exploit.—*The Merchant of Venice*, iii, 2, 60.

15
Look you for any other issue?
Much Ado about Nothing. Act ii, sc. 2, l. 30. [Borachio]

Grow to what adverse issue it can, I will put it in practice.
Much Ado about Nothing. Act iii, sc. 2, l. 52. [Don John]

Let the issue show itself.
Much Ado about Nothing. Act iii, sc. 2, l. 133. [Don John]

16
Well, well, I see the issue of these arms.
Richard II. Act ii, sc. 3, l. 152. [York]

See the issue of his search.
The Merry Wives of Windsor. Act iii, sc. 3, l. 186. [Page]

See but the issue of my jealousy.
The Merry Wives of Windsor. Act iv, sc. 2, l. 207. [Ford]

See the issue.—*The Winter's Tale*, v, 3, 128.

17
No doubt we 'll bring it to a happy issue.
Richard III. Act iii, sc. 7, l. 54. [Gloucester]

Happy be the issue.—*Henry V*, v, 2, 12.

Gracious be the issue!—*The Winter's Tale,* iii, 1, 22.

1
The issue is embracement.
Troilus and Cressida. Act iv, sc. 5, l. 148. [Hector]

2
I would most gladly know the issue of it.
The Winter's Tale. Act v, sc. 2, l. 9. [Autolycus]

Better issue.—*Antony and Cleopatra,* i, 2, 97.
Certain issue.—*Macbeth,* v, 4, 20.
Cruel issue.—*Julius Cæsar,* iii, 1, 294.
Different issues.—*King Lear,* iv, 3, 37.
Fair issue.—*The Tempest,* iv, 1, 24.
Fearful bloody issue.—*King John,* i, 1, 38.
Fine issues.—*Measure for Measure,* i, 1, 37.
Grosser issues.—*Othello,* iii, 3, 219.
Luckier issue.—*Much Ado about Nothing,* v, 3, 32.
Most poor issue.—*Henry VIII,* i, 1, 87.
Thriving issue.—*The Winter's Tale,* ii, 2, 45.

II—Issue: Child

3
I shall never have the blessing of God till I have issue o' my body; for they say barnes are blessings.
All's Well that Ends Well. Act i, sc. 3, l. 26. [Clown]

A barne; a very pretty barne!—*The Winter's Tale,* iii, 3, 70. The only uses of "barne."
Issue of their bodies.—*III Henry VI,* iii, 2, 131.

4
All the unlawful issue that their lust
Since then hath made between them.
Antony and Cleopatra. Act iii, sc. 6, l. 7. [Cæsar]

5
They are the issue of your loins, my liege,
And blood of your begetting.
Cymbeline. Act v, sc. 5, l. 330. [Belarius]

Issue of a king.—*I Henry VI,* v, 5, 72; *Macbeth,* iv, 1, 87; *The Rape of Lucrece,* l. 37.
Issue to a faithless Jew.—*The Merchant of Venice,* ii, 4, 38.
Issue of Polixenes.—*Winter's Tale,* ii, 3, 93.
Banquo's issue.—*Macbeth,* iii, 1, 65; iv, 1, 102.

6
Thou seest that I no issue have.
I Henry VI. Act ii, sc. 5, l. 94. [Mortimer]

Without issue.—*Henry VIII,* i, 2, 134.

7
Our issues . . . will scarce be gentlemen.
Henry VIII. Act iii, sc. 2, l. 291. [Surrey]

Thou art the issue of my dear offence.
King John, i, 1, 257. See under SEDUCTION.

8
Why had I not with charitable hand
Took up a beggar's issue at my gates?
Much Ado about Nothing. Act iv, sc. 1, l. 134. [Leonato]

9
The issue was not his begot.
Richard III, iii, 5, 90. See under BASTARD.

Thy issue blurred with nameless bastardy.
The Rape of Lucrece, l. 522.

10
Your sweet issue your sweet form should bear.
Sonnets. No. xiii.

Sweet issue of a more sweet-smelling sire.
Venus and Adonis, l. 1178. The only use of "sweet-smelling." "Sweet smell" occurs in *II Henry VI,* i, 1, 255.

Abundant issue.—*Sonnets,* xcvii.
Male issue.—*Henry VIII,* ii, 4, 191.
Removed issue.—*King John,* ii, 1, 186.
Sequent issue.—*All's Well that Ends Well,* v, 3, 197.
Succeeding issue.—*Richard II,* i, 3, 20.

11
Bless this twain, that they may prosperous be
And honour'd in their issue.
The Tempest. Act iv, sc. 1, l. 104. [Juno]

12
Of this was Tamora delivered;
The issue of an irreligious Moor.
Titus Andronicus. Act v, sc. 3, l. 120. [Marcus]

Aaron: A joyful issue.
Nurse: A joyless, dismal, black, and sorrowful issue.
Titus Andronicus. Act iv, sc. 2, l. 65.

13
I had rather glib myself than they
Should not produce fair issue.
The Winter's Tale. Act ii, sc. 1, l. 149. [Antigonus] The only use of "glib" in the sense of geld.

No, I 'll not rear Another's issue.
Winter's Tale. Act ii, sc. 3, l. 192. [Leontes]

Care not for issue.—*Winter's Tale,* v, 1, 46.

ITALY

14
Those girls of Italy, take heed of them:
They say, our French lack language to deny,
If they demand.
All's Well that Ends Well. Act ii, sc. 1, l. 19. [King]

The shes of Italy should not betray
Mine interest and his honour.
Cymbeline. Act i, sc. 3, l. 29. [Imogen]

Some jay of Italy . . . hath betray'd him.
Cymbeline. Act iii, sc. 4, l. 51. [Imogen]

15
Our Italy Shines o'er with civil swords.
Antony and Cleopatra. Act i, sc. 3, l. 44. [Antony]

O, from Italy!—*Antony and Cleopatra,* ii, 5, 23.
Bound for Italy.—*Cymbeline,* iii, 6, 42.

16
There 's an Italian come.
Cymbeline. Act ii, sc. 1, l. 40. [Lord]

I 'll go see this Italian.—*Cymbeline,* ii, 1, 53.
False Italian.—*Cymbeline,* iii, 2, 4.
Italian gentry.—*Cymbeline,* v, 1, 18.

17
That drug-damn'd Italy hath out-craftied him,
And he 's at some hard point.
Cymbeline. Act iii, sc. 4, l. 15. [Imogen] The only use of "drug-damn'd" and "out-craftied."

We fear not What can from Italy annoy us.
Cymbeline. Act iv, sc. 3, l. 33. [Cymbeline]

Mine Italian brain
'Gan in your duller Britain operate
Most vilely.
Cymbeline. Act v, sc. 5, l. 196. [Iachimo]

1 Fruitful Lombardy,
The pleasant garden of great Italy.
The Taming of the Shrew. Act i, sc. 1, l. 3. [Lucentio] The only mention of Lombardy.

Proud Italy.—*Richard II,* ii, 1, 21.

ITCH

2 Rubbing the poor itch of your opinion,
Make yourselves scabs.
Coriolanus. Act i, sc. 1, l. 169. [Marcius]

Itch of his affection.—*Antony and Cleopatra,* iii, 13, 7.

3
My elbow itched; I thought there would a scab follow.
Much Ado about Nothing. Act iii, sc. 3, l. 106. [Borachio] The only use of "itched."

Mine eyes do itch.—*Othello,* iv, 3, 58.

Itching palm.—*Julius Cæsar,* iv, 3, 10; 12. See under BRIBERY. The only use of "itching."

4
Ajax: My fingers itch.
Thersites: I would thou didst itch from head to foot and I had the scratching of thee; I would make thee the loathsomest scab in Greece.
Troilus and Cressida. Act ii, sc. 1, l. 29. The only use of "loathsomest."

My finger itches.—*The Merry Wives of Windsor,* ii, 3, 48.

My fingers itch.—*Romeo and Juliet,* iii, 5, 165.

5
She loved not the savour of tar nor of pitch,
Yet a tailor might scratch her where'er she did itch.
The Tempest. Act ii, sc. 2, l. 54. [Stephano] See under TAILOR.

J

JACK

6
Take hence this Jack, and whip him.
Antony and Cleopatra. Act iii, sc. 13, l. 93. [Antony]

This Jack of Cæsar's.—*Antony and Cleopatra,* iii, 13, 103.

7
But long I will not be Jack out of office.
I Henry VI. Act i, sc. 1, l. 175. [Bishop of Winchester] A phrase used in the first play and never repeated.

A Jack guardant cannot office me from my son.
Coriolanus. Act v, sc. 2, l. 67. [Menenius] "Guardant" (guardian) is repeated in *I Henry VI,* iv, 7, 9: "Angry guardant."

8
I am no proud Jack.
I Henry IV, ii, 4, 12. See under CHARACTER.

He called you Jack.—*I Henry IV,* iii, 3, 158.

Blown Jack.—*I Henry IV,* iv, 2, 53.

Lean Jack.—*I Henry IV,* ii, 4, 358.

Old Jack.—*I Henry IV,* ii, 4, 41; 207; *The Merry Wives of Windsor,* ii, 2, 144.

Plump Jack.—*I Henry IV,* ii, 4, 527.

Swearing Jack.—*The Taming of the Shrew,* ii, 1, 290.

Sweet Jack.—*II Henry IV,* ii, 4, 410.

Twangling Jack.—*Taming of the Shrew,* ii, 1, 290. "Twangling" is repeated in *The Tempest,* iii, 2, 146: "Twangling instruments."

9
If I be not Jack Falstaff, then am I a Jack.
I Henry IV. Act v, sc. 4, l. 142. [Falstaff]

10
You little Jack-a-Lent, have you been true to us?
The Merry Wives of Windsor, iii, 3, 27; v, 5, 134. A Jack-a-Lent was a puppet thrown at during the Lenten fairs.

Jackanapes.—*Henry V,* v, 2, 148, and six times in later plays.

Jack-dog.—*The Merry Wives of Windsor,* ii, 3, 65; iii, 1, 85.

Jack o' the clock.—*Richard II,* v, 5, 60. The mechanical figure which struck the bell.

Jack priest.—*The Merry Wives of Windsor,* i, 4, 123; ii, 3, 32.

Jack-slave.—*Cymbeline,* ii, 1, 22.

11
Do you play the flouting Jack?
Much Ado about Nothing. Act i, sc. 1, l. 186. [Benedick]

12
Silken, sly, insinuating Jacks.
Richard III, i, 3, 53. See under SLANDER.

Bragging Jacks.—*The Merchant of Venice,* iii, 4, 77.

Saucy Jacks.—*Sonnets,* cxxviii.

13
Since every Jack became a gentleman,
There 's many a gentle person made a Jack.
Richard III. Act i, sc. 3, l. 72. [Gloucester]

Like a Jack, thou keep'st the stroke
Betwixt thy begging and my meditation.
Richard III. Act iv, sc. 2, l. 117. [King Richard]

14
As hot a Jack . . . as any in Italy.
Romeo and Juliet, iii, 1, 12. See under FELLOW.

15
Be the jacks fair within, the jills fair without.
The Taming of the Shrew. Act iv, sc. 1, l. 51. [Grumio]

Jack shall have Jill
Nought shall go ill;
The man shall have his mare again, and all shall be well.
A Midsummer-Night's Dream. Act iii, sc. 2, l. 461. [Puck]

1
Your fairy . . . has done little better than played the Jack with us.
Tempest. Act iv, sc. 1, l. 196. [Stephano]

JADE

See also Horse

2
Poor jade, is wrung in the withers out of all cess.
I Henry IV. Act ii, sc. 1, l. 7. [Carrier] The only use of "cess" (calculation).
Let the galled jade wince, our withers are unwrung.
Hamlet. Act iii, sc. 2, l. 253. The only uses of "withers."
3 Their poor jades
Lob down their heads, dropping the hides and hips,
The gum down-roping from their pale-dead eyes.
And in their pale dull mouths the gimmal bit
Lies foul with chew'd grass, still and motionless.
Henry V. Act iv, sc. 2, l. 46. [Lord Grandpré] The only use of "down-roping," "pale-dead," "gimmal" (double), and "motionless."
Give poor jades the bots.—*I Henry IV,* ii, 1, 11. "Bots" is repeated in *The Taming of the Shrew,* iii, 2, 56, and in *Pericles,* ii, 1, 124.
Poor jade.—*II Henry IV,* i, 1, 45.
4
He is indeed a horse; and all other jades you may call beasts.
Henry V. Act iii, sc. 7, l. 25. [Dauphin]
5 Hollow pamper'd jades of Asia,
Which cannot go but thirty mile a day.
II Henry IV. Act ii, sc. 4, l. 178. [Pistol]
Deceitful jades.—*Julius Cæsar,* iv, 2, 26.
Sur-rein'd jades.—*Henry V,* iii, 5, 19. The only use of "sur-rein'd" (over-ridden).
Tired jades.—*Taming of the Shrew,* iv, 1, 1.
Unruly jades.—*Richard II,* iii, 3, 179.
6
Let carman whip his jade.
Measure for Measure. Act ii, sc. 1, l. 269. The only use of "carman." "Carmen" occurs in *II Henry IV,* iii, 2, 341.
7
Sir, give him head: I know he'll prove a jade.
The Taming of the Shrew. Act i, sc. 2, l. 249. [Lucentio]
8
How like a jade he stood, tied to the tree,
Servilely master'd with a leathern rein!
Venus and Adonis, l. 391. The only use of "servilely."
Jade's tricks. See under TRICK.

JEALOUSY

See also Envy

9
I will be more jealous of thee than a Barbary cock-pigeon over his hen.
As You Like It. Act iv, sc. 1, l. 150. [Rosalind] The only use of "cock-pigeon."
Jealous in honour.—*As You Like It,* ii, 7, 151. See under SOLDIER.

10
Self-harming jealousy! fie, beat it hence!
The Comedy of Errors. Act ii, sc. 1, l. 102. [Luciana] The only use of "self-harming."
How many fond fools serve mad jealousy!
The Comedy of Errors. Act ii, sc. 1, l. 116. [Luciana]
Who would be jealous then of such a one?
The Comedy of Errors. Act iv, sc. 2, l. 23. [Luciana]
11
The venom clamours of a jealous woman
Poisons more deadly than a mad dog's tooth.
The Comedy of Errors. Act v, sc. 1, l. 69. [Abbess]
Thy jealous fits
Have scared thy husband from the use of wits.
The Comedy of Errors. Act v, sc. 1, l. 85. [Abbess]
12
We'll slip you for a season; but our jealousy
Does yet depend.
Cymbeline. Act iv, sc. 3, l. 22. [Cymbeline]
Beshrew my jealousy!—*Hamlet,* ii, 1, 113.
Artless jealousy.—*Hamlet,* iv, 5, 19.
Needless jealousy.—*Cymbeline,* v, 4, 66.
13
O, how hast thou with jealousy infected
The sweetness of affiance!
Henry V. Act ii, sc. 2, l. 126. [King Henry]
Fell jealousy,
Which troubles oft the bed of blessed marriage.
Henry V. Act v, sc. 2, l. 391. [Queen Isabel]
Jealous of your absence.—*Henry V,* iv, 1, 302.
14
And be not jealous on me, gentle Brutus.
Julius Cæsar. Act i, sc. 2, l. 71. [Cæsar]
That you do love me, I am nothing jealous.
Julius Cæsar. Act i, sc. 2, l. 162. [Brutus]
15
Each jealous of the other, as the stung
Are of the adder.
King Lear. Act v, sc. 1, l. 56. [Edmund]
16
Let not my jealousies be your dishonours,
But mine own safeties.
Macbeth. Act iv, sc. 3, l. 29. [Malcolm] The only use of "safeties."
17
I shall grow jealous of you shortly, Launcelot, if you thus get my wife into corners.
The Merchant of Venice. Act iii, sc. 5, l. 31. [Lorenzo]
18
Green-eyed jealousy!
The Merchant of Venice. Act iii, sc. 2, l. 110. [Portia]
O, beware, my lord, of jealousy;
It is the green-eyed monster which doth mock
The meat it feeds on: that cuckold lives in bliss
Who, certain of his fate, loves not his wronger;
But, O, what damned minutes tells he o'er
Who dotes, yet doubts, suspects, yet strongly loves!
Othello. Act iii, sc. 3, l. 165. [Iago] These two uses of "green-eyed" are the only ones in the plays.

1
I will possess him with yellowness.
The Merry Wives of Windsor. Act i, sc. 3, l. 10. [Nym] The only use of "yellowness."

Civil as an orange, and something of that jealous complexion.
Much Ado about Nothing. Act ii, sc. 1, l. 304. [Beatrice]

2
He 's as far from jealousy as I am from giving him cause; and that I hope is an unmeasurable distance.
The Merry Wives of Windsor. Act ii, sc. 1, l. 107. [Mrs. Page] "Unmeasurable" is repeated in *Timon of Athens,* iv, 3, 178.

Alas! the sweet woman leads an ill life with him: he 's a very jealousy man: she leads a very frampold life with him, good heart.
The Merry Wives of Windsor. Act ii, sc. 2, l. 92. [Mistress Quickly] The only use of "frampold" (quarrelsome).

That same knave Ford, her husband, hath the finest mad devil of jealousy in him, Master Brook, that ever governed frenzy.
The Merry Wives of Windsor. Act v, sc. 1, l. 18. [Falstaff]

As jealous as Ford, that searched a hollow walnut for his wife's leman.
The Merry Wives of Windsor. Act iv, sc. 2, l. 170. [Ford] The only use of "walnut." "Leman" is repeated in *II Henry IV,* v, 3, 49, and in *Twelfth Night,* ii, 3, 26.

Who says this is improvident jealousy?
Merry Wives of Windsor. Act ii, sc. 2, l. 302. [Ford] "Improvident" is repeated in *I Henry VI,* ii, 1, 58: "Improvident soldiers."

He will trust his wife; he will not be jealous.
The Merry Wives of Windsor. Act ii, sc. 2, l. 315. [Ford]

3
God be praised for my jealousy!
The Merry Wives of Windsor. Act ii, sc. 2, l. 324. [Ford]

My jealousy is reasonable.
The Merry Wives of Windsor. Act iv, sc. 2, l. 155. [Ford]

This is fery fantastical humours and jealousies.
The Merry Wives of Windsor. Act iii, sc. 3, l. 181. [Evans]

This is jealousies.—*The Merry Wives of Windsor,* iv, 2, 164.

Leave your jealousies.—*The Merry Wives of Windsor,* v, 5, 139.

I never saw him so gross in his jealousy till now.
The Merry Wives of Windsor. Act iii, sc. 3, l. 201. [Mrs. Ford]

Dwelling in a continual 'larum of jealousy.
The Merry Wives of Windsor. Act iii, sc. 5, l. 72. [Falstaff]

4
These are the forgeries of jealousy.
A Midsummer-Night's Dream. Act ii, sc. 1, l. 81. [Titania]

Jealousy shall be called assurance.
Much Ado about Nothing. Act ii, sc. 2, l. 50. [Borachio]

5
A jealousy so strong
That judgement cannot cure.
Othello. Act ii, sc. 1, l. 310. [Iago]

Oft my jealousy Shapes faults that are not.
Othello. Act iii, sc. 3, l. 147. [Iago]

'Tis not to make me jealous
To say my wife is fair, feeds well, loves company,
Is free of speech, sings, plays and dances well.
Othello. Act iii, sc. 3, l. 183. [Othello]

6
Emilia: Is not this man jealous?
Desdemona: I ne'er saw this before.
Othello. Act iii, sc. 4, l. 99.

Desdemona: But my noble Moor
Is true of mind and made of no such baseness
As jealous creatures are, it were enough
To put him to ill thinking.
Emilia: Is he not jealous?
Desdemona: Who, he? I think the sun where he was born
Drew all such humours from him.
Othello. Act iii, sc. 4, l. 26.

One not easily jealous, but, being wrought,
Perplex'd in the extreme.
Othello. Act v, sc. 2, l. 345. [Othello]

7
Jealous souls will not be answer'd so;
They are not ever jealous for the cause,
But jealous for they are jealous: 'tis a monster
Begot upon itself, born on itself.
Othello. Act iii, sc. 4, l. 159. [Emilia]

The souls of all my tribe defend
From jealousy!
Othello. Act iii, sc. 3, l. 175. [Iago]

8
Think'st thou I 'ld make a life of jealousy,
To follow still the changes of the moon
With fresh suspicions?
Othello. Act iii, sc. 3, l. 177. [Othello]

You are jealous now
That this is from some mistress, some remembrance.
Othello. Act iii, sc. 4, l. 185. [Cassio]

He, when he hears of her, cannot refrain
From the excess of laughter.
Othello. Act iv, sc. 1, l. 99. [Iago]

His unbookish jealousy.—*Othello,* iv, 1, 102. The only use of "unbookish."

9
A jealous-hood, a jealous-hood!
Romeo and Juliet. Act iv, sc. 4, l. 13. [Capulet] The only use of the phrase.

The scope and tenour of thy jealousy.
Sonnets. No. lxi.

10
Our first merriment hath made thee jealous.
The Taming of the Shrew. Act iv, sc. 5, l. 76. [Petruchio]

11
But jealousy what might befall your travel,
Being skilless in these parts; which to a stranger,
Unguided and unfriended, often prove
Rough and unhospitable.
Twelfth Night. Act iii, sc. 3, l. 8. [Antonio] The only use of "unhospitable." "Unguided" is repeated in *II Henry IV,* iv, 4, 59, and "unfriended" in *King Lear,* i, 1, 206.

1
Love, thou know'st, is full of jealousy.
The Two Gentlemen of Verona. Act ii, sc. 4, l. 177. [Valentine]

A kind of godly jealousy—
Which, I beseech you, call a virtuous sin.
Troilus and Cressida. Act iv, sc. 4, l. 82. [Troilus]

A savage jealousy
That sometime savours nobly.
Twelfth Night, v, 1, 122. See under LOVE.

2
Jealousy, that sour unwelcome guest.
Venus and Adonis, l. 449.

For where Love reigns, disturbing Jealousy
Doth call himself Affection's sentinel;
Gives false alarms, suggesteth mutiny,
And in a peaceful hour doth cry "Kill, kill!"
Distempering gentle Love in his desire,
As air and water do abate the fire.
Venus and Adonis, l. 649. "Disturbing" is repeated in *Coriolanus,* iv, 5, 57, and "distempering" in *Othello,* i, 1, 99: "Distempering draughts."

This sour informer, this bate-breeding spy,
This canker that eats up Love's tender spring,
This carry-tale, dissentious Jealousy,
That sometime true news, sometime false doth bring,
Knocks at my heart and whispers in mine ear.
Venus and Adonis, l. 655. The only use of "bate-breeding" (strife-breeding). "Carry-tale" occurs again in *Love's Labour 's Lost,* v, 2, 463; and "informer" in *Sonnets,* cxxv.

3
This jealousy
Is for a precious creature: as she 's rare,
Must it be great, and as his person 's mighty,
Must it be violent.
The Winter's Tale, i, 2, 451. [Polixenes]

Transported by my jealousies
To bloody thoughts.
Winter's Tale. Act iii, sc. 2, l. 159. [Leontes]

Fond jealousies.—*The Winter's Tale,* iv, 1, 18.

Little jealousies.—*Antony and Cleopatra,* ii, 2, 134.

Peevish jealousies.—*Othello,* iv, 3, 90.

JESTING

See also Foolery, Humour

4
They may jest
Till their own scorn return to them unnoted
Ere they can hide their levity in honour.
All's Well that Ends Well. Act i, sc. 2, l. 33. [King] "Unnoted" is repeated in *Timon of Athens,* iii, 5, 21.

5
A trusty villain, sir, that very oft,
When I am dull with care and melancholy,
Lightens my humour with his merry jests.
The Comedy of Errors. Act i, sc. 2, l. 19. [Antipholus of Syracuse] The only use of "merry jests." "Merry jest" occurs in *Titus Andronicus,* v, 2, 175.

I pray you, jest, sir, as you sit at dinner.
The Comedy of Errors. Act i, sc. 2, l. 62. [Dromio of Ephesus]

6
These jests are out of season;
Reserve them till a merrier hour than this.
The Comedy of Errors. Act i, sc. 2, l. 68. [Antipholus of Syracuse]

If you will jest with me, know my aspect
And fashion your demeanour to my looks.
The Comedy of Errors. Act ii, sc. 2, l. 32. [Antipholus of Syracuse]

What means this jest?—*The Comedy of Errors,* ii, 2, 21.

Think'st thou I jest?—*The Comedy of Errors,* ii, 2, 23.

7
Now your jest is earnest.
The Comedy of Errors. Act ii, sc. 2, l. 24. [Dromio of Syracuse]

This jest shall cost me some expense.
The Comedy of Errors. Act iii, sc. 1, l. 123. [Antipholus of Ephesus]

8
How now, mad wag! what, in thy quips and thy quiddities?
I Henry IV. Act i, sc. 2, l. 51. [Falstaff]

Where be his quiddities now?
Hamlet. Act v, sc. 1, l. 107. [Hamlet] The only uses of "quiddities" (quibbles).

No quips now, Pistol!
The Merry Wives of Windsor. Act i, sc. 3, l. 45. [Falstaff]

The Quip Modest.—*As You Like It,* v, 4, 79; 97.

Sudden quips.—*The Two Gentlemen of Verona,* iv, 2, 12.

Quips and sentences.—*Much Ado about Nothing,* ii, 3, 249. The only uses of "quip" and "quips."

9
Once in my days I 'll be a madcap.
I Henry IV. Act i, sc. 2, l. 159. [Prince of Wales]

Why, what a madcap hath heaven lent us here!
King John. Act i, sc. 1, l. 84. [King John]

That last is Biron, the merry mad-cap lord.
Love's Labour 's Lost. Act ii, sc. 1, l. 215. [Maria]

Come on, you madcap.—*The Two Gentlemen of Verona,* ii, 5, 8.

Madcap duke.—*I Henry IV,* i, 3, 244.

Mad-cap ruffian.—*The Taming of the Shrew,* ii, 1, 290.

Nimble-footed madcap.—*I Henry IV,* iv, 1, 95. The only uses of "madcap."

10
I have a jest to execute that I cannot manage alone.
I Henry IV. Act i, sc. 2, l. 180. [Poins]

In the reproof of this lies the jest.
I Henry IV. Act i, sc. 2, l. 213. [Poins]

When a jest is so forward, and afoot too! I hate it.
I Henry IV. Act ii, sc. 2, l. 50. [Falstaff]

It would be argument for a week, laughter for a month and a good jest for ever.
I Henry IV. Act ii, sc. 2, l. 100. [Prince]

11
He ambled up and down
With shallow jesters and rash bavin wits,
Soon kindled and soon burnt.
I Henry IV. Act iii, sc. 2, l. 60. [King Henry] The only use of "ambled" and "bavin" (brushwood).

The king's jester.—*Hamlet,* v, 1, 199.

The prince's jester.—*Much Ado about Nothing,* ii, 1, 142; 251.

1
A pretty slight drollery.
II Henry IV. Act ii, sc. 1, l. 156. [Falstaff]

A living drollery.—*The Tempest,* iii, 3, 21. The only uses of "drollery."

2
O, it is much that a lie with a slight oath and a jest with a sad brow will do with a fellow that never had the ache in his shoulders!
II Henry IV. Act v, sc. 1, l. 92. [Falstaff]

Reply not to me with a fool-born jest.
II Henry IV. Act v, sc. 5, l. 59. [King Henry V] The only use of "fool-born."

3
His jest will savour but of shallow wit,
When thousands weep more than did laugh at it.
Henry V. Act i, sc. 2, l. 295. [King Henry]

4
A proper jest, and never heard before.
II Henry VI. Act i, sc. 1, l. 132. [Gloucester]

Jest on, brothers.—*III Henry VI,* iii, 2, 116.

They do but jest.—*Hamlet,* iii, 2, 244.

I did but jest.—*Venus and Adonis,* l. 997.

5
None but I shall turn his jest to sorrow.
III Henry VI. Act iii, sc. 3, l. 261. [Warwick]

Turn it to a jest.—*Love's Labour 's Lost,* v, 2, 390.

6
Did he make the jest against his will?
III Henry VI. Act v, sc. 1, l. 30. [Gloucester]

So jest with heaven.—*King John,* iii, 1, 242.

7
Jesters do oft prove prophets.
King Lear. Act v, sc. 3, l. 71. [Regan]

8
By yea and nay, sir, then I swore in jest.
Love's Labour 's Lost. Act i, sc. 1, l. 54. [Biron]

Maria: Not a word with him but a jest.
Boyet: And every jest but a word.
Love's Labour 's Lost. Act ii, sc. 1, l. 216.

9
A pox of that jest!
Love's Labour 's Lost. Act v, sc. 2, l. 46. [Katharine]

This jest is dry to me.
Love's Labour 's Lost. Act v, sc. 2, l. 373. [Biron]

Sir Andrew: But what 's your jest?
Maria: A dry jest, sir.
Sir Andrew: Are you full of them?
Maria: Ay, sir, I have them at my fingers' ends: marry, now I let go your hand, I am barren.
Twelfth Night. Act i, sc. 3, l. 80.

10
A jest 's prosperity lies in the ear
Of him that hears it, never in the tongue
Of him that makes it.
Love's Labour 's Lost. Act v, sc. 2, l. 871. [Rosaline]

A twelvemonth! well; befall what will befall,
I 'll jest a twelvemonth in an hospital.
Love's Labour 's Lost. Act v, sc. 2, l. 880. [Biron] The only use of "hospital."

11
That were a jest indeed!
The Merry Wives of Windsor. Act ii, sc. 2, l. 116. [Mistress Quickly]

'Od's heartlings, that 's a pretty jest indeed!
Merry Wives of Windsor. Act iii, sc. 4, l. 59. [Slender] The only use of "heartlings."

A pretty jest.—*Much Ado about Nothing,* ii, 3, 141.

12
Let me be your jest; I deserve it.
The Merry Wives of Windsor. Act iii, sc. 3, l. 161. [Ford]

My uncle can tell you good jests of him.
The Merry Wives of Windsor. Act iii, sc. 4, l. 38. [Slender]

Methinks there would be no period to the jest.
The Merry Wives of Windsor. Act iv, sc. 2, l. 236. [Mrs. Ford]

The image of the jest
I 'll show you here at large.
The Merry Wives of Windsor. Act iv, sc. 6, l. 17. [Fenton]

I pray you, come, hold up the jest no higher.
The Merry Wives of Windsor. Act v, sc. 5, l. 109. [Mrs. Page]

'Tis no jest.—*A Midsummer-Night's Dream,* iii, 2, 280.

13
Huddling jest upon jest.
Much Ado about Nothing. Act ii, sc. 1, l. 252. [Benedick] The only use of "huddling." "Huddled" occurs in *The Merchant of Venice,* iv, 1, 28.

14
The man doth fear God, howsoever it seems not in him by some large jests he will make.
Much Ado about Nothing. Act ii, sc. 3, l. 204. [Don Pedro]

Nay, but his jesting spirit; which is now crept into a lute-string and now governed by stops.
Much Ado about Nothing. Act iii, sc. 2, l. 60. [Claudio] The only use of "lute-string."

You break jests as braggarts do their blades, which, God be thanked, hurt not.
Much Ado about Nothing. Act v, sc. 1, l. 189. [Benedick]

15
Yet in the midst of all her pure protestings,
Her faith, her oaths, her tears, and all were jestings.
The Passionate Pilgrim, l. 95. The only use of "protestings." "Protesting" occurs in *The Taming of the Shrew,* ii, 1, 311.

16
This would have been a biting jest.
Richard III. Act ii, sc. 4, l. 30. [York]

17
He jests at scars that never felt a wound.
Romeo and Juliet. Act ii, sc. 2, l. 1. [Romeo]

18
To see, now, how a jest shall come about!
Romeo and Juliet. Act i, sc. 3, l. 45. [Nurse]

19
O single-soled jest, solely singular for the singleness!
Romeo and Juliet. Act ii, sc. 4, l. 69. [Ro-

meo] The only use of "single-soled." "Singleness" is repeated in *Sonnets,* viii.

I will bite thee by the ear for that jest.
Romeo and Juliet. Act ii, sc. 4, l. 81. [Mercutio]

Look to 't, think on 't, I do not use to jest.
Romeo and Juliet. Act iii, sc. 5, l. 191. [Capulet]

1
Manage well the jest.
The Taming of the Shrew. Ind., sc. 1, l. 45. [Lord]

'Tis no time to jest.
The Taming of the Shrew. Act i, sc. 1, l. 231. [Lucentio]

I will continue that I broach'd in jest.
The Taming of the Shrew. Act i, sc. 2, l. 84. [Hortensio]

Nay then you jest, and now I well perceive
You have but jested with me all this while.
The Taming of the Shrew. Act ii, sc. 1, l. 19. [Bianca] The only use of "jested."

But is this true? or is it else your pleasure,
Like pleasant travellers, to break a jest
Upon the company you overtake?
The Taming of the Shrew. Act iv, sc. 5, l. 71. [Vincentio]

2
Have at you for a bitter jest or two!
The Taming of the Shrew. Act v, sc. 2, l. 45. [Petruchio]

Bitter jests.—*Taming of the Shrew,* iii, 2, 13.

Too bitter is thy jest.—*Love's Labour's Lost,* iv, 3, 174.

3
Come, you are so full of cony-catching!
The Taming of the Shrew. Act iv, sc. 1, l. 45. [Curtis] "Cony-catching" occurs again in *Merry Wives of Windsor,* i, 1, 128.

4
And, as the jest did glance away from me,
'Tis ten to one it maim'd you two outright.
The Taming of the Shrew. Act v, sc. 2, l. 61. [Petruchio]

She says you have some goodly jest in hand.
The Taming of the Shrew. Act v, sc. 2, l. 91. [Biondello]

5
I thank thee for that jest.
The Tempest. Act iv, sc. 1, l. 241. [Stephano]

I know thou dost but jest.
Titus Andronicus. Act ii, sc. 3, l. 253. [Saturninus]

Here 's no sound jest!
Titus Andronicus. Act iv, sc. 2, l. 26. [Aaron]

I have govern'd our determined jest.
Titus Andronicus. Act v, sc. 2, l. 139. [Tamora]

Scurril jests.—*Troilus and Cressida,* i, 3, 145. The only use of "scurril." "Scurrility" occurs twice and "scurrilous" once.

6
Sir Toby: I could marry this wench for this device.
Sir Andrew: So could I too.
Sir Toby: And ask no other dowry with her but such another jest.
Sir Andrew: Nor I neither.
Twelfth Night. Act ii, sc. 5, l. 199.

Some excellent jests, fire-new from the mint.
Twelfth Night. Act iii, sc. 2, l. 23. [Fabian] "Fire-new" is used four times.

7
O jest unseen, inscrutable, invisible,
As a nose on a man's face, or a weathercock on a steeple!
The Two Gentlemen of Verona. Act ii, sc. 1, l. 141. [Speed] The only use of "inscrutable." "Weathercock" is repeated in *Love's Labour's Lost,* iv, 1, 97, and in *The Merry Wives of Windsor,* iii, 2, 18.

Do you not perceive the jest?
The Two Gentlemen of Verona. Act ii, sc. 1, l. 159. [Speed]

8
Was not my lord The verier wag o' the two?
Winter's Tale. Act i, sc. 2, l. 65. [Hermione]

We . . . are wags too.—*II Henry IV,* i, 2, 200.

Bold wag.—*Love's Labour's Lost,* v, 2, 108.

Mad wag.—*I Henry IV,* i, 2, 50; iv, 2, 55.

Sweet wag.—*I Henry IV,* i, 2, 18; 26.

Why, wag!—*The Two Gentlemen of Verona,* v, 4, 86. The only uses of "wag" in this sense.

JESUS, see Christ

JEW

9
I am a Jew else, an Ebrew Jew.
I Henry IV. Act ii, sc. 4, l. 198. [Falstaff] The only use of "Ebrew."

Thou art an Hebrew, a Jew, and not worth the name of a Christian.
The Two Gentlemen of Verona. Act ii, sc. 5, l. 57. [Launce]

The Hebrew will turn Christian: he grows kind.
The Merchant of Venice. Act i, sc. 3, l. 180. [Antonio]

Wealthy Hebrew.—*The Merchant of Venice,* i, 3. 58. The only uses of "Hebrew."

10
Sufferance is the badge of all our tribe.
You call me misbeliever, cut-throat dog,
And spit upon my Jewish gaberdine.
The Merchant of Venice. Act i, sc. 3, l. 111. [Shylock] The only use of "misbeliever." "Cut-throat" is repeated in *Macbeth,* iii, 4, 17; and "gaberdine" is used twice more, both times in *The Tempest,* ii, 2, 40; 115.

Here comes another of the tribe: a third cannot be matched, unless the devil himself turn Jew.
The Merchant of Venice. Act iii, sc. 1, l. 80. [Salanio]

11
There is much kindness in the Jew.
The Merchant of Venice. Act i, sc. 3, l. 154. [Antonio]

Now, by my hood, a Gentile and no Jew.
The Merchant of Venice. Act ii, sc. 6, l. 51. The only use of Gentile.

In converting Jews to Christians, you raise the price of pork.
The Merchant of Venice. Act iii, sc. 5, l. 37. [Jessica]

12
The Jew my master, who, God bless the mark, is a kind of devil. . . . Certainly the Jew is the very devil incarnal.
The Merchant of Venice. Act ii, sc. 2, l. 24.

[Launcelot] The only use of "incarnal." Some editors give "incarnate," which occurs twice, in *Henry V*, ii, 3, 34: "Devils incarnate"; and in *Titus Andronicus*, v, 1, 40: "Incarnate devils."

My master 's a very Jew.
The Merchant of Venice. Act ii, sc. 2, l. 111. [Launcelot]

I am a Jew, if I serve the Jew any longer.
The Merchant of Venice. Act ii, sc. 2, l. 120. [Launcelot]

If I do not love her, I am a Jew.
Much Ado about Nothing. Act ii, sc. 3, l. 272. [Benedick]

1
Most beautiful pagan, most sweet Jew! if a Christian did not play the knave and get thee, I am much deceived.
The Merchant of Venice. Act ii, sc. 3, l. 11. [Launcelot]

My incony Jew!—*Love's Labour 's Lost*, iii, 1, 137. "Incony" (rare, fine) occurs again in the same play, iv, 1, 144, "Incony wit," and nowhere else.

Most lovely Jew.—*A Midsummer-Night's Dream*, iii, 1, 97.

2
If e'er the Jew her father come to heaven,
It will be for his gentle daughter's sake.
The Merchant of Venice. Act ii, sc. 4, l. 34. [Lorenzo]

There is no mercy for me in heaven, because I am a Jew's daughter.
The Merchant of Venice. Act iii, sc. 5, l. 35. [Jessica]

3
I am a Jew. Hath not a Jew eyes? hath not a Jew hands, organs, dimensions, senses, affections, passions? fed with the same food, hurt with the same weapons, subject to the same diseases, healed by the same means, warmed and cooled by the same winter and summer, as a Christian is? If you prick us, do we not bleed? if you tickle us, do we not laugh? If you poison us, do we not die? and if you wrong us, shall we not revenge? If we are like you in the rest, we will resemble you in that. If a Jew wrong a Christian, what is his humility? Revenge. If a Christian wrong a Jew, what should his sufferance be by Christian example? Why, revenge.
The Merchant of Venice. Act iii, sc. 1, l. 61. [Shylock]

The curse never fell upon our nation till now; I never felt it till now.
The Merchant of Venice. Act iii, sc. 1, l. 89. [Shylock]

Than which what 's harder? His Jewish heart.
The Merchant of Venice, iv, 1, 80. See under HEART for full quotation.

4
The Jew shall have all justice.
The Merchant of Venice. Act iv, sc. 1, l. 321. [Portia]

Why doth the Jew pause?
The Merchant of Venice. Act iv, sc. 1, l. 335. [Portia]

Blaspheming Jew.—*Macbeth*, iv, 1, 26.

Currish Jew.—*Merchant of Venice*, iv, 1, 292.

Dog Jew.—*The Merchant of Venice*, ii, 8, 14.

The circumcised dog.—*Othello*, v, 2, 355. The only use of "circumcised."

Rich Jew.—*The Merchant of Venice*, ii, 2, 130; 156; v, 1, 292.

Villain Jew.—*The Merchant of Venice*, ii, 8, 4.

Wealthy Jew.—*The Merchant of Venice*, v, 1, 15. "Jew" occurs sixty times in *The Merchant of Venice*, and only seven times in all the other plays. "Jewess" is used only once, in *The Merchant of Venice*, ii, 5, 43.

5
What a Herod of Jewry is this!
The Merry Wives of Windsor. Act ii, sc. 1, l. 20. [Mrs. Page] "Herod of Jewry" is repeated three times in *Antony and Cleopatra*, i, 1, 28; iii, 3, 3, and iii, 6, 73.

Stubborn Jewry.—*Richard II*, ii, 1, 55.

The wives of Jewry.—*Henry V*, iii, 3, 40.

JEWEL

See also Diamond, Gem, Pearl, Stone

6
We lost a jewel of her; and our esteem
Was made the poorer by it.
All's Well that Ends Well. Act v, sc. 3, l. 1. [King]

7
The jeweller that owes the ring is sent for.
All's Well that Ends Well, v, 3, 297.

Th' other 's a jeweller.—*Timon of Athens*, i, 1, 8. The only uses of "jeweller."

8
Let 's away,
And get our jewels and our wealth together.
As You Like It. Act i, sc. 3, l. 135. [Celia]

From the east to western Ind,
No jewel is like Rosalind.
As You Like It. Act iii, sc. 2, l. 93. [Rosalind, reading]

9
I see the jewel best enamelled
Will lose his beauty.
The Comedy of Errors. Act ii, sc. 1, l. 109. [Adriana]

Jewels lose their glory if neglected.
Pericles. Act ii, sc. 2, l. 12. [Simonides]

10
A carbuncle entire, as big as thou art,
Were not so rich a jewel.
Coriolanus. Act i, sc. 4, l. 55. [Titus] Carbuncle is used five times.

11
Not comforted to live,
But that there is this jewel in the world
That I may see again.
Cymbeline. Act i, sc. 1, l. 90. [Imogen]

She your jewel, this your jewel, and my gold are yours.
Cymbeline. Act i, sc. 4, l. 165. [Iachimo]

Jewels Of rich and exquisite form.
Cymbeline. Act i, sc. 6, l. 189. [Iachimo]

Go bid my woman
Search for a jewel that too casually
Hath left mine arm.
Cymbeline. Act ii, sc. 3, l. 145. [Imogen] The only use of "casually."

Bear her this jewel, pledge of my affection.
I Henry VI. Act v, sc. 3, l. 47. [King Henry]

1
We 'll see your trinkets here all forthcoming.
II Henry VI. Act i, sc. 4, l. 56. [Buckingham] "Trinkets" is repeated in *The Winter's Tale,* iv, 4, 613, and "forthcoming" in *II Henry VI,* iii, 1, 179, and *The Taming of the Shrew,* v, 1, 96.

My jewels trifles are.—*Sonnets,* xlviii.

2
I took a costly jewel from my neck,
A heart it was, bound in with diamonds,
And threw it towards thy land.
II Henry VI. Act iii, sc. 2, l. 107. [Queen]

3
Master o' the jewel-house.
Henry VIII, iv, 1, 111; v, 1, 34. "Jewel-house" is repeated in v, 1, 34, and occurs in no other play.

4
A jewel Well worth a poor man's taking.
King Lear. Act iv, sc. 6, l. 28. [Gloucester]

5
Paled pearls and rubies red as blood.
A Lover's Complaint, l. 198. The only use of "paled" in this sense.

Rubies unparagoned.—*Cymbeline,* ii, 2, 17. "Unparagoned" is repeated in i, 4, 87, and occurs in no other play. "Ruby" or "rubies" is used seven times.

6
The diamond,—why, 'twas beautiful and hard,
Whereto his invised properties did tend;
The deep-green emerald, in whose fresh regard
Weak sights their sickly radiance do amend;
The heaven-hued sapphire and the opal blend
With objects manifold: each several stone,
With wit well blazon'd, smiled or made some moan.
Lover's Complaint, l. 211. The only use of "invised" (invisible?), "deep-green," "heaven-hued," "opal," and of "emerald" as a noun. It is used as an adjective in *Merry Wives of Windsor,* v, 5, 74: "Emerald tufts." "Radiance" is repeated in *All's Well that Ends Well,* i, 1, 99, and in *King Lear,* i, 1, 111.

Embellished with rubies, carbuncles, sapphires.
The Comedy of Errors, iii, 2, 138. See under Nose.

Like sapphire.—*The Merry Wives of Windsor,* v, 5, 75. The only references to the sapphire.

7
I knew her by this jewel on her sleeve.
Love's Labour's Lost. Act v, sc. 2, l. 455. [King]

8
The jewel that we find, we stoop and take 't
Because we see it; but what we do not see
We tread upon, and never think of it.
Measure for Measure. Act ii, sc. 1, l. 24. [Angelo]

Stones whose rates are either rich or poor
As fancy values them.
Measure for Measure. Act ii, sc. 2, l. 150. [Isabella] See also under Stone.

9
It was my turquoise; I had it of Leah when I was a bachelor.
The Merchant of Venice. Act iii, sc. 1, l. 126. [Shylock] The only mention of turquoise and of Leah.

10
And I have found Demetrius like a jewel,
Mine own, and not mine own.
A Midsummer-Night's Dream. Act iv, sc. 1, l. 195. [Helena]

11
Benedick: Would you buy her, that you inquire after her?
Claudio: Can the world buy such a jewel?
Benedick: Yea, and a case to put it into.
Much Ado about Nothing. Act i, sc. 1, l. 181.

12
An agate very vilely cut.
Much Ado about Nothing. Act iii, sc. 1, l. 65. [Hero]

I was never manned with an agate till now.
II Henry IV. Act i, sc. 2, l. 19. [Falstaff]

Like an agate.—*Love's Labour's Lost,* ii, 1, 236.

Agate-ring.—*I Henry IV,* ii, 4, 78.

Agate-stone.—*Romeo and Juliet,* i, 4, 55. The only uses of "agate."

13
The jewels you have had from me . . . would half have corrupted a votarist.
Othello. Act iv, sc. 2, l. 187. [Roderigo]

If she will return me my jewels, I will give over my suit and repent my unlawful solicitation.
Othello. Act iv, sc. 2, l. 200. [Roderigo] The only use of "solicitation."

14
And, spite of all the rapture of the sea,
This jewel holds his building on my arm.
Pericles. Act ii, sc. 1, l. 161. [Pericles]

15
That rich jewel he should keep unknown
From thievish ears, because it is his own.
The Rape of Lucrece, l. 34.

Rich jewel.—*Romeo and Juliet,* i, 5, 48; *Timon of Athens,* iii, 4, 23; *Twelfth Night,* ii, 5, 67; *Pericles,* v, 3, 24.

16
I 'll give my jewels for a set of beads.
Richard II, iii, 3, 147. See under Grave.

17
In those holes
Where eyes did once inhabit, there were crept,
As 'twere in scorn of eyes, reflecting gems,
Which woo'd the slimy bottom of the deep,
And mock'd the dead bones that lay scatter'd by.
Richard III. Act i, sc. 4, l. 29. [Clarence] The only use of "reflecting."

They shall fetch thee jewels from the deep.
A Midsummer-Night's Dream. Act iii, sc. 1, l. 161. [Titania]

18
A base foul stone, made precious by the foil
Of England's chair, where he is falsely set.
Richard III. Act v, sc. 3, l. 250. [Richmond]

19
Well thou know'st to my dear doting heart

Thou art the fairest and most precious jewel.
Sonnets. No. cxxxi.

Precious jewel.—*As You Like It,* ii, 1, 14; *The Merchant of Venice,* iii, 1, 91; *Richard II,* i, 3, 267; *Venus and Adonis,* l. 824.
Basest jewel.—*Sonnets,* xcvi. See under QUEEN.
Best jewel.—*Sonnets,* lxv.
Captain jewels in the carcanet.—*Sonnets,* lii. "Carcanet" (collar set with jewels) is repeated in *The Comedy of Errors,* iii, 1, 4.
Dear jewel.—*The Rape of Lucrece,* l. 1191.
False jewel.—*A Lover's Complaint,* l. 154.
Heavenly jewel.—*The Merry Wives of Windsor,* iii, 3, 45; *Pericles,* iii, 2, 99.
Little jewel.—*The Two Gentlemen of Verona,* iv, 4, 51.

1
He hath the jewel of my life in hold.
The Taming of the Shrew. Act i, sc. 2, l. 119. [Hortensio]

Jewel of life.—*King John,* v, 1, 40.
Jewel of children.—*Winter's Tale,* v, 1, 116.
Jewels of our father.—*King Lear,* i, 1, 271.

2
You mend the jewel by the wearing it.
Timon of Athens. Act i, sc. 1, l. 172. [Jeweller]

He wears jewels now of Timon's gift,
For which I wait for money.
Timon of Athens. Act iii, sc. 4, l. 19. [Titus]

He gave me a jewel th' other day, and now he has beat it out of my hat: did you see my jewel?
Timon of Athens. Act iii, sc. 6, l. 122. [Lord]

3
She is mine own,
And I as rich in having such a jewel
As twenty seas, if all their sand were pearl,
The water nectar, and the rocks pure gold.
The Two Gentlemen of Verona. Act ii, sc. 4, l. 168. [Valentine] "Nectar" occurs once again in the plays, in *Troilus and Cressida,* iii, 2, 23 and once in the poems, in *Venus and Adonis,* l. 572.

Dumb jewels often in their silent kind
More than quick words do move a woman's mind.
The Two Gentlemen of Verona. Act iii, sc. 1, l. 90. [Valentine]

4
Jewels [are made] to wear.
Venus and Adonis, l. 163.

JOLLITY

See also Merriment

5
Be jolly, lords.
Antony and Cleopatra. Act ii, sc. 7, l. 65. [Pompey]

This life is most jolly.
As You Like It. Act ii, sc. 7, l. 183. [Amiens]

What! I will be jovial.—*King Lear,* iv, 6, 203.
Be bright and jovial.—*Macbeth,* iii, 2, 28.
Jovial face.—*Cymbeline,* iv, 2, 311.
Jovial star.—*Cymbeline,* v, 4, 109. The only uses of "jovial," the two from *Cymbeline* capitalized, as referring to JOVE.

6
The plainer dealer, the sooner lost: yet he loseth it in a kind of jollity.
The Comedy of Errors. Act ii, sc. 2, l. 89. [Dromio of Syracuse]

Triumphs for nothing and lamenting toys
Is jollity for apes and grief for boys.
Cymbeline. Act iv, sc. 2, l. 193. [Guiderius]

7
There shall the pairs of faithful lovers be
Wedded, with Theseus, all in jollity.
A Midsummer-Night's Dream. Act iv, sc. 1, l. 95. [Oberon]

A fortnight hold we this solemnity,
In nightly revels and new jollity.
A Midsummer-Night's Dream. Act v, sc. 1, l. 376. [Theseus]

8
Don Pedro: By my troth, a pleasant-spirited lady.
Leonato: There 's little of the melancholy element in her, my lord: she is never sad but when she sleeps, and not ever sad then; for I have heard my daughter say, she hath often dreamed of unhappiness and waked herself with laughing.
Much Ado about Nothing. Act ii, sc. 1, l. 355. The only use of "pleasant-spirited."

9
Needy nothing trimm'd in jollity.
Sonnets. No. lxvi.

10
I promise you, my soul is very jocund.
Richard III. Act v, sc. 3, l. 232. [Richmond]

As . . . jocund as to jest Go I to fight.
Richard II. Act i, sc. 3, l. 95. [Mowbray]

Then be thou jocund.—*Macbeth,* iii, 2, 40.
Let us be jocund.—*The Tempest,* iii, 2, 126.
Most jocund.—*Twelfth Night,* v, 1, 135. "Jocund" occurs nine times.

11
Apprehend Nothing but jollity.
Winter's Tale. Act iv, sc. 4, l. 24. [Florizel] All the uses of "jollity" are given in this section.

JOURNEY

12
Cæsar through Syria Intends his journey.
Antony and Cleopatra. Act v, sc. 2, l. 200. [Dolabella]

13
You have well saved me a day's journey.
Coriolanus. Act iv, sc. 3, l. 12. [Volsce]

'Twill be Two long days' journey.
King John. Act iv, sc. 3, l. 19. [Salisbury]

His day's hard journey.—*Macbeth,* i, 7, 62.
Day's journey.—*Romeo and Juliet,* ii, 5, 10.
Half a day's journey.—*Pericles,* ii, 1, 112.

14
Go we to attire you for the journey.
II Henry VI. Act ii, sc. 4, l. 106. [Stanley]

Great journey.—*Henry VIII,* i, 1, 85.
French journey.—*Henry VIII,* i, 2, 155.
Shorter journey.—*Othello,* ii, 1, 284.

15
I have a journey, sir, shortly to go;
My master calls me, I must not say no.
King Lear. Act v, sc. 3, l. 321. [Kent]

Look forward on the journey you shall go.
Measure for Measure. Act iv, sc. 3, l. 61. [Duke Vincentio]

Make a journey.—*Cymbeline,* ii, 4, 43.
Spur on my journey.—*Coriolanus,* i, 10, 33.

1
My lord, whoever journeys to the prince,
For God's sake, let not us two be behind.
Richard III. Act ii, sc. 2, l. 146. [Buckingham]

2
What a jaunt have I had!
Romeo and Juliet. Act ii, sc. 5, l. 26. [Nurse] The only use of "jaunt."
Jaunting up and down.
Romeo and Juliet. Act ii, sc. 5, l. 53. [Nurse] The only use of "jaunting."

3
How heavy do I journey on the way.
Sonnets. No. l.
Then begins a journey.—*Sonnets,* xxvii.
Travelling some journey.—*The Taming of the Shrew,* Ind., 1, 76.

4
Trip no further, pretty sweeting;
Journeys end in lovers meeting,
Every wise man's son doth know.
Twelfth Night. Act ii, sc. 3, l. 43. [Clown]

5 Tell me some good mean
How, with my honour, I may undertake
A journey to my loving Proteus.
The Two Gentlemen of Verona. Act ii, sc. 7, l. 5. [Julia]
Take a note of what I stand in need of,
To furnish me upon my longing journey.
The Two Gentlemen of Verona. Act ii, sc. 7, l. 84. [Julia]
Julia: But tell me, wench, how will the world repute me
For undertaking so unstaid a journey? . . .
Lucetta: If Proteus like your journey when you come,
No matter who's displeased when you are gone.
The Two Gentlemen of Verona. Act iii, sc. 1, l. 59. "Unstaid" is repeated in *Richard II,* ii, 1, 2, and in *Twelfth Night,* ii, 4, 18.

JOY

See also Happiness, Merriment, Rejoicing

6
Bliss in our brows' bent; none our parts so poor,
But was a race of heaven.
Antony and Cleopatra. Act i, sc. 3, l. 36. [Cleopatra]
Bliss and goodness on you!
Measure for Measure. Act iii, sc. 2, l. 228. [Duke]
Bliss be upon you!—*Romeo and Juliet,* v, 3, 124.
Heaven's bliss.—*II Henry VI,* iii, 3, 27.
Heavenly bliss.—*III Henry VI,* iii, 3, 182.
Bliss and joy.—*III Henry VI,* i, 2, 31.

7 To our noble consul
Wish we all joy and honour.
Coriolanus. Act ii, sc. 2, l. 156. [Coriolanus]
I wish you joy.—*Antony and Cleopatra,* v, 2, 261; 281.
Joy, gentle friends! joy and fresh days of love
Accompany your hearts!
A Midsummer-Night's Dream. Act v, sc. 1, l. 29. [Theseus]
All joy befal your grace.—*Cymbeline,* iii, 5, 9.
Joy to you!—*Measure for Measure,* v, 1, 532.
Much joy and favour to you.—*Henry VIII,* ii, 2, 118.
Joy and all comfort in your sacred breast!—*Pericles,* i, 2, 33.
New joy wait on you!—*Pericles,* v, Gower, 102.
Joy be the consequence!—*The Merchant of Venice,* iii, 2, 107.

8 The gods do mean to strike me
To death with mortal joy.
Cymbeline. Act v, sc. 5, l. 234. [Cymbeline]
Overcome with joy.—*Hamlet,* ii, 2, 72.
It is too much of joy.—*Othello,* ii, 1, 199.

9
There did seem in him a kind of joy.
Hamlet. Act iii, sc. 1, l. 18. [Rosencrantz]
There appears much joy in him.
Much Ado about Nothing. Act i, sc. 1, l. 21. [Messenger]
Full of joy.—*A Midsummer-Night's Dream,* v, 1, 28.

10
Bonny sweet Robin is all my joy.
Hamlet. Act iv, sc. 5, l. 187. [Ophelia]

11
If he be sick with joy, he'll recover without physic.
II Henry IV. Act iv, sc. 5, l. 15. [Prince of Wales]
It did infect my blood with joy.
II Henry IV. Act iv, sc. 5, l. 170. [Prince]

12
I speak of Africa and golden joys.
II Henry IV. Act v, sc. 3, l. 104. [Pistol] The only mention of Africa. African occurs in *The Tempest,* ii, 1, 125.
Earthly joys.—*Pericles,* i, 1, 49.
Everlasting joy.—*II Henry VI,* ii, 1, 18.
Fleeting joy.—*The Rape of Lucrece,* l. 212.
Gentle joy.—*A Midsummer-Night's Dream,* iv, 1, 4.
Lively joy.—*Venus and Adonis,* l. 498.
Lucky joys.—*II Henry IV,* 4, 3, 99.
Proud joy.—*Richard II,* v, 5, 59.
Joy of liberty.—*III Henry VI,* iv, 6, 63.
Joys of love.—*II Henry VI,* i, 1, 251.
Joys in bed.—*The Passionate Pilgrim,* l. 345.

13
Right joyous are we to behold your face.
Henry V. Act v, sc. 2, l. 9. [French King]
Who will of thy arrival be full joyous.
The Taming of the Shrew, iv, 5, 70. The only uses of "joyous."

14
How joyful am I made by this contract!
I Henry VI. Act iii, sc. 1, l. 143. [King Henry]
God make your majesty joyful as you have been!
Richard III, i, 3, 19.
O, make them joyful!—*Richard III,* iii, 7, 203.
I am joyful of your sights.—*Timon of Athens,* i, 1, 255.

15 Live thou to joy thy life;
Myself no joy in nought but that thou livest.
II Henry VI. Act iii, sc. 2, l. 365. [Suffolk]

16 Never henceforth shall I joy again,
Never, O never, shall I see more joy!
III Henry VI. Act ii, sc. 1, l. 77. [Edward]

I will joy no more.—*Antony and Cleopatra,* iv, 6, 20.

1 I cannot joy, until I be resolved
Where our right valiant father is become.
III Henry VI. Act ii, sc. 1, l. 9. [Richard]

This earth affords no joy to me,
But to command, to check, to o'erbear such
As are of better person than myself.
III Henry VI . Act iii, sc. 2, l. 165. [Gloucester]

There 's nothing in this world can make me joy.
King John. Act iii, sc. 4, l. 107. [Dauphin]

2 Such as fill my heart with unhoped joys.
III Henry VI. Act iii, sc. 3, l. 172. [Queen Margaret] The only use of "unhoped."

Unlook'd for joy.—*Sonnets,* xxv.

3 Now, all my joy Trace the conjunction!
Henry VIII. Act iii, sc. 2, l. 44. [Surrey]

I am stifled With the mere rankness of their joy.
Henry VIII. Act iv, sc. 1, l. 59. [Gentleman]

4 And leap for joy, though they are lame with blows.
Love's Labour 's Lost. Act v, sc. 2, l. 291. [Boyet]

Hark, how they joy!—*Coriolanus,* v, 4, 60.

5 In measure rein thy joy.
The Merchant of Venice, iii, 2, 113. See under LOVE.

Bassanio: Every something, being blent together,
Turns to a wild of nothing, save of joy,
Express'd and not express'd. . . .
Nerissa: My lord and lady, it is now our time . . .
To cry good joy: good joy, my lord and lady. . . .
Gratiano: I wish you all the joy that you can wish.
The Merchant of Venice. Act iii, sc. 2, l. 183.

He finds the joys of heaven here on earth.
The Merchant of Venice. Act iii, sc. 5, l. 81. [Jessica]

6 Though that his joy be joy,
Yet throw such changes of vexation on 't,
As it may lose some colour.
Othello. Act i, sc. 1, l. 71. [Iago]

7 Led on by heaven, and crown'd with joy at last.
Pericles. Act v, Gower, l. 90.

Give me a gash, put me to present pain;
Lest this great sea of joys rushing upon me
O'erbear the shores of my mortality,
And drown me with their sweetness.
Pericles. Act v, sc. 1, l. 193. [Pericles]

8 Her joy with heaved-up hand she doth express.
The Rape of Lucrece, l. 111. "Heaved-up hands" is repeated in l. 638.

9 For ever will I walk upon my knees,
And never see day that the happy sees,
Till thou give joy.
Richard II. Act v, sc. 3, l. 93. [Duchess of York]

10 Much it joys me too.
Richard III. Act i, sc. 2, l. 220. [Anne]

Wherein dost thou joy?—*Richard III,* iv, 4, 93.

11 And so most joyfully we take our leave.
Richard III. Act iii, sc. 7, l. 245. [Buckingham] "Joyfully" occurs twice more in the plays, in *Henry V,* iv, 3, 8, and in *Hamlet,* ii, 2, 42.

12 Although I joy in thee,
I have no joy of this contract to-night.
Romeo and Juliet. Act ii, sc. 2, l. 116. [Juliet]

Ah, Juliet, if the measure of thy joy
Be heap'd like mine and that thy skill be more
To blazon it, then sweeten with thy breath
This neighbour air, and let rich music's tongue
Unfold the imagined happiness that both
Receive in either by this dear encounter.
Romeo and Juliet. Act ii, sc. 6, l. 24. [Romeo]

Lady Capulet: But now I'll tell the joyful tidings, girl.
Juliet: And joy comes well in such a needy time.
Romeo and Juliet. Act iii, sc. 5, l. 105. "Joyful tidings" also occurs in *II Henry IV,* i, 1, 35.

13 Sweets with sweets war not, joy delights in joy.
Sonnets. No. viii.

14 God give thee joy of him!
Love's Labour 's Lost. Act v, sc. 2, l. 448. [Princess of France]

I wish him joy of her.
Much Ado about Nothing. Act ii, sc. 1, l. 200. [Claudio]

God give him joy!—*The Taming of the Shrew,* iv, 2, 52.

God give his lordship joy!—*Titus Andronicus,* iv, 3, 76.

God give me joy.—*Much Ado about Nothing,* iii, 4, 24.

God give thee joy!—*Much Ado about Nothing,* ii, 1, 312; 350; *Titus Andronicus,* i, 1, 400.

God give you joy!—*Pericles,* ii, 5, 87.

God send you joy!
The Taming of the Shrew, ii, 1, 321.

Well, the gods give us joy!
As You Like It. Act iii, sc. 3, l. 48. [Audrey]

The gods give you joy.—*Coriolanus,* ii, 3, 118; 142.

Heaven give thee joy!—*The Merry Wives of Windsor,* v, 5, 250.

15 O joy, e'en made away ere 't can be born!
Timon of Athens. Act i, sc. 2, l. 110. [Timon]

Joy had the like conception in our eyes
And at that instant like a babe sprung up.
Timon of Athens. Act i, sc. 2, l. 115. [Lord]

16 Swooning destruction, or some joy too fine,
Too subtle-potent, tuned too sharp in sweetness,
For the capacity of my ruder powers:

I fear it much; and I do fear besides,
That I shall lose distinction in my joys.
Troilus and Cressida. Act iii, sc. 2, l. 24. [Troilus] The only use of "subtle-potent." "Swooning" is repeated in *A Lover's Complaint,* l. 305.

1 What joy is joy, if Silvia be not by?
The Two Gentlemen of Verona. Act iii, sc. 1, l. 175. [Valentine]

2 Take advantage on presented joy.
Venus and Adonis, l. 405.

3 Reviving joy bids her rejoice.
Venus and Adonis, l. 977.

4 Ready to leap out of himself for joy.
The Winter's Tale. Act v, sc. 2, l. 54. [Third Gentleman]

II—Joy and Sorrow

5 I have felt so many quirks of joy and grief,
That the first face of neither, on the start,
Can woman me unto 't.
All's Well that Ends Well. Act iii, sc. 2, l. 51. [Countess]

6 If you find him sad,
Say I am dancing; if in mirth, report
That I am sudden sick.
Antony and Cleopatra. Act i, sc. 3, l. 3. [Cleopatra]

7 With mirth in funeral and with dirge in marriage,
In equal scale weighing delight and dole.
Hamlet. Act i, sc. 2, l. 12. [King]

Our wedding cheer to a sad burial feast.
Romeo and Juliet, iv, 5, 87. [Capulet]

8 The violence of either grief or joy
Their own enactures with themselves destroy:
Where joy most revels, grief doth most lament;
Grief joys, joy grieves, on slender accident.
Hamlet. Act iii, sc. 2, l. 206. [Player King] The only use of "enactures."

9 From wondering fall to weeping joys.
II Henry VI. Act i, sc. 1, l. 34. [King Henry]

My sorrows unto joys.—*III Henry VI,* iv, 6, 4.

10 Sound drums and trumpets! farewell sour annoy!
For here, I hope, begins our lasting joy.
III Henry VI. Act v, sc. 7, l. 45. [King Edward]

That time offer'd sorrow; This, general joy.
Henry VIII. Act iv, sc. 1, l. 6. [Gentleman]

11 My plenteous joys,
Wanton in fulness, seek to hide themselves
In drops of sorrow.
Macbeth. Act i, sc. 4, l. 33. [Duncan]

12 Joy could not show itself modest enough without a badge of bitterness.
Much Ado about Nothing. Act i, sc. 1, l. 22. [Messenger]

How much better is it to weep at joy than to joy at weeping!
Much Ado about Nothing. Act i, sc. 1, l. 28. [Leonato]

13 Momentary joy breeds months of pain.
The Rape of Lucrece, l. 690.

Their light joy seemed to appear,
Like bright things stain'd, a kind of heavy fear.
The Rape of Lucrece, l. 1434.

14 John of Gaunt: Thy grief is but thy absence for a time.
Bolingbroke: Joy absent, grief is present for that time.
John of Gaunt: What is six winters? they are quickly gone.
Bolingbroke: To men in joy; but grief makes one hour ten.
Richard II. Act i, sc. 3, l. 258.

Lady: Madam, we'll tell tales.
Queen: Of sorrow or of joy?
Lady: Of either, madam.
Queen: Of neither, girl:
For if of joy, being altogether wanting,
It doth remember me the more of sorrow;
Of if of grief, being altogether had,
It adds more sorrow to my want of joy.
Richard II. Act iii, sc. 4, l. 10.

15 Drown desperate sorrow in dead Edward's grave,
And plant your joys in living Edward's throne.
Richard III. Act ii, sc. 2, l. 99. [Rivers]

Eighty odd years of sorrow have I seen,
And each hour's joy wreck'd with a week of teen.
Richard III. Act iv, sc. 1, l. 96. [Duchess of York] The only use of "eighty."

16 Come what sorrow can,
It cannot countervail the exchange of joy
That one short minute gives me in her sight.
Romeo and Juliet. Act ii, sc. 6, l. 3. [Romeo] "Countervail" is repeated in *Pericles,* ii, 3, 56.

Call thee back
With twenty hundred thousand times more joy
Than thou went'st forth in lamentation.
Romeo and Juliet. Act iii, sc. 3, l. 152. [Friar Laurence]

17 My grief lies onward and my joy behind.
Sonnets. No. l.

18 Let grief and sorrow still embrace his heart
That doth not wish you joy!
The Tempest. Act v, sc. 1, l. 214. [Alonso]

19 But sorrow, that is couch'd in seeming gladness,
Is like that mirth fate turns to sudden sadness.
Troilus and Cressida. Act i, sc. 1, l. 39. [Troilus]

He is melancholy without cause, and merry against the hair.
Troilus and Cressida. Act i, sc. 2, l. 26. [Alexander]

1
The wisest beholder, that knew no more but seeing, could not say if the importance were joy or sorrow; but in the extremity of the one, it must needs be.
The Winter's Tale. Act v, sc. 2, l. 19. [First Gentleman]

There might you have beheld one joy crown another, so and in such manner that it seemed sorrow wept to take leave of them, for their joy waded in tears.
The Winter's Tale. Act v, sc. 2, l. 48. [Third Gentleman]

But O, the noble combat that 'twixt joy and sorrow.
The Winter's Tale. Act v, sc. 2, l. 79. [Third Gentleman]

JUDGE

2
By the Lord, I 'll be a brave judge.
I Henry IV. Act i, sc. 2, l. 72. [Falstaff]

3
Let me be umpire in this doubtful strife.
I Henry VI. Act iv, sc. 1, l. 151. [King Henry]

A man of complements, whom right and wrong
Have chose as umpire of their mutiny.
Love's Labour 's Lost. Act i, sc. 1, l. 169. [King Ferdinand]

There is three umpires in this matter, as I understand.
The Merry Wives of Windsor. Act i, sc. 1, l. 139. [Evans]

Kind umpire.—*I Henry VI,* ii, 5, 29.
Play the umpire.—*Romeo and Juliet,* iv, 1, 63.
The only uses of "umpire" and "umpires."

4
Having here
No judge indifferent, nor no more assurance
Of equal friendship and proceeding.
Henry VIII. Act ii, sc. 4, l. 16. [Queen Katharine]

I do believe, . . .
You are mine enemy, and make my challenge
You shall not be my judge.
Henry VIII. Act ii, sc. 4, l. 75. [Queen Katharine]

I utterly abhor, yea, from my soul
Refuse you for my judge.
Henry VIII. Act i, sc. 4, l. 81. [Queen Katharine]

I do refuse you for my judge; and here,
Before you all, appeal unto the pope,
To bring my whole cause 'fore his holiness,
And to be judged by him.
Henry VIII. Act ii, sc. 4, l. 118. [Queen Katharine]

I shall both find your lordship judge and juror.
Henry VIII. Act v, sc. 3, l. 60. [Cranmer]

5
Heaven is above all yet; there sits a judge
That no king can corrupt.
Henry VIII. Act iii, sc. 1, l. 100. [Queen Katharine]

That supernal judge, that stirs good thoughts
In any breast of strong authority,
To look into the blots and stains of right.
King John. Act ii, sc. 1, l. 112. [King Philip] The only use of "supernal."

6
Thou robed man of justice, take thy place;
And thou, his yoke-fellow of equity,
Bench by his side.
King Lear. Act iii, sc. 6, l. 38. [King Lear] "Yoke-fellow" is repeated in *Henry V,* ii, 3, 56; iv, 6, 9. The only use of "bench" as a verb.

7
No; I would tell what 'twere to be a judge,
And what a prisoner.
Measure for Measure. Act ii, sc. 2, l. 69. [Isabella]

He who the sword of heaven will bear
Should be as holy as severe;
Pattern in himself to know,
Grace to stand, and virtue go.
Measure for Measure. Act iii, sc. 2, l. 275. [Duke]

8
To offend, and judge, are distinct offices
And of opposed natures.
The Merchant of Venice. Act ii, sc. 9, l. 61. [Portia]

Thou shalt be both the plaintiff and the judge
Of thine own cause.
Twelfth Night. Act v, sc. 1, l. 362. [Olivia]

Be you judge Of your own cause.
Measure for Measure. Act v, sc. 1, l. 166. [Duke]

Play judge and executioner all himself.
Cymbeline. Act iv, sc. 2, l. 128. [Guiderius]

Be judge yourself.—*King John,* i, 1, 79; *Othello,* i, 1, 38.
Let him be judge.—*As You Like It,* iv, 1, 220.
Judge of Israel.—*Hamlet,* ii, 2, 422.

9
A Daniel come to judgement! yea, a Daniel!
O wise young judge, how do I honour thee!
The Merchant of Venice. Act iv, sc. 1, l. 223. [Shylock]

A second Daniel!—*The Merchant of Venice,* iv, 1, 333; 340. Daniel is mentioned only in this scene.

It doth appear you are a worthy judge;
You know the law, your exposition
Hath been most sound: I charge you by the law,
Whereof you are a well-deserving pillar,
Proceed to judgement.
The Merchant of Venice. Act iv, sc. 1, l. 236. [Shylock] "Well-deserving" is used four times.

O wise and upright judge!
The Merchant of Venice. Act iv, sc. 1, l. 250. [Shylock]

O upright judge! Mark, Jew: O learned judge!
The Merchant of Venice. Act iv, sc. 1, l. 313. [Gratiano]

Learned judge.—*The Merchant of Venice,* iv, 1, 304; 317.
Upright judge.—*Richard II,* iv, 1, 118.
Noble judge!—*The Merchant of Venice,* iv, 1, 246; 253; *Henry VIII,* v, 3, 101.

10
My bloody judge forbade my tongue to speak.
The Rape of Lucrece, l. 1648.

Frowning judge.—*Richard III,* i, 4, 190.

11
When the judge is robb'd the prisoner dies.
The Rape of Lucrece, l. 1652.

1
Thieves for their robbery have authority
When judges steal themselves.
Measure for Measure. Act ii, sc. 2, l. 176. [Angelo]

JUDGEMENT

See also Doom

2
Never trust my judgement in any thing.
All's Well that Ends Well. Act iii, sc. 6, l. 34. [Second Lord]

3 Men's judgements are
A parcel of their fortunes.
Antony and Cleopatra. Act iii, sc. 13, l. 31. [Enobarbus]

In our own filth drop our clear judgements; make us
Adore our errors; laugh at 's, while we strut
To our confusion.
Antony and Cleopatra. Act iii, sc. 13, l. 113. [Antony]

Green in judgement.—*Antony and Cleopatra,* i, 5, 74.

4 Weed your better judgements
Of all opinion that grows rank in them.
As You Like It. Act ii, sc. 7, l. 45. [Jaques] "Better judgement" is repeated in *Othello,* iii, 3, 236, and *Sonnets,* lxxxvii.

He disabled my judgement.
As You Like It. Act v, sc. 4, l. 80. [Touchstone]

Defect of judgement.—*Coriolanus,* iv, 7, 39.

5
Upon my mended judgement—if I offend not to say it is mended.
Cymbeline. Act i, sc. 4, l. 49. [Posthumus]

Honour'd with confirmation your great judgement
In the election of a sir so rare.
Cymbeline. Act i, sc. 6, l. 174. [Iachimo]

6
Take each man's censure, but reserve thy judgement.
Hamlet. Act i, sc. 3, l. 69. [Polonius]

Others, whose judgements in such matters, cried to the top of mine.
Hamlet. Act ii, sc. 2, l. 458. [Hamlet]

Frankly judge.—*Hamlet,* iii, 1, 34.

7 Blest are those
Whose blood and judgement are so well commingled,
That they are not a pipe for fortune's finger
To sound what stop she please.
Hamlet. Act iii, sc. 2, l. 73. [Hamlet] The only use of "commingled."

8
We will both our judgements join.
Hamlet. Act iii, sc. 2, l. 91. [Hamlet]

Divided from herself and her fair judgement,
Without the which we are pictures, or mere beasts.
Hamlet. Act iv, sc. 5, l. 85. [King]

It shall as level to your judgement pierce
As day does to your eye.
Hamlet. Act iv, sc. 5, l. 151. [King]

Make choice of whom your wisest friends you will,
And they shall hear and judge 'twixt you and me:
If by direct or by collateral hand
They find us touch'd, we will our kingdom give,
Our crown, our life, and all that we call ours,
To you in satisfaction.
Hamlet. Act iv, sc. 5, l. 204. [King] "Collateral" is repeated in *All's Well that Ends Well,* i, 1, 99: "Collateral light."

9
Struck me in my very seat of judgement.
II Henry IV. Act v, sc. 2, l. 80. [Chief Justice]

My judgement is, we should not step too far.
II Henry IV. Act i, sc. 3, l. 20. [Bardolph]

In my judgement.—*The Two Gentlemen of Verona,* iv, 4, 156.

I have no judgement.—*II Henry IV,* i, 2, 16.

You have no judgement.—*Troilus and Cressida,* i, 2, 99.

I cannot judge.—*III Henry VI,* ii, 1, 128.

10
You have good judgement.
Henry V. Act iii, sc. 7, l. 58. [Constable]

In his good judgements.—*Henry V,* iv, 7, 50.

The fellow has good judgement.—*Antony and Cleopatra,* iii, 3, 28.

Of an excellent
And unmatch'd wit and judgement.
Henry VIII. Act ii, sc. 4, l. 46. [Queen Katharine]

My best judgement.—*Othello,* 2, 3, 206. The only use of this phrase.

By all men's judgements.—*The Two Gentlemen of Verona,* iv, 4, 167.

Unpartial judging.—*Henry VIII,* ii, 2, 107. The only use of "unpartial." "Impartial" occurs five times. The only use of "judging."

11
Judge you, my Lord of Warwick, then, between us.
I Henry VI. Act ii, sc. 4, l. 10. [Somerset]

Then judge, great lords, if I have done amiss.
I Henry VI. Act iv, sc. 1, l. 27. [Talbot]

If I may judge.—*II Henry VI,* 1, 3, 207.

You shall judge.—*The Two Gentlemen of Verona,* iv, 4, 18.

12
Forbear to judge, for we are sinners all.
II Henry VI. Act iii, sc. 2, l. 31. [King Henry]

13
If my suspect be false, forgive me, God,
For judgement only doth belong to Thee.
II Henry VI. Act iii, sc. 2, l. 139. [King Henry]

14
In choosing for yourself, you show'd your judgement,
Which being shallow, you shall give me leave
To play the broker in mine own behalf.
III Henry VI. Act iv, sc. 1, l. 61. [Clarence]

Weak . . . in judgement.—*III Henry VI,* iv, 1, 12.

15
This was a judgement on me.
Henry VIII. Act ii, sc. 4, l. 194. [King Henry]

16
It shall be said, his judgement ruled our hands.
Julius Cæsar. Act ii, sc. 1, l. 147. [Metellus]

1
O judgement! thou art fled to brutish beasts,
And men have lost their reason.
Julius Cæsar. Act iii, sc. 2, l. 109. [Antony]
Where is my judgement fled
That censures falsely?
Sonnets. No. cxlviii.
What, are men mad? Hath nature given them eyes
To see this vaulted arch, and the rich crop
Of sea and land, which can distinguish 'twixt
The fiery orbs above and the twinn'd stones
Upon the number'd beach? and can we not
Partition make with spectacles so precious
'Twixt fair and foul?
Cymbeline. Act i, sc. 6, l. 32. [Iachimo]

2
He was brought again to the bar, to hear
His knell rung out, his judgement.
Henry VIII, ii, 1, 31. See under KNELL.
Came to the bar.—*Henry VIII,* ii, 1, 12.
Throng to the bar.—*Richard III,* v, 3, 199.

3
Judge, O you gods, how dearly Cæsar loved him!
Julius Cæsar. Act iii, sc. 2, l. 186. [Antony]
Judge me, you gods!—*Julius Cæsar,* iv, 2, 38.

4
Answer my life my judgement.
King Lear. Act i, sc. 1, l. 153. [Kent]
Judge it meet.—*King Lear,* i, 2, 97.

5
This judgement of the heavens, that makes us tremble,
Touches us not with pity.
King Lear. Act v, sc. 3, l. 231. [Albany]

6
We still have judgement here.
Macbeth. Act i, sc. 7, l. 7. [Macbeth]
Heavy judgement.—*Macbeth,* i, 3, 110.

7
Let mine own judgement pattern out my death.
Measure for Measure. Act ii, sc. 1, l. 30. [Angelo]
How would you be,
If He, which is the top of judgement, should
But judge you as you are?
Measure for Measure. Act ii, sc. 2, l. 75. [Isabella]

8
Some god direct my judgement!
The Merchant of Venice. Act ii, sc. 7, l. 13. [Prince of Morocco]
Seven times tried that judgement is,
That did never choose amiss.
The Merchant of Venice. Act ii, sc. 9, l. 64. [Prince of Arragon, reading]

9
With all brief and plain conveniency
Let me have judgement.
The Merchant of Venice. Act iv, sc. 1, l. 82. [Antonio] "Conveniency" is repeated in *Othello,* iv, 2, 178.
What judgement shall I dread, doing no wrong?
The Merchant of Venice. Act iv, sc. 1, l. 89. [Shylock]
It could not be judged.—*The Merry Wives of Windsor,* i, 1, 93.

10
Lysander: I had no judgement when to her I swore.
Helena: Nor none, in my mind, now you give her o'er.
A Midsummer-Night's Dream. Act iii, sc. 2, l. 134.

11
I pray thee speak in sober judgement.
Much Ado about Nothing. Act i, sc. 1, l. 171. [Claudio] The only use of "sober judgement."
She cannot be so much without true judgement—
Having so swift and excellent a wit
As she is prized to have.
Much Ado about Nothing. Act iii, sc. 1, l. 88. [Ursula]
True judgement.—*Much Ado about Nothing,* i, 1, 168; *Coriolanus,* iii, 1, 158.
Purged judgement.—*Henry V,* ii, 2, 136.
Safer judgement.—*Coriolanus,* ii, 3, 226.
Temper'd judgement.—*Measure for Measure,* v, 1, 478.
Make the judgement good.—*Pericles,* iv, 6, 100.

12
Thieves are not judged but they are by to hear,
Although apparent guilt be seen in them;
And shall the figure of God's majesty,
His captain, steward, deputy-elect,
Anointed, crowned, planted many years,
Be judged by subject and inferior breath,
And he himself not present?
Richard II. Act iv, sc. 1, l. 123. [Bishop of Carlisle] The only use of "deputy-elect."
Common judgement-place.—*Romeo and Juliet,* i, 1, 109. The only use of "judgement-place."

13
It shows but little . . . judgement in him.
Timon of Athens. Act iii, sc. 3, l. 10. [Sempronius]

14
If, after two days' shine, Athens contain thee,
Attend our weightier judgement.
Timon of Athens. Act iii, sc. 5, l. 101. [Senator]
He tempts judgement.—*Troilus and Cressida,* v, 7, 22.
He 's one o' the soundest judgements in Troy.
Troilus and Cressida. Act i, sc. 2, l. 208. [Pandarus]
His head unmellow'd, but his judgement ripe.
The Two Gentlemen of Verona. Act ii, sc. 4, l. 70. [Valentine] The only use of "unmellow'd."
In judgement old.—*The Merchant of Venice,* ii, 7, 71.

15
Being judge in love, she cannot right her cause.
Venus and Adonis, l. 220.

16
With thoughts so qualified as your charities
Shall best instruct you, measure me.
The Winter's Tale. Act ii, sc. 1, l. 113. [Hermione]

I wish, my liege,
You had only in your silent judgement tried it,
Without more overture.
The Winter's Tale. Act ii, sc. 1, l. 170. [Antigonus]

II—Judgement-Day

1 The dreadful judgement-day
So dreadful will not be as was his sight.
I Henry VI. Act i, sc. 1, l. 29. [Winchester]

He shall never wake till the judgement-day.
Richard III. Act i, sc. 4, l. 105. [Murderer]

At the day of judgement!—*The Merry Wives of Windsor,* iii, 3, 227.

The general all-ending day.—*Richard III,* iii, 1, 78. See under TRUTH.

2 O, let the vile world end,
And the premised flames of the last day
Knit earth and heaven together!
Now let the general trumpet blow his blast.
II Henry VI. Act v, sc. 2, l. 40. [Young Clifford] The only use of "premised."

Then, dreadful trumpet, sound the general doom!
Romeo and Juliet. Act iii, sc. 2, l. 67. [Juliet]

3
Men, wives and children stare, cry out and run
As it were doomsday.
Julius Cæsar. Act iii, sc. 1, l. 97. [Trebonius]

What less than dooms-day is the prince's doom?
Romeo and Juliet, iii, 3, 9. See under DOOM.

Doomsday is near.—*I Henry IV,* iv, 1, 134.
Then is doomsday near.—*Hamlet,* ii, 2, 243.
Almost to doomsday.—*Hamlet,* i, 1, 120.
Last till doomsday.—*Hamlet,* v, 1, 67.
Lives till doomsday.—*The Comedy of Errors,* iii, 2, 101.
Play till doomsday.—*Antony and Cleopatra,* v, 2, 232.
Talk till doomsday.—*Love's Labour's Lost,* iv, 3, 274.
My body's doomsday.—*Richard III,* v, 1, 12.
Tybalt's dooms-day.—*Romeo and Juliet,* v, 3, 234. The only uses of "doomsday."
Day of doom.—*III Henry VI,* v, 6, 93; *Richard II,* iii, 2, 189; *Titus Andronicus,* ii, 3, 42.

4
What, will the line stretch out to the crack of doom?
Macbeth. Act iv, sc. 1, l. 117. [Macbeth]

JURY

5
The jury, passing on the prisoner's life,
May in the sworn twelve have a thief or two
Guiltier than him they try.
Measure for Measure. Act ii, sc. 1, l. 19. [Angelo] The only use of "guiltier."

His noble jury.—*Henry VIII,* iii, 2, 269. The only uses of "jury."

6
In christening shalt thou have two godfathers:
Had I been judge, thou shouldst have had ten more,
To bring thee to the gallows, not the font.
The Merchant of Venice. Act iv, sc. 1, l. 398. [Gratiano] "Font" is repeated in *Richard II,* iv, 1, 256.

7
Fabian: I will prove it legitimate, sir, upon the oaths of judgement and reason.
Sir Toby: And they have been grand-jurymen since before Noah was a sailor.
Twelfth Night. Act iii, sc. 2, l. 15. The only use of "grand-jurymen."

You are grand-jurors, are ye? we'll jure ye, faith.
I Henry IV. Act ii, sc. 2, l. 96. [Falstaff] The only use of "grand-jurors."

Jurors on thy life.—*Timon of Athens,* iv, 3, 345. The only use of "jurors."

Judge and juror.—*Henry VIII,* v, 3, 60. The only use of "juror."

JUSTICE

8
Justice, most gracious due, O, grant me justice!
The Comedy of Errors. Act v, sc. 1, l. 190. [Antipholus of Ephesus]

Justice, sweet prince, against that woman there!
The Comedy of Errors. Act v, sc. 1, l. 197. [Antipholus of Ephesus]

O worthy prince, dishonour not your eye
By throwing it on any other object
Till you have heard me in my true complaint
And given me justice, justice, justice, justice!
Measure for Measure. Act v, sc. 1, l. 22. [Isabella]

Now, good my lord, give me the scope of justice.
Measure for Measure. Act v, sc. 1, l. 234. [Angelo]

Let loose on me the justice of the state.
Othello. Act i, sc. 1, l. 140. [Roderigo]

I beg for justice, which thou, prince, must give.
Romeo and Juliet. Act iii, sc. 1, l. 185. [Lady Capulet]

Justice on the doers!—*All's Well that Ends Well,* v, 3, 154.

9
If he slay me, He does fair justice.
Coriolanus. Act iii, sc. 4, l. 24. [Coriolanus]

Justice . . . could not be so cruel.—*Cymbeline,* iii, 2, 40.

10
Deal justly with me.
Hamlet. Act ii, sc. 2, l. 284. [Hamlet]

I will deal in this
As secretly and justly as your soul
Should with your body.
Much Ado about Nothing, iv, 1, 249. See BODY AND SOUL.

I do not find thou dealest justly with me.
Othello. Act iv, sc. 2, l. 173. [Roderigo]

Let us deal justly.—*King Lear,* iii, 6, 42.
He is justly served.—*Hamlet,* v, 2, 338.
Look you speak justly.—*Measure for Measure,* v, 1, 298.
Spoken . . . justly.—*Henry VIII,* ii, 4, 65.
Justly weigh'd.—*II Henry IV,* iv, 1, 67; *Twelfth Night,* v, 1, 375; *Pericles,* v, 1, 89.

11
In the corrupted currents of this world
Offence's gilded hand may shove by justice,
And oft 'tis seen the wicked prize itself

Buys out the law: but 'tis not so above;
There is no shuffling, there the action lies
In his true nature; and we ourselves compell'd,
Even to the teeth and forehead of our faults,
To give in evidence.

Hamlet. Act iii, sc. 3, l. 57. [King] The only use of "shove." "Shuffling" is repeated in iv, 7, 138, and in *I Henry IV,* iii, 1, 135.

1 Justice hath liquored her.

I Henry IV. Act ii, sc. 1, l. 94. [Gadshill] The only use of "liquored" (to dress with oil or grease).

2 Now, for our consciences, the arms are fair,
When the intent of bearing them is just.

I Henry IV. Act v, sc. 2, l. 88. [Hotspur]

3 To pluck down justice from your awful bench.

II Henry IV. Act v, sc. 2, l. 86. [Chief Justice]

Happy am I, that have a man so bold,
That dares do justice on my proper son;
And not less happy, having such a son,
That would deliver up his greatness so
Into the hands of justice.

II Henry IV. Act v, sc. 2, l. 108. [King Henry V]

And poise the cause in justice' equal scales,
Whose beam stands sure, whose rightful cause prevails.

II Henry VI. Act ii, sc. 1, l. 204. [King Henry]

4 What stronger breastplate than a heart untainted!
Thrice is he arm'd that hath his quarrel just,
And he but naked, though lock'd up in steel,
Whose conscience with injustice is corrupted.

II Henry VI. Act iii, sc. 2, l. 232. [King Henry] The only use of "breastplate."

5 Justice with favour have I always done.

II Henry VI. Act iv, sc. 7, l. 72. [Lord Say]

6 You fight in justice.

III Henry VI. Act v, sc. 4, l. 81. [Queen Margaret]

The justice of our cause.—*III Henry VI,* ii, 1, 133; *Titus Andronicus,* i, 1, 2.

7 The law I bear no malice for my death;
'Twas done, upon the premises, but justice.

Henry VIII. Act ii, sc. 1, l. 62. [Buckingham]

8 Do justice
For truth's sake and his conscience.

Henry VIII. Act iii, sc. 2, l. 396. [Wolsey]

Be just, and fear not.

Henry VIII. Act iii, sc. 2, l. 446. [Wolsey]

9 Did not great Julius bleed for justice' sake?
What villain touch'd his body, that did stab,
And not for justice?

Julius Cæsar. Act iv, sc. 3, l. 19. [Brutus]

10 Through tatter'd clothes small vices do appear;
Robes and furr'd gowns hide all. Plate sin with gold,
And the strong lance of justice hurtless breaks;
Arm it in rags, a pigmy's straw does pierce it.

King Lear. Act iv, sc. 6, l. 168. [King Lear] The only use of "hurtless."

11 Draw thy sword,
That, if my speech offend a noble heart,
Thy arm may do thee justice.

King Lear. Act v, sc. 3, l. 126. [Edgar]

I 'll do you justice.—*Othello,* ii, 3, 90.

To do you justice.—*Antony and Cleopatra,* iii, 6, 88.

Give you justice.—*Measure for Measure,* v, 1, 27.

12 Justice always whirls in equal measure.

Love's Labour 's Lost. Act iv, sc. 3, l. 384. [Biron]

Even-handed justice.—*Macbeth,* i, 7, 10. See under RETRIBUTION for full quotation.

Common justice.—*Measure for Measure,* i, 1, 12.

Regular justice.—*Timon of Athens,* v, 4, 61. The only use of "regular."

13 Justice had with valour arm'd
Compell'd these skipping kerns to trust their heels.

Macbeth. Act i, sc. 2, l. 29. [Sergeant]

You may be rightly just,
Whatever I shall think.

Macbeth. Act iv, sc. 3, l. 30. [Malcolm]

14 It rested in your grace
To unloose this tied-up justice when you pleased.

Measure for Measure. Act i, sc. 3, l. 31. [Friar Thomas] The only use of "tied-up."

What 's open made to justice,
That justice seizes.

Measure for Measure. Act ii, sc. 1, l. 21. [Angelo]

Which is the wiser here? Justice or Iniquity?

Measure for Measure. Act ii, sc. 1, l. 180. [Escalus]

15 His life is parallel'd
Even with the stroke and line of his great justice.

Measure for Measure. Act iv, sc. 2, l. 82. [Duke] The only use of "parallel'd."

The very siege of justice.—*Measure for Measure,* iv, 2, 101.

We hear
Such goodness of your justice, that our soul
Cannot but yield you forth to public thanks,
Forerunning more requital.

Measure for Measure. Act v, sc. 1, l. 5. [Duke] The only use of "forerunning."

My brother had but justice,
In that he did the thing for which he died.

Measure for Measure. Act v, sc. 1, l. 453. [Isabella]

16 He . . . doth impeach the freedom of the state,

If they deny him justice.
The Merchant of Venice. Act iii, sc. 2, l. 280. [Salerio]

For, as thou urgest justice, be assured
Thou shalt have justice, more than thou desirest.
The Merchant of Venice. Act iv, sc. 1, l. 315. [Portia]

1
My parts, my title and my perfect soul
Shall manifest me rightly.
Othello. Act i, sc. 2, l. 31. [Othello]

'Tis meet I should be used so, very meet.
Othello. Act iv, sc. 2, l. 107. [Desdemona]

2
If justice cannot tame you, she shall ne'er weigh more reasons in her balance.
Much Ado about Nothing. Act v, sc. 1, l. 210. [Dogberry]

3
When shall he think to find a stranger just,
When he himself himself confounds, betrays
To slanderous tongues and wretched hateful days?
The Rape of Lucrece, l. 159.

Justice is feasting while the widow weeps.
The Rape of Lucrece, l. 906.

Sparing justice feeds iniquity.
The Rape of Lucrece, l. 1687.

4
Since we can not atone you, we shall see
Justice design the victor's chivalry.
Richard II. Act i, sc. 1, l. 202. [King Richard]

Why at our justice seem'st thou then to lour?
Richard II. Act i, sc. 3, l. 235. [King Richard]

For he is just and always loved us well.
Richard II. Act ii, sc. 1, l. 221. [King Richard]

Cries . . . to me for justice.—*Richard II,* i, 1, 106.

5
O God, I fear thy justice will take hold
On me, and you, and mine, and yours for this!
Richard III. Act ii, sc. 1, l. 131. [King Edward]

6
Thus hath the course of justice wheel'd about,
And left thee but a very prey to time.
Richard III. Act iv, sc. 4, l. 105. [Queen Margaret]

Though justice be thy plea, consider this,
That, in the course of justice, none of us
Should see salvation.
The Merchant of Venice. Act iv, sc. 1, l. 198. [Portia]

Cut off by course of justice.—*Measure for Measure,* v, 1, 35.

7 Be as just and gracious unto me
As I am confident and kind to thee.
Titus Andronicus. Act i, sc. 1, l. 60. [Saturninus]

Whose friend in justice thou hast ever been.
Titus Andronicus. Act i, sc. 1, l. 180. [Marcus]

8
Go sound the ocean, and cast your nets, . . .
Yet there 's as little justice as at land.
Titus Andronicus. Act iv, sc. 3, l. 7. [Titus]

We may go pipe for justice.
Titus Andronicus. Act iv, sc. 3, l. 24. [Titus]

Marry, for Justice, she is so employ'd,
He thinks, with Jove in heaven, or somewhere else,
So that perforce you must needs stay a time.
Titus Andronicus. Act iv, sc. 3, l. 39. [Publius]

And, sith there 's no justice in earth nor hell,
We will solicit heaven and move the gods
To send down Justice for to wreak our wrongs.
Titus Andronicus. Act iv, sc. 3, l. 49. [Titus]

Shall I have justice?—*Titus Andronicus,* iv, 3, 79.

Thou shalt have justice.—*Titus Andronicus,* iv, 3, 104.

He and his shall know that justice lives.
Titus Andronicus. Act iv, sc. 4, l. 23. [Saturninus]

See justice done on Aaron, that damned Moor.
Titus Andronicus. Act v, sc. 3, l. 201. [Lucius]

9
We may not think the justness of each act
Such and no other than event doth form it.
Troilus and Cressida, ii, 2, 119. See under Act. The only use of "justness."

10 Do not count it holy
To hurt by being just: it is as lawful,
For we would give much, to use violent thefts,
And rob in the behalf of charity.
Troilus and Cressida. Act v, sc. 3, l. 19. [Andromache]

11
Be certain what you do, sir, lest your justice
Prove violence.
The Winter's Tale. Act ii, sc. 1, l. 127. [Antigonus]

Let us be clear'd
Of being tyrannous, since we so openly
Proceed in justice, which shall have due course,
Even to the guilt or the purgation.
Winter's Tale. Act iii, sc. 2, l. 4. [Leontes]

Thou
Shalt feel our justice, in whose easiest passage
Look for no less than death.
The Winter's Tale. Act iii, sc. 2, l. 90. [Leontes] The only use of "easiest."

II—Justice of the Peace

12 And then the justice,
In fair round belly with good capon lined,
With eyes severe and beard of formal cut,
Full of wise saws and modern instances.
As You Like It. Act ii, sc. 7, l. 153. [Jaques]

13
You are right, justice, and you weigh this well;
Therefore still bear the balance and the sword.
II Henry IV. Act v, sc. 2, l. 102. [King Henry V]

Foolish justices.—*II Henry IV,* v, 1, 75.

Starved justice.—*II Henry IV,* iii, 2, 327.

1
See how yond justice rails upon yond simple thief. Hark, in thine ear: change places; and, handy-dandy, which is the justice, which is the thief?
King Lear. Act iv, sc. 6, l. 155. [King Lear] The only use of "handy-dandy."

2
My brother justice have I found so severe, that he hath forced me to tell him he is indeed Justice.
Measure for Measure. Act iii, sc. 2, l. 266. [Escalus]

3
Slender: In the county of Gloucester, justice of peace and 'Coram.'
Shallow: Ay, cousin Slender, and 'Custalorum.'
Slender: Ay, and 'Rato-lorum' too; and a gentleman born, master parson; who writes himself 'Armigero,' in any bill, warrant, quittance, or obligation, 'Armigero.'
The Merry Wives of Windsor. Act i, sc. 1, l. 5. The only use of "Coram (addenda)," "Custalorum (custos rotulorum, keeper of the rolls)," "Rato-lorum (rotolorum)," and "Armigero (dative of armiger, esquire)."

He 's a justice of peace in his country.
The Merry Wives of Windsor. Act i, sc. 1, l. 225. [Slender]

Justice of peace.—*II Henry VI,* iv, 7, 45; *II Henry IV*, iii, 2, 64; *The Merry Wives of Windsor,* i, 1, 283.

False justicer.—*King Lear,* iii, 6, 59.

Most learned justicer.—*King Lear,* iii, 6, 23.

Upright justicer.—*Cymbeline,* v, 5, 214. The only uses of "justicer."

You justicers.—*King Lear,* iv, 2, 79. The only use of "justicers."

K

KEY

4
Wear . . . bunches of keys at their girdles.
II Henry IV. Act i, sc. 2, l. 45. [Falstaff]

5
Thou didst bear the key of all my counsels.
Henry V, ii, 2, 96. See under TRAITOR.

Key of villanous secrets.—*Othello,* iv, 2, 22.

6
These counties are the keys of Normandy.
II Henry VI. Act i, sc. 1, l. 114. [Salisbury] Normandy is mentioned five times in this play, once in *Love's Labour 's Lost,* ii, 1, 43, and once in *Hamlet,* iv, 7, 83.

7
What! fear not, man, but yield me up the keys.
III Henry VI. Act iv, sc. 7, l. 37. [King Edward]

Deliver me the key.—*The Merchant of Venice,* ii, 7, 59.

Give her this key.—*The Comedy of Errors,* iv, 1, 103.

Give up your keys.—*Measure for Measure,* v, 1, 467.

There 's my key.—*King Lear,* i, 2, 186.

Here are the keys.—*Richard III,* i, 4, 96.

Here be my keys.—*The Merry Wives of Windsor,* iii, 3, 172.

There are my keys.—*The Merchant of Venice,* ii, 5, 12.

Under his key.—*Macbeth,* iii, 6, 18.

8
Give me a key for this,
And instantly unlock my fortunes here.
The Merchant of Venice. Act ii, sc. 9, l. 51. [Arragon]

9
I will use her as the key of the cuckoldly rogue's coffer; and there 's my harvest-home.
The Merry Wives of Windsor. Act ii, sc. 2, l. 285. [Falstaff] "Harvest-home" is repeated in *I Henry IV,* i, 3, 35.

10
In what key shall a man take you, to go in the song?
Much Ado about Nothing, i, 1, 188. See under SONG.

Both in one key.—*A Midsummer-Night's Dream,* iii, 2, 206.

In another key.—*A Midsummer-Night's Dream,* i, 1, 18.

In a bondman's key.—*The Merchant of Venice,* i, 3, 124.

Selfsame key.—*Troilus and Cressida,* i, 3, 53. The only uses of "key" in this sense.

11
They say he wears a key in his ear and a lock hanging by it.
Much Ado about Nothing. Act v, sc. 2, l. 318. [Dogberry]

12
Give me leave that I may turn the key,
That no man enter till my tale be done.
Richard II. Act v, sc. 3, l. 36. [Aumerle]

If wolves had at thy gate howl'd that stern time,
Thou shouldst have said 'Good porter, turn the key.'
King Lear. Act iii, sc. 7, l. 63. [Gloucester]

I pray you, turn the key and keep our counsel.
Othello. Act iv, sc. 2, l. 94. [Othello]

Turn you the key.—*Measure for Measure,* i, 4, 8.

Turning the key.—*Macbeth,* ii, 3, 3.

Turns the key.—*King Lear,* ii, 4, 53.

Bigger key.—*Measure for Measure,* iv, 1, 31.

Blessed key.—*Sonnets,* lii.

Feeble key.—*The Comedy of Errors,* v, 1, 310.

Key . . . of office.—*The Tempest,* i, 2, 83.

Life's key.—*All 's Well that Ends Well,* i, 1, 76.

13
I could have filed keys off that hung in chains.
The Winter's Tale. Act iv, sc. 4, l. 624. [Autolycus]

KILLING

See also Execution, Murder

1
I kill thee, make thee away, translate thy life into death, thy liberty into bondage . . . I will kill thee a hundred and fifty ways.
As You Like It. Act v, sc. 1, l. 58. [Touchstone]

Henceforth guard thee well;
For I 'll not kill thee there, nor there, nor there;
But, by the forge that stithied Mars his helm,
I 'll kill thee every where, yes, o'er and o'er.
Troilus and Cressida. Act iv, sc. 5, l. 253. [Hector] The only use of "stithied." "As foul as Vulcan's stithy" occurs in *Hamlet,* iii, 2, 89.

I would have him nine years a-killing.
Othello. Act iv, sc. 1, l. 188. [Othello]

2
Aufidius: Insolent villain!
Conspirators: Kill, kill, kill, kill, kill him!
Coriolanus. Act v, sc. 6, l. 131.

In a peaceful hour doth cry "Kill, kill!"
Venus and Adonis, l. 652. See under JEALOUSY.

3
He Hath widow'd and unchilded many a one.
Coriolanus. Act v, sc. 6, l. 153. [Aufidius] The only use of "widow'd" and "unchilded."

4
Was it for me to kill the heir-apparent?
I Henry IV. Act ii, sc. 4, l. 297. [Falstaff] "Heir-apparent" is used six times.

5
By this sword, he that makes the first thrust I 'll kill him.
Henry V. Act ii, sc. 1, l. 104. [Bardolph]

6
Kill me with thy sword,
And not with such a cruel threatening look.
III Henry VI. Act i, sc. 3, l. 16. [Rutland]

Ah, kill me with thy weapon, not with words!
III Henry VI. Act v, sc. 6, l. 26. [King Henry]

Kill with looks.—*Richard II,* iii, 2, 165.

Kill it with a groan.—*Richard II,* v, 1, 100.

7
Let 's kill him boldly, but not wrathfully;
Let 's carve him as a dish fit for the gods,
Not hew him as a carcass fit for hounds.
Julius Cæsar. Act ii, sc. 1, l. 172. [Brutus] The only use of "wrathfully," and of the phrase, "a dish fit for the gods."

Kill him in the shell.—*Julius Cæsar,* ii, 1, 34.

8
How 'scaped I killing when I cross'd you so?
Julius Cæsar. Act iv, sc. 3, l. 150. [Cassius]

Kill me straight.
Kill Brutus, and be honour'd in his death.
Julius Cæsar. Act v, sc. 4, l. 13. [Lucilius]

I 'll rather kill myself.—*Julius Cæsar,* v, 5, 7.

'To kill myself,' quoth she, 'alack, what were it,
But with my body my poor soul's pollution?'
The Rape of Lucrece, l. 1156.

Bid me kill myself, and I will do it.
Richard III. Act i, sc. 2, l. 187. [Gloucester] See also under SUICIDE.

9
See that Claudio be executed.
Measure for Measure. Act ii, sc. 1, l. 34. [Angelo] See under DEATH.

He shall be executed presently.
Timon of Athens. Act iii, sc. 5, l. 103. [Senator]

Be executed.—*Measure for Measure,* iv, 2, 124; 133; 182; *Twelfth Night,* iii, 4, 30; *Henry V,* iii, 6, 106; *Richard III,* v, 3, 96; *Coriolanus,* iv, 5, 232; *Titus Andronicus,* ii, 3, 303; v, 2, 15.

Claudio, whom here you have warrant to execute.
Measure for Measure. Act iv, sc. 2, l. 166. [Duke]

Execute the noble duke.—*Richard II,* iv, 1, 82.

Execute upon him.—*Othello,* ii, 3, 228. See also EXECUTION.

10
Bassanio: Do all men kill the things they do not love?
Shylock: Hates any man the thing he would not kill?
The Merchant of Venice. Act iv, sc. 1, l. 66.

11
By gar, I vill kill de Jack priest.
The Merry Wives of Windsor. Act i, sc. 4, l. 123. [Caius]

By gar, me vill kill de priest.
The Merry Wives of Windsor. Act ii, sc. 3, l. 85. [Caius]

Monster, I will kill this man.
The Tempest. Act iii, sc. 2, l. 114. [Stephano]

12
How many hath he killed and eaten in these wars? But how many hath he killed? for indeed I promised to eat all of his killing.
Much Ado about Nothing. Act i, sc. 1, l. 43. [Beatrice]

It will not kill a fly.—*As You Like It,* iv, 1, 110. "Kill a fly" is repeated in *Titus Andronicus,* iii, 2, 77; v, 1, 142. See under FLY.

13
If you go on thus, you will kill yourself.
Much Ado about Nothing. Act v, sc. 1, l. 1. [Antonio]

Leonato: If thou kill'st me, boy, thou shalt kill a man.
Antonio: He shall kill two of us, and men indeed.
Much Ado about Nothing. Act v, sc. 1, l. 79.

14
Othello: I would not kill thy unprepared spirit;
No; heaven forfend! I would not kill thy soul.
Desdemona: Talk you of killing?
Othello: Ay, I do.
Desdemona: Then heaven
Have mercy on me.
Othello: Amen, with all my heart!
Desdemona: If you say so, I hope you will not kill me. . . .
O, banish me, my lord, but kill me not! . . .
Kill me to-morrow, let me live tonight! . . .
But half an hour! . . . But while I say one prayer!
Othello: It is too late. [*He stifles her*]
Othello. Act v, sc. 2, l. 31.

1 Since I am near slain,
Kill me outright with looks and rid my pain.
Sonnets. No. cxxxix.

2
He kills her in her own humour.
The Taming of the Shrew. Act iv, sc. 1, l. 183. [Peter]

This is a way to kill a wife with kindness.
The Taming of the Shrew. Act iv, sc. 1, l. 211. [Petruchio]

I should kill thee with much cherishing.
Romeo and Juliet. Act ii, sc. 2, l. 184. [Juliet]

Thou hast kill'd the sweetest innocent
That e'er did lift up eye.
Othello. Act v, sc. 2, l. 199. [Emilia]

3
To kill, I grant, is sin's extremest gust;
But, in defence, by mercy, 'tis most just.
Timon of Athens. Act iii, sc. 5, l. 54. [Alcibiades]

4
Kill a man, or else devise his death.
Titus Andronicus. Act v, sc. 1, l. 128. [Aaron]

5
I will waylay thee going home; where if it be thy chance to kill me, . . . thou killest me like a rogue and a villain.
Twelfth Night. Act iii, sc. 4, l. 176. [Sir Toby Belch, reading] The only use of "waylay" in the plays. "Waylaid" occurs in *I Henry IV*, i, 2, 183.

They will kill each other by the look, like cockatrices.
Twelfth Night, iii, 4, 214. See under DUELLING for full quotation. "Cockatrice" occurs twice more in the plays, in *Richard III,* iv, 1, 55, and in *Romeo and Juliet,* iii, 2, 47.

Come, basilisk,
And kill the innocent gazer with thy sight.
II Henry VI, iii, 2, 53. For other uses of "basilisk," see EYE: BASILISK AND COCKATRICE.

6
I kill'd a man, whose death I much repent;
But yet I slew him manfully in fight,
Without false vantage or base treachery.
The Two Gentlemen of Verona. Act iv, sc. 1, l. 27. [Valentine] "Manfully" is repeated in *Titus Andronicus,* i, 1, 196.

7
O, thou didst kill me: kill me once again.
Venus and Adonis, l. 499.

KIN

See also Family

8
Cymbeline: Is he thy kin, thy friend?
Imogen: He is a Roman; no more kin to me
Than I to your highness.
Cymbeline. Act v, sc. 5, l. 111.

He 's not thy kinsman.—*As You Like It,* ii, 4, 67.

Nothing kin.—*Measure for Measure,* ii, 4, 113.

No kin else.—*Timon of Athens,* i, 1, 121.

9
A little more than kin, and less than kind.
Hamlet. Act i, sc. 2, l. 65. [Hamlet]

Kin with kin and kind with kind.
Richard II, iv, 1, 141. See under WAR.

10
Nay, they will be kin to us, or they will fetch it from Japhet.
II Henry IV. Act ii, sc. 2, l. 128. [Prince] The only mention of Japhet.

Even such kin as the parish heifers are to the town bull.
II Henry IV. Act ii, sc. 2, l. 171. [Prince of Wales]

Kin to the king.—*II Henry IV*, ii, 2, 120.

11
So little kin to the purpose.
Henry V. Act iii, sc. 7, l. 72. [Constable]

12
It is a peerless kinsman.
Macbeth. Act i, sc. 4, l. 58. [Duncan]

I am his kinsman and his subject.
Macbeth, i, 7, 13. See under TRUST.

Dear kinsman.—*Romeo and Juliet,* iii, 1, 153.

Gentle kinsman.—*King John,* iv, 2, 166.

Great kinsman.—*Romeo and Juliet,* iv, 3, 53.

Kind kinsman.—*Henry V*, iv, 3, 10.

Little kinsman.—*King John,* iii, 3, 18.

Noble kinsman.—*The Merchant of Venice,* i, 1, 57; *Richard II,* ii, 1, 262.

Valiant kinsman.—*King John,* v, 3, 5.

13
Were he my kinsman, brother, or my son,
It should be thus with him.
Measure for Measure. Act ii, sc. 2, l. 81. [Angelo]

I am half afeard
Thou wilt say anon he is some kin to thee.
The Merchant of Venice. Act ii, sc. 9, l. 96. [Portia]

14
In that thou art like to be my kinsman, live unbruised and love my cousin.
Much Ado about Nothing. Act v, sc. 4, l. 112. [Benedick]

Why, how now, kinsman!—*Romeo and Juliet,* i, 5, 62.

Kinsmen of mine.—*Henry VIII,* i, 1, 81.

15
Hence comes it that your kindred shuns
your house.
The Taming of the Shrew. Induction, sc. 2, l. 30. [Lord]

No kindred weep for me.—*Henry VIII,* iii, 1, 150.

Dull kindred.—*As You Like It,* iii, 2, 32.

Great kindred.—*Measure for Measure,* iii, 2, 109.

Proud kindred.—*Richard III,* ii, 2, 150.

Kindred of the king.—*Richard II,* i, 1, 70.

Guilty kindred of the queen.—*Richard III,* ii, 1, 135.

Mine own kindred.—*Cymbeline,* v, 5, 429.

16
She is my kinswoman.
Troilus and Cressida, i, 1, 44. "Kinswoman" occurs again in *II Henry IV*, ii, 2, 169, and in *Much Ado about Nothing,* iv, 1, 305.

17
Because she 's kin to me, therefore she 's not so fair as Helen: an she were not kin to me, she would be as fair on Friday as Helen is on Sunday.
Troilus and Cressida. Act i, sc. 1, l. 75. [Pandarus]

What kin are you to me?—*Twelfth Night,* v, i, 237.
Near'st of kin.—*The Winter's Tale,* iii, 2, 54.
Kin to Jove's thunder.—*Winter's Tale,* iii, i, 10.

1
One touch of nature makes the whole world kin.
Troilus and Cressida. Act iii, sc. 3, l. 175. [Ulysses]

2
I know no touch of consanguinity;
No kin, no love, no blood.
Troilus and Cressida. Act iv, sc. 2, l. 103. [Cressida] The only use of "consanguinity."

3 We 'll bar thee from succession;
Not hold thee of our blood, no, not our kin,
Far than Deucalion off.
The Winter's Tale. Act iv, sc. 4, l. 439. [Polixenes] Deucalion is mentioned again in *Coriolanus,* ii, i, 102.

KINDNESS

See also Mildness

4
You are too indulgent.
Antony and Cleopatra. Act i, sc. 4, l. 16. [Cæsar] The only use of "indulgent."

5
Kindness, nobler ever than revenge.
As You Like It. Act iv, sc. 3, l. 129. [Oliver]

6
Use her with more kindness.
The Comedy of Errors, iii, 2, 6. For "use kindly" see under Use.
Deep kindness.—*Sonnets,* clii.
Fair kindness.—*Twelfth Night,* iii, 4, 376.
Much kindness.—*Merchant of Venice,* i, 3, 154.
Pure kindness.—*King Lear,* ii, 4, 127.
Selfsame kindness.—*The Taming of the Shrew,* v, 2, 5.

7
O, he is grown most kind of late.
Coriolanus. Act iv, sc. 6, l. 11. [Sicinius]
He grows kind.—*Merchant of Venice,* i, 3, 179.
Ever most kind.—*Measure for Measure,* iii, i, 229.
Wondrous kind.—*All 's Well that Ends Well,* v, 3, 311.
Be kind.—*Henry V,* iii, Prol., 34; *Sonnets,* cxliii.
I will be very kind.—*The Taming of the Shrew,* i, i, 98.
Thou 'rt kind.—*Macbeth,* i, 3, 12.
Kind and comfortable.—*King Lear,* i, 4, 328.
Kind and courteous.—*A Midsummer-Night's Dream,* iii, i, 167.
Kind and dear.—*King Lear,* iv, 7, 29.
Kind and honest.—*Othello,* iii, i, 43.
Kind and noble.—*Pericles,* v, i, 68.
Kind and tame.—*A Lover's Complaint,* l. 311.
Kind and true.—*Sonnets,* cv.

8
You o'er-rate my poor kindness.
Cymbeline. Act i, sc. 4, l. 41. [Frenchman] The only use of "o'er-rate" and "poor kindness."
I shall unfold equal discourtesy
To your best kindness.
Cymbeline. Act ii, sc. 3, l. 101. [Imogen] The only use of "discourtesy" and "best kindness."

9 When a world of men
Could not prevail with all their oratory,
Yet hath a woman's kindness over-ruled.
I Henry VI. Act ii, sc. 2, l. 48. [Talbot]

10
You do not use me with that affability as in discretion you ought to use me.
Henry V. Act iii, sc. 2, l. 138. [Fluellen] "Affability" is repeated in *Julius Cæsar,* ii, i, 82, and *The Taming of the Shrew,* ii, i, 49.

11 I may live to do you kindness if
You do it her.
II Henry VI. Act ii, sc. 4, l. 83. [Gloucester]

12
I come, in kindness and unfeigned love.
III Henry VI. Act iii, sc. 3, l. 51. [Warwick] "Unfeigned" is repeated in l. 202 of the same scene, "Unfeigned friend"; and in *The Taming of the Shrew,* iv, 2, 32, "Unfeigned oath."
Yet shall you have all kindness at my hand
That your estate requires and mine can yield.
III Henry VI. Act iii, sc. 3, l. 149. [King Lewis]
Nay, be thou sure I 'll well requite thy kindness.
III Henry VI. Act iv, sc. 6, l. 10. [King Henry]
If fortune serve me, I 'll requite this kindness.
III Henry VI. Act iv, sc. 7, l. 78. [King Edward]
Give him all kindness.—*Julius Cæsar,* v, 4, 28.

13
There 's a great abatement of kindness appears as well in the general dependants as in the duke himself also and your daughter.
King Lear. Act i, sc. 4, l. 64. [Knight]
The gods reward your kindness!
King Lear. Act iii, sc. 6, l. 5. [Kent]

14 Yet do I fear thy nature;
It is too full o' the milk of human kindness
To catch the nearest way.
Macbeth. Act i, sc. 5, l. 17. [Lady Macbeth]

15
Truly, sir, for your kindness I owe you a good turn.
Measure for Measure. Act iv, sc. 2, l. 62. [Pompey]
Bassanio: This were kindness.
Shylock: This kindness will I show.
The Merchant of Venice. Act i, sc. 3, l. 144.

16
A kind overflow of kindness.
Much Ado about Nothing. Act i, sc. i, l. 26. [Leonato]
Your over-kindness doth wring tears from me!
Much Ado about Nothing. Act v, sc. i, l. 303. [Claudio] The only use of "over-kindness."
The sincerity of love and honest kindness.
Othello. Act ii, sc. 3, l. 333. [Iago]

17
I never spake bad word, nor did ill turn
To any living creature: believe me, la,
I never kill'd a mouse, nor hurt a fly:

I trod upon a worm against my will,
But I wept for it.
Pericles. Act iv, sc. 1, l. 1. [Marina]

If thou hadst drunk to him, 't had been a kindness
Becoming well thy fact.
Pericles. Act iv, sc. 3, l. 11. [Cleon]

Since your kindness
We have stretch'd thus far, let us beseech you
That for our gold we may provision have,
Wherein we are not destitute for want,
But weary for the staleness.
Pericles. Act v, sc. 1, l. 54. [Helicanus] The only use of "staleness."

Your present kindness
Makes my past miseries sports.
Pericles. Act v, sc. 3, l. 40. [Pericles]

1
Be brief, lest that the process of thy kindness
Last longer telling than my kindness' date.
Richard III. Act iv, sc. 4, l. 253. [Queen Elizabeth]

I cannot make you what amends I would,
Therefore accept such kindness as I can.
Richard III. Act iv, sc. 4, l. 309. [King Richard]

Thy kindness freezeth.—*Richard III,* iv, 2, 22.

2
Be, as thy presence is, gracious and kind,
Or to thyself at least kind-hearted prove.
Sonnets. No. x. The only use of "kind-hearted."

3
This do and do it kindly, gentle sirs.
The Taming of the Shrew. Induction, sc. 1, l. 66. [Lord]

Why, this is kindly done!—*Troilus and Cressida,* iii, 1, 105.

4
To express the like kindness, myself that have been more kindly beholding to you than any, freely give unto you this young scholar, that hath been long studying at Rheims.
The Taming of the Shrew. Act ii, sc. 1, l. 77. [Gremio] Rheims is mentioned again in *I Henry VI,* i, 1, 60; 92.

5
This is the way to kill a wife with kindness.
The Taming of the Shrew. Act iv, sc. 1, l. 211. [Petruchio]

6
Kindness in women, not their beauteous looks,
Shall win my love.
The Taming of the Shrew. Act iv, sc. 2, l. 41. [Hortensio]

Is she kind as she is fair?
For beauty lives with kindness.
The Two Gentlemen of Verona. Act iv, sc. 2, l. 44. [Song]

If there be a kind woman in Windsor, she is one.
The Merry Wives of Windsor. Act ii, sc. 2, l. 126. [Mistress Quickly] The only use of "kind woman."

7
He outgoes The very heart of kindness.
Timon of Athens. Act i, sc. 1, l. 285. [Lord]

I have received some small kindnesses from him.
Timon of Athens. Act iii, sc. 2, l. 22. [Lucius] "Kindnesses" is repeated in *The Comedy of Errors,* iv, 3, 5; in *Twelfth Night,* iii, 4, 385; and in *Cymbeline,* i, 6, 23.

Is not my kindness subtle, covetous,
If not a usuring kindness?
Timon of Athens. Act iv, sc. 3, l. 515. [Timon] "Usuring" is repeated in iii, 5, 110, "Usuring senate," and occurs in no other play.

To ease them of their griefs,
Their fears of hostile strokes, their aches, losses,
Their pangs of love, with other incident throes
That nature's fragile vessel doth sustain
In life's uncertain voyage, I will some kindness do them.
Timon of Athens. Act v, sc. 1, l. 201. [Timon]

8
Lending your kind commiseration.
Titus Andronicus. Act v, sc. 3, l. 93. [Marcus] "Commiseration" occurs also in *Love's Labour's Lost,* iv, 1, 64, and in *The Merchant of Venice,* iv, 1, 30.

9
Yet is the kindness but particular.
Troilus and Cressida, iv, 5, 20. See under KISS.

10
My bosom is full of kindness.
Twelfth Night. Act ii, sc. 1, l. 40. [Sebastian]

He did me kindness, sir.—*Twelfth Night,* v, 1, 69.

Do him that kindness.—*Titus Andronicus,* v, 3, 171.

KING

See also Crown, Emperor, Majesty, Monarch, Prince, Sovereign

11
Kings have been your fellows.
Antony and Cleopatra. Act iv, sc. 2, l. 13. [Antony]

12
Our great king himself doth woo me oft
For my confections.
Cymbeline. Act i, sc. 5, l. 14. [Queen]

That confection Which I gave him for cordial.
Cymbeline. Act v, sc. 5, l. 246. [Cornelius] "Confection" is used in no other play.

13
Hail, great king!
To sour your happiness, I must report
The queen is dead.
Cymbeline. Act v, sc. 5, l. 25. [Cornelius] "Great king" is repeated twenty-one times.

14
If the king like not the comedy,
Why then, belike, he likes it not, perdy.
Hamlet. Act iii, sc. 2, l. 304. [Hamlet] "Perdy" is used four times.

Guildenstern: The king, sir,—
Hamlet: Ay, sir, what of him?
Guildenstern: Is in his retirement marvellous distempered.
Hamlet: With drink, sir?
Guildenstern: No, my lord, rather with choler.
Hamlet: Your wisdom should show itself more richer to signify this to his doctor; for, for

me to put him to his purgation would perhaps plunge him into far more choler.
Hamlet. Act iii, sc. 2, l. 310.

1
The king shall drink to Hamlet's better breath;
And in the cup an union shall he throw,
Richer than that which four successive kings
In Denmark's crown have worn. Give me the cups; . . .
'Now the king drinks to Hamlet.'
Hamlet. Act v, sc. 2, l. 282. [King]

Danish king.—*Hamlet,* iv, 4, 1.

2
The king himself is to be feared as the lion.
I Henry IV. Act iii, sc. 3, l. 169. [Falstaff]

Vernon: The king himself in person is set forth,
Or hitherwards intended speedily,
With strong and mighty preparation.
Hotspur: He shall be welcome too.
I Henry IV. Act iv, sc. 1, l. 91.

The king hath drawn
The special head of all the land together.
I Henry IV. Act iv, sc. 4, l. 27. [Archbishop of York]

The king will give you battle presently.
I Henry IV. Act v, sc. 2, l. 31. [Worcester]

The king comes on apace.—*I Henry IV,* v, 2, 90.

3
Blunt: If that the king
Have any way your good deserts forgot,
Which he confesseth to be manifold,
He bids you name your griefs; and with all speed
You shall have your desires with interest. . . .
Hotspur: The king is kind; and well we know the king
Knows at what time to promise, when to pay.
I Henry IV. Act iv, sc. 3, l. 45.

It is not possible, it cannot be,
The king should keep his word in loving us.
I Henry IV. Act v, sc. 2, l. 4. [Worcester]

4
Hotspur: The king hath many marching in his coats.
Earl of Douglas: Now, by my sword, I will kill all his coats;
I 'll murder all his wardrobe, piece by piece,
Until I meet the king.
I Henry IV. Act v, sc. 3, l. 25.

Douglas: What art thou,
That counterfeit'st the person of a king?
King Henry: The king himself; who, Douglas, grieves at heart
So many of his shadows thou hast met
And not the very king. . . .
Douglas: I fear thou art another counterfeit;
And yet, in faith, thou bear'st thee like a king.
I Henry IV. Act v, sc. 4, l. 27.

Yet looks he like a king: behold, his eye,
As bright as is the eagle's, lightens forth
Controlling majesty.
Richard II. Act iii, sc. 3, l. 68. [York]

5
So is the unfirm king In three divided.
II Henry IV. Act i, sc. 3, l. 73. [Hastings]

O earth, yield us that king again,
And take thou this!
II Henry IV. Act i, sc. 3, l. 106. [Archbishop]

O, when the king did throw his warder down,
His own life hung upon the staff he threw;
Then threw he down himself and all their lives.
II Henry IV. Act iv, sc. 1, l. 125. [Mowbray]

The king hath wasted all his rods
On late offenders, that he now doth lack
The very instruments of chastisement.
II Henry IV. Act iv, sc. 1, l. 215. [Hastings]

6
I hear the king my father is sore sick.
II Henry IV. Act iv, sc. 3, l. 83.

How doth the king?—*II Henry IV,* iv, 5, 10; v, 2, 2.

The king recovers.—*II Henry IV,* iv, 4, 129.

The king your father is disposed to sleep.
II Henry IV. Act iv, sc. 5, l. 17. [Warwick]

7
And, as you are a king, speak in your state
What I have done that misbecame my place,
My person, or my liege's sovereignty.
II Henry IV. Act v, sc. 2, l. 99. [Lord Chief-Justice] The only use of "misbecame."

Why, there spoke a king.
II Henry IV. Act v, sc. 3, l. 73. [Shallow]

8
She hath herself not only well defended
But taken and impounded as a stray
The King of Scots.
Henry V. Act i, sc. 2, l. 159. [Canterbury] The only use of "impounded" and "King of Scots."

She clepes him king of graves.
Venus and Adonis, l. 995. See under DEATH.

King of this country.—*The Tempest,* iv, 1, 243.

Kings o' the earth.—*Antony and Cleopatra,* iii, 6, 68.

King of good fellows.—*Henry V,* v, 2, 261.

King of infinite space.—*Hamlet,* ii, 2, 261.

King o' the isle.—*The Tempest,* v, 1, 288.

Island kings.—*Troilus and Cressida,* iii, 1, 167.

Indian king.—*A Midsummer-Night's Dream,* ii, 1, 22.

Sparta's king.—*Troilus and Cressida,* ii, 2, 183.

Of all kingdoms king.—*As You Like It,* v, 4, 10.

Foreign kings.—*II Henry VI,* iv, 7, 82.

9
Suppose that you have seen
The well-appointed king at Hampton pier
Embark his royalty.
Henry V. Act iii, Prol., l. 4. [Chorus]

Thou wouldst find me such a plain king that thou wouldst think I had sold my farm to buy my crown.
Henry V. Act v, sc. 2, l. 128. [King Henry]

10
This is in traffic of a king.
I Henry VI. Act v, sc. 3, l. 164. [Suffolk]

11
Great King of England and my gracious lord.
II Henry VI. Act i, sc. 1, l. 24. [Queen]

"Great king" occurs twenty-one times in the plays, and there are seventeen references to the King of England.

And now to London with triumphant march,
There to be crowned England's royal king.
III Henry VI. Act ii, sc. 6, l. 87. [Warwick] "England's royal king" is repeated in *I Henry VI,* v, 3, 115; and *Richard III,* iii, 7, 22. "Royal kings" occurs in *Richard II,* ii, 1, 51; iii, 1, 8; and *Antony and Cleopatra,* v, 2, 330.

Great England's lawful king.—*II Henry VI,* v, 1, 4. "Lawful king" is repeated in *III Henry VI,* i, 1, 137; v, 1, 88; in *King John,* ii, 1, 222; and in *Richard* II, iii, 3, 74.

Who loves the king and will embrace his pardon,
Fling up his cap, and say 'God save his majesty!'
II Henry VI. Act iv, sc. 8, l. 14. [Clifford]

God save the king! Will no man say amen?
Richard II. Act iv, sc. 1, l. 172. [King Richard]

God save the king!—*II Henry VI,* iv, 8, 19; iv, 9, 22; *Macbeth,* i, 2, 47. See under ENGLAND.

God bless the king!—*Love's Labour's Lost,* iv, 3, 189.

Salisbury and Warwick: Long live our sovereign Richard, England's king!
York: We thank you, lords. But I am not your king
Till I be crown'd.
II Henry VI. Act ii, sc. 2, l. 63.

Long live the king!—*Hamlet,* i, 1, 3. The only use of the phrase.

Sir king, all hail! the gods preserve you!
Hail, royal sir!
Pericles. Act v, sc. 1, l. 39. [Lysimachus]

Good angels preserve the king.
The Tempest. Act ii, sc. 1, l. 306. [Gonzalo]

1 Pernicious protector, dangerous peer,
That smooth'st it so with king and commonweal!
II Henry VI. Act ii, sc. 1, l. 21. [Beaufort] "King and commonweal" is repeated in l. 191, and in *Titus Andronicus,* i, 1, 114.

King and commander of our commonweal,
The wide world's emperor.
Titus Andronicus. Act i, sc. 1, l. 247. [Titus]

2 I see no reason why a king of years
Should be to be protected like a child.
God and King Henry govern England's realm.
II Henry VI. Act ii, sc. 3, l. 28. [Queen]

Queen: Help, lords! the king is dead.
Somerset: Rear up his body; wring him by the nose.
II Henry VI. Act iii, sc. 2, l. 33.

I am far better born than is the king,
More like a king, more kingly in my thoughts.
II Henry VI. Act v, sc. 1, l. 28. [York] The only use of the phrase "far better."

3 Falstaff: My king! my Jove! I speak to thee, my heart!
King Henry V: I know thee not, old man: fall to thy prayers;
Presume not that I am the thing I was;
For God doth know, so shall the world perceive,
That I have turn'd away my former self;
So will I those that kept me company.
II Henry VI. Act v, sc. 5, l. 50.

4 King Henry: Tell me, may not the king adopt an heir?
York: What then?
King Henry: An if he may, then am I lawful king. . . .
Exeter: My conscience tells me he is lawful king.
III Henry VI. Act i, sc. 1, l. 135.

Art thou king, and wilt be forced?
III Henry VI. Act i, sc. 1, l. 230. [Queen Margaret]

I will be king, or die.—*III Henry VI,* i, 2, 35.

5 What! was it you that would be England's king?
III Henry VI. Act i, sc. 4, l. 70. [Queen Margaret]

Queen Margaret: Becomes it thee to be thus bold in terms
Before thy sovereign and thy lawful king?
Edward: I am his king, and he should bow his knee; . . .
You, that are king, though he do wear the crown,
Have caused him, by new act of parliament,
To blot out me, and put his own son in.
III Henry VI. Act ii, sc. 2, l. 85.

How will the country for these woful chances
Misthink the king and not be satisfied!
III Henry VI. Act ii, sc. 5, l. 108. [King Henry] The only use of "misthink."

6 This is the quondam king; let's seize upon him.
III Henry VI. Act iii, sc. 1, l. 23. [Keeper]

Keeper: Say, what are thou that talk'st of kings and queens?
King Henry: More than I seem, and less than I was born to:
A man at least, for less I should not be;
And men may talk of kings, and why not I?
Keeper: Ay, but thou talk'st as if thou wert a king.
King Henry: Why, so I am, in mind; and that's enough.
III Henry VI. Act iii, sc. 1, l. 55.

7 Thou setter up and plucker down of kings.
III Henry VI. Act ii, sc. 3, l. 37. [Edward] The only use of "plucker."

Proud setter up and puller down of kings!
III Henry VI. Act iii, sc. 3, l. 157. [Queen Margaret] The only use of "puller," and of "setter" in this sense.

Who lived king, but I could dig his grave?
III Henry VI. Act v, sc. 2, l. 21. [Warwick]

8 In despite of all mischance,
Of thee thyself and all thy complices,
Edward will bear himself as king.
III Henry VI. Act iv, sc. 3, l. 43. [King Edward]

Be true king indeed, thou but the shadow.
III Henry VI. Act iv, sc. 3, l. 50. [Warwick]

1 The two kings,
Equal in lustre, were now best, now worst,
As presence did present them.
Henry VIII. Act i, sc. 1, l. 28. [Norfolk]

A pair of kings.—*The Winter's Tale,* v, 3, 146.

2 Seek the king;
That sun, I pray, may never set!
Henry VIII. Act iii, sc. 2, l. 414. [Wolsey]

3 In the name of God
How comes it then that thou art call'd a king,
When living blood doth in these temples beat,
Which owe the crown that thou o'ermasterest?
King John. Act ii, sc. 1, l. 106. [King Philip] The only use of "o'ermasterest."

Your king, whose labour'd spirits,
Forwearied in this action of swift speed,
Crave harbourage within your city walls.
King John. Act ii, sc. 1, l. 233. [King John] The only use of "forwearied." "Harbourage" is repeated in *Pericles,* i, 4, 100.

King o'er him and all that he enjoys.
King John. Act ii, sc. 1, l. 240. [King Philip]

He that proves the king,
To him will we prove loyal.
King John. Act ii, sc. 1, l. 270. [First Citizen]

Our kingdom's king.—*King John,* ii, 1, 286.

Your king and England's.—*King John,* ii, 1, 313.

4
France, shall we knit our powers
And lay this Angiers even with the ground;
Then after fight who shall be king of it?
King John. Act ii, sc. 1, l. 398. [King John]

The king, I fear, is poison'd by a monk.
King John. Act v, sc. 6, l. 23. [Hubert]

The king
Yet speaks and peradventure may recover.
King John. Act v, sc. 6, l. 30. [Hubert]

5
Call not your stocks for me: I serve the king.
King Lear. Act ii, sc. 2, l. 135. [Kent]

6
King Lear: I am a king,
My masters, know you that.
Gentleman: You are a royal one, and we obey you.
King Lear. Act iv, sc. 6, l. 203.

Ay, every inch a king.
King Lear. Act iv, sc. 6, l. 109. [King Lear]

7
Princess: Was that the king that spurr'd his horse so hard
Against the steep uprising of the hill?
Boyet: I know not; but I think it was not he.
Princess: Whoe'er a' was, a' show'd a mounting mind.
Love's Labour's Lost. Act iv, sc. 1, l. 1. The only use of "uprising."

But will you hear? the king is my love sworn.
Love's Labour's Lost. Act v, sc. 2, l. 282. [Rosaline]

O me, with what strict patience have I sat,
To see a king transformed to a gnat!
Love's Labour's Lost, iv, 3, 165. [Biron]

8 To be king
Stands not within the prospect of belief.
Macbeth. Act i, sc. 3, l. 73. [Macbeth]

He chid the sisters
When first they put the name of king upon me.
Macbeth. Act iii, sc. 1, l. 57. [Macbeth]

9
The king doth keep his revels here to-night:
Take heed the queen come not within his sight.
A Midsummer-Night's Dream. Act ii, sc. 1, l. 18. [Puck]

10
They do abuse the king that flatter him.
Pericles. Act i, sc. 2, l. 38. [Helicanus]

Heaven forbid
That kings should let their ears hear their faults hid!
Pericles. Act i, sc. 2, l. 61. [Pericles]

For though
This king were great, his greatness was no guard
To bar heaven's shaft, but sin had his reward.
Pericles. Act ii, sc. 4, l. 13. [Helicanus]

Kings' misdeeds cannot be hid in clay.
The Rape of Lucrece, l. 609.

11
Think not the king doth banish thee,
But thou the king.
Richard II. Act i, sc. 3, l. 279. [Gaunt]

How art thou a king
But by fair sequence and succession?
Richard II. Act ii, sc. 1, l. 198. [York]

The king is not himself.—*Richard II,* ii, 1, 241.

12
Green: Our nearness to the king in love
Is near the hate of those love not the king. . . .
Bagot: We ever have been near the king.
Richard II. Act ii, sc. 2, l. 127.

I am the king's friend, and will rid his foe.
Richard II. Act v, sc. 4, l. 11. [Exton]

13 We thought ourself thy lawful king:
And if we be, how dare thy joints forget
To pay their awful duty to our presence?
Richard II. Act iii, sc. 3, l. 74. [King]

14
What must the king do now? must he submit?
The king shall do it: must he be deposed?
The king shall be contented: must he lose
The name of king? o' God's name, let it go.
Richard II. Act iii, sc. 3, l. 143. [King]

Servant: What, think you then the king shall be deposed?
Gardener: Depress'd he is already, and deposed
'Tis no doubt he will be.
Richard II. Act iii, sc. 4, l. 68. The only use of "depress'd."

O that I were a mockery king of snow,
Standing before the sun of Bolingbroke,
To melt myself away in water-drops!
Richard II. Act iv, sc. 1, l. 260. [King Richard] "Water-drops" is repeated in *King Lear,* ii, 4, 280, and in *Troilus and Cressida,* iii, 2, 193. The only use of "mockery" as an adjective.

1
Queen: Wilt thou, pupil-like,
Take thy correction mildly, . . .
Which art a lion and a king of beasts?
King Richard: A king of beasts, indeed; if aught but beasts,
I had been still a happy king of men.
Richard II. Act v, sc. 1, l. 31. The only use of "pupil-like," and "king of beasts."

King of cats.—*Romeo and Juliet,* iii, 1, 80.
King of courtesy.—*I Henry IV,* ii, 4, 11.
King of heaven.—*Richard III,* i, 2, 105; *Richard II,* iii, 3, 101.
King of honour.—*I Henry IV,* iv, 1, 10.
King of men.—*Richard II,* v, 1, 36; *Pericles,* ii, 3, 45.
King of shadows.—*A Midsummer-Night's Dream,* iii, 2, 347.
King of smiles.—*I Henry IV,* i, 3, 246.

2
This dead king to the living king I 'll bear:
Take hence the rest, and give them burial here.
Richard II. Act v, sc. 5, l. 118. [Exton]

Late king.—*I Henry VI,* ii, 4, 91; *II Henry IV,* iv, 1, 58.

3
Poor key-cold figure of a holy king!
Richard III. Act i, sc. 2, l. 5. [Lady Anne] The only use of "key-cold" in the plays. It occurs again in *The Rape of Lucrece,* l. 1774: "Key-cold Lucrece."

Dear brother, live, and be a king.
Richard III. Act ii, sc. 1, l. 113. [King Edward]

And who is England's king but great York's heir?
Richard III. Act iv, sc. 4, l. 473. [King Richard]

4
The king's name is a tower of strength.
Richard III. Act v, sc. 3, l. 12. [King Richard] "King's name" is repeated in *III Henry VI,* iii, 1, 99, and also in *Richard II,* iii, 2, 85.

King's coin.—*Henry VIII,* iii, 2, 325.
King's crown.—*Measure for Measure,* ii, 2, 60.
King's English.—*The Merry Wives of Windsor,* i, 4, 6.
King's highway.—*Richard II,* iii, 3, 155.
King's King.—*Richard III,* iv, 4, 346.
King's majesty.—*Henry VIII,* ii, 3, 60.
King's press.—*I Henry IV,* iv, 2, 13.

5
Live, and beget a happy race of kings.
Richard III. Act v, sc. 3, l. 157. [Ghosts]

The king enacts more wonders than a man,
Daring an opposite to every danger.
Richard III. Act v, sc. 4, l. 2. [Catesby]

6
The harlot king
Is quite beyond mine arm, out of the blank
And level of my brain, plot-proof.
The Winter's Tale. Act ii, sc. 3, l. 4. [Leontes] The only use of "plot-proof."

The penitent king, my master, hath sent for me.
Winter's Tale. Act iv, sc. 2, l. 7. [Camillo]

That unhappy king, my master.—*The Winter's Tale,* iv, 4, 523.

Absent king.—*I Henry IV,* iv, 3, 86; v, 1, 49.
Christian king.—*Henry V,* i, 2, 241; ii, Prol., 6.
Contending kings.—*Rape of Lucrece,* l. 939.
Crowned king.—*I Henry IV,* iii, 2, 54. See Crown.
Dread King.—*II Henry VI,* iii, 2, 154.
Easy-melting king.—*III Henry VI,* ii, 1, 171. The only use of "easy-melting."
Enemy king.—*King Lear,* v, 3, 220.
Fairy king.—*A Midsummer-Night's Dream,* iv, 1, 98.
Fearful king.—*III Henry VI,* i, 1, 25.
Fool-hardy king.—*Richard II,* v, 3, 43.
Our hard-ruled king.—*Henry VIII,* iii, 2, 101. The only use of "hard-ruled."
Incensed kings.—*King John,* iii, 1, 238.
Lunatic king.—*King Lear,* iii, 7, 46.
Mad kings.—*King John,* ii, 1, 561.
Mighty king.—*King John,* i, 1, 59; *Pericles,* ii, Gower, 1; v, 1, 92.
Miserable king.—*King Lear,* v, 3, 46.
Native king.—*Richard II,* iii, 2, 25.
Natural king.—*III Henry VI,* i, 1, 82.
New-made king.—*Richard II,* v, 2, 45.
Offended king.—*Cymbeline,* i, 1, 75.
Poor king.—*II Henry VI,* i, 1, 111; *III Henry VI,* v, 6, 63; *King Lear,* iii, 6, 50.
Prisoner kings.—*Henry V,* i, 2, 162.
Proud king.—*I Henry IV,* i, 3, 184.
Reconciled king.—*Winter's Tale,* iv, 2, 26.
Rightful king.—*I Henry VI,* iv, 1, 60; *II Henry VI,* ii, 2, 24; *Richard II,* v, 1, 50.
Silent king.—*Richard II,* iv, 1, 290.
Sovereign king.—*Henry VIII,* i, 1, 202; *Rape of Lucrece,* l. 652. See under Sovereign.
Subtle king.—*I Henry IV,* i, 3, 169.
Superfluous kings.—*Antony and Cleopatra,* iii, 12, 5.
True king.—*III Henry VI,* iii, 3, 114; iv, 3, 50; *Richard II,* iv, 1, 318; v, 1, 6.
Unhappy king.—*I Henry IV,* i, 3, 148.
Unthankful king.—*I Henry IV,* i, 3, 136. The only use of "unthankful."
Wasteful king.—*Richard II,* iii, 4, 55.
Well-wish'd king.—*Measure for Measure,* ii, 4, 27. The only use of "well-wish'd."

II—The Good King

7
So excellent a king; that was, to this,
Hyperion to a satyr.
Hamlet. Act i, sc. 2, l. 139. [Hamlet] Hyperion is mentioned six times in the plays. The only use of "satyr."

He was a goodly king.—*Hamlet,* i, 2, 186.

A king
Upon whose property and most dear life
A damn'd defeat was made.
Hamlet. Act ii, sc. 2, l. 596. [Hamlet]

Never alone
Did the king sigh, but with a general groan.
Hamlet. Act iii, sc. 3, l. 22. [Rosencrantz]

8
The king is full of grace and fair regard.
Henry V. Act i, sc. 1, l. 22. [Canterbury]

The king is a good king: but it must be as it may; he passes some humours and careers.
Henry V. Act ii, sc. 1, l. 131. [Nym] "Good king" is used seven times.

The king 's a bawcock, and a heart of gold,
A lad of life, an imp of fame;
Of parents good, of fist most valiant.
Henry V. Act iv, sc. 1, l. 44. [Pistol] "Bawcock" (*beau coq,* fine fellow) occurs

again in *Henry V,* iii, 2, 26, and also in *Twelfth Night,* iii, 4, 125, and in *The Winter's Tale,* i, 2, 121.

1
Bedford: King Henry the Fifth, too famous to live long!
England ne'er lost a king of so much worth.
Gloucester: England ne'er had a king until his time. . . .
Winchester: He was a king bless'd of the King of kings.
I Henry VI. Act i, sc. 1, l. 6.

Take heed you dally not before your king;
Lest he that is the supreme King of kings
Confound your hidden falsehood.
Richard III. Act ii, sc. 1, l. 12. [King Edward] "King of kings" is used also in *Richard III,* i, 4, 200, and *Antony and Cleopatra,* iii, 6, 13.

2
The presence of a king engenders love
Amongst his subjects and his loyal friends,
As it disanimates his enemies.
I Henry VI. Act iii, sc. 1, l. 181. [Gloucester] The only use of "disanimates."

3
A gracious king that pardons all offences.
Henry VIII. Act ii, sc. 2, l. 68. [Norfolk]

The king is a noble gentleman.
Love's Labour's Lost. Act v, sc. 1, l. 100. [Armado]

4
Malcolm: Comes the king forth, I pray you?
Doctor: Ay, sir; there are a crew of wretched souls
That stay his cure: their malady convinces
The great assay of art; but at his touch—
Such sanctity hath heaven given his hand—
They presently amend.
Macbeth. Act iv, sc. 3, l. 140.

Holy king.—*Richard III,* i, 2, 5; *Macbeth,* iii, 6, 30.
Sainted king.—*Macbeth,* iv, 3, 109.

5
First Fisherman: This is called Pentapolis, and our king the good Simonides.
Pericles: The good King Simonides, do you call him?
First Fisherman: Ay, sir; and he deserves so to be called for his peaceable reign and good government.
Pericles: He is a happy king, since he gains from his subjects the name of good by his government.
Pericles. Act ii, sc. 1, l. 103.

6
Thou seem'st not what thou art, a god, a king;
For kings like gods should govern every thing.
The Rape of Lucrece, l. 601.

Royal kings,
Fear'd by their breed and famous by their birth,
Renowned for their deeds as far from home,
For Christian service and true chivalry.
Richard II. Act ii, sc. 1, l. 51. [Gaunt]

Good king, great king, and yet not greatly good.
Richard II. Act iv, sc. 1, l. 263. [King Richard]

Gentle king.—*III Henry VI,* ii, 2, 161; 172.
Loving king.—*Love's Labour's Lost,* v, 2, 4.
Noble king.—*Richard III,* i, 2, 215.
Sweet king.—*I Henry VI,* iii, 1, 131.
Worthy king.—*II Henry IV,* ii, 4, 38.

7
The king
Is wise and virtuous, and his noble queen
Well struck in years, fair, and not jealous.
Richard III. Act i, sc. 1, l. 90. [Gloucester]

III—The Bad King

8
A vice of kings;
A cutpurse of the empire and the rule,
That from a shelf the precious diadem stole,
And put it in his pocket!
Hamlet. Act iii, sc. 4, l. 98. [Hamlet] The only use of "shelf."

A king of shreds and patches.
Hamlet. Act iii, sc. 4, l. 102. [Hamlet] The only use of the phrase.

Let the bloat king tempt you again to bed;
Pinch wanton on your cheek; call you his mouse;
And let him, for a pair of reechy kisses,
Or paddling in your neck with his damn'd fingers,
Make you to ravel all this matter out.
Hamlet. Act iii, sc. 4, l. 182. [Hamlet] The only use of "bloat." "Reechy" is repeated in *Much Ado about Nothing,* iii, 3, 143, and in *Coriolanus,* ii, 1, 225; and "ravel" in *The Two Gentlemen of Verona,* iii, 2, 52, and in *Richard II,* iv, 1, 228.

Hamlet: The king is a thing—
Guildenstern: A thing, my lord!
Hamlet: Of nothing.
Hamlet. Act iv, sc. 2, l. 30.

Horatio: Why, what a king is this! . . .
Hamlet: He that hath kill'd my king and whored my mother.
Hamlet. Act v, sc. 2, l. 62. The only use of "whored."

9
The skipping king, he ambled up and down
With shallow jesters and rash bavin wits,
Soon kindled and soon burnt; carded his state,
Mingled his royalty with capering fools,
Had his great name profaned with their scorns
And gave his countenance, against his name,
To laugh at gibing boys and stand the push
Of every beardless vain comparative.
I Henry IV. Act iii, sc. 2, l. 60. [King Henry] The only use of "ambled," "bavin," and "carded." "Gibing" occurs again in *Love's Labour's Lost,* v, 2, 868: "Gibing spirit"; and "beardless" in *King John,* v, 1, 69: "Beardless boy." "Skipping" occurs five times.

10
A worthless king,
Having neither subject, wealth, nor diadem.
II Henry VI. Act iv, sc. 1, l. 81. [Captain]

King did I call thee? no, thou art not king,
Not fit to govern and rule multitudes,

Which darest not, no, nor canst not rule a traitor.
That head of thine doth not become a crown;
Thy hand is made to grasp a palmer's staff,
And not to grace an awful princely sceptre.
That gold must round engirt these brows of mine,
Whose smile and frown, like to Achilles' spear,
Is able with the change to kill and cure.
Here is a hand to hold a sceptre up
And with the same to act controlling laws.
II Henry VI. Act v, sc. 1, l. 93. [York]

1
Farewell, faint-hearted and degenerate king,
In whose cold blood no spark of honour bides.
III Henry VI. Act i, sc. 1, l. 183. [Westmoreland] "Faint-hearted" is repeated in *I Henry VI*, i, 3, 22, and in *Titus Andronicus*, iii, 1, 65.

His noble kinsman: most degenerate king!
Richard II. Act ii, sc. 1, l. 262. [Northumberland]

Bloody king.—*Richard III*, iv, 3, 22.
Perjured kings.—*King John*, iii, 1, 111.
Vile king.—*Hamlet*, iv, 5, 115.

2
Then they for sudden joy did weep,
And I for sorrow sung,
That such a king should play bo-peep,
And go the fools among.
King Lear. Act i, sc. 4, l. 191. [Fool] The only use of "bo-peep" in the plays.

IV—Kings: Their Tribulations

3
Canst thou, O partial sleep, give thy repose
To the wet sea-boy in an hour so rude,
And in the calmest and most stillest night,
With all appliances and means to boot,
Deny it to a king? Then happy low, lie down!
Uneasy lies the head that wears a crown.
II Henry IV. Act iii, sc. 1, l. 26. [King Henry] The only use of "sea-boy" and "calmest."

4
I think the king is but a man, as I am: the violet smells to him as it doth to me; the element shows to him as it doth to me; all his senses have but human conditions: his ceremonies laid by, in his nakedness he appears but a man.
Henry V. Act iv, sc. 1, l. 105. [King Henry]

I live with bread, like you, feel want,
Taste grief, need friends: subjected thus,
How can you say to me, I am a king?
Richard II. Act iii, sc. 2, l. 175. [King Richard]

5
Upon the king! let us our lives, our souls,
Our debts, our careful wives,
Our children and our sins lay on the king!
We must bear all. O hard condition,
Twin-born with greatness, subject to the breath
Of every fool, whose sense no more can feel
But his own wringing! What infinite heart's-ease
Must kings neglect, that private men enjoy!
And what have kings, that privates have not too,
Save ceremony, save general ceremony?
Henry V. Act iv, sc. 1, l. 247. [King Henry]

No, thou proud dream,
That play'st so subtly with a king's repose;
I am a king that find thee, and I know
'Tis not the balm, the sceptre and the ball,
The sword, the mace, the crown imperial,
The intertissued robe of gold and pearl,
The farced title running 'fore the king,
The throne he sits on, nor the tide of pomp
That beats upon the high shore of this world,
No, not all these, thrice-gorgeous ceremony,
Not all these, laid in bed majestical,
Can sleep so soundly as the wretched slave,
Who with a body fill'd and vacant mind
Gets him to rest, cramm'd with distressful bread;
Never sees horrid night, the child of hell,
But, like a lackey, from the rise to set
Sweats in the eye of Phœbus and all night
Sleeps in Elysium; next day after dawn
Doth rise and help Hyperion to his horse,
And follows so the ever-running year,
With profitable labour, to his grave.
Henry V. Act iv, sc. 1, l. 274. [King Henry] The only use of "intertissued," "farced," "thrice-gorgeous," and "ever-running." "Subtly" is repeated in *Romeo and Juliet*, iv, 3, 25, and in *Troilus and Cressida*, iii, 3, 232.

Gross brain little wots
What watch the king keeps to maintain the peace,
Whose hours the peasant best advantages.
Henry V. Act iv, sc. 1, l. 299. [King Henry]

Was ever king that joy'd an earthly throne,
And could command no more content than I? . . .
Was never subject long'd to be a king
As I do long and wish to be a subject.
II Henry VI. Act iv, sc. 9, l. 1. [King Henry]

6
Gives not the hawthorn-bush a sweeter shade
To shepherds looking on their silly sheep,
Than doth a rich embroider'd canopy
To kings that fear their subjects' treachery?
O, yes, it doth; a thousand-fold it doth.
And to conclude, the shepherd's homely curds,
His cold thin drink out of his leather bottle,
His wonted sleep under a fresh tree's shade,
All which secure and sweetly he enjoys,
Is far beyond a prince's delicates,
His viands sparkling in a golden cup,
His body couched in a curious bed,
When care, mistrust, and treason waits on him.
III Henry VI. Act ii, sc. 5, l. 42. [King Henry] The only use of "hawthorn-bush" and "delicates." "Embroider'd" is repeated in *The Passionate Pilgrim*, l. 364.

Sad-hearted men, much overgone with care,
Here sits a king more woful than you are.
III Henry VI. Act ii, sc. 5, l. 123. [King Henry] The only use of "sad-hearted."

1
It is the curse of kings to be attended
By slaves that take their humours for a warrant
To break within the bloody house of life,
And on the winking of authority
To understand a law, to know the meaning
Of dangerous majesty, when perchance it frowns
More upon humour than advised respect.
King John. Act iv, sc. 2, l. 208. [King John]

What surety of the world, what hope, what stay,
When this was now a king, and now is clay?
King John. Act v, sc. 7, l. 68. [Prince Henry]

2
For God's sake, let us sit upon the ground
And tell sad stories of the death of kings:
How some have been deposed; some slain in war;
Some haunted by the ghosts they have deposed;
Some poison'd by their wives; some sleeping kill'd;
All murder'd: for within the hollow crown
That rounds the mortal temples of a king
Keeps Death his court and there the antic sits,
Scoffing his state and grinning at his pomp,
Allowing him a breath, a little scene,
To monarchize, be fear'd and kill with looks,
Infusing him with self and vain conceit,
As if this flesh which walls about our life
Were brass impregnable, and humour'd thus
Comes at the last and with a little pin
Bores through his castle wall, and farewell king!
Richard II. Act iii, sc. 2, l. 155. [King Richard] The only use of "monarchize." "Infusing" is repeated in *Venus and Adonis,* l. 928.

Go to Flint castle: there I 'll pine away;
A king, woe's slave, shall kingly woe obey.
Richard II. Act iii, sc. 2, l. 209. [King Richard]

3
The king is sickly, weak and melancholy,
And his physicians fear him mightily.
Richard III. Act i, sc. 1, l. 136. [Hastings]

Rivers: We follow'd then our lord, our lawful king:
So should we you, if you should be our king.
Gloucester: If I should be! I had rather be a pedlar:
Far be it from my heart, the thought of it!
Queen Elizabeth: As little joy, my lord, as you suppose
You should enjoy, were you this country's king,
As little joy may you suppose in me,
That I enjoy, being the queen thereof.
Richard III. Act i, sc. 3, l. 147.

If not by war, by surfeit die your king,
As ours by murder, to make him a king!
Richard III. Act i, sc. 3, l. 197. [Queen Margaret]

4
Kings are no less unhappy, their issue not being gracious, than they are in losing them when they have approved their virtues.
The Winter's Tale. Act iv, sc. 2, l. 29. [Polixenes]

V—King and Beggar

5
The king 's a beggar, now the play is done.
All's Well that Ends Well. Epilogue, l. 1. [King]

6
Then are our beggars bodies, and our monarchs and outstretched heroes the beggars' shadows.
Hamlet. Act ii, sc. 2, l. 269. [Hamlet]

Your fat king and your lean beggar is but variable service, two dishes, but to one table: that 's the end.
Hamlet. Act iv, sc. 3, l. 24. [Hamlet]

A king may go a progress through the guts of a beggar.
Hamlet. Act iv, sc. 3, l. 32. [Hamlet]

7
Our scene is alter'd from a serious thing,
And now chang'd to 'The Beggar and the King.'
Richard II. Act v, sc. 3, l. 79. [Bolingbroke]

Sometimes am I king;
Then treasons make me wish myself a beggar,
And so I am; then crushing penury
Persuades me I was better when a king;
Then am I king'd again; and by and by
Think that I am unking'd by Bolingbroke,
And straight am nothing.
Richard II. Act v, sc. 5, l. 32. [King Richard] The only use of "crushing." "Unking'd" is repeated in iv, 1, 220, and occurs in no other play.

8
Thus have I had thee, as a dream doth flatter,
In sleep a king, but waking no such matter.
Sonnets. No. lxxxvii.

9
The king lies by a beggar, if a beggar dwell near him.
Twelfth Night. Act iii, sc. 1, l. 8. [Viola]

VI—King and Subject

10
Doth not the king lack subjects?
II Henry IV, i, 2, 86. See under BEGGAR.

11
We know enough if we know we are the king's subjects: if his cause be wrong, our obedience to the king wipes the crime of it out of us.
Henry V. Act iv, sc. 1, l. 137. [Bates]

Every subject's duty is the king's; but every subject's soul is his own.
Henry V. Act iv, sc. 1, l. 186. [King Henry]

12
Was ever king so grieved for subjects' woe?
III Henry VI. Act ii, sc. 5, l. 111. [King Henry]

King Henry: You were sworn true subjects unto me. . . .
Keeper: We were subjects but while you were king.
III Henry VI. Act iii, sc. 1, l. 78.
We are true subjects to the king.
III Henry VI. Act iii, sc. 1, l. 94. [Keeper]
I am a subject fit to jest withal,
But far unfit to be a sovereign.
III Henry VI. Act iii, sc. 2, l. 91. [Lady Grey]

1
Subjects may challenge nothing of their sovereigns.
III Henry VI. Act iv, sc. 6, l. 6. [Lieutenant]
What subject can give sentence on his king?
And who sits here that is not Richard's subject?
Richard II. Act iv, sc. 1, l. 121. [Bishop of Carlisle]

2
Lear: What art thou?
Kent: A very honest-hearted fellow, and as poor as the king.
Lear: If thou be as poor for a subject as he is for a king, thou art poor indeed.
King Lear. Act i, sc. 4, l. 19. The only use of "honest-hearted."
When I do stare, see how the subject quakes.
King Lear. Act iv, sc. 6, l. 110. [King Lear]
Poor grooms are sightless night, kings glorious day.
The Rape of Lucrece, l. 1013.

3 I am greater than a king:
For when I was a king, my flatterers
Were then but subjects; being now a subject,
I have a king here to my flatterer.
Richard II. Act iv, sc. 1, l. 305. [King Richard]

4
For I am all the subjects that you have,
Which first was mine own king.
The Tempest. Act i, sc. 2, l. 341. [Caliban]
How fares the king and 's followers?
The Tempest. Act v, sc. 1, l. 7. [Prospero]

VII—Divine Right

5
There 's such divinity doth hedge a king,
That treason can but peep to what it would.
Hamlet. Act iv, sc. 5, l. 123. [King]

6
I am a king, and privileged to speak.
III Henry VI. Act ii, sc. 2, l. 120. [King Henry]

7 I will keep my state,
Be like a king and show my sail of greatness.
Henry V. Act i, sc. 2, l. 273. [King Henry]
This grace of kings must die,
If hell and treason hold their promises.
Henry V. Act ii, Prologue, l. 28. [Chorus]

8
I was anointed king at nine months old.
III Henry VI. Act iii, sc. 1, l. 76. [King Henry] "Anointed king" is repeated in *Richard II,* ii, 3, 96, and iii, 2, 55, and in *The Winter's Tale,* i, 2, 358.
Let not the heavens hear these tell-tale women
Rail on the Lord's anointed.
Richard III. Act iv, sc. 4, l. 149. [King Richard] "Lord's anointed" occurs once again in *Macbeth,* ii, 3, 73.
The king before the Douglas' rage
Stoop'd his anointed head as low as death.
II Henry IV. Induction, l. 31. [Rumour]
England's true-anointed lawful king.—*III Henry VI,* iii, 3, 29. The only use of "true-anointed."

9
What earthy name to interrogatories
Can task the free breath of a sacred king?
King John. Act iii, sc. 1, l. 147. [King John]
We still retain
The name, and all the additions to a king.
King Lear. Act i, sc. 1, l. 137. [King Lear]

10
Kings are earth's gods; in vice their law 's their will;
And if Jove stray, who dares say Jove doth ill?
Pericles. Act i, sc. 1, l. 103. [Pericles]
If a king bid a man be a villain, he 's bound by the indenture of his oath to be one.
Pericles. Act ii, sc. 3, l. 8. [Thaliard]

11
Not all the water in the rough rude sea
Can wash the balm off from an anointed king;
The breath of worldly men cannot depose
The deputy elected by the Lord.
Richard II. Act iii, sc. 2, l. 54. [King Richard]
For I may never lift
An angry arm against His minister
Richard II. Act i, sc. 2, l. 40. [Gaunt]

12
Weigh you the worth and honour of a king
So great as our dread father in a scale
Of common ounces? will you with counters sum
The past proportion of his infinite?
And buckle in a waist most fathomless
With spans and inches so diminutive
As fears and reasons? fie, for godly shame!
Troilus and Cressida. Act ii, sc. 2, l. 26. [Troilus] The only use of "fathomless."

KINGDOM

13
To give a kingdom for a mirth.
Antony and Cleopatra. Act i, sc. 4, l. 18. [Cæsar]
Kiss'd away Kingdoms.—*Antony and Cleopatra,* iii, 10, 8.

14
Our kingdom is stronger than it was.
Cymbeline. Act iii, sc. 1, l. 35. [Cloten]

15 This great work,
Which is almost to pluck a kingdom down
And set another up.
II Henry IV. Act i, sc. 3, l. 48. [Bardolph]
You may perceive the body of our kingdom
How foul it is; what rank diseases grow,
And with what danger, near the heart of it.
II Henry IV. Act iii, sc. 1, l. 38. [King Henry]

O my poor kingdom, sick with civil blows!
II Henry IV. Act iv, sc. 5, l. 134. [King Henry]
Chastised kingdom.—*King John,* v, 2, 84.
Conquer'd kingdoms.—*Antony and Cleopatra,* iii, 6, 36.
Fairy kingdom.—*Midsummer-Night's Dream,* ii, 1, 144.
Large kingdom.—*Richard II,* iii, 3, 153.
Little kingdom.—*King John,* iv, 2, 98; *II Henry IV,* iv, 3, 118; *Julius Cæsar,* ii, 1, 58.
Peopled kingdom.—*Henry V,* i, 2, 189.
Scatter'd kingdom.—*King Lear,* iii, 1, 31.
Unfurnish'd kingdom.—*Henry V,* i, 2, 148.

1
A kingdom for a stage, princes to act,
And monarchs to behold the swelling scene!
Henry V. Prologue, l. 3. [Chorus]

But we our kingdom's safety must so tender,
Whose ruin you have sought, that to her laws
We do deliver you.
Henry V. Act ii, sc. 2, l. 175. [King Henry]

So be there 'twixt your kingdoms such a spousal,
That never may ill office.
Henry V. Act v, sc. 2, l. 390. [Queen Isabel] "Spousal" is repeated in *Titus Andronicus,* i, 1, 337.

2
All the wealthy kingdoms of the west.
II Henry VI. Act i, sc. 1, l. 154. [Cardinal]
Christian kingdoms.—*Henry VIII,* ii, 2, 93.

3
Warwick: 'Twas I that gave the kingdom to thy brother.
King Edward: Why then 'tis time, if but by Warwick's gift.
III Henry VI. Act v, sc. 1, l. 34.

By her I claim the kingdom.
II Henry VI. Act ii, sc. 2, l. 47. [York]

4
To thee and thine hereditary ever
Remain this ample third of our fair kingdom.
King Lear. Act i, sc. 1, l. 81. [King Lear]

The half o' the kingdom thou hast not forgot,
Wherein I thee endow'd.
King Lear. Act ii, sc. 4, l. 183. [King Lear]

5
I see thee compass'd with thy kingdom's pearl,
That speak my salutation in their minds.
Macbeth. Act v, sc. 8, l. 56. [Macduff]

6
This kingdom is without a head.
Pericles. Act ii, sc. 4, l. 35. [Lord]

7
My kingdom stands on brittle glass.
Richard III. Act iv, sc. 2, l. 62. [King Richard]

If I did take the kingdom from your sons,
To make amends, I 'll give it to your daughter.
Richard III. Act iv, sc. 4, l. 294. [King Richard]
Kingdom of perpetual night.—*Richard III,* i, 4, 47.
Kingdom of perpetual rest.—*Richard III,* ii, 2, 46.

8
This will prove a brave kingdom to me.
The Tempest. Act iii, sc. 2, l. 153. [Stephano]

I 'll turn you out of my kingdom.
The Tempest. Act iv, sc. 1, l. 253. [Stephano]

KISS

See also Lip

9
Strangers and foes do sunder, and not kiss.
All's Well that Ends Well. Act ii, sc. 5, l. 91. [Helena]
Kiss like native things.—*All's Well that Ends Well,* i, 1, 238.

10
Last thing he did, dear queen,
He kiss'd,—the last of many doubled kisses,—
This orient pearl.
Antony and Cleopatra. Act i, sc. 5, l. 39. [Alexas]

We have kiss'd away Kingdoms and provinces.
Antony and Cleopatra. Act iii, sc. 10, l. 7. [Scarus]

Give me a kiss; Even this repays me.
Antony and Cleopatra. Act iii, sc. 11, l. 70. [Antony]

11
Bestow'd his lips on that unworthy place,
As it rain'd kisses.
Antony and Cleopatra. Act iii, sc. 13, l. 84. [Cleopatra]

This is a soldier's kiss.
Antony and Cleopatra. Act iv, sc. 4, l. 30. [Antony]

That kiss Which is my heaven to have.
Antony and Cleopatra. Act v, sc. 2, l. 305. [Cleopatra]

12
I here importune death awhile, until
Of many thousand kisses the poor last
I lay upon thy lips.
Antony and Cleopatra. Act iv, sc. 15, l. 19. [Antony]

And welcome, welcome! die where thou hast lived:
Quicken with kissing: had my lips that power,
Thus would I wear them out.
Antony and Cleopatra. Act iv, sc. 15, l. 38. [Cleopatra]

13
I remember the kissing of her batlet and the cow's dugs that her pretty chopt hands had milked.
As You Like It. Act ii, sc. 4, l. 49. [Touchstone] The only use of "batlet" (a small bat for beating clothes), "chopt" (chapped), and "milked."

14
Orlando: I would kiss before I spoke.
Rosalind: Nay, you were better speak first, and when you were gravelled for lack of matter, you might take occasion to kiss.
As You Like It. Act iv, sc. 1, l. 72. The only use of "gravelled" (nonplussed).

For lovers lacking—God warn us!—matter, the cleanliest shift is to kiss.
As You Like It. Act iv, sc. 1, l. 76. [Rosalind] The only use of "cleanliest."

If I were a woman I would kiss as many of you as had beards that pleased me, complexions that liked me and breaths that I defied not.
As You Like It. Epilogue, l. 19. [Rosalind]

1 O, a kiss
Long as my exile, sweet as my revenge!
Now, by the jealous queen of heaven, that kiss
I carried from thee, dear; and my true lip
Hath virgin'd it e'er since.

Coriolanus. Act v, sc. 3, l. 44. [Coriolanus] The only use of "virgin'd."

2
Give him that parting kiss which I had set
Betwixt two charming words.

Cymbeline. Act i, sc. 3, l. 34. [Imogen]

But kiss; one kiss! Rubies unparagon'd,
How dearly they do 't!

Cymbeline. Act ii, sc. 2, l. 17. [Iachimo] "Unparagoned" occurs again in the same play, i, 4, 87, and in no other.

3
I understand thy kisses and thou mine,
And that 's a feeling disputation.

I Henry IV. Act iii, sc. 1, l. 205. [Mortimer]

4
Didst thou not kiss me and bid me fetch thee thirty shillings?

II Henry IV. Act ii, sc. 1, l. 110. [Hostess]

Kiss me, Doll.—*II Henry IV,* ii, 4, 285.

5
Falstaff: Thou dost give me flattering busses.
Doll Tearsheet: By my troth, I kiss thee with a most constant heart.

II Henry IV. Act ii, sc. 4, l. 291.

Buss thee as my wife.—*King John,* iii, 4, 35.
Buss the clouds.—*Troilus and Cressida,* iv, 5, 220. The only uses of "buss" and "busses."

6
O, tell me when my lips do touch his cheeks,
That I may kindly give one fainting kiss.

I Henry VI. Act ii, sc. 5, l. 39. [Mortimer]

Kindly kiss'd my cheek.—*Richard III,* ii, 2, 24.

7
I can express no kinder sign of love
Than this kind kiss.

II Henry VI. Act i, sc. 1, l. 18. [King Henry]

Soft kiss.—*The Winter's Tale,* i, 2, 95.
Dainty kisses.—*Troilus and Cressida,* v, 2, 81.
Lawful kiss.—*The Rape of Lucrece,* l. 387.
Righteous kiss.—*Romeo and Juliet,* v, 3, 114.

8
Fain would I go to chafe his paly lips
With twenty thousand kisses.

II Henry VI. Act iii, sc. 2, l. 141. [King Henry] "Paly" is repeated in *Henry V,* iv, Prol., 8: "Paly flames"; and in *Romeo and Juliet,* iv, 1, 100: "Paly ashes."

Let them kiss one another, for they loved well when they were alive.

II Henry VI. Act iv, sc. 7, l. 137. [Cade]

At every corner have them kiss.

II Henry VI. Act iv, sc. 7, l. 145. [Cade]

9
See, see! they join, embrace, and seem to kiss,
As if they vow'd some league inviolable.

III Henry VI. Act ii, sc. 1, l. 29. [Richard] "Inviolable" is repeated in *King John,* v, 2, 7.

After we had embraced, kissed, protested, and, as it were, spoke the prologue of our comedy.

The Merry Wives of Windsor. Act iii, sc. 5, l. 74. [Falstaff]

With kind embracements, tempting kisses.

The Taming of the Shrew. Induction, sc. 1, l. 118. [Lord]

10
And that I love the tree from whence thou sprang'st,
Witness the loving kiss I give the fruit.
[Aside] To say the truth, so Judas kiss'd his master,
And cried 'all hail!' when as he meant all harm.

III Henry VI. Act v, sc. 7, l. 31. [Gloucester]

Celia: His kisses are Judas's own children . . .
Rosalind: And his kissing is as full of sanctity as the touch of holy bread . . .
Celia: A nun of winter's sisterhood kisses not more religiously.

As You Like It. Act iii, sc. 4, l. 10.

11
He would kiss you twenty with a breath.

Henry VIII. Act i, sc. 4, l. 30. [Sands]

Sweetheart,
I were unmannerly, to take you out,
And not to kiss you.

Henry VIII. Act i, sc. 4, l. 94. [King Henry]

12
They would go and kiss dead Cæsar's wounds.

Julius Cæsar. Act iii, sc. 2, l. 137. [Antony]

13
Upon thy cheek lay I this zealous kiss,
As seal to this indenture of my love.

King John. Act ii, sc. 1, l. 19. [Austria]

Kiss him with a glorious victory.

King John, ii, 1, 394. See under FORTUNE.

14 This kiss, if it durst speak,
Would stretch thy spirits up into the air.

King Lear. Act iv, sc. 2, l. 22. [Goneril]

15
O my dear father! Restoration hang
Thy medicine on my lips; and let this kiss
Repair those violent harms that my two sisters
Have in thy reverence made!

King Lear. Act iv, sc. 7, l. 26. [Cordelia] The only use of "restoration."

Kiss the honour'd gashes whole.

Antony and Cleopatra, iv, 8, 10. See under WOUND.

And thus I search it with a sovereign kiss.

The Two Gentlemen of Verona. Act i, sc. 2, l. 116. [Julia]

16
Kisses the base ground with obedient breast.

Love's Labour 's Lost. Act iv, sc. 3, l. 224. [Biron]

Kiss the ground.—*Macbeth,* v, 8, 28.
Kiss the earth.—*The Winter's Tale,* v, 1, 199.
Kiss'd the Cretan strand.—*The Taming of the Shrew,* i, 1, 175.
Kiss the valleys.—*The Winter's Tale,* v, 1, 206.

17
He would mouth with a beggar, though she smelt brown bread and garlic.

Measure for Measure. Act iii, sc. 2, l. 194. [Lucio]

Marry, garlic, To mend her kissing with!
Winter's Tale. Act iv, sc. 4, l. 162. [Dorcas]

Would you have us kiss tar?
As You Like It. Act iii, sc. 2, l. 64. [Corin]

Reechy kisses.—*Hamlet,* iii, 4, 184.

1
But my kisses bring again, bring again;
Seals of love, but seal'd in vain.
Measure for Measure. Act iv, sc. 1, l. 5. [Song]

2
Turn you where your lady is
And claim her with a loving kiss.
The Merchant of Venice. Act iii, sc. 2, l. 138. [Bassanio, reading]

3
Come, sit thee down upon this flowery bed,
While I thy amiable cheeks do coy,
And stick musk-roses in thy sleek smooth head,
And kiss thy fair large ears, my gentle joy.
A Midsummer-Night's Dream. Act iv, sc. 1, l. 1. [Titania] Musk-roses are mentioned again in ii, 1, 252, and in ii, 2, 3, and in no other play.

Pyramus: O, kiss me through the hole of this vile wall!
Thisbe: I kiss the wall's hole, not your lips at all.
A Midsummer-Night's Dream. Act v, sc. 1, l. 202.

4
I will depart unkissed.
Much Ado about Nothing. Act v, sc. 2, l. 54. [Beatrice] The only use of "unkissed."

I will not kiss thee.—*Timon of Athens,* iv, 3, 64.

5
Very good; well kissed! an excellent courtesy! 'tis so, indeed.
Othello. Act ii, sc. 1, l. 176. [Iago]

I found not Cassio's kisses on her lips.
Othello. Act iii, sc. 3, l. 341. [Othello]

Iago: To kiss in private?
Othello: An unauthorized kiss.
Othello. Act iv, sc. 1, l. 2. The only use of "unauthoriz'd."

6
Kiss me hard,
As if he pluck'd up kisses by the roots
That grew upon my lips.
Othello. Act iii, sc. 3, l. 422. [Iago]

You 'll kiss me hard and speak to me as if
I were a baby still.
The Winter's Tale. Act ii, sc. 1, l. 5. [Mamillius]

7
I kiss'd thee ere I kill'd thee: no way but this;
Killing myself, to die upon a kiss.
Othello. Act v, sc. 2, l. 358. [Othello]

Thus with a kiss I die.
Romeo and Juliet. Act v, sc. 3, l. 120. [Romeo]

8
Ah, that I had my lady at this bay,
To kiss and clip me till I run away!
The Passionate Pilgrim, l. 155.

9
King Richard: One kiss shall stop our mouths, and dumbly part;
Thus give I mine, and thus take I thy heart.
Queen: Give me mine own again; 'twere no good part
To take on me to keep and kill thy heart.
Richard II. Act v, sc. 1, l. 95. "Dumbly" is repeated in *A Midsummer-Night's Dream,* v, 1, 98.

Speak, cousin; or, if you cannot, stop his mouth with a kiss.
Much Ado about Nothing. Act ii, sc. 1, l. 321. [Beatrice]

10
And bid my friend, for joy of this good news,
Give Mistress Shore one gentle kiss the more.
Richard III. Act iii, sc. 1, l. 184. [Gloucester] "Gentle kiss" is repeated in *The Two Gentlemen of Verona,* ii, 7, 29.

Bear her my true love's kiss.
Richard III. Act iv, sc. 4, l. 430. [King Richard]

Give him for my sake but one loving kiss.
Love's Labour 's Lost. Act ii, sc. 1, l. 248. [Boyet]

11
Ladies . . . who straight on kisses dream.
Romeo and Juliet. Act i, sc. 4, l. 74. [Mercutio]

Palm to palm is holy palmers' kiss.
Romeo and Juliet, i, 5, 102. See under HAND.

12
You kiss by the book.
Romeo and Juliet. Act i, sc. 5, l. 113. [Juliet]

Keep this holy kiss.
Romeo and Juliet. Act iv, sc. 1, l. 43. [Paris]

I dreamt my lady came and found me dead, . . .
And breathed such life with kisses in my lips,
That I revived, and was an emperor.
Romeo and Juliet. Act v, sc. 1, l. 6. [Romeo]

13 He took the bride about the neck
And kiss'd her lips with such a clamorous smack
That at the parting all the church did echo.
The Taming of the Shrew. Act iii, sc. 2, l. 179. [Gremio] The only use of "smack" in this sense. It is used nine times in the phrase "smack of" something.

One, Kate, that you must kiss, and be acquainted with.
The Taming of the Shrew. Act iv, sc. 1, l. 155. [Petruchio]

Nay, I will give thee a kiss.
The Taming of the Shrew. Act v, sc. 1, l. 153. [Katharina]

Kiss him for that, good widow.
The Taming of the Shrew. Act v, sc. 2, l. 25. [Petruchio]

14
Petruchio: First kiss me, Kate. . . .
Katherina: What, in the midst of the street?
Petruchio: What, art thou ashamed of me?
Katherina: No, sir, God forbid; but ashamed to kiss.
Taming of the Shrew. Act v, sc. 1, l. 148.

Art thou ashamed to kiss?
Venus and Adonis, l. 121.

1
I will kiss thy foot.
The Tempest. Act ii, sc. 2, l. 153. [Caliban]
Kissing my foot.—*II Henry IV*, iv, 3, 54.
Kissing Cæsar's feet.—*Julius Cæsar*, v, 1, 42.

2
For my tidings gave me twenty kisses.
Titus Andronicus. Act v, sc. 1, l. 120. [Aaron]

That kiss is comfortless
As frozen water to a starved snake.
Titus Andronicus. Act iii, sc. 1, l. 251. [Marcus]

3
So, so; rub on, and kiss the mistress. How now! a kiss in fee-farm! build there, carpenter; the air is sweet.
Troilus and Cressida. Act iii, sc. 2, l. 52. [Pandarus] The only use of "fee-farm."
Kiss my lady.—*II Henry IV*, i, 2, 232.
Kiss fair ladies' brows.—*Romeo and Juliet*, i, 1, 236.
Kiss her face.—*Venus and Adonis*, l. 872.
Kiss the book.—*The Tempest*, ii, 2, 135; 145.
Kiss'd the clouds.—*Pericles*, i, 4, 24.
Kiss the moon.—*Pericles*, iii, 1, 46.
Kiss the rod.—*The Two Gentlemen of Verona*, i, 2, 59; *Richard II*, v, 1, 32.
Kiss his shadow.—*Venus and Adonis*, l. 162.
Kiss the turrets.—*Rape of Lucrece*, l. 1372.
Kiss your princely nephew.—*III Henry VI*, v, 7, 27.
Kissed your keeper's daughter.—*The Merry Wives of Windsor*, i, 1, 116.

4
'Twas not my purpose, thus to beg a kiss:
I am ashamed.
Troilus and Cressida. Act iii, sc. 2, l. 145. [Cressida]

He . . . scants us with a single famish'd kiss,
Distasted with the salt of broken tears.
Troilus and Cressida. Act iv, sc. 4, l. 49. [Troilus] The only use of "distasted."

5
Nestor: Our general doth salute you with a kiss.
Ulysses: Yet is the kindess but particular;
'Twere better she were kiss'd in general.
Nestor: And very courtly counsel: I 'll begin.
So much for Nestor.
Achilles: I 'll take that winter from your lips, fair lady. . . .
Patroclus: The first was Menelaus' kiss; this, mine:
Patroclus kisses you.
Menelaus: O, this is trim!
Patroclus: Paris and I kiss evermore for him.
Menelaus: I 'll have my kiss, sir. Lady, by your leave.
Cressida: In kissing, do you render or receive?
Patroclus: Both take and give.
Cressida: I 'll make my match to live,
The kiss you take is better than you give;
Therefore no kiss.
Troilus and Cressida. Act iv, sc. 5, l. 19.

Ulysses: May I, sweet lady, beg a kiss of you?
Cressida: You may.
Ulysses: I do desire it. . . .
Cressida: I am your debtor, claim it when 'tis due.
Ulysses: Never 's my day, and then a kiss of you.
Troilus and Cressida. Act iv, sc. 5, l. 47.

6
Then come kiss me, sweet and twenty.
Twelfth Night. Act ii, sc. 3, l. 52. [Clown]
Kiss me, be kind.—*Sonnets*, cxliii.

7
I 'll kiss each several paper for amends.
The Two Gentlemen of Verona. Act i, sc. 2, l. 108. [Julia]

Now kiss, embrace, contend, do what you will.
The Two Gentlemen of Verona. Act i, sc. 2, l. 129. [Julia]

Now should I kiss my father.
The Two Gentlemen of Verona. Act ii, sc. 3, l. 28. [Launce]

8
Seal the bargain with a holy kiss.
The Two Gentlemen of Verona. Act ii, sc. 2, l. 7. [Julia]

Seal the title with a lovely kiss.
The Taming of the Shrew. Act iii, sc. 2, l. 125. [Petruchio]

9
Here come and sit, where never serpent hisses,
And being set, I 'll smother thee with kisses.
Venus and Adonis, l. 17.

Ten kisses short as one, one long as twenty.
Venus and Adonis, l. 22.

He saith she is immodest, blames her 'miss;
What follows more she murders with a kiss.
Venus and Adonis, l. 53.

She kissed his brow, his cheek, his chin,
And where she ends she doth anew begin.
Venus and Adonis, l. 59.

One sweet kiss shall pay this countless debt.
Venus and Adonis, l. 84.

10
'O, pity,' 'gan she cry, 'flint-hearted boy!
'Tis but a kiss I beg; why art thou coy?'
Venus and Adonis, l. 95. The only use of "flint-hearted."

Give me one kiss, I 'll give it thee again,
And one for interest, if thou wilt have twain.
Venus and Adonis, l. 209.

Men will kiss even by their own direction.
Venus and Adonis, l. 216. See under MAN.

He kisses her; and she, by her good will,
Will never rise, so he will kiss her still.
Venus and Adonis, l. 479.

A thousand kisses buys my heart from me;
And pay them at thy leisure, one by one.
Venus and Adonis, l. 517.

Say, for non-payment that the debt should double,
Is twenty hundred kisses such a trouble?
Venus and Adonis, l. 521. The only use of "non-payment."

11
'Now let me say "Good night," and so say you;
If you will say so, you shall have a kiss.'
'Good night,' quoth she, and, ere he says 'Adieu,'

The honey fee of parting tender'd is.
Venus and Adonis, l. 535.
The warm effects which she in him finds missing
She seeks to kindle with continual kissing.
Venus and Adonis, l. 605.
And all is but to rob thee of a kiss.
Venus and Adonis, l. 723.
Steal a kiss.—*Venus and Adonis,* l. 726.
The kiss I give you is bestow'd in vain.
Venus and Adonis, l. 771.
With kissing him I should have kill'd him.
Venus and Adonis, l. 1118.

1
Kissing with the inside lip.
Winter's Tale. Act i, sc. 2, l. 286. [Leontes]
Let no man mock me, For I will kiss her.
Winter's Tale. Act v, sc. 3, l. 79. [Leontes]

II—Kissing the Hand

2
I kiss his conquering hand.
Antony and Cleopatra. Act iii, sc. 13, l. 75. [Cleopatra]
Sweet knight, I kiss thy neif.
II Henry IV. Act ii, sc. 4, l. 200. [Pistol] "Neif" (neaf, hand) occurs again in *A Midsummer-Night's Dream,* iv, 1, 20: "Give me your neaf."

3
I kiss your hand and call you my queen.
Henry V. Act v, sc. 2, l. 271. [King Henry]
Humbly to kiss your hand.—*III Henry VI,* iii, 3, 61.
I kiss your highness' hand.—*III Henry VI,* iv, 8, 26.
I 'll kiss thy hand.—*Richard III,* i, 3, 280.
Let him kiss your hand.—*Richard III,* ii, 1, 21. Repeated in various forms many times throughout the plays.

4
O, could this kiss be printed in thy hand,
That thou mightst think upon these by the seal,
Through whom a thousand sighs are breathed for thee!
II Henry VI. Act iii, sc. 2, l. 343. [Queen Margaret] "Printed" is used only once more, in *Much Ado about Nothing,* iv, 1, 124: "Printed in her blood."
O, let me kiss that hand!—*King Lear,* iv, 6, 135.
Kiss the tender inward of thy hand.—*Sonnets,* cxxviii.

5
To see him kiss his hand! and how most sweetly a' will swear!
Love's Labour 's Lost. Act iv, sc. 1, l. 148. [Costard]

6
O, let me kiss
This princess of pure white, this seal of bliss!
A Midsummer-Night's Dream, iii, 2, 143. See under Hand.
Kisses the hands Of your fresh princess.
The Winter's Tale. Act iv, sc. 4, l. 560. [Camillo]

7
Why dost thou . . . kiss thy hand so oft?
Twelfth Night. Act iii, sc. 4, l. 36. [Olivia]
It had been better you had not kissed your three fingers so oft.
Othello. Act ii, sc. 1, l. 174. [Iago]
I kiss these fingers.—*I Henry VI,* v, 3, 48.
I will kiss thy royal finger.—*Love's Labour 's Lost,* v, 2, 891.

8
Give me that hand of yours to kiss.
Winter's Tale. Act v, sc. 3, l. 46. [Perdita]

III—Kissing the Lips

9
King Henry: I 'll kiss your lips, Kate. . . . It is not a fashion for the maids in France to kiss before they are married, would she say?
Alice: Oui, vraiment.
King Henry: O Kate, nice customs curtsy to great kings. Dear Kate, you and I cannot be confined within the weak list of a country's fashion: we are the makers of manners, Kate.
Henry V. Act v, sc. 2, l. 274.
I will kiss thy lips;
Haply some poison yet doth hang on them.
Romeo and Juliet. Act v, sc. 3, l. 164. [Juliet] See under Poison.

10
Give them thy fingers, me thy lips to kiss.
Sonnets. No. cxxviii.
Let me kiss thy lips.—*Titus Andronicus,* iii, 1, 120.
Kiss my parched lips.—*King John,* v, 7, 40.
Kiss the lips.—*King John,* iii, 4, 166.
Kiss these lips.—*Antony and Cleopatra,* iii, 13, 174.
Kiss'd his lips.—*Henry V,* iv, 6, 25.

11
O, take this warm kiss on thy pale cold lips.
Titus Andronicus. Act v, sc. 3, l. 153. [Lucius]
Loving kiss for kiss,
Thy brother Marcus tenders on thy lips:
O, were the sum of these that I should pay
Countless and infinite, yet would I pay them!
Titus Andronicus. Act v, sc. 3, l. 156. [Marcus]

12
Touch but my lips with those fair lips of thine,—
Though mine be not so fair, yet are they red—
The kiss shall be thine own as well as mine.
Venus and Adonis, l. 115.

KNAVE

See also Fool and Knave; Rascal; Rogue

13
Wilt thou ever be a foul-mouthed and calumnious knave?
All's Well that Ends Well. Act i, sc. 3, l. 60. [Countess] "Foul-mouthed" occurs again in *I Henry IV,* iii, 3, 122. "Calumnious" is used twice more in the plays, "calumnious strokes" in *Hamlet,* i, 3, 38, and "calumnious tongues" in *Henry VIII,* v, 1, 112.

You are not worth another word, else I 'ld call you knave.
All's Well that Ends Well. Act ii, sc. 3, l. 280. [Lafeu]

Parolles: Away! thou 'rt a knave.
Clown: You should have said, sir, before a knave thou 'rt a knave; that 's, before me thou 'rt a knave: this had been truth, sir.
All's Well that Ends Well. Act ii, sc. 4, l. 28.

A good knave, i' faith, and well fed.
All's Well that Ends Well. Act ii, sc. 4, l. 39. [Parolles] "Good knave" is repeated in *Twelfth Night,* iv, 2, 22.

I know that knave; hang him!
All's Well that Ends Well. Act iii, sc. 5, l. 17. [Mariana]

A shrewd knave and an unhappy.
All's Well that Ends Well. Act iv, sc. 5, l. 66 [Lafeu]

Here is a purr of fortune's, sir, or of fortune's cat,—but not a musk-cat,—that has fallen into the unclean fishpond of her displeasure, and, as he says, is muddied withal: pray you, sir, use the carp as you may; for he looks like a poor, decayed, ingenious, foolish, rascally knave.
All's Well that Ends Well. Act v, sc. 2, l. 20. [Clown] "Purr" occurs again in *King Lear,* iii, 6, 47. The only use of "musk-cat," and "fishpond." "Carp" is repeated in *Hamlet,* ii, 1, 63, and *King Lear,* i, 4, 222 .

Thou art a knave, and no knave. What an equivocal companion is this!
All's Well that Ends Well. Act v, sc. 3, l. 249. [King] "Equivocal" is used again in *Othello,* i, 3, 217.

1
Wherein have you played the knave?
All's Well that Ends Well, v, 2, 32. See under FORTUNE.

I will speak to him like a saucy lackey and under that habit play the knave with him.
As You Like It. Act iii, sc. 2, l. 313. [Rosalind]

Play the knave.—*The Merchant of Venice,* ii, 3, 12.

2 Stand the buffet
With knaves that smell of sweat.
Antony and Cleopatra. Act i, sc. 4, l. 20. [Cæsar]

3
Touchstone: Stand you both forth now: stroke your chins, and swear by your beards that I am a knave.
Celia: By our beards, if we had them, thou art.
Touchstone: By my knavery, if I had it, then I were.
As You Like It. Act i, sc. 2, l. 75.

4
What should such fellows as I do crawling between earth and heaven? we are arrant knaves, all; believe none of us.
Hamlet. Act iii, sc. 1, l. 130. [Hamlet]

He 's an arrant knave.
Hamlet, i, 5, 124. See under VILLAIN.

That arrant malmsey-nose knave.
II Henry IV. Act ii, sc. 1, l. 43. [Hostess] The only use of "malmsey-nose."

They are arrant knaves, and will backbite.
II Henry IV. Act v, sc. 1, l. 35. [Shallow] The only use of "backbite."

Shallow: That Visor is an arrant knave, on my knowledge.
Davy: I grant your worship that he is a knave, sir; but yet, God forbid, sir, but a knave should have some countenance at his friend's request. An honest man, sir, is able to speak for himself, when a knave is not. . . . The knave is mine honest friend, sir; therefore, I beseech your worship, let him be countenanced.
II Henry IV. Act v, sc. 1, l. 45. "Arrant knave" is repeated in v, 4, 1.

What an arrant, rascally, beggarly, lousy knave it is.
Henry V. Act iv, sc. 8, l. 36. [Fluellen]

A couple of as arrant knaves as any in Messina.
Much Ado about Nothing. Act iii, sc. 5, l. 34. [Verges]

I leave an arrant knave with your worship; which I beseech your worship to correct yourself, for the example of others.
Much Ado about Nothing. Act v, sc. 1, l. 331. [Dogberry]

5 This counsellor
Is now most still, most secret and most grave,
Who was in life a foolish prating knave.
Hamlet. Act iii, sc. 4, l. 213. [Hamlet]

How the knave jowls it to the ground.
Hamlet. Act v, sc. 1, l. 84. [Hamlet] The only use of "jowls."

6
He call'd them untaught knaves.
I Henry IV, i, 3, 43. See BODY, 118:13.

Farewell, you muddy knave.
I Henry IV. Act ii, sc. 1, l. 106. [Gadshill]

Ah! whoreson caterpillars! bacon-fed knaves!
I Henry IV. Act ii, sc. 2, l. 88. [Falstaff] The only use of "bacon-fed."

Hang ye, gorbellied knaves.
I Henry IV. Act ii, sc. 2, l. 93. [Falstaff] The only use of "gorbellied" (fat-bellied).

Three misbegotten knaves in Kendal green.
I Henry IV. Act ii, sc. 4, l. 246. [Falstaff] "Kendal green" is repeated in l. 257. It is a coarse woolen cloth, so called from the town in England where it was first made.

Discarded unjust serving-men, younger sons to younger brothers, revolted tapsters and ostlers trade-fallen, the cankers of a calm world and a long peace, ten times more dishonourable ragged than an old faced ancient.
I Henry IV. Act iv, sc. 2, l. 30. [Falstaff] The only use of "trade-fallen."

7
The rascally, scauld, beggarly, lousy, pragging knave.
Henry V. Act v, sc. 1, l. 5. [Fluellen] The only use of "pragging." "Scauld knave" occurs twice more in the same play, v, 1, 33, and v, 1, 55, and nowhere else.

You scurvy, lousy knave, God pless you!
Henry V. Act v, sc. 1, l. 18. [Fluellen]

That scurvy doting foolish young knave.
Troilus and Cressida. Act v, sc. 4, l. 4. [Thersites]

Scurvy knave.—*Romeo and Juliet,* ii, 4, 161; 171.

Scurvy railing knave.—*Troilus and Cressida,* v, 4, 31. "Scurvy," a favourite adjective with Shakespeare, was used twenty-five times.

The lousy knave.—*The Merry Wives of Windsor,* iii, 3, 256. "Lousy knave" occurs five times in the plays; "lousy footboy" once (*Henry VIII,* v, 3, 139); and "he is lousy" once (*All's Well that Ends Well,* iv, 3, 220).

1

You are a counterfeit cowardly knave.

Henry V. Act v, sc. 1, l. 73. [Gower]

He is a knave besides; a cowardly knave as you would desires to be acquainted withal.

The Merry Wives of Windsor. Act iii, sc. 1, l. 68. [Evans]

Beastly knave.—*King Lear,* ii, 2, 75.

Drunken knaves.—*The Merry Wives of Windsor,* i, 1, 190; *Pericles,* ii, 1, 61.

Fantastical knave.—*As You Like It,* iii, 3, 109.

Foolish knave.—*The Taming of the Shrew,* iv, 1, 130.

Foul knave.—*Antony and Cleopatra,* i, 2, 76.

Naughty knave.—*Julius Cæsar,* i, 1, 16.

Poor knave.—*Julius Cæsar,* iv, 3, 241; *Coriolanus,* ii, 1, 76.

Poor gallant knave.—*All's Well that Ends Well,* iv, 3, 117.

Rascal knaves.—*The Taming of the Shrew,* iv, 1, 134.

Rude knave.—*Hamlet,* v, 1, 109.

Sly and constant knave.—*Cymbeline,* i, 5, 75.

Unjust knave.—*Troilus and Cressida,* v, 1, 96.

Unthrifty knave.—*The Merchant of Venice,* i, 3, 177.

Untoward knave.—*King John,* i, 1, 243.

Wrangling knave.—*All's Well that Ends Well,* ii, 2, 27.

2

A crafty knave does need no broker.

II Henry VI. Act i, sc. 2, l. 100. [Hume]

You shall go near
To call them both a pair of crafty knaves.

II Henry VI. Act i, sc. 2, l. 102. [Hume]

3

The lyingest knave in Christendom.

II Henry VI, ii, 1, 125. [Gloucester]

If she say I am not fourteen pence on the score for sheer ale, score me up for the lyingest knave in Christendom.

The Taming of the Shrew. Induction, sc. 2, l. 24. [Sly] The only uses of "lyingest."

They are lying knaves.

Much Ado about Nothing. Act v, sc. 1, l. 223. [Dogberry]

4

Ye are lazy knaves;
And here ye lie baiting of bombards, when
Ye should do service.

Henry VIII. Act v, sc. 4, l. 84. [Lord Chamberlain] "Lazy knaves" is repeated in l. 74 of the same scene, and occurs nowhere else.

5

Though this knave came something saucily into the world before he was sent for, yet was his mother fair; there was good sport at his making, and the whoreson must be acknowledged.

King Lear. Act i, sc. 1, l. 21. [Gloucester] "Saucily" occurs again in ii, 4, 41, and in no other play. It is used a third time in *The Rape of Lucrece,* l. 1348.

How now, my pretty knave! how dost thou?

King Lear. Act i, sc. 4, l. 107. [King Lear]

Friendly knave.—*King Lear,* i, 4, 103.

Gentle knave.—*Julius Cæsar,* iv, 3, 269.

Sweet knaves.—*Timon of Athens,* i, 1, 258.

6

A knave; a rascal; an eater of broken meats; a base, proud, shallow, beggarly, three-suited, hundred-pound, filthy, worsted-stocking knave; a lily-livered, action-taking knave, a whoreson, glass-gazing, superserviceable, finical rogue; one-trunk-inheriting slave; one that wouldst be a bawd, in way of good service, and art nothing but the composition of a knave, beggar, coward, pandar, and the son and heir of a mongrel bitch: one whom I will beat into clamorous whining, if thou deniest the least syllable of thy addition.

King Lear. Act ii, sc. 2, l. 15. [Kent] This is a masterpiece of unique invective, for "three-suited," "hundred-pound," "worsted-stocking," "action-taking," "glass-gazing," "superserviceable," "finical," and "one-trunk-inheriting," appear nowhere else in the plays. "Lily-livered" appears only once again, in *Macbeth,* v, 3, 15, and "bitch" in *The Merry Wives of Windsor,* iii, 5, 11.

He that beguiled you in a plain accent was a plain knave; which for my part I will not be, though I should win your displeasure to entreat me to 't.

King Lear. Act ii, sc. 2, l. 117. [Kent]

You stubborn ancient knave, you reverend braggart.

King Lear. Act ii, sc. 2, l. 133. [Cornwall]

7

Cornwall: Why dost thou call him knave?
What 's his offence?
Kent: His countenance likes me not.

King Lear. Act ii, sc. 2, l. 95.

Timon: Why dost thou call them knaves? thou know'st them not.
Apemantus: Are they not Athenians?

Timon of Athens. Act i, sc. 1, l. 181.

Yet, on my conscience, there are verier knaves desire to live, for all he is a Roman.

Cymbeline. Act v, sc. 4, l. 208. [Gaoler] "Verier" is used again in *The Winter's Tale,* i, 2, 66: "The verier wag of the two."

8

Thou art the first knave that e'er madest a duke.

Measure for Measure. Act v, sc. 1, l. 361. [Duke]

9

Hang him, poor cuckoldly knave, I know him not: yet I wrong him to call him poor; they say the jealous wittolly knave hath masses of money.

The Merry Wives of Windsor. Act ii, sc. 2, l. 281. [Falstaff] The only use of "wittolly" (cuckoldly).

Cuckoldly knave.—*The Merry Wives of Windsor,* v, 5, 114.

Jealous knave.—*The Merry Wives of Windsor,* iii, 5, 102.

Jealous rascally knave.—*The Merry Wives of Windsor,* ii, 2, 276.

1
Dogberry: You are to bid any man stand, in the prince's name.
Second Watch: How if a' will not stand?
Dogberry: Why, then, take no note of him, but let him go; and presently call the rest of the watch together and thank God you are rid of a knave.
Much Ado about Nothing. Act iii, sc. 3, l. 26.

Masters, it is proved already that you are little better than false knaves: and it will go near to be thought so shortly.
Much Ado about Nothing. Act iv, sc. 2, l. 22. [Dogberry]

Sir, I say to you, it is thought you are false knaves.
Much Ado about Nothing. Act iv, sc. 2, l. 29. [Dogberry] The only uses of "false knaves."

2
You shall mark
Many a duteous and knee-crooking knave,
That, doting on his own obsequious bondage,
Wears out his time, much like his master's ass,
For nought but provender, and when he 's old, cashier'd:
Whip me such honest knaves.
Othello. Act i, sc. 1, l. 44. [Iago] The only use of "knee-crooking."

A knave of common hire, a gondolier.
Othello. Act i, sc. 1, l. 126. [Roderigo] The only use of "gondolier."

A knave very voluble.
Othello. Act ii, sc. 1, l. 242. [Iago] "Voluble" occurs twice more, in *The Comedy of Errors,* ii, 1, 92, and in *Love's Labour 's Lost,* ii, 1, 76.

A slipper and subtle knave, a finder of occasions, that has an eye can stamp and counterfeit advantages, though true advantage never present itself; a devilish knave. Besides, the knave is handsome, young, and hath all those requisites in him that folly and green minds look after: a pestilent complete knave.
Othello. Act ii, sc. 1, l. 247. [Iago] The only use of "slipper" (slippery) as an adjective. "Requisite" occurs only once more, in *The Winter's Tale,* iv, 4, 687. "Finder" is repeated in *Twelfth Night,* iii, 4, 154: "Finder of madmen." "Finder out" is used in *The Winter's Tale,* v, 2, 131: "Finder out of this secret."

A knave teach me my duty!
I 'll beat the knave into a twiggen bottle.
Othello. Act ii, sc. 3, l. 151. [Cassio] The only use of "twiggen." A twiggen bottle is one covered with wicker.

And, for I know thou 'rt full of honesty, . . .
Therefore these stops of thine fright me the more:
For such things in a false disloyal knave
Are tricks of custom, but in a man that 's just
They are close delations, working from the heart
That passion cannot rule.
Othello. Act iii, sc. 3, l. 118. [Othello] The only use of "delations" (accusations).

The Moor 's abused by some most villanous knave,
Some base notorious knave, some scurvy fellow.
O heaven, that such companions thou 'ldst unfold,
And put in every honest hand a whip
To lash the rascals naked through the world
Even from the east to the west!
Othello. Act iv, sc. 2, l. 139. [Emilia]

3
So dissolute a crew.
Richard II. Act v, sc. 3, l. 12. [Bolingbroke]

As dissolute as desperate.—*Richard II,* v, 3, 20.
Dissolute disease.—*The Merry Wives of Windsor,* iii, 3, 204. The only uses of "dissolute." "Dissolutely" also occurs three times.

4
Thou must stand by too, and suffer every knave to use me at his pleasure?
Romeo and Juliet. Act ii, sc. 4, l. 163. [Nurse]

What a pestilent knave is this same!
Romeo and Juliet. Act iv, sc. 5, l. 147. [Musician]

5
She may perhaps call him half a score knaves or so: why, that 's nothing.
The Taming of the Shrew. Act i, sc. 2, l. 111. [Grumio]

Hortensio: Madame, 'tis now in tune.
Lucentio: All but the base.
Hortensio: The base is right; 'tis the base knave that jars.
Taming of the Shrew. Act iii, sc. 1, l. 46.

A whoreson beetle-headed, flap-ear'd knave!
The Taming of the Shrew. Act iv, sc. 1, l. 160. [Petruchio] The only use of "beetle-headed" and "flap-ear'd."

Call forth an officer. Carry this mad knave to the gaol.
The Taming of the Shrew. Act v, sc. 1, l. 95. [Tranio]

Lunatic knave.—*The Merry Wives of Windsor,* iii, 5, 104.

6
Timon: Away! what art thou? . . .
Flavius: An honest poor servant of yours.
Timon: Then I know thee not:
I never had honest men about me, I; all
I kept were knaves, to serve in meat to villains.
Timon of Athens. Act iv, sc. 3, l. 479.

There 's never a one of you but trusts a knave,
That mightily deceives you.
Timon of Athens. Act v, sc. 1, l. 96. [Timon]

7
Sir Andrew: Let our catch be, 'Thou knave.'
Clown: 'Hold thy peace, thou knave,' knight? I shall be constrained in 't to call thee knave, knight.
Sir Andrew: 'Tis not the first time I have constrained one to call me knave.
Twelfth Night. Act ii, sc. 3, l. 66.

The knave counterfeits well; a good knave.
Twelfth Night. Act iv, sc. 2, l. 22. [Sir Toby]

An ass-head and a coxcomb and a thin-faced knave, a gull!
Twelfth Night. Act v, sc. 1, l. 212. [Sir

Toby] The only use of "thin-faced." "Ass-head" is repeated in *A Midsummer-Night's Dream,* iii, 1, 119.

But when I came to man's estate, . . .
'Gainst knaves and thieves men shut their gate.
Twelfth Night. Act v, sc. 1, l. 402. [Clown]

II—Knavery

1
Marshal me to knavery.
Hamlet. Act iii, sc. 4, l. 205. [Hamlet]
O royal knavery!—*Hamlet,* v, 2, 19.
Double knavery.—*Othello,* i, 3, 400.

2
'Tis as arrant a piece of knavery, mark you now, as can be offer 't.
Henry V. Act iv, sc. 7, l. 2. [Fluellen]
Hume's knavery will be the duchess' wreck.
II Henry VI. Act i, sc. 2, l. 105. [Hume]
By holy Mary, Butts, there 's knavery.
Henry VIII. Act v, sc. 2, l. 33. [King Henry]
It is . . . fery honest knaveries.
The Merry Wives of Windsor. Act iv, sc. 5, l. 81. [Evans]
Full . . . of knaveries.—*Henry V,* iv, 7, 52.

3
This is a knavery of them to make me afeard. . . .
I see their knavery.
A Midsummer-Night's Dream. Act iii, sc. 1, l. 115. [Bottom]

4
Knavery cannot, sure, hide himself in such reverence.
Much Ado about Nothing. Act ii, sc. 3, l. 124. [Benedick]
Knavery's plain face is never seen till used.
Othello. Act ii, sc. 1, l. 321. [Iago]

5
[I will in] to sound the depth of this knavery.
The Taming of the Shrew. Act v, sc. 1, l. 141. [Baptista]
Here 's no knavery!—*The Taming of the Shrew,* i, 2, 138.
This is flat knavery.—*The Taming of the Shrew,* v, 1, 37.
I hold it the more knavery.—*The Winter's Tale,* iv, 4, 697.
All this knavery.—*The Taming of the Shrew,* iv, 3, 58.
By my knavery.—*As You Like It,* i, 2, 80.

6
Here is such patchery, such juggling and such knavery!
Troilus and Cressida. Act ii, sc. 3, l. 77. [Thersites]
Know his gross patchery.—*Timon of Athens,* v, 1, 99. The only uses of "patchery."

7
I would we were well rid of this knavery.
Twelfth Night. Act iv, sc. 2, l. 72. [Sir Toby]

KNEE

See also Humility

8
Before the gods my knee shall bow my prayers
To them for you.
Antony and Cleopatra. Act ii, sc. 3, l. 3. [Octavia]

9
Thy knee bussing the stones.
Coriolanus. Act iii, sc. 2, l. 75. [Volumnia] The only use of "bussing."

My arm'd knees,
Who bow'd but in my stirrup, bend like his
That hath received an alms.
Coriolanus. Act iii, sc. 2, l. 118. [Coriolanus]
Down, ladies! let us shame him with our knees.
Coriolanus. Act v, sc. 3, l. 169. [Volumnia]
Here 's my knee.—*Cymbeline,* v, 5, 325.

10
His knees knocking each other.
Hamlet, ii, 1, 81. See under FEAR.

11
Crook the pregnant hinges of the knee.
Hamlet. Act iii, sc. 2, l. 66. [Hamlet] The only use of "crook."

Hinge thy knee,
And let his very breath, whom thou 'lt observe,
Blow off thy cap; praise his most vicious strain,
And call it excellent.
Timon of Athens. Act iv, sc. 3, l. 211. [Apemantus]

12
Bow, stubborn knees; and, heart with strings of steel,
Be soft as sinews of the new-born babe!
Hamlet. Act iii, sc. 3, l. 70. [King]
Then jointly to the ground their knees they bow.
The Rape of Lucrece, l. 1846.
Bow his knee.—*III Henry VI,* ii, 2, 87.
Bow thy knee.—*Richard II,* i, 3, 47.
Bow your knees.—*Cymbeline,* v, 5, 19.
Knees humbly bow'd.—*Romeo and Juliet,* iii, 1, 161.

13
How long is 't ago, Jack, since thou sawest thine own knee?
I Henry IV. Act ii, sc. 4, l. 359. [Prince of Wales]
Sit on my knee, Doll.—*II Henry IV,* ii, 4, 247.
Then I felt to his knees, and they were as cold as any stone.
Henry V. Act ii, sc. 3, l. 26. [Hostess]

14
Canst thou, when thou command'st the beggar's knee,
Command the health of it?
Henry V. Act iv, sc. 1, l. 273. [King Henry]

15
I beseech God on my knees.
II Henry VI, iv, 10, 62. "On my knees," "On his knees," etc., are repeated frequently.

16
Why, Warwick, hath thy knee forgot to bow?
II Henry VI. Act v, sc. 1, l. 161. [King Henry]
For shame! in duty bend thy knee to me.
II Henry VI, v, 1, 173. See under AGE.
O Warwick, I do bend my knee with thine; . . .
And, ere my knee rise from the earth's cold face,
I throw my hands, mine eyes, my heart to thee.
III Henry VI. Act ii, sc. 3, l. 33. [Edward]

Bend thy knee.—*I Henry VI,* v, 1, 61.
I bend my knee.—*Richard II,* v, 3, 97.
Bended knee.—*II Henry VI,* i, 1, 10; *The Two Gentlemen of Verona,* iii, 1, 229.
Fair knighthood's bending knee.—*The Merry Wives of Windsor,* v, 5, 76.

1
My knee, Made hard with kneeling.
King John. Act iii, sc. 1, l. 309. [Constance]
Oftener upon her knees than on her feet.
Macbeth, iv, 3, 110. See under QUEEN.

2
To-morrow you must die; go to your knees and make ready.
Measure for Measure. Act iii, sc. 1, l. 171. [Duke]

3
Lend me your knees, and all my life to come
I 'll lend you all my life to do you service.
Measure for Measure. Act v, sc. 1, l. 436. [Mariana]
O Isabel, will you not lend a knee?
Measure for Measure. Act v, sc. 1, l. 447. [Mariana]
Ye men of Cyprus, let her have your knees.
Othello, ii, 1, 84. See under BLESSING.

4
Down upon her knees she falls.
Much Ado about Nothing. Act ii, sc. 3, l. 152. [Claudio]
Down on your knees.—*As You Like It,* iii, 5, 57.
Fall upon your knees.—*Julius Cæsar,* i, 1, 58.

5
A brace of draymen bid God speed him well
And had the tribute of his supple knee.
Richard II. Act i, sc. 4, l. 32. [King Richard] "Drayman" occurs in *Troilus and Cressida,* i, 2, 270.
Supple knees
Feed arrogance and are the proud man's fees.
Troilus and Cressida. Act iii, sc. 3, l. 48. [Ulysses]
Courtiers' knees.—*Romeo and Juliet,* i, 4, 72.

6
We are amazed; and thus long have we stood
To watch the fearful bending of thy knee.
Richard II. Act iii, sc. 3, l. 72. [King Richard]
Fair cousin, you debase your princely knee
To make the base earth proud with kissing it.
Richard II. Act iii, sc. 3, l. 190. [King Richard]
For ever may my knees grow to the earth.
Richard II, v, 3, 30. See under PARDON.
His weary joints would gladly rise, I know;
Our knees shall kneel till to the ground they grow.
Richard II. Act v, sc. 3, l. 105. [Duchess of York]
O happy vantage of a kneeling knee!
Richard II. Act v, sc. 3, l. 132. [Duchess of York]

7
With his knees he kiss'd the Cretan strand.
The Taming of the Shrew. Act i, sc. 1, l. 175. [Lucentio]

8
He drops down The knee before him.
Timon of Athens. Act i, sc. 1, l. 60. [Poet]
Feeble knee.—*Titus Andronicus,* ii, 3, 288.

9
A thousand knees
Ten thousand years together, naked, fasting,
Upon a barren mountain, and still winter
In storm perpetual, could not move the gods
To look that way thou wert.
The Winter's Tale. Act iii, sc. 2, l. 211. [Paulina]

KNEELING

10
I would you had kneel'd, my lord, to ask me mercy,
And that at my bidding you could so stand up.
All's Well that Ends Well. Act ii, sc. 1, l. 66. [Lafeu]
At thy feet I kneel.—*Titus Andronicus,* i, 1, 161.
Kneel'd at my feet.—*Richard III,* ii, 1, 107.
Kneeling at our feet.—*Henry V,* iii, 6, 140.
Kneel'd down at the board.—*II Henry VI,* iv, 1, 57.

11
I Will kneel to him with thanks.
Antony and Cleopatra. Act v, sc. 2, l. 20. [Cleopatra]
Cæsar: Arise, you shall not kneel:
I pray you, rise; rise, Egypt.
Cleopatra: Sir, the gods
Will have it thus; my master and my lord
I must obey.
Antony and Cleopatra. Act v, sc. 2, l. 112.
I kneel'd before him;
'Twas very faintly he said 'Rise.'
Coriolanus. Act v, sc. 1, l. 65. [Cominius]

12
O, stand up blest!
Whilst, with no softer cushion than the flint,
I kneel before thee.
Coriolanus. Act v, sc. 3, l. 52. [Volumnia]
Kneel not to me.—*Cymbeline,* v, 5, 417.
You must not kneel.—*King Lear,* iv, 7, 59.

13
Somerset: Kneel for grace.
York: Wouldst thou have me kneel? First let me ask of these,
If they can brook I bow a knee to man.
II Henry VI. Act v, sc. 1, l. 108.
Kneel for grace and mercy at my feet.
III Henry VI. Act i, sc. 1, l. 75. [King Henry]
Kneel for grace.—*III Henry VI,* ii, 2, 81; *Titus Andronicus,* i, 1, 480.
Kneel for peace.—*The Taming of the Shrew,* v, 2, 162.
Nay, we must longer kneel.—*Henry VIII,* i, 2, 9.

14
Come, Warwick, take the time; kneel down, kneel down.
III Henry VI. Act v, sc. 1, l. 48. [Gloucester]
Kneel down before you.—*II Henry IV,* Epil., 35.

15
She kneel'd, and saint-like
Cast her fair eyes to heaven and pray'd devoutly.
Then rose again and bow'd her to the people.
Henry VIII. Act iv, sc. 1, l. 83. [Third Gentleman] "Devoutly" is repeated in *A Mid-*

summer-Night's Dream, i, 1, 109, and in *Hamlet,* iii, 1, 64.

1
Doth not Brutus bootless kneel?
Julius Cæsar. Act ii, sc. 1, l. 75. [Cæsar]

2
Kneel down before him, hang upon his gown.
Measure for Measure. Act ii, sc. 2, l. 44. [Lucio]
Now is your time: speak loud and kneel before him.
Measure for Measure. Act v, sc. 1, l. 19. [Friar Peter]

3
Sweet Isabel, do yet but kneel by me;
Hold up your hands, say nothing; I 'll speak all.
Measure for Measure. Act v, sc. 1, l. 442. [Mariana]
Kneel with me and help to bear thy part,
To rouse our Roman gods with invocations.
The Rape of Lucrece, l. 1830.
Kneel we together.—*II Henry VI,* ii, 2, 59.
Look, who kneels here!—*Pericles,* v, 3, 46.

4
You were kneel'd to and importuned otherwise
By all of us.
The Tempest. Act ii, sc. 1, l. 128. [Sebastian]
I will kneel to him.—*The Tempest,* ii, 2, 123.

5 What, wilt thou kneel with me?
Do, then, dear heart.
Titus Andronicus. Act iii, sc. 1, l. 210. [Titus]
My lord, kneel down with me; Lavinia, kneel;
And kneel, sweet boy, the Roman Hector's hope.
Titus Andronicus. Act iv, sc. 1, l. 87. [Marcus]
Kneel in the streets.—*Titus Andronicus,* i, 1, 455. See under QUEEN.
Stoop and kneel.—*Titus Andronicus,* v, 2, 118.

6
Like a lowly lover down she kneels.
Venus and Adonis, l. 350.
We all kneel.—*The Winter's Tale,* ii, 3, 153.
They kneel, they kiss the earth.—*The Winter's Tale,* v, 1, 199.

KNELL

7
Be this sweet Helen's knell, and now forget her.
All's Well that Ends Well. Act v, sc. 3, l. 67. [King]

8
He was brought again to the bar, to hear
His knell rung out, his judgement.
Henry VIII. Act ii, sc. 1, l. 31. [Gentleman]
Cause the musicians play me that sad note
I named my knell, whilst I sit meditating
On that celestial harmony I go to.
Henry VIII. Act iv, sc. 2, l. 78. [Katharine]

9 It is a knell
That summons thee to heaven or to hell.
Macbeth. Act ii, sc. 1, l. 63. [Macbeth]
The dead man's knell
Is there scarce ask'd for who.
Macbeth. Act iv, sc. 3, l. 170. [Ross]
His knell is knoll'd.
Macbeth. Act v, sc. 8, l. 50. [Siward] "Knoll'd" is repeated in *As You Like It,* ii, 7, 114; 121: "Knoll'd to church."
Doleful knell.—*The Rape of Lucrece,* l. 1495; *The Passionate Pilgrim,* l. 272.

10
Let us all ring fancy's knell:
I 'll begin it,—Ding, dong, bell.
The Merchant of Venice. Act iii, sc. 2, l. 70. [Song]
Sea-nymphs hourly ring his knell:
Ding-dong, . . . Ding-dong, bell.
The Tempest. Act i, sc. 2, l. 402. [Ariel] The only use of "sea-nymphs" and of "ding-dong."

KNIFE

See also Dagger, Weapon

11
Edgar: What means that bloody knife?
Gentleman: 'Tis hot, it smokes;
It came even from the heart of—O, she 's dead!
King Lear. Act v, sc. 3, l. 223.
'Twixt my extremes and me this bloody knife
Shall play the umpire, arbitrating that
Which the commission of thy years and art
Could to no issue of true honour bring.
Romeo and Juliet. Act iv, sc. 1, l. 62. [Juliet]
Bloody knife.—*The Rape of Lucrece,* l. 1840; *Macbeth,* iii, 6, 35.
Butcher's knife.—*III Henry VI,* v, 6, 9.

12
A short knife and a thong!
The Merry Wives of Windsor. Act ii, sc. 2, l. 18. [Falstaff]
Little knife.—*Titus Andronicus,* iii, 2, 16.
Crooked knife.—*Sonnets,* c.

13
Even here she sheathed in her harmless breast
A harmful knife, that thence her soul unsheathed.
The Rape of Lucrece, l. 1723. "Unsheathed" is repeated in *II Henry IV,* iv, 4, 86: "Rebel's sword unsheathed."
Sheathe his knife.—*Henry VIII,* i, 2, 210.
Ill-sheathed knife.—*I Henry IV,* i, 1, 17. The only use of "ill-sheathed." See under WAR.

14
I fear'd by Tarquin's falchion to be slain,
Yet for the self-same purpose seek a knife.
The Rape of Lucrece, l. 1046.
Biting falchion.—*King Lear,* v, 3, 276.
Murderous falchion.—*Richard III,* i, 2, 94.
Purple falchion.—*III Henry VI,* i, 4, 12. The only uses of "falchion."

15
Wretched I, . . . against my heart
Will fix a sharp knife to affright mine eye.
The Rape of Lucrece, l. 1136. "Sharp knife" is repeated in l. 1047.
Sharp-ground knife.—*Romeo and Juliet,* iii, 3, 44. The only use of "sharp-ground."

16
And from the purple fountain Brutus drew
The murderous knife, and, as it left the place,

Her blood, in poor revenge, held it in chase.
The Rape of Lucrece, l. 1734.
Cruel knife.—*Sonnets,* lxiii.
Fatal knife.—*The Rape of Lucrece,* l. 1843.

1
Fool, fool! thou whet'st a knife to kill thyself.
Richard III. Act i, sc. 3, l. 244. [Queen Margaret]
No doubt the murderous knife was dull and blunt
Till it was whetted on thy stone-hard heart,
To revel in the entrails of my lambs.
Richard III. Act iv, sc. 4, l. 226. [Queen Elizabeth] The only use of "stone-hard."
Bassanio: Why dost thou whet thy knife so earnestly?
Shylock: To cut the forfeiture from that bankrupt there.
Gratiano: Not on thy sole, but on thy soul, harsh Jew,
Thou makest thy knife keen.
The Merchant of Venice. Act iv, sc. 1, l. 121.
Daggers . . .
Which thou hast whetted on thy stony heart.
II Henry IV. Act iv, sc. 5, l. 107. [King Henry]

2
The hardest knife ill-used doth lose his edge.
Sonnets. No. xcv. The only use of "ill-used." "Hardest" is repeated in *The Merry Wives of Windsor,* i, 3, 51: "Hardest voice."

3
Their knives care not
While you have throats to answer.
Timon of Athens. Act v, sc. 1, l. 180. [Timon]
Out with your knives.—*Timon of Athens,* iv, 1, 9.
Draw his knives.—*Cymbeline,* v, 3, 73.
Hired knife.—*Antony and Cleopatra,* v, 1, 21.
Treason's knife.—*Pericles,* iv, Gower, 14.
Treason's secret knife.—*II Henry VI,* iii, 1, 174.

4
Sirrah, hast thou a knife? come, let me see it.
Here, Marcus, fold it in the oration.
Titus Andronicus. Act iv, sc. 3, l. 115. [Titus]
Where 's thy knife?—*Cymbeline,* iii, 4, 99.

KNIGHTHOOD

See also Champion, Chivalry

5
Arise my knights o' the battle: I create you
Companions to our person and will fit you
With dignities becoming your estates.
Cymbeline. Act v, sc. 5, l. 20. [Cymbeline]
Thy Cæsar knighted me.—*Cymbeline,* iii, 1, 70.

6
The adventurous knight shall use his foil and target.
Hamlet. Act ii, sc. 2, l. 334. [Hamlet]
This all-praised knight.—*I Henry IV,* iii, 2, 140. The only use of "all-praised."
Dear knight.—*Twelfth Night,* i, 3, 95; ii, 3, 156.
Gallant knight.—*I Henry IV,* v, 3, 20; *The Passionate Pilgrim,* l. 216.
Good knight.—*II Henry IV,* iii, 2, 70; v, 5, 9.
Good old knight.—*Henry V,* iv, 1, 303.
Lovely knights.—*Sonnets,* cvi.
Sweet knight.—*II Henry IV,* ii, 4, 200; v, 3, 91.
Trusty knight.—*The Passionate Pilgrim,* l. 221.
Worthy knight.—*Love's Labour 's Lost,* v, 2, 890.

7
Two and twenty knights,
Balk'd in their own blood did Sir Walter see
On Holmedon's plains.
I Henry IV. Act i, sc. 1, l. 68. [King Henry] "Balked" is repeated in *Twelfth Night,* iii, 2, 26. Holmedon is mentioned five times in this play, and in no other.

8
Sir John Colevile of the dale, a most furious knight and valorous enemy.
II Henry IV. Act iv, sc. 3, l. 42. [Falstaff]

9
I would not take a knighthood for my fortune.
II Henry IV, v, 3, 133. See under FORTUNE.
Gently laid my knighthood on my shoulder.
Richard II, i, 1, 79. See under SWORD.
Bound in knighthood.—*The Rape of Lucrece,* l. 1697.
By knighthood.—*The Rape of Lucrece,* l. 569.
On thy knighthood.—*Richard II,* i, 3, 14.
You promised knighthood.—*III Henry VI,* ii, 2, 59. See below.
Setting thy knighthood aside.—*I Henry IV,* iii, 3, 137. Also *II Henry IV,* i, 2, 93.
Ornament of knighthood.—*I Henry VI,* iv, 1, 29.
Rites of knighthood.—*Richard II,* i, 1, 75.
Rule of knighthood.—*King Lear,* v, 3, 145.
Shame to knighthood.—*The Rape of Lucrece,* l. 197.
Fair knighthood.—*The Merry Wives of Windsor,* v, 5, 76. The only uses of "knighthood."
Knighthoods and honours.—*Cymbeline,* v, 2, 6. The only use of "knighthoods."

10
Come, come, you she knight-errant, come.
II Henry IV. Act v, sc. 4, l. 25. [Beadle] The only use of "knight-errant."

11
The fat knight with the great-belly doublet.
Henry V. Act iv, sc. 7, l. 50. [Fluellen] The only use of "great-belly" as a hyphenated adjective. "Great-bellied" occurs twice.
The poor unvirtuous fat knight.
The Merry Wives of Windsor, iv, 3, 232. The only use of "unvirtuous."
Fat knight.—*The Merry Wives of Windsor,* iv, 2, 29; 37.
Greasy knight.—*The Merry Wives of Windsor,* ii, 1, 112.
Merry knight.—*The Merry Wives of Windsor,* ii, 1, 228.
Unclean knight.—*The Merry Wives of Windsor,* iv, 4, 57.
Bully knight! Bully Sir John!—*The Merry Wives of Windsor,* iv, 5, 16.

12
Great is the rumour of this dreadful knight,
And his achievements of no less account.
I Henry VI. Act ii, sc. 3, l. 7. [Countess] The Countess is referring to Talbot.

13
I vow'd, base knight, when I did meet thee next,
To tear the garter from thy craven's leg.
I Henry VI. Act iv, sc. 1, l. 14. [Talbot]

O shame to knighthood and to shining arms!
The Rape of Lucrece, l. 197.

Cowardly knight.—*I Henry VI,* iii, 2, 109.

Dissembling knight!—*The Merry Wives of Windsor,* iii, 3, 152.

Paltry knight.—*The Merry Wives of Windsor,* ii, 1, 164.

1
Knights of the garter were of noble birth,
Valiant and virtuous, full of haughty courage,
Such as were grown to credit by the wars;
Not fearing death, nor shrinking for distress,
But always resolute in most extremes.
He then that is not furnish'd in this sort
Doth but usurp the sacred name of knight.
I Henry VI. Act iv, sc. 1, l. 34. [Talbot]

Knight of the noble order of Saint George,
Worthy Saint Michael and the Golden Fleece.
I Henry VI. Act iv, sc. 7, l. 68. [Sir William Lucy]

2
Doubtless he would have made a noble knight;
See, where he lies inhearsed in the arms
Of the most bloody nurser of his harms!
I Henry VI. Act iv, sc. 7, l. 44. [Burgundy] The only use of "inhearsed" and "nurser."

What though I be enthrall'd? he seems a knight,
And will not any way dishonour me.
I Henry VI. Act v, sc. 3, l. 101. [Margaret]

3 Lord marquess, kneel down:
We here create thee the first duke of Suffolk,
And gird thee with the sword.
II Henry VI. Act i, sc. 1, l. 63. [King Henry]

Iden, kneel down. Rise up a knight.
II Henry VI. Act v, sc. 1, l. 78. [King Henry]

Queen Margaret: Edward, kneel down.
King Henry: Edward Plantagenet, arise a knight;
And learn this lesson, draw thy sword in right.
III Henry VI. Act ii, sc. 2, l. 60.

Kneel thou down Philip, but rise more great,
Arise sir Richard and Plantagenet.
King John. Act i, sc. 1, l. 161. [King John]

Knight is your degree.—*II Henry IV,* iv, 3, 6.

He is but a knight, is a'? . . . To equal him, I will make myself a knight presently.
II Henry VI. Act iv, sc. 2, l. 125. [Cade]

4
You promised knighthood to our forward son:
Unsheathe your sword, and dub him presently.
III Henry VI. Act ii, sc. 2, l. 59. [Queen Margaret]

Do me right, And dub me knight: Samingo.
II Henry IV. Act v, sc. 3, l. 77. [Silence] The only use of "Samingo," a drunken abbreviation of San Domingo, a frequent refrain of drinking-songs.

Knight, knight, good mother, Basilico-like.
What! I am dubb'd! I have it on my shoulder.
King John. Act i, sc. 1, l. 244. [Bastard] The only use of "Basilico-like," a reference to Kyd's *Soliman and Perseda,* i, 3, 169: "I, the aforesaid Basilico—Knight, good fellow, Knight, Knight."

Dubb'd knights.—*Henry V,* iv, 8, 91.

5
A soldier, by the honour-giving hand
Of Cœur-de-lion knighted in the field.
King John. Act i, sc. 1, l. 53. [Bastard] The only use of "honour-giving." Cœur-de-lion is mentioned six times.

Knighted in field.—*Titus Andronicus,* i, 1, 196.

6
Go, Faulconbridge: now hast thou thy desire;
A landless knight makes thee a landed squire.
King John. Act i, sc. 1, l. 176. [King John] The only use of "landless."

7
His knights grow riotous.
King Lear. Act i, sc. 3, l. 6. [Goneril]

Riotous knights.—*King Lear,* ii, 1, 96.

8
Thine own true knight,
By day or night,
Or any kind of light,
With all his might
For thee to fight.
The Merry Wives of Windsor. Act ii, sc. 1, l. 15. [Mrs. Page]

True knight.—*Romeo and Juliet,* iii, 2, 142; *Richard II,* i, 3, 34; *II Henry IV,* i, 2, 50; *Twelfth Night,* ii, 3, 54; *Troilus and Cressida,* iv, 5, 96; *Cymbeline,* v, 5, 186.

9
If I would but go to hell for an eternal moment or so,
I could be knighted.
The Merry Wives of Windsor. Act ii, sc. 1, l. 49. [Mrs. Ford]

Here, read, read; perceive how I might be knighted.
The Merry Wives of Windsor. Act ii, sc. 1, l. 54. [Mrs. Ford]

10
These knights will hack; and so thou shouldst not alter the article of thy gentry.
The Merry Wives of Windsor. Act ii, sc. 1, l. 52. [Mrs. Page]

11
Quince: Flute, you must take Thisby on you.
Flute: What is Thisby? a wandering knight?
A Midsummer-Night's Dream. Act i, sc. 2, l. 46.

12
A whole bookful of these quondam carpet-mongers.
Much Ado about Nothing. Act v, sc. 2, l. 32. [Benedick] The only use of "bookful" and "carpet-mongers."

He is knight, dubbed with unhatched rapier and on carpet consideration.
Twelfth Night. Act iii, sc. 4, l. 257. [Sir Toby] "Unhatched" (immature) is repeated in *Othello,* iii, 4, 141: "Unhatch'd practice."

13
There are princes and knights come from

all parts of the world to just and tourney for her love.

Pericles. Act ii, sc. 1, l. 116. [First Fisherman] "Tourney" is repeated in l. 150, and occurs in no other scene. The only use of "just" in this sense. "Joust" does not appear.

Simonides: Who is the first that doth prefer himself?
Thaisa: A knight of Sparta, my renowned father;
And the device he bears upon his shield
Is a black Ethiope reaching at the sun:
The word, 'Lux tua vita mihi.'
Simonides: He loves you well that holds his life of you.
Who is the second that presents himself?
Thaisa: A prince of Macedon, my royal father;
And the device he bears upon his shield
Is an arm'd knight that 's conquer'd by a lady:
The motto thus, in Spanish, 'Piu por dulzura que por fuerza.'
Simonides: And what 's the third?
Thaisa: The third of Antioch;
And his device a wreath of chivalry;
The word, 'Me pompæ provexit apex.'
Simonides: What is the fourth?
Thaisa: A burning torch that 's turned upside down;
The word, 'Quod me alit, me extinguit.'
Simonides: Which shows that beauty hath his power and will,
Which can as well inflame as it can kill.
Thaisa: The fifth, a hand environed with clouds,
Holding out gold that 's by the touchstone tried;
The motto thus, 'Sic spectanda fides.'
Simonides: And what 's
The sixth and last, the which the knight himself
With such a graceful courtesy deliver'd?
Thaisa: He seems to be a stranger; but his present is
A wither'd branch, that 's only green at top;
The motto, 'In hac spe vivo.'
Simonides: A pretty moral;
From the dejected state wherein he is,
He hopes by you his fortunes yet may flourish.

Pericles. Act ii, sc. 2, l. 17. All the mottoes are unique: "Lux tua vita mihi," Thy light is my life; "Piu por dulzura que por fuerza," More by gentleness than by force: "Me pompæ provexit apex," The crown of honour has led me on; "Quod me alit, me extinguit," That which feeds me, extinguishes me; "Sic spectanda fides," So faith is to be tested; and "In hac spe vivo," In this hope I live. "Device," in the sense of motto, is used once again in *King John,* i, 1, 210.

Knight of Tyre.—*Pericles,* ii, 5, 43.

1
You are right courteous knights.

Pericles. Act ii, sc. 3, l. 27. [Pericles]

A knight well-spoken, neat and fine.

The Two Gentlemen of Verona. Act i, sc. 1, l. 10. [Lucetta] "Well-spoken" is repeated in *Richard III,* i, 1, 29; i, 3, 348.

2
Yon knight doth sit too melancholy,
As if the entertainment in our court
Had not a show might countervail his worth.

Pericles. Act ii, sc. 3, l. 54. [Simonides] "Countervail" is repeated in *Romeo and Juliet,* ii, 6, 4.

Do you know the French knight that cowers i' the hams?

Pericles. Act iv, sc. 2, l. 112. [Boult] The only use of "cowers."

3
Knights, by their oaths, should right poor ladies' charms.

The Rape of Lucrece, l. 1694.

4
Marshal, ask yonder knight in arms,
Both who he is and why he cometh hither.

Richard II. Act i, sc. 3, l. 26. [King Richard]

5
Many a time hath banish'd Norfolk fought
For Jesu Christ in glorious Christian field,
Streaming the ensign of the Christian cross
Against black pagans, Turks, and Saracens;
And toil'd with works of war, retired himself
To Italy; and there at Venice gave
His body to that pleasant country's earth,
And his pure soul unto his captain Christ,
Under whose colours he had fought so long.

Richard II. Act iv, sc. 1, l. 92. [Bishop of Carlisle] The only use of "streaming" and mention of Saracens.

6
Call some knight to arms
That hath a stomach.

Troilus and Cressida. Act ii, sc. 1, l. 136. [Achilles]

Come knights from east to west,
And cull their flower, Ajax shall cope the best.

Troilus and Cressida. Act ii, sc. 3, l. 274. [Ulysses]

Will you the knights
Shall to the edge of all extremity
Pursue each other?

Troilus and Cressida. Act iv, sc. 5, l. 67. [Æneas]

Half heart, half hand, half Hector comes to seek
This blended knight, half Trojan and half Greek.

Troilus and Cressida. Act iv, sc. 5, l. 85. [Æneas] "Blended" is repeated in *Coriolanus,* iii, 1, 103.

Go, gentle knight, Stand by our Ajax.

Troilus and Cressida. Act iv, sc. 5, l. 88. [Agamemnon]

Gentle knight.—*Henry V,* ii, 2, 14.

7
I have chastised the amorous Trojan,
And am her knight by proof.

Troilus and Cressida. Act v, sc. 5, l. 4. [Diomedes]

8
A foolish knight that you brought in one night here to be her wooer.

Twelfth Night. Act i, sc. 3, l. 16. [Maria]

Foolish knight.—*Twelfth Night,* ii, 5, 86.

Poor knight.—*A Midsummer-Night's Dream,* v, 1, 282; *All's Well that Ends Well,* i, 3, 120; *King Lear,* iii, 2, 86.

Stranger knight.—*Pericles,* ii, 3, 67; ii, 5, 16.

Tender-smelling knight.—*Love's Labour 's Lost,* v, 2, 569. The only use of "tender-smelling."

Virgin knight.—*Much Ado about Nothing,* v, 3, 13.
Wounded knight.—*As You Like It,* iii, 2, 254.

KNOCKING

1
Dromio of Ephesus: Master, knock the door hard.
Luce: [Within] Let him knock till it ache.
The Comedy of Errors. Act iii, sc. 1, l. 58.
Knock at my chamber-window.—*All's Well that Ends Well,* iv, 2, 54.

2
To the court I'll knock her back, foot her home again.
Cymbeline. Act iii, sc. 5, l. 148. [Cloten]

3
Knock but at the gate,
And he himself will answer.
II Henry IV. Act i, sc. 1, l. 5. [Porter]
There's knocking at the gate.—*Macbeth,* v, 1, 73.
Knocking at the taverns.—*II Henry IV,* ii, 4, 388.

4
Who knocks so loud at door?
II Henry IV. Act ii, sc. 4, l. 381. [Hostess]
More knocking at the door!
II Henry IV. Act ii, sc. 4, l. 399. [Falstaff]
Look who's at the door there, ho! who knocks?
II Henry IV. Act v, sc. 3, l. 75. [Shallow]
Open locks, Whoever knocks!—*Macbeth,* iv, 1, 47.
Knock and enter.—*Romeo and Juliet,* i, 4, 33.

5
I have an humour to knock you indifferently well.
Henry V. Act ii, sc. 1, l. 58. [Nym] The only use of "indifferently well."
Would he were knock'd i' the head!
Troilus and Cressida. Act iv, sc. 2, l. 35. [Cressida]
I'll knock you o'er the mazzard.
Othello. Act ii, sc. 3, l. 155. [Cassio]
Knocked about the mazzard.—*Hamlet,* v, 1, 97. The only uses of "mazzard" (head).
Knock him about the sconce.—*Hamlet,* v, 1, 110. "Sconce" is used seven times.
Knocking out his brains.—*Othello,* iv, 2, 236; *Troilus and Cressida,* ii, 1, 110.
'Twere good you knocked him.—*The Two Gentlemen of Verona,* ii, 4, 7. See also under FIGHTING.

6
Who's that that knocks so imperiously?
I Henry VI. Act i, sc. 3, l. 5. [Warder] "Imperiously" is repeated in *Venus and Adonis,* l. 265.
What's he that knocks as he would beat down the gate?
The Taming of the Shrew. Act v, sc. 1, l. 17. [Pedant]
Who knocks so hard? whence come you? what's your will?
Romeo and Juliet. Act iii, sc. 3, l. 78. [Friar Laurence]
Who's that knocks?—*Julius Cæsar,* ii, 1, 309.
Who's there that knocks?—*Cymbeline,* ii, 3, 82.

7
My liege, I'll knock once more to summon them.
III Henry VI. Act iv, sc. 7, l. 16. [Hastings]
We'll knock.—*I Henry VI,* iii, 2, 12.
Somebody knocks.—*Julius Cæsar,* ii, 1, 60.
Hark, hark! one knocks.—*Julius Cæsar,* ii, 1, 304.
Hark! More knocking.—*Macbeth,* ii, 2, 57.
Hark! who is't that knocks?—*Othello,* iv, 3, 53.

8
I hear a knocking
At the south entry: retire we to our chamber.
Macbeth. Act ii, sc. 2, l. 65. [Lady Macbeth]
Here's a knocking indeed! If a man were porter of hell-gate, he should have old turning the key. Knock, knock, knock!
Macbeth. Act ii, sc. 3, l. 1. [Porter] The only use of "hell-gate."
Knock, knock! Who's there in the other devil's name?
Macbeth. Act ii, sc. 3, l. 9. [Porter]
Cressida: How earnestly they knock! . . .
Pandarus: Who's there? What's the matter? will you beat down the door?
Troilus and Cressida. Act iv, sc. 2, l. 41. Loud knocking at the door to usher in a crisis in the play was a favourite device with Shakespeare.

9
Knock him down there.
II Henry VI. Act iv, sc. 6, l. 9. [Cade]
Knock down.—*II Henry VI,* iv, 8, 2.
Knock 'em down by the dozens.—*Henry VIII,* v, 4, 32.

10
Petruchio: I trow this is his house.
Here, sirrah Grumio; knock, I say.
Grumio: Knock, sir! Whom should I knock? is there any man has abused your worship?
Petruchio: Villain, I say, knock me here soundly.
Grumio: Knock you here, sir! why, sir, what am I, sir, that I should knock you here, sir?
Petruchio: Villain, I say, knock me at this gate
And rap me well, or I'll knock your knave's pate.
Grumio: My master is grown quarrelsome.
I should knock you first,
And then I know after who comes by the worst.
Petruchio: Will it not be?
Faith, sirrah, an you'll not knock, I'll ring it;
I'll try how you can sol, fa, and sing it.
The Taming of the Shrew. Act i, sc. 2, l. 4.
Petruchio: I bade the rascal knock upon your gate
And could not get him for my heart to do it.
Grumio: Knock at the gate! O Heavens! Spake you not these words plain, 'Sirrah, knock me here, rap me here, knock me well, and knock me soundly'? And come you now with, 'knocking at the gate'?
The Taming of the Shrew. Act i, sc. 2, l. 36.
Knock at your ear.—*The Taming of the Shrew,* iv, 1, 67.
Knock at my door.—*Titus Andronicus,* iv, 3, 119.
Knock at his study.—*Titus Andronicus,* v, 2, 5.

KNOT

1
I would he had continued to his country
As he began, and not unknit himself
The noble knot he made.
Coriolanus. Act iv, sc. 2, l. 30. [Sicinius]
Unknit This churlish knot.—*I Henry IV,* v, 1, 16.
Unknit that sorrow-wreathen knot.—*Titus Andronicus,* iii, 2, 4. The only use of "sorrow-wreathen." "Unknit" is used a fourth time in *The Taming of the Shrew,* v, 2, 136: "Unknit that threatening unkind brow."
Ancient knot.—*Richard III,* iii, 1, 182.
Gordian knot.—*Henry V,* i, 1, 46; *Cymbeline,* ii, 2, 34.
Nuptial knot.—*III Henry VI,* iii, 3, 55.
Sad knot.—*The Tempest,* i, 2, 224.
Self-figured knot.—*Cymbeline,* ii, 3, 124. The only use of "self-figured."
True-love knots.—*The Two Gentlemen of Verona,* ii, 7, 46.
Unslipping knot.—*Antony and Cleopatra,* ii, 2, 129. The only use of "unslipping."
Virgin knot.—*Pericles,* iv, 2, 160.
Knot of amity.—*I Henry VI,* v, 1, 16.
Knot of his scarf.—*All's Well that Ends Well,* iv, 3, 163.
Strong knots of love.—*Macbeth,* iv, 3, 27.
This knot intrinsicate.—*Antony and Cleopatra,* v, 2, 307. The only use of "intrinsicate."
Another knot, five-finger-tied.—*Troilus and Cressida,* 157. The only use of the phrase.

2 By this knot thou shalt so surely tie
Thy now unsured assurance to the crown,
That yon green boy shall have no sun to ripe
The bloom that promiseth a mighty fruit.
King John. Act ii, sc. 1, l. 470. [Queen Elinor] The only use of "unsured."

3
Trust me, a good knot.
The Merry Wives of Windsor. Act iii, sc. 2, l. 52. [Ford]
There's a knot . . . against me.—*The Merry Wives of Windsor,* iv, 2, 123.
A knot you are of damned blood-suckers.
Richard III, iii, 3, 6. See under Blood.
Knot of mouth-friends!—*Timon of Athens,* iii, 6, 99. The only use of "mouth-friends."

4
I'll have this knot knit up to-morrow morning.
Romeo and Juliet. Act iv, sc. 2, l. 24. [Capulet]
He shall not knit a knot.
The Merry Wives of Windsor, iii, 2, 76. See under Fortune.

5 Knots, by the conflux of meeting sap,
Infect the sound pine and divert his grain
Tortive and errant from his course of growth.
Troilus and Cressida. Act i, sc. 3, l. 7. [Agamemnon] The only use of "conflux," "tortive," and "errant."

6
O time! thou must untangle this, not I;
It is too hard a knot for me to untie!
Twelfth Night. Act ii, sc. 2, l. 41. [Viola] The only use of "untangle."

Hard knots.—*Troilus and Cressida,* i, 3, 316.
Knotted . . . locks.—*Hamlet,* i, 5, 18.
Knotted oaks.—*Troilus and Cressida,* i, 3, 50. The only uses of "knotted."
Knotty entrails.—*The Tempest,* i, 2, 295.
Knotty oaks.—*Julius Cæsar,* i, 3, 6.
Knotty-pated.—*I Henry IV,* ii, 4, 251. The only uses of "knotty."

KNOWLEDGE

See also Learning

7
He was skilful enough to have lived still, if knowledge could be set up against mortality.
All's Well that Ends Well. Act i, sc. 1, l. 34. [Lafeu]

8
Countess: Dost thou believe 't?
Helena: Ay, madam, knowingly.
All's Well that Ends Well. Act i, sc. 3, l. 256.
Felt them knowingly.—*Cymbeline,* iii, 3, 46. The only uses of "knowingly."

9
But what at full I know, thou know'st no part,
I knowing all my peril, thou no art.
All's Well that Ends Well. Act ii, sc. 1, l. 135. [King]
It is not so with Him that all things knows
As 'tis with us that square our guess by shows.
All's Well that Ends Well. Act ii, sc. 1, l. 152. [Helena]
He is very great in knowledge and accordingly valiant.
All's Well that Ends Well. Act ii, sc. 5, l. 8. [Bertram]

10
In mine own direct knowledge.
All's Well that Ends Well. Act iii, sc. 6, l. 9. [Lord]
On my knowledge.—*II Henry IV,* v, 1, 46.
To my knowledge.—*Richard III,* i, 3, 309; *Richard II,* ii, 3, 38.
Upon my knowledge.—*All's Well that Ends Well,* iv, 3, 220.
I would I knew.—*All's Well that Ends Well,* iii, 6, 18.
I would I knew his mind.—*The Two Gentlemen of Verona,* i, 2, 33.
I would you knew.—*Love's Labour's Lost,* v, 2, 31.
Knew my business.—*The Taming of the Shrew,* iii, 2, 193.
Knew my heart.—*As You Like It,* iii, 1, 13.
She never knew harm-doing.—*Henry VIII,* ii, 3, 5. The only use of "harm-doing."

11
Faith, I know more than I'll speak.
All's Well that Ends Well. Act v, sc. 3, l. 256. [Parolles]
Things which would derive me ill will to speak of; therefore I will not speak what I know.
All's Well that Ends Well. Act v, sc. 3, l. 266. [Parolles]
I speak not this in estimation,
As what I think might be, but what I know.
I Henry IV. Act i, sc. 3, l. 272. [Worcester]
Here I am to speak what I do know.
Julius Cæsar. Act iii, sc. 2, l. 106. [Antony]

I 'll call upon you ere you go to bed,
And tell you what I know.
Hamlet. Act iii, sc. 3, l. 34. [Polonius]

1 Leave unexecuted
Your own renowned knowledge.
Antony and Cleopatra. Act iii, sc. 7, l. 45. [Enobarbus] The only use of "unexecuted."
Mine own knowledge.—*Antony and Cleopatra,* ii, 2, 91.
Mature in knowledge.—*Antony and Cleopatra,* i, 4, 31.
Of great . . . knowledge.—*Henry V,* iii, 2, 83.

2
How prove you that, in the great heap of your knowledge?
As You Like It. Act i, sc. 2, l. 72. [Celia]
O knowledge ill-inhabited, worse than Jove in a thatched house!
As You Like It. Act iii, sc. 3, l. 10. [Jaques] The only use of "ill-inhabited."
I speak not this that you should bear a good opinion of my knowledge.
As You Like It. Act v, sc. 2, l. 59. [Rosalind]

3
Be it known unto all men by these presents.
As You Like It. Act i, sc. 2, l. 131. [Rosalind, reading]

4
I know what I know.
The Comedy of Errors. Act iii, sc. 1, l. 11. [Dromio of Ephesus] Repeated in *Measure for Measure,* iii, 2, 161.
We know what we know.
Love's Labour's Lost. Act v, sc. 2, l. 490. [Costard]
This you know I know.
A Midsummer-Night's Dream. Act iii, sc. 2, l. 163. [Lysander]

5
You know neither me, yourselves, nor any thing.
Coriolanus. Act ii, sc. 1, l. 75. [Menenius]
Before I know myself, seek not to know me.
Venus and Adonis, l. 525.
Knowing myself.—*Coriolanus,* ii, 3, 155.
Knowledge of themselves.—*King Lear,* iv, 6, 291.

6
Oft-times not knowing why.
Cymbeline. Act i, sc. 6, l. 63. [Imogen]
Knowing nought.—*King Lear,* ii, 2, 86.
Nought knowing.—*The Tempest,* i, 2, 18.
Great knowing.—*Cymbeline,* ii, 3, 102.
Timely knowing.—*Cymbeline,* i, 6, 97.

7
Iachimo: More particulars
Must justify my knowledge.
Posthumus: So they must,
Or do your honour injury.
Cymbeline. Act ii, sc. 4, l. 78.

8
Take you, as 'twere, some distant knowledge of him.
Hamlet. Act ii, sc. 1, l. 13. [Polonius]
Knowledge of myself.—*Twelfth Night,* v, 1, 21.
Knowledge of thyself.—*King John,* v, 2, 35.
Knowledge of the broil.—*Macbeth,* i, 2, 6.
Knowledge of his chin.—*As You Like It,* iii, 2, 222.
Knowledge of my fault.—*As You Like It,* i, 3, 48.
Knowledge of your mistress.—*Cymbeline,* ii, 4, 51.
Knowledge of my parentage.—*The Taming of the Shrew,* ii, 1, 96.

9
To know a man well, were to know himself.
Hamlet. Act v, sc. 2, l. 146. [Hamlet]
Before I knew thee, Hal, I knew nothing.
I Henry IV, i, 2, 104. See HARM, 671:3.
I knew the man.—*Julius Cæsar,* iv, 3, 5.

10
That 's more than we know.
Henry V. Act iv, sc. 1, l. 135. [Williams]

11
Good knowledge and literatured in the wars.
Henry V. Act iv, sc. 8, l. 157. [Fluellen] The only use of "literatured." "Literature" does not occur in the plays.
Let us have knowledge.—*I Henry VI,* ii, 1, 4.
I knew her well.—*II Henry VI,* iv, 2, 45.
I know it well.—*III Henry VI,* ii, 1, 157, and four times in later plays.
I knew not what I did!—*III Henry VI,* ii, 5, 69.

12
Knowledge the wing wherewith we fly to heaven.
II Henry VI, iv, 7, 79. See under IGNORANCE.

13
You know no more than others; but you frame
Things that are known alike; which are not wholesome
To those which would not know them.
Henry VIII. Act i, sc. 2, l. 44. [Queen Katharine]
Has he had knowledge of it?—*Henry VIII,* v, 3, 4.

14
Tut, I am in their bosoms, and I know
Wherefore they do it.
Julius Cæsar. Act v, sc. 1, l. 7. [Antony]

15
We know the worst.
King John. Act iv, sc. 3, l. 27. [Salisbury]
I am bent to know,
By the worst means, the worst.
Macbeth. Act iii, sc. 4, l. 134. [Macbeth]

16 I know you what you are;
And like a sister am most loath to call
Your faults as they are named.
King Lear. Act i, sc. 1, l. 272. [Cordelia]
What a brazen-faced varlet art thou, to deny thou knowest me!
King Lear. Act ii, sc. 2, l. 30. [Kent] The only use of "brazen-faced." "Brazen-face" occurs in *Merry Wives of Windsor,* iv, 2, 141.

17
Be govern'd by your knowledge, and proceed
I' the sway of your own will.
King Lear. Act iv, sc. 7, l. 19. [Cordelia]
Knowledge and assurance.—*King Lear,* iii, 1, 41.

18
Too much to know is to know nought but fame.
Love's Labour's Lost. Act i, sc. 1, l. 92. [Biron]

If knowledge be the mark, to know thee shall suffice.
Love's Labour's Lost. Act iv, sc. 2, l. 115. [Sir Nathaniel] Also in *The Passionate Pilgrim,* l. 63.
That angel knowledge.—*Love's Labour's Lost,* i, 1, 113.

1
They have more in them than mortal knowledge.
Macbeth. Act i, sc. 5, l. 3. [Lady Macbeth, reading]
Be innocent of the knowledge, dearest chuck,
Till thou applaud the deed.
Macbeth. Act iii, sc. 2, l. 45. [Macbeth]
You have known what you should not.
Macbeth. Act v, sc. 1, l. 51. [Doctor]

2
If your knowledge be more it is much darkened in your malice.
Measure for Measure. Act iii, sc. 2, l. 156. [Duke] "Darkened" is repeated in *Coriolanus,* iv, 7, 5.
He knows too much.—*The Merry Wives of Windsor,* iii, 2, 75.
I know you of old.—*Much Ado about Nothing,* i, 1, 145.

3
You know my inwardness and love.
Much Ado about Nothing. Act iv, sc. 1, l. 247. [Benedick] The only use of "inwardness."

What, man! I know them, yea,
And what they weigh, even to the utmost scruple.
Much Ado about Nothing. Act v, sc. 1, l. 92. [Antonio]
Best known to you.—*Othello,* i, 3, 223. The only use of this phrase.

4
I swear 'tis better to be much abused
Than but to know 't a little.
Othello. Act iii, sc. 3, l. 336. [Othello]

There may be in the cup
A spider steep'd, and one may drink, depart,
And yet partake no venom, for his knowledge
Is not infected: but if one present
The abhorr'd ingredient to his eye, make known
How he hath drunk, he cracks his gorge, his sides,
With violent hefts. I have drunk, and seen the spider.
The Winter's Tale. Act ii, sc. 1, l. 39. [Leontes] The only use of "hefts" (retching).

5
Duke of Gloucester: But what 's the matter, Clarence? may I know?
Duke of Clarence: Yea, Richard, when I know; for I protest
As yet I do not.
Richard III. Act i, sc. 1, l. 51.

6
You know not what you do.
Romeo and Juliet. Act i, sc. 1, l. 72. [Benvolio]

7
Thou art as fair in knowledge as in hue.
Sonnets. No. lxxxii.

8
O, that once more you knew but what you are!
The Taming of the Shrew. Induction, sc. 2, l. 80. [Second Servant]

More to know
Did never meddle with my thoughts.
The Tempest. Act i, sc. 1, l. 21. [Miranda]

9
I know not, Marcus; but I know it is.
Titus Andronicus. Act i, sc. 1, l. 394. [Titus]
'Tis sure enough, an you knew how.
Titus Andronicus. Act iv, sc. 1, l. 95. [Titus]

10
Pandarus: You know me, do you not?
Servant: Faith, sir, superficially.
Troilus and Cressida. Act iii, sc. 1, l. 9. "Superficially" is repeated in ii, 2, 165, and occurs in no other play.
He knew his man.—*Troilus and Cressida,* ii, 1, 141.

11
Call my thought a certain knowledge.
Troilus and Cressida. Act iv, sc. 1, l. 41. [Paris]
Certain knowledge.—*King John,* i, 1, 61.

12
Beguile the time and feed your knowledge.
Twelfth Night. Act iii, sc. 3, l. 41. [Antonio]
You shall know more hereafter.
Twelfth Night. Act iii, sc. 4, l. 137. [Malvolio]

13
Camillo: I dare not know, my lord.
Polixenes: How! dare not! do not. Do you know, and dare not?
The Winter's Tale. Act i, sc. 2, l. 376.

What you do know, you must,
And cannot say, you dare not.
The Winter's Tale. Act i, sc. 2, l. 379. [Polixenes]

I cannot speak, nor think,
Nor dare to know that which I know.
The Winter's Tale. Act iv, sc. 4, l. 461. [Shepherd]

14
Let him have knowledge who I am.
Winter's Tale. Act ii, sc. 2, l. 2. [Paulina]
Have knowledge.—*Coriolanus,* v, 1, 61.
Come to knowledge.—*Measure for Measure,* v, 1, 153.
Gain'd knowledge.—*Othello,* i, 3, 390.

15
Alack, for lesser knowledge!
Winter's Tale. Act ii, sc. 1, l. 38. [Leontes]
Better knowledge.—*Measure for Measure,* iii, 2, 159.
Clearer knowledge.—*Winter's Tale,* ii, 1, 97.
Particular knowledge.—*Henry V,* iii, 2, 83.
Seeming knowledge.—*All's Well that Ends Well,* ii, 3, 5.
True knowledge.—*Coriolanus,* ii, 2, 15.
Knowledge from others' eyes.—*II Henry IV,* i, 1, 86.

L

LABOUR

See also Toil, Work

1
All labour
Mars what it does; yea, very force entangles
Itself with strength.
Antony and Cleopatra. Act iv, sc. 14, l. 47. [Antony] The only use of "entangles."

2
Sir, I am a true labourer: I earn that I eat, get that I wear, owe no man hate, envy no man's happiness, glad of other men's good, content with my harm.
As You Like It. Act iii, sc. 2, l. 77. [Corin] "Labourer" occurs only once more in the plays, in *All's Well that Ends Well,* i, 2, 67. "Labouring men" is used in *II Henry VI,* iv, 2, 19.

3
Duke Senior: Go, seek him: tell him I would speak with him.
First Lord: He saves my labour by his own approach.
As You Like It. Act ii, sc. 7, l. 7.
That labour may you save.—*The Comedy of Errors,* iv, 1, 14.
To save labour.—*Coriolanus,* i, 3, 90.
Save thou thy labour.—*Henry V,* iv, 3, 121.
I 'll save you That labour.—*Henry VIII,* ii, 1, 4.
Save that labour.—*Rape of Lucrece,* l. 1290.
Save you your labour.—*Othello,* v, 1, 101.
A labour saved!—*Troilus and Cressida,* iii, 3, 241.

4
This fool's speed
Be cross'd with slowness; labour be his meed!
Cymbeline. Act iii, sc. 5, l. 167. [Pisanio]

5
We thank you for your well-took labour.
Hamlet. Act ii, sc. 2, l. 83. [King]
Well took, i' faith.—*Romeo and Juliet,* ii, 4, 131. The only uses of "well-took."

6
Labour shall refresh itself with hope.
Henry V. Act ii, sc. 2, l. 37. [Lord Scroop]

7
He talks of wood: it is some carpenter.
I Henry VI. Act v, sc. 3, l. 90. [Margaret]
Flavius: What trade art thou?
First Commoner: Why, sir, a carpenter.
Marullus: Where is thy leather apron and thy rule?
Julius Cæsar. Act i, sc. 1, l. 5.
A rare carpenter.—*Much Ado about Nothing,* i, 1, 187.
Build there, carpenter.—*Troilus and Cressida,* iii, 2, 53.
Builds stronger than . . . a carpenter.—*Hamlet,* v, 1, 48; 58. The only uses of "carpenter."

8
Is all our travail turn'd to this effect?
I Henry VI. Act v, sc. 4, l. 102. [York]
Thirty-three years have I but gone in travail.
The Comedy of Errors. Act v, sc. 1, l. 400. [Abbess] The only use of "thirty-three."
I have had my labour for my travail.
Troilus and Cressida. Act i, sc. 1, l. 71. [Pandarus]
He and myself
Have travail'd in the great shower of your gifts,
And sweetly felt it.
Timon of Athens. Act v, sc. 1, l. 72. [Painter] The only use of "travail'd."

9
While these do labour for their own preferment,
Behoves it us to labour for the realm.
II Henry VI. Act i, sc. 1, l. 181. [Salisbury]

10
Labour in thy vocation.
II Henry VI. Act iv, sc. 2, l. 17. [Holland]
Why, Hal, 'tis my vocation, Hal; 'tis no sin for a man to labour in his vocation.
I Henry IV. Act i, sc. 2, l. 116. [Falstaff]
Base vocation.—*I Henry VI,* i, 2, 80. The only uses of "vocation."

11
He was an honest man, and a good bricklayer.
II Henry VI. Act iv, sc. 2, l. 42. [Dick]
Ignorant of his birth and parentage,
Became a bricklayer.
II Henry VI, iv, 2, 153. The only uses of "bricklayer."

12
Your labour is but lost.
III Henry VI. Act iii, sc. 1, l. 32. [King Henry]
You do but lose your labour.
Measure for Measure. Act v, sc. 1, l. 433. [Duke]
Cold, indeed; and labour lost:
Then, farewell, heat, and welcome, frost!
The Merchant of Venice. Act ii, sc. 7, l. 74. [Prince of Morocco]
If I find her honest, I lose not my labour; if she be otherwise, 'tis labour well bestowed.
The Merry Wives of Windsor. Act ii, sc. 1, l. 247. [Ford]
Lose my labour.—*Comedy of Errors,* v, 1, 97.
Thou hast lost thy labour.—*The Winter's Tale,* iv, 4, 786.
Thou losest labour.—*Macbeth,* v, 8, 8.
We have lost our labour.—*All's Well that Ends Well,* iii, 5, 7.

13
We 'll set thee to school to an ant, to teach thee there 's no labouring i' the winter.
King Lear. Act ii, sc. 4, l. 68. [Fool]
Full of labours.—*King Lear,* i, 4, 7.

14
He labour'd in his country's wreck.
Macbeth. Act i, sc. 3, l. 114. [Angus]
Labour'd in their minds.—*A Midsummer-Night's Dream,* v, 1, 73.
Laboured to dissuade him.—*As You Like It,* i, 1, 146.
Labour'd after him.—*Timon of Athens,* i, 1, 86.
Labour'd much.—*Hamlet,* v, 2, 34.

Labouring to save his life.—*Measure for Measure,* v, 1, 396.
Full of labour.—*Twelfth Night,* iii, 1, 73.

1
The labour we delight in physics pain.
Macbeth. Act ii, sc. 3, l. 55. [Macbeth] See also under BUSINESS.
Labour Delight in them sets off.
The Tempest, iii, 1, 1. See under SPORT.
Their very labour Was to them as a painting.
Henry VIII. Act i, sc. 1, l. 25. [Norfolk]
Makes my labours pleasures.—*The Tempest,* iii, 1, 7.
A blessed labour.—*Richard III,* ii, 1, 52.
Guiltless labour.—*Measure for Measure,* iv, 2, 69.
Profitable labour.—*Henry V,* iv, 1, 294. See under KING.

2
A crew of patches, rude mechanicals,
That work for bread upon Athenian stalls.
A Midsummer-Night's Dream. Act iii, sc. 2, l. 9. [Puck]
Being mechanical, you ought not to walk
Upon a labouring day.
Julius Cæsar. Act i, sc. 1, l. 3. [Flavius] See under PROFESSION.
Mechanical . . . rogue.—*The Merry Wives of Windsor,* ii, 2, 290.
Base dunghill villain and mechanical.—*II Henry VI,* i, 3, 196.
Most mechanical.—*II Henry IV,* v, 5, 38. The only uses of "mechanical" and "mechanicals."
Mechanic slaves
With greasy aprons, rules, and hammers.
Antony and Cleopatra, v, 2, 209. [Cleopatra]
The poor mechanic porters.—*Henry V,* i, 2, 200.
Rome's mechanics.—*Coriolanus,* v, 3, 83.
Mechanic compliment.—*Antony and Cleopatra,* iv, 4, 32. The only uses of "mechanic" and "mechanics."

3
Hard-handed men that work in Athens here.
A Midsummer-Night's Dream. Act v, sc. 1, l. 72. [Philostrate] The only use of "hard-handed." "Hard hand" occurs twice, in *II Henry VI,* iv, 2, 22, and in *Julius Cæsar,* iv, 3, 74.
Lean unwash'd artificer.—*King John,* iv, 2, 201. The only use of "artificer."

4
Suit ill spent and labour ill bestowed.
Much Ado about Nothing. Act iii, sc. 2, l. 103. [Don John]
Bootless labour.—*III Henry VI,* i, 4, 20.
Grievous labour.—*The Two Gentlemen of Verona,* i, 1, 33.
Hard labour.—*I Henry IV,* iv, 3, 23.
Incessant . . . labour.—*II Henry IV,* iv, 4, 118.
Lasting labour.—*Romeo and Juliet,* iv, 5, 45.
Monstrous labour.—*Antony and Cleopatra,* ii, 7, 105.
Painful labour.—*The Taming of the Shrew,* v, 2, 149.
Sore labour.—*Macbeth,* ii, 2, 38.
Sweating labour.—*Antony and Cleopatra,* i, 3, 93.
Treacherous labour.—*I Henry IV,* v, 4, 57.
'Tis a double labour.—*I Henry IV,* iii, 3, 202.

5
It is written, that the shoemaker should meddle with his yard, and the tailor with his last, the fisher with his pencil, and the painter with his nets.
Romeo and Juliet. Act i, sc. 2, l. 39. [Servant] The only use of "shoemaker."

6
Leave that labour to great Hercules;
And let it be more than Alcides' twelve.
The Taming of the Shrew. Act i, sc. 2, l. 257. [Gremio] Hercules is mentioned thirty-six times in the plays and Alcides seven times.
Hercules' labours.—*Much Ado about Nothing,* ii, 1, 380. The labours of Hercules are referred to again in *Coriolanus,* iv, 1, 18.

7
I will fetch off my bottle, though I be o'er ears for my labour.
The Tempest. Act iv, sc. 1, l. 213. [Stephano]
Gone between and between, but small thanks for my labour.
Troilus and Cressida. Act i, sc. 1, l. 72. [Pandarus]
You mar our labour.—*The Tempest,* i, 1, 15.

8
Shortly shall all my labours end.
The Tempest. Act iv, sc. 1, l. 265. [Prospero]

9
Why, if it please you, take it for your labour.
The Two Gentlemen of Verona. Act ii, sc. 3, l. 139. [Silvia]
Take it for thy labour.—*I Henry IV,* iv, 2, 7; *Timon of Athens,* i, 1, 213; *Cymbeline,* i, 5, 61.
There 's for thy labour.—*Henry V,* iii, 6, 167.
Nothing for my labour.—*The Two Gentlemen of Verona,* i, 1, 104.
Pay thee for thy labour.—*Timon of Athens,* i, 1, 232.
Pay thy labour richly.—*Antony and Cleopatra,* iv, 14, 37.
Labour's recompense.—*Richard II,* ii, 3, 62.

II—Labour in Childbirth

See also Birth

10 The queen 's in labour,
They say, in great extremity; and fear'd
She 'll with the labour end.
Henry VIII. Act v, sc. 1, l. 18. [Lovell]
My Muse labours, And thus she is deliver'd.
Othello, ii, 1, 128. See under INVENTION.
With labour.—*Antony and Cleopatra,* iii, 7, 81.
On this travail look for greater birth.
Much Ado about Nothing. Act iv, sc. 1, l. 215. [Friar] See also under BIRTH.
Gentle travail.—*Henry VIII,* v, 1, 71.

11
The lady shrieks, and well-a-near
Does fall in travail with her fear.
Pericles. Act iii, Gower, l. 51. The only use of "well-a-near."

12 Lucina, O
Divinest patroness, and midwife gentle, . . .
Make swift the pangs Of my queen's travails!
Pericles. Act iii, sc. 1, l. 10. [Pericles]
Lucina lent me not her aid,
But took me in my throes;

That from me was Posthumus ript,
Came crying 'mongst his foes.
Cymbeline. Act v, sc. 4, l. 43. [Mother]
Till Lucina reign'd.—*Pericles,* i, 1, 8. The only references to Lucina, the Roman goddess who presided over childbirth.

1
Aaron: But say, again, how many saw the child?
Nurse: Cornelia the midwife and myself;
And no one else but the deliver'd empress.
Aaron: The empress, the midwife, and yourself:
Two may keep counsel when the third 's away.
Titus Andronicus. Act iv, sc. 2, l. 140.
Send the midwife presently to me.
The midwife and the nurse well made away,
Then let the ladies tattle what they please.
Titus Andronicus. Act iv, sc. 2, l. 166. [Aaron]
The midwife wonder'd and the women cried.
III Henry VI, v, 6, 74. See under Tooth.
She was a midwife.—*II Henry VI,* iv, 2, 46.
She is the fairies' midwife.—*Romeo and Juliet,* i, 4, 54.
Midwife to my woe.—*Richard II,* ii, 2, 60.
Lady Margery, your midwife there.—*The Winter's Tale,* ii, 3, 160.

LACKEY, see Servant

LAD

See also Boy

2 Two striplings—lads more like to run
The country base than to commit such slaughter.
Cymbeline. Act v, sc. 3, l. 19. [Posthumus] "Base" in this sense is repeated in *The Two Gentlemen of Verona,* i, 2, 97, and in *Venus and Adonis,* l. 303: "Bid a base."
A handsome stripling.—*Richard III,* i, 3, 101.
A proper stripling.—*Taming of the Shrew,* i, 2, 144. The only uses of "stripling" and "striplings."

3
Good lads, how do ye both?
Hamlet. Act ii, sc. 2, l. 229. [Hamlet] "Good lads" is repeated in *I Henry IV,* ii, 4, 15, and in *Cymbeline,* v, 5, 101.
Dear lad.—*Twelfth Night,* i, 4, 20.
Golden lads.—*Cymbeline,* iv, 2, 262.
Honest lads.—*The Merry Wives of Windsor,* i, 3, 42.
Lusty lads.—*II Henry IV,* v, 3, 21.
Sweet rosy lad.—*Cymbeline,* v, 5, 121.
A lad of life.—*Henry V,* iv, 1, 45. See under King.
A lad of mettle.—*I Henry IV,* ii, 4, 13.
Lads of peace.—*The Merry Wives of Windsor,* iii, 1, 113.

4
My old lad of the castle.
I Henry IV. Act i, sc. 2, l. 47. [Prince of Wales] Referring to Falstaff.
Well, go thy ways, old lad.
The Taming of the Shrew. Act v, sc. 2, l. 181. [Lucentio]
There are yet missing of your company
Some few odd lads that you remember not.
The Tempest. Act v, sc. 1, l. 254. [Prospero]
Old lad, I am thine own.
Titus Andronicus. Act iv, sc. 2, l. 121. [Aaron]

5
This pretty lad will prove our country's bliss.
III Henry VI. Act iv, sc. 6, l. 70. [King Henry] See under Prophecy.
Fearful lad.—*III Henry VI,* v, 4, 7.
Knavish lad.—*A Midsummer-Night's Dream,* iii, 2, 440.
Mad lad.—*Twelfth Night,* iv, 2, 139.
Untutor'd lad.—*III Henry VI,* v, 5, 32.

6
Young lad, come forth; I have to say with you.
King John. Act iv, sc. 1, l. 8. [Hubert]
Here 's a young lad framed of another leer.
Titus Andronicus. Act iv, sc. 2, l. 119. [Aaron] The only uses of "young lad."

7
Where are these lads? where are these hearts?
A Midsummer-Night's Dream. Act iv, sc. 2, l. 25. [Bottom]
How now, lad!—*I Henry IV,* iii, 3, 102.
Ha' to thee, lad!—*The Taming of the Shrew,* v, 2, 37.

8
I like you, lads; about your business straight;
Go, go, dispatch.
Richard III. Act i, sc. 3, l. 355. [Gloucester]

9
Two lads that thought there was no more behind
But such a day to-morrow as to-day,
And to be boy eternal.
The Winter's Tale. Act i, sc. 2, l. 63. [Polixenes]

LADDER

10
Northumberland, thou ladder wherewithal
The mounting Bolingbroke ascends my throne.
Richard II. Act v, sc. 1, l. 55. [King Richard] Quoted in *II Henry IV,* iii, 1, 70. "Wherewithal" is repeated in *Henry VIII,* i, 3, 59.

11
Cords made like a tackled stair;
Which to the high top-gallant of my joy
Must be my convoy in the secret night.
Romeo and Juliet. Act ii, sc. 4, l. 201. [Romeo] The only use of "tackled" and "top-gallant."
Hie you to church; I must another way,
To fetch a ladder, by the which your love
Must climb a bird's nest soon when it is dark.
Romeo and Juliet. Act ii, sc. 5, l. 74. [Nurse]
Get me a ladder.—*Titus Andronicus,* v, 1, 53.
Ladders, ho!—*Coriolanus,* i, 4, 22.
Ambition's ladder.—*Julius Cæsar,* ii, 1, 22.
12 I must climb her window,
The ladder made of cords.
The Two Gentlemen of Verona. Act ii, sc. 4, l. 181. [Valentine]

This night he meaneth with a corded ladder
To climb celestial Silvia's chamber window.
The Two Gentlemen of Verona. Act ii, sc. 6, l. 33. [Proteus]

Know, noble lord, they have devised a mean
How he her chamber-window will ascend
And with a corded ladder fetch her down.
The Two Gentlemen of Verona. Act iii, sc. 1, l. 38. [Proteus] The only uses of "corded."

Why then, a ladder quaintly made of cords,
To cast up, with a pair of anchoring hooks,
Would serve to scale another Hero's tower,
So bold Leander would adventure it.
Two Gentlemen of Verona. Act iii, sc. 1, l. 117. [Valentine] "Anchoring" is repeated in *King Lear,* iv, 6, 18: "Anchoring bark."

Here 's the ladder for the purpose.
The Two Gentlemen of Verona. Act iii, sc. 1, l. 152. [Duke]

LADY

See also Gentlewoman; Lord and Lady; Woman

1
Parolles: O, my knave, how does my old lady?
Clown: So that you had her wrinkles and I her money,
I would she did as you say.
All's Well that Ends Well. Act ii, sc. 4, l. 18. "Old lady" is repeated in *I Henry IV,* iii, 3, 4.

Farewell, ancient lady.—*Romeo and Juliet,* ii, 4, 150.

2
Helena: I know his lady.
Diana: There is a gentleman that serves the count
Reports but coarsely of her.
All's Well that Ends Well. Act iii, sc. 5, l. 58. The only use of "coarsely."

Your lady being so easy.—*Cymbeline,* ii, 4, 47.

3
Lafeu: 'Twas a good lady, 'twas a good lady: we may pick a thousand salads ere we light on such another herb.
Clown: Indeed, sir, she was the sweet-marjoram of the salad, or rather, the herb of grace.
All's Well that Ends Well. Act iv, sc. 5, l. 14. "Sweet marjoram" is used again in *King Lear,* iv, 6, 94.

She 's a most triumphant lady, if report be square to her.
Antony and Cleopatra. Act ii, sc. 2, l. 189. [Mecænas]

She 's my good lady, and will conceive, I hope,
But the worst of me.
Cymbeline. Act ii, sc. 3, l. 158. [Imogen]

So good a lady that no tongue could ever
Pronounce dishonour of her.
Henry VIII. Act ii, sc. 3, l. 3. [Anne Bullen]

So good a lady.—*Much Ado about Nothing,* ii, 3, 216.

Good lady.—*Romeo and Juliet,* i, 5, 116, and four times in later plays.

A goodly lady, trust me.—*Titus Andronicus,* i, 1, 261.

Bounteous lady.—*The Tempest,* iv, 1, 60.

Dear lady.—*Love's Labour's Lost,* ii, 1, 95, and nine times in later plays.

Most dear lady.—*Hamlet,* ii, 2, 123.

Lady dear!—*A Midsummer-Night's Dream,* i, 2, 56.

Fortunate lady!—*All's Well that Ends Well,* ii, 4, 14.

4 A more unhappy lady,
If this division chance, ne'er stood between,
Praying for both parts.
Antony and Cleopatra. Act iii, sc. 4, l. 12. [Octavia]

O miserable lady!—*Winter's Tale,* i, 2, 351.

Wretched lady.—*Henry VIII,* iii, 1, 106; 146.

5 O, thy vile lady!
She has robb'd me of my sword.
Antony and Cleopatra. Act iv, sc. 14, l. 22. [Antony]

Disloyal lady.—*The Winter's Tale,* ii, 3, 203.

Naughty lady.—*King Lear,* iii, 7, 37.

Uncivil lady.—*Twelfth Night,* v, 1, 115.

Unmerciful lady.—*King Lear,* iii, 7, 33. The only use of "unmerciful."

6 If ladies be but young and fair,
They have the gift to know it.
As You Like It. Act ii, sc. 7, l. 37. [Jaques]

Young lady.—*Romeo and Juliet,* i, 3, 75; i, 3, 101; ii, 4, 173, and five times in later plays.

My young lady and mistress.—*Hamlet,* ii, 2, 444.

7
She is a virtuous and a reverend lady.
The Comedy of Errors. Act v, sc. 1, l. 134. [Duke]

Virtuous lady.—*I Henry VI,* ii, 2, 38.

Honourable ladies.—*The Merchant of Venice,* iii, 4, 70.

Honour'd lady.—*Cymbeline,* v, 5, 232.

Sacred lady!—*The Winter's Tale,* i, 2, 50.

The rarest of our ladies.—*Cymbeline,* i, 4, 66.

8
My as fair as noble ladies,—and the moon, were she earthly, no nobler.
Coriolanus. Act ii, sc. 1, l. 107. [Menenius]

Noble lady (ladies).—*Taming of the Shrew,* Ind., 1, 111, and six times in later plays.

9 A lady
So fair, and fasten'd to an empery,
Would make the great'st king double.
Cymbeline. Act i, sc. 6, l. 119. [Iachimo]

Your lady
Is one of the fairest that I have look'd upon.
Cymbeline. Act ii, sc. 4, l. 31. [Iachimo]

By this day! she 's a fair lady: I do spy some marks of love in her.
Much Ado about Nothing. Act ii, sc. 3, l. 254. [Benedick]

Fair lady (ladies).—*I Henry VI,* ii, 3, 73, and twenty-three times in later plays.

Thrice-fair lady.—*The Merchant of Venice,* iii, 2, 147. "Thrice-fair" is repeated in *Venus and Adonis,* l. 7.

10 She 's a lady
So tender of rebukes that words are strokes
And strokes death to her.
Cymbeline. Act iii, sc. 5, l. 39. [Queen]

Tender lady.—*The Winter's Tale,* ii, 2, 24.

1
The lady shall say her mind freely or the blank verse shall halt for 't.
Hamlet. Act ii, sc. 2, l. 338. [Hamlet]
Like a lady as thou art.—*I Henry IV*, iii, 1, 258.
A lady like me.—*The Winter's Tale,* iii, 2, 66.

2
I see the lady hath a thing to grant,
Before the king will grant her humble suit.
III Henry VI. Act iii, sc. 2, l. 12. [Gloucester]

3
Lead in your ladies, every one: sweet partner,
I must not yet forsake you.
Henry VIII. Act i, sc. 4, l. 103. [King Henry]
I will go to meet the ladies.—*Coriolanus,* v, 4, 55.
Here comes the lady.—*Romeo and Juliet,* ii, 6, 16; iv, 1, 17; *Othello,* i, 3, 170.

4
Alas, poor lady!
She 's a stranger now again.
Henry VIII. Act ii, sc. 3, l. 16. [Old Lady]
Alas, poor lady, desolate and left!
I weep myself to think upon thy words.
The Two Gentlemen of Verona. Act iv, sc. 4, l. 179. [Silvia] "Poor lady" is repeated five times in later plays.
Poor wronged lady.—*Measure for Measure,* iii, 1, 206.

5
Blush for shame;
For your own ladies and pale-visaged maids
Like Amazons come tripping after drums,
Their thimbles into armed gauntlets change,
Their needles to lances, and their gentle hearts
To fierce and bloody inclination.
King John. Act v, sc. 2, l. 153. [Bastard] The only use of "pale-visaged" and "thimbles." "Thimble" occurs in *The Taming of the Shrew,* iv, 3, 108; 149.

6
Of all these bounds, even from this line to this, . . .
We make thee lady.
King Lear. Act i, sc. 1, l. 64. [King Lear]
Royal lady.—*Henry VIII,* ii, 4, 153.
Sovereign lady.—*II Henry VI,* iii, 1, 161; 178; *Timon of Athens,* i, 1, 68.

7
Lord, Lord, how the ladies and I have put him down!
Love's Labour 's Lost. Act iv, sc. 1, l. 143. [Costard]

8
She is a most sweet lady.
Love's Labour 's Lost. Act ii, sc. 1, l. 207. [Longaville]
Sweet lady (or ladies).—*III Henry VI,* iii, 2, 150, and twenty-seven times in later plays.
So sweet a lady.—*All 's Well that Ends Well,* iv, 3, 9.
In mine eye she is the sweetest lady that ever I looked on.
Much Ado about Nothing. Act i, sc. 1, l. 189. [Claudio]
Sweetest lady.—*Romeo and Juliet,* ii, 4, 212.

9
She 's an excellent sweet lady; and, out of all suspicion, she is virtuous.
Much Ado about Nothing. Act ii, sc. 3, l. 165. [Don Pedro]
Most excellent accomplished lady.
Twelfth Night. Act iii, sc. 1, l. 95. [Viola]
Excellent ladies.—*As You Like It,* i, 2, 197.

10
Some men must love my lady and some Joan.
Love's Labour 's Lost. Act iii, sc. 1, l. 207. [Biron]
Well, now can I make any Joan a lady.
King John. Act i, sc. 1, l. 184. [Bastard]

11
Costard: Pray you, which is the head lady?
. . . Which is the greatest lady, the highest?
Princess: The thickest and the tallest.
Costard: The thickest and the tallest! it is so; truth is truth.
Love's Labour 's Lost. Act iv, sc. 1, l. 42. The only use of "tallest."

12
O gentle lady,
'Tis not for you to hear what I can speak:
The repetition, in a woman's ear,
Would murder as it fell.
Macbeth. Act ii, sc. 3, l. 88. [Macduff]
Gentle lady.—*A Midsummer-Night's Dream,* iii, 2, 152.

13
You know the lady; she is fast my wife.
Measure for Measure. Act i, sc. 2, l. 151. [Claudio]
I have heard of the lady, and good words went with her name.
Measure for Measure. Act iii, sc. 1, l. 219. [Isabella]

14
Well, tell me now what lady is the same
To whom you swore a secret pilgrimage?
The Merchant of Venice. Act i, sc. 1, l. 119. [Antonio]
That 's the lady.—*The Merchant of Venice,* ii, 7, 31; 38.

15
Falstaff: I 'll speak it before the best lord; I would make thee my lady.
Mrs. Ford: I your lady, Sir John! alas, I should be a pitiful lady!
Merry Wives of Windsor. Act iii, sc. 3, l. 54.
My lady the hostess!—*I Henry IV,* ii, 4, 315.
Seeming lady.—*The Winter's Tale,* v, 1, 191.

16
Will not the ladies be afeard of the lion?
A Midsummer-Night's Dream, iii, 1, 28. See under Lion.
Ladies shall be frighted,
And, gladly quaked, hear more.
Coriolanus. Act i, sc. 9, l. 5. [Cominius]
I quaked for fear.—*The Merry Wives of Windsor,* iii, 5, 104. The only uses of "quaked."

17
A sweet Athenian lady is in love
With a disdainful youth.
A Midsummer-Night's Dream. Act ii, sc. 1, l. 260. [Oberon]
Roman ladies.—*Coriolanus,* v, 4, 41.
Lovely Roman ladies.—*Titus Andronicus,* ii, 1, 113.

Welsh lady.—*I Henry IV*, iii, 1, 247.

1
Truly, the lady fathers herself. Be happy, lady; for you are like an honourable father.
Much Ado about Nothing. Act i, sc. 1, l. 112. [Don Pedro]

The lady is very well worthy.
Much Ado about Nothing. Act i, sc. 1, l. 224. [Don Pedro]

Worthy lady.—*The Two Gentlemen of Verona,* iv, 3, 7; iv, 4, 166; *The Winter's Tale,* ii, 2, 5.

Ladies of esteem.—*Romeo and Juliet,* i, 3, 70.

Truly an obedient lady.—*Othello,* iv, 1, 259.

2
I did never think that lady would have wed any man.
Much Ado about Nothing. Act ii, sc. 3, l. 96. [Claudio]

Wedded lady.—*Cymbeline,* i, 6, 2; v, 5, 261. See under WIFE.

New-married ladies.—*Titus Andronicus,* ii, 2, 15. "New-married" is repeated in *Henry V,* v, 2, 190: "New-married wives"; and in *Measure for Measure,* v, 1, 405: "New-married man."

3
You have killed a sweet lady, and her death shall fall heavy on you.
Much Ado about Nothing. Act v, sc. 1, l. 149. [Benedick]

You have among you killed a sweet and innocent lady.
Much Ado about Nothing. Act v, sc. 1, l. 193. [Benedick]

4
Unless thy lady prove unjust,
Press never thou to choose anew.
The Passionate Pilgrim, l. 331.

5
Your lady seeks my life; come you between,
And save poor me, the weaker.
Pericles. Act iv, sc. 1, l. 90. [Marina]

Look to the lady; O, she 's but o'erjoy'd.
Early in blustering morn this lady was
Thrown upon this shore.
Pericles. Act v, sc. 3, l. 21. [Cerimon]

6
Lysimachus: O here is
The lady that I sent for. Welcome, fair one!
Is 't not a goodly presence?
Helicanus: She 's a gallant lady.
Pericles. Act v, sc. 1, l. 64.

Gallant lady.—*Love's Labour 's Lost,* ii, 1, 194; 196.

7
She is the hopeful lady of my earth.
Romeo and Juliet. Act i, sc. 2, l. 15. [Capulet]

My lady and my wife.—*Romeo and Juliet,* iv, 1, 18.

She is my lady.—*Twelfth Night,* ii, 5, 128. "My lady" is used frequently throughout the plays, twenty-seven times in *Twelfth Night* alone.

By 'r lady.—*Richard III,* ii, 3, 4, and twelve times in later plays.

8
What lady is that, which doth enrich the hand
Of yonder knight?
Romeo and Juliet. Act i, sc. 5, l. 43. [Romeo]

So shows a snowy dove trooping with crows,
As yonder lady o'er her fellows shows.
Romeo and Juliet. Act i, sc. 5, l. 51. [Romeo]

It is my lady, O, it is my love!
O, that she knew she were!
Romeo and Juliet. Act ii, sc. 2, l. 10. [Romeo]

God's lady dear!—*Romeo and Juliet,* ii, 5, 63.

9
You do not know the lady's mind.
Romeo and Juliet. Act iv, sc. 1, l. 4. [Friar Laurence]

10
Thou hast a lady far more beautiful
Than any woman in this waning age.
The Taming of the Shrew. Induction, sc. 2, l. 64. [Lord]

Beauteous ladies.—*The Two Gentlemen of Verona,* v, 2, 12.

Lovely lady.—*II Henry VI,* i, 4, 77; *A Midsummer-Night's Dream,* ii, 2, 18.

Pretty lady.—*Much Ado about Nothing,* iv, 1, 99; *Hamlet,* iv, 5, 40; *All's Well that Ends Well,* i, 1, 88.

11
Full many a lady
I have eyed with best regard.
Tempest. Act iii, sc. 1, l. 39. [Ferdinand]

12
Servant: Please you, my lord, there are certain ladies most desirous of admittance.
Timon: Ladies! what are their wills?
Servant: There comes with them a forerunner, my lord, which bears that office, to signify their pleasures.
Timon: I pray, let them be admitted.
Timon of Athens. Act i, sc. 2, l. 121.

There 's a forerunner come.—*The Merchant of Venice,* i, 2, 136.

Great forerunner.—*King John,* ii, 1, 2. The only uses of "forerunner."

13
He hath a lady, wiser, fairer, truer,
Than ever Greek did compass in his arms.
Troilus and Cressida. Act i, sc. 3, l. 275. [Æneas]

There is no lady of more softer bowels,
More spongy to suck in the sense of fear.
Troilus and Cressida. Act ii, sc. 2, l. 11. [Hector]

Spongy April.—*The Tempest,* iv, 1, 65.

Spongy officers.—*Macbeth,* i, 7, 71.

Spongy south.—*Cymbeline,* iv, 2, 349. The only uses of "spongy."

14
Tell you the lady what she is to do,
And haste her to the purpose.
Troilus and Cressida. Act iv, sc. 3, l. 4. [Paris]

Is the lady ready?—*Troilus and Cressida,* iv, 4, 51.

15
Hey, Robin, jolly Robin,
Tell me how thy lady does.
Twelfth Night. Act iv, sc. 2, l. 78. [Clown]

Talkest thou nothing but of ladies?
Twelfth Night. Act iv, sc. 2, l. 29. [Clown]

1
How does your lady? and how thrives your love?
The Two Gentlemen of Verona. Act ii, sc. 4, l. 125. [Valentine]

2
A lady's 'Verily' 's As potent as a lord's.
Winter's Tale. Act i, sc. 2, l. 50. [Hermione]

3
Paulina: How fares our gracious lady?
Emilia: As well as one so great and so forlorn
May hold together.
The Winter's Tale. Act ii, sc. 2, l. 21.

Gracious lady.—*Henry VIII,* v, 5, 7.
Lady gracious.—*I Henry VI,* i, 2, 74.
Lady daughter.—*Cymbeline,* i, 1, 154.
Lady Disdain.—*Much Ado about Nothing,* i, 1, 119.
Lady Fortune.—*The Winter's Tale,* iv, 4, 51.
Lady mother.—*Romeo and Juliet,* iii, 5, 39; 66; *All's Well that Ends Well,* iv, 3, 102.
Lady of the house.—*Romeo and Juliet,* i, 5, 115; *Twelfth Night,* i, 5, 177; 183.
Lady Tongue.—*Much Ado about Nothing,* ii, 1, 284.
Lady widow.—*Romeo and Juliet,* i, 2, 69.
Widow lady.—*King John,* ii, 1, 548.

4
There is no lady living
So meet for this great errand.
Winter's Tale. Act ii, sc. 2, l. 45. [Emilia]

Away with that audacious lady! Antigonus,
I charged thee that she should not come about me:
I knew she would.
Winter's Tale. Act ii, sc. 3, l. 42. [Leontes]

LAKE

5
Descend to darkness and the burning lake!
II Henry VI. Act i, sc. 4, l. 42. [Bolingbroke]

Lake of darkness.—*King Lear,* iii, 6, 8.
Pluto's damned lake.—*II Henry IV,* ii, 4, 170.

I 'll dive into the burning lake below,
And pull her out of Acheron by the heels.
Titus Andronicus. Act iv, sc. 3, l. 43. [Titus]

Black as Acheron.—*A Midsummer-Night's Dream,* iii, 2, 357.
The pit of Acheron.—*Macbeth,* iii, 5, 15. The only uses of Acheron.

6
Pool! Sir Pool! lord!
Ay, Kennel, puddle, sink.
II Henry VI. Act iv, sc. 1, l. 70. [Captain]

Thy sea within a puddle's womb is hearsed,
And not the puddle in thy sea dispersed.
The Rape of Lucrece, l. 657. "Hearsed" is repeated in *The Merchant of Venice,* iii, 1, 93, and in *Hamlet,* i, 4, 47.

Gilded puddle.—*Antony and Cleopatra,* i, 4, 62. The only uses of "puddle."

7
At last I left them
I' the filthy-mantled pool beyond your cell,
There dancing up to the chins, that the foul lake
O'erstunk their feet.
The Tempest. Act iv, sc. 1, l. 181. [Ariel] The only use of "filthy-mantled" and "o'erstunk."

Great pool.—*Cymbeline,* iii, 4, 142.
Standing pool.—*King Lear,* iii, 4, 139. "Pool" is used a fifth time in *The Tempest,* iv, 1, 208.
Standing lakes.—*The Tempest,* v, 1, 33.

8
And his pond fish'd by his next neighbour, by
Sir Smile, his neighbour.
Winter's Tale. Act i, sc. 2, l. 195. [Leontes]

Strange fowl light upon neighbouring ponds.
Cymbeline. Act i, sc. 4, l. 98. [Iachimo]

Standing pond.—*Merchant of Venice,* i, 1, 89.
A pond as deep as hell.—*Measure for Measure,* iii, 1, 94.
As fish are in a pond.—*II Henry IV,* i, 1, 200. The only uses of "pond" and "ponds."

LAMB

See also Fox, Lion, Sheep, Wolf

9
Brutus: He 's a lamb indeed, that baes like a bear.
Menenius: He 's a bear indeed, that lives like a lamb.
Coriolanus. Act ii, sc. 1, l. 12. "Baes" is repeated in *Much Ado about Nothing,* iii, 3, 75.

I am a lamb.—*Titus Andronicus,* iv, 2, 137.

10
The lamb entreats the butcher: where 's thy knife?
Thou art too slow to do thy master's bidding,
When I desire it too.
Cymbeline. Act iii, sc. 4, l. 99. [Imogen]

11
Thy tender lambkin now is king.
II Henry IV. Act v, sc. 3, l. 122. [Pistol] "Lambkin" occurs only once again in the plays, in *Henry V,* ii, 1, 133.

12
I will sit as quiet as a lamb.
King John. Act iv, sc. 1, l. 80. [Arthur]

Gentle as a lamb.—*Romeo and Juliet,* ii, 5, 45.
Gentle lambs.—*Richard III,* iv, 4, 22.

13
Now serves the season that they may surprise
The silly lambs.
The Rape of Lucrece, l. 166.

Silly lamb.—*Venus and Adonis,* l. 1098.
Harmless lambs.—*III Henry VI,* ii, 5, 75.
Innocent lamb.—*II Henry VI,* iv, 2, 87.
Poor lamb.—*The Rape of Lucrece,* l. 677.
Slaughter'd lamb.—*Titus Andronicus,* ii, 3, 223.
Sucking lamb.—*II Henry VI,* iii, 1, 71.
Sweet lamb.—*Love's Labour 's Lost,* ii, 1, 220.
Trembling lamb.—*III Henry VI,* i, 1, 242.
Wearied lamb.—*The Rape of Lucrece,* l. 737.
Wolvish-ravening lamb!—*Romeo and Juliet,* iii, 2, 76. The only use of "wolvish-ravening."

14
What, lamb! what, lady-bird!
Romeo and Juliet. Act i, sc. 3, l. 3. [Nurse] The only use of "lady-bird." "Lamb," as a term of endearment, is used seven times.

Tut, she 's a lamb, a dove, a fool to him!
The Taming of the Shrew. Act iii, sc. 2, l. 159. [Gremio]

How now, lambs?—*Troilus and Cressida,* iv, 4, 25.

LAMENTATION

See also Mourning

1
Moderate lamentation is the right of the dead, excessive grief the enemy to the living.
All's Well that Ends Well. Act i, sc. 1, l. 64. [Lafeu]
But yet let me lament.—*Antony and Cleopatra,* v, 1, 40.

2 You do draw my spirits from me
With new lamenting ancient oversights.
II Henry IV. Act ii, sc. 3, l. 46. [Northumberland] The only use of "oversights."
Lament therefore.—*II Henry IV,* v, 3, 113.

3
Still lamenting and mourning.
II Henry VI. Act iv, sc. 4, l. 22. [King Henry]
Christian-like laments.—*II Henry VI,* iii, 2, 58.

4
Alack, alack the day!
King Lear. Act iv, sc. 6, l. 185. [Gloucester]
Alack the day! *Passionate Pilgrim,* l. 227.
Alack the heavy day!—*Richard II,* iv, 1, 257.
Alack, alack!—*A Midsummer-Night's Dream,* iv, 1, 172. "Alack" is used sixteen times.
Alas the day!—*As You Like It,* iii, 2, 231, and five times in later plays.
Alas the heavy day!—*Othello,* iv, 2, 42.
Alas the while!—*The Merchant of Venice,* ii, 1, 31. "Alas" occurs twenty-two times.
Ah, well-a-day!—*Romeo and Juliet,* iii, 2, 37, and six times in later plays.

5
Her own lamentation, which she yet wears for his sake.
Measure for Measure. Act iii, sc. 1, l. 237. [Duke]
She laments, sir, for it, that it would yearn your heart to see it.
The Merry Wives of Windsor. Act iii, sc. 5, l. 44. [Mistress Quickly]

6 She . . .
Shall be lamented, pitied and excused
Of every hearer.
Much Ado about Nothing. Act iv, sc. 1, l. 216. [Friar]
Lamented by the king.—*Winter's Tale,* v, 2, 93.
Very much lamented.—*Julius Cæsar,* i, 2, 55.

7
Whom she finds forlorn she doth lament.
The Rape of Lucrece, l. 1500.
My laments would be drawn out too long,
To tell them all with one poor tired tongue.
The Rape of Lucrece, l. 1616.
Do not steep thy heart
In such relenting dew of lamentations.
The Rape of Lucrece, l. 1828.

8
Whilst I awhile obsequiously lament.
Richard III. Act i, sc. 2, l. 3. [Lady Anne] The only use of "obsequiously."
Why lament you, pretty one?—*Pericles,* iv, 2, 72.
Hear the lamentations of poor Anne.
Richard III. Act i, sc. 2, l. 9. [Lady Anne]
Lamentation of the French.—*Henry V,* Prol., 36.
Mother's lamentation.—*Richard III,* iv, 4, 14.

9
Give me no help in lamentation.
Richard III. Act ii, sc. 2, l. 66. [Queen Elizabeth]
Which modern lamentation might have moved.
Romeo and Juliet. Act iii, sc. 2, l. 120. [Juliet]

10
O noble father, you lament in vain.
Titus Andronicus. Act iii, sc. 1, l. 27. [Lucius]
Let reason govern thy lament.
Titus Andronicus. Act iii, sc. 1, l. 219. [Marcus]
Leave these bitter deep laments.
Titus Andronicus. Act iii, sc. 2, l. 46. [Boy]
Leave this faint puling and lament as I do,
In anger, Juno-like.
Coriolanus. Act iv, sc. 2, l. 32. [Volumnia] The only use of "Juno-like."
To speak puling.—*The Two Gentlemen of Verona,* ii, 1, 26.
Puling cuckold.—*Troilus and Cressida,* iv, 1, 61.
Puling fool.—*Romeo and Juliet,* iii, 5, 185. The only uses of "puling."

11
Your dire-lamenting elegies.
The Two Gentlemen of Verona. Act iii, sc. 2, l. 82. [Proteus] The only use of "dire-lamenting."

LAMP, see Torch

LAND

See also Sea and Land

12
The land bids me tread no more upon 't;
It is ashamed to bear me!
Antony and Cleopatra. Act iii, sc. 11, l. 1. [Antony]

13 If to-morrow
Our navy thrive, I have an absolute hope
Our landmen will stand up.
Antony and Cleopatra. Act iv, sc. 3, l. 9. [Fourth Soldier] The only use of "landmen."

14
Thy lands and all things that thou dost call thine
Worth seizure do we seize into our hands.
As You Like It. Act iii, sc. 1, l. 9. [Duke]
And all their lands restored to them again
That were with him exiled.
As You Like It. Act v, sc. 4, l. 170. [Jaques]
To one his lands withheld, and to the other
A land itself at large, a potent dukedom.
As You Like It. Act v, sc. 4, l. 174. [Duke Senior]

15
First Lord: Stand you! You have land enough of your own: but he added to your having; gave you some ground.
Second Lord [Aside]: As many inches as you have oceans. Puppies!
Cymbeline. Act i, sc. 2, l. 18.

16
He hath much land, and fertile.
Hamlet. Act v, sc. 2, l. 87. [Hamlet]

Fertile land.—*I Henry IV,* iii, 1, 77.
Fruitful land.—*Taming of the Shrew,* ii, 1, 372.

1
You may buy land now as cheap as stinking mackerel.
I Henry IV. Act ii, sc. 4, l. 394. [Falstaff]
The only mention of mackerel.

2
The land is burning; Percy stands on high;
And either we or they must lower lie.
I Henry IV. Act iii, sc. 3, l. 227. [Prince Henry]

Blustering land.—*King John,* v, 1, 21.
Revolting land.—*Richard II,* iii, 3, 163.

3 He doth bestride a bleeding land,
Gasping for life.
II Henry IV. Act i, sc. 1, l. 207. [Mortimer]

Bewailing land.—*Henry VIII,* iii, 2, 255.
Declining land.—*Richard II,* ii, 1, 240.
Dirty lands.—*Twelfth Night,* ii, 4, 85.
Fearful land.—*Richard II,* iii, 2, 110.
Gleaned land.—*Henry V,* i, 2, 151.
Sickly land.—*Richard III,* ii, 3, 30.
Woeful land.—*Richard II,* ii, 2, 99.
Salique land.—*Henry V,* i, 2, 39.

4
All the temporal lands which men devout
By testament have given to the church
Would they strip from us.
Henry V. Act i, sc. 1, l. 9. [Canterbury]

Christian land.—*Richard III,* iii, 7, 116.
Duteous land.—*I Henry IV,* iv, 3, 44.
Fair land.—*Richard III,* v, 5, 38.
Fair King Richard's land.—*Richard II,* iii, 3, 47.
Fairy land.—*The Comedy of Errors,* ii, 2, 191; *A Midsummer-Night's Dream,* ii, 1, 65; 122; iv, 1, 66. See under FAIRY.
Great land.—*Cymbeline,* ii, 1, 70.
Green land.—*The Tempest,* iv, 1, 130.
Happier lands.—*Richard II,* ii, 1, 49.
Holy Land.—*II Henry IV,* iii, 1, 108.
Narrow lands.—*Comedy of Errors,* iv, 2, 38.
Noiseless land.—*King Lear,* iv, 2, 56.

5
From Scotland am I stol'n, even of pure love,
To greet mine own land with my wishful sight.
No, Harry, Harry, 'tis no land of thine.
III Henry VI. Act iii, sc. 1, l. 13. [King Henry]

All the land knows that.
Henry VIII. Act iv, sc. 1, l. 105. [Gentleman]

6
Lord of thy presence and no land beside.
King John. Act i, sc. 1, l. 137. [Queen Elinor]

A land remote.—*King John,* v, 2, 31.

7
Thy death-bed is no lesser than thy land
Wherein thou liest in reputation sick.
Richard II. Act ii, sc. 1, l. 95. [Gaunt]
Why, cousin, wert thou regent of the world,
It were a shame to let this land by lease.
Richard II. Act ii, sc. 1, l. 109. [Gaunt]

8
Landlord of England art thou, not king.
Richard II. Act ii, sc. 1, l. 113. [John of Gaunt]

Gouty landlord.—*A Lover's Complaint,* l. 140.
The universal landlord.—*Antony and Cleopatra,* iii, 13, 72. The only uses of "landlord."

9
His land 's put to their books.
Timon of Athens. Act i, sc. 2, l. 206. [Flavius]
Timon: All the lands thou hast
Lie in a pitch'd field.
Alcibiades: Ay, defiled land, my lord.
Timon of Athens. Act i, sc. 2, l. 231.

Land and living.—*Winter's Tale,* iv, 3, 104.
Land rats.—*The Merchant of Venice,* i, 3, 23.
Land thieves.—*Merchant of Venice,* i, 3, 24.

LANGUAGE

For English Language, see under England; for French Language, under France

10
Parolles: My lord! my master!
Lafeu: Ay, is it not a language I speak?
Parolles: A most harsh one, and not to be understood without bloody succeeding.
All's Well that Ends Well. Act ii, sc. 3, l. 196.

Speak what terrible language you will: though you understand it not yourselves.
All's Well that Ends Well. Act iv, sc. 1, l. 3. [Second Lord]

11
He hath a smack of all neighbouring languages; therefore we must every one be a man of his own fancy, not to know what we speak one to another; so we seem to know, is to know straight our purpose: choughs' language, gabble enough, and good enough.
All's Well that Ends Well. Act iv, sc. 1, l. 18. [Second Lord]

I . . . Took pains to make thee speak, taught thee each hour
One thing or other: when thou didst not, savage,
Know thine own meaning, but wouldst gabble like
A thing most brutish.
The Tempest. Act i, sc. 2, l. 354. [Prospero]

Gabble like tinkers.—*Twelfth Night,* ii, 3, 95. See under MANNERS for full quotation. The only uses of "gabble."

12
Parolles: I shall lose my life for want of language.
Soldier: I understand thee and can speak thy tongue.
All's Well that Ends Well. Act iv, sc. 1, l. 76.

13
Ill school'd In bolted language.
Coriolanus, iii, 1, 322. See under CANDOUR.

14 He did provoke me
With language that would make me spurn the sea,
If it could so roar to me.
Cymbeline. Act v, sc. 5, l. 293. [Guiderius]

This is not the hunters' language.—*Cymbeline,* iii, 3, 74.
Language unmannerly.—*Henry VIII,* i, 2, 27.
Disdainful language.—*Henry V,* iii, 6, 118.

Lustful language.—*Venus and Adonis,* l. 47.

1
But I will never be a truant, love,
Till I have learn'd thy language; for thy tongue
Makes Welsh as sweet as ditties highly penn'd,
Sung by a fair queen in a summer's bower,
With ravishing division, to her lute.
I Henry IV. Act iii, sc. 1, l. 207. [Mortimer] The Welsh language is referred to six times in this scene, and nowhere else.

2
Thy speaking of my tongue, and I thine, most truly-falsely, must needs be granted to be at one.
Henry V. Act v, sc. 2, l. 203. [King Henry] The only use of "truly-falsely."

I will upon all hazards well believe
Thou art my friend, that know'st my tongue so well.
King John. Act v, sc. 6, l. 7. [Hubert]

I have no tongue but one, gentle my lord,
Let me entreat you speak the former language.
Measure for Measure. Act ii, sc. 4, l. 139. [Isabella]

I'll swear that I do know your tongue.
The Merchant of Venice. Act i, sc. 6, l. 27. [Jessica]

Is't not possible to understand in another tongue?
You will do't, sir, really.
Hamlet. Act v, sc. 2, l. 132. [Horatio] The only use of "really."

He speaks the common tongue,
Which all men speak with him.
Timon of Athens. Act i, sc. 1, l. 174. [Merchant]

I would I had bestowed that time in the tongues that I have in fencing, dancing and bear-baiting.
Twelfth Night. Act i, sc. 3, l. 97. [Sir Andrew]

A strange tongue.—*II Henry IV,* iv, 4, 69.

3 Be not too rough in terms;
For he is fierce and cannot brook hard language.
II Henry VI. Act iv, sc. 9, l. 44. [King Henry]

4 The king hath found
Matter against him that for ever mars
The honey of his language.
Henry VIII. Act iii, sc. 2, l. 20. [Norfolk]

Gardiner: I shall remember this bold language.
Cromwell: Do. Remember your bold life too.
Henry VIII. Act v, sc. 3, l. 84.

5
My dialect, which you discommend so much.
King Lear. Act ii, sc. 2, l. 115. [Kent] "Dialect" occurs again in *Measure for Measure,* i, 2, 188. The only use of "discommend."

6
They have been at a great feast of languages, and stolen the scraps.
Love's Labour's Lost. Act v, sc. 1, l. 39. [Moth]

7
Nerissa: What say you, then, to Falconbridge, the young baron of England?
Portia: You know I say nothing to him, for he understands not me, nor I him: he hath neither Latin, French, nor Italian, and you will come into the court and swear that I have a poor pennyworth in the English.
The Merchant of Venice. Act i, sc. 2, l. 71.

Cunning in Greek, Latin, and other languages.
The Taming of the Shrew. Act ii, sc. 1, l. 81. [Gremio]

8
There is not chastity enough in language
Without offence to utter them.
Much Ado about Nothing. Act iv, sc. 1, l. 98. [Don John]

9 We commit no crime
To use one language in each several clime.
Pericles. Act iv, sc. 4, l. 5. [Gower]

10 The red plague rid you
For learning me your language!
The Tempest. Act i, sc. 2, l. 364. [Caliban]

My language! heavens!
I am the best of them that speak this speech,
Were I but where 'tis spoken.
The Tempest. Act i, sc. 2, l. 428. [Ferdinand]

It is a sleepy language and thou speak'st
Out of thy sleep.
The Tempest. Act ii, sc. 1, l. 211. [Sebastian]

Where the devil should he learn our language?
The Tempest. Act ii, sc. 2, l. 69. [Stephano]

11
I read it in the grammar long ago.
Titus Andronicus. Act iv, sc. 2, l. 23. [Chiron] The only use of "grammar." "Grammar school" occurs in *II Henry VI,* iv, 7, 37.

Priscian a little scratched, 'twill serve.
Love's Labour's Lost. Act v, sc. 1, l. 31. [Holofernes] The only use of "Priscian" (a grammarian).

12
There's language in her eye, her cheek, her lip.
Troilus and Cressida. Act iv, sc. 5, l. 55. [Ulysses]

There was . . . language in their very gesture.
Winter's Tale. Act v, sc. 2, l. 14. [Gentleman]

13
Second Outlaw: Have you the tongues?
Valentine: My youthful travel therein made me happy. . . .
First Outlaw: A linguist and a man of such perfection
As we do in your quality much want.
Two Gentlemen of Verona. Act iv, sc. 1, l. 33.

The manifold linguist and the armipotent soldier.
All's Well that Ends Well. Act iv, sc. 3, l. 265. [Lord] The only uses of "linguist." "Armipotent" is repeated in *Love's Labour's Lost,* v, 2, 650: "Armipotent Mars."

14
Lest barbarism, making me a precedent,
Should a like language use to all degrees
And mannerly distinguishment leave out
Betwixt the prince and beggar.
The Winter's Tale. Act ii, sc. 1, l. 84. [Leontes] The only use of "distinguishment."

You speak a language that I understand not.
The Winter's Tale. Act iii, sc. 2, l. 81. [Hermione]

LANGUISHING, see Sickness

LARK

1
Hark, hark! the lark at heaven's gate sings.
Cymbeline, ii, 3, 21. See under RISING.

2
From the rising of the lark to the lodging of the lamb.
Henry V. Act iii, sc. 7, l. 34. [Dauphin]

Stir with the lark to-morrow.—*Richard III,* v, 3, 56.

Waked by the lark.—*Troilus and Cressida,* iv, 2, 9.

3
Look up a-height; the shrill-gorged lark so far
Cannot be seen or heard.
King Lear. Act iv, sc. 6, l. 57. [Edgar] The only use of "a-height" and "shrill-gorged."

4
Merry larks are ploughmen's clocks.
Love's Labour's Lost, v, 2, 914. See under SPRING.

5
Fairy king, attend, and mark:
I do hear the morning lark.
A Midsummer-Night's Dream. Act iv, sc. 1, l. 97. [Puck]

Morning lark.—*The Taming of the Shrew,* Ind., 2, 46.

Mounting larks.—*Richard II,* iii, 3, 183.

I could o'ermount the lark.—*Henry VIII,* ii, 3, 94. The only use of "o'ermount."

6
Romeo: It was the lark, the herald of the morn. . . .
I 'll say yon grey is not the morning's eye, . . .
Nor that is not the lark, whose notes do beat
The vaulty heaven so high above our heads. . . .
Juliet: It is the lark that sings so out of tune,
Straining harsh discords and unpleasing sharps.
Some say the lark makes sweet division;
This doth not so, for she divideth us:
Some say the lark and loathed toad change eyes;
O, now I would they had changed voices too!
Since arm from arm that voice doth us affray,
Hunting thee hence with hunt's-up to the day.
Romeo and Juliet. Act iii, sc. 5, l. 6. The only use of "hunt's-up."

7 The lark at break of day arising
From sullen earth, sings hymns at heaven's gate.
Sonnets. No. xxix.

Lo, here the gentle lark, weary of rest,
From his moist cabinet mounts up on high,
And wakes the morning, from whose silver breast
The sun ariseth in his majesty.
Venus and Adonis, l. 853.

The lark, that tirra-lyra chants.
The Winter's Tale. Act iv, sc. 3, l. 9. [Autolycus] The only use of "tirra-lyra."

Tuned like the lark.—*The Passionate Pilgrim,* l. 198.

LASCIVIOUSNESS, see Wantonness

LATENESS

See also under Rising

8
I am come, I dread, too late.
Antony and Cleopatra. Act iv, sc. 14, l. 127. [Diomedes]

Marcius: Come I too late?
Cominius: Ay, if you come not in the blood of others,
But mantled in your own.
Coriolanus. Act i, sc. 6, l. 27. The only use of "mantled."

Supper is done, and we shall come too late.
Romeo and Juliet. Act i, sc. 4, l. 105. [Benvolio]

Then do we sin against our own estate,
When we may profit meet, and come too late.
Timon of Athens. Act v, sc. 1, l. 44. [Poet]

He comes too late.—*The Comedy of Errors,* iii, 1, 49; *The Merchant of Venice,* ii, 8, 6; *Richard II,* i, 4, 64.

I hope I am not too late.—*Henry VIII,* v, 2, 1.

Be not too late.—*The Tempest,* iv, 1, 133.

You come too late.—*Richard III,* iii, 5, 69.

It is too late.—*I Henry VI,* iv, 4, 1, and frequently in later plays.

'Tis too late.—*Measure for Measure,* ii, 2, 57.

All too late.—*The Rape of Lucrece,* l. 1686; *Titus Andronicus,* ii, 3, 264.

Better once than never, for never too late.
The Taming of the Shrew. Act v, sc. 1, l. 155. [Petruchio]

9
An you be so tardy, come no more in my sight.
As You Like It. Act iv, sc. 1, l. 51. [Rosalind]

Be not ta'en tardy.—*Richard III,* iv, 1, 52.

You 're tardy.—*Henry VIII,* i, 4, 7.

Tardy and remiss.—*Troilus and Cressida,* iv, 4, 143.

Come tardy off.—*Hamlet,* iii, 2, 28.

10
'Tis very late, i' faith.
II Henry IV. Act ii, sc. 4, l. 175. [Hostess]

'Tis very late.—*Romeo and Juliet,* iii, 4, 5; *Venus and Adonis,* l. 531.

It grows late.—*II Henry IV,* ii, 4, 299.

It grows very late.—*Romeo and Juliet,* iii, 3, 164.

It waxes late.—*Romeo and Juliet,* i, 5, 128.

It is so very, very late.—*Romeo and Juliet,* iii, 4, 34.

11
Now, Falstaff, where have you been all this while?
When every thing is ended, then you come:
These tardy tricks of yours will, on my life,
One time or other break some gallows' back.
II Henry IV. Act iv, sc. 3, l. 29. [Lancaster]

Early and late.—*II Henry VI,* i, 1, 91.

We shall be late.—*Henry VIII,* i, 3, 65.

1
Good hour of night, Sir Thomas! Whither so late?
Henry VIII. Act v, sc. 1, l. 5. [Gardiner]
Men must not walk too late.
Macbeth. Act iii, sc. 6, l. 7. [Lennox]
2
For my own part, I came in late.
Troilus and Cressida. Act iv, sc. 2, l. 55. [Pandarus]
3
To be up late is to be up late.
Twelfth Night. Act ii, sc. 3, l. 5. [Sir Andrew]
Come, come, I'll go burn some sack; 'tis too late to go to bed now.
Twelfth Night. Act ii, sc. 3, l. 206. [Sir Toby]

LATIN

See also Language

4
Thus in Latin, Præclarissimus filius noster Henricus, Rex Angliæ, et Hæres Francia.
Henry V. Act v, sc. 2, l. 369. [Exeter]
Dick, the Butcher: What say you of Kent?
Lord Say: Nothing but this; 'tis 'bona terra, mala gens.'
Cade: Away with him, away with him! he speaks Latin.
II Henry VI. Act iv, sc. 7, l. 60.
5
O, good my lord, no Latin.
Henry VIII, iii, 1, 42. See under ENGLISH for full quotation.
6
O, I smell false Latin; dunghill for unguem.
Love's Labour's Lost. Act v, sc. 1, l. 83. [Holofernes] The only use of "unguem."
7
He hath neither Latin, French, nor Italian.
The Merchant of Venice, i, 2, 75. See under LANGUAGE.
Lacks Latin.—*As You Like It*, iii, 2, 337.
8
Ay, you spake in Latin then too; but 'tis no matter.
The Merry Wives of Windsor. Act i, sc. 1, l. 185. [Slender]
Nay, 'tis no matter, sir, what he 'leges in Latin.
The Taming of the Shrew. Act i, sc. 2, l. 29. [Grumio] The only use of "'leges."
Cunning in . . . Latin.—*The Taming of the Shrew*, ii, 1, 81.
9
'Hang-hog' is Latin for bacon.
The Merry Wives of Windsor. Act iv, sc. 1, l. 50. [Mistress Quickly] The only use of "hang-hog."
Remuneration! O, that's the Latin word for three farthings.
Love's Labour's Lost, iii, 1, 138. See under REWARD.

LAUGHTER

10
O, for the love of laughter.
All's Well that Ends Well. Act iii, sc. 6, l. 36. [First Lord]
Increase of laughter.—*All's Well that Ends Well*, ii, 4, 38.
11
I laugh'd him out of patience; and that night
I laugh'd him into patience.
Antony and Cleopatra. Act ii, sc. 5, l. 19. [Cleopatra]
12
When I did hear
The motley fool thus moral on the time,
My lungs began to crow like chanticleer,
That fools should be so deep-contemplative,
And did I laugh sans intermission
An hour by his dial.
As You Like It. Act ii, sc. 7, l. 28. [Jaques] The only use of "deep-contemplative."
You were wont, when you laughed, to crow like a cock.
The Two Gentlemen of Verona, ii, 1, 27. See under LOVE.
13
I will laugh like a hyen, and that when thou art inclined to sleep.
As You Like It. Act iv, sc. 1, l. 157. [Rosalind] The only use of "hyen." "Hyena" does not occur at all.
14
Laughs from 's free lungs, cries 'O, Can my sides hold.'
Cymbeline. Act i, sc. 6, l. 68. [Iachimo]
His eyes in flood with laughter.
Cymbeline. Act i, sc. 6, l. 74. [Iachimo]
Move laughter.—*Coriolanus*, iii, 3, 52.
Tends to laughter.—*II Henry IV*, i, 2, 10.
Make her laugh at that.—*Hamlet*, v, 1, 215.
15
Were 't not for laughing, I should pity him.
I Henry IV. Act ii, sc. 2, l. 117. [Prince of Wales]
Come out of that fat room and lend me thy hand to laugh a little.
I Henry IV. Act ii, sc. 4, l. 1. [Prince of Wales]
16
A' shall laugh without intervallums. . . . O, you shall see him laugh till his face be like a wet cloak ill laid up!
II Henry IV. Act v, sc. 1, l. 91. [Falstaff] The only use of "intervallums."
Continual laughter.—*II Henry IV*, v, 1, 89.
A man cannot make him laugh.—*II Henry IV*, iv, 3, 95.
Laugh'd in his face.—*III Henry VI*, ii, 1, 60.
17
Were I a common laugher.
Julius Cæsar, i, 2, 72. [Cassius] "Laugher" is repeated in *The Rape of Lucrece*, l. 124.
I durst not laugh, for fear of opening my lips and receiving the bad air.
Julius Cæsar. Act i, sc. 2, l. 251. [Casca]
I'll use you . . . for my laughter.—*Julius Cæsar*, iv, 3, 49.
Laughter and contempt.—*King Lear*, i, 4, 309.
Lust and laughter.—*Timon of Athens*, iv, 3, 492.
Mirth and laughter.—*The Merchant of Venice*, i, 1, 80; *Julius Cæsar*, iv, 3, 114.
18
Making that idiot, laughter, keep men's eyes,
And strain their cheeks to idle merriment.
King John. Act iii, sc. 3, l. 45. [King John]

1
Biron: To hear? or forbear laughing?
Longaville: To hear meekly, sir, and to laugh moderately; or to forbear both.
Love's Labour's Lost. Act i, sc. 1, l. 198. The only use of "meekly."

By virtue, thou enforcest laughter.
Love's Labour's Lost. Act iii, sc. 1, l. 75. [Armado] The only use of "enforcest."

2
O, I am stabb'd with laughter!
Love's Labour's Lost. Act v, sc. 2, l. 80. [Boyet]

With such a zealous laughter, so profound,
That in this spleen ridiculous appears,
To check their folly, passion's solemn tears.
Love's Labour's Lost. Act v, sc. 2, l. 116. [Boyet]

To move wild laughter in the throat of death?
It cannot be; it is impossible.
Love's Labour's Lost. Act v, sc. 2, l. 865. [Biron] See under WIT.

Shallow laughing.—*Love's Labour's Lost,* v, 2, 870.

3
There 's one did laugh in 's sleep.
Macbeth. Act ii, sc. 2, l. 23. [Macbeth]

Laugh and leap.—*The Merchant of Venice,* i, 1, 49; *Love's Labour's Lost,* iv, 3, 148.

Laugh like parrot.—*The Merchant of Venice,* i, 1, 53.

4
When shall we laugh? say, when?
The Merchant of Venice. Act i, sc. 1, l. 66. [Bassanio]

If you tickle us, do we not laugh?—*The Merchant of Venice,* iii, 1, 68. See under JEW.

5
I shall never laugh but in that maid's company!
The Merry Wives of Windsor. Act i, sc. 4, l. 162. [Mistress Quickly]

6
And then the whole quire hold their hips and laugh,
And waxen in their mirth and neeze and swear
A merrier hour was never wasted there.
A Midsummer-Night's Dream. Act ii, sc. 1, l. 55. [Puck] The only use of "neeze" (sneeze).

7
Did he never make you laugh?
Much Ado about Nothing. Act ii, sc. 1, l. 140. [Beatrice]

Laugh at him.—*Much Ado about Nothing,* ii, 1, 147.

Laugh me Out of myself.—*Much Ado about Nothing,* iii, 1, 75.

8
How now! interjections? Why then, some be of laughing, as, ah, ha, he!
Much Ado about Nothing. Act iv, sc. 1, l. 22. [Benedick] The only use of "interjections."

9
He, when he hears of her, cannot refrain
From the excess of laughter.
Othello. Act iv, sc. 1, l. 100. [Iago]

10
I shall laugh at this a twelve-month hence.
Richard III. Act iii, sc. 2, l. 57. [Hastings]

He will live, and laugh at this hereafter.
Julius Cæsar. Act ii, sc. 1, l. 191. [Trebonius]

Laughter for a month.—*I Henry IV,* ii, 2, 101. See under JESTING.

11
I cannot choose but laugh.
Romeo and Juliet. Act i, sc. 3, l. 50. [Nurse]

Pandarus: I cannot choose but laugh to think how she tickled his chin. . . . And she takes it upon her to spy a white hair on his chin.
Cressida: Alas, poor chin! many a wart is richer.
Pandarus: But there was such laughing! Queen Hecuba laughed that her eyes ran o'er.
Cressida: With mill-stones.
Pandarus: And Cassandra laughed.
Cressida: But there was more temperate fire under the pot of her eyes: did her eyes run o'er too? . . . At what was all this laughing?
Pandarus: Marry, at the white hair that Helen spied on Troilus' chin.
Troilus and Cressida. Act i, sc. 2, l. 149. "Mill-stones" is repeated in *Richard III,* i, 3, 354; i, 4, 246.

12
Went they not quickly, I should die with laughing.
The Taming of the Shrew. Act iii, sc. 2, l. 243. [Gremio]

Wink and laugh.—*The Taming of the Shrew,* iv, 4, 75.

13
Of such sensible and nimble lungs that they always use to laugh at nothing. . . . So you may continue and laugh at nothing still.
The Tempest. Act ii, sc. 1, l. 174. [Gonzalo]

Will you laugh me asleep, for I am very heavy?
The Tempest. Act ii, sc. 1, l. 188. [Gonzalo]

14
It may prove an argument of laughter.
Timon of Athens. Act iii, sc. 3, l. 20. [Sempronius] See FOOL, 564:13.

15
Why dost thou laugh? it fits not with this hour.
Titus Andronicus. Act iii, sc. 1, l. 266. [Marcus]

Madam, why laugh you at such a barren rascal?
Twelfth Night. Act v, sc. 1, l. 383. [Clown]

16
Almost broke my heart with extreme laughter.
Titus Andronicus. Act v, sc. 1, l. 113. [Aaron]

If you desire the spleen, and will laugh yourselves into stitches, follow me.
Twelfth Night. Act iii, sc. 2, l. 72. [Maria] The only use of "stitches."

17
Unless you laugh and minister occasion to him, he is gagged.
Twelfth Night. Act i, sc. 5, l. 93. [Malvolio] "Gagged" occurs again in the same play, v, 1, 384, and nowhere else.

How with a sportful malice it was follow'd,
May rather pluck on laughter than revenge;
If that the injuries be justly weigh'd
That have on both sides pass'd.
Twelfth Night. Act v, sc. 1, l. 373. [Fabian]

Present laughter.—*Twelfth Night,* ii, 3, 49.
To be laughed at, see under Ridicule.

II—Laughter and Tears

1
Wouldst thou have laugh'd had I come coffin'd home,
That weep'st to see me triumph?
Coriolanus. Act ii, sc. 1, l. 193. [Coriolanus]
I could weep
And I could laugh, I am light and heavy.
Coriolanus. Act ii, sc. 1, l. 200. [Menenius]

2
For his advantage still did wake and sleep:
To make the weeper laugh, the laugher weep.
A Lover's Complaint, l. 123.

3
More merry tears
The passion of loud laughter never shed.
A Midsummer-Night's Dream, v, 1, 69. See Eye: The Weeping Eye, 447:10.

4
Romeo: Dost thou not laugh?
Benvolio: No, coz, I rather weep.
Romeo and Juliet. Act i, sc. 1, l. 189.

5
Strange times, that weep with laughing, not with weeping!
Timon of Athens. Act iv, sc. 3, l. 493. [Timon]

6
Beheld his tears, and laugh'd so heartily,
That both mine eyes were rainy like to his.
Titus Andronicus. Act v, sc. 1, l. 116. [Aaron] "Rainy" is used four times.

7
Stopping the career
Of laughter with a sigh.
The Winter's Tale, i, 2, 287. See under Sigh.

LAW
See also Statute

8
Make thine own edict for thy pains, which we
Will answer as a law.
Antony and Cleopatra. Act iii, sc. 12, l. 32. [Cæsar]
Takes on him to reform
Some certain edicts and some strait decrees
That lie too heavy on the commonwealth.
I Henry IV. Act iv, sc. 3, l. 78. [Hotspur]
Our late edict shall strongly stand in force.
Love's Labour's Lost. Act i, sc. 1, l. 11. [King]
Spurn at his edict.—*Richard III,* i, 4, 203.
The edict infringe.—*Measure for Measure,* ii, 2, 92.
It stands as an edict in destiny.—*A Midsummer-Night's Dream,* i, 1, 151.
Edicts for usury.—*Coriolanus,* i, 1, 84.
Strait edict.—*II Henry VI,* iii, 2, 258.
Strict edict.—*Pericles,* i, 1, 111.
Contrary to thy established proclaimed edict and continent canon.
Love's Labour's Lost. Act i, sc. 1, l. 261. [King Ferdinand] The only uses of "edict."
The canon of the law.—*King John,* ii, 1, 180.
Canon 'gainst self-slaughter.—*Hamlet,* i, 2, 132. See under Suicide.
Most inhibited sin in the canon.—*All's Well that Ends Well,* i, 1, 158. See Virginity, 1605:3.
'Twas from the canon.—*Coriolanus,* iii, 1, 90.
Hospitable canon.—*Coriolanus,* i, 10, 26. The only uses of "canon."
Religious canons.—*Timon of Athens,* iv, 3, 60. The only use of "canons."

9
I shall have law in Ephesus,
To your notorious shame.
The Comedy of Errors. Act iv, sc. 1, l. 83. [Angelo]
He hath resisted law,
And therefore law shall scorn him further trial.
Coriolanus. Act iii, sc. 1, l. 267. [Sicinius]

10
You wear out a good wholesome forenoon in hearing a cause between an orange-wife and a fosset-seller; and then rejourn the controversy of three pence to a second day of audience. When you are hearing a matter between party and party, if you chance to be pinched with the colic, you make faces like mummers; set up the bloody flag against all patience; and, in roaring for a chamber-pot, dismiss the controversy bleeding, the more entangled by your hearing; all the peace you make in their cause is, calling both the parties knaves.
Coriolanus. Act ii, sc. 1, l. 77. [Menenius] The only use of "orange-wife," "fosset-seller," "rejourn," "mummers," and "chamber-pot." "Forenoon" is repeated in *Antony and Cleopatra,* i, 2, 26.
The law's delay.—*Hamlet,* iii, 1, 72.

11
The law
Protects not us: then why should we be tender . . .
For we do fear the law?
Cymbeline. Act iv, sc. 2, l. 125. [Guiderius]

12
For the law of writ and the liberty, these are the only men.
Hamlet. Act ii, sc. 2, l. 419. [Polonius]
Bonds of law.—*Hamlet,* i, 2, 24.

13
How dangerous is it that this man goes loose!
Yet must not we put the strong law on him.
Hamlet. Act iv, sc. 3, l. 2. [King]
Angry law.—*Measure for Measure,* iii, 1, 208.
Just law.—*Measure for Measure,* ii, 4, 52.

14
Second Clown: The crowner hath sat on her, and finds it Christian burial. . . . But is this law?
First Clown: Ay, marry, is't; crowner's quest law.
Hamlet. Act v, sc. 1, l. 4.
Go thou and seek the crowner, and let him sit o' my coz.
Twelfth Night. Act i, sc. 5, l. 142. The only uses of "crowner" (coroner).

15
Hamlet: Is not parchment made of sheep-skins?
Horatio: Ay, my lord, and of calf-skins too.

Hamlet: They are sheep and calves which seek out assurance in that.
Hamlet. Act v, sc. 1, l. 123. The only use of "sheep-skins." "Calf-skins" occurs five times.

1
The rusty curb of old father antic the law.
I Henry IV. Act i, sc. 2, l. 68. [Falstaff]

2
The majesty and power of law and justice.
II Henry IV. Act v, sc. 2, l. 78. [Chief Justice]
See your most dreadful laws so loosely slighted.
II Henry IV. Act v, sc. 2, l. 94. [Chief Justice] "Loosely" is used again, in ii, 2, 9, and occurs in no other play.
The laws of England are at my commandment.
II Henry IV. Act v, sc. 3, l. 143. [Falstaff]
Contrary to the law.—*II Henry IV,* ii, 4, 373.

3 Justly and religiously unfold
Why the law Salique that they have in France
Or should, or should not, bar us in our claim.
Henry V. Act i, sc. 2, l. 10. [King Henry]
'In terram Salicam mulieres ne succedant:'
'No woman shall succeed in Salique land.'
Henry V. Act i, sc. 2, l. 38. [Canterbury]
All appear
To hold in right and title of the female: . . .
Howbeit they would hold up this Salique law
To bar your highness claiming from the female.
Henry V. Act i, sc. 2, l. 89. [Canterbury]
The Salique law.—*Henry V,* i, 2, 54.

4
Arrest them to the answer of the law;
And God acquit them of their practices!
Henry V. Act ii, sc. 2, l. 143. [King Henry]
King's laws.—*Henry V,* iv, 1, 180.
Public laws.—*Timon of Athens,* v, 4, 62.
Recorded law.—*Measure for Measure,* ii, 4, 61.

5
I 'll be no breaker of law.
I Henry VI. Act i, sc. 4, l. 80. [Gloucester] "Breaker" is repeated in *I Henry IV,* i, 2, 132: "Breaker of proverbs."
I am not partial to infringe our laws.
Comedy of Errors. Act i, sc. 1, l. 4. [Duke]
I am loath to break our country's laws.
Richard II. Act ii, sc. 3, l. 169. [York]
I stand here for law.—*The Merchant of Venice,* iv, 1, 142.
I crave the law.—*Merchant of Venice,* iv, 1, 206.
We are for law.—*Timon of Athens,* iii, 5, 86.

6
Faith, I have been a truant in the law,
And never yet could frame my will to it;
And therefore frame the law unto my will.
I Henry VI. Act ii, sc. 4, l. 7. [Suffolk]
Between two hawks, which flies the higher pitch;
Between two dogs, which hath the deeper mouth;
Between two blades, which bears the better temper;
Between two horses, which doth bear him best;
Between two girls, which hath the merriest eye;
I have perhaps some shallow spirit of judgement;
But in these nice sharp quillets of the law,
Good faith, I am no wiser than a daw.
I Henry VI. Act ii, sc. 4, l. 11. [Warwick] "Quillets" occurs six times in the plays.

7
Thy cruelty in execution
Upon offenders hath exceeded law
And left thee to the mercy of the law.
II Henry VI. Act i, sc. 3, l. 135. [Buckingham]
I lie open to the law.—*II Henry VI,* i, 3, 159.
Let him have all the rigour of the law.
II Henry VI. Act i, sc. 3, l. 199. [York]
The law, thou see'st, hath judged thee:
I cannot justify whom the law condemns.
II Henry VI. Act ii, sc. 3, l. 15. [Gloucester]
This is the law.—*II Henry VI,* i, 3, 214.

8
'Tis meet he be condemn'd by course of law.
II Henry VI. Act iii, sc. 1, l. 237. [Beaufort]
The duke cannot deny the course of law:
For the commodity that strangers have
With us in Venice, if it be denied,
Will much impeach the justice of his state.
The Merchant of Venice. Act iii, sc. 3, l. 26. [Antonio]
To trip the course of law.—*II Henry IV,* v, 2, 87.
Convict by course of law.—*Richard III,* i, 4, 192. The only use of "convict."
By order of law.—*King Lear,* i, 1, 19.
Form of law.—*II Henry VI,* iii, 1, 58; *Richard III,* iii, 5, 42.
Breach of law.—*II Henry VI,* ii, 4, 66.

9
Now art thou within point-blank of our jurisdiction regal.
II Henry VI. Act iv, sc. 7, l. 28. [Cade] "Point-blank" is repeated in *The Merry Wives of Windsor,* iii, 2, 34, and "jurisdiction" in *Henry VIII,* iii, 2, 312.

10
We must not rend our subjects from our laws,
And stick them in our will.
Henry VIII. Act i, sc. 2, l. 93. [King Henry]
If the trial of the law o'ertake ye,
You 'll part away disgraced.
Henry VIII. Act iii, sc. 1, l. 96. [Campeius]
Defeat the law.—*Henry VIII,* ii, 1, 14.

11 Not ever
The justice and truth o' the question carries
The due o' the verdict with it: at what ease
Might corrupt minds procure knaves as corrupt
To swear against you? such things have been done.
Henry VIII. Act v, sc. 1, l. 129. [King Henry]
But quickly on his side the verdict went.
A Lover's Complaint, l. 113.
By their verdict.—*Sonnets,* xlvi.
Given their verdict.—*Richard III,* i, 4, 189.
Giving my verdict.—*I Henry VI,* ii, 4, 48.
Is 't a verdict?—*Coriolanus,* i, 1, 11.
Bold verdict.—*I Henry VI,* iii, 1, 63. The only uses of "verdict."

12 When law can do no right,
Let it be lawful that law bar no wrong:
Law cannot give my child his kingdom here,

For he that holds his kingdom holds the law;
Therefore, since law itself is perfect wrong,
How can the law forbid my tongue to curse?
King John. Act iii, sc. 1, l. 185. [Constable]
Must I rob the law?—*King John*, iv, 3, 78.

1 The laws are mine, not thine:
Who can arraign me for 't?
King Lear. Act v, sc. 3, l. 158. [Goneril]
Will nothing stick our person to arraign.
Hamlet, iv, 5, 93. See under SLANDER.
Summon a session that we may arraign
Our most disloyal lady.
The Winter's Tale. Act ii, sc. 3, l. 202. [Leontes]
Arraign her first.—*King Lear*, iii, 6, 48.
I will arraign them straight.—*King Lear*, iii, 6, 22.
Arraign your conscience.—*Measure for Measure*, ii, 3, 21. The only uses of "arraign."

2
A dangerous law against gentility!
Love's Labour's Lost. Act i, sc. 1, l. 129. [Biron] "Gentility" occurs only once more in the plays, in *As You Like It*, i, 1, 22: "Mines my gentility."
So to the laws at large I write my name:
And he that breaks them in the least degree
Stands in attainder of eternal shame.
Love's Labour's Lost. Act i, sc. 1, l. 156. [Biron]
Attainder of his slanderous lip.—*Richard II*, iv, 1, 24.
Attainder of suspect.—*Richard III*, iii, 5, 32. The only uses of "attainder."

3
I keep her as a vessel of thy law's fury; and shall, at the least of thy sweet notice, bring her to trial.
Love's Labour's Lost. Act i, sc. 1, l. 277. [King] See also under TRIAL.

4 Your scope is as mine own,
So to enforce or qualify the laws
As to your soul seems good.
Measure for Measure. Act i, sc. 1, l. 65. [Duke]
Bidding the law make court'sy to their will.
Measure for Measure. Act ii, sc. 4, l. 175. [Isabella]

5 Use and liberty,
Which have for long run by the hideous law,
As mice by lions.
Measure for Measure. Act i, sc. 4, l. 62. [Lucio]
We must not make a scarecrow of the law,
Setting it up to fear the birds of prey,
And let it keep one shape, till custom make it
Their perch and not their terror.
Measure for Measure. Act ii, sc. 1, l. 1. [Angelo] "Scarecrow" occurs twice more in the plays, in *I Henry VI*, i, 4, 43, and in *I Henry IV*, iv, 2, 41.
Pull'd the law upon you.
Measure for Measure. Act ii, sc. 1, l. 16. [Escalus]
What know the laws
That thieves do pass on thieves?
Measure for Measure. Act ii, sc. 1, l. 22. [Angelo]
The law hath not been dead, though it hath slept.
Measure for Measure. Act ii, sc. 2, l. 90. [Angelo]
Laws for all faults,
But faults so countenanced, that the strong statutes
Stand like the forfeits in a barber's shop,
As much in mock as mark.
Measure for Measure. Act v, sc. 1, l. 321. [Duke] "Countenanced" is repeated in *II Henry IV*, v, 1, 35; 57.

6
If this law hold in Vienna ten year, I 'll rent the fairest house in it after three-pence a bay.
Measure for Measure. Act ii, sc. 1, l. 254. [Pompey]
O just but severe law!—*Measure for Measure*, ii, 2, 41.
Sore law.—*II Henry VI*, iv, 7, 7.
Stinking law.—*II Henry VI*, iv, 7, 13.

7
It is the law, not I condemn your brother.
Measure for Measure. Act ii, sc. 2, l. 80. [Angelo]
The manacles of the all-building law.
Measure for Measure. Act ii, sc. 4, l. 93. [Angelo] The only use of "all-building."
You seem'd of late to make the law a tyrant.
Measure for Measure. Act ii, sc. 4, l. 114. [Angelo]
Has he affections in him,
That thus can make him bite the law by the nose,
When he would force it?
Measure for Measure. Act iii, sc. 1, l. 108. [Claudio]
By order of law.—*Measure for Measure*, iii, 2, 8.
He hath offended the law.—*Measure for Measure*, iii, 2, 16.

8
In law, what plea so tainted and corrupt
But, being season'd with a gracious voice,
Obscures the show of evil?
The Merchant of Venice. Act iii, sc. 2, l. 75. [Bassanio]
And oft 'tis seen the wicked prize itself
Buys out the law.
Hamlet, iii, 3, 60. See under JUSTICE.

9
The law hath yet another hold on you.
The Merchant of Venice. Act iv, sc. 1, l. 347. [Portia]
Fie upon your law!—*The Merchant of Venice*, iv, 1, 101.
The law allows it.—*The Merchant of Venice*, iv, 1, 303.
Is that the law?—*The Merchant of Venice*, iv, 1, 314.

10
I will make a Star-chamber matter of it.
Merry Wives of Windsor. Act i, sc. 1, l. 1. [Shallow] The only use of "Star-chamber."

11 According to our law,
Immediately provided in that case.
A Midsummer-Night's Dream. Act i, sc. 1, l. 44. [Egeus]
According to our law.—*Richard II*, i, 3, 20.

1
I beg the law, the law, upon his head.
A Midsummer-Night's Dream. Act iv, sc. 1, l. 159. [Lysander]
Law of Athens.—*Midsummer-Night's Dream,* i, 1, 119.
Athenian law.—*A Midsummer-Night's Dream,* iv, 1, 158.
Sharp Athenian law.—*A Midsummer-Night's Dream,* i, 1, 162.
Mantua's law.—*Romeo and Juliet,* v, 1, 66.
Laws of Rome.—*Titus Andronicus,* i, 1, 407.
Laws of Venice.—*The Merchant of Venice,* iv, 1, 311; 348.
Venetian law.—*Merchant of Venice,* iv, 1, 178.
The world's law.—*Romeo and Juliet,* v, 1, 72.

2
The bloody book of law
You shall yourself read in the bitter letter.
Othello. Act i, sc. 3, l. 67. [Duke]

3
Thy state of law is bondslave to the law.
Richard II. Act ii, sc. 1, l. 114. [Gaunt] "Bondslave" is repeated in *Othello,* i, 2, 99, and in *Twelfth Night,* ii, 5, 209.
I challenge law.—*Richard II,* ii, 3, 134.
I know no law.—*Measure for Measure,* ii, 1, 43.

4
O good! convey? conveyers are you all,
That rise thus nimbly by a true king's fall.
Richard II. Act iv, sc. 1, l. 317. [King Richard] The only use of "conveyers."

5
Villain, thou know'st no law of God nor man.
Richard III. Act i, sc. 2, l. 70. [Lady Anne]
How canst thou urge God's dreadful law to us,
When thou hast broke it in so dear degree?
Richard III. Act i, sc. 4, l. 214. [Murderer]
Tables of his law.—*Richard III,* i, 4, 201.

6
Let us take the law of our sides.
Romeo and Juliet. Act i, sc. 1, l. 44. [Sampson]
Is the law of our side?
Romeo and Juliet. Act i, sc. 1, l. 54. [Sampson]
If I see . . . the law on my side.
Romeo and Juliet. Act ii, sc. 4, l. 169. [Peter] The only play in which this phrase is used.

7
Thy fault our law calls death; but the kind prince,
Taking thy part hath rush'd aside the law.
Romeo and Juliet. Act iii, sc. 3, l. 25. [Friar Laurence]
Ay, by my troth, the case may be amended.
Romeo and Juliet. Act iv, sc. 5, l. 101. [First Musician]

8
If aught in this
Miscarried by my fault, let my old life
Be sacrificed, some hour before his time,
Unto the rigour of severest law.
Romeo and Juliet. Act v, sc. 3, l. 266. [Friar Laurence]

9
Hostess: I must go fetch the third-borough.
Sly: Third, or fourth, or fifth borough, I'll answer him by law.
The Taming of the Shrew. Induction, sc. 1, l. 11. The only use of "third-borough" (constable).

10
The law shall bruise him.
Timon of Athens. Act iii, sc. 5, l. 4. [Senator]
The law hath ta'en revenge on them.
Titus Andronicus. Act iii, sc. 1, l. 117. [Titus]
For law is strict.—*Timon of Athens,* iii, 5, 85.
Civil laws are cruel.—*Timon of Athens,* iv, 3, 60.

11
If this law
Of nature be corrupted through affection,
And that great minds, of partial indulgence
To their benumbed wills, resist the same,
There is a law in each well-order'd nation
To curb those raging appetities that are
Most disobedient and refractory.
Troilus and Cressida. Act ii, sc. 2, l. 176. [Hector] The only use of "benumbed," "well-ordered," and "refractory."
These moral laws
Of nature and of nations speak aloud.
Troilus and Cressida. Act ii, sc. 2, l. 184. [Hector] The only use of "moral laws."
The law and process of great nature.
Winter's Tale. Act ii, sc. 2, l. 60. [Paulina]
Law of nature.—*II Henry IV,* iii, 2, 357; *Henry V,* ii, 4, 80; *All's Well that Ends Well,* iv, 5, 65; *Venus and Adonis,* l. 171.
Nature's law.—*Cymbeline,* v, 4, 38.
Human law.—*The Rape of Lucrece,* l. 571.
Martial law.—*Henry V,* iv, 8, 46.
Law of arms.—*I Henry VI,* iii, 4, 38; iv, 1, 100; *Henry V,* iv, 7, 2; *King Lear,* v, 3, 152.
Law of friendship.—*The Two Gentlemen of Verona,* iii, 1, 5.
Laws of war.—*Henry V,* iv, 1, 68; *Henry VIII,* i, 4, 52.

12
That keeps you from the blow of the law.
Twelfth Night. Act iii, sc. 4, l. 168. [Fabian]
Still you keep o' the windy side of the law.
Twelfth Night. Act iii, sc. 4, l. 181. [Fabian]
Let the law go whistle.
Winter's Tale. Act iv, sc. 4, l. 714. [Clown]
Opposing laws with strokes.—*Troilus and Cressida,* iii, 3, 79.

13
I'll have an action of battery against him, if there be any law in Illyria.
Twelfth Night. Act iv, sc. 1, l. 36. [Sir Andrew]
Elbow: Prove this, thou wicked Hannibal, or I'll have mine action of battery on thee.
Escalus: If he took you a box o' the ear, you might have your action of slander too.
Measure for Measure. Act ii, sc. 1, l. 186.
His action of battery.—*Hamlet,* v, 1, 111. The only uses of the phrase.

LAWYER

14
I will make
One of her women lawyer to me, for
I yet not understand the case myself.
Cymbeline. Act ii, sc. 3, l. 78. [Cloten]

15
Why may not that be the skull of a lawyer? Where be his quiddities now, his quillets, his cases, his tenures, and his tricks?
Hamlet. Act v, sc. 1, l. 106. [Hamlet]

"Quiddities" (quibbles) is repeated in *I Henry IV*, i, 2, 51: "Thy quips and thy quiddities." The only use of "tenures."

Crack the lawyer's voice,
That he may never more false title plead,
Nor sound his quillets shrilly.

Timon of Athens. Act iv, sc. 3, l. 153. [Timon] "Shrilly" is repeated in *Titus Andronicus,* ii, 3, 18: "Replying shrilly." For "quillets" see under CHEATING.

1
I was then advised by my learned counsel in the laws.

II Henry IV. Act i, sc. 2, l. 153. [Falstaff]

Good counsellors lack no clients.

Measure for Measure. Act i, sc. 2, l. 109. [Pompey]

You are a counsellor.—*Henry VIII,* v, 3, 49; *The Tempest,* i, 1, 23.

Noble counsellor.—*Pericles,* v, 1, 184. See under COUNSEL.

2
I could be well content
To be mine own attorney in this case.

I Henry VI. Act v, sc. 3, l. 165. [Suffolk]

And will have no attorney but myself.

The Comedy of Errors. Act v, sc. 1, l. 100. [Adriana]

Attorneys are denied me.

Richard II, ii, 3, 134. See under INHERITANCE.

Not changing heart with habit, I am still
Attorney'd at your service.

Measure for Measure. Act v, sc. 1, l. 389. [Duke]

Royally attorneyed.—*The Winter's Tale,* i, 1, 30. The only uses of "attorneyed."

I, by attorney, bless thee.—*Richard III,* v, 3, 83.

Die by attorney.—*As You Like It,* iv, 1, 94.

The king's attorney.—*Henry VIII,* ii, 1, 15.

Windy attorneys.—*Richard III,* iv, 4, 127. See under WORDS.

Attorney of my love.—*Richard III,* iv, 4, 413. The only uses of "attorney" and "attorneys."

3
Dick: The first thing we do, let 's kill all the lawyers.
Cade: Nay, that I mean to do. Is not this a lamentable thing, that of the skin of an innocent lamb should be made parchment? that parchment, being scribbled o'er, should undo a man? Some say the bee stings: but I say, 'tis the bee's wax; for I did but seal once to a thing, and I was never mine own man since.

II Henry VI. Act iv, sc. 2, l. 83. The only use of "bee's wax."

4
Lawyers . . . who straight dream on fees.

Romeo and Juliet. Act i, sc. 4, l. 73. [Mercutio]

'Tis like the breath of an unfee'd lawyer; you gave me nothing for 't.

King Lear. Act i, sc. 4, l. 142. [Fool] The only use of "unfee'd."

5
One that knows the law.

Much Ado about Nothing. Act iv, sc. 2, l. 86. [Dogberry]

6
Do as adversaries do in law,
Strive mightily, but eat and drink as friends.

The Taming of the Shrew. Act i, sc. 2, l. 278. [Tranio]

7
Autolycus: What advocate hast thou to him?
Shepherd: I know not, an 't like you.
Clown: Advocate 's the court-word for a pheasant: say you have none.
Shepherd: None, sir; I have no pheasant, cock nor hen.

The Winter's Tale. Act iv, sc. 4, l. 765.

I 'll undertake to be
Her advocate to the loud'st.

Winter's Tale. Act ii, sc. 2, l. 38. [Paulina]

I will be known your advocate.

Cymbeline. Act i, sc. 1, l. 76. [Queen]

Advocate for thee.—*The Comedy of Errors,* i, 1, 146.

An earnest advocate to plead for him.

Richard III. Act i, sc. 3, l. 87. [Queen Elizabeth]

Thy adverse party is thy advocate—
And 'gainst myself a lawful plea commence.

Sonnets. No. xxxv.

What! An advocate for an impostor! hush!

The Tempest. Act i, sc. 2, l. 477. [Prospero]

Step forth mine advocate.—*The Winter's Tale,* v, 1, 221. The only uses of "advocate."

LEAD

8
Love, I am full of lead.

Antony and Cleopatra. Act iii, sc. 11, l. 72. [Antony]

A brooch of lead.—*Love's Labour 's Lost,* v, 2, 621.

Feather of lead.—*Romeo and Juliet,* i, 1, 186.

Fins of lead.—*Coriolanus,* i, 1, 184.

Soul of lead.—*Romeo and Juliet,* i, 4, 15.

9
To melt the city leads upon your pates.

Coriolanus. Act iv, sc. 6, l. 82. [Cominius]

Leads fill'd.—*Coriolanus,* ii, 1, 227.

Go, go; up to the leads.—*Richard III,* iii, 7, 55.

10
The loss of those great towns will make him burst his lead and rise from death.

I Henry VI. Act i, sc. 1, l. 63. [Bedford]

Lapp'd in lead.—*Passionate Pilgrim,* l. 396.

11
Armado: The way is but short; away!
Moth: As swift as lead, sir.
Armado: The meaning, pretty ingenious?
Is not lead a metal heavy, dull, and slow?
Moth: Minimè, honest master; or rather, master, no.
Armado: I say lead is slow.
Moth: You are too swift to say so:
Is that lead slow which is fired from a gun?

Love's Labour 's Lost. Act iii, sc. 1, l. 57. The only use of "minimè" (not at all).

12
What says this leaden casket?
'Who chooseth me must give and hazard all he hath.'
Must give: for what? for lead? hazard for lead? . . .

I 'll then nor give nor hazard aught for lead. . . .
Is 't like that lead contains her? 'Twere damnation
To think so base a thought: it were too gross
To rib her cerecloth in the obscure grave.
Or shall I think in silver she 's immured,
Being ten times undervalued to tried gold?
O sinful thought! Never so rich a gem
Was set in worse than gold.
The Merchant of Venice. Act ii, sc. 7, l. 15. The only use of "cerecloth."

Thou meagre lead,
Which rather threatenest than dost promise aught,
Thy paleness moves me more than eloquence;
And here choose I: joy be the consequence!
The Merchant of Venice. Act iii, sc. 2, l. 104. [Bassanio]

Base lead.—*The Merchant of Venice,* ii, 9, 20.
Dull lead.—*The Merchant of Venice,* ii, 7, 8.
Dull and heavy lead.—*II Henry IV,* i, 1, 118.
Meagre lead.—*Merchant of Venice,* iii, 2, 104.
Molten lead.—*I Henry IV,* v, 3, 34; *King Lear,* iv, 7, 48.

1
I had as lief bear so much lead.
The Merry Wives of Windsor. Act iv, sc. 2, l. 118. [Servant]
Lies like lead.—*Macbeth,* ii, 1, 6.
Heavy and pale as lead.—*Romeo and Juliet,* ii, 5, 17.

2
If he be leaden, . . . be thou so too.
Richard III, iii, 1, 176. See under COLDNESS. "Leaden" is repeated sixteen times, always in the other instances directly modifying a noun.

3
Let us be lead within thy bosom, Richard,
And weigh thee down to ruin, shame, and death!
Richard III. Act v, sc. 3, l. 152. [Ghosts]

4
Mine eyes are turn'd to fire, my heart to lead:
Heavy heart's lead, melt at mine eyes' red fire!
So shall I die by drops of hot desire.
Venus and Adonis, l. 1072.

LEADER

5
They have a leader . . . that will put you to 't.
Coriolanus. Act i, sc. 1, l. 232. [Marcius]

6
Our guider, come; to the Roman camp conduct us.
Coriolanus. Act i, sc. 7, l. 7. [Lartius] The only use of "guider."

Became his guide,
Led him, begg'd for him, saved him from despair.
King Lear. Act v, sc. 3, l. 190. [Edgar]
Be your guide.—*Measure for Measure,* iv, 2, 181.
A guide, a goddess.—*All's Well that Ends Well,* i, 1, 183.
My stay, my guide.—*II Henry VI,* ii, 3, 25.
Former guides.—*Antony and Cleopatra,* iii, 13, 145.
Safer guides.—*Othello,* ii, 3, 205.
Unsavoury guide!—*Romeo and Juliet,* v, 3, 116.

7
What well-appointed leader fronts us here?
II Henry IV. Act iv, sc. 1, l. 25. [Archbishop of York] "Well-appointed" is used five times in the plays.
A most gallant leader.
II Henry IV. Act iii, sc. 2, l. 68. [Bardolph]
A knight, a captain and a leader.
I Henry VI. Act iv, sc. 1, l. 32. [Gloucester]
True leaders.—*Venus and Adonis,* l. 503.
Worthy leader.—*I Henry VI,* i, 1, 143.
Men of leading.—*I Henry IV,* iv, 3, 17.

8
The ringleader and head of all this rout.
II Henry VI. Act ii, sc. 1, l. 170. [Buckingham] The only use of "ringleader."

9
Who did guide,
I mean, who set the body and the limbs
Of this great sport together, as you guess?
Henry VIII. Act i, sc. 1, l. 45. [Buckingham]
The prime man of the state.
Henry VIII. Act iii, sc. 2, l. 162. [King Henry]
Conductor of his people.
King Lear. Act iv, sc. 7, l. 88. [Gentleman] The only use of "conductor."

10
Thou marshall'st me the way that I was going.
Macbeth. Act ii, sc. 1, l. 42. [Macbeth]

11
You were wont to be a follower, but now you are a leader.
The Merry Wives of Windsor. Act iii, sc. 2, l. 2. [Mrs. Page]
We must follow the leaders.
Much Ado about Nothing. Act ii, sc. 1, l. 157. [Beatrice]

12
The sinew and the forehand of our host.
Troilus and Cressida. Act i, sc. 3, l. 143. [Ulysses] "Forehand" is used four times.
Which is that god in office, guiding men?
Troilus and Cressida. Act i, sc. 3, l. 231. [Æneas]
He is their god: he leads them like a thing
Made by some other deity than nature,
That shapes man better; and they follow him,
Against us brats, with no less confidence
Than boys pursuing summer butterflies,
Or butchers killing flies.
Coriolanus. Act iv, sc. 6, l. 90. [Cominius]

II—Leading

13
Westmoreland: Come, my lord, I 'll lead you to your tent.
Prince: Lead me, my lord? I do not need your help.
I Henry IV. Act v, sc. 4, l. 9.
I 'll lead you to some biding.—*King Lear,* iv, 6, 228.
Lead him to my bower.—*Midsummer-Night's Dream,* iii, 1, 202.
Lead me to my chamber.—*Antony and Cleopatra,* ii, 5, 119.

1
We will our youth lead on to higher fields.
II Henry IV. Act iv, sc. 4, l. 3. [King]
Please it your grace lead on?
Much Ado about Nothing. Act i, sc. 1, l. 160. [Leonato]
Lead on, o' God's name.
Henry VIII. Act ii, sc. 1, l. 78. [Buckingham]
Lead them on.—*All's Well that Ends Well,* ii, 4, 17.

2
My lord, most humbly on my knee I beg
The leading of the vaward.
Henry V. Act iv, sc. 3, l. 129. [York] "Vaward" (vanguard) is repeated in *II Henry IV,* i, 2, 199; *I Henry VI,* i, 1, 132; *Coriolanus,* i, 6, 53; and *A Midsummer-Night's Dream,* iv, 1, 110.
Lead the way.—*II Henry VI,* ii, 4, 110, and six times in later plays.

3
Then lead me hence; with whom I leave my my curse.
I Henry VI. Act v, sc. 4, l. 86. [La Pucelle]
Lead him hence.—*II Henry IV,* iv, 3, 81.
Lead me from hence.—*Antony and Cleopatra,* ii, 5, 109.
Lead us from hence.—*Winter's Tale,* v, 3, 152.
Lead him off.—*Othello,* ii, 3, 254.
Lead off this ground.—*The Tempest,* ii, 1, 323.
We'll lead you thither.—*As You Like It,* iv, 3, 162.
He leads himself.—*King Lear,* ii, 4, 301.

4
Didst thou not lead him through the glimmering night?
A Midsummer-Night's Dream. Act ii, sc. 1, l. 77. [Oberon]
Up and down, up and down,
I will lead them up and down:
I am fear'd in field and town:
Goblin, lead them up and down.
A Midsummer-Night's Dream. Act iii, sc. 2, l. 396. [Puck]
I'll lead you about a round.—*A Midsummer-Night's Dream,* iii, 1, 109.
Lead you even to death.—*Romeo and Juliet,* v, 3, 220.

5
The smallest twine may lead me.
Much Ado about Nothing. Act iv, sc. 1, l. 252. [Leonato] The only use of "twine" as a noun. As a verb, it is repeated in *Coriolanus,* iv, 5, 112, and in *Venus and Adonis,* l. 873.

6
I will lead forth my soldiers to the plain.
Richard III. Act v, sc. 3, l. 291. [King Richard]
Lead forth.—*Measure for Measure,* i, 1, 75.
Lead him forth.—*I Henry IV,* ii, 3, 75.

7
How many gazers mightst thou lead away,
If thou wouldst use the strength of all thy state!
Sonnets. No. xcvi.

8
Nor lead me, like a firebrand, in the dark
Out of my way.
The Tempest. Act ii, sc. 2, l. 6. [Caliban]

LEAGUE

See also Alliance

9
Keep then fair league and truce with thy true bed.
The Comedy of Errors. Act ii, sc. 2, l. 147. [Adriana]
Blessed league.—*The Rape of Lucrece,* l. 383.
Fair-faced league.—*King John,* ii, 1, 417. "Fair-faced" is used once again in *Much Ado about Nothing,* iii, 1, 61.
Incorporate league.—*Henry V,* v, 2, 394.
Some league inviolable.—*III Henry VI,* ii, 1, 30.
League of amity.—*III Henry VI,* iii, 3, 53.
League and amity.—*Richard III,* i, 3, 281.

10 Now he has crack'd the league
Between us and the emperor.
Henry VIII. Act ii, sc. 2, l. 25. [Norfolk]
Flaw'd the league.—*Henry VIII,* i, 1, 95.
Conclude . . . A league.—*Henry VIII,* iii, 2, 323.
O, make a league with me!—*King John,* iv, 2, 126.
Vows a league.—*The Rape of Lucrece,* l. 287.

11 This league that we have made
Will give her sadness very little cure.
King John. Act ii, sc. 1, l. 545. [King Philip]
This royal hand and mine are newly knit,
And the conjunction of our inward souls
Married in league, coupled and link'd together
With all religious strength of sacred vows;
The latest breath that gave the sound of words
Was deep-sworn faith, peace, amity, true love.
King John. Act iii, sc. 1, l. 226. [King Philip] The only use of "deep-sworn."

12
There is such a league between my good man and he!
The Merry Wives of Windsor. Act iii, sc. 2, l. 25. [Mrs. Page]
League whose date till death shall never end.
A Midsummer-Night's Dream. Act iii, sc. 2, l. 373. [Oberon]
I Will keep a league till death.
Richard II, v, 1, 22. See under NECESSITY.

13
This forced league doth force a further strife.
The Rape of Lucrece, l. 689.
Shameful is this league!—*II Henry VI,* i, 1, 98.
Inglorious league!—*King John,* v, 1, 65.

14
You peers, continue this united league.
Richard III. Act ii, sc. 1, l. 2. [King Edward]
Seal thou this league
With thy embracements to my wife's allies.
Richard III. Act ii, sc. 1, l. 29. [King Edward]

15
They . . . Bore us some leagues to sea.
The Tempest. Act i, sc. 2, l. 145. [Prospero]
A league below the city.—*Measure for Measure,* iv, 3, 103.
A league from Epidamnum.—*The Comedy of Errors,* i, 1, 63.
A league without the town.—*A Midsummer-Night's Dream,* i, 1, 165.
Swim a league.—*A Midsummer-Night's Dream,* ii, 1, 174.

He was not three leagues off when I left him.
Much Ado about Nothing. Act i, sc. 1, l. 4. [Messenger]
Three leagues.—*The Two Gentlemen of Verona,* v, 1, 11.
He lies to-night within seven leagues of Rome.
Julius Cæsar. Act iii, sc. 1, l. 286. [Servant]
Seven leagues.—*A Midsummer-Night's Dream,* i, 1, 159.
Twice five leagues.—*The Comedy of Errors,* i, 1, 101.
Ten leagues.—*The Tempest,* ii, 1, 247.
Twelve leagues.—*Henry V,* iii, 2, 46.
Five and thirty leagues.—*The Tempest,* iii, 2, 17.
Thousand leagues.—*I Henry IV,* iii, 1, 227.
Longest leagues make short.—*Pericles,* iv, 4, 1.

1
When we join in league,
I am a lamb: but if you brave the Moor,
The chafed boar, the mountain lioness,
The ocean swells not so as Aaron storms.
Titus Andronicus. Act iv, sc. 2, l. 136. [Aaron]
Deeply still in league.—*Titus Andronicus,* iv, 1, 98.

LEANNESS, see THINNESS

LEARNING

See also Knowledge, Scholar, Wisdom

2
Learn of the wise, and perpend.
As You Like It. Act iii, sc. 2, l. 69. [Touchstone] "Perpend" (consider) is used five times.
I shall be glad to learn of noble men.
Julius Cæsar. Act iv, sc. 3, l. 54. [Brutus]

3
The burden of lean and wasteful learning.
As You Like It. Act iii, sc. 2, l. 341. [Rosalind]

4
Art thou learned? . . . Then learn this of me.
As You Like It. Act v, sc. 1, l. 42. [Touchstone]
It shall do you no harm to learn.
All's Well that Ends Well. Act ii, sc. 2, l. 39. [Clown]
I'll gladly learn.—*Measure for Measure,* ii, 3, 23.
I do desire to learn.—*Measure for Measure,* iv, 2, 59.
I am too old to learn.—*King Lear,* ii, 2, 134.

5
Puts to him all the learnings that his time
Could make him the receiver of; which he took,
As we do air, fast as 'twas minister'd.
Cymbeline. Act i, sc. 1, l. 43. [Gentleman]
Those twins of learning that he raised in you,
Ipswich and Oxford!
Henry VIII. Act iv, sc. 2, l. 58. [Griffith]
Course of learning.—*The Taming of the Shrew,* i, 1, 9.

6
Whose learning and good letters peace hath tutor'd.
II Henry IV. Act iv, sc. 1, l. 44. [Westmoreland]
Learning a mere hoard of gold kept by the devil.
II Henry IV, iv, 3, 124. See under SACK.

7
The even mead, that erst brought sweetly forth
The freckled cowslip, burnet and green clover,
Wanting the scythe, all uncorrected, rank,
Conceives by idleness and nothing teems
But hateful docks, rough thistles, kecksies, burs,
Losing both beauty and utility.
And as our vineyards, fallows, meads and hedges,
Defective in their natures, grow to wildness,
Even so our houses and ourselves and children
Have lost, or do not learn for want of time,
The sciences that should become our country.
Henry V. Act v, sc. 2, l. 48. [Burgundy] The only use of "burnet," "uncorrected," "kecksies," and "utility." "Docks" is repeated in *The Tempest,* ii, 1, 144.

8
The gentleman is learn'd, and a most rare speaker;
To nature none more bound.
Henry VIII. Act i, sc. 2, l. 111. [King Henry]
Very learned.—*Love's Labour's Lost,* iv, 2, 106.
Well learned.—*Love's Labour's Lost,* iv, 2, 116.
Learned without opinion.—*Love's Labour's Lost,* v, 1, 5.
Learn'd and valiant.—*Twelfth Night,* i, 5, 279.
So learned and so wise.—*Measure for Measure,* v, 1, 475.
Never schooled and yet learned.—*As You Like It,* i, 1, 173.
Learned it without book.—*Romeo and Juliet,* i, 2, 61.

9
Much He spoke, and learnedly.
Henry VIII. Act ii, sc. 1, l. 27. [Gentleman]
Learnedly delivered.—*The Tempest,* ii, 1, 44.
Learnedly handle.—*The Winter's Tale,* iv, 4, 207. The only uses of "learnedly."

10
I'll talk a word with this same learned Theban.
King Lear. Act iii, sc. 4, l. 162. [King Lear] The only use of "Theban." Thebes is mentioned in *A Midsummer-Night's Dream,* v, 1, 51.
Learned clerks.—*II Henry VI,* iv, 7, 76.
Learned council.—*II Henry VI,* i, 1, 89.
Learned counsel.—*II Henry IV,* i, 2, 152.
Learned doctor.—*The Merchant of Venice,* iv, 1, 105; *All's Well that Ends Well,* ii, 1, 119.
Learned fool.—*Love's Labour's Lost,* v, 2, 72.
Learned judge.—*The Merchant of Venice,* iv, 1, 308; 317.
Learned man.—*Henry VIII,* ii, 2, 124; iii, 2, 395.
Learned pate.—*Timon of Athens,* iv, 3, 17.
Learned priest.—*Henry VIII,* ii, 2, 97.

1
Learn . . . by heart.
Love's Labour's Lost. Act iii, sc. 1, l. 36. [Moth]

2
For as it would ill become me to be vain, indiscreet, or a fool,
So were there a patch set on learning, to see him in a school.
Love's Labour's Lost. Act iv, sc. 2, l. 31. [Sir Nathaniel]

You hear his learning.—*Love's Labour's Lost,* v, 1, 54.

3
Learning is but an adjunct to ourself
And where we are our learning likewise is:
Then when ourselves we see in ladies' eyes,
Do we not likewise see our learning there?
Love's Labour's Lost. Act iv, sc. 3, l. 314. [Biron] "Adjunct" occurs only once more in the plays, in *King John,* iii, 2, 57.

4
Monsieur, are you not lettered?
Love's Labour's Lost. Act v, sc. 1, l. 47. [Armado] The only use of "lettered."

5 The nature of our people,
Our city's institutions, and the terms
For common justice, you 're as pregnant in
As art and practice hath enriched any
That we remember.
Measure for Measure. Act i, sc. 1, l. 10. [Duke] The only use of "institutions."

His own learning, the greatness whereof I cannot enough commend.
The Merchant of Venice. Act iv, sc. 1, l. 158. [Clerk, reading]

6
The thrice three Muses mourning for the death
Of Learning, late deceased in beggary.
A Midsummer-Night's Dream. Act v, sc. 1, l. 52. [Theseus, reading]

7
O, what learning is!
Romeo and Juliet. Act iii, sc. 3, l. 160. [Nurse]

O this learning, what a thing it is!
The Taming of the Shrew. Act i, sc. 2, l. 160. [Gremio]

I must to the learned.
Romeo and Juliet. Act i, sc. 2, l. 45. [Servant]

8
The vacant leaves thy mind's imprint will bear,
And of this book this learning mayst thou taste.
Sonnets. No. lxxvii.

LECHERY

See also Lewdness; Love and Lust; Lust; Wantonness

9
I am rough and lecherous.
King Lear. Act i, sc. 2, l. 142. [Edmund] See under DESTINY.

Lecherous as a monkey.—*II Henry IV,* iii, 2, 338. See under CHARACTER.

Remorseless, treacherous, lecherous.—*Hamlet,* ii, 2, 609.

Sparrows must not build in his house-eaves because they are lecherous.
Measure for Measure. Act iii, sc. 2, l. 185. [Lucio] The only uses of "house-eaves" and "lecherous."

10
Lucio: What 's thy offence, Claudio? . . . Lechery?
Claudio: Call it so. . . .
Lucio: Is lechery so look'd after?
Claudio: Thus stands it with me: upon a true contract
I got possession of Julietta's bed.
Measure for Measure. Act i, sc. 2. l. 139.

11
Lucio: A little more levity to lechery would do no harm to him: something too crabbed that way, friar.
Duke: It is too general a vice, and severity must cure it.
Lucio: Yes, in good sooth, the vice is of a general kindred; it is well allied: but it is impossible to extirp it quite, friar, till eating and drinking be put down.
Measure for Measure. Act iii, sc. 2, l. 103. The only use of "extirp." "Extirpate" occurs in *The Tempest,* i, 2, 125: "Extirpate me and mine."

12
I will now take the lecher; he is at my house.
The Merry Wives of Windsor. Act iii, sc. 5, l. 146. [Ford]

Like a lecher, out of whorish loins.
Troilus and Cressida, iv, 1, 63. The only use of "whorish." See under COMPARISON.

Murderous lechers.—*King Lear,* iv, 6, 282.

Old lecher.—*King Lear,* iii, 4, 117.

Lecher in my sight.—*King Lear,* iv, 6, 115. The only uses of "lecher."

13
We have here recovered the most dangerous piece of lechery that ever was known in the commonwealth.
Much Ado about Nothing. Act iii, sc. 3, l. 179. [Second Watch]

Lechery, by this hand; an index and obscure prologue to the history of lust and foul thoughts.
Othello. Act ii, sc. 1, l. 263. [Iago]

14
Nothing but lechery! all incontinent varlets!
Troilus and Cressida. Act v, sc. 1, l. 106. [Thersites]

The parrot will not do more for an almond than he for a commodious drab. Lechery, lechery; still, wars and lechery; nothing else holds fashion.
Troilus and Cressida. Act v, sc. 2, l. 194. [Thersites] The only use of "almond" and "commodious."

War and lechery.—*Troilus and Cressida,* ii, 3, 81.

In a sort, lechery eats itself.
Troilus and Cressida. Act v, sc. 4, l. 37. [Thersites]

Fry, lechery, fry!—*Troilus and Cressida,* v, 2, 57.

Lechery! I defy lechery.—*Twelfth Night,* i, 5, 133.

LECTURE

1
I have heard him read many lectures.
As You Like It. Act iii, sc. 2, l. 365. [Rosalind]
Say we read lectures to you.
Coriolanus. Act ii, sc. 3, l. 243. [Brutus]
See you read no other lectures to her.
The Taming of the Shrew. Act i, sc. 2, l. 148. [Gremio]
Read a lecture.—*Richard II,* iv, 1, 232.
Former lecture.—*Hamlet,* ii, 1, 67.
2
And when in music we have spent an hour,
Your lecture shall have leisure for as much.
The Taming of the Shrew. Act iii, sc. 1, l. 7. [Hortensio]
Bianca: His lecture will be done ere you have tuned.
Hortensio: You 'll leave his lecture when I am in tune?
The Taming of the Shrew. Act iii, sc. 1, l. 24. The only uses of "lecture."

LEG

See also Limb

3
His legs bestrid the ocean: his rear'd arm
Crested the world.
Antony and Cleopatra. Act v, sc. 2, l. 82. [Cleopatra] See under MAN: GREAT MEN. The only use of "crested."
4
Your legs are young.
Cymbeline. Act iii, sc. 3, l. 11. [Belarius]
I know the shape of 's leg.
Cymbeline. Act iv, sc. 2, l. 309. [Imogen]
5
A leg of Rome shall not return to tell
What crows have peck'd them here.
Cymbeline. Act v, sc. 3, l. 93. [Second Captain] The only use of "peck'd."
English legs.—*Henry V,* iii, 6, 158.
Capon's leg.—*I Henry IV,* i, 2, 129; *The Two Gentlemen of Verona,* iv, 4, 10.
Left legs.—*The Taming of the Shrew,* iv, 1, 95. There is no reference to right legs.
Maids' legs.—*Hamlet,* iii, 2, 126.
Spinners' legs.—*Romeo and Juliet,* i, 4, 59.
6
We 'll walk afoot awhile, and ease our legs.
I Henry IV. Act ii, sc. 2, l. 84. [Traveller]
He had no legs that practised not his gait.
II Henry IV. Act ii, sc. 3, l. 23. [Lady Percy]
7
I would fain see the man, that has but two legs.
Henry V. Act iv, sc. 7, l. 169. [Fluellen]
Went on four legs.—*Tempest,* ii, 2, 63; 68; 93.
8
We must have you find your legs.
II Henry VI. Act ii, sc. 1, l. 148. [Gloucester]
Throws away his crutch
Before his legs be firm to bear his body.
II Henry VI. Act iii, sc. 1, l. 189. [Gloucester]
9
When you and I met at Saint Alban's last,
Your legs did better service than your hands.
III Henry VI. Act ii, sc. 2, l. 103. [Queen Margaret]
If my tongue cannot entreat you to acquit me, will you command me to use my legs?
II Henry IV. Epilogue, l. 18. [Dancer]
Your hands than mine are quicker for a fray,
My legs are longer though, to run away.
A Midsummer-Night's Dream. Act iii, sc. 2, l. 342. [Helena] "Quicker" occurs only once more, in *Sonnets,* xl.
Use your legs, take the start, run away.
The Merchant of Venice. Act ii, sc. 2, l. 5. [Launcelot]
Every man betake him to his legs.
Romeo and Juliet. Act i, sc. 4, l. 34. [Benvolio] See under DISCRETION.
10
Shape my legs of an unequal size.
III Henry VI. Act iii, sc. 1, l. 159. [Gloucester]
Their legs are both of a bigness.
II Henry IV. Act ii, sc. 4, l. 266. [Falstaff] The only use of "bigness."
King: I think Hector was not so clean-timbered.
Longaville: His leg is too big for Hector's.
Dumain: More calf, certain.
Love's Labour 's Lost. Act v, sc. 2, l. 642. The only use of "clean-timbered" and of "calf" in this sense.
Legged like a man!—*The Tempest,* ii, 2, 36. The only use of "legged."
11
They have all new legs, and lame ones.
Henry VIII. Act i, sc. 3, l. 11. [Lord Sands]
My legs, like loaden branches, bow to earth,
Willing to leave their burthen.
Henry VIII. Act iv, sc. 2, l. 2. [Katharine]
12
Horses are tied by the heads, dogs and bears by the neck, monkeys by the loins, and men by the legs: when a man's over-lusty at legs, then he wears wooden nether-stocks.
King Lear. Act ii, sc. 4, l. 7. [Fool] "Over-lusty" occurs again in *Henry V,* iv, Prol., 18; and "nether-stocks" in *I Henry IV,* ii, 4, 130.
How is 't? Feel you your legs?
King Lear. Act iv, sc. 6, l. 65. [Edgar]
13
My legs can keep no pace with my desires.
A Midsummer-Night's Dream. Act iii, sc. 2, l. 445. [Hermia]
Leaden legs.—*A Midsummer-Night's Dream,* iii, 2, 365.
Weary legs.—*Venus and Adonis,* l. 705.
14
And would in glorious action I had lost
Those legs that brought me to a part of it!
Othello. Act ii, sc. 3, l. 186. [Iago]
My leg is cut in two.—*Othello,* v, 1, 72.
Lost his leg.—*Twelfth Night,* v, 1, 66.
15
Laid his leg
Over my thigh, and sigh'd, and kiss'd.
Othello. Act iii, sc. 3, l. 423. [Iago]
Straight leg and quivering thigh,
And the demesnes that there adjacent lie.
Romeo and Juliet. Act ii, sc. 1, l. 19. [Mercutio] See under CHARM.
Straight legs.—*Venus and Adonis,* l. 297.
Legs and thighs.—*Twelfth Night,* i, 3, 149.

1
'Tis the better for you that your resorters stand upon sound legs.
Pericles. Act iv, sc. 6, l. 26. [Lysimachus] The only use of "resorters."
2
Why have those banish'd and forbidden legs
Dared once to touch a dust of England's ground?
Richard II. Act ii, sc. 3, l. 90. [York]
Bad legs.—*Much Ado about Nothing,* ii, 1, 81.
Black legs.—*Titus Andronicus,* iv, 2, 102.
Craven's leg.—*I Henry VI,* iv, 1, 15.
3
I came hither on my legs.
Richard III. Act i, sc. 4, l. 87. [Murderer]
4
Though his face be better than any man's, yet his leg excels all men's.
Romeo and Juliet. Act ii, sc. 5, l. 40. [Nurse]
His leg is but so so; and yet 'tis well.
As You Like It. Act iii, sc. 5, l. 119. [Phebe]
She did praise my leg.—*Twelfth Night,* ii, 5, 182.
5
I 'll pull thee by the lesser legs.
The Tempest. Act ii, sc. 2, l. 107. [Stephano]
A decreasing leg.—*II Henry IV,* i, 2, 205.
6
I doubt whether their legs be worth the sums
That are given for 'em.
Timon of Athens. Act i, sc. 2, l. 238. [Apemantus]
7
The elephant hath joints, but none for courtesy: his legs are legs for necessity, not for flexure.
Troilus and Cressida. Act ii, sc. 3, l. 113. [Ulysses]
Make this leg.—*King John,* i, 1, 240.
8
Sir Toby: I did think, by the excellent constitution of thy leg, it was formed under the star of a galliard.
Sir Andrew: Ay, 'tis strong, and it does indifferent well in a flame-coloured stock.
Twelfth Night. Act i, sc. 3, l. 141. "Constitution" is repeated in *The Merchant of Venice,* iii, 2, 249, and "flame-coloured" in *I Henry IV,* i, 2, 11: "Flame-coloured taffeta." "Galliard" (a quick and lively dance) is used four times. See under DANCE.
I had rather than forty shillings I had such a leg.
Twelfth Night. Act ii, sc. 3, l. 20. [Sir Andrew]
Huge legs.—*Julius Cæsar,* i, 2, 137.
Sound legs.—*Timon of Athens,* i, 2, 240.
9
Sir Toby: Taste your legs, sir; put them to motion.
Viola: My legs do better understand me, sir, than I understand what you mean by bidding me taste my legs.
Sir Toby: I mean, to go, sir, to enter.
Twelfth Night. Act iii, sc. 1, l. 87.
10
Proteus: And yet she takes exceptions at your person.
Thurio: What, that my leg is too long?
Proteus: No; that it is too little.
Thurio: I 'll wear a boot, to make it somewhat rounder.
The Two Gentlemen of Verona. Act v, sc. 2, l. 3. The only use of "rounder."
11
Stands on his hinder legs with listening ear.
Venus and Adonis, l. 698. The only use of "hinder" in this sense.

LEGACY, see Inheritance

LEISURE

See also Ease

12
I would not, in plain terms, from this time forth,
Have you so slander any moment leisure,
As to give words or talk with the Lord Hamlet.
Hamlet. Act i, sc. 3, l. 132. [Polonius]
13
No leisure had he to enrank his man.
I Henry VI. Act i, sc. 1, l. 115. [Messenger] The only use of "enrank."
Leisure to be sick.—*I Henry IV,* iv, 1, 17.
Leisure to make love.—*The Taming of the Shrew,* i, 2, 136.
Leisure to repent.—*Richard III,* iv, 4, 293.
14
I will attend upon your lordship's leisure.
I Henry VI. Act v, sc. 1, l. 55. [Legate]
I shall attend your leisure.
Measure for Measure. Act iv, sc. 1, l. 57. [Duke]
We 'll make our leisures to attend on yours.
The Merchant of Venice. Act i, sc. 1, l. 68. [Salarino]
Attend his leisure.—*Macbeth,* iii, 2, 3.
Attend The leisure.—*King Lear,* ii, 4, 37.
We will stay your leisure.
I Henry IV. Act i, sc. 3, l. 258. [Worcester]
We stay upon your leisure.
Macbeth. Act i, sc. 3, l. 148. [Banquo]
I thank you, and will stay upon your leisure.
All's Well that Ends Well. Act iii, sc. 5, l. 48. [Helena]
He shall stay my leisure.
The Taming of the Shrew. Act iii, sc. 2, l. 219. [Katharina]
Stays thy leisure.—*The Taming of the Shrew,* iv, 3, 59.
15
Are you not at leisure?
I Henry VI. Act v, sc. 3, l. 97. [Margaret]
Not at leisure.—*I Henry VI,* ii, 3, 26.
16
Duke: Might you dispense with your leisure, I would by and by have some speech with you.
Isabella: I have no superfluous leisure.
Measure for Measure. Act iii, sc. 1, l. 154.
Good leisure.—*Measure for Measure,* iii, 2, 261.
Sovereign leisure.—*Antony and Cleopatra,* i, 3, 60.
Spiritual leisure.—*Henry VIII,* iii, 2, 140.
17
I am sorry that your leisure serves you not.
The Merchant of Venice, iv, 1, 405.

If your leisure served, I would speak with you.
Much Ado about Nothing, iii, 2, 84.
Juliet: Are you at leisure, holy father, now?
Friar Laurence: My leisure serves me, pensive daughter, now.
Romeo and Juliet. Act iv, sc. 1, l. 37.
Leisure answers Leisure.—*Measure for Measure,* v, 1, 415.

1
Come to me at your convenient leisure.
The Merry Wives of Windsor. Act iii, sc. 5, l. 137. [Falstaff]
At your leisure.—*The Merchant of Venice,* v, 1, 267.
At your best leisure.—*Julius Cæsar,* iii, 1, 5.
At your kind'st leisure.—*Macbeth,* ii, 1, 24.
At more leisure.—*The Comedy of Errors,* iv, 1, 100; *Taming of the Shrew,* iii, 2, 110; *II Henry IV,* iv, 4, 89; *Hamlet,* v, 2, 26.
At our more leisure.—*Measure for Measure,* i, 3, 49.
At their leisure.—*All 's Well that Ends Well,* i, 2, 75.
At pick'd leisure.—*The Tempest,* v, 1, 247.

2
Wait for no man's leisure.
Much Ado about Nothing, i, 3, 17. See under CANDOR.

3
Expedient manage must be made, my liege,
Ere further leisure yield them further means
For their advantage and your highness' loss.
Richard II. Act i, sc. 4, l. 39. [Green]
The leisure and the fearful time.—*Richard III,* v, 3, 97.
The leisure and enforcement of the time.—*Richard III,* v, 3, 238.

LENDING

See also Borrowing and Lending

4
Falstaff: Will your lordship lend me a thousand pound to furnish me forth?
Chief Justice: Not a penny, not a penny.
II Henry IV. Act i, sc. 3, l. 250.
I will not lend thee a penny.
The Merry Wives of Windsor. Act ii, sc. 2, l. 1. [Falstaff]
Lend less than thou owest.
King Lear, i, 4, 133. See under BEHAVIOUR.

5
In low simplicity
He lends out money gratis and brings down
The rate of usance here with us in Venice.
The Merchant of Venice. Act i, sc. 3, l. 44. [Shylock] "Usance" is repeated in l. 109 and l. 142, and occurs in no other scene.
If thou wilt lend this money, lend it not
As to thy friends; . . .
But lend it rather to thine enemy.
The Merchant of Venice. Act i, sc. 3, l. 133. [Antonio]
He was wont to lend money for a Christian courtesy.
The Merchant of Venice. Act iii, sc. 1, l. 51. [Shylock]

6
I think myself in better plight for a lender than you are.
The Merry Wives of Windsor. Act ii, sc. 2, l. 171. [Ford]

Neither a borrower nor a lender be.
Hamlet, i, 3, 75. See under BORROWING.
Keep . . . thy pen from lenders' books.
King Lear, iii, 4, 100. See under BEHAVIOUR.
The only uses of "lender."

7
Received eight thousand nobles
In name of lendings.
Richard II. Act i, sc. 1, l. 88. [Bolingbroke] "Lendings" is used a second time in *King Lear,* iii, 4, 113: "Off, off, you lendings!"
Lending me this acquaintance.—*King Lear,* iv, 3, 56.
Lending soft audience.—*A Lover's Complaint,* l. 278.
Lending your kind commiseration.—*Titus Andronicus,* v, 3, 93.
Lending grace.—*All 's Well that Ends Well,* ii, 1, 163.
Lending him wit.—*The Rape of Lucrece,* l. 964.
The only uses of "lending."

8
This is no time to lend money, especially upon bare friendship, without security.
Timon of Athens, iii, 1, 44. [Lucullus]

9
For the fair kindness you have show'd me here,
And, part, being prompted by your present trouble,
Out of my lean and low ability
I 'll lend you something.
Twelfth Night. Act iii, sc. 4, l. 376. [Viola]

LENITY, see under Mercy

LESSON, see under Teaching

LETTER

10
First Lord: You have not given him his mother's letter?
Second Lord: I have delivered it an hour since: there is something in 't that stings his nature.
All 's Well that Ends Well. Act iv, sc. 3, l. 1.
Letters from my mother.—*All 's Well that Ends Well,* ii, 3, 293.
Letters of commendation.—*All 's Well that Ends Well,* iv, 3, 92.
Letters of commission.—*I Henry VI,* v, 4, 95.
Letters of entreaty.—*Timon of Athens,* v, 2, 11.
Letters of the selfsame tenour.—*Julius Cæsar,* iv, 3, 171.
Letters of strange tenour.—*Measure for Measure,* iv, 2, 215.
Pocket up my letters.—*Antony and Cleopatra,* ii, 2, 73.

11
I 'll write to him a very taunting letter.
As You Like It. Act iii, sc. 5, l. 134. [Phebe] The only use of "taunting."
Bitter letter.—*Othello,* i, 3, 68.
Feigned letter.—*Cymbeline,* v, 5, 279.
Forged letters.—*Cymbeline,* iv, 2, 318.

12
And, look you, here 's your letter.
All 's Well that Ends Well. Act v, sc. 3, l. 312. [Helena]
This is a letter of your own device.
As You Like It, iv, 3, 20. [Rosalind]

Will you hear the letter?—*As You Like It,* iv, 3, 36.

1
A letter for me! it gives me an estate of seven years' health; in which time I will make a lip at the physician.
Coriolanus. Act ii, sc. 1, l. 125. [Menenius]

2 Write, my queen,
And with mine eyes I'll drink the words you send,
Though ink be made of gall.
Cymbeline. Act i, sc. 1, l. 99. [Posthumus]

3 As the winds give benefit
And convoy is assistant, do not sleep,
But let me hear from you.
Hamlet. Act i, sc. 3, l. 2. [Laertes]

Letters congruing to that effect.
Hamlet. Act iv, sc. 3, l. 66. [King] The only use of "congruing."

4
My lord, I'll steep this letter in sack and make him eat it.
II Henry IV. Act ii, sc. 2, l. 147. [Poins]

5
Have you perused the letters from the pope?
I Henry VI. Act v, sc. 1, l. 1. [King Henry]

Madam, please you peruse this letter.
The Two Gentlemen of Verona. Act iv, sc. 4, l. 126. [Julia]

Peruse this letter!—*King Lear,* ii, 2, 172.

Peruse that letter.—*Twelfth Night,* v, 1, 338.

6
Let there be letters writ to every shire.
Henry VIII. Act i, sc. 2, l. 103. [Wolsey] The only use of "shire."

I have writ my letters.—*All's Well that Ends Well,* ii, 5, 26.

I have writ your letter.—*The Two Gentlemen of Verona,* ii, 1, 110.

7
Thou whoreson zed! thou unnecessary letter!
King Lear. Act ii, sc. 2, l. 69. [Kent] The only use of "zed," the English name for the last letter of the alphabet.

Nurse: Doth not rosemary and Romeo begin both with one letter?
Romeo: Ay, nurse; what of that? both with an R.
Nurse: Ah, mocker! that's the dog's name; R is for the— No; I know it begins with some other letter:—and she hath the prettiest sententious of it, of you and rosemary, that it would do you good to hear it.
Romeo and Juliet. Act ii, sc. 4, l. 219. The nurse is supposed to be referring to the old saying that R is the dog's letter. Ben Jonson, in his grammar, says, "R is the dog's letter, and hurreth in the sound."

Foulest letters.—*II Henry IV,* iv, 4, 104.

Golden letters.—*King John,* iii, 1, 85; *Love's Labour's Lost,* v, 2, 44.

Red letters.—*II Henry VI,* iv, 2, 98.

Roman letters.—*Titus Andronicus,* v, 1, 139.

8
I have received a letter this night; 'tis dangerous to be spoken; I have locked the letter in my closet.
King Lear. Act iii, sc. 3, l. 10. [Gloucester]

I have a letter guessingly set down,
Which came from one that's of a neutral heart,
And not from one opposed.
King Lear. Act iii, sc. 7, l. 47. [Gloucester] The only use of "guessingly."

Ope this letter.—*King Lear,* v, 1, 40.

Unseal the letter.—*King Lear,* iv, 5, 22.

Unseal this letter soon.—*The Merchant of Venice,* v, 1, 275.

9
This letter will tell you more.
Love's Labour's Lost. Act i, sc. 1, l. 189. [Dull]

Here he hath framed a letter to a sequent of the stranger queen's, which accidentally, or by the way of progression, hath miscarried.
Love's Labour's Lost. Act iv, sc. 2, l. 144. [Holofernes] The only use of "progression." "Accidentally" is repeated in *The Comedy of Errors,* v, 1, 361, and in *Coriolanus,* iv, 3, 40.

Let this letter be read.—*Love's Labour's Lost,* iv, 3, 193.

The letter is too long by half a mile.
Love's Labour's Lost. Act v, sc. 2, l. 54. [Maria]

10
We have received your letters full of love; . . .
And, in our maiden council, rated them
At courtship, pleasant jest and courtesy,
As bombast and as lining to the time.
Love's Labour's Lost. Act v, sc. 2, l. 787. [Princess] Bombast occurs twice more in the plays, in *I Henry IV,* ii, 4, 359, and *Othello,* i, 1, 13. "Lining" is repeated in *Richard II,* i, 4, 61.

11 We shall write to you,
As time and our concernings shall importune,
How it goes with us, and do look to know
What doth befall you here.
Measure for Measure. Act i, sc. 1, l. 56. [Duke]

Dear concernings.—*Hamlet,* iii, 4, 191. The only uses of "concernings."

12
Every letter he hath writ hath disvouched other.
Measure for Measure. Act iv, sc. 4, l. 1. [Escalus] The only use of "disvouched."

Wend you with this letter.—*Measure for Measure,* iv, 3, 150. "Wend" is repeated in *The Comedy of Errors,* i, 1, 158, and in *A Midsummer-Night's Dream,* iii, 2, 372.

13 Here is a letter, lady;
The paper as the body of my friend,
And every word in it a gaping wound,
Issuing life-blood.
The Merchant of Venice. Act iii, sc. 2, l. 266. [Bassanio]

Letters sadly penn'd in blood.—*A Lover's Complaint,* l. 47.

14
There's a post come from my master, with his horn full of good news.
The Merchant of Venice. Act v, sc. 1, l. 46. [Launcelot]

The post is come.
Titus Andronicus. Act iv, sc. 3, l. 77. [Titus]

She that from Naples
Can have no note, unless the sun were post—
The man i' the moon 's too slow.

The Tempest. Act ii, sc. 1, l. 247. [Antonio]

I fear my Julia would not deign my lines,
Receiving them from such a worthless post.

The Two Gentlemen of Verona. Act i, sc. 1, l. 160. [Proteus]

Get posts and letters.—*II Henry IV*, i, 1, 214.

Where is the post?—*III Henry VI*, v, 1, 1.

Met'st thou my posts?—*Antony and Cleopatra*, i, 5, 61.

A post with packets.—*Henry VIII*, v, 2, 32.

1

Falstaff: I have writ me here a letter to her [Ford's wife]: and here 's another to Page's wife. . . . Go bear thou this letter to Mistress Page; and thou this to Mistress Ford: we will thrive, lads, we will thrive. . . .

Nym: Here, take the humour-letter: I will keep the haviour of reputation.

Falstaff: Hold, sirrah, bear you these letters tightly.

The Merry Wives of Windsor. Act i, sc. 3, l. 65. The only use of "humour-letter." "Tightly" is repeated in ii, 3, 67, and occurs in no other play.

I should save borne the humoured letter to her.

The Merry Wives of Windsor. Act ii, sc. 1, l. 135. [Nym] "Humoured" is repeated in *Richard II*, iii, 2, 168.

2

Letter for letter, but that the name of Page and Ford differs! To my great comfort in this mystery of ill opinions, here 's the twin-brother of thy letter: but let thine inherit first; for, I protest, mine never shall. I warrant he hath a thousand of these letters, writ with blank space for different names, —sure, more,—and these are of the second edition; he will print them, out of doubt; for he cares not what he puts into the press.

The Merry Wives of Windsor. Act ii, sc. 1, l. 71. [Mrs. Page] The only use of "twin-brother," "edition," and of "press" in this sense.

Letter after letter.—*The Merry Wives of Windsor*, ii, 2, 66.

3

O, that my husband saw this letter! it would give eternal food to his jealousy.

The Merry Wives of Windsor. Act ii, sc. 1, l. 103. [Mrs. Ford]

Marry, she has received your letter, for the which she thanks you a thousand times.

The Merry Wives of Windsor. Act ii, sc. 2, l. 83. [Mistress Quickly]

What, Sir John Falstaff! Are these your letters, knight?

The Merry Wives of Windsor. Act iii, sc. 3, l. 148. [Mrs. Page]

And did he send you both these letters at an instant?

The Merry Wives of Windsor. Act iv, sc. 4, l. 3. [Page]

4

Why, this boy will carry a letter twenty mile, as easy as a cannon will shoot point-blank twelve score.

The Merry Wives of Windsor. Act iii, sc. 2, l. 32. [Ford] "Point-blank" occurs again in *II Henry VI*, iv, 7, 28.

5

She tore the letter into a thousand half-pence; railed at herself, that she should be so immodest to write to one that she knew would flout her.

Much Ado about Nothing. Act ii, sc. 3, l. 146. [Leonato]

6

Her letter now is seal'd, and on it writ
'At Ardea to my lord.'

The Rape of Lucrece, l. 1331. Ardea is mentioned again in l. 1.

7

Call in the letters-patent that he hath.

Richard II. Act ii, sc. 1, l. 202. [York]

I am denied to sue my livery here,
And yet my letters-patent give me leave.

Richard II. Act ii, sc. 3, l. 129. [Bolingbroke]

To confirm his goodness,
Tied it by letters-patent.

Henry VIII. Act iii, sc. 2, l. 249. [Wolsey] The only uses of "letters-patent."

8

Any man that can write may answer a letter.

Romeo and Juliet. Act ii, sc. 4, l. 10. [Mercutio]

9

Seest thou this letter? take it up, I pray thee,
And give the king this fatal-plotted scroll.

Titus Andronicus. Act ii, sc. 3, l. 46. [Aaron] The only use of "fatal-plotted."

Your letter is with Jupiter by this.

Titus Andronicus. Act iv, sc. 3, l. 66. [Marcus]

10

Here 's a letter come from yond poor girl.

Troilus and Cressida. Act v, sc. 3, l. 99. [Pandarus]

Here 's a letter for thee.—*Troilus and Cressida*, v, 1, 7.

Here 's a letter from him.—*Coriolanus*, ii, 1, 118.

Here are letters for you.—*Cymbeline*, ii, 4, 35.

11

I will drop in his way some obscure epistles of love.

Twelfth Night. Act ii, sc. 3, l. 169. [Maria]

As a madman's epistles are no gospels, so it skills not much when they are delivered.

Twelfth Night. Act v, sc. 1, l. 294. [Clown] The only use of "gospels." "Gospell'd" occurs in *Macbeth*, iii, 1, 88. "Epistle" is used in no other play.

12

Jove and my stars be praised! Here is yet a postscript.

Twelfth Night. Act ii, sc. 5, l. 187. [Malvolio] "Postscript" occurs again in *Hamlet*, iv, 7, 53.

13

We shall have a rare letter from him: but you 'll not deliver 't?

Twelfth Night. Act iii, sc. 2, l. 60. [Fabian]

Good letters.—*II Henry IV*, iv, 1, 44.

Great letters.—*Much Ado about Nothing,* i, 1, 267.
Honourable letter.—*Timon of Athens,* i, 1, 97.
Important letters.—*The Comedy of Errors,* v, 1, 138.
New-dated letters.—*II Henry IV,* iv, 1, 8. The only use of "new-dated."

1
If this letter move him not, his legs cannot.
Twelfth Night. Act iii, sc. 4, l. 188. [Sir Toby]

This letter, being so excellently ignorant, will breed no terror in the youth: he will find it comes from a clodpole.
Twelfth Night. Act iii, sc. 4, l. 206. [Sir Toby] The only use of "clodpole."

2 Let me hear from thee by letters
Of thy success in love and what news else
Betideth here in absence of thy friend;
And I likewise will visit thee with mine.
The Two Gentlemen of Verona. Act i, sc. 1, l. 57. [Valentine]

And yet I would I had o'erlooked the letter.
The Two Gentlemen of Verona. Act i, sc. 2, l. 50. [Julia]

3
How now! what letter are you reading there? . . .
Lend me the letter: let me see what news.
The Two Gentlemen of Verona. Act i, sc. 3, l. 51. [Antonio]

What letters hast thou there?—*I Henry IV,* iv, 1, 13.
Let me see his letter.—*Twelfth Night,* v, 1, 2.

4
Speed: Why, she hath given you a letter.
Valentine: That 's the letter I writ to her friend.
Speed: And that letter hath she delivered, and there an end.
Two Gentlemen of Verona. Act ii, sc. 1, l. 165.

What say you to a letter from your friends
Of much good news?
The Two Gentlemen of Verona. Act ii, sc. 4, l. 51. [Duke]

What letter is this same?—*The Two Gentlemen of Verona,* iii, 1, 137.

5
Thy letters may be here, though thou art hence;
Which, being writ to me, shall be deliver'd.
The Two Gentlemen of Verona. Act iii, sc. 1, l. 248. [Proteus]

Now will he be swinged for reading my letter.
The Two Gentlemen of Verona. Act iii, sc. 1, l. 392. [Launce]

LEVITY

6
Ere they can hide their levity.
All's Well that Ends Well, i, 2, 35. See under Jesting.

7
Let me request you off: our graver business
Frowns at this levity.
Antony and Cleopatra. Act ii, sc. 7, l. 127. [Cæsar]

He is already Traduced for levity.
Antony and Cleopatra. Act iii, sc. 7, l. 13. [Enobarbus]

Disvalued in levity.—*Measure for Measure,* v, 1, 222. The only use of "disvalued."

8
Our own precedent passions do instruct us
What levity 's in youth.
Timon of Athens, i, 1, 132. See under Youth.

9
Else might the world convince of levity
As well my undertakings as your counsels.
Troilus and Cressida. Act ii, sc. 2, l. 130. [Paris] The only uses of "levity." See also Lightness, under Inconstancy.

LEWDNESS

See also Lechery, Lust, Wantonness

10
How dearly would it touch thee to the quick,
Shouldest thou but hear I were licentious.
The Comedy of Errors. Act ii, sc. 2, l. 132. [Adriana]

Licentious ear.—*Pericles,* v, 3, 30.
Licentious measure.—*Timon of Athens,* v, 4, 4.
Licentious wickedness.—*Henry V,* iii, 3, 22. The only uses of "licentious."

11
You have been so lewd.
II Henry IV. Act ii, sc. 2, l. 66. [Poins]

A sort of naughty persons, lewdly bent.
II Henry VI. Act ii, sc. 1, l. 167. [Buckingham]

Thunder shall not so awake the beds of eels as my giving out her beauty stir up the lewdly-inclined.
Pericles. Act iv, sc. 2, l. 154. [Boult]

Lewdly given.—*I Henry IV,* ii, 4, 469. The only uses of "lewdly."

12
They may, 'cum privilegio,' wear away
The lag end of their lewdness.
Henry VIII. Act i, sc. 3, l. 34. [Lovell] "Lewdness" is repeated in *Hamlet,* i, 5, 54. See under Lust.

Cum privilegio ad imprimendum solum.—*The Taming of the Shrew,* iv, 4, 93. The only uses of "cum privilegio" (with exclusive right). The second phrase means "with exclusive copyright."

13
Against such lewdsters and their lechery
Those that betray them do no treachery.
Merry Wives of Windsor. Act v, sc. 3, l. 23. [Mrs. Page] The only use of "lewdsters."

14
Fie, fie! 'tis lewd and filthy.
The Taming of the Shrew. Act iv, sc. 3, l. 65. [Petruchio] See under Cap.

Lewd attempts.—*I Henry IV,* 3, 2, 14.
Lewd complaints.—*Richard III,* i, 3, 61.
Lewd day-bed.—*Richard III,* iii, 7, 72. "Day-bed" is repeated in *Twelfth Night,* ii, 5, 54.
Lewd employments.—*Richard II,* i, 1, 90.
Lewd eyes.—*Rape of Lucrece,* l. 392; l. 971.
Lewd fellow.—*Measure for Measure,* v, 1, 515; *Much Ado about Nothing,* v, 1, 341.
Lewd interpreter.—*The Merchant of Venice,* iii, 4, 80.
Lewd minx.—*Othello,* iii, 3, 476.
Lewd pranks.—*I Henry VI,* iii, 1, 15.
Lewd-tongued.—*The Winter's Tale,* ii, 3, 172. The only use of the phrase.

LIBERALITY

See also Bounty, Generosity

1
She hath been liberal and free.
I Henry VI. Act v, sc. 4, l. 82. [Warwick]
Liberal, full of spirit.—*III Henry VI,* i, 2, 43.
She is too liberal.—*The Two Gentlemen of Verona,* iii, 1, 355.
Something too liberal.—*The Merchant of Venice,* ii, 2, 194.

2
Men of his way should be most liberal;
They are set here for examples.
Henry VIII. Act i, sc. 3, l. 61. [Lord Sands]

3
I see, sir, you are liberal in offers.
The Merchant of Venice. Act iv, sc. 1, l. 438. [Portia]
I will become as liberal as you;
I'll not deny him any thing I have,
No, not my body nor my husband's bed.
The Merchant of Venice. Act v, sc. 1, l. 226. [Portia]

4
A liberal rewarder of his friends.
Richard III. Act i, sc. 3, l. 124. [Gloucester] The only use of "rewarder."

5
Liberal
To mine own children in good bringing up.
The Taming of the Shrew. Act i, sc. 1, l. 98. [Baptista]

6
Over and beside Signior Baptista's liberality,
I'll mend it with a largess.
The Taming of the Shrew. Act i, sc. 2, l. 149. [Gremio]
Liberal largess.—*Richard II,* i, 4, 44.
Liberality, and such like, the spice and salt that season a man.
Troilus and Cressida. Act i, sc. 2, l. 277. [Pandarus] See under MAN.
Fair looks, and liberality.—*Titus Andronicus,* ii, 1, 92. The only uses of "liberality."

7
And this is all a liberal course allows;
Who cannot keep his wealth must keep his house.
Timon of Athens. Act iii, sc. 3, l. 41. [Servant]

LIBERTINE

8
For thou thyself hast been a libertine,
As sensual as the brutish sting itself.
As You Like It. Act ii, sc. 7, l. 65. [Duke Senior]
I have begun,
And now I give my sensual race the rein.
Measure for Measure. Act ii, sc. 4, l. 159. [Angelo]
Sensual fault.—*Sonnets,* xxxv.
Sensual feast.—*Sonnets,* cxli. The only uses of "sensual."
Savage sensuality.—*Much Ado about Nothing,* iv, 1, 62. "Sensuality" is repeated in *Othello,* i, 3, 331.

9
Cousin, I think thou art enamoured
On his follies: never did I hear
Of any prince so wild a libertine.
I Henry IV. Act v, sc. 2, l. 70. [Hotspur]
None but libertines delight in him.
Much Ado about Nothing. Act ii, sc. 1, l. 144. [Beatrice]
Charter'd libertine.—*Henry V,* i, 1, 48. See under SPEECH.
Reckless libertine.—*Hamlet,* i, 3, 49.
Tie up the libertine.—*Antony and Cleopatra,* ii, 1, 23. The only uses of "libertine."

10
Ay, you have been a mouse-hunt in your time.
Romeo and Juliet. Act iv, sc. 4, l. 11. [Lady Capulet] The only use of "mouse-hunt."

11
Out upon him! prig, for my life, prig: he haunts wakes, fairs and bear-baitings.
The Winter's Tale. Act iv, sc. 3, l. 108. [Clown] The only use of "prig."

LIBERTY

See also Freedom

12
Now go we in content
To liberty and not to banishment.
As You Like It. Act i, sc. 3, l. 139. [Celia]
I must have liberty
Withal, as large a charter as the wind,
To blow on whom I please.
As You Like It. Act ii, sc. 7, l. 47. [Jaques]

13
A man is master of his liberty.
The Comedy of Errors. Act ii, sc. 1, l. 7. [Luciana]
Headstrong liberty is lash'd with woe.
The Comedy of Errors. Act ii, sc. 1, l. 15. [Luciana] The only use of "lash'd."

14
You are at point to lose your liberties.
Coriolanus. Act iii, sc. 1, l. 194. [Sicinius]
Take their liberties.—*Coriolanus,* ii, 3, 223.
I lost my liberty and they their lives.
I Henry VI. Act ii, sc. 5, l. 81. [Mortimer]
They quite forgot their loss of liberty.
III Henry VI, iv, 6, 15. See under BIRD.

15
Il est content de vous donner la liberté, la franchisement.
Henry V. Act iv, sc. 4, l. 56. [Boy] The only use of "liberté" and "franchisement."

16
Now show yourselves men; 'tis for liberty.
II Henry VI. Act iv, sc. 2, l. 193. [Cade]
Princely liberty.—*I Henry VI,* v, 3, 140.

17
Turn'd my captive state to liberty.
III Henry VI. Act iv, sc. 6, l. 3. [King Henry]
I give thee thy liberty, set thee from durance.
Love's Labour's Lost. Act iii, sc. 1, l. 129. [Armado]
Gain your liberty.—*I Henry VI,* v, 3, 32.
He brings me liberty.—*Antony and Cleopatra,* v, 2, 237.
Delivered him to his liberty.—*Measure for Measure,* iv, 2, 137.
Liberty of flight.—*I Henry VI,* iv, 2, 24.
Liberty of gazing.—*Comedy of Errors,* v, 1, 53.
Liberty of the prison.—*Measure for Measure,* iv, 2, 156.
Liberties of sin.—*Comedy of Errors,* i, 2, 102.

1
I am sorry To see you ta'en from liberty.
Henry VIII. Act i, sc. 1, l. 204. [Brandon]
Pent from liberty.—*Richard III,* i, 4, 267.

2
Cinna: Liberty! Freedom! Tyranny is dead!
Run hence, proclaim, cry it about the streets.
Cassius: Some to the common pulpits, and cry out
'Liberty, freedom, and enfranchisement!' . . .
Brutus: Let 's all cry 'Peace, freedom and liberty!'
Julius Cæsar. Act iii, sc. 1, l. 78.
So often shall the knot of us be call'd
The men that gave their country liberty.
Julius Cæsar. Act iii, sc. 1, l. 17. [Cassius]

3
I envy at their liberty.
King John. Act iii, sc. 4, l. 73. [Constance]
By my sweet soul, I mean setting thee at liberty, enfreedoming thy person.
Love's Labour 's Lost. Act iii, sc. 1, l. 125. [Armado] The only use of "enfreedoming."
I muse why she 's at liberty.
Richard III. Act i, sc. 3, l. 305. [Rivers]
At liberty.—*II Henry VI,* v, 1, 87; *Richard III,* i, 1, 133; *Coriolanus,* ii, 3, 31; *The Tempest,* v, 1, 235.
Free, at liberty.—*Richard III,* iii, 6, 9.
Set at liberty.—*King John,* iii, 3, 9.
Full liberty.—*Othello,* ii, 2, 10.
Great liberty.—*III Henry VI,* iv, 5, 6.

4
Lucio: Why, how now, Claudio! whence comes this restraint?
Claudio: From too much liberty, my Lucio, liberty.
Measure for Measure. Act i, sc. 2, l. 128.
Liberty plucks justice by the nose.
Measure for Measure. Act i, sc. 3, l. 29. [Duke]

5
My master . . . hath threatened to put me into everlasting liberty; . . . he swears he 'll turn me away.
The Merry Wives of Windsor. Act iii, sc. 3, l. 29. [Robin]

6
If I had my liberty, I would do my liking.
Much Ado about Nothing. Act i, sc. 3, l. 37. [Don John]
Ne'er look on liberty!—*Romeo and Juliet,* iii, 2, 58.

7
This liberty is all that I request.
The Taming of the Shrew, ii, 1, 95. See under Wooing.
Derive a liberty From heartiness.
The Winter's Tale, i, 2, 112. See under Entertainment. The only use of "heartiness."

LICENSE

8
We license your departure with your son.
I Henry IV. Act i, sc. 3, l. 123. [King Henry]
Thou shalt have a license to kill.
II Henry VI. Act iv, sc. 3, l. 8. [Cade]
Full license.—*Antony and Cleopatra,* i, 2, 112.
By his license.—*Hamlet,* iv, 4, 2.
License of free foot.—*As You Like It,* ii, 7, 68.
License of ink.—*Twelfth Night,* iii, 2, 48.

9
For the fifth Harry from curb'd license plucks
The muzzle of restraint, and the wild dog
Shall flesh his tooth on every innocent.
II Henry IV. Act iv, sc. 5, l. 131. [King Henry] "Muzzle" is repeated in *Much Ado about Nothing,* i, 3, 34, and in *Henry VIII,* i, 1, 121.
Did give ourself To barbarous license.
Henry V. Act i, sc. 2, l. 270. [King Henry]

10
I come to thee for charitable license.
Henry V. Act iv, sc. 7, l. 74. [Montjoy]

LIE AND LYING

See also Falsehood; Truth and Falsehood

11
To return and swear the lies he forges.
All's Well that Ends Well. Act iv, sc. 1, l. 26. [Second Lord]
Tells a lie and swears it.—*Much Ado about Nothing,* iv, 1, 324.
Forged lies.—*Venus and Adonis,* l. 804.

12
He will lie, sir, with such volubility, that you would think truth were a fool.
All's Well that Ends Well. Act iv, sc. 3, l. 283. [Parolles]
I 'll commend her volubility.—*The Taming of the Shrew,* ii, 1, 176. The only uses of "volubility."

13
Messenger: Should I lie, madam?
Cleopatra: O, I would thou didst!
Antony and Cleopatra. Act ii, sc. 5, l. 93.
Something given to lie.—*Antony and Cleopatra,* v, 2, 253.

14
You lie, up to the hearing of the gods.
Antony and Cleopatra. Act v, sc. 2, l. 95. [Cleopatra]
Nut-hook, nut-hook, you lie.
II Henry IV. Act v, sc. 4, l. 8. [Doll Tearsheet] "Nut-hook" (beadle, constable) occurs again in *The Merry Wives of Windsor,* i, 1, 171. "You lie" is repeated ten times in the plays.

15
O, for shame, for shame, Lie not.
As You Like It. Act iii, sc. 5, l. 18. [Phebe]
These are all lies.—*As You Like It,* iv, 1, 107.

16
Touchstone: I have had four quarrels, and like to have fought one.
Jaques: How was that ta'en up?
Touchstone: Faith, we met, and found the quarrel was upon the seventh cause.
Jaques: How seventh cause? . . .
Touchstone: Upon a lie seven times removed. . . . I did dislike the cut of a certain courtier's beard: he sent me word, if I said his beard was not cut well, he was in mind it was: this is called the Retort Courteous. If I sent him word again 'it was not well cut,' he would send me word, he cut it to please himself: this is called the Quip

Modest. If again 'it was not well cut,' he disabled my judgement: this is called the Reply Churlish. If again 'it was not well cut,' he would answer I spake not true: this is called the Reproof Valiant. If again 'it was not well cut,' he would say, I lied: this is called the Countercheck Quarrelsome: and so to the Lie Circumstantial and the Lie Direct.
Jaques: And how often did you say his beard was not well cut?
Touchstone: I durst go no further than the Lie Circumstantial, nor he durst not give me the Lie Direct; and so we measured swords and parted.
Jaques: Can you nominate in order now the degrees of the lie? . . . .
Touchstone: I will name you the degrees. The first, the Retort Courteous; the second, the Quip Modest; the third, the Reply Churlish; the fourth, the Reproof Valiant; the fifth, the Countercheck Quarrelsome; the sixth, the Lie with Circumstance; the seventh, the Lie Direct. All these you may avoid but the Lie Direct.

As You Like It. Act v, sc. 4, l. 48. [Touchstone] "Countercheck" is repeated in *King John,* ii, 1, 224.

The lie deadly.—*Coriolanus,* ii, 1, 67.

1
Faith, sir, if you had told as many lies in his behalf as you have uttered words in your own, you should not pass here; no, though it were as virtuous to lie as to live chastely.

Coriolanus. Act v, sc. 2, l. 24. [Sentinel] "Chastely" is repeated in *All's Well that Ends Well,* i, 3, 218: "Wish chastely"; and in iii, 7, 34: "Chastely absent."

Unless you would devise some virtuous lie.
Sonnets. No. lxxii.

2
Will poor folks lie,
That have afflictions on them, knowing 'tis
A punishment or trial? Yes; no wonder,
When rich ones scarce tell true. To lapse in fulness
Is sorer than to lie for need, and falsehood
Is worse in kings than beggars.
Cymbeline. Act iii, sc. 6, l. 9. [Imogen]

If I do lie and do
No harm by it, though the gods hear, I hope
They 'll pardon it.
Cymbeline. Act iv, sc. 2, l. 377. [Imogen]

What lies I have heard!—*Cymbeline,* iv, 2, 32.

3
'Tis as easy as lying.
Hamlet. Act iii, sc. 2, l. 372. [Hamlet]

4
Hamlet: Whose grave 's this, sirrah?
Clown: Mine, sir. . . .
Hamlet: I think it is thine, indeed; for thou liest in 't.
Clown: You lie out on 't, sir, and therefore it is not yours: for my part, I do not lie in 't, and yet it is mine.
Hamlet: Thou dost lie in 't, to be in 't and say it is thine: 'tis for the dead, not for the quick; therefore thou liest.
Clown: 'Tis a quick lie, sir; 'twill away again, from me to you.
Hamlet. Act v, sc. 1, l. 127.

Desdemona: Do you know, sirrah, where Lieutenant Cassio lies?
Clown: I dare not say he lies any where. . . . He 's a soldier, and for one to say a soldier lies, is stabbing.
Othello. Act iii, sc. 4, l. 1. "Stabbing" is repeated in *The Winter's Tale,* iv, 4, 748. See below, under To GIVE THE LIE.

5
The virtue of this jest will be, the incomprehensible lies that this same fat rogue will tell us when we meet at supper.
I Henry IV. Act i, sc. 2, l. 208. [Poins] The only use of "incomprehensible."

If I tell thee a lie, spit in my face, call me horse.
I Henry IV. Act ii, sc. 4, l. 214. [Falstaff]

Say you so, say you so? I say unto you again, you are a shallow cowardly hind, and you lie.
I Henry IV. Act ii, sc. 3, l. 16. [Hotspur]

These lies are like their father that begets them: gross as a mountain, open, palpable.
I Henry IV. Act ii, sc. 4, l. 249. [Prince of Wales]

6
For my part, if a lie may do thee grace,
I 'll gild it with happiest terms I have.
I Henry IV. Act v, sc. 4, l. 161. [Prince of Wales]

How this world is given to lying!
I Henry IV. Act v, sc. 4, l. 148. [Falstaff]

Every third word a lie, duer paid to the hearer than the Turk's tribute.
II Henry IV. Act iii, sc. 2, l. 330. [Falstaff] The only use of "duer."

7
Proud lord, thou liest:
Within these forty hours Surrey durst better
Have burnt that tongue than said so.
Henry VIII. Act iii, sc. 2, l. 252. [Wolsey]

8
Detested kite! thou liest.
King Lear. Act i, sc. 4, l. 284. [King Lear]

This sword, this arm, and my best spirits, are bent
To prove upon thy heart, whereto I speak,
Thou liest.
King Lear. Act v, sc. 3, l. 139. [Edgar]

I say, thou liest,
And will maintain what thou hast said is false
In thy heart-blood.
Richard II. Act iv, sc. 1, l. 26. [Aumerle]

If thou deny'st it twenty times, thou liest;
And I will turn thy falsehood to thy heart,
Where it was forged, with my rapier's point.
Richard II. Act iv, sc. 1, l. 38. [Fitzwater]

Thou liest, abhorred tyrant; with my sword
I 'll prove the lie thou speak'st.
Macbeth. Act v, sc. 7, l. 10. [Young Siward]

Thou liest, thou thread, thou thimble,
Thou yard, three-quarters, half-yard, quarter, nail!
Thou flea, thou nit, thou winter-cricket thou!
Taming of the Shrew. Act iv, sc. 3, l. 106. [Petruchio] "Thimble" occurs once more in *Taming of the Shrew,* iv, 3, 149, and in *King*

John, v, 2, 156. "Three-quarters" is used in *Comedy of Errors,* iii, 2, 111, and in *Winter's Tale,* iv, 4, 814. The only use of "half-yard" and "winter-cricket." "Nit" occurs only once again, in *Love's Labour 's Lost,* iv, 1, 150.

Thou liest, thou jesting monkey, thou.
Tempest. Act iii, sc. 2, l. 52. [Caliban] "Thou liest" occurs twenty-eight times in the plays.

1
Whose tongue soe'er speaks false,
Not truly speaks; who speaks not truly, lies.
King John. Act iv, sc. 3, l. 91. [Hubert]

2
Keep a schoolmaster that can teach thy fool to lie:
I would fain learn to lie.
King Lear. Act i, sc. 4, l. 195. [Fool]

They told me I was every thing; 'tis a lie, I am not ague-proof.
King Lear. Act iv, sc. 6, l. 106. [King Lear] The only use of "ague-proof."

3
What in the world he is
That names me traitor, villain-like he lies.
King Lear. Act v, sc. 3, l. 97. [Edmund]

Villain-like, I lie.
Cymbeline. Act v, sc. 5, l. 218. [Posthumus] The only uses of "villain-like."

4
With the hell-hated lie o'erwhelm thy heart.
King Lear. Act v, sc. 3, l. 147. [Edmund] The only use of "hell-hated."

5
How you delight, my lords, I know not, I;
But, I protest, I love to hear him lie.
Love's Labour 's Lost. Act i, sc. 1, l. 175. [King]

6
Twenty of these puny lies I 'll tell.
The Merchant of Venice. Act iii, sc. 4, l. 74. [Portia]

Tell quaint lies.—*Merchant of Venice,* iii, 4, 69.

If I could add a lie unto a fault, I would deny it.
The Merchant of Venice. Act v, sc. 1, l. 186. [Bassanio]

7
I like not the humour of lying.
The Merry Wives of Windsor. Act ii, sc. 1, l. 132. [Nym]

Shall I tell you a lie?—*The Merry Wives of Windsor,* i, 1, 69.

I will not lie to you.—*The Merry Wives of Windsor,* iii, 5, 65.

I lie not.—*Much Ado about Nothing,* iv, 1, 273; *Timon of Athens,* i, 1, 226.

I do not lie.—*The Tempest,* iii, 2, 53.

And now I should not lie.—*Henry VIII,* iv, 2, 143.

Lie and cog.—*Much Ado about Nothing,* v, 1, 95.

8
They have spoken untruths.
Much Ado about Nothing. Act v, sc. 1, l. 220. [Dogberry]

Let all untruths stand by thy stained name,
And they 'll seem glorious.
Troilus and Cressida. Act v, sc. 2, l. 179. [Troilus]

He would say untruths.—*Henry VIII,* iv, 2, 38. The only uses of "untruths."

My untruth.—*Richard II,* ii, 2, 101. The only use of "untruth."

9
He lies to the heart.
Othello. Act v, sc. 2, l. 156. [Emilia]

You told a lie; an odious, damned lie;
Upon my soul, a lie, a wicked lie.
Othello. Act v, sc. 2, l. 180. [Emilia]

Fantastical lies.—*Othello,* ii, 1, 226.

10
By all my hopes, most falsely doth he lie.
Richard II. Act i, sc. 1, l. 68. [Mowbray]

Now swallow down that lie.
Richard II. Act i, sc. 1, l. 132. [Mowbray]

11
And spur thee on with full as many lies
As may be holloa'd in thy treacherous ear
From sun to sun.
Richard II. Act iv, sc. 1, l. 53. [Lord] The only use of "holloa'd."

Dishonourable boy!
That lie shall lie so heavy on my sword,
That it shall render vengeance and revenge
Till thou the lie-giver and that lie do lie
In earth as quiet as thy father's skull.
Richard II. Act iv, sc. 1, l. 65. [Surrey] The only use of "lie-giver."

If I dare eat, or drink, or breathe, or live,
I dare meet Surrey in a wilderness,
And spit upon him, whilst I say he lies,
And lies, and lies.
Richard II. Act iv, sc. 1, l. 73. [Fitzwater]

12
Lies well steel'd with weighty arguments.
Richard III. Act i, sc. 1, l. 148. [Gloucester]

I will . . . lie for you.—*Richard III,* i, 1, 115.

Yet I lie.—*Richard III,* v, 3, 191.

In faith, I lie.—*Troilus and Cressida,* iii, 2, 129.

13
When my love swears that she is made of truth
I do believe her, though I know she lies,
That she might think me some untutor'd youth,
Unlearned in the world's false subtleties. . . .
Therefore I lie with her and she with me,
And in our faults by lies we flatter'd be.
Sonnets. No. cxxxviii. Repeated, with a few variations, in *The Passionate Pilgrim,* l. 1.

Iago: Lie—
Othello: With her?
Iago: With her, on her; what you will.
Othello: Lie with her! Lie on her! We say lie on her, when they belie her. Lie with her! that 's fulsome.
Othello. Act iv, sc. 1, l. 35.

14
One
Who having into truth, by telling of it,
Made such a sinner of his memory,
To credit his own lie.
The Tempest. Act i, sc. 2, l. 99. [Prospero]

You 'll lie like dogs and yet say nothing neither.
The Tempest. Act iii, sc. 2, l. 22. [Trinculo]

Wilt thou tell a monstrous lie, being but half a fish and half a monster?
The Tempest. Act iii, sc. 2, l. 32. [Trinculo]

So foul a lie.—*Sonnets,* clii.

15
Shall I not lie in publishing a truth?
Troilus and Cressida. Act v, sc. 2, l. 119. [Troilus] The only use of "publishing."

1
As many lies as will lie in thy sheet of paper, although the sheet were big enough for the bed of Ware in England, set 'em down.
Twelfth Night. Act iii, sc. 2, l. 49. [Sir Toby] The great bed of Ware, 10 ft. 9 in. in length and breadth, is still in existence and was exhibited in London in 1931. It dates from the 16th century, and belonged to the Saracen's Head Inn, at Ware.
The wanton lies.—*The Two Gentlemen of Verona,* v, 2, 10.

2
Why should I carry lies abroad?
The Winter's Tale. Act iv, sc. 4, l. 274. [Autolycus]

II—To Give the Lie

3
Must I with base tongue give my noble heart
A lie that it must bear?
Coriolanus. Act iii, sc. 2, l. 100. [Coriolanus]
Giving itself the lie.—*Coriolanus,* ii, 2, 37.
Give this cur the lie.—*Coriolanus,* v, 6, 107.
Give the lie.—*As You Like It,* iii, 2, 410; *A Midsummer-Night's Dream,* iii, 1, 138; *Sonnets,* cl.

4
Who . . . gives me the lie i' the throat,
As deep as to the lungs? who does me this?
Hamlet. Act ii, sc. 2, l. 601. [Hamlet] See under COWARDICE.
Giving him the lie.—*Macbeth,* ii, 3, 40.
Gave thee the lie.—*Macbeth,* ii, 3, 41.

5
Stephano: As you like this, give me the lie another time.
Trinculo: I did not give the lie.
The Tempest. Act iii, sc. 2, l. 85.

6
Clown: We are but plain fellows, sir.
Autolycus: A lie; you are rough and hairy. Let me have no lying: it becomes none but tradesmen, and they often give us soldiers the lie: but we pay them for it with stamped coin, not stabbing steel; therefore they do not give us the lie.
Clown: Your worship had like to have given us one, if you had not taken yourself with the manner.
The Winter's Tale. Act iv, sc. 4, l. 742.
Give me the lie, do.—*Winter's Tale,* v, 2, 144.

III—Lie in the Throat

7
I had lied in my throat if I had said so.
II Henry IV. Act i, sc. 2, l. 94. [Falstaff]
You lie in your throat.
II Henry IV. Act i, sc. 2, l. 97. [Servant]
That 's a lie in thy throat.
Henry V. Act iv, sc. 8, l. 17. [Fluellen]

8
I do nothing in the world but lie, and lie in my throat.
Love's Labour 's Lost. Act iv, sc. 3, l. 12. [Biron]

9
For me to devise a lodging and say he lies here or he lies there, were to lie in mine own throat.
Othello. Act iii, sc. 4, l. 11. [Clown]

10
Even in his throat . . . I return the lie.
Pericles. Act ii, sc. 5, l. 56. [Pericles]

11
Then, Bolingbroke, as low as to thy heart,
Through the false passage of thy throat, thou liest.
Richard II. Act i, sc. 1, l. 124. [Mowbray]
In thy foul throat thou liest.
Richard III. Act i, sc. 2, l. 93. [Lady Anne]
Thou liest in thy throat.
Twelfth Night. Act iii, sc. 4, l. 172. [Sir Toby]
Lies in 's throat.—*The Taming of the Shrew,* iv, 3, 133.

IV—The Liar

12
I know him a notorious liar.
All 's Well that Ends Well. Act i, sc. 1, l. 111. [Helena]
I am full sorry
That he approves the common liar.
Antony and Cleopatra. Act i, sc. 1, l. 59. [Demetrius]
Greatest liar.—*Antony and Cleopatra,* i, 3, 39.
An infinite and endless liar.—*All 's Well that Ends Well,* iii, 6, 11.
Measureless liar.—*Coriolanus,* v, 6, 103.
A very liar.—*Taming of the Shrew,* ii, 1, 246.
Liars and adulterers.—*King Lear,* i, 2, 134.
Liar and slave!—*Macbeth,* v, 5, 35.
Liars and swearers.—*Macbeth,* iv, 2, 57.

13
I do despise a liar as I do despise one that is false, or as I despise one that is not true.
The Merry Wives of Windsor. Act i, sc. 1, l. 69. [Evans]
God and good men hate so foul a liar.
Richard II. Act i, sc. 1, l. 114. [Mowbray]

14
You 're liars all.
Winter's Tale. Act ii, sc. 3, l. 146. [Leontes]
You have been his liar.—*Coriolanus,* v, 2, 32.
There be liars.—*Troilus and Cressida,* ii, 1, 109; *The Winter's Tale,* iv, 4, 240.

LIFE

I—Definitions

15
The web of our life is of a mingled yarn, good and ill together: our virtues would be proud, if our faults whipped them not; and our crimes would despair, if they were not cherished by our virtues.
All 's Well that Ends Well. Act iv, sc. 3, l. 83. [First Lord] "Yarn" is repeated in *Coriolanus,* i, 3, 93.

16
Life 's but a walking shadow, a poor player
That struts and frets his hour upon the stage
And then is heard no more: it is a tale
Told by an idiot, full of sound and fury,
Signifying nothing.
Macbeth. Act v, sc. 5, l. 24. [Macbeth] The only use of "signifying."

17
Life is a shuttle.
The Merry Wives of Windsor. Act v, sc. 1, l. 25. [Falstaff] The only use of "shuttle."

1
Sir Toby: Does not our life consist of the four elements?
Sir Andrew: Faith, so they say; but I think it rather consists of eating and drinking.
Twelfth Night. Act ii, sc. 3, l. 9.

II—Familiar Phrases

2
Rogue, thou hast lived too long.
Antony and Cleopatra. Act ii, sc. 5, l. 73. [Cleopatra]
A noble life before a long.
Coriolanus. Act iii, sc. 1, l. 153. [Coriolanus]
Biron: Now, God save thy life!
Rosaline: And yours from long living!
Love's Labour 's Lost. Act ii, sc. 1, l. 191.
God save your life.—*Love's Labour 's Lost,* iv, 2, 150.

3
Live a little; comfort a little; cheer thyself a little.
As You Like It. Act ii, sc. 6, l. 5. [Orlando]
My full life.—*As You Like It,* iii, 2, 4.
'Od 's my little life!—*As You Like It,* iii, 5, 43.
Hard life.—*Cymbeline,* iv, 4, 27.
Former life.—*The Winter's Tale,* v, 2, 123.
Past life.—*The Winter's Tale,* iii, 2, 34.

4
The lives of all your loving complices
Lean on your health.
II Henry IV. Act i, sc. 1, l. 163. [Morton]
Come to life.—*II Henry IV,* iii, 1, 84.

5
For mine own part, I have not a case of lives.
Henry V. Act iii, sc. 2, l. 4. [Nym]
Let us on heaps go offer up our lives.
Henry V. Act iv, sc. 5, l. 18. [Constable]
Sell every man his life as dear as mine.
I Henry VI. Act iv, sc. 2, l. 53. [Talbot]

6
By me they nothing gain an if I stay;
'Tis but the shortening of my life one day.
I Henry VI. Act iv, sc. 6, l. 36. [Talbot] The only use of "shortening."
No prince nor peer shall have just cause to say,
God shorten Harry's happy life one day!
II Henry IV. Act v, sc. 2, l. 144. [King Henry]
An chud ha' bin zwaggered out of my life, 'twould not ha' bin zo long as 'tis by a vortnight.
King Lear. Act iv, sc. 6, l. 243. [Edgar] The only use of "zwaggered."

7
Thy life to me is sweet.
I Henry VI, iv, 6, 55. See DEATH, 306:2.
How long fairly shall her sweet life last?
Richard III. Act iv, sc. 4, l. 352. [Queen Elizabeth] "Sweet life" is repeated in *The Two Gentlemen of Verona,* i, 3, 45; *King John,* iv, 3, 65; 106; and *A Midsummer-Night's Dream,* ii, 2, 61.

8
Soldiers, this day have you redeem'd your lives.
II Henry VI. Act iv, sc. 9, l. 15. [Clifford]

9
Let me for this my life-time reign as king.
III Henry VI. Act i, sc. 1, l. 171. [King Henry] The only use of "life-time."

10
If any spark of life be yet remaining,
Down, down to hell; and say I sent thee thither.
III Henry VI. Act v, sc. 6, l. 66. [Gloucester] "Sparks of life" occurs in *Julius Cæsar,* i, 3, 57.
Bloody house of life.—*King John,* iv, 2, 210. See KINGS: THEIR TRIBULATIONS.
Book of life.—*Richard II,* i, 3, 202.
Pith of life.—*Hamlet,* iv, 1, 23.
Strings of life.—*King Lear,* v, 3, 216.
Thread of life.—*Pericles,* i, 2, 108.
Time of life.—*Julius Cæsar,* v, 1, 106.

11
Whiles warm life plays in that infant's veins.
King John, iii, 4, 132. See under REST.
Warm life.—*The Winter's Tale,* v, 3, 35.

12
Man's life 's as cheap as beast's.
King Lear. Act ii, sc. 4, l. 270. [King Lear]
No man's life Was to be trusted with them.
Macbeth. Act ii, sc. 3, l. 110. [Lennox]
Ten leagues beyond man's life.
The Tempest. Act ii, sc. 1, l. 247. [Antonio]

13
Then there 's life in 't.
King Lear. Act iv, sc. 6, l. 203. [King Lear]
Tut, there 's life in 't, man.
Twelfth Night. Act i, sc. 3, l. 117. [Sir Toby]

14
The life to come.
Macbeth, i, 7, 7 (see RETRIBUTION); *Measure for Measure,* v, 1, 437; *Winter's Tale,* iv, 3, 30.
Eternal life.—*Romeo and Juliet,* iv, 5, 70.
Immortal life.—*Sonnets,* lxxxi. See IMMORTALITY.

15
I bear a charmed life.
Macbeth. Act v, sc. 8, l. 12. [Macbeth] See under CHARM for full quotation.

16
Thou hast contrived against the very life
Of the defendant.
The Merchant of Venice. Act iv, sc. 1, l. 360. [Portia]
Even he that did uphold the very life
Of my dear friend.
The Merchant of Venice. Act v, sc. 1, l. 214. [Bassanio]

17
Sweet lady, you have given me life and living.
The Merchant of Venice. Act v, sc. 1, l. 286. [Antonio]
Life and liberty.—*The Taming of the Shrew,* iv, 2, 113.

18
I have lived fourscore years and upward.
The Merry Wives of Windsor. Act iii, sc. 1, l. 56. [Shallow]
Stretched-out life.—*Troilus and Cressida,* i, 3, 61. The only use of "stretched-out."

19
Be ready, as your lives shall answer it.
Richard II. Act i, sc. 1, l. 198. [King Richard]
Duchess: What is the matter, Aumerle?
Aumerle: Good mother, be content; it is no more

Than my poor life must answer.
Duchess: Thy life answer!
Richard II. Act v, sc. 2, l. 81.
Answer with their lives.—*Titus Andronicus,* ii, 3, 298.

1
By great preservation, We live to tell it you.
Richard III. Act iii, sc. 5, l. 36. [Buckingham]
Tender preservation of our person.
Henry V. Act ii, sc. 2, l. 59. [King Henry]
Give us particulars of thy preservation.
The Tempest. Act v, sc. 1, l. 135. [Alonso]
For preservation cased.—*Cymbeline,* v, 3, 22.
Times of preservation.—*Henry VIII,* iii, 2, 147.
Our preservation.—*The Tempest,* ii, 1, 7. The only uses of "preservation."

2
O dear account! my life is my foe's debt.
Romeo and Juliet. Act i, sc. 5, l. 120. [Romeo]

3
Where is the life that late I led?
The Taming of the Shrew. Act iv, sc. 1, l. 143. [Petruchio, singing]
'Where is the life that late I led?' say they:
Why, here it is; welcome these pleasant days!
II Henry IV. Act v, sc. 3, l. 147. [Pistol]
Why, thou globe of sinful continents, what a life dost thou lead!
II Henry IV. Act ii, sc. 4, l. 309. [Prince of Wales]
Lead my life.—*The Comedy of Errors,* iii, 2, 67.

4
Is it for fear to wet a widow's eye
That thou consumest thyself in single life?
Sonnets. No. ix.
The single and peculiar life is bound,
With all the strength and armour of the mind,
To keep itself from noyance.
Hamlet. Act iii, sc. 3, l. 11. [Rosencrantz] The only use of "noyance."
Single life.—*A Midsummer-Night's Dream,* i, 1, 90; 121; *Much Ado about Nothing,* v, 4, 116. See MARRIAGE AND CELIBACY.
For this twelvemonth she 'll not undertake
A married life.
Pericles. Act ii, sc. 5, l. 3. [Simonides]
Such a life, with such a wife, were strange!
The Taming of the Shrew. Act i, sc. 2, l. 194. [Gremio]

5
Gonzalo: Here is every thing advantageous to life.
Antonio: True; save means to live.
The Tempest. Act ii, sc. 1, l. 49.
Advantageous care.—*Troilus and Cressida,* v, 4, 22. The only uses of "advantageous."

6
I Have given you here a third of mine own life,
Or that for which I live.
The Tempest. Act iv, sc. 1, l. 3. [Prospero] The only use of "third."
For term of life thou art assured mine,
And life no longer than thy love shall stay.
Sonnets. No. xcii. See LOVE AND LIFE.

7
To me can life be no commodity.
Winter's Tale. Act iii, sc. 2, l. 94. [Hermione]
O, hear me breathe my life
Before this ancient sir.
Winter's Tale. Act iv, sc. 4, l. 371. [Florizel]

III—Hazarding Life

See also Hazard

8
Sir, my life is yours;
I humbly set it at your will.
Cymbeline. Act iv, sc. 3, l. 12. [Pisanio]

9
I dare pawn down my life for him.
King Lear. Act i, sc. 2, l. 93. [Edmund]
I 'll lay my life.—*Troilus and Cressida,* iii, 1, 95.
My life upon 't.—*Twelfth Night,* ii, 4, 24.
My life for yours.—*A Midsummer-Night's Dream,* iii, 1, 43.

10
By my life, my troth.
Love's Labour 's Lost. Act v, sc. 2, l. 450. [King] "By my life" is repeated twenty times in later plays.
For my life.—*Richard III,* iv, 1, 3, and five times in later plays.
On my life.—*Richard III,* iii, 2, 46, and twelve times in later plays.
Upon my life.—*II Henry VI,* iii, 1, 46, and twelve times in later plays.
Not for my life.—*Taming of the Shrew,* iv, 3, 1.
Not for thy life.—*The Taming of the Shrew,* iv, 3, 160.

11
I would set my life on any chance,
To mend it, or be rid on 't.
Macbeth. Act iii, sc. 1, l. 113. [Murderer]

12
I will plead against it with my life.
Measure for Measure. Act iv, sc. 2, l. 193. [Duke]
In peril of my life.—*The Merchant of Venice,* ii, 2, 173.
Careless of your life.—*The Taming of the Shrew,* iv, 2, 79.

13
If ever you disturb our streets again,
Your lives shall pay the forfeit of the peace.
Romeo and Juliet. Act i, sc. 1, l. 103. [Prince]
Keep peace, upon your lives.—*King Lear,* ii, 2, 52.
Hold, for your lives!—*Othello,* ii, 3, 165.

14
Oft thou shouldst hazard thy life.
Timon of Athens. Act iv, sc. 3, l. 338. [Timon]
Hazard life.—*The Two Gentlemen of Verona,* v, 4, 21.
Hazard of his life.—*The Two Gentlemen of Verona,* iii, 1, 116.

15
Pay thy life thou owest me.
Troilus and Cressida. Act v, sc. 6, l. 7. [Troilus]

IV—Losing Life

16
The worthy gentleman did lose his life.
III Henry VI. Act iii, sc. 2, l. 7. [King Edward]
Lose my life.—*II Henry VI,* iv, 7, 71; *All's Well that Ends Well,* iv, 1, 77.

17
Thy life, who I would be sorry should be thus foolishly lost.
Measure for Measure. Act i, sc. 2, l. 195. [Lucio]

1
My husband lost his life to get the crown.
Richard III. Act ii, sc. 4, l. 57. [Duchess of York] "Lost his life" is repeated in *Pericles,* i, Gower, 38.
Well-lost life.—*All's Well that Ends Well,* i, 3, 254. The only use of "well-lost."

V—Saving Life

2
French Soldier: Gardez ma vie, et je vous donnerai deux cent écus.
Pistol: What are his words?
Boy: He prays you to save his life.
Henry V. Act iv, sc. 4, l. 44.

3
The king will labour still to save his life,
The commons haply rise to save his life.
II Henry VI. Act iii, sc. 1, l. 239. [Suffolk]
Admit no other way to save his life.
Measure for Measure. Act ii, sc. 4, l. 88. [Angelo] "Save her life" occurs in *Richard III,* iv, 4, 212.

4
Therefore yet relent, and save my life.
II Henry VI. Act iv, sc. 7, l. 124. [Lord Say] "Save my life" is repeated in *The Comedy of Errors,* v, 1, 283; and "saved my life" in *I Henry IV,* v, 4, 123, and *Sonnets,* cxlv.
Safeguard thine own life.—*Richard II,* i, 2, 35.

5
Your fellow Tranio here, to save my life,
Puts my apparel and my countenance on, . . .
While I make way from hence to save my life.
The Taming of the Shrew. Act i, sc. 1, l. 233. [Lucentio]
To save your life in this extremity,
This favour will I do you.
The Taming of the Shrew. Act iv, sc. 2, l. 102. [Tranio] "Save your life" is repeated in *Much Ado about Nothing,* v, 4, 96; and "save thy life" in *III Henry VI,* i, 3, 3; *The Comedy of Errors,* v, 1, 193; and "saving of thy life" in *Julius Cæsar,* v, 3, 38.

6
Leontes: You that have been so tenderly officious . . .
To save this bastard's life, . . . what will you adventure
To save this brat's life? . . .
Antigonus: I 'll pawn the little blood which I have left
To save the innocent.
The Winter's Tale. Act ii, sc. 2, l. 159.

VI—Sparing Life

7
O lord, sir! spare not me.
All's Well that Ends Well. Act ii, sc. 2, l. 53. [Clown] "Spare not me" is repeated in l. 55, and in ii, 2, 47; also in *The Taming of the Shrew,* iv, 3, 153.
Spare me not.—*Richard II,* ii, 1, 124.
Spare us not.—*Coriolanus,* ii, 3, 243.
Spare not.—*Richard III,* i, 3, 114; *Twelfth Night,* ii, 3, 120; *Passionate Pilgrim,* l. 324.
Spare not the babe.—*Timon of Athens,* iv, 3, 118.
Spare not the old father.—*Cymbeline,* v, 5, 327.
Spare not any man.—*Pericles,* ii, 1, 137.

8
The general is content to spare thee yet;
And hoodwink'd as thou art, will lead thee on
To gather from thee.
All's Well that Ends Well. Act iv, sc. 1, l. 89. [Soldier] "Hoodwink'd" is repeated in *Romeo and Juliet,* i, 4, 4, and in *Cymbeline,* v, 2, 16.
I pray you, spare me.—*Cymbeline,* ii, 3, 100; *Henry VIII,* ii, 4, 54; *Rape of Lucrece,* l. 582.

9
Captain: What, think you much to pay two thousand crowns,
And bear the name and port of gentlemen?
Cut both the villains' throats; for die you shall:
The lives of those which we have lost in fight
Be counterpoised with such a petty sum!
Gentleman: I 'll give it, sir; and therefore spare my life.
II Henry VI. Act iv, sc. 1, l. 18. "Spare my life" was used in the first play and never again. "Counterpoised" is repeated in iii, 3, 137, and in *Coriolanus,* ii, 2, 91.

10
We will not leave one lord, one gentleman:
Spare none but such as go in clouted shoon.
II Henry VI. Act iv, sc. 2, l. 194. [Cade]
He 'll spare none.—*Timon of Athens,* i, 1, 177.
York not our old men spares;
No more will I their babes.
II Henry VI. Act v, sc. 2, l. 51. [Young Clifford]
He will spare neither man, woman, nor child.
II Henry IV. Act ii, sc. 1, l. 18. [Hostess]

11
Spare him, spare him!
He's not prepared for death.
Measure for Measure. Act ii, sc. 2, l. 83. [Isabella]
Spare my first-born son.—*Titus Andronicus,* i, 1, 120.
Spare my guiltless wife.—*Richard III,* i, 4, 72.

VII—Seeking Life

12
All to make away my guiltless life.
II Henry VI. Act iii, sc. 1, l. 167. [Gloucester]
Have my life.—*II Henry VI,* iii, 1, 147.

13
What, did my father's godson seek your life?
King Lear. Act ii, sc. 1, l. 93. [Regan] The only use of "godson." "Seek thy life" occurs in *The Comedy of Errors,* i, 1, 152.
He seeks my life.—*The Merchant of Venice,* iii, 3, 21.
He sought my life.—*King Lear,* iii, 4, 172.
Doth he so seek his life?—*Measure for Measure,* i, 4, 72.
Seek the life of any citizen.—*The Merchant of Venice,* iv, 1, 351.

14
Myself would, on the rearward of reproaches,
Strike at thy life.
Much Ado about Nothing. Act iv, sc. 1, l. 128. [Leonato]

Level not to hit their lives.
Richard III. Act iv, sc. 4, l. 202. [Queen Elizabeth]

VIII—Taking Life

1
He will . . . never leave thee till he hath ta'en thy life by some indirect means or other.
As You Like It. Act i, sc. 1, l. 157. [Oliver]
Take their life.—*Romeo and Juliet,* Prol., l. 6.
Take thy life.—*Pericles,* i, 2, 57.
Take away your life.—*Pericles,* i, 2, 105.

2
Let thine own hands take away her life.
Cymbeline. Act iii, sc. 4, l. 28. [Imogen, reading]
Take her life.—*The Tempest,* i, 2, 267.

3
What have we to lose,
But that he swore to take, our lives?
Cymbeline. Act iv, sc. 2, l. 124. [Guiderius]
For Imogen's dear life take mine; and though
'Tis not so dear, yet 'tis a life; you coin'd it.
Cymbeline. Act v, sc. 4. l. 22. [Posthumus] "Dear life" is repeated in *Hamlet,* ii, 2, 597, and in *The Winter's Tale,* v, 3, 103.
If you will take this audit, take this life,
And cancel these cold bonds.
Cymbeline. Act v, sc. 4, l. 27. [Posthumus]
Take that life, beseech you,
Which I so often owe.
Cymbeline. Act v, sc. 5, l. 414. [Iachimo]
Take my life.—*I Henry VI,* iii, 1, 22; *The Tempest,* v, 1, 274.

4
Why, what a ruthless thing is this in him, for the rebellion of a codpiece to take away the life of a man!
Measure for Measure. Act iii, sc. 2, l. 121. [Lucio] See under CODPIECE.

IX—Love of Life

5
My life, sir, in any case: not that I am afraid to die; but that, my offences being many, I would repent out the remainder of nature: let me live, sir, in a dungeon, i' the stocks, or any where, so I may live.
All's Well that Ends Well. Act iv, sc. 3, l. 270. [Parolles]

6
I love long life better than figs!
Antony and Cleopatra. Act i, sc. 2, l. 32. [Charmian] "Long life" is repeated in *II Henry IV,* iv, 3, 54; *Hamlet,* iii, 1, 69; and *The Tempest,* iv, 1, 24.
Faith, I will live so long as I may, that 's the certain of it; and when I cannot live any longer, I will do as I may: that is my rest, that is the rendezvous of it.
Henry V. Act ii, sc. 1, l. 15. [Nym]
Long live Queen Margaret.—*II Henry VI,* i, 1, 37. "Long live" is repeated thirteen times in later plays.

7
Lucius: I do not bid thee beg my life, good lad;
And yet I know thou wilt. . . .
Imogen: Your life, good master,
Must shuffle for itself.
Cymbeline. Act v, sc. 5, l. 101.
Beg his life.—*Measure for Measure,* ii, 4, 69.

8
One that grasp'd And tugg'd for life.
II Henry VI. Act iii, sc. 2, l. 173. [Warwick]
Gasping for life.—*II Henry IV,* i, 1, 208.
I pant for life.—*King Lear,* v, 3, 243.

9
It is a life that I have desired: I will thrive.
The Merry Wives of Windsor. Act i, sc. 3, l. 21. [Bardolph]

10
I life would wish, and that I might
Waste it for you, like taper-light.
Pericles. Act i, Gower, l. 15. [Gower] "Taper-light" is repeated in *King John,* iv, 2, 14.

11
Which of you, if you were a prince's son,
Being pent from liberty, as I am now,
If two such murderers as yourselves came to you,
Would not entreat for life?
Richard III. Act i, sc. 4, l. 266. [Clarence]
The proudest of you all
Have been beholding to him in his life;
Yet none of you would once plead for his life.
Richard III. Act ii, sc. 1, l. 128. [King Edward]

12
I hold my life as dear as you do yours;
And never in my life, I do protest,
Was it more precious to me than 'tis now.
Richard III. Act iii, sc. 2, l. 80. [Hastings]
God lend me life.—*The Taming of the Shrew,* iv, 2, 76.

13
If of life you keep a care,
Shake off slumber, and beware.
The Tempest. Act ii, sc. 1, l. 303. [Ariel]

X—Life: Its Briefness

14
How brief the life of man
Runs his erring pilgrimage,
That the stretching of a span
Buckles in his sum of age.
As You Like It. Act iii, sc. 2, l. 137. [Celia]
Timon is dead, who hath outstretch'd his span.
Timon of Athens. Act v, sc. 3, l. 3. [Soldier]
My life is spann'd already.
Henry VIII. Act i, sc. 1, l. 223. [Buckingham] The only use of "spann'd."
A life 's but a span.—*Othello,* ii, 3, 74.
Brief span.—*Henry VIII,* iii, 2, 140.

15
A man's life 's no more than to say 'One.'
Hamlet. Act v, sc. 2, l. 74. [Hamlet]

16
O, gentlemen, the time of life is short!
To spend that shortness basely were too long,
If life did ride upon a dial's point,
Still ending at the arrival of an hour.
I Henry IV. Act v, sc. 2, l. 82. [Hotspur]

17
Good men's lives
Expire before the flowers in their caps,
Dying or ere they sicken.
Macbeth. Act iv, sc. 3, l. 171. [Ross]

This carol they began that hour,
With a hey, and a ho, and a hey nonino,
How that a life was but a flower.
As You Like It. Act v, sc. 3, l. 27. [Song]

1
King Richard: Why, uncle, thou hast many years to live.
John of Gaunt: But not a minute, king, that thou canst give:
Shorten my days thou canst with sullen sorrow,
And pluck nights from me, but not lend a morrow.
Richard II. Act i, sc. 3, l. 225.

2
We are such stuff
As dreams are made on, and our little life
Is rounded with a sleep.
The Tempest. Act iv, sc. 1, l. 156. [Prospero]

3
Life's uncertain voyage.
Timon of Athens. Act v, sc. 1, l. 205. [Timon] The only use of this phrase.

XI—The Good Life

4
I dare defend
My innocent life against an emperor.
King John. Act iv, sc. 3, l. 88. [Hubert]

5
If his own life answer the straitness of his proceeding, it shall become him well.
Measure for Measure. Act iii, sc. 2, l. 269. [Duke] The only use of "straitness."

6
It is very meet
The Lord Bassanio lead an upright life.
The Merchant of Venice. Act iii, sc. 5, l. 78. [Jessica]

Upright as the cedar.—*Love's Labour's Lost,* iv, 3, 89.
Austere insociable life.—*Love's Labour's Lost,* v, 2, 809. "Insociable" is repeated in v, 1, 20, and occurs in no other play. "Unsociable" is not used at all.
Chaste life.—*Sonnets,* cliv.
Clear life.—*The Tempest,* iii, 3, 82.
Fair life.—*The Rape of Lucrece,* l. 661.
Religious life.—*As You Like It,* v, 4, 187. See under RELIGION.
True life.—*Cymbeline,* ii, 4, 76.
The life of purity.—*The Rape of Lucrece,* l. 780.

7
Our holy lives must win a new world's crown,
Which our profane hours here have stricken down.
Richard II. Act v, sc. 1, l. 24. [King Richard]

8
Ay, ay, I care not for a good life.
Twelfth Night. Act ii, sc. 3, l. 37. [Sir Andrew] "Good life" is repeated in *As You Like It,* iii, 2, 14; *The Merry Wives of Windsor,* iii, 3, 127; and *The Tempest,* iii, 3, 86.

XII—The Evil Life

9
Ah, what a sign it is of evil life,
Where death's approach is seen so terrible!
II Henry VI. Act iii, sc. 3, l. 5. [King Henry] "Evil life" was used in the first play, and never again.

Base life.—*King Lear,* ii, 4, 218.
Baser life.—*Antony and Cleopatra,* v, 2, 293.
Bold life.—*Henry VIII,* v, 3, 85.
Dishonour'd life.—*Measure for Measure,* iv, 4, 34; *The Rape of Lucrece,* l. 1186.
Lawless lives.—*The Two Gentlemen of Verona,* iv, 1, 54.
Monstrous life.—*II Henry VI,* iii, 3, 30.
Pernicious lives.—*Richard II,* iii, 1, 4.
Shamed life.—*Richard II,* v, 3, 71.
Wicked life.—*Titus Andronicus,* v, 3, 145.

10
May all the building in my fancy pluck
Upon my hateful life.
King Lear. Act iv, sc. 2, l. 85. [Goneril]

Hateful life.—*King John,* iii, 1, 179.

11
Duke: Say to thyself,
From their abominable and beastly touches
I drink, I eat, array myself, and live.
Canst thou believe thy living is a life,
So stinkingly depending? Go mend, go mend.
Pompey: Indeed, it does stink in some sort, sir.
Measure for Measure. Act iii, sc. 2, l. 24. The only use of "stinkingly."

Life of passion.—*Much Ado about Nothing,* ii, 3, 110.

12
My bad life reft me so much of friends.
Much Ado about Nothing. Act iv, sc. 1, l. 198. [Leonato]

Upon this bad life to make all this good.
Richard II. Act i, sc. 1, l. 99. [Bolingbroke] "Bad life" is repeated in *Coriolanus,* i, 6, 71.

13
Her life was beast-like, and devoid of pity;
And, being so, shall have like want of pity.
Titus Andronicus. Act v, sc. 3, l. 199. [Lucius] The only use of "beast-like."

XIII—The Happy Life

14
Thy life is dear; for all that life can rate
Worth name of life in thee hath estimate,
Youth, beauty, wisdom, courage, all
That happiness and prime can happy call.
All's Well that Ends Well. Act ii, sc. 1, l. 182. [King]

15
O, this life
Is nobler than attending for a check,
Richer than doing nothing for a bauble,
Prouder than rustling in unpaid-for silk:
Such gain the cap of him that makes 'em fine,
Yet keeps his book uncross'd: no life to ours.
Cymbeline. Act iii, sc. 3, l. 21. [Belarius] The only use of "unpaid-for" and "uncross'd."

What pleasure, sir, find we in life, to lock it
From action and adventure?
Cymbeline. Act iv, sc. 4, l. 2. [Arviragus]

16
O God! methinks it were a happy life,
To be no better than a homely swain;
To sit upon a hill as I do now,
To carve out dials quaintly, point by point.
III Henry VI. Act ii, sc. 5, l. 21. [King Henry]

Ah, what a life were this! how sweet! how lovely!
III Henry VI. Act ii, sc. 5, l. 41. [King Henry]
What a life is this!—*As You Like It*, ii, 7, 9.
This life is most jolly.—*As You Like It,* ii, 7, 183.

1
Heaven, from thy endless goodness, send
prosperous life, long, and ever happy.
Henry VIII. Act v, sc. 5, l. 1. [Garter]

2 So we 'll live,
And pray, and sing, and tell old tales, and laugh
At gilded butterflies, and hear poor rogues
Talk of court news.
King Lear. Act v, sc. 3, l. 11. [King Lear]

XIV—The Unhappy Life

3 Her life,
Which, being cruel to the world, concluded
Most cruel to herself.
Cymbeline. Act v, sc. 5, l. 31. [Cornelius]

4 Who would fardels bear,
To grunt and sweat under a weary life.
Hamlet. Act iii, sc. 1, l. 76. [Hamlet] For "Fardel," see BURDEN.

5
I cannot tell what you and other men
Think of this life; but, for my single self,
I had as lief not be as live to be
In awe of such a thing as I myself.
Julius Cæsar. Act i, sc. 2, l. 93. [Cassius]

6
Life is as tedious as a twice-told tale
Vexing the dull ear of a drowsy man.
King John. Act iii, sc. 4, l. 108. [Dauphin] The only use of "twice-told tale" and "vexing."
I see a man's life is a tedious one.
Cymbeline. Act iii, sc. 6, l. 1. [Imogen]

7 Edmund, I think, is gone,
In pity of his misery, to dispatch
His nighted life.
King Lear. Act iv, sc. 5, l. 11. [Regan] "Nighted" is repeated in *Hamlet,* i, 2, 68: "Nighted colour."

8
Alas! the sweet woman leads an ill life with him: she leads a very frampold life with him, good heart!
The Merry Wives of Windsor. Act ii, sc. 2, l. 91. [Mistress Quickly] The only use of "frampold" (disagreeable).

9
All is but toys: renown and grace is dead;
The wine of life is drawn, and the mere lees
Is left this vault to brag of.
Macbeth. Act ii, sc. 3, l. 99. [Macbeth] "Lees" occurs only once more, in *Troilus and Cressida,* iv, 1, 62.

XV—The Quiet Life

10
And this our life, exempt from public haunt,
Finds tongues in trees, books in the running brooks,
Sermons in stones, and good in every thing.
As You Like It. Act ii, sc. 1, l. 15. [Duke senior]

11
Corin: And how like you this shepherd's life, Master Touchstone?
Touchstone: Truly, shepherd, in respect of itself, it is a good life; but in respect that it is a shepherd's life, it is naught. In respect that it is solitary, I like it very well; but in respect that it is private, it is a very vile life. Now, in respect it is in the fields, it pleaseth me well; but in respect it is not in the court, it is tedious. As it is a spare life, look you, it fits my humour well: but as there is no more plenty in it, it goes much against my stomach.
As You Like It. Act iii, sc. 2, l. 11.

12 Haply this life is best,
If quiet life be best; sweeter to you
That have a sharper known; well corresponding
With your stiff age: but unto us it is
A cell of ignorance; travelling a-bed;
A prison for a debtor.
Cymbeline. Act iii, sc. 3, l. 29. [Guiderius] The only use of "corresponding."
Fie upon this quiet life.
I Henry IV. Act ii, sc. 4, l. 117. [Prince of Wales]
Quiet life.—*The Taming of the Shrew,* v, 2, 108.
Wholesome life.—*Hamlet,* iii, 2, 271.

13
I know my life so even.
Henry VIII. Act iii, sc. 1, l. 38. [Queen Katharine]
His life was gentle.—*Julius Cæsar,* v, 5, 73. See under MAN.

14
I have ever loved the life removed
And held in idle price to haunt assemblies
Where youth, and cost, and witless bravery keeps.
Measure for Measure. Act i, sc. 3, l. 8. [Duke]
In some reclusive and religious life,
Out of all eyes, tongues, minds and injuries.
Much Ado about Nothing. Act iv, sc. 1, l. 244. [Friar Francis] The only use of "reclusive."

15
Here 's a simple line of life.
The Merchant of Venice. Act ii, sc. 2, l. 169. [Launcelot]

16
Now, mild may be thy life!
Pericles. Act iii, sc. 1, l. 27. [Lychorida]

XVI—Weariness of Life

17
The poisonous damp of night disponge upon me,
That life, a very rebel to my will,
May hang no longer on me.
Antony and Cleopatra. Act iv, sc. 9, l. 13. [Enobarbus] The only use of "disponge."

18
No reason I, since of your lives you set
So slight a valuation, should reserve

My crack'd one to more care.
Cymbeline. Act iv, sc. 4, l. 48. [Belarius] "Valuation" is repeated in *II Henry IV,* iv, 1, 189.

1
I do not set my life at a pin's fee.
Hamlet. Act i, sc. 4, l. 65. [Hamlet]

2
Ere I lead this life long, I 'll sew nether socks and mend them and foot them too.
I Henry IV. Act ii, sc. 4, l. 129. [Falstaff] "Socks" occurs again in *The Merry Wives of Windsor,* iii, 5, 91.

3
My life I never held but as a pawn
To wage against thy enemies; nor fear to lose it.
King Lear. Act i, sc. 1, l. 157. [Kent]

4
I have lived long enough: my way of life
Is fall'n into the sear, the yellow leaf.
Macbeth. Act v, sc. 3, l. 22. [Macbeth]

I am so out of love with life that I will sue to be rid of it.
Measure for Measure. Act iii, sc. 1, l. 173. [Claudio]

5
For life, I prize it
As I weigh grief, which I would spare.
The Winter's Tale. Act iii, sc. 2, l. 43. [Hermione]

My life stands in the level of your dreams,
Which I 'll lay down.
The Winter's Tale. Act iii, sc. 2, l. 82. [Hermione]

Life, I prize it not a straw.
The Winter's Tale. Act iii, sc. 2, l. 110. [Hermione]

XVII—The End of Life

6
I am afeard the life of Helen, lady,
Was foully snatch'd.
All's Well that Ends Well. Act v, sc. 3, l. 153. [King]

7
In thee there is not half an hour of life.
Hamlet. Act v, sc. 2, l. 326. [Laertes]

8
He . . .
Yields up his life unto a world of odds.
I Henry VI. Act iv, sc. 4, l. 24. [Lucy]

I yield thee up my life.
Antony and Cleopatra. Act v, sc. 1, l. 12. [Dercetas]

9
These great lords and Margaret our queen
Do seek subversion of thy harmless life.
II Henry VI. Act iii, sc. 1, l. 207. [King Henry] The only use of "subversion."

Shamefully bereft of life.
II Henry VI, iii, 2, 269.

Deprived him of his life.—*I Henry IV,* iv, 3, 91.

10
Their thread of life is spun.
II Henry VI. Act iv, sc. 2, l. 31. [Bevis] "Spun" is repeated in *Coriolanus,* i, 3, 93.

Farewell life!—*II Henry VI,* iii, 2, 356.

11
The sands are number'd that make up my life;
Here must I stay, and here my life must end.
III Henry VI. Act i, sc. 4, l. 25. [York]

But wherefore dost thou come, is 't for my life?
III Henry VI. Act v, sc. 6, l. 29. [King Henry]

12
For further life in this world I ne'er hope.
Henry VIII. Act ii, sc. 1, l. 69. [Buckingham]

If heaven had pleased to have given me longer life
And able means, we had not parted thus.
Henry VIII. Act iv, sc. 2, l. 152. [Katharine]

13
This day I breathed first: time is come round,
And where I did begin, there shall I end;
My life is run his compass.
Julius Cæsar. Act v, sc. 3, l. 23. [Cassius]

14
Have I not hideous death within my view,
Retaining but a quantity of life,
Which bleeds away, even as a form of wax
Resolveth from his figure 'gainst the fire?
King John. Act v, sc. 4, l. 22. [Melun]

15
'Tis wonder that thy life and wits at once
Had not concluded all.
King Lear. Act iv, sc. 7, l. 41. [Cordelia]

16
We have done our course.
Othello. Act iv, sc. 2, l. 93. [Othello]

17
'Tis all as easy
Falsely to take away a life true made
As to put metal in restrained means
To make a false one.
Measure for Measure. Act ii, sc. 4, l. 46. [Angelo]

18
You take my house when you do take the prop
That doth sustain my house; you take my life
When you do take the means whereby I live.
The Merchant of Venice. Act iv, sc. 1, l. 375. [Shylock]

19
'In vain,' quoth she, 'I live, and seek in vain
Some happy mean to end a hapless life.'
The Rape of Lucrece, l. 1044.

'Daughter, dear daughter,' old Lucretius cries,
'That life was mine which thou hast here deprived.'
The Rape of Lucrece, l. 1751.

'O,' quoth Lucretius, 'I did give that life
Which she too early and too late hath spill'd.'
The Rape of Lucrece, l. 1800.

20
Dissolve the bands of life.
Richard II, ii, 2, 71. See under HOPE.

Abridge thy life.—*The Two Gentlemen of Verona,* iii, 1, 245.

Abridge my doleful days.—*II Henry IV,* ii, 4, 211. The only uses of "abridge."

Resign thy life.—*Titus Andronicus,* i, 1, 191.

Shorten thy life.—*The Winter's Tale,* iv, 4, 433.

She render'd life.—*Antony and Cleopatra,* iv, 14, 33.

21
Queen Elizabeth: How long fairly shall her sweet life last?

King Richard: So long as heaven and nature lengthens it.
Richard III. Act iv, sc. 4, l. 352.

1
I reck not though I end my life to-day.
Troilus and Cressida. Act v, sc. 6, l. 26. [Troilus]
End her life.—*Richard II,* i, 2, 55.

2
Even with the vail and darking of the sun,
To close the day up, Hector's life is done.
Troilus and Cressida. Act v, sc. 8, l. 7. [Achilles] The only use of "darking."

3
And were I not immortal, life were done
Between this heavenly and earthly sun.
Venus and Adonis, l. 197.

XVIII—Life and Death

4
Uncertain life, and sure death.
All's Well that Ends Well. Act ii, sc. 3, l. 20. [Lafeu]

Rather I'll expect victorious life
Than death and honour.
Antony and Cleopatra. Act iv, sc. 2, l. 43. [Antony]

5
But here must end the story of my life;
And happy were I in my timely death.
Comedy of Errors. Act i, sc. 1, l. 138. [Ægeon] "Story of my life," see under STORY.

6
Brave death outweighs bad life.
Coriolanus. Act i, sc. 6, l. 71. [Marcius] See under PATRIOTISM.

7
I am merrier to die than thou art to live.
Cymbeline. Act v, sc. 4, l. 175. [Posthumus]
I had rather thou shouldst live while nature will
Than die ere I hear more.
Cymbeline. Act v, sc. 5, l. 151. [Cymbeline]

8
He that is not guilty of his own death shortens not his own life.
Hamlet. Act v, sc. 1, l. 21. [First Clown]

9
An if we live, we live to tread on kings;
If die, brave death, when princes die with us!
I Henry IV. Act v, sc. 2, l. 86. [Hotspur]

10
For he hath found to end one doubt by death
Revives two greater in the heirs of life.
II Henry IV. Act iv, sc. 1, l. 199. [Archbishop of York]
Thy life did manifest thou lovedst me not,
And thou wilt have me die assured of it.
II Henry IV. Act iv, sc. 5, l. 105. [King Henry]

11
Where they feared the death, they have borne life away.
Henry V. Act iv, sc. 1, l. 184. [King Henry]

12
I gave thee life and rescued thee from death.
I Henry VI. Act iv, sc. 6, l. 5. [Talbot]
O, that I could but call these dead to life!
I Henry VI. Act iv, sc. 7, l. 81. [Lucy]

13
For in the shade of death I shall find joy;
In life but double death.
II Henry VI. Act iii, sc. 2, l. 54. [King Henry]
Life in death.—*II Henry VI,* iii, 2, 152; *Venus and Adonis,* l. 413.
Dead life.—*Richard III,* iv, 4, 26.
Deadly life.—*Twelfth Night,* i, 5, 284.
Dying life.—*The Rape of Lucrece,* l. 1055.
Lifeless life.—*The Rape of Lucrece,* l. 1374.

14
He shall die, an it be but for pleading so well for his life.
II Henry VI. Act iv, sc. 7, l. 112. [Cade]

15
Dark cloudy death o'ershades his beams of life,
And he nor sees nor hears us what we say.
III Henry VI. Act ii, sc. 6, l. 62. [Warwick]

16
No certain life achieved by others' death.
King John. Act iv, sc. 2, l. 105. [King John]

17
Life and death! I am ashamed
That thou hast power to shake my manhood thus;
That these hot tears, which break from me perforce,
Should make thee worth them.
King Lear. Act i, sc. 4, l. 318. [King Lear]

O, our lives' sweetness!
That we the pain of death would hourly die
Rather than die at once!
King Lear. Act v, sc. 3, l. 184. [Edgar]

18
I have drugg'd their possets,
That death and nature do contend about them,
Whether they live or die.
Macbeth. Act ii, sc. 2, l. 6. [Lady Macbeth] The only use of "drugg'd."
[He] shall live the lease of nature, pay his breath
To time and mortal custom.
Macbeth. Act iv, sc. 1, l. 99. [Macbeth]

19
Claudio: I've hope to live, and am prepared to die.
Duke: Be absolute for death; either death or life
Shall thereby be the sweeter. Reason thus with life:
If I do lose thee, I do lose a thing
That none but fools would keep: a breath thou art,
Servile to all the skyey influences,
That dost this habitation, where thou keep'st,
Hourly afflict: merely, thou art death's fool;
For him thou labour'st by thy flight to shun
And yet runn'st toward him still. Thou art not noble;
For all the accommodations that thou bear'st
Are nursed by baseness. Thou 'rt by no means valiant;
For thou dost fear the soft and tender fork
Of a poor worm. Thy best of rest is sleep,
And that thou oft provokest; yet grossly fear'st

Thy death, which is no more. Thou art not thyself;
For thou exist'st on many a thousand grains
That issue out of dust. Happy thou art not;
For what thou hast not, still thou strivest to get,
And what thou hast, forget'st. Thou art not certain;
For thy complexion shifts to strange effects,
After the moon. If thou art rich, thou 'rt poor;
For, like an ass whose back with ingots bows,
Thou bear'st thy heavy riches but a journey,
And death unloads thee. Friend hast thou none;
For thine own bowels, which do call thee sire,
The mere effusion of thy proper loins,
Do curse the gout, serpigo, and the rheum,
For ending thee no sooner. Thou hast nor youth nor age,
But, as it were, an after-dinner's sleep,
Dreaming on both; for all thy blessed youth
Becomes as aged, and doth beg the alms
Of palsied eld; and when thou art old and rich,
Thou hast neither heat, affection, limb, nor beauty,
To make thy riches pleasant. What 's yet in this
That bears the name of life? Yet in this life
Lie hid moe thousand deaths: yet death we fear,
That makes these odds all even.
Claudio: I humbly thank you.
To sue to live, I find I seek to die;
And, seeking death, find life: let it come on.

Measure for Measure. Act iii, sc. 1, l. 4. The only use of "skyey" and "ingots." "Serpigo" (skin eruption) is repeated in *Troilus and Cressida,* ii, 3, 81; and "after-dinner" in *Troilus and Cressida,* ii, 3, 121.

Isabella: O, I do fear thee, Claudio; and I quake
Lest thou a feverous life shouldst entertain,
And six or seven winters more respect
Than a perpetual honour. . . .
If I would yield him my virginity
Thou mightst be freed. . . .
Claudio: Thou shalt not do 't.
Isabella: O, were it but my life,
I 'ld throw it down for your deliverance
As frankly as a pin. . . .
Claudio: Death is a fearful thing.
Isabella: And shamed life a hateful. . . .
Claudio: The weariest and most loathed worldly life
That age, ache, penury and imprisonment
Can lay on nature is a paradise
To what we fear of death. . . . Sweet sister, let me live. . . .
Isabella: O faithless coward! O dishonest wretch!
Wilt thou be made a man out of my vice?
Is 't not a kind of incest, to take life
From thine own sister's shame?

Measure for Measure. Act iii, sc. 1, l. 74.

That life is better life, past fearing death,
Than that which lives to fear.

Measure for Measure. Act iv, sc. 1, l. 402. [Duke] "Better life" is repeated in *The Merry Wives of Windsor,* ii, 2, 122; and in *Antony and Cleopatra,* v, 2, 2.

Unfit to live or die.

Measure for Measure. Act iv, sc. 3, l. 68. [Duke]

1

It is silliness to live when to live is torment; and then have we a prescription to die when death is our physician.

Othello. Act i, sc. 3, l. 309. [Roderigo] The only use of "silliness."

I 'ld have thee live;
For, in my sense, 'tis happiness to die.

Othello. Act v, sc. 2, l. 289. [Othello]

2

Thus ready for the way of life or death,
I wait the sharpest blow.

Pericles. Act i, sc. 1, l. 54. [Pericles]

3

Showing life's triumph in the map of death,
And death's dim look in life's mortality.

The Rape of Lucrece, l. 402.

Life lived in death, and death in life.

The Rape of Lucrece, l. 406.

O, that is gone for which I sought to live,
And therefore now I need not fear to die.

The Rape of Lucrece, l. 1051.

To live or die which of the twain were better,
When life is shamed, and death reproach's debtor.

The Rape of Lucrece, l. 1155.

4

Even through the hollow eyes of death
I spy life peering.

Richard II. Act ii, sc. 1, l. 270. [Northumberland]

5

My babes were destined to a fairer death,
If grace had bless'd thee with a fairer life.

Richard III. Act iv, sc. 4, l. 219. [Queen Elizabeth]

6

Lavinia: For 'tis not life that I have begg'd so long;
Poor I was slain when Bassianus died.
Tamora: What begg'st thou, then? fond woman, let me go.
Lavinia: 'Tis present death I beg.

Titus Andronicus. Act ii, sc. 3, l. 170.

7

That ever death should let life bear his name,
Where life hath no more interest but to breathe!

Titus Andronicus. Act iii, sc. 1, l. 249. [Lucius]

Would I were dead, so you did live again!

Titus Andronicus. Act v, sc. 3, l. 173. [Young Lucius]

8

Jove, let Æneas live,
If to my sword his fate be not the glory,
A thousand complete courses of the sun!
But, in mine emulous honour, let him die,

With every joint a wound, and that to-morrow.
Troilus and Cressida. Act iv, sc. 1, l. 25. [Diomedes]

1
I fly not death, to fly his deadly doom:
Tarry I here, I but attend on death:
But, fly I hence, I fly away from life.
The Two Gentlemen of Verona. Act iii, sc. 1, l. 185. [Valentine]

2
Do I delight to die, or life desire?
But now I lived, and life was death's annoy;
But now I died, and death was lively joy.
Venus and Adonis, l. 496.

3
Either for life or death.
The Winter's Tale. Act iii, sc. 3, l. 45. [Antigonus]
Bequeath to death your dumbness, for from him
Dear life redeems you.
The Winter's Tale. Act v, sc. 3, l. 102. [Paulina]

LIGHT

4
For what obscured light the heavens did grant
Did but convey into our fearful minds
A doubtful warrant of immediate death.
The Comedy of Errors. Act i, sc. 1, l. 67. [Ægeon]
Obscured lights.—*The Two Gentlemen of Verona,* v, 3, 15.
Grey light.—*A Midsummer-Night's Dream,* iii, 2, 419.
Smoky light.—*Cymbeline,* i, 6, 109.
Smother'd light.—*The Rape of Lucrece,* l. 783.
Unwilling light.—*Venus and Adonis,* l. 1051.

5
Light is an effect of fire.
The Comedy of Errors, iv, 3, 56. See under WENCH.
Giving more light than heat.
Hamlet, i, 3, 118. See under APPEARANCE.

6
By this light, I am well spoke on.
II Henry IV. Act ii, sc. 2, l. 69. [Poins]
By this good light.—*The Winter's Tale,* ii, 3, 82.
By this day and this light.—*Henry V,* iv, 8, 66.
A phrase, in one of these forms, frequently repeated throughout the plays.
Light in darkness.—*II Henry VI,* ii, 1, 67. See under DARKNESS.
Collateral light.—*All's Well that Ends Well,* i, 1, 99.
Enclosed lights.—*Cymbeline,* ii, 2, 21.
Ever-burning lights.—*Othello,* iii, 3, 463. See under VOW.
Fair and natural light.—*I Henry IV,* v, 1, 18.
Flaming light.—*The Rape of Lucrece,* l. 1627.
Free and offer'd light.—*Timon of Athens,* v, 1, 48.
Gracious light.—*Sonnets,* vii.
Growing light.—*III Henry VI,* ii, 5, 2.
Lesser lights.—*Pericles,* ii, 3, 41.
Living light.—*Macbeth,* ii, 4, 10.
Piercing light.—*The Rape of Lucrece,* l. 1091.
Tyrannous and damned light.—*Hamlet,* ii, 2, 482.

7
We . . . Should join our lights together
And over-shine the earth.
III Henry VI. Act ii, sc. 1, l. 35. [Edward]

8
Clarence, beware; thou keep'st me from the light,
But I will sort a pitchy day for thee.
III Henry VI. Act v, sc. 6, l. 86. [Gloucester]

9
These exhalations whizzing in the air
Give so much light that I may read by them.
Julius Cæsar. Act ii, sc. 1, l. 44. [Brutus]
The only use of "whizzing."
Give light.—*Love's Labour's Lost,* iv, 3, 32.
Give him light.—*Love's Labour's Lost,* i, 1, 83.

10
Light seeking light doth light of light beguile:
So, ere you find where light in darkness lies,
Your light grows dark by losing of your eyes.
Love's Labour's Lost. Act i, sc. 1, l. 77. [Biron]
Rosaline: We need more light to find your meaning out.
Katharine: You'll mar the light by taking it in snuff.
Love's Labour's Lost. Act v, sc. 2, l. 21. "Snuff" in the sense of huff, resentment, is used four times.
By light we lose light.—*Love's Labour's Lost,* v, 2, 376.

11
A light for Monsieur Judas! it grows dark, he may stumble.
Love's Labour's Lost, v, 2, 635. [Boyet]
Malvolio: Help me to some light and some paper. . . .
Clown: I will fetch you light and paper and ink.
Twelfth Night. Act iv, sc. 2, l. 113.
Give us a light there, ho!—*Macbeth,* iii, 3, 9.
Light, I say! light!—*Othello,* i, 1, 145.
More light, you knaves.—*Romeo and Juliet,* i, 5, 29; 89.
Light to my chamber, ho!—*Romeo and Juliet,* iii, 4, 33.
Now some light.—*Julius Cæsar,* v, 3, 31.

12
Who did strike out the light?
Macbeth. Act iii, sc. 3, l. 18. [Murderer]
Doctor: How came she by that light?
Gentleman: Why, it stood by her: she has light by her continually; 'tis her command.
Macbeth. Act v, sc. 1, l. 25. "Continually" is repeated in *Richard III,* v, 3, 84, and in *I Henry IV,* ii, 1, 88.

13
They wilfully exile themselves from light
And must for aye consort with black-brow'd night.
A Midsummer-Night's Dream. Act iii, sc. 2, l. 386. [Puck] "Black-brow'd night" is repeated in *Romeo and Juliet,* iii, 2, 20.
Through the house goes glimmering light,
By the dead and drowsy fire.
A Midsummer-Night's Dream. Act v, sc. 1, l. 398. [Oberon] "Glimmering" is repeated in ii, 1, 77, and in iii, 2, 61, and occurs in no other play.

1 These things, come thus to light,
Smother her spirits up.
Much Ado about Nothing. Act iv, sc. 1, l. 112. [Don John]

Come to light.—*Henry V,* iv, 8, 23; *The Merchant of Venice,* ii, 2, 83; *Titus Andronicus,* iv, 2, 125; *Henry VIII,* iii, 2, 29.

Bring to light.—*II Henry VI,* iii, 1, 65; *Measure for Measure,* iii, 2, 189; *The Rape of Lucrece,* l. 940.

Brought to light.—*Henry V,* ii, 2, 185; *Much Ado about Nothing,* v, 1, 240.

2
Put out the light, and then put out the light:
If I quench thee, thou flaming minister,
I can again thy former light restore,
Should I repent me: but once put out thy light,
Thou cunning'st pattern of excelling nature,
I know not where is that Promethean heat
That can thy light relume.
Othello. Act v, sc. 2, l. 6. [Othello] The only use of "cunning'st" and "relume." "Promethean" occurs also in *Love's Labour's Lost,* iv, 3, 304; 351.

What lights come yond?—*Othello,* i, 2, 28.

Lend me a light.—*Othello,* v, 1, 88.

Lend thee light.—*Venus and Adonis,* l. 864.

Give me the light.—*Romeo and Juliet,* v, 3, 25.

3
No light, no fire: the unfriendly elements
Forget thee utterly.
Pericles. Act iii, sc. 1, l. 58. [Pericles]

Keep them from the light.—*Pericles,* i, 1, 136.

4
Fair torch, burn out thy light, and lend it not
To darken her whose light excelleth thine.
The Rape of Lucrece, l. 190.

Small lights are soon blown out.
The Rape of Lucrece, l. 647. See under FIRE.

This said, he sets his foot upon the light,
For light and lust are deadly enemies.
The Rape of Lucrece, l. 673.

5
But, soft! what light through yonder window breaks?
Romeo and Juliet, ii, 2, 2. See under SUN.

Eastern light.—*The Rape of Lucrece,* l. 773.

Morning light.—*The Rape of Lucrece,* l. 745.

Streaks of light.—*Romeo and Juliet,* ii, 3, 2. The only use of the phrase. "Streaks of day" occurs in *Macbeth,* iii, 3, 5.

6
Yond light is not day-light, I know it, I;
It is some meteor that the sun exhales,
To be to thee this night a torch-bearer,
And light thee on thy way.
Romeo and Juliet. Act iii, sc. 5, l. 12. [Juliet] "Torch-bearer" is used five times in the plays and "daylight" twelve.

Juliet: O, now be gone; more light and light it grows.
Romeo: More light and light; more dark and dark our woes!
Romeo and Juliet. Act iii, sc. 5, l. 35.

Full of light.—*Romeo and Juliet,* v, 3, 86.

7
Upon mine honour, he shall never know
That I had any light from thee of this.
Two Gentlemen of Verona, iii, 1, 48. [Duke]

What light is light, if Silvia be not seen?
The Two Gentlemen of Verona. Act iii, sc. 1, l. 174. [Valentine]

Reason's light.—*The Two Gentlemen of Verona,* ii, 4, 210.

Heaven's lights.—*Love's Labour's Lost,* i, 1, 88; *Venus and Adonis,* l. 533.

Heavenly light.—*Othello,* iv, 3, 65. See under DEED.

Light of heaven.—*Othello,* iv, 2, 150.

Light of truth.—*Love's Labour's Lost,* i, 1, 75.

World's light.—*Othello,* i, 3, 410.

LIGHTNESS, see Inconstancy

LIGHTNING

See also Thunder

8
Now he 'll outstare the lightning.
Antony and Cleopatra. Act iii, sc. 13, l. 195. [Enobarbus]

I would outstare the sternest eyes that look.
The Merchant of Venice, ii, 1, 27. See under WOOING.

I 'll follow and outstare him.
Henry VIII. Act i, sc. 1, l. 129. [Buckingham] The only uses of "outstare."

Harmless lightning.—*Cymbeline,* v, 5, 394.

9 Never till to-night, never till now,
Did I go through a tempest dropping fire.
Julius Cæsar. Act i, sc. 3, l. 9. [Casca]

When the cross blue lightning seem'd to open
The breast of heaven, I did present myself
Even in the aim and very flash of it.
Julius Cæsar. Act i, sc. 3, l. 50. [Casca]

10
Be thou as lightning in the eyes of France.
King John. Act i, sc. 1, l. 24. [King John]

Like to lightning.—*III Henry VI,* ii, 1, 129.

Go like lightning.—*Romeo and Juliet,* iii, 1, 177.

Swift like lightning.—*Richard II,* i, 3, 79.

11
You nimble lightnings, dart your blinding flames
Into her scornful eyes!
King Lear. Act ii, sc. 4, l. 167. [King Lear]

In the most terrible and nimble stroke
Of quick, cross lightning.
King Lear. Act iv, sc. 7, l. 34. [Cordelia]

12
Brief as the lightning in the collied night,
That, in a spleen, unfolds both heaven and earth,
And ere a man hath power to say 'Behold!'
The jaws of darkness do devour it up.
A Midsummer-Night's Dream. Act i, sc. 1, l. 145. [Lysander] "Collied" (black, grimy) occurs again in *Othello,* ii, 3, 206, as a verb: "Passion, having my best judgement collied, Assays to lead the way."

Too like the lightning, which doth cease to be
Ere one can say 'It lightens.'
Romeo and Juliet. Act ii, sc. 2, l. 119. [Juliet] "Lightens" in this sense is used again in *Julius Cæsar,* i, 3, 74: "Thunders, lightens."

1
Lightning strike the murderer dead.
Richard III, i, 2, 64. See EARTH, 397:13.
Lightning before death.—*Romeo and Juliet,* v, 3, 90.

I would the lightning had
Burnt up those logs that you are enjoin'd to pile!
The Tempest. Act iii, sc. 1, l. 16. [Miranda]

2 Jove's lightnings, the precursors
O' the dreadful thunder-claps.
The Tempest. Act i, sc. 2, l. 201. [Ariel] The only use of "precursors" and "thunder-claps."
Jove's lightning.—*Love's Labour's Lost,* iv, 2, 119; *The Passionate Pilgrim,* l. 67.
Lightning from the sky.—*Venus and Adonis,* l. 348.

LIKENESS

See also Resemblance

3
What was he like? I have forgot him.
All's Well that Ends Well. Act i, sc. 1, l. 92. [Helena]
A crow o' the same nest.
All's Well that Ends Well. Act iv, sc. 3, l. 319. [Parolles]

Mine eye doth his effigies witness
Most truly limn'd and living in your face.
As You Like It. Act ii, sc. 7, l. 193. [Duke] The only use of "effigies" and "limn'd." "Limning" occurs in *Venus and Adonis,* l. 290.

4
Like one another as half-pence are.
As You Like It, iii, 2, 372. See under WOMAN.
One sand another Not more resembles.
Cymbeline. Act v, sc. 5, l. 120. [Arviragus]
These hands are not more like.
Hamlet. Act i, sc. 2, l. 212. [Horatio]
'Tis alike as my fingers is to my fingers.
Henry V. Act iv, sc. 7, l. 32. [Fluellen]
'Tis as like you As cherry is to cherry.
Henry VIII. Act v, sc. 1, l. 168. [Old Lady]
She 's as like this as a crab 's like an apple. . . . She will taste as like this as a crab does to a crab.
King Lear. Act i, sc. 5, l. 15. [Fool]
He is as like thee as a man may be.
Richard II. Act v, sc. 2, l. 108. [Duchess of York]
As like Hermione as is her picture.
The Winter's Tale. Act v. sc. 1, l. 74. [Paulina]

5
Two godly sons . . . the one so like the other
As could not be distinguish'd but by names.
The Comedy of Errors. Act i, sc. 1, l. 51. [Ægeon]
I know not which is which.
The Comedy of Errors. Act v, sc. 1, l. 364. [Duke] "Which is which" is repeated in *A Midsummer-Night's Dream,* ii, 1, 114; in *Timon of Athens,* ii, 2, 82; and in *Macbeth,* iii, 4, 127.
One of these men is Genius to the other;
And so of these. Which is the natural man,
And which the spirit? who deciphers them?
The Comedy of Errors. Act v, sc. 1, l. 332. [Duke] "Decipher" is repeated in *The Merry Wives of Windsor,* v, 2, 10.
These two so like.—*The Comedy of Errors,* v, 1, 357.

6
Methinks you are my glass, and not my brother:
I see by you I am a sweet-faced youth.
The Comedy of Errors. Act v, sc. 1, l. 417. [Dromio of Ephesus] "Sweet-faced" occurs also in *A Midsummer-Night's Dream,* i, 2, 88.
Thou art thy mother's glass, and she in thee
Calls back the lovely April of her prime.
Sonnets. No. iii.

7
Creatures may be alike.
Cymbeline. Act v, sc. 5, l. 125. [Belarius]
Most like.—*Julius Cæsar,* i, 3, 73; *Hamlet,* i, 1, 43; ii, 2, 365; 437; *Antony and Cleopatra,* i, 1, 25; *Cymbeline,* iii, 4, 119; v, 5, 259.
Very like.—*Hamlet,* i, 2, 237; iii, 2, 399; *Cymbeline,* ii, 4, 36; *The Tempest,* v, 1, 265.
Something like.—*Timon of Athens,* ii, 2, 115.

8
Marcellus: Is it not like the king?
Horatio: As thou art to thyself.
Hamlet. Act i, sc. 1, l. 58.
I shall not look upon his like again.
Hamlet, i, 2, 188. See under MAN.

9
I am, my lord, but as my betters are.
II Henry IV. Act iv, sc. 3, l. 71. [Colevile]
Be like them.—*II Henry IV,* ii, 3, 4.
Seem like him.—*II Henry IV,* ii, 3, 28.
Remain alike.—*Coriolanus,* i, 4, 63.

10
Helen, the mother of great Constantine,
Nor yet Saint Philip's daughters, were like thee.
I Henry VI. Act i, sc. 2, l. 142. [Charles] "Like thee" is repeated in i, 4, 95.
Am I not witch'd like her? or thou not false like him?
II Henry VI. Act iii, sc. 2, l. 119. [Queen]

11
The like yet never heard of.
III Henry VI. Act ii, sc. 1, l. 33. [Richard] See under OMEN.
Was ever heard the like?—*Titus Andronicus,* ii, 3, 276.
Didst ever see the like?—*The Taming of the Shrew,* iv, 1, 182.
I never saw the like.—*Coriolanus,* ii, 1, 284.

12
'Good Gloucester' and 'good devil' were alike,
And both preposterous.
III Henry VI. Act v, sc. 6, l. 4. [King Henry]

13
Queen Elinor: He hath a trick of Cœur-de-lion's face;
The accent of his tongue affecteth him.
Do you not read some tokens of my son
In the large composition of this man?
King John: Mine eye hath well examined his parts
And finds them perfect Richard.
King John. Act i, sc. 1, l. 85.

This boy
Liker in feature to his father Geffrey
Than thou and John in manners; being as like
As rain to water, or devil to his dam.
King John. Act ii, sc. 1, l. 125. [Constance] "Liker" occurs again in *Love's Labour's Lost,* v, 2, 846.

Both are alike; and both alike we like.
King John. Act ii, sc. 1, l. 331. [Citizen]

Both alike.—*Comedy of Errors,* i, 1, 56; *Henry V,* iv, 7, 27; *Romeo and Juliet,* Prol., 1; *Troilus and Cressida,* iv, 1, 54; *Cymbeline,* iv, 2, 5.

1
Thou art too like the spirit of Banquo; down!
Macbeth. Act iv, sc. 1, l. 112. [Macbeth]

2
Well, there went but a pair of shears between us.
Measure for Measure. Act i, sc. 2, l. 28. [First Gentleman]

As like almost to Claudio as himself.
Measure for Measure. Act v, sc. 1, l. 494. [Provost]

3
Here he comes in the likeness of a Jew.
The Merchant of Venice. Act iii, sc. 1, l. 24. [Salanio]

In likeness of a new untrimmed bride.—*King John,* iii, 1, 209. The only use of "untrimmed."

In very likeness of a roasted crab.—*A Midsummer-Night's Dream,* ii, 1, 48.

In likeness of a filly foal.—*A Midsummer-Night's Dream,* ii, 1, 46. The only use of "filly foal."

In the likeness of your grace.—*Much Ado about Nothing,* i, 1, 100.

In the likeness of an old fat man.—*I Henry IV,* ii, 4, 493.

Likeness of a man.—*Sonnets,* cxli.

In likeness of a coal-black Moor.—*Titus Andronicus,* iii, 2, 78.

In the likeness of a sigh.—*Romeo and Juliet,* ii, 1, 8.

In thy likeness.—*Love's Labour's Lost,* iv, 3, 46.

Old Adam's likeness.—*Richard II,* iii, 4, 73.

Borrow'd likeness.—*Romeo and Juliet,* iv, 1, 104.

True likeness.—*Henry V,* v, 2, 317; 321.

4 The bosom lover of my lord,
Must needs be like my lord.
The Merchant of Venice. Act iii, sc. 4, l. 17. [Portia]

5
Balthasar: I would you did like me.
Margaret: So would not I, for your own sake.
Much Ado about Nothing. Act ii, sc. 1, l. 103.

Did the like.—*Macbeth,* iii, 4, 18.

Do the like.—*I Henry IV,* ii, 4, 339; *Coriolanus,* i, 4, 45.

Do you the like.—*Julius Cæsar,* iv, 2, 50.

Done the like.—*Titus Andronicus,* iv, 1, 111.

Perform the like.—*Titus Andronicus,* v, 3, 45.

Such like.—*The Two Gentlemen of Verona,* iv, 1, 52.

6
All men are not alike; alas, good neighbour!
Much Ado about Nothing. Act iii, sc. 5, l. 43. [Dogberry]

Not alike.—*Cymbeline,* i, 6, 148.

Nothing like.—*All's Well that Ends Well,* iii, 2, 15.

It is not very like.—*Romeo and Juliet,* iv, 3, 36.

7 My brother hath a daughter,
Almost the copy of my child that 's dead.
Much Ado about Nothing. Act v, sc. 1, l. 298. [Leonato]

There never came her like in Mytilene.
Pericles. Act iv, sc. 6, l. 31. [Bawd]

In the child the father's image lies.
The Rape of Lucrece, l. 1753.

8 I did infer your lineaments,
Being the right idea of your father,
Both in your form and nobleness of mind.
Richard III. Act iii, sc. 7, l. 12. [Buckingham]

9
Apemantus: Do not assume my likeness.
Timon: Were I like thee, I 'ld throw away myself.
Apemantus: Thou hast cast away thyself, being like thyself.
Timon of Athens. Act iv, sc. 3, l. 218.

Like itself.—*II Henry IV,* iv, 1, 33; *Richard II,* ii, 1, 295; *Antony and Cleopatra,* ii, 7, 47.

Like myself.—*King Lear,* i, 4, 179; *Cymbeline,* iv, 4, 39.

All alike.—*Love's Labour's Lost,* iv, 3, 126; *Measure for Measure,* i, 1, 35; *Macbeth,* iii, 1, 101; *Antony and Cleopatra,* iii, 13, 34; *Sonnets,* cv.

Alike in all.—*Titus Andronicus,* i, 1, 174.

Like to.—*II Henry VI,* iv, 9, 32, and twenty-seven times in later plays.

Too like the sire for ever being good.
Titus Andronicus. Act v, sc. 1, l. 50. [Lucius]

10
Parallels, as like as Vulcan and his wife.
Troilus and Cressida. Act i, sc. 3, l. 168. [Ulysses]

He parallels Nessus.—*All's Well that Ends Well,* iv, 2, 281.

Stand up his parallel.—*Cymbeline,* v, 4, 54.

Lack a parallel.—*All's Well that Ends Well,* v, 3, 193.

Without a parallel.—*The Tempest,* i, 2, 74.

Parallel course.—*Othello,* ii, 3, 355.

11
One face, one voice, one habit, and two persons,
A natural perspective, that is and is not!
Twelfth Night. Act v, sc. 1, l. 223. [Duke]

How have you made division of yourself?
An apple, cleft in two, is not more twin
Than these two creatures.
Twelfth Night. Act v, sc. 1, l. 229. [Antonio]

12
How like, methought, I then was to this kernel,
This squash, this gentleman.
The Winter's Tale. Act i, sc. 2, l. 159. [Leontes] "Squash" occurs twice more in the plays, in *A Midsummer-Night's Dream,* iii, 1, 191, and in *Twelfth Night,* i, 5, 166.

Leontes: This brat is none of mine; . . .
Paulina: It is yours;
And, might we lay the old proverb to your charge,

So like you, 'tis the worse. Behold, my lords,
Although the print be little, the whole matter
And copy of the father.
The Winter's Tale. Act ii, sc. 3, l. 92.

The copy of my child that 's dead.—*Much Ado about Nothing,* v, 1, 298.

Leave the world no copy.—*Twelfth Night,* i, 5, 261.

Not let that copy die.—*Sonnets,* xi.

A copy out of mine.—*Winter's Tale,* i, 2, 122.

Nature's copy.—*Macbeth,* iii, 2, 38. See also under EXAMPLE.

1
Leontes: How now, you wanton calf!
Art thou my calf?
Mamillius: Yes, if you will, my lord.
Leontes: Thou want'st a rough pash and the shoots that I have,
To be full like me: yet they say we are
Almost as like as eggs; women say so,
That will say anything: but were they false
As o'er-dyed blacks, as wind, as waters, false
As dice are to be wish'd by one that fixes
No bourn 'twixt his and mine, yet were it true
To say this boy were like me.
The Winter's Tale. Act i, sc. 2, l. 126. The only use of "pash" in the sense of head or face, and of "o'er-dyed."

He had pair'd Well with this lord.
The Winter's Tale. Act v, sc. 1, l. 116. [Paulina] The only use of "pair'd."

2
Her dead likeness, I do well believe,
Excels whatever yet you looked upon
Or hand of man hath done.
Winter's Tale. Act v, sc. 3, l. 15. [Paulina]

Comes it not something near?
Winter's Tale. Act v, sc. 3, l. 23. [Paulina]

LIKING

3
Is it possible, on such a sudden, you should fall into so strong a liking?
As You Like It. Act i, sc. 3, l. 27. [Celia]

Is 't possible that on so little acquaintance you should like her?
As You Like It, v, 2, 1. See under LOVE.

Would now like him, now loathe him.
As You Like It. Act iii, sc. 2, l. 436. [Rosalind]

4
Take her away; I do not like her now.
All 's Well that Ends Well. Act v, sc. 3, l. 282. [King]

Being no other but she is, I do not like her.
Much Ado about Nothing. Act i, sc. 1, l. 177. [Benedick]

I do not like the man.—*Measure for Measure,* v, 1, 128.

I do not like thy look.—*Much Ado about Nothing,* iv, 2, 46.

I like him not.—*Hamlet,* iii, 3, 1.

I like it not.—*I Henry VI,* iii, 2, 110. "Like it not" is repeated four times in later plays.

I like you not.—*As You Like It,* iii, 5, 74.

I like not.—*III Henry VI,* iv, 6, 89, and thirteen times in later plays.

Against his liking.—*All 's Well that Ends Well,* iii, 5, 57.

5
Jaques: Good my lord, like this fellow.
Duke Senior: I like him very well.
As You Like It. Act v, sc. 4, l. 53.

I like him well.—*All 's Well that Ends Well,* iii, 5, 84; iv, 5, 72.

I like it well.—*III Henry VI,* iii, 3, 167; *The Taming of the Shrew,* iv, 3, 21; *King John,* ii, 1, 398; *Richard II,* iii, 2, 4.

I like it very well.—*As You Like It,* iii, 2, 16.

Well I like it.—*The Two Gentlemen of Verona,* i, 3, 35.

I like that well.—*Pericles,* ii, 5, 19.

I like thee well.—*The Two Gentlemen of Verona,* iv, 5, 44; *King John,* i, 1, 148.

I like you, lads.—*Richard III,* i, 3, 355.

I like them all.—*II Henry IV,* iv, 2, 53.

I like this well.—*Timon of Athens,* v, 1, 207; *King Lear,* iv, 2, 84.

I like the work well.—*Othello,* iii, 4, 189.

I like your work.—*Timon of Athens,* i, 1, 160.

Do you not like it?—*The Two Gentlemen of Verona,* ii, 1, 127.

6
King Henry: Do you like me, Kate?
Katharine: Pardonnez-moi, I cannot tell vat is 'like me.'
King Henry: An angel is like you, Kate, and you are like an angel.
Henry V. Act v, sc. 2, l. 107.

7
An 't like your lordly lord-protectorship.
II Henry VI. Act ii, sc. 1, l. 30. [Suffolk] The only use of "lord-protectorship." "An 't like you" is repeated frequently in later plays.

Likes me better.—*Henry V,* iv, 1, 16; iv, 3, 77. A phrase used only in this play.

It likes me well.—*King John,* ii, 1, 533; *Taming of the Shrew,* iv, 4, 62; *Hamlet,* ii, 2, 80.

This likes me well.—*Hamlet,* v, 2, 276.

Likes me not.—*The Two Gentlemen of Verona,* iv, 2, 57; *King Lear,* ii, 2, 96.

8
If he see aught in you that makes him like,
That any thing he sees, which moves his liking,
I can with ease translate it to my will.
King John. Act ii, sc. 1, l. 511. [Blanch]

9
Avert your liking a more worthier way.
King Lear. Act i, sc. 1, l. 214. [King Lear] The only use of "avert."

If I like thee no worse after dinner, I will not part from thee yet.
King Lear. Act iii, sc. 4, l. 44. [King Lear]

10
Lorenzo: How dost thou like the Lord Bassanio's wife?
Jessica: Past all expressing.
The Merchant of Venice. Act iii, sc. 5, l. 77.

Now, good Sir John, how like you the Windsor wives?
The Merry Wives of Windsor. Act v, sc. 5, l. 110. [Mrs. Page]

11
If matters grow to your likings.
The Merry Wives of Windsor. Act i, sc. 1, l. 79. [Evans]

I like it never the better for that.
The Merry Wives of Windsor. Act ii, sc. 1, l. 186. [Ford]
What didst not like?—*Othello,* iii, 3, 110.

1
Drive liking to the name of love.
Much Ado about Nothing, i, 1, 302. See under EYE.
Claudio: Lest my liking might too sudden seem
I would have salved it with a longer treatise.
Don Pedro: What need the bridge much broader than the flood?
Much Ado about Nothing. Act i, sc. 1, l. 316.

2
If you like her, so; if not, I have lost my earnest.
Pericles. Act iv, sc. 2, l. 48. [Boult]
Your treatise makes me like you worse and worse.
Venus and Adonis, l. 773.

3
If you like me, you shall have me and mine.
The Taming of the Shrew. Act ii, sc. 1, l. 385. [Gremio]

4 You have broken from his liking
Where you were tied in duty.
The Winter's Tale. Act v, sc. 1, l. 212. [Leontes]
Do my liking.—*Much Ado About Nothing,* i, 3, 38.
In my liking.—*Henry VIII,* ii, 4, 33.
In their liking.—*Coriolanus,* i, 1, 199.
In your liking.—*King Lear,* i, 1, 236.
In some liking.—*I Henry IV,* iii, 3, 6.
Own liking.—*All's Well that Ends Well,* i, 1, 164.
Father's liking.—*The Taming of the Shrew,* iii, 2, 131.
Men's liking.—*The Merry Wives of Windsor,* ii, 1, 57.

LILY

5
How bravely thou becomest thy bed, fresh lily,
And whiter than the sheets!
Cymbeline. Act ii, sc. 2, l. 15. [Iachimo]
O sweetest, fairest lily!
My brother wears thee not the one half so well
As when thou grew'st thyself.
Cymbeline. Act iv, sc. 2, l. 201. [Guiderius]

6 Like the lily,
That once was mistress of the field and flourish'd,
I 'll hang my head and perish.
Henry VIII. Act iii, sc. 1, l. 151. [Queen Katharine]

7
To paint the lily.
King John, iv, 2, 11. See under EXCESS.

8
Lilies that fester smell far worse than weeds.
Sonnets. No. xciv.

9 Lilies of all kinds,
The flower-de-luce being one!
The Winter's Tale, iv, 4, 126. See under FLOWER.
A most unspotted lily.—*Henry VIII,* v, 5, 62.
Unsullied lily.—*Love's Labour 's Lost,* v, 2, 352.
Gather'd lily.—*Titus Andronicus,* iii, 1, 113.
Lily-beds.—*Troilus and Cressida,* iii, 2, 13. The only use of the phrase.

LIMB

See also Arm, Leg

10 Expose
Those tender limbs of thine to the event
Of the none-sparing war.
All's Well that Ends Well. Act iii, sc. 2, l. 106. [Helena] The only use of "none-sparing."
Gentle limbs.—*All's Well that Ends Well,* v, 1, 4.
Young limbs.—*II Henry IV,* i, 2, 257.
Young in limbs.—*The Merchant of Venice,* ii, 7, 71.

11
He 's a limb that has but a disease.
Coriolanus, iii, 1, 296. See under DISEASE.

12 My limbs,
Weaken'd with grief, being now enraged with grief,
Are thrice themselves.
II Henry IV. Act i, sc. 1, l. 143. [Northumberland]
Feeble limbs.—*Richard III,* ii, 2, 58.
Old limbs.—*As You Like It,* ii, 3, 41; *I Henry IV,* v, 1, 13.
Recreant limbs.—*King John,* iii, 1, 129; 131; 133; 199.
Weary limbs.—*Henry V,* v, 1, 89.
War-wearied limbs.—*I Henry VI,* iv, 4, 18.
Weak unable limbs.—*I Henry VI,* iv, 5, 4.

13
Care I for the limb, the thewes . . . of a man?
II Henry IV, iii, 2, 276. See MAN, 914:4.
Thews and limbs.—*Julius Cæsar,* i, 3, 81.
Thews and bulk.—*Hamlet,* i, 3, 12. The only uses of "thews."

14 Good yeomen,
Whose limbs were made in England.
Henry V. Act iii, sc. 1, l. 25. [King Henry]
So do our vulgar drench their peasant limbs
In blood of princes.
Henry V. Act iv, sc. 7, l. 80. [King Henry]

15
Even like a man new haled from the rack,
So fare my limbs with long imprisonment
I Henry VI. Act ii, sc. 5, l. 3. [Mortimer]

16
Set limb to limb, and thou art far the lesser.
II Henry VI. Act iv, sc. 10, l. 50. [Iden]
And so he comes, to rend his limbs asunder.
III Henry VI, i, 3, 15. See under LION.

17
Our course will seem too bloody, Caius Cassius,
To cut the head off and then hack the limbs, . . .
For Antony is but a limb of Cæsar.
Julius Cæsar. Act ii, sc. 1, l. 162. [Brutus]
Mincing with his sword her husband's limbs.
Hamlet. Act ii, sc. 2, l. 537. [First Player]

18
To whom am I beholding for these limbs?
King John, i, 1, 239. See under SON.

This swain, because of his great limb or joint, shall pass Pompey the Great.
Love's Labour 's Lost. Act v, sc. 1, l. 134. [Holofernes]
Proper limbs.—*Richard III,* iii, 7, 125.
Strong-knit limbs.—*I Henry VI,* ii, 3, 21.
Strong-knit sinews.—*III Henry VI,* ii, 3, 4. The only uses of "strong-knit."

1
Let them keep their limbs whole.
The Merry Wives of Windsor. Act iii, sc. 1, l. 79. [Host]
Couch his limbs.—*Romeo and Juliet,* ii, 3, 38.
Their limbs may halt.—*Timon of Athens,* iv, 1, 24.

2
Away with him! and make a fire straight;
And with our swords, upon a pile of wood,
Let 's hew his limbs till they be clean consumed.
Titus Andronicus. Act i, sc. 1, l. 127. [Lucius]
Hew his limbs.—*Titus Andronicus,* i, 1, 97.

3
Alarbus' limbs are lopp'd.
Titus Andronicus. Act i, sc. 1, l. 143. [Lucius]
A limb lopp'd off.—*II Henry VI,* ii, 3, 42; *I Henry IV,* iv, 1, 43.

4
O, let me teach you how to knit again . . .
These broken limbs again into one body.
Titus Andronicus. Act v, sc. 3, l. 70. [Marcus]
New-transformed limbs.—*Titus Andronicus,* ii, 3, 64. The only use of "new-transformed."
Broken limb.—*As You Like It,* i, 1, 134; *II Henry IV,* iv, 1, 222.
Break my limbs.—*King John,* iv, 3, 6.
Bend my limbs.—*Richard II,* iv, 1, 165.

5 Limbs are his instruments,
In no less working than are swords and bows
Directive by the limbs.
Troilus and Cressida. Act i, sc. 3, l. 354. [Nestor] The only use of "directive."

I will the second time,
As I would buy thee, view thee limb by limb.
Troilus and Cressida. Act iv, sc. 5, l. 238. [Achilles]
Each several limb is doubled.—*Venus and Adonis,* l. 1067.

LIMIT

6 I 'll limit thee this day
To seek thy life by beneficial help.
The Comedy of Errors. Act i, sc. 1, l. 151. [Duke]

7
You have stood your limitation.
Coriolanus. Act ii, sc. 3, l. 146. [Menenius]

Am I yourself
But, as it were, in sort or limitation?
Julius Cæsar, ii, 1, 282. See under Wife. The only uses of "limitation."

8
Out of limit . . . You stand.
I Henry IV. Act iv, sc. 3, l. 39. [Blunt]
Out of all sanctified limit.—*All's Well that Ends Well,* i, 1, 152.
Give no limits.—*III Henry VI,* ii, 2, 119.
Without limit.—*Much Ado about Nothing,* i, 3, 5.

9
The farthest limit of my embassy.
King John. Act i, sc. 1, l. 22. [Chatillon]
Dateless limit.—*Richard II,* i, 3, 151.
Sparing limit.—*Richard III,* iii, 7, 94.
Limits far remote.—*Sonnets,* xliv.
Above his limits.—*Richard II,* iii, 2, 109.
Beyond all limit.—*The Tempest,* iii, 1, 72.
Within the limit.—*Love's Labour 's Lost,* ii, 1, 67; *Richard II,* iii, 3, 26.

10
Dispatch; the limit of your lives is out.
Richard III. Act iii, sc. 3, l. 8. [Ratcliff]

11
Limit each leader to his several charge.
Richard III. Act v, sc. 3, l. 25. [Richmond]

12
Stony limits cannot hold love out.
Romeo and Juliet, ii, 2, 67. See under Love.

13
You must confine yourself within the modest limits of order.
Twelfth Night. Act i, sc. 3, l. 8. [Maria]
Within this limit is relief enough.
Venus and Adonis, l. 235.

14 Hurried
Here to this place, i' the open air, before
I have got strength of limit.
The Winter's Tale. Act iii, sc. 2, l. 107. [Hermione]

LINE

15
He sends you this most memorable line.
Henry V. Act ii, sc. 4, l. 88. [Exeter]
Accursed line.—*III Henry VI,* i, 3, 32.
Heroic line.—*I Henry VI,* ii, 5, 78.
True line.—*Henry V,* i, 2, 71.
Line of kings.—*Macbeth,* i, 3, 112.

16
Give him line and scope.
II Henry IV. Act iv, sc. 4, l. 39. [King Henry]

17
Comest thou with deep premeditated lines,
With written pamphlets studiously devised?
I Henry VI. Act iii, sc. 1, l. 1. [Bishop of Winchester] The only use of "pamphlets" and "studiously."

18
All that stand about him are under the line, they need no other penance.
Henry VIII. Act v, sc. 4, l. 44. [Man]

19 Yon grey lines
That fret the clouds are messengers of day.
Julius Cæsar. Act ii, sc. 1, l. 103. [Cinna]

20
I fear these stubborn lines lack power to move.
Love's Labour 's Lost. Act iv, sc. 3, l. 55. [Longaville]
What, did these rent lines show some love of thine?
Love's Labour 's Lost. Act iv, sc. 3, l. 220. [King]
His lines shall ravish savage ears.
Love's Labour 's Lost, iv, 3, 348. See Poetry: The Poet, 1171:11.

1 In top of rage the lines she rents,
Big discontent so breaking their contents.
A Lover's Complaint, l. 55.

2
What, will the line stretch out to the crack of doom?
Macbeth. Act iv, sc. 1, l. 117. [Macbeth]

3
Go to, here 's a simple line of life.
The Merchant of Venice. Act ii, sc. 2, l. 169. [Launcelot]

Lines of life.—*Sonnets,* xvi.

4
Lines of fair comfort and encouragement.
Richard III. Act v, sc. 2, l. 6. [Richmond]

Lines of favour.—*Cymbeline,* iv, 2, 104.

Eternal lines.—*Sonnets,* xviii.

These poor rude lines.—*Sonnets,* xxxii. See under POET.

Black lines.—*Sonnets,* lxiii.

5
Nay, if you read this line, remember not
The hand that writ it.
Sonnets. No. lxxi. See under MOURNING.

Those lines that I before have writ do lie,
Even those that said I could not love you dearer:
Yet then my judgement knew no reason why
My most full flame should afterwards burn clearer.
Sonnets. No. cxv.

6
Come, hang them on this line.
The Tempest. Act iv, sc. 1, l. 193. [Prospero]

7
Here 's no sound jest! the old man hath found their guilt;
And sends them weapons wrapp'd about with lines,
That wound, beyond their feeling, to the quick.
Titus Andronicus. Act iv, sc. 2, l. 26. [Aaron]

What I mean to do
See here in bloody lines I have set down.
Titus Andronicus. Act v, sc. 2, l. 13. [Titus]

Crimson lines.—*Titus Andronicus,* v, 2, 22.

8
Last night she enjoined me to write some lines to one she loves.
The Two Gentlemen of Verona. Act ii, sc. 1, l. 94. [Valentine]

Frame some feeling line.—*The Two Gentlemen of Verona,* iii, 2, 76.

Sweet lines.—*The Two Gentlemen of Verona,* i, 3, 45.

Wanton lines.—*The Two Gentlemen of Verona,* i, 2, 42.

A volume of enticing lines.—*I Henry VI,* v, 5, 14. See under PERFECTION.

9
I will not look upon your master's lines:
I know they are stuff'd with protestations
And full of new-found oaths; which he will break
As easily as I will tear this paper.
The Two Gentlemen of Verona. Act iv, sc. 4, l. 133. [Silvia] The only use of "new-found."

LINEN

10
They 'll find linen enough on every hedge.
I Henry IV, iv, 2, 52. See under SHIRT.

Get linen.—*Pericles,* iii, 2, 109.

11
It is a low ebb of linen with thee.
II Henry IV. Act ii, sc. 2, l. 22. [Prince Henry]

Want of linen.—*Love's Labour 's Lost,* v, 2, 719.

12
They have marvellous foul linen.
II Henry IV. Act v, sc. 1, l. 38. [Davy]

Throw foul linen upon him, as if it were going to bucking.
The Merry Wives of Windsor. Act iii, sc. 3, l. 138. [Mrs. Page] The only use of "bucking" (washing).

This 'tis to have linen and buck-baskets!
The Merry Wives of Windsor. Act iii, sc. 5, l. 145. [Ford] "Buck-basket" (dirty linen basket) is repeated in iii, 3, 2, iii, 5, 88, and v, 2, 139, and occurs in no other play.

13
I 'll bring linen for him straight.
The Merry Wives of Windsor. Act iv, sc. 2, l. 102. [Mrs. Ford]

Linen for your head. *The Merry Wives of Windsor,* iv, 2, 83.

Fine linen.—*Taming of the Shrew,* ii, 1, 355.

Senseless linen!—*Cymbeline,* i, 3, 7.

Linen cheeks.—*Macbeth,* v, 3, 16.

14
In any case, let Thisby have clean linen.
A Midsummer-Night's Dream. Act iv, sc. 2, l. 40. [Bottom]

15
With the nightly linen that she wears
He pens her piteous clamours in her head.
The Rape of Lucrece, l. 680.

16
My traffic is sheets; when the kite builds, look to lesser linen.
The Winter's Tale. Act iv, sc. 3, l. 23. [Autolycus]

LION

17 Better 'twere
I met the ravin lion when he roar'd
With sharp constraint of hunger.
All 's Well that Ends Well. Act iii, sc. 2, l. 119. [Helena] "Ravin" (ravenous) occurs twice more in the plays, in *Measure for Measure,* i, 2, 133, and in *Macbeth,* ii, 4, 28.

18
'Tis better playing with a lion's whelp
Than with an old one dying.
Antony and Cleopatra. Act iii, sc. 13, l. 94. [Enobarbus] "Lion's whelp" is repeated five times.

19
Oliver: A lioness, with udders all drawn dry,
Lay couching, head on ground, with catlike watch,
When that the sleeping man should stir; for 'tis
The royal disposition of that beast
To prey on nothing that doth seem as dead. . . .

Rosalind: Did he leave him there,
Food to the suck'd and hungry lioness?
Oliver: Twice did he turn his back and purposed so;
But kindness, nobler ever than revenge,
And nature, stronger than his just occasion,
Made him give battle to the lioness,
Who quickly fell before him.
As You Like It. Act iv, sc. 3, l. 115. The only use of "udders" and "catlike."

And here upon his arm,
The lioness had torn some flesh away.
As You Like It. Act iv, sc. 3, l. 148. [Oliver]

A lioness hath whelped in the streets.
Julius Cæsar. Act ii, sc. 2, l. 17. [Calpurnia] "Whelped" is repeated in *Timon of Athens,* ii, 2, 90.

Mountain lioness.—*Titus Andronicus,* iv, 2, 138. "Lioness" is used once again in *King John,* ii, 1, 291. See below.

1 O, the blood more stirs
To rouse a lion than to start a hare!
I Henry IV. Act i, sc. 3, l. 197. [Hotspur]

2
The lion will not touch the true prince.
I Henry IV. Act ii, sc. 4, l. 300. [Falstaff]

3
The man that once did sell the lion's skin
While the beast lived, was killed with hunting him.
Henry V. Act iv, sc. 3, l. 93. [King Henry]

4 Like lions wanting food,
Do rush upon us as their hungry prey.
I Henry VI. Act i, sc. 2, l. 27. [Reignier]

Like a hungry lion.—*I Henry VI,* iv, 7, 7.

5
Great men tremble when the lion roars.
II Henry VI. Act iii, sc. 1, l. 19. [Queen]

O, tremble, for you hear the lion roar.
King John. Act ii, sc. 1, l. 294. [Bastard]

Thus dost thou hear the Nemean lion roar.
Love's Labour 's Lost. Act iv, sc. 1, l. 90. [Boyet] "Nemean lion" is repeated in *Hamlet,* i, 4, 83.

Now the hungry lion roars,
And the wolf behowls the moon.
A Midsummer-Night's Dream. Act v, sc. 1, l. 378. [Puck] The only use of "behowls."

Have not I in my time heard lions roar?
The Taming of the Shrew, i, 2, 201. See under Wooing for full quotation.

Sebastian: Even now, we heard a hollow burst of bellowing
Like bulls, or rather lions. . . .
Antonio: Sure, it was the roar
Of a whole herd of lions.
Tempest. Act ii, sc. 1, l. 311. "Bellowing" is repeated in *The Merchant of Venice,* v, 1, 73.

Roaring lions.—*King John,* ii, 1, 459.

Roars As doth the lion.—*Julius Cæsar,* i, 3, 75.

6
So looks the pent-up lion o'er the wretch
That trembles under his devouring paws;
And so he walks, insulting o'er his prey,
And so he comes, to rend his limbs asunder.
III Henry VI. Act i, sc. 3, l. 12. [Rutland]

Close pent-up guilts.—*King Lear,* iii, 2, 57. The only uses of "pent-up."

To whom do lions cast their gentle looks?
Not to the beast that would usurp their den.
III Henry VI. Act ii, sc. 2, l. 11. [Clifford]

7
O piteous spectacle! O bloody times!
Whiles lions war and battle for their dens,
Poor harmless lambs abide their enmity.
III Henry VI. Act ii, sc. 5, l. 73. [King Henry]

When the lion fawns upon the lamb,
The lamb will never cease to follow him.
III Henry VI. Act iv, sc. 8, l. 49. [King Henry]

8
Against the Capitol I met a lion,
Who glared upon me, and went surly by,
Without annoying me.
Julius Cæsar. Act i, sc. 3, l. 20. [Casca] The only use of "glared" and "annoying."

9
We are two lions litter'd in one day,
And I the elder and more terrible.
Julius Cæsar. Act ii, sc. 2, l. 46. [Cæsar]

In Rome litter'd.—*Coriolanus,* iii, 1, 239.

Littered under Mercury.—*The Winter's Tale,* iv, 3, 25. The only uses of "littered."

10
Richard, that robb'd the lion of his heart
And fought the holy wars in Palestine.
King John. Act ii, sc. 1, l. 3. [Dauphin]

11
Blanch: O, well did he become that lion's robe
That did disrobe the lion of that robe!
Bastard: It lies as sightly on the back of him
As great Alcides' shows upon an ass.
King John. Act ii, sc. 1, l. 141. The only use of "sightly."

Sirrah, were I at home,
At your den, sirrah, with your lioness,
I would set an ox-head to your lion's hide,
And make a monster of you.
King John. Act ii, sc. 1, l. 290. [Bastard] The only use of "ox-head."

Thou wear a lion's hide! doff it for shame,
And hang a calf's-skin on those recreant limbs.
King John. Act iii, sc. 1, l. 128. [Constance]

What, shall they seek the lion in his den,
And fright him there? and make him tremble there?
King John. Act v, sc. 1, l. 57. [Bastard]

12
The lion and the belly-pinched wolf
Keep their fur dry.
King Lear, iii, 1, 13. See under Night. The only use of "belly-pinched."

13
Your lion, that holds his poll-axe sitting on a close-stool, will be given to Ajax: he will be the ninth Worthy.
Love's Labour 's Lost. Act v, sc. 2, l. 580. [Costard] The only use of "poll-axe." "Close-stool" (a chamber-pot placed in a stool with cover) occurs again in *All's Well that Ends Well,* v, 2, 18.

14
Quince: Snug, the joiner; you, the lion's part: and I hope, here is a play fitted.
Snug: Have you the lion's part written?

pray you, if it be, give it me, for I am slow of study.
Quince: You may do it extempore, for it is nothing but roaring.
Bottom: Let me play the lion too: I will roar, that I will do any man's heart good to hear me; I will roar, that I will make the duke say 'Let him roar again, let him roar again.'
Quince: An you should do it too terribly, you would fright the duchess and the ladies, that they would shriek; and that were enough to hang us all.
All: That would hang us, every mother's son. . . .
Bottom: I will aggravate my voice so that I will roar you as gently as any sucking dove; I will roar you as 'twere any nightingale.
A Midsummer-Night's Dream. Act i, sc. 2, l. 66. "Terribly" is repeated in *The Tempest,* ii, 1, 313, and in *Timon of Athens,* iv, 3, 136.
I will aggravate his style.—*The Merry Wives of Windsor,* ii, 2, 296.
Aggravate the note.—*Richard II,* i, 1, 43. The only uses of "aggravate."
Snout: Will not the ladies be afeard of the lion?
Starveling: I fear it, I promise you.
Bottom: Masters, you ought to consider with yourselves: to bring in—God shield us!—a lion among ladies, is a most dreadful thing, for there is not a more fearful wild-fowl than your lion living.
A Midsummer-Night's Dream. Act iii, sc. 1, l. 28. "Wild-fowl" is repeated in *Twelfth Night,* iv, 2, 55.

1

This grisly beast, which Lion hight by name,
The trusty Thisby coming first by night,
Did scare away, or rather did affright;
And as she fled, her mantle she did fall,
Which Lion vile with bloody mouth did stain.
A Midsummer-Night's Dream. Act v, sc. 1, l. 140. [Quince, as Prologue] "Grisly" is repeated in *I Henry VI,* i, 4, 47: "Grisly countenance."

In such a night
Did Thisbe fearfully o'ertrip the dew
And saw the lion's shadow ere himself
And ran dismay'd away.
The Merchant of Venice. Act v, sc. 1, l. 7. [Jessica] The only use of "o'ertrip."

2

Lysander: This lion is a very fox for his valour.
Theseus: True; and a goose for his discretion.
Demetrius: Not so, my lord; for his valour cannot carry his discretion; and the fox carries the goose.
A Midsummer-Night's Dream. Act v, sc. 1, l. 233.
O wherefore, Nature, didst thou lions frame?
A Midsummer-Night's Dream. Act v, sc. 1, l. 296. [Pyramus]

Well moused, Lion.—*A Midsummer-Night's Dream,* v, 1, 274. The only use of "moused."
Well roared, Lion.—*A Midsummer-Night's Dream,* v, 1, 270.

3

As the grim lion fawneth o'er his prey,
Sharp hunger by the conquest satisfied.
The Rape of Lucrece, l. 421.
To tame the . . . lion wild.
The Rape of Lucrece, l. 956.
Lion proud.—*Venus and Adonis,* l. 884.
Chafed lion.—*King John,* iii, 1, 259.
Couching lion.—*I Henry IV,* iii, 1, 153. The only use of "couching" as an adjective.

4

King Richard: Lions make leopards tame.
Mowbray: Yea, but not change his spots.
Richard II. Act i, sc. 1, l. 174. "Leopard" is repeated in *I Henry VI,* i, 5, 31, and in *Timon of Athens,* iv, 3, 343. The reference is to the Old Testament: Jeremiah, xiii, 23: "Can the Ethiopian change his skin, or the leopard his spots?"
In war was never lion raged more fierce,
In peace was never gentle lamb more mild,
Than was that young and princely gentleman.
Richard II. Act ii, sc. 1, l. 173. [York]

5

The lion dying thrusteth forth his paw,
And wounds the earth, if nothing else, with rage
To be o'erpower'd.
Richard II. Act v, sc. 1, l. 29. [Queen] "O'erpowered" is repeated in *Antony and Cleopatra,* ii, 3, 22.
Dead lions.—*King John,* ii, 1, 138.
Fangless lion.—*II Henry IV,* iv, 1, 218. The only use of "fangless."
Old lion.—*I Henry IV,* i, 2, 84.

6

A lion and a king of beasts.
Richard II, v, 1, 34. See under KING.
Kingly lion.—*III Henry VI,* v, 7, 11.
Imperious lion.—*Othello,* ii, 3, 276.

7

The lion moved with pity did endure
To have his princely paws pared all away.
Titus Andronicus, ii, 3, 151. [Lavinia]
The dam will wake; and, if she wind you once,
She 's with the lion deeply still in league,
And lulls him whilst she playeth on her back,
And when he sleeps will she do what she list.
Titus Andronicus. Act iv, sc. 1, l. 97. [Titus]

8

Diomedes: When contention and occasion meet,
By Jove, I 'll play the hunter for thy life
With all my force, pursuit and policy.
Æneas: And thou shalt hunt a lion, that will fly
And thou shalt hunt a lion, that will fly
With his face backward.
Troilus and Cressida. Act iv, sc. 1, l. 19.
He is a lion That I am proud to hunt.
Coriolanus. Act i, sc. 1, l. 239. [Marcius]

9

If one should be a prey, how much the better
To fall before the lion than the wolf!
Twelfth Night. Act iii, sc. 1, l. 139. [Olivia]

LIPS

See also Kiss, Mouth

1
There was a pretty redness in his lip,
A little riper and more lusty red
Than that mix'd in his cheek: 'twas just the difference
Betwixt the constant red and mingled damask.
As You Like It. Act iii, sc. 5, l. 120. [Phebe]
The only use of "redness" and "riper."

2
I will make a lip at the physician.
Coriolanus, ii, 1, 127. See under LETTER.
Bristled lips.—*Coriolanus,* ii, 2, 96.

3
Here hung those lips that I have kissed I know not how oft. Where be your gibes now? your gambols? your songs? your flashes of merriment, that were wont to set the table on a roar?
Hamlet. Act v, sc. 1, l. 207. [Hamlet]

4
My love, give me thy lips.
Henry V. Act ii, sc. 3, l. 49. [Pistol]
You have witchcraft in your lips, Kate: there is more eloquence in a sugar touch of them than in the tongues of the French council.
Henry V. Act v, sc. 2, l. 301. [King Henry]

5
Seal up your lips, and give no words but mum.
II Henry VI. Act i, sc. 2, l. 89. [Hume]
Seal the accuser's lips.—*King Lear,* iv, 6, 174.
I had rather seal my lips.—*Antony and Cleopatra,* v, 2, 146.
Your . . . lips must seal it too.—*Pericles,* ii, 5, 85.
Set thy seal-manual on my wax-red lips.
Venus and Adonis, l. 516. The only use of "seal-manual" and "wax-red."

6
To have thee with thy lips to stop my mouth;
So shouldst thou either turn my flying soul,
Or I should breathe it so into thy body,
And then it lived in sweet Elysium.
II Henry VI. Act iii, sc. 2, l. 396. [Suffolk]
Thy lips that kiss'd the queen shall sweep the ground.
II Henry VI. Act iv, sc. 1, l. 75. [Captain]

7
Take my hand,
And with thy lips keep in my soul awhile!
III Henry VI. Act v, sc. 2, l. 34. [Warwick]

8
His coward lips did from their colour fly.
Julius Cæsar. Act i, sc. 2, l. 122. [Cassius]
Murmuring lips.—*King John,* iv, 2, 53.
Parched lips.—*King John,* v, 7, 40.
Slanderous lips.—*Richard II,* iv, 1, 24.

9
King Philip: Young princes, close your hands.
Austria: And your lips too.
King John. Act ii, sc. 1, l. 533.
Hold close thy lips.—*III Henry VI,* ii, 2, 118.
I will not open my lips.—*Twelfth Night,* i, 5, 2.
Open not thy lips.—*As You Like It,* i, 3, 84.
Lips, do not move.—*Twelfth Night,* ii, 5, 109.
Attested by the closing of the lips.—*Twelfth Night,* v, 1, 161.

10
Boyet: No sheep, sweet lamb, unless we feed on your lips.
Margaret: You sheep, and I pasture: shall that finish the jest?
Boyet: So you grant pasture for me. [Offering to kiss her.]
Margaret: Not so, gentle beast:
My lips are no common, though several they be.
Love's Labour's Lost. Act ii, sc. 1, l. 220.
Slaver with lips as common as the stairs
That mount the Capitol.
Cymbeline. Act i, sc. 6, l. 105. [Iachimo]
The only use of "slaver."

11
Take, O, take those lips away,
That so sweetly were forsworn.
Measure for Measure. Act iv, sc. 1, l. 1. [Song]

12
Here are sever'd lips,
Parted with sugar breath: so sweet a bar
Should sunder such sweet friends.
The Merchant of Venice. Act iii, sc. 2, l. 119. [Bassanio]

13
Let us command to know that of your mouth or of your lips; for divers philosophers hold that the lips is parcel of the mouth.
The Merry Wives of Windsor. Act i, sc. 1, l. 235. [Evans]

14
O, how ripe in show
Thy lips, those kissing cherries, tempting grow!
A Midsummer-Night's Dream. Act iii, sc. 2, l. 139. [Demetrius]
My cherry lips have often kiss'd thy stones.
A Midsummer-Night's Dream. Act v, sc. 1, l. 192. [Thisbe]
A cherry lip.—*Richard III,* i, 1, 94.
Rosed lips.—*Titus Andronicus,* ii, 4, 24.
Rosy lips.—*Sonnets,* no. cxvi.
Her scarlet lip.—*Romeo and Juliet,* ii, 1, 18.
Two lips, indifferent red.—*Twelfth Night,* i, 5, 265.

15
These lily lips, This cherry nose.
These yellow cowslip cheeks,
Are gone, are gone.
A Midsummer-Night's Dream. Act v, sc. 1, l. 337. [Thisbe]

16
They met so near with their lips that their breaths embraced together.
Othello. Act ii, sc. 1, l. 265. [Iago]

17
'Even thus,' quoth she, 'he seized on my lips,'
And with her lips on his did act the seizure.
The Passionate Pilgrim, l. 151.

18
Teach not thy lips such scorn, for they were made
For kissing, lady, not for such contempt.
Richard III. Act i, sc. 2, l. 172. [Gloucester]
A lip of much contempt.
The Winter's Tale. Act i, sc. 2, l. 373. [Polixenes]

1
The King is angry: see, he bites the lip.
Richard III. Act iv, sc. 2, l. 27. [Catesby] "Bites the lip" is repeated five times in later plays.
He hangs the lip at something.
Troilus and Cressida. Act iii, sc. 1, l. 152. [Helen]
Alas, why gnaw you so your nether lip?
Othello. Act v, sc. 2, l. 43. [Desdemona]
Hanging of thy nether lip.—*I Henry IV,* ii, 4, 447.
A touch of his nether lip.—*Othello,* iv, 3, 40. "Nether" is used a fourth time in *King Lear,* iv, 2, 79: "Nether crimes."

2
Their lips were four red roses on a stalk,
Which in their summer beauty kiss'd each other.
Richard III. Act iv, sc. 3, l. 12. [Tyrrel]

3
My lips, two blushing pilgrims, ready stand
To smooth that rough touch with a tender kiss.
Romeo and Juliet. Act i, sc. 5, l. 97. [Romeo]
Romeo: Have not saints lips, and holy palmers too?
Juliet: Ay, pilgrim, lips that they must use in prayer.
Romeo and Juliet. Act i, sc. 5, l. 103.
Romeo: Thus from my lips, by yours, my sin is purged.
Juliet: Then have my lips the sin that they have took.
Romeo: Sin from my lips? O trespass sweetly urged!
Give me my sin again.
Romeo and Juliet. Act i, sc. 5, l. 109.
And steal immortal blessing from her lips,
Who, even in pure and vestal modesty,
Still blush, as thinking their own kisses sin.
Romeo and Juliet. Act iii, sc. 3, l. 37. [Romeo]

4
Lips, O you
The doors of breath, seal with a righteous kiss
A dateless bargain to engrossing death!
Romeo and Juliet. Act v, sc. 3, l. 113. [Romeo] "Dateless" is repeated in *Richard II,* i, 3, 151: "Dateless limit." The only use of "engrossing."
His gates of breath.—*II Henry IV,* iv, 5, 31.

5
I will kiss thy lips;
Haply some poison yet doth hang on them,
To make me die with a restorative.
Thy lips are warm.
Romeo and Juliet. Act v, sc. 3, l. 164. [Juliet] "Restoratives" occurs in *Pericles,* i, Gower, 8.
Come then, and take the last warmth of my lips.
Antony and Cleopatra. Act v, sc. 2, l. 294. [Cleopatra]

6
How oft, when thou, my music, music play'st,
Upon that blessed wood whose motion sounds
With thy sweet fingers, when thou gently sway'st
The wiry concord that mine ear confounds,
Do I envy those jacks that nimble leap
To kiss the tender inward of thy hand,
Whilst my poor lips, which should that harvest reap,
At the wood's boldness by thee blushing stand!
To be so tickled, they would change their state
And situation with those dancing chips,
O'er whom thy fingers walk with gentle gait,
Making dead wood more blest than living lips.
Since saucy jacks so happy are in this,
Give them thy fingers, me thy lips to kiss.
Sonnets. No. cxxviii. The only use of "chips." "Wiry" is repeated in *King John,* iii, 4, 64: "Wiry friends."
Those lips of thine,
That have profaned their scarlet ornaments
And seal'd false bonds of love as oft as mine.
Sonnets. No. cxlii.
Those lips that Love's own hand did make
Breathed forth the sound that said 'I hate.'
Sonnets. No. cxlv.

7
I saw her coral lips to move.
The Taming of the Shrew. Act i, sc. 1, l. 179. [Lucentio]
Coral lips.—*The Rape of Lucrece,* l. 420.
Coral is far more red than her lips' red.
Sonnets. No. cxxx. "Coral" is used a fourth time in *The Tempest,* i, 2, 397: "Of his bones are coral made."

8
I 'll take that winter from your lips, fair lady.
Troilus and Cressida. Act iv, sc. 5, l. 24. [Achilles]

9
Diana's lip Is not more smooth and rubious.
Twelfth Night. Act i, sc. 4, l. 31. [Duke] The only use of "rubious."
Ruby lips.—*Julius Cæsar,* iii, 1, 260.
Rubies unparagon'd!—*Cymbeline,* ii, 2, 17. "Unparagon'd" is repeated in i, 4, 87, and occurs in no other play.

10
And yet not cloy thy lips with loathed satiety,
But rather famish them amid their plenty,
Making them red and pale with fresh variety.
Venus and Adonis, l. 19. "Amid" is used only once more, in *The Taming of the Shrew,* iv, 1, 206; and "variety" once more, in *Antony and Cleopatra,* ii, 2, 241.
Soon she stops his lips.—*Venus and Adonis,* l. 46.
But when her lips were ready for his pay,
He winks, and turns his lips another way.
Venus and Adonis, l. 89.
What were thy lips the worse for one poor kiss?
Venus and Adonis, l. 207.
Long may they kiss each other, for this cure!
O, never let their crimson liveries wear!
Venus and Adonis, l. 505.

Pure lips, sweet seals in my soft lips imprinted.
Venus and Adonis, l. 511.
Ripe lip.—*King Lear,* iv, 3, 22.
Sweet lips.—*Venus and Adonis,* l. 633.
Tempting lip.—*Venus and Adonis,* l. 127.
True lip.—*Coriolanus,* v, 3, 47.

1

He with her plenty press'd, she faint with dearth,
Their lips together glued, fall to the earth.
Venus and Adonis, l. 545.

Her lips are conquerors, his lips obey,
Paying what ransom the insulter willeth.
Venus and Adonis, l. 549. The only use of "insulter."

She will draw his lips' rich treasure dry.
Venus and Adonis, l. 552.

So do thy lips
Make modest Dian cloudy and forlorn,
Lest she should steal a kiss and die forsworn.
Venus and Adonis, l. 724.

2

She looks upon his lips, and they are pale.
Venus and Adonis, l. 1123.
Pale cold lips.—*Titus Andronicus,* v, 3, 153.
Cold lips.—*Troilus and Cressida,* iv, 4, 29.
Waned lip.—*Antony and Cleopatra,* ii, 1, 21.
Lips new-waxen pale.—*The Rape of Lucrece,* l. 1663. The only use of "new-waxen."

3

Leontes: I might have look'd upon my queen's full eyes,
Have taken treasure from her lips—
Paulina: And left them
More rich for what they yielded.
The Winter's Tale. Act v, sc. 1, l. 53.

The ruddiness upon her lip is wet;
You'll mar it if you kiss it.
The Winter's Tale. Act v, sc. 3, l. 81. [Paulina] The only use of "ruddiness."

Kissing with inside lip.—*The Winter's Tale,* i, 2, 286. See under Kiss.

LITTLENESS

4

Melted from
The smallness of a gnat to air.
Cymbeline, i, 3, 21. See under Gnat. The only use of "smallness."

Much smaller than the smallest of his thoughts.
II Henry IV, i, 3, 30. See under Power. "Smaller" is used three times, and "smallest" eighteen times.

Small things make base men proud.
II Henry VI, iv, 1, 106. See under Trifle.

Things small as nothing.—*Troilus and Cressida,* ii, 3, 179..
These things seem small.—*A Midsummer-Night's Dream,* iv, 1, 192.
Small things.—*King John,* iv, 1, 95.
By small and small.—*Richard II,* iii, 2, 198. "Small" is used eighty-one times.

5

The blessedness of being little.
Henry VIII, iv, 2, 66. See under Overthrow.

6

Armado: Pretty, because little.
Moth: Little pretty, because little.
Love's Labour's Lost. Act i, sc. 2, l. 22.

Little darlings.—*Pericles,* i, 4, 44.
Little souls.—*Richard III,* iv, 4, 191.
Little thing.—*Twelfth Night,* iii, 4, 331; *Coriolanus,* v, 3, 195. A few examples of Shakespeare's use of this adjective, which occurs 325 times in the plays and poems.
Littlest doubts.—*Hamlet,* iii, 2, 181. The only use of "littlest."

7

Helena: Though she be but little, she is fierce.
Hermia: 'Little' again! nothing but 'low' and 'little.'
A Midsummer-Night's Dream. Act iii, sc. 2, l. 325.

It is too little.—*Richard II,* v, 1, 61.
Much too little.—*Love's Labour's Lost,* ii, 1, 62.
Threefold too little.—*The Two Gentlemen of Verona,* i, 1, 116.

8

Because that I am little, like an ape,
He thinks that you should bear me on your shoulders.
Richard III. Act iii, sc. 1, l. 130. [York]

Drawn in little.—*Twelfth Night,* iii, 4, 95.

9

When that I was and a little tiny boy.
Twelfth Night, v, 1, 398. See under Rain.

Little tiny kickshaws.—*II Henry IV,* v, 1, 29.
Little tiny thief.—*II Henry IV,* v, 3, 60.
Little tiny wit.—*King Lear,* iii, 2, 74. The only uses of "tiny."

LIVER

10

This way will I take upon me to wash your liver as clean as a sound sheep's heart.
As You Like It. Act iii, sc. 2, l. 443. [Rosalind]

11

Left the liver white and pale, which is the badge of pusillanimity.
II Henry IV, iv, 3, 113. The only use of "pusillanimity." See under Sack.

Livers pale.—*Troilus and Cressida,* ii, 2, 50.
Livers white as milk.—*The Merchant of Venice,* iii, 2, 86.

12

My knight, I will inflame thy noble liver,
And make thee rage.
II Henry IV. Act v, sc. 5, l. 33. [Pistol]

Dirt-rotten livers.—*Troilus and Cressida,* v, 1, 24. The only use of "dirt-rotten."
Spotted livers.—*Troilus and Cressida,* v, 3, 18.
Liver of blaspheming Jew.—*Macbeth,* iv, 1, 26. "Blaspheming" is repeated in *II Henry VI,* iii, 2, 372.

13

And let my liver rather heat with wine
Than my heart cool with mortifying groans.
The Merchant of Venice. Act i, sc. 1, l. 81. [Gratiano] "Mortifying" is repeated in *Much Ado about Nothing,* i, 3, 13: "Mortifying mischief."

Heat my liver.—*Antony and Cleopatra,* i, 2, 23.
Heat of our livers.—*II Henry IV,* i, 2, 198.
Hot livers.—*I Henry IV,* ii, 4, 355.
Liver burning hot.—*The Merry Wives of Windsor,* ii, 1, 121.
Ardour of my liver.—*The Tempest,* iv, 1, 56.
No motion of the liver.—*Twelfth Night,* ii, 4, 101.

1 Liver, brain and heart,
These sovereign thrones.
Twelfth Night. Act i, sc. 1, l. 37. [Duke]
Liver, heart and brain.—*Cymbeline*, v, 5, 14.
Wife's liver.—*The Winter's Tale*, i, 2, 304.

LIVERY

2
O, if I had had time to have made new liveries, I would have bestowed the thousand pound I borrowed of you.
II Henry IV. Act iv, sc. 5, l. 7. [Falstaff]
Put the liveries to making.—*The Merchant of Venice*, ii, 2, 124.
Rare new liveries.—*The Merchant of Venice*, ii, 2, 117.
3
I will apparel them all in one livery.
II Henry VI. Act iv, sc. 2, l. 81. [Cade]
4
O, 'tis the cunning livery of hell,
The damned'st body to invest and cover
In prenzie guards!
Measure for Measure. Act iii, sc. 1, l. 95. [Isabella] The only use of "damned'st." "Prenzie" (a doubtful word) is repeated in line 94, and occurs nowhere else.
Destined livery.—*Measure for Measure*, ii, 4, 138.
Good livery.—*All's Well that Ends Well*, iv, 5, 106.
Light and careless livery.—*Hamlet*, iv, 7, 80. See AGE AND YOUTH, 21:7.
Proud livery.—*Sonnets*, ii.
Shadow'd livery.—*The Merchant of Venice*, ii, 1, 2. See under COMPLEXION.
Wonted liveries.—*Midsummer-Night's Dream*, ii, 1, 113.
Nature's livery.—*Hamlet*, i, 4, 32.
Slander's livery.—*The Rape of Lucrece*, l. 1054.
Sorrow's livery.—*The Rape of Lucrece*, l. 1222.
5 Give him a livery
More guarded than his fellows': see it done.
The Merchant of Venice. Act ii, sc. 2, l. 163. [Bassanio]
6
One twelve moons more she 'll wear Diana's livery;
This by the eye of Cynthia hath she vow'd,
And on her virgin honour will not break it.
Pericles. Act ii, sc. 5, l. 10. [Simonides]
A vestal livery will I take me to,
And never more have joy.
Pericles. Act iii, sc. 4, l. 10. [Thaisa]
Her vestal livery is but sick and green
And none but fools do wear it; cast it off.
Romeo and Juliet. Act ii, sc. 2, l. 8. [Romeo] See under SUN.
Livery of a nun.—*Midsummer-Night's Dream*, i, 1, 70. See under NUN.
7
A maid-child call'd Marina; who, O goddess,
Wears yet thy silver livery.
Pericles. Act v, sc. 3, l. 6. [Pericles] The only use of "maid-child."
Silver livery.—*II Henry VI*, v, 2, 47. See under AGE.
8
I am denied to sue my livery here.
Richard II. Act ii, sc. 3, l. 129.
Sue his livery.—*I Henry IV*, iv, 3, 62; *Richard II*, ii, 1, 204. The only uses of "sue livery," meaning to institute a suit to obtain delivery of property.
9 I think it is our way,
If we will keep in favour with the king,
To be her men and wear her livery.
Richard III. Act i, sc. 1, l. 78. [Gloucester]
10
Tybalt: Here comes my man.
Mercutio: But I 'll be hang'd, sir, if he wear your livery.
Romeo and Juliet. Act iii, sc. 1, l. 59.
Yet do our hearts wear Timon's livery.
Timon of Athens. Act iv, sc. 2, l. 17. [Servant]
In his livery Walk'd crowns and crownets.
Antony and Cleopatra, v, 2, 90. See under MAN: GREAT MEN.
11
It appears, by their bare liveries, that they live by your bare words.
The Two Gentlemen of Verona. Act ii, sc. 4, l. 45. [Valentine]
12
O, never let their crimson liveries wear!
Venus and Adonis, l. 506.
Ne'er saw the beauteous livery that he wore.
Venus and Adonis, l. 1107.

LOAD

See also Burden, Weight

13
I have loaden me with many spoils.
I Henry VI, ii, 1, 80. See under NAME.
Loaden with their heads.—*Titus Andronicus*, v, 2, 53.
Loaden with honour.—*Coriolanus*, v, 3, 164.
Loaden with irons.—*Timon of Athens*, iii, 5, 50.
Loaden with heavy news.—*I Henry IV*, i, 1, 37.
Loaden branches.—*Henry VIII*, iv, 2, 2. The only uses of "loaden."
14 Unburthens with his tongue
The envious load that lies upon his heart.
II Henry VI. Act iii, sc. 1, l. 156. [Gloucester]
Heavy load.—*Pericles*, i, 4, 91.
Living load.—*II Henry VI*, v, 2, 64.
Slanderous loads.—*Julius Cæsar*, iv, 1, 20.
Ceres' plenteous load.—*II Henry VI*, i, 2, 2. Ceres is mentioned four times.
15 From these shoulders,
These ruin'd pillars, out of pity, taken
A load would sink a navy.
Henry VIII. Act iii, sc. 2, l. 381. [Wolsey]
Take down his load.—*Julius Cæsar*, iv, 1, 25.
Load him with his desert!—*Henry V*, iii, 7, 85.
Load my she with knacks.—*The Winter's Tale*, iv, 4, 360.
16
She bears the load of lust he left behind.
The Rape of Lucrece, l. 734.
This load of wrath that burning Troy doth bear.
The Rape of Lucrece, l. 1474.
17
Set down, set down your honourable load.
Richard III. Act i, sc. 2, l. 1. [Anne]
Come, now towards Chertsey with your holy load,

Taken from Paul's to be interred there.
Richard III. Act i, sc. 2, l. 29. [Anne] Chertsey is mentioned again in l. 215, and l. 226, and in no other scene.

1
You cloudy princes and heart-sorrowing peers,
That bear this mutual heavy load of moan.
Richard III. Act ii, sc. 2, l. 112. [Buckingham] The only use of "heart-sorrowing."

Loads o' gravel.—*Troilus and Cressida,* v, 1, 22.
Load of sorrow.—*Much Ado about Nothing,* v, 1, 28.
Load of title.—*Henry VIII,* ii, 3, 39.

2
I had my load before, now press'd with bearing.
Venus and Adonis, l. 430.

LOATHING, see Hate

LONDON

3
Made Lud's town with rejoicing fires bright
And Britons strut with courage.
Cymbeline. Act iii, sc. 1, l. 32. [Cloten]

On the gates of Lud's-town set your heads.
Cymbeline. Act iv, sc. 2, l. 99. [Cloten] The only uses of "Lud's-town."

4
Hath my sword therefore broke through London gates, that you should leave me at the White Hart in Southwark?
II Henry VI. Act iv, sc. 8, l. 23. [Cade] Southwark is mentioned again in iv, 2, 27, and in no other play.

London bridge.—*I Henry VI,* iii, 1, 23; *II Henry VI,* iv, 4, 49; iv, 6, 16.
London road.—*I Henry IV,* ii, 1, 16.
London-stone.—*II Henry VI,* iv, 6, 2.
London streets.—*II Henry VI,* iv, 8, 47; *Richard II,* v, 5, 77.

5
I hope to see London once ere I die.
II Henry IV. Act v, sc. 3, l. 64. [Davy]

Proud London.—*II Henry IV,* i, 3, 104.

6
How doth London pour out her citizens!
Henry V. Act v, Prologue, l. 24. [Chorus]

Among the Londoners.—*Henry VIII,* i, 2, 154. The only use of the word.

7
Thou shalt to London presently.
III Henry VI. Act i, sc. 2, l. 36. [York]

Why, Via! to London will we march amain,
And once again bestride our foaming steeds,
And once again cry 'Charge upon our foes!'
But never once again turn back and fly.
III Henry VI. Act ii, sc. 1, l. 182. [Warwick] The only use of "foaming steeds."

And now to London with triumphant march.
III Henry VI. Act ii, sc. 6, l. 87. [Warwick]

Now to London.—*III Henry VI,* ii, 1, 174; ii, 6, 109.

What now remains, my lords, for us to do
But march to London?
III Henry VI. Act iv, sc. 3, l. 60. [Oxford]

March amain to London.—*III Henry VI,* iv, 8, 4.
Comes to London.—*III Henry VI,* iv, 4, 26; *I Henry IV,* ii, 1, 47.
Go merrily to London.—*I Henry IV,* ii, 2, 100.
I 'll hence to London.—*III Henry VI,* v, 5, 47.
Let 's away to London.—*III Henry VI,* v, 5, 88.
Meet at London.—*Richard II,* iii, 4, 97.
Post to London.—*III Henry VI,* i, 2, 55; *Richard II,* iii, 4, 90.
Set on towards London.—*Richard II,* iii, 3, 204.
Set out for London.—*Henry VIII,* ii, 2, 5.

8
From London by the king was I press'd forth.
III Henry VI. Act ii, sc. 5, l. 64. [Son]

9
London hath received,
Like a kind host, the Dauphin and his powers.
King John. Act v, sc. 1, l. 31. [Bastard]

Welcome to London!—*II Henry IV,* ii, 4, 316; *Richard III,* iii, 1, 1.

10
Towards London they do bend their course.
Richard III. Act iv, sc. 5, l. 14. [Christopher]

LONELINESS, see Solitude

LONGING

11
I have Immortal longings in me.
Antony and Cleopatra. Act v, sc. 2, l. 283. [Cleopatra]

Nice longing.—*Cymbeline,* ii, 5, 26. See under Woman.

12
Ne'er long'd my mother so
To see me first, as I have now.
Cymbeline. Act iii, sc. 4, l. 2. [Imogen]

I never longed to hear a word till now.
Richard II, v, 3, 115. See under Pardon.

Longed to be a king.—*II Henry VI,* iv, 9, 5.
Longed to eat adders.—*The Winter's Tale,* iv, 4, 267.
Longed long.—*Hamlet,* iii, 1, 94. The only uses of "longed." "Longed-for" occurs in *King John,* iv, 2, 8: "Longed-for change."

13
All which we pine for now.
Macbeth. Act iii, sc. 6, l. 37. [Lord]

I alone must sit and pine.
The Rape of Lucrece, l. 795.

Dwindle, peak and pine.—*Macbeth,* i, 3, 23.
I pine and die.—*Love's Labour 's Lost,* i, 1, 31.
I pine, I perish.—*The Taming of the Shrew,* i, 1, 160.
There I 'll pine away.—*Richard II,* iii, 2, 209.
Though the body pine.—*Love's Labour 's Lost,* i, 1, 25; *Pericles,* i, 2, 31.

14
Now do I wish it, love it, long for it.
A Midsummer-Night's Dream, iv, 1, 180. "Long for" occurs five times in the plays.

Long to hear.—*II Henry VI,* ii, 2, 6, and eight times in later plays.
Long to know—*The Comedy of Errors,* iv, 4, 146; *Troilus and Cressida,* iv, 1, 31.
Long to see.—*II Henry VI,* ii, 4, 110, and six times in later plays.
Long to talk.—*All's Well that Ends Well,* iv, 5, 109.
He did long in vain.—*II Henry IV,* ii, 3, 14.
Long with all my heart.—*Richard III,* ii, 4, 4.

1
Cytherea, all in love forlorn,
A longing tarriance for Adonis made
Under an osier growing by a brook,
A brook where Adon used to cool his spleen.
The Passionate Pilgrim, l. 73. Cytherea is mentioned five times. "Tarriance" is repeated in *The Two Gentlemen of Verona,* ii, 7, 90. The only use of "Adon."

2
Longing to hear the hateful foe bewray'd.
The Rape of Lucrece, l. 1698.
Longing for what it had not.—*Antony and Cleopatra,* iii, 6, 48.
Longing for that food.—*The Two Gentlemen of Verona,* ii, 7, 17.
Longing . . . for stewed prunes.—*Measure for Measure,* ii, 1, 92; 102.
Vainly longing.—*Henry VIII,* i, 2, 81.

3
Sir, you have saved my longing.
Timon of Athens. Act i, sc. 1, l. 1. [Alcibiades]
Longing and liking.—*As You Like It,* iii, 2, 431.
Longing, wavering.—*Twelfth Night,* ii, 4, 35.

4
I have a woman's longing,
An appetite that I am sick withal.
Troilus and Cressida. Act iii, sc. 3, l. 237. [Achilles]
I shall review Sicilia, for whose sight
I have a woman's longing.
Winter's Tale. Act iv, sc. 4, l. 679. [Camillo] "Review" is repeated in *Sonnets,* lxxiv.
We do our longing stay.—*Pericles,* v, 3, 83.

LOOK

I—Familiar Phrases

5
He did look far
Into the service of the time and was
Discipled of the bravest.
All's Well that Ends Well. Act i, sc. 2, l. 26. [King] The only use of "discipled."
A far-off look.—*II Henry VI,* iii, 1, 10.

6
By his looks methinks 'Tis warm at 's heart.
Coriolanus. Act ii, sc. 3, l. 159. [Sicinius]

7
How look I,
That I should seem to lack humanity?
Cymbeline. Act iii, sc. 2, l. 15. [Pisanio]
How look you?—*King Lear,* iii, 7, 94.
Thy looks are humble.—*Richard III,* i, 4, 173.

8
Looking before and after.
Hamlet. Act iv, sc. 4, l. 37. [Hamlet]
Look after.—*II Henry VI,* iii, 1, 219, and five times in later plays.
Look back.—*Richard III,* iii, 5, 6, and seven times in later plays.
Backward look.—*Sonnets,* lix.
Looking back.—*Antony and Cleopatra,* iii, 11, 53.
Look behind.—*Richard III,* i, 4, 275; *Othello,* ii, 1, 158.
Look beyond.—*II Henry IV,* iv, 4, 67.
Look forward.—*Measure for Measure,* iv, 3, 61.

9
I understand thy looks.
I Henry IV. Act iii, sc. 1, l. 201. [Mortimer]
What seest thou in our looks?
Pericles. Act i, sc. 2, l. 51. [Pericles]
Thy looks are full of speed.—*I Henry IV,* iii, 2, 162.
Speaking looks.—*King Lear,* iv, 5, 25.

10
My heart's dear Harry
Threw many a northward look to see his father
Bring up his powers.
II Henry IV. Act ii, sc. 3, l. 12. [Lady Percy] "Northward" is repeated in *I Henry IV,* iii, 1, 79, and in *The Merchant of Venice,* ii, 1, 4.

11
Durst not presume to look once in the face.
I Henry VI, i, 1, 140. See under ENEMY.
I 'll ne'er look you in the face again.
Julius Cæsar. Act i, sc. 2, l. 284. [Casca]
Abide me, if thou darest for well I wot . . .
Thou darest not stand, nor look me in the face.
A Midsummer-Night's Dream. Act iii, sc. 2, l. 422. [Demetrius]

12
His looks are full of peaceful majesty.
III Henry VI. Act iv, sc. 6, l. 71. [King Henry]
Looks of an empress.—*Henry V,* v, 2, 254.

13
Buckingham Shall lessen this big look.
Henry VIII. Act i, sc. 1, l. 119. [Wolsey]
Nay, look not big.—*The Taming of the Shrew,* iii, 2, 230.
Look big.—*I Henry IV,* iv, 1, 58.
Look too lofty.—*Richard II,* iii, 4, 35.
Looks proudly.—*Richard III,* iv, 3, 42.

14
I read in 's looks Matter against me.
Henry VIII. Act i, sc. 1, l. 125. [Buckingham]
Now, by thy looks I guess thy message.
Henry VIII. Act v, sc. 1, l. 161. [King Henry]
Yea, the illiterate, that know not how
To cipher what is writ in learned books,
Will quote my loathsome trespass in my looks.
The Rape of Lucrece, l. 810. "Illiterate" is repeated in *The Two Gentlemen of Verona,* iii, 1, 296: "Illiterate loiterer."
Let not our looks put on our purposes,
But bear it as our Roman actors do,
With untired spirits and formal constancy.
Julius Cæsar. Act ii, sc. 1, l. 225. [Brutus] "Untired" is repeated in *Richard III,* iv, 2, 44.

15
Yon Cassius hath a lean and hungry look.
Julius Cæsar. Act i, sc. 2, l. 194. [Cæsar]
Meagre were his looks.—*Romeo and Juliet,* v, 1, 40.
Goose look.—*Macbeth,* v, 3, 12.

16
You look not well, Signior Antonio.
The Merchant of Venice. Act i, sc. 1, l. 73. [Gratiano]
You look not well.—*Troilus and Cressida,* ii, 1, 69.
You look very ill. . . . Faith, but you do.
The Merry Wives of Windsor. Act ii, sc. 1, l. 36. [Mrs. Page]

Look ill.—*All's Well that Ends Well,* i, 1, 175; *Timon of Athens,* i, 2, 58.
Look so poorly.—*Richard II,* iii, 3, 128.

1
O, teach me how you look, and with what art
You sway the motion of Demetrius' heart.
A Midsummer-Night's Dream. Act i, sc. 1, l. 192. [Helena]

2
I do not like thy look, I promise thee.
Much Ado about Nothing. Act iv, sc. 2, l. 46. [Dogberry]

3
O ill-starr'd wench!
Pale as thy smock! when we shall meet at compt,
This look of thine will hurl my soul from heaven,
And fiends will snatch at it.
Othello. Act v, sc. 2, l. 272. [Othello] The only use of "ill-starr'd."

4
Even so, this pattern of the worn-out age
Pawn'd honest looks, but laid no words to gage.
The Rape of Lucrece, l. 1350. The only use of "worn-out."

5
I 'll look to like, if looking liking move.
Romeo and Juliet. Act i, sc. 3, l. 97. [Juliet]

6
Master, master, look about you.
The Taming of the Shrew. Act i, sc. 2, l. 141. [Grumio] "Look about" is repeated six times in later plays.

Thou canst not look askance.
The Taming of the Shrew. Act ii, sc. 1, l. 249. [Petruchio] The only use of "askance."

Look down.—*Titus Andronicus,* ii, 3, 215, and six times in later plays.
Looking down.—*Julius Cæsar,* iii, 1, 219.
Looking all downwards.—*Titus Andronicus,* iii, 1, 124.
Look for.—*III Henry VI,* iii, 2, 127, and twenty-two times in later plays.
Look further.—*The Merry Wives of Windsor,* ii, 1, 245; *King Lear,* i, 4, 76.
Look in.—*II Henry VI,* v, 1, 142, and fourteen times in later plays.
Look into.—*II Henry VI,* ii, 1, 202, and nine times in later plays.
Look like.—*Love's Labour 's Lost,* iv, 3, 266, and eighteen times in later plays.
Look on.—*II Henry VI,* iv, 1, 29, and seventy-six times in later plays.
Look out.—*The Taming of the Shrew,* v, 1, 57, and ten times in later plays.
Look over.—*A Midsummer-Night's Dream,* iv, 2, 38; *Antony and Cleopatra,* ii, 2, 5.
Look round about.—*Titus Andronicus,* v, 2, 98.
Look there.—*Henry VIII,* v, 3, 98; *King Lear,* v, 3, 311.
Look through.—*The Taming of the Shrew,* Ind., 2, 12, and six times in later plays.
Look to it.—*II Henry VI,* i, 1, 156, and twenty times in later plays.
Look upon.—*II Henry VI,* ii, 4, 38, and sixty times in later plays.
Look you.—*Richard III,* iii, 7, 47, and twenty-one times in later plays.
Look you here.—*Julius Cæsar,* iii, 2, 200.
Look you there.—*Hamlet,* iii, 4, 134; *Troilus and Cressida,* ii, 1, 91.
Look you yonder.—*Troilus and Cressida,* i, 2, 223; 231.

7
She, poor soul,
Knows not which way to look.
The Taming of the Shrew. Act iv, sc. 1, l. 187. [Curtis]

Look that way.—*The Merry Wives of Windsor,* iii, 1, 9.
Which way looks he?—*Much Ado about Nothing,* i, 3, 55.
Looking out at the window.—*The Taming of the Shrew,* v, 1, 32.

8
Lift up thy looks.
Winter's Tale. Act iv, sc. 4, l. 489. [Florizel]

Look up.—*I Henry VI,* i, 4, 89, and eleven times in later plays.

9
O, what a war of looks there was between them!
Venus and Adonis, l. 355. See under Eye.

II—Angry Looks

10
Why tender'st thou that paper to me with a look untender?
Cymbeline. Act iii, sc. 4, l. 12. [Imogen] "Untender" is repeated in *King Lear,* i, 1, 108.

Ungentle looks.—*Julius Cæsar,* ii, 1, 242.

11
Let thy looks be stern.
I Henry VI. Act i, sc. 2, l. 62. [Charles]

Why look you still so stern and tragical?
I Henry VI. Act iii, sc. 1, l. 125. [Warwick]

Stern looks.—*Henry V,* v, 2, 61; *King John,* iv, 1, 88.
Bold stern looks.—*The Rape of Lucrece,* l. 1252.

12
Look not upon me, for thine eyes are wounding.
II Henry VI, iii, 2, 51. See under Eye.

Nay, do not fright us with an angry look.
II Henry VI. Act v, sc. 1, l. 26. [York]

13
Gentle my lord, sleek o'er your rugged looks.
Macbeth. Act iii, sc. 2, l. 27. [Lady Macbeth]

Your cat-a-mountain looks.—*Merry Wives of Windsor,* ii, 2, 27. See under Honour for full quotation. The only use of "cat-a-mountain."
Bloody looks.—*I Henry IV,* i, 3, 104.
Cloudy looks.—*The Passionate Pilgrim,* l. 312.
Cold looks.—*King Lear,* ii, 4, 37.
Colder looks.—*King Lear,* i, 3, 22.
Dissembling looks.—*Richard III,* i, 2, 237.
Distasteful looks.—*Timon of Athens,* ii, 2, 220. The only use of "distasteful."
Envious looks.—*II Henry VI,* ii, 4, 12.
Fierce looks.—*King John,* iv, 1, 74.
Hateful looks.—*II Henry VI,* ii, 4, 23.
Mortal looks.—*Sonnets,* vii.
Parling looks.—*The Rape of Lucrece,* l. 100. The only use of "parling" (alarming).
Threatening looks.—*The Comedy of Errors,* i, 1, 10; *Titus Andronicus,* i, 1, 134.
Warp'd looks.—*King Lear,* iii, 6, 56.

Wild looks.—*Romeo and Juliet,* v, 3, 240.
Looking wildly.—*The Merry Wives of Windsor,* iii, 3, 94.
Looks so wildly.—*Richard II,* v, 3, 24.
Looking scornfully.—*Rape of Lucrece,* l. 187.
Looking awry.—*Richard II,* ii, 2, 21

1
Look grim as hell!
Othello. Act iv, sc. 2, l. 64. [Othello]
Grim looks.—*Coriolanus,* i, 4, 58; *Pericles,* i, Gower, 40.
Look grimly.—*Antony and Cleopatra,* iv, 12, 5.

2
How tartly that gentleman looks! I never can see him but I am heart-burned an hour after.
Much Ado about Nothing. Act ii, sc. 1, l. 3. [Beatrice] The only use of "tartly." "Heart-burned" occurs again in *I Henry IV,* iii, 3, 59: "Sure to be heart-burned."

3
How angerly I taught my brow to frown!
The Two Gentlemen of Verona. Act i, sc. 2, l. 62. [Julia]
You look angerly.—*Macbeth,* iii, 5, 1.
Nor look . . . angerly.—*King John,* iv, 1, 82. The only uses of "angerly."

4
And at his look she flatly falleth down,
For looks kill love and love by looks reviveth.
Venus and Adonis, l. 463.

III—Friendly Looks

5
Sweet Cytherea, sitting by a brook
With young Adonis, lovely, fresh, and green,
Did court the lad with many a lovely look,
Such looks as none could look but beauty's queen.
The Passionate Pilgrim, l. 43.
Looks of love.—*I Henry IV,* i, 3, 290.

6 Look thou but sweet,
And I am proof against their enmity.
Romeo and Juliet. Act ii, sc. 2, l. 72. [Romeo]
Thy looks should nothing thence but sweetness tell.
Sonnets. No. xciii. See HYPOCRISY, 745:4.
Sweet look.—*A Midsummer-Night's Dream,* ii, 2, 127; *Venus and Adonis,* l. 371.
Look sweetly.—*Much Ado about Nothing,* ii, 1, 91.

7 Ah! my love well knows
Her pretty looks have been mine enemies,
And therefore from my face she turns my foes,
That they elsewhere might dart their injuries.
Yet do not so; but since I am near slain,
Kill me outright with looks and rid my pain.
Sonnets. No. cxxxix. "Kill with looks," See under KILLING.
Puts on his pretty looks.—*King John,* iii, 4, 95.

8
Look cheerfully upon me.
The Taming of the Shrew. Act iv, sc. 3, l. 38. [Petruchio] See also under CHEERFULNESS.

Then, at my suit, look graciously on him; . . .
Nor with sour looks afflict his gentle heart.
Titus Andronicus. Act i, sc. 1, l. 439. [Tamora]
You must not look so sour.
The Taming of the Shrew. Act ii, sc. 1, l. 229. [Petruchio]
Meantime look gracious.—*I Henry VI,* i, 2, 117.
Look friendly.—*Pericles,* iv, 6, 97.

9
O, know'st thou not his looks are my soul's food?
Pity the dearth that I have pined in,
By longing for that food so long a time.
The Two Gentlemen of Verona. Act ii, sc. 7, l. 15. [Julia]
I gave him gentle looks.
The Two Gentlemen of Verona. Act iii, sc. 1, l. 31. [Duke]
Gentle looks.—*III Henry VI,* ii, 2, 11.

10
Vouchsafe me, for my meed, but one fair look;
A smaller boon than this I cannot beg
And less than this, I am sure, you cannot give.
The Two Gentlemen of Verona. Act v, sc. 4, l. 23. [Proteus]
Fair looks.—*The Taming of the Shrew,* v, 2, 153; *Titus Andronicus,* ii, 1, 92.
Calm looks.—*Romeo and Juliet,* iii, 1, 161; *The Rape of Lucrece,* l. 1508.
Cherubin look.—*Timon of Athens,* iv, 3, 63.
Ever-harmless looks.—*The Tempest,* iv, 1, 129. The only use of "ever-harmless."
Good looks.—*Richard III,* iii, 4, 100. The only use of this phrase.
Over-partial looks.—*Sonnets,* cxxxvii. The only use of "over-partial."
Peaceful looks.—*III Henry VI,* ii, 6, 32.

IV—Merry Looks

11
His company must do his minions grace,
Whilst I at home starve for a merry look.
The Comedy of Errors. Act ii, sc. 1, l. 87. [Adriana]
See where she comes from shrift with merry look.
Romeo and Juliet. Act iv, sc. 2, l. 15. [Nurse]
Looks so merrily.—*The Merry Wives of Windsor,* ii, 1, 198.

12 My decayed fair
A sunny look of his would soon repair.
The Comedy of Errors. Act ii, sc. 1, l. 98. [Adriana]

13
Prithee, man, look cheerly.
Timon of Athens. Act ii, sc. 2, l. 223. [Timon]
Cheerful look.—*I Henry IV,* ii, 4, 465.
Saucy looks.—*Love's Labour's Lost,* i, 1, 85.

V—Pale Looks

14
Ay me, poor man, how pale and wan he looks!
The Comedy of Errors. Act iv, sc. 4, l. 111. [Luciana]

As I am an honest man, he looks pale. Art thou sick, or angry?
Much Ado about Nothing. Act v, sc. 1, l. 130. [Don Pedro]
Look so green and pale.—*Macbeth,* i, 7, 37.
Look not so pale.—*Macbeth,* v, 1, 60.
Gilded pale looks.—*Cymbeline,* v, 3, 34.

1 How now! why look'st thou pale?
II Henry VI. Act iii, sc. 2, l. 27. [King Henry] "Look pale" is used nineteen times in the plays.
Why is your cheek so pale?—*A Midsummer-Night's Dream,* i, 1, 128.
Look paler and paler.—*As You Like It,* iv, 3, 178.
Looks a little paler.—*The Merchant of Venice,* v, 1, 125.
Paler . . . than her milk-white dove.—*The Passionate Pilgrim,* l. 119. The only uses of "paler."
Look not pale.—*Taming of the Shrew,* v, 1, 143.

2 Thy paleness moves me more than eloquence.
The Merchant of Venice. Act iii, sc. 2, l. 106. [Bassanio]
The paleness of this flower.—*I Henry VI,* iv, 1, 106.
Swooning paleness.—*A Lover's Complaint,* l. 305. The only uses of "paleness."

3 Buckingham: Look I so pale, Lord Dorset, as the rest?
Dorset: Ay, my good lord; and no one in this presence
But his red colour hath forsook his cheeks.
Richard III. Act ii, sc. 1, l. 83.

VI—Sad Looks

4 Looking on it with lack-lustre eye.
As You Like It, ii, 7, 21. The only use of "lack-lustre." See Time: Its Flight, 1534:8.

5 Piteous they will look, like drowned mice.
I Henry VI. Act i, sc. 2, l. 12. [Alençon] See under England.
With a look so piteous in purport
As if he had been loosed out of hell
To speak of horrors.
Hamlet. Act ii, sc. 1, l. 82. [Ophelia] The only use of "purport."
Piteous looks.—*The Rape of Lucrece,* l. 1502.

6 What art thou, whose heavy looks foretell
Some dreadful story hanging on thy tongue?
III Henry VI. Act ii, sc. 1, l. 43. [Richard]
Heavy looks.—*Romeo and Juliet,* ii, 2, 158.
Why looks your grace so heavily to-day?
Richard III. Act i, sc. 4, l. 1. [Brakenbury]

7 He will look as hollow as a ghost.
King John, iii, 4, 84. See under Ghost.
Death's dim look.—*Rape of Lucrece,* l. 403.
Looks of care.—*Timon of Athens,* iv, 3, 205.

8 Why looks your highness sad?
Love's Labour's Lost. Act v, sc. 2, l. 391. [Princess]
She looks very sad.—*III Henry VI,* iii, 2, 110.
Why dost thou look so sadly?—*King John,* iii, 1, 20.
Looks sadly.—*Richard III,* v, 3, 287.
Look you sad, friends?—*Antony and Cleopatra,* v, 1, 26.
Looks so sad.—*Julius Cæsar,* i, 2, 217.
Look not sad.—*Antony and Cleopatra,* iii, 11, 17; *King John,* iii, 3, 2.

9 And sorts a sad look to her lady's sorrow.
The Rape of Lucrece, l. 1221.
Sad looks.—*A Midsummer-Night's Dream,* iii, 2, 237; *Richard II,* iii, 4, 98.

VII—Strange Looks

10 Why do you look so strange?
All's Well that Ends Well. Act v, sc. 3, l. 168. [Diana]
Ægeon: Why look you strange on me? you know me well.
Antipholus of Ephesus: I never saw you in my life till now.
The Comedy of Errors. Act v, sc. 1, l. 295.
You all look strangely on me.
II Henry IV. Act v, sc. 2, l. 63. [King Henry]
Look strange.—*Sonnets,* lxxxix.

11 Why look you so upon me?
As You Like It. Act iii, sc. 5, l. 70. [Rosalind] Repeated in *The Winter's Tale,* iv, 4, 473.
Nay, look not so upon me.
All's Well that Ends Well. Act iv, sc. 3, l. 221. [First Lord]

12 Wherefore this ghastly looking?
The Tempest. Act ii, sc. 1, l. 309. [Alonso]
Ghastly looks.—*Richard III,* iii, 5, 8.
Staring full ghastly.—*II Henry VI,* iii, 2, 170.

13 How may
A stranger to those most imperial looks
Know them from eyes of other mortals?
Troilus and Cressida. Act i, sc. 3, l. 223. [Æneas]
How he looks!—*Troilus and Cressida,* i, 2, 254.

LOOKER ON, see under Spectator

LORD

See also Ancestry

14 Scurvy, old, filthy, scurvy lord. . . . I'll beat him, an he were double and double a lord.
All's Well that Ends Well. Act ii, sc. 3, l. 250. [Parolles]
Scurvy lord.—*Troilus and Cressida,* ii, 1, 56.
False lord.—*The Rape of Lucrece,* l. 50.
Faultful lord.—*The Rape of Lucrece,* l. 715. The only use of "faultful."
Lustful lord.—*The Rape of Lucrece,* l. 169.
Poor lord.—*Richard III,* i, 2, 28; i, 3, 139; *All's Well that Ends Well,* iii, 2, 105.
Sweating lord.—*Richard III,* iii, 1, 24.
Talking lord.—*Henry VIII,* iii, 2, 265.
Undone lord.—*Timon of Athens,* iv, 3, 488.
A most unworthy and unnatural lord.
Winter's Tale. Act ii, sc. 3, l. 113. [Paulina]

1 She deserves a lord
That twenty such rude boys might tend upon
And call her hourly mistress.
All's Well that Ends Well. Act iii, sc. 2, l. 83. [Countess] See also under HUSBAND.

2
How heavy weighs my lord!
Antony and Cleopatra. Act iv, sc. 15, l. 32. [Cleopatra]

Distress'd lord.—*I Henry VI*, iv, 3, 30; *Pericles*, i, 4, 7.

3
Lords of the wide world and wild watery seas.
The Comedy of Errors, ii, 1, 21. See under MAN.

Here's the lord of the soil come to seize me for a stray.
II Henry VI. Act iv, sc. 10, l. 26. [Cade]

I did not think thee lord of such a spirit.
I Henry IV. Act v, sc. 4, l. 18. [Prince of Wales]

Lord of all.—*II Henry VI*, i, 1, 187.
Lord of folded arms.—*Love's Labour's Lost*, iii, 1, 183. See under CUPID.
Lord of beasts.—*Hamlet*, v, 2, 88.
Lord of duty.—*Othello*, i, 3, 184.
Lord of his fortunes.—*Antony and Cleopatra*, iii, 12, 11.
Lord of his reason.—*Antony and Cleopatra*, iii, 13, 4.
Lord of hosts.—*I Henry VI*, i, 1, 31.
Lord of imbecility.—*Troilus and Cressida*, i, 3, 114. The only use of "imbecility."
Lord of lords.—*Antony and Cleopatra*, iv, 8, 16.
Lord of my life.—*Titus Andronicus*, iv, 4, 28.
Lord of my love.—*Sonnets*, xxvi.
Lord of this fair mansion.—*The Merchant of Venice*, iii, 2, 169.
Lord of our presence.—*King John*, ii, 1, 367.
Lord of thy presence.—*King John*, i, 1, 137.

4
Lords and heads o' the state.
Coriolanus. Act v, sc. 6, l. 91. [Aufidius]

Lord of this city.—*II Henry VI*, iv, 6, 1; *Coriolanus*, v, 6, 1.
Lords and rulers.—*I Henry VI*, iii, 2, 11.

5 This is a lord! O noble misery,
To be i' the field, and ask 'what news?' of me!
Cymbeline. Act v, sc. 3, l. 64. [Posthumus]

6
Pisanio: O, my all-worthy lord!
Cloten: All-worthy villain! . . . no more of 'worthy lord.'
Cymbeline. Act iii, sc. 5, l. 93. The only use of "all-worthy."

No, this thrice worthy and right valiant lord
Must not so stale his palm, nobly acquired.
Troilus and Cressida. Act ii, sc. 3, l. 200. [Ulysses]

Worthy lord.—*Timon of Athens*, i, 1, 9; *Coriolanus*, v, 6, 62.

7
Four of their lords I'll change for one of ours.
I Henry VI. Act i, sc. 1, l. 151. [Bedford]

English lords.—*King John*, v, 5, 10.
Lords of England.—*Henry V*, iv, 1, 30; v, 2, 359; *Richard II*, ii, 3, 140.
French lord.—*The Merchant of Venice*, i, 2, 58.
Grecian lords.—*Troilus and Cressida*, iii, 3, 138.
Lord of Greece.—*Troilus and Cressida*, i, 3, 307; iv, 4, 125.
Holy lord of Milan.—*King John*, v, 2, 120.
Lord of Rome.—*The Rape of Lucrece*, l. 1818.
Roman lord.—*The Rape of Lucrece*, l. 301; *Titus Andronicus*, iv, 1, 62.
Rome's imperial lord.—*Titus Andronicus*, i, 1, 250.
Scottish lord.—*Merchant of Venice*, i, 2, 83.
A lord of Trojan blood.—*Troilus and Cressida*, i, 2, 13.
Trojan lords.—*Troilus and Cressida*, iii, 3, 236.
Lords of Tyre.—*Pericles*, i, 3, 30.
Volscian lords.—*Coriolanus*, v, 3, 3.
Native lords.—*Henry V*, iii, 5, 26.

8
But I remember, when the fight was done,
When I was dry with rage and extreme toil,
Breathless and faint, leaning upon my sword,
Came there a certain lord, neat, and trimly dress'd,
Fresh as a bridegroom; and his chin new reap'd
Show'd like a stubble-land at harvest-home;
He was perfumed like a milliner.
I Henry IV. Act i, sc. 3, l. 30. [Hotspur] The only use of "new reap'd" and "stubble-land." "Harvest-home" is repeated in *The Merry Wives of Windsor*, ii, 2, 287; and "milliner" in *The Winter's Tale*, iv, 4, 192.

9
Servant: Villains, answer you so the lord protector?
Warder: The lord protect him! . . .
Gloucester: There's none protector of the realm but I.
I Henry VI. Act i, sc. 3, l. 8. "Lord protector" (never hyphenated) is used seven times in *I Henry VI*, eight times in *II Henry VI*, once in *III Henry VI*, and four times in *Richard III*.

Brakenbury: I mean the lord protector.
Queen Elizabeth: The Lord protect him from that kingly title.
Richard III. Act iv, sc. 1, l. 19. A play upon words used in the third and fourth plays, and never again.

Lordly lord-protectorship.—*II Henry VI*, ii, 1, 30. The only use of "lord-protectorship."
Lordly monarch.—*I Henry VI*, v, 3, 6.
Lordly nation.—*I Henry VI*, iii, 3, 62.
Lordly peers.—*II Henry VI*, i, 1, 11.
Lordly sir.—*I Henry VI*, iii, 1, 43. The only uses of "lordly," which occurs only in these two plays. "Lordly crew" is used in *The Rape of Lucrece*, l. 1731.

10 Return, thou wandering lord;
Charles and the rest will take thee in their arms.
I Henry VI. Act iii, sc. 3, l. 76. [La Pucelle]

Banish'd lord.—*Cymbeline*, ii, 1, 70.

11
Welcome, brave captain and victorious lord!
I Henry VI. Act iii, sc. 4, l. 16. [King Henry]

Brave lord.—*Antony and Cleopatra*, iii, 13, 177.

Blood-thirsty lord.—*I Henry VI*, ii, 3, 34. The only use of "blood-thirsty."
Dreadful lord.—*I Henry VI*, i, 1, 110.
Great lord.—*Timon of Athens*, i, 1, 20.
Mighty lord.—*II Henry VI*, iv, 1, 80; *The Taming of the Shrew*, Ind., 1, 65; *The Two Gentlemen of Verona*, ii, 4, 136.
Noble lord.—*II Henry VI*, v, 2, 6, and frequently thereafter.
Noble honour'd lord.—*Winter's Tale*, v, 1, 158.
War-like lords.—*I Henry VI*, ii, 5, 70.

1

It was the pleasure of my lord the king.
II Henry VI. Act i, sc. 1, l. 138. [Beaufort]

My lord the king.—*II Henry VI*, iii, 1, 93; v, 1, 124; *The Winter's Tale*, iii, 2, 143.
Our lord the king.—*Richard II*, iii, 3, 101.
The king his lord.—*Henry VIII*, ii, 4, 178.
My lord and sovereign.—*III Henry VI*, iii, 3, 50.
Royal lord.—*King Lear*, iv, 7, 44.
Sovereign lord.—*Henry V*, iv, 3, 68; *The Winter's Tale*, iii, 2, 17.
My lord the emperor.—*Titus Andronicus*, iii, 1, 150.
Imperial lord.—*Henry V*, Epil., 8; *Titus Andronicus*, i, 1, 250.
My lord and father.—*Titus Andronicus*, i, 1, 142; 158; *Romeo and Juliet*, iii, 5, 121; v, 3, 24; *Coriolanus*, i, 1, 158.
My lord and husband.—*The Taming of the Shrew*, Ind., 2, 108; *Coriolanus*, v, 3, 37; *Antony and Cleopatra*, iii, 4, 16.
My lord your husband.—*The Merchant of Venice*, iii, 4, 7.
Lord and master.—*All's Well that Ends Well*, ii, 3, 194; 257; *King Lear*, v, 3, 78; *Timon of Athens*, iii, 1, 11; *Twelfth Night*, i, 5, 271; *Henry VIII*, iii, 2, 414.
My lord your master.—*I Henry VI*, v, 1, 41.
My master and my lord.—*Antony and Cleopatra*, v, 2, 116. See under MASTER.
My lord your son.—*Richard III*, ii, 2, 40; *II Henry IV*, i, 1, 15; 83; *All's Well that Ends Well*, i, 3, 168; 238; iv, 5, 74: 99; *Cymbeline*, i, 1, 160.

2

Revelling like lords.
II Henry VI. Act i, sc. 1, l. 224. [York] See PIRATE, 1155:4.

His lordship.—*II Henry VI*, i, 3, 16. A phrase used in the first act of the first play, and repeated (sometimes as "your lordship") 116 times.

3

Ah, thou say, thou serge, nay, thou buckram lord!
II Henry VI. Act iv, sc. 7, l. 27. [Cade] The only use of "serge."

4

Ay, my good lord:—my lord, I should say rather;
'Tis sin to flatter; 'good' was little better.
III Henry VI. Act v, sc. 6, l. 2. [King Henry] "Good lord" is repeated ten times in later plays.

Good sweet honey lord.—*I Henry IV*, i, 2, 179.
Goodly lord.—*Merchant of Venice*, iii, 5, 55.
Him who you term'd, sir, 'The good old lord.'
The Tempest. Act v, sc. 1, l. 15. [Ariel]
Old lord.—*I Henry IV*, i, 2, 94; *The Tempest*, iii, 3, 4.
Ancient lords.—*I Henry IV*, iii, 2, 104.
Young lords.—*All's Well that Ends Well*, i, 2, 33; ii, 1, 1; iii, 2, 3; v, 3, 12; *Titus Andronicus*, ii, 1, 69; iv, 2, 32. The phrase is used only in these two plays.
Youthful lord.—*Romeo and Juliet*, iv, 2, 25.

5

An honest country lord, as I am, beaten
A long time out of play, may bring his plain-song
And have an hour of hearing.
Henry VIII. Act i, sc. 3, l. 44. [Sands] "Plain-song" (simple melody) occurs also in *Henry V*, iii, 2, 6, and in *A Midsummer-Night's Dream*, iii, 1, 134.

Honest lord.—*Timon of Athens*, iv, 2, 37.
Honourable lord.—*Timon of Athens*, iii, 6, 3.
Honourable virtuous lord.—*Timon of Athens*, iii, 2, 32.
Sensible lord.—*II Henry IV*, i, 2, 220.

6

Some merry mocking lord, belike; is 't so?
Love's Labour 's Lost. Act ii, sc. 1, l. 52. [Princess of France]

Merry mad-cap lord.—*Love's Labour 's Lost*, ii, 1, 215. "Madcap" occurs seven times in the plays.
Mad lord.—*Timon of Athens*, iii, 6, 121.

7

Is not your lord honourable without marriage?
Much Ado about Nothing. Act iii, sc. 4, l. 31. [Margaret]

New-trothed lord.—*Much Ado about Nothing*, iii, 1, 38. The only use of "new-trothed."
Wedded lord.—*Pericles*, iii, 4, 9.

8

Is my lord well, that he doth speak so wide?
Much Ado about Nothing. Act iv, sc. 1, l. 63. [Hero]

9

My lord shall never rest;
I 'll watch him tame and talk him out of patience;
His bed shall seem a school, his board a shrift.
Othello. Act iii, sc. 3, l. 22. [Desdemona]

My lord is not my lord; nor should I know him,
Were he in favour as in humour alter'd.
Othello. Act iii, sc. 4, l. 125. [Desdemona]

Commend me to my kind lord.
Othello. Act v, sc. 2, l. 125. [Desdemona]

My lord, my love, my dear.—*The Rape of Lucrece*, l. 1293.
Mine own lord.—*Hamlet*, iv, 1, 5.
Dear lord.—*Richard III*, iv, 1, 77; *All's Well that Ends Well*, i, 3, 164; *The Rape of Lucrece*, l. 1191; l. 1676.
Dearer lord.—*Romeo and Juliet*, iii, 2, 66.
Fair lords.—*III Henry VI*, ii, 1, 95, six times in later plays, and twice in *The Rape of Lucrece*.
First lord.—*Hamlet*, iii, 2, 225; *Timon of Athens*, iv, 3, 513.
Friendly lord.—*Coriolanus*, ii, 3, 198.
Gracious lord.—*Richard III*, i, 1, 122.
Kind lord.—*Timon of Athens*, iv, 2, 44.
Loving lord.—*The Taming of the Shrew*, v, 2, 160; *As You Like It*, i, 1, 106.
Precedent lord.—*Hamlet*, iii, 4, 98.

Sweet lord.—*III Henry VI,* ii, 3, 48, and eighteen times in later plays.

1 Thou worthy lord
Of this unworthy wife that greeteth thee,
Health to thy person!
The Rape of Lucrece, l. 1303.

2
Northumberland: My lord—
King Richard: No lord of thine, thou haught insulting man,
Nor no man's lord; I have no name, no title.
Richard II. Act iv, sc. 1, l. 253. "Haught" (for haughty) is repeated in *III Henry VI,* ii, 1, 169, and in *Richard III,* ii, 3, 28.

My hard-hearted lord,
That set'st the word itself against the word!
Richard II, v, 3, 121. [Duchess of York]

3
My bosom's lord sits lightly in his throne.
Romeo and Juliet. Act v, sc. 1, l. 3. [Romeo] See under HEART.

4
There is a lord will hear you play to-night.
The Taming of the Shrew. Induction, sc. 1, l. 93. [Lord]

Upon my life, I am a lord indeed.
The Taming of the Shrew. Induction, sc. 2, l. 74. [Sly]

Here 's a lord.—*Troilus and Cressida,* ii, 3, 274.

5 This lord of weak remembrance, this,
Who shall be of as little memory
When he is earth'd.
The Tempest. Act ii, sc. 1, l. 236. [Antonio] The only use of "earth'd."

Lords that can prate
As amply and unnecessarily
As this Gonzalo.
The Tempest. Act ii, sc. 1, l. 263. [Antonio] The only use of "unnecessarily."

My brace of lords.—*The Tempest,* v, 1, 126.

6
Apemantus: Heavens, that I were a lord!
Timon: What wouldst do then, Apemantus?
Apemantus: E'en as Apemantus does now; hate a lord with my heart. . . .
Timon: Wherefore?
Apemantus: That I had no angry wit to be a lord.
Timon of Athens. Act i, sc. 1, l. 234.

How fairly this lord strives to appear foul! takes virtuous copies to be wicked, like those that under hot ardent zeal would set whole realms on fire.
Timon of Athens. Act iii, sc. 3, l. 31. [Servant] The only use of "ardent."

7
This lord, . . . who wears his wit in his belly and his guts in his head.
Troilus and Cressida. Act ii, sc. 1, l. 79. [Thersites]

Mongrel beef-witted lord!—*Troilus and Cressida,* ii, 1, 14. The only use of "beef-witted."

Blunt-witted lord!—*II Henry VI,* iii, 2, 210. The only use of "blunt-witted."

Sodden-witted lord!—*Troilus and Cressida,* ii, 1, 47. The only use of "sodden-witted."

8
Shall the proud lord . . . be worshipped
Of that we hold an idol more than he?
Troilus and Cressida. Act ii, sc. 3, l. 194. [Ulysses]

Proud lords.—*The Rape of Lucrece,* l. 1259.

Proud northern lord.—*II Henry VI,* v, 2, 6.

9 No man is the lord of any thing,
Though in and of him there be much consisting,
Till he communicate his parts to others.
Troilus and Cressida. Act iii, sc. 3, l. 115. [Ulysses]

II—Lord and Lady

10
It is not the fashion to see the lady the epilogue; but it is no more unhandsome than to see the lord the prologue.
As You Like It. Epilogue, l. 1. [Rosalind]

11
Costard: From my lord to my lady.
Princess: From which lord to which lady?
Love's Labour 's Lost. Act iv, sc. 1, l. 104.

12
You need not fear, lady, the having any of these lords.
The Merchant of Venice. Act i, sc. 2, l. 109. [Nerissa]

Take him for thy lord.—*The Taming of the Shrew,* iii, 1, 75.

13
Servant: Where is my lady?
Portia: Here: what would my lord?
The Merchant of Venice. Act ii, sc. 9, l. 85.

Got 's lords and his ladies!—*The Merry Wives of Windsor,* i, 1, 243.

14
Oberon: Tarry, rash wanton: am not I thy lord?
Titania: Then I must be thy lady.
A Midsummer-Night's Dream. Act ii, sc. 1, l. 63.

There is two or three lords and ladies more married.
A Midsummer-Night's Dream. Act iv, sc. 2, l. 16. [Snug]

15
Emilia: Good madam, what 's the matter with my lord?
Desdemona: With who?
Emilia: Why, with my lord, madam.
Desdemona: Who is thy lord?
Emilia: He that is yours, sweet lady.
Desdemona: I have none: do not talk to me, Emilia.
Othello. Act iv, sc. 2, l. 98.

My lord and lady.—*Othello,* v, 1, 127.

16
Here stands a lord, and there a lady weeping.
Pericles. Act i, sc. 4, l. 47. [Cleon]

17
Thou art a lord and nothing but a lord:
Thou hast a lady.
The Taming of the Shrew. Induction, sc. 2, l. 63. [Lord]

Am I a lord? and have I such a lady?
The Taming of the Shrew. Induction, sc. 2, l. 70. [Sly]

1
Timon: Wilt dine with me, Apemantus?
Apemantus: No; I eat not lords.
Timon: An thou shouldst, thou 'ldst anger ladies.
Apemantus: O, they eat lords; so they come by great bellies.
Timon: That 's a lascivious apprehension.
Timon of Athens. Act i, sc. 1, l. 206.

2
I love thee not a jar o' the clock behind
What lady-she her lord.
The Winter's Tale. Act i, sc. 2, l. 43. [Hermione] The only use of "lady-she."

III—The Lord

3
Salisbury: O Lord, have mercy on us, wretched sinners!
Gargrave: O Lord, have mercy on me, woeful man!
I Henry VI. Act i, sc. 4, l. 70.
Lord have mercy on thee for a hen!
All's Well that Ends Well. Act ii, sc. 3, l. 223. [Lafeu]
Write 'Lord have mercy on us' on those three.
Love's Labour 's Lost. Act v, sc. 2, l. 419. [Biron]
O Lord, have mercy upon me!—*II Henry VI,* i, 3, 219; *Othello,* v, 2, 57.
Lord have mercy on us!—*Love's Labour 's Lost,* v, 2, 419.

4
Good fellow, tell us here the circumstance,
That we for thee may glorify the Lord.
II Henry VI. Act ii, sc. 1, l. 74. [King Henry]
Lord worshipped might he be!—*The Merchant of Venice,* ii, 2, 98.

5
O Lord bless me! I pray God!
II Henry VI. Act ii, sc. 3, l. 77. [Peter]
The Lord in heaven bless thee!—*Henry V,* iv, 1, 33.
The Lord lighten thee!—*II Henry IV,* ii, 1, 208.
The Lord preserve thy good grace!—*II Henry IV,* ii, 4, 315.
The Lord protect him!—*II Henry VI,* i, 3, 5. Used frequently in later plays.
The Lord increase this business!—*Henry VIII,* iii, 2, 161.
Lord warrant us!—*As You Like It,* iii, 3, 5.
By the Lord!—*I Henry IV,* i, 2, 44, and frequently thereafter.
Lord, Lord!—*Richard III,* i, 4, 21; *The Two Gentlemen of Verona,* i, 2, 15; *Love's Labour 's Lost,* iv, 1, 143; *Romeo and Juliet,* ii, 4, 185; 212; *II Henry IV,* iii, 2, 325; *The Merry Wives of Windsor,* ii, 2, 56.
O Lord!—*II Henry VI,* i, 1, 19. Used in the first scene of the first play, and frequently thereafter.

6
Now Lord be thanked for my good amends!
The Taming of the Shrew. Induction, sc. 2, l. 99. [Sly]
The Lord be praised!—*Troilus and Cressida,* iii, 1, 8.
Good Lord deliver us!—*The Taming of the Shrew,* i, 1, 66.

LOSS

7
How mightily sometimes we make us comforts of our losses!
All's Well that Ends Well. Act iv, sc. 3, l. 76. [First Lord]
Fare you well: had you such a loss as I,
I could give better comfort than you do.
King John. Act iii, sc. 4, l. 99. [Constance]

8
Take from his heart, take from his brain, from 's time,
What should not then be spared.
Antony and Cleopatra. Act iii, sc. 7, l. 12. [Enobarbus]
Like a right gipsy, hath, at fast and loose,
Beguiled me to the very heart of loss.
Antony and Cleopatra. Act iv, sc. 12, l. 28. [Antony]

9
Make not, sir, Your loss your sport.
Cymbeline. Act ii, sc. 4, l. 47. [Posthumus]

10
Your loss is great, so your regard should be;
My worth unknown, no loss is known to me.
I Henry VI. Act iv, sc. 5, l. 22. [John Talbot]
Your loss is as yourself, great; and you bear it
As answering to the weight.
Antony and Cleopatra. Act v, sc. 2, l. 101. [Dolabella]
Sir, you may thank yourself for this great loss.
The Tempest. Act ii, sc. 1, l. 123. [Sebastian]
Dear loss.—*Cymbeline,* v, 5, 345.
Utter loss.—*I Henry VI,* v, 4, 112.
All is lost.—*II Henry VI,* iii, 1, 85.
All lost! . . . All lost!—*The Tempest,* i, 1, 54.
All, all lost, quite lost!—*Tempest,* iv, 1, 190.
All losses are restored.—*Sonnets,* xxx. See under FRIEND.

11
I can give the loser leave to chide.
II Henry VI. Act iii, sc. 1, l. 182. [Queen Margaret]
Beshrew the winners, for they play'd me false!
And well such losers may have leave to speak.
II Henry VI. Act iii, sc. 1, l. 184. [Gloucester]
Losers will have leave
To ease their stomachs with their bitter tongues.
Titus Andronicus. Act iii, sc. 1, l. 233. [Titus]
Thus losers part.—*The Merchant of Venice,* ii, 7, 77.
Neither party loser.—*II Henry IV,* iv, 2, 91.
Repute yourself such a loser.—*Othello,* ii, 3, 272.
With the losers let it sympathise.—*II Henry IV,* v, 1, 7.
Winner and loser.—*Hamlet,* iv, 5, 143. The only uses of "loser" and "losers."

12
Great lords, wise men ne'er sit and wail their loss,
But cheerly seek how to redress their harms.
III Henry VI. Act v, sc. 4, l. 1. [Queen Margaret]
It were lost sorrow to wail one that 's lost.
Richard III. Act ii, sc. 2, l. 11. [Duchess of York]

Even so great men great losses should endure.
Julius Cæsar. Act iv, sc. 3, l. 193. [Messala]

1
O insupportable and touching loss!
Julius Cæsar. Act iv, sc. 3, l. 151. [Cassius]
O insupportable!—*Othello,* v, 2, 98.
Insupportable vexation.—*All 's Well that Ends Well,* ii, 3, 243. The only uses of "insupportable."

2
Thou losest here, a better where to find.
King Lear. Act i, sc. 1, l. 264. [King of France]
Seeking to give Losses their remedies.
King Lear. Act ii, sc. 2, l. 176. [Kent]

3
We have lost Best half of our affair.
Macbeth. Act iii, sc. 3, l. 20. [Murderer]

4
Salanio: Why, the end is, he hath lost a ship.
Salarino: I would it might prove the end of his losses.
The Merchant of Venice. Act iii, sc. 1, l. 18.
These griefs and losses have so bated me,
That I shall hardly spare a pound of flesh
To-morrow to my bloody creditor.
The Merchant of Venice. Act iii, sc. 3, l. 32. [Antonio]
Glancing an eye of pity on his losses,
That have of late so huddled on his back,
Enow to press a royal merchant down.
The Merchant of Venice. Act iv, sc. 1, l. 27. [Duke] The only use of "glancing" and "huddled."
Loss upon loss!—*The Merchant of Venice,* iii, 1, 96.

5
For it so falls out
That what we have we prize not to the worth
Whiles we enjoy it, but being lack'd and lost,
Why, then we rack the value, then we find
The virtue that possession would not show us
Whiles it was ours.
Much Ado about Nothing. Act iv, sc. 1, l. 219. [Friar Francis]
They that lose half with greater patience bear it
Than they whose whole is swallow'd in confusion.
The Rape of Lucrece, l. 1158.

6
The worst is worldly loss thou canst unfold.
Richard II. Act iii, sc. 2, l. 94. [King Richard]
Light loss.—*King John,* iii, 1, 206.
Little loss.—*Henry V,* iv, 8, 115; *King John,* ii, 1, 307.
Merest loss.—*The Taming of the Shrew,* Ind., 1, 23. The only use of "merest."

7
Queen Elizabeth: Was never widow had so dear a loss!
Children: Were never orphans had so dear a loss!
Duchess: Was never mother had so dear a loss!
Richard III. Act ii, sc. 2, l. 77.
They Match not the high perfection of my loss.
Richard III. Act iv, sc. 4, l. 65. [Queen Margaret]
Bettering thy loss makes the bad causer worse.
Richard III. Act iv, sc. 4, l. 122. [Queen Margaret] "Bettering" is repeated in *The Tempest,* i, 2, 90; "causer" in *Richard III,* i, 2, 117, and in *Love's Labour 's Lost,* iv, 3, 311.

8
Tut, I have lost myself; I am not here.
Romeo and Juliet. Act i, sc. 1, l. 203. [Romeo]
Come, civil night, . . .
And learn me how to lose a winning match,
Play'd for a pair of stainless maidenhoods.
Romeo and Juliet. Act iii, sc. 2, l. 11. [Juliet] "Stainless" is repeated in *Twelfth Night,* i, 5, 278: "Stainless youth."

9
If I lose thee, my loss is my love's gain,
And losing her, my friend hath found that loss;
Both find each other, and I lose both twain,
And both for my sake lay on me the cross.
Sonnets. No. xlii.

10
There is not only disgrace and dishonour in that, monster, but an infinite loss.
The Tempest. Act iv, sc. 1, l. 209. [Stephano]
Infinite loss.—*Cymbeline,* i, 1, 120.

11
We shall lose our time.
The Tempest. Act iv, sc. 1, l. 248. [Caliban]
Lose the tide, and the voyage, and the master, and the service, and the tied!
The Two Gentlemen of Verona. Act ii, sc. 3, l. 56. [Launce]

12
Alonso: I have lost . . .
My dear son Ferdinand.
Prospero: I am woe for 't, sir.
Alonso: Irreparable is the loss, and patience
Says it is past her cure.
Prospero: I rather think
You have not sought her help, of whose soft grace
For the like loss I have her sovereign aid
And rest myself content.
Alonso: You the like loss!
Prospero: As great to me as late; and, supportable
To make the dear loss, have I means much weaker
Than you may call to comfort you, for I
Have lost my daughter.
The Tempest. Act v, sc. 1, l. 137. The only use of "irreparable" and "supportable."
The loss you have is but a son being king,
And by that loss your daughter is made queen.
Richard III. Act iv, sc. 4, l. 307. [King Richard]

13
This loss of blood,
As from a conduit with three issuing spouts.
Titus Andronicus. Act iii, sc. 1, l. 29. [Marcus]
Loss of liberty.—*III Henry VI,* iv, 6, 15.
Loss of life.—*I Henry IV,* v, 4, 78.
Loss of maidenhead.—*Pericles,* iii, Gower, 10.

Maiden loss.—*Measure for Measure,* iv, 4, 27.
Loss of men.—*All's Well that Ends Well,* iii, 2, 44.
Loss of time.—*The Two Gentlemen of Verona,* i, 3, 19; *Coriolanus,* iii, 1, 285.
Loss of virginity.—*All's Well that Ends Well,* i, 1, 138.
Loss of wealth.—*Troilus and Cressida,* iv, 1, 60.

1
I am a foul way out.
Twelfth Night. Act ii, sc. 3, l. 200. [Sir Andrew]

II—Loss and Gain

2
First Lord: Your lordship is the most patient man in loss, the most coldest that ever turned up ace.
Cloten: It would make any man cold to lose.
First Lord: But not every man patient after the noble temper of your lordship. You are most hot and furious when you win.
Cloten: Winning will put any man into courage.
Cymbeline. Act ii, sc. 3, l. 1.

3
Cymbeline: Thou hast lost by this a kingdom.
Imogen: No, my lord;
I have got two worlds by 't.
Cymbeline. Act v, sc. 5, l. 373.
Losing a mite, a mountain gain.—*Pericles,* ii, Gower, 8.

4
That, swoopstake, you will draw both friend and foe,
Winner and loser?
Hamlet. Act iv, sc. 5, l. 142. [King] The only use of "swoopstake" (an indiscriminate person).

5
Didst thou at first, to flatter us withal,
Make us partakers of a little gain,
That now our loss might be ten times so much?
I Henry VI. Act ii, sc. 1, l. 51. [Charles]

6
Whoever wins, on that side shall I lose;
Assured loss before the match be play'd.
King John. Act iii, sc. 1, l. 335. [Blanch]
Assured loss.—*King Lear,* iii, 6, 102.

7
Who loses and who wins; who 's in, who 's out.
King Lear. Act v, sc. 3, l. 15. [King Lear]
No sooner got but lost.—*Troilus and Cressida,* iv, 2, 76.

8
The loss, the gain, the ordering on 't, is all
Properly ours.
Winter's Tale. Act ii, sc. 1, l. 169. [Leontes]
Gain and loss.—*Richard III,* ii, 4, 59.
Gains or loses.—*Cymbeline,* ii, 4, 59.

LOVE

See also Affection, Devotion, Liking

I—Definitions

9
Love is merely a madness, and, I tell you, deserves as well a dark house and a whip as madmen do: and the reason why they are not so punished and cured is, that the lunacy is so ordinary that the whippers are in love too.
As You Like It. Act iii, sc. 2, l. 420. [Rosalind] The only use of "whippers."

10
Phebe: Good shepherd, tell this youth what 'tis to love.
It is to be all made of sighs and tears . . .
It is to be all made of faith and service . . .
It is to be all made of fantasy,
All made of passion and all made of wishes,
All adoration, duty, and observance,
All humbleness, all patience and impatience,
All purity, all trial, all observance.
As You Like It. Act v, sc. 2, l. 89.
For love is crowned with the prime
In spring time, the only pretty ring time.
As You Like It. Act v, sc. 3, l. 33. [Song]

11
This is the very ecstasy of love,
Whose violent property fordoes itself
And leads the will to desperate undertakings
As oft as any passion under heaven
That does afflict our natures.
Hamlet. Act ii, sc. 1, l. 102. [Polonius] "Fordoes" is repeated in *Othello,* v, 1, 129.
By the Lord, this love is as mad as Ajax.
Love's Labour 's Lost. Act iv, sc. 3, l. 6. [Biron]

12
Love 's not love
When it is mingled with regards that stand
Aloof from the entire point.
King Lear. Act i, sc. 1, l. 241. [King of France]

13
How can that be true love which is falsely attempted?
Love is a familiar; Love is a devil: there is no evil angel but Love.
Love's Labour 's Lost. Act i, sc. 2, l. 176. [Armado]

14
But love, first learned in a lady's eyes,
Lives not alone immured in the brain;
But, with the motion of all elements,
Courses as swift as thought in every power,
And gives to every power a double power,
Above their functions and their offices.
It adds a precious seeing to the eye;
A lover's eyes will gaze an eagle blind;
A lover's ear will hear the lowest sound,
When the suspicious head of theft is stopp'd:
Love's feeling is more soft and sensible
Than are the tender horns of cockled snails;
Love's tongue proves dainty Bacchus gross in taste:
For valour, is not Love a Hercules,
Still climbing trees in the Hesperides?
Love's Labour 's Lost. Act iv, sc. 3, l. 327. [Biron] The only use of "cockled." "Cockle hat" occurs in *Hamlet,* iv, 5, 25. The Hesperides are mentioned again in *Pericles,* i, 1, 27.
And when Love speaks, the voice of all the gods

Make heaven drowsy with the harmony.
Love's Labour 's Lost. Act iv, sc. 3, l. 344. [Biron]

1

Love doth approach disguised,
Armed in arguments.
Love's Labour 's Lost. Act v, sc. 2, l. 83. [Boyet]

Yet, since love's argument was first on foot,
Let not the cloud of sorrow justle it
From what it purposed.
Love's Labour 's Lost. Act v, sc. 2, l. 757. [King Ferdinand]

This was a great argument of love in her toward you.
Twelfth Night. Act iii, sc. 2, l. 12. [Fabian]

2

Love is full of unbefitting strains,
All wanton as a child, skipping and vain,
Form'd by the eye, and therefore like the eye,
Full of strange shapes, of habits and of forms,
Varying in subject as the eye doth roll
To every varied object in his glance.
Love's Labour 's Lost. Act v, sc. 2, l. 770. [Biron] The only use of "unbefitting."

Love is like a child,
That longs for everything that he can come by.
The Two Gentlemen of Verona. Act iii, sc. 1, l. 124. [Duke]

Love is a babe.—*Sonnets,* cxv.

3

The love that follows us sometime is our trouble,
Which still we thank as love.
Macbeth. Act i, sc. 6, l. 11. [Duncan]

4

Love talks with better knowledge, and knowledge with dearer love.
Measure for Measure. Act iii, sc. 2, l. 159. [Duke]

5

Lysander: Ay me! for aught that I could ever read,
Could ever hear by tale or history,
The course of true love never did run smooth;
But, either it was different in blood,—
Hermia: O cross! too high to be enthrall'd to low.
Lysander: Or else misgraffed in respect of years,—
Hermia: O spite! too old to be engaged to young.
Lysander: Or else it stood upon the choice of friends,—
Hermia: O hell! to choose love by another's eyes.
Lysander: Or, if there were a sympathy in choice,
War, death or sickness did lay siege to it,
Making it momentany as a sound,
Swift as a shadow, short as any dream;
Brief as the lightning in the collied night,
That, in a spleen, unfolds both heaven and earth,
And ere a man hath power to say 'Behold!'
The jaws of darkness do devour it up:
So quick bright things come to confusion.
Hermia: If then true lovers have been ever cross'd,
It stands as an edict in destiny:
Then let us teach our trial patience,
Because it is a customary cross,
As due to love as thoughts and dreams and sighs,
Wishes and tears, poor fancy's followers.
A Midsummer-Night's Dream. Act i, sc. 1, l. 132. The only use of "misgraffed" and "momentany." "Course of love" is repeated in *Romeo and Juliet,* v, 3, 287, and in *Othello,* i, 3, 91. "Collied" (murky, darkened) is repeated in *Othello,* ii, 3, 206: "My best judgement collied."

Whom best I love I cross; to make my gift,
The more delay'd, delighted.
Cymbeline. Act v, sc. 4, l. 101. [Jupiter]

O injurious love,
That respites me a life, whose very comfort
Is still a dying horror!
Measure for Measure. Act ii, sc. 3, l. 40. [Juliet]

6

Love is a smoke raised with the fume of sighs;
Being purged, a fire sparkling in lovers' eyes;
Being vex'd, a sea nourish'd with lovers' tears:
What is it else? a madness most discreet,
A choking gall and a preserving sweet.
Romeo and Juliet. Act i, sc. 1, l. 196. [Romeo]

Romeo: Is love a tender thing? it is too rough,
Too rude, too boisterous, and it pricks like thorn.
Mercutio: If love be rough with you, be rough with love.
Romeo and Juliet. Act i, sc. 4, l. 25.

Prick love for pricking, and you beat love down.
Romeo and Juliet. Act i, sc. 4, l. 28. [Mercutio]

Love goes toward love, as schoolboys from their books,
But love from love, toward school with heavy looks.
Romeo and Juliet. Act ii, sc. 2, l. 157. [Romeo]

This drivelling love is like a great natural, that runs lolling up and down to hide his bauble in a hole.
Romeo and Juliet. Act ii, sc. 4, l. 95. [Mercutio] The only use of "drivelling."

7

O, learn to read what silent love hath writ:
To hear with eyes belongs to love's fine wit.
Sonnets. No. xxiii.

Two loves I have of comfort and despair,
Which like two spirits do suggest me still.
Sonnets. No. cxliv. Repeated in *The Passionate Pilgrim,* l. 15.

Love is too young to know what conscience is.
Sonnets. No. cli. See under CONSCIENCE.

My love is as a fever.—*Sonnets,* cxlvii. See under DISEASE: FEVER.

1
O spirit of love! how quick and fresh art thou,
That, notwithstanding thy capacity
Receiveth as the sea, nought enters there,
Of what validity and pitch soe'er,
But falls into abatement and low price,
Even in a minute.
Twelfth Night. Act i, sc. 1, l. 9. [Duke]

What is love? 'tis not hereafter;
Present mirth hath present laughter;
What 's to come is still unsure;
In delay there lies no plenty;
Then come kiss me, sweet and twenty.
Youth 's a stuff will not endure.
Twelfth Night. Act ii, sc. 3, l. 48. [Clown, singing]

2
Fie, fie, how wayward is this foolish love
That, like a testy babe, will scratch the nurse
And presently all humbled kiss the rod!
The Two Gentlemen of Verona. Act i, sc. 2, l. 57. [Julia]

O, how this spring of love resembleth
The uncertain glory of an April day,
Which now shows all the beauty of the sun,
And by and by a cloud takes all away!
The Two Gentlemen of Verona. Act i, sc. 3, l. 84. [Proteus]

3
I have done penance for contemning Love,
Whose high imperious thoughts have punish'd me
With bitter fasts, with penitential groans,
With nightly tears and daily heart-sore sighs;
For in revenge of my contempt of love,
Love hath chased sleep from my enthralled eyes
And made them watchers of mine own heart's sorrow.
O gentle Proteus, Love 's a mighty lord
And hath so humbled me as I confess
There is no woe to his correction,
Nor to his service no such joy on earth.
Now no discourse, except it be of love;
Now can I break my fast, dine, sup and sleep,
Upon the very naked name of love.
The Two Gentlemen of Verona. Act ii, sc. 4, l. 129. [Valentine] The only use of "penitential." "Heart-sore" is repeated in i, 1, 30, and occurs in no other play.

O, flatter me; for love delights in praises.
The Two Gentlemen of Verona. Act ii, sc. 4, l. 148. [Valentine]

4
Love is a spirit all compact of fire,
Not gross to sink, but light, and will aspire.
Venus and Adonis, l. 149.

Is love so light, sweet boy, and may it be
That thou shouldst think it heavy unto thee?
Venus and Adonis, l. 155.

Love can comment upon every woe.
Venus and Adonis, l. 714.

Love makes young men thrall and old men dote;
. . . Love is wise in folly, foolish-witty.
Venus and Adonis, l. 837. The only use of "foolish-witty."

O hard-believing love, how strange it seems
Not to believe, and yet too credulous!
Thy weal and woe are both of them extremes.
Venus and Adonis, l. 985. The only use of "hard-believing."

II—Familiar Phrases

5
O, for the love of laughter!
All's Well that Ends Well. Act iii, sc. 6, l. 43. [Lord]

For love of God.—*Hamlet,* v, 1, 296; *Twelfth Night,* ii, 3, 92; v, 1, 175; 180.

For the love of mockery.—*Twelfth Night,* ii, 5, 21.

Love of grace.—*Hamlet,* iii, 4, 144.

Love of soul.—*King John,* v, 1, 10.

6
Why do people love you?
As You Like It. Act ii, sc. 2, l. 5. [Adam]

But, mistress, know yourself: down on your knees,
And thank heaven, fasting, for a good man's love.
As You Like It. Act iii, sc. 5, l. 57. [Rosalind]

7
He is one of the patterns of love.
As You Like It. Act iv, sc. 1, l. 99. [Rosalind]

The extremity of love.
As You Like It. Act iv, sc. 3, l. 23. [Rosalind]

He is far gone, far gone: and truly in my youth I suffered much extremity for love; very near this.
Hamlet. Act ii, sc. 2, l. 190. [Polonius]

8
I shall be loved when I am lack'd.
Coriolanus. Act iv, sc. 1, l. 15. [Coriolanus]

9
How should I your true love know
From another one?
By his cockle hat and staff,
And his sandal shoon.
Hamlet. Act iv, sc. 5, l. 23. [Ophelia] "True love" occurs twenty-nine times in the plays and poems. The only use of "sandal."

10
Love, whose month is ever May.
Love's Labour 's Lost. Act iv, sc. 3, l. 102. [Dumain] Repeated in *The Passionate Pilgrim,* l. 228.

11
Sweet heart, let that pass.
Love's Labour 's Lost. Act v, sc. 1, l. 110. [Holofernes] "Sweet heart" is used four times in this scene, and thirteen times in later plays, sometimes as one word, sometimes as two.

Trip no further, pretty sweeting.—*Twelfth Night,* ii, 3, 43. "Sweeting" is repeated in *I Henry VI,* iii, 3, 21; *The Taming of the Shrew,* iv, 3, 36; *Romeo and Juliet,* ii, 4, 83; and *Othello,* ii, 3, 252.

Dearest chuck.—*Macbeth,* iii, 2, 45.

Sweet chuck.—*Henry V,* iii, 2, 26; *Love's Labour 's Lost,* v, 1, 117; v, 2, 667. "Chuck," by itself, is used four times.

O dainty duck! O dear!—*A Midsummer-Night's Dream,* v, 1, 286.

Ah, sweet ducks!—*Troilus and Cressida,* iv, 4, 12.

Most best, most dearest.—*King Lear,* i, 1, 219.

Most dear'st! my collop!—*The Winter's Tale,* i, 2, 137. "Collop" (piece of flesh) is repeated in *I Henry VI,* iv, 4, 18.

Who, young and simple, would not be so lover'd?
A Lover's Complaint, l. 320. The only use of "lover'd."

1
Love like a shadow flies when substance love pursues;
Pursuing that that flies, and flying what pursues.
The Merry Wives of Windsor. Act ii, sc. 2, l. 215. [Ford]

2
Loving goes by haps.
Much Ado about Nothing. Act iii, sc. 1, l. 105. [Hero]

3
One that loved not wisely but too well.
Othello. Act v, sc. 2, l. 344. [Othello]

4
Love and Fortune be my gods, my guide!
The Rape of Lucrece, l. 351.

5
How many a holy and obsequious tear
Hath dear religious love stol'n from mine eye.
Sonnets. No. xxxi.

Our love was new and then but in the spring.
Sonnets. No. cii.

6
In sadness, cousin, I do love a woman.
Romeo and Juliet. Act i, sc. 1, l. 210. [Romeo]

But can you affection the 'oman?
The Merry Wives of Windsor. Act i, sc. 1, l. 234. [Evans]

7
If love have touch'd you, nought remains but so,
'Redime te captum quam queas minimo.'
The Taming of the Shrew. Act i, sc. 1, l. 166. [Tranio] A misquotation of Terence's line (*Eunuchus,* i, 1, 29), "Quid agas? nisi ut te redimas captum quam queas minumo, Ransom yourself from captivity as cheaply as you can." The misquotation was copied from Lilly's *Latin Grammar.*

8
Our fine musician groweth amorous.
The Taming of the Shrew. Act iii, sc. 1, l. 63. [Lucentio]

Sure my brother is amorous on Hero.
Much Ado about Nothing. Act ii, sc. 1, l. 161. [Don John]

9
Now, if you love me, stay.
The Taming of the Shrew. Act iii, sc. 2, l. 205. [Katharina]

An you love me.—*Twelfth Night,* ii, 3, 63.

As you love our favour.—*I Henry VI,* iv, 1, 135.

This do thou for my love.—*Titus Andronicus,* v, 2, 129.

10
Love me or love me not.
The Taming of the Shrew. Act iv, sc. 3, l. 84. [Katherina]

Love me, and leave me not.
The Merchant of Venice. Act v, sc. 1, l. 150. [Gratiano]

11
Lass-lorn.
The Tempest. Act iv, sc. 1, l. 68. [Iris] The only use of the phrase.

12
Of such a nature is his politic love.
Timon of Athens. Act iii, sc. 3, l. 35. [Servant]

13
Love's thrice repured nectar.
Troilus and Cressida. Act iii, sc. 2, l. 23. [Troilus] The only use of "repured."

What, billing again?
Troilus and Cressida. Act iii, sc. 2, l. 61. [Pandarus] The only use of "billing."

More vindicative than jealous love.
Troilus and Cressida. Act iv, sc. 5, l. 107. [Ulysses] The only use of "vindicative."

14
Valentine: Since thou lovest, love still and thrive therein,
Even as I would were I to love begin. . . .
Proteus: Upon some book I love I'll pray for thee.
Valentine: That's on some shallow story of deep love;
How young Leander cross'd the Hellespont.
Proteus: That's a deep story of a deeper love;
For he was more than over shoes in love.
Valentine: 'Tis true; for you are over boots in love,
And yet you never swum the Hellespont.
The Two Gentlemen of Verona. Act i, sc. 1, l. 9. "Swum" is repeated in *The Tempest,* ii, 2, 133: "Swum ashore."

We'll draw thee from the mire
Of this sir-reverence love, wherein thou stick'st
Up to the ears.
Romeo and Juliet. Act i, sc. 4, l. 41. [Mercutio] "Sir-reverence" is used again in *The Comedy of Errors,* iii, 2, 93.

In love, i' faith, to the very tip of the nose.
Troilus and Cressida. Act iii, sc. 1, l. 138. [Helen]

Full of love.—*Titus Andronicus,* iv, 2, 43.

Horribly in love.—*Troilus and Cressida,* iii, 1, 106.

15
'Tis love you cavil at.
The Two Gentlemen of Verona. Act i, sc. 1, l. 38. [Proteus]

16
Julia: Wouldst thou then counsel me to fall in love?
Lucette: Ay, madam, so you stumble not unheedfully.
The Two Gentlemen of Verona. Act i, sc. 2, l. 2. The only use of "unheedfully." "Fall in love" is repeated eight times in later plays.

Rosalind: Let me see; what think you of falling in love?
Celia: Marry, I prithee, do, to make sport

withal: but love no man in good earnest; nor no further in sport neither than with safety of a pure blush thou mayst in honour come off again.

As You Like It. Act i, sc. 2, l. 27.

I do much wonder that one man, seeing how much another man is a fool when he dedicates his behaviours to love, will, after he hath laughed at such shallow follies in others, become the argument of his own scorn by falling in love.

Much Ado about Nothing. Act ii, sc. 3, l. 7. [Benedick]

He 's fallen in love.—*As You Like It,* iii, 5, 66.
Honeying and making love.—*Hamlet,* iii, 4, 93.
Made love to you.—*Pericles,* ii, 5, 70.
Make love.—*Macbeth,* iii, 1, 124.

1
For love is still most precious in itself.

The Two Gentlemen of Verona. Act ii, sc. 6, l. 24. [Proteus]

Love, lend me wings to make my purpose swift,
As thou hast lent me wit to plot this drift!

The Two Gentlemen of Verona. Act ii, sc. 6, l. 42. [Proteus]

Only deserve my love by loving him.

The Two Gentlemen of Verona. Act ii, sc. 7, l. 82. [Julia]

2
Twenty odd-conceited true-love knots.

The Two Gentlemen of Verona. Act ii, sc. 7, l. 46. [Julia] The only use of either phrase.

3
Pox of your love-letters!

The Two Gentlemen of Verona. Act iii, sc. 1, l. 390. [Speed]

What, have I scaped love-letters in the holiday-time of my beauty, and am I now a subject for them?

The Merry Wives of Windsor. Act ii, sc. 1, l. 1. [Mrs. Page] The only uses of "love-letters" and of "holiday-time."

Love-affair.—*The Two Gentlemen of Verona,* iii, 1, 254.
Love-broker.—*Twelfth Night,* iii, 2, 39.
Love-feat.—*Love's Labour 's Lost,* v, 2, 123.
Love-god.—*Sonnets,* cliv.
Love-kindling.—*Sonnets,* cliii.
Love-lacking.—*Venus and Adonis,* l. 752.
Love-monger.—*Love's Labour 's Lost,* ii, 1, 253.
Love-shaft.—*A Midsummer-Night's Dream,* ii, 1, 159.
Love-sick.—*Titus Andronicus,* v, 3, 82; *Antony and Cleopatra,* ii, 2, 199; *Venus and Adonis,* l. 175; 328.
Love-song.—*The Two Gentlemen of Verona,* ii, 1, 20, and four times in later plays.
Love-suit.—*Sonnets,* cxxxvi.
Love-token.—*A Midsummer-Night's Dream,* i, 1, 29. None of these phrases is used more than once except "love-sick" and "love-song."

4
Loving-jealous.—*Romeo and Juliet,* ii, 2, 82. The only use of the phrase.
Lovingly.—*Titus Andronicus,* i, 1, 165. The only use of the word.

5
Alas, how love can trifle with itself!

The Two Gentlemen of Verona. Act iv, sc. 4, l. 188. [Julia]

6
He that wears her like her medal, hanging
About his neck.

The Winter's Tale. Act i, sc. 2, l. 307. [Leontes] The only use of "medal."

Over-fond of the shepherd's daughter.

The Winter's Tale. Act v, sc. 2, l. 126. [Autolycus] The only use of "over-fond."

III—Love: Its Power

7
What power is it which mounts my love so high,
That makes me see, and cannot feed mine eye?

All 's Well that Ends Well. Act i, sc. 1, l. 235. [Helena]

Our blood to us, this to our blood is born;
It is the show and seal of nature's truth,
Where love's strong passion is impress'd in youth.

All 's Well that Ends Well. Act i, sc. 3, l. 137. [Countess]

8
Her love to both
Would, each to other and all loves to both,
Draw after her.

Antony and Cleopatra. Act ii, sc. 2, l. 137. [Agrippa]

9
I 'll wrestle with you in my strength of love:
Look, here I have you; thus I let you go,
And give you to the gods.

Antony and Cleopatra. Act iii, sc. 2, l. 62. [Antony]

10
Silvius: O Corin, that thou knew'st how I do love her!
Corin: I partly guess; for I have loved ere now. . . .
Silvius: If thy love was ever like to mine—
As sure I think did never man love so—
How many actions most ridiculous
Hast thou been drawn to by thy fantasy?
Corin: Into a thousand that I have forgotten.
Silvius: O, thou didst then ne'er love so heartily!
If thou remember'st not the slightest folly
That ever love did make thee run into,
Thou hast not loved:
Or if thou hast not sat as I do now,
Wearying thy hearer in thy mistress' praise,
Thou hast not loved:
Or if thou hast not broke from company
Abruptly, as my passion now makes me,
Thou hast not loved.

As You Like It. Act ii, sc. 4, l. 23. [Silvius]

I see love hath made thee a tame snake.

As You Like It. Act iv, sc. 3, l. 70. [Rosalind]

11
Polonius: Mad for thy love?
Ophelia: My lord, I do not know;
But truly, I do fear it.

Hamlet. Act ii, sc. 1, l. 85.

1
Her virtues graced with external gifts
Do breed love's settled passions in my heart:
And like as rigour of tempestuous gusts
Provokes the mightiest hulk against the tide,
So am I driven by breath of her renown
Either to suffer shipwreck or arrive
Where I may have fruition of her love.

I Henry VI. Act v, sc. 5, l. 3. [King Henry] The only use of "fruition."

High tempestuous gusts.—*Titus Andronicus*, v, 3, 69. The only uses of "tempestuous."

2
Needs must you lay your heart at his dispose,
Subjected tribute to commanding love,
Against whose fury and unmatched force
The aweless lion could not wage the fight,
Nor keep his princely heart from Richard's hand.
He that perforce robs lions of their hearts
May easily win a woman's.

King John. Act i, sc. 1, l. 263. [Bastard] "Aweless" is repeated in *Richard III*, ii, 4, 52: "Aweless throne."

3 Deny himself to Jove
Turning mortal for thy love.

Love's Labour's Lost. Act iv, sc. 3, l. 117. [Dumain, reading] Also *The Passionate Pilgrim*, l. 244.

Remember, Jove, thou wast a bull for thy Europa; love set on thy horns. O powerful love! that, in some respects, makes a beast a man, in some other, a man a beast. You were also, Jupiter, a swan for the love of Leda. O omnipotent Love! how near the god drew to the complexion of a goose!

The Merry Wives of Windsor. Act v, sc. 5, l. 3. [Falstaff]

4
Love lack'd a dwelling, and made him her place;
And when in his fair parts she did abide,
She was new lodged and newly deified.

A Lover's Complaint, l. 84. The only use of "deified."

O most potential love! vow, bond, nor space,
In thee hath neither sting, knot, nor confine,
For thou art all, and all things else are thine.

A Lover's Complaint, l. 264. "Potential" is repeated in *King Lear*, ii, 1, 78, and in *Othello*, i, 2, 13.

Love's arms are peace, 'gainst rule, 'gainst sense, 'gainst shame,
And sweetens, in the suffering pangs it bears,
The aloes of all forces, shocks, and fears.

A Lover's Complaint, l. 271. The only use of "aloes."

5
In love the heavens themselves do guide the state.

The Merry Wives of Windsor. Act v, sc. 5, l. 245. [Ford]

6
O, then, what graces in my love do dwell,
That he hath turn'd a heaven unto a hell!

A Midsummer-Night's Dream. Act i, sc. 1, l. 206. [Hermia]

7
Things base and vile, holding no quantity,
Love can transpose to form and dignity.

A Midsummer-Night's Dream. Act i, sc. 1, l. 232. [Helena] "Transpose" is repeated in *Macbeth*, iv, 3, 21.

Love takes the meaning in love's conference.

A Midsummer-Night's Dream. Act ii, sc. 2, l. 46. [Lysander]

8
Whom love hath turn'd almost the wrong side out.

Othello. Act ii, sc. 3, l. 54. [Iago]

9
Benvolio: Alas, that love, so gentle in his view,
Should be so tyrannous and rough in proof!
Romeo: Alas, that love, whose view is muffled still,
Should, without eyes, see pathways to his will!

Romeo and Juliet. Act i, sc. 1, l. 175.

Alike bewitched by the charm of looks.

Romeo and Juliet. Act ii, Prologue, l. 6. [Chorus]

10
With love's light wings did I o'er-perch these walls;
For stony limits cannot hold love out,
And what love can do that dares love attempt.

Romeo and Juliet. Act ii, sc. 2, l. 66. [Romeo] The only use of "o'er-perch."

11
So true a fool is love that in your will,
Though you do any thing, he thinks no ill.

Sonnets. No. lvii.

Love wrought these miracles.

The Taming of the Shrew. Act v, sc. 1, l. 127. [Lucentio]

12
Our old love made a particular force,
And made us speak like friends.

Timon of Athens. Act v, sc. 2, l. 8. [Messenger] "Old love" is repeated in *Coriolanus*, v, 3, 12.

Do it for ancient love.—*King Lear*, iv, 1, 45.

13
Helen: Let thy song be love: this love will undo us all. O Cupid, Cupid, Cupid!
Pandarus: Love! ay, that it shall, i' faith.
Paris: Ay, good now, love, love, nothing but love.
Pandarus: In good troth, it begins so. [Sings]
Love, love, nothing but love, still more!
For, O, love's bow
Shoots buck and doe:
The shaft confounds,
Not that it wounds,
But tickles still the sore.
These lovers cry Oh! oh! they die!
Yet that which seems the wound to kill,
Doth turn oh! oh! to ha! ha! he!
So dying love lives still.

Troilus and Cressida. Act iii, sc. 1, l. 119.

14 Time, force, and death,
Do to this body what extremes you can;

But the strong base and building of my love
Is as the very centre of the earth,
Drawing all things to it.
Troilus and Cressida. Act iv, sc. 2, l. 107. [Cressida]

1
Love is your master, for he masters you.
The Two Gentlemen of Verona. Act i, sc. 1, l. 39. [Valentine]

Yet writers say, as in the sweetest bud
The eating canker dwells, so eating love
Inhabits in the finest wits of all.
The Two Gentlemen of Verona. Act i, sc. 1, l. 42. [Proteus]

2 By love the young and tender wit
Is turn'd to folly.
The Two Gentlemen of Verona. Act i, sc. 1, l. 47. [Valentine]

Once more I 'll mark how love can vary wit.
Love's Labour 's Lost. Act iv, sc. 3, l. 100. [Biron]

3
I leave myself, my friends and all, for love.
The Two Gentlemen of Verona. Act i, sc. 1, l. 65. [Proteus]

Julia: Didst thou but know the inly touch of love,
Thou wouldst as soon go kindle fire with snow
As seek to quench the fire of love with words.
Lucetta: I do not seek to quench your love's hot fire,
But qualify the fire's extreme rage,
Lest it should burn above the bounds of reason.
Julia: The more thou damm'st it up, the more it burns.
Two Gentlemen of Verona. Act ii, sc. 7, l. 18.

4
Sorrow on love hereafter shall attend:
It shall be waited on with jealousy,
Find sweet beginning, but unsavoury end.
Venus and Adonis, l. 1136.

It shall be fickle, false and full of fraud,
Bud and be blasted in a breathing-while;
The bottom poison and, the top o'erstraw'd
With sweets that shall the truest sight beguile:
The strongest body shall it make most weak,
Strike the wise dumb and teach the fool to speak.
It shall be sparing and too full of riot,
Teaching decrepit age to tread the measures;
The staring ruffian shall it keep in quiet,
Pluck down the rich, enrich the poor with treasures;
It shall be raging-mad and silly-mild,
Make the young old, the old become a child.
It shall suspect where is no cause of fear;
It shall not fear where it should most mistrust;
It shall be merciful and too severe,
And most deceiving when it seems most just;
Perverse it shall be where it shows most toward,
Put fear to valour, courage to the coward.
It shall be cause of war and dire events,
And set dissension 'twixt the son and sire;
Subject and servile to all discontents,
As dry combustious matter is to fire.
Venus and Adonis, l. 1141. The only use of "o'erstraw'd," "raging-mad," "silly-wild," and "combustious." "Breathing-while" is repeated in *Richard III,* i, 3, 60: "Cannot be quiet scarce a breathing-while."

IV—Love: Its Manifestations

5
Rosalind: He seems to have the quotidian of love upon him.
Orlando: I am he that is so love-shaked: I pray you, tell me your remedy.
Rosalind: There is none of my uncle's marks upon you: he taught me how to know a man in love: in which cage of rushes I am sure you are not prisoner.
Orlando: What were his marks?
Rosalind: A lean cheek, which you have not, a blue eye and sunken, which you have not, an unquestionable spirit, which you have not, a beard neglected, which you have not; but I pardon you for that, for simply your having in beard is a younger brother's revenue: then your hose should be ungartered, your bonnet unbanded, your sleeve unbuttoned, your shoe untied and every thing about you demonstrating a careless desolation.
As You Like It. Act iii, sc. 2, l. 383. "Quotidian" occurs again in *Henry V,* ii, 1, 124. The only use of "love-shaked," "unquestionable," "unbanded," "unbuttoned," and "demonstrating." "Sunken" is repeated in *Henry V,* i, 2, 165: "Sunken wreck;" and "untied" in *Pericles,* 4, 2, 160.

6
All fancy-sick she is and pale of cheer,
With sighs of love, that costs the fresh blood dear.
A Midsummer-Night's Dream. Act iii, sc. 2, l. 96. [Oberon] The only use of "fancy-sick."

7
By heaven, I do love: and it hath taught me to rhyme and to be melancholy.
Love's Labour 's Lost. Act iv, sc. 3, l. 13. [Biron]

As much love in rhyme
As would be cramm'd up in a sheet of paper.
Love's Labour 's Lost. Act v, sc. 2, l. 6. [Princess of France]

8
Benedick: Gallants, I am not as I have been.
Leonato: So say I: methinks you are sadder.
Claudio: I hope he be in love.
Don Pedro: Hang him, truant! There 's no true drop of blood in him, to be truly touched with love: if he be sad, he wants money. . . .
Claudio: Yet say I, he is in love. . . . If he be not in love with some woman, there is no believing old signs: a' brushes his hat o' mornings; what should that bode? . . .
Don Pedro: Nay, a' rubs himself with civet: can you smell him out by that?
Claudio: That 's as much as to say, the sweet youth 's in love.
Don Pedro: The greatest note of it is his

melancholy: . . . Conclude, conclude the youth 's in love.
Much Ado about Nothing. Act iii, sc. 2, l. 14.

Paris: He eats nothing but doves, love, and that breeds hot blood, and hot blood begets hot thoughts, and hot thoughts beget hot deeds, and hot deeds is love.
Pandarus: Is this the generation of love? hot blood, hot thoughts, and hot deeds? Why, they are vipers: is love a generation of vipers?
Troilus and Cressida. Act iii, sc. 1, l. 140.

1
To be in love, where scorn is bought with groans;
Coy looks with heart-sore sighs; one fading moment's mirth
With twenty watchful, weary, tedious nights:
If haply won, perhaps a hapless gain;
If lost, why then a grievous labour won;
However, but a folly bought with wit,
Or else a wit by folly vanquished.
Two Gentlemen of Verona. Act i, sc. 1, l. 29. [Valentine] "Heart-sore sighs" is repeated in ii, 4, 132, and occurs in no other play.

Valentine: Why, how know you that I am in love?
Speed: Marry, by these special marks: first, you have learned, like Sir Proteus, to wreathe your arms, like a malecontent; to relish a love-song, like a robin-redbreast; to walk alone, like one that had the pestilence; to sigh, like a schoolboy that had lost his A B C; to weep, like a young wench that had buried her grandam; to fast, like one that takes diet; to watch, like one that fears robbing; to speak puling, like a beggar at Hallowmas. You were wont, when you laughed, to crow like a cock; when you walked, to walk like one of the lions; when you fasted, it was presently after dinner; when you looked sadly, it was for want of money: and now you are metamorphosed with a mistress, that, when I look on you, I can hardly think you my master.
The Two Gentlemen of Verona. Act ii, sc. 1, l. 17. The only use of "robin-redbreast" and "fasted." "Metamorphosed" occurs again in the same play, i, 1, 66, and in no other. Hallowmas is mentioned again in *Measure for Measure,* ii, 1, 128, and in *Richard II,* v, 1, 80.

2 He says he loves my daughter:
I think so too; for never gazed the moon
Upon the water as he 'll stand and read
As 'twere my daughter's eyes: and, to be plain,
I think there is not half a kiss to choose
Who loves another best.
The Winter's Tale. Act iv, sc. 4, l. 171. [Shepherd]

V—Love: Constant

3 I love thee
By love's own sweet constraint, and will for ever.
All's Well that Ends Well. Act iv, sc. 2, l. 15. [Bertram]

If she had partaken of my flesh, and cost me the dearest groans of a mother, I could not have owed her a more rooted love.
All's Well that Ends Well. Act iv, sc. 5, l. 10. [Countess] The only use of "partaken."

4
Rosalind: Now tell me how long you would have her after you have possessed her.
Orlando: For ever and a day.
Rosalind: Say 'a day,' without the 'ever.'
As You Like It. Act iv, sc. 1, l. 143. "For ever and a day" is repeated in *The Taming of the Shrew,* iv, 4, 97.

You and you no cross shall part:
You and you are heart in heart: . . .
You and you are sure together,
As the winter to foul weather.
As You Like It. Act v, sc. 4, l. 137. [Hymen]

Love Unseparable.—*Coriolanus,* iv, 4, 15. The only use of "unseparable."

Undivided loves.—*Sonnets,* xxxvi. The only use of "undivided." "Undividable" occurs in *The Comedy of Errors,* ii, 2, 124.

5
I have not been common in my love.
Coriolanus, ii, 3, 101. See under PEOPLE.

This last old man,
Whom with a crack'd heart I have sent to Rome,
Loved me above the measure of a father;
Nay, godded me, indeed.
Coriolanus. Act v, sc. 3, l. 8. [Coriolanus] The only use of "godded."

6 Whose love was of that dignity
That it went hand in hand even with the vow
I made to her in marriage.
Hamlet. Act i, sc. 5, l. 48. [Ghost]

So many journeys may the sun and moon
Make us again count o'er ere love be done!
Hamlet. Act iii, sc. 2, l. 171. [Player Queen]

Love between them like the palm might flourish.
Hamlet. Act v, sc. 2, l. 40. [Hamlet]

7
His love was an eternal plant.
III Henry VI, iii, 3, 124. [Warwick]

8
Her that loves him with that excellence
That angels love good men with.
Henry VIII. Act ii, sc. 2, l. 34. [Norfolk]

He loves me well; and I have given him reasons.
Julius Cæsar. Act ii, sc. 1, l. 219. [Brutus]

9 She, sweet lady, dotes,
Devoutly dotes, dotes in idolatry,
Upon this spotted and inconstant man.
A Midsummer-Night's Dream. Act i, sc. 1, l. 108. [Lysander]

I never knew a woman so dote upon a man.
The Merry Wives of Windsor. Act ii, sc. 2, l. 105. [Mistress Quickly]

Followed her with a doting observance.
The Merry Wives of Windsor. Act ii, sc. 2, l. 202. [Ford]

As you on him, Demetrius dote on you!
A Midsummer-Night's Dream. Act i, sc. 1, l. 225. [Lysander]

Dote on thee.—*A Midsummer-Night's Dream,* iv, 1, 50.

Dote upon my love.—*The Two Gentlemen of Verona,* ii, 4, 173.

You dote on her.—*Two Gentlemen of Verona,* iv, 4, 87; *Much Ado about Nothing,* ii, 3, 219.

All alike do dote.—*Love's Labour's Lost,* iv, 3, 126.

1
Thy love ne'er alter till thy sweet life end!
A Midsummer-Night's Dream. Act ii, sc. 2, l. 61. [Hermia]

Best love.—*All's Well that Ends Well,* iii, 3, 2; *Antony and Cleopatra,* iii, 4, 21.
Comely love.—*Much Ado about Nothing,* iv, 1, 55.
Equal love.—*Henry V,* v, 2, 23.
Ever-preserved love.—*Hamlet,* ii, 2, 296. The only use of "ever-preserved."
Everlasting love.—*King John,* v, 4, 20.
Fair love.—*Richard III,* ii, 1, 50; *Love's Labour's Lost,* iv, 3, 380; *A Midsummer-Night's Dream,* ii, 2, 35; *Troilus and Cressida,* v, 1, 45; *The Rape of Lucrece,* l. 7.
Faithful love.—*Richard III,* iii, 7, 149; *King John,* iii, 4, 66.
Firm love.—*Troilus and Cressida,* i, 2, 320.
First best love.—*The Two Gentlemen of Verona,* v, 4, 46.
Gentle love.—*Taming of the Shrew,* iv, 2, 46; *Othello,* ii, 3, 250; *Venus and Adonis,* l. 653.
Good love.—*King John,* iv, 1, 49; *Coriolanus,* iii, 2, 84.
Great love.—*All's Well that Ends Well,* ii, 3, 91; *Hamlet,* iii, 2, 182; iv, 7, 18; *Macbeth,* i, 6, 23; *The Merry Wives of Windsor,* i, 1, 254; *Troilus and Cressida,* iii, 3, 221; *King Lear,* i, 4, 335; *Othello,* ii, 1, 207; *The Tempest,* ii, 1, 123.
Ingrafted love.—*Julius Cæsar,* ii, 1, 184. The only use of "ingrafted."
Innocent love.—*Hamlet,* iii, 4, 43.
Kind love.—*The Two Gentlemen of Verona,* ii, 7, 2; *Julius Cæsar,* iii, 1, 176.
Love-sick Love.—*Venus and Adonis,* l. 328.
Perfect love.—*I Henry VI,* v, 5, 50; *Richard III,* ii, 1, 16; iii, 7, 90; *The Taming of the Shrew,* iv, 3, 12.
Perfect'st love.—*Sonnets,* li.
Pure love.—*III Henry VI,* iii, 1, 13; *Romeo and Juliet,* ii, 3, 92; *As You Like It,* ii, 7, 131; *All's Well that Ends Well,* iii, 4, 38; *Antony and Cleopatra,* i, 2, 152.
Pure heart's love.—*Richard III,* iv, 1, 4; iv, 4, 403.
Unfeigned love.—*III Henry VI,* iii, 3, 51.
Unstained love.—*King John,* ii, 1, 16.
Well-meant honest love.—*III Henry VI,* iii, 3, 67. The only use of "well-meant."

2
She loves him with an enraged affection; it is past the infinite of thought.
Much Ado about Nothing. Act ii, sc. 3, l. 105. [Leonato]

Iago: I never knew woman love man so.
Cassio: Alas, poor rogue! I think, i' faith, she loves me.
Othello. Act iv, sc. 1, l. 111.

3
The heavens forbid
But that our loves and comforts should increase,
Even as our days do grow!
Othello. Act ii, sc. 1, l. 195. [Desdemona]

4
I wot your love pursues A banish'd traitor.
Richard II. Act ii, sc. 3, l. 59. [Bolingbroke]

5
Buckingham: You and he are near in love.
Hastings: I thank his grace, I know he loves me well.
Richard III. Act iii, sc. 4, l. 13.

Near in love.—*Richard II,* iii, 1, 17.
Love me dearly.—*Richard III,* ii, 2, 26.

6
Say, I will love her everlastingly.
Richard III. Act iv, sc. 4, l. 349. [King Richard]

7
Now Romeo is beloved and loves again.
Romeo and Juliet. Act ii, Prol., l. 5. [Chorus]

Then happy I, that love and am beloved.
Sonnets. No. xxv.

8
Therefore love moderately; long love doth so.
Romeo and Juliet. Act ii, sc. 6, l. 14. [Friar Laurence]

O love, Be moderate; allay thy ecstasy;
In measure rein thy joy; scant this excess.
I feel too much thy blessing: make it less,
For fear I surfeit.
The Merchant of Venice. Act iii, sc. 2, l. 111. [Portia]

Wish chastely and love dearly.
All's Well that Ends Well. Act i, sc. 3, l. 218. [Helena]

9
For thy sweet love remember'd such wealth brings
That then I scorn to change my state with kings.
Sonnets. No. xxix.

Sweet love.—*The Comedy of Errors,* iii, 2, 58, and seventeen times in later plays and poems.

There reigns love and all love's loving parts.
Sonnets. No. xxxi.

10
Kind is my love to-day, to-morrow kind,
Still constant in a wondrous excellence.
Sonnets. No. cv.

'Fair, kind, and true,' have often lived alone,
Which three till now never kept seat in one.
Sonnets. No. cv.

11
Love is not love
Which alters when it alteration finds,
Or bends with the remover to remove:
O, no! it is an ever-fixed mark
That looks on tempests and is never shaken;
It is the star to every wandering bark,
Whose worth's unknown, although his height be taken,
Love's not Time's fool, though rosy lips and cheeks
Within his bending sickle's compass come;
Love alters not with his brief hours and weeks,
But bears it out even to the edge of doom.
If this be error and upon me proved,
I never writ, nor no man ever loved.
Sonnets. No. cxvi. The only use of "remover." "Ever-fixed" is repeated in *Othello,* ii, 1, 15: "Ever-fixed pole."

So that eternal love in love's fresh case
Weighs not the dust and injury of age,
Nor gives to necessary wrinkles place,

But makes antiquity for aye his page,
Finding the first conceit of love there bred
Where time and outward form would show it dead.
Sonnets. No. cviii.

And ruin'd love, when it is built anew,
Grows fairer than at first, more strong, far greater.
Sonnets. No. cxix.

Restored love.—*II Henry IV,* iv, 2, 65.

1 I did strive to prove
The constancy and virtue of your love.
Sonnets. No. cxvii.

2
A contract of true love.
The Tempest. Act iv, sc. 1, l. 84. [Iris] Repeated in l. 133. "True love" is used thirty times.

A contract of eternal bond of love.
Twelfth Night. Act v, sc. 1, l. 159. [Priest]

True in love.—*Troilus and Cressida,* i, 3, 279; *Sonnets,* xxi.

True-betrothed love.—*Titus Andronicus,* i, 1, 406. The only use of "true-betrothed."

True-confirmed love.—*The Two Gentlemen of Verona,* iv, 4, 108. The only use of "true-confirmed."

3 Affection chains thy tender days
To the sweet glances of thy honour'd love.
The Two Gentlemen of Verona. Act i, sc. 1, l. 3. [Valentine]

His love sincere.—*The Two Gentlemen of Verona,* ii, 7, 76.

4
O, learn to love; the lesson is but plain,
And once made perfect, never lost again.
Venus and Adonis, l. 407.

5
I loved him as in honour he required,
With such a kind of love as might become
A lady like me, with a love even such,
So and no other, as yourself commanded.
The Winter's Tale. Act iii, sc. 2, l. 64. [Hermione]

Women will love her, that she is a woman
More worth than any man; men, that she is
The rarest of all women.
The Winter's Tale. Act v, sc. 1, l. 110. [Gentleman]

VI—Love: Inconstant

6
There shall your master have a thousand loves,
A mother and a mistress and a friend,
A phœnix, captain and an enemy,
A guide, a goddess, and a sovereign,
A counsellor, a traitress, and a dear.
All's Well that Ends Well. Act i, sc. 1, l. 180. [Helena]

7
I had seen this hot love on the wing.
Hamlet. Act ii, sc. 2, l. 132. [Polonius]

Hamlet: I did love you once.
Ophelia: Indeed, my lord, you made me believe so.
Hamlet: You should not have believed me; . . . I loved you not.
Ophelia: I was the more deceived.
Hamlet. Act iii, sc. 1, l. 116.

Ophelia: 'Tis brief, my lord.
Hamlet: As woman's love.
Hamlet. Act iii, sc. 2, l. 163.

8
This world is not for aye, nor 'tis not strange
That even our loves should with our fortunes change;
For 'tis a question left us yet to prove,
Whether love lead fortune, or else fortune love.
Hamlet. Act iii, sc. 2, l. 210. [Player King]

Hitherto doth love on fortune tend.
Hamlet. Act iii, sc. 2, l. 216. [Player King]

Love cools.—*King Lear,* i, 2, 115. See under OMEN.

9
Nay, you may think my love was crafty love
And call it cunning.
King John. Act iv, sc. 1, l. 53. [Arthur]

Cunning love.—*Sonnets,* cxlviii; *Venus and Adonis,* l. 471.

10
He, he, and you, and you, my liege, and I,
Are pick-purses in love, and we deserve to die.
Love's Labour's Lost. Act iv, sc. 3, l. 208. [Biron] The only use of "pick-purses." "Pick-purse" occurs three times.

11
Lysander: You have her father's love, Demetrius;
Let me have Hermia's: do you marry him.
Egeus: Scornful Lysander! true, he hath my love,
And what is mine my love shall render him. . . .
Lysander: My love is more than his. .
Demetrius, I'll avouch it to his head,
Made love to Nedar's daughter, Helena,
And won her soul.
A Midsummer-Night's Dream. Act i, sc. 1 l. 93. Nedar is mentioned again in iv, 1, 135 and in no other play.

If e'er I loved her, all that love is gone.
A Midsummer-Night's Dream. Act iii, sc. 2, l. 170. [Demetrius]

Lysander: Why should he stay, whom love doth press to go?
Hermia: What love could press Lysander from my side?
Lysander: Lysander's love, that would not let him bide.
A Midsummer-Night's Dream. Act iii, sc. 2, l. 184.

Since night you loved me; yet since night you left me.
A Midsummer-Night's Dream. Act iii, sc. 2, l. 275. [Hermia]

O me! you juggler! you canker-blossom!
You thief of love! what, have you come by night
And stolen my love's heart from him?
A Midsummer-Night's Dream. Act iii, sc. 2, l. 282. [Hermia] The only use of "canker-blossom." "Juggler" occurs four times.

I with the morning's love have oft made sport.
A Midsummer-Night's Dream. Act iii, sc. 2, l. 389. [Oberon]

1
Margaret: I 'll dance it.
Beatrice: Ye light o' love, with your heels! then, if your husband have stables enough, you 'll see he shall lack no barns.
Much Ado about Nothing. Act iii, sc. 4, l. 47.

2
My fortunes against any lay worth naming, this crack of your love shall grow stronger than it was before.
Othello. Act ii, sc. 3, l. 330. [Iago]

I call'd my love false love; but what said he then?
Sing willow, willow, willow;
If I court moe women, you 'll couch with moe men.
Othello. Act iv, sc. 3, l. 55. [Desdemona, singing]

False love.—*III Henry VI,* iii, 3, 160; *The Comedy of Errors,* iii, 2, 8; *Othello,* iv, 3, 55; *Antony and Cleopatra,* i, 3, 62.
Despiteful love.—*The Taming of the Shrew,* iv, 2, 14.
Feigning love.—*A Midsummer-Night's Dream,* i, 1, 31.
Forged love.—*I Henry VI,* iii, 1, 190.
Light love.—*Romeo and Juliet,* ii, 2, 105.

3
Romeo: My heart 's dear love is set
On the fair daughter of rich Capulet:
As mine on hers, so hers is set on mine:
And all combined, save what thou must combine
By holy marriage. . . .
Friar Laurence: Holy Saint Francis, what a change is here!
Is Rosaline, whom thou didst love so dear,
So soon forsaken? young men's love then lies
Not truly in their hearts, but in their eyes. . . .
Romeo: Thou chid'st me oft for loving Rosaline.
Friar Laurence: For doting, not for loving, pupil mine.
Romeo: And bad'st me bury love.
Friar Laurence: Not in a grave
To lay one in, another out to have.
Romeo: I pray thee, chide not: she whom I love now
Doth grace for grace and love for love allow;
The other did not so.
Friar Laurence: O, she knew well
Thy love did read by rote and could not spell.
Romeo and Juliet. Act ii, sc. 3, l. 57.

What says
My conceal'd lady to our cancell'd love?
Romeo and Juliet. Act iii, sc. 3, l. 97. [Romeo]

4
The master, the swabber, the boatswain and I,
The gunner and his mate
Loved Mall, Meg and Marian and Margery.
But none of us cared for Kate.
The Tempest. Act ii, sc. 2, l. 48. [Stephano]
"Gunner" is repeated in *Henry V,* iii, Prol., 32; "swabber" in *Twelfth Night,* i, 5, 217.

5
The chameleon Love can feed on air.
The Two Gentlemen of Verona, ii, 1, 179.
See under Food.

VII—Protestations

6
Countess: Do you love my son?
Helena: Your pardon, noble mistress!
Countess: Love you my son?
Helena: Do you not love him, madam?
Countess: Go not about; my love hath in 't a bond
Whereof the world takes note: come, come, disclose
The state of your affection. . . .
Helena: Then, I confess,
Here on my knees, before high heaven and you,
That before you, and next unto high heaven,
I love your son.
My friends were poor but honest; so 's my love:
Be not offended; for it hurts not him
That he is loved of me.
All's Well that Ends Well. Act i, sc. 3, l. 192.

Now, Dian, from thy altar do I fly,
And to imperial Love, that god most high,
Do my sighs stream.
All's Well that Ends Well. Act ii, sc. 3, l. 80. [Helena]

As thou lovest her, Thy love 's to me religious.
All's Well that Ends Well. Act ii, sc. 3, l. 189. [King]

Love is holy.—*All's Well that Ends Well,* iv, 2, 32.

7
I begin to love him for this.
All's Well that Ends Well. Act iv, sc. 3, l. 293. [Lord]

Let me love him for that, and do you love him because I do.
As You Like It. Act i, sc. 3, l. 40. [Rosalind]

Thou dost love her because thou know'st I love her.
Sonnets. No. xlii.

That love I begg'd for you he begg'd of me.
The Comedy of Errors. Act iv, sc. 2, l. 12. [Luciana]

8
Cleopatra: If it be love indeed, tell me how much.
Antony: There 's beggary in the love that can be reckon'd.
Cleopatra: I 'll set a bourn how far to be beloved.
Antony: Then must thou needs find out new heaven, new earth.
Antony and Cleopatra. Act i, sc. 1, l. 14.

Kingdoms are clay: our dungy earth alike
Feeds beast as man: the nobleness of life
Is to do thus.
Antony and Cleopatra. Act i, sc. 1, l. 35.

[Antony] "Dungy earth" is repeated in *The Winter's Tale,* ii, 1, 157.

Ho! hearts, tongues, figures, scribes, bards, poets, cannot
Think, speak, cast, write, sing, number, ho!
His love for Antony.

Antony and Cleopatra. Act iii, sc. 2, l. 16. [Enobarbus] "Bard" is repeated in *Richard III,* iv, 2, 109: "Bard of Ireland"; and "scribe" in *The Two Gentlemen of Verona,* ii, 1, 146, and in *Titus Andronicus,* ii, 4, 4.

1
I thank thee for thy love to me, which thou shalt find I will most kindly requite.

As You Like It. Act i, sc. 1, l. 144. [Oliver]

I do receive your offer'd love like love,
And will not wrong it.

Hamlet. Act v, sc. 2, l. 262. [Laertes]

2
Orlando: Fair youth, I would I could make thee believe I love.
Rosalind: Me believe it! you may as soon make her that you love believe it; which, I warrant, she is apter to do than to confess she does.

As You Like It. Act iii, sc. 2, l. 404. "Apter" is repeated in *II Henry IV,* i, 1, 69.

Rosalind: But are you so much in love as your rhymes speak?
Orlando: Neither rhyme nor reason can express how much.

As You Like It. Act iii, sc. 2, l. 416.

Rosalind: Ask me what you will, I will grant it.
Orlando: Then love me, Rosalind.
Rosalind: Yes, faith, will I, Fridays and Saturdays and all.
Orlando: And wilt thou have me?
Rosalind: Ay, and twenty such.

As You Like It. Act iv, sc. 1, l. 113.

3
Phebe: Thou hast my love: is not that neighbourly?
Silvius: I would have you.
Phebe: Why, that were covetousness.
Silvius, the time was that I hated thee,
And yet it is not that I bear thee love;
But since that thou canst talk of love so well,
Thy company, which erst was irksome to me,
I will endure, and I 'll employ thee too. . . .
Silvius: So holy and so perfect is my love,
And I in such a poverty of grace,
That I shall think it a most plenteous crop
To glean the broken ears after the man
That the main harvest reaps.

As You Like It. Act iii, sc. 5, l. 90.

O coz, coz, coz, my pretty little coz, that thou didst know how many fathom deep I am in love! But it cannot be sounded: my affection hath an unknown bottom, like the bay of Portugal.

As You Like It. Act iv, sc. 1, l. 209. [Rosalind] The only mention of Portugal.

He that brings this love to me
Little knows this love in me.

As You Like It. Act iv, sc. 3, l. 56. [Rosalind, reading]

4
It is thyself, mine own self's better part,
Mine eye's clear eye, my dear heart's dearer heart,
My food, my fortune and my sweet hope's aim,
My sole earth's heaven and my heaven's claim.

The Comedy of Errors. Act iii, sc. 2, l. 61. [Antipholus of Syracuse]

5
Know thou first, I loved the maid I married.

Coriolanus. Act iv, sc. 5, l. 119. [Aufidius]

6
Cloten: I swear I love you.
Imogen: If you but said so, 'twere as deep with me:
If you swear still, your recompense is still
That I regard it not.

Cymbeline. Act ii, sc. 3, l. 95.

This imperceiverant thing loves him in my despite.

Cymbeline. Act iv, sc. 1, l. 15. [Cloten] The only use of "imperceiverant."

I love thee: I have spoke it:
How much the quantity, the weight as much,
As I do love my father.

Cymbeline. Act iv, sc. 2, l. 16. [Guiderius]

I love thee more and more.—*Cymbeline,* v, 5, 109.

7
Doubt that the stars are fire;
Doubt that the sun doth move;
Doubt truth to be a liar;
But never doubt I love.
O dear Ophelia, I am ill at these numbers; I have not art to reckon my groans: but that I love thee best, O most best, believe it.

Hamlet. Act ii, sc. 2, l. 116. [Polonius, reading letter from Hamlet to Ophelia]

Best love.—*Antony and Cleopatra,* iii, 4, 21.

8
Rosencrantz: My lord, you once did love me.
Hamlet: So I do still, by these pickers and stealers.

Hamlet. Act iii, sc. 2, l. 347. The only use of "pickers" and "stealers." "Stealer" occurs in *Much Ado about Nothing,* ii, 1, 233, and in *Cymbeline,* ii, 3, 75.

So much was our love,
We would not understand what was most fit.

Hamlet. Act iv, sc. 1, l. 19. [King]

She 's so conjunctive to my life and soul,
That, as the star moves not but in his sphere,
I could not but by her.

Hamlet. Act iv, sc. 7, l. 14. [King] "Conjunctive" occurs again in *Othello,* i, 3, 374.

In youth, when I did love, did love,
Methought it was very sweet.

Hamlet. Act v, sc. 1, l. 69. [Clown]

9
Falstaff: I am old, I am old.
Doll: I love thee better than I love e'er a scurvy young boy of them all.

II Henry IV. Act ii, sc. 4, l. 294.

10
I loved thee as a brother, John.

II Henry IV. Act v, sc. 4, l. 19. [Prince]

I love thee brotherly.—*Cymbeline,* iv, 2, 158. "Brother-love" occurs in *Henry VIII,* v, 3,

173; "brother's love" is used frequently throughout the plays.

1

A man that I love and honour with my soul and my heart, and my duty, and my life, and my living, and my uttermost power.

Henry V. Act iii, sc. 6, l. 7. [Fluellen]

From heart-string I love the lovely bully.

Henry V, iv, 1, 47. See under KING.

I love him well.—*I Henry IV*, iii, 3, 107.

2

King Henry: Canst thou love me?

Katharine: I cannot tell.

King Henry: Can any of your neighbours tell, Kate? I'll ask them. Come, I know thou lovest me. . . . I love thee cruelly. . . . By mine honour, in true English, I love thee, Kate: by which honour I dare not swear thou lovest me; yet my blood begins to flatter me that thou dost. . . . Take me by the hand and say 'Harry of England, I am thine.'

Henry V. Act v, sc. 2, l. 206.

If you will love me soundly with your French heart, I will be glad to hear you confess it brokenly with your English tongue.

Henry V. Act v, sc. 2, l. 104. [King Henry] The only use of "brokenly."

3

A wilderness is populous enough,
So Suffolk had thy heavenly company:
For where thou art, there is the world itself,
With every several pleasure in the world,
And where thou art not, desolation.

II Henry VI. Act iii, sc. 2, l. 360. [Suffolk]

Sole possessor of my love.

III Henry VI. Act iii, sc. 3, l. 24. [Queen Margaret] "Possessor" is repeated in *The Merchant of Venice*, i, 3, 75.

Loved him next heaven.—*Henry VIII*, iii, 1, 130.

Heavenly love.—*Love's Labour's Lost*, iv, 3, 66, *The Passionate Pilgrim*, l. 35.

4

If lusty love should go in quest of beauty,
Where should he find it fairer than in Blanch?
If zealous love should go in search of virtue,
Where should he find it purer than in Blanch?
If love ambitious sought a match of birth,
Whose veins bound richer blood than Lady Blanch?

King John. Act ii, sc. 1, l. 426. [Citizen]

All I see in you is worthy love.

King John. Act ii, sc. 1, l. 517. [Blanch]

5

King John: Speak then, prince Dauphin; can you love this lady?
Lewis the Dauphin: Nay, ask me if I can refrain from love;
For I do love her most unfeignedly.

King John. Act ii, sc. 1, l. 524.

Shallow: Can you love the maid?

Slender: I will marry her, sir, at your request: but if there be no great love in the beginning, yet heaven may decrease it upon better acquaintance, when we are married and have more occasion to know one another.

The Merry Wives of Windsor. Act i, sc. 1, l. 252.

The valiant Paris seeks you for his love. . . .
What say you? can you love the gentleman? . . .
Speak briefly, can you like of Paris' love?

Romeo and Juliet. Act i, sc. 4, l. 74. [Lady Capulet]

6

I love thee well;
And, by my troth, I think thou lovest me well.

King John. Act iii, sc. 3, l. 54. [King John]

The like tender of our love we make,
To rest without a spot for evermore.

King John. Act v, sc. 7, l. 106. [Salisbury]

7

I must love you, and sue to know you better.

King Lear. Act i, sc. 1, l. 31. [Kent]

I love you more than words can wield the matter;
Dearer than eye-sight, space, and liberty;
Beyond what can be valued, rich or rare;
No less than life, with grâce, health, beauty, honour;
As much as child e'er loved, or father found;
A love that makes breath poor, and speech unable;
Beyond all manner of so much I love you.

King Lear. Act i, sc. 1, l. 56. [Goneril]

In my true heart
I find she names my very deed of love;
Only she comes too short: that I profess
Myself an enemy to all other joys,
Which the most precious square of sense possesses;
And find I am alone felicitate
In your dear highness' love.

King Lear. Act i, sc. 1, l. 72. [Regan] The only use of "felicitate."

My love 's More richer than my tongue. . . .
Unhappy that I am, I cannot heave
My heart into my mouth: I love your majesty
According to my bond; nor more nor less. . . .
You have begot me, bred me, loved me: I
Return those duties back as are right fit,
Obey you, love you, and most honour you.

King Lear. Act i, sc. 1, l. 79. [Cordelia]

Whoop, Jug! I love thee.—*King Lear*, i, 4, 245.

I 'll love thee much.—*King Lear*, iv, 5, 21.

8

I will hereupon confess I am in love: and as it is base for a soldier to love, so am I in love with a base wench.

Love's Labour's Lost. Act i, sc. 2, l. 60. [Armado] The only use of "hereupon."

My spirit grows heavy in love.

Love's Labour's Lost. Act i, sc. 2, l. 127. [Armado]

I do affect the very ground, which is base, where her shoe, which is baser, guided by her foot, which is basest, doth tread.

Love's Labour's Lost. Act i, sc. 2, l. 172. [Armado]

Adieu, valour! rust, rapier! be still, drum! for your manager is in love; yea, he loveth.

Love's Labour's Lost. Act i, sc. 2, l. 187. [Armado] "Manager" is used a second time in *A Midsummer-Night's Dream*, v, 1, 35.

1
My love is most immaculate white and red.
Love's Labour 's Lost. Act i, sc. 2, l. 95. [Armado]

King Ferdinand: By heaven, thy love is black as ebony.
Biron: Is ebony like her? O wood divine!
Love's Labour 's Lost. Act iv, sc. 3, l. 247.

2
And I, forsooth, in love! I, that have been love's whip;
A very beadle to a humorous sigh;
A critic, nay, a night-watch constable;
A domineering pedant o'er the boy;
Than whom no mortal so magnificent!
Love's Labour 's Lost. Act iii, sc. 1, l. 176. [Biron] The only use of "night-watch" and "domineering."

Well, I will love, write, sigh, pray, sue and groan:
Some men must love my lady and some Joan.
Love's Labour 's Lost. Act iii, sc. 1, l. 206. [Biron]

3
Shall I command thy love? I may: shall I enforce thy love? I could: shall I entreat thy love? I will.
Love's Labour 's Lost. Act iv, sc. 1, l. 81. [Boyet]

Celestial as thou art, O, pardon love this wrong,
That sings heaven's praise with such an earthly tongue.
Love's Labour 's Lost. Act iv, sc. 2, l. 121. [Sir Nathaniel]

This will I send and something else more plain,
That shall express my true love's fasting pain.
Love's Labour 's Lost. Act iv, sc. 3, l. 121. [Dumain]

Good heart, what grace hast thou, thus to reprove
These worms for loving, that art most in love?
Love's Labour 's Lost. Act iv, sc. 3, l. 153. [Biron]

King: But what of this? are we not all in love?
Biron: Nothing so sure; and thereby all forsworn.
King: Then leave this chat; and, good Biron, now prove
Our loving lawful.
Love's Labour 's Lost. Act iv, sc. 3, l. 282.

Lawful promised love.—*Titus Andronicus,* i, 1, 298.

4
My love to thee is sound, sans crack or flaw.
Love's Labour 's Lost. Act v, sc. 2, l. 415. [Biron]

Our love being yours, the error that love makes
Is likewise yours.
Love's Labour 's Lost. Act v, sc. 2, l. 781. [Biron]

Grant us your loves.—*Love's Labour 's Lost,* v, 2, 798.

5
We love him highly,
And shall continue our graces towards him.
Macbeth. Act i, sc. 6, l. 29. [Duncan]

6
Angelo: Plainly conceive, I love you.
Isabella: My brother did love Juliet,
And you tell me that he shall die for it.
Angelo: He shall not, Isabel, if you give me love.
Measure for Measure. Act ii, sc. 4, l. 141.

7
I love thee, and it is my love that speaks.
The Merchant of Venice. Act i, sc. 1, l. 87. [Gratiano]

My love indeed, For who love I so much?
The Merchant of Venice. Act ii, sc. 6, l. 29. [Jessica]

Beshrew me but I love her heartily.
The Merchant of Venice, ii, 6, 52. See under CHARACTER.

8
If you do love me, you will find me out.
The Merchant of Venice. Act iii, sc. 2, l. 41. [Portia]

You loved, I loved for intermission.
The Merchant of Venice. Act iii, sc. 2, l. 201. [Gratiano]

Since you are dear bought, I will love you dear.
The Merchant of Venice. Act iii, sc. 2, l. 316. [Portia]

Rightly love.—*Merchant of Venice,* i, 2, 36.

9
Ford: Love my wife!
Pistol: With liver burning hot.
Merry Wives of Windsor. Act ii, sc. 1, l. 120.

You have brought her into such a canaries as 'tis wonderful. The best courtier of them all, when the court lay at Windsor, could never have brought her to such a canary.
The Merry Wives of Windsor. Act ii, sc. 2, l. 61. [Mistress Quickly] Canary is probably an intentional blunder for quandary. Its only use in this sense.

I have long loved her.—*The Merry Wives of Windsor,* ii, 2, 201.

I would not break with her for more money than I 'll speak of.
The Merry Wives of Windsor. Act iii, sc. 2, l. 56. [Slender]

10
I love thee; none but thee; and thou deservest it.
The Merry Wives of Windsor. Act iii, sc. 3, l. 80. [Falstaff]

What made me love thee? let that persuade thee there 's something extraordinary in thee.
The Merry Wives of Windsor. Act iii, sc. 3, l. 74. [Falstaff]

Well, heaven knows how I love you; and you shall one day find it.
The Merry Wives of Windsor. Act iii, sc. 3, l. 87. [Mrs. Ford]

He tells me 'tis a thing impossible
I should love thee but as a property.
The Merry Wives of Windsor. Act iii, sc. 4, l. 10. [Fenton]

I see you are obsequious in your love, and I profess requital to a hair's breadth; not only, Mistress Ford, in the simple office of love, but in all the accoutrement, complement and ceremony of it.
The Merry Wives of Windsor. Act iv, sc. 2, l. 2. [Falstaff]

11
And thy fair virtue's force perforce doth move me

On the first view to say, to swear, I love thee.
A Midsummer-Night's Dream. Act iii, sc. 1, l. 143. [Titania]

I do love thee, therefore go with me.
A Midsummer-Night's Dream. Act iii, sc. 1, l. 159. [Titania]

My mistress with a monster is in love.
A Midsummer-Night's Dream. Act iii, sc. 2, l. 6. [Puck]

1
When his love he doth espy,
Let her shine as gloriously
As the Venus of the sky.
A Midsummer-Night's Dream. Act iii, sc. 2, l. 105. [Oberon] "Gloriously" is repeated in *Venus and Adonis,* l. 857.

Look, where thy love comes; yonder is thy dear.
A Midsummer-Night's Dream. Act iii, sc. 2, l. 176. [Demetrius]

Lysander: My love, my life, my soul, fair Helena!
. . . I love thee; by my life I do:
I swear by that which I will lose for thee,
To prove him false that says I love thee not.
Demetrius: I say I love thee more than he can do.
A Midsummer-Night's Dream. Act iii, sc. 2, l. 246.

So doth the woodbine the sweet honeysuckle
Gentle entwist; the female ivy so
Enrings the barky fingers of the elm.
O, how I love thee! how I dote on thee!
A Midsummer-Night's Dream. Act iv, sc. 1, l. 44. [Titania] The only use of "entwist," "enrings," and "barky."

2
It is certain I am loved of all ladies, only you excepted.
Much Ado about Nothing. Act i, sc. 1, l. 126. [Benedick]

That I love her, I feel.
Much Ado about Nothing. Act i, sc. 1, l. 230. [Claudio]

Lady, as you are mine, I am yours: I give away myself for you and dote upon the exchange.
Much Ado about Nothing. Act ii, sc. 1, l. 319. [Claudio]

I will be horribly in love with her.
Much Ado about Nothing. Act ii, sc. 3, l. 244. [Benedick]

He is in love.—*Much Ado about Nothing,* i, 1, 214.

3
My love is thine to teach: teach it but how,
And thou shalt see how apt it is to learn
Any hard lesson that may do thee good.
Much Ado about Nothing. Act i, sc. 1, l. 293. [Don Pedro]

I will teach you how to humour your cousin, that she shall fall in love with Benedick; and I, with your two helps, will so practise on Benedick that, in despite of his quick wit and his queasy stomach, he shall fall in love with Beatrice.
Much Ado about Nothing. Act ii, sc. 1, l. 396. [Don Pedro]

4
Benedick is sick in love with Beatrice.
Much Ado about Nothing. Act iii, sc. 1, l. 20. [Hero]

And, Benedick, love on; I will requite thee,
Taming my wild heart to thy loving hand:
If thou dost love, my kindness shall incite thee
To bind our loves up in a holy band.
Much Ado about Nothing. Act iii, sc. 1, l. 111. [Beatrice] The only use of "taming."

You may think perchance that I think you are in love: nay, by 'r lady, . . . I cannot think . . . that you are in love or that you will be in love or that you can be in love. Yet Benedick was such another, and now is he become a man: . . . and how you may become converted I know not, but methinks you look with your eyes as other women do.
Much Ado about Nothing. Act iii, sc. 4, l. 81. [Margaret]

Benedick: I do love nothing in the world so well as you: is not that strange?
Beatrice: As strange as the thing I know not. It were as possible for me to say I loved nothing so well as you: but believe me not; and yet I lie not. . . .
Benedick: By my sword, Beatrice, thou lovest me.
Beatrice: Do not swear, and eat it.
Benedick: I will swear by it that you love me; and I will make him eat it that says I love not you. . . .
Beatrice: You have stayed me in a happy hour: I was about to protest I loved you.
Benedick: And do it with all thy heart.
Beatrice: I love you with so much of my heart that none is left to protest.
Much Ado about Nothing. Act iv, sc. 1, l. 269.

Benedick: Tell me for which of my bad parts didst thou fall in love with me?
Beatrice: For them all together; . . . But for which of my good parts did you first suffer love for me?
Benedick: Suffer love! a good epithet! I do suffer love indeed, for I love thee against my will.
Beatrice: In spite of your heart, I think; alas, poor heart! If you spite it for my sake, I will spite it for yours.
Much Ado about Nothing. Act v, sc. 2, l. 60.

5
For thee I 'll lock up all the gates of love,
And on my eyelids shall conjecture hang,
To turn all beauty into thoughts of harm,
And never shall it more be gracious.
Much Ado about Nothing. Act iv, sc. 1, l. 106. [Claudio]

By this hand, I love thee.—*Much Ado about Nothing,* iv, 1, 328.

The god of love, That sits above,
And knows me, and knows me,
How pitiful I deserve.
Much Ado about Nothing. Act v, sc. 2, l. 26. [Benedick, singing]

Serve God, love me and mend.
Much Ado about Nothing. Act v, sc. 2, l. 95. [Benedick]

I will live in thy heart, die in thy lap and be buried in thy eyes.
Much Ado about Nothing. Act v, sc. 2, l. 104. [Benedick]

1
That I did love the Moor to live with him,
My downright violence and storm of fortunes
May trumpet to the world.
Othello. Act i, sc. 3, l. 249. [Desdemona]
Iago: I think you think I love you.
Cassio: I have well approved it, sir.
Othello. Act ii, sc. 3, l. 316.
You do love my lord:
You have known him long.
Othello. Act iii, sc. 3, l. 10. [Desdemona]

2
Excellent wretch! Perdition catch my soul,
But I do love thee! and when I love thee not,
Chaos is come again.
Othello. Act iii, sc. 3, l. 90. [Othello]
Othello: If thou dost love me,
Show me thy thought.
Iago: My lord, you know I love you.
Othello: I think thou dost; . . .
I know thou 'rt full of love and honesty.
Othello. Act iii, sc. 3, l. 115.
I humbly do beseech you of your pardon
For too much loving you.
Othello. Act iii, sc. 3, l. 212. [Iago]
I greet thy love,
Not with vain thanks, but with acceptance bounteous.
Othello. Act iii, sc. 3, l. 469. [Othello]
My love doth so approve him,
That even his stubbornness, his checks, his frowns,— . . .
Have grace and favour in them.
Othello. Act iv, sc. 3, l. 19. [Desdemona]

3
He loves you well that holds his life of you.
Pericles, ii, 2, 22. See under KNIGHTHOOD.
Thaisa: If you love me, sir.
Pericles: Even as my life my blood that fosters it.
Pericles. Act ii, sc. 5, l. 89.

4
He loves you, on my life, and holds you dear.
Richard II. Act ii, sc. 1, l. 143. [York]
Little are we beholding to your love,
And little look'd for at your helping hands.
Richard II. Act iv, sc. 1, l. 160. [Bolingbroke]
And yet I love him.—*Richard II,* v, 2, 110.

5
I do love thee so,
That I will shortly send thy soul to heaven,
If heaven will take the present at our hands.
Richard III. Act i, sc. 1, l. 118. [Gloucester]
He lives that loves thee better than he could.
Richard III. Act i, sc. 2, l. 141. [Gloucester]
With my hand I seal my true heart's love.
Richard III. Act ii, sc. 1, l. 10. [Rivers]
This interchange of love, I here protest,
Upon my part shall be unviolable.
Richard III. Act ii, sc. 1, l. 26. [Dorset] The only use of "unviolable." "Inviolable" occurs twice, in *III Henry VI,* ii, 1, 30, and in *King John,* v, 2, 7.
Cheer each other in each other's love.
Richard III. Act ii, sc. 2, l. 114. [Buckingham]
The tender love I bear your grace, my lord,
Makes me most forward.
Richard III. Act iii, sc. 4, l. 65. [Hastings]
By heaven, I come in perfect love to him.
Richard III. Act iii, sc. 7, l. 90. [Buckingham]
Refuse not, mighty lord, this proffered love.
Richard III. Act iii, sc. 7, l. 202. [Buckingham]

6
King Richard: Then know, that from my soul I love thy daughter.
Queen Elizabeth: My daughter's mother thinks it with her soul.
King Richard: What do you think?
Queen Elizabeth: That thou dost love my daughter from thy soul:
So from thy soul's love didst thou love her brothers;
And from my heart's love I do thank thee for it.
King Richard: Be not so hasty to confound my meaning:
I mean, that with my soul I love thy daughter.
Richard III. Act iv, sc. 4, l. 255.

7
This love that thou hast shown
Doth add more grief to too much of mine own.
Romeo and Juliet. Act i, sc. 1, l. 194. [Romeo]
I cannot bound a pitch above dull woe:
Under love's heavy burden do I sink.
Romeo and Juliet. Act i, sc. 4, l. 21. [Romeo]
Prodigious birth of love it is to me,
That I must love a loathed enemy.
Romeo and Juliet. Act i, sc. 5, l. 142. [Juliet]
Be but sworn my love,
And I 'll no longer be a Capulet.
Romeo and Juliet. Act ii, sc. 1, l. 35. [Romeo]
Call me but love, and I 'll be new baptized.
Romeo and Juliet. Act ii, sc. 2, l. 50. [Romeo] The only use of "baptized."
My heart's dear love.—*Romeo and Juliet,* ii, 2, 115. "Dear love" is repeated eighteen times in later plays and poems.
Dearest love.—*Macbeth,* i, 5, 59; *Sonnets,* cxvii.

8
In truth, fair Montague, I am too fond.
Romeo and Juliet. Act ii, sc. 2, l. 98. [Juliet]
You see how simple and how fond I am.
A Midsummer-Night's Dream. Act iii, sc. 2, l. 317. [Helena]
I laugh to see your ladyship so fond.
I Henry VI. Act ii, sc. 3, l. 45. [Talbot]
It is my shame to be so fond.
Othello. Act i, sc. 3, l. 320. [Roderigo]

9
This bud of love, by summer's ripening breath,
May prove a beauteous flower when next we meet.
Romeo and Juliet. Act ii, sc. 2, l. 121. [Juliet] The only use of "ripening."
My bounty is as boundless as the sea,
My love as deep; the more I give to thee,
The more I have, for both are infinite.
Romeo and Juliet. Act ii, sc. 2, l. 133. [Juliet]

But my true love is grown to such excess
I cannot sum up sum of half my wealth.
Romeo and Juliet. Act ii, sc. 6, l. 33. [Juliet]

1
Hood my unmann'd blood, . . . till strange love, grown bold,
Think true love acted simple modesty.
Romeo and Juliet. Act iii, sc. 2, l. 14. [Juliet] "Hood" as a verb is repeated in *The Merchant of Venice,* ii, 2, 202: "Hood mine eyes." "Unmann'd" occurs again in *Macbeth,* iii, 4, 73.

O, I have bought the mansion of a love,
But not possess'd it, and, though I am sold,
Not yet enjoy'd.
Romeo and Juliet. Act iii, sc. 2, l. 26. [Juliet]

By heaven, I love thee better than myself.
Romeo and Juliet. Act v, sc. 3, l. 64. [Romeo]

2
Take all my loves, my love, yea, take them all;
What hast thou then more than thou hadst before?
Sonnets. No. xl.

Is it thy will thy image should keep open
My heavy eyelids to the weary night?
Dost thou desire my slumbers should be broken,
While shadows like to thee do mock my sight? . . .
O, no! thy love, though much, is not so great:
It is my love that keeps mine eye awake;
Mine own true love that doth my rest defeat,
To play the watchman ever for thy sake:
For thee watch I whilst thou dost wake elsewhere,
From me far off, with others all too near.
Sonnets. No. lxi.

For as the sun is daily new and old,
So is my love still telling what is told.
Sonnets. No. lxxvi.

Such is my love, to thee I so belong,
That for thy right myself will bear all wrong.
Sonnets. No. lxxxviii.

3
Thy love is better than high birth to me,
Richer than wealth, prouder than garments' cost,
Of more delight than hawks or horses be;
And having thee, of all men's pride I boast.
Sonnets. No. xci.

I love thee in such sort
As, thou being mine, mine is thy good report.
Sonnets. No. xcvi.

And yet, by heaven, I think my love as rare
As any she belied with false compare.
Sonnets. No. cxxx.

No want of conscience hold it that I call
Her 'love' for whose dear love I rise and fall.
Sonnets. No. cli.

4
I will love thee ne'er the less, my girl.
The Taming of the Shrew. Act i, sc. 1, l. 77. [Baptista] "Ne'er the less" occurs again in *Troilus and Cressida,* ii, 2, 189.

I love her ten times more than e'er I did.
The Taming of the Shrew. Act ii, sc. 1, l. 162. [Petruchio]

I tell you, 'tis incredible to believe
How much she loves me.
Taming of the Shrew. Act ii, sc. 1, l. 308. [Petruchio] The only use of "incredible."

I am one that love Bianca more
Than words can witness, or your thoughts can guess.
The Taming of the Shrew. Act ii, sc. 1, l. 337. [Tranio]

Gremio: Youngling, thou canst not love so dear as I.
Tranio: Greybeard, thy love doth freeze.
The Taming of the Shrew. Act ii, sc. 1, l. 339. "Youngling" is repeated in *Titus Andronicus,* ii, 1, 73; iv, 2, 93. "Greybeard" occurs five times.

She 's the choice love of Signior Gremio.
The Taming of the Shrew. Act i, sc. 2, l. 237. [Gremio]

Take in your love, and then let me alone.
The Taming of the Shrew. Act iv, sc. 2, l. 71. [Tranio]

5
No, noble mistress; 'tis fresh morning with me
When you are by at night.
The Tempest. Act iii, sc. 1, l. 33. [Ferdinand]

Miranda: Do you love me?
Ferdinand: O heaven, O earth, bear witness, . . . I
Beyond all limit of what else i' the world
Do love, prize, honour you.
The Tempest. Act iii, sc. 1, l. 67.

6
Timon: Love you the maid?
Lucilius: Ay, my good lord, and she accepts of it.
Timon of Athens. Act i, sc. 1, l. 134.

Look you, I love you well; I 'll give you gold.
Timon of Athens. Act v, sc. 1, l. 103. [Timon]

7
Her to whom my thoughts are humbled all.
Titus Andronicus. Act i, sc. 1, l. 51. [Bassianus]

I love Lavinia more than all the world.
Titus Andronicus. Act ii, sc. 1, l. 72. [Chiron]

Ah, my sweet Moor, sweeter to me than life!
Titus Andronicus. Act ii, sc. 3, l. 51. [Tamora]

8
Sweet, above thought I love thee.
Troilus and Cressida. Act iii, sc. 1, l. 172. [Paris]

Cressida: I have loved you night and day
For many weary months.
Troilus: Why was my Cressid then so hard to win?
Cressida: Hard to seem won: but I was won, my lord,
With the first glance.
Troilus and Cressida. Act iii, sc. 2, l. 122. The only use of the phrase "first glance."

I love you now; but not, till now, so much
But I might master it.
Troilus and Cressida. Act iii, sc. 2, l. 128. [Cressida]

I know what 'tis to love.
Troilus and Cressida. Act iv, sc. 3, l. 10. [Paris]

My love admits no qualifying dross.
Troilus and Cressida, iv, 4, 9. The only use of "qualifying." See under GRIEF.

I love thee in so strain'd a purity,
That the bless'd gods, as angry with my fancy,
More bright in zeal than the devotion which
Cold lips blow to their deities, take thee from me.

Troilus and Cressida. Act iv, sc. 4, l. 26. [Troilus]

Cressida: O heavens! you love me not.
Troilus: Die I a villain, then!

Troilus and Cressida. Act iv, sc. 4, l. 84.

1
O, she that hath a heart of that fine frame
To pay this debt of love but to a brother,
How will she love, when the rich golden shaft
Hath kill'd the flock of all affections else
That live in her!

Twelfth Night. Act i, sc. 1, l. 33. [Duke]

O, then unfold the passion of my love,
Surprise her with discourse of my dear faith.

Twelfth Night. Act i, sc. 4, l. 24. [Duke]

Viola: My lord and master loves you: O, such love
Could be but recompensed, though you were crown'd
The nonpareil of beauty!
Olivia: How does he love me?
Viola: With adorations, fertile tears,
With groans that thunder love, with sighs of fire.

Twelfth Night. Act i, sc. 5, l. 271.

2
She loves me, sure; the cunning of her passion
Invites me in this churlish messenger. . . .
Poor lady, she were better love a dream. . . .
How will this fadge? my master loves her dearly;
And I, poor monster, fond as much on him;
And she, mistaken, seems to dote on me.
What will become of this? As I am man,
My state is desperate for my master's love;
As I am woman,—now alas the day!—
What thriftless sighs shall poor Olivia breathe!

Twelfth Night. Act ii, sc. 2, l. 23. [Viola] "Fadge" (fit) is repeated in *Love's Labour 's Lost,* v, 1, 154.

'Tis pity love should be so contrary.

The Two Gentlemen of Verona. Act iv, sc. 4, l. 88. [Julia]

3
Alas, their love may be call'd appetite.
No motion of the liver, but the palate.

Twelfth Night, ii, 4, 100. See under WOMAN.

Duke: Make no compare
Between that love a woman can bear me
And that I owe Olivia.
Viola: Ay, but I know—
Duke: What dost thou know?
Viola: Too well what love women to men may owe:
In faith, they are as true of heart as we.
My father had a daughter loved a man,
As it might be, perhaps, were I a woman,
I should your lordship.
Duke: And what 's her history?
Viola: A blank, my lord. She never told her love,
But let concealment, like a worm i' the bud,
Feed on her damask cheek: she pined in thought,
And with a green and yellow melancholy
She sat like patience on a monument,
Smiling at grief. Was not this love indeed?
We men say more, swear more: but indeed
Our shows are more than will; for still we prove
Much in our vows, but little in our love.
Duke: But died thy sister of her love, my boy?
Viola: I am all the daughters of my father's house,
And all the brothers too: and yet I know not.
Sir, shall I to this lady?
Duke: Ay, that 's the theme.
To her in haste; give her this jewel, say,
My love can give no place, bide no denay.

Twelfth Night. Act ii, sc. 4, l. 104. The only use of "denay." "Denay'd" occurs in *II Henry VI,* i, 3, 107.

Him I love
More than I love these eyes, more than my life,
More, by all mores, than e'er I shall love wife.
If I do feign, you witnesses above
Punish my life for tainting of my love!

Twelfth Night. Act v, sc. 1, l. 137. [Viola]

4
Except I be by Silvia in the night,
There is no music in the nightingale;
Unless I look on Silvia in the day,
There is no day for me to look upon;
She is my essence, and I leave to be,
If I be not by her fair influence
Foster'd, illumined, cherish'd, kept alive.

The Two Gentlemen of Verona. Act iii, sc. 1, l. 178. [Valentine] The only use of "illumined."

He lives not now that knows me to be in love; yet I am in love.

The Two Gentlemen of Verona. Act iii, sc. 1, l. 264. [Launce]

And notwithstanding all her sudden quips,
The least whereof would quell a lover's hope,
Yet, spaniel-like, the more she spurns my love,
The more it grows and fawneth on her still.

Two Gentlemen of Verona. Act iv, sc. 2, l. 12. [Proteus] The only use of "spaniel-like."

You know that love
Will creep in service where it cannot go.

The Two Gentlemen of Verona. Act iv, sc. 2, l. 19. [Proteus]

He loved her out of all nick.

The Two Gentlemen of Verona. Act iv, sc. 2, l. 76. [Host] The only use of the phrase.

O, Heaven be judge how I love Valentine,
Whose life 's as tender to me as my soul!

The Two Gentlemen of Verona. Act v, sc. 4, l. 36. [Silvia]

They love me well.—*The Two Gentlemen of Verona,* iv, 4, 16.

5
Though neither eyes nor ears, to hear nor see,
Yet should I be in love by touching thee.

Venus and Adonis, l. 437.

Look how he can, she cannot choose but love.

Venus and Adonis, l. 79.

1 Or I 'll be thine, my fair,
Or not my father's. For I cannot be
Mine own, nor any thing to any, if
I be not thine.

Winter's Tale. Act iv, sc. 4, l. 42. [Florizel]

Thou hast sworn my love to be.

Winter's Tale. Act iv, sc. 4, l. 312. [Dorcas]

Were I crown'd the most imperial monarch,
Thereof most worthy, were I the fairest youth
That ever made eye swerve, had force and knowledge
More then was ever man's, I would not prize them
Without her love; for her employ them all;
Commend them and condemn them to her service
Or to their own perdition.

Winter's Tale. Act iv, sc. 4, l. 382. [Florizel]

You; whom he loves—
He bade me say so—more than all the sceptres
And those that bear them living.

Winter's Tale. Act v, sc. 1, l. 145. [Florizel]

VIII—Love at First Sight

2
Dead shepherd, now I find thy saw of might,
'Who ever loved that loved not at first sight?'

As You Like it. Act iii, sc. 5, l. 81. [Phebe] An allusion to Christopher Marlowe, who died in 1593, six years before *As You Like It* was written, and from whose *Hero and Leander* (Sestiad i, l. 176) the quotation is taken.

Orlando: Is 't possible that on so little acquaintance you should like her? that but seeing you should love her? and loving woo? and, wooing, she should grant? and will you persever to enjoy her?

Oliver: Neither call the giddiness of it in question, the poverty of her, the small acquaintance, my sudden wooing, nor her sudden consenting; but say with me, I love Aliena.

As You Like It. Act v, sc. 2, l. 1. The only use of "giddiness."

Your brother and my sister no sooner met but they looked, no sooner looked but they loved, no sooner loved but they sighed, no sooner sighed but they asked one another the reason, no sooner knew the reason but they sought the remedy; and in these degrees have they made a pair of stairs to marriage which they will climb incontinent, or else be incontinent before marriage: they are in the very wrath of love and they will together; clubs cannot part them.

As You Like It. Act v, sc. 2, l. 35. [Rosalind]

3
How sweetly you do minister to love,
That know love's grief by his complexion!
But lest my liking might too sudden seem,
I would have salved it with a longer treatise.

Much Ado about Nothing. Act i, sc. 1, l. 314. [Claudio] The only use of "salved."

4
Tranio: I pray, sir, tell me, is it possible
That love should of a sudden take such hold?
Lucentio: O Tranio, till I found it to be true,
I never thought it possible or likely;
But see, while idly I stood looking on,
I found the effect of love in idleness. . . .
Tranio, I burn, I pine, I perish, Tranio.

The Taming of the Shrew. Act i, sc. 1, l. 151.

The very instant that I saw you, did
My heart fly to your service.

The Tempest. Act iii, sc. 1, l. 64. [Ferdinand]

5
Even so quickly may one catch the plague?
Methinks I feel this youth's perfections
With an invisible and subtle stealth
To creep in at mine eyes.

Twelfth Night. Act i, sc. 5, l. 314. [Olivia]

6
O, how quick is love!

Venus and Adonis, l. 38.

IX—Love: Its Perjuries

7
If I should swear by God's great attributes,
I loved you dearly, would you believe my oaths,
When I did love you ill?

All's Well that Ends Well. Act iv, sc. 2, l. 25. [Diana]

8
For his verity in love, I do think him as concave as a covered goblet or a worm-eaten nut.

As you Like It. Act iii, sc. 4, l. 25. [Celia] "Concave" is used again in *Julius Cæsar,* i, 1, 52. Both "goblet" and "worm-eaten" occur twice more.

9
Myself have often heard him say and swear
That this his love was an eternal plant,
Whereof the root was fix'd in virtue's ground,
The leaves and fruit maintain'd with beauty's sun,
Exempt from envy, but not from disdain.

III Henry VI. Act iii, sc. 3, l. 123. [Warwick]

10
If love make me forsworn, how shall I swear to love?

Love's Labour's Lost. Act iv, sc. 2, l. 109. [Sir Nathaniel]

Madam, he swore that he did hold me dear
As precious eyesight, and did value me
Above this world; adding thereto moreover
That he would wed me, or else die my lover.

Love's Labour's Lost. Act v, sc. 2, l. 444. [Rosaline]

11
When my love swears that she is made of truth
I do believe her, though I know she lies,
That she might think me some untutor'd youth,
Unlearned in the world's false subtleties.
Thus vainly thinking that she thinks me young,
Although she knows my days are past the best,
Simply I credit her false-speaking tongue:
On both sides thus is simple truth suppress'd.
But wherefore says she not she is unjust?

And wherefore say not I that I am old?
O, love's best habit is in seeming trust,
And age in love loves not to have years told.
Therefore I lie with her and she with me,
And in our faults by lies we flatter'd be.
Sonnets. No. cxxxviii. This sonnet is repeated, with a few variations, at the beginning of *The Passionate Pilgrim.* "False speaking" (unhyphenated) occurs in *Macbeth,* iv, 3, 130.

If I might teach thee wit, better it were,
Though not to love, yet, love, to tell me so:
As testy sick men, when their deaths be near,
No news but health from their physicians know.
Sonnets. No. cxl.

1
At lovers' perjuries, They say, Jove laughs.
Romeo and Juliet. Act ii, sc. 2, l. 92. [Juliet] An echo of the famous line of Ovid (*Ars Amatoria,* bk. i, l. 633), "Juppiter ex alto perjuria ridet amantum."

If you should deal double with her, truly it were an ill thing to be offered to any gentlewoman, and very weak dealing.
Romeo and Juliet. Act ii, sc. 4, l. 178. [Nurse]

Thy dear love sworn but hollow perjury,
Killing that love which thou hast vow'd to cherish.
Romeo and Juliet. Act iii, sc. 3, l. 128. [Friar Laurence]

2
Love bade me swear and Love bids me forswear.
The Two Gentlemen of Verona. Act ii, sc. 6, l. 6. [Proteus]

X—Blind Love

3
If you like elsewhere, do it by stealth:
Muffle your false love with some show of blindness.
The Comedy of Errors. Act iii, sc. 2, l. 7. [Luciana]

4
Burgundy: Love . . . must appear naked and blind. . . . A naked blind boy.
King Henry: She must be blind too.
Burgundy: As love is, my lord, before it loves.
Henry V. Act v, sc. 2, l. 316.

This is the liver-vein, which makes flesh a deity,
A green goose a goddess.
Love's Labour's Lost. Act iv, sc. 3, l. 74. [Biron] The only use of "liver-vein," the old name for the basilic vein.

5
But love is blind and lovers cannot see
The pretty follies that themselves commit.
The Merchant of Venice. Act ii, sc. 6, l. 36. [Jessica]

6
Love looks not with the eyes, but with the mind;
And therefore is wing'd Cupid painted blind.
Nor hath Love's mind of any judgement taste;
Wings and no eyes figure unheedy haste:
And therefore is Love said to be a child,
Because in choice he is so oft beguiled.
A Midsummer-Night's Dream. Act i, sc. 1, l. 234. [Helena] The only use of "unheedy."

7
Benvolio: Blind is his love and best befits the dark.
Mercutio: If love be blind, love cannot hit the mark.
Romeo and Juliet. Act ii, sc. 1, l. 32.

If love be blind, It best agrees with night.
Romeo and Juliet. Act iii, sc. 2, l. 9. [Juliet]

8
Valentine: I have loved her ever since I saw her; and still I see her beautiful.
Speed: If you love her, you cannot see her.
Valentine: Why?
Speed: Because Love is blind. . . . You, being in love, cannot see to put on your hose.
Valentine: Belike, boy, then you are in love; for last morning you could not see to wipe my shoes.
Speed: True, sir; I was in love with my bed; I thank you, you swinged me for my love, which makes me the bolder to chide you for yours.
Two Gentlemen of Verona. Act ii, sc. 1, l. 73.

Valentine: Why, lady, Love hath twenty pair of eyes.
Thurio: They say that Love hath not an eye at all.
Two Gentlemen of Verona. Act ii, sc. 4, l. 95.

Upon a homely object Love can wink.
The Two Gentlemen of Verona. Act ii, sc. 4, l. 98. [Valentine]

What should it be that he respects in her
But I can make respective in myself,
If this fond Love were not a blinded god?
The Two Gentlemen of Verona. Act iv, sc. 4, l. 199. [Julia]

XI—Silent Love

9
The ostentation of our love, which, left unshown,
Is often left unloved.
Antony and Cleopatra. Act iii, sc. 6, l. 52. [Cæsar] "Unloved" is used only once more, in *A Midsummer-Night's Dream,* iii, 2, 234: "To love unloved." "Unloving" occurs in *III Henry VI,* ii, 2, 25: "Unloving father."

10
Love, and be silent.
King Lear. Act i, sc. 1, l. 63. [Cordelia]

11
Let us be wary, let us hide our loves.
Othello. Act iii, sc. 3, l. 420. [Iago]

A murderous guilt shows not itself more soon
Than love that would seem hid: love's night is noon.
Twelfth Night. Act iii, sc. 1, l. 159. [Olivia]

12
My love is strengthen'd, though more weak in seeming;
I love not less, though less the show appear:
That love is merchandised whose rich esteeming

The owner's tongue doth publish every where.

Sonnets. No. cii. The only use of "Merchandised" and "esteeming."

Gremio, 'tis now no time to vent our love.

The Taming of the Shrew. Act i, sc. 2, l. 179. [Hortensio]

1
Jove knows I love: But who?
Lips, do not move; No man must know.

Twelfth Night. Act ii, sc. 5, l. 107. [Malvolio]

2
Julia: And wouldst thou have me cast my love on him?
Lucetta: Ay, if you thought your love not cast away.
Julia: Why he, of all the rest, hath never moved me.
Lucetta: Yet he, of all the rest, I think, best loves ye.
Julia: His little speaking shows his love but small.
Lucetta: Fire that 's closest kept burns most of all.
Julia: They do not love that do not show their love.
Lucetta: O, they love least that let men know their love.

Two Gentlemen of Verona. Act i, sc. 2, l. 25.

What, gone without a word?
Ay, so true love should do: it cannot speak.

The Two Gentlemen of Verona. Act ii, sc. 2, l. 16. [Proteus]

XII—Love and Fear

3
What my love is, proof hath made you know;
And as my love is sized, my fear is so:
Where love is great, the littlest doubts are fear;
Where little fears grow great, great love grows there.

Hamlet. Act iii, sc. 2, l. 179. [Player Queen] The only use of "sized" and "littlest."

4
My love and fear glued many friends to thee.

III Henry VI. Act ii, sc. 6, l. 5. [Clifford] "Glued" is used once more in *Titus Andronicus,* ii, 1, 41.

I love him not, nor fear him: there 's my creed.

Henry VIII. Act ii, sc. 2, l. 51. [Suffolk] The only use of "creed."

5
When she seem'd to shake and fear your looks,
She loved them most.

Othello. Act iii, sc. 3, l. 207. [Iago]

6
Love thrives not in the heart that shadows dreadeth.

The Rape of Lucrece, l. 270.

Against love's fire fear's frost hath dissolution.

The Rape of Lucrece, l. 355.

7
And she steal love's sweet bait from fearful hooks.

Romeo and Juliet. Act ii, Prologue, l. 8.

8
Fie, fie, fond love, thou art so full of fear
As one with treasure laden, hemm'd with thieves.

Venus and Adonis, l. 1021.

XIII—Love and Hate

9
Let not your hate encounter with my love.

All 's Well that Ends Well. Act i, sc. 3, l. 214. [Helena]

I shall prove
A lover of my drum, hater of love.

All 's Well that Ends Well. Act iii, sc. 3, l. 11. [Bertram]

10
The hated, grown to strength,
Are newly grown to love.

Antony and Cleopatra. Act i, sc. 3, l. 48. [Antony]

11
I love him not nor hate him not; and yet
I have more cause to hate him than to love him.

As You Like It. Act iii, sc. 5, l. 127. [Phebe]

12
If they love they know not why, they hate upon no better a ground.

Coriolanus. Act ii, sc. 2, l. 11. [Officer]

13
I love and hate her: for she 's fair and royal.

Cymbeline. Act iii, sc. 5, l. 70. [Cloten]

She never loved you, only
Affected greatness got by you, not you:
Married your royalty, was wife to your place;
Abhorr'd your person.

Cymbeline. Act v, sc. 5, l. 37. [Cornelius]

14
How love to me and to her son
Hath made her break out into terms of rage!

III Henry VI. Act i, sc. 1, l. 264. [King Henry]

These words have turn'd my hate to love.

III Henry VI. Act iii, sc. 3, l. 199. [Queen Margaret]

15
When thou didst hate him worst, thou lovedst him better
Than ever thou lovedst Cassius.

Julius Cæsar. Act iv, sc. 3, l. 106. [Cassius]

Hated by one he loves.—*Julius Cæsar,* iv, 3, 96.

16
I would not from your love make such a stray,
To match you where I hate.

King Lear. Act i, sc. 1, l. 212. [King Lear]

Drew from my heart all love,
And added to the gall.

King Lear. Act i, sc. 4, l. 291. [King Lear]

17
Bassanio: Do all men kill the things they do not love?
Shylock: Hates any man the thing he would not kill?
Bassanio: Every offence is not a hate at first.

The Merchant of Venice. Act iv, sc. 1, l. 66.

Why should I not, had I the heart to do it,
Like to the Egyptian thief at point of death,
Kill what I love?—a savage jealousy

That sometime savours nobly.
Twelfth Night. Act v, sc. 1, l. 120. [Duke]
That death 's unnatural that kills for loving.
Othello. Act v, sc. 2, l. 42. [Desdemona]

1
Hermia: The more I hate, the more he follows me.
Helena: The more I love, the more he hateth me.
A Midsummer-Night's Dream. Act i, sc. 1, l. 198.
An if she did not hate him deadly, she would love him dearly.
Much Ado about Nothing. Act v, sc. 1, l. 178. [Don Pedro]

2
Though I do hate him as I do hell-pains,
Yet, for necessity of present life,
I must show out a flag and sign of love.
Othello. Act i, sc. 1, l. 155. [Iago] "Hell-pains" is repeated in *All's Well that Ends Well,* ii, 3, 245: "I would it were hell-pains for thy sake."
She, in spite of nature,
Of years, of country, credit, every thing,
To fall in love with what she fear'd to look on!
Othello. Act i, sc. 3, l. 96. [Brabantio]
Yield up, O love, thy crown and hearted throne
To tyrannous hate!
Othello. Act iii, sc. 3, l. 448. [Othello] "Hearted" is repeated in *Othello,* i, 3, 373, and in *Antony and Cleopatra,* iii, 13, 178.

3
There is no hate in loving.
The Rape of Lucrece, l. 240.
Yield to my love; if not, enforced hate,
Instead of love's coy touch, shall rudely tear thee.
The Rape of Lucrece, l. 668.

4
Their love
Lies in their purses, and whoso empties them
By so much fills their hearts with deadly hate.
Richard II. Act ii, sc. 2, l. 129. [Bagot]
Sweet love, I see, changing his property,
Turns to the sourest and most deadly hate.
Richard II. Act iii, sc. 2, l. 135. [Scroop] "Sourest" is repeated in *As You Like It,* iii, 2, 115: "Sourest rind"; and in *Antony and Cleopatra,* ii, 2, 24: "Sourest points." "Sourest-natured" occurs in *The Two Gentlemen of Verona,* ii, 3, 6.

5
Dissemble not your hatred, swear your love.
Richard III. Act ii, sc. 1, l. 8. [King Edward]
God punish me
With hate in those where I expect most love!
Richard III. Act ii, sc. 1, l. 34. [Buckingham]
Made peace of enmity, fair love of hate,
Between these swelling wrong-incensed peers.
Richard III. Act ii, sc. 1, l. 50. [King Edward] The only use of "wrong-incensed."
King Richard: Say that I did all this for love of her.
Queen Elizabeth: Nay, then indeed she cannot choose but hate thee,
Having bought love with such a bloody spoil.
Richard III. Act iv, sc. 4, l. 288.
King Richard: Say, I, her sovereign, am her subject love.
Queen Elizabeth: But she, your subject, loathes such sovereignty.
Richard III. Act iv, sc. 4, l. 355.

6
Here 's much to do with hate, but more with love.
Why, then, O brawling love! O loving hate! . . .
This love feel I, that feel no love in this.
. . . Such is love's transgression.
Romeo and Juliet. Act i, sc. 1, l. 181. [Romeo]
My only love sprung from my only hate!
Too early seen unknown, and known too late!
Romeo and Juliet. Act i, sc. 5, l. 140. [Juliet]
My life were better ended by their hate,
Than death prorogued, wanting of thy love.
Romeo and Juliet. Act ii, sc. 2, l. 77. [Romeo] The only use of "prorogued."
Proud can I never be of what I hate;
But thankful even for hate, that is meant love.
Romeo and Juliet. Act iii, sc. 5, l. 148. [Juliet]
See, what a scourge is laid upon your hate,
That heaven finds means to kill your joys with love.
Romeo and Juliet. Act v, sc. 3, l. 292. [Prince]

7
Shall hate be fairer lodged than gentle love?
Sonnets. No. x.
Such civil war is in my love and hate
That I an accessary needs must be
To that sweet thief which sourly robs from me.
Sonnets. No. xxxv. "Sourly" is repeated in *Sonnets,* xli, and also in *Coriolanus,* v, 3, 13.
And yet, love knows, it is a greater grief
To bear love's wrong than hate's known injury
Sonnets. No. xl.
I must ne'er love him whom thou dost hate.
Sonnets. No. lxxxix.
Love is my sin and thy dear virtue hate.
Sonnets. No. cxlii.
But, love, hate on, for now I know thy mind;
Those that can see thou lovest, and I am blind.
Sonnets. No. cxlix.
In act thy bed-vow broke and new faith torn
In vowing new hate after new love bearing.
Sonnets. No. clii. The only use of "bed-vow."

8
Apemantus: I love thee better now than e'er I did.
Timon: I hate thee worse.
Timon of Athens. Act iv, sc. 3, l. 233.
Use her as you will,
The worse to her, the better loved of me.
Titus Andronicus. Act ii, sc. 3, l. 166. [Tamora]

9
The noblest hateful love, that e'er I heard of.
Troilus and Cressida. Act iv, sc. 1, l. 33. [Paris]
Hark, Greek: as much as I do Cressid love,
So much by weight hate I her Diomed.
Troilus and Cressida. Act v, sc. 2, l. 167. [Troilus]

1
To plead for love deserves more fee than hate.
The Two Gentlemen of Verona. Act i, sc. 2, l. 48. [Lucetta]

For love of you, not hate unto my friend,
Hath made me publisher of this pretence.
The Two Gentlemen of Verona. Act iii, sc. 1, l. 46. [Proteus] "Publisher" is repeated in *The Rape of Lucrece,* l. 33.

But love will not be spurr'd to what it loathes.
The Two Gentlemen of Verona. Act v, sc. 2, l. 7. [Julia]

2
His love, perceiving how he is enraged,
Grew kinder, and his fury was assuaged.
Venus and Adonis, l. 317. The only use of "perceiving" and "assuaged." "Assuage" occurs three times.

XIV—Love and Pity

3
But miserable most to love unloved?
This you should pity rather than despise.
A Midsummer-Night's Dream. Act iii, sc. 2, l. 234. [Helena]

She loved me for the dangers I had pass'd,
And I loved her that she did pity them.
Othello. Act i, sc. 3, l. 167. [Othello]

4 There is no creature loves me;
And if I die, no soul shall pity me:
Nay, wherefore should they, since that I myself
Find in myself no pity to myself?
Richard III. Act v, sc. 3, l. 200. [King Richard]

5
Viola: I pity you.
Olivia: That 's a degree to love.
Viola: No, not a grize; for 'tis a vulgar proof,
That very oft we pity enemies.
Twelfth Night. Act iii, sc. 1, l. 134. "Grize" (step) is repeated in *Timon of Athens,* iv, 3, 16, and in *Othello,* i, 3, 200.

6
Because he loves her, he despiseth me;
Because I love him, I must pity him.
The Two Gentlemen of Verona. Act iv, sc. 4, l. 100. [Julia]

XV—Love and Reason

7
Love's reason 's without reason.
Cymbeline. Act iv, sc. 2, l. 22. [Arviragus]

8
The expedition of my violent love
Outrun the pauser, reason.
Macbeth. Act ii, sc. 3, l. 116. [Macbeth] The only use of "pauser."

Ask me no reason why I love you; for though Love use Reason for his physician, he admits him not for his counsellor.
The Merry Wives of Windsor. Act ii, sc. 1, l. 4. [Mrs. Page]

9
To say the truth, reason and love keep little company together now-a-days.
A Midsummer-Night's Dream. Act iii, sc. 1, l. 146. [Bottom] "Now-a-days" is repeated in *Hamlet,* v, 1, 181, and in *Pericles,* ii, 1, 73.

10
Benedick: Do you not love me?
Beatrice: Why, no; no more than reason.
. . . Do you not love me?
Benedick: Troth, no; no more than reason.
Much Ado about Nothing. Act v, sc. 4, l. 74.

11
My reason, the physician to my love,
Angry that his prescriptions are not kept,
Hath left me.
Sonnets. No. cxlvii.

12 To be wise and love
Exceeds man's might; that dwells with gods above.
Troilus and Cressida. Act iii, sc. 2, l. 163. [Cressida]

13
Every reason excites to this, that my lady loves me.
Twelfth Night. Act ii, sc. 5, l. 180. [Malvolio]

14
Cesario, by the roses of the spring,
By maidhood, honour, truth and every thing,
I love thee so, that, maugre all my pride,
Nor wit nor reason can my passion hide.
Do not extort thy reasons from this clause,
For that I woo, thou therefore hast no cause;
But rather reason thus with reason fetter,
Love sought is good, but given unsought is better.
Twelfth Night. Act iii, sc. 1, l. 161. [Olivia] "Maidhood" is repeated in *Othello,* i, 1, 173; and "maugre" in *Titus Andronicus,* iv, 2, 110: "Maugre all the world"; and in *King Lear,* v, 3, 131: "Maugre thy strength."

XVI—Vain Love

15 'Twere all one
That I should love a bright particular star
And think to wed it, he is so above me:
In his bright radiance and collateral light
Must I be comforted, not in his sphere.
The ambition in my love thus plagues itself:
The hind that would be mated by the lion
Must die for love.
All's Well that Ends Well. Act i, sc. 1, l. 96. [Helena] "Collateral" occurs again in *Hamlet,* iv, 5, 206.

I know I love in vain, strive against hope;
Yet in this captious and intenible sieve
I still pour in the waters of my love
And lack not to lose still.
All's Well that Ends Well. Act i, sc. 3, l. 207. [Helena] The only use of "intenible."

Love make your fortunes twenty times above
Her that so wishes and her humble love!
All's Well that Ends Well. Act ii, sc. 3, l. 88. [Helena]

Humble love.—*Othello,* iii, 3, 458.

16
I cannot love her, nor will strive to do 't.
All's Well that Ends Well. Act ii, sc. 3, l. 152. [Bertram]

Say that you love me not, but say not so
In bitterness.
As You Like It. Act iii, sc. 5, l. 2. [Silvius]

I would love you, if I could.
As You Like It. Act v, sc. 2, l. 121. [Rosalind]

You love me not.—*Julius Cæsar,* iv, 3, 89.

I will not love: if I do, hang me; i' faith, I will not.
Love's Labour 's Lost. Act iv, sc. 3, l. 8. [Biron]

He loves us not; He wants the natural touch.
Macbeth. Act iv, sc. 2, l. 8. [Lady Macduff]

Cassio: Not that I love you not.
Bianca: But that you do not love me.
Othello. Act iii, sc. 4, l. 196.

1
You shall be more beloving than beloved.
Antony and Cleopatra. Act i, sc. 2, l. 22. [Soothsayer] The only use of "beloving."

Madam, methinks, if you did love him dearly,
You do not hold the method to enforce
The like from him.
Antony and Cleopatra. Act i, sc. 3, l. 6. [Charmian]

Thou lovest me not with the full weight that I love thee.
As You Like It. Act i, sc. 2, l. 8. [Celia]

I warrant I love you more than you do me.
King John. Act iv, sc. 1, l. 31. [Arthur]

If he love me to madness, I shall never requite him.
The Merchant of Venice. Act i, sc. 2, l. 69. [Portia]

But miserable most, to love unloved.
A Midsummer-Night's Dream. Act iii, sc. 2, l. 234. [Helena] "Unloved" is repeated in *Antony and Cleopatra,* iii, 6, 53.

O, 'tis the curse in love, and still approved,
When women cannot love where they 're beloved!
The Two Gentlemen of Verona. Act v, sc. 4, l. 43. [Proteus]

She 's Love, she loves, and yet she is not loved.
Venus and Adonis, l. 610.

2
I pray you, do not fall in love with me,
For I am falser than vows made in wine:
Besides, I like you not.
As You Like It. Act iii, sc. 5, l. 72. [Rosalind]

3
The pangs of despised love.
Hamlet. Act iii, sc. 1, l. 72. [Hamlet]

Pangs of love.—*Timon of Athens,* v, 1, 203.

4
The origin and commencement of his grief
Sprung from neglected love.
Hamlet. Act iii, sc. 1, l. 185. [Polonius] "Origin" is repeated in i, 4, 26, in *King Lear,* iv, 2, 32, and in *A Lover's Complaint,* l. 222; "commencement" in *Othello,* i, 3, 350: "It was a violent commencement."

5
Hotspur: Away, you trifler! Love! I love thee not,
I care not for thee, Kate. . . .
Lady Percy: Do you not love me? do you not, indeed?
Well, do not then; for since you love me not,
I will not love myself. Do you not love me?
Nay, tell me if you speak in jest or no.
Hotspur: Come, wilt thou see me ride?
And when I am o' horseback, I will swear
I love thee infinitely.
I Henry IV. Act ii, sc. 3, l. 93.

He loves me not.—*I Henry IV,* ii, 3, 67.

6
He loves thee, and thou dost neglect him. . . .
Therefore omit him not; blunt not his love.
II Henry IV. Act iv, sc. 4, l. 21. [King Henry]

7
Why, love forswore me in my mother's womb.
III Henry VI. Act iii, sc. 2, l. 153. [Gloucester]

And am I then a man to be beloved?
O monstrous fault, to harbour such a thought!
III Henry VI. Act iii, sc. 2, l. 163. [Gloucester]

And this word 'love,' which greybeards call divine,
Be resident in men like one another
And not in me: I am myself alone.
III Henry VI. Act v, sc. 6, l. 81. [Gloucester]

8
Drawn in the flattering table of her eye!
Hang'd in the frowning wrinkle of her brow!
And quarter'd in her heart! he doth espy
Himself love's traitor: this is pity now,
That, hang'd and drawn and quarter'd, there should be
In such a love so vile a lout as he.
King John. Act ii, sc. 1, l. 504. [Bastard]

9
Oswald: Prithee, if thou lovest me, tell me.
Kent: I love thee not.
Oswald: Why, then, I care not for thee.
Kent: If I had thee in Lipsbury pinfold, I would make thee care for me.
King Lear. Act ii, sc. 2, l. 6. The only use of "Lipsbury pinfold," whose meaning is unexplained. "Pinfold" is repeated in *The Two Gentlemen of Verona,* i, 1, 114, meaning a pound for stray cattle.

10
Believe not that the dribbling dart of love
Can pierce a complete bosom.
Measure for Measure. Act i, sc. 3, l. 2. [Duke] The only use of "dribbling."

11
I love thee not, therefore pursue me not.
A Midsummer-Night's Dream. Act ii, sc. 1, l. 188. [Demetrius]

Demetrius: Do I not in plainest truth
Tell you, I do not, nor I cannot love you?
Helena: And even for that do I love you the more. . . .
I 'll follow thee and make a heaven of hell
To die upon the hand I love so well.
A Midsummer-Night's Dream. Act ii, sc. 1, l. 200.

Of thy misprision must perforce ensue

Some true love turn'd and not a false turn'd true.
A Midsummer-Night's Dream. Act iii, sc. 2, l. 90. [Oberon]

1
I had rather hear my dog bark at a crow than a man swear he loves me.
Much Ado about Nothing. Act i, sc. 1, l. 132. [Beatrice]

Don Pedro: I shall see thee, ere I die, look pale with love.
Benedick: With anger, with sickness, or with hunger, my lord, not with love.
Much Ado about Nothing. Act i, sc. 1, l. 249.

I will not be sworn but love may transform me to an oyster; but I 'll take my oath on it, till he have made an oyster of me, he shall never make me such a fool.
Much Ado about Nothing. Act ii, sc. 3, l. 25. [Benedick]

There 's no true drop of blood in him, to be truly touched with love.
Much Ado about Nothing. Act iii, sc. 2, l. 18. [Don Pedro]

Then shall he mourn,
If ever love had interest in his liver.
Much Ado about Nothing. Act iv, sc. 1, l. 232. [Friar Francis]

There is no love in you.
Much Ado about Nothing. Act iv, sc. 1, l. 295. [Beatrice]

2
Hath love in thy old blood no living fire?
Richard II. Act i, sc. 2, l. 10. [Duchess of Gloucester]

Love loving not itself none other can.
Richard II. Act v, sc. 3, l. 88. [Duchess of York]

Hath he set bounds betwixt their love and me?
Richard III. Act iv, sc. 1, l. 21. [Queen Elizabeth]

3
She hath forsworn to love, and in that vow
Do I live dead that live to tell it now.
Romeo and Juliet. Act i, sc. 1, l. 229. [Romeo]

I cannot love,
I am too young; I pray you, pardon me.
Romeo and Juliet. Act iii, sc. 5, l. 187. [Juliet]

4
Pandarus: He esteems her no more than I esteem an addle egg.
Cressida: If you love an addle egg as well as you love an idle head, you would eat chickens i' the shell.
Troilus and Cressida. Act i, sc. 2, l. 144.

5
Your lord does know my mind; I cannot love him. . . .
He might have took his answer long ago. . . .
I cannot love him: let him send no more;
Unless, perchance, you come to me again,
To tell me how he takes it.
Twelfth Night. Act 1, sc. 5, l. 276. [Olivia]

Love make his heart of flint that you shall love;
And let your fervour, like my master's, be
Placed in contempt!
Twelfth Night. Act i, sc. 5, l. 305. [Viola]

6
I cannot leave to love, and yet I do;
But there I leave to love where I should love.
The Two Gentlemen of Verona. Act ii, sc. 6. l. 17. [Proteus]

I hold him but a fool that will endanger
His body for a girl that loves him not.
The Two Gentlemen of Verona. Act v, sc. 4, l. 133. [Thurio] "Endanger" is repeated in *The Merry Wives of Windsor,* ii, 2, 16.

7
Art thou a woman's son, and canst not feel
What 'tis to love? how want of love tormenteth?
Venus and Adonis, l. 201.

Poor queen of love, in thine own law forlorn,
To love a cheek that smiles at thee in scorn!
Venus and Adonis, l. 251.

XVII—Lost Love

8
The brains of my Cupid 's knocked out, and I begin to love as an old man loves money, with no stomach.
All 's Well that Ends Well. Act iii, sc. 2, l. 16. [Clown]

Ambitious love hath so in me offended,
That barefoot plod I the cold ground upon,
With sainted vow my faults to have amended.
All 's Well that Ends Well. Act iii, sc. 4, l. 5. [Steward]

Love that comes too late,
Like a remorseful pardon slowly carried,
To the great sender turns a sour offence,
Crying, 'That 's good that 's gone.'
All 's Well that Ends Well. Act v, sc. 3, l. 57. [King]

9
Let not the piece of virtue, which is set
Betwixt us as the cement of our love,
To keep it builded, be the ram to batter
The fortress of it.
Antony and Cleopatra. Act iii, sc. 2, l. 28. [Cæsar] The only use of "builded."

10
Shall love, in building, grow so ruinous?
The Comedy of Errors. Act iii, sc. 2, l. 4. [Luciana]

Belike you thought our love would last too long,
If it were chain'd together.
The Comedy of Errors. Act iv, sc. 1, l. 25. [Antipholus of Ephesus]

11
Love is begun by time;
And that I see, in passages of proof,
Time qualifies the spark and fire of it.
There lives within the very flame of love
A kind of wick or snuff that will abate it.
Hamlet. Act iv, sc. 7, l. 112. [King] The only use of "wick."

12
See already how he doth begin
To make us strangers to his looks of love.
I Henry IV. Act i, sc. 3, l. 289. [Worcester]

In respect of the love he bears our house: he shows in this, he loves his own barn better than he loves our house.
I Henry IV. Act ii, sc. 3, l. 4. [Hotspur]

13
Their over-greedy love hath surfeited.
II Henry IV. Act i, sc. 3, l. 88. [Archbishop of York] The only use of "over-greedy."

When love begins to sicken and decay,
It useth an enforced ceremony.
Julius Cæsar. Act iv, sc. 2, l. 20. [Brutus]

Gods, gods! 'tis strange that from their cold'st neglect
My love should kindle to inflamed respect.
King Lear. Act i, sc. 1, l. 257. [King of France]

1
If frosts and fasts, hard lodging and thin weeds
Nip not the gaudy blossoms of your love.
Love's Labour 's Lost. Act v, sc. 2, l. 811. [Princess of France]

2
And will you rent our ancient love asunder?
A Midsummer-Night's Dream. Act iii, sc. 2, l. 215. [Helena]

My love to Hermia,
Melted as the snow, seems to me now
As the remembrance of an idle gawd
Which in my childhood I did dote upon.
A Midsummer-Night's Dream. Act iv, sc. 1, l. 169. [Demetrius]

3
And from hence
I 'll love no friend, sith love breeds such offence.
Othello. Act iii, sc. 3, l. 379. [Iago]

All my fond love thus do I blow to heaven.
'Tis gone.
Othello. Act iii, sc. 3, l. 445. [Othello]

4
She burn'd with love, as straw with fire flameth;
She burn'd out love, as soon as straw out-burneth.
The Passionate Pilgrim, l. 97. The only use of "out-burneth."

5
Troilus: What too curious dreg espies my lady in the fountain of our love?
Cressida: More dregs than water, if my fears have eyes.
Troilus and Cressida. Act iii, sc. 2, l. 69.

She was beloved, she loved: she is, and doth:
But still sweet love is food for fortune's tooth.
Troilus and Cressida. Act iv, sc. 5, l. 292. [Troilus]

6
Even as one heat another heat expels,
Or as one nail by strength drives out another,
So the remembrance of my former love
Is by a newer object quite forgotten.
The Two Gentlemen of Verona. Act ii, sc. 4, l. 192. [Proteus]

Now my love is thaw'd;
Which, like a waxen image 'gainst a fire,
Bears no impression of the thing it was.
The Two Gentlemen of Verona. Act ii, sc. 4, l. 200. [Proteus] "Thaw'd" is repeated in *Julius Cæsar,* iii, 1, 41.

I love him not as I was wont.
O, but I love his lady too too much,
And that 's the reason I love him so little.
The Two Gentlemen of Verona. Act ii, sc. 4, l. 204. [Proteus]

My love to her is dead.
The Two Gentlemen of Verona. Act ii, sc. 6, l. 28. [Proteus]

Dead love.—*Twelfth Night,* i, 1, 31.

Death-mark'd love.—*Romeo and Juliet,* Prol., 9. The only use of "death-mark'd."

7
Therefore as you unwind her love from him,
Lest it should ravel and be good to none,
You must provide to bottom it on me.
The Two Gentlemen of Verona. Act iii, sc. 2, l. 51. [Thurio] "Unwind" is repeated in *Henry V,* i, 2, 101; and "ravel" in *Richard II* iv, 1, 228, and in *Hamlet,* iii, 4, 186.

This weak impress of love is as a figure
Trenched in ice, which with an hour's heat
Dissolves to water and doth lose his form.
The Two Gentlemen of Verona. Act iii, sc. 2, l. 6. [Duke] "Trenched" is repeated in *Macbeth,* iii, 4, 27: "Trenched gashes."

8
Fie, no more of love!
Venus and Adonis, l. 185.

XVIII—Love and Lust

See also Lechery, Lust, Wantonness

9
The great prerogative and rite of love,
Which, as your due, time claims, he does acknowledge;
But puts it off to a compell'd restraint;
Whose want, and whose delay, is strew'd with sweets,
Which they distil now in the curbed time,
To make the coming hour o'erflow with joy
And pleasure drown the brim.
All 's Well that Ends Well. Act ii, sc. 4, l. 42. [Parolles]

Time goes on crutches till love have all his rites.
Much Ado about Nothing. Act ii, sc. 1, l. 372. [Claudio]

God give us leisure for these rites of love!
Richard III. Act v, sc. 3, l. 101. [Derby]

Lovers can see to do their amorous rites
By their own beauties.
Romeo and Juliet. Act iii, sc. 2, l. 8. [Juliet]

I must not yield to any rites of love.
I Henry VI. Act i, sc. 2, l. 113. [La Pucelle]

10
King: Did he love this woman?
Parolles: Faith, sir, he did love her; but how?
King: How, I pray you?
Parolles: He did love her, sir, as a gentleman loves a woman.
King: How is that?
Parolles: He loved her, sir, and he loved her not. . . . Indeed he was mad for her, and talked of Satan and of Limbo and of Furies and I know not what.
All 's Well that Ends Well. Act v, sc. 3, l. 241.

11
The country copulatives.
As You Like It. Act v, sc. 4, l. 58. [Touchstone] The only use of "copulatives."

Let copulation thrive.—*King Lear,* iv, 6, 116. "Copulation" occurs again in *As You Like It,* iii, 2, 84. See under Bawd.

1
Some love that drew him oft from home.
The Comedy of Errors. Act v, sc. 1, l. 56. [Adriana]
Such love must needs be treason in my breast.
Hamlet. Act iii, sc. 2, l. 188. [Player Queen]
Contemned love.—*Twelfth Night,* i, 5, 289.
Erring love.—*The Two Gentlemen of Verona,* ii, 4, 213.
Free love.—*Timon of Athens,* i, 2, 188.
Inflaming love.—*I Henry VI,* v, 5, 82; *Pericles,* iv, 1, 5.
Loose love.—*Love's Labour 's Lost,* v, 2, 776.
Unlawful love.—*The Comedy of Errors,* v, 1, 51.
Untaught love.—*Measure for Measure,* ii, 4, 29.
Unthrift love.—*Merchant of Venice,* v, 1, 16.

2
By Gis and by Saint Charity,
Alack, and fie for shame!
Young men will do 't, if they come to 't;
By cock, they are to blame.
Quoth she, before you tumbled me,
You promised me to wed.
So would I ha' done, by yonder sun,
And thou hadst not come to my bed.
Hamlet. Act iv, sc. 5, l. 59. [Ophelia] The only use of "Gis," short for Jesus.

3
It was Alençon that enjoyed my love.
I Henry VI. Act v, sc. 4, l. 73. [La Pucelle]
My soul intends . . . to enjoy thee for my love.
III Henry VI. Act iii, sc. 2, l. 94. [King Edward]
No, he hath enjoy'd her: . . .
She hath been colted by him.
Cymbeline. Act ii, sc. 4, l. 126. [Posthumus] "Colted" is used again in *I Henry IV,* ii, 2, 41.

4
Surfeiting in joys of love.
II Henry VI. Act i, sc. 1, l. 251. [York]

5
You love the breeder better than the male.
III Henry VI. Act ii, sc. 1, l. 42. [Richard]
Breeder of these dire events.—*Titus Andronicus,* v, 3, 178.
Breeder of all good.—*The Two Gentlemen of Verona,* iii, 1, 243.
Breeder of sinners.—*Hamlet,* iii, 1, 123.
Breeder of my sorrow.—*III Henry VI,* iii, 3, 43.
Fair breeder.—*Venus and Adonis,* l. 282.
Unback'd breeder.—*Venus and Adonis,* l. 320. The only uses of "breeder." "Unback'd" is repeated in *The Tempest,* iv, 1, 176: "Unback'd colts."
Woolly breeders.—*Merchant of Venice,* i, 3, 84.
Fairest breeders.—*Titus Andronicus,* iv, 2, 68. The only uses of "breeders."

6
King Edward: But stay thee, 'tis the fruits of love I mean.
Lady Grey: The fruits of love I mean, my loving liege.
King Edward: Ay, but, I fear me, in another sense.
What love think'st thou I sue so much to get?
Lady Grey: My love till death, my humble thanks, my prayers;
That love which virtue begs and virtue grants.
King Edward: No, by my troth, I did not mean such love. . . .
To tell thee plain, I aim to lie with thee.
Lady Grey: To tell you plain, I had rather lie in prison.
III Henry VI. Act iii, sc. 2, l. 58.

7
Regan: Tell me—but truly—but then speak the truth,
Do you not love my sister?
Edmund: In honour'd love.
Regan: But have you never found my brother's way
To the forfended place?
Edmund: That thought abuses you.
Regan: I am doubtful that you have been conjunct
And bosom'd with her.
King Lear. Act v, sc. 1, l. 8. The only use of "bosom'd." "Conjunct" is repeated in ii, 2, 125, and occurs in no other play.

8
Duke Vincentio: Love you the man that wrong'd you?
Juliet: Yes, as I love the woman that wrong'd him.
Measure for Measure. Act ii, sc. 3, l. 24.
I had him in mine arms
With all the effect of love.
Measure for Measure. Act v, sc. 1, l. 198. [Mariana]

9
Make love's quick pants in Desdemona's arms.
Othello. Act ii, sc. 1, l. 80. [Cassio]
O thou day o' the world,
Chain mine arm'd neck; leap thou, attire and all,
Through proof of harness to my heart, and there
Ride on the pants triumphing!
Antony and Cleopatra. Act iv, sc. 8, l. 13. [Antony]

10
I do love her too;
Not out of absolute lust, though peradventure
I stand accountant for as great a sin.
Othello. Act ii, sc. 1, l. 300. [Iago]
She with Cassio hath the act of shame
A thousand times committed; Cassio confess'd it:
And she did gratify his amorous works
With that recognizance and pledge of love
Which I first gave her.
Othello. Act v, sc. 2, l. 211. [Othello] The only use of "recognizance." "Recognizances" occurs in *Hamlet,* v, 1, 113.

11
Was this a lover, or a lecher whether?
Bad in the best, though excellent in neither.
The Passionate Pilgrim, l. 101.

12
Let fair humanity abhor the deed
That spots and stains love's modest snow-white weed.
The Rape of Lucrece, l. 195.

One that will do the deed
Though Argus were her eunuch and her guard.
Love's Labour's Lost. Act iii, sc. 1, l. 200. [Biron]

1
Go, get thee to thy love, as was decreed,
Ascend her chamber, hence and comfort her.
Romeo and Juliet. Act iii, sc. 3, l. 146. [Friar Laurence]

Ah me! how sweet is love itself possess'd,
When but love's shadows are so rich in joy.
Romeo and Juliet. Act v, sc. 1, l. 10. [Romeo]

2
Do not give dalliance Too much the rein.
The Tempest. Act iv, sc. 1, l. 51. [Prospero]

Silken dalliance.—*Henry V,* ii, Prol., 2.
Wanton dalliance.—*I Henry VI,* v, 1, 23.
Primrose path of dalliance.—*Hamlet,* i, 3, 50.
See PREACHER, 1190:13.

3 Conflict such as was supposed
The wandering prince and Dido once enjoy'd,
When with a happy storm they were surprised
And curtain'd with a counsel-keeping cave.
Titus Andronicus. Act ii, sc. 3, l. 21. [Tamora] The only use of "counsel-keeping."

Let her joy her raven-colour'd love.
Titus Andronicus. Act ii, sc. 3, l. 83. [Lavinia] The only use of "raven-colour'd."

4
This is the monstruosity in love, lady, that the will is infinite and the execution confined, that the desire is boundless and the act a slave to limit.
Troilus and Cressida. Act iii, sc. 2, l. 87. [Troilus] The only use of "monstruosity."

They say all lovers swear more performance than they are able and yet reserve an ability that they never perform, vowing more than the perfection of ten and discharging less than the tenth part of one. They that have the voice of lions and the act of hares, are they not monsters?
Troilus and Cressida. Act iii, sc. 2, l. 91. [Cressida] The only use of "discharging."

5
O sweet-suggesting Love, if thou hast sinn'd,
Teach me, thy tempted subject, to excuse it!
The Two Gentlemen of Verona. Act ii, sc. 6, l. 7. [Proteus] The only use of "sweet-suggesting."

6
Love keeps his revels where there are but twain.
Venus and Adonis, l. 123.

Who sees his true-love in her naked bed,
Teaching the sheets a whiter hue than white,
But, when his glutton eye so full hath fed,
His other agents aim at like delight.
Venus and Adonis, l. 397.

Now is she in the very lists of love,
Her champion mounted for the hot encounter.
Venus and Adonis, l. 595.

7
I hate not love, but your device in love,
That lends embracements unto every stranger.
You do it for increase: O strange excuse,
When reason is the bawd to lust's abuse!
Venus and Adonis, l. 789.

Call it not love, for Love to heaven is fled,
Since sweating Lust on earth usurp'd his name;
Under whose simple semblance he hath fed
Upon fresh beauty, blotting it with blame;
Which the hot tyrant stains and soon bereaves,
As caterpillars do the tender leaves.
Love comforteth like sunshine after rain,
But Lust's effect is tempest after sun;
Love's gentle spring doth always fresh remain,
Lust's winter comes ere summer half be done;
Love surfeits not, Lust like a glutton dies;
Love is all truth, Lust full of forged lies.
Venus and Adonis, l. 793.

8
I am not bookish, yet I can read waiting-gentlewoman in the 'scape. This has been some stair-work, some trunk-work, some behind-door-work: they were warmer that got this than the poor thing is here.
The Winter's Tale. Act iii, sc. 3, l. 74. [Shepherd] The only use of "stair-work," "trunk-work," and "behind-door-work." "Bookish" is repeated in *II Henry VI,* i, 1, 259, and in *Othello,* i, 1, 24. "Waiting-gentlewoman" occurs four times.

A bank for love to lie and play on.
Winter's Tale. Act iv, sc. 4, l. 130. [Perdita]

XIX—Love and Death

9
The poor world is almost six thousand years old, and in all this time there was not any man died in his own person, videlicet, in a love-cause.
As You Like It. Act iv, sc. 1, l. 94. [Rosalind] The only use of "love-cause." "Videlicet" occurs four times.

Men have died from time to time and worms have eaten them, but not for love.
As You Like It. Act iv, sc. 1, l. 108. [Rosalind]

10 Espoused to death, with blood he seal'd
A testament of noble-ending love.
Henry V. Act iv, sc. 6, l. 26. [Exeter] The only use of "noble-ending."

If thou canst love me for this, take me; if not, to say to thee that I shall die, is true; but for thy love, by the Lord, no; yet I love thee too.
Henry V. Act v, sc. 2, l. 157. [King Henry]

11 And tell quaint lies,
How honourable ladies sought my love,
Which I denying, they fell sick and died.
The Merchant of Venice. Act iii, sc. 4, l. 69. [Portia]

12
Claudio: Hero thinks surely she will die; for she says she will die if he love her not, and she will die ere she make her love known, and she will die, if he woo her, rather than she will bate one breath of her accustomed crossness.
Don Pedro: She doth well: if she should make tender of her love, 'tis very possible he'll scorn it. . . . I am sorry for your

niece. Shall we go seek Benedick, and tell him of her love? . . .
Claudio: If he do not dote upon her upon this, I will never trust my expectation.
Much Ado about Nothing. Act ii, sc. 3, l. 180. The only use of "crossness."

1
Be thus when thou art dead, and I will kill thee,
And love thee after.
Othello. Act v, sc. 2, l. 18. [Othello]

2
All our evening sport from us is fled,
All our love is lost, for Love is dead.
The Passionate Pilgrim, l. 291.
O love! O life! not life, but love in death!
Romeo and Juliet. Act iv, sc. 5, l. 58. [Paris]

3
Let your love even with my life decay.
Sonnets. No. lxxi.

4
No man alive can love in such a sort
The thing he means to kill more excellently.
Troilus and Cressida. Act iv, sc. 1, l. 23. [Æneas]

5
My love to love is love but to disgrace it;
For I have heard it is a life in death,
That laughs and weeps, and all but with a breath.
Venus and Adonis, l. 412.
Love's golden arrow at him should have fled,
And not Death's ebon dart, to strike him dead.
Venus and Adonis, l. 947
Sith in his prime Death doth my love destroy,
They that love best their loves shall not enjoy.
Venus and Adonis, l. 1163.

XX—The Lover

6
We that are true lovers run into strange capers.
As You Like It. Act ii, sc. 4, l. 54. [Touchstone]
True lover.—*A Midsummer-Night's Dream,* i, 1, 150; and six times in later plays.

7
And then the lover,
Sighing like furnace, with a woeful ballad
Made to his mistress' eyebrow.
As You Like It. Act ii, sc. 7, l. 147. [Jaques]
It is as easy to count atomies as to resolve the propositions of a lover.
As You Like It. Act iii, sc. 2, l. 245. [Celia] "Atomies" is repeated in iii, 5, 13, and in *Romeo and Juliet,* i, 4, 57. "Atomy" occurs in *II Henry IV,* v, 4, 33.
Lovers are given to poetry, and what they swear in poetry may be said as lovers they do feign.
As You Like It. Act iii, sc. 3, l. 20. [Touchstone]

8
The sight of lovers feedeth those in love.
As You Like It. Act iii, sc. 4, l. 60. [Rosalind]
Here comes a lover of mine and a lover of hers.
As You Like It. Act v, sc. 2, l. 82. [Rosalind]
It was a lover and his lass.
As You Like It. Act v, sc. 3, l. 17. [Song]

9
All lovers young, all lovers must
Consign to thee, and come to dust.
Cymbeline. Act iv, sc. 2, l. 274. [Guiderius and Arviragus]

10
The lover shall not sigh gratis.
Hamlet. Act ii, sc. 2, l. 335. [Hamlet]

11
King: A true man or a thief that gallops so?
Biron: I post from love: good lover, let me go.
Love's Labour's Lost. Act iv, sc. 3, l. 187.
No great good lover.—*Henry VIII,* iv, 1, 104.
Best lover.—*Julius Cæsar,* iii, 2, 49.
Blest lovers.—*The Tempest,* iv, 1, 86.
Bosom lover.—*Merchant of Venice,* iii, 4, 17.
Deceased lover.—*Sonnets,* xxxii.
Faithful lover.—*Love's Labour's Lost,* v, 2, 50; *A Midsummer-Night's Dream,* iv, 1, 96.
Gentle lover.—*A Midsummer-Night's Dream,* iii, 2, 452.
Hollow lover.—*As You Like It,* iv, 1, 197.
Lowly lover.—*Venus and Adonis,* l. 350.
Poor lovers.—*The Two Gentlemen of Verona,* ii, 2, 21.
Sweet lovers.—*As You Like It,* v, 3, 22; *Love's Labour's Lost,* iv, 3, 214.
Youthful lover.—*The Two Gentlemen of Verona,* iii, 1, 41.
Lover dear.—*A Midsummer-Night's Dream,* i, 2, 55.

12
Lovers and madmen have such seething brains,
Such shaping fantasies, that apprehend
More than cool reason ever comprehends.
A Midsummer-Night's Dream. Act v, sc. 1, l. 4. [Theseus] The only use of "shaping." "Seething" is repeated in *Sonnets,* cliii.
The lover, all as frantic,
Sees Helen's beauty in a brow of Egypt.
A Midsummer-Night's Dream. Act v, sc. 1, l. 10. [Theseus]

13
From forth the fatal loins of these two foes
A pair of star-cross'd lovers take their life;
Whose misadventured piteous overthrows
Do with their death bury their parents' strife.
Romeo and Juliet, Prol., l. 5. The only use of "star-cross'd" and "misadventured."

14
Clubs, clubs! these lovers will not keep the peace.
Titus Andronicus. Act ii, sc. 1, l. 37. [Aaron]

15
Come hither, boy: if ever thou shalt love,
In the sweet pangs of it remember me;
For such as I am all true lovers are,
Unstaid and skittish in all motions else,
Save in the constant image of the creature
That is beloved.
Twelfth Night. Act ii, sc. 4, l. 15. [Duke] "Unstaid" and "skittish" both occur three times in the plays.

16
Speed: My master is become a notable lover.
Launce: I never knew him otherwise.
Speed: Than how?

Launce: A notable lubber, as thou reportest him to be.
Speed: Why, thou whoreson ass, thou mistakest me. . . . I tell thee my master is become a hot lover.
Launce: Why, I tell thee, I care not though he burn himself in love.
Two Gentlemen of Verona. Act ii, sc. 5, l. 43.

1 Lovers break not hours,
Unless it be to come before their time.
Two Gentlemen of Verona. Act v, sc. 1, l. 4. [Eglamour]

Gratiano: Lovers ever run before the clock.
Salarino: O, ten times faster Venus' pigeons fly
To seal love's bonds new-made, than they are wont
To keep obliged faith unforfeited!
The Merchant of Venice. Act ii, sc. 6, l. 4. The only use of "obliged" and "unforfeited."

Orlando: My fair Rosalind, I come within an hour of my promise.
Rosalind: Break an hour's promise in love! He that will divide a minute into a thousand parts and break but a part of the thousandth part of a minute in the affairs of love, it may be said of him that Cupid hath clapped him o' the shoulder, but I 'll warrant him heart-whole.
As You Like It. Act iv, sc. 1, l. 42. The only use of "heart-whole."

2
Lovers' hours are long, though seeming short.
Venus and Adonis, l. 842.

LOYALTY

See also Fidelity

3
The loyalty well held to fools does make
Our faith mere folly.
Antony and Cleopatra. Act iii, sc. 13, l. 42. [Enobarbus]

4
Master, go on, and I will follow thee,
To the last gasp, with truth and loyalty.
As You Like It. Act ii, sc. 3, l. 69. [Adam]

Fight till the last gasp.—*I Henry VI,* i, 2, 127.
At last gasp.—*Cymbeline,* i, 5, 53.
To the latest gasp.—*III Henry VI,* v, 2, 41.
His latest gasp.—*III Henry VI,* ii, 1, 108.
My latter gasp.—*I Henry VI,* ii, 5, 38.
Makes him gasp.—*II Henry VI,* iii, 2, 371.
Gasp out my eloquence.—*Henry V,* v, 2, 149. The only uses of "gasp." "Gasping" occurs three times.

5
A loyal sir To him thou follow'st.
The Tempest. Act v, sc. 1, l. 69. [Prospero]

Remains loyal.—*Cymbeline,* iii, 2, 47.
Still kept loyal.—*I Henry IV,* iii, 2, 43.

6
I dare be bound he 's true and shall perform
All parts of his subjection loyally
Cymbeline. Act iv, sc. 3, l. 18. [First Lord] The only use of "loyally."

7
O, where is faith? O, where is loyalty?
If it be banish'd from the frosty head,
Where shall it find a harbour in the earth?
II Henry VI. Act v, sc. 1, l. 166. [King Henry]

8 While life upholds this arm,
This arm upholds the house of Lancaster.
III Henry VI. Act iii, sc. 3, l. 106. [Earl of Oxford]

My loyalty,
Which ever has and ever shall be growing,
Till death, that winter, kill it.
Henry VIII. Act iii, sc. 2, l. 177. [Cardinal Wolsey]

To him will we prove loyal.—*King John,* ii, 1, 271.

9
Nature thus gives way to loyalty.
King Lear. Act iii, sc. 5, l. 4. [Edmund]

I will persevere in my course of loyalty, though the conflict be sore between that and my blood.
King Lear. Act iii, sc. 5, l. 22. [Edmund]

And then end life when I end loyalty!
A Midsummer-Night's Dream. Act ii, sc. 2, l. 63. [Lysander]

10
To-day shalt thou behold a subject die
For truth, for duty, and for loyalty.
Richard III. Act iii, sc. 3, l. 3. [Lord Rivers]

Loyalty . . . To God.—*Richard II,* i, 3, 19.
Loyalty . . . Toward the king.—*Henry VIII,* iii, 2, 272.
Constant loyalty.—*III Henry VI,* iii, 3, 241; *Henry V,* iii, 2, 5.
Firm loyalty.—*III Henry VI,* iii, 3, 240.
Submissive loyalty of heart.—*I Henry VI,* iii, 4, 10.

11
Yet do our hearts wear Timon's livery,
That see I by our faces.
Timon of Athens. Act iv, sc. 2, l. 17. [Servant]

12
Be bold in us: we 'll follow where thou lead'st,
Like stinging bees in hottest summer's day
Led by their master to the flowered fields.
Titus Andronicus. Act v, sc. 1, l. 13. [First Goth] "Flowered" is repeated in *Romeo and Juliet,* ii, 4, 64.

13
Longer than I prove loyal to your grace
Let me not live to look upon your grace.
The Two Gentlemen of Verona. Act iii, sc. 2, l. 20. [Proteus]

I protest true loyalty to her.
The Two Gentlemen of Verona. Act iv, sc. 2. l. 7. [Proteus]

I beseech you hear me, who profess
Myself your loyal servant, your physician,
Your most obedient counsellor.
The Winter's Tale. Act ii, sc. 3, l. 53. [Paulina]

Loyal servant.—*Coriolanus,* v, 6, 142; *Cymbeline,* iv, 3, 16.
Loyal bosom.—*Richard II,* ii, 3, 98.
Loyal breast.—*Richard II,* i, 1, 181; *Henry VIII,* iii, 2, 200; *The Phœnix and the Turtle,* l. 57.
Loyal dame.—*The Rape of Lucrece,* l. 1034.
Loyal friends.—*I Henry VI,* iii, 1, 182.
Loyal gentleman.—*Richard II,* i, 1, 148; i, 3, 87.
Loyal subject.—*III Henry VI,* iv, 7, 44; *Henry V,* i, 2, 127; *Henry VIII,* iii, 2, 180.

LUCK

See also Chance, Fortune

I—Good Luck

1
Good luck go with thee!
Henry V. Act iv, sc. 3, l. 11. [Bedford]
As good luck would have it.—*The Merry Wives of Windsor,* iii, 5, 84.
Good luck grant thee!—*A Midsummer-Night's Dream,* i, 1, 221.
They shall have good luck.—*A Midsummer-Night's Dream,* ii, 1, 41.
Good luck, an 't be thy will!—*The Winter's Tale,* iii, 3, 70.
Good luck To my proceedings.—*Richard III,* iv, 4, 402.
Natural luck.—*Antony and Cleopatra,* ii, 3, 26.
Luck of Cæsar.—*Antony and Cleopatra,* v, 2, 289.

2
This comes off well.
Measure for Measure. Act ii, sc. 1, l. 57. [Escalus]

3
If it be my luck, so; if not, happy man be his dole!
The Merry Wives of Windsor. Act iii, sc. 4, l. 67. [Slender] "Happy man be his dole" is used four times in the plays. It is a proverb, cited by John Heywood in 1546 ("Happy man, happy dole") meaning, "May his dole (or lot) be that of a happy man."

This is the third time; I hope good luck lies in odd numbers. Away! go. They say there is divinity in odd numbers, either in nativity, chance, or death.
The Merry Wives of Windsor. Act v, sc. 1, l. 2. [Falstaff] This is the first reference in English literature to the proverb, "There 's luck in odd numbers."

Strew good luck, ouphes, on every sacred room:
That it may stand till the perpetual doom.
The Merry Wives of Windsor. Act v, sc. 5, l. 61. [Mistress Quickly] "Ouphes," an obsolete spelling of oafs, which Shakespeare uses again in iv, 4, 49, but in no other play.

Unearned luck.—*A Midsummer-Night's Dream,* v, 1, 439. The only use of "unearned."

4
Luck, in very spite of cunning,
Bade him win all.
Troilus and Cressida. Act v, sc. 5, l. 41. [Ulysses]

5
We are lucky, boy; and to be so still requires nothing but secrecy.
The Winter's Tale. Act iii, sc. 3, l. 129. [Shepherd]

'Tis a lucky day, boy, and we 'll do good deeds on 't.
The Winter's Tale. Act iii, sc. 3, l. 142. [Shepherd]

Lucky joys.—*II Henry IV,* v, 3, 99.
Lucky ruler.—*II Henry VI,* iii, 1, 291.
Lucky war.—*Henry V,* ii, 2, 184.
Nice and lucky.—*Antony and Cleopatra,* iii, 13, 180. The only uses of "lucky."
Luckier issue.—*Much Ado about Nothing,* v, 3, 32.
Luckiest stars.—*All's Well that Ends Well,* i, 3, 252. The only use of "luckier" and "luckiest."

II—Bad Luck

6
I ne'er had worse luck in my life.
All's Well that Ends Well. Act ii, sc. 2, l. 59. [Clown]

I have but lean luck.
The Comedy of Errors. Act iii, sc. 2, l. 93. [Dromio of Syracuse]

7
Hapless Ægeon, whom the fates have mark'd
To bear the extremity of dire mishap!
The Comedy of Errors. Act i, sc. 1, l. 141. [Duke]

Hapless Valentine!—*The Two Gentlemen of Verona,* iii, 1, 260.
The hapless male to one sweet bird.—*III Henry VI,* v, 6, 15.
Hapless father.—*III Henry VI,* i, 4, 156.
Hapless gain.—*The Two Gentlemen of Verona,* i, 1, 32.
Hapless hands.—*II Henry VI,* i, 1, 226.
Hapless life.—*The Rape of Lucrece,* l. 1045.
Hapless time.—*I Henry VI,* iii, 1, 201. The only uses of "hapless."

8
Was there ever man had such luck! when I kissed the jack, upon an up-cast to be hit away!
Cymbeline. Act ii, sc. 1, l. 1. [Cloten] The only use of "up-cast," a throw at the game of bowls.

Well, forward, forward! thus the bowl should run,
And not unluckily against the bias.
The Taming of the Shrew. Act iv, sc. 5, l. 24. [Petruchio]

Things have fall'n out, sir, so unluckily.
Romeo and Juliet. Act iii, sc. 4, l. 1. [Capulet]

How unluckily it happened!—*Timon of Athens,* iii, 2, 51.
Come unluckily home.—*II Henry IV,* Epil., 13.
Starr'd most unluckily.—*The Winter's Tale,* iii, 2, 100. The only use of "starr'd." "Unluckily" is used twice more, in *Comedy of Errors,* v, 1, 125, and in *Julius Cæsar,* iii, 3, 2.
O, much I fear some ill unlucky thing.
Romeo and Juliet, v, 3, 136. See under FEAR.
Unlucky deeds.—*Othello,* v, 2, 341.
Unlucky hour.—*Titus Andronicus,* ii, 3, 251.
Unlucky manage.—*Romeo and Juliet,* iii, 1, 148.
Unlucky Irish wars.—*I Henry IV,* v, 1, 53. The only uses of "unlucky."
Luckless realm.—*III Henry VI,* ii, 6, 18.
Luckless time.—*III Henry VI,* v, 6, 45. The only play in which "luckless" occurs.

9
He told me that rebellion had bad luck.
II Henry IV. Act i, sc. 1, l. 41. [Travers] The only use of "bad luck."

Ween you of better luck.
Henry VIII. Act v, sc. 1, l. 135. [King] The only use of "better luck" and of "ween." "Weening" occurs in *I Henry VI,* ii, 5, 88.

10
Shylock: No ill luck stirring but what lights on my shoulders. . . .
Tubal: Yes, other men have ill luck too.

Antonio, as I heard in Genoa,—
Shylock: What, what, what? ill luck, ill luck?
Tubal: Hath an argosy cast away, coming from Tripolis.
The Merchant of Venice. Act iii, sc. 1, l. 98. Shakespeare was fond of "lights on," which is repeated frequently throughout the plays. Tripolis is mentioned three times in this play and nowhere else. Tripoli is used in *The Taming of the Shrew,* iv, 2, 76.

Sir John, we have had ill luck.
The Merry Wives of Windsor. Act v, sc. 5, l. 120. [Mrs. Ford]

Met ill luck.—*II Henry IV,* i, 1, 51. The only uses of "ill-luck."

1
'Twere hard luck, being in so preposterous estate as we are.
The Winter's Tale. Act v, sc. 2, l. 158. [Clown] The only use of "hard luck."

Good or evil luck.—*Sonnets,* xiv. The only use of "evil luck."

LUNACY

See also Madness

2
The lunacy is so ordinary that the whippers are in love too.
As You Like It, iii, 2, 423. See under LOVE.

3
Being lunatic, He rush'd into my house.
The Comedy of Errors. Act iv, sc. 3, l. 94. [Courtezan]

4
The terms of our estate may not endure
Hazard so near us as doth hourly grow
Out of his lunacies.
Hamlet. Act iii, sc. 3, l. 5. [King]

Turbulent and dangerous lunacy.—*Hamlet,* iii, 1, 4. "Turbulent" is repeated in *Timon of Athens,* v, 1, 221, and in *Pericles,* iii, 2, 4.

Hamlet's lunacy.—*Hamlet,* ii, 2, 49.

Strange lunacy.—*The Taming of the Shrew,* Ind., 2, 31.

5
Why, this is lunatics! this is mad as a mad dog!
The Merry Wives of Windsor. Act iv, sc. 2, l. 130. [Evans]

6
Dispute not with her, she is lunatic.
Richard III. Act i, sc. 3, l. 254. [Dorset]

Persuade him that he hath been lunatic.
The Taming of the Shrew. Induction, sc. 1, l. 63. [Lord]

'Oman, art thou lunatics?—*The Merry Wives of Windsor,* iv, 1, 71.

What, is the man lunatic?—*The Taming of the Shrew,* v, 1, 74.

Half lunatic.—*The Taming of the Shrew,* ii, 1, 289.

Lunatic bans.—*King Lear,* ii, 3, 19.

Lunatic fool.—*Richard II,* ii, 1, 115.

Lunatic king.—*King Lear,* iii, 7, 46.

Lunatic knave.—*The Merry Wives of Windsor,* iii, 5, 105.

Malvolio the lunatic.—*Twelfth Night,* iv, 2, 26.

7
This closing with him fits his lunacy:
Whate'er I forge to feed his brain-sick fits,
Do you uphold and maintain in your speeches.
Titus Andronicus. Act v, sc. 2, l. 70. [Tamora]

8
These dangerous unsafe lunes i' the king, beshrew them!
Winter's Tale. Act ii, sc. 2, l. 30. [Paulina]

Your husband is in his old lunes again.
The Merry Wives of Windsor, Act iv, sc. 2, l. 22. [Mrs. Page]

Pettish lunes.—*Troilus and Cressida,* ii, 3, 139. The only uses of "lunes" (fits of lunacy).

LUNGS

9
My lungs began to crow like chanticleer.
As You Like It, ii, 7, 30. See under LAUGHTER.

The heaving of my lungs provokes me to ridiculous smiling.
Love's Labour 's Lost. Act iii, sc. 1, l. 77. [Armado]

Laughs from 's free lungs.—*Cymbeline,* i, 6, 68.

Hateful lungs.—*Henry V,* ii, 1, 52.

Infected lungs.—*Pericles,* iv, 6, 179.

Sensible and nimble lungs.—*The Tempest,* ii, 1, 174.

Spongy lungs.—*A Lover's Complaint,* l. 326.

Wheezing lungs.—*Troilus and Cressida,* v, 1, 24. The only use of "wheezing."

Lungs and rotten ones.—*The Tempest,* ii, 1, 47.

Lungs are tickle o' the sere.—*Hamlet,* ii, 2, 337.

10
So shall my lungs Coin words.
Coriolanus, iii, 1, 77. See under DISEASE.

11
My lungs are wasted so
That strength of speech is utterly denied me.
II Henry IV. Act iv, sc. 5, l. 217. [King Henry]

Thou but offend'st thy lungs to speak so loud.
The Merchant of Venice. Act iv, sc. 1, l. 140. [Shylock]

Bully knight! bully Sir John! speak from thy lungs military.
The Merry Wives of Windsor. Act v, sc. 1, l. 18. [Hostess]

12
God bless thy lungs, good knight.
II Henry IV, v, 5, 9. See GOD, 620:11.

13
Let vultures vile seize on his lungs also!
II Henry IV. Act v, sc. 3, l. 146. [Pistol]

14
Now crack thy lungs.
Troilus and Cressida. Act iv, sc. 5, l. 7. [Ajax]

LUST

See also Desire; Lechery; Lewdness; Love and Lust; Wantonness

15
But, O strange men!
That can such sweet use make of what they hate,
When saucy trusting of the cozen'd thoughts
Defiles the pitchy night: so lust doth play
With what it loathes for that which is away.
All's Well that Ends Well. Act iv, sc. 4,

l. 21. [Helena] "Pitchy" is repeated in *I Henry VI,* ii, 2, 2: "Pitchy mantle"; and in *III Henry VI,* v, 6, 85: "Pitchy day."

1 His captain's heart,
Which in the scuffles of great fights hath burst
The buckles on his breast, reneges all temper,
And is become the bellows and the fan
To cool a gipsy's lust.

Antony and Cleopatra. Act i, sc. 1, l. 7. [Philo] The only use of "scuffles." "Renege" is repeated in *King Lear,* ii, 2, 84.

2 That this body, consecrate to thee,
By ruffian lust should be contaminate!

The Comedy of Errors. Act ii, sc. 2, l. 134. [Adriana] "Contaminate" is repeated in *Julius Cæsar,* iv, 3, 24: "Contaminate our fingers." "Contaminated" occurs five times.

I am possess'd with an adulterate blot;
My blood is mingled with the crime of lust.

The Comedy of Errors. Act ii, sc. 2, l. 142. [Adriana]

3
When my lust hath dined, . . . to the court
I 'll knock her back, foot her home again.

Cymbeline. Act iii, sc. 5, l. 146. [Cloten]

4
Virtue, as it never will be moved,
Though lewdness court it in a shape of heaven,
So lust, though to a radiant angel link'd,
Will sate itself in a celestial bed,
And prey on garbage.

Hamlet. Act i, sc. 5, l. 53. [Ghost] "Garbage" occurs again in *Cymbeline,* i, 6, 50. The only use of "sate."

5
You must not put another scandal on him,
That he is open to incontinency.

Hamlet. Act ii, sc. 1, l. 29. [Polonius]

The cognizance of her incontinency
Is this: she hath bought the name of whore thus dearly.

Cymbeline. Act ii, sc. 5, l. 127. [Posthumus]

Thou didst accuse him of incontinency.

Cymbeline. Act iii, sc. 4, l. 49. [Imogen] The only uses of "incontinency." "Incontinence" does not occur at all.

Be incontinent.—*As You Like It,* v, 2, 42.
Turn incontinent.—*Timon of Athens,* iv, 1, 3.
Incontinent varlets.—*Troilus and Cressida,* v, 1, 106. The only uses of "incontinent" in the sense of lecherous.

6
Polluted with your lusts.

I Henry VI. Act v, sc. 4, l. 43. [La Pucelle]

Wanton lust.—*III Henry VI,* iii, 3, 210.

7
Served the lust of my mistress' heart, and did the act of darkness with her.

King Lear. Act iii, sc. 4, l. 89. [Edgar]

Do the deed of darkness.—*Pericles,* iv, 6, 32.
The loathsome act of lust.—*The Rape of Lucrece,* l. 1636.

8
One that slept in the contriving of lust, and waked to do it.

King Lear. Act iii, sc. 4, l. 92. [Edgar]

In woman out-paramoured the Turk.

King Lear. Act iii, sc. 4, l. 94. [Edgar] The only use of "out-paramoured."

A serviceable villain;
As duteous to the vices of thy mistress
As badness would desire.

King Lear. Act iv, sc. 6, l. 257. [Edgar]

9
The superfluous and lust-dieted man.

King Lear. Act iv, sc. 1, l. 70. [Gloucester] The only use of "lust-dieted."

Lust-breathed.—*The Rape of Lucrece,* l. 3.
Lust-stained.—*Othello,* v, 1, 36.
Lust-wearied.—*Antony and Cleopatra,* ii, 1, 38. The only use of these phrases.

10
Their saucy sweetness that do coin heaven's image
In stamps that are forbid.

Measure for Measure, ii, 4, 45. [Angelo]

By gift of my chaste body
To his concupiscible intemperate lust.

Measure for Measure. Act v, sc. 1, l. 97. [Isabella] The only use of "concupiscible." "Intemperate" occurs only once more, in *Much Ado about Nothing,* iv, 1, 60.

Summer-seeming lust.—*Macbeth,* iv, 3, 86. The only use of "summer-seeming."

11
Duke: Know you this woman?
Lucio: Carnally, she says.

Measure for Measure. Act v, sc. 1, l. 214. The only use of "carnally."

12
Till the wicked fire of lust have melted him in his own grease.

The Merry Wives of Windsor. Act ii, sc. 1, l. 68. [Mrs. Ford]

Fie on lust and luxury!
Lust is but a bloody fire,
Kindled with unchaste desire,
Fed in heart, whose flames aspire
As thoughts do blow them, higher and higher.

The Merry Wives of Windsor. Act v, sc. 5. l. 98. [Song]

This is enough to be the decay of lust and late-walking through the realm.

The Merry Wives of Windsor. Act v, sc. 5, l. 152. [Falstaff] The only use of "late-walking."

13
Your daughter and the Moor are now making the beast with two backs.

Othello. Act i, sc. 1, l. 117. [Iago]

The gross clasps of a lascivious Moor.

Othello. Act i, sc. 1, l. 127. [Roderigo]

We have reason to cool our raging motions, our carnal stings, our unbitted lusts, whereof I take this that you call love to be a sect or scion.

Othello. Act i, sc. 3, l. 334. [Iago] The only use of "unbitted." "Carnal" is repeated in *Richard III,* iv, 4, 56: "Carnal cur"; and in *Hamlet,* v, 2, 392: "Carnal acts." "Scion" occurs again in *Henry V,* iii, 5, 7, and in *The Winter's Tale,* iv, 4, 93.

It is merely a lust of the blood and a permission of the will.

Othello. Act i, sc. 3, l. 339. [Iago]

Prompture of the blood.—*Measure for Measure,* ii, 4, 178. The only use of "prompture."

1
When the blood is made dull with the act of sport, there should be, again to inflame it and to give satiety a fresh appetite, loveliness in favour, sympathy in years, manners and beauties.
Othello. Act ii, sc. 1, l. 230. [Iago]
2
I 'll pour this pestilence into his ear,
That she repeals him for her body's lust.
Othello. Act ii, sc. 3, l. 362. [Iago]
What sense had I of her stol'n hours of lust?
I saw 't not, thought it not, it harm'd not me.
Othello. Act iii, sc. 3, l. 338. [Othello]
Would you, the supervisor, grossly gape on—
Behold her topp'd?
Othello. Act iii, sc. 3, l. 395. [Iago] The only use of "supervisor" and of "topp'd" in this sense.
As prime as goats, as hot as monkeys,
As salt as wolves in pride.
Othello. Act iii, sc. 3, l. 403. [Iago]
3
O rash false heat, wrapp'd in repentant cold,
Thy hasty spring still blasts, and ne'er grows old!
The Rape of Lucrece, l. 48.
His naked armour of still-slaughter'd lust.
The Rape of Lucrece, l. 188. The only use of "still-slaughter'd."
As corn o'ergrown with weeds, so heedful fear
Is almost choked by unresisted lust.
The Rape of Lucrece, l. 281. The only use of "unresisted."
His servile powers, . . .
Stuff up his lust, as minutes fill up hours.
The Rape of Lucrece, l. 295.
His rage of lust by gazing qualified.
The Rape of Lucrece, l. 424.
And wilt thou be the school where Lust shall learn?
Must he in thee read lectures of such shame?
The Rape of Lucrece, l. 617.
Black lust, dishonour, shame, misgoverning,
Who seek to stain the ocean of thy blood.
The Rape of Lucrece, l. 654. The only use of "misgoverning."
Seducing lust, thy rash relier.
The Rape of Lucrece, l. 639. The only use of "relier."
4
While Lust is in his pride, no exclamation
Can curb his heat or rein his rash desire.
The Rape of Lucrece, l. 705.
One man's lust these many lives confounds.
The Rape of Lucrece, l. 1489.
His scarlet lust came evidence to swear
That my poor beauty had purloin'd his eyes.
The Rape of Lucrece, l. 1650. The only use of "purloin'd."
5
She bears the load of lust he left behind.
The Rape of Lucrece, l. 734.
Cistern of my lust.—*Macbeth,* iv, 3, 63.
Engines of lust.—*All's Well that Ends Well,* iii, 5, 21.
Heat of lust.—*The Rape of Lucrece,* l. 1473.
Pillow to our lust.—*Titus Andronicus,* ii, 3, 130.
6
His . . . bestial appetite in change of lust;
Which stretched to their servants, daughters, wives,
Even where his lustful eye or savage heart,
Without control, listed to make his prey.
Richard III. Act iii, sc. 5, l. 81. [Gloucester] The only use of "listed." "Bestial" is repeated in *Hamlet,* iv, 4, 40: "Bestial oblivion"; and in *Othello,* ii, 3, 264: "What remains is bestial."
This lustful lord leap'd from his bed.
The Rape of Lucrece, l. 169.
Lustful bed.—*The Taming of the Shrew.* Induction, sc. 2, l. 40.
Lustful eye.—*The Rape of Lucrece,* l. 179.
Lustful language.—*Venus and Adonis,* l. 47.
Lustful paramours.—*I Henry VI,* iii, 2, 53.
Lustful sons.—*Titus Andronicus,* iv, 1, 79.
Lustful Edward.—*III Henry VI,* iii, 2, 129.
The only uses of "lustful."
7
The expense of spirit in a waste of shame
Is lust in action; and till action, lust
Is perjured, murderous, bloody, full of blame,
Savage, extreme, rude, cruel, not to trust,
Enjoy'd no sooner but despised straight,
Past reason hated, as a swallow'd bait
On purpose laid to make the taker mad;
Mad in pursuit and in possession so;
Had, having, and in quest to have, extreme;
A bliss in proof, and proved, a very woe;
Before, a joy proposed; behind, a dream.
All this the world well knows; yet none knows well
To shun the heaven that leads men to this hell.
Sonnets. No. cxxix.
8
The murkiest den,
The most opportune place, the strong'st suggestion
Our worser genius can, shall never melt
Mine honour into lust.
The Tempest. Act iv, sc. 1, l. 25. [Ferdinand] The only use of "murkiest." "Opportune" is repeated in *The Winter's Tale,* iv, 4, 511.
9
Melted down thy youth
In different beds of lust.
Timon of Athens. Act iv, sc. 3, l. 256. [Timon]
Lust and liberty
Creep in the minds and marrows of our youth.
Timon of Athens, iv, 1, 25. See under YOUTH.
Lust and laughter.—*Timon of Athens,* iv, 3, 492.
Lust and foul thoughts.—*Othello,* ii, 1, 264.
Lust and rank thoughts.—*Cymbeline,* ii, 5, 24.
10
There serve your lusts, shadow'd from heaven's eye.
Titus Andronicus. Act ii, sc. 1, l. 130. [Aaron]
O, keep me from their worse than killing lust,
And tumble me into some loathsome pit,
Where never man's eye may behold my body:
Do this, and be a charitable murderer.
Titus Andronicus. Act ii, sc. 3, l. 175. [Lavinia]

Let them satisfy their lust on thee.
Titus Andronicus. Act ii, sc. 3, l. 180. [Tamora]

Aaron: Did you not use his daughter very friendly?
Demetrius: I would we had a thousand Roman dames
At such a bay, by turn to serve our lust.
Titus Andronicus. Act iv, sc. 2, l. 40.

Here 's the base fruit of his burning lust.
Titus Andronicus. Act v, sc. 1, l. 43. [Lucius]

Absolute lust.—*Othello,* ii, 1, 301.
Prone lust.—*The Rape of Lucrece,* l. 684.
Shameful lust.—*Hamlet,* i, 5, 45.
Sweating Lust.—*Venus and Adonis,* l. 794.
Epicurism and lust.—*King Lear,* i, 4, 265. The only use of "Epicurism."
Lust of English youth.—*Henry V,* iii, 5, 30.

1
When I am hence, I 'll answer to my lust.
Troilus and Cressida. Act iv, sc. 4, l. 134. [Diomedes]

2
Backward she push'd him, as she would be thrust,
And govern'd him in strength, though not in lust.
Venus and Adonis, l. 41.

And careless lust stirs up a desperate courage;
Planting oblivion, beating reason back,
Forgetting shame's pure blush and honour's wrack.
Venus and Adonis, l. 556.

LUXURY

3
To 't, luxury, pell-mell!
King Lear. Act iv, sc. 6, l. 119. [King Lear]

4
One all of luxury, an ass, a madman.
Measure for Measure, v, 1, 506. See under DESERVING.

Hateful luxury.—*Richard III,* iii, 5, 80.
Heart-wish'd luxury.—*A Lover's Complaint,* l. 314. The only use of "heart-wish'd."
Lust and luxury.—*The Merry Wives of Windsor,* v, 5, 98.
Fathers' luxury.—*Henry V,* iii, 5, 6.
Couch for luxury.—*Hamlet,* i, 5, 83.

5
How the devil Luxury, with his fat rump and potato-finger, tickles these together!
Troilus and Cressida. Act v, sc. 2, l. 55. [Thersites] The only use of "rump" and "potato-finger." "Potatoes" occurs only once in the plays, in *The Merry Wives of Windsor,* v, 5, 21, the reference being to the Spanish or sweet potato, supposed to have aphrodisiac qualities. All the uses of "luxury" are given above.

6
Luxurious, avaricious, false.
Macbeth, iv, 3, 58. See under CHARACTER.

Luxurious bed.—*Much Ado about Nothing,* iv, 1, 42.
Luxurious drab.—*Troilus and Cressida,* v, 4, 9.
Luxurious goat.—*Henry V,* iv, 4, 20.
Luxurious woman.—*Titus Andronicus,* v, 1, 88. The only uses of "luxurious." "Luxuriously" occurs once, in *Antony and Cleopatra,* iii, 13, 120: "Besides what hotter hours, . . . you have Luxuriously pick'd out."

LYING, see Lie and Lying

M

MADNESS

See also Anger, Distraction, Ecstasy, Lunacy, Wits

7
He was mad for her.
All's Well that Ends Well, v, 3, 260. See under LOVE for full quotation.

Mad in folly.—*All's Well that Ends Well,* v, 3, 3.

8
Though I am mad, I will not bite him.
Antony and Cleopatra. Act ii, sc. 5, l. 80. [Cleopatra]

Exceeding mad, in love too:
But he would bite none.
Henry VIII. Act i, sc. 4, l. 28. [Lord Sands]

9
I drave my suitor from his mad humour of love to a living humour of madness.
As You Like It. Act iii, sc. 2, l. 438. [Rosalind]

Born of madness.—*As You Like It,* iv, 1, 218.

10
Sure, he is stark mad.
The Comedy of Errors. Act ii, sc. 1, l. 59. [Dromio of Ephesus]

I think you are all mated or stark mad.
The Comedy of Errors. Act v, sc. 1, l. 281. [Duke] "Mated" in the sense of confounded or stupefied is repeated in *The Comedy of Errors,* iii, 2, 54: "not mad, but mated"; in *The Taming of the Shrew,* iii, 2, 246: "Madly mated"; and in *Macbeth,* v, 1, 86: "My mind she has mated."

Run mad indeed, stark mad!
Winter's Tale. Act iii, sc. 2, l. 184. [Paulina]

Stark mad.—*The Taming of the Shrew,* i, 1, 69.
Frantic-mad.—*Sonnets,* cxlvii. The only use of the phrase.
Raging mad.—*II Henry VI,* iii, 2, 394.

11
Wast thou mad,
That thus so madly thou didst answer me?
The Comedy of Errors. Act ii, sc. 2, l. 11. [Antipholus of Syracuse]

Benvolio: Why, Romeo, art thou mad?
Romeo: Not mad, but bound more than a madman is.
Romeo and Juliet. Act i, sc. 2, l. 54.

What, art thou mad, old fellow?
King Lear. Act ii, sc. 2, l. 91. [Cornwall] Also *Cymbeline,* i, 1, 147.

My masters, are you mad? or what are you?
Twelfth Night. Act ii, sc. 3, l. 93. [Malvolio]
What, art mad?—*King Lear,* iv, 6, 153.
What, are men mad?—*Cymbeline,* i, 6, 32.
Are all the people mad?—*Twelfth Night,* iv, 1, 29.
Why, are ye mad?—*Titus Andronicus,* ii, 1, 75.
What, are you mad?—*Romeo and Juliet,* iii, 5, 158; *Othello,* v, 2, 194.

1 How comes it,
That thou art thus estranged from thyself?
The Comedy of Errors. Act ii, sc. 2, l. 121. [Adriana]
How come you thus estranged?
Love's Labour's Lost, v, 2, 213. The only uses of "estranged."

2
Now out of doubt Antipholus is mad,
Else would he never so demean himself. . . .
The reason that I gather he is mad, . . .
Is a mad tale he told to-day at dinner.
The Comedy of Errors. Act iv, sc. 3, l. 82. [Courtezan]
Hold, hurt him not, for God's sake! he is mad.
The Comedy of Errors. Act v, sc. 1, l. 33. [Adriana]

3 Both man and master is possess'd;
I know it by their pale and deadly looks.
The Comedy of Errors. Act iv, sc. 4, l. 95. [Pinch]
I was possess'd.—*Comedy of Errors,* v, 1, 245.
He is, sure, possessed, madam.
Twelfth Night. Act iii, sc. 4, l. 9. [Maria]
If all the devils of hell be drawn in little, and Legion himself possessed him, yet I'll speak to him.
Twelfth Night. Act iii, sc. 4, l. 94. [Sir Toby] The only uses of "possessed" in this sense.

4
Antipholus of Ephesus: Peace, doting wizard, peace! I am not mad.
Adriana: O, that thou wert not, poor distressed soul!
The Comedy of Errors. Act iv, sc. 4, l. 61.
I am not mad; I know thee well enough:
Witness this wretched stump, witness these crimson lines; . . .
I know them all, though they suppose me mad.
Titus Andronicus. Act v, sc. 2, l. 21. [Titus]
I am no more mad than you are: make the trial of it in any constant question.
Twelfth Night. Act iv, sc. 2, l. 51. [Malvolio]
Clown: Tell me true, are you not mad indeed? or do you but counterfeit?
Malvolio: Believe me, I am not; I tell thee true.
Twelfth Night. Act iv, sc. 2, l. 121.
Do not think I am mad.—*Twelfth Night,* iv, 2, 33.
I am not mad.—*Twelfth Night,* iv, 2, 44; v, 1, 382.

5
And thereof came it that the man was mad.
The Comedy of Errors. Act v, sc. 1, l. 68. [Abbess]
Sure, the man is mad.—*I Henry VI,* v, 3, 85.

6 This ill day
A most outrageous fit of madness took him;
That desperately he hurried through the street—
With him his bondman, all as mad as he,—
Doing displeasure to the citizens.
The Comedy of Errors. Act v, sc. 1, l. 138. [Adriana] "Fit of madness" is repeated in l. 76, and occurs only in this scene.
If he were mad, he would not plead so coldly.
The Comedy of Errors. Act v, sc. 1, l. 272. [Duke]

7
To leave you in your madness, 'twere my sin.
Cymbeline. Act ii, sc. 3, l. 103. [Cloten]
A madness, of which her life 's in danger.
Cymbeline. Act iv, sc. 3, l. 3. [Cymbeline]

8 Not frenzy, not
Absolute madness could so far have raved.
Cymbeline. Act iv, sc. 2, l. 134. [Belarius]
In a frenzy, . . . away he posts.
Cymbeline. Act v, sc. 5, l. 282. [Pisanio]
His untimely frenzy thus awaketh.
The Rape of Lucrece, l. 1675.
A most extracting frenzy of mine own
From my remembrance clearly banish'd his.
Twelfth Night. Act v, sc. 1, l. 288. [Olivia] "Extracting" is repeated in *Measure for Measure,* iii, 2, 49.
Distraction, frenzy and amazement.—*Troilus and Cressida,* v, 3, 85.
His fits, his frenzy.—*Titus Andronicus,* iv, 4, 12.
Some fit or frenzy.—*Titus Andronicus,* iv, 1, 17.
Fine frenzy.—*A Midsummer-Night's Dream,* v, 1, 12.

9 Some other horrible form
Which might deprive your sovereignty of reason
And draw you into madness.
Hamlet. Act i, sc. 4, l. 72. [Horatio]

10 Your noble son is mad:
Mad call I it; for to define true madness,
What is 't but to be nothing else but mad?
Hamlet. Act ii, sc. 2, l. 92. [Polonius]
That he is mad, 'tis true: 'tis true 'tis pity;
And pity 'tis 'tis true.
Hamlet. Act ii, sc. 2, l. 97. [Polonius]
Alas, he 's mad!—*Hamlet,* iii, 4, 105.
He . . . fell into a sadness, then into a fast,
Thence to a watch, thence into a weakness,
Thence to a lightness, and, by this declension,
Into the madness wherein now he raves.
Hamlet. Act ii, sc. 2, l. 146. [Polonius] "Declension" is repeated in *Richard III,* iii, 7, 189, and in *The Merry Wives of Windsor,* iv, 1, 76.

11
Though this be madness, yet there is method in 't.
Hamlet. Act ii, sc. 2, l. 207. [Polonius]
What he spake, though it lack'd form a little.
Was not like madness.
Hamlet, iii, 1, 171. See under SPEECH.

12
How pregnant sometimes his replies are! a happiness that often madness hits on, which reason and sanity could not so prosperously be delivered of.
Hamlet. Act ii, sc. 2, l. 212. [Polonius] The only use of "sanity." "Prosperously" is repeated in *Coriolanus,* v, 6, 75.

Her madness hath the oddest frame of sense,
Such a dependency of thing on thing,
As e'er I heard in madness.
Measure for Measure. Act v, sc. 1, l. 61. [Duke] The only use of "oddest." "Dependency" is repeated in *Measure for Measure,* v, 1, 62, and in *Antony and Cleopatra,* v, 2, 26.

O, matter and impertinency mix'd!
Reason in madness!
King Lear. Act iv, sc. 6, l. 178. [Edgar] The only use of "impertinency."

His very madness, like some ore
Among a mineral of metals base,
Shows itself pure.
Hamlet. Act iv, sc. 1, l. 25. [Queen]

A madness most discreet.—*Romeo and Juliet,* i, 1, 199.

1
I am but mad, north-north-west: when the wind is southerly, I know a hawk from a handsaw.
Hamlet. Act ii, sc. 2, l. 396. [Hamlet] The only use of "southerly." "Handsaw" is supposed by some commentators to be a corruption of hernshaw, a heron, but the proverb, as Hamlet speaks it, is included in John Ray's *English Proverbs,* 1670. "Hand-saw" occurs again in *I Henry IV,* ii, 4, 187, in its usual meaning, and with a hyphen.

2
Go to, I 'll no more on 't; it hath made me mad.
Hamlet. Act iii, sc. 1, l. 153. [Hamlet]

It will make us mad.—*Macbeth,* ii, 2, 34.

3
Madness in great ones must not unwatch'd go.
Hamlet. Act iii, sc. 1, l. 196 [King] The only use of "unwatch'd."

I like him not, nor stands it safe with us
To let his madness range.
Hamlet. Act iii, sc. 3, l. 1. [King]

4
Madness would not err.
Hamlet, iii, 4, 73. See under CHOICE.

It is not madness
That I have utter'd: bring me to the test,
And I the matter will re-word; which madness
Would gambol from.
Hamlet. Act iii, sc. 4, l. 141. [Hamlet] The only use of "re-word." "Re-worded" occurs in *A Lover's Complaint,* l. 1.

I essentially am not in madness,
But mad in craft.
Hamlet. Act iii, sc. 4, l. 187. [Hamlet]

A crafty madness.—*Hamlet,* iii, 1, 8.

5
Mad as the sea and wind, when both contend
Which is the mightier.
Hamlet. Act iv, sc. 1, l. 7. [Queen]

As mad as the vex'd sea; singing aloud.
King Lear. Act iv, sc. 4, l. 2. [Cordelia]

6
By heaven, thy madness shall be paid with weight,
Till our scale turn the beam.
Hamlet. Act iv, sc. 5, l. 156. [Laertes]

A document in madness, thoughts and remembrance fitted.
Hamlet. Act iv, sc. 5, l. 178. [Laertes] The only use of the word "document."

7
Clown: Young Hamlet, . . . he that is mad, and sent into England.
Hamlet: Ay, marry, why was he sent into England?
Clown: Why, because he is mad: he shall recover his wits there; or, if he do not, it 's no great matter there. . . . There the men are as mad as he.
Hamlet: How came he mad? . . .
Clown: Faith, e'en with losing his wits.
Hamlet. Act v, sc. 1, l. 161.

A whoreson mad fellow.
Hamlet. Act v, sc. 1, l. 193. [First Clown] "Mad fellow" is also used twice in *I Henry IV,* ii, 4, 369, and iv, 2, 39.

8
This is mere madness:
And thus awhile the fit will work on him.
Hamlet. Act v, sc. 1, l. 307. [Queen]

9
What I have done,
That might your nature, honour and exception
Roughly awake, I here proclaim was madness.
Hamlet. Act v, sc. 2, l. 241. [Hamlet]

His madness is poor Hamlet's enemy.
Hamlet. Act v, sc. 2, l. 250. [Hamlet]

10
Thou art essentially mad, without seeming so.
I Henry IV. Act ii, sc. 4, l. 540. [Falstaff] "Essentially" is repeated in *II Henry VI,* v, 2, 39, and in *Hamlet,* iii, 4, 187.

11
Nay, if you melt, then will she run mad.
I Henry IV. Act iii, sc. 1, l. 212. [Glendower]

He will sure run mad.
Romeo and Juliet. Act ii, sc. 4, l. 5. [Mercutio]

He ran mad and died.—*Henry VIII,* ii, 2, 130.

Runs presently mad.—*Much Ado about Nothing,* i, 1, 88.

Poor lady, she 'll run mad.—*Othello,* iii, 3, 317.

Leonato: You will never run mad, niece.
Beatrice: No, not till a hot January.
Much Ado about Nothing. Act i, sc. 1, l. 93. January is mentioned once again, in *The Winter's Tale,* iv, 4, 111.

Run mad.—*I Henry IV,* iii, 1, 145; *The Rape of Lucrece,* l. 997; *Romeo and Juliet,* iv, 3, 48; iv, 5, 76; *Troilus and Cressida,* v, 1, 53; *Twelfth Night,* ii, 5, 213.

Straight fall mad.—*Titus Andronicus,* ii, 3, 104.

O fool, I shall go mad.—*King Lear,* ii, 4, 289.

Go mad.—*Troilus and Cressida,* iv, 2, 78.

If I should despair, I should grow mad.
Sonnets. No. cxl.

12
My lord, this is a poor mad soul.
II Henry IV. Act ii, sc. 1, l. 114. [Falstaff] The only use of "mad soul."

Being a little intoxicates in his prains.
Henry V. Act iv, sc. 7, l. 39. [Fluellen] The only use of "intoxicates."

1
Good Lord, what madness rules in brain-sick men,
When for so slight and frivolous a cause
Such factious emulations shall arise!
I Henry VI. Act iv, sc. 1, l. 111. [King Henry]

The bedlam brain-sick duchess.
II Henry VI. Act iii, sc. 1, l. 51. [Suffolk]

Brain-sick fits.—*Titus Andronicus,* v, 2, 71.
Brain-sick raptures.—*Troilus and Cressida,* ii, 2, 122.
Brain-sick son.—*II Henry VI,* v, 1, 163. The only uses of "brain-sick." "Brainsickly" occurs once, in *Macbeth,* ii, 2, 46.

2
To Bedlam with him! is the man grown mad?
II Henry VI. Act v, sc. 1, l. 131. [Clifford]

Ha! art thou bedlam?
Henry V. Act v, sc. 1, l. 20. [Pistol]

Bedlam, have done.—*King John,* ii, 1, 183.
Get the Bedlam to lead him.—*King Lear,* iii, 7, 103. "Bedlam" occurs eight times in the plays.

3
What, is the fellow mad?
Julius Cæsar. Act iii, sc. 1, l. 10. [Cæsar]

Alack, sir, he is mad.—*King Lear,* iv, 1, 47.
Mad with terror.—*Richard III,* iii, 5, 4.
Mad in pursuit.—*Sonnets,* cxxix.
Mad and merry.—*The Taming of the Shrew,* iii, 2, 228.
Mad with misery.—*Titus Andronicus,* iii, 2, 9.

4
Shall I be frighted when a madman stares?
Julius Cæsar. Act iv, sc. 3, l. 40. [Brutus]

One sees more devils than vast hell can hold,
That is, the madman.
A Midsummer-Night's Dream. Act v, sc. 1, l. 9. [Theseus]

Help, help, help! here 's a madman will murder me.
The Taming of the Shrew. Act v, sc. 1, l. 61. [Biondello]

The fool shall look to the madman.
Twelfth Night. Act i, sc. 5, l. 145. [Clown]

Nay, I 'll ne'er believe a madman till I see his brains.
Twelfth Night. Act iv, sc. 2, l. 125. [Clown] "Madman" is used twenty-five times, and "madmen" twelve times.

5
Mad world! mad kings! mad composition!
King John. Act ii, sc. 1, l. 561. [Bastard] The only use of any of these phrases.

Mad ass.—*The Taming of the Shrew,* v, 1, 87.
Mad-brain.—*Taming of the Shrew,* iii, 2, 10.
Mad-brained.—*I Henry VI,* i, 2, 15; *The Taming of the Shrew,* iii, 2, 165; *Timon of Athens,* v, 1, 177.
Mad devil.—*The Merry Wives of Windsor,* v, 1, 19.
Mad dog.—*The Comedy of Errors,* v, 1, 70; *The Merry Wives of Windsor,* iv, 2, 131.
Mad folks.—*Cymbeline,* ii, 3, 106.
Mad-headed.—*I Henry IV,* ii, 3, 80.
Mad knave.—*Taming of the Shrew,* v, 1, 95.
Mad masters.—*Taming of the Shrew,* iv, 1, 1.
Mad mothers.—*Henry V,* iii, 3, 39.
Mad rogue.—*Hamlet,* v, 1, 196.
Mad sister.—*Troilus and Cressida,* ii, 2, 98.
Mad soul.—*II Henry IV,* ii, 1, 113.
Mad spirit.—*A Midsummer-Night's Dream,* iii, 2, 4.
Mad wag.—*I Henry IV,* i, 2, 50; iv, 2, 55.
Mad woman.—*Richard II,* v, 2, 95; *The Merchant of Venice,* iv, 1, 445; *Timon of Athens,* i, 2, 138.

6
Lady, you utter madness, and not sorrow.
King John. Act iii, sc. 4, l. 43. [Pandulph]

I am not mad: this hair I tear is mine; . . .
I am not mad: I would to heaven I were!
For then, 'tis like I should forget myself:
O, if I could, what grief should I forget!
Preach some philosophy to make me mad . . .
I am not mad; too well, too well I feel
The different plague of each calamity.
King John. Act iii, sc. 4, l. 45. [Constance]

7
O, let me not be mad, not mad, sweet heaven!
Keep me in temper: I would not be mad!
King Lear. Act i, sc. 5, l. 50. [King Lear]

That way madness lies.
King Lear. Act iii, sc. 4, l. 21. [King Lear]

Thou say'st the king grows mad; I 'll tell thee, friend,
I am almost mad myself.
King Lear. Act iii, sc. 4, l. 170. [Gloucester]

His roguish madness Allows itself to any thing.
King Lear. Act iii, sc. 7, l. 104. [Servant] The only use of "roguish."

8
Fool: Prithee, nuncle, tell me whether a madman be a gentleman or a yeoman?
Lear: A king, a king!
King Lear. Act iii, sc. 6, l. 10. "Nuncle" is used by the Fool fifteen times in *King Lear,* and occurs in no other play.

9
To deal plainly,
I fear I am not in my perfect mind.
King Lear. Act iv, sc. 7, l. 62. [King Lear]

10
It insinuateth me of insanie: anne intellegis domine? to make frantic, lunatic.
Love's Labour 's Lost. Act v, sc. 1, l. 28. [Holofernes] The only use of "insanie." "Insanity" does not occur in the plays.

Were such things here as we do speak about?
Or have we eaten on the insane root
That takes the reason prisoner?
Macbeth. Act i, sc. 3, l. 83. [Banquo] The only use of "insane."

11
Some say he 's mad: others that lesser hate him
Do call it valiant fury.
Macbeth. Act v, sc. 2, l. 13. [Caithness]

His actions show much like to madness: pray heaven his wisdom be not tainted!
Measure for Measure. Act iv, sc. 4, l. 4. [Angelo]

12
She speaks this in the infirmity of sense.
Measure for Measure. Act v, sc. 1, l. 47. [Duke]

Madly spoken.—*Measure for Measure,* v, 1, 89.
Madly-used.—*Twelfth Night,* v, 1, 319.

1 Neglect me not, with that opinion
That I am touch'd with madness!
Measure for Measure. Act v, sc. 1, l. 50. [Isabella]

2
Any madness I ever yet beheld seemed but tameness, civility and patience, to this his distemper he is in now.
The Merry Wives of Windsor. Act iv, sc. 2, l. 27. [Mrs. Page] "Tameness" is repeated in *King Lear,* iii, 6, 19.

I would not ha' your distemper in this kind for the wealth of Windsor Castle.
The Merry Wives of Windsor. Act iii, sc. 3, l. 31. [Page]

Provoked and instigated by his distemper.
The Merry Wives of Windsor. Act iii, sc. 5, l. 77. [Falstaff] The only use of "instigated."

He hath found
The head and source of all your son's distemper.
Hamlet. Act ii, sc. 2, l. 54. [King]

What is your cause of distemper?—*Hamlet,* iii, 2, 351.

Heat and flame of thy distemper.—*Hamlet,* iii, 4, 123. See under PATIENCE.

Drive away distemper.—*Cymbeline,* iii, 4, 194.

Proceeding on distemper.—*Henry V,* ii, 2, 54.

Puts some of us in distemper.—*The Winter's Tale,* i, 2, 385. "Distemper" is used once again, as a verb, in *Twelfth Night,* ii, 1, 5.

3
Fetter strong madness in a silken thread.
Much Ado about Nothing. Act v, sc. 1, l. 25. [Leonato]

4 Practising upon his peace and quiet
Even to madness.
Othello. Act ii, sc. 1, l. 319. [Iago]

Savage madness.—*Othello,* iv, 1, 56.

5 If I should despair, I should grow mad,
And in my madness might speak ill of thee.
Sonnets. No. cxl.

6
What, would you make me mad?
The Taming of the Shrew. Induction, sc. 2, l. 18. [Sly]

Why, how now, Kate! I hope thou art not mad.
The Taming of the Shrew. Act iv, sc. 5, l. 43. [Petruchio]

I have made you mad.—*The Tempest,* iii, 3, 58.

I fear, a madness held me.
The Tempest. Act v, sc. 1, l. 116. [Alonso]

Hiss me into madness.—*The Tempest,* ii, 2, 14.

7
Like madness is the glory of this life.
Timon of Athens, i, 2, 139. See under GLORY.

8
He is not with himself.
Titus Andronicus. Act i, sc. 1, l. 368. [Martius]

No man should be mad but I.
Titus Andronicus. Act iii, sc. 2, l. 24. [Titus]

I tell thee I am mad.
Troilus and Cressida. Act i, sc. 1, l. 51. [Troilus]

I'm worse than mad.—*Timon of Athens,* iii, 5, 106.

Am I mad?—*Romeo and Juliet,* v, 3, 80.

I think thou 'rt mad.—*Antony and Cleopatra,* ii, 7, 62.

For I have heard my grandsire say full oft,
Extremity of griefs would make men mad;
And I have read that Hecuba of Troy
Ran mad for sorrow.
Titus Andronicus. Act iv, sc. 1, l. 18. [Young Lucius]

9
With too much blood and too little brain, these two may run mad; but, if with too much brain and too little blood they do, I 'll be a curer of madmen.
Troilus and Cressida. Act v, sc. 1, l. 53. [Thersites] "Curer" is repeated in *The Merry Wives of Windsor,* ii, 3, 40: "Curer of bodies."

Of this madness cured.—*II Henry IV,* iv, 2, 41.

My negation hath no taste of madness.
Troilus and Cressida. Act v, sc. 2, l. 127. [Troilus] The only use of "negation." "Negative" occurs twice, in *Twelfth Night,* v, 1, 24, and *The Winter's Tale,* i, 2, 274.

O plague and madness!—*Troilus and Cressida,* v, 2, 35.

Madness of discourse.—*Troilus and Cressida.* v, 2, 142.

10
Why, this is very midsummer madness.
Twelfth Night. Act iii, sc. 4, l. 61. [Olivia] The only use of the phrase. "Midsummer" occurs twice more in the plays, in *As You Like It,* iv, 1, 103, and in *I Henry IV,* iv, 1, 102.

More matter for a May morning.
Twelfth Night. Act iii, sc. 4, l. 156. [Fabian]

11
My niece is already in the belief that he 's mad: we may carry it thus, for our pleasure and his penance, till our very pastime, tired out of breath, prompt us to have mercy on him: at which time we will bring the device to the bar and crown thee for a finder of madmen.
Twelfth Night. Act iii, sc. 4, l. 149. [Sir Toby] "Finder" is repeated in *Othello,* ii, 1, 246: "A finder of occasions."

The man grows mad: away with him.
Twelfth Night. Act iii, sc. 4, l. 405. [Officer]

12
My reason that persuades me
To any other trust but that I am mad
Or else the lady 's mad.
Twelfth Night. Act iv, sc. 3, l. 14. [Sebastian]

They say she 's mad.—*Coriolanus,* iv, 2, 9.

Being mad before, how doth she now for wits?
Venus and Adonis, l. 249. See also under WITS.

13
No settled senses of the world can match
The pleasure of that madness.
Winter's Tale. Act v, sc. 3, l. 72. [Leontes]

MAGIC

See also Charm, Conjuring, Witchcraft

14
I have, since I was three year old, conversed with a magician, most profound in his art and yet not damnable.
As You Like It. Act v, sc. 2, l. 66. [Rosalind]

I am a magician. Therefore, put on your best array.
As You Like It. Act v, sc. 2, l. 78. [Rosalind]

A great magician,
Obscured in the circle of this forest.
As You Like It. Act v, sc. 4, l. 33. [Orlando]
Great magician.—*I Henry IV*, i, 3, 85.
Black magician.—*Richard III*, i, 2, 34. The only uses of "magician."

1
They say this town is full of cozenage,
As, nimble jugglers that deceive the eye,
Dark-working sorcerers that change the mind,
Soul-killing witches that deform the body,
Disguised cheaters, prating mountebanks,
And many such-like liberties of sin.
The Comedy of Errors. Act i, sc. 2, l. 97. [Antipholus of Syracuse] The only use of "dark-working," "soul-killing," and "deform." "Cozenage" is repeated in *The Merry Wives of Windsor*, iv, 5, 64, and in *Hamlet*, v, 2, 67.
Stale juggler.—*II Henry IV*, ii, 4, 141.
Threadbare juggler.—*The Comedy of Errors*, v, 1, 239.
You juggler!—*A Midsummer-Night's Dream*, iii, 2, 282. The only uses of "juggler." "Juggled" occurs once, and "juggling" five times.
Sure, these are but imaginary wiles
And Lapland sorcerers inhabit here.
The Comedy of Errors. Act iv, sc. 3, l. 10. [Antipholus of Syracuse] The only mention of Lapland.
Conjurers and sorcerers, that afraid of him
By magic verses have contrived his end.
I Henry VI. Act i, sc. 1, l. 26. [Exeter]
Subject to a sorcerer.—*The Tempest*, iii, 2, 49. The only uses of "sorcerer."

2
Thou art, as you are all, a sorceress:
I conjure thee to leave me and be gone.
The Comedy of Errors. Act iv, sc. 3, l. 67. [Antipholus of Syracuse]
Bring forth that sorceress condemn'd to burn.
I Henry VI. Act v, sc. 4, l. 1. [York]
Damned sorceress.—*I Henry VI*, iii, 2, 38. The only uses of "sorceress."

3
Fell banning hag, enchantress.
I Henry VI. Act v, sc. 3, l. 42. [York] The only use of "banning" and "enchantress."

4
This is the foul fiend Flibbertigibbet: he begins at curfew, and walks till the first cock; he gives the web and the pin, squints the eye, and makes the hare-lip; mildews the white wheat, and hurts the poor creature of earth.
King Lear. Act iii, sc. 4, l. 120. [Edgar] Flibbertigibbet is mentioned again in iv, 1, 64; "hare-lip" in *A Midsummer-Night's Dream*, v, 1, 418. "Curfew" is repeated in *Measure for Measure*, iv, 2, 78, and in *The Tempest*, v, 1, 40. "Curfew-bell" occurs in *Romeo and Juliet*, iv, 4, 4.
Distill'd by magic sleights
Shall raise some artificial sprites.
Macbeth. Act iii, sc. 5, l. 26. [Hecate] The only use of "sleights." "Sleight" occurs in *III Henry VI*, iv, 2, 20.

5
We are simple men; we do not know what 's brought to pass under the profession of fortune-telling. She works by charms, by spells, by the figure, and such daubery as this is, beyond our element: we know nothing.
The Merry Wives of Windsor. Act iv, sc. 2, l. 182. [Ford] The only use of "daubery."
I 'll conjure you, I 'll fortune-tell you!
The Merry Wives of Windsor. Act iv, sc. 2, l. 196. [Ford]
A thread-bare juggler and a fortune-teller.
The Comedy of Errors. Act v, sc. 1, l. 239. [Angelo] The only uses of "fortune-telling," "fortune-tell," and "fortune-teller." "Thread-bare" is repeated in *II Henry VI*, iv, 2, 8.

6
I'll refer me to all things of sense,
If she in chains of magic were not bound.
Othello. Act i, sc. 2, l. 64. [Brabantio]
I therefore apprehend and do attach thee
For an abuser of the world, a practiser
Of arts inhibited and out of warrant.
Othello. Act i, sc. 2, l. 77. [Brabantio] The only use of "abuser." "Practiser" is repeated in *All's Well that Ends Well*, ii, 1, 188: "Sweet practiser." "Practisers" occurs in *Love's Labour's Lost*, iv, 3, 325: "Barren practisers." "Inhibited" is used again in *All 's Well that Ends Well*, i, 1, 157.

7
There 's magic in the web of it:
A sibyl, that had number'd in the world
The sun to course two hundred compasses,
In her prophetic fury sew'd the work;
The worms were hallow'd that did breed the silk;
And it was dyed in mummy which the skilful
Conserved of maidens' hearts.
Othello. Act iii, sc. 4, l. 69. [Othello] The only use of "conserved." "Mummy" is repeated in *The Merry Wives of Windsor*, iii, 5, 18, and in *Macbeth*, iv, 1, 23.
The nine sibyls of old Rome.—*I Henry VI*, i, 2, 56.
Sibyl's leaves.—*Titus Andronicus*, iv, 1, 105.
As old as Sibyl.—*The Taming of the Shrew*, i, 2, 70. The only uses of Sibyl.
As old as Sibylla.—*The Merchant of Venice*, i, 2, 116. The only use of Sibylla.

8
I say, by sorcery he got this isle.
The Tempest. Act iii, sc. 2, l. 60. [Caliban]
Baleful sorcery.—*I Henry VI*, ii, 1, 15.
Sorceries terrible.—*The Tempest*, i, 2, 264. The only uses of "sorcery" and "sorcerers."

9
Pluck my magic garment from me.
The Tempest. Act i, sc. 2, l. 24. [Prospero]
This rough magic I here abjure.
The Tempest. Act v, sc. 1, l. 50. [Prospero]
And there is in this business more than nature
Was ever conduct of.
The Tempest. Act v, sc. 1, l. 243. [Alonso]

10
O royal piece, There 's magic in thy majesty.
Winter's Tale. Act v, sc. 3, l. 38. [Leontes]
If this be magic, let it be an art
Lawful as eating.
Winter's Tale. Act v, sc. 3, l. 110. [Leontes]
Mighty magic.—*Othello*, i, 3, 92.
Natural magic.—*Hamlet*, iii, 2, 270.
Magic of bounty!—*Timon of Athens*, i, 1, 6.

Magical word.—*Antony and Cleopatra,* iii, 1, 31. The only use of "magical."

MAID

See also Girl

1
I 'll like a maid the better, whilst I have a tooth in my head.
All's Well that Ends Well. Act ii, sc. 3, l. 47. [Lafeu]

If thou canst like this creature as a maid,
I can create the rest: virtue and she
Is her own dower; honour and wealth from me.
All's Well that Ends Well. Act ii, sc. 3, l. 149. [King]

A maid too virtuous
For the contempt of empire.
All's Well that Ends Well, iii, 2, 33. See under RASHNESS.

2 This young maid might do her
A shrewd turn.
All's Well that Ends Well. Act iii, sc. 5, l. 70. [Widow]

Here 's a young maid with travel much oppress'd
And faints for succour.
As You Like It. Act ii, sc. 4, l. 74. [Rosalind]

O heavens! is 't possible, a young maid's wits
Should be as mortal as an old man's life?
Hamlet. Act iv, sc. 5, l. 159. [Laertes]

A fair young maid that yet wants baptism.
Henry VIII. Act v, sc. 3, l. 162. [King] "Young maid" is repeated in *As You Like It,* iii, 2, 331, and in *Othello,* i, 3, 112.

3 But, fair soul,
In your fine frame hath love no quality?
If the quick fire of youth light not your mind,
You are no maiden, but a monument.
All's Well that Ends Well. Act iv, sc. 2, l. 3. [Bertram]

Since Frenchmen are so braid,
Marry that will, I live and die a maid.
All's Well that Ends Well. Act iv, sc. 2, l. 73. [Diana] The only use of "braid" in this sense (deceitful).

Cold maids.—*Hamlet,* iv, 7, 172.

4
You are come A market-maid to Rome.
Antony and Cleopatra. Act iii, sc. 6, l. 51. [Cæsar] The only use of "market-maid."

Country maid.—*Love's Labour's Lost,* iii, 1, 132.

5
Alas, what danger will it be to us,
Maids as we are, to travel forth so far!
As You Like It. Act i, sc. 3, l. 110. [Rosalind]

Speak, sad brow and true maid.
As You Like It. Act iii, sc. 2, l. 226. [Rosalind] The only use of "true maid."

6
Maids are May when they are maids, but the sky changes when they are wives.
As You Like It. Act iv, sc. 1, l. 148. [Rosalind]

O rose of May! Dear maid.
Hamlet. Act iv, sc. 5, l. 157. [Laertes] "Dear maid" is used only once again, in *Measure for Measure,* v, 1, 393.

7
The chariest maid is prodigal enough,
If she unmask her beauty to the moon.
Hamlet. Act i, sc. 3, l. 36. [Laertes] The only use of "chariest."

8
Yet here she is allow'd her virgin crants,
Her maiden strewments.
Hamlet. Act v, sc. 1, l. 255. [First Priest] The only use of "crants" and "strewments." The former was a garland carried before the bier of a maid and hung over her grave; the latter, flowers strewn on a grave. "Strewings" in the same sense occurs in *Cymbeline,* iv, 2, 285.

I thought thy bride-bed to have deck'd, sweet maid,
And not have strew'd thy grave.
Hamlet. Act v, sc. 1, l. 268. [Queen] "Bride-bed" is repeated in *A Midsummer-Night's Dream,* v, 1, 410; and "sweet maid" in *The Winter's Tale,* iv, 4, 92.

9
A maid yet rosed over with the virgin crimson of modesty.
Henry V. Act v, sc. 2, l. 323. [Burgundy] "Rosed" is repeated in *Titus Andronicus,* ii, 4, 24: "Rosed lips."

Maids, well summered and warm kept, are like flies at Bartholomew-tide, blind, though they have their eyes; and then they will endure handling, which before would not abide looking on.
Henry V. Act v, sc. 2, l. 335. [Burgundy] The only use of "summered" and "Bartholomew-tide" (24 August).

10
What is 't to me, when you yourselves are cause,
If your pure maidens fall into the hand
Of hot and forcing violation?
Henry V. Act iii, sc. 3, l. 19. [King Henry] The only use of "pure maidens." "Pure maid" occurs in *A Lover's Complaint,* l. 315.

Yet they do wink and yield, as love is blind and enforces.
Henry V. Act v, sc. 2, l. 327. [King Henry]

11
A holy maid hither with me I bring,
Which by a vision sent to her from heaven
Ordained is to raise this tedious siege
And drive the English forth from the bounds of France.
I Henry VI. Act i, sc. 2, l. 51. [Bastard] "Holy maid" is repeated in v, 4, 65, and occurs in no other play.

Burgundy: What 's that Pucelle whom they term so pure?
Talbot: A maid, they say.
Bedford: A maid! and be so martial!
Burgundy: Pray God she prove not masculine ere long,
If underneath the standard of the French
She carry armour as she hath begun.
I Henry VI. Act ii, sc. 1, l. 20. "Masculine" is repeated in *Troilus and Cressida,* v, 1, 20: "Masculine whore"; and in *Twelfth Night,* v, 1, 257: "Masculine attire."

12
Thou maiden youth, be vanquish'd by a maid.
I Henry VI. Act iv, sc. 7, l. 38. [La Pucelle]

In maiden meditation fancy-free.
A Midsummer-Night's Dream. Act ii, sc. 1, l. 164. [Oberon] The only use of either "maiden meditation" or "fancy-free."

Maiden pride, adieu!
Much Ado about Nothing. Act iii, sc. 1, l. 109. [Beatrice]

Maiden battle.—*Troilus and Cressida,* iv, 5, 87.
Maiden bed.—*All's Well that Ends Well,* iv, 2, 57.
Maiden blood.—*I Henry VI,* v, 4, 52; *Titus Andronicus,* ii, 3, 232.
Maiden blossom.—*I Henry VI,* ii, 4, 47; 75.
Maiden blush.—*Romeo and Juliet,* ii, 2, 86; *Henry V,* v, 2, 253.
Maiden cities.—*Henry V,* v, 2, 353.
Maiden council.—*Love's Labour's Lost,* v, 2, 789.
Maiden honour.—*Love's Labour's Lost,* v, 2, 351.
Maiden modesty.—*Much Ado about Nothing,* iv, 1, 181.
Maiden pilgrimage.—*A Midsummer-Night's Dream,* i, 1, 75.
Maiden presence.—*Hamlet,* i, 3, 121.
Maiden shame.—*Midsummer-Night's Dream,* iii, 2, 285.
Maiden sword.—*I Henry IV,* v, 4, 134.
Maiden virtue.—*King John,* ii, 1, 98; *Sonnets,* lxvi.
Maiden weeds.—*Twelfth Night,* v, 1, 262.

1 He that wins of all,
Of kings, of beggars, old men, young men, maids,
Who, having no external thing to lose
But the word 'maid,' cheats the poor maid of that.
King John. Act ii, sc. 1, l. 569. [Bastard]

Poor lowly maid.—*The Winter's Tale,* iv, 4, 9.

2
The gods to their dear shelter take thee, maid,
That justly think'st, and hast most rightly said!
King Lear. Act i, sc. 1, l. 184. [Kent]

Not all the dukes of waterish Burgundy
Can buy this unprized precious maid of me.
King Lear. Act i, sc. 1, l. 261. [King of France] "Waterish" occurs again in *Othello,* iii, 3, 15. The only use of "unprized."

3
A maid of grace and complete majesty.
Love's Labour's Lost. Act i, sc. 1, l. 137. [Biron]

An honest maid as ever broke bread.
The Merry Wives of Windsor. Act i, sc. 4, l. 160. [Mistress Quickly] The only use of "honest maid."

A very virtuous maid.
Measure for Measure. Act ii, sc. 2, l. 20. [Provost] Also *Twelfth Night,* i, 2, 36.

Never could the strumpet,
With all her double vigour, art and nature,
Once stir my temper: but this virtuous maid
Subdues me quite.
Measure for Measure. Act ii, sc. 2, l. 183. [Angelo]

Fire-eyed maid.—*I Henry IV,* iv, 1, 114. "Fire-eyed" is repeated in *Romeo and Juliet,* iii, 1, 129: "Fire-eyed fury."

Gentle maid.—*All's Well that Ends Well,* iii, 5, 100; *A Lover's Complaint,* l. 177.
Gentle maiden.—*The Winter's Tale,* iv, 4, 85.
Kind maid.—*All's Well that Ends Well,* ii, 1, 148; *Measure for Measure,* v, 1, 398.
Lovely maid.—*King John,* ii, 1, 425.
Proper maid.—*All's Well that Ends Well,* iv, 3, 240.

4
Ere long espied a fickle maid full pale,
Tearing of papers, breaking rings a-twain,
Storming her world with sorrow's wind and rain.
A Lover's Complaint, l. 5. "A-twain" is repeated in *King Lear,* ii, 2, 80.

False maids.—*Troilus and Cressida,* iii, 2, 197.

5
He preached pure maid, and praised cold chastity.
A Lover's Complaint, l. 315.

6 When maidens sue,
Men give like gods; but when they weep and kneel,
All their petitions are as freely theirs
As they themselves would owe them.
Measure for Measure. Act i, sc. 4, l. 80. [Lucio]

Fasting maids whose minds are dedicate
To nothing temporal.
Measure for Measure, ii, 2, 154. See under PRAYER.

7
This forenamed maid hath yet in her the continuance of her first affection.
Measure for Measure. Act iii, sc. 1, l. 248. [Duke] The only use of "forenamed."

The maid will I frame and make fit for his attempt.
Measure for Measure. Act iii, sc. 1, l. 268. [Duke]

I pray you, be acquainted with this maid;
She comes to do you good.
Measure for Measure. Act iv, sc. 1, l. 51. [Duke]

8 I am not solely led
By nice direction of a maiden's eyes.
The Merchant of Venice. Act ii, sc. 1, l. 13. [Portia]

A maiden hath no tongue but thought.
The Merchant of Venice. Act iii, sc. 2, l. 8. [Portia]

9 Go you, and where you find a maid
That, ere she sleep, has thrice her prayers said,
Raise up the organs of her fantasy;
Sleep she as sound as careless infancy.
The Merry Wives of Windsor. Act v, sc. 5, l. 53. [Evans]

10
This is he, my master said,
Despised the Athenian maid;
And here the maiden, sleeping sound,
On the dank and dirty ground.
Pretty soul! she durst not lie
Near this lack-love, this kill-courtesy.
A Midsummer-Night's Dream. Act ii, sc. 2, l. 72. [Puck] The only use of "lack-love" and "kill-courtesy."

Reason says you are the worthier maid.
A Midsummer-Night's Dream, ii, 2, 116. See under REASON.

'Tis not maidenly.—*A Midsummer-Night's Dream,* iii, 2, 217. "Maidenly" is repeated in *II Henry IV,* ii, 2, 82: "Maidenly man-at-arms."

1
Leonato: Well, then, go you into hell?
Beatrice: No, but to the gate; and there will the devil meet me, like an old cuckold, with horns on his head, and say 'Get you to heaven, Beatrice, get you to heaven; here 's no place for you maids.'
Much Ado about Nothing. Act ii, sc. 1, l. 44.

Beatrice: I am stuffed, cousin; I cannot smell.
Margaret: A maid, and stuffed! there 's goodly catching of cold.
Beatrice: O, God help me! God help me! how long have you professed apprehension?
Much Ado about Nothing. Act iii, sc. 4, l. 64.

2 Would you not swear,
All you that see her, that she were a maid?
Much Ado about Nothing. Act iv, sc. 1, l. 39. [Claudio]

And surely as I live, I am a maid.
Much Ado about Nothing. Act v, sc. 4, l. 64. [Hero]

I am a simple maid, and therein wealthiest,
That I protest I simply am a maid.
All's Well that Ends Well. Act ii, sc. 3, l. 72. [Helena] The only use of "wealthiest."

I am a right maid for my cowardice.
A Midsummer-Night's Dream. Act iii, sc. 2, l. 302. [Helena]

I am a maid,
My lord, that ne'er before invited eyes,
But have been gazed on like a comet.
Pericles. Act v, sc. 1, l. 85. [Marina]

3
Whether a maid so tender, fair and happy,
So opposite to marriage . . .
Would ever have, to incur a general mock,
Run from her guardage to the sooty bosom
Of such a thing as thou.
Othello. Act i, sc. 2, l. 66. [Brabantio] The only use of "guardage" and "sooty."

A maiden never bold;
Of spirit so still and quiet, that her motion
Blush'd at herself.
Othello. Act i, sc. 3, l. 94. [Brabantio]

A maid
That paragons description and wild fame;
One that excels the quirks of blazoning pens,
And in the essential vesture of creation
Does tire the ingener.
Othello. Act ii, sc. 1, l. 61. [Cassio] The only use of "essential" and "ingener."

4
My mother had a maid call'd Barbara:
She was in love, and he she loved proved mad
And did forsake her.
Othello. Act iv, sc. 3, l. 26. [Desdemona]

5 For me,
That am a maid, though most ungentle fortune
Have placed me in this sty, where, since I came,
Diseases have been sold dearer than physic,
O, that the gods
Would set me free from this unhallow'd place,
Though they did change me to the meanest bird
That flies i' the purer air!
Pericles. Act iv, sc. 6, l. 102. [Marina]

Lord: We have a maid in Mytilene, I durst wager,
Would win some words of him.
Lysimachus: 'Tis well bethought.
She questionless with her sweet harmony
And other chosen attractions, would allure,
And make a battery through his deafen'd parts.
Pericles. Act v, sc. 1, l. 43. "Questionless" is repeated in *Merchant of Venice,* i, 1, 176.

6 Ay me! poor maid,
Born in a tempest, when my mother died.
Pericles. Act iv, sc. 1, l. 18. [Marina]

A maid-child call'd Marina.—*Pericles,* v, 3, 6. The only use of "maid-child."

Poor maid.—*A Midsummer-Night's Dream,* iii, 2, 158; *All 's Well that Ends Well,* v, 3, 146; *King John,* ii, 1, 572; *Measure for Measure,* iii, 1, 241.

7
I, a maid, die maiden-widowed.
Romeo and Juliet. Act iii, sc. 2, l. 135. [Juliet] The only use of "maiden-widowed."

8 In the other's silence do I see
Maid's mild behavior and sobriety.
The Taming of the Shrew. Act i, sc. 1, l. 70. [Lucentio] "Sobriety" is repeated in *Henry V,* 4, 1, 74.

Master, you look'd so longly on the maid,
Perhaps you mark'd not what 's the pith of all.
The Taming of the Shrew. Act i, sc. 1, l. 170. [Tranio] The only use of "longly."

If you love the maid,
Bend thoughts and wits to achieve her. Thus it stands:
Her elder sister is so curst and shrewd
That till the father rid his hands of her,
Master, your love must live a maid at home;
And therefore he has closely mewed her up.
The Taming of the Shrew. Act i, sc. 1, l. 183. [Tranio]

Katharine the curst!
A title for maid of all titles the worst.
The Taming of the Shrew. Act i, sc. 2, l. 129. [Grumio]

Why, then the maid is mine from all the world.
The Taming of the Shrew. Act ii, sc. 1, l. 386. [Tranio]

9
Fair lovely maid, once more good day to thee.
The Taming of the Shrew. Act iv, sc. 5, l. 33. [Petruchio]

The maid is fair, o' the youngest for a bride.
Timon of Athens, i, 1, 123. See under DAUGHTER.

I am slain by a fair cruel maid.
Twelfth Night. Act ii, sc. 4, l. 55. [Song]

Fair maid.—*I Henry VI,* i, 2, 64; *Romeo and Juliet,* iv, 5, 67; *All 's Well that Ends Well,* ii, 3, 58; *Measure for Measure,* ii, 2, 79; ii, 4, 30; *A Midsummer-Night's Dream,* i, 1, 46.

Fair French maid.—*Henry V,* v, 2, 345.

1
Ferdinand: My prime request,
Which I do last pronounce, is, O you wonder!
If you be maid or no?
Miranda: No wonder, sir;
But certainly a maid.
The Tempest. Act i, sc. 2, l. 425.
What is this maid with whom thou wast at play?
The Tempest. Act v, sc. 1, l. 185. [Alonso]
This maid is mine.—*Titus Andronicus,* i, 1, 276.
Free maids.—*Twelfth Night,* ii, 4, 46.
Pale-visaged maids.—*King John,* v, 2, 154. The only use of "pale-visaged."
Pining maidens.—*Henry V,* ii, 4, 107.
Reconciled maid.—*A Lover's Complaint,* l. 329.
Tongue-tied maidens.—*Troilus and Cressida,* iii, 2, 219. See under CUPID.

II—Maid and No Maid

2
He knows I am no maid, and he 'll swear to 't;
I 'll swear I am a maid, and he knows not.
Great king, I am no strumpet, by my life;
I am either maid, or else this old man's wife.
All's Well that Ends Well. Act v, sc. 3, l. 291. [Diana]
I confess besides I am no maid.
Measure for Measure. Act v, sc. 1, l. 185. [Mariana]
3
Then up he rose, and donn'd his clothes,
And dupp'd the chamber door;
Let in the maid, that out a maid
Never departed more.
Hamlet. Act iv, sc. 5, l. 52. [Ophelia] The only use of "dupp'd" (opened).
She that 's a maid now, and laughs at my departure,
Shall not be a maid long, unless things be cut shorter.
King Lear. Act i, sc. 5, l. 55. [Fool]
4
Costard: I deny her virginity: I was taken with a maid.
King: This maid will not serve your turn, sir.
Costard: This maid will serve my turn, sir.
Love's Labour 's Lost. Act i, sc. 1, l. 298.
5
Duke Vincentio: What, are you married?
Mariana: No, my lord.
Duke Vincentio: Are you a maid?
Mariana: No, my lord.
Duke Vincentio: A widow, then?
Mariana: Neither, my lord.
Duke Vincentio: Why, you are nothing then: neither maid, widow, nor wife?
Lucio: My lord, she may be a punk; for many of them are neither maid, widow, nor wife.
Measure for Measure. Act v, sc. 1, l. 171.
A deflower'd maid.—*Measure for Measure,* iv, 4, 24. See also under RAPE.
Wronged maid.—*Measure for Measure,* iii, 1, 260.

6
Falstaff: Good maid, then.
Mistress Quickly: I 'll be sworn,
As my mother was, the first hour I was born.
Merry Wives of Windsor. Act ii, sc. 2, l. 37.
Cozened with the semblance of a maid.
Much Ado about Nothing. Act ii, sc. 2, l. 39. [Borachio]
7
Did you by indirect and forced courses
Subdue and poison this young maid's affections?
Or came it by request and such fair question
As soul to soul affordeth?
Othello. Act i, sc. 3, l. 111. [First Senator]
8
This is the hag, when maids lie on their backs,
That presses them and learns them first to bear,
Making them women of good carriage.
Romeo and Juliet. Act i, sc. 4, l. 92. [Mercutio]
9
'Tis a milkmaid; yet 'tis not a maid, for she hath had gossips; yet 'tis a maid, for she is her master's maid, and serves for wages.
The Two Gentlemen of Verona. Act iii, sc. 1, l. 268. [Launce] "Milkmaid" occurs only once more in the plays, in *Measure for Measure,* i, 2, 177.

MAIDENHEAD

See also Virginity

10
Why, then, it is like, if there come a hot June and this civil buffeting hold, we shall buy maidenheads as they buy hob-nails, by the hundreds.
I Henry IV. Act ii, sc. 4, l. 396. [Prince of Wales] The only use of "buffeting." June is mentioned again in the same play, iii, 2, 75, and in *Antony and Cleopatra,* iii, 10, 14. "Hobnails" occurs again in *II Henry VI,* iv, 10, 63.
Is 't such a matter to get a pottle-pot's maidenhead?
II Henry IV. Act ii, sc. 2, l. 83. [Bardolph] "Pottle-pot" occurs again in v, 3, 68, and in no other play.
Maidenhead of our affairs.—*I Henry IV,* iv, 1, 59.
11
Drew blood
From thee, my boy, and had the maidenhood
Of thy first fight.
I Henry VI. Act iv, sc. 6, l. 16. [Talbot]
Wreck of maidenhood.—*All's Well that Ends Well,* iii, 5, 24. The only uses of "maidenhood." "Maidhood" occurs twice, in *Twelfth Night,* iii, 1, 162, and in *Othello,* i, 1, 173.
A pair of stainless maidenhoods.—*Romeo and Juliet,* iii, 2, 13. The only use of "maidenhoods."
12
There shall not a maid be married, but she shall pay to me her maidenhead ere they have it.
II Henry VI. Act iv, sc. 7, l. 129. [Cade]
Venture maidenhead.—*Henry VIII,* ii, 3, 25.

1
Such a maidenhead were no cheap thing, if men were as they have been.
Pericles. Act iv, sc. 2, l. 64. [Bawd]
I must have your maidenhead taken off, or the common hangman shall execute it.
Pericles. Act iv, sc. 6, l. 136. [Boult]
Loss of maidenhead.—*Pericles,* iii, Gower, 10.
2
If fires be hot, knives sharp, or waters deep,
Untied I still my virgin knot will keep.
Pericles. Act iv, sc. 2, l. 159. [Marina]
If thou dost break her virgin-knot before
All sanctimonious ceremonies may
With full and holy rite be minister'd . . . barren hate,
Sour-eyed disdain and discord shall bestrew
The union of your bed with weeds so loathly
That you shall hate it both.
The Tempest. Act iv, sc. 1, l. 15. [Prospero]
The only uses of "virgin-knot" and "sour-eyed." "Sanctimonious" is repeated in *Measure for Measure,* i, 2, 7: "Sanctimonious pirate"; and "loathly" in *II Henry IV,* iv, 4, 122, and in *King Lear,* ii, 1, 51.
3
Sampson: When I have fought with the men, I will be cruel with the maids, and cut off the heads.
Gregory: The heads of the maids?
Sampson: Ay, the heads of the maids, or their maidenheads; take it in what sense thou wilt.
Gregory: They must take it in the sense that feel it.
Sampson: Me they shall feel while I am able to stand and 'tis known I am a pretty piece of flesh.
Romeo and Juliet. Act i, sc. 1, l. 27.
Now, by my maidenhead.
Romeo and Juliet. Act i, sc. 3, l. 2. [Nurse]
By my troth and maidenhead.
Henry VIII. Act ii, sc. 3, l. 23. [Anne]
I 'll to my wedding-bed;
And death, not Romeo, take my maidenhead!
Romeo and Juliet. Act iii, sc. 2, l. 136. [Juliet]
4
Carouse full measure to her maidenhead.
The Taming of the Shrew. Act iii, sc. 2, l. 227. [Petruchio]
How go maidenheads?—*Troilus and Cressida,* iv, 2, 23.
As secret as maidenhead.—*Twelfth Night,* i, 5, 232.
5
I would I had some flowers o' the spring that might
Become your time of day; and yours, and yours,
That wear upon your virgin branches yet
Your maidenheads growing.
Winter's Tale. Act iv, sc. 4, l. 113. [Perdita]

MAJESTY

See also King

6 Dull of tongue, and dwarfish!
What majesty is in her gait? Remember,
If e'er thou look'dst on majesty.
Antony and Cleopatra. Act iii, sc. 3, l. 19. [Cleopatra]
The man hath seen some majesty, and should know.
Antony and Cleopatra. Act iii, sc. 3, l. 45. [Cleopatra]
Majesty, to keep decorum, must
No less beg than a kingdom.
Antony and Cleopatra. Act v, sc. 2, l. 17. [Cleopatra]
7 The cease of majesty
Dies not alone; but, like a gulf, doth draw
What 's near it with it: it is a massy wheel,
Fix'd on the summit of the highest mount,
To whose huge spokes ten thousand lesser things
Are mortised and adjoin'd; which, when it falls,
Each small annexment, petty consequence,
Attends the boisterous ruin.
Hamlet. Act iii, sc. 3, l. 15. [Rosencrantz]
The only use of "mortised," "adjoin'd," and "annexment." "Mortise" occurs in *Othello,* ii, 1, 9.
Where is the beauteous majesty of Denmark?
Hamlet. Act v, sc. 1, l. 21. [Ophelia] "Majesty of buried Denmark" occurs in i, 1, 48.
8 Majesty might never yet endure
The moody frontier of a servant brow.
I Henry IV. Act i, sc. 3, l. 18. [King Henry]
Majestically, both in word and matter.
I Henry IV. Act ii, sc. 4, l. 479. [Falstaff]
The only use of "majestically."
9 O majesty!
When thou dost pinch thy bearer, thou dost sit
Like a rich armour worn in heat of day
That scalds with safety.
II Henry IV. Act iv, sc. 5, l. 28. [Prince of Wales]
This new and gorgeous garment, majesty,
Sits not so easy on me as you think.
II Henry IV. Act v, sc. 2, l. 44. [King Henry V]
10
For that I have laid by my majesty
And plodded like a man for working-days.
Henry V. Act i, sc. 2, l. 276. [King Henry]
"Plodded" is repeated in *II Henry VI,* iv, 1, 54. "Working-days" occurs four times.
11
I need not to be ashamed of your majesty, praised be God, so long as your majesty is an honest man.
Henry V. Act iv, sc. 7, l. 118. [Fluellen]
God save your majesty!—*Richard II,* ii, 2, 41; *II Henry VI,* iv, 2, 77; iv, 8, 15; *Henry V,* v, 2, 307.
God save his majesty.—*The Tempest,* ii, 1, 168.
"His majesty" and "your majesty" are repeated many times throughout the plays.
12
Methought I sat in seat of majesty
In the cathedral church of Westminster,
And in that chair where kings and queens are crown'd.
II Henry VI. Act i, sc. 2, l. 36. [Duchess of Gloucester]

With what a majesty he bears himself.
II Henry VI. Act iii, sc. 1, l. 6. [Queen Margaret]

Ah! sancta majestas, who would not buy thee dear?
II Henry VI. Act v, sc. 1, l. 5. [York] The only use of "sancta majestas."

1
Chatillon: The majesty,
The borrow'd majesty, of England here.
Queen Elinor: A strange beginning: 'borrow'd majesty!'
King John. Act i, sc. 1, l. 3.

Ha, majesty! how high thy glory towers,
When the rich blood of kings is set on fire!
King John. Act ii, sc. 1, l. 350. [Bastard]

King Philip: Have I not pawn'd to you my majesty?
Constance: You have beguiled me with a counterfeit
Resembling majesty, which, being touch'd and tried,
Proves valueless.
King John. Act iii, sc. 1, l. 98. The only use of "valueless."

2
Power,
Pre-eminence, and all the large effects
That troop with majesty.
King Lear. Act i, sc. 1, l. 132. [King Lear] "Pre-eminence" occurs again in *The Comedy of Errors*, ii, 1, 23.

To plainness honour 's bound,
When majesty stoops to folly.
King Lear. Act i, sc. 1, l. 150. [Kent]

3
I sue for exiled majesty's repeal;
Let him return, and flattering thoughts retire.
The Rape of Lucrece, l. 640.

O fair return of banish'd majesty!
King John. Act iii, sc. 1, l. 321. [Constance]

Anointed majesty.—*I Henry IV*, iv, 3, 40.
Complete majesty.—*Love's Labour 's Lost*, i, 1, 137.
Dangerous majesty.—*King John*, iv, 2, 213.
Dear majesty.—*Hamlet*, ii, 2, 135.
Formal majesty.—*II Henry IV*, v, 2, 133.
Gentle majesty.—*Venus and Adonis*, l. 278.
Good majesty.—*Antony and Cleopatra*, iii, 3, 2.
Grim majesty.—*II Henry VI*, iii, 2, 50.
High majesty.—*Richard II*, ii, 1, 295.
Imperial majesty.—*II Henry VI*, i, 1, 1; *Henry V*, v, 2, 26.
Peaceful majesty.—*III Henry VI*, iv, 6, 71.
Proud majesty.—*Richard II*, iv, 1, 252.
Royal majesty.—*II Henry VI*, i, 2, 70; i, 3, 215; *Richard II*, ii, 1, 120.
Sacred majesty.—*Sonnets*, vii.
Sun-like majesty.—*I Henry IV*, iii, 2, 79. The only use of "sun-like."
Sweet majesty.—*Love's Labour 's Lost*, v, 2, 888; *Richard II*, ii, 2, 20; *Henry V*, iv, Prol., 40.
Tired majesty.—*Richard II*, iv, 1, 178.

4
Awake, thou coward majesty! thou sleepest.
Richard II. Act iii, sc. 2, l. 84. [King Richard]

I am unfit for state and majesty.
Richard III. Act iii, sc. 7, l. 205. [Gloucester]

MALADY, see Disease

MALICE

5
His malice 'gainst the lady
Will suddenly break forth.
As You Like It. Act i, sc. 2, l. 294. [Le Beau]

6
Speak not maliciously.
Coriolanus. Act i, sc. 1, l. 35. [Citizen]

Fight maliciously.—*Antony and Cleopatra*, iii, 13, 179.
Work Maliciously.—*The Winter's Tale*, i, 2, 321. The only uses of "maliciously."

7
A malice, that, giving itself the lie, would pluck reproof and rebuke from every ear that heard it.
Coriolanus. Act ii, sc. 2, l. 36. [Officer]

Translate his malice towards you into love.
Coriolanus. Act ii, sc. 3, l. 197. [Brutus]

Spend my malice.—*Coriolanus*, ii, 1, 58.

8
A thing more made of malice than of duty.
Cymbeline. Act iii, sc. 5, l. 33. [Cymbeline]

One of her malice.—*Cymbeline*, i, 5, 35.

Malice and lucre in them
Have laid this woe here.
Cymbeline. Act iv, sc. 2, l. 324. [Imogen] "Lucre" is used only once again, in *I Henry VI*, v, 4, 141.

9
Beside, I fear me, if thy thoughts were sifted,
The king, thy sovereign, is not quite exempt
From envious malice of thy swelling heart.
I Henry VI. Act iii, sc. 1, l. 24. [Gloucester] The only use of "sifted."

Ancient malice.—*Coriolanus*, ii, 1, 244; iv, 5, 100; *Richard II*, i, 1, 9.
Deepest malice.—*Coriolanus*, iv, 6, 41.
Grounded malice.—*Richard III*, i, 3, 29.
Heart's malice.—*II Henry VI*, iii, 1, 154.
Inveterate malice.—*Richard II*, i, 1, 14.
Poor malice.—*Macbeth*, iii, 2, 14.
Private malice.—*Henry VIII*, iii, 2, 268.
Sportful malice.—*Twelfth Night*, v, 1, 373.
Fortune's malice.—*III Henry VI*, iv, 3, 46; iv, 6, 28.
Cardinal's malice.—*Henry VIII*, i, 1, 105.
Servant's malice.—*II Henry VI*, i, 3, 213.
Malice and displeasure.—*Coriolanus*, ii, 2, 24; iv, 5, 78.
The malice of this age.—*II Henry IV*, i, 2, 195.

10
I have heard you preach
That malice was a great and grievous sin.
I Henry VI. Act iii, sc. 1, l. 127. [King Henry]

Gloucester: Churchmen so hot? good uncle, hide such malice;
With such holiness can you do it?
Suffolk: No malice, sir; no more than well becomes
So good a quarrel and so bad a peer.
II Henry VI. Act ii, sc. 1, l. 23.

God forbid any malice should prevail,
That faultless may condemn a nobleman!
II Henry VI. Act iii, sc. 2, l. 23. [Queen] "Faultless" is repeated in ii, 1, 189, and in *Richard III*, i, 3, 78. It occurs only in these earliest plays.

1 Malicious censurers; which ever,
As ravenous fishes, do a vessel follow
That is new-trimm'd.
Henry VIII. Act i, sc. 2, l. 78. [Wolsey]
The only use of "censurers" and "new-trimm'd." "Malicious" occurs twelve times.

2
If ever any malice in your heart
Were hid against me, now to forgive me frankly.
Henry VIII. Act ii, sc. 1, l. 80. [Lovell]
Out of malice.—*Henry VIII,* ii, 1, 157.
More out of malice than integrity.—*Henry VIII,* v, 3, 145.

3
You are potently opposed; and with a malice
Of as great size.
Henry VIII. Act v, sc. 1, l. 134. [King Henry]
This is a piece of malice.
Henry VIII. Act v, sc. 1, l. 8. [Doctor Butts]
Men that make
Envy and crooked malice nourishment
Dare bite the best.
Henry VIII. Act v, sc. 3, l. 43. [Cranmer]

4
God turn their hearts! I never sought their malice.
Henry VIII. Act v, sc. 2, l. 15. [Cranmer]
I bear no malice.—*Henry VIII,* ii, 1, 62.
Malice ne'er meant.—*Henry VIII,* ii, 2, 69.
Without any malice.—*All's Well that Ends Well,* iii, 6, 9.

5
You shall do small respect, show too bold malice
Against the grace and person of my master.
King Lear. Act ii, sc. 2, l. 137. [Kent]

6
In the great hand of God I stand; and thence
Against the undivulged pretence I fight
Of treasonous malice.
Macbeth. Act ii, sc. 3, l. 136. [Banquo]
"Undivulged" occurs again in *King Lear,* iii, 2, 52.
Malice domestic.—*Macbeth,* iii, 2, 25.

7
Thou but lead'st this fashion of thy malice
To the last hour of act.
The Merchant of Venice. Act iv, sc. 1, l. 18. [Duke]
Malice bears down truth.
The Merchant of Venice. Act iv, sc. 1, l. 214. [Bassanio]
What malice was between you?
Othello. Act v, sc. 1, l. 102. [Iago]

8
Speak of me as I am; nothing extenuate,
Nor set down aught in malice.
Othello. Act v, sc. 2, l. 342. [Othello]

9
Deep malice makes too deep incision.
Richard II. Act i, sc. 1, l. 155. [King Richard]
The new-heal'd wound of malice.
Richard III. Act ii, sc. 2, l. 125. [Buckingham]

10 No levell'd malice
Infects one comma in the course I hold.
Timon of Athens. Act i, sc. 1, l. 47. [Poet]
"Comma" occurs again in *Hamlet,* v, 2, 42.
'Tis in the malice of mankind that he thus advises us.
Timon of Athens. Act iv, sc. 3, l. 456. [Bandit]

11
Some devil whisper curses in my ear,
And prompt me, that my tongue may utter forth
The venomous malice of my swelling heart!
Titus Andronicus. Act v, sc. 3, l. 11. [Aaron]
Malice forced with wit.—*Troilus and Cressida,* v, 1, 63.
I think there is not in the world either malice or matter to alter it.
The Winter's Tale. Act i, sc. 1, l. 36. [Archidamus]

MAN

See also Character; Gods and Men; Master and Man; Wife: Man and Wife

I—Definitions

12 All the world 's a stage,
And all the men and women merely players:
They have their exits and their entrances;
And one man in his time plays many parts,
His acts being seven ages. At first the infant,
Mewling and puking in the nurse's arms.
And then the whining school-boy, with his satchel
And shining morning face, creeping like snail
Unwillingly to school. And then the lover,
Sighing like furnace, with a woeful ballad
Made to his mistress' eyebrow. Then the soldier,
Full of strange oaths and bearded like the pard,
Jealous in honour, sudden and quick in quarrel,
Seeking the bubble reputation
Even in the cannon's mouth. And then the justice,
In fair round belly with good capon lined,
With eyes severe and beard of formal cut,
Full of wise saws and modern instances:
And so he plays his part. The sixth age shifts
Into the lean and slipper'd pantaloon,
With spectacles on nose and pouch on side,
His youthful hose, well saved, a world too wide
For his shrunk shank; and his big manly voice,
Turning again toward childish treble, pipes
And whistles in his sound. Last scene of all,
That ends this strange eventful history,
Is second childishness and mere oblivion,
Sans teeth, sans eyes, sans taste, sans every thing.
As You Like It. Act ii, sc. 7, l. 139. [Jaques]
The only use of "mewling," "puking," "satchel," and "slipper'd." "Pantaloon" occurs again in *The Taming of the Shrew,* iii, 1, 37. "Pard" (leopard) is repeated in *A*

Midsummer-Night's Dream, ii, 2, 31; *The Tempest,* iv, 1, 262; and *Troilus and Cressida,* iii, 2, 201. "Sans" is used eleven times.

1
What a piece of work is man! how noble in reason! how infinite in faculty! in form and moving how express and admirable! in action how like an angel! in apprehension how like a god! the beauty of the world! the paragon of animals! And yet, to me, what is this quintessence of dust? man delights not me; no, nor woman neither.

Hamlet. Act ii, sc. 2, l. 316. [Hamlet] "Quintessence" is used a second time in *As You Like It,* iii, 2, 147: "The quintessence of every sprite."

What is a man,
If his chief good and market of his time
Be but to sleep and feed? a beast, no more.

Hamlet. Act iv, sc. 4, l. 33. [Hamlet]

2
'Homo' is a common name to all men.

I Henry IV. Act ii, sc. 1, l. 104. [Gadshill] The only use of "homo."

3
This little kingdom, man.

II Henry IV, iv, 3, 118. See under SACK.

This foolish-compounded clay, man.

II Henry IV, i, 2, 9. See under INVENTION. The only use of "foolish-compounded."

Men are but gilded loam or painted clay.

Richard II, i, 1, 179. See REPUTATION, 1266:12.

Men of mould.—*Henry V,* iii, 2, 23.

4
Will you tell me, Master Shallow, how to choose a man? Care I for the limb, the thewes, the stature, bulk, and big assemblance of a man! Give me the spirit, Master Shallow.

II Henry IV. Act iii, sc. 2, l. 275. [Falstaff] "Thews," so spelled, is repeated in *Julius Cæsar,* i, 3, 81: "Thews and limbs"; and in *Hamlet,* i, 3, 12: "Thews and bulk."

O, give me the spare men, and spare me the great ones.

II Henry IV, iii, 2, 288. See under THINNESS.

5
So in the world; 'tis furnish'd well with men,
And men are flesh and blood, and apprehensive.

Julius Cæsar. Act iii, sc. 1, l. 66. [Cæsar]

6
Is man no more than this?

King Lear. Act iii, sc. 4, l. 107. [King Lear]

Unaccommodated man is no more but such a poor, bare, forked animal as thou art.

King Lear. Act iii, sc. 4, l. 112. [King Lear] The only use of "unaccommodated."

7
The earth hath bubbles, as the water has,
And these are of them.

Macbeth. Act i, sc. 3, l. 79. [Banquo]

First Murderer: We are men, my liege.
Macbeth: Ay, in the catalogue ye go for men;
As hounds and greyhounds, mongrels, spaniels, curs,
Shoughs, water-rugs and demi-wolves are clept
All by the name of dogs.

Macbeth. Act iii, sc. 1, l. 91. The only use of "shoughs," "water-rats," "demi-wolves," and "clept."

8
But man, proud man,
Drest in a little brief authority,
Most ignorant of what he 's most assured,
His glassy essence, like an angry ape,
Plays such fantastic tricks before high heaven
As make the angels weep.

Measure for Measure. Act ii, sc. 2, l. 117. [Isabella] "Glassy" is repeated in *I Henry VI,* v, 3, 62, and in *Hamlet,* iv, 7, 168, in both cases "glassy stream."

How some men creep in skittish fortune's hall,
Whiles others play the idiots in her eyes!

Troilus and Cressida. Act iii, sc. 3, l. 134. [Ulysses] "Skittish" is repeated in the Prologue, l. 20: "Skittish spirits"; and in *Twelfth Night,* ii, 4, 18: "Unstaid and skittish."

9
Man is but an ass. . . . Man is but a patched fool.

A Midsummer-Night's Dream, iv, 1, 212. See under DREAM for full quotation.

Man is a giddy thing.

Much Ado about Nothing. Act v, sc. 4, l. 110. [Benedick]

Therein do men from children nothing differ.

Much Ado about Nothing. Act v, sc. 1, l. 33. [Antonio]

10
'Tis not a year or two shows us a man:
They are all but stomachs, and we all but food;
They eat us hungerly, and when they are full,
They belch us.

Othello. Act iii, sc. 4, l. 103. [Emilia] "Hungerly" is repeated in *Taming of the Shrew,* iii, 2, 177, and in *Timon of Athens,* i, 1, 262.

We must think men are not gods.

Othello. Act iii, sc. 4, l. 148. [Desdemona]

11
In men, as in a rough-grown grove, remain
Cave-keeping evils that obscurely sleep.

Rape of Lucrece, l. 1249. The only use of "rough-grown" and "cave-keeping." "Cave-keeper" occurs in *Cymbeline,* iv, 2, 298. "Obscurely" is repeated in *Julius Cæsar,* i, 2, 323.

There 's no trust,
No faith, no honesty in men; all perjured,
All forsworn, all naught, all dissemblers.

Romeo and Juliet. Act iii, sc. 2, l. 85. [Nurse] "Dissembler" is repeated in *Richard III,* i, 2, 185, and in *Much Ado about Nothing,* v, 1, 53.

12
Men as plants increase,
Cheered and check'd even by the self-same sky,
Vaunt in their youthful sap, at height decrease,
And wear their brave state out of memory.

Sonnets. No. xv.

13
I have, in this rough work, shaped out a man,
Whom this beneath world doth embrace and hug
With amplest entertainment.

Timon of Athens. Act i, sc. 1, l. 43 [Poet]

The strain of man's bred out
Into baboon and monkey.
Timon of Athens, i, 1, 259. [Apemantus]
Such summer-birds are men.
Timon of Athens. Act iii, sc. 6, l. 34. [Timon] The only use of "summer-birds."

1
Pandarus: Have you any eyes? Do you know what a man is? Is not birth, beauty, good shape, discourse, manhood, learning, gentleness, virtue, youth, liberality, and such like, the spice and salt that season a man? Cressida: Ay, a minced man: and then to be baked with no date in the pie, for then the man's date 's out.
Troilus and Cressida. Act i, sc. 2, l. 274. The only use of "minced." "Liberality" occurs only twice more in two plays, in *The Taming of the Shrew,* i, 2, 150, and in *Titus Andronicus,* ii, 1, 92.

II—Familiar Phrases

2
O, strange men!
That can such sweet use make of what they hate.
All's Well that Ends Well, iv, 4, 21. See under LUST.

3
I saw the man to-day, if man he be.
All's Well that Ends Well. Act v, sc. 3, l. 203. [Lafeu]
This is the man.—*All's Well that Ends Well,* ii, 3, 111.

4
Third Soldier: What man is this?
Second Soldier: Stand close, and list him.
Antony and Cleopatra. Act iv, sc. 9, l. 6.
Guard: This is the man.
Cleopatra: Avoid, and leave him.
Antony and Cleopatra. Act v, sc. 2, l. 241.
'Tis the man.—*Antony and Cleopatra,* i, 5, 54.
Behold this man.—*Antony and Cleopatra,* iv, 8, 22.
This is not the man.—*II Henry IV,* Epil., 34.

5
What shall I call thee when thou art a man?
As You Like It. Act i, sc. 3, l. 125. [Celia]

6
Most shallow man! . . . God help thee, shallow man!
As You Like It. Act iii, sc. 2, l. 67. [Touchstone]
Is the single man therefore blessed?
As You Like It, iii, 3, 59. See under MARRIAGE AND CELIBACY. "Single man" in another sense occurs in *Coriolanus,* iv, 1, 42.
When that the sleeping man should stir.
As You Like It, iv, 3, 117. See under LION. "Sleeping men" occurs in *II Henry VI,* iii, 2, 197; 226.
Drowsy man.—*King John,* iii, 4, 109.
Rich man.—*As You Like It,* iii, 2, 337, and four times in later plays. See under RICHES.

7
Know of me
What man I am, and how, and why, and where.
As You Like It. Act iv, sc. 3, l. 96. [Oliver]

You a man! you lack a man's heart. . . . Take a good heart and counterfeit to be a man.
As You Like It, iv, 3, 164. See under COUNTERFEIT.
Thou art no man, though of a man's complexion,
For men will kiss even by their own direction.
Venus and Adonis, l. 215.
They shall yet belie thy happy years,
That say thou art a man.
Twelfth Night. Act i, sc. 4, l. 30. [Duke]

8
You are a merry man, sir.
The Comedy of Errors. Act iii, sc. 2, l. 183. [Angelo] "Merry man" is repeated four times in later plays. See under MERRIMENT.
Which is the natural man, And which the spirit?
The Comedy of Errors, v, 1, 333. See under LIKENESS. "Natural man" is repeated in *Timon of Athens,* i, 1, 157.

9
Make of him a formal man again.
The Comedy of Errors. Act v, sc. 1, l. 105. [Abbess]
Not like a formal man.—*Antony and Cleopatra,* ii, 5, 41. See FURY, 596:10.

10
I sprang not more in joy at first hearing he was a man-child than now in first seeing he had proved himself a man.
Coriolanus. Act i, sc. 3, l. 17. [Volumnia] The only use of "sprang" and "man-child."
He proved best man i' the field.
Coriolanus. Act ii, sc. 2, l. 101. [Cominius] "Best man" is used six times.

11
I will counterfeit the bewitchment of some popular man.
Coriolanus, ii, 3, 109. See under PEOPLE.
You might have been enough the man you are,
With striving less to be so.
Coriolanus. Act iii, sc. 2, l. 19. [Volumnia]

12
He 's as like to do 't as any man I can imagine.
Coriolanus. Act iv, sc. 5, l. 216. [Servant]

13
'Tween man and man they weigh not every stamp.
Cymbeline. Act v, sc. 4, l. 24. [Posthumus]

14
The humorous man shall end his part in peace.
Hamlet. Act ii, sc. 2, l. 335. [Hamlet]
Inward man.—*Hamlet,* ii, 2, 6; *Pericles,* ii, 2, 57.
Forgetful man.—*I Henry IV,* i, 3, 161.

15
O monstrous! eleven buckram men grown out of two!
I Henry IV. Act ii, sc. 4, l. 243. [Prince of Wales]
Men in Kendal green.—*I Henry IV,* ii, 4, 257.

16
What manner of man is he?
I Henry IV. Act ii, sc. 4, l. 323. [Falstaff]
Now, by my holidame,
What manner of man are you?
Henry VIII. Act v, sc. 1, l. 117. [King Henry] "By my holidame" is repeated in *The Taming of the Shrew,* v, 2, 99, and in *Romeo and Juliet,* i, 3, 43.

What manner of man?—*I Henry IV*, ii, 4, 462; *As You Like It*, iii, 2, 216.
What men have I!—*I Henry VI*, i, 2, 22.
All manner of men.—*I Henry VI*, i, 3, 74.
Men of all sorts.—*II Henry IV*, i, 2, 7.

1
He gave you all the duties of a man.
I Henry IV. Act v, sc. 2, l. 56. [Vernon]
Benedick: May a man do it?
Beatrice: It is a man's office, but not yours.
Much Ado about Nothing. Act iv, sc. 1, l. 267.

2
Have you provided me here half a dozen sufficient men?
II Henry IV. Act iii, sc. 2, l. 103. [Falstaff]
You'll never meet a more sufficient man.
Othello. Act iii, sc. 4, l. 91. [Desdemona]

3
There are other men fitter to go out than I.
II Henry IV. Act iii, sc. 2, l. 126. [Mouldy]
They are your likeliest men.
II Henry IV. Act iii, sc. 2, l. 273. [Shallow] The only use of "likeliest."

4
No man is too good to serve 's prince.
II Henry IV. Act iii, sc. 2, l. 253. [Feeble]
I did not think Master Silence had been a man of this mettle.
II Henry IV. Act v, sc. 3, l. 40. [Falstaff]
What is the trust or strength of foolish man?
I Henry VI. Act iii, sc. 2, l. 112. [Bedford]

5
They have demean'd themselves Like men.
III Henry VI. Act i, sc. 4, l. 7. [York]
Play the men.—*The Tempest*, i, 1, 11.
Play'd the men.—*I Henry VI*, i, 6, 16.
Show yourselves men.—*II Henry VI*, iv, 2, 193.
Come, be a man.—*Othello*, i, 3, 340; iv, 1, 66.

6
I was never mine own man since.
II Henry VI, iv, 2, 91. See under LAWYER.

7
He is a man, and, Clifford, cope with him.
III Henry VI. Act i, sc. 3, l. 24. [Rutland]
He was a man.—*III Henry VI*, v, 5, 56.
I am a man again.—*Macbeth*, iii, 4, 108.
Thou art a man.—*Pericles*, v, 1, 137.

8
This imperious man will work us all.
Henry VIII. Act ii, sc. 2, l. 47. [Norfolk]
They have sent me such a man I would have wish'd for.
Henry VIII. Act ii, sc. 2, l. 101. [King Henry]

9
Those men are happy; and so are all near her.
Henry VIII. Act iv, sc. 1, l. 50. [Gentleman] "Those men are happy" is repeated in iv, 2, 147. "Happy man" occurs eight times. See under HAPPINESS.
There's no man happy.—*Othello*, iv, 2, 18.

10
He was a man
Of an unbounded stomach, ever ranking
Himself with princes.
Henry VIII. Act iv, sc. 2, l. 33. [Katharine] The only use of "unbounded."
Let me lose the fashion of a man!
Henry VIII. Act iv, sc. 2, l. 159. [Capucius]
Thou hast made me now a man!
Henry VIII. Act v, sc. 5, l. 65. [King Henry]
We are all men.—*Henry VIII*, v, 3, 10. See under FRAILTY.
We are but men.—*Henry VIII*, v, 4, 79.
Men are men.—*Othello*, ii, 3, 241.

11
I had thought I had men of some understanding
And wisdom of my council; but I find none.
Henry VIII. Act v, sc. 3, l. 185. [King Henry]
He is the wiser man.—*The Merry Wives of Windsor*, ii, 3, 39.
You are the wiser man.—*All's Well that Ends Well*, ii, 4, 23. "Wise man" is used twenty-six times. See under WISDOM.

12
You are not wood, you are not stones, but men.
Julius Cæsar. Act iii, sc. 2, l. 147. [Antony]
O, you are men of stones!—*King Lear*, v, 3, 257.

13
Having more man than wit about me.
King Lear. Act ii, sc. 4, l. 42. [Kent]
What a pretty thing man is when he goes in his doublet and hose and leaves off his wit!
Much Ado about Nothing. Act v, sc. 1, l. 202. [Don Pedro]

14
O, the difference of man and man!
King Lear. Act iv, sc. 2, l. 26. [Goneril]
All men are not alike; alas, good neighbour!
Much Ado about Nothing. Act iii, sc. 5, l. 43. [Dogberry]

15
That thing you speak of,
I took it for a man.
King Lear. Act iv, sc. 6, l. 77. [Gloucester]
Know thou this, that men Are as the time is.
King Lear. Act v, sc. 3, l. 30. [Edmund]

16
I am the very man.
King Lear. Act v, sc. 3, l. 286. [Kent]
The very same man.—*The Merry Wives of Windsor*, iv, 5, 37.
This very man.—*Measure for Measure*, ii, 1, 104; *Much Ado about Nothing*, ii, 1, 123.

17
A man in all the world's new fashion planted,
That hath a mint of phrases in his brain;
One whom the music of his own vain tongue
Doth ravish like enchanting harmony.
A man of complements, whom right and wrong
Have chose as umpire of their mutiny.
Love's Labour's Lost. Act i, sc. 1, l. 165. [King Ferdinand]

18
A man of travel, that hath seen the world.
Love's Labour's Lost, v, 1, 113. See under TRAVEL.
A man of fourscore pound a year.
Measure for Measure. Act ii, sc. 1, l. 127. [Pompey]
A man of my kidney.
The Merry Wives of Windsor. Act iii, sc. 5, l. 117. [Falstaff] The only use of "kidney."

19
Princess of France: Doth this man serve God?
Biron: Why ask you?

Princess of France: He speaks not like a man of God's making.
Love's Labour's Lost. Act v, sc. 2, l. 527.

God made him, and therefore let him pass for a man.
The Merchant of Venice. Act i, sc. 2, l. 60. [Portia]

1
I must be one of these same dumb wise men,
For Gratiano never lets me speak.
The Merchant of Venice. Act i, sc. 1, l. 106. [Lorenzo]

I have seen the dumb men throng to him.
Coriolanus, ii, 1, 278. See under APPLAUSE.

Dumb man.—*Much Ado about Nothing,* i, 1, 212.

Men of few words.—*Henry V,* iii, 2, 38. See under WORD AND DEED.

Blind man.—*I Henry VI,* ii, 4, 24; *II Henry VI,* ii, 1, 63; *The Merchant of Venice,* v, 1, 112; *Much Ado about Nothing,* ii, 1, 205. See under BLINDNESS.

Blind men.—*King Lear,* ii, 4, 71.

2
He is every man in no man.
The Merchant of Venice. Act i, sc. 2, l. 64. [Portia]

3
But, stay; I smell a man of middle-earth.
The Merry Wives of Windsor. Act v, sc. 5, l. 84. [Evans] The only use of "middle-earth," the earth viewed as being between heaven and hell.

4
You were best to call them generally, man by man.
A Midsummer-Night's Dream. Act i, sc. 2, l. 3. [Bottom]

Man by man.—*I Henry IV,* iii, 3, 65.

Every man of them.—*I Henry IV,* ii, 4, 197; *Julius Cæsar,* ii, 1, 90.

To the last man.—*II Henry IV,* iv, 2, 44.

5
We'll try no manhood here.
A Midsummer-Night's Dream. Act iii, sc. 2, l. 412. [Puck]

Makes much against my manhood.—*Henry V,* iii, 2, 53.

Saving your manhoods.—*II Henry IV,* ii, 1, 29.

Saving your majesty's manhood.—*Henry V,* iv, 8, 36. "Manhood" occurs twenty-seven times.

6
Hard-handed men that work in Athens here.
A Midsummer-Night's Dream, v, 1, 72. The only use of "hard-handed." See under LABOUR.

Labouring man.—*II Henry VI,* iv, 2, 19.

7
Here you may see Benedick the married man.
Much Ado about Nothing, i, 1, 270. The phrase is repeated three times in this play and "married man" occurs four times.

8
Men were deceivers ever.
Much Ado about Nothing, ii, 3, 65. See under INCONSTANCY.

9
God's a good man; an two men ride of a horse, one must ride behind.
Much Ado about Nothing. Act iii, sc. 5, l. 39. [Dogberry]

10
Are you a man? have you a soul or sense?
Othello. Act iii, sc. 3, l. 374. [Iago]

There is no such man; it is impossible.
Othello. Act iv, sc. 2, l. 134. [Iago]

O, these men, these men!—*Othello,* iv, 3, 60.

11
Men should be what they seem.
Othello, iii, 3, 129. See SEEMING, 1330:9.

Be every man himself.—*Coriolanus,* iii, 1, 265.

12
Disprove this villain, if thou be'st a man.
Othello. Act v, sc. 2, l. 172. [Emilia]

13
Wind, rain, and thunder, remember, earthly man
Is but a substance that must yield to you.
Pericles. Act ii, sc. 1, l. 2. [Pericles]

What a man cannot get, he may lawfully deal for.
Pericles. Act ii, sc. 1, l. 120. [Fisherman]

14
As I am a Christian faithful man.
Richard III. Act i, sc. 4, l. 4. [Clarence]

As I am a man.—*The Merry Wives of Windsor,* iv, 2, 151; *King Lear,* iv, 7, 69.

As I am an honest man.—*Much Ado about Nothing,* v, 1, 130; *Othello,* ii, 3, 266.

As thou'rt a man.—*Hamlet,* v, 2, 353.

15
Duke of Clarence: In God's name, what art thou?
Second Murderer: A man, as you are.
Duke of Clarence: But not, as I am, royal.
Second Murderer: Nor you, as we are, loyal.
Richard III. Act i, sc. 4, l. 169.

I am a man as other men are.
A Midsummer-Night's Dream. Act iii, sc. 1, l. 45. [Bottom]

16
A man, young lady! lady, such a man
As all the world—why, he's a man of wax.
Romeo and Juliet. Act i, sc. 3, l. 75. [Nurse]

Stand up, stand up; stand, an you be a man.
Romeo and Juliet. Act iii, sc. 3, l. 88. [Nurse]

You'll be the man!—*Romeo and Juliet,* i, 5, 83.

17
If I can by any means light on a fit man,
. . . I will wish him to her father.
The Taming of the Shrew. Act i, sc. 1, l. 111. [Gremio] "Light on" was a favourite phrase with Shakespeare, and was used many times.

The most senseless and fit man.—*Much Ado about Nothing,* iii, 3, 23. The only uses of "fit man."

Picked man.—*King John,* i, 1, 193.

18
This
Is the third man that e'er I saw, the first
That e'er I sigh'd for.
The Tempest. Act i, sc. 2, l. 444. [Miranda]

To the most of men this is a Caliban
And they to him are angels.
The Tempest. Act i, sc. 2, l. 480. [Prospero]

How beauteous mankind is! O brave new world.

That has such people in 't!
The Tempest. Act v, sc. 1, l. 183. [Miranda] "Mankind" is used nineteen times.

Handsome man.—*Antony and Cleopatra,* i, 2, 75.

A well-favoured man.
Much Ado about Nothing, iii, 3, 15. See under EDUCATION for full quotation.

A most ugly man.—*King John,* iii, 1, 37.

Hairy men.—*The Comedy of Errors,* ii, 2, 87.

1 I was the first man
That e'er received gift from him.
Timon of Athens. Act iii, sc. 3, l. 16. [Sempronius]

The king's son . . .
Was the first man that leap'd.
The Tempest. Act i, sc. 2, l. 212. [Ariel] The only uses of "first man."

2
Why do fond men expose themselves to battle?
Timon of Athens, iii, 5, 42. See under ENDURANCE. The only use of "fond men." "Fond man" occurs in *I Henry VI,* v, 2, 80.

More man? plague, plague!
Timon of Athens. Act iv, sc. 3, l. 197. [Timon]

Moe things like men! Eat, Timon, and abhor them.
Timon of Athens. Act iv, sc. 3, l. 398. [Timon]

Living men.—*Timon of Athens,* v, 4, 72.

Living man.—*Titus Andronicus,* v, 3, 127.

3
Come, come, thou reverend man of Rome,
And bring our emperor gently in thy hand.
Titus Andronicus. Act v, sc. 3, l. 137. [Æmilius]

Cruel men of Rome.—*Julius Cæsar,* i, 1, 41.

Giddy men of Rome.—*Titus Andronicus,* iv, 4, 87.

Men of Angiers.—*King John,* ii, 1, 199.

Men of Bury.—*II Henry VI,* iii, 2, 240.

Men of Cyprus.—*Othello,* ii, 1, 84.

Men of Harfleur.—*Henry V,* iii, 3, 27.

Men of Kent.—*II Henry VI,* iv, 7, 59.

Men of Troy.—*Troilus and Cressida,* i, 3, 233.

Foreign man.—*Henry VIII,* ii, 2, 129.

Northern man.—*Love's Labour 's Lost,* v, 2, 701.

Seafaring men.—*The Comedy of Errors,* i, 1, 81. The only use of "seafaring." See under SAILOR.

"Man i' the moon," see under MOON.

4
This man, lady, hath robbed many beasts of their particular additions.
Troilus and Cressida. Act i, sc. 2, l. 18. [Alexander] See under CHARACTER.

How should this man, that makes me smile, make Hector angry?
Troilus and Cressida. Act i, sc. 2, l. 32. [Cressida]

Pandarus: Do you know a man if you see him?
Cressida: Ay, if I ever saw him before and knew him.
Troilus and Cressida. Act i, sc. 2, l. 67.

5
I do hate a proud man, as I hate the engendering of toads.
Troilus and Cressida, ii, 3, 169. "Proud man" occurs seven times. See under PRIDE.

Arrogant man.—*Timon of Athens,* iv, 3, 180.

Haught insulting man.—*Richard II,* iv, 1, 255. The only use of "haught" for "haughty."

Vain man.—*II Henry IV,* v, 5, 48.

6
I would have been much more a fresher man,
Had I expected thee.
Troilus and Cressida. Act v, sc. 6, l. 21. [Hector]

This is the man I seek.—*Troilus and Cressida,* v, 8, 10.

7
I am the man: if it be so, as 'tis.
Twelfth Night. Act ii, sc. 2, l. 26. [Viola]

8
'There dwelt a man in Babylon, lady, lady!'
Twelfth Night. Act ii, sc. 3, l. 84. [Sir Toby]

This is a dear manakin to you, Sir Toby.
Twelfth Night. Act iii, sc. 2, l. 57. [Fabian] The only use of "manakin."

No worse man than Sir Toby to look to me!
Twelfth Night. Act iii, sc. 4, l. 72. [Malvolio]

A little thing would tell them how much I lack of a man.
Twelfth Night. Act iii, sc. 4, l. 333. [Viola]

9
Black men are pearls in beauteous ladies' eyes.
The Two Gentlemen of Verona. Act v, sc. 2, l. 12. [Proteus] See under FACE.

III—Good Men
See also Goodness

10
The best of men.
Antony and Cleopatra, ii, 2, 131; iii, 7, 27. This is the only use of this phrase.

He is simply the rarest man i' the world.
Coriolanus. Act iv, sc. 5, l. 168. [Servant]

The man is noble.—*Coriolanus,* v, 6, 126.

Soft-conscienced men.—*Coriolanus,* i, 1, 38. The only use of "soft-conscienced."

11 Give me that man
That is not passion's slave, and I will wear him
In my heart's core, ay, in my heart of heart.
Hamlet. Act iii, sc. 2, l. 76. [Hamlet] The only use of the phrases "heart's core" and "heart of heart."

12
Turn true man and leave these rogues.
I Henry IV. Act ii, sc. 2, l. 24. [Falstaff] "True man" is used twelve times, five times in connection with THIEF, q. v.

I am no true man.—*Julius Cæsar,* i, 2, 263.

13
Falstaff: There is a virtuous man whom I have often noted in thy company, but I know not his name.

Prince: What manner of man, an it like your majesty?

Falstaff: A goodly portly man, i' faith, and a corpulent; of a cheerful look, a pleasing eye and a most noble carriage; and, as I think, his age some fifty, or, by 'r lady, inclining to three score; and now I remember me, his name is Falstaff: if that man

should be lewdly given, he deceiveth me; for, Harry, I see virtue in his looks.
I Henry IV. Act ii, sc. 4, l. 460. The only use of "virtuous man" and "corpulent." "Lewdly" is repeated in *II Henry VI,* ii, 1, 167: "Lewdly bent."

He is a man . . . of comely virtues.
Timon of Athens. Act iii, sc. 4, l. 14. [Alcibiades]

1 It is but eight years since
This Percy was the man nearest my soul.
II Henry IV. Act iii, sc. 1, l. 60. [King Henry]

2 We know your grace to be a man
Just and upright.
I Henry VI. Act iii, sc. 1, l. 94. [Servant]

Justest men.—*Antony and Cleopatra,* ii, 1, 2. "Just men" does not occur in the plays.

3
The Lord protect him, for he 's a good man.
II Henry VI. Act i, sc. 3, l. 6. [Petitioner] "Good man" occurs thirty-seven times.

The good old man were fain that all were well.
III Henry VI. Act iv, sc. 7, l. 31. [Hastings] "Good old man" is used nine times.

I 'll tell you there is good men porn at Monmouth.
Henry V. Act iv, sc. 7, l. 56. [Fluellen]

They should be good men; their affairs as righteous:
But all hoods make not monks.
Henry VIII. Act iii, sc. 1, l. 22. [Queen Katharine] The queen is quoting an epigram dating back to 1387, when it appeared in Thomas Usk's *Testament of Love:* "Habit maketh no monk."

Are you good men and true?—*Much Ado about Nothing,* iii, 3, 1. The only use of the phrase.
Good easy man.—*Henry VIII*, iii, 2, 356.
That good man of worship.—*Richard III*, i, 1, 66.

4
Men of singular integrity and learning.
Henry VIII, ii, 4, 58. See under CHARACTER.

Men of gravity and learning.—*Henry VIII*, iii, 1, 73.
Grave man.—*Romeo and Juliet*, iii, 1, 102.
Reverend grave men.—*Coriolanus*, ii, 1, 66.
Sage, grave men.—*Richard III*, iii, 7, 227.
A learned man.—*Henry VIII*, ii, 2, 124; iii, 2, 395; *The Passionate Pilgrim,* l. 225. See under LEARNING.
Learned men.—*Love's Labour 's Lost,* v, 2, 895; *Henry VIII*, iv, 1, 32.

5 Nor is there living . . .
A man that more detests, more stirs against,
Both in his private conscience and his place,
Defacers of a public peace, than I do.
Henry VIII. Act v, sc. 3, l. 37. [Cranmer]

Foul defacer of God's handiwork.
Richard III, iv, 4, 51. The only uses of "defacer" and "defacers."

6
His life was gentle, and the elements
So mix'd in him that Nature might stand up
And say to all the world 'This was a man!'
Julius Cæsar. Act v, sc. 5, l. 73. [Antony]

7
A man of stricture and firm abstinence.
Measure for Measure. Act i, sc. 3, l. 12. [Duke] The only use of "stricture."

8
Your honour is accounted a merciful man.
Measure for Measure. Act iii, sc. 2, l. 203. [Mistress Overdone] "Merciful man" is repeated in *Much Ado about Nothing,* iii, 3, 64. See under MERCY.

9
O excellent young man!
The Merchant of Venice, iv, 1, 246; *As You Like It,* i, 2, 225.

They may pass for excellent men.
A Midsummer-Night's Dream. Act v, sc. 1, l. 220. [Theseus]

Blessed man.—*Romeo and Juliet,* ii, 3, 53.
Charitable men.—*Timon of Athens,* iii, 2, 82.
Chaste man.—*The Merry Wives of Windsor,* ii, 1, 83. See under CHASTITY.
Constant man.—*Merchant of Venice,* iii, 2, 250.
Discreet man.—*Twelfth Night,* i, 5, 103.
High-resolved men.—*Titus Andronicus,* iv, 4, 64. The only use of "high-resolved."
Noble man.—*Coriolanus,* v, 3, 154; *Troilus and Cressida,* i, 3, 294.
Noble men.—*Julius Cæsar,* iv, 3, 54.
Noblest of men.—*Antony and Cleopatra,* iv, 15, 59.
Reasonable man.—*The Winter's Tale,* iv, 4, 617.
Reverend man.—*A Lover's Complaint,* l. 57.
Sensible man.—*Othello,* ii, 3, 309.
Sound man.—*King Lear,* ii, 4, 113.
Worthy man.—*Measure for Measure,* v, 1, 309; *Coriolanus,* ii, 2, 40; 126.
Worthy men.—*Coriolanus,* iii, 3, 35.
There never was a worthier man.—*Coriolanus,* ii, 3, 43. See also under WORTH.
Men of heart.—*Coriolanus,* v, 6, 99.
Men of peace.—*Love's Labour 's Lost,* v, 1, 37.
Men of trust.—*Coriolanus,* i, 6, 52.
Men of their words.—*King Lear,* iv, 6, 106.

10
Here stand a pair of honourable men.
Much Ado about Nothing. Act v, sc. 1, l. 276. [Leonato]

For Brutus is an honourable man;
So are they all, all honourable men.
Julius Cæsar. Act iii, sc. 2, l. 87. [Antony]

Bawd: First, I would have you note, this is an honourable man.
Marina: I desire to find him so, that I may worthily note him.
Bawd: Next, he 's the governor of this country, and a man whom I am bound to.
Marina: If he govern the country, you are bound to him indeed; but how honourable he is in that, I know not.
Pericles. Act iv, sc. 6, l. 53.

Honourable man.—*Measure for Measure,* ii, 1, 89; *Timon of Athens,* iii, 2, 20; *The Tempest,* v, 1, 62.

11 When I met this holy man,
Those men you talk of came into my mind.
Richard III. Act iii, sc. 3, l. 117. [Hastings] "Holy man" is used seven times. See under HOLINESS.

Holy and devout religious men.
Richard III. Act iii, sc. 7, l. 92. [Buckingham]

We still have known thee for a holy man.
Romeo and Juliet. Act v, sc. 3, l. 270. [Prince]

So holy a man.—*Measure for Measure,* iv, 3, 117.

Man o' the church.—*II Henry VI,* i, 1, 186.

1
O admirable man!
Troilus and Cressida. Act i, sc. 2, l. 258. [Pandarus]

A man distill'd Out of our virtues.
Troilus and Cressida. Act i, sc. 3, l. 350. [Nestor]

A man of such perfection
As we do in our quality much want.
The Two Gentlemen of Verona. Act iv, sc. 1, l. 57. [First Outlaw]

IV—Men: Good, Better, Best

2
He shall be encountered with a man as good as himself.
II Henry VI. Act iv, sc. 2, l. 124. [Cade]

Vernon: Sirrah, thy lord I honour as he is.
Basset: Why, what is he? as good a man as York?
Vernon: Hark ye, not so.
I Henry VI. Act iii, sc. 4, l. 35.

As good a man as he, sir, whoe'er I am.
II Henry IV. Act iv, sc. 3, l. 12. [Falstaff]

Being as good a man as yourself.
Henry V. Act iii, sc. 2, l. 140. [Fluellen]

He 's a man good enough.
Troilus and Cressida. Act i, sc. 2, l. 207. [Pandarus]

Great Hector was a man as good as he.
Troilus and Cressida. Act v, sc. 9, l. 6. [Ajax]

I have no ambition To see a goodlier man.
The Tempest. Act i, sc. 2, l. 482. [Miranda] "Goodlier" is repeated in *All 's Well that Ends Well,* iii, 5, 83.

3
That I 'll prove on better men than Somerset.
I Henry VI. Act ii, sc. 4, l. 98. [Plantagenet]

I could have better spared a better man.
I Henry IV. Act v, sc. 4, l. 104. [Prince of Wales]

Mariana: I crave no other, nor no better man.
Duke: Never crave him; we are definitive.
Measure for Measure. Act v, sc. 1, l. 431. The only use of "definitive."

Sampson: I serve as good a man as you.
Abraham: No better. . . .
Gregory: Say 'better.' . . .
Sampson: Yes, better, sir.
Romeo and Juliet. Act i, sc. 1, l. 61.

Hector is not a better man than Troilus.
Troilus and Cressida. Act i, sc. 2, l. 86. [Pandarus]

Troilus is the better man of the two.
Troilus and Cressida. Act i, sc. 2, l. 64. [Pandarus]

Among ourselves
Give him allowance for the better man.
Troilus and Cressida. Act i, sc. 3, l. 376. [Ulysses]

If he fail,
Yet go we under our opinion still
That we have better men.
Troilus and Cressida. Act i, sc. 3, l. 384. [Ulysses]

Ajax: Do you not think he thinks himself a better man than I am?
Agamemnon: No question.
Troilus and Cressida. Act ii, sc. 3, l. 153. See under COMPARISON.

He hath stayed for a better man than thee.
The Two Gentlemen of Verona. Act iii, sc. 1, l. 385. [Launce] Shakespeare used the phrase "better man," or "better men" twelve times, six times in *Troilus and Cressida* alone.

This man is better than the man he slew,
As well descended as thyself.
Cymbeline. Act v, sc. 5, l. 302. [Belarius]

4
Tell Kent from me, she hath lost her best man.
II Henry VI. Act iv, sc. 10, l. 79. [Cade] "Best man," or "best men" occurs six times in the plays.

All the best men are ours.—*Henry VIII,* Epil., 13.

Let him choose
Out of my files, his projects to accomplish,
My best and freshest men.
Coriolanus. Act v, sc. 6, l. 33. [Aufidius]

V—Bad Men

5 Hollow men, like horses hot at hand,
Make gallant show and promise of their mettle;
But when they should endure the bloody spur,
They fall their crests, and, like deceitful jades,
Sink in the trial.
Julius Cæsar. Act iv, sc. 2, l. 23. [Brutus]

6
Humanity must perforce prey on itself,
Like monsters of the deep.
King Lear. Act iv, sc. 2, l. 49. [Albany]

7
What bloody man is that?
Macbeth. Act i, sc. 2, l. 1. [Duncan] "Bloody man" occurs four times.

Man of blood.—*Macbeth,* iii, 4, 126.

8 Those men
Blush not in actions blacker than the night,
Will shun no course to keep them from the light.
Pericles. Act i, sc. 1, l. 134. [Pericles]

9
All men are bad, and in their badness reign.
Sonnets. No. cxxi. Shakespeare is paraphrasing the maxim of Bias of Priene, "Most men are bad."

Bad men.—*Richard II,* v, 1, 71.
This bold bad man.—*Henry VIII,* ii, 2, 44.
Awful men.—*The Two Gentlemen of Verona,* iv, 1, 46.
Base man.—*Richard II,* iv, 1, 20.
Base men.—*II Henry VI,* iv, 1, 106.
Cruel men.—*Henry VIII,* v, 3, 100.
Cunning man.—*II Henry VI,* iv, 1, 34.
Cunning men.—*Taming of the Shrew,* i, 1, 97.
Men cautelous.—*Julius Cæsar,* ii, 1, 129. "Cautelous" (crafty) is repeated in *Coriolanus,* iv, 1, 33: "Cautelous baits."
Cursed man.—*Richard II,* iii, 4, 76.
Deceitful men.—*The Two Gentlemen of Verona,* ii, 7, 72.
Defused infection of a man.—*Richard III,* i, 2,

78. "Defused" is repeated in *Henry V*, v, 2, 61.
Desartless man.—*Much Ado about Nothing*, iii, 3, 10.
Dishonest man.—*Twelfth Night*, i, 5, 50.
Man of falsehood.—*I Henry IV*, ii, 1, 71.
False man.—*Macbeth*, ii, 3, 143.
Foul-mouthed man.—*I Henry IV*, iii, 3, 123. "Foul-mouthed" is repeated in *All's Well that Ends Well*, i, 3, 60: "Foul-mouthed knaves."
Fraudful man.—*II Henry VI*, iii, 1, 81. The only use of "fraudful."
Graceless men.—*II Henry VI*, iv, 4, 38.
Hard-hearted man.—*Richard II*, v, 3, 87. "Hard-hearted" is used seven times.
Lascivious men.—*The Two Gentlemen of Verona*, ii, 7, 41.
Lust-dieted man.—*King Lear*, iv, 1, 70. The only use of the phrase.
Milk-liver'd man!—*King Lear*, iv, 2, 50. The only use of "milk-liver'd."
Naughty man.—*Much Ado about Nothing*, v, 1, 307; *Troilus and Cressida*, iv, 2, 34.
Perjured men.—*Love's Labour 's Lost*, v, 2, 346.
A rude and savage man.—*Love's Labour 's Lost*, iv, 3, 222. See under INDIA.
Sanctuary men.—*Richard III*, iii, 1, 55.
Simular man of virtue.—*King Lear*, iii, 2, 54. See under HYPOCRISY.
Spotted and inconstant man.—*A Midsummer-Night's Dream*, i, 1, 110.
Men of inconstancy.—*Love's Labour 's Lost*, iv, 3, 180.
Unjust man.—*I Henry IV*, iii, 3, 144.
Villanous man.—*I Henry IV*, ii, 4, 139.
Whoremaster man.—*King Lear*, i, 2, 138.
Wicked men.—*Richard III*, v, 1, 23; *Richard II*, v, 1, 66.
Wilful men.—*King Lear*, ii, 4, 305.
Men of malice.—*Henry VIII*, iii, 2, 243.
Men of sin.—*The Tempest*, iii, 3, 53.
Usurers' men.—*Timon of Athens*, ii, 2, 61; 101.
The worst of men.—*Timon of Athens*, iv, 3, 275.

1

Sirs, I will practise on this drunken man.
The Taming of the Shrew. Induction, sc. 1, l. 36. [Lord] "Drunken man" is repeated in *Twelfth Night*, i, 5, 138. See under DRINKING: DRUNKENNESS.

O, that a mighty man of such descent,
Of such possessions and so high esteem,
Should be infused with so foul a spirit!
The Taming of the Shrew. Induction, sc. 2, l. 15. [Lord]

2

I wonder men dare trust themselves with men:
Methinks they should invite them without knives;
Good for their meat, and safer for their lives.
Timon of Athens. Act i, sc. 2, l. 44. [Apemantus]

Timon will to the woods; where he shall find
The unkindest beast more kinder than mankind.
Timon of Athens. Act iv, sc. 1, l. 35. [Timon]

Excellent workman! thou canst not paint a man so bad as is thyself.
Timon of Athens. Act v, sc. 1, l. 32. [Timon]

3

Ingrateful man, with liquorish draughts
And morsels unctuous, greases his pure mind,
That from it all consideration slips!
Timon of Athens. Act iv, sc. 3, l. 194. [Timon] The only use of "liquorish" and "unctuous." "Ingrateful man" is repeated in *King Lear*, iii, 2, 9.

VI—Great Men

See also Greatness

4

My man of men.
Antony and Cleopatra. Act i, sc. 5, l. 72. [Cleopatra]

He 's the Jupiter of men.
Antony and Cleopatra. Act iii, sc. 2, l. 9. [Enobarbus]

The fullest man, and worthiest.
Antony and Cleopatra. Act iii, sc. 13, l. 87. [Thyreus] The only use of "fullest."

I dream'd there was an Emperor Antony:
O, such another sleep, that I might see
But such another man! . . .
His face was as the heavens; and therein stuck
A sun and moon, which kept their course, and lighted
The little O, the earth. . . .
His legs bestrid the ocean: his rear'd arm
Crested the world; his voice was propertied
As all the tuned spheres, and that to friends;
But when he meant to quail and shake the orb,
He was as rattling thunder. For his bounty,
There was no winter in 't; an autumn 'twas
That grew the more by reaping: his delights
Were dolphin-like; they show'd his back above
The element they lived in: in his livery
Walk'd crowns and crownets; realms and islands were
As plates dropp'd from his pocket. . . .
Think you there was, or might be, such a man
As this I dream'd of? . . .
But, if there be, or ever were, one such,
It 's past the size of dreaming: nature wants stuff
To vie strange forms with fancy.
Antony and Cleopatra. Act v, sc. 2, l. 76. [Cleopatra] The only use of "crested" and "dolphin-like." "Crownets" is repeated in iv, 12, 27, and in *Troilus and Cressida*, Prol., 6.

5

The man I speak of cannot in the world
Be singly counterpoised.
Coriolanus, ii, 2, 90. See under VALOUR.

6

Great men
That had a court no bigger than this cave,
That did attend themselves and had the virtue
Which their own conscience seal'd them—laying by
That nothing-gift of differing multitudes—
Could not out-peer these twain.
Cymbeline. Act v, sc. 4, l. 127. [Posthumus] The only use of "nothing-gift" and "out-peer."

7

He was a man, take him for all in all,
I shall not look upon his like again.
Hamlet. Act i, sc. 2, l. 187. [Hamlet]

1
I am not in the roll of common men.
I Henry IV, iii, 1, 43. See under GREATNESS.

2 And him, O wondrous him!
O miracle of men!
II Henry IV. Act ii, sc. 3, l. 32. [Lady Percy]

Thou wondrous man.—*The Tempest*, ii, 2, 168.
Full-fraught man.—*Henry V*, ii, 2, 139. "Full-fraught" is repeated in *The Two Gentlemen of Verona*, iii, 2, 70.

3 She hath beheld the man
Whose glory fills the world with loud report.
I Henry VI. Act ii, sc. 2, l. 42. [Messenger]

That ever living man of memory.
I Henry VI. Act iv, sc. 3, l. 51. [Lucy]

4
Richard shall live to make the Earl of Warwick
The greatest man in England but the king.
II Henry VI. Act ii, sc. 2, l. 81. [York]

The greatest man in the realm.—*II Henry IV*, v, 3, 92.

5
Great men oft die by vile bezonians.
II Henry VI, iv, i, 134. See under GREATNESS.

Great men have reaching hands.
II Henry VI. Act iv, sc. 7, l. 86. [Lord Say]

6 This man so complete,
Who was enroll'd 'mongst wonders.
Henry VIII. Act i, sc. 2, l. 118. [King Henry]

A man in much esteem with the king.
Henry VIII. Act iv, sc. 1, l. 109. [Gentleman]

7
Now could I, Casca, name to thee a man
Most like this dreadful night,
That thunders, lightens, opens graves, and roars
As doth the lion in the Capitol,
A man no mightier than thyself or me
In personal action, yet prodigious grown
And fearful, as these strange eruptions are.
Julius Cæsar. Act i, sc. 3, l. 72. [Cassius] "Strange eruptions" is repeated in *I Henry IV*, iii, 1, 28, and "strange eruption" occurs in *Hamlet*, i, 1, 69. "Eruptions" is used once more in *Love's Labour 's Lost*, v, 1, 121: "Such eruptions."

The foremost man of all the world.
Julius Cæsar. Act iv, sc. 3, l. 22. [Brutus]

Men of note.—*Love's Labour 's Lost*, iii, 1, 25.
Man of quality.—*Othello*, ii, 3, 110.

8
Base men by his endowments are made great.
Richard II. Act ii, sc. 3, l. 139. [Willoughby]

9
What men of name resort to him?
Richard III. Act iv, sc. 5, l. 8. [Derby]

What men of name are slain on either side?
Richard III. Act v, sc. 5, l. 12. [Richmond]

Why this it is to have a name in great men's fellowship.
Antony and Cleopatra. Act ii, sc. 7, l. 12. [Servant]

10
Petruchio: A man well known throughout all Italy. . . .
Baptista: A mighty man of Pisa.
Taming of the Shrew. Act ii, sc. 1, l. 69; 105.

Mighty man.—*King John*, i, 1, 225.
Mighty men.—*Henry V*, Epil., 3.
Chiefest men.—*King John*, ii, 1, 39.
Famous man.—*Richard III*, iii, 1, 84.
Royal man.—*I Henry IV*, ii, 4, 321.
Men of royal siege.—*Othello*, i, 2, 22.

11
Heavens, what a man is there! a very horse,
That has he knows not what.
Troilus and Cressida. Act iii, sc. 3, l. 126. [Ulysses]

Thou great and complete man.—*Troilus and Cressida*, iii, 3, 181.
Great and growing men.—*Richard II*, iii, 4, 61. See under PRUDENCE. "Great man (or men)" is used nineteen times in the plays.

12
That I may call thee something more than man.
Winter's Tale. Act iv, sc. 4, l. 545. [Florizel]

VII—Common Men

13 Let him breathe between the heavens and earth,
A private man in Athens.
Antony and Cleopatra. Act iii, sc. 12, l. 14. [Euphronius]

Being but a private man again,
You shall know how many dare accuse you boldly,
More than, I fear, you are provided for.
Henry VIII. Act v, sc. 3, l. 55. [Gardiner]

Private man.—*I Henry VI*, v, 4, 136; *Titus Andronicus*, iv, 4, 75.
Private men.—*Henry V*, iv, 1, 254.

14
You appeared to me but as a common man.
Henry V. Act iv, sc. 8, l. 54. [Williams]

Common man (or men).—*I Henry VI*, iv, 1, 31, and six times in later plays.
A common and an outward man.—*All 's Well that Ends Well*, iii, 1, 11.
Homely man.—*Macbeth*, iv, 2, 68.
A plain man.—*Richard III*, i, 3, 51, and three times in later plays.
A plain, blunt man.—*Julius Cæsar*, iii, 2, 222.

15
And Humphrey is no little man in England.
II Henry VI. Act iii, sc. 1, l. 20. [Queen]

Petty men.—*Julius Cæsar*, i, 2, 136.

16
We are simple men.
The Merry Wives of Windsor. Act iv, sc. 2, l. 183. [Ford]

Simple man.—*I Henry VI*, iv, 1, 187.
Simple men.—*III Henry VI*, iii, 1, 83. See under SIMPLICITY.
An ordinary man.—*Twelfth Night*, i, 3, 90.
Ordinary men.—*Julius Cæsar*, iii, 1, 37; *King Lear*, i, 4, 36.

17
I will some other be, some Florentine,
Some Neapolitan, or meaner man of Pisa.
The Taming of the Shrew. Act i, sc. 1, l. 209. [Lucentio]

Meaner man.—*Coriolanus*, i, 6, 27.

Mean-born man.—*II Henry VI,* iii, 1, 335. "Mean-born" is repeated in *Richard III,* iv, 2, 54: "Mean-born gentleman."

A man not worth her pains.—*The Winter's Tale,* v, 1, 155. See under WORTH.

VIII—Honest Men

See also Honesty

1
True honest men being heard, like false Æneas,
Were in his time thought false.
Cymbeline. Act iii, sc. 4, l. 60. [Imogen]

2
Do not cast away an honest man for a villain's accusation.
II Henry VI. Act i, sc. 3, l. 206. [Horner]

3
Ye speak like honest men; pray God ye prove so!
Henry VIII. Act iii, sc. 1, l. 69. [Queen]

4
Mistress Quickly: The young man is an honest man.
Caius: What shall de honest man do in my closet? dere is no honest man dat shall come in my closet.
Merry Wives of Windsor. Act i, sc. 4, l. 75.

I cannot be said to be a flattering honest man.
Much Ado about Nothing, i, 3, 32. See under CANDOUR.

5
I do proclaim
One honest man—mistake me not—but one;
No more, I pray,—and he 's a steward.
Timon of Athens. Act iv, sc. 3, l. 509. [Timon]

Have I once lived to see two honest men?
Timon of Athens. Act v, sc. 1, l. 59. [Timon] "Honest man (men)" is used fifty-two times in the plays.

6
To be said an honest man and a good housekeeper goes as fairly as to say a careful man and a great scholar.
Twelfth Night. Act iv, sc. 2, l. 9. [Clown] "Housekeeper" occurs twice more in the plays, in *Coriolanus,* i, 3, 55, and in *Macbeth,* iii, 1, 97.

7
You seem to be honest plain men.
The Winter's Tale. Act iv, sc. 4, l. 824. [Autolycus]

Honest plain-dealing man.—*II Henry VI,* iv, 2, 111.

Honest old man.—*The Merchant of Venice,* ii, 2, 148. See also under HONESTY.

Free and honest men.—*Henry VIII,* iii, 1, 60.

Free men.—*Julius Cæsar,* iii, 2, 26.

Thrifty honest men.—*II Henry VI,* iv, 2, 196.

IX—Valiant Men

See also Valour

8
Many moe corrivals and dear men
Of estimation and command in arms.
I Henry IV. Act iv, sc. 4, l. 31. [Archbishop of York] "Corrival" (rival, competitor) is used again in *I Henry IV,* i, 3, 207.

9
Our present musters grow upon the file
To five and twenty thousand men of choice.
II Henry IV. Act i, sc. 3, l. 11. [Hastings]

Men of merit.—*II Henry IV,* ii, 4, 405.

Man of action.—*II Henry IV,* ii, 4, 406.

Men of courage.—*Henry V,* ii, 4, 8.

10
I knew him a good backsword man.
II Henry IV. Act iii, sc. 2, l. 71. [Shallow] The only use of "backsword man" (fencer at single-stick).

11
Of fighting men we have full three score thousand.
Henry V. Act iv, sc. 3, l. 3. [Westmoreland]

Thou shalt have twelve thousand fighting men.
Richard II. Act iii, sc. 2, l. 70. [Salisbury] The only uses of "fighting men."

12
O that we now had here
But one ten thousand of those men in England
That do no work to-day!
Henry V. Act iv, sc. 3, l. 16. [Westmoreland]

The French have reinforced their scatter'd men.
Henry V. Act iv, sc. 6, l. 36. [King Henry]

13
Mirror of all martial men.
I Henry VI. Act i, sc. 4, l. 74. [Talbot]

A martial man to be soft fancy's slave!
The Rape of Lucrece, l. 200.

An iron man.—*II Henry IV,* iv, 2, 8.

A man of steel.—*Antony and Cleopatra,* iv, 4, 33.

14
Lo, there thou stand'st, a breathing valiant man,
Of an invincible unconquer'd spirit!
I Henry VI. Act iv, sc. 2, l. 31. [General]

15
'Tis not his wont to be the hindmost man,
Whate'er occasion keeps him from us now.
II Henry VI. Act iii, sc. 1, l. 2. [King Henry] "Hindmost" is repeated in *Troilus and Cressida,* iii, 3, 160.

No man alive so fain as I!
II Henry VI. Act iii, sc. 1, l. 244. [Suffolk]

16
The man is a proper man, of mine honour.
II Henry VI, iv, 2, 102. The phrase "a proper man" was used in the first play, and fifteen times in later ones.

Upon my life, she finds, although I cannot,
Myself to be a marvellous proper man.
Richard III. Act i, sc. 2, l. 254. [Gloucester]

Pyramus is a sweet-faced man; a proper man, as one shall see in a summer's day; a most lovely gentleman-like man.
A Midsummer-Night's Dream. Act i, sc. 2, l. 88. [Quince] "Sweet-faced" is used again in *The Comedy of Errors,* v, 1, 418: "Sweet-faced youth." "Gentleman-like" is repeated four other times in the plays.

He is a proper man's picture.
The Merchant of Venice. Act i, sc. 2, l. 77. [Portia]

A proper man of person.
Troilus and Cressida. Act i, sc. 2, l. 209. [Pandarus]

As proper men as ever trod upon neat's leather.
Julius Cæsar. Act i, sc. 1, l. 29. [Commoner] "Neat's leather" is repeated in *The Tempest,* ii, 2, 73.
As proper a man as ever went on four legs.
The Tempest. Act ii, sc. 2, l. 63. [Stephano]
The properest man in Italy.—*Much Ado about Nothing,* v, 1, 173. The only use of "properest."
Paris is the properer man.—*Romeo and Juliet,* ii, 4, 217. "Properer man" is repeated in *As You Like It,* iii, 5, 51.

1
I will fill the house with armed men.
III Henry VI. Act i, sc. 1, l. 167. [York] "Armed men" is repeated in *I Henry VI,* ii, 2, 24, and in *Much Ado about Nothing,* v, 4, 128.
Man-at-arms.—*III Henry VI,* v, 4, 42; *II Henry IV,* ii, 2, 82.
Man of arms.—*I Henry VI,* i, 4, 30.
Men of war.—*Richard II,* ii, 1, 286; ii, 3, 52; *II Henry IV,* v, 1, 31.
The rapier and dagger man.—*Measure for Measure,* iv, 3, 15.
Military man.—*Henry V,* iii, 2, 86.
Military men.—*II Henry IV,* iv, 1, 62.
Stout men.—*Timon of Athens,* iv, 3, 32.

2
I dare do all that may become a man;
Who dares do more is none.
Macbeth. Act i, sc. 7, l. 46. [Macbeth]
When you durst do it, then you were a man;
And, to be more than what you were, you would
Be so much more the man.
Macbeth. Act i, sc. 7, l. 49. [Lady Macbeth]
Lady Macbeth: Are you a man?
Macbeth: Ay, and a bold one, that dare look on that
Which might appal the devil.
Macbeth. Act iii, sc. 4, l. 58.
Malcolm: Dispute it like a man.
Macduff: I shall do so;
But I must also feel it as a man.
Macbeth. Act iv, sc. 3, l. 220.

3
Why should a man whose blood is warm within,
Sit like his grandsire cut in alabaster?
Sleep when he wakes and creep into the jaundice
By being peevish?
The Merchant of Venice. Act i, sc. 1, l. 83. [Gratiano] "Alabaster" occurs twice more in the plays, in *Richard III,* iv, 3, 11, and in *Othello,* v, 2, 5. "Jaundice" is repeated in *Troilus and Cressida,* i, 3, 2.

4
Thy prime of manhood daring, bold, and venturous.
Richard III. Act iv, sc. 4, l. 170. [Duchess of York]

5 We are but shrubs, no cedars we,
No big-boned men framed of the Cyclops' size;
But metal, Marcus, steel to the very back.
Titus Andronicus. Act iv, sc. 3, l. 45. [Titus] The only use of "big-boned."

6
Alexander: They say he is a very man per se,
And stands alone.
Cressida: So do all men, unless they are drunk, sick, or have no legs.
Troilus and Cressida. Act i, sc. 2, l. 15. The only use of "per se."

7
That 's Æneas: is not that a brave man?
Troilus and Cressida. Act i, sc. 2, l. 202. [Pandarus]
Go thy way, Hector! There 's a brave man, niece.
O brave Hector! Look how he looks! . . . is 't not a brave man?
Troilus and Cressida. Act i, sc. 2, l. 216. [Pandarus]
That 's a brave man.—*As You Like It,* iii, 4, 43.
O, a brave man!—*Troilus and Cressida,* i, 2, 220. See also under COURAGE.

8
Look ye yonder, niece: is 't not a gallant man too, is 't not?
Troilus and Cressida. Act i, sc. 2, l. 231. [Pandarus]
Gallant man.—*Troilus and Cressida,* i, 2, 40.

X—Ruined Men

9 Stay there, sir,
And see the noble ruin'd man you speak of.
Henry VIII. Act ii, sc. 1, l. 54. [Gentleman]
Thou art the ruins of the noblest man
That ever lived in the tide of times.
Julius Cæsar. Act iii, sc. 1, l. 256. [Antony]

10
I am a poor fall'n man.
Henry VIII, iii, 2, 413. See under FALL.
Falling man.—*Henry VIII,* iii, 2, 333; v, 3, 77.
Weak men must fall.—*Richard II,* iii, 2, 62.
Broken man.—*Richard II,* ii, 1, 257.
Condemned man.—*Coriolanus,* iv, 5, 186.
Discarded men.—*The Merry Wives of Windsor,* ii, 1, 182.
Ebb'd man.—*Antony and Cleopatra,* i, 4, 43.
Ebbing men.—*The Tempest,* ii, 1, 226.

11
He shall live a man forbid.
Macbeth. Act i, sc. 3, l. 21. [Witch]
Henceforth be never number'd among men
A Midsummer-Night's Dream. Act iii, sc. 2, l. 67. [Hermia]

12
Our men are vanquish'd ere they do resist.
Pericles. Act i, sc. 2, l. 27. [Pericles]
Vanquish'd men.—*Passionate Pilgrim,* l. 280.

13
Thou art a banish'd man.
Richard II, ii, 3, 110. See under BANISHMENT.
These banish'd men that I have kept withal
Are men endued with worthy qualities.
The Two Gentlemen of Verona. Act v, sc. 4, l. 153. [Valentine] The only use of "endued."
Because you are a banish'd man,
Therefore, above the rest, we parley to you.
The Two Gentlemen of Verona. Act iv, sc. 1, l. 59. [Outlaw]
They are free men, but I am banished.
Romeo and Juliet, iii, 3, 42. See under BANISHMENT.

Banish'd man.—*III Henry VI,* iii, 3, 25; *Titus Andronicus,* iii, 1, 99; *Cymbeline,* v, 5, 319.

XI—Wretched Men

1
I am a poor man.
All's Well that Ends Well, v, 3, 251. See also under POVERTY.

Poor man (or men).—*II Henry VI,* iv, 7, 46, and thirty times in later plays.
Poor banish'd man.—*King Lear,* iii, 4, 169.
Poor famish'd man.—*II Henry VI,* iv, 10, 47.

My men; they are the poorest,
But poverty could never draw 'em from me.
Henry VIII. Act iv, sc. 2, l. 148. [Katharine]

2
A wretched ragged man, o'ergrown with hair.
As You Like It. Act iv, sc. 3, l. 107. [Oliver]

O, how wretched
Is that poor man that hangs on princes' favours!
Henry VIII. Act iii, sc. 2, l. 367. [Wolsey] See under PRINCE.

Wretched man.—*II Henry VI,* iii, 2, 72, and five times in later plays.
A living-dead man.—*The Comedy of Errors,* v, 1, 241. See under CHARACTER.

3
The shales and husks of men.
Henry V. Act iv, sc. 2, l. 18. [Constable of France] The only use of "shales."

4
Sad-hearted men, much overgone with care.
III Henry VI, ii, 5, 123. See under KING. The only use of "sad-hearted."

Sad-faced men.—*Titus Andronicus,* v, 3, 67. The only use of the phrase.
Sad man.—*Titus Andronicus,* v, 2, 28.
Brainsick men.—*I Henry VI,* iv, 1, 111.
Desperate man.—*Romeo and Juliet,* v, 3, 59.
Desperate men.—*Romeo and Juliet,* v, 1, 36; *King John,* iii, 1, 32.
Fearful man.—*III Henry VI,* v, 4, 44; *Romeo and Juliet,* iii, 3, 1.
Feeble man.—*Julius Cæsar,* ii, 4, 36.
Frantic man.—*Richard II,* iii, 3, 185.
Hungry-starved men.—*I Henry VI,* i, 5, 16. The only use of "hungry-starved."
Melancholy man.—*All's Well that Ends Well,* iii, 2, 4.
Needy man.—*Romeo and Juliet,* v, 1, 50.
Woful man.—*I Henry VI,* i, 4, 71.

5
Here is a sick man that would speak with you.
Julius Cæsar. Act ii, sc. 1, l. 310. [Lucius] "Sick man" is repeated five times.

Testy sick men.—*Sonnets,* cxl.
Men diseased.—*Sonnets,* cliv.

6
I am a man
More sinn'd against than sinning.
King Lear. Act iii, sc. 2, l. 59. [King Lear] The only use of "sinning."

Why, this would make a man a man of salt,
To use his eyes for garden water-pots,
Ay, and laying autumn's dust.
King Lear. Act iv, sc. 6, l. 199. [King Lear] The only use of "water-pots."

7
Where is this rash and most unfortunate man?
Othello. Act v, sc. 2, l. 283. [Lodovico]

8
A man whom both the waters and the wind,
In that vast tennis-court, have made the ball
For them to play upon.
Pericles. Act ii, sc. 1, l. 62. [Pericles] The only use of "tennis-court," in a scene probably not by Shakespeare. "Tennis" occurs in *Hamlet,* ii, 1, 59, and *Henry VIII,* i, 3, 30; "tennis-balls" in *Much Ado about Nothing,* iii, 2, 47, and *Henry V,* i, 2, 258.

9
We worldly men
Have miserable, mad, mistaking eyes.
Titus Andronicus. Act v, sc. 2, l. 65. [Titus]

Worldly men.—*Richard II,* iii, 2, 56.
Man of this world.—*II Henry IV,* v, 3, 102.

XII—Old and Young Men

See also Age and Youth

10
Parolles: You are too old, sir; let it satisfy you, you are too old.
Lafeu: I must tell thee, sirrah, I write man; to which title age cannot bring thee.
All's Well that Ends Well. Act ii, sc. 3, l. 208.

11
An old religious uncle, . . . who was in his youth an inland man.
As You Like It. Act iii, sc. 2, l. 362. [Rosalind]

Aged man.—*The Rape of Lucrece,* l. 855.
Gentle aged men.—*Titus Andronicus,* iii, 1, 23.
Goodly aged men.—*Timon of Athens,* v, 1, 175.
Gracious aged man.—*King Lear,* iv, 2, 41.
Venerable man.—*Cymbeline,* ii, 5, 3.

12
What, ye knaves! young men must live.
I Henry IV, ii, 2, 96. [Falstaff] "Young men" or "young man" is used thirty-seven times in the plays. See under YOUTH.

Lusty young men.—*Romeo and Juliet,* i, 2, 26.
Mad young man.—*Hamlet,* iv, 1, 19.
Younger man.—*As You Like It,* ii, 3, 54; *Coriolanus,* iv, 1, 22.
Youthful men.—*Comedy of Errors,* v, 1, 52.

13
York not their old men spares;
No more will I their babes.
II Henry VI. Act v, sc. 2, l. 51. [Young Clifford] "Old men" or "old man" is used fifty-nine times.

Idle old man.—*King Lear,* i, 3, 16.
Old religious man.—*As You Like It,* v, 4, 166.
Poor old man.—*King Lear,* ii, 4, 275.

14
'An old man, broken with the storms of state,
Is come to lay his weary bones among ye;
Give him a little earth for charity!'
Henry VIII. Act iv, sc. 2, l. 21. [Griffith, quoting Wolsey]

A poor, infirm, weak, and despised old man.
King Lear. Act iii, sc. 2, l. 20. [King Lear]

15
Tell him of Nestor, one that was a man

When Hector 's grandsire suck'd: he is old now.
Troilus and Cressida. Act i, sc. 3, l. 291. [Nestor]

1
'Tis a fair young man, and well attended.
Twelfth Night. Act i, sc. 5, l. 110. [Maria]

A young man
More fit to do another such offence
Than die for this.
Measure for Measure, ii, 3, 13. [Provost]

Young men, whom Aristotle thought
Unfit to hear moral philosophy.
Troilus and Cressida, ii, 2, 166. [Hector] A reference to the *Nicomachean Ethics,* bk. i, ch. 3, sec. 5.

XIII—Dead Men

2
The strait pass was damm'd
With dead men hurt behind.
Cymbeline. Act v, sc. 3, l. 11. [Posthumus]

He 's but a dead man.—*The Merry Wives of Windsor,* iv, 2, 44. "Dead man (or men)" occurs nineteen times.
Dying man.—*Henry VIII,* ii, 1, 125.
Dying men.—*Julius Cæsar,* ii, 2, 23; *King John,* ii, 1, 5; *Richard II,* ii, 1, 88.
Carrion men.—*Julius Cæsar,* iii, 1, 275.
Decayed men.—*The Comedy of Errors,* iv, 3, 26. See under OFFICER.
Mortal man.—*III Henry VI,* ii, 5, 29.
Mortal men.—*I Henry IV,* iv, 2, 73.
Slaughter'd men.—*King John,* iii, 1, 302.
Strangled man.—*II Henry VI,* iii, 2, 170.
Unburied men.—*Coriolanus,* iii, 3, 122.

3
That headless man
I thought had been my lord.
Cymbeline. Act v, sc. 5, l. 299. [Imogen] "Headless man" is repeated in iv, 2, 308; and "headless" in *II Henry VI,* i, 2, 65: "Headless necks"; *A Midsummer-Night's Dream,* iii, 1, 112: "Headless bear"; and *Titus Andronicus,* i, 1, 186: "Headless Rome."

4
Go thy ways, old Jack; die when thou wilt, if manhood, good manhood, be not forgot upon the face of the earth, then am I a shotten herring.
I Henry IV. Act ii, sc. 4, l. 141. [Falstaff] The only use of "shotten," referring to a herring which has shot or shed its roe, and which is therefore worthless.

Lancaster: Did you not tell me this fat man was dead?
Prince: I did; I saw him dead,
Breathless and bleeding on the ground. . . .
Thou art not what thou seem'st.
Falstaff: No, that 's certain; I am not a double man.
I Henry IV. Act v, sc. 4, l. 135.

Fat men.—*Merry Wives of Windsor,* ii, 1, 56.
Gross fat man.—*I Henry IV,* ii, 4, 560.
Whoreson round man.—*I Henry IV,* ii, 4, 155.
Thin man.—*II Henry IV,* v, 4, 20.

5
If these men do not die well, it will be a black matter for the king that led them to it.
Henry V. Act iv, sc. 1, l. 151. [Williams]

Can I make men live, whether they will or no?
II Henry VI. Act iii, sc. 3, l. 10. [Cardinal]

Why, am I dead? do I not breathe a man?
III Henry VI. Act iii, sc. 1, l. 82. [King Henry]

XIV—Man and Woman

6
That man should be at woman's command, and yet no hurt done!
All 's Well that Ends Well. Act i, sc. 3, l. 96. [Clown]

Men are to mell with, boys are not to kiss.
All 's Well that Ends Well. Act iv, sc. 3, l. 257. [Soldier] The only use of "mell" (copulate).

7
You are a thousand times a properer man
Than she a woman.
As You Like It. Act iii, sc. 5, l. 51. [Rosalind]

He is A man worth any woman.
Cymbeline. Act i, sc. 1, l. 145. [Imogen]

She is a woman More worth than any man.
The Winter's Tale, v, 1, 110. See under LOVE.

8
The beasts, the fishes and the winged fowls
Are their males' subjects and at their controls:
Men, more divine, the masters of all these,
Lords of the wide world and wild watery seas,
Indued with intellectual sense and souls,
Of more pre-eminence than fish and fowls,
Are masters to their females, and their lords.
The Comedy of Errors. Act ii, sc. 1, l. 18. [Luciana] "Pre-eminence" is repeated in *King Lear,* i, 1, 133.

9
Dromio of Syracuse: I am a woman's man. . . .
Antipholus of Syracuse: What woman's man? . . .
Dromio of Syracuse: I am due to a woman; one that claims me, one that haunts me, one that will have me.
The Comedy of Errors. Act iii, sc. 2, l. 77.

We are women's men.—*Antony and Cleopatra,* iii, 7, 71.

10
To think that man, who knows
By history, report, or his own proof,
What woman is, yea, what she cannot choose
But must be, will his free hours languish for
Assured bondage?
Cymbeline. Act i, sc. 6, l. 69. [Iachimo]

Is there no way for men to be but women
Must be half-workers?
Cymbeline. Act ii, sc. 5, l. 1. [Posthumus] The only use of "half-workers."

11
Man delights not me; no, nor woman neither.
Hamlet. Act ii, sc. 2, l. 323. [Hamlet]

12
Charles: Then come, o' God's name. I fear no woman.
La Pucelle: And while I live, I 'll ne'er fly from a man.
I Henry VI. Act i, sc. 2, l. 102.

1
I have a man's mind, but a woman's might.
Julius Cæsar. Act ii, sc. 4, l. 8. [Portia]

2
He is the half part of a blessed man,
Left to be finished by such as she;
And she a fair divided excellence,
Whose fulness of perfection lies in him.
King John. Act ii, sc. 1, l. 437. [Citizen]

3
It is the manner of a man to speak to a woman.
Love's Labour's Lost. Act i, sc. 1, l. 212. [Costard]

4
Nerissa: Why, shall we turn to men?
Portia: Fie, what a question 's that,
If thou wert near a lewd interpreter!
The Merchant of Venice. Act iii, sc. 4, l. 78.

5
I went to her, Master Brook, as you see, like a poor old man: but I came from her, Master Brook, like a poor old woman.
The Merry Wives of Windsor. Act v, sc. 1, l. 16. [Falstaff]

He beat me grievously, in the shape of a woman; for in the shape of man, Master Brook, I fear not Goliath with a weaver's beam.
The Merry Wives of Windsor. Act v, sc. 1, l. 21. [Falstaff] The only mention of Goliath in the plays, except for "Sampsons and Goliasas" in *I Henry VI,* i, 2, 33.

6
If you were men, as men you are in show,
You would not use a gentle lady so.
A Midsummer-Night's Dream. Act iii, sc. 2, l. 151. [Helena]

He for a man, God warrant us; she for a woman, God bless us.
A Midsummer-Night's Dream. Act v, sc. 1, l. 325. [Demetrius]

7
O that I were a man!
Much Ado about Nothing. Act iv, sc. 1, l. 305. [Beatrice]

O that I were a man for his sake! or that I had any friend would be a man for my sake! But manhood is melted into courtesies, valour into compliment, and men are only turned into tongue, and trim ones too.
Much Ado about Nothing. Act iv, sc. 1, l. 319. [Beatrice]

I cannot be a man with wishing, therefore I will die a woman with grieving.
Much Ado about Nothing. Act iv, sc. 1, l. 325. [Beatrice]

She wish'd
That heaven had made her such a man.
Othello. Act i, sc. 3, l. 162. [Othello]

I wish'd myself a man.—*Troilus and Cressida,* iii, 2, 136. See under WOOING.

8
Men have marble, women waxen, minds.
The Rape of Lucrece, l. 1240.

Though men can cover crimes with bold stern looks,
Poor women's faces are their own faults' books.
The Rape of Lucrece, l. 1252.

O, let it not be hild
Poor women's faults, that they are so fulfill'd
With men's abuses: those proud lords, to blame,
Make weak-made women tenants to their shame.
The Rape of Lucrece, l. 1257. The only use of "hild" (held) and "weak-made."

9
No less! nay, bigger; women grow by men.
Romeo and Juliet. Act i, sc. 3, l. 95. [Nurse]

And art thou changed? pronounce this sentence then,
Women may fall, when there 's no strength in men.
Romeo and Juliet. Act ii, sc. 3, l. 79. [Friar Laurence]

10
Art thou a man? thy form cries out thou art:
Thy tears are womanish; thy wild acts denote
The unreasonable fury of a beast:
Unseemly woman in a seeming man!
Or ill-beseeming beast in seeming both!
Romeo and Juliet. Act iii, sc. 3, l. 109. [Friar Laurence] The only use of "unseemly."

11
Surely, this man Was born of woman.
Timon of Athens. Act iv, sc. 3, l. 500. [Timon]

Man that 's of a woman born.—*Macbeth,* v, 7, 13.

Think like a man, but of no woman bred.
Venus and Adonis, l. 214. See under IDOLATRY.

12
A woman impudent and mannish grown
Is not more loathed than an effeminate man
In time of action.
Troilus and Cressida. Act iii, sc. 3, l. 217. [Patroclus] "Mannish" is repeated in *As You Like It,* i, 3, 129: "Mannish cowards"; and in *Cymbeline,* iv, 2, 236: "Mannish crack."

13
As I am man,
My state is desperate for my master's love;
As I am woman,—now alas the day!—
What thriftless sighs shall poor Olivia breathe!
Twelfth Night. Act ii, sc. 2, l. 37. [Viola]

However we do praise ourselves,
Our fancies are more giddy and unfirm,
More longing, wavering, sooner lost and worn,
Than women's are.
Twelfth Night. Act ii, sc. 4, l. 33. [Duke]

MANNERS

See also Behaviour, Court, Courtesy

14
Countess: Come on, sir; I shall now put you to the height of your breeding.
Clown: I will show myself highly fed and lowly taught.
All's Well that Ends Well. Act ii, sc. 2, l. 1.

So far beneath your soft and tender breeding.
Twelfth Night. Act v, sc. 1, l. 331. [Duke]

What is breeding
That changeth thus his manners.
The Winter's Tale. Act i, sc. 2, l. 374. [Polixenes]

Good breeding.—*As You Like It,* iii, 2, 31; *Twelfth Night,* iii, 4, 204.
Higher breeding.—*II Henry IV,* ii, 2, 39.
Virtuous breeding.—*Henry VIII,* iv, 2, 134.
Of excellent breeding.—*The Merry Wives of Windsor,* ii, 2, 234.
Want of breeding.—*Cymbeline,* iv, 4, 26.

1 A rude despiser of good manners.
As You Like It. Act ii, sc. 7, l. 92. [Duke Senior] The only use of "despiser."

You have books for good manners.
As You Like It. Act v, sc. 4, l. 95. [Touchstone]

Well, I am school'd: good manners be your speed!
I Henry IV. Act iii, sc. 1, l. 190. [Hotspur]

When good manners shall lie all in one or two men's hands and they unwashed too, 'tis a foul thing.
Romeo and Juliet. Act i, sc. 5, l. 4. [Servant]

Good manners.—*As You Like It,* iii, 2, 42; 43; 47; *Henry VIII,* v, 2, 29.
Dishonest manners.—*Henry V,* i, 2, 49.
Lavish manners.—*II Henry IV,* iv, 4, 64.
Plausive manners.—*Hamlet,* i, 4, 30.

2 She says . . . that I lack manners.
As You Like It. Act iv, sc. 3, l. 15. [Rosalind]

3 I 'll view the manners of the town.
The Comedy of Errors. Act i, sc. 2, l. 12. [Antipholus of Syracuse]

4 I am much sorry, sir,
You put me to forget a lady's manners,
By being so verbal.
Cymbeline. Act ii, sc. 3, l. 109. [Imogen] "Verbal" occurs again in *All's Well that Ends Well,* v, 3, 137, and in *King Lear,* iv, 3, 26.

My fears forgetting manners.
Hamlet. Act v, sc. 2, l. 17. [Hamlet]

5 What foolish master taught you these manners, Sir John?
II Henry IV. Act ii, sc. 1, l. 202. [Chief Justice]

I 'll teach you differences.
King Lear. Act i, sc. 4, l. 99. [Kent]

6 Garnish'd and deck'd in modest complement.
Henry V, ii, 2, 134. See under CHARACTER.

Complement extern.—*Othello,* i, 1, 63. "Extern" is repeated in *Sonnets,* cxxv.
Complement and ceremony.—*The Merry Wives of Windsor,* iv, 2, 5. The only uses of "complement," that which completes the manners and demeanour of a gentleman.

7 O, he is the courageous captain of complements.
Romeo and Juliet. Act ii, sc. 4, l. 20. [Mercutio]

A man of complements.—*Love's Labour 's Lost,* i, 1, 169.
These are complements.—*Love's Labour 's Lost,* iii, 1, 23. The only uses of "complements."

8 You and I cannot be confined within the weak list of a country's fashion: we are the makers of manners.
Henry V. Act v, sc. 2, l. 294. [King Henry]

9 Foul indigested lump,
As crooked in thy manners as thy shape!
II Henry VI. Act v, sc. 1, l. 158. [Clifford]

An indigested and deformed lump.—*III Henry VI,* v, 6, 51. The only uses of "indigested."

He is as disproportion'd in his manners
As in his shape.
The Tempest. Act v, sc. 1, l. 290. [Prospero] "Disproportion'd" is used again in *Othello,* i, 3, 2.

10 Men's evil manners live in brass; their virtues
We write in water.
Henry VIII. Act iv, sc. 2, l. 45. [Griffith]

11 Our country manners give our betters way.
King John. Act i, sc. 1, l. 156. [Bastard]

Comely-distant sits he by her side.
A Lover's Complaint, l. 65. The only use of "comely-distant."

Are you so formal, sir?
The Taming of the Shrew. Act iii, sc. 1, l. 61. [Lucentio]

Here 's a million of manners.
The Two Gentlemen of Verona. Act ii, sc. 1, l. 104. [Speed]

12 Quite athwart Goes all decorum.
Measure for Measure. Act i, sc. 3, l. 30. [Duke]

Keep decorum.—*Antony and Cleopatra,* i, 2, 77. Repeated in v, 2, 17. "Decorum" occurs again in *Measure for Measure,* i, 3, 31.

13 My manners tell me
We have your wrong rebuke.
Othello. Act i, sc. 1, l. 130. [Roderigo]

Let it not gall your patience, good Iago,
That I extend my manners; 'tis my breeding
That gives me this bold show of courtesy.
Othello. Act ii, sc. 1, l. 98. [Cassio]

These bloody accidents must excuse my manners,
That so neglected you.
Othello. Act v, sc. 1, l. 94. [Iago]

14 Be Kent unmannerly, When Lear is mad.
King Lear. Act i, sc. 1, l. 147. [Kent]

I 'll rather be unmannerly than troublesome.
The Merry Wives of Windsor. Act i, sc. 1, l. 325. [Slender]

An unmannerly slave, that will thrust himself into secrets!
The Two Gentlemen of Verona. Act iii, sc. 1, l. 393. [Launce]

This apish and unmannerly approach.
King John. Act v, sc. 2, l. 131. [Bastard]

Their manners are so apish.—*King Lear,* i, 4, 184.
Apish courtesy.—*Richard III,* i, 3, 49.
Apish nation.—*Richard II,* ii, 1, 22.
Apish, shallow, inconstant.—*As You Like It,* iii, 2, 432. The only uses of "apish."

Unmannerly intruder as thou art!
Titus Andronicus. Act ii, sc. 3, l. 65. [Tamora] "Unmannerly" is used thirteen times.

Go, base intruder!—*The Two Gentlemen of*

Verona, iii, 1, 157. The only uses of "intruder" in the plays.
Unmanner'd dog!—*Richard III,* i, 2, 39.
Unmanner'd slaves!—*Taming of the Shrew,* iv, i, 169. The only uses of "unmanner'd."

1
Public means which public manners breeds.
Sonnets. No. cxi.

2
Frame your manners to the time.
The Taming of the Shrew. Act i, sc. 1, l. 232. [Lucentio]
Use your manners discreetly in all kind of companies.
The Taming of the Shrew. Act i, sc. 1, l. 247. [Tranio]
Let them curtsy with their left legs and not presume to touch a hair of my master's horse-tail till they kiss their hands.
The Taming of the Shrew. Act iv, sc. 1, l. 95. [Grumio] The only use of "horse-tail."

3
Their manners are more gentle-kind than of
Our human generation you shall find
Many, nay, almost any.
The Tempest. Act iii, sc. 3, l. 32. [Gonzalo] The only use of "gentle-kind."

4
Thou dost affect my manners, and dost use them.
Timon of Athens. Act iv, sc. 3, l. 199. [Apemantus]

5
Have you no wit, manners, nor honesty, but to gabble like tinkers at this time of night?
Twelfth Night. Act ii, sc. 3, l. 94. [Malvolio] "Gabble" is repeated in *All's Well that Ends Well,* iv, 1, 22, and in *The Tempest,* i, 2, 356.

6
Lucetta, as thou lovest me, let me have
What thou thinkest meet and is most mannerly.
The Two Gentlemen of Verona. Act ii, sc. 7, l. 57. [Julia]
Comes so mannerly.—*The Merchant of Venice,* ii, 9, 100.
Mannerly demand.—*Cymbeline,* iii, 6, 92.
Mannerly devotion.—*Romeo and Juliet,* i, 5, 100.
Mannerly distinguishment.—*The Winter's Tale,* ii, 1, 86. The only use of "distinguishment."
Mannerly forbearance.—*I Henry VI,* ii, 4, 19. The only uses of "mannerly."
Mannerly-modest.—*Much Ado about Nothing,* ii, 1, 79. The only use of the phrase.

7
We stand upon our manners.
Winter's Tale. Act iv, sc. 4, l. 164. [Clown]
Is there no manners left among maids?
Winter's Tale. Act iv, sc. 4, l. 244. [Clown]

MANSION

See also House

8
Her house is sack'd, her quiet interrupted,
Her mansion batter'd by the enemy;
Her sacred temple spotted, spoil'd, corrupted,
Grossly engirt with daring infamy.
The Rape of Lucrece, l. 1170.
Accursed The mansion!—*Cymbeline,* v, 5, 155.

9
O, what a mansion have those vices got!
Sonnets. No. lxv.
Everlasting mansion.—*Timon of Athens,* v, 1, 218. See under GRAVE.
Fading mansion.—*Sonnets,* cxlvi.
Fair mansion.—*Merchant of Venice,* iii, 2, 170.
Hateful mansion.—*Romeo and Juliet,* iii, 3, 108.
Innocent mansion.—*Cymbeline,* iii, 4, 70.
Marble mansion.—*Cymbeline,* v, 4, 87.
Marbled mansion.—*Timon of Athens,* iv, 3, 191. The only use of "marbled."

10
Leave not the mansion so long tenantless.
The Two Gentlemen of Verona, v, 4, 8. See under ABSENCE.

MAP

11
Glendower: Come, here 's the map: shall we divide our right
According to our three-fold order ta'en?
Mortimer: The archdeacon hath divided it
Into three limits very equally.
I Henry IV. Act iii, sc. 1, l. 70. The only use of "archdeacon."
Give me the map, there.—*King Lear,* i, 1, 38.

12
If you look in the maps of the 'orld, I warrant you sall find, in the comparisons between Macedon and Monmouth, that the situations, look you, is both alike.
Henry V. Act iv, sc. 7, l. 24. [Fluellen]
Map of days.—*Sonnets,* lxviii.
Map of death.—*The Rape of Lucrece,* l. 402.
Map of honour.—*II Henry VI,* iii, 1, 203; *Richard II,* v, 1, 12.
Map of my microcosm.—*Coriolanus,* ii, 1, 68. The only use of "microcosm." See CHARACTER, 174:2.
Map of woe.—*Titus Andronicus,* iii, 2, 12.

13
Peering in maps for ports and piers and roads.
The Merchant of Venice. Act i, sc. 1, l. 19. [Salanio]
The new map with the augmentation of the Indies.
Twelfth Night, iii, 2, 85. See under SMILE.

MARINER, see Sailor

MARK

14
To be the mark Of mouldy muskets.
All's Well that Ends Well. Act iii, sc. 2, l. 110. [Helena]

15
There is none of my uncle's marks upon you.
As You Like It, iii, 2, 387. See under LOVE.
What were his marks?—*As You Like It,* iii, 2, 391.

16
Told me what privy marks I had about me, as, the mark of my shoulder.
The Comedy of Errors. Act iii, sc. 2, l. 147. [Dromio of Syracuse]
Some marks Of secret on her person.
Cymbeline. Act v, sc. 5, l. 205. [Iachimo]

1
Her enemies' marks upon me.
Coriolanus. Act iii, sc. 3, l. 111. [Coriolanus]
Foemen's marks.—*Titus Andronicus,* iv, 1, 127.
2
He was the mark and glass, copy and book
That fashion'd others.
II Henry IV, ii, 3, 31. See under EXAMPLE.
3
Call we to mind, and mark but this.
I Henry VI. Act iii, sc. 3, l. 68. [La Pucelle]
Attend, and mark.—*A Midsummer-Night's Dream,* iv, 1, 98.
Mark a little while.—*Winter's Tale,* v, 3, 118.
Mark, I say, instantly.—*King Lear,* v, 3, 36.
Mark her well.—*The Winter's Tale,* ii, 1, 65.
Mark him.—*Julius Cæsar,* iii, 1, 18; iii, 2, 122; *Troilus and Cressida,* i, 2, 251.
Mark it.—*Hamlet,* i, 1, 43; *King Lear,* i, 4, 130; *Cymbeline,* i, 1, 58.
Mark me.—*The Merchant of Venice,* ii, 2, 51, and six times in later plays.
Mark what I say.—*Measure for Measure,* iv, 3, 130; *Troilus and Cressida,* v, 7, 2.
Mark ye me.—*I Henry IV,* iii, 1, 139.
Mark you.—*Hamlet,* ii, 1, 41.
Mark you but that! *The Merchant of Venice,* v, 1, 243.
Mark you that?—*Coriolanus,* ii, 2, 150; *Hamlet,* v, 1, 19.
Mark you this.—*The Merchant of Venice,* i, 3, 98; *Much Ado about Nothing,* i, 1, 213; *Coriolanus,* iii, 3, 74.
Mark you now.—*Henry V,* iv, 7, 3; 44.
Pray you, mark.—*The Merry Wives of Windsor,* iv, 1, 45; *Hamlet,* iv, 5, 38.
Didst not mark?—*Othello,* ii, 1, 260.
Do you mark me, sir?—*Tempest,* ii, 1, 169.
Do you mark that?—*Hamlet,* iii, 2, 118; *King Lear,* i, 4, 333; *Macbeth,* v, 1, 46.
I did not mark it.—*Julius Cæsar,* i, 2, 236.
They do not mark me.—*Love's Labour 's Lost,* v, 2, 172.
Thou dost not mark me.—*Romeo and Juliet,* ii, 4, 188.
Nobody marks you.—*Much Ado about Nothing,* i, 1, 118.

If they did hear,
They would not mark me, or if they did mark,
They would not pity me.
Titus Andronicus. Act iii, sc. 1, l. 33. [Titus]
4
That 's the golden mark I seek to hit.
II Henry VI, i, 1, 243. See under CROWN.
Princes, it is too late to talk of love;
And that 's the mark I know you level at.
Pericles. Act ii, sc. 3, l. 113. [Simonides]
5
Hast thou a mark to thyself, like an honest plain-dealing man?
II Henry VI, iv, 2, 110. See under EDUCATION.
6
By no means I may discover them
By any mark of favour.
Julius Cæsar. Act ii, sc. 1, l. 75. [Lucius]
Marks of love.—*Much Ado about Nothing,* ii, 3, 255.
Marks of merit.—*Coriolanus,* ii, 3, 172.
Mark of modesty.—*Rape of Lucrece,* l. 1220.
Marks of sovereignty.—*King Lear,* i, 4, 252.
Mark of thought.—*Antony and Cleopatra,* iii, 6, 87.
Mark of virtue.—*Merchant of Venice,* iii, 2, 82.
Mark of wonder.—*Cymbeline,* v, 5, 365.
Mark prodigious.—*A Midsummer-Night's Dream,* v, 1, 419.
7
Maria: A mark marvellous well shot, for they did both hit it.
Boyet: A mark! O, mark but that mark! A mark, says my lady!
Let the mark have a prick in 't, to mete at, if it may be.
Love's Labour 's Lost. Act iv, sc. 1, l. 133.
You have hit the mark.—*Henry VIII,* ii, 1, 165.
Hits the mark.—*Pericles,* i, 1, 164. See under Bow.
8
The scornful mark of every open eye.
The Rape of Lucrece, l. 520.
9
Benvolio: I aim'd so near, when I supposed you loved.
Romeo: A right good mark-man! And she 's fair I love.
Benvolio: A right fair mark, fair coz, is soonest hit.
Romeo and Juliet. Act i, sc. 1, l. 211. The only use of "mark-man."
10
Methinks he hath no drowning mark upon him.
The Tempest, i, 1, 31. See under HANGING.
11
Nor set A mark so bloody on the business.
The Tempest. Act i, sc. 2, l. 141. [Prospero]
Bloody marks.—*III Henry VI,* ii, 5, 71.
Ever-fixed mark.—*Sonnets,* cxvi. "Ever-fixed" is repeated in *Othello,* ii, 1, 15: "Ever-fixed pole."
Eye-offending marks.—*King John,* iii, 1, 47. "Eye-offending" is repeated in *Twelfth Night,* i, 1, 30: "Eye-offending brine."
Official marks.—*Coriolanus,* ii, 3, 148.
Slander's mark.—*Sonnets,* lxx.
12
Stand, stand, thou Greek; thou art a goodly mark.
Troilus and Cressida. Act v, sc. 6, l. 27. [Hector]
Graceful marks.—*Pericles,* iv, Gower, 36.
Gracious mark.—*The Winter's Tale,* iv, 4, 8.
Bless the mark.—*The Two Gentlemen of Verona,* iv, 4, 21; *The Merchant of Venice,* ii, 2, 25; *Othello,* i, 1, 33.
Save the mark!—*I Henry IV,* i, 3, 56; *Romeo and Juliet,* iii, 2, 53.
13
Thy mark is feeble age.
Venus and Adonis, l. 941. See under DEATH.

MARKET

14
Sell when you can: you are not for all markets.
As You Like It. Act iii, sc. 5, l. 60. [Rosalind]
We shall be the more marketable.
As You Like It, i, 2, 103. See under NEWS.
No doubt, marketable.—*The Tempest,* v, 1, 266. The only uses of "marketable."

1
In open market-place produced they me.
I Henry VI, i, 4, 40. See under ENTERTAINMENT. "Market-place" occurs twenty-two times in the plays, always merely as the designation as the place for a meeting or ceremony.
I 'll meet with you upon the mart.
The Comedy of Errors. Act i, sc. 2, l. 27. [Merchant] "Mart" is used twelve times in this play, and five times in all the others.
Desperate mart.—*The Taming of the Shrew,* ii, 1, 329.
Foreign mart.—*Hamlet,* i, 1, 74.
Syracusan marts.—*Comedy of Errors,* i, 1, 18.
2
Market men That come to gather money.
I Henry VI, iii, 2, 4. See under WORD. "Market-men" (hyphenated) is repeated in v, 5, 54, and occurs in no other play.
Poor market folks that come to sell their corn.
I Henry VI. Act iii, sc. 2, l. 14. [La Pucelle] The only use of "market folks."
Go in; the market bell is rung.
I Henry VI. Act iii, sc. 2, l. 16. [Watchman] The only use of "market bell."
Proclaim'd at market-crosses, read in churches.
I Henry IV. Act v, sc. 1, l. 73. [King Henry] The only use of "market-crosses."
Market-days.—*II Henry VI,* iv, 2, 62. The only use of the phrase.
Market-maid.—*Antony and Cleopatra,* iii, 6, 51. The only use of the phrase.
Market-price.—*All's Well that Ends Well,* v, 3, 219. The only use of the phrase.
Market-town.—*II Henry VI,* ii, 1, 159; *King Lear,* iii, 6, 78.
3
Bawd: Hast thou cried her through the market?
Boult: I have cried her almost to the number of her hairs; I have drawn her picture with my voice.
Pericles. Act iv, sc. 2, l. 98.
Search the market narrowly.—*Pericles,* iv, 2, 3.
Shall I search the market?—*Pericles,* iv, 2, 18.
Idle markets.—*Twelfth Night,* iii, 3, 46.

MARRIAGE

See also Match, Nuptial, Wedlock

4
Countess: Tell me thy reason why thou wilt marry.
Clown: My poor body, madam, requires it: I am driven on by the flesh.
All's Well that Ends Well. Act i, sc. 3, l. 29.
I do marry that I may repent.
All's Well that Ends Well. Act i, sc. 3, l. 39. [Clown]
If men could be contented to be what they are, there were no fear in marriage.
All's Well that Ends Well. Act i, sc. 3, l. 54. [Clown]
5
Good fortune and the favour of the king
Smile upon this contract; whose ceremony
Shall seem expedient on the now-born brief,
And be perform'd to-night: the solemn feast
Shall more attend upon the coming space,
Expecting absent friends.
All's Well that Ends Well. Act ii, sc. 3, l. 184. [King]
A contract of true love to celebrate.
The Tempest. Act iv, sc. 1, l. 84. [Iris] Repeated in l. 133.
A contract of eternal bond of love.—*Twelfth Night,* v, 1, 159. See also under BETROTHAL.
6
A young man married is a man that 's marr'd.
All's Well that Ends Well. Act ii, sc. 3, l. 315. [Parolles]
7
If you shall marry,
You give away this hand, and that is mine;
You give away heaven's vows, and those are mine;
You give away myself, which is known mine;
For I by vow am so embodied yours,
That she which marries you must marry me,
Either both or none.
All's Well that Ends Well. Act v, sc. 3, l. 169. [Diana] The only use of "embodied."
8
Let me be married to three kings in a forenoon, and widow them all.
Antony and Cleopatra. Act i, sc. 2, l. 26. [Charmian]
9
By this marriage,
All little jealousies, which now seem great,
And all great fears, which now import their dangers,
Would then be nothing.
Antony and Cleopatra. Act ii, sc. 2, l. 133. [Agrippa]
Though I make this marriage for my peace,
I' the east my pleasure lies.
Antony and Cleopatra. Act ii, sc. 3, l. 39. [Antony]
10
Cleopatra: [Antony is] thou say'st free.
Messenger: Free, madam! no; I made no such report:
He 's bound unto Octavia.
Cleopatra: For what good turn?
Messenger: For the best turn i' the bed. . . .
Madam, he 's married to Octavia.
Antony and Cleopatra. Act ii, sc. 5, l. 56.
He married but his occasion here.
Antony and Cleopatra. Act ii, sc. 6, l. 139. [Enobarbus]
11
Jaques: Will you be married, motley?
Touchstone. As the ox hath his bow, sir, the horse his curb and the falcon her bells, so man hath his desires; and as pigeons bill, so wedlock would be nibbling.
Jaques: And will you, being a man of your breeding, be married under a bush like a beggar? Get you to church, and have a good priest that can tell you what marriage is: this fellow will but join you together as they join wainscot; then one of you will prove a shrunk panel and, like green timber, warp, warp.

Touchstone (Aside): I am not in the mind but I am better to be married of him than of another; for he is not like to marry me well; and not being well married, it will be a good excuse for me hereafter to leave my wife. . . .

Come, sweet Audrey:
We must be married, or we must live in bawdry. . . .
Wind away, Begone, I say,
I will not to wedding with thee.

As You Like It. Act iii, sc. 3, l. 79. The only use of "wainscot" and "panel." "Nibbling" is repeated in *The Tempest,* iv, 1, 62.

Touchstone: We shall find a time, Audrey; patience, gentle Audrey.
Audrey: Faith, the priest was good enough, for all the old gentleman's saying.

As You Like It. Act v, sc. 1, l. 1.

I will marry you, if ever I marry woman, and I'll be married to-morrow.

As You Like It. Act v, sc. 2, l. 122. [Rosalind]

To-morrow is the joyful day, Audrey; to-morrow will we be married.

As You Like It. Act v, sc. 3, l. 1. [Touchstone]

To couple us.—*As You Like It,* iii, 3, 45.

1
According as marriage binds and blood breaks.

As You Like It. Act v, sc. 4, l. 59. [Touchstone]

2
Adriana: This servitude makes you to keep unwed.
Luciana: Not this, but troubles of the marriage-bed.

The Comedy of Errors. Act ii, sc. 1, l. 26. "Unwed" is repeated in *The Passionate Pilgrim,* l. 304; "marriage-bed" occurs twice in *King John,* iii, 1, 245; v, 2, 93.

Marriage-day.—*Romeo and Juliet,* v, 3, 233; *All's Well that Ends Well,* v, 3, 70; *Pericles,* v, 3, 76.
Marriage-dowry.—*Measure for Measure,* iii, 1, 230.
Marriage-feast.—*Love's Labour's Lost,* ii, 1, 40; *Pericles,* iii, Gower, 4.
Marriage-hour.—*The Two Gentlemen of Verona,* ii, 4, 179.
Marriage joys.—*Richard III,* iv, 4, 330.
Marriage-pleasures.—*Pericles,* i, Gower, 34.
Marriage-rite.—*Pericles,* i, Gower, 17.
Marriage-vow.—*The Merry Wives of Windsor,* ii, 2, 258.

3
What, was I married to her in my dream?
Or sleep I now and think I hear all this?

The Comedy of Errors. Act ii, sc. 2, l. 184. [Antipholus of Syracuse]

4
Give out Conjectural marriages.

Coriolanus, i, 1, 198. See under RUMOUR. "Conjectural" is repeated in *All's Well that Ends Well,* v, 3, 114: "Conjectural fears."

Bad marriage.—*Twelfth Night,* i, 5, 21.
Blessed marriage.—*Henry V,* v, 2, 392.
Forced marriage.—*The Merry Wives of Windsor,* v, 5, 243.
Holy marriage.—*Romeo and Juliet,* ii, 3, 61. The only use of the phrase.
Home-bred marriage.—*III Henry VI,* iv, 1, 38. "Home-bred" is repeated in *Richard II,* i, 3, 187: "Home-bred hate."
Intended marriage.—*Much Ado about Nothing,* i, 3, 47.
Sweet marriage.—*The Tempest,* ii, 1, 72.
Twofold marriage.—*Richard II,* v, 1, 72.

5
If thou wilt needs marry, marry a fool; for wise men know well enough what monsters you make of them.

Hamlet. Act iii, sc. 1, l. 142. [Hamlet]

We will have no more marriages: those that are married already, all but one, shall live; the rest shall keep as they are.

Hamlet. Act iii, sc. 1, l. 154. [Hamlet]

6
Mistress Ursula, whom I have weekly sworn to marry since I perceived the first white hair on my chin.

II Henry IV. Act i, sc. 2, l. 269. [Falstaff] The only use of "weekly."

7
When they marry, they get wenches.

II Henry IV. Act iv, sc. 3, l. 101. [Falstaff]

On whom there is no more dependency
But brats and beggary, in self-figured knot.

Cymbeline. Act ii, sc. 3, l. 123. [Cloten] The only use of "self-figured."

8
Make this marriage to be solemnized.

I Henry VI. Act v, sc. 3, l. 168. [Suffolk]

For at Saint Mary's chapel presently
The rites of marriage shall be solemnized.

King John. Act ii, sc. 1, l. 538. [King Philip]

9
Marriage is a matter of more worth
Than to be dealt in by attorneyship.

I Henry VI. Act v, sc. 5, l. 55. [Suffolk] The only use of "attorneyship."

Fatal this marriage, cancelling your fame.

II Henry VI. Act i, sc. 1, l. 99. [Gloucester]

10 Fall by war's mischance,
For mocking marriage.

III Henry VI. Act iii, sc. 3, l. 254. [King Lewis]

With marriage wherefore was he mocked?

Cymbeline. Act v, sc. 4, l. 58. [Mother]

11
Matter of marriage was the charge he gave me.

III Henry VI. Act iii, sc. 3, l. 258. [Warwick]

Hasty marriage seldom proveth well.

III Henry VI. Act iv, sc. 1, l. 18. [Gloucester]

Our overhasty marriage.—*Hamlet,* ii, 2, 57. The only use of "overhasty."

12
No, God forbid that I should wish them sever'd
Whom God hath join'd together; ay, and 'twere pity
To sunder them that yoke so well together.

III Henry VI. Act iv, sc. 1, l. 21. [Gloucester]

God, the best maker of all marriages.

Henry V. Act v, sc. 2, l. 387. [Queen Isabel]

1
Though I want a kingdom, yet in marriage
I may not prove inferior to yourself.
III Henry VI. Act iv, sc. 1, l. 121. [Clarence]

2
Prove but our marriage lawful, by my life
And kingly dignity, we are contented.
Henry VIII. Act ii, sc. 4, l. 226. [King Henry]

Deem'd our marriage lawful.—*Henry VIII,* ii, 4, 53.

Lawful marriage.—*III Henry VI,* iii, 3, 57.

3
I was once before him for getting a wench with child; . . . but I was fain to forswear it; they would else have married me to the rotten medlar.
Measure for Measure. Act iv, sc. 3, l. 179. [Lucio]

Lucio: Marrying a punk, my lord, is pressing to death, whipping, and hanging.
Duke: Slandering a prince deserves it.
Measure for Measure. Act v, sc. 1, l. 528. "Punk" occurs four times in the plays.

I marry her! what? a customer!
Othello. Act iv, sc. 1, l. 122. [Cassio]

4
Consenting to the safeguard of your honour,
I thought your marriage fit; else imputation,
For that he knew you, might reproach your life
And choke your good to come.
Measure for Measure. Act v, sc. 1, l. 424. [Duke]

5
I had rather be married to a death's-head with a bone in his mouth.
The *Merchant of Venice.* Act i, sc. 2, l. 55. [Portia] "Death's-head" occurs also in *I Henry IV,* iii, 3, 34, and in *II Henry IV,* ii, 4, 255.

If I should marry him, I should marry twenty husbands.
The Merchant of Venice. Act i, sc. 2, l. 67. [Portia]

If he have the condition of a saint and the complexion of a devil, I had rather he should shrive me than wive me.
The Merchant of Venice. Act i, sc. 2, l. 142. [Portia]

6
Swear before you choose, if you choose wrong
Never to speak to lady afterward
In way of marriage.
The Merchant of Venice. Act ii, sc. 1, l. 40. [Portia]

Never in my life
To woo a maid in way of marriage.
The Merchant of Venice. Act ii, sc. 9, l. 12. [Arragon]

7
I am half yourself.
The Merchant of Venice. Act iii, sc. 2, l. 251. [Portia]

I would have daffed all other respects and made her half myself.
Much Ado about Nothing. Act ii, sc. 3, l. 176. [Don Pedro] "Daffed" occurs again in *I Henry IV,* iv, 1, 96.

8
The ancient saying is no heresy,
Hanging and wiving goes by destiny.
The Merchant of Venice. Act ii, sc. 9, l. 82. [Nerissa] "Wiving" occurs once again in *Cymbeline,* v, 5, 167.

For I the ballad will repeat,
Which men full true shall find;
Your marriage comes by destiny,
Your cuckoo sings by kind.
All's Well that Ends Well. Act i, sc. 3, l. 64. [Clown]

9
I will marry her upon any reasonable demands.
The Merry Wives of Windsor. Act i, sc. 1, l. 232. [Slender]

This 'tis to be married!
The Merry Wives of Windsor. Act iii, sc. 5, l. 144. [Ford]

In the lawful name of marrying,
To give our hearts united ceremony.
The Merry Wives of Windsor. Act iv, sc. 6, l. 50. [Fenton]

Desire a marriage.—*The Merry Wives of Windsor,* i, 1, 57.

In the way of marriage.—*The Merry Wives of Windsor,* i, 4, 89.

10 In the temple, by and by, with us
These couples shall eternally be knit.
A Midsummer-Night's Dream. Act iv, sc. 1, l. 184. [Theseus] The only use of "eternally."

11
Benedick, the married man.
Much Ado about Nothing, i, 1, 270; v, 1, 185; v, 4, 100.

A married man! that's most intolerable.—*I Henry VI,* v, 4, 79.

Are you a married man or a bachelor?—*Julius Cæsar,* iii, 3, 8.

If he be a married man, he's his wife's head.—*Measure for Measure,* iv, 2, 4.

Married calm.—*Troilus and Cressida,* i, 3, 100.

Married ear.—*Love's Labour's Lost,* v, 2, 921.

Married life.—*Pericles,* ii, 5, 4.

Married mankind.—*The Merry Wives of Windsor,* 4, 2, 23.

Married men.—*Love's Labour's Lost,* v, 2, 909.

Married ones.—*Cymbeline,* v, 1, 2.

Married woman.—*Antony and Cleopatra,* i, 3, 20.

New-married ladies.—*Titus Andronicus,* ii, 2, 15.

New-married man.—*Measure for Measure,* v, 1, 405.

New-married wife.—*Henry V,* v, 2, 190. The only uses of "new-married."

12
I would not marry her, though she were endowed with all that Adam had left him before he transgressed.
Much Ado about Nothing. Act ii, sc. 1, l. 258. [Benedick]

Name the day of marriage, and God give thee joy!
Much Ado about Nothing. Act ii. sc. 1, l. 312. [Don Pedro]

I have railed so long against marriage.
Much Ado about Nothing. Act ii, sc. 3, l. 246. [Benedick]

1
Don Pedro: I do but stay till your marriage be consummate, and then go I toward Arragon.
Claudio: I 'll bring you thither, my lord, if you 'll vouchsafe me.
Don Pedro: Nay, that would be as great a soil in the new gloss of your marriage as to show a child his new coat and forbid him to wear it.
Much Ado about Nothing. Act iii, sc. 2, l. 1.

Come, Friar Francis, be brief; only to the plain form of marriage, and you shall recount their particular duties afterwards.
Much Ado about Nothing. Act iv, sc. 1, l. 1. [Leonato]

In brief, since I do purpose to marry, I will think nothing to any purpose that the world can say against it.
Much Ado about Nothing. Act v, sc. 4, l. 106. [Benedick]

2
Iago: 'Faith, he to-night hath boarded a land carack:
If it prove lawful prize, he 's made for ever.
Cassio: I do not understand.
Iago: He 's married.
Othello. Act i, sc. 2, l. 50. "Carack" occurs again in *The Comedy of Errors,* iii, 2, 140.

3
O curse of marriage,
That we can call these delicate creatures ours,
And not their appetites!
Othello. Act iii, sc. 3, l. 268. [Othello]

4
This siege that hath engirt his marriage.
The Rape of Lucrece, l. 221. "Engirt" is repeated in *II Henry VI,* iii, 1, 200 and v, 1, 99. It occurs in no other play.

5
What, marry, may she! marry with a king, . . .
I wis your grandam had a worser match.
Richard III. Act i, sc. 3, l. 100. [Gloucester] "Wis" is used four times.

Bound with triumphant garlands will I come
And lead thy daughter to a conqueror's bed.
Richard III. Act iv, sc. 4, l. 333. [King Richard]

O, now, let Richmond and Elizabeth, . . .
By God's fair ordinance conjoin together!
Richard III. Act v, sc. 5, l. 29. [Richmond] "Conjoin" is repeated in *II Henry IV,* iv, 5, 64.

6
An I might live to see thee married once,
I have my wish.
Romeo and Juliet. Act i, sc. 3, l. 61. [Nurse]

Lady Capulet: How stands your disposition to be married?
Juliet: It is an honour that I dream not of.
Nurse: An honour! were not I thy only nurse,
I would say thou hadst suck'd wisdom from thy teat.
Lady Capulet: Well think of marriage now: younger than you,
Here in Verona, ladies of esteem
Are made already mothers.
Romeo and Juliet. Act i, sc. 3, l. 65. "Teat" is repeated in *Titus Andronicus,* ii, 3, 145.

7
If that thy bent of love be honourable,
Thy purpose marriage, send me word to-morrow.
Romeo and Juliet. Act ii, sc. 2, l. 143. [Juliet]

Is not marriage honourable in a beggar?
Much Ado about Nothing. Act iii, sc. 4, l. 30. [Margaret]

The state of honourable marriage.
Much Ado about Nothing. Act v, sc. 4, l. 30. [Benedick]

8
This I pray,
That thou consent to marry us to-day.
Romeo and Juliet. Act ii, sc. 3, l. 63. [Romeo]

Do thou but close our hands with holy words,
Then love-devouring death do what he dare;
It is enough I may but call her mine.
Romeo and Juliet. Act ii, sc. 6, l. 6. [Romeo] The only use of "love-devouring."

I 'll have this knot knit up to-morrow morning.
Romeo and Juliet. Act iv, sc. 2, l. 24. [Capulet]

Shrived and married.—*Romeo and Juliet,* ii, 4, 194.

9
She 's not well married that lives married long;
But she 's best married that dies married young.
Romeo and Juliet. Act iv, sc. 5, l. 77. [Friar Laurence]

10
Let me not to the marriage of true minds
Admit impediments.
Sonnets. No. cxvi.

11
Haply to wive and thrive as best I may.
The Taming of the Shrew. Act i, sc. 2, l. 56. [Petruchio]

Will you, nill you, I will marry you . . .
Thou must be married to no man but me;
For I am he am born to tame you, Kate.
The Taming of the Shrew. Act ii, sc. 1, l. 273. [Petruchio] The only use of "will you, nill you."

12
To me she 's married, not unto my clothes.
The Taming of the Shrew. Act iii, sc. 2, l. 119. [Petruchio]

'Twere good, methinks, to steal our marriage;
Which once perform'd, let all the world say no.
The Taming of the Shrew. Act iii, sc. 2, l. 142. [Lucentio]

Such a mad marriage never was before.
The Taming of the Shrew. Act iii, sc. 2, l. 184. [Gremio]

13
And, honest company, I thank you all,
That have beheld me give away myself.
The Taming of the Shrew. Act iii, sc. 2, l. 195. [Petruchio]

Sir Oliver: Is there none here to give the woman?
Touchstone: I will not take her on gift of any man.

Sir Oliver: Truly, she must be given or the marriage is not lawful.
As You Like it. Act iii, sc. 3, l. 67.

1
I knew a wench married in an afternoon as she went to the garden for parsley to stuff a rabbit.
The Taming of the Shrew. Act iv, sc. 4, l. 99. [Biondello] The only mention of parsley.

2
Honour, riches, marriage-blessing.
The Tempest. Act iv, sc. 1, l. 106. [Juno] The only use of "marriage-blessing."

3 Here I swear by all the Roman gods,
Sith priest and holy water are so near
And tapers burn so bright and every thing
In readiness for Hymenæus stand,
I will not re-salute the streets of Rome,
Or climb my palace, till from forth this place
I lead espoused my bride along with me.
Titus Andronicus. Act i, sc. 1, l. 322. [Saturninus] The only use of Hymenæus. "Hymen" is used ten times. "Re-salute" occurs again in *Titus Andronicus,* i, 1, 75.

And in the sacred Pantheon her espouse.
Titus Andronicus. Act i, sc. 1, l. 242. [Saturninus] "Espouse" occurs four times.

I was espoused.—*II Henry VI,* i, 1, 9.
Espoused to death.—*Henry V,* iv, 6, 26.

4 Let still the woman take
An elder than herself; so wears she to him,
So sways she level in her husband's heart.
Twelfth Night. Act ii, sc. 4, l. 30. [Duke]

A solemn combination shall be made
Of our dear souls.
Twelfth Night. Act v, sc. 1, l. 392. [Duke]

II—Marriage and Love

5
Why did he marry Fulvia, and not love her?
Antony and Cleopatra. Act i, sc. 1, l. 41. [Cleopatra]

I think the policy of that purpose made more in the marriage than the love of the parties.
Antony and Cleopatra, ii, 6, 126. [Menas]

6 Haply, when I shall wed,
That lord whose hand must take my plight shall carry
Half my love with him, half my care and duty:
Sure, I shall never marry like my sisters,
To love my father all.
King Lear. Act i, sc. 1, l. 102. [Cordelia]

If you will marry, make your loves to me,
My lady is bespoke.
King Lear. Act v, sc. 3, l. 88. [Albany]

7
You would have married her most shamefully,
Where there was no proportion held in love.
The Merry Wives of Windsor. Act v, sc. 5, l. 234. [Fenton]

8
But that I love the gentle Desdemona,
I would not my unhoused free condition
Put into circumscription and confine
For the sea's worth.
Othello. Act i, sc. 2, l. 25. [Othello] "Unhoused" occurs again in *Timon of Athens,* iv, 3, 229. The only use of "circumscription."

III—Marriage and Money
See also Dowry

9
Yet is she a wondrous fat marriage.
The Comedy of Errors. Act iii, sc. 2, l. 94. [Dromio of Syracuse]

10 To be partner'd
With tomboys hired with that self exhibition
Which your own coffers yield!
Cymbeline. Act i, sc. 6. l. 121. [Iachimo] The only use of "partner'd" and "tomboys."

11 So abject, base and poor,
To choose for wealth and not for perfect love.
I Henry VI. Act v, sc. 5, l. 49. [Suffolk]

12
I tell you, he that can lay hold of her
Shall have the chinks.
Romeo and Juliet. Act i, sc. 5, l. 118. [Nurse] The only use of "chinks."

13
I come to wive it wealthily in Padua;
If wealthily, then happily in Padua.
The Taming of the Shrew. Act i, sc. 2, l. 75. [Petruchio] The only use of "wealthily."

Give him gold enough and marry him to a puppet or an aglet-baby.
The Taming of the Shrew. Act i, sc. 2, l. 78. [Grumio] The only use of "aglet-baby" (a small image on the end of a lace).

IV—Marriage and Celibacy

14
Fair maid, send forth thine eye: this youthful parcel
Of noble bachelors stand at my bestowing.
All's Well that Ends Well. Act ii, sc. 3, l. 58. [King]

15
Is the single man therefore blessed? No: as a walled town is more worthier than a village, so is the forehead of a married man more honourable than the bare brow of a bachelor.
As You Like It. Act iii, sc. 3, l. 58. [Touchstone]

Contracted bachelors, such as had been asked twice on the banns.
I Henry IV. Act iv, sc. 2, l. 17. [Falstaff]

He 'll be crowing as if he had writ man ever since his father was a bachelor.
II Henry IV. Act i, sc. 2, l. 30. [Falstaff]

16
Cinna: Wisely I say, I am a bachelor.
Citizen: That 's as much as to say, they are fools that marry.
Julius Cæsar. Act iii, sc. 3, l. 17.

17 On Dian's altar to protest
For aye austerity and single life.
A Midsummer-Night's Dream. Act i, sc. 1, l. 89. [Theseus]

If thou live, remember'd not to be,
Die single, and thine image dies with thee.
Sonnets. No. iii.

1
Shall I never see a bachelor of threescore again?
Much Ado about Nothing. Act i, sc. 1, l. 201. [Benedick]
I will live a bachelor.
Much Ado about Nothing. Act i, sc. 1, l. 248. [Benedick]
Away to Saint Peter for the heavens; he shows me where the bachelors sit, and there live we as merry as the day is long.
Much Ado about Nothing. Act ii, sc. 1, l. 49. [Beatrice]
When I said I would die a bachelor, I did not think I should live till I were married.
Much Ado about Nothing. Act ii, sc. 3, l. 252. [Benedick]

2
A bachelor, a handsome stripling too.
Richard III. Act i, sc. 3, l. 101. [Gloucester] "Stripling" occurs also in *The Taming of the Shrew,* i, 2, 144, and in *Cymbeline,* v, 3, 19.

3
Broom-groves,
Whose shadow the dismissed bachelor loves.
The Tempest. Act iv, sc. 1, l. 66. [Iris] The only use of "broom-groves." "Broom" occurs only once in the plays, in *A Midsummer-Night's Dream,* v, 1, 396. "Broom-staff" is used in *Henry VIII,* v, 4, 57.

4
Sure as death I swore
I would not part a bachelor from the priest.
Titus Andronicus. Act i, sc. 1, l. 487. [Saturninus]
He was a bachelor then.
Twelfth Night. Act i, sc. 2, l. 29. [Viola]

V—Promise of Marriage

5
He had sworn to marry me
When his wife 's dead; therefore I 'll lie with him
When I am buried.
All's Well that Ends Well. Act iv, sc. 2, l. 71. [Diana]
Diana: Do you know he promised me marriage? . . .
Parolles: I knew of their going to bed, and of other motions, as promising her marriage.
All's Well that Ends Well. Act v, sc. 3, l. 255.
Claims marriage of me.—*The Comedy of Errors,* iv, 4, 159.

6
Before you tumbled me,
You promised me to wed.
Hamlet, iv, 5, 64. See under Love.

7
I was contracted to them both: all three
Now marry in an instant.
King Lear. Act v, sc. 3, l. 228. [Edmund]

8
He promised her marriage.
Measure for Measure. Act iii, sc. 2, l. 213. [Mistress Overdone]
He promised me marriage.—*All's Well that Ends Well,* v, 3, 225.
And five years since there was some speech of marriage
Betwixt myself and her; which was broke off.
Measure for Measure. Act v, sc. 1, l. 217. [Angelo]

9
She is persuaded I will marry her, out of her own love and flattery, not out of my promise.
Othello. Act iv, sc. 1, l. 132. [Cassio]

VI—Second Marriage

10
The main consents are had: and here we 'll stay
To see our widower's second marriage-day.
All's Well that Ends Well. Act v, sc. 3, l. 69. [King] "Marriage-day" is used three times.

11
The instances that second marriage move
Are base respects of thrift, but none of love.
Hamlet. Act iii, sc. 2, l. 192. [Player Queen] See also under Husband.

12
Shortly, I believe,
His second marriage shall be publish'd.
Henry VIII. Act iii, sc. 2, l. 67. [Suffolk]

13
I think you are happy in this second match,
For it excels your first.
Romeo and Juliet. Act iii, sc. 5, l. 224. [Nurse]
Then comes she to me,
And, with wild looks, bid me devise some mean
To rid her from this second marriage,
Or in my cell there would she kill herself.
Romeo and Juliet. Act v, sc. iii, l. 239. [Friar Laurence]

14
What holier than, for royalty's repair,
For present comfort and for future good,
To bless the bed of majesty again
With a sweet fellow to 't?
The Winter's Tale. Act v, sc. 1, l. 31. [Dion]

MART, see Market

MARVEL

See also Admiration, Wonder

15
Deliver . . . this marvel to you.
Hamlet. Act i, sc. 2, l. 193. [Horatio]

16
Here cometh Charles: I marvel how he sped.
I Henry VI. Act ii, sc. 1, l. 48. [Alençon] "I marvel" is repeated twelve times in the plays.
Thou marvell'st at my words.
Macbeth, iii, 2, 54. The only use of "marvell'st."
That 's great marvel.—*Love's Labour 's Lost,* i, 2, 128.
'Tis marvel.—*Taming of the Shrew,* iv, 2, 86.
We marvel much.—*All 's Well that Ends Well,* iii, 1, 7.
You make me marvel.—*Timon of Athens,* ii, 2, 133.
You may marvel.—*Measure for Measure,* v, 1, 395.

17
It is marvel he out-dwells his hour.
The Merchant of Venice, ii, 6, 3. See under Lover. The only use of "out-dwells."

18
She finds, although I cannot,
Myself to be a marvellous proper man.
Richard III. Act i, sc. 2, l. 255. [Gloucester] "Marvellous" occurs twenty-one times, always followed by a noun.

1
Strike all that look upon with marvel.
The Winter's Tale. Act v, sc. 3, l. 100. [Paulina]
Marvel not.—*Troilus and Cressida,* iii, 3, 181.
That 's no marvel.—*II Henry IV,* iv, 3, 96. "No marvel" occurs eight times.
You must not marvel.—*All 's Well that Ends Well,* ii, 5, 63.
Who marvels then?—*Troilus and Cressida,* ii, 2, 42.

MASK

See also Visor

2
Biron: Now fair befall your mask!
Rosaline: Fair fall the face it covers!
Love's Labour 's Lost. Act ii, sc. 1, l. 124.
Fair ladies mask'd are roses in their bud;
Dismask'd, their damask sweet commixture shown,
Are angels vailing clouds, or roses blown.
Love's Labour 's Lost. Act v, sc. 2, l. 295. [Boyet] The only use of "dismask'd." "Commixture" is repeated in *III Henry VI,* ii, 6, 6.
Masks and merry hours.—*Love's Labour 's Lost,* iv, 3, 379.
3 These black masks
Proclaim an enshield beauty ten times louder
Than beauty could, display'd.
Measure for Measure. Act ii, sc. 4, l. 79. [Angelo] The only use of "enshield."
Ugliest mask.—*II Henry IV,* i, 1, 66.
4
My husband bids me; now I will unmask.
Measure for Measure. Act v, sc. 1, l. 206. [Mariana] "Unmask" is repeated in *Hamlet,* i, 3, 37.
5
Will you prepare you for this masque to-night?
The Merchant of Venice. Act ii, sc. 4, l. 22. [Lorenzo]
What, are there masques?—*The Merchant of Venice,* ii, 5, 28.
No masque to-night.—*The Merchant of Venice,* ii, 6, 64.
6
What masques, what dances shall we have?
A Midsummer-Night's Dream. Act v, sc. 1, l. 32. [Theseus]
What Masque? what music?—*A Midsummer-Night's Dream,* v, i, 40.
The masque Was cried incomparable.
Henry VIII. Act i, sc. 1, l. 26. [Norfolk]
I delight in masques and revels.
Twelfth Night, i, 3, 120. See Revelry.
Harness'd masque.—*King John,* v, 2, 132.
7
When I send for you, come hither mask'd.
Much Ado about Nothing. Act v, sc. 4, l. 12. [Leonato]
We will every one be mask'd.
Love's Labour 's Lost. Act v, sc. 2, l. 127. [Princess of France]
Mask'd and vizarded.—*The Merry Wives of Windsor,* iv, 6, 40.
8
These happy masks that kiss fair ladies' brows
Being black put us in mind they hide the fair.
Romeo and Juliet. Act i, sc. 1, l. 236. [Romeo]
Mask their brows.—*The Rape of Lucrece,* l. 794.
9
Give me a case to put my visage in:
A visor for a visor!
Romeo and Juliet. Act i, sc. 4, l. 29. [Romeo]
Mask thy monstrous visage.—*Julius Cæsar,* ii, 1, 81.
10
Threw her sun-expelling mask away.
The Two Gentlemen of Verona. Act iv, sc, 4, l. 158. [Julia] The only use of "sun-expelling."
My mask, to defend my beauty.
Troilus and Cressida, i, 2, 286. See under Woman.
Masks for faces.—*The Winter's Tale,* iv, 4, 223.

MASTER

11
Parolles: Whom I serve above is my master.
Lafeu: Who? God?
Parolles: Ay, sir.
Lafeu: The devil it is that 's thy master.
All 's Well that Ends Well. Act ii, sc. 3, l. 260.
12
By sea He is an absolute master.
Antony and Cleopatra. Act ii, sc. 2, l. 166. [Cæsar]
Complete master.—*Love's Labour 's Lost,* iii, 1, 11.
13 Perchance to-morrow
You 'll serve another master.
Antony and Cleopatra. Act iv, sc. 2, l. 27. [Antony]
He was my master; and I wore my life
To spend upon his haters.
Antony and Cleopatra. Act v, sc. 1, l. 8. [Dercetas] The only use of "haters." "Hater" occurs in *All 's Well that Ends Well,* iii, 3, 11: "Hater of love."
14
What, my young master? O my gentle master!
O my sweet master!
As You Like It. Act ii, sc. 3, l. 2. [Adam] "Young master" is repeated in *The Merchant of Venice,* ii, 5, 19, and in *King Lear,* ii, 2, 49. "Sweet master (or masters)" occurs three times and "gentle master" five.
15
My master is of churlish disposition.
As You Like It. Act ii, sc. 4, l. 80. See under Welcome, 1653:2.
Testy master.—*Venus and Adonis,* l. 319.
Tardy master.—*Comedy of Errors,* ii, 1, 44.
16
A man is master of his liberty.
The Comedy of Errors. Act ii, sc. 1, l. 7. [Luciana]
Men at some time are masters of their fates.
Julius Cæsar. Act i, sc. 2, l. 139. [Cassius]
17
Make him master of thy bed.
The Comedy of Errors. Act v, sc. 1, l. 163. [Duke]
Master of the citadel.—*Othello,* ii, 1, 211.
Master of the feast.—*Cymbeline,* iii, 6, 29.

Master of fence.—*The Merry Wives of Windsor*, i, 1, 295.
Masters of the field.—*Troilus and Cressida*, v, 10, 1.
Master of a full poor cell.—*Tempest*, i, 2, 20.
Master of his heart.—*Troilus and Cressida*, i, 1, 4.
Master O' the jewel house.—*Henry VIII*, iv, 1, 110.
Masters o' the people.—*Coriolanus*, ii, 2, 55; 81.
Master O' the rolls.—*Henry VIII*, v, 1, 34.
Master of my servants.—*The Merchant of Venice*, iii, 2, 170.
Master of my speeches.—*Cymbeline*, i, 4, 152.
Master of my state.—*The Comedy of Errors*, ii, 1, 95.
I 'll be master of it.—*Troilus and Cressida*, v, 6, 30.
I am your master.—*The Comedy of Errors*, v, 1, 411.

1
O, my old master! who hath bound him here?
The Comedy of Errors. Act v, sc. 1, l. 338. [Dromio of Syracuse] "Old master" occurs six times in the plays.
Old worshipful old master.—*The Taming of the Shrew*, v, 1, 56.
New master.—*The Merchant of Venice*, ii, 3, 6.

2 It cannot be
But that my master is abused.
Cymbeline. Act iii, sc. 4, l. 122. [Pisanio]
Alas!
There is no more such masters: I may wander
From east to occident, cry out for service,
Try many, all good, serve truly, never
Find such another master.
Cymbeline. Act iv, sc. 2, l. 370. [Imogen] "Occident" occurs once more in *Richard II*, iii, 3, 67.

3
How doth the martlemas, your master?
II Henry IV. Act ii, sc. 2, l. 110. [Poins] The only use of "martlemas" (a corruption of Martinmas).

4 Must I needs forgo
So good, so noble and so true a master?
Henry VIII. Act iii, sc. 2, l. 422. [Cromwell]
My noble master will appear Such as he is.
Julius Cæsar. Act iv, sc. 2, l. 11. [Pindarus]
My very noble and approved good masters.
Othello. Act i, sc. 3, l. 77. [Othello]
Noble masters.—*Coriolanus*, v, 6, 133.
Our late noble master.—*Timon of Athens*, v, 1, 58.
So noble a master!—*Timon of Athens*, iv, 2, 6.
That 's my noble master!—*Tempest*, i, 2, 299.
Hail to thee, noble master!—*King Lear*, ii, 4, 4.
All hail, great master!—*The Tempest*, i, 2, 189.

5
Thy master is a wise and valiant Roman.
Julius Cæsar. Act iii, sc. 1, l. 138. [Brutus]
Elder masters.—*Hamlet*, v, 2, 259.
Grave masters.—*Timon of Athens*, iv, 1, 11.
Subtle masters.—*Julius Cæsar*, ii, 1, 175.

6
Take thou my soldiers, prisoners, patrimony;
Dispose of them, of me; the walls are thine:
Witness the world, that I create thee here
My lord and master.
King Lear. Act v, sc. 3, l. 75. [Regan]
My master and my lord.—*Antony and Cleopatra*, v, 2, 116; 190. See also under LORD.

7
A good master of mine.
Love's Labour 's Lost. Act iv, sc. 1, l. 106. [Costard] "Good master" is repeated in *King Lear*, v, 3, 267; *Othello*, i, 3, 77; *The Winter's Tale*, v, 2, 188.
Master mine.—*The Merry Wives of Windsor*, i, 1, 164.
Dear master.—*As You Like It*, ii, 6, 1.
Dearest master.—*All's Well that Ends Well*, iii, 4, 9; *Timon of Athens*, iv, 3, 478.
Great master.—*Henry V*, iv, 8, 100; *King Lear*, iv, 2, 75; *The Tempest*, i, 2, 189.
Honest master.—*Love's Labour 's Lost*, iii, 1, 61; *The Merry Wives of Windsor*, i, 1, 67.
Royal master.—*Richard II*, v, 5, 75, and three times in later plays.
Valiant master.—*The Tempest*, iii, 2, 53.
Worthy master.—*Timon of Athens*, iv, 3, 518

8
Call up the right master constable.
Much Ado about Nothing, iii, 3, 178. "Master constable" occurs five times in this play, and in no other. See CONSTABLE.
That 's my master, master doctor.
The Merry Wives of Windsor. Act iii, sc. 4, l. 89. [Mistress Quickly] "Master doctor" is repeated six times in later scenes, and occurs in no other play.
Master gentleman.—*Much Ado about Nothing*, iv, 2, 17.
Master guest.—*The Merry Wives of Windsor*, ii, 3, 76.
Master-gunner.—*I Henry VI*, i, 4, 6.
Master schoolmaster.—*Love's Labour 's Lost*, iv, 2, 87.
Master parson.—*Love's Labour 's Lost*, iv, 2, 84; *Twelfth Night*, iv, 2, 13; *The Merry Wives of Windsor*, i, 1, 9; 3, 1, 45.
Master spirits.—*Julius Cæsar*, iii, 1, 163.
Master steward.—*Timon of Athens*, iv, 2, 1.
Master tapster.—*Measure for Measure*, ii, 1, 223.
Master young gentleman.—*The Merchant of Venice*, ii, 2, 40.
Master young man.—*The Merchant of Venice*, ii, 2, 34.

9
We cannot all be masters, nor all masters
Cannot be truly follow'd.
Othello. Act i, sc. 1, l. 43. [Iago]

10 You must be her master,
And she will be your scholar.
Pericles. Act ii, sc. 5, l. 38. [Simonides]
Thy master dies thy scholar.
Antony and Cleopatra. Act iv, sc. 14, l. 102. [Antony]

11
Dickon thy master is bought and sold.
Richard III. Act v, sc. 3, l. 305. [King Richard] The only use of "Dickon."

12
My master is the great rich Capulet.
Romeo and Juliet. Act i, sc. 2, l. 83. [Servant]

Am I the master here, or you?
Romeo and Juliet. Act i, sc. 5, l. 80. [Capulet]

1
My master is grown quarrelsome.
The Taming of the Shrew. Act i, sc. 2, l. 13. [Grumio]
My master is mad.—*The Taming of the Shrew,* i, 2, 18.
Mad masters.—*Taming of the Shrew,* iv, 1, 2.
Foolish master.—*II Henry IV,* ii, 1, 202.

2
I must believe my master.
The Taming of the Shrew. Act iii, sc. 1, l. 54. [Bianca]

3
I will be master of what is mine own.
Taming of the Shrew. Act iii, sc. 2, l. 231. [Petruchio] See also under POSSESSIONS.

4
What would my potent master? here I am.
The Tempest. Act iv, sc. 1, l. 34. [Ariel]
Weak masters.—*The Tempest,* v, 1, 41.
False masters.—*Timon of Athens,* iii, 4, 50.

5
For many so arrive at second masters,
Upon their first lord's neck.
Timon of Athens. Act iv, sc. 3, l. 512. [Timon]

6
What news with your mastership?
The Two Gentlemen of Verona. Act iii, sc. 1, l. 280. [Speed]
An 't please your mastership.—*The Merchant of Venice,* ii, 2, 61.
Show'd mastership.—*Coriolanus,* iv, 1, 7. The only uses of "mastership."

7
That rare Italian master, Julio Romano.
The Winter's Tale, v, 2, 105. See under STATUE.
Love's master.—*Venus and Adonis,* l. 585

II—Master and Man

8
My master, my dear lord is he; and I
His servant live, and will his vassal die.
All's Well that Ends Well. Act i, sc. 3, l. 164. [Helena]

9
Man and master laugh my woes to scorn.
The Comedy of Errors. Act ii, sc. 2, l. 207. [Adriana]
Servants must their masters' minds fulfil.
The Comedy of Errors. Act iv, sc. 1, l. 113. [Dromio of Syracuse]
Both man and master is possess'd.
The Comedy of Errors, iv, 4, 95. See under MADNESS.

10
I must die;
And if I do not by thy hand, thou art
No servant of thy master's.
Cymbeline. Act iii, sc. 4, l. 76. [Imogen]

11
I would curry with Master Shallow that no man could better command his servants.
II Henry IV. Act v, sc. 1, l. 82. [Falstaff] The only use of "curry" (to use flattery).
If a servant, under his master's command transporting a sum of money, be assailed by robbers and die in many irreconciled iniquities, you may call the business of the master the author of the servant's damnation: but this is not so: . . . the master [is not bound to answer the particular endings] of his servant; for they purpose not their death, when they purpose their services.
Henry V. Act iv, sc. 1, l. 158. [King Henry] The only use of "irreconciled."

12
Neither man nor master would take aught.
The Merchant of Venice. Act v, sc. 1, l. 183. [Gratiano]

13
Nor can we be distinguish'd by our faces
For man or master.
The Taming of the Shrew. Act i, sc. 1, l. 205. [Lucentio]
Was it fit for a servant to use his master so?
The Taming of the Shrew. Act i, sc. 2, l. 32. [Grumio]

14
Bianca: And you may prove, sir, master of your art.
Lucentio: While you, sweet dear, prove mistress of my heart!
The Taming of the Shrew. Act iv, sc. 2, l. 9.

15
No more dams I 'll make for fish;
Nor fetch in firing
At requiring;
Nor scrape trencher, nor wash dish:
'Ban, 'Ban, Cacaliban
Has a new master: get a new man.
The Tempest. Act ii, sc. 2, l. 184. [Caliban] The only use of "firing."

16
Unless the master were the man.
Twelfth Night. Act i, sc. 5, l. 313. [Olivia]

17
How many masters would do this for his servant?
The Two Gentlemen of Verona. Act iv, sc. 4, l. 32. [Launce]
I am my master's true-confirmed love;
But cannot be true servant to my master,
Unless I prove false traitor to myself.
The Two Gentlemen of Verona. Act iv, sc. 4, l. 108. [Julia] The only use of "true-confirmed."

MATCH

I—Match: Contest

See also Contest

18
Half won is match well made; match, and well make it.
All's Well that Ends Well. Act iv, sc. 3, l. 255. [Soldier]
I dare you to this match.—*Cymbeline,* i, 4, 158.
'Tis our match.—*Cymbeline,* iii, 6, 30.
Set a match.—*I Henry IV,* i, 2, 119.

19
What cunning match have you made?
I Henry IV. Act ii, sc. 4, l. 101. [Poins]
Tell him he hath made a match with such a wrangler
That all the courts of France will be disturb'd
With chaces.
Henry V. Act i, sc. 2, l. 264. [King Henry] The only use of "chaces" (tennis-plays).

1
Match to match I have encounter'd him
And made a prey for carrion kites and crows
Even of the bonny beast he loved so well.
II Henry VI. Act v, sc. 2, l. 10. [York.]
Easy match.—*King John,* v, 2, 106.
2
There I have had another bad match.
The Merchant of Venice. Act iii, sc. 1, l. 46. [Shylock] The only use of "bad match."
Heavenly match.—*The Merchant of Venice,* iii, 5, 84.
3
Switch and spurs, switch and spurs; or I 'll cry a match.
Romeo and Juliet. Act ii, sc. 4, l. 73. [Romeo]
Lose a winning match.—*Romeo and Juliet,* iii, 2, 12. See under Loss.
4
Cressida: I 'll make my match to live,
The kiss you take is better than you give. . . .
Menelaus: I 'll give you boot, I 'll give you three for one.
Cressida: You 're an odd man; give even or give none.
Menelaus: An odd man, lady! every man is odd.
Cressida: No, Paris is not; for you know, 'tis true.
That you are odd, and he is even with you.
Menelaus: You fillip me o' the head.
Cressida: No, I 'll be sworn.
Ulysses: It were no match, your nail against his horn.
Troilus and Cressida. Act iv, sc. 5, l. 37.
Wilt thou make the match?—*Venus and Adonis,* l. 586.

II—Match: Marriage

See also Marriage, Nuptial, Wedlock

5 Had he match'd according to his state,
He might have kept that glory to this day.
III Henry VI. Act ii, sc. 2, l. 152. [Edward]
Day, night, hour, tide, time, work, play,
Alone, in company, still my care hath been
To have her match'd.
Romeo and Juliet. Act iii, sc. 5, l. 178. [Capulet]
Match'd in marriage.—*Richard III,* iv, 3, 37.
6
The match is made; she seals it with a curtsy.
III Henry VI. Act iii, sc. 2, l. 57. [Gloucester]
Make some pretty match.—*Richard II,* iii, 3, 165.
Then shall we have a match.—*All 's Well that Ends Well,* v, 3, 30.
7
Citizen: If love ambitious sought a match of birth,
Whose veins bound richer blood than Lady Blanch? . . .
This union shall do more than battery can
To our fast-closed gates; for at this match,
With swifter spleen than powder can enforce,
The mouth of passage shall we fling wide ope,
And give you entrance: but without this match
The sea enraged is not half so deaf, . . .
As we to keep this city. . . .
Elinor: Son, list to this conjunction, make this match.
King John. Act ii, sc. 1, l. 430. The only use of "fast-closed."
She is no match for you.—*The Merry Wives of Windsor,* iii, 4, 77.
8
I hold it a sin to match in my kindred.
Much Ado about Nothing. Act ii, sc. 1, l. 68. [Beatrice]
His grace hath made the match, and all grace say Amen to it.
Much Ado about Nothing. Act ii, sc. 1, l. 314. [Leonato]
I would fain have it a match.
Much Ado about Nothing. Act ii, sc. 1, l. 383. [Don Pedro]
9 Matches
Of her own clime, complexion, and degree,
Whereto we see in all things nature tends.
Othello. Act iii, sc. 3, l. 229. [Iago]
Noble matches.—*Othello,* iv, 2, 125.
Thy match was mortal to him.—*Othello,* v, 2, 205.
10
Mates, maid! how mean you that? no mates for you,
Unless you were of gentler, milder mould.
The Taming of the Shrew. Act i, sc. 1, l. 59. [Hortensio]
Mated with an equal husband.
Timon of Athens. Act i, sc. 1, l. 140. [Timon]
11
God send you joy, Petruchio! 'tis a match.
The Taming of the Shrew. Act ii, sc. 1, l. 321. [Baptista]
Was ever match clapp'd up so suddenly?
The Taming of the Shrew. Act ii, sc. 1, l. 327. [Gremio]
Of all mad matches never was the like.
The Taming of the Shrew. Act iii, sc. 2, l. 244. [Tranio]
Pass my daughter a sufficient dower,
The match is made.
The Taming of the Shrew. Act iv, sc. 4, l. 46. [Baptista] See under Dowry.
12 In this match
I hold me highly honour'd of your grace.
Titus Andronicus. Act i, sc. 1, l. 244. [Titus]
She 'll not match above her degree, neither in estate, years, nor wit.
Twelfth Night. Act i, sc. 3, l. 115. [Sir Toby]
13
Speed: But tell me true, will 't be a match?
Launce: Ask my dog: if he say ay, it will; if he say no, it will; if he shake his tail and say nothing, it will.
Two Gentlemen of Verona. Act ii, sc. 5, l. 35.
The match Were rich and honourable.
The Two Gentlemen of Verona. Act iii, sc. 1, l. 63. [Valentine]

To keep me from a most unholy match,
Which heaven and fortune still rewards with plagues.
The Two Gentlemen of Verona. Act iv, sc. 3, l. 30. [Silvia]

1
O, peace, Paulina!
Thou shouldst a husband take by my consent,
As I by thine a wife: this is a match,
And made between 's by vows.
The Winter's Tale. Act v, sc. 3, l. 136. [Leontes]

MATTER

2
We 'll sift this matter further.
All's Well that Ends Well. Act v, sc. 3, l. 124. [King]

3
I do not much dislike the matter, but
The manner of his speech.
Antony and Cleopatra. Act ii, sc. 2, l. 113. [Cæsar]

4
I love to cope him in these sullen fits,
For then he 's full of matter.
As You Like It. Act ii, sc. 1, l. 67. [Duke Senior]

5
Adriana: Why, man, what is the matter?
Dromio of Syracuse: I do not know the matter.
The Comedy of Errors. Act iv, sc. 2, l. 41.
What is the matter with thee?—*Twelfth Night,* iii, 4, 27.
What 's the matter?—*II Henry VI,* iii, 2, 28, and frequently throughout the plays.

6
We need not put new matter to his charge.
Coriolanus. Act iii, sc. 3, l. 76. [Sicinius]
New matter still?—*Pericles,* v, 5, 243.

7
More matter, with less art.
Hamlet, ii, 2, 95. See under ART.
There 's matter in these sighs, these profound heaves:
You must translate.
Hamlet. Act iv, sc. 1, l. 1. [King] The only use of "heaves" as a noun.
We 'll put the matter to the present push.
Hamlet. Act v, sc. 1, l. 318. [King]

8
I 'll read you matter deep and dangerous.
I Henry IV, i, 3, 190. See under BOOK.
A black matter.—*Henry V,* iv, 1, 151.
Covert matters.—*Julius Cæsar,* iv, 1, 46.
Doleful matter.—*The Winter's Tale,* iv, 4, 189.
Heavy matters!—*The Winter's Tale,* iii, 3, 115.
Hideous matter.—*Twelfth Night,* i, 5, 221.
Impossible matter.—*The Tempest,* ii, 1, 88.
Monstrous matter.—*Antony and Cleopatra,* ii, 2, 187.
Strange matters.—*Macbeth,* i, 5, 64.

9
There were matters against you for your life.
II Henry IV. Act i, sc. 2, l. 151. [Chief Justice]
Matters of this consequence.—*Henry V,* ii, 4, 146.

10
I will devise matter enough out of this Shallow to keep Prince Harry in continual laughter the wearing out of six fashions, which is four terms, or two actions.
II Henry IV. Act v, sc. 1, l. 86. [Falstaff]

11
You take the matter otherwise than is meant.
Henry V. Act iii, sc. 2, l. 137. [Fluellen]
You mistake the matter.—*Richard III,* i, 3, 62.

12
These are no women's matters.
II Henry VI. Act i, sc. 3, l. 120. [Gloucester]
I meddle with no . . . women's matters.
Julius Cæsar. Act i, sc. 1, l. 25. [Commoner]

13
But, to the matter that we have in hand.
II Henry VI. Act i, sc. 3, l. 162. [Gloucester]
I never said nor thought any such matter.
II Henry VI. Act i, sc. 3, l. 191. [Horner]
'Tis no matter.—*II Henry VI,* iii, 1, 263. "No matter" is repeated frequently throughout the plays.
It 's no great matter.—*Hamlet,* v, 1, 167.
'Tis no great matter.—*Coriolanus,* ii, 1, 31.
'Tis no such matter.—*Much Ado about Nothing,* v, 4, 82.

14
I have great matters to impart to thee.
II Henry VI. Act iii, sc. 2, l. 299. [King Henry]
There 's some great matter she 'ld employ me in.
The Two Gentlemen of Verona. Act iv, sc. 3, l. 3. [Eglamour]
I thought she had some great matter there in hand.
The Winter's Tale. Act v, sc. 2, l. 113. [Gentleman]
Great matter.—*II Henry VI,* iii, 2, 299, and seven times in later plays.

15
I 'll hence to London on a serious matter.
III Henry VI. Act v, sc. 5, l. 47. [Gloucester]
'Faith, he is posted hence on serious matter.
King Lear. Act iv, sc. 5, l. 8. [Regan]
Serious matters.—*Timon of Athens,* ii, 2, 219.
Matter of heavy consequence.—*All's Well that Ends Well,* ii, 5, 49.
Matters of great moment.—*Richard III,* iii, 7, 67.
Matter of some moment.—*Henry VIII,* i, 2, 163.
Matters of needful value.—*Measure for Measure,* i, 1, 56.

16
Casca will tell us what the matter is.
Julius Cæsar. Act i, sc. 1, l. 189. [Cassius]
I know not what the matter is.
King Lear. Act i, sc. 4, l. 61. [Knight]

17
And O, what better matter breeds for you
Than I have named!
King John. Act iii, sc. 4, l. 170. [Pandulph]
Fitter matter.—*All's Well that Ends Well,* iv, 5, 81.

18
Matter and impertinency mixed.
King Lear, iv, 6, 178. See under MADNESS. The only use of "impertinency."

1
In him a plenitude of subtle matter
Applied to cautels, all strange forms receives.
A Lover's Complaint, l. 302. The only use of "plenitude." "Cautel" (deceit) is repeated in *Hamlet,* i, 3, 15. "Cautelous" occurs in *Coriolanus,* iv, 1, 33, and in *Julius Cæsar,* ii, 1, 129.
Base matter.—*Julius Cæsar,* i, 3, 110.
Baser matter.—*Hamlet,* i, 5, 104.
Vile matter.—*Romeo and Juliet,* iii, 2, 83.
2
The matter being afoot, keep your instruction.
Measure for Measure. Act iv, sc. 5, l. 3. [Duke]
As the matter now stands.—*Measure for Measure,* iii, 1, 201.
As the matter falls.—*The Merchant of Venice,* iii, 2, 204.
3
I will make a Star-Chamber matter of it.
Merry Wives of Windsor. Act i, sc. 1, l. 2. [Shallow] The only use of "Star-Chamber."
4
Falstaff: What matter have you against me?
Slender: Marry, sir I have matter in my head against you.
Merry Wives of Windsor. Act i, sc. 1, l. 125.
The matter will be known to-night, or never.
The Merry Wives of Windsor. Act v, sc. 1, l. 11. [Falstaff]
A matter of small consequence.—*Richard II,* v, 2, 61.
Some eight-penny matter.—*I Henry IV,* iii, 3, 119. The only use of "eight-penny."
5
Take up this mangled matter at the best.
Othello. Act i, sc. 3, l. 172. [Duke]
Mince this matter.—*Othello,* ii, 3, 247.
6
Go with me to make the matter good.
The Taming of the Shrew. Act iv, sc. 2, l. 113. [Tranio]
Good matter.—*Taming of the Shrew,* i, 1, 255.
7
Most poor matters Point to rich ends.
The Tempest. Act iii, sc. 1, l. 3. [Ferdinand]
8
More matter for a May morning.
Twelfth Night. Act iii, sc. 4, l. 156. [Fabian]
Here is more matter for a hot brain.
The Winter's Tale. Act iv, sc. 4, l. 699. [Autolycus]
9
Pray you, sir, do you know of this matter?
Twelfth Night. Act iii, sc. 4, l. 284. [Viola]
Let him let the matter slip.
Twelfth Night. Act iii, sc. 4, l. 314. [Sir Andrew]
10
How stands the matter with them?
The Two Gentlemen of Verona. Act ii, sc. 5, l. 21. [Speed]
There may be matter in it.—*The Winter's Tale,* iv, 4, 874.
Combustious matter.—*Venus and Adonis,* l. 1162. The only use of "combustious."
Forgotten matter.—*Twelfth Night,* ii, 3, 174.
Matter of marriage.—*III Henry VI,* iii, 3, 258.
Something-settled matter.—*Hamlet,* iii, 1, 181. The only use of "something-settled."
Worldly matters.—*Othello,* i, 3, 300.

MAW, see Stomach

MAY

11
To do observance to a morn of May.
A Midsummer-Night's Dream. Act i, sc. 1, l. 167. [Lysander]
May morning.—*Twelfth Night,* iii, 4, 156.
No doubt they rose up early to observe
The rite of May.
A Midsummer-Night's Dream. Act iv, sc. 1, l. 136. [Theseus]
Impossible . . . as 'tis to make 'em sleep
On May-day morning; which will never be.
Henry VIII. Act v, sc. 4, l. 12. [Man] May-day is mentioned again in *All's Well that Ends Well,* ii, 2, 25; May-morn in *Henry V,* i, 2, 120; maypole in *A Midsummer-Night's Dream,* iii, 2, 296.
First of May.—*Much Ado about Nothing,* i, 1, 194.
Thirtieth of May.—*II Henry VI,* i, 1, 49. The only use of "thirtieth."
12
She came adorned hither like sweet May.
Richard II. Act v, sc. 1, l. 79. [King Richard]
Love, whose month was ever May.—*Love's Labour's Lost,* iv, 3, 102. Repeated in *The Passionate Pilgrim,* l. 228.
In the merry month of May.—*The Passionate Pilgrim,* l. 374.
Month of May.—*I Henry IV,* iv, 1, 101.
Buds of May.—*Sonnets,* xviii.
O rose of May!—*Hamlet,* iv, 5, 157.
As flush as May.—*Hamlet,* iii, 3, 81.
His May of youth.—*Much Ado about Nothing,* v, 1, 76.

MAYOR

13
How London doth pour out her citizens!
The mayor and all his brethren in best sort,
Like to the senators of the antique Rome,
With the plebeians swarming at their heels,
Go forth and fetch their conquering Cæsar in.
Henry V. Act v, Prologue, l. 24. [Chorus]
14
Mayor, farewell: thou dost but what thou mayst.
I Henry VI. Act i, sc. 3, l. 86. [Gloucester]
Peace, mayor!—*I Henry VI,* i, 3, 59.
15
The lord mayor craves aid of your honour.
II Henry VI. Act iv, sc. 5, l. 4. [Citizen]
Lord mayor.—*Richard III,* iii, 5, 14; iii, 7, 55; *Henry VIII,* ii, 1, 151; v, 5, 70.
Master mayor.—*III Henry VI,* iv, 7, 20; 27.
16
My lord, the mayor of London comes to greet you.
Richard III. Act iii, sc. 1, l. 17. [Gloucester]
He brings the mayor along.—*Richard III,* iii, 5, 13.

1
The mayor towards Guildhall hies him in all post.
Richard III. Act iii, sc. 5, l. 73. [Gloucester] The Guildhall is mentioned again in l. 102, and in no other scene.

2
Gloucester: Will not the mayor then and his brethren come?
Buckingham: The mayor is here at hand.
Richard III. Act iii, sc. 7, l. 44.
The mayor and citizens . . .
Are come to have some conference with his grace.
Richard III. Act iii, sc. 7, l. 66. [Buckingham]

3 When last I was at Exeter,
The mayor in courtesy show'd me the castle.
Richard III. Act iv, sc. 2, l. 105. [King Richard] "Mayor" is used eighteen times in the plays, nine times in *Richard III* alone.

MEAL, see Eating

MEANING

See also Intention

4
Wicked meaning in a lawful deed
And lawful meaning in a lawful act,
Were both not sin, and yet a sinful fact.
All's Well that Ends Well. Act iii, sc. 7, l. 45. [Helena]
My meaning in 't, I protest, was very honest.
All's Well that Ends Well. Act iv, sc. 3, l. 246. [Parolles]
Pompey: I have fair meanings, sir.
Antony: And fair words to them.
Antony and Cleopatra. Act ii, sc. 6, l. 67.

5
Now the witch take me, if I meant it thus!
Antony and Cleopatra. Act iv, sc. 2, l. 37. [Antony]
You take me in too dolorous a sense.
Antony and Cleopatra. Act iv, sc. 2, l. 39. [Antony] The only use of "dolorous."
Meaning me a beast.—*As You Like It,* iv, 3, 49.
Meaning you.—*Troilus and Cressida,* ii, 1, 142.

6
What is the drift of your compact?
The Comedy of Errors. Act ii, sc. 2, l. 163. [Antipholus of Syracuse]
Marry, sir, here 's my drift.
Hamlet. Act ii, sc. 1, l. 37. [Polonius]
Hold you ever to our special drift.
Measure for Measure. Act iv, sc. 5, l. 4. [Duke]
O, understand my drift.
The Merry Wives of Windsor. Act ii, sc. 2, l. 251. [Ford]
I will tell you my drift.
Much Ado about Nothing. Act ii, sc. 1, l. 403. [Don Pedro]
My free drift Halts not particularly.
Timon of Athens. Act i, sc. 1, l. 45. [Poet] "Particularly" is repeated in *Coriolanus,* i, 1, 21.
We know your drift.—*Coriolanus,* iii, 3, 116.
Know our drift.—*Romeo and Juliet,* iv, 1, 114.
Cunning drift.—*The Two Gentlemen of Verona,* iv, 2, 83.
Intended drift.—*The Two Gentlemen of Verona,* iii, 1, 18.
Sole drift of my purpose.—*Tempest,* v, 1, 29.

7
The folded meaning of your words' deceit.
The Comedy of Errors. Act iii, sc. 2, l. 36. [Antipholus of Syracuse]
Read, and declare the meaning.—*Cymbeline,* v, 5, 434.

8
That 's not my meaning.
Hamlet. Act ii, sc. 1, l. 31. [Polonius]
'Tis not my meaning.—*Richard II,* ii, 3, 74.

9
Aunchient Pistol, I do partly understand your meaning.
Henry V. Act iii, sc. 6, l. 53. [Fluellen]
Teach her to know my meaning.
Henry V. Act v, sc. 2, l. 334. [Burgundy]

10
Reignier: Shall we disturb him, since he keeps no mean?
Alençon: He may mean more than we poor men do know.
I Henry VI. Act i, sc. 2, l. 121.
Her meaning is,
No way to that, for weakness, which she entered.
I Henry VI. Act iii, sc. 2, l. 24. [Reignier]

11
Why, then you mean not as I thought you did.
III Henry VI. Act iii, sc. 2, l. 65. [Lady Grey]
'Tis wisdom to conceal our meaning.
III Henry VI. Act iv, sc. 7, l. 60. [King Edward]
Well guess'd, believe me; for that was my meaning.
III Henry VI. Act iv, sc. 5, l. 22. [Gloucester]

12 To know the meaning
Of dangerous majesty.
King John, iv, 2, 212. See under KING.

13
What 's your dark meaning, mouse, of this light word? . . .
We need more light to find your meaning out.
Love's Labour 's Lost. Act v, sc. 2, l. 19. [Rosaline] The only use of "dark meaning."
The meaning, pretty ingenious?—*Love's Labour 's Lost,* iii, 1, 59.

14
That is the very defect of the matter, sir.
The Merchant of Venice. Act ii, sc. 2, l. 152. [Gobbo]
I pray thee, understand a plain man in his plain meaning.
The Merchant of Venice. Act iii, sc. 5, l. 62. [Lorenzo]

15
Ay, I think my cousin meant well.
The Merry Wives of Windsor. Act i, sc. 1, l. 265. [Shallow]
What, sovereign sir,
I did not well I meant well.
Winter's Tale. Act v, sc. 3, l. 2. [Paulina]

16
O illegitimate construction!
Much Ado about Nothing. Act iii, sc. 4,

l. 50. [Margaret] "Illegitimate" occurs only once more in the plays, in *Troilus and Cressida,* v, 7, 18.

I have no moral meaning.
Much Ado about Nothing. Act iii, sc. 4, l. 79. [Margaret]

By my troth, there 's one meaning well suited.
Much Ado about Nothing. Act v, sc. 1, l. 230. [Claudio]

Not meaning any harm?—*Othello,* iv, 1, 4.

1
And would not take her meaning nor her pleasure.
The Passionate Pilgrim, l. 154.

2
He has found the meaning;
But I will gloze with him.
Pericles. Act i, sc. 1, l. 109. [Antiochus] Also i, 1, 143.

3
Come, come, we know your meaning.
Richard III. Act i, sc. 3, l. 74. [Queen Elizabeth]

Thou know'st our meaning.
Titus Andronicus. Act ii, sc. 3, l. 271. [Saturninus]

Widow: And now you know my meaning.
Katharina: A very mean meaning.
The Taming of the Shrew. Act v, sc. 2, l. 30.

Thou hast most kindly hit it.
Romeo and Juliet. Act ii, sc. 4, l. 59. [Mercutio]

4
I will not reason what is meant hereby,
Because I will be guiltless of the meaning.
Richard III. Act i, sc. 4, l. 94. [Brakenbury]

Be not so hasty to confound my meaning.
Richard III. Act iv, sc. 4, l. 261. [King Richard]

5
Thus, like thc formal vice, Iniquity,
I moralize two meanings in one word.
Richard III. Act iii, sc. 1, l. 82. [Gloucester]

Ever double Both in his words and meaning.
Henry VIII. Act iv, sc. 2, l. 38. [Katharine]

Biondello: Expound the meaning or moral of his signs and tokens.
Lucentio: I pray thee, moralize them.
Taming of the Shrew. Act iv, sc. 4, l. 79.

Duke: Did he not moralize the spectacle?
First Lord: O, yes, into a thousand similes.
As You Like It. Act ii, sc. 1, l. 44. The only uses of "moralize."

6
Take our good meaning, for our judgement sits
Five times in that ere once in our five wits.
Romeo and Juliet. Act i, sc. 4, l. 46. [Mercutio]

I am no honest man if there be any good meaning towards you.
King Lear. Act i, sc. 2, l. 189. [Edmund] The only uses of "good meaning."

We are not the first
Whom with best meaning, have incurr'd the worst.
King Lear. Act v, sc. 3, l. 3. [Edmund]

His meaning is good.—*The Merry Wives of Windsor,* i, 1, 263.

Noble meaning.—*Timon of Athens,* v, 4, 59.

7
I pray you, tell me what you meant by that.
The Taming of the Shrew. Act v, sc. 2, l. 27. [Katharina]

8
Write down thy mind, bewray thy meaning so.
Titus Andronicus. Act ii, sc. 4, l. 3. [Chiron]

Thou shalt not sigh, nor hold thy stumps to heaven,
Nor wink, nor nod, nor kneel, nor make a sign,
But I of these will wrest an alphabet
And by still practice learn to know thy meaning.
Titus Andronicus. Act iii, sc. 2, l. 42. [Titus] The only use of "alphabet."

9
I do not strain at the position,—
It is familiar.
Troilus and Cressida. Act iii, sc. 3, l. 112. [Ulysses]

10
His meaning struck her ere his words begun.
Venus and Adonis, l. 462.

MEASURE

See also Dancing, Moderation

11
This is hard and undeserved measure.
As You Like It. Act ii, sc. 3, l. 273. [Parolles]

12
With measure heap'd in joy.
As You Like It. Act v, sc. 4, l. 185. See BRIDE, 141:5.

The measure of thy joy Be heap'd like mine.
Romeo and Juliet. Act ii, sc. 6, l. 24. [Romeo]

Fill up the measure.—*King John,* ii, 1, 556.

13
I have no strength in measure, yet a reasonable measure in strength.
Henry V. Act v, sc. 2, l. 140. [King Henry]

14
Measure for measure must be answered.
III Henry VI. Act ii, sc. 6, l. 55. [Warwick]

MEASURE still FOR MEASURE.
Measure for Measure, v, 1, 416. See under COMPENSATION.

15
King: Say to her we have measured many miles
To tread a measure with you on the grass. . . .
Rosaline: Curtsy, sweet hearts; and so the measure ends.
King: More measure of this measure; be not nice.
Love's Labour's Lost. Act v, sc. 2, l. 184.

But let them measure us by what they will;
We'll measure them a measure, and be gone.
Romeo and Juliet. Act i, sc. 4, l. 9. [Benvolio]

I have trod a measure.—*As You Like It,* v, 4, 45.

Dancing measures.—*As You Like It,* v, 4, 199.

Delightful measures.—*Richard III,* i, 1, 8; i, 3, 291.

Tripping measure.—*Twelfth Night,* v, 1, 41.

1 We 'll drink a measure The table round.
Macbeth, iii, 4, 11. See under DRINKING.

A measure to the health of Black Othello.
Othello. Act ii, sc. 3, l. 32. [Iago]

2 There is measure in every thing.
Much Ado about Nothing. Act ii, sc. 1, l. 74. [Beatrice]

3 'I measure him,' says she, 'by my own spirit.'
Much Ado about Nothing. Act ii, sc. 3, l. 149. [Leonato]

4 Shrewd and froward, so beyond all measure.
The Taming of the Shrew. Act i, sc. 2, l. 90. [Hortensio]

In all fair measure.—*Troilus and Cressida,* iii, 1, 47.
In some measure.—*II Henry IV,* i, 1, 139.
In some large measure.—*Richard II,* i, 2, 26.
In some little measure.—*As You Like It,* v, 2, 63.
In some slight measure.—*A Midsummer-Night's Dream,* iii, 2, 86.

5 Fill'd the time With all licentious measure.
Timon of Athens, v, 4, 4. See under WILL.

Equal measure.—*Love's Labour 's Lost,* iv, 3, 384.
Little measure.—*Julius Cæsar,* iii, 1, 150.
Narrow measure.—*Antony and Cleopatra,* iii, 4, 8.
Sinister measure.—*Measure for Measure,* iii, 2, 257.
Tedious measures.—*The Merchant of Venice,* ii, 6, 11.

MEAT

See also Flesh

6 I think, sir, you can eat none of this homely meat.
All's Well that Ends Well. Act ii, sc. 2, l. 48. [Countess]

I will eat no meat.—*Antony and Cleopatra,* v, 2, 49.

7 It is meat and drink to me.
As You Like It. Act v, sc. 1, l. 11. [Touchstone]

That 's meat and drink to me, now.
The Merry Wives of Windsor. Act i, sc. 1, l. 306. [Slender]

8 She is so hot because the meat is cold;
The meat is cold because you come not home.
The Comedy of Errors, i, 2, 47. See under STOMACH.

'Your meat doth burn,' quoth I; 'My gold!' quoth he.
The Comedy of Errors. Act ii, sc. 1, l. 63. [Dromio of Ephesus]

Dromio of Syracuse: I think the meat wants that I have.
Antipholus of Syracuse: In good time, sir; what 's that?
Dromio of Syracuse: Basting.
Antipholus of Syracuse: Well, sir, then 't will be dry.
Dromio of Syracuse: If it be, sir, I pray you, eat none of it.
Antipholus of Syracuse: Your reason?
Dromio of Syracuse: Lest it make you choleric and purchase me another dry basting.
The Comedy of Errors. Act ii, sc. 2, l. 57. The only uses of "basting."

Dress meat.—*The Taming of the Shrew,* iv, 3, 40; *The Merry Wives of Windsor,* i, 4, 102.

9 Thou say'st his meat was sauced with thy upbraidings.
The Comedy of Errors. Act v, sc. 1, l. 73. [Abbess]

I have too long borne Your blunt upbraidings.
Richard III. Act i, sc. 3, l. 104. [Queen Elizabeth] The only uses of "upbraidings."

10 There is cold meat i' the cave; we 'll browse on that.
Cymbeline. Act iii, sc. 6, l. 38. [Guiderius] The only use of "browse."

You come in faint for want of meat, depart reeling with too much drink; sorry that you have paid too much, and sorry that you are paid too much; purse and brain both empty; the brain the heavier for being too light, the purse too light, being drawn of heaviness.
Cymbeline. Act v, sc. 4, l. 163. [Gaoler]

11 I am meat for your master.
II Henry IV. Act ii, sc. 4, l. 135. [Doll]

12 What 's a joint of mutton or two in a whole Lent?
II Henry IV. Act ii, sc. 4, l. 375. [Hostess] "Joint of mutton" is repeated in v, 1, 28.

The duke, I say to you again, would eat mutton on Fridays.
Measure for Measure. Act iii, sc. 2, l. 192. [Lucio]

What 's this? mutton?—*The Taming of the Shrew,* iv, 1, 163. Mutton is referred to thirteen times.

13 Too much cloyed with fat meat.
II Henry IV. Epilogue, l. 28. [Dancer]

14 I have eat no meat these five days.
II Henry VI. Act iv, sc. 10, l. 41. [Cade]

She eat no meat to-day, nor none shall eat.
The Taming of the Shrew. Act iv, sc. 1, l. 200. [Petruchio]

Who abstains from meat that is not gaunt?
Richard II. Act ii, sc. 1, l. 76. [Gaunt]

15 Lorenzo: Serve in the meat. . . .
Launcelot: For the meat, sir, it shall be covered.
The Merchant of Venice. Act iii, sc. 5, l. 64.

16 He eats his meat without grudging.
Much Ado about Nothing. Act iii, sc. 4, l. 89. [Margaret]

17 Look to the baked meats, good Angelica.
Romeo and Juliet. Act iv, sc. 4, l. 5. [Capulet]

Funeral baked meats.
Hamlet, i, 2, 180. See under THRIFT for full quotation.

Broken meats.—*King Lear,* ii, 2, 16.
Worms' meat.—*Romeo and Juliet,* iii, 1, 112.

1
'Tis burnt; and so is all the meat.
The Taming of the Shrew. Act iv, sc. 1, l. 164. [Petruchio]

Katharina: The meat was well, if you were so contented.
Petruchio: I tell thee, Kate, 'twas burnt and dried away;
And I expressly am forbid to touch it,
For it engenders choler, planteth anger;
And better 'twere that both of us did fast,
Since, of ourselves, ourselves are choleric,
Than feed it with such over-roasted flesh.
The Taming of the Shrew. Act iv, sc. 1, l. 172. [Petruchio] "Over-roasted" is repeated in *Cymbeline,* v, 4, 154.

Grumio: What say you to a neat's foot?
Katharina: 'Tis passing good: I prithee let me have it.
Grumio: I fear it is too choleric a meat. . . .
Katharina: Go, get thee gone, thou false deluding slave,
That feed'st me with the very name of meat.
The Taming of the Shrew. Act iv, sc. 3, l. 17. The only use of "neat's foot."

2
Timon: Prithee, let my meat make thee silent.
Apemantus: I scorn thy meat; 'twould choke me, for I should ne'er flatter thee.
Timon of Athens. Act i, sc. 2, l. 36.

Make the meat be beloved more than the man that gives it.
Timon of Athens. Act iii, sc. 6, l. 85. [Timon]

MEDDLING

3
Servant: How, sir! do you meddle with my master?
Coriolanus: Ay; 'tis an honester service than to meddle with thy mistress.
Coriolanus. Act iv, sc. 5, l. 50.

4
Thou find'st to be too busy is some danger.
Hamlet. Act iii, sc. 4, l. 33. [Hamlet]

5
O, beat away the busy meddling fiend.
II Henry VI. Act iii, sc. 3, l. 21. [King Henry]

Meddling friar.—*Measure for Measure,* v, 1, 127.
Meddling monkey.—*A Midsummer-Night's Dream,* ii, 1, 181.
Meddling priest.—*King John,* iii, 1, 163. The only uses of "meddling."

6
The devil speed him; no man's pie is freed
From his ambitious finger.
Henry VIII. Act i, sc. 1, l. 52. [Buckingham]

7
I meddle with no tradesmen's matters, nor women's matters.
Julius Cæsar. Act i, sc. 1, l. 25. [Commoner] See SHOE, 1356:9.

8
Not scurvy, nor a temporary meddler.
Measure for Measure. Act v, sc. 1, l. 145. [Friar Peter] The only use of "temporary."

An thou hadst hated meddlers sooner, thou wouldst have loved thyself better now.
Timon of Athens. Act iv, sc. 3, l. 309. [Apemantus] The only uses of "meddler."

9
You were best meddle with buck-washing.
The Merry Wives of Windsor. Act iii, sc. 3, l. 165. The only use of "buck-washing."

10
They are to meddle with none but the prince's subjects.
Much Ado about Nothing. Act iii, sc. 3, l. 34. [Dogberry]

The less you meddle or make with them, why, the more is for your honesty.
Much Ado about Nothing. Act iii, sc. 3, l. 55. [Dogberry]

I'll not meddle nor make no further.
Troilus and Cressida. Act i, sc. 1, l. 14. [Pandarus]

I'll meddle nor make no more i' the matter.
Troilus and Cressida. Act i, sc. 1, l. 84. [Pandarus]

Meddle or make.—*The Merry Wives of Windsor,* i, 4, 116.

11
Do you not meddle.
Much Ado about Nothing. Act v, sc. 1, l. 101. [Antonio]

Meddle not with her.—*The Taming of the Shrew,* ii, 1, 25.
We will not meddle with him.—*All's Well that Ends Well,* iv, 3, 41.
Meddle you must, that's certain.—*Twelfth Night,* iii, 4, 275.
Pox on 't, I'll not meddle with him.—*Twelfth Night,* iii, 4, 308.
No, I'll not meddle.—*Coriolanus,* v, 1, 38.
Faith, I'll not meddle in 't.—*Troilus and Cressida,* i, 1, 66.
I'll not meddle with it.—*Richard III,* i, 4, 137.
Meddle with my thoughts.—*Tempest,* i, 2, 22.
Durst never meddle.—*Troilus and Cressida,* iii, 3, 202.

12
Let him call me rogue for being so far officious; for I am proof against that title and what shame else belongs to 't.
The Winter's Tale. Act iv, sc. 4, l. 871. [Autolycus]

You are too officious.—*A Midsummer-Night's Dream,* iii, 2, 330.
So tenderly officious.—*Winter's Tale,* ii, 3, 159.
Officious, and not valiant.—*Coriolanus,* i, 8, 14.
Be every one officious.—*Titus Andronicus,* v, 2, 202.
Officious lords.—*Henry VIII,* iii, 2, 237. The only uses of "officious."

MEDIATION, see Compromise

MEDICINE

See also Doctor, Physic, Remedy

13
I have seen a medicine
That's able to breathe life into a stone,
Quicken a rock, and make you dance canary
With spritely fire and motion; whose simple touch
Is powerful to araise King Pepin, nay,
To give great Charlemain a pen in 's hand

And write to her a love-line.
All's Well that Ends Well. Act ii, sc. 1, l. 75. [Lafeu] The only use of "araise" and "love-line." Charlemain is mentioned again in *Henry V,* i, 2, 75, and Pepin is referred to five times.

The tinct and multiplying medicine.
All's Well that Ends Well. Act v, sc. 3, l. 102. [King] "Tinct" and "multiplying" both occur four times in the plays.

That great medicine hath
With his tinct gilded thee.
Antony and Cleopatra. Act i, sc. 5, l. 36. [Cleopatra]

1
Wholesome syrups, drugs and holy prayers.
The Comedy of Errors. Act v, sc. 1, l. 104. [Abbess] "Syrups" occurs again in *Othello,* iii, 3, 331.

He hath a drug of mine.
Cymbeline. Act iii, sc. 5, l. 57. [Queen]

The drug he gave me, which he said was precious
And cordial to me, have I not found it
Murderous to the senses?
Cymbeline. Act iv, sc. 2, l. 326. [Imogen]

O true apothecary! Thy drugs are quick.
Romeo and Juliet. Act v, sc. 3, l. 119. [Romeo]

I 'll now taste of thy drug.—*Cymbeline,* iv, 2, 38.

A drug of such damned nature.—*Cymbeline,* i, 5, 36.

Mortal drugs.—*Romeo and Juliet,* v, 1, 66.

Passive drugs.—*Timon of Athens,* iv, 3, 254. The only use of "passive."

2
By medicine life may be prolonged.
Cymbeline, v, 5, 29. See under DOCTOR.

No medicine in the world can do thee good.
Hamlet. Act v, sc. 2, l. 325. [Laertes]

Labouring art can never ransom nature
From her inaidible estate.
All's Well that Ends Well. Act ii, sc. 1, l. 121. [King] The only use of "inaidible."

3
Telling me the sovereign'st thing on earth
Was parmaceti for an inward bruise.
I Henry IV. Act i, sc. 3, l. 57. [Hotspur] The only use of "sovereign'st" and "parmaceti" (spermaceti).

4
If the rascal have not given me medicines to make me love him, I 'll be hanged; it could not be else; I have drunk medicines.
I Henry IV. Act ii, sc. 2, l. 19. [Falstaff]

5
It is but as a body yet distemper'd;
Which to his former strength may be restored
With good advice and little medicine.
II Henry IV. Act iii, sc. 1, l. 41. [Warwick]

To diet rank minds sick of happiness
And purge the obstructions which begin to stop
Our very veins of life.
II Henry IV. Act iv, sc. 1, l. 64. [Archbishop of York]

Preserving life in medicine potable.
II Henry IV. Act iv, sc. 5, l. 163. [Prince of Wales] The only use of "potable."

6
Provide
A salve for any sore that may betide.
III Henry VI. Act iv, sc. 6, l. 87. [Warwick]

Earth's sovereign salve to do a goddess good.
Venus and Adonis, l. 28.

No man well of such a salve can speak
That heals the wound and cures not the disgrace.
Sonnets. No. xxxiv.

The humble salve which wounded bosoms fits!
Sonnets. No. cxx.

To see the salve doth make the wound ache more.
The Rape of Lucrece, l. 1116.

Salve The long-grown wounds.
I Henry IV, iii, 2, 155. See under INTEMPERANCE.

No salve in the mail. . . . No salve, sir, but a plantain.
Love's Labour 's Lost, iii, 1, 74. See under RIDDLE.

Salve for perjury.—*Love's Labour 's Lost,* iv, 3, 289.

You may salve so.—*Coriolanus,* iii, 2, 70.

7
The present time 's so sick,
That present medicine must be minister'd,
Or overthrow incurable ensues.
King John. Act v, sc. 1, l. 14. [King John]

Regan: Sick, O, sick!
Goneril: If not, I 'll ne'er trust medicine.
King Lear. Act v, sc. 3, l. 95.

8
Many simples operative, whose power
Will close the eye of anguish.
King Lear. Act iv, sc. 1, l. 14. [Doctor] The only use of "operative."

Collected from all simples that have virtue
Under the moon.
Hamlet, iv, 7, 145. See under POISON.

Culling of simples.—*Romeo and Juliet,* v, 1, 40.

Compounded of many simples.—*As You Like It,* iv, 1, 16.

Dere is some simples in my closet.
The Merry Wives of Windsor. Act i, sc. 4, l. 65. [Evans] The only uses of "simples."

9
Meet we the medicine of the sickly weal,
And with him pour we in our country's purge
Each drop of us.
Macbeth. Act v, sc. 2, l. 27. [Caithness]

10
What rhubarb, senna, or what purgative drug,
Would scour these English hence?
Macbeth. Act v, sc. 3, l. 55. [Macbeth] The only mention of rhubarb and senna (sometimes written cyme), and the only use of "purgative."

11
I wonder that thou, being, as thou sayest thou art, born under Saturn, goest about to apply a moral medicine to a mortifying mischief.
Much Ado about Nothing. Act i, sc. 3, l. 11. [Don John]

Beatrice: By my troth, I am sick.
Margaret: Get you some of this distilled Car-

duus Benedictus, and lay it to your heart: it is the only thing for a qualm.
Hero: There thou prickest her with a thistle.
Beatrice: Benedictus! why Benedictus? you have some moral in this Benedictus.
Margaret: Moral! no, by my troth, I have no moral meaning; I meant plain holy-thistle.
Much Ado about Nothing. Act iii, sc. 4, l. 72. Carduus benedictus, or holy thistle, was one of the great medicines of the age. It was given to Martin Luther during a heart attack.

Loathed medicine!—*A Midsummer-Night's Dream,* iii, 2, 64.

Preceptial medicine.—*Much Ado about Nothing,* v, 1, 24. The only use of "preceptial," consisting of precepts.

Medicines bought of mountebanks.—*Othello,* i, 3, 61.

1
Work on, My medicine, work!
Othello. Act iv, sc. 1, l. 45. [Iago]

2
'Tis known, I ever
Have studied physic, through which secret art,
By turning o'er authorities, I have
Together with my practice, made familiar
To me and to my aid the blest infusions
That dwell in vegetives, in metals, stones;
And I can speak of the disturbances
That Nature works, and of her cures.
Pericles. Act iii, sc. 2, l. 31. [Cerimon] The only use of "infusions" and of "vegetives."

O, mickle is the powerful grace that lies
In herbs, plants, stones, and their true qualities.
Romeo and Juliet. Act ii, sc. 3, l. 15. [Friar Laurence]

Within the infant rind of this small flower
Poison hath residence and medicine power:
For this, being smelt, with that part cheers each part;
Being tasted, slays all senses with the heart.
Romeo and Juliet. Act ii, sc. 3, l. 23. [Friar Laurence]

3
Romeo: Your plantain-leaf is excellent for that.
Benvolio: For what, I pray thee?
Romeo: For your broken shin.
Romeo and Juliet. Act i, sc. 2, l. 52. The only mention of plantain-leaf. Plantain is referred to in *Love's Labour's Lost,* iii, 1, 74.

4
Is this the poultice for my aching bones?
Romeo and Juliet. Act ii, sc. 5, l. 65. [Nurse] The only use of "poultice."

A goodly medicine for my aching bones!
Troilus and Cressida. Act v, sc. 10, l. 35. [Pandarus]

5
Like a willing patient, I will drink
Potions of eisel 'gainst my strong infection.
Sonnets. No. cxi. Eisel (vinegar) is mentioned again in *Hamlet,* v, 1, 299.

Minister'st a potion unto me
That thou wouldst tremble to receive thyself.
Pericles. Act i, sc. 2, l. 68. [Pericles]

Drink off this potion.—*Hamlet,* v, 2, 337.

Hated potion.—*A Midsummer-Night's Dream,* iii, 2, 64.

Poisonous potions.—*I Henry IV,* v, 4, 56.

Rash potion.—*The Winter's Tale,* i, 2, 319.

Sleeping potion.—*Romeo and Juliet,* v, 3, 244.

Potion of imprisonment.—*II Henry IV,* i, 2, 145.

6
Ills that were not, grew to faults assured
And brought to medicine a healthful state
Which, rank of goodness, would by ill be cured:
But thence I learn, and find the lesson true,
Drugs poison him that fell so sick of you.
Sonnets. No. cxviii.

To prevent our maladies unseen,
We sicken to shun sickness when we purge.
Sonnets. No. cxviii.

7
Gonzalo: You rub the sore,
When you should bring in the plaster. . . .
Antonio: And most chirurgeonly.
The Tempest. Act ii, sc. 1, l. 137. The only use of "chirurgeonly."

I am not glad that such a sore of time
Should seek a plaster.
King John. Act v, sc. 2, l. 13. [Salisbury] The only uses of "plaster" in this sense.

8
When I was sick, you gave me bitter pills,
And I must minister the like to you.
The Two Gentlemen of Verona. Act ii, sc. 4, l. 149. [Proteus]

Swallowed snowballs for pills.
The Merry Wives of Windsor, iii, 5, 24. The only uses of "pills."

9
Preserver of my father, now of me,
The medicine of our house.
The Winter's Tale. Act iv, sc. 4, l. 596. [Florizel]

Recovered again with aqua-vitæ or some other hot infusion.
Winter's Tale. Act iv, sc. 4, l. 814. [Autolycus] Aqua-vitæ is mentioned six times. "Infusion" is repeated in *Hamlet,* v, 2, 122. "Infusions" is used once, in *Pericles,* iii, 2, 35. See above.

II—Medicine: Prescriptions

10
My father left me some prescriptions
Of rare and proved effects, such as his reading
And manifest experience had collected
For general sovereignty.
All's Well that Ends Well. Act i, sc. 3, l. 227. [Helena]

Many receipts he gave me; chiefly one,
Which, as the dearest issue of his practice,
And of his old experience the only darling,
He bade me store up, as a triple eye,
Safer than mine own two, more dear.
All's Well that Ends Well. Act ii, sc. 1, l. 108. [Helena] The only use of "receipts" in this sense.

11
The most sovereign prescription in Galen is but empiricutic, and, to this preservative, of no better report than a horse-drench.
Coriolanus. Act ii, sc. 1, l. 127. [Menenius] The only use of "empiricutic" (quackish),

"preservative," and "horse-drench." Galen is mentioned five times.

1
How I should be your patient to follow your prescriptions, the wise may make some dram of a scruple, or indeed a scruple itself.
II Henry IV. Act i, sc. 2, l. 147. [Falstaff]

I 'll go along by your prescription.
Henry VIII. Act i, sc. 1, l. 151. [Buckingham]

Make prescription.—*III Henry VI,* iii, 3, 94.

2
Then have we a prescription to die when death is our physician.
Othello. Act i, sc. 3, l. 310. [Roderigo]

Angry that his prescriptions are not kept.
Sonnets. No. cxlvii. This section includes all the uses of "prescription" and "prescriptions."

3
This we prescribe, though no physician.
Richard II, i, 1, 154. See under DOCTOR.

You prescribe to yourself very preposterously.
The Merry Wives of Windsor. Act ii, sc. 2, l. 249. [Falstaff]

Make each
Prescribe to other as each other's leech.
Timon of Athens. Act v, sc. 4, l. 83. [Alcibiades] The only use of "leech."

Prescribe not us our duties.
King Lear. Act i, sc. 1, l. 279. [Regan] The only uses of "prescribe." "Prescript" occurs three times.

MEDITATION

See also Contemplation, Reflection, Thought

4
I and my bosom must debate a while,
And then I would no other company.
Henry V. Act iv, sc. 1, l. 31. [King Henry] See also DEBATE.

Nothing do but meditate.—*Henry V,* v, 2, 60.

I will meditate the while.—*Twelfth Night,* iii, 4, 219. The only uses of "meditate."

Look, he meditates.—*Julius Cæsar,* v, 5, 12. The only use of "meditates."

5
Here is my scabbard, meditating that
Shall dye your white rose in a bloody red.
I Henry VI. Act ii, sc. 4, l. 60. [Somerset]

Whilst I sit meditating.—*Henry VIII,* iv, 2, 79.

Meditating on virginity.—*All's Well that Ends Well,* i, 1, 121. See under VIRGINITY.

6
Close up his eyes and draw the curtain close;
And let us all to meditation.
II Henry VI. Act iii, sc. 3, l. 32. [King Henry]

7 How dare you thrust yourselves
Into my private meditations?
Henry VIII. Act ii, sc. 2, l. 66. [King Henry]

And so we 'll leave you to your meditations
How to live better.
Henry VIII. Act iii, sc. 2, l. 345. [Norfolk]

Continual meditations.—*Henry VIII,* iv, 2, 28.

8
Consider it not so deeply.
Macbeth. Act ii, sc. 2, l. 30. [Lady Macbeth]

9
In maiden meditation, fancy-free.
A Midsummer-Night's Dream. Act ii, sc. 1, l. 164. [Oberon] The only use of "fancy-free."

Meditations lawful.—*Othello,* iii, 3, 143.

10
Divinely bent to meditation.
Richard III. Act iii, sc. 7, l. 62. [Catesby]

He is not lolling on a lewd day-bed,
But on his knees at meditation;
Not dallying with a brace of courtezans,
But meditating with two deep divines.
Richard III. Act iii, sc. 7, l. 72. [Buckingham] "Day-bed" is repeated in *Twelfth Night,* ii, 5, 54.

O fearful meditation!—*Sonnets,* lxv.

11
I was much wrapt in this.
Troilus and Cressida. Act iii, sc. 3, l. 123. [Ulysses] The only use of "wrapt" in this sense. "Wrapp'd in dismal thinkings" occurs in *All's Well that Ends Well,* v, 3, 128.

MEED

See also Reward

12 For his meed
Was brow-bound with the oak.
Coriolanus, ii, 2, 101. See under COURAGE. The only use of "brow-bound."

In his meed he 's unfellowed.
Hamlet, v, 2, 149. See under WEAPON. The only use of "unfellowed."

13
Each one already blazing by our meeds.
III Henry VI, ii, 1, 36. See under LIGHT.

My meed hath got me fame.
III Henry VI, iv, 8, 38. See under FAME.

14
Receive the meed of punishment.
Love's Labour's Lost. Act i, sc. 1, l. 270. [King]

Meed, I am sure, I have received none; unless experience be a jewel that I have purchased at an infinite rate.
The Merry Wives of Windsor. Act ii, sc. 2, l. 211. [Ford]

15
Great treasure is the meed proposed.
Rape of Lucrece, l. 132.

16
For his meed, poor lord, he is mew'd up.
Richard III. Act i, sc. 3, l. 138. [Gloucester]

Labour be his meed!—*Cymbeline,* iii, 5, 168.

Want his meed.—*The Two Gentlemen of Verona,* ii, 4, 112.

17
If you be hired for meed, go back again.
Richard III. Act i, sc. 4, l. 234. [Clarence]

When I have my meed, I must away.
Richard III. Act i, sc. 4, l. 289. [Murderer]

18 No meed, but he repays
Sevenfold above itself.
Timon of Athens, i, 1, 288. See GENEROSITY, 605:8. "Sevenfold" is repeated in *Antony and Cleopatra,* iv, 14, 38: "Seven-fold shield."

1
There 's meed for meed, death for a deadly deed!
Titus Andronicus, v, 3, 66. See under RETRIBUTION.
Honourable meed.—*Titus Andronicus,* i, 1, 216.
2
If thou wilt deign this favour, for thy meed
A thousand honey secrets shalt thou know.
Venus and Adonis, l. 15.
For my meed.—*The Two Gentlemen of Verona,* v, 4, 23. All the uses of "meed" in both plays and poems are given in this section.

MEEKNESS

See also Humility

3
Doing the honour of thy lordliness
To one so meek.
Antony and Cleopatra. Act v, sc. 2, l. 161. [Cleopatra] The only use of "lordliness."
4
They can be meek that have no other cause.
The Comedy of Errors, ii, 1, 33. [Adriana]
5
Hadst thou been meek, our title still had slept.
III Henry VI. Act ii, sc. 2, l. 160. [Edward]
6
You 're meek and humble-mouthed.
Henry VIII, ii, 4, 107. See under ARROGANCE. The only use of "humble-mouthed." "Humble-visaged" occurs in *Love's Labour 's Lost,* i, 1, 34.
Borne his faculties so meek.—*Macbeth,* i, 7, 17.
Meek and gentle.—*Julius Cæsar,* iii, 1, 255.
Poor, and meek.—*The Rape of Lucrece,* l. 710. The only uses of "meek."
7
God bless thee; and put meekness in thy mind,
Love, charity, obedience, and true duty!
Richard III. Act ii, sc. 2, l. 107. [Duchess of York]
Thy meekness saint-like.—*Henry VIII,* ii, 4, 138. See under WIFE.
Meekness and humility.—*Henry VIII,* ii, 4, 109.
Love and meekness.—*Henry VIII,* v, 3, 62. The only uses of "meekness."
To hear meekly.—*Love's Labour's Lost,* i, 1, 199. The only use of "meekly."

MEETING

See also Encounter

8
Let 's meet as little as we can.
As You Like It, iii, 2, 273. [Jaques]
By two o'clock I will be with thee again.
As You Like It. Act iv, sc. 1, l. 183. [Orlando]
I would fain see this meeting.
As You Like It. Act iii, sc. 3, l. 46. [Jaques]
First meeting.—*Cymbeline,* v, 5, 379; *The Tempest,* v, 1, 165.
Second meeting.—*Macbeth,* iii, 1, 86.
9
You know the rendezvous.
Hamlet. Act iv, sc. 4, l. 4. [Fortinbras]
That is the rendezvous.—*Henry V,* ii, 1, 18.
My rendezvous is quite cut off.—*Henry V,* v, 1, 88.
A rendezvous, a home to fly unto.—*I Henry IV,* iv, 1, 57. The only uses of "rendezvous."
10
Appoint them a place of meeting.
I Henry IV. Act i, sc. 2, l. 190. [Poins]
Let 's appoint him a meeting.
The Merry Wives of Windsor. Act ii, sc. 1, l. 97. [Mrs. Page]
Appoint a meeting with this old fat fellow.
The Merry Wives of Windsor. Act iv, sc. 4, l. 15. [Page]
Appoint the meeting Even at his father's house.
Titus Andronicus. Act iv, sc. 4, l. 102. [Tamora] The only uses of "appoint a meeting."
Meetings and appointments.—*The Merry Wives of Windsor,* iii, 1, 92.
11
Peace to this meeting, wherefore we are met!
Henry V. Act v, sc. 2, l. 1. [King Henry]
Fairly met!—*Henry V,* v, 2, 10; *Measure for Measure,* v, 1, 1.
Happily met.—*Taming of the Shrew,* iv, 5, 59.
Well met.—*Richard III,* iii, 2, 110, and seventeen times in later plays.
Very well met.—*As You Like It,* iii, 3, 75.
12
I will meet thee, if thou stir abroad.
III Henry VI. Act v, sc. 1, l. 96. [Clarence]
13
If we do meet again, why, we shall smile;
If not, why then, this parting was well made.
Julius Cæsar. Act v, sc. 1, l. 118. [Brutus]
If we do meet again, we 'll smile indeed;
If not, 'tis true this parting was well made.
Julius Cæsar. Act v, sc. 1, l. 121. [Cassius]
14
First Witch: When shall we three meet again
In thunder, lightning, or in rain?
Second Witch: When the hurlyburly 's done,
When the battle 's lost and won.
Third Witch: That will be ere the set of sun.
Macbeth. Act i, sc. 1, l. 1. "We three" is repeated in *Twelfth Night,* ii, 3, 17; and "hurlyburly" in *I Henry IV,* v, 1, 78.
15
I 'll come to you anon.
Macbeth. Act iii, sc. 1, l. 139. [Macbeth]
'Tide life, 'tide death, I come without delay.
A Midsummer-Night's Dream. Act v, sc. 1, l. 205. [Thisbe]
Thou canst not come to me: I come to thee.
Titus Andronicus. Act ii, sc. 3, l. 245. [Quintus]
16
Good hearts, what ado here is to bring you together!
The Merry Wives of Windsor. Act iv, sc. 5, l. 128. [Mistress Quickly]
17
If a merry meeting may be wished, God prohibit it!
Much Ado about Nothing. Act v, sc. 1, l. 336. [Dogberry] The only use of "prohibit."
All our merry meetings on the plains.
The Passionate Pilgrim, l. 290.

Merry meetings.—*Richard III*, i, 1, 7.
Good meeting.—*Macbeth*, iii, 4, 109.
Gracious meeting.—*Henry V*, v, 2, 13.
Fearful meeting.—*II Henry IV*, iv, 1, 16.

1
Both stood, like old acquaintance in a trance,
Met far from home, wondering each other's chance.
The Rape of Lucrece, l. 1595.

2
Methinks King Richard and myself should meet
With no less terror than the elements
Of fire and water, when their thundering shock
At meeting tears the cloudy cheeks of heaven.
Be he the fire, I 'll be the yielding water:
The rage be his, whilst on the earth I rain
My waters.
Richard II. Act iii, sc. 3, l. 54. [Bolingbroke] The only use of "thundering."

3
I think oxen and wainropes cannot hale them together.
Twelfth Night. Act iii, sc. 2, l. 63. [Sir Toby] The only use of "wainropes."

4
Tell me, Love's master, shall we meet to-morrow?
Venus and Adonis, l. 585.

5
Did you see the meeting of the two kings?
The Winter's Tale. Act v, sc. 2, l. 43. [Gentleman]

Meeting of the petty gods.—*The Winter's Tale*, iv, 4, 4.
Lovers meeting.—*Twelfth Night*, ii, 3, 44.
Meeting-place.—*Cymbeline*, iv, 1, 26. The only use of the phrase.

MELANCHOLY

See also Sadness

6 'Let me not live,'—
This his good melancholy oft began,
On the catastrophe and heel of pastime.
All's Well that Ends Well. Act i, sc. 2, l. 55. [King]

Clown: By my troth, I take my young lord to be a very melancholy man.
Countess: By what observance, I pray you?
Clown: Why, he will look upon his boot and sing; mend the ruff and sing; ask questions and sing; pick his teeth and sing. I know a man that had this trick of melancholy sold a goodly manor for a song.
All's Well that Ends Well. Act iii, sc. 2, l. 3.

Diana: Why is he melancholy?
Helena: Perchance he 's hurt i' the battle.
All's Well that Ends Well. Act iii, sc. 5, l. 89.

How is it that the clouds still hang on you?
Hamlet. Act i, sc. 2, l. 66. [King]

7
He has a cloud in 's face.
Antony and Cleopatra. Act iii, sc. 2, l. 51. [Agrippa]

8
I can suck melancholy out of a song, as a weasel sucks eggs.
As You Like It. Act ii, sc. 5, l. 12. [Jaques]

Adieu, good Monsieur Melancholy.
As You Like It. Act iii, sc. 2, l. 311. [Orlando]

Rosalind: They say you are a melancholy fellow.
Jaques: I am so; I do love it better than laughing.
As You Like It. Act iv, sc. 1, l. 3.

I have neither the scholar's melancholy, which is emulation, nor the musician's, which is fantastical, nor the courtier's, which is proud, nor the soldier's, which is ambitious, nor the lawyer's, which is politic, nor the lady's, which is nice, nor the lover's, which is all these: but it is a melancholy of mine own, compounded of many simples, extracted from many objects, and indeed the sundry contemplation of my travels, in which my often rumination wraps me in a most humorous sadness.
As You Like It. Act iv, sc. 1, l. 10. [Jaques] The only use of "extracted" and "rumination."

Make you melancholy.—*As You Like It*, ii, 5, 10.

9
Sweet recreation barr'd, what doth ensue
But moody and dull melancholy,
Kinsman to grim and comfortless despair,
And at her heels a huge infectious troop
Of pale distemperatures and foes to life?
The Comedy of Errors. Act v, sc. 1, l. 78. [Abbess]

Being moody, give him line and scope.
II Henry IV. Act iv, sc. 4, l. 39. [King Henry]

He 's moody.—*Henry VIII*, iii, 2, 75.

As soon moved to be moody, and as soon moody to be moved.
Romeo and Juliet, iii, 1, 14. See under FELLOW.

How now? moody?—*The Tempest*, i, 2, 244.
Moody beggars.—*I Henry IV*, i, 3, 19.
Moody food.—*Antony and Cleopatra*, ii, 5, 1.
Moody frontier.—*I Henry IV*, i, 3, 19.
Moody fury.—*I Henry VI*, iii, 1, 123.
Moody heaviness.—*Rape of Lucrece*, l. 1602.
Moody Pluto.—*The Rape of Lucrece*, l. 533.
Moody souls.—*Richard III*, v, 1, 7.
Moody thoughts.—*III Henry VI*, iv, 6, 13. The only uses of "moody."

10 O melancholy!
Who ever yet could sound thy bottom? find
The ooze, to show what coast thy sluggish crare
Might easiliest harbour in? Thou blessed thing!
Jove knows what man thou mightst have made; but I,
Thou diedst, a most rare boy, of melancholy.
Cymbeline. Act iv, sc. 2, l. 203. [Belarius] The only use of "sluggish," "crare" (trading-vessel), "easiliest," and "diedst."

11 There 's something in his soul,
O'er which his melancholy sits on brood.
Hamlet. Act iii, sc. 1, l. 172. [King]

1
Falstaff: I am as melancholy as a gib cat or a lugged bear.
Prince: Or an old lion, or a lover's lute.
Falstaff: Yea, or the drone of a Lincolnshire bagpipe.
Prince: What sayest thou to a hare, or the melancholy of Moor-ditch?
I Henry IV. Act i, sc. 2, l. 83. The only use of "gib cat," "lugged," and "Moor-ditch." "Bagpipe" is used four times.

2
Tell me, sweet lord, what is 't that takes from thee
Thy stomach, pleasure and thy golden sleep?
Why dost thou bend thine eyes upon the earth,
And start so often when thou sit'st alone?
Why hast thou lost the fresh blood in thy cheeks;
And given my treasures and my rights of thee
To thick-eyed musing and cursed melancholy?
I Henry IV. Act ii, sc. 3, l. 43. [Lady Percy] The only use of "thick-eyed."

Yesternight, at supper
You suddenly arose, and walk'd about,
Musing and sighing, with your arms across,
And when I ask'd you what the matter was,
You stared upon me with ungentle looks.
Julius Cæsar. Act ii, sc. 1, l. 239. [Portia]

Allicholy and musing.—*The Merry Wives of Windsor*, i, 4, 164. See below.

Musing the morning is so much o'erworn.
Venus and Adonis, l. 866.

Made wit with musing weak.—*The Two Gentlemen of Verona*, i, 1, 69. The only uses of "musing."

He should still Dwell in his musings.
Henry VIII. Act iii, sc. 2, l. 132. [King Henry]

Drew . . . musings into my mind.—*Pericles*, i, 2, 97. The only uses of "musings."

3
Clarence: I am here, brother, full of heaviness.
Prince: How now! rain within doors, and none abroad!
II Henry IV. Act iv, sc. 5, l. 8.

Heaviness foreruns the good event.
II Henry IV, iv, 2, 82. See under CHANCE.

But, lady, if your maid may be so bold,
She would request to know your heaviness.
The Rape of Lucrece, l. 1282.

Lay aside life-harming heaviness.
Richard II. Act ii, sc. 2, l. 3. [Bushy] The only use of "life-harming."

To-night she is mew'd up to her heaviness.
Romeo and Juliet. Act iii, sc. 4, l. 11. [Lady Capulet]

The strangeness of your story put
Heaviness in me.
The Tempest. Act i, sc. 2, l. 306. [Miranda]

Put thee from thy heaviness.—*Romeo and Juliet*, iii, 5, 109.

Drawn of heaviness.—*Cymbeline*, v, 4, 168.

Gone into heaviness.—*Antony and Cleopatra*, iv, 14, 33.

Embraced heaviness.—*The Merchant of Venice*, ii, 8, 52.

Moody heaviness.—*Rape of Lucrece*, l. 1602.

Pleasing heaviness.—*I Henry IV*, iii, 1, 218.

Sorrow's heaviness.—*A Midsummer-Night's Dream*, iii, 2, 84.

Grandsire's heaviness.—*Titus Andronicus*, iii, 2, 49.

Heaviness of his sleep.—*King Lear*, iv, 7, 21.

Heaviness and guilt.—*Cymbeline*, v, 2, 1.

A heaviness that 's gone.—*The Tempest*, v, 1, 200. The only uses of "heaviness."

4
My mind was troubled with deep melancholy.
II Henry VI. Act v, sc. 1, l. 34. [York]

Dull-eyed melancholy.—*Pericles*, i, 2, 2. "Dull-eyed" is repeated in *The Merchant of Venice*, iii, 3, 14: "Dull-eyed fool."

Green and yellow melancholy.—*Twelfth Night*, ii, 4, 116. See under PATIENCE.

Sable-coloured melancholy.—*Love's Labour 's Lost*, i, 1, 233. The only use of "sable-coloured."

Sour melancholy.—*Richard II*, v, 6, 20.

After his sour fashion.—*Julius Cæsar*, i, 2, 180.

True melancholy.—*Antony and Cleopatra*, iv, 9, 12. See under MOON.

Melancholy state.—*Pericles*, v, 1, 222.

All disconsolate.—*Julius Cæsar*, v, 3, 55. The only use of "disconsolate."

5
That surly spirit, melancholy.
King John. Act iii, sc. 3, l. 42. [King John]

6
Pat he comes like the catastrophe of the old comedy: my cue is villanous melancholy, with a sigh like Tom o' Bedlam.
King Lear. Act i, sc. 2, l. 146. [Edmund] The only mention of Tom o' Bedlam.

For thee . . . am I cast down.
King Lear. Act v, sc. 3, l. 5. [Cordelia]

That low-spirited swain.
Love's Labour 's Lost, i, 1, 250. The only use of "low-spirited."

7
Armado: Boy, what sign is it when a man of great spirit grows melancholy?
Moth: A great sign, sir, that he will look sad.
Armado: Why, sadness is one and the self-same thing, dear imp.
Moth: No, no; O Lord, sir, no.
Armado: How canst thou part sadness and melancholy, my tender juvenal?
Moth: By a familiar demonstration of the working, my tough senior.
Love's Labour 's Lost. Act i, sc. 2, l. 1. "Demonstration" is repeated in *King Lear*, iv, 3, 12: "Demonstration of grief."

Most rude melancholy, valour gives thee place.
Love's Labour 's Lost. Act iii, sc. 1, l. 69. [Armado]

He made her melancholy, sad, and heavy;
And so she died.
Love's Labour 's Lost. Act v, sc. 2, l. 14. [Katharine]

Be melancholy.—*Love's Labour 's Lost*, iv, 3, 13.

1
You should have heard him so loud and so melancholy.
The Merry Wives of Windsor. Act i, sc. 4, l. 95. [Mistress Quickly]
Mrs. Ford: How now, sweet Frank! why art thou melancholy?
Ford: I melancholy! I am not melancholy.
Merry Wives of Windsor. Act ii, sc. 1, l. 155.
How melancholies I am!
The Merry Wives of Windsor. Act iii, sc. 1, l. 13. [Evans] Only use of "melancholies."

2
Turn melancholy forth to funerals.
A Midsummer-Night's Dream. Act i, sc. 1, l. 14. [Theseus]
Turn thy solemness out o' door.
Coriolanus. Act i, sc. 3, l. 120. [Valeria] The only use of "solemnness."

3
He is of a very melancholy disposition.
Much Ado about Nothing. Act ii, sc. 1, l. 6. [Hero]
Not marked or not laughed at, strikes him into melancholy.
Much Ado about Nothing. Act ii, sc. 1, l. 153. [Beatrice]
I found him here as melancholy as a lodge in a warren.
Much Ado about Nothing. Act ii, sc. 1, l. 221. [Benedick] The only use of "warren."
We are high-proof melancholy and would fain have it beaten away.
Much Ado about Nothing. Act v, sc. 1, l. 123. [Claudio] The only use of "high-proof" (in the highest degree).
Made you melancholy.—*Richard III,* iii, 1, 3.

4
My life . . .
Sinks down to death, oppress'd with melancholy.
Sonnets. No. xlv.

5
Melancholy is the nurse of frenzy.
The Taming of the Shrew. Induction, sc. 2, l. 135. [Messenger]

6
How now, daughter Katharine! in your dumps?
The Taming of the Shrew. Act ii, sc. 1, l. 286. [Baptista]
Distress likes dumps when time is kept with tears.
The Rape of Lucrece, l. 1127.
Step out of these dreary dumps.
Titus Andronicus. Act i, sc. 1, l. 391. [Marcus] The only use of "dreary."
Dumps so dull and heavy.—*Much Ado about Nothing,* ii, 3, 73.
Doleful dumps.—*Romeo and Juliet,* iv, 5, 129. See under MUSIC. The only uses of "dumps."
Deploring dump.—*The Two Gentlemen of Verona,* iii, 2, 85.
Merry dump.—*Romeo and Juliet,* iv, 5, 108.
Not a dump.—*Romeo and Juliet,* iv, 5, 109. The only uses of "dump."

7
This is in thee a nature but infected;
A poor unmanly melancholy sprung
From change of fortune.
Timon of Athens. Act iv, sc. 3, l. 202. [Apemantus]

8
What signifies my deadly-standing eye,
My silence and my cloudy melancholy?
Titus Andronicus. Act ii, sc. 3, l. 32. [Aaron] The only use of "deadly-standing."
Our melancholy upon your head!
Troilus and Cressida. Act iii, sc. 1, l. 76. [Helen]
Now, the melancholy god protect thee.
Twelfth Night. Act ii, sc. 4, l. 75. [Clown]
Boiled to death with melancholy.—*Twelfth Night,* ii, 5, 3.
Addicted to a melancholy.—*Twelfth Night,* ii, 5, 223.
Melancholy without cause.—*Troilus and Cressida,* i, 2, 27.

9
She is lumpish, heavy, melancholy.
The Two Gentlemen of Verona. Act iii, sc. 2, l. 62. [Duke] The only use of "lumpish."
Host: Now, my young guest, methinks you 're allycholy: I pray you, why is it?
Julia: Marry, mine host, because I cannot be merry.
Two Gentlemen of Verona. Act iv, sc. 2, l. 26.
But indeed she is given too much to allicholy and musing.
The Merry Wives of Windsor. Act i, sc. 4, l. 163. [Mistress Quickly] The only uses of "allicholy."

10
A melancholy malcontent.
Venus and Adonis, l. 313.
Melancholy bait.—*The Merchant of Venice,* i, 1, 101.
Melancholy bells.—*Romeo and Juliet,* iv, 5, 86.
Melancholy boughs.—*As You Like It,* ii, 7, 111.
Melancholy flood.—*Richard III,* i, 4, 45.
Melancholy Jaques.—*As You Like It,* ii, 1, 26; 41.
Melancholy lord.—*Richard III,* v, 3, 68.
Melancholy night.—*II Henry VI,* iv, 1, 4.
Melancholy vale.—*Comedy of Errors,* v, 1, 120.

11
He is gone aboard a new ship to purge melancholy and air himself: for, if thou beest capable of things serious, thou must know the king is full of grief.
The Winter's Tale. Act iv, sc. 4, l. 788. [Autolycus]

MEMORY

See also Remembrance

12
Yet hath my night of life some memory.
Comedy of Errors, v, 1, 314. See under AGE.

13
Yea, my memory is tired.
Coriolanus. Act i, sc. 9, l. 91. [Coriolanus]
Yet he shall have a noble memory.
Coriolanus. Act v, sc. 6, l. 155. [Aufidius] "Noble memory" is repeated in v, 1, 17.
Famous memory.—*Henry V,* iv, 7, 95.
Good memory.—*Coriolanus,* iv, 5, 77.
Hateful memory.—*Antony and Cleopatra,* iv, 9, 9.

Worthy memory.—*The Taming of the Shrew,* iv, 1, 84.

1
Why should I write this down, that 's riveted,
Screw'd to my memory?
Cymbeline. Act ii, sc. 2, l. 43. [Iachimo] The only use of "screwed." "Riveted" occurs three times.

2
Though yet of Hamlet our dear brother's death
The memory be green.
Hamlet. Act i, sc. 2, l. 1. [King]

'Tis in my memory lock'd,
And you yourself shall keep the key of it.
Hamlet. Act i, sc. 3, l. 85. [Ophelia]

Remember thee!
Ay, thou poor ghost, while memory holds a seat
In this distracted globe. Remember thee!
Yea, from the table of my memory
I 'll wipe away all trivial fond records,
All saws of books, all forms, all pressures past,
That youth and observation copied there;
And thy commandment all alone shall live
Within the book and volume of my brain.
Hamlet. Act i, sc. 5, l. 95. [Hamlet] "Pressure" occurs once again in iii, 2, 27, and in no other play.

I 'll note you in my book of memory.
I Henry VI, ii, 4, 101.

Books of memory.—*II Henry VI,* i, 1, 100.

Live in your memory.—*Hamlet,* ii, 2, 470.

3
O heavens! die two months ago, and not forgotten yet? There there 's hope a great man's memory may outlive his life half a year: but, by 'r lady, he must build churches then.
Hamlet. Act iii, sc. 2, l. 39. [Hamlet]

4
Whose memory is written on the earth.
II Henry IV, iv, 1, 81. See under DANGER.

Keep no tell-tale to his memory.
II Henry IV, iv, 1, 202. See under REMEMBRANCE.

5
Their memory
Shall as a pattern or a measure live.
II Henry IV. Act iv, sc. 4, l. 75. [Warwick]

That action, hence borne out,
May waste the memory of former days.
II Henry IV. Act iv. sc. 5, l. 215. [King Henry]

6
In memory of her when she is dead,
Her ashes, in an urn more precious
Than the rich-jewel'd coffer of Darius,
Transported shall be at high festivals
Before the kings and queens of France.
I Henry VI. Act i, sc. 6, l. 23. [Charles] The only use of "rich-jewel'd," and the only mention of Darius.

7
Some little memory of me will stir him.
Henry VIII. Act iii, sc. 2, l. 417. [Wolsey]

Little memory.—*The Tempest,* ii, 1, 233.

I thank my memory.—*Henry VIII,* iii, 2, 303.

Your memory is bad.—*Love's Labour 's Lost,* iv, 1, 99.

Begot in the ventricle of memory.—*Love's Labour 's Lost,* iv, 2, 71. The only use of "ventricle."

8
Memory, the warder of the brain,
Shall be a fume, and the receipt of reason
A limbeck only.
Macbeth. Act i, sc. 7, l. 65. [Lady Macbeth] "Limbeck" (still) occurs again in *Sonnets,* cxix.

9
He is a good sprag memory.
The Merry Wives of Windsor. Act iv, sc. 1, l. 84. [Evans] The only use of "sprag" (sprack, alert).

10
And now have toil'd their unbreath'd memories.
A Midsummer-Night's Dream. Act v, sc. 1, l. 74. [Philostrate] The only use of "unbreath'd."

11
I would forget it fain;
But, O, it presses to my memory,
Like damned guilty deeds to sinners' minds.
Romeo and Juliet. Act iii, sc. 2, l. 109. [Juliet]

12
When wasteful war shall statues overturn,
And broils root out the work of masonry,
Nor Mars his sword nor war's quick fire shall burn
The living record of your memory.
Sonnets. No. lv. "Masonry" is repeated in *All's Well that Ends Well,* ii, 1, 31.

Never cut from memory
My love's sweet beauty.
Sonnets. No. lxiii.

Look, what thy memory can not contain
Commit to these waste blanks, and thou shalt find
Those children nursed, deliver'd from thy brain,
To take a new acquaintance of thy mind.
Sonnets. No. lxxvii.

From hence your memory death cannot take.
Sonnets. No. lxxxi.

Full character'd with lasting memory.
Sonnets. No. cxxii. "Character'd" is repeated in *II Henry VI,* iii, 1, 300, and in *The Two Gentlemen of Verona,* ii, 7, 4.

13
Of whose memory Hereafter more.
Timon of Athens. Act v, sc. 4, l. 80. [Alcibiades]

14
Let memory . . . Upbraid my falsehood!
Troilus and Cressida, iii, 2, 196. See under FALSENESS.

Leave no memory.—*The Two Gentlemen of Verona,* v, 4, 10.

15
To make a recordation to my soul
Of every syllable that here was spoke.
Troilus and Cressida. Act v, sc. 2, l. 116. [Troilus] "Recordation" occurs again in *II Henry IV,* ii, 3, 61.

O, that record is lively in my soul!
Twelfth Night. Act v, sc. 1, l. 253. [Sebastian]

1
I call to mind your gracious favours.
The Two Gentlemen of Verona. Act iii, sc. 1, l. 6. [Proteus]
Call to mind That I have been your wife.
Henry VIII. Act ii, sc. 4, l. 34. [Queen Katharine]
At last she calls to mind.
The Rape of Lucrece, l. 1366. The only uses of "call to mind."

2 Good Paulina,
Who hast the memory of Hermione
I know, in honour.
Winter's Tale. Act v, sc. 1, l. 49. [Leontes]
O you memory Of old Sir Rowland!—*As You Like It,* ii, 3, 3.
Memory of my womb.—*Antony and Cleopatra,* iii, 13, 163.

3 Thou know 'st
He dies to me again when talk'd of.
Winter's Tale. Act v, sc. 1, l. 119. [Leontes]

MEND

I—Mend: Reform

See also Reformation

4
And so God mend me.
As You Like It. Act iv, sc. 1, l. 193. [Rosalind]
God mend him!—*II Henry IV,* i, 2, 124.
God shall mend my soul!—*Romeo and Juliet,* i, 5, 81.
God mend all!—*Henry VIII,* i, 2, 201.
Heaven mend all!—*Cymbeline,* v, 5, 68.

5
I see a good amendment of life in thee; from praying to purse-taking.
I Henry IV. Act i, sc. 2, l. 114. [Prince of Wales] The only use of "purse-taking."
What likelihood of his amendment, lords?
Richard III. Act i, sc. 3, l. 33. [Queen Elizabeth]
His majesty's amendment.—*All's Well that Ends Well,* i, 1, 14.
Hearing your amendment.—*The Taming of the Shrew,* Ind., 2, 131. The only uses of "amendment."
What is done cannot be now amended.
Richard III, iv, 4, 291. See under DEED.
Cannot be amended.—*Coriolanus,* iv, 7, 12; *The Rape of Lucrece,* l. 578.
The case may be amended.—*Romeo and Juliet,* iv, 5, 101.
Faults to have amended.—*All's Well that Ends Well,* iv, 5, 101. The only uses of "amended."
Give the fault amending.—*The Rape of Lucrece,* l. 1614. The only use of "amending."

6
Do thou amend thy face, and I 'll amend my life.
I Henry IV. Act iii, sc. 3, l. 27. [Falstaff]
Clown: Thou wilt amend thy life?
Autolycus: Ay, an it like your good worship.
The Winter's Tale. Act v, sc. 2, l. 166.
It is I
That all the abhorred things o' the earth amend
By being worse than they.
Cymbeline. Act v, sc. 5, l. 215. See REMORSE, 1259:14.
Amend your drunkenness.—*Twelfth Night,* ii, 5, 81.
Amend that fault.—*Richard III,* iii, 7, 115.
Amend this fault.—*I Henry IV,* iii, 1, 180.
Do you amend it then.—*A Midsummer-Night's Dream,* ii, 1, 118.

7
Mend when thou canst; be better at thy leisure.
King Lear. Act ii, sc. 4, l. 232. [King Lear]
Mend him who can: the ladies call him sweet.
Love's Labour's Lost. Act v, sc. 2, l. 328. [Biron]
Go mend, go mend.—*Measure for Measure,* iii, 2, 28.
If you pardon, we will mend.—*A Midsummer-Night's Dream,* v, 1, 437.

8
God amend us, God amend! we are much out o' the way.
Love's Labour's Lost. Act iv, sc. 3, l. 76. [Biron]

9 Neither wish I
You take much pains to mend.
Timon of Athens. Act v, sc. 1, l. 91. [Timon]

II—Mend: Repair

10
Thus I mend it.
The Comedy of Errors. Act ii, sc. 2, l. 107. [Dromio of Syracuse]

11
I would thou wert a man's tailor, that thou mightst mend him and make him fit to go.
II Henry IV. Act iii, sc. 2, l. 175. [Falstaff]
Mend the ruff.—*All's Well that Ends Well,* iii, 2, 7.
Mend stocks.—*I Henry IV,* ii, 4, 130.

12
We have now a broken banquet; but we 'll mend it.
Henry VIII. Act i, sc. 4, l. 61. [Wolsey]

13
Since it is as it is, mend it for your own good.
Othello. Act ii, sc. 3, l. 304. [Iago]

14
I cannot mend it, I must needs confess.
Richard II. Act ii, sc. 3, l. 153. [York]
That we cannot mend.
Richard II. Act iii, sc. 2, l. 100. [King Richard]

15
Were it not sinful then, striving to mend,
To mar the subject that before was well?
Sonnets. No. ciii.

16
'Tis not well mended so, it is but botch'd.
Timon of Athens. Act iv, sc. 3, l. 285. [Timon]
Botch'd up.—*Twelfth Night,* iv, 1, 60. The only uses of "botched."

17
Will this gear ne'er be mended?
Troilus and Cressida. Act i, sc. 1, l. 6. [Pandarus]

18
Any thing that 's mended is but patched.
Twelfth Night. Act i, sc. 5, l. 52. [Clown]
See under PATCH.

MERCHANDISE

1
The merchandise which thou hast brought from Rome
Are all too dear for me: lie they upon thy hand,
And be undone by 'em!
Antony and Cleopatra. Act ii, sc. 5, l. 104. [Cleopatra]
Sent about merchandise.—*Henry V,* iv, 1, 155.
2
Salarino: But tell not me; I know, Antonio
Is sad to think upon his merchandise.
Antonio: Believe me, no: I thank my fortune for it,
My ventures are not in one bottom trusted,
Nor to one place; nor is my whole estate
Upon the fortune of this present year;
Therefore my merchandise makes me not sad.
The Merchant of Venice. Act i, sc. 1, l. 39.
Were he out of Venice, I can make what merchandise I will.
The Merchant of Venice. Act iii, sc. 1, l. 133. [Shylock]
Rich with merchandise.—*A Midsummer-Night's Dream,* ii, 1, 134.
3
I would adventure for such merchandise.
Romeo and Juliet, ii, 2, 84. See under PILOT.

MERCHANT

4
This very day a Syracusian merchant
Is apprehended for arrival here;
And not being able to buy out his life,
According to the statute of the town,
Dies ere the weary sun set in the west.
The Comedy of Errors. Act i, sc. 2, l. 3. [Merchant]
A reverend Syracusian merchant,
Who put unluckily into this bay
Against the laws and statutes of this town.
The Comedy of Errors. Act v, sc. 1, l. 124. [Merchant]
Merchant of Syracuse.—*The Comedy of Errors,* i, 1, 3.
5
I am invited, sir, to certain merchants,
Of whom I hope to make much benefit.
The Comedy of Errors. Act i, sc. 2, l. 24. [Merchant]
Perhaps some merchant hath invited him
And from the mart he's somewhere gone to dinner.
The Comedy of Errors. Act ii, sc. 1, l. 4. [Luciana]
6
You minion, you, are these your customers?
The Comedy of Errors. Act iv, sc. 4, l. 63. [Antipholus of Ephesus]
Give way to customers.—*Pericles,* iv, 6, 21.
Old customers.—*Measure for Measure,* iv, 3, 4.
Customers with gloves.—*The Winter's Tale,* iv, 4, 192. The only uses of "customers."
I think thee now some common customer.
All's Well that Ends Well. Act v, sc. 3, l. 287. [King] "Customer" is used a second time in *Othello,* iv, 1, 122.
7
There where merchants most do congregate.
Merchant of Venice. Act i, sc. 3, l. 50. [Shylock] The only use of "congregate." "Congregated" occurs twice, in *All's Well that Ends Well,* ii, 1, 120, and in *Othello,* ii, 1, 69.
Which is the merchant here, and which the Jew?
The Merchant of Venice. Act iv, sc. 1, l. 174. [Portia]
8
Huge rocks, high winds, strong pirates, shelves and sands,
The merchant fears, ere rich at home he lands.
The Rape of Lucrece, l. 335.
Lo, here, the hopeless merchant of this loss,
With head declined, and voice damm'd up with woe.
The Rape of Lucrece, l. 1661.
9
What saucy merchant was this, that was so full of his ropery?
Romeo and Juliet. Act ii, sc. 4, l. 153. [Nurse] The only use of "ropery" (trickery).
Poor merchant.—*Merchant of Venice,* iv, 1, 23.
Riddling merchant.—*I Henry VI,* ii, 3, 57.
Royal merchant.—*The Merchant of Venice,* iii, 2, 242; iv, 1, 29.
10
A merchant of great traffic through the world.
The Taming of the Shrew. Act i, sc. 1, l. 12. [Lucentio]
A merchant of incomparable wealth.
The Taming of the Shrew. Act iv, sc. 2, l. 98. [Pedant]
11
Faith, gentlemen, now I play a merchant's part,
And venture madly on a desperate mart.
The Taming of the Shrew. Act ii, sc. 1, l. 328. [Baptista]
12
Let us, like merchants, show our foulest wares,
And think, perchance, they 'll sell; if not,
The lustre of the better yet to show,
Shall show the better.
Troilus and Cressida. Act i, sc. 3, l. 299. [Ulysses]
We turn not back the silks upon the merchant,
When we have soil'd them.
Troilus and Cressida. Act ii, sc. 2, l. 69. [Troilus]

MERCY

13
Whip him, fellows,
Till, like a boy, you see him cringe his face,
And whine aloud for mercy.
Antony and Cleopatra. Act iii, sc. 13, l. 99. [Antony] The only use of "cringe."
Wert thou a man,
Thou wouldst have mercy on me.
Antony and Cleopatra. Act v, sc. 2, l. 174. [Cleopatra]
We are all undone, unless
The noble man have mercy.
Coriolanus. Act iv, sc. 6, l. 107. [Menenius]

Have mercy on him.—*Twelfth Night,* iii, 4, 152.

Have mercy.—*Henry VIII,* iii, 2, 262.

1 Were I not the better part made mercy,
I should not seek an absent argument
Of my revenge, thou present.

As You Like It. Act iii, sc. 1, l. 2. [Duke]

Now, trust me, were it not against our laws,
Against my crown, my oath, my dignity,
Which princes, would they, may not disannul,
My soul should sue as advocate for thee.

The Comedy of Errors. Act i, sc. 1, l. 143. [Duke] "Disannul" occurs again in *III Henry VI,* iii, 3, 81.

2
Vagabond exile, flaying, pent to linger
But with a grain a day, I would not buy
Their mercy at the price of one fair word.

Coriolanus. Act iii, sc. 3, l. 89. [Coriolanus]

This mercy we have showed.—*Coriolanus,* v, 3, 137.

Stooping to your clemency.—*Hamlet,* iii, 2, 160. The only use of "clemency."

3
There is no more mercy in him than there is milk in a male tiger.

Coriolanus. Act v, sc. 4, l. 30. [Menenius]

There is no seeming mercy in the king.

I Henry IV. Act v, sc. 2, l. 35. [Worcester]

There 's no hoped-for mercy with the brothers
More than with ruthless waves, with sands and rocks.

III Henry VI. Act v, sc. 4, l. 35. [Queen Margaret] "Hoped-for" is repeated in iv, 8, 61, and occurs in no other play.

There 's no mercy left.—*Macbeth,* ii, 3, 152.

4 Whereto serves mercy
But to confront the visage of offence?

Hamlet. Act iii, sc. 3, l. 46. [King]

They have dealt with me like thieves of mercy.

Hamlet. Act iv, sc. 6, l. 20. [Horatio]

5
Rouse up fear and trembling, and do observance to my mercy.

II Henry IV. Act iv, sc. 3, l. 15. [Falstaff]

6
That 's mercy, but too much security.

Henry V. Act ii, sc. 2, l. 44. [Scroop]

The mercy that was quick in us but late,
By your own counsel is suppress'd and kill'd:
You must not dare, for shame, to talk of mercy.

Henry V. Act ii, sc. 2, l. 79. [King Henry]

The gates of mercy shall be all shut up.

Henry V. Act iii, sc. 3, l. 10. [King Henry]

Not a man of them . . . shall taste our mercy.

Henry V. Act iv, sc. 7, l. 68. [King Henry]

God quit you in his mercy!

Henry V. Act ii, sc. 2, l. 166. [King Henry]

God take mercy on brave Talbot's soul.

I Henry VI. Act iv, sc. 3, l. 34. [Sir William Lucy]

Take mercy on the poor souls.—*Henry V,* ii, 4, 103. See also under SOUL.

God for his mercy!—*Richard II,* ii, 2, 98.

God's mercy!—*All's Well that Ends Well,* i, 3, 155.

Name of mercy!—*The Winter's Tale,* ii, 1, 73.

O mercy, God!—*The Taming of the Shrew,* iv, 3, 87.

Have mercy, Jesu!—*Richard III,* v, 3, 178. "Jesu" is used fourteen times and "Jesu Christ" three times.

Heaven Have mercy on me!—*Othello,* v, 2, 33.

Juno have mercy!—*Troilus and Cressida,* i, 2, 133.

Lord have mercy upon us!

II Henry VI, i, 3, 219. See under LORD.

I cry you (thee) mercy.—*II Henry VI,* i, 3, 142, and fifteen times in later plays.

Mercy on me!—*King John,* iv, 1, 12; *The Merry Wives of Windsor,* iii, 1, 22; *Henry VIII,* v, 4, 71.

Mercy on us!—*The Winter's Tale,* iii, 3, 70; *The Tempest,* i, 1, 63; iii, 2, 141.

7
To our best mercy give yourselves.

Henry V. Act iii, sc. 3, l. 3. [King Henry]

8
We yield our town and lives to thy soft mercy.

Henry V. Act iii, sc. 3, l. 48. [Governor]

9
Use mercy to them all.

Henry V. Act iii, sc. 3, l. 54. [King Henry]

As I suck blood, I will some mercy show.

Henry V. Act iv, sc. 4, l. 68. [Pistol]

10 Will ye relent,
And yield to mercy whilst 'tis offer'd you?

II Henry VI. Act iv, sc. 8, l. 11. [Clifford]

Northumberland: Yield to our mercy, proud Plantagenet.
Clifford: Ay, to such mercy as his ruthless arm,
With downright payment, show'd unto my father.

III Henry VI. Act i, sc. 4, l. 30.

11
Open Thy gate of mercy, gracious God!
My soul flies through these wounds to seek out Thee.

III Henry VI. Act i, sc. 4, l. 177. [York]

12
What makes robbers bold but too much lenity?

III Henry VI. Act ii, sc. 6, l. 22. [Clifford]

This is too much lenity.—*III Henry VI,* ii, 2, 9.

A little more lenity to lechery would do no harm in him: something too crabbed that way, friar.

Measure for Measure. Act iii, sc. 2, l. 103. [Lucio] "Crabbed" occurs twice more in the plays, in *The Winter's Tale,* i, 2, 102, and in *The Tempest,* iii, 1, 8.

Use lenity, sweet chuck!—*Henry V,* iii, 2, 26.

Away to heaven, respective lenity!

Romeo and Juliet, iii, 1, 128. See under FURY.

Awake your dangerous lenity.—*Coriolanus,* iii, 1, 99.

Gives consent . . . of lenity.—*I Henry VI,* v, 4, 125.

Lenity and cruelty.—*Henry V,* iii, 6, 118. The only uses of "lenity."

13
Revoke that doom of mercy.

III Henry VI. Act ii, sc. 6, l. 46. [Richard]

14
My mercy dried their water-flowing tears.

III Henry VI. Act iv, sc. 8, l. 43. [King Henry] The only use of "water-flowing."

1
If I talk to him, with his innocent prate
He will awake my mercy which lies dead.
King John. Act iv, sc. 1, l. 25. [Hubert]
You do lack
That mercy which fierce fire and iron extends,
Creatures of note for mercy-lacking uses.
King John. Act iv, sc. 1, l. 119. [Arthur] The only use of "mercy-lacking."
The infinite and boundless reach Of mercy.
King John, iv, 3, 118. See under DEED.
2 Now mercy goes to kill,
And shooting well is then accounted ill.
Love's Labour 's Lost. Act iv, sc. 1, l. 24. [Princess of France]
3
Mercy is not itself, that oft looks so.
Measure for Measure. Act ii, sc. 1, l. 297. [Escalus]
When vice makes mercy, mercy 's so extended,
That for the fault's love is the offender friended.
Measure for Measure. Act iv, sc. 2, l. 115. [Duke]
4
No ceremony that to great ones 'longs,
Not the king's crown, nor the deputed sword,
The marshal's truncheon, nor the judge's robe,
Become them with one half so good a grace
As mercy does.
Measure for Measure. Act ii, sc. 2, l. 59. [Isabella] The only use of "deputed."
O, think on that;
And mercy then will breathe within your lips,
Like man new made.
Measure for Measure. Act ii, sc. 2, l. 77. [Isabella]
Ignomy in ransom and free pardon
Are of two houses: lawful mercy
Is nothing kin to foul redemption.
Measure for Measure. Act ii, sc. 4, l. 111. [Isabella] "Ignomy" is repeated in *Titus Andronicus,* iv, 2, 115, and in *Troilus and Cressida,* v, 10, 33. "Ignominy" occurs once, in *I Henry IV,* v, 4, 100.
5
There is a devilish mercy in the judge,
If you 'll implore it, that will free your life,
But fetter you till death.
Measure for Measure. Act iii, sc. 1, l. 65. [Isabella]
Mercy to thee would prove itself a bawd.
Measure for Measure. Act iii, sc. 1, l. 150. [Isabella]
He had some feeling of the sport; he knew the service, and that instructed him to mercy.
Measure for Measure. Act iii, sc. 2, l. 126. [Lucio]
This would make mercy swear and play the tyrant.
Measure for Measure. Act iii, sc. 2, l. 206. [Escalus]
Pray thee take this mercy to provide
For better times to come.
Measure for Measure. Act v, sc. 1, l. 489. [Duke] The only use of "better times."
6
Tell not me of mercy.
The Merchant of Venice. Act iii, sc. 3, l. 1. [Shylock]

Thou 'lt show thy mercy and remorse more strange
Than is thy strange apparent cruelty.
The Merchant of Venice. Act iv, sc. 1, l. 20. [Duke]
How shalt thou hope for mercy, rendering none?
The Merchant of Venice. Act iv, sc. 1, l. 88. [Duke]
7
The quality of mercy is not strain'd,
It droppeth as the gentle rain from heaven
Upon the place beneath: it is twice blest;
It blesseth him that gives and him that takes:
'Tis mightiest in the mightiest: it becomes
The throned monarch better than his crown;
His sceptre shows the force of temporal power,
The attribute to awe and majesty,
Wherein doth sit the dread and fear of kings;
But mercy is above this sceptred sway;
It is enthroned in the hearts of kings,
It is an attribute to God himself;
And earthly power doth then show likest God's
When mercy seasons justice. Therefore, Jew,
Though justice be thy plea, consider this,
That, in the course of justice, none of us
Should see salvation: we do pray for mercy;
And that same prayer doth teach us all to render
The deeds of mercy.
The Merchant of Venice. Act iv, sc. 1, l. 184. [Portia]
8
Down therefore and beg mercy.
The Merchant of Venice. Act iv, sc. 1, l. 363. [Portia]
Beg mercy.—*III Henry VI,* v, 1, 23.
Ask mercy.—*III Henry VI,* ii, 6, 69.
I cry your worships mercy.—*A Midsummer-Night's Dream,* iii, 1, 182.
Cry the man mercy.—*As You Like It,* iii, 5, 61.
9
Portia: What mercy can you render him, Antonio?
Gratiano: A halter gratis; nothing else, for God's sake.
The Merchant of Venice. Act iv, sc. 1, l. 378.
10
I that am cruel am yet merciful.
Othello. Act v, sc. 2, l. 86. [Othello]
You have always been called a merciful man.
Much Ado about Nothing. Act iii, sc. 3, l. 64. [Verges] "Merciful man" is repeated in *Measure for Measure,* iii, 2, 203.
Merciful Heaven!—*Measure for Measure,* ii, 2, 114; *Macbeth,* iv, 3, 207.
Merciful powers!—*Macbeth,* ii, 1, 7.
11
Mercy but murders, pardoning those that kill.
Romeo and Juliet. Act iii, sc. 1, l. 202. [Prince]
Nothing emboldens sin so much as mercy.
Timon of Athens. Act iii, sc. 5, l. 3. [Senator] The only use of "emboldens."

1
This is dear mercy, and thou seest it not.
Romeo and Juliet. Act iii, sc. 3, l. 28. [Friar Laurence]
Stay not, be gone; live, and hereafter say,
A madman's mercy bade thee run away.
Romeo and Juliet. Act v, sc. 3, l. 66. [Romeo]
2
But when she saw my woeful state,
Straight in her heart did mercy come.
Sonnets. No. cxlv.
3
I 'll turn my mercy out o' doors and make a stock-fish of thee.
The Tempest. Act iii, sc. 2, l. 78. [Stephano]
4
Wilt thou draw near the nature of the gods?
Draw near them then in being merciful:
Sweet mercy is nobility's true badge.
Titus Andronicus. Act i, sc. 1, l. 117. [Tamora]
O, let us yet be merciful.—*Henry V,* ii, 2, 47.
Be merciful.—*Romeo and Juliet,* iii, 3, 12; *The Merchant of Venice,* iv, 1, 233; *Henry V,* iii, 2, 23.
5
And at thy mercy shall they stoop and kneel,
And on them shalt thou ease thy angry heart.
Titus Andronicus. Act v, sc. 2, l. 118. [Tamora]
6 You have a vice of mercy in you,
Which better fits a lion than a man.
Troilus and Cressida. Act v, sc. 3, l. 37. [Troilus]

MERIT

7 Who ever strove
To show her merit, that did miss her love?
All's Well that Ends Well. Act i, sc. 1, l. 241. [Helena]
Inspired merit so by breath is barr'd.
All's Well that Ends Well. Act ii, sc. 1, l. 151. [Helena]
The merit of service is seldom attributed to the true and exact performer.
All's Well that Ends Well. Act iii, sc. 6, l. 63. [Parolles]
For the sake of merit.—*Antony and Cleopatra,* ii, 7, 61.
He has a merit.—*Coriolanus,* iv, 7, 48.
8
I . . . am bound To load thy merit richly.
Cymbeline. Act i, sc. 5, l. 72. [Queen]
9 The spurns
That patient merit of the unworthy takes.
Hamlet. Act iii, sc. 1, l. 73. [Hamlet]
10
O, if men were to be saved by merit, what hole in hell were hot enough for him?
I Henry IV. Act i, sc. 2, l. 119. [Falstaff]
Saved by merit.—*Love's Labour 's Lost,* iv, 1, 21.
11
You see, my good wenches, how men of merit are sought after: the undeserver may sleep, when the man of action is called on.
II Henry IV. Act ii, sc. 4, l. 404. [Falstaff] "Undeserver" is repeated in *Julius Cæsar,* iv, 3, 12, and in *Henry VIII,* iii, 2, 175.
No petter than a fellow, look you now, of no merits.
Henry V. Act v, sc. 1, l. 8. [Fluellen]
12
There 's in him stuff that puts him to these ends.
Henry VIII. Act i, sc. 1, l. 58. [Norfolk]
The force of his own merit makes his way.
Henry VIII. Act i, sc. 1, l. 64. [Norfolk]
13
This is a slight unmeritable man,
Meet to be sent on errands.
Julius Cæsar. Act iv, sc. 1, l. 12. [Antony] "Unmeritable" occurs once again in *Richard III,* iii, 7, 155.
14
And meritorious shall that hand be call'd.
King John, iii, 1, 176. See under HAND.
The deed is meritorious.—*II Henry VI,* iii, 1, 270.
Meritorious fair design.—*The Rape of Lucrece,* l. 1692.
Meritorious service.—*The Merry Wives of Windsor,* iv, 2, 217. The only uses of "meritorious."
15
A provoking merit, set a-work by a reproveable badness in himself.
King Lear. Act iii, sc. 5, l. 8. [Cornwall] The only use of "reproveable." "Provoking" is repeated in *Othello,* i, 2, 7: "Provoking term," and "a-work" in *II Henry IV,* iv, 3, 124, and in *Hamlet,* ii, 2, 510.
16
What a merit were it in death to take this poor maid from the world!
Measure for Measure. Act iii, sc. 1, l. 240. [Isabella]
17 Who shall go about
To cozen fortune and be honourable
Without the stamp of merit?
The Merchant of Venice. Act ii, sc. 9, l. 37. [Arragon]
Marks of merit.—*Coriolanus,* ii, 3, 172.
O, that estates, degrees and offices
Were not derived corruptly, and that clear honour
Were purchased by the merit of the wearer!
How many then should cover that stand bare!
How many be commanded that command!
The Merchant of Venice. Act ii, sc. 9, l. 41. [Arragon] The only use of "corruptly."
18
Whatsoever I have merited, either in my mind or in my means, meed, I am sure, I have received none.
The Merry Wives of Windsor. Act ii, sc. 2, l. 210. [Ford]
More hath it merited.—*Titus Andronicus,* iii, 1, 197.
More of thee merited.—*Cymbeline,* v, 5, 304.
How merited.—*The Winter's Tale,* iii, 2, 49.
Merited some love.—*Henry V,* iii, 6, 25.
Merited benefit.—*Measure for Measure,* iii, 1, 206. The only uses of "merited."
19
Nor from mine own weak merits will I draw
The smallest fear or doubt of her revolt.
Othello. Act iii, sc. 3, l. 187. [Othello]
Without merit.—*Othello,* ii, 3, 270.

1 A dearer merit . . .
Have I deserved at your highness' hands.
Richard II, i, 3, 156. See under DESERVING.
More merit.—*Hamlet,* ii, 2, 558.
Desert and merit.—*Henry V,* ii, 2, 34.
Simpleness and merit.—*Much Ado about Nothing,* iii, 1, 70.

2
Right noble is thy merit, well I wot.
Richard II. Act v, sc. 6, l. 18. [Bolingbroke]
Hear all, all see,
And like her most whose merit most shall be.
Romeo and Juliet. Act i, sc. 2, l. 30. [Capulet]

3
Lord of my love, to whom in vassalage
Thy merit hath my duty strong knit,
To thee I send this written embassage,
To witness duty, not to show my wit.
Sonnets. No. xxvi. "Vassalage" is repeated in *Troilus and Cressida,* iii, 2, 40. "Embassage" occurs six times.
Place my merit in the eye of scorn.
Sonnets. No. lxxxviii.
What 's new to speak, what new to register,
That may express my love or thy dear merit?
Sonnets. No. cviii.

4
You bate too much of your own merits.
Timon of Athens. Act i, sc. 2, l. 212. [Timon]

5
Both merits poised, each weighs nor less nor more.
Troilus and Cressida, iv, 1, 65. See under COMPARISON.
Assubjugate his merit.—*Troilus and Cressida,* ii, 3, 202. The only use of "assubjugate."
Affected merit.—*Troilus and Cressida,* ii, 2, 60.
Purposed merit.—*Othello,* iii, 4, 117.
Unrival'd merit.—*The Two Gentlemen of Verona,* v, 4, 144. The only use of "unrival'd."
Merit of vile gold.—*King John,* iii, 1, 165.

6
Our head shall go bare till merit crown it.
Troilus and Cressida. Act iii, sc. 2, l. 99. [Troilus]
He merits well to have her, that doth seek her.
Troilus and Cressida. Act iv, sc. 1, l. 55. [Diomedes]
I do not call your faith in question
So mainly as my merit.
Troilus and Cressida. Act iv, sc. 4, l. 84. [Troilus]

MERMAID

7
Her gentlewomen, like the Nereides,
So many mermaids, tended her i' the eyes,
And made their bends adornings: at the helm
A seeming mermaid steers.
Antony and Cleopatra. Act ii, sc. 2, l. 211. [Enobarbus] The only mention of the Nereides, and use of "adornings."

8
O, train me not, sweet mermaid, with thy note,
To drown me in thy sister's flood of tears:
Sing, siren, for thyself and I will dote:
Spread o'er the silver waves thy golden hairs,
And as a bed I 'll take them and there lie,
And in that glorious supposition think
He gains by death that hath such means to die:
Let Love, being light, be drowned if she sink!
The Comedy of Errors. Act iii, sc. 2, l. 45. [Antipholus of Syracuse]
I 'll stop mine ears against the mermaid's song.
The Comedy of Errors. Act iii, sc. 2, l. 169. [Antipholus of Syracuse]
As if some mermaid did their ears entice.
The Rape of Lucrece, l. 1411.

9 Once I sat upon a promontory,
And heard a mermaid on a dolphin's back
Uttering such dulcet and harmonious breath
That the rude sea grew civil at her song
And certain stars shot madly from their spheres,
To hear the sea-maid's music.
A Midsummer-Night's Dream. Act ii, sc. 1, l. 149. [Oberon] "Sea-maid" occurs again in *Measure for Measure,* iii, 2, 115.

MERRIMENT

See also Jollity, Mirth

10
She 's very merry; but yet she is not well.
All's Well that Ends Well. Act ii, sc. 4, l. 4. [Clown]

11
Celia: I pray thee, Rosalind, sweet my coz, be merry.
Rosalind: Dear Celia, I show more mirth than I am mistress of; and would you yet I were merrier?
As You Like It. Act i, sc. 2, l. 1.
Celia: My sweet Rose, my dear Rose, be merry.
Rosalind: From henceforth I will, coz, and devise sports.
As You Like it. Act i, sc. 2, l. 25.
God rest you merry, sir.
As You like It. Act v, sc. 1, l. 65. [William]
Rest you merry!—*Romeo and Juliet,* i, 2, 86.

12
I am glad to see you in this merry vein.
The Comedy of Errors. Act ii, sc. 2, l. 20. [Dromio of Syracuse]
You are a merry man, sir.
The Comedy of Errors. Act iii, sc. 2, l. 183. [Angelo] "Merry man" is repeated four times in later plays.
A merrier man,
Within the limit of becoming mirth,
I never spent an hour's talk withal.
Love's Labour's Lost. Act ii, sc. 1 l. 66. [Rosaline]
Mass, and well said; a merry whoreson, ha!
Romeo and Juliet. Act iv, sc. 4, l. 19. [Capulet]
Heaven give you many, many merry days!
The Merry Wives of Windsor. Act v, sc. 5, l. 254. [Mrs. Page] "Merry days" is repeated in *Love's Labour 's Lost,* i, 2, 164, and in *Richard II,* iv, 1, 344. Shakespeare was fond of "merry" and applied it to 51 nouns.

1
Your man and you are marvellous merry.
The Comedy of Errors. Act iv, sc. 3, l. 59. [Courtezan]

2
O God, your only jig-maker. What should a man do but be merry?
Hamlet. Act iii, sc. 2, l. 132. [Hamlet] The only use of "jig-maker."

Flashes of merriment, that were wont to set the table on a roar.
Hamlet. Act v, sc. 1, l. 210. See LIPS, 880:3.

3
Prince of Wales: Shall we be merry?
Poins: As merry as crickets, my lad.
I Henry IV. Act ii, sc. 4, l. 99.

What, shall we be merry? shall we have a play extempore?
I Henry IV. Act ii, sc. 4, l. 308. [Falstaff]

It is extempore.—*The Taming of the Shrew,* ii, 1, 265.

You may do it extempore.—*A Midsummer-Night's Dream,* i, 2, 70.

We may do anything extempore.—*The Winter's Tale,* iv, 4, 692.

Blushed extempore.—*I Henry IV,* ii, 4, 347. The only uses of "extempore."

4
He will . . . turn all to a merriment.
II Henry IV. Act ii, sc. 4, l. 324. [Poins]

Idle merriment.—*King John,* iii, 3, 46.

Mocking merriment.—*Love's Labour 's Lost,* v, 2, 139.

Reason's merriment.—*Romeo and Juliet,* iv, 5, 83.

5
Therefore be merry, coz; since sudden sorrow
Serves to say thus, 'some good thing comes to-morrow.'
II Henry IV. Act iv, sc. 2, l. 83. [Westmoreland]

I have been merry twice and once ere now.
II Henry IV. Act v, sc. 3, l. 42. [Silence]

Lack nothing: be merry.
II Henry IV. Act v, sc. 3, l. 73. [Shallow]

Though my mocks come home by me, I will now be merry.
Love's Labour 's Lost. Act v, sc. 2, l. 638. [Dumain]

To be merry best becomes you; for, out of question, you were born in a merry hour.
Much Ado about Nothing. Act ii, sc. 1, l. 346. [Don Pedro]

Be merry, for our time of stay is short.
Richard II, ii, 1, 223.

Beseech you, sir, be merry; you have cause.
The Tempest. Act ii, sc. 1, l. 1. [Gonzalo]

Be merry, Peter.—*II Henry VI,* ii, 3, 70.

Let 's be merry.—*Henry VIII,* i, 4, 104.

Be mad and merry.—*The Taming of the Shrew,* iii, 2, 228.

Say I am merry.—*Julius Cæsar,* ii, 4, 45.

6
He would have all as merry
As, first, good company, good wine, good welcome,
Can make good people.
Henry VIII. Act i, sc. 4, l. 5. [Guildford]

That noble lady,
Or gentleman, that is not freely merry,
Is not my friend.
Henry VIII. Act i, sc. 4, l. 35. [Wolsey]

7
Good gentlemen, look fresh and merrily.
Julius Cæsar Act ii, sc. 1, l. 224. [Brutus]

What, you look merrily!—*As You Like It,* ii, 7, 11.

There is either liquor in his pate or money in his purse when he looks so merrily.
The Merry Wives of Windsor. Act ii, sc. 1, l. 197. [Page]

Full merrily.—*Love's Labour 's Lost,* v, 2, 481; *Troilus and Cressida,* v, 10, 42.

8
I could be merry now.
King John. Act iii, sc. 3, l. 67. [King John]

I 'll be merry.—*Cymbeline,* iii, 5, 150.

9
By my christendom,
So I were out of prison and kept sheep,
I should be as merry as the day is long.
King John. Act iv, sc. 1, l. 16. [Arthur]

As merry as the day is long.
Much Ado about Nothing, ii, 1, 52. See under MARRIAGE AND CELIBACY. The only uses of this phrase.

As merry as when our nuptial day was done.
Coriolanus, i, 6, 31. See NUPTIAL, 1077:10.

10
Here was a consent,
Knowing aforehand of our merriment,
To dash it like a Christmas comedy.
Love's Labour 's Lost. Act v, sc. 2, l. 460. [Biron] The only use of "aforehand."

We . . . met your loves
In their own fashion, like a merriment.
Love's Labour 's Lost. Act v, sc. 2, l. 793. [Princess of France]

Thou interrupt'st our merriment.—*Love's Labour 's Lost,* v, 2, 725.

Climb in the merriness.—*Love's Labour 's Lost,* i, 1, 202. The only use of "merriness."

11
And rather proved the sliding of your brother
A merriment than a vice.
Measure for Measure. Act ii, sc. 4, l. 115. [Angelo] The only use of "sliding."

Rather rejoicing to see another merry, than merry at any thing which professed to make him rejoice.
Measure for Measure. Act iii, sc. 2, l. 251. [Escalus]

12
I would have stay'd till I had made you merry,
If worthier friends had not prevented me.
The Merchant of Venice. Act i, sc. 1, l. 60. [Salarino]

13
Stir up Athenian youth to merriments.
A Midsummer-Night's Dream. Act i, sc. 1, l. 13. [Theseus]

O spite! O hell! I see you all are bent
To set against me for your merriment.
A Midsummer-Night's Dream. Act iii, sc. 2, l. 145. [Helena]

14
I am not merry; but I do beguile
The thing I am, by seeming otherwise.
Othello. Act ii, sc. 1, l. 123. [Desdemona]

Indeed, I have been merrier.—*King John,* iv, 1, 12.

1
Simonides: What, are you merry, knights?
Knights: Who can be other in this royal presence?
Pericles. Act ii, sc. 3, l. 48.

2
How oft when men are at the point of death
Have they been merry! which their keepers call
A lightning before death.
Romeo and Juliet. Act v, sc. 3, l. 88. [Romeo]

3
Thou makest me merry; I am full of pleasure.
The Tempest. Act iii, sc. 2, l. 125. [Caliban]
Make me merry.—*I Henry IV,* iii, 3, 16.
Make us merry.—*Titus Andronicus,* iii, 2, 65.
Make merry, man.—*II Henry VI,* i, 2, 85. Used in the first scene of the first play, and frequently thereafter.

4
Merrily, merrily shall I live now
Under the blossom that hangs on the bough.
The Tempest. Act v, sc. 1, l. 93. [Ariel]
Lives merrily.—*As You Like It,* iii, 2, 340.
Die merrily.—*I Henry IV,* iv, 1, 134.
Merrily hent the stile-a.—*The Winter's Tale,* iv, 3, 133. See under HEART.
Go merrily to London.—*I Henry IV,* ii, 2, 100.
Now merrily to horse.—*I Henry IV,* ii, 2, 111.

5
Come, we 'll have you merry.
The Two Gentlemen of Verona. Act iv, sc. 2, l. 30. [Host]

6
I know his lordship is but merry with me.
Timon of Athens. Act iii, sc. 2, l. 42. [Lucius]

7
Hath learn'd to sport and dance,
To toy, to wanton, dally, smile and jest.
Venus and Adonis, l. 105.

MESSAGE

8
He hath not fail'd to pester us with message.
Hamlet. Act i, sc. 2, l. 22. [King] The only use of "pester."

9
Exeter: This was a merry message.
King Henry: We hope to make the sender blush at it.
Henry V. Act i, sc. 2, l. 298.
On what submissive message art thou sent?
I Henry VI. Act iv, sc. 7, l. 53. [Charles]

10
Go tell this heavy message to the king.
II Henry VI. Act iii, sc. 2, l. 379. [Queen]
I go of message from the queen to France.
II Henry VI. Act iv, sc. 1, l. 113. [Suffolk]
I sent your message.—*Henry VIII,* v, 1, 64.
I guess thy message.—*Henry VIII,* v, 1, 162.

11
Deliver a plain message bluntly.
King Lear. Act i, sc. 4, l. 36. [Kent]
Unfold his message.—*Macbeth,* iii, 6, 47.
A message well sympathized.—*Love's Labour's Lost,* iii, 1, 52.

12
I come
With message unto princely Pericles;
But since my landing I have understood
Your lord has betook himself to unknown travels,
My message must return from whence it came.
Pericles. Act i, sc. 4, l. 33. [Thaliard]
My message is to you.—*Richard II,* ii, 3, 69.

13
Henceforth do your messages yourself.
Romeo and Juliet. Act ii, sc. 5, l. 66. [Nurse]
Titus: Come, come; thou 'lt do thy message, wilt thou not?
Young Lucius: Ay, with my dagger in their bosoms, grandsire.
Titus Andronicus. Act iv, sc. 1, l. 117.
Do this message honourably.—*Titus Andronicus,* iv, 4, 104.

14
May one, that is a herald and a prince,
Do a fair message to his kingly ears?
Troilus and Cressida. Act i, sc. 3, l. 218. [Æneas]
Gracious message.—*Antony and Cleopatra,* ii, 5, 86.
Humble message.—*Timon of Athens,* v, 4, 20.
Private message.—*Measure for Measure,* v, 1, 465.
Speechless messages.—*The Merchant of Venice,* i, 1, 164.

15
Chiron: Here 's the son of Lucius;
He hath some message to deliver us.
Aaron: Ay, some mad message from his mad grandfather.
Titus Andronicus. Act iv, sc. 2, l. 1.
Horrid message.—*Twelfth Night,* iii, 4, 220.

16
Your message done, hie home unto my chamber.
The Two Gentlemen of Verona. Act iv, sc. 4, l. 93. [Proteus]
Speak the message.—*The Two Gentlemen of Verona,* iv, 4, 117.

MESSENGER

17
Dispatch the most convenient messenger.
All's Well that Ends Well. Act iii, sc. 4, l. 34. [Count]
Provide this messenger.—*All's Well that Ends Well,* iii, 4, 40.

18
Call in the messengers . . . The messengers!
Antony and Cleopatra. Act i, sc. 1, l. 29.
No messenger, but thine.—*Antony and Cleopatra,* i, 1, 52.

19
Cleopatra: Met'st thou my posts?
Alexas: Ay, madam, twenty several messengers.
Why do you send so thick?
Cleopatra: Who 's born that day
When I forget to send to Antony,
Shall die a beggar.
Antony and Cleopatra. Act i, sc. 5, l. 61.
A reeking post,
Stew'd in his haste, half breathless.
King Lear. Act ii, sc. 4, l. 30. [King Lear]
For "post" see under LETTER.

20
My messenger He hath whipp'd with rods.
Antony and Cleopatra. Act iv, sc. 1, l. 2. [Cæsar]

A messenger from Cæsar.—*Antony and Cleopatra,* iii, 13, 37.
Most kind messenger.—*Antony and Cleopatra,* iii, 13, 73.
Too slow a messenger.—*Antony and Cleopatra,* v, 2, 324.

1
I am but as a guiltless messenger.
As You Like It. Act iv, sc. 3, l. 12. [Silvius]
Were you made the messenger?—*As You Like It,* i, 2, 62.

2
For God's sake, send some other messenger.
The Comedy of Errors. Act ii, sc. 1, l. 77. [Dromio of Ephesus]
I must go send some better messenger.
The Two Gentlemen of Verona. Act i, sc. 1, l. 159. [Proteus]

3
Reason with the fellow,
Before you punish him, where he heard this,
Lest you shall chance to whip your information
And beat the messenger who bids beware
Of what is to be dreaded.
Coriolanus. Act iv, sc. 6, l. 51. [Menenius]
Admit no messengers.—*Hamlet,* ii, 2, 144.

4
Thou baleful messenger, out of my sight!
II Henry VI. Act iii, sc. 2, l. 48. [King Henry]
York: Art thou a messenger, or come of pleasure?
Buckingham: A messenger from Henry, our dread liege,
To know the reason of these arms in peace.
II Henry VI. Act v, sc. 1, l. 16.

5
Urge it no more; lest that, instead of words,
I send thee, Warwick, such a messenger
As shall revenge his death before I stir.
III Henry VI. Act i, sc. 1, l. 98. [Lord Clifford]
Come, cousin, you shall be the messenger.
III Henry VI. Act i, sc. 1, l. 272. [King Henry]

6
He perhaps shall need
Some messenger betwixt me and the peers;
And be thou he.
King John. Act iv, sc. 2, l. 178. [King John]

7
The several messengers
From hence attend dispatch.
Macbeth. Act ii, sc. 1, l. 126. [Regan]
Yet I have not seen
So likely an ambassador of love:
A day in April never came so sweet,
To show how costly summer was at hand,
As this fore-spurrer comes before his lord.
The Merchant of Venice. Act ii, sc. 9, l. 91. [Servant] The only use of "fore-spurrer."
With an absolute 'Sir, not I,'
The cloudy messenger turns me his back.
Macbeth. Act iii, sc. 6, l. 40. [Lord]
Here stays without A messenger.—*The Merchant of Venice,* iv, 1, 108.
There is come a messenger.—*The Merchant of Venice,* v, 1, 117.
Here comes my messenger.—*A Midsummer-Night's Dream,* iii, 2, 4.

8
Look who comes yonder: she shall be our messenger to this paltry knight.
The Merry Wives of Windsor. Act ii, sc. 1, l. 162. [Mrs. Page]
I have another messenger.—*The Merry Wives of Windsor,* ii, 2, 98.

9
Messengers Of strong prevailment.
A Midsummer-Night's Dream, i, 1, 34. See under Wooing. The only use of "prevailment."
Messengers of day.—*Julius Cæsar,* ii, 1, 104.
Messengers of war.—*King John,* ii, 1, 260.

10
My good she-Mercury.
Merry Wives of Windsor. Act ii, sc. 2, l. 81. [Falstaff] The only use of "she-Mercury."
Winged messenger.—*Romeo and Juliet,* ii, 2, 28.
Speedy messenger.—*King John,* ii, 1, 554.
Swift messengers.—*Sonnets,* xlv.

11
The galleys
Have sent a dozen sequent messengers
This very night at one another's heels.
Othello. Act i, sc. 2, l. 40. [Cassio]
A messenger from the galleys.—*Othello,* i, 3, 13.
The messengers of Venice stay the meat.
Othello. Act iv, sc. 2, l. 170. [Iago]

12
But now the mindful messenger comes back,
Brings home his lord and other company.
The Rape of Lucrece, l. 1583. The only use of "mindful."

13
To tread the ooze Of the salt deep,
To run upon the sharp wind of the north,
To do me business in the veins o' the earth
When it is baked with frost.
The Tempest. Act i, sc. 2, l. 252. [Prospero]
Hail, many-colour'd messenger.
The Tempest. Act iv, sc. 1, l. 76. [Ceres] "Many-colour'd" is repeated in *All's Well that Ends Well,* i, 3, 158.

14
I hope it remains not unkindly with your lordship that I returned you an empty messenger.
Timon of Athens. Act iii, sc. 6, l. 39. [Lord]

15
He shent our messengers; and we lay by
Our appertainments, visiting of him.
Troilus and Cressida. Act ii, sc. 3, l. 86. [Agamemnon] "Shent" (reproved) is used five times. The only use of "appertainments."

16
Viola: Tell me your mind: I am a messenger.
Olivia: Sure, you have some hideous matter to deliver, when the courtesy of it is so fearful.
Twelfth Night. Act i, sc. 5, l. 219.
Run after this same peevish messenger.
Twelfth Night. Act i, sc. 5, l. 319. [Olivia]
Churlish messenger.—*Twelfth Night,* ii, 2, 24.
Distemper'd messenger.—*All's Well that Ends Well,* i, 3, 157.
Leaden messengers.—*All's Well that Ends Well,* iii, 2, 111.

Pure messengers.—*The Two Gentlemen of Verona,* ii, 7, 77.

1 I will be thankful
To any happy messenger from thence.
The Two Gentlemen of Verona. Act ii, sc. 4, l. 52. [Valentine]
And now am I, unhappy messenger,
To plead for that which I would not obtain.
The Two Gentlemen of Verona. Act iv, sc. 4, l. 104. [Julia]

METAL

See also Gold, Iron, Lead, Silver, Steel

2
That you were made of is metal to make virgins.
All's Well that Ends Well. Act i, sc. 1, l. 141. [Parolles] See under VIRGINITY.
Good sparks and lustrous, a word, good metals.
All's Well that Ends Well. Act ii, sc. 1, l. 41. [Parolles]

3
To what metal this counterfeit lump of ore will be melted.
All's Well that Ends Well. Act iii, sc. 6, l. 39. [Lord]
Like some ore
Among a mineral of metals base,
Shows itself pure.
Hamlet. Act iv, sc. 1, l. 25. [Queen] The only uses of ore.
Mortal mineral.—*Cymbeline,* v, 5, 50.
Poisonous mineral.—*Othello,* ii, 1, 306. The only uses of "mineral."
Drugs or minerals.—*Othello,* i, 2, 74. The only use of minerals.

4
Queen: Come hither, my dear Hamlet, sit by me.
Hamlet: No, good mother, here 's metal more attractive.
Hamlet. Act iii, sc. 2, l. 113. Hamlet is referring to Ophelia.

5
For from his metal was his party steel'd.
II Henry IV. Act i, sc. 1, l. 116. [Morton]
Metal, Marcus, steel to the very back.
Titus Andronicus. Act iv, sc. 3, l. 47. [Titus]

6 Now I feel
Of what coarse metal ye are moulded.
Henry VIII. Act iii, sc. 2, l. 238. [Wolsey]
Barren metal.—*Merchant of Venice,* i, 3, 135.
Bright metal.—*I Henry IV,* i, 2, 236.
Golden metal.—*Richard III,* iv, 1, 60.
Imperial metal.—*Richard III,* iv, 4, 382. See under CROWN.
Twisted metal.—*A Lover's Complaint,* l. 205.

7
See whether their basest metal be not moved.
Julius Cæsar. Act i, sc. 1, l. 66. [Flavius]
They have all been touch'd and found base metal.
Timon of Athens. Act iii, sc. 3, l. 6. [Servant]
Let there be some test made of my metal.
Measure for Measure, i, 1, 49. See under TRIAL.

8
Thy honourable metal may be wrought
From that it is disposed.
Julius Cæsar, i, 2, 313. See under NOBILITY.

9 O, it grieves my soul,
That I must draw this metal from my side
To be a widow-maker!
King John. Act v, sc. 2, l. 15. [Salisbury] The only use of "widow-maker."

10 Sir, I am made
Of the self-same metal that my sister is,
And prize me at her worth.
King Lear. Act i, sc. 1, l. 70. [Regan]
That metal . . . that fashion'd thee
Made him a man.
Richard II, i, 2, 23. See under BROTHER.

11
Our copper buys no better treasure.
Love's Labour 's Lost. Act iv, sc. 3, l. 386. [Biron]
Copper crowns.—*Troilus and Cressida,* iv, 4, 107.
Copper nose.—*Troilus and Cressida,* i, 2, 115.
Copper ring.—*I Henry IV,* iii, 3, 98; 162. The only mention of copper.

12
How now, my metal of India!
Twelfth Night. Act ii, sc. 5, l. 17. [Sir Toby]

METHOD

See also Way

13
I will beat this method into your sconce.
The Comedy of Errors. Act ii, sc. 2, l. 34. [Antipholus of Syracuse]
You do not hold the method.—*Antony and Cleopatra,* i, 3, 7. See under LOVE.

14
Though this be madness, yet there is method in 't.
Hamlet, ii, 2, 208. See under MADNESS.
An honest method, as wholesome as sweet.
Hamlet, ii, 2, 465. See under STYLE.

15 I am not able
Verbatim to rehearse the method of my pen.
I Henry VI. Act iii, sc. 1, l. 12. [Gloucester] The only use of "verbatim."
What sayest thou to this . . . method? Is 't not drowned i' the last rain, ha?
Measure for Measure. Act iii, sc. 2, l. 50. [Lucio]

16
Fall somewhat into a slower method.
Richard III. Act i, sc. 2, l. 117. [Gloucester]
New-found methods.—*Sonnets,* lxxvi. The entries under this section are the only uses of "method" in the plays.

METTLE

See also Courage, Spirit

17
I do think there is mettle in death.
Antony and Cleopatra, i, 2, 147. See under DEATH.

18
Of unimproved mettle hot and full.
Hamlet. Act i, sc. 1, l. 96. [Horatio] The only use of "unimproved."

19
Well, that rascal hath good mettle in him; he will not run . . . afoot he will not budge a foot.
I Henry IV. Act ii, sc. 4, l. 383. [Falstaff]
A lad of mettle.—*I Henry IV,* ii, 4, 13.

A man of this mettle.—*II Henry IV,* v, 3, 41.
1 Show us here
The mettle of your pasture.
Henry V, iii, 1, 26. See under ANCESTRY.
The mettle of a king.—*King John,* ii, 1, 401.
Mettle of your sex.—*Twelfth Night,* v, 1, 330.
Mettle of my speech.—*As You Like It,* ii, 7, 82.
2
Dieu de batailles! where have they this mettle?
Henry V. Act iii, sc. 5, l. 15. [Constable] The only use of "Dieu de batailles."
The fellow has mettle enough in his belly.
Henry V. Act iv, sc. 8, l. 66. [Fluellen]
3
The insuppressive mettle of our spirits.
Julius Cæsar, ii, 1, 134. See under OATH. The only use of "insuppressive."
Make promise of their mettle.—*Julius Cæsar,* iv, 2, 24.
Brave mettle.—*The Tempest,* ii, 1, 182.
Quick mettle.—*Julius Cæsar,* i, 2, 300.
4
Thy undaunted mettle should compose
Nothing but males.
Macbeth. Act i, sc. 7, l. 73. See CHILD, 187:5.
Our mettle is bred out.—*Henry V,* iii, 5, 29. See WIFE, 1668:10.
5
If you take it not patiently, why, your mettle is the more.
Measure for Measure. Act iii, sc. 2, l. 79. [Lucio]
6
Thou hast mettle enough in thee to kill care.
Much Ado about Nothing, v, 1, 133. See under CARE.
Now I see there's mettle in thee.
Othello. Act iv, sc. 2, l. 207. [Iago]
Even of your mettle.—*Richard III,* iv, 4, 302.
7 [The] self-same mettle,
Whereof thy proud child, arrogant man, is puff'd,
Engenders the black toad and adder blue.
Timon of Athens, iv, 3, 179. See under NATURE.
8
I am one that had rather go with sir priest than sir knight: I care not who knows so much of my mettle.
Twelfth Night. Act iii, sc. 4, l. 297. [Viola]

MIDNIGHT

See also Night

9
'Tis now struck twelve; get thee to bed,
Francisco.
Hamlet. Act i, sc. 1, l. 7. [Bernardo]
The Windsor bell hath struck twelve; the minute draws on.
The Merry Wives of Windsor. Act v, sc. 5, l. 1. [Falstaff]
The iron tongue of midnight hath told twelve.
A Midsummer-Night's Dream. Act v, sc. 1, l. 370. [Theseus] See also under BELL.
Twelve o'clock at midnight.—*I Henry IV,* ii, 4, 107.
10
In the dead vast and middle of the night.
Hamlet. Act i, sc. 2, l. 198. [Horatio]
Upon the heavy middle of the night.
Measure for Measure. Act iv, sc. 1, l. 35. [Isabella]
About the mid of night.—*Richard III,* v, 3, 77.
11
'Tis now the very witching time of night,
When churchyards yawn and hell itself
breathes out
Contagion to this world.
Hamlet. Act iii, sc. 2, l. 406. [Hamlet] The only use of "witching."
Now it is the time of night
That the graves all gaping wide,
Every one lets forth his sprite,
In the church-way paths to glide.
A Midsummer-Night's Dream. Act v, sc. 1, l. 386. [Puck] The only use of "church-way.
12
We have heard the chimes at midnight, Master Shallow.
II Henry IV. Act iii, sc. 2, l. 228. [Falstaff]
13
Let us go, For it is after midnight.
Julius Cæsar. Act i, sc. 3, l. 162. [Cassius]
After midnight.—*All's Well that Ends Well,* iv, 3, 34; *Twelfth Night,* ii, 3, 2; 7.
'Tis midnight.—*Henry V,* iii, 7, 97; *Henry VIII,* v, 1, 72.
14
Macbeth: What is the night?
Lady Macbeth: Almost at odds with morning, which is which.
Macbeth. Act iii, sc. 4, l. 126.
15
Midnight, assist our moan;
Help us to sigh and groan,
Heavily, heavily.
Much Ado about Nothing. Act v, sc. 3, l. 16. [Song]
16 The lights burn blue.
It is now dead midnight.
Richard III. Act v, sc. 3, l. 180. [King Richard]
The dreadful dead of dark midnight.
The Rape of Lucrece, l. 1625.
'Tis now dark midnight.—*Measure for Measure,* iv, 2, 67.
Dead midnight still.—*Henry V,* iii, Prol., 9.
Deep midnight.—*A Midsummer-Night's Dream,* i, 1, 223.
Still midnight.—*The Merry Wives of Windsor,* iv, 4, 30.
Hush'd as midnight.—*The Tempest,* iv, 1, 207.
17
One midnight, fated to the purpose.
The Tempest. Act i, sc. 2, l. 128. [Prospero]
Thou call'dst me up at midnight.—*The Tempest,* i, 2, 228.

MIDWIFE, see under Labour

MIGHT

See also Power, Right, Strength

18
Cleopatra . . . Submits her to thy might.
Antony and Cleopatra. Act iii, sc. 12, l. 17. [Euphronius]
19
I will from henceforth rather be myself,
Mighty and to be fear'd.
I Henry IV. Act i, sc. 3, l. 5. [King Henry]

Thou art mighty yet.—*Julius Cæsar,* v, 3, 94.
His person 's mighty.—*Winter's Tale,* i, 2, 455.
In himself too mighty.—*The Winter's Tale,* ii, 3, 20. "Mighty" is used 102 times.

1
How mighty then you are, O, hear me tell!
A Lover's Complaint, l. 253.
Thyself art mighty; for thine own sake leave me:
Myself a weakling; do not then ensnare me.
The Rape of Lucrece, l. 583. "Weakling" is repeated in *III Henry VI,* v, 1, 37.
Most mighty for thy place and sway.
Troilus and Cressida. Act i, sc. 3, l. 60. [Ulysses]
Most mighty.—*The Tempest,* i, 2, 204.

2
I to conquer sought with all my might.
The Rape of Lucrece, l. 488.
With all his might.—*The Merry Wives of Windsor,* ii, 1, 18; *Othello,* i, 2, 16.

3
O, from what power hast thou this powerful might?
Sonnets. No. cl.
Conquering might.—*Love's Labour 's Lost,* v, 2, 566.
Former might.—*Sonnets,* lvi.
Mickle might.—*Henry V,* ii, 1, 70.
Newer might.—*Sonnets,* cxxiii.
Almighty dreadful little might.—*Love's Labour 's Lost,* iii, 1, 205. See under CUPID.
Man's might.—*Troilus and Cressida,* iii, 2, 164.
Woman's might.—*Julius Cæsar,* ii, 4, 8.

4
O, be not proud, nor brag not of thy might.
Venus and Adonis, l. 113.

MILDNESS

See also Gentleness

5
She never reprehended him but mildly.
The Comedy of Errors, v, 1, 87. See under REPROOF.
Cominius: Arm yourself To answer mildly. . . .
Coriolanus: The word is 'mildly.' . . . I
Will answer in mine honour.
Menenius: Ay, but mildly.
Coriolanus: Well, mildly be it then. Mildly!
Coriolanus. Act iii, sc. 2, l. 138.
Deal mildly with his youth.
Richard II, ii, 1, 69. See under YOUTH.
Take thy correction mildly.
Richard II. Act v, sc. 1, l. 32. [Queen]
We did as mildly as we might.—*Titus Andronicus,* i, 1, 475. The only uses of "mildly."

6
As mild and gentle as the cradle-babe.
II Henry VI, iii, 2, 392. See under DEATH. The only use of "cradle-babe."
Mild and gentle.—*Richard III,* iv, 4, 160.
Mild as a dove.—*The Passionate Pilgrim,* l. 86.
Be thou mild.—*II Henry VI,* iii, 4, 48.
Mild, or come not near me.—*Much Ado about Nothing,* ii, 3, 34.
Mild may be thy life!—*Pericles,* iii, 1, 27.
I should have been more mild.—*Richard II,* i, 3, 240.
More mild.—*Richard II,* ii, 1, 174; *Richard III,* iv, 4, 172.

7
He is famed for mildness, peace, and prayer.
III Henry VI, ii, 1, 156. See under HAND.
My mildness hath allayed their swelling griefs.
III Henry VI. Act iv, sc. 8, l. 42. [King Henry]
Bear with mildness.—*III Henry VI,* iv, 4, 20.

8
You are much more attask'd for want of wisdom
Than praised for harmful mildness.
King Lear. Act i, sc. 4, l. 366. [Goneril] The only use of "attask'd."
Let mild women to him lose their mildness.
Rape of Lucrece, l. 979. See under WOMAN.

9
So mild, that Patience seem'd to scorn his woes.
The Rape of Lucrece, l. 1505.
So sober-sad, so weary, and so mild.
The Rape of Lucrece, l. 1542. The only use of "sober-sad."

10
In the mildness of your sleepy thoughts.
Richard III, iii, 7, 123. See under THOUGHT.
Hearing thy mildness praised in every town.
The Taming of the Shrew, ii, 1, 192. See under WOOING.
Thou with mildness entertain'st thy wooers.
The Taming of the Shrew, ii, 1, 252. See under CHARACTER.

11
You will be more mild and tractable.
Titus Andronicus. Act i, sc. 1, l. 470. [Tamora] For "tractable" see OBEDIENCE.
Mild and affable.—*II Henry VI,* iii, 1, 9.
Mild and beautiful.—*The Two Gentlemen of Verona,* iv, 4, 185.
Mild, and virtuous.—*Richard III,* i, 2, 104.
Mild, pitiful and flexible.—*III Henry VI,* i, 4, 141.

12
O, sir, I find her milder than she was.
The Two Gentlemen of Verona. Act v, sc. 2, l. 2. [Proteus]
Why did you wish me milder?
Coriolanus. Act iii, sc. 2, l. 14. [Coriolanus]
Change you to a milder form.—*The Two Gentlemen of Verona,* v, 4, 56.
Of milder mould.—*The Taming of the Shrew,* i, 1, 60. The only uses of "milder." "Mildest" occurs twice, in *All's Well that Ends Well,* iii, 4, 18, and in *Titus Andronicus,* iv, 1, 85.

MILK

13
I would the milk
Thy mother gave thee when thou suck'dst her breast,
Had been a little ratsbane for thy sake!
I Henry VI. Act v, sc. 4, l. 27. [Shepherd] "Ratsbane" occurs again in *II Henry IV,* i, 2, 48, and in *King Lear,* iii, 4, 55.
Come to my woman's breasts,
And take my milk for gall.
Macbeth. Act i, sc. 5, l. 48. [Lady Macbeth]
The milk thou suck'dst from her did turn to marble.
Titus Andronicus, ii, 3, 144. See under TYRANNY.
Mother's milk.—*Twelfth Night,* i, 5, 171.

1
Milk comes frozen home in pail.
Love's Labour's Lost, v, 2, 925. See under WINTER.

2
Too full o' the milk of human kindness.
Macbeth, i, 5, 18. See under KINDNESS for full quotation.

Sweet milk of concord.—*Macbeth,* iv, 3, 98. See under CHAOS for full quotation.

Sweet milk.—*Romeo and Juliet,* iii, 3, 55.

Skim milk.—*I Henry IV,* ii, 3, 36; *A Midsummer-Night's Dream,* ii, 1, 36. "Skim" is used in no other connection.

Milk of Burgundy.—*King Lear,* i, 1, 86.

3
'Item: She can milk'; look you, a sweet virtue in a maid with clean hands.
The Two Gentlemen of Verona. Act iii, sc. 1, l. 277. [Launce] "She can milk" is repeated in l. 302.

Milk my ewes.—*The Winter's Tale,* iv, 4, 461.

Milking-time.—*Winter's Tale,* iv, 4, 246. The only use of the phrase. See SECRECY, 1328:18.

Milkmaid.—*The Two Gentlemen of Verona,* iii, 1, 268; *Measure for Measure,* i, 2, 177.

Milk-pap.—*Timon of Athens,* iv, 3, 115.

Milksop.—*Richard III,* v, 3, 325; *Much Ado about Nothing,* v, 1, 91.

Milk-white.—*II Henry VI,* i, 1, 254, and five times in later plays.

White as milk.—*The Merchant of Venice,* iii, 2, 86; *Pericles,* iv, Gower, 22.

Milky gentleness.—*King Lear,* i, 4, 364.

Milky head.—*Hamlet,* ii, 2, 500.

Milky heart.—*Timon of Athens,* iii, 1, 57. The only uses of "milky."

4
The innocent milk in its most innocent
mouth.
The Winter's Tale. Act iii, sc. 2, l. 101. [Hermione]

MIND

See also Brain, Wits

5
Where an unclean mind carries virtuous qualities, there commendations go with pity.
All's Well that Ends Well, i, 1, 48. See under CHARACTER.

Beastly mind.—*Cymbeline,* i, 6, 153.

The mind growing once corrupt.—*Henry VIII,* i, 2, 116. See under BENEFIT.

Ill-breeding minds.—*Hamlet,* iv, 5, 15. The only use of "ill-breeding."

Rancorous mind.—*II Henry VI,* iii, 1, 24.

Rank minds.—*II Henry IV,* iv, 1, 64.

Sinners' minds.—*Romeo and Juliet,* iii, 2, 111.

Villain's mind.—*Merchant of Venice,* i, 3, 181.

Wicked mind.—*The Rape of Lucrece,* l. 1540.

6
He and his physicians are of a mind.
All's Well that Ends Well, i, 3, 244. See under DOCTOR.

I would not have Rosalind of this mind.
As You Like It. Act iv, sc. 1, l. 108. [Orlando]

I would we were all of one mind, and one mind good.
Cymbeline. Act v, sc. 4, l. 212. [Gaoler]

An captains were of my mind, they would truncheon you out.
II Henry IV. Act ii, sc. 4, l. 153. [Doll] The only use of "truncheon" as a verb.

There is but one mind in all these men.
Julius Cæsar. Act ii, sc. 3, l. 5. [Artemidorus]

Our sister,
Whose mind and mine, I know, in that are one.
King Lear. Act i, sc. 3, l. 15. [Goneril]

O, that you bore The mind that I do!
The Tempest. Act ii, sc. 1, l. 266. [Antonio]

An all men were of my mind.—*Troilus and Cressida,* ii, 3, 225.

That 's my mind too.—*Troilus and Cressida,* iv, 1, 6.

They themselves are o' the mind.—*The Winter's Tale,* iv, 4, 337.

Not of my mind.—*I Henry IV,* iii, 1, 22.

I am not in the mind.—*As You Like It,* iii, 3, 91.

7
An thy mind stand to 't, boy, steal away
bravely.
All's Well that Ends Well. Act ii, sc. 1, l. 29. [Parolles]

Rouse up a brave mind.
The Merchant of Venice. Act ii, sc. 2, l. 12. [Launce] "Brave mind" is repeated in *II Henry VI,* iv, 2, 22.

8
Let no fair be kept in mind
But the fair of Rosalind.
As You Like It. Act iii, sc. 2, l. 99. [Rosalind, reading]

9
Seal up thy mind.
As You Like It. Act iv, sc. 3, l. 58. [Rosalind]

10
Your minds,
Pre-occupied with what you rather must do
Than what you should, made you against
the grain
To voice him consul.
Coriolanus. Act ii, sc. 3, l. 239. [Brutus] The only use of "pre-occupied" and "against the grain."

11
The heavens . . . keep unshaked
That temple, thy fair mind.
Cymbeline. Act ii, sc. 1, l. 67. [Lord]

She bore a mind that envy could not but call fair.
Twelfth Night. Act ii, sc. 1, l. 30. [Sebastian]

Fair minds.—*Henry V,* Epil., 14.

12
It is a mind
That shall remain a poison where it is,
Not poison any further.
Coriolanus. Act iii, sc. 1, l. 86. [Sicinius]

Thy mind to her is now as low as were
Thy fortunes.
Cymbeline. Act iii, sc. 2, l. 10. [Pisanio]

If you could wear a mind
Dark as your fortune is, and but disguise
That which, to appear itself, must not yet be
But by self-danger, you should tread a course
Pretty and full of view.
Cymbeline. Act iii, sc. 4, l. 146. [Pisanio] The only use of "self-danger."

1 What is in thy mind
That makes thee stare thus?
Cymbeline. Act iii, sc. 3, l. 4. [Imogen]

2
Think us no churls, nor measure our good minds
By this rude place we live in.
Cymbeline. Act iii, sc. 6, l. 65. [Belarius]
Good mind.—*The Winter's Tale,* iii, 2, 163.

3
O, what a noble mind is here o'erthrown!
The courtier's, soldier's, scholar's, eye, tongue, sword;
The expectancy and rose of the fair state.
Hamlet. Act iii, sc. 1, l. 158. [Ophelia]
"Expectancy" is repeated in *Othello,* ii, 1, 41.
It is meet
That noble minds keep ever with their likes.
Julius Cæsar, i, 2, 314. See under NOBILITY.
The noblest mind he carries
That ever govern'd man.
Timon of Athens. Act i, sc. 1, l. 291. [Lord]
Noble mind.—*II Henry VI,* ii, 4, 10, and five times in later plays.
Right noble mind.—*Timon of Athens,* iii, 2, 87.
Noblest minds.—*Timon of Athens,* iv, 3, 471.

4
If your mind dislike anything, obey it.
Hamlet. Act v, sc. 2, l. 227. [Horatio]
Taint not thy mind.—*Hamlet,* i, 5, 85.
A mind impatient.—*Hamlet,* i, 2, 96.
Men's minds are wild.—*Hamlet,* v, 2, 405.
Giddy minds.—*II Henry IV,* iv, 5, 214.
Green minds.—*Othello,* ii, 1, 251.
Inconstant mind.—*Sonnets,* xcii.
Quick minds.—*Antony and Cleopatra,* i, 2, 114.

5
I knew of this before; but, to speak truth,
This present grief had wiped it from my mind.
II Henry IV. Act i, sc. 1, l. 210. [Northumberland]

6
God put it in thy mind to take it hence.
II Henry IV. Act iv, sc. 5, l. 179. [King Henry]
It were well
The general were put in mind of it.
Othello. Act ii, sc. 3, l. 136. [Montano]
Put in mind.—*Coriolanus,* v, 6, 118.
Put us in mind.—*Romeo and Juliet,* i, 1, 237.
Put you in mind.—*Twelfth Night,* v, 1, 42.
Bear you it in mind.—*Pericles,* iv, 4, 15.
Call to mind, see under MEMORY.

7
Grapple your minds to sternage of this navy.
Henry V. Act iii, Prol., l. 18. [Chorus]
The only use of "sternage."
King Henry: All things are ready, if our minds be so.
Westmoreland: Perish the man whose mind is backward now!
Henry V. Act iv, sc. 3, l. 71.

8
When the mind is quicken'd, out of doubt,
The organs, though defunct and dead before,
Break up their drowsy grave and newly move,
With casted slough and fresh legerity.
Henry V. Act iv, sc. 1, l. 20. [King Henry]
The only use of "casted" and "legerity." "Defunct" is repeated in *Othello,* i, 3, 265, and in *Cymbeline,* iv, 2, 358.
Vacant mind.—*Henry V,* iv, 1, 286.

9
Humble lowliness of mind.
I Henry VI. Act v, sc. 5, l. 18. [Suffolk]
This base and humble mind.
II Henry VI. Act i, sc. 2, l. 62. [Duchess of Gloucester]
'Tis but a base ignoble mind
That mounts no higher than a bird can soar.
II Henry VI. Act ii, sc. 1, l. 13. [Gloucester]
I 'll ne'er bear a base mind.
II Henry IV. Act iii, sc. 2, l. 251. [Feeble]
Faith, I'll bear no base mind.—*II Henry IV,* iii, 2, 257.

10
By this I shall perceive the commons' mind.
II Henry IV. Act iii, sc. 1, l. 374. [York]
King Edward: But now you partly may perceive my mind.
Lady Grey: My mind will never grant what I perceive
Your highness aims at, if I aim aright.
III Henry VI. Act iii, sc. 2, l. 66.
You perceive my mind?—*I Henry VI,* ii, 2, 59.

11 Let thy dauntless mind
Still ride in triumph over all mischance.
III Henry VI. Act iii, sc. 3, l. 17. [King Lewis]
Fearless minds climb soonest unto crowns.
III Henry VI. Act iv, sc. 7, l. 62. [Gloucester]
Fiery mind.—*Hamlet,* ii, 1, 33.
Haughty mind.—*Richard III,* iv, 2, 37.
Royal minds.—*Henry VIII,* iv, 1, 8.
Unmatched mind.—*Timon of Athens,* iv, 3, 523.

12
Though fortune's malice overthrow my state,
My mind exceeds the compass of her wheel.
III Henry VI. Act iv, sc. 3, l. 46. [King Edward]

13
You bear a gentle mind.
Henry VIII, ii, 3, 57. See under GENTLENESS.
Gentle mind.—*The Rape of Lucrece,* l. 1148.
Bounteous mind.—*Henry VIII,* i, 3, 55.
Serious mind.—*Henry VIII,* iii, 2, 80.
Strong minds.—*Sonnets,* cxv.
Thrifty mind.—*Merchant of Venice,* ii, 5, 55.
A mind of honour.—*Measure for Measure,* ii, 4, 179.
A mind so rare.—*Cymbeline,* i, 6, 16. See under BEAUTY.

14
My mind 's not on it.
Henry VIII. Act v, sc. 1, l. 57. [King Henry]

15
Yet have I a mind That fears him much.
Julius Cæsar. Act iii, sc. 1, l. 144. [Cassius]
Fearful minds.—*Comedy of Errors,* i, 1, 68.
My mind misgives.—*Romeo and Juliet,* i, 4, 106; *Othello,* iii, 4, 89.

16
He bears too great a mind.
Julius Cæsar. Act v, sc. 1, l. 113. [Brutus]
Great minds.—*Troilus and Cressida,* ii, 2, 177; *Sonnets,* cxiv.

1
Your mind is all as youthful as your blood.
King John. Act iii, sc. 4, l. 125. [Pandulph]

You have slander'd nature in my form,
Which, howsoever rude exteriorly,
Is yet the cover of a fairer mind.
King John. Act iv, sc. 2, l. 256. [Hubert] The only use of "exteriorly."

2
My mind as generous, and my shape as true.
King Lear. Act i, sc. 2, l. 8. [Edmund]

An honest mind and plain.—*King Lear,* ii, 2, 105.

3
One minded like the weather, most unquietly.
King Lear. Act iii, sc. 1, l. 2. [Gentleman] The only use of "unquietly."

So many so minded.—*Coriolanus,* i, 6, 73.

Were I so minded.—*The Tempest,* v, 1, 126.

4
I fear I am not in my perfect mind.
King Lear, iv, 7, 63. See under MADNESS.

5
Being of an old father's mind.
Love's Labour's Lost. Act iv, sc. 2, l. 33. [Sir Nathaniel]

A' show'd a mounting mind.—*Love's Labour's Lost,* iv, 1, 4.

6
Henceforth my wooing mind shall be express'd
In russet yeas and honest kersey noes.
Love's Labour's Lost. Act v, sc. 2, l. 412. [Biron] "Russet" is repeated in *Hamlet,* i, 1, 166, and "russet-pated" occurs in *A Midsummer-Night's Dream,* iii, 2, 21. "Kersey" is used in *Measure for Measure,* i, 2, 35: "English kersey"; and in *The Taming of the Shrew,* iii, 2, 68: "Kersey boot-hose."

I wish you the peace of mind, most royal couplement!
Love's Labour's Lost. Act v, sc. 2, l. 534. The only use of "couplement" (couple).

Rest your minds in peace.—*I Henry VI,* i, 1, 44.

7
For Banquo's issue have I filed my mind.
Macbeth. Act iii, sc. 1, l. 65. [Macbeth] The only use of "filed" in the sense of defiled.

8
Better be with the dead,
Whom we, to gain our peace, have sent to peace,
Than on the torture of the mind to lie
In restless ecstasy.
Macbeth. Act iii, sc. 2, l. 19. [Macbeth]

O, full of scorpions is my mind!
Macbeth. Act iii, sc. 2, l. 36. [Macbeth] "Scorpion" is used again in *II Henry VI,* iii, 2, 86, and in *Cymbeline,* v, 5, 45.

Infected minds
To their deaf pillows will discharge their secrets.
Macbeth. Act v, sc. 1, l. 80. [Doctor]

No mind that's honest
But in it shares some woe.
Macbeth. Act iv, sc. 3, l. 197. [Ross]

Hurt minds.—*Macbeth,* ii, 2, 39.

9
Canst thou not minister to a mind diseased,
Pluck from the memory a rooted sorrow,
Raze out the written troubles of the brain
And with some sweet oblivious antidote
Cleanse the stuff'd bosom of that perilous stuff
Which weighs upon the heart?
Macbeth. Act v, sc. 2, l. 40. [Macbeth] The only use of "oblivious." "Antidote" occurs again in *Timon of Athens,* iv, 3, 435.

10
My mind promises with my habit no loss shall touch her by my company.
Measure for Measure. Act iii, sc. 1, l. 181. [Duke]

Fit his mind to death.—*Measure for Measure,* ii, 4, 187.

11
Your mind is tossing on the ocean.
The Merchant of Venice. Act i, sc. 1, l. 8. [Salarino]

12
I pray you, have in mind where we must meet.
The Merchant of Venice. Act i, sc. 1, l. 71. [Lorenzo]

Now methinks I have a mind to it.
The Merchant of Venice. Act iv, sc. 1, l. 433. [Portia]

I have no mind of feasting forth to-night.
The Merchant of Venice. Act ii, sc. 5, l. 37. [Shylock.]

I have no mind to Isbel.—*All's Well that Ends Well,* iii, 2, 13.

13
A golden mind stoops not to shows of dross.
The Merchant of Venice. Act ii, sc. 7, l. 20. [Prince of Morocco]

My mind was never yet more mercenary.
The Merchant of Venice. Act iv, sc. 1, l. 418. [Portia]

14
Not sick, my lord, unless it be in mind;
Nor well, unless in mind.
The Merchant of Venice. Act iii, sc. 2, l. 237. [Salerio]

My mind is heavy.—*The Merry Wives of Windsor,* iv, 6, 2.

Heavy mind.—*Richard II,* ii, 4, 18.

15
So Got udge me, that is a virtuous mind.
The Merry Wives of Windsor. Act i, sc. 1, l. 191. [Evans]

16
Falstaff: Keep in that mind; I'll deserve it.
Mrs. Ford: Nay, I must tell you, so you do; or else I could not be in that mind.
Merry Wives of Windsor. Act iii, sc. 3, l. 89.

God keep your ladyship still in that mind.
Much Ado about Nothing. Act i, sc. 1, l. 135. [Benedick]

God keep your lordship in that gracious mind!
Richard III. Act iii, sc. 2, l. 56. [Catesby]

17
All their minds transfigured.
A Midsummer-Night's Dream, v, 1, 24. See under STORY. The only use of "transfigured."

Never labour'd in their minds till now.
A Midsummer-Night's Dream. Act v, sc. 1, l. 73. [Philostrate]

1
I 'll hold my mind, were she an Ethiope.
Much Ado about Nothing. Act v, sc. 4, l. 38. [Claudio]

2
I saw Othello's visage in his mind,
And to his honours and his valiant parts
Did I my soul and fortunes consecrate.
Othello. Act i, sc. 3, l. 253. [Desdemona]
Be free and bounteous to her mind.
Othello. Act i, sc. 3, l. 265. [Othello]
Good faith, how foolish are our minds!
Othello. Act iv, sc. 3, l. 23. [Desdemona]
Farewell the tranquil mind!—*Othello,* iii, 3, 348. See under WAR.

3
Now to Marina bend your mind.
Pericles. Act iii, Gower, l. 5.
Had I brought hither a corrupted mind,
Thy speech had alter'd it.
Pericles. Act iv, sc. 6, l. 111. [Lysander]

4
In his inward mind he doth debate
What following sorrow may on this arise.
The Rape of Lucrece, l. 185.
She bears the load of lust he left behind,
And he the burthen of a guilty mind.
The Rape of Lucrece, l. 734.
Guilty mind.—*III Henry VI,* v, 6, 11.

5
Men have marble, women waxen, minds.
The Rape of Lucrece, l. 1240.

6
Though my gross blood be stain'd with this abuse,
Immaculate and spotless is my mind.
The Rape of Lucrece, l. 1655.
May my pure mind with the foul act dispense,
My low-declined honour to advance?
The Rape of Lucrece, l. 1704. The only use of "low-declined."
So pure a mind.—*The Rape of Lucrece,* l. 761.
Pure mind.—*Timon of Athens,* iv, 3, 195.

7
Sweet York, sweet husband, be not of that mind.
Richard II. Act v, sc. 2, l. 107. [Duchess]

8
Thou wast provoked by thy bloody mind,
Which never dreamt on aught but butcheries.
Richard III. Act i, sc. 2, l. 99. [Lady Anne] The only use of "butcheries."
That bloody mind, I think, they learn'd of me.
Titus Andronicus. Act v, sc. 1, l. 101. [Aaron]

9
My lord, you shall o'er-rule my mind for once.
Richard III. Act iii, sc. 1, l. 57. [Bourchier]
Those men you talk of came into my mind.
Richard III. Act iii, sc. 3, l. 118. [Hastings]

10
A troubled mind drave me to walk abroad.
Romeo and Juliet. Act i, sc. 1, l. 127. [Benvolio]
Achilles: My mind is troubled, like a fountain stirr'd;
And I myself see not the bottom of it.
Thersites: Would the fountain of your mind were clear again, that I might water an ass at it!
Troilus and Cressida. Act iii, sc. 3, l. 311.
A turn or two I 'll walk,
To still my beating mind.
The Tempest. Act iv, sc. 1, l. 162. [Prospero]
Disturbed mind.—*Venus and Adonis,* l. 340.
Troubled minds.—*The Rape of Lucrece,* l. 126.

11
They look into the beauty of thy mind,
And that, in guess, they measure by thy deeds.
Sonnets. No. lxix.
My most true mind thus makes my eye untrue.
Sonnets. No. cxiii. See under EYE.
True minds.—*Sonnets,* cxvi.

12
I have frequent been with unknown minds.
Sonnets. No. cxvii.

13
My mind hath been as big as one of yours.
The Taming of the Shrew. Act v, sc. 2, l. 170. [Katharina]

14
But how is it
That this lives in thy mind?
The Tempest. Act i, sc. 2, l. 48. [Prospero]
Perchance he will not mind me.
The Tempest. Act ii, sc. 2, l. 17. [Caliban]
Do not infest your mind with beating on
The strangeness of this business.
The Tempest. Act v, sc. 1, l. 246. [Prospero]
Have you a mind to sink?—*Tempest,* i, 1, 42.

15
All minds,
As well of glib and slippery creatures as
Of grave and austere quality.
Timon of Athens. Act i, sc. 1, l. 52. [Poet]
Never mind Was so unwise to be so kind.
Timon of Athens. Act ii, sc. 2, l. 5. [Flavius]
I 'll ever serve his mind with my best will.
Timon of Athens. Act iv, sc. 2, l. 49. [Flavius]

16
Arm the minds of infants to exclaims.
Titus Andronicus, iv, 1, 86. See under WRITING.

17
Your mind is the clearer, Ajax.
Troilus and Cressida, ii, 3, 163. See under PRIDE.
A mind
That doth renew swifter than blood decays.
Troilus and Cressida. Act iii, sc. 2, l. 169. See WOMAN, 1704:4.
Let your mind be coupled with your words.
Troilus and Cressida. Act v, sc. 2, l. 15. [Diomedes]
Minds swayed by eyes are full of turpitude.
Troilus and Cressida, v, 2, 112. See under EYE. "Turpitude" is repeated in *Antony and Cleopatra,* iv, 6, 33.
My mind is now turn'd whore.
Troilus and Cressida. Act v, sc. 2, l. 114. [Thersites]

18
I will believe thou hast a mind that suits
With this thy fair and outward character.
Twelfth Night. Act i, sc. 2, l. 50. [Viola]
Thy mind is a very opal.
Twelfth Night. Act ii, sc. 4, l. 77. [Clown] The only mention of opal in the plays. It occurs in *A Lover's Complaint,* l. 215.

1
Not black in my mind, though yellow in my legs.
Twelfth Night. Act iii, sc. 4, l. 28. [Malvolio]
The mind too, 'mongst all colours
No yellow in't.
The Winter's Tale. Act ii, sc. 3, l. 106. [Paulina]
2
In nature there 's no blemish but the mind.
Twelfth Night. Act iii, sc. 4, l. 401. [Antonio]
3
I see you have a month's mind to them.
The Two Gentlemen of Verona. Act i, sc. 2, l. 137. [Julia]
He bears an honourable mind.
The Two Gentlemen of Verona. Act v, sc. 3, l. 13. [Outlaw]
So hard a mind.—*Venus and Adonis,* l. 203.
4
Not noted, is 't,
But of the finer natures? by some severals
Of head-piece extraordinary?
The Winter's Tale. Act i, sc. 2, l. 225. [Leontes] "Head-piece" occurs again in *Henry V,* iii, 7, 149, and in *King Lear,* iii, 2, 26.

II—Changing the Mind

5
With every minute you do change a mind.
Coriolanus, i, 1, 186. See under People.
Change my mind.—*Sonnets,* x.
Change the mind.—*Comedy of Errors,* i, 2, 99.
6
Their minds may change.
Julius Cæsar. Act ii, sc. 2, l. 96. [Brutus]
Now I change my mind,
And partly credit things that do presage.
Julius Cæsar. Act v, sc. 1, l. 78. [Cassius]
7
It would better fit your honour to change your mind.
Much Ado about Nothing, iii, 2, 119. See under Marriage.
Your mind perhaps may change.
Othello. Act iii, sc. 3, l. 452. [Iago]
8
My mind is changed, sir, my mind is changed.
Richard III. Act iv, sc. 4, l. 456. [King Richard]
9
Cannot soon revolt and change your mind.
The Two Gentlemen of Verona. Act iii, sc. 2, l. 59. [Duke]
Julia: It is the lesser blot, modesty finds,
Women to change their shapes than men their minds.
Proteus: Than men their minds! 'tis true.
The Two Gentlemen of Verona. Act v, sc. 4, l. 108.

III—Knowing the Mind

10
Adriana: Know'st thou his mind?
Dromio of Ephesus: Ay, ay, he told his mind upon mine ear.
The Comedy of Errors. Act ii, sc. 1, l. 48.
11
Call thither all the officers of the town,
Where they shall know our mind.
Coriolanus. Act i, sc. 5, l. 28. [Lartius]
Come some other time to know our mind.
III Henry VI. Act iii, sc. 2, l. 18. [King Edward]
12
King Henry: What shall I know of thee?
Montjoy: My master's mind.
King Henry: Unfold it.
Henry V. Act iii, sc. 6, l. 122.
Now I know thy mind.—*Sonnets,* cxlix.
I know your mind.—*II Henry VI,* i, 1, 139, and frequently in later plays.
13
To know How you stand minded.
Henry VIII. Act iii, sc. 1, l. 58. [Wolsey]
14
What would these strangers? know their minds, Boyet.
Love's Labour 's Lost. Act v, sc. 2, l. 174. [Rosaline]
15
My people do already know my mind.
The Merchant of Venice. Act iii, sc. 4, l. 37. [Portia]
Knowing my mind, you wrong me.
The Merry Wives of Windsor. Act iii, sc. 4, l. 80. [Page]
I know Anne's mind.—*The Merry Wives of Windsor,* i, 4, 112; 137.
16
In any case have a nay-word, that you may know one another's mind.
The Merry Wives of Windsor. Act ii, sc. 2, l. 131. [Mistress Quickly]
We have a nay-word how to know each other.
The Merry Wives of Windsor. Act v, sc. 2, l. 5. [Slender]
Gull him into a nay-word.—*Twelfth Night,* ii, 3, 146. The only uses of "nay-word" (watch-word).
17
Send quickly to Sir John to know his mind.
The Merry Wives of Windsor. Act iv, sc. 5, l. 83. [Mrs. Page]
18
Buckingham: Who knows the lord protector's mind herein?
Who is most inward with the noble duke?
Ely: Your grace, we think, should soonest know his mind.
Buckingham: Who, I, my lord? we know each other's faces,
But for our hearts, he knows no more of mine,
Than I of yours;
Nor I no more of his, than you of mine.
Richard III. Act iii, sc. 4, l. 7.
Let me know your mind.
Richard III. Act iv, sc. 4, l. 446. [Catesby]
19
You say you do not know the lady's mind.
Romeo and Juliet. Act iv, sc. 1, l. 4. [Friar Laurence]
You know my mind.—*Troilus and Cressida,* iii, 3, 56.
Your lord does know my mind.—*Twelfth Night,* i, 5, 276.
I would I knew his mind.—*The Two Gentlemen of Verona,* i, 2, 33.
Knew his mind.—*Venus and Adonis,* l. 308.

I partly know his mind.—*The Winter's Tale,* v, 3, 142.

1
This is the hour that Madam Silvia
Entreated me to call and know her mind.
The Two Gentlemen of Verona. Act iv, sc. 3, l. 1. [Eglamour]

IV—Speaking the Mind

See also Candour

2
The lady shall say her mind freely.
Hamlet. Act ii, sc. 2, l. 338. [Hamlet]

Say my mind.—*The Taming of the Shrew,* iv, 3, 75. See under CANDOUR.

Say your mind.—*All's Well that Ends Well,* ii, 1, 98.

Break thy mind to me.—*Henry V,* v, 2, 265.

3
Had I first been put to speak my mind,
I think I should have told your Grace's tale.
II Henry VI. Act iii, sc. 1, l. 43. [Suffolk] "Speak my mind" is repeated frequently in later plays.

There are that dare; and I myself have ventured
To speak my mind of him.
Henry VIII. Act v, sc. 1, l. 40. [Gardiner]

Nay, speak thy mind.—*Richard II,* ii, 1, 230.

Tell me your mind.—*Twelfth Night,* i, 5, 219.

Tell on thy mind.—*Titus Andronicus,* v, 1, 69.

Ease my mind.—*Titus Andronicus,* ii, 4, 35.

Write down thy mind.—*Titus Andronicus,* ii, 4, 3.

I'll write my mind.—*I Henry VI,* v, 3, 66.

4
Helen, to you our minds we will unfold.
A Midsummer-Night's Dream. Act i, sc. 1, l. 208. [Lysander]

5
He tells you flatly what his mind is.
The Taming of the Shrew. Act i, sc. 2, l. 77. [Grumio] "Flatly" is used in similar phrases in three other plays: "He tells me flatly," *The Merchant of Venice,* iii, 5, 34; "Tell me flatly," *I Henry IV,* ii, 4, 12; "He flatly says," *King John,* v, 2, 126. These are the only uses of "flatly" in the plays, but it occurs once in *Venus and Adonis,* l. 463: "Flatly falleth down."

Tell me thy mind.—*The Taming of the Shrew,* i, 1, 21.

I will tell him my mind.—*Henry V,* iii, 6, 89.

6 I'll show my mind
According to my shallow simple skill.
The Two Gentlemen of Verona. Act i, sc. 2, l. 7. [Lucetta]

V—Mind and Body

7 I will not do 't,
Lest I surcease to honour mine own truth
And by my body's action teach my mind
A most inherent baseness.
Coriolanus. Act iii, sc. 2, l. 120. [Coriolanus] The only use of "inherent."

8
The incessant care and labour of his mind
Hath wrought the mure that should confine it in
So thin that life looks through and will break out.
II Henry IV. Act iv, sc. 4, l. 118. [Clarence] The only use of "mure."

A weak mind and an able body.
II Henry IV, ii, 4, 273. See under CHARACTER.

Weak and silly mind.—*Venus and Adonis,* l. 1016.

9
Since the heavens have shaped my body so,
Let hell make crook'd my mind to answer it.
III Henry VI. Act v, sc. 6, l. 78. [Gloucester]

10 We are not ourselves
When nature, being oppress'd, commands the mind
To suffer with the body.
King Lear. Act ii, sc. 4, l. 108. [King Lear]

I . . . am fall'n out with my more headier will,
To take the indisposed and sickly fit
For the sound man.
King Lear. Act ii, sc. 4, l. 110. [King Lear] The only use of "headier" and "indisposed."

When the mind 's free,
The body 's delicate: the tempest in my mind
Doth from my senses take all feeling else
Save what beats there.
King Lear. Act iii, sc. 4, l. 11. [King Lear]

11
The mind shall banquet, though the body pine.
Love's Labour 's Lost. Act i, sc. 1, l. 25. [Longaville]

12
Her body's stain her mind untainted clears.
The Rape of Lucrece, l. 1710.

13
Our purses shall be proud, our garments poor;
For 'tis the mind that makes the body rich.
The Taming of the Shrew. Act iv, sc. 3, l. 173. [Petruchio]

14 The still and mental parts, . . .
Why, this hath not a finger's dignity:
They call this bed-work, mappery, closet-war;
So that the ram that batters down the wall, . . .
They place before his hand that made the engine.
Troilus and Cressida. Act i, sc. 3, l. 200. [Ulysses] The only use of "bed-work," "mappery," and "closet-war."

MINISTER

15 His coin, ships, legions,
May be a coward's; whose ministers would prevail
Under the service of a child.
Antony and Cleopatra. Act iii, sc. 13, l. 22. [Antony]

16
Break thou in pieces and consume to ashes,
Thou foul accursed minister of hell!
I Henry VI. Act v, sc. 4, l. 92. [York]

Avaunt, thou dreadful minister of hell!
Richard III. Act i, sc. 2, l. 46. [Anne]

Flaming minister.—*Othello,* v, 2, 8.

1 For a minister of my intent,
I have seduced a headstrong Kentishman,
John Cade of Ashford.
II Henry VI. Act iii, sc. 1, l. 355. [York] The only use of "Kentishman." "Kentishmen" occurs in *III Henry* VI, i, 2, 41. "Kentish" is used twice.

Master Dumbe, our minister.—*II Henry IV,* ii, 4, 95. The only reference to Dumbe.

Your master, Whose minister you are.
Henry VIII. Act v, sc. 1, l. 136. [King Henry]

2
But yet I call you servile ministers.
King Lear. Act iii, sc. 2, l. 21. [King Lear]

Debile minister.—*All 's Well that Ends Well,* ii, 3, 40.

Weakest minister.—*All 's Well that Ends Well,* ii, 1, 140. See under TRIFLE.

3 You murdering ministers,
Wherever in your sightless substances
You wait on nature's mischief!
Macbeth. Act i, sc. 5, l. 49. [Lady Macbeth]

The cruel ministers
Of this dead butcher and his fiend-like queen.
Macbeth. Act v, sc. 8, l. 68. [Malcolm] "Fiend-like" is repeated in *Titus Andronicus,* v, 1, 45: "Fiend-like face."

We two shall be the ministers.—*The Merry Wives of Windsor,* iv, 2, 234.

4
How sweetly do you minister to love!
Much Ado about Nothing, i, 1, 314. See under LOVE. "Minister," as a verb, is used nineteen times.

5
Who made thee, then, a bloody minister,
When gallant-springing brave Plantagenet
That princely novice, was struck dead by thee?
Richard III. Act i, sc. 4, l. 227. [First Murderer] The only use of "gallant-springing."

6
Make us thy ministers of chastisement!
Richard III. Act v, sc. 3, l. 113. [Richmond] See under PRAYER.

I and my fellows are ministers of fate.
The Tempest, iii, 3, 61. See under FATE.

Ministers of grace.—*Hamlet,* i, 4, 39.

Minister of honour.—*Winter's Tale,* ii, 2, 50.

Public minister of justice.—*Antony and Cleopatra,* v, 1, 20.

Ministers . . . of war.—*Troilus and Cressida,* Prol., 4.

7
Ministers for the purpose hurried thence
Me and thy crying self.
The Tempest. Act i, sc. 2, l. 131. [Prospero]

8
My meaner ministers
Their several kinds have done.
The Tempest. Act iii, sc. 3, l. 87. [Prospero]

Potent ministers.—*The Tempest,* i, 2, 275.

Blessed ministers.—*Measure for Measure,* v, 1, 115.

9
Tamora: These are my ministers, and come with me.
Titus: Are these thy ministers? what are they call'd?
Tamora: Rapine and Murder, therefore called so,
Cause they take vengeance of such kind of men. . . .
Now I will hence about thy business,
And take my ministers along with me.
Titus Andronicus. Act v, sc. 2, l. 61.

10
I chose Camillo for the minister.
Winter's Tale. Act iii, sc. 2, l. 161. [Leontes]

MINSTREL

11
I will use him for my minstrelsy.
Love's Labour 's Lost. Act i, sc. 1, l. 177. [King]

Every room . . . bray'd with minstrelsy.
Timon of Athens. Act ii, sc. 2, l. 170. [Flavius] The only use of "bray'd."

What minstrelsy and pretty din.—*Pericles,* v, 2, 272. The only uses of "minstrelsy."

12
Tush! none but minstrels like of sonneting!
Love's Labour 's Lost, iv, 3, 158. See under POETRY. The only use of "sonneting." "Tush" is repeated in *The Taming of the Shrew,* i, 2, 211, and in *Much Ado about Nothing,* iii, 3, 130.

Feast-finding minstrels.—*The Rape of Lucrece,* l. 817. The only use of "feast-finding."

13
What, dost thou make us minstrels? an thou make minstrels of us, look to hear nothing but discords.
Romeo and Juliet. Act iii, sc. 1, l. 51. [Mercutio]

As we do the minstrels.—*Much Ado about Nothing,* v, 1, 129.

I will give you the minstrel.—*Romeo and Juliet,* iv, 5, 116.

14
Hark, hark! I hear the minstrels play.
The Taming of the Shrew. Act iii, sc. 2, l. 185. [Gremio] These are the only uses of "minstrel" and "minstrels."

MINUTE

See also under Moment, Time

15
Or four and twenty times the pilot's glass
Hath told the thievish minutes how they pass.
All's Well that Ends Well, ii, 1, 168. See under TIME.

Brief minutes.—*Sonnets,* xiv.

Damned minutes.—*Othello,* iii, 3, 169.

Tedious minutes.—*A Midsummer-Night's Dream,* ii, 2, 112.

Watchful minutes.—*King John,* iv, 1, 46.

Wretched minutes.—*Sonnets,* cxxvi.

16
But of a minute old.
Cymbeline. Act ii, sc. 5, l. 31. [Posthumus]

The minute I was born.—*Pericles,* v, 1, 160.

The minute I began.—*Pericles,* v, 1, 214.

17 I have entreated him along
With us to watch the minutes of this night.
Hamlet. Act i, sc. 1, l. 26. [Marcellus]

1 Every minute now
Should be the father of some stratagem.
II Henry IV. Act i, sc. 1, l. 7. [Northumberland]

2
The latest minute of the hour.
Love's Labour's Lost. Act v, sc. 2, l. 797. [King]
One minute behind your hour.—*As You Like It,* iv, 1, 195.
The minute draws on.—*The Merry Wives of Windsor,* v, 5, 2.
The third part of a minute.—*A Midsummer-Night's Dream,* ii, 2, 2.
The thousandth part of a minute.—*As You Like It,* iv, 1, 46.

3
To spite me now, each minute seems a moon.
The Passionate Pilgrim, l. 207.

4
Till every minute pays the hour his debt.
The Rape of Lucrece, l. 229.
One poor retiring minute in an age
Would purchase thee a thousand thousand friends.
The Rape of Lucrece, l. 962.
Minutes fill up hours.—*The Rape of Lucrece,* l. 297.

5
In a minute there are many days.
Romeo and Juliet. Act iii, sc. 5, l. 45. [Juliet]
One short minute.—*Romeo and Juliet,* ii, 6, 5.
Even in a minute.—*Twelfth Night,* i, 1, 14.

6
Like as the waves make towards the pebbled shore,
So do our minutes hasten to their end.
Sonnets. No. lx. The only use of "pebbled."
Thy dial [will show] how thy precious minutes waste.
Sonnets. No. lxxvii.

MIRACLE

See also Wonder

7 Seas have dried
When miracles have by the greatest been denied.
All's Well that Ends Well. Act ii, sc. 1, l. 143. [Helena]
They say miracles are past; and we have our philosophical persons, to make modern and familiar, things supernatural and causeless.
All's Well that Ends Well. Act ii, sc. 3, l. 1. [Lafeu] The only use of "philosophical." "Supernatural" occurs again in *Macbeth,* i, 3, 130.
It must be so; for miracles are ceased.
Henry V. Act i, sc. 1, l. 67. [Archbishop of Canterbury]

8
You are come by miracle.
The Comedy of Errors. Act v, sc. 1, l. 264. [Merchant]
I have 'scaped by miracle.
I Henry IV. Act ii, sc. 4, l. 184. [Falstaff]

9 Who this should be,
Doth miracle itself, loved before me.
Cymbeline. Act iv, sc. 2, l. 28. [Belarius]

10
The greatest miracle that e'er ye wrought.
I Henry VI, v, 4, 66. See under PREGNANCY.
Exceeding miracles.—*I Henry VI,* v, 4, 41.

11
Gloucester: Fellow, what miracle dost thou proclaim?
Townsman: A miracle! a miracle!
Suffolk: Come to the king and tell him what miracle. . . .
Gloucester: Saint Alban here hath done a miracle. . . .
Cardinal: Duke Humphrey here has done a miracle to-day.
Suffolk: True; made the lame to leap and fly away.
Gloucester: But you have done more miracles than I;
You made in a day, my lord, whole towns to fly.
II Henry VI. Act ii, sc. 1, l. 60.

12
Nothing almost sees miracles But misery.
King Lear, ii, 2, 172. See under MISERY.
Reason without miracle.—*King Lear,* i, 1, 225.
Thy life's a miracle.—*King Lear,* iv, 6, 55.

13
A miracle! here's our own hands against our hearts.
Much Ado about Nothing, v, 4, 91. [Benedick]
A most high miracle!—*The Tempest,* v, 1, 177.
Wondrous miracle.—*King John,* ii, 1, 497.

14
It was a miracle to 'scape suffocation.
The Merry Wives of Windsor, iii, 5, 119. [Falstaff] The only use of "suffocation."
The miracle, I mean our preservation.
The Tempest. Act ii, sc. 1, l. 6. [Gonzalo]

15
Now do I long to hear . . . who to thank,
Besides the gods, for this grand miracle.
Pericles. Act v, sc. 3, l. 56. [Pericles]
I would laugh at that miracle.—*Troilus and Cressida,* v, 4, 37.
Love wrought these miracles.—*The Taming of the Shrew,* v, 1, 127. See under LOVE.

16 Unless this miracle have might,
That in black ink my love may still shine bright.
Sonnets. No. lxv.

17
His word is more than the miraculous harp; he hath raised the wall and houses too.
The Tempest. Act ii, sc. 1, l. 86. [Sebastian]
Miraculous organ.—*Hamlet,* ii, 2, 623.
Miraculous work.—*Macbeth,* iv, 3, 147. The only uses of "miraculous."

18 'Tis that miracle and queen of gems
That nature pranks her in attracts my soul.
Twelfth Night, ii, 4, 88. See under WOOING.
Nature's miracle.—*I Henry VI,* v, 3, 54.
A miracle in nature.—*The Merchant of Venice,* iii, 2, 90.
O miracle of men!—*II Henry IV,* ii, 3, 33.

19
May this, almost a miracle, be done?
The Winter's Tale. Act iv, sc. 4, l. 544. [Florizel] All the uses of "miracle" and "miracles" are cited in this section.

MIRROR

1
When such a spacious mirror 's set before him,
He needs must see himself.
Antony and Cleopatra. Act v, sc. 1, l. 34. [Mecænas]
Hold the mirror up to nature.—*Hamlet,* iii, 2, 24. See under ACTING for full quotation.
Mirror of all courtesy.—*Henry VIII,* ii, 1, 53.
Mirror of all Christian kings.—*Henry V,* ii, Prol., 6.
Mirror of all martial men.—*I Henry VI,* i, 4, 74.

2
Methinks you are my glass, and not my brother:
I see by you I am a sweet-faced youth.
The Comedy of Errors, v, 1, 417. See under LIKENESS.
I my brother know Yet living in my glass.
Twelfth Night, iii, 4, 415. See under BROTHER.

3
He was indeed the glass
Wherein the noble youth did dress themselves.
II Henry IV. Act ii, sc. 3, l. 21. [Lady Percy]
He was the mark and glass, copy and book,
That fashion'd others.
II Henry IV. Act ii, sc. 3, l. 31. [Lady Percy] See under EXAMPLE.
Glass of fashion.—*Hamlet,* iii, 1, 161.
The glass, the school, the book.—*The Rape of Lucrece,* l. 615.

4
That never looks in his glass for love of any thing he sees there.
Henry V. Act v, sc. 2, l. 155. [King Henry]

5
It is very much lamented, Brutus,
That you have no such mirrors as will turn
Your hidden worthiness into your eye,
That you might see your shadow.
Julius Cæsar. Act i, sc. 2, l. 55. [Cassius]
I, your glass,
Will modestly discover to yourself
That of yourself which you yet know not of.
Julius Cæsar. Act i, sc. 2, l. 68. [Cassius] See under CANDOUR.
You go not till I set you up a glass
Where you may see the inmost part of you.
Hamlet. Act iii, sc. 4, l. 19. [Hamlet]
Give me the glass, and therein will I read.
Richard II. Act iv, sc. 1, l. 276. [King Richard]

6
Poor broken glass, I often did behold
In thy sweet semblance my old age new born;
But now that fair fresh mirror, dim and old,
Shows me a bare-boned death by time outworn;
O, from thy cheeks my image thou hast torn,
And shiver'd all the beauty of my glass,
That I no more can see what once I was!
The Rape of Lucrece, l. 1758. The only use of "bare-boned." "Bare-bone" occurs in *I Henry IV,* ii, 4, 358.

7
O flattering glass,
Like to my followers in prosperity,
Thou dost beguile me!
Richard II. Act iv, sc. 1, l. 279. [King Richard]
'Tis not her glass, but you, that flatters her.
As You Like It. Act iii, sc. 5, l. 54. See under FLATTERY.

8
King Richard: An if my word be sterling yet in England,
Let it command a mirror hither straight,
That it may show me what a face I have,
Since it is bankrupt of his majesty.
Bolingbroke: Go some of you and fetch a looking-glass.
Richard II. Act iv, sc. 1, l. 264.
I, that am not shaped for sportive tricks,
Nor made to court an amorous looking-glass.
Richard III. Act i, sc. 1, l. 14. [Gloucester]
I 'll be at charges for a looking-glass.
Richard III. Act i, sc. 2, l. 256. [Gloucester]
She did neglect her looking-glass.
The Two Gentlemen of Verona. Act iv, sc. 4, l. 157. [Julia]
Lend me a looking-glass.—*King Lear,* v, 3, 261.
As in a looking-glass.—*The Winter's Tale,* i, 2, 117. The only uses of "looking-glass."

9
But now two mirrors of his princely semblance
Are crack'd in pieces by malignant death,
And I for comfort have but one false glass,
Which grieves me when I see my shame in him.
Richard III. Act ii, sc. 2, l. 51. [Duchess]
Watery glass.—*A Midsummer-Night's Dream,* i, 1, 210.
Wicked and dissembling glass.—*A Midsummer-Night's Dream,* ii, 2, 98.
Glasses of thine eyes.—*Richard II,* i, 3, 208.
Glasses of my sight.—*Coriolanus,* iii, 2, 117.

10
Thy glass will show thee how thy beauties wear.
Sonnets. No. lxxvii.
Your own glass shows you when you look in it.
Sonnets. No. ciii.

MIRTH

See also Merriment

11
He was disposed to mirth.
Antony and Cleopatra. Act i, sc. 2, l. 86. [Cleopatra]
In mirth.—*Antony and Cleopatra,* i, 3, 4.

12
Then is there mirth in heaven,
When earthly things made even
Atone together.
As You Like It. Act v, sc. 4, l. 114. [Hymen]

13
In despite of mirth, mean to be merry.
The Comedy of Errors. Act iii, sc. 1, l. 108. [Antipholus of Ephesus]
As she is now, she will but disease our better mirth.
Coriolanus. Act i, sc. 3, l. 116. [Volumnia]
I wish you much mirth.—*Coriolanus,* i, 3, 123.

1
Imogen: Is he disposed to mirth? I hope he is.
Iachimo: Exceeding pleasant; none a stranger there
So merry and so gamesome: he is call'd
The Briton reveller.
Cymbeline. Act i, sc. 6, l. 58.
Pleasant, gamesome.—*The Taming of the Shrew,* ii, 1, 247.
I am not gamesome.—*Julius Cæsar,* i, 2, 28. The only uses of "gamesome."
2
I have of late—but wherefore I know not—lost all my mirth.
Hamlet. Act ii, sc. 2, l. 307. [Hamlet]
Mirth in funeral.—*Hamlet,* i, 2, 12.
3
Laughest thou, wretch? thy mirth shall turn to moan.
I Henry VI. Act ii, sc. 3, l. 44. [Countess of Auvergne]
Present mirth hath present laughter;
What 's to come is still unsure.
Twelfth Night. Act ii, sc. 3, l. 49. [Clown]
Mirth and laughter.—*Julius Cæsar,* iv, 3, 114; *The Merchant of Venice,* i, 1, 80.
Mirth and joy.—*I Henry VI,* i, 6, 15.
Mirthful comic shows.—*III Henry VI,* v, 7, 43. The only use of "mirthful."
Mirth-moving jest.—*Love's Labour 's Lost,* ii, 1, 71. The only use of "mirth-moving."
4
Make yourself mirth with your particular fancy.
Henry VIII. Act ii, sc. 3, l. 101. [Anne]
Full of . . . mirth.—*King John,* v, 2, 59.
New-fangled mirth.—*Love's Labour 's Lost,* i, 1, 106.
5
That base minnow of thy mirth.
Love's Labour 's Lost. Act i, sc. 1, l. 250. [King] The only use of "minnow." "Minnows" occurs in *Coriolanus,* iii, 1, 89: "Triton of the minnows."
Eruptions and sudden breaking out of mirth.
Love's Labour 's Lost. Act v, sc. 1, l. 121. [Armado]
Mirth is in his face.
Love's Labour 's Lost. Act v, sc. 2, l. 79. [Princess of France]
Mirth cannot move a soul in agony.
Love's Labour 's Lost. Act v, sc. 2, l. 867. [Biron] See under WIT for full quotation.
6
Be large in mirth.
Macbeth. Act iii, sc. 4, l. 11. [Macbeth]
7
My mirth it much displeased, but pleased my woe.
Measure for Measure. Act iv, sc. 1, l. 13. [Mariana]
8
Put on
Your boldest suit of mirth, for we have friends
That purpose merriment.
The Merchant of Venice. Act ii, sc. 2, l. 210. [Bassanio]
9
I was then frugal of my mirth.
The Merry Wives of Windsor. Act ii, sc. 1, l. 28. [Mrs. Page] "Frugal" is repeated in *Much Ado about Nothing,* iv, 1, 130: "Frugal nature's frame."
She enlargeth her mirth so far that there is shrewd construction made of her.
The Merry Wives of Windsor. Act ii, sc. 2, l. 231. [Ford]
10
Awake the pert and nimble spirit of mirth.
A Midsummer-Night's Dream. Act i, sc. 1, l. 13. [Theseus]
11
Where is our usual manager of mirth?
A Midsummer-Night's Dream. Act v, sc. 1, l. 35. [Theseus]
'Very tragical mirth.'
Merry and tragical! tedious and brief!
A Midsummer-Night's Dream. Act v, sc. 1, l. 57. [Theseus]
12
From the crown of his head to the sole of his foot, he is all mirth.
Much Ado about Nothing. Act iii, sc. 2, l. 9. [Don Pedro] The only use of the phrase.
13
How well this honest mirth becomes their labour!
Pericles. Act ii, sc. 1, l. 99. [Pericles]
Becoming mirth.—*Love's Labour 's Lost,* ii, 1, 67.
Prepare for mirth, for mirth becomes a feast.
Pericles. Act ii, sc. 3, l. 7. [Simonides]
14
Who buys a minute's mirth to wail a week?
The Rape of Lucrece, l. 213.
Mirth doth search the bottom of annoy;
Sad souls are slain in merry company.
The Rape of Lucrece, l. 1109.
15
And frame your mind to mirth and merriment,
Which bars a thousand harms and lengthens life.
The Taming of the Shrew. Induction, sc. 2, l. 137. [Messenger]
16
We will include all jars
With triumphs, mirth and rare solemnity.
The Two Gentlemen of Verona. Act v, sc. 4, l. 160. [Duke]
17
See, your guests approach:
Address yourself to entertain them sprightly,
And let 's be red with mirth.
Winter's Tale. Act iv, sc. 4, l. 52. [Florizel]

MISANTHROPY

18
He 's opposite to humanity.
Timon of Athens. Act i, sc. 1, l. 283. [Lord]
Alcibiades: Is man so hateful to thee,
That art thyself a man?
Timon: I am Misanthropos, and hate mankind.
Timon of Athens. Act iv, sc. 3, l. 51. The only use of Misanthropos.
Hate all, curse all, show charity to none,
But let the famish'd flesh slide from the bone,
Ere thou relieve the beggar; give to dogs
What thou deny'st to men; let prisons swallow 'em,

Debts wither 'em to nothing; be men like blasted woods,
And may diseases lick up their false bloods!
Timon of Athens. Act iv, sc. 3, l. 534. [Timon]

MISCARRIAGE

See also Disaster, Misfortune

1
An the child I go with do now miscarry, thou wert better thou hadst struck thy mother.
II Henry IV. Act v, sc. 4, l. 11. [Doll]
I pray God the fruit of her womb miscarry.
II Henry IV. Act v, sc. 4, l. 16. [Hostess] The only use of "fruit of her womb."
2
If he miscarry, farewell wars in France.
I Henry VI. Act iv, sc. 3, l. 16. [York]
If they miscarry, we miscarry too.
King John. Act v, sc. 4, l. 3. [Pembroke]
3
Better ten thousand base-born Cades miscarry
Than you should stoop unto a Frenchman's mercy.
II Henry VI. Act iv, sc. 8, l. 49. [Clifford] "Base-born" is repeated in *II Henry VI,* i, 3, 86: "Base-born callet"; and in *III Henry VI,* ii, 2, 143: "Base-born heart." It occurs only in these two plays.
4 If you miscarry,
Your business of the world hath so an end.
King Lear. Act v, sc. 1, l. 44. [Edgar]
I may miscarry in 't.—*Othello,* v, 1, 6.
5 There miscarried
A vessel of our country, richly fraught.
The Merchant of Venice. Act ii, sc. 8, l. 29. [Salarino]
My ships have all miscarried.—*The Merchant of Venice,* iii, 2, 318.
Accidentally . . . miscarried.—*Love's Labour's Lost,* iv, 2, 144.
Certainly miscarried.—*King Lear,* v, 4, 3.
Quite miscarried.—*The Merchant of Venice,* v, 1, 251.
Have since miscarried.—*II Henry IV,* iv, 1, 129.
Miscarried by my fault.—*Romeo and Juliet,* v, 3, 267.
Miscarried By underhand corrupted foul injustice.—*Richard III,* v, 1, 5.
Miscarried at sea.—*Measure for Measure,* iii, 1, 217.
The letters . . . miscarried.—*Henry VIII,* iii, 2, 30. The only uses of "miscarried." "Miscarrying" occurs once, in *Troilus and Cressida,* i, 3, 351.
Miscarry upon the sea.—*Henry V,* iv, 1, 155.
6
I would not have him miscarry for the half of my dowry.
Twelfth Night. Act iii, sc. 4, l. 69. [Olivia]

MISCHANCE

See also Misfortune

7 By misfortunes was my life prolong'd,
To tell sad stories of my own mishaps.
The Comedy of Errors. Act i, sc. 1, l. 120. [Ægeon]
Languisheth in her mishaps.—*Venus and Adonis,* l. 603.
Worldly mishaps.—*Titus Andronicus,* i, 1, 152. The only uses of "mishaps."
The extremity of dire mishap!
Comedy of Errors. Act i, sc. 1, l. 142. [Duke]
What! shall we curse the planets of mishap
That plotted thus our glory's overthrow?
I Henry VI. Act i, sc. 1, l. 23. [Exeter] The only uses of "mishap."
8
He never can meet more mischance than come
To be but named of thee.
Cymbeline. Act ii, sc. 3, l. 137. [Imogen]
9 The devil and mischance look big
Upon the maidenhead of our affairs.
I Henry IV. Act iv, sc. 1, l. 58. [Hotspur]
10
Never come mischance between us twain!
Hamlet, iii, 2, 238. See under SLEEP.
But let this same be presently perform'd,
Even while men's minds are wild; lest more mischance,
On plots and errors, happen.
Hamlet. Act v, sc. 2, l. 404. [Horatio]
Met with some mischance.—*I Henry IV,* i, 3, 232.
11
My thoughts do hourly prophesy Mischance.
II Henry VI. Act iii, sc. 2, l. 283. [King]
12
But now mischance hath trod my title down,
And with dishonour laid me on the ground.
III Henry VI. Act iii, sc. 3, l. 8. [Queen Margaret]
In despite of all mischance.—*III Henry VI,* iv, 3, 43.
War's mischance.—*III Henry VI,* iii, 3, 254.
13
'Tis some mischance; the cry is very direful.
Othello. Act v, sc. 1, l. 38. [Gratiano]
14
Let there bechance him pitiful mischances.
Rape of Lucrece, l. 976. "Bechance" is repeated in *Two Gentlemen of Verona,* i, 1, 61.
With some mischance cross Tarquin in his flight.
The Rape of Lucrece, l. 968.
15
Nimble mischance, that art so light of foot.
Richard II. Act iii, sc. 4, l. 92. [Queen]
Bad mischance.—*I Henry VI,* i, 1, 89.
Foul mischance.—*The Two Gentlemen of Verona,* ii, 2, 11.
Sad mischance.—*Richard III,* iv, 4, 114.
Mad mischances.—*Venus and Adonis,* l. 738.
16
Let mischance be slave to patience.
Romeo and Juliet. Act v, sc. 3, l. 221. [Verona.]
The mischance of the hour.—*The Tempest,* i, 1, 28.
17
A thousand more mischances than this one
Have learn'd me how to brook this patiently.
The Two Gentlemen of Verona. Act v, sc. 3, l. 3. [Silvia]

MISCHIEF

See also Evil, Harm, Injury, Prank

1
This is miching mallecho; it means mischief.
Hamlet. Act iii, sc. 2, l. 147. [Hamlet] The only use of "miching mallecho" (sneaking villainy).
Mean mischief.—*The Winter's Tale,* iv, 4, 197. See under SONG.
Bode no mischief.—*Much Ado about Nothing,* ii, 3, 83.

2
He cares not what mischief he does, if his weapon be out.
II Henry IV. Act ii, sc. 1, l. 16. [Hostess]
Alack, what mischiefs might be set abroach
In shadow of such greatness!
II Henry IV, iv, 2, 14. See under TREACHERY.
The secret mischiefs that I set abroach
I lay unto the grievous charge of others.
Richard III. Act i, sc. 3, l. 325. [Gloucester]
Who set this ancient quarrel new abroach?
Romeo and Juliet, i, 1, 111. The only uses of "abroach."
Broached mischief.—*I Henry IV,* v, 1, 21.

3
Some sudden mischief may arise of it.
Henry V. Act iv, sc. 7, l. 186. [King Henry]
Had your watch been good,
This sudden mischief never could have fall'n.
I Henry VI. Act ii, sc. 1, l. 58. [La Pucelle]

4
You see what mischief and what murder too
Hath been enacted through your enmity;
Then be at peace, except ye thirst for blood.
I Henry VI. Act iii, sc. 1, l. 115. [Warwick]
Pucelle, that witch, that damned sorceress,
Hath wrought this hellish mischief unawares.
I Henry VI. Act iii, sc. 2, l. 38. [Talbot]
A plaguing mischief light on Charles and thee!
I Henry VI, v, 3, 39. See under CURSE.

5
My heart 's on future mischief set.
II Henry VI. Act v, sc. 2, l. 84. [Young Clifford]
There 's mischief in this man.
Henry VIII. Act i, sc. 2, l. 187. [King Henry]
Prone to mischief.—*Henry VIII,* i, 1, 160.
Made this mischief.—*Henry VIII,* ii, 1, 22.

6
Yet let 'em look they glory not in mischief,
Nor build their evils on the graves of great men.
Henry VIII. Act ii, sc. 1, l. 66. [Buckingham]
Foreseeing these fell mischiefs.—*Henry VIII,* v, 1, 49. The only use of "foreseeing."

7
Mischief, thou art afoot,
Take thou what course thou wilt!
Julius Cæsar. Act iii, sc. 2, l. 265. [Antony]
Do some mischief.—*Julius Cæsar,* iii, 1, 93.
Millions of mischiefs.—*Julius Cæsar,* iv, 1, 51.

8
Some airy devil hovers in the sky
And pours down mischief.
King John. Act iii, sc. 2, l. 2. [Bastard]

9
Demetrius: If thou follow me, do not believe
But I shall do thee mischief in the wood.
Helena: Ay, in the temple, in the town, the field,
You do me mischief.
A Midsummer-Night's Dream. Act ii, sc. 1, l. 236.
Done their mischief.—*King Lear,* iv, 2, 55.

10
Will it serve for any model to build mischief on?
Much Ado about Nothing. Act i, sc. 3, l. 48. [Don John]
Mortifying mischief.—*Much Ado about Nothing,* i, 3, 13. "Mortifying" is repeated in *The Merchant of Venice,* i, 1, 82: "Mortifying groans."
O mischief strangely thwarting!—*Much Ado about Nothing,* iii, 2, 135.

11
To mourn a mischief that is past and gone
Is the next way to draw new mischief on.
Othello. Act i, sc. 3, l. 204. [Duke]

12
O mischief, thou art swift
To enter in the thoughts of desperate men!
Romeo and Juliet. Act v, sc. 1, l. 35. [Romeo]

13
Invert What best is boded me to mischief!
The Tempest. Act iii, sc. 1, l. 70. [Ferdinand] "Invert" is repeated in *Troilus and Cressida,* v, 2, 122.
Do that good mischief which may make this island
Thine own for ever.
The Tempest. Act iv, sc. 1, l. 217. [Caliban]
Mischiefs manifold.—*The Tempest,* i, 2, 264.

14
Grant I may ever love, and rather woo
Those that would mischief me than those that do!
Timon of Athens, iv, 3, 474. See under ENEMY. The only use of "mischief" as a verb.

15
And what not done, that thou hast cause to rue,
Wherein I had no stroke of mischief in it?
Titus Andronicus. Act v, sc. 1, l. 109. [Aaron]
Complots of mischief.—*Titus Andronicus,* v, 1, 65.
Mischief and despair.—*I Henry VI,* v, 4, 90.
Great hurt and mischief.—*Coriolanus,* iv, 5, 73.

16
My thoughts are ripe in mischief.
Twelfth Night. Act v, sc. 1, l. 132. [Duke]

MISCONSTRUCTION

See also Mistake

17
He misconstrues all that you have done.
As You Like It. Act i, sc. 2, l. 277. [Le Beau]
Be not dismay'd, fair lady; nor misconstrue
The mind of Talbot.
I Henry VI. Act ii, sc. 3, l. 73. [Talbot]
Haply may Misconstrue us.—*Richard III,* iii, 5, 61. The only uses of "misconstrue."

18
So much misconstrued in his wantonness.
I Henry IV, v, 2, 69. See under HOPE.

Alas, thou hast misconstrued every thing!
Julius Cæsar. Act v, sc. 3, l. 84. [Titinius]
Lest . . . I be misconstrued.—*The Merchant of Venice,* ii, 2, 197. The only uses of "misconstrued."

1 It pleased the king . . .
To strike at me, upon his misconstruction.
King Lear, ii, 2, 124. See under OFFENCE. The only use of "misconstruction."
No, misconceived!—*I Henry VI,* v, 4, 49. The only use of "misconceived."

2
I am altogether misprised: but it shall not be so long.
As You Like It. Act i, sc. 1, l. 177. [Oliver]
Your reputation shall not therefore be misprised.
As You Like It, i, 2, 192. See under REPUTATION.
A misprised mood.—*A Midsummer-Night's Dream,* iii, 2, 74. The only uses of "misprised."
Misprising of a maid too virtuous.—*All's Well that Ends Well,* iii, 2, 33.
A . . . great deal misprising.—*Troilus and Cressida,* iv, 5, 74.
Misprising what they look on.—*Much Ado about Nothing,* iii, 1, 52. The only uses of "misprising."

MISERY

See also Wretchedness

3
Thus misery doth part The flux of company.
As You Like It. Act ii, sc. 1, l. 51. [Lord] "Flux" is repeated in iii, 2, 70, "Flux of a cat," and occurs in no other play.

4
Make my misery serve thy turn.
Coriolanus. Act iv, sc. 5, l. 94. [Coriolanus]
Your misery increase with your age!
Coriolanus. Act v, sc. 2, l. 113. [Menenius]
Live, and love thy misery.
Timon of Athens. Act iv, sc. 3, l. 396. [Apemantus]

5
To exchange one misery with another.
Cymbeline. Act i, sc. 5, l. 55. [Queen]
O noble misery,
To be i' the field, and ask 'what news?' of me!
Cymbeline. Act v, sc. 3, l. 64. [Posthumus]
O misery on 't!—*Antony and Cleopatra,* iii, 13, 112.

6
A naked subject to the weeping clouds
And waste for churlish winter's tyranny.
II Henry IV. Act i, sc. 3, l. 61. [Bardolph]
Get you therefore hence,
Poor miserable wretches, to your death:
The taste whereof, God of his mercy give
You patience to endure.
Henry V. Act ii, sc. 2, l. 177. [King Henry]
Engirt with misery.—*II Henry VI,* iii, 1, 200.
Further misery.—*Titus Andronicus,* iii, 1, 134.
Hellish misery.—*Merchant of Venice,* iii, 4, 21.
Human misery.—*I Henry VI,* iii, 2, 137.
Intermissive miseries.—*I Henry VI,* i, 1, 88. The only use of "intermissive."
Men's miseries.—*I Henry VI,* ii, 5, 29.

7
I will not wish ye half my miseries;
I have more charity.
Henry VIII. Act iii, sc. 1, l. 108. [Queen Katharine]

8
Nothing almost sees miracles But misery.
King Lear. Act ii, sc. 2, l. 172. [Kent]
I 'll repair the misery thou dost bear
With something rich about me.
King Lear. Act iv, sc. 1, l. 79. [Gloucester]
Duke of Albany: How have you known the miseries of your father?
Edgar: By nursing them, my lord.
King Lear. Act v, sc. 3, l. 180.

9
Second Murderer: I am one, my liege,
Whom the vile blows and buffets of the world
Have so incensed that I am reckless what
I do to spite the world.
First Murderer: And I another
So weary with disasters, tugg'd with fortune,
That I would set my life on any chance,
To mend it, or be rid on 't.
Macbeth. Act iii, sc. 1, l. 108.

10
It easeth some, though none it ever cured,
To think their dolour others have endured.
The Rape of Lucrece, l. 1581. The nearest approach to "misery loves company." For "dolour" see under GRIEF.

11
Misery makes sport to mock itself.
Richard II. Act ii, sc. 1, l. 85. [Gaunt]

12
O ill-dispersing wind of misery!
Richard III. Act iv, sc. 1, l. 53. [Duchess of York] The only use of "ill-dispersing."
So many miseries have crazed my voice,
That my woe-wearied tongue is mute and dumb.
Richard III. Act iv, sc. 4, l. 17. [Duchess of York] The only use of "woe-wearied."
Sharp misery had worn him to the bones.
Romeo and Juliet, v, 1, 41. See under DOCTOR.

13
Misery acquaints a man with strange bedfellows.
The Tempest. Act ii, sc. 2, l. 41. [Trinculo]

14 Willing misery
Outlives incertain pomp, is crown'd before:
The one is filling still, never complete.
Timon of Athens. Act iv, sc. 3, l. 242. [Apemantus]
Apemantus: Thou shouldst desire to die, being miserable.
Timon: Not by his breath that is more miserable.
Timon of Athens. Act iv, sc. 3, l. 248.
I made thee miserable.—*Titus Andronicus,* iv, 3, 18.
Made miserable.—*Titus Andronicus,* iii, 2, 28.
Be miserable.—*Richard III,* i, 3, 258. "Miserable" is used thirty-three times in the plays. It does not occur in the poems.

1
If there were reason for these miseries,
Then into limits could I bind my woes.
Titus Andronicus. Act iii, sc. 1, l. 220. [Titus]
These miseries are more than may be borne.
Titus Andronicus. Act iii, sc. 1, l. 244. [Marcus]
2
O miserable, unhappy that I am!
The Two Gentlemen of Verona. Act v, sc. 4, l. 28. [Silvia]
3
Misery is trodden on by many,
And being low never relieved by any.
Venus and Adonis, l. 707.
The flatness of my misery.
The Winter's Tale. Act iii, sc. 2, l. 123. [Hermione] The only use of "flatness."

MISFORTUNE

See also Mischance

4
I am he, that unfortunate he.
As You Like It. Act iii, sc. 2, l. 414. [Orlando]
Unfortunate beggar.—*Timon of Athens,* iii, 6, 47; *King Lear,* iv, 6, 68.
Unfortunate man.—*Othello,* v, 2, 283.
Unfortunate son.—*All's Well that Ends Well,* iii, 2, 28.
Unfortunate souls.—*Macbeth,* iv, 1, 152.
Unfortunate in the infirmity.—*Othello,* ii, 3, 42.
Gentle, but unfortunate.—*Cymbeline,* iv, 2, 59.
More unfortunate.—*Coriolanus,* v, 3, 97.
Howe'er unfortunate.—*I Henry VI,* i, 4, 4.
Was unfortunate.—*III Henry VI,* iii, 3, 118. The only uses of "unfortunate." "Unfortunately" occurs once, in *Venus and Adonis,* l. 1029.
5
By misfortunes was my life prolong'd.
The Comedy of Errors. Act i, sc. 1, l. 120. [Ægeon]
By misfortune.—*Pericles,* ii, 3, 88.
Hard misfortune.—*Rape of Lucrece,* l. 1713.
6
'Twill go hard with you.
II Henry VI. Act iv, sc. 2, l. 108. [Dick]
If law, authority and power deny not,
It will go hard with poor Antonio.
The Merchant of Venice. Act iii, sc. 2, l. 292. [Jessica] "Go hard" is repeated in *The Merchant of Venice,* i, 1, 86; *The Taming of the Shrew,* iv, 4, 109; *The Two Gentlemen of Verona,* i, 1, 86.
7 Are you yet to learn
What late misfortune is befall'n King Edward?
III Henry VI. Act iv, sc. 4, l. 2. [Queen Elizabeth]
8
Bear with mildness my misfortune's cross.
III Henry VI. Act iv, sc. 4, l. 20. [Queen Elizabeth]
One silly cross Wrought all my loss.
The Passionate Pilgrim, l. 258.
To mourn thy crosses, with thy daughter's, call
And give them repetition to the life.
Pericles. Act v, sc. 1, l. 246. [Diana]
I see what crosses my attempt will bring.
The Rape of Lucrece, l. 491.
Our crosses on the way
Have made it tedious, wearisome, and heavy.
Richard III. Act iii, sc. 1, l. 4. [Prince]
Crosses love not him.—*Love's Labour's Lost,* i, 2, 36.
Crosses, cares and grief.—*Richard II,* ii, 2, 79.
Sour cross.—*Richard II,* iv, 1, 241.
What crosses to ensue.—*II Henry IV,* iii, 1, 55.
9 The worst is not
So long as we can say 'This is the worst.'
King Lear. Act iv, sc. 1, l. 29. [Edgar]
10 Every object that might make me fear
Misfortune to my ventures, out of doubt
Would make me sad.
The Merchant of Venice. Act i, sc. 1, l. 20. [Salanio]
11
And never dare misfortune cross her foot.
The Merchant of Venice. Act ii, sc. 4, l. 36. [Lorenzo]
12
There is some ill a-brewing towards my rest.
The Merchant of Venice. Act ii, sc. 5, l. 17. [Shylock] The only use of "a-brewing."
Lead to any ill.—*Much Ado about Nothing,* ii, 1, 159.
Complot any ill.—*Richard II,* i, 1, 86.
Second ills with ills.—*Cymbeline,* v, 1, 14. See also under Evil.
13
What dreadful dole is here!
A Midsummer-Night's Dream. Act v, sc. 1, l. 283. [Pyramus]
Pitiful dole.—*As You Like It,* i, 2, 139.
Dole and woe.—*Pericles,* iii, Gower, 42.
14 Make misfortune drunk
With candle-wasters.
Much Ado about Nothing. Act v, sc. 1, l. 17. [Leonato] The only use of "candle-wasters."
15
Now, by the gods, I pity his misfortune,
And will awake him from his melancholy.
Pericles. Act ii, sc. 3, l. 90. [Simonides]
16
Bearing their own misfortunes on the back
Of such as have before endured the like.
Richard II. Act v, sc. 5, l. 29. [King Richard]
How comest thou hither,
Where no man never comes but that sad dog
That brings me food to make misfortune live?
Richard II. Act v, sc. 5, l. 69. [King Richard]
17
Your looks are pale and wild, and do import
Some misadventure.
Romeo and Juliet. Act v, sc. 1, l. 28. [Balthasar] "Misadventure" occurs again in v, 3, 188, and in no other play.
Much misfortune bodes.—*Romeo and Juliet,* i, 4, 91.
18
One writ with me in sour misfortune's book!
Romeo and Juliet. Act v, sc. 3, l. 82. [Romeo]
19 To do't, or no, is certain
To me a break-neck.
The Winter's Tale. Act i, sc. 2, l. 362. [Camillo] The only use of "break-neck."

MISPRISION

1
Misprision is guilty of this fault.
I Henry IV. Act i, sc. 3, l. 27. [Northumberland]
Sweet misprision.—*Love's Labour's Lost,* iv, 3, 98.
Vile misprision.—*All's Well that Ends Well,* ii, 3, 159.

2
Of thy misprision must perforce ensue
Some true love turn'd.
A Midsummer-Night's Dream. Act iii, sc. 2, l. 90. [Oberon]

3
There is some strange misprision in the princes.
Much Ado about Nothing. Act iv, sc. 1, l. 187. [Friar]
Misprision in the highest degree!
Twelfth Night. Act i, sc. 5, l. 61. [Clown]
Upon misprision growing.—*Sonnets,* lxxxvii.
These are the only uses of "misprision" (misunderstanding, contempt).

MISTAKE

See also Error, Misconstruction

4
Gentlemen both, you will mistake each other.
Henry V. Act iii, sc. 2, l. 146. [Gower]
It will be noted from the quotations which follow that "mistake" is used throughout the plays as a verb, never as a noun.
You did mistake
The outward composition of his body.
I Henry VI. Act ii, sc. 3, l. 74. [Talbot]
I mistake your shape and meaning quite.
A Midsummer-Night's Dream. Act ii, sc. 1, l. 32. [Fairy]
I mistake you.—*The Winter's Tale,* i, 2, 99.
Thou hast mistaken quite.—*A Midsummer-Night's Dream,* iii, 2, 88.
You are mistaken.—*Cymbeline,* i, 4, 89.
You are too much mistaken.—*Henry V,* ii, 4, 30.
You have mistaken him.—*All's Well that Ends Well,* ii, 5, 43.
Mistaken all this while.—*Coriolanus,* v, 3, 55.
Something mistaken.—*Henry VIII,* i, 1, 195.
Pardon me if I be mistaken.—*King Lear,* i, 4, 70.
Thou mistakest.—*II Henry VI,* v, 1, 130; *The Two Gentlemen of Verona,* ii, 5, 49; *A Midsummer-Night's Dream,* iii, 2, 345. The only uses of "mistakest."
I do not mistake.—*II Henry VI,* v, 1, 129.
If I mistake not.—*I Henry IV,* v, 4, 59.

5
Thou hast misspoke, misheard.
King John. Act iii, sc. 1, l. 4. [Constance]
The only use of "misspoke" and "misheard."

6
The better act of purposes mistook
Is to mistake again.
King John. Act iii, sc. 1, l. 274. [Pandulph]
Oberon: This is thy negligence: still thou mistakest,
Or else committ'st thy knaveries wilfully.
Puck: Believe me, king of shadows, I mistook.
A Midsummer-Night's Dream. Act iii, sc. 2, l. 345.
You mistook, sir.—*The Two Gentlemen of Verona,* i, 1, 120.
You have been mistook.—*Twelfth Night,* v, 1, 266.
You have but mistook me.—*Richard II,* iii, 2, 174.
You may be marvellously mistook.—*Henry V,* iii, 6, 85.
I have mistook.—*The Two Gentlemen of Verona,* v, 4, 94.
How am I mistook!—*The Merry Wives of Windsor,* iii, 3, 111.

7
You must not, sir, mistake my niece.
Much Ado about Nothing. Act i, sc. 1, l. 61. [Leonato]

8
Yet sinn'd I not But in mistaking.
Much Ado about Nothing. Act v, sc. 1, l. 284. [Claudio]
Pardon, I pray thee, for my mad mistaking.
The Taming of the Shrew, iv, 5, 49.
For thy mistaking so, we pardon thee.
II Henry VI. Act v, sc. 1, l. 128. [York]
Mistaking the place.—*The Merry Wives of Windsor,* ii, 2, 225.
Mistaking his purpose.—*King Lear,* i, 2, 90.
Mistaking eyes.—*Taming of the Shrew,* iv, 5, 45; *Titus Andronicus,* v, 2, 66. "Mistaking" is used eleven times.
Made thee no mistakings.—*Tempest,* i, 2, 248. The only use of "mistakings."

9
Bolingbroke: Mistake not, uncle, further than you should.
York: Take not, good cousin, further than you should,
Lest you mistake the heavens are o'er our heads.
Richard II. Act iii, sc. 3, l. 15.
Mistake me not.—*The Taming of the Shrew,* ii, 1, 66; *As You Like It,* i, 3, 66; *Richard II,* ii, 3, 74; *The Winter's Tale,* iii, 2, 110.
Mistake no more.—*The Taming of the Shrew,* iv, 2, 16.

10
You mistake the matter.
Richard III. Act i, sc. 3, l. 62. [Queen]
Mistake the truth.—*The Tempest,* ii, 1, 57.
Mistake the word.—*The Two Gentlemen of Verona,* iii, 1, 283.
You mistake.—*The Two Gentlemen of Verona,* i, 1, 113, and frequently thereafter.
You mistake me much.—*Richard III,* ii, 2, 8.
You do mistake me, sir.—*Twelfth Night,* iii, 4, 362.
You did mistake him, sure.—*Cymbeline,* iv, 2, 102.

11
Hermione: You, my lord, Do but mistake.
Leontes: You have mistook, my lady.
The Winter's Tale. Act ii, sc. 1, l. 80.
Hermione: You scarce can right me throughly then to say
You did mistake.
Leontes: No; if I did mistake
In those foundations which I build upon,
The centre is not big enough to bear
A school-boy's top.
The Winter's Tale. Act ii, sc. 1, l. 99.

MISTRESS

1
To each of you one fair and virtuous mistress
Fall, when Love please! marry, to each, but one!
All's Well that Ends Well. Act ii, sc. 3, l. 63. [Helena]

Show me a mistress that is passing fair.
Romeo and Juliet, i, 1, 240. See under BEAUTY.

Fair mistress.—*Love's Labour's Lost,* iv, 3, 376; *The Taming of the Shrew,* i, 1, 119; *Cymbeline,* i, 4, 114.

2
'My mistress, sir,' quoth I; 'Hang up thy mistress!
I know not thy mistress; out on thy mistress!' . . .
'I know,' quoth he, 'no house, no wife, no mistress.'
The Comedy of Errors. Act ii, sc. 1, l. 67. [Dromio of Ephesus]

Some other mistress hath thy sweet aspects.
The Comedy of Errors. Act ii, sc. 2, l. 113. [Adriana]

3
Your unparagoned mistress is dead, or she 's outprized by a trifle.
Cymbeline. Act i, sc. 4, l. 87. [Iachimo] The only use of "unparagoned" and "outprized."

My mistress exceeds in goodness the hugeness of your unworthy thinking.
Cymbeline. Act i, sc. 4, l. 156. [Posthumus] The only use of "hugeness."

Auspicious mistress.—*All's Well that Ends Well,* iii, 3, 8; *King Lear,* ii, 1, 42.
Beloved mistress.—*As You Like It,* iv, 1, 83.
Buskin'd mistress.—*A Midsummer-Night's Dream,* ii, 1, 71. The only use of "buskin'd."
Country mistresses.—*Cymbeline,* i, 4, 62.
Most dear mistress.—*The Tempest,* iii, 1, 21.
Fortunate mistress.—*Winter's Tale,* iv, 4, 662.
Gentle mistress.—*The Comedy of Errors,* v, 1, 370; *The Taming of the Shrew,* iv, 5, 27; *Othello,* i, 3, 178.
Good mistress.—*Henry VIII,* v, 1, 77.
Gracious mistress.—*Winter's Tale,* i, 2, 233.
Honourable mistress.—*All's Well that Ends Well,* i, 3, 145.
Merry mistress.—*The Taming of the Shrew,* iv, 5, 53.
Precious mistress.—*Winter's Tale,* v, 1, 223.
Pretty mistress.—*Love's Labour's Lost,* v, 2, 286; *The Merry Wives of Windsor,* i, 4, 146.
Proud mistress.—*As You Like It,* iii, 5, 48.
Wedded mistress.—*Coriolanus,* iv, 5, 123.
White-handed mistress.—*Love's Labour's Lost,* v, 2, 230. The only use of "white-handed."
Young mistress.—*Hamlet,* ii, 2, 140; *Othello,* ii, 3, 53.

4
I have enjoyed the dearest bodily part of your mistress.
Cymbeline. Act i, sc. 4, l. 161. [Iachimo]

I 'll point you . . . where you may
Enjoy your mistress.
The Winter's Tale. Act iv, sc. 4, l. 536. [Camillo]

5
Dauphin: My horse is my mistress.
Orleans: Your mistress bears well.
Dauphin: Me well; which is the prescript praise and perfection of a good and particular mistress.
Constable: Nay, for methought yesterday your mistress shrewdly shook your back.
Dauphin: So perhaps did yours.
Constable: Mine was not bridled.
Dauphin: O then belike she was old and gentle; and you rode, like a kern of Ireland, your French hose off and in your strait strossers. . . . Be warned by me, then: they that ride so and ride not warily, fall into foul bogs. I had rather have my horse to my mistress.
Constable: I had as lief have my mistress a jade.
Dauphin: I tell thee, constable, my mistress wears her own hair.
Constable: I could make as true a boast as that, if I had a sow to my mistress.
Henry V. Act iii, sc. 7, l. 47. The only use of "strossers" (trousers). "Warily" is used only once again, in *Love's Labour's Lost,* v, 2, 93.

6
Or study where to meet some mistress fine,
When mistresses from common sense are hid.
Love's Labour's Lost. Act i, sc. 1, l. 63. [Biron]

My love, her mistress, is a gracious moon;
She an attending star, scarce seen a light.
Love's Labour's Lost. Act iv, sc. 3, l. 230. [King]

7
How doth my dear morsel, thy mistress?
Measure for Measure. Act iii, sc. 2, l. 56. [Lucio]

8
You saw the mistress, I beheld the maid.
The Merchant of Venice. Act iii, sc. 2, l. 200. [Gratiano]

Valentine: Sweet lady, entertain him
To be my fellow-servant to your ladyship.
Silvia: Too low a mistress for so high a servant.
Proteus: Not so, sweet lady: but too mean a servant
To have a look of such a worthy mistress.
The Two Gentlemen of Verona. Act ii, sc. 4, l. 105. The only use of "fellow-servant."

Maid, to thy master's bed;
Thy mistress is o' the brothel!
Timon of Athens. Act iv, sc. 1, l. 12. [Timon]

9
I am the mistress of my fate.
The Rape of Lucrece, l. 1069.

Mistress of your charms.—*Macbeth,* iii, 5, 6.
Mistress of the feast.—*The Winter's Tale,* iv, 3, 42; iv, 4, 68.
Mistress of the field.—*Henry VIII,* iii, 1, 152.
Mistress of the house.—*The Merchant of Venice,* v, 1, 38.

1
My mistress is the sweetest lady. . . . O, there is a nobleman in town, one Paris, that would fain lay knife aboard; but she, good soul, had as lief see a toad, a very toad, as see him. I anger her sometimes and tell her that Paris is the properer man; but, I 'll warrant you, when I say so, she looks as pale as any clout in the versal world.
Romeo and Juliet. Act ii, sc. 4, l. 211. [Nurse]
The only use of "versal."

2
The mistress which I serve quickens what 's dead
And makes my labours pleasures.
The Tempest. Act iii, sc. 1, l. 6. [Ferdinand]
My sweet mistress
Weeps when she sees me work.
Tempest. Act iii, sc. 1, l. 11. [Ferdinand]
Sweet mistress.—*The Comedy of Errors,* iii, 2, 29, and four times in later plays.

3
Servants: How does your mistress?
Fool: She 's e'en setting on water to scald such chickens as you are.
Timon of Athens. Act ii, sc. 1, l. 69.

4
Rome's royal mistress, mistress of my heart.
Titus Andronicus. Act i, sc. 1, l. 241. [Saturninus]
Mistress of my heart.—*The Taming of the Shrew,* iv, 2, 10.
Mistress of his heart.—*A Lover's Complaint,* l. 142.
Imperial mistress.—*Titus Andronicus,* ii, 1, 13.
Sovereign mistress.—*Othello,* i, 3, 225; *The Winter's Tale,* i, 2, 280; *Antony and Cleopatra,* iv, 9, 12; *Sonnets,* cxxvi.

5
Demetrius: Wilt thou betray thy noble mistress thus?
Aaron: My mistress is my mistress; this myself.
Titus Andronicus. Act iv, sc. 2, l. 106.
Noble mistress.—*All's Well that Ends Well,* i, 3, 192; *Titus Andronicus,* iv, 2, 106; *The Tempest,* iii, 1, 33; *Cymbeline,* iii, 4, 190.
Noble and chaste mistress.—*I Henry IV,* i, 2, 32.

6
[He] loves his mistress more than in confession,
With truant vows to her own lips he loves,
And dare avow her beauty and her worth
In other arms than hers.
Troilus and Cressida. Act i, sc. 3, l. 269. [Æneas]
To Diomed
You shall be mistress, and command him wholly.
Troilus and Cressida. Act iv, sc. 4, l. 121. [Diomed]

7
O mistress mine, where are you roaming?
O, stay and hear; your true love 's coming,
That can sing both high and low.
Twelfth Night. Act ii, sc. 3, l. 40. [Clown]
Orsino's mistress and his fancy's queen.
Twelfth Night. Act v, sc. 1, l. 397. [Duke]

8
Now you are metamorphosed with a mistress.
The Two Gentlemen of Verona, ii, 1, 32. See under LOVE for full quotation.
Silvia: You are welcome to a worthless mistress.
Proteus: I 'll die on him that says so but yourself.
Two Gentlemen of Verona. Act ii, sc. 4, l. 113.
Dread mistress.—*The Winter's Tale,* i, 2, 322.
Poor mistress.—*The Two Gentlemen of Verona,* iv, 4, 175; *Henry VIII,* iii, 1, 47.

MISTRUST

See also Distrust

9
Mistrust cannot make me a traitor.
As You Like It, i, 3, 58. See under TRAITOR.
That ugly treason of mistrust.—*The Merchant of Venice,* iii, 2, 28. See under TREASON.
Mistrust, and treason.—*III Henry VI,* ii, 5, 54.

10
Mistrust, that shows him worthy death.
II Henry VI. Act iii, sc. 1, l. 242. [Suffolk]

11
I hold it cowardice to rest mistrustful.
III Henry VI, iv, 2, 8. See under COWARDICE.
Mistrustful wood.—*Venus and Adonis,* l. 826.
The only uses of "mistrustful."

12
Titinius: Mistrust of my success hath done this deed.
Messala: Mistrust of good success hath done this deed.
Julius Cæsar. Act v, sc. 3, l. 65.

13
He needs not our mistrust, since he delivers
Our offices and what we have to do
To the direction just.
Macbeth. Act iii, sc. 3, l. 2. [Murderer]

14
I will never mistrust my wife again.
The Merry Wives of Windsor, v, 5, 141. See under WOOING.
Mistrust Ensuing dangers.—*Richard III,* ii, 3, 42.
Mistrust no parcel.—*III Henry VI,* v, 6, 38.
No cause to mistrust.—*Richard III,* iii, 2, 87.
Full of fond mistrust.—*The Rape of Lucrece,* l. 284.
Kindled her mistrust.—*Rape of Lucrece,* l. 1352.

15
Bianca: In time I may believe, yet I mistrust.
Lucentio: Mistrust it not.
The Taming of the Shrew. Act iii, sc. 1, l. 51.
Mistrust me not.—*Richard III,* iv, 4, 479.

16
It shall not fear where it should most mistrust.
Venus and Adonis, l. 1154. See under LOVE.

17
All 's true that is mistrusted.
Winter's Tale, ii, 1, 48. See under TRUTH.
It had been vicious To have mistrusted her.
Cymbeline. Act v, sc. 5, l. 66. [Cymbeline]
I mistrusted not.—*Much Ado about Nothing,* ii, 1, 189. The only uses of "mistrusted."
Mistrusting them.—*Richard III,* iv, 4, 528.
The only use of "mistrusting."

MOAN

1 He is gone, he is gone,
And we cast away moan.
Hamlet. Act iv, sc. 5, l. 197. [Ophelia, singing]

2
The fresh streams ran by her, and murmur'd her moans.
Othello. Act iv, sc. 3, l. 45. [Desdemona] See under SONG.

3
Poor wasting monuments of lasting moans.
The Rape of Lucrece, l. 798.
Longest moans.—*Richard II,* v, 1, 90.

4 My father York and Edward wept,
To hear the piteous moan that Rutland made.
Richard III. Act i, sc. 2, l. 157. [Gloucester]
Alas, I am the mother of these moans!
Their woes are parcell'd, mine are general.
Richard III. Act ii, sc. 2, l. 80. [Duchess of York] The only use of "parcell'd."

5
Then can I grieve at grievances foregone,
And heavily from woe to woe tell o'er
The sad account of fore-bemoaned moan,
Which I new pay as if not paid before.
Sonnets. No. xxx. The only use of "fore-bemoaned."

6
Virgins and boys, mid-age and wrinkled eld,
Soft infancy, that nothing can but cry,
Add to my clamours! let us pay betimes
A moity of that mass of moan to come.
Troilus and Cressida. Act ii, sc. 2, l. 104. [Cassandra] The only use of "mid-age."

7
Mark the moan she makes.
The Two Gentlemen of Verona. Act ii, sc. 3, l. 33. [Launce]
Make moan.—*The Merchant of Venice,* i, 1, 126; *Midsummer-Night's Dream,* v, 1, 341.
Made moan.—*Merchant of Venice,* iii, 3, 23.
Sigh and moan.—*Much Ado about Nothing,* v, 3, 16.

MOCKERY

See also Ridicule

8
An you mean to mock me after, you should not have mocked me before.
As You Like It. Act i, sc. 2, l. 220. [Orlando]
The devil take mocking.—*As You Like It,* iii, 2, 227.
Afflict me with thy mocks.—*As You Like It,* iii, 5, 33.

9
Thou art a mocker of my labour.
As You Like It. Act ii, sc. 6, l. 13. [Orlando]
Our very priests must become mockers.
Coriolanus. Act ii, sc. 1, l. 93. [Menenius]
In truth, I know it is a sin to be a mocker.
The Merchant of Venice. Act i, sc. 2, l. 61. [Portia]
Never did mockers waste more idle breath.
A Midsummer-Night's Dream. Act iii, sc. 2, l. 168. [Helena]
Ah, mocker!—*Romeo and Juliet,* ii, 4, 223.
Old mocker.—*Love's Labour's Lost,* v, 2, 552. The only uses of "mocker" and "mockers."

10
The gods begin to mock me.
Coriolanus. Act i, sc. 9, l. 79. [Coriolanus]
Mock, bestow Your sued-for tongues.
Coriolanus. Act ii, sc. 3, l. 215. [Brutus] The only use of "sued-for."
He did but mock us.—*Coriolanus,* ii, 3, 169.
Mock us with our bareness.—*All's Well that Ends Well,* iv, 2, 20. See under SEDUCTION.
Mock our eyes with air.—*Antony and Cleopatra,* iv, 14, 7. See under CLOUD.
What an infinite mock is this!
Cymbeline, v, 4, 195.

11
Was not this mockery?
Coriolanus. Act ii, sc. 3, l. 181. [Citizen]
Vent it for a mockery.—*Cymbeline,* v, 3, 56.
What a mockery!—*King John,* iii, 1, 285.
What mockery will it be!—*The Taming of the Shrew,* iii, 2, 4.
As in mockery.—*A Midsummer-Night's Dream,* ii, 1, 111.
Injury a mockery makes.—*Othello,* i, 3, 207.
For the love of mockery.—*Twelfth Night,* ii, 5, 22.
Malicious mockery.—*Hamlet,* i, 1, 146.
Monumental mockery.—*Troilus and Cressida,* iii, 3, 153.
Unreal mockery.—*Macbeth,* iii, 4, 107.
Mockery king of snow!—*Richard II,* iv, 1, 260.
Mockery of unquiet slumbers.—*Richard III,* iii, 2, 27.

12
I pray thee, do not mock me, fellow-student.
Hamlet. Act i, sc. 2, l. 177. [Hamlet] The only use of "fellow-student."
Pray do not mock me.—*King Lear,* iv, 7, 59.
Look you mock him not.—*Hamlet,* ii, 2, 571.

13
Not one now, to mock your own grinning? quite chap-fallen?
Hamlet. Act v, sc. 1, l. 212. [Hamlet] The only use of "chap-fallen."
You mock me, sir.—*Hamlet,* v, 2, 268.

14
For now a time is come to mock at form.
II Henry IV. Act iv, sc. 5, l. 119. [King Henry]
Nay, more, to spurn at your most royal image
And mock your workings in a second body.
II Henry IV. Act v, sc. 2, l. 89. [Chief Justice]
And with this spirit sadly I survive,
To mock the expectation of the world.
II Henry IV. Act v, sc. 2, l. 125. [Chief Justice]

15 This mock of his
Hath turn'd his balls to gun-stones.
Henry V. Act i, sc. 2, l. 281. [King Henry] The only use of "gun-stones."
Sweeten the bitter mock.
Henry V. Act ii, sc. 4, l. 122. [Exeter]
Return your mock.—*Henry V,* ii, 4, 125. See under RETRIBUTION.

16 Yet sit and see,
Minding true things by what their mockeries be.
Henry V. Act iv, Prol., l. 52. [Chorus]
Good God! why should they mock poor fellows thus?
Henry V. Act iv, sc. 3, l. 92. [King Henry]

Will you mock at ancient tradition, begun upon an honourable respect.
Henry V. Act v, sc. 1, l. 74. [Gower]
He was full of . . . mocks.—*Henry V,* iv, 7, 52.

1 If you can mock a leek, you can eat a leek.
Henry V. Act v, sc. 1, l. 39. [Fluellen]
When you take occasions to see leeks hereafter, I pray you, mock at 'em.
Henry V. Act v, sc. 1, l. 58. [Fluellen]

2 Your majesty shall mock at me.
Henry V. Act v, sc. 2, l. 102. [Katharine]
Mock me mercifully.—*Henry V,* v, 2, 214. The only use of "mercifully."

3 I, to make thee mad, do mock thee thus.
III Henry VI. Act i, sc. 4, l. 90. [Queen Margaret]
They mock thee, Clifford.—*III Henry VI,* ii, 6, 76.

4 Mock'd or carp'd at.
Henry VIII. Act i, sc. 2, l. 86. [Wolsey] The only use of "carp'd."
Let it alone; my state now will but mock me.
Henry VIII. Act ii, sc. 1, l. 101. [Buckingham]

5 It were a mock
Apt to be render'd, for some one to say
'Break up the senate till another time,
When Cæsar's wife shall meet with better dreams.'
Julius Cæsar. Act ii, sc. 2, l. 96. [Brutus]
Mock the deep-mouth'd thunder.—*King John,* v, 2, 173. See under Drum.

6 One side will mock another; the other too.
King Lear. Act iii, sc. 7, l. 71. [Regan]

7 Princess: We are wise girls to mock our lovers so.
Rosaline: They are worse fools to purchase mocking so.
Love's Labour's Lost. Act v, sc. 2, l. 58.
They do it but in mocking merriment;
And mock for mock is only my intent.
Love's Labour's Lost. Act v, sc. 2, l. 139. [Princess]
So shall we stay, mocking intended game,
And they, well mock'd, depart away with shame.
Love's Labour's Lost. Act v, sc. 2, l. 155. [Princess]
They 'll mock us now downright.
Love's Labour's Lost. Act v, sc. 2, l. 389. [King]
Let 's mock them still.—*Love's Labour's Lost,* v, 2, 301.

8 Mock the time with fairest show.
Macbeth, i, 7, 81. See under Face.

9 He hath . . . laughed at my losses, mocked at my gains, scorned my nation.
The Merchant of Venice. Act iii, sc. 1, l. 56. [Shylock]

10 Trust me, we 'll mock him.
The Merry Wives of Windsor. Act iii, sc. 3, l. 244. [Page]
His gibes and his mockeries!
The Merry Wives of Windsor. Act iii, sc. 3, l. 259. [Evans]
The truth being known,
We 'll all present ourselves, dis-horn the spirit,
And mock him home to Windsor.
Merry Wives of Windsor. Act iv, sc. 4, l. 62. [Mrs. Page] The only use of "dis-horn."
Mrs. Ford: That cannot choose but amaze him.
Mrs. Page: If he be not amazed, he will be mocked; if he be amazed, he will every way be mocked.
Merry Wives of Windsor. Act v, sc. 3, l. 18.

11 Wherefore was I to this keen mockery born?
A Midsummer-Night's Dream. Act ii, sc. 2, l. 123. [Helena]
Can you not hate me, as I know you do,
But you must join in souls to mock me too?
A Midsummer-Night's Dream. Act iii, sc. 2, l. 149. [Helena]
I pray you, though you mock me, gentlemen,
Let her not hurt me.
A Midsummer-Night's Dream. Act iii, sc. 2, l. 299. [Helena]
Thou mock'st me.—*A Midsummer-Night's Dream,* iii, 2, 426.
Nay, mock not, mock not.—*Much Ado about Nothing,* i, 1, 287.

12 She mocks all her wooers out of suit.
Much Ado about Nothing. Act ii, sc. 1, l. 364. [Leonato]
She would mock me into air: O, she would laugh me
Out of myself, press me to death with wit.
Therefore let Benedick, like cover'd fire,
Consume away in sighs, waste inwardly:
It were a better death than die with mocks,
Which is as bad as die with tickling.
Much Ado about Nothing. Act iii, sc. 1, l. 75. [Hero]
Dost thou mock me?—*Othello,* iv, 1, 61.
Incur a general mock.—*Othello,* i, 2, 69.

13 O, I am mock'd,
And thou by some incensed god sent hither
To make the world to laugh at me.
Pericles. Act v, sc. 1, l. 143. [Pericles]
Mock the mind.—*The Rape of Lucrece,* l. 1414.

14 Mock not my senseless conjuration, lords.
Richard II. Act iii, sc. 2, l. 23. [King Richard]

15 Uncle, my brother mocks both you and me.
Richard III. Act iii, sc. 2, l. 129. [York]
If that your moody discontented souls
Do through the clouds behold this present hour,
Even for revenge mock my destruction!
Richard III. Act v, sc. 1, l. 7. [Buckingham]
Come, come, you mock me.—*Richard III,* iv, 4, 284.
Come, come, you 're mocking.—*The Taming of the Shrew,* v, 2, 132.
Mocking the air.—*King John,* v, 1, 72.
Mocking birds.—*The Rape of Lucrece,* l. 1121. See under Bird. The only use of the phrase.
Lo, how he mocks me!
The Tempest. Act iii, sc. 2, l. 34. [Caliban]

1
It is a pretty mocking of the life.
Timon of Athens, i, 1, 35. See under PAINTING.

2
For this proud mock I 'll be thy slaughterman.
Titus Andronicus. Act iv, sc. 4, l. 58. [Saturninus] "Slaughter-man" (or -men) occurs five times in the plays.

3
In his tent Lies mocking our designs.
Troilus and Cressida. Act i, sc. 3, l. 145. [Ulysses]

Now will he be mocking:
I shall have such a life!
Troilus and Cressida. Act iv, sc. 2, l. 21. [Cressida]

My lord, come you again into my chamber:
You smile and mock me, as if I meant naughtily.
Troilus and Cressida. Act iv, sc. 2, l. 37. [Cressida] The only use of "naughtily."

Mock not, that I affect the untraded oath.
Troilus and Cressida. Act iv, sc. 5, l. 178. [Hector] The only use of "untraded" (unhackneyed).

O, sir, to such as boasting show their scars
A mock is due.
Troilus and Cressida. Act iv, sc. 5, l. 290. [Troilus]

Thou never shalt mock Diomed again.
Troilus and Cressida. Act v, sc. 2, l. 99. [Diomedes]

Nay, that 's a mock.—*Winter's Tale,* ii, 1, 14.

MODERATION

See also Measure, Temperance

4
Distribution should undo excess,
And each man have enough.
King Lear. Act iv, sc. 1, l. 73. [Gloucester] "Distribution" occurs only once again in the plays, in *Coriolanus,* i, 9, 35.

5
Laugh moderately.—*Love's Labour's Lost,* i, 1, 200.

Love moderately.—*Romeo and Juliet,* ii, 6, 14. The only uses of "moderately."

6
It is no mean happiness therefore, to be seated in the mean: superfluity comes sooner by white hairs, but competency lives longer.
The Merchant of Venice. Act i, sc. 2, l. 7. [Nerissa] "Competency" occurs again in *Coriolanus,* i, 1, 143. "Superfluity" is used four times.

7
Pandarus: Be moderate, be moderate.
Cressida: Why tell you me of moderation?
Troilus and Cressida. Act iv, sc. 4, l. 1. The only use of "moderation."

O love, Be moderate; allay thy ecstasy;
In measure rein thy joy.
The Merchant of Venice, iii, 2, 112. See under LOVE.

Moderate haste.—*Hamlet,* i, 2, 238.
Moderate pace.—*Twelfth Night,* ii, 2, 3.
Moderate table.—*Timon of Athens,* iii, 4, 117. The only uses of "moderate" as an adjective. As a verb, it is used once, in *Troilus and Cressida,* iv, 4, 5: "How can I moderate it?"

MODESTY

8
Too modest are you;
More cruel to your good report than grateful
To us that give you truly.
Coriolanus. Act i, sc. 9, l. 53. [Cominius]

9
Me of my lawful pleasure she restrain'd
And pray'd me oft forbearance; did it with
A pudency so rosy the sweet view on 't
Might well have warm'd old Saturn.
Cymbeline. Act ii, sc. 5, l. 9. [Posthumus] The only use of "pudency." "Rosy" is repeated in v, 5, 121, and occurs in no other play. Saturn is mentioned five times.

10
Though peril to my modesty, not death on 't,
I would adventure.
Cymbeline. Act iii, sc. 4, l. 155. [Imogen]

Bashful modesty.—*The Taming of the Shrew,* ii, 1, 49.
Beauteous modesty.—*The Taming of the Shrew,* i, 2, 255.
Cold modesty.—*Julius Cæsar,* iii, 1, 213; *A Lover's Complaint,* l. 293.
Dear modesty.—*A Lover's Complaint,* l. 202.
Maiden modesty.—*Much Ado about Nothing,* iv, 1, 181.
Simple modesty.—*Romeo and Juliet,* iii, 2, 16.
Vestal modesty.—*Romeo and Juliet,* iii, 3, 38.
Women's modesty.—*The Merry Wives of Windsor,* ii, 1, 58.
Modesty of fearful duty.—*A Midsummer-Night's Dream,* v, 1, 101.
Sad Lucretia's modesty.—*As You Like It,* iii, 2, 156.
Modesty of honour.—*Twelfth Night,* v, 1, 343.
The modesty of it.—*Henry V,* iv, 1, 75.

11
Her looks do argue her replete with modesty.
III Henry VI. Act iii, sc. 2, l. 84. [King Edward]

12
Win straying souls with modesty again,
Cast none away.
Henry VIII. Act v, sc. 3, l. 64. [Cranmer]

13
Can it be
That modesty may more betray our sense
Than woman's lightness?
Measure for Measure. Act ii, sc. 2, l. 168. [Angelo]

I have laboured for the poor gentleman to the extreme shore of my modesty.
Measure for Measure. Act iii, sc. 2, l. 265. [Escalus]

14
Pray thee, take pain
To allay with some cold drops of modesty
Thy skipping spirit.
The Merchant of Venice. Act ii, sc. 2, l. 194 [Bassanio]

Pluck the borrowed veil of modesty from the so seeming Mistress Page.
The Merry Wives of Windsor. Act iii, sc. 2, l. 42. [Ford]

15
You do impeach your modesty too much,
To leave the city and commit yourself
Into the hands of one that loves you not;

To trust the opportunity of night
And the ill counsel of a desert place
With the rich worth of your virginity.
A Midsummer-Night's Dream. Act ii, sc. 1, l. 214. [Demetrius]

But, gentle friend, for love and courtesy
Lie further off; in human modesty,
Such separation as may well be said
Becomes a virtuous bachelor and a maid.
A Midsummer-Night's Dream. Act ii, sc. 2, l. 56. [Hermia]

Have you no modesty, no maiden shame,
No touch of bashfulness?
A Midsummer-Night's Dream. Act iii, sc. 2, l. 285. [Helena] The only use of "bashfulness."

1 Is she not a modest young lady?
Much Ado about Nothing. Act i, sc. 1, l. 166. [Claudio]

Modest assurance.—*Twelfth Night,* i, 5, 192.
Modest doubt.—*Troilus and Cressida,* ii, 2, 15.
Modest eloquence.—*Rape of Lucrece,* l. 563.
Modest evidence.—*Much Ado about Nothing,* iv, 1, 38.
Modest eyes.—*Antony and Cleopatra,* iv, 15, 27; *The Rape of Lucrece,* l. 683.
Modest gaze.—*Merchant of Venice,* v, 1, 78.
Modest girl.—*Taming of the Shrew,* i, 1, 161.
Modest haste.—*King Lear,* ii, 4, 25.
Modest nature.—*Henry VIII,* iv, 2, 135.
Modest office.—*Much Ado about Nothing,* ii, 1, 390.
Modest smile.—*Henry V,* iii, Prol., 33.
Modest stillness.—*Henry V,* iii, 1, 4.
Modest terms.—*Twelfth Night,* iv, 2, 36.
Modest truth.—*King Lear,* iv, 7, 5.
Modest wife.—*The Merry Wives of Windsor,* ii, 2, 102; iv, 2, 136.
Modest wisdom.—*Macbeth,* v, 3, 119. A few examples of the use of "modest," which occurs forty-five times.

2 O, sir, I can be modest.
Pericles. Act iv, sc. 6, l. 41. [Boult]

Thou look'st Modest as Justice.
Pericles. Act v, sc. 1, l. 121. [Pericles]

Modest as morning when she coldly eyes
The youthful Phœbus.
Troilus and Cressida. Act i, sc. 3, l. 229. [Æneas]

3 O modest wantons! wanton modesty!
The Rape of Lucrece, l. 401.

4 So much is my poverty of spirit,
So mighty and so many my defects,
As I had rather hide me from my greatness,
Being a bark to brook no mighty sea,
Than in my greatness covet to be hid,
And in the vapour of my glory smother'd.
Richard III. Act iii, sc. 7, l. 159. [Gloucester]

5 She will not stay the siege of loving terms,
Nor bide the encounter of assailing eyes,
Nor ope her lap to saint-seducing gold.
Romeo and Juliet. Act i, sc. 1, l. 218. [Romeo] The only use of "saint-seducing."

Not stepping o'er the bounds of modesty.
Romeo and Juliet. Act iv, sc. 2, l. 27. [Juliet] The only use of "stepping."

O'erstep not the modesty of nature.
Hamlet, iii, 2, 21. The only use of "o'erstep."

6 But I am doubtful of your modesties.
The Taming of the Shrew. Induction, sc. 1, l. 94. [Lord]

She 's not froward, but modest as the dove.
The Taming of the Shrew. Act ii, sc. 1, l. 295. [Petruchio]

7 My modesty, The jewel in my dower.
The Tempest. Act iii, sc. 1, l. 53. [Miranda]

I perceive in you so excellent a touch of modesty.
Twelfth Night. Act ii, sc. 1, l. 12. [Sebastian]

By my modesty.—*The Two Gentlemen of Verona,* i, 2, 41.
In modesty.—*The Two Gentlemen of Verona,* i, 2, 55; ii, 1, 171.
With modesty.—*I Henry VI,* ii, 2, 39; *Henry VIII,* ii, 2, 137; *Timon of Athens,* i, 2, 97.
With as much modesty as cunning.—*Hamlet,* ii, 2, 461.
With modesty enough.—*Hamlet,* v, 1, 230.

8 You are retired,
As if you were a feasted one and not
The hostess of the meeting.
The Winter's Tale. Act iv, sc. 4, l. 62. [Shepherd]

MOLE

9 The mole in my neck.
The Comedy of Errors, iii, 2, 147.

On her left breast
A mole cinque-spotted, like the crimson drops
I' the bottom of a cowslip.
Cymbeline. Act ii, sc. 2, l. 37. [Iachimo] The only use of "cinque-spotted" (having five spots).

Under her breast—
Worthy the pressing—lies a mole, right proud
Of that most delicate lodging: by my life,
I kiss'd it; and it gave me present hunger
To feed again, though full.
Cymbeline. Act ii, sc. 4, l. 134. [Iachimo]

Upon his neck a mole, a sanguine star;
It was a mark of wonder.
Cymbeline. Act v, sc. 5, l. 364. [Cymbeline]

My father had a mole upon his brow.
Twelfth Night, v, 1, 249.

Patch'd with foul moles.—*King John,* iii, 1, 47. See under Ugliness.
Never mole, hare lip, nor scar.—*A Midsummer-Night's Dream,* v, 1, 418.
Vicious mole of nature.—*Hamlet,* i, 4, 24.

10 Well said, old mole! canst work i' the earth so fast?
A worthy pioneer!
Hamlet. Act i, sc. 5, l. 162. [Hamlet]

I will bring these two moles, these blind ones, aboard him.
The Winter's Tale. Act iv, sc. 4, l. 867. [Autolycus] "Blind mole" also in *The Tempest,* iv, 1, 194, and *Pericles,* i, 1, 100.

11 Come, make him stand upon this molehill here,

That raught at mountains with outstretched arms.
III Henry VI. Act i, sc. 4, l. 67. [Queen Margaret] "Raught," as the past of "reach," is used five times.
Here on this molehill will I sit me down.
III Henry VI. Act ii, sc. 5, l. 14. [King Henry]
Olympus to a molehill.—*Coriolanus,* v, 3, 30. The only uses of "molehill."

MOMENT

See also Minute

1
To hear from him a matter of some moment.
Henry VIII, i, 2, 163. See under MATTER.
Something of moment.—*Othello,* iii, 4, 138.
Of moment.—*Cymbeline,* i, 6, 182.
Of great moment.—*Richard III,* iii, 7, 67; *Hamlet,* iii, 1, 86.
Of more moment.—*Henry VIII,* v, 3, 51.
Of no moment.—*III Henry VI,* i, 2, 22.
Mighty moment.—*Henry VIII,* ii, 4, 213.
Far poorer moment.—*Antony and Cleopatra,* i, 2, 147.
2
For an eternal moment or so.
The Merry Wives of Windsor, ii, 1, 50. See under KNIGHTHOOD.
Fading moment.—*The Two Gentlemen of Verona,* i, 1, 30.
Little moment.—*Sonnets,* xv.
3
On the moment Follow his strides.
Timon of Athens. Act i, sc. 1, l. 79. [Poet]
Upon the moment.—*A Lover's Complaint,* l. 248.
To the very moment.—*Othello,* i, 3, 133.
4
In this extant moment.
Troilus and Cressida. Act iv, sc. 5, l. 168. [Agamemnon]
In a moment.—*As You Like It,* i, 2, 135; *King John,* ii, 1, 391; *Henry V,* iii, 3, 33; *I Henry VI,* ii, 3, 66; iv, 2, 12; *Henry VIII,* Prol., 29; *Macbeth,* ii, 3, 115; *The Rape of Lucrece,* l. 250; 868.
In that moment.—*A Midsummer-Night's Dream,* iii, 2, 33.
5
At this moment is so implacable.
Twelfth Night. Act iii, sc. 4, l. 260. [Sir Toby]
At that very moment.—*Henry V,* i, 1, 27.
From this moment.—*Macbeth,* iv, 1, 146.

MONARCH

See also King, Sovereign

6 Broad-fronted Cæsar,
When thou wast here above the ground, I was
A morsel for a monarch.
Antony and Cleopatra. Act i, sc. 5, l. 29. [Cleopatra] The only use of "broad-fronted."
7 Two mighty monarchies,
Whose high upreared and abutting fronts
The perilous narrow ocean parts asunder.
Henry V. Prologue, l. 20. [Chorus] The only use of "monarchies" and "abutting."
Let them know
Of what a monarchy you are the head.
Henry V. Act ii, sc. 4, l. 72. [Dauphin]
Worth a monarchy.—*II Henry VI,* iv, 10, 21.
Dark monarchy.—*Richard III,* i, 4, 51.
Last monarchy.—*All's Well that Ends Well,* ii, 1, 14.
His monarchy.—*A Lover's Complaint,* l. 196.
This monarchy.—*Richard III,* i, 1, 83. The only uses of "monarchy."
8
Never was monarch better fear'd and loved
Than is your majesty.
Henry V. Act ii, sc. 2, l. 25. [Cambridge]
9
Hath that poor monarch taught thee to insult?
III Henry VI. Act i, sc. 4, l. 124. [York]
Such it seems
As may beseem a monarch like himself.
III Henry VI. Act iii, sc. 3, l. 121. [Warwick]
The greatest monarch now alive.
Henry VIII. Act v, sc. 3, l. 164. [Cranmer]
Imperial monarch.—*Winter's Tale,* iv, 4, 383.
Lordly monarch.—*I Henry VI,* v, 3, 6.
New-crowned monarch.—*The Merchant of Venice,* iii, 2, 50. "New crowned" (unhyphenated) is repeated in *King John,* iv, 2, 35.
Throned monarch.—*The Merchant of Venice,* iv, 1, 189.
10
The gallant monarch is in arms.
King John. Act v, sc. 2, l. 148. [Bastard]
My fair, sweet, honey monarch.
Love's Labour's Lost. Act v, sc. 2, l. 530. [Armado]
11
This deed will make thee only loved for fear;
But happy monarchs still are fear'd for love.
The Rape of Lucrece, l. 610.
12
Sole monarch of the universal earth.
Romeo and Juliet, iii, 2, 94. See under SHAME.
Monarch of the vine.—*Antony and Cleopatra,* ii, 7, 120.

MONEY

See also Angel, Gold, Riches

13
I think you have no money in your purse.
As You Like It. Act ii, sc. 4, l. 13. [Touchstone] See also under PURSE.
No eyes in your head, nor no money in your purse? Your eyes are in a heavy case, your purse in a light.
King Lear. Act iv, sc. 6, l. 148. [King Lear]
Money in his purse.—*The Merry Wives of Windsor,* ii, 1, 198.
14
There is your money that I was to keep.
The Comedy of Errors. Act i, sc. 2, l. 8. [Merchant]
Antipholus of Syracuse: Where have you left the money that I gave you?

Dromio of Ephesus: O,—sixpence, that I had o' Wednesday last
To pay the saddler for my mistress' crupper?
The saddler had it, sir; I kept it not.
The Comedy of Errors. Act i, sc. 2, l. 56. The only use of "saddler."

A woman's crupper of velure.—*The Taming of the Shrew,* iii, 2, 61.

How I lost my crupper.—*The Taming of the Shrew,* iv, 1, 84. The only uses of "crupper."

1
Antipholus of Syracuse: Tell me, and dally not, where is the money? . . .
Where is the gold I gave in charge to thee?
Dromio of Ephesus: To me, sir? you gave no gold to me. . . .
Antipholus of Syracuse: Answer me
In what safe place you have bestow'd my money? . . .
Where is the thousand marks you had of me?
Dromio of Ephesus: I have some marks of yours upon my pate,
Some of my mistress' marks upon my shoulders,
But not a thousand marks between you both. . . .
Antipholus of Syracuse: Upon my life, by some device or other,
The villain is o'er-raught of all my money. . . .
I greatly fear my money is not safe.
The Comedy of Errors. Act i, sc. 2, l. 59. "O'er-raught is repeated in *Hamlet,* iii, 1, 17.

Angelo: Soon at supper-time I 'll visit you
And then receive my money for the chain.
Antipholus of Syracuse: I pray you, sir, receive the money now,
For fear you ne'er see chain nor money more.
The Comedy of Errors. Act iii, sc. 2, l. 179.

At five o'clock I shall receive the money.
The Comedy of Errors. Act iv, sc. 1, l. 11. [Angelo]

I am not furnish'd with the present money.
The Comedy of Errors. Act iv, sc. 1, l. 34. [Antipholus of Ephesus]

Disburse the sum on the receipt thereof.
The Comedy of Errors. Act iv, sc. 1, l. 38. [Antipholus of Ephesus] The only use of "disburse."

Fetch your money.—*The Comedy of Errors,* iv, 1, 54.

Save the money.—*Comedy of Errors,* ii, 2, 98.

2
There 's the money, bear it straight.
The Comedy of Errors. Act iv, sc. 2, l. 63. [Adriana]

There 's money for thee.—*King Lear,* iv, 6, 134; *Twelfth Night,* iv, 1, 20.

3
I 'll give thee, ere I leave thee, so much money,
To warrant thee.
The Comedy of Errors. Act iv, sc. 4, l. 2. [Antipholus of Ephesus]

Tender money to me.—*The Comedy of Errors,* iv, 3, 4.

4
Antipholus of Ephesus: Thou hast suborn'd the goldsmith to arrest me.
Adriana: Alas, I sent you money to redeem you,
By Dromio here, who came in haste for it.
Dromio of Ephesus: Money by me! heart and good-will you might;
But surely, master, not a rag of money.
The Comedy of Errors. Act iv, sc. 4, l. 86.

5 Here 's money for my meat:
I would have left it on the board so soon
As I had made my meal, and parted
With prayers for the provider.
Cymbeline. Act iii, sc. 6, l. 53. [Imogen] The only use of "provider."

Here 's money for thy charges.
Titus Andronicus. Act iv, sc. 3, l. 105. [Titus]

6
And for my means, I 'll husband them so well,
They shall go far with little.
Hamlet. Act iv, sc. 5, l. 138. [Laertes]

7
There 's money of the king's coming down the hill; 'tis going to the king's exchequer.
I Henry IV. Act ii, sc. 2, l. 56. [Bardolph]

The money shall be paid back again with advantage.
I Henry IV. Act ii, sc. 4, l. 599. [Prince of Wales]

Prince: The money is paid back again.
Falstaff: O, I do not like that paying back; 'tis a double labour.
I Henry IV. Act iii, sc. 3, l. 200.

8
Bardolph: Will you give me money, captain?
Falstaff: Lay out, lay out.
Bardolph: This bottle makes an angel.
Falstaff: An if it do, take it for thy labour; and if it make twenty, take them all; I 'll answer the coinage.
I Henry IV. Act iv, sc. 2, l. 4. "Coinage" is repeated in *Hamlet,* iii, 4, 137: "Coinage of your brain." See also under ANGEL.

9
I shall receive money o' Thursday.
II Henry IV. Act ii, sc. 4, l. 298. [Falstaff]

Sterling money.—*II Henry IV,* ii, 1, 131. "Sterling" is used only twice more in the plays, in *Richard II,* iv, 1, 264, and in *Hamlet,* i, 3, 107.

10
Nym: I shall have my noble?
Pistol: In cash most justly paid.
Henry V. Act ii, sc. 1, l. 120. The only use of "cash."

Want guilders for my voyage.
The Comedy of Errors. Act iv, sc. 1, l. 4. [Merchant] The only use of "guilders."

11 You shall first receive
The sum of money which I promised
Should be deliver'd to his holiness
For clothing me in these grave ornaments.
I Henry VI. Act v, sc. 1, l. 51. [King Henry] The only use of "clothing."

Sum of money.—*Henry V,* iv, 1, 159.

Great sums of money.—*II Henry VI,* iii, 1, 61.

1
Here, Tom, take all the money that I have.
II Henry VI. Act iii, sc. 3, l. 76. [Peter]
I will none of your money.
Henry V. Act iv, sc. 8, l. 72. [Williams]
There shall be no money; all shall eat and drink on my score.
II Henry VI. Act iv, sc. 2, l. 79. [Cade]
2
I can raise no money by vile means.
Julius Cæsar. Act iv, sc. 3, l. 71. [Brutus]
3
I do it for some piece of money.
Measure for Measure. Act ii, sc. 1, l. 284. [Elbow]
Fond shekels of the tested gold.
Measure for Measure. Act ii, sc. 2, l. 149. [Isabella] The only use of "shekels" and "tested."
Ready money.—*Measure for Measure*, iv, 3, 8. The only use of the phrase.
4
Neither have I money nor commodity
To raise a present sum. . . .
Go, presently inquire, and so will I,
Where money is.
The Merchant of Venice. Act i, sc. 1, l. 178. [Antonio]
Signior Antonio, many a time and oft
In the Rialto you have rated me
About my moneys and my usances.
The Merchant of Venice. Act i, sc. 3, l. 107. [Shylock] "Usance" occurs twice more in this scene and in no other play.
You come to me, and you say
'Shylock, we would have moneys:' you say so;
You, that did void your rheum upon my beard.
The Merchant of Venice. Act i, sc. 3, l. 116. [Shylock]
5
I will go and purse the ducats straight.
The Merchant of Venice. Act i, sc. 3, l. 175. [Shylock]
I will make fast the doors, and gild myself
With some more ducats.
The Merchant of Venice. Act ii, sc. 6, l. 49. [Jessica] "Ducats" is used fifty-one times, twenty-six times in *The Merchant of Venice* alone.
6
If he had
The present money to discharge the Jew,
He would not take it.
The Merchant of Venice. Act iii, sc. 2, l. 275. [Salerio]
Portia: Is he not able to discharge the money?
Bassanio: Yes, here I tender it for him in the court;
Yea, twice the sum: if that will not suffice,
I will be bound to pay it ten times o'er,
On forfeit of my hands, my head, my heart.
The Merchant of Venice. Act iv, sc. 1, l. 208.
7
Seven hundred pounds of moneys, and gold and silver.
The Merry Wives of Windsor. Act i, sc. 1, l. 52. [Evans]
8
Tester I'll have in pouch when thou shalt lack,
Base Phrygian Turk!
The Merry Wives of Windsor. Act i, sc. 3, l. 96. [Pistol]
Hold, there's a tester for thee.—*II Henry IV*, iii, 2, 296. The only uses of "tester" (sixpence).
9
If money go before, all ways do lie open.
The Merry Wives of Windsor. Act ii, sc. 2, l. 175. [Ford]
Troth, I have a bag of money here troubles me.
The Merry Wives of Windsor. Act ii, sc. 2, l. 177. [Ford]
Money is a good soldier, sir, and will on.
The Merry Wives of Windsor. Act ii, sc. 2, l. 176. [Falstaff]
There is money; spend it, spend it; spend more; spend all I have.
The Merry Wives of Windsor. Act ii, sc. 2, l. 240. [Ford]
I will first make bold with your money.
The Merry Wives of Windsor. Act ii, sc. 2, l. 262. [Falstaff]
They say the jealous wittolly knave hath masses of money.
The Merry Wives of Windsor. Act ii, sc. 2, l. 283. [Falstaff] The only use of "wittolly" (cuckoldy).
I like his money well.
The Merry Wives of Windsor. Act iii, sc. 5, l. 59. [Falstaff]
The doctor is well money'd.
The Merry Wives of Windsor, iv, 4, 88. The only use of "money'd."
Money enough.—*Much Ado about Nothing*, ii, 1, 16.
10
If he be sad, he wants money.
Much Ado about Nothing. Act iii, sc. 2, l. 20. [Don Pedro]
When you looked sadly it was for want of money.
The Two Gentlemen of Verona, ii, 1, 31. See under LOVE.
11
Put money in thy purse.
Othello. Act i, sc. 3, l. 45. [Iago] Repeated in lines 47, 49, 52, 59.
Make all the money thou canst.
Othello. Act i, sc. 3, l. 361. [Iago]
With no money at all.—*Othello*, ii, 3, 374.
12
How shall we do for money for these wars?
Richard II. Act ii, sc. 2, l. 104. [York]
You shall have your money.—*Pericles*, iv, 2, 58.
13
Nothing comes amiss, so money comes withal.
The Taming of the Shrew. Act i, sc. 2, l. 82. [Grumio]
14
Will money buy 'em?
The Tempest. Act v, sc. 1, l. 265. [Sebastian]
15
Fly, damned baseness,
To him that worships thee!
Timon of Athens. Act iii, sc. 1, l. 50. [Flaminius]
Titus: Your lord sends now for money.
Hortensius: Most true, he does.
Titus: And he wears jewels now of Timon's gift,
For which I wait for money. . . .

Servant: Mark, how strange it shows,
Timon in this should pay more than he owes:
And e'en as if your lord should wear rich jewels,
And send for money for 'em. . . .
Titus: We wait for certain money here, sir.
Flavius: Ay, if money were as certain as your waiting,
'Twere sure enough.
Timon of Athens. Act iii, sc. 4, l. 18.

Importune him for my moneys.—*Timon of Athens,* ii, 1, 16.

What, you come for money?—*Timon of Athens,* ii, 2, 10.

Told their money.—*Timon of Athens,* iii, 5, 107.

How much money must I have?—*Titus Andronicus,* iv, 4, 46.

1 Thou hadst need send for more money.
Twelfth Night. Act ii, sc. 3, l. 198. [Sir Toby]

Send for money, knight.—*Twelfth Night,* ii, 3, 202.

You can fool no more money out of me at this throw.
Twelfth Night. Act v, sc. 1, l. 44. [Duke]

2 Speed: Less than a pound shall serve me for carrying your letter.
Proteus: You mistake; I mean the pound,—a pinfold.
Speed: From a pound to a pin?
The Two Gentlemen of Verona. Act i, sc. 1, l. 111. "Pinfold" is repeated in *King Lear,* ii, 2, 9: "Lipsbury pinfold." A pinfold is a pound for stray cattle.

3 Will you take eggs for money?
The Winter's Tale. Act i, sc. 2, l. 161. [Leontes]

Clown: Dost lack any money? I have a little money for thee. . . .
Autolycus: Offer me no money, I pray you; that kills my heart.
The Winter's Tale. Act iv, sc. 3, l. 82.

Will you buy any tape, Or lace for your cape,
My dainty duck, my dear-a?
Any silk, any thread, Any toys for your head,
Of the new'st and finest, finest wear-a?
Come to the peddler; Money 's a medler,
That doth utter all men's ware-a.
The Winter's Tale. Act iv, sc. 4, l. 322. [Autolycus] "Tape" is repeated in the same scene, l. 610, and occurs nowhere else. The only use of "medler."

MONK

4 All hoods make not monks.
Henry VIII. Act iii, sc. 1, l. 23. [Queen Katharine] A proverb introduced by Thomas Usk, in his *Testament of Love,* c. 1387: "For habit maketh no monk"; and repeated in *The Romaunt of the Rose* (l. 6192), about 1400. It should be noted that the word "monk" appears only in *King John* and *Henry VIII.*

The monk might be deceived.—*Henry VIII,* i, 2, 79.

That devil-monk.—*Henry VIII,* ii, 1, 22.

Holy monk.—*Henry VIII,* i, 2, 160.

A monk o' the Chartreux.—*Henry VIII,* i, 1, 221.

5 The king, I fear, is poison'd by a monk; . . .
A monk, I tell you; a resolved villain,
Whose bowels suddenly burst out.
King John. Act v, sc. 6, l. 23. [Hubert]

MONKEY

See also Ape

6 More giddy in my desires than a monkey.
As You Like It. Act iv, sc. 1, l. 153. [Rosalind]

Hot as monkeys.—*Othello,* iii, 3, 403.

Lecherous as a monkey.—*II Henry IV,* iii, 2, 338. See under CHARACTER.

Jesting monkey.—*The Tempest,* iii, 2, 52.

Poor monkey.—*Macbeth,* iv, 2, 59.

7 Monkeys [are tied] by the loins.
King Lear, ii, 4, 8. See under LEG.

8 I would not have given it for a wilderness of monkeys.
The Merchant of Venice. Act iii, sc. 1, l. 127. [Shylock]

On meddling monkey, or on busy ape.
A Midsummer-Night's Dream. Act ii, sc. 1, l. 181. [Oberon]

9 This is the monkey's own giving out.
Othello. Act iv, sc. 1, l. 131. [Cassio]

Apes and monkeys.—*Cymbeline,* i, 6, 39.

Baboon and monkey.—*Timon of Athens,* i, 1, 260.

Goats and monkeys!—*Othello,* iv, 1, 274.

MONSTER

10 Make a monster of the multitude.
Coriolanus, ii, 3, 11. See under INGRATITUDE.

Turn monster.—*As You Like It,* i, 2, 23.

11 The imperious seas breed monsters.
Cymbeline. Act iv, sc. 2, l. 35. [Imogene]

Monsters of the deep—*King Lear,* iv, 2, 50.

Abominable monster.—*The Tempest,* ii, 2, 163.

Brave monster.—*The Tempest,* ii, 2, 192; iii, 2, 12.

Carrion monster.—*King John,* iii, 4, 33.

Civil monster.—*Othello,* iv, 1, 64.

Ignorant monster.—*The Tempest,* iii, 2, 28.

Lean abhorred monster.—*Romeo and Juliet,* v, 3, 104.

Monsieur Monster.—*The Tempest,* iii, 2, 21.

Poor monster.—*The Tempest,* iii, 2, 42; *Twelfth Night,* ii, 2, 35.

12 Thou changed and self-cover'd thing, for shame
Be-monster not thy feature.
King Lear. Act iv, sc. 2, l. 62. [Albany] The only use of "self-cover'd" and "be-monster."

He cannot be such a monster.—*King Lear,* i, 2, 102.

13 I will show you a monster.
The Merry Wives of Windsor. Act iii, sc. 2, l. 82. [Ford]

Have with you to see this monster.
The Merry Wives of Windsor. Act iii, sc. 2, l. 93. [All]

1
No, no, I am as ugly as a bear;
For beasts that meet me run away for fear;
Therefore no marvel though Demetrius
Do, as a monster, fly my presence thus.
A Midsummer-Night's Dream. Act ii, sc. 2, l. 94. [Helena]

2 The Cannibals that each other eat,
The Anthropophagi and men whose heads
Do grow beneath their shoulders.
Othello. Act i, sc. 3, l. 143. [Othello] The only use of "Anthropophagi." "Anthropophagirian" occurs in *The Merry Wives of Windsor,* iv, 5, 10.

When we were boys,
Who would believe that there were mountaineers
Dew-lapp'd like bulls, whose throats had hanging at 'em
Wallets of flesh? or that there were such men
Whose heads stood in their breasts?
The Tempest. Act iii, sc. 3, l. 43. [Gonzalo] "Dew-lapp'd" occurs again in *A Midsummer-Night's Dream,* iv, 1, 126; "wallet" in *Troilus and Cressida,* iii, 3, 145.

3
Emilia: 'Tis a monster,
Begot upon itself, born on itself.
Desdemona: Heaven keep that monster from Othello's mind.
Othello. Act iii, sc. 4, l. 161. Referring to jealousy.

Green-eyed monster.—*Othello,* iii, 3, 166. See under JEALOUSY.

That monster, custom.—*Hamlet,* iii, 4, 161. See under CUSTOM.

Monster envy.—*Pericles,* iv, Gower, 12.

Monster Ignorance.—*Love's Labour's Lost,* iv, 2, 24.

A great-sized monster of ingratitudes.
Troilus and Cressida, iii, 3, 147. See under TIME. "Great-sized" is repeated in v, 10, 26: "Great-sized coward," and ocurs in no other play.

4
Monsters and things indigest.
Sonnets. No. cxiv. "Indigest" occurs again in *King John,* v, 7, 26.

A monster, a very monster.—*The Taming of the Shrew,* iii, 2, 71.

5
A freckled whelp hag-born—not honour'd with
A human shape.
The Tempest. Act i, sc. 2, l. 283. [Prospero] The only use of "hag-born."

There would this monster make a man.
The Tempest. Act ii, sc. 2, l. 32. [Trinculo]

This is some monster of the isle with four legs, who hath got, as I take it, an ague.
The Tempest. Act ii, sc. 2, l. 67. [Stephano]

Four legs and two voices: a most delicate monster!
The Tempest. Act ii, sc. 2, l. 93. [Stephano]

This is a very shallow monster! . . . A very weak monster! . . . A most poor credulous monster! . . . a most perfidious and drunken monster!
The Tempest. Act ii, sc. 2, l. 147. [Trinculo]

I shall laugh myself to death at this puppy-headed monster. A most scurvy monster!
The Tempest. Act ii, sc. 2, l. 158. [Trinculo] The only use of "puppy-headed."

A most ridiculous monster.
The Tempest. Act ii, sc. 2, l. 169. [Trinculo]

A howling monster; a drunken monster!
The Tempest. Act ii, sc. 2, l. 183. [Trinculo]

Half a fish and half a monster.—*The Tempest,* iii, 2, 33.

6
That a monster should be such a natural!
The Tempest. Act iii, sc. 2, l. 36. [Trinculo]

The poor monster's my subject and he shall not suffer indignity.
The Tempest. Act iii, sc. 2, l. 42. [Stephano]

7
Stephano: Do you hear, monster? If I should take a displeasure against you, look you,—
Trinculo: Thou wert but a lost monster.
The Tempest. Act iv, sc. 1, l. 201.

A murrain on your monster!—*The Tempest,* iii, 2, 88.

Teem with new monsters.—*Timon of Athens,* iv, 3, 190.

8
O, had the monster seen those lily hands.
Titus Andronicus, ii, 4, 44. See under HAND.

9
Troilus: In all Cupid's pageant there is presented no monster.
Cressida: Nor nothing monstrous neither?
Troilus: Nothing, but our undertakings. . . .
Cressida: They that have the voice of lions and the act of hares, are they not monsters?
Troilus: Are there such? such are not we.
Troilus and Cressida. Act iii, sc. 2, l. 80. "Monstrous" is used sixty-two times; "monstrously" once, in *The Comedy of Errors,* v, 1, 11; "monstrousness" once, in *Timon of Athens,* iii, 2, 79; and "monstruosity" once, in *Troilus and Cressida,* iii, 2, 87.

He's grown a very land-fish, languageless, a monster.
Troilus and Cressida. Act iii, sc. 3, l. 264. [Thersites] The only use of "land-fish" and "languageless."

MONTH

10
But two months dead: nay, not so much, not two.
Hamlet. Act i, sc. 2, l. 138. [Hamlet]

Within these two months, that's a month before
This bond expires, I do expect return
Of thrice three times the value of this bond.
The Merchant of Venice. Act i, sc. 3, l. 158. [Antonio]

Some two months since.—*All's Well that Ends Well,* iv, 3, 56.

Some two months hence.—*Julius Cæsar,* ii, 1, 109; *Troilus and Cressida,* v, 10, 53.

Two months ago.—*Hamlet,* iii, 2, 139.

Two months since.—*Hamlet,* iv, 7, 82.

But for two months.—*As You Like It,* v, 4, 198.

These two months.—*Henry VIII,* v, 4, 90.

Two months on her way.—*Love's Labour's Lost,* v, 2, 679.
'Tis twice two months.—*Hamlet,* iii, 2, 136.

1
Thou naughty varlet, tell me, where hast thou been this month?
I Henry IV. Act ii, sc. 4, l. 475. [Falstaff]
I would detain you here some month or two.
The Merchant of Venice. Act iii, sc. 1, l. 9. [Portia]
I tell him we shall stay here at least a month.
Much Ado about Nothing. Act i, sc. 1, l. 150. [Don Pedro]
A month ago I went from hence.
Twelfth Night. Act i, sc. 2, l. 31. [Captain] "A month ago" is repeated in *The Winter's Tale,* iv, 4, 300.

I 'll give him my commission
To let him there a month behind the gest
Prefix'd for 's parting.
The Winter's Tale. Act i, sc. 2, l. 40. [Hermione] The only use of "gest" (the time alloted for a halt).

There was not full a month
Between their births.
The Winter's Tale. Act v, sc. 1, l. 117. [Paulina]
I 'll follow thee a month.—*Coriolanus,* iv, 1, 38.
Within a month.—*Hamlet,* i, 2, 145.
Within this month.—*Hamlet,* iv, 3, 38.
A little month.—*Hamlet,* i, 2, 147.
A month before the day.—*The Merchant of Venice,* i, 3, 183.
I 'll stay a month longer.—*Twelfth Night,* i, 3, 119.
Once in a month.—*The Tempest,* i, 2, 262.

2
The first of this next month.
II Henry VI. Act ii, sc. 4, l. 71. [Herald]
The eleventh of this month.—*I Henry IV,* iii, 2, 166.
By the ninth of next month.—*I Henry IV,* ii, 3, 30.
The last of next month.—*II Henry VI,* i, 3, 225.

3
What was a month old at Cain's birth?
Love's Labour's Lost, iv, 2, 36. "A month old" is repeated in l. 40 and l. 47. See under MOON.
But a month old.—*Winter's Tale,* iv, 4, 270.
Not six months old.—*The Comedy of Errors,* i, 1, 45.
Nine months old.—*II Henry VI,* iv, 9, 4; *III Henry VI,* i, 1, 112; iii, 1, 76; *Richard III,* ii, 3, 17.
Twelve month old.—*I Henry IV,* i, 1, 28.

4
How many months do you desire?
The Merchant of Venice. Act i, sc. 3, l. 59. [Shylock]
Weary months.—*Troilus and Cressida,* iii, 2, 123.
Whole months.—*Titus Andronicus,* ii, 4, 55.

5
I must needs be gone;
My twelve months are expired.
Pericles. Act iii, sc. 3, l. 1. [Pericles] See under YEAR for "twelvemonth."

6
Our doctors say this is no month to bleed.
Richard II. Act i, sc. 1, l. 157. [King Richard]

7
'Tis full three months since I did see him last.
Richard II, v, 3, 2. See under SON.
Three crabbed months had sour'd themselves to death.
The Winter's Tale, i, 2, 102. See under BETROTHAL.
For three months.—*The Merchant of Venice,* i, 3, 2; 9; 67; 68; 105.
This three months.—*Pericles,* v, 1, 24.
Some three months since.—*Richard III,* i, 2, 241.
Three months before.—*Twelfth Night,* v, 1, 97.
Some six months since.—*All's Well that Ends Well,* i, 2, 71.
Some sixteen months.—*The Two Gentlemen of Verona,* iv, 1, 21.
For eighteen months.—*II Henry VI,* i, 1, 42.

II—The Months

See also April, May

8
Not till a hot January.
Much Ado about Nothing, i, 1, 94. January is mentioned only once again, in *The Winter's Tale,* iv, 4, 111.
Such a February face.
Much Ado about Nothing, v, 4, 41. The only mention of February.

9
March is wasted fourteen days.
Julius Cæsar. Act ii, sc. 1, l. 59. [Lucius]
Remember March, the ides of March remember.
Julius Cæsar. Act iv, sc. 3, l. 18. [Brutus]
Beware the ides of March.—*Julius Cæsar,* i, 2, 18; 19. "Ides of March" is repeated in ii, 1, 40; iii, 1, 1, and v, 1, 114. March is mentioned only twice more in the plays, in *I Henry IV,* iv, 1, 111, and in *The Winter's Tale,* iv, 4, 120.

10
It is like, if there come a hot June.
I Henry IV, ii, 4, 397. June is mentioned again in iii, 2, 75, and only once more in the plays, in *Antony and Cleopatra,* iii, 10, 14. It is referred to once in the poems, in *Sonnets,* civ.
He makes a July's day short as December.
The Winter's Tale, i, 2, 169. July is mentioned only once again, in *Henry VIII,* i, 1, 154.
The tenth of August last.
I Henry VI, i, 1, 110. There is only one other reference to August, in *The Tempest,* iv, 1, 134. September is not mentioned at all, nor is October or November.
O, the twelfth day of December.
Twelfth Night, ii, 3, 90. December is mentioned five times in the plays and once in *Sonnets,* xcvii.

MONUMENT

11
Charmian: To the monument!
There lock yourself, and send him word you are dead.
Cleopatra: To the monument! . . . To the monument!
Antony and Cleopatra. Act iv, sc. 13, l. 3.

1 O bill, sore-shaming
Those rich-left heirs that let their fathers lie
Without a monument.
Cymbeline. Act iv, sc. 2, l. 225. [Arviragus] The only use of "sore-shaming" and "rich-left."

2
This grave shall have a living monument.
Hamlet. Act v, sc. 1, l. 320. [King]

Gilded monuments.—*Sonnets,* lv.
Marble monument.—*Measure for Measure,* v, 1, 233.
Old monument.—*Much Ado about Nothing,* iv, 1, 208.
Stately monuments.—*Rape of Lucrece,* l. 946.
Valour's monuments.—*I Henry VI,* iii, 2, 120.
Wasting monuments.—*Rape of Lucrece,* l. 798.
Woful monuments.—*II Henry VI,* iii, 2, 342.

3
Defacing monuments of conquer'd France,
Undoing all, as all had never been.
II Henry VI. Act i, sc. 1, l. 102. [Gloucester] The only use of "defacing."

This monument of the victory will I bear.
II Henry VI. Act iv, sc. 3, l. 12. [Cade]

4
If charnel-houses and our graves must send
Those that we bury back, our monuments
Shall be the maws of kites.
Macbeth. Act iii, sc. 4, l. 71. [Macbeth] "Charnel-house" occurs again in *Romeo and Juliet,* iv, 1, 81.

5 For a monument upon thy bones,
And e'er remaining lamps, the belching whale
And humming water must o'erwhelm thy corpse,
Lying with simple shells.
Pericles. Act iii, sc. 1, l. 62. [Pericles] "Belching whale" is repeated in *Troilus and Cressida,* v, 5, 23, and "humming" in *The Tempest,* ii, 1, 317.

Her monument is almost finish'd.
Pericles, iv, 3, 42. See under EPITAPH.

Where, like a virtuous monument, she lies,
To be admired of lewd unhallow'd eyes.
The Rape of Lucrece, l. 391.

6
In that dim monument where Tybalt lies.
Romeo and Juliet. Act iii, sc. 5, l. 203. [Juliet]

7
Unswept stone besmear'd with sluttish time.
Sonnets. No. lv.

Your monument shall be my gentle verse.
Sonnets. No. lxxi.

8 Wherefore gaze this goodly company,
As if they saw some wondrous monument,
Some comet or unusual prodigy?
The Taming of the Shrew. Act iii, sc. 2, l. 96. [Petruchio]

Monument . . . of good deeds.—*Timon of Athens,* iv, 3, 466.

9
This monument five hundred years hath stood,
Which I have sumptuously re-edified:
Here none but soldiers and Rome's servitors
Repose in fame.
Titus Andronicus. Act i, sc. 1, l. 350. [Titus] The only use of "sumptuously." "Re-edified" occurs again in *Richard III,* iii, 1, 71.

Closed in our household's monument.
Titus Andronicus. Act v, sc. 3, l. 194. [Lucius]

Capel's monument.—*Romeo and Juliet,* v, 1, 18; v, 3, 127.

MOOD

10
Abetting him to thwart me in my mood.
The Comedy of Errors. Act ii, sc. 2, l. 172. [Adriana] The only use of "abetting."

One on 's father's moods.—*Coriolanus,* i, 3, 72.
Fortune's mood.—*All's Well that Ends Well,* v, 2, 5; *Pericles,* iii, Gower, 46.
Woman's mood.—*I Henry IV,* i, 3, 237.

11
She is importunate, indeed distract:
Her mood will needs be pitied.
Hamlet. Act iv, sc. 5, l. 2. [Gentleman]

12
His moods, and his displeasures.
Henry V, iv, 7, 38. See under ALEXANDER.

That close aspect of his
Does show the mood of a much troubled breast.
King John. Act iv, sc. 2, l. 72. [Pembroke]

13
You are but now cast in his mood.
Othello. Act ii, sc. 3, l. 274. [Iago]

Albeit unused to the melting mood.
Othello. Act v, sc. 2, l. 349. See EYE, 447:11.

14
Wayward once, his mood with nought agrees.
The Rape of Lucrece, l. 1095.

Wayward mood.—*Comedy of Errors,* iv, 4, 4.
Angry mood.—*Richard III,* i, 2, 242.
Colder moods.—*King Lear,* ii, 2, 83.
Encrimson'd mood.—*A Lover's Complaint,* l. 201. The only use of "encrimson'd."
Misprised mood.—*A Midsummer-Night's Dream,* iii, 2, 74.
Rash mood.—*King Lear,* ii, 4, 172.
It small avails my mood.—*The Rape of Lucrece,* l. 1273.
Change of mood.—*Timon of Athens,* i, 1, 84.

15
He must observe their mood on whom he jests.
Twelfth Night, iii, 1, 69. See under WISDOM.

For "moody" see under MELANCHOLY.

MOON

See also Sun and Moon

16
Alack, our terrene moon Is now eclipsed!
Antony and Cleopatra. Act iii, sc. 13, l. 153. [Antony] The only use of "terrene."

Moon and stars!—*Antony and Cleopatra,* iii, 13, 95.

17
Be witness to me, O thou blessed moon,
When men revolted shall upon record
Bear hateful memory, poor Enobarbus did
Before thy face repent!
Antony and Cleopatra. Act iv, sc. 9, l. 7. [Enobarbus]

O sovereign mistress of true melancholy.
Antony and Cleopatra. Act iv, sc. 9, l. 12. [Enobarbus]

1
And thou, thrice-crowned queen of night, survey
With thy chaste eye, from thy pale sphere above,
Thy huntress' name that my full life doth sway.
As You Like It. Act iii, sc. 2, l. 2. [Orlando] The only use of "thrice-crowned" and "huntress."

This pale queen of night.—*The Two Gentlemen of Verona,* iv, 2, 100.

The silver-shining queen.—*The Rape of Lucrece,* l. 786. The only use of "silver-shining."

Cynthia for shame obscures her silver shine.
Venus and Adonis, l. 728. Cynthia is mentioned twice more, in *Romeo and Juliet,* iii, 5, 20, and in *Pericles,* ii, 5, 11.

2
The moist star
Upon whose influence Neptune's empire stands.
Hamlet. Act i, sc. 1, l. 118. [Horatio]

But I might see young Cupid's fiery shaft
Quench'd in the chaste beams of the watery moon,
And the imperial votaress passed on,
In maiden meditation, fancy-free.
A Midsummer-Night's Dream. Act ii, sc. 1, l. 161. [Oberon] The only use of "fancy-free." "Watery moon" is repeated in *Richard III,* ii, 2, 69.

The moon methinks looks with a watery eye;
And when she weeps, weeps every little flower,
Lamenting some enforced chastity.
A Midsummer-Night's Dream. Act iii, sc. 1, l. 203. [Titania]

Nine changes of the watery star hath been
The shepherd's note since we have left our throne
Without a burthen.
Winter's Tale. Act i, sc. 2, l. 1. [Polixenes]

Changes of the moon.—*Othello,* iii, 3, 178.

Change their moons.—*Richard II,* i, 3, 220. See under DEATH.

3
What may this mean,
That thou, dead corse, again in complete steel
Revisit'st thus the glimpses of the moon?
Hamlet. Act i, sc. 4, l. 51. [Hamlet] The only use of "revisit'st." "Revisit" does not occur.

And thirty dozen moons with borrow'd sheen
About the world have times twelve thirties been.
Hamlet. Act iii, sc. 2, l. 167. [Player King] The only use of "thirties."

Till now some nine moons wasted.
Othello. Act i, sc. 3, l. 84. [Othello] See under ARMS.

Not many moons gone by.—*Antony and Cleopatra,* iii, 12, 6.

Twelve moons more.—*Pericles,* ii, 5, 10.

Twice six moons.—*Pericles,* iii, Gower, 31.

Each minute seems a moon.—*The Passionate Pilgrim,* l. 207. See under MINUTE.

4
Let us be Diana's foresters, gentlemen of the shade, minions of the moon; and let men say we be men of good government, being governed, as the sea is, by our noble and chaste mistress the moon.
I Henry IV. Act i, sc. 2, l. 28. [Falstaff]

The fortune of us that are the moon's men doth ebb and flow like the sea, being governed, as the sea is, by the moon.
I Henry IV. Act i, sc. 2, l. 35. [Prince of Wales]

5
My lord, they say five moons were seen to-night;
Four fixed, and the fifth did whirl about
The other four in wondrous motion.
King John. Act iv, sc. 2, l. 182. [Hubert]

6
Dull: Can you tell me by your wit
What was a month old at Cain's birth, that 's not five weeks old as yet?
Holofernes: Dictynna, goodman Dull; Dictynna, goodman Dull.
Dull: What is Dictynna?
Sir Nathaniel: A title to Phœbe, to Luna, to the moon.
Holofernes: The moon was a month old when Adam was no more,
And raught not to five weeks when he came to five-score.
The allusion holds in the exchange.
Dull: 'Tis true indeed; the collusion holds in the exchange.
Holofernes: God comfort thy capacity! I say, the allusion holds in the exchange.
Dull: And I say, the pollusion holds in the exchange; for the moon is never but a month old.
Love's Labour 's Lost. Act iv, sc. 2, l. 35. The only use of "Dictynna," "Luna," "collusion," and "pollusion." "Fivescore" occurs again in iv, 3, 242, and in no other play.

When Phœbe doth behold
Her silver visage in the watery glass.
A Midsummer-Night's Dream. Act i, sc. 1, l. 209. [Lysander]

7
Rosaline: Thus change I like the moon. . . .
You took the moon at full, but now she 's changed.
King: Yet still she is the moon.
Love's Labour 's Lost. Act v, sc. 2, l. 212.

You would lift the moon out of her sphere, if she would continue in it five weeks without changing.
The Tempest. Act ii, sc. 1, l. 183. [Gonzalo]

8
Upon the corner of the moon
There hangs a vaporous drop profound.
Macbeth. Act iii, sc. 5, l. 23. [Hecate]

Horns o' the moon.—*Antony and Cleopatra,* iv, 12, 45; *Coriolanus,* i, 1, 217.

9
Four happy days bring in
Another moon: but, O, methinks how slow
This old moon wanes!
A Midsummer-Night's Dream. Act i, sc. 1, l. 2. [Theseus]

The moon, like to a silver bow
New-bent in heaven.
A Midsummer-Night's Dream. Act i, sc. 1, l. 9. [Hyppolyta] The only use of "new-bent."

The moon, the governess of floods,
Pale in her anger, washes all the air.
A Midsummer-Night's Dream. Act ii, sc. 1, l. 103. [Titania] "Governess" is repeated in *The Rape of Lucrece,* l. 443.

Moon, take thy flight.—*A Midsummer-Night's Dream,* v, 1, 310.

1
Moonshine: This lanthorn doth the horned moon present,
Myself the man i' the moon do seem to be.
Theseus: This is the greatest error of all the rest: the man should be put into the lanthorn. How is it else the man i' the moon? . . .
Hippolyta: I am aweary of this moon: would he would change!
Theseus: It appears, by his small light of discretion, that he is in the wane. . . .
Lysander: Proceed, Moon.
Moonshine: All that I have to say, is, to tell you than the lanthorn is the moon; I, the man in the moon; this thorn-bush, my thorn-bush; and this dog, my dog.
A Midsummer-Night's Dream. Act v, sc. 1, l. 248. The only use of "thorn-bush."

Stephano: I was the man i' the moon when time was.
Caliban: I have seen thee in her and I do adore thee:
My mistress show'd me thee and thy dog and thy bush. . . .
Trinculo: The man i' the moon! A most poor credulous monster!
The Tempest. Act ii, sc. 2, l. 142.

The man i' the moon 's too slow.
The Tempest. Act ii, sc. 1, l. 249. [Antonio] The only references to the man in the moon.

2
Sweet Moon, I thank thee for thy sunny beams;
I thank thee, Moon, for shining now so bright;
For, by thy gracious, golden, glittering gleams
I trust to take of truest Thisby sight.
A Midsummer-Night's Dream. Act v, sc. 1, l. 279. [Pyramus] The only use of "gleams."

The moon shines bright.—*The Merchant of Venice,* v, 1, 1.

Though it be night, yet the moon shines.
King Lear. Act ii, sc. 2, l. 33. [Kent]

So pale did shine the moon on Pyramus
When he by night lay bathed in maiden blood.
Titus Andronicus. Act ii, sc. 3, l. 231. [Martius]

The pale moon shines by night.
The Winter's Tale. Act iv, sc. 3, l. 16. [Autolycus]

The moon shines fair.—*I Henry IV,* iii, 1, 142.

3
Banquo: How goes the night, boy?
Fleance: The moon is down; I have not heard the clock.
Banquo: And she goes down at twelve.
Macbeth. Act ii, sc. 1, l. 1.

It is the very error of the moon;
She comes more nearer earth than she was wont,
And makes men mad.
Othello. Act v, sc. 2, l. 110. [Othello]

The moon winks.—*Othello,* iv, 2, 77.

4
The moon being clouded presently is miss'd.
Rape of Lucrece, l. 1007. See under STAR.

5
Romeo: Lady, by yonder blessed moon I swear
That tips with silver all these fruit-tree tops—
Juliet: O, swear not by the moon, the inconstant moon,
That monthly changes in her circled orb,
Lest that thy love prove likewise variable.
Romeo and Juliet. Act iii, sc. 2, l. 107.

By yonder moon I swear you do me wrong.
The Merchant of Venice. Act v, sc. 1, l. 142. [Gratiano]

6
The mortal moon hath her eclipse endured.
Sonnets. No. cvii.

Cold moon.—*A Midsummer-Night's Dream,* ii, 1, 156.

Cold fruitless moon.—*A Midsummer-Night's Dream,* i, 1, 73.

Fleeting moon.—*Antony and Cleopatra,* v, 2, 240.

Full moon.—*II Henry IV,* iv, 3, 57; *King Lear,* iv, 6, 70.

Gazing moon.—*Henry V,* iv, Prol., 27.

Modest moon.—*Coriolanus,* i, 1, 261.

Pale-faced moon.—*Richard II,* ii, 4, 10; *I Henry IV,* i, 3, 202.

Silver moon.—*The Rape of Lucrece,* l. 371.

Visiting moon.—*Antony and Cleopatra,* iv, 15, 68.

Wandering moon.—*A Midsummer-Night's Dream,* iv, 1, 103.

Half-moon.—*I Henry IV,* ii, 4, 30; iii, 1, 100; *The Winter's Tale,* ii, 1, 11.

Moon of Rome.—*Coriolanus,* v, 3, 65.

7
This moon-calf.
The Tempest. Act ii, sc. 2, l. 111. [Stephano]

How now, moon-calf?—*The Tempest,* ii, 2, 139.

Thou beest a good moon-calf.—*The Tempest,* iii, 2, 25. "Moon-calf" is repeated in iii, 2, 25; 26. It is used only in this play.

8
The moon 's an arrant thief,
And her pale fire she snatches from the sun.
Timon of Athens, iv, 3, 440. See under THEFT.

9
My lord, I aim a mile beyond the moon.
Titus Andronicus. Act iv, sc. 3, l. 65. [Marcus]

II—Moonlight

10
How sweet the moonlight sleeps upon this bank!
The Merchant of Venice. Act v, sc. 1, l. 54. [Lorenzo]

The moon sleeps with Endymion
And would not be awaked.
The Merchant of Venice. Act v, sc. 1, l. 109. [Portia] The only mention of Endymion.

1
Thou hast by moonlight at her window sung.
A Midsummer-Night's Dream, i, 1, 30. See under WOOING.

Meet me in the palace wood . . . by moonlight.
A Midsummer-Night's Dream. Act i, sc. 2, l. 104. [Quince]

Ill met by moonlight.—*A Midsummer-Night's Dream,* ii, 1, 60.

Moonlight revels.—*A Midsummer-Night's Dream,* ii, 1, 141.

It is not moonlight now.—*The Taming of the Shrew,* iv, 5, 3.

2
Quince: There is two hard things; that is, to bring the moonlight into a chamber; for, you know, Pyramus and Thisby meet by moonlight.
Snout: Doth the moon shine that night we play our play?
Bottom: A calendar, a calendar! look in the almanac; find out moonshine, find out moonshine.
Quince: Yes, it doth shine that night.
Bottom: Why, then may you leave a casement of the great chamber window, where we play, open, and the moon may shine in at the casement.
Quince: Ay; or else one must come in with a bush of thorns and a lanthorn, and say he comes to disfigure, or to present, the person of Moonshine.
A Midsummer-Night's Dream. Act iii, sc. 1, l. 48.

This man, with lanthorn, dog, and bush of thorn,
Presenteth Moonshine; for, if you will know,
By moonshine did these lovers think no scorn
To meet at Ninus' tomb, there, there to woo.
A Midsummer-Night's Dream. Act v, sc. 1, l. 136. [Quince] "Moonshine" is repeated in v, 1, 151; 318; 355. "By moonshine" is repeated in *The Tempest,* v, 1, 37.

King: Vouchsafe, bright moon, and these thy stars, to shine,
Those clouds removed, upon our watery eyne.
Rosaline: O vain petitioner! beg a greater matter;
Thou now request'st but moonshine in the water.
Love's Labour's Lost. Act v, sc. 2, l. 205.

I am some twelve or fourteen moonshines
Lag of a brother.
King Lear. Act i, sc. 2, l. 5. [Edmund]

I 'll make a sop o' the moonshine of you.
King Lear, ii, 2, 35. See under THREAT.

Till . . . moonshine be out.—*The Merry Wives of Windsor,* v, 5, 106.

Moonshine's watery beams.—*Romeo and Juliet,* i, 4, 62.

Moonshine revellers.—*The Merry Wives of Windsor,* v, 5, 42. All the uses of both "moonlight" and "moonshine" are given in this section.

3
Fan the moonbeams from her sleeping eyes.
A Midsummer-Night's Dream, iii, 1, 176. See under BUTTERFLY. The only use of "moonbeams."

MORNING

See also Dawn, Sunrise

4
This morning, like the spirit of a youth
That means to be of note, begins betimes.
Antony and Cleopatra. Act iv, sc. 4, l. 26. [Antony]

The morn is fair.—*Antony and Cleopatra,* iv, 2, 24.

Fair was the morn.—*The Passionate Pilgrim,* l. 117.

It is great morning.—*Troilus and Cressida,* iv, 3, 1; *Cymbeline,* iv, 2, 142.

5
But, look, the morn, in russet mantle clad,
Walks o'er the dew of yon high eastward hill.
Hamlet. Act i, sc. 1, l. 166. [Horatio] "Russet" occurs again in *Love's Labour 's Lost,* v, 2, 413. The only use of "eastward."

Methinks I scent the morning air.
Hamlet. Act i, sc. 5, l. 58. [Ghost] "Morning air" is repeated in *Rape of Lucrece,* l. 778.

Morning cock.—*Hamlet,* i, 2, 218.

Morning dew.—*Titus Andronicus,* ii, 3, 201; *A Midsummer-Night's Dream,* iv, 1, 126.

Morning drops.—*Love's Labour 's Lost,* iv, 3, 27.

Morning face.—*As You Like It,* ii, 7, 146.

Morning field.—*Henry V,* iv, 2, 40.

Morning lark.—*The Taming of the Shrew,* Ind., 2, 46; *A Midsummer-Night's Dream,* iv, 1, 99.

Morning light.—*The Rape of Lucrece,* l. 745.

Morning roses.—*The Taming of the Shrew,* ii, 1, 174.

Morning story.—*Comedy of Errors,* v, 1, 356.

Morning sun.—*III Henry VI,* iv, 7, 80; *Sonnets,* cxxxii.

Morning taste.—*Timon of Athens,* iv, 3, 226.

6
Be with me betimes in the morning.
I Henry IV, ii, 4, 600. "In the morning" is repeated frequently throughout the plays.

7
Will it never be morning?
Henry V. Act iii, sc. 7, l. 6. [Orleans]

I would it were morning.—*Henry V,* iii, 7, 90.

The Dauphin longs for morning.—*Henry V,* iii, 7, 98.

Drowsy morning.—*Henry V,* iv, Prol., 16.

8
Is not that the morning which breaks yonder?
Henry V. Act iv, sc. 1, l. 87. [Court]

9
Be it in the morn,
When every one will give the time of day.
II Henry VI. Act iii, sc. 1, l. 13. [Queen]

10
See how the morning opes her golden gates,
And takes her farewell of the glorious sun!
How well resembles it the prime of youth,
Trimm'd like a younker prancing to his love!
III Henry VI. Act ii, sc. 1, l. 21. [Richard]

"Younker" is repeated in *The Merchant of Venice,* ii, 6, 14, and in *I Henry IV*, iii, 3, 92. The only use of "prancing."

1
The morning comes upon 's.
Julius Cæsar. Act ii, sc. 1, l. 221. [Cassius]
Is it physical
To walk unbraced and suck up the humours
Of the dank morning?
Julius Cæsar. Act ii, sc. 1, l. 261. [Portia] "Physical" is repeated in *Coriolanus,* i, 5, 19; and "unbraced" in *Julius Cæsar,* i, 3, 48, and in *Hamlet,* ii, 1, 78.
Raw cold morning.—*Julius Cæsar,* ii, 1, 236.
The morn is cold.—*Troilus and Cressida,* iv, 2, 1.
Blustering morn.—*Pericles,* v, 3, 22.

2
You shall hear more ere morning.
Measure for Measure, iv, 2, 98. "Ere morning" is repeated in *The Merchant of Venice,* v, 1, 48.

3
Good morning to you, fair and gracious daughter.
Measure for Measure. Act iv, sc. 3, l. 116. [Duke]
When you have given good morning to your mistress,
Attend the queen.
Cymbeline. Act ii, sc. 3, l. 66. [Cymbeline] The only uses of "good morning." "Good morrow" occurs twenty-one times.

4
He plies the duke at morning and at night.
The Merchant of Venice. Act iii, sc. 2, l. 279. [Salerio]
From morn till even.—*Henry V,* iii, 1, 20.
From morn till night.—*Love's Labour's Lost,* v, 2, 660.

5 In the morning early we will both
Fly toward Belmont.
The Merchant of Venice. Act iv, sc. 1, l. 456. [Antonio]
In the morning early.—*As You Like It,* ii, 2, 6; *I Henry IV,* iv, 3, 110.
Early in the morning.—*Richard III,* v, 3, 88; *Romeo and Juliet,* v, 3, 23.
Betimes i' the morn.—*Measure for Measure,* iv, 4, 18.
The next morn betimes.—*Measure for Measure,* v, 1, 101.

6
It is almost morning.
The Merchant of Venice, v, 1, 295. "It is almost morning" is repeated in *Romeo and Juliet,* ii, 2, 177; *Cymbeline,* ii, 3, 10.
By the mass, 'tis morning.—*Othello,* ii, 3, 384.

7
I do invite you to-morrow morning.
The Merry Wives of Windsor, iii, 3, 246. "To-morrow morning" is used fifteen times.
Swore he would meet her . . . next morning.
Much Ado about Nothing, iii, 3, 172. "Next morning" is repeated in *All's Well that Ends Well,* iv, 3, 91; *Timon of Athens,* ii, 2, 25.
Next morn.—*Antony and Cleopatra,* ii, 5, 20.
Coming morn.—*Midsummer-Night's Dream,* v, 1, 372.

8
Scarce had the sun dried up the dewy morn.
The Passionate Pilgrim, l. 71. "Dewy" is repeated in *Richard III,* v, 3, 284, and in *The Rape of Lucrece,* l. 1232.

9 The silent hours steal on,
And flaky darkness breaks within the east.
Richard III. Act v, sc. 3, l. 85. [Derby] The only use of "flaky."
How far into the morning is it, lords?
Richard III. Act v, sc. 3, l. 234. [Richmond]
Infant morn.—*Richard III,* iv, 4, 16.

10
This found I on my tent this morning.
Richard III, v, 3, 308. "This morning" occurs twenty-two times in the plays.
To-day morning.—*Twelfth Night,* v, 1, 294.

11
The grey-eyed morn smiles on the frowning night,
Chequering the eastern clouds with streaks of light,
And flecked darkness like a drunkard reels
From forth day's path and Titan's fiery wheels.
Romeo and Juliet. Act ii, sc. 3, l. 1. [Friar Laurence] The only use of "grey-eyed," "chequering," and "flecked."
Yon grey is not the morning's eye,
'Tis but the pale reflex of Cynthia's brow.
Romeo and Juliet. Act iii, sc. 5, l. 19. [Romeo] "Reflex" is repeated in *I Henry VI,* v, 4, 87.
The morn is bright and grey.
Titus Andronicus, ii, 2, 1. See under HUNTING.

12
A glooming peace this morning with it brings.
Romeo and Juliet. Act v, sc. 3, l. 305. [Verona] The only use of "glooming."

13
Full many a glorious morning have I seen
Flatter the mountain-tops with sovereign eye,
Kissing with golden face the meadows green,
Gilding pale streams with heavenly alchemy.
Sonnets. No. xxxiii. "Alchemy" occurs again in *Sonnets,* cxiv, and *Julius Cæsar,* i, 3, 159.
Many a morning.—*Romeo and Juliet,* i, 1, 137.
Every morning.—*The Taming of the Shrew,* i, 1, 137; *Much Ado about Nothing,* ii, 1, 31.

14
The morning wears, 'tis time we were at church.
The Taming of the Shrew. Act iii, sc. 2, l. 113. [Petruchio]
The morning now is something worn.
A Midsummer-Night's Dream. Act iv, sc. 1, l. 186. [Theseus]
Musing the morning is so much overworn.
Venus and Adonis, l. 866.

15 The morning steals upon the night,
Melting the darkness.
The Tempest. Act v, sc. 1, l. 65. [Prospero]
Last morning—*The Two Gentlemen of Verona,* ii, 1, 86.

16
Like a red morn, that ever yet betoken'd
Wreck to the seaman, tempest to the field,

Sorrow to shepherds, woe unto the birds,
Gusts and foul flaws to herdmen and to herds.
Venus and Adonis, l. 453. The only use of "betoken'd" and "herdmen."

MORTALITY

1
All is mortal in nature.
As You Like It. Act ii, sc. 4, l. 56. [Touchstone]
Most mortal.—*Coriolanus,* v, 3, 189.
2
What mortality is!
Cymbeline. Act iv, sc. 1, l. 16. [Cloten]
Brief mortality.—*Henry V,* i, 2, 28.
Life's mortality.—*The Rape of Lucrece,* l. 403.
3
Exposing what is mortal and unsure
To all that fortune, death and danger dare.
Hamlet. Act iv, sc. 4, l. 51. [Hamlet]
Things mortal.—*Hamlet,* ii, 2, 539.
Mortal things.—*Venus and Adonis,* l. 996.
4
Here on my knee I beg mortality,
Rather than life preserved with infamy.
I Henry VI. Act iv, sc. 5, l. 32. [John Talbot]
Wing'd through the lither sky,
In thy despite shall 'scape mortality.
I Henry VI. Act iv, sc. 7, l. 21. [Talbot] The only use of "lither" (soft).
My brethren mortal.—*Henry VIII,* iii, 2, 148.
5
We cannot hold mortality's strong hand.
King John. Act iv, sc. 2, l. 82. [King John]
6
Gloucester: O, let me kiss that hand!
King Lear: Let me wipe it first; it smells of mortality.
King Lear. Act iv, sc. 6, l. 135.
7
Mortality and mercy in Vienna
Live in thy tongue and heart.
Measure for Measure. Act i, sc. 1, l. 45. [Duke]
Insensible of mortality.—*Measure for Measure,* iv, 2, 152.
8
Had I but died an hour before this chance,
I had lived a blessed time; for, from this instant,
There 's nothing serious in mortality.
Macbeth. Act ii, sc. 3, l. 96. [Macbeth]
In them nature's copy 's not eterne.
Macbeth. Act iii, sc. 2, l. 38. [Lady Macbeth] "Eterne" occurs again in *Hamlet,* ii, 2, 512.
9
We are all mortal.
Much Ado about Nothing. Act i, sc. 1, l. 59. [Beatrice]
You are mortal.—*Richard III,* i, 2, 44.
I was mortal.—*Richard III,* v, 3, 124.
10
Cover your heads and mock not flesh and blood
With solemn reverence.
Richard II. Act iii, sc. 2, l. 171. [King Richard]

MOTHER

11
Countess: You know, Helen,
I am a mother to you.
Helena: Mine honourable mistress.
Countess: Nay, a mother:
Why not a mother? When I said 'a mother,'
Methought you saw a serpent: what 's in 'mother'
That you start at it? I say, I am your mother;
And put you in the catalogue of those
That were enwombed mine: 'tis often seen
Adoption strives with nature and choice breeds
A native slip to us from foreign seeds:
You ne'er oppress'd me with a mother's groan,
Yet I express to you a mother's care:
God's mercy, maiden! does it curd thy blood
To say I am thy mother? . . .
Helena: You are my mother, madam; would you were,—
So that my lord your son were not my brother,—
Indeed my mother!
All's Well that Ends Well. Act i, sc. 3, l. 143. The only use of "enwombed."
And now you should be as your mother was
When your sweet self was got.
All's Well that Ends Well. Act iv, sc. 2, l. 9. [Bertram]
O my dear mother, do I see you living?
All's Well that Ends Well. Act v, sc. 3, l. 320. [Helena]
Dearest mother.—*Coriolanus,* iv, 1, 48.
12
She became
A joyful mother of two goodly sons.
The Comedy of Errors. Act i, sc. 1, l. 51. [Ægeon]
A gasping, new-deliver'd mother.
Richard II, ii, 2, 65. See under WOE.
13
He did it to please his mother.
Coriolanus. Act i, sc. 1, l. 39. [Citizen]
My mother,
Who has a charter to extol her blood,
When she does praise me grieves me.
Coriolanus. Act i, sc. 9, l. 13. [Marcius]
Let Thy mother rather feel thy pride than fear
Thy dangerous stoutness.
Coriolanus. Act iii, sc. 2, l. 125. [Volumnia] "Stoutness" is repeated in v, 6, 27, and occurs in no other play.
14
The honour'd mould
Wherein this trunk was framed, and in her hand
The grandchild to her blood.
Coriolanus. Act v, sc. 3, l. 22. [Coriolanus] The only use of "grandchild."
I holp to frame thee.
Coriolanus. Act v, sc. 3, l. 63. [Volumnia]
15
My mother bows;
As if Olympus to a molehill should
In supplication nod.
Coriolanus. Act v, sc. 3, l. 29. [Coriolanus]

You gods! I prate,
And the most noble mother of the world
Leave unsaluted: sink, my knee, i' the earth.
Coriolanus. Act v, sc. 3, l. 48. [Coriolanus] The only use of "unsaluted."

There 's no man in the world
More bound to 's mother; yet here he lets me prate
Like one i' the stocks.
Thou hast never in thy life
Show'd thy dear mother any courtesy,
When she, poor hen, fond of no second brood,
Has cluck'd thee to the wars and safely home,
Loaden with honour.
Coriolanus. Act v, sc. 3, l. 158. [Volumnia] The only use of "cluck'd."

O mother, mother!
What have you done? . . . O my mother, mother! Oh!
You have won a happy victory to Rome;
But, for your son,—believe it, O, believe it,
Most dangerously you have with him prevail'd,
If not most mortal to him.
Coriolanus. Act v, sc. 3, l. 182. [Coriolanus]

Sicinius: He loved his mother dearly.
Menenius: So did he me: and he no more remembers his mother now than an eight-year-old horse.
Coriolanus. Act v, sc. 4, l. 15. The only use of "eight-year-old."

1
You shall not find me, daughter,
After the slander of most stepmothers,
Evil-eyed unto you.
Cymbeline. Act i, sc. 1, l. 70. [Queen] The only use of "stepmothers" and "evil-eyed."

A mother hourly coining plots.—*Cymbeline,* ii, 1, 64.

2
Thou wast their nurse; they took thee for their mother,
And every day do honour to her grave.
Cymbeline. Act iii, sc. 3, l. 104. [Belarius]

O, what, am I
A mother to the birth of three? Ne'er mother
Rejoiced deliverance more.
Cymbeline. Act v, sc. 5, l. 368. [Cymbeline]

3 So loving to my mother
That he might not beteem the winds of heaven
Visit her face too roughly.
Hamlet. Act i, sc. 2, l. 140. [Hamlet] "Beteem" occurs again in *A Midsummer-Night's Dream,* i, 1, 131.

Taint not thy mind, nor let thy soul contrive
Against thy mother aught.
Hamlet. Act i, sc. 5, l. 85. [Ghost]

How cheerfully my mother looks, and my father died within these two hours.
Hamlet. Act iii, sc. 2, l. 34. [Hamlet]

A mother, Since nature makes them partial.
Hamlet. Act iii, sc. 3, l. 31. [Polonius]

Would it were not so!—you are my mother.
Hamlet. Act iii, sc. 4, l. 16. [Hamlet]

His mother Lives almost by his looks.
Hamlet. Act iv, sc. 7, l. 11. [King]

Whored my mother.—*Hamlet,* v, 2, 64. The only use of "whored."

4
Your naked infants spitted upon pikes,
Whiles the mad mothers with their howls confused
Do break the clouds, as did the wives of Jewry
At Herod's bloody-hunting slaughtermen.
Henry V. Act iii, sc. 3, l. 38. [King Henry] The only use of "spitted" and "bloody-hunting."

5
All my mother came into mine eyes
And gave me up to tears.
Henry V, iv, 6, 31.

O, how this mother swells up toward my heart!
King Lear. Act ii, sc. 4, l. 56. [King Lear]

6
God's mother deigned to appear to me.
I Henry VI, i, 2, 78. See under VISION.

Christ's mother helps me.—*I Henry VI,* i, 2, 106.

God's Mother.—*II Henry VI,* ii, 1, 51; *III Henry VI,* iii, 2, 103.

God's blest mother.—*Henry VIII,* v, 1, 153.

God's holy mother.—*Richard III,* i, 3, 306.

Holy mother of our Lord.—*Richard III,* iii, 7, 2.

Our holy mother.—*King John,* iii, 1, 141.

7 O, if you love my mother,
Dishonour not her honourable name,
To make a bastard and a slave of me!
I Henry VI. Act iv, sc. 5, l. 13. [Talbot]

Dishonour not your mothers; now attest
That those whom you call'd fathers did beget you.
Henry V. Act iii, sc. 1, l. 22. [King Henry]

8
Lord Talbot: Shall all thy mother's hopes lie in one tomb?
John Talbot: Ay, rather than I 'll shame my mother's womb.
I Henry VI. Act iv, sc. 5, l. 34.

9
Suffolk: Thy mother took into her blameful bed
Some stern untutor'd churl, and noble stock
Was graft with crab-tree slip. . . .
Warwick: Say it was thy mother that thou mean'st,
That thou thyself wast born in bastardy,
II Henry VI. Act iii, sc. 2, l. 212. See under BASTARD. "Blameful" is repeated in *Richard III,* i, 2, 119, and in *A Midsummer-Night's Dream,* v, 1, 147; "untutor'd" in *III Henry VI,* v, 5, 32, and in *Pericles,* i, 4, 74; "crab-tree" in *Coriolanus,* ii, 1, 205, and in *Henry VIII,* v, 4, 8.

Like ambitious Sylla, overgorged
With gobbets of thy mother's bleeding heart.
II Henry VI. Act iv, sc. 1, l. 84. [Captain] The only mention of Sylla, and the only use of "overgorged." "Gobbets" occurs again in *II Henry VI,* v, 2, 58, and in no other play.

10
How will my mother for a father's death
Take on with me and ne'er be satisfied!
III Henry VI. Act ii, sc. 5, l. 103. [Son]

O Ned, sweet Ned! speak to thy mother, boy!
III Henry VI. Act v, sc. 5, l. 51. [Queen Margaret]

1
Cassius: Have not you love enough to bear with me,
When that rash humour which my mother gave me
Makes me forgetful?
Brutus: Yes, Cassius; and, from henceforth,
When you are over-earnest with your Brutus,
He 'll think your mother chides, and leave you so.
Julius Cæsar. Act iv, sc. 3, l. 119. The only use of "over-earnest."

2
King John: Is that the elder, and art thou the heir?
You came not of one mother then, it seems.
Bastard: Most certain of one mother, mighty king;
That is well known; and, as I think, one father:
But for the certain knowledge of that truth
I put you o'er to heaven and to my mother:
Of that I doubt, as all men's children may.
Queen Elinor: Out on thee, rude man! thou dost shame thy mother
And wound her honour with this diffidence.
King John. Act i, sc. 1, l. 57.

Heaven guard my mother's honour!
King John. Act i, sc. 1, l. 70. [Bastard]

O me! it is my mother. How now, good lady!
What brings you here to court so hastily?
King John. Act i, sc. 1, l. 220. [Bastard]

There 's a good mother, boy, that blots thy father.
King John. Act ii, sc. 1, l. 132. [Queen Elinor]

Good mother.—*Richard III,* iv, 4, 161; 412; *King John,* i, 1, 6; i, 1, 224; *The Merry Wives of Windsor,* iii, 4, 87; *All's Well that Ends Well,* v, 3, 296; *Richard II,* v, 2, 82; *Coriolanus,* ii, 1, 218; *Hamlet,* i, 2, 77; iii, 2, 116; iii, 4, 28.

3
His mother shames him so, poor boy, he weeps.
King John. Act ii, sc. 1, l. 166. [Queen Elinor]

This day hath made
Much work for tears in many an English mother,
Whose sons lie scattered on the bleeding ground.
King John. Act ii, sc. 1, l. 301. [French Herald] The only use of the phrase "English mother" in the plays.

Mothers that lack sons.—*Coriolanus,* ii, 1, 196.

4
O, this will make my mother die with grief!
King John. Act iii, sc. 3, l. 5. [Arthur]

5
Turn all her mother's pains and benefits
To laughter and contempt.
King Lear. Act i, sc. 4, l. 308. [King Lear]

6
Heaven shield my mother play'd my father fair!
Measure for Measure. Act iii, sc. 1, l. 141. [Isabella]

I am much afeard my lady his mother played false with a smith.
The Merchant of Venice. Act i, sc. 2, l. 47. [Portia]

I am sure Margery your wife is my mother.
The Merchant of Venice. Act ii, sc. 2, l. 94. [Launcelot]

7
Those mothers who, to nousel up their babes,
Thought nought too curious, are ready now
To eat those little darlings whom they loved.
Pericles. Act i, sc. 4, l. 42. [Cleon] The only use of "nousel" (nuzzle).

8
That mother tries a merciless conclusion
Who, having two sweet babes, when death takes one,
Will slay the other and be nurse to none.
The Rape of Lucrece, l. 1160.

9
My dangerous cousin, let your mother in:
I know she is come to pray for your foul sin.
Richard II. Act v, sc. 3, l. 81. [Bolingbroke]

Your mother well hath pray'd, and prove you true.
Richard II. Act v, sc. 3, l. 145. [Bolingbroke]

Richmond: How fares our loving mother?
Derby: I, by attorney, bless thee from thy mother,
Who prays continually for Richmond's good.
Richard III. Act v, sc. 3, l. 82.

10
Thou art a widow; yet thou art a mother,
And hast the comfort of thy children left thee.
Richard III. Act ii, sc. 2, l. 55. [Duchess of York]

Duchess: Was never mother had so dear a loss!
Alas, I am the mother of these moans! . . .
Dorset: Comfort, dear mother; God is much displeased
That you take with unthankfulness his doing. . . .
Rivers: Madam, bethink you, like a careful mother,
Of the young prince your son. . . .
Gloucester: Madam, my mother, I do cry you mercy.
Richard III. Act ii, sc. 2, l. 79.

But yet let mothers doubt.
Richard III. Act ii, sc. 4, l. 22. [Duchess of York]

11
A care-crazed mother of a many children.
Richard III. Act iii, sc. 7, l. 184. [Buckingham] The only use of "care-crazed."

Queen Elizabeth: I am their mother; who should keep me from them?
Duchess: I am their father's mother; I will see them.
Richard III. Act iv, sc. 1, l. 22.

A mother only mock'd with two sweet babes.
Richard III. Act iv, sc. 4, l. 87. [Queen Margaret]

For joyful mother, one that wails the name.
Richard III. Act iv, sc. 4, l. 99. [Queen Margaret]

12
King Richard: Who intercepts my expedition?

Duchess of York: O, she that might have intercepted thee,
By strangling thee in her accursed womb,
From all the slaughters, wretch, that thou hast done!
Richard III. Act iv, sc. 4, l. 136.

Again shall you be mother to a king.
Richard III. Act iv, sc. 4, l. 317. [King Richard]

King Richard: Go, then, my mother, to thy daughter go;
Make bold her bashful years with your experience. . . .
Queen Elizabeth: Shall I go win my daughter to thy will?
King Richard: And be a happy mother by the deed.
Richard III. Act iv, sc. 4, l. 325.

Happy mother.—*Sonnets,* viii.
Earthly mother.—*Venus and Adonis,* l. 863.
Gracious mother.—*Titus Andronicus,* ii, 3, 89. *Cymbeline,* ii, 3, 41.
Hopeful mother.—*Richard III,* i, 2, 24.
Lady mother.—*All's Well that Ends Well,* iv, 3, 102; *Romeo and Juliet,* iii, 5, 39; 66.
Noble mother.—*King John,* iv, 2, 121; *Coriolanus,* v, 1, 71; v, 3, 49; *Titus Andronicus,* ii, 1, 51.
Queen mother.—*Hamlet,* iii, 1, 190; *Cymbeline,* v, 5, 362.
Subtle mother.—*Richard III,* iii, 1, 152.
Trojan mothers.—*The Rape of Lucrece,* l. 1431.
True mother.—*Hamlet,* iv, 5, 150.
Wise mother.—*The Merchant of Venice,* i, 3, 74.
Witty mother.—*The Taming of the Shrew,* ii, 1, 266.

1
Paris: Younger than she are happy mothers made.
Capulet: And too soon marr'd are those so early made.
Romeo and Juliet. Act i, sc. 2, l. 12.

I was your mother much upon these years
That you are now a maid.
Romeo and Juliet. Act i, sc. 3, l. 72. [Lady Capulet]

Her mother is the lady of the house,
And a good lady, and a wise and virtuous.
Romeo and Juliet. Act i, sc. 5, l. 115. [Nurse]

O, sweet my mother, cast me not away.
Romeo and Juliet. Act iii, sc. 5, l. 200. [Juliet]

2
Play the mother's part, kiss me, be kind.
Sonnets. No. cxliii.

3
Good wombs have borne bad sons.
The Tempest. Act i, sc. 2, l. 119. [Miranda]

4
Painter: You 're a dog.
Apemantus: Thy mother 's of my generation: what 's she, if I be a dog?
Timon of Athens. Act i, sc. 1, l. 203.

Yet every mother breeds not sons alike.
Titus Andronicus. Act ii, sc. 3, l. 146. [Lavinia]

5
Aaron: Here lacks but your mother for to say amen.
Chiron: And that would she for twenty thousand more.
Demetrius: Come, let us go; and pray to all the gods
For our beloved mother in her pains.
Titus Andronicus. Act iv, sc. 2, l. 44.

A mother to his youth.—*Titus Andronicus,* i, 1, 332.

6
Chiron: Thou hast undone our mother.
Aaron: Villain, I have done thy mother. . . .
Demetrius: By this our mother is for ever shamed.
Chiron: Rome will despise her for this foul escape.
Titus Andronicus. Act iv, sc. 2, l. 75.

7
Hold thee dearly for thy mother's sake.
Titus Andronicus. Act v, sc. 1, l. 36. [Goth]

You know your mother means to feast with me,
And calls herself Revenge, and thinks me mad.
Titus Andronicus. Act v, sc. 2, l. 185. [Titus]

8
O, had thy mother borne so hard a mind,
She had not brought forth thee, but died unkind.
Venus and Adonis, l. 203.

Think, we had mothers.—*Troilus and Cressida,* v, 2, 130.

9
Your mother was most true to wedlock, prince;
For she did print your royal father off,
Conceiving you.
The Winter's Tale. Act v, sc. 1, l. 124. [Leontes]

Mother to a hopeful prince.—*The Winter's Tale,* iii, 2, 41.
Mother of fools.—*Much Ado about Nothing,* ii, 1, 295.

MOTION

10
Her motion and her station are as one.
Antony and Cleopatra. Act iii, sc. 3, l. 22. [Messenger]

11
My wife, not meanly proud of two such boys,
Made daily motions for our home return.
The Comedy of Errors. Act i, sc. 1, l. 59. [Ægeon]

12
From face to foot
He was a thing of blood, whose every motion
Was timed with dying cries.
Coriolanus. Act ii, sc. 2, l. 112. [Cominius]
The only use of "timed."

13
It lifted up its head and did address
Itself to motion.
Hamlet. Act i, sc. 2, l. 116. [Horatio]

In your motion you are hot and dry.
Hamlet. Act iv, sc. 7, l. 158. [King]

14
Thus with imagined wing our swift scene flies
In motion of no less celerity
Than that of thought.
Henry V. Act iii, Prol., l. 2. [Chorus]

15
How doth your grace affect their motion?
I Henry VI. Act v, sc. 1, l. 7. [King Henry]

Doth this motion please thee?
Titus Andronicus. Act i, sc. 1, l. 243. [Saturninus]

1
Meanwhile must be an earnest motion
Made to the queen.
Henry VIII. Act ii, sc. 4, l. 233. [Campeius]

Unshaked of motion.—*Julius Cæsar,* iii, 1, 70.
Free from motion.—*King John,* ii, 1, 453.
Sway of motion.—*King John,* ii, 1, 578.

2
O, I am scalded with my violent motion,
And spleen of speed to see your majesty!
King John. Act v, sc. 7, l. 49. [Bastard] See also under Speed. The only use of "scalded."

Borrow'd motion.—*A Lover's Complaint,* l. 327.
Continual motion.—*Henry V,* i, 2, 185; *The Rape of Lucrece,* l. 591.
Corporal motion.—*Julius Cæsar,* iv, 1, 33.
Dreadful motion.—*King John,* iv, 2, 255.
Excellent motion.—*The Merry Wives of Windsor,* iii, 3, 68; *The Taming of the Shrew,* i, 2, 280; *The Two Gentlemen of Verona,* ii, 1, 100.
Fell motion.—*King Lear,* ii, 1, 52.
First motion.—*Julius Cæsar,* ii, 1, 64.
Good motion.—*The Merry Wives of Windsor,* i, 1, 55.
Heavy motion.—*The Rape of Lucrece,* l. 1326.
Inward motion.—*King John,* i, 1, 212.
Loving motion.—*Coriolanus,* ii, 3, 57.
Mortal motion.—*Twelfth Night,* iii, 4, 304.
Perpetual motion.—*II Henry IV,* i, 2, 247.
Poor and old motion.—*II Henry IV,* iv, 3, 37.
Raging motions.—*Othello,* i, 3, 335.
Self-unable motion.—*All's Well that Ends Well,* iii, 1, 13. The only use of "self-unable."
Sincere motions.—*Henry VIII,* i, 1, 153.
Trivial motion.—*Coriolanus,* ii, 1, 56.
Wild motion.—*Cymbeline,* i, 6, 103.
Wondrous motion.—*King John,* iv, 2, 184.
Motion of all elements.—*Love's Labour's Lost,* iv, 3, 329. See under Love.
Motion of a school-boy's tongue.—*Love's Labour's Lost,* v, 2, 403.
No motion of the liver.—*Twelfth Night,* ii, 4, 101.

3
He is a motion generative: that's infallible.
Measure for Measure. Act iii, sc. 2, l. 119. [Lucio] The only use of "generative."

I have a motion much imports your good.
Measure for Measure. Act v, sc. 1, l. 541. [Duke]

4
The motions of his spirit are dull as night.
The Merchant of Venice. Act v, sc. 1, l. 86. [Lorenzo]

5
Your father and my uncle hath made motions.
The Merry Wives of Windsor. Act iii, sc. 4, l. 67. [Slender]

End motion here!—*Romeo and Juliet,* iii, 2, 59.

6
Incite them to quick motion.
The Tempest. Act iv, sc. 1, l. 39. [Prospero]

Spritely motion.—*All's Well that Ends Well,* ii, 1, 78.
Swift motion.—*Sonnets,* xlv.
Swift in motion.—*Romeo and Juliet,* ii, 5, 13.
What, all in motion?—*Timon of Athens,* iii, 6, 112.
I'll make the motion.—*Twelfth Night,* iii, 4, 316.

7 Things in motion sooner catch the eye
Than what not stirs.
Troilus and Cressida. Act iii, sc. 3, l. 183. [Ulysses]

MOTIVE

8
This was your motive, was it?
All's Well that Ends Well. Act i, sc. 3, l. 236. [Countess]

It hath fated her to be my motive.—*All's Well that Ends Well,* iv, 4, 20.
Motives of mere fancy.—*All's Well that Ends Well,* v, 3, 215.
Ignorant motive.—*Antony and Cleopatra,* ii, 2, 96.
Precious motives.—*Macbeth,* iv, 3, 27.

9 The accusation
Which they have often made against the senate,
All cause unborn, could never be the motive
Of our so frank donation.
Coriolanus. Act iii, sc. 1, l. 127. [Coriolanus]

10
Though you did love this youth, I blame ye not;
You had a motive for it.
Cymbeline. Act v, sc. 5, l. 267. [Belarius]

11 This, I take it,
Is the main motive of our preparations.
Hamlet. Act i, sc. 1, l. 104. [Horatio]

What would he do
Had he the motive . . . That I have?
Hamlet, ii, 2, 586. See under Actor.

I am satisfied in nature,
Whose motive, in this case, should stir me most
To my revenge.
Hamlet. Act v, sc. 2, l. 255. [Laertes]

Without more motive.—*Hamlet,* i, 4, 76.

12
If these be motives weak, break off betimes.
Julius Cæsar. Act ii, sc. 1, l. 116. [Brutus]

What motive may
Be stronger with thee than the name of wife?
King John. Act iii, sc. 1, l. 315. [Blanch]

13 Desires to know
In brief the grounds and motives of her woe.
A Lover's Complaint, l. 62.

14
Albeit I confess thy father's wealth
Was the first motive that I woo'd thee, Anne.
The Merry Wives of Windsor. Act iii, sc. 4, l. 13. [Fenton]

15
Am I the motive of these tears, my lord?
Othello. Act iv, sc. 2, l. 43. [Desdemona]

16
The slavish motive of recanting fear.
Richard II, i, 1, 193. See under Tongue.

1 Nor are they living
Who were the motives that you first went out.
Timon of Athens. Act v, sc. 4, l. 26. [Senator]

MOUNTAIN

2
O Lord, Lord! it is a hard matter for friends to meet; but mountains may be removed with earthquakes and so encounter.
As You Like It. Act iii, sc. 2, l. 194. [Celia]

3
Up to the mountains!
Cymbeline. Act iii, sc. 3, l. 73. [Belarius]
We'll higher to the mountains.—*Cymbeline,* iv, 4, 8.
Aspiring mountains.—*Rape of Lucrece,* l. 548.
Barren mountain.—*I Henry IV,* i, 3, 89; 159; *The Winter's Tale,* iii, 2, 213.
Craggy mountains.—*The Passionate Pilgrim,* l. 356.
Envious mountain.—*III Henry VI,* iii, 2, 157.
Far-off mountains.—*A Midsummer-Night's Dream,* iv, 1, 193.
Flat mountain.—*Hamlet,* v, 1, 275.
Forked mountain.—*Antony and Cleopatra,* iv, 14, 5.
Huge mountain.—*Julius Cæsar,* ii, 4, 7.
Liquid mountains.—*Troilus and Cressida,* i, 3, 40.
Rocky mountains.—*II Henry IV,* iv, 1, 188.
Mountain of affection.—*Much Ado about Nothing,* ii, 1, 382.
Mountain of mad flesh.—*The Merry Wives of Windsor,* iv, 4, 158.
Mountain of mummy.—*The Merry Wives of Windsor,* iii, 5, 18. "Mummy" is repeated in *Macbeth,* iv, 1, 23, and in *Othello,* iii, 4, 74.

4
Could you on this fair mountain leave to feed,
And batten on this moor?
Hamlet. Act iii, sc. 4, l. 66. [Hamlet]
And, if thou prate of mountains, let them throw
Millions of acres on us, till our ground,
Singeing his pate against the burning zone,
Make Ossa like a wart!
Hamlet. Act v, sc. 1, l. 303. [Hamlet] The only use of "singeing" and "zone," and the only mention of Ossa.

5
Ha, thou mountain-foreigner!
The Merry Wives of Windsor. Act i, sc. 1, l. 164. [Pistol] The only use of "mountain-foreigner."

6
The frozen ridges of the Alps.
Richard II. Act i, sc. 1, l. 64. [Mowbray]
The Alps and Apennines, the Pyrenean.—*King John,* i, 1, 202. The Alps are mentioned also in *Henry V,* iii, 5, 52, and *Antony and Cleopatra,* i, 4, 66. The only mention of the Apennines and the Pyrenees.

7 As mountains are for winds,
That shake not, though they blow perpetually.
The Taming of the Shrew. Act ii, sc. 1, l. 141. [Petruchio]

MOURNING

See also Lamentation, Sorrow

8
What willingly he did confound he wail'd,
Believe 't, till I wept too.
Antony and Cleopatra. Act iii, sc. 2, l. 58. [Enobarbus]

9
They bore him barefaced on the bier;
Hey non nonny, nonny, hey nonny;
And in his grave rain'd many a tear.
Hamlet. Act iv, sc. 5, l. 164. [Ophelia] "Barefaced" occurs also in *A Midsummer-Night's Dream,* i, 2, 100, and in *Macbeth,* iii, 1, 119. "Hey nonny nonny" is repeated in *Much Ado about Nothing,* ii, 3, 71. "Ha, no, nonny" occurs in *King Lear,* iii, 4, 103.

10
For this I shall have time enough to mourn.
II Henry IV. Act i, sc. 1, l. 136. [Northumberland]
Mourn you for him.—*Coriolanus,* v, 6, 144.

11
Pistol: My manly heart doth yearn. . . .
For Falstaff he is dead,
And we must yearn therefore.
Bardolph: Would I were with him, wheresome'er he is, either in heaven or in hell!
Henry V. Act ii, sc. 3, l. 3. The only use of "wheresome'er."

12
Hung be the heavens with black, yield day to night!
I Henry VI. Act i, sc. 1, l. 1. [Bedford]
We mourn in black: why mourn we not in blood?
I Henry VI. Act i, sc. 1, l. 17. [Exeter]
In black mourn I.—*Passionate Pilgrim,* l. 264.
Clad in mourning black.—*The Rape of Lucrece,* l. 1585.
And some will mourn in ashes, some coal-black.
Richard II. Act v, sc. 1, l. 49. [King Richard]
Come, mourn with me for that I do lament,
And put on sullen black incontinent.
Richard II. Act v, sc. 6, l. 47. [Bolingbroke]

13
Away with these disgraceful wailing robes!
Wounds will I lend the French instead of eyes,
To weep their intermissive miseries.
I Henry VI. Act i, sc. 1, l. 86. [Bedford] The only use of "disgraceful" and "intermissive."

14
I would be blind with weeping, sick with groans,
Look pale as primrose with blood-drinking sighs.
II Henry VI. Act iii, sc. 2, l. 62. [Queen Margaret] "Blood-drinking" is repeated in *I Henry VI,* ii, 4, 108, and in *Titus Andronicus,* ii, 3, 224.
King Henry: How now, madam!
Still lamenting and mourning for Suffolk's death?
I fear me, love, if that I had been dead,
Thou wouldest not have mourn'd so much for me.

Queen: No, my love, I should not mourn, but die for thee.
II Henry VI. Act iv, sc. 4, l. 21.

Mourn I not for thee?—*II Henry VI*, iii, 2, 383.

1 Shall we go throw away our coats of steel,
And wrap our bodies in black mourning gowns,
Numbering our Ave-Maries with our beads?
III Henry VI. Act ii, sc. 1, l. 160. [Richard] "Ave-Maries" is repeated in *II Henry VI*, i, 3, 59.

My mourning weeds are laid aside,
And I am ready to put armour on.
III Henry VI. Act iii, sc. 3, l. 229. [Queen Margaret] "Mourning weeds" is repeated in iv, 1, 104, and in *Titus Andronicus*, i, 1, 70, and v, 3, 196.

2 You all did love him once, not without cause:
What cause withholds you then, to mourn for him?
Julius Cæsar. Act iii, sc. 2, l. 107. [Antony]

3 Howl, howl, howl, howl! O, you are men of stones:
Had I your tongues and eyes, I 'ld use them so
That heaven's vault should crack.
King Lear. Act v, sc. 3, l. 257. [King Lear]

4 We shall make our griefs and clamour roar
Upon his death.
Macbeth. Act i, sc. 7, l. 78. [Lady Macbeth]

Maintain a mourning ostentation.
Much Ado about Nothing. Act iv, sc. 1, l. 207. [Friar]

5 'Tis stale to sigh, to weep, and groan.
The Rape of Lucrece, l. 1362.

She her plaints a little while doth stay,
Pausing for means to mourn some newer way.
The Rape of Lucrece, l. 1364.

6 March sadly after; grace my mournings here;
In weeping after this untimely bier.
Richard II. Act v, sc. 6, l. 51. [Bolingbroke]

We wept after her hearse, And yet we mourn.
Pericles. Act iv, sc. 3, l. 41. [Dionyza]

7 Told the sad story of my father's death,
And twenty times made pause to sob and weep,
That all the standers-by had wet their cheeks,
Like trees bedash'd with rain.
Richard III. Act i, sc. 2, l. 161. [Gloucester] The only use of "bedash'd."

'Tis sweet and commendable in your nature, Hamlet,
To give these mourning duties to your father.
Hamlet. Act i, sc. 2, l. 87. [King]

8 Leave these sad designs
To him that hath more cause to be a mourner.
Richard III. Act i, sc. 2, l. 211. [Gloucester]

Let no mourner say
He weeps for her, for she was only mine,
And only must be wail'd by Collatine.
The Rape of Lucrece, l. 1797.

Another flap-mouth'd mourner, black and grim.
Venus and Adonis, l. 920. The only use of "flap-mouth'd."

I am no mourner.—*Richard III*, iii, 2, 51.

Tarry for the mourners.—*Romeo and Juliet*, iv, 5, 150.

9 Oh, who shall hinder me to wail and weep,
To chide my fortune, and torment myself?
Richard III. Act ii, sc. 2, l. 34. [Queen Elizabeth]

O, what cause have I,
Thine being but a moiety of my grief,
To overgo thy plaints and drown thy cries!
Richard III. Act ii, sc. 2, l. 59. [Duchess of York] The only use of "overgo."

O, who hath any cause to mourn but I?
Richard III. Act iv, sc. 4, l. 34. [Queen Elizabeth]

10 No longer mourn for me when I am dead
Than you shall hear the surly sullen bell
Give warning to the world that I am fled
From this vile world, with vilest worms to dwell:
Nay, if you read this line, remember not
The hand that writ it; for I love you so
That I in your sweet thoughts would be forgot
If thinking on me then should make you woe.
Sonnets. No. lxxi.

O, let it then as well beseem thy heart
To mourn for me, since mourning doth thee grace.
Sonnets. No. cxxxii.

11 Do not draw back, for we will mourn with thee:
O, could our mourning ease thy misery!
Titus Andronicus. Act ii, sc. 4, l. 56. [Marcus]

No funeral rite, nor man in mourning weeds,
No mournful bell shall ring her burial.
Titus Andronicus. Act v, 3, 196. [Lucius]

Mournful crocodile.—*II Henry VI*, iii, 1, 226.

Mournful death.—*I Henry VI*, ii, 2, 16.

Mournful hymns.—*Sonnets*, cii.

Mournful epitaphs.—*Much Ado about Nothing*, iv, 1, 209.

Mournful tears.—*II Henry VI*, iii, 2, 340. The only uses of "mournful."

12 But shall I go mourn for that, my dear?
The Winter's Tale. Act iv, sc. 3, l. 15. [Autolycus, singing]

MOUSE

13 Bernardo: Have you had a quiet guard?
Francisco: Not a mouse stirring.
Hamlet. Act i, sc. 1, l. 10.

14 But mice and rats, and such small deer,
Have been Tom's food for seven long year.
King Lear. Act iii, sc. 4, l. 144. [Edgar]

Look, look, a mouse! Peace, peace; this piece of toasted cheese will do 't.
King Lear. Act iv, sc. 6, l. 89. [King Lear]

1
You, ladies, you, whose gentle hearts do fear
The smallest monstrous mouse that creeps on floor.
A Midsummer-Night's Dream. Act v, sc. 1, l. 222. [Lion]

Not a mouse
Shall disturb this hallow'd house.
A Midsummer-Night's Dream. Act v, sc. 1, l. 394. [Puck]

2
Dun 's the mouse, the constable's own word.
Romeo and Juliet. Act i, sc. 4, l. 40. [Mercutio] "Dun" occurs again in i, 4, 41 and in no other play. It is used also in *Sonnets*, cxxx.

MOUTH

3
You must borrow me Gargantua's mouth.
As You Like It. Act iii, sc. 2, l. 238. [Celia] The only mention of Gargantua.

4
You being their mouths, why rule you not their teeth?
Coriolanus. Act iii, sc. 1, l. 36. [Coriolanus]

It is spoke freely out of many mouths.
Coriolanus. Act iv, sc. 6, l. 64. [Messenger]

5
Makes mouths at the invisible event.
Hamlet, iv, 4, 50. See PRINCE, 1201:1.

This makes bold mouths.
Henry VIII. Act i, sc. 2, l. 60. [Queen Katharine]

Make mouths.—*Midsummer-Night's Dream*, iii, 2, 238. See under RIDICULE.

Made mouths in a glass.—*King Lear*, iii, 2, 36.

6
In thy hateful lungs, yea, in thy maw, perdy,
And, which is worse, within thy nasty mouth!
Henry V. Act ii, sc. 1, l. 52. [Pistol] "Nasty" occurs again in *Hamlet*, iii, 4, 94. "Perdy" is used four times.

Foul mouth.—*Romeo and Juliet*, iv, 3, 34; *Measure for Measure*, v, 1, 309.

Foul-mouthed.—*I Henry IV*, iii, 3, 122; *All's Well that Ends Well*, i, 3, 60.

Foul-mouthed'st.—*II Henry IV*, ii, 4, 77.

Venom-mouth'd.—*Henry VIII*, i, 1, 120. The only use of the phrase.

7
Touch her soft mouth, and march.
Henry V. Act ii, sc. 3, l. 61. [Pistol]

Innocent mouth.—*Winter's Tale*, iii, 2, 101.

Minikin mouth.—*King Lear*, iii, 6, 43. See under SHEEP for full quotation.

8
Now will I dam up this thy yawning mouth
For swallowing the treasure of the realm.
II Henry VI. Act iv, sc. 1, l. 73. [Captain] "Yawning" occurs twice more in the plays, in *Henry V*, i, 2, 204, and in *Macbeth*, iii, 2, 43.

My mouth shall be the parliament of England.
II Henry VI. Act iv, sc. 7, l. 17. [Cade]

9
Suppose that I am now my father's mouth.
III Henry VI. Act v, sc. 5, l. 18. [Prince of Wales]

Butter-woman's mouth.—*All's Well that Ends Well*, iv, 1, 45. "Butter-women" occurs in *As You Like It*, iii, 2, 103.

Cannon's mouth.—*As You Like It*, ii, 7, 153.

Friar's mouth.—*All's Well that Ends Well*, ii, 2, 28.

Greyhound's mouth.—*Much Ado about Nothing*, v, 2, 12.

Oven's mouth.—*Pericles*, iv, 2, 108.

People's mouths.—*Coriolanus*, iii, 1, 271.

Thunder's mouth.—*King John*, iii, 4, 38.

Villain's mouth.—*Measure for Measure*, v, 1, 304.

World's wide mouth.—*I Henry IV*, i, 3, 153.

10
Have your mouth fill'd up
Before you open it.
Henry VIII. Act ii, sc. 3, l. 87. [Old Lady]

With open mouth swallowing a tailor's news.
King John, iv, 2, 195. See TAILOR, 1486:2.

Ope my mouth.—*Titus Andronicus*, v, 3, 175.

Open'd their mouths.—*Venus and Adonis*, l. 248.

Open your mouth.—*The Tempest*, ii, 2, 85; 87.

11
The mouth of passage shall we fling wide ope,
And give you entrance.
King John. Act ii, sc. 1, l. 449. [Citizen]

Here 's a large mouth, indeed,
That spits forth death and mountains, rocks and seas,
Talks as familiarly of roaring lions
As maids of thirteen do of puppy-dogs!
King John. Act ii, sc. 1, l. 457. [Bastard] The only use of "puppy-dogs." "Puppy-dog" occurs in *Henry V*, iii, 2, 78.

12
Will not a calf's-skin stop that mouth of thine?
King John. Act iii, sc. 1, l. 299. [Bastard]

Peace! I will stop your mouth.
Much Ado about Nothing. Act v, sc. 4, l. 98. [Benedick]

Nay, then I 'll stop your mouth.
Titus Andronicus. Act ii, sc. 3, l. 185. [Chiron]

Stop his mouth, and let him speak no more.
Titus Andronicus. Act v, sc. 1, l. 151. [Lucius]

Stop close their mouths, let them not speak a word.
Titus Andronicus. Act v, sc. 2, l. 165. [Publius]

Stop their mouths, let them not speak to me.
Titus Andronicus. Act v, sc. 2, l. 168. [Titus]

Stop his mouth.—*Much Ado about Nothing*, ii, 1, 322.

Stop my mouth.—*II Henry VI*, iii, 2, 396; *Troilus and Cressida*, iii, 2, 141.

Stop our mouths.—*Richard II*, v, 1, 95; *Henry VIII*, ii, 2, 9.

Stop the mouth.—*Timon of Athens*, ii, 2, 156.

Stop their mouths.—*Henry VIII*, v, 3, 23.

His mouth is stopp'd.—*Othello*, v, 2, 71.

Shut your mouth, dame.
King Lear. Act v, sc. 3, l. 154. [Albany]

1
Be thy mouth or black or white.
King Lear, iii, 6, 69. See under Dog.
Black mouth.—*Henry VIII,* i, 3, 58.
Bloody mouth.—*Midsummer-Night's Dream,* v, 1, 144.
Brazen mouth.—*King John,* iii, 3, 38.
Common mouth.—*Coriolanus,* iii, 1, 22.
Congeal'd mouths.—*Richard III,* i, 2, 56.
Deeper mouth.—*I Henry VI,* ii, 4, 12.
Dumb mouths.—*Julius Cæsar,* iii, 1, 260; iii, 2, 229.
Fatal mouths.—*Henry V,* iii, Prol., 27.
Full mouth.—*Henry V,* i, 2, 230.
Misty mouth.—*Titus Andronicus,* ii, 3, 236.
Pale dull mouths.—*Henry V,* iv, 2, 49.
Rotten mouth.—*Richard III,* iv, 4, 2.
Ungracious mouth.—*Richard II,* ii, 3, 89.

2
Say, if thou 'dst rather hear it from our mouths,
Or from our masters?
Macbeth. Act iv, sc. 1, l. 62. [Witch]

3
O perilous mouths,
That bear in them one and the self-same tongue,
Either of condemnation or approof!
Measure for Measure. Act ii, sc. 4, l. 172. [Isabella] "Condemnation" is used three times in the plays and "approof" four times.
If I had my mouth, I would bite.
Much Ado about Nothing. Act i, sc. 3, l. 36. [Don John]

4
These mouths, who but of late, earth, sea, and air,
Were all too little to content and please, . . .
They are now starved for want of exercise.
Pericles. Act i, sc. 4, l. 34. [Cleon]
A Spaniard's mouth so watered.—*Pericles,* iv, 2, 108. See under Inclination. The only use of the phrase.

5
From your own mouth, my lord, did I this deed.
Richard II. Act v, sc. 6, l. 37. [Exton]
Seal up the mouth of outrage for a while.
Romeo and Juliet, v, 3, 216. See under Mystery.
Mouths of men.—*Sonnets,* lxxxi.
Mouth of honour.—*Henry VIII,* i, 1, 137.

6
What, must our mouths be cold?
The Tempest. Act i, sc. 1, l. 56. [Boatswain]
Hast thou no mouth by land?
Tempest. Act v, sc. 1, l. 220. [Gonzalo]

7
Ajax . . . foams at mouth.
Troilus and Cressida, v, 5, 36. See also *Othello,* iv, 1, 55; *Julius Cæsar,* i, 2, 255; *Cymbeline,* v, 5, 276.

8
The ruby-colour'd portal.
Venus and Adonis, l. 451. The only use of "ruby-colour'd."
That sweet coral mouth,
Whose precious taste her thirsty lips well knew.
Venus and Adonis, l. 542.
Sweet mouth.—*The Two Gentlemen of Verona,* iii, 1, 330.

9
Whose frothy mouth, bepainted all with red,
Like milk and blood being mingled both together.
Venus and Adonis, l. 901. The only use of "frothy." "Bepaint" occurs in *Romeo and Juliet,* ii, 2, 86.

MULTITUDE

See also Citizen, Mob, People

10
Ingratitude is monstrous, and for the multitude to be ingrateful, were to make a monster of the multitude.
Coriolanus. Act ii, sc. 3, l. 10. [Citizen]
The mutable, rank-scented many.
Coriolanus. Act iii, sc. 1, l. 66. [Coriolanus] The only use of "mutable" and "rank-scented."

11
He 's loved of the distracted multitude,
Who like not in their judgement, but their eyes.
Hamlet. Act iv, sc. 3, l. 4. [King]

12
Follow'd him
Even at the heels in golden multitudes.
I Henry IV. Act iv, sc. 3, l. 72. [Hotspur]
This bisson multitude.
Coriolanus. Act iii, sc. 1, l. 131. [Coriolanus] "Bisson" (blind) occurs three times in the plays.
The buzzing pleased multitude.
The Merchant of Venice. Act iii, sc. 2, l. 182. [Bassanio]
Barbarous multitudes.—*The Merchant of Venice,* ii, 9, 33. See under Choice for full quotation.
Differing multitudes.—*Cymbeline,* iii, 6, 86.
Fair multitude.—*King John,* iii, 4, 62.
Ragged multitude.—*II Henry VI,* iv, 4, 32.
Rude multitude.—*II Henry VI,* iii, 2, 135; *Love's Labour 's Lost,* v, 1, 95.

13
The blunt monster with uncounted heads,
The still-discordant wavering multitude.
II Henry IV. Induction, l. 18. [Rumour] The only use of "still-discordant."
First Citizen: He himself stuck not to call us the many-headed multitude.
Third Citizen: We have been called so of many; not that our heads are some brown, some black, some auburn, some bald, but that our wits are so diversely coloured: and truly I think if all our wits were to issue out of one skull, they would fly east, west, north, south, and their consent of one direct way should be at once to all the points o' the compass.
Coriolanus. Act ii, sc. 3, l. 17. The only use of "many-headed."
The beast With many heads butts me away.
Coriolanus. Act iv, sc. 1, l. 1. [Coriolanus]

14
See how the giddy multitude do point,
And nod their heads, and throw their eyes on thee!
II Henry VI. Act ii, sc. 4, l. 21. [Duchess of Gloucester]
Was ever feather so lightly blown to and fro as this multitude?
II Henry VI. Act iv, sc. 8, l. 57. [Cade]

1
Mercy o' me, what a multitude are here!
They grow still too; from all parts they are
coming,
As if we kept a fair here!
Henry VIII. Act v, sc. 4, l. 71. [Chamberlain]

2
The common herd.
Julius Cæsar. Act i, sc. 2, l. 290. [Casca]
Are these your herd? Must these have voices?
Coriolanus. Act iii, sc. 1, l. 33. [Coriolanus]
Stoop to the herd.
Coriolanus. Act iii, sc. 2, l. 32. [Menenius]

3
The fool multitude, that choose by show,
Not learning more than the fond eye doth
teach.
The Merchant of Venice. Act ii, sc. 9, l. 26. [Arragon]

MURDER

See also Killing

4
He will have other means to cut you off.
As You Like It. Act ii, sc. 3, l. 25. [Adam]
Cut him off.—*Measure for Measure,* v, 1, 112; *Julius Cæsar,* iv, 3, 210; *King Lear,* iv, 5, 38; iv, 6, 268.
Cut me off.—*Merchant of Venice,* iv, 1, 272.
Cut them off.—*II Henry IV,* iv, 5, 210.

5
You 'll rejoice That he is thus cut off.
Coriolanus. Act v, sc. 6, l. 140. [Aufidius]
We would have all offenders so cut off.
Henry V. Act iii, sc. 6, l. 114. [King Henry]
Cut off by course of justice.—*Measure for Measure,* v, 1, 35.
Cut off my lord.—*Cymbeline,* iv, 2, 16.

6
How! that I should murder her?
Upon the love and truth and vows which I
Have made to thy command? I, her? her
blood?
Cymbeline. Act iii, sc. 2, l. 11. [Pisanio]
Murder in heaven?—*Cymbeline,* iv, 2, 312.

7
Foul deeds will rise,
Though all the earth o'erwhelm them, to
men's eyes.
Hamlet. Act i, sc. 2, l. 257. [Hamlet]
Murder, though it have no tongue, will speak
With most miraculous organ.
Hamlet. Act ii, sc. 2, l. 622. [Hamlet]
Murder cannot be hid long.
The Merchant of Venice. Act ii, sc. 2, l. 83. [Launcelot]

8
Ghost: Revenge his foul and most unnatural
murder.
Hamlet: Murder!
Ghost: Murder most foul, as in the best it is;
But this most foul, strange and unnatural.
Hamlet. Act i, sc. 5, l. 25.
Thus was I, sleeping, by a brother's hand
Of life, of crown, of queen, at once dispatch'd:
Cut off even in the blossoms of my sin,
Unhousel'd, disappointed, unaneled,
No reckoning made, but sent to my account
With all my imperfections on my head.
Hamlet. Act i, sc. 5, l. 74. [Ghost] The only use of "unhousel'd," "disappointed," and "unaneled."

9
What wilt thou do? thou wilt not murder
me?
Help, help, ho!
Hamlet. Act iii, sc. 4, l. 21. [Queen]
What, will you murder me?—*The Comedy of Errors,* iv, 4, 112.

10
Northumberland: The unhappy king . . .
did return
To be deposed and shortly murdered.
Worcester: And for whose death we in the
world's wide mouth
Live scandalized and foully spoken of.
I Henry IV. Act i, sc. 3, l. 148. [Worcester] "Scandalized" occurs again in *The Two Gentlemen of Verona,* ii, 7, 61.
Pray God you have not murdered some of them.
I Henry IV. Act ii, sc. 4, l. 210. [Prince]

11
God let me not live, but I will murder your ruff for this.
II Henry IV. Act ii, sc. 4, l. 144. [Pistol]

12
Men may sleep, and they may have their throats about them at that time; and some say knives have edges.
Henry V. Act ii, sc. 1, l. 23. [Nym]
Laertes: To cut his throat i' the church.
King: No place, indeed, should murder sanc-
tuarize.
Hamlet. Act iv, sc. 7, l. 127. The only use of "sanctuarize." The cutting of throats is referred to nineteen times in the plays. See under THROAT.

13
O well a day, Lady, if he be not drawn now! we shall see wilful adultery and murder committed.
Henry V. Act ii, sc. 1, l. 39. [Hostess]
The guilt of premeditated and contrived murder.
Henry V. Act iv, sc. 1, l. 172. [King Henry] The phrase "contrived murder" occurs again in *Othello,* i, 2, 3.

14
Salisbury is a desperate homicide.
I Henry VI, i, 2, 25. See under FIGHTING.
A bloody tyrant and a homicide.
Richard III, v, 3, 246. See under TYRANT.
Bloody homicide.—*I Henry VI,* v, 4, 62; *Richard III,* v, 2, 18. "Homicide" is used a fifth time in *Richard III,* i, 2, 125.

15
Murder indeed, that bloody sin, I tortured
Above the felon or what trespass else.
II Henry VI. Act iii, sc. 1, l. 131. [Gloucester]
Do not stand on quillets how to slay him:
Be it by gins, by snares, by subtlety,
Sleeping or waking, 'tis no matter how,
So he be dead.
II Henry VI. Act iii, sc. 1, l. 261. [Suffolk] The only use of "subtlety." For "quillets" see under LAW.

1
It is reported, mighty sovereign,
That good Duke Humphrey traitorously is murder'd.
II Henry VI. Act iii, sc. 2, l. 122. [Warwick]
Warwick: It cannot be that he was murder'd here. . . .
Suffolk: Why, Warwick, who should do the duke to death?
Myself and Beaufort had him in protection;
And we, I hope, sir, are no murderers.
II Henry VI. Act iii, sc. 2, l. 177.
A Roman sworder and banditto slave
Murder'd sweet Tully.
II Henry VI. Act iv, sc. 1, l. 135. [Suffolk]
See DEATH, 307:2.
Murder'd traitorously.—*II Henry VI,* ii, 2, 27.
Murder'd wrongfully.—*II Henry VI,* ii, 3, 107.
Murdered for our pains.—*II Henry IV,* iv, 5, 79.

2
Pernicious blood-sucker of sleeping men!
II Henry VI. Act iii, sc. 2, l. 226. [Warwick] "Blood-sucker" occurs again in *Richard III,* iii, 3, 6.
Unless you be possess'd with devilish spirits,
You cannot but forbear to murder me.
II Henry VI. Act iv, sc. 7, l. 80. [Say]

3
Straight be done to death.
II Henry VI. Act iii, sc. 2, l. 244. [Salisbury]
Done to death by slanderous tongues.—*Much Ado about Nothing,* v, 3, 3.
Done to death.—*III Henry VI,* ii, 1, 103; iii, 3, 103. The only uses of the phrase.

4
King Henry: Gentle son Edward, thou wilt stay with me?
Queen Margaret: Ay, to be murder'd by his enemies.
III Henry VI. Act i, sc. 1, l. 259.
Take me from the world:
My soul to heaven, my blood upon your heads!
III Henry VI. Act i, sc. 4, l. 167. [York]

5 Not contented that he lopp'd the branch
In hewing Rutland when his leaves put forth,
But set his murdering knife unto the root
From whence that tender spray did sweetly spring.
III Henry VI. Act ii, sc. 6, l. 47. [Richard] The only use of "hewing."
Murdering basilisks.—*II Henry VI,* iii, 2, 324; *Henry V,* v, 2, 17.
Murdering innocents.—*III Henry VI,* v, 6, 32.
Murdering ministers.—*Macbeth,* i, 5, 49.

6
Butchers and villains! bloody cannibals!
How sweet a plant have you untimely cropp'd!
III Henry VI. Act v, sc. 5, l. 61. [Queen Margaret]
Murder is thy alms-deed;
Petitioners for blood thou ne'er put'st back.
III Henry VI. Act v, sc. 5, l. 79. [Queen Margaret] The only use of "alms-deed."

7 Here wast thou bay'd, brave hart;
Here didst thou fall; and here thy hunters stand,
Sign'd in thy spoil, and crimson'd in thy lethe.
Julius Cæsar. Act iii, sc. 1, l. 204. [Antony] The only use of "crimson'd" and of "lethe" as a common noun in the sense of death.
Slaying is the word; It is a deed in fashion.
Julius Cæsar. Act v, sc. 5, l. 4. [Brutus] The only use of "slaying." "Slay" occurs twenty-six times, "slayeth" once.

8
King John: Death.
Hubert: My lord?
King John: A grave.
Hubert: He shall not live.
King John. Act iii, sc. 3, l. 66.
Thy hand hath murder'd him: I had a mighty cause
To wish him dead, but thou hadst none to kill him.
King John. Act iv, sc. 2, l. 205. [King John]
Hadst thou not been by, . . .
This murder would not have come into my mind.
King John. Act iv, sc. 2, l. 220. [King John]
And thou, to be endeared to a king,
Made it no conscience to destroy a prince.
King John. Act iv, sc. 2, l. 228. [King John]

9
Pembroke: O death, made proud with pure and princely beauty!
The earth had not a hole to hide this deed.
Salisbury: Murder, as hating what himself hath done,
Doth lay it open to urge on revenge.
King John. Act iv, sc. 3, l. 35.
This is the very top,
The height, the crest, or crest unto the crest,
Of murder's arms.
King John. Act iv, sc. 3, l. 45. [Salisbury]
All murders past do stand excused in this:
And this, so sole and so unmatchable,
Shall give a holiness, a purity,
To the yet unbegotten sin of times;
And prove a deadly bloodshed but a jest,
Exampled by this heinous spectacle.
King John. Act iv, sc. 3, l. 51. [Pembroke] The only use of "unbegotten." "Bloodshed" is repeated in *II Henry IV,* iv, 5, 195.
They found him dead and cast into the streets,
An empty casket, where the jewel of life
By some damn'd hand was robb'd and ta'en away.
King John. Act v, sc. 1, l. 39. [Bastard]

10 The revenging gods
'Gainst parricides did all their thunders bend.
King Lear. Act ii, sc. 1, l. 47. [Edmund] "Parricide" occurs again in *Macbeth,* iii, 1, 32.

11 Wither'd murder,
Alarum'd by his sentinel, the wolf,
Whose howl's his watch, thus with his stealthy pace,
With Tarquin's ravishing strides, towards his design
Moves like a ghost.
Macbeth. Act ii, sc. 1, l. 52. [Macbeth] The only use of "stealthy."

There 's one did laugh in 's sleep, and one cried 'Murder!'
That they did wake each other.
Macbeth. Act ii, sc. 2, l. 23. [Macbeth]

1
Ring the alarum-bell. Murder and treason!
Macbeth. Act ii, sc. 3, l. 79. [Macduff] "Ring the alarum-bell" is repeated in v, 5, 51. "Alarum-bell" is used in no other play.

Macduff: Your royal father 's murdered.
Malcolm: O, by whom?
Lennox: Those of his chamber, as it seem'd, had done it.
Macbeth. Act ii, sc. 3, l. 105.

2
Blood hath been shed ere now, i' the olden time,
Ere human statute purged the gentle weal;
Ay, and since too, murders have been perform'd
Too terrible for the ear.
Macbeth. Act iii, sc. 4, l. 75. [Macbeth] The only use of "olden."

Stones have been known to move and trees to speak;
Augurs and understood relations have
By magot-pies and choughs and rooks brought forth
The secret'st man of blood.
Macbeth. Act iii, sc. 4, l. 123. [Macbeth] The only use of "augurs," "magot-pies," and "secret'st."

Your castle is surprised; your wife and babes
Savagely slaughtered.
Macbeth. Act iv, sc. 3, l. 204. [Ross] The only use of "savagely."

3 Now does he feel
His secret murders sticking on his hands.
Macbeth. Act v, sc. 2, l. 16. [Angus]

4
He murder cries and help from Athens calls.
A Midsummer-Night's Dream. Act iii, sc. 2, l. 26. [Puck]

5
Though in the trade of war I have slain men,
Yet do I hold it very stuff o' the conscience
To do no contrived murder.
Othello. Act i, sc. 2, l. 1. [Iago]

How shall I murder him?
Othello. Act iv, sc. 1, l. 178. [Othello]

6 Kill men i' the dark!—
Where be these bloody thieves?—
How silent is this town!—Ho! murder! murder!
Othello. Act v, sc. 1, l. 63. [Iago]

Help ho! murder! murder!—*Othello,* v, 1, 27.
Murder! murder!—*Othello,* v, 1, 37.
Ho! murder! murder!—*Othello,* v, 1, 64.

7
O my good lord, yonder 's foul murder done.
Othello. Act v, sc. 2, l. 106. [Emilia]

Search, seek, and know how this foul murder comes.
Romeo and Juliet. Act v, sc. 3, l. 198. [Verona]

I am the greatest, able to do least,
Yet most suspected, as the time and place
Doth make against me, of this direful murder.
Romeo and Juliet. Act v, sc. 3, l. 223. [Friar Laurence]

Foul murder.—*Hamlet,* iii, 3, 52.
Heady murder.—*Henry V,* iii, 3, 32.
Shameful murder.—*II Henry VI,* iv, 1, 95.
Murders fell.—*The Rape of Lucrece,* l. 766.

8
Othello: Murder 's out of tune,
And sweet revenge grows harsh.
Desdemona: O, falsely, falsely murder'd! . . .
Othello: Why, how should she be murder'd?
Emilia: Alas, who knows?
Othello: You heard her say herself, it was not I.
Othello. Act v, sc. 2, l. 115.

Help! help, ho! help!
The Moor hath kill'd my mistress! Murder! murder!
Othello. Act v, sc. 2, l. 166. [Emilia]

O, are you come, Iago? you have done well,
That men must lay their murders on your neck.
Othello. Act v, sc. 2, l. 169. [Emilia]

My mistress here lies murder'd in her bed, . . .
And your reports have set the murder on.
Othello. Act v, sc. 2, l. 185. [Emilia]

9
Murder 's as near to lust as flame to smoke.
Pericles. Act i, sc. 1, l. 138. [Pericles]

10 Like a traitor coward,
Sluiced out his innocent soul through streams of blood.
Richard II. Act i, sc. 1, l. 102. [Bolingbroke] "Sluiced" occurs once again in *The Winter's Tale,* i, 2, 194.

In suffering thus thy brother to be slaughter'd,
Thou showest the naked pathway to thy life,
Teaching stern murder how to butcher thee.
Richard II. Act i, sc. 2, l. 30. [Duchess of Gloucester]

Murders, treasons and detested sins,
The cloak of night being pluck'd from off their backs,
Stand bare and naked, trembling at themselves.
Richard II. Act iii, sc. 2, l. 44. [King Richard]

11
With Cain go wander thorough shades of night,
And never show thy head by day nor light.
Richard II. Act v, sc. 6, l. 43. [Bolingbroke]

Cain's jaw-bone, that did the first murder!
Hamlet. Act v, sc. 1, l. 85. [Hamlet] The only use of "jaw-bone." Cain is mentioned six times.

12
Take him over the costard with the hilts of thy sword, and then we will chop him in the malmsey-butt in the next room.
Richard III. Act i, sc. 4, l. 159. [Murderer] "Malmsey-butt" is repeated in l. 277.

Erroneous vassal! the great King of kings
Hath in the tables of his law commanded
That thou shalt do no murder.
Richard III. Act i, sc. 4, l. 200. [Clarence] "Erroneous" occurs again in *III Henry VI,* ii, 5, 90.

1
How fain, like Pilate, would I wash my hands
Of this most grievous guilty murder done!
Richard III. Act i, sc. 4, l. 279. [Murderer]
Done a drunken slaughter, and defaced
The precious image of our dear Redeemer.
Richard III. Act ii, sc. 1, l. 122. [King Edward]

2
The tyrannous and bloody deed is done,
The most arch act of piteous massacre
That ever yet this land was guilty of.
Richard III. Act iv, sc. 3, l. 1. [Tyrrel]
I 'll find a day to massacre them all
And raze their faction and their family.
Titus Andronicus. Act i, sc. 1, l. 450. [Tamora]
Massacres, Acts of black night.—*Titus Andronicus,* v, 1, 63.
General wreck and massacre.—*I Henry VI,* i, 1, 135.
Triumph in massacres.—*I Henry IV,* v, 4, 14.
Welcome . . . massacre.—*Richard III,* ii, 4, 53.

3
This ruthless piece of butchery.
Richard III. Act iv, sc. 3, l. 5. [Tyrrel]
Civil butchery.—*I Henry IV,* i, 1, 13. "Butchery" is used a third time in *As You Like It,* ii, 3, 27.

4
York: I shall not sleep quiet at the Tower.
Gloucester: Why, what should you fear?
York: Marry, my uncle Clarence' angry ghost:
My grandam told me he was murder'd there.
Richard III. Act iii, sc. 1, l. 142.
Tell her thou madest away her uncle Clarence,
Her uncle Rivers; yea, and for her sake,
Madest quick conveyance with her good aunt.
Richard III. Act iv, sc. 4, l. 283. [Queen Elizabeth]
Murder, stern murder, in the direst degree.
Richard III. Act v, sc. 3, l. 197. [King Richard]

5
When I was mortal, my anointed body
By thee was punched full of deadly holes.
Richard III. Act v, sc. 3, l. 124. [Ghost of Henry VI] The only use of "punched."
Most sacrilegious murder hath broke ope
The Lord's anointed temple, and stole thence
The life o' the building!
Macbeth. Act ii, sc. 3, l. 72. [Macduff] "Sacrilegious" occurs again in *Cymbeline,* v, 5, 220.

6
Tamora: Where is thy brother Bassianus? . . .
Saturninus: Poor Bassianus here lies murdered. . . .
Look, sirs, if you can find the huntsman out
That should have murder'd Bassianus here.
Tamora: How easily murder is discovered!
Titus Andronicus. Act ii, sc. 3, l. 261.
O, he hath murdered his master!
The Taming of the Shrew. Act v, sc. 1, l. 90. [Vincentio]

7
There thou mayst brain him,
Having first seized his books, or with a log
Batter his skull, or paunch him with a stake,
Or cut his wezand with thy knife.
The Tempest. Act iii, sc. 2, l. 96. [Caliban] The only use of "wezand" and of "paunch" as a verb.
Let 's alone And do the murder first.
The Tempest. Act iv, sc. 1, l. 231. [Caliban]

8
Confer with me of murder and of death:
There 's not a hollow cave or lurking-place,
No vast obscurity or misty vale,
Where bloody murder or detested rape
Can couch for fear, but I will find them out.
Titus Andronicus. Act v, sc. 2, l. 34. [Tamora] The only use of "lurking-place." "Obscurity" is repeated in *Venus and Adonis,* l. 760.
The one is Murder, Rape is the other's name.
Titus Andronicus. Act v, sc. 2, l. 157. [Titus]
Rapine and murder.—*Titus Andronicus,* v, 2, 59; 62; 83.

9
Pray thee, do on them some violent death.
Titus Andronicus. Act v, sc. 2, l. 108. [Titus]

10
I must believe you, sir:
I do; and will fetch off Bohemia for 't.
The Winter's Tale. Act i, sc. 2, l. 333. [Camillo]
I am appointed him to murder you.
Winter's Tale. Act i, sc. 2, l. 412. [Camillo]
Incense me To murder her I married.
Winter's Tale. Act v, sc. 1, l. 61. [Leontes]

II—The Murderer

11
A murderer and a villain.
Hamlet. Act iii, sc. 4, l. 96. [Hamlet]
What 's worse than murderer, that I may name it?
III Henry VI. Act v, sc. 5, l. 58. [Queen Margaret]

12
We shall be call'd purgers, not murderers.
Julius Cæsar. Act ii, sc. 1, l. 180. [Brutus] The only use of "purgers."
Play the murderer.—*Love's Labour 's Lost,* iv, 1, 8.

13
The murderers,
Steep'd in the colours of their trade, their daggers
Unmannerly breech'd with gore.
Macbeth. Act ii, sc. 3, l. 120. [Macbeth] The only use of "breech'd."
The one has my pity; not a jot the other,
Being a murderer, though he were my brother.
Measure for Measure. Act iv, sc. 2, l. 64. [Provost]

14
It cannot be but thou hast murder'd him;
So should a murderer look, so dead, so grim.
A Midsummer-Night's Dream. Act iii, sc. 2, l. 56. [Hermia]
Yet you, the murderer, look as bright, as clear,
As yonder Venus in her glittering sphere.
A Midsummer-Night's Dream. Act iii, sc. 2, l. 60. [Demetrius]

1
An honourable murderer, if you will;
For nought I did in hate, but all in honour.
Othello. Act v, sc. 2, l. 294. [Othello]
Bloody murderer.—*II Henry VI,* iii, 1, 128.
Charitable murderer.—*Titus Andronicus,* ii, 3, 178.
Crafty murderer.—*II Henry VI,* iii, 1, 254.
Egregious murderer.—*Cymbeline,* v, 5, 211.
Present murderer.—*Pericles,* iv, Gower, 38.
Traitor murderer.—*Romeo and Juliet,* iii, 5, 85.

2
That foul defacer of God's handiwork.
Richard III. Act iv, sc. 4, l. 51. [Queen Margaret] The only use of "defacer." "Defacers" occurs in *Henry VIII,* v, 3, 41: "Defacers of a public peace."
Strike the murderer dead.—*Richard III,* i, 2, 64. See under EARTH.

3
Doth she not think me an old murderer,
Now I have stain'd the childhood of our joy
With blood removed but little from her own?
Romeo and Juliet. Act iii, sc. 3, l. 94. [Romeo]

4
Find out murderers in their guilty caves.
Titus Andronicus. Act v, sc. 2, l. 52. [Titus]
Show me a murderer, I 'll deal with him.
Titus Andronicus. Act v, sc. 2, l. 93. [Demetrius]
When thou find'st a man that 's like thyself,
Good Murder, stab him; he 's a murderer.
Titus Andronicus. Act v, sc. 2, l. 99. [Titus]

MUSIC

See also Harmony

5
Music, moody food Of us that trade in love.
Antony and Cleopatra. Act ii, sc. 5, l. 1. [Cleopatra]
Make battery to our ears with loud music.
Antony and Cleopatra. Act ii, sc. 7, l. 115. [Enobarbus]
Loud music is too harsh for ladies' heads,
Since they love men in arms as well as beds.
Pericles. Act ii, sc. 3, l. 97. [Simonides]

6
The trumpets, sackbuts, psalteries and fifes,
Tabors and cymbals and the shouting Romans,
Make the sun dance.
Coriolanus. Act v, sc. 4, l. 52. [Messenger] The only use of "sackbuts," "psalteries," and "cymbals."

7
I would this music would come: I am advised to give her music o' mornings; they say it will penetrate. Come on; tune: if you can penetrate her with your fingering, so; we 'll try with tongue too.
Cymbeline. Act ii, sc. 3, l. 12. [Cloten]
If this penetrate, I will consider your music the better: if it do not, it is a vice in her ears, which horse-hairs and calves'-guts, nor the voice of unpaved eunuch to boot, can never amend.
Cymbeline. Act ii, sc. 3, l. 31. [Cloten] The only use of "horse-hairs," "calves'-guts," and "unpaved."
Is it not strange that sheeps' guts should hale souls out of men's bodies?
Much Ado about Nothing. Act ii, sc. 3, l. 61. [Benedick]
What music will be in him when Hector has knocked out his brains, I know not; but, I am sure, none, unless the fiddler Apollo get his sinews to make catlings on.
Troilus and Cressida. Act iii, sc. 3, l. 303. [Thersites] The only use of "catlings" (catgut). Catling is the name of a musician in *Romeo and Juliet,* iv, 5, 132.

8
I have assailed her with music.
Cymbeline. Act ii, sc. 3, l. 44. [Cloten]
Music, awake her; strike!
Winter's Tale. Act v, sc. 3, l. 98. [Paulina]
Strike up, pipers.—*Much Ado about Nothing,* v, 4, 131. The only mention of pipers.

9
If that his head have ear in music.
Cymbeline. Act iii, sc. 4, l. 178. [Pisanio]

10
Come, come music! come, the recorders!
Hamlet. Act iii, sc. 2, l. 302. [Hamlet] "Recorders" is repeated in l. 360.
Whisper music to my weary spirit.
II Henry IV. Act iv, sc. 5, l. 3. [King Henry]
Let the music knock it.
Henry VIII. Act i, sc. 4, l. 108. [King Henry]
Now, music, sound, and sing your solemn hymn.
Much Ado about Nothing. Act v, sc. 3, l. 11. [Claudio]
Give me some music.—*Twelfth Night,* ii, 4, 1.
Give us some music.—*As You Like It,* ii, 7, 173.
Let him ply his music.—*Hamlet,* ii, 1, 73.
Let music sound.—*The Merchant of Venice,* iii, 2, 43.
Sound, music.—*A Midsummer-Night's Dream,* iv, 1, 90.
Louder the music there!—*King Lear,* iv, 7, 25.
Play, music.—*As You Like It,* v, 4, 184.
Musicians, play.—*Romeo and Juliet,* i, 5, 27.

11
Lull'd with sound of sweetest melody.
II Henry IV, iii, 1, 14. See under SLEEP.
Pretty buzzing melody.—*Titus Andronicus,* iii, 2, 64.
Sweet melody.—*Midsummer-Night's Dream,* i, 1, 189.

12
Orpheus with his lute made trees,
And the mountain tops that freeze,
Bow themselves when he did sing:
To his music plants and flowers
Ever sprung; as sun and showers
There had made a lasting spring.

Every thing that heard him play,
Even the billows of the sea,
Hung their heads, and then lay by.
In sweet music is such art,
Killing care and grief of heart
Fall asleep, or hearing, die.
Henry VIII. Act iii, sc. 1, l. 3. [Song]

Lorenzo: With sweetest touches pierce your mistress' ear
And draw her home with music.
Jessica: I am never merry when I hear sweet music.
Lorenzo: The reason is, your spirits are attentive:
For do but note a wild and wanton herd,
Or race of youthful and unhandled colts,
Fetching mad bounds, bellowing and neighing loud,
Which is the hot condition of their blood;
If they but hear perchance a trumpet sound,
Or any air of music touch their ears,
You shall perceive them make a mutual stand,
Their savage eyes turn'd to a modest gaze
By the sweet power of music: therefore the poet
Did feign that Orpheus drew trees, stones and floods;
Since nought so stockish, hard and full of rage,
But music for the time doth change his nature.
The man that hath no music in himself,
Nor is not moved with concord of sweet sounds,
Is fit for treasons, stratagems and spoils.

The Merchant of Venice. Act v, sc. 1, l. 67. The only use of "stockish." "Unhandled" is repeated in *Henry VIII,* iii, 2, 58.

For Orpheus' lute was strung with poets' sinews,
Whose golden touch could soften steel and stones,
Make tigers tame and huge leviathans
Forsake unsounded deeps to dance on sands.

The Two Gentlemen of Verona. Act iii, sc. 2, l. 78. [Proteus] "Unsounded" is repeated in *II Henry VI,* iii, 1, 57.

To recreate himself when he hath sung,
The tiger would be tame and gently hear him.

Venus and Adonis, l. 1095. The only use of "recreate." "Recreation" occurs in *Julius Cæsar,* iii, 2, 256.

1 Bid the music leave,
They are harsh and heavy to me.

Henry VIII. Act iv, sc. 2, l. 94. [Katharine]

Heavy music.—*I Henry VI,* iv, 2, 40.

2 As sweet and musical
As bright Apollo's lute, strung with his hair.

Love's Labour's Lost. Act iv, sc. 3, l. 342. [Biron]

3
Mariana: I cry you mercy, sir; and well could wish
You had not found me here so musical:
Let me excuse me, and believe me so,
My mirth it much displeased, but pleased my woe.
Duke: 'Tis good; though music oft hath such a charm
To make bad good, and good provoke to harm.

Measure for Measure. Act iv, sc. 1, l. 10.

Then should you be nothing but musical, for you are altogether governed by humours.

I Henry IV. Act iii, sc. 1, l. 236. [Lady Percy]

4
The vile squealing of the wry-neck'd fife.

The Merchant of Venice. Act ii, sc. 5, l. 30. [Shylock] The only use of "squealing" and "wry-neck'd."

5
And what is music then? Then music is
Even as the flourish when true subjects bow
To a new-crowned monarch.

The Merchant of Venice. Act iii, sc. 2, l. 48. [Portia] "New-crowned" occurs again in *King John,* iv, 2, 35.

Here will we sit and let the sounds of music
Creep in our ears.

The Merchant of Venice. Act v, sc. 1, l. 55. [Lorenzo]

6
There 's not the smallest orb which thou behold'st
But in his motion like an angel sings,
Still quiring to the young-eyed cherubins.

The Merchant of Venice. Act v, sc. 1, l. 60. [Lorenzo] The only use of "quiring" and "young-eyed."

Music from the spheres.—*Twelfth Night,* iii, 1, 121.

The music of the spheres!—*Pericles,* v, 1, 231.

7
Titania: What, wilt thou hear some music, my sweet love?
Bottom: I have a reasonable good ear in music. Let 's have the tongs and the bones.

A Midsummer-Night's Dream. Act iv, sc. 1, l. 29. The only use of the phrase "good ear," and of "tongs" and "bones" in the sense of rude musical instruments.

Music, ho! music, such as charmeth sleep!

A Midsummer-Night's Dream. Act iv, sc. 1, l. 87. [Titania]

8
I have known when there was no music with him but the drum and the fife; and now had he rather hear the tabor and the pipe.

Much Ado about Nothing. Act ii, sc. 3, l. 13. [Benedick]

9
The general so likes your music, that he desires you, for love's sake, to make no more noise with it. . . . to hear music the general does not greatly care.

Othello. Act iii, sc. 1, l. 12. [Clown]

He hears no music.—*Julius Cæsar,* i, 2, 204.

10
If you have any music that may not be heard, to 't again.

Othello. Act iii, sc. 1, l. 16. [Clown]

11
The rough and woeful music that we have,
Cause it to sound, beseech you.
The viol once more.

Pericles. Act iii, sc. 2, l. 88. [Cerimon] The viol is mentioned again in i, 1, 81, and in *Richard* II, i, 3, 162.

Most heavenly music!
It nips me unto listening.

Pericles. Act v, sc. 1, l. 234. [Pericles]

Heavenly music.—*The Tempest,* v, 1, 52.

Excellent music.—*Much Ado about Nothing,* ii, 3, 87.

Healthful music.—*Hamlet,* iii, 4, 141.

Softest music.—*Romeo and Juliet,* ii, 2, 167.

12 Music do I hear?
Ha, ha! keep time: how sour sweet music is,

When time is broke and no proportion kept!
So is it in the music of men's lives.
And here have I the daintiness of ear
To check time broke in a disorder'd string;
But for the concord of my state and time
Had not an ear to hear my true time broke.
Richard II. Act v, sc. 5, l. 41. [King Richard] The only use of "daintiness."

This music mads me; let it sound no more;
For though it have holp madmen to their wits,
In me it seems it will make wise men mad.
Richard II. Act v, sc. 5, l. 61. [King Richard]

1
Thou sing'st sweet music.
Richard III. Act iv, sc. 2, l. 79. [King Richard]

Deep-sweet music.—*Venus and Adonis,* l. 432. The only use of "deep-sweet."

Marvellous sweet music.—*The Tempest,* iii, 3, 19. "Sweet music" occurs eight times in the plays.

Rich music's tongue.
Romeo and Juliet. Act ii, sc. 6, l. 27. [Romeo]

2
Music to hear, why hear'st thou music sadly?
Sonnets. No. viii.

The true concord of well-tuned sounds.
Sonnets. No. viii. "Well-tuned" is repeated in *Titus Andronicus,* ii, 3, 18: "Well-tuned horns"; and in *Othello,* ii, 1, 202: "You are well tuned now!"

Mark how one string, sweet husband to another,
Strikes each in each by mutual ordering.
Sonnets. No. viii.

That wild music burthens every bough.
Sonnets. No. cii.

How oft, when thou, my music, music play'st,
Upon that blessed wood whose motion sounds
With thy sweet fingers, when thou gently sway'st
The wiry concord that mine ear confounds,
Do I envy those jacks that nimble leap
To kiss the tender inward of thy hand,
Whilst my poor lips, which should that harvest reap,
At the wood's boldness by thee blushing stand!
To be so tickled, they would change their state
And situation with those dancing chips,
O'er whom thy fingers walk with gentle gait,
Making dead wood more blest than living lips.
Since saucy jacks so happy are in this,
Give them thy fingers, me thy lips to kiss.
Sonnets. No. cxxviii. The only use of "chips." "Situation" is repeated in *II Henry IV,* i, 3, 51, and in *Henry V,* iv, 7, 27.

3
Procure me music ready when he wakes,
To make a dulcet and a heavenly sound.
The Taming of the Shrew. Induction, sc. 1, l. 50. [Lord]

Wilt thou have music? hark! Apollo plays.
The Taming of the Shrew. Induction, sc. 2, l. 37. [Lord]

Music and poesy use to quicken you.
The Taming of the Shrew. Act i, sc. 1, l. 36. [Tranio]

4
I did but tell her she mistook her frets,
And bow'd her hand to teach her fingering.
The Taming of the Shrew. Act ii, sc. 1, l. 150. [Hortensio] "Frets" in this sense is used again in l. 153, and occurs in no other scene.

To learn the order of my fingering,
I must begin with rudiments of art.
The Taming of the Shrew. Act iii, sc. 1, l. 65. [Hortensio]

You would be fingering.—*The Two Gentlemen of Verona,* i, 2, 101. "Fingering" is used a fourth time in *Cymbeline,* ii, 3, 15. See above.

5
To know the cause why music was ordain'd!
Was it not to refresh the mind of man
After his studies or his usual pain?
The Taming of the Shrew. Act iii, sc. 1, l. 10. [Lucentio]

6
Where should this music be? i' the air or the earth?
It sounds no more: and, sure, it waits upon
Some god o' the island. Sitting on a bank,
Weeping again the king my father's wreck,
This music crept by me upon the waters,
Allaying both their fury and my passion
With its sweet air.
Tempest. Act i, sc. 2, l. 387. [Ferdinand]

Music i' the air.—*Antony and Cleopatra,* iv, 3, 13.

7
Upon mine honour, sir, I heard a humming,
And that a strange one too, which did awake me.
The Tempest. Act ii, sc. 1, l. 317. [Gonzalo] "Humming" is repeated in *Pericles,* iii, 1, 64.

Then I beat my tabor;
At which, like unback'd colts, they prick'd their ears,
Advanced their eyelids, lifted up their noses
As they smelt music: so I charm'd their ears
That calf-like they my lowing follow'd through
Tooth'd briars, sharp furzes, pricking goss and thorns,
Which enter'd their frail shins.
The Tempest. Act iv, sc. 1, l. 175. [Ariel] The only use of "unback'd," "calf-like," "tooth'd," "furzes," and "goss." "Lowing" is repeated in iv, 1, 179; and "furze" occurs in i, 1, 70; neither is used in any other play.

Come with better music.—*Timon of Athens,* i, 2, 252.

The music would not please.—*Titus Andronicus,* ii, 1, 70.

8
Pandarus: What music is this?
Servant: I do but partly know, sir: it is music in parts.
Pandarus: Know you the musicians?
Servant: Wholly, sir.
Pandarus: Who play they to?
Servant: To the hearers, sir.
Pandarus: At whose pleasure, friend?
Servant: At mine, sir, and theirs that love music.
Troilus and Cressida. Act iii, sc. 1, l. 18.

Here is good broken music.
Troilus and Cressida, iii, 1, 52. [Pandarus]

Broken music.—*As You Like It,* i, 2, 150; *Henry V,* v, 2, 263.
Current music.—*Henry VIII,* i, 3, 47.
Defunctive music.—*The Phœnix and the Turtle,* l. 14.
Lawful music.—*Pericles,* i, 1, 82.

1
If music be the food of love, play on;
Give me excess of it, that, surfeiting,
The appetite may sicken, and so die.
That strain again! it had a dying fall:
O, it came o'er my ear like the sweet sound,
That breathes upon a bank of violets,
Stealing and giving odour.
Twelfth Night. Act i, sc. 1, l. 1. [Duke]
I can sing
And speak to him in many sorts of music.
Twelfth Night. Act i, sc. 2, l. 57. [Viola]
We shall hear music.—*Troilus and Cressida,* i, 3, 74.

2 To their instruments
Tune a deploring dump.
Two Gentlemen of Verona. Act iii, sc. 2, l. 84. [Proteus] The only use of "deploring."
'When griping grief the heart doth wound,
And doleful dumps the mind oppress,' . . .
'Then music with her silver sound
With speedy help doth lend redress.'
Romeo and Juliet. Act iv, sc. 5, l. 128. [Peter] For "dumps" see under MELANCHOLY.

3
Now must we to her window,
And give some evening music to her ear.
The Two Gentlemen of Verona. Act iv, sc. 2, l. 16. [Proteus]
Let's tune, and to it lustily awhile.
The Two Gentlemen of Verona. Act iv, sc. 2, l. 25. [Thurio]

4
The music likes you not.
The Two Gentlemen of Verona. Act iv, sc. 2, l. 55. [Host]
Host: I perceive you delight not in music.
Julia: Not a whit, when it jars so.
The Two Gentlemen of Verona. Act iv, sc. 2, l. 66.

II—The Musician

5
And those musicians that shall play to you
Hang in the air a thousand leagues from hence.
I Henry IV. Act iii, sc. 1, l. 226. [Glendower]

6
Balthazar: There 's not a note of mine that 's worth the noting.
Don Pedro: Why, these are very crotchets that he speaks;
Note, notes, forsooth, and nothing.
Much Ado about Nothing. Act ii, sc. 3, l. 57.
I will carry no crotchets: I 'll re you, I 'll fa you; do you note me?
Romeo and Juliet. Act iv, sc. 5, l. 120. [Peter]
Ut, re, sol, la, mi, fa.—*Love's Labour's Lost,* iv, 2, 102.
A re; . . . B mi.—*The Taming of the Shrew,* iii, 1, 74.
D sol re: . . . E la mi.—*The Taming of the Shrew,* iii, 1, 77.

7
Peter: Musicians, O, musicians, 'Heart's ease, Heart's ease:' O, an you will have me live, play 'Heart's ease.'
First Musician: Why 'Heart's ease'?
Peter: O, musicians, because my heart itself plays 'My heart is full of woe:' O, play me some merry dump, to comfort me.
Romeo and Juliet. Act iv, sc. 5, l. 102.

8
A fine musician to instruct our mistress.
The Taming of the Shrew. Act i, sc. 2, l. 174. [Hortensio] "Fine musician" is repeated in iii, 1, 63.
Admirable musician.—*Othello,* iv, 1, 199.
Excellent musician.—*Much Ado about Nothing,* ii, 3, 36.
Good musician.—*The Taming of the Shrew,* ii, 1, 145.
Quaint musician.—*The Taming of the Shrew,* iii, 2, 149.

9
While she did call me rascal fiddler
And twangling Jack.
The Taming of the Shrew. Act ii, sc. 1, l. 158. [Hortensio] "Twangling" is repeated in *The Tempest,* iii, 2, 146.
Fiddler, forbear.—*The Taming of the Shrew,* iii, 1, 1. "Fiddler" is used a third time in *Troilus and Cressida,* iii, 3, 305: "Fiddler Apollo."

10
Some gentlemen well skill'd in music.
The Two Gentlemen of Verona. Act iii, sc. 2, l. 92. [Thurio]

MUSING, see under Melancholy

MUTE

11
All the rest is mute.
All's Well that Ends Well. Act ii, sc. 3, l. 83. [Helena]

12
Thou wilt be a voluntary mute to my design.
Cymbeline. Act iii, sc. 5, l. 158. [Cloten]
In my hearing be you mute and dumb.
The Rape of Lucrece, l. 1123.
Mute and dumb.—*Hamlet,* ii, 2, 137.
Hush, and be mute.—*The Tempest,* iv, 1, 126.
My servant straight was mute.—*Love's Labour's Lost,* v, 2, 277.
Your mute I 'll be.—*Twelfth Night,* i, 2, 62.
Turkish mute.—*Henry V,* i, 2, 232.

13
The duke was dumb and could not speak a word.
II Henry VI. Act iii, sc. 2, l. 32. [Cardinal]
I am dumb.—*Merchant of Venice,* v, 1, 279.
Quite dumb?—*A Midsummer-Night's Dream,* v, 1, 334.

14
I left him almost speechless.
King John. Act v, sc. 6, l. 24. [Hubert]
He . . . was speechless.—*Julius Cæsar,* i, 2, 255.
Speechless tongues.—*Pericles,* i, 1, 36.

15 They spake not a word;
But, like dumb statuas or breathing stones,
Gazed each on other, and look'd deadly pale.
Richard III, iii, 7, 24. [Buckingham]

1
You should have banged the youth into dumbness.
Twelfth Night. Act iii, sc. 2, l. 24. [Fabian] "Banged" is repeated in *Othello,* ii, 1, 21.
Bequeath to death your dumbness.
The Winter's Tale, v, 3, 102. See 870: 3.
Dumbness of the gesture.—*Timon of Athens,* i, 1, 33.
Cunning in dumbness.—*Troilus and Cressida,* iii, 2, 140.
Speech in their dumbness.—*The Winter's Tale,* v, 2, 15.
Prince of dumbness.—*King Lear,* iv, 1, 63. The only uses of "dumbness."
Dumb action.—*Titus Andronicus,* iii, 2, 40.
Dumb discourse.—*The Tempest,* iii, 3, 39.
Dumb innocent.—*All's Well that Ends Well,* iv, 3, 214.
Dumb man.—*Much Ado about Nothing,* i, 1, 212; *Coriolanus,* ii, 1, 278.
Dumb mouths.—*Julius Cæsar,* iii, 1, 260; iii, 2, 229.
Dumb silence.—*The Two Gentlemen of Verona,* iii, 1, 207.

MUTINY

2 Worshipful mutiners,
Your valour puts well forth.
Coriolanus. Act i, sc. 1, l. 254. [Marcius]
If you prove a mutineer,—the next tree!
The Tempest. Act iii, sc. 2, l. 41. [Stephano] The only uses of "mutiners" and "mutineer."
3
This mutiny were better put in hazard,
Than stay, past doubt, for greater.
Coriolanus. Act ii, sc. 3, l. 264. [Brutus]
4
I 'll either make thee stoop and bend thy knee,
Or sack this country with a mutiny.
I Henry VI. Act v, 3, 61. [Winchester]
Myself have calm'd their spleenful mutiny.
II Henry VI. Act iii, sc. 2, l. 128. [Warwick] "Spleenful" is repeated in *Titus Andronicus,* ii, 3, 191: "Spleenful sons."
5
There is a mutiny in 's mind.
Henry VIII. Act iii, sc. 2, l. 120. [King]
6
Good friends, sweet friends, let me not stir you up
To such a sudden flood of mutiny.
Julius Cæsar. Act iii, sc. 2, l. 213. [Antony]
Ruffle up your spirits and put a tongue
In every wound of Cæsar that should move
The stones of Rome to rise and mutiny.
Julius Cæsar. Act iii, sc. 2, l. 232. [Antony]
We 'll mutiny.—*Julius Cæsar,* iii, 2, 235.
7
Away, I say; go out, and cry a mutiny.
Othello. Act ii, sc. 3, l. 157. [Iago]
From ancient grudge break to new mutiny.
Romeo and Juliet. Prologue, l. 3.
You 'll make a mutiny among my guests!
Romeo and Juliet. Act i, 5, 82. [Capulet]
8
With herself is she in mutiny.
The Rape of Lucrece, l. 1153.
What mutiny!—*Troilus and Cressida,* i, 3, 96.
9
This mutiny each part doth so surprise
That from their dark beds once more leap her eyes.
Venus and Adonis, l. 1049.
Mutinous members.—*Coriolanus,* i, 1, 153.
Mutinous parts.—*Coriolanus,* i, 1, 115.
Mutinous people.—*Coriolanus,* i, 2, 11.
Mutinous winds.—*Coriolanus,* v, 3, 59; *The Tempest,* v, 1, 42. "Mutinous" occurs seven times in the plays, four times in *Coriolanus.*

MYSTERY

10
Why, what an intricate impeach is this!
I think you all have drunk of Circe's cup.
The Comedy of Errors. Act v, sc. 1, l. 269. [Duke] The only use of "intricate." "Impeach" is used once more as a noun in *III Henry VI,* i, 4, 60: "Impeach of valour." Circe is mentioned again in *I Henry VI,* v, 3, 35.
11 Those mysteries which heaven
Will not have earth to know.
Coriolanus. Act iv, sc. 2, l. 35. [Volumnia]
Nature's mystery.—*All's Well that Ends Well,* v, 3, 103.
12
You would pluck out the heart of my mystery.
Hamlet. Act iii, sc. 2, l. 381. [Hamlet]
13
And take upon 's the mystery of things,
As if we were God's spies.
King Lear. Act v, sc. 3, l. 16. [Cordelia]
Mysteries of Hecate.—*King Lear,* i, 1, 112. Hecate is mentioned seven times in the plays.
Strange mysteries.—*Henry VIII,* i, 3, 2.
14
Provost: Sirrah, here 's a fellow will help you to-morrow in your execution. . . . He hath been a bawd.
Abhorson: A bawd, sir? fie upon him! he will discredit our mystery. . . .
Pompey: Do you call, sir, your occupation a mystery?
Abhorson: Ay, sir; a mystery.
Pompey: Painting, sir, I have heard say, is a mystery; and your whores, sir, being members of my occupation, using painting, do prove my occupation a mystery: but what mystery there should be in hanging, if I should be hanged, I cannot imagine.
Abhorson: Sir, it is a mystery.
Measure for Measure. Act iv, sc. 2, l. 23.
15
Your mystery, your mystery: nay, dispatch.
Othello. Act iv, sc. 2, l. 30. [Othello]
16
Seal up the mouth of outrage for a while,
Till we can clear these ambiguities,
And know their spring, their head, their true descent.
Romeo and Juliet, v, 3, 216. [Verona] "Ambiguities" occurs again in *Henry V,* v, 1, 48. "Ambiguous" is used in *Hamlet,* i, 5, 178.
17
This mystery remains undiscovered.
Winter's Tale, v, 2, 130. [Autolycus]

N

NAIL

1
'Tis too late to pare her nails now.
All's Well that Ends Well, v, 2, 31. See under FORTUNE for full quotation.
Every one may pare his nails with a wooden dagger.
Henry V. Act iv, sc. 4, l. 76. [Boy]
Let not him that plays the lion pare his nails, for they shall hang out for the lion's claws.
A Midsummer-Night's Dream. Act iv, sc. 2, l. 41. [Bottom]
Like a mad lad, Pare thy nails, dad.
Twelfth Night. Act iv, sc. 2, l. 139. [Clown]
2
Some devils ask but the parings of one's nail.
The Comedy of Errors, iv, 3, 72. See under DEVIL for full quotation.
The very parings of our nails.—*I Henry VI,* iii, 1, 102. "Parings" is used a third time in *King Lear,* i, 4, 206.
3
Katharine: Comment appelez-vous les ongles?
Alice: Les ongles? nous les appelons de nails.
Henry V. Act iii, sc. 4, l. 16. [Alice] The only uses of "ongles."
4
And with my nails digg'd stones out of the ground,
To hurl at the beholders of my shame.
I Henry VI. Act i, sc. 4, l. 45. [Talbot]
5
Could I come near your beauty with my nails,
I 'ld set my ten commandments in your face.
II Henry VI. Act i, sc. 3, l. 144. [Duchess of Gloucester] This is the only instance in the plays where "ten commandments" is used to indicate the finger-nails, but the phrase, in its usual meaning, occurs in *Measure for Measure,* i, 2. 8.
If I thought that, I tell thee, homicide,
These nails should rend that beauty from my cheeks.
Richard III. Act i, sc. 2, l. 125. [Lady Anne]
But that still use of grief makes wild grief tame,
My tongue should to thy ears not name my boys
Till that my nails were anchor'd in thine eyes.
Richard III. Act iv, sc. 4, l. 229. [Queen Elizabeth] The only use of "anchor'd."
With her nails She'll flay thy wolvish visage.
King Lear. Act i, sc. 4, l. 329. [King Lear] The only use of "flay." "Wolvish" occurs again in *The Merchant of Venice,* iv, 1, 138.
Let Patient Octavia plough thy visage up
With her prepared nails.
Antony and Cleopatra. Act iv, sc. 12, l. 37. [Cleopatra]
6
How these vain weak nails
May tear a passage through the flinty ribs
Of this hard world, my ragged prison walls,
And, for they cannot, die in their own pride.
Richard II. Act v, sc. 5, l. 19. [King Richard]
7
We may blow our nails together, and fast it fairly out.
The Taming of the Shrew. Act i, sc. 1, l. 108. [Gremio]
The shepherd, blowing of his nails.
III Henry VI, ii, 5, 3. See under DAWN.
Dick the shepherd blows his nail.
Love's Labour's Lost, v, 2, 923. See under WINTER.
8
Thou mayst knock a nail into his head.
The Tempest. Act iii, sc. 2, l. 69. [Caliban]
9
As one nail by strength drives out another.
The Two Gentlemen of Verona, ii, 4, 193. See under LOVE for full quotation.
One fire drives out one fire; one nail, one nail.
Coriolanus, iv, 7, 54.

NAKEDNESS

10 Rather on Nilus' mud
Lay me stark naked.
Antony and Cleopatra. Act v, sc. 2, l. 58. [Cleopatra]
And stood stark naked on the brook's green brim.
The Passionate Pilgrim, l. 80.
Strip your sword stark naked.
Twelfth Night. Act iii, sc. 4, l. 274. [Sir Toby] The only uses of "stark naked."
All naked.—*Sonnets,* xxvi.
Being naked.—*Coriolanus,* i, 10, 20.
Naked to mine enemies.—*Henry VIII,* iii, 2, 457.
Naked as I am.—*Othello,* v, 2, 258.
11
I am set naked on your kingdom.
Hamlet. Act iv, sc. 7, l. 44. [King]
Leave you naked.—*Measure for Measure,* iii, 1, 73.
12 With presented nakedness out-face
The winds and persecutions of the sky.
King Lear. Act ii, sc. 3, l. 11. [Edgar]
13 Nothing I'll bear from thee
But nakedness, thou detestable town!
Timon of Athens. Act iv, sc. 1, l. 32. [Timon]
Go naked.—*Timon of Athens,* v, 1, 70.

NAME

14
I am from humble, he from honour'd name.
All's Well that Ends Well. Act i, sc. 3, l. 162. [Helena]
My low and humble name to propagate.
All's Well that Ends Well. Act ii, sc. 1, l. 200. [Helena]
His name with zealous fervour sanctify.
All's Well that Ends Well. Act iii, sc. 4, l. 11. [Steward]

1 Pompey's name strikes more
Than could his war resisted.
Antony and Cleopatra. Act i, sc. 4, l. 54. [Messenger] See under INFLUENCE.

More laugh'd at, that I should
Once name you derogately, when to sound your name
It not concern'd me.
Antony and Cleopatra. Act ii, sc. 2, l. 33. [Cæsar] The only use of "derogately." "Derogation" occurs in *Cymbeline,* ii, 1, 47, and "derogate" twice in *Cymbeline* and once in *King Lear.*

2 The last she spake
Was 'Antony! most noble Antony!'
Then in the midst a tearing groan did break
The name of Antony; it was divided
Between her heart and lips: she render'd life,
Thy name so buried in her.
Antony and Cleopatra. Act iv, sc. 14, l. 30. [Mardian]

3
She robs thee of thy name.
As You Like It. Act i, sc. 3, l. 82. [Duke]

Nay, I care not for their names; they owe me nothing.
As You Like It. Act ii, sc. 5, l. 21. [Jaques]

4 No man hath a name,
By falsehood and corruption doth it shame.
The Comedy of Errors. Act ii, sc. 1, l. 112. [Adriana]

5
How can she thus call us by our names?
Unless it be by inspiration.
The Comedy of Errors. Act ii, sc. 2, l. 168. [Antipholus of Syracuse]

Sweet mistress,—what your name is else I know not,
Nor by what wonder you do hit of mine.
The Comedy of Errors. Act iii, sc. 2, l. 29. [Antipholus of Syracuse]

Every one doth call me by my name.
The Comedy of Errors. Act iv, sc. 3, l. 3. [Antipholus of Syracuse]

Yet one time he did call me by my name.
Coriolanus. Act v, sc. 1, l. 9. [Cominius]

6
O villain! thou hast stolen both mine office and my name.
The one ne'er got me credit, the other mickle blame.
If thou hadst been Dromio to-day in my place,
Thou wouldst have changed thy face for a name or thy name for an ass.
The Comedy of Errors. Act iii, sc. 1, l. 44. [Dromio of Ephesus]

Dost thou think
I 'll grace thee with that robbery, thy stol'n name?
Coriolanus. Act v, sc. 6, l. 88. [Aufidius]

They would truncheon you out, for taking their names upon you before you had earned them.
II Henry IV. Act ii, sc. 4, l. 153. [Doll] The only use of "truncheon" as a verb.

7
Know, Rome, that all alone Marcius did fight
Within Corioli gates; where he hath won,
With fame, a name to Caius Marcius; these
In honour follows Coriolanus.
Welcome to Rome, renowned Coriolanus!
Coriolanus. Act ii, sc. 1, l. 179. [Herald]

Aufidius: Whence comest thou? what wouldst thou? thy name?
Coriolanus: If, Tullus,
Not yet thou knowest me, and, seeing me, dost not
Think me for the man I am, necessity
Commands me name myself.
Aufidius: What is thy name?
Coriolanus: A name unmusical to the Volscians' ears,
And harsh in sound to thine.
Aufidius: Say, what 's thy name? . . .
Coriolanus: My name is Caius Marcius, who hath done
To thee particularly and to all the Volsces
Great hurt and mischief; thereto witness may
My surname, Coriolanus; the painful service,
The extreme dangers and the drops of blood
Shed for my thankless country are requited
But with that surname: a good memory,
And witness of the malice and displeasure
Which thou shouldst bear me: only that name remains.
Coriolanus. Act iv, sc. 5, l. 58. The only use of "unmusical." "Particularly" is repeated in *Timon of Athens,* i, 1, 46.

Tullus Aufidius,
The second name of men, obeys his points
As if he were his officer.
Coriolanus. Act iv, sc. 6, l. 125. [Cominius]

Coriolanus
He would not answer to; forbade all names;
He was a kind of nothing, titleless,
Till he had forged himself a name o' the fire
Of burning Rome.
Coriolanus. Act v, sc. 1, l. 11. [Cominius] The only use of "titleless."

The man was noble,
But with his last attempt he wiped it out;
Destroy'd his country, and his name remains
To the ensuing age abhorr'd.
Coriolanus. Act v, sc. 3, l. 145. [Volumnia]

8
Thou, Leonatus, art the lion's whelp;
The fit and apt construction of thy name
Being Leo-natus, doth import so much.
The piece of tender air, thy virtuous daughter,
Which we call 'mollis aer;' and 'mollis aer'
We term it 'mulier:' which 'mulier' I divine
Is this most constant wife.
Cymbeline. Act v, sc. 5, l. 378. [Soothsayer] The only use of "mollis aer" and "mulier." "Mulieres" occurs in *Henry V,* i, 2, 38: "Mulieres ne succedant."

9
Horatio: And your poor servant ever.
Hamlet: Sir, my good friend; I 'll change that name with you.
Hamlet. Act i, sc. 2, l. 162.

As school-maids change their names
By vain though apt affection.
Measure for Measure. Act i, sc. 4, l. 47. [Isabella] The only use of "school-maids."

1
Trembling even at the name of Mortimer.
I Henry IV. Act i, sc. 3, l. 144. [Hotspur]

Good cousin Hotspur,
For by that name as oft as Lancaster
Doth speak of you, his cheek looks pale.
I Henry IV. Act ii, sc. 1, l. 7. [Glendower]

2
Renowned Douglas, whose . . . great name in arms
Holds from all soldiers chief majority.
I Henry IV. Act iii, sc. 2, l. 107. [King Henry]

Take the odds Of his great name.
I Henry IV, v, 1, 98. See under DUELLING.

Would to God
Thy name in arms were now as great as mine!
I Henry IV. Act v, sc. 4, l. 69. [Hotspur]

Your name is great
In mouths of wisest censure.
Othello. Act ii, sc. 3, l. 192. [Othello]

3
An adopted name of privilege,
A hare-brain'd Hotspur, govern'd by a spleen.
I Henry IV. Act v, sc. 2, l. 18. [Worcester] "Hare-brain'd" is repeated in *I Henry VI*, i, 2, 37: "Hare-brain'd slaves."

A field
Where nothing but the sound of Hotspur's name
Did seem defensible.
II Henry IV. Act ii, sc. 3, l. 36. [Lady Percy] "Defensible" is repeated in *Henry V*, iii, 3, 50.

4
If we, with thrice such powers left at home,
Cannot defend our own doors from the dog,
Let us be worried and our nation lose
The name of hardiness and policy.
II Henry IV. Act i, sc. 2, l. 217. [Canterbury] "Hardiness" is repeated in *Cymbeline*, iii, 6, 22.

Name of craft.—*The Merry Wives of Windsor*, v, 5, 239.

5
We fortify in paper and in figures,
Using the names of men instead of men:
Like one that draws the model of a house
Beyond his power to build it.
II Henry IV. Act i, sc. 3, l. 56. [Bardolph]

6
I would to God my name were not so terrible to the enemy as it is.
II Henry IV. Act i, sc. 3, l. 244. [Falstaff]

What a disgrace is it to me to remember thy name!
II Henry IV. Act ii, sc. 2, l. 15. [Prince of Wales]

I . . . told John a Gaunt he beat his own name.
II Henry IV. Act iii, sc. 2, l. 348. [Falstaff]

7
King Henry: Doth any name particular belong
Unto the lodging where I first did swoon?
Warwick: 'Tis call'd Jerusalem, my noble lord.
King Henry: Laud be to God! even there my life must end.
It hath been prophesied to me many years,
I should not die but in Jerusalem,
Which vainly I supposed the Holy Land.
II Henry IV. Act iv, sc. 5, l. 233.

8
Such fellows are perfect in the great commanders' names.
Henry V. Act iii, sc. 6, l. 75. [Gower]

9
We shall much disgrace
With four or five most vile and ragged foils,
Right ill-disposed in brawl ridiculous,
The name of Agincourt.
Henry V. Act iv, Prologue, l. 49. [Chorus] "Ill disposed" (unhyphenated) is repeated in *Troilus and Cressida*, ii, 3, 84.

Rouse him at the name of Crispian.—*Henry V*, iv, 3, 43. See GLORY, 616:7.

10
Our names,
Familiar in his mouth as household words.
Henry V. Act iv, sc. 3, l. 51. [King Henry]

Our household's name.—*I Henry VI*, iv, 6, 38.

11
So great fear of my name 'mongst them was spread
That they supposed I could rend bars of steel
And spurn in pieces posts of adamant.
I Henry VI. Act i, sc. 4, l. 50. [Talbot]

The cry of Talbot serves me for a sword;
For I have loaden me with many spoils,
Using no other weapon but his name.
I Henry VI. Act ii, sc. 1, l. 79. [Soldier]

Is this the Talbot, so much fear'd abroad
That with his name the mothers still their babes?
I Henry VI. Act ii, sc. 3, l. 16. [Countess]

O young John Talbot, I did send for thee
To tutor thee in stratagems of war,
That Talbot's name might be in thee revived
When sapless age and weak unable limbs
Shall bring thy father to his drooping chair.
I Henry VI. Act iv, sc. 5, l. 1. [Talbot] "Sapless" is repeated in ii, 5, 12, "Sapless branches," and occurs in no other play.

Is my name Talbot? and am I your son?
And shall I fly?
I Henry VI. Act iv, sc. 5, l. 12. [John Talbot]

12
Blotting your names from books of memory.
II Henry VI. Act i, sc. 1, l. 100. [Gloucester]

13
Richard: Richard, I bear thy name; I'll venge thy death. . . .
Edward: His name that valiant duke hath left with thee;
His dukedom and his chair with me is left.
III Henry VI. Act ii, sc. 1, l. 87.

Bear the name.—*I Henry VI*, iv, 4, 9; *II Henry VI*, iv, 1, 19; *Measure for Measure*, iii, 1, 39.

14
Out of ruins,
Made my name once more noble.
Henry VIII. Act ii, sc. 1, l. 114. [Buckingham]

His honour and the greatness of his name
Shall be, and make new nations.
Henry VIII. Act v, sc. 5, l. 52. [Cranmer]

1
You must be seeing christenings. . . . On my Christian conscience, this one christening will beget a thousand.
Henry VIII. Act v, sc. 4, l. 10. [Porter]
They 're come already from the christening.
Henry VIII. Act v, sc. 4. l. 87. [Chamberlain]
In christening shalt thou have two godfathers.
The Merchant of Venice. Act iv, sc. 1, l. 398. [Gratiano] See under JURY. The only uses of "christening."

2
Pluck but his name out of his heart, and turn him going.
Julius Cæsar. Act iii, sc. 3, l. 38. [Citizen]
These many, then, shall die; their names are prick'd.
Julius Cæsar. Act iv, sc. 1, l. 1. [Antony]
I will proclaim my name about the field.
Julius Cæsar. Act v, sc. 4, l. 3. [Young Cato]

3
Melun: Lead me to the revolts of England here.
Salisbury: When we were happy we had other names.
King John. Act v, sc. 4, l. 7.
These earthly godfathers of heaven's lights
That give a name to every fixed star
Have no more profit of their shining nights
Than those that walk and wot not what they are.
Love's Labour 's Lost. Act i, sc. 1, l. 88. [Biron]
Every godfather can give a name.
Love's Labour 's Lost. Act i, sc. 1, l. 93. [Biron]
Here is his name.—*Love's Labour 's Lost,* iv, 3, 203.

4
When tongues speak sweetly, then they name her name.
Love's Labour 's Lost. Act iii, sc. 1, l. 167. [Biron]
Nay, you must name his name. . . . Let him name his name, and tell them plainly he is Snug the joiner.
A Midsummer-Night's Dream. Act iii, sc. 1, l. 37. [Bottom]
Name them.—*The Comedy of Errors,* ii, 2, 97.
Name it.—*Love's Labour 's Lost,* v, 2, 239; *Richard II,* iv, 1, 304.
I will not name it.—*The Two Gentlemen of Verona,* ii, 1, 123.
Never name her.—*The Merry Wives of Windsor,* iv, 1, 65.

5
Brave Macbeth—well he deserves that name.
Macbeth. Act i, sc. 2, l. 16. [Sergeant]

6 Thou call'st thyself a hotter name
Than any is in hell.
Macbeth. Act v, sc. 7, l. 6. [Young Siward]

7
'Tis surely for a name.
Measure for Measure. Act i, sc. 2, l. 175. [Claudio]
In the ambush of my name, strike home.
Measure for Measure. Act i, sc. 3, l. 41. [Duke]

8 What 's yet in this
That bears the name of life?
Measure for Measure. Act iii, sc. 1, l. 39. [Duke] See under LIFE: LIFE AND DEATH.
He gains from his subjects the name of good by his government.
Pericles, ii, 1, 109. See under KING.
Name of action.—*Hamlet,* iii, 1, 88.
Name of death.—*Coriolanus,* iii, 1, 260.
Name of dogs.—*Macbeth,* iii, 1, 95.
Name of fault.—*The Winter's Tale,* iii, 2, 61.
Name of gentlemen.—*II Henry VI,* iv, 1, 19.
Name of God.—*Richard III,* i, 4, 210.
Name of help.—*Pericles,* i, 4, 31.
Name of honour.—*Julius Cæsar,* i, 2, 89; ii, 1, 317.
Name of jesting.—*Twelfth Night,* iii, 5, 23.
Name of magistrate.—*The Tempest,* ii, 1, 149.
Name of mercy.—*The Winter's Tale,* iii, 3, 105.
Name of pitch.—*II Henry IV,* ii, 4, 455.
Name of right.—*King John,* v, 2, 67.
Name of sanctity.—*Twelfth Night,* iii, 4, 93.
Name of traitor.—*II Henry IV,* ii, 2, 100.
Name of valour.—*II Henry VI,* v, 2, 40.
Name of wife.—*King John,* iii, 1, 314.

9
Leonato: How many gentlemen have you lost in this action?
Messenger: But few of any sort, and none of name. . . .
Beatrice: I pray you, is Signior Mountanto returned from the wars or no?
Messenger: I know none of that name, lady: there was none such on the army of any sort.
Much Ado about Nothing. Act i, sc. 1, l. 5.
None else of name; and of all other men
But five and twenty.
Henry V. Act iv, sc. 8, l. 110. [King Henry]
None else of name and noble estimate.
Richard II. Act ii, sc. 3, l. 56. [Percy]

10 Who can blot that name
With any just reproach?
Much Ado about Nothing. Act iv, sc. 1, l. 81. [Hero]

11
Fie, fie! they are not to be named, my lord,
Not to be spoken of.
Much Ado about Nothing. Act iv, sc. 1, l. 96. [Don John]
What you will have it named, even that it is.
The Taming of the Shrew. Act iv, sc. 5, l. 21. [Katharina]
He is already named.—*Macbeth,* ii, 4, 31.
Newly named.—*Coriolanus,* ii, 1, 190.
Nobly named.—*Coriolanus,* ii, 3, 251.

12
Whose names yet run smoothly in the even road of a blank verse.
Much Ado about Nothing. Act v, sc. 2, l. 33. [Margaret]

13
Ask him his name and orderly proceed
To swear him in the justice of his cause.
Richard II. Act i, sc. 3, l. 9. [King Richard]
Can sick men play so nicely with their names? . . .
Since thou dost seek to kill my name in me,

I mock my name, great king, to flatter thee.
Richard II. Act ii, sc. 1, l. 84. [King Richard]

1
Is not the king's name twenty thousand names?
Arm, arm, my name! a puny subject strikes
At thy great glory.
Richard II. Act iii, sc. 2, l. 85. [King Richard]

Must he lose
The name of king? o' God's name, let it go.
Richard II, iii, 3, 146. See under KING. "Name of King" is repeated in *King John,* ii, 1, 349; *Macbeth,* iii, 1, 58; *The Tempest,* i, 1, 18.

Sacred name of knight.—*I Henry VI,* iv, 1, 40.

2
York: Long live Henry, fourth of that name!
Bolingbroke: In God's name, I 'll ascend the regal throne.
Richard II. Act iv, sc. 1, l. 112.

The name of Henry the Fifth hales them to an hundred mischiefs.
II Henry VI. Act iv, sc. 8, l. 58. [Cade]

God save King Henry, of that name the sixth!
I Henry VI. Act iv, sc. 1, l. 2. [Winchester]

3
I have no name, no title,
No, not that name was given me at the font,
But 'tis usurp'd: alack the heavy day,
That I have worn so many winters out,
And know not now what name to call myself.
Richard II. Act iv, sc. 1, l. 255. [King Richard] "Font" occurs once again in *The Merchant of Venice,* iv, 1, 400.

4
Gloucester: He lives that loves thee better than he could.
Anne: Name him.
Gloucester: Plantagenet.
Anne: Why that was he.
Gloucester: The selfsame name, but one of better nature.
Richard III. Act i, sc. 2, l. 141.

I cry thee mercy then, for I had thought
That thou hadst call'd me all these bitter names.
Richard III. Act i, sc. 3, l. 235. [Gloucester]

Richmond! When last I was at Exeter,
The mayor in courtesy show'd me the castle,
And call'd it Rougemont: at which name I started,
Because a bard of Ireland told me once,
I should not live long after I saw Richmond.
Richard III. Act iv, sc. 2, l. 106. [King Richard]

5
The king's name is a tower of strength.
Richard III. Act v, sc. 3, l. 12. [King Richard]

Here 's the midwife's name to 't, one Mistress Tale-porter.
The Winter's Tale. Act iv, sc. 4, l. 272. [Autolycus]

Rob me of a happy mother's name.
Richard II, v, 2, 93. See under SON.

Thy mother's name is ominous to children.
Richard III. Act iv, sc. 1, l. 41. [Queen]

Beauty's name.—*Sonnets,* cxxvii.
Cupid's name.—*Love's Labour 's Lost,* v, 2, 9.
Devils' names.—*I Henry IV,* iii, 1, 157; *The Merry Wives of Windsor,* ii, 1, 24.
Dog's name.—*Romeo and Juliet,* ii, 4, 223.
Pleasure's name.—*King Lear,* iv, 6, 123.
Prince's name.—*II Henry IV,* iv, 2, 25.
Traitor's name.—*Troilus and Cressida,* iii, 3, 6.

6
Capulet: Find those persons out
Whose names are written there. . . .
Servant: Find them out whose names are written here! . . . I am sent to find those persons whose names are here writ, and can never find what names the writing person here hath writ. I must to the learned.
Romeo and Juliet. Act i, sc. 2, l. 35.

7
Juliet: What 's he that now is going out of door?
Nurse: Marry, that, I think be young Petruchio.
Juliet: What 's he that follows there, that would not dance?
Nurse: I know not.
Juliet: Go ask his name: if he be married,
My grave is like to be my wedding bed.
Nurse: His name is Romeo, and a Montague;
The only son of your great enemy.
Romeo and Juliet. Act i, sc. 5, l. 132.

Juliet: O Romeo, Romeo! wherefore art thou Romeo?
Deny thy father and refuse thy name;
Or, if thou wilt not, be but sworn my love,
And I 'll no longer be a Capulet. . . .
'Tis but thy name that is my enemy;
Thou art thyself, though not a Montague.
What 's Montague? it is nor hand nor foot,
Nor arm, nor face, nor any other part
Belonging to a man. O, be some other name!
What 's in a name? that which we call a rose
By any other name would smell as sweet;
So Romeo would, were he not Romeo call'd,
Retain that dear perfection which he owes
Without that title. Romeo, doff thy name,
And for that name which is no part of thee
Take all myself.
Romeo: I take thee at thy word:
Call me but love, and I 'll be new baptized;
Henceforth I never will be Romeo.
Juliet: What man art thou that thus bescreen'd in night
So stumblest on my counsel?
Romeo: By a name
I know not how to tell thee who I am:
My name, dear saint, is hateful to myself,
Because it is an enemy to thee;
Had I it written, I would tear the word.
Juliet: My ears have not yet drunk a hundred words
Of that tongue's utterance, yet I know the sound:
Art thou not Romeo and a Montague?
Romeo: Neither, fair saint, if either thee dislike.
Romeo and Juliet. Act ii, sc. 2, l. 33. The only use of "bescreen'd."

1
Ah, poor my lord, what tongue shall smooth thy name,
When I, thy three-hours wife, have mangled it?
Romeo and Juliet. Act iii, sc. 2, l. 98. [Juliet]
The only use of "three-hours" as a hyphenated phrase.
As if that name,
Shot from the deadly level of a gun,
Did murder her; as that name's cursed hand
Murder'd her kinsman. O, tell me, friar, tell me,
In what vile part of this anatomy
Doth my name lodge? tell me, that I may sack
The hateful mansion.
Romeo and Juliet. Act iii, sc. 3, l. 102. [Romeo]

2
Your name from hence immortal life shall have.
Sonnets. No. lxxxi.
In my tongue
Thy sweet beloved name no more shall dwell,
Lest I, too much profane, should do it wrong
And haply of our old acquaintance tell.
Sonnets. No. lxxxix.
Naming thy name blesses an ill report.
Sonnets. No. xcv.
Budding name.—*Sonnets,* xcv.

3
And twenty more such names and men as these
Which never were nor no man ever saw.
The Taming of the Shrew. Induction, sc. 2, l. 97. [Servant]

4
He does it under name of perfect love.
The Taming of the Shrew. Act v, sc. 3, l. 12. [Katharina]
Feed'st me with the very name of meat.
The Taming of the Shrew. Act v, sc. 3, l. 32. [Katharina]
Name of love.—*Much Ado about Nothing,* i, 1, 302.

5
Jeweller: You know me, Apemantus?
Apemantus: Thou know'st I do: I call'd thee by thy name.
Timon of Athens. Act i, sc. 1, l. 185.
Seek not my name.—*Timon of Athens,* v, 4, 71.
Advance Thy name.—*Titus Andronicus,* i, 1, 238.

6 I have writ my name
Without the help of any hand at all.
Titus Andronicus. Act iv, sc. 1, l. 70. [Marcus]
I can write my name.—*II Henry VI,* iv, 2, 113. See under EDUCATION.
I write my name.—*Love's Labour's Lost,* i, 1, 156.
I'll write my name.—*Love's Labour's Lost,* i, 1, 117.
Elves, list your names.—*The Merry Wives of Windsor,* v, 5, 46.
Subscribe your names.—*Love's Labour's Lost,* i, 1, 19.

7
Brave slip, sprung from the great Andronicus,
Whose name was once our terror, now our comfort.
Titus Andronicus. Act v, sc. 1, l. 9. [Goth]

8
I'll tell you them all by their names as they pass by.
Troilus and Cressida. Act i, sc. 2, l. 198. [Pandarus]
O you gods divine!
Make Cressid's name the very crown of falsehood,
If ever she leave Troilus!
Troilus and Cressida. Act iv, sc. 2, l. 105. [Cressida]
Lose their names.—*Troilus and Cressida,* i, 3, 118.

9
Be pleased that I shake off these names you give me.
Twelfth Night. Act v, sc. 1, l. 76. [Antonio]

10
What means this passion at his name?
The Two Gentlemen of Verona. Act i, sc. 2, l. 16. [Julia]
As in revenge of thy ingratitude,
I throw thy name against the bruising stones
The Two Gentlemen of Verona. Act i, sc. 2, l. 110. [Julia]
Poor wounded name! my bosom as a bed
Shall lodge thee till thy wound be throughly heal'd.
The Two Gentlemen of Verona. Act i, sc. 2, l. 114. [Julia]
Mine own name.—*The Two Gentlemen of Verona,* i, 2, 120.

11
Now she adds honours to his hateful name.
Venus and Adonis, l. 994.

12
Let me be unrolled and my name put in the book of virtue.
The Winter's Tale. Act iv, sc. 3, l. 131. [Autolycus]
Common name.—*I Henry IV,* ii, 1, 104.
Complaining names.—*The Two Gentlemen of Verona,* i, 2, 127.
Conquering name.—*I Henry VI,* ii, 1, 26.
Different names.—*The Merry Wives of Windsor,* ii, 1, 77.
General name.—*Titus Andronicus,* ii, 3, 183; *Troilus and Cressida,* i, 3, 322.
Naked name.—*The Two Gentlemen of Verona,* ii, 4, 142.
Old name.—*Henry VIII,* iv, 1, 98.
Sole name.—*Macbeth,* iv, 3, 12.

II—Good Name

13
I would to God thou and I knew where a commodity of good names were to be bought.
I Henry IV. Act i, sc. 2, l. 92. [Falstaff]

14
I am in good name and fame with the very best.
II Henry IV. Act ii, sc. 4, l. 81. [Hostess]
He will keep that good name still.
Henry V, iii, 7, 111. See under HARM.
Good name.—*I Henry IV,* iv, 3, 35; *Timon of Athens,* v, 1, 165.
Of good name.—*II Henry IV,* i, 1, 26.

1 Hero: Indeed, he had an excellent good name.
Ursula: His excellence did earn it ere he had it.
Much Ado about Nothing. Act iii, sc. 1, l. 98.

God hath blessed you with a good name.
Much Ado about Nothing. Act iii, sc. 3, l. 13. [Dogberry]

2 Good name in man and woman, dear my lord,
Is the immediate jewel of our souls:
Who steals my purse steals trash; 'tis something, nothing;
'Twas mine, 'tis his, and has been slave to thousands;
But he that filches from me my good name
Robs me of that which not enriches him
And makes me poor indeed.
Othello. Act iii, sc. 3, l. 155. [Iago] The only use of "filches." "Filch" occurs in l. 315, and in no other play. "Filched" is used in *A Midsummer-Night's Dream,* i, 1, 36.

My good name, that senseless reputation.
The Rape of Lucrece, l. 820.

3 My unsoil'd name, the austereness of my life,
My vouch against you, and my place i' the state,
Will so your accusation overweigh,
That you shall stifle in your own report
And smell of calumny.
Measure for Measure. Act ii, sc. 4, l. 155. [Angelo] The only use of "unsoil'd" and "austereness." "Overweigh" is repeated in l. 170 of the same scene, and in *Hamlet,* iii, 2, 31.

4 My fair name,
Despite of death that lives upon my grave,
To dark dishonour's use thou shalt not have.
Richard II. Act i, sc. 1, l. 167. [Mowbray]

Fair name.—*Richard II,* i, 1, 167; *As You Like It,* v, 1, 24; *Sonnets,* cviii.
Fairer name.—*Love's Labour 's Lost,* iii, 1, 142.
High name.—*The Rape of Lucrece,* l. 108.
Honest name.—*II Henry VI,* ii, 1, 199.
Honourable name.—*I Henry VI,* iv, 5, 14.
Lawful name.—*The Merry Wives of Windsor,* iv, 6, 50.
Noble names.—*The Winter's Tale,* i, 2, 393.
Princely name.—*The Rape of Lucrece,* l. 599.
Renowned name.—*I Henry VI,* iv, 5, 41.
Royal name.—*I Henry VI,* v, 3, 160.
Sovereign name.—*The Winter's Tale,* v, 1, 26.

III—Ill Name

5 What a wounded name,
Things standing thus unknown, shall live behind me!
Hamlet. Act v, sc. 2, l. 355. [Hamlet]

6 You are in an ill name.
II Henry IV. Act ii, sc. 4, l. 98. [Hostess] The only use of "ill name."

Odious is the name.—*The Merry Wives of Windsor,* ii, 1, 123.

7 Her name, that was as fresh
As Dian's visage, is now begrimed and black
As mine own face.
Othello. Act iii, sc. 3, l. 386. [Othello] The only use of "begrimed."

Desdemona: Am I that name, Iago?
Iago: What name, fair lady?
Desdemona: Such as she says my lord did say I was.
Emilia: He call'd her whore: a beggar in his drink
Could not have laid such terms upon his callet.
Othello. Act iv, sc. 2, l. 118.

She hath bought the name of whore thus dearly.
Cymbeline. Act ii, sc. 4, l. 128. [Posthumus]

8 Do not so much as my poor name rehearse.
Sonnets. No. lxxi.

My name be buried where my body is,
And live no more to shame nor me nor you.
Sonnets. No. lxxii.

Thence comes it that my name receives a brand.
Sonnets. No. cxi.

Dreadful name.—*Titus Andronicus,* v, 2, 39.
Earthy name.—*King John,* iii, 1, 147.
Grosser name.—*Hamlet,* iv, 7, 171.
Hateful name.—*I Henry IV,* v, 2, 41.
Low names.—*Richard III,* i, 4, 82.
Poor name.—*Henry VIII,* iv, 2, 126.
Stained name.—*Troilus and Cressida,* v, 2, 178.
Vile name.—*A Midsummer-Night's Dream,* ii, 2, 107.

9 My name
Be yoked with his that did betray the Best!
Winter's Tale. Act i, sc. 2, l. 418. [Polixenes]

IV—Individual Names

10 What 's her name, Since she was Cleopatra?
Antony and Cleopatra. Act iii, sc. 13, l. 98. [Antony]

11 Bertram: They told me that your name was Fontibell.
Diana: No, my good lord, Diana.
All's Well that Ends Well. Act iv, sc. 2, l. 1.

12 I 'll have no worse a name than Jove's own page;
And therefore look you call me Ganymede.
As You Like It. Act i, sc. 3, l. 126. [Rosalind] Ganymede is mentioned five times in this play, and in no other.

Jaques: Rosalind is your love's name?
Orlando: Yes, just.
Jaques: I do not like her name.
Orlando: There was no thought of pleasing you when she was christened.
As You Like It. Act iii, sc. 2, l. 280. The only use of "christened."

There is a man haunts the forest, that abuses our young plants with carving 'Rosalind' on their barks; hangs odes upon hawthorns and elegies on brambles, all, forsooth, deifying the name of Rosalind.
As You Like It, iii, 2, 379. The only use of "deifying."

Didst thou hear without wondering how thy name should be hanged and carved upon these trees?

As You Like It. Act iii, sc. 2, l. 181. [Celia]

1

Touchstone: Is thy name William?
William: William, sir.
Touchstone: A fair name.

As You Like It. Act v, sc. 1, l. 22.

Make but my name thy love, and love that still,
And then thou lovest me, for my name is 'Will.'

Sonnets. No. cxxxvi.

2

Dromio of Ephesus: Maud, Bridget, Marian, Cicely, Gillian, Ginn!
Dromio of Syracuse: [Within] Mome, malt-horse, capon, coxcomb, idiot, patch!

The Comedy of Errors. Act iii, sc. 1, l. 31. The only use of Maud, Gillian, and Ginn, and of "mome." Cicely occurs twice, Bridget thrice, and Marian six times.

Antipholus of Syracuse: What 's her name?
Dromio of Syracuse: Nell, sir; but her name and three quarters, that 's an ell and three quarters, will not measure her from hip to hip.

The Comedy of Errors. Act iii, sc. 2, l. 110.

Is not your name, sir, call'd Antipholus?

The Comedy of Errors, v, 1, 286.

3

I know you well, sir, and you know me; your name,
I think, is Adrian.

Coriolanus. Act iv, sc. 3, l. 1. [Roman]

Menenius: It is lots to blanks,
My name hath touch'd your ears: it is Menenius.
Sentinel: Be it so; go back: the virtue of your name
Is not here passable. . . .
Menenius: Prithee, fellow, remember my name is Menenius, always factionary to the party of your general.

Coriolanus. Act v, sc. 2, l. 11. The only use of "factionary." "Passable" is repeated in *Cymbeline,* i, 2, 10: "His body 's a passable carcass."

First Sentinel: Now, sir, is your name Menenius?
Second Sentinel: 'Tis a spell, you see, of much power.

Coriolanus. Act v, sc. 2, l. 101.

4

Belarius: What 's your name?
Imogen: Fidele, sir.

Cymbeline. Act iii, sc. 6, l. 60.

Thy name [Fidele] well fits thy faith, thy faith thy name.

Cymbeline. Act iv, sc. 2, l. 381. [Caius Lucius]

5

Cloten: Thou injurious thief,
Hear but my name, and tremble.
Guiderius: What 's thy name?
Cloten: Cloten, thou villain.
Guiderius: Cloten, thou double villain, be thy name,
I cannot tremble at it: were it Toad, or Adder, Spider,
'Twould move me sooner.

Cymbeline. Act iv, sc. 2, l. 86.

6

I am sworn brother to a leash of drawers; and can call them all by their christen names, as Tom, Dick, and Francis.

I Henry IV. Act ii, sc. 4, l. 7. [Prince of Wales] The only use of "christen names."

Name of Ned.—*I Henry IV,* ii, 4, 24.

Doll Tearsheet she by name.—*II Henry IV,* ii, 1, 81.

7

Blunt: What is thy name, that in the battle thus
Thou crossest me? What honour dost thou seek
Upon my head?
Douglas: Know then, my name is Douglas;
And I do haunt thee in the battle thus
Because some tell me that thou art a king.

I Henry IV. Act v, sc. 3, l. 1.

His name was Blunt.—*I Henry IV,* v, 3, 20.

8

Hotspur: If I mistake not, thou art Harry Monmouth.
Prince: Thou speak'st as if I would deny my name.
Hotspur: My name is Harry Percy.
Prince: Why, then I see
A very valiant rebel of the name.

I Henry IV. Act v, sc. 4, l. 59.

9

Jack Falstaff with my familiars, John with my brothers and sisters, and Sir John with all Europe.

II Henry IV. Act ii, sc. 2, l. 145. [Falstaff]

His name is Falstaff.—*I Henry IV,* ii, 4, 468.

Mrs. Page: I cannot tell you what the dickens his name is. . . . What do you call your knight's name, sirrah?
Robin: Sir John Falstaff. . . .
Mrs. Page: He, he; I can never hit on 's name.

The Merry Wives of Windsor. Act iii, sc. 2, l. 19. The only use of "dickens," a variation of deuce.

Fluellen: Harry Monmouth, being in his right wits and his good judgements, turned away the fat knight with the great-belly doublet: he was full of jests, and gipes, and knaveries, and mocks; I have forgot his name.
Gower: Sir John Falstaff.

Henry V. Act iv, sc. 7, l. 49. The only use of "gipes."

I have forgot your name.—*The Taming of the Shrew,* Ind., 1, 86.

I know not his name.—*I Henry IV,* ii, 4, 461.

10

Falstaff: What 's your name, sir? of what condition are you, and of what place, I pray?
Coleville: I am a knight, sir; and my name is Coleville of the dale.
Falstaff: Well, then, Coleville is your name, a knight is your degree, and your place the dale. Coleville shall still be your name, a traitor your degree, and the dungeon your place, a place deep enough; so shall you be still Coleville of the dale.

II Henry IV. Act iv, sc. 3, l. 1.

1 That black name, Edward,
Black Prince of Wales.
Henry V. Act ii, sc. 4, l. 56. [French King]
King Henry: What is thy name? I know thy quality.
Montjoy: Montjoy.
King Henry: Thou dost thy office fairly.
Henry V. Act iii, sc. 6, l. 146.
What is thy name? discuss.
Henry V. Act iv, sc. 4, l. 5. [Pistol]

2
Come hither, boy: ask me this slave in French
What is his name.
Henry V. Act iv, sc. 4, l. 25. [Pistol]
Pistol: What is thy name?
King Henry: Harry le Roy.
Pistol: Le Roy! a Cornish name: art thou of Cornish crew?
King Henry: No, I am a Welshman.
Henry V. Act iv, sc. 1, l. 48.
Pistol: My name is Pistol call'd.
King Henry: It sorts well with your fierceness.
Henry V. Act iv, sc. 1, l. 62.

3
Suffolk: Who art thou? say, that I may honour thee.
Margaret: Margaret my name, and daughter to a king,
The King of Naples, whoso'er thou art.
Suffolk: An earl I am, and Suffolk am I call'd.
I Henry VI. Act v, sc. 3, l. 50.

4
Gloucester: Tell me, sirrah, what's my name?
Simpcox: Alas, master, I know not. . . .
Gloucester: What's thine own name?
Simpcox: Saunder Simpcox, an if it please you, master.
II Henry VI. Act ii, sc. 1, l. 117.
Whitmore: My name is Walter Whitmore. . . .
Suffolk: Thy name affrights me, in whose sound is death. . . .
Thy name is Gaultier, being rightly sounded.
Whitmore: Gaultier or Walter, which it is, I care not.
II Henry VI. Act iv, sc. 1, l. 31.

5
Gartner: The high and mighty princess of England, Elizabeth! . . .
King Henry: What is her name?
Cranmer: Elizabeth.
Henry VIII. Act v, sc. 5, l. 3.

6
Brutus and Cæsar: what should be in that 'Cæsar'?
Why should that name be sounded more than yours?
Write them together, yours is as fair a name:
Sound them, it doth become the mouth as well;
Weigh them, it is as heavy; conjure with 'em,
Brutus will start a spirit as soon as Cæsar.
Julius Cæsar. Act i, sc. 2, l. 142. [Cassius]
Citizen: What is your name? . . .
Cinna: What is my name? . . .
Citizen: Your name, sir, truly.
Cinna: Truly, my name is Cinna. . . . I am Cinna the poet. . . . I am not Cinna the conspirator.
Citizen: It's no matter, his name's Cinna; pluck but his name out of his heart, and turn him going.
Julius Cæsar. Act iii, sc. 3, l. 5.

7
King John: What is thy name?
Bastard: Philip, my liege, so is my name begun;
Philip, good old sir Robert's wife's eldest son.
King John: From henceforth bear his name whose form thou bear'st:
Kneel thou down Philip, but rise more great,
Arise sir Richard and Plantagenet.
King John. Act i, sc. 1, l. 156.
'Good den, sir Richard!'—'God-a-mercy, fellow!'—
And if his name be George, I'll call him Peter;
For new-made honour doth forget men's names.
King John. Act i, sc. 1, l. 185. [Bastard]
My name is Constance; I was Geffrey's wife;
Young Arthur is my son, and he is lost.
King John. Act iii, sc. 4, l. 46. [Constance]

8
Herald: What are you?
Your name, your quality? . . .
Edgar: Know, my name is lost;
By treason's tooth bare-gnawn and canker-bit:
Yet am I noble as the adversary
I come to cope.
King Lear. Act v, sc. 3, l. 119. The only use of "bare-gnawn" and "canker-bit."
In wisdom I should ask thy name.
King Lear. Act v, sc. 3, l. 142. [Edmund]
Your name, fair gentlewoman?—*King Lear,* i, 4, 257.

9
Dumain: Sir, I pray you, a word: what lady is that same?
Boyet: The heir of Alençon, Katharine her name. . . .
Longaville: I beseech you a word: what is she in white?
Boyet: A woman sometimes, an you saw her in the light.
Longaville: Perchance light in the light. I desire her name.
Boyet: She hath but one for herself: to desire that were a shame. . . .
Biron: What's her name in the cap?
Boyet: Rosaline, by good hap.
Love's Labour's Lost. Act ii, sc. 1, l. 194.

10
My name is Elbow: I do lean upon justice.
Measure for Measure. Act ii, sc. 1, l. 48. [Elbow]
O thou caitiff! O thou varlet! O thou wicked Hannibal!
Measure for Measure. Act ii, sc. 1, l. 182. [Elbow] Hannibal is mentioned four times in the plays.

What's your name?—*Measure for Measure,* ii, 1, 45.

I pray you, your name?—*Measure for Measure,* iii, 2, 168.

1
Portia: Is your name Shylock?
Shylock: Shylock is my name.
The Merchant of Venice. Act iv, sc. 1, l. 176.

Lorenzo: Your name, I pray you, friend.
Stephano: Stephano is my name.
The Merchant of Venice. Act v, sc. 1, l. 27.

2
Mistress Quickly: Peter Simple, you say your name is?
Simple: Ay, for fault of a better.
Merry Wives of Windsor. Act i, sc. 4, l. 16.

My name is Corporal Nym; I speak and I avouch; 'tis true: my name is Nym.
The Merry Wives of Windsor. Act ii, sc. 1, l. 137. [Nym]

Names! Amaimon sounds well; Lucifer, well; Barbason, well; yet they are devils' additions, the names of fiends: but Cuckold! Wittol!—Cuckold! the devil himself hath not such a name.
The Merry Wives of Windsor. Act ii, sc. 2, l. 311. [Ford] Amaimon occurs again in *I Henry IV,* ii, 4, 370, and Barbason in *Henry V,* ii, 1, 57. Lucifer is mentioned six times. The only use of "wittol" (a contented cuckold).

3
Bottom: I beseech your worship's name.
Cobweb: Cobweb.
Bottom: I shall desire you of more acquaintance, good Master Cobweb: if I cut my finger, I shall make bold with you. Your name, honest gentleman?
Peaseblossom: Peaseblossom.
Bottom: I pray you, commend me to Mistress Squash, your mother and to Master Peascod, your father. Good Master Peaseblossom, I shall desire you of more acquaintance too. Your name, I beeseech you, sir?
Mustardseed: Mustardseed.
Bottom: Good Master Mustardseed, I know your patience well: that same cowardly, giant-like ox-beef hath devoured many a gentleman of your house: I promise you your kindred hath made my eyes water ere now. I desire your more acquaintance, good Master Mustardseed.
A Midsummer-Night's Dream. Act iii, sc. 1, l. 183. "Giant-like" is repeated in *Hamlet,* iv, 5, 121. The only use of "ox-beef."

4
Thus answer I in name of Benedick.
Much Ado about Nothing. Act ii, sc. 1, l. 179. [Claudio]

Benedick: Which is Beatrice?
Beatrice: I answer to that name.
Much Ado about Nothing. Act v, sc. 4, l. 73.

Answer truly to your name.—*Much Ado about Nothing,* iv, 1, 80.

5
Simonides: We desire to know of him,
Of whence he is, his name and parentage. . . .
Pericles: A gentleman of Tyre; my name, Pericles;
My education been in arts and arms.
Pericles. Act ii, sc. 3, l. 73.

Marina who,
For she was born at sea, I have named so.
Pericles. Act iii, sc. 3, l. 12. [Pericles]

Pericles: Thy name, my most kind virgin?
Recount, I do beseech thee: come, sit by me.
Marina: My name is Marina. . . . The name
Was given me by one that had some power,
My father, and a king. . . . Call'd Marina
For I was born at sea.
Pericles. Act v, sc. 1, l. 141.

Pericles: What was thy mother's name? tell me but that. . . .
Marina: Is it no more to be your daughter than
To say my mother's name was Thaisa?
Thaisa was my mother, who did end
The minute I began.
Pericles. Act v, sc. 1, l. 202.

6
What is thy name? and wherefore comest thou hither?
Richard II. Act i, sc. 3, l. 31. [Marshal]

And furbish new the name of John a Gaunt,
Even in the lusty haviour of his son.
Richard II. Act i, sc. 3, l. 76. [Bolingbroke] The only use of "furbish."

O, how that name befits my composition!
Richard II. Act ii, sc. 1, l. 73. [Gaunt]

No name fits thy nature but thy own!
Titus Andronicus. Act ii, sc. 3, l. 119. [Lavinia]

7
Clarence: My name is George.
Gloucester: Alack, my lord, that fault is none of yours.
Richard III. Act i, sc. 1, l. 46.

He . . . says a wizard told him that by G
His issue disinherited should be;
And, for my name of George begins with G,
It follows in his thought that I am he.
Richard III. Act i, sc. 1, l. 56. [Clarence]

8
Tell me her father's name and 'tis enough.
The Taming of the Shrew. Act i, sc. 2, l. 94. [Petruchio]

Baptista: What may I call your name?
Petruchio: Petruchio is my name; Antonio's son.
The Taming of the Shrew. Act ii, sc. 1, l. 67.

You lie, in faith; for you are call'd plain Kate,
And bonny Kate and sometimes Kate the curst;
But Kate, the prettiest Kate in Christendom,
Kate of Kate Hall, my super-dainty Kate,
For dainties are all Kates.
Taming of the Shrew. Act ii, sc. 1, l. 186. [Petruchio] The only use of "super-dainty."

Baptista: Pray, what do you think is his name?
Vincentio: His name? as if I knew not his name: I have brought him up ever since he was three years old, and his name is Tranio.
The Taming of the Shrew. Act v, sc. 1, l. 83.

My name is call'd Vincentio.—*The Taming of the Shrew,* iv, 5, 55.

9
Ferdinand: What is your name?
Miranda: Miranda.—O my father,
I have broke your hest to say so!
The Tempest. Act iii, sc. 1, l. 36.

1
Agamemnon: Sir, you of Troy, call you yourself Æneas?
Æneas: Ay, Greek, that is my name.
Troilus and Cressida. Act i, sc. 3, l. 245.
Æneas: If not Achilles, sir,
What is your name?
Achilles: If not Achilles, nothing.
Troilus and Cressida. Act iv, sc. 5, l. 75.
What name? what parentage?—*Twelfth Night,* v, 1, 238.
2
O, would her name were Grace!
The Winter's Tale. Act i, sc. 2, l. 99. [Hermione]

V—In the Name of

3
That is intended in the general's name.
II Henry IV. Act iv, sc. 1, l. 166. [Westmoreland]
4
I charge you in his majesty's name, apprehend him.
Henry V. Act iv, sc. 8, l. 18. [Fluellen]
5
Wretched shall France be only in my name.
I Henry VI. Act i, sc. 4, l. 97. [Talbot]
I' the name of me.—*Winter's Tale,* iv, 3, 54.
In his name.—*King John,* iii, 1, 140.
In our name.—*Antony and Cleopatra,* iii, 12, 28.
In thy name.—*Much Ado about Nothing,* ii, 1, 310.
In your name.—*The Two Gentlemen of Verona,* i, 2, 40.
6
I do arrest you in his highness' name.
II Henry VI. Act iii, sc. 1, l. 136. [Suffolk]
In his highness' name.—*I Henry VI,* i, 3, 77.
In the prince's name.—*Much Ado about Nothing,* iii, 3, 27; 177; iv, 2, 40. *Romeo and Juliet,* iii, 1, 145.
7
First Keeper: We charge you, in God's name, and the king's,
To go with us unto the officers.
King Henry: In God's name, lead; your king's name be obey'd:
And what God will, then let your king perform.
III Henry VI. Act iii, sc. 1, l. 97.
In God's name and the king's.
Richard II. Act i, sc. 3, l. 11. [Marshal]
Keep your way, i' God's name: I have done.
Much Ado about Nothing. Act i, sc. 1, l. 144. [Benedick]
In God's name, cheerly on, courageous friends.
Richard III. Act v, sc. 2, l. 14. [Richmond] "In God's name" is repeated in i, 4, 169; iii, 4, 3; *II Henry IV,* i, 4, 12; iv, 1, 227; *Much Ado about Nothing,* v, 1, 319; *The Taming of the Shrew,* i, 2, 195; iv, 5, 1.
In the name of God.—*I Henry IV,* iii, 2, 153; *King John,* ii, 1, 106; *Hamlet,* ii, 1, 76; *Henry VIII,* ii, 4, 56.
In the name of God Almighty.—*Henry V,* ii, 4, 77.
In the name of Jesu Christ!—*Henry V,* iv, 1, 65.

8
Now, in the names of all the gods at once.
Julius Cæsar, i, 2, 148. See under Greatness.
9
Who 's there, i' the name of Beelzebub? . . .
Who 's there, in the other devil's name?
Macbeth. Act ii, sc. 3, l. 4. [Porter]
In Apollo's name.—*Winter's Tale,* iii, 2, 119.
In Cæsar's name.—*Cymbeline,* iii, 1, 67.
In the devil's name.—*I Henry IV,* iii, 1, 69; *The Taming of the Shrew,* iv, 3, 92.
I' the name of fame and honour.—*Cymbeline,* iii, 3, 51.
In the name of justice.—*All 's Well that Ends Well,* ii, 3, 172.
In the name o' the people.—*Coriolanus,* iii, 3, 99.
I' the name of something holy.—*The Tempest,* iii, 3, 94.
I' the name of thrift.—*Henry VIII,* iii, 2, 109.
In the name of Time.—*Winter's Tale,* iv, 1, 3.
I' the name of truth.—*Macbeth,* i, 3, 52.
10
But what, o' God's name, doth become of this?
Richard II. Act ii, sc. 1, l. 251. [Willoughby] "O' God's name" is repeated in *II Henry VI,* ii, 3, 34; iv, 7, 115; *Henry V,* i, 2, 102.

NAPKIN, see Handkerchief

NATION

11
Methinks they are a gentle nation.
The Comedy of Errors. Act iv, sc. 4, l. 158. [Dromio of Syracuse]
Best govern'd nation.—*II Henry IV,* v, 2, 137.
English nation.—*II Henry IV,* i, 2, 241. See under England.
Neighbouring nation.—*Pericles,* i, 4, 65.
New nations.—*Henry VIII,* v, 5, 53.
Well-ordered nation.—*Troilus and Cressida,* ii, 2, 180. The only use of "well-ordered."
O nation miserable.—*Macbeth,* iv, 3, 103.
12
The nation holds it no sin to tarre them to controversy.
Hamlet. Act ii, sc. 2, l. 370. [Rosencrantz] "Tarre" (incite) is repeated in *King John,* iv, 1, 117, and in *Troilus and Cressida,* i, 3, 392.
Fluellen: There is not many of your nation—
Macmorris: Of my nation! What ish my nation? Ish a villain, and a bastard, and a knave, and a rascal— What ish my nation? Who talks of my nation?
Henry V. Act iii, sc. 2, l. 130.
13
He hates our sacred nation.
The Merchant of Venice. Act i, sc. 3, l. 49. [Shylock]
14
A nation strong, train'd up in arms.
Titus Andronicus. Act i, sc. 1, l. 30. [Marcus]

NATURE

See also Character. For Art and Nature see under Art

15
The mightiest space in fortune nature brings
To join like likes and kiss like native things.
All 's Well that Ends Well. Act i, sc. 1, l. 237. [Helena]

Frank nature, rather curious than in haste,
Hath well composed thee.
All's Well that Ends Well. Act i, sc. 2, l. 20. [King]

'Tis often seen
Adoption strives with nature and choice breeds
A native slip to us from foreign seeds.
All's Well that Ends Well. Act i, sc. 3, l. 150. [Countess]

I have kept them tame, and know their natures.
All's Well that Ends Well. Act ii, sc. 5, l. 49. [Lafeu]

1
In nature's infinite book of secrecy
A little I can read.
Antony and Cleopatra. Act i, sc. 2, l. 9. [Soothsayer]

It cannot be thus long, the sides of nature
Will not sustain it.
Antony and Cleopatra. Act i, sc. 3, l. 16. [Cleopatra]

Nature, stronger than his just occasion.
As You Like It. Act iv, sc. 3, l. 130. [Oliver]

2
It would have gall'd his surly nature,
Which easily endures not article
Tying him to aught.
Coriolanus. Act ii, sc. 3, l. 203. [Sicinius]

Thou crusty batch of nature.
Troilus and Cressida. Act v, sc. 1, l. 5. [Achilles] The only use of "crusty" and "batch."

Abused nature.—*King Lear,* iv, 7, 15.
Baser nature.—*Hamlet,* v, 2, 60.
Cursed natures.—*Timon of Athens,* iv, 3, 19.
Damn'd nature.—*Cymbeline,* i, 5, 36.
Dissembling nature.—*Richard III,* i, 1, 19.
Drenched natures.—*Macbeth,* i, 7, 68.
Evil nature.—*The Tempest,* i, 2, 92.
Forging Nature.—*Venus and Adonis,* l. 729. The only use of "forging."
Opposed natures.—*The Merchant of Venice,* ii, 9, 62.
Overbearing nature.—*Othello,* i, 3, 56.
Strange nature.—*The Merchant of Venice,* iv, 1, 177; *Romeo and Juliet,* ii, 1, 25; *Troilus and Cressida,* v, 2, 148.
Thankless natures.—*Timon of Athens,* v, 1, 63.
Wilder nature.—*Henry VIII,* v, 1, 15.

3
His nature is too noble for this world.
Coriolanus. Act iii, sc. 1, l. 255. [Menenius] See under NOBILITY.

I know his noble nature.
Henry VIII. Act iii, sc. 2, l. 418. [Cardinal Wolsey] "Noble" was a favourite adjective with Shakespeare, who used it nearly 500 times.

Noble nature.—*Timon of Athens,* ii, 2, 217; *Othello,* ii, 1, 298; iii, 3, 199; *Cymbeline,* iv, 2, 364; *Henry VIII,* iii, 1, 62.
Noble modest nature.—*Henry VIII,* iv, 2, 135.
Better nature.—*Richard III,* i, 2, 143; *The Tempest,* i, 2, 496.
Divine nature.—*Cymbeline,* iv, 2, 170.
Finer natures.—*The Winter's Tale,* i, 2, 226.
Frugal nature.—*Much Ado about Nothing,* iv, 1, 130. "Frugal" is used only once more in the plays, in *The Merry Wives of Windsor,* ii, 1, 28: "Frugal of my mirth."
Good nature.—*Othello,* ii, 3, 138; *The Tempest,* i, 2, 359.
Gracious nature.—*Coriolanus,* ii, 3, 195; *Timon of Athens,* i, 1, 56.
Great nature.—*Coriolanus,* v, 3, 33; *Macbeth,* ii, 2, 39; *The Winter's Tale,* ii, 2, 60; *Cymbeline,* v, 4, 48.
Great creating nature.—*The Winter's Tale,* iv, 4, 88.
Kind nature.—*Titus Andronicus,* v, 3, 168.
Primy nature.—*Hamlet,* i, 3, 7. The only use of "primy."
Repairing nature.—*II Henry VI,* v, 3, 22.
True nature.—*Hamlet,* iii, 3, 62; iv, 5, 17.
Well-derived nature.—*All's Well that Ends Well,* iii, 2, 90.
Wise nature.—*Cymbeline,* v, 5, 367.

4
To this end
He bow'd his nature, never known before
But to be rough, unswayable and free.
Coriolanus. Act v, sc. 6, l. 24. [Aufidius] The only use of "unswayable."

5
How hard it is to hide the sparks of nature!
Cymbeline. Act iii, sc. 3, l. 79. [Belarius]

Nature prompts them
In simple and low things to prince it much
Beyond the trick of others.
Cymbeline. Act iii, sc. 3, l. 84. [Belarius]

For nature doth abhor to make his bed
With the defunct, or sleep upon the dead.
Cymbeline. Act iv, sc. 2, l. 357. [Lucius]

6
For nature, crescent, does not grow alone
In thews and bulk, but, as this temple waxes,
The inward service of the mind and soul
Grows wide withal.
Hamlet. Act i, sc. 3, l. 11. [Laertes]

Nature is fine in love, and where 'tis fine,
It sends some precious instance of itself
After the thing it loves.
Hamlet. Act iv, sc. 5, l. 161. [Laertes]

7
Diseased nature oftentimes breaks forth
In strange eruptions.
I Henry IV, iii, 1, 27. See under EARTHQUAKE.

According to their firm proposed natures.
Henry V. Act v, sc. 2, l. 362. [Westmoreland]

8
Nature makes me suddenly relent.
I Henry VI. Act iii, sc. 3, l. 59. [Burgundy]

9
You know his nature, That he 's revengeful.
Henry VIII. Act i, sc. 1, l. 108. [Norfolk]

Thou hast a cruel nature and a bloody.
Henry VIII. Act v, sc. 3, l. 129. [King Henry]

Bloody nature.—*Twelfth Night,* iii, 3, 30.

10
The nature of it? in what kind, let 's know,
Is this exaction?
Henry VIII. Act i, sc. 2, l. 53. [King Henry]

All of one nature.—*I Henry IV,* i, 1, 11.

11
Nature does require
Her times of preservation.
Henry VIII, iii, 2, 146. See under TIME.

1
How that might change his nature, there 's the question.
Julius Cæsar. Act ii, sc. 1, l. 13. [Brutus] See also under CHANGE.
Change his nature.—*The Merchant of Venice*, v, 1, 82.

2
I have as much of this in art as you,
But yet my nature could not bear it so.
Julius Cæsar. Act iv, sc. 3, l. 194. [Cassius] See also ART AND NATURE.
Nature must obey necessity.
Julius Cæsar. Act iv, sc. 3, l. 227. [Brutus]

3
Thou, nature, art my goddess; to thy law
My services are bound.
King Lear. Act i, sc. 2, l. 1. [Edmund]
Hear, nature, hear; dear goddess, hear!
King Lear, i, 4, 297. See under CURSE.
Good goddess Nature.—*The Winter's Tale*, ii, 3, 103.

4
Thy tender-hefted nature shall not give
Thee o'er to harshness.
King Lear. Act ii, sc. 4, l. 174. [King Lear] The only use of "tender-hefted."
Allow not nature more than nature needs.
King Lear. Act ii, sc. 4, l. 269. [King Lear]
I will forget my nature.—*King Lear*, i, 5, 35.
Oppressed nature sleeps.—*King Lear*, iii, 6, 104.
O ruin'd piece of nature!—*King Lear*, iv, 6, 137.

5
Fair nature is both kind and tame.
A Lover's Complaint, l. 311.
Fair nature.—*Henry V*, iii, 1, 8.

6
Yet do I fear thy nature.
Macbeth, i, 5, 17. See under KINDNESS.
A good and virtuous nature may recoil
In an imperial charge.
Macbeth. Act iv, sc. 3, l. 19. [Malcolm]
'Gainst nature still!—*Macbeth*, ii, 4, 27.

7
Nature never lends
The smallest scruple of her excellence
But, like a thrifty goddess, she determines
Herself the glory of a creditor,
Both thanks and use.
Measure for Measure. Act i, sc. 1, l. 37. [Duke]

8
Nature hath framed strange fellows in her time.
The Merchant of Venice. Act i, sc. 1, l. 51. [Salarino]

9
The Moor, howbeit that I endure him not,
Is of a constant, loving, noble nature.
Othello. Act ii, sc. 1, l. 297. [Iago]
I would not have your free and noble nature,
Out of self-bounty, be abused.
Othello. Act iii, sc. 3, l. 199. [Iago] The only use of "self-bounty."
Of a free and open nature.—*Othello*, i, 3, 405.

10
Is this the nature
Whom passion could not shake?
Othello, iv, 1, 276. See under CHARACTER.
Nature would not invest herself in such shadowing passion without some instruction.
Othello. Act iv, sc. 1, l. 40. [Othello]
Mortal natures.—*Othello*, ii, 1, 72.

11
Thou cunning'st pattern of excelling nature.
Othello, v, 2, 11. See under LIGHT.
When nature framed this piece, she meant thee a good turn; therefore see what a paragon she is.
Pericles. Act iv, sc. 2, l. 150. [Bawd]

12
Though fond nature bids us all lament,
Yet nature's tears are reason's merriment.
Romeo and Juliet. Act iv, sc. 5, l. 82. [Friar Laurence]

13
Nature calls thee to be gone.
Sonnets. No. iv.
Nature's bequest gives nothing but doth lend,
And being frank she lends to those are free.
Sonnets. No. iv. The only use of "bequest."
Now bankrupt Nature is.
Sonnets. No. lxvii.
My nature is subdued
To what it works in, like the dyer's hand.
Sonnets. No. cxi.
Nature, sovereign mistress over wrack.
Sonnets. No. cxxvi.

14
All things in common nature should produce
Without sweat or endeavour: . . . Nature should bring forth,
Of its own kind, all foison, all abundance.
The Tempest. Act ii, sc. 1, l. 159. [Gonzalo]

15
Nature,
To whom all sores lay siege, can bear great fortune,
But by contempt of nature.
Timon of Athens. Act iv, sc. 3, l. 6. [Timon]
That nature, being sick of man's unkindness,
Should yet be hungry! Common mother, thou,
Whose womb unmeasurable, and infinite breast,
Teems, and feeds all; whose self-same mettle,
Whereof thy proud child, arrogant man, is puff'd,
Engenders the black toad and adder blue,
The gilded newt and eyeless venom'd worm,
With all the abhorred births below crisp heaven
Whereon Hyperion's quickening fire doth shine.
Timon of Athens. Act iv, sc. 3, l. 176. [Timon] "Unmeasurable" is repeated in *The Merry Wives of Windsor*, ii, 1, 109.

16
The bounteous housewife, nature.
Timon of Athens. Act iv, sc. 3, l. 423. [Timon]
Bounteous nature.—*Macbeth*, ii, 1, 98.
Niggard nature.—*Timon of Athens*, v, 4, 77.
Mere nature.—*Timon of Athens*, iv, 3, 231.
Naked natures.—*Timon of Athens*, iv, 3, 228.

17
I will make thee Do thy right nature.
Timon of Athens. Act iv, sc. 3, l. 43. [Timon]
It almost turns my dangerous nature mild.
Timon of Athens. Act iv, sc. 3, l. 499. [Timon]

18
O, why should nature build so foul a den?
Titus Andronicus. Act iv, sc. 1, l. 59. [Marcus]

1 Nature craves
All dues be render'd to their owners.
Troilus and Cressida. Act ii, sc. 2, l. 173. [Hector]

2
One touch of nature makes the whole world kin.
Troilus and Cressida. Act iii, sc. 3, l. 175. [Ulysses]

3
Now Nature cares not for thy mortal vigour,
Since her best work is ruin'd with thy rigour.
Venus and Adonis, l. 953.

4
How sometimes nature will betray its folly,
Its tenderness, and make itself a pastime
To harder bosoms!
The Winter's Tale. Act i, sc. 2, l. 151. [Leontes]

Let nature crush the sides o' the earth together
And mar the seeds within!
Winter's Tale, iv, 4, 449. See under FAITH.

NAVY, see Ship

NEATNESS

5 A certain lord, neat, and trimly dress'd,
Fresh as a bridegroom; and his chin new reap'd
Show'd like a stubble-land at harvest-home.
I Henry IV. Act i, sc. 3, l. 33. [Hotspur] The only use of "trimly" and "stubble-land." "Harvest-home" occurs again in *The Merry Wives of Windsor,* ii, 2, 287.

Neat and cleanly.—*II Henry IV,* ii, 4, 502.

6
Now, my spruce companions, is all ready, and all things neat?
The Taming of the Shrew. Act iv, sc. 1, l. 116. [Grumio]

He is too spruce.—*Love's Labour's Lost,* v, 1, 14.

Spruce affectation.—*Love's Labour's Lost,* v, 2, 407. The only uses of "spruce."

7
We must be neat; not neat, but cleanly, captain:
And yet the steer, the heifer and the calf
Are all call'd neat.
Winter's Tale. Act i, sc. 2, l. 123. [Leontes]

Herd of neat.—*III Henry VI,* ii, 1, 14.

NECESSITY

See also Need

8
The strong necessity of time commands
Our services awhile.
Antony and Cleopatra. Act i, sc. 3, l. 42. [Antony]

Be you not troubled with the time, which derives
O'er your content these strong necessities.
Antony and Cleopatra. Act iii, sc. 6, l. 82. [Cæsar]

Real necessities.—*Coriolanus,* iii, 1, 147.

Royal necessities.—*The Winter's Tale,* i, 1, 28.

Necessitied to help.—*All's Well that Ends Well,* v, 3, 85. The only use of "necessitied."

9
Thither I must, although against my will.
The Comedy of Errors. Act iv, sc. 1, l. 112. [Dromio of Syracuse]

Whither I must, I must.
I Henry IV. Act ii, sc. 3, l. 108. [Hotspur]

Juliet: What must be shall be.
Friar Laurence: That 's a certain text.
Romeo and Juliet. Act iv, sc. 1, l. 21.

What you will have, I 'll give, and willing too;
For do we must what force will have us do.
Richard II. Act iii, sc. 3, l. 206. [King Richard]

Needs must.—*Richard II,* iii, 2, 4, and frequently throughout the plays.

10 Necessity so bow'd the state
That I and greatness were compell'd to kiss.
II Henry IV. Act iii, 1, 73. [King Henry]

11
Are these things then necessities?
Then let us meet them like necessities.
II Henry IV. Act iii, 1, 92. [King Henry]

Now sit we close about this taper here,
And call in question our necessities.
Julius Cæsar. Act iv, sc. 3, l. 164. [Brutus]

The art of our necessities is strange,
That can make vile things precious.
King Lear. Act iii, sc. 2, l. 70. [King Lear]

12
Yet that is but a crush'd necessity,
Since we have locks to safeguard necessaries.
Henry V. Act i, sc. 2, l. 175. [Exeter]

I must unto the road
To disembark some necessaries.
The Two Gentlemen of Verona. Act ii, sc. 4, l. 188. [Proteus]

Such necessaries As are behoveful for our state.
Romeo and Juliet, iv, 3, 7. The only use of "behoveful."

My necessaries are embark'd.—*Hamlet,* i, 3, 1.

I must fetch his necessaries ashore.—*Othello,* ii, 1, 292.

Stuffs and necessaries.—*The Tempest,* i, 2, 164. The only uses of "necessaries."

13
It must and shall be so: content thyself.
III Henry VI. Act i, sc. 1, l. 85. [York]

14
Necessity will cause discreet proceeding.
King Lear. Act i, sc. 4, l. 232. [Goneril]

Necessity's sharp pinch!
King Lear. Act ii, sc. 4, l. 214. [King Lear]

15
King: She must lie here on mere necessity.
Biron: Necessity will make us all forsworn. . . .
If I break faith, this word shall speak for me,
I am forsworn on 'mere necessity.'
Love's Labour's Lost. Act i, sc. 1, l. 149.

16
I 'll rather dwell in my necessity.
The Merchant of Venice. Act i, sc. 3, l. 156. [Bassanio]

The fairest grant is the necessity.
Much Ado about Nothing. Act i, sc. 1, l. 319. [Don Pedro]

1
Teach thy necessity to reason thus;
There is no virtue like necessity.
Richard II. Act i, sc. 3, l. 277. [Gaunt]
To make a virtue of necessity.
The Two Gentlemen of Verona. Act iv, sc. 1, l. 62. [Outlaw]

2
I am sworn brother, sweet,
To grim Necessity, and he and I
Will keep a league till death.
Richard II. Act v, sc. 1, l. 20. [King Richard]

3
Urge the necessity and state of times.
Richard III. Act iv, sc. 4, l. 416. [King Richard]

4
Bid him suppose some good necessity
Touches his friend, which craves to be remember'd.
Timon of Athens. Act ii, sc. 2, l. 236. [Timon]
Had his necessity made use of me,
I would have put my wealth into donation,
And the best half would have returned to him.
Timon of Athens. Act iii, sc. 2, l. 89. [Stranger]

5
My necessity
Makes me to ask you for my purse.
Twelfth Night. Act iii, sc. 4, l. 368. [Antonio]

6
One of these two must be necessities,
Which then will speak, that you must change this purpose,
Or I my life.
Winter's Tale. Act iv, sc. 4, l. 38. [Perdita]
Thou must think there 's a necessity in 't.
Winter's Tale. Act iv, sc. 4, l. 648. [Camillo]

7
Though it be great pity, yet it is necessary.
The Winter's Tale. Act iv, sc. 4, l. 803. [Autolycus]
It is necessary.—*Henry V,* iv, 7, 146.
It were but necessary.—*II Henry VI,* iii, 2, 261.
'Tis necessary.—*Timon of Athens,* iii, 5, 2.

NECK

8
He 'll beat Aufidius' head below his knee
And tread upon his neck.
Coriolanus. Act i, sc. 3, l. 49. [Volumnia]
Napes of your necks.—*Coriolanus,* ii, 1, 43. The only use of "napes."

9
Paddling in your neck with his damned fingers.
Hamlet. Act iii, sc. 4, l. 185. See KING, 806:8.

10
Gadshill: Sirrah, if they meet not with Saint Nicholas' clerks, I 'll give thee this neck.
Chamberlain: No, I 'll none of it: I pray thee, keep that for the hangman.
I Henry IV. Act ii, sc. 1, l. 68. See under HANGING.

11
Had my sweet Harry had but half their numbers,
To-day might I, hanging on Hotspur's neck,
Have talk'd of Monmouth's grave.
II Henry IV. Act ii, sc. 3, l. 43. [Lady Percy]
Cassio: By this hand, she falls me thus about my neck—
Othello: Crying 'O dear Cassio!' as it were: his gesture imports it.
Cassio: So hangs, and lolls, and weeps upon me, so hales, and pulls me: ha, ha, ha!
Othello. Act iv, sc. 1, l. 139. The only use of "lolls." "Lolling" occurs four times.
On his neck her yoking arms she throws.
Venus and Adonis, l. 592. The only use of "yoking."
She hung about my neck.—*The Taming of the Shrew,* ii, 1, 310.
She hangs about his neck.—*The Winter's Tale,* v, 3, 112.
Like a jewel has hung twenty years
About his neck.—*Henry VIII,* ii, 2, 33.

12
Katharine: Comment appelez-vous le col?
Alice: De neck, madame.
Henry V. Act iii, sc. 4, l. 34.

13
Let his neck answer for it.
Henry V. Act iv, sc. 8, l. 45. [Fluellen]
Up to the neck.—*Henry V,* iv, 1, 120.

14
He yoketh your rebellious necks.
I Henry VI. Act ii, sc. 3, l. 64. [Talbot]
Yield not your necks To fortune's yoke.
III Henry VI. Act iii, sc. 3, l. 16. [King Lewis]
An thou wilt needs thrust thy neck into a yoke, wear the print of it and sigh away Sundays.
Much Ado about Nothing. Act i, sc. 1, l. 202. [Benedick]
Ay, while you live, draw your neck out o' the collar.
Romeo and Juliet. Act i, sc. 1, l. 5. [Gregory]

15
Break your necks or hang yourselves.
I Henry VI. Act v, sc. 4, l. 91. [La Pucelle]
Make poor men's cattle break their necks.
Titus Andronicus. Act v, sc. 1, l. 132. [Aaron]
I had as lief thou didst break his neck as his finger.
As You Like It, i, 1, 153.
I would they had broke 's neck!—*Troilus and Cressida,* iv, 2, 79.
A plague break thy neck for fighting me!—*Troilus and Cressida,* v, 4, 34.
Break his neck.—*Coriolanus,* iii, 3, 30.
Break his neck or hazard mine.—*Coriolanus,* iv, 7, 25.
Returning to break our necks.—*Coriolanus,* v, 4, 37.

16
His neck will come to your waist,—a cord, sir.
Measure for Measure. Act iii, sc. 2, l. 42. [Elbow]

17
With signs of war about his aged neck.
Richard II. Act ii, sc. 2, l. 74. [Queen]
His short thick neck cannot be easily harm'd.
Venus and Adonis, l. 627.
Halter'd neck.—*Antony and Cleopatra,* iii, 13, 130.
Headless necks.—*II Henry VI,* i, 2, 65.
Humbled neck.—*As You Like It,* iii, 5, 5.

Lion's neck.—*A Midsummer-Night's Dream,* iii, 1, 38.
Reechy neck.—*Coriolanus,* ii, 1, 225.
Soldier's neck.—*Romeo and Juliet,* i, 4, 82.

NEED

See also Necessity

1
He must needs go that the devil drives.
All's Well that Ends Well. Act i, sc. 3, l. 31. [Clown] A proverb quoted first in English literature about 1420 by John Lydgate, *The Assembly of Gods,* st. 3. John Heywood included it in his *Proverbs* in 1533, and it was in frequent use thereafter.
She must needs go in.
The Merry Wives of Windsor, iii, 4, 96. "Must needs" is used frequently throughout the plays.
It must needs be.—*The Winter's Tale,* v, 2, 21.
Thou hast need.—*Romeo and Juliet,* iv, 3, 13.
I have no need.—*Richard II,* iv, 1, 309.
It needs not.—*III Henry VI,* i, 4, 125, and frequently thereafter.
She needs it not.—*Love's Labour's Lost,* iv, 3, 239; *Two Gentlemen of Verona,* v, 2, 21.
We need it not.—*Romeo and Juliet,* iii, 5, 176.
You need it not.—*Cymbeline,* ii, 4, 66; *Measure for Measure,* i, 2, 111.
He shall not need.—*Winter's Tale,* iv, 4, 426.
It shall not need.—*The Comedy of Errors,* v, 1, 390.
You shall not need.—*Pericles,* i, 3, 11.
So had you need.—*The Taming of the Shrew,* i, 1, 215; *As You Like It,* ii, 7, 169.
So you had need.—*I Henry VI,* i, 1, 157.
'Tis more than need.—*Love's Labour's Lost,* iv, 3, 259; *King John,* i, 1, 179.
What 's the need?—*Henry VIII,* ii, 4, 2.
What needs all that?—*The Comedy of Errors,* iii, 1, 60.

2
Between these main parcels of dispatch effected many nicer needs.
All's Well that Ends Well. Act iv, sc. 3, l. 103. [Bertram]

3
We shall presently have need of you.
I Henry IV. Act iii, sc. 2, l. 3. [King Henry]

4
There is no need of any such redress;
Or if there were, it not belongs to you.
II Henry IV. Act iv, sc. 1, l. 97. [Westmoreland]
Never yet more need.—*II Henry IV,* i, 1, 215.

5
Alas, sir, we did it for pure need.
II Henry VI. Act ii, sc. 1, l. 157. [Wife]
Greatest need.—*Richard III,* v, 2, 21.
Present need.—*Antony and Cleopatra,* ii, 2, 101.
Probable need.—*All's Well that Ends Well,* ii, 4, 52.
True need.—*King Lear,* ii, 4, 273.

6
O, then, tread down my need.
King John, iii, 1, 215. See under FAITH.
Thou shalt not need.—*King John,* iii, 1, 320.

7
O, reason not the need: our basest beggars
Are in the poorest thing superfluous.
King Lear. Act ii, sc. 4, l. 267. [King Lear]
What should you need of more?—*King Lear,* ii, 4, 241.

8
Well then, it now appears you need my help
The Merchant of Venice. Act i, sc. 3, l. 115. [Shylock]
Nor shall we need his help.—*I Henry IV,* iii, 1, 88.
I do not need your help.—*I Henry IV,* v, 4, 10.
Need you my help?—*Romeo and Juliet,* iv, 3, 6.

9
God grant we never may have need of you!
Richard III. Act i, sc. 3, l. 76. [Queen Elizabeth]
But, God be thanked, there 's no need of me,
And much I need to help you, if need were.
Richard III. Act iii, sc. 7, l. 165. [Gloucester]
God send me no need of thee!
Romeo and Juliet. Act iii, sc. 1, l. 7. [Mercutio]

10
They may chance to need thee at home.
The Taming of the Shrew. Act v, sc. 1, l. 3. [Lucentio]

11
Immediate are my needs, and my relief
Must not be toss'd and turn'd to me in words,
But find supply immediate.
Timon of Athens. Act ii, sc. 1, l. 25. [Senator]

12 The emperor needs her not,
Nor her, nor thee, nor any of thy stock.
Titus Andronicus. Act i, sc. 1, l. 299. [Saturninus]
Whenever you have need.—*Titus Andronicus,* iv, 2, 15.

13
I have need of such a youth.
The Two Gentlemen of Verona. Act iv, sc. 4, l. 69. [Proteus] See under YOUTH.
Forced by need.—*The Winter's Tale,* v, 1, 92.

NEEDLE

14
I do but say what she is: so delicate with her needle.
Othello. Act iv, sc. 1, l. 199. [Othello]

15
When she would with sharp needle wound
The cambric, which she made more sound
By hurting it.
Pericles. Act iv, Gower, l. 23.

16
It is as hard to come as for a camel
To thread the postern of a small needle's eye.
Richard II. Act v, sc. 5, l. 16. [King Richard]

17
Go ply thy needle.
The Taming of the Shrew. Act ii, sc. 1, l. 25. [Baptista]
Tailor: How did you desire it should be made?
Grumio: Marry, sir, with needle and thread.
Taming of the Shrew. Act iv, sc. 3, l. 120.
With our needles created both one flower.
A Midsummer-Night's Dream. Act iii, sc. 2, l. 204. [Helena]
Live honestly by the prick of their needles.
Henry V. Act ii, sc. 1, l. 37. [Hostess]
Helen's needle.—*Troilus and Cressida,* ii, 1, 87.

NEGLECT

1
Sleeping neglection doth betray to loss
The conquest of our scarce-cold conqueror.
I Henry VI. Act iv, sc. 3, l. 49. [Lucy] "Scarce-cold" is repeated in *Cymbeline,* v, 5, 469.
And this neglection of degree it is
That by a pace goes backward, with a purpose
It hath to climb.
Troilus and Cressida. Act i, sc. 3, l. 127. [Ulysses]
If neglection Should herein make me vile.
Pericles. Act iii, sc. 3, l. 20. [Cleon] The only uses of "neglection."

2
Nor construe any further my neglect,
Than that poor Brutus, with himself at war,
Forgets the shows of love to other men.
Julius Cæsar. Act i, sc. 2, l. 45. [Brutus]

3
I have perceived a most faint neglect of late; which I have rather blamed as mine own jealous curiosity than as a very pretence and purpose of unkindness.
King Lear. Act i, sc. 4, l. 73. [King Lear]

4
His honour, his affairs, his friends, his state,
Neglected all.
The Rape of Lucrece, l. 45.
Strangely neglected.—*Henry VIII,* iii, 2, 11.

5
So then we do neglect The thing we have.
The Rape of Lucrece, l. 152.

6
Neglecting it may do much danger.
Romeo and Juliet. Act v, sc. 2, l. 19. [Friar Laurence]
Neglecting an attempt of ease and gain.
Othello. Act i, sc. 3, l. 29. [Senator]
Neglecting worldly ends.—*The Tempest,* i, 2, 89. The only uses of "neglecting."

7
Mark how with my neglect I do dispense:
You are so strongly in my purpose bred
That all the world besides methinks are dead.
Sonnets. No. cxii.

NEGLIGENCE

8
To this point I stand,
That both the worlds I give to negligence.
Hamlet. Act iv, sc. 5, l. 133. [Hamlet]

9
O negligence! Fit for a fool to fall by.
Henry VIII. Act iii, sc. 2, l. 213. [Wolsey]

10
Put on what weary negligence you please,
You and your fellows.
King Lear. Act i, sc. 3, l. 12. [Goneril]
Wise in our negligence.
King Lear. Act iii, sc. 1, l. 32. [Kent]

11
This is my negligence.
A Midsummer-Night's Dream. Act iii, sc. 2, l. 345. [Oberon]
My sluggard negligence.
The Rape of Lucrece, l. 1278. "Sluggard" is repeated in *Richard III,* v, 3, 225.

12
My rest and negligence befriends thee now.
Troilus and Cressida, v, 6, 17. [Achilles]
You either fear his humour or my negligence.
Twelfth Night. Act i, sc. 4, l. 5. [Viola]

13
I may be negligent, foolish and fearful;
In every one of these no man is free,
But that his negligence, his folly, fear,
Among the infinite doings of the world,
Sometime puts forth. In your affairs, my lord,
If ever I were wilful-negligent,
It was my folly; if industriously
I play'd the fool, it was my negligence,
Not weighing well the end.
The Winter's Tale. Act i, sc. 2, l. 250. [Camillo] The only use of "wilful-negligent" and "industriously."

NEIGHBOUR

14
Is not that neighbourly?
As You Like It. Act iii, sc. 5, l. 90. [Phebe] "Neighbourly" occurs once again in *The Merchant of Venice,* i, 2, 85.

15
So we will home to Rome,
And die among our neighbours.
Coriolanus. Act v, sc. 3, l. 172. [Volumnia]

16
I must live among my neighbours.
II Henry IV. Act ii, sc. 4, l. 80. [Hostess]
A giddy neighbour to us.—*Henry V,* i, 2, 145.
Ill neighbourhood.—*Henry V,* i, 2, 153. "Neighbourhood" is repeated in v, 2, 381, and in *Timon of Athens,* iv, 1, 17.

17
For our bad neighbour makes us early stirrers,
Which is both healthful and good husbandry:
Besides, they are our outward consciences,
And preachers to us all, admonishing
That we should dress us fairly for our end.
Thus may we gather honey from the weed,
And make a moral of the devil himself.
Henry V. Act iv, sc. 1, l. 6. [King Henry] The only use of "admonishing." "Early stirrer" is repeated in *II Henry IV,* iii, 2, 3.

18
He is a marvellous good neighbour, faith, and a very good bowler.
Love's Labour's Lost. Act v, sc. 2, l. 585. [Costard] The only use of "bowler."
Gentle neighbours.—*Pericles,* iii, 2, 107.
Good neighbour.—*Much Ado about Nothing,* iii, 5, 44.
Honest neighbours.—*A Midsummer-Night's Dream,* iii, 1, 149, and four times in later plays.
Kind neighbours.—*Coriolanus,* iv, 6, 24.
Neighbours and friends.—*The Taming of the Shrew,* iii, 2, 248.

NEPTUNE

19
Neptune's salt wash.
Hamlet. Act iii, sc. 2, l. 166. [Player King]
Neptune's billow.—*Pericles,* iii, Gower, 45.
Neptune's ear.—*Troilus and Cressida,* v, 2, 174.
Neptune's hips.—*II Henry IV,* iii, 1, 51.

Neptune's ocean.—*Macbeth,* ii, 2, 60.
Neptune's park.—*Cymbeline,* iii, 1, 19.
Neptune's triumphs.—*Pericles,* v, 1, 17.
Neptune's yellow sands.—*Midsummer-Night's Dream,* ii, 1, 126.

1 The most mighty Neptune
Seem to besiege and make his bold waves tremble,
Yea, his dread trident shake.
The Tempest. Act i, sc. 2, l. 204. [Ariel]

He would not flatter Neptune for his trident. *Coriolanus,* iii, 1, 256. The only uses of "trident."

2 With printless foot
Do chase the ebbing Neptune.
The Tempest, v, 1, 34. See under FAIRY.

God Neptune.—*Pericles,* v, Gower, 17.
The green Neptune.—*Antony and Cleopatra,* iv, 14, 58; *The Winter's Tale,* iv, 4, 28.
Mask'd Neptune.—*Pericles,* iii, 3, 36.
Vast Neptune.—*Timon of Athens,* v, 4, 78.
Watery Neptune.—*Richard II,* ii, 1, 63.

3 The fearful usage,
At least ungentle, of the dreadful Neptune.
Winter's Tale. Act v, sc. 1, l. 153. [Leontes]

NEST

4
Your æry buildeth in our æry's nest.
Richard III. Act i, sc. 3, l. 270. [Queen Margaret]

Birds' nest.—*Romeo and Juliet,* ii, 5, 76; *Much Ado about Nothing,* ii, 1, 230; 238.
Jay's nest.—*The Tempest,* ii, 2, 173.
Phœnix' nest.—*Phœnix and the Turtle,* l. 56.
Puttock's nest.—*II Henry VI,* iii, 2, 191.
Scorpion's nest.—*II Henry VI,* iii, 2, 86.
Swan's nest.—*Cymbeline,* iii, 4, 142.
Unguárded nest.—*Henry V,* i, 2, 170.
Wasp's nest.—*The Winter's Tale,* iv, 4, 814.
Watery nest.—*The Rape of Lucrece,* l. 1611.

5
Lady, come from that nest Of death.
Romeo and Juliet. Act v, sc. 3, l. 151. [Friar Laurence]

Nest of hollow bosoms.—*Henry V,* ii, Prol., 21.
Nest of spicery.—*Richard III,* iv, 4, 424.
Nest of traitors.—*The Winter's Tale,* ii, 3, 81.

NEWS

See also Tidings

6
My news I might have told hereafter.
Antony and Cleopatra. Act iii, sc. 5, l. 22. [Eros]

With news the time's with labour, and throes forth,
Each minute, some.
Antony and Cleopatra. Act iii, sc. 7, l. 81. [Canidius]

The news is true.—*Antony and Cleopatra,* iii, 7, 55.
Your news is not true.—*Hamlet,* ii, 2, 243.

7
Oliver: What's the new news at the new court?
Charles: There's no news at the court, sir, but the old news.
As You Like It. Act i, sc. 1, l. 101.

Polixenes: What is the news i' the court?
Camillo: None rare, my lord.
The Winter's Tale. Act i, sc. 2, l. 367.

Give me my pardon, sir: if, sir, you come with news from the court, I take it there's but two ways, either to utter them, or to conceal them.
II Henry IV. Act v, sc. 3, l. 114. [Shallow]

Now, Hal, to the news at court.—*I Henry IV,* iii, 3, 197.
Court news.—*King Lear,* v, 3, 14.

8
Touchstone: Here comes Monsieur Le Beau.
Rosalind: With his mouth full of news.
Celia: Which he will put on us, as pigeons feed their young.
Rosalind: Then shall we be news-crammed.
Celia: All the better; we shall be the more marketable.
As You Like It. Act i, sc. 2, l. 97. The only use of "news-crammed." "Marketable" is repeated in *The Tempest,* v, 1, 266.

Yonder comes news.—*Coriolanus,* i, 4, 1.
Here comes more news.—*II Henry IV,* i, 1, 59.
Look, here's more news.—*II Henry IV,* iv, 4, 93.

9
How couldst thou in a mile confound an hour,
And bring thy news so late?
Coriolanus. Act i, sc. 6, l. 17. [Cominius]

The augurer tells me we shall have news to-night.
Coriolanus. Act ii, sc. 1, l. 1. [Menenius]

10
O slaves, I can tell you news,—news, you rascals! . . . The bottom of the news is, our general is cut i' the middle.
Coriolanus. Act iv, sc. 5, l. 181. [Servant]

Polonius: My lord, I have news to tell you.
Hamlet: My lord, I have news to tell you.
Hamlet. Act ii, sc. 2, l. 408.

But wherefore do I tell these news to thee?
I Henry IV. Act iii, sc. 2, l. 121. [King]

Come, cousin, let us tell the queen these news.
III Henry VI. Act i, sc. 1, l. 182. [Clifford]

Well, old man, I will tell you news of your son.
The Merchant of Venice. Act ii, sc. 2, l. 82. [Launcelot]

I have news to tell you.—*Henry VIII,* v, 1, 94.
I'll tell the news.—*Julius Cæsar,* v, 4, 17.

11
Pray God my news be worth a welcome.
I Henry IV. Act iv, sc. 1, l. 87. [Vernon]

This is the news at full.—*II Henry IV,* i, 1, 135.
News of peace.—*II Henry IV,* iv, 2, 70.

12
Our news shall go before us to his majesty.
II Henry IV. Act iv, sc. 3, l. 84. [Lancaster]

13
Falstaff: O base Assyrian knight, what is thy news?
Let King Cophetua know the truth thereof.
Silence: And Robin Hood, Scarlet, and John.
II Henry IV. Act v, sc. 3, l. 104. Robin Hood is mentioned also in *Two Gentlemen of Verona,* iv, 1, 36, and in *As You Like it,* i, 1, 122, and King Cophetua in *Love's Labour's Lost,* iv, 1, 66, and *Romeo and Juliet,* ii, 1, 14.

1
Where 's the Prince Dauphin? I have
News for him.
I Henry VI. Act i, sc. 2, l. 46. [Bastard]
These news, my lords, may cheer our drooping spirits.
I Henry VI. Act v, sc. 2, l. 1. [Charles the Dauphin]
2
Had he been ta'en, we should have heard the news;
Had he been slain, we should have heard the news;
Or had he 'scaped, methinks we should have heard
The happy tidings of his good escape.
III Henry VI. Act ii, sc. 1, l. 4. [Prince of Wales]
Even now we heard the news.
III Henry VI. Act v, sc. 2, l. 32. [Somerset]
Be sure to hear some news.—*III Henry VI,* v, 5, 48.
3
These news are every where; every tongue speaks 'em.
Henry VIII. Act ii, sc. 2, l. 39. [Chamberlain]
Marry, this is yet but young, and may be left
To some ears unrecounted.
Henry VIII. Act iii, sc. 2, l. 47. [Suffolk]
The only use of "unrecounted."
Latest news.—*Richard II,* v, 6, 1.
That 's news indeed.—*Henry VIII,* iii, 2, 402.
4
This news was brought to Richard but even now.
King John. Act v, sc. 3, l. 12. [Messenger]
You breathe these dead news in as dead an ear.
King John. Act v, sc. 7, l. 65. [Salisbury]
5
The news is not so tart.
King Lear. Act iv, sc. 2, l. 88. [Goneril]
So tart a favour.—*Antony and Cleopatra,* ii, 5, 38. The only uses of "tart."
6
The king hath happily received, Macbeth,
The news of thy success.
Macbeth. Act i, sc. 3, l. 89. [Ross]
7
This news is old enough, yet it is every day's news.
Measure for Measure. Act iii, sc. 2, l. 243. [Duke]
Master, master! news, old news, and such news as you never heard of!
The Taming of the Shrew. Act iii, sc. 2, l. 30. [Biondello]
Old news.—*Taming of the Shrew,* iii, 2, 42.
8
There is no composition in these news
That gives them credit.
Othello. Act i, sc. 3, l. 1. [Duke]
News, lads! our wars are done.
Othello. Act ii, sc. 1, l. 20. [Third Gentleman]
9
What news, what news, in this our tottering state?
Richard III. Act iii, sc. 2, l. 37. [Hastings]
"What news?" occurs thirty-six times in the plays.
What news on the Rialto?
The Merchant of Venice. Act i, sc. 3, l. 39. [Shylock] Salanio repeats the same phrase in iii, 1, 1.
How now, Shylock! what news among the merchants?
The Merchant of Venice. Act iii, sc. 1, l. 25. [Salanio]
How now, Tubal, what news from Genoa?
The Merchant of Venice. Act iii, sc. 1, l. 83. [Shylock]
What news, Æneas, from the field to-day?
Troilus and Cressida. Act i, sc. 1, l. 111. [Troilus]
What news with you so early?
Troilus and Cressida. Act iv, sc. 2, l. 48. [Pandarus]
What news from France?—*II Henry VI,* iii, 1, 83.
What news from Oxford?—*Richard II,* v. 2, 52.
News from Verona?—*Romeo and Juliet,* v, 1, 12.
What news more?—*Macbeth,* v, 3, 30.
What 's the news from Venice?—*The Merchant of Venice,* iii, 2, 241.
What 's the news in Rome?—*Coriolanus,* iv, 3, 10.
What 's the news with thee?—*A Midsummer-Night's Dream,* i, 1, 21.
What 's the news with you?—*Measure for Measure,* i, 2, 86; iv, 3, 41; *Hamlet,* i, 2, 42; *Othello,* iii, 4, 109. "What 's the news?" occurs eighteen times in the plays.
What are thy news?—*III Henry VI,* iii, 3, 171.
What is the news?—*Measure for Measure,* iv, 1, 27; *Henry VIII,* v, 1, 61.
These are news indeed.—*Romeo and Juliet,* iii, 5, 124.
10
Second Citizen: Hear you the news abroad?
First Citizen: Ay, that the king is dead.
Second Citizen: Bad news, by 'r lady.
Richard III. Act ii, sc. 3, l. 3.
Hear'st thou the news abroad?
King John. Act iv, sc. 2, l. 160. [King John]
You have heard of the news abroad; I mean the whispered ones?
King Lear. Act ii, sc. 1, l. 7. [Curan]
What news abroad?—*III Henry VI,* ii, 1, 95, and four times in later plays.
11
Good news or bad, that thou comest in so bluntly?
Richard III. Act iv, sc. 3, l. 45. [King Richard]
Am I happy in thy news?—*Richard III,* iv, 3, 24.
12
Though news be sad, yet tell them merrily;
If good, thou shamest the music of sweet news
By playing it to me with so sour a face. . . .
Is thy news good, or bad? answer to that;
Say either, and I 'll stay the circumstance:
Let me be satisfied, is 't good or bad?
Romeo and Juliet. Act ii, sc. 5, l. 22. [Juliet]
If 't be summer news,
Smile to 't before; if winterly, thou need'st

But keep that countenance still.
Cymbeline. Act iii, sc. 4, l. 12. [Imogen] The only use of "winterly."

Pour out the pack of matter to mine ear,
The good and bad together.
Antony and Cleopatra. Act ii, sc. 5, l. 54. [Cleopatra]

1
Curtis: Good Grumio, the news.
Grumio: Why, 'Jack, boy! ho! boy!' and as much news as will thaw.
Taming of the Shrew. Act iv, sc. 1, l. 41.

I pray thee, news.—*The Taming of the Shrew,* iv, 1, 55.

2
News, news from heaven! Marcus, the post is come.
Titus Andronicus. Act iv, sc. 3, l. 77. [Titus]

There is no news.—*The Two Gentlemen of Verona,* i, 3, 55.

I know no news, my lord.—*King Lear,* i, 2, 29.

No news of them?—*The Merchant of Venice,* iii, 1, 94.

Let Time's news
Be known when 'tis brought forth.
Winter's Tale. Act iv, sc. 1, l. 26. [Time]

This news which is called true is so like an old tale, that the verity of it is in strong suspicion.
The Winter's Tale. Act v, sc. 2, l. 29. [Gentleman]

Tailor's news.—*King John,* iv, 2, 195.

II—Good News

3
Valeria: In truth, la, go with me; and I'll tell you excellent news of your husband.
Virginia: O, good madam, there can be none yet.
Valeria: Verily, I do not jest with you; there came news from him last night.
Coriolanus. Act i, sc. 3, l. 100.

4
My news shall be the fruit to that great feast.
Hamlet. Act ii, sc. 2, l. 52. [Polonius]

5
He hath brought us smooth and welcome news.
I Henry IV. Act i, sc. 1, l. 66. [King Henry]

Bardolph: I bring you certain news from Shrewsbury.
Northumberland: Good, an God will!
Bardolph: As good as heart can wish.
II Henry IV. Act i, sc. 1, l. 12.

What! I do bring good news.
II Henry IV. Act v, sc. 3, l. 134. [Pistol]

He brings great news.
Macbeth. Act i, sc. 5, l. 39. [Lady Macbeth]

I should be glad to hear such news as this
Once every hour.
Henry VIII. Act iii, sc. 2, l. 24. [Surrey]

6
I'll be myself the harbinger and make joyful
The hearing of my wife with your approach.
Macbeth. Act i, sc. 4, l. 45. [Macbeth]

7
I have better news in store for you
Than you expect.
The Merchant of Venice. Act v, sc. 1, l. 274. [Portia]

I have heard better news.
II Henry IV. Act ii, sc. 1, l. 179. [Chief Justice]

Bring me better news.—*Richard III,* iv, 4, 510.

8
The news is very fair and good, my lord.
Richard II. Act iii, sc. 3, l. 5. [Northumberland]

Beneficial news.—*Othello,* ii, 2, 7.

Best news.—*Richard III,* iv, 5, 534; *The Tempest,* v, 1, 221.

Joyful news.—*Romeo and Juliet,* v, 1, 2.

9
And thereupon he sends you this good news.
Richard III. Act iii, sc. 2, l. 48. [Catesby]

And wherefore should these good news make me sick? . . .
I should rejoice now at this happy news.
II Henry IV. Act iv, sc. 4, l. 102. [King]

Prince: Heard he the good news yet?
Tell it him.
Gloucester: He alter'd much upon the hearing it.
II Henry IV. Act iv, sc. 5, l. 11.

Shall good news be baffled?
Then, Pistol, lay thy head in Furies' lap.
II Henry IV. Act v, sc. 3, l. 109. [Pistol]

Thou still hast been the father of good news.
Hamlet. Act ii, sc. 2, l. 42. [King]

I know, by that same eye, there's some good news.
Antony and Cleopatra. Act i, sc. 3, l. 19. [Cleopatra] "Good news" is used eighteen times in the plays.

10
Indeed, I am no mourner for that news.
Richard III. Act iii, sc. 2, l. 51. [Hastings]

11
I'll tell you news indifferent good for either.
The Taming of the Shrew. Act i, sc. 2, l. 181. [Hortensio]

III—Bad News

12
Messenger: The nature of bad news infects the teller.
Antony: When it concerns the fool or coward.
Antony and Cleopatra. Act i, sc. 2, l. 99. The only use of "teller."

Though it be honest, it is never good
To bring bad news: give to a gracious message
An host of tongues; but let ill tidings tell
Themselves when they be felt.
Antony and Cleopatra. Act ii, sc. 5, l. 85. [Cleopatra]

13
Some news is come
That turns our countenances.
Coriolanus. Act iv, sc. 6, l. 58. [Messenger]

I do not like this news.—*Coriolanus,* iv, 6, 158.

14
More uneven and unwelcome news
Came from the north.
I Henry IV. Act i, sc. 1, l. 50. [Westmoreland]

Yet the first bringer of unwelcome news
Hath but a losing office, and his tongue
Sounds ever after as a sullen bell,
Remember'd tolling a departed friend.
II Henry IV. Act i, sc. 1, l. 100. [Morton] The only use of "tolling."
I think 'tis no unwelcome news to you.
The Two Gentlemen of Verona. Act ii, sc. 4, l. 81. [Duke] The only uses of "unwelcome news."

1
There 's villanous news abroad.
I Henry IV. Act ii, sc. 4, l. 366. [Falstaff]
Baleful news.—*III Henry VI*, ii, 1, 97.
Fearful news.—*Coriolanus*, iv, 6, 139.
Foul shrewd news.—*King John*, v, 5, 14.
Hard news.—*The Rape of Lucrece*, l. 255.
Stiff news.—*Antony and Cleopatra*, i, 2, 104.
Unsavoury news.—*III Henry VI*, iv, 6, 80.

2
These news,
Having been well, that would have made me sick,
Being sick, have in some measure made me well.
II Henry IV. Act i, sc. 1, l. 137. [Northumberland]
If Henry were recall'd to life again,
These news would cause him once more yield the ghost.
I Henry VI. Act i, sc. 1, l. 66. [Gloucester]
This news, I think, hath turn'd your weapon's edge.
II Henry VI. Act ii, sc. 1, l. 180. [Beaufort]

3
Cold news for me.
II Henry VI. Act i, sc. 1, l. 237. [York]
Cold news, Lord Somerset: but God's will be done!
II Henry VI. Act iii, sc. 1, l. 86. [King Henry]

4
Ay me! what is this world! what news are these!
II Henry VI. Act iii, sc. 2, l. 380. [Queen Margaret]
These news I must confess are full of grief.
III Henry VI. Act iv, sc. 4, l. 13. [Rivers]

5
Bastard: Come, come; sans compliment, what news abroad? . . .
Hubert: O, my sweet sir, news fitting to the night,
Black, fearful, comfortless and horrible.
Bastard: Show me the very wound of this ill news:
I am no woman, I 'll not swoon at it.
King John. Act v, sc. 6, l. 16.
Fellow, be gone: I cannot brook thy sight:
This news hath made thee a most ugly man.
King John. Act iii, sc. 1, l. 36. [Constance]

6
The news I bring Is heavy in my tongue.
Love's Labour's Lost. Act v, sc. 2, l. 726. [Mercade]
A post from Wales loaden with heavy news.
I Henry IV. Act i, sc. 1, l. 37. [Westmoreland]
Yonder is heavy news.—*All's Well that Ends Well*, ii, 3, 258.

7
This news distracts me!
The Merry Wives of Windsor. Act ii, sc. 2, l. 139. [Falstaff]

8
Antonio: I can tell you strange news that you yet dreamt not of.
Leonato: Are they good?
Antonio: As the event stamps them.
Much Ado about Nothing. Act i, sc. 2, l. 4.
I have heard strange news.
King Lear. Act ii, sc. 1, l. 89. [Cornwall]
There 's strange news come.—*Antony and Cleopatra*, iii, 5, 2.

9
Gardener, for telling me these news of woe,
Pray God the plants thou graft'st may never grow.
Richard II. Act iii, sc. 4, l. 100. [Queen]

10
Now, by Saint Paul, this news is bad indeed.
Richard III. Act i, sc. 1, l. 138. [Gloucester]
Archbishop of York: What news?
Messenger: Such news, my lord, as grieves me to unfold.
Richard III. Act ii, sc. 4, l. 38.
Queen Elizabeth: I swoon
With this dead-killing news!
Anne: Despiteful tidings! O unpleasing news!
Richard III. Act iv, sc. 1, l. 35. The only use of "dead-killing."
Unpleasing news.—*Richard II*, iii, 4, 74.

11
O, pardon me for bringing these ill news,
Since you did leave it for my office, sir.
Romeo and Juliet. Act v, sc. 1, l. 22. [Balthasar]
Ill news.—*Much Ado about Nothing*, ii, 1, 180.

12
Speed: What news, then, in your paper?
Launce: The blackest news that ever thou heardest.
Speed: Why, man, how black?
Launce: Why, as black as ink.
The Two Gentlemen of Verona. Act iii, sc. 1, l. 284.

13
This news is mortal to the queen.
Winter's Tale. Act iii, sc. 2, l. 149. [Paulina]

NIGHT

See also Day and Night; Midnight

I—Familiar Phrases

14
A great cause of the night is lack of sun.
As You Like It. Act iii, sc. 2, l. 29. [Corin]
O grim-look'd night! O night with hue so black!
O night, which ever art when day is not!
A Midsummer-Night's Dream. Act v, sc. 1, l. 171. [Pyramus] The only use of "grim-look'd."
When the sun sets, who doth not look for night?
Richard III. Act ii, sc. 3, l. 34. [Citizen]

15
As good to wink, sweet love, as look on night.
The Comedy of Errors. Act iii, sc. 2, l. 58. [Antipholus of Syracuse]

1
Making night hideous.
Hamlet. Act i, sc. 4, l. 54. [Hamlet]
The nights are wholesome.
Hamlet, i, 1, 162. See under TIME.

2
It now draws toward night.
Henry V. Act iii, sc. 6, l. 179. [King Henry]
'Tis almost night.—*Cymbeline*, iii, 6, 67.
'Tis now near night.—*Romeo and Juliet*, iv, 2, 39.
The night comes on.—*King Lear*, ii, 4, 303.
I am glad 'tis night.—*The Merchant of Venice*, ii, 6, 34.
How goes the night?—*Macbeth*, ii, 1, 1.
What is the night?—*Macbeth*, iii, 4, 126.

3
This night the siege assuredly I 'll raise.
I Henry VI. Act i, sc. 2, l. 130. [La Pucelle] "This night" is repeated frequently.
This very night.—*The Two Gentlemen of Verona*, iii, 1, 124; *Othello*, i, 2, 42.
That night.—*Much Ado about Nothing*, ii, 1, 56; *Antony and Cleopatra*, ii, 5, 19.
That very night.—*Romeo and Juliet*, iv, 1, 116.
The very night.—*Much Ado about Nothing*, ii, 2, 46.
Ensuing night.—*Henry VIII*, i, 1, 27.
Last night.—*Richard III*, ii, 4, 1, and twenty-nine times in later plays.
Next night.—*The Merchant of Venice*, v, 1, 302; *Othello*, iii, 3, 340; iv, 2, 219; *Romeo and Juliet*, iv, 5, 5.
The night before.—*King Lear*, ii, 4, 3; *The Rape of Lucrece*, l. 15.
To-morrow night.—*II Henry VI*, i, 4, 84, and nine times in later plays.
Three nights ago.—*King John*, v, 3, 11.
Monday night.—*I Henry IV*, i, 2, 39; *Much Ado about Nothing*, v, 1, 169.
Tuesday night.—*Measure for Measure*, v, 1, 229; *Othello*, iii, 3, 60.
Winter's night.—*II Henry VI*, iii, 2, 335; v, 5, 25; v, 7, 17.

4 Creeping murmur and the poring dark
Fills the wide vessel of the universe.
Henry V. Act iv, Prologue, l. 2. [Chorus] The only use of "poring" and "universe."
Deep night, dark night, the silent of the night.
II Henry VI, i, 4, 19. See WITCH, 1692:13.
The dragon wing of night o'erspreads the earth.
Troilus and Cressida. Act v, sc. 8, l. 17. [Achilles]
The vaporous night approaches.
Measure for Measure. Act iv, sc. 1, l. 58. [Duke] "Vaporous" occurs again in *Macbeth*, iii, 5, 24.

5 I have watch'd the night,
Ay, night by night, in studying good for England.
II Henry VI. Act iii, sc. 1, l. 110. [Gloucester]

6
Night's coverture.
III Henry VI. Act iv, sc. 2, l. 13. [Warwick]
Well cover'd with the night's black mantle.
III Henry VI. Act iv, sc. 2, l. 22. [Warwick]
I have night's cloak to hide me from their sight.
Romeo and Juliet. Act ii, sc. 2, l. 75. [Romeo]
Muffle me, night, awhile.
Romeo and Juliet. Act v, sc. 3, l. 21. [Paris]

7
The deep of night is crept upon our talk.
Julius Cæsar. Act iv, sc. 3, l. 226. [Brutus]
In deep of night to walk.—*The Merry Wives of Windsor*, iv, 4, 40.

8
I must become a borrower of the night
For a dark hour or twain.
Macbeth. Act iii, sc. 1, l. 26. [Banquo]
To black Hecate's summons
The shard-borne beetle with his drowsy hums
Hath rung night's yawning peal.
Macbeth. Act iii, sc. 2, l. 41. [Macbeth] The only use of "shard-borne."

9
The night is long that never finds the day.
Macbeth. Act iv, sc. 3, l. 240. [Malcolm]

10
The close night doth play the runaway.
The Merchant of Venice. Act ii, sc. 6, l. 47. [Lorenzo]

11
Come you to me at night.
The Merry Wives of Windsor. Act ii, sc. 2, l. 276. [Falstaff] "At night" is repeated in *Measure for Measure*, i, 4, 88; *Romeo and Juliet*, iii, 2, 140; *Hamlet*, ii, 2, 84.
By night.—*The Two Gentlemen of Verona*, iii, 2, 83; *Titus Andronicus*, ii, 3, 232; *Romeo and Juliet*, ii, 2, 166; *Timon of Athens*, i, 1, 117; *Julius Cæsar*, ii, 1, 78; *Pericles*, iii, 1, 12; *Venus and Adonis*, l. 732; 755; *Sonnets*, lxxxvi.
All night.—*Measure for Measure*, iv, 3, 49; 57; *Henry V*, iv, 1, 77; iv, 4, 10; *Julius Cæsar*, ii, 1, 88; *King Lear*, ii, 2, 142; *Cymbeline*, iv, 2, 294.
All night long.—*Hamlet*, i, 1, 160.
All the night.—*Romeo and Juliet*, iii, 3, 159; *King Lear*, ii, 4, 90.
The livelong night.—*Macbeth*, ii, 3, 65. "Livelong" is used only twice more in the plays, in *Julius Cæsar*, i, 1, 46, and in *Troilus and Cressida*, i, 3, 147, both "The livelong day."
Ere night.—*III Henry VI*, ii, 5, 59; v, 4, 69; *I Henry IV*, v, 2, 73; *Henry V*, iv, 3, 116; *Julius Cæsar*, v, 3, 109; *The Passionate Pilgrim*, l. 312.
Till night.—*King Lear*, ii, 2, 142.

12
The night is dark; light and spirits will become it well.
The Merry Wives of Windsor. Act v, sc. 2, l. 13. [Page]
Dark night.—*Love's Labour's Lost*, i, 1, 42; *Much Ado about Nothing*, iii, 3, 167; *Romeo and Juliet*, ii, 2, 106; *The Rape of Lucrece*, l. 729.
Dark dismal-dreaming night.—*The Passionate Pilgrim*, l. 200. The only use of "dismal-dreaming."
Darkest night.—*Hamlet*, v, 2, 267.
Dark-eyed night.—*King Lear*, ii, 1, 121. The only use of "dark-eyed."

1
No night is now with hymn or carol blest.
A Midsummer-Night's Dream. Act ii, sc. 1, l. 102. [Titania]
Dark night, that from the eye his function takes,
The ear more quick of apprehension makes;
Wherein it doth impair the seeing sense,
It pays the hearing double recompense.
A Midsummer-Night's Dream. Act iii, sc. 2, l. 177. [Hermia]

2
In this time of the night!
Othello. Act i, sc. 2, l. 94. [Brabantio]
It is now high supper-time, and the night grows to waste.
Othello. Act iv, sc. 2, l. 249. [Iago]
This is the night
That either makes me or fordoes me quite.
Othello. Act v, sc. 1, l. 128. [Iago] "Fordoes" is repeated in *Hamlet,* ii, 1, 103.

3
She sung, and made the night-bird mute.
Pericles. Act iv, Gower, l. 26. The only use of "night-bird."
Night-brawler.—*Othello,* ii, 3, 196.
Night-cap.—*Julius Cæsar,* i, 2, 247; *Othello,* ii, 1, 316.
Night-crow.—*III Henry VI,* v, 6, 45.
Night-dogs.—*The Merry Wives of Windsor,* v, 5, 252.
Night-foes.—*III Henry VI,* iv, 3, 22.
Night-gown.—*Much Ado about Nothing,* iii, 4, 18; *Macbeth,* ii, 2, 70; v, 1, 5; 69; *Othello,* iv, 3, 34.
Night-mare.—*King Lear,* iii, 4, 126.
Night-owl.—*Richard II,* iii, 3, 183; *Twelfth Night,* ii, 3, 60.
Night-raven.—*Much Ado about Nothing,* ii, 3, 84.
Night-wanderers.—*A Midsummer-Night's Dream,* ii, 1, 39; *Venus and Adonis,* l. 825.

4
Wore out the night.
The Rape of Lucrece, l. 123.

5
The eye of heaven is out, and misty night
Covers the shame that follows sweet delight.
The Rape of Lucrece, l. 356.

6
Now stole upon the time the dead of night.
The Rape of Lucrece, l. 162; l. 449.
Dead of night.—*II Henry IV,* i, 1, 72; *Twelfth Night,* i, 5, 290. See also MIDNIGHT.
Aged night.—*Richard III,* iv, 4, 16.

7
Shuts up his windows, locks fair daylight out
And makes himself an artificial night.
Romeo and Juliet. Act i, sc. 1, l. 145. [Montague]
Night by night.—*Romeo and Juliet,* i, 4, 70.
Bescreen'd in night.—*Romeo and Juliet,* ii, 2, 52. The only use of "bescreen'd."

8 Come, civil night,
Thou sober-suited matron, all in black,
And learn me how to lose a winning match,
Play'd for a pair of stainless maidenhoods.
Romeo and Juliet. Act iii, sc. 2, l. 10. [Juliet] The only use of "sober-suited."
Come, gentle night, come, loving, black-brow'd night,
Give me my Romeo.
Romeo and Juliet. Act iii, sc. 2, l. 20. [Juliet] "Black-brow'd night" is repeated in *A Midsummer-Night's Dream,* iii, 2, 387.
Here walk I in the black brow of night.
King John. Act v, sc. 6, l. 17. [Hubert]
Black-corner'd night.—*Timon of Athens,* v, 1, 47. The only use of "black-corner'd."
Black-faced night.—*Venus and Adonis,* l. 773. "Black-faced" is repeated in *Richard III,* i, 2, 159: "Black-faced Clifford"; *The Rape of Lucrece,* l. 547: "Black-faced cloud"; and *The Rape of Lucrece,* l. 1518: "Black-faced storms."
Black night.—*Richard III,* i, 2, 131; *Sonnets,* lxxiii; *Titus Andronicus,* v, 1, 64.
Blind concealing night.—*The Rape of Lucrece,* l. 675.
Cloudy night.—*Romeo and Juliet,* iii, 2, 4.
Collied night.—*A Midsummer-Night's Dream,* i, 1, 145. "Collied" (darkened) is repeated in *Othello,* ii, 3, 206.
Death's dateless night.—*Sonnets,* xxx.
Dim night.—*Romeo and Juliet,* v, 3, 107.
Eyeless night.—*King John,* v, 6, 12.
Glimmering night.—*A Midsummer-Night's Dream,* ii, 1, 77.
Hot midsummer night.—*As You Like It,* iv, 1, 103.
Secret night.—*Romeo and Juliet,* ii, 4, 203.
Sightless night.—*The Rape of Lucrece,* l. 1013.
Steepy night.—*Sonnets,* lxiii. "Steepy" is repeated in *Timon of Athens,* i, 1, 75.
Stumbling night.—*King John,* v, 5, 18.
Swart-complexion'd night.—*Sonnets,* xxviii. The only use of "swart-complexion'd."

9
All the frosty nights that I have watch'd.
Titus Andronicus. Act iii, sc. 1, l. 5. [Titus]
It hath been the longest night
That e'er I watch'd and the most heaviest.
The Two Gentlemen of Verona. Act iv, sc. 2, l. 140. [Julia]
This will last out a night in Russia,
When nights are longest there.
Measure for Measure. Act ii, sc. 1, l. 139. [Angelo]
Endless night.—*Richard II,* i, 3, 177; 223.
Eternal night.—*Richard III,* iv, 3, 62.
Lasting night.—*King John,* iii, 4, 27.
Perpetual night.—*The Rape of Lucrece,* l. 784.
Watchful night.—*II Henry IV,* iv, 5, 25.

10 'The night is spent.'
'Why, what of that?' quoth she.
Venus and Adonis, l. 717.

II—Pleasant Night

11
Let's have one other gaudy night.
Antony and Cleopatra. Act iii, sc. 13, l. 183. [Antony]
Burn this night with torches: know, my hearts,
I hope well of to-morrow.
Antony and Cleopatra. Act iv, sc. 2, l. 41. [Antony]

12
Ha! 'twas a merry night.
II Henry IV. Act iii, sc. 2, l. 210. [Shallow]

An we shall be merry, now comes in the sweet o' the night.
II Henry IV. Act v, sc. 3, l. 52. [Silence]

1
I wish your highness A quiet night.
Henry VIII. Act v, sc. 1, l. 76. [Duke of Suffolk]

Blessed night.—*Romeo and Juliet,* ii, 2, 139.
Brave night.—*King Lear,* iii, 2, 79.
Calmest and most stillest Night.—*II Henry IV,* iii, 1, 28. The only use of "calmest" and "stillest."
Careful night.—*Pericles,* i, 2, 81.
Happy night.—*I Henry VI,* ii, 1, 11; *Romeo and Juliet,* i, 3, 106.
Peaceful night.—*Pericles,* i, 2, 4.

2
Casca: What night is this!
Cassius: A very pleasing night to honest men.
Julius Cæsar. Act i, sc. 3, l. 42.

3
Come, seeling night,
Scarf up the tender eye of pitiful day;
And with thy bloody and invisible hand
Cancel and tear to pieces that great bond
Which keeps me pale!
Macbeth. Act iii, sc. 2, l. 46. [Macbeth]
The only use of "seeling," a term in falconry meaning to close a hawk's eyes by drawing the upper eyelids down with a thread.

4
Lorenzo: The moon shines bright: in such a night as this, . . .
Troilus methinks mounted the Trojan walls
And sigh'd his soul toward the Grecian tents,
Where Cressid lay that night.
Jessica: In such a night
Did Thisbe fearfully o'ertrip the dew. . . .
Lorenzo: In such a night
Stood Dido with a willow in her hand
Upon the wild sea banks and waft her love
To come again to Carthage.
Jessica: In such a night
Medea gather'd the enchanted herbs
That did renew old Æson.
Lorenzo: In such a night
Did Jessica steal from the wealthy Jew
And with an unthrift love did run from Venice
As far as Belmont.
Jessica: In such a night
Did young Lorenzo swear he loved her well,
Stealing her soul with many vows of faith
And ne'er a true one.
Lorenzo: In such a night
Did pretty Jessica, like a little shrew,
Slander her love, and he forgave it her.
Jessica: I would out-night you, did no body come.
The Merchant of Venice. Act v, sc. 1, l. 1.
The only use of "out-night."

The night Is shiny.—*Antony and Cleopatra,* iv, 9, 2. The only use of "shiny."
Shining nights.—*Love's Labour's Lost,* i, 1, 90.

5
All this while hath revell'd in the night.
Richard II. Act iii, sc. 2, l. 48. [King Richard]

Consorted with the humorous night.
Romeo and Juliet. Act ii, sc. 1, l. 31. [Benvolio]

Dewy night.—*The Rape of Lucrece,* l. 1232.

III—Unpleasant Night

6
The foul womb of night.
Henry V. Act iv, Prologue, l. 4. [Chorus]

Horrid night, the child of hell.
Henry V. Act iv, sc. 1, l. 288. [King Henry]

Solemn night with slow sad gait descended
To ugly hell.
The Rape of Lucrece, l. 1081.

Hell-black night.—*King Lear,* iv, 1, 34. The only use of "hell-black."

7
The cripple tardy-gaited night
Who, like a foul and ugly witch, doth limp
So tediously away.
Henry V. Act iv, Prologue, l. 20. [Chorus]
The only use of "tardy-gaited." "Tediously" occurs only once more in the plays, in *Troilus and Cressida,* iv, 2, 13.

The weary and all-watched night.
Henry V. Act iv, Prologue, l. 38. [Chorus]
The only use of "all-watched."

O weary night, O long and tedious night,
Abate thy hours!
A Midsummer-Night's Dream. Act iii, sc. 2, l. 431. [Helena]

Tedious nights.—*Richard III,* iii, 2, 6; *The Two Gentlemen of Verona,* i, 1, 31; *The Rape of Lucrece,* l. 1379; *Richard II,* v, 1, 40.

8
For my part, I have walk'd about the streets,
Submitting me unto the perilous night.
Julius Cæsar. Act i, sc. 3, l. 46. [Cassius]

This dreadful night,
That thunders, lightens, opens graves, and roars.
Julius Cæsar. Act i, sc. 3, l. 70. [Cassius]

For now, this fearful night,
There is no stir or walking in the streets;
And the complexion of the element
In favour's like the work we have in hand,
Most bloody, fiery, and most terrible.
Julius Cæsar. Act i, sc. 3, l. 126. [Cassius]

9
This night, whose black contagious breath
Already smokes about the burning crest
Of the old, feeble and day-wearied sun.
King John. Act v, sc. 4, l. 33. [Melun] The only use of "day-wearied."

10
This night, wherein the cub-drawn bear would couch,
The lion and the belly-pinched wolf
Keep their fur dry, unbonneted he runs,
And bids what will take all.
King Lear. Act iii, sc. 1, l. 12. [Gentleman]
The only use of "cub-drawn" and "belly-pinched." "Unbonneted" is repeated in *Othello,* i, 2, 23. "Fur" is used only once again in the plays, in *Troilus and Cressida,* ii, 2, 38.

Here's a night pities neither wise man nor fool.
King Lear. Act iii, sc. 2, l. 13. [Fool]

Things that love night
Love not such nights as these.
King Lear. Act iii, sc. 2, l. 42. [Kent]

In such a night
To shut me out! . . . In such a night as this!
King Lear. Act iii, sc. 4, l. 17. [King Lear]

This cold night will turn us all to fools and madmen.
King Lear. Act iii, sc. 4, l. 80. [Fool]

'Tis a naughty night to swim in.
King Lear. Act iii, sc. 4, l. 115. [Fool]

What a night's this!—*King Lear,* iii, 4, 175.

'Tis a wild night.—*King Lear,* ii, 4, 311.

1 Come, thick night,
And pall thee in the dunnest smoke of hell,
That my keen knife see not the wound it makes,
Nor heaven peep through the blanket of the dark,
To cry 'Hold, hold!'
Macbeth. Act i, sc. 5, l. 51. [Lady Macbeth] The only use of "dunnest." "Pall" occurs again in *Hamlet,* v, 2, 9.

The night has been unruly.
Macbeth, ii, 3, 59. See under OMEN.

Macbeth: 'Twas a rough night.
Lennox: My young remembrance cannot parallel
A fellow to it.
Macbeth. Act ii, sc. 3, l. 66.

This sore night Hath trifled former knowings.
Macbeth. Act ii, sc. 4, l. 3. [Old Man] The only use of "trifled."

It is a heavy night.—*Othello,* v, 1, 42.

2
Cermino: 'T has been a turbulent and stormy night.
Servant: I have been in many; but such a night as this,
Till now, I ne'er endured.
Pericles. Act iii, sc. 2, l. 3.

3
Sable Night, mother of Dread and Fear,
Upon the world dim darkness doth display,
And in her vaulty prison stows the Day.
The Rape of Lucrece, l. 117.

O comfort-killing Night, image of hell!
Dim register and notary of shame!
Black stage for tragedies and murders fell!
Vast sin-concealing chaos! nurse of blame!
Blind muffled bawd! dark harbour for defame!
Grim cave of death! whispering conspirator
With close-tongued treason and the ravisher.
The Rape of Lucrece, l. 764. The only use of "comfort-killing," "sin-concealing," and "close-tongued."

O hateful, vaporous and foggy Night!
The Rape of Lucrece, l. 771.

O Night, thou furnace of foul-reeking smoke.
The Rape of Lucrece, l. 799. The only use of "foul-reeking."

O, this dread night, wouldst thou one hour come back,
I could prevent this storm and shun thy wrack!
The Rape of Lucrece, l. 965.

4
O, I have pass'd a miserable night,
So full of ugly sights, of ghastly dreams,
That, as I am a Christian faithful man,
I would not spend another such a night,
Though 'twere to buy a world of happy days,
So full of dismal terror was the time!
Richard III. Act i, sc. 4, l. 2. [Clarence]

5
The merciless and pitchy night.
Venus and Adonis, l. 821.

Pitchy night.—*All's Well that Ends Well,* iv, 4, 24.

Baleful burning night.—*Titus Andronicus,* v, 3, 83.

Cursed crimeful night.—*The Rape of Lucrece,* l. 970. "Crimeful" is repeated in *Hamlet,* iv, 7, 7.

Dead night.—*Sonnets,* xliii.

Deadly night.—*I Henry VI,* ii, 4, 127.

Dire night.—*Romeo and Juliet,* v, 3, 247.

Direful night.—*The Rape of Lucrece,* l. 741.

False night.—*The Rape of Lucrece,* l. 1075.

Frowning night.—*Romeo and Juliet,* ii, 3, 1.

Ghastly night.—*Sonnets,* xxvii.

Hideous night.—*Sonnets,* xii.

Mortal night.—*Pericles,* v, 1, 37.

Numb cold night.—*Richard III,* ii, 1, 117.

Sullied night.—*Sonnets,* xv. "Sullied" is repeated in *I Henry VI,* iv, 4, 6.

Tyrannous night.—*King Lear,* iii, 4, 156.

Ugly night.—*Troilus and Cressida,* v, 8, 6; *The Rape of Lucrece,* l. 925; *Venus and Adonis,* l. 1041.

Uncheerful night.—*The Rape of Lucrece,* l. 1024. The only use of "uncheerful."

Weary night.—*Sonnets,* lxi.

Windy night.—*Sonnets,* xc.

Night of sorrow.—*Venus and Adonis,* l. 481.

Night of woe.—*Sonnets,* cxx.

IV—Night and Love

6
I'll make a journey twice as far, to enjoy
A second night of such sweet shortness which
Was mine in Britain.
Cymbeline. Act ii, sc. 4, l. 43. [Iachimo]

7
It is not night when I do see your face,
Therefore I think I am not in the night.
A Midsummer-Night's Dream. Act ii, sc. 1, l. 221. [Helena]

Were I with her, the night would post too soon;
But now are minutes added to the hours.
The Passionate Pilgrim, l. 205.

8
Gallop apace, you fiery-footed steeds,
Towards Phœbus' lodging: such a waggoner
As Phaëton would whip you to the west,
And bring in cloudy night immediately.
Spread thy close curtain, love-performing night,
That runaways' eyes may wink, and Romeo
Leap to these arms, untalk'd of and unseen.
Romeo and Juliet. Act iii, sc. 2, l. 1. [Ju-

liet] The only use of "fiery-footed" and "love-performing." Shakespeare mentions Phœbus eighteen times and Phaëton five.

Phœbus' steeds are founder'd
Or night kept chain'd below.

Tempest. Act iv, sc. 1, l. 31. [Ferdinand]

1
Troilus: Dreaming night will hide our joys no longer. . . .
Cressida: Night hath been too brief.
Troilus: Beshrew the witch! with venomous wights she stays
As tediously as hell, but flies the grasps of love
With wings more momentary-swift than thought.

Troilus and Cressida. Act iv, sc. 2, l. 10. The only use of "momentary-swift."

2
Duke: No man hath access by day to her.
Valentine: Why, then, I would resort to her by night.

The Two Gentlemen of Verona. Act iii, sc. 1, l. 110.

The night's dead silence
Will well become such sweet-complaining grievance.

The Two Gentlemen of Verona. Act iii, sc. 2, l. 85. [Proteus] The only use of "sweet-complaining."

Now of this dark night I perceive the reason.
Venus and Adonis, l. 727.

NIGHTINGALE

3
The nightingale, if she should sing by day,
When every goose is cackling, would be thought
No better a musician than the wren.

The Merchant of Venice. Act v, sc. 1, l. 104. [Portia]

4
Every thing did banish moan,
Save the nightingale alone:
She, poor bird, as all forlorn,
Lean'd her breast up-till a thorn,
And there sung the dolefull'st ditty,
That to hear it was great pity:
'Fie, fie, fie,' now would she cry;
'Tereu, tereu!' by and by.

The Passionate Pilgrim, l. 379. The only use of "up-till" and "dolefull'st."

5
It was the nightingale, and not the lark,
That pierced the fearful hollow of thine ear;
Nightly she sings on yond pomegranate-tree.

Romeo and Juliet. Act iii, sc. 5, l. 2. [Juliet] The only use of "pomegranate-tree." "Pomegranate" occurs in *All's Well that Ends Well,* ii, 3, 276.

Twenty caged nightingales do sing.
The Taming of the Shrew. Induction, sc. 2, l. 38. [Lord]

6
His Philomel must lose her tongue to-day.
Titus Andronicus. Act ii, sc. 3, l. 43. [Aaron]

Philomel in summer's front doth sing
And stops her pipe in growth of riper days.
Sonnets. No. cii. Philomel is used nine times.

7
Fair Philomela, she but lost her tongue,
And in a tedious sampler sew'd her mind.

Titus Andronicus. Act ii, sc. 4, l. 38. [Marcus] Philomela is used again in iv, 1, 52.

While Philomela sits and sings, I sit and mark,
And wish her lays were tuned like the lark;
For she doth welcome daylight with her ditty.

The Passionate Pilgrim, l. 197.

8
Nightingales answer daws.
Twelfth Night. Act iii, sc. 4, l. 38. [Malvolio]

My nightingale.—*Antony and Cleopatra,* iv, 8, 18.

NOBILITY

See also Ancestry, Quality

9
When I consider
What great creation and what dole of honour
Flies where you bid it, I find that she, which late
Was in my nobler thoughts most base, is now
The praised of the king; who, so ennobled,
Is as 'twere born so.

All's Well that Ends Well. Act ii, sc. 3, l. 175. [Bertram] The only use of "ennobled."

10
The nobleness of life Is to do thus.
Antony and Cleopatra. Act i, sc. 1, l. 36. [Antony]

Nobleness of birth.—*The Two Gentlemen of Verona,* i, 3, 33. See under Ancestry.
Nobleness of mind.—*Richard III,* iii, 7, 14.

11
'Tis your noblest course.
Antony and Cleopatra. Act iii, sc. 13, l. 78. [Thyreus]

Noblest love.—*Troilus and Cressida,* iv, 1, 33.
Noblest man.—*Julius Cæsar,* iii, 1, 256.
Noblest mind.—*Timon of Athens,* i, 1, 291.
Noblest-minded.—*Julius Cæsar,* i, 3, 122.
Noblest of men.—*Antony and Cleopatra,* iv, 15, 59.

12
Thrice-nobler than myself!
Antony and Cleopatra. Act iv, sc. 14, l. 95. [Antony] The only use of the phrase.

Thrice-noble.—*II Henry VI,* iii, 1, 266, and three times in later plays.

13
What 's brave, what 's noble,
Let 's do it after the high Roman fashion,
And make death proud to take us.

Antony and Cleopatra. Act iv, sc. 15, l. 86. [Cleopatra]

'Tis noble.—*Antony and Cleopatra,* ii, 3, 30.
Be noble to myself.—*Antony and Cleopatra,* v, 2, 192.

14
O Antony,
Nobler than my revolt is infamous,
Forgive me in thine own particular.

Antony and Cleopatra. Act iv, sc. 9, l. 18. [Enobarbus] "Infamous" is used only once again in the plays, in *I Henry VI,* iv, 1, 30. See under Fact.

Let the world see His nobleness well acted.
Antony and Cleopatra. Act v, sc. 2, l. 44. [Proculeius]

1 I sin in envying his nobility,
And were I any thing but what I am,
I would wish me only he.
Coriolanus. Act i, sc. 1, l. 234. [Caius]
He 's right noble.—*Coriolanus,* ii, 2, 133.
You do the nobler.—*Coriolanus,* iii, 2, 6.
The man is noble.—*Coriolanus,* v, 6, 126.
The man was noble.—*Coriolanus,* v, 3, 145.

2 The god of soldiers . . . inform
Thy thoughts with nobleness; that thou mayst prove
To shame unvulnerable.
Coriolanus. Act v, sc. 3, l. 71. [Coriolanus] The only use of "unvulnerable." "Invulnerable" occurs three times.

3 He is one of the noblest note.
Cymbeline. Act i, sc. 6, l. 21. [Imogen, reading]
I had rather not be so noble as I am; they dare not fight with me.
Cymbeline. Act ii, sc. 1, l. 19. [Cloten]
A nobler sir ne'er lived 'Twixt sky and ground.
Cymbeline. Act v, sc. 5, l. 145. [Iachimo]
Noble in reason.—*Hamlet,* ii, 2, 316.

4 How many nobles then should hold their places,
That must strike sail to spirits of vile sort!
II Henry IV. Act v, sc. 2, l. 17. [Warwick]
Cowardly nobles.—*Coriolanus,* iv, 6, 122.
Dastard nobles.—*Coriolanus,* iv, 5, 81.
Factious nobles.—*Troilus and Cressida,* ii, 2, 209.
Let him be a noble.—*Henry VIII,* iv, 2, 146. "Noble," in the sense of a member of the nobility, is used frequently throughout the plays.

5 True nobility is exempt from fear:
More can I bear than you dare execute.
II Henry VI. Act iv, sc. 1, l. 129. [Suffolk]
True nobility warrants these words.—*Titus Andronicus,* i, 1, 271.
Like her true nobility.—*Henry VIII,* ii, 4, 142.

6 If we live thus tamely, . . .
Farewell nobility; let his grace go forward,
And dare us with his cap like larks.
Henry VIII. Act iii, sc. 2, l. 279. [Surrey]

7 The nobility think scorn to go in leather aprons.
II Henry VI. Act iv, sc. 2, l. 13. [Holland]
The nobility Held in contempt.
Richard III. Act i, sc. 3, l. 79. [Gloucester]
Despised nobility.—*Henry VIII,* iii, 2, 291.
Stain'd nobility.—*I Henry IV,* v, 4, 13.
Awake, English nobility!—*I Henry VI,* i, 1, 78.
Noble English.—*King John,* v, 4, 10; *Henry V,* i, 2, 111.
Noblest English.—*Henry V,* iii, 1, 17.
French nobility.—*Henry V,* i, 2, 110.
The nobility of Rome.—*Coriolanus,* iv, 7, 29.

Stand aside, nobility.—*I Henry IV,* ii, 4, 429.

8 Your grace must needs deserve all strangers' loves,
You are so noble.
Henry VIII. Act ii, sc. 2, l. 102. [Campeius]
Your grace is noble.—*Henry VIII,* i, 4, 38.
I might call him
A thing divine, for nothing natural
I ever saw so noble.
The Tempest. Act i, sc. 2, l. 417. [Miranda]
So noble.—*Troilus and Cressida,* ii, 2, 158; *Coriolanus,* iii, 1, 56; *Timon of Athens,* iv, 2, 6; *The Winter's Tale,* iv, 4, 21; *Henry VIII,* i, 4, 67; v, 3, 74.
So noble and so great.—*Measure for Measure,* i, 1, 50.
So noble and so true.—*Henry VIII,* iii, 2, 423.

9 When did he regard
The stamp of nobleness in any person
Out of himself?
Henry VIII. Act iii, sc. 2, l. 11. [Suffolk]

10 Well, Brutus, thou art noble; yet, I see,
Thy honourable metal may be wrought
From that it is disposed: therefore it is meet
That noble minds keep ever with their likes;
For who so firm that cannot be seduced?
Julius Cæsar. Act i, sc. 2, l. 312. [Cassius]
This was the noblest Roman of them all.
Julius Cæsar. Act v, sc. 5, l. 68. [Antony]

11 A noble temper dost thou show in this;
And great affections wrestling in thy bosom
Doth make an earthquake of nobility.
King John. Act v, sc. 2, l. 40. [Dauphin]

12 But signs of nobleness, like stars, shall shine
On all deservers.
Macbeth. Act i, sc. 4, l. 41. [Duncan]
In his royalty of nature
Reigns that which would be fear'd.
Macbeth. Act iii, sc. 1, l. 50. [Macbeth]

13 Thou art too noble to conserve a life
In base appliances.
Measure for Measure. Act iii, sc. 1, l. 88. [Isabella]
His nature is too noble for the world.
Coriolanus. Act iii, sc. 1, l. 255. [Menenius Agrippa]
Too noble.—*Coriolanus,* iii, 2, 40.

14 He is of a noble strain, of approved valour and confirmed honesty.
Much Ado about Nothing. Act ii, sc. 1, l. 394. [Don Pedro]

15 Base men being in love have then a nobility in their natures more than is native to them.
Othello. Act ii, sc. 1, l. 217. [Iago]
Nobility of love.—*Hamlet,* i, 2, 110.

16 Would God that any in this noble presence
Were enough noble to be upright judge
Of noble Richard! then true noblesse would
Learn him forbearance from so foul a wrong.
Richard II. Act iv, sc. 1, l. 117. [Bishop of Carlisle] The only use of "noblesse."

1 Many fair promotions
Are daily given to ennoble those
That scarce, some two days since, were worth a noble.
Richard III. Act i, sc. 3, l. 80. [Gloucester] The only use of "ennoble."
A noble shalt thou have.—*Henry V,* ii, 1, 112.
I shall have my noble?—*Henry V,* ii, 1, 119.
Let it be but twenty nobles.—*II Henry VI,* ii, 1, 167.

2
O, that your young nobility could judge
What 'twere to lose it, and be miserable!
Richard III. Act i, sc. 3, l. 257. [Queen Margaret]

3 You
Whose star-like nobleness gave life and influence
To their whole being!
Timon of Athens. Act v, sc. 1, l. 66. [Poet] "Star-like" is repeated in *Henry VIII,* v, 5, 47.
The affection of nobleness which nature shows above her breeding.
The Winter's Tale. Act v, sc. 2, l. 40. [Gentleman]
To see his nobleness!
Winter's Tale. Act ii, sc. 3, l. 12. [Leontes]

4
A nobler man, a braver warrior,
Lives not this day within the city walls.
Titus Andronicus. Act i, sc. 1, l. 25. [Marcus]
No doubt he 's noble.—*Henry VIII,* i, 3, 57.
Noble as he is.—*II Henry VI,* v, 3, 14.
Noble she is.—*II Henry VI,* ii, 1, 194.
Noble she was.—*All 's Well that Ends Well,* v, 3, 95.
You have been noble.—*Pericles,* v, 1, 264.
Noble and true-hearted.—*King Lear,* i, 2, 126.
Noble and valiant.—*Othello,* ii, 2, 1.
Noble and young.—*Timon of Athens,* v, 4, 13.
Noble, wise, judicious.—*Macbeth,* iv, 2, 16.
How noble.—*Much Ado about Nothing,* iii, 1, 60.
Most noble.—*Julius Cæsar,* iii, 1, 199.
Right noble.—*Richard II,* v, 6, 18.
Very noble.—*Othello,* i, 3, 77.
More noble than the world.—*Twelfth Night,* ii, 4, 84.
Noblest of thy strain.—*Julius Cæsar,* v, 1, 59.

5
He seems to be the more noble in being fantastical.
Winter's Tale. Act iv, sc. 4, l. 778. [Clown]
No less noble.—*Troilus and Cressida,* ii, 3, 159.
Less noble.—*Richard III,* ii, 1, 91.

NOISE

See also Clamour, Sound

6
Why, these balls bound, there 's noise in it.
All 's Well that Ends Well. Act ii, sc. 3, l. 314. [Parolles]

7
Cleopatra, catching but the least noise of this, dies instantly.
Antony and Cleopatra. Act i, sc. 2, l. 145. [Enobarbus]
Noises it against us.—*Antony and Cleopatra,* iii, 6, 96.
The noise goes.—*Troilus and Cressida,* i, 2, 12.

8
Who is that at the door that keeps all this noise?
The Comedy of Errors. Act iii, sc. 1, l. 61. [Adriana]

9
Marcius: O, they are at it!
Lartius: Their noise be our instruction.
Coriolanus. Act i, sc. 4, l. 21.
But hark, what noise the general makes!
Coriolanus. Act i, sc. 5, l. 10. [Marcius]
Before him he carries noise, and behind him he leaves tears.
Coriolanus. Act ii, sc. 1, l. 174. [Volumnia]
Unshout the noise that banish'd Marcius.
Coriolanus, v, 5, 4. See under WELCOME.
He returns, Splitting the air with noise.
Coriolanus. Act v, sc. 6, l. 51. [Conspirator]
Dreadful noise.—*Richard III,* i, 4, 22.
Loudest noise.—*Cymbeline,* iii, 5, 44.

10
See if thou canst find out Sneak's noise; Mistress Tearsheet would fain hear some music.
II Henry IV. Act ii, sc. 4, l. 12. [Drawer]

11
The hum of either army stilly sounds.
Henry V. Act iv, Prologue, l. 5. [Chorus] The only use of "stilly."

12
What noise is this? what traitors have we here?
I Henry VI. Act i, sc. 3, l. 15. [Woodville]
What noise is this?—*II Henry VI,* iii, 2, 236; *Troilus and Cressida,* ii, 2, 97; *Othello,* v, 1, 48.
What noise is here?—*Romeo and Juliet,* iv, 5, 17.
What noise there, ho?—*The Winter's Tale,* ii, 3, 39.
What means this noise?—*II Henry VI,* ii, 1, 59.
What is that noise?—*Macbeth,* v, 5, 7.
But, hark, what noise?—*Measure for Measure,* iv, 2, 72.
Who makes that noise there?—*Measure for Measure,* iv, 3, 27.
Wherefore 's this noise?—*Antony and Cleopatra,* v, 2, 233.
What was the second noise for?—*Julius Cæsar,* i, 2, 224.

13
What stir is this? what tumult 's in the heavens?
Whence cometh this alarum and the noise?
I Henry VI. Act i, sc. 5, l. 98. [Talbot]
What halloing and what stir is this to-day?
The Two Gentlemen of Verona. Act v, sc. 4, l. 13. [Valentine] "Halloing" is repeated in *II Henry IV,* i, 2, 213.

14 The noise of thy cross-bow
Will scare the herd, and so my shoot is lost.
III Henry VI. Act iii, sc. 1, l. 6. [First Keeper] "Cross-bow" is repeated in *Henry V,* iv, 8, 99.
Noise of targets.—*Henry VIII,* Prol., 15.

1 Such a noise arose
As the shrouds make at sea in a stiff tempest,
As loud, and to as many tunes.
Henry VIII. Act iv, sc. 1, l. 71. [Gentleman]

You 'll leave your noise anon, ye rascals.
Henry VIII. Act v, sc. 4, l. 1. [Porter]

2 Bid every noise be still: peace yet again!
Julius Cæsar. Act i, sc. 2, l. 14. [Casca]

Make no noise, make no noise; draw the curtains: so, so, so.
King Lear. Act iii, sc. 6, l. 89. [King Lear]

You shall also make no noise in the streets.
Much Ado about Nothing. Act iii, sc. 3, l. 36. [Dogberry]

Make no noise.—*The Merchant of Venice,* iv, 1, 76; v, 1, 3.
Make no more noise.—*Othello,* iii, 1, 13.
No noise.—*The Tempest,* iv, 1, 216.
Here are . . . no noise.—*Titus Andronicus,* i, 1, 155.

3 How is 't with me, when every noise appals me?
Macbeth. Act ii, sc. 2, l. 58. [Macbeth]

Didst thou not hear a noise?—*Macbeth,* ii, 2, 15.
That way the noise is.—*Macbeth,* v, 7, 14.
The noise was here.—*Othello,* v, 2, 93.
I hear some noise within.—*Romeo and Juliet,* ii, 2, 36; v, 3, 151.
There was a noise, That 's verity.—*The Tempest,* ii, 1, 320.
Mark the high noises.—*King Lear,* iii, 6, 118.

4 He goes but to see a noise that he heard.
A Midsummer-Night's Dream. Act iii, sc. 1, l. 93. [Quince]

The noise they make
Will cause Demetrius to awake.
A Midsummer-Night's Dream. Act iii, sc. 2, l. 116. [Oberon]

5 No noise but owls' and wolves' death-boding cries.
The Rape of Lucrece, l. 165. The only use of "death-boding."

6 Let 's march without the noise of threatening drum.
Richard II, iii, 3, 51. See under DRUM.

7 With the very noise I trembling waked.
Richard III, i, 4, 60. See under DREAM.

8 Think you a little din can daunt mine ears?
The Taming of the Shrew, i, 2, 200. See under WOOING for full quotation.

O, 'twas a din to fright a monster's ear,
To make an earthquake!
The Tempest. Act ii, sc. 1, l. 314. [Antonio]

Brazen din.—*Antony and Cleopatra,* iv, 8, 36.
The din of war.—*Coriolanus,* ii, 2, 119.
A din confused.—*Coriolanus,* iii, 3, 20.

9 Be not afeard; the isle is full of noises.
The Tempest. Act iii, sc. 2, l. 144. [Caliban]

With strange and several noises
Of roaring, shrieking, howling, jingling chains,
And moe diversity of sounds, all horrible.
Tempest. Act v, sc. 1, l. 232. [Boatswain] The only use of "jingling" and "diversity."

10 Let us sit down and mark their yelping noise.
Titus Andronicus. Act ii, sc. 3, l. 20. [Tamora] "Yelping" is repeated in *I Henry VI,* iv, 2, 47: "Yelping kennel."

When he hath ceased his ill-resounding noise.
Venus and Adonis, l. 919. The only use of "ill-resounding."

NOON

11 Now Phaëthon hath tumbled from his car,
And made an evening at the noontide prick.
III Henry VI. Act i, sc. 4, l. 33. [Clifford] "Noontide" occurs four times in the plays and once in the poems. Phaëthon is mentioned five times.

12 Lear: We 'll go to supper i' the morning. . . .
Fool: And I 'll go to bed at noon.
King Lear. Act iii, sc. 6, l. 90.

At noon.—*Coriolanus,* i, 1, 265; *Cymbeline,* i, 3, 31; *King John,* iv, 2, 151; 156; *The Rape of Lucrece,* l. 784.
After noon.—*I Henry IV,* i, 2, 4.
Ere noon.—*Macbeth,* iii, 5, 22.
'Fore noon.—*Measure for Measure,* ii, 2, 160.
Till noon.—*King Lear,* ii, 2, 141.
Tuesday noon.—*Othello,* iii, 3, 61.

13 The bawdy hand of the dial is now upon the prick of noon.
Romeo and Juliet. Act ii, sc. 4, l. 118. [Mercutio]

Now is the sun upon the highmost hill
Of this day's journey.
Romeo and Juliet. Act ii, sc. 5, l. 9. [Juliet] "Highmost" is repeated in *Sonnets,* vii.

NORTH

14 The lordly monarch of the north.
I Henry VI. Act v, sc. 3, l. 6. [La Pucelle]

The frozen bosom of the north.—*Romeo and Juliet,* i, 4, 101.
The Hotspur of the north.—*I Henry IV,* ii, 4, 115.
That same Mad fellow of the north.—*I Henry IV,* ii, 4, 369.
The Percies of the north.—*I Henry VI,* ii, 5, 67. The only mention of Percies.
Toward the north.—*Julius Cæsar,* ii, 1, 109.
From north to south.—*King John,* ii, 1, 413; *I Henry IV,* i, 3, 196.

15 Entreat the north
To make his bleak winds kiss my parched lips
And comfort me with cold.
King John. Act v, sc. 7, l. 39. [King John]

16 Northward born,
Where Phœbus' fire scarce thaws the icicles.
The Merchant of Venice. Act ii, sc. 1, l. 5. [Morocco] "Northward" is repeated in *I Henry IV,* iii, 1, 79, and in *II Henry IV,* ii, 3, 13.

17 The grisled north
Disgorges such a tempest forth,

That, as a duck for life that dives,
So up and down the poor ship drives.
Pericles. Act iii, Gower, l. 47. The only use of "grisled."

1 The north,
Where shivering cold and sickness pines the clime.
Richard II. Act v, sc. 1, l. 76. [King Richard]

2
By the north pole.
Love's Labour's Lost. Act v, sc. 2, l. 699. [Armado] The only use of "north pole." "Pole" by itself, referring to the north pole, is used twice, in *Hamlet,* i, 1, 36, and in *Othello,* ii, 1, 15.

North star.—*Much Ado about Nothing,* ii, 1, 258.
Northern star.—*Julius Cæsar,* iii, 1, 60.
North-north-east.—*Love's Labour's Lost,* i, 1, 248.
North-north-west.—*Hamlet,* ii, 2, 396.

NOSE

3
Clown: Prithee, allow the wind.
Parolles: Nay, you need not to stop your nose, sir.
All's Well that Ends Well. Act v, sc. 2, l. 10.

Stops the nose at it.—*Othello,* iv, 2, 77.
Stop their nose.—*Antony and Cleopatra,* iii, 13, 39.

4
Her nose, all o'er embellished with rubies, carbuncles, sapphires.
The Comedy of Errors. Act iii, sc. 2, l. 137. [Dromio of Syracuse] The only use of "embellished" and of "sapphires." "Sapphire" occurs in *The Merry Wives of Windsor,* v, 5, 75.

Marian's nose looks red and raw.
Love's Labour's Lost, v, 2, 934. See under WINTER.

5
I have not wash'd My nose that bled.
Coriolanus. Act i, sc. 9, l. 47. [Marcius]

It was not for nothing my nose fell a-bleeding.
The Merchant of Venice, ii, 5, 24. See under OMEN.

Tickle our noses with spear-grass to make them bleed.
I Henry IV. Act ii, sc. 4, l. 340. [Bardolph] The only mention of spear-grass.

Bloody noses.—*I Henry IV,* ii, 3, 96.
Crook'd noses.—*Cymbeline,* iii, 1, 37.
Hook-nosed.—*II Henry IV,* iv, 3, 45. The only use of the phrase. See under CONQUEROR.
Innocent nose.—*As You Like It,* ii, 1, 39.
Meeting noses.—*The Winter's Tale,* i, 2, 285.

6
You shall nose him as you go up the stairs into the lobby.
Hamlet. Act iv, sc. 3, l. 38. [Hamlet]

7
And 'twixt his finger and his thumb he held
A pouncet-box, which ever and anon
He gave his nose and took 't away again;
Who therewith angry, when it next came there,
Took it in snuff.
I Henry IV. Act i, sc. 3, l. 37. [Hotspur] The only use of "pouncet-box."

8
Thou art our admiral, thou bearest the lantern in the poop, but 'tis in the nose of thee; thou art the Knight of the Burning Lamp.
I Henry IV. Act iii, sc. 3, l. 28. [Falstaff] "Poop" is used a second time in *Antony and Cleopatra,* ii, 2, 197: "The poop was beaten gold." "Pooped" occurs in *Pericles,* iv, 2, 25: "She quickly pooped him."

9
I have maintained that salamander of yours with fire any time this two and thirty years; God reward me for it!
I Henry IV. Act iii, sc. 3, l. 52. [Falstaff] The only use of "salamander."

Honest Bardolph, whose zeal burns in his nose.
II Henry IV. Act ii, sc. 4, l. 357. [Prince of Wales]

His lips blows at his nose, and it is like a coal of fire, sometimes plue, and sometimes red; but his nose is executed, and his fire 's out.
Henry V. Act iii, sc. 6, l. 109. [Fluellen]

I had as lief Helen's golden tongue had commended
Troilus for a copper nose.
Troilus and Cressida. Act i, sc. 2, l. 114. [Cressida]

10
His nostrils stretched with struggling.
II Henry VI. Act iii, sc. 2, l. 171. [Warwick] "Struggling" is repeated in *Hamlet,* iii, 3, 68.

His nostrils drink the air.—*Venus and Adonis,* l. 273.
Breathes at nostrils.—*The Tempest,* ii, 2, 65. "Nostrils" is used a fourth time in *Cymbeline,* v, 5, 477.
Stretch the nostril wide.—*Henry V,* iii, 1, 15.
Nostril wide.—*Venus and Adonis,* l. 296.
Dullest nostril.—*The Winter's Tale,* i, 2, 421.
Offended nostril.—*The Merry Wives of Windsor,* iii, 5, 94. The only uses of "nostril."

11 You would swear
Their very noses had been counsellors
To Pepin or Clotharius, they keep state so.
Henry VIII. Act i, sc. 3, l. 8. [Chamberlain] The only mention of Clotharius. Pepin is referred to five times.

Three times was his nose discharged against me.
Henry VIII. Act v, sc. 4, l. 47. [Man]

12
Thou canst tell why one's nose stands i' the middle on 's face? . . . Why, to keep one's eyes of either side 's nose; that what a man cannot smell out, he may spy into.
King Lear. Act i, sc. 5, l. 19. [Fool]

All that follow their noses are led by their eyes but blind men; and there 's not a nose among twenty but can smell him that 's stinking.
King Lear. Act ii, sc. 4, l. 70. [Fool]

He had a thousand noses.—*King Lear,* iv, 6, 70.

13
Did I not pluck thee by the nose?
Measure for Measure, v, 1, 342. [Lucio]

Wrings her nose.—*Venus and Adonis,* l. 475.
Wring him by the nose.—*II Henry VI,* iii, 2, 34.

1 We had like to have had our two noses snapped off with two old men without teeth.
Much Ado about Nothing. Act v, sc. 1, l. 115. [Claudio]

2 [He] will as tenderly be led by the nose
As asses are.
Othello. Act i, sc. 3, l. 407. [Iago]

Led by the nose with gold.
The Winter's Tale, iv, 4, 832. The only uses of this phrase.

3 His nose being shadow'd by his neighbour's ear.
The Rape of Lucrece, l. 1416.

4 Sometime she gallops o'er a courtier's nose.
Romeo and Juliet, i, 5, 77. See under FAIRY.

Dead man's nose.—*Winter's Tale,* ii, 1, 152.
Keeper's nose.—*Titus Andronicus,* ii, 1, 94.
Parson's nose.—*Romeo and Juliet,* i, 4, 80.
Nose of Turk.—*Macbeth,* iv, 1, 29.

5 Receives not thy nose court odour from me?
Winter's Tale, iv, 4, 757. See under COURT.

6 I 'll slit the villain's nose.
The Taming of the Shrew. Act v, sc. 1, l. 134. [Vincentio] The only use of "slit."

7 Down with the nose,
Down with it flat; take the bridge quite away
Of him that, his particular to foresee,
Smells from the general weal.
Timon of Athens. Act iv, sc. 3, l. 157. [Timon]

8 Malvolio's nose is no whipstock.
Twelfth Night. Act ii, sc. 3, l. 27. [Clown] "Whipstock" is used again in *Pericles,* ii, 2, 51.

9 What, hast smutch'd thy nose?
They say it is a copy out of mine.
Winter's Tale. Act i, sc. 2, l. 121. [Leontes] The only use of "smutch'd."

NOTE

10 Note him, good Charmian, 'tis the man; but note him.
Antony and Cleopatra, i, 5, 53. See under TEMPERAMENT.

Mark him; note him.—*Troilus and Cressida,* i, 2, 251.
Note him.—*As You Like It,* iii, 2, 267.
I did very well note him.—*Hamlet,* iii, 2, 301.

11 The note was very untuneable.
As You Like It, v, 3, 36. See under SONG.

Sigh a note and sing a note.
Love's Labour 's Lost, iii, 1, 14. See under SINGING.

Relish your nimble notes to pleasing ears.
The Rape of Lucrece, l. 1126.

'D sol re,' one clef, two notes have I.
Taming of the Shrew. Act iii, sc. 1, l. 77. [Bianca, reading] The only use of "clef."

At last, though long, our jarring notes agree.
The Taming of the Shrew. Act v, sc. 2, l. 1. [Lucentio]

One pleasing note do sing.—*Sonnets,* viii.
Sweet varied notes, enchanting every ear.
Titus Andronicus, iii, 1, 86. See under TONGUE.

Sweet notes.—*Troilus and Cressida,* v, 10, 45.
Complaining notes.—*The Two Gentlemen of Verona,* v, 4, 5.
Loud note.—*Troilus and Cressida,* iv, 5, 3.
Merry note.—*Love's Labour 's Lost,* v, 2, 929; *As You Like It,* ii, 5, 3.
A raven's note.—*II Henry VI,* iii, 1, 21.
Sad note.—*Henry VIII,* iv, 2, 78.
Shepherd's note.—*The Winter's Tale,* i, 2, 2.
Wailing note.—*Venus and Adonis,* l. 835.
Warbling note.—*Midsummer-Night's Dream,* v, 1, 405.

12 Creatures of note for mercy-lacking uses.
King John. Act iv, sc. 1, l. 121. [Arthur] The only use of "mercy-lacking."

He is of note.—*Antony and Cleopatra,* iv, 9, 32.
Men of note.—*Love's Labour 's Lost,* iii, 1, 25.
Some sir of note.—*Twelfth Night,* iii, 4, 82.
Be of note.—*Antony and Cleopatra,* iv, 4, 27.
Of a crescent note.—*Cymbeline,* i, 4, 2.
One of greatest note.—*Macbeth,* v, 7, 21.
Of holiest note.—*A Lover's Complaint,* l. 233.
Of mighty note.—*All's Well that Ends Well,* v, 3, 14.
Of most rare note.—*Winter's Tale,* iv, 2, 48.
Dreadful note.—*Henry V,* iv, Prol., 14; *Macbeth,* iii, 2, 44.
Due note.—*King Lear,* ii, 1, 85.
Good note.—*Twelfth Night,* iii, 4, 168.
Greatest note.—*Much Ado about Nothing,* iii, 2, 54.
High note.—*Henry VIII,* ii, 3, 59.
Natural notes.—*Cymbeline,* ii, 2, 28.
Perjured note.—*Love's Labour 's Lost,* iv, 3, 125.
Precious note.—*Cymbeline,* ii, 3, 127.

13 Take note of what is done.
Measure for Measure. Act ii, sc. 2, l. 94. [Angelo]

I have ta'en a due and wary note upon 't.
Measure for Measure, iv, 1, 38. [Isabella]

By the Lord, Horatio, these three years I have taken note of it.
Hamlet. Act v, sc. 1, l. 150. [Hamlet]

Take note of him.—*Julius Cæsar,* v, 3, 50.
Take note of it.—*Measure for Measure,* v, 1, 80; *Twelfth Night,* iii, 2, 38.
Take angry note.—*Winter's Tale,* v, 1, 173.
Take good note.—*Julius Cæsar,* ii, 4, 14.
Take but good note.—*Antony and Cleopatra,* i, 1, 11.
Take No note at all.—*The Merchant of Venice,* v, 1, 120.
Take no note of him.—*Much Ado about Nothing,* iii, 3, 29; *Romeo and Juliet,* i, 5, 73.
What need you note it?—*Henry VIII,* ii, 4, 128.
They have ta'en note of us.—*Coriolanus,* iv, 2, 10.
Take note, take note, O world.—*Othello,* iii, 3, 377.
Let the world take note.—*Hamlet,* i, 2, 108.
The world takes note.—*All's Well that Ends Well,* i, 3, 195.

But note me, signior.—*The Merchant of Venice,* i, 3, 98.
Note me this.—*Coriolanus,* i, 1, 131.
Do you note me?—*Romeo and Juliet,* iv, 5, 121.
Note this.—*II Henry IV,* iv, 1, 197.
Give him heedful note.—*Hamlet,* iii, 2, 89.

1
That is the very note of it.
The Merry Wives of Windsor. Act i, sc. 1, l. 172. [Nym]
Notes of admiration.—*Winter's Tale,* v, 2, 12.
Note of expectation.—*Macbeth,* iii, 3, 10.
Note of judgement.—*Troilus and Cressida,* ii, 3, 134.

2
What could he see but mightily he noted?
What did he note but strongly he desired?
The Rape of Lucrece, l. 414.
I have noted it well.—*King Lear,* i, 4, 81.
Noted well.—*Love's Labour 's Lost,* iv, 3, 140.
Well noted.—*Love's Labour 's Lost,* iv, 3, 88; *King John,* iv, 2, 21.
Richly noted.—*The Winter's Tale,* v, 3, 145.
This is noted, and generally.—*Henry VIII,* ii, 1, 46.
We have noted it.—*Cymbeline,* iii, 5, 34.
She 's noted.—*Troilus and Cressida,* v, 2, 11.
I noted her not.—*Much Ado about Nothing,* i, 1, 165.
Not noted.—*The Winter's Tale,* i, 2, 225.
Missingly noted.—*Winter's Tale,* iv, 2, 35. The only use of "missingly."

NOTHINGNESS

3
To say nothing, to do nothing, to know nothing, and to have nothing, is to be a great part of your title; which is within a very little of nothing.
All's Well that Ends Well. Act ii, sc. 4, l. 25. [Clown]

4
Naught, naught, all naught!
Antony and Cleopatra. Act iii, sc. 10, l. 1. [Enobarbus]
All 's but naught.—*Antony and Cleopatra,* iv, 15, 78.
Be naught awhile.—*As You Like It,* i, 1, 39.
A thing of naught.—*A Midsummer-Night's Dream,* iv, 2, 14.
You are naught.—*Hamlet,* iii, 2, 157.

5
That harsh, noble, simple nothing.
Cymbeline. Act iii, sc. 4, l. 135. [Imogen]
'Twas but a bolt of nothing, shot at nothing,
Which the brain makes of fumes.
Cymbeline. Act iv, sc. 2, l. 300. [Imogen]
I am nothing: or if not,
Nothing to be were better.
Cymbeline. Act iv, sc. 2, l. 367. [Imogen]

6
This nothing 's more than matter.
Hamlet. Act iv, sc. 5, l. 174. [Laertes]

7
Nay, an a' do nothing but speak nothing, a' shall be nothing here.
II Henry IV. Act ii, sc. 4, l. 207. [Falstaff]
More than my all is nothing.
Henry VIII. Act ii, sc. 3, l. 67. [Anne]

8
Nothing will come of nothing.
King Lear. Act i, sc. 1, l. 92. [King Lear]
The quality of nothing hath not such need to hide itself.
King Lear. Act i, sc. 2, l. 33. [Gloucester]
Fool: Can you make no use of nothing, nuncle?
King Lear: Why, no, boy; nothing can be made out of nothing.
King Lear. Act i, sc. 4, l. 143.
Now thou art an O without a figure.
King Lear. Act i, sc. 4, l. 211. [Fool]

9
Nothing is But what is not.
Macbeth. Act i, sc. 3, l. 141. [Macbeth]

10
If he be less, he 's nothing.
Measure for Measure. Act v, sc. 1, l. 58. [Isabella]
I was worse than nothing.
The Merchant of Venice. Act iii, sc. 2, l. 263. [Bassanio]

11
Mine were the very cipher of a function.
Measure for Measure, ii, 2, 39. See under FAULT.
Either a fool or a cipher.—*As You Like It,* iii, 2, 308.
Like a cipher.—*The Winter's Tale,* i, 2, 6. The only uses of "cipher" as a noun. As a verb it occurs in *The Rape of Lucrece,* ll. 207, and 811. "Cipher'd" is used once, in *The Rape of Lucrece,* l. 1396.
Ciphers to this great accompt.—*Henry V,* Prol., 17. The only use of "ciphers."

12
It is nothing, nothing in the world.
A Midsummer-Night's Dream. Act v, sc. 1, l. 78. [Philostrate]

13
Ay, no; no, ay; for I must nothing be;
Therefore no no, for I resign to thee.
Richard II. Act iv, sc. 1, l. 201. [King Richard]
Whate'er I be,
Nor I nor any man that but man is
With nothing shall be pleased, till he be eased
With being nothing.
Richard II, v, 5, 38. [King Richard]

14
My long sickness
Of health and living now begins to mend,
And nothing brings me all things.
Timon of Athens. Act v, sc. 1, l. 189. [Timon]

15
With what 's unreal thou coactive art,
And fellow'st nothing: then 'tis very credent
Thou mayst co-join with something.
Winter's Tale. Act i, sc. 2, l. 141. [Leontes] The only use of "coactive" (acting in concert), "fellow'st," and "co-join."
Be impudently negative,
To have nor eyes nor ears nor thought.
Winter's Tale. Act i, sc. 2, l. 274. [Leontes] The only use of "negative." "Negatives" occurs in *Twelfth Night,* v, 1, 24.
Is this nothing?
Why, then the world and all that 's in't is nothing;
The covering sky is nothing; Bohemia nothing;
My wife is nothing; nor nothing have these nothings,
If this be nothing.
Winter's Tale. Act i, sc. 2, l. 292. [Leontes]

NOVELTY

1
It is a novelty to the world.
All's Well that Ends Well. Act ii, sc. 3, l. 22. [Lafeu]
Novelty is only in request.
Measure for Measure. Act iii, sc. 2, l. 237. [Duke]

2
If there be nothing new, but that which is
Hath been before, how are our brains beguiled,
Which, labouring for invention, bear amiss
The second burthen of a former child.
Sonnets. No. lix.
Why with the time do I not glance aside
To new-found methods and to compounds strange?
Sonnets. No. lxxvi. "New-found" occurs again in *The Two Gentlemen of Verona,* iv, 4, 135.

3
All with one consent praise new-born gawds,
Though they are made and moulded of things past,
And give to dust that is a little gilt
More laud than gilt o'er-dusted.
Troilus and Cressida. Act iii, sc. 3, l. 176. [Ulysses] The only use of "o'er-dusted."

4
How novelty may move, and parts with person,
Alas, a kind of godly jealousy—
Which, I beseech you, call a virtuous sin—
Makes me afeard.
Troilus and Cressida. Act iv, sc. 4, l. 81. [Troilus]

5
O, you are novices!
The Taming of the Shrew. Act ii, sc. 1, l. 313. [Petruchio]
That princely novice.—*Richard III,* i, 4, 228.
Mars dote on you for his novices!—*All's Well that Ends Well,* ii, 1, 48.
A novice of this place.—*Measure for Measure,* i, 4, 19.
Sold me to this novice.—*Antony and Cleopatra,* iv, 12, 14. The only uses of "novice" and "novices."

NUMBER

See also Figure

6
Take
Convenient numbers to make good the city.
Coriolanus. Act i, sc. 5, l. 13. [Marcius]
A certain number,
Though thanks to all, must I select from all.
Coriolanus. Act i, sc. 7, l. 80. [Marcius] "Select" is repeated in *Hamlet,* i, 3, 74.
Behold Dissentious numbers pestering streets.
Coriolanus. Act iv, sc. 6, l. 7. [Sicinius]

7
The number of the king exceedeth ours.
I Henry IV. Act iv, sc. 3, l. 28. [Worcester]

8
Shall we draw our numbers and set on?
II Henry IV. Act i, sc. 3, l. 109. [Mowbray]
When you have drawn your number,
Repair to the Capitol.
Coriolanus. Act ii, sc. 3, l. 261. [Brutus]

9
The muster of his kingdom too faint a number.
Henry V. Act iii, sc. 6, l. 139. [Montjoy]
Command our present numbers Be mustered.
Cymbeline. Act iv, sc. 2, l. 343. [Lucius]

10
Sorry am I his numbers are too few.
Henry V. Act iii, sc. 5, l. 56. [Constable]
My numbers lessened.—*Henry V,* iii, 6, 155.
Poor number.—*Twelfth Night,* i, 2, 10.

11
Proud of their numbers and secure in soul.
Henry V. Act iv, Prol., l. 17.
Full numbers.—*Much Ado about Nothing,* i, 1, 9.
Fuller number.—*Julius Cæsar,* iv, 3, 208.
Great number.—*Twelfth Night,* iii, 3, 29.
Happy number.—*As You Like It,* v, 4, 178.
Honour'd number.—*Coriolanus,* iii, 1, 72.
Opposed numbers.—*Henry V,* iv, 1, 308.
Terrible numbers.—*Macbeth,* i, 2, 51.

12
Bring me just notice of the numbers dead
On both our parts.
Henry V. Act iv, sc. 7, l. 122. [King Henry]
King Henry: Are the dead numbered?
Herald: Here is the number of the slaughter'd French. . . .
King Henry: This note doth tell me of ten thousand French
That in the field lie slain. . . .
Where is the number of our English dead? . . .
But five and twenty. O God, thy arm was here!
Henry V. Act iv, sc. 8, l. 78. The king is referring to the dead at the battle of Agincourt.
Number of the dead.—*Richard III,* iv, 1, 45.
Numbers of the fear'd.—*II Henry IV,* iii, 1, 98.
Number of the foe.—*Richard III,* v, 3, 9.
Numbers of our foes.—*II Henry IV,* iv, 1, 4.
Number of her hairs.—*Pericles,* iv, 2, 100.
Numbers of our host.—*Macbeth,* v, 4, 6.
Number of our men.—*Pericles,* i, 4, 86.
Number of the ships.—*Antony and Cleopatra,* iii, 9, 3.

13
Make up no factious numbers for the matter.
II Henry VI. Act ii, sc. 1, l. 40. [Gloucester]

14
The little number of your doubtful friends.
King John. Act v, sc. 1, l. 36. [Bastard]
So great a number.—*King Lear,* ii, 4, 243.

15
Moth: I am sure you know how much the gross sum of deuce-ace amounts to.
Armado: It doth amount to one more than two.
Moth: Which the base vulgar do call three.
Love's Labour's Lost. Act i, sc. 2, l. 48. The only use of "deuce-ace."
Armado: The fox, the ape, the humble-bee,
Were still at odds, being but three.
Moth: Until the goose came out of door,
And stay'd the odds by adding four.
Love's Labour's Lost. Act iii, sc. 1, l. 90.
Now the number is even.
Love's Labour's Lost. Act iv, sc. 3, l. 211. [Dumain]
And three times thrice is nine.
Love's Labour's Lost. Act v, sc. 2, l. 488. [Biron]

1
Let me supervise the canzonet. Here are only numbers ratified.
Love's Labour's Lost. Act iv, sc. 2, l. 125. [Holofernes] The only use of "canzonet." "Supervise" is repeated in *Hamlet,* v, 2, 23.
These numbers will I tear, and write in prose.
Love's Labour's Lost. Act iv, sc. 3, l. 57. [Longaville]
Soft! here follows prose.
Twelfth Night. Act ii, sc. 5, l. 154. [Malvolio] The only uses of "prose."
2
Nay, I have verses too, . . . The numbers true.
Love's Labour's Lost. Act v, sc. 2, l. 34. [Rosaline]
Now is he for the numbers that Petrarch flowed in: Laura to his lady was but a kitchen-wench; marry, she had a better love to be-rhyme her
Romeo and Juliet. Act ii, sc. 4, l. 40. [Mercutio] The only mention of Petrarch. "Kitchen-wench" is repeated in *The Comedy of Errors,* iii, 2, 96. The only use of "be-rhyme." "Be-rhymed" occurs in *As You Like It,* iii, 2, 186.
And in fresh numbers number all your graces.
Sonnets. No. xvii. See under Face.
And he that calls on thee, let him bring forth
Eternal numbers to outlive long date.
Sonnets. No. xxxviii.
But now my gracious numbers are decay'd
And my sick Muse doth give another place.
Sonnets. No. lxxix.
I am ill at these numbers.
Hamlet, ii, 2, 120. [Polonius, reading]
Fiery numbers.—*Love's Labour's Lost,* iv, 3, 322.
3
Evans: How many numbers is in nouns?
William: Two.
Mistress Quickly: Truly, I thought there had been one number more, because they say ''Od's nouns.'
Merry Wives of Windsor. Act iv, sc. 1, l. 21.
Good luck lies in odd numbers. . . . There is divinity in odd numbers.
The Merry Wives of Windsor. Act v, sc. 1, l. 2. [Falstaff]
4
Among a number one is reckon'd none.
Sonnets. No. cxxxvi.
5
May these add to the number that may scald thee!
Timon of Athens. Act iii, sc. 1, l. 53. [Flaminius]

NUN

6
A nun of winter's sisterhood.
As You Like It, iii, 4, 7. See under Kiss.
Come, I'll dispose of thee
Among a sisterhood of holy nuns.
Romeo and Juliet. Act v, sc. 3, l. 156. [Friar Laurence]
To be shortly of a sisterhood.—*Measure for Measure,* ii, 2, 21.
In probation of a sisterhood.—*Measure for Measure,* v, 1, 72. "Sisterhood" is used a fifth time in *Measure for Measure,* i, 4, 5.
7
Get thee to a nunnery. . . . Go thy ways to a nunnery. . . . Get thee to a nunnery, go: farewell. . . . To a nunnery, go, and quickly too. Farewell.
Hamlet. Act iii, sc. 1, l. 122. [Hamlet] "Nunnery" is used these four times in this scene and nowhere else.
8
Lo, this device was sent me from a nun,
Or sister sanctified, of holiest note.
A Lover's Complaint, l. 233. The only use of "holiest."
A sacred nun, . . . disciplined, ay, dieted in grace.
A Lover's Complaint, l. 260.
Praying nuns.—*Richard III,* iv, 4, 201.
Self-loving nuns.—*Venus and Adonis,* l. 752.
9
The livery of a nun,
For aye to be in shady cloister mew'd,
To live a barren sister all your life,
Chanting faint hymns to the cold fruitless moon.
A Midsummer-Night's Dream. Act i, sc. 1, l. 70. [Theseus]

NUPTIAL

See also Marriage, Match, Wedlock

10
O, let me clip ye
In arms as sound as when I woo'd, in heart
As merry as when our nuptial day was done,
And tapers burn'd to bedward!
Coriolanus. Act i, sc. 6, l. 29. [Marcius] The only use of "bedward." "Nuptial-day" is repeated in *A Midsummer-Night's Dream,* iii, 2, 12. "Theseus' nuptial-day."
11
The catastrophe is a nuptial.
Love's Labour's Lost. Act iv, sc. 1, l. 77. [Boyet]
12
Straight shall our nuptial rites be solemnized.
The Merchant of Venice. Act ii, sc. 9, l. 6. [Portia]
Nuptial ceremony.—*A Midsummer-Night's Dream,* v, 1, 55.
Nuptial knot.—*III Henry VI,* iii, 3, 55.
Nuptial bed.—*I Henry VI,* v, 5, 58.
Nuptial vow.—*Titus Andronicus,* ii, 3, 125.
13
Our nuptial hour Draws on apace.
A Midsummer-Night's Dream. Act i, sc. 1, l. 1. [Theseus]
This looks not like a nuptial.
Much Ado about Nothing. Act iv, sc. 1, l. 69. [Benedick]
14
The celebration of his nuptial.
Othello. Act ii, sc. 2, l. 8. [Herald]
We'll celebrate their nuptials.
Pericles. Act v, sc. 3, l. 8. [Pericles] The only use of "nuptials."
15
I have hope to see the nuptial
Of our dear-beloved solemnized.
The Tempest. Act v, sc. 1, l. 308. [Prospero] The only use of "dear-beloved."

NURSE

1
A nursery to our gentry.
All's Well that Ends Well, i, 2, 16. See under WAR.
Nursery of evil.—*Troilus and Cressida,* i, 3, 319.
Kind nursery.—*King Lear,* i, 1, 126.
Nursery of arts.—*Taming of the Shrew,* i, 1, 2. "Nursery" is used a fifth time in *Cymbeline,* i, 1, 59: "From their nursery Were stol'n."
Dear nurse of arts.—*Henry V,* v, 2, 35.
Nurse of blame.—*The Rape of Lucrece,* l. 767.
Nurse of judgement.—*Henry VIII,* ii, 2, 94.
Nature's soft nurse.—*II Henry IV,* iii, 1, 6.
Sorrow's nurse.—*Richard III,* ii, 2, 87.
2
Belarius: First pay me for the nursing of thy sons;
And let it be confiscate all, so soon
As I have received it.
Cymbeline: Nursing of my sons!
Cymbeline. Act v, sc. 5, l. 322.
Careful nursing.—*Pericles,* iii, 1, 81. "Nursing" is repeated in *Measure for Measure,* iii, 2, 126, and in *King Lear,* v, 3, 181.
3
Here nursed up and bred.
Measure for Measure. Act iv, sc. 2, l. 134. [Provost]
Nursed by baseness.—*Measure for Measure,* iii, 1, 15.
4
There dwells one Mistress Quickly, which is in the manner of his nurse, or his dry nurse, or his cook, or his laundry, his washer, and his wringer.
The Merry Wives of Windsor. Act i, sc. 2, l. 2. [Evans] The only use of the phrase, "dry nurse" and of "laundry," "washer," and "wringer."
5
You have A nurse of me.
Pericles. Act iv, sc. 1, l. 24. [Dionyza]
Nurses are not the fates To foster it.
Pericles. Act iv, sc. 3, l. 14. [Dionyza]
6
The nurse, to still her child, will tell my story,
And fright her crying babe with Tarquin's name.
The Rape of Lucrece, l. 813.
7
The nurse cursed in the pantry.
Romeo and Juliet. Act i, sc. 3, l. 102. [Servant] The only use of "pantry."
Here comes my nurse.—*Romeo and Juliet,* iii, 2, 31.
Thou wast their nurse.—*Cymbeline,* iii, 3, 104.
8
She will a handmaid be to his desires,
A loving nurse, a mother to his youth.
Titus Andronicus. Act i, 1, 331. [Tamora]
Dear nurse.—*Coriolanus,* v, 3, 110; *Romeo and Juliet,* ii, 4, 207.
Gentle nurse.—*Romeo and Juliet,* iv, 3, 1.
Foul nurse.—*Venus and Adonis,* l. 773.
Good nurse.—*Romeo and Juliet,* ii, 2, 137; ii, 4, 199; *Pericles,* v, 1, 161.
Good, sweet nurse.—*Romeo and Juliet,* ii, 5, 55.
Honest nurse.—*Romeo and Juliet,* ii, 5, 80.
Honey nurse.—*Romeo and Juliet,* ii, 5, 18.
Prattling nurse.—*Coriolanus,* ii, 1, 222. "Prattling" is repeated in *The Merry Wives of Windsor,* iv, 1, 1: "No more prattling."
Sweet, sweet, sweet nurse.—*Romeo and Juliet,* ii, 5, 55.

NUT

9
There can be no kernel in this light nut.
All's Well that Ends Well. Act ii, sc. 5, l. 47. [Lafeu]
New nuts.—*A Midsummer-Night's Dream,* iv, 1, 40.
10
Sweetest nut hath sourest rind.
As You Like It. Act iii, sc. 2, l. 115. [Touchstone] "Rind" is repeated in *Romeo and Juliet,* ii, 3, 23: "Infant rind."
11
I could be bounded in a nutshell.
Hamlet, ii, 2, 260. See under DREAM.
No stronger than a nutshell.—*The Tempest,* i, 1, 50. The only uses of "nutshell."
12
I with my long nails will dig thee pig-nuts.
The Tempest. Act ii, sc. 2, l. 172. [Caliban] The only mention of pig-nuts.

NYMPH

13
Modest Dian circled with her nymphs.
III Henry VI. Act iv, sc. 8, l. 21. [Warwick]
The stately Phœbe 'mongst her nymphs.
Titus Andronicus, i, 1, 316. See under QUEEN.
14
Fare thee well, nymph: ere he do leave this grove,
Thou shalt fly him and he shall seek thy love.
A Midsummer-Night's Dream. Act ii, sc. 1, l. 245. [Oberon]
15
But, soft! what nymphs are these?
A Midsummer-Night's Dream. Act iv, sc. 1, l. 131. [Theseus]
Nymphs back peeping fearfully.
The Passionate Pilgrim, l. 287.
Nymphs that vow'd chaste life to keep.
Sonnets. No. cliv.
16
You nymphs, call'd Naiads, of the windring brooks,
With your sedged crowns and ever-harmless looks,
Leave your crisp channels. . . . Come, temperate nymphs.
The Tempest. Act iv, sc. 1, l. 128. [Iris] The only use of "Naiads," "windring" (winding?), "sedged," and "ever-harmless."
To make cold nymphs chaste crowns.
The Tempest. Act iv, sc. 1, l. 66. [Iris]
Fresh nymphs.—*The Tempest,* iv, 1, 137.
Wanton ambling nymph.—*Richard III,* i, 1, 17.
17
Go make thyself like a nymph o' the sea.
The Tempest. Act i, sc. 2, l. 301. [Prospero]
Thou gentle nymph, cherish thy forlorn swain!
The Two Gentlemen of Verona. Act v, sc. 4, l. 12. [Valentine]

O

OAK

1
An oak whose antique root peeps out.
As You Like It. Act ii, sc. 1, l. 31. [Lord]
An oak, whose boughs were moss'd with age
And high top bald with dry antiquity.
As You Like It. Act iv, sc. 3, l. 105. [Oliver]
"Moss'd" is repeated in *Timon of Athens,* iv, 3, 223: "Moss'd trees."
Hardest-timber'd oak.—*III Henry VI,* ii, 1, 55. The only use of the phrase.
Knotted oaks.—*Troilus and Cressida,* i, 3, 50.
The knotty oaks.—*Julius Cæsar,* i, 3, 6.
Old oak.—*The Rape of Lucrece,* l. 950.
Unwedgeable and gnarled oak.—*Measure for Measure,* ii, 2, 116. The only use of either adjective.

2
To a cruel war I sent him; from which he returned, his brows bound with oak.
Coriolanus. Act ii, sc. 3, l. 15. [Volumnia]
For his meed Was brow-bound with the oak.
Coriolanus. Act ii, sc. 2, l. 102. [Cominius]
The only use of "brow-bound."
He comes the third time home with the oaken garland.
Coriolanus. Act ii, sc. 1, l. 138. [Volumnia]
The only use of "oaken."

3
At the duke's oak we meet.
A Midsummer-Night's Dream. Act i, sc. 2, l. 113. [Quince]
The oak Of Herne the hunter.—*The Merry Wives of Windsor,* v, 5, 79.
Herne's oak.—*The Merry Wives of Windsor,* iv, 4, 40; iv, 6, 19; v, 1, 12; v, 3, 15.
Jove's stout oak.—*The Tempest,* v, 1, 45.

4
An oak with but one green leaf on it would have answered her.
Much Ado about Nothing. Act ii, sc. 1, l. 247. [Benedick]

OATH

See also Vow, Word

5
Three great oaths would scarce make that be believed.
All's Well that Ends Well. Act iv, sc. 1, l. 64. [Lord]
Your oaths
Are words and poor conditions, but unseal'd.
All's Well that Ends Well. Act iv, sc. 2, l. 29. [Diana] The only use of "unseal'd."
When he swears oaths, bid him drop gold, and take it.
All's Well that Ends Well. Act iv, sc. 3, l. 252. [Soldier]

6
The oath of a lover is no stronger than the word of a tapster; they are both the confirmer of false reckonings.
As You Like It. Act iii, sc. 4, l. 32. [Celia]
"Confirmer" is used only once again, in *King John,* iii, 1, 24.

7
I will not eat my word.
As You Like It. Act v, sc. 4, l. 155. [Phebe]
Beatrice: Will you not eat your word?
Benedick: With no sauce that can be devised to it.
Much Ado about Nothing. Act iv, sc. 1, l. 280.
Now to my word;
It is 'Adieu, adieu! remember me.'
I have sworn 't.
Hamlet. Act i, sc. 5, l. 110. [Hamlet]
Sufficeth, I am come to keep my word.
The Taming of the Shrew. Act iii, sc. 2, l. 108. [Petruchio]

8
It is a branch and parcel of mine oath.
The Comedy of Errors. Act v, sc. 1, l. 106. [Abbess]
Bound with an oath.—*Coriolanus,* v, 1, 69.
Your hand; a covenant.
Cymbeline. Act i, sc. 4, l. 177. [Iachimo]
Hark you, he swears; by Jupiter he swears.
Cymbeline. Act ii, sc. 4, l. 122. [Posthumus]

9
Hamlet: Give me one poor request.
Horatio: What is 't, my lord? we will.
Hamlet: Never make known what you have seen to-night.
Horatio and Marcellus: My lord, we will not.
Hamlet: Nay, but swear 't. . . .
Marcellus: We have sworn, my lord, already.
Hamlet: Indeed, upon my sword, indeed.
Ghost [Beneath]: Swear.
Hamlet: Ah, ha, boy! Say'st thou so? art thou there, truepenny?
Come on—you hear this fellow in the cellarage—
Consent to swear.
Horatio: Propose the oath, my lord.
Hamlet: Never to speak of this that you have seen,
Swear by my sword.
Ghost [Beneath]: Swear.
Hamlet: Hic et ubique? then we 'll shift our ground.
Come hither, gentlemen,
And lay your hands again upon my sword:
Never to speak of this that you have heard,
Swear by my sword.
Ghost [Beneath]: Swear.
Hamlet. Act i, sc. 5, l. 142. The only use of "truepenny," "cellarage," and "hic et ubique."

10
I put thee now to thy book-oath.
II Henry IV. Act ii, sc. 1, l. 112. [Hostess]
The only use of "book-oath."
O, who can give an oath? where is a book?
Love's Labour's Lost, iv, 3, 250. See under Blackness.

I 'll be sworn on a book, she loves you.
The Merry Wives of Windsor. Act i, sc. 4, l. 155. [Mistress Quickly]

Come, swear to that; kiss the book.
The Tempest. Act ii, sc. 2, l. 145. [Stephano] "Kiss the book" is repeated in l. 134, and occurs in no other scene.

1
Sword is an oath, and oaths must have their course.
Henry V. Act ii, sc. 1, l. 106. [Pistol]

An oath of mickle might.
Henry V. Act ii, sc. 1, l. 70. [Pistol]

A dreadful oath, sworn with a solemn tongue.
II Henry VI. Act iii, sc. 2, l. 158. [Suffolk]

A good mouth-filling oath.—*I Henry IV,* iii, 1, 259. The only use of "mouth-filling." See under SWEARING.

Strong-bonded oath.—*A Lover's Complaint,* l. 279. The only use of "strong-bonded."

Terrible oath.—*Twelfth Night,* iii, 4, 197.

Untraded oath.—*Troilus and Cressida,* iv, 5, 178. The only use of "untraded" (un-hackneyed).

2
Trust none;
For oaths are straws, men's faiths are wafer-cakes.
Henry V. Act ii, sc. 3, l. 52. [Pistol] The only use of "wafer-cakes."

False oaths.—*Cymbeline,* iii, 3, 66.

Ordinary oaths.—*Julius Cæsar,* i, 2, 73.

Slight oath.—*II Henry IV,* v, 1, 92.

Strange oaths.—*As You Like It,* ii, 7, 150.

Unlawful oaths.—*I Henry VI,* v, 5, 30.

Dicers' oaths.—*Hamlet,* iii, 4, 45.

Vehement oaths.—*Merchant of Venice,* v, 1, 171.

Whore's oath.—*King Lear,* iii, 6, 21.

3
King Henry: Is it fit this soldier keep his oath?
Fluellen: He is a craven and a villain else.
Henry V. Act iv, sc. 7, l. 138.

Though he be as good a gentleman as the devil is, as Lucifer and Belzebub himself, it is necessary, look your grace, that he keep his vow and his oath.
Henry V. Act iv, sc. 7, l. 144. [Fluellen] Belzebub is mentioned again in *Twelfth Night,* v, 1, 291. Lucifer is mentioned six times.

I cannot look greenly nor gasp out my eloquence, nor I have no cunning in protestation; only downright oaths, which I never use till urged, nor never break for urging.
Henry V. Act v, sc. 2, l. 149. [King Henry] "Greenly" is repeated in *Hamlet,* iv, 5, 83: "We have done but greenly."

4
We 'll take your oath,
And all the peers', for surety of our leagues.
Then shall I swear to Kate, and you to me;
And may our oaths well kept and prosperous be!
Henry V. Act v, sc. 2, l. 399. [King Henry]

Take your oath.—*I Henry VI,* iv, 1, 3.

Hath ta'en his oath.—*The Merchant of Venice,* ii, 9, 2.

5
Had I but said, I would have kept my word,
But when I swear, it is irrevocable.
II Henry VI. Act iii, sc. 2, l. 293. [King Henry]

Therefore delay not, give thy hand to Warwick;
And, with thy hand, thy faith irrevocable.
III Henry VI. Act iii, sc. 3, l. 246. [Queen Margaret] "Irrevocable" is used a third time in *As You Like It,* i, 3, 85: "Firm and irrevocable."

6
Against thy oath and true allegiance sworn.
II Henry VI. Act v, sc. 1, l. 20. [Buckingham]

Against my oath.—*The Comedy of Errors,* i, 1, 144; *Measure for Measure,* iv, 2, 194.

7
It is great sin to swear unto a sin,
But greater sin to keep a sinful oath.
Who can be bound by any solemn vow
To do a murderous deed, to rob a man,
To force a spotless virgin's chastity,
To reave the orphan of his patrimony,
To wring the widow from her custom'd right,
And have no other reason for this wrong
But that he was bound by a solemn oath?
II Henry VI. Act v, sc. 1, l. 182. [Salisbury] "Reave" is used only once again, in *All's Well that Ends Well,* v, 3, 86.

Perhaps thou wilt object my holy oath:
To keep that oath were more impiety
Than Jepthah's, when he sacrificed his daughter.
III Henry VI. Act v, sc. 1, l. 89. [Clarence] Jepthah is mentioned three times in the plays.

Holy oath.—*III Henry VI,* i, 4, 405.

8
King Henry: Take an oath
To cease this civil war. . . .
York: This oath I willingly take and will perform.
III Henry VI. Act i, sc. 1, l. 196.

I here take my oath before this honourable assembly.
King Lear. Act iii, sc. 6, l. 48. [King Lear]

I 'll take my oath on it.—*Much Ado about Nothing,* ii, 3, 26.

9
Trust not simple Henry nor his oaths.
III Henry VI. Act i, sc. 2, l. 59. [York] See also TRUST: LACK OF TRUST.

Ah, simple men, you know not what you swear!
III Henry VI. Act iii, sc. 1, l. 83. [King Henry]

10
Brutus: Give me your hands all over, one by one.
Cassius: And let us swear our resolution.
Brutus: No, not an oath: . . .
What need we any spur but our own cause,
To prick us to redress? . . . what other oath
Than honesty to honesty engaged,
That this shall be, or we will fall for it?
Swear priests and cowards and men cautelous,
Old feeble carrions and such suffering souls

That welcome wrongs; unto bad causes swear
Such creatures as men doubt; but do not stain
The even virtue of our enterprise,
Nor the insuppressive mettle of our spirits,
To think that or our cause or our performance
Did need an oath.

Julius Cæsar. Act ii, sc. 1, l. 112. The only use of "insuppressive" (insuppressible). "Cautelous" (crafty) is repeated in *Coriolanus,* iv, 1, 33: "Cautelous baits."

Come now, keep thine oath.—*Julius Cæsar,* v, 3, 40.

1 Like a civil war set'st oath to oath,
Thy tongue against thy tongue.

King John. Act iii, sc. 1, l. 264. [Pandulph]

By what thou swear'st against the thing thou swear'st,
And makest an oath the surety for thy truth
Against an oath.

King John. Act iii, sc. 1, l. 281. [Pandulph]

My good friend, thy voluntary oath
Lives in this bosom, dearly cherished.

King John. Act iii, sc. 3, l. 23. [King John]

Oath of service.—*King John,* v, 1, 23.
Oath of loyalty.—*Cymbeline,* i, 6, 102.
King's oath.—*King John,* iii, 1, 10.

2
Thou swear'st thy gods in vain.

King Lear. Act i, sc. 1, l. 163. [Kent]

3
Your oaths are pass'd; and now subscribe your names,
That his own hand may strike his honour down
That violates the smallest branch herein:
If you are arm'd to do as sworn to do,
Subscribe to your deep oaths, and keep it too.

Love's Labour's Lost. Act i, sc. 1, l. 19. [King]

Your oath is pass'd.—*Love's Labour's Lost,* i, 1, 49.

4
But I believe, although I seem so loath,
I am the last that will last keep his oath.

Love's Labour's Lost. Act i, sc. 1, l. 160. [Biron]

These oaths . . . will prove an idle scorn.

Love's Labour's Lost, i, 1, 311. See under WAGER.

'Tis deadly sin so keep that oath, my lord,
And sin to break it.

Love's Labour's Lost. Act ii, sc. 1, l. 105. [Princess of France]

What mean you, madam? by my life, my troth,
I never swore this lady such an oath.

Love's Labour's Lost. Act v, sc. 2, l. 450. [King]

Your oath I will not trust.—*Love's Labour's Lost,* v, 2, 804.

5 Think'st thou thy oaths,
Though they would swear down each particular saint,
Were testimonies against his worth and credit
That 's seal'd in approbation?

Measure for Measure. Act v, sc. 1, l. 242. [Duke]

6
I am enjoin'd by oath to observe three things.

The Merchant of Venice. Act ii, sc. 9, l. 9. [Arragon]

I 'll keep my oath,
Patiently to bear my wroth.

The Merchant of Venice. Act ii, sc. 9, l. 77. [Arragon, reading] The only use of "wroth" (ruin).

7
I have sworn an oath that I will have my bond.

The Merchant of Venice. Act iii, sc. 3, l. 5. [Shylock]

Swearing till my very roof was dry
With oaths of love.

The Merchant of Venice. Act iii, sc. 2, l. 206. [Gratiano]

Her lips to mine how often hath she joined,
Between each kiss her oaths of true love swearing!

The Passionate Pilgrim, l. 91.

8
By our holy Sabbath have I sworn.

The Merchant of Venice. Act iv, sc. 1, l. 36. [Shylock]

An oath, an oath, I have an oath in heaven.

The Merchant of Venice. Act iv, sc. 1, l. 228. [Shylock]

Bassanio: I swear to thee, even by thine own fair eyes,
Wherein I see myself—
Portia: Mark you but that!
In both my eyes he doubly sees himself;
In each eye, one: swear by your double self,
And there 's an oath of credit.

The Merchant of Venice. Act v, sc. 1, l. 242

9
I do believe the swearer.

The Merry Wives of Windsor. Act ii, sc. 2, l. 40. [Falstaff] The only use of "swearer."

The swearers are fools.—*Macbeth,* iv, 2, 56.
Make our swearers priests.—*Pericles,* iv, 6, 13. The only uses of "swearers."

10
Two bosoms interchained with an oath;
So then two bosoms and a single troth.

A Midsummer-Night's Dream. Act ii, sc. 2, l. 49. [Lysander] The only use of "interchained."

Weigh oath with oath, and you will nothing weigh:
Your vows to her and me, put in two scales,
Will even weigh, and both as light as tales.

A Midsummer-Night's Dream. Act iii, sc. 2, l. 131. [Helena]

11 Come, swear it, damn thyself;
Lest, being like one of heaven, the devils themselves
Should fear to seize thee: therefore be double damn'd:
Swear thou art honest.

Othello. Act iv, sc. 2, l. 35. [Othello] The only use of "double damn'd."

Thy oath remember; thou hast sworn to do it.

Pericles. Act iv, sc. 1, l. 1. [Dionyza]

1
I will not wrong thy true affection so,
To flatter thee with an infringed oath.
The Rape of Lucrece, l. 1060.

2
According to thy oath and band.
Richard II. Act i, sc. 1, l. 2. [King Richard]
My oath—
Which God defend a knight should violate!
Richard II. Act i, sc. 3, l. 17. [Mowbray]
Return again, and take an oath with thee.
Richard II. Act i, sc. 3, l. 178. [King Richard]
To keep the oath that we administer:
You never shall, so help you truth and God!
Richard II. Act i, sc. 3, l. 182. [King Richard] The only use of "administer."
This swears he, as he is a prince, is just;
And, as I am a gentleman, I credit him.
Richard II. Act iii, sc. 3, l. 119. [Northumberland]
I am bound by oath.—*Richard III,* iv, 1, 28.

3
Let me unkiss the oath 'twixt thee and me;
And yet not so, for with a kiss 'twas made.
Richard II. Act v, sc. 1, l. 74. [King Richard] The only use of "unkiss."

4
I have sworn deep oaths of thy deep kindness,
Oaths of thy love, thy truth, thy constancy.
Sonnets. No. clii.
Protesting oath on oath.—*The Taming of the Shrew,* ii, 1, 311. See under Wooing.

5 The strongest oaths are straw
To the fire i' the blood.
The Tempest. Act iv, sc. 1, l. 52. [Prospero]

6
You are not oathable.
Timon of Athens, iv, 3, 135. The only use of "oathable."
Spare your oaths.—*Timon of Athens,* iv, 3, 138.

7
What should I swear by? thou believest no god:
That granted, how canst thou believe an oath?
Titus Andronicus. Act v, sc. 1, l. 71. [Lucius]

8
Swear the oaths now to her that you have sworn to me.
Troilus and Cressida. Act iii, sc. 2, l. 43. [Pandarus]
Taxing me and gaging me to keep
An oath that I have sworn.
Troilus and Cressida. Act v, sc. 1, l. 46. [Achilles] The only use of "gaging."
I prithee, do not hold me to mine oath.
Troilus and Cressida. Act v, sc. 2, l. 26. [Cressida]

9
Duke: Boy, thou hast said to me a thousand times
Thou never shouldst love woman like to me.
Viola: And all those sayings will I over-swear;
And all those swearings keep as true in soul
As doth that orbed continent the fire
That severs day from night.
Twelfth Night. Act v, sc. 1, l. 274. The only use of "over-swear."
Pray God, he keep his oath!—*Twelfth Night,* iii, 4, 341.
Oaths of judgement.—*Twelfth Night,* iii, 2, 16.

10
Here is her oath for love, her honour's pawn.
The Two Gentlemen of Verona. Act i, sc. 3, l. 47. [Proteus]
Twenty thousand soul-confirming oaths.
The Two Gentlemen of Verona. Act ii, sc. 6, l. 16. [Proteus] The only use of "soul-confirming."
Julia: A thousand oaths, an ocean of his tears
And instances of infinite of love
Warrant me welcome to my Proteus.
Lucetta: All these are servants to deceitful men.
The Two Gentlemen of Verona. Act ii, sc. 7, l. 69.
His oaths are oracles.—*The Two Gentlemen of Verona,* ii, 7, 75.
Full of new-found oaths.—*The Two Gentlemen of Verona,* iv, 4, 135. The only use of "new-found."
New-tuned oaths.—*Henry V,* iii, 6, 80. The only use of "new-tuned."

11
Behold her that gave aim to all thy oaths,
And entertain'd 'em deeply in her heart.
The Two Gentlemen of Verona. Act v, sc. 4, l. 101. [Julia]

12
You would seek to unsphere the stars with oaths.
The Winter's Tale. Act i, sc. 2, l. 48. [Hermione] The only use of "unsphere."
Most accursed am I
To be by oath enjoin'd to this.
The Winter's Tale. Act iii, sc. 3, l. 52. [Antigonus]
According to thine oath.—*The Winter's Tale,* iii, 3, 30.
Bear witness to his oath.—*The Winter's Tale,* v, 1, 72.

13 I 'll swear 't. If word nor oath
Prevail not, go and see.
The Winter's Tale. Act iii, sc. 2, l. 204. [Paulina]
Let boors and franklins say it, I 'll swear it.
The Winter's Tale. Act v, sc. 2, l. 173. [Clown] The only use of "boors" and "franklins." "Boor" occurs in *The Merry Wives of Windsor,* iv, 5, 1, and "franklin" (freeholder) in *I Henry IV,* ii, 1, 60, and in *Cymbeline,* iii, 2, 79.

II—Broken Oaths

See also Perjury

14
He professes not keeping of oaths; in breaking 'em he is stronger than Hercules.
All's Well that Ends Well. Act iv, sc. 3, l. 282. [Parolles]
You have broken
The article of your oath; which you shall never
Have tongue to charge me with.
Antony and Cleopatra. Act ii, sc. 2, l. 81. [Cæsar]

Antony: But on, Cæsar; The article of my oath.
Cæsar: To lend me arms and aid when I required them;
The which you both denied.
Antony and Cleopatra. Act ii, sc. 2, l. 86.

1
When I break that oath, let me turn monster.
As You Like It. Act i, sc. 2, l. 23. [Celia]

Not for Bohemia, nor the pomp that may
Be thereat glean'd, for all the sun sees or
The close earth wombs or the profound seas hide
In unknown fathoms, will I break my oath
To this my fair beloved.
The Winter's Tale. Act iv, sc. 4, l. 498. [Florizel]

2
Breaking his oath and resolution like
A twist of rotten silk.
Coriolanus. Act v, sc. 6, l. 95. [Aufidius]

Broke oath on oath.—*I Henry IV,* iv, 3, 101.

3
York: I took an oath that he should quietly reign.
Edward: But for a kingdom any oath may be broken:
I would break a thousand oaths to reign one year.
Richard: No; God forbid your grace should be forsworn.
III Henry VI. Act i, sc. 2, l. 15. "A thousand oaths" is repeated in *The Two Gentlemen of Verona,* ii, 7, 69, and v, 4, 48.

An oath is of no moment, being not took
Before a true and lawful magistrate,
That hath authority over him that swears.
III Henry VI. Act i, sc. 2, l. 22. [Richard]

Your oath, my lord, is vain and frivolous.
III Henry VI. Act i, sc. 2, l. 27. [Richard]

4
King Henry: But did you never swear, and break an oath?
Keeper: No, never such an oath; nor will not now.
III Henry VI. Act iii, sc. 1, l. 72.

But do not break your oaths; for of that sin
My mild entreaty shall not make you guilty.
III Henry VI. Act iii, sc. 1, l. 90. [King Henry]

5
Tell me, then, have you not broke your oaths?
III Henry VI. Act iii, sc. 1, l. 79. [King Henry]

Broke his solemn oath.—*III Henry VI,* i, 4, 100.

His oath is broke.—*III Henry VI,* ii, 2, 89.

Break my oath.—*Love's Labour's Lost,* v, 2, 348.

6
Clarence: Didst thou not hear me swear I would not do it?
Queen Margaret: Ay, but thou usest to forswear thyself.
III Henry VI. Act v, sc. 5, l. 74.

To swear and to forswear.
As You Like It. Act v, sc. 4, l. 58. [Touchstone]

Forswear not thyself.—*The Two Gentlemen of Verona,* ii, 5, 3.

I was fain to forswear it.—*Measure for Measure,* iv, 3, 183.

You 'll forswear this again.—*Measure for Measure,* iii, 2, 177.

Forswear myself.—*Titus Andronicus,* v, 1, 130. "Forswear" is used twenty-nine times in the plays. It does not occur in the poems.

His oath-breaking; which he mended thus,
By now forswearing that he is forsworn.
I Henry IV. Act v, sc. 2, l. 38. [Worcester] The only use of "oath-breaking." "Forswearing" is repeated in *Richard III,* i, 4, 207.

7
You are forsworn, forsworn.
King John. Act iii, sc. 1, l. 101. [Constance]

But thou dost swear only to be forsworn;
And most forsworn, to keep what thou dost swear.
King John. Act iii, sc. 1, l. 286. [Pandulph]

I am forsworn on 'mere necessity.'
Love's Labour's Lost, i, 1, 155. See under NECESSITY.

I am forsworn!—*Love's Labour's Lost,* iv, 3, 47; 116; *The Merchant of Venice,* iii, 2, 11; *Sonnets,* clii.

King: Hear me, dear lady; I have sworn an oath.
Princess: Our Lady help my Lord! he 'll be forsworn.
Love's Labour's Lost. Act ii, sc. 1, l. 97.

It is religion to be thus forsworn.
Love's Labour's Lost. Act iv, sc. 3, l. 363. [Biron]

We are again forsworn, in will and error.
Love's Labour's Lost, v, 2, 471. See under PERJURY.

Swear not, lest ye be forsworn again.
Love's Labour's Lost. Act v, sc. 2, l. 842. [Katharine]

If you swear, my lord, you shall not be forsworn.
Much Ado about Nothing. Act i, sc. 1, l. 154. [Leonato]

Foh, foh! come, tell a pin: you are forsworn.
Troilus and Cressida. Act v, sc. 2, l. 22. [Diomedes]

She bids me think how I have been forsworn.
The Two Gentlemen of Verona, iv, 2, 10. See under BEAUTY.

Do you think I 'll be forsworn?
Henry V. Act iv, sc. 8, l. 13. [Williams]

I shall be forsworn.—*Love's Labour's Lost,* i, 2, 175.

I shall be much forsworn.—*The Two Gentlemen of Verona,* ii, 6, 1.

I 'll not be forsworn.—*Romeo and Juliet,* iii, 5, 197.

He is forsworn.—*King John,* v, 4, 31; *I Henry IV,* v, 2, 39.

They are both forsworn.—*The Comedy of Errors,* v, 1, 212.

All perjured, All forsworn.—*Romeo and Juliet,* iii, 2, 86.

To myself forsworn.—*Love's Labour's Lost,* iv, 2, 111; *The Passionate Pilgrim,* l. 59. "Forsworn" is used sixty-one times.

He forswore most monstrously.
The Comedy of Errors. Act v, sc. 1, l. 11. [Angelo] The only use of "monstrously."

I never prospered since I forswore myself at primero.
The Merry Wives of Windsor. Act iv, sc. 5, l. 103. [Falstaff] Primero, a card game, is mentioned again in *Henry VIII,* v, 1, 7.

Forswore himself.—*Richard III,* i, 3, 136.

I forswore not thee.—*The Passionate Pilgrim,* l. 33. "Forswore" is used nine times.

1

Swore as many oaths as I spake words, and broke them in the sweet face of heaven.
King Lear. Act iii, sc. 4, l. 90. [Edgar]

2

Or, having sworn too hard a keeping oath,
Study to break it and not break my troth.
Love's Labour's Lost. Act i, sc. 1, l. 65. [Biron]

What fool is not so wise
To lose an oath to win a paradise?
Love's Labour's Lost. Act iv, sc. 3, l. 72. [Longaville] Repeated in *The Passionate Pilgrim,* l. 41.

For wisdom's sake, a word that all men love,
Or for love's sake, a word that loves all men,
Or for men's sake, the authors of these women,
Or women's sake, by whom we men are men,
Let us once lose our oaths to find ourselves,
Or else we lose ourselves to keep our oaths.
Love's Labour's Lost. Act iv, sc. 3, l. 357. [Biron]

So much I hate a breaking cause to be
Of heavenly oaths, vow'd with integrity.
Love's Labour's Lost. Act v, sc. 2, l. 355. [Princess of France]

Your oath once broke, you force not to forswear.
Love's Labour's Lost. Act v, sc. 2, l. 440. [Princess of France]

3

Have misbecomed our oaths and gravities.
Love's Labour's Lost. Act v, sc. 2, l. 778. [Biron] The only use of "misbecomed" and "gravities." "Misbecome" occurs in *Henry V,* ii, 4, 118, and "misbecame" in *II Henry IV,* v, 2, 100. "Gravity" is used thirteen times.

Play'd foul play with our oaths.—*Love's Labour's Lost,* v, 2, 766.

4

For ere Demetrius look'd on Hermia's eyne,
He hail'd down oaths that he was only mine;
And when this hail some heat from Hermia felt,
So he dissolved, and showers of oaths did melt.
A Midsummer-Night's Dream. Act i, sc. 1, l. 242. [Helena]

5

Let him ne'er see joy that breaks that oath!
Richard II. Act ii, sc. 3, l. 151. [Northumberland]

God pardon all oaths that are broke to me!
Richard II. Act iv, sc. 1, l. 214. [King Richard]

Cracking the strong warrant of an oath.
Richard II, iv, 1, 235. [King Richard]

6

But why of two oaths' breach do I accuse thee,
When I break twenty?
Sonnets. No. clii.

7

For whose dear sake thou didst then rend thy faith
Into a thousand oaths; and all those oaths
Descended into perjury.
The Two Gentlemen of Verona. Act v, sc. 4, l. 47. [Silvia]

III—Some Examples

8

Ay, by my sceptre and my hopes of heaven.
All's Well that Ends Well. Act ii, sc. 1, l. 195. [King]

By my sceptre and my soul to boot.
I Henry IV. Act iii, sc. 2, l. 97. [King Henry]

9

Touchstone: By mine honour. . . .
Rosalind: Where learned you that oath, fool?
Touchstone: Of a certain knight that swore by his honour they were good pancakes and swore by his honour the mustard was naught: now I 'll stand to it, the pancakes were naught and the mustard was good, and yet was not the knight forsworn.
Celia: How prove you that, in the great heap of your knowledge? . . .
Touchstone: If you swear by that that is not, you are not forsworn: no more was this knight, swearing by his honour, for he never had any; or if he had, he had sworn it away before ever he saw those pancakes or that mustard.
As You Like It. Act i, sc. 2, l. 63. The only uses of "pancakes." "Pancake" occurs in *All's Well that Ends Well,* ii, 2, 25: "A pancake for Shrove Tuesday."

By my troth, and in good earnest, and so God mend me, and by all pretty oaths that are not dangerous.
As You Like It, iv, 1, 192. [Rosalind]

By these pickers and stealers.
Hamlet. Act iii, sc. 2, l. 349. [Hamlet] The only use of "pickers" and "stealers." "Stealer" occurs in *Much Ado about Nothing,* ii, 1, 233, and in *Cymbeline,* ii, 3, 75.

10

My oath should be 'By this fire, that 's God's angel.'
I Henry IV, iii, 3, 39. See under FACE.

Nay, an I do, I pray God my girdle break.
I Henry IV. Act iii, sc. 3, l. 171. [Falstaff]

11

By cock and pie, sir, you shall not away to-night.
II Henry IV. Act v, sc. 1, l. 1. [Shallow]

By cock and pie, you shall not choose, sir!
The Merry Wives of Windsor. Act i, sc. 1, l. 316. [Page]

By God's liggens, I thank thee.
II Henry IV. Act v, sc. 3, l. 69. [Shallow] The only use of "liggens," a word without special meaning.

12

Orleans: By the white hand of my lady, he 's a gallant prince.

Constable: Swear by her foot, that she may tread out the oath.
Henry V. Act iii, sc. 7, l. 101.

By this hand I swear,
That sways the earth this climate overlooks,
Before we will lay down our just-borne arms,
We 'll put thee down, 'gainst whom these arms we bear.
King John. Act ii, sc. 1, l. 345. [King Philip] The only use of "just-borne."

1
By the sacred radiance of the sun,
The mys eries of Hecate, and the night;
By all the operation of the orbs
From whom we do exist, and cease to be.
King Lear. Act i, sc. 1, l. 111. [King Lear]

2
By welkin and her star!
The Merry Wives of Windsor. Act i, sc. 3, l. 101. [Nym]

Ay, be-gar.—*The Merry Wives of Windsor,* iii, 2, 65.
By 'r lady.—*Richard III,* ii, 3, 4, and thirteen times in later plays.
By 'r lakin.—*A Midsummer-Night's Dream,* iii, 1, 14; *The Tempest,* iii, 3, 1.
By my fay.—*The Taming of the Shrew,* Induction, 2, 83; *Romeo and Juliet,* i, 5, 128; *Hamlet,* ii, 2, 272.
'Od's heartlings!—*The Merry Wives of Windsor,* iii, 4, 59.
'Od's lifelings!—*Twelfth Night,* v, 1, 187.
'Od's me!—*The Merry Wives of Windsor,* i, 4, 64.
'Od's my little life!—*As You Like It,* iii, 5, 43.
'Od's my will!—*As You Like It,* iv, 3, 17.
'Od's nouns!—*The Merry Wives of Windsor,* iv, 1, 25.
'Od's pittikins!—*Cymbeline,* iv, 2, 293.
'Od's plessed will!—*The Merry Wives of Windsor,* i, 1, 273.

3
By knighthood, gentry, and sweet friendship's oath.
The Rape of Lucrece, l. 369.

4
Swear by the duty that you owe to God.
Richard II. Act i, sc. 3, l. 180. [King Richard]

Swear by this bottle.
The Tempest. Act ii, sc. 2, l. 124. [Stephano]

I 'll swear upon that bottle.
The Tempest. Act ii, sc. 2, l. 129. [Caliban]

5
King Richard: Now, by my George, my garter, and my crown,—
Queen Elizabeth: Profaned, dishonour'd, and the third usurp'd.
King Richard: I swear—
Queen Elizabeth: By nothing, for this is no oath:
The George, profaned, hath lost his holy honour;
The garter, blemish'd, pawn'd his knightly virtue;
The crown, usurp'd, disgraced his kingly glory.
If something thou wilt swear to be believed,
Swear then by something that thou hast not wrong'd.
King Richard: Now, by the world,—
Queen Elizabeth: 'Tis full of thy foul wrongs.
King Richard: My father's death—
Queen Elizabeth: Thy life hath that dishonour'd.
King Richard: Then, by myself—
Queen Elizabeth: Thyself thyself misusest.
King Richard: Well then, by God—
Queen Elizabeth: God's wrong is most of all.
If thou hadst fear'd to break an oath by Him,
The unity the king thy brother made
Had not been broken, nor thy brother slain:
If thou hadst fear'd to break an oath by Him,
The imperial metal, circling now thy brow,
Had graced the tender temples of my child. . . .
What canst thou swear by now?
King Richard: The time to come.
Queen Elizabeth: That thou hast wronged in the time o'erpast; . . .
Swear not by time to come; for that thou hast
Misused ere used, by time misused o'erpast.
Richard III. Act iv, sc. 4, l. 366.

6
By the bare scalp of Robin Hood's fat friar.
The Two Gentlemen of Verona. Act iv, sc. 1, l. 36. [Outlaw]

By my halidom.—*The Two Gentlemen of Verona,* iv, 2, 136. The only use of "halidom."
By my holidame.—*Romeo and Juliet,* i, 3, 43. [Nurse] Repeated in *The Taming of the Shrew,* v, 2, 99, and *Henry VIII,* v, 1, 116.

OBEDIENCE

See also Disobedience

7
Sir, I can nothing say,
But that I am your most obedient servant.
All's Well that Ends Well. Act ii, sc. 5, l. 77. [Helena]

Your most obedient subject.—*Richard III,* iv, 2, 68.
A loyal and obedient subject.—*Henry VIII,* iii, 2, 180.
Obedient as the scabbard.—*Cymbeline,* iii, 4, 82.
Obedient to the stream.—*The Comedy of Errors,* i, 1, 87.

8
I hourly learn A doctrine of obedience.
Antony and Cleopatra. Act v, sc. 2, l. 30. [Cleopatra]

9
Ere I learn love, I 'll practise to obey.
The Comedy of Errors. Act ii, sc. 1, l. 29. [Luciana]

10
As weeds before
A vessel under sail, so men obey'd
And fell below his stem.
Coriolanus. Act ii, sc. 2, l. 109. [Coriolanus]

Have we not had a taste of his obedience?
Coriolanus. Act iii, sc. 1, l. 318. [Sicinius]

1
You sin against Obedience.
Cymbeline. Act ii, sc. 3, l. 116. [Cloten]

Their obedience fails.—*Coriolanus,* iii, 1, 166.

You have obedience scanted.—*King Lear,* i, 1, 281.

Enforced obedience.—*King Lear,* i, 2, 135.

Plausible obedience.—*Measure for Measure.* Act iii, sc. 1, l. 253. The only use of "plausible."

Contending 'gainst obedience.—*Macbeth,* ii, 4, 17.

Will not be obedient.—*The Taming of the Shrew,* iv, 1, 199.

Not obedient.—*The Taming of the Shrew,* v, 2, 158.

Obedience fail in children.—*Timon of Athens,* iv, 1, 4.

2 We both obey,
And here give up ourselves, in the full bent
To lay our service freely at your feet,
To be commanded.
Hamlet. Act ii, sc. 2, l. 29. [Guildenstern]

3
Let me no more from this obedience rise.
II Henry IV. Act iv, sc. 5, l. 147. [Prince]

4
Therefore doth heaven divide
The state of man in divers functions,
Setting endeavour in continual motion;
To which is fixed, as an aim or butt,
Obedience.
Henry V. Act i, sc. 1, l. 183. [Archbishop of Canterbury]

5
Bring him in obedience to your yoke.
I Henry VI. Act i, sc. 1, l. 164. [Exeter]

6
We do no otherwise than we are will'd.
I Henry VI. Act i, sc. 3, l. 10. [Warder] The only use of "no otherwise."

Obey our will, which travails in thy good.
All's Well that Ends Well. Act ii, sc. 3, l. 165. [King]

In every thing I wait upon his will.
All's Well that Ends Well. Act ii, sc. 4, l. 55. [Helena]

Knowing thy will,
I will acquaintance strangle and look strange.
Sonnets. No. lxxxix.

7
Let them obey that know not how to rule.
II Henry VI. Act v, sc. 1, l. 6. [York]

8
What your pleasure is, shall satisfy me.
III Henry VI. Act iii, sc. 2, l. 20. [Lady Grey]

Always obedient to your grace's will,
I come to know your pleasure.
Measure for Measure. Act i, sc. 1, l. 26. [Angelo]

I wait upon his pleasure.
The Two Gentlemen of Verona. Act ii, sc. 4, l. 117. [Silvia]

9
If you mind to hold your true obedience,
Give me assurance with some friendly vow,
That I may never have you in suspect.
III Henry VI. Act iv, sc. 1, l. 140. [King Edward]

And true obedience, of this madness cured,
Stoop tamely to the foot of majesty.
II Henry IV. Act iv, sc. 2, l. 41. [Archbishop of York]

Fair looks, and true obedience.—*The Taming of the Shrew,* v, 2, 153.

10 I do not know
What kind of my obedience I should tender.
More than my all is nothing.
Henry VIII. Act ii, sc. 3, l. 65. [Anne]

11
When Cæsar says 'do this,' it is perform'd.
Julius Cæsar. Act i, sc. 2, l. 10. [Antony]

What he bids be done is finished with his bidding.
Coriolanus. Act v, sc. 4, l. 24. [Menenius]

12 She is bound in honour still to do
What you in wisdom still vouchsafe to say.
King John. Act ii, sc. 1, l. 522. [Blanch]

Make them tame to their obedience!
King John. Act iv, sc. 2, l. 262. [King John]

The king:
From whose obedience I forbid my soul.
King John. Act iv, sc. 3, l. 63. [Salisbury]

We will untread the steps of damned flight,
And like a bated and retired flood,
Leaving our rankness and irregular course,
Stoop low within those bounds we have o'erlook'd
And calmly run on in obedience
Even to our ocean.
King John. Act v, sc. 4, l. 52. [Salisbury] "Untread" is repeated in *The Merchant of Venice,* ii, 6, 10.

13
Give obedience where 'tis truly owed.
Macbeth. Act v, sc. 2, l. 26. [Caithness]

14 Her gentle spirit
Commits itself to yours to be directed,
As from her lord, her governor, her king.
The Merchant of Venice. Act iii, sc. 2, l. 165. [Portia]

Madam, with all my heart;
I shall obey you in all fair commands.
The Merchant of Venice. Act iii, sc. 4, l. 35. [Lorenzo]

Seemingly obedient.—*The Merry Wives of Windsor,* iv, 6, 33. The only use of "seemingly."

15
Benedick: Sweet Beatrice, wouldst thou come when I called thee?
Beatrice: Yes, signior, and depart when you bid me.
Much Ado about Nothing. Act v, sc. 2, l. 42.

16 Come hither, gentle mistress:
Do you perceive in all this company
Where most you owe obedience?
Othello. Act i, sc. 3, l. 178. [Brabantio]

Be as your fancies teach you;
Whate'er you be, I am obedient.
Othello. Act iii, sc. 3, l. 88. [Desdemona]

She 's obedient, as you say, obedient,
Very obedient.
Othello. Act iv, sc. 1, l. 266. [Othello]

17 Let him command,
And to obey shall be in me remorse.
Othello. Act iii, sc. 3, l. 467. [Iago]

1
Without or yea or no.
The Rape of Lucrece, l. 1340.
Swift obedience.—*The Rape of Lucrece,* l. 1215.

2
Obedience bids I should not bid again.
Richard II. Act i, sc. 1, l. 163. [Gaunt]

3
We are the queen's abjects, and must obey.
Richard III. Act i, sc. 1, l. 106. [Gloucester] "Abjects," as a noun, is repeated in *Julius Cæsar,* iv, 1, 37: "Feeds On abjects, orts."
Commend my best obedience to the queen.
The Winter's Tale, ii, 2, 36.

4
If thou dost find him tractable to us,
Encourage him.
Richard III. Act iii, sc. 1, l. 174. [Buckingham]
This tractable obedience is a slave
To each incensed will.
Henry VIII. Act i, sc. 2, l. 64. [Queen Katharine]
Altogether more tractable.—*Troilus and Cressida,* ii, 3, 160.
Mild and tractable.—*Titus Andronicus,* i, 1, 470.
Tractable enough.—*Pericles,* iv, 6, 211.
Tractable to any honest reason.—*I Henry IV,* iii, 3, 194.

5
Henceforward I am ever ruled by you.
Romeo and Juliet. Act iv, sc. 2, l. 22. [Juliet]

6
Speak of my lameness, and I straight will halt.
Sonnets. No. lxxxix.

7
I am tied to be obedient.
The Taming of the Shrew. Act i, sc. 1, l. 217. [Tranio]
Most obedient.—*Taming of the Shrew,* v, 2, 67.
Obedient to their dooms.—*Pericles,* iii, Gower, 32.

8
Her obedience,
Her new-built virtue and obedience.
The Taming of the Shrew. Act v, sc. 2, l. 117. [Petruchio] "New-built" is repeated in *Cymbeline,* i, 5, 19.
In all obedience.—*The Taming of the Shrew,* Ind., 2, 109; *Henry VIII,* v, 3, 117.

9
Prospero: Hast thou, spirit,
Perform'd to point the tempest that I bade thee?
Ariel: To every article.
The Tempest. Act i, sc. 2, l. 193.
Ariel, thy charge Exactly is perform'd.
The Tempest. Act i, sc. 2, l. 237. [Prospero]
I will be correspondent to command
And do my spiriting gently.
Tempest. Act i, sc. 2, l. 297. [Ariel] The only use of "correspondent" and "spiriting."
Prospero: Exactly do
All points of my command.
Ariel: To the syllable.
The Tempest. Act i, sc. 2, l. 499.

10
I must obey: his art is of such power,
It would control my dam's god, Setebos,
And make a vassal of him.
The Tempest. Act i, sc. 2, l. 372. [Caliban] Setebos is mentioned again in v, 1, 261.
Weigh'd between loathness and obedience, at
Which end o' the beam should bow.
Tempest. Act ii, sc. 1, l. 130. [Sebastian] "Loathness" is repeated in *Antony and Cleopatra,* iii, 11, 18, and in *Cymbeline,* i, 1, 108.

11
Your bidding shall I do effectually.
Titus Andronicus. Act iv, sc. 4, l. 107. [Æmilius] "Effectually" is repeated in *Sonnets,* cxiii.
I will do everything that thou wilt have me.
Twelfth Night. Act ii, sc. 5, l. 194. [Malvolio]

12
Or like the froward infant still'd with dandling.
He now obeys and now no more resisteth.
Venus and Adonis, l. 562. The only use of "dandling."

13
Obedience to a master, one
Who in rebellion with himself will have
All that are his so too.
Winter's Tale. Act i, sc. 2, l. 354. [Camillo]

OBLIVION

14
O, my oblivion is a very Antony,
And I am all forgotten.
Antony and Cleopatra. Act i, sc. 3, l. 90. [Cleopatra]

15
The dust of old oblivion.
Henry V. Act ii, sc. 4, l. 87. [Exeter]

16
To feed oblivion with decay of things.
The Rape of Lucrece, l. 947.

17
Almost shoulder'd in the swallowing gulf
Of blind forgetfulness and dark oblivion.
Richard III. Act iii, sc. 7, l. 128. [Buckingham] The only use of "shoulder'd."

18
Many things of worthy memory, which now shall die in oblivion and thou return unexperienced to thy grave.
The Taming of the Shrew. Act iv, sc. 1, l. 84. [Grumio] The only use of "unexperienced."
Lives But in oblivion and hateful griefs.
Titus Andronicus. Act iii, sc. 1, l. 295. [Lucius]

19
And blind oblivion swallow'd cities up.
Troilus and Cressida. Act iii, sc. 2, l. 194. [Cressida]
Bestial oblivion.—*Hamlet,* iv, 4, 40.
Mere oblivion.—*As You Like It,* ii, 7, 165.
Formless ruin of oblivion.—*Troilus and Cressida,* iv, 5, 167.
Razure of oblivion.—*Measure for Measure,* v, 1, 13.
Razed oblivion.—*Sonnets.* No. cxxii.

OBSCURITY

20
I was of late as petty to his ends
As is the morn-dew on the myrtle-leaf
To his grand sea.
Antony and Cleopatra. Act iii, sc. 12, l. 8.

[Euphronius] The only use of "morn-dew" and "myrtle-leaf."

Lesser than a little.
Coriolanus. Act i, sc. 4, l. 15. [Senator]

1
To apprehend thus,
Draws us a profit from all things we see;
And often, to our comfort, shall we find
The sharded beetle in a safer hold
Than is the full-wing'd eagle.
Cymbeline. Act iii, sc. 3, l. 17. [Belarius]
The only use of "sharded" and "full-wing'd."

I am ashamed
To look upon the holy sun, to have
The benefit of his blest beams, remaining
So long a poor unknown.
Cymbeline. Act iv, sc. 4, l. 40. [Arviragus]

O base and obscure vulgar!—*Love's Labour's Lost,* iv, 1, 69.

Obscure funeral.—*Hamlet,* iv, 5, 213.

Obscure grave.—*Richard II,* iii, 3, 154; *The Merchant of Venice,* ii, 7, 51.

Obscure and lowly swain.—*II Henry VI,* iv, 1, 50.

2
Even since then hath Richard been obscured.
I Henry VI. Act ii, sc. 5, l. 26. [Mortimer]

Why, 'tis an office of discovery, love;
And I should be obscured.
The Merchant of Venice. Act ii, sc. 6, l. 43. [Jessica]

You may marvel why I obscured myself.
Measure for Measure. Act v, sc. 1, l. 395. [Duke]

3
And sleep in dull cold marble, where no mention
Of me more must be heard of.
Henry VIII. Act iii, sc. 2, l. 433. [Wolsey]

4
Destroy them not in dark obscurity.
Venus and Adonis, l. 760.

Vast obscurity.—*Titus Adronicus,* v, 2, 36.
The only uses of "obscurity."

OBSERVANCE

5
Relish it with good observance.
As You Like It. Act iii, sc. 2, l. 247. [Celia]

Due observance.—*Troilus and Cressida,* i, 3, 31.

Special observance.—*Hamlet,* iii, 2, 21.

True observance.—*All's Well that Ends Well,* ii, 5, 79.

Strict observances.—*Love's Labour's Lost,* i, 1, 36. "Observances" is used twice more, in *Othello,* iii, 4, 149, and in *Timon of Athens,* iv, 1, 19.

6
Use all observance of civility.
The Merchant of Venice. Act ii, sc. 2, l. 204. [Gratiano]

7
Followed her with a doting observance.
The Merry Wives of Windsor, ii, 2, 203. See under LOVE.

8
To do observance to a morn of May.
A Midsummer-Night's Dream. Act i, sc. 1, l. 167. [Lysander]

Do observance to my mercy.—*II Henry IV,* iv, 3, 16.

9
Such sweet observance in this work was had,
That one might see those far-off eyes look sad.
The Rape of Lucrece, l. 1385.

10
Without observance or respect.
Troilus and Cressida. Act ii, sc. 3, l. 175. [Ulysses]

Unsure observance.—*Othello,* iii, 3, 151.

I have no observance.—*Antony and Cleopatra,* iii, 3, 25.

OBSERVATION

11
He hath strange places cramm'd
With observation.
As You Like It, ii, 7, 41. See under BRAIN.

12
What observation madest thou in this case?
The Comedy of Errors. Act iv, sc. 2, l. 5. [Adriana]

13
Observe his inclination in yourself.
Hamlet. Act ii, sc. 1, l. 71. [Polonius]

Even with the very comment of thy soul
Observe mine uncle.
Hamlet. Act iii, sc. 2, l. 84. [Hamlet]

I'll observe his looks.—*Hamlet,* ii, 2, 625.

14
The observed of all observers.
Hamlet. Act iii, sc. 1, l. 162. [Ophelia]

15
Tut, that's a foolish observation.
III Henry VI. Act ii, sc. 6, l. 108. [Warwick]

16
I do observe you now of late.
Julius Cæsar. Act i, sc. 2, l. 32. [Cassius]

Must I observe you?—*Julius Cæsar,* iv, 3, 45.

He is a great observer and he looks
Quite through the deeds of men.
Julius Cæsar. Act i, sc. 2, l. 202. [Cæsar]

17
For he is but a bastard to the time
That doth not smack of observation;
And so am I, whether I smack or no;
And not alone in habit and device,
Exterior form, outward accoutrement,
But from the inward motion to deliver
Sweet, sweet, sweet poison for the age's tooth.
King John. Act i, sc. 1, l. 207. [Bastard]

18
The observation we have made of it hath been but little.
King Lear. Act i, sc. 1, l. 292. [Goneril]

19
My observation, which very seldom lies.
Love's Labour's Lost. Act ii, sc. 1, l. 228. [Boyet]

My penny of observation.
Love's Labour's Lost, iii, 1, 28. See under EXPERIENCE.

20
Wait the season and observe the times.
Love's Labour's Lost. Act v, sc. 2, l. 63. [Rosaline]

21
Now our observation is perform'd.
A Midsummer-Night's Dream. Act iv, sc. 1, l. 108. [Theseus]

Trust not my observations.—*Much Ado about Nothing,* iv, 1, 167. See under ERROR.

1 You shall observe him,
And his own courses will denote him so
That I may save my speech.
Othello. Act iv, sc. 1, l. 289. [Iago]

2
With good life And observation strange.
The Tempest. Act iii, sc. 3, l. 87. [Prospero]

3
Let me stay at thine apperil, Timon: I come to observe; I give thee warning on 't.
Timon of Athens. Act i, sc. 2, l. 32. [Apemantus] The only use of "apperil" (risk).

4
Observe him, for the love of mockery.
Twelfth Night. Act ii, sc. 5, l. 21. [Maria]
I shall observe him with all care and love.
II Henry IV. Act iv, sc. 4, l. 49. [Clarence]
Observe, observe, he 's moody.
Henry VIII. Act iii, sc. 2, l. 75. [Norfolk]
Observe his construction of it.—*Twelfth Night,* ii, 3, 190.
Observe her; stand close.—*Macbeth,* v, 1, 23.
Observe her well.—*Othello,* iii, 3, 197.
I observe her now.—*All's Well that Ends Well,* i, 3, 141.
Hast thou observed that?—*The Two Gentlemen of Verona,* ii, 1, 48.
Well observed.—*II Henry IV,* iv, 4, 36.

OBSTACLE, see Impediment

OBSTINACY

See also Stubbornness

5 Only sin
And hellish obstinacy tie thy tongue.
All's Well that Ends Well. Act i, sc. 3, l. 182. [Countess]
You do not well in obstinacy To cavil.
I Henry VI, v, 4, 17. The only uses of "obstinacy."

6
In bed he slept not for my urging it;
At board he fed not for my urging it;
Alone, it was the subject of my theme;
In company I often glanced it;
Still did I tell him it was vile and bad.
The Comedy of Errors. Act v, sc. 1, l. 63. [Adriana]

7
You are too absolute.
Coriolanus. Act iii, sc. 2, l. 39. [Volumnia]
How absolute the knave is!
Hamlet. Act v, sc. 1, l. 148. [Hamlet]
How absolute she 's in 't.
Pericles. Act ii, sc. 5, l. 19. [Simonides]
Be absolute.—*Measure for Measure,* iii, 1, 5.

8
Let it be virtuous to be obstinate.
Coriolanus. Act v, sc. 3, l. 26. [Coriolanus]

9
Fie, Joan, that thou wilt be so obstacle!
I Henry VI. Act v, sc. 4, l. 17. [Shepherd]

10 Never Hydra-headed wilfulness
So soon did lose his seat and all at once.
Henry V. Act i, sc. 1, l. 35. [Archbishop of Canterbury] The only use of "Hydra-headed" and "wilfulness."

11 If when you make your prayers,
God should be so obdurate as yourselves,
How would it fare with your departed souls?
II Henry VI. Act iv, sc. 7, l. 121. [Say]
Thou thinkest me as far in the devil's book as thou and Falstaff for obduracy and persistency.
II Henry IV. Act ii, sc. 2, l. 48. [Prince of Wales] The only use of "obduracy" and "persistency."
Be not obdurate, open thy deaf ears.
Titus Andronicus. Act ii, sc. 3, l. 160. [Lavinia]
He stands obdurate.—*The Merchant of Venice,* iv, 1, 8.

12
The sea enraged is not half so deaf,
Lions more confident, mountains and rocks
More free from motion, no, not Death himself
In mortal fury half so peremptory,
As we to keep this city.
King John. Act ii, sc. 1, l. 451. [Citizen]
I am as peremptory as she is proud-minded.
Taming of the Shrew, ii, 1, 132. [Petruchio] The only use of "proud-minded."
I am peremptory.—*The Two Gentlemen of Verona,* i, 3, 71.
We are peremptory.—*Coriolanus,* iii, 1, 286.
Are you so peremptory?—*Pericles,* ii, 5, 73.
How peremptory!—*II Henry VI,* iii, 1, 8.
Too peremptory.—*I Henry IV,* i, 3, 17. See also under COMMAND.

13
The Dauphin is too wilful-opposite.
King John. Act v, sc. 2, l. 124. [Pandulph] The only use of "wilful-opposite."

14
How unremoveable and fix'd he is
In his own course.
King Lear. Act ii, sc. 4, l. 94. [Gloucester] The only use of "unremoveable."
He 's irremoveable.—*The Winter's Tale,* iv, 4, 517. The only use of "irremoveable."
'Tis best to give him way; he leads himself.
King Lear. Act ii, sc. 4, l. 301. [Cornwall]

15
You are too senseless-obstinate, my lord,
Too ceremonious and traditional.
Richard III. Act iii, sc. 1, l. 44. [Buckingham] The only use of "senseless-obstinate" and "traditional."

OCCASION

See also Fate, Destiny

16 Goaded with most sharp occasions,
Which lay nice manners by.
All's Well that Ends Well. Act v, sc. 1, l. 14. [Helena]

17 Look, here he comes,
And brings the dire occasion in his arms
Of what we blame him for.
Cymbeline. Act iv, sc. 2, l. 195. [Belarius]

18
Occasion smiles upon a second leave.
Hamlet. Act i, sc. 3, l. 54. [Laertes]
To gather
So much as from occasion you may glean.
Hamlet. Act ii, sc. 2, l. 15. [King]
How all occasions do inform against me,
And spur my dull revenge!
Hamlet. Act iv, sc. 4, l. 32. [Hamlet]

1 From this swarm of fair advantages
You took occasion to be quickly woo'd.
I Henry IV. Act v, sc. 1, l. 55. [Worcester]

2
Mowbray: I well allow the occasion of our arms. . . .
Archbishop: Let us on,
And publish the occasion of our arms.
II Henry IV. Act i, sc. 3, l. 5.

[We] are enforced from our most quiet there
By the rough torrent of occasion.
II Henry IV. Act iv, sc. 1, l. 71. [Archbishop of York]

3
I sall quit you with gud leve, as I may pick occasion.
Henry V. Act iii, sc. 2, l. 110. [Jamy]

There is occasions and causes why and wherefore in all things.
Henry V. Act v, sc. 1, l. 3. [Fluellen]

4
That winter lion, who in rage forgets
Aged contusions and all brush of time,
And, like a gallant in the brow of youth,
Repairs him with occasion.
II Henry VI. Act v, sc. 3, l. 2. [York] The only use of "contusions."

5
I seek occasion how to rise.
III Henry VI. Act i, sc. 2, l. 45. [York]

Find occasion.—*The Taming of the Shrew,* ii, 1, 36.
Minister occasion.—*Twelfth Night,* i, 5, 94; *The Tempest,* ii, 1, 173.
Take occasion.—*I Henry VI,* iv, 1, 130; *Henry V,* v, 1, 58· *As You Like It,* iv, 1, 75.
Embrace the occasion.—*The Merchant of Venice,* i, 1, 64.
The occasion shall instruct you.—*Henry VIII,* v, 1, 149.

6 When I give occasion of offence,
Then let me die.
III Henry VI. Act i, sc. 3, l. 44. [Rutland]

As occasion serves.
III Henry VI. Act iii, sc. 3, l. 236. [King Lewis]

7
I am joyful To meet the least occasion.
Henry VIII. Act iii, sc. 2, l. 7. [Surrey]

Upon the least occasion.—*Twelfth Night,* ii, 1, 42. The only uses of "least occasion."

8
Withhold thy speed, dreadful occasion!
O, make a league with me.
King John. Act iv, sc. 2, l. 125. [King John]

Beshrew my soul
But I do love the favour and the form
Of this most fair occasion.
King John. Act v, sc. 4, l. 49. [Salisbury]

Compelling occasion.—*Antony and Cleopatra,* i, 2, 141.
Good occasion.—*Troilus and Cressida,* iv, 1, 3; *Henry VIII,* v, 1, 109.
Great occasion.—*Othello,* iv, 1, 59.
Great and instant occasion.—*Timon of Athens,* iii, 1, 19.
Just occasion.—*As You Like It,* iv, 3, 130.
Light occasion.—*A Lover's Complaint,* l. 86.
Like occasion.—*The Winter's Tale,* i, 1, 2.
Near occasions.—*Timon of Athens,* iii, 6, 12.
Present occasion.—*II Henry IV,* iv, 1, 206; *Timon of Athens,* iii, 2, 39.
Sad occasion.—*Twelfth Night,* iii, 4, 20.

9
I would breed from hence occasions.
King Lear. Act i, sc. 3, l. 24. [Goneril]

Occasions, noble Gloucester, of some poise,
Wherein we must have use of your advice.
King Lear. Act ii, sc. 1, l. 122. [Regan]

10
Get on your nightgown, lest occasion call us,
And show us to be watchers.
Macbeth. Act ii, sc. 2, l. 70. [Macbeth] "Watchers" is used a second time in *The Two Gentlemen of Verona,* ii, 4, 135.

11
Yet more quarrelling with occasion!
The Merchant of Venice. Act iii, sc. 5, l. 60. [Lorenzo]

12
Fee'd every slight occasion.
The Merry Wives of Windsor. Act ii, sc. 2, l. 204. [Ford]

On the wing of occasions.
The Merry Wives of Windsor, ii, 2, 210. See under WOOING.

13
He heartily prays some occasion may detain us longer.
Much Ado about Nothing. Act i, sc. 1, l. 150. [Don Pedro]

14 He protests he loves you
And needs no other suitor but his likings
To take the safest occasion by the front
To bring you in again.
Othello. Act iii, sc. 1, l. 50. [Emilia]

15
By the way, I'll sort occasion.
Richard III. Act ii, sc. 2, l. 148. [Buckingham]

On what occasion, God he knows, not I.
Richard III. Act iii, sc. 1, l. 26. [Hastings]

16
Tybalt: You will find me apt enough to that, sir, an you will give me occasion.
Mercutio: Could you not take some occasion without giving?
Romeo and Juliet. Act iii, sc. 1, l. 45.

17 What occasion of import
Hath all so long detain'd you from your wife,
And sent you hither so unlike yourself?
Taming of the Shrew. Act iii, sc. 2, l. 104.

The occasion speaks thee.
The Tempest. Act ii, sc. 1, l. 207. [Antonio]

18
My master is awaked by great occasion.
Timon of Athens. Act i, sc. 2, l. 21. [Caphis]

I am proud, say, that my occasions have found time to use 'em toward a supply of money.
Timon of Athens. Act ii, sc. 2, l. 199. [Timon]

I should ne'er have denied his occasion.
Timon of Athens. Act iii, sc. 2, l. 26. [Lucius]

If his occasion were not virtuous,
I should not urge it half so faithfully.
Timon of Athens. Act iii, sc. 2, l. 45. [Servilius]

His occasions might have woo'd me first.
Timon of Athens, iii, 3, 15. [Sempronius]

1
I had made mine own occasion mellow.
Twelfth Night. Act i, sc. 2, l. 43. [Viola]
You may have very fit occasion for 't.
Twelfth Night. Act iii, sc. 4, l. 190. [Maria]
We intended
To keep in darkness what occasion now
Reveals before 'tis ripe.
Twelfth Night. Act v, sc. 1, l. 155. [Olivia]
2
I am courted now with a double occasion.
The Winter's Tale. Act iv, sc. 4, l. 864. [Autolycus]

OCCUPATION

See also Trade

3
An I had been a man of any occupation, if I would not have taken him at a word, I would I might go to hell among the rogues.
Julius Cæsar. Act i, sc. 2, l. 268. [Casca]
4
'Tis my occupation to be plain.
King Lear. Act ii, sc. 2, l. 98. [Kent]
5
Angelo: What are you, sir?
Elbow: He, sir! a tapster, sir; parcel-bawd; one that serves a bad woman; whose house, sir, was, as they say, plucked down in the suburbs.
Measure for Measure. Act ii, sc. 1, l. 63. The only use of "parcel-bawd."
6
Do you call, sir, your occupation a mystery?
Measure for Measure, iv, 2, 40. See under MYSTERY.
7
Othello's occupation 's gone!
Othello. Act iii, sc. 3, l. 357. [Othello]
No occupation.—*The Tempest,* ii, 1, 154.
Occupations perish!—*Coriolanus,* iv, 1, 14.
'Tis my occupation.—*The Winter's Tale,* iv, 4, 302.
Royal occupation.—*Antony and Cleopatra,* iv, 4, 17.

OCEAN

8
The beachy girdle of the ocean
Too wide for Neptune's hips.
II Henry IV. Act iii, sc. 1, l. 50. [King Henry] The only use of "beachy."
9
Swill'd with the wild and wasteful ocean.
Henry V. Act iii, sc. 1, l. 14. [King Henry] The only use of "swill'd."
Perilous narrow ocean.—*Henry V*, Prol., l. 22.
Salt-waved ocean.—*The Rape of Lucrece,* l. 1231. The only use of "salt-waved."
Troubled ocean.—*The Rape of Lucrece,* l. 589.
Wild ocean.—*The Two Gentlemen of Verona,* ii, 7, 32.
The deep bosom of the ocean.—*Richard III,* i, 1, 4.
Ocean of his tears.—*The Two Gentlemen of Verona,* ii, 7, 69.
Ocean of salt tears.—*II Henry VI,* iii, 2, 143.
Ocean of thy blood.—*Rape of Lucrece,* l. 655.
10
I have seen
The ambitious ocean swell and rage and foam,
To be exalted with the threatening clouds.
Julius Cæsar. Act i, sc. 3, l. 6. [Casca]
11
Will all great Neptune's ocean wash this blood
Clean from my hand? No, this my hand will rather
The multitudinous seas incarnadine,
Making the green one red.
Macbeth. Act ii, sc. 2, l. 60. [Macbeth] The only use of "incarnadine." "Multitudinous" is used again in *Coriolanus,* iii, 1, 156.
12 I have seen the hungry ocean gain
Advantage on the kingdom of the shore.
Sonnets. No. lxiv.

ODDITY

13
How strange or odd soe'er I bear myself.
Hamlet. Act i, sc. 5, l. 170. [Hamlet]
But this is something odd.—*Coriolanus,* ii, 3, 88.
14
No, not to be so odd and from all fashions
As Beatrice is, cannot be commendable.
Much Ado About Nothing. Act iii, sc. 1, l. 72. [Hero]
15
How oddly thou repliest.
Romeo and Juliet. Act ii, sc. 5, l. 61. [Juliet]
How oddly he is suited!—*The Merchant of Venice,* i, 2, 79.
How oddly will it sound.—*Tempest,* v, 1, 197.
Oddly poised.—*Troilus and Cressida,* i, 3, 339. The only uses of "oddly."
16
Cressida: You 're an odd man; . . .
Menelaus: An odd man, lady! every man is odd.
Troilus and Cressida. Act iv, sc. 5, l. 41.
There is such odds in the man.
As You Like It. Act i, sc. 2, l. 169. [Duke]
Odd angle.—*The Tempest,* i, 2, 223.
Odd behaviour.—*The Taming of the Shrew,* Ind., i, 95.
Odd-conceited.—*The Two Gentlemen of Verona,* ii, 7, 46.
Odd humour.—*The Taming of the Shrew,* iii, 2, 74.
Odd quirks.—*Much Ado about Nothing,* ii, 3, 244.
Odd sayings.—*Merchant of Venice,* ii, 2, 66.
Odd tricks.—*Antony and Cleopatra,* iv, 2, 14.
Odd worm.—*Antony and Cleopatra,* v, 2, 259. It will be noted that none of these phrases is used twice.

ODDS

See also Gaming, Wager

17
His quails ever
Beat mine, inhoop'd, at odds.
Antony and Cleopatra. Act ii, sc. 3, l. 36. [Antony] The only use of "inhoop'd." Quails are mentioned again in *Troilus and Cressida,* v, 1, 57: "One that loves quails."
18
'Tis odds beyond arithmetic.
Coriolanus. Act iii, sc. 1, l. 245. [Cominius]

1
I shall win at the odds.
Hamlet. Act v, sc. 2, l. 222. [Hamlet]
Your grace hath laid the odds o' the weaker side.
Hamlet. Act v, sc. 2, l. 272. [Hamlet]
2
I will lay odds.
II Henry IV. Act v, sc. 5, l. 111. [Lancaster]
I would allow him odds.
Richard II. Act i, sc. 1, l. 62. [Mowbray]
Exeter: There 's five to one; . . .
Salisbury: God's arm strike with us! 'tis a fearful odds.
Henry V. Act iv, sc. 3, l. 4.
Take the odds.—*I Henry IV,* v, 1, 97.
3
I desire Nothing but odds with England.
Henry V. Act ii, sc. 4, l. 128. [Dauphin]
4
As doth a ruler with unlawful oaths;
Or one that, at a triumph having vow'd
To try his strength, forsaketh yet the lists
By reason of his adversary's odds:
A poor earl's daughter is unequal odds,
And therefore may be broke without offence.
I Henry VI. Act v, sc. 5, l. 30. [Suffolk]
Took odds to combat a poor famish'd man.
II Henry VI. Act iv, sc. 10, l. 47. [Iden]
5
Five men to twenty! though the odds be great,
I doubt not, uncle, of our victory.
Many a battle have I won in France,
When as the enemy hath been ten to one.
III Henry VI. Act i, sc. 2, l. 71. [York]
Hercules himself must yield to odds.
III Henry VI. Act ii, sc. 1, l. 53. [Messenger]
6
That makes these odds all even.
Measure for Measure. Act iii, sc. 1, l. 41. See LIFE, 868:19.
Odd-even.—*Othello,* i, 1, 124.
Even or odd.—*Romeo and Juliet,* i, 3, 16.
7
I cannot speak
Any beginning to this peevish odds.
Othello. Act ii, sc. 3, l. 184. [Iago]
With that odds he weighs King Richard down.
Richard II. Act iii, sc. 4, l. 89. [Gardener]
8
And pity 'tis you have lived at odds so long.
Romeo and Juliet. Act i, sc. 2, l. 5. [Paris]
At odds.—*Richard III,* ii, 1, 70; *Timon of Athens,* iii, 5, 116; *Macbeth,* iii, 4, 127; *King Lear,* i, 3, 5.
9
Then he shall have no odds.
The Taming of the Shrew. Act iv, sc. 3, l. 155. [Hortensio]
The odds is gone.—*Antony and Cleopatra,* iv, 15, 66.
There 's no odds.—*Timon of Athens,* i, 2, 61.
Confounding odds.—*Timon of Athens,* iv, 3, 392.
10
Thou hast the odds of me.
Titus Andronicus. Act v, sc. 2, l. 19. [Titus]
The odds of multitude.—*Troilus and Cressida,* v, 4, 23.
11
The stars, I see, will kiss the valleys first:
The odds for high and low 's alike.
The Winter's Tale. Act v, sc. 1, l. 206. [Florizel]

OFFENCE

12
Methinks, thou art a general offence, and every man should beat thee: I think thou wast created for men to breathe themselves upon thee.
All's Well that Ends Well. Act ii, sc. 3, l. 269. [Lafeu]
The young lord
Did to his majesty, his mother and his lady
Offence of mighty note; but to himself
The greatest wrong of all.
All's Well that Ends Well. Act v, sc. 3, l. 12. [Lafeu]
13
The nature of his great offence is dead,
And deeper than oblivion we do bury
The incensing relics of it.
All's Well that Ends Well. Act v, sc. 3, l. 23. [King] The only use of "incensing."
If there be
No great offence belongs to 't, give your friend
Some touch of your late business.
Henry VIII. Act v, sc. 1, l. 11. [Gardiner] The only uses of "great offence."
14
Take no offence that I would not offend you.
Antony and Cleopatra. Act ii, sc. 5, l. 99. [Messenger]
But 'twould offend him; and in his offence
Should my performance perish.
Antony and Cleopatra. Act iii, sc. 1, l. 26. [Ventidius]
15
I will no further offend you than becomes me for my good.
As You Like It. Act i, sc. 1, l. 83. [Orlando]
Never so much as in a thought unborn
Did I offend your highness.
As You Like It. Act i, sc. 3, l. 53. [Rosalind]
16
No more of this; it does offend my heart.
Coriolanus. Act ii, sc. 1, l. 185. [Coriolanus]
They do offend our sight.—*Henry V,* iv, 7, 62.
Offend thine ear.—*Sonnets,* viii.
17
His last offences to us
Shall have judicious hearing.
Coriolanus. Act v, sc. 6, l. 127. [Lord]
18
Lord: It is not fit your lordship should undertake every companion that you give offence to.
Cloten: No, I know that: but it is fit I should commit offence to my inferiors.
Cymbeline. Act ii, sc. 1, l. 28.
19
Horatio: There 's no offence, my lord.
Hamlet: Yes, by Saint Patrick, but there is, Horatio,
And much offence too.
Hamlet. Act i, sc. 5, l. 135. The only mention of Saint Patrick.

King: Have you heard the argument? Is there no offence in 't?
Hamlet: No, no, they do but jest, poison in jest; no offence i' the world.
Hamlet. Act iii, sc. 2, l. 242.
Banish all offence.—*I Henry VI,* v, 5, 96.
Without offence.—*I Henry VI,* v, 5, 35; *II Henry IV,* iv, 5, 103; *Much Ado about Nothing,* iv, 1, 99; *Cymbeline,* i, 5, 6.

1
O, my offence is rank, it smells to heaven;
It hath the primal eldest curse upon 't.
Hamlet. Act iii, sc. 3, l. 36. [King] "Primal" occurs only once more in the plays, in *Antony and Cleopatra,* i, 4, 41.
Rank offence.—*Measure for Measure,* iii, 1, 100.
Foul offence.—*The Rape of Lucrece,* l. 1852.
Giddy offences.—*As You Like It,* iii, 2, 367.
Heinous capital offence.—*Pericles,* ii, 4, 5.
Slow offence.—*Sonnets,* li.
Vile offence.—*The Comedy of Errors,* i, 1, 35; *King Lear,* iv, 2, 47.

2
May one be pardon'd and retain the offence?
Hamlet. Act iii, sc. 3, l. 56. [King]
Where the offence is let the great axe fall.
Hamlet. Act iv, sc. 5, l. 218. [King]

3
I 'll so offend, to make offence a skill;
Redeeming time when men think least I will.
I Henry IV. Act i, sc. 2, l. 239. [Prince of Wales]
What you have done hath not offended me.
I Henry VI. Act ii, sc. 3, l. 76. [Talbot]
You shall hardly offend.—*II Henry IV,* ii, 4, 126.

4 I would I could
Quit all offences with as clear excuse
As well as I am doubtless I can purge
Myself of many I am charged withal.
I Henry IV. Act iii, sc. 2, l. 18. [Prince of Wales]
All his offences live upon my head.
I Henry IV. Act v, sc. 2, l. 20. [Worcester]

5
All offences, my lord, come from the heart.
Henry V. Act iv, sc. 8, l. 49. [Williams]

6
Be not offended, nature's miracle,
Thou art allotted to be ta'en by me.
I Henry VI. Act v, sc. 3, l. 54. [Suffolk]
Be not offended.—*All's Well that Ends Well,* i, 3, 202; *Twelfth Night,* iv, 1, 54; *Macbeth,* iv, 3, 37.

7
I must offend before I be attainted.
II Henry VI. Act ii, sc. 4, l. 59. [Gloucester] "Attainted" is repeated in *I Henry VI,* ii, 4, 92; 96.
Tell me wherein have I offended most?
II Henry VI. Act iv, sc. 7, l. 103. [Say]

8 So weak of courage and in judgement
That they 'll take no offence at our abuse.
III Henry VI. Act iv, sc. 1, l. 12. [Clarence]
They take offence without a cause.
III Henry VI. Act iv, sc. 1, l. 14. [King Edward]

9
There cannot be those numberless offences
'Gainst me, that I cannot take peace with.
Henry VIII. Act ii, sc. 1, l. 84. [Buckingham]
In what have I offended you? what cause
Hath my behaviour given to your displeasure?
Henry VIII. Act ii, sc. 4, l. 19. [Queen Katharine]

10 That which would appear offence in us,
His countenance, like richest alchemy,
Will change to virtue and to worthiness.
Julius Cæsar. Act i, sc. 3, l. 158. [Casca]
You have some sick offence within your mind.
Julius Cæsar. Act ii, sc. 1, l. 268. [Portia]
Who is here so base that would be a bondman?
If any, speak; for him I have offended. . . .
Who is here so vile that will not love his country? If any, speak; for him have I offended.
Julius Cæsar. Act iii, sc. 2, l. 31. [Brutus]
Nor his offences enforced, for which he suffered death.
Julius Cæsar. Act iii, sc. 2, l. 43. [Brutus]
In such a time as this it is not meet
That every nice offence should bear his comment.
Julius Cæsar. Act iv, sc. 3, l. 7. [Cassius]
Mere offence.—*Cymbeline,* v, 5, 334.

11 Her offence
Must be of such unnatural degree,
That monsters it.
King Lear. Act i, sc. 1, l. 221. [King of France]
His offence, honesty!
King Lear. Act i, sc. 2, l. 128. [Gloucester]

12
Cornwall: What was the offence you gave him?
Oswald: I never gave him any:
It pleased the king his master very late
To strike at me, upon his misconstruction.
King Lear. Act ii, sc. 2, l. 121. The only use of "misconstruction."
Gentleman: Made you no more offence but what you speak of?
Kent: None.
King Lear. Act ii, sc. 4, l. 61.
All 's not offence that indiscretion finds
And dotage terms so.
King Lear. Act ii, sc. 4, l. 199. [Goneril]

13
Bethink yourself wherein you may have offended him.
King Lear. Act i, sc. 2, l. 175. [Edmund]
None does offend, none, I say, none.
King Lear. Act iv, sc. 6, l. 172. [King Lear]
How have I offended?—*King Lear,* ii, 4, 198; *Pericles,* iv, 1, 80.
All have not offended.—*Timon of Athens,* v, 4, 35.

14
All my offences that abroad you see
Are errors of the blood, none of the mind.
A Lover's Complaint, l. 183.

15 If you much note him,
You shall offend him and extend his passion.
Macbeth. Act iii, sc. 4, l. 56. [Lady Macbeth]

1
Lucio: What 's thy offence, Claudio?
Claudio: What but to speak of would offend again.
Lucio: What, is 't murder? . . . Lechery?
Claudio: Call it so.
Measure for Measure. Act i, sc. 2, l. 139.
Duke: What offence hath this man made you, sir?
Elbow: Marry, sir, he hath offended the law.
Measure for Measure. Act iii, sc. 2, l. 14.
Claudio: Hearken after their offence, my lord.
Don Pedro: Officers, what offence have these men done? . . . I ask thee what 's their offence. . . . Who have you offended, masters, that you are thus bound to your answer? . . . What 's your offence?
Much Ado about Nothing. Act v, sc. 1, l. 216.
For what offence?—*Richard III,* ii, 4, 45.
What 's his offence?—*King Lear,* ii, 2, 95.
What is my offence?—*Richard III,* i, 4, 187.

2
You may not so extenuate his offence.
Measure for Measure. Act ii, sc. 1, l. 27. [Angelo]
He hath but as offended in a dream!
Measure for Measure. Act ii, sc. 2, l. 4. [Provost]
Who is it that hath died for this offence?
There 's many have committed it.
Measure for Measure. Act ii, sc. 2, l. 88. [Isabella]
Self-offences.—*Measure for Measure,* iii, 2, 280. The only use of "self-offences."

3
The watch ought to offend no man: and it is an offence to stay a man against his will.
Much Ado about Nothing. Act iii, sc. 3, l. 87. [Dogberry]

4
Hence hath offence his quick celerity,
When it is borne in high authority.
Measure for Measure. Act iv, sc. 2, l. 113. [Duke Vincentio]
The offence pardons itself.
Measure for Measure. Act v, sc. 1, l. 540. [Duke]

5
Every offence is not a hate at first.
The Merchant of Venice. Act iv, sc. 1, l. 68. [Bassanio]

6
The offence is holy that she hath committed.
The Merry Wives of Windsor. Act v, sc. 5, l. 238. [Fenton]
Dear offence.—*King John,* i, 1, 257; *Henry V,* ii, 2, 181.

7
If we offend, it is with our good will.
That you should think, we come not to offend.
A Midsummer-Night's Dream. Act v, sc. 1, l. 108. [Quince]
I 'll offend nobody.—*Much Ado about Nothing,* iii, 4, 34.

8
The very head and front of my offending
Hath this extent, no more.
Othello. Act i, sc. 3, l. 80. [Othello]
If my offence be of such mortal kind
That nor my service past, nor present sorrows,
Nor purposed merit in futurity,
Can ransom me into his love again,
But to know so much be my benefit.
Othello. Act iii, sc. 4, l. 115. [Cassio] The only use of "futurity."

9
He that is approved in this offence,
Though he had twinn'd with me, both at a birth,
Shall lose me.
Othello. Act ii, sc. 3, l. 211. [Othello] "Twinn'd" is used again in *Timon of Athens,* iv, 3, 3: "Twinn'd brothers"; in *The Winter's Tale,* i, 2, 67: "Twinn'd lambs"; and in *Cymbeline,* i, 6, 35: "Twinn'd stones."

10
The business of the state does him offence.
Othello. Act iv, sc. 2, l. 166. [Iago]

11
Who takes offence at what would make me glad?
Pericles. Act ii, sc. 5, l. 72. [Thaisa]

12
He scowls and hates himself for his offence.
The Rape of Lucrece, l. 738.
With my trespass never will dispense,
Till life to death acquit my forced offence.
The Rape of Lucrece, l. 1070.
For one's offence why should so many fall,
To plague a private sin in general?
The Rape of Lucrece, l. 1483.

13
If thy offences were upon record,
Would it not shame thee in so fair a troop
To read a lecture of them?
Richard II. Act iv, sc. 1, l. 230. [King Richard]

14
Wherein, my friends, have I offended you?
Richard III. Act i, sc. 4, l. 182. [Clarence]
With no man here he is offended;
For, were he, he had shown it in his looks.
Richard III. Act iii, sc. 4, l. 58. [Hastings]
I do suspect I have done some offence
That seems disgracious in the city's eyes.
Richard III. Act iii, sc. 7, l. 111. [Gloucester] "Disgracious" is repeated in iv, 4, 177, and occurs in no other play.

15
You break into some merry passion
And so offend him.
The Taming of the Shrew. Induction, sc. 1, l. 97. [Lord]
Is it any offence?—*The Taming of the Shrew,* i, 3, 231.

16
Take no unkindness of his hasty words.
The Taming of the Shrew. Act iv, sc. 3, l. 169. [Hortensio]

17
To make a sweet lady sad is a sour offence.
Troilus and Cressida. Act iii, sc. 1, l. 79. [Helen] "Sour offence" is repeated in *All's Well that Ends Well,* v, 3, 59.
What offends you, lady?—*Troilus and Cressida,* iii, 2, 151.
O, pardon; I offend.—*Troilus and Cressida,* iv, 5, 182.
I am offended with you.—*Troilus and Cressida,* v, 3, 77.

You train me to offend you.—*Troilus and Cressida,* v, 3, 4.

1
I beseech you, do me this courteous office, as to know of the knight what my offence to him is: it is something of my negligence, nothing of my purpose.
Twelfth Night. Act iii, sc. 4, l. 277. [Viola]

If this young gentleman
Have done offence, I take the fault on me:
If you offend him, I for him defy you.
Twelfth Night. Act iii, sc. 4, l. 343. [Antonio]

I am so far in offence with my niece that I cannot pursue with any safety this sport to the upshot.
Twelfth Night. Act iv, sc. 2, l. 75. [Sir Toby] "Upshot" is used a second time in *Hamlet,* v, 2, 395.

2
The offences we have made you do we 'll answer.
Winter's Tale. Act i, sc. 2, l. 83. [Hermione]

Their offences being so capital.—*The Winter's Tale,* iv, 4, 822.

II—The Offender

3
A desperate offendress against nature.
All's Well that Ends Well. Act i, sc. 1, l. 153. [Parolles] The only use of "offendress."

4
Bind the offender,
And take him from our presence.
Cymbeline. Act v, sc. 5, l. 300. [Cymbeline]

5
The offender's scourge is weigh'd,
But never the offence.
Hamlet. Act iv, sc. 3, l. 6. [King]

6
Other offenders we will pause upon.
I Henry IV. Act v, sc. 5, l. 15. [King Henry]

Late offenders.—*II Henry IV,* iv, 1, 216.

7
We would have all such offenders so cut off.
Henry V. Act iii, sc. 6, l. 113. [King Henry]

Chief offender.—*I Henry VI,* iii, 1, 130.

Great offender.—*Henry VIII,* v, 3, 121.

8
You yourself know how easy it is to be such an offender.
The Merry Wives of Windsor. Act ii, sc. 2, l. 195. [Ford]

Which are the offenders that are to be examined?
Much Ado about Nothing. Act iv, sc. 2, l. 7. [Sexton]

9
With foul offenders thou perforce must bear,
When they in thee the like offences prove.
The Rape of Lucrece, l. 612.

Foul offenders.—*II Henry VI,* ii, 1, 203; *Titus Andronicus,* v, 2, 40; *The Rape of Lucrece,* l. 612.

10
The offender's sorrow lends but weak relief
To him that bears the strong offence's cross.
Sonnets. No. xxxiv.

Loving offenders, thus I will excuse ye.
Sonnets. No. xlii.

We 're offenders now.—*The Winter's Tale,* v, 1, 59.

OFFER

11
Lepidus: Be pleased to tell us . . . how you take
The offers we have sent you. . . .
Pompey: I come before you here a man prepared
To take this offer.
Antony and Cleopatra. Act ii, sc. 6, l. 29.

Take his offer.—*As You Like It,* iii, 5, 61; *King Lear,* iii, 4, 161.

I take your offer.—*The Two Gentlemen of Verona,* iv, 1, 70; *The Merchant of Venice,* iv, 1, 318.

We 'll take your offer kindly.—*All's Well that Ends Well,* iii, 5, 104.

12
These offers,
Which serve not for his vantage, he shakes off;
And so should you.
Antony and Cleopatra. Act iii, sc. 7, l. 33. [Canidius]

13
Well you know we of the offering side
Must keep aloof from strict arbitrement.
I Henry IV. Act iv, sc. 1, l. 69. [Worcester] "Arbitrement" is used six times, always with this, the original, spelling.

Faithfull'st offerings.—*Twelfth Night,* v, 1, 117. The only use of "faithfull'st."

Polluted offerings.—*Troilus and Cressida,* v, 3, 17.

Rich offerings.—*I Henry IV,* i, 2, 141.

14
We offer fair; take it advisedly.
I Henry IV. Act v, sc. 1, l. 114. [King Henry] "Advisedly" is repeated in *The Merchant of Venice,* v, 1, 253.

Thou offer'st fairly.—*As You Like It,* v, 4, 173.

Fairly offer'd.—*The Winter's Tale,* iv, 4, 389.

This offer comes from mercy, not from fear.
II Henry IV. Act iv, sc. 1, l. 150. [Westmoreland]

He hath forced us to compel this offer.
II Henry IV. Act iv, sc. 1, l. 147. [Mowbray]

15
I have made an offer to his majesty.
Henry V. Act i, sc. 1, l. 75. [Canterbury]

The offer likes not.—*Henry V,* iii, Prol., 32.

16
'Come, offer at my shrine, and I will help thee.'
II Henry VI. Act ii, sc. 1, l. 92. [Simpcox]

Offer up.—*I Henry VI,* i, 1, 46; *Henry V,* iv, 5, 18; *Romeo and Juliet,* iii, 2, 104; *Macbeth,* iv, 3, 16.

17
We must embrace
This gentle offer of the perilous time.
King John. Act iv, sc. 3, l. 12. [Salisbury]

I embrace your offer.—*Much Ado about Nothing,* v, 5, 304; *Twelfth Night,* v, 1, 328; *Pericles,* iii, 3, 38.

Gentle offer.—*The Passionate Pilgrim,* l. 54.

Gentlemanlike offer.—*Romeo and Juliet,* ii, 4, 190. "Gentlemanlike" is used five times.

Gracious offers.—*I Henry IV*, iv, 3, 30.
Heavy offer.—*The Tempest*, ii, 1, 194.
Liberal and kind offer.—*I Henry IV*, v, 2, 2.
Most noble offer.—*The Winter's Tale*, ii, 2, 48.
Proffer'd offer.—*King John*, ii, 1, 258.

1
Change not your offer made in heat of blood.
Love's Labour's Lost. Act v, sc. 2, l. 810. [Princess]

Make no more offers.—*The Merchant of Venice*, iv, 1, 81.
Offer them instances.—*Much Ado about Nothing*, ii, 2, 41.

2
An offer, uncle, that we will accept.
Richard II. Act ii, sc. 3, l. 162. [Bolingbroke]

3
Nay, I have offer'd all, I have no more.
The Taming of the Shrew. Act ii, sc. 1, l. 383. [Gremio]

I must confess your offer is the best.
The Taming of the Shrew. Act ii, sc. 1, l. 388. [Baptista]

4
What, didst thou offer her this from me?
The Two Gentlemen of Verona. Act iv, sc. 4, l. 58. [Proteus]

OFFICE

5
I will no more enforce mine office on you.
All's Well that Ends Well. Act ii, sc. 1, l. 129. [Helena]

Declare thine office.—*Antony and Cleopatra*, iii, 12, 10.
I must attend mine office.—*Antony and Cleopatra*, iv, 6, 27.

6
Time was, I did him a desired office,
Dear almost as his life.
All's Well that Ends Well. Act iv, sc. 4, l. 5. [Helena]

I wish I could do a good office between you.
The Merry Wives of Windsor. Act i, sc. 1, l. 102. [Page]

We are come to do you a good office, master parson.
The Merry Wives of Windsor. Act iii, sc. 1, l. 49. [Page] These are the only uses of "good office," which occurs only in this play.

Noble offices.—*II Henry IV*, iv, 4, 24.

7
Let the high office and the honour go.
Coriolanus. Act ii, sc. 3, l. 129. [Coriolanus]

Great office.—*Antony and Cleopatra*, ii, 3, 1; *Macbeth*, i, 7, 18.

8
We charge you, that you have contrived to take
From Rome all season'd office and to wind
Yourself into a power tyrannical.
Coriolanus. Act iii, sc. 3, l. 63. [Sicinius]

What are your offices?—*Coriolanus*, iii, 1, 35.

9
It is an office of the gods to venge it,
Not mine to speak on 't.
Cymbeline. Act i, sc. 6, l. 92. [Iachimo]

10 In short time
All offices of nature should again
Due their due functions.
Cymbeline. Act v, sc. 5, l. 256. [Cornelius]

Offices of nature.—*King Lear*, ii, 4, 181.

11
The insolence of office.
Hamlet. Act iii, sc. 1, l. 73. [Hamlet]

God in office.—*Troilus and Cressida*, i, 3, 231.
Office of God.—*All's Well that Ends Well*, v, 2, 52.
A dog's obeyed in office.—*King Lear*, iv, 6, 163. See under AUTHORITY.

12 My office is
To noise abroad that Harry Monmouth fell
Under the wrath of noble Hotspur's sword.
II Henry IV. Induction, l. 28. [Rumour]

13
Do your offices, do your offices: Master Fang and Master Snare, do me, do me, do me your offices.
II Henry IV. Act ii, sc. 1, l. 44. [Hostess]

Do you your office, or give up your place,
And you shall be well spared.
Measure for Measure. Act ii, sc. 2, l. 13. [Angelo]

Fail not to do your office.
Measure for Measure. Act iv, sc. 2, l. 129. [Provost, reading]

Do thy office.—*Sonnets*, ci; *Twelfth Night*, iii, 4, 359.
Do you the office, friar.—*Measure for Measure*, v, 1, 383.
They shall do their office.—*I Henry IV*, v, 1, 112.
Do their best office.—*Winter's Tale*, iv, 4, 582.
Thou dost thy office fairly.—*Henry V*, iii, 6, 148.

14
A foutre for thine office!
II Henry IV. Act v, sc. 3, l. 121. [Pistol]

A foutre for the world!—*II Henry IV*, v, 3, 103. "Foutre" is used in no other play. It is a gross term of contempt, presumably deriving from the Latin *futuere*, to have sexual intercourse with.

15
Choose what office thou wilt in the land, 'tis thine.
II Henry IV. Act v, sc. 3, l. 129. [Falstaff]

16 My office hath so far prevail'd
That, face to face and royal eye to eye,
You have congreeted.
Henry V. Act v, sc. 2, l. 29. [Burgundy] The only use of "congreeted."

17
The office did Distinctly his full function.
Henry VIII. Act i, sc. 1, l. 44. [Norfolk]

Your office, sergeant; execute it.
Henry VIII. Act i, sc. 1, l. 198. [Brandon]

18
You were the duke's surveyor, and lost your office
On the complaint o' the tenants.
Henry VIII. Act i, sc. 2, l. 172. [Queen Katharine] "Surveyor" is used six times.

19
For holy offices I have a time.
Henry VIII, iii, 2, 144. See under TIME.

Holy office.—*Cymbeline*, iii, 3, 4.

20
That 's not an office for a friend, my lord.
Julius Cæsar. Act v, sc. 5, l. 29. [Volumnius]

1
Edmund, I hear that you have shown your
father
A child-like office.
King Lear. Act ii, sc. 1, l. 107. [Cornwall]
"Child-like" is repeated in *The Two Gentlemen of Verona,* iii, 1, 75: "Child-like duty."

2
I have on Angelo imposed the office.
Measure for Measure. Act i, sc. 3, l. 40. [Duke]

I thought, by your readiness in the office, you had continued in it some time.
Measure for Measure. Act ii, sc. 1, l. 275. [Escalus]

3 I do discharge you of your office:
Give up your keys.
Measure for Measure. Act v, sc. 1, l. 466. [Duke]

4
It is a man's office, but not yours.
Much Ado about Nothing. Act iv, sc. 1, l. 268. [Beatrice]

'Tis all men's office.—*Much Ado about Nothing,* v, 1, 27.
Fortune's office.—*As You Like It,* i, 2, 44.
Husband's office.—*Comedy of Errors,* iii, 2, 2.
Time's office.—*The Rape of Lucrece,* l. 936.
Tongue's office.—*Richard II,* i, 3, 256.
Virtue's office.—*Love's Labour 's Lost,* v, 2, 350.

5
It is thought abroad that 'twixt my sheets
He hath done my office.
Othello. Act i, sc. 3, l. 393. [Iago]

Take mine office.—*Othello,* iii, 3, 375.

6
I do not like the office.
Othello. Act iii, sc. 3, l. 410. [Iago]

You . . . have the office opposite to Saint Peter,
And keep the gate of hell!
Othello. Act iv, sc. 2, l. 90. [Othello]

7
Not daring trust the office of mine eyes.
Passionate Pilgrim, l. 196. See under Eye.

Office of mine eyes.—*All's Well that Ends Well,* v, 3, 306.
Offices of life.—*Henry VIII,* ii, 4, 190.
Office of love.—*Much Ado About Nothing,* ii, 1, 183; *Merry Wives of Windsor,* iv, 2, 5.
Offices of man.—*Coriolanus,* i, 1, 141.
Offices of pity.—*The Winter's Tale,* ii, 3, 189.
Offices of tender courtesy.—*The Merchant of Venice,* iv, 1, 33.
Courteous office.—*Twelfth Night,* iii, 4, 278.
Offices of truth.—*The Tempest,* v, 1, 156.
Office of a warming pan.—*Henry V,* ii, 1, 88.
Offices that profit us.—*The Tempest,* i, 2, 312.

8
I would wish no better office than to be beadle.
Pericles, ii, 1, 97. See under Begging.

9
Thy princely office how canst thou fulfil?
The Rape of Lucrece, l. 628.

Bloody office.—*Richard II,* iv, 1, 5.
Charitable office.—*The Winter's Tale,* iv, 3, 81.
Desired office.—*All's Well that Ends Well,* iv, 4, 5.
Distinct offices.—*Merchant of Venice,* ii, 9, 61.
Hateful office.—*II Henry VI,* iii, 2, 93.
Hot office.—*The Taming of the Shrew,* iv, 1, 34.
Little office.—*Richard II,* ii, 2, 137.
Losing office.—*II Henry IV,* i, 1, 101.
Modest office.—*Much Ado about Nothing,* ii, 1, 390.
Required office.—*All's Well that Ends Well* ii, 5, 65.
Scepter'd office.—*Richard III,* iii, 7, 119.
Unpeopled offices.—*Richard II,* i, 2, 69.

10 Both are ready in their offices
At any time.
Richard III, iii, 5, 10. See under Acting.

Each one to his office.—*The Taming of the Shrew,* Ind., 1, 73.
Each in his office.—*The Taming of the Shrew.* Ind., 2, 36.
All offices are open.—*Othello,* ii, 2, 9.
You know your office, brother.—*Much Ado about Nothing,* v, 4, 14.
Then to your offices.—*A Midsummer-Night's Dream,* ii, 2, 8.

11
These offices, so oft as thou wilt look,
Shall profit thee and much enrich my book.
Sonnets. No. lxxvii.

12
Hortensio: That 's my office.
Petruchio: Spoke like an officer: ha' to thee,
lad!
The Taming of the Shrew. Act v, sc. 2, l. 36.

It is my office.—*II Henry VI,* ii, 4, 102; *The Comedy of Errors,* v, 1, 99.
That is my office.—*III Henry VI,* i, 4, 109.
This is my office.—*Much Ado. about Nothing,* iii, 1, 12.

13 Would I were gently put out of office
Before I were forced out!
Timon of Athens. Act i, sc. 2, l. 207. [Flavius]

Jack out of office.—*I Henry VI,* i, 1, 175.

14
Timon: Why dost thou seek me out?
Apemantus: To vex thee.
Timon: Always a villain's office or a fool's.
Dost please thyself in 't?
Timon of Athens. Act iv, sc. 3, l. 236.

'Tis an ill office.—*The Two Gentlemen of Verona,* iii, 2, 40.
Ill office.—*Henry V,* v, 2, 391.

15 'Tis an office of great worth
And you an officer fit for the place.
The Two Gentlemen of Verona. Act i, sc. 2. l. 44. [Julia]

Therefore the office is indifferent,
Being entreated to it by your friend.
The Two Gentlemen of Verona. Act iii, sc. 2, l. 44. [Duke]

16 The office
Becomes a woman best; I 'll take 't upon me.
Winter's Tale. Act ii, sc. 2, l. 31. [Paulina]

OFFICER

See also Soldier: Officers

17
A filthy officer he is in those suggestions for the young earl.
All's Well that Ends Well. Act iii, sc. 5, l. 18. [Mariana]

The duke knows him for no other but a poor officer of mine. . . . He had the honour to be

the officer at a place there called Mile-end, to instruct for the doubling of files.
All's Well that Ends Well. Act iv, sc. 3, l. 226. [Parolles] "Mile-end" is mentioned again in *II Henry IV*, iii, 2, 298.

1
Antipholus of Syracuse: What Adam dost thou mean? . . .
Dromio of Syracuse: That Adam that keeps the prison: . . . he that came behind you, sir, like an evil angel, and bid you forsake your liberty.
Antipholus of Syracuse: I understand thee not.
Dromio of Syracuse: No? why, 'tis a plain case: he that went, like a bass-viol, in a case of leather; the man, sir, that when gentlemen are tired, gives them a sob and 'rests them; he, sir, that takes pity on decayed men and gives them suits of durance; he that sets up his rest to do more exploits with his mace than a morris-pike.
Antipholus of Syracuse: What, thou meanest an officer?
Dromio of Syracuse: Ay, sir, the sergeant of the band; he that brings any man to answer it that breaks his band; one that thinks a man always going to bed and says 'God give you good rest!'
Comedy of Errors. Act iv, sc. 3, l. 14. The only use of "bass-viol" and "morris-pike."

What wilt thou do, thou peevish officer?
The Comedy of Errors. Act iv, sc. 4, l. 117. [Adriana]

I'll leave him to the officer.—*The Comedy of Errors,* iv, 1, 61.

I'll attach you by this officer.—*The Comedy of Errors,* iv, 1, 6.

Arrest him, officer.—*The Comedy of Errors,* iv, 1, 76.

Well, officer, arrest him.—*The Comedy of Errors,* iv, 1, 69.

He did arrest me with an officer.—*The Comedy of Errors,* v, 1, 230.

2
Call thither all the officers of the town.
Coriolanus. Act i, sc. 5, l. 28. [Lartius]

Officer of state.—*Coriolanus,* v, 2, 3.

Officers of sorts.—*Henry V,* i, 2, 190.

3 Have you thus
Given Hydra here to chose an officer?
Coriolanus. Act iii, sc. 1, l. 92. [Coriolanus]

Be you then as the people's officer.
Coriolanus. Act iii, sc. 1, l. 330. [Sicinius]

Caius Marcius was A worthy officer in the war.
Coriolanus. Act iv, sc. 6, l. 30. [Brutus]

4
Wilt thou kill God's officers and the king's?
II Henry IV. Act ii, sc. 1, l. 56. [Hostess]

Pluck down my officers.—*II Henry IV,* iv, 5, 118.

5 Art thou officer?
Or art thou base, common and popular?
Henry V. Act iv, sc. 1, l. 37. [Pistol]

6
Here's a wise officer.
Measure for Measure. Act ii, sc. 1, l. 58. [Escalus]

Domestic officers.—*Cymbeline,* iii, 1, 65.
Expert officers.—*I Henry VI,* iii, 2, 127.
Foolish officers.—*II Henry IV,* ii, 1, 177.
Ill officers.—*Julius Cæsar,* iv, 2, 7.
Mortal officer.—*Pericles,* v, 3, 62.
Petty officer.—*Measure for Measure,* ii, 2, 112.
So indiscreet an officer.—*Othello,* ii, 3, 280.
Spongy officers.—*Macbeth,* i, 7, 71.

7
Go, Tubal, fee me an officer.
The Merchant of Venice. Act iii, sc. 1, l. 131. [Shylock]

8
Your husband's coming hither, woman, with all the officers in Windsor.
The Merry Wives of Windsor. Act iii, sc. 3, l. 114. [Mrs. Page]

9
We are the poor duke's officers.
Much Ado about Nothing. Act iii, sc. 5, l. 22. [Dogberry]

Prince's officer.—*Much Ado about Nothing,* iv, 2, 73.

The sweet grace's officer, Anthony Dull.—*Love's Labour's Lost,* i, 1, 271.

10
This is your charge: you shall comprehend all vagrom men.
Much Ado about Nothing. Act iii, sc. 3, l. 25. [Dogberry] Only use of "vagrom" (vagrant).

11 In conclusion,
Nonsuits my mediators; for, 'Certes,' says he,
'I have already chose my officer.'
Othello. Act i, sc. 1, l. 17. [Iago] The only use of "nonsuits" and "mediators."

Cassio, I love thee;
But never more be officer of mine.
Othello. Act ii, sc. 3, l. 248. [Othello]

12 Get weapons, ho!
And raise some special officers of night.
Othello. Act i, sc. 1, l. 182. [Brabantio]

Special officers.—*Love's Labour's Lost,* ii, 1, 162.

OMEN

See also Superstition

13
Nay, if an oily palm be not a fruitful prognostication,
I cannot scratch mine ear.
Antony and Cleopatra. Act i, sc. 2, l. 53. [Charmian] "Prognostication" is repeated in *The Winter's Tale,* iv, 4, 817.

14 In the gross and scope of my opinion,
This bodes some strange eruption to our state.
Hamlet. Act i, sc. 1, l. 68. [Horatio]

In the most high and palmy state of Rome,
A little ere the mightiest Julius fell,
The graves stood tenantless and the sheeted dead
Did squeak and gibber in the Roman streets.
Hamlet. Act i, sc. 1, l. 113. [Horatio] The only use of "palmy," "sheeted," and "gibber." "Squeak" is repeated in *Twelfth Night,* ii, 3, 97, and "tenantless" in *The Two Gentlemen of Verona,* v, 4, 8.

Stars with trains of fire and dews of blood,
Disasters in the sun.
Hamlet. Act i, sc. 1, l. 117. [Horatio]

Harbingers preceding still the fates
And prologue to the omen coming on,
Have heaven and earth together demonstrated
Unto our climatures and countrymen.

Hamlet. Act i, sc. 1, l. 122. [Horatio] The only use of "demonstrated" and "climatures." "Preceding" is repeated in *All's Well that Ends Well,* v, 3, 196. "Harbinger" occurs six times.

My father's spirit in arms! all is not well.

Hamlet. Act i, sc. 2, l. 255. [Hamlet]

To my sick soul, as sin's true nature is,
Each toy seems prologue to some great amiss.

Hamlet. Act iv, sc. 5, l. 17. [Queen]

1

O, what portents are these?

I Henry IV. Act ii, sc. 3, l. 65. [Lady Percy]

Be no more an exhaled meteor,
A prodigy of fear and a portent
Of broached mischief to the unborn times.

I Henry IV. Act v, sc. 1, l. 19. [King Henry] The only use of "exhaled."

These are portents; but yet I hope, I hope,
They do not point on me.

Othello. Act v, sc. 2, l. 45. [Desdemona]

Warnings and portents.—*Julius Cæsar,* ii, 2, 80. The only uses of "portent" and "portents."

2

Bardolph: My lord, do you see these meteors? do you behold these exhalations?
Prince of Wales: I do.
Bardolph: What think you they portend?
Prince of Wales: Hot livers and cold purses.

I Henry IV. Act ii, sc. 4, l. 351.

3

The people fear me; for they do observe
Unfather'd heirs and loathly births of nature:
The seasons change their manners, as the year
Had found some months asleep and leap'd them over.

II Henry IV. Act iv, sc. 4, l. 121. [Humphrey] The only use of "unfather'd."

4

Comets, importing change of times and states,
Brandish your crystal tresses in the sky.

I Henry VI. Act i, sc. 1, l. 2. [Bedford] "Comets" is repeated in *Julius Cæsar,* ii, 2, 30.

Some comet or unusual prodigy.—*The Taming of the Shrew,* iii, 2, 98.

Like a comet I was wonder'd at.—*I Henry IV,* iii, 2, 47.

Gazed on like a comet.—*Pericles,* v, 1, 87.

Comet of revenge.—*I Henry VI,* i, 1, 2. The only uses of "comet."

5

Now help, ye charming spells and periapts;
And ye choice spirits that admonish me
And give me signs of future accidents.

I Henry VI, v, 3, 2. [Pucelle] The only use of "periapts" (amulets) and "admonish."

6

What boded this, but well forewarning wind
Did seem to say 'Seek not a scorpion's nest,
Nor set no footing on this unkind shore?'

II Henry VI. Act iii, sc. 2, l. 85. [Queen Margaret] The only use of "forewarning."

7

Richard: In this the heaven figures some event.
Edward: 'Tis wondrous strange, the like yet never heard of.

III Henry VI. Act ii, sc. 1, l. 32.

Tush, man, abodements must not now affright us.

III Henry VI. Act iv, sc. 7, l. 13. [King Edward] The only use of "abodements."

8

There were drawn
Upon a heap a hundred ghastly women,
Transformed with their fear; who swore they saw
Men all in fire walk up and down the streets.

Julius Cæsar. Act i, sc. 3, l. 22. [Casca]

When these prodigies
Do so conjointly meet, let not men say
'These are their reasons; they are natural;'
For, I believe, they are portentous things
Unto the climate that they point upon.

Julius Cæsar. Act i, sc. 3, l. 28. [Casca] "Conjointly" is repeated in *King John,* ii, 1, 379.

Fierce fiery warriors fought upon the clouds,
In ranks and squadrons and right form of war,
Which drizzled blood upon the Capitol;
The noise of battle hurtled in the air,
Horses did neigh, and dying men did groan,
And ghosts did shriek and squeal about the streets.

Julius Cæsar. Act ii, sc. 2, l. 19. [Calpurnia] The only use of "hurtled" and "squeal." "Drizzled" is repeated in *The Comedy of Errors,* v, 1, 312.

9

Sullen presage of your own decay.

King John. Act i, sc. 1, l. 28. [King John]

10

No natural exhalation in the sky,
No scope of nature, no distemper'd day,
No common wind, no customed event,
But they will pluck away his natural cause
And call them meteors, prodigies and signs,
Abortives, presages and tongues of heaven.

King John. Act iii, sc. 4, l. 153. [Pandulph] The only use of "abortives." "Abortive" occurs four times.

11

These late eclipses in the sun and moon portend no good to us: though the wisdom of nature can reason it thus and thus, yet nature finds itself scourged by the sequent effects: love cools, friendship falls off, brothers divide: in cities, mutinies; in countries, discord; in palaces, treason; and the bond cracked 'twixt son and father.

King Lear. Act i, sc. 2, l. 112. [Gloucester]

O, these eclipses do portend these divisions!

King Lear. Act i, sc. 2, l. 148. [Edmund]

Edmund: I am thinking, brother, of a prediction I read this other day, what should follow these eclipses.
Edgar: Do you busy yourself about that?
Edmund: I promise you, the effects he writes of succeed unhappily; as of naturalness between the child and the parent; death, dearth, dissolutions of ancient amities; divisions in

state, menaces and maledictions against king and nobles; needless diffidences, banishment of friends, dissipation of cohorts, nuptial breaches, and I know not what.

King Lear. Act i, sc. 2, l. 152. The only use of "maledictions," "dissipation," "cohorts."

Something deeper,
Whereof perchance these are but furnishings.

King Lear. Act iii, sc. 1, l. 28. [Kent] The only use of "furnishings."

1 The night has been unruly: where we lay,
Our chimneys were blown down; and, as they say,
Lamentings heard i' the air; strange screams of death,
And prophesying with accents terrible
Of dire combustion and confused events
New hatch'd to the woeful time: the obscure bird
Clamour'd the livelong night: some say, the earth
Was feverous and did shake.

Macbeth. Act ii, sc. 3, l. 59. [Lennox] The only use of "clamour'd." "Combustion" is repeated in *Henry VIII*, v, 4, 51. "Scream" is repeated in ii, 2, 16, and occurs in no other play. "Feverous" is used four times.

2 It was not for nothing that my nose fell a-bleeding on Black-Monday last at six o'clock i' the morning, falling out that year on Ash-Wednesday was four year, in the afternoon.

The Merchant of Venice. Act ii, sc. 5, l. 24. [Launcelot] The only use of "Black-Monday" and "Ash-Wednesday."

By the pricking of my thumbs,
Something wicked this way comes.
Open, locks, Whoever knocks!

Macbeth. Act iv, sc. 1, l. 44. [Second Witch]

3 It comes o'er my memory,
As doth the raven o'er the infected house,
Boding to all.

Othello. Act iv, sc. 1, l. 20. [Othello]

4 The bay-trees in our country are all wither'd
And meteors fright the fixed stars of heaven:
The pale-faced moon looks bloody on the earth
And lean-look'd prophets whisper fearful change;
Rich men look sad and ruffians dance and leap,
The one in fear to lose what they enjoy,
The other to enjoy by rage and war:
These signs forerun the death or fall of kings.

Richard II. Act ii, sc. 4, l. 8. [Captain] The only use of "bay-trees" and "lean-look'd."

Stanley did dream the boar did raze his helm;
But I disdain'd it, and did scorn to fly:
Three times to-day my foot-cloth horse did stumble,
And startled, when he look'd upon the Tower,
As loath to bear me to the slaughter-house.

Richard III. Act iii, sc. 4, l. 84. [Hastings]

5 Cassandra doth foresee; and I myself
Am like a prophet suddenly enrapt
To tell thee that this day is ominous.

Troilus and Cressida. Act v, sc. 3, l. 64. [Priam] The only use of "enrapt."

6 What should that alphabetical position portend?

Twelfth Night. Act ii, sc. 5, l. 130. [Malvolio] The only use of "alphabetical."

7 Look, how the world's poor people are amazed
At apparitions, signs and prodigies,
Whereon with fearful eyes they long have gazed,
Infusing them with dreadful prophecies.

Venus and Adonis, l. 925. "Infusing" is used a second time in *Richard II*, iii, 2, 166.

Disturb'd with prodigies on earth.

Titus Andronicus, i, 1, 101. [Lucius]

OPINION

See also Mind

8 Let us rear
The higher our opinion, that our stirring
Can from the lap of Egypt's widow pluck
The ne'er-lust-wearied Antony.

Antony and Cleopatra. Act ii, sc. 1, l. 35. [Pompey] The only use of "ne'er-lust-wearied."

Opinion that so sticks on Marcius shall
Of his demerits rob Cominius.

Coriolanus. Act i, sc. 1, l. 275. [Sicinius]

9 Opinion, that did help me to the crown,
Had still kept loyal to possession
And left me in reputeless banishment,
A fellow of no mark nor likelihood.

I Henry IV. Act iii, sc. 2, l. 42. [King Henry] The only use of "reputeless."

Thou hast redeem'd thy lost opinion.

I Henry IV. Act v, sc. 4, l. 48. [King Henry]

10 I pray you all, Speak plainly your opinions.

II Henry IV. Act i, sc. 3, l. 3. [Archbishop]

Let me have your express opinions.

I Henry VI. Act i, sc. 4, l. 64. [Salisbury]

Deliver,
Like free and honest men, our just opinions.

Henry VIII. Act iii, sc. 1, l. 59. [Wolsey]

And now, good sweet, say thy opinion.

The Merchant of Venice. Act iii, sc. 5, l. 76. [Lorenzo]

What's your opinion?—*The Taming of the Shrew*, iii, 2, 245.

11 Partly to satisfy my opinion, and partly for the satisfaction, look you, of my mind.

Henry V. Act iii, sc. 2, l. 105. [Fluellen]

12 Yield the other in the right opinion.

I Henry VI. Act ii, sc. 4, l. 42. [Vernon]

If I, my lord, for my opinion bleed,
Opinion shall be surgeon to my hurt.

I Henry VI. Act ii, sc. 4, l. 52. [Vernon]

1
In my opinion yet thou see'st not well.
II Henry VI. Act ii, sc. 1, l. 107. [Gloucester]
Truly, sir, in my poor opinion, they will to 't then.
Measure for Measure. Act ii, sc. 1, l. 245. [Pompey]
In mine opinion.—*Richard III,* iii, 1, 52.
In my opinion.—*Richard III,* ii, 2, 131; *All's Well that Ends Well,* iv, 2, 31; *Cymbeline,* i, 4, 119.
In our opinions.—*I Henry VI,* v, 5, 61; *Hamlet,* ii, 1, 115.
This is mine opinion.—*III Henry VI,* iv, 1, 29; *Richard III,* iii, 4, 45.
My own opinion.—*I Henry IV,* ii, 4, 445.

2
Give me leave
In this close walk to satisfy myself,
In craving your opinion.
II Henry VI. Act ii, sc. 2, l. 2. [York]

3
Norfolk: When returns Cranmer?
Suffolk: He is return'd in his opinions.
Henry VIII. Act iii, sc. 2, l. 62.
His own opinion was his law.
Henry VIII. Act iv, sc. 2, l. 37. [Katharine]
New opinions,
Divers and dangerous; which are heresies,
And, not reform'd, may prove pernicious.
Henry VIII. Act v, sc. 3, l. 17. [Lord Chancellor]

4
Believe me, there's an ill opinion spread then
Even of yourself.
Henry VIII. Act ii, sc. 2, l. 125. [Campeius]
Ill opinion.—*The Merry Wives of Windsor,* ii, 1, 73; *Troilus and Cressida,* v, 4, 19; *Cymbeline,* i, 4, 175.
Base opinion.—*Henry VIII,* iii, 1, 36.
Foul opinion.—*Cymbeline,* ii, 4, 58.
Hard opinions.—*II Henry IV,* Epil., 33; *The Two Gentlemen of Verona,* ii, 7, 81.
Hideous opinion.—*Twelfth Night,* iii, 4, 212.

5
Writings all tending to the great opinion
Rome holds of his name.
Julius Cæsar. Act i, sc. 3, l. 322. [Cassius]
Great opinion.—*I Henry IV,* iv, 1, 77; *Troilus and Cressida,* iv, 4, 105.
Good opinion.—*As You Like It,* v, 2, 60; *Julius Cæsar,* ii, 1, 145; *Henry VIII,* ii, 3, 61.
Rich opinion.—*Othello,* ii, 3, 195.

6
Everyone doth wish
You had but that opinion of yourself
That every noble Roman bears of you.
Julius Cæsar. Act ii, sc. 1, l. 91. [Cassius]

7
Makes sound opinion sick and truth suspected.
King John. Act iv, sc. 2, l. 26. [Salisbury]

8
His very opinion in the letter!
King Lear. Act i, sc. 2, l. 80. [Gloucester]
When false opinion, whose wrong thought defiles thee,
In thy just proof, repeals and reconciles thee.
King Lear. Act iii, sc. 6, l. 119. [Edgar]

9
I have bought
Golden opinions from all sorts of people,
Which would be worn now in their newest gloss,
Not cast aside so soon.
Macbeth. Act i, sc. 7, l. 32. [Macbeth]

10
But fish not, with this melancholy bait,
For this fool gudgeon, this opinion.
The Merchant of Venice. Act i, sc. 1, l. 101. [Gratiano] The only use of "gudgeon."
Nay, but ask my opinion too of that.
The Merchant of Venice. Act iii, sc. 5, l. 90. [Jessica]
He is furnished with my opinion.—*The Merchant of Venice,* iv, 1, 157.

11
I cannot put off my opinion so easily.
The Merry Wives of Windsor. Act ii, sc. 1, l. 242. [Ford]
The opinion that fire cannot melt out of me: I will die in it at the stake.
Much Ado about Nothing. Act i, sc. 1, l. 234. [Benedick]

12
Come, let them be opinioned.
Much Ado about Nothing. Act iv, sc. 2, l. 69. [Dogberry] The only use of "opinioned."

13
Opinion, a sovereign mistress of effects.
Othello. Act i, sc. 3, l. 225. [Duke]
How have I been behaved, that he might stick
The small'st opinion on my least misuse.
Othello. Act iv, sc. 2, l. 108. [Desdemona]
Even from this instant do build on thee a better opinion than ever before.
Othello. Act iv, sc. 2, l. 208. [Iago]
Better opinion.—*II Henry IV,* iv, 5, 189.

14
Opinion's but a fool, that makes us scan
The outward habit by the inward man.
Pericles. Act ii, sc. 2, l. 56. [Simonides]
Men's opinions.—*Richard II,* iii, 1, 26.

15
I do now let loose my opinion; hold it no longer.
The Tempest. Act ii, sc. 2, l. 37. [Trinculo]
Acibiades: What friendship may I do thee?
Timon: None, but to Maintain my opinion.
Timon of Athens. Act iv, sc. 3, l. 70.

16
To steel a strong opinion to themselves.
Troilus and Cressida. Act i, sc. 3, l. 353. [Nestor]
We did our main opinion crush
In taint of our best man. . . .
Yet go we under our opinion still
That we have better men.
Troilus and Cressida. Act i, sc. 3, l. 373. [Ulysses]
Main opinion.—*Julius Cæsar,* ii, 1, 196.

17
Hector's opinion Is this in way of truth.
Troilus and Cressida. Act ii, sc. 2, l. 188. [Hector]
A plague of opinion! a man may wear it on both sides, like a leather jerkin.
Troilus and Cressida. Act iii, sc. 3, l. 266. [Thersites]

1
Think of me as you please.
Twelfth Night. Act v, sc. 1, l. 318. [Fabian]

2
Once remove
The root of his opinion, which is rotten
As ever oak or stone was sound.
Winter's Tale. Act ii, sc. 3, l. 88. [Paulina]

Good my lord, be cured
Of this diseased opinion, and betimes;
For 'tis most dangerous.
Winter's Tale. Act i, sc. 2, l. 296. [Camillo]

How blest am I
In my just censure, in my true opinion!
Winter's Tale. Act ii, sc. 1, l. 36. [Leontes]

OPPORTUNITY

See also Occasion

3
Let 's take the instant by the forward top;
For we are old, and on our quick'st decrees
The inaudible and noiseless foot of Time
Steals ere we can effect them.
All's Well that Ends Well. Act v, sc. 3, l. 39. [King] The only use of "inaudible." "Noiseless" occurs again in *King Lear,* iv, 2, 56.

To take the present time by the top.
Much Ado about Nothing. Act i, sc. 2, l. 15. [Antonio]

4
Who seeks, and will not take when once 'tis offer'd,
Shall never find it more.
Antony and Cleopatra. Act ii, sc. 7, l. 89. [Menas]

Sell when you can: you are not for all markets.
As You Like It. Act iii, sc. 5, l. 60. [Rosalind]

5
That opportunity . . . We have again.
Cymbeline. Act iii, sc. 1, l. 14. [Queen]

Had I . . . opportunity.—*Cymbeline,* i, 4, 116.

I shall give thee opportunity.—*Cymbeline,* iii, 4, 29.

6
By time, by means and place.
Hamlet. Act ii, sc. 2, l. 127. [Polonius]

Thoughts black, hands apt, drugs fit, and time agreeing;
Confederate season, else no creature seeing.
Hamlet. Act iii, sc. 2, l. 266. [Lucianus]

Weigh what convenience both of time and means
May fit us to our shape.
Hamlet. Act iv, sc. 7, l. 150. [King]

7
Come pat betwixt too early and too late.
Henry VIII. Act ii, sc. 3, l. 84. [Old Lady]

8
Embrace we then this opportunity.
I Henry VI. Act ii, sc. 1, l. 13. [Talbot]

If once it be neglected, ten to one
We shall not find like opportunity.
I Henry VI. Act v, sc. 4, l. 157. [Reignier]

Better opportunity.—*Henry V,* iii, 2, 151.

Good opportunities.—*The Merry Wives of Windsor,* iii, 1, 15.

9
There is a tide in the affairs of men,
Which, taken at the flood, leads on to fortune;
Omitted, all the voyage of their life
Is bound in shallows and in miseries.
On such a full sea are we now afloat;
And we must take the current when it serves,
Or lose our ventures.
Julius Cæsar. Act iv, sc. 3, l. 218. [Brutus] "Afloat" is used a second time in *Sonnets,* lxxx: "Hold me up afloat."

10
You have many opportunities to cut him off.
King Lear. Act iv, sc. 6, l. 268. [Edgar, reading]

11
Nor time nor place
Did then adhere, and yet you would make both.
Macbeth. Act i, sc. 7, l. 51. [Lady Macbeth]

The perfect spy o' the time, The moment on 't.
Macbeth. Act iii, sc. 1, l. 130. [Macbeth]

12
Engrossed opportunities to meet her.
The Merry Wives of Windsor. Act ii, sc. 2, l. 203. [Ford]

Opportunity . . . Cannot attain it.—*The Merry Wives of Windsor,* iii, 4, 20.

Opportunity of night.—*A Midsummer-Night's Dream,* ii, 1, 217.

Opportunity of sharp revenge.—*Titus Andronicus,* i, 1, 137.

13
O Opportunity, thy guilt is great!
'Tis thou that executest the traitor's treason:
Thou set'st the wolf where he the lamb may get;
Whoever plots the sin, thou 'point'st the season;
'Tis thou that spurn'st at right, at law, at reason;
And in thy shady cell, where none may spy him,
Sits Sin, to seize the souls that wander by him.

Thou makest the vestal violate her oath;
Thou blow'st the fire when temperance is thaw'd;
Thou smother'st honesty, thou murder'st troth;
Thou foul abettor! thou notorious bawd!
Thou plantest scandal and displacest laud:
Thou ravisher, thou traitor, thou false thief,
Thy honey turns to gall, thy joy to grief!

Thy secret pleasure turns to open shame,
Thy private feasting to a public fast,
Thy smoothing titles to a ragged name,
Thy sugar'd tongue to bitter wormwood taste:
Thy violent vanities can never last.
How comes it then, vile Opportunity,
Being so bad, such numbers seek for thee?
The Rape of Lucrece, l. 876. The only use of "abettor."

The poor, lame, blind, halt, creep, cry out for thee;
But they ne'er meet with Opportunity.
The Rape of Lucrece, l. 902.

Wrath, envy, treason, rape, and murder's rages,
Thy heinous hours wait on them as their pages.
The Rape of Lucrece, l. 909.
When Truth and Virtue have to do with thee,
A thousand crosses keep them from thy aid:
They buy thy help; but Sin ne'er gives a fee,
He gratis comes.
The Rape of Lucrece, l. 911.
Why hath thy servant, Opportunity,
Betray'd the hours thou gavest to repose,
Cancell'd my fortunes, and enchained me
To endless date of never-ending woes?
The Rape of Lucrece, l. 932. The only use of "enchained" and "never-ending."
In vain I rail at Opportunity.
The Rape of Lucrece, l. 1023.
Ill-annexed Opportunity.
The Rape of Lucrece, l. 874. The only use of "ill-annexed."

1
The double guilt of this opportunity you let time wash off.
Twelfth Night. Act iii, sc. 2, l. 27. [Fabian]

2
Make use of time, let not advantage slip.
Venus and Adonis, l. 129. See under ADVANTAGE.

OPPOSITION

3
He . . . found no opposition
But what he look'd for should oppose.
Cymbeline. Act ii, sc. 5, l. 17. [Posthumus]
More remarkable in single oppositions.
Cymbeline. Act iv, sc. 1, l. 14. [Cloten]
In single opposition, hand to hand.
I Henry IV, i, 3, 99. See under FIGHTING.
So great an opposition.—*I Henry IV,* ii, 3, 15.
Disobedient opposition.—*Romeo and Juliet,* iv, 2, 18.
Liberal opposition.—*Love's Labour's Lost,* v, 2, 743.
Peevish opposition.—*Hamlet,* i, 2, 100.
Opposition bloody.—*Macbeth,* ii, 3, 184.
Opposition of your person.—*Hamlet,* v, 2, 178.
Great opposer.—*Coriolanus,* iv, 3, 36. "Opposer" is used four times.

4
Doubt not, my lord, they shall be well opposed.
I Henry IV. Act iv, sc. 4, l. 33. [Michael]
Be no more opposed.—*I Henry IV,* i, 1, 15.

5 We stand opposed by such means
As you yourself have forged against yourself.
I Henry IV. Act v, sc. 1, l. 67. [Worcester]
You are potently opposed.—*Henry VIII,* v, 1, 134.

6
I . . . oppose not myself against their will.
Richard II. Act iii, sc. 3, l. 18. [Bolingbroke]
Oppose my will.—*Macbeth,* iv, 3, 65.
She opposes her against my will.—*The Two Gentlemen of Verona,* iii, 2, 26.
Oppose against their wills.—*The Winter's Tale,* v, 1, 46.
Oppose his hatred.—*Coriolanus,* iii, 1, 20.

7
In general part we were opposed.
Timon of Athens. Act v, sc. 2, l. 7. [Messenger]
They are opposed already.—*Troilus and Cressida,* iv, 5, 94.
Half to half the world opposed.—*Antony and Cleopatra,* iii, 13, 9.

8
Oppose not Scythia to ambitious Rome.
Titus Andronicus. Act i, sc. 1, l. 132. [Demetrius]
Whom may you else oppose, . . .
If not Achilles?
Troilus and Cressida. Act i, sc. 3, l. 333. [Nestor]

OPPRESSION

9
Our oppression Exceeds what we expected.
Antony and Cleopatra. Act iv, sc. 7, l. 2. [Agrippa]
Our oppression hath made up this league.
King John. Act iii, sc. 1, l. 106. [Constable]

10
Free from oppression or the stroke of war.
I Henry VI. Act v, sc. 3, l. 155. [Suffolk]

11
Nor much oppress'd them with great subsidies.
III Henry VI, iv, 8, 45. See under WEALTH.
You ne'er oppress'd me.—*All's Well that Ends Well,* i, 3, 153.
Why dost thou so oppress me?—*Troilus and Cressida,* iv, 5, 241.
Oppress our nest.—*I Henry IV,* v, 1, 61.
Oppress'd with melancholy.—*Sonnets,* xlv.
Oppress'd With riotous feeders.—*Timon of Athens,* ii, 2, 167.
Oppress'd with travel.—*The Tempest,* iii, 3, 15.
With travel much oppress'd.—*As You Like It,* ii, 4, 74.
Oppress'd with two weak evils.—*As You Like It,* ii, 7, 132.
Oppress'd with wrongs.—*King John,* iii, 1, 13.

12 You remember
How under my oppression I did reek
When I first moved you.
Henry VIII. Act ii, sc. 4, l. 207. [King Henry]

13 The poor mole casts
Copp'd hills towards heaven, to tell the earth is throng'd
By man's oppression; and the poor worm doth die for 't.
Pericles. Act i, sc. 1, l. 100. [Pericles] The only use of "copp'd" (peaked).
Stoop with oppression.—*Richard II,* iii, 4, 31.

14
Too great oppression for a tender thing.
Romeo and Juliet. Act i, sc. 4, l. 24. [Mercutio]
Heart's oppression.—*Romeo and Juliet,* i, 1, 90.

15
Day's oppression is not eased by night.
Sonnets, xxviii. See under DAY AND NIGHT.

ORACLE

16
Answering the letter of the oracle.
Cymbeline. Act v, sc. 5, l. 450. [Soothsayer]

17
These oracles are hardly attain'd,
And hardly understood.
II Henry VI. Act i, sc. 4, l. 74. [York]

1 One
Hath crawl'd into the favour of the king,
And is his oracle.
Henry VIII. Act iii, sc. 2, l. 102. [Wolsey]

2
May they not be my oracles as well,
And set me up in hope?
Macbeth. Act iii, sc. 1, l. 9. [Banquo]

3 I am Sir Oracle,
And when I ope my lips let no dog bark!
The Merchant of Venice. Act i, sc. 1, l. 93. [Gratiano]

4
Some oracle Must rectify our knowledge.
The Tempest. Act v, sc. 1, l. 244. [Alonso]

5
Wert thou an oracle to tell me so,
I 'ld not believe thee.
Troilus and Cressida. Act iv, sc. 5, l. 252. [Hector]

Bold as an oracle.—*Troilus and Cressida,* i, 3, 192.

6
From the oracle They will bring all.
Winter's Tale. Act ii, sc. 1, l. 185. [Leontes]
Yet shall the oracle
Give rest to the minds of others, such as he
Whose ignorant credulity will not
Come up to the truth.
The Winter's Tale. Act ii, sc. 1, l. 190. [Leontes] The only use of "credulity."
When the oracle,
Thus by Apollo's great divine seal'd up,
Shall the contents discover.
The Winter's Tale. Act iii, sc. 1, l. 18. [Dion]

7
I do refer me to the oracle:
Apollo be my judge!
Winter's Tale. Act iii, 2, 116. [Hermione]
Therefore bring forth,
And in Apollo's name, his oracle.
Winter's Tale. Act iii, sc. 2, l. 118. [Lord]
You, Cleomenes and Dion, have
Been both at Delphos, and from thence have brought
This seal'd-up oracle, by the hand deliver'd
Of great Apollo's priest.
The Winter's Tale. Act iii, sc. 2, l. 126. [Officer] "Seal'd-up" is repeated in *Love's Labour's Lost,* iii, 1, 170: "Seal'd up counsel."

8
There is no truth at all i' the oracle.
Winter's Tale. Act iii, sc. 2, l. 141. [Leontes]
Apollo, pardon
My great profaneness 'gainst thine oracle!
The Winter's Tale. Act iii, sc. 2, l. 154. [Leontes] The only use of "profaneness."
For has not the divine Apollo said,
Is 't not the tenour of his oracle?
Winter's Tale. Act v, sc. 1, l. 37. [Paulina]
The oracle is fulfilled.
Winter's Tale. Act v, sc. 2, l. 24. [Gentleman]
The oracle Gave hope thou wast in being.
Winter's Tale. Act v, sc. 3, l. 126. [Hermione]

ORATOR AND ORATORY

9
He 's a good drum, my lord, but a naughty orator.
All's Well that Ends Well. Act v, sc. 3, l. 253. [Lafeu]
Very good orators, when they are out, they will spit.
As You Like It. Act iv, 1, 75. [Rosalind]

10 Nay, an thou 'lt mouth,
I 'll rant as well as thou.
Hamlet. Act v, sc. 1, l. 306. [Hamlet] The only use of "rant." "Ranting" occurs once, in *The Merry Wives of Windsor* ii, 1, 196.

11
Prettily, methought, did play the orator.
I Henry VI. Act iv, sc. 1, l. 175. [Warwick]
I can better play the orator.
III Henry VI. Act i, sc. 2, l. 2. [Edward]
I 'll play the orator as well as Nestor.
III Henry VI. Act iii, 2, 188. [Gloucester]
Full well hath Clifford play'd the orator,
Inferring arguments of mighty force.
III Henry VI. Act ii, sc. 2, l. 43. [King Henry]
Fear not, my lord, I 'll play the orator
As if the golden fee for which I plead
Were for myself.
Richard III. Act iii, 5, 95. [Buckingham]

12
How quaint an orator you are.
II Henry VI. Act iii, sc. 2, l. 274. [Suffolk]
Breathing orators.—*Richard III,* iv, 4, 129.
Prevailing orators.—*Titus Andronicus,* iii, 1, 26.
Subtle orator.—*III Henry VI,* iii, 1, 33.

13
I am no orator, as Brutus is.
Julius Cæsar, iii, 2, 221. See under CHARACTER.

14
The orator, to deck his oratory.
The Rape of Lucrece, l. 815.
Mine oratory grew to an end.
Richard III. Act iii, sc. 7, l. 20. [Buckingham]
Weak oratory.—*Richard III,* iii, 1, 37.
Drown my oratory.—*Titus Andronicus,* v, 3, 90.
All their oratory.—*I Henry VI,* ii, 2, 49. The only uses of "oratory."

15
That is as fit as can be to serve for your oration.
Titus Andronicus. Act iv, sc. 3, l. 95. [Marcus]
Deliver an oration.—*Titus Andronicus,* iv, 3, 98.

16 'Hem, and stroke thy beard,
As he being drest to some oration.'
Troilus and Cressida. Act i, sc. 3, l. 165. [Ulysses] "Oration" is used seven times.

ORDER

17
I 'll order take my mother shall not hear.
All's Well that Ends Well. Act iv, sc. 2, l. 55. [Diana]
I will take order for her keeping close.
Richard III. Act iv, sc. 2, l. 52. [King Richard]

18
See High order in this great solemnity.
Antony and Cleopatra. Act v, sc. 2, l. 368. [Cæsar]

19
Orleans: We are enow yet living in the field
To smother up the English in our throngs,

If any order might be thought upon.
Bourbon: The devil take order now! I 'll to the throng.
Henry V. Act iv, sc. 5, l. 19.

1
Now will we take some order in the town.
I Henry VI. Act iii, sc. 2, l. 126. [Talbot]

Provide me soldiers, lords,
Whiles I take order for mine own affairs.
II Henry VI. Act iii, sc. 1, l. 319. [York]

There is order ta'en for you.—*Richard II,* v, 1, 53.

This order hath Baptista ta'en.—*The Taming of the Shrew,* i, 2, 126.

2
I would have him dead, my Lord of Suffolk,
Ere you can take due orders for a priest.
II Henry VI. Act iii, sc. 1, l. 273. [Cardinal]

The noble order of Saint George.—*I Henry VI,* iv, 7, 68.

Holy order.—*Romeo and Juliet,* iii, 3, 114; *Measure for Measure,* iv, 3, 152.

A votaress of my order.—*A Midsummer-Night's Dream,* ii, 1, 123.

A brother of gracious order.—*Measure for Measure,* iii, 2, 232.

Blest order.—*Measure for Measure,* ii, 3, 3.

Honourable order.—*I Henry VI,* iv, 1, 41.

3
Dick: They are all in order and march toward us.
Cade: But then are we in order when we are most out of order.
II Henry VI. Act iv, sc. 2, l. 198.

Things are set in order.—*I Henry VI,* ii, 2, 32.

Every thing in order.—*The Taming of the Shrew,* iv, 1, 53.

4
Order gave everything view.
Henry VIII. Act i, sc. 1, l. 44. [Norfolk]

5
Out of your grace, devise, ordain, impose
Some gentle order.
King John. Act iii, sc. 1, l. 250. [King Philip] The only use of "ordain."

All form is formless, order orderless.
King John. Act iii, sc. 1, l. 253. [Pandulph] "Formless" occurs again in *Troilus and Cressida,* iv, 5, 167. The only use of "orderless."

By cold gradation and well-balanced form.
Measure for Measure. Act iv, sc. 3, l. 104. [Duke] The only use of "well-balanced." "Gradation" occurs again in *Othello,* i, 1, 37.

Keep law and form and due proportion.
Richard II. Act iii, sc. 4, l. 41. [Servant] The only use of the phrase "due proportion."

6
Have thou the ordering of this present time.
King John. Act v, sc. 1, l. 77. [King John]

The ordering on 't, is . . . Properly ours.
The Winter's Tale. Act ii, sc. 1, l. 169. [Leontes]

Ordering of the mind.—*The Winter's Tale,* ii, 3, 106.

Ordering your affairs.—*The Winter's Tale,* iv, 4, 139.

7
Stand not upon the order of your going,
But go at once.
Macbeth. Act iii, sc. 4, l. 119. [Lady Macbeth]

Order of the field.—*Troilus and Cressida,* iv, 5, 70.

Order of their fight.—*Troilus and Cressida,* iv, 5, 90.

Order of his funeral.—*Julius Cæsar,* iii, 1, 230.

Order of law.—*Measure for Measure,* iii, 2, 8.

Order of proscription.—*Julius Cæsar,* iv, 3, 180.

8
We
Shall take upon 's what else remains to do,
According to our order.
Macbeth. Act v, sc. 6, l. 4. [Malcolm]

9
There are pretty orders beginning, I can tell you.
Measure for Measure. Act ii, sc. 1, l. 249. [Escalus]

Hadst thou not order?
Why dost thou ask again?
Measure for Measure. Act ii, sc. 2, l. 8. [Angelo]

There shall be order for 't.
Measure for Measure, ii, 2, 25. [Angelo]

10
Lock hand in hand; yourselves in order set.
The Merry Wives of Windsor. Act v, sc. 5, l. 81. [Evans]

11
If I know how or which way to order these affairs
Thus thrust disorderly into my hands,
Never believe me.
Richard II. Act ii, sc. 2, l. 109. [York]

12
Now will I in, to take some privy order.
Richard III. Act iii, sc. 5, l. 106. [Gloucester]

Private order.—*Measure for Measure,* v, 1, 471.

Fair order.—*King John,* v, 2, 4.

Fair-play orders.—*King John,* v, 1, 67.

Threefold order.—*I Henry IV,* iii, 1, 71.

True order.—*II Henry IV,* iv, 4, 100.

13
Make it orderly and well.
The Taming of the Shrew, iv, 3, 94. See under FASHION.

Go to it orderly.—*The Taming of the Shrew,* ii, 1, 45.

Orderly proceed.—*Richard II,* i, 3, 9.

Very orderly.—*The Two Gentlemen of Verona,* i, 1, 130. "Orderly" is used eight times.

14
Tailor: Grumio gave order how it should be done.
Grumio: I gave him no order.
Taming of the Shrew. Act iv, sc. 3, l. 118.

I have . . . given order.—*All's Well that Ends Well,* ii, 5, 27.

15
The heavens themselves, the planets and this centre
Observe degree, priority and place,
Insisture, course, proportion, season, form,
Office and custom, in all line of order.
Troilus and Cressida. Act i, sc. 3, l. 85. [Ulysses] "Priority" occurs again in *Coriolanus,* i, 1, 251. The only use of "insisture."

ORDNANCE, see Cannon

ORNAMENT

1
This ornament of knighthood.
I Henry VI. Act iv, sc. 1, l. 29. [Talbot]
Ornament of life.—*Macbeth,* i, 7, 42.
Thou that art now the world's fresh ornament.
Sonnets. No. i.
Gracious Lavinia, Rome's rich ornament.
Titus Andronicus, i, 1, 52. [Bassianus]
Sweet ornament that decks a thing divine!
The Two Gentlemen of Verona. Act ii, sc. 1, l. 4. [Valentine]
Sweet ornaments.—*Titus Andronicus,* ii, 4, 18.
Bedecking ornaments.—*Love's Labour's Lost,* ii, 1, 79.
Fair ornament.—*Merchant of Venice,* iii, 2, 80.
Helpful ornament.—*I Henry IV,* iii, 1, 125.
True ornaments.—*Richard III,* iii, 7, 99.
2
Deck my body in gay ornaments.
III Henry VI. Act iii, 2, 149. [Gloucester]
Clothing me in these grave ornaments.
I Henry VI. Act v, sc. 1, l. 54. [Winchester]
Grave beseeming ornaments.—*Romeo and Juliet,* i, 1, 100.
3
So may the outward shows be least themselves:
The world is still deceived with ornament.
The Merchant of Venice. Act iii, sc. 2, l. 73. [Bassanio]
Thus ornament is but the guiled shore
To a most dangerous sea; the beauteous scarf
Veiling an Indian beauty.
The Merchant of Venice. Act iii, sc. 2, l. 97. [Bassanio] Only use of "guiled" and "veiling."
4
This ornament Makes me look dismal.
Pericles. Act v, sc. 3, l. 73. [Pericles]
5
Help me sort such needful ornaments
As you think fit to furnish me to-morrow.
Romeo and Juliet. Act iv, sc. 2, l. 34. [Juliet]

ORPHAN

6
To reave the orphan of his patrimony.
II Henry VI. Act v, sc. 1, l. 187. [Salisbury] "Reave" is repeated in *All's Well that Ends Well,* v, 3, 86.
7 Orphans . . .
Shall rue the hour that ever thou wast born.
III Henry VI. Act v, sc. 6, l. 42. [King]
8
Each new morn . . . new orphans cry.
Macbeth. Act iv, sc. iii, l. 4. [Macduff]
9
The orphan pines while the oppressor feeds.
The Rape of Lucrece, l. 905. "Oppressor" is repeated in *Hamlet,* iii, 1, 71.
Orphans and unfather'd fruit.
Sonnets. No. xcvii.
Unfather'd heirs.—*II Henry IV,* iv, 4, 122. The only uses of "unfather'd."
Orphan heirs.—*The Merry Wives of Windsor,* v, 5, 43.
10
Were never orphans had so dear a loss!
Richard III. Act ii, sc. 2, l. 78. [Children]

OUTRAGE

11
I fear some outrage.
King John, iii, 4, 106. [King Philip]
12 'Tis worse than murder,
To do upon respect such violent outrage.
King Lear. Act ii, sc. 4, l. 23. [King Lear]
Desperate outrage.—*Much Ado about Nothing,* ii, 3, 159.
Immodest clamorous outrage.—*I Henry VI,* iv, 1, 126.
Rancorous outrage.—*The Comedy of Errors,* i, 1, 6.
13 O, preposterous
And frantic outrage, end thy damned spleen.
Richard III. Act ii, sc. 4, l. 63. [Duchess of York]
14
Gentlemen, for shame, forbear this outrage!
Romeo and Juliet, iii, 1, 90. [Romeo]
15 Do no outrages
On silly women or poor passengers.
The Two Gentlemen of Verona. Act iv, sc. 1, l. 71. [Valentine]
They love me well; yet I have much to do
To keep them from uncivil outrages.
The Two Gentlemen of Verona. Act v, sc. 4, l. 17. [Valentine]

OVERTHROW

See also Mischance

16
We are like to have the overthrow again.
I Henry VI. Act iii, sc. 2, l. 106. [Fastolfe]
I fear thy overthrow
More than my body's parting with my soul!
III Henry VI. Act ii, sc. 6, l. 3. [Clifford]
17
His overthrow heap'd happiness upon him;
For then, and not till then, he felt himself,
And found the blessedness of being little.
Henry VIII. Act iv, sc. 2, l. 64. [Griffith]
18
Sudden push gives them the overthrow.
Julius Cæsar. Act v, sc. 2, l. 5. [Brutus]
Thine own trip shall be thine overthrow.
Twelfth Night. Act v, sc. 1, l. 170. See DISSEMBLING, 364:7.
19
You 're overthrown, you 're undone for ever!
The Merry Wives of Windsor, iii, 3, 102. See SHAME, 1347:6.
Thou art overthrown!—*As You Like It,* i, 2, 271.
All o'erthrown.—*The Tempest,* Epil., 1.
Quite overthrown!—*Romeo and Juliet,* iv, 5, 57. "Overthrown" is used seventeen times.
20
Mutual overthrow of mortal kind!
Venus and Adonis, l. 1018.
Assured overthrow.—*Henry V,* iv, 3, 81.
Dire overthrow.—*Richard II,* v, 6, 16.
Late overthrow.—*I Henry VI,* i, 2, 49.
Misadventured piteous overthrows.—*Romeo and Juliet,* Prol., 7. The only use of "misadventured."
Purposed overthrow.—*Sonnets,* xc.
Enemies' overthrow.—*I Henry VI,* iii, 2, 111.
Glory's overthrow.—*I Henry VI,* i, 1, 24.
Overthrow incurable.—*King John,* v, 1, 16.

OWL

1
They say the owl was a baker's daughter.
Hamlet. Act iv, sc. 5, l. 41. [Ophelia]

2
Thou ominous and fearful owl of death.
I Henry VI. Act iv, sc. 2, l. 15. [General]
Out on you, owls! nothing but songs of death?
Richard III. Act iv, sc. 4, l. 509. [King Richard]

3
Bring forth that fatal screech-owl to our house,
That nothing sung but death to us and ours.
III Henry VI. Act ii, sc. 6, l. 56. [Edward]
The time when screech-owls cry.—*II Henry VI,* i, 4, 21.
Boding screech-owls.—*II Henry VI,* iii, 2, 327.
The screech-owl, screeching loud.—*A Midsummer-Night's Dream,* v, 1, 383.
A screech-owl aye be call'd.—*Troilus and Cressida,* v, 10, 16. The only uses of "screech-owl" and "screech-owls."

4
Yesterday the bird of night did sit
Even at noon-day upon the market-place,
Hooting and shrieking.
Julius Cæsar. Act i, sc. 3, l. 26. [Casca] The only use of "noon-day."
The owl shrieked at thy birth.
III Henry VI, v, 6, 44. See BIRTH, 99:9.
It was the owl that shriek'd, the fatal bellman,
Which gives the stern'st good-night.
Macbeth. Act ii, sc. 2, l. 3. [Lady Macbeth] The only use of "bellman."
I heard the owl scream and the crickets cry.
Macbeth. Act ii, sc. 2, l. 16. [Lady Macbeth]

5
Good night, my good owl!
Love's Labour 's Lost. Act iv, sc. 1, l. 141. [Boyet]
I bade the vile owl go.
Troilus and Cressida. Act ii, sc. 1, l. 99. [Ajax]
Mousing owl.—*Macbeth,* ii, 4, 13.
Nightly owl.—*Titus Andronicus,* ii, 3, 97.
Staring owl.—*Love's Labour 's Lost,* v, 2, 936.

6
The clamorous owl that nightly hoots and wonders
At our quaint spirits.
A Midsummer-Night's Dream. Act ii, sc. 2, l. 6. [Titania]

7
For night-owls shriek where mounting larks should sing.
Richard II. Act iii, sc. 3, l. 183. [King Richard] The only use of "night-owls."
Shall we rouse the night-owl in a catch?—*Twelfth Night.* Act ii, sc. 3, l. 60. [Sir Toby]
Like the night-owl's lazy flight.—*III Henry VI,* ii, 1, 130. The only uses of "night-owl."

8
The owl, night's herald, shrieks, " 'Tis very late."
Venus and Adonis, l. 531.

OX

9 We shall feed like oxen at a stall,
The better cherish'd, still the nearer death.
I Henry IV. Act v, sc. 2, l. 14. [Worcester]

10
Katharine: Veal, quoth the Dutchman. Is not 'veal' a calf?
Longaville: A calf, fair lady!
Katharine: No, a fair lord calf.
Longaville: Let 's part the word.
Katharine: No, I 'll not be your half:
Take all, and wean it; it may prove an ox.
Longaville: Look, how you butt yourself in these sharp mocks!
Will you give horns, chaste lady? do not so.
Katharine: Then die a calf, before your horns do grow.
Love's Labour 's Lost. Act v, sc. 2, l. 247. The only uses of "veal."

11
The ox hath therefore stretch'd his yoke in vain,
The ploughman lost his sweat.
A Midsummer-Night's Dream. Act ii, sc. 1, l. 93. [Titania]

12
And yet the steer, the heifer and the calf
Are all call'd neat.
Winter's Tale. Act i, sc. 2, l. 123. [Leontes]
Herd of neat.—*III Henry VI,* ii, 1, 14.
Neat-herd.—*The Winter's Tale,* iv, 4, 332; *Cymbeline,* i, 1, 149.

P

PACE

13
He has no pace, but runs where he will.
All's Well that Ends Well. Act iv, sc. 5, l. 70. [Countess]
In pace another Juno.—*Pericles,* v, 1, 112.
Keep pace.—*Sonnets,* li.
Mend his pace.—*Hamlet,* v, 1, 64.

14
She 's not paced yet: you must take some pains to work her to your manage.
Pericles. Act iv, sc. 6, l. 68. [Bawd]
We paced along.—*Richard III,* i, 4, 16.
Paced back again.—*Henry VIII,* iv, 1, 93. The only uses of "paced."

15
With slow but stately pace kept on his course.
Richard II. Act v, sc. 2, l. 10. [York]
With his stealthy pace.—*Macbeth,* ii, 1, 54.
Pace easy.—*Antony and Cleopatra,* ii, 2, 64.
Pace forth.—*Sonnets,* lv.
Pace softly.—*The Winter's Tale,* iv, 3, 121.

1
On a moderate pace I have since arrived but hither.
Twelfth Night. Act ii, sc. 2, l. 3. [Viola]
Divers paces.—*As You Like It,* iii, 2, 327.
Hostile paces.—*I Henry IV,* i, 1, 9.
Modest paces.—*Henry VIII,* iv, 1, 82.
Petty pace.—*Macbeth,* v, 5, 20.
Slow pace.—*Henry VIII,* i, 1, 132.
Strengthless pace.—*The Rape of Lucrece,* l. 709. "Strengthless" is repeated in *II Henry IV,* i, 1, 141: "Strengthless hinges"; and in *I Henry VI,* ii, 5, 13: "Strengthless stay."
Swift pace.—*Henry V,* v, Prol., 15.
Trembling paces.—*The Rape of Lucrece,* l. 1391.
Violent pace.—*Othello,* iii, 3, 457.
Wonted pace.—*Hamlet,* ii, 2, 354.

PAGEANT

2
Corin: If you will see a pageant truly play'd,
Between the pale complexion of true love
And the red glow of scorn and proud disdain,
Go hence a little and I shall conduct you,
If you will mark it.
Rosalind: O, come, let us remove.
As You Like It. Act iii, sc. 4, l. 55.
Shall we their fond pageant see?
A Midsummer-Night's Dream. Act iii, sc. 2, l. 114. [Puck]
Cupid's pageant.—*Troilus and Cressida,* iii, 2, 81.

3
Some delightful ostentation, or show, or pageant, or antique, or firework.
Love's Labour 's Lost. Act v, sc. 1, l. 117. [Armado]
Pageants and sights of honour.—*Henry VIII,* iv, 1, 11.
Pageants of delight.—*The Two Gentlemen of Verona,* iv, 4, 164.

4
This cannot be,
By no assay of reason: 'tis a pageant,
To keep us in false gaze.
Othello. Act 1, sc. 3, l. 17. [Senator]

5
What pageantry, what feats, what shows,
What ministrelsy, and pretty din,
The regent made in Mytilene
To greet the king.
Pericles. Act v, sc. 2, l. 6. [Gower] The only use of "pageantry."

6
A woeful pageant have we here beheld.
Richard II, iv, 1, 321. See under Woe.
Woeful pageants.—*As You Like It,* ii, 7, 138.
Direful pageant.—*Richard III,* iv, 4, 85.

7
With ridiculous and awkward action,
Which, slanderer, he imitation calls,
He pageants us.
Troilus and Cressida. Act i, sc. 3, l. 146. [Ulysses] The only use of "pageants" as a verb.

8
You shall see the pageant of Ajax.
Troilus and Cressida. Act iii, sc. 3, l. 273. [Thersites]
Pageants of the sea.—*The Merchant of Venice,* i, 1, 11.
Black vesper's pageants.—*Antony and Cleopatra,* iv, 14, 8.
Fortune's pageant.—*II Henry VI,* i, 2, 67.
Insubstantial pageant.—*The Tempest,* iv, 1, 155. The only use of "insubstantial."

PAIN

9
The other lives merrily because he feels no pain.
As You Like It. Act iii, sc. 2, l. 339. [Rosalind]
So thou wilt let me live, and feel no pain.
II Henry VI. Act iii, sc. 3, l. 4. [Cardinal]

10
'Tis good for men to love their present pains
Upon example; so the spirit is eased.
Henry V. Act iv, sc. 1, l. 18. [King Henry]

11
He shall not breathe infection in this air
But three days longer, on the pain of death.
II Henry VI. Act iii, sc. 2, l. 287. [King Henry]
Pain of death.—*II Henry VI,* iii, 2, 257; *I Henry VI,* i, 3, 79; iv, 1, 47; *Richard III,* i, 3, 167; *Romeo and Juliet,* i, 1, 110; *II Henry IV,* v, 5, 67; *Richard II,* i, 3, 42; *King Lear,* v, 3, 185.
Pain of life.—*Richard II,* i, 3, 153.
Pain of punishment.—*Antony and Cleopatra,* i, 1, 39.
On pain of their perpetual displeasure.—*King Lear,* iii, 3, 4.
On pain of losing her tongue.—*Love's Labour 's Lost,* i, 1, 124.

12
How light and portable my pain seems now,
When that which makes me bend makes the king bow!
King Lear. Act iii, sc. 6, l. 115. [Edgar] "Portable" is repeated in *Macbeth,* iv, 3, 89, and in *Troilus and Cressida,* ii, 3, 144.

13
Where lies thy pain?
And where my liege 's? all about the breast:
A caudle, ho!
Love's Labour 's Lost. Act iv, sc. 3, l. 172. [Biron] "Caudle" (a warm drink given to sick people) is repeated in *II Henry VI,* iv, 7, 95, and in *Timon of Athens,* iv, 3, 226.

14
Herein mean I to enrich my pain.
A Midsummer-Night's Dream. Act i, sc. 1, l. 250. [Helena]
Extremely stretch'd and conn'd with cruel pain.
A Midsummer-Night's Dream. Act v, sc. 1, l. 80. [Philostrate]
Accepted pain.—*Troilus and Cressida,* iii, 3, 30.
Common pain.—*II Henry IV,* iv, 5, 224.
Fasting pain.—*Love's Labour 's Lost,* iv, 3, 122.
Personal pain.—*Pericles,* iii, 2, 46.
Present pain.—*Pericles,* v, 1, 193.
Pain perpetual.—*The Rape of Lucrece,* l. 726.

15
Othello: I have a pain upon my forehead here.
Desdemona: 'Faith, that 's with watching; 'twill away again;

Let me but bind it hard, within this hour
It will be well.
Othello. Act iii, sc. 3, l. 284.
I would not have thee linger in thy pain.
Othello. Act v, sc. 2, l. 87. [Othello]
More mickle was the pain.—*The Passionate Pilgrim,* l. 219.

1
Pain pays the income of each precious thing.
The Rape of Lucrece, l. 334. The only use of "income."

2
One pain is lessen'd by another's anguish.
Romeo and Juliet. Act i, sc. 2, l. 47. [Benvolio]
Pity-wanting pain.—*Sonnets,* cxl. The only use of "pity-wanting."

3
Sirs, drag them from the pit unto the prison:
There let them bide until we have devised
Some never-heard-of torturing pain for them.
Titus Andronicus. Act ii, sc. 3, l. 283. [Saturninus] The only use of "never-heard-of."
A hell of pain.—*Troilus and Cressida,* iv, 1, 57.
Pains of hell.—*Richard II,* iii, 1, 34.

PAINS

See also Trouble

4
Lord, how we lose our pains!
All's Well that Ends Well. Act v, sc. 1, l. 24. [Widow]
On whom my pains,
Humanly taken, all, all lost, quite lost.
Tempest. Act iv, sc. 1, l. 189. [Prospero]

5 You lay out too much pains
For purchasing but trouble.
Cymbeline. Act ii, sc. 3, l. 92. [Imogen]

6 If you knew what pains
I have bestow'd to breed this present peace,
You would drink freely.
II Henry IV. Act iv, sc. 2, l. 73. [Westmoreland]

7 Your pains
Are register'd where every day I turn
The leaf to read them.
Macbeth. Act i, sc. 3, l. 150. [Macbeth]
I commend your pains.—*Macbeth,* iv, 1, 39.
I will content your pains.—*Othello,* iii, 1, 1.

8 Lend him your kind pains
To find out this abuse.
Measure for Measure. Act v, sc. 1, l. 246. [Duke]
We freely cope your courteous pains withal.
The Merchant of Venice. Act iv, sc. 1, l. 412. [Bassanio]
It is worth the pains.—*The Merchant of Venice,* ii, 6, 33.
It may be worth thy pains.—*Twelfth Night,* i, 2, 57.
Not worth her pains.—*The Winter's Tale,* iv, 1, 155.

9
I must entreat your pains, I think.
Much Ado about Nothing. Act v, sc. 4, l. 18. [Benedick]
I'll deserve your pains.—*Othello,* i, 1, 184.

10
You must take some pains to work her to your manage.
Pericles. Act iv, sc. 6, l. 69. [Bawd]
Take pains.—*Henry V,* iv, 1, 69; *King John,* i, 1, 219; *The Merchant of Venice,* ii, 2, 194; *A Midsummer-Night's Dream,* i, 2, 111; *Much Ado about Nothing,* ii, 3, 260; *Timon of Athens,* v, 1, 92.
Ta'en great pains.—*The Merchant of Venice,* iv, 1, 7; *Twelfth Night,* i, 5, 186.
Ta'en much pain.—*Henry VIII,* iii, 2, 72.
Took some pains.—*The Merchant of Venice,* v, 1, 182.

11
Thy pains, Fitzwater, shall not be forgot.
Richard II. Act v, sc. 6, l. 17. [Bolingbroke]
I'll quit thy pains.—*Romeo and Juliet,* ii, 4, 204.

12
All my pains is sorted to no proof.
The Taming of the Shrew. Act iv, sc. 3, l. 43. [Petruchio]
You might have saved me my pains.—*Twelfth Night,* ii, 2, 6.

13
Having nothing but the word 'noddy' for my pains.
The Two Gentlemen of Verona. Act i, sc. 1, l. 131. [Speed] "Noddy" (simpleton) is repeated in l. 119 and l. 122 of the same scene, and occurs nowhere else.
Now you have taken the pains to set it together, take it for your pains.
The Two Gentlemen of Verona. Act i, sc. 1, l. 123. [Speed]
Proteus: What said she? nothing?
Speed: No, not so much as 'Take this for thy pains.'
Two Gentlemen of Verona. Act i, sc. 1, l. 150.
Here is for your pains.—*Two Gentlemen of Verona,* i, 1, 139; *Romeo and Juliet,* ii, 4, 194.
I thank you for your pains.—*The Taming of the Shrew,* iii, 2, 186; *Much Ado about Nothing,* ii, 3, 258; *Twelfth Night,* i, 5, 302.
There's for thy pains.—*The Merry Wives of Windsor,* iii, 4, 104; *Much Ado about Nothing,* v, 1, 326; *Twelfth Night,* ii, 4, 68; *Othello,* iv, 2, 93.

PAINTING

See also Picture

14
Though he be painted one way like a Gorgon,
The other way 's a Mars.
Antony and Cleopatra. Act ii, sc. 5, l. 116. [Cleopatra] "Gorgon" is repeated in *Macbeth,* ii, 3, 77.
I paint him in the character.—*Coriolanus,* v, 4, 28.
Paint himself.—*Much Ado about Nothing,* iii, 2, 58.
Paint the meadows.—*Love's Labour's Lost,* v, 2, 907.
Paint the white rose red.—*I Henry VI,* ii, 4, 50.

15
I have heard of your paintings too, well enough.
Hamlet, iii, 1, 148. See under FACE.

1
For thy walls, a pretty slight drollery, or the story of the Prodigal, or the German hunting in water-work, is worth a thousand of these bed-hangings and these fly-bitten tapestries.

II Henry IV. Act ii, sc. 1, l. 156. [Falstaff] The only use of "water-work," "bed-hangings," and "fly-bitten." "Drollery" occurs once again in *The Tempest*, iii, 3, 21: "A living drollery."

'Tis painted about with the story of the Prodigal, fresh and new.

The Merry Wives of Windsor. Act iv, sc. 5, l. 7. [Hostess]

2
Does Bridget paint still, Pompey, ha?

Measure for Measure. Act iii, sc. 2, l. 83. [Lucio] Bridget is mentioned twice more in the plays, in *The Comedy of Errors*, iii, 1, 31, and *The Merry Wives of Windsor*, ii, 1, 11. See FACE: THE PAINTED FACE.

3
A piece Of skilful painting.

The Rape of Lucrece, l. 1367.

This well-painted piece.

The Rape of Lucrece, l. 1443. "Well-painted" is repeated in *Othello*, iv, 1, 268: "Well-painted passion."

Painted imagery.—*Richard II*, v, 2, 16. The only use of "imagery."

4
Perspective it is best painter's art.

Sonnets. No. xxiv.

Perspectives, which rightly gazed upon
Show nothing but confusion, eyed awry
Distinguish form.

Richard II. Act ii, sc. 2, l. 18. [Bushy]

Natural perspective.—*Twelfth Night*, v, 1, 224.

Scornful perspective.—*All's Well that Ends Well*, v. 3, 48. The only uses of "perspective."

5
Why should false painting imitate his cheek
And steal dead seeing of his living hue?

Sonnets. No. lxvii.

And their gross painting might be better used
Where cheeks need blood; in thee it is abused.

Sonnets. No. lxxxii.

I never saw that you did painting need
And therefore to your fair no painting set.

Sonnets. No. lxxxiii. See under WORTH.

6
We 'll show thee Io as she was a maid,
And how she was beguiled and surprised,
As lively painted as the deed was done.

The Taming of the Shrew. Ind., sc. 2, l. 56. [Lord] The only mention of Io.

7
Painter: 'Tis a good piece.
Poet: So 'tis: this comes off well and excellent.
Painter: Indifferent.
Poet: Admirable: how this grace
Speaks his own standing! what a mental power
This eye shoots forth! how big imagination
Moves in this lip! to the dumbness of the gesture
One might interpret.
Painter: It is a pretty mocking of the life.
Here is a touch; is 't good?
Poet: I will say of it,
It tutors nature: artificial strife
Lives in these touches, livelier than life.

Timon of Athens. Act i, sc. 1, l. 28.

A thousand moral paintings I can show
That shall demonstrate these quick blows of Fortune's
More pregnantly than words.

Timon of Athens. Act i, sc. 1, l. 90. [Painter] The only use of "pregnantly."

Oily painting.—*The Winter's Tale*, v, 3, 83.

Old painting.—*Love's Labour 's Lost*, iii, 1, 21.

Reechy painting.—*Much Ado about Nothing*, iii, 1, 21.

8
The painting is almost the natural man;
For since dishonour traffics with man's nature,
He is but outside: these pencill'd figures are
Even such as they give out.

Timon of Athens. Act i, sc. 1, l. 157. [Timon] "Pencill'd" is repeated in *The Rape of Lucrece*, l. 1497.

II—The Painter

9
The red blood reek'd, to show the painter's strife.

The Rape of Lucrece, l. 1377.

In her the painter had anatomized
Time's ruin, beauty's wreck, and grim care's reign.

The Rape of Lucrece, l. 1450.

This picture she advisedly perused,
And chid the painter for his wondrous skill.

The Rape of Lucrece, l. 1527. "Advisedly" is repeated in *The Merchant of Venice*, v, 1, 253, and in *I Henry IV*, v, 1, 114.

Conceited painter.—*The Rape of Lucrece*, l. 1371.

The painter was no good.—*The Rape of Lucrece*, l. 1461.

The painter was so nice.—*The Rape of Lucrece*, l. 1412.

10
Through the painter must you see his skill.

Sonnets. No. xxiv.

11
And yet the painter flatter'd her a little.

The Two Gentlemen of Verona. Act iv, sc. 4, l. 192. [Julia]

12
Look, when a painter would surpass the life,
In limning out a well-proportioned steed,
His art with nature's workmanship at strife,
As if the dead the living should exceed.

Venus and Adonis, l. 289. The only use of "surpass" and "limning." "Well-proportioned" is repeated in *II Henry VI*, iii, 2, 175.

PALACE

13
Had our great palace the capacity
To camp this host, we all would sup together.

Antony and Cleopatra. Act iv, sc. 8, l. 32. [Antony]

1
This is the palace of the fearful king,
And this the regal seat.
III Henry VI. Act i, sc. 1, l. 25. [Warwick]

Palace of our king.—*II Henry VI,* iv, 1, 102.
Bishop's palace.—*III Henry VI,* v, 1, 45.
Emperor's palace.—*Titus Andronicus,* ii, 1, 46.
Princes' palaces.—*The Merchant of Venice,* i, 2, 15.
Soul's palace.—*III Henry VI,* ii, 1, 74.

2
Bring us to our palace; where we 'll show
What 's yet behind, that 's meet you all should know.
Measure for Measure. Act v, sc. 1, l. 544. [Duke]

3
Where 's that palace whereinto foul things
Sometimes intrude not?
Othello, iii, 3, 137. See APPREHENSION, 49:5.

4 Thou seem'st a palace
For the crown'd Truth to dwell in.
Pericles. Act v, sc. 1, l. 122. [Pericles]

5
My gorgeous palace for a hermitage.
Richard II, iii, 3, 148. See under GRAVE.

Gorgeous palace.—*Romeo and Juliet,* iii, 2, 85; *The Tempest,* iv, 1, 152.
Golden palaces.—*I Henry VI,* v, 3, 170.
Graced palace.—*King Lear,* i, 4, 267.
Palace crystalline.—*Cymbeline,* v, 4, 113. The only use of "crystalline."
Palace of dim night.—*Romeo and Juliet,* v, 3, 107.

6
The palace full of tongues, of eyes, and ears.
Titus Andronicus, ii, 1, 127. See under COURT.

PALENESS

7
How now! why look'st thou pale? why tremblest thou?
II Henry VI. Act iii, sc. 2, l. 27. [King Henry]

Juliet: Either my eyesight fails, or thou look'st pale.
Romeo: And trust me, love, in my eyes so do you.
Romeo and Juliet. Act iii, sc. 5, l. 57.

Ay me, poor man, how pale and wan he looks!
The Comedy of Errors. Act iv, sc. 4, l. 111. [Luciana]

He looks pale.—*Much Ado about Nothing,* v, 1, 131. "Looks pale" is used frequently throughout the plays.
Look'st thou pale?—*King John,* iii, 1, 195.
Why look you pale?—*Love's Labour 's Lost,* v, 2, 392.
Why dost thou look so pale?—*The Taming of the Shrew,* ii, 1, 143.
Look not pale.—*Taming of the Shrew,* v, 1, 143.
Look not so pale.—*Macbeth,* v, 1, 69. See under LOOK.
What, pale again?—*All 's Well that Ends Well,* i, 3, 175.
Then, if you can, Be pale.—*Cymbeline,* ii, 4, 96.
I am pale, Charmian.—*Antony and Cleopatra,* ii, 5, 59.
Pale at heart.—*Measure for Measure,* iv, 3, 157.
Pale for woe.—*The Two Gentlemen of Verona,* iii, 1, 228.
Pale in her anger.—*A Midsummer-Night's Dream,* ii, 1, 104.
Pale with envy.—*Henry V,* v, 2, 378.
Pale with fear.—*The Rape of Lucrece,* l. 183.
Pale with grief.—*Romeo and Juliet,* ii, 2, 5.
Pale with love.—*Much Ado about Nothing,* i, 1, 250.

8
Thy paleness moves me more than eloquence.
The Merchant of Venice. Act iii, sc. 2, l. 106. [Bassanio]

Paleness of the flower.—*I Henry VI,* iv, 1, 106.
Swooning paleness.—*A Lover's Complaint,* l. 305. The only uses of "paleness." "Swooning" is repeated in *Troilus and Cressida,* iii, 2, 24: "Swooning destruction."

9
Have I not reason to look pale and dead?
Richard II, iii, 2, 79. See under BLOOD.

Pale and dead.—*I Henry VI,* iv, 2, 38.
Deadly pale.—*Richard III,* iii, 7, 26.
Pale and faint.—*Venus and Adonis,* l. 739.
Pale and wan.—*Titus Andronicus,* ii, 3, 90.
Pale and wild.—*Romeo and Juliet,* v, 1, 28.
Pining and pale.—*Henry V,* iv, Prol., 14.
White and pale.—*II Henry IV,* iv, 3, 113.
Very pale.—*Hamlet,* i, 2, 233.

10
She looks as pale as any clout in the versal world.
Romeo and Juliet, ii, 4, 218. See under MISTRESS. The only use of "versal."

Pale as ashes.—*Romeo and Juliet,* iii, 2, 55.
Ashy pale.—*The Rape of Lucrece,* l. 1512.
Pale as lead.—*Romeo and Juliet,* ii, 5, 17.
Pale as milk.—*A Midsummer-Night's Dream,* v, 1, 345.
Pale as primrose.—*II Henry VI,* iii, 2, 63.
Pale as his shirt.—*Hamlet,* ii, 1, 81.
Pale as thy smock.—*Othello,* v, 2, 273.

11 With this dear sight
Struck pale and bloodless.
Titus Andronicus, iii, 1, 258. See under HORROR. "Pale and bloodless" is repeated in *II Henry VI,* iii, 2, 162, and in *Troilus and Cressida,* i, 3, 134.

Bloodless fear.—*Venus and Adonis,* l. 891.
Bloodless hand.—*The Rape of Lucrece,* l. 1597.
Bloodless remnant.—*Richard III,* i, 2, 7.
Bloodless stroke.—*Twelfth Night,* ii, 5, 117.
Bloodless white.—*A Lover's Complaint,* l. 201. The only uses of "bloodless."

12 A sudden pale,
Like lawn being spread upon the blushing rose,
Usurps her cheek.
Venus and Adonis, l. 589.

PALM

I—Palm Tree

13
Look here what I found on a palm-tree.
As You Like It, iii, 2, 186. The only use of "palm-tree."

14 Ye gods, it doth amaze me
A man of such a feeble temper should
So get the start of the majestic world

And bear the palm alone.
Julius Cæsar. Act i, sc. 2, l. 128. [Cassius]
Bear the palm.—*Coriolanus,* v, 3, 117.

1 You shall see him a palm in Athens again, and flourish with the highest.
Timon of Athens. Act v, sc. 1, l. 12. [Painter]

II—Palm of the Hand

2 Iras: There 's a palm presageth chastity, if nothing else.
Charmian: E'en as the overflowing Nilus presageth famine.
Iras: Go, you wild bedfellow, you cannot soothsay.
Charmian: Nay, if an oily palm be not a fruitful prognostication, I cannot scratch mine ear.
Antony and Cleopatra. Act i, sc. 2, l. 47. The only use of "soothsay." "Prognostication" is repeated in *The Winter's Tale,* iv, 4, 817.

3 Lean but upon a rush,
The cicatrice and capable impressure
Thy palm some moments keeps.
As You Like It, iii, 5, 23. See under SCAR.

4 Do not dull thy palm with entertainment.
Hamlet, i, 3, 64. See under FRIEND.

5 Brutus: You yourself
Are much condemn'd to have an itching palm. . . .
Cassius: I an itching palm!
Julius Cæsar, iv, 3, 9. See under BRIBERY.
Not that I have the power to clutch my hand,
When his fair angels would salute my palm.
King John. Act ii, sc. 1, l. 589. [Bastard]

6 He takes her by the palm.
Othello. Act ii, sc. 1, l. 168. [Iago]
Didst thou not see her paddle with the palm of his hand?
Othello. Act ii, sc. 1, l. 259. [Iago] The only use of "paddle."
Palm of the hand.—*The Comedy of Errors,* iii, 2, 124; *II Henry IV,* i, 2, 24.
Paddling palms.—*The Winter's Tale,* i, 2, 115. "Paddling" is repeated in *Hamlet,* iii, 4, 185.

7 Palm to palm is holy palmers' kiss.
Romeo and Juliet, i, 5, 102. See under HAND.
Snatch our palm from palm.—*King John,* iii, 1, 244.

8 Still virginalling Upon his palm!
The Winter's Tale. Act i, sc. 2, l. 125. [Leontes] The only use of "virginalling," playing on the virginals, fingering.
Virgin palm.—*Love's Labour 's Lost,* v, 2, 816.
Virginal palms.—*Coriolanus,* v, 2, 46.
Palm of ploughman.—*Troilus and Cressida,* i, 1, 59.

9 With this she seizeth on his sweating palm,
The precedent of pith and livelihood.
Venus and Adonis, l. 25.

PANDAR

See also Bawd

10 Thou art the pandar to her dishonour and equally to me disloyal.
Cymbeline. Act iii, sc. 4, l. 32. [Imogen, reading]
You should have been a pandar.
The Merry Wives of Windsor, v, 5, 176.
Ah, you precious pandar!—*Cymbeline,* iii, 5, 81.
O you pandarly rascals!—*The Merry Wives of Windsor,* iv, 2, 122. The only use of "pandarly."

11 With his cap in hand,
Like a base pandar, hold the chamber-door
Whilst by a slave, no gentler than my dog,
His fairest daughter is contaminated.
Henry V. Act iv, sc. 5, l. 13. [Bourbon]

12 Shall I Sir Pandarus of Troy become?
The Merry Wives of Windsor. Act i, sc. 3, l. 83. [Pistol]
I would play Lord Pandarus of Phrygia, sir, to bring a Cressida to this Troilus.
Twelfth Night. Act iii, sc. 1, l. 58. [Clown]

13 Troilus the first employer of pandars.
Much Ado about Nothing. Act v, sc. 2, l. 31. The only use of "employer."

14 I cannot come to Cressid but by Pandar.
Troilus and Cressida. Act i, sc. 1, l. 98. [Troilus]
Since I have taken such pains to bring you together let all pitiful goers-between be called to the world's end after my name; call them all Pandars; . . . all brokers-between Pandars.
Troilus and Cressida. Act iii, sc. 2, l. 207. [Pandarus] The only use of "goers-between" and "brokers-between."
As many as be here of pandar's hall,
Your eyes, half out, weep out at Pandar's fall; . . .
Brethren and sisters of the hold-door trade.
Troilus and Cressida. Act v, sc. 10, l. 48. [Pandar] The only use of "hold-door."

PAPER

15 Parolles: Pray you, sir, deliver me this paper.
Clown: Foh! prithee, stand away: a paper from fortune's close-stool to give to a nobleman!
All's Well that Ends Well. Act v, sc. 2, l. 16.

16 O damn'd paper!
Black as the ink that 's on thee!
Cymbeline. Act iii, sc. 2, l. 19. [Pisanio]
Why tender'st thou that paper to me, with
A look untender?
Cymbeline. Act iii, sc. 4, l. 11. [Imogen] "Untender" is repeated in *King Lear,* i, 1, 108.
What shall I need to draw my sword? the paper
Hath cut her throat already.
Cymbeline. Act iii, sc. 4, l. 34. [Pisanio]
This paper is the history of my knowledge
Touching her flight.
Cymbeline. Act iii, sc. 5, l. 99. [Pisanio]

1
What see you in those papers that you lose
So much complexion? Look ye, how they change!
Their cheeks are paper.
Henry V. Act ii, sc. 2, l. 72. [King Henry]
The rest the paper tells.—*II Henry IV*, ii, 1, 147.

2
With this ungracious paper strike the sight
Of the death-practised duke.
King Lear. Act iv, sc. 6, l. 283. [Edgar] The only use of "death-practised."

3
Deliver this paper into the royal hand of the king:
It may concern much.
Love's Labour's Lost. Act iv, sc. 2, l. 145. [Holofernes]
He comes in like a perjure, wearing papers. *Love's Labour's Lost*, iv, 3, 48.
Sheet of paper.—*Love's Labour's Lost*, v, 2, 7; *Much Ado about Nothing*, ii, 3, 138; 140; *Twelfth Night*, iii, 2, 50.
Brown paper.—*Measure for Measure*, iv, 3, 6.
Fair paper.—*Othello*, iv, 2, 71.
Vulgar paper.—*Sonnets*, xxxviii.
Papers of state.—*Henry VIII*, iii, 2, 121.

4
Baille me some paper.
The Merry Wives of Windsor. Act i, sc. 4, l. 92. [Caius] The only use of "baille," from the French *bailler*, to give.
Go get me hither paper, ink, and pen.
The Rape of Lucrece, l. 1289. See under INK.

5
Now here 's another discontented paper,
Found in his pocket too.
Othello. Act v, sc. 2, l. 314. [Lodovico]

6 What presence must not know,
From where you do remain let paper show.
Richard II. Act i, sc. 3, l. 249. [Aumerle]

7
So should my papers yellow'd with their age
Be scorn'd like old men of less truth than tongue.
Sonnets. No. xvii.

PARADISE

8
The air of paradise did fan the house
And angels officed all.
All's Well that Ends Well, iii, 2, 128. [Helena] "Officed" is repeated in *Othello*, i, 3, 271, and in *The Winter's Tale*, i, 2, 172.

9
You would for paradise break faith and troth.
Love's Labour's Lost, iv, 3, 143. [King]
Win a paradise.—*Love's Labour's Lost*, iv, 3, 73; *The Passionate Pilgrim*, l. 42.
Kept the Paradise.—*Comedy of Errors*, iv, 3, 16.

10
A paradise To what we fear of death.
Measure for Measure, iii, 1, 131. See under DEATH.

11
Before the time I did Lysander see,
Seem'd Athens as a paradise to me.
A Midsummer-Night's Dream. Act i, sc. 1, l. 204. [Hermia]

12
If ye should lead her into a fool's paradise, as they say, it were a very gross kind of behaviour, as they say.
Romeo and Juliet. Act ii, sc. 4, l. 175. [Nurse] The only use of "fool's paradise."
Mortal paradise.—*Romeo and Juliet*, iii, 2, 82.

13 Let me live here ever;
So rare a wonder'd father and a wife
Makes this place Paradise.
Tempest. Act iv, sc. 1, l. 122. [Ferdinand]

PARASITE

14
Like to a step-dame or a dowager
Long withering out a young man's revenue.
Midsummer-Night's Dream. Act i, sc. 1, l. 5. [Theseus] "Withering" is repeated in l. 77 of the same scene, and occurs nowhere else.

15
The caterpillars of the commonwealth,
Which I have sworn to weed and pluck away.
Richard II, ii, 3, 166. [Bolingbroke]
Caterpillars eat my leaves away.
II Henry VI. Act iii, sc. 1, l. 190. [York]
Swarming with caterpillars.—*Richard II*, iii, 4, 47.
As caterpillars do.—*Venus and Adonis*, l. 798.
False caterpillars.—*II Henry VI*, iv, 4, 37.
Whoreson caterpillar.—*I Henry IV*, ii, 2, 88.
Send a caterpillar.—*Pericles*, v, 1, 60. The only uses of "caterpillar" and "caterpillars."

16
The ivy which had hid my princely trunk,
And suck'd my verdure out on 't.
The Tempest. Act i, sc. 2, l. 86. [Prospero] "Verdure" is repeated in *The Two Gentlemen of Verona*, i, 2, 87, and in *Venus and Adonis*, l. 507.
Female ivy.—*A Midsummer-Night's Dream*, iv, 1, 48.
Usurping ivy.—*Comedy of Errors*, ii, 2, 180.
Browning of ivy.—*Winter's Tale*, iii, 3, 69. The only uses of "ivy."

PARDON

See also Excuse, Forgiveness

17 This I must say,
But first I beg my pardon.
All's Well that Ends Well, v, 3, 11. [Lafeu]
Octavia: I begg'd His pardon for return.
Cæsar: Which soon he granted,
Being an obstruct 'tween his lust and him.
Antony and Cleopatra. Act iii, sc. 6, l. 59. The only use of "obstruct."
Exactly begg'd
Your grace's pardon, and I hope I had it.
Richard II. Act i, sc. 1, l. 140. [Mowbray]
Beg pardon.—*II Henry VI*, iii, 2, 221; *As You Like It*, iii, 5, 6; *Romeo and Juliet*, iii, 3, 152.
Beg thy pardon.—*Richard II*, v, 2, 113.
Beg your pardons.—*II Henry IV*, Epil., 4.
Cried he? and begg'd a pardon?—*Antony and Cleopatra*, iii, 13, 132.

1
For they have pardons, being ask'd, as free
As words to little purpose.
Coriolanus. Act iii, sc. 2, l. 88. [Menenius]
Let him not ask our pardon.—*All's Well that Ends Well,* v, 3, 22.
Ask pardon.—*Measure for Measure,* iii, 1, 173; *Othello,* v, 2, 300.
I cry you gentle pardon.—*Othello,* v, 1, 93.
Find pardon.—*I Henry IV,* iii, 2, 28.
Imploring pardon.—*Henry V,* iv, 1, 322.
Pardon absolute.—*I Henry IV,* iv, 3, 50.
Promised pardon.—*Henry VIII,* i, 2, 56.
Special pardon.—*III Henry VI,* iv, 1, 87.
Under your pardon.—*Julius Cæsar,* iv, 3, 213.

2
I minded him how royal 'twas to pardon
When it was less expected.
Coriolanus. Act v, sc. 1, l. 18. [Cominius]

3
Give me your pardon, sir: I've done you wrong;
But pardon 't, as you are a gentleman.
Hamlet. Act v, sc. 2, l. 237. [Hamlet]

4
On his more advice we pardon him.
Henry V. Act ii, sc. 2, l. 43. [King Henry]
I pardon thee thy life before thou ask it.
The Merchant of Venice. Act iv, sc. 1, l. 369. [Duke]
I pardon you for that.—*As You Like It,* iii, 2, 395.
I will pardon you.—*The Two Gentlemen of Verona,* iii, 2, 98.
I pardon them and thee.—*The Two Gentlemen of Verona,* v, 4, 158.

5
We . . . here pronounce free pardon to them all.
II Henry VI. Act iv, sc. 8, l. 9. [Buckingham]
Did not we send grace,
Pardon and terms of love to all of you?
I Henry IV. Act v, sc. 5, l. 2. [King Henry]
Pardon's the word to all.
Cymbeline. Act v, sc. 5, l. 422. [Cymbeline]
Send our . . . Free pardon to each man.
Henry VIII. Act i, sc. 2, l. 100. [King Henry]

6
Pardon me, God, I knew not what I did!
III Henry VI. Act ii, sc. 5, l. 69. [Son]
Beseeching you and God to pardon me.
Henry V. Act ii, sc. 2, l. 160. [Cambridge]
I pray you, pardon me; pray heartily, pardon me.
The Merry Wives of Windsor. Act iii, sc. 3, l. 243. [Ford]
Pardon me, if you please; if not, I, pleased
Not to be pardon'd, am content withal.
Richard II. Act ii, sc. 1, l. 187. [York]
Give me your pardon.—*Cymbeline,* i, 6, 162.
O, pardon me, my stars!—*Love's Labour's Lost,* iii, 1, 78.
O, pardon me that I descend so low!—*I Henry IV,* i, 3, 149.
O, pardon love this wrong.—*Love's Labour's Lost,* iv, 2, 121.
Pardon me.—*II Henry VI,* i, 1, 54. Used in the first scene of the first play, and fifty-six times thereafter.
Would you'ld pardon me.—*Twelfth Night,* iii, 3, 24.

7
But if an humble prayer may prevail,
I then crave pardon of your majesty.
III Henry VI. Act iv, sc. 6, l. 7. [Lieutenant]
Crave pardon.—*The Comedy of Errors,* i, 2, 26; *Coriolanus,* iii, 1, 65; *Measure for Measure,* ii, 2, 14; *Macbeth,* iv, 3, 20; *Antony and Cleopatra,* ii, 5, 98; *Passionate Pilgrim,* l. 141.

8
He shall pardon thee these outrages.
III Henry VI. Act v, sc. 1, l. 24. [King Edward]
O, God forgive my sins, and pardon thee!
III Henry VI, v, 6, 60. [King Henry]

9
I humbly do entreat your highness' pardon.
Henry VIII. Act iv, sc. 2, l. 104. [Messenger]
I do entreat your grace to pardon me.
A Midsummer-Night's Dream. Act i, sc. 1, l. 58. [Hermia]
I do beseech your grace to pardon me.
Richard II. Act v, sc. 2, l. 60. [Aumerle]
I beseech your graces both to pardon me.
Richard III. Act i, sc. 1, l. 84. [Brakenbury]

10 By the merit of vile gold, dross, dust,
Purchase corrupted pardon of a man,
Who in that sale sells pardon from himself.
King John. Act iii, sc. 1, l. 165. [King John]

11
Pardon is still the nurse of second woe.
Measure for Measure. Act ii, sc. 1, l. 298. [Escalus]
Yes; I do think that you might pardon him,
And neither heaven nor man grieve at the mercy.
Measure for Measure. Act ii, sc. 2, l. 49. [Isabella]
Sign me a present pardon for my brother.
Measure for Measure. Act ii, sc. 4, l. 152. [Isabella]
I hope it is some pardon or reprieve
For the most gentle Claudio.
Measure for Measure. Act iv, sc. 2, l. 74. [Provost]
This is his pardon, purchased by such sin
For which the pardoner himself is in.
Measure for Measure. Act iv, sc. 2, l. 111. [Duke] The only use of "pardoner."

12
Pardon, good father! good my mother, pardon!
The Merry Wives of Windsor. Act v, sc. 5, l. 230. [Anne]
I . . . am enjoin'd
By holy Laurence to fall prostrate here,
And beg your pardon: pardon, I beseech you.
Romeo and Juliet, iv, 2, 19. [Juliet]

13
Desdemona: Heaven pardon him!
Emilia: A halter pardon him! and hell gnaw his bones!
Othello. Act iv, sc. 2, l. 135.

14
Aumerle: For ever may my knees grow to the earth,
My tongue cleave to my roof within my mouth,

Unless a pardon ere I rise or speak.
Bolingbroke: Intended or committed was this fault?
If on the first, how heinous e'er it be,
To win thy after-love I pardon thee.
Richard II. Act v, sc. 3, l. 30. "After-love" is repeated in *The Two Gentlemen of Verona,* iii, 1, 95.

If thou do pardon, whosoever pray,
More sins for this forgiveness prosper may.
Richard II. Act v, sc. 3, l. 83. [York]

Duchess of York: An if I were thy nurse, thy tongue to teach,
'Pardon' should be the first word of thy speech.
I never long'd to hear a word till now;
Say 'pardon,' king; let pity teach thee how:
The word is short, but not so short as sweet;
No word like 'pardon' for kings' mouths so meet.
York: Speak it in French, king; say 'pardonne moi.'
Duchess of York: Dost thou teach pardon pardon to destroy? . . .
Speak 'pardon' as 'tis current in our land;
The chopping French we do not understand. . . .
Pardon is all the suit I have in hand.
Bolingbroke: I pardon him, as God shall pardon me. . . .
Duchess of York: Twice saying 'pardon' does not pardon twain,
But makes one pardon strong.
Bolingbroke: With all my heart I pardon him.
Richard II. Act v, sc. 3, l. 113. The only use of "pardonne moi" and "chopping."

French Soldier: O pardonnez-moi!
Pistol: Say'st thou me so? is that a ton of moys?
Henry V. Act iv, sc. 4, l. 23. The only use of "ton." "Pardonnez-moi" is repeated in v, 2, 108, and occurs in no other play.

1
Some tardy cripple bore the countermand,
That came too lag to see him buried.
Richard III. Act ii, sc. 1, l. 89. [Gloucester]

Duke: Have you no countermand for Claudio yet,
But he must die to-morrow?
Provost: None, sir, none.
Duke: As near the dawning, provost, as it is,
You shall hear more ere morning. . . .
Provost: I believe there comes
No countermand.
Measure for Measure. Act iv, sc. 2, l. 95. The only uses of "countermand" as a noun. As a verb, it occurs in *The Comedy of Errors,* iv, 2, 37, and in *Rape of Lucrece,* l. 276.

2
You straight are on your knees for pardon, pardon;
And I, unjustly too, must grant it you.
Richard III. Act ii, sc. 1, l. 124. [King Edward]

3
To you it doth belong
Yourself to pardon of self-doing crime.
Sonnets. No. lviii. Only use of "self-doing."

4
Pardon me in what I have to say.
The Taming of the Shrew. Act iv, sc. 4, l. 38. [Baptista]

Give pardon to my speech.—*Troilus and Cressida,* i, 3, 357.
Pardon what I have spoke.—*Antony and Cleopatra,* ii, 2, 139.
What you have spoke I pardon.—*Measure for Measure,* v, 1, 366.

5
As you from crimes would pardon'd be,
Let your indulgence set me free.
The Tempest. Epilogue, l. 19. [Prospero]

6
At my suit, sweet, pardon what is past.
Titus Andronicus. Act i, sc. 1, l. 431. [Tamora]

By my advice, all humbled on your knees,
You shall ask pardon of his majesty.
Titus Andronicus. Act i, sc. 1, l. 472. [Tamora]

PARENTS

See also Father, Mother

7
He asked me of what parentage I was; I told him, of as good as he.
As You Like It. Act iii, sc. 4, l. 39 [Rosalind]

Graceless! wilt thou deny thy parentage?
I Henry VI. Act v, sc. 4, l. 14. [Warwick]

Time hath rooted out my parentage.
Pericles. Act v, sc. 1, l. 93. [Marina]

My lord, if you did know my parentage,
You would not do me violence.
Pericles. Act v, sc. 1, l. 100. [Marina]

Report thy parentage.—*Pericles,* v, 1, 130.
What parentage?—*Twelfth Night,* v, 1, 238.
Good parentage.—*Pericles,* v, 1, 98.
Noble parentage.—*Romeo and Juliet,* iii, 5, 181.

8
Their parents were exceeding poor.
The Comedy of Errors. Act i, sc. 1, l. 57. [Ægeon]

9
A father cruel, and a step-dame false.
Cymbeline. Act i, sc. 6, l. 1. [Imogen]

10
Father and mother is man and wife; man and wife is one flesh; and so, my mother.
Hamlet. Act iv, sc. 3, l. 53. [Hamlet]

11
Obey thy parents.
King Lear. Act iii, sc. 4, l. 82. [Edgar]

Praise him that got thee, she that gave thee suck.
Troilus and Cressida. Act ii, sc. 3, l. 252. [Ulysses]

12
We are their parents and original.
A Midsummer-Night's Dream. Act ii, sc. 1, l. 117. [Titania]

13
The parents live, whose children thou hast butcher'd,
Old wither'd plants, to wail it with their age.
Richard III. Act iv, sc. 4, l. 393. [Queen Elizabeth]

Good parent.—*The Tempest,* i, 2, 94.

14
My mother's blood
Runs on the dexter cheek, and this sinister
Bounds in my father's.
Troilus and Cressida. Act iv, sc. 5, l. 127.

[Hector] The only use of "dexter." "Sinister cheek" occurs in *All's Well that Ends Well,* ii, 1, 44.

PARLEY

1
Well, by my will we shall admit no parley.
II Henry IV. Act iv, sc. 1, l. 159. [Mowbray]
Break off the parley.—*III Henry VI,* ii, 2, 110.
2
The town sounds a parley.
Henry V. Act iii, sc. 2, l. 149. [Gower]
Sounds a parley.—*Othello,* ii, 3, 23; *The Rape of Lucrece,* l. 471.
3 At your father's castle walls
We 'll crave a parley, to confer with him.
I Henry VI. Act v, sc. 3, l. 129. [Suffolk]
Calls to parley.—*Macbeth,* ii, 3, 87.
Command to parley.—*Hamlet,* i, 3, 123.
Summon a parley.—*I Henry VI,* iii, 3, 35.
4 I myself,
Rather than bloody war shall cut them short,
Will parley with Jack Cade.
II Henry VI. Act iv, sc. 4, l. 11. [King Henry]
5
They stand, and would have parley.
Julius Cæsar. Act v, sc. 1, l. 21. [Brutus]
They are at hand, To parley or to fight.
King John. Act ii, sc. 1, l. 77. [Chatillon]
Parley with sin.—*King John,* iv, 2, 238.
6
Say that the emperor requests a parley.
Titus Andronicus. Act iv, sc. 4, l. 101. [Tamora]
He craves a parley at your father's house.
Titus Andronicus. Act v, sc. 1, l. 159. [Æmilius]
7
Indeed, because you are a banish'd man,
Therefore, above the rest, we parley to you.
The Two Gentlemen of Verona. Act iv, sc. 1, l. 59. [Outlaw]

PARSON, see Preacher

PART

8 Thy father's moral parts
Mayst thou inherit too.
All's Well that Ends Well. Act i, sc. 2, l. 21. [King]
Thou wert best set thy lower part where thy nose stands.
All's Well that Ends Well. Act ii, sc. 3, l. 267. [Lafeu]
9
You take from me a great part of myself.
Antony and Cleopatra. Act iii, sc. 2, l. 24. [Cæsar]
For the most part.—*Antony and Cleopatra,* iii, 3, 34; *As You Like It,* iii, 2, 435; *Hamlet,* iii, 2, 13; *The Winter's Tale,* iv, 2, 5.
For my part.—*II Henry VI,* i, 3, 104, and thirty nine times in later plays.
Mine own poor part.—*Hamlet,* i, 5, 131.
10 My better parts
Are all thrown down, and that which here stands up
Is but a quintain, a mere lifeless block.
As You Like It. Act i, sc. 2, l. 261. [Orlando] The only use of "quintain," a post set up as a mark to be tilted at.
The better part of valour is discretion; in which better part I have saved my life.
I Henry IV. Act v, sc. 4, l. 121. [Falstaff]
Undividable, incorporate,
Am better than thy dear self's better part.
The Comedy of Errors. Act ii, sc. 2, l. 124. [Adriana] The only use of "undividable."
Mine own self's better part.—*The Comedy of Errors,* iii, 2, 61. "Better part" occurs twelve times.
11
The discontented members, the mutinous parts.
Coriolanus. Act i, sc. 1, l. 115. [Menenius]
I . . . stand upon my common part with those
That have beheld the doing.
Coriolanus. Act i, sc. 9, l. 39. [Marcius]
12
The greater part carries it.
Coriolanus. Act ii, sc. 3, l. 41. [Citizen]
Greater part.—*Julius Cæsar,* iv, 2, 29.
Greatest part.—*III Henry VI,* iii, 3, 82.
Great part.—*All's Well that Ends Well,* ii, 4, 26; *Coriolanus,* v, 6, 147; *Antony and Cleopatra,* iii, 2, 24; *Cymbeline,* iv, 3, 5.
Main part.—*Macbeth,* iv, 3, 198; *Cymbeline,* v, 4, 16.
Major part.—*Coriolanus,* ii, 1, 64.
13
You . . . that love the fundamental part of state more than you doubt the change on 't.
Coriolanus. Act iii, sc. 1, l. 151. [Coriolanus] "Fundamental" is repeated in *All's Well that Ends Well,* iii, 1, 2.
14
I have enjoyed the dearest bodily part of your mistress.
Cymbeline. Act i, sc. 4, l. 161. [Iachimo]
Fair parts.—*A Lover's Complaint,* l. 83.
Fair parts of woman.—*Henry VIII,* ii, 3, 27.
Loving parts.—*Sonnets,* xxxi.
Private part.—*Troilus and Cressida,* ii, 2, 125.
Secret parts.—*Hamlet,* ii, 2, 239.
15
Could I find out The woman's part in me!
Cymbeline, ii, 5, 20. See under WOMAN.
All is semblative a woman's part.
Twelfth Night. Act i, sc. 4, l. 34. [Duke] The only use of "semblative." "Woman's part" is used a third time in *Cymbeline,* ii, 5, 22.
Mother's part.—*Coriolanus,* v, 3, 168; *Sonnets,* cxliii.
This is a Roman's part.—*Julius Cæsar,* v, 3, 89.
16
I have resumed again The part I came in.
Cymbeline. Act v, sc. 3, l. 75. [Posthumus]
17 Your sum of parts
Did not together pluck such envy from him
As did that one.
Hamlet. Act iv, sc. 7, l. 74. [King]
18
Every part about you blasted with antiquity.
II Henry IV, i, 2, 207. See under AGE AND YOUTH.
'Tis 'semper idem,' for 'obsque hoc nihil est': 'tis all in every part.
II Henry IV. Act v, sc. 5, l. 30. [Pistol] The only use of either Latin phrase.

1
Marry, the immortal part needs a physician.
II Henry IV, ii, 2, 112. See under SOUL.
I have lost the immortal part of myself, and what remains is bestial.
Othello, ii, 3, 264. See under REPUTATION.
Immortal part.—*II Henry IV*, ii, 2, 112; *Romeo and Juliet,* v, 1, 19; *Othello,* ii, 3, 263.
Blessed part.—*Henry VIII,* iv, 2, 30.
2
Leaving their earthly parts to choke your clime,
The smell whereof shall breed a plague in France.
Henry V. Act iv, sc. 3, l. 102. [King Henry]
Brute part.—*Hamlet,* iii, 2, 110.
3
It is the part of men to fear and tremble.
Julius Cæsar, i, 3, 54. See GODS, 621:12.
4
Three parts of him Is ours already.
Julius Cæsar, i, 3, 154. See under ACCOMPLICE.
Half part.—*King John,* ii, 1, 437.
Ninth part.—*Troilus and Cressida,* ii, 1, 78.
Tenth part.—*Troilus and Cressida,* iii, 2, 95.
Third part.—*Antony and Cleopatra,* ii, 7, 96; *Coriolanus,* v, 6, 78.
Thousandth part.—*Pericles,* v, 1, 136.
Twentieth part.—*Hamlet,* iii, 4, 97.
5
Mine eye hath well examined his parts
And finds them perfect Richard.
King John, i, 1, 89. See under LIKENESS.
Remembers me of all his gracious parts.
King John, iii, 4, 96. See under GRIEF.
Choice and rarest parts.—*King Lear,* i, 4, 285.
Best part.—*King John,* v, 7, 61; *I Henry IV,* i, 3, 100; *Henry VIII,* iii, 2, 258.
Finest part.—*Antony and Cleopatra,* i, 2, 152.
Gentle part.—*Richard III,* iii, 4, 21.
Sound parts.—*All's Well that Ends Well,* ii, 1, 170.
Spacious and dilated parts.—*Troilus and Cressida,* ii, 3, 261.
Valiant parts.—*Othello,* i, 3, 254.
6
My snuff and loathed part of nature should
Burn itself out.
King Lear. Act iv, sc. 6, l. 39. [Gloucester]
Dull part.—*The Winter's Tale,* v, 1, 64.
Duller parts.—*Love's Labour 's Lost,* iv, 2, 28.
Feeble parts.—*Henry V,* ii, 4, 22.
Sickly part.—*Hamlet,* iii, 4, 80.
Slavish parts.—*Merchant of Venice,* iv, 1, 92.
Vile part.—*Romeo and Juliet,* iii, 3, 106.
Worser part.—*Hamlet,* iii, 4, 157; *The Rape of Lucrece,* l. 294.
7
A man of sovereign parts he is esteem'd.
Love's Labour 's Lost. ii, 1, 44. See under CHARACTER.
My parts had power to charm a sacred nun.
A Lover's Complaint, l. 260.
8
Your highness' part Is to receive our duties.
Macbeth. Act i, sc. 4, l. 23. [Macbeth]
It is our part.—*Timon of Athens,* v, 1, 123.
That is your part.—*Measure for Measure,* iv, 6, 3.
9
Thou art too wild, too rude and bold of voice;
Parts that become thee happily enough
And in such eyes as ours appear not faults;
But where thou art not known, why, there they show
Something too liberal.
The Merchant of Venice. Act ii, sc. 2, l. 190. [Bassanio]
10
Examined my parts with most judicious œillades.
The Merry Wives of Windsor. Act i, sc. 3, l. 67. [Falstaff] "Œillades" is repeated in *King Lear,* iv, 5, 25: "Strange œillades."
I thy parts admire.—*Love's Labour 's Lost,* iv, 2, 118; *The Passionate Pilgrim,* l. 66.
External parts.—*The Taming of the Shrew,* v, 2, 168.
Outward parts.—*King John,* v, 7, 15; *Love's Labour 's Lost,* iv, 1, 32; *The Merchant of Venice,* iii, 2, 82; *Sonnets,* xlvi; *Venus and Adonis,* l. 435.
11
A part to tear a cat in.
A Midsummer-Night's Dream, i, 2, 32. See under ACTING.
Remember your parts.—*The Merry Wives of Windsor,* v, 4, 2.
12
[He] never could maintain his part but in the force of his will.
Much Ado about Nothing. Act i, sc. 1, l. 238. [Claudio]
I will assume my part in some disguise.
Much Ado about Nothing. Act i, sc. 1, l. 323. [Don Pedro]
You may do the part of an honest man.
Much Ado about Nothing. Act ii, sc. 1, l. 172. [Don John]
Let it be thy part.—*Much Ado about Nothing,* iii, 1, 18.
13
Benedick: Tell me for which of my bad parts didst thou first fall in love with me?
Beatrice: For them all together; which maintained so politic a state of evil that they will not admit any good part to intermingle with them. But for which of my good parts did you first suffer love for me?
Much Ado about Nothing. Act v, sc. 2, l. 60. "Intermingle" is repeated in *Othello,* iii, 3, 25.
Good parts.—*As You Like It,* i, 1, 150; *Merchant of Venice,* i, 2, 46; *The Merry Wives of Windsor,* ii, 2, 110; *Much Ado about Nothing,* v, 2, 65; *Timon of Athens,* iii, 1, 40.
14
He with thee doth bear a part.
The Passionate Pilgrim, l. 428.
I can bear my part.—*Winter's Tale,* iv, 4, 301.
Never call'd to bear my part.—*Macbeth,* iii, 5, 8.
Help to bear my part.—*The Rape of Lucrece,* l. 1830.
Thou 'lt bear a part.—*Winter's Tale,* iv, 4, 299.
15
I hear say you are of honourable parts.
Pericles. Act iv, sc. 6, l. 86. [Marina]
Stuff'd, as they say, with honourable parts.
Romeo and Juliet, iii, 5, 183. See under GENTLEMAN.
She hath all courtly parts.—*Cymbeline,* iii, 5, 71.

1
Make a battery through his deafen'd parts.
Pericles, v, 1, 47. See under MAID.

2
How came you in these parts?
Pericles. Act v, sc. 1, l. 171. [Pericles]
These parts, which . . . often prove
Rough and inhospitable.
Twelfth Night. Act iii, sc. 3, l. 9. [Antonio]
In these parts.—*I Henry VI*, iv, 1, 163; *Henry V*, iii, 1, 20.
Parts remote.—*Coriolanus*, iv, 5, 148.

3
When every part a part of woe doth bear.
'Tis but a part of sorrow that we hear.
The Rape of Lucrece, l. 1327.

4
Our part therein we banish with yourselves.
Richard II. Act i, sc. 3, l. 181. [King Richard]

5
Came more and more and fought on part and part,
Till the prince came, who parted either part.
Romeo and Juliet. Act i, sc. 1, l. 121. [Benvolio]

6
Sure, that part
Was aptly fitted and naturally performed.
The Taming of the Shrew. Induction, sc. 1, l. 86. [Lord]

7
My master . . . humbly prays you
That with your other noble parts you 'll suit
In giving him his right.
Timon of Athens. Act ii, sc. 1, l. 21. [Caphis]
Noble parts.—*Timon of Athens*, ii, 2, 23.
Nobler parts.—*King John*, iii, 1, 291; *Sonnets*, cli.

8
The still and mental parts,
That do contrive how many hands shall strike,
When fitness calls them on.
Troilus and Cressida. Act i, sc. 3, l. 200. [Ulysses]
'Twixt his mental and his active parts
Kingdom'd Achilles in commotion rages.
Troilus and Cressida, ii, 3, 184. See under WORTH. The only use of "kingdom'd."

9
The parts that fortune hath bestow'd upon her,
Tell her, I hold as giddily as fortune.
Twelfth Night, ii, 4, 86. See under WOOING. "Giddily" is repeated in *Much Ado about Nothing*, iii, 3, 140.

10
Some stubborn and uncourteous parts
We had conceived against him.
Twelfth Night. Act v, sc. 1, l. 369. [Fabian]
Contrary parts.—*I Henry VI*, iii, 1, 81.
Extreme parts.—*Love's Lavour's Lost*, v, 2, 750.
Feeling part.—*Venus and Adonis*, l. 892.
Inmost part.—*Hamlet*, iii, 4, 20.
Latter part.—*Antony and Cleopatra*, iv, 6, 39.
Lion's part.—*A Midsummer-Night's Dream*, i, 2, 66; 68.
Present parts.—*II Henry VI*, v, 2, 87.
Puppet's part.—*King Lear*, ii, 2, 40.
Smallest part.—*I Henry VI*, ii, 3, 52.
Parts of man.—*The Winter's Tale*, i, 2, 400.

II—Playing a Part

11
It is a part That I shall blush in acting.
Coriolanus. Act ii, sc. 2, l. 148. [Coriolanus]
You have put me now to such a part which never
I shall discharge to the life.
Coriolanus. Act iii, sc. 2, l. 105. [Coriolanus]
Perform a part Thou hast not done before.
Coriolanus. Act iii, sc. 2, l. 109. [Volumnia]

12
Pucelle hath bravely played her part in this,
And doth deserve a coronet of gold.
I Henry VI. Act iii, sc. 3, l. 88. [Alencon]

13
I will not be slack
To play my part in Fortune's pageant.
II Henry VI. Act i, sc. 2, l. 66. [Duchess of Gloucester]

14
I would have play'd
The part my father meant to act upon
The usurper.
Henry VIII. Act i, sc. 2, l. 194. [Surveyor]
Play a part.—*The Merchant of Venice*, i, 1, 78.
Played the part.—*Much Ado about Nothing*, ii, 1, 220.
Played their parts.—*Much Ado about Nothing*, iii, 2, 79.

15
My lord, I warrant you we will play our part.
The Taming of the Shrew. Induction, sc. 1, l. 69. [Huntsman]
Play a merchant's part.—*The Taming of the Shrew*, ii, 1, 328.
Plays many parts.—*As You Like It*, ii, 7, 142.
And so he plays his part.—*As You Like It*, ii, 7, 157. See MAN, 940:12.

16
To have no screen between this part he play'd
And him he play'd it for, he needs will be
Absolute Milan.
The Tempest. Act i, sc. 2, l. 107. [Prospero]

17
Our youth got me to play the woman's part.
The Two Gentlemen of Verona. Act iv, sc. 4, l. 165. [Julia]
I did play a lamentable part.—*The Two Gentlemen of Verona*, iv, 4, 171.

III—Taking One's Part

18
All the beholders take his part with weeping.
As You Like It. Act i, sc. 2, l. 139. [Le Beau]
Take the part.—*As You Like It*, i, 3, 22.

19
You take my part from me, sir.
Coriolanus. Act iv, sc. 3, l. 55. [Volsce]

20
Your son 's my father's friend; he takes his part.
Cymbeline. Act i, sc. 1, l. 165. [Imogen]
Reignier, Duke of Anjou, doth take his part.
I Henry VI. Act i, sc. 1, l. 94. [Messenger]

21
Such
As would, but that they dare not, take our parts.
II Henry VI. Act iv, sc. 2, l. 195. [Cade]

1
Fool: Sirrah, you were best take my coxcomb.
Kent: Why, fool?
Fool: Why, for taking one's part that 's out of favour.
King Lear. Act i, sc. 4, l. 108.
Make it your cause; send down, and take my part!
King Lear, ii, 4, 195. See under AGE.
Take his part.—*King Lear,* iii, 6, 63.
Take their part.—*Macbeth,* iv, 3, 224.
2
Sweet Isabel, take my part;
Lend me your knees.
Measure for Measure. Act v, sc. 1, l. 435. [Mariana]
Take not her part.—*A Midsummer-Night's Dream,* iii, 2, 333.
3
Many a time,
When I have spoken of you dispraisingly,
Hath ta'en your part.
Othello. Act iii, sc. 3, l. 71. [Desdemona] The only use of "dispraisingly."
Taking my part.—*Romeo and Juliet,* iii, 3, 26.
Take part.—*The Tempest,* v, 1, 27.
Take them in good part.—*The Comedy of Errors,* iii, 1, 28. "Good part" is repeated in *Much Ado about Nothing,* v, 2, 64, and in *Richard II,* v, 1, 97.

PARTING

See also Departure, Farewell, Separation

4
Our parting is a tortured body.
All's Well that Ends Well. Act ii, sc. 1, l. 37. [Bertram]
5
Nay, pray you, seek no colour for your going,
But bid farewell, and go.
Antony and Cleopatra. Act i, sc. 3, l. 32. [Cleopatra]
Stand not upon the order of your going.
Macbeth, iii, 4, 119. See under DISMISSAL.
6
Sir, you and I must part, but that 's not it:
Sir, you and I have loved, but there 's not it;
That you know well.
Antony and Cleopatra. Act i, sc. 3, l. 87. [Cleopatra]
We will here part.—*Antony and Cleopatra,* iii, 2, 38.
7
Shall we be sunder'd? shall we part, sweet girl?
As You Like It. Act i, sc. 3, l. 100. [Celia]
Even as a splitted bark, so sunder we.
II Henry VI. Act iii, sc. 2, l. 411. [Suffolk]
'Twere pity
To sunder them that yoke so well together.
III Henry VI, iv, 1, 23. See under MARRIAGE.
8
Orlando: Why, whither, Adam, wouldst thou have me go?
Adam: No matter whither, so you come not here.
As You Like It. Act ii, sc. 3, l. 29.
Go thy way(s).—*The Taming of the Shrew,* iv, 5, 23, and sixteen times in later plays.
Ay, go your ways, go your ways.—*As You Like It,* iv, 1, 185; *The Merry Wives of Windsor,* i, 2, 1; iv, 1, 81.
9
Ah, do not tear away thyself from me!
For know, my love, as easy mayst thou fall
A drop of water in the breaking gulf
And take unmingled thence that drop again,
Without addition or diminishing,
As take from me thyself and not me too.
The Comedy of Errors. Act ii, sc. 2, l. 126. [Adriana] "Unmingled" is repeated in *Troilus and Cressida,* i, 3, 30.
10
Posthumus: Should we be taking leave
As long a term as yet we have to live,
The loathness to depart would grow. Adieu!
Imogen: Nay, stay a little:
Were you but riding forth to air yourself,
Such parting were too petty.
Cymbeline. Act i, sc. 1, l. 106.
11
There cannot be a pinch in death
More sharp than this is.
Cymbeline. Act i, sc. 1, l. 130. [Imogen]
Imogen: What was the last
That he spake to thee?
Pisanio: It was his queen, his queen!
Imogen: Then waved his handkerchief?
Pisano: And kiss'd it, madam.
Imogen: Senseless linen! happier therein than I!
And that was all?
Pisano: No madam; for so long
As he could make me with his eye or ear
Distinguish him from others, he did keep
The deck, with glove, or hat, or handkerchief,
Still waving, as the fits and stirs of 's mind
Could best express how slow his soul sail'd on,
How swift his ship.
Cymbeline. Act i, sc. 3, l. 4.
12
Without more circumstance at all,
I hold it fit that we shake hands and part.
Hamlet. Act i, sc. 5, l. 127. [Hamlet]
Even here Do we shake hands.—*Antony and Cleopatra,* iv, 12, 20. The only uses of "shake hands." "Shook hands" occurs four times: *III Henry VI,* i, 4, 102; *As You Like It,* v, 4, 107; *Macbeth,* i, 2, 21; *The Winter's Tale,* i, 1, 32.
13
Thou art going to the wars; and whether I shall ever see thee again or no, there is nobody cares.
II Henry IV. Act ii, sc. 4, l. 72. [Doll]
Haply you shall not see me more.
Antony and Cleopatra. Act iv, sc. 2, l. 26. [Antony]
14
My lady craves
To know the cause of your abrupt departure.
I Henry VI. Act ii, sc. 3, l. 29. [Messenger] The only use of "abrupt."
15
O, go not yet! Even thus two friends condemn'd

Embrace and kiss and take ten thousand leaves,
Loather a hundred times to part than die.
Yet now farewell; and farewell life with thee!
II Henry VI. Act iii, sc. 2, l. 353. [Queen Margaret] The only use of "loather."

Away! Though parting be a fretful corrosive,
It is applied to a deathful wound.
II Henry VI. Act iii, sc. 2, l. 403. [Queen Margaret] The only use of "deathful." "Corrosive" is repeated in *I Henry VI,* iii, 3, 3.

1
Take leave until we meet again,
Where'er it be, in heaven or in earth.
III Henry VI. Act ii, sc. 3, l. 42. [Edward] "Take leave" or "take my leave" occurs twenty-two times in the plays.

Let us all embrace:
And take our leave, until we meet in heaven.
Richard III. Act iii, sc. 3, l. 24. [Rivers]

The last leave of thee takes my weeping eye.
Richard II. Act i, sc. 2, l. 74. [Duchess of Gloucester]

Take leave and part; for you must part forthwith.
Richard II. Act v, sc. 1, l. 70. [Northumberland]

I have too grieved a heart
To take a tedious leave.
The Merchant of Venice. Act ii, sc. 7, l. 76. [Morocco]

Polonius: My honourable lord, I will most humbly take my leave of you.
Hamlet: You cannot, sir, take from me any thing that I will more willingly part withal: except my life, except my life, except my life.
Hamlet. Act ii, sc. 2, l. 217.

My wish receive,
Which great Love grant! and so, I take my leave.
All's Well that Ends Well. Act ii, sc. 3, l. 90. [Helena]

Let that be left Which leaves itself.
Antony and Cleopatra. Act iii, sc. 11, l. 19. [Antony]

Wipe not out the rest of thy services by leaving me now.
The Winter's Tale. Act iv, sc. 2, l. 11. [Polixenes]

2
So part we sadly in this troublous world,
To meet with joy in sweet Jerusalem.
III Henry VI. Act v, sc. 5, l. 7. [Queen Margaret]

'Tis time to part.—*Julius Cæsar,* ii, 1, 193.
Dumbly part.—*Richard II,* v, 1, 95.

3
Let us not be dainty of leave-taking,
But shift away.
Macbeth. Act ii, sc. 3, l. 150. [Malcolm]

Why in that rawness left you wife and child,
Those precious motives, those strong knots of love,
Without leave-taking?
Macbeth. Act iv, sc. 3, l. 26. [Malcolm] The only use of "rawness." "Leave-taking" occurs five times in the plays.

4
Turning his face, he put his hand behind him,
And with affection wondrous sensible
He wrung Bassanio's hand; and so they parted.
The Merchant of Venice. Act ii, sc. 8, l. 47. [Salarino]

5
We must starve our sight
From lovers' food till morrow deep midnight.
A Midsummer-Night's Dream. Act i, sc. 1, l. 222. [Hermia]

Alas! this parting strikes poor lovers dumb.
The Two Gentlemen of Verona. Act ii, sc. 2, l. 21. [Proteus]

6
At my parting sweetly did she smile,
In scorn or friendship, nill I construe whether.
The Passionate Pilgrim, l. 187.

7
Come on our queen: to-morrow must we part;
Be merry, for our time of stay is short.
Richard II. Act ii, sc. 1, l. 222. [King Richard]

Farewell: if heart's presages be not vain,
We three here part that ne'er shall meet again.
Richard II. Act ii, sc. 2, l. 142. [Bagot]

Queen: And must we be divided? must we part?
King Richard: Ay, hand from hand, my love, and heart from heart.
Richard II. Act v, sc. 1, l. 81.

8
Good night, good night! as sweet repose and rest
Come to thy heart as that within my breast!
Romeo and Juliet. Act ii, sc. 2, l. 123. [Juliet]

I would have thee gone:
And yet no further than a wanton's bird;
Who lets it hop a little from her hand,
Like a poor prisoner in his twisted gyves,
And with a silk thread plucks it back again,
So loving-jealous of his liberty.
Romeo and Juliet. Act ii, sc. 2, l. 177. [Juliet] The only use of "loving-jealous."

Good night, good night! parting is such sweet sorrow,
That I shall say good night till it be morrow.
Romeo and Juliet. Act ii, sc. 2, l. 185. [Juliet]

But that a joy past joy calls out on me,
It were a grief, so brief to part with thee.
Romeo and Juliet. Act iii, sc. 3, l. 173. [Romeo]

I have more care to stay than will to go.
Romeo and Juliet. Act iii, sc. 5, l. 23. [Romeo]

9
Eyes, look your last!
Arms, take your last embrace! and, lips, O you
The doors of breath, seal with a righteous kiss.
Romeo and Juliet. Act v, sc. 3, l. 113.

As easy might I from myself depart
As from my soul, which in thy breast doth lie.
Sonnets. No. cix.

10
We must all part Into this sea of air.
Timon of Athens. Act iv, sc. 2, l. 21. [Servant]

Thus part we rich in sorrow, parting poor.
Timon of Athens. Act iv, sc. 2, l. 29. [Flavius]

1
Let 's kiss and part, for we have much to do.
Titus Andronicus. Act iii, sc. 1, l. 288. [Titus]
Come, kiss; and let us part.
Troilus and Cressida. Act iv, sc. 4, l. 100. [Troilus]
2
I am gone, sir, And anon, sir,
I 'll be with you again, In a trice.
Twelfth Night. Act iv, sc. 2, l. 130. [Clown]
Direct thy feet
Where thou and I henceforth may never meet.
Twelfth Night. Act v, sc. 1, l. 171. [Duke]
3
A Jew would have wept to have seen our parting.
The Two Gentlemen of Verona. Act ii, sc. 3, l. 12. [Launce]
Hollow parting.—*Richard II,* i, 4, 9.
Present parting.—*All's Well that Ends Well,* ii, 5, 61.
4
They parted very fairly in jest.
The Two Gentlemen of Verona. Act ii, sc. 5, l. 14. [Launce]
Peace! stand aside: the company parts.
The Two Gentlemen of Verona. Act iv, sc. 2, l. 81. [Julia]
5
Part and bid good night.
Venus and Adonis, l. 534.
Let us part.—*Venus and Adonis,* l. 421.

PASS

6 Please you to give quiet pass
Through your dominions.
Hamlet. Act ii, sc. 2, l. 77. [Voltimand]
Gentle pass.—*Henry V,* ii, Prol., 39.
Permissive pass.—*Measure for Measure,* i, 3, 38. The only use of "permissive."
Strait pass.—*Cymbeline,* v, 3, 11.
Worthy pass.—*All's Well that Ends Well,* ii, 5, 58.
7
If we may pass, we will.
Henry V. Act iii, sc. 6, l. 169. [King Henry]
8
O, stay! I have no power to let her pass.
I Henry VI. Act v, sc. 3, l. 60. [Suffolk]
Let her pass by.—*II Henry VI,* ii, 4, 18.
9
Your request shall make me let it pass.
Henry V. Act v, sc. 2, l. 372. [King Henry]
For what is inward between us, let it pass.
Love's Labour's Lost. Act v, sc. 1, l. 102. [Armado]
Let it pass.—*Pericles,* ii, 3, 35.
Bid it pass.—*I Henry IV,* iv, 1, 97.
It might pass.—*All's Well that Ends Well,* ii, 3, 213.
Pray you, pass on.—*Henry VIII,* ii, 4, 130.
10
Till thou speak, thou shalt not pass from hence.
II Henry VI. Act i, sc. 4, l. 30. [Margery]
You may not pass, you must return.
Coriolanus. Act v, sc. 2, l. 5. [Sentinel]
You cannot pass. Therefore, go back.
Coriolanus. Act v, sc. 2, l. 34. [Sentinel]
Let him not pass, But kill him rather.
Othello. Act v, sc. 2, l. 241. [Montano]
You pass not here.—*Titus Andronicus,* i, 1, 290.
Thou canst not pass.—*Romeo and Juliet,* iii, 3, 149.
He shall not pass.—*Measure for Measure,* iv, 6, 12.
Pass no further.—*Coriolanus,* iii, 1, 24.
I pass not.—*II Henry VI,* iv, 2, 136.
11
Disturb him not; let him pass peaceably.
II Henry VI. Act iii, sc. 3, l. 25. [Salisbury]
O, let him pass!—*King Lear,* v, 3, 313.
Let me pass quietly.—*Timon of Athens,* iii, 4, 54.
Pass away.—*Henry VIII,* i, 4, 33.
12
Who hateth him and honours not his father, . . .
Shake he his weapon at us and pass by.
II Henry VI. Act iv, sc. 8, l. 16. [Clifford]
'Pass by and curse thy fill, but pass and stay not here thy gait.'
Timon of Athens. Act v, sc. 4, l. 73. [Alcibiades, reading] See under Epitaph.
Pass by.—*Julius Cæsar,* i, 2, 179; *Romeo and Juliet,* i, 1, 46; *Timon of Athens,* ii, 1, 12; *Troilus and Cressida,* i, 2, 199.
They pass by strangely.—*Troilus and Cressida,* iii, 3, 71.
Strangely pass.—*Sonnets,* xlix.
13
Did I let pass the abuse done to my niece?
III Henry VI. Act iii, sc. 3, l. 188. [Warwick]
14
Of great import indeed, too, but let that pass
Love's Labour's Lost. Act v, sc. 1, l. 106. [Armado]
Let that pass.—*Richard III,* iv, 2, 88; *The Merry Wives of Windsor,* i, 4, 15.
15
A thing not in his power to bring to pass.
The Merchant of Venice, i, 3, 93. See under Providence.
Bring to pass.—*The Taming of the Shrew,* iii, 2, 131.
16
We do not know what 's brought to pass.
The Merry Wives of Windsor, iv, 2, 183. See under Magic.
Lord, let me never have a cause to sigh,
Till I be brought to such a silly pass!
The Taming of the Shrew. Act v, sc. 2, l. 123. [Widow]
Brought him to this pass.—*King Lear,* iii, 4, 65.
17
How came these things to pass?
A Midsummer-Night's Dream. Act iv, sc. 1, l. 83. [Titania]
It came to pass, as most like it was.
Hamlet. Act ii, sc. 2, l. 437. [Hamlet]
It came to pass.—*A Midsummer-Night's Dream,* iii, 2, 33.
Come to pass.—*All's Well that Ends Well,* iv, 3, 371; *Antony and Cleopatra;* iv, 14, 121; *As You Like It,* ii, 5, 52; *Twelfth Night,* iii, 4, 196; *Measure for Measure,* ii, 1, 256; *Henry VIII,* i, 2, 63.
Pass away the time.—*Richard III,* i, 1, 25.

1
My lord, will 't please you pass along?
Richard III. Act iii, sc. 1, l. 136. [Gloucester]
So shall we pass along And never stir assailants.
As You Like It. Act i, sc. 3, l. 115. [Celia]
On, there; pass along!—*Antony and Cleopatra,* iii, 1, 37.
Pass along.—*III Henry VI,* ii, 1, 195; *The Two Gentlemen of Verona,* v, 4, 168; *Troilus and Cressida,* iii, 3, 51.
2
Nay, an thou pass upon me, I 'll no more with thee.
Twelfth Night. Act iii, sc. 1, l. 48. [Viola]
3
Let me pass The same I am.
The Winter's Tale. Act iv, sc. 9, l. 9. [Time]
Pass this way.—*The Winter's Tale,* iv, 4, 20.

PASSAGE

4
O, that 'had'! how sad a passage 'tis!
All's Well that Ends Well. Act i, sc. 1, l. 20. [Countess]
5
Now in the stirring passage of the day.
The Comedy of Errors. Act iii, sc. 1, l. 99. [Balthazar]
There is gallant and most prave passages.
Henry V. Act iii, sc. 6, l. 97. [Fluellen]
Bloody passage.—*Coriolanus,* v, 6, 70.
Bright passage.—*Richard II,* iii, 3, 67.
Common passage.—*Cymbeline,* iii, 4, 94.
Easiest passage.—*The Winter's Tale,* iii, 2, 91.
False passage.—*Richard II,* i, 1, 125.
Foreign passages.—*Richard II,* i, 3, 272.
Hollow passage.—*I Henry VI,* v, 4, 121.
Honey passage.—*Venus and Adonis,* l. 452.
Impossible passages.—*Twelfth Night,* iii, 2, 77.
Muddy passages.—*Richard II,* v, 3, 62.
Sweet passage.—*III Henry VI,* ii, 3, 41.
Swift passage.—*The Winter's Tale,* iv, 1, 5.
Unhidden passages.—*Henry V,* i, 1, 86. The only use of "unhidden."
6
Now she is there, how will she specify
Where is the best and safest passage in?
I Henry VI. Act iii, sc. 2, l. 21. [Bastard]
7
Like valour's minion carved out his passage.
Macbeth. Act i, sc. 2, l. 19. [Sargeant]
Cut their passage.—*Henry V,* ii, 2, 16.
Make good the passage.—*Cymbeline,* v, 3, 23.
Passage free.—*Othello,* i, 2, 98.
8
The sullen passage of thy weary steps.
Richard II, i, 3, 265. See under BANISHMENT.
The fearful passage of their death-mark'd love.
Romeo and Juliet. Prologue, l. 9. The only use of "death-mark'd."
How sad a passage.—*All's Well that Ends Well,* i, 1, 20.
9
Keep then this passage to the Capitol.
Titus Andronicus. Act i, sc. 1, l. 12. [Bassianus]
No passage.—*Othello,* v, 1, 37.
Stopp'd the passage.—*III Henry VI,* i, 3, 22.
Struggling for passage.—*Venice and Adonis,* l. 1047.
Passage to remorse.—*Macbeth,* i, 5, 45.
Passages of alleys.—*Comedy of Errors,* iv, 2, 38.
Passages of life.—*I Henry IV,* iii, 2, 8.
Passages of proof.—*Hamlet,* iv, 7, 113.

PASSENGER

10
Fellows, stand fast; I see a passenger.
The Two Gentlemen of Verona. Act iv, sc. 1, l. 1. [Outlaw]
My mates . . .
Have some unhappy passenger in chase.
The Two Gentlemen of Verona. Act v, sc. 4, l. 14. [Valentine]
Poor passengers.—*II Henry VI,* iii, 1, 129; *The Two Gentlemen of Verona,* iv, 1, 72.
Relenting passengers.—*II Henry VI,* iii, 1, 227
Rob our passengers.—*Richard II,* v, 3, 9.
11
Never did passenger in summer's heat
More thirst for drink than she for this good turn.
Venus and Adonis, l. 91.

PASSION

See also Anger

12
Your passions Have to the full appeach'd.
All's Well that Ends Well. Act i, sc. 3, l. 196. [Countess] The only use of "appeach'd," to give accusatory evidence.
Her passions are made of nothing but the finest part of pure love.
Antony and Cleopatra. Act i, sc. 2, l. 151. [Enobarbus]
What 's thy passion?—*Antony and Cleopatra,* iii, 10, 5.
13
What passion hangs these weights upon my tongue?
As You Like It. Act i, sc. 2, l. 269. [Orlando]
Jove, Jove! this shepherd's passion
Is much upon my fashion.
As You Like It. Act ii, sc. 4, l. 61. [Rosalind]
For every passion something and for no passion truly any thing.
As You Like It. Act iii, sc. 2, l. 433. [Rosalind]
14 Till this afternoon his passion
Ne'er brake into extremity of rage.
The Comedy of Errors. Act v, sc. 1, l. 47. [Adriana]
15
Tear a passion to tatters.
Hamlet. Act iii, sc. 2, l. 11. [Hamlet] The only use of "tatters." See ACTING, 10:11.
What to ourselves in passion we propose,
The passion ending, doth the purpose lose.
Hamlet. Act iii, sc. 2, l. 204. [Player King]
16
This strained passion doth you wrong.
II Henry IV. Act i, sc. 1, l. 161. [Travers]
Base passions.—*I Henry VI,* v, 2, 18.
Cock's passion.—*The Taming of the Shrew,* iv, 1, 121.
Gross passion.—*Henry V,* ii, 2, 132.
Hot passion.—*Troilus and Cressida,* ii, 2, 169.
Ireful passion.—*Comedy of Errors,* v, 1, 151.
Merry passion.—*The Taming of the Shrew,* Ind., 1, 97.
Poor passion.—*Antony and Cleopatra,* iv, 15, 74.
Precedent passions.—*Timon of Athens,* i, 1, 133.
Settled passions.—*I Henry VI,* v, 5, 4.

Stormy passion.—*II Henry IV*, i, 1, 165.

Strong passion.—*All's Well that Ends Well*, i, 3, 139.

Towering passion.—*Hamlet*, v, 2, 80.

1
His passions, like a whale on ground,
Confound themselves with working.
II Henry IV, iv, 4, 40. See under BEHAVIOUR.

2 Had the passions of thy heart burst out,
I fear we should have seen decipher'd there
More rancorous spite, more furious raging broils,
Than yet can be imagined or supposed.
I Henry VI. Act iv, sc. 1, l. 183. [Exeter]

3
Beshrew me, but this passion moves me so
That hardly can I check my eyes from tears.
III Henry VI. Act i, sc. 4, l. 150. [Northumberland]

For lo, his passion, but an art of craft,
Even then, resolved my reason into tears.
A Lover's Complaint, l. 295.

4
This is it that makes me bridle passion.
III Henry VI. Act iv, sc. 4, l. 19. [Queen Elizabeth]

5 Vexed I am
Of late with passions of some difference.
Julius Cæsar. Act i, sc. 2, l. 39. [Brutus]

I have much mistook your passion.—*Julius Cæsar*, i, 2, 48.

Passion, I see, is catching.
Julius Cæsar, iii, 1, 283. See EYE, 452:11.

6
His passion is so ripe, it needs must break.
King John. Act iv, sc. 2, l. 79. [Salisbury]

7
I heard your guilty rhymes, observed your fashion,
Saw sighs reek from you, noted well your passion.
Love's Labour's Lost. Act iv, sc. 3, l. 139. [King]

Move him to passion.—*Love's Labour's Lost*, iv, 3, 202.

8 This noble passion,
Child of integrity, hath from my soul
Wiped the black scruples.
Macbeth. Act iv, sc. 3, l. 114. [Malcolm]

Notable passion.—*The Winter's Tale*, v, 2, 17.

9
I never heard a passion so confused,
So strange, outrageous, and so variable.
The Merchant of Venice. Act ii, sc. 8, l. 13. [Salanio] "Variable" is used six times.

All other passions fleet to air,
As doubtful thoughts.
The Merchant of Venice. Act iii, sc. 2, l. 108. [Portia]

10
You spend your passion on a misprised mood.
A Midsummer-Night's Dream. Act iii, sc. 2, l. 74. [Demetrius]

This passion, and the death of a dear friend, would go near to make a man look sad.
A Midsummer-Night's Dream. Act v, sc. 1, l. 293. [Theseus]

Her passion ends the play.
A Midsummer-Night's Dream. Act v, sc. 1, l. 321. [Theseus]

11
No; rather I will go to Benedick
And counsel him to fight against his passion.
Much Ado about Nothing. Act iii, sc. 1, l. 82. [Hero]

12
My blood begins my safer guides to rule;
And passion, having my best judgement collied,
Assays to lead the way.
Othello. Act ii, sc. 3, l. 205. [Othello] "Collied" (darkened) is repeated in *A Midsummer-Night's Dream* i, 1, 145: "Collied night."

You are eaten up with passion.
Othello. Act iii, sc. 3, l. 391. [Othello]

O well-painted passion!
Othello. Act iv, sc. 1, l. 268. [Othello] "Well-painted" is repeated in *Venus and Adonis*, l. 212, and in *The Rape of Lucrece*, l. 1443.

Some bloody passion shakes your very frame.
Othello. Act v, sc. 2, l. 44. [Desdemona]

13 The passions of the mind,
That have their first conception by mis-dread,
Have after-nourishment and life by care.
Pericles. Act i, sc. 2, l. 12. [Pericles] The only use of "mis-dread" and "after-nourishment."

This borrow'd passion stands for true old woe.
Pericles. Act iv, sc. 4, l. 24. [Gower]

14 The life and feeling of her passion
She hoards.
The Rape of Lucrece, l. 1317.

Such passion her assails,
That patience is quite beaten from her breast.
The Rape of Lucrece, l. 1562.

15
Passion lends them power.
Romeo and Juliet. Act ii, Prologue, l. 13. [Chorus]

Thou overheard'st, ere I was ware,
My true love's passion.
Romeo and Juliet. Act ii, sc. 2, l. 103. [Juliet]

16
Ferdinand: Your father's in some passion
That works him strongly.
Miranda: Never till this day
Saw I him touch'd with anger so distemper'd.
The Tempest. Act iv, sc. 1, l. 143.

17
O, you gods, I feel my master's passion!
Timon of Athens. Act iii, sc. 1, l. 58. [Flaminius]

With such sober and unnoted passion
He did behave his anger.
Timon of Athens. Act iii, sc. 5, l. 21. [Alcibiades]

18
Is not my sorrow deep, having no bottom?
Then be my passions bottomless with them.
Titus Andronicus. Act iii, sc. 1, l. 217. [Titus] "Bottomless" is repeated in *As You Like It*, iv, 1, 214.

1
Even such a passion doth embrace my bosom.
Troilus and Cressida. Act iii, sc. 2, l. 37. [Troilus]
Your passion draws ears hither.
Troilus and Cressida. Act v, sc. 2, l. 181. [Ulysses]
2
Trembling in her passion.
Venus and Adonis, l. 27.
Swelling passion doth provoke a pause.
Venus and Adonis, l. 218.
Passion on passion deeply is redoubled.
Venus and Adonis, l. 832.
Variable passions throng her constant woe,
As striving who should best become her grief.
Venus and Adonis, l. 967.
Dumbly she passions, franticly she doteth.
Venus and Adonis, l. 1059. "Franticly" is repeated in *Titus Andronicus,* iii, 2, 31.
3
Fear you his tyrannous passion more, alas,
Than the queen's life?
Winter's Tale. Act ii, sc. 3, l. 28. [Paulina]

PAST

4
Things that are past are done with me.
Antony and Cleopatra. Act i, sc. 2, l. 101. [Antony]
Things past.—*Sonnets,* xxx; *Troilus and Cressida,* iii, 3, 177.
5
O thoughts of men accursed!
Past and to come seems best; things present worst.
II Henry IV. Act i, sc. 3, l. 107. [Archbishop of York]
Not wondering at the present nor the past.
Sonnets. No. cxxiii.
What they do in present,
Though less than yours in past, much o'ertop yours.
Troilus and Cressida. Act iii, sc. 3, l. 163. [Ulysses]
Every present time doth boast itself
Above a better gone.
The Winter's Tale. Act v, sc. 1, l. 96. [Paulina]
6
Pick'd from the worm-holes of long-vanish'd days.
Henry V. Act ii, sc. 4, l. 86. [Duke of Exeter] The only use of "long-vanish'd." "Worm-holes" is repeated in *The Rape of Lucrece,* l. 946.
His days and times are past.
Timon of Athens. Act i, sc. 2, l. 21. [Senator]
In the times past.—*Macbeth,* iii, 1, 77.
Thou seest what 's past.—*III Henry VI,* iii, 3, 226.
That is past.—*Richard III,* iv, 4, 364; *Henry VIII,* iv, 1, 95.
'Tis past.—*King Lear,* v, 3, 164; *Troilus and Cressida,* v, 2, 97.
Past and gone.—*Othello,* i, 3, 204.
7
What 's past and what 's to come she can descry.
I Henry VI. Act i, sc. 2, l. 57. [Bastard]
What 's past and what 's to come is strew'd with husks
And formless ruin of oblivion.
Troilus and Cressida. Act iv, sc. 5, l. 166. [Agamemnon]
8
To-morrow, and to-morrow, and to-morrow,
Creeps in this petty pace from day to day
To the last syllable of recorded time,
And all our yesterdays have lighted fools
The way to dusty death.
Macbeth. Act v, sc. 5, l. 19. [Macbeth]
9
Queen Elizabeth: What canst thou swear by now?
King Richard: The time to come.
Queen Elizabeth: That thou hast wronged in the time o'erpast;
For I myself have many tears to wash
Hereafter time, for time past wrong'd by thee. . . .
Swear not by time to come; for that thou hast
Misused ere used, by time misused o'erpast.
Richard III. Act iv, sc. 4, l. 387. The only use of "o'erpast."
10
Our dates are brief, and therefore we admire
What thou dost foist upon us that is old.
Sonnets. No. cxxiii. The only use of "foist."
11
I must
Once in a month recount what thou hast been,
Which thou forget'st.
The Tempest. Act i, sc. 2, l. 261. [Prospero]
What 's past is prologue.
The Tempest. Act ii, sc. 1, l. 253. [Antonio]
The best is past.
The Tempest. Act iii, sc. 3, l. 51. [Alonso]

PASTIME

12
Make pastime with us a day or two, or longer.
Cymbeline. Act iii, sc. 1, l. 78. [Cloten]
13
We have had pastimes here and pleasant game.
Love's Labour 's Lost. Act v, sc. 2, l. 360. [Princess of France]
We will with some strange pastime solace them.
Love's Labour 's Lost. Act iv, sc. 3, l. 377. [Biron]
Here 's some good pastime toward.—*The Taming of the Shrew,* i, 1, 68.
Did you assay him To any pastime?—*Hamlet,* iii, 1, 15.
14
It will be pastime passing excellent,
If it be husbanded with modesty.
The Taming of the Shrew. Induction, sc. 1, l. 67. [Lord]
15
Make a pastime of every weary step.
The Two Gentlemen of Verona. Act ii, sc. 7, l. 35. [Julia]

PASTURE

1 Anon a careless herd,
Full of the pasture, jumps along by him.
As You Like It. Act ii, sc. 1, l. 52. [Lord]

2
Good pasture makes fat sheep.
As You Like It. Act iii, sc. 2, l. 28. [Corin]

It is the pasture lards the rother's sides.
Timon of Athens. Act iv, sc. 3, l. 12. [Timon] The only use of "rother" (ox).

Graze as you find pasture.—*Cymbeline,* v, 4, 2.

3
They sell the pasture now to buy the horse.
Henry V. Act ii, Prol., l. 5. [Chorus]

4
Too small a pasture for such store of muttons.
The Two Gentlemen of Verona. Act i, sc. 1, l. 105. [Proteus]

PATCH

5
O madam, yonder 's my lord your son with a patch of velvet on 's face: . . . a goodly patch of velvet.
All's Well that Ends Well. Act iv, sc. 5, l. 99. [Clown]

6
Antony: If you 'll patch a quarrel,
As matter whole you have not to make it with,
It must not be with this. . . .
Cæsar: You patch'd up your excuses.
Antony and Cleopatra. Act ii, sc. 2, l. 52.

Patch a wall.—*Hamlet,* v, 1, 239.

7
What patch is made our porter?
The Comedy of Errors. Act iii, sc. 1, l. 36. [Dromio of Ephesus]

The patch is kind enough, but a huge feeder.
The Merchant of Venice. Act ii, sc. 5, l. 46. [Shylock]

A crew of patches.—*A Midsummer-Night's Dream,* iii, 2, 9.

Scurvy patch!—*The Tempest,* iii, 2, 71.

8 This must be patch'd
With cloth of any colour.
Coriolanus. Act iii, sc. 1, l. 252. [Menenius]

Patch'd with foul moles.—*King John,* iii, 1, 47.

9
We go to gain a little patch of ground
That hath in it no profit but the name.
To pay five ducats, five, I would not farm it.
Hamlet. Act iv, sc. 4, l. 18. [Captain]

10
Patches set upon a little breech
Discredit more in hiding of the fault
Than did the fault before it was so patched.
King John, iv, 2, 32. See under FAULT.

Patch-breech.—*Pericles,* ii, 1, 14. The only use of the phrase.

11
Anything that 's mended is but patched: virtue that transgresses is but patched with sin; and sin that amends is but patched with virtue.
Twelfth Night. Act i, sc. 5, l. 52. [Clown]

PATE

See also Head

12
I have some marks of yours upon my pate.
The Comedy of Errors. Act i, sc. 2, l. 82. [Dromio of Ephesus]

Adriana: Back, slave, or I will break thy pate across.
Dromio of Ephesus: And he will bless that cross with other beating;
Between you I shall have a holy head.
The Comedy of Errors. Act ii, sc. 1, l. 78.

Breaks my pate across.—*Hamlet,* ii, 2, 599. See also *The Comedy of Errors,* ii, 2, 220; iii, 1, 74; *All's Well that Ends Well,* ii, 1, 68; *Cymbeline,* ii, 1, 8.

Peat his pate.—*Henry V,* v, 1, 43.

I 'll knock your knave's pate.—*The Taming of the Shrew,* i, 2, 12.

13
Is this the fine of his fines, and the recovery of his recoveries, to have his fine pate full of fine dirt?
Hamlet. Act v, sc. 1, l. 113. [Hamlet]

14
There is a groat to heal your pate. . . . God be w' you, and keep you, and heal your pate.
Henry V. Act v, sc. 1, l. 61. [Fluellen]

15
A curled pate will grow bald.
Henry V. Act v, sc. 2, l. 169. [King Henry]

Bald pate.—*The Comedy of Errors,* ii, 2, 71.

Lean pates.—*Love's Labour 's Lost,* i, 1, 26.

Singeing his pate.—*Hamlet,* v, 1, 305. The only use of "singeing."

16
The bishop and the Duke of Gloucester's men . . .
Do pelt so fast at one another's pate
That many have their giddy brains knocked out.
I Henry VI. Act iii, sc. 1, l. 78. [Mayor]

17
Chop away that factious pate of his.
II Henry VI. Act v, sc. 1, l. 135. [Clifford]

PATH

See also Course, Way

18
We walk not in the trodden paths.
As You Like It. Act i, sc. 3, l. 15. [Rosalind]

Familiar paths.—*Henry V,* ii, 4, 52.

19
And ask him why, that hour of fairy revel,
In their so sacred paths he dares to tread
In shape profane.
The Merry Wives of Windsor. Act iv, sc. 4, l. 58. [Mrs. Page]

Church-way paths.—*A Midsummer-Night's Dream,* v, 1, 389. The only use of "church-way."

Good path.—*Measure for Measure,* iv, 3, 138.

20
Tread the stranger paths of banishment.
Richard II. Act i, sc. 3, l. 143. [King Richard]

Go, tread the path that thou shalt ne'er return.
Richard III. Act i, sc. 1, l. 117. [Gloucester]

She treads the path that she untreads again.
Venus and Adonis, l. 908.

1
I have found the path.
Titus Andronicus. Act ii, sc. 1, l. 110. [Aaron]
Here is a path.—*Cymbeline,* iii, 6, 18.
2
The path is smooth that leadeth on to danger.
Venus and Adonis, l. 788.
The primrose path of dalliance.—*Hamlet,* i, 3, 50. See PREACHER, 1190:13, for full quotation.
Keep then the path.—*Troilus and Cressida,* iii, 3, 155.
Out of the path.—*King John,* iii, 4, 129.

PATIENCE

3
With patience more
Than savages could suffer.
Antony and Cleopatra. Act i, sc. 4, l. 59. [Cæsar]
Be ever known to patience.
Antony and Cleopatra. Act iii, sc. 6, l. 98. [Cæsar]
Think upon patience.—*All's Well that Ends Well,* iii, 2, 50.
4
Patience is sottish, and impatience does
Become a dog that 's mad.
Antony and Cleopatra. Act iv, sc. 15, l. 79. [Cleopatra] The only use of "sottish."
5
Her very silence and her patience
Speak to the people.
As You Like It. Act i, sc. 3, l. 80. [Duke]
Patience herself would startle at this letter
And play the swaggerer.
As You Like It. Act iv, sc. 3, l. 13. [Rosalind]
6
So thou, that hast no unkind mate to grieve thee,
With urging helpless patience wouldst relieve me;
But, if thou live to see like right bereft,
This fool-begg'd patience in thee will be left.
The Comedy of Errors. Act ii, sc. 1, l. 38. [Adriana] The only use of "fool-begg'd."
My master preaches patience to him.
The Comedy of Errors. Act v, sc. 1, l. 174. [Servant]
Patience unmoved!—*Comedy of Errors,* ii, 1, 32.
7
Luciana: Have patience, I beseech.
Adriana: I cannot, nor I will not, hold me still.
The Comedy of Errors. Act iv, sc. 2, l. 16.
Have patience and endure.
Much Ado about Nothing. Act iv, sc. 1, l. 256. [Friar Francis]
I do beseech you, sir, have patience.
Romeo and Juliet. Act v, sc. 1, l. 27. [Balthasar]
Beseech your patience.—*Cymbeline,* i, 1, 153.
Entreat your patience.—*The Two Gentlemen of Verona,* iv, 4, 116.
Bid them have patience.—*Troilus and Cressida,* iv, 4, 54.
Have patience.—*I Henry VI,* i, 3, 18, and frequently in later plays.

You must have patience.—*Macbeth,* iv, 2, 2.
God's patience.—*The Merry Wives of Windsor,* i, 4, 5.
Great patience.—*Henry VIII,* iii, 1, 137.
Mild patience.—*The Rape of Lucrece,* l. 1268.
Strict patience.—*Love's Labour's Lost,* iv, 3, 165.
Tender patience.—*Richard II,* ii, 1, 207.
Tongue-tied patience.—*Sonnets,* cxl.
8
A very little thief of occasion will rob you of a great deal of patience.
Coriolanus. Act ii, sc. 1, l. 31. [Menenius]
Were I as patient as the midnight sleep,
By Jove, 'twould be my mind!
Coriolanus. Act iii, sc. 1, l. 85. [Coriolanus]
9
'Twere good
You lean'd unto his sentence with what patience
Your wisdom may inform you.
Cymbeline. Act i, sc. 1, l. 77. [Queen]
If you'll be patient, I'll no more be mad;
That cures us both.
Cymbeline. Act ii, sc. 3, l. 108. [Imogen]
Quite besides The government of patience.
Cymbeline. Act ii, sc. 4, l. 149. [Philario]
10
Upon the heat and flame of thy distemper
Sprinkle cool patience.
Hamlet. Act iii, sc. 4, l. 123. [Queen]
Be you content to lend your patience to us.
Hamlet. Act iv, sc. 5, l. 210. [King]
Strengthen your patience in our last night's speech.
Hamlet. Act v, sc. 1, l. 317. [King]
11
You tread upon my patience.
I Henry IV. Act i, sc. 3, l. 4. [King Henry]
Your coming hither have done enough
To put him quite beside his patience.
I Henry IV. Act iii, sc. 1, l. 178. [Worcester]
12
I am as poor as Job, my lord, but not so patient.
II Henry IV. Act i, sc. 2, l. 144. [Falstaff]
13
I was lately here . . . to pray your patience.
II Henry IV. Epilogue, l. 10.
I know not how to pray your patience.
Much Ado about Nothing. Act v, sc. 1, l. 281. [Claudio]
I pray you, sir, take patience.—*King Lear,* ii, 4, 140.
14
Linger your patience on.
Henry V. Act ii, Prologue, l. 31. [Chorus]
Sit patiently.—*Henry V,* iv, Prol., 24.
I took all patiently.—*Rape of Lucrece,* l. 1641.
15
Though patience be a tired mare, yet she will plod.
Henry V. Act ii, sc. 1, l. 26. [Nym]
16
I pray thee, sort thy heart to patience.
II Henry VI. Act ii, sc. 4, l. 68. [Gloucester]
Your humble patience pray.—*Henry V,* Prol., 33.
Pray you, use your patience.—*The Merry Wives of Windsor,* iii, 1, 84.

1
Patience is for poltroons.
III Henry VI. Act i, sc. 1, l. 62. [Clifford] The only use of "poltroons."

Who can be patient in such extremes?
III Henry VI. Act i, sc. 1, l. 215. [Queen Margaret]

Why art thou patient, man? thou shouldst be mad.
III Henry VI. Act i, sc. 4, l. 89. [Queen Margaret]

2
With patience calm the storm.
III Henry VI. Act iii, sc. 3, l. 38. [King Lewis]

Sends me a paper to persuade me patience.
III Henry VI. Act iii, sc. 3, l. 176. [King Lewis]

3 I am much too venturous
In tempting of your patience.
Henry VIII. Act i, sc. 2, l. 54. [Queen Katharine]

Sweetly
In all the rest show'd a most noble patience.
Henry VIII. Act ii, sc. 1, l. 35. [Gentleman]

You must take
Your patience to you and be well contented.
Henry VIII. Act v, sc. 1, l. 104. [King]

Lay all the weight ye can upon my patience.
Henry VIII. Act v, sc. 3, l. 66. [Cranmer]

I attend with patience.—*Henry VIII,* v, 2, 19.

I 'll stay with patience.—*Love's Labour 's Lost,* v, 2, 845.

4 Many a time and oft
Have you climb'd up to walls and battlements,
To towers and windows, yea, to chimney-tops,
Your infants in your arms, and there have sat
The live-long day, with patient expectation.
Julius Cæsar. Act i, sc. 1, l. 42. [Marullus] The only use of "chimney-tops." "Chimney's top" occurs in *III Henry VI,* v, 6, 47.

Can I bear that with patience?
Julius Cæsar. Act ii, sc. 1, l. 301. [Portia]

Arming myself with patience.
Julius Cæsar. Act v, sc. 1, l. 106. [Brutus]

5
He is more patient Than when you left him.
King John. Act v, sc. 7, l. 11. [Pembroke]

6
I will be the pattern of all patience.
King Lear. Act iii, sc. 2, l. 37. [King Lear]

Where is the patience now,
That you so oft have boasted to retain?
King Lear. Act iii, sc. 6, l. 61. [Kent] The only use of "boasted."

Patience and sorrow strove
Who should express her goodliest.
King Lear. Act iv, sc. 3, l. 18. [Gentleman] "Goodliest" is repeated in *Titus Andronicus,* iv, 2, 11: "Goodliest weapons"; and in *Henry VIII,* iv, 1, 69: "Goodliest woman."

7
I thank God I have as little patience as another man; and therefore I can be quiet.
Love's Labour 's Lost. Act i, sc. 2, l. 170. [Costard]

8
God grant us patience!
Love's Labour 's Lost. Act i, sc. 1, l. 196. [Longaville]

God give me patience.
Much Ado about Nothing. Act ii, sc. 3, l. 154. [Claudio]

O you blessed ministers above
Keep me in patience.
Measure for Measure. Act v, sc. 1, l. 115. [Isabella]

You heavens, give me that patience, patience I need!
King Lear. Act ii, sc. 4, l. 274. [King Lear]

Patience, be near me still.
Henry VIII. Act iv, sc. 2, l. 76. [Katharine]

9 Do you find
Your patience so predominant in your nature?
Macbeth. Act iii, sc. 1, l. 86. [Macbeth]

10
My patience here is touch'd.
Measure for Measure. Act v, sc. 1, l. 235. [Angelo]

11
Still have I borne it with a patient shrug.
The Merchant of Venice. Act i, sc. 3, l. 110. [Shylock] "Shrug" is used four times.

I do oppose
My patience to his fury, and am arm'd
To suffer, with a quietness of spirit,
The very tyranny and rage of his.
The Merchant of Venice. Act iv, sc. 1, l. 10. [Antonio]

12
At most odds with his own gravity and patience.
The Merry Wives of Windsor. Act iii, sc. 1, l. 54. [Page]

13
She in mild terms begg'd my patience.
A Midsummer-Night's Dream. Act iv, sc. 1, l. 61. [Oberon]

I know your patience well.—*A Midsummer-Night's Dream,* iii, 1, 197.

14
Out, dog! out, cur! thou drivest me past the bounds
Of maiden's patience.
A Midsummer-Night's Dream. Act iii, sc. 2, l. 65. [Hermia]

They vex me past my patience!
Henry VIII. Act ii, sc. 4, l. 130. [Queen Katharine]

I'm out of patience.—*The Tempest,* i, 1, 58.

Laugh'd him out of patience.—*Antony and Cleopatra,* ii, 5, 19.

Talk him out of patience.—*Othello,* iii, 3, 23.

15
Bring me a father that so loved his child,
Whose joy of her is overwhelm'd like mine,
And bid him speak of patience.
Much Ado about Nothing. Act v, sc. 1, l. 8. [Leonato]

I of him will gather patience.
Much Ado about Nothing. Act v, sc. 1, l. 19. [Leonato]

'Tis all men's office to speak patience
To those that wring under the load of sorrow,
But no man's virtue nor sufficiency

To be so moral when he shall endure
The like himself.
Much Ado about Nothing. Act v, sc. 1, l. 27. [Leonato]

Gentlemen both, we will not wake your patience.
Much Ado about Nothing. Act v, sc. 1, l. 102. [Don Pedro]

1 What cannot be preserved when fortune takes,
Patience her injury a mockery makes.
Othello. Act i, sc. 3, l. 206. [Duke]

He bears the sentence well that nothing bears
But the free comfort which from thence he hears,
But he bears both the sentence and the sorrow
That, to pay grief, must of poor patience borrow.
Othello. Act i, sc. 3, l. 212. [Brabantio]

How poor are they that have not patience!
Othello. Act ii, sc. 3, l. 376. [Iago]

Confine yourself but in a patient list.
Othello. Act iv, sc. 1, l. 76. [Iago]

I will be found most cunning in my patience;
But—dost thou hear?—most bloody.
Othello. Act iv, sc. 1, l. 91. [Othello]

Patience, thou young and rose-lipp'd cherubin.
Othello. Act iv, sc. 2, l. 63. [Othello] The only use of "rose-lipp'd."

2 Marry, patience;
Or I shall say you are all in all in spleen,
And nothing of a man.
Othello. Act iv, sc. 1, l. 88. [Iago]

Patience, good lady.—*II Henry VI,* i, 4, 18. "Patience" is used in this way frequently in later plays.

Patience, I pray you.—*The Taming of the Shrew,* iv, 1, 159.

Patience awhile.—*Coriolanus,* i, 1, 130; *Othello,* v, 1, 87.

3 Yet can I not of such tame patience boast
As to be hush'd and nought at all to say.
Richard II. Act i, sc. 1, l. 52. [Thomas Mowbray]

Patience is stale, and I am weary of it.
Richard II. Act v, sc. 5, l. 104. [King Richard]

4 I can no longer hold me patient.
Richard III. Act i, sc. 3, l. 157. [Queen Margaret]

How long shall I be patient? ah, how long?
Richard II. Act ii, sc. 1, l. 163. [York]

5 Either be patient, and entreat me fair,
Or with the clamorous report of war
Thus will I drown your exclamations.
Richard III. Act iv, sc. 4, l. 151. [King Richard]

Be patient, for the world is broad and wide.
Romeo and Juliet. Act iii, sc. 3, l. 16. [Friar Laurence]

Cardinal Wolsey: Be patient yet.
Queen Katharine: I will, when you are humble.
Henry VIII. Act ii, sc. 4, l. 73.

Will you be patient?—*Julius Cæsar,* iii, 2, 154.

Be patient till the last.—*Julius Cæsar,* iii, 2, 12.

Nay, good, be patient.—*The Tempest,* i, 1, 16.

Be patient.—*II Henry VI,* i, 3, 68, and twenty times in later plays.

Patient yourself, madam.—*Titus Andronicus,* i, 1, 121.

6 Patiently hear my impatience.
Richard III. Act iv, sc. 4, l. 156. [Duchess of York]

By your patience.—*Richard III,* iv, 1, 15, and seven times in later plays.

7 Patience perforce with wilful choler meeting
Makes my flesh tremble in their different greeting.
Romeo and Juliet. Act i, sc. 5, l. 91. [Tybalt]

Hear me with patience.—*Romeo and Juliet,* iii, 5, 160; *The Taming of the Shrew,* i, 2, 239; *Cymbeline,* iii, 4, 115.

8 Bear this work of heaven with patience.
Romeo and Juliet. Act v, sc. 3, l. 261. [Friar Laurence]

Bear with patience
Such griefs as you yourself do lay upon yourself.
Pericles. Act i, sc. 2, l. 65. [Helicanus]

I shall with aged patience bear your yoke.
Pericles. Act ii, sc. 4, l. 48. [Helicanus]

9 Patience, tame to sufferance.
Sonnets. No. lviii.

Patience herself, what goddess e'er she be,
Doth lesser blench at sufferance than I do.
Troilus and Cressida. Act i, sc. 1, l. 27. [Troilus]

10 For patience she will prove a second Grissel.
The Taming of the Shrew. Act ii, sc. 1, l. 297. [Petruchio] The only reference to Grissel in the plays—the patient Griselda, of course, of Boccaccio.

11 Patience Says it is past her cure.
The Tempest. Act v, sc. 1, l. 140. [Alonso]

Why have I patience to endure all this?
Titus Andronicus. Act ii, sc. 3, l. 88. [Tamora]

12 Pandarus: He that will have a cake out of the wheat must needs tarry the grinding.
Trojan: Have I not tarried?
Pandarus: Ay, the grinding; but you must tarry the bolting.
Troilus: Have I not tarried?
Pandarus: Ay, the bolting, but you must tarry the leavening.
Troilus: Still have I tarried.
Pandarus: Ay, to the leavening; but here's yet in the word 'hereafter' the kneading, the making of the cake, the heating of the oven and the baking; nay, you must stay the cooling too, or you may chance to burn your lips.
Troilus and Cressida. Act i, sc. 1, l. 15. The only use of "baking."

13 Whose patience Is, as a virtue.
Troilus and Cressida. Act i, sc. 2, l. 4. [Alexander]

There is between my will and all offences
A guard of patience.
Troilus and Cressida. Act v, sc. 2, l. 53. [Troilus]

I will not be myself, nor have cognition
Of what I feel: I am all patience.
Troilus and Cressida. Act v, sc. 2, l. 63. [Troilus] The only use of "cognition."

You have sworn patience.—*Troilus and Cressida,* v, 2, 62.

I did swear patience.—*Troilus and Cressida,* v, 2, 84.

1
I will be patient; outwardly I will.
Troilus and Cressida. Act v, sc. 2, l. 68. [Troilus]

I 'll be as patient as a gentle stream.
The Two Gentlemen of Verona. Act ii, sc. 7, l. 34. [Julia]

As patient as the female dove.
Hamlet. Act v, sc. 1, l. 309. [Queen]

Nay, I 'll be patient.—*Pericles,* v, 1, 146.

I will be patient.—*The Merry Wives of Windsor,* ii, 1, 130.

I can be patient.—*King Lear,* ii, 4, 233.

2
She pined in thought,
And with a green and yellow melancholy
She sat like Patience on a monument,
Smiling at grief.
Twelfth Night. Act ii, sc. 4, l. 115. [Viola]

Thou dost look
Like Patience gazing on kings' graves, and smiling
Extremity out of act.
Pericles. Act v, sc. 1, l. 138. [Pericles]

3
Well, I perceive I must be fain to bear with you.
The Two Gentlemen of Verona. Act i, sc. 1, l. 127. [Speed]

My patience, more than thy desert,
Is privilege for thy departure hence.
The Two Gentlemen of Verona. Act iii, sc. 1, l. 159. [Duke]

Lend me patience to forbear awhile.
The Two Gentlemen of Verona. Act v, sc. 4, l. 27. [Valentine]

4
I must be patient till the heavens look
With an aspect more favourable.
The Winter's Tale. Act ii, sc. 1, l. 106. [Hermione]

I must be patient.—*All 's Well that Ends Well,* ii, 3, 251; v, 3, 219.

Thou must be patient.—*Measure for Measure,* iv, 3, 159; *King Lear,* iv, 6, 182.

We must be patient.—*Hamlet,* iv, 5, 69.

You must awhile be patient.—*Othello,* iii, 4, 129.

5
Take patience to you, And I 'll say nothing.
The Winter's Tale. Act iii, sc. 2, l. 232. [Paulina]

PATRICIAN

6
We are accounted poor citizens, the patricians good.
Coriolanus. Act i, sc. 1, l. 15. [Citizen]

Most charitable care Have the patricians of you.
Coriolanus. Act i, sc. 1, l. 68. [Menenius]

Where great patricians shall attend and shrug.
Coriolanus. Act i, sc. 9, l. 4. [Cominius]

I am known to be a humorous patrician.
Coriolanus. Act ii, sc. 1, l. 51. [Menenius]

Ere in my own house I do shade my head,
The good patricians must be visited.
Coriolanus. Act ii, sc. 1, l. 211. [Coriolanus]

O Good but most unwise patricians!
Coriolanus. Act iii, sc. 1, l. 91. [Coriolanus]

7
Noble patricians, patrons of my right.
Titus Andronicus. Act i, sc. 1, l. 1. [Saturninus]

The patricians . . .
Upon a just survey, take Titus' part.
Titus Andronicus. Act i, sc. 1, l. 455. [Tamora] "Patrician" occurs only in *Coriolanus* and in the first scene of *Titus Andronicus.*

Patricians and plebeians.—*Titus Andronicus,* i, 1, 231.

PATRIOTISM

8
Consider you what services he has done for his country?
Coriolanus. Act i, sc. 1, l. 31. [Citizen]

If any fear
Lesser his person than an ill report;
If any think brave death outweighs bad life
And that his country's dearer than himself;
Let him alone, or so many so minded,
Wave thus, to express his disposition,
And follow Marcius.
Coriolanus. Act i, sc. 6, l. 69. [Marcius]

He hath deserved worthily of his country.
Coriolanus. Act ii, sc. 2, l. 27. [Officer]

Fourth Citizen: You have deserved nobly of your country, and you have not deserved nobly.
Coriolanus: Your enigma?
Fourth Citizen: You have been a scourge to her enemies, you have been a rod to her friends.
Coriolanus. Act ii, sc. 3, l. 95. "Enigma" is repeated in *Love's Labour 's Lost,* iii, 1, 72.

You have received many wounds for your country.
Coriolanus. Act ii, sc. 3, l. 114. [Citizen] Also l. 171.

Be that you seem, truly your country's friend.
Coriolanus. Act iii, sc. 1, l. 218. [Menenius]

I do love
My country's good with a respect more tender,
More holy and profound than mine own life.
Coriolanus. Act iii, sc. 3, l. 111. [Cominius]

9
These present wars shall find I love my country.
Cymbeline. Act iv, sc. 3, l. 43. [Pisanio]

If in your country wars you chance to die,
That is my bed too, lads, and there I 'll lie.
Cymbeline. Act iv, sc. 4, l. 51. [Belarius]

Striking in our country's cause
Fell bravely and were slain.
Cymbeline. Act v, sc. 4, l. 71. [Brother]

10
One drop of blood drawn from thy country's bosom
Should grieve thee more than streams of foreign gore.
I Henry VI. Act iii, sc. 3, l. 54. [La Pucelle]

Is all our travail turn'd to this effect?
After the slaughter of so many peers,

So many captains, gentlemen and soldiers,
That in this quarrel have been overthrown
And sold their bodies for their country's benefit.
I Henry VI. Act v, sc. 4, l. 102. [York]

1
So God help Warwick, as he loves the land,
And common profit of his country!
II Henry VI. Act i, sc. 1, l. 205. [Warwick]

God in mercy so deal with my soul,
As I in duty love my king and country!
II Henry VI. Act i, sc. 3, l. 160. [Gloucester]

I 'll yield myself to prison willingly,
Or unto death, to do my country good.
II Henry VI. Act iv, sc. 9, l. 42. [Somerset]

2
From Scotland am I stol'n, even of pure love,
To greet mine own land with my wishful sight.
III Henry VI. Act iii, sc. 1, l. 13. [King Henry] The only use of "wishful."

3
As I slew my best lover for the good of Rome, I have the same dagger for myself, when it shall please my country to need my death.
Julius Cæsar. Act iii, sc. 2, l. 49. [Brutus]

4
I weep for joy
To stand upon my kingdom once again,
Dear earth, I do salute thee with my hand,
Though rebels wound thee with their horses' hoofs:
As a long-parted mother with her child
Plays fondly with her tears and smiles in meeting,
So, weeping, smiling, greet I thee, my earth,
And do thee favours with my royal hands.
Feed not thy sovereign's foe, my gentle earth,
Nor with thy sweets comfort his ravenous sense.
Richard II. Act iii, sc. 2, l. 4. [King Richard] The only use of "long-parted."

5
If you do fight against your country's foes,
Your country's fat shall pay your pains the hire.
Richard III. Act v, sc. 3, l. 257. [Richmond]

6
But yet I love my country, and am not
One that rejoices in the common wreck.
Timon of Athens. Act v, sc. 1, l. 194. [Timon]

7
To the love and favour of my country
Commit myself, my person and the cause.
Titus Andronicus. Act i, sc. 1, l. 58. [Saturninus]

O, if to fight for king and commonweal
Were piety in thine, it is in these.
Titus Andronicus. Act i, sc. 1, l. 114. [Tamora]

8
It is fifteen years since I saw my country: though I have for the most part been aired abroad, I desire to lay my bones there.
Winter's Tale. Act iv, sc. 2, l. 4. [Camillo]

PATRON

9
Twenty years
Have I been patron to Antipholus.
Comedy of Errors. Act v, sc. 1, l. 326. [Duke]

10
Confess who set thee up and pluck'd thee down,
Call Warwick patron.
III Henry VI. Act v, sc. 1, l. 26. [Warwick]

11
My great patron thought on in my prayers.
King Lear. Act i, sc. 1, l. 144. [Kent]

My worthy arch and patron comes to-night.
King Lear. Act ii, sc. 1, l. 61. [Gloucester]

My soul's earth's god, and body's fostering patron.
Love's Labour 's Lost. Act i, sc. 1, l. 222. [King] The only use of "fostering."

12
The patroness of heavenly harmony.
The Taming of the Shrew. Act iii, sc. 1, l. 5. [Hortensio]

Behold our patroness!—*Coriolanus,* v, 5, 1.
O Divinest patroness!—*Pericles,* iii, 1, 11.

13
O sir, I . . . will repute you ever
The patron of my life and liberty.
The Taming of the Shrew. Act iv, sc. 2, l. 112. [Pedant]

The five best senses
Acknowledge thee their patron.
Timon of Athens. Act i, sc. 2, l. 129. [Cupid]

Patron of virtue.—*Titus Andronicus,* i, 1, 65.
Patron of all light.—*Venus and Adonis,* l. 860.
Patrons of my right.—*Titus Andronicus,* i, 1, 1.

PAUSE

14
No marvel though she pause.
The Comedy of Errors. Act ii, sc. 1, l. 32. [Adriana]

Give us pause.—*Hamlet,* iii, 1, 68. See DEATH, 304:6.
Deliberate pause.—*Hamlet,* iv, 3, 9.
Sad pause.—*The Rape of Lucrece,* l. 277.

15
Pause, and take thy breath.
I Henry VI. Act iv, sc. 6, l. 4. [Talbot]

Take time to pause.—*A Midsummer-Night's Dream,* i, 1, 83.
Pause awhile.—*Much Ado about Nothing,* iv, 1, 202; *I Henry IV,* i, 3, 129.
Pause a day or two.—*The Merchant of Venice,* iii, 2, 1.
Pause, or be more temperate.—*King John,* ii, 1, 195.
Pause, if thou wilt.—*Troilus and Cressida,* v, 6, 14.
Pause there.—*The Merchant of Venice,* ii, 7, 24.
Yet pause awhile.—*Pericles,* ii, 3, 53.

16
But yet I 'll make a pause.
III Henry VI. Act iii, sc. 2, l. 10. [King Edward]

But yet I 'll pause.—*Richard II,* ii, 3, 168.
I 'll never pause again.—*III Henry VI,* ii, 3, 30.
Then mightst thou pause.—*Venus and Adonis,* l. 137.
Then pause not.—*King John,* v, 1, 14.
Nay, do not pause.—*Richard III,* i, 2, 180.
There is no pause.—*Othello,* v, 2, 82.

1
We coldly pause for thee.
King John. Act ii, sc. 1, l. 53. [King Philip]
I pause for a reply.—*Julius Cæsar,* iii, 2, 36.

2
Hadst thou but shook thy head or made a pause.
King John. Act iv, sc. 2, l. 231. [King John]

3
Too long a pause for that which you find there.
The Merchant of Venice. Act ii, sc. 9, l. 53. [Portia]

4
Without any pause or staggering.
Merry Wives of Windsor. Act iii, sc. 3, l. 12. [Mrs. Ford] The only use of "staggering."

5
Give me some breath, some little pause, my lord.
Richard III. Act iv, sc. 2, l. 24. [Buckingham]
And I have seen thee pause and take thy breath,
When that a ring of Greeks have hemm'd thee in,
Like an Olympian wrestling.
Troilus and Cressida. Act iv, sc. 5, l. 192. [Nestor] Speaking to Hector. "Olympian" occurs again in *III Henry VI,* ii, 3, 53: "Olympian games."

6
He rouseth up himself and makes a pause.
The Rape of Lucrece, l. 541.

PAYMENT

7
Take this purse of gold,
And let me buy your friendly help thus far,
Which I will over-pay and pay again
When I have found it.
All's Well that Ends Well. Act iii, sc. 7, l. 14. [Helena]
Your very goodness and your company
O'erpays all I can do.
Cymbeline. Act ii, sc. 4, l. 9. [Philario] The only uses of "overpay" and "overpays."
To be acknowledged, madam, is o'erpaid.
King Lear. Act iv, sc. 7, l. 4. [Kent] The only use of "o'erpaid."
Pay and yet pay still.—*Cymbeline,* i, 4, 39.
You have paid too much.—*Cymbeline,* v, 4, 165.

8
After he scores, he never pays the score: . . .
He ne'er pays after-debts, take it before.
All's Well that Ends Well. Act iv, sc. 3, l. 254. [Soldier] The only use of "after-debts."
For count of this, the count's a fool, I know it,
Who pays before, but not when he does owe it.
All's Well that Ends Well. Act iv, sc. 3, l. 258. [Soldier]
Paid his score.—*Macbeth,* v, 8, 52.
Pay your fees.—*The Winter's Tale,* i, 2, 53.
Pay a fine.—*The Comedy of Errors,* ii, 2, 76.
Paying the fine.—*King John,* v, 4, 37.
Pay the price.—*Henry V,* ii, 2, 154.
Pay the theft.—*Hamlet,* iii, 2, 94.

9
If he come to-morrow, I'll give him his payment.
As You Like It. Act i, sc. 1, l. 168. [Charles]
King: Give her an hundred marks. I'll to the queen.
Old Lady: An hundred marks! By this light, I'll ha' more.
An ordinary groom is for such payment.
I will have more, or scold it out of him.
Henry VIII. Act v, sc. 1, l. 170.
Fair payment for foul words is more than due.
Love's Labour's Lost. Act iv, sc. 1, l. 19. [Princess of France]
He humbly prays your speedy payment.
Timon of Athens. Act ii, sc. 2, l. 28. [Servant]
There's payment for you.—*Timon of Athens,* v, 1, 116.
Black payment.—*The Rape of Lucrece,* l. 576.
Bloody payment.—*I Henry IV,* i, 3, 186.
Downright payment.—*III Henry VI,* i, 4, 32.

10
Angelo: Either consent to pay this sum for me
Or I attach you by this officer.
Antipholus of Ephesus: Consent to pay thee what I never had!
Arrest me, foolish fellow, if thou darest.
The Comedy of Errors. Act iv, sc. 1, l. 72.
Pay the sum.—*The Comedy of Errors,* v, 1, 131; 284.
The sum is paid.—*Henry V,* ii, Prol., 33.

11
Prince: Did I ever call for thee to pay thy part?
Falstaff: No; I'll give thee thy due, thou hast paid all there.
I Henry IV. Act i, sc. 2, l. 57.
We, as the spring of all, shall pay for all.
I Henry IV. Act v, sc. 2, l. 23. [Worcester]
He pays the whole.—*Sonnets,* cxxxiv.

12
Two I am sure I have paid, two rogues in buckram suits.
I Henry IV. Act ii, sc. 4, l. 213. [Falstaff]
And with a thought seven of the eleven I paid.
I Henry IV. Act ii, sc. 4, l. 241. [Falstaff]

13
Paid money that I borrowed, three or four times.
I Henry IV, iii, 3, 20. See under VIRTUE.
Paid back again with advantage.—*I Henry IV,* ii, 4, 599.
Paid with weight.—*Hamlet,* iv, 5, 156.
Pays interest.—*Timon of Athens,* i, 2, 206.

14
Prince: The money is paid back. . . .
Falstaff: O, I do not like that paying back; 'tis a double labour.
I Henry IV. Act iii, sc. 3, l. 199.
Paid down.—*The Winter's Tale,* v, 1, 3.
Paid home.—*The Winter's Tale,* v, 3, 4.

15
I have paid Percy, I have made him sure.
I Henry IV. Act v, sc. 3, l. 47. [Falstaff]
Though I could 'scape shot-free at London, I fear the shot here; here's no scoring but upon the pate.
I Henry IV. Act v, sc. 3, l. 30. [Falstaff] The only use of "shot-free" and "scoring."

Never welcome to a place till some certain shot be paid and the hostess say 'Welcome!'
The Two Gentlemen of Verona. Act ii, sc. 5, l. 6. [Launce]

Pays the shot.—*Cymbeline,* v, 4, 158.

1

That hot termagant Scot had paid me scot and lot.
I Henry IV, v, 4, 115. See under COUNTERFEIT. "Termagant" is repeated in *Hamlet,* iii, 2, 15.

2

Who never promiseth but he means to pay.
I Henry IV. Act v, sc. 4, l. 43. [Prince of Wales]

Bate me some and I will pay you some and, as most debtors do, promise you infinitely.
II Henry IV. Epilogue, l. 15.

3

Pray thee, peace. Pay her the debt you owe her, and unpay the villany you have done her: the one you may do with sterling money, and the other with current repentance.
II Henry IV. Act ii, sc. 1, l. 130. [Chief Justice] The only use of "unpay."

You shall have gold
To pay the petty debt twenty times over.
The Merchant of Venice. Act iii, sc. 2, l. 309. [Portia] See also under DEBT.

Paid as debts.—*Pericles,* iv, Gower, 34.

4

Hostess: You 'll pay me all together?
Falstaff: Will I live?
II Henry IV. Act ii, sc. 1, l. 172.

Pay thee plenteously.—*II Henry IV,* iv, 5, 40. The only use of "plenteously."

5

Let them have pay, and part.
II Henry IV. Act iv, sc. 2, l. 70. [Hastings]

Davy: Here is now the smith's note for shoeing and plough-irons.
Shallow: Let it be cast and paid.
II Henry IV. Act v, sc. 1, l. 19. The only use of "shoeing" and "plough-irons."

Let him pay.—*I Henry IV,* iii, 3, 87.

I meant indeed to pay you.—*II Henry IV,* Epil., 12.

6

Base is the slave that pays.
Henry V. Act ii, sc. 1, l. 100. [Pistol]

Let senses rule; the word is 'Pitch and Pay.'
Henry V. Act ii, sc. 3, l. 51. [Pistol]

Ay 'll pay 't as valorously as I may.
Henry V. Act iii, sc. 2, l. 125. [Macmorris] The only use of "valorously."

7

Princess: Confess receipt
Of that which hath so faithfully been paid.
King: I do protest I never heard of it;
And if you so prove it, I 'll repay it back.
Love's Labour's Lost. Act ii, sc. 1, l. 156.

If you repay me not on such a day,
In such a place, such sum or sums as are
Express'd in the condition, let the forfeit
Be nominated for an equal pound
Of your fair flesh.
The Merchant of Venice. Act i, sc. 3, l. 147. [Shylock]

To repay that money will be a biting affliction.
The Merry Wives of Windsor. Act v, sc. 5, l. 178. [Ford]

No meed, but he repays Sevenfold above itself.
Timon of Athens. Act i, sc. 1, l. 188. [Lord] "Sevenfold" is repeated in *Antony and Cleopatra,* iv, 14, 38.

This repays me.—*Antony and Cleopatra,* iii, 11, 71.

8

He disbursed at Saint Colme's inch
Ten thousand dollars to our general use.
Macbeth. Act i, sc. 2, l. 61. [Ross] The only other instance of the use of "dollar" is in *The Tempest,* ii, 1, 18. Probably referring to the German thaler.

9

The service and the loyalty I owe,
In doing it, pays itself.
Macbeth. Act i, sc. 4, l. 22. [Macbeth]

He pays himself.—*Coriolanus,* i, 1, 33.

Pay ourselves.—*Hamlet,* iii, 2, 203.

10

You have paid the heavens your function.
Measure for Measure. Act iii, sc. 2, l. 263. [Escalus]

Paying for them very honestly.—*Measure for Measure,* ii, 1, 105.

Pay down.—*Measure for Measure,* i, 2, 125.

11

He shall pay for this.
The Merchant of Venice. Act ii, sc. 8, l. 26. [Salanio]

If this prove true, they 'll pay for it.—*The Winter's Tale,* ii, 1, 146.

You shall pay well for 'em.—*The Winter's Tale,* iv, 4, 321.

I 'll make them pay.—*The Merry Wives of Windsor,* iv, 3, 11.

I am paid for 't now.—*Antony and Cleopatra,* ii, 5, 108.

Then I am paid.—*The Two Gentlemen of Verona,* v, 4, 77.

So, you 're paid.—*The Tempest,* ii, 1, 36.

12

He is well paid that is well satisfied;
And I, delivering you, am satisfied
And therein do account myself well paid.
The Merchant of Venice. Act iv, sc. 1, l. 415. [Portia]

Well-paid.—*Antony and Cleopatra,* iii, 1, 32.

13

I paid nothing for it neither, but was paid for my learning.
The Merry Wives of Windsor. Act iv, sc. 5, l. 62. [Falstaff]

We will nothing pay.—*Cymbeline,* iii, 1, 13.

14

Pay you with unthankfulness in thought.
Pericles. Act i, sc. 4, l. 102. [Cleon]

I 'll pay your bounties.—*Pericles,* ii, 1, 149.

Pay him tribute.—*I Henry VI,* v, 4, 130. See under TRIBUTE.

15

Thy sacred physic shall receive such pay
As thy desires can wish.
Pericles. Act v, sc. 1, l. 74. [Lysimachus]

Heavenly pay.—*Richard II,* iii, 2, 60.

High pay.—*III Henry VI,* ii, 1, 134.

Large pay.—*III Henry VI,* iv, 7, 88.

Present pay.—*Henry V,* ii, 1, 112.

Soldiers' pay.—*II Henry VI,* iii, 1, 62; 105.
True pay.—*Hamlet,* i, 3, 106.
Uncurrent pay.—*Twelfth Night,* iii, 3, 16.
Yearly pay.—*Henry V,* iv, 1, 315.

1
Then thank him not for that which he doth say,
Since what he owes thee thou thyself dost pay.
Sonnets. No. lxxix.

Have I not seen dwellers on form and favour
Lose all, and more, by paying too much rent?
Sonnets. No. cxxv.

2
Hostess: You will not pay for the glasses you have burst?
Sly: No, not a denier. Go by, Jeronimy.
The Taming of the Shrew. Induction, i, l. 8. The only use of Jeronimy.

I 'll not pay a denier.—*I Henry IV,* iii, 3, 91. "Denier," a small French coin, the twelfth of a sou, is used a third time in *Richard III,* i, 2, 252: "My dukedom to a beggarly denier."

3
Say thou wilt see the tailor paid.
The Taming of the Shrew. Act iv, sc. 3, l. 166. [Petruchio]

Duly paid.—*Henry VIII,* iv, 2, 150.
In cash most justly paid.—*Henry V,* ii, 1, 120.
He was paid for that.—*Cymbeline,* iv, 2, 246.
Paid for.—*Henry V,* iii, 6, 117; *Timon of Athens,* iii, 1, 65.

4
He shall pay for him that hath him, and that soundly.
The Tempest. Act ii, sc. 2, l. 81. [Stephano]

He shall pay for me ere he has me.
Troilus and Cressida. Act iii, sc. 3, l. 298. [Thersites]

5
If I should pay you for 't as 'tis extoll'd,
It would unclew me quite.
Timon of Athens. Act i, sc. 1, l. 67. [Timon] The only use of "extoll'd" and "unclew."

6
Timon's money
Has paid his men their wages.
Timon of Athens. Act iii, sc. 2, l. 77. [Stranger]

Mark, how strange it shows,
Timon in this should pay more than he owes.
Timon of Athens. Act iii, sc. 4, l. 21. [Servant]

7
Ill art thou repaid.
Titus Andronicus. Act iii, sc. 1, l. 235. [Messenger]

8
I 'll pay thee bounteously.
Twelfth Night. Act i, sc. 2, l. 52. [Viola] The only use of "bounteously."

Paid me richly.—*Much Ado about Nothing,* v, 1, 255.

9
For which . . . I shall pay dear.
Twelfth Night. Act iii, sc. 3, l. 36. [Antonio]

You pay a great deal too dear for what 's given freely.
Winter's Tale. Act i, sc. 1, l. 18. [Camillo]

Pays dear.—*Cymbeline,* i, 1, 106.
Pay full dearly.—*I Henry IV,* v, 1, 84.

10
He pays you as surely as your feet hit the ground they step on.
Twelfth Night, iii, 4, 305. See under DUELLING.

There 's money for thee: if you tarry longer, I shall give worse payment.
Twelfth Night. Act iv, sc. 1, l. 20. [Sebastian]

The third pays for all.—*Twelfth Night,* v, 1, 40.

11
He hath paid you all he promised you: may be he has paid you more.
Winter's Tale. Act iv, sc. 4, l. 241. [Mopsa]

Paid ere he promised.—*Henry VIII,* i, 1, 186.
Pay them at thy leisure.—*Venus and Adonis,* l. 518.

PEACE

See also War and Peace

12
Second Lord: I hear there is an overture of peace.
First Lord: Nay, I assure you, a peace concluded.
All 's Well that Ends Well. Act iv, sc. 3, l. 46.

13
What peace you 'll make, advise me.
Coriolanus. Act v, sc. 3, l. 197. [Coriolanus]

Perchance the cardinal cannot make your peace.
King John. Act v, sc. 1, l. 74. [Bastard]

I will make your peace with him if I can.
Twelfth Night. Act iii, sc. 4, l. 296. [Fabian]

Make thy peace.—*Antony and Cleopatra,* ii, 5, 70.
Make your peace with Cæsar.—*Antony and Cleopatra,* iii, 11, 6.
Making his peace.—*Julius Cæsar,* iii, 1, 197.

14
The time of universal peace is near:
Prove this a prosperous day, the three-nook'd world
Shall bear the olive freely.
Antony and Cleopatra. Act iv, sc. 6, l. 5. [Cæsar] The only use of "three-nook'd."

Universal peace.—*Macbeth,* iv, 3, 99.

Peace puts forth her olive every where.
II Henry IV. Act iv, sc. 4, l. 87. [Westmoreland]

Peace proclaims olives of endless age.
Sonnets. No. cvii.

I hold the olive in my hand; my words are as full of peace as matter.
Twelfth Night. Act i, sc. 5, l. 225. [Viola]

15
All the swords In Italy . . .
Could not have made this peace.
Coriolanus. Act v, sc. 3, l. 207. [Coriolanus]

We have made peace
With no less honour to the Antiates
Than shame to the Romans.
Coriolanus. Act v, sc. 6, l. 79. [Coriolanus]

King Richard: I warrant they have made peace with Bolingbroke.
Scroop: Peace have they made with him indeed, my lord. . . .
King Richard: Would they make peace? terrible hell make war
Upon their spotted souls for this offence!
Richard II. Act iii, sc. 2, l. 127.

Made his peace.—*King John,* v, 2, 92; 96.
Made peace of enmity.—*Richard III,* ii, 1, 50.

1
Plenty and peace breeds cowards: hardness ever
Of hardiness is mother.
Cymbeline. Act iii, sc. 6, l. 21. [Imogen] "Hardiness" is repeated in *Henry V,* i, 2, 220.

Peace and plenty.—*Cymbeline,* v, 4, 145; v, 5, 442; 458.

In the temple of great Jupiter
Our peace we'll ratify; seal it with feasts.
Cymbeline. Act v, sc. 5, l. 482. [Cymbeline]

2
This is the imposthume of much wealth and peace,
That inward breaks, and shows no cause without.
Hamlet. Act iv, sc. 4, l. 27. [Hamlet] "Imposthume" (purulent swelling) is repeated in *Troilus and Cressida,* v, 1, 24.

As peace should still her wheaten garland wear
And stand a comma 'tween their amities.
Hamlet. Act v, sc. 2, l. 41. [Hamlet] The only use of "wheaten."

3
Find we a time for frighted peace to pant,
And breathe short-winded accents of new broils.
I Henry IV. Act i, sc. 1, l. 2. [King Henry] "Short-winded" is repeated in *II Henry IV,* ii, 2, 136, and occurs nowhere else.

March all one way and be no more opposed.
I Henry IV. Act i, sc. 1, l. 15. [King Henry]

4
Not to break peace or any branch of it,
But to establish here a peace indeed,
Concurring both in name and quality.
II Henry IV. Act iv, sc. 1, l. 87. [Archbishop] The only use of "concurring."

We come within our awful banks again
And knit our powers to the arm of peace.
II Henry IV. Act iv, sc. 1, l. 176. [Archbishop of York]

There is a thing within my bosom tells me
That no conditions of our peace can stand.
II Henry IV. Act iv, sc. 1, l. 183. [Mowbray]

If we can make our peace
Upon such large terms and so absolute
As our conditions shall consist upon,
Our peace shall stand as firm as rocky mountains.
II Henry IV. Act iv, sc. 1, l. 185. [Hastings]

If we do now make our atonement well,
Our peace will, like a broken limb united,
Grow stronger for the breaking.
II Henry IV. Act iv, sc. 1, l. 221. [Archbishop of York] "Atonement" is used only three times in the plays, as above, and in *Richard III,* i, 3, 36, and *The Merry Wives of Windsor,* i, 1, 33.

5
The word of peace is render'd: hark, how they shout!
II Henry IV. Act iv, sc. 2, l. 87. [Lancaster]

A peace is of the nature of a conquest;
For then both parties nobly are subdued,
And neither party loser.
II Henry IV. Act iv, sc. 2, l. 89. [Archbishop of York]

6
Lancaster: Peace be with him that hath made us heavy!
Chief Justice: Peace be with us, lest we be heavier!
II Henry IV. Act v, sc. 2, l. 25.

Now peace be here.—*Cymbeline,* iii, 6, 35.
Peace and content be here!—*Timon of Athens,* v, 1, 130.
Peace be amongst them.—*I Henry VI,* v, 2, 6.
Peace be in this place!—*Measure for Measure,* i, 4, 6.
Peace be with him!—*Much Ado about Nothing,* v, 1, 196; *Measure for Measure,* v, 1, 401; *Henry VIII,* iv, 2, 75.
Peace be with you!—*Romeo and Juliet,* iii, 1, 59, and three times in later plays.
Peace be to your labour.—*Pericles,* ii, 1, 56.
Peace to the lords of Tyre!—*Pericles,* i, 3, 30.
Peace to your highness!—*Henry VIII,* iii, 1, 23.
We wish your peace.—*The Tempest,* iv, 1, 163.

7
The slave, a member of the country's peace,
Enjoys it; but in gross brain little wots
What watch the king keeps to maintain the peace.
Henry V. Act iv, sc. 1, l. 298. [King Henry]

Naked, poor and mangled Peace,
Dear nurse of arts, plenties and joyful births.
Henry V. Act v, sc. 2, l. 34. [Burgundy] The only use of "plenties."

If . . . you would the peace, . . . you must buy that peace
With full accord to all our just demands.
Henry V. Act v, sc. 2, l. 68. [King Henry]

8 Without expense at all,
By guileful fair words peace may be obtain'd.
I Henry VI. Act i, sc. 1, l. 76. [Messenger] "Guileful" is repeated in *Titus Andronicus,* v, 1, 104: "Guileful hole."

9
Contumeliously should break the peace.
I Henry VI. Act i, sc. 3, l. 58. [Mayor] The only use of "contumeliously."

The troubler of the poor world's peace.
Richard III. Act i, sc. 3, l. 221. [Queen Margaret] "Troubler" is repeated in *Richard III,* i, 3, 221: "Troubler of the poor."

10 As we hither came in peace,
So let us still continue peace and love.
I Henry VI. Act iv, sc. 1, l. 160. [King Henry]

I would have peace and quietness.
Troilus and Cressida. Act ii, sc. 1, l. 90. [Thersites]

Peace and quiet.—*Othello,* ii, 1, 319.

11
They humbly sue your excellence
To have a godly peace concluded of.
I Henry VI. Act v, sc. 1, l. 4. [Gloucester]

12
And therefore are we certainly resolved
To draw conditions of a friendly peace.
I Henry VI. Act v, sc. 3, l. 38. [King Henry]

The states of Christendom,
Moved with remorse of these outrageous broils

Have earnestly implored a general peace.
I Henry VI. Act v, sc. 4, l. 95. [Cardinal Beaufort]
Shall we at last conclude effeminate peace?
I Henry VI. Act v, sc. 4, l. 107. [York]
Conclude a peace.—*I Henry VI,* v, 4, 113.

1 So, now dismiss your army when ye please;
Hang up your ensigns, let your drums be still,
For here we entertain a solemn peace.
I Henry VI. Act v, sc. 4, l. 173. [York]
Celestial peace.—*I Henry VI,* v, 5, 65.
Christian peace.—*Henry VIII,* iv, 2, 156.
Civil peace.—*I Henry IV,* iv, 3, 43; *II Henry IV,* iv, 1, 42.
Contracted peace.—*II Henry VI,* i, 1, 40.
Convenient peace.—*Coriolanus,* v, 3, 191.
Eternal peace.—*I Henry VI,* v, 3, 48.
Friendly peace.—*Richard III,* ii, 1, 59.
Fruitful peace.—*I Henry VI,* v, 4, 127.
Gentle-sleeping peace.—*Richard III,* i, 3, 288. The only use of "gentle-sleeping."
Glooming peace.—*Romeo and Juliet,* v, 3, 305. The only use of "glooming."
Honourable peace.—*II Henry VI,* ii, 3, 38.
Long peace.—*I Henry IV,* iv, 2, 33; *Timon of Athens,* i, 2, 3.
Maid-pale peace.—*Richard II,* iii, 3, 98. The only use of "maid-pale."
Perpetual peace.—*Richard III,* v, 2, 15.
Present peace.—*Coriolanus,* iv, 6, 2; *II Henry IV,* iv, 2, 74.
Proffer'd peace.—*I Henry VI,* iv, 2, 9.
Public peace.—*Henry VIII,* v, 3, 41.
Smiling peace.—*King John,* iii, 1, 246.
Smooth-faced peace.—*Richard III,* v, 5, 33.
Sweet peace.—*A Midsummer-Night's Dream,* v, 1, 425; *Richard II,* iv, 1, 103.
Peace of mind.—*Love's Labour's Lost,* v, 2, 534.
Peace with honour.—*Coriolanus,* iii, 2, 49. See WAR: WAR AND PEACE.

2 King Henry: Blessed are the peacemakers on earth.
Cardinal: Let me be blessed for the peace I make.
II Henry VI. Act ii, sc. 1, l. 35. "Peacemakers" is repeated in *As You Like It,* v, 4, 108, and in *Henry VIII,* iii, 1, 167.
To be a make-peace shall become my age.
Richard II. Act i, sc. 1, l. 160. [John of Gaunt] The only use of "make-peace."

3 Go in peace.
II Henry VI. Act ii, sc. 3, l. 26. [King Henry]
Get you hence in peace.—*Henry V,* i, 2, 294.

4 A proper title of a peace; and purchased
At a superfluous rate!
Henry VIII. Act i, sc. 1, l. 98. [Abergavenny]

5 Heaven's peace be with him!
That 's Christian care enough: for living murmurers
There 's places of rebuke.
Henry VIII. Act ii, sc. 2, l. 131. [Campeius] The only use of "murmurers."
God's peace be with him!—*Henry VIII,* ii, 1, 111.
God's peace!—*I Henry VI,* i, 3, 75; *Henry V,* iv, 3, 31.
A peace above all earthly dignities.
Henry VIII, iii, 2, 379. See under CONSCIENCE.

6 Still in thy right hand carry gentle peace,
To silence envious tongues.
Henry VIII. Act iii, sc. 2, l. 445. [Wolsey]
Gentle peace.—*Henry V,* v, 2, 65.

7 Every man shall eat in safety,
Under his own vine, what he plants; and sing
The merry songs of peace to all his neighbours.
Henry VIII. Act v, sc. 5, l. 34. [Cranmer]

8 Nor heaven nor earth have been at peace tonight.
Julius Cæsar. Act ii, sc. 2, l. 1. [Cæsar]
Be at peace.—*I Henry VI,* iii, 1, 117; iv, 1, 115.

9 Peace, freedom and liberty!
Julius Cæsar. Act iii, sc. 1, l. 110. [Brutus]

10 The peace of heaven is theirs that lift their swords
In such a just and charitable war.
King John. Act ii, sc. 1, l. 35. [Austria]
Leave your children, wives and you in peace.
King John. Act ii, sc. 1, l. 257. [King Philip]

11 King John: Peace be to France, if France in peace permit
Our just and lineal entrance to our own;
If not, bleed France, and peace ascend to heaven,
Whiles we, God's wrathful agent, do correct
Their proud contempt that beats His peace to heaven.
King Philip: Peace be to England, if that war return
From France to England, there to live in peace.
King John. Act ii, sc. 1, l. 84.
I shall show you peace and fair-faced league.
King John. Act ii, sc. 1, l. 417. [Citizen] "Fair-faced" is repeated in *Much Ado about Nothing,* iii, 1, 61.
France, thou mayst hold a serpent by the tongue,
A chafed lion by the mortal paw,
A fasting tiger safer by the tooth,
Than keep in peace that hand which thou dost hold.
King John. Act iii, sc. 1, l. 258. [Pandulph]

12 With unhack'd swords and helmets all unbruised,
We will bear home that lusty blood again.
King John. Act ii, sc. 1, l. 254. [King Philip]
To part with unhack'd edges, and bear back
Our targes undinted.
Antony and Cleopatra. Act ii, sc. 6, l. 38. [Pompey] The only uses of "unhack'd" and of "undinted."

1 The fat ribs of peace
Must by the hungry now be fed upon.
King John. Act iii, sc. 3, l. 9. [King John]
Arm you against your other enemies,
I 'll make a peace between your soul and you.
King John. Act iv, sc. 2, l. 249. [Hubert]

2
Give to our tables meat, sleep to our nights,
Free from our feasts and banquets bloody knives,
Do faithful homage and receive free honours.
Macbeth. Act iii, sc. 6, l. 34. [Lord]
Macduff: The tyrant has not batter'd at their peace?
Ross: No; they were well at peace when I did leave 'em.
Macbeth. Act iv, sc. 3, l. 178.

3
Heaven grant us its peace!
Measure for Measure. Act i, sc. 2, l. 4. [Gentleman]
God send us peace!—*II Henry IV,* iii, 2, 313.
All things shall be peace.—*A Midsummer-Night's Dream,* iii, 2, 377.

4
If he do fear God, a' must necessarily keep peace: if he break the peace, he ought to enter into a quarrel with fear and trembling.
Much Ado about Nothing. Act ii, sc. 3, l. 201. The only use of "necessarily."
Keep peace.—*King Lear,* ii, 2, 52; *Macbeth,* i, 5, 47.

5
A moth of peace.
Othello. Act i, sc. 3, l. 257. [Desdemona]
Men of peace.—*Love's Labour 's Lost,* v, 1, 37.
Now a man of peace.—*The Merry Wives of Windsor,* ii, 3, 45.

6
Iago: Come, hold your peace.
Emilia: 'Twill out, 'twill out: I peace!
Othello. Act v, sc. 2, l. 219.
Held my peace.—*The Winter's Tale,* i, 2, 28.
Hold my peace.—*Hamlet,* i, 2, 246.
Holding my peace.—*King Lear,* i, 4, 202.
Hold thy peace.—*Twelfth Night,* ii, 3, 73.
Peace, ho! no outrage; peace!—*Coriolanus,* v, 6, 125.
Pray thee, fellow, peace.—*Much Ado about Nothing,* iv, 2, 46.

7 I bequeath a happy peace to you
And all good men.
Pericles. Act i, sc. 1, l. 50. [Pericles]
Happy peace.—*King John,* v, 1, 63.

8
Tyrus stands in a litigious peace.
Pericles. Act iii, sc. 3, l. 2. [Pericles] The only use of "litigious," in a scene probably not by Shakespeare.

9
To wake our peace, which in our country's cradle
Draws the sweet infant breath of gentle sleep.
Richard II. Act i, sc. 3, l. 132. [King Richard]
Might from our quiet confines fright fair peace.
Richard II. Act i, sc. 3, l. 137. [King Richard]

10
Now are our brows bound with victorious wreaths;
Our bruised arms hung up for monuments;
Our stern alarums changed to merry meetings,
Our dreadful marches to delightful measures.
Richard III. Act i, sc. 1, l. 5. [Gloucester]
In this weak piping time of peace.
Richard III. Act i, sc. 1, l. 24. [Gloucester] "Piping" is repeated in *A Midsummer-Night's Dream,* ii, 1, 88.

11
Make peace with God, for you must die, my lord.
Richard III. Act i, sc. 4, l. 256. [Murderer]
Make my peace with God.—*Richard III,* i, 4, 258.
My peace is made.—*Richard III.* Act i, sc. 2, l. 198. [Gloucester]
Their peace is made
With heads, and not with hands.
Richard II. Act iii, sc. 2, l. 137. [Scroop]

12
I entreat true peace of you.
Richard III. Act ii, sc. 1, l. 62. [Gloucester]
Pursue him, and entreat him to a peace.
Twelfth Night. Act v, sc. 1, l. 388. [Duke]
With thee in true peace live!—*II Henry IV,* iv, 5, 220.
Live at peace.—*Twelfth Night,* iv, 3, 28.
Live in peace.—*III Henry VI,* i, 1, 188; *Richard II,* iii, 3, 95.

13
The perfect period of this peace.
Richard III. Act ii, sc. 1, l. 44. [King Edward]
I do not know that Englishman alive
With whom my soul is any jot at odds
More than the infant that is born to-night.
Richard III. Act ii, sc. 1, l. 69. [Gloucester]
Now civil wounds are stopp'd, peace lives again:
That she may long live here, God say amen!
Richard III. Act v, sc. 5, l. 40. [Richmond]
England's peace.—*Richard III,* iv, 4, 343.
Peace of England.—*Richard III,* iii, 5, 45.

14
I do but keep the peace.
Romeo and Juliet. Act i, sc. 1, l. 75. [Benvolio]
Keep the peace, I say.
King John. Act iv, sc. 3, l. 93. [Bastard]
Keep the peace.—*I Henry VI,* iii, 1, 87; *Titus Andronicus,* ii, 1, 37.

15
What, drawn, and talk of peace! I hate the word,
As I hate hell.
Romeo and Juliet. Act i, sc. 1, l. 77. [Tybalt]
Canker'd with peace.—*Romeo and Juliet,* i, 1, 102.

16
Marry, peace it bodes, and love and quiet life,
And awful rule and right supremacy;

And, to be short, what not, that 's sweet and happy?
The Taming of the Shrew. Act v, sc. 2, l. 108. [Petruchio]
Kneel for peace.—*The Taming of the Shrew,* v, 2, 162.

1 Treason, felony,
Sword, pike, knife, gun, or need of any engine,
Would I not have.
The Tempest. Act ii, sc. 1, l. 160. [Gonzalo]

PEARL

2 This treasure of an oyster.
Antony and Cleopatra. Act i, sc. 5, l. 44. [Alexas]
I 'll . . . hail rich pearls upon thee.
Antony and Cleopatra. Act ii, sc. 5, l. 46. [Cleopatra]
Heaps of pearl.—*Richard III,* i, 4, 26.
Brinish pearl.—*The Rape of Lucrece,* l. 1213.
Heaven-moving pearls.—*King John,* ii, 1, 69. See under TEAR.
Liquid pearl.—*A Midsummer-Night's Dream,* i, 1, 211.
Melting pearl.—*The Two Gentlemen of Verona,* iii, 1, 224.
Paled pearls.—*A Lover's Complaint,* l. 198. "Paled" is repeated in *Cymbeline,* iii, 1, 19.
Round clear pearls.—*The Rape of Lucrece,* l. 1553.

3 Pearl enough for a swine.
Love's Labour 's Lost. Act iv, sc. 2, l. 90. [Holofernes]

4 Hang a pearl in every cowslip's ear.
A Midsummer-Night's Dream, ii, 1, 15. See under DEW.

5 One whose hand,
Like the base Indian, threw a pearl away
Richer than all his tribe.
Othello. Act v, sc. 2, l. 346. [Othello]

6 Bright orient pearl, alack, too timely shaded!
The Passionate Pilgrim, l. 133. The only use of "shaded."
Orient pearl.—*Richard III,* iv, 4, 322; *A Midsummer-Night's Dream,* iv, 1, 59.

7 Why, sir, what 'cerns it you if I wear pearl and gold?
The Taming of the Shrew. Act v, sc. 1, l. 77. [Tranio]
Boss'd with pearl.—*The Taming of the Shrew,* ii, 1, 355. The only use of "boss'd."
Set with pearls.—*Much Ado about Nothing,* iii, 4, 20.

8 This is the pearl that pleased your empress' eye.
Titus Andronicus. Act v, sc. 1, l. 42. [Lucius]
Those are pearls that were his eyes.—*The Tempest,* i, 2, 398.

9 Her bed is India; there she lies, a pearl.
Troilus and Cressida. Act i, sc. 1, l. 103. [Troilus]

10 This pearl she gave me, I do feel 't and see 't.
Twelfth Night. Act iv, sc. 3, l. 2. [Sebastian]
These pearls to me sent Longaville.—*Love's Labour 's Lost,* v, 2, 53.

PEASANT

11 You have trained me like a peasant.
As You Like It. Act i, sc. 1, l. 72. [Orlando]

12 Our peasants,
Who in unnecessary actions warm
About our squares of battle were enow
To purge this field of such a hilding foe.
Henry V. Act iv, sc. 2, l. 26. [Constable]

13 Like peasant foot-boys do they keep the walls.
I Henry VI, iii, 2, 69. See under FIGHTING.
Like me to the peasant boys of France.
I Henry VI. Act iv, sc. 6, l. 48. [John Talbot]

14 So worthless peasants bargain for their wives,
As market-men for oxen, sheep, or horse.
I Henry VI. Act v, sc. 5, l. 53. [Suffolk] "Market men" (unhyphenated) is repeated in iii, 2, 4, and occurs in no other play.

15 Give me thy sword. A peasant stand up thus!
King Lear. Act iii, sc. 7, l. 80. [Regan]
I will predominate over the peasant.
The Merry Wives of Windsor. Act ii, sc. 2, l. 294. [Falstaff] "Predominate" is used a second time in *Timon of Athens,* iv, 3, 142.
Bold peasant.—*King Lear,* iv, 6, 235.
Briton peasant.—*Cymbeline,* v, 1, 24.

16 A sort of vagabonds, rascals, and runaways,
A scum of Bretons, and base lackey peasants,
Whom their o'er-cloyed country vomits forth
To desperate ventures and assured destruction.
Richard III. Act v, sc. 3, l. 316. [King Richard] The only use of "o'er-cloyed."
Base peasants.—*II Henry VI,* iv, 8, 21.
Dullest peasant.—*II Henry IV,* i, 1, 113.
Heartless peasants.—*The Rape of Lucrece,* l. 1392.
Prating peasant.—*Comedy of Errors,* ii, 1, 81.
Whoreson peasant.—*The Two Gentlemen of Verona,* iv, 4, 47.
Low peasantry.—*The Merchant of Venice,* ii, 9, 46. The only use of "peasantry."
Peasant limbs.—*Henry V,* iv, 7, 80.
Peasant slave.—*Hamlet,* ii, 2, 576.
Peasant swain.—*The Taming of the Shrew,* iv, 1, 132.
Peasant towns.—*II Henry IV,* Ind., 33.
Slaves and peasants.—*Timon of Athens,* ii, 2, 174.

17 How my men will stay themselves from laughter
When they do homage to this simple peasant.
The Taming of the Shrew. Ind., sc. 1, l. 134. [Lord]

PEDANT

1
How fiery and forward our pedant is!
The Taming of the Shrew. Act iii, sc. 1, l. 48. [Hortensio]
Pedascule, I 'll watch you better yet.
Taming of the Shrew. Act iii, sc. 1, l. 50. [Hortensio] The only use of "pedascule."
But I have cause to pry into this pedant:
Methinks he looks as though he were in love.
The Taming of the Shrew. Act iii, sc. 1, l. 87. [Hortensio]
A mercatante, or a pedant,
I know not what; but formal in apparel.
The Taming of the Shrew. Act iv, sc. 2, l. 63. [Biondello] The only use of "mercatante" (foreign trader).
Domineering pedant.—*Love's Labour 's Lost,* iii, 1, 179. The only use of "domineering."
Wrangling pedant.—*The Taming of the Shrew,* iii, 1, 4.
2
Sir Toby: And cross-gartered?
Maria: Most villanously; like a pedant that keeps a school i' the church.
Twelfth Night. Act iii, sc. 2, l. 79.

PEDLAR

3
He is wit's pedlar.
Love's Labour 's Lost, v, 2, 317. See under WIT.
I had rather be a pedlar.—*Richard III,* i, 3, 149. See under KING.
By birth a pedlar.—*The Taming of the Shrew,* Ind., 2, 20.
4
O master, if you did but hear the pedlar at the door, you would never dance again.
The Winter's Tale. Act iv, sc. 4, l. 181. [Servant]
These pedlars, that have more in them than you 'ld think.
The Winter's Tale. Act iv, sc. 4, l. 217. [Clown]
Let me pocket up my pedlar's excrement.
The Winter's Tale. Act iv, sc. 4, l. 732. [Autolycus] Referring to his beard.

PEN

See also Ink, Writing

5
I . . . am not able
Verbatim to rehearse the method of my pen.
I Henry VI. Act iii, sc. 1, l. 12. [Gloucester] The only use of "verbatim."
6
Keep . . . thy pen from lenders' books.
King Lear. Act iii, sc. 4, l. 100. [Edgar]
7
Write, pen; for I am for whole volumes in folio.
Love's Labour 's Lost. Act i, sc. 2, l. 191. [Armado] The only use of "folio."
8
I 'll mar the young clerk's pen.
The Merchant of Venice. Act v, sc. 1, l. 237. [Gratiano]
Author's pen.—*Troilus and Cressida,* Prol., 24.
Ballad-maker's pen.—*Much Ado about Nothing,* i, 1, 255.
Beauty's pen.—*Romeo and Juliet,* i, 3, 82.
Poet's pen.—*A Midsummer-Night's Dream,* v, 1, 15.
Great Charlemain's pen.—*All 's Well that Ends Well,* ii, 1, 80. Charlemain is mentioned again in *Henry V,* i, 2, 75.
9
Bid him bring his pen and inkhorn.
Much Ado about Nothing. Act iii, sc. 5, l. 63.
Pen and ink-horn.—*II Henry VI,* iv, 2, 117.
Inkhorn mate.—*I Henry VI,* iii, 1, 99. The only uses of "ink-horn."
Help me to a candle, and pen, ink and paper.
Twelfth Night. Act iv, sc. 2, l. 87. [Malvolio]
Give me pen and ink.—*Titus Andronicus,* iv, 3, 106.
Pen and ink.—*I Henry VI,* v, 3, 66; *Twelfth Night,* iv, 2, 15.
10
She would with rich and constant pen
Veil to her mistress Dian.
Pericles. Act iv, Gower, l. 28.
11
Every alien pen hath got my use
And under thee their poesy disperse.
Sonnets. No. lxxviii.
I see their antique pen would have express'd
Even such a beauty as you master now.
Sonnets. No. cvi.
Antique pen.—*Sonnets,* xix.
All-unable pen.—*Henry V,* Epil., 1. The only use of "all-unable."
Blazoning pens.—*Othello,* ii, 1, 63. "Blazoning" is repeated in *Titus Andronicus,* iv, 4, 18.
Pupil pen.—*Sonnets,* xvi.
Snow-white pen.—*Love's Labour 's Lost,* i, 1, 245.
Well-refined pen.—*Sonnets,* lxxxv. The only use of "well-refined."
Worthier pen.—*Sonnets,* lxxix.

PENALTY

12
Here feel we but the penalty of Adam,
The seasons' difference.
As You Like It. Act ii, sc. 1, l. 5. [Duke senior]
13
Biron: Let 's see the penalty. . . . Who devised this penalty?
Longaville: Marry, that did I.
Biron: Sweet lord, and why?
Longaville: To fright them hence with that dread penalty.
Love's Labour 's Lost. Act i, sc. 1, l. 123.
14
The enrolled penalties
Which have like unscour'd armour, hung by the wall
So long that nineteen zodiacs have gone round
And none of them been worn.
Measure for Measure. Act i, sc. 2, l. 170. [Claudio] The only use of "unscour'd" and "zodiacs." "Zodiac" occurs in *Titus Andronicus,* ii, 1, 7.
Grievous penalties.—*The Merchant of Venice,* iv, 1, 410.
Under penalty.—*Measure for Measure,* iv, 2, 177.

1 Thou now exact'st the penalty,
Which is a pound of this poor merchant's flesh.
The Merchant of Venice. Act iv, sc. 1, l. 22. [Duke]

Exact the penalty.—*The Merchant of Venice,* i, 3, 138.

I crave . . . the penalty.—*The Merchant of Venice,* iv, 1, 207.

He shall have nothing but the penalty.—*The Merchant of Venice,* iv, 1, 322.

2
Montague is bound as well as I,
In penalty alike.
Romeo and Juliet. Act i, sc. 2, l. 1. [Capulet]

PENANCE

3
After three days' open penance done.
II Henry VI. Act ii, sc. 3, l. 11. [King Henry]

Double penance.—*Sonnets,* cxi.

Lingering penance.—*The Merchant of Venice,* iv, 1, 271.

4
Let not her penance exceed the king's commission.
II Henry VI. Act ii, sc. 4, l. 75. [Gloucester]

Madam, your penance done, throw off this sheet.
II Henry VI, ii, 4, 105.

5
Sands: By my life,
They are a sweet society of fair ones.
Lovell: O, that your lordship were but now confessor
To one or two of these!
Sands: I would I were;
They should find easy penance.
Lovell: Faith, how easy?
Sands: As easy as a down-bed would afford it.
Henry VIII. Act i, sc. 4, l. 14. The only use of "down-bed."

Gentlemen,
The penance lies on you, if these fair ladies
Pass away frowning.
Henry VIII. Act i, sc. 4, l. 31. [Chamberlain]

They need no other penance.—*Henry VIII,* v, 4, 45.

6
Yet confident I 'll keep what I have swore
And bide the penance of each three years' day.
Love's Labour 's Lost. Act i, sc. 1, l. 114. [Biron]

7
My penance is to call Lucetta back
And ask remission for my folly past.
The Two Gentlemen of Verona. Act i, sc. 2, l. 64. [Julia]

8 Friar Laurence met them both,
As he in penance wander'd through the forest.
The Two Gentlemen of Verona. Act v, sc. 2, l. 37. [Duke]

PENITENCE, see Repentance

PENNY

9
I shall never hold that man my friend
Whose tongue shall ask me for one penny.
I Henry IV. Act i, sc. 3, l. 90. [King Henry]

Penny in purse.—*II Henry IV,* v, 1, 34.

Penny cord.—*Henry V,* iii, 6, 50; *Cymbeline,* v, 4, 170.

Penny of observation.—*Love's Labour 's Lost,* iii, 1, 28.

10
To the last penny.
Henry VIII. Act iii, sc. 2, l. 452. [Wolsey]

11
An I had but one penny in the world, thou shouldst have it to buy gingerbread.
Love's Labour 's Lost. Act v, sc. 1, l. 74. [Costard] The only use of "gingerbread."

Her father is make her a petter penny.
The Merry Wives of Windsor. Act i, sc. 1, l. 61. [Evans]

12
I will not lend thee a penny.
The Merry Wives of Windsor. Act ii, sc. 2, l. 1. [Falstaff]

Not a penny.—*II Henry IV,* i, 2, 252; *Romeo and Juliet,* ii, 4, 195; *The Merry Wives of Windsor,* ii, 2, 4.

A single penny more.—*All's Well that Ends Well,* v, 2, 39.

13
Now by Saint Jamy, I hold you a penny.
The Taming of the Shrew, iii, 2, 84. See under HORSE.

PENNYWORTH

14
Your pennyworth is good, an your goose be fat.
Love's Labour 's Lost. Act iii, sc. 1, l. 103. [Costard]

Cheap pennyworths.—*II Henry VI,* i, 1, 222.

Poor pennyworth.—*The Merchant of Venice,* i, 2, 77.

15
We 'll fit the kid-fox with a pennyworth.
Much Ado about Nothing. Act ii, sc. 3, l. 44. [Claudio] Only use of "kid-fox" (cub fox).

Take your pennyworths now.—*Romeo and Juliet,* iv, 5, 4.

Pennyworth of sugar.—*I Henry IV,* ii, 4, 25.

Pennyworth of sugar-candy.—*I Henry IV,* iii, 3, 180. The only use of "sugar-candy."

16
Though the pennyworth on his side be the worst, yet hold thee, there 's some boot.
Winter's Tale. Act iv, sc. 4, l. 648. [Camillo]

PENURY, see Poverty

PEOPLE

See also Citizen; Man: Common Man; Mob; Multitude; Rabble; Vulgarity

17 Our slippery people,
Whose love is never link'd to the deserver
Till his deserts are past.
Antony and Cleopatra. Act i, sc. 2, l. 192. [Antony] "Deserver" is repeated in *Troilus and Cressida,* iii, 2, 14, and *Macbeth,* i, 4, 42.

1
The people love me, and the sea is mine.
Antony and Cleopatra. Act ii, sc. 1, l. 9. [Pompey]

Why do people love you?—*As You Like It,* ii, 3, 5.

We love our people well.—*I Henry IV,* v, 1, 104.

2
Marcius: What 's the matter, you dissentious rogues?
That, rubbing the poor itch of your opinion,
Make yourselves scabs?
Citizen: We have ever your good word.
Marcius: He that will give good words to thee will flatter
Beneath abhorring. . . . He that trusts to you,
Where he should find you lions, finds you hares;
Where foxes, geese: you are no surer, no,
Than is the coal of fire upon the ice,
Or hailstone in the sun. . . . Who deserves greatness
Deserves your hate; and your affections are
A sick man's appetite, who desires most that
Which would increase his evil. He that depends
Upon your favours swims with fins of lead
And hews down oaks with rushes. Hang ye! Trust ye?
With every minute you do change a mind,
And call him noble that was now your hate,
Him vile that was your garland.

Coriolanus. Act i, sc. 1, l. 168. The only use of "hailstone." "Hailstones" occurs in *The Merry Wives of Windsor,* i, 3, 90: "Vanish like hailstones."

3
Supple and courteous to the people.
Coriolanus. Act ii, sc. 1, l. 30. [Officer]

Nor, showing, as the manner is, his wounds
To the people, beg their stinking breaths.
Coriolanus. Act ii, sc. 1, l. 251. [Brutus]

We must suggest the people in what hatred
He still hath held them; that to's power he would
Have made them mules, silenced their pleaders and
Dispropertied their freedoms, holding them,
In human action and capacity,
Of no more soul nor fitness for the world
Than camels in the war, who have their provand
Only for bearing burdens, and sore blows
For sinking under them.

Coriolanus. Act ii, sc. 1, l. 261. [Brutus] The only use of "dispropertied" and "provand." "Pleaders" is repeated in v, 1, 36, and occurs in no other play.

4
There have been many great men that have flattered the people, who ne'er loved them; and there be many that they have loved, they know not wherefore.
Coriolanus. Act ii, sc. 2, l. 8. [Officer]

To seem to affect the malice and displeasure of the people is as bad as that which he dislikes, to flatter them for their love.
Coriolanus. Act ii, sc. 2, l. 24. [Officer]

The people Must have their voices.
Coriolanus. Act ii, sc. 2, l. 143. [Sicinius]

You see how he intends to use the people.
Coriolanus. Act ii, sc. 2, l. 159. [Brutus]

5 He loves your people;
But tie him not to be their bedfellow.
Coriolanus. Act ii, sc. 2, l. 68. [Menenius]

Your people, I love them as they weigh.
Coriolanus. Act ii, sc. 2, l. 77. [Coriolanus]

Citizen: You have not indeed loved the common people.
Coriolanus: You should account me the more virtuous that I have not been common in my love. I will, sir, flatter my sworn brother, the people, to earn a dearer estimation of them; 'tis a condition they account gentle: and since the wisdom of their choice is rather to have my hat than my heart, I will practise the insinuating nod and be off to them most counterfeitly; that is, sir, I will counterfeit the bewitchment of some popular man and give it bountiful to the desirers.

Coriolanus. Act ii, sc. 3, l. 100. The only use of "counterfeitly" and "desirers."

6
Malignantly remain Fast foe to the plebeii.
Coriolanus. Act ii, sc. 3, l. 190. [Brutus] The only use of "plebeii." "Plebs" is used in *Titus Andronicus,* iv, 3, 92; "plebeian" eight times in various plays.

The fusty plebeians.—*Coriolanus,* i, 9, 7.

The hungry plebeians.—*Coriolanus,* ii, 1, 10.

The beastly plebeians.—*Coriolanus,* ii, 1, 106.

The people, your multiplying spawn.—*Coriolanus,* ii, 2, 81. The only use of "spawn."

The mutable, rank-scented many.—*Coriolanus,* iii, 1, 66. The only use of "mutable" and "rank-scented."

7
The people are incensed against him.
Coriolanus. Act iii, sc. 1, l. 32. [Brutus]

The people cry you mock'd them.
Coriolanus. Act iii, sc. 1, l. 42. [Brutus]

The people are abused; set on.
Coriolanus. Act iii, sc. 1, l. 58. [Cominius]

You speak o' the people,
As if you were a god to punish, not
A man of their infirmity.
Coriolanus. Act iii, sc. 1, l. 80. [Brutus]

The people are the city.—*Coriolanus,* iii, 1, 200.

8 Will you hence,
Before the tag return? whose rage doth rend
Like interrupted waters and o'erbear
What they are used to bear.
Coriolanus. Act iii, sc. 1, l. 247. [Cominius] The only use of "tag."

The tag-rag people.—*Julius Cæsar,* i, 2, 260. The only use of "tag-rag."

9 Woollen vassals, things created
To buy and sell with groats, to show bare heads
In congregations, to yawn, be still and wonder.
Coriolanus. Act iii, sc. 2, l. 9. [Coriolanus] "Woollen" is repeated in *The Merchant of Venice,* iv, 1, 56, and in *Much Ado about Nothing,* ii, 1, 33.

The fires i' the lowest hell fold-in the people!
Coriolanus. Act iii, sc. 3, l. 68. [Coriolanus] "Fold-in" is repeated in v, 6, 126, and occurs in no other play.

You common cry of curs! whose breath I hate
As reek o' the rotten fens, whose loves I prize
As the dead carcasses of unburied men
That do corrupt my air, I banish you.
Coriolanus. Act iii, sc. 3, l. 120. [Coriolanus]

1 He has,
As much as in him lies, from time to time
Envied against the people, seeking means
To pluck away their power.
Coriolanus. Act iii, sc. 3, l. 93. [Sicinius]

The cruelty and envy of the people.
Coriolanus. Act iv, sc. 5, l. 80. [Coriolanus]

2
You and your apron-men; you that stood so much
Upon the voice of occupation and
The breath of garlic-eaters!
Coriolanus. Act iv, sc. 6, l. 96. [Menenius] Only use of "apron-men" and "garlic-eaters."

The people
Deserve such pity of him as the wolf
Does of the shepherds.
Coriolanus. Act iv, sc. 6, l. 109. [Cominius]

You are they
That made the air unwholesome, when you cast
Your stinking greasy caps.
Coriolanus. Act iv, sc. 6, l. 129. [Menenius]

3
The groundlings, who for the most part are capable of nothing but inexplicable dumb-shows and noise.
Hamlet. Act iii, sc. 2, l. 12. [Hamlet] The only use of "groundlings" and "inexplicable."

The people muddied,
Thick and unwholesome in their thoughts.
Hamlet. Act iv, sc. 5, l. 81. [King] "Muddied" is repeated in *All's Well that Ends Well,* v, 2, 4, and 23.

The great love the general gender bear him;
Who, dripping all his faults in their affection,
Would, like the spring that turneth wood to stone,
Covert his gyves to graces.
Hamlet. Act iv, sc. 7, l. 18. [King] The only use of "dripping."

4
An habitation giddy and unsure
Hath he that buildeth on the vulgar heart.
II Henry IV. Act i, sc. 3, l. 89. [Archbishop of York] See also under VULGARITY.

5
Here comes the townsmen on procession.
II Henry VI, ii, 1, 68. [Cardinal] "Townsmen" is repeated in *King John,* ii, 1, 361.

The commons, like an angry hive of bees
That want their leader, scatter up and down.
II Henry VI. Act iii, sc. 2, l. 125. [Warwick]

The hateful commons.—*Richard II,* ii, 2, 138.
The wavering commons.—*Richard II,* ii, 2, 129.

Doubt not the commoners.
Coriolanus. Act ii, sc. 1, l. 243. [Sicinius]

The vital commoners.—*II Henry IV,* iv, 3, 119.
O thou public commoner!—*Othello,* iv, 2, 73.
Commoner o' the camp.—*All's Well that Ends Well,* v, 3, 194. The only uses of "commoner" and "commoners."

6
Rebellious hinds, the filth and scum of Kent,
Mark'd for the gallows.
II Henry VI. Act iv, sc. 2, l. 130. [Stafford]

What, art thou drawn among these heartless hinds?
Romeo and Juliet. Act i, sc. 1, l. 73. [Tybalt] The only use of "heartless."

Cowardly hind.—*I Henry IV,* ii, 3, 16.
Rational hind.—*Love's Labour's Lost,* i, 2, 123.
Rude unpolish'd hinds.—*II Henry VI,* iii, 2, 271.
Veriest hind.—*Cymbeline,* v, 3, 77.
Out upon thee, hind!—*The Comedy of Errors,* iii, 1, 77.

7
The rascal people, thirsting after prey.
II Henry VI. Act iv, sc. 4, l. 51. [Messenger]

8
The common people swarm like summer flies;
And whither fly the gnats but to the sun?
III Henry VI. Act ii, sc. 6, l. 8. [Clifford]

The common people by numbers swarm to us.
III Henry VI. Act iv, sc. 2, l. 2. [Warwick]

Many giddy people flock to him.
III Henry VI. Act iv, sc. 8, l. 5. [Warwick]

The common people.—*II Henry VI,* i, 1, 158; *Titus Andronicus,* iv, 4, 73; *Richard II,* i, 4, 24; *Coriolanus,* ii, 2, 6.
The common lag of people.—*Timon of Athens,* iii, 6, 91.
Abject people.—*II Henry VI,* ii, 4, 11.
Barbarous people.—*Henry V,* iii, 5, 4.
Envious people.—*II Henry VI,* ii, 4, 35.
Frosty people.—*Henry V,* iii, 5, 24.
Gentle people.—*Titus Andronicus,* v, 3, 149.
Innocent people.—*The Tempest,* ii, 1, 164.
Lighter people.—*Twelfth Night,* v, 1, 347. "Lighter" is used only once more, in *Richard III,* v, 3, 3.
Starved people.—*The Merchant of Venice,* v, 1, 295.
Poor people.—*II Henry IV,* ii, 1, 108; *Henry VIII,* iv, 2, 157; *Venus and Adonis,* l. 925.
Wise people.—*Antony and Cleopatra,* v, 2, 267.
Mine own people.—*The Merry Wives of Windsor,* ii, 2, 52; iv, 2, 14.
People of Rome.—*Titus Andronicus,* i, 1, 20; 179; 217; v, 3, 67.

9 All good people,
You that thus far have come to pity me,
Hear what I say, and then go home and lose me.
Henry VIII. Act ii, sc. 1, l. 55. [Buckingham]

Good people.—*Measure for Measure,* ii, 1, 41; *Henry VIII,* i, 4, 7; ii, 1, 131.

10
First Gentleman: God save you, sir! where have you been broiling?
Third Gentleman: Among the crowd i' the Abbey; where a finger
Could not be wedged in more.
Henry VIII. Act iv, sc. 1, l. 56. The only use of "broiling."

11
The people fell a-hooting,
Love's Labour's Lost. Act iv, sc. 2, l. 61. [Holofernes] The only use of "a-hooting."

Strangely-visited people,
All swoln and ulcerous.
Macbeth, iv, 3, 150. See under DISEASE. The only use of "strangely-visited."

1 The body public be
A horse whereon the governor doth ride,
Who, newly in the seat, that it may know
He can command, lets it straight feel the spur.
Measure for Measure. Act i, sc. 2, l. 163. [Claudio] The only use of "body public." "Public body" occurs in *Timon of Athens,* v, 1, 148.

So play the foolish throngs with one that swoons;
Come all to help him, and so stop the air
By which he should revive: and even so
The general, subject to a well-wish'd king,
Quit their own part, and in obsequious fondness
Crowd to his presence, where their untaught love
Must needs appear offence.
Measure for Measure. Act ii, sc. 4, l. 24. [Angelo] The only use of "well-wish'd."

2
The rout is coming.
The Taming of the Shrew. Act iii, sc. 2, l. 183. [Gremio]

Base and abject routs.—*II Henry IV,* iv, 1, 33.
The common rout.—*The Comedy of Errors,* iii, 1, 101.
Traitorous rout.—*I Henry VI,* iv, 1, 173.
Rout of rebels.—*II Henry IV,* iv, 2, 9.

3
You see this confluence, this great flood of visitors.
Timon of Athens. Act i, sc. 1, l. 42. [Poet] The only use of "confluence."

In the plainer and simpler kind of people, the deed of saying is quite out of use.
Timon of Athens. Act v, sc. 1, l. 27. [Painter]

4 Would thou wert shipp'd to hell,
Rather than rob me of the people's hearts!
Titus Andronicus. Act i, sc. 1, l. 206. [Saturninus]

I will restore to thee
The people's hearts, and wean them from themselves.
Titus Andronicus. Act i, sc. 1, l. 210. [Titus]

You heavy people, circle me about,
That I may turn me to each one of you,
And swear unto my soul to right your wrongs.
Titus Andronicus. Act iii, sc. 1, l. 277. [Titus]

PERFECTION

5
Whose high respect and rich validity
Did lack a parallel.
All's Well that Ends Well. Act v, sc. 3, l. 192. [Diana]

When once he was mature for man,
In Britain where was he
That could stand up his parallel?
Cymbeline. Act v, sc. 4, l. 52. [First Brother]

Well may we fight for her whom, we know well,
The world's large spaces cannot parallel.
Troilus and Cressida. Act ii, sc. 2, l. 161. [Paris]

If, one by one, you wedded all the world,
Or from the all that are took something good,
To make a perfect woman, she you kill'd
Would be unparallel'd.
Winter's Tale. Act v, sc. 1, l. 13. [Paulina]

A lass unparallel'd.—*Antony and Cleopatra,* v, 2, 319.
Fame unparallel'd.—*Coriolanus,* v, 2, 16. The only uses of "unparallel'd."
Without a parallel.—*The Tempest,* i, 2, 74.

6 I bind,
On pain of punishment, the world to weet
We stand up peerless.
Antony and Cleopatra. Act i, sc. 1, l. 38. [Antony] The only use of "weet" (know).

Stand peerless.—*Pericles,* iv, Gower, 40.

But you, O you,
So perfect and so peerless, are created
Of every creature's best.
The Tempest. Act iii, sc. 1, l. 46. [Ferdinand] See under WOMAN for full quotation.

Leontes: His princess, say you, with him?
Gentleman: Ay, the most peerless piece of earth, I think,
That e'er the sun shone bright on.
The Winter's Tale. Act v, sc. 1, l. 93.

She lived peerless.—*The Winter's Tale,* v, 3, 14.
Peerless dame.—*The Rape of Lucrece,* l. 21.
Peerless feature.—*I Henry VI,* v, 5, 68.
Peerless kinsman.—*Macbeth,* i, 4, 58. The only uses of "peerless."

7
The demi-Atlas of this earth, the arm
And burgonet of men.
Antony and Cleopatra. Act i, sc. 5, l. 23. [Cleopatra] The only use of "demi-Atlas." "Burgonet" (steel casque) occurs four times.

A creature such
As, to seek through the regions of the earth
For one his like, there would be something failing
In him that should compare. I do not think
So fair an outward and such stuff within
Endows a man but he.
Cymbeline. Act i, sc. 1, l. 19. [Gentleman]

The gods made you, Unlike all others, chaffless.
Cymbeline. Act i, sc. 6, l. 177. [Iachimo] The only use of "chaffless."

8 My mother seem'd
The Dian of that time: so doth my wife
The nonpareil of this.
Cymbeline. Act ii, sc. 5, l. 6. [Posthumus]

He himself Calls her a nonpareil.
The Tempest. Act iii, sc. 2, l. 107. [Caliban]

Nonpareil of beauty.—*Twelfth Night,* i, 5, 273.
Thou art the nonpareil.—*Macbeth,* iii, 4, 19.
The nonpareil!—*Antony and Cleopatra,* iii, 2, 11. The only uses of "nonpareil."

9
The chief perfections of that lovely dame,
Had I sufficient skill to utter them,
Would make a volume of enticing lines,
Able to ravish any dull conceit.
I Henry VI. Act v, sc. 5, l. 12. [Suffolk]

All her perfections challenge sovereignty.
III Henry VI, iii, 2, 86. [King Edward]

The primest creature
That's paragon'd o' the world.
Henry VIII. Act ii, sc. 4, l. 229. [King] The only use of "primest" and "paragon'd."

1
Crack nature's moulds, all germens spill at once,
That make ingrateful man!
King Lear. Act iii, sc. 2, l. 8. [King Lear] "Germens" (germs) occurs again in *Macbeth,* iv, 1, 59.
All perfections that a man may owe.
Love's Labour 's Lost. Act ii, sc. 1, l. 5. [Boyet]
We will turn it finely off, sir.
Love's Labour 's Lost. Act v, sc. 2, l. 511. [Costard]
2 I had else been perfect,
Whole as the marble, founded as the rock,
As broad and general as the casing air.
Macbeth. Act iii, sc. 4, l. 21. [Macbeth] The only use of "casing." "Founded" is repeated in *Othello,* iii, 4, 94.
Be perfect.—*Measure for Measure,* v, 1, 82.
I am perfect.—*Macbeth,* iv, 2, 66; *Cymbeline,* iii, 1, 73; iv, 2, 118.
I hope I was perfect.—*Love's Labour 's Lost,* v, 2, 562.
Thou art perfect.—*I Henry IV,* ii, 4, 39; iii, 1, 229; *The Winter's Tale,* iii, 3, 1.
Thou hast been godlike perfect.—*Pericles,* v, 1, 208.
Perfect, divine.—*A Midsummer-Night's Dream,* iii, 2, 137.
So perfect.—*As You Like It,* iii, 5, 99.
For ever perfect.—*Timon of Athens,* i, 2, 90.
3
I trust it will grow to a most prosperous perfection.
Measure for Measure. Act iii, sc. 1, l. 274. [Isabella]
Angel-like perfection.—*The Two Gentlemen of Verona,* ii, 4, 66.
Best perfections.—*Pericles,* i, 1, 11.
Dear perfection.—*All's Well that Ends Well,* v, 3, 18; *Romeo and Juliet,* ii, 2, 46.
Divine perfection.—*The Two Gentlemen of Verona,* ii, 7, 13.
High perfection.—*Richard III,* iv, 4, 66.
Pure perfection.—*Venus and Adonis,* l. 735.
Sweet perfections.—*Twelfth Night,* i, 1, 39.
True perfection.—*The Two Gentlemen of Verona,* ii, 4, 197; *Merchant of Venice,* v, 1, 108.
4
Cassio: She 's a most exquisite lady.
Iago: And, I 'll warrant her, full of game.
Cassio: Indeed, she 's a most fresh and delicate creature.
Iago: What an eye she has! methinks it sounds a parley of provocation.
Cassio: An inviting eye, and yet methinks right modest.
Iago: And when she speaks, is it not an alarum to love?
Cassio: She is indeed perfection.
Othello. Act ii, sc. 3, l. 18.
The most replenished sweet work of nature,
That from the prime creation e'er she framed.
Richard III. Act iv, sc. 3, l. 18. [Tyrrel]
5 No perfection is so absolute,
That some impurity doth not pollute.
The Rape of Lucrece, l. 853. The only use of "impurity."
6 Every thing that grows
Holds in perfection but a little moment.
Sonnets. No. xv.
Right perfection wrongfully disgraced.
Sonnets. No. lxvi.
Best is best, if never intermix'd.
Sonnets. No. ci. "Intermix'd" is repeated in *Richard II,* v, 5, 12.
7
In thy dumb action will I be as perfect
As begging hermits in their holy prayers.
Titus Andronicus. Act iii, sc. 2, l. 40. [Titus]
8
No perfection in reversion shall have a praise in present.
Troilus and Cressida. Act iii, sc. 2, l. 99. [Troilus]
9
Methinks I feel this youth's perfections
With an invisible and subtle stealth
To creep in at mine eyes.
Twelfth Night. Act i, sc. 5, l. 315. [Olivia]
10
Thy soft hands, sweet lips and crystal eyne,
Whose full perfection all the world amazes.
Venus and Adonis, l. 633.

PERFUME

11
A strange invisible perfume hits the sense.
Antony and Cleopatra. Act ii, sc. 2, l. 217. [Enobarbus]
April perfumes.—*Sonnets,* civ.
Diseased perfumes.—*Timon of Athens,* iv, 3, 207.
Excellent perfume.—*Much Ado about Nothing,* iii, 4, 63.
12
He was perfumed like a milliner.
I Henry IV. Act i, sc. 3, l. 36. [Hotspur]
Perfumed with civet.—*As You Like It,* iii, 2, 65.
Well perfumed.—*The Taming of the Shrew,* i, 2, 152.
13
Thou owest . . . the cat no perfume.
King Lear. Act iii, sc. 4, l. 110. [King Lear]
14
Here 's the smell of blood still: all the perfumes of Arabia will not sweeten this little hand.
Macbeth. Act v, sc. 1, l. 56. [Lady Macbeth]
15
Being entertained for a perfumer.
Much Ado about Nothing. Act i, sc. 3, l. 60. [Borachio] The only use of "perfumer."
16
The rose looks fair, but fairer we it deem
For that sweet odour which doth in it live . . .
Of their sweet deaths are sweetest odours made.
Sonnets. No. liv.
Cerimon: Soft! it smells most sweetly in my sense.
Sec. Gentleman: A delicate odour.
Cerimon: As ever hit my nostril.
Pericles. Act iii, sc. 2, l. 60.
The heavens rain odours on you!
Twelfth Night. Act iii, sc. 1, l. 95. [Viola]
Bottom: Thisby, with flowers of odious savours sweet,—

Quince: Odours, odours.
Bottom: —odours savours sweet.
A Midsummer-Night's Dream. Act iii, sc. 1, l. 84.

1
Burn sweet wood to make the lodging sweet.
The Taming of the Shrew. Induction, sc. 1, l. 49. [Lord]
Let one attend him with a silver basin
Full of rose-water and bestrew'd with flowers;
Another bear the ewer, the third a diaper.
The Taming of the Shrew. Induction, sc. 1, l. 55. [Lord] The only use of "rose-water" and "diaper."
She is sweeter than perfume itself.
The Taming of the Shrew. Act i, sc. 2, l. 153. [Gremio]

2
Smoke, like incense, doth perfume the sky.
Titus Andronicus. Act i, sc. 1, l. 145. [Lucius]

PERIL

See also Danger

3
Unknown,
Pitied nor hated, to the face of peril
Myself I 'll dedicate.
Cymbeline. Act v, sc. 1, l. 27. [Posthumus]
Fronting peril.—*II Henry IV,* iv, 4, 66.
Full of peril.—*I Henry IV,* i, 3, 191.

4
You knew he walk'd o'er perils, on an edge,
More likely to fall in than to get o'er.
II Henry IV. Act i, sc. 1, l. 170. [Morton]
For certainly thou art so near the gulf,
Thou needs must be englutted.
Henry V. Act iv, sc. 3, l. 82. [Montjoy] "Englutted" is repeated in *Timon of Athens,* ii, 2, 175. "Englut" is used in *Othello,* i, 3, 57.

5
Perils did
Abound, as thick as thought could make 'em, and
Appear in forms more horrid.
Henry VIII. Act iii, sc. 2, l. 194. [Wolsey]

6
Let us presently go sit in council,
How covert matters may be best disclosed,
And open perils surest answered.
Julius Cæsar. Act iv, sc. 1, l. 45. [Antony]
Dear peril.—*Timon of Athens,* v, 1, 231.
Likely peril.—*II Henry IV,* i, 1, 184.
Royal peril.—*Antony and Cleopatra,* iv, 8, 35.
Utmost peril.—*Coriolanus,* iii, 1, 326.

7
The peril of our curses light on thee.
King John, iii, 2, 295. See under CURSE.
On peril of a curse.—*King John,* iii, 1, 191.
Peril of the . . . law.—*A Midsummer-Night's Dream,* iv, 1, 158.

8
'Gainst her own content,
To put the by-past perils in her way?
A Lover's Complaint, l. 157. The only use of "by-past."
Perils past.—*II Henry IV,* iii, 1, 55.
Perils overblown.—*The Taming of the Shrew,* v, 2, 3.

9
There is the peril of waters, winds and rocks.
The Merchant of Venice. Act i, sc. 3, l. 25. [Shylock]

10
Lest, to thy peril, thou aby it dear.
A Midsummer-Night's Dream. Act iii, sc. 2, l. 175. [Demetrius]
Thou shalt aby it.—*A Midsummer-Night's Dream,* iii, 2, 335. "Aby" (pay the penalty for) is used only in this scene.
At his peril.—*Othello,* i, 2, 81.
At thy peril.—*Merchant of Venice,* iv, 1, 344.
At your peril.—*Measure for Measure,* iv, 2, 130.
On my peril.—*Richard III,* iv, 1, 26.
On thy peril.—*A Midsummer-Night's Dream,* ii, 2, 87.
On your displeasure's peril.—*The Winter's Tale,* ii, 3, 45.
On your own peril.—*Cymbeline,* v, 4, 189.
To my peril.—*Antony and Cleopatra,* v, 2, 146.
Upon his peril.—*Antony and Cleopatra,* v, 2, 143.

11
There stand I in much peril.
Othello. Act v, sc. 1, l. 21. [Iago]
In peril of my life.—*The Merchant of Venice,* ii, 2, 173.
Peril to my soul.—*Measure for Measure,* ii, 4, 65.
On thy soul's peril.—*Winter's Tale,* ii, 3, 181.
I knowing all my peril.—*All 's Well that Ends Well,* ii, 1, 136.
You know the peril.—*Cymbeline,* i, 1, 80.

12
That the extreme peril of the case,
The peace of England and our persons' safety,
Enforced us to this execution.
Richard III. Act iii, sc. 5, l. 44. [Gloucester]
Without peril.—*Richard III,* v, 3, 39.
Free from peril.—*As You Like It,* ii, 1, 4.

PERJURY

13
There 's for twitting me with perjury.
III Henry VI. Act v, sc. 5, l. 40. [Clarence] The only use of "twitting."

14
That same purpose-changer, that sly devil,
That broker, that still breaks the pate of faith,
That daily break-vow.
King John. Act ii, sc. 1, l. 567. [Bastard] The only use of "purpose-changer" and "break-vow."
Thou art perjured too,
And soothest up greatness.
King John. Act iii, sc. 1, l. 120. [Constance] The only use of "soothest."

15
You 'll prove perjured if you make me stay.
Love's Labour 's Lost. Act ii, sc. 1, l. 113. [Princess of France]
Nay, to be perjured, which is worst of all.
Love's Labour 's Lost. Act iii, sc. 1, l. 196. [Biron]
Longaville: Am I the first that have been perjured so?
Biron: I could put thee in comfort. Not by two that I know:
Thou makest the triumviry.
Love's Labour 's Lost. Act iv, sc. 3, l. 51. The only use of "triumviry." "Triumvirate" occurs in *Antony and Cleopatra,* iii, 6, 28.

You 'll not be perjured, 'tis a hateful thing.
Love's Labour's Lost. Act iv, sc. 3, l. 157. [Biron]
False and perjured.—*Cymbeline,* iii, 4, 65.
Perjured and unjust.—*III Henry VI,* v, 1, 106.

1
Nor God, nor I, delights in perjured men.
Love's Labour's Lost. Act v, sc. 2, l. 346. [Princess of France]
False, fleeting, perjured Clarence.
Richard III. Act i, sc. 4, l. 55. [Clarence]
Perjured kings.—*King John,* iii, 1, 107; 111.
False perjured Proteus.—*The Two Gentlemen of Verona,* v, 4, 39.
Perjured Henry!—*III Henry VI,* ii, 2, 81.
Perjured Sinon.—*The Rape of Lucrece,* l. 1521.
O perjured woman!—*The Comedy of Errors,* v, 1, 212; *Othello,* v, 2, 63.

2
Thus pour the stars down plagues for perjury.
Love's Labour's Lost. Act v, sc. 2, l. 394. [Biron]
Now, to our perjury to add more terror,
We are again forsworn, in will and error.
Love's Labour's Lost. Act v, sc. 2, l. 470. [Biron]
You are attaint with faults and perjury.
Love's Labour's Lost. Act v, sc. 2, l. 829. [Rosaline]
Some salve for perjury.—*Love's Labour's Lost,* iv, 3, 289.

3
Faith, here 's an equivocator, that could swear in both the scales against either scale.
Macbeth. Act ii, sc. 3, l. 10. [Porter] "Equivocator" is repeated in lines 13 and 35 of the same scene, and occurs nowhere else.

4
Shall I lay perjury upon my soul?
No, not for Venice.
The Merchant of Venice. Act iv, sc. 1, l. 229. [Shylock]

5
What a Herod of Jewry is this!
The Merry Wives of Windsor. Act ii, sc. 1, l. 20. [Mrs. Page] "Herod of Jewry" is used again in *Antony and Cleopatra,* i, 2, 28; iii, 3, 3; and iii, 6, 73.
It out-Herods Herod.—*Hamlet,* iii, 2, 16. The only use of "out-Herods."

6
Why, this is flat perjury.
Much Ado about Nothing. Act iv, sc. 2, l. 44. [Dogberry]
Take heed of perjury.
Othello. Act v, sc. 2, l. 51. [Othello]

7
What scourge for perjury
Can this dark monarchy afford?
Richard III. Act i, sc. 4, l. 50. [Clarence]
Perjury, perjury, in the high'st degree.
Richard III. Act v, sc. 3, l. 196. [King Richard]

8
How oft hast thou with perjury cleft the root!
The Two Gentlemen of Verona. Act v, sc. 4, l. 103. [Julia]
Threefold perjury.—*The Two Gentlemen of Verona,* ii, 6, 5.

9
I have sworn thee fair; more perjured I,
To swear against the truth so foul a lie!
Sonnets. No. clii.

PERPLEXITY

10
I rest perplexed with a thousand cares.
I Henry VI. Act v, sc. 5, l. 95. [King Henry]
Perplex'd in the extreme.—*Othello,* v, 2, 346.
Perplex'd in all.—*Cymbeline,* iv, 3, 41.

11
King Philip: I am perplex'd and know not what to say.
Pandulph: What canst thou say but will perplex thee more?
King John. Act iii, sc. 1, l. 221. The only use of "perplex."

12
All our house in a great perplexity.
The Two Gentlemen of Verona, ii, 3, 9. See under TEAR.
In perplexity and doubtful dilemma.
The Merry Wives of Windsor. Act iv, sc. 5, l. 85. [Host]
Avaunt, perplexity!—*Love's Labour's Lost,* v, 2, 298. The only uses of "perplexity."

PERSEVERANCE

13
Instruct my daughter how she shall persever.
All's Well that Ends Well. Act iii, sc. 7, l. 37. [Widow]
He persists As if his life lay on 't.
All's Well that Ends Well. Act iii, sc. 7, l. 42. [Widow] The only use of "persists." "Persist" occurs in *Troilus and Cressida,* ii, 2, 186.

14
Shepherd, ply her hard.
As You Like It. Act iii, sc. 5, l. 76. [Rosalind]

15
I 'll say as they say and persever so
And in this mist at all adventures go.
The Comedy of Errors. Act ii, sc. 2, l. 217. [Antipholus of Syracuse]
Persever not.—*King John,* ii, 1, 421.

16
Persever in that clear way thou goest,
And the gods strengthen thee!
Pericles. Act iv, sc. 6, l. 113. [Lysimachus]

17
Perseverance, dear my lord,
Keeps honour bright: to have done is to hang
Quite out of fashion, like a rusty mail
In monumental mockery.
Troilus and Cressida. Act iii, sc. 3, l. 150. [Ulysses] "Perseverance" is used only once again, in *Macbeth,* iv, 3, 93: "The king-becoming graces, . . . perseverance."

18
Tell then, there thy fixed foot shall grow
Till thou have audience. . . .
Be clamorous and leap all civil bounds.
Twelfth Night. Act i, sc. 4, l. 17. [Duke]

19
Ay, and perversely she persevers so.
The Two Gentlemen of Verona. Act iii, sc. 2, l. 28. [Duke] The only use of "perversely."

PERSON

1 For her own person,
It beggar'd all description.
Antony and Cleopatra. Act ii, sc. 2, l. 202. [Enobarbus]

2 Of all things upon the earth he hated
Your person most.
Coriolanus. Act iii, sc. 1, l. 14. [Lartius]

Lady: What 's your lordship's pleasure?
Cloten: Your lady's person.
Cymbeline. Act ii, sc. 3, l. 84.

Thus did I keep my person fresh and new;
My presence, like a robe pontifical,
Ne'er seen but wonder'd at.
I Henry IV. Act iii, sc. 2, l. 55. [King Henry] The only use of "pontifical."

3
I then did use the person of your father.
II Henry IV. Act v, sc. 2, l. 64. [Chief Justice]

Not to come near our person by ten mile.
II Henry IV. Act v, sc. 5, l. 69. [King Henry]

4
Therefore take heed how you impawn our person.
Henry V. Act i, sc. 2, l. 21. [King Henry] The only use of "impawn." "Impaw'd" occurs twice, in *I Henry IV*, iv, 3, 108, and *The Winter's Tale,* i, 2, 436.

5
In thine own person answer thy abuse.
II Henry VI. Act ii, sc. 1, l. 41. [Gloucester]

His own person.—*As You Like It,* iv, 1, 97; *Henry V,* iii, 6, 140.

Mine own person.—*As You Like It,* iv, 1, 92; *Coriolanus,* v, 6, 35.

6
A sort of naughty persons, lewdly bent.
II Henry VI. Act ii, sc. 1, l. 167. [Buckingham]

Dishonest person.—*Measure for Measure,* v, 1, 262.

7
Me seemeth then it is no policy . . .
That he should come about your royal person.
II Henry VI. Act iii, sc. 1, l. 23. [Queen] "Royal person" is repeated twice in subsequent scenes of this play, and five times in later plays.

Best person.—*A Midsummer-Night's Dream,* iv, 2, 11.
Better person.—*III Henry VI,* iii, 3, 167.
Free person.—*The Winter's Tale,* ii, 1, 194.
Gentle person.—*Richard III,* i, 3, 73.
Good person.—*Henry VIII,* ii, 4, 155.
Graced person.—*Macbeth,* iii, 4, 41.
Gracious person.—*Measure for Measure,* iii, 1, 208; *Twelfth Night,* i, 5, 281.
Great person.—*The Tempest,* i, 2, 237.
High person.—*Henry VIII,* i, 2, 140.
Imagined person.—*Measure for Measure,* v, 1, 213.
Noble person.—*Henry VIII,* i, 2, 174.
Noble and natural person.—*Cymbeline,* iii, 5, 140.
Philosophical persons.—*All 's Well that Ends Well,* ii, 3, 2. The only use of "philosophical."
Respected person.—*Measure for Measure,* ii, 1, 173.
Unvalued persons.—*Hamlet,* i, 3, 19. "Unvalued" is repeated in *Richard III,* i, 4, 27: "Unvalued jewels."

8
So might your grace's person be in danger.
II Henry VI. Act iv, sc. 4, l. 45. [Say]

9 Think ye see
The very persons of our noble story.
Henry VIII. Prologue, l. 26.

It is that fery person.—*The Merry Wives of Windsor,* i, 1, 50.

10
We live not to be griped by meaner persons.
Henry VIII. Act ii, sc. 2, l. 136. [Wolsey] The only use of "griped."

Unsolicited
I left no reverend person in this court.
Henry VIII. Act ii, sc. 4, l. 219. [King Henry] "Unsolicited" is repeated in *Titus Andronicus,* iv, 3, 60.

11 Evermore they pointed
To the good of your most sacred person.
Henry VIII. Act iii, sc. 2, l. 172. [Wolsey]

Sacred person.—*Henry VIII,* ii, 4, 41.

12
Good reverend father, make my person yours,
And tell me how you would bestow yourself.
King John. Act iii, sc. 1, l. 224. [King Philip]

13
Dull: Which is the duke's own person?
Biron: This, fellow: what wouldst?
Dull: I myself reprehend his own person, for I am his grace's tharborough; but I would see his own person in flesh and blood.
Love's Labour 's Lost. Act i, sc. 1, l. 182. The only use of "tharborough" (third-borough, constable).

The prince's own person.—*Much Ado about Nothing,* iii, 3, 79.

Enfreedoming thy person.—*Love's Labour 's Lost,* iii, 1, 125. The only use of "enfreedoming."

14
You must, sir, change persons with me.
Measure for Measure. Act v, sc. 1, l. 339. [Duke]

15
With her personage, her tall personage, . . .
She hath prevail'd with him.
A Midsummer-Night's Dream, iii, 2, 292. See under STATURE.

Of what personage . . . is he?—*Twelfth Night,* i, 5, 164.

Honourable personages.—*All 's Well that Ends Well,* ii, 3, 278. The only uses of "personage" and "personages."

16
Our watch, sir, have indeed comprehended two aspicious persons.
Much Ado about Nothing. Act iii, sc. 5, l. 49. [Dogberry]

17
He hath a person and a smooth dispose
To be suspected, framed to make women false.
Othello. Act i, sc. 3, l. 403. [Iago]

1
Set thy person forth to sell.
The Passionate Pilgrim, l. 310. See under WOOING.

2
My dukedom to a beggarly denier,
I do mistake my person all this while.
Richard III. Act i, sc. 2, l. 252. [Gloucester]
Nay, for a need, thus far come near my person.
Richard III. Act iii, sc. 5, l. 85. [Gloucester]

3
What misadventure is so early up,
That calls our person from our morning's rest?
Romeo and Juliet. Act v, sc. 3, l. 188. [Prince]

4
Thou mightst call him A goodly person.
The Tempest. Act i, sc. 2, l. 415. [Prospero]
Goodly person.—*Pericles,* v, 1, 36.

5
Procure safe-conduct for his person.
Troilus and Cressida. Act iii, sc. 3, l. 275. [Achilles]
Convey them with safe-conduct.—*Henry V,* i, 2, 297. The only uses of "safe-conduct."

6
She takes exceptions at your person.
The Two Gentlemen of Verona. Act v, sc. 2, l. 3. [Proteus]

7
Tender your person to his presence.
The Winter's Tale. Act iv, sc. 4, l. 826. [Autolycus]
His person 's mighty.—*Winter's Tale,* i, 2, 453.

II—In Person

8
Why should not we Be there in person?
Antony and Cleopatra. Act iii, sc. 7, l. 5. [Cleopatra]
Can he be there in person?—*Antony and Cleopatra,* iii, 7, 57.
Himself in person there?—*King Lear,* iv, 5, 2.
There in person.—*Troilus and Cressida,* iii, 1, 33; iv, 1, 2.

9
Myself in person will straight follow you.
III Henry VI. Act iv, sc. 1, l. 133. [King Edward]
We will ourself in person to this war.
Richard II. Act i, sc. 4, l. 42. [King Richard]

10
Here comes his grace in person.
Richard II. Act ii, sc. 3, l. 82. [Bolingbroke]
In person.—*Comedy of Errors,* v, 1, 119; *I Henry IV,* iv, 1, 91; *II Henry IV,* ii, 1, 127; *Henry VIII,* i, 2, 5; *Measure for Measure,* i, 3, 47.
Appear in person.—*Winter's Tale,* iii, 2, 10.
Come in person.—*Comedy of Errors,* v, 1, 116.
Go in person.—*Comedy of Errors,* v, 1, 234.
Is he in person ready?—*Henry VIII,* i, 1, 117.

PERSONALITY

See Also Identity

11
We know what we are, but know not what we may be.
Hamlet. Act iv, sc. 5, l. 42. [Ophelia]
You are, and do not know 't.
Macbeth. Act ii, sc. 3, l. 102. [Macbeth]

12
I shall hereafter, my thrice gracious lord,
Be more myself.
I Henry IV. Act iii, sc. 2, l. 92. [Prince of Wales]
Be thou still like thyself.
III Henry VI. Act iii, sc. 3, l. 15. [King Lewis]
Why, thou must be thyself.
The Merry Wives of Windsor. Act iii, sc. 4, l. 3. [Fenton]

13
Near or far off, well won is still well shot,
And I am I, howe'er I was begot.
King John. Act i, sc. 1, l. 174. [Bastard]
I am that I am.—*Sonnets,* cxxi.

14
Let me be that I am and seek not to alter me.
Much Ado about Nothing. Act i, sc. 3, l. 38. [Don John]

15
He 's that he is: I may not breathe my censure
What he might be: if what he might he is not,
I would to heaven he were!
Othello. Act iv, sc. 1, l. 281. [Iago]

16
Nurse: O, tell me, did you see Aaron the Moor?
Aaron: Well, more or less, or ne'er a whit at all,
Here Aaron is; and what with Aaron now?
Titus Andronicus. Act iv, sc. 2, l. 52.

17
Cressida: 'Tis just to each of them; he is himself. . . .
Pandar: Himself! no, he's not himself: would a' were himself.
Troilus and Cressida. Act i, sc. 2, l. 75.
Led . . . a little from himself.—*Troilus and Cressida,* ii, 3, 191.
You cannot shun Yourself.—*Troilus and Cressida,* iii, 2, 152.

PERSUASION

18
With what persuasion did he tempt thy love?
The Comedy of Errors. Act iv, sc. 2, l. 13. [Adriana]

19
God give thee the spirit of persuasion and him the ears of profiting.
I Henry IV. Act i, sc. 2, l. 170. [Falstaff]
Better consider what you have to do
Than I, that have not well the gift of tongue,
Can lift your blood up with persuasion.
I Henry IV. Act v, sc. 2, l. 77. [Hotspur]

20
Fair persuasions mix'd with sugar'd words.
I Henry VI. Act iii, sc. 3, l. 18. [La Pucelle]
A good persuasion.—*A Midsummer-Night's Dream,* i, 1, 156.
Womanly persuasion.—*The Taming of the Shrew,* v, 2, 120.

21
I doubt not, I, but we shall soon persuade
Both him and all his brothers unto reason.
III Henry VI. Act ii, sc. 7, l. 33. [Hastings]
I cannot persuade thee.—*Coriolanus,* v, 3, 120.
I persuade myself.—*Othello,* ii, 3, 223.

Let me persuade you.—*I Henry VI,* iii, 1, 105; iv, 1, 132.
Let us persuade you.—*I Henry VI,* iii, 2, 93.
Let that persuade thee.—*The Merry Wives of Windsor,* iii, 3, 74.
Persuade yourself.—*Measure for Measure,* iv, 1, 53.
We will persuade him.—*The Taming of the Shrew,* iii, 2, 127.
Cease to persuade.—*The Two Gentlemen of Verona,* i, 1, 1.
Persuade me not.—*The Merry Wives of Windsor,* i, 1, 1.

1
The best persuasions to the contrary
Fail not to use, and with what vehemency
The occasion shall instruct you.
Henry VIII. Act v, sc. 1, l. 147. [Cranmer]

Cross him with their opposite persuasion.
The Rape of Lucrece, l. 286.

2
It may be . . . the persuasion of his augurers
May hold him from the Capitol to-day.
Julius Cæsar. Act ii, sc. 1, l. 198. [Cassius]

3 She hath prosperous art
When she will play with reason and discourse,
And well she can persuade.
Measure for Measure. Act i, sc. 2, l. 189. [Claudio]

Such a fellow is not to be talked withal.
Measure for Measure. Act v, sc. 1, l. 348. [Escalus]

4 The magnificoes
Of greatest port, have all persuaded with him.
The Merchant of Venice. Act iii, sc. 2, l. 283. [Salerio] The only use of "magnificoes." "Magnifico" occurs in *Othello,* i, 2, 12.

I have persuaded him.—*Twelfth Night,* iii, 4, 321.
I persuaded them.—*Much Ado about Nothing,* iii, 1, 41.
Are you now persuaded?—*I Henry VI,* ii, 3, 61.
She is persuaded.—*Othello,* iv, 1, 132.
We are well persuaded.—*Henry V,* ii, 2, 20.
Mightily persuaded.—*As You Like It,* i, 2, 219.
Soon persuaded.—*III Henry VI,* iv, 7, 30.
Thoroughly persuaded.—*Coriolanus,* i, 1, 205.
Nor am I yet persuaded.—*Othello,* iv, 2, 180.
O, be persuaded!—*Troilus and Cressida,* v, 3, 19.

5
For he 's a spirit of persuasion, only
Professes to persuade.
The Tempest. Act ii, sc. 1, l. 235. [Antonio]

Persuasion could but thus convince me.
Troilus and Cressida. Act iii, sc. 2, l. 171. [Troilus]

You may temper her by your persuasion.
The Two Gentlemen of Verona. Act iii, sc. 2, l. 64. [Duke]

PERVERSITY

See also Obstinacy

6 You do not well
To bear with their perverse objections.
I Henry VI. Act iv, sc. 1, l. 128. [Gloucester]

7
What most he should dislike seems pleasant to him;
What like, offensive.
King Lear. Act iv, sc. 2, l. 10. [Oswald]

8 I never yet saw man,
How wise, how noble, young, how rarely featured,
But she would spell him backward: if fair-faced,
She would swear the gentleman should be her sister;
If black, why, Nature, drawing of an antique,
Made a foul blot; if tall, a lance ill-headed;
If low, an agate very vilely cut;
If speaking, why, a vane blown with all winds;
If silent, why, a block moved with none.
So turns she every man the wrong side out
And never gives to truth and virtue that
Which simpleness and merit purchaseth.
Much Ado about Nothing. Act iii, sc. 1, l. 59. [Hero] "Fair-faced" is repeated in *King John,* ii, 1, 417. The only use of "ill-headed." "Agate" is repeated in *II Henry IV,* i, 2, 19, and in *Love's Labour's Lost,* ii, 1, 236; and "vane" in *Much Ado about Nothing,* iii, 3, 138, and in *Love's Labour's Lost,* iv, 1, 97.

9 Like a misbehaved and sullen wench,
Thou pout'st upon thy fortune and thy love:
Take heed, take heed, for such die miserable.
Romeo and Juliet. Act iii, sc. 3, l. 143. [Friar Laurence] The only use of "misbehaved" and "pout'st." "Pout" occurs in *Coriolanus,* v, 1, 52: "We pout upon the morning"; and "pouted" in *Venus and Adonis,* l. 33: "Pouted in a dull disdain."

I 'll frown and be perverse.—*Romeo and Juliet,* ii, 2, 96. See under Wooing.

10
Duke: Still so cruel?
Olivia: Still so constant, lord.
Duke: What, to perverseness?
Twelfth Night. Act v, sc. 1, l. 113. The only use of "perverseness."

PESTILENCE

See also Infection, Plague

11
The most infectious pestilence upon thee!
Antony and Cleopatra. Act ii, sc. 5, l. 61. [Cleopatra]

The token'd pestilence, Where death is sure.
Antony and Cleopatra. Act iii, sc. 10, l. 9. [Scarus] The only use of "token'd."

12
Now the red pestilence strike all trades in Rome,
And occupations perish!
Coriolanus. Act iv, sc. 1, l. 13. [Volumnia]

A pestilence on him!—*Hamlet,* v, 1, 196; *Troilus and Cressida,* iv, 2, 21.

13
Devouring pestilence hangs in our air
And thou art flying to a fresher clime.
Richard II. Act i, sc. 3, l. 284. [Gaunt]

1
Suspecting that we both were in a house
Where the infectious pestilence did reign.
Romeo and Juliet. Act v, sc. 2, l. 9. [Friar John] The only use of "suspecting."
Life-poisoning pestilence.—*Venus and Adonis,* l. 740. The only use of "life-poisoning."

PETITION

See also Prayer, Request

2
Nay, I prithee now with most petitionary vehemence, tell me who it is.
As You Like It. Act iii, sc. 2, l. 199. [Rosalind] The only use of "vehemence."
Petitionary countrymen.—*Coriolanus,* v, 2, 82. The only uses of "petitionary."

3
A petition granted them, a strange one.
Coriolanus. Act i, sc. 1, l. 214. [Marcius]
It was a bare petition of a state
To one whom they had punish'd.
Coriolanus. Act v, sc. 1, l. 20. [Cominius]
This boy . . .
Does reason our petition with more strength
Than thou hast to deny 't.
Coriolanus. Act v, sc. 3, l. 174. [Volumnia]

4
You have, I know, petition'd all the gods
For my prosperity!
Coriolanus. Act ii, sc. 1, l. 187. [Coriolanus] The only use of "petition'd."

5
He hath, my lord, wrung from me my slow leave
By laboursome petition.
Hamlet. Act i, sc. 2, l. 58. [Polonius] "Laboursome" is repeated in *Cymbeline,* iii, 4, 167.

6
And that is my petition, noble lord.
I Henry VI. Act iv, sc. 1, l. 101. [Vernon]

7
I am but a poor petitioner of our whole township.
II Henry VI. Act i, sc. 3, l. 26. [Petitioner]
Let us, that are poor petitioners, speak too.
The Taming of the Shrew. Act ii, sc. 1, l. 72. [Gremio]
Poor petitioner.—*II Henry VI,* i, 3, 26; *Richard III,* iii, 7, 183.

8
Petitioners for blood thou ne'er put'st back.
III Henry VI. Act v, sc. 5, l. 80. [Queen Margaret]

9
What, urge you your petitions in the street?
Come to the Capitol.
Julius Cæsar. Act iii, sc. 1, l. 11. [Cassius]

10
Melted by the windy breath Of soft petitions.
King John, ii, 1, 478. See under ZEAL.
Full petition.—*Julius Cæsar,* ii, 1, 58.
General petition.—*Henry V,* v, 2, 305.
Poor petition.—*All's Well that Ends Well,* v, 1, 19; *Henry VIII,* iv, 2, 138.

11
O vain petitioner! beg a greater matter;
Thou now request'st but moonshine in the water.
Love's Labour's Lost. Act v, sc. 2, l. 207. See under MOON.

12
All their petitions are . . . freely theirs.
Measure for Measure, i, 4, 82. See under MAID.

13
Consort with me in loud and dear petition.
Troilus and Cressida. Act v, sc. 3, l. 9. [Andromache]

14
Your petition Is yet unanswer'd.
The Winter's Tale. Act v, sc. 1, l. 228. [Leontes] The only use of "unanswer'd."

PHILOMELA, see Nightingale

PHILOSOPHY

15
Hast any philosophy in thee, shepherd?
As You Like It. Act iii, sc. 2, l. 22. [Touchstone]
Such a one is a natural philosopher.
As You Like It. Act iii, sc. 2, l. 34. [Touchstone]
Heathen philosopher.—*As You Like It,* v, 1, 36.

16
There are more things in heaven and earth, Horatio,
Than are dreamt of in your philosophy.
Hamlet. Act i, sc. 5, l. 166. [Hamlet]
'Sblood, there is something in this more than natural, if philosophy could find it out.
Hamlet. Act ii, sc. 2, l. 384. [Hamlet]

17
It shall go hard but I will make him a philosopher's two stones to me.
II Henry IV. Act iii, sc. 2, l. 354. [Falstaff]

18
Of your philosophy you make no use,
If you give place to accidental evils.
Julius Cæsar. Act iv, sc. 3, l. 145. [Cassius]
That philosophy
By which I did blame Cato for the death
Which he did give himself.
Julius Cæsar. Act v, sc. 1, l. 101. [Brutus]

19
First let me talk with this philosopher.
King Lear. Act iii, sc. 4, l. 159. [King Lear]
Noble philosopher, your company.
King Lear. Act iii, sc. 4, l. 177. [King Lear]
I will still keep with my philosopher.
King Lear. Act iii, sc. 4, l. 181. [King Lear]

20
To love, to wealth, to pomp, I pine and die;
With all these living in philosophy.
Love's Labour's Lost. Act i, sc. 1, l. 31. [Dumain]

21
For there was never yet philosopher
That could endure the toothache patiently,
However they have writ the style of gods
And made a push at chance and sufferance.
Much Ado about Nothing. Act v, sc. 1, l. 35. [Leonato]

22
Adversity's sweet milk, philosophy.
Romeo and Juliet. Act iii, sc. 3, l. 55. [Friar Laurence]

Hang up philosophy!
Unless philosophy can make a Juliet,
Displant a town, reverse a prince's doom,
It helps not, it prevails not: talk no more.
Romeo and Juliet. Act iii, sc. 3, l. 59. [Romeo] The only use of "displant."

1
I fear he will prove the weeping philosopher when he grows old, being so full of unmannerly sadness in his youth.
The Merchant of Venice. Act i, sc. 2, l. 52. [Portia]

Sometime the philosopher.—*Timon of Athens,* ii, 2, 131.

2
Lucentio: For the time I study,
Virtue and that part of philosophy
Will I apply that treats of happiness
By virtue specially to be achieved.
Tell me thy mind. . . .
Tranio: Mi perdonato, gentle master mine,
I am in all affected as yourself;
Glad that you thus continue your resolve
To suck the sweets of sweet philosophy.
Only, good master, while we do admire
This virtue and this moral discipline,
Let 's be no stoics nor no stocks, I pray;
Or so devote to Aristotle's checks
As Ovid be an outcast quite abjured:
Balk logic with acquaintance that you have.
And practise rhetoric in your common talk;
Music and poesy use to quicken you;
The mathematics and the metaphysics,
Fall to them as you find your stomach serves you;
No profit grows where is no pleasure ta'en:
In brief, sir, study what you most affect.
The Taming of the Shrew. Act i, sc. 1, l. 17. The only use of "mi perdonato," "stoics," and "metaphysics." Aristotle is mentioned again in *Troilus and Cressida,* ii, 2, 166; and Ovid in *As You Like It,* iii, 3, 8, in *Titus Andronicus,* iv, 1, 42, and in *Love's Labour 's Lost,* iv, 2, 127, where he is referred to as Ovidius Naso. "Abjured" is repeated in *Twelfth Night,* i, 2, 40; and "balk" in *The Rape of Lucrece,* l. 696. "Balked" occurs twice, in *I Henry IV,* i, 1, 69, and in *Twelfth Night,* iii, 2, 26; and "metaphysical" once, in *Macbeth,* i, 5, 30.

Then give me leave to read philosophy.
The Taming of the Shrew. Act iii, sc. 1, l. 13. [Lucentio]

Moral philosophy.—*Troilus and Cressida,* ii, 2, 167.

PHŒBUS, see Sun

PHŒNIX

3 From their ashes shall be rear'd
A phœnix that shall make all France afeard.
I Henry VI. Act iv, sc. 7, l. 93. [Sir William Lucy]

When
The bird of wonder dies, the maiden phœnix,
Her ashes new create another heir,
As great in admiration as herself.
Henry VIII. Act v, sc. 5, l. 41. [Cranmer] See under PROPHECY.

4
Burn the long-lived phœnix in her blood.
Sonnets. No. xix. The only use of "long-lived."

5 In Arabia
There is one tree, the phœnix' throne, one phœnix
At this hour reigning there.
The Tempest. Act iii, sc. 3, l. 22. [Sebastian]

Rare as phœnix.—*As You Like It,* iv, 3, 17.
Phœnix is used three times in *The Comedy of Errors* as the name of an inn, and once in *Twelfth Night* as the name of a ship.

PHRASE

6
The gallant militarist—that was his own phrase.
All's Well that Ends Well, iv, 3, 162. The only use of "militarist."

Her very phrases.—*Twelfth Night,* ii, 5, 102.

7
Not to crack the wind of the poor phrase.
Hamlet. Act i, sc. 3, l. 108. [Polonius]

'Good sir,' or so, or 'friend,' or 'gentleman,'
According to the phrase or the addition
Of man and country.
Hamlet. Act ii, sc. 1, l. 46. [Polonius]

8
That 's an ill phrase, a vile phrase; 'beautified' is a vile phrase.
Hamlet. Act ii, sc. 2, l. 111. [Polonius] "Beautified" is repeated in *The Two Gentlemen of Verona,* iv, 1, 55: "Beautified with goodly shape."

Swinish phrase.—*Hamlet,* i, 4, 19. "Swinish" is repeated in *Macbeth,* i, 7, 67: "Swinish sleep."

Phrase of sorrow.—*Hamlet,* v, 1, 278.

9
The phrase would be more german to the matter.
Hamlet. Act v, sc. 2, l. 165. [Hamlet]

The phrase is to the matter.
Measure for Measure. Act v, sc. 1, l. 90. [Isabella]

10
Shallow: Good phrases are surely, and ever were, very commendable. Accommodated! it comes of 'accommodo': very good; a good phrase.
Bardolph: Pardon me, sir; I have heard the word. Phrase call you it? by this good day, I know not the phrase; but I will maintain the word with my sword to be a soldier-like word, and a word of exceeding good command, by heaven. Accommodated; that is, when a man is, as they say, accommodated; or when a man is, being, whereby a' may be thought to be accommodated: which is an excellent thing.
II Henry IV. Act iii, sc. 2, l. 76. The only use of "accommodo."

'Tis not a soldier-like phrase.
Merry Wives of Windsor. Act ii, sc. 1, l. 13. [Mrs. Page] The only uses of "soldier-like."

A good phrase.—*II Henry IV,* iii, 2, 79.

1
The pig, or the great, or the mighty, or the huge, or the magnanimous, are all one reckonings, save the phrase is a little variations.
Henry V. Act iv, sc. 7, l. 16. [Fluellen]
So they phrase 'em.—*Henry VIII,* i, 1, 34.

2 Thou speak'st
In better phrase and manner than thou didst.
King Lear. Act iv, sc. 6, l. 7. [Gloucester]

3
The epithets are sweetly varied, like a scholar at the least.
Love's Labour's Lost. Act iv, sc. 2, l. 8. [Sir Nathaniel]
A most singular and choice epithet.
Love's Labour's Lost. Act v, sc. 1, l. 17. [Sir Nathaniel]
A good epithet!—*Much Ado about Nothing,* v, 2, 67.
Stuff'd with epithets.—*Othello,* i, 1, 14.
Answer to that epithet.—*Love's Labour's Lost,* v, 2, 170. The only uses of "epithet" and "epithets."

4
'Convey,' the wise it call. 'Steal!' foh! a fico for the phrase!
The Merry Wives of Windsor. Act i, sc. 3, l. 32. [Pistol] The only use of "fico."

5
Little bless'd with the soft phrase of peace.
Othello, i, 3, 82. See under RUDENESS.
Precious phrase by all the Muses filed.
Sonnets. No. lxxxv.
Red-lattice phrases.—*The Merry Wives of Windsor,* ii, 2, 28. "Red lattice" (unhyphenated) occurs in *II Henry IV,* ii, 2, 86.
Taffeta phrases.—*Love's Labour's Lost,* v, 2, 406. See under RHETORIC.
There's a stewed phrase indeed!—*Troilus and Cressida,* iii, 1, 45.
A mint of phrases in his brain.—*Love's Labour's Lost,* i, 1, 166. See MAN, 943:17.

PHYSIC

See also Medicine, Remedy

6
Sweet practiser, thy physic I will try,
That ministers thine own death, if I die.
All's Well that Ends Well. Act ii, sc. 1, l. 188. [King] "Practiser" is repeated in *Love's Labour's Lost,* iv, 3, 325, and in *Othello,* i, 2, 78.
The younger of our nature,
That surfeit on their ease, will day by day
Come here for physic.
All's Well that Ends Well, iii, 1, 17. [Lord]

7
I will physic your rankness.
As You Like It. Act i, sc. 1, l. 91. [Oliver] "Rankness" occurs twice more, in *King John,* v, 4, 54, and *Henry VIII,* iv, 1, 59.
I will not cast away my physic but on those that are sick.
As You Like It, iii, 2, 376. [Rosalind]

8 Jump a body with a dangerous physic
That's sure of death without it.
Coriolanus. Act iii, sc. 1, l. 154. [Coriolanus]
The violent fit o' the time craves it as physic
For the whole state.
Coriolanus. Act iii, sc. 2, l. 33. [Menenius]

9
This physic but prolongs thy sickly days.
Hamlet. Act iii, sc. 3, l. 96. [Hamlet]

10
I will see what physic the tavern affords.
I Henry VI. Act iii, sc. 1, l. 147. [Servant]

11
'Tis time to give 'em physic, their diseases
Are grown so catching.
Henry VIII. Act i, sc. 3, l. 36. [Sands]
Give physic to the sick.—*The Rape of Lucrece,* l. 901.
Give physic to my grief.—*Sonnets,* xxxiv.
I have given her physic.—*Titus Andronicus,* iv, 2, 162.
Physic your cold breast.—*A Lover's Complaint,* l. 259.
Take thy physic first.—*Timon of Athens,* iii, 6, 110.
Take physic.—*King Lear,* iii, 4, 33.

12 He brings his physic
After his patient's death.
Henry VIII. Act iii, sc. 2, l. 40. [Chamberlain]
That gentle physic, given in time, had cured me;
But now I am past all comforts here, but prayers.
Henry VIII. Act iv, sc. 2, l. 122. [Katharine]

13
Throw physic to the dogs; I'll none of it.
Macbeth. Act v, sc. 3, l. 47. [Macbeth]
Farewell all physic.—*Henry VIII,* v, 3, 27.

14
Rosaline: Alack, let it blood.
Biron: Would that do it good?
Rosaline: My physic says 'ay.'
Love's Labour's Lost. Act ii, sc. 1, l. 186.

15
'Tis a physic That's bitter to sweet end.
Measure for Measure. Act iv, sc. 6, l. 7. [Isabella]

16 'Tis known, I ever
Have studied physic, through which secret art,
By turning o'er authorities, I have,
Together with my practice, made familiar
To me and to my aid the blest infusions
That dwell in vegetives, in metals, stones;
And I can speak of the disturbances
That nature works, and of her cures.
Pericles. Act iii, sc. 2, l. 37. [Cerimon] The only use of "vegetives" and "disturbances."
Holy physic.—*Romeo and Juliet,* ii, 3, 52.

17
That will physic the great Myrmidon.
Troilus and Cressida. Act i, sc. 3, l. 378. [Ulysses]
I know my physic will work with him.
Twelfth Night. Act ii, sc. 3, l. 187. [Maria]

18
Physic for 't there is none.
Winter's Tale. Act i, sc. 2, l. 200. [Leontes]

PHYSICIAN, see Doctor

PICTURE

1
All the pictures fairest lined
Are but black to Rosalind.
As You Like It. Act iii, sc. 2, l. 97. [Rosalind, reading]

2
What, have you got the picture of old Adam new-apparelled?
The Comedy of Errors. Act iv, sc. 3, l. 13. [Dromio of Syracuse] The only use of "new-apparelled."

3
Who was he
That, otherwise than noble nature did,
Hath alter'd that good picture?
Cymbeline. Act iv, sc. 2, l. 363. [Lucius]

He began
His mistress' picture; which by his tongue being made,
And then a mind put in 't, either our brags
Were crack'd of kitchen-trulls, or his description
Proved us unspeaking sots.
Cymbeline, v, 5, 174. [Iachimo] The only use of "kitchen-trulls" and "unspeaking."

4
Those that would make mows at him while my father lived, give twenty, forty, fifty, an hundred ducats a-piece for his picture in little.
Hamlet. Act ii, sc. 2, l. 381. [Hamlet]

Look here, upon this picture, and on this,
The counterfeit presentment of two brothers.
Hamlet. Act iii, sc. 4, l. 53. [Hamlet] "Presentment" is repeated in *Timon of Athens,* i, 1, 27.

5
Long time thy shadow hath been thrall to me,
For in my gallery thy picture hangs.
I Henry VI. Act ii, sc. 3, l. 36. [Countess]

Your gallery
Have we pass'd through, not without much content
In many singularities.
Winter's Tale. Act v, sc. 3, l. 10. [Leontes]

Avoid the gallery.—*Henry VIII,* v, 1, 86.
Withdraw into the gallery.—*Pericles,* ii, 2, 59. The only uses of "gallery."

6
Were but his picture left amongst you here,
It would amaze the proudest of you all.
I Henry VI. Act iv, sc. 7, l. 83. [Lucy]

7
His picture
I will send far and near, that all the kindom
May have due note of him.
King Lear. Act ii, sc. 1, l. 83. [Gloucester]

8
O, he hath drawn my picture in his letter!
Love's Labour's Lost. Act v, sc. 2, l. 38. [Rosaline]

I have drawn her picture with my voice.
Pericles. Act iv, sc. 2, l. 101. [Boult]

9
Many there were that did his picture get,
To serve their eyes, and in it put their mind.
A Lover's Complaint, l. 134.

He is a proper man's picture.—*The Merchant of Venice,* i, 2, 78.

10
You may come and see the picture, she says, that you wot of.
The Merry Wives of Windsor. Act ii, sc. 2, l. 89. [Mrs. Quickly]

I will go get her picture.—*Much Ado about Nothing,* ii, 3, 273.

11
You are pictures out of doors.
Othello, ii, 1, 110. See under WOMAN.

12
Your painted counterfeit.
Sonnets. No. xvi.

Your true image pictured lies;
Which in my bosom's shop is hanging still,
That hath his windows glazed with thine eyes.
Sonnets. No. xxiv.

With my love's picture then my eye doth feast
And to the painted banquet bids my heart.
Sonnets. No. xlvii. See under EYE.

Thy picture in my sight,
Awakes my heart to heart's and eye's delight.
Sonnets. No. xlvii.

13
Hang it round with all my wanton pictures.
The Taming of the Shrew. Induction, sc. 1, l. 47. [Lord]

Dost thou love pictures?
The Taming of the Shrew. Induction, sc. 2, l. 51. [Servant]

14
Timon: How likest thou this picture, Apemantus?
Apemantus: The best, for the innocence.
Timon: Wrought he not well that painted it?
Apemantus: He wrought better than made the painter; and yet he 's but a filthy piece of work.
Timon of Athens. Act i, sc. 1, l. 198.

The picture of my youth.—*Titus Andronicus,* iv, 2, 108.

15
Come, draw this curtain, and let 's see your picture.
Troilus and Cressida. Act iii, sc. 2, l. 49. [Pandarus]

We will draw the curtain and show you the picture.
Twelfth Night. Act i, sc. 5, l. 248. [Olivia]

16
Thou picture of what thou seemest.
Troilus and Cressida. Act v, sc. 1, l. 6. [Thersites]

Lifeless picture.—*Venus and Adonis,* l. 211.

17
Did you never see the picture of 'we three'?
Twelfth Night. Act ii, sc. 3, l. 16. [Clown]

Here, wear this jewel for me, 'tis my picture;
Refuse it not; it hath no tongue to vex you.
Twelfth Night. Act iii, sc. 4, l. 228. [Olivia]

Mine own picture.—*II Henry IV,* iv, 3, 53.

18
'Tis but her picture I have yet beheld,
And that hath dazzled my reason's light;
But when I look on her perfections,
There is no reason but I shall be blind.
The Two Gentlemen of Verona. Act ii, sc. 4, l. 209. [Proteus]

Vouchsafe me yet your picture for my love,
The picture that is hanging in your chamber;

To that I 'll speak, to that I 'll sigh and weep.
The Two Gentlemen of Verona. Act iv, sc. 2, l. 121. [Proteus]

Tell my lady
I claim the promise for her heavenly picture.
The Two Gentlemen of Verona. Act iv, sc. 4, l. 91. [Proteus]

Heavenly picture.—*The Merchant of Venice,* ii, 7, 48.

Julia: I do entreat your patience
To hear me speak the message I am sent on.
Silvia: From whom?
Julia: From my master, Sir Proteus, madam.
Silvia: O, he sends you for a picture.
Julia: Ay, madam.
Silvia: Ursula, bring my picture there.
Go give your master this: tell him from me,
One Julia, that his changing thoughts forget,
Would better fit his chamber than this shadow.
The Two Gentlemen of Verona. Act iv, sc. 4, l. 116.

Here is her picture.—*The Two Gentlemen of Verona,* iv, 4, 189.

PIETY

1
Is not this course pious?
Henry VIII. Act ii, sc. 2, l. 38. [Norfolk]

Pious innocent.—*Pericles,* iv, 3, 17.
Pious sir.—*Measure for Measure,* i, 3, 16.

2
Thou art full of piety, as shall be proved upon thee by good witness.
Much Ado about Nothing. Act iv, sc. 2, l. 81. [Dogberry]

The picture of pure piety.
The Rape of Lucrece, l. 542.

Glistering semblances of piety.—*Henry V,* ii, 2, 117.

3
Look you get a prayer-book in your hand,
And stand betwixt two churchmen, good my lord;
For on that ground I 'll build a holy descant.
Richard III. Act iii, sc. 7, l. 47. [Buckingham] "Descant" is repeated in i, 1, 27, and in *The Two Gentlemen of Verona,* i, 2, 94.

Wear prayer-books in my pocket.—*The Merchant of Venice,* ii, 2, 201. The only uses of "prayer-book" and "prayer-books."

4
O cruel, irreligious piety!
Titus Andronicus. Act i, sc. 1, l. 130. [Tamora]

5
How his piety
Does my deeds make the blacker!
Winter's Tale. Act iii, sc. 2, l. 172. [Leontes]

PILGRIM

6
God save you, pilgrim! whither are you bound?
All's Well that Ends Well. Act iii, sc. 5, l. 35. [Widow]

I am Saint Jaques' pilgrim, thither gone.
All's Well that Ends Well. Act iii, sc. 4, l. 4. [Steward]

A pilgrimage to Saint Jaques le Grand.—*All's Well that Ends Well,* iv, 3, 57.

7
There are pilgrims going to Canterbury with rich offerings.
I Henry IV. Act i, sc. 2, l. 140. [Poins]

8
For Mowbray and myself are like two men
That vow a long and weary pilgrimage.
Richard II. Act i, sc. 3, l. 48. [Bolingbroke]

An inforced pilgrimage.—*Richard II,* i, 3, 264.
Erring pilgrimage.—*As You Like It,* iii, 2, 138.
Golden pilgrimage.—*Sonnets,* vii.
Maiden pilgrimage.—*A Midsummer-Night's Dream,* i, 1, 75.
Secret pilgrimage.—*The Merchant of Venice,* i, 1, 120.
Zealous pilgrimage.—*Sonnets,* xxvii.

9
A true-devoted pilgrim is not weary
To measure kingdoms with his feeble steps.
The Two Gentlemen of Verona. Act ii, sc. 7, l. 9. [Julia] The only use of "true-devoted."

Blushing pilgrims.—*Romeo and Juliet,* i, 5, 97.
Good pilgrim.—*Romeo and Juliet,* i, 5, 99.
Holy pilgrim.—*All's Well that Ends Well,* iii, 5, 42.

PILLOW

10
Have I my pillow left unpress'd in Rome?
Antony and Cleopatra. Act iii, sc. 13, l. 106. [Antony] The only use of "unpress'd."

11
Who is this Thou makest thy bloody pillow?
Cymbeline. Act iv, sc. 2, l. 362. [Lucius]

12
A good soft pillow for that good white head
Were better than a churlish turf of France.
Henry V. Act iv, sc. 1, l. 14. [King Henry]

One turf shall serve as pillow for us both.
A Midsummer-Night's Dream. Act ii, sc. 2, l. 41. [Lysander]

13
That pillow . . .
Where thou wast wont to rest thy weary head.
The Rape of Lucrece, l. 1620.

A pillow for his head.—*Pericles,* v, 1, 237.

14
Here I 'll fling the pillow, there the bolster.
The Taming of the Shrew. Act iv, sc. 1, l. 204. [Petruchio] The only use of "bolster" in this sense.

15
Pluck stout men's pillows from below their heads.
Timon of Athens. Act iv, sc. 3, l. 32. [Timon]

16
Make his dead trunk pillow to our lust.
Titus Andronicus, ii, 3, 130. See under HUSBAND.

His loving breast thy pillow.—*Titus Andronicus,* v, 3, 163. See under GRANDFATHER.
Deaf pillows.—*Macbeth,* v, 1, 81.
Down pillow.—*Cymbeline,* iii, 6, 35.
Fair pillow.—*Troilus and Cressida,* iii, 1, 49.
Midnight pillow.—*As You Like It,* ii, 4, 27.

PILOT

17
What though the mast be now blown overboard,
The cable broke, the holding-anchor lost,

And half our sailors swallow'd in the flood?
Yet lives our pilot still.
III Henry VI. Act v, sc. 4, l. 3. [Queen Margaret] The only use of "holding-anchor."

1 His pilot
Of very expert and approved allowance.
Othello. Act ii, sc. 1, l. 48. [Cassio]

Skilful pilot.—*III Henry VI*, v, 4, 20.

Traded pilots.—*Troilus and Cressida*, ii, 2, 64. "Traded" is used only once more, in *King John*, iv, 3, 109.

2
I am no pilot; yet, wert thou as far
As that vast shore wash'd with the farthest sea,
I would adventure for such merchandise.
Romeo and Juliet. Act ii, sc. 2, l. 82. [Romeo]

Thou desperate pilot, now at once run on
The dashing rocks thy sea-sick weary bark!
Romeo and Juliet. Act v, sc. 3, l. 117. [Romeo]

3
Be pilot to me and thy places shall
Still neighbour mine.
The Winter's Tale. Act i, sc. 2, l. 448. [Polixenes]

PIN

4
Which show like pins' heads to her.
II Henry IV. Act iv, sc. 3, l. 58. [Falstaff]

Pins' heads.—*I Henry IV*, iv, 2, 24. The only uses of "pins' heads."

5
I would not care a pin, if the other three were in.
Love's Labour 's Lost. Act iv, sc. 3, l. 18. [Biron]

Not worth a pin.—*The Two Gentlemen of Verona*, ii, 7, 56.

6 If you should need a pin,
You could not with more tame a tongue desire it.
Measure for Measure. Act ii, sc. 2, l. 46. [Lucio]

Tut, a pin!—*Merry Wives of Windsor*, i, 1, 117.

7 And with a little pin
Bores through his castle wall.
Richard II, iii, 2, 169. See under KING.

Great pin.—*II Henry VI*, iv, 10, 32.

Row of pins.—*Richard II*, iii, 4, 26.

Pins and poking-sticks of steel.—*The Winter's Tale*, iv, 4, 228. The only use of "poking-sticks."

PINCH

8
Here 's the pang that pinches.
Henry VIII. Act ii, sc. 3, l. 1. [Anne]

Sharp pinch.—*King Lear*, ii, 4, 214.

Lover's pinch.—*Antony and Cleopatra*, v, 2, 298.

9
There pinch the maids as blue as bilberry.
The Merry Wives of Windsor. Act v, sc. 5, l. 49. [Pistol] The only use of "bilberry" (whortle-berry).

Pinch us black and blue.—*The Comedy of Errors*, ii, 2, 194. See under FAIRY.

10
But those as sleep and think not on their sins,
Pinch them, arms, legs, backs, shoulders, sides and shins.
The Merry Wives of Windsor. Act v, sc. 5, l. 57. [Evans]

Pinch him, fairies, mutually; Pinch him for his villainy;
Pinch him, and burn him, and turn him about,
Till candles and starlight and moonshine be out.
The Merry Wives of Windsor. Act v, sc. 5, l. 103. [Song]

Pinch her by the hand.—*The Merry Wives of Windsor*, iv, 6, 44.

Pinch one another.—*Antony and Cleopatra*, ii, 7, 7.

11 Thou shalt be pinch'd
As thick as honeycomb, each pinch more stinging
Than bees that made 'em.
The Tempest. Act i, sc. 2, l. 328. [Prospero] The only use of "honeycomb."

He 'll fill our skins with pinches.
The Tempest. Act iv, sc. 1, l. 233. [Caliban]

I shall be pinch'd to death.
The Tempest. Act v, sc. 1, l. 276. [Caliban]

Pinched with the colic.—*Coriolanus*, ii, 1, 82.

With a kind of colic pinch'd.—*I Henry IV*, iii, 1, 29.

What, have I pinch'd you?—*The Taming of the Shrew*, ii, 1, 373.

Pinched a placket.—*The Winter's Tale*, iv, 4, 622. See PURSE, 1225:4.

PINE

12 This pine is bark'd,
That overtopp'd them all.
Antony and Cleopatra. Act iv, sc. 12, l. 24. [Antony] The only use of "overtopp'd."

13
Ay me! the bark peel'd from the lofty pine,
His leaves will wither and his sap decay.
The Rape of Lucrece, l. 1167.

14
Thus droops this lofty pine and hangs his sprays.
II Henry VI. Act ii, sc. 3, l. 45. [Suffolk]

Eastern pines.—*Richard II*, iii, 2, 42.

Mountain pines.—*The Merchant of Venice*, iv, 1, 75; *Cymbeline*, iv, 2, 175.

Sound pine.—*Troilus and Cressida*, i, 3, 8.

Tuft of pines.—*The Winter's Tale*, ii, 1, 34.

15 She did confine thee,
By help of her most potent ministers, . . .
Into a cloven pine; . . . it was mine art,
When I arrived and heard thee, that made gape
The pine and let thee out.
The Tempest. Act i, sc. 2, l. 274. [Prospero]

The strong-based promontory
Have I made shake and by the spurs pluck'd up
The pine and cedar.
The Tempest. Act v, sc. 1, l. 46. [Prospero] The only use of "strong-based."

For pine in the sense of languish, see under LONGING.

PIRATE

1
Menecrates and Menas, famous pirates,
Make the sea serve them, which they ear and wound
With keels of every kind.
Antony and Cleopatra. Act i, sc. 4, l. 48. [Messenger] The only mention of Menecrates. Menas is mentioned five times.
Bargulus the strong Illyrian pirate.—*II Henry VI,* iv, 1, 108. The only mention of Bargulus.
The great pirate Valdes.—*Pericles,* iv, 1, 97. The only mention of Valdes.
2
I must Rid all the sea of pirates.
Antony and Cleopatra. Act ii, sc. 6, l. 35. [Pompey]
3
A pirate of very warlike appointment.
Hamlet. Act iv, sc. 6, l. 15. [Horatio]
4
Pirates may make cheap pennyworths of their pillage
And purchase friends and give to courtezans,
Still revelling like lords till all be gone;
While as the silly owner of the goods
Weeps over them and wrings his hapless hands
And shakes his head and trembling stands aloof,
While all is shared and all is borne away,
Ready to starve and dare not touch his own.
II Henry VI. Act i, sc. 1, l. 222. [York]
Suffolk dies by pirates.—*II Henry VI,* iv, 1, 138.
Boarded with a pirate.—*II Henry VI,* iv, 9, 33.
5
Water-thieves and land-thieves, I mean pirates.
The Merchant of Venice. Act i, sc. 3, l. 24. [Shylock] The only use of either phrase.
6
Hear me, you wrangling pirates, that fall out
In sharing that which you have pill'd from me!
Richard III. Act i, sc. 3, l. 158. [Queen Margaret] "Pill'd" occurs again in *Richard II,* ii, 1, 246.
Notable pirate! thou salt-water thief!
Twelfth Night. Act v, sc. 1, l. 72. [Duke]
Notorious pirate.—*Measure for Measure,* iv, 3, 75.
Sanctimonious pirate.—*Measure for Measure,* i, 2, 8. "Sanctimonious" is repeated in *The Tempest,* iv, 1, 16: "Sanctimonious ceremonies."
Strong pirates.—*The Rape of Lucrece,* l. 335.
A crew of pirates.—*Pericles,* v, 1, 176.
7
Antonio never yet was thief or pirate.
Twelfth Night. Act v, sc. 1, l. 77. [Antonio]

PITY

See also Compassion; Love and Pity

8 Give pity
To her, whose state is such that cannot choose
But lend and give where she is sure to lose.
All's Well that Ends Well. Act i, sc. 3, l. 219. [Helena]
9
Pity me, Charmian, But do not speak to me.
Antony and Cleopatra. Act ii, sc. 5, l. 118. [Cleopatra]
Our care and pity is so much upon you,
That we remain your friend.
Antony and Cleopatra. Act v, sc. 2, l. 188. [Cæsar]
10 Wiped our eyes
Of drops that sacred pity hath engender'd.
As You Like It. Act ii, sc. 7, l. 122. [Duke senior]
Pity me not;
As till that time I shall not pity thee.
As You Like It. Act iii, sc. 5, l. 33. [Phebe]
Pity me not.—*Hamlet,* i, 5, 5.
11
Do you pity him? no, he deserves no pity.
As You Like It. Act iv, sc. 3, l. 66. [Rosalind]
The more pity.—*As You Like It,* i, 2, 92.
The more the pity.—*I Henry IV,* ii, 4, 514; *A Midsummer-Night's Dream,* iii, 1, 148.
12
Iachimo: Whilst I am bound to wonder, I am bound
To pity too.
Imogen: What do you pity, sir?
Iachimo: Two creatures heartily.
Imogen: Am I one, sir?
You look on me: what wreck discern you in me
Deserves your pity?
Cymbeline. Act i, sc. 6, l. 81.
If there be
Yet left in heaven as small a drop of pity
As a wren's eye, fear'd gods, a part of it!
Cymbeline. Act iv, sc. 2, l. 303. [Imogen]
A thing of pity.—*Cymbeline,* v, 4, 47.
13
'Tis true 'tis pity; and pity 'tis 'tis true.
Hamlet. Act ii, sc. 2, l. 97. [Polonius]
Pity 'tis.—*Romeo and Juliet,* i, 2, 5.
'Tis pity.—*The Comedy of Errors,* v, 1, 27, and frequently in later plays.
'Tis pity of him.—*Antony and Cleopatra,* i, 4, 71; *Measure for Measure,* ii, 3, 42; *Othello,* ii, 3, 130.
'Twere pity.—*III Henry VI,* iv, 1, 22, and frequently in later plays.
That were pity.—*Merchant of Venice,* ii, 2, 209.
What pity it is!—*Richard II,* iii, 4, 55.
Is 't not pity?—*King John,* v, 2, 24.
14
Pitiful-hearted Titan, that melted at the sweet tale of the sun's!
I Henry IV. Act ii, sc. 4, l. 134. [Prince] The only use of "pitiful-hearted."
15
It was great pity, so it was.
I Henry IV, i, 3, 59. See under CANNON.
Great pity.—*Othello,* ii, 3, 143; *The Winter's Tale,* iv, 4, 804; *Passionate Pilgrim,* l. 384.
Childish pity.—*Henry VIII,* v, 3, 25.
Feeling pity.—*A Lover's Complaint,* l. 178.
Holy pity.—*Henry VIII,* iii, 2, 263.

1
Pity the city of London, pity us!
I Henry VI. Act iii, sc. 1, l. 77. [Mayor]
Pity me.—*III Henry VI*, i, 3, 40.

2
Who should be pitiful, if you not be?
I Henry VI. Act iii, sc. 1, l. 109. [King Henry]

He was never,
But where he meant to ruin, pitiful.
Henry VIII. Act iv, sc. 2, l. 39. [Katharine]

She swore, in faith, 'twas strange, 'twas passing strange,
'Twas pitiful, 'twas wondrous pitiful.
Othello. Act i, sc. 3, l. 159. [Othello]

Be pitiful.—*III Henry VI*, iii, 2, 32; *Titus Andronicus*, iii, 1, 8.
'Tis pitiful.—*Othello*, v, 2, 210.

3
Pity was all the fault that was in me;
For I should melt at an offender's tears,
And lowly words were ransom for their fault.
II Henry VI. Act iii, sc. 1, l. 125. [Gloucester]

Full of foolish pity.—*II Henry VI*, iii, 1, 224.

4
Henceforth I will not have to do with pity.
II Henry VI. Act v, sc. 2, l. 56. [Clifford]

Nor let pity, which
Even women have cast off, melt thee.
Pericles. Act iv, sc. 1, l. 6. [Dionyza]

Devoid of pity.—*Titus Andronicus*, v, 3, 199. The only use of "devoid."
Void of pity.—*II Henry VI*, iv, 7, 69.
Out of pity.—*Henry VIII*, iii, 2, 382.
Uncapable of pity.—*The Merchant of Venice*, iv, 1, 5. "Uncapable" is repeated in *Othello*, iv, 2, 235.

5
Rutland: To thee I pray; sweet Clifford, pity me!
Clifford: Such pity as my rapier's point affords.
III Henry VI. Act i, sc. 3, l. 36.

This too much lenity
And harmful pity must be laid aside.
III Henry VI. Act ii, sc. 2, l. 9. [Clifford]

6
O, pity, pity, gentle heaven, pity!
III Henry VI. Act ii, sc. 5, l. 96. [King Henry]

Pity my case.—*II Henry VI*, i, 3, 218.
Bestow your pity on me.—*Henry VIII*, ii, 4, 14.
Have pity.—*The Tempest*, i, 2, 474.
Have some pity.—*Henry VIII*, iv, 2, 139.

7
At their hands I have deserved no pity.
III Henry VI. Act ii, sc. 6, l. 26. [Clifford]

Thou pitied'st Rutland; I will pity thee.
III Henry VI. Act ii, sc. 6, l. 74. [Edward]

My pity hath been balm to heal their wounds.
III Henry VI. Act iv, sc. 8, l. 41. [King Henry]

8
All Was either pitied in him or forgotten.
Henry VIII. Act ii, sc. 1, l. 29. [Gentleman]

Freshly pitied in our memories.
Henry VIII. Act v, sc. 3, l. 31. [Gardiner]

We . . . are therefore to be pitied.
Antony and Cleopatra. Act v, sc. 2, l. 179. [Cleopatra]

Pitied nor hated.—*Cymbeline*, v, 1, 28.

9
O, this is full of pity!
Henry VIII. Act ii, sc. 1, l. 137. [Gentleman]

To give her the avaunt! it is a pity
Would move a monster.
Henry VIII. Act ii, sc. 3, l. 10. [Anne]

Pity drop upon her.
Henry VIII. Act ii, sc. 3, l. 18. [Anne]

10
As fire drives out fire, so pity pity.
Julius Cæsar. Act iii, sc. 1, l. 171. [Brutus]

All pity choked with custom of fell deeds.
Julius Cæsar. Act iii, sc. 1, l. 269. [Antony] The only use of the phrase "fell deeds."

I perceive, you feel The dint of pity.
Julius Cæsar. Act iii, sc. 2, l. 197. [Antony] "Dint" is repeated in *II Henry IV*, iv, 1, 128.

11
A most poor man, made tame to fortune's blows;
Who, by the art of known and feeling sorrows,
Am pregnant to good pity.
King Lear. Act iv, sc. 6, l. 225. [Edgar]

I should e'en die with pity
To see another thus.
King Lear. Act iv, sc. 7, l. 53. [King Lear]

Let pity not be believed!—*King Lear*, iv, 3, 31.

12
Pity, like a naked new-born babe,
Striding the blast, or heaven's cherubim, horsed
Upon the sightless couriers of the air,
Shall blow the horrid deed in every eye,
That tears shall drown the wind.
Macbeth. Act i, sc. 7, l. 21. [Macbeth] The only use of "striding." "Courier" is repeated in *Timon of Athens*, v, 2, 6. The only use of "cherubim." "Cherubin" occurs seven times.

13
Courage! there will be pity taken on you.
Measure for Measure. Act i, sc. 2, l. 112. [Pompey]

None takes pity on thy pain.
The Passionate Pilgrim, l. 392.

Take pity.—*The Comedy of Errors*, iv, 3, 25; *Much Ado about Nothing*, ii, 3, 271; *Henry V*, iii, 2, 28.

14
It is pity of her life.
Measure for Measure, ii, 1, 77. [Elbow]

It is pity of our lives.—*Twelfth Night*, ii, 5, 14.
It were pity of my life.—*A Midsummer-Night's Dream*, iii, 1, 44.
'Twere pity on my life.—*A Midsummer-Night's Dream*, v, 1, 229.
In pity of his misery.—*King Lear*, iv, 5, 12.
In pity of his tender years.—*Venus and Adonis*, l. 1091.

15
Isabella: Yet show some pity.
Angelo: I show it most of all when I show justice;
For then I pity those I do not know.
Measure for Measure. Act ii, sc. 2, l. 99.

1
And pluck commiseration of his state
From brassy bosoms and rough hearts of flint.
The Merchant of Venice. Act iv, sc. 1, l. 30. [Duke] The only use of "brassy."
Have commiseration.—*Love's Labour 's Lost,* iv, 1, 64.
Kind commiseration.—*Titus Andronicus,* v, 3, 93. The only uses of "commiseration."
2
Her dotage now I do begin to pity.
A Midsummer-Night's Dream. Act iv, sc. 1, l. 50. [Oberon]
If I do not take pity of her, I am a villain.
Much Ado about Nothing. Act ii, sc. 3, l. 271. [Benedick]
I cannot choose but pity her.
The Two Gentlemen of Verona. Act iv, sc. 4, l. 82. [Julia]
They seem to pity the lady.—*Much Ado about Nothing,* ii, 3, 231.
3
Come, I will have thee; but, by this light, I take thee for pity.
Much Ado about Nothing. Act v, sc. 4, l. 92. [Benedick]
4
The pity of it, Iago! O Iago, the pity of it, Iago!
Othello. Act iv, sc. 1, l. 206. [Othello]
5
Soft pity enters at an iron gate.
The Rape of Lucrece, l. 595.
6
No good at all that I can do for him;
Unless you call it good to pity him.
Richard II. Act ii, sc. 1, l. 235. [Ross]
Barbarism itself have pitied him.
Richard II. Act v, sc. 2, l. 36. [York]
Alas, poor fool! why do I pity him
That with his very heart despiseth me?
The Two Gentlemen of Verona. Act iv, sc. 4, l. 98. [Julia]
Beshrew my heart, but I pity the man.
A Midsummer-Night's Dream. Act v, sc. 1, l. 295. [Hippolyta]
Forget to pity him, lest pity prove
A serpent that will sting thee to the heart.
Richard II. Act v, sc. 3, l. 57. [York]
7
Pity may move thee 'pardon' to rehearse.
Richard II. Act v, sc. 3, l. 128. [Duchess]
We may pity, though not pardon thee.
The Comedy of Errors. Act i, sc. 1, l. 98. [Duke]
8
No beast so fierce but knows some touch of pity.
Richard III. Act i, sc. 2, l. 71. [Lady Anne]
Clarence is well-spoken, and perhaps
May move your hearts to pity, if you mark him.
Richard III. Act i, sc. 3, l. 348. [Gloucester]
Move thy pity.—*The Rape of Lucrece,* l. 1553.
9
My friend, I spy some pity in thy looks.
Richard III. Act i, sc. 4, l. 270. [Clarence]
Tear-falling pity dwells not in this eye.
Richard III. Act iv, sc. 2, l. 66. [King Richard] The only use of "tear-falling."
10
Is there no pity sitting in the clouds,
That sees into the bottom of my grief?
Romeo and Juliet. Act iii, sc. 5, l. 198. [Juliet]
11
Pity me then and wish I were renew'd; . . .
Pity me then, dear friend, and I assure ye
Even that your pity is enough to cure me.
Sonnets. No. cxi.
Root pity in thy heart, that when it grows
Thy pity may deserve to pitied be.
Sonnets. No. cxlii.
12
Show pity, or I die.
The Taming of the Shrew. Act iii, sc. 1, l. 78. [Bianca]
13
Pity move my father To be inclined my way!
The Tempest. Act i, sc. 2, l. 446. [Miranda]
Alack, for pity!—*The Tempest,* i, 2, 132.
14
Men must learn now with pity to dispense.
Timon of Athens. Act iii, sc. 2, l. 93. [Stranger]
For pity is the virtue of the law,
And none but tyrants use it cruelly.
Timon of Athens. Act iii, sc. 5, l. 8. [Alcibiades]
Pity 's sleeping.—*Timon of Athens,* iv, 3, 492.
15
Do thou entreat her show a woman pity.
Titus Andronicus. Act ii, sc. 3, l. 147. [Chiron]
O, be to me, though thy hard heart say no,
Nothing so kind, but something pitiful!
Titus Andronicus. Act ii, sc. 3, l. 155. [Lavinia]
I know not what it [pity] means.
Titus Andronicus. Act ii, sc. 3, l. 157. [Tamora]
16
Let 's leave the hermit pity with our mothers,
And when we have our armours buckled on,
The venom'd vengeance ride upon our swords,
Spur them to ruthful work, rein them from ruth.
Troilus and Cressida. Act v, sc. 3, l. 45. [Troilus] "Ruthful" is repeated in *III Henry VI,* ii, 5, 95: "Ruthful deeds"; and in *Titus Andronicus,* v, 1, 66: "Ruthful to hear."
17 O, you should not rest
Between the elements of air and earth,
But you should pity me!
Twelfth Night. Act i, sc. 5, l. 293. [Viola]
18
For pity now she can no more detain him.
Venus and Adonis, l. 577.

PLACE

See also Time and Place

19
Lord: You are loved, sir. . . .
King: I fill a place, I know 't.
All's Well that Ends Well. Act i, sc. 2, l. 67.
Place in the commonwealth.—*Julius Cæsar,* iii, 2, 47.
Place i' the state.—*Measure for Measure,* ii, 4, 156.

1
There 's place and means for every man alive.
All's Well that Ends Well. Act iv, sc. 3, l. 375. [Parolles]

2
Here is the place appointed for the wrestling.
As You Like It. Act i, sc. 2, l. 154. [Le Beau]

Look you, this is the place appointed.
The Merry Wives of Windsor. Act iii, sc. 1, l. 96. [Evans]

In that same place thou hast appointed me,
To-morrow truly will I meet with thee.
A Midsummer-Night's Dream. Act i, sc. 1, l. 177. [Hermia]

My merry host . . . hath appointed them contrary places.
The Merry Wives of Windsor. Act ii, sc. 1, l. 217. [Shallow]

Here is the place.—*King Lear,* iii, 4, 1; iv, 6, 11.
This is the place.—*Romeo and Juliet,* v, 3, 171.
Show me the place.—*As You Like It,* ii, 1, 66.

3
I like this place,
And willingly could waste my time in it.
As You Like It. Act ii, sc. 4, l. 94. [Celia]

4
Nay, keep your place.
Coriolanus. Act ii, sc. 2, l. 70. [Menenius]

Keep place together.—*The Merry Wives of Windsor,* ii, 1, 63.
Keeps place.—*Troilus and Cressida,* iii, 3, 199.
Here 's no place for you.—*Coriolanus,* iv, 5, 33.

5
It is place which lessens and sets off.
Cymbeline. Act iii, sc. 3, l. 13. [Belarius]

6
I am near to the place where they should meet, if Pisanio have mapped it truly.
Cymbeline. Act iv, sc. 1, l. 1. [Cloten] The only use of "mapped."

7
I think he would change places with his officer.
Cymbeline. Act v, sc. 4, l. 180. [Gaoler]

Change places.—*King Lear,* iv, 6, 156.
Change your place.—*Measure for Measure,* i, 2, 110.
Changing place.—*Sonnets,* lx.

8
Bestow this place on us a little while.
Hamlet. Act iv, sc. 1, l. 4. [Queen]

Give us the place alone.
Twelfth Night. Act i, sc. 5, l. 235. [Olivia] See under DISMISSAL.

Fly this place.—*King Lear,* ii, 1, 22.
Leave this place.—*As You Like It,* i, 2, 274.
Quit this place.—*The Tempest,* ii, 1, 322.
Let 's from this place.—*Winter's Tale,* v, 3, 146.

9
He holds his place; for look you how he writes.
II Henry IV. Act ii, sc. 2, l. 116. [Prince]

Hold their places.—*II Henry IV,* v, 2, 17.
Hold his place.—*Julius Cæsar,* iii, 1, 65.

10
Each hath his place and function to attend:
I am left out; for me nothing remains.
I Henry VI. Act i, sc. 1, l. 173. [Winchester]

11
Appoint them a place of meeting.
I Henry VI. Act i, sc. 2, l. 190. [Poins]

Place of death and sorry execution.
The Comedy of Errors. Act v, sc. 1, l. 121. [Merchant]

Place of execution.—*II Henry VI,* ii, 3, 6.
Place of peace.—*Romeo and Juliet,* v, 3, 143.
Place of potency.—*Coriolanus,* ii, 3, 190.
Place of stand.—*Romeo and Juliet,* i, 5, 52.

12
Thy place shall be honourable.
I Henry IV. Act ii, sc. 4, l. 596. [Prince]

We shall employ thee in a worthier place.
Measure for Measure. Act v, sc. 1, l. 537. [Duke]

13
Sirs, take your places and be vigilant.
I Henry VI. Act ii, sc. 1, l. 1. [Sergeant]

In our coronation take your place.
I Henry VI. Act iii, sc. 4, l. 27. [King Henry] "Take your place" is used ten times.

Take place by us.—*Henry VIII,* i, 2, 10.

14
We will bestow you in some better place.
I Henry VI. Act iii, sc. 2, l. 88. [Talbot]

I will . . . advise him for a better place.
Measure for Measure. Act iv, sc. 2, l. 223. [Duke]

I would prefer him to a better place.
King Lear. Act i, sc. 1, l. 277. [Cordelia] "Better place" is repeated in *The Merchant of Venice,* iii, 5, 73; *As You Like It,* ii, 4, 17; and *II Henry IV,* iv, 4, 22.

15
Thy place is fill'd.
III Henry VI. Act iii, sc. 1, l. 16. [King Henry]

This place becomes thee not.—*Henry VIII,* v, 3, 133.
Is this a place to roar in?—*Henry VIII,* v, 4, 7.
I made good my place.—*Henry VIII,* v, 4, 57.

16
I 'll get me to a place more void, and there
Speak to great Cæsar as he comes along.
Julius Cæsar. Act ii, sc. 4, l. 37. [Soothsayer]

No place will please me so . . .
As here by Cæsar.
Julius Cæsar. Act iii, sc. 1, l. 161. [Antony]

17
Would I might never stir from off this place.
King John, i, 1, 145. See under APPEARANCE.

I will not stir from this place, do what they can.
A Midsummer-Night's Dream. Act iii, sc. 1, l. 125. [Bottom]

18
What 's he that hath so much thy place mistook
To set thee here?
King Lear. Act ii, sc. 4, l. 12. [King Lear]

The dark and vicious place where thee he got
Cost him his eyes.
King Lear. Act v, sc. 3, l. 172. [Edgar]

Fix'd place.—*King Lear,* i, 4, 291.
Fixed places.—*The Rape of Lucrece,* l. 1525.

19
Then for the place where; . . . the place where: it standeth north-north-east and by east from the west corner of thy curious-knotted garden.
Love's Labour 's Lost. Act i, sc. 1, l. 243.

[King, reading] The only use of "north-north-east" (see under Direction) and "curious-knotted."

An I had thee in place where, thou shouldst know it.
The Taming of the Shrew. Act iv, sc. 3, l. 150. [Tailor]

1 First Witch: Where the place?
Second Witch: Upon the heath.
Third Witch: There to meet with Macbeth.
Macbeth. Act i, sc. 1, l. 6.

2 Dispose of her
To some more fitter place, and that with speed.
Measure for Measure. Act ii, sc. 2, l. 16. [Angelo]

We'll borrow place of him.—*Measure for Measure,* v, 1, 367.

3 O place, O form,
How often dost thou with thy case, thy habit,
Wrench awe from fools and tie the wiser souls
To thy false seeming!
Measure for Measure. Act ii, sc. 4, l. 12. [Angelo]

4 I will search impossible places.
The Merry Wives of Windsor. Act iii, sc. 5, l. 151. [Ford]

5 Here 's a marvellous convenient place for our rehearsal.
A Midsummer-Night's Dream. Act iii, sc. 1, l. 2. [Quince]

The most convenient place that I can think of.
Henry VIII. Act ii, sc. 2, l. 138. [King Henry]

Convenient place.—*II Henry VI,* i, 3, 212.

The place answer to convenience.—*Measure for Measure,* iii, 1, 258.

6 'Tis great pity that the noble Moor
Should hazard such a place as his own second
With one of an ingraft infirmity.
Othello. Act ii, sc. 3, l. 143. [Montano] The only use of "ingraft." "Ingrafted" occurs in *Julius Cæsar,* ii, 1, 184.

7 I will ask him for my place again.
Othello. Act ii, sc. 3, l. 306. [Cassio]

Importune her help to put you in your place again.
Othello. Act ii, sc. 3, l. 324. [Iago]

Cassio: I being absent and my place supplied,
My general will forget my love and service.
Desdemona: Do not doubt that; before Emilia here
I give thee warrant of thy place.
Othello. Act iii, sc. 2, l. 17.

Though it be fit that Cassio have his place,
For, sure, he fills it up with great ability,
Yet, if you please to hold him off awhile,
You shall by that perceive him and his means.
Othello. Act iii, sc. 3, l. 246. [Iago]

Cassio shall have my place.
Othello. Act iv, sc. 1, l. 272. [Othello]

8 Marshal: Sir, yonder is your place.
Pericles: Some other is more fit.
Pericles. Act ii, sc. 3, l. 23.

Fitter place.—*King Lear,* v, 3, 59.

Come, bring me to some private place.
Pericles. Act iv, sc. 6, l. 97. [Lysimachus]

Private place.—*Romeo and Juliet,* iii, 1, 54.

Secret place.—*Richard II,* v, 6, 25.

9 O, that the gods
Would set me free from this unhallow'd place! . . . O, that the gods
Would safely deliver me from this place!
Pericles. Act iv, sc. 6, l. 106. [Marina]

10 Thou hold'st a place, for which the pained'st fiend
Of hell would not in reputation change.
Pericles. Act iv, sc. 6, l. 173. [Marina] The only use of "pained'st."

Helicanus: What is your place?
Lysimachus: I am the governor of this place you lie before.
Pericles. Act v, sc. 1, l. 20.

11 Keep still possession of thy gloomy place.
The Rape of Lucrece, l. 803.

Barren place.—*The Tempest,* i, 2, 338.

Common place.—*Sonnets,* cxxxvii.

Forfended place.—*King Lear,* v, 1, 11. The only use of "forfended."

Less place.—*Henry VIII,* ii, 2, 112.

Little place.—*Henry V,* Prol., 16.

Lower place.—*Antony and Cleopatra,* iii, 1, 12.

Lowest place.—*All's Well that Ends Well,* ii, 3, 133.

Old place.—*II Henry IV,* ii, 2, 161.

Prepared place.—*Henry VIII,* iv, 1, 64.

Rival place.—*The Merchant of Venice,* i, 1, 174.

Rude place.—*Cymbeline,* iii, 6, 66.

Slippery place.—*King John,* iii, 4, 137. See Danger, 285:8.

Strange places.—*As You Like It,* ii, 7, 40.

Tainted place.—*The Rape of Lucrece,* l. 1746.

Tender place.—*Henry VIII,* ii, 2, 144.

Ulcerous place.—*Hamlet,* iii, 4, 147.

Unworthy place.—*Antony and Cleopatra,* iii, 13, 84.

Wrong places.—*The Merry Wives of Windsor,* iii, 1, 110.

12 Fellow, give place; here is no longer stay.
Richard II. Act v, sc. 5, l. 95. [Keeper] "Give place" is used eight times.

Let all the rest give place.
Twelfth Night. Act ii, sc. 4, l. 82. [Duke]

Give up your place.—*Measure for Measure,* ii, 2, 13.

Give another place.—*Sonnets,* lxxix.

Give no place.—*Twelfth Night,* ii, 4, 127.

13 The place [is] death, considering who thou art.
Romeo and Juliet. Act ii, sc. 2, l. 64. [Juliet]

A very fatal place it seems to me.—*Titus Andronicus,* ii, 3, 202.

This place is dangerous.—*Troilus and Cressida,* v, 2, 38.

14 Thou didst usurp my place.
Richard III, iv, 4, 109. See under Usurpation.

Usurp the place.—*III Henry VI,* i, 2, 25.

Claim the place.—*Richard III,* iii, 1, 50.
Deserved the place.—*Richard III,* iii, 1, 49.
Earns a place.—*Antony and Cleopatra,* iii, 13, 46.
Supply his place.—*III Henry VI,* iv, 6, 50.
Resign my place.—*II Henry VI,* i, 3, 124.

1
Here on this grass-plot, in this very place.
The Tempest. Act iv, sc. 1, l. 73. [Iris] The only use of "grass-plot."

The very place.—*Hamlet,* i, 4, 75.
This very place.—*Twelfth Night,* i, 2, 23.

2
Enforce them to this place, And presently.
The Tempest. Act v, sc. 1, l. 100. [Prospero]

3
Ay, such a place there is, where we did hunt . . .
Pattern'd by that the poet here describes,
By nature made for murders and for rapes.
Titus Andronicus. Act iv, sc. 1, l. 55. [Titus] The only use of "pattern'd."

4
Here 's an excellent place; here we may see most bravely.
Troilus and Cressida. Act i, sc. 2, l. 197. [Pandarus]

Native place.—*Troilus and Cressida,* ii, 2, 96.

5
I know my place as I would they should do theirs.
Twelfth Night. Act ii, sc. 5, l. 60. [Malvolio]

You know your places well.—*All's Well that Ends Well,* iii, 1, 21; *Henry V,* iv, 3, 78.
Get you a place.—*Hamlet,* iii, 2, 96.
Go in your place.—*Measure for Measure,* iii, 1, 261.

6
Like a cipher, Yet standing in rich place.
Winter's Tale. Act i, sc. 2, l. 6. [Polixenes]

Authentic in your place.—*The Merry Wives of Windsor,* ii, 2, 236.
Authentic place.—*Troilus and Cressida,* i, 3, 108.
Best place.—*I Henry VI,* i, 4, 65.
Civil'st place.—*II Henry VI,* iv, 7, 66.
First place.—*Timon of Athens,* iii, 6, 75.
A place below the first.—*Coriolanus,* i, 1, 270.
Great place.—*Measure for Measure,* ii, 4, 92; v, 1, 294. Used only in this play.
Holy place.—*I Henry VI,* iii, 3, 14; *Julius Cæsar,* iii, 2, 259.
Privileged place.—*I Henry VI,* i, 3, 46.
Safe place.—*The Comedy of Errors,* i, 2, 78.
Settled place.—*I Henry VI,* ii, 5, 106.
True place.—*Twelfth Night,* v, 1, 126.

7
Bear it
To some remote and desert place quite out
Of our dominions. . . . I do in justice charge thee,
On thy soul's peril and thy body's torture,
That thou command it strangely to some place
Where chance may nurse or end it.
The Winter's Tale. Act ii, sc. 3, l. 175. [Leontes]

Desert place.—*As You Like It,* ii, 4, 72; iv, 3, 142; *A Midsummer-Night's Dream,* ii, 1, 218.

8
This place is famous for the creatures
Of prey that keep upon 't.
The Winter's Tale. Act iii, sc. 3, l. 12. [Mariner]

Places remote enough are in Bohemia.
The Winter's Tale. Act iii, sc. 3, l. 31. [Antigonus]

9
Have you thought on
A place whereto you 'll go?
The Winter's Tale. Act iv, sc. 4, l. 546. [Camillo]

PLAGUE

See also Infection, Pestilence

10
'Twas pretty, though a plague
To see him every hour.
All's Well that Ends Well. Act i, sc. 1, l. 103. [Helena]

11
The hoarded plague o' the gods
Requite your love!
Coriolanus. Act iv, sc. 2, l. 11. [Volumnia]

A plague o' both your houses!
Romeo and Juliet. Act iii, sc. 1, l. 94. [Mercutio]

The plague of Greece upon thee.—*Troilus and Cressida,* ii, 1, 13.
A plague upon you all!—*Richard III,* i, 3, 58.
A plague upon them!—*II Henry VI,* iii, 2, 309.
A phrase used, with variations, throughout the plays. See under CURSE.

12
Thou wast born to be a plague to men.
III Henry VI. Act v, sc. 5, l. 28. [Queen Margaret]

13
Pray to the gods to intermit the plague
That needs must light on this ingratitude.
Julius Cæsar. Act i, sc. 2, l. 59. [Marullus] The only use of "intermit."

Plagued for her sin.—*King John,* ii, 1, 184.
Plague of custom.—*King Lear,* i, 2, 3.

14
O plague right well prevented!
Much Ado about Nothing. Act iii, sc. 2, l. 136. [Don John]

15
This forked plague is fated to us
When we do quicken.
Othello. Act iii, sc. 3, l. 276. [Othello]

Grievous plague.—*Richard III,* i, 3, 217.
Strumpet's plague.—*Othello,* iv, 1, 97.

16
Only my plague thus far I count my gain,
That she that makes me sin awards me pain.
Sonnets. No. cxli.

17
I will plague them all, Even to roaring.
The Tempest. Act iv, sc. 1, l. 192. [Prospero]

I 'll plague him.—*The Merchant of Venice,* iii 1, 121.
I shall be plagued.—*Troilus and Cressida,* v, 2, 105.

18
Plagues, incident to men,
Your potent and infectious fevers heap
On Athens, ripe for stroke!
Timon of Athens. Act iv, sc. 1, l. 21. [Timon]

Be as a planetary plague, when Jove
Will o'er some high-viced city hang his poison
In the sick air.
Timon of Athens. Act iv, sc. 3, l. 108. [Timon] The only use of "high-viced." "Planetary" occurs again in *King Lear,* i, 2, 135.

1
Let your brief plagues be mercy.
Troilus and Cressida. Act v, sc. 10, l. 8. [Troilus]

2
How now?
Even so quickly may one catch the plague?
Twelfth Night. Act i, sc. 5, l. 313. [Olivia]

PLAINNESS, see Candour

PLAINT, see Complaint

PLAY

See also Acting, Comedy, Stage, Tragedy

3
Play one scene Of excellent dissembling.
Antony and Cleopatra. Act i, sc. 3, l. 78. See DISSEMBLING, 363:16.

Cleopatra: Let 's to billiards: come, Charmian.
Charmian: My arm is sore; best play with Mardian.
Cleopatra: As well a woman with an eunuch play'd
As with a woman. Come, you 'll play with me, sir?
Mardian: As well as I can, madam.
Antony and Cleopatra. Act ii, sc. 5, l. 3. The only mention of "billiards."

Play for lack of work.—*All 's Well that Ends Well,* i, 1, 23.

4
And, when thou hast done this chare, I 'll give thee leave
To play till doomsday.
Antony and Cleopatra. Act v, sc. 2, l. 231. [Cleopatra]

The maid . . . that does the meanest chares.
Antony and Cleopatra, iv, 15, 75. The only uses of "chare" and "chares" (chores).

5
The play, I remember, pleased not the million: 'twas caviare to the general: but it was . . . an excellent play, well digested in the scenes, set down with as much modesty as cunning.
Hamlet. Act ii, sc. 2, l. 456. [Hamlet] The only mention of "caviare."

The play may please.—*As You Like It,* Epil., 18.

Displeasing play.—*II Henry IV,* Epil., 10.

Good play.—*As You Like It,* Epil., 9; *Twelfth Night,* v, 1, 39.

Old play.—*Love's Labour 's Lost,* v, 2, 884; *Henry V,* iv, 4, 76.

An old infant play.—*Love's Labour 's Lost,* iv, 3, 78.

Tragic play.—*Richard III,* iv, 4, 68. See TRAGEDY.

6
Hamlet: We 'll hear a play to-morrow. Dost thou hear me, old friend; can you play the Murder of Gonzago?
Player: Ay, my lord.
Hamlet: We 'll ha 't to-morrow night.
Hamlet. Act ii, sc. 2, l. 560.

I 'll have these players
Play something like the murder of my father
Before mine uncle: I 'll observe his looks;
I 'll tent him to the quick: if he but blench,
I know my course. . . . The play 's the thing
Wherein I 'll catch the conscience of the king.
Hamlet, ii, 2, 623.

There is a play to-night before the king;
One scene of it comes near the circumstance
Which I have told thee of my father's death:
I prithee when thou seest that act afoot,
Even with the very comment of thy soul
Observe my uncle.
Hamlet. Act iii, sc. 2, l. 80. [Hamlet]

I 'll mark the play.—*Hamlet,* iii, 2, 158.

7
King: What do you call the play?
Hamlet: The Mouse-trap. Marry, how? Tropically. This play is the image of a murder done in Vienna: Gonzago is the duke's name; his wife, Baptista: you shall see anon; 'tis a knavish piece of work: but what o' that? your majesty and we that have free souls, it touches us not: let the galled jade wince, our withers are unwrung.
Hamlet. Act iii, sc. 2, l. 246. The only use of "mouse-trap" and "tropically" (figuratively).

Give o'er the play.—*Hamlet,* iii, 2, 279.

8
Hamlet: Will you play upon this pipe?
Guildenstern: My lord, I cannot.
Hamlet: I pray you. . . .
Guildenstern: I know no touch of it, my lord.
Hamlet: 'Tis as easy as lying; govern these ventages with your fingers and thumb, give it breath with your mouth, and it will discourse most eloquent music. Look you, these are the stops.
Guildenstern: But these cannot I command to any utterance of harmony; I have not the skill.
Hamlet: Why, look you now, how unworthy a thing you make of me! You would play upon me; you would seem to know my stops; you would pluck out the heart of my mystery; you would sound me from the lowest note to the top of my compass: and there is much music, excellent voice, in this little organ; yet cannot you make it speak. 'Sblood, do you think I am easier to be played on than a pipe? Call me what instrument you will, though you can fret me, yet you cannot play upon me.
Hamlet. Act iii, sc. 2, l. 366. The only use of "ventage."

9
They cry 'hem!' and bid you play it off.
I Henry IV. Act ii, sc. 4, l. 18. [Prince]

Shall we have a play extempore?
I Henry IV. Act ii, sc. 4, l. 308. [Falstaff]

Play out the play.—*I Henry IV,* ii, 4, 531.

Play our play.—*A Midsummer-Night's Dream,* iii, 1, 53.

Be bold to play.—*Venus and Adonis,* l. 124.
Frankly play.—*Hamlet,* v, 2, 264.
Go, play, boy, play.—*The Winter's Tale,* i, 2, 187. See under ACTING.

1
Nay, you shall find no boy's play here, I can tell you.
I Henry IV. Act v, sc. 4, l. 75. [Falstaff] The only use of "boy's play."

2
If we may,
We 'll not offend one stomach with our play.
Henry V. Act ii, Prologue, l. 39. [Chorus]

3
Play with your fancies.
Henry V. Act iii, Prologue, l. 7.
Play with flowers.—*Henry V,* ii, 3, 15.
Play with mammets.—*I Henry IV,* ii, 3, 95. "Mammet" (doll) is repeated in *Romeo and Juliet,* iii, 5, 186: "Whining mammet."
Play with reason.—*Measure for Measure,* i, 2, 190.
Play with sparrows.—*The Tempest,* iv, 1, 100.

4
Like thee, Nero,
Play on the lute, beholding the towns burn.
I Henry VI. Act i, sc. 4, l. 95. [Talbot]
He plays o' the viol de gamboys.
Twelfth Night, i, 3, 26. See under CHARACTER.
Play On the tabor.—*Love's Labour 's Lost,* v, 1, 160.
Play the trumpet.—*I Henry IV,* v, 1, 4.
Play the tune.—*Twelfth Night,* ii, 4, 14.

5
I come no more to make you laugh: things now,
That bear a weighty and a serious brow,
Sad, high, and working, full of state and woe,
Such noble scenes as draw the eye to flow,
We now present. Those that can pity, here
May, if they think it well, let fall a tear;
The subject will deserve it. Such as give
Their money out of hope they may believe,
May here find truth too. Those that come to see
Only a show or two, and so agree
The play may pass, if they be still and willing,
I 'll undertake may see away their shilling
Richly in two short hours. Only they
That come to hear a merry bawdy play,
A noise of targets, or to see a fellow
In a long motley coat guarded with yellow,
Will be deceived; for, gentle hearers, know
To rank our chosen truth with such a show
As fool and fight is, beside forfeiting
Our own brains, and the opinion that we bring,
To make that only true we now intend,
Will leave us never an understanding friend.
Henry VIII, Prol., 1.
'Tis ten to one this play can never please
All that are here: some come to take their ease,
And sleep an act or two . . . others, to hear the city
Abused extremely, and to cry "That 's witty!"
Henry VIII, Epil., 1.

6
King: I will play no more to-night;
My mind 's not on 't; you are too hard for me.
Suffolk: Sir, I did never win of you before.
King: But little, Charles;
Nor shall not when my fancy 's on my play.
Henry VIII. Act v, sc. 1, l. 56.
We 'll play with them for the first boy for a thousand ducats.
The Merchant of Venice. Act iii, sc. 2, l. 216. [Gratiano]
Make my play.—*Henry VIII,* i, 4, 46.

7
He loves no plays, As thou dost, Antony.
Julius Cæsar. Act i, sc. 2, l. 203. [Cæsar]

8
I 'ld play incessantly upon these jades.
King John, ii, 1, 385. See under CANNON.
I 'll play no more with you.
Love's Labour 's Lost. Act v, sc. 2, l. 235. [Princess]
Go your ways, and play.—*The Merry Wives of Windsor,* iv, 1, 81.
Play a set.—*Henry V,* i, 2, 262.
Play fast and loose.—*King John,* iii, 1, 242.
Play for a kingdom.—*Henry V,* iii, 6, 119.

9
And Nestor play at push-pin with the boys.
Love's Labour 's Lost. Act iv, sc. 3, l. 169. [Biron] The only use of "push-pin" (a child's game).
Madam, we 'll play at bowls.
Richard II. Act iii, sc. 4, l. 3. [Lady]
Challenge her to bowl.—*Love's Labour 's Lost,* iv, 1, 140.
Play at cherry-pit.—*Twelfth Night,* iii, 4, 129.
Play at dice.—*The Merchant of Venice,* ii, 1, 32. See GAMING, 601:5.
Play at loggats.—*Hamlet,* v, 1, 100. The only use of "loggats" (a game in which sticks are thrown at a stake).
Plays at quoits.—*II Henry IV,* ii, 4, 266. The only use of "quoits." "Quoit" occurs in the same scene, l. 206: "Quoit him down," and is used nowhere else.
Play at subtle games.—*Troilus and Cressida,* iv, 4, 89.
Play at that game.—*Timon of Athens,* i, 2, 12.
Plays at tables.—*Love's Labour 's Lost,* v, 2, 326.
Play at will.—*The Winter's Tale,* ii, 1, 52.

10
If any of the audience hiss, you may cry 'Well done!'
Love's Labour 's Lost. Act v, sc. 1, l. 145. [Moth]
Dismiss this audience.—*Love's Labour 's Lost,* iv, 3, 210.
Let the audience look to their eyes.—*A Midsummer-Night's Dream,* i, 2, 28. For "give me audience" see under FAMILIAR PHRASES.

11
King Ferdinand: Come, sir, it wants a twelvemonth and a day,
And then 'twill end.
Biron: That 's too long for a play.
Love's Labour 's Lost. Act v, sc. 2, l. 887.

1
What, a play toward! I 'll be an auditor;
An actor, too, perhaps, if I see cause.
A Midsummer-Night's Dream. Act iii, sc. 1, l. 81. [Puck] "Auditor" is repeated in *I Henry IV*, ii, 1, 63, and "auditors" occurs in *Timon of Athens*, ii, 2, 165.

Met together to rehearse a play
Intended for great Theseus' nuptial-day.
A Midsummer-Night's Dream. Act iii, sc. 2, l. 11. [Puck] "Nuptial-day" is repeated in *Coriolanus*, i, 6, 31.

2
Is there no play,
To ease the anguish of a torturing hour?
A Midsummer-Night's Dream. Act v, sc. 1, l. 36. [Theseus]

A play there is, my lord, some ten words long,
Which is as brief as I have known a play;
But by ten words, my lord, it is too long,
Which makes it tedious; for in all the play
There is not one word apt, one player fitted.
A Midsummer-Night's Dream. Act v, sc. 1, l. 61. [Philostrate]

This palpable-gross play hath well beguiled
The heavy gait of night.
A Midsummer-Night's Dream, v, 1, 374. [Theseus] The only use of "palpable-gross."

3
That 's the scene that I would see, which will be merely a dumb-show.
Much Ado about Nothing. Act ii, sc. 3, l. 225. [Don Pedro] "Dumb-show" occurs four times.

Dumb play.—*Venus and Adonis*, l. 359.

4
Madly play with my forefathers' joints.
Romeo and Juliet. Act iv, sc. 3, l. 51. [Juliet]

Play and trifle.—*Othello*, i, 1, 133.

5
Servant: My lord, you nod; you do not mind the play.
Sly: Yes, by Saint Anne, do I. A good matter, surely: comes there any more of it?
Page: My lord, 'tis but begun.
Sly: 'Tis a very excellent piece of work, madam lady: would 'twere done!
The Taming of the Shrew. Act i, sc. 1, l. 254. Saint Anne is mentioned again in *Twelfth Night*, ii, 3, 126.

6
Our play
Leaps o'er the vaunt and firstlings of those broils,
Beginning in the middle, starting thence away
To what may be digested in a play.
Troilus and Cressida, Prol., 26. "Firstlings" is repeated in *Macbeth*, iv, 1, 147.

7
But that 's all one, our play is done,
And we 'll strive to please you every day.
Twelfth Night. Act v, sc. 1, l. 416. [Clown]

New joy wait on you!
Here our play has ending.
Pericles. Act v, sc. 3, l. 102. [Gower]

8
Methinks I play as I have seen them do
In Whitsun pastorals.
Winter's Tale, iv, 1, 33. [Perdita] Whitsun is repeated in *Henry V*, ii, 4, 25.

II—Play Fair and Foul

9
I doubt some foul play.
Hamlet. Act i, sc. 2, l. 256. [Hamlet]

It is apparent foul play; and 'tis shame
That greatness should so grossly offer it.
King John. Act iv, sc. 2, l. 93. [Salisbury]

Do me no foul play, friends.
King Lear. Act iii, sc. 7, l. 21. [Gloucester]

10
She died at night; I 'll say so. Who can cross it?
Unless you play the pious innocent,
And for an honest attribute cry out
'She died by foul play.'
Pericles. Act iv, sc. 3, l. 16. [Dionyza]

What foul play had we, that we came from thence?
The Tempest. Act i, sc. 2, l. 60. [Miranda]

Play 's foul play.—*Love's Labour 's Lost*, v, 2, 766.

Foul play.—*I Henry IV*, iii, 2, 169; *The Tempest*, i, 2, 63.

11
According to the fair play of the world,
Let me have audience.
King John. Act v, sc. 2, l. 118. [Bastard]

Hector: O, 'tis fair play.
Troilus: Fool's play, by heaven.
Troilus and Cressida. Act v, sc. 3, l. 43.

Fair-play orders.—*King John*, v, 1, 67.

Simony was fair play.—*Henry VIII*, iv, 2, 36. The only use of "simony."

12
Miranda: Sweet lord, you play me false.
Ferdinand: No, my dear'st love,
I would not for the world.
Miranda: Yes, for a score of kingdoms you should wrangle,
And I would call it fair play.
The Tempest. Act v, sc. 1, l. 172.

Julia: He plays false, father.
Host: How? out of tune on the strings?
Julia: Not so; but yet so false that he grieves my very heart-strings. . . .
Host: You would have them always play but one thing?
Julia: I would always have one play but one thing.
Two Gentlemen of Verona. Act iv, sc. 2, l. 59.

Play false.—*The Comedy of Errors*, ii, 2, 144; *King John*, i, 1, 118; *Macbeth*, i, 5, 22. See FALSENESS, 468:9.

Play false strains.—*As You Like It*, iv, 3, 68.

III—Play a Part

See also Part: Playing a Part

13
Shall 's have a play of this? Thou scornful page,
There lie thy part.
Cymbeline. Act v, sc. 5, l. 228. [Posthumus]

14
I prithee, call in Falstaff. I 'll play Percy and that damned brawn shall play Dame Mortimer his wife.
I Henry IV. Act ii, sc. 4, l. 121. [Prince]

Play me Nestor; hem, and stroke thy beard.
Troilus and Cressida. Act i, sc. 3, l. 165. [Ulysses]

Faith, unless you play the honest Troyan, the poor wench is cast away.
Love's Labour's Lost. Act v, sc. 2, l. 681. [Costard]

I would play Lord Pandarus of Phrygia.
Twelfth Night. Act iii, sc. 1, l. 58. [Clown]

1 Give me leave
To play the broker in my own behalf.
III Henry VI. Act iv, sc. 1, l. 62. [Clarence]

Plays the alchemist.—*King John,* iii, 1, 78.
Play the Amazon.—*III Henry VI,* iv, 1, 106.
Play bo-peep.—*King Lear,* i, 4, 193. The only use of "bo-peep."
Play the cook.—*Titus Andronicus,* v, 2, 205; *Cymbeline,* iii, 6, 30; iv, 2, 164.
Play the coward.—*I Henry IV,* ii, 4, 52.
Play the cur.—*The Two Gentlemen of Verona,* iv, 4, 1.
Play the devil.—*Richard III,* i, 3, 338; *King John,* ii, 1, 135.
Play the dog.—*III Henry VI,* v, 6, 77.
Play the eaves-dropper.—*Richard III,* v, 3, 221. The only use of "eaves-dropper."

2
Why should I play the Roman fool?
Macbeth. Act v, sc. 8, l. 1. [Macbeth]

Let me play the fool.
The Merchant of Venice, i, 1, 79. See under FOOL.

Play the god.—*Othello,* ii, 3, 353.
Play the humble host.—*Macbeth,* iii, 4, 4.

3
By Jove, I 'll play the hunter for thy life
With all my force, pursuit and policy.
Troilus and Cressida, iv, 1, 17. See under THREAT.

Play the good husband.—*The Taming of the Shrew,* v, 1, 71.

4
I 'll play the housewife for this once.
Romeo and Juliet. Act iv, sc. 2, l. 43. [Capulet]

Play the idle huswife with me this afternoon.
Coriolanus. Act i, sc. 3, l. 76. [Valeria]

Play the huswife.—*Henry V,* v, 1, 85.
Play the noble housewife.—*All's Well that Ends Well,* ii, 2, 62.

5
Or do you play the flouting Jack?
Much Ado about Nothing, i, 1, 185. See under SPEECH.

Play judge and executioner.—*Cymbeline,* iv, 2, 128.
Play the knave.—*As You Like It,* iii, 2, 314. See under KNAVE.

6
I play the man I am.
Coriolanus. Act iii, sc. 2, l. 15. [Coriolanus]

Play the men.—*The Tempest,* i, 1, 11.
Play a merchant's part.—*The Taming of the Shrew,* ii, 1, 328.
Play the mother's part.—*Sonnets,* cxliii.
Play the murderer.—*Love's Labour's Lost,* iv, 1, 8.
Play the noble beast.—*Much Ado about Nothing,* v, 4, 47.
Play the orator.—*I Henry VI,* iv, 1, 175. See under ORATOR.

7
As nearly as I may I 'll play the penitent.
Antony and Cleopatra. Act ii, sc. 2, l. 91. [Antony]

Play the porter.—*Comedy of Errors,* ii, 2, 213.
Play the recanter.—*Timon of Athens,* v, 1, 149. The only use of "recanter."
Plays the rogue.—*II Henry IV,* i, 2, 274.
Play the ruffian.—*II Henry VI,* v, 1, 164.
Play the runaway.—*The Merchant of Venice,* ii, 6, 47.
Play the saucy cuttle.—*II Henry IV,* ii, 4, 139.
Play the scribe.—*Titus Andronicus,* ii, 4, 4.

8
Which now again you are most apt to play the sir in.
Othello. Act ii, sc. 1, l. 175. [Iago]

Play the spaniel.—*Henry VIII,* v, 3, 126.
Plays the spider.—*The Merchant of Venice,* iii, 2, 121.
Play the swaggerer.—*As You Like It,* iv, 3, 14.
Play the swan.—*Othello,* v, 2, 247.
Play the torturer.—*Richard II,* iii, 2, 198.
Play the touch.—*Richard III,* iv, 2, 8.
Play truant.—*Love's Labour's Lost,* ii, 1, 74.
Play the tyrant.—*Measure for Measure,* iii, 2, 207; *Troilus and Cressida,* iii, 2, 127.
Play the umpire.—*Romeo and Juliet,* iv, 1, 63.
Play the villain.—*Othello,* ii, 3, 342.
Play the wantons.—*Richard II,* iii, 2, 164.
Play the watchman ever for thy sake.
Sonnets. No. lxi.

9
Bottom: First, good Peter Quince, say what the play treats on, then read the names of the actors, and so grow to a point.
Quince: Marry, our play is, The most lamentable comedy, and the most cruel death of Pyramus and Thisby.
Bottom: A very good piece of work, I assure you, and a merry. . . .
Flute: Let me not play a woman; I have a beard coming.
Quince: That 's all one: you shall play it in a mask. . . .
Bottom: An I may hide my face, let me play Thisby too. I 'll speak in a monstrous little voice,—'Thisne, Thisne;'—'Ay Pyramus, my lover dear! thy Thisby dear, and lady dear!'
Quince: No, no; you must play Pyramus. . . . Robin Starveling, you must play Thisby's mother. . . . Snug, the joiner; you the lion's part: and, I hope, here is a play fitted.
A Midsummer-Night's Dream. Act i, sc. 2, l. 8. For "lion's part" see under LION.

You will play barefaced.—*A Midsummer-Night's Dream,* i, 2, 100.

10
Our youth got me to play a woman's part.
The Two Gentlemen of Verona. Act iv, sc. 4, l. 165. [Julia]

Play the woman.—*Macbeth,* iv, 3, 230; *Henry VIII,* iii, 2, 430.
Play the workman.—*Cymbeline,* iv, 1, 7.

11
I see the play so lies That I must bear a part.
The Winter's Tale. Act iv, sc. 4, l. 668. [Perdita]

PLAYER, see Acting and Actor

PLAYFELLOW

1
It is your fault that I have loved Posthumus:
You bred him as my playfellow.
Cymbeline. Act i, sc. 1, l. 144. [Imogen]

2
Playfellows to keep you company.
II Henry VI, iii, 2, 302. See under CURSE.
My playfellow, your hand.—*Antony and Cleopatra,* iii, 13, 125.

3
Farewell, sweet playfellow; pray thou for us!
A Midsummer-Night's Dream. Act i, sc. 1, l. 220. [Hermia]
Old playfellows.—*Henry VIII,* i, 3, 33.
Sullen playfellow!—*Richard III,* iv, 1, 102.

4
In marriage-pleasures play-fellow.
Pericles, i, Gower, 34. The only use of "marriage-pleasures."
Young play-fellow.—*The Winter's Tale,* i, 2, 80. The only instances in which "play-fellow" is hyphenated, the former almost certainly not by Shakespeare.

5 Two tender playfellows for dust,
Thy broken faith hath made a prey for worms.
Richard III. Act iv, sc. 4, l. 385. [Queen Elizabeth]
Shall I be your playfellow?—*The Winter's Tale,* ii, 1, 3.

PLEASING

6
Herod of Jewry dare not look upon you
But when you are well pleased.
Antony and Cleopatra. Act iii, sc. 3, l. 3. [Alexas]
Be well pleased with this.
The Merchant of Venice. Act iii, sc. 2, l. 136. [Bassanio, reading]
I am well pleased.—*The Merchant of Venice,* iii, 4, 43. "Well pleased" is repeated in *II Henry VI,* iv, 10, 25; and *Coriolanus,* ii, 2, 136.
It pleaseth me well.—*As You Like It,* iii, 2, 18.
It shall please me well.—*Julius Cæsar,* iv, 3, 53.
It will please plentifully.—*The Winter's Tale,* iv, 4, 328.

7
Thou shouldst have better pleased me with this deed.
As You Like It. Act i, sc. 2, l. 239. [Duke] "Better pleased" is repeated in *The Winter's Tale,* iv, 4, 495. "Better please" occurs in *Measure for Measure,* ii, 4, 32, and in *Henry VIII,* i, 4, 13.
I know not which pleases me better.
The Merry Wives of Windsor. Act iii, sc. 3, l. 189. [Mrs. Ford]
Now, by the gods, he could not please me better.
Pericles. Act ii, sc. 3, l. 72. [Thaisa]

8
Amiens: I know I cannot please you.
Jaques: I do not desire you to please me.
As You Like It. Act ii, sc. v, l. 15.

9
It seems he hath great care to please his wife.
The Comedy of Errors. Act ii, sc. 1, l. 56. [Adriana]
Please your wife, withal.—*The Comedy of Errors,* iii, 2, 178.
Please his grandam.—*The Merchant of Venice,* ii, 2, 206.

10
I will please you what you will demand.
The Comedy of Errors. Act iv, sc. 4, l. 52. [Adriana]

11
Do as you please.
Hamlet. Act iii, sc. 1, l. 188. [Polonius]

12
King Henry: Wilt thou have me?
Katharine: Dat is as it sall please de roi mon père.
King Henry: Nay, it will please him well, Kate; it shall please him, Kate.
Katharine: Den it sall also content me.
Henry V. Act v, sc. 2, l. 265.

13
Nay, be not angry; I am pleased again.
II Henry VI. Act i, sc. 2, l. 55. [Gloucester]
If you be pleased, retire into my cell
And there repose.
The Tempest. Act iv, sc. 1, l. 161. [Prospero]
I fear me, he will scarce be pleased withal.
The Two Gentlemen of Verona. Act ii, sc. 7, l. 67. [Lucetta]
Be pleased awhile.—*Cymbeline,* v, 5, 356.
She will be pleased.—*The Taming of the Shrew,* iv, 4, 107.

14
An if what pleases him shall pleasure you.
Fight closer, or, good faith, you'll catch a blow.
III Henry VI. Act iii, sc. 2, l. 22. [Gloucester]

15
Till God please to send the rest.
III Henry VI. Act iv, sc. 7, l. 47. [King Edward]
If God please.—*Henry V,* iv, 3, 120.
Please God.—*Henry V,* iv, 7, 171; *Much Ado about Nothing,* ii, 3, 37.
God doth please.—*Love's Labour's Lost,* v, 2, 316.
When Heaven please.—*I Henry VI,* iii, 2, 110.

16
Surrey: May it please your grace—
King Henry: No, sir, it does not please me.
Henry VIII. Act v, sc. 3, l. 134.
And if it please you, so; if not, why, so.
The Two Gentlemen of Verona. Act ii, sc. 1, l. 137. [Silvia]
I am not bound to please thee.—*The Merchant of Venice,* iv, 1, 65.
An't please you.—*II Henry VI,* ii, 1, 77, and ten times in later plays.
As it please me.—*Much Ado about Nothing,* ii, 1, 59.
As it please you.—*Much Ado about Nothing,* ii, 1, 56.
If it please you.—*II Henry VI,* ii, 1, 124, and five times in later plays.
If you please.—*Love's Labour's Lost,* i, 1, 50, and eleven times in later plays.

May it please you.—*The Two Gentlemen of Verona,* i, 3, 39, and six times in later plays.
Please you.—*The Comedy of Errors,* i, 2, 27, and twenty-four times in later plays.
So please you.—*II Henry IV,* iv, 2, 93, and twenty-one times in later plays.
Will it please you?—*The Two Gentlemen of Verona,* i, 2, 140, and nine times in later plays.
This may please you.—*II Henry IV,* iv, 2, 60.
Will these please you?—*Henry VIII,* v, 3, 170.
I know it will well please them.—*II Henry IV,* iv, 2, 71.
We 'll strive to please.—*Twelfth Night,* v, 1, 417.

1
It will please his grace, by the world, sometime to lean upon my poor shoulder.
Love's Labour 's Lost. Act v, sc. 1, l. 107. [Armado]

2
Those things do best please me
That befal preposterously.
A Midsummer-Night's Dream. Act iii, sc. 2, l. 120. [Puck]

I am best pleased to be from such a deed.
King John. Act iv, sc. 1, l. 86. [Executioner]
I am best pleased with that.—*Love's Labour 's Lost,* v, 2, 229. "Best pleased" is used a third time in *The Two Gentlemen of Verona,* i, 2, 102. "Best pleases" occurs in *Love's Labour 's Lost,* v, 2, 517, and in *A Midsummer-Night's Dream,* iii, 2, 120.

3
He both pleases men and angers them, and then they laugh at him and beat him.
Much Ado about Nothing. Act ii, sc. 1, l. 146. [Beatrice]

4
If she and I be pleased, what 's that to you?
The Taming of the Shrew. Act ii, sc. 1, l. 305. [Petruchio]

5
I 'll . . . learn my lessons as I please myself.
The Taming of the Shrew. Act iii, sc. 1, l. 20. [Bianca]

I will not go to-day,
No, nor to-morrow, not till I please myself. . . .
For me, I 'll not be gone till I please myself.
The Taming of the Shrew. Act iii, sc. 2, l. 210. [Katharina]

Please himself.—*Richard III,* ii, 2, 129; *As You Like It,* v, 4, 78.
Please myself.—*As You Like It,* ii, 5, 23.
Please themselves.—*Pericles,* iv, 1, 101.
Please thyself.—*Timon of Athens,* iv, 3, 238.
Please yourself.—*The Comedy of Errors,* iii, 2, 175; *Henry VIII,* ii, 4, 114.

6
Buckingham: To-morrow will it please you to be crown'd?
Gloucester: Even when you please.
Richard III. Act iii, sc. 7, l. 242.

That that likes not you pleases me best.
Troilus and Cressida. Act v, sc. 2, l. 102. [Thersites]

7
If it please the eye of one, it is with me as the very true sonnet is, 'Please one, and please all.'
Twelfth Night, iii, 4, 23. See under DRESS.

Please his eye.—*Comedy of Errors,* ii, 1, 114.
Please the eye.—*I Henry IV,* v, 1, 75; *Love's Labour 's Lost,* i, 1, 80.
Please your eyes.—*Pericles,* i, Gower, 4.
Pleased his ear.—*The Tempest,* i, 2, 85.

PLEASURE

8
There 's not a minute of our lives should stretch
Without some pleasure now.
Antony and Cleopatra. Act i, sc. 1, l. 46. [Antony]

The present pleasure,
By revolution lowering, does become
The opposite of itself.
Antony and Cleopatra. Act i, sc. 2, l. 128. [Antony] The only use of "lowering." "Present pleasure" is repeated in i, 4, 32, and occurs in no other play.

9
I dedicate myself to your sweet pleasure.
Cymbeline. Act i, sc. 6, l. 136. [Iachimo]

At your sweet pleasure.—*Love's Labour 's Lost,* v, 1, 89.
Most sweet pleasure.—*Love's Labour 's Lost,* v, 1, 92.
At your pleasure.—*The Taming of the Shrew,* i, 1, 54; *Troilus and Cressida,* Prol., 30.
At your grace's pleasure.—*Pericles,* ii, 3, 112.
At your noble pleasure.—*Antony and Cleopatra,* i, 2, 116. The only use of "noble pleasure."
Be it his pleasure.—*All 's Well that Ends Well,* iii, 1, 16.
It was your pleasure.—*As You Like It,* i, 3, 72.

10
Me of my lawful pleasure she restrain'd.
Cymbeline, ii, 5, 9. See under MODESTY.

Just pleasure.—*Sonnets,* cxxi.

11
I know your master's pleasure and he mine.
Cymbeline. Act iii, sc. 1, l. 86. [Cymbeline]

Your pleasure was my mere offence.
Cymbeline. Act v, sc. 5, l. 334. [Belarius]

12
Their pleasures here are past, so is their pain.
Cymbeline. Act iv, sc. 2, l. 290. [Belarius]

You make your pleasure of pains.
Twelfth Night. Act iii, sc. 3, l. 2. [Sebastian]

13
By your companies
To draw him on to pleasures.
Hamlet. Act ii, sc. 2, l. 14. [King]

Both your majesties
Might, by the sovereign power you have of us,
Put your dread pleasures more into command
Than to entreaty.
Hamlet. Act ii, sc. 2, l. 26. [Rosencrantz]

14
What is your good pleasure?
II Henry IV. Act iii, sc. 2, l. 65. [Shallow]

I would desire the duke to use his good pleasure.
Henry V. Act iii, sc. 6, l. 57. [Fluellen]

Dwell I but in the suburbs
Of your good pleasure?
Julius Cæsar. Act ii. sc. 1, l. 285. [Portia]

God's good pleasure.—*II Henry VI,* iii, 3, 26.
The only uses of "good pleasure."

Best pleasure.—*The Tempest,* i, 2, 190.

1

Hast thou not worldly pleasure at command,
Above the reach or compass of thy thought?
II Henry VI. Act i, sc. 2, l. 45. [Gloucester]

What other pleasure can the world afford?
III Henry VI. Act iii, sc. 2, l. 147. [Gloucester]

Remote from all the pleasures of the world.
Love's Labour's Lost. Act v, sc. 2, l. 806. [Princess]

Never to taste the pleasures of the world.
King John. Act iv, sc. 3, l. 68. [Salisbury]

Pleasures of the world.—*Love's Labour's Lost,* v, 2, 807; *King John,* iii, 3, 35; *Cymbeline,* iv, 2, 296.

World's pleasure.—*All's Well that Ends Well,* ii, 4, 37.

2

By my life, This is against our pleasure.
Henry VIII. Act i, sc. 2, l. 68. [King Henry]

I' the name of God,
Your pleasure be fulfill'd!
Henry VIII. Act ii, sc. 4, l. 56. [Queen Katharine]

Their pleasures
Must be fulfill'd, and I attend with patience.
Henry VIII. Act v, sc. 2, l. 18. [Cranmer]

Fulfil your pleasure.—*Julius Cæsar,* iii, 1, 159.

3

So please you, we will stand and watch your pleasure.
Julius Cæsar. Act iv, sc. 3, l. 249. [Varro]

4

Your royal pleasure must be done.
King John. Act iv, sc. 2, l. 17. [Pembroke]

We come To know your royal pleasure.
Henry VIII. Act ii, sc. 2, l. 71. [Norfolk]
The only uses of "royal pleasure."

5

'Tis not in thee To grudge my pleasures.
King Lear. Act ii, sc. 4, l. 176. [King Lear]

Let fall Your horrible pleasure.
King Lear. Act iii, sc. 2, l. 18. [King Lear]

Methinks our pleasure might have been demanded,
Ere you had spoke so far.
King Lear. Act v, sc. 3, l. 62. [Regan]

6

He hath been in unusual pleasure.
Macbeth. Act ii, sc. 1, l. 13. [Banquo]

Extraordinary pleasure.—*As You Like It,* i, 2, 7.

7

I come to know your pleasure.
Measure for Measure. Act i, sc. 1, l. 27. [Angelo]

Isabella: I have come to know your pleasure.
Angelo: That you might know it, would much better please me
Than to demand what 'tis.
Measure for Measure. Act ii, sc. 4, l. 31.

I'll know his pleasure.—*Measure for Measure,* ii, 2, 3.

We will know your pleasures.—*Julius Cæsar,* iii, 1, 98; *Henry VIII,* v, 3, 8.

8

What I do is to pleasure you.
The Merry Wives of Windsor. Act i, sc. 1, l. 251. [Shallow]

Will you pleasure me?—*The Merchant of Venice,* i, 3, 7.

9

It is admirable pleasures and fery honest knaveries.
The Merry Wives of Windsor. Act iv, sc. 4, l. 80. [Evans]

10

Pleasure and action make the hours seem short.
Othello. Act ii, sc. 3, l. 385. [Iago]

11

Here pleasures court mine eyes, and mine eyes shun them.
Pericles. Act i, sc. 2, l. 6. [Pericles]

You shall live in pleasure.
Pericles. Act iv, sc. 2, l. 81. [Bawd]

Incestuous pleasure.—*Hamlet,* iii, 3, 90.

12

Thy secret pleasure turns to open shame.
The Rape of Lucrece, l. 890.

Why should the private pleasure of some one
Become the public plague of many moe?
The Rape of Lucrece, l. 1478.

13

And hate the idle pleasures of these days.
Richard III. Act i, sc. 1, l. 31. [Gloucester]

Barren pleasures.—*I Henry IV,* iii, 2, 14.

14

I have not sounded him, nor he deliver'd
His gracious pleasure any way therein.
Richard III. Act iii, sc. 4, l. 16. [Hastings]

What is your gracious pleasure?—*Macbeth,* v, 3, 30.

15

Gloucester: What is your grace's pleasure?
Buckingham: Even that, I hope, which pleaseth God above.
Richard III. Act iii, sc. 7, l. 108.

Your grace's pleasure.—*Pericles,* ii, 3, 112; ii, 5, 29.

Duke's pleasure.—*King Lear,* ii, 2, 159.

What is't your highness' pleasure?
Richard III. Act iv, sc. 4, l. 452. [Ratcliff]
"Highness' pleasure" is repeated frequently.

Hear the king's pleasure, cardinal.
Henry VIII. Act iii, sc. 2, l. 228. [Norfolk]
"King's pleasure" is repeated in l. 337, in i, 1, 215 and v, 3, 90. Also in *Hamlet,* v, 2, 209, and *Love's Labour's Lost,* v, 1, 92.

He sends to know your lordship's pleasure.
Richard III. Act iii, sc. 2, l. 15. [Messenger]

What's your lordship's pleasure?—*Cymbeline,* ii, 3, 85.

Lordships' pleasures.—*Henry VIII,* v, 2, 31.

He attends your ladyship's pleasure.—*Twelfth Night,* iii, 4, 65.

What is't your worship's pleasure?—*Measure For Measure,* ii, 1, 192.

What is your pleasure?—*All's Well that Ends Well,* i, 3, 143, and five times in later plays.

What are your pleasures with me?—*Henry VIII,* iii, 1, 26.

16

Your grace may do your pleasure.
Richard III. Act iv, sc. 2, l. 21. [Buckingham]

Like or find fault; do as your pleasures are.
Troilus and Cressida, Prol., 30.

Do thy pleasure.—*King Lear,* iv, 1, 49.

Do your pleasure.—*King John,* iii, 1, 252.

Use your pleasure.—*The Merchant of Venice,* iii, 2, 323.

1 Come you this afternoon,
To know our further pleasure.
Romeo and Juliet. Act i, sc. 1, l. 108. [Prince]

Attend his further pleasure.—*All's Well that Ends Well,* ii, 4, 54.

2
Nurse: Thou must stand by too, and suffer every knave to use me at his pleasure.
Peter: I saw no man use you at his pleasure; if I had, my weapon should quickly have been out, I warrant you.
Romeo and Juliet. Act ii, sc. 4, l. 163.

Use her at thy pleasure.—*Pericles,* iv, 6, 151.

3
Blunting the fine point of seldom pleasure.
Sonnets. No. lii. "Blunting" is repeated in *A Lover's Complaint,* l. 161.

Common pleasures.—*Julius Cæsar,* iii, 2, 255.
Constant pleasure.—*King Lear,* v, 1, 4.
Curious pleasures.—*Pericles,* i, 1, 16.
Different pleasures.—*Timon of Athens,* i, 1, 264.
Greater pleasures.—*King Lear,* v, 3, 2.

4
Sir, to your pleasure humbly I subscribe.
The Taming of the Shrew. Act i, sc. 1, l. 81. [Bianca]

5 I propose not merely to myself
The pleasures such a beauty brings with it.
Troilus and Cressida. Act ii, sc. 2, l. 146. [Paris]

Pleasure and revenge
Have ears more deaf than adders to the voice
Of any true decision.
Troilus and Cressida. Act ii, sc. 2, l. 171. [Hector]

6
You speak your fair pleasure.
Troilus and Cressida. Act iii, sc. 1, l. 51. The only use of "fair pleasure."

You speak your pleasures.—*Henry VIII,* iii, 2, 13.

7
Clown: I take pleasure in singing, sir.
Duke: I'll pay thy pleasure then.
Clown: Truly, sir, and pleasure will be paid, one time or another.
Twelfth Night. Act ii, sc. 4, l. 70. "Take pleasure" is repeated in *Much Ado about Nothing,* ii, 3, 262.

PLEDGE

See also Promise

8
I pledge your grace.
II Henry IV. Act iv, sc. 2, l. 73. [Westmoreland]

I'll pledge you a mile to the bottom.
II Henry IV, v, 3, 57. See under DRINKING.

Pledge him freely.—*Pericles,* ii, 3, 78.

9 Answer me one doubt,
What pledge have we of thy firm loyalty?
III Henry VI. Act iii, sc. 3, l. 238. [King Lewis]

Pledge of my affection.—*I Henry VI,* v, 1, 47.
Pledges of my fealty.—*II Henry VI,* v, 1, 50.
Pledge of love.—*Othello,* v, 2, 214.
Pledge my vow.—*III Henry VI,* iii, 3, 250.

10
My heart is thirsty for that noble pledge.
Julius Cæsar. Act iv, sc. 3, l. 160. [Cassius]

11
Petruchio, patience; I am Grumio's pledge.
The Taming of the Shrew. Act i, sc. 2, l. 45. [Hortensio]

Pledge for his truth.—*Richard II,* v, 2, 41.
I'll pledge it for him.—*Antony and Cleopatra,* ii, 7, 91.

12
He leaves his pledges dearer than his life.
Titus Andronicus. Act iii, sc. 1, l. 292. [Lucius]

If he stand on hostage for his safety,
Bid him demand what pledge will please him best.
Titus Andronicus. Act iv, sc. 4, l. 106. [Saturninus]

Let the emperor give his pledges
Unto my father and my uncle Marcus.
Titus Andronicus. Act v, sc. 1, l. 163. [Lucius]

Now the pledge.—*Troilus and Cressida,* v, 2, 65.
There is my pledge.—*I Henry VI,* iv, 1, 120; *King Lear,* v, 3, 93.
Pretty pledge.—*Troilus and Cressida,* v, 2, 77.

PLOT

See also Conspiracy, Device, Practice

13
If it be so, you have wound a goodly clew.
All's Well that Ends Well. Act i, sc. 3, l. 188. [Countess] The only use of "clew."

14
Why then to-night Let us assay our plot.
All's Well that Ends Well. Act iii, sc. 7, l. 43. [Helena]

Who cannot be crushed with a plot?
All's Well that Ends Well. Act iv, sc. 3, l. 360. [Parolles]

I fall Under this plot.—*Antony and Cleopatra,* iv, 12, 49.

15
It is a purposed thing, and grows by plot.
Coriolanus. Act iii, sc. 1, l. 38. [Coriolanus]

Call 't not a plot.—*Coriolanus,* iii, 1, 41.
Coining plots.—*Cymbeline,* ii, 1, 64.

16
It cannot choose but be a noble plot.
I Henry IV. Act i, sc. 3, l. 279. [Hotspur]

Your whole plot too light for the counterpoise of so great an opposition.
I Henry IV. Act ii, sc. 3, l. 14. [Hotspur]

By the Lord, our plot is a good plot as ever was laid; our friends true and constant: a good plot, good friends, and full of expectation; an excellent plot, very good friends.
I Henry IV. Act ii, sc. 3, l. 18. [Hotspur]

Thou layest the plot how.
I Henry IV. Act ii, sc. 1, l. 57. [Gadshill]

John lays you plots; the times conspire with you.
King John. Act iii, sc. 4, l. 146. [Pandulph]

I will lay a plot to try that.—*The Merry Wives of Windsor,* iii, 3, 202.

Plots have I laid, inductions dangerous,
By drunken prophecies, libels and dreams.
Richard III. Act i, sc. 1, l. 32. [Gloucester] The only use of "libels" and "inductions." "Induction" occurs in *Richard III,* iv, 4, 5, and in *I Henry IV,* iii, 1, 2.

This plot of death which sadly she had laid.
The Rape of Lucrece, l. 1212.
The plot is laid.—*I Henry VI,* ii, 3, 4.
Good plots, they are laid.—*The Merry Wives of Windsor,* iii, 2, 39.

1
He hath heard of our confederacy.
I Henry IV. Act iv, sc. 4, l. 38. [Archbishop]
I stood i' the level
Of a full-charged confederacy, and give thanks
To you that choked it.
Henry VIII. Act i, sc. 2, l. 3. [King] The only use of "full-charged."
What confederacy have you with the traitors
Late footed in the kingdom?
King Lear. Act ii, sc. 7, l. 44. [Cornwall]
Lo, she is one of this confederacy!
Now I perceive they have conjoin'd all three
To fashion this false sport in spite of me.
A Midsummer-Night's Dream. Act iii, sc. 2, l. 192. [Helena]
Confederacy of Lady Eleanor.—*II Henry VI,* ii, 1, 168. The only uses of "confederacy."

2
A pretty plot, well chosen to build upon!
II Henry VI. Act i, sc. 4, l. 59. [York]
In this private plot be we the first.
II Henry VI. Act ii, sc. 2, l. 60. [Warwick]

3
I know their complot is to have my life.
II Henry VI. Act iii, sc. 1, l. 147. [Gloucester]
Nor never by advised purpose meet
To plot, contrive, or complot any ill.
Richard II. Act i, sc. 3, l. 188. [King]
Lay a complot.—*Titus Andronicus,* v, 2, 147.
Complots of mischief.—*Titus Andronicus,* v, 1, 65.
Complot of this timeless tragedy.—*Titus Andronicus,* ii, 3, 265.
Digest our complots.—*Richard III,* iii, 1, 200.
Yield to our complots.—*Richard III,* iii, 1, 192.
The only uses of "complot" and "complots."

4
I see them lay their heads together to surprise me.
II Henry VI. Act iv, sc. 8, l. 60. [Cade]
How the young folks lay their heads together!
The Taming of the Shrew. Act i, sc. 2, l. 139. [Grumio] The only uses of "lay their heads together."

5
These are the limbs o' the plot.
Henry VIII. Act i, sc. 1, l. 220. [Buckingham]

6
Ligarius: What 's to do?
Brutus: A piece of work that will make sick men whole.
Julius Cæsar. Act ii, sc. 1, l. 326.

7
Call for our chiefest men of discipline,
To cull the plots of best advantages.
King John. Act ii, sc. 1, l. 39. [King Philip]
Methinks I see this hurly all on foot.
King John. Act iii, sc. 4, l. 169. [Pandulph]
"Hurly" is repeated in *II Henry IV,* iii, 1, 25, and in *The Taming of the Shrew,* iv, 1, 206.

8
Had he a hand to write this? a heart and brain to breed it in?
King Lear. Act i, sc. 2, l. 60. [Gloucester]
Thy suggestion, plot, and damned practice.
King Lear. Act ii, sc. 1, l. 75. [Edmund]
I have o'erheard a plot of death upon him.
King Lear. Act iii, sc. 6, l. 96. [Gloucester]
A plot upon her virtuous husband's life.
King Lear. Act iv, sc. 6, l. 279. [Edgar]

9
Machination ceases.
King Lear. Act v, sc. 1, l. 46. [Edgar]
Machinations, hollowness.—*King Lear,* i, 2, 122. The only uses of "machination."

10
Strange things I have in head, that will to hand;
Which must be acted ere they may be scann'd.
Macbeth. Act iii, sc. 4, l. 139. [Macbeth]

11
The provost knows our purpose and our plot.
Measure for Measure. Act iv, 5, 2. [Duke]
Unburden all my plots and purposes.
Merchant of Venice, i, 1, 133. [Bassanio]

12
Then she plots, then she ruminates.
The Merry Wives of Windsor, ii, 2, 320. See under WIFE.
Ruminate strange plots.—*Titus Andronicus,* v, 2, 6.
Deep plots.—*Hamlet,* v, 2, 9.
Devilish plots.—*Richard III,* iii, 4, 62.

13
Let our plot go forward.
The Merry Wives of Windsor. Act iv, sc. 4, l. 13. [Page]
What is your plot?—*The Merry Wives of Windsor,* iv, 4, 45.

14
Let there be the same net spread for her.
Much Ado about Nothing. Act ii, sc. 3, l. 221. [Don Pedro]
So will I turn her virtue into pitch,
And out of her own goodness make the net
That shall enmesh them all.
Othello. Act ii, sc. 3, l. 366. [Iago] The only use of "enmesh."

15
Once did I lay an ambush for your life,
A trespass that doth vex my grieved soul.
Richard II. Act i, sc. 1, l. 137. [Mowbray]
Who would have suspected an ambush where I was taken?
All's Well that Ends Well. Act iv, sc. 3, l. 335. [Parolles]
See the ambush of our friends be strong;
I fear the emperor means no good to us.
Titus Andronicus. Act v, sc. 3, l. 9. [Lucius]
In secret ambush.—*III Henry VI,* iv, 6, 83.
I fear some ambush.—*Cymbeline,* iv, 2, 65.

16
Is there no plot
To rid the realm of this pernicious blot?
Richard II. Act iv, sc. 1, l. 324. [Aumerle]
Come home with me to supper; and I 'll lay
A plot shall show us all a merry day.
Richard II. Act iv, sc. 1, l. 333. [Abbot]
They do plot Unlikely wonders.
Richard II, v, 5, 18. See under THOUGHT.

17
'Tis hatch'd and shall be so.
Taming of the Shrew, i, 1, 211. [Lucentio]
And now 'tis plotted.—*The Taming of the Shrew,* i, 1, 193.

1
We 'll over-reach the greybeard, Gremio.
The Taming of the Shrew. Act iii, sc. 2, l. 147. [Tranio]
O'erreach them.—*Titus Andronicus,* v, 2, 143. "O'er-reaches" occurs in *Hamlet,* v, 1, 87.
Gross o'erreaching.—*The Merry Wives of Windsor,* v, 5, 145. The only use of "o'erreaching."

2
The setting of thine eye and cheek proclaim
A matter from thee, and a birth indeed
Which throes thee much to yield.
The Tempest. Act ii, sc. 1, l. 233. [Sebastian]
Dost thou like the plot, Trinculo?
The Tempest. Act iii, sc. 2, l. 117. [Stephano]
The minute of their plot Is almost come.
The Tempest. Act iv, sc. 1, l. 141. [Prospero]

3
You do but plot your deaths By this device.
Titus Andronicus. Act ii, sc. 1, l. 78. [Aaron]
This way, or not at all, stand you in hope.
Titus Andronicus. Act ii, sc. 1, l. 119. [Aaron]
Chief architect and plotter of these woes.
Titus Andronicus. Act v, sc. 3, l. 122. [Marcus] The only use of "plotter."

4
Myself am one made privy to the plot.
The Two Gentlemen of Verona. Act iii, sc. 1, l. 12. [Proteus]
Privy to their late escape.—*The Winter's Tale,* ii, 1, 94.
Privy to your wishes.—*Antony and Cleopatra,* i, 2, 42.

5
Know, noble lord, they have devised a mean.
The Two Gentlemen of Verona. Act iii, sc. 1, l. 38. [Proteus]

6
There is a plot against my life, my crown.
Winter's Tale. Act ii, sc. 1, l. 47. [Leontes]

II—Plot of Ground

7
Let us
Find out the prettiest daisied plot we can.
Cymbeline, iv, 2, 398. See under GRAVE.

8
Fight for a plot
Whereon the numbers cannot try the cause.
Hamlet. Act iv, sc. 4, l. 62. [Hamlet]

9
Many unfrequented plots there are
Fitted by kind for rape and villainy.
Titus Andronicus. Act ii, sc. 1, l. 115. [Aaron] "Unfrequented" is repeated in *The Two Gentlemen of Verona,* v, 4, 2: "Unfrequented woods."
Blessed plot.—*Richard II,* ii, 1, 50.
Green plot.—*A Midsummer-Night's Dream,* iii, 1, 3.
Obscure plot.—*Titus Andronicus,* ii, 3, 77.
Sandy plot.—*Titus Andronicus,* iv, 1, 69.
Survey the plot.—*II Henry IV,* i, 3, 42; 51.
Plot of ground.—*I Henry VI,* ii, 4, 89.

PLOUGH

10
He plough'd her, and she cropp'd.
Antony and Cleopatra. Act ii, sc. 2, l. 233. [Agrippa]
She shall be ploughed.—*Pericles,* iv, 6, 154. See under VIRGINITY.

11
Let the Volces
Plough Rome and harrow Italy.
Coriolanus. Act v, sc. 3, l. 33. [Coriolanus]
The coulter rusts
That should deracinate such savagery.
Henry V. Act v, sc. 2, l. 46. [Burgundy] The only use of "coulter." "Deracinate" is repeated in *Troilus and Cressida,* i, 3, 99.

12
I have vowed to Jaquenetta to hold the plough for her sweet love three years.
Love's Labour's Lost. Act v, sc. 2, l. 893. [Armado]

13
Whilst the heavy ploughman snores,
All with weary task fordone.
A Midsummer-Night's Dream. Act v, sc. 1, l. 380. [Puck] "Ploughman" occurs also in ii, 1, 94, in *Troilus and Cressida,* i, 1, 59 and in *The Rape of Lucrece,* l. 958.

14
Yoke you like draught-oxen and make you plough.
Troilus and Cressida. Act ii, sc. 1, l. 116. [Thersites] The only use of "draught-oxen."

15
'Tis thou that rigg'st the bark and plough'st the foam.
Timon of Athens. Act v, sc. 1, l. 53. [Timon]

POCKET

16
Falstaff: Have you inquired yet who picked my pocket? . . . I 'll be sworn my pocket was picked. . . . Shall I not take mine ease in mine inn but I shall have my pocket picked? . . . I fell asleep behind the arras and had my pocket picked. This house is turned bawdy-house; they pick pockets. . . .
Prince of Wales: Charge an honest woman with picking thy pocket! why, thou whoreson, impudent, embossed rascal, if there was anything in thy pocket but tavern-reckonings, memorandums of bawdy-houses, and one poor penny-worth of sugar-candy to make thee long-winded, if thy pocket were enriched with any other injuries than these, I am a villain: and yet you will stand to it; you will not pocket up wrong. . . .
Falstaff: You confess then, you picked my pocket?
Prince of Wales: It appears so by the story.
I Henry IV. Act iii, sc. 3, l. 60. "Pocket up wrongs" is repeated in *King John,* iii, 1, 200. The phrase "picked my pocket" occurs only in this scene. The only use of "tavern-reckonings," "memorandums," "sugar-candy," and "long-winded."
Search his pockets.—*I Henry IV,* ii, 4, 580.

17
They would have me as familiar with other men's pockets as their gloves or their handkerchers; which makes much against my manhood, if I should take from another's pocket to put into mine; for it is plain pocketing up of wrongs.
Henry V. Act iii, sc. 2, l. 50. [Boy] Shakespeare uses "handkercher" six times and

"handkerchief" twenty-seven. "Napkin" occurs sixteen times, always in the sense of handkerchief. The only use of "pocketing."
Fill'd their pockets.—*I Henry VI,* iii, 1, 80.
Put it in the pocket of my gown.—*Julius Cæsar,* iv, 3, 253.
Put it in his pocket.—*Hamlet,* iii, 4, 101.
Found in his pocket.—*Othello,* v, 2, 309; 315.

1
Antonio: If but one of his pockets could speak, would it not say he lies?
Sebastian: Ay, or very falsely pocket up his report.
The Tempest. Act ii, sc. 1, l. 65.
Pocket up.—*I Henry IV,* iii, 3, 183; *King John,* iii, 1, 200; *The Winter's Tale,* iv, 4, 734; *Antony and Cleopatra,* ii, 2, 73.

POETRY

See also Ballad, Numbers, Rhyme, Verse

2
Hangs odes upon hawthorns and elegies on brambles.
As You Like It. Act iii, sc. 2, l. 379. [Rosalind]
Once more I 'll read the ode that I have writ.
Love's Labour 's Lost, iv, 3, 99. The only uses of "ode" and "odes."
Dire-lamenting elegies.
The Two Gentlemen of Verona, iii, 2, 82. The only uses of "elegies."

3
Touchstone: Truly I wish the gods had made thee poetical.
Audrey: I do not know what 'poetical' is; is it honest in deed and word? is it a true thing?
Touchstone: No, truly; for the truest poetry is the most feigning. . . .
Audrey: Do you wish then that the gods had made me poetical?
Touchstone: I do, truly; for thou swearest to me thou art honest: now, if thou wert a poet, I might have some hope that thou didst feign.
As You Like It. Act iii, sc. 3, l. 15.

4
Scene individable, or poem unlimited.
Hamlet, ii, 2, 418. See under ACTOR. The only use of "poem."
Mincing poetry.—*I Henry IV,* iii, 1, 129. See under BALLAD.

5
The elegancy, facility, and golden cadence of poesy.
Love's Labour 's Lost. Act iv, sc. 2, l. 125. [Holofernes] The only use of "elegancy" and "cadence."
Music and poesy use to quicken you.
The Taming of the Shrew. Act i, sc. 1, l. 36. [Tranio]
Our poesy is as a gum, which oozes
From whence 'tis nourish'd.
Timon of Athens. Act i, sc. 1, l. 21. [Poet]
Much is the force of heaven-bred poesy.
The Two Gentlemen of Verona. Act iii, sc. 2, l. 72. [Duke] The only use of "heaven-bred."

6
Tush, none but minstrels like of sonneting!
Love's Labour 's Lost. Act iv, sc. 3, l. 158. [Biron] The only use of "sonneting."

7
Time's pencil, or my pupil pen,
Neither in inward worth nor outward fair,
Can make you live yourself in eyes of men.
Sonnets. No. xvi.
So long as men can breathe or eyes can see,
So long lives this and this gives life to thee.
Sonnets. No. xviii.
His beauty shall in these black lines be seen,
And they shall live, and he in them still green.
Sonnets. No. lxiii.
Return, forgetful Muse, and straight redeem
In gentle numbers time so idly spent;
Sing to the ear that doth thy lays esteem
And gives thy pen both skill and argument. . . .
Give my love fame faster than Time wastes life;
So thou prevent'st his scythe and crooked knife.
Sonnets. No. c.
Because he needs no praise, wilt thou be dumb?
Excuse not silence so; for 't lies in thee
To make him much outlive a gilded tomb,
And to be praised of ages yet to be.
Then do thy office, Muse; I teach thee how
To make him seem long hence as he shows now.
Sonnets. No. ci.

8
Our gentle flame
Provokes itself and like the current flies
Each bound it chafes.
Timon of Athens. Act i, sc. 1, l. 23. [Poet]

II—The Poet

9
That fancy-monger.
As You Like It. Act iii, sc. 2, l. 382. [Rosalind] The only use of this phrase.
All that poets feign.—*III Henry VI,* i, 2, 31.
As poets feign.—*Passionate Pilgrim,* l. 115.

10
The most capricious poet, honest Ovid.
As You Like It. Act iii, sc. 3, l. 8. [Touchstone] Ovid is mentioned again in *The Taming of the Shrew,* i, 1, 33, and in *Titus Andronicus,* iv, 1, 42. Ovidius Naso occurs in *Love's Labour 's Lost,* iv, 2, 127. The only use of "capricious."
Thracian poet.—*Titus Andronicus,* ii, 4, 51.

11
Never durst poet touch a pen to write
Until his ink were temper'd with Love's sighs;
O, then his lines would ravish savage ears
And plant in tyrants mild humility.
Love's Labour 's Lost. Act iv, sc. 3, l. 346. [Biron]

12
The poet's eye, in a fine frenzy rolling,
Doth glance from heaven to earth, from earth to heaven;
And as imagination bodies forth
The forms of things unknown, the poet's pen
Turns them to shapes and gives to airy nothing
A local habitation and a name.
A Midsummer-Night's Dream. Act v, sc. 1,

l. 12. [Theseus] "Local" is repeated in *Troilus and Cressida,* iv, 5, 244.

1
If thou survive my well-contented day,
When that churl Death my bones with dust shall cover,
And shalt by fortune once more re-survey
These poor rude lines of thy deceased lover,
Compare them with the bettering of the time,
And though they be outstripp'd by every pen,
Reserve them for my love, not for their rhyme,
Exceeded by the height of happier men.
O, then vouchsafe me but this loving thought:
'Had my friend's Muse grown with this growing age,
A dearer birth than this his love had brought,
To march in ranks of better equipage:
But since he died and poets better prove,
Theirs for their style I 'll read, his for his love.'

Sonnets. No. xxxii. The only use of "well-contented" and "equipage." "Re-survey" occurs again in *Henry V,* v, 2, 81.

POINT

2
It remains,
As the main point of this our after-meeting.

Coriolanus. Act ii, sc. 2, l. 42. [Menenius] The only use of "main point."

Ample point.—*Troilus and Cressida,* iii, 3, 89.
Extremest point.—*Richard II,* iv, 1, 47.
Fatal points.—*Romeo and Juliet,* iii, 1, 171.
Fine point.—*Sonnets,* lii.
Highest point.—*Henry VIII,* iii, 2, 223.
Incensed points.—*Hamlet,* v, 2, 61.
Leaden points.—*Julius Cæsar,* iii, 1, 173.
Sourest points.—*Antony and Cleopatra,* ii, 2, 24.
Steely point.—*III Henry VI,* ii, 3, 16.
Thorny point.—*As You Like It,* ii, 7, 94.
All the points o' the compass.—*Coriolanus,* ii, 3, 25.

3
You are at point to lose your liberties.

Coriolanus. Act iii, sc. 1, l. 194. [Sicinius]

Almost at point to enter.—*Coriolanus,* v, 4, 64.
At point . . . to master Cæsar's sword.

Cymbeline. Act iii, sc. 1, l. 30. [Queen]

Who . . . are at point
To show their open banner.

King Lear. Act iii, sc. 1, l. 33. [Kent]

He 's at some hard point.—*Cymbeline,* iii, 4, 16.
At point to sink for food.—*Cymbeline,* iii, 6, 17.
Already at a point.—*Macbeth,* iv, 3, 135.
At all points.—*Richard II,* i, 3, 2.

4
Falstaff: Thou knowest my old ward; here I lay, and thus I bore my point. . . . I made no more ado but took all their seven points in my target thus. . . . Their points being broken,—
Poins: Down fell their hose.

I Henry IV. Act ii, sc. 4, l. 215. Points were tagged laces for attaching hose to the doublet, and fastening various parts of the dress where buttons are now used.

Upon mine honour, for a silken point
I'll give my barony.

II Henry IV. Act i, sc. 1, l. 53. [Bardolph] The only use of "barony."

Points more than all the lawyers in Bohemia can learnedly handle, though they come to him by the gross.

The Winter's Tale. Act iv, sc. 4, l. 207 [Servant]

Ties his points.—*Antony and Cleopatra,* iii, 13. 157.

5
Come we to full points here; and are etceteras nothing?

II Henry IV. Act ii, sc. 4, l. 198. [Pistol]

6
Here lies the point: why, being son to me, art thou so pointed at?

I Henry IV. Act ii, sc. 4, l. 448. [Falstaff]

Shallow: Ay, there 's the point, sir.
Evans: Marry, is it; the very point of it.

Merry Wives of Windsor. Act i, sc. 1, l. 229.

Well, then, here 's the point.—*Cymbeline,* iii. 4, 156.
Here lies the point.—*Hamlet,* v, 1, 10.
That is the point.—*Henry V,* iii, 2, 108.
This is the point.—*Measure for Measure,* i, 4. 49.
There 's the point.—*II Henry IV,* i, 3, 18; *The Merry Wives of Windsor,* i, 1, 229; *Othello,* iii, 3, 228; *Antony and Cleopatra,* ii, 6, 31.

7
Vows . . . humble service till the point of death.

I Henry VI. Act iii, sc. 1, l. 168. [Plantagenet] "Point of death" is repeated in *II Henry VI,* iii, 2, 369; *Romeo and Juliet,* v, 3, 88; *Twelfth Night,* v, 1, 121.

Point of battle.—*Coriolanus,* i, 1, 166.
Point of envy.—*Cymbeline,* ii, 3, 133.
Point of friendship.—*I Henry IV,* v, 1, 122.
Point of honour.—*Richard II,* v, 3, 11.
Point of ignorance.—*Henry VIII,* i, 3, 26.
Point of war.—*II Henry IV,* iv, 1, 52.
Point of weight.—*Henry VIII,* iii, 1, 71.
Point of wisdom.—*Richard III,* i, 4, 99. Of these phrases only "point of death" is used more than once.

8
I saw him hold Lord Percy at the point.

I Henry IV. Act v, sc. 4, l. 21. [King Henry]

Keep At point.—*King Lear,* i, 4, 347.
Point against point.—*Macbeth,* i, 2, 56.

9
The state of Normandy
Stands on a tickle point.

II Henry VI. Act i, sc. 1, l. 215. [York]

Why, brother, wherefore stand you on nice points?

III Henry VI. Act iv, sc. 7, l. 58. [Gloucester]

10
The sharp thorny points
Of my alleged reasons, drive this forward

Henry VIII. Act ii, sc. 4, l. 224. [King]

11
My point and period will be throughly wrought.

Or well or ill, as this day's battle 's fought.
King Lear. Act iv, sc. 7, l. 98. [Kent]
This fellow doth not stand upon points.
A Midsummer-Night's Dream. Act v, sc. 1, l. 118. [Theseus]
1
Examine him upon that point.
Much Ado about Nothing. Act v, sc. 1, l. 322. [Dogberry]
Let me know the point.—*Measure for Measure,* iii, 1, 73.
There's a fearful point!—*Romeo and Juliet,* iv, 3, 32.
2
Tell him O'er, point by point.
Pericles. Act v, sc. 1, l. 227. [Pericles]
Point by point.—*III Henry VI,* ii, 5, 24; *Henry VIII,* i, 2, 7.
From point to point.—*All's Well that Ends Well,* iii, 1, 1; v, 3, 325.
Point from point.—*All's Well that Ends Well,* iv, 3, 72.
Point to point.—*King John,* ii, 1, 390; *Romeo and Juliet,* iii, 1, 165.
3 Thou know'st not what it is
With javelin's point a churlish swine to gore.
Venus and Adonis, l. 616.
Bodkin's point.—*The Winter's Tale,* iii, 3, 87.
Dagger's point.—*III Henry VI,* v, 6, 27; *Titus Andronicus,* iv, 2, 70.
Dial's point.—*I Henry IV,* v, 2, 84; *Richard II,* v, 5, 53.
Enemy's point.—*Titus Andronicus,* v, 3, 111.
Knife's point.—*Much Ado about Nothing,* ii, 3, 264.
Knife's sharp point.—*Titus Andronicus,* v, 3, 63.
Lance's point.—*Richard II,* i, 3, 74.
Rapier's point.—*III Henry VI,* i, 3, 37; i, 4, 80; *Richard II,* iv, 1, 40; *Titus Andronicus,* iv, 2, 85; *Romeo and Juliet,* iv, 3, 57.
Spear's point.—*Venus and Adonis,* l. 626.
4
But that 's not to the point.
Winter's Tale. Act iii, sc. 3, l. 91. [Clown]
To the point.—*I Henry IV,* iv, 3, 89; *Measure for Measure,* ii, 1, 100; iii, 1, 254.
Grow to a point.—*A Midsummer-Night's Dream,* i, 2, 10.
Let me know the point.—*Measure for Measure,* iii, 1, 73.
No point.—*Love's Labour 's Lost,* ii, 1, 190; v, 2, 277.

POISON

See also Venom

5
I would poison that vile rascal.
All's Well that Ends Well. Act iii, sc. 5, l. 87. [Diana]
Now I feed myself With most delicious poison.
Antony and Cleopatra. Act i, sc. 5, l. 26. [Cleopatra]
6
Have I the aspic in my lips?
Antony and Cleopatra. Act v, sc. 2, l. 296. [Cleopatra]
Swell, bosom, with thy fraught,
For 'tis of aspics' tongues!
Othello. Act iii, sc. 3, l. 449. [Othello]
7
With thy sharp teeth this knot intrinsicate
Of life at once untie: poor venomous fool,
Be angry, and dispatch.
Antony and Cleopatra. Act v, sc. 2, l. 307. [Cleopatra] The only use of "intrinsicate."
Serpent's poison.—*Antony and Cleopatra,* i, 2, 201.
8
He will practise against thee by poison.
As You Like It. Act i, sc. 1, l. 157. [Oliver]
I will deal in poison with thee.
As You Like It. Act v, sc. 1, l. 59. [Touchstone]
9
Thou 'rt poison to my blood.
Cymbeline. Act i, sc. 1, l. 128. [Cymbeline]
10 These most poisonous compounds,
Which are the movers of a languishing death;
But though slow, deadly.
Cymbeline. Act i, sc. 5, l. 8. [Cornelius]
Strange lingering poisons.
Cymbeline. Act i, sc. 5, l. 34. [Cornelius]
Such boil'd stuff As well might poison poison!
Cymbeline. Act i, sc. 6, l. 125. [Iachimo]
A mortal mineral; which, being took,
Should by the minute feed on life and lingering
By inches waste you.
Cymbeline. Act v, sc. 5, l. 50. [Cornelius]
Poisonous mineral.—*Othello,* ii, 1, 306.
The poisonous simple sometimes is compacted
In a pure compound.
The Rape of Lucrece, l. 530.
Poisonous damp.—*Antony and Cleopatra,* iv, 9, 13.
Poisonous potions.—*I Henry IV,* v, 4, 56.
Poisonous toad.—*Richard III,* i, 3, 246.
Poisonous-tongued.—*Cymbeline,* iii, 2, 5.
11 We will fear no poison, which attends
In place of greater state.
Cymbeline. Act iii, sc. 3, l. 77. [Belarius]
Thou gavest me poison: dangerous fellow, hence!
Breathe not where princes are.
Cymbeline. Act v, sc. 5, l. 237. [Imogen]
Ta'en off by poison.—*Cymbeline,* v, 5, 47.
12
Upon my secure hour thy uncle stole,
With juice of cursed hebenon in a vial,
And in the porches of my ears did pour
The leperous distilment; whose effect
Holds such an enmity with blood of man
That swift as quicksilver it courses through
The natural gates and alleys of the body,
And with a sudden vigour it doth posset
And curd, like eager droppings into milk
The thin and wholesome blood.
Hamlet. Act i, sc. 5, l. 61. [Ghost] The only use of "hebenon" (henbane), "leperous," and "distilment." "Quicksilver" is mentioned again in *II Henry IV,* ii, 4, 248.
Poison in jest.—*Hamlet,* iii, 2, 244.
13
Thou mixture rank, of midnight weeds collected,
With Hecate's ban thrice blasted, thrice infected,
Thy natural magic and dire property,

On wholesome life usurp immediately.
Hamlet. Act iii, sc. 2, l. 268. [Lucianus]
I bought an unction of a mountebank,
So mortal that, but dip a knife in it,
Where it draws blood no cataplasm so rare,
Collected from all simples that have virtue
Under the moon, can save the thing from death
That is but scratch'd withal: I 'll touch my point
With this contagion, that, if I gall him slightly,
It may be death.
Hamlet. Act iv, sc. 7, l. 142. [Lærtes] The only use of "cataplasm." "Unction" occurs again in *Hamlet,* iii, 4, 145, and in no other play.
I 'll have prepared him
A chalice for the nonce, whereon but sipping,
If he by chance escape your venom'd stuck,
Our purpose may hold there.
Hamlet. Act iv, sc. 7, l. 160. [King] The only use of "sipping."
The drink, the drink! I am poison'd.
Hamlet. Act v, sc. 2, l. 321. [Queen]
The potent poison quite o'er-crows my spirit.
Hamlet. Act v, sc. 2, l. 364. [Hamlet] The only use of "o'er-crows."

1
I would have him poison'd with a pot of ale.
I Henry IV. Act i, sc. 3, l. 233. [Hotspur]

2
In poison there is physic.
II Henry IV. Act i, sc. 1, l. 137. [Northumberland]

3
Hide not thy poison with such sugar'd words.
II Henry VI. Act iii, sc. 2, l. 45. [King Henry]
Your grace attended to their sugar'd words,
But look'd not on the poison of their hearts.
Richard III. Act iii, sc. 1, l. 13. [Gloucester]

4
What! art thou, like the adder, waxen deaf?
Be poisonous too and kill thy forlorn queen.
II Henry VI. Act iii, sc. 2, l. 76. [Queen]
You might condemn us as poisonous.
Coriolanus. Act v, sc. 3, l. 135. [Volumnia]

5
Give me some drink; and bid the apothecary
Bring the strong poison that I bought of him.
II Henry VI. Act iii, sc. 3, l. 17. [Beaufort]

6
From the inward motion to deliver
Sweet, sweet, sweet poison for the age's tooth.
King John. Act i, sc. 1, l. 212. [Bastard]
The burning quality
Of that fell poison which assaileth him.
King John. Act v, sc. 7, l. 8. [Pembroke]

7
Poison'd,—ill fare—dead, forsook, cast off.
King John. Act v, sc. 7, l. 35. [King John]
Poison'd by a monk.—*King John,* v, 6, 23.
Poison'd by their wives.—*Richard II,* iii, 2, 159.

8
Within me is a hell; and there the poison
Is as a fiend confined to tyrannize
On unreprievable condemned blood.
King John. Act v, sc. 7, l. 46. [King John] The only use of "unreprievable."

9
If you have poison for me, I will drink it.
King Lear. Act iv, sc. 7, l. 72. [King Lear]
Her sister
By her is poisoned; she hath confess'd it.
King Lear. Act v, sc. 3, l. 226. [Gentleman]
The one the other poison'd for my sake.
King Lear. Act v, sc. 3, l. 240. [Edmund]

10
I will incense Page to deal with poison.
The Merry Wives of Windsor. Act i, sc. 3, l. 9. [Nym]

11
The poison of that lies in you to temper.
Much Ado about Nothing. Act ii, sc. 2, l. 21. [Borachio]
I have drunk poison.—*Much Ado about Nothing,* v, 1, 253.

12
Othello: Get me some poison, Iago; this night: . . . this night, Iago.
Iago: Do it not with poison, strangle her in her bed, even the bed she hath contaminated.
Othello: Good, good: the justice of it pleases: very good.
Othello. Act iv, sc. 1, l. 216.
Poison his delight.—*Othello,* i, 1, 68.

13
Poison and treason are the hands of sin.
Pericles. Act i, sc. 1, l. 39. [Pericles]

14
I will not poison thee with my attaint.
The Rape of Lucrece, l. 1072.

15
They love not poison that do poison need.
Richard II. Act v, sc. 6, l. 38. [Bolingbroke]

16
Gloucester: Why dost thou spit at me?
Lady Anne: Would it were mortal poison, for thy sake!
Gloucester: Never came poison from so sweet a place.
Lady Anne: Never hung poison on a fouler toad.
Richard III. Act i, sc. 2, l. 145.

17
Say thou but 'I,'
And that bare vowel 'I' shall poison more
Than the death-darting eye of cockatrice.
Romeo and Juliet. Act iii, sc. 2, l. 45. [Juliet] The only use of "death-darting."

18
Hadst thou no poison mix'd, no sharp-ground knife,
No sudden mean of death, though ne'er so mean?
Romeo and Juliet. Act iii, sc. 3, l. 44. [Romeo] The only use of "sharp-ground."
Rank poison.—*Romeo and Juliet,* i, 2, 51.

19
If you could find out but a man
To bear a poison, I would temper it.
Romeo and Juliet. Act iii, sc. 5, l. 97. [Juliet]
Temper poisons.—*Cymbeline,* v, 5, 250.

1 What if it be a poison, which the friar
Subtly hath minister'd to have me dead?
Romeo and Juliet. Act iv, sc. 3. l. 24. [Juliet]

2 If a man did need a poison now,
Whose sale is present death in Mantua,
Here lives a caitiff wretch would sell it him.
Romeo and Juliet. Act v, sc. 1, l. 50. [Romeo]

Let me have
A dram of poison, such soon-speeding gear
As will disperse itself through all the veins
That the life-weary taker may fall dead
And that the trunk may be discharged of breath
As violently as hasty powder fired
Doth hurry from the fatal cannon's womb.
Romeo and Juliet. Act v, sc. 1, l. 59. [Romeo] The only use of "soon-speeding" and "life-weary."

Put this in any liquid thing you will,
And drink it off; and, if you had the strength
Of twenty men, it would dispatch you straight.
Romeo and Juliet. Act v, sc. 1, l. 77. [Apothecary]

Come, cordial and not poison, go with me
To Juliet's grave; for there must I use thee.
Romeo and Juliet. Act v, sc. 1, l. 85. [Romeo]

Poison, I see, hath been his timeless end:
O churl! drunk all, and left no friendly drop
To help me after?
Romeo and Juliet. Act v, sc. 3, l. 162. [Juliet]

Drugs poison him.—*Sonnets,* cxviii.

3 Timon: Would poison were obedient and knew my mind!
Apemantus: Where wouldst thou send it?
Timon: To sauce thy dishes.
Timon of Athens. Act iv, sc. 3, l. 296.

What dish o' poison has she dressed him!
Twelfth Night. Act ii, sc. 5, l. 123. [Fabian]

4 Leontes: Bespice a cup,
To give mine enemy a lasting wink;
Which draught to me were cordial.
Camillo: Sir, my lord,
I could do this, and that with no rash potion,
But with a lingering dram that should not work
Maliciously like poison.
The Winter's Tale. Act i, sc. 2, l. 316. The only use of "bespice."

I am his cupbearer:
If from me he have wholesome beverage,
Account me not your servant.
The Winter's Tale. Act i, sc. 2, l. 345. [Camillo] The only use of "beverage." "Cupbearer" is repeated in l. 313 of the same scene, and occurs nowhere else.

I must be the poisoner Of good Polixenes.
The Winter's Tale. Act i, sc. 2, l. 352. [Camillo] The only use of "poisoner."

POLICY

See also Cunning

5 I will o'er-run thee with policy.
As You Like It. Act v, sc. 1, l. 61. [Touchstone]

Shrewdness of policy.—*Antony and Cleopatra,* ii, 2, 69. The only use of "shrewdness."

6 I have been politic with my friend, smooth with mine enemy.
As You Like It. Act v, sc. 4, l. 46. [Touchstone]

Hugely politic.—*Sonnets,* cxxiv. "Hugely" is repeated in *As You Like It,* ii, 7, 72.

Am I politic? am I subtle? am I a Machiavel?
The Merry Wives of Windsor. Act iii, sc. 1, l. 103. [Host]

Murderous Machiavel.—*III Henry VI,* iii, 2, 193.

Notorious Machiavel!—*I Henry VI,* v, 4, 74. The only references to Machiavel.

7 Never did base and rotten policy
Colour her working with such deadly wounds.
I Henry IV. Act i, sc. 3, l. 108. [Hotspur]

It proceeds from policy, not love.
II Henry IV. Act iv, sc. 1, l. 148. [Mowbray]

That were some love but little policy.
Richard II, v, 1, 84. [Northumberland]

8 Turn him to any cause of policy,
The Gordian knot of it he will unloose,
Familiar as his garter.
Henry V. Act i, sc. 1, l. 45. [Canterbury]

As slippery as the Gordian knot was hard!
Cymbeline, ii, 2, 34. The only mention of the "Gordian knot."

9 Search out thy wit for secret policies.
I Henry VI. Act iii, sc. 3, l. 12. [Bastard]

10 And did my brother Bedford toil his wits,
To keep by policy what Henry got?
II Henry VI. Act i, sc. 1, l. 83. [Gloucester]

That he should die is worthy policy.
II Henry VI. Act iii, sc. 1, l. 235. [Beaufort]

By devilish policy art thou grown great.
II Henry VI. Act iv, sc. 1, l. 83. [Captain]

His far-fet policy.—*II Henry VI,* iii, 1, 293. The only use of "far-fet," an abbreviation of far-fetched.

Military policy.—*All's Well that Ends Well,* i, 1, 132.

Pale policy.—*Henry V,* ii, Prol., 14.

Powerful policy.—*III Henry VI,* i, 2, 58.

Policy of mind.—*Much Ado about Nothing,* iv, 1, 200.

11 That policy may either last so long,
Or feed upon such nice and waterish diet,
Or breed itself so out of circumstance.
Othello. Act iii, sc. 3, l. 14. [Cassio] "Waterish" is repeated in *King Lear,* i, 1, 261: "Waterish Burgundy."

12 Policy, that heretic,
Which works on leases of short-number'd hours.
Sonnets. No. cxxiv. The only use of "short-number'd."

13 If she be curst, it is for policy.
The Taming of the Shrew. Act ii, sc. 1, l. 294. [Petruchio]

'Tis but his policy.—*III Henry VI,* ii, 6, 65.

It is his policy.—*III Henry VI,* v, 4, 62.
Plague of your policy!—*Henry VIII,* iii, 2, 259.
That were no policy.—*II Henry VI,* iii, 1, 238.

1 Policy sits above conscience.
Timon of Athens. Act iii, sc. 2, l. 94. [Stranger]

The devil knew not what he did when he made man politic; he crossed himself by 't: and I cannot think but, in the end, the villanies of man will set him clear.
Timon of Athens. Act iii, sc. 3, l. 28. [Servant]

2 'Tis policy and stratagem must do
That you affect.
Titus Andronicus. Act ii, sc. 1, l. 104. [Aaron]

O Lord, sir, 'tis a deed of policy.
Titus Andronicus. Act iv, sc. 2, l. 148. [Aaron]

3 The policy of those crafty swearing rascals.
Troilus and Cressida. Act v, sc. 4, l. 10. [Thersites]

Policy, that mongrel cur.—*Troilus and Cressida,* v, 4, 14.

POLITICIAN

4 Statist though I am none.
Cymbeline. Act ii, sc. 4, l. 16. [Posthumus] "Statist occurs again in *Hamlet,* v, 2, 33.

5 It might be the pate of a politician, . . . one that would circumvent God.
Hamlet. Act v, sc. 1, l. 86. [Hamlet] The only use of "circumvent."

Hear him debate of commonwealth affairs,
You would say it hath been all in all his study.
Henry V. Act i, sc. 1, l. 41. [Canterbury]

6 Get thee glass eyes;
And, like a scurvy politician, seem
To see the things thou dost not.
King Lear. Act iv, sc. 6, l. 174. [King Lear]

Vile politician.—*I Henry IV,* i, 3, 241.

7 I had as lief be a Brownist as a politician.
Twelfth Night. Act ii, sc. 2, l. 33. [Sir Andrew] The only use of Brownist, a follower of Robert Brown, a Puritan.

We are politicians.—*Twelfth Night,* ii, 3, 80.

POMP

8 O, behold, How pomp is follow'd!
Antony and Cleopatra. Act v, sc. 2, l. 150. [Cleopatra]

9 The tide of pomp
That beats upon the high shore of this world.
Henry V. Act iv, sc. 1, l. 281. [King Henry]

To think upon my pomp shall be my hell.
II Henry VI. Act ii, sc. 4, l. 41. [Duchess of Gloucester]

10 Why, what is pomp, rule, reign, but earth and dust?
III Henry VI. Act v, sc. 2, l. 27. [Warwick]

11 Till this time pomp was single, but now married
To one above itself.
Henry VIII. Act i, sc. 1, l. 15. [Norfolk]

Every man that stood
Show'd like a mine. Their dwarfish pages were
As cherubins, all gilt: the madams too,
Not used to toil, did almost sweat to bear
The pride upon them.
Henry VIII. Act i, sc. 1, l. 21. [Norfolk]

12 Vain pomp and glory of this world, I hate ye.
Henry VIII. Act iii, sc. 2, l. 365. [Wolsey]

Pomps and vain-glories.—*Timon of Athens,* i, 2, 249.
Absurd pomp.—*Hamlet,* iii, 2, 65.
Dreadful pomp.—*King John,* iv, 2, 173.
Funeral pomp.—*Titus Andronicus,* i, 1, 176.
Incertain pomp.—*Timon of Athens,* iv, 3, 243.
Painted pomp.—*As You Like It,* ii, 1, 3.
Wrested pomp.—*King John,* iv, 3, 154.

13 Shall braying trumpets and loud churlish drums,
Clamours of hell, be measures to our pomp?
King John. Act iii, sc. 1, l. 303. [Blanch] The only use of "braying."

Therefore, to be possess'd of double pomp,
To guard a title that was rich before, . . .
Is wasteful and ridiculous excess.
King John. Act iv, sc. 2, l. 9. [Salisbury]

14 Take physic, pomp;
Expose thyself to feel what wretches feel,
That thou mayst shake the superflux to them,
And show the heavens more just.
King Lear. Act iii, sc. 4, l. 33. [King Lear] The only use of "superflux."

15 I give this heavy weight from off my head
And this unwieldy sceptre from my hand,
The pride of kingly sway from out my heart;
With mine own tears I wash away my balm,
With mine own hands I give away my crown,
With mine own tongue deny my sacred state,
With mine own breath release all duty's rites:
All pomp and majesty I do forswear.
Richard II. Act iv, sc. 1, l. 204. [King Richard]

POND, POOL, see Lake

POPULARITY

16 All tongues speak of him, and the bleared sights
Are spectacled to see him: your prattling nurse
Into a rapture lets her baby cry
While she chats him: the kitchen malkin pins
Her richest lockram 'bout her reechy neck,
Clambering the walls to eye him: stalls, bulks, windows,

Are smother'd up, leads fill'd, and ridges horsed
With variable complexions, all agreeing
In earnestness to see him: seld-shown flamens
Do press among the popular throngs and puff
To win a vulgar station.
Coriolanus. Act ii, sc. 1, l. 221. [Junius Brutus] The only use of "lockram" (coarse linen) and "seld-shown." "Malkin" (slattern) occurs again in *Pericles*, iv, 3, 34, and "reechy" (filthy) in *Much Ado about Nothing*, iii, 3, 143: "Reechy painting," and in *Hamlet*, iii, 4, 184: "Reechy kisses." "Flamens" (priests) is repeated in *Timon of Athens*, iv, 3, 155.

1
That nothing-gift of differing multitudes.
Cymbeline. Act iii, sc. 6, l. 86. [Imogen] The only use of "nothing-gift."

2
Enfeoff'd himself to popularity.
I Henry IV. Act iii, sc. 2, l. 69. [King Henry] The only use of "enfeoff'd."

3 I love the people,
But do not like to stage me to their eyes:
Though it do well, I do not relish well
Their loud applause and Aves vehement;
Nor do I think the man of safe discretion
That does affect it.
Measure for Measure. Act i, sc. 1, l. 68. [Duke] The only use of "Aves."

4
Ourself and Bushy, Bagot here and Green
Observed his courtship to the common people;
How he did seem to dive into their hearts
With humble and familiar courtesy,
What reverence he did throw away on slaves,
Wooing poor craftsmen with the craft of smiles
And patient underbearing of his fortune,
As 'twere to banish their affects with him.
Richard II. Act i, sc. 4, l. 23. [King Richard] The only use of "craftsmen" and "underbearing."

PORT

5 No port is free; no place,
That guard, and most unusual vigilance,
Does not attend my taking.
King Lear. Act ii, sc. 3, l. 3. [Edgar]
Descend, and open your uncharg'd ports.
Timon of Athens. Act v, sc. 4, l. 55. [Alcibiades] The only use of "uncharg'd."
All ports I'll bar.—*King Lear*, ii, 1, 82.
Keep house and port.—*The Taming of the Shrew*, i, 1, 208.
Let the ports be guarded.—*Coriolanus*, i, 7, 1.
City ports.—*Coriolanus*, v, 6, 6.
Port of Rome.—*Antony and Cleopatra*, i, 3, 46.
Ports of slumber.—*II Henry IV*, iv, 5, 24.

6
'Tis not unknown to you, Antonio,
How much I have disabled mine estate
By something showing a more swelling port
Than my faint means would grant continuance.
The Merchant of Venice. Act i, sc. 1, l. 122. [Bassanio]
Magnificoes Of greatest port.—*The Merchant of Venice*, iii, 2, 283. The only use of "magnificoes." "Magnifico" occurs in *Othello*, i, 2, 12.
The port of gentlemen.—*II Henry VI*, iv, 1, 19.
Assume the port of Mars.—*Henry V*, Prol., 6.
Bearing my port.—*The Taming of the Shrew*, iii, 1, 36.
Sprightly port.—*Antony and Cleopatra*, iv, 14, 52.

7
All places that the eye of heaven visits
Are to a wise man ports and happy havens.
Richard II. Act i, sc. 3, l. 275. [Gaunt]
The very ports they blow,
All the quarters that they know
I' the shipman's card.
Macbeth. Act i, sc. 3, l. 15. [First Witch]
The anchor 's in the port.—*Titus Andronicus*, iv, 4, 38.
He touch'd the ports desired.—*Troilus and Cressida*, ii, 2, 76.
Here beside the port.—*All 's Well that Ends Well*, iii, 5, 39.
Port of Athens.—*Troilus and Cressida*, Prol., 3.
Best ports.—*King Lear*, iii, 1, 33.
For barons of the Cinque-ports.
Henry VIII, iv, 1, 48. The only mention of the Cinque-ports.

PORTENT, see Omen

POSSESSIONS

8
This is the brief of money, plate, and jewels,
I am possess'd of: 'tis exactly valued.
Antony and Cleopatra. Act v, sc. 2, l. 138. [Cleopatra]

9
An ill-favoured thing, sir, but mine own.
As You Like It. Act v, sc. 4, l. 60. [Touchstone]
All for use of that which is mine own.
The Merchant of Venice. Act i, sc. 3, l. 114. [Shylock]
An easy task it is to win our own.
Richard II. Act iii, sc. 2, l. 191. [King Richard]
I 'll keep mine own, despite of all the world.
The Taming of the Shrew. Act iii, sc. 2, l. 144. [Lucentio]
'Suum cuique' is our Roman justice:
This prince in justice seizeth but his own.
Titus Andronicus. Act i, sc. 1, l. 280. [Marcus]
Have I not reason to prefer mine own?
The Two Gentlemen of Verona. Act ii, sc. 4, l. 156. [Proteus]

10 I am still possess'd
Of those effects for which I did the murder,
My crown, mine own ambition and my queen.
Hamlet. Act iii, sc. 3, l. 53. [King] The only use of "effects" in this sense.

11
Now has he land and beefs.
II Henry IV. Act iii, sc. 2, l. 352. [Falstaff]

1
We lose the better half of our possessions.
Henry V. Act i, sc. 1, l. 8. [Canterbury]

2
Look to my chattels and my movables.
Henry V. Act ii, sc. 3, l. 50. [Pistol] "Moveables" (spelled thus except in the quotation from above) is repeated in *Richard III,* iii, 1, 195; iv, 2, 93; *Richard II,* ii, 1, 161; *The Taming of the Shrew,* ii, 1, 198; *Cymbeline,* ii, 2, 29.

She is my goods, my chattels.
The Taming of the Shrew. Act iii, sc. 2. l. 232. [Petruchio]

Forfeit all your chattels.—*Henry VIII,* iii, 2, 343. The only uses of "chattels."

3
I 'll rather keep
That which I have than, coveting for more,
Be cast from possibility of all.
I Henry VI. Act v, sc. 4, l. 144. [Charles]

I wish but for the thing I have.
Romeo and Juliet. Act ii, sc. 2, l. 132. [Juliet]

To have, is to have.
As You Like It. Act v, sc. 1, l. 44. [Touchstone]

And have is have, however men do catch.
King John. Act i, sc. 1, l. 173. [Bastard]

4
My parks, my walks, my manors that I had,
Even now forsake me, and of all my lands
Is nothing left me but my body's length.
III Henry VI. Act v, sc. 2, l. 24. [Warwick]

5
Rich stuffs, and ornaments of household; which
I find at such proud rate, that it out-speaks
Possession of a subject.
Henry VIII. Act iii, sc. 2, l. 126. [King] The only use of "out-speaks."

6
King John: Our strong possession and our right for us.
Queen Elinor: Your strong possession much more than your right.
King John. Act i, sc. 1, l. 39.

What in rest you have in right you hold.
King John. Act iv, sc. 2, l. 55. [Pembroke]

7
Who hath had three suits to his back, six shirts to his body, horse to ride, and weapon to wear.
King Lear. Act iii, sc. 4, l. 141. [Edgar]

8
Fear not yet
To take upon you what is yours.
Macbeth. Act iv, sc. 3, l. 69. [Macduff]

What is yours to bestow is not yours to reserve.
Twelfth Night. Act i, sc. 5, l. 200. [Viola]

9
What 's mine is yours and what is yours is mine.
Measure for Measure. Act v, sc. 1, l. 543. [Duke]

Myself and what is mine to you and yours
Is now converted: but now I was the lord
Of this fair mansion, master of my servants,
Queen o'er myself; and even now, but now,
This house, these servants and this same myself
Are yours, my lord.
The Merchant of Venice. Act iii, sc. 2, l. 168. [Portia]

10
I ken the wight: he is of substance good.
The Merry Wives of Windsor. Act i, sc. 3, l. 40. [Pistol]

I should love thee but as a property.
The Merry Wives of Windsor. Act iii, sc. 4, l. 10. [Fenton]

Property was thus appalled,
That the self was not the same;
Single nature's double name
Neither two nor one was called.
The Phœnix and the Turtle, l. 37.

11
We have no good that we can say is ours.
The Rape of Lucrece, l. 873.

Nothing this wide universe I call,
Save thou, my rose; in it thou art my all.
Sonnets. No. cix.

12
So shall you share all that he doth possess,
By having him, making yourself no less.
Romeo and Juliet. Act i, sc. 3, l. 93. [Lady Capulet]

13
Crowns in my purse I have and goods at home.
The Taming of the Shrew. Act i, sc. 2, l. 57. [Petruchio]

My hangings all of Tyrian tapestry;
In ivory coffers I have stuff'd my crowns;
In cypress chests my arras counterpoints,
Costly apparel, tents, and canopies,
Fine linen, Turkey cushions boss'd with pearl,
Valance of Venice gold in needlework,
Pewter and brass and all things that belong
To house or housekeeping: then, at my farm
I have a hundred milch-kine to the pail,
Sixscore fat oxen standing in my stalls,
And all things answerable to this portion.
The Taming of the Shrew. Act ii, sc. 1, l. 351. [Gremio] The only use of "counterpoints," "boss'd," "valance," "needlework," and "sixscore." "Tyrian" is repeated in *Pericles,* v, Gower, 28: "Tyrian ship"; and "milch-kine" in *The Merry Wives of Windsor,* iv, 4, 33.

Mellow hangings.—*Cymbeline,* iii, 3, 63.

Rich hangings.—*II Henry VI,* v, 3, 12. The only uses of "hangings."

14
I am possess'd of that is mine.
Titus Andronicus. Act i, sc. 1, l. 408. [Bassianus]

Then, good my liege, let me have what is mine.
King John, i, 1, 114. [Faulconbridge]

Mine I loved and mine I praised
And mine that I was proud on.
Much Ado about Nothing. Act iv, sc. 1, l. 138. [Leonato]

15
I do enjoy
At ample point all that I did possess.
Troilus and Cressida. Act iii, sc. 3, l. 88. [Achilles]

16
She was mine and not mine, twice or thrice in that last article. Rehearse that once more.
The Two Gentlemen of Verona. Act iii, sc. 1, l. 364. [Launce]

Thurio: Considers she my possessions?
Proteus: O, ay; and pities them.
Thurio: Wherefore?

Julia: That such an ass should owe them.
Two Gentlemen of Verona. Act v, sc. 2, l. 25.
My possessions she esteems not.—*The Two Gentlemen of Verona,* iii, 1, 79.
His possessions are so huge.—*The Two Gentlemen of Verona,* ii, 4, 175.

1
He hath ribbons of all the colours i' the rainbow; points more than all the lawyers in Bohemia can learnedly handle, though they come to him by the gross: inkles, caddisses, cambrics, lawns: why, he sings 'em over as they were gods and goddesses; you would think a smock were a she-angel, he so chants to the sleeve-hand and the work about the square on 't.
The Winter's Tale. Act iv, sc. 4, l. 205. [Servant] The only use of "caddisses" (worsted ribbons), "she-angel," and "sleeve-hand." "Inkles" (a kind of tape) is repeated in *Love's Labour 's Lost,* iii, 1, 140, and in *Pericles,* v, Gower, 8; "cambric" in *Coriolanus,* i, 3, 95, and in *Pericles,* iv, Gower, 24; and "lawn" in *The Winter's Tale,* iv, 4, 220, and in *Othello,* iv, 3, 73.

Lawn as white as driven snow;
Cyprus black as e'er was crow;
Gloves as sweet as damask roses;
Masks for faces and for noses;
Bugle bracelet, necklace amber,
Perfume for a lady's chamber;
Golden quoits and stomachers,
For my lads to give their dears:
Pins and poking-sticks of steel,
What maids lack from head to heel:
Come, buy of me, come; come buy, come buy;
Buy, lads, or else your lasses cry:
Come buy.
The Winter's Tale. Act iv, sc. 4, l. 220. [Autolycus] The only use of "driven snow," "necklace," and "poking-sticks."

POST, see Letter

POSTERITY

2
Virgilia: He 'ld make an end of thy posterity.
Volumnia: Bastards and all.
Coriolanus. Act iv, sc. 2, l. 26.

3
Posterity, await for wretched years,
When at their mothers' moist eyes babes shall suck,
Our isle be made a nourish of salt tears,
And none but women left to wail the dead.
I Henry VI. Act i, sc. 1, l. 48. [Bedford]

4
Cut off the sequence of posterity.
King John. Act ii, sc. 1, l. 96. [King Philip]
Leaving no posterity,
'Twas not their infirmity,
It was married chastity.
The Phœnix and the Turtle, l. 59.

5
My posterity, shamed with the note,
Shall curse my bones, and hold it for no sin
To wish that I their father had not been.
The Rape of Lucrece, l. 208.

6 Who is he so fond will be the tomb
Of his self-love, to stop posterity?
Sonnets. No. iii.
What could death do, if thou shouldst depart,
Leaving thee living in posterity?
Sonnets. No. vi.
All posterity
That wear this world out to the ending doom.
Sonnets. No. lv.

7
What is thy body but a swallowing grave,
Seeming to bury that posterity
Which by the rights of time thou needs must have,
If thou destroy them not in dark obscurity?
Venus and Adonis, l. 757.

POVERTY

8 Mistake me not so much
To think my poverty is treacherous.
As You Like It. Act i, sc. 3, l. 66. [Rosalind]
Heavy tedious penury.—*As You Like It,* iii, 2, 342.
Crushing penury.—*Richard II,* v, 5, 34.

9 I in such a poverty of grace,
That I shall think it a most plenteous crop
To glean the broken ears after the man
That the main harvest reaps.
As You Like It. Act iii, sc. 5, l. 100. [Silvius]
Poverty of spirit.—*Richard III,* iii, 7, 159.
Poverty in wit.—*Love's Labour 's Lost,* v, 2, 269.

10
Why should the poor be flatter'd?
Hamlet, iii, 2, 64. See under FLATTERY.

11
Alas, he is poor; he hath nothing.
I Henry IV. Act iii, sc. 3, l. 88. [Hostess]
Having nothing, nothing can he lose.
III Henry VI. Act iii, sc. 3, l. 152. [Warwick]

12
Westmoreland: Methinks they are exceeding poor and bare, too beggarly.
Falstaff: 'Faith, for their poverty, I know not where they had that; and for their bareness, I am sure they never learned that of me.
I Henry IV. Act iv, sc. 2, l. 74.
As poor as Job.—*II Henry IV,* i, 2, 144; *The Merry Wives of Windsor,* v, 5, 164.
Poor, but honest.—*All 's Well that Ends Well,* i, 3, 201.

13 His coffers sound
With hollow poverty and emptiness.
II Henry IV. Act i, sc. 3, l. 74. [Hastings]
Poverty hath distracted her.
II Henry IV. Act ii, sc. 1, l. 117. [Falstaff]
Houseless poverty.—*King Lear,* iii, 4, 26. "Houseless" is repeated in l. 30, and occurs in no other scene.
Full of poverty.—*Love's Labour 's Lost,* v, 2, 380.

14
Five hundred poor I have in yearly pay,
Who twice a-day their wither'd hands hold up
Toward heaven.
Henry V. Act iv, sc. 2, l. 315. [King Henry]

1 If I were covetous, ambitious or perverse,
As he will have me, how am I so poor?
I Henry VI. Act iii, sc. 1, l. 29. [Winchester]

2 Fortune, that arrant whore,
Ne'er turns the key to the poor.
King Lear. Act ii, sc. 4, l. 52. [Fool]

3 I know him not: yet I wrong him to call him poor; they say the jealous wittolly knave hath masses of money.
The Merry Wives of Windsor. Act ii, sc. 2, l. 281. [Falstaff] The only use of "wittolly."

4 Come hither, man. I see that thou art poor:
Hold, there is forty ducats.
Romeo and Juliet. Act v, sc. 1, l. 58. [Romeo]

My poverty, but not my will, consents.
Romeo and Juliet. Act v, sc. 1, l. 75. [Apothecary]

5 Alack, what poverty my Muse brings forth!
Sonnets. No. ciii.

6 He 's poor, and that 's revenge enough. Who can speak broader than he that has no house to put his head in? such may rail against great buildings.
Timon of Athens. Act iii, sc. 4, l. 62. [Servant]

Let me be recorded by the righteous gods,
I am as poor as you.
Timon of Athens. Act iv, sc. 2, l. 4. [Flavius]

His poor self,
A dedicated beggar to the air,
With his disease of all-shunn'd poverty,
Walks, like contempt, alone.
Timon of Athens. Act iv, sc. 2, l. 12. [Servant] The only use of "all-shunn'd." "Dedicated" is repeated in *The Tempest,* i, 2, 89.

7 O world, how apt the poor are to be proud!
Twelfth Night. Act iii, sc. 1, l. 138. [Olivia]

8 Autolycus: I am a poor fellow, sir.
Camillo: Why, be so still; here 's nobody will steal that from thee.
The Winter's Tale. Act iv, sc. 4, l. 644.

II—Poverty and Riches

9 'Tis not so well that I am poor, though many of the rich are damned.
All 's Well that Ends Well. Act i, sc. 3, l. 17. [Clown]

Poor and content is rich and rich enough,
But riches fineless is as poor as winter
To him that ever fears he shall be poor.
Othello. Act iii, sc. 3, l. 172. [Iago] The only use of "fineless" (infinite).

10 Repeal daily any wholesome act established against the rich, and provide more piercing statutes daily, to chain up and restrain the poor.
Coriolanus. Act i, sc. 1, l. 84. [Citizen]

11 Well, whiles I am a beggar, I will rail
And say there is no sin but to be rich;
And being rich, my virtue then shall be
To say there is no vice but beggary.
King John. Act ii, sc. 1, l. 593. [Bastard]

12 If thou art rich, thou 'rt poor;
For, like an ass whose back with ingots bows,
Thou bear'st thy heavy riches but a journey,
And death unloads thee.
Measure for Measure. Act iii, sc. 1, l. 25. [Duke] The only use of "ingots."

Most rich, being poor.—*King Lear,* i, 1, 253. See under VIRTUE.

Poorly rich.—*The Rape of Lucrece,* l. 97.

13 It is still her use
To let the wretched man outlive his wealth,
To view with hollow eye and wrinkled brow
An age of poverty.
The Merchant of Venice. Act iv, sc. 1, l. 268. [Antonio]

14 And high and low beguiles the rich and poor.
The Merry Wives of Windsor. Act i, sc. 3, l. 95. [Pistol]

15 Rich men sin, and I eat root.
Timon of Athens. Act i, sc. 2, l. 72. [Apemantus]

16 Pluck down the rich, enrich the poor with treasures.
Venus and Adonis, l. 1150. See under LOVE.

POWER

See also Might, Puissance

I—Earthly Power

17 In a most weak and debile minister, great power, great transcendence.
All 's Well that Ends Well. Act ii, sc. 3, l. 39. [Lafeu] The only use of "transcendence." "Debile" is repeated in *Coriolanus,* i, 9, 48 "Debile wretch."

Great power.—*I Henry VI,* i, 4, 103; *III Henry VI,* v, 2, 50; *II Henry IV,* iv, 4, 98; *Coriolanus,* iii, 3, 80; *Cymbeline,* v, 4, 26.

Absolute power.—*Coriolanus,* iii, 1, 116; *Measure for Measure,* i, 3, 13; *Timon of Athens* v, 1, 165; *King Lear,* v, 3, 300.

Ample power.—*Troilus and Cressida,* ii, 2, 140.

Mighty power.—*II Henry VI,* iv, 9, 25; *Richard III,* iv, 4, 535; v, 3, 38; *Julius Cæsar,* iv, 3, 169.

Sovereign power.—*All 's Well that Ends Well,* ii, 3, 60; *Hamlet,* ii, 2, 27.

18 My powers are crescent, and my auguring hope
Says it will come to the full.
Antony and Cleopatra. Act ii, sc. 1, l. 10. [Pompey] The only use of "auguring."

Had I great Juno's power,
The strong-wing'd Mercury should fetch thee up,
And set thee by Jove's side.
Antony and Cleopatra. Act iv, sc. 15, l. 35. [Cleopatra] The only use of "strong-wing'd."

1
Make bold power look pale.
Coriolanus. Act i, sc. 1, l. 216. [Marcius]
Bloody power.—*I Henry VI,* iv, 2, 8; *King John,* ii, 1, 221.
Malignant power.—*The Two Gentlemen of Verona,* iii, 1, 238.
Rebel powers.—*Sonnets,* cxlvi.
Ruder powers.—*Troilus and Cressida,* iii, 2, 26.
Servile powers.—*The Rape of Lucrece,* l. 295.
Splitting power.—*Henry VIII,* ii, 4, 183.
Wicked powers.—*The Winter's Tale,* v, 3, 91.

2
First Citizen: Once, if he do require our voices, we ought not to deny him.
Second Citizen: We may, sir, if we will.
First Citizen: We have power in ourselves to do it, but it is a power that we have no power to do.
Coriolanus. Act ii, sc. 3, l. 1.
I would have had you put your power well on,
Before you had worn it out.
Coriolanus. Act iii, sc. 2, l. 17. [Volumnia]
Now we have shown our power,
Let us seem humbler after it is done
Than when it was a-doing.
Coriolanus. Act iv, sc. 2, l. 3. [Brutus]
And power, unto itself most commendable,
Hath not a tomb so evident as a chair
To extol what it hath done.
Coriolanus. Act iv, sc. 7, l. 51. [Aufidius]

3
The power I have on you is to spare you.
Cymbeline. Act v, sc. 5, l. 418. [Posthumus]

4
The power of beauty will sooner transform honesty.
Hamlet, iii, 1, 111. See under BEAUTY.
Power of fancy.—*As You Like It,* iii, 5, 29.
Power of the king.—*The Winter's Tale,* iv, 4, 37.
Power of law and justice.—*II Henry IV,* v, 2, 78.
Power of life.—*Cymbeline,* v, 5, 256.
Power of music.—*Merchant of Venice,* v, 1, 79.
Power of speech.—*Julius Cæsar,* iii, 2, 226.
Power of his wits.—*King Lear,* iii, 6, 4.
Your power legatine.—*Henry VIII,* iii, 2, 339. The only use of "legatine."
Power tyrannical.—*Coriolanus,* iii, 3, 65.
Tyrannical power.—*Coriolanus,* iii, 3, 2. The phrase is used nowhere else.
Nature's power.—*Sonnets,* cxxvii.

5
His power, like to a fangless lion,
May offer, but not hold.
II Henry IV. Act iv, sc. 1, l. 218. [Hastings] The only use of "fangless."
Free power to ratify, Augment, or alter.
Henry V. Act v, sc. 2, l. 86. [King Henry]
Powers are your retainers.—*Henry VIII,* ii, 4, 113.
Charmed power.—*A Lover's Complaint,* l. 146.
Domestic powers.—*Antony and Cleopatra,* i, 3, 47.
Earthly power.—*Merchant of Venice,* iv, 1, 196.
Guiding power.—*All's Well that Ends Well,* ii, 3, 111.
Human powers.—*Coriolanus,* ii, 1, 236.
Lawful power.—*King John,* iii, 1, 172.
Main power.—*Henry VIII,* ii, 2, 7.
Mental power.—*Timon of Athens,* i, 1, 31.
Personal power.—*Hamlet,* i, 2, 36.
Public power.—*Coriolanus,* iii, 1, 269.
Temporal power.—*The Merchant of Venice,* iv, 1, 190.
Utmost power.—*Richard III,* v, 3, 10.
Uttermost power.—*Henry V,* iii, 6, 10.
Vital powers.—*II Henry VI,* iii, 2, 41.

6
O, stay! I have no power to let her pass.
I Henry VI. Act v, sc. 3, l. 60. [Suffolk]
I have no power upon you.—*Antony and Cleopatra,* i, 3, 23.
He hath no power to ask her how she fares.
The Rape of Lucrece, l. 1594.

7
So under Him that great supremacy,
Where we do reign, we will alone uphold,
Without the assistance of a mortal hand.
King John. Act iii, sc. 1, l. 156. [King John]
Use all your power.—*King John,* v, 1, 6.

8
Though well we may not pass upon his life
Without the form of justice, yet our power
Shall do a courtesy to our wrath, which men
May blame, but not control.
King Lear. Act iii, sc. 7, l. 24. [Cornwall]

9
I could
With barefaced power sweep him from my sight.
Macbeth. Act iii, sc. 1, l. 118. [Macbeth]

10
Assay the power you have.
Measure for Measure. Act i, sc. 4, l. 76. [Lucio]
Make rash remonstrance of my hidden power.
Measure for Measure. Act v, sc. 1, l. 397. [Duke] The only use of "remonstrance."

11
I would to heaven I had your potency.
Measure for Measure, ii, 2, 67. [Isabella]
Changeful potency.—*Troilus and Cressida,* iv, 4, 99.
Wondrous potency.—*Hamlet,* iii, 4, 170.
Our potency made good.—*King Lear,* i, 1, 175.
A place of potency.—*Coriolanus,* ii, 3, 190. "Potency" is used a sixth time in *Henry VIII,* i, 1, 105.

12
Leave you your power to draw,
And I shall have no power to follow you.
A Midsummer-Night's Dream. Act ii, sc. 1, l. 197. [Helena]
Power to be kind.—*Timon of Athens,* iii, 2, 61.
Power to bid you welcome.—*The Merchant of Venice,* iii, 2, 225.
Power to choose.—*All's Well that Ends Well,* ii, 3, 62.
Power to crush.—*Coriolanus,* ii, 3, 211.
Power to die.—*Romeo and Juliet,* iii, 5, 242.
Power to speak.—*Henry VIII,* iii, 2, 373.
Power to steal.—*Merchant of Venice,* iii, 2, 125.
Power to tell.—*Richard II,* iii, 2, 120.
Power to thunder.—*Coriolanus,* iii, 1, 257.

13
By that fatherly and kindly power
That you have in her, bid her answer truly.
Much Ado about Nothing, iv, 1, 75. [Claudio]

14
Pericles: Thou know'st I have power
To take thy life from thee.

Helicanus: I have ground the axe myself;
Do you but strike the blow.
Pericles. Act i, sc. 2, l. 56.

1
They are both in each other's powers.
The Tempest. Act i, sc. 2, l. 450. [Prospero]
They are in my power.—*The Tempest,* iii, 3, 90.

2
Everything includes itself in power.
Troilus and Cressida, i, 3, 119. See under APPETITE.
You might do much.—*Twelfth Night,* i, 5, 295.
Use power with power.—*Sonnets,* cxxxix.

3
Hearing him, thy power had lost his power.
Venus and Adonis, l. 944.

4 'Tis powerful, think it,
From east, west, north and south.
Winter's Tale. Act i, sc. 2, l. 202. [Leontes]

5 It is in my power
To o'erthrow law and in one self-born hour
To plant and o'erwhelm custom.
The Winter's Tale. Act iv, sc. 1, l. 7. [Time] "Self-born" is repeated in *Richard II,* ii, 3, 80: "Self-born arms."

II—Divine Power

6
Some blessed power deliver us from hence!
The Comedy of Errors. Act iv, sc. 3, l. 44. [Antipholus of Syracuse]
Blessed power.—*A Midsummer-Night's Dream,* iv, 1, 77.

7
O heavenly powers, restore him!
Hamlet. Act iii, sc. 1, l. 147. [Ophelia]
O heaven! O heavenly powers!—*Othello,* v, 2, 218.
Some heavenly power guide us!—*The Tempest,* v, 1, 105.
The higher powers forbid!—*The Winter's Tale,* iii, 2, 203.

8
A greater power than we denies all this.
King John. Act ii, sc. 1, l. 368. [Citizen]
High powers.—*Julius Cæsar,* v, 1, 107.
Merciful powers.—*Macbeth,* ii, 1, 8.
Sweet powers.—*Othello,* ii, 1, 197.
Unknown power.—*Macbeth,* iv, 1, 69.
Wise powers.—*Antony and Cleopatra,* ii, 1, 6.
Power divine.—*Measure for Measure,* v, 1, 374.
Th' eternal power.—*The Rape of Lucrece,* l. 345.

9
The powers above Put on their instruments.
Macbeth. Act iv, sc. 3, l. 238. [Malcolm]
We cannot but obey the powers above us.
Pericles. Act iii, sc. 3, l. 9. [Pericles]

10 That Power that made you king
Hath power to keep you king in spite of all.
Richard II. Act iii, sc. 2, l. 27. [Carlisle]
The power that made me.—*King Lear,* i, 1, 210.

11 O you powers
That give heaven countless eyes to view men's acts.
Pericles. Act i, sc. 1, l. 72. [Pericles]
The powers to whom I pray abhor this fact.
The Rape of Lucrece, l. 349.

12
A greater power than we can contradict
Hath thwarted our intents.
Romeo and Juliet. Act v, sc. 3, l. 153. [Friar] Laurence]

13
If any power pities wretched tears,
To that I call!
Titus Andronicus. Act iii, sc. 1, l. 209. [Titus]

III—Armed Power

14
Forthwith a power of English shall we levy.
I Henry IV. Act i, sc. 1, l. 22. [King Henry]
Great power of English.—*II Henry IV,* iv, 4, 98.
Power of France.—*Henry V,* i, 2, 107; *King John,* iii, 1, 193; iv, 2, 129.
Power of Greece.—*The Rape of Lucrece,* l. 1368.
British power.—*King Lear,* iv, 4, 21.
English power.—*Macbeth,* v, 2, 1.
Roman power.—*Coriolanus,* i, 3, 109.
Scottish power.—*I Henry IV,* iii, 1, 85.

15
The king with mighty and quick-raised power
Meets with Lord Harry: . . .
I fear the power of Percy is too weak
To wage an instant trial with the king.
I Henry IV. Act iv, sc. 4, l. 12. [Archbishop] The only use of "quick-raised."

16 The king . . . hath sent out
A speedy power to encounter you.
II Henry IV. Act i, sc. 1, l. 132. [Morton]
Flattering himself in project of a power
Much smaller than the smallest of his thoughts:
And so, with great imagination
Proper to madness, led his powers to death,
And winking leap'd into destruction.
II Henry IV. Act i, sc. 3, l. 29. [Bardolph]

17
We 'll follow them with all the power we have.
I Henry VI. Act ii, sc. 2, l. 33. [Burgundy]
Keep not back your powers in dalliance.
I Henry VI. Act v, sc. 2, l. 5. [Alençon]

18
Their power, I think, is thirty thousand strong.
III Henry VI. Act ii, sc. 1, l. 177. [Warwick]
Never such a power
For any foreign preparation
Was levied in the body of a land.
King John. Act iv, sc. 2, l. 110. [Messenger]
Where be your powers?—*King John,* v, 7, 75.
Weary powers.—*King John,* v, 5, 18.

19
I saw the tyrant's power a-foot.
Macbeth. Act iv, sc. 3, l. 185. [Ross] "Tyrant's power" is repeated in v, 6, 7.
Our power is ready.—*Macbeth,* iv, 3, 236.

20 For us to levy power
Proportionable to the enemy
Is all unpossible.
Richard II. Act ii, sc. 2, l. 125. [Bushy] The only use of "proportionable."
My power is weak and all ill left.
Richard II. Act ii, sc. 3, l. 154. [York]

PRACTICE

1
No practice had In the brave squares of war.
Antony and Cleopatra. Act iii, sc. 11, l. 39. [Antony]

2
I overheard him and his practices.
As You Like It. Act ii, sc. 2, l. 26. [Adam]
God acquit them of their practices!
Henry V, ii, 2, 144. See under LAW.
How came His practices to light?
Henry VIII. Act iii, sc. 2, l. 28. [Surrey]
Driven To find out practices of cunning hell.
Othello. Act i, sc. 3, l. 101. [Brabantio]
Devilish practices.—*II Henry VI*, iii, 1, 46.
Malicious practices.—*I Henry VI*, iv, 1, 7.

3
I have been in continual practice.
Hamlet. Act v, sc. 2, l. 221. [Hamlet]

4
Wouldst thou have practised on me for thy use!
Henry V, ii, 2, 99. See under TRAITOR.
Practised dangerously against your state.
II Henry VI. Act ii, sc. 1, l. 171. [Buckingham]
Practise on my state.—*Antony and Cleopatra*, ii, 2, 39.
Practised on man's life.—*King Lear*, iii, 2, 57.
Practised well.—*The Merry Wives of Windsor*, iv, 4, 65.
I never practised it.—*Pericles*, ii, 1, 71.

5
He did bewray his practice.
King Lear. Act ii, sc. 1, l. 109. [Gloucester]
This is practice, Gloucester.—*King Lear*, v, 3, 151.
Active practice.—*Much Ado about Nothing*, v, 1, 75.
Cunning practice.—*Titus Andronicus*, v, 2, 77.
Damned practice.—*King Lear*, ii, 1, 75.
Foul practice.—*Hamlet*, v, 2, 328.
Present practice.—*Pericles*, iv, 2, 136.
Unhatch'd practice.—*Othello*, iii, 4, 141.

6
Thou art suborn'd against his honour
In hateful practice.
Measure for Measure. Act v, sc. 1, l. 106. [Duke]
This needs must be a practice.—*Measure for Measure*, v, 1, 123.

7
In practice let us put it presently.
Much Ado about Nothing. Act i, sc. 1, l. 330. [Don Pedro]
I will put it in practice.—*Much Ado about Nothing*, ii, 2, 53.
Put in practice.—*Love's Labour's Lost*, i, 1, 308; *The Passionate Pilgrim*, l. 217.

8
I will practise on this drunken man.
Taming of the Shrew. Ind., sc 1, l. 36. [Lord]
Practise an answer.—*I Henry IV*, ii, 4, 412.
Practise how to bride it.—*The Taming of the Shrew*, iii, 2, 253.
Practise rhetoric.—*The Taming of the Shrew*, i, 1, 35.
Practise stratagems.—*Romeo and Juliet*, iii, 5, 211.
Practise the insinuating nod.—*Coriolanus*, ii, 3, 106.
I'll practise to obey.—*The Comedy of Errors*, ii, 1, 29.
Let them practise.—*I Henry VI*, ii, 1, 25.

9
He, . . . to my kingly guest
Unclasp'd my practice.
Winter's Tale. Act iii, sc. 2, l. 167. [Leontes]
Unclasp'd
To thee the book even of my secret soul.
Twelfth Night, i, 4, 13. The only uses of "unclasp'd."

PRAISE

See also Applause, Commendation

10
The rather will I spare my praises towards him;
Knowing him is enough.
All's Well that Ends Well. Act ii, sc. 1, l. 106. [Helena]

11
I never loved you much; but I ha' praised ye.
Antony and Cleopatra. Act ii, sc. 6, l. 78. [Enobarbus]
I will praise any man that will praise me.
Antony and Cleopatra. Act ii, sc. 6, l. 91. [Enobarbus]
He plied them both with excellent praises.
Antony and Cleopatra. Act iii, sc. 2, l. 14. [Agrippa]

12
Your praise is come too swiftly home before you.
As You Like It. Act ii, sc. 3, l. 9. [Adam]
Wearying thy hearer in thy mistress' praise.
As You Like It. Act ii, sc. 4, l. 38. [Silvius] The only use of "wearying."

13
First he did praise my beauty, then my speech.
The Comedy of Errors. Act iv, sc. 2, l. 15. [Luciana]
Praise of my beauty.—*Much Ado about Nothing*, v, 2, 5.
Praise my eyes.—*Midsummer-Night's Dream*, iii, 2, 223.
Praise my noble act.—*Antony and Cleopatra*, v, 2, 228.
Praise new-born gauds.—*Troilus and Cressida*, iii, 3, 176.
Praise thy wisdom.—*Troilus and Cressida*, ii, 3, 259.
Praise her liquor.—*The Two Gentlemen of Verona*, iii, 1, 350.
Praised cold chastity.—*Lover's Complaint*, l. 315.

14
To the spire and top of praises.
Coriolanus. Act i, sc. 9, l. 24. [Cominius] The only use of "spire."
You shout me forth
In acclamations hyperbolical;
As if I loved my little should be dieted
In praises sauced with lies.
Coriolanus. Act i, sc. 9, l. 50. [Marcius] The only use of "acclamations." "Hyperbolical" is repeated in *Twelfth Night*, iv, 2, 29: "Fiend hyperbolical."

My praises made thee first a soldier, so
To have my praise for this, perform a part
Thou hast not done before.
Coriolanus. Act iii, sc. 2, l. 108. [Volumnia]
With all praise.—*Coriolanus,* ii, 2, 94.

1
First Gentleman: I do not think
So fair an outward and such stuff within
Endows a man but he.
Second Gentleman: You speak him far.
First Gentleman: I do extend him, sir, within himself,
Crush him together rather than unfold
His measure duly.
Cymbeline. Act i, sc. 1, l. 22.
Most praised, most loved.—*Cymbeline,* i, 1, 47.
Well praised!—*Othello,* ii, 1, 132.

2 Worse than the sun in March,
This praise doth nourish agues.
I Henry IV. Act iv, sc. 1, l. 111. [Hotspur]
Adieu, and take thy praise with thee to heaven!
I Henry IV. Act v, sc. 4, l. 99. [Prince]

3
Trimm'd up your praises with a princely tongue,
Spoke your deservings like a chronicle,
Making you ever better than his praise
By still dispraising praise valued with you.
I Henry IV. Act v, sc. 2, l. 57. [Vernon]
Dispraise those parts in me that you love with your heart!
Henry V. Act v, sc. 2, l. 213. [King Henry]
Not dispraising whom we praised.
Cymbeline. Act v, sc. 5, l. 173. [Iachimo] The only uses of "dispraising."

4 Make her chronicle as rich with praise
As is the ooze and bottom of the sea
With sunken wreck and sumless treasuries.
Henry V. Act i, sc. 2, l. 163. [Archbishop of Canterbury] The only use of "sumless."
Praise and glory on his head!
Henry V. Act iv, Prologue, l. 31. [Chorus]

5
All the priests and friars in my realm
Shall in procession sing her endless praise.
I Henry VI. Act i, sc. 6, l. 19. [Charles]

6
This is the latest glory of thy praise
That I, thy enemy, due thee withal.
I Henry VI. Act iv, sc. 2, l. 33. [General]
Solicit Henry with her wondrous praise.
I Henry VI. Act v, sc. 3, l. 190. [Suffolk]
Added praise.—*Sonnets,* ciii.
Common praise.—*The Winter's Tale,* iii, 1, 3.
Deserved praise.—*Henry V,* iii, 7, 35.
Earned praise.—*Pericles,* iv, Gower, 13.
Fair praise.—*Love's Labour's Lost,* iv, 1, 23; *Much Ado about Nothing,* i, 1, 174.

7
The argument of your praise, balm of your age.
King Lear. Act i, sc. 1, l. 218. [French King]

8
Moth: Speak you this in my praise, master?
Armado: In thy condign praise.
Love's Labour's Lost. Act i, sc. 2, l. 26. "Condign" occurs again in *II Henry VI,* iii, 1, 130.

God bless my ladies! are they all in love,
That every one her own hath garnished
With such bedecking ornaments of praise?
Love's Labour's Lost. Act ii, sc. 1, l. 77. [Princess of France] The only use of "bedecking."
Nay, never paint me now:
Where fair is not, praise cannot mend the brow.
Love's Labour's Lost. Act iv, sc. 1, l. 16. [Princess of France]
When shall you hear that I
Will praise a hand, a foot, a face, an eye,
A gait, a state, a brow, a breast, a waist,
A leg, a limb?
Love's Labour's Lost. Act iv, sc. 3, l. 183. [Biron]
She passes praise; then praise too short doth blot.
Love's Labour's Lost. Act iv, sc. 3, l. 241 [Biron]
With that, all laugh'd and clapp'd him on the shoulder,
Making the bold wag by their praises bolder.
Love's Labour's Lost. Act v, sc. 2, l. 107 [Boyet]

9
I praise God for you, sir.
Love's Labour's Lost. Act v, sc. 1, l. 2. [Nathaniel]
Praise God.—*II Henry IV,* v, 3, 19; *Henry V.* iii, 6, 25.
I praise God for you.—*Much Ado about Nothing,* v, 1, 325; *All's Well that Ends Well,* v. 2, 59.
God be praised!—*II Henry VI,* ii, 1, 66, and frequently in later plays.
Praised be God!—*Henry V,* iv, 7, 90; 119; iv. 8, 21.
Praise the gods!—*Coriolanus,* v, 5, 2.
Praised be the gods!—*As You Like It,* iii, 2, 40.
I praise heaven for it.—*The Merry Wives of Windsor,* i, 4, 150.
I give heaven praise.—*The Merry Wives of Windsor,* iii, 4, 62.
Sings heaven's praises.—*Love's Labour's Lost.* iv, 2, 122.
Jove and my stars be praised!—*Twelfth Night* ii, 5, 188.
Great Jupiter be praised!—*Cymbeline,* v, 3, 84.
I praise the Lord.—*Love's Labour's Lost,* iv 2, 75.
The lord be praised!—*Troilus and Cressida,* iii, 1, 7.
Praise my Maker.—*Henry VIII,* v, 5, 69.
Creator's praise.—*III Henry VI,* iv, 6, 44.
Heaven's praise.—*The Passionate Pilgrim,* l. 70.
Virtue's praise.—*Titus Andronicus,* i, 1, 168.

10
His wonders and his praises do contend
Which should be thine or his.
Macbeth. Act i, sc. 3, l. 92. [Ross]
As thick as hail
Came post with post; and every one did bear
Thy praises in his kingdom's great defence,
And pour'd them down before him.
Macbeth. Act i, sc. 3, l. 97. [Ross]

11
I remember him worthy of thy praise.
The Merchant of Venice. Act i, sc. 2, l. 132. [Portia]
Worthy praise.—*I Henry VI,* v, 5, 11; *II Henry VI,* iii, 1, 68.

Worth praise.—*Troilus and Cressida,* v, 3, 93.

1

Thou spend'st such high-day wit in praising him.

The Merchant of Venice. Act ii, sc. 9, l. 98. [Portia] The only use of "high-day."

Giddy in spirit, still gazing in a doubt
Whether those peals of praise be his or no.

The Merchant of Venice. Act iii, sc. 2, l. 145. [Bassanio]

Nay, let me praise you while I have a stomach.

The Merchant of Venice. Act iii, sc. 5, l. 92. [Jessica]

2

I shall be rather praised for this than mocked.

The Merry Wives of Windsor. Act iii, sc. 2, l. 48. [Ford]

3

Why, i' faith, methinks she 's too low for a high praise, too brown for a fair praise and too little for a great praise.

Much Ado about Nothing. Act i, sc. 1, l. 173. [Benedick]

When I do name him, let it be thy part
To praise him more than ever man did merit.

Much Ado about Nothing. Act iii, sc. 1, l. 18. [Hero]

Thus far can I praise him.—*Much Ado about Nothing,* ii, 1, 394.

4

What praise couldst thou bestow on a deserving woman indeed, one that, in the authority of her merit, did justly put on the vouch of very malice itself?

Othello. Act ii, sc. 1, l. 145. [Desdemona]

5

All praises, which are paid as debts,
And not as given.

Pericles, iv, Gower, 34.

6

The niggard prodigal that praised her so.

The Rape of Lucrece, l. 79.

Therefore that praise which Collatine doth owe
Enchanted Tarquin answers with surmise.

The Rape of Lucrece, l. 82.

Decks with praises Collatine's high name.

The Rape of Lucrece, l. 108.

7

Praises, of whose taste the wise are fond,
Lascivious metres, to whose venom sound
The open ear of youth doth always listen.

Richard II. Act ii, sc. 1, l. 18. [York] The only use of "metres." "Metre" occurs in *I Henry IV,* iii, 1, 130, and in *Measure for Measure,* i, 2, 22.

8

Is it more sin to wish me thus forsworn,
Or to dispraise my lord with that same tongue
Which she hath praised him with above compare
So many thousand times?

Romeo and Juliet. Act iii, sc. 5, l. 236. [Juliet]

9

Let them say more that like of hearsay well;
I will not praise that purpose not to sell.

Sonnets. No. xxi. "Hearsay" is repeated in *Much Ado about Nothing,* iii, 1, 23.

The pain be mine, but thine shall be the praise.

Sonnets. No. xxxviii.

Your praise shall still find room
Even in the eyes of all posterity.

Sonnets. No. lv.

O, sure I am, the wits of former days
To subjects worse have given admiring praise.

Sonnets. No. lix.

Those parts of thee that the world's eye doth view
Want nothing that the thought of hearts can mend;
All tongues, the voice of souls, give thee that due,
Uttering bare truth, even so as foes commend.
The outward thus with outward praise is crown'd;
But those same tongues that give thee so thine own
In other accents do this praise confound
By seeing further than the eye hath shown.

Sonnets. No. lxix.

And hang more praise upon deceased I
Than niggard truth would willingly impart.

Sonnets. No. lxxii.

He can afford
No praise to thee but what in thee doth live.

Sonnets. No. lxxix.

Who is it that says most? which can say more
Than this rich praise, that you alone are you?

Sonnets. No. lxxxiv.

You to your beauteous blessings add a curse,
Being fond on praise, which makes your praises worse.

Sonnets. No. lxxxiv.

Hearing you praised, I say ''Tis so, 'tis true,'
And to the most of praise add something more.

Sonnets. No. lxxxv.

All their praises are but prophecies.

Sonnets. No. cvi.

Praised of ages yet to be.—*Sonnets,* ci.

10

Praise in departing.

The Tempest. Act iii, sc. 3, l. 39. [Prospero]

Thou shalt find she will outstrip all praise
And make it halt behind her.

The Tempest. Act iv, sc. 1, l. 10. [Prospero]

11

Timon: Sir, your jewel
Hath suffer'd under praise.
Jeweler: What, my lord! dispraise?
Timon: A mere satiety of commendations.

Timon of Athens. Act i, sc. 1, l. 164. See also COMMENDATION.

I know, no man
Can justly praise but what he does affect.

Timon of Athens. Act i, sc. 2, l. 220. [Timon]

Ah, when the means are gone that buy this praise,
The breath is gone whereof this praise is made:
Feast-won, fast-lost; one cloud of winter showers,
These flies are couch'd.

Timon of Athens. Act ii, sc. 2, l. 178. [Flavius] The only use of the phrases "feast-won" and "fast-lost."

Praise his most vicious strain
And call it excellent.

Timon of Athens. Act iv, sc. 3, l. 213. [Apemantus]

Citing my worthless praise.—*Titus Andronicus,* v, 3, 117. The only use of "citing."
Poor praise.—*All's Well that Ends Well,* i, 2, 45.
Thriftless praise.—*Sonnets,* ii.
Undeserving praise.—*Love's Labour's Lost,* v, 2, 366.

1
The worthiness of praise distains his worth,
If that the praised himself bring the praise forth:
But what the repining enemy commends,
That breath fame blows; that praise, sole pure, transcends.
Troilus and Cressida. Act i, sc. 3, l. 241. [Æneas] The only use of "repining" and "transcends."

Seeks his praise more than he fears his peril.
Troilus and Cressida. Act i, sc. 3, l. 267. [Æneas]

He's not yet through warm: force him with praises: pour in, pour in; his ambition is dry.
Troilus and Cressida. Act ii, sc. 3, l. 232. [Nestor]

Praise us as we are tasted, allow us as we prove.
Troilus and Cressida. Act iii, sc. 2, l. 98. [Troilus]

She is as far high-soaring o'er thy praises
As thou unworthy to be call'd her servant.
Troilus and Cressida. Act iv, sc. 4, l. 126. [Troilus] The only use of "high-soaring."

I forgive you the praise.—*Twelfth Night,* i, 5, 205.

2
Flatter and praise, commend, extol their graces.
The Two Gentlemen of Verona, iii, 1, 102. See under FLATTERY.

Extol her blood.—*Coriolanus,* i, 9, 14.
Extol me thus.—*Measure for Measure,* v, 1, 508.
Extol what it hath done.—*Coriolanus,* iv, 7, 53. The only uses of "extol."
As 'tis extoll'd.—*Timon of Athens,* i, 1, 167. The only use of "extoll'd."
In the verity of extolment.—*Hamlet,* v, 2, 121. The only use of "extolment."

3
Good things should be praised.
The Two Gentlemen of Verona. Act iii, sc. 1, l. 353. [Launce]

To praise his faith which I would have dispraised.
The Two Gentlemen of Verona. Act iv, sc. 4, l. 107. [Julia]

4
Cram 's with praise, and make 's
As fat as tame things.
The Winter's Tale. Act i, sc. 2, l. 91. [Hermione]

Our praises are our wages: you may ride 's
With one soft kiss a thousand furlongs ere
With spur we heat an acre.
The Winter's Tale. Act i, sc. 2, l. 94. [Hermione]

Praise her but for this her without-door form.
The Winter's Tale. Act ii, sc. 1, l. 69. [Leontes] The only use of "without-door."

Your praises are too large.
The Winter's Tale. Act iv, sc. 4, l. 147. [Perdita]

They cannot praise us.—*The Winter's Tale,* i, 1, 17.

II—Self-Praise

5
You praise yourself
By laying defects of judgement to me.
Antony and Cleopatra. Act ii, sc. 2, l. 54. [Cæsar]

6
This comes too near the praising of myself.
The Merchant of Venice. Act iii, sc. 4, l. 22. [Portia]

Praise myself for charity.—*Cymbeline,* iv, 2, 169.

7
There's not one wise man among twenty that will praise himself.
Much Ado about Nothing. Act v, sc. 2, l. 76. [Beatrice]

Therefore is it most expedient for the wise, if Don Worm, his conscience, find no impediment to the contrary, to be the trumpet of his own virtues, as I am to myself. So much for praising myself, who, I myself will bear witness, is praiseworthy.
Much Ado about Nothing. Act v, sc. 2, l. 85. [Benedick] The only use of "praiseworthy."

8
Little shall I grace my cause
In speaking for myself.
Othello. Act i, sc. 3, l. 88. [Othello]

9
What can mine own praise to mine own self bring?
Sonnets. No. xxxix.

'Tis thee, myself, that for myself I praise,
Painting my age with beauty of thy days.
Sonnets. No. lxii.

10
When no friends are by, men praise themselves.
Titus Andronicus. Act v, sc. 3, l. 118. [Lucius]

11
Whatever praises itself but in the deed, devours the deed in the praise.
Troilus and Cressida. Act ii, sc. 3, l. 166. [Agamemnon]

PRANK

See also Mischief

12
Tell him his pranks have been too broad to bear with,
And that your grace hath screen'd and stood between
Much heat and him.
Hamlet. Act iii, sc. 4, l. 2. [Polonius] The only use of "screen'd."

13
Lewd, pestiferous and dissentious pranks.
I Henry VI, iii, 1, 15. See under WICKEDNESS. "Pestiferous" is repeated in *All's Well that Ends Well,* iv, 3, 340: "Pestiferous reports."

Foul pranks.—*Othello,* ii, 1, 143.
Idle pranks.—*The Comedy of Errors,* ii, 2, 210.
New pranks.—*King Lear,* i, 4, 259.

1
In Venice they do let heaven see the pranks
They dare not show their husbands.
Othello. Act iii, sc. 3, l. 202. [Iago]
2 Go with me to my house,
And hear thou there how many fruitless pranks
This ruffian hath botch'd up.
Twelfth Night. Act iv, sc. 1, l. 58. [Olivia] "Botch'd" is repeated in *Timon of Athens,* iv. 3, 285.
3
I will tell the king all, every word, yea, and his son's pranks too.
The Winter's Tale. Act iv, sc. 4, l. 716. [Shepherd]

PRATTLE

See also Gossip

4
Why pratest thou to thyself?
The Comedy of Errors. Act ii, sc. 2, l. 195. [Luciana]
Thou pratest, and pratest.—*Coriolanus,* iv, 5, 53.
Why stay we prating here?
Coriolanus. Act i, sc. 1, l. 49. [Citizen]
Will she love him still for prating? let not thy discreet heart think it.
Othello. Act ii, sc. 1, l. 226. [Iago]
We must give folks leave to prate.
The Merry Wives of Windsor. Act i, sc. 4, l. 128. [Mistress Quickly]
Dost thou prate, rogue?
Othello. Act ii, sc. 3, l. 153. [Cassio]
Audacious prate!—*I Henry VI,* iv, 1, 124.
Leave your prating.—*Winter's Tale,* iv, 4, 349.
Prating boy.—*Merchant of Venice,* v, 1, 164.
Prating coxcomb.—*Henry V,* iv, 1, 79.
Prating knave.—*Hamlet,* iii, 4, 215.
Prating mountebanks.—*Comedy of Errors,* i, 2, 101. "Mountebank" occurs again in *Comedy of Errors,* v, 1, 238; in *Coriolanus,* iii, 2, 132; *Hamlet,* iv, 7, 142; and *Othello,* i, 3, 61.
5
Poor prattler, how thou talk'st!
Macbeth. Act iv, sc. 2, l. 64. [Lady Macduff] The only use of "prattler."
6
Prithee, no more prattling.
Merry Wives of Windsor. Act v, sc. 1, l. 1. [Falstaff] "Prattling" occurs once again in *Coriolanus,* ii, 1, 222: "Prattling nurse."
7
Mere prattle, without practice.
Othello. Act i, sc. 1, l. 26. [Iago]
I prattle out of fashion.
Othello. Act ii, sc. 1, l. 208. [Othello]
I prattle Something too wildly.
The Tempest. Act iii, sc. 1, l. 57. [Miranda]
8
What great ones do the less will prattle of.
Twelfth Night. Act i, sc. 2, l. 33. [Captain]

PRAYER

See also Knee, Petition

9
When thou hast leisure, say thy prayers.
All's Well that Ends Well. Act i, sc. 1, l. 227. [Parolles]
You had my prayers to lead them on; and to keep them on, have them still.
All's Well that Ends Well. Act ii, sc. 4, l. 17. [Parolles]
He cannot thrive,
Unless her prayers, whom heaven delights to hear
And loves to grant, reprieve him from the wrath
Of greatest justice.
All's Well that Ends Well. Act iii, sc. 4, l. 26. [Count]
10
Charmian: Hear me this prayer, though thou deny me a matter of more weight. . . .
Iras: Amen. Hear that prayer of the people!
Antony and Cleopatra. Act i, sc. 2, l. 70.
We, ignorant of ourselves,
Beg often our own harms, which the wise powers
Deny us for our good; so find we profit
By losing of our prayers.
Antony and Cleopatra. Act ii, sc. 1, l. 5. [Menecrates]
The good gods will mock me presently,
When I shall pray.
Antony and Cleopatra. Act iii, sc. 4, l. 15. [Octavia]
So bad a prayer as his Was never yet for sleep.
Antony and Cleopatra. Act iv, sc. 9, l. 27. [Soldier]
11
Whiles you chid me, I did love;
How then might your prayers move!
As You Like It. Act iv, sc. 3, l. 54. [Rosalind]
12
I will . . . visit her with my prayers.
Coriolanus. Act i, sc. 3, l. 88. [Virgilia]
Prayers to the gods, which is a comfort
That all but we enjoy.
Coriolanus. Act v, sc. 3, l. 105. [Volumnia]
You have pray'd well to-day.
Coriolanus. Act v, sc. 4, l. 58. [Menenius]
13
Then I am in heaven for him.
Cymbeline. Act i, sc. 3, l. 32. [Imogen]
14 Lovers
And men in dangerous bonds pray not alike:
Though forfeiters you cast in prison, yet
You clasp young Cupid's tables.
Cymbeline. Act iii, sc. 2, l. 36. [Imogen] The only use of "forfeiters."
15 For mine own poor part,
Look you, I 'll go pray.
Hamlet. Act i, sc. 5, l. 131. [Hamlet]
Pray can I not,
Though inclination be as sharp as will.
Hamlet. Act iii, sc. 3, l. 38. [King]
And what 's in prayer but this two-fold force,
To be forestalled ere we come to fall,
Or pardon'd being down?
Hamlet. Act iii, sc. 3, l. 48. [King]
But, O, what form of prayer
Can serve my turn?
Hamlet. Act iii, sc. 3, l. 51. [King]
16
My words fly up, my thoughts remain below:

Words without thoughts never to heaven go.
Hamlet. Act iii, sc. 3, l. 97. [King]
When I would pray and think, I think and pray
To several subjects. Heaven hath my empty words.
Measure for Measure. Act ii, sc. 4, l. 1. [Angelo]

1
Nay, that 's past praying for.
I Henry IV. Act ii, sc. 4, l. 211. [Falstaff]
Watch to-night, pray to-morrow.
I Henry IV. Act ii, sc. 4, l. 306. [Falstaff]
Say thy prayers, and farewell.
I Henry IV. Act v, sc. 1, l. 124. [Prince]

2 Hearty prayers
That your attempts may overlive the hazard
And fearful meeting of their opposite.
II Henry IV. Act iv, sc. 1, l. 14. [Archbishop of York] The only use of "overlive."

3
They have said their prayers, and they stay for death.
Henry V. Act iv, sc. 2, l. 56. [Constable]

4
Pray for me, I pray you, for I think I have taken my last draught in this world.
II Henry VI. Act ii, sc. 3, l. 73. [Peter] "I pray you (thee)" is repeated thirty-seven times in later plays.
I prithee.—*II Henry VI,* ii, 1, 33, and thirty-one times in later plays.
I prithee, pray for me.—*Measure for Measure,* iii, 2, 191.
Pray thou for us.—*A Midsummer-Night's Dream,* i, 1, 220.
Pray for thee.—*Richard III,* v, 3, 137; 166.
I pray the gods.—*The Taming of the Shrew,* iv, 4, 67.
I 'll send my prayers with him.—*Macbeth,* iii, 6, 49.
Take my prayers with you.—*Coriolanus,* iv, 2, 44.
Make your prayers.—*II Henry VI,* iv, 7, 121.
O, pray, pray, pray.—*All's Well that Ends Well,* iv, 1, 86.

5
O, let me pray before I take my death!
III Henry VI. Act i, sc. 3, l. 35. [Rutland]

6
Nay, stay; let 's hear the orisons he makes.
III Henry VI. Act i, sc. 4, l. 110. [Queen]
I have need of many orisons
To move the heavens to smile upon my state.
Romeo and Juliet. Act iv, sc. 3, l. 3. [Juliet]
Nymph, in thy orisons
Be all my sins remember'd.
Hamlet. Act iii, sc. 1, l. 89. [Hamlet]
At the sixth hour of morn, at noon, at midnight,
To encounter me with orisons.
Cymbeline. Act i, sc. 3, l. 31. [Imogen]
Heavy orisons.—*Henry V,* ii, 2, 53. The only uses of "orisons."

7
As the long divorce of steel falls on me,
Make of your prayers one sweet sacrifice,
And lift my soul to heaven.
Henry VIII. Act ii, 1, 76. [Buckingham]
My prayers
Are not words duly hallow'd, nor my wishes
More worth than empty vanities; yet prayers and wishes
Are all I can return.
Henry VIII. Act ii, sc. 3, l. 67. [Anne]
He has my heart yet; and shall have my prayers
While I shall have my life.
Henry VIII. Act iii, sc. 1, l. 180. [Queen Katharine]
The king shall have my service; but my prayers
For ever and for ever shall be yours.
Henry VIII. Act iii, sc. 2, l. 426. [Cromwell]

8
Prithee to bed; and in thy prayers remember
The estate of my poor queen.
Henry VIII. Act v, sc. 1, l. 73. [King Henry]
I will . . . remember in my prayers.—*Henry VIII,* v, 1, 76.

9
I could be well moved, if I were as you;
If I could pray to move, prayers would move me.
Julius Cæsar. Act iii, sc. 1, l. 58. [Cæsar]

10
Upon which better part our prayers come in,
If thou vouchsafe them.
King John. Act iii, sc. 1, l. 293. [Pandulph]
I had rather pray a month with mutton and porridge.
Love's Labour's Lost. Act i, sc. 1, l. 304. [Costard]

11 Are you so gospell'd
To pray for this good man and for his issue,
Whose heavy hand hath bow'd you to the grave
And beggar'd yours for ever?
Macbeth. Act iii, sc. 1, l. 88. [Macbeth] The only use of "gospell'd."

12 True prayers
That shall be up at heaven and enter there
Ere sun-rise, prayers from preserved souls,
From fasting maids whose minds are dedicate
To nothing temporal.
Measure for Measure. Act ii, sc. 2, l. 151. [Isabella]
I 'll pray a thousand prayers for thy death,
No word to save thee.
Measure for Measure. Act iii, sc. 1, l. 146. [Isabella]
Clap into your prayers.
Measure for Measure. Act iv, sc. 3, l. 43. [Abhorson]
I am come to advise you, comfort you and pray with you.
Measure for Measure. Act iv, sc. 3, l. 54. [Duke]

13
I 'll follow him no more with bootless prayers.
The Merchant of Venice. Act iii, sc. 3, l. 20. [Antonio]
Trouble deaf heaven with my bootless cries.
Sonnets. No. xxix.
Bootless prayer.—*Titus Andronicus,* iii, 1, 75.
Base prayers.—*Titus Andronicus,* v, 3, 185.
Borrowing prayers.—*All's Well that Ends Well,* iii, 1, 9.

Charitable prayers.—*Hamlet,* v, 1, 253.
Holy prayers.—*The Comedy of Errors,* iv, 4, 58; v, 1, 104; *The Two Gentlemen of Verona,* i, 1, 17; *Titus Andronicus,* iii, 2, 41; *Macbeth,* iv, 3, 154.
Morn prayer.—*Measure for Measure,* ii, 4, 71.
Unfruitful prayer.—*The Rape of Lucrece,* l. 344.
Vehement prayers.—*The Rape of Lucrece,* l. 475.
Weak prayers.—*Midsummer-Night's Dream,* iii, 2, 250.

1
Gratiano: Can no prayers pierce thee?
Shylock: No, none that thou hast wit enough to make.
The Merchant of Venice. Act iv, sc. 1, l. 126.

2
She doth stray about
By holy crosses, where she kneels and prays
For happy wedlock hours.
The Merchant of Venice. Act v, sc. 1, l. 30. [Stephano]

We have been praying for our husbands' healths.
The Merchant of Venice. Act v, sc. 1, l. 114. [Portia]

3
His worst fault is, that he is given to prayer; he is something peevish that way.
The Merry Wives of Windsor. Act i, sc. 4, l. 13. [Mistress Quickly]

4
O that my prayers could such affection move!
A Midsummer-Night's Dream. Act i, sc. 1, l. 197. [Helena]

The more my prayer, the lesser is my grace.
A Midsummer-Night's Dream. Act ii, sc. 2, l. 89. [Helena]

5
Found good means
To draw from her a prayer of earnest heart.
Othello. Act i, sc. 3, l. 151. [Othello]

6
The people's prayers still fall upon you.
Pericles. Act iii, sc. 3, l. 19. [Cleon]

Pray; but be not tedious,
For the gods are quick of ear.
Pericles. Act iv, sc. 1, l. 69. [Leonine]

Sigh a prayer.—*Phœnix and the Turtle,* l. 67.

7
That for his prey to pray he doth begin,
As if the heavens should countenance his sin.
The Rape of Lucrece, l. 342.

His ear her prayers admits, but his heart granteth
No penetrable entrance to her plaining.
The Rape of Lucrece, l. 558.

8
Add proof unto mine armour with thy prayers.
Richard II. Act i, sc. 3, l. 73. [Bolingbroke]

Unto my mother's prayers I bend my knee.
Richard II. Act v, sc. 3, l. 97. [Aumerle]

9
What shrill-voiced suppliant makes this eager cry?
Richard II. Act v, sc. 3, l. 75. [Bolingbroke] The only use of "shrill-voiced."

Thou hast made it like an humble suppliant.
Titus Andronicus. Act iv, sc. 3, l. 117. [Titus]

Humble suppliant.—*Richard III,* i, 1, 74, *The Rape of Lucrece,* l. 897.
Devoted suppliant.—*Richard III,* i, 2, 207.
Poor suppliant.—*All's Well that Ends Well,* v, 3, 134. The only uses of "suppliant." "Suppliants" occurs in *Coriolanus,* iii, 1, 44: "Suppliants for the people," and "supplicant" in *A Lover's Complaint,* l. 276.

10
His prayers are in jest.
Richard II. Act v, 3, 101. [Duchess of York]

He prays but faintly and would be denied;
We pray with heart and soul and all beside.
Richard II. Act v, 3, 103. [Duchess of York]

His prayers are full of false hypocrisy;
Ours of true zeal and deep integrity.
Our prayers do out-pray his; then let them have
That mercy which true prayer ought to have.
Richard II. Act v, sc. 3, l. 107. [Duchess of York] The only use of "out-pray."

11
To your good prayers will scarcely say amen.
Richard III. Act i, 3, 21. [Queen Elizabeth]

Amen, amen, to that fair prayer, say I!
A Midsummer-Night's Dream. Act ii, sc. 2, l. 62. [Lysander] "Fair prayer" is repeated in *Measure for Measure,* i, 4, 69.

Let me say 'amen' betimes, lest the devil cross my prayer.
Merchant of Venice, iii, 1, 22. [Salanio]

Margaret: I say my prayers aloud.
Balthazar: I love you the better: the hearers may cry, Amen.
Much Ado about Nothing. Act ii, sc. 1, l. 108.

I have said my prayers and devil Envy say Amen.
Troilus and Cressida. Act ii, sc. 3, l. 22. [Thersites]

I could not say 'Amen,'
When they did say 'God bless us!'
Macbeth. Act ii, sc. 2, l. 28. [Macbeth] "Amen" is used forty times.

12
A virtuous and a Christian-like conclusion,
To pray for them that have done scathe to us.
Richard III. Act i, sc. 3, l. 316. [Rivers]

God will revenge it; whom I will importune
With daily prayers all to that effect.
Richard III. Act ii, sc. 2, l. 14. [Boy]

O, remember, God,
To hear her prayers for them, as now for us!
Richard III. Act iii, sc. 3, l. 18. [Rivers]

Not sleeping, to engross his idle body,
But praying, to enrich his watchful soul.
Richard III. Act iii, sc. 7, l. 76. [Buckingham]

My prayers on the adverse party fight.
Richard III. Act iv, sc. 4, l. 190. [Duchess of York]

13
O Thou, whose captain I account myself,
Look on my forces with a gracious eye;
Put in their hands thy bruising irons of wrath,
That they may crush down with a heavy fall
The usurping helmets of our adversaries!

Make us thy ministers of chastisement,
That we may praise thee in the victory!
To thee I do commend my watchful soul,
Ere I let fall the windows of mine eyes:
Sleeping and waking, O, defend me still!
Richard III. Act v, sc. 3, l. 108. [Richmond]

The prayers of holy saints and wronged souls,
Like high-rear'd bulwarks, stand before our faces.
Richard III. Act v, sc. 3, l. 241. [Richmond] The only use of "high-rear'd."

1
Look you get a prayer-book in your hand.
Richard III. Act iii, sc. 7, l. 47. [Buckingham]

Wear prayer-books in my pockets.—*The Merchant of Venice,* ii, 2, 201. The only mention of prayer-books.

A book of prayers in his hand.—*Richard III,* iii, 7, 98.

A book of prayers on their pillow lay.—*Richard III,* iv, 3, 14.

2 Like prayers divine,
I must each day say o'er the very same.
Sonnets. No. cviii.

3
She prayed, that never prayed before.
The Taming of the Shrew. Act iv, sc. 1, l. 81. [Grumio]

4
And my ending is despair,
Unless I be relieved by prayer
Which pierces so that it assaults
Mercy itself and frees all faults.
The Tempest. Epilogue, l. 15. [Prospero]

5
Immortal gods, I crave no pelf;
I pray for no man but myself.
Timon of Athens. Act i, sc. 2, l. 63. [Apemantus]

6
Heaven shall hear our prayers.
Titus Andronicus. Act iii, sc. 1, l. 211. [Titus]

My prayers to heaven for you.—*Henry VIII,* iii, 2, 177.

Pray heaven!—*The Two Gentlemen of Verona,* ii, 7, 79; *As You Like It,* i, 2, 209; *Measure for Measure,* ii, 2, 125; iv, 4, 4.

7
Sirrah, can you with a grace deliver a supplication?
Titus Andronicus. Act iv, sc. 3, l. 106. [Titus]

Deliver our supplications.—*II Henry VI,* i, 3, 3.
In supplication nod.—*Coriolanus,* v, 3, 31.
Here is a supplication for you.—*Titus Andronicus,* iv, 3, 109.
Rebels' supplication.—*II Henry VI,* iv, 4, 2.
Supplications to his lordship.—*II Henry VI,* i, 3, 16. The only uses of "supplication" and "supplications."

8
Get him to say his prayers, good Sir Toby, get him to pray.
Twelfth Night. Act iii, sc. 4, l. 131. [Maria]

9
Upon some book I love I'll pray for thee.
The Two Gentlemen of Verona. Act i, sc. 1, l. 20. [Proteus]

Thy horse will sooner con an oration than thou learn a prayer without book.
Troilus and Cressida. Act ii, sc. 1, l. 18. [Thersites]

10 And have in vain said many
A prayer upon her grave.
Winter's Tale. Act v, sc. 3, l. 140. [Leontes]

PREACHER

See also Priest

11
We'ld find no fault with the tithe-woman, if I were the parson.
All's Well that Ends Well, i, 3, 89. The only use of "tithe-woman."

I hear the parson is no jester.
The Merry Wives of Windsor. Act ii, sc. 1, l. 218. [Shallow]

Sometime comes she with a tithe-pig's tail
Tickling a parson's nose as a' lies asleep,
Then dreams he of another benefice.
Romeo and Juliet. Act i, sc. 4, l. 79. [Mercutio] Only use of "tithe-pig" and "benefice."

Master Parson, quasi pers-on.
Love's Labour's Lost. Act iv, sc. 2, l. 85. [Holofernes] The only use of "quasi."

Master parson.—*The Merry Wives of Windsor,* i, 1, 9; iii, 1, 43; 50; 75; *Twelfth Night,* iv, 2, 13; 17; 31. "Parson" is used fifteen times.

12
O most gentle pulpiter! what tedious homily of love have you wearied your parishioners withal, and never cried 'Have patience, good people'!
As You Like It. Act iii, sc. 2, l. 163. [Rosalind] The only use of "pulpiter" and "homily." "Parishioners" occurs again in *Love's Labour's Lost,* iv, 2, 76.

A most vile Martext.
As You Like It. Act v, sc. 1, l. 6. [Touchstone] Sir Oliver Martext is the name of the vicar.

13
Do not, as some ungracious pastors do,
Show me the steep and thorny way to heaven;
Whiles, like a puff'd and reckless libertine,
Himself the primrose path of dalliance treads,
And recks not his own rede.
Hamlet. Act i, sc. 3, l. 47. [Ophelia] The only use of "pastors" and "rede" (counsel).

His form and cause conjoin'd, preaching to stones,
Would make them capable.
Hamlet. Act iii, sc. 4, l. 126. [Hamlet] The only use of "preaching."

14
Your flock, assembled by the bell,
Encircled you to hear with reverence
Your exposition on the holy text.
II Henry IV. Act iv, sc. 2, l. 5. [Lancaster] The only use of "encircled." "Encircle" occurs in *Merry Wives of Windsor,* iv, 4, 56.

Who hath not heard it spoken
How deep you were within the books of God?
To us the speaker in his parliament;
To us the imagined voice of God himself;

The very opener and intelligencer
Between the grace, the sanctities of heaven
And our dull workings.
II Henry IV. Act iv, sc. 2, l. 16. [Lancaster] The only use of "opener." "Intelligencer" is repeated in *Richard III,* iv, 4, 71: "Hell's black intelligencer."

1 A clergyman of holy reverence.
Richard II. Act iii, sc. 3, l. 28. [Percy]

Mayor: See, where he stands between two clergymen!
Buckingham: Two props of virtue for a Christian prince,
To stay him from the fall of vanity.
Richard III. Act iii, sc. 7, l. 95.

Holy clergymen.—*Richard II,* iv, 1, 324. "Clergymen" occurs again in *King John,* iv, 2, 141. "Clergy" is used four times.

2 Come, sermon me no further.
Timon of Athens. Act ii, sc. 2, l. 181. [Timon] The only use of "sermon" as a verb.

Making a sermon of continency to her.
The Taming of the Shrew, iv, 1, 185.

Sermons in stones.—*As You Like It,* ii, 1, 17. The only uses of "sermon" and "sermons."

PRECEDENT

See also Example

3 I 'll show thee a precedent.
I Henry IV. Act ii, sc. 4, l. 37. [Prince]

Make them your precedent.
III Henry VI. Act ii, sc. 2, l. 33. [Clifford]

Have you a precedent Of this commission?
Henry VIII. Act i, sc. 2, l. 91. [King Henry]

Your grace has given a precedent of wisdom
Above all princes.
Henry VIII. Act ii, sc. 2, l. 86. [Wolsey]

4 In this the antique and well noted face
Of plain old form is much disfigured.
King John, iv, 2, 21. [Salisbury] "Disfigured" is repeated in *Richard II,* iii, 1, 10.

5 I may example my digression by some mighty precedent.
Love's Labour's Lost, i, 2, 121. [Armado]

6 But, ah, who ever shunn'd by precedent
The destined ill she must herself assay?
A Lover's Complaint, l. 155.

7 'Twill be recorded for a precedent,
And many an error by the same example
Will rush into the state.
Merchant of Venice, iv, 1, 220. [Portia]

8 Thy case, dear friend,
Shall be my precedent.
Tempest. Act ii, sc. 1, l. 290. [Sebastian]

A pattern, precedent, and lively warrant,
For me, most wretched, to perform the like.
Titus Andronicus. Act v, sc. 3, l. 44. [Titus]

The pattern of all patience.—*King Lear,* iii, 2, 37.

A pattern to all princes.—*Henry VIII,* v, 5, 23.

A pattern of celestial peace.—*I Henry VI,* v, 5, 65.

Pattern of mine own thoughts.—*The Winter's Tale,* iv, 4, 393.

Pattern of our shame.—*King John,* iii, 4, 16.

Patterns of love.—*As You Like It,* iv, 1, 100.

Cunning'st pattern.—*Othello,* v, 2, 11.

PRECEPT

9 I will bestow some precepts of this virgin
Worthy the note.
All's Well that Ends Well. Act iii, sc. 5, l. 103. [Helena]

10 You were used to load me
With precepts that would make invincible
The heart that conn'd them.
Coriolanus. Act iv, sc. 1, l. 9. [Coriolanus]

11 These few precepts in thy memory
See thou character.
Hamlet. Act i, sc. 3, l. 58. [Polonius]

Those precepts cannot be served.
II Henry IV. Act v, sc. 1, l. 14. [Davy]

Send precepts to the leviathan.
Henry V. Act iii, sc. 3, l. 26. [King Henry]

What are precepts worth?—*A Lover's Complaint,* l. 267.

12 In action all of precept, he did show me
The way twice o'er.
Measure for Measure. Act iv, sc. 1, l. 40. [Isabella]

13 My father's precepts I therein do forget.
The Tempest. Act iii, sc. 1, l. 58. [Miranda]

Icy precepts of respect.—*Timon of Athens,* iv, 3, 258.

PREFERMENT

14 I 'll move the king
To any shape of thy preferment such
As thou 'lt desire.
Cymbeline. Act i, sc. 5, l. 69. [Queen]

Be but duteous, and true preferment shall tender itself to thee.
Cymbeline. Act iii, sc. 5, l. 159. [Cloten]

Labour for thine own preferment.
II Henry VI. Act i, sc. 1, l. 181. [Salisbury]

Seek preferment.—*The Two Gentlemen of Verona,* i, 3, 7.

Stands in the gap and trade of moe preferments.
Henry VIII. Act v, sc. 1, l. 36. [Lovell] "Moe" instead of more is used twenty-eight times in the plays.

15 If you do chance to hear of that blind traitor,
Preferment falls on him that cuts him off.
King Lear. Act iv, sc. 5, l. 37. [Regan]

16 She may help you to many fair preferments;
And then deny her aiding hand therein,
And lay those honours on your high deserts.
Richard III. Act i, sc. 3, l. 95. [Gloucester]

17 Preferment goes by letter and affection,
And not by old gradation.
Othello. Act i, sc. 1, l. 36. [Iago]

By cold gradation.—*Measure for Measure,* iv, 3, 104. The only uses of "gradation."

18 Now, had I not the dash of my former life in me, would preferment drop on my head.
The Winter's Tale. Act v, sc. 2, l. 123. [Autolycus]

PREGNANCY

See also Womb

1
He knows himself my bed he hath defiled;
And at that time he got his wife with child:
Dead though she be, she feels her young one kick.
All's Well that Ends Well. Act v, sc. 3, l. 301. [Diana]
The pleasing punishment that women bear.
The Comedy of Errors. Act i, sc. 1, l. 47. [Ægeon]
2
Conception is a blessing: but not as your daughter may conceive.
Hamlet, ii, 2, 185. See under DAUGHTER. "Conception" in this sense is used only once again in *Pericles,* i, 1, 8, a scene probably not by Shakespeare.
Widow: Thus I conceive by him.
Petruchio: Conceives by me! How likes Hortensio that?
Hortensio: My widow says, thus she conceives her tale.
The Taming of the Shrew. Act v, sc. 2, l. 22.
She . . . will conceive, I hope.—*Cymbeline,* ii, 3, 158.
3
Pregnancy is made a tapster, and hath his quick wit wasted in giving reckonings.
II Henry IV. Act i, sc. 2, l. 192. The only use of "pregnancy."
O, 'tis pregnant, pregnant!
Cymbeline. Act iv, sc. 2, l. 325. [Imogen]
'Tis very pregnant.—*Measure for Measure,* ii, 1, 23. "Pregnant" is used fourteen times in the plays, always in the sense of weighty, or full of meaning.
4
La Pucelle: I am with child, ye bloody homicides:
Murder not then the fruit within my womb,
Although ye hale me to a violent death.
York: Now heaven forfend! the holy maid with child!
Warwick: The greatest miracle that e'er ye wrought:
Is all your strict preciseness come to this?
I Henry VI. Act v, sc. 4, l. 62. The only use of "preciseness."
She's quick; the child brags in her belly already.
Love's Labour's Lost. Act v, sc. 2, l. 682. [Costard]
The getting up of the negro's belly: the Moor is with child by you, Launcelot.
The Merchant of Venice. Act iii, sc. 5, l. 41. [Lorenzo] The only use of "negro."
5
Let wives with child
Pray that their burthens may not fall this day,
Lest that their hopes prodigiously be cross'd.
King John. Act iii, sc. 1, l. 89. [Constance] The only use of "prodigiously."
6
Mrs. Overdone: But what's his offence?
Pompey: Groping for trouts in a peculiar river.
Mrs. Overdone: What, is there a maid with child by him?
Pompey: No, but there's a woman with maid by him.
Measure for Measure. Act i, sc. 2, l. 90. The only use of "groping."
Claudio: But it chances
The stealth of our most mutual entertainment
With character too gross is writ on Juliet.
Lucio: With child perhaps?
Claudio: Unhappily, even so.
Measure for Measure. Act i, sc. 2, l. 157.
7
Being, as I say, with child, and being great-bellied.
Measure for Measure. Act ii, sc. 1, l. 101. [Pompey]
Great-bellied women,
That had not half a week to go.
Henry VIII, iv, 1, 76. The only uses of "great-bellied."
When we have laugh'd to see the sails conceive
And grow big-bellied with the wanton wind.
A Midsummer-Night's Dream. Act ii, sc. 1, l. 128. [Titania] The only use of "big-bellied."
She grew round-wombed.—*King Lear,* i, 1, 14. The only use of the phrase. See under SON.
8
What shall be done, sir, with the groaning Juliet?
She's very near her hour.
Measure for Measure. Act ii, sc. 2, l. 15. [Provost]
A gentlewoman of mine,
Who, falling in the flaws of her own youth,
Hath blister'd her report: she is with child.
Measure for Measure. Act ii, sc. 3, l. 10. [Provost]
9
This blue-eyed hag was hither brought with child.
Tempest. Act i, sc. 2, l. 269. [Prospero]
10
Unless it swells past hiding, and then it's past watching.
Troilus and Cressida. Act i, sc. 2, l. 295. [Cressida]
11
The queen your mother rounds apace.
Winter's Tale. Act ii, sc. 1, l. 16. [Lady]
She is spread of late
Into a goodly bulk: good time encounter her!
Winter's Tale. Act ii, sc. 1, l. 19. [Lady]
Let her sport herself
With what she's big with; for 'tis Polixenes
Has made thee swell thus.
Winter's Tale. Act ii, sc. 1, l. 60. [Leontes]

PRELATE, see Priest

PREPARATION

12
I will . . . put myself into my mortal preparation.
All's Well that Ends Well. Act iii, sc. 6, l. 81. [Parolles]
Dreadful preparation.—*Henry V,* ii, Prol., 13.
Dreadful note of preparation.—*Henry V,* iv, Prol., 14.

Foreign preparation.—*King John,* iv, 2, 111.
Mighty preparation.—*Othello,* i, 3, 221.
Royal preparation.—*Macbeth,* v, 3, 57.
Strong and mighty preparation.—*I Henry IV,* iv, 1, 93.

1
I 'll raise the preparation of a war
Shall stain your brother.
Antony and Cleopatra. Act iii, sc. 4, l. 26. [Antony]
Their preparation is to-day by sea;
We please them not by land.
Antony and Cleopatra, iv, 10, 1.
That 's the way
To fool their preparation, and to conquer
Their most absurd intents.
Antony and Cleopatra. Act v, sc. 2, l. 224. [Cleopatra]

2
You 'll find They 've not prepared for us.
Coriolanus. Act i, sc. 2, l. 29. [Senator]
He 's not prepared for death.
Measure for Measure. Act ii, sc. 2, l. 84. [Isabella]
Prepared I was not.—*All's Well that Ends Well,* ii, 5, 66.

3
They are in most warlike preparation.
Coriolanus. Act iv, sc. 3, l. 17. [Volsce]
Lead on this preparation.—*Coriolanus,* i, 2, 15.

4
Your preparation can affront no less
Than what you hear of: come more, for more you 're ready.
Cymbeline. Act iv, sc. 3, l. 29. [Lord]

5
Defences, musters, preparations,
Should be maintain'd.
Henry V. Act ii, sc. 4, l. 18. [Dauphin]
Go about my preparation.—*I Henry VI,* i, 1, 166.
Preparation for a bloody siege.—*King John,* ii, 1, 213.

6
Advise the duke, where you are going, to a most festinate preparation.
King Lear. Act iii, sc. 7, l. 9. [Cornwall] The only use of "festinate" (hasty).
Our preparation stands
In expectation of them.
King Lear. Act iv, sc. 4, l. 22. [Cordelia]

7
Prepare, madam, prepare!
Arm, wenches, arm! encounters mounted are
Against your peace.
Love's Labour 's Lost. Act v, sc. 2, l. 81. [Boyet]
Against this coming end you should prepare.
Sonnets. No. xiii.
Prepare thyself.—*Hamlet,* iv, 3, 45.
Prepare yourself.—*King John,* iv, 1, 90; *Measure for Measure,* iii, 1, 169; iv, 2, 72; *Richard II,* iv, 1, 320.
Bid him prepare.—*Henry V,* iv, 4, 34; *The Rape of Lucrece,* l. 1294.
Bid them prepare.—*Love's Labour 's Lost,* v, 2, 510; *Julius Cæsar,* ii, 2, 118.
Prepare for dinner.—*The Merchant of Venice,* iii, 5, 52; *King Lear,* i, 3, 26.
Prepare for mirth.—*Pericles,* ii, 3, 7.
Prepare for war.—*III Henry VI,* iv, 1, 131.
Prepare to chide.—*Romeo and Juliet,* iii, 3, 162.
Prepare to die.—*Richard III,* i, 4, 185; *A Midsummer-Night's Dream,* i, 1, 86.
Prepare to fight.—*Troilus and Cressida,* ii, 3, 238.
Prepare To follow.—*Romeo and Juliet,* iv, 5, 92.
Prepares to write.—*The Rape of Lucrece,* l. 1296.
Modestly prepares.—*The Rape of Lucrece,* l. 1607.
Prepare my horses.—*King Lear,* i, 4, 280.
Prepare the body.—*Julius Cæsar,* iii, 1, 253.
Prepare This body.—*Pericles,* i, 1, 43.
Prepare thy brow to frown.—*Coriolanus,* iv, 5, 69.
Prepare thy grave.—*Timon of Athens,* iv, 3, 378.
Prepare your bosom.—*The Merchant of Venice,* iv, 1, 245.
Prepare your throats.—*Titus Andronicus,* v, 2, 197.

8
Let him be furnished with divines, and have all charitable preparation.
Measure for Measure. Act iii, sc. 2, l. 221. [Escalus]
We have not made good preparations.
The Merchant of Venice. Act ii, sc. 4, l. 4. [Gratiano]

9
I make bold to press with so little preparation upon you.
The Merry Wives of Windsor. Act ii, sc. 2, l. 163. [Ford]
Your many war-like, court-like, and learned preparations.
The Merry Wives of Windsor. Act ii, sc. 2, l. 237. [Ford] The only use of "court-like"

10
He hath made great preparation.
Much Ado about Nothing. Act i, sc. 1, l. 280. [Don Pedro]
All the preparation overthrown.—*Much Ado about Nothing,* ii, 2, 50.

11
For that I am prepared and full resolved.
Titus Andronicus. Act ii, sc. 1, l. 57. [Chiron]
I am prepared.—*I Henry VI,* i, 2, 98.
He is prepared.—*King John,* v, 2, 130.
They are prepared.—*Coriolanus,* iii, 2, 139.
We are prepared.—*I Henry IV,* ii, 3, 37; *King John,* ii, 1, 83.
Be prepared.—*Julius Cæsar,* i, 2, 66; *Antony and Cleopatra,* i, 3, 66.
Let him be prepared.—*Measure for Measure,* ii, 1, 35.
Better prepared.—*Much Ado about Nothing,* i, 2, 23.
Well prepared.—*Henry V,* i, 2, 234; *King John,* v, 2, 134; *The Merchant of Venice,* iv, 1, 264.
Prepared for land.—*Antony and Cleopatra,* iii, 7, 41.
Prepared for war.—*Antony and Cleopatra,* iii, 6, 58.
Prepared to die.—*Measure for Measure,* iii, 1, 4.
Prepared to the spit.—*Titus Andronicus,* iv, 2, 146.

1
Be yare in thy preparation.
Twelfth Night, iii, 4, 245. See under DUELLING. "Yare" (nimble, brisk) is used ten times and "yarely" twice.

PREROGATIVE

2
Insisting on the old prerogative.
Coriolanus. Act iii, sc. 3, l. 17. [Sicinius] The only use of "insisting."

3
The true and auncient prerogatifes and laws of the wars is not kept.
Henry V. Act iv, sc. 1, l. 67. [Fluellen]

Prerogative of age.—*Troilus and Cressida*, i, 3, 107.

Prerogative of love.—*All's Well that Ends Well*, ii, 4, 42. See under LOVE.

Prerogative of speech.—*Twelfth Night*, ii, 5, 78.

4
Then give me leave to have prerogative.
The Taming of the Shrew. Act iii, sc. 1, l. 6. [Hortensio]

Our prerogative Calls not your counsels.
Winter's Tale. Act ii, sc. 1, l. 163. [Leontes]

With all prerogative.—*The Tempest*, i, 2, 105. "Prerogative" is used an eighth time in *I Henry VI*, v, 4, 142. "Prerogatived" occurs once, in *Othello*, iii, 3, 274.

PRESENCE

See also Absence, Appearance

5
Bear a fair presence, though your heart be tainted.
The Comedy of Errors, iii, 2, 13. See under APPEARANCE.

6
Be somewhat scanter of your maiden presence.
Hamlet. Act i, sc. 3, l. 121. [Polonius] The only use of "scanter."

7
Had I so lavish of my presence been.
I Henry IV. Act iii, sc. 2, l. 39. [King Henry]

Being with his presence glutted, gorged and full.
I Henry IV. Act iii, sc. 2, l. 84. [King Henry] The only use of "glutted." "Glut" occurs in *The Tempest*, i, 1, 63. "Gorged" is repeated in *Romeo and Juliet*, v, 3, 46.

8
The presence of a king engenders love.
I Henry VI, iii, 1, 181. See under KING.

In presence of the Kings of France and Sicil.
II Henry VI, i, 1, 6. [Suffolk] "Sicil" is used three times, and Sicilia fourteen.

Presence of the king.—*Richard III*, i, 3, 115.

9
My sovereign's presence makes me mild.
II Henry VI. Act iii, sc. 2, l. 219. [Warwick]

Ross: Your presence makes us rich, most noble lord.
Willoughby: And far surmounts our labour to attain it.
Richard II. Act ii, sc. 3, l. 63.

10
Your royal presences be ruled by me.
King John. Act ii, sc. 1, l. 377. [Bastard]

Yet of your royal presence I'll adventure
The borrow of a week.
Winter's Tale. Act i, sc. 2, l. 38. [Hermione]

Royal presence.—*Richard III*, i, 2, 58; ii, 1, 78; *Richard II*, iv, 1, 115; *Pericles*, ii, 3, 49.

High presence.—*The Winter's Tale*, v, 1, 88.

Noble presence.—*Richard III*, iii, 4, 66; *Richard II*, iv, 1, 117.

Princely presence.—*Richard II*, i, 1, 34.

Stately presence.—*I Henry VI*, i, 1, 21.

Excepting your worship's presence.—*Much Ado about Nothing*, iii, 5, 34.

11
The king by me requests your presence straight.
King John. Act iv, sc. 3, l. 22. [Bastard]

He is in presence here.—*II Henry IV*, iv, 4, 17.

You were in presence then.—*Richard II*, iv, 1, 62.

Not here in presence.—*Henry V*, i, 2, 2.

12
And ever and anon they made a doubt
Presence majestical would put him out.
Love's Labour's Lost, v, 2, 101. [Boyet]

13
And from thy hated presence part I so.
A Midsummer-Night's Dream. Act iii, sc. 2, l. 80. [Hermia]

Fly my presence.—*A Midsummer-Night's Dream*, ii, 2, 97.

14
Your presence glads our days.
Pericles. Act ii, sc. 3, l. 21. [Simonides]

Is 't not a goodly presence?
Pericles. Act v, sc. 1, l. 66. [Lysimachus]

Enchanting presence.—*The Comedy of Errors*, iii, 2, 166.

Feasting presence.—*Romeo and Juliet*, v, 3, 86.

Good presence.—*Love's Labour's Lost*, v, 2, 536.

Of excellent presence.—*As You Like It*, i, 2, 130.

15
Call them to our presence; face to face,
And frowning brow to brow.
Richard II. Act i, sc. 1, l. 15. [King Richard]

16
Her presence still renew his sorrows.
Titus Andronicus, v, 3, 42. [Saturninus]

Her presence
Shall quite strike off all service I have done,
In most accepted pain.
Troilus and Cressida. Act iii, sc. 3, l. 28. [Calchas]

17
I will put on his presence.
Troilus and Cressida. Act iii, sc. 3, l. 272. [Thersites]

18
Repair me with thy presence, Silvia.
The Two Gentlemen of Verona. Act v, sc. 4, l. 11. [Valentine]

19
From his presence
I am barr'd, like one infectious.
The Winter's Tale, iii, 2, 98. [Hermione]

How
Should I, in these my borrow'd flaunts, behold
The sternness of his presence?
Winter's Tale. Act iv, sc. 4, l. 22. [Perdita] The only use of "flaunts" and "sternness."

PRESENT

See also Past

1
'Was' is not 'is.'
As You Like It. Act iii, sc. 4, l. 32. [Celia]
Therefore take the present time.
As You Like It. Act v, sc. 3, l. 31. [Song]
"Present time" is used seven times.
Present day.—*Richard III,* i, 1, 69; *Sonnets,* cvi.
Present evening.—*King Lear,* ii, 1, 103.
Present hour.—*Richard III,* v, 1, 8, and four times in later plays.
Present winter.—*Cymbeline,* ii, 4, 5.
Present year.—*The Merchant of Venice,* i, 1, 44.
2
Thy letters have transported me beyond
This ignorant present, and I feel now
The future in the instant.
Macbeth. Act i, sc. 5, l. 57. [Lady Macbeth]
Crowning the present, doubting of the rest.
Sonnets. No. cxv.
3
Make stale The glistering of this present.
Winter's Tale. Act iv, sc. 1, l. 13. [Time]

PRESENTS

See also Gift

4
To mend the petty present, I will piece
Her opulent throne with kingdoms.
Antony and Cleopatra. Act i, sc. 5, l. 45. [Alexas] "Opulent" occurs again in *King Lear,* i, 1, 88.
5
Some dozen Romans of us . . . have mingled sums
To buy a present for the emperor.
Cymbeline. Act i, sc. 6, l. 185. [Iachimo]
Presents well worthy Rome's imperial lord.
Titus Andronicus. Act i, sc. 1, l. 250. [Titus]
He 's a present for any emperor that ever trod on neat's-leather.
The Tempest. Act ii, sc. 2, l. 72. [Stephano]
As proper men as ever trod upon neat's-leather.
Julius Cæsar, i, 1, 29. The only uses of neat's-leather."
6
What present hast thou there?
Love's Labour 's Lost. Act iv, sc. 3, l. 189. [King]
Gobbo: How dost thou and thy master agree? I have brought him a present. . . .
Launcelot: Give him a present! give him a halter. . . . Give me your present to one Master Bassanio.
The Merchant of Venice. Act ii, sc. 2, l. 107.
7
She did scorn the present that I sent her.
The Two Gentlemen of Verona. Act iii, sc. 1, l. 92. [Duke]
Presents that I intend to send them both.
Titus Andronicus. Act iv, sc. 1, l. 116. [Titus]
Give them to his master for a present.
Titus Andronicus. Act iv, sc. 3, l. 75. [Marcus]
Not only brought many presents to give her, but have given largely to many to know what she would have given.
The Merry Wives of Windsor. Act ii, sc. 2, l. 206. [Ford]

PRESUMPTION

See also Impudence

8
But most it is presumption in us when
The help of heaven we count the act of men.
All's Well that Ends Well. Act ii, sc. 1, l. 154. [Helena]
9
Let my presumption not provoke thy wrath.
I Henry VI. Act ii, sc. 3, l. 70. [Countess]
Tut, this was nothing but an argument
That he that breaks a stick of Gloucester's grove
Shall lose his head for his presumption.
II Henry VI. Act i, sc. 2, l. 32. [Duchess]
That is too much presumption on thy part.
II Henry VI. Act v, sc. 1, l. 38. [Buckingham]
10
Makes thee thus presumptuous and proud.
III Henry VI, i, 1, 157.
Presumptuous dame.—*II Henry VI,* i, 2, 42.
Presumptuous priest!—*I Henry IV,* iii, 1, 8.
Presumptuous suit.—*All's Well that Ends Well,* i, 3, 204.
Presumptuous vassals.—*I Henry VI,* iv, 1, 125.
The only uses of "presumptuous."
11
They shall have wars and pay for their presumption.
III Henry VI. Act iv, sc. 1, l. 114. [King Edward]
Gloucester: Thy son I kill'd for his presumption.
King Henry: Hadst thou been kill'd when first thou didst presume,
Thou hadst not lived to kill a son of mine.
III Henry VI. Act v, sc. 6, l. 34.
Dare he presume?—*III Henry VI,* iii, 3, 178.
I will not so presume.—*I Henry VI,* v, 3, 185.
Let none presume.—*The Merchant of Venice,* ii, 9, 39.
Do not presume.—*Julius Cæsar,* iv, 3, 63.
12
A very forward March-chick!
Much Ado about Nothing. Act i, sc. 3, l. 58. [Don John] The only use of "March-chick."
Forward child.—*As You Like It,* iii, 3, 14.
Forward guest.—*Taming of the Shrew,* ii, 1, 51.
Forward son.—*III Henry VI,* i, 1, 203; ii, 2, 58.
Forward spirit.—*II Henry IV,* i, 1, 173.
13
But on thy side I may not be too forward.
Richard III. Act v, sc. 3, l. 94. [Derby]
Baccare! you are marvellous forward.
Taming of the Shrew, ii, 1, 73. [Gremio]
The only use of "baccare" (stand back).
You grow too forward.—*The Taming of the Shrew,* iii, 1, 1.
You 'll still be too forward.—*The Two Gentlemen of Verona,* ii, 1, 11.
They are ever forward.—*Henry VIII,* iv, 1, 9.
14 Thou dost over-ween in all;
And so in this, to bear me down with braves.
Titus Andronicus. Act ii, sc. 1, l. 29. [Chiron]
You overween to take it so.—*II Henry IV,* iv, 1, 149.
I o'erween to think so.—*The Winter's Tale,* iv, 2, 9. The only uses of "overween."
My heart o'erweens too much.—*III Henry VI,* iii, 2, 144. The only use of "o'erweens."

PRETENCE

See also Dissembling, Seeming

1
Keep your great pretences veil'd till when
They needs must show themselves.
Coriolanus. Act i, sc. 2, l. 20. [Aufidius]
Why hast thou abused
So many miles with a pretence?
Cymbeline. Act iii, sc. 4, l. 105. [Imogen]
Still pretending.—*Cymbeline,* v, 5, 250. "Pretending" is repeated in *Measure for Measure,* iii, 1, 236.
Under pretence.—*Henry VIII,* i, 1, 177.
2 If I do feign,
O let me in my present wildness die!
II Henry IV. Act iv, sc. 5, l. 152. [Prince]
If I do feign you witnesses above
Punish my life.
Twelfth Night. Act v, sc. 1, l. 140. [Viola]
Feigned ashes.—*I Henry VI,* iii, 1, 190.
Feigned ecstasies.—*Titus Andronicus,* iv, 4, 21.
Feigned friend.—*III Henry VI,* iv, 2, 11.
Feigned prayer.—*Richard III,* v, 1, 21.
Sung
With feigning voice verses of feigning love.
A Midsummer-Night's Dream, i, 1, 30. See under Wooing.
'Twas never merry world
Since lowly feigning was call'd compliment.
Twelfth Night. Act iii, sc. 1, l. 109. [Olivia]
Most friendship is feigning.—*As You Like It,* ii, 7, 181.
The truest poetry is the most feigning.—*As You Like It,* iii, 3, 20. The only uses of "feigning."
3 Insulted, rail'd,
And put upon him such a deal of man,
That worthied him, got praises of the king
For him attempting who was self-subdued.
King Lear. Act ii, sc. 2, l. 126. [Oswald] The only use of "worthied" and "self-subdued."
No further pretence.—*King Lear,* i, 2, 95.
Make pretence.—*Pericles,* i, 2, 91.
4
His givings-out were of an infinite distance
From his true-meant design.
Measure for Measure. Act i, sc. 4, l. 54. [Lucio] The only use of "givings-out" and "true-meant."
Ambiguous giving out.—*Hamlet,* i, 5, 178.
Giving out her beauty.—*Pericles,* iv, 2, 155.
The monkey's own giving out.—*Othello,* iv, 1, 131. The only uses of "giving out."
5
He is no less than a stuffed man.
Much Ado about Nothing. Act i, sc. 1, l. 58. [Beatrice]
6 Now he throws that shallow habit by,
Wherein deep policy did him disguise.
The Rape of Lucrece, l. 1814.
7 There is boundless theft
In limited professions.
Timon of Athens. Act iv, sc. 3, l. 430. [Timon]
8
Whom you pretend to honour and adore.
Titus Andronicus. Act i, sc. 1, l. 42. [Marcus]
Pretended flight.—*The Two Gentlemen of Verona,* ii, 6, 37. The only use of "pretended."
9
How angerly I taught my brow to frown,
When inward joy enforced my heart to smile!
The Two Gentlemen of Verona. Act i, sc. 2, l. 62. [Julia] "Angerly" is repeated in *King John,* iv, 1, 81, and in *Macbeth,* iii, 5, 1.

PRICE

10
He might have bought me at a common price.
All's Well that Ends Well. Act v, sc. 3, l. 190. [Diana]
At our own price.—*Coriolanus,* i, 1, 11.
Easy price.—*Titus Andronicus,* iii, 1, 199.
Little price.—*Henry V,* iii, 6, 47.
Trivial price.—*All's Well that Ends Well,* v, 3, 61.
Pay the price.—*Henry V,* ii, 2, 154.
11 She got the ring;
And I had that which any inferior might
At market-price have bought.
All's Well that Ends Well. Act v, sc. 3, l. 217. [Bertram] The only use of "market-price."
Now her price is fall'n.
King Lear. Act i, sc. 1, l. 200. [King Lear]
12
Coriolanus: Well then, I pray, your price o' the consulship.
Citizen: The price is to ask it kindly.
Coriolanus. Act ii, sc. 3, l. 79.
Set your entreatments at a higher rate
Than a command to parley.
Hamlet. Act i, sc. 3, l. 122. [Polonius] The only use of "entreatments."
13
Poor fellow, never joyed since the price of oats rose; it was the death of him.
I Henry IV. Act ii, sc. 1, l. 13. [Carrier]
Price of hogs.—*Merchant of Venice,* iii, 5, 26.
Price of pork.—*Merchant of Venice,* iii, 5, 38.
14
King: More measure of this measure; be not nice.
Rosaline: We can afford no more at such a price.
Love's Labour's Lost. Act v, sc. 2, l. 222.
15
I know my price.
Othello. Act i, sc. 1, l. 11. [Iago]
16
If heaven would make me such another world
Of one entire and perfect chrysolite,
I 'ld not have sold her for it.
Othello. Act v, sc. 2, l. 144. [Othello] The only use of "chrysolite."
17
The cheapest of us is ten groats too dear.
Richard II. Act v, sc. 5, l. 68. [King Richard]
Let what is dear in Sicily be cheap.
Winter's Tale. Act i, sc. 2, l. 175. [Leontes]
Dear-bought.—*II Henry VI,* i, 1, 252; *The Merchant of Venice,* iii, 2, 315.
18
That if he overhold his price so much,
We 'll none of him.
Troilus and Cressida. Act ii, sc. 3, l. 142. [Agamemnon] The only use of "overhold."

PRICK, see under Hound

PRIDE

See also Arrogance

1
My pride fell with my fortunes.
As You Like It. Act i, sc. 2, l. 264. [Rosalind]
Why, who cries out on pride,
That can therein tax any private party?
As You Like It. Act ii, sc. 7, l. 70. [Jaques]
Must you be therefore proud and pitiless?
As You Like It. Act iii, sc. 5, l. 40. [Rosalind]
And be not proud: though all the world could see,
None could be so abused in sight as he.
As You Like It. Act iii, sc. 5, l. 78. [Rosalind]
But, sure, he 's proud, and yet his pride becomes him.
As You Like It. Act iii, sc. 5, l. 114. [Phebe]
She calls me proud, and that she could not love me,
Were man as rare as phœnix.
As You Like It. Act iv, sc. 3, l. 16. [Rosalind]
2
'Fly pride,' says the peacock.
The Comedy of Errors. Act iv, sc. 3, l. 81. [Dromio of Syracuse]
Like a peacock sweep along his tail.
I Henry VI. Act iii, sc. 3, l. 6. [La Pucelle]
He stalks up and down like a peacock,—a stride and a stand.
Troilus and Cressida. Act iii, sc. 3, l. 251. [Thersites]
3
He pays himself with being proud.
Coriolanus. Act i, sc. 1, l. 33. [Citizen]
Proud; which he is, even to the altitude of his virtue.
Coriolanus. Act i, sc. 1, l. 40. [Citizen] "Altitude" is repeated in *Hamlet,* ii, 2, 446, and in *King Lear,* iv, 6, 53.
Sicinius: Was ever man so proud as is this Marcius?
Brutus: He has no equal.
Coriolanus. Act i, sc. 1, l. 257.
Junius Brutus: He is grown
Too proud to be so valiant.
Sicinius: Such a nature,
Tickled with good success, disdains the shadow
Which he treads on at noon.
Coriolanus. Act i, sc. 1, l. 262.
You talk of pride: O that you could turn your eyes toward the napes of your necks, and make but an interior survey of your good selves! O that you could! . . . Then you should discover a brace of unmeriting, proud, violent, testy magistrates, alias fools, as any in Rome.
Coriolanus. Act ii, sc. 1, l. 41. [Menenius] The only use of "napes" and "unmeriting." "Alias" is repeated in *All 's Well that Ends Well,* iv, 5, 44.
He 's vengeance proud, and loves not the common people.
Coriolanus. Act ii, sc. 2, l. 5. [Officer]
He bears himself more proudlier,
Even to my person, than I thought he would
When first I did embrace him: yet his nature
In that 's no changeling.
Coriolanus. Act iv, sc. 7, l. 8. [Aufidius] The only use of "proudlier."
O'ercome with pride, ambitious past all thinking.
Coriolanus. Act iv, sc. 6, l. 31. [Brutus]
Pride,
Which out of daily fortune ever taints
The happy man.
Coriolanus. Act iv, sc. 7, l. 37. [Aufidius]
He lost By lack of stooping.
Coriolanus. Act v, sc. 6, l. 28. [Conspirator]
4
Prick'd on by a most emulate pride.
Hamlet. Act i, sc. 1, l. 83. [Horatio] The only use of "emulate" as an adjective. It is used as a verb in *The Merry Wives of Windsor,* iii, 3, 58: "Emulate the diamond."
Fair pride.—*The Passionate Pilgrim,* l. 22.
Foul pride.—*Sonnets,* cxliv.
Imprison'd pride.—*Sonnets,* lii.
Maiden pride.—*Much Ado about Nothing,* iii, 1, 109.
Modest pride.—*Venus and Adonis,* l. 278.
New pride.—*Sonnets,* lxxvi.
Short-lived pride!—*Love's Labour 's Lost,* iv, 1, 15. "Short-lived" occurs again in the same play, ii, 1, 54, and in no other.
Pride of France.—*Henry V,* i, 2, 112; *I Henry VI,* iii, 2, 40.
Pride of Gallia.—*I Henry VI,* iv, 6, 15.
Pride of place.—*Macbeth,* ii, 4, 12.
Pride of truth.—*A Lover's Complaint,* l. 105.
Take a pride.—*II Henry IV,* i, 2, 7.
Took some pride.—*Coriolanus,* v, 6, 37.
5
Pride went before, ambition follows him.
II Henry VI. Act i, sc. 1, l. 180. [Salisbury]
To bridle and suppress the pride of Suffolk.
II Henry VI. Act i, sc. 1, l. 201. [Salisbury]
Ill can thy noble mind abrook
The abject people gazing on thy face.
II Henry VI. Act ii, sc. 4, l. 10. [Gloucester] The only use of "abrook."
Let it make thee crest-fall'n,
Ay, and allay this thy abortive pride.
II Henry VI. Act iv, sc. 1, l. 59. [Suffolk] "Crest-fall'n" is repeated in *Merry Wives of Windsor,* iv, 5, 102, and in *Richard II,* i, 1, 188.
6
What hath broach'd this tumult but thy pride?
III Henry VI. Act ii, sc. 2, l. 159. [Edward]
Proud-hearted.—*III Henry VI,* v, 1, 98. The only use of the phrase.
Proud in heart and mind.—*King Lear,* iii, 4, 87.
7
I can see his pride
Peep through each part of him.
Henry VIII. Act i, sc. 1, l. 68. [Abergavenny]
This top-proud fellow,
Whom from the flow of gall I name not.
Henry VIII. Act i, sc. 1, l. 151. [Buckingham] The only use of "top-proud."
My high-blown pride At length broke under me.
Henry VIII, iii, 2, 361. See under FALL. The only use of "high-blown."
Pride must have a fall, and break the neck
Of that proud man that did usurp his back.
Richard II. Act v, sc. 5, l. 88. [King Richard] A proverb which appeared first in Alexander Barclay's *Ship of Folys,* in 1509.
8
He will never follow any thing
That other men begin.
Julius Cæsar. Act ii, sc. 1, l. 151. [Brutus]

1
I will instruct my sorrows to be proud;
For grief is proud and makes his owner stoop.
To me and to the state of my great grief
Let kings assemble.
King John. Act iii, sc. 1, l. 68. [Constance]

2
Let pride, which she calls plainness, marry her.
King Lear. Act i, sc. 1, l. 131. [King Lear]

With strain'd pride
To come between our sentence and our power.
King Lear. Act i, sc. 1, l. 172. [King Lear]

Blast her pride.—*King Lear,* ii, 4, 170.

3
Set not thy sweet heart on proud array.
King Lear. Act iii, sc. 4, l. 84. [Edgar]

4
All pride is willing pride.
Love's Labour's Lost. Act ii, sc. 1, l. 36. [Princess of France]

5
Proud was his form, in his eye pride express'd.
Love's Labour's Lost. Act ii, sc. 1, l. 237. [Boyet]

He of tall building and of goodly pride.
Sonnets. No. lxxx.

6
But Nature never framed a woman's heart
Of prouder stuff than that of Beatrice.
Much Ado about Nothing. Act iii, sc. 1, l. 49. [Hero]

I must not seem proud.—*Much Ado about Nothing,* ii, 3, 237.

7
'Tis pride that pulls the country down;
Then take thine auld cloak about thee.
Othello. Act ii, sc. 3, l. 98. [Iago] A scrap from an old ballad, *Take Thine Auld Cloak about Thee,* given in Percy's *Reliques,* Ser. i, bk. ii, no. 7.

Loving his own pride.—*Othello,* i, 1, 12.

8
Pride so great
The name of help grew odious to repeat.
Pericles. Act i, sc. 4, l. 30. [Cleon]

So their pride doth grow,
Paying more slavish tribute than they owe.
The Rape of Lucrece, l. 298.

9
The eagle-winged pride
Of sky-aspiring and ambitious thoughts.
Richard II. Act i, sc. 3, l. 129. [King Richard] The only use of either phrase.

The pride of kingly sway.—*Richard II,* iv, 1, 206.

All souls that will be safe fly from my side,
For time hath set a blot upon my pride.
Richard II. Act iii, sc. 2, l. 80. [King Richard]

10
So proudly as if he disdain'd the ground.
Richard II. Act v, sc. 5, l. 83. [Groom]

I will bear myself proudly.—*Much Ado about Nothing,* ii, 3, 234.

Securely done, A little proudly.—*Troilus and Cressida,* iv, 5, 74.

11
The queen's sons and brothers haught and proud.
Richard III. Act ii, sc. 3, l. 28. [Citizen] "Haught" is repeated in *III Henry VI,* ii, 1, 169, and in *Richard II,* iv, 1, 254.

12
Proud me no prouds.
Romeo and Juliet. Act iii, sc. 5, l. 153. [Capulet]

Proud of his pride.
Sonnets. No. cli.

13
The purple pride
Which on thy soft cheek for complexion dwells.
Sonnets. No. xcix.

14
The seeded pride
That hath to this maturity blown up . . .
Must . . . now be cropp'd.
Troilus and Cressida. Act i, sc. 3, l. 316. [Ulysses] The only use of "maturity." "Seeded" is repeated in *The Rape of Lucrece,* l. 603: "Seeded in thine age."

An a' be proud with me, I 'll pheeze his pride.
Troilus and Cressida. Act ii, sc. 3, l. 215. [Ajax] "Pheeze" (frighten away) occurs again in *The Taming of the Shrew,* Ind., i, 1.

15
Lion-sick, sick of proud heart: you may call it melancholy, if you will favour the man; but, by my head, 'tis pride.
Troilus and Cressida. Act ii, sc. 3, l. 93. [Ajax] The only use of "lion-sick."

We think him over-proud And under-honest.
Troilus and Cressida. Act ii, sc. 3, l. 132. [Agamemnon] The only use of "under-honest." "Over-proud occurs again in *Richard II,* iii, 4, 59.

Ajax: Why should a man be proud? How doth pride grow? I know not what pride is.
Agamemnon: Your mind is the clearer, Ajax, and your virtues the fairer. He that is proud eats up himself: pride is his own glass, his own trumpet, his own chronicle.
Troilus and Cressida. Act ii, sc. 3, l. 161.

Pride hath no other glass
To show itself but pride.
Troilus and Cressida. Act iii, sc. 3, l. 47. [Ulysses]

16
I do hate a proud man, as I hate the engendering of toads.
Troilus and Cressida. Act ii, sc. 3, l. 169. [Ajax] The only use of "engendering."

He . . . speaks not to himself but with a pride
That quarrels at self-breath.
Troilus and Cressida. Act ii, sc. 3, l. 181. [Ulysses] The only use of "self-breath."

He is so plaguy proud that the death-tokens of it
Cry 'No recovery.'
Troilus and Cressida. Act ii, sc. 3, l. 187. [Ulysses] The only use of "plaguy" and "death-tokens."

That were to enlard his fat already pride.
Troilus and Cressida. Act ii, sc. 3, l. 205. [Ulysses] The only use of "enlard."

17
A' should not bear it so, a' should eat swords first: shall pride carry it?
Troilus and Cressida. Act ii, sc. 3, l. 227. [Ajax]

How one man eats into another's pride,
While pride is fasting in his wantonness!
Troilus and Cressida, iii, 3, 136. [Ulysses]

1
I see what you are, you are too proud.
Twelfth Night. Act i, sc. 5, l. 269. [Viola]
Maugre all thy pride.—*Twelfth Night,* iii, 1, 163.

2
This pride of hers,
Upon advice, hath drawn my love from her.
The Two Gentlemen of Verona. Act iii, sc. 1, l. 72. [Duke]
Speed: 'She is proud.'
Launce: Out with that too; it was Eve's legacy, and cannot be ta'en from her.
The Two Gentlemen of Verona. Act iii, sc. 1, l. 341.

PRIEST

See also Preacher

3
Faithfully confirmed by the rector of the place.
All's Well that Ends Well. Act iv, sc. 3, l. 68. [First Lord] The only use of "rector." "Rectorship" occurs in *Coriolanus,* ii, 3, 213.

4
Have a good priest that can tell you what marriage is.
As You Like It, iii, 3, 86. See under MARRIAGE. The only use of "good priest."
You shall be the priest and marry us.
As You Like It. Act iv, sc. 1, l. 123. [Rosalind]
The priest was good enough.—*As You Like It,* v, 1, 3.

5
Our very priests must become mockers, if they shall encounter such ridiculous subjects as you are.
Coriolanus. Act ii, sc. 1, l. 93. [Menenius]

6
Hear him but reason in divinity,
And all-admiring with an inward wish
You would the king were made a prelate.
Henry V. Act i, sc. 1, l. 38. [Archbishop of Canterbury] The only use of "all-admiring."
Gloucester: Am I not protector, saucy priest?
Winchester: And am I not a prelate of the church?
Gloucester: Yes, as an outlaw in a castle keeps
And useth it to patronage his theft.
I Henry VI. Act iii, sc. 1, l. 45. The only use of "patronage."
Haughty prelate.—*I Henry VI,* i, 3, 23; *Richard III,* iv, 4, 502.
Noble prelate.—*I Henry IV,* i, 3, 267.
Proud prelate.—*II Henry VI,* i, 1, 142.

7
I have built
Two chantries, where the sad and solemn priests
Sing still for Richard's soul.
Henry V. Act iv, sc. 2, l. 317. [King Henry] The only use of "chantries." "Chantry" occurs in *Twelfth Night,* iv, 3. 24.
We of the spirituality.—*Henry V,* i, 2, 132. The only use of spirituality.

8
All the priests and friars in my realm
Shall in procession sing her endless praise.
I Henry VI. Act i, sc. 6, l. 19. [Charles]
'Tis a meddling friar; I do not like the man.
Measure for Measure. Act v, sc. 1, l. 127. [Lucio]
A saucy friar, A very scurvy fellow.
Measure for Measure. Act v, sc. 1, l. 135. [Lucio]
We shall find this friar a notable fellow.
Measure for Measure. Act v, sc. 1, l. 268. [Escalus]
Unreverend and unhallow'd friar.—*Measure for Measure,* v, 1, 307.

9
It was the friar of orders grey,
As he forth walked on his way.
The Taming of the Shrew. Act iv, sc. 1, l. 148. [Petruchio, singing] A fragment of an old ballad. See Percy's RELIQUES, Series i, bk. ii, no. 18.

10
This cardinal's more haughty than the devil.
I Henry VI. Act i, sc. 3, l. 85. [Mayor]
Let us watch the haughty cardinal.—*II Henry VI,* i, 1, 174.
What! is my Lord of Winchester install'd,
And call'd unto a cardinal's degree?
Then I perceive that will be verified
Henry the Fifth did sometime prophesy,
'If once he come to be a cardinal,
He 'll make his cap co-equal with the crown.'
I Henry VI. Act v, sc. 1, l. 28. [Exeter] The only use of "co-equal."
This is the cardinal's doing, the king-cardinal.
Henry VIII. Act ii, sc. 2, l. 20. [Norfolk] The only use of "king-cardinal."
Upon my soul, two reverend cardinal virtues;
But cardinal sins and hollow hearts I fear ye:
Mend 'em, for shame, my lords.
Henry VIII. Act iii, sc. 1, l. 103. [Queen Katharine]
This cardinal,
Though from an humble stock, undoubtedly
Was fashion'd to much honour from his cradle.
Henry VIII. Act iv, sc. 2, l. 48. [Griffith] The only use of "undoubtedly."

11
What, cardinal, is your priesthood grown peremptory?
Tantæne animis cœlestibus iræ?
Churchmen so hot? good uncle, hide such malice.
II Henry VI. Act ii, sc. 1, l. 23. [Gloucester] The Latin (Can there be such passions in heavenly minds?) is a quotation from Vergil, *Æneid,* i, 15.
Chaplain, away! thy priesthood saves thy life.
III Henry VI. Act i, sc. 3, l. 3. [Clifford] "Chaplain" is used four times. The only uses of "priesthood."
Who should be pitiful, if you be not?
Or who should study to prefer a peace,
If holy churchmen take delight in broils?
I Henry VI. Act iii, sc. 1, l. 109. [King Henry]
That churchman bears a bounteous mind indeed.
Henry VIII. Act i, sc. 3, l. 55. [Lovell]
Love and meekness, lord,
Become a churchman better than ambition.
Henry VIII. Act v, sc. 3, l. 62. [Cranmer]

Sir Hugh hath shown himself a wise and patient churchman.
The Merry Wives of Windsor. Act ii, sc. 3, l. 57. [Shallow]
We are justices and doctors and churchmen.
The Merry Wives of Windsor. Act ii, sc. 3, l. 49. [Shallow]
Art thou a churchman?—*Twelfth Night,* iii, 1, 4.
You are a churchman.—*Henry VIII,* i, 4, 88.
Ambitious churchman.—*II Henry VI,* ii, 1, 182.
Holy churchmen.—*I Henry VI,* iii, 1, 111.
Imperious churchman.—*II Henry VI,* i, 3, 72.
Religious churchmen.—*I Henry VI,* i, 1, 40.

1
Presumptuous priest! this place commands my patience,
Or thou shouldst find thou hast dishonour'd me.
I Henry VI. Act iii, sc. 1, l. 8. [Gloucester]
Brother priest.—*Troilus and Cressida,* ii, 2, 37.
Churlish priest.—*Hamlet,* v, 1, 263.
False priest.—*II Henry VI,* ii, 4, 53.
Hedge-priest.—*Love's Labour's Lost,* v, 2, 545. The only use of the phrase.
Just and learned priest.—*Henry VIII,* ii, 2, 97.
Maiden priests.—*Pericles,* v, 1, 243.
Peel'd priest.—*I Henry VI,* i, 3, 30.
Sir priest.—*Twelfth Night,* iii, 4, 298.
Solemn priest.—*All's Well that Ends Well,* ii, 3, 286.
Welsh priest.—*The Merry Wives of Windsor,* ii, 1, 209.
Great Apollo's priest.—*The Winter's Tale,* iii, 2, 129.
God Bel's priests.—*Much Ado about Nothing,* iii, 3, 144. See under FASHION.
Diana's priest.—*Cymbeline,* i, 6, 133.

2
Suffolk: Say but the word, and I will be his priest.
Beaufort: But I would have him dead, my Lord of Suffolk,
Ere you can take due orders for a priest.
II Henry VI. Act iii, sc. 1, l. 272.
Priests pray for enemies, but princes kill.
II Henry VI. Act v, sc. 2, l. 71. [Richard]

3
Norfolk: This priest has no pride in him?
Suffolk: Not to speak of.
Henry VIII. Act ii, sc. 2, l. 82.

4
No Italian priest
Shall tithe or toll in our dominions.
King John. Act iii, sc. 1, l. 153. [King John]
You and all the kings of Christendom
Are led so grossly by this meddling priest,
Dreading the curse that money may buy out.
King John. Act iii, sc. 1, l. 162. [King John]

5
When priests are more in word than matter.
King Lear, iii, 2, 81. See under PROPHECY.

6
I will teach a scurvy jack-a-nape priest to meddle or make.
The Merry Wives of Windsor. Act i, sc. 4, l. 115. [Caius]
He is de coward Jack priest of de vorld.
The Merry Wives of Windsor. Act ii, sc. 3, l. 32. [Caius] "Jack priest" is repeated in i, 4, 123.
Scurvy jack-dog priest! by gar, me vill cut his ears.
The Merry Wives of Windsor. Act ii, sc. 3, l. 66. [Caius] "Jack-dog" occurs again in iii, 1, 85, and in no other play.

7
Shall I lose my parson, my priest?
The Merry Wives of Windsor. Act iii, sc. 1, l. 106. [Host]
Bring you the maid, you shall not lack a priest.
The Merry Wives of Windsor. Act iv, sc. 6, l. 53. [Host]
Am I both priest and clerk?—*Richard II,* iv, 1, 173.

8
O, now I want the priest that spake to me:
I now repent.
Richard III. Act iii, sc. 4, l. 89. [Hastings]

9
A divine, a ghostly confessor,
A sin-absolver.
Romeo and Juliet. Act iii, sc. 3, l. 49. [Romeo] The only use of "sin-absolver."

10
All-amazed, the priest let fall the book;
And, as he stoop'd again to take it up,
This mad-brain'd bridegroom took him such a cuff
That down fell priest and book and book and priest.
Taming of the Shrew. Act iii, sc. 2, l. 163. [Gremio] The only use of "all-amazed."
The old priest of Saint Luke's church is at your command at all hours. . . . My master hath appointed me to go to Saint Luke's, to bid the priest be ready to come against you come with your appendix.
The Taming of the Shrew. Act iv, sc. 4, l. 88. [Biondello]
The priest is ready.—*The Taming of the Shrew,* v, 1, 1.

PRINCE

11
Clown: Well, sir, if I cannot serve you, I can serve as great a prince as you are. . . .
Lafeu: What prince is that?
Clown: The black prince, sir; alias the prince of darkness.
All's Well that Ends Well. Act iv, sc. 5, l. 36. See under DEVIL. "Alias" is repeated in *Coriolanus,* ii, 1, 44.
The Black Prince, that young Mars of men.
Richard II. Act ii, sc. 3, l. 101. [York]
Edward the Black Prince.—*Henry V,* i, 2, 105; ii, 4, 56; *II Henry VI,* ii, 2, 18.

12
The greatest prince o' the world,
The noblest.
Antony and Cleopatra, iv, 15, 54. See under CHANGE.

13
Their blood thinks scorn,
Till it fly out and show them princes born.
Cymbeline. Act iv, sc. 4, l. 53. [Belarius]
Cymbeline: He was a prince.
Guiderius: A most incivil one.
Cymbeline. Act v, sc. 5, l. 291. The only use of "incivil."

1 A delicate and tender prince,
Whose spirit with divine ambition puff'd
Makes mouths at the invisible event,
Exposing what is mortal and unsure
To all that fortune, death and danger dare,
Even for an egg-shell.
Hamlet. Act iv, sc. 4, l. 48. [Hamlet] The only use of "egg-shell."

Tender prince.—*Richard III,* iii, 1, 28; iv, 1, 4; 103.

2
The most comparative, rascalliest, sweet young prince.
I Henry IV. Act i, sc. 2, l. 90. [Falstaff] The only use of "rascalliest."

Sweet young prince.—*III Henry VI,* v, 5, 67.
Sweet prince.—*I Henry VI,* iii, i, 152, and eleven times in later plays.

3
I 'll tickle ye for a young prince, i' faith.
I Henry IV. Act ii, sc. 4, l. 489. [Falstaff]

Young prince.—*III Henry VI,* iii, 3, 241, and seventeen times in later plays.
Youthful prince.—*II Henry IV,* i, 2, 163.

4
That same sword-and-buckler Prince of Wales.
I Henry IV. Act i, sc. 3, l. 230. [Hotspur] The only use of "sword-and-buckler."

The nimble-footed madcap Prince of Wales.
I Henry IV. Act iv, sc. 1, l. 95. [Hotspur] "Nimble-footed" is repeated in *The Two Gentlemen of Verona,* v, 3, 7.

Edward, Black Prince of Wales.—*Henry V,* ii, 4, 56; iv, 7, 97; *II Henry VI,* ii, 2, 11. The Prince of Wales is mentioned fourteen times in the plays.

5
The true prince may, for recreation sake, prove a false thief.
I Henry IV. Act i, sc. 2, l. 173. [Falstaff] "True prince" is repeated five times in ii, 4. It occurs nowhere else except in *Pericles,* i, 2, 124, probably not by Shakespeare.

The prince is a Jack, a sneak-cup: 'sblood, an he were here, I would cudgel him like a dog.
I Henry IV. Act iii, sc. 3, l. 99. [Falstaff] The only use of "sneak-cup" (one who shirks his liquor).

A prince should not be so loosely studied as to remember so weak a composition.
II Henry IV. Act ii, sc. 2, l. 9. [Poins] "Loosely" is repeated in v, 2, 94, and occurs in no other play.

Wild prince.—*The Merry Wives of Windsor,* iii, 2, 74.

6
The prince but studies his companions
Like a strange tongue, wherein, to gain the language,
'Tis needful that the most immodest word
Be look'd upon and learn'd; which once attain'd,
Your highness knows, comes to no further use
But to be known and hated. So, like gross terms,
The prince will in the perfectness of time
Cast off his followers; and their memory
Shall as a pattern or a measure live,
By which his grace must mete the lives of others,
Turning past evils to advantages.
II Henry IV. Act iv, sc. 4, l. 68. [Warwick]

7
Strong-fixed is the house of Lancaster
And like a mountain, not to be removed.
But now thy uncle is removing hence;
As princes do their courts, when they are cloy'd
With long continuance in a settled place.
I Henry VI. Act ii, sc. 5, l. 102. [Mortimer] The only use of "strong-fixed."

8
By the white hand of my lady, he 's a gallant prince.
Henry V. Act iii, sc. 7, l. 102. [Orleans]

Gallant princes.—*Henry V,* iv, 2, 15.

The wisest prince that there had reign'd.
Henry VIII. Act ii, sc. 4, l. 49. [Queen Katharine]

Such a prince;
Not only good and wise, but most religious.
Henry VIII. Act v, sc. 3, l. 115. [Gardiner]

Wise prince.—*III Henry VI,* iii, 3, 85.
Beloved prince.—*Merchant of Venice,* iii, 2, 181.
Christian prince.—*I Henry VI,* v, 3, 172; *Richard III,* iii, 7, 96.
Fair prince.—*Troilus and Cressida,* iii, 1, 52.
Gentle princes.—*Richard III,* iv, 1, 10; *Cymbeline,* iv, 5, 336.
Good prince.—*Pericles,* ii, Gower, 33.
Great princes.—*Henry V,* iii, 5, 46; *Troilus and Cressida,* iii, 3, 27.
High-illustrious prince.—*King Lear,* v, 3, 135. The only use of the phrase.
Kind prince.—*Romeo and Juliet,* iii, 3, 25.
Mighty prince.—*Richard II,* iii, 3, 172.
Noble prince.—*Richard III,* iii, 5, 64, and five times in later plays.
Pleasant prince.—*Henry V,* i, 2, 281.
Renowned prince.—*III Henry VI,* iii, 3, 214; *The Merchant of Venice,* ii, 1, 20.
Royal prince.—*Measure for Measure,* v, 1, 37; *Richard II,* ii, 1, 239; v, 5, 67.
Worthy prince.—*The Two Gentlemen of Verona,* iii, 1, 10; *Measure for Measure,* v, 1, 22; *King Lear,* v, 3, 178; *Pericles,* i, 2, 88.
Most worthy prince.—*Cymbeline,* v, 5, 358.
A prince most prudent.—*Henry VIII,* ii, 4, 46.
A prince of the blood.—*Troilus and Cressida,* iii, 3, 26.
Princes of my blood.—*I Henry IV,* iii, 2, 35.
A prince of power.—*The Tempest,* i, 1, 57.
Prince of cats.—*Romeo and Juliet,* ii, 4, 19.
Prince of chivalry.—*Troilus and Cressida,* i, 2, 249.
Prince of darkness.—*All's Well that Ends Well,* iv, 5, 44; *King Lear,* iii, 4, 148.
Prince of fiends.—*Henry V,* iii, 3, 16.
Prince of palfreys.—*Henry V,* iii, 7, 29.

9
For many of our princes—woe the while!—
Lie drown'd and soak'd in mercenary blood.
Henry V. Act iv, sc. 7, l. 78. [Montjoy]

10
King Henry: Princes French, and peers, health to you all! . . .

French King: Fairly met, . . . princes English. . . .
Queen Isabella: You English princes all, I do salute you.
Henry V. Act v, sc. 2, l. 8.

You princes of the Goths,
The Roman emperor greets you all by me.
Titus Andronicus. Act v, sc. 1, l. 56. [Æmilius] "Princes of the Goths" is repeated in v, 2, 125.

Nerissa: There is the Neapolitan prince.
Portia: Ay, there 's a colt indeed, for he doth nothing but talk of his horse; and he makes it a great appropriation to his own good parts, that he can shoe him himself. I am much afeard my lady his mother played false with a smith.
The Merchant of Venice. Act i, sc. 2, l. 43. The only use of "appropriation."

Prince of Arragon.—*The Merchant of Venice,* ii, 9, 2.
Prince of Ithaca.—*Troilus and Cressida,* i, 3, 70.
Prince of Morocco.—*The Merchant of Venice,* i, 2, 137.
Persian prince.—*The Merchant of Venice,* ii, 1, 25.
Prince Dauphin.—*Henry V,* iii, 5, 64.
Prince Florizel.—*The Winter's Tale,* iv, 2, 29; v, 1, 85.
Prince Lucifer.—*King John,* iv, 3, 122.
Prince Paris.—*Troilus and Cressida,* iv, 1, 4.
Foreign princes.—*I Henry VI,* iv, 1, 144; *Henry VIII,* i, 4, 56.

1
None do you like but an effeminate prince,
Whom, like a school-boy, you may overawe.
I Henry VI. Act i, sc. 1, l. 35. [Gloucester] The only use of "over-awe."

2
Third Servant: My lord, we know your grace to be a man
Just and upright; and, for your royal birth,
Inferior to none but to his majesty:
And ere that we will suffer such a prince,
So kind a father of the commonweal,
To be disgraced by an inkhorn mate,
We and our wives and children all will fight
And have our bodies slaughter'd by thy foes.
First Servant: Ay, and the very parings of our nails
Shall pitch a field when we are dead.
I Henry VI. Act iii, sc. 1, l. 94. "Inkhorn" is repeated in *II Henry VI,* iv, 2, 117, and in *Much Ado about Nothing,* iii, 5, 63.

All: Welcome, high prince, the mighty Duke of York!
Somerset: Perish, base prince, ignoble Duke of York!
I Henry VI. Act iii, sc. 1, l. 177.

Rude prince.—*II Henry IV,* i, 2, 218.

3
Princes should be free.
I Henry VI. Act v, sc. 3, l. 114. [Margaret]

4
Sometime I 'll say, I am Duke Humphrey's wife,
And he a prince and ruler of the land:
Yet so he ruled and such a prince he was
As he stood by whilst I, his forlorn duchess,
Was made a wonder and a pointing-stock
To every idle rascal follower.
II Henry VI. Act ii, sc. 4, l. 42. [Duchess of Gloucester] The only use of "pointing-stock."

5
Why, that is spoken like a toward prince.
III Henry VI. Act ii, sc. 2, l. 66. [Clifford]

A prince soon won with moving words.
III Henry VI. Act iii, sc. 1, l. 34. [King Henry]

Thou no more art prince than she is queen.
II Henry VI. Act iii, sc. 3. l. 80. [Warwick]

6
The hearts of princes kiss obedience,
So much they love it; but to stubborn spirits
They swell, and grow as terrible as storms.
Henry VIII. Act iii, sc. 1, l. 162. [Wolsey]

O, how wretched
Is that poor man that hangs on princes' favours!
There is, betwixt that smile we would aspire to,
That sweet aspect of princes, and their ruin,
More pangs and fears than wars or women have.
Henry VIII. Act iii, sc. 2, l. 366. [Cardinal Wolsey]

Great princes' favourites their fair leaves spread
But as the marigold at the sun's eye,
And in themselves their pride lies buried,
For at a frown they in their glory die.
Sonnets. No. xxv.

7
Now these her princes are come home again,
Come the three corners of the world in arms,
And we shall shock them.
King John. Act v, sc. 7, l. 115. [Bastard]

8
Yon sometimes famous princes, like thyself,
Drawn by report, adventurous by desire.
Pericles. Act i, sc. 1, l. 34. [Antiochus]

This prince, the fair-betrothed of your daughter.
Pericles. Act v, sc. 3, l. 71. [Pericles] The only use of "fair-betrothed."

9
Princes in this should live like gods above,
Who freely give to every one that comes
To honour them:
And princes not doing so are like to gnats,
Which make a sound, but kill'd are wonder'd at.
Pericles. Act ii, sc. 3, l. 59. [Simonides]

Princes are
A model, which heaven makes like to itself:
As jewels lose their glory if neglected,
So princes their renown if not respected.
Pericles. Act ii, sc. 2, l. 12. [Simonides]

Princes are the glass, the school, the book,
Where subjects' eyes do learn, do read, do look.
The Rape of Lucrece, l. 615.

1
Princes have but their titles for their glories,
And outward honour for an inward toil;
And, for unfelt imagination,
They often feel a world of restless cares:
So that, betwixt their titles and low names,
There 's nothing differs but the outward fame.
Richard III. Act i, sc. 4, l. 78. [Brakenbury]

2
O, if thine eye be not a flatterer,
Come thou on my side, and entreat for me,
As you would beg, were you in my distress:
A begging prince what beggar pities not?
Richard III. Act i, sc. 4, l. 271. [Clarence]

Butcher'd princes.—*Richard III,* v, 3, 122.
Cloudy princes.—*Richard III,* ii, 2, 112.
Dying prince.—*I Henry VI,* iii, 2, 86.
Living prince.—*The Tempest,* v, 1, 108.
Wandering prince.—*Titus Andronicus,* ii, 3, 22.

3
I long with all my heart to see the prince:
I hope he is much grown since last I saw him.
Richard III. Act ii, sc. 4, l. 4. [Duchess of York]

How fares the prince?—*Richard III,* ii, 4, 40.

God keep the prince from all the pack of you!
Richard III. Act iii, sc. 3, l. 5. [Grey]

Ah, ha, my lord, this prince is not an Edward!
He is not lolling on a lewd day-bed,
But on his knees at meditation;
Not dallying with a brace of courtezans,
But meditating with two deep divines;
Not sleeping, to engross his idle body,
But praying, to enrich his watchful soul:
Happy were England, would this gracious prince
Take on himself the sovereignty thereof. . . .
Famous Plantagenet, most gracious prince,
Lend favourable ears to our request.
Richard III. Act iii, sc. 7, l. 71. [Buckingham] "Day-bed" is repeated in *Twelfth Night,* ii, 5, 54, and "dallying" in *Hamlet,* iii, 2, 257.

4 Think you not how dangerous
It is to jet upon a prince's right?
Titus Andronicus. Act ii, sc. 1, l. 63. [Aaron] "Jet" in the sense of encroach upon is repeated in *The Comedy of Errors,* ii, 2, 28, and in *Richard III,* ii, 4, 51.

5
Princes orgulous, their high blood chafed.
Troilus and Cressida. Prologue, l. 2. The only use of "orgulous" (proud).

The prince must think me tardy and remiss,
That swore to ride before him to the field.
Troilus and Cressida. Act iv, sc. 4, l. 144. [Æneas]

6
Princely shall be thy usage every way.
Titus Andronicus. Act i, sc. 1, l. 266. [Saturninus]

Prince-like.—*Cymbeline,* v, 5, 298. The only use of the phrase.

7
Are you so fond of your young prince as we
Do seem to be of ours?
The Winter's Tale. Act i, sc. 2, l. 164. [Leontes]

We shall
Present our services to a fine new prince
One of these days.
The Winter's Tale. Act ii, sc. 1, l. 17. [Lady]

O cursed wretch,
Thou knew'st this was the prince, and wouldst adventure
To mingle faith with him!
The Winter's Tale. Act iv, sc. 4, l. 470. [Shepherd]

Had our prince,
Jewel of children, seen this hour, he had pair'd
Well with this lord.
The Winter's Tale. Act v, sc. 1, l. 115. [Paulina]

II—Princess

8 Fitting for a princess
Descended of so many royal kings.
Antony and Cleopatra. Act v, sc. 2, l. 329. [Charmian]

9 The truest princess
That ever swore her faith.
Cymbeline. Act v, sc. 5, l. 416. [Iachimo]

A most virtuous princess.—*Pericles,* ii, 5, 34.
A princess to equal any.—*Pericles,* iv, 3, 7.
Princess of pure white.—*A Midsummer-Night's Dream,* iii, 2, 144.
Admired princess.—*Love's Labour 's Lost,* i, 1, 141.
Dear princess.—*Love's Labour 's Lost,* ii, 1, 150.
Fair princess.—*Love's Labour 's Lost,* ii, 1, 90, and four times in later plays.
Fresh princess.—*The Winter's Tale,* iv, 4, 562.
Gentle princess.—*I Henry VI,* v, 3, 110.
Mighty princess.—*Cymbeline,* i, 6, 172.
Poor princess.—*Cymbeline,* ii, 1, 61.
Spotted princess.—*The Rape of Lucrece,* l. 721.

10
The preyful princess pierced and prick'd a pretty pleasing pricket.
Love's Labour 's Lost. Act iv, sc. 2, l. 58. [Holofernes] The only use of "preyful." "Pricket" (a buck in its second year) occurs four times in this scene, and nowhere else.

PRISON

See also Captivity

11
We will bind and hoodwink him.
All's Well that Ends Well. Act iii, sc. 6, l. 25. [Lord]

Till then I 'll keep him dark and safely lock'd.
All's Well that Ends Well. Act iv, sc. 1, l. 105. [Lord]

In a dark and dankish vault at home
There left me and my man, both bound together.
The Comedy of Errors. Act v, sc. 1, l. 247. [Antipholus of Ephesus] The only use of "dankish."

Come, we 'll have him in a dark room and bound.
Twelfth Night. Act iii, sc. 4, l. 148. [Sir Toby]

1
Hamlet: What have you, my good friends, deserved at the hands of fortune, that she sends you to prison hither?
Guildenstern: Prison, my lord?
Hamlet: Denmark 's a prison.
Rosencrantz: Then is the world one.
Hamlet: A goodly one, in which there are many confines, wards and dungeons, Denmark being one o' the worst.
Rosencrantz: We think not so, my lord.
Hamlet: Why, then, 'tis none to you; for there is nothing either good or bad, but thinking makes it so: to me it is a prison.
Rosencrantz: Why then, your ambition makes it one; 'tis too narrow for your mind.
Hamlet. Act ii, sc. 2, l. 245.

No court in Europe is too good for thee;
What dost thou then in prison?
The Winter's Tale. Act ii, sc. 2, l. 3. [Paulina]

2
Your lordship may minister the potion of imprisonment to me in respect of poverty.
II Henry IV. Act i, sc. 2, l. 145. [Falstaff]

Hold himself safe in his prisonment.
King John. Act iii, sc. 4, l. 161. [Pandulph] The only use of "prisonment."

It was proclaimed a year's imprisonment, to be taken with a wench.
Love's Labour 's Lost. Act i, sc. 1, l. 289. [King]

Imprison him: if imprisonment be the due of a bawd, why, 'tis his right.
Measure for Measure. Act iii, sc. 2, l. 69. [Lucio]

Imprison him.—*King John,* iv, 2, 155; *Richard III,* ii, 2, 22.

You shall have your full time of imprisonment.
Measure for Measure. Act iv, sc. 2, l. 13. [Provost]

Your imprisonment shall not be long.
Richard III. Act i, sc. 1, l. 114. [Gloucester]

Long imprisonment.—*I Henry VI,* ii, 5, 4.

Easy-held imprisonment.—*I Henry VI,* v, 3, 139. The only use of "easy-held."

Late imprisonment.—*Richard III,* i, 3, 91.

3
Thy Doll, and Helen of thy noble thoughts,
Is in base durance and contagious prison;
Haled thither
By most mechanical and dirty hand.
II Henry IV. Act v, sc. 5, l. 35. [Pistol]

He upon some action Is now in durance.
Twelfth Night, v, 1, 283.

Claudio: Perpetual durance?
Isabella: Ay, just; perpetual durance, a restraint,
Though all the world's vastidity you had,
To a determined scope.
Measure for Measure. Act iii, sc. 1, l. 67. The only use of "vastidity."

Set thee from durance.—*Love's Labour 's Lost,* iii, 1, 130. The only use of "durance" in this sense. "Suits of durance" occurs in *The Comedy of Errors,* iv, 3, 27.

4
Carry Sir John Falstaff to the Fleet.
II Henry IV. Act v, sc. 5, l. 97. [Chief Justice] The only mention of the Fleet.

I 'll find
A Marshalsea shall hold ye play these two months.
Henry VIII. Act v, sc. 4, l. 90. [Lord Chamberlain] The only mention of the Marshalsea.

I have some of 'em in Limbo Patrum, and there they are like to dance these three days.
Henry VIII. Act v, sc. 4, l. 67. [Porter] The only use of "Limbo Patrum," the abode of the just who died before Christ's coming.

5
In prison hast thou spent a pilgrimage
And like a hermit overpass'd thy days.
I Henry VI. Act ii, sc. 5, l. 116. [Plantagenet] The only use of "overpass'd."

6
Let them be clapp'd up close.
II Henry VI. Act i, sc. 4, l. 53. [Buckingham]

To close prison he commanded her,
With many bitter threats of biding there.
The Two Gentlemen of Verona. Act iii, sc. 1, l. 235. [Proteus]

Darksome prison.—*The Rape of Lucrece,* l. 379. The only use of "darksome."

Earthy prison.—*Titus Andronicus,* i, 1, 99.

Hollow prison.—*Titus Andronicus,* iii, 2, 10.

Polluted prison.—*The Rape of Lucrece,* l. 1726.

Vaulty prison.—*The Rape of Lucrece,* l. 119.

Prison gates.—*A Midsummer-Night's Dream,* i, 2, 36.

Prison-house.—*Hamlet,* i, 5, 14.

Prison walls.—*Richard II,* v, 5, 21.

7
You four, from hence to prison back again;
From thence unto the place of execution.
II Henry VI. Act ii, sc. 3, l. 5. [King Henry]

Take him to prison;
And see our pleasure herein executed.
Measure for Measure. Act v, sc. 1, l. 526. [Duke]

Away with her to prison!—*Measure for Measure,* iii, 2, 201; *The Winter's Tale,* ii, 1, 103.

Away with him to prison.—*Measure for Measure,* v, 1, 325.

Away with them to prison.—*II Henry VI,* i, 3, 223.

Take him to prison.—*Measure for Measure,* iii, 2, 32.

Thou shalt to prison.—*Love's Labour 's Lost,* i, 2, 163.

To prison with her!—*Measure for Measure,* v, 1, 121; *All's Well that Ends Well,* v, 3, 283.

Let prison swallow 'em.—*Timon of Athens,* iv, 3, 537.

Roughly send to prison.—*II Henry IV,* v, 2, 70.

8
Go, lead the way; I long to see my prison.
II Henry VI. Act ii, sc. 4, l. 110. [Duchess of Gloucester]

Ah, let me live in prison all my days.
III Henry VI. Act i, sc. 3, l. 43. [Rutland]

Bear me to prison.—*Measure for Measure,* i, 2, 121.

Commend me to the prison.—*Measure for Measure,* iii, 2, 73.

On, officer, to prison.—*The Comedy of Errors,* iv, 1, 108.

1 Come, let 's away to prison:
We two alone will sing like birds i' the cage.
King Lear. Act v, sc. 3, l. 8. [King Lear]
We 'll wear out,
In a wall'd prison, packs and sects of great ones,
That ebb and flow by the moon.
King Lear. Act v, sc. 3, l. 17. [King Lear]
Our cage
We make a quire, as doth the prison'd bird,
And sing our bondage freely.
Cymbeline. Act iii, sc. 3, l. 42. [Arviragus] The only use of "prison'd."
I am trusted with a muzzle and enfranchised with a clog; therefore I have decreed not to sing in my cage.
Much Ado about Nothing. Act i, sc. 3, l. 34. [Don John]

2
There 's one yonder arrested and carried to prison was worth five thousand of you all.
Measure for Measure. Act i, sc. 2, l. 60. [Mistress Overdone]
Cast in prison.—*Cymbeline,* iii, 2, 38.

3
Othello: Where will you that I go
To answer this your charge?
Brabantio: To prison, till fit time
Of law and course of direct session
Call thee to answer.
Othello. Act i, sc. 2, l. 84.

4
I have been studying how I may compare
This prison where I live unto the world:
And for because the world is populous
And here is not a creature but myself,
I cannot do it.
Richard II. Act v, sc. 5, l. 1. [King Richard]

5 O thou bloody prison,
Fatal and ominous to noble peers!
Within the guilty closure of thy walls
Richard the second here was hack'd to death;
And, for more slander to thy dismal seat,
We give thee up our guiltless blood to drink.
Richard III. Act iii, sc. 3, l. 9. [Rivers] Referring to the Tower of London.
Then was I going prisoner to the Tower.
Richard III. Act iii, sc. 2, l. 102. [Hastings]
It stands agreed,
I take it, by all voices, that forthwith
You be convey'd to the Tower a prisoner.
Henry VIII. Act v, sc. 3, l. 87. [Chancellor]

6
Why will you mew her up?
The Taming of the Shrew. Act i, sc. 1, l. 87. [Gremio]
Mew up Your tender kinsman.
King John, iv, 2, 57. The only uses of "mew up."
Here you sty me In this hard rock.
The Tempest. Act i, sc. 2, l. 342. [Caliban] The only use of "sty" as a verb.

7
Tranio: Carry this mad knave to the gaol. . . .
Vincentio: Carry me to the gaol!
Gremio: Stay, officer; he shall not go to prison.
Baptista: I say he shall go to prison. . . .
Away with the dotard! to the gaol with him!
The Taming of the Shrew. Act v, sc. 1, l. 95.
I 'll slit the villain's nose that would have me sent to the gaol.
The Taming of the Shrew, v, 1, 135.
Meet me at the gaol.—*Much Ado about Nothing,* iii, 5, 69. "Gaol" is used eight times.
Naughty gaoler.—*The Merchant of Venice,* iii, 3, 9.
Steeled gaoler.—*Measure for Measure,* iv, 2, 90.
Gaoler to his pity.—*Coriolanus,* v, 1, 65. "Gaoler" is used thirteen times.

8
My father's loss, the weakness which I feel,
The wreck of all my friends, nor this man's threats,
To whom I am subdued, are but light to me,
Might I but through my prison once a day
Behold this maid: all corners else o' the earth
Let liberty make use of; space enough
Have I in such a prison.
Tempest. Act i, sc. 2, l. 487. [Ferdinand]

9
Sperr up the sons of Troy.
Troilus and Cressida. Prologue, l. 19. The only use of "sperr" (shut).

10
Peace in this prison!
Twelfth Night. Act iv, sc. 2, l. 21. [Clown]
Why have you suffer'd me to be imprison'd,
Kept in a dark house, visited by a priest?
Twelfth Night. Act v, sc. 1, l. 349. [Malvolio]

11 Here 's ado,
To lock up honesty and honour from
The access of gentle visitors!
Winter's Tale. Act ii, sc. 2, l. 9. [Paulina]

II—Prisoner

See also Captive

12 You 're my prisoner, but
Your gaoler shall deliver you the keys
That lock up your restraint.
Cymbeline. Act i, sc. 1, l. 72. [Queen]
Thou art my prisoner.—*I Henry VI,* v, 3, 45.
He is my prisoner.—*The Comedy of Errors,* iv, 4, 115.
He is your prisoner.—*II Henry VI,* iii, 1, 187.
I am thy prisoner.—*I Henry VI,* v, 3, 74; *The Comedy of Errors,* iv, 4, 113.
Then am I the prisoner.—*King Lear,* iv, 6, 271.

13
You shall not now be stol'n, you have locks upon you;
So graze as you find pasture.
Cymbeline. Act v, sc. 4, l. 1. [Gaoler]

14
Knock off his manacles; bring your prisoner.
Cymbeline. Act v, sc. 4, l. 199. [Messenger]

We'll put you . . . in manacles.—*Coriolanus,* i, 9, 57.
Led With manacles through our streets.—*Coriolanus,* v, 3, 115.
Manacles of the all-building law.—*Measure for Measure,* ii, 4, 93. The only uses of "manacles."
I'll manacle thy neck and feet together.
The Tempest, i, 2, 461. See under PUNISHMENT.
Manacle the bear-ward.—*II Henry VI,* v, 1, 149.
Manacle of love.—*Cymbeline,* i, 1, 122. The only uses of "manacle."

1
Like prisoners wildly over-grown with hair.
Henry V. Act v, sc. 2, l. 43. [Burgundy]

2
Talbot: I go to certify her Talbot's here.
Countess: If thou be he, then art thou prisoner.
Talbot: Prisoner! to whom?
Countess: To me, blood-thirsty lord;
And for that cause I train'd thee to my house.
I Henry VI. Act ii, sc. 3, l. 32.
Lucy: I come to know what prisoners thou hast ta'en
And to survey the bodies of the dead.
Charles: For prisoners ask'st thou? hell our prison is.
I Henry VI. Act iv, sc. 7, l. 56.
Rivers: Then is my sovereign slain?
Queen Elizabeth: Ay, almost slain, for he is taken prisoner.
III Henry VI. Act iv, sc. 4, l. 6.
Ta'en prisoner.—*II Henry IV,* i, 1, 126; *King John,* iii, 4, 7; *The Rape of Lucrece,* l. 1608.
Taken prisoners.—*I Henry VI,* iv, 1, 26.
Took prisoner.—*I Henry VI,* i, 1, 145.

3
Master, this prisoner freely give I thee.
II Henry VI. Act iv, sc. 1, l. 12. [Captain]
The prisoner is a prince.—*II Henry VI,* iv, 1, 44.

4
Break open the gaols and let out the prisoners.
II Henry VI. Act iv, sc. 3, l. 18. [Dick]
Ransomless here we set our prisoners free.
Titus Andronicus, i, 1, 274. [Saturninus]
Deliver him
Up to his pleasure, ransomless and free.
I Henry IV. Act v, sc. 5, l. 27. [Prince of Wales] The only uses of "ransomless."

5
I was my chamber's prisoner.
Henry VIII. Act i, sc. 1, l. 13. [Buckingham]

6
It is not for prisoners to be too silent in their words; and therefore I will say nothing.
Love's Labour 's Lost, i, 2, 168. [Costard]

7
Thou wert immured, restrained, captivated, bound.
Love's Labour 's Lost. Act iii, sc. 1, l. 125. [Armado] The only use of "captivated."
Immured in the brain.—*Love's Labour 's Lost,* iv, 3, 328.
Immured within your walls.—*Richard III,* iv, 1, 100.
In silver she's immured.—*The Merchant of Venice,* ii, 7, 52.

8
One that is a prisoner nine years old.
Measure for Measure. Act iv, sc. 2, l. 135. [Provost]
Imprison'd thou didst painfully remain
A dozen years.
The Tempest. Act i, sc. 2, l. 278. [Prospero]
Else you had looked through the grate, like a geminy of baboons.
Merry Wives of Windsor. Act ii, sc. 2, l. 8. [Falstaff] The only use of "geminy" (pair).

9
You shall close prisoner rest,
Till that the nature of your fault be known
To the Venetian state.
Othello. Act v, sc. 2, l. 335. [Lodovico]
Doom'd a prisoner.—*Richard II,* v, 1, 4.
Prisoner to the palsy.—*Richard II,* i, 3, 104.

10
Gloucester: How hath your lordship brook'd imprisonment?
Hastings: With patience, noble lord, as prisoners must.
Richard III. Act i, sc. 1, l. 125.
He is frank'd up to fatting for his pains.
Richard III. Act i, sc. 3, l. 314. [Gloucester] The only use of "frank'd" and "fatting."
Shut up in prison, kept without my food,
Whipp'd and tormented.
Romeo and Juliet. Act i, sc. 2, l. 57. [Romeo]

11
Like a poor prisoner in his twisted gyves.
Romeo and Juliet, ii, 2, 180. See under PARTING.
In gyves.—*Cymbeline,* v, 4, 14.
Redeem you from your gyves.—*Measure for Measure,* iv, 2, 12.
Convert his gyves to graces.—*Hamlet,* iv, 7, 21.
As if they had gyves on.—*I Henry IV,* iv, 2, 44.
Unconstrained gyves.—*A Lover's Complaint.* The only uses of "gyves."
I will gyve thee.—*Othello,* ii, 1, 171. The only use of "gyve."

12
A liquid prisoner pent in walls of glass.
Sonnets. No. v.
Fairest prisoner.—*Cymbeline,* i, 1, 123.
Noble prisoner.—*Julius Cæsar,* v, 4, 15.
Poor prisoner.—*The Winter's Tale,* ii, 2, 28.
Scottish prisoners.—*I Henry IV,* i, 3, 259.
Trojan prisoner.—*Troilus and Cressida,* iii, 3, 18.

13
Give us the proudest prisoner of the Goths,
That we may hew his limbs, and on a pile
Ad manes fratrum sacrifice his flesh.
Titus Andronicus. Act i, sc. 1, l. 96. [Lucius] The only use of "ad manes fratrum." "Manes" is repeated in ii, 1, 135: "Per manes vehor."
Mount her pitch, whom thou in triumph long
Hast prisoner held, fetter'd in amorous chains.
Titus Andronicus. Act ii, sc. 1, l. 14. [Aaron]
Leading him prisoner in a red-rose chain.
Venus and Adonis, l. 110. The only use of "red-rose."

1
Force me to keep you as a prisoner,
Not like a guest.
The Winter's Tale, i, 2, 52. [Hermione]
To be your prisoner should import offending;
Which is for me less easy to commit
Than you to punish.
The Winter's Tale, i, 2, 57. [Polixenes]

PRIVACY

2
Tell him privily of our intent.
III Henry VI. Act i, sc. 2, l. 39. [York]
I 'll privily away.—*Measure for Measure*, i, 1, 68.
I will privily relieve him.—*King Lear*, iii, 3, 15.
He privily Deals.—*Henry VIII*, i, 1, 183. The only uses of "privily."
3
And yet the king not privy to my drift.
III Henry VI. Act i, sc. 2, l. 46. [York]
Privy to thy country's fate.—*Hamlet*, i, 1, 133.
Privy to their late escape.—*The Winter's Tale*, ii, 1, 94.
Privy to those faults.—*II Henry VI*, iii, 1, 47.
Privy to the marriage.—*Romeo and Juliet*, v, 3, 266.
Privy to the plot.—*The Two Gentlemen of Verona*, iii, 1, 12.
Privy to your wishes.—*Antony and Cleopatra*, i, 2, 42.
Privy to none of this.—*Winter's Tale*, ii, 1, 95.
4
I myself will lead a private life.
III Henry VI. Act iv, sc. 6, l. 42. [King Henry]
Let me enjoy my private.—*Twelfth Night*, iii, 4, 100.
I left him private.—*Henry VIII*, ii, 2, 15.
Private in his chamber.—*Romeo and Juliet*, i, 1, 144.
5
We are too open here to argue this;
Let 's think in private more.
Henry VIII. Act ii, sc. 1, l. 168. [Gentleman]
6
Fie! privacy? fie!
The Merry Wives of Windsor. Act iv, sc. 5, l. 24. [Host]
Achilles: Of this my privacy
I have strong reasons.
Ulysses: But 'gainst your privacy
The reasons are more potent and heroical.
Troilus and Cressida. Act iii, sc. 3, l. 190. The only uses of "privacy."
7
This night,
We 'll pass the business privately and well.
The Taming of the Shrew. Act iv, sc. 4, l. 57. [Tranio]
Be it as you shall privately determine.
Othello. Act i, sc. 3, l. 276. [Duke]
Speak it privately.—*The Merchant of Venice*, ii, 4, 21.
He hears nought privately.—*Troilus and Cressida*, i, 3, 249.
Handled her privately.—*Measure for Measure*, v, 1, 277.
Privately twice or thrice.—*The Winter's Tale*, v, 2, 114. The only uses of "privately."

PRIVILEGE

8
You need but plead your honourable privilege.
All's Well that Ends Well. Act iv, sc. 5, l. 95. [Countess]
9
Thou hast lost thy princely privilege
With vile participation.
I Henry IV. Act iii, sc. 2, l. 86. [King Henry] "Participation" is repeated in *II Henry IV*, v, 1, 77.
10
He bears him on the place's privilege.
I Henry VI. Act ii, sc. 4, l. 86. [Plantagenet]
Adorn his temples with a coronet,
And yet, in substance and authority,
Retain but privilege of a private man?
I Henry VI. Act v, sc. 4, l. 134. [Alençon]
11
I beg the ancient privilege of Athens.
A Midsummer-Night's Dream. Act i, sc. 1, l. 41. [Egeus]
Demetrius: What should I get therefore?
Hermia: A privilege never to see me more.
A Midsummer-Night's Dream. Act iii, sc. 2, l. 78.
12
Such neighbour nearness to our sacred blood
Should nothing privilege him.
Richard II. Act i, sc. 1, l. 119. [King Richard] "Nearness" is repeated in ii, 2, 127, and occurs in no other play.
Presuming on an ague's privilege.
Richard II. Act ii, sc. 1, l. 116. [King Richard]
13
You break no privilege nor charter there.
Richard III. Act iii, sc. 1, l. 54. [Buckingham]
14
Nor age nor honour shall shape privilege.
Titus Andronicus. Act iv, sc. 4, l. 57. [Saturninus]
15
He is a privileged man.
Troilus and Cressida. Act ii, sc. 3, l. 61. [Achilles]
You 're privileged.—*Henry VIII*, i, 4, 52.
Cum privilegio.—*The Taming of the Shrew*, iv, 4, 93; *Henry VIII*, i, 3, 34.
16
The child-bed privilege denied, which 'longs
To women of all fashion.
The Winter's Tale. Act iii, sc. 2, l. 104. [Hermione]
Holy privilege of blessed sanctuary.—*Richard III*, iii, 1, 41.
Privilege of age.—*Much Ado about Nothing*, v, 1, 60.
Privilege of antiquity.—*All's Well that Ends Well*, ii, 3, 220.
Privilege of mine honours.—*King Lear*, v, 3, 129.
Privilege of nature.—*Coriolanus*, v, 3, 25.
Privilege your beauty bears.—*Titus Andronicus*, iv, 2, 116.
Men's privilege.—*Troilus and Cressida*, iii, 2, 136.
Rotten privilege.—*Coriolanus*, i, 10, 23.

PRIZE

See also Reward

1
If beauty, wisdom, modesty, can settle
The heart of Antony, Octavia is
A blessed lottery to him.
Antony and Cleopatra. Act ii, sc. 2, l. 246. [Mecænas]

2
And is not this an honourable spoil?
A gallant prize? ha, cousin, is it not?
I Henry IV. Act i, sc. 1, l. 74. [King Henry]

3
A goodly prize, fit for the devil's grace!
I Henry VI. Act v, sc. 3, l. 33. [York]
He brought home noble prize.—*Troilus and Cressida,* ii, 2, 86.
A proclaim'd prize!—*King Lear,* iv, 6, 230.
Lawful prize.—*Othello,* i, 2, 51.
Wicked prize.—*Hamlet,* iii, 3, 59.

4
My lord, a prize, a prize! here 's the Lord Say, which sold the towns in France; he that made us pay one and twenty fifteens, and one shilling to the pound, the last subsidy.
II Henry VI. Act iv, sc. 7, l. 22. [Messenger] "Subsidy" is repeated in *III Henry VI,* iv, 8, 45.
A prize! a prize!—*The Two Gentlemen of Verona,* v, 4, 121; *The Winter's Tale,* iv, 3, 31; *Pericles,* iv, 1, 94.

5
It is war's prize to take all vantages.
III Henry VI, i, 4, 59. See under WAR.

6
This is not Brutus, friend; but, I assure you,
A prize no less.
Julius Cæsar. Act v, sc. 4, l. 27. [Antony]

7
I come by note, to give and to receive.
Like one of two contending in a prize,
That thinks he hath done well in people's eyes.
The Merchant of Venice. Act iii, sc. 2, l. 141. [Bassanio]

8
Give fire: she is my prize, or ocean whelm them all!
The Merry Wives of Windsor. Act ii, sc. 2, l. 143. [Pistol] The only use of "whelm."
He is my prize.—*Troilus and Cressida,* v, 6, 10.

9
Bound for the prize of all too precious you.
Sonnets. No. lxxxvi.
But, rising at thy name, doth point out thee
As his triumphant prize.
Sonnets. No. cli.

10
This swift business
I must uneasy make, lest too light winning
Make the prize light.
The Tempest. Act i, sc. 2, l. 450. [Prospero]
For the prize I 'll bring thee to
Shall hoodwink this mischance.
The Tempest. Act iv, sc. 1, l. 205. [Caliban]

11
You have play'd your prize.
Titus Andronicus. Act i, sc. 1, l. 399. [Saturninus]

PROBABILITY

12
The least of all these signs was probable.
II Henry VI. Act iii, sc. 2, l. 178. [Warwick]
How probable I do not know.
Coriolanus. Act iv, sc. 6, l. 65. [Messenger]
'Tis . . . very probable!—*As You Like It,* iii, 5, 11.
It may be probable.—*Cymbeline,* ii, 4, 115.
Most probable.—*Antony and Cleopatra,* v, 2, 356.
Yet is 't not probable.—*Cymbeline,* iv, 2, 141.

13
'Tis probable and palpable to thinking.
Othello. Act i, sc. 2, l. 76. [Brabantio]
Which to you shall seem probable.—*The Tempest,* v, 1, 249.
Probable lies.—*All 's Well that Ends Well,* iii, 6, 107.
Probable need.—*All 's Well that Ends Well,* ii, 4, 52. The only uses of "probable."

PROCEEDING

14
Come, we 'll inform them
Of our proceedings.
Coriolanus. Act ii, sc. 2, l. 163. [Brutus]
I'll acquaint our duteous citizens
With all your just proceedings.
Richard III. Act iii, sc. 5, l. 65. [Mayor]

15
Is this proceeding just and honourable?
II Henry IV. Act iv, sc. 2, l. 110. [Mowbray]
Just proceeding.—*All 's Well that Ends Well,* v, 3, 236.
I like this fair proceeding.—*II Henry IV,* v, 5, 103.
Fair proceedings.—*King John,* iii, 1, 97.
Contrary proceedings.—*Henry VIII,* iii, 2, 26.
Discreet proceeding.—*King Lear,* i, 4, 233.
Dull proceeding.—*The Two Gentlemen of Verona,* ii, 6, 41.
Foul proceedings.—*Titus Andronicus,* v, 3, 8; *Othello,* i, 3, 65.
Manifest proceeding.—*The Merchant of Venice,* iv, 1, 358.
Merciless proceeding.—*King John,* ii, 1, 214.
Quick proceeders, marry.—*The Taming of the Shrew,* iv, 2, 11. The only use of "proceeders."

16
What plain proceeding is more plain than this?
II Henry VI. Act ii, sc. 2, l. 53. [Warwick]

17
Proceeded well to stop all good proceeding!
Love's Labour's Lost. Act i, sc. 1, l. 95. [Dumain]
Good proceeding.—*All 's Well that Ends Well,* ii, 4, 50.

18
To these violent proceedings all my neighbours shall cry aim.
The Merry Wives of Windsor. Act iii, sc. 2, l. 44. [Ford]
Push on this proceeding.—*The Winter's Tale,* ii, 1, 179.
Proceedings of a drunken brain.—*Venus and Adonis,* l. 910.

PROCESS

1 Proceed by process;
Lest parties, as he is beloved, break out
And sack great Rome with Romans.
Coriolanus. Act iii, sc. 1, l. 314. [Menenius]

2
Behind the arras I 'll convey myself
To hear the process.
Hamlet. Act iii, sc. 3, l. 29. [Polonius]

3 Thou mayst not coldly set
Our sovereign process.
Hamlet. Act iv, sc. 3, l. 64. [King]

Forged process.—*Hamlet,* i, 5, 37.
Needless process.—*Measure for Measure,* v, 1, 92.

4 After this process,
To give her the avaunt! it is a pity.
Henry VIII. Act ii, sc. 3, l. 9. [Anne]

5
And often at his very loose decides
That which long process could not arbitrate.
Love's Labour 's Lost. Act v, sc. 2, l. 752. [King]

6
Tell her the process of Antonio's end.
The Merchant of Venice. Act iv, sc. 1, l. 274. [Antonio]

Thou shalt tell the process of their death.
Richard III. Act iv, sc. 3, l. 32. [King Richard]

Process of thy kindness.—*Richard III,* iv, 4, 253.
Process of great nature.—*The Winter's Tale,* ii, 2, 60.
Process of the seasons.—*Sonnets,* civ.
Process of your speech.—*Troilus and Cressida,* iv, 1, 8.
Process of my travel.—*Richard II,* ii, 3, 12.
Such was the process.—*Othello,* i, 3, 142.

PROCLAMATION

7
Worcester: Was not he proclaim'd
By Richard that dead is the next of blood?
Northumberland: He was; I heard the proclamation.
I Henry IV. Act i, sc. 3, l. 145.

8
Nought rests for me in this tumultuous strife
But to make open proclamation.
I Henry VI. Act i, sc. 3, l. 70. [Mayor]

9
Sound trumpet; Edward shall be here proclaim'd:
Come, fellow-soldier, make thou proclamation
III Henry VI. Act iv, sc. 7, l. 69. [Hastings]

Is proclamation made?—*III Henry VI,* v, 5, 9.
Such proclamation hath been made.—*Richard III,* iv, 4, 519.

10
Chamberlain: What news, Sir Thomas Lovell?
Lovell: I hear of none, but the new proclamation
That 's clapp'd upon the court-gate.
Chamberlain: What is 't for?
Lovell: The reformation of our travell'd gallants.
Henry VIII. Act i, sc. 3, l. 16. "Court-gate" is repeated in *II Henry IV,* iii, 2, 33.

11
King: Did you hear the proclamation?
Costard: I do confess much of the hearing it, but little of the marking of it.
King: It was proclaimed a year's imprisonment to be taken with a wench.
Costard: I was taken with none, sir: I was taken with a damsel.
King: Well, it was proclaimed 'damsel.'
Costard: This was no damsel neither, sir; she was a virgin.
King: It is so varied too: for it was proclaimed 'virgin.'
Love's Labour 's Lost. Act i, sc. 1, l. 286.

Agreeing with the proclamation.—*Measure for Measure,* i, 2, 81.
Better proclamation.—*Measure for Measure,* iii, 2, 152.
Bloody proclamation.—*King Lear,* v, 3, 183.
Proclamation of thy passion.—*All 's Well that Ends Well,* i, 3, 180.

12
Ajax: Toadstool, learn me the proclamation.
Thersites: Dost thou think I have no sense, thou strikest me thus?
Ajax: The proclamation!
Thersites: Thou art proclaimed a fool, I think. . . .
Ajax: I say, the proclamation! . . . I bade the vile owl go learn me the tenour of the proclamation. . . .
Achilles: Marry, this, sir, is proclaim'd through all our host:
That Hector, by the fifth hour of the sun,
Will with a trumpet 'twixt our tents and Troy
To-morrow morning call some knight to arms
That hath a stomach.
Troilus and Cressida. Act ii, sc. 1, l. 22. The only use of "toadstool."

13
There is a proclamation that you are vanished.
The Two Gentlemen of Verona. Act iii, sc. 1, l. 216. [Launce]

Is your countryman
According to our proclamation gone?
The Two Gentlemen of Verona. Act iii, sc. 2, l. 11. [Duke]

14 These proclamations,
So forcing faults upon Hermione,
I little like.
The Winter's Tale. Act iii, sc. 1, l. 15. [Cleomenes]

PRODIGALITY

15
Shall I keep your hogs and eat husks with them? What prodigal portion have I spent, that I should come to such penury?
As You Like It. Act i, sc. 1, l. 40. [Orlando]

A hundred and fifty tattered prodigals lately come from swine-keeping, from eating draff and husks.

I Henry IV. Act iv, sc. 2, l. 37. [Falstaff] The only use of "swine-keeping." "Draff" (hog-wash) is repeated in *The Merry Wives of Windsor*, iv, 2, 109: "Still swine eats all the draff."

1
We may boldly spend upon the hope of what
Is to come in.

I Henry IV. Act iv, sc. 1, l. 54. [Douglas]

Look, what an unthrift in the world doth spend
Shifts but his place, for still the world enjoys it.

Sonnets. No. ix.

While I play the good husband at home, my son and my servant spend all at the university.

The Taming of the Shrew. Act v, sc. 1, l. 71. [Vincentio]

2 So sicken'd their estates, that never
They shall abound as formerly.

Henry VIII. Act i, sc. 1, l. 82. [Abergavenny]

My noble gossips, ye have been too prodigal.

Henry VIII. Act v, sc. 5, l. 13. [King Henry]

3
I have wasted myself out of my means.

Othello. Act iv, sc. 2, l. 186. [Roderigo]

4
If that one be prodigal,
Bountiful they will him call,
And with such-like flattering,
'Pity but he were a king.'

The Passionate Pilgrim, l. 411.

Prodigality of nature.—*Richard III*, i, 2, 244. The only use of "prodigality." See under GENTLEMAN.

5
He 's a very fool and a prodigal.

Twelfth Night. Act i, sc. 3, l. 25. [Maria]

A bankrupt, a prodigal.—*The Merchant of Venice*, iii, 1, 46.

I was No prodigal.—*Timon of Athens*, iv, 3, 278.

Niggard prodigal.—*The Rape of Lucrece*, l. 79.

Prodigal enough.—*Hamlet*, i, 3, 36.

6
I have received my proportion, like the prodigious son.

The Two Gentlemen of Verona. Act ii, sc. 3, l. 3. [Launce]

7
Be prodigal: the lamp that burns by night
Dries up his oil to lend the world his light.

Venus and Adonis, l. 755.

Spare not to spend.—*The Passionate Pilgrim*, l. 324.

PROFESSION

See also Occupation, Trade

8
He was famous, sir, in his profession.

All's Well that Ends Well. Act i, sc. 1, l. 29. [Countess]

The greatest Of his profession.—*All's Well that Ends Well*, i, 3, 250.

High profession.—*Henry VIII*, ii, 4, 117.

9
I . . . would not change that calling.

As You Like It. Act i, sc. 2, l. 246. [Orlando]

Ne'er a fantastical knave of them all shall flout me out of my calling.

As You Like It. Act iii, sc. 3, l. 107. [Sir Oliver]

I seek not to advance
Or raise myself, but keep my wonted calling.

I Henry VI. Act iii, sc. 1, l. 31. [Winchester]

10
Which for sport sake are content to do the profession some grace.

I Henry IV. Act ii, sc. 1, l. 78. [Gadshill]

My profession 's sacred.—*I Henry VI*, i, 2, 114.

11
Woe upon ye And all such false professors!

Henry VIII. Act iii, sc. 1, l. 115. [Queen Katharine]

Professors of one faith.—*I Henry VI*, v, 1, 14.

The zeal of all professors.—*The Winter's Tale*, v, 1, 108. The only uses of "professors."

Knavish professions.—*The Winter's Tale*, iv, 3, 105.

Limited professions.—*Timon of Athens*, iv, 3, 431.

12
Is this a holiday? what! know you not,
Being mechanical, you ought not walk
Upon a labouring day without the sign
Of your profession?

Julius Cæsar. Act i, sc. 1, l. 2. [Flavius]

13
I had thought to have let in some of all professions.

Macbeth. Act ii, sc. 3, l. 21. [Porter]

14
We do not know what 's brought to pass under the profession of fortune-telling.

Merry Wives of Windsor, iv, 2, 184. See under MAGIC. The only use of "fortune-telling."

15
Lysimachus: How long have you been at this profession?
Marina: E'er since I can remember.
Lysimachus: Did you go to 't so young?
Were you a gamester at five or at seven?

Pericles. Act iv, sc. 6, l. 78.

She makes our profession as it were to stink afore the face of the gods.

Pericles. Act iv, sc. 6, l. 144. [Boult]

16
He has almost charmed me from my profession, by persuading me to it.

Timon of Athens. Act iv, sc. 3, l. 454. [Bandit]

Therein am I constant to my profession.

The Winter's Tale. Act iv, sc. 4, l. 698. [Autolycus]

PROFIT

See also Gain

17 To apprehend thus,
Draws us a profit from all things we see.

Cymbeline, iii, 3, 17. See under SERVICE.

18
Profits will accrue.

Henry V. Act ii, sc. 1, l. 117. [Pistol] The only use of "accrue."

Has not the boy profited?—*II Henry IV*, ii, 2, 90.

For profit's sake.—*I Henry VI*, iii, 3, 63.

1 The profits of my death
Were very pregnant and potential spurs
To make thee seek it.
King Lear. Act ii, sc. 1, l. 77. [Edmund] "Potential" is repeated in *Othello,* i, 2, 13: "A voice potential."

2
Profit again should hardly draw me here.
Macbeth. Act v, sc. 3, l. 62. [Doctor]

3
Snail-slow in profit.
The Merchant of Venice. Act ii, sc. 5, l. 47. [Shylock] The only use of "snail-slow."
But little for my profit.—*Henry VIII,* iii, 1, 83.
I profit not by thy talk.—*Troilus and Cressida,* v, 1, 16.
There 's no profit.—*Cymbeline,* iv, 2, 163.
Without profit.—*Richard II,* iii, 4, 38.
Mere profit.—*Pericles,* iv, 2, 132.
Peculiar profit.—*Othello,* iii, 3, 79.
Profit of excess.—*The Rape of Lucrece,* l. 138.
Profit of our hope.—*Hamlet,* ii, 2, 24.
Profit of the city.—*The Merchant of Venice,* iii, 3, 30.
Profit of the state.—*Henry VIII,* iii, 2, 174.
Profit of this land.—*Richard II,* iv, 1, 225.

4
The purchase made, the fruits are to ensue;
That profit 's yet to come 'tween me and you.
Othello. Act ii, sc. 3, l. 9. [Othello]
I thank you for this profit.
Othello. Act iii, sc. 3, l. 379. [Iago]
Do yourself a profit.—*Othello,* iv, 2, 238.
Made thee more profit.—*The Tempest,* i, 2, 172.

5
Thou canst not do a thing in the world so soon,
To yield thee so much profit.
Pericles. Act iv, sc. 1, l. 3. [Leonine]
How have I offended,
Wherein my death might yield her any profit?
Pericles. Act iv, sc. 1, l. 81. [Marina]
Mark me: you must seem to . . . despise profit where you have most gain.
Pericles. Act iv, sc. 2, l. 127. [Bawd]

6
No profit grows where is no pleasure ta'en.
The Taming of the Shrew. Act i, sc. 1, l. 39. [Tranio]

PROGRESS

7
Of that and all the progress, more and less,
Resolvedly more leisure shall express.
All's Well that Ends Well. Act v, sc. 3, l. 331. [King] The only use of "resolvedly."

8
The king is now in progress towards Saint Alban's.
II Henry VI. Act i, sc. 4, l. 76. [York]
In progress to be hatch'd.—*Measure for Measure,* ii, 2, 97.
I' the progress of this business.—*Henry VIII,* ii, 4, 175.

9
A peaceful progress to the ocean.
King John. Act ii, sc. 1, l. 340. [King John]
Golden progress.—*I Henry IV,* iii, 1, 222.
Native progress.—*Romeo and Juliet,* iv, 1, 97.
Time's thievish progress.—*Sonnets,* lxxvii.

PROJECT

See also Shift

10
My project may deceive me.
All's Well that Ends Well. Act i, sc. 1, l. 243. [Helena]

11 This project
Should have a back or second, that might hold,
If this should blast in proof.
Hamlet. Act iv, sc. 7, l. 153. [King]

12
Always bending Towards their project.
The Tempest. Act iv, sc. 1, l. 174. [Ariel]
Now does my project gather to a head.
The Tempest. Act v, sc. 1, l. 1. [Prospero]

13
Our project's life this shape of sense assumes.
Troilus and Cressida. Act i, sc. 3, l. 385. [Ulysses]

14
Else his project dies.
The Tempest. Act ii, sc. 1, l. 299. [Ariel]
Else my project fails.—*The Tempest,* Epil., 12.
Settled project.—*The Winter's Tale,* iv, 4, 535.
Project of affection.—*Much Ado about Nothing,* iii, 1, 55.
So dire a project.—*Troilus and Cressida,* ii, 2, 134.

15 Determine on some course,
More than a wild exposture to each chance
That starts i' the way before thee.
Coriolanus. Act iv, sc. 1, l. 36. [Volumnia] The only use of "exposture."

16
In deep designs and matters of great moment.
Richard III. Act iii, sc. 7, l. 67. [Buckingham]
Be not peevish-fond in great designs.
Richard III. Act iv, sc. 4, l. 417. [King Richard] The only use of "peevish-fond."
Why, there you touch'd the life of our design.
Troilus and Cressida. Act ii, sc. 2, l. 194. [Troilus]

PROLOGUE

17
Thus he his special nothing ever prologues.
All's Well that Ends Well. Act ii, sci 1, l. 95. [King]

18
Is this a prologue, or the posy of a ring?
Hamlet. Act iii, sc. 2, l. 162. [Hamlet]
Ere I could make a prologue to my brains,
They had begun the play.
Hamlet. Act v, sc. 2, l. 30. [Hamlet]
Prologues to a bad voice.—*As You Like It,* v, 3, 13.
Prologue to his sleep.—*Othello,* ii, 3, 134.

19
Prologue-like your humble patience pray,
Gently to hear, kindly to judge, our play.
Henry V. Prologue, l. 33. [Chorus]

20
But mine is made the prologue to their play;
For thousands more, that yet suspect no peril,

Will not conclude their plotted tragedy.
II Henry VI. Act iii, sc. 1, l. 151. [Gloucester]

Prologue vilely penn'd.—*Love's Labour 's Lost,* v, 2, 305.

Happy prologues.—*Macbeth,* i, 3, 128.

1

Bottom: Write me a prologue; and let the prologue seem to say, we will do no harm with our swords and that Pyramus is not killed indeed; and, for the more better assurance, tell them that I Pyramus am not Pyramus, but Bottom the weaver: this will put them out of fear.
Quince: Well, we will have such a prologue; and it shall be written in eight and six.
Bottom: No, make it two more; let it be written in eight and eight.
Snout: Will not the ladies be afeard of the lion? . . . Another prologue must tell he is not a lion.
Bottom: Nay, you must name his name.
A Midsummer-Night's Dream. Act iii, sc. 1, l. 18.

Lysander: He hath rid his prologue like a rough colt; he knows not the stop. . . .
Hippolyta: Indeed he hath played on his prologue like a child on a recorder; a sound, but not to government.
A Midsummer-Night's Dream. Act v, sc. 1, l. 119.

2

No without-book prologue, faintly spoke
After the prompter, for our entrance.
Romeo and Juliet. Act i, sc. 4, l. 7. [Benvolio] The only use of "without-book."

A prologue arm'd, but not in confidence
Of author's pen or actor's voice.
Troilus and Cressida. Prologue, l. 23.

PROMISE

See also Pledge

3

From Antony win Cleopatra: promise,
And in our name, what she requires; add more,
From thine invention, offers.
Antony and Cleopatra. Act iii, sc. 12, l. 27. [Cæsar]

I have performed . . . my promise.
Antony and Cleopatra. Act v, sc. 2, l. 203. [Dolabella]

4

If you do keep your promises in love
But justly, as you have exceeded all promise,
Your mistress shall be happy.
As You Like It. Act i, sc. 2, l. 255. [Celia]

Keep promise, love.—*A Midsummer-Night's Dream,* i, 1, 179; *The Merchant of Venice,* ii, 3, 20.

You do not keep your promise.—*Twelfth Night,* v, 1, 106.

If promises be kept.—*I Henry IV,* iii, 2, 168.

5

If you break one jot of your promise or come one minute behind your hour, I will think you the most pathetical break-promise and the most hollow lover and the most unworthy of her you call Rosalind that may be chosen out of the gross band of the unfaithful: therefore beware my censure and keep your promise.
As You Like It. Act iv, sc. 1, l. 194. [Rosalind] The only use of "break-promise" and "unfaithful."

You might excuse His broken promise.
As You Like It. Act iv, sc. 3, l. 154. [Oliver]

To break promise with him.
Twelfth Night, ii, 3, 137. [Sir Andrew]

An hourly promise-breaker.—*All 's Well that Ends Well,* iii, 6, 12.

Worse than a promise-breaker.—*Coriolanus,* i, 8, 2. The only uses of the phrase.

6

You use this dalliance to excuse
Your breach of promise.
The Comedy of Errors. Act iv, sc. 1, l. 48. [Antipholus of Ephesus] The only use of "breach of promise."

7

Is this the promise that you made your mother?
Coriolanus. Act iii, sc. 3, l. 86. [Menenius]

Is this your promise?—*King John,* iv, 1, 97.

Former promise.—*Coriolanus,* i, 1, 242.

Deceiving promises.—*Measure for Measure,* iii, 2, 260.

As good as promise.—*Cymbeline,* v, 4, 137.

8

These promises are fair.
I Henry IV. Act iii, sc. 1, l. 1. [Mortimer]

Firm promise.—*The Taming of the Shrew,* ii, 1, 387.

Gracious promise.—*Coriolanus,* ii, 3, 201.

Greatest promise.—*The Winter's Tale,* i, 1, 39.

Wonderful promise.—*Twelfth Night,* iii, 4, 290.

9

This, in the name of God, I promise here:
The which if He be pleased I shall perform.
I Henry IV. Act iii, sc. 2, l. 153. [Prince of Wales]

I have promised to make all this matter even.
As You Like It. Act v, sc. 4, l. 18. [Rosalind]

I have pass'd
My word and promise to the emperor.
Titus Andronicus. Act i, sc. 1, l. 468. [Tamora]

I promise thee (you).—*I Henry VI,* iv, i, 174, and fifteen times in later plays.

I make thee promise.—*Julius Cæsar,* ii, 1, 56.

Made promise.—*The Merry Wives of Windsor,* iv, 6, 34.

It is my promise.—*The Tempest,* iv, 1, 41.

Promise you infinitely.—*II Henry IV,* Epil., 17.

What do you promise me?—*All 's Well that Ends Well,* ii, 1, 193.

I cannot promise.—*Henry VIII,* iii, 2, 4.

10

Who never promiseth but he means to pay.
I Henry IV. Act v, sc. 4, l. 43. See under Payment.

Promiseth a mighty fruit.—*King John,* ii, 1, 473.

Promiseth successful fortune.—*III Henry VI,* ii, 2, 40. The only uses of "promiseth."

1
'Tis hereafter to know, but now to promise: do but now promise, Kate, you will endeavour for your French part of such a boy.
Henry V. Act v, sc. 2, l. 226. [King Henry]

2
Thy promises are like Adonis' gardens
That one day bloom'd and fruitful were the next.
I Henry VI. Act i, sc. 6, l. 6. [Charles]

3
I cheer'd them up with justice of our cause,
With promise of high pay and great rewards.
III Henry VI. Act ii, sc. 1, l. 133. [Warwick]

'Tis but reason that I be released
From giving aid which late I promised.
III Henry VI. Act iii, sc. 3, l. 147. [King Lewis]

Promise aid.—*The Rape of Lucrece,* l. 1696.
Promises assurance.—*Antony and Cleopatra,* iii, 7, 47.
Promise noble service.—*Cymbeline,* iv, 2, 339.
Promises royal peril.—*Antony and Cleopatra,* iv, 8, 35.
Promise them success.—*Richard III,* iv, 4, 193.

4
Every drop of blood
That every Roman bears, and nobly bears,
Is guilty of a several bastardy,
If he do break the smallest particle
Of any promise that hath pass'd from him.
Julius Cæsar. Act ii, sc. 1, l. 136. [Brutus] "Particle" is repeated in *Twelfth Night,* i, 5, 264.

5
If that from him there may be aught applied
Which may her suffering ecstasy assuage,
'Tis promised in the charity of age.
A Lover's Complaint, l. 68.

6
Be these juggling fiends no more believed,
That palter with us in a double sense;
That keep the word of promise to our ear,
And break it to our hope.
Macbeth. Act v, sc. 8, l. 19. [Macbeth]

7
He was ever precise in promise-keeping.
Measure for Measure. Act i, sc. 2, l. 76. [Lucio] The only use of "promise-keeping."

8
Have you received no promise of satisfaction at her hands?
The Merry Wives of Windsor. Act ii, sc. 2, l. 217. [Falstaff]

Give him promise of satisfaction.—*Measure for Measure,* iii, 1, 275.
Promise of his life.—*All's Well that Ends Well,* iii, 6, 30.
Promise me life.—*The Merchant of Venice,* iii, 2, 34.

9
To build upon a foolish woman's promise.
The Merry Wives of Windsor. Act iii, sc. 5, l. 42. [Falstaff]

10
Desdemona: Come now, your promise.
Othello: What promise, chuck?
Othello. Act iii, sc. 4, l. 48.

Remember, as thou read'st, thy promise pass'd.
Richard II. Act v, sc. 3, l. 51. [Aumerle]

Thou didst promise to bate me a full year.
The Tempest. Act i, sc. 2, l. 249. [Ariel]

I claim the promise.—*The Two Gentlemen of Verona,* iv, 4, 92.
I'll claim that promise.—*Richard III,* iii, 1, 197.

11
'Twere as good a deed as to drink when a man's a-hungry, to challenge him the field, and then to break promise with him and make a fool of him.
Twelfth Night. Act ii, sc. 3, l. 135. [Sir Andrew]

He has promised me, as he is a gentleman and a soldier.
Twelfth Night. Act iii, sc. 4, l. 338. [Sir Toby]

He hath promised you more than that, or there be liars.
Winter's Tale. Act iv, sc. 4, l. 239. [Dorcas]

12
Upon this promise did he raise his chin,
Like a dive-dapper peering through a wave,
Who, being look'd on, ducks as quickly in;
So offers he to give what she did crave.
Venus and Adonis, l. 86. The only use of "dive-dapper" (dabchick).

13
I can smooth and fill his aged ear
With golden promises.
Titus Andronicus. Act iv, sc. 4, l. 96. [Tamora]

II—Promise and Performance

14
The duchess, I tell you, expects performance of your promises.
II Henry VI. Act i, sc. 4, l. 1. [Hume]

His promises were, as he then was, mighty;
But his performance, as he is now, nothing.
Henry VIII. Act iv, sc. 2, l. 41. [Katharine]

15
His promises fly so beyond his state
That what he speaks is all in debt.
Timon of Athens. Act i, sc. 2, l. 203. [Flavius]

Promise me friendship, but perform none: if thou wilt not promise, the gods plague thee, for thou art a man! if thou dost perform, confound thee, for thou art a man!
Timon of Athens. Act iv, sc. 3, l. 72. [Timon]

Promising is the very air o' the time: it opens the eyes of expectation: performance is ever the duller for his act; . . . To promise is most courtly and fashionable: performance is a kind of will or testament which argues a great sickness in his judgement that makes it.
Timon of Athens. Act v, sc. 1, l. 24. [Painter]

16
He will spend his mouth, and promise, like Brabbler the hound; but when he performs, astronomers foretell it.
Troilus and Cressida. Act v, sc. 1, l. 98. [Thersites] The only reference to Brabbler.

Why should our endeavour be so loved and the performance so loathed?
Troilus and Cressida. Act v, sc. 10, l. 39. [Pandarus]

PROOF

See also Testimony

1
The particular confirmations, point from point, to the full arming of the verity.
All's Well that Ends Well. Act iv, sc. 3, l. 71. [Lord]

Let heaven
Witness how dear I hold this confirmation.
Henry VIII. Act v, sc. 3, l. 174. [Cranmer]
Confirmation of my promised gift.—*All's Well that Ends Well,* ii, 3, 56.
Better confirmation.—*II Henry IV,* iv, 5, 189.
Greater confirmation.—*The Winter's Tale,* iii, 1, 180.
Jealous confirmations.—*Othello,* iii, 3, 323.

2
My fore-past proofs, howe'er the matter fall,
Shall tax my fears of little vanity.
All's Well that Ends Well. Act v, sc. 3, l. 121. [King] The only use of "fore-past."
This is his wife; That ring 's a thousand proofs.
All's Well that Ends Well. Act v, sc. 3, l. 198. [Count]

3
Here 's a voucher,
Stronger than ever law could make.
Cymbeline. Act ii, sc. 2, l. 39. [Iachimo]
His double vouchers.—*Hamlet,* v, 1, 114.
Will his vouchers vouch him?—*Hamlet,* v, 1, 117. The only uses of "vouchers."

4
Let proof speak.
Cymbeline. Act iii, sc. 1, l. 77. [Lucius]
Out of your proof you speak.
Cymbeline. Act iii, sc. 3, l. 27. [Guiderius]

5
This was sometime a paradox, but now the time gives it proof.
Hamlet. Act iii, sc. 1, l. 114. [Hamlet]

6
Well, we leave that to the proof.
I Henry IV. Act ii, sc. 2, l. 72. [Prince of Wales]
I 'll put 't in proof.—*King Lear,* iv, 6, 189.
Mark but this for proof.—*I Henry VI,* iii, 3, 68.

7
Only this proof I 'll of thy valour make.
I Henry VI. Act i, sc. 2, l. 94. [Charles]
Proof of arms.—*I Henry IV,* v, 2, 55.
Proofs of holy writ.—*Othello,* iii, 3, 324.
Proofs for sin.—*Measure for Measure,* iii, 2, 31.

8
Proofs as clear as founts in July when
We see each grain of gravel.
Henry VIII. Act i, sc. 1, l. 154. [Buckingham]
I do pronounce him in that very shape
He shall appear in proof.
Henry VIII. Act i, sc. 1, l. 196. [Buckingham]

9
His fact . . . came not to an undoubtful proof.
Measure for Measure. Act iv, sc. 2, l. 142. [Provost] The only use of "undoubtful."
We 'll leave a proof.—*The Merry Wives of Windsor,* iv, 2, 106.
Both the proofs are extant.—*The Merry Wives of Windsor,* v, 5, 126.

10
Confirm'd, confirm'd! O, that is stronger made
Which was before barr'd up with ribs of iron!
Much Ado about Nothing. Act iv, sc. 1, l. 152. [Leonato]
She was charged with nothing
But what was true and very full of proof.
Much Ado about Nothing. Act v, sc. 1, l. 104. [Don Pedro]

11
To vouch this, is no proof,
Without more wider and more overt test
Than these thin habits and poor likelihoods
Of modern seeming do prefer against him.
Othello. Act i, sc. 3, l. 106. [Duke] The only use of "overt."
Othello: I 'll see before I doubt; when I doubt, prove;
And on the proof, there is no more but this,—
Away at once with love or jealousy! . . .
Iago: I speak not yet of proof. . . .
Othello: Give me the ocular proof.
Othello. Act iii, sc. 3, l. 190. The only use of "ocular."

So prove it,
That the probation bear no hinge nor loop
To hang a doubt on.
Othello. Act iii, sc. 3, l. 364. [Othello]
This may help to thicken other proofs
That do demonstrate thinly.
Othello. Act iii, sc. 3, l. 430. [Iago]
I 'll have some proof.—*Othello,* iii, 3, 386.

12
And on just proof surmise accumulate.
Sonnets. No. cxvii.
Just proof.—*King Lear,* iii, 6, 120.
Childhood proof.—*The Merchant of Venice,* i, 1, 144.
Better proof.—*Venus and Adonis,* l. 626.
Common proof.—*Julius Cæsar,* ii, 1, 21.
Cruel proof.—*As You Like It,* i, 2, 184.
Hourly proof.—*Much Ado about Nothing,* ii, 1, 188.
Newer proof.—*Sonnets,* cx.
Others' proof.—*A Lover's Complaint,* l. 163.
Simular proof.—*Cymbeline,* v, 5, 200. "Simular" (counterfeited) is repeated in *King Lear,* iii, 2, 54.
Strong proof.—*Romeo and Juliet,* i, 1, 216; *Julius Cæsar,* ii, 1, 299.
True proof.—*Troilus and Cressida,* i, 3, 34.
Vulgar proof.—*Twelfth Night,* iii, 1, 135.
Proofs new-bleeding.—*A Lover's Complaint,* l. 153. The only use of "new-bleeding."

13
That I 'll prove upon thee, though thy little finger be armed in a thimble.
The Taming of the Shrew. Act iv, sc. 3, l. 148. [Grumio]
Make your proof.—*Twelfth Night,* i, 5, 67.
Ay, to the proof.—*The Taming of the Shrew,* ii, 1, 141.
I 'll bide your proof.—*Twelfth Night,* i, 5, 71.

14
Call me before the exactest auditors
And set me on the proof.
Timon of Athens. Act ii, sc. 2, l. 165. [Flavius]

1 Here, there, and every where, he leaves and takes,
Dexterity so obeying appetite
That what he will he does, and does so much
That proof is call'd impossibility.
Troilus and Cressida. Act v, sc. 5, l. 26. [Nestor]

2 That which I shall report will bear no credit,
Were not the proof so nigh.
The Winter's Tale. Act v, sc. 1, l. 179. [Lord]

That which you hear you'll swear you see, there is such unity in the proofs.
The Winter's Tale. Act v, sc. 2, l. 34. [Gentleman]

PROPERTY, see Possessions

PROPHECY

3 The prophecy like the parrot, 'beware the rope's end.'
The Comedy of Errors. Act iv, sc. 4, l. 45. [Dromio of Ephesus]

4 I will prophesy he comes to tell me of the players.
Hamlet. Act ii, sc. 2, l. 405. [Hamlet]

I do prophesy the election lights
On Fortinbras.
Hamlet. Act v, sc. 2, l. 366. [Hamlet]

O, I could prophesy,
But that the earthy and cold hand of death
Lies on my tongue.
I Henry IV. Act v, sc. 4, l. 83. [Hotspur]

And thus I prophesy, that many a thousand,
Which now mistrust no parcel of my fear,
And many an old man's sigh and many a widow's,
And many an orphan's water-standing eye—
Men for their sons, wives for their husbands,
And orphans for their parents' timeless death—
Shall rue the hour that ever thou wast born.
III Henry VI. Act v, sc. 6, l. 37. [King Henry] The only use of "water-standing."

Over thy wounds now do I prophesy.
Julius Cæsar. Act iii, sc. 1, l. 259. [Antony]

I prophesy thy death, my living sorrow.
Venus and Adonis, l. 671.

Since thou art dead, lo, here I prophesy.
Venus and Adonis, l. 1135.

Here I prophesy.—*I Henry VI,* ii, 4, 124; *Richard III,* iii, 4, 106.

Let me prophesy.—*Richard II,* iv, 1, 136.

Hourly prophesy.—*II Henry VI,* iii, 2, 283.

What of her ensues I list not prophesy.
The Winter's Tale. Act iv, sc. 1, l. 26. [Time]

I would not prophesy.—*Antony and Cleopatra,* ii, 6, 125.

5 Tell thou an earl his divination lies,
And I will take it as a sweet disgrace
And make thee rich for doing me such wrong.
II Henry IV. Act i, sc. 1, l. 88 [Northumberland]

Do not these high strains
Of divination in our sister work
Some touches of remorse?
Troilus and Cressida. Act ii, sc. 2, l. 113. [Hector]

Abuse my divination.—*Cymbeline,* iv, 2, 351. The only uses of "divination."

Darest thou, thou little better thing than earth,
Divine his downfall?
Richard II. Act iii, sc. 4, l. 78. [Queen]

6 Lordlings, farewell; and say, when I am gone,
I prophesied France will be lost ere long.
II Henry VI. Act i, sc. 1, l. 145. [Gloucester]

I prophesied.—*The Tempest,* v, 1, 217.

Prophesied thou shouldst be king.—*Richard III,* v, 3, 129.

It hath been prophesied.—*II Henry IV,* iv, 5, 237.

7 Did speak these words, now proved a prophecy.
II Henry IV. Act iii, sc. 1, l. 69. [King]

Foretelling this same time's condition.
II Henry IV. Act iii, sc. 1, l. 78. [King] The only use of "foretelling."

A man may prophesy,
With a near aim, of the main chance of things
As yet not come to life, which in their seeds
And weak beginnings lie intreasured.
II Henry IV. Act iii, sc. 1, l. 82. [Warwick] The only use of "intreasured."

8 And now I fear that fatal prophecy . . .
Was in the mouth of every sucking babe.
I Henry VI. Act iii, sc. 1, l. 197. [Exeter]

Infusing them with dreadful prophecies.
Venus and Adonis, l. 928.

Drunken prophecies.—*Richard III,* i, 1, 33.

Frustrate prophecies.—*II Henry IV,* v, 2, 127.

Presaging prophecy.—*III Henry VI,* iv, 6, 92. The only use of "presaging."

Vain prophecy.—*Henry VIII,* i, 2, 147.

O'er-ruled by prophecies.—*I Henry IV,* iv, 4, 18.

9 If secret powers
Suggest but truth to my divining thoughts,
This pretty lad will prove our country's bliss.
III Henry VI. Act iv, sc. 6, l. 68. [King Henry] The only use of "divining."

This royal infant—heaven still move about her!—
Though in her cradle, yet now promises
Upon this land a thousand thousand blessings,
Which time shall bring to ripeness: she shall be—
But few now living can behold that goodness—
A pattern to all princes living with her,
And all that shall succeed: Saba was never
More covetous of wisdom and fair virtue
Than this pure soul shall be: all princely graces
That mould up such a mighty piece as this is,
With all the virtues that attend the good,
Shall still be doubled on her: truth shall nurse her,
Holy and heavenly thoughts still counsel her:
She shall be loved and fear'd: her own shall bless her;
Her foes shake like a field of beaten corn,
And hang their heads with sorrow: good grows with her:

In her days every man shall eat in safety,
Under his own vine, what he plants; and sing
The merry songs of peace to all his neighbours:
Good shall be truly known; and those about her
From her shall read the perfect ways of honour,
And by those claim their greatness, not by blood.
Nor shall this peace sleep with her: but as when
The bird of wonder dies, the maiden phœnix,
Her ashes new create another heir,
As great in admiration as herself;
So shall she leave her blessedness to one,
When heaven shall call her from this cloud of darkness,
Who, from the sacred ashes of her honour
Shall star-like rise, as great in fame as she was,
And so stand fix'd: peace, plenty, love, truth, terror,
That were the servants to this chosen infant,
Shall then be his, and like a vine grow to him:
Wherever the bright sun of heaven shall shine,
The honour and the greatness of his name
Shall be, and make new nations: he shall flourish,
And, like a mountain cedar, reach his branches
To all the plains about him: our children's children
Shall see this, and bless heaven.
Henry VIII. Act v, sc. 5, l. 18. [Cranmer] The only mention of Saba. "Star-like" is repeated in *Timon of Athens,* v, 1, 66: "Star-like nobleness."

1
I will buzz abroad such prophecies
That Edward shall be fearful of his life.
III Henry VI. Act v, sc. 6, l. 86. [Gloucester]
Buzz these conjurations.—*II Henry VI,* i, 2, 99.
Buzz lamenting doings.—*Titus Andronicus,* iii, 2, 62.

2
Now hear me speak with a prophetic spirit.
King John. Act iii, sc. 4, l. 126. [Pandulph]
The prophetic soul
Of the wide world dreaming on things to come.
Sonnets. No. cvii.
O my prophetic soul! My uncle!
Hamlet. Act i, sc. 5, l. 40. [Hamlet]
Prophetic fury.—*Othello,* iii, 4, 72.
Prophetic tears.—*Troilus and Cressida,* ii, 2, 102.

3
Foreknowing that the truth will fall out so.
King John. Act iv, sc. 2, l. 154. [Peter]
Happily, foreknowing may avoid.
Hamlet. Act i, sc. 1, l. 133. [Horatio] The only uses of "foreknowing."
He seems to have a foreknowledge of that.
Twelfth Night. Act i, sc. 5, l. 151. [Malvolio] The only use of "foreknowledge."
Her foresight could not forestall their will.
The Rape of Lucrece, l. 728. The only use of "foresight."

4
We had a kind of light what would ensue.
King John. Act iv, sc. 3, l. 61. [Salisbury]
I 'll speak a prophecy ere I go:
When priests are more in word than matter;
When brewers mar their malt with water;
When nobles are their tailors' tutors;
No heretics burn'd, but wenches' suitors;
When every case in law is right;
No squire in debt, nor no poor knight;
When slanders do not live in tongues;
Nor cutpurses come not to throngs;
When usurers tell their gold i' the field;
And bawds and whores do churches build;
Then shall the realm of Albion
Come to great confusion:
Then comes the time, who lives to see 't,
That going shall be used with feet.
King Lear. Act iii, sc. 2, l. 80. [Fool] The only use of "malt."

5
If you can look into the seeds of time,
And say which grain will grow and which will not,
Speak then to me, who neither beg nor fear
Your favours nor your hate.
Macbeth. Act i, sc. 3, l. 58. [Banquo]

6
If you live to see this come to pass, say
Pompey told you so.
Measure for Measure. Act ii, sc. 1, l. 255. [Pompey]
Like a prophet,
Looks in a glass, that shows what future evils . . .
Are now to have no successive degrees,
But, ere they live, to end.
Measure for Measure. Act ii, sc. 2, l. 94. [Angelo]

7
He hearkens after prophecies and dreams.
Richard III. Act i, sc. 1, l. 54. [Clarence]
O, thou didst prophesy the time would come
That I should wish for thee to help me curse
That bottled spider, that foul bunch-back'd toad!
Richard III. Act iv, sc. 4, l. 79. [Queen Elizabeth] The only use of "bunch-back'd."

8
Her brain-sick raptures.
Troilus and Cressida. Act ii, sc. 2, l. 122. [Troilus]

9
My prophecy is but half his journey yet.
Troilus and Cressida. Act iv, sc. 5, l. 218. [Ulysses]
How often have I told you 'twould be thus!
The Winter's Tale, iv, 4, 484. [Perdita]
Fortunate mistress,—let my prophecy
Come home to ye!
The Winter's Tale, iv, 4, 661. [Camillo]

II—The Prophet

10
A prophet I, madam; and I speak the truth the next way.
All's Well that Ends Well. Act i, sc. 3, l. 62. [Clown]

11
Where 's the soothsayer that you praised so?
Antony and Cleopatra, i, 2, 3. [Charmian]
Call forth your soothsayer.—*Cymbeline,* v, 5, 426.
A soothsayer bids you beware the ides of March.
Julius Cæsar. Act i, sc. 2, l. 19. [Brutus]
Go, you wild bedfellow, you cannot soothsay.
Antony and Cleopatra. Act i, sc. 2, l. 51. [Iras] The only use of "soothsay."

1
Yea, this man's brow, like to a title-leaf,
Foretells the nature of a tragic volume.
II Henry IV. Act i, sc. 1, l. 60. [Northumberland] The only use of "title-leaf."
The spirit of deep prophecy she hath,
Exceeding the nine sibyls of old Rome.
I Henry VI. Act i, sc. 2, l. 55. [Bastard]
No prophet will I trust, if she prove false.
I Henry VI. Act i, sc. 2, l. 150. [Charles]
'When he,' quoth she, 'shall split thy heart with sorrow,
Remember Margaret was a prophetess.'
Richard III. Act v, sc. 1, l. 26. [Buckingham]
Glorious prophetess.—*I Henry VI*, i, 6, 8.
Holy prophetess.—*I Henry VI*, i, 4, 102. The only uses of "prophetess."
A prophet to the fall of all our foes!
I Henry VI. Act iii, sc. 2, l. 32. [Charles]
Prophets and apostles.—*II Henry VI*, i, 3, 60.
Your prophet the Nazarite.—*The Merchant of Venice*, i, 3, 35. The only use of "Nazarite."
2
I'll hear no more: die, prophet, in thy speech.
III Henry VI. Act v, sc. 6, l. 57. [Gloucester]
Did not the prophet
Say that before Ascension-day at noon
My crown I should give off?
King John. Act v, sc. 1, l. 25. [King John] Ascension-day is mentioned again in v, 1, 22 and 26, and in no other play.
3
How long have you been a sectary astronomical?
King Lear. Act i, sc. 2, l. 164. [Edgar] The only use of "astronomical." "Sectary" occurs again in *Henry VIII*, v, 3, 70.
Prophet-like
They hail'd him father to a line of kings.
Macbeth. Act iii, sc. 1, l. 59. [Macbeth] The only use of "prophet-like."
He hath a heavenly gift of prophecy.
Macbeth. Act iv, sc. 3, l. 157. [Malcolm]
4
Methinks I am a prophet new inspired.
Richard II. Act ii, sc. 1, l. 31. [Gaunt]
Lean-look'd prophets.—*Richard II*, ii, 4, 11. The only use of "lean-look'd." See under OMEN.
5
My other self, my counsel's consistory,
My oracle, my prophet!
Richard III. Act ii, sc. 2, l. 151. [Gloucester] "Consistory" is repeated in *Henry VIII*, ii, 4, 92.
How chance the prophet could not at that time
Have told me, I being by, that I should kill him?
Richard III. Act iv, sc. 2, l. 103. [King Richard]
6
Nor can I fortune to brief minutes tell,
Pointing to each his thunder, rain and wind,
Or say with princes if it shall go well,
By oft predict that I in heaven find.
Sonnets. No. xiv.
7
The sad augurs mock their own presage.
Sonnets. No. cvii. "Augurs" is used a second time in *Macbeth*, iii, 4, 124. "Augur" occurs once, in *The Phœnix and Turtle*, l. 7.
What say the augurers?—*Julius Cæsar*, ii, 2, 37. "Augurers" is repeated in ii, 1, 200.
The augurers say They know not.—*Antony and Cleopatra*, iv, 12, 4.
The augurer tells me we shall have news to-night.—*Coriolanus*, ii, 1, 1.
You are too sure an augurer.—*Antony and Cleopatra*, v, 2, 337. The only uses of "augurer" and "augurers."
If my augury deceive me not.—*The Two Gentlemen of Verona*, iv, 4, 73.
We defy augury.—*Hamlet*, v, 2, 230. The only uses of "augury."
8
I myself
Am like a prophet suddenly enrapt.
Troilus and Cressida, v, 3, 64. [Priam]
Prophet may you be!
Troilus and Cressida. Act iii, sc. 2, l. 190. [Cressida]

PROPORTION

9
The just proportion that we gave them out.
II Henry IV. Act iv, sc. 1, l. 23. [Mowbray]
Just proportion.—*Richard III*, iv, 4, 110; v, 3, 26.
Due proportion.—*Richard II*, iii, 4, 41.
First proportion.—*I Henry IV*, iv, 4, 15.
Large proportion.—*I Henry VI*, ii, 3, 21.
Least proportion.—*I Henry VI*, ii, 3, 53.
Like proportion.—*The Merchant of Venice*, iii, 4, 14.
10
We must not only arm to invade the French,
But lay down our proportions to defend
Against the Scot, who will make road upon us
With all advantages.
Henry V. Act i, sc. 2, l. 136. [King Henry]
Let our proportions for these wars
Be soon collected.
Henry V. Act i, sc. 2, l. 307. [King Henry]
So the proportions of defence are fill'd.
Henry V. Act ii, sc. 4, l. 45. [Dauphin]
The lists and full proportions, are all made
Out of his subject.
Hamlet. Act i, sc. 2, l. 32. [King]
11
Methinks the realms of England, France and Ireland
Bear that proportion to my flesh and blood
As did the fatal brand Althea burn'd
Unto the prince's heart of Calydon.
II Henry VI. Act i, sc. 1, l. 232. [York] The only mention of Calydon. Althea is referred to again in *II Henry IV*, ii, 2, 93; 96.
Bear the same proportion.—*Henry VIII*, v, 1, 129.
12
Her promised proportions
Came short of composition.
Measure for Measure. Act v, sc. 1, l. 219. [Angelo]
No proportion held in love.—*The Merry Wives of Windsor*, v, 5, 235.

1
Three or four thousand chequins were as pretty a proportion to live quietly.
Pericles. Act iv, sc. 2, l. 28. [Pandar] The only use of "chequins" (sequins).

2
I, that am curtail'd of this fair proportion.
Richard III. Act i, sc. 1, l. 18. [Gloucester]

Keep . . . proportion.—*Romeo and Juliet,* ii, 4, 22.
No proportion kept.—*Richard II,* v, 5, 43.
'Gainst all proportion.—*Henry V,* ii, 2, 109; iv, 1, 153.
In any proportion.—*Measure for Measure,* i, 2, 23.

3 Will you with counters sum
The past proportion of his infinite?
Troilus and Cressida, ii, 2, 28. See under KING.

4
I have received my proportion, like the prodigious son.
The Two Gentlemen of Verona. Act ii, sc. 3, l. 3. [Launce]

PROSPERITY

See also Adversity

5
Bold gentleman, Prosperity be thy page!
Coriolanus. Act i, sc. 5, l. 23. [Titus]

The glorious gods sit in hourly synod about thy particular prosperity!
Coriolanus. Act v, sc. 2, l. 74. [Menenius]

6 Thou shalt thrust thy hand as deep
Into the purse of rich prosperity
As Lewis himself.
King John. Act v, sc. 2, l. 60. [Dauphin]

7
That sir which serves and seeks for gain,
And follows but for form,
Will pack when it begins to rain,
And leave thee in the storm.
King Lear. Act ii, sc. 4, l. 79. [Fool]

8
Fairies and gods Prosper it with thee!
King Lear. Act iv, sc. 6, l. 29. [Gloucester]

Well may you prosper!—*King Lear,* i, 1, 285.
God prosper your affairs!—*II Henry IV,* iii, 2, 313.
Prosper you, sweet sir!—*The Winter's Tale,* iv, 3, 126.
Prosper him.—*King Lear,* iii, 7, 92.
Prosper our colours.—*I Henry VI,* iv, 2, 56.
Prosper this realm.—*I Henry VI,* i, 1, 53.
Prosper best.—*III Henry VI,* ii, 5, 18.
Prosper better.—*I Henry VI,* v, 5, 106.
We prosper well.—*The Tempest,* ii, 1, 72.
We shall never prosper.—*Pericles,* iv, 2, 13.

9
Welcome the sour cup of prosperity! Affliction may one day smile again; and till then, sit thee down, sorrow!
Love's Labour's Lost. Act i, sc. 1, l. 315. [Costard]

10
I intend to thrive in this new world.
Richard II. Act iv, sc. 1, l. 78. [Fitzwater]

We will thrive, lads, we will thrive.
The Merry Wives of Windsor. Act i, sc. 3, l. 81. [Falstaff]

We shall thrive, I trust.—*I Henry IV,* i, 3, 300.
We shall thrive now.—*Antony and Cleopatra,* iv, 4, 9.
Thrive as best I may.—*The Merchant of Venice,* ii, 7, 60.
So thrive it in your game!—*King John,* iv, 2, 95.
Thrive well.—*Richard III,* iii, 5, 98.
Live and thrive!—*Coriolanus,* iv, 6, 23.

11
So, now prosperity begins to mellow
And drop into the rotten mouth of death.
Richard III. Act iv, sc. 4, l. 1. [Queen Margaret]

12
Smiling plenty.
Richard III. Act v, sc. 5, l. 34. [Richmond]

Spacious plenty.—*Timon of Athens,* iv, 3, 71.
Peace and plenty.—*Cymbeline,* v, 4, 145; v, 5, 442; 458. The only play in which this phrase occurs.
Peace and prosperity!—*Measure for Measure,* i, 4, 15.

13
Live, and be prosperous.
Romeo and Juliet. Act v, sc. 3, l. 42. [Romeo]

Bless this twain, that they may prosperous be.
The Tempest. Act iv, sc. 1, l. 104. [Juno]

Mayst thou prove prosperous!—*Pericles,* i, 1, 59.
Prosperous be thy life.—*I Henry VI,* ii, 5, 114.
The gods make her prosperous.—*Pericles,* v, 1, 80.

14
Prosperity 's the very bond of love,
Whose fresh complexion and whose heart together
Affliction alters.
The Winter's Tale. Act iv, sc. 4, l. 583. [Camillo]

PROTESTATION

15
The lady doth protest too much, methinks.
Hamlet. Act iii, sc. 2, l. 240. [Queen]

I protest.—*I Henry VI,* iv, 2, 19, and forty-two times in later plays.

16
I can but say their protestation over.
Love's Labour's Lost. Act i, sc. 1, l. 33. [Biron]

I have no cunning in protestation.—*Henry V,* v, 2, 150. See under OATH.

17
But she, that yet her sad task hath not said,
The protestation stops.
The Rape of Lucrece, l. 1699.

And to his protestation urged the rest.
The Rape of Lucrece, l. 1844.

18
Here is a coil with protestation!
The Two Gentlemen of Verona. Act i, sc. 2, l. 99. [Julia]

Stuff'd with protestations.
The Two Gentlemen of Verona. Act iv, sc. 4, l. 134. [Silvia]

New protester.—*Julius Cæsar,* i, 2, 74. The only use of "protester."

PROVERB

See also Familiar Phrases

1
Full of wise saws and modern instances.
As You Like It. Act ii, sc. 7, l. 156. [Jaques]
We'll whisper o'er a couplet or two of most sage saws.
Twelfth Night. Act iii, sc. 4, l. 412. [Sir Toby]
Who fears a sentence or an old man's saw
Shall by a painted cloth be kept in awe.
The Rape of Lucrece, l. 244.

2
Have at you with a proverb.
The Comedy of Errors. Act iii, sc. 1, l. 51. [Dromio of Ephesus]
The ancient proverb.—*II Henry VI,* iii, 1, 170.
The proverb is something musty.—*Hamlet,* iii, 2, 359.

3
They said they were an-hungry; sigh'd forth proverbs,
That hunger broke stone walls, that dogs must eat,
That meat was made for mouths, that the gods sent not
Corn for the rich men only.
Coriolanus. Act i, sc. 1, l. 209. [Marcius] The only use of "an-hungry."
Orleans: Ill will never said well.
Constable: I will cap that proverb with 'There is flattery in friendship.'
Orleans: And I will take up that with 'Give the devil his due.' . . .
Constable: Have at the very eye of that proverb with 'A pox of the devil.'
Orleans: You are the better at proverbs, by how much 'A fool's bolt is soon shot.'
Henry V. Act iii, sc. 7, l. 124. "Evil will never said well" appeared first in the prologue of Wager's *Mary Magdalene,* in 1566. "There is flattery in friendship" was probably coined by Shakespeare. "A fool's bolt is soon shot" appeared first in *The Proverbs of Alfred* in 1270. The origins of the other two are unknown.

4
An old saying, that was a man when King
Pepin of France was a little boy.
Love's Labour's Lost. Act iv, sc. 1, l. 121. [Rosaline]
There's a saying very old and true.
Henry V. Act i, sc. 2, l. 166. [Westmoreland]
I can tell thee where that saying was born.
Twelfth Night. Act i, sc. 5, l. 9. [Maria]
That's true enough;
Though 'tis a saying, sir, not due to me.
The Winter's Tale. Act iii, sc. 2, l. 58. [Hermione]
The old saying.—*The Two Gentlemen of Verona,* v, 2, 11; *Twelfth Night,* v, 1, 40.
The ancient saying.—*The Merchant of Venice,* ii, 9, 82.
A proper saying!—*Much Ado about Nothing,* iv, 1, 312.
'Tis a foolish saying.—*Henry V,* iv, 1, 215.

5
Fast bind, fast find;
A proverb never stale in thrifty mind.
The Merchant of Venice. Act ii, sc. 5, l. 54. [Shylock]

6
He gives me the proverbs and the no-verbs.
The Merry Wives of Windsor. Act iii, sc. 1, l. 107. [Host] The only use of "no-verbs."

7
And the country proverb known
That every man should take his own.
A Midsummer-Night's Dream. Act iii, sc. 2, l. 458. [Puck]

8
I am proverb'd with a grandsire phrase.
Romeo and Juliet. Act i, sc. 4, l. 37. [Romeo] The only use of "proverb'd."

9
If that this simple syllogism will serve, so; if it will not, what remedy?
Twelfth Night. Act i, sc. 5, l. 55. [Clown] The only use of "syllogism."

PROVIDENCE

See also Power: Divine Power

10
But yet heaven's bounty towards him might
Be used more thankfully.
Cymbeline. Act i, sc. 6, l. 78. [Iachimo]
The heavens still must work.
Cymbeline. Act iv, sc. 3, l. 41. [Pisanio]
All was lost, But that the heavens fought.
Cymbeline. Act v, sc. 3, l. 3. [Posthumus]

11
There's a divinity that shapes our ends,
Rough-hew them how we will.
Hamlet. Act v, sc. 2, l. 10. [Hamlet] The only use of "rough-hew."
There's a special providence in the fall of a sparrow.
Hamlet. Act v, sc. 2, l. 230. [Hamlet]

12 The providence of some high powers
That govern us below.
Julius Cæsar. Act v, sc. 1, l. 107. [Brutus]

13
We were villains by necessity; fools by heavenly compulsion; knaves, thieves and treachers, by spherical predominance; drunkards, liars, and adulterers, by an enforced obedience of planetary influence; and all that we are evil in, by a divine thrusting on.
King Lear. Act i, sc. 2, l. 133. [Edmund] The only use of "treachers." "Planetary" is repeated in *Timon of Athens,* iv, 3, 108: "Planetary plague."

14
A thing not in his power to bring to pass,
But sway'd and fashion'd by the hand of heaven.
The Merchant of Venice. Act i, sc. 3, l. 93. [Antonio]
All is in his hands above.
The Merry Wives of Windsor. Act i, sc. 4, l. 154. [Mistress Quickly]

15
He, that hath the steerage of my course,
Direct my sail!
Romeo and Juliet. Act i, sc. 4, l. 112. [Romeo]

1
Providence divine.
The Tempest. Act i, sc. 2, l. 159. [Prospero]
Sir, she is mortal;
But by immortal Providence she 's mine.
The Tempest. Act v, sc. 1, l. 188. [Ferdinand]

2
The providence that 's in a watchful state
Knows almost every grain of Plutus' gold,
Finds bottom in the uncomprehensive deeps,
Keeps place with thought and almost, like the gods,
Does thoughts unveil in their dumb cradles.
Troilus and Cressida. Act iii, sc. 3, l. 196. [Ulysses] The only use of "uncomprehensive" and "unveil." Plutus is mentioned four times.

3
It is Jove's doing, and Jove make me thankful!
Twelfth Night. Act iii, sc. 4, l. 82. [Malvolio]

PRUDENCE

See also Caution

4
Chief Justice: Wake not a sleeping wolf.
Falstaff: To wake a wolf is as bad as to smell a fox.
II Henry IV. Act i, sc. 2, l. 174.

5
It fits us then to be as provident
As fear may teach us out of late examples.
Henry V. Act ii, sc. 4, l. 11. [French King]
Most provident in peril.
Twelfth Night. Act i, sc. 2, l. 12. [Captain] The only uses of "provident."

6
But yet be wary in thy studious care.
I Henry VI. Act ii, sc. 5, l. 97. [Mortimer] "Studious" is repeated in *The Two Gentlemen of Verona,* i, 3, 10.
It behoves men to be wary.—*Winter's Tale,* iv, 4, 257. "Be wary" is repeated six times.

7
Be wise and circumspect.
II Henry VI. Act i, sc. 1, l. 157. [Beaufort]
High-reaching Buckingham grows circumspect.
Richard III. Act iv, sc. 2, l. 31. [King Richard] The only use of "high-reaching" and the only uses of "circumspect."

8
Let us be keen, and rather cut a little,
Than fall, and bruise to death.
Measure for Measure. Act ii, sc. 1, l. 5. [Escalus]

9
Let it cool the while.
Much Ado about Nothing. Act ii, sc. 3, l. 212. [Don Pedro]

10
O, what pity is it
That he had not so trimm'd and dress'd his land
As we this garden! We at time of year
Do wound the bark, the skin of our fruit-trees,
Lest, being over-proud in sap and blood,
With too much riches it confound itself:
Had he done so to great and growing men,
They might have lived to bear and he to taste
Their fruits of duty: superfluous branches
We lop away, that bearing boughs may live:
Had he done so, himself had borne the crown,
Which waste of idle hours hath quite thrown down.
Richard II. Act iii, sc. 4, l. 55. [Gardener] "Over-proud" is repeated in *Troilus and Cressida,* ii, 3, 132.

11
This Sir Prudence.
The Tempest. Act ii, sc. 1, l. 286. [Antonio]

12
I am sure 'tis safer to
Avoid what 's grown than question how 'tis born.
The Winter's Tale. Act i, sc. 2, l. 432. [Camillo]

PUISSANCE

See also Might, Power

13
That he should draw his several strengths together
And come against us in full puissance,
Need not be dreaded.
II Henry IV. Act i, sc. 3, l. 76. [Archbishop]
O, fly to Scotland
Till that the nobles and the armed commons
Have of their puissance made a little taste.
II Henry IV. Act ii, sc. 3, l. 50. [Lady Northumberland]
Puissance of the king.—*II Henry IV,* i, 3, 9.

14
Then forth, dear countrymen: let us deliver
Our puissance into the hand of God.
Henry V. Act ii, sc. 2, l. 189. [King Henry]
Pith and puissance.—*Henry V,* iii, Prol., 21.
Imaginary puissance.—*Henry V,* Prol., 25.
Thrice-puissant.—*Henry V,* i, 2, 119. The only use of the phrase.

15
Go draw our puissance together.
King John. Act iii, sc. 1, l. 338. [King John]

16
We will follow
In the main battle, whose puissance on either side
Shall be well winged with our chiefest horse.
Richard III. Act v, sc. 3, l. 298. [King Richard]

PULSE, see Heart

PUNISHMENT

See also Beating, Condemnation, Correction, Retribution, Threat, Torture

17
There is no remedy, sir, but you must die: the general says. you that have so traitorously discovered the secrets of your army and made such pestiferous reports of men very nobly held, can serve the world for no honest use; therefore you must die.
All's Well that Ends Well. Act iv, sc. 3.

l. 337. [Soldier] "Pestiferous" is repeated in *I Henry VI,* iii, 1, 15: "Pestiferous pranks."

1
To punish me for what you make me do
Seems much unequal.
Antony and Cleopatra. Act ii, sc. 5, l. 100. [Messenger]

Bid that welcome
Which comes to punish us, and we punish it
Seeming to bear it lightly.
Antony and Cleopatra. Act iv, sc. 14, l. 136. [Antony]

On pain of punishment.—*Antony and Cleopatra,* i, 1, 39.

2
First Servant: He scotched him and notched him like a carbonado.
Second Servant: An he had been cannibally given, he might have broiled and eaten him too.
Coriolanus, iv, 5, 198. The only use of "notched," and "cannibally." "Scotched" occurs again in *Macbeth,* iii, 2, 13.

3
She 's punish'd for her truth, and undergoes,
More goddess-like than wife-like, such assaults
As would take in some virtue.
Cymbeline. Act iii, sc. 2, l. 7. [Pisanio] "Goddess-like" is repeated in *The Winter's Tale,* iv, 4, 10, and in *Pericles,* v, Gower, 4; "wife-like" in *Henry VIII,* ii, 4, 138.

Having received the punishment before
For that which I did then.
Cymbeline. Act v, sc. 5, l. 343. [Belarius]

4
Heaven hath pleased it so,
To punish me with this and this with me,
That I must be their scourge and minister.
Hamlet. Act iii, sc. 4, l. 173. [Hamlet]

5
Hang me up by the heels for a rabbit-sucker or a poulter's hare.
I Henry IV. Act ii, sc. 4, l. 480. [Falstaff] The only use of "rabbit-sucker" (a very young rabbit) and "poulter."

Thou art only mark'd
For the hot vengeance and the rod of heaven
To punish my mistreadings.
I Henry IV. Act iii, sc. 2, l. 9. [King Henry] The only use of "mistreadings."

6
For the which I think thou wilt howl.
II Henry IV. Act ii, sc. 4, l. 373. [Falstaff]

I have him already tempering between my finger and my thumb, and shortly will I seal with him.
II Henry IV. Act iv, sc. 3, l. 140. [Falstaff]

7
I will have you as soundly swinged for this . . . If you be not swinged, I'll forswear half-kirtles.
II Henry IV. Act v, sc. 4, l. 21. [Doll Tearsheet] The only use of "half-kirtles" (jackets).

I had swinged him soundly.
Measure for Measure. Act v, sc. 1, l. 130. [Lucio]

If it had not been i' the church, I would have swinged him, or he would have swinged me.
The Merry Wives of Windsor. Act v, sc. 5, l. 196. [Slender]

If they deny to come,
Swinge me them soundly forth.
The Taming of the Shrew. Act v, sc. 2, l. 103. [Petruchio]

You swinged me for my love.—*The Two Gentlemen of Verona,* ii, 1, 88.

Now will he be swinged.—*The Two Gentlemen of Verona,* iii, 1, 392.

8
Here men are punish'd for before-breach of the king's laws.
Henry V. Act iv, sc. 1, l. 179. [King Henry] The only use of "before-breech."

Punish'd ere they have done their mischief.—*King Lear,* iv, 2, 54.

Subjects punish'd that ne'er thought offence.—*Pericles,* i, 2, 27.

9
Give him chastisement for this abuse.
I Henry VI. Act iv, sc. 1, l. 69. [King Henry] "Give him chastisement" is repeated in *Richard II,* iv, 1, 22.

The name of Cassius honours this corruption,
And chastisement doth therefore hide his head.
Julius Cæsar. Act iv, sc. 3, l. 15. [Brutus]

Rough chastisement.—*Richard II,* i, 1, 106.

10
Thy sale of offices and towns in France,
If they were known, as the suspect is great,
Would make thee quickly hop without thy head.
II Henry VI. Act i, sc. 3, l. 138. [Queen Margaret]

Till the axe of death
Hang over thee, as, sure, it shortly will.
II Henry VI. Act ii, sc. 4, l. 49. [Duchess of Gloucester]

Your great goodness, out of holy pity,
Absolved him with an axe.
Henry VIII. Act iii, sc. 2, l. 263. [Surrey]

11
Did he not, contrary to form of law,
Devise strange deaths for small offences done?
II Henry VI. Act iii, sc. 1, l. 58. [Beaufort]

I never gave them condign punishment.
II Henry VI. Act iii, sc. 1, l. 130. [Gloucester] "Condign" is repeated in *Love's Labour's Lost,* i, 2, 27: "Condign praise."

12
The honour of it
Does pay the act of it; as, i' the contrary,
The foulness is the punishment.
Henry VIII. Act iii, sc. 2, l. 181. [Wolsey]

13
I will punish home.
King Lear. Act iii, sc. 4, l. 16. [King Lear]

He . . . quit the house on purpose, that their punishment
Might have the freer scope.
King Lear. Act iv, sc. 2, l. 94. [Messenger]

Judicious punishment!—*King Lear,* iii, 4, 76.

14
Thou shalt be heavily punished.
Love's Labour's Lost. Act i, sc. 2, l. 155. [Armado]

Him I . . . have sent to thee, to receive the meed of punishment.
Love's Labour 's Lost. Act i, sc. 1, l. 268. [King, reading]

1 Fond fathers,
Having bound up the threatening twigs of birch,
Only to stick it in their children's sight
For terror, not to use, in time the rod
Becomes more mock'd than fear'd.
Measure for Measure. Act i, sc. 3, l. 23. [Duke]

Those many had not dared to do that evil,
If the first that did the edict infringe
Had answer'd for his deed.
Measure for Measure. Act ii, sc. 2, l. 91. [Angelo]

Punish them to your height of pleasure.
Measure for Measure. Act v, sc. 1, l. 240. [Duke]

2
That were a punishment too good for them.
Much Ado about Nothing. Act iii, sc. 3, l. 4. [Dogberry]

I 'll devise thee brave punishments for him.
Much Ado about Nothing. Act v, sc. 4, l. 129. [Benedick]

3
Some of us will smart for it.
Much Ado about Nothing. Act v, sc. 1, l. 109. [Antonio]

Made me smart.—*I Henry VI,* iv, 6, 42.

Ease thy smart.—*Troilus and Cressida,* iv, 4, 20.

Earth-vexing smart.—*Cymbeline,* v, 4, 42. The only use of the phrase.

4
A punishment more in policy than in malice; even so as one would beat his offenceless dog to affright an imperious lion.
Othello. Act ii, sc. 3, l. 274. [Iago] A paraphrase of the French proverb, "Battre le chien devant le lion," which means, as Cotgrave explains it, "To punish a mean person in the presence, and to the terror, of a great one." Chaucer used it in his *The Squieres Tale,* l. 491, c. 1386. The only use of "offenceless."

5 If there be cords, or knives,
Poison, or fire, or suffocating streams,
I 'll not endure it.
Othello. Act iii, sc. 3, l. 388. [Othello]

6
God punish me.
Richard III. Act ii, sc. 1, l. 34. [Buckingham]

God will punish me.—*Henry VIII,* ii, 4, 75.

7
But I 'll amerce you with so strong a fine
That you shall all repent.
Romeo and Juliet. Act iii, sc. 1, l. 195. [Prince] The only use of "amerce."

I for winking at your discords too
Have lost a brace of kinsmen: all are punish'd.
Romeo and Juliet. Act v, sc. 3, l. 294. [Prince]

Some shall be pardon'd, and some punished.
Romeo and Juliet. Act v, sc. 3, l. 308. [Prince]

8
Fright me with urchin-shows, pitch me i' the mire.
The Tempest. Act ii, sc. 2, l. 5. [Caliban] The only use of "urchin-shows" (self-like apparitions).

Go charge my goblins that they grind their joints
With dry convulsions, shorten up their sinews
With aged cramps, and more pinch-spotted make them
Than pard or cat o' mountain.
Tempest. Act iv, sc. 1, l. 259. [Prospero] The only use of "convulsions" and "pinch-spotted." "Cat o' mountain" occurs again in *The Merry Wives of Windsor,* ii, 2, 27.

9
Reverse the doom of death.
Titus Andronicus. Act iii, sc. 1, l. 24. [Titus]

Hither hale that misbelieving Moor,
To be adjudged some direful slaughtering death,
As punishment for his most wicked life.
Titus Andronicus. Act v, sc. 3, l. 143. [Marcus] The only use of "misbelieving."

Set him breast-deep in earth, and famish him;
There let him stand, and rave, and cry for food.
Titus Andronicus. Act v, sc. 3, l. 179. [Lucius] The only use of "breast-deep."

10
Let me be punish'd, that have minded you
Of what you should forget.
The Winter's Tale. Act iii, sc. 2, l. 226. [Paulina]

PURITY

See also Chastity

11
I could drive her then from the ward of her purity, her reputation, her marriage-vow, and a thousand other her defences, which now are too too strongly embattled against me.
The Merry Wives of Windsor. Act ii, sc. 2, l. 257. [Ford] "Marriage-vow" occurs again in *Hamlet,* iii, 4, 44.

12
Thou pure impiety and impious purity!
Much Ado about Nothing. Act iv, sc. 1, l. 105. [Claudio]

Such a winnow'd purity.
Troilus and Cressida. Act iii, sc. 2, l. 174. [Troilus]

All purity.—*As You Like It,* v, 2, 104.

Purity of manhood.—*Timon of Athens,* iv, 3, 14.

13
Offer pure incense to so pure a shrine.
The Rape of Lucrece, l. 194.

14
Be they as pure as grace.
Hamlet. Act i, sc. 4, l. 33. [Hamlet]

Pure as the unsullied lily.—*Love's Labour 's Lost,* v, 2, 351. The only use of "unsullied."

As pure as sin.—*Henry V,* i, 2, 32.

As pure as snow.—*Hamlet,* iii, 1, 141; *Macbeth,* iv, 3, 53.

Purest snow.—*Coriolanus,* v, 3, 66.

Innocent and pure.—*The Tempest,* ii, 1, 155.

Pure for his love.—*Twelfth Night,* v, 1, 86.

1
O, when mine eyes did see Olivia first,
Methought she purged the air of pestilence!
Twelfth Night. Act i, sc. 1, l. 19. [Duke]

PURPOSE

See also Aim, End, Intention

2
Now I see The bottom of your purpose.
All's Well that Ends Well. Act iii, sc. 7, l. 28. [Widow]
I had no such purpose.—*All's Well that Ends Well,* iv, 1, 40.

3
Come, come, to the purpose.
All's Well that Ends Well. Act v, sc. 3, l. 241. [King]
But to the purpose.—*The Two Gentlemen of Verona,* iv, 1, 53, and five times in later plays.
What's that to the purpose?—*Twelfth Night,* i, 3, 21.
To better purpose.—*Winter's Tale,* i, 2, 89.
To every purpose.—*Timon of Athens,* 14, 3, 390.
To little purpose.—*Coriolanus,* iii, 2, 89.
To some purpose.—*As You Like It,* v, 2, 58.
To this purpose.—*Troilus and Cressida,* i, 3, 264.
To what purpose?—*Richard II,* i, 3, 253.
Not to the purpose.—*Romeo and Juliet,* ii, 4, 46; *Hamlet,* v, 1, 44.

4
I am sorry to give breathing to my purpose.
Antony and Cleopatra. Act i, sc. 3, l. 14. [Antony]
My purposes do draw me much about.
Antony and Cleopatra. Act ii, sc. 4, l. 8. [Lepidus]

5
It serves my purpose.
Coriolanus. Act i, sc. 1, l. 94. [Menenius]
Win our purpose.—*Coriolanus,* i, 6, 50.

6 I wish no better
Than have him hold that purpose and to put it
In execution.
Coriolanus. Act ii, sc. 1, l. 255. [Sicinius]
We'll execute your purpose.—*Henry VIII,* iii, 3, 50.

7 Purpose so barr'd, it follows,
Nothing is done to purpose.
Coriolanus. Act iii, sc. 1, l. 148. [Coriolanus]

8 I crossed the seas on purpose
To see your grace.
Cymbeline. Act i, sc. 6, l. 202. [Iachimo]
On purpose.—*The Comedy of Errors,* iv, 3, 92; *Much Ado about Nothing,* ii, 3, 41; *The Taming of the Shrew,* Ind., 2, 41; *Twelfth Night,* iii, 4, 74; *I Henry IV,* ii, 4, 334; *King Lear,* iv, 2, 94; *Sonnets,* cxxix.
Of purpose.—*Henry VIII,* v, 2, 14.

9 If I were as wise as honest, then
My purpose would prove well.
Cymbeline. Act iii, sc. 4, l. 121. [Pisanio]

10 Give him a further edge,
And drive his purpose on to these delights.
Hamlet. Act iii, sc. 1, l. 26. [King]
Purpose is but the slave to memory,
Of violent birth, but poor validity.
Hamlet. Act iii, sc. 2, l. 198. [Player King]
Whet thy almost blunted purpose.
Hamlet. Act iii, sc. 4, l. 111. [Ghost]
King: So is it, if thou knew'st our purposes.
Hamlet: I see a cherub that sees them.
Hamlet. Act iv, sc. 3, l. 49. The only use of "cherub."
I am constant to my purposes.
Hamlet. Act v, sc. 2, l. 208. [Hamlet]
Purposes mistook.—*Hamlet,* v, 2, 395.

11
But this our purpose now is twelve month old.
I Henry IV. Act i, sc. 1, l. 28. [King Henry]
You start away
And lend no ear unto my purposes.
I Henry IV. Act i, sc. 3, l. 216. [Worcester]
The purpose you undertake is dangerous.
I Henry IV. Act ii, sc. 3, l. 12. [Hotspur]

12
In every thing the purpose must weigh the folly.
II Henry IV. Act ii, sc. 2, l. 195. [Prince of Wales]

13
Our purposes God justly hath discover'd.
Henry V. Act ii, sc. 2, l. 151. [Scroop]

14
Your purpose is both good and reasonable.
I Henry VI. Act v, sc. 1, l. 36. [Exeter]
'Tis for a good purpose.—*Measure for Measure,* ii, 1, 155.
Good purpose.—*Antony and Cleopatra,* ii, 2, 147; v, 2, 131.
Advised purpose.—*Richard II,* i, 3, 188.
Graver purpose.—*Cymbeline,* i, 4, 151.
Great purpose.—*Troilus and Cressida,* v, 1, 43.
Holy purpose.—*I Henry IV,* i, 1, 102.
Noble purpose.—*All's Well that Ends Well,* iii, 2, 73.
Self-same purpose.—*Rape of Lucrece,* l. 1047.
Set purpose.—*Pericles,* ii, 2, 54.
Special purpose.—*Othello,* v, 2, 322.
Strong purpose.—*Richard II,* v, 2, 34.
Studied purposes.—*Henry VIII,* iii, 2, 168.
Written purposes.—*Antony and Cleopatra,* ii, 6, 4.

15
A cold premeditation for my purpose!
III Henry VI. Act iii, sc. 2, l. 133. [Gloucester] The only use of "premeditation."

16 There's his period,
To sheathe his knife in us.
Henry VIII. Act i, sc. 2, l. 209. [King]
'Twas not my purpose.—*Henry VIII,* iii, 2, 145.

17 This shall make
Our purpose necessary and not envious.
Julius Cæsar. Act ii, sc. 1, l. 178. [Brutus]
I fear our purpose is discovered.
Julius Cæsar. Act iii, sc. 1, l. 17. [Cassius]

18 Meantime
We shall express our darker purpose.
King Lear. Act i, sc. 1, l. 37. [King Lear]
Angry purpose.—*Cymbeline,* ii, 3, 61.
Fell purpose.—*Macbeth,* i, 5, 47. The only use of the phrase.
Most pernicious purpose!—*Measure for Measure,* ii, 4, 150.
Secret purposes.—*The Winter's Tale,* v, 1, 36.
Sore purpose.—*Cymbeline,* iv, 1, 25.

Unlawful purpose.—*All's Well that Ends Well,* iii, 5, 73.
Unnatural purpose.—*King Lear,* ii, 1, 52.
Vile purpose.—*The Rape of Lucrece,* l. 220.

1 I do beseech you
To understand my purposes aright.
King Lear. Act i, sc. 4, l. 259. [Goneril]
Suspend thy purpose.—*King Lear,* i, 4, 298.
Make your own purpose.—*King Lear,* ii, 1, 113.
There was no purpose in them.—*King Lear,* ii, 4, 3.

2
Know of the duke if his last purpose hold,
Or whether since he is advised by aught
To change the course.
King Lear. Act v, sc. 1, l. 1. [Edmund]
Ask him his purposes.—*King Lear,* v, 3, 118.

3 'Tis our will
That some plain man recount their purposes:
Know what they would.
Love's Labour's Lost. Act v, sc. 2, l. 175. [Rosaline]

4
Infirm of purpose!
Macbeth. Act ii, sc. 2, l. 52. [Lady Macbeth]
The flighty purpose never is o'ertook
Unless the deed go with it.
Macbeth. Act iv, sc. 1, l. 145. [Macbeth] The only use of "flighty."

5 A purpose
More grave and wrinkled than the aims and ends
Of burning youth.
Measure for Measure. Act i, sc. 3, l. 4. [Vincentio]

6
Here is the heart of my purpose.
The Merry Wives of Windsor. Act ii, sc. 2, l. 233. [Ford]
He'll tell me all his purpose.
The Merry Wives of Windsor. Act iv, sc. 4, l. 77. [Ford]
Assist me in my purpose.—*The Merry Wives of Windsor,* iv, 6, 3.
I knew of your purpose.—*The Merry Wives of Windsor,* v, 5, 214.

7
Since I do purpose to marry, I will think nothing to any purpose that the world can say against it.
Much Ado about Nothing. Act v, sc. 4, l. 106. [Benedick]

8 He holds me well;
The better shall my purpose work on him.
Othello. Act i, sc. 3, l. 396. [Iago]
He, swift of foot, Outran my purpose.
Othello. Act ii, sc. 3, l. 232. [Iago]

9
I will make them acquainted with your purpose, and I doubt not but I shall find them tractable enough.
Pericles. Act iv, sc. 6, l. 209. [Boult]
My purpose was for Tarsus, there to strike
The inhospitable Cleon; but I am
For other service first.
Pericles. Act v, sc. 1, l. 254. [Pericles] The only use of "inhospitable."

10 What pricks you on
To take advantage of the absent time
And fright our native peace with self-born arms.
Richard II. Act ii, sc. 3, l. 78. [Berkeley] "Self-born" occurs again in *The Winter's Tale,* iv, 1, 8. "Pricks me on" is used three times, in *I Henry IV,* v, 1, 131; *Love's Labour's Lost,* i, 1, 269; and *The Two Gentlemen of Verona,* iii, 1, 8.

11 For his purpose . . .
I have not sounded him.
Richard III. Act iii, sc. 4, l. 16. [Hastings]
Left nothing fitting for the purpose
Untouch'd, or slightly handled, in discourse.
Richard III. Act iii, sc. 7, l. 18. [Buckingham] "Untouch'd" is repeated in *Julius Cæsar,* iii, 1, 142.
The better for our purpose.
Richard III. Act v, sc. 3, l. 274. [Ratcliff]
For what purpose?—*Romeo and Juliet,* ii, 2, 130.

12
If you but knew how you the purpose cherish
Whiles thus you mock it! how, in stripping it,
You more invest it!
The Tempest. Act ii, sc. 1, l. 228. [Antonio] The only use of "stripping."
Do not, for one repulse, forego the purpose
That you resolved to effect.
The Tempest. Act iii, sc. 3, l. 12. [Antonio]

13
It is very likely to load our purposes with what they travail for.
Timon of Athens. Act v, sc. 1, l. 17. [Painter]
Fits the purpose.—*Titus Andronicus,* ii, 3, 84.

14
The purpose is perspicuous even as substance,
Whose grossness little characters sum up.
Troilus and Cressida. Act i, sc. 3, l. 324. [Nestor] The only use of "perspicuous."
It is the purpose that makes strong the vow;
But vows to every purpose must not hold.
Troilus and Cressida. Act v, sc. 3, l. 23. [Cassandra]

15
My purpose is, indeed, a horse of that colour.
Twelfth Night. Act ii, sc. 3, l. 181. [Maria]

16
To your own bents dispose you.
The Winter's Tale. Act i, sc. 2, l. 179. [Leontes] The only use of "bents."
Full bent.—*Hamlet,* ii, 2, 30; *Much Ado about Nothing,* ii, 3, 232. *Pericles,* ii, Gower, 23.
True bent.—*Julius Cæsar,* ii, 1, 210.
Divinely bent.—*Richard III,* iii, 7, 62.
Lewdly bent.—*II Henry VI,* ii, 1, 167.
Bent of love.—*Romeo and Juliet,* ii, 2, 143.

17 On our knees we beg,
As recompense of our dear services
Past and to come, that you do change this purpose,
Which being so horrible, so bloody, must
Lead on to some foul issue.
The Winter's Tale. Act ii, sc. 3, l. 149. [Lord]

PURSE

See also Money

1
A purse of gold most resolutely snatched on Monday night and most dissolutely spent on Tuesday morning; got with swearing 'Lay by' and spent with crying 'Bring in.'
I Henry IV. Act i, sc. 2, l. 38. [Prince of Wales]

Purse of gold.—*Richard III,* i, 4, 144; *All's Well that Ends Well,* iii, 7, 14.
Purse of ducats.—*The Comedy of Errors,* iv, 1, 105; iv, 4, 90; v, 1, 385.
Purse the ducats.—*The Merchant of Venice,* i, 3, 175.
Empty purses.—*Timon of Athens,* iv, 2, 12; *Cymbeline,* iv, 2, 113; v, 4, 166.
His purse is empty.—*Hamlet,* v, 2, 136.
Fat purses.—*I Henry IV,* i, 2, 142.
Halfpenny purse.—*Love's Labour's Lost,* v, 1, 77; *Merry Wives of Windsor,* iii, 5, 149.
Foreign purse.—*Henry V,* ii, 2, 10.
Free purses.—*I Henry VI,* i, 3, 64.
Prodigal's purse.—*Troilus and Cressida,* v, 1, 37.

2
Falstaff: What money is in my purse?
Page: Seven groats and two pence.
Falstaff: I can get no remedy against this consumption of the purse: borrowing only lingers and lingers it out, but the disease is incurable.
II Henry IV. Act i, sc. 2, l. 262. [Falstaff]

Leanness of purse.—*II Henry VI,* i, 1, 112.

3
Help to waste His borrow'd purse.
The Merchant of Venice. Act ii, sc. 5, l. 50. [Shylock]

4
Falstaff: Pistol, did you pick Master Slender's purse?
Slender: Ay, by these gloves did he, or I would I might never come in mine own great chamber again else, of seven groats in mill-sixpences, and two Edward shovel-boards.
The Merry Wives of Windsor. Act i, sc. 1, l. 154. The only use of "mill-sixpences" (stamped by the mill), and "shovel-boards" (shillings used in the game of shove-board).

They throng who should buy first: . . . by which means I saw whose purse was best in picture; and what I saw, to my good use I remembered. . . . You might have pinched a placket, it was senseless; 'twas nothing to geld a codpiece of a purse; I could have filed keys off that hung in chains. . . . I picked and cut most of their festival purses; and had not the old man come in with a whoo-bub against his daughter, . . . I had not left a purse alive in the whole army.
The Winter's Tale. Act iv, sc. 4, l. 611. [Autolycus] The only use of "whoo-bub."

Picking of purses.—*I Henry IV,* ii, 1, 56.
Who steals my purse steals trash.—*Othello,* iii, 3, 157. See NAME, 1050:2.
Cutpurse, see under THEFT.

5
She has all the rule of her husband's purse.
The Merry Wives of Windsor. Act i, sc. 3, l. 58. [Falstaff]

She bears the purse too; she is a region in Guiana, all gold and bounty.
Merry Wives of Windsor. Act i, sc. 3, l. 76. [Falstaff] The only mention of Guiana.

6
Thou . . . hast had my purse
As if the strings were thine.
Othello. Act i, sc. 1, l. 2. [Roderigo]

Believe me, I had rather have lost my purse
Full of crusadoes.
Othello. Act iii, sc. 4, l. 26. [Desdemona] The only use of "crusadoes" (a Portuguese gold coin bearing the figure of a cross).

Fill thy purse with money.
Othello. Act i, sc. 3, l. 353. [Iago]

Our purses shall be proud.—*The Taming of the Shrew,* iv, 3, 173. See under MIND.

7
I fear 'tis deepest winter in Lord Timon's purse.
Timon of Athens. Act iii, sc. 4, l. 14. [Servant]

Cold purses.—*I Henry IV,* ii, 4, 355. See under OMEN.

8
Olivia: I thank you for your pains: spend this for me.
Viola: I am no fee'd post, lady; keep your purse.
Twelfth Night. Act i, sc. 5, l. 302.

Antonio: Hold, sir, here's my purse. . . .
Sebastian: Why I your purse?
Antonio: Haply your eye may light upon some toy
You have desire to purchase: and your store,
I think, is not for idle markets, sir.
Sebastian: I'll be your purse-bearer and leave you
For an hour.
Twelfth Night. Act iii, sc. 3, l. 38. The only use of "purse-bearer."

Here's my purse.—*Cymbeline,* iii, 5, 124.
There's my purse.—*Richard III,* iv, 4, 516, and four times in later plays.
Take my purse.—*King Lear,* iv, 6, 252.

9
Denied me mine own purse,
Which I had recommended to his use
Not half an hour before.
Twelfth Night. Act v, sc. 1, l. 94. [Antonio] The only use of "recommended." "Recommend" occurs three times.

10
Open your purse, that the money and the matter may be both at once delivered.
The Two Gentlemen of Verona. Act i, sc. 1, 137. [Speed]

11
Your purse is not hot enough to purchase your spice.
The Winter's Tale. Act iv, sc. 3, l. 127. [Autolycus]

Show the inside of your purse to the outside of his hand, and no more ado.
The Winter's Tale. Act iv, sc. 4, l. 833. [Clown]

PURSUIT

1
Whilst yet with Parthian blood thy sword is warm,
The fugitive Parthians follow; spur through Media,
Mesopotamia, and the shelters whither
The routed fly.
Antony and Cleopatra. Act iii, sc. 1, l. 6. Shakespeare's only use of "that blessed word" Mesopotamia, and of "routed."

2 A hue and a cry
Hath follow'd certain men unto this house.
I Henry IV. Act ii, sc. 4, l. 556. [Sheriff]
Hue and cry, villain, go!—*The Merry Wives of Windsor,* iv, 5, 92. The only uses of the phrase.

3
Turn head, and stop pursuit.
Henry V. Act ii, sc. 4, l. 69. [Dauphin]
Cease our hot pursuit.—*I Henry VI,* ii, 2, 3.
Pursuit would be in vain.—*All's Well that Ends Well,* iii, 4, 25.
Slow pursuit.—*The Rape of Lucrece,* l. 696.

4 All things that are,
Are with more spirit chased than enjoy'd.
The Merchant of Venice. Act ii, sc. 6, l. 12. [Gratiano]

5
Clap on more sails; pursue; up with your fights.
The Merry Wives of Windsor. Act ii, sc. 2, l. 142. [Pistol]

6
She shall pursue it with a soul of love.
A Midsummer-Night's Dream. Act ii, sc. 1, l. 182. [Oberon]
Pursue me not.—*Midsummer-Night's Dream,* ii, 1, 188.
Set forth in your pursuit.—*Twelfth Night,* iii, 3, 13.

PYRAMID

7
I have heard the Ptolemies' pyramises are very goodly things; without contradiction, I have heard that.
Antony and Cleopatra. Act ii, sc. 7, l. 39. [Lepidus] The only use of "pyramises."

A statelier pyramis to her I'll rear
Than Rhodope's or Memphis' ever was.
I Henry VI. Act i, sc. 6, l. 21. [Charles] The only use of "statelier" and "pyramis," and the only mention of Rhodope and Memphis.

8 Rather make
My country's pyramids my gibbet,
And hang me up in chains.
Antony and Cleopatra. Act v, sc. 2, l. 60. [Cleopatra]
Palaces and pyramids do slope
Their heads to their foundations.
Macbeth. Act iv, sc. 1, l. 57. [Macbeth]

9
Thy pyramids built up with newer might
To me are nothing novel, nothing strange.
Sonnets. No. cxxiii. The only use of "novel."

PYTHAGORAS

10
I was never so berhymed since Pythagoras' time, that I was an Irish rat, which I can hardly remember.
As You Like It. Act iii, sc. 2, l. 186. [Rosalind] The only use of "berhymed."

11
Thou almost makest me waver in my faith
To hold opinion with Pythagoras,
That souls of animals infuse themselves
Into the trunks of men.
The Merchant of Venice. Act iv, sc. 1, l. 130. [Gratiano] The only use of "waver."

12
Clown: What is the opinion of Pythagoras concerning wild fowl?
Malvolio: That the soul of our grandam might haply inhabit a bird.
Clown: What thinkest thou of his opinion?
Malvolio: I think nobly of the soul, and no way approve his opinion.
Twelfth Night. Act iv, sc. 2, l. 54.
Thou shalt hold the opinion of Pythagoras ere I will allow of thy wits, and fear to kill a woodcock, lest thou dispossess the soul of thy grandam.
Twelfth Night. Act iv, sc. 2, l. 62. [Clown]

Q

QUALITY

13
His qualities being at this poor price, I need not ask you if gold will corrupt him to revolt.
All's Well that Ends Well. Act iv, sc. 3, l. 308. [First Soldier]

14 Whose quality, going on,
The sides o' the world may danger.
Antony and Cleopatra. Act i, sc. 2, l. 198. [Antony]

15
A shop of all the qualities that man
Loves woman for, besides that hook of wiving.
Cymbeline. Act v, sc. 5, l. 166. [Iachimo]
Qualities Beseeming such a wife.—*The Two Gentlemen of Verona,* iii, 1, 65.

16
Come, give us a taste of your quality.
Hamlet. Act ii, sc. 2, l. 452. [Hamlet]
A quality Wherein, they say, you shine.
Hamlet. Act iv, sc. 7, l. 73. [King]

17 You are not of our quality,
But stand against us like an enemy.
I Henry IV. Act iv, sc. 3, l. 36. [Hotspur]

1
Which swims against your stream of quality.
II Henry IV. Act v, sc. 2, l. 34. [Clarence]

2
Thou 'lt not believe
With how depraved a quality.
King Lear. Act ii, sc. 4, l. 38. [King Lear]
I have many ill qualities.—*Much Ado about Nothing*, ii, 1, 106.
Baser quality.—*Henry V*, i, 1, 62.
Monstrous quality.—*Julius Cæsar*, i, 3, 68.
Vicious qualities.—*I Henry VI*, v, 4, 35.

3
You know the fiery quality of the duke.
King Lear. Act ii, sc. 4, l. 93. [Gloucester]
Burning quality.—*King John*, v, 7, 8.
Fierce quality.—*King Lear*, i, 2, 12.

4
What is thy name? I know thy quality.
Henry V. Act iii, sc. 6, l. 147. [King Henry]
What are you? Your name, your quality?
King Lear. Act v, sc. 3, l. 119. [Herald]
What quality are they of?
Measure for Measure. Act ii, sc. 1, l. 59. [Angelo]
What quality?—*King Lear*, ii, 4, 97.
Of quality.—*Othello*, ii, 3, 110.
Of quality or degree.—*King Lear*, v, 3, 110.

5
His qualities were beauteous as his form.
A Lover's Complaint, l. 99.
Gentlemen-like qualities.—*As You Like It*, i, 1, 73.
Grave and austere quality.—*Timon of Athens*, i, 1, 54.
True quality.—*Julius Cæsar*, iii, 1, 41; *Romeo and Juliet*, ii, 3, 16; *The Rape of Lucrece*, l. 1313.
Virtuous qualities.—*All's Well that Ends Well*, i, 1, 49.
Wondrous qualities.—*The Taming of the Shrew*, ii, 1, 50.
Worthy qualities.—*The Two Gentlemen of Verona*, v, 4, 153.

6
What is the quality of mine offence?
The Rape of Lucrece, l. 1702.
Quality of flesh.—*Timon of Athens*, iv, 3, 156.
Quality of her passion.—*Antony and Cleopatra*, v, 1, 63.
Qualities of people.—*Antony and Cleopatra*, i, 1, 54.
Quality of persons.—*Twelfth Night*, iii, 1, 70.
Quality of the time.—*Twelfth Night*, iii, 3, 31.

7
She hath more qualities than a water-spaniel.
The Two Gentlemen of Verona. Act iii, sc. 1, l. 271. [Launce] The only use of "water-spaniel."
Bawd: Boult, has she any qualities?
Boult: She has a good face, speaks well, and has excellent good clothes: there 's no further necessity of qualities.
Pericles. Act iv, sc. 2, l. 50.

QUANTITY

8
Methinks my moiety, north from Burton here,
In quantity equals not one of yours.
I Henry IV. Act iii, sc. 1, l. 96. [Hotspur]

9
If I were sawed into quantities, I should make four dozen of such bearded hermits' staves as Master Shallow.
II Henry IV. Act v, sc. 1, l. 70. [Falstaff]
The only use of "sawed."
He is not quantity enough for that Worthy's thumb.
Love's Labour's Lost. Act v, sc. 1, l. 137. [Armado]
Holding no quantity.—*A Midsummer-Night's Dream*, i, 1, 232.
Thou quantity, thou remnant!—*The Taming of the Shrew*, iv, 3, 112.

10
A quantity of life, Which bleeds away.
King John. Act v, sc. 4, l. 23. [Melun]
Quantity of choice.—*Hamlet*, iii, 4, 75.
Quantity of dirty lands.—*Twelfth Night*, ii, 4, 85.
Quantity of love.—*Hamlet*, v, 1, 293.

11
He likewise enriched poor straggling soldiers with great quantity.
Timon of Athens. Act v, sc. 1, l. 7. [Painter]
The only use of "great quantity."
Above their quantity.—*Timon of Athens*, v, 4, 18.
How much the quantity.—*Cymbeline*, iv, 2, 17.

QUARREL

See also Contention, Discord, Dissension

12
Holy seems the quarrel
Upon your grace's part; black and fearful
On the opposer.
All's Well that Ends Well. Act iii, sc. 1, l. 4. [Lord]

13
Look here, and at thy sovereign leisure read
The garboils she awaked.
Antony and Cleopatra. Act i, sc. 3, l. 60. [Antony]
So much uncurable, her garboils.—*Antony and Cleopatra*, ii, 2, 67. "Garboils" (brawls) is used in no other play.

14
'Tis not a time For private stomaching.
Antony and Cleopatra. Act ii, sc. 2, l. 8. [Lepidus] The only use of "stomaching."
Quarrel no more.—*Antony and Cleopatra*, i, 3, 66.
Patch a quarrel.—*Antony and Cleopatra*, ii, 2, 52.

15
You shall have time to wrangle in when you have nothing else to do.
Antony and Cleopatra. Act ii, sc. 2, l. 105. [Enobarbus]
You to a long and well-deserved bed:
And you to wrangling.
As You Like It. Act v, sc. 4, l. 196. [Jaques]
The only use of "well-deserved."
You still wrangle with her.
Love's Labour's Lost. Act iv, sc. 1, l. 119. [Maria]
Let us not wrangle.—*Julius Cæsar*, iv, 2, 45.

1
I have had four quarrels, and like to have fought one.
As You Like It. Act v, sc. 4, l. 48. [Touchstone]
The quarrel was upon the seventh cause.
As You Like It, v, 4, 51. See LIE, 857:16.
We quarrel in print, by the book.
As You Like It. Act v, sc. 4, l. 94. [Touchstone]

2
Had we no quarrel else to Rome, but that
Thou art thence banish'd, we would muster all
From twelve to seventy.
Coriolanus. Act iv, sc. 5, l. 133. [Aufidius]
Rome's quarrel.—*Titus Andronicus,* v, 3, 102.

3
My quarrel was not altogether slight.
Cymbeline. Act i, sc. 4, l. 51. [Posthumus]

4
Beware
Of entrance to a quarrel, but being in,
Bear 't that the opposed may beware of thee.
Hamlet. Act i, sc. 3, l. 65. [Polonius]
Find quarrel in a straw.—*Hamlet,* iv, 4, 55. See under GREATNESS.

5
You pick a quarrel to beguile me.
I Henry IV. Act iii, sc. 3, l. 76. [Hostess] The only use of "pick a quarrel."
O, would the quarrel lay upon their heads!
I Henry IV. Act v, sc. 2, l. 48. [Hotspur]

6
Shall we fall foul for toys?
II Henry IV. Act ii, sc. 4, l. 183. The only use of "fall foul."
I did upbraid her and fall out with her.
A Midsummer-Night's Dream. Act iv, sc. 1, l. 53. [Oberon] "Fall out" in this sense is repeated in *Richard III,* i, 3, 158; *Troilus and Cressida,* iii, 1, 93; *Romeo and Juliet,* i, 3, 32; iii, 1, 29; *Cymbeline,* v, 4, 32.

7
Be it thy course to busy giddy minds
With foreign quarrels.
II Henry IV. Act iv, sc. 5, l. 214. [King Henry]
I make my quarrel in particular.
II Henry IV. Act iv, sc. 1, l. 96. [Archbishop]
The quarrel of a true inheritor.—*II Henry IV,* iv, 5, 169.

8
Why the devil should we keep knives to cut one another's throats?
Henry V. Act ii, sc. 1, l. 95. [Bardolph] See THROAT, 1523:6.
Be friends, you English fools, be friends: we have French quarrels enow, if you could tell how to reckon.
Henry V. Act iv, sc. 1, l. 239. [Bates]

9
King Henry: I should be angry with you, if the time were convenient.
Williams: Let it be a quarrel between us, if you live.
King Henry: I embrace it. . . . I will make it my quarrel.
Henry V. Act iv, sc. 1, l. 217.

10
Cease, cease these jars and rest your minds in peace.
I Henry VI. Act i, sc. 1, l. 44. [Bedford]
O, what a scandal is it to our crown,
That two such noble peers as ye should jar!
I Henry VI. Act iii, sc. 1, l. 69. [King]
Fall'n at jars.—*II Henry VI,* i, 1, 253.
You live at jar.—*II Henry VI,* iv, 8, 43.
Endless jar.—*Troilus and Cressida,* i, 3, 117.
Mortal and intestine jars.—*The Comedy of Errors,* i, 1, 11. "Intestine" is repeated in *I Henry IV,* i, 1, 12: "Intestine shock."

11
I dare say
This quarrel will drink blood another day.
I Henry VI, ii, 4, 133. See under ROSE.
The quarrel toucheth none but us alone;
Betwixt ourselves let us decide it then.
I Henry VI. Act iv, sc. 1, l. 118. [Somerset]

12
If I longer stay,
We shall begin our ancient bickerings.
II Henry VI. Act i, sc. 1, l. 143. [Gloucester] The only use of "bickerings."
Purposely, therefore,
Left I the court, to see this quarrel tried.
II Henry VI. Act ii, sc. 3, l. 52. [Queen]

13
Thrice is he arm'd that hath his quarrel just.
II Henry VI, iii, 2, 233. See under JUSTICE.
His quarrel honourable.—*Henry V,* iv, 1, 133.

14
York: What is your quarrel? how began it first?
Edward: No quarrel, but a slight contention.
III Henry VI, i, 2, 5. See under CONTENTION.
What stratagems, how fell, how butcherly,
Erroneous, mutinous and unnatural,
This deadly quarrel daily doth beget!
III Henry VI. Act ii, sc. 5, l. 89. [Father] The only use of "butcherly." "Erroneous" occurs again in *Richard III,* i, 4, 200.
Bad quarrel.—*Titus Andronicus,* i, 1, 342.
Damned quarrel.—*Macbeth,* i, 2, 14.
Great quarrel.—*Titus Andronicus,* iii, 1, 4.
Known quarrel.—*Henry V,* ii, 4, 17.
Wrongful quarrel.—*Titus Andronicus,* i, 1, 293.

15
My quarrel and this English queen's are one.
III Henry VI. Act iii, sc. 3, l. 216. [Bona]

16
Do hourly Carp and quarrel.
King Lear. Act i, sc. 4, l. 222. [Goneril] The only use of "carp" in this sense. The fish of that name is twice referred to, in *All's Well that Ends Well,* v, 2, 24, and in *Hamlet,* ii, 1, 63.
Fall
To quarrel with your great opposeless wills.
King Lear. Act iv, sc. 6, l. 37. [Gloucester] The only use of "opposeless."
The best quarrels, in the heat, are cursed
By those that feel their sharpness.
King Lear. Act v, sc. 3, l. 56. [Edmund]
How grew your quarrel?—*King Lear,* ii, 2, 66.

17
I should forge
Quarrels unjust against the good and loyal,

Destroying them for wealth.
Macbeth. Act iv, sc. 3, l. 82. [Macbeth]
It is a rupture that you may easily heal.
Measure for Measure. Act iii, sc. 1, l. 244. [Duke] "Rupture" is repeated in *Troilus and Cressida,* v, 1, 22.

1
This their jangling I esteem a sport.
A Midsummer-Night's Dream. Act iii, sc. 2, l. 353. [Puck]
Good wits will be jangling.—*Love's Labour's Lost,* ii, 1, 225.
Jangling of the bells.—*Pericles,* ii, 1, 45. The only uses of "jangling."

2
Don Pedro: The Lady Beatrice hath a quarrel to you: the gentleman that danced with her told her she is much wronged by you.
Benedick: O, she misused me past the endurance of a block!
Much Ado about Nothing. Act ii, sc. 1, l. 245.

3
In the managing of quarrels you may say he is wise; for either he avoids them with great discretion, or undertakes them with a most Christian-like fear.
Much Ado about Nothing. Act ii, sc. 3, l. 196. [Don Pedro]
Don Pedro: Nay, do not quarrel with us, good old man.
Antonio: If he could right himself with quarrelling,
Some of us would lie low.
Much Ado about Nothing. Act v, sc. 1, l. 50.

4
As full of quarrel and offence
As my young mistress' dog.
Othello. Act ii, sc. 3, l. 52. [Iago]
What! in a town of war,
Yet wild, the people's hearts brimful of fear,
To manage private and domestic quarrel,
In night, and on the court and guard of safety!
'Tis monstrous.
Othello. Act ii, sc. 3, l. 213. [Othello]
I remember a mass of things, but nothing distinctly; a quarrel, but nothing wherefore.
Othello. Act ii, sc. 3, l. 289. [Cassio]

5
Thus cavils she with every thing she sees.
The Rape of Lucrece, l. 1093. See under ARGUMENT.

6
Say who thou art, . . .
Against what man thou comest, and what thy quarrel.
Richard II. Act i, sc. 3, l. 13. [Marshal]
What 's thy quarrel?—*Richard II,* i, 3, 33.
God's is the quarrel.—*Richard II,* i, 2, 37.

7
Gloucester: It is a quarrel most unnatural,
To be revenged on him that loveth you.
Lady Anne: It is a quarrel just and reasonable,
To be revenged on him that slew my husband.
Richard III. Act i, sc. 2, l. 134.
Take not the quarrel from his powerful arm.
Richard III. Act i, sc. 4, l. 223. [Clarence]

8
You have been factious one against the other.
Richard III. Act ii, sc. 1, l. 20. [King Edward]
Be factious for redress.—*Julius Cæsar,* i, 3, 118.
I will bandy with thee in faction.
As You Like It. Act v, sc. 1, l. 61. [Touchstone]
Their fraction is more our wish than their faction.
Troilus and Cressida. Act ii, sc. 3, l. 107. [Nestor]
After distasteful looks and these hard fractions.
Timon of Athens. Act ii, sc. 2, l. 220. [Flavius]

9
The quarrel is between our masters and us their men.
Romeo and Juliet. Act i, sc. 1, l. 23. [Gregory]
Quarrel, I will back thee.
Romeo and Juliet. Act i, sc. 1, l. 39. [Sampson]
Abraham: Do you bite your thumb at us, sir? . . .
Sampson: No, sir, I do not bite my thumb at you, sir, but I bite my thumb, sir.
Gregory: Do you quarrel, sir?
Abraham: Quarrel, sir! no, sir.
Sampson: If you do, sir, I am for you.
Romeo and Juliet. Act i, sc. 1, l. 51.
Who set this ancient quarrel new abroach?
Romeo and Juliet. Act i, sc. 1, l. 111. [Montague]
Ancient quarrels.—*Richard II,* ii, 1, 248.

10
I dare draw as soon as another man, if I see occasion in a good quarrel, and the law on my side.
Romeo and Juliet. Act ii, sc. 4, l. 167. [Peter]
Thou wilt quarrel with a man that hath a hair more, or a hair less, in his beard, than thou hast; . . . what eye but such an eye would spy out such a quarrel? Thy head is as full of quarrels as an egg is full of meat . . . thou hast quarrelled with a man for coughing in the street, because he hath wakened thy dog that hath lain asleep in the sun.
Romeo and Juliet. Act iii, sc. 1, l. 18. [Mercutio]
An I were so apt to quarrel as thou art, any man should buy the fee-simple of my life for an hour and a quarter.
Romeo and Juliet. Act iii, sc. 1, l. 34. [Benvolio] "Fee-simple" is used six times in the plays.
A great quarreller; and but he hath the gift of a coward to allay the gust he hath in quarrelling, 'tis thought among the prudent he would quickly have the gift of a grave.
Twelfth Night. Act i, sc. 3, l. 31. [Maria] The only use of "quarreller."
As quarrelous as the weasel.
Cymbeline. Act iii, sc. 4, l. 162. [Pisanio] The only use of "quarrelous."

11
The nature of our quarrel yet never brooked parle.
The Taming of the Shrew. Act i, sc. 1, l. 116. [Hortensio]

We will compound this quarrel.
The Taming of the Shrew. Act i, sc. 2, l. 27. [Hortensio]

1 How fares my Kate? What, sweeting, all amort?
The Taming of the Shrew. Act iv, sc. 3, l. 36. [Petruchio]

What, all amort?—*I Henry VI,* iii, 2, 124. The only uses of "amort."

2 Your words have took such pains as if they labour'd
To bring manslaughter into form and set quarreling
Upon the head of valour; which indeed
Is valour misbegot.
Timon of Athens. Act iii, sc. 5, l. 26. [First Senator] The only use of "manslaughter."

3 You are very short with us;
But, if we live, we 'll be as sharp with you.
Titus Andronicus. Act i, sc. 1, l. 409. [Saturninus]

This day all quarrels die.
Titus Andronicus, i, 1, 465. [Tamora]

Such quarrels may be broach'd
Without controlment, justice, or revenge.
Titus Andronicus. Act ii, sc. 1, l. 67. [Aaron] "Controlment" is repeated in *King John,* i, 1, 20, and in *Much Ado about Nothing,* i, 3, 21.

These quarrels must be quietly debated.
Titus Andronicus. Act v, sc. 3, l. 20. [Marcus]

4 This petty brabble will undo us all.
Titus Andronicus. Act ii, sc. 1, l. 62. [Aaron]

Here in the streets, desperate of shame and state,
In private brabble did we apprehend him.
Twelfth Night. Act v, sc. 1, l. 67. [Officer] The only use of "brabble."

Apprehend him.—*Henry V,* iv, 7, 165; iv, 8, 18; *King Lear,* i, 2, 83; ii, 1, 110.

Apprehend her.—*Othello,* i, 1, 178.

Apprehend thee.—*Romeo and Juliet,* v, 3, 56; 69; *Othello,* i, 2, 77.

Apprehend you.—*III Henry VI,* iii, 1, 71. The only uses of "apprehend" in this sense.

5 Be cross with him.
Titus Andronicus. Act ii, sc. 3, l. 53. [Aaron]

Why do you cross me in this exigent?
Julius Cæsar. Act v, sc. 1, l. 19. [Antony] "Exigent" is repeated in *I Henry VI,* ii, 5, 9, and in *Antony and Cleopatra,* iv, 14, 63.

Why should Titania cross her Oberon?
A Midsummer-Night's Dream. Act ii, sc. 1, l. 119. [Oberon]

If I can cross him any way, I bless myself every way.
Much Ado about Nothing. Act i, sc. 3, l. 69. [Don John]

6 What 's the quarrel?
Troilus and Cressida. Act ii, sc. 1, l. 98. [Achilles]

A good quarrel to draw emulous factions and bleed to death upon.
Troilus and Cressida. Act ii, sc. 3, l. 79. [Thersites]

Take heed, the quarrel 's most ominous to us.
Troilus and Cressida. Act v, sc. 7, l. 20. [Thersites]

Rank feud.—*Troilus and Cressida,* iv, 5, 132. The only use of "feud."

7 I am sure no man hath any quarrel to me: my remembrance is very free and clear from any image of offence done to any man.
Twelfth Night. Act iii, sc. 4, l. 247. [Viola]

And let no quarrel nor no brawl to come
Taint the condition of this present hour.
Twelfth Night. Act v, sc. 5, l. 364. [Fabian] See also under FIGHTING.

Take up the quarrel.—*Twelfth Night,* iii, 4, 320.

QUEEN

See also King

8 Fie, wrangling queen!
Whom every thing becomes, to chide, to laugh,
To weep; whose every passion fully strives
To make itself, in thee, fair and admired!
Antony and Cleopatra. Act i, sc. 1, l. 48. [Antony]

Absolute queen.—*Antony and Cleopatra,* iii, 6, 11.

Bloody-minded queen.—*III Henry VI,* ii, 6, 33.

Dread queen.—*Titus Andronicus,* v, 3, 26; *Antony and Cleopatra,* iii, 3, 9.

Fiend-like queen.—*Macbeth,* v, 8, 69.

Insulting queen.—*III Henry VI,* ii, 1, 168.

Jealous queen.—*Coriolanus,* v, 3, 46.

Ruthless queen.—*III Henry VI,* i, 4, 156; ii, 1, 61.

Ungentle queen.—*II Henry VI,* iii, 2, 290.

Warlike queen.—*III Henry VI,* ii, 1, 123.

Wicked queen.—*Cymbeline,* v, 5, 463.

9 I must from this enchanting queen break off.
Antony and Cleopatra. Act i, sc. 2, l. 132. [Antony]

O, never was there queen
So mightily betray'd!
Antony and Cleopatra. Act i, sc. 3, l. 24. [Cleopatra]

The queen my mistress,
Confined in all she has, her monument,
Of thy intents desires instruction,
That she preparedly may frame herself
To the way she 's forced to.
Antony and Cleopatra. Act v, sc. 1, l. 55. [Egyptian] The only use of "preparedly."

10 Our queen,
The imperial jointress to this warlike state.
Hamlet. Act i, sc. 2, l. 8. [King] The only use of "jointress."

First Player: 'But who, O, who had seen the mobled queen—'
Hamlet: 'The mobled queen?'
Polonius: That 's good; 'mobled queen' is good.
Hamlet. Act ii, sc. 2, l. 524. The only use of "mobled" (veiled).

You are the queen, your husband's brother's wife.
Hamlet. Act iii, sc. 4, l. 15. [Hamlet]

Who, that 's but a queen, fair, sober, wise,
Would from a paddock, from a bat, a gib,
Such dear concernings hide?
Hamlet. Act iii, sc. 4, l. 189. [Hamlet] The only use of "gib" (cat). "Paddock" (toad) occurs again in *Macbeth,* i, 1, 9.

The queen carouses to thy fortune.
Hamlet. Act v, sc. 2, l. 300. [Queen]

Seeming-virtuous queen.—*Hamlet,* i, 5, 46. The only use of the phrase.

1
Upon that I kiss your hand, and I call you my queen.
Henry V. Act v, sc. 2, l. 271. [King Henry]

Bear me witness all,
That here I kiss her as my sovereign queen.
Henry V. Act v, sc. 2, l. 385. [King Henry]

2
He doth intend she shall be England's queen.
I Henry VI. Act v, sc. 1, l. 45. [Gloucester]

Small joy have I in being England's queen.
Richard III. Act i, sc. 3, l. 110. [Queen Elizabeth]

England's queen.—*Richard III,* i, 3, 209.
England's counted queen.—*Richard III,* iv, 1, 47.
England's royal queen.—*I Henry VI,* v, 5, 24.
Great Albion's queen.—*III Henry VI,* iii, 3, 7.

3
Suffolk: Say, gentle princess, would you not suppose
Your bondage happy, to be made a queen?
Margaret: To be a queen in bondage is more vile
Than is a slave in base servility.
I Henry VI. Act v, sc. 3, l. 110.

I 'll undertake to make thee Henry's queen,
To put a golden sceptre in thy hand
And set a precious crown upon thy head.
I Henry VI. Act v, sc. 3, l. 117. [Suffolk]

4
The fairest queen that ever king received.
II Henry VI. Act i, sc. 1, l. 16. [Suffolk]

Fair queen.—*III Henry VI,* iii, 3, 12, and eleven times in later plays.
Dear queen.—*Antony and Cleopatra,* v, 2, 185.
Dear-bought queen.—*II Henry VI,* i, 1, 252. "Dear bought" occurs again in *The Merchant of Venice,* iii, 2, 315.
Gentle queen.—*II Henry VI,* iii, 2, 305, and five times in later plays.
Gracious queen.—*The Winter's Tale,* i, 2, 459.
Thrice-gracious queen.—*Richard II,* ii, 2, 24. "Thrice-gracious" is repeated in *I Henry IV,* iii, 2, 92: "Thrice-gracious lord."
Lovely queen.—*III Henry VI,* v, 7, 26.
Noble queen.—*III Henry VI,* iii, 3, 195; *Richard III,* i, 1, 91.
Precious queen.—*Antony and Cleopatra,* i, 3, 73; *The Winter's Tale,* iv, 2, 27.
Radiant queen.—*The Merry Wives of Windsor,* v, 5, 50.
Silver-shining queen.—*The Rape of Lucrece,* l. 786. The only use of the phrase.
Sweet queen.—*Troilus and Cressida,* iii, 1, 51. Used five times in this scene, and five times in other plays.
Honey-sweet queen.—*Troilus and Cressida,* iii, 1, 154. "Honey-sweet" is repeated in *Troilus and Cressida,* iii, 1, 71: "Honey-sweet lord"; and in *Henry V,* ii, 3, 1: "Honey-sweet husband."

5
Am I a queen in title and in style,
And must be made a subject to a duke?
II Henry VI. Act i, sc. 3, l. 51. [Queen]

Ay me, unhappy! To be a queen, and crown'd with infamy!
II Henry VI. Act iii, sc. 2, l. 70. [Queen]

6
One way or other, she is for a king;
And she shall be my love, or else my queen.
III Henry VI. Act iii, sc. 2, l. 87. [King Edward]

I know I am too mean to be your queen,
And yet too good to be your concubine.
III Henry VI. Act iii, sc. 2, l. 97. [Lady Grey] The only use of "concubine."

Our quondam queen.—*III Henry VI,* iii, 3, 153. Shakespeare uses "quondam" six times.

7
Anne: By my troth and maidenhead,
I would not be a queen.
Old Lady: Beshrew me, I would,
And venture maidenhead for 't.
Henry VIII. Act ii, sc. 3, l. 23.

Old Lady: You would not be a queen?
Anne: No, not for all the riches under heaven.
Old Lady: 'Tis strange: a three-pence bow'd would hire me,
Old as I am, to queen it.
Henry VIII. Act ii, sc. 3, l. 34.

I swear again, I would not be a queen
For all the world.
Henry VIII. Act ii, sc. 3, l. 45. [Anne]

There was a lady once, 'tis an old story,
That would not be a queen, that would she not,
For all the mud in Egypt: have you heard it?
Henry VIII. Act ii, sc. 4, l. 90. [Old Lady]

8
I am about to weep; but, thinking that
We are a queen, or long have dream'd so, certain
The daughter of a king, my drops of tears
I 'll turn to sparks of fire.
Henry VIII. Act ii, sc. 4, l. 70. [Queen Katharine]

The queen is obstinate,
Stubborn to justice, apt to accuse it, and
Disdainful to be tried by 't.
Henry VIII. Act ii, sc. 4, l. 121. [Campeius]

9
The queen of earthly queens: she 's noble born;
And, like her true nobility, she has
Carried herself towards me.
Henry VIII. Act ii, sc. 4, l. 141. [King]

The late queen's gentlewoman, a knight's daughter,
To be her mistress' mistress! the queen's queen!
Henry VIII. Act iii, sc. 2, l. 94. [Wolsey]

O queen of queens! how far dost thou excel,
No thought can think, nor tongue of mortal tell.
Love's Labour 's Lost. Act iv, sc. 3, l. 40. [King]

High and mighty queen.—*Richard III,* iv, 4, 347.
Princely queen.—*II Henry VI,* i, 1, 72.
Proud queen.—*III Henry VI,* i, 4, 118, and frequently thereafter.
Renowned queen.—*III Henry VI,* iii, 3, 38.

Royal queen.—*Antony and Cleopatra,* v, 2, 37.

1 She had all the royal makings of a queen.
Henry VIII. Act iv, sc. 1, l. 87. [Gentleman]

Although unqueen'd, yet like
A queen, and daughter to a king, inter me.
Henry VIII. Act iv, sc. 2, l. 171. [Katharine] The only use of "unqueen'd."

2 Out, insolent! thy bastard shall be king,
That thou mayst be a queen, and check the world!
King John. Act ii, sc. 1, l. 122. [Queen Elinor]

3 It seem'd she was a queen
Over her passion; who, most rebel-like,
Sought to be king o'er her.
King Lear. Act iv, sc. 3, l. 15. [Gentleman] The only use of "rebel-like."

Queen o'er myself.—*The Merchant of Venice,* iii, 2, 171.

4 The queen that bore thee,
Oftener upon her knees than on her feet,
Died every day she lived.
Macbeth. Act iv, sc. 3, l. 109. [Macduff]

5 My Nan shall be the queen of all the fairies.
The Merry Wives of Windsor. Act iv, sc. 4, l. 71. [Mrs. Page] Fairy queen, see under FAIRY.

6 This queen will live: nature awakes; a warmth
Breathes out of her: she hath not been entranced
Above five hours: see how she 'gins to blow
Into life's flower again!
Pericles. Act iii, sc. 2, l. 94. [Cerimon] The only use of "entranced."

Dead queen.—*Pericles,* iii, 1, 18.

Drown'd queen.—*Pericles,* v, 1, 207.

7 I had rather be a country servant-maid
Than a great queen, with this condition,
To be thus taunted, scorn'd and baited at.
Richard III. Act i, sc. 3, l. 107. [Queen Elizabeth] The only use of "servant-maid."

A little joy enjoys the queen thereof;
For I am she, and altogether joyless.
Richard III. Act i, sc. 3, l. 155. [Queen Margaret] "Joyless" is repeated in *Titus Andronicus,* iv, 2, 66.

Thyself a queen, for me that was a queen,
Outlive thy glory, like my wretched self!
Richard III. Act i, sc. 3, l. 202. [Queen Margaret]

Poor painted queen!
Richard III. Act i, sc. 3, l. 241. [Queen Margaret]

I call'd thee then poor shadow, painted queen;
The presentation of but what I was.
Richard III. Act iv, sc. 4, l. 83. [Queen Margaret] "Presentation" is repeated in *As You Like It,* v, 4, 112.

A queen in jest, only to fill the scene.
Richard III. Act iv, sc. 4, l. 91. [Queen Margaret]

Queen of sad mischance.—*Richard III,* iv, 4, 114.

Forlorn queen.—*II Henry VI,* iii, 2, 77.

Poor queen.—*II Henry VI,* ii, 2, 25; *III Henry VI,* i, 1, 264; iii, 1, 32; *Richard II,* iii, 4, 102; *Henry VIII,* v, 1, 74.

Tristful queen.—*I Henry IV,* ii, 4, 431.

Weeping queen.—*Richard II,* iii, 4, 107.

Woeful queen.—*Pericles,* iv, Gower, 3.

Wretched queen.—*Hamlet,* v, 2, 344; *Pericles,* iii, 1, 55.

8 Anointed let me be with deadly venom,
And die, ere men can say, God save the queen!
Richard III. Act iv, sc. 1, l. 62. [Anne]

Who sues to thee and cries 'God save the queen'?
Where be the bending peers that flatter'd thee?
Where be the thronging troops that follow'd thee?
Richard III. Act iv sc. 4, l. 94. [Queen Margaret] "Thronging" is repeated in *Much Ado about Nothing,* i, 1, 305.

9 As on the finger of a throned queen
The basest jewel will be well esteem'd.
Sonnets. No. xcvi.

10 Lovely Tamora, queen of Goths,
That like the stately Phœbe 'mongst her nymphs
Dost overshine the gallant'st dames of Rome.
Titus Andronicus. Act i, sc. 1, l. 315. [Saturninus] The only use of "gallant'st." "Queen of Goths" is repeated five times in this scene.

And make them know what 'tis to let a queen
Kneel in the streets and beg for grace in vain.
Titus Andronicus. Act i, sc. 1, l. 454. [Tamora]

This queen,
This goddess, this Semiramis, this nymph,
This siren.
Titus Andronicus. Act ii, sc. 1, l. 21. [Aaron]

11 A Grecian queen, whose youth and freshness
Wrinkles Apollo's, and makes stale the morning.
Troilus and Cressida. Act ii, sc. 2, l. 78. [Troilus] "Freshness" is repeated in *The Tempest,* ii, 1, 63.

Love-sick queen.—*Venus and Adonis,* l. 175.

Silly queen.—*The Passionate Pilgrim,* l. 123.

Ransack'd queen.—*Troilus and Cressida,* ii, 2, 150.

Strange queen.—*Love's Labour's Lost,* iv, 2, 134.

Stranger queen.—*Love's Labour's Lost,* iv, 2, 143.

Menelaus' queen.—*Troilus and Cressida,* Prol., 9.

Queen of Troy.—*Titus Andronicus,* i, 1, 136.

Carthage queen.—*Midsummer-Night's Dream,* i, 1, 173.

Queen of Carthage.—*The Taming of the Shrew,* i, 1, 159.

Egypt's queen.—*Antony and Cleopatra,* i, 1, 29.

Queen of Egypt.—*Antony and Cleopatra,* v, 2, 112.

Queen of Ptolemy.—*Antony and Cleopatra,* i, 4, 6.

Queen of Tunis.—*The Tempest,* ii, 1, 246.

12 Paulina: I come from your good queen.
Leontes: Good queen!

Paulina: Good queen, my lord
Good queen; I say good queen;
And would by combat make her good, so were I
A man, the worst about you. . . . The good queen,
For she is good, hath brought you forth a daughter.
The Winter's Tale. Act ii, sc. 3, l. 58.

Good queen.—*The Winter's Tale,* i, 2, 200; *Henry VIII,* ii, 1, 158; v, 5, 5; *Antony and Cleopatra,* v, 2, 158; 206; *Venus and Adonis,* l. 607.

1
I dare my life lay down and will do 't, sir,
Please you to accept it, that the queen is spotless.
Winter's Tale. Act ii, sc. 1, l. 130. [Lord]

Give me the office
To choose you a queen: she shall not be so young
As was your former; but she shall be such
As, walk'd your first queen's ghost, it should take joy
To see her in your arms.
Winter's Tale. Act v, sc. 1, l. 77. [Paulina]

2
Good sooth, she is
The queen of curds and cream.
Winter's Tale. Act iv, sc. 4, l. 160. [Camillo]

Queen o' the feast.—*Pericles,* ii, 3, 17.
Queen of gems.—*Twelfth Night,* ii, 4, 88.
Queen of love.—*The Passionate Pilgrim,* l. 117.
Queen of music.—*Passionate Pilgrim,* l. 112.
Queen of night.—*As You Like It,* iii, 2, 2; *The Two Gentlemen of Verona,* iv, 2, 100.
Queen o' the sky.—*The Tempest,* iv, 1, 70.
High'st queen of state.—*The Tempest,* iv, 1, 101.
Queen of virgins.—*All's Well that Ends Well,* i, 3, 119.
Beauty's queen.—*The Passionate Pilgrim,* l. 46.

QUESTION

See also Answer

3
Let me ask you a question.
All's Well that Ends Well. Act i, sc. 1, l. 123. [Helena]

More should I question thee, and more I must,
Though more to know could not be more to trust.
All's Well that Ends Well. Act ii, sc. 1, l. 208. [King]

Ask questions.—*All's Well that Ends Well,* iii, 2, 7.
I'll question her.—*All's Well that Ends Well,* iii, 5, 35.
I'll question you.—*The Winter's Tale,* i, 2, 60.

4
I beseech you, let me answer to the particular of the inter'gatories.
All's Well that Ends Well. Act iv, sc. 3, l. 206. [Parolles]

Nor the time nor place
Will serve our long inter'gatories.
Cymbeline. Act v, sc. 5, l. 391. [Cymbeline]

Charge us there upon inter'gatories,
And we will answer all things faithfully.
The Merchant of Venice. Act v, sc. 1, l. 298. [Portia] The only uses of "inter'gatories." "Interrogatories" occurs once, in *King John,* iii, 1, 147.

First inter'gatory.—*The Merchant of Venice,* v, 1, 300. The only use of "inter'gatory."

5
Whiles a wedlock-hymn we sing,
Feed yourselves with questioning.
As You Like It, v, 4, 144. [Hymen] The only use of "questioning," and "wedlock-hymn."

6
That 's a question: how shall we try it?
The Comedy of Errors. Act v, sc. 1, l. 421. [Dromio of Ephesus]

There 's the question.—*II Henry VI,* iv, 2, 149; *Julius Cæsar,* ii, 1, 13.
That is not the question.—*The Merry Wives of Windsor,* i, 1, 227.

7
I wonder, doctor,
Thou ask'st me such a question.
Cymbeline. Act i, sc. 5, l. 10. [Queen]

8
Let me question more in particular.
Hamlet. Act ii, sc. 2, l. 244. [Hamlet]

Queen: Come, come, you answer with an idle tongue.
Hamlet: Go, go, you question with a wicked tongue.
Hamlet. Act iii, sc. 4, l. 11.

I must call 't in question.
Hamlet. Act iv, sc. 5, l. 217. [Laertes]

Call in question.—*As You Like It,* v, 2, 6; *Julius Cæsar,* iv, 3, 165; *Twelfth Night,* i, 4, 6; *Troilus and Cressida,* iii, 2, 60.

9
I 'll put another question to thee.
Hamlet. Act v, sc. 1, l. 43. [Clown]

Question further.—*Cymbeline,* ii, 4, 52.
Further to question.—*Pericles,* i, 3, 12.

10
'Tis a question left us yet to prove,
Whether love lead fortune, or else fortune love.
Hamlet. Act iii, sc. 2. l. 212. [Player King]

Niggard of question.—*Hamlet,* iii, 1, 13.

11
Come, come, you paraquito, answer me
Directly unto this question that I ask.
I Henry IV. Act ii, sc. 3, l. 88. [Lady Percy] The only use of "paraquito."

Shall the blessed sun of heaven prove a micher and eat blackberries? a question not to be asked. Shall the son of England prove a thief and take purses? a question to be asked.
I Henry IV. Act ii, sc. 4, l. 449. [Falstaff] The only use of "micher" (truant).

12
Wherefore do I this? so the question stands.
II Henry IV. Act iv, sc. 1, l. 53. [Archbishop]

I muse you make so slight a question.
II Henry IV, iv, 1, 167. [Westmoreland]

13
Marry, I wad full fain hear some question 'tween you tway.
Henry V. Act iii, sc. 2, l. 127. [Jamy]

Out of question.—*Love's Labour 's Lost,* iv, 1, 30, and five times in later plays.
No question of that.—*II Henry VI,* iv, 2, 61.
No question but he was.—*Measure for Measure,* iii, 2, 146.

No question.—*Troilus and Cressida,* ii, 3, 155; *Othello,* iv, 3, 63; *Twelfth Night,* i, 3, 92.
Past question.—*Twelfth Night,* i, 3, 104.
Sans question.—*Love's Labour 's Lost,* v, 1, 91.
In contempt of question.—*Twelfth Night,* ii, 5, 98.

1
Ask me what question thou canst possible,
And I will answer unpremeditated.
I Henry VI. Act i, sc. 2, l. 87. [La Pucelle] The only use of "unpremeditated."

2
The question did at first so stagger me,
Bearing a state of mighty moment in 't
And consequence of dread, that I committed
The daring'st counsel which I had to doubt.
Henry VIII. Act ii, sc. 4, l. 212. [Bishop of Lincoln] The only use of "daring'st."

3
How needless was it then to ask the question!
Love's Labour 's Lost. Act ii, sc. 1, l. 117. [Rosaline]
'Tis 'long of you that spur me with such questions.
Love's Labour 's Lost. Act ii, sc. 1, l. 119. [Rosaline]
Question enrages him.
Macbeth. Act iii, sc. 4, l. 118. [Lady Macbeth]

4
I 'll stay no longer question.
The Merchant of Venice. Act iv, sc. 1, l. 346. [Shylock]
I will not stay thy questions.
A Midsummer-Night's Dream. Act ii, sc. 1, l. 235. [Demetrius]
Stay not to question.—*Romeo and Juliet,* 4, 3, 158.

5
And then comes answer like an Absey book:
'O sir,' says answer, 'at your best command;
At your employment; at your service, sir:'
'No, sir,' says question, 'I, sweet sir, at yours:'
And so, ere answer knows what question would,
Saving in dialogue of compliment,
And talking of the Alps and Appenines,
The Pyrenean and the river Po,
It draws toward supper in conclusion so.
King John. Act i, sc. 1, l. 196. [Bastard] The only use of "Absey," "Appenines," "Pyrenean" and "river Po."

6
Give me leave to question; you shall see how I 'll handle her.
Measure for Measure. Act v, sc. 1, l. 272. [Escalus]
First in question.—*Measure for Measure,* i, 1, 47.
Let them question.—*Merry Wives of Windsor,* iii, 1, 78.
Question him yourself.—*Much Ado about Nothing,* i, 2, 20.

7
Do you question me, as an honest man should do, for my simple true judgement; or would you have me speak after my custom?
Much Ado about Nothing. Act i, sc. 1, l. 167. [Benedick]
Let me but move one question to your daughter.
Much Ado about Nothing. Act iv, sc. 1, l. 74. [Claudio]
What kind of catechising call you this?
Much Ado about Nothing. Act iv, sc. 1, l. 79. [Hero] The only use of "catechising."

8
I wonder in my soul,
What you would ask me, that I should deny,
Or stand so mammering on.
Othello. Act iii, sc. 3, l. 68. [Desdemona] The only use of "mammering" (muttering).
Make questions.—*Othello,* iii, 4, 17.

9
Well demanded, wench:
My tale provokes that question.
The Tempest. Act i, sc. 2, l. 139. [Prospero]
Still 'tis beating in my mind.
The Tempest. Act i, sc. 2, l. 176. [Miranda]
Here cease more questions.—*The Tempest,* i, 2, 184.
Question me no more.—*Titus Andronicus,* ii, 3, 48.

10
Cressida: This is her question.
Pandar: That 's true; make no question of that.
Troilus and Cressida. Act i, sc. 2, l. 173.
I 'll decline the whole question.—*Troilus and Cressida,* ii, 3, 55.
Certain question.—*I Henry VI,* iv, 1, 95.
Constant question.—*Twelfth Night,* iv, 2, 53.
Facile question.—*Othello,* i, 3, 23.
Fair question.—*Othello,* i, 3, 113.
Meered question.—*Antony and Cleopatra,* iii, 13, 10. The only use of "meered" (only).
Necessary question.—*Hamlet,* iii, 2, 47.
Present question.—*The Merchant of Venice,* iv, 1, 172.
Queasy question.—*King Lear,* ii, 1, 19.

11
That question 's out of my part.
Twelfth Night. Act i, sc. 5, l. 191. [Viola]

QUICK

12
How dearly would it touch thee to the quick.
The Comedy of Errors. Act ii, sc. 2, l. 132. [Adriana]
I am struck to the quick.—*The Tempest,* v, 1, 25.

13
Brutus: He was quick mettle when he went to school.
Cassius: So is he now in execution
Of any bold or noble enterprise,
However he puts on this tardy form.
Julius Cæsar. Act i, sc. 2, l. 300.

14
'Tis for the dead, not for the quick.
Hamlet. Act v, sc. 1, l. 137. [Hamlet]
Now pile your dust upon the quick and dead,
Till of this flat a mountain you have made,
To o'ertop old Pelion, or the skyish head
Of blue Olympus.
Hamlet. Act v, sc. 1, l. 274. [Laertes] The only use of "skyish." Pelion is mentioned again in *The Merry Wives of Windsor,* ii, 1, 82, and Olympus six times in various plays.

Be buried quick with her, and so will I.
Hamlet. Act v, sc. 1, l. 302. [Hamlet]

So there's my riddle: one that's dead is quick.
All's Well that Ends Well. Act v, sc. 3, l. 304. [Diana]

Not to be buried, But quick and in mine arms.
The Winter's Tale. Act iv, sc. 4, l. 131. [Perdita]

Alas, I had rather be set quick i' the earth
And bowl'd to death with turnips!
The Merry Wives of Windsor. Act iii, sc. 4, l. 90. [Anne] The only mention of turnips.

Thou 'rt quick, But yet I 'll bury thee.
Timon of Athens. Act iv, sc. 3, l. 44. [Timon]

1
You must not be so quick.
Love's Labour's Lost. Act ii, sc. 1, l. 118. [Biron]

Short, quick, snap.—*Merry Wives of Windsor,* iv, 5, 3.

Snip, snap, quick.—*Love's Labour's Lost,* v, 1, 62.

Be quick.—*The Tempest,* i, 2, 366. See also under HASTE.

2
The poor wench is cast away: she 's quick.
Love's Labour's Lost. Act v, sc. 2, l. 682. [Costard]

Quick by him.—*Love's Labour's Lost,* v, 2, 687. See under PREGNANCY.

QUIET

3
An hour of quiet shortly shall we see;
Till then, in patience our proceeding be.
Hamlet. Act v, sc. 1, l. 321. [King]

4
Pistol, I would be quiet.
II Henry IV. Act ii, sc. 4, l. 199. [Falstaff]

Be quiet then as men should be,
Till he hath pass'd necessity.
Pericles. Act ii, Gower, l. 5.

Be quiet.—*II Henry VI,* i, 3, 146, and frequently in later plays.

Be quiet, people.—*Comedy of Errors,* v, 1, 38.

Be quiet and depart.—*The Comedy of Errors,* v, 1, 112.

I can be quiet.—*Love's Labour's Lost,* i, 2, 171.

Keep quiet.—*Henry V,* i, 2, 79.

Quiet yourselves.—*I Henry VI,* iv, 1, 115.

Better quiet.—*II Henry IV,* iv, 5, 188.

5
To stop effusion of our Christian blood
And stablish quietness on every side.
I Henry VI. Act v, sc. 1, l. 9. [Gloucester] The only use of "stablish."

Give me quietness.—*III Henry VI,* iv, 3, 16.

Quietness of spirit.—*The Merchant of Venice,* iv, 1, 12.

And quietness, grown sick of rest, would purge
By any desperate change.
Antony and Cleopatra. Act i, sc. 3, l. 53. [Antony]

6
Thy greatest help is quiet.
II Henry VI. Act ii, sc. 4, l. 67. [Gloucester]

7
I am glad he is so quiet.
The Merry Wives of Windsor. Act i, sc. 4, l. 95. [Mrs. Quickly]

Let me quiet go.—*Midsummer-Night's Dream,* iii, 2, 314.

8
Her house is sack'd, her quiet interrupted.
Rape of Lucrece, l. 1170. See under MANSION.

9
Lo! thus, by day my limbs, by night my mind,
For thee and for myself no quiet find.
Sonnets. No. xxvii.

Never at quiet!—*Macbeth,* ii, 3, 18.

She is much out of quiet.—*Twelfth Night,* ii, 3, 144.

R

RABBLE

See also People

10
The rabble should have first unroof'd the city,
Ere so prevail'd with me.
Coriolanus. Act i, sc. 1, l. 222. [Marcius] The only use of "unroof'd."

The rabble . . . that can judge as fitly of his worth
As I can of those mysteries which heaven
Will not have earth to know.
Coriolanus. Act iv, sc. 2, l. 33. [Volumnia]

11
The rabble call him lord.
Hamlet. Act iv, sc. 5, l. 102. [Gentleman]

12 Follow'd with a rabble that rejoice
To see my tears.
II Henry VI. Act ii, sc. 4, l. 32. [Duchess]

At his heels a rabble.—*The Merry Wives of Windsor,* iii, 5, 76.

There 's a trim rabble.—*Henry VIII,* v, 4, 75.

13
The rabblement hooted and clapped their chopped hands and threw up their sweaty night-caps and uttered such a deal of stinking breath.
Julius Cæsar. Act i, sc. 2, l. 246. [Casca] The only use of "rabblement." "Night-cap" is repeated in *Othello,* ii, 1, 316; and "sweaty" in *Hamlet,* i, 1, 77: "Sweaty haste."

14 Your disorder'd rabble
Make servants of their betters.
King Lear. Act i, sc. 4, l. 277. [Goneril]

To be baited with the rabble's curse.
Macbeth. Act v, sc. 8, l. 29. [Macbeth]

15
Go bring the rabble.
The Tempest. Act iv, sc. 1, l. 37. [Prospero]

RACE

1 None our parts so poor,
But was a race of heaven.
Antony and Cleopatra. Act i, sc. 3, l. 36. [Cleopatra]
2
Now I give my sensual race the rein.
Measure for Measure. Act ii, sc. 4, l. 160. [Angelo]
Drowsy race.—*King John,* iii, 3, 39.
Fiery race.—*Sonnets,* li.
Happy race.—*Richard III,* v, 3, 157.
Lawful race.—*Antony and Cleopatra,* iii, 13, 107.
Noble race.—*II Henry VI,* iii, 2, 215; *Pericles,* v, Gower, 9.
Nobler race.—*The Winter's Tale,* iv, 4, 95.
Valiant race.—*Cymbeline,* v, 4, 83.
3
Thy vile race . . . had that in 't which good natures
Could not abide to be with.
The Tempest. Act i, sc. 2, l. 358. [Prospero]
Whole race of mankind.—*Timon of Athens,* iv, 1, 40.
4
A race or two of ginger.
The Winter's Tale, iv, 3, 50. See under Food.
Two razes of ginger.—*I Henry IV,* ii, 2, 27. The only uses of "race" or "raze" in the sense of root.

RAGE

See also Anger, Fury, Wrath

5 O, that I were
Upon the hill of Basan, to outroar
The horned herd! for I have savage cause.
Antony and Cleopatra. Act iii, sc. 13, l. 126. [Antony] The only mention of Basan.
When one so great begins to rage, he 's hunted
Even to falling.
Antony and Cleopatra. Act iv, sc. 1, l. 7. [Mecænas]
6
Put not your worthy rage into your tongue.
Coriolanus. Act iii, sc. 1, l. 241. [Menenius]
This tiger-footed rage, when it shall find
The harm of unscann'd swiftness, will too late
Tie leaden pounds to 's heels.
Coriolanus. Act iii, sc. 1, l. 312. [Menenius] The only use of "tiger-footed" and "unscann'd."
Appertaining rage.—*Romeo and Juliet,* iii, 1, 66.
Barren rage.—*Sonnets,* xiii.
Blunt rage.—*The Rape of Lucrece,* l. 1398.
Desperate rage.—*The Rape of Lucrece,* l. 219.
Extreme rage.—*The Two Gentlemen of Verona,* ii, 7, 22.
Extremity of rage.—*The Comedy of Errors,* v, 1, 48.
Eyeless rage.—*King Lear,* iii, 1, 8.
Harsh rage.—*I Henry IV,* iii, 1, 183.
High rage.—*King Lear,* ii, 4, 299.
Mortal rage.—*Sonnets,* lxiv.
Old rage.—*Love's Labour 's Lost,* v, 2, 417.
Pernicious rage.—*Romeo and Juliet,* i, 1, 91.
Staring rage.—*King John,* iv, 3, 49.
Unmitigable rage.—*The Tempest,* i, 2, 276. The only use of "unmitigable."
Warlike rage.—*I Henry VI,* iv, 6, 13.
Wild rage.—*Henry V,* iv, 7, 82.
Wildest rage.—*A Midsummer-Night's Dream,* v, 1, 225.
7
The fire of rage is in him.
Cymbeline. Act i, sc. 1, l. 77. [Queen]
He rages; none Dare come about him.
Cymbeline. Act iii, sc. 5, l. 67. [Cloten]
Rages like a chafed bull.—*III Henry VI,* ii, 5, 126.
Doth he still rage?—*King John,* v, 7, 11.
My rage is gone.—*Coriolanus,* v, 6, 148.
8
Like the hectic in my blood he rages.
Hamlet. Act iv, sc. 3, l. 68. [King] The only use of "hectic" (fever).
How much I had to do to calm his rage!
Hamlet. Act iv, sc. 7, l. 193. [King]
9
Disguise fair nature with hard-favour'd rage.
Henry V. Act iii, sc. 1, l. 8. [King Henry]
Abate thy rage, abate thy manly rage,
Abate thy rage, great duke!
Good bawcock, bate thy rage; use lenity, sweet chuck!
Henry V. Act iii, sc. 2, l. 24. [Pistol]
His rages, and his furies, and his wraths, and his cholers, and his moods, and his displeasures, and his indignations.
Henry V. Act iv, sc. 7, l. 36. [Fluellen]
Stop the rage betime.—*II Henry VI,* iii, 1, 285.
10
Bid'st thou me rage? why, now thou hast thy wish.
III Henry VI. Act i, sc. 4, l. 143. [York]
Your rage mistakes us.—*Henry VIII,* iii, 1, 101.
11
Or shall we give the signal to our rage
And stalk in blood to our possession?
King John. Act ii, sc. 1, l. 265. [King Philip]
12 In their rage, . . .
They whirl asunder and dismember me.
King John. Act iii, sc. 1, l. 329. [Blanch]
Thy rage shall burn thee up, and thou shalt turn
To ashes, ere our blood shall quench that fire.
King John. Act iii, sc. 1, l. 344. [King Philip]
My rage was blind.—*King John,* iv, 2, 264.
13
Throw this report on their incensed rage.
King John. Act iv, sc. 2, l. 261. [King John]
His incensement at this moment is so implacable.
Twelfth Night. Act iii, sc. 4, l. 260. [Sir Toby] The only use of "incensement."
14 Seek, seek for him;
Lest his ungovern'd rage dissolve the life
That wants the means to lead it.
King Lear. Act iv, sc. 4, l. 18. [Cordelia]
The great rage, You see, is kill'd in him.
King Lear. Act iv, sc. 7, l. 78. [Doctor]
Great rage of heart.—*I Henry VI,* iv, 7, 11.
In top of rage.—*A Lover's Complaint,* l. 55.
15 Did he not straight
In pious rage the two delinquents tear,
That were the slaves of drink and thralls of sleep?
Macbeth. Act iii, sc. 6, l. 11. [Lennox] The only use of "delinquents."

Full of rage.—*The Merchant of Venice,* v, 1, 81.
1
Preceptial medicine to rage.
Much Ado about Nothing. Act v, sc. 1, l. 24. [Leonato] The only use of "preceptial."
2
Men in rage strike those that wish them best.
Othello. Act ii, sc. 3, l. 243. [Iago]
To rage the city turn.—*Pericles,* v, 3, 97.
3
In fell battle's rage.
The Rape of Lucrece, l. 145.
Frenchmen's rage.—*I Henry VI,* iv, 6, 34.
Rage of France.—*I Henry VI,* iv, 6, 3.
Heaven's fell rage.—*A Lover's Complaint,* l. 13.
Parents' rage.—*Romeo and Juliet,* Prol., 10.
Poet's rage.—*Sonnets,* xvii.
Sorrow's rage.—*Richard III,* i, 3, 278.
Traitors' rage.—*II Henry VI,* iii, 1, 174.
Tyrant's rage.—*King Lear,* iv, 6, 63.
4
This moves in him more rage and lesser pity.
The Rape of Lucrece, l. 468.
In rage sent out, recall'd in rage, being past.
The Rape of Lucrece, l. 1671.
Rage of lust.—*The Rape of Lucrece,* l. 424.
5
Rage must be withstood.
Richard II. Act i, sc. 1, l. 173. [King Richard] The only use of "withstood."
The rage be his.—*Richard II,* iii, 3, 59.
Fawn on rage.—*Richard II,* v, 1, 33.
6
Tush, that was in thy rage.
Richard III. Act i, sc. 2, l. 188. [Gloucester]
Replete with too much rage.
Sonnets. No. xxiii.
7
He 's flung in rage from this ungrateful seat
Of monstrous friends.
Timon of Athens. Act iv, sc. 2, l. 45. [Flavius]
Then the thing of courage
As roused with rage with rage doth sympathize.
Troilus and Cressida. Act i, sc. 3, l. 51. [Nestor]

RAILING

8
Let me rail so high,
That the false housewife Fortune break her wheel.
Antony and Cleopatra. Act iv, sc. 15, l. 43. [Cleopatra]
We two will rail against our mistress the world and all our misery.
As You Like It. Act iii, sc. 2, l. 295. [Jaques]
9
Rosalind: Can a woman rail thus?
Silvius: Call you this railing?
As You Like It. Act iv, sc. 3, l. 42.
Did you ever hear such railing?—*As You Like It,* iv, 3, 46.
His railing is intolerable.—*II Henry VI,* iii, 1, 172.
10
There was a haberdasher's wife of small wit . . . that railed upon me till her pinked porringer fell off her head.
Henry VIII. Act v, sc. 4, l. 49. [Man] The only use of "haberdasher" and "pinked." "Porringer" occurs again in *The Taming of the Shrew,* iv, 3, 64.
Rail'd at me.—*The Two Gentlemen of Verona,* ii, 2, 4.
Rail'd against our person.—*Henry V,* ii, 2, 41.
Railed at herself.—*Much Ado about Nothing,* ii, 3, 147.
Thou hast railed on thyself.—*As You Like It,* i, 1, 65.
I have railed so long.—*Much Ado about Nothing,* ii, 3, 246.
11
Like a poor beggar, raileth on the rich.
King John. Act ii, sc. 1, l. 592. [Bastard] The only use of "raileth."
12
Why, what a monstrous fellow art thou, thus to rail on one that is neither known to thee nor knows thee!
King Lear. Act ii, sc. 2, l. 27. [Oswald]
He . . . rails against all married mankind.
The Merry Wives of Windsor. Act iv, sc. 2, l. 23. [Mrs. Page]
He rails upon me.—*Troilus and Cressida,* ii, 1, 98.
13
Sometime rail thou like Demetrius.
A Midsummer-Night's Dream. Act iii, sc. 2, l. 362. [Oberon]
She 'll rail in the street.—*Othello,* iv, 1, 170.
In vain I rail.—*The Rape of Lucrece,* l. 1023.
14
And rail on Phyrrus that hath done him wrong.
The Rape of Lucrece, l. 1467.
Rail on the Lord's anointed.—*Richard III,* iv, 4, 150.
15
And rail upon the hostess of the house;
And say you would present her at the leet.
The Taming of the Shrew. Induction, sc. ii, l. 88. [First Servant] The only use of "leet" (a special court of record).
An he begin once, he 'll rail in his rope-tricks.
The Taming of the Shrew. Act i, sc. 2, l. 112. [Grumio] The only use of "rope-tricks" (an illiterate distortion of rhetoric).
And rails, and swears, and rates, that she, poor soul,
Knows not which way to stand, to look, to speak.
The Taming of the Shrew. Act iv, sc. 1, l. 187. [Curtis]
16
Nay, an you begin to rail on society once, I am sworn not to give regard to you. Farewell; and come with better music.
Timon of Athens. Act i, sc. 2, l. 250. [Timon]
17
O, that I knew thy heart; and knew the beast,
That I might rail at him, to ease my mind!
Titus Andronicus. Act ii, sc. 4, l. 34. [Marcus]
18
Thou grumblest and railest every hour.
Troilus and Cressida. Act ii, sc. 1, l. 35. [Thersites] The only use of "grumblest."
Come in and rail.—*Troilus and Cressida,* ii, 3, 26.

1
I rail'd on thee, fearing thy love's decrease.
Venus and Adonis, l. 1002.

RAIMENT, see Dress

RAIN

2
How now! rain within doors, and none abroad!
II Henry IV, iv, 5, 9. See MELANCHOLY, 979:3.

3
For raging wind blows up incessant showers,
And when the rage allays, the rain begins.
III Henry VI. Act i, sc. 4, l. 145. [York]

Shower of rain.—*Antony and Cleopatra,* i, 2, 156.

Drops of rain.—*Titus Andronicus,* ii, 3, 141.

4
You cataracts and hurricanoes, spout
Till you have drench'd our steeples, drown'd the cocks!
King Lear. Act iii, sc. 2, l. 2. [King Lear] The only use of "cataracts." "Hurricano" occurs again in *Troilus and Cressida,* v, 2, 172.

Let the sky rain potatoes.
The Merry Wives of Windsor, v, 5, 21. The only mention of potatoes.

Spout, rain!—*King Lear,* iii, 2, 15.

Gentle rain.—*Merchant of Venice,* iv, 1, 185.

5
Stand thee close, then, under this penthouse, for it drizzles rain.
Much Ado about Nothing. Act iii, sc. 3, l. 110. [Borachio] Pent-house" occurs also in *The Merchant of Venice,* ii, 6, 1, and in *Macbeth,* i, 3, 20. "Penthouse-like" is used in *Love's Labour's Lost,* iii, 1, 17. The only use of "drizzles." "Drizzle" occurs in *Romeo and Juliet,* iii, 5, 127: "Drizzle dew."

Begins to rain.—*King Lear,* ii, 4, 81.

Rains downright.—*Romeo and Juliet,* iii, 5, 129.

6
No flood by raining slaketh.
The Rape of Lucrece, l. 1677. The only use of "slaketh." "Slake" occurs in *III Henry VI,* i, 3, 29.

7
Dry the rain on my storm-beaten face.
Sonnets. No. xxxiv. The only use of "storm-beaten."

8
When that I was and a little tiny boy,
With hey, ho, the wind and the rain,
A foolish thing was but a toy,
For the rain it raineth every day.
Twelfth Night. Act v, sc. 1, l. 398. [Clown] The refrain is repeated in *King Lear,* iii, 2, 75.

9
Rain added to a river that is rank
Perforce will force it overflow the bank.
Venus and Adonis, l. 71.

But through the flood-gates breaks the silver rain.
Venus and Adonis, l. 959. See under TEAR.

II—Rainbow

10
Add another hue unto the rainbow.
King John, iv, 2, 14. See under EXCESS.

All the colours of the rainbow.—*The Merry Wives of Windsor,* iv, 5, 119; *The Winter's Tale,* iv, 4, 206.

Like rainbows in the sky.—*The Rape of Lucrece,* l. 1587. The only uses of "rainbow" and "rainbows."

11
With each end of thy blue bow dost crown
My bosky acres and my unshrubb'd down,
Rich scarf to my proud earth.
The Tempest. Act iv, sc. 1, l. 80. [Ceres] The only use of "bosky" and "unshrubb'd."

Heavenly bow.—*The Tempest,* iv, 1, 86.

Watery arch.—*The Tempest,* iv, 1, 71.

RANCOUR

See also Anger, Hatred

12
Rancour will out.
II Henry VI. Act i, sc. 1, l. 142. [Gloucester]

13
Put rancours in the vessel of my peace.
Macbeth. Act iii, sc. 1, l. 67. [Macbeth]

14
It issues from the rancour of a villain.
Richard II. Act i, sc. 1, l. 143. [Mowbray]

15
The broken rancour of your high-swoln hearts,
But lately splinter'd, knit, and join'd together,
Must gently be preserved, cherish'd, and kept.
Richard III. Act ii, sc. 2, l. 117. [Buckingham] The only use of "high-swoln" and "splinter'd."

This sudden stab of rancour I misdoubt.
Richard III. Act iii, sc. 2, l. 89. [Stanley]

Unmitigated rancour.—*Much Ado about Nothing,* iv, 1, 308. The only use of "unmitigated."

Rancorous enemy.—*Richard III,* i, 3, 50.

Rancorous heart.—*II Henry VI,* iii, 1, 24.

Rancorous mind.—*II Henry VI,* iii, 1, 24.

Rancorous outrage.—*The Comedy of Errors,* i, 1, 6.

Rancorous spite.—*I Henry VI,* iv, 1, 185. The only uses of "rancorous." It will be noted that the word does not occur after the fifth play.

RANK

16
With . . . his well-paid ranks,
The ne'er-yet-beaten horse of Parthia
We have jaded out o' the field.
Antony and Cleopatra. Act iii, sc. 1, l. 32. [Ventidius] The only use of "well-paid" and "ne'er-yet-beaten."

Low ranks.—*All's Well that Ends Well,* i, 2, 43.

Smoky ranks.—*The Rape of Lucrece,* l. 783.

Pure ranks.—*The Rape of Lucrece,* l. 73.

Well-beseeming ranks.—*I Henry IV,* i, 1, 14.

17
Would he had been of my rank!
Cymbeline. Act ii, sc. 1, l. 17. [Cloten]

Best rank.—*Hamlet,* i, 3, 73.

Equal rank.—*II Henry IV,* v, 2, 137.

First rank.—*Troilus and Cressida,* iii, 3, 161.

Worst rank.—*Macbeth,* iii, 1, 103.

18
Our ranks are broke, and ruin follows us.
III Henry VI. Act ii, sc. 3, l. 10. [George]

All our ranks are broke.—*Henry V*, iv, 5, 6.

1
He finds thee in the stout Norwegian ranks
Nothing afeard.
Macbeth. Act i, sc. 3, l. 95. [Ross]

Fill up her enemies' ranks.—*King John*, v, 2, 29.

2
Rank me with the barbarous multitudes.
The Merchant of Venice, ii, 9, 33. See under CHOICE.

3
Their ranks began
To break upon the galled shore, and than
Retire again, till, meeting greater ranks,
They join and shoot their foam at Simois' banks.
The Rape of Lucrece, l. 1439.

4
Bring in thy ranks, but leave without thy rage.
Timon of Athens. Act v, sc. 4, l. 39. [Senator]

Ranks of better equipage.—*Sonnets*, xxxii.
Ranks of blue veins.—*Rape of Lucrece*, l. 440.
Ranks of death.—*King Lear*, ii, 4, 261.
Ranks of foreign powers.—*King John*, iv, 2, 244.
Ranks of Greekish youth.—*Troilus and Cressida*, iv, 5, 185.
Ranks of people.—*Othello*, ii, 1, 54.
Ranks and squadrons.—*Julius Cæsar*, ii, 2, 20.

Rank and file, see under SOLDIER, OFFICER.

II—Rankness

5
Touchstone: If I keep not my rank,—
Rosalind: Thou loseth thy old smell.
As You Like It. Act i, sc. 2, l. 113.

Rank of gross diet.—*Antony and Cleopatra*, v, 2, 212.
Rank as any flax-wench.—*The Winter's Tale*, i, 2, 277. The only use of "flax-wench."
Rank as a fox.—*Twelfth Night*, ii, 5, 136.

6
Ha! what, so rank? Ah ha!
Henry VIII. Act i, sc. 2, l. 186. [King Henry]

Something rank.—*The Merry Wives of Windsor*, iv, 6, 22.
Most rank.—*Othello*, iii, 2, 232.
None so rank.—*Hamlet*, ii, 1, 20.

RANSOM

7
O, ransom, ransom! do not hide mine eyes.
All's Well that Ends Well. Act iv, sc. 1, l. 74. [Parolles]

Use me well; You shall have ransom.
King Lear. Act iv, sc. 6, l. 195. [King Lear]

8
His goods confiscate to the duke's dispose,
Unless a thousand marks be levied,
To quit the penalty and to ransom him.
Comedy of Errors. Act i, sc. 1, l. 21. [Duke]

Let him be ransom'd.—*Cymbeline*, v, 5, 85.
Exchanged and ransomed.—*I Henry VI*, i, 4, 29.
Ransom home.—*I Henry IV*, i, 3, 92.
Prisoners' ransom.—*I Henry IV*, ii, 3, 57.
Sufficient ransom.—*The Two Gentlemen of Verona*, iv, 4, 75.
Willing ransom.—*Henry V*, iii, 5, 63.

9
Bid him therefore consider of his ransom; which must proportion the losses we have borne, the subjects we have lost, the disgrace we have digested; which in weight to re-answer, his pettiness would bow under. For our losses, his exchequer is too poor; for the effusion of our blood, the muster of his kingdom is too faint a number; and for our disgrace, his own person, kneeling at our feet, but a weak and worthless satisfaction.
Henry V. Act iii, sc. 6, l. 132. [Montjoy]
The only use of "re-answer," and "pettiness."

My ransom is this frail and worthless trunk.
Henry V. Act iii, sc. 6, l. 163. [King Henry]

Montjoy: Once more I come to know of thee, King Harry,
If for thy ransom thou wilt now compound,
Before thy most assured overthrow. . . .
King Henry: I pray thee, bear my former answer back:
Bid them achieve me and then sell my bones. . . .
Come thou no more for ransom, gentle herald:
They shall have none, I swear, but these my joints;
Which if they have as I will leave 'em them,
Shall yield them little, tell the constable.
Henry V. Act iv, sc. 3, l. 79.

Exeter: Here comes the herald of the French, my liege.
Gloucester: His eyes are humbler than they used to be.
King Henry: How now? what means this, herald? know'st thou not
That I have fined these bones of mine for ransom?
Comest thou again for ransom?
Montjoy: No, great king:
I come to thee for charitable license,
That we may wander o'er this bloody field
To look our dead and then to bury them.
Henry V. Act iv, sc. 7, l. 69.

10
Pistol: O Signieur Dew, thou diest on point of fox,
Except, O signieur, thou do give to me
Egregious ransom. . . .
Boy: For his ransom he will give you two hundred crowns.
Pistol: Tell him my fury shall abate, and I the crowns will take.
Henry V. Act iv, sc. 4, l. 9.

11
His ransom there is none but I shall pay:
I 'll hale the Dauphin headlong from his throne:
His crown shall be the ransom of my friend;
Four of their lords I 'll change for one of ours.
I Henry VI. Act i, sc. 1, l. 148. [Bedford]

What ransom must I pay before I pass?
For I perceive I am thy prisoner. . . .
Wilt thou accept of ransom? yea, or no.
I Henry VI. Act v, sc. 3, l. 73. [Margaret]

12
If, after three days' space, thou here be'st found
On any ground that I am ruler of,

The world shall not be ransom for thy life.
II Henry VI. Act iii, sc. 2, l. 295. [King Henry]

Captain: Bring forth the soldiers of our prize;
For, whilst our pinnace anchors in the Downs,
Here shall they make their ransom on the sand,
Or with their blood stain this discolour'd shore. . . .
Gentleman: What is my ransom, master? let me know.
Master: A thousand crowns, or else lay down your head.
II Henry VI. Act iv, sc. 1, l. 8.

1
The world's ransom, blessed Mary's Son.
Richard II. Act ii, sc. 1, l. 56. [Gaunt]

2
For me, the ransom of my bold attempt
Shall be this cold corpse on the earth's cold face.
Richard III. Act v, sc. 3, l. 265. [Richmond]

I will send his ransom.—*Timon of Athens,* i, 1, 105.

3
Aaron: Titus Andronicus, my lord the emperor
Sends thee this word,—that, if thou love thy sons,
Let Marcus, Lucius, or thyself, old Titus,
Or any one of you, chop off your hand,
And send it to the king: he for the same
Will send thee hither both thy sons alive:
And that shall be the ransom for their fault. . . .
Titus: With all my heart, I'll send the emperor
My hand:
Good Aaron, wilt thou help to chop it off?
Titus Andronicus. Act iii, sc. 1, l. 150.

RAPE

4
For rapes and ravishments he parallels Nessus.
All's Well that Ends Well. Act iv, sc. 3, l. 281. [Parolles] The only use of "ravishments."

5
With that suit upon my back will I ravish her.
Cymbeline. Act iii, sc. 5, l. 142. [Cloten]

'Faith I must ravish her, or she'll disfurnish us of all our cavaliers, and make our swearers priests.
Pericles. Act iv, sc. 6, l. 11. [Boult] "Disfurnish" occurs three times.

We must either get her ravished, or be rid of her.
Pericles. Act iv, sc. 6, l. 5. [Boult]

6
Ravish your wives and daughters before your faces.
II Henry VI. Act iv, sc. 8, l. 31. [Cade]

Ravish our daughters?—*Richard III,* v, 3, 337.

You have holp to ravish your own daughters.—*Coriolanus,* iv, 6, 81.

Ravish a maid, or plot the way to do it.
Titus Andronicus. Act v, sc. 1, l. 129. [Aaron]

7
Under that colour am I come to scale
Thy never-conquer'd fort.
The Rape of Lucrece, l. 481. The only use of "never-conquer'd."

'Lucrece,' quoth he, 'this night I must enjoy thee:
If thou deny, then force must work my way.'
The Rape of Lucrece, l. 512.

8 Quoth he, 'I must deflower:
The powers to whom I pray abhor this fact,
How can they then assist me in the act?'
The Rape of Lucrece, l. 348.

Now will I hence to seek my lovely Moor,
And let my spleenful sons this trull deflour.
Titus Andronicus. Act ii, sc. 3, l. 190. [Tamora] "Spleenful" occurs again in *II Henry VI,* iii, 2, 128. The only uses of "deflour," spelled, it will be noted, in different ways.

But, sure, some Tereus hath deflowered thee,
And, lest thou shouldst detect him, cut thy tongue.
Titus Andronicus. Act ii, sc. 4, l. 26. [Marcus]

Enforced, stain'd and deflowered.—*Titus Andronicus,* v, 3, 38.

Flower as she was, deflowered by him.—*Romeo and Juliet,* iv, 5, 37. See under DEATH.

Deflower'd my dear.—*A Midsummer-Night's Dream,* v, 1, 297.

Deflower'd maid.—*Measure for Measure,* iv, 4, 24.

9 Her subjects with foul insurrection
Have batter'd down her consecrated wall.
The Rape of Lucrece, l. 722.

Late-sack'd island.—*Rape of Lucrece,* l. 1740. The only use of "late-sack'd."

10
Saturninus: Traitor, if Rome have law or we have power,
Thou and thy faction shall repent this rape.
Bassianus: Rape, call you it, my lord, to seize my own,
My true-betrothed love and now my wife?
Titus Andronicus. Act i, sc. 1, l. 403. The only use of "true-betrothed."

11
Ravish'd and wrong'd, as Philomela was,
Forced in the ruthless, vast, and gloomy woods.
Titus Andronicus. Act iv, sc. 1, l. 52. [Titus] "Gloomy" is repeated in *I Henry VI,* v, 4, 89, and in *The Rape of Lucrece,* l. 803.

Aaron: They cut thy sister's tongue and ravish'd her
And cut her hands and trimm'd her as thou saw'st.
Lucius: O detestable villain! call'st thou that trimming?
Aaron: Why, she was wash'd and cut and trimm'd, and 'twas
Trim sport for them that had the doing of it.
Titus Andronicus. Act v, sc. 1, l. 92. "Trimming" is repeated in *Antony and Cleopatra,* v, 2, 345.

They it were that ravish'd our sister.—*Titus Andronicus,* v, 3, 99.

What, was she ravish'd? tell who did the deed.
Titus Andronicus. Act v, sc. 3, l. 53. [Saturninus]

When it is thy hap
To find another that is like to thee,
Good Rapine, stab him; he 's a ravisher.
Titus Andronicus. Act v, sc. 2, l. 101. [Titus]
Said to be a ravisher.—*Coriolanus,* iv, 5, 243.
Thou ravisher.—*The Rape of Lucrece,* l. 888. The only uses of "ravisher."

1
Show me a villain that hath done a rape,
And I am sent to be revenged on him.
Titus Andronicus. Act v, sc. 2, l. 94. [Chiron]
Mark'd with rape.—*Titus Andronicus,* iv, 2, 9.
Detested rape.—*Titus Andronicus,* v, 2, 37.

2 I would have the soil of her fair rape
Wiped off, in honourable keeping her.
Troilus and Cressida, ii, 2, 147. [Paris]
Helen's rape.—*The Rape of Lucrece,* l. 1369.
Lucrece's rape.—*Titus Andronicus,* iv, 1, 91.

RAPIER, see Sword

RARITY

3 My state,
Seldom but sumptuous, showed like a feast
And won by rareness such solemnity.
I Henry IV. Act iii, sc. 2, l. 57. [King Henry]
Strain of rareness.—*Cymbeline,* iii, 4, 95.
Infusion of such rareness.—*Hamlet,* v, 2, 123. The only uses of "rareness."

4
Sir Nathaniel: A rare talent!
Dull: If a talent be a claw, look how he claws him with a talent.
Love's Labour's Lost. Act iv, sc. 2, l. 64.

5
Gonzalo: The rarity of it is—which is indeed almost beyond credit,—
Sebastian: As many vouched rarities are.
The Tempest. Act ii, sc. 1, l. 58.
Rarity redeems him.—*All's Well that Ends Well,* iv, 3, 306.
A rarity most beloved.—*King Lear,* iv, 3, 25.
What particular rarity?—*Timon of Athens,* i, 1, 4.
Beauty, truth and rarity.—*The Phœnix and Turtle,* l. 53. The only uses of "rarity."
Rarities of nature's truth.—*Sonnets,* lx. The only use of "rareties."

6
Think on thy Proteus, when thou haply seest
Some rare note-worthy object in thy travel.
Two Gentlemen of Verona. Act i, sc. 1, l. 12. [Proteus] The only use of "note-worthy."
Something rare
Even then will rush to knowledge.
The Winter's Tale. Act iii, sc. 1, l. 20. [Dion]

7
She 's rare.
The Winter's Tale. Act i, sc. 2, l. 452. [Polixenes]
Most rare.—*Pericles,* iii, 2, 107.
Divine and rare.—*Midsummer-Night's Dream,* iii, 2, 226.
Rare as phœnix.—*As You Like It,* iv, 3, 17.
Rare, pleasant, speedy.—*Winter's Tale,* iii, 1, 13.

RASCAL

See also Knave, Rogue

8
Peace, ye fat-kidneyed rascal! what a brawling dost thou keep!
I Henry IV. Act ii, sc. 2, l. 5. [Prince of Wales] The only use of "fat-kidneyed."
What a pagan rascal is this! an infidel!
I Henry IV. Act ii, sc. 3, l. 32. [Hotspur]
Thou whoreson, impudent, embossed rascal.
I Henry IV. Act iii, sc. 3, l. 177. [Prince]

9
Falstaff: You make fat rascals, Mistress Doll.
Doll: I make them! gluttony and diseases make them; I make them not.
II Henry IV. Act ii, sc. 4, l. 45.
I cannot endure such a fustian rascal.
II Henry IV. Act ii, sc. 4, l. 203. [Doll]
Thou damned tripe-visaged rascal.
II Henry IV. Act v, sc. 4, l. 9. [Doll] The only use of "tripe-visaged."

10
Hostess: Ay, come, you starved bloodhound.
Doll: Goodman death, goodman bones!
Hostess: Thou atomy, thou!
Doll: Come, you thin thing; come, you rascal.
II Henry IV. Act v, sc. 4, l. 31. The only use of "bloodhound" and "atomy."

11
Why, this is an arrant counterfeit rascal; I remember him now; a bawd, a cut-purse.
Henry V. Act iii, sc. 6, l. 64. [Gower]
Bald-pated, lying rascal.—*Measure for Measure,* v, 1, 357. The only use of "bald-pated."
Bottle-ale rascal.—*II Henry IV,* ii, 4, 140. The only use of "bottle-ale."
Cony-catching rascals.—*The Merry Wives of Windsor,* i, 1, 128. "Cony-catching" (cheating) is repeated in *The Taming of the Shrew,* iv, 1, 45.
Cowardly rascals.—*Henry V,* iv, 7, 6; *King Lear,* ii, 2, 59.
Crafty swearing rascals.—*Troilus and Cressida,* v, 4, 11.
Cut-purse rascal.—*II Henry IV,* ii, 4, 137.
Dishonest rascal.—*The Merry Wives of Windsor,* iii, 3, 196.
Flattering rascal.—*Cymbeline,* i, 5, 27.
Lean raw-boned rascals.—*I Henry VI,* i, 2, 35. The only use of "raw-boned."
Muddy rascal.—*II Henry IV,* ii, 4, 43.
Muddy-mettled rascal.—*Hamlet,* ii, 2, 594. The only use of "muddy-mettled."
Oily rascal.—*I Henry IV,* ii, 4, 575.
Pandarly rascals.—*The Merry Wives of Windsor,* iv, 2, 122. The only use of "pandarly."
Pitiful rascals.—*I Henry IV,* iv, 2, 70.
Rude rascals.—*Henry VIII,* v, 4, 11.
Stretch-mouthed rascal.—*The Winter's Tale,* iv, 4, 197. The only use of "stretch-mouthed."
Swaggering rascal.—*II Henry IV,* ii, 4, 76.
Traitorly rascals.—*The Winter's Tale,* iv, 4, 821. The only use of "traitorly."
Vile rascal.—*All's Well that Ends Well,* iii, 5, 87.
Wide-chapp'd rascal.—*The Tempest,* i, 1, 60. The only use of "wide-chapp'd."

1 What a damned Epicurean rascal is this!
The Merry Wives of Windsor. Act ii, sc. 2, l. 300. [Ford]

2 Hector: Art thou of blood and honour?
Thersites: No, no, I am a rascal; a scurvy railing knave; a very filthy rogue.
Troilus and Cressida. Act v, sc. 4, l. 29.

3 I marvel your ladyship takes delight in such a barren rascal.
Twelfth Night. Act i, sc. 5, l. 89. [Malvolio] "Barren rascal" is repeated in v, 1, 383.

RASHNESS

See also Boldness

4 This is not well, rash and unbridled boy,
To fly the favours of so good a king;
To pluck his indignation on thy head
By the misprising of a maid too virtuous
For the contempt of empire.
All's Well that Ends Well. Act iii, sc. 2, l. 30. [Countess] "Unbridled children" occurs in *Troilus and Cressida,* iii, 2, 130.

5 Nor heady-rash, provoked with raging ire.
The Comedy of Errors, v, 1, 216. [Antipholus of Ephesus] The only use of "heady-rash."

6 Fool-hardiness; not I.
Coriolanus, i, 4, 46. The only use of "fool-hardiness" in the plays. "Foolhardy" appears twice, in *All's Well that Ends Well,* iv, 1, 32; and *Richard II,* v, 3, 43.

Manhood is call'd foolery, when it stands
Against a falling fabric.
Coriolanus. Act iii, sc. 1, l. 246. [Cominius]

7 Our indiscretion sometimes serves us well.
Hamlet. Act v, sc. 2, l. 8. [Hamlet] "Indiscretion" is used only once again, in *King Lear,* ii, 4, 199.

8 We may outrun,
By violent swiftness, that which we run at,
And lose by over-running.
Henry VIII. Act i, sc. 1, l. 141. [Norfolk] The only use of "over-running."

9 Reverse thy doom;
And, in thy best consideration, check
This hideous rashness.
King Lear. Act i, sc. 1, l. 151. [Kent]

Be not so rash.—*II Henry VI,* iv, 1, 28.
I might be too rash.—*Measure for Measure,* ii, 2, 9.

10 He is rash and very sudden in choler.
Othello. Act ii, sc. 1, l. 279. [Iago]

Thou art rash as fire.—*Othello,* v, 2, 134.
Rash and most unfortunate.—*Othello,* v, 2, 282.

11 This is the fruit of rashness!
Richard III. Act ii, sc. 1, l. 134. [Gloucester]

Against the form of law,
Proceed thus rashly to the villain's death.
Richard III. Act iii, sc. 5, l. 42. [Gloucester]

Too rashly plotted.—*I Henry VI,* iv, 4, 3.
Rashly, and praised be rashness.—*Hamlet,* v, 2, 5.

12 Too rash, too unadvised, too sudden.
Romeo and Juliet. Act ii, sc. 2, l. 118. [Juliet]

13 Who cannot condemn rashness in cold blood?
Timon of Athens. Act iii, sc. 5, l. 53. [Alcibiades]

Forgive my general and exceptless rashness,
You perpetual-sober gods!
Timon of Athens. Act iv, sc. 3, l. 502. [Timon] The only use of "exceptless" and "perpetual-sober."

A rashness that I ever yet have shunn'd.
The Two Gentlemen of Verona. Act iii, sc. 1, l. 30. [Duke]

14 Alas! I have show'd too much
The rashness of a woman.
Winter's Tale. Act iii, sc. 2, l. 221. [Paulina]

RAT

15 She is served As I would serve a rat.
Cymbeline. Act v, sc. 5, l. 247. [Cornelius]

16 How now! a rat? Dead, for a ducat, dead!
Hamlet. Act iii, sc. 4, l. 24. [Hamlet]

A rat, a rat!—*Hamlet,* iv, 1, 10.
You rat-catcher.—*Romeo and Juliet,* iii, 1, 78. The only use of the phrase.

17 Rats that ravin down their proper bane.
Measure for Measure, i, 2, 133. See under Evil.

Irish rat.—*As You Like It,* iii, 2, 188.
Old rat.—*King Lear,* iii, 4, 138.
Poor rats.—*Richard III,* v, 3, 331.

18 There be land-rats and water-rats.
The Merchant of Venice. Act i, sc. 3, l. 23. [Shylock] The only use of either phrase.

What if my house be troubled with a rat
And I be pleased to give ten thousand ducats
To have it baned?
The Merchant of Venice. Act iv, sc. 1, l. 44. [Shylock] The only use of "baned."

19 A rotten carcass of a boat, not rigg'd,
Nor tackle, sail, nor mast; the very rats
Instinctively have quit it.
The Tempest. Act i, sc. 2, l. 146. [Prospero] The only use of "instinctively."

RAVEN

20 The croaking raven doth bellow for revenge.
Hamlet. Act iii, sc. 2, l. 264. [Hamlet] The only use of "croaking."

I would croak like a raven; I would bode, I would bode.
Troilus and Cressida. Act v, sc. 2, l. 191. [Thersites]

Dove-feather'd raven!—*Romeo and Juliet,* iii, 2, 76. The only use of the phrase.
Fatal raven.—*Titus Andronicus,* ii, 3, 97.
Hateful raven.—*II Henry VI,* iii, 1, 76.
Moulten raven.—*I Henry IV,* iii, 1, 152. The only use of "moulten."

21 Ravens, crows and kites,
Fly o'er our heads and downward look on us,

As we were sickly prey.
Julius Cæsar. Act v, sc. 1, l. 85. [Cassius]

1
An amber-colour'd raven was well noted.
Love's Labour's Lost. Act iv, sc. 3, l. 88. [Biron] The only use of "amber-colour'd."
Raven-colour'd.—*Titus Andronicus,* ii, 3, 83. The only use of the phrase.

2 The raven himself is hoarse
That croaks the fatal entrance of Duncan
Under my battlements.
Macbeth. Act i, sc. 5, l. 39. [Lady Macbeth]

3
Young ravens must have food.
The Merry Wives of Windsor. Act i, sc. 3, l. 38. [Pistol]

4
I had as lief have heard the night-raven, come what plague could have come after it.
Much Ado about Nothing. Act ii, sc. 3, l. 83. [Benedick] The only use of "night-raven."

5
The raven doth not hatch a lark.
Titus Andronicus. Act ii, sc. 3, l. 149. [Lavinia]
Some say the ravens foster forlorn children,
The while their own birds famish in their nests.
Titus Andronicus. Act ii, sc. 3, l. 153. [Lavinia]
Did ever raven sing so like a lark,
That gives sweet tidings of the sun's uprise?
Titus Andronicus. Act iii, sc. 1, l. 158. [Titus]

6
The raven chides blackness.
Troilus and Cressida. Act ii, sc. 3, l. 221. [Ulysses]

RAVISH, see Rape

READINESS

7
Make you ready with your stiff bats and clubs.
Coriolanus. Act i, sc. 1, l. 165. [Menenius]
She 's making her ready, she 'll come straight.
Troilus and Cressida. Act iii, sc. 2, l. 31. [Pandarus]
Make yourself ready in your cabin for the mischance of the hour.
The Tempest. Act i, sc. 1, l. 27. [Boatswain]
Deiphobus: Let us make ready straight.
Æneas: Yea, with a bridegroom's fresh alacrity,
Let us address to tend on Hector's heels.
Troilus and Cressida. Act iv, sc. 4, l. 146.
Go make thee ready.—*Antony and Cleopatra,* iii, 3, 40.
Go, make you ready.—*Hamlet,* iii, 2, 50.
Make her ready straight.—*The Taming of the Shrew,* iv, 4, 63.
Make ready.—*I Henry IV,* iii, 3, 192; *Measure for Measure,* iii, 1, 172.

8
Make them be strong and ready for this hint,
When we shall hap to give 't them.
Coriolanus. Act iii, sc. 3, l. 23. [Sicinius]

9
I am joyful to hear of their readiness.
Coriolanus. Act iv, sc. 3, l. 51. [Roman]

10
Gaoler: Are you ready for death?
Posthumus: Over-roasted rather; ready long ago.
Cymbeline, v, 4, 152. See under Hanging.
Are we all ready?—*Julius Cæsar,* iii, 1, 31.
Are you ready?—*Twelfth Night,* ii, 4, 50.
Is he ready?—*Henry VIII,* iii, 2, 82.
Is he in person ready?—*Henry VIII,* i, 1, 117.
Is my lord ready?—*Timon of Athens,* iii, 4, 35.
Is she ready?—*Cymbeline,* ii, 3, 86.
Will you be ready?—*Romeo and Juliet,* iii, 4, 22.

11
The readiness is all.
Hamlet, v, 2, 234. See under Destiny.

12
We ready are to try our fortunes.
II Henry IV, iv, 2, 43. See under Fortune.
Thou shalt find us ready for thee still.
I Henry VI. Act ii, sc. 5, l. 104. [Somerset]
Ready, so please your grace.
The Merchant of Venice. Act iv, sc. 1, l. 2. [Antonio] "Ready" is used in this way frequently throughout the plays.
We are ready.—*Henry VIII,* iii, 1, 173; *Pericles,* ii, 2, 4.
He is ready at the door.—*The Merchant of Venice,* iv, 1, 15.
I am ready.—*III Henry VI,* iii, 3, 230, and frequently in later plays.
I am almost ready.—*King Lear,* v, 3, 203.
Almost ready.—*The Merry Wives of Windsor,* ii, 1, 88.
They are ready.—*As You Like It,* i, 2, 155; *King Lear,* v, 3, 52.
Ready at thy beck.—*The Taming of the Shrew,* Ind., 2, 36.
Ready and willing.—*The Taming of the Shrew,* iv, 4, 34.
Very ready.—*Measure for Measure,* iv, 3, 40.

13
All things are ready, if our minds be so.
Henry V, iv, 3, 71. See under Mind.

14
Royal commanders, be in readiness.
III Henry VI. Act ii, sc. 2, l. 67. [Messenger]
Be in readiness.—*Cymbeline,* iii, 5, 23.

15
Somerset: We are in readiness.
Queen Margaret: This cheers my heart, to see your forwardness.
III Henry VI. Act v, sc. 4, l. 64.
All things are in readiness.
Richard III. Act v, sc. 3, l. 52. [Catesby]
Every thing in readiness.—*Titus Andronicus,* i, 1, 325.
We could at once put us in readiness.
The Taming of the Shrew. Act i, sc. 1, l. 43. [Lucentio]
To-morrow be in readiness to go.
The Two Gentlemen of Verona. Act i, sc. 3, l. 70. [Antonio]
In readiness.—*I Henry VI,* iii, 1, 186; *The Merchant of Venice,* ii, 4, 33; *Timon of Athens,* i, 2, 172; *Cymbeline,* iv, 2, 336.

16
Let 's briefly put on manly readiness.
Macbeth. Act ii, sc. 3, l. 139. [Macbeth]

Readiness in the office.—*Measure for Measure,* ii, 1, 275.

1
Be ready at the farthest by five of the clock.
The Merchant of Venice. Act ii, sc. 2, l. 122. [Bassanio]
Be ready here hard by in the brew-house.
The Merry Wives of Windsor. Act iii, sc. 3, l. 10. [Mrs. Ford] The only use of "brew-house."
Be ready, as your lives shall answer it.
Richard II. Act i, sc. 1, l. 198. [King Richard]
They shall be ready at your highness' will.
Titus Andronicus, ii, 3, 297. See under RETRIBUTION.
Be ready.—*Julius Cæsar,* iv, 3, 81; *Measure for Measure,* iii, 1, 107; *Richard II,* i, 1, 205; *The Taming of the Shrew,* Ind., 1, 59; iv, 4, 104.
Be ready straight.—*The Taming of the Shrew,* Ind., 1, 52.
He shall in time be ready.—*Antony and Cleopatra,* v, 1, 72.
They be ready.—*The Taming of the Shrew,* iii, 2, 207.

2
One . . . That cannot tread the way out readily.
Rape of Lucrece, l. 1152. "Readily" is used only once again, in *II Henry VI,* v, 2, 83. "May readily be stopp'd."

3
The readiest way to make the wench amends.
Richard III, i, 1, 155. See under HUSBAND.
Tell me, I beseech you, which is the readiest way?
The Taming of the Shrew. Act i, sc. 2, l. 220. [Tranio]
Readiest champions.—*Titus Andronicus,* i, 1, 151.
Readiest man.—*Timon of Athens,* i, 2, 49. The only uses of "readiest."

4
Grumio: Are they all ready?
Curtis: They are.
Grumio: Call them forth.
Taming of the Shrew. Act iv, sc. 1, l. 97.
All ready.—*The Taming of the Shrew,* iv, 1, 54.

5
I 'll get 'em all three all ready.
Twelfth Night. Act iii, sc. 1, l. 102. [Sir Andrew]
Go get it ready.—*King Lear,* i, 4, 9.
I 'll see them ready.—*Titus Andronicus,* v, 2, 206.
I have it ready.—*The Merchant of Venice,* iv, 1, 337.
I have them ready.—*The Merchant of Venice,* iv, 1, 256.
'Tis ready.—*Coriolanus,* iii, 3, 10; *The Merry Wives of Windsor,* i, 4, 63.
'Tis time you were ready.—*Much Ado about Nothing,* iii, 4, 53.
Ready now.—*Pericles,* i, 4, 43.
Not ready yet.—*I Henry IV,* iii, 1, 87.

READING

See also Books, Writing

6
Nay, I 'll read it first.
All's Well that Ends Well. Act iv, sc. 3, l. 244. [Soldier]
Read it again.—*All's Well that Ends Well,* iii, 4, 3.

7
Teaching all that read to know
The quintessence of every sprite.
As You Like It. Act iii, sc. 2, l. 146. [Celia] "Quintessence" is repeated in *Hamlet,* ii, 2, 321: "Quintessence of dust."
Reading ill-favouredly.—*As You Like It,* iii, 2, 279.
Read it not.—*Coriolanus,* v, 6, 84.

8
So far I read aloud.
Cymbeline. Act i, sc. 6, l. 26. [Imogen]
Reading aloud.—*Twelfth Night,* ii, 5, 94.

9
Read, and declare the meaning.
Cymbeline. Act v, sc. 5, l. 434. [Lucius]
Read here.—*King John,* iv, 1, 33.

10
Look, where sadly the poor wretch comes reading.
Hamlet. Act ii, sc. 2, l. 168. [Queen]
Read on this book;
That show of such exercise may colour
Your loneliness.
Hamlet. Act iii, sc. 1, l. 44. [Polonius]
Read it at more leisure.—*Hamlet,* v, 2, 26.
Read it at your leisure.—*The Merchant of Venice,* v, 1, 267.
Read it instantly.—*Julius Cæsar,* iii, 1, 9.

11
What read you there,
That hath so cowarded and chased your blood?

What read you there,
That hath so cowarded and chased your blood?
Henry V. Act ii, sc. 2, l. 74. [King Henry] The only use of "cowarded."
Fashion, wrest, or bow your reading.
Henry V. Act i, sc. 2, l. 14. [King Henry]
Every one may read.—*I Henry VI,* ii, 2, 14.
I can read no further.—*II Henry VI,* i, 1, 55.
As I have read.—*II Henry VI,* ii, 2, 40; *Love's Labour's Lost,* i, 2, 88.

12
But stay, I 'll read it over once again.
II Henry VI. Act iv, sc. 4, l. 14. [King Henry]
Read o'er this.—*Henry VIII,* iii, 2, 201.
Reading it over.—*Much Ado about Nothing,* ii, 3, 142.

13
Because they could not read, thou hast hanged them; when, indeed, only for that cause they have been most worthy to live.
II Henry VI. Act iv, sc. 7, l. 49. [Cade]
Canst not read?—*Timon of Athens,* ii, 2, 85.
I cannot read.—*I Henry IV,* v, 2, 81.
Read not.—*Antony and Cleopatra,* ii, 3, 5.
Fie on thee, jolt-head! thou canst not read.
The Two Gentlemen of Verona. Act iii, sc. 1, l. 291. [Launce]
You heedless joltheads!—*The Taming of the Shrew,* iv, 1, 169. The only uses of "jolt-head" and "joltheads."

1
He reads much; He is a great observer.
Julius Cæsar. Act i, sc. 2, l. 201. [Cæsar]

2
Is not the leaf turn'd down
Where I left reading?
Julius Cæsar. Act iv, sc. 3, l. 273. [Brutus]

Fold down the leaf where I have left.—*Cymbeline,* ii, 2, 4.

Here the leaf 's turn'd down. *Cymbeline,* ii, 2, 45.

3
Painfully to pore upon a book
To seek the light of truth; while truth the while
Doth falsely blind the eyesight of his look.
Love's Labour 's Lost. Act i, sc. 1, l. 74. [Biron]

4
How well he 's read!
Love's Labour 's Lost. Act i, sc. 1, l. 94. [King]

Exceedingly well read.—*I Henry IV,* iii, 1, 166.

Well read in poetry.—*The Taming of the Shrew,* i, 2, 170.

Thou art deeper read.—*Titus Andronicus,* iv, 1, 33.

5
I 'll read the writing.
The Merchant of Venice. Act ii, sc. 7, l. 64. [Morocco]

Trust not my reading.—*Much Ado about Nothing,* iv, 1, 167.

6
Tarquin's eye may read the mot afar.
The Rape of Lucrece, l. 830. The only use of "mot." "Mots" is used five times, always in a French sentence.

7
Northumberland: Read o'er this paper. . . .
King Richard: I 'll read enough,
When I do see the very book indeed
Where all my sins are writ, and that 's myself.
Richard II. Act iv, sc. 1, l. 273.

8
Servant: I pray, sir, can you read?
Romeo: Ay, mine own fortune in my misery.
Servant: Perhaps you have learned it without book: but, I pray, can you read any thing you see?
Romeo: Ay, if I know the letters and the language.
Romeo and Juliet. Act i, sc. 2, l. 59.

I can read.—*Romeo and Juliet,* i, 2, 66.

Read by rote.—*Romeo and Juliet,* ii, 3, 88.

O, learn to read.—*Sonnets,* xxiii.

9
Gremio: What will you read to her?
Lucentio: Whate'er I read to her, I 'll plead for you
As for my patron, stand you so assured.
The Taming of the Shrew. Act i, sc. 2, l. 154.

Lucentio: Now, mistress, profit you in what you read?
Bianca: What, master, read you? first resolve me that.
Lucentio: I read what I profess, the Art to Love.
Bianca: And may you prove, sir, master of your art!
Lucentio: While you, sweet dear, prove mistress of my heart!
Taming of the Shrew. Act iv, sc. 2, l. 6.

My son profits nothing in the world at his book.
The Merry Wives of Windsor. Act iv, sc. 1, l. 15. [Mrs. Page]

10
Page: Read me the superscription of these letters: I know not which is which.
Apemantus: Canst not read?
Page: No.
Apemantus: There will little learning die then, that day thou art hanged.
Timon of Athens. Act ii, sc. 2, l. 81. "Superscription" is repeated in *I Henry VI,* iv, 1, 53: "Churlish superscription."

11
Thy sight is young,
And thou shalt read when mine begin to dazzle.
Titus Andronicus. Act iii, sc. 2, l. 84. [Titus]

Ah, boy, Cornelia never with more care
Read to her sons than she hath read to thee
Sweet poetry.
Titus Andronicus. Act iv, sc. 1, l. 12. [Titus]

O, do ye read, my lord, what she has writ?
'Stuprum. Chiron. Demetrius.'
Titus Andronicus. Act iv, sc. 1, l. 77. [Titus]

12
O, like a book of sport thou 'lt read me o'er.
Troilus and Cressida. Act iv, sc. 5, l. 239. [Hector]

Let me read.—*Troilus and Cressida,* v, 3, 100.

13
I will read politic authors.
Twelfth Night, ii, 5, 175. See under BEHAVIOUR.

Do but read.—*Twelfth Night,* iii, 4, 161.

14
And when it 's writ, for my sake read it over.
The Two Gentlemen of Verona. Act ii, sc. 1, l. 136. [Silvia]

Read on.—*The Two Gentlemen of Verona,* iii, 1, 329.

REALM

See also Kingdom

15
Realms and islands were
As plates dropp'd from his pocket.
Antony and Cleopatra. Act v, sc. 2, l. 91. [Cleopatra]

16
This realm dismantled was Of Jove himself.
Hamlet. Act iii, sc. 2, l. 293. [Hamlet] The only use of "dismantled."

17
Prosper this realm, keep it from civil broils.
I Henry VI. Act i, sc. 1, l. 53. [Bedford]

Destroy the realm.—*I Henry VI,* iii, 1, 114. "Realm" is used sixteen times in this play, and seventeen times in *II Henry VI,* against twenty-eight times in all the other plays together.

18
I foresee with grief
The utter loss of all the realm of France.
I Henry VI. Act v, sc. 4, l. 112. [Beaufort]

"Realm of France" is repeated seven times in this and later plays.
Realms of England and of France.—*I Henry VI*, v, 1, 6.
The realms of England, France and Ireland.—*II Henry VI*, i, 1, 232.
England's realm.—*II Henry VI*, ii, 3, 30.
Realm of Albion.—*King Lear*, iii, 2, 91.

1
All the realm shall be in common.
II Henry VI. Act iv, sc. 2, l. 74. [Cade]
Luckless realm.—*III Henry VI*, ii, 6, 18.
His realm a slaughter-house.—*III Henry VI*, v, 4, 78.

2
The Earl of Wiltshire hath the realm in farm.
Richard II. Act ii, sc. 1, l. 256. [Ross]
Royal realm.—*Richard II*, i, 4, 45.
Whole realms.—*Timon of Athens*, iii, 3, 34; *Henry VIII*, v, 3, 16.

REASON

See also Rhyme and Reason

3
Countess: Is this all your worship's reason?
Clown: Faith, madam, I have other holy reasons, such as they are.
Countess: May the world know them?
All's Well that Ends Well. Act i, sc. 3, l. 33.
Tell me thy reason.—*All's Well that Ends Well*, i, 3, 29.

4
The reasons of our state I cannot yield.
All's Well that Ends Well. Act iii, sc. 1, l. 10. [Lord]
No reason Can found his state in safety.
Timon of Athens. Act ii, sc. 1, l. 12. [Senator]

5
My reasons are most strong.
All's Well that Ends Well. Act iv, sc. 2, l. 59. [Diana]
I have reasons strong and forcible.
III Henry VI. Act i, sc. 2, l. 3. [Montague]
Strong reasons make strong actions.
King John. Act iii, sc. 4, l. 182. [Dauphin]
My reasons are both good and weighty.
The Taming of the Shrew. Act i, sc. 1, l. 252. [Lucentio]
A reason mighty, strong, and effectual.
Titus Andronicus. Act v, sc. 3, l. 43. [Titus]
Strong reasons.—*Troilus and Cressida*, iii, 3, 191.

Reason strong,
For his advantage still did wake and sleep.
A Lover's Complaint, l. 123.

6
My reason Sits in the wind against me.
Antony and Cleopatra. Act iii, sc. 10, l. 36. [Enobarbus]

7
Come, lame me with reasons.
As You Like It. Act i, sc. 3, l. 6. [Celia]
No sooner knew the reason than they sought the remedy.
As You Like It, v, 2, 39. See under Love.

8
Antipholus of Syracuse: For what reason?
Dromio of Syracuse: For two; and sound ones too.
Antipholus: Nay, not sound, I pray you.
Dromio: Sure ones then.
Antipholus: Nay, not sure, in a thing falsing.
Dromio: Certain ones then.
The Comedy of Errors. Act ii, sc. 2, l. 91. The only use of "falsing."
Your reason was not substantial.
The Comedy of Errors. Act ii, sc. 2, l. 105. [Antipholus of Syracuse]
Know the reason.—*The Comedy of Errors*, iii, 1, 97.
Know you the reason?—*King Lear*, iv, 3, 2.

9
What, are you mad, that you do reason so?
The Comedy of Errors. Act iii, sc. 2, l. 53. [Luciana]
How fondly dost thou reason!
The Comedy of Errors. Act iv, sc. 2, l. 57. [Adriana]
Hath he not reason?—*The Comedy of Errors*, iv, 2, 62.

10
If 'gainst yourself you be incensed, we 'll put you
Like one that means his proper harm, in manacles,
Then reason safely with you.
Coriolanus. Act i, sc. 9, l. 56. [Cominius]
Reason with the fellow.—*Coriolanus*, iv, 6, 51.

11
Desire not
To allay my rages and revenges with
Your colder reasons.
Coriolanus. Act v, sc. 3, l. 84. [Coriolanus]
Bury His reasons with his body.
Coriolanus. Act v, sc. 6, l. 59. [Conspirator]

12
That 's the reason I was up so early.
Cymbeline. Act ii, sc. 3, l. 38. [Cloten]
That 's the reason.—*The Two Gentlemen of Verona*, ii, 4, 206.

13
You cannot speak of reason to the Dane,
And lose your voice.
Hamlet. Act i, sc. 2, l. 44. [King]
By my fay, I cannot reason.
Hamlet. Act ii, sc. 2, l. 271. [Hamlet]
Reason pandars will.
Hamlet. Act iii, sc. 4, l. 88. [Hamlet]

14
The o'ergrowth of some complexion,
Oft breaking down the pales and forts of reason.
Hamlet. Act i, sc. 4, l. 27. [Hamlet] The only use of "o'ergrowth."
Now see that noble and most sovereign reason,
Like sweet bells jangled, out of tune and harsh.
Hamlet. Act iii, sc. 1, l. 165. [Ophelia] The only use of "jangled." "Jangling" occurs three times.
Sure, he that made us with such large discourse,
Looking before and after, gave us not
That capability and god-like reason
To fust in us unused.
Hamlet. Act iv, sc. 4, l. 36. [Hamlet] The

only use of "fust" (to grow mouldy). "Unused" is repeated in *Othello,* v, 2, 349.
Human reason.—*The Comedy of Errors,* v, 1, 189.

1 For two special reasons;
Which may to you, perhaps, seem much unsinew'd,
But yet to me they are strong.
Hamlet. Act iv, sc. 7, l. 9. [King] The only use of "unsinew'd."
Larded with many several sorts of reasons.
Hamlet. Act v, sc. 2, l. 20. [Hamlet]

2
What is the reason that you use me thus?
Hamlet. Act v, sc. 1, l. 312. [Hamlet]
What is the reason of this terrible summons?
Othello. Act i, sc. 1, l. 82. [Brabantio]
Tranio: For what reason, I beseech you?
Gremio: For this reason, if you 'll know.
The Taming of the Shrew. Act i, sc. 2, l. 235.
What 's his reason?—*The Merchant of Venice,* iii, 1, 60.
What 's the reason?—*II Henry VI,* iv, 9, 37.
What was his reason?—*Richard II,* ii, 3, 28.
What reason have you for 't?—*Love's Labour 's Lost,* v, 2, 715.

3
I will lay down such reasons for this adventure that he shall go.
I Henry IV. Act i, sc. 2, l. 168. [Poins]
Prince of Wales: Come, tell us your reason: what sayest thou to this?
Poins: Come, your reason, Jack, your reason.
Falstaff: What, upon compulsion? 'Zounds, an I were at the strappado, or all the racks in the world, I would not tell you on compulsion. Give you a reason on compulsion! if reasons were as plentiful as blackberries, I would give no man a reason upon compulsion, I.
I Henry IV. Act ii, sc. 4, l. 258. The only use of "strappado."
So can I give no reason, nor I will not.
The Merchant of Venice. Act iv, sc. 1, l. 59. [Shylock]

4
Thou shalt find me tractable to any honest reason.
I Henry IV. Act iii, sc. 3, l. 194. [Falstaff]

5
Many thousand reasons hold me back.
II Henry IV. Act ii, sc. 4, l. 66. [Northumberland]
For divers reasons.—*I Henry IV,* i, 3, 262.
Divers unknown reasons.—*Richard III,* i, 2, 218.
Sundry weighty reasons.—*Macbeth,* iii, 1, 126.

6
Every idle, nice and wanton reason.
II Henry IV. Act iv, sc. 1, l. 191. [Mowbray]
Better reasons.—*II Henry VI,* iii, 1, 37.
Clearer reason.—*The Tempest,* v, 1, 68.
Common reason.—*Othello,* iii, 3, 64.
Cool reason.—*A Midsummer-Night's Dream,* v, 1, 6.
Fundamental reasons.—*All 's Well that Ends Well,* iii, 1, 2. "Fundamental" is repeated in *Coriolanus,* iii, 1, 151: "Fundamental part."
Lawful reasons.—*Sonnets,* xlix.
Loud reason.—*Othello,* i, 1, 151.
Pretty reason.—*King Lear,* i, 5, 38.
Public reasons.—*Julius Cæsar,* iii, 2, 7.
Safe reason.—*Cymbeline,* iv, 2, 131.
Sharp reasons.—*Henry VIII,* ii, 1, 14.
Small reason.—*Love's Labour 's Lost,* i, 2, 92.

7
Your own reasons turn into your bosoms,
As dogs upon their masters, worrying you.
Henry V. Act ii, sc. 2, l. 82. [King Henry]

8
You have great reason to do Richard right.
I Henry VI. Act iii, sc. 1, l. 154. [Gloucester]
You have great reason to be sad.
As You Like It. Act iv, sc. 1, l. 21. [Rosalind]
Great reason why.—*Richard III,* v, 3, 185.
Great reason.—*Love's Labour 's Lost,* v, 2, 28; *Titus Andronicus,* ii, 3, 81.
Greater reason.—*Othello,* iv, 2, 217.

9
There 's reason he should be displeased at it.
II Henry VI. Act i, sc. 1, l. 155. [Beaufort]

10
Peace, son! and show some reason.
II Henry VI. Act i, sc. 3, l. 116. [Salisbury]
Give me leave To show some reason.
II Henry VI. Act i, sc. 3, l. 166. [Suffolk]
'Tis but reason.—*III Henry VI,* iii, 3, 147.
No more than reason.—*Much Ado about Nothing,* v, 4, 74; 77.
Within reason.—*Othello,* iv, 2, 223.
Without all reason.—*Coriolanus,* iii, 1, 144.
In all reason.—*Measure for Measure,* iii, 1, 250; *A Midsummer-Night's Dream,* v, 1, 259.
In any reason.—*The Merry Wives of Windsor,* i, 1, 249.

11
Tell me some reason why.
III Henry VI. Act iv, sc. 1, l. 25. [King Edward]

12
It fits thee not to ask the reason why.
Pericles. Act i, sc. 1, l. 157. [Antiochus]
The reason why.—*As You Like It,* iii, 2, 422.

13
Had I not reason, think ye, to make haste?
III Henry VI. Act v, sc. 6, l. 72. [Gloucester]
Have I not reason to look pale and dead?
Richard II. Act iii, sc. 2, l. 79. [King Richard]
Have I not reason, think you, to look pale?
Titus Andronicus. Act ii, sc. 3, l. 91. [Tamora]
Have I not reason?—*Macbeth,* iii, 5, 2.
Had he not reason?—*Titus Andronicus,* iv, 2, 39.
He has some reason.—*King Lear,* iv, 1, 33.

14
Let your reason with your choler question.
Henry VIII. Act i, sc. 1, l. 130. [Norfolk]
If with the sap of reason you would quench,
Or but allay, the fire of passion.
Henry VIII. Act i, sc. 1, l. 148. [Norfolk]

15
I have not known when his affections sway'd
More than his reason.
Julius Cæsar. Act ii, sc. 1, l. 20. [Brutus]

16
Antony: You shall give me reasons
Why and wherein Cæsar was dangerous.

Brutus: Or else were this a savage spectacle:
Our reasons are so full of good regard
That were you, Antony, the son of Cæsar,
You should be satisfied.
Julius Cæsar. Act iii, sc. 1, l. 221.

Give him reasons.—*Julius Cæsar,* ii, 1, 219.

Give me a living reason.
Othello. Act iii, sc. 3, l. 409. [Othello]

He hath given me satisfying reasons.
Othello. Act v, sc. 1, l. 9. [Roderigo]

I 'll give him reasons for 't.—*Twelfth Night,* i, 5, 325.

1
Methinks there is much reason in his sayings.
Julius Cæsar. Act iii, sc. 2, l. 113. [Citizen]

There thou speak'st reason.—*Much Ado about Nothing,* v, 1, 41.

2
Good reasons must, of force, give place to better.
Julius Cæsar. Act iv, sc. 3, l. 203. [Brutus]

Good reason.—*II Henry VI,* iv, 2, 171.

3 Being not mad but sensible of grief,
My reasonable part produces reason
How I may be deliver'd of these woes,
And teaches me to kill or hang myself.
King John. Act iii, sc. 4, l. 53. [Constance]

Reason not the need.—*King Lear,* ii, 4, 267.

Hear reason.—*King Lear,* v, 3, 82.

4
Dumain: In reason nothing.
Biron: Something then in rhyme.
Love's Labour 's Lost. Act i, sc. 1, l. 99. See RHYME AND REASON.

5
Dear princess, were not his requests so far
From reason's yielding, your fair self should make
A yielding 'gainst some reason in my breast.
Love's Labour 's Lost. Act ii, sc. 1, l. 150. [King]

All liberal reason I will yield unto.
Love's Labour 's Lost. Act ii, sc. 1, l. 168. [King]

6
Your reasons at dinner have been sharp and sententious: pleasant without scurrility, witty without affection, audacious without impudency, learned without opinion, and strange without heresy.
Love's Labour 's Lost. Act v, sc. 1, l. 1. [Sir Nathaniel] The only use of "impudency." "Scurrility" occurs once more, in the same play, iv, 2, 55. "Sententious" occurs twice more, in *As You Like It,* v, 4, 66, and *Romeo and Juliet,* ii, 4, 225.

His reasons are as two grains of wheat hid in two bushels of chaff: you shall seek all day ere you find them, and when you have them, they are not worth the search.
The Merchant of Venice. Act i, sc. 1, l. 114. [Bassanio] The only use of "bushels."

7 Moe reasons for this action
At our more leisure shall I render you.
Measure for Measure. Act i, sc. 3, l. 48. [Duke]

8 Do not banish reason
For inequality; but let your reason serve
To make the truth appear where it seems hid,
And hide the false seems true.
Measure for Measure. Act v, sc. 1, l. 64. [Isabella] The only use of "inequality."

9 Many that are not mad
Have, sure, more lack of reason.
Measure for Measure. Act v, sc. 1, l. 67. [Duke]

Reason in madness!—*King Lear,* iv, 6, 179.

10
I reason'd with a Frenchman yesterday.
The Merchant of Venice. Act ii, sc. 8, l. 27. [Salarino]

Why is this reason'd?—*King Lear,* v, 1, 28.

Rightly reasoned.—*Much Ado about Nothing,* v, 1, 229. The only uses of "reasoned."

11
There is no firm reason to be render'd.
The Merchant of Venice. Act iv, sc. 1, l. 53. [Shylock]

12
Ay, sir, you shall find me reasonable; if it be so, I shall do that that is reason.
The Merry Wives of Windsor. Act i, sc. 1, l. 217. [Slender]

I will do as it shall become one that would do reason.
The Merry Wives of Windsor. Act i, sc. 1, l. 241. [Slender]

Reason, you rogue, reason.
The Merry Wives of Windsor. Act ii, sc. 2, l. 15. [Falstaff]

I will do reason, any reason.
Tempest. Act iii, sc. 2, l. 128. [Stephano]

13
The will of man is by his reason sway'd.
A Midsummer-Night's Dream. Act ii, sc. 2, l. 115. [Lysander]

And touching now the point of human skill,
Reason becomes the marshal to my will.
A Midsummer-Night's Dream. Act ii, sc. 2, l. 119. [Lysander]

14
You should have little reason for that.
A Midsummer-Night's Dream, iii, 1, 146. See under LOVE.

You have no reason.—*Much Ado about Nothing,* iv, 1, 260.

15
It is all the wealth that he hath left, to be known a reasonable creature.
Much Ado about Nothing. Act i, sc. 1, l. 70. [Beatrice]

16
Conrade: You should hear reason.
Don John: And when I have heard it, what blessing brings it?
Conrade: If not a present remedy, at least a patient sufferance.
Much Ado about Nothing. Act i, sc. 3, l. 6.

17
We have reason to cool our raging motions.
Othello, i, 3, 334. See under LUST.

With my nobler reason 'gainst my fury
Do I take part.
The Tempest. Act v, sc. 1, l. 26. [Prospero]

The pauser, reason.—*Macbeth,* ii, 3, 117. The only use of "pauser."

1
I will hear further reason for this.
Othello. Act iv, sc. 2, l. 251. [Roderigo]

2
Let reason rule things worthy blame.
The Passionate Pilgrim, l. 301.

3
Now do I see he had some reason for 't.
Pericles. Act i, sc. 3, l. 8. [Thaliard]

I have reason for it.—*The Merchant of Venice,* iii, 2, 234.

I have no reason for it.—*King John,* i, 1, 66.

4
Her reason to herself is only known.
Pericles. Act ii, sc. 5, l. 5. [Simonides]

She has her quirks, her reasons, her master reasons.
Pericles. Act iv, sc. 6, l. 8. [Bawd]

5
First let 's reason with him.
Richard III. Act i, sc. 4, l. 164. [Murderer]

Let 's reason with the worst that may befall.
Julius Cæsar. Act v, sc. 1, l. 97. [Cassius]

While we reason here,
A royal battle might be won and lost.
Richard III. Act iv, sc. 4, l. 537. [King Richard]

6
Thou know'st our reasons urged upon the way.
Richard III. Act iii, sc. 1, l. 160. [Buckingham]

King Richard: Your reasons are too shallow and too quick.
Queen Elizabeth: O no, my reasons are too deep and dead.
Richard III. Act iv, sc. 4, l. 361.

7 The reason that I have to love thee
Doth much excuse the appertaining rage.
Romeo and Juliet. Act iii, sc. 1, l. 65. [Romeo]

Now do you know the reason of this haste.
Romeo and Juliet. Act iv, sc. 1, l. 15. [Paris]

8
Now reason is past cure.
Sonnets. No. cxlvii.

9
Your reason For raising this sea-storm?
The Tempest. Act i, sc. 2, l. 176. [Miranda] The only use of "sea-storm."

The reason?—*II Henry IV,* ii, 2, 53.

Your reason?—*As You Like It,* iii, 2, 40; *The Comedy of Errors,* ii, 2, 62; *Love's Labour 's Lost,* ii, 1, 233; *Titus Andronicus,* v, 3, 40.

10
Fool: The reason of this?
Servant: I could render one.
Apemantus: Do it then, that we may account thee a whoremaster and a knave.
Timon of Athens. Act ii, sc. 2, l. 108.

11
Marcus: But yet let reason govern thy lament.
Titus: If there were reason for these miseries,
Then into limits could I bind my woes.
Titus Andronicus. Act iii, sc. 1, l. 219.

12
Wilt thou have a reason for this coil?
Titus Andronicus. Act iii, sc. 1, l. 225. [Titus]

Who was so firm, so constant, that this coil
Would not infect his reason?
The Tempest. Act i, sc. 2, l. 207. [Prospero]

13
No marvel, though you bite so sharp at reasons,
You are so empty of them.
Troilus and Cressida. Act ii, sc. 2, l. 33. [Helenus]

You fur your gloves with reason.
Troilus and Cressida. Act ii, sc. 2, l. 38. [Troilus]

14 Nay, if we talk of reason,
Let 's shut our gates and sleep: manhood and honour
Should have hare-hearts, would they but fat their thoughts
With this cramm'd reason: reason and respect
Make livers pale and lustihood deject.
Troilus and Cressida. Act ii, sc. 2, l. 46. [Troilus] The only use of "hare-hearts." "Lustihood" occurs again in *Much Ado about Nothing,* v, 1, 76.

The reasons you allege do more conduce
To the hot passion of distemper'd blood
Than to make up a free determination
'Twixt right and wrong.
Troilus and Cressida. Act ii, sc. 2, l. 168. [Hector] The only use of "allege." "Conduce" appears again in v, 2, 147, and in no other play.

15
Sir Toby: Thy exquisite reason, dear knight?
Sir Andrew: I have no exquisite reason for 't, but I have reason good enough.
Twelfth Night. Act ii, sc. 3, l. 155.

Thy reason, dear venom, give thy reason.
Twelfth Night. Act iii, sc. 2, l. 2. [Sir Toby]

I will show thee no reason for 't.
Twelfth Night. Act iii, sc. 1, l. 167. [Sir Toby]

16
I have no other but a woman's reason:
I think him so because I think him so.
The Two Gentlemen of Verona. Act i, sc. 2, l. 22. [Lucetta]

17
What are you reasoning with yourself?
The Two Gentlemen of Verona. Act ii, sc. 1, l. 147. [Valentine]

This reasoning is not in the fashion to choose me a husband.
The Merchant of Venice. Act i, sc. 2, l. 23. [Portia] The only uses of "reasoning."

18
Reasonless to reason thus?
The Two Gentlemen of Verona. Act ii, sc. 4, l. 198. [Proteus]

This proffer is absurd and reasonless.
I Henry VI. Act v, sc. 4, l. 137. [Alençon] The only uses of "reasonless."

1
'Fie, fie,' he says, 'you crush me; let me go;
You have no reason to withhold me so.'
Venus and Adonis, l. 611.
Reason is the bawd to lust's abuse.
Venus and Adonis, l. 792. See under LUST.
2
If my reason
Will thereto be obedient, I have reason;
If not, my senses, better pleased with madness,
Do bid it welcome.
The Winter's Tale. Act iv, sc. 4, l. 492. [Florizel]

REBELLION

See also Revolt, Revolution, Usurpation

3
Now, God delay our rebellion!
All's Well that Ends Well. Act iv, sc. 3, l. 23. [Lord]
Natural rebellion, done i' the blaze of youth;
When oil and fire, too strong for reason's force,
O'erbears it and burns on.
All's Well that Ends Well. Act v, sc. 3, l. 6. [Countess]
4
We nourish 'gainst our senate
The cockle of rebellion, insolence, sedition,
Which we ourselves have plough'd for, sow'd, and scatter'd.
Coriolanus. Act iii, sc. 1, l. 69. [Coriolanus]
The vulture of sedition.—*I Henry VI,* iv, 3, 47.
Heap'd sedition.—*III Henry VI,* ii, 2, 158. The only uses of "sedition."
5
In a rebellion,
When what 's not meet, but what must be, was law.
Coriolanus. Act iii, sc. 1, l. 167. [Coriolanus]
6
Rebellion looks so giant-like.
Hamlet. Act iv, sc. 5, l. 121. [King] "Giant-like" occurs again in *A Midsummer-Night's Dream,* iii, 1, 197.
7
A mighty and a fearful head they are,
If promises be kept on every hand,
As ever offer'd foul play in a state.
I Henry IV. Act iii, sc. 2, l. 167. [Blunt]
If we without his help can make a head
To push against a kingdom, with his help
We shall o'erturn it topsy-turvy down.
I Henry IV. Act iv, sc. 1, l. 80. [Hotspur] The only use of "topsy-turvy." "O'erturn is repeated in *Henry V,* 4, 2, 24.
You conjure from the breast of civil peace
Such bold hostility, teaching his duteous land
Audacious cruelty.
I Henry IV. Act iv, sc. 3, l. 43. [Blunt]
Rebellion lay in his way, and he found it.
I Henry IV. Act v, sc. 1, l. 28. [Falstaff]
To face the garment of rebellion
With some fine colour that may please the eye.
I Henry IV. Act v, sc. 1, l. 74. [King Henry]
8
And never yet did insurrection want
Such water-colours to impaint his cause;
Nor moody beggars, starving for a time
Of pellmell havoc and confusion.
I Henry IV. Act v, sc. 1, l. 79. [King Henry] The only use of "water-colours" and "impaint."
For that same word, rebellion, did divide
The action of their bodies from their souls; . . .
This word, rebellion, it had froze them up,
As fish are in a pond. But now the bishop
Turns insurrection to religion.
II Henry IV. Act i, sc. 1, l. 194. [Morton]
If that rebellion
Came like itself, in base and abject routs,
Led on by bloody youth, guarded with rags,
And countenanced by boys and beggary,
I say, if damn'd commotion so appear'd,
In his true, native and most proper shape,
You, reverend father, and these noble lords
Had not been here, to dress the ugly form
Of base and bloody insurrection
With your fair honours.
II Henry IV. Act iv, sc. 1, l. 32. [Westmoreland]
The state of man,
Like to a little kingdom, suffers then
The nature of an insurrection.
Julius Cæsar. Act ii, sc. 1, l. 67. [Brutus]
Strange insurrections.—*Coriolanus,* iv, 3, 13.
9
Thus ever did rebellion find rebuke.
I Henry IV. Act v, sc. 5, l. 1. [King Henry]
Rebellion in this land shall lose his sway,
Meeting the check of such another day.
I Henry IV. Act v, sc. 5, l. 41. [King Henry]
10
Quenching the flame of bold rebellion
Even with the rebels' blood.
II Henry IV. Induction, l. 26. [Rumour]
11
What peer hath been suborn'd to grate on you,
That you should seal this lawless bloody book
Of forged rebellion with a seal divine?
II Henry IV. Act iv, sc. 1, l. 90. [Westmoreland]
But for you, rebels, look to taste the due
Meet for rebellion and such acts as yours.
Most shallowly did you these arms commence,
Fondly brought here and foolishly sent hence.
II Henry IV. Act iv, sc. 2, l. 116. [Lancaster] The only use of "shallowly."
That rebellion had bad luck.—*II Henry IV,* i, 1, 41
12
Bringing rebellion broached on his sword.
Henry V. Act v, Prologue, l. 32. [Chorus]
13
Such which breaks
The sides of loyalty, and almost appears
In loud rebellion.
Henry VIII. Act i, sc. 2, l. 27. [Queen Katharine]
14
Rebellion, flat rebellion!
King John. Act iii, sc. 1, l. 298. [Austria]
Gross rebellion.—*Richard II,* ii, 3, 109.
Wise rebellion.—*Coriolanus,* i, 1, 162.
Rebellion of a codpiece.—*Measure for Measure,* iii, 2, 122.
15
This must not be thus borne: this will break out

To all our sorrows, and ere long I doubt.
King John. Act iv, sc. 2, l. 101. [Pembroke]
Unthread the rude eye of rebellion
And welcome home again discarded faith.
King John. Act v, sc. 4, l. 11. [Melun] The only use of "unthread."

1 Rebellion's head, rise never till the wood
Of Birnam rise.
Macbeth. Act iv, sc. 1, l. 96. [Macbeth]

2 This earth shall have a feeling and these stones
Prove armed soldiers, ere her native king
Shall falter under foul rebellion's arms.
Richard II. Act iii, sc. 2, l. 24. [King Richard] The only use of "falter."
Yea, distaff-women manage rusty bills
Against thy seat: both young and old rebel,
And all goes worse than I have power to tell.
Richard II. Act iii, sc. 2, l. 118. [Sir Stephen Scroop] The only use of "distaff-women."

3 Rebellious subjects, enemies to peace,
Profaners of this neighbour-stained steel.
Romeo and Juliet. Act i, sc. 1, l. 88. [Prince] The only use of "neighbour-stained" and "profaners."
Rebellious earth.—*Richard II,* v, 1, 5.
Rebellious hell.—*Hamlet,* iii, 4, 82.
Rebellious hinds.—*II Henry VI,* iv, 2, 130.
Rebellious liquors.—*As You Like It,* ii, 3, 49.
Rebellious necks.—*I Henry VI,* ii, 3, 64.

II—Rebels

4 A hundred thousand rebels die in this.
I Henry VI. Act iii, sc. 2, l. 160. [King Henry]
English rebels.—*I Henry IV,* iii, 2, 165.
Kentish rebels.—*II Henry VI,* iv, 4, 42.

5 God be thanked for these rebels, they offend none but the virtuous.
I Henry IV. Act iii, sc. 3, l. 214. [Falstaff]

6 A very valiant rebel of the name.
I Henry IV. Act v, sc. 4, l. 62. [Prince of Wales]
A famous rebel art thou.—*II Henry IV,* iv, 3, 69.

7 Pause us, till these rebels, now afoot,
Come underneath the yoke of government.
II Henry IV. Act iv, sc. 4, l. 9. [King Henry]

8 I come amain,
To signify that rebels there are up.
II Henry VI. Act iii, sc. 1, l. 283.
The rebels have assay'd to win the Tower.
II Henry VI. Act iv, sc. 5, l. 9. [Scales]

9 Look where the sturdy rebel sits,
Even in the chair of state.
III Henry VI. Act i, sc. 1, l. 50. [King Henry] "Sturdy" is repeated in *Venus and Adonis,* l. 152.

10 Upon these taxations,
The clothiers all, not able to maintain
The many to them 'longing, have put off
The spinsters, carders, fullers, weavers, who,
Unfit for other life, compell'd by hunger
And lack of other means, in desperate manner
Daring the event to the teeth, are all in uproar,
And danger serves among them.
Henry VIII. Act i, sc. 2, l. 30. [Norfolk] The only use of "carders," and "fullers."

11 Worthy to be a rebel, for to that
The multiplying villanies of nature
Do swarm upon him.
Macbeth. Act i, sc. 2, l. 10. [Sergeant]

12 Now for the rebels which stand out in Ireland.
Richard II. Act i, sc. 4, l. 38. [Green]

13 And you that do abet him in this kind
Cherish rebellion and are rebels all.
Richard II. Act ii, sc. 3, l. 146. [York] The only use of "abet."

14 You bow like subjects,
Yet that, by you deposed, you quake like rebels?
Richard III. Act i, sc. 3, l. 161. [Queen Margaret]
Petty rebel.—*Richard III,* iv, 4, 332.

REBUKE

See also Reproach, Reproof

15 Why bear you these rebukes and answer not?
The Comedy of Errors. Act v, sc. 1, l. 89. [Luciana]

16 Rebuke and dread correction wait on us.
I Henry IV. Act v, sc. 1, l. 111. [King Henry]
This dear and deep rebuke.—*II Henry IV,* iv, 5, 141.

17 Rebuke me not for that which you provoke.
Love's Labour's Lost. Act v, sc. 2, l. 347. [King]
O, why rebuke you him that loves you so?
Lay breath so bitter on your bitter foe.
A Midsummer-Night's Dream. Act iii, sc. 2, l. 43. [Demetrius]

RECKONING

18 I will tear the reckoning from his heart.
I Henry IV. Act iii, sc. 2, l. 152. [Prince]
False reckonings.—*As You Like It,* iii, 4, 35.
Heavy reckoning.—*Henry V,* iv, 1, 141; *Cymbeline,* v, 4, 159.
Trim reckoning!—*I Henry IV,* v, 1, 137.
O weary reckoning!—*Othello,* iii, 4, 176.

19 I am ill at reckoning;
It fitteth the spirit of a tapster.
Love's Labour's Lost. Act i, sc. 2, l. 42. [Armado]
Called her to a reckoning.—*I Henry IV,* i, 2, 53. See under HOSTESS.
How goes our reckoning?—*Timon of Athens,* ii, 2, 159.

It were pity you should get your living by reckoning, sir.
Love's Labour 's Lost. Act v, sc. 2, l. 497. [Costard]

1
Of honourable reckoning are you both.
Romeo and Juliet. Act i, sc. 2, l. 4. [Paris]

RECOMPENSE

See also Compensation, Payment, Reward

2
But do not look for further recompense
Than thine own gladness that thou art employ'd.
As You Like It. Act iii, sc. 5, l. 97. [Phebe]
Look for recompense.—*Sonnets,* xxiii.

3
When I have chased all my foes from hence,
Then will I think upon a recompense.
I Henry VI. Act i, sc. 2, l. 115. [Charles]

4
He means to recompense the pains you take
By cutting off your heads: thus hath he sworn.
King John. Act v, sc. 4, l. 15. [Melun]

5 Thou art so far before
That swiftest wing of recompense is slow
To overtake thee.
Macbeth. Act i, sc. 4, l. 16. [Duncan]

6
It may compel him to her recompense.
Measure for Measure. Act iii, sc. 2, l. 263. [Duke]

7
So shall I evermore be bound to thee;
Besides, I 'll make a present recompense.
The Merry Wives of Windsor. Act iv, sc. 6, l. 54. [Fenton]
Bad recompense.—*Twelfth Night,* ii, 1, 7.
Double recompense.—*A Midsummer-Night's Dream,* iii, 2, 180.
Friendly recompense.—*Much Ado about Nothing,* v, 4, 83.
God-like recompense.—*Love's Labour 's Lost,* i, 1, 58.

8
My recompense is thanks, that 's all;
Yet my good will is great, though the gift small.
Pericles. Act iii, sc. 4, l. 17. [Thaisa]

9
As my fortune ripens with my love,
It shall be still thy true love's recompense.
Richard II. Act ii, sc. 3, l. 48. [Bolingbroke]
Labour's recompense.—*Richard II,* ii, 3, 62.

10 A recompense more fruitful
Than their offence can weigh down by the dram.
Timon of Athens. Act v, sc. 1, l. 153. [Senator]

11
Now, princes, for the service I have done you,
The advantage of the time prompts me aloud
To call for recompense.
Troilus and Cressida. Act iii, sc. 3, l. 1. [Calchas]
As recompense of our dear services.
Winter's Tale, ii, 3, 150. See under PURPOSE.

12
My master, not myself, lacks recompense.
Twelfth Night. Act i, sc. 5, l. 304. [Viola]

RECONCILIATION

13
We are reconciled, and the first view shall kill
All repetition.
All 's Well that Ends Well. Act v, sc. 3, l. 21. [King]
Repetition cannot make it less.
The Rape of Lucrece, l. 1285.

14
The Jove of power make me . . .
Your reconciler.
Antony and Cleopatra. Act iii, sc. 4, l. 29. [Octavia] The only use of "reconciler."

15 In my terms of honour
I stand aloof; and will no reconcilement
Till by some elder masters, of known honour,
I have a voice and precedent of peace,
To keep my name ungored.
Hamlet. Act v, sc. 2, l. 257. [Laertes] The only use of "reconcilement" and "ungored."

16
And I, I hope, shall reconcile them all.
III Henry VI. Act i, sc. 1, l. 273. [Exeter]
We 'll devise a means to reconcile you.—*II Henry VI,* iv, 8, 72.
Our suit Is, that you reconcile them.—*Coriolanus,* v, 3, 136.
I shall be reconciled to him again.—*Richard III,* i, 4, 184.
I desire To reconcile me.—*Richard III,* ii, 1, 59.
I 'll reconcile me.—*Winter's Tale,* iii, 2, 156.

17
If I have any grace or power to move you,
His present reconciliation take.
Othello. Act iii, sc. 3, l. 46. [Desdemona] The only use of "reconciliation."

18
And let it be mine honour, good my lord,
That I have reconciled your friends and you.
Titus Andronicus. Act i, sc. 1, l. 466. [Tamora]
Reconcile your friends.—*Romeo and Juliet,* iii, 3, 151.

RECOVERY

19
Bertram: Some dishonour we had in the loss of that drum; but it is not to be recovered.
Parolles: It might have been recovered.
Bertram: It might; but it is not now.
Parolles: It is to be recovered.
All's Well that Ends Well. Act iii, sc. 6, l. 59.

20
Those that do die of it do seldom or never recover.
Antony and Cleopatra, v, 2, 247. See under WORM.

21
Brief, I recover'd him, bound up his wound.
As You Like It. Act iv, sc. 3, l. 151. [Oliver]

1 Bind him fast
And bear him home for his recovery.
The Comedy of Errors. Act v, sc. 1, l. 41. [Adriana]
He 'll recover without physic.—*II Henry IV,* iv, 5, 14.

2
Lost, and recover'd in a day again!
I Henry VI. Act iii, sc. 2, l. 115. [Talbot]
Wert thou as we are,
We might recover all our loss again.
III Henry VI. Act v, sc. 2, l. 29. [Somerset]

3
What, doth she swoon? use means for her recovery.
III Henry VI. Act v, sc. 5, l. 45. [King Edward]

4
With the help of a surgeon he might yet recover.
A Midsummer-Night's Dream. Act v, sc. 1, l. 317. [Theseus]
He may recover yet.—*Antony and Cleopatra,* iv, 9, 35.
Look, he recovers.—*As You Like It,* iv, 3, 161.
He will recover straight.—*Othello,* iv, 1, 58.

5
Why, but you are now well enough: how came you thus recovered?
Othello. Act ii, sc. 3, l. 295. [Iago]

6
Your master will be dead ere you return;
There 's nothing can be minister'd to nature
That can recover him.
Pericles. Act iii, sc. 2, l. 7. [Cerimon]
Sure, all 's effectless; yet nothing we 'll omit
That bears recovery's name.
Pericles. Act v, sc. 1, l. 53. [Helicanus] "Effectless" is repeated in *Titus Andronicus,* iii, 1, 76.
No recovery.—*Troilus and Cressida,* ii, 3, 188.
Past recovery.—*II Henry VI,* i, 1, 116.

7
I heard of an Egyptian
That had nine hours lien dead,
Was by good appliance recovered.
Pericles. Act iii, sc. 2, l. 84. [Cerimon]
Sir, I will use
My utmost skill in his recovery, Provided
That none but I and my companion maid
Be suffer'd to come near him.
Pericles. Act v, sc. 1, l. 75. [Marina]

8 There 's no doubt his majesty
Will soon recover his accustom'd health.
Richard III. Act i, sc. 3, l. 1. [Rivers]
The king . . . peradventure may recover.
King John. Act v, sc. 6, l. 31. [Hubert]
The king recovers.—*II Henry IV,* iv, 4, 129.
Recovery of the king.—*All 's Well that Ends Well,* ii, 3, 42.
She hath recover'd the king, and undone me.
All 's Well that Ends Well. Act iii, sc. 2, l. 22. [Countess, reading]

9
If I can recover him and keep him tame and get to Naples with him, he 's a present for any emperor that ever trod on neat's leather. . . . If I can recover him and keep him tame, I will not take too much for him. . . . If all the wine in my bottle will recover him, I will help his ague.
The Tempest. Act ii, sc. 2, l. 71. [Stephano]

10
Kill him whom you have recovered.
Twelfth Night. Act ii, sc. 1, l. 39. [Sebastian]
If I cannot recover your niece, I am a foul way out.
Twelfth Night. Act ii, sc. 3, l. 200. [Sir Andrew]

11
Her heart is but o'ercharged; she will recover.
Winter's Tale. Act iii, sc. 2, l. 151. [Leontes]

RECREANT, see Falseness

RECREATION

12
Sweet recreation barr'd, what doth ensue
But moody and dull melancholy?
The Comedy of Errors, v, 1, 78. See under MELANCHOLY.

13
It is a recreation to be by
And hear him mock.
Cymbeline. Act i, sc. 6, l. 75. [Iachimo]

14
'Tis the breathing time of day with me.
Hamlet. Act v, sc. 2, l. 181. [Hamlet]

15 Common pleasures,
To walk abroad, and recreate yourselves.
Julius Cæsar. Act iii, sc. 2, l. 255. [Antony] The only use of "recreate."

16
Is there no quick recreation granted?
Love's Labour 's Lost. Act i, sc. 1, l. 162. [Biron]
We will to our recreation.
Love's Labour 's Lost. Act iv, sc. 2, l. 172. [Holofernes]

REDEMPTION

See also Salvation

17
Will you send him, mistress, redemption, the money in his desk?
The Comedy of Errors. Act iv, sc. 2, l. 46. [Dromio of Syracuse]
Redeem'd I was as I desired.—*I Henry VI,* i, 4, 34.

18
You bid me seek redemption of the devil.
Measure for Measure. Act v, sc. 1, l. 29. [Isabella]

19
O villains, vipers, damn'd without redemption!
Richard II. Act iii, sc. 2, l. 129. [King Richard]
Thou wilt be condemned into everlasting redemption for this.
Much Ado about Nothing. Act iv, sc. 2, l. 58. [Dogberry]

20
I every day expect an embassage
From my Redeemer to redeem me hence.
Richard III. Act ii, sc. 1, l. 3. [King Edward] "Redeemer" is repeated in l. 123 of the same scene and occurs in no other play.

REDRESS

1
I beseech you I may have redress against them.
II Henry IV. Act ii, sc. 1, l. 118. [Falstaff]
I promised you redress of these same grievances
Whereof you did complain; which, by mine honour,
I will perform with a most Christian care.
II Henry IV. Act iv, sc. 2, l. 113. [Lancaster]
2
No way canst thou turn thee for redress.
I Henry VI. Act iv, sc. 2, l. 25. [General]
No, not a man comes for redress of thee.
III Henry VI. Act iii, sc. 1, l. 20. [King]
3
Sir, I had thought by making this well known unto you,
To have found a safe redress.
King Lear. Act i, sc. 4, l. 223. [Goneril]
4
Good night to your redress!
Measure for Measure, v, 1, 301. [Duke]
Wring redress from you.—*Measure for Measure,* v, 1, 32.
Redress of injustice.—*Measure for Measure,* iv, 4, 10.
Succour and redress.—*Richard II,* iii, 2, 32.
5
Unmask, my dear, this moody heaviness,
And tell thy grief, that we may give redress.
The Rape of Lucrece, l. 1602.
Lend redress.—*Romeo and Juliet,* iv, 5, 146.
6
Things past redress are now with me past care.
Richard II. Act ii, sc. 3, l. 171. [York]
7
Now he writes to heaven for his redress.
Titus Andronicus, iv, 4, 13. [Saturninus]

REFLECTION

See also Consideration

8
You weigh this well.
II Henry IV. Act v, sc. 2, l. 102. [King Henry V]
9
'Twas dangerous for him
To ruminate on this.
Henry VIII. Act i, sc. 2, l. 179. [Surveyor]
Ruminates like an hostess that hath no arithmetic but her brain to set down her reckoning.
Troilus and Cressida. Act iii, sc. 3, l. 252. [Thersites]
That you may ruminate.
The Two Gentlemen of Verona. Act i, sc. 2, l. 49. [Lucetta]
Then she ruminates.—*The Merry Wives of Windsor,* ii, 2, 321.
Inly ruminate.—*Henry V,* iv, Prol., 24.
Ruminate himself.—*Troilus and Cressida,* ii, 3, 198.
Ruminate my grief.—*I Henry VI,* v, 5, 101.
Ruminate strange plots.—*Titus Andronicus,* v, 2, 6.
As thou dost ruminate.—*Othello,* iii, 3, 132.
Thus to ruminate.—*Sonnets,* lxiv. The only uses of "ruminate" and "ruminates."
Ruminated, plotted and set down.—*I Henry IV,* i, 3, 274.
By duty ruminated.—*Antony and Cleopatra,* ii, 2, 141. The only uses of "ruminated."
10
Lay hand on heart, advise.
Romeo and Juliet. Act iii, 5, 192. [Capulet]
11
Please you, deliberate a day or two.
The Two Gentlemen of Verona. Act i, sc. 3, l. 73. [Proteus]
Not to deliberate.—*II Henry IV,* v, 5, 22.

REFORMATION

See also Mending

12
I do not shame
To tell you what I was, since my conversion
So sweetly tastes, being the thing I am.
As You Like It, iv, 3, 136. [Oliver] "Conversion" is repeated in *King John,* i, 1, 189.
And to the skirts of this wild wood he came;
Where meeting with an old religious man,
After some question with him, was converted
Both from his enterprise and from the world.
As You Like It. Act v, sc. 4, l. 165. [Jaques]
May I be so converted.—*Much Ado about Nothing,* ii, 3, 23.
How you may be converted I know not.
Much Ado about Nothing. Act iii, sc. 4, l. 91. [Margaret]
13
Out of these convertites
There is much matter to be heard and learn'd.
As You Like It. Act v, sc. 4, l. 190. [Jaques]
He thence departs, a heavy convertite.
The Rape of Lucrece, l. 743.
A gentle convertite.—*King John,* v, 1, 19. The only uses of "convertite" and "convertites."
14
I must give over this life, and I will give it over: by the Lord, an I do not, I am a villain: I 'll be damned for never a king's son in Christendom.
I Henry IV. Act i, sc. 2, l. 106. [Falstaff]
An 'twere not as good a deed as drink, to turn true man and to leave these rogues, I am the veriest varlet that ever chewed with a tooth.
I Henry IV. Act ii, sc. 2, l. 24. [Falstaff]
I 'll purge and leave sack, and live cleanly as a nobleman should do.
I Henry IV. Act v, sc. 4, l. 168. [Falstaff]
15
So, when this loose behaviour I throw off
And pay the debt I never promised,
By how much better than my word I am,
By so much shall I falsify men's hopes;
And like bright metal on a sullen ground,
My reformation, glittering o'er my fault,
Shall show more goodly and attract more eyes
Than that which hath no foil to set it off.
I Henry IV. Act i, sc. 2, l. 231. [Prince of Wales] The only use of "falsify."
Presume not that I am the thing I was;
For God doth know, so shall the world perceive,
That I have turn'd away my former self.
II Henry IV, v, 5, 60. [King Henry V]
Never came reformation in a flood,
With such a heady currance, scouring faults.
Henry V. Act i, sc. 1, l. 33. [Canterbury] The only use of "currance" (current).

1
Thou whoreson little tidy Bartholomew boar-pig, when wilt thou leave fighting o' days and foining o' nights, and begin to patch up thine old body for heaven?
II Henry IV. Act ii, sc. 4, l. 250. [Doll] The only use of "tidy" and "boar-pig." "Bartholomew-tide" occurs in *Henry V*, v, 2, 336, and "foining" (thrusting) is repeated in *Much Ado about Nothing*, v, 1, 84.

As we hear you do reform yourselves,
We will, according to your strengths and qualities,
Give you advancement.
II Henry IV. Act v, sc. 5, l. 72. [King Henry V]

2
Let me persuade you take a better course.
I Henry VI. Act iv, sc. 1, l. 132. [Gloucester]

3
Your captain is brave, and vows reformation.
II Henry VI. Act iv, sc. 2, l. 70. [Cade]
Reformation must be sudden.—*Henry VIII*, v, 3, 20.

4 Throw away that spirit,
And I shall find you empty of that fault,
Right joyful of your reformation.
Love's Labour's Lost. Act v, sc. 2, l. 877. [Rosaline]

5
They are reformed, civil, full of good
And fit for great employment, worthy lord.
The Two Gentlemen of Verona. Act v, sc. 4, l. 156. [Valentine]

6 Priest-like, thou
Hast cleansed my bosom, I from thee departed
Thy penitent reform'd.
The Winter's Tale. Act i, sc. 2, l. 237. [Leontes] "Priest-like" is repeated in *Coriolanus*, v, 1, 56: "Priest-like fasts."

REFUSAL

See also Denial

7
Fall in rage With their refusal.
Coriolanus. Act ii, sc. 3, l. 267. [Brutus] The only use of "refusal."

8
Who shall say me nay?
I Henry IV. Act iii, sc. 1, l. 117. [Hotspur]
You shall not say me nay.
Love's Labour's Lost. Act iv, sc. 2, l. 171. [Holofernes]
I can say nay.—*Richard III*, iii, 7, 53.
I say nay to that.—*Comedy of Errors*, v, 1, 371.
I'll . . . say thee nay.—*Romeo and Juliet*, ii, 2, 96.
Dares not answer nay.—*A Midsummer-Night's Dream*, iii, 1, 136.
Still answer nay.—*Richard III*, iii, 7, 51.
Past all saying nay.—*The Merchant of Venice*, iii, 2, 232.

9
Again I do refuse you.
Henry VIII. Act ii, sc. 4, l. 118. [Queen Katharine]
Refuse your aid.—*Coriolanus*, v, 1, 33.
Refuse thy name.—*Romeo and Juliet*, ii, 2, 34.
Refuse to marry me.—*As You Like It*, v, 4, 13.
Heaven's offer we refuse.—*Richard II*, iii, 2, 31.
Refuse it not.—*Twelfth Night*, iii, 4, 229.
Refuse not.—*Richard III*, iii, 7, 202.
Refuse none.—*The Merchant of Venice*, i, 2, 28.

10
He hath refused it in the open court.
The Merchant of Venice. Act iv, sc. 1, l. 338. [Portia]
Refused the crown.—*Julius Cæsar*, i, 2, 248; 266.

11
You will reject her.
Love's Labour's Lost, v, 2, 438. The only use of "reject."

12
Refuse me, hate me, torture me to death!
Much Ado about Nothing. Act iv, sc. 1, l. 186. [Hero]

13 In wholesome wisdom
He might not but refuse you.
Othello. Act iii, sc. 1, l. 49. [Emilia]

REJOICING

14
It rejoices me, that I hope I shall see him ere I die.
All's Well that Ends Well. Act iv, sc. 5, l. 89. [Countess]
Rejoice with him.—*The Comedy of Errors*, v, 1, 413.

15
You'll rejoice That he is thus cut off.
Coriolanus. Act v, sc. 6, l. 139. [Aufidius]
Freelier rejoice.—*Coriolanus*, i, 3, 3. The only use of "freelier."
I . . . heartily will rejoice.—*Henry V*, ii, 2, 159.

16
Pistol: Rejoice therefore. . . .
Fluellen: It is not a thing to rejoice at.
Henry V. Act iii, sc. 6, l. 53.
Wherefore rejoice?—*Julius Cæsar*, i, 1, 37.
I rejoice at it.—*Julius Cæsar*, iii, 2, 27.
Rejoice to see my tears.—*II Henry VI*, ii, 4, 32.

17
Rejoice, you men of Angiers, ring your bells.
King John. Act ii, sc. 1, l. 312. [Herald]

18
'So, so,' quoth he, 'these lets attend the time,
Like little frosts that sometimes threat the spring,
To add a more rejoicing to the prime,
And give the sneaped birds more cause to sing.'
The Rape of Lucrece, l. 330. The only use of "sneaped" (pinched with cold).

19
I'll go along no such sight to be shown,
But to rejoice in splendour of mine own.
Romeo and Juliet. Act i, sc. 2, l. 105. [Romeo]

20 O, rejoice
Beyond a common joy, and set it down
With gold on lasting pillars.
The Tempest. Act v, sc. 1, l. 206. [Gonzalo]
My rejoicing At nothing can be more.—*The Tempest*, iii, 1, 93.

21
Shall we thither and with our company piece the rejoicing?
The Winter's Tale. Act v, sc. 2, l. 117. [Gentleman]

RELENTING

1 Can you . . . behold
My sighs and tears and will not once relent?
I Henry VI. Act iii, sc. 1, l. 107. [King Henry]
Will ye relent?—*II Henry VI*, iv, 8, 11.
Suddenly relent.—*I Henry VI*, iii, 3, 59.
Relent and sigh.—*The Merchant of Venice*, iii, 3, 15.

2
May be he will relent.
Measure for Measure. Act ii, sc. 2, l. 3. [Provost]
He will relent.—*Measure for Measure*, ii, 2, 124.
I do relent.—*The Merry Wives of Windsor*, ii, 2, 31.

3
Fierce Andronicus would not relent.
Titus Andronicus. Act ii, sc. 3, l. 165. [Tamora]
He . . . relents not.—*Measure for Measure*, iii, 1, 239.

RELIGION

4
The duke hath put on a religious life
And thrown into neglect the pompous court.
As You Like It. Act v, sc. 4, l. 187. [Jaques] "Religious life" is repeated in *Much Ado about Nothing*, iv, 1, 244.
Religious love put out Religion's eye.
A Lover's Complaint, l. 250.
Religious canons.—*Timon of Athens*, iv, 3, 60.
Religious churchmen.—*I Henry VI*, i, 1, 40.
Religious fear.—*Hamlet*, iii, 3, 8.
Religious house.—*Richard II*, v, 1, 23.
Religious man.—*As You Like It*, v, 4, 166.
Religious men.—*Richard III*, iii, 7, 92.
Religious strength.—*King John*, iii, 1, 229.
Religious truth.—*Henry VIII*, iv, 2, 74.
Religious uncle.—*As You Like It*, iii, 2, 362.

5
I see you have some religion in you.
Cymbeline. Act i, sc. 4, l. 148. [Iachimo]

6 Seeks to overthrow religion,
Because he is protector of the realm.
I Henry VI. Act i, sc. 3, l. 65. [Gloucester]

7
Methinks my lord should be religious.
I Henry VI. Act iii, sc. 1, l. 54. [Somerset]
Seem they religious? Why, so didst thou.
Henry V. Act ii, sc. 2, l. 130. [King Henry]

8
A spleeny Lutheran.
Henry VIII. Act iii, sc. 2, l. 99. [Wolsey] The only use of "spleeny" and "Lutheran."

9
It is religion that doth make vows kept;
But thou hast sworn against religion.
King John. Act iii, sc. 1, l. 279. [Pandulph]

10 In religion,
What damned error, but some sober brow
Will bless it and approve it with a text,
Hiding the grossness with fair ornament?
The Merchant of Venice. Act iii, sc. 2, l. 77. [Bassanio]
Religion groans at it.—*Timon of Athens*, iii, 2, 83.

11 I know thou art religious
And hast a thing within thee called conscience,
With twenty popish tricks and ceremonies,
Which I have seen thee careful to observe.
Titus Andronicus. Act v, sc. 1, l. 74. [Aaron] The only use of "popish."

REMEDY

See also Cure, Medicine

12
Our remedies oft in ourselves do lie,
Which we ascribe to heaven.
All's Well that Ends Well. Act i, sc. 1, l. 231. [Helena]
There is a remedy, approved, set down,
To cure the desperate languishings whereof
The king is render'd lost.
All's Well that Ends Well. Act i, sc. 3, l. 234. [Helena] The only use of "languishings." "Languishing" occurs in *Cymbeline*, i, 5, 9: "Languishing death."

13
I pray you, tell me your remedy.
As You Like It, iii, 2, 386. [Orlando]
Beg of her for remedy.—*A Midsummer-Night's Dream*, iii, 2, 109.
A remedy presents itself.—*Measure for Measure*, iii, 1, 204.
There is remedy enough.—*I Henry VI*, v, 3, 135.
I will fit thee with a remedy.—*Much Ado about Nothing*, i, 1, 321.
I know my remedy.—*The Taming of the Shrew*, Ind., 1, 11.
Instant remedy.—*King Lear*, i, 4, 268.

14
His remedies are tame i' the present peace.
Coriolanus. Act iv, sc. 6, l. 2. [Sicinius]

15 This must be patch'd
With cloth of any colour.
Coriolanus. Act iii, sc. 1, l. 252. [Menenius]

16 To gather . . .
Whether aught, to us unknown, afflicts him thus,
That, open'd, lies within our remedy.
Hamlet. Act ii, sc. 2, l. 15. [King]

17
I can get no remedy against this consumption of the purse.
II Henry IV, i, 2, 264. See under PURSE.
There 's no remedy.—*I Henry VI*, ii, 2, 57, and frequently in later plays.
Here is no remedy.—*The Merry Wives of Windsor*, v, 5, 244.
Is there no remedy?—*King John*, iv, 1, 91; *Measure for Measure*, iii, 1, 61.
I know no wise remedy.—*As You Like It*, i, 1, 26.
Past remedy.—*Titus Andronicus*, iv, 3, 31.

18 Thus hulling in
The wild sea of my conscience, I did steer
Toward this remedy.
Henry VIII. Act ii, sc. 4, l. 199. [King Henry] The only use of "hulling."

19 Things done without all remedy
Should be without regard.
Macbeth. Act iii, sc. 2, l. 11. [Lady Macbeth]

1
Why, all the souls that were were forfeit once;
And He that might the vantage best have took
Found out the remedy.
Measure for Measure. Act ii, sc. 2, l. 73. [Isabella]

2
I 'll apply To your eye,
Gentle lover, remedy.
A Midsummer-Night's Dream. Act iii, sc. 2, l. 450. [Puck]

3
When remedies are past, the griefs are ended
By seeing the worst, which late on hopes depended.
Othello. Act i, sc. 3, l. 202. [Duke] The only use of "depended."

4
The remedy indeed to do me good
Is to let forth my foul-defiled blood.
The Rape of Lucrece, l. 1028. The only use of "foul-defiled."

5
Our remedies
Within thy help and holy physic lies.
Romeo and Juliet. Act ii, sc. 3, l. 51. [Romeo]

I long to die,
If what thou speak'st speak not of remedy.
Romeo and Juliet. Act iv, sc. 1, l. 66. [Juliet]
If thou darest, I 'll give thee remedy.
Romeo and Juliet. Act iv, sc. 1, l. 76. [Friar Laurence]

6
The nature of the sickness found, . . .
What is the remedy?
Troilus and Cressida. Act i, sc. 3, l. 140. [Agamemnon]
What remedy?—*I Henry VI,* v, 3, 132; *The Merry Wives of Windsor,* v, 5, 250; *Twelfth Night,* i, 5, 56.

7
Beseech you, tenderly apply to her
Some remedies for life.
The Winter's Tale. Act iii, sc. 2, l. 153. [Leontes]

REMEMBRANCE

See also Memory

8
His good remembrance, sir,
Lies richer in your thoughts than on his tomb;
So in approof lives not his epitaph
As in your royal speech.
All's Well that Ends Well. Act i, sc. 2, l. 48. [Bertram]
Clear remembrance.—*Pericles,* v, 3, 12.
Self-gracious remembrance.—*All's Well that Ends Well,* iv, 5, 78.
Weak remembrance.—*The Tempest,* ii, 1, 236.
Young remembrance.—*Macbeth,* ii, 3, 67.

9
Little Helen, farewell: if I can remember thee, I will think of thee at court.
All's Well that Ends Well. Act i, sc. 2, l. 203. [Parolles]
I can hardly remember.—*As You Like It,* iii, 2, 188.
I cannot remember.—*The Merry Wives of Windsor,* i, 1, 174.
Remember not.—*The Tempest,* v, 1, 255.
No remembrances.—*Sonnets,* v.

10
Praising what is lost
Makes the remembrance dear.
All's Well that Ends Well. Act v, sc. 3, l. 19. [King]
In our heart's table.
All's Well that Ends Well, i, 1, 106. [Helena]

11
The time shall not
Out-go my thinking on you.
Antony and Cleopatra, iii, 2, 60. [Cæsar]

12
You must learn me how to remember.
As You Like It. Act i, sc. 2, l. 6. [Rosalind]
As I remember.—*As You Like It,* i, 1, 1; *Love's Labour 's Lost,* i, 1, 258; *Romeo and Juliet,* v, 1, 55.
As I do remember.—*King Lear,* iv, 7, 74.
As I may remember.—*II Henry IV,* iii, 1, 66.

13
Ægeus: I am sure you both of you remember me.
Dromio of Ephesus: Ourselves we do remember, sir, by you;
For lately we were bound, as you are now.
The Comedy of Errors. Act v, sc. 1, l. 291.

14
The remembrancer of her to hold
The hand-fast to her lord.
Cymbeline. Act i, sc. 5, l. 77. [Queen] "Hand-fast" is repeated in *The Winter's Tale,* iv, 4, 795.
Sweet remembrancer!—*Macbeth,* iii, 4, 37. The only uses of "remembrancer."

15
Praise Be given to your remembrance.
Cymbeline. Act ii, sc. 4, l. 92. [Posthumus]
Many years . . . not wore him
From my remembrance.
Cymbeline. Act iv, sc. 4, l. 22. [Arviragus]

16
I forgot to ask him one thing: I 'll remember 't anon.
Cymbeline. Act iii, sc. 5, l. 133. [Cloten]

17
Heaven and earth! Must I remember?
Hamlet. Act i, sc. 2, l. 142. [Hamlet]

18
Laertes: Remember well
What I have said to you.
Ophelia: 'Tis in my memory lock'd,
And you yourself shall keep the key of it.
Hamlet. Act i, sc. 3, l. 84.
If this but answer to my just belief,
I 'll well remember you.
Pericles. Act v, sc. 1, l. 239. [Lysimachus]
Remember well.—*King John,* v, 1, 22.
I well remember.—*Richard II,* iv, 1, 167; *King Lear,* iv, 6, 108; *Pericles,* iii, 4, 5.
I remember it well.—*Romeo and Juliet,* i, 3, 22.
I can remember well.—*Macbeth,* ii, 4, 1.
I remember them too well.—*Richard III,* i, 3, 118.

19
Marry, well bethought.
Hamlet. Act i, sc. 3, l. 90. [Polonius]
'Tis well bethought.—*Pericles,* v, 1, 44.

1
Ghost: Adieu, adieu! Hamlet, remember me. . . .
Hamlet: Remember thee!
Ay, thou poor ghost.
Hamlet. Act i, sc. 5, l. 91. See under MEMORY.

I beseech you, remember.—*Hamlet,* v, 2, 108.

2
My lord, I have remembrances of yours
That I have longed long to re-deliver.
Hamlet. Act iii, sc. 1, l. 93. [Ophelia] "Re-deliver" is repeated in v, 2, 186, and in *Measure for Measure,* iv, 4, 6.

There 's rosemary, that 's for remembrance.
Hamlet. Act iv, sc. 5, l. 175. [Ophelia] See under FLOWERS.

3 Therefore will he wipe his tables clean
And keep no tell-tale to his memory
That may repeat and history his loss
To new remembrance.
II Henry IV. Act iv, sc. 1, l. 201. [York]

Do not bid me remember.—*II Henry IV,* ii, 4, 255.

4
Porter, remember what I gave in charge.
I Henry VI. Act ii, sc. 3, l. 1. [Countess]

Remember this.—*Richard III,* i, 3, 299; v, 3, 239.

Remember what I have said.—*Pericles,* iv, 1, 47.

Remember what I tell you.—*King Lear,* i, 3, 21.

Remember what I told you.—*Much Ado about Nothing,* ii, 1, 69.

Remember where we are.—*I Henry VI,* iv, 1, 137. "Remember," as a simple imperative, is used frequently throughout the plays.

5
I remember it to my grief.
III Henry VI. Act i, sc. 1, l. 93. [Northumberland] "I remember" is used frequently.

I do remember it.—*I Henry VI,* i, 1, 165, and frequently in later plays.

I must remember you.—*I Henry IV,* v, 1, 32.

I remember him now.—*Henry V,* iii, 6, 65.

I remember Of such a time.—*Henry VIII,* i, 2, 190.

6 Remember me
In all humility unto his highness.
Henry VIII. Act iv, sc. 2, l. 160. [Katharine]

Remember me.—*Twelfth Night,* ii, 4, 16.

Now I remember me.—*Twelfth Night,* v, 1, 286.

Something over to remember me by.—*Henry VIII,* iv, 2, 151.

7
Gardiner: I shall remember this bold language.
Cromwell: Do. Remember your bold life too.
Henry VIII. Act v, sc. 3, l. 84.

I shall remember.—*Julius Cæsar,* i, 2, 9.

We shall remember.—*Antony and Cleopatra,* v, 2, 119.

8
Remember that you call on me to-day:
Be near me, that I may remember you.
Julius Cæsar. Act ii, sc. 2, l. 122. [Cæsar]

9
Unkind remembrance! thou and eyeless night
Have done me shame.
King John. Act v, sc. 6, l. 12. [Hubert]

10
I cannot but remember such things were,
That were most precious to me.
Macbeth. Act iv, sc. 3, l. 222. [Macduff]

11
Lucio: Do you remember what you said of the duke?
Duke: Most notedly, sir.
Measure for Measure. Act v, sc. 1, l. 335. The only use of "notedly."

12
Nerissa: Do you not remember, lady, in your father's time, a Venetian, a scholar and a soldier, that came hither in company of the Marquis of Montferrat? . . .
Portia: I remember him well, and I remember him worthy of thy praise.
The Merchant of Venice. Act 1, sc. 2, l. 123.

Do you not remember?—*Henry V,* ii, 3, 42.

Do you remember?—*Measure for Measure,* v, 1, 333; *Twelfth Night,* v, 1, 382.

Can you remember?—*As You Like It,* iii, 2, 369.

Canst thou remember?—*The Tempest,* i, 2, 38.

13
Take some remembrance of us as a tribute,
Not as a fee.
The Merchant of Venice. Act iv, sc. 1, l. 422. [Bassanio]

This was her first remembrance from the Moor.
Othello. Act iii, sc. 3, l. 291. [Emilia]

Keep this remembrance for thy Julia's sake.
The Two Gentlemen of Verona. Act ii, sc. 2, l. 5. [Julia]

Keep it safe for our remembrance.—*King John,* v, 2, 2.

14
How say you? O, I should remember him.
The Merry Wives of Windsor. Act i, sc. 4, l. 29. [Mrs. Quickly]

I pray you, know me when we meet again.
The Merchant of Venice. Act iv, sc. 1, l. 419. [Portia]

I pray you, remember in your prain.
The Merry Wives of Windsor. Act iv, sc. 1, l. 36. [Evans]

I pray you, have your remembrance, child.
The Merry Wives of Windsor. Act iv, sc. 1, l. 48. [Evans]

15
Neither press, coffer, chest, trunk, well, vault, but he hath an abstract for the remembrance of such places, and goes to them by his note.
The Merry Wives of Windsor. Act iv, sc. 2, l. 62. [Mrs. Ford]

16
As you hear of me, so think of me.
Much Ado about Nothing. Act iv, sc. 1, l. 337. [Benedick]

17
Aumerle: Remember who you are.
King Richard: I had forgot myself.
Richard II. Act iii, sc. 2, l. 82.

Briefly thyself remember.—*King Lear,* iv, 6, 233.

1
The setting sun, and music at the close,
As the last taste of sweets, is sweetest last,
Writ in remembrance more than things long past.
Richard II. Act ii, sc. 1, l. 12. [Gaunt]

2
Let me put in your minds, if you forget,
What you have been ere now, and what you are;
Withal, what I have been, and what I am.
Richard III. Act i, sc. 3, l. 131. [Gloucester]

3 Nurse, come back again;
I have remember'd me.
Romeo and Juliet. Act i, sc. 3, l. 9. [Lady Capulet]

Be remember'd.—*The Rape of Lucrece,* l. 607.
Be you remembered.—*Titus Andronicus,* iv, 3, 5.
If you be remember'd.—*Measure for Measure,* ii, 1, 110; 114.
Craves to be remember'd.—*Timon of Athens,* ii, 2, 237.
Now I am remember'd.—*As You Like It,* iii, 5, 131.
Let it be remembered.—*Much Ado about Nothing,* v, 1, 315.
Equally remembered.—*Much Ado about Nothing,* i, 1, 13.
Freshly remember'd.—*Henry V,* iv, 3, 55.
Well remember'd.—*II Henry IV,* iv, 1, 112; *The Merchant of Venice,* ii, 8, 26.

4
Juliet: I have forgot why I did call thee back.
Romeo: Let me stand here till thou remember it.
Juliet: I shall forget to have thee still stand there,
Remembering how I love thy company.
Romeo and Juliet. Act ii, sc. 2, l. 171.

5
When to the sessions of sweet silent thought
I summon up remembrance of things past,
I sigh the lack of many a thing I sought,
And with old woes new wail my dear time's waste.
Sonnets. No. xxx.

6
Of any thing the image tell me that
Hath kept with thy remembrance.
The Tempest. Act i, sc. 2, l. 43. [Prospero]
If thou remember'st aught ere thou camest here,
How thou camest here thou mayst.
The Tempest. Act i, sc. 2, l. 51. [Prospero]

7
How sharp the point of this remembrance is!
The Tempest. Act v, sc. 1, l. 138. [Alonso]
Let us not burthen our remembrance with
A heaviness that 's gone.
The Tempest. Act v, sc. 1, l. 199. [Prospero]
Call me to your remembrances.—*Timon of Athens,* iii, 5, 92.

8
Remembrance of my father's death.
Titus Andronicus. Act iii, sc. 1, l. 241. [Messenger]
For your father's remembrance.—*As You Like It,* i, 1, 67.
Remembrance of her father.—*All 's Well that Ends Well,* i, 1, 56.

9
Pandar: You 'll remember your brother's excuse?
Paris: To a hair.
Troilus and Cressida. Act iii, sc. 1, l. 154.
Diomedes: Will you remember?
Cressida: Remember! yes.
Diomedes: Nay, but do, then. . . .
Troilus: What should she remember?
Troilus and Cressida. Act v, sc. 2, l. 12.

10 O pretty, pretty pledge!
Thy master now lies thinking in his bed
Of thee and me, and sighs, and takes my glove,
And gives memorial dainty kisses to it,
As I kiss thee.
Troilus and Cressida. Act v, sc. 2, l. 77. [Cressida]

11
A brother's dead love, which she would keep fresh
And lasting in her sad remembrance.
Twelfth Night. Act i, sc. 1, l. 31. [Valentine]
She is drowned already, sir, with salt water, though I seem to drown her remembrance again with more.
Twelfth Night. Act ii, sc. 1, l. 31. [Sebastian]

12
I 'll not remember you of my own lord,
Who is lost too.
The Winter's Tale. Act iii, sc. 2, l. 231. [Paulina]
Whose very naming punishes me with the remembrance.
The Winter's Tale. Act iv, sc. 2, l. 24. [Polixenes]

13
What I saw, to my good use I remembered.
The Winter's Tale. Act iv, sc. 4, l. 615. [Autolycus]

REMORSE

14 When thou shalt be disedged by her
That now thou tirest on, how thy memory
Will then be pang'd by me.
Cymbeline. Act iii, sc. 4, l. 96. [Imogen]
The only use of "disedged" and "pang'd."
O, give me cord, or knife, or poison,
Some upright justicer! Thou, king, send out
For torturers ingenious: it is I
That all the abhorr'd things o' the earth amend
By being worse than they.
Cymbeline. Act v, sc. 5, l. 213. [Posthumus]
"Justicer" is repeated in *King Lear,* iii, 6, 23; 59; iv, 2, 79.
The gods throw stones of sulphur on me.
Cymbeline. Act v, sc. 5, l. 240. [Pisanio]

15 Leave her to heaven
And to those thorns that in her bosom lodge,
To prick and sting her.
Hamlet. Act i, sc. 5, l. 86. [Ghost]
And never did the Cyclops' hammers fall
On Mars's armour forged for proof eterne
With less remorse.
Hamlet. Act ii, sc. 2, l. 511. [First Player]

The Cyclops are mentioned again in *Titus Andronicus,* iv, 3, 46. "Eterne" is repeated in *Macbeth,* iii, 2, 38. Mars is mentioned no less than 38 times.

1
What says Monsieur Remorse?
I Henry IV. Act i, sc. 2, l. 124. [Poins]

I feel remorse in myself with his words; but I 'll bridle it.
II Henry VI. Act iv, sc. 7, l. 111. [Cade]

2
Nero will be tainted with remorse,
To hear and see her plaints, her brinish tears.
III Henry VI. Act iii, sc. 1, l. 40. [King Henry] "Brinish" occurs again in *Titus Andronicus,* iii, 1, 97.

You have no children, butchers! if you had,
The thought of them would have stirr'd up remorse.
III Henry VI. Act v, sc. 5, l. 63. [Queen Margaret]

Thrill'd with remorse.—*King Lear,* iv, 2, 73. The only use of "thrill'd."

3
That gave to me Many a groaning throe.
Henry VIII. Act ii, sc. 4, l. 198. [King]

4
Nay, in the body of this fleshly land,
This kingdom, this confine of blood and breath,
Hostility and civil tumult reigns
Between my conscience and my cousin's death.
King John. Act iv, sc. 2, l. 245. [King John] The only use of "fleshly."

5
Stop up the access and passage to remorse,
That no compunctious visitings of nature
Shake my fell purpose.
Macbeth. Act i, sc. 5, l. 45. [Lady Macbeth] The only use of "compunctious."

Who then shall blame
His pester'd senses to recoil and start,
When all that is within him does condemn
Itself for being there?
Macbeth. Act v, sc. 2, l. 22. [Menteith]

6
If so your heart were touch'd with that remorse
As mine is to him.
Measure for Measure. Act ii, sc. 2, l. 54. [Angelo]

7
The rogues slighted me into the river with as little remorse as they would have drowned a blind bitch's puppies, fifteen i' the litter.
The Merry Wives of Windsor. Act iii, sc. 5, l. 9. [Falstaff]

8
Never pray more; abandon all remorse.
Othello. Act iii, sc. 3, l. 369. [Othello]

Whip me, ye devils, . . .
Blow me about in winds! roast me in sulphur!
Wash me in steep-down gulfs of liquid fire!
Othello. Act v, sc. 2, l. 277. [Othello] The only use of "steep-down."

9
Will not my tongue be mute, my frail joints shake,
Mine eyes forego their light, my false heart bleed?
The Rape of Lucrece, l. 227.

Poor wretches have remorse in poor abuses.
The Rape of Lucrece, l. 269.

10
The urging of that word 'judgement' hath bred a kind of remorse in me.
Richard III. Act i, sc. 4, l. 109. [Murderer]

Gentle, kind, effeminate remorse.
Richard III. Act iii, sc. 7, l. 211. [Buckingham]

With conscience and remorse;
They could not speak.
Richard III. Act iv, sc. 3, l. 20. [Tyrrel]

11
Is there a murderer here? No. Yes, I am:
Then fly. What, from myself? Great reason why:
Lest I revenge. What, myself upon myself?
Richard III. Act v, sc. 3, l. 184. [King Richard]

12
Methought the billows spoke and told me of it;
The winds did sing it to me, and the thunder,
That deep and dreadful organ-pipe, pronounced
The name of Prosper: it did bass my trespass.
The Tempest. Act iii, sc. 3, l. 96. [Alonso] "Organ-pipe" occurs again in *King John,* v, 7, 23.

Inward pinches.—*The Tempest,* v, 1, 77.

13
'Pity,' she cries, 'some favour, some remorse.'
Venus and Adonis, l. 257.

14
She I kill'd! I did so: but thou strikest me
Sorely, to say I did; it is as bitter
Upon thy tongue as in my thought.
Winter's Tale. Act v, sc. 1, l. 17. [Leontes]

REMUNERATION, see Reward

RENOWN

See also Fame, Reputation

15
Quick accumulation of renown,
Which he achieved by the minute.
Antony and Cleopatra. Act iii, sc. 1, l. 19. [Ventidius] The only use of "accumulation."

16
Honour . . . was no better than picture-like to hang by the wall, if renown made it not stir.
Coriolanus. Act i, sc. 3, l. 11. [Volumnia] The only use of "picture-like."

17
Thou never hadst renown, nor canst not lose it.
I Henry VI. Act iv, sc. 5, l. 40. [Talbot]

Razing the characters of your renown.
II Henry VI. Act i, sc. 1, l. 101. [Gloucester] The only use of "razing."

With modesty admiring thy renown.—*I Henry VI,* ii, 2, 39.

1
Such strong renown as time shall ne'er decay.
Pericles. Act iii, sc. 2, l. 48. [Gentleman]
Great renown.—*The Passionate Pilgrim,* l. 420.
2
Renowned for their deeds as far from home.
Richard II. Act ii, sc. 1, l. 53. [Gaunt]
Most renown'd.—*Antony and Cleopatra,* iii, 13, 53.
Most fine, most honour'd, most renown'd.—*II Henry IV,* iv, 5, 164.
Three-fold renown'd.—*III Henry VI,* v, 7, 5.

REPENTANCE

3
I repent me much That so I harried him.
Antony and Cleopatra. Act iii, sc. 3, l. 43. [Cleopatra] The only use of "harried."
I do repent me.—*Othello,* iii, 3, 392.
I repent me.—*Richard III,* i, 4, 285.
I now repent.—*Richard III,* iii, 4, 90.
Then I'll repent.—*The Merchant of Venice,* iii, 4, 72.
4
Try what repentance can: what can it not?
Yet what can it when one can not repent?
Hamlet. Act iii, sc. 3, l. 65. [King]
Repent what's past; avoid what is to come.
Hamlet. Act iii, sc. 4, l. 150. [Hamlet]
For this same lord,
I do repent; but heaven hath pleased it so.
Hamlet. Act iii, sc. 4, l. 172. [Hamlet]
5
Well, I'll repent, and that suddenly, while I am in some liking; I shall be out of heart shortly, and then I shall have no strength to repent.
I Henry IV. Act iii, sc. 3, l. 5. [Falstaff]
The young lion repents; marry, not in ashes and sackcloth, but in new silk and old sack.
II Henry IV. Act i, sc. 2, l. 221. [Falstaff]
He puts on sackcloth.—*Pericles,* iv, 4, 29. The only uses of "sackcloth."
6
Repent at idle times as thou mayest; and so, farewell.
II Henry IV. Act ii, sc. 2, l. 140. [Poins]
7
My penitence comes after all,
Imploring pardon.
Henry V. Act iv, sc. 1, l. 321. [King Henry] The only use of "imploring."
The constable desires thee thou wilt mind
Thy followers of repentance; that their souls
May make a peaceful and a sweet retire
From off these fields, where, wretches, their poor bodies
Must lie and fester.
Henry V. Act iv, sc. 3, l. 84. [Montjoy]
8
Didst ever hear a man so penitent?
II Henry VI. Act iii, sc. 2, l. 4. [Murderer]
In faith, he's penitent.—*Othello,* iii, 3, 63.
9
Thou and thy house shall rue it.
III Henry VI. Act i, sc. 1, l. 94. [Northumberland]
Thou shalt rue this hour within this hour.
King John. Act iii, sc. 1, l. 323. [King John]
Rue the hour that ever thou wast born.—*III Henry VI,* v, 6, 43.
Rue my shame.—*II Henry VI,* ii, 4, 24.
Rue this treason.—*I Henry VI,* iii, 2, 36.
Rue, even for ruth.—*Richard II,* iii, 4, 106. See under TEAR.
Rue with a difference.—*Hamlet,* iv, 5, 181.
10
Repent in bootless penitence.
III Henry VI, Act ii, sc. 6, l. 70. [Edward]
Repent my fault.—*Henry V,* ii, 2, 152.
Repent his folly.—*Henry V,* iii, 6, 131.
Repent the loss.—*Romeo and Juliet,* iii, l. 196.
Repent this rape.—*Titus Andronicus,* i, l. 404.
Repent the sin.—*Romeo and Juliet,* iv, 2, 17.
11
Implor'd your highness' pardon and set forth
A deep repentance.
Macbeth. Act i, sc. 4, l. 6. [Malcolm]
12
I have seen,
When, after execution, judgement hath
Repented o'er his doom.
Measure for Measure. Act ii, sc. 2, l. 10. [Provost]
Duke: Repent you, fair one, of the sin you carry?
Juliet: I do; and bear the shame most patiently.
Measure for Measure. Act ii, sc. 3, l. 19.
I'll teach you how you shall arraign your conscience,
And try your penitence if it be sound,
Or hollowly put on.
Measure for Measure. Act ii, sc. 3, l. 21. [Duke] "Hollowly" is repeated in *The Tempest,* iii, 1, 70.
Hath he borne himself penitently in prison?
Measure for Measure. Act iv, sc. 2, l. 147. [Duke] The only use of "penitently."
13
I never did repent for doing good,
Nor shall not now.
The Merchant of Venice. Act iii, sc. 4, l. 10. [Portia]
14
If my wind were but long enough to say my prayers,
I would repent.
The Merry Wives of Windsor. Act iv, sc. 5, l. 104. [Falstaff]
15
Thou shalt aby it.
A Midsummer-Night's Dream. Act iii, sc. 2, l. 175; 335. The only uses of "aby" (atone for).
You should here repent you.—*A Midsummer-Night's Dream,* v, 1, 115.
Happily repent.—*Othello,* iii, 3, 238.
16
Fear, and not love, begets his penitence.
Richard II. Act v, sc. 3, l. 56. [York]
17
Much it joys me too,
To see you are become so penitent.
Richard III. Act i, sc. 2, l. 220. [Lady Anne]
18
She hath had too much wrong; and I repent
My part thereof that I have done to her.
Richard III. Act i, sc. 3, l. 307. [Gloucester]
If I unwittingly, or in my rage,
Have aught committed that is hardly borne
By any in this presence, I desire
To reconcile me to his friendly peace.
Richard III. Act ii, sc. 1, l. 56. [Gloucester]

"Unwittingly" occurs once again in *Henry VIII,* iii, 2, 123.

Men shall deal unadvisedly sometimes,
Which after hours give leisure to repent.
Richard III. Act iv, sc. 4, l. 292. [King Richard] The only use of "unadvisedly." "Unadvised" occurs six times.

As I intend to prosper and repent,
So thrive I in my dangerous attempt
Of hostile arms]
Richard III. Act iv, sc. 4, l. 397. [King Richard]

1
Clarence: Relent, and save your souls.
Murderer: Relent! 'tis cowardly and womanish.
Clarence: Not to relent is beastly, savage, devilish.
Richard III. Act i, sc. 4, l. 263.

I do relent: what would thou more of man?
The Merry Wives of Windsor. Act ii, sc. 2, l. 31. [Pistol]

2
I am no baby, I, that with base prayers
I should repent the evils I have done.
Titus Andronicus. Act v, sc. 3, l. 185. [Aaron]

If one good deed in all my life I did,
I do repent it from my very soul.
Titus Andronicus. Act v, sc. 3, l. 189. [Aaron]

3
Ne'er repent it.
The Two Gentlemen of Verona. Act iv, sc. 1, l. 30. [First Outlaw]

Then I repent not.—*Timon of Athens,* i, 1, 184.

4
Return, return, and make thy love amends.
The Two Gentlemen of Verona. Act iv, sc. 2, l. 99. [Silvia]

He will make thee amends.—*The Merry Wives of Windsor,* ii, 3, 70.

I will one way or other make you amends.—*The Merry Wives of Windsor,* iii, 5, 49.

I 'll make you amends.—*The Comedy of Errors,* ii, 2, 54.

I will make amends.—*III Henry VI,* v, 1, 100.

I cannot make you what amends I would.—*Richard III,* iv, 4, 309.

We will make amends ere long.—*A Midsummer-Night's Dream,* v, 1, 441.

Make amends now.—*Macbeth,* iii, 5, 14.

Make her amends.—*Othello,* iv, 1, 255.

You make amends.—*Cymbeline,* i, 6, 168.

Make amends.—*Richard III,* iv, 4, 295; *The Rape of Lucrece,* l. 961.

Makes amends.—*The Tempest,* iv, 1, 2; *The Two Gentlemen of Verona,* iii, 1, 331.

Maketh us amends.—*III Henry VI,* iv, 7, 2.

Good amends.—*The Taming of the Shrew,* Ind., 2, 99.

5
Who by repentance is not satisfied
Is nor of heaven nor earth, for these are pleased.
By penitence the Eternal's wrath 's appeased.
The Two Gentlemen of Verona. Act v, sc. 4, l. 79. [Valentine]

6
Paid down
More penitence than done trespass.
The Winter's Tale. Act v, sc. 1, l. 3. [Cleomenes]

REPLY

See also Answer

7
Pray you, look not sad,
Nor make replies of loathness.
Antony and Cleopatra. Act iii, sc. 11, l. 17. [Antony] "Loathness" is repeated in *The Tempest,* ii, 1, 130, and in *Cymbeline,* i, 1, 108.

The Reply Churlish.—*As You Like It,* v, 4, 80: 98.

Threateningly replies.—*All's Well that Ends Well,* ii, 3, 87.

8
Why, 'tis a loving and a fair reply.
Hamlet. Act i, sc. 2, l. 121. [King]

How pregnant sometimes his replies are!
Hamlet. Act ii, sc. 2, l. 212. [Polonius] See under MADNESS.

Most free in his reply.—*Hamlet,* iii, 1, 14.

9
We will not now be troubled with reply.
I Henry IV. Act v, sc. 1, l. 113. [King Henry]

Take leave and stand not to reply.
III Henry VI. Act iv, sc. 8, l. 23. [Warwick]

Look'd for no reply.—*Richard III,* i, 3, 237.

Reply not.—*Romeo and Juliet,* iii, 5, 164; *Troilus and Cressida,* i, 1, 50.

Not replying.—*Richard III,* iii, 7, 145.

Replying shrilly.—*Titus Andronicus,* ii, 3, 18. The only uses of "replying."

10
Vouchsafe
To give me hearing what I shall reply.
I Henry VI. Act iii, sc. 1, l. 27. [Winchester]

11
I pause for a reply.
Julius Cæsar. Act iii, sc. 2, l. 37. [Brutus]

What reply, ha?—*Measure for Measure,* iii, 2, 50.

I shall reply amazedly.—*A Midsummer-Night's Dream,* iv, 1, 151.

Make reply.—*King John,* iii, 3, 49; *Richard II,* ii, 3, 73.

Reply, reply.—*The Merchant of Venice,* iii, 2, 66.

Faint reply.—*Timon of Athens,* iii, 3, 25.

12
He knows not me: I said 'Good morrow, Ajax;' and he replies 'Thanks, Agamemnon.'
Troilus and Cressida. Act iii, sc. 3, l. 261. [Thersites]

13
Often have you writ to her, and she, in modesty,
Or else for want of idle time, could not again reply.
The Two Gentlemen of Verona. Act ii, sc. 1, l. 171. [Speed]

1
And here she meets another sadly scowling,
To whom she speaks, and he replies with
howling.
Venus and Adonis, l. 917. The only use of "scowling."

2
You were straited For a reply.
The Winter's Tale. Act iv, sc. 4, l. 365. [Polixenes] The only use of "straited."

REPORT

See also Gossip, Rumour

3 I must thank him only,
Lest my remembrance suffer ill report.
Antony and Cleopatra. Act ii, sc. 2, l. 159. [Antony]

Ill report.—*Coriolanus,* i, 6, 70; *Hamlet,* ii, 2, 550; *Sonnets,* xcv.

Too bad for bad report.—*Cymbeline,* i, 1, 17.

Pestiferous reports.—*All's Well that Ends Well,* iv, 3, 340. "Pestiferous" occurs again in *I Henry VI,* iii, 1, 15.

Clamorous report.—*Richard III,* iv, 4, 152.

Loud report.—*I Henry VI,* ii, 2, 43.

4
My reporter devised well for her.
Antony and Cleopatra. Act ii, sc. 2, l. 193. [Agrippa] The only use of "reporter."

5
Read not my blemishes in the world's report.
Antony and Cleopatra. Act ii, sc. 3, l. 5. [Antony]

I made no such report.—*Antony and Cleopatra,* ii, 5, 57.

This I 'll report.—*Antony and Cleopatra,* v, 2, 32.

6
Report speaks goldenly of his profit.
As You Like It. Act i, sc. 1, l. 6. [Orlando] The only use of "goldenly."

7 I have adventured
To try your taking of a false report.
Cymbeline. Act i, sc. 6, l. 172. [Iachimo]

Stuffing the ears of men with false reports.
II Henry IV. Induction, l. 8. [Rumour]

I 'll fill these dogged spies with false reports.
King John. Act iv, sc. 1, l. 129. [Hubert]

They have committed false report.—*Much Ado about Nothing,* v, 1, 220.

Made a false report.—*Coriolanus,* iv, 5, 157.

8
Cloten: There is gold for you;
Sell me your good report.
Lady: How! my good name? or to report of
you
What I shall think is good?
Cymbeline. Act ii, sc. 3, l. 87.

Stand my good lord, pray, in your good report.
II Henry IV. Act iv, sc. 3, l. 89. [Falstaff]

I love thee in such sort
As, thou being mine, mine is thy good report.
Sonnets. No. xxxvi. Repeated in No. xcvi.

Good report I hear of you.—*The Taming of the Shrew,* iv, 4, 28.

Give me your good report.—*The Winter's Tale,* v, 2, 162.

Cruel to your good report.—*Coriolanus,* i, 9, 54.

Masterly report.—*Hamlet,* iv, 7, 97.

Perfectest report.—*Macbeth,* i, 5, 2. "Perfectest" is repeated in *Much Ado about Nothing,* ii, 1, 317.

Rare reports.—*I Henry VI,* ii, 3, 10.

9 Though his actions were not visible, yet
Report should render him hourly to your
ear
As truly as he moves.
Cymbeline. Act iii, sc. 4, l. 152. [Pisanio]

After his own report.—*Cymbeline,* iv, 2, 119.

10
I see report is fabulous and false.
I Henry VI. Act ii, sc. 3, l. 18. [Countess] "Fabulous" is used only once again, in *Henry VIII,* i, 1, 36: "Fabulous story."

Report is changeable.
King Lear. Act iv, sc. 7, l. 92. [Kent]

11 Thrusting this report
Into his ears; I may say, thrusting it;
For piercing steel and darts envenomed
Shall be as welcome to the ears of Brutus
As tidings of this sight.
Julius Cæsar. Act v, sc. 3, l. 74. [Messala]

12
I . . . can perceive no truth in your report.
Macbeth. Act v, sc. 1, l. 2. [Doctor]

13
Sir, the duke is marvellous little beholding to your reports; but the best is, he lives not in them.
Measure for Measure. Act iv, sc. 3, l. 166. [Duke]

14
Salarino: If my gossip Report be an honest woman of her word.
Salanio: I would she were as lying a gossip in that as ever knapped ginger or made her neighbours believe she wept for the death of a third husband.
The Merchant of Venice. Act iii, sc. 1, l. 7. The only use of "knapped" (with this meaning, to bite noisily). It is repeated in *King Lear,* ii, 4, 125, with the meaning of to strike.

15 Signior Benedick,
For shape, for bearing, argument and valour
Goes foremost in report through Italy.
Much Ado about Nothing. Act iii, sc. 1, l. 95. [Ursula]

16
If you do find me foul in her report,
The trust, the office I do hold of you,
Not only take away, but let your sentence
Even fall upon my life.
Othello. Act i, sc. 3, l. 117. [Othello]

17
If she be accused in true report,
Bear with her weakness.
Richard III. Act i, sc. 3, l. 27. [Derby]

I must needs report the truth. . . .
Your reports have set the murder on.
Othello. Act v, sc. 2, l. 128. [Emilia]

Report him truly.—*Coriolanus,* v, 4, 27.

True report.—*Timon of Athens,* v, 1, 18; *Antony and Cleopatra,* ii, 2, 47.

Just and true report.—*Timon of Athens,* v, 1, 18.

My report is just.—*Titus Andronicus,* v, 3, 115.

1
'Twas told me you were rough and coy and sullen,
And now I find report a very liar.
The Taming of the Shrew. Act ii, sc. 1, l. 245. [Petruchio]
By report I know him well.—*The Taming of the Shrew,* ii, 1, 105.
2
I have it
Upon his own report and I believe it.
The Winter's Tale. Act iv, sc. 4, l. 169. [Shepherd]
By their own report.—*The Winter's Tale,* iv, 4, 345.
By her own report.—*Measure for Measure,* v, 1, 274.
By your own report.—*The Two Gentlemen of Verona,* iv, l. 56.
3
Though I report it, That should be silent.
The Winter's Tale. Act iv, sc. 4, l. 177. [Shepherd]

REPOSE

See also Rest

4
Sport and repose lock from me day and night!
Hamlet. Act iii, sc. 2, l. 227. [Player Queen]
5
For this night we will repose us here.
II Henry VI. Act ii, sc. 1, l. 200. [King]
Repose you for this night.—*Richard II,* ii, 3, 161.
Repose myself.—*III Henry VI,* iv, 6, 47.
6
These should be hours for necessities,
Not for delights; times to repair our nature
With comforting repose.
Henry VIII. Act v, sc. 1, l. 2. [Gardiner]
7
Our foster-nurse of nature is repose.
King Lear. Act iv, sc. 4, l. 12. [Doctor] "Foster-nurse" is repeated in *As You Like It,* ii, 3, 40.
8
Some day or two
Your highness shall repose you at the Tower.
Richard III. Act iii, sc. 1, l. 65. [Gloucester]
9
Good night, good night! as sweet repose and rest
Come to thy heart as that within my breast!
Romeo and Juliet. Act ii, sc. 2, l. 123. [Juliet]
Dear repose.—*Sonnets,* xxvii.
Good repose.—*Julius Cæsar,* iv, 3, 233; *Macbeth,* ii, 1, 29.
10
This is a strange repose, to be asleep
With eyes wide open; standing, speaking, moving,
And yet so fast asleep.
The Tempest. Act ii, sc. 1, l. 213. [Sebastian]
Retire into my cell And there repose.
The Tempest. Act iv, sc. 1, l. 162. [Prospero]
11
Repose you here in rest.
Titus Andronicus, i, 1, 151. See under GRAVE.
Repose in fame.—*Titus Andronicus,* i, 1, 353.
Repose and rest.—*The Rape of Lucrece,* l. 757.
Means . . . to repose him here.—*The Taming of the Shrew,* Ind., l. 75.
Repose you there.—*King Lear,* iii, 2, 63.

REPROACH

See also Blame, Rebuke, Upbraiding

12
I 'll warrant she 'll tax him home.
Hamlet. Act iii, sc. 3, l. 29. [Polonius]
Tax him with injustice.—*Measure for Measure,* v, 1, 312.
I tax not you.—*King Lear,* iii, 2, 16.
13
In confutation of which rude reproach.
I Henry VI. Act iv, sc. 1, l. 98. [Basset] The only use of "confutation."
Foul-faced reproach.—*Richard III,* iii, 7, 231. The only use of "foul-faced."
Undeserved reproach.—*The Rape of Lucrece,* l. 824.
Vile reproach.—*Henry V,* iii, 6, 50.
14
O, whither shall we fly from this reproach?
I Henry VI. Act i, sc. 1, l. 97. [Exeter]
15
Wouldst thou have me rescue thee from this reproach?
II Henry VI. Act ii, sc. 4, l. 64. [Gloucester]
I am but reproach:
And shall I then be used reproachfully?
II Henry VI. Act ii, sc. 4, l. 96. [Duchess of Gloucester] The only use of "reproachfully."
Reproach and beggary
Is crept into the palace of our king.
II Henry VI. Act iv, sc. 1, l. 101. [Captain]
Injurious Margaret!
III Henry VI. Act iii, sc. 3, l. 78. [Warwick]
16
They vent reproaches most bitterly on you.
Henry VIII. Act i, sc. 2, l. 23. [Queen Katharine]
Just reproach.—*Much Ado about Nothing,* iv, 1, 82.
17
Et tu, Brute! Then fall, Cæsar!
Julius Cæsar. Act iii, sc. 1, l. 77. [Cæsar]
18
Many worthy and chaste dames even thus,
All guiltless, meet reproach.
Othello. Act iv, sc. 1, l. 47. [Iago]
19
I 'll not expostulate with her, lest her body and beauty unprovide my mind again.
Othello. Act iv, sc. 1, l. 217. [Othello] The only use of "unprovide."
The time now serves not to expostulate.
The Two Gentlemen of Verona. Act iii, sc. 1, l. 251. [Proteus]
Stay not to expostulate.—*III Henry VI,* ii, 5, 135.
Bitterly could I expostulate.—*Richard III,* iii, 7, 192.
To expostulate.—*Hamlet,* ii, 2, 86. The only uses of "expostulate."
Nay, we must use expostulation kindly.
Troilus and Cressida. Act iv, sc. 4, l. 62. [Troilus] The only use of "expostulation."

1
Thou back'st reproach against long-living laud.
The Rape of Lucrece, l. 622. The only use of "long-living."
Reproach, disdain, and deadly enmity.
The Rape of Lucrece, l. 503.
Reproach is stamp'd in Collatinus' face.
The Rape of Lucrece, l. 829.
2
Reproach and dissolution hangeth over him.
Richard II. Act ii, sc. 1, l. 258. [Northumberland]
3
Thrust these reproachful speeches down his throat
That he hath breathed in my dishonour here.
Titus Andronicus. Act ii, sc. 1, l. 55. [Demetrius]
Reproachful words.—*Titus Andronicus,* i, 1, 308. The only uses of "reproachful."
4
Fie on him, Jezebel!
Twelfth Night. Act ii, sc. 5, l. 46. [Sir Andrew] The only mention of Jezebel.
O, fie, fie, fie!
What dost thou, or what art thou, Angelo?
Measure for Measure. Act ii, sc. 2, l. 172. [Angelo] "Fie" as a term of reproach is used twenty-six times in the plays and five times in the poems.

REPROOF

See also Chiding

5 Your reproof
Were well deserved of rashness.
Antony and Cleopatro. Act ii, sc. 2, l. 123. [Cæsar]
The Reproof Valiant.—*As You Like It,* 5, 4, 98. See under LIE.
6
You should for that have reprehended him.
The Comedy of Errors. Act v, sc. 1, l. 57. [Abbess]
She never reprehended him but mildly.
The Comedy of Errors. Act v, sc. 1, l. 87. [Luciana]
I reprehended him.—*Richard III,* iii, 7, 27.
Pardon me for reprehending thee,
For thou hast done a charitable deed.
Titus Andronicus. Act iii, sc. 2, l. 69. [Titus] The only use of "reprehending."
Sharply he did think to reprehend her.
Venus and Adonis, l. 470.
7
She did betray me to my own reproof.
The Comedy of Errors. Act v, sc. 1, l. 90. [Luciana]
8
I will not undergo this sneap without reply.
II Henry IV. Act ii, sc. 1, l. 133. [Falstaff] The only use of "sneap" (reproof).
9
Your reproof is something too round.
Henry V. Act iv, sc. 1, l. 216. [King Henry]
10
Orderly and well-behaved reproof to all uncomeliness.
The Merry Wives of Windsor. Act ii, sc. 1, l. 59. [Mrs. Ford] The only use of "well-behaved" and "uncomeliness."
Reproof, obedient and in order, Fits kings.
Pericles. Act i, sc. 2, l. 42. [Helicanus]
11
I know not whether to depart in silence,
Or bitterly to speak in your reproof.
Richard III. Act iii, sc. 7, l. 141. [Gloucester]
I have a touch of your condition,
Which cannot brook the accent of reproof.
Richard III. Act iv, sc. 4, l. 157. [King Richard]
12
You must contrary me!
Romeo and Juliet. Act i, sc. 5, l. 87. [Capulet]
Nor no railing in a known discreet man, though he do nothing but reprove.
Twelfth Night. Act i, sc. 5, l. 102. [Olivia]
See also RAILING.

REPUTATION

See also Credit; Name: Good Name

13
Common speech Gives him a worthy pass.
All's Well that Ends Well. Act ii, sc. 5, l. 57. [Bertram]
I am well spoke on.
II Henry IV. Act ii, sc. 2, l. 69. [Poins]
14
[I] would not put my reputation now
In any staining act.
All's Well that Ends Well. Act iii, sc. 7, l. 6. [Widow] The only use of "staining."
Upon my reputation and credit and as I hope to live.
All's Well that Ends Well. Act iv, sc. 3, l. 153. [Parolles]
15 I have offended reputation,
A most unnoble swerving.
Antony and Cleopatra. Act iii, sc. 11, l. 49. [Antony] The only use of "unnoble."
Your reputation shall not therefore be misprised.
As You Like It. Act i, sc. 2, l. 191. [Rosalind]
The bubble reputation.—*As You Like It,* ii, 7, 152. See MAN, 940:12.
16
Herein you war against your reputation.
The Comedy of Errors. Act iii, sc. 1, l. 86. [Balthazar]
This touches me in reputation.
The Comedy of Errors. Act iv, sc. 1, l. 71. [Angelo]
Of very reverend reputation, sir,
Of credit infinite, highly beloved,
Second to none that lives here in the city.
The Comedy of Errors. Act v, sc. 1, l. 5. [Angelo]
17
He was then of a crescent note.
Cymbeline. Act i, sc. 4, l. 2. [Iachimo]
18 Restore yourselves
Into the good thoughts of the world again.
I Henry IV. Act i, sc. 3, l. 181. [Hotspur]
I better brook the loss of brittle life
Than those proud titles thou hast won of me.
I Henry IV. Act v, sc. 4, l. 78. [Hotspur]

1
Answer in the effect of your reputation.
II Henry IV. Act ii, sc. 1, l. 142. [Chief Justice]

2
His reputation is as arrant a villain and a Jacksauce, as ever his black shoe trod upon God's ground and his earth, in my conscience, la!
Henry V. Act iv, sc. 7, l. 149. [Fluellen] The only use of "Jacksauce."

3
He is a man of no estimation in the world.
Henry V. Act iii, sc. 6, l. 15. [Fluellen]

And are you grown so high in his esteem,
Because I am so dwarfish and so low?
A Midsummer-Night's Dream. Act iii, sc. 2, l. 294. [Hermia]

'Tis better to be vile than vile esteem'd.
Sonnets. No. cxxi.

Vile esteem'd.—*I Henry VI,* i, 4, 33.

Of good esteem.—*The Two Gentlemen of Verona,* i, 3, 40.

4
What know I how the world may deem of me?
II Henry VI. Act iii, sc. 2, l. 65. [Queen Margaret]

For yet I am not look'd on in the world.
III Henry VI. Act v, sc. 7, l. 22. [Gloucester]

Yourself, held precious in the world's esteem.
Love's Labour 's Lost. Act ii, sc. 1, l. 4. [Boyet]

How will the world repute me?
The Two Gentlemen of Verona. Act ii, sc. 7, l. 59. [Julia]

5
O, he sits high in all the people's hearts.
Julius Cæsar. Act i, sc. 3, l. 157. [Casca]

6
You will lose your reputation.
Love's Labour 's Lost. Act v, sc. 2, l. 708. [Moth]

7
The very stream of his life and the business he hath helmed must upon a warranted need give him a better proclamation. Let him be but testimonied in his own bringings-forth, and he shall appear to the envious a scholar, a statesman and a soldier.
Measure for Measure. Act iii, sc. 2, l. 150. [Duke Vincentio] The only uses of "helmed" and "bringings-forth."

Her reputation was disvalued In levity.
Measure for Measure. Act v, sc. 1, l. 221. [Angelo] The only use of "disvalued."

8
I will keep the haviour of reputation.
The Merry Wives of Windsor. Act i, sc. 3, l. 86. [Nym]

Defend your reputation, or bid farewell to your good life for ever.
The Merry Wives of Windsor. Act iii, sc. 3, l. 126. [Mrs. Page]

9
Her wounded reputation.
Much Ado about Nothing. Act iv, sc. 1, l. 243. [Friar Francis]

In reputation sick.—*Richard II,* ii, 1, 96.

My reputation stain'd.—*Romeo and Juliet,* iii, 1, 116.

Slender reputation.—*The Two Gentlemen of Verona,* i, 3, 6.

10
What 's the matter,
That you unlace your reputation thus
And spend your rich opinion for the name
Of a night-brawler?
Othello. Act ii, sc. 3, l. 193. [Othello] The only use of "unlace" and "night-brawler."

Cassio: Reputation, reputation, reputation! O, I have lost my reputation! I have lost the immortal part of myself, and what remains is bestial . . .

Iago: Reputation is an idle and most false imposition; oft got without merit, and lost without deserving.
Othello. Act ii, sc. 3, l. 262.

11
Makest fair reputation but a bawd.
The Rape of Lucrece, l. 623.

12
The purest treasure mortal times afford
Is spotless reputation: that away,
Men are but gilded loam or painted clay.
Richard II. Act i, sc. 1, l. 177. [Mowbray]

Spoke like a tall fellow that respects his reputation.
Richard III. Act i, sc. 4, l. 156. [Murderer]

13
So reputed
In dignity, and for the liberal arts
Without a parallel.
The Tempest. Act i, sc. 2, l. 72. [Prospero]

Dear'st repute.—*Troilus and Cressida,* i, 3, 337.

14
The cry went once on thee,
And still it might, and yet it may again,
If thou wouldst not entomb thyself alive
And case thy reputation in thy tent.
Troilus and Cressida. Act iii, sc. 3, l. 184. [Ulysses]

I see my reputation is at stake;
My fame is shrewdly gored.
Troilus and Cressida. Act iii, sc. 3, l. 227. [Achilles]

15
Turn then my freshest reputation to
A savour that may strike the dullest nostril
Where I arrive, and my approach be shunn'd,
Nay, hated too, worse than the great'st infection
That e'er was heard or read!
The Winter's Tale. Act i, sc. 2, l. 420. [Polixenes]

REQUEST

See also Petition

16
I have no ears to his request.
Antony and Cleopatra. Act iii, sc. 12, l. 20. [Cæsar]

Say my request 's unjust, And spurn me back.
Coriolanus. Act v, sc. 3, l. 164. [Volumnia]

A small request, And yet of moment too.
Cymbeline. Act i, sc. 6, l. 181. [Iachimo]

17
As you are friends, scholars and soldiers,
Give me one poor request.
Hamlet. Act i, sc. 5. l. 141. [Hamlet]

Well shall you perceive how willingly
I will both hear and grant you your requests.
King John. Act iv, sc. 2, l. 45. [King John]
Upon his mere request.—*Measure for Measure,* v, 1, 152.
Fair request.—*Troilus and Cressida,* ii, 3, 177.
High request.—*Richard III,* iii, 7, 155.

1
'Tis done at your request.
Othello. Act iii, sc. 3, l. 474. [Iago]
At your request
My father will grant precious things as trifles.
The Winter's Tale. Act v, sc. 1, l. 221. [Florizel]
At your request.—*The Merry Wives of Windsor,* i, 1, 253; *Troilus and Cressida,* ii, 3, 191; *Twelfth Night,* iii, 4, 38.
Upon your request.—*The Merry Wives of Windsor,* i, 1, 249.
At my request.—*III Henry VI,* iv, 3, 51; *The Two Gentlemen of Verona,* ii, 1, 132; *The Winter's Tale,* i, 2, 87.
At our request.—*III Henry VI,* iii, 3, 110.
At thy request.—*The Tempest,* iii, 2, 128.
In our request.—*Coriolanus,* v, 3, 90.
In request.—*Coriolanus,* iii, 1, 251; *Measure for Measure,* iv, 3, 9; *The Winter's Tale,* iv, 4, 297.
In no request.—*Coriolanus,* iv, 3, 37.
By request.—*Othello,* i, 3, 113.

2
Lend favourable ears to our request.
Richard III. Act iii, sc. 7, l. 101. [Buckingham]

3
What shall you ask of me that I 'll deny,
That honour saved may upon asking give?
Twelfth Night. Act iii, sc. 4, l. 231. [Olivia]
Grant me another request.—*Twelfth Night,* v, 1, 4.

4
This your request is altogether just.
The Winter's Tale. Act iii, sc. 2, l. 117. [Lord]

RESCUE

5
Without rescue in the first assault or ransom afterward.
All's Well that Ends Well. Act i, sc. 3, l. 121. [Steward]

6
Wilt thou suffer them To make a rescue?
The Comedy of Errors. Act iv, sc. 4, l. 114. [Antipholus of Ephesus]
How comes 't that you
Have holp to make this rescue?
Coriolanus. Act iii, sc. 1, l. 276. [Sicinius]
Makes the rescue.—*Antony and Cleopatra,* ii, 11, 48.
Fair rescue.—*I Henry IV,* v, 4, 50.
Honourable rescue.—*King John,* v, 2, 18.

7
Fang: A rescue! A rescue!
Hostess: Good people, bring a rescue or two.
II Henry IV. Act ii, sc. 1, l. 61.
Rescue, my Lord of Norfolk, rescue, rescue!
Richard III. Act v, sc. 4, l. 1. [Cate]
Spur to the rescue.—*I Henry VI,* iv, 3, 19.

8
Too late comes rescue: he is ta'en or slain.
I Henry VI. Act iv, sc. 4, l. 42. [Lucy]
No rescue? What, a prisoner?—*King Lear,* iv, 6, 194.

9
I gave thee life and rescued thee from death. . . .
From the pride of Gallia rescued thee.
I Henry VI. Act iv, sc. 6, l. 5. [Talbot]
Here, purposing the Bastard to destroy,
Came in strong rescue.
I Henry VI. Act iv, sc. 6, l. 25. [Talbot]
The only use of "purposing."

10
When Oxford had me down, he rescued me,
And said, 'Dear brother, live, and be a king.'
Richard III. Act ii, sc. 1, l. 112. [King Edward]
I rescued her.—*King John,* iii, 2, 7.
Was 't you he rescued?—*As You Like It,* iv, 3, 134.

RESEMBLANCE

See also Likeness

11 Something have you heard
Of Hamlet's transformation; so call it,
Sith nor the exterior nor the inward man
Resembles that it was.
Hamlet. Act ii, sc. 2, l. 4. [King]

12
In face, in gait, in speech, he doth resemble.
II Henry VI. Act iii, sc. 2, l. 373. [York]
If we are like you in the rest, we will resemble you in that.
The Merchant of Venice, iii, 1, 70. See under JEW.

13
How well resembles it the prime of youth!
III Henry VI, ii, 1, 23. See under MORNING.
Well resembles.—*III Henry VI,* ii, 5, 99; *The Rape of Lucrece,* l. 1392.
More resembles.—*Cymbeline,* v, 5, 121.
Most resemble.—*Timon of Athens,* i, 2, 103.

14
His resemblance, being not like the duke.
Richard III. Act iii, sc. 7, l. 11. [Buckingham]
Not a resemblance, but a certainty.
Measure for Measure, iv, 2, 203. See under CERTAINTY.
Resemblance of the mother.—*Winter's Tale,* v, 2, 39. The only uses of "resemblance."

15
Resembling sire and child and happy mother.
Sonnets. No. viii.
Resembling dew of night.—*The Rape of Lucrece,* l. 396.
Resembling well his pale cheeks.—*Venus and Adonis,* l. 1169.
Resembling majesty.—*King John,* iii, 1, 100.
Resembling parasites.—*Venus and Adonis,* l. 848.
Resembling spirits of light.—*Love's Labour 's Lost,* iv, 3, 257.
Resembling strong youth.—*Sonnets,* vii. The only uses of "resembling."

1
Tranio: He is my father, sir; and, sooth to say,
In countenance somewhat doth resemble you.
Biondello: As much as an apple doth an oyster, and all one.
The Taming of the Shrew. Act iv, sc. 2, l. 99.
Well mayst thou know her by thy own proportion,
For up and down she doth resemble thee.
Titus Andronicus. Act v, sc. 2, l. 106. [Titus]
2
It was said she much resembled me.
Twelfth Night, ii, 1, 27. See under BEAUTY.
Resembled thee.—*II Henry VI,* i, 3, 56.
Resembled my father.—*Macbeth,* ii, 2, 13. The only uses of "resembled."
3
I could make that resemble something in me.
Twelfth Night. Act ii, sc. 5, l. 131. [Malvolio]

RESOLUTION

4 We have no friend
But resolution, and the briefest end.
Antony and Cleopatra. Act iv, sc. 15, l. 90. [Cleopatra] The only use of "briefest."
5
Let them pull all about mine ears, present me
Death on the wheel or at wild horses' heels,
Or pile ten hills on the Tarpeian rock,
That the precipitation might down stretch
Below the beam of sight, yet will I still
Be thus to them.
Coriolanus. Act iii, sc. 2, l. 1. [Coriolanus] "Precipitation" is repeated in iii, 3, 102, and occurs in no other play. The Tarpeian rock is mentioned five times, also only in this play.
He will shake Your Rome about your ears.
Coriolanus. Act iv, sc. 6, l. 98. [Cominius]
6 I should be sick,
But that my resolution helps me.
Cymbeline. Act iii, sc. 6, l. 3. [Imogen]
7 Would to God
You were of our determination!
I Henry IV. Act iv, sc. 3, l. 33. [Hotspur]
Did she change her determination?
The Merry Wives of Windsor. Act iii, sc. 5, l. 69. [Ford]
Free determination.—*Troilus and Cressida,* ii, 2, 170.
Quick determination.—*Hamlet,* iii, 1, 176.
What are you then determined to do?
Julius Cæsar. Act v, sc. 1, l. 100. [Cassius]
Are you yet determined?—*Much Ado about Nothing,* v, 4, 36.
I am determined.—*Richard III,* i, 1, 30.
It is determined.—*Richard III,* i, 3, 15.
Well determined.—*Measure for Measure,* v, 1, 258.
8
Terrible in constant resolution.
Henry V. Act ii, sc. 4, l. 35. [Constable]
Determinate resolution.—*Henry VIII,* ii, 4, 176.
Due resolution.—*King Lear,* i, 2, 108.
Resolution thus fobbed.—*I Henry IV,* i, 2, 68. The only use of "fobbed" (cheated).
Insinew'd to this action.—*II Henry IV,* iv, 1, 172. The only use of "insinew'd."
9
Now set the teeth and stretch the nostril wide,
Hold hard the breath and bend up every spirit
To his full height.
Henry V. Act iii, sc. 1, l. 15. [King Henry]
10
Resolve on this, thou shalt be fortunate.
I Henry VI. Act i, sc. 2, l. 91. [La Pucelle]
11
Nay, stand thou back; I will not budge a foot:
This be Damascus, be thou cursed Cain,
To slay thy brother Abel, if thou wilt.
I Henry VI. Act i, sc. 3, l. 38. [Bishop of Winchester] The only mention of "Damascus."
12
Do what ye dare, we are as resolute.
I Henry VI. Act iii, sc. 1, l. 91. [Servant]
Be always resolute.—*I Henry VI,* iv, 1, 38.
Be bloody, bold, and resolute.—*Macbeth,* iv, 1, 79.
He is resolute.—*As You Like It,* i, 1, 147.
Therefore be resolute.—*III Henry VI,* v, 4, 61.
You are resolute, then?—*Twelfth Night,* i, 5, 23.
13 Steel thy fearful thoughts,
And change misdoubt to resolution:
Be that thou hopest to be, or what thou art
Resign to death.
II Henry VI. Act iii, sc. 1, l. 331. [York]
14
I am resolved for death or dignity.
II Henry VI. Act v, sc. 1, l. 194. [York]
I am resolved.—*II Henry VI,* v, 1, 198; *III Henry VI,* ii, 2, 124; *The Two Gentlemen of Verona,* i, 3, 66; *Love's Labour's Lost,* i, 1, 24; *The Taming of the Shrew,* i, 1, 90; *Twelfth Night,* i, 5, 24; *Pericles,* iv, 1, 12.
Citizen: You are all resolved rather to die than famish?
All: Resolved, resolved.
Coriolanus. Act i, sc. 1, l. 4.
Resolved to die.—*Measure for Measure,* iii, 2, 262.
15
The soldiers should have toss'd me on their pikes
Before I would have granted to that act.
III Henry VI. Act i, sc. 1, l. 244. [Queen Margaret]
16
Let us hear your firm resolve.
III Henry VI. Act iii, sc. 3, l. 129. [King Lewis]
Firm resolve.—*Taming of the Shrew,* ii, 1, 93.
High resolve.—*I Henry VI,* v, 5, 75.
High-resolved men.—*Titus Andronicus,* iv, 4, 64. The only use of "high-resolved."
17
Ah, that thy father had been so resolved!
III Henry VI. Act v, sc. 5, l. 22. [Queen Margaret]

1 I am fresh of spirit and resolved
To meet all perils very constantly.
Julius Cæsar. Act v, sc. 1, l. 91. [Cassius]
Let us swear our resolution.—*Julius Cæsar,* ii, 1, 113.

2 I am settled, and bend up
Each corporal agent to this terrible feat.
Macbeth. Act i, sc. 7, l. 79. [Macbeth]
He 's settled, Not to come off.—*Henry VIII,* iii, 2, 22.

3
Think you I can a resolution fetch
From flowery tenderness?
Measure for Measure. Act iii, sc. 1, l. 82. [Claudio]
I am freely dissolved, and dissolutely.
The Merry Wives of Windsor. Act i, sc. 1, l. 260. [Slender]

4
To be once in doubt Is once to be resolved.
Othello. Act iii, sc. 3, l. 179. [Othello]
It makes us, or it mars us; think on that,
And fix most firm thy resolution.
Othello. Act v, sc. 1, l. 4. [Iago]

5
Ever to obtain his will resolving.
The Rape of Lucrece, l. 129. The only use of "resolving."
My resolution, love, shall be thy boast,
By whose example thou revenged mayst be.
The Rape of Lucrece, l. 1193.
My resolution, husband, do thou take.
The Rape of Lucrece, l. 1200.

6
How high a pitch his resolution soars!
Richard II. Act i, sc. 1, l. 109. [King Richard]
He was not so resolved when last we spake together.
Richard II. Act ii, sc. 3, l. 29. [Northumberland]
I thought thou hadst been resolute.
Richard III. Act i, sc. 4, l. 115. [First Murderer]

7
In this resolution here we leave you.
Richard III. Act iii, sc. 7, l. 218. [Buckingham]
So I take my leave,
In resolution as I swore before.
The Taming of the Shrew. Act iv, sc. 2, l. 42. [Hortensio]

8
Do thou but call my resolution wise,
And with this knife I 'll help it presently.
Romeo and Juliet. Act iv, sc. 1, l. 53. [Juliet]

9
Be strong and prosperous In this resolve.
Romeo and Juliet. Act iv, sc. 1, l. 122. [Friar Laurence]

10
How I firmly am resolved you know.
The Taming of the Shrew. Act i, sc. 1, l. 49. [Baptista]
I firmly am resolved.—*III Henry VI,* iii, 3, 219.
I am thus resolved.—*The Taming of the Shrew,* ii, 1, 395.
I now am full resolved.—*The Two Gentlemen of Verona,* iii, 1, 76.
Now are we well resolved.—*Henry V,* i, 2, 222.
Certainly resolved.—*I Henry VI,* v, 1, 37.
Full resolved.—*Titus Andronicus,* ii, 1, 57.
Resolved for flight.—*Winter's Tale,* iv, 4, 519.
Resolved upon a course.—*Antony and Cleopatra,* iii, 11, 9.

11
Stand resolved, but hope withal.
Titus Andronicus. Act i, sc. 1, l. 135. [Demetrius]
Resolved withal
To do myself this reason and this right.
Titus Andronicus. Act i, sc. 1, l. 278. [Bassianus]
So must you resolve,
That what you cannot as you would achieve,
You must perforce accomplish as you may.
Titus Andronicus. Act ii, sc. 1, l. 105. [Aaron]

12
Your resolution cannot hold.
The Winter's Tale. Act iv, sc. 4, l. 36. [Perdita]

RESPECT

13
I attend them with all respect.
As You Like It. Act i, sc. 2, l. 177. [Orlando]
They respect not us.—*Coriolanus,* v, 4, 37.

14 My condition;
Which hath been as smooth as oil, soft as young down,
And therefore lost that title of respect
Which the proud soul ne'er pays but to the proud.
I Henry IV. Act i, sc. 3, l. 6. [King Henry]
Vouchsafe me hearing and respect.
I Henry IV. Act iv, sc. 3, l. 31. [Blunt]
Before, I loved thee as a brother, John;
But now, I do respect thee as my soul.
I Henry IV. Act v, sc. 4, l. 19. [Prince of Wales]

15 Men so noble,
However faulty, should yet find respect
For what they have been.
Henry VIII. Act v, sc. 3, l. 74. [Cromwell]
Respect him;
Take him, and use him well, he 's worthy of it.
Henry VIII. Act v, sc. 3, l. 154. [King Henry]

16
According to his virtue let us use him,
With all respect and rites of burial.
Julius Cæsar. Act v, sc. 5, l. 76. [Octavius]

17
By heaven, Hubert, I am almost ashamed
To say what good respect I have of thee.
King John. Act iii, sc. 3, l. 27. [King John]
Good respect.—*II Henry IV,* ii, 2, 109; *Julius Cæsar,* v, 5, 45.
Advised respects.—*Sonnets,* xlix.
Best respect.—*Julius Cæsar,* i, 2, 59.
Dear respect.—*Henry VIII,* v, 3, 119.
Fair respect.—*King John,* iii, 1, 58.
High respect.—*I Henry IV,* iii, 1, 170; *All's Well that Ends Well,* v, 3, 192; *Macbeth,* iii, 6, 29; *Midsummer-Night's Dream,* ii, 1, 209.
Honourable respect.—*Henry V,* v, 1, 75.
Noble respect.—*A Midsummer-Night's Dream,* v, 1, 91.
Profound respect.—*King John,* iii, 1, 318.
Pure respect.—*Henry VIII,* ii, 3, 95.
Sweet respect.—*Sonnets,* xxvi.

1
More than all the world I did respect her.
Love's Labour's Lost. Act v, sc. 2, l. 437. [King]

2
This is a respected fellow; and his mistress is a respected woman.
Measure for Measure. Act ii, sc. 1, l. 170. [Elbow]

The time is yet to come that she was ever respected with man, woman, or child.
Measure for Measure. Act ii, sc. 1, l. 175. [Elbow]

I respected with her before I was married to her! If ever I was respected with her, or she with me, let not your worship think me the poor duke's officer.
Measure for Measure. Act ii, sc. 1, l. 183. [Elbow]

3
Duke: Do you persuade yourself that I respect you?
Mariana: Good friar, I know you do.
Measure for Measure. Act iv, sc. 1, l. 53.

4
Respect to your great place!
Measure for Measure. Act v, sc. 1, l. 294. [Duke]

Dost thou not suspect my place? dost thou not suspect my years?
Much Ado about Nothing. Act iv, sc. 2, l. 76. [Dogberry]

5
Nothing is good, I see, without respect.
The Merchant of Venice. Act v, sc. 1, l. 99. [Portia]

6
I never heard a man of his place, gravity and learning so wide of his own respect.
The Merry Wives of Windsor. Act iii, sc. 1, l. 57. [Shallow]

7
True respect will prison false desire.
The Rape of Lucrece, l. 642.

True respect.—*Rape of Lucrece,* l. 201; 1347.

8
Throw away respect,
Tradition, form and ceremonious duty.
Richard II, iii, 2, 172. [King Richard]

9
Do him obeisance.
The Taming of the Shrew. Induction, sc. 1, l. 108. [Lord] The only use of "obeisance."

The icy precepts of respect.
Timon of Athens, iv, 3, 258. [Timon]

10
Is there no respect of place, persons, nor time in you?
Twelfth Night. Act ii, sc. 3, l. 97. [Malvolio]

She uses me with a more exalted respect than any one else that follows her.
Twelfth Night. Act ii, sc. 5, l. 30. [Malvolio]

11
What should it be that he respects in her
But I can make respective in myself?
The Two Gentlemen of Verona. Act iv, sc. 4, l. 199. [Julia]

You should have been respective.—*The Merchant of Venice,* v, 1, 156.

'Tis too respective.—*King John,* i, 1, 188. "Respective" is used a fourth time in *Romeo and Juliet,* iii, 1, 128: "Respective lenity."

12
Full of respects, yet nought at all respecting.
Venus and Adonis, l. 911.

Base respects.—*Hamlet,* iii, 2, 193.
Inflamed respect.—*King Lear,* i, 1, 258.
Less respect.—*Measure for Measure,* ii, 2, 86.
Small respect.—*King Lear,* ii, 2, 137.
Trifling respect.—*The Merry Wives of Windsor,* ii, 1, 45.

13
I will respect thee as a father if
Thou bear'st my life off hence.
The Winter's Tale. Act i, sc. 2, l. 461. [Polixenes]

She respects me as her only son.—*A Midsummer-Night's Dream,* i, 1, 160.

REST

See also Repose, Sleep

14
I 'll follow thee a month, devise with thee
Where thou shalt rest.
Coriolanus. Act iv, sc. 1, l. 38. [Cominius]

15
The crickets sing, and man's o'er-labour'd sense
Repairs itself by rest.
Cymbeline. Act ii, sc. 2, l. 11. [Iachimo] The only use of "o'er-labour'd."

Go in and rest.—*Cymbeline,* iv, 2, 43.
Go to your rest.—*Hamlet,* ii, 2, 84.
Full of rest.—*I Henry IV,* iv, 3, 27.
Gets him to rest.—*Henry V,* iv, 1, 287.
Rest your minds in peace.—*I Henry VI,* i, 1, 44.

16
Spite of spite needs must I rest awhile.
III Henry VI. Act ii, sc. 3, l. 5. [Warwick]

Here at the palace will I rest awhile.
III Henry VI. Act iv, sc. 8, l. 33. [King Henry]

Sat down
To rest awhile, some half hour or so,
In a rich chair of state.
Henry VIII. Act iv, sc. 1, l. 65. [Gentleman]

Lie here and rest awhile.—*King Lear,* iii, 6, 87.
I 'll rest.—*As You Like It,* iii, 2, 73.
I 'll to my rest.—*Romeo and Juliet,* i, 5, 129.
Rest myself.—*The Tempest,* v, 1, 144.
Rest himself.—*I Henry VI,* ii, 5, 2.

17
So many hours must I take my rest.
III Henry VI, ii, 5, 32. See under Time.

You shall take your rest For this one night.
The Tempest. Act v, sc. 1, l. 301. [Prospero]

Take your rest.—*The Tempest,* ii, 1, 197.

Lo, in this hollow cradle take thy rest.
Venus and Adonis, l. 1185.

18
Night hangs upon mine eyes; my bones would rest,
That have but labour'd to attain this hour.
Julius Cæsar. Act v, sc. 5, l. 41. [Brutus]

Come, poor remains of friends, rest on this rock.
Julius Cæsar. Act v, sc. 5, l. 1. [Brutus]

19
It cannot be
That, whiles warm life plays in that infant's veins,
The misplaced John should entertain an hour,

One minute, nay, one quiet breath of rest.
King John. Act iii, sc. 4, l. 131. [Pandulph]

1
How do you do, sir? Stand you not so amazed:
Will you lie down and rest upon the cushions?
King Lear. Act iii, sc. 6, l. 35. [Kent]

This rest might yet have balm'd thy broken sinews.
King Lear. Act iii, sc. 6, l. 105. [Kent]

2
What, sir, not yet at rest?
Macbeth. Act ii, sc. 1, l. 12. [Banquo]

At rest.—*King John,* v, 7, 82.

3
As I have set up my rest to run away, so I will not rest till I have run some ground.
The Merchant of Venice. Act ii, sc. 2, l. 110. [Launcelot]

'Till I come again,
No bed shall e'er be guilty of my stay,
No rest be interposer 'twixt us twain.
The Merchant of Venice. Act iii, sc. 2, l. 329. [Bassanio] The only use of "interposer."

4
We 'll rest us, Hermia, if you think it good.
A Midsummer-Night's Dream. Act ii, sc. 2, l. 37. [Lysander]

Rest us here.—*Pericles,* i, 4, 1.
Rest my head.—*A Midsummer-Night's Dream,* ii, 2, 40.
Rest thy weary head.—*The Rape of Lucrece,* l. 1621.

5
Here will I rest me till the break of day.
A Midsummer-Night's Dream. Act iii, sc. 2, l. 445. [Hermia]

I needs must rest me.—*The Tempest,* iii, 3, 4.
Let me rest.—*A Midsummer-Night's Dream,* ii, 2, 8; *Pericles,* v, 1, 236.
Let her rest.—*II Henry VI,* i, 3, 95.
Let it rest.—*I Henry VI,* iv, 1, 121; 180.
Let them rest.—*Richard III,* iii, 1, 157.

6
Therefore each one betake him to his rest;
To-morrow all for speeding do their best.
Pericles. Act ii, sc. 3, l. 115. [Simonides]

And every one to rest themselves betake,
Save thieves, and cares, and troubled minds, that wake.
The Rape of Lucrece, l. 125.

7
Disturb his hours of rest with restless trances.
The Rape of Lucrece, l. 974.

Disturb your rest.—*II Henry VI,* iii, 2, 256.

8
Here let us rest, if this rebellious earth
Have any resting for her true king's queen.
Richard II. Act v, sc. 1, l. 5. [Queen]

9
Set down, set down your honourable load, . . .
And still, as you are weary of the weight,
Rest you, whiles I lament King Henry's corse.
Richard III. Act i, sc. 2, l. 1. [Anne]

Pray, set it down and rest you.
The Tempest. Act iii, sc. 1, l. 18. [Miranda]

Pray now, rest yourself.—*Tempest,* iii, 1, 20.
Sit you down, father; rest you.—*King Lear,* iv, 6, 260.
Sit down, and rest.—*The Tempest,* iii, 3, 6.
Rest you fair.—*Merchant of Venice,* i, 3, 60.
Rest you happy!—*Antony and Cleopatra,* i, 1, 62.
Rest you merry.—*As You Like It,* v, 1, 65; *Romeo and Juliet,* i, 2, 65; 86.
Rest you well.—*Measure for Measure,* iv, 3, 186.
Rest secure.—*III Henry VI,* iv, 4, 33.
So may he rest.—*Henry VIII,* iv, 2, 31.

10
Anne: Ill rest betide the chamber where thou liest!
Gloucester: So will it, madam, till I lie with you.
Anne: I hope so.
Gloucester: I know so.
Richard III. Act i, sc. 2, l. 112.

Ill rest.—*The Passionate Pilgrim,* l. 8.

11
God give your grace good rest!
Richard III. Act i, sc. 4, l. 75. [Brakenbury]

God give her good rest!—*Titus Andronicus,* iv, 2, 63.
God give you good rest!—*The Comedy of Errors,* iv, 3, 33.
He took good rest.—*Winter's Tale,* ii, 3, 10.
And so, good rest.—*The Two Gentlemen of Verona,* iv, 2, 133
Good rest.—*The Passionate Pilgrim,* l. 181.

12
God give you quiet rest to-night!
Richard III. Act v, sc. 3, l. 43. [Blount]

Idle rest.—*The Passionate Pilgrim,* l. 195.
Life-preserving rest.—*The Comedy of Errors,* v, 1, 83. The only use of "life-preserving."
Morning's rest.—*Romeo and Juliet,* v, 3, 189.
Natural rest.—*III Henry VI,* iv, 3, 5.
Purposed rest.—*Love's Labour 's Lost,* v, 2, 91.

13
His new kingdom of perpetual rest.
Richard III. Act ii, sc. 2, l. 46. [Queen Elizabeth]

Lasting rest.—*King John,* v, 7, 24. See under Swan.
Rest for ever.—*King Lear,* v, 3, 150.
Closed up in rest!—*III Henry VI,* ii, 1, 76.
Goes to rest.—*Titus Andronicus,* i, 1, 133.

14
Rest thy unrest on England's lawful earth.
Richard III. Act iv, sc. 4, l. 29. [Duchess of York]

Let her rest in her unrest awhile.
Titus Andronicus. Act iv, sc. 2, l. 31. [Aaron]

So sweet to rest!—*Romeo and Juliet,* ii, 2, 188.

15
Get thee to bed and rest, for thou hast need.
Romeo and Juliet. Act iv, sc. 3, l. 13. [Lady Capulet]

You shall rest but little.—*Romeo and Juliet,* iv, 5, 7.
Little rest.—*Julius Cæsar,* iv, 3, 228.

16
How can I then return in happy plight,
That am debarr'd the benefit of rest?
Sonnets. No. xxviii. The only use of "debarr'd."

Nor night nor day no rest.
The Winter's Tale. Act ii, sc. 3, l. 1. [Leontes]
Takes no rest.—*Venus and Adonis,* l. 647.
I cannot rest.—*III Henry VI,* i, 2, 32.

1 There I 'll rest as after much turmoil
A blessed soul doth in Elysium.
The Two Gentlemen of Verona. Act ii, sc. 7, l. 37. [Julia] The only use of "turmoil."
God rest his soul.—*The Merchant of Venice,* ii, 2, 76. See Boy, 132:4.
Soul's rest.—*Measure for Measure,* ii, 4, 187.
Heaven rest them now!—*Macbeth,* iv, 3, 227.
See also under Heaven.

RESTITUTION

2
He calls me to a restitution large
Of gold and jewels that I bobb'd from him.
Othello. Act v, sc. 1, l. 15. [Iago] "Bobb'd" is repeated in *Richard III,* v, 3, 334, and in *Troilus and Cressida,* ii, 1, 76, always in the sense of cheated.
He makes restitution.—*The Merry Wives of Windsor,* v, 5, 33.
Hopeless restitution.—*Coriolanus,* iii, 1, 16.
Never ask'd for restitution.—*II Henry VI,* iii, 1, 118.

RESULT

See also Consequence, Event

3
We may march in England or in France,
Not seeing what is likely to ensue.
I Henry VI. Act iii, sc. 1, l. 187. [Exeter]
I foretold you then what would ensue.
Troilus and Cressida. Act iv, sc. 5, l. 217. [Ulysses]
We had a kind of light what would ensue.
King John. Act iv, sc. 3, l. 61. [Salisbury]
What will ensue hereof, there 's none can tell.
Richard II, ii, 1, 212. See under Event.
Bear up against what should ensue.
The Tempest, i, 2, 158. See under Stomach.
What doth ensue.—*The Comedy of Errors,* v, 1, 78.
Doth it therefore ensue?—*As You Like It,* i, 3, 32.
This will ensue.—*Comedy of Errors,* ii, 2, 193.
What ensues.—*Cymbeline,* iii, 2, 81; *Pericles,* i, Gower, 41; iii, Gower, 53.
The fruits are to ensue.—*Othello,* ii, 3, 9.

4
More depends on it than we must yet deliver.
Measure for Measure. Act iv, sc. 2, l. 128. [Provost]
There 's more depends on this.—*The Merchant of Venice,* iv, 1, 434.

5
This falls out better than I could devise.
A Midsummer-Night's Dream. Act iii, sc. 2, l. 35. [Oberon]
It oft falls out.—*Measure for Measure,* ii, 4, 117.
Fall out right.—*I Henry VI,* ii, 3, 4.
Fall out so.—*King John,* iv, 2, 154.
It so falls out.—*Much Ado about Nothing,* iv, 1, 219.
So falls it out.—*Richard III,* iii, 2, 66.
So it must fall out.—*Coriolanus,* ii, 1, 259.

6
But what, o' God's name, doth become of this?
Richard II. Act ii, sc. 1, l. 251. [Willoughby]
What shall become of this? what will this do?
Much Ado about Nothing. Act iv, sc. 1, l. 211. [Leonato]
What will become of this?
Twelfth Night. Act ii, sc. 2, l. 37. [Viola]
What will become of me now, wretched lady!
Henry VIII. Act iii, sc. 1, l. 146. [Queen Katharine]
What becomes of me?—*King John,* iii, 1, 35.
What shall become of me?—*Measure for Measure,* i, 2, 108.

7
I told you what would come of this.
Winter's Tale. Act iv, sc. 4, l. 457. [Perdita]
O, what would come of it!
Julius Cæsar. Act iii, sc. 2, l. 151. [Antony] "Come of" is used eleven times. The word "result" does not appear in Shakespeare.

RETIREMENT

8
Retire, we have engaged ourselves too far.
Antony and Cleopatra. Act iv, sc. 7, l. 1. [Agrippa]
Virgilia: Give me leave to retire myself.
Volumnia: Indeed, you shall not.
Coriolanus. Act i, sc. 3, l. 30.
Retire to your chamber.—*Antony and Cleopatra,* iv, 4, 35.
Retire with me to my lodging.—*King Lear,* i, 2, 183.

9 Come on, my fellows:
He that retires, I 'll take him for a Volsce,
And he shall feel mine edge.
Coriolanus. Act i, sc. 4, l. 27. [Marcius]
Cowardly in retire.—*Coriolanus,* i, 6, 3.

10 Then began
A stop i' the chaser, a retire, anon
A rout, confusion thick; forthwith they fly
Chickens, the way which they stoop'd eagles; slaves,
The strides they victors made.
Cymbeline. Act v, sc. 3, l. 39. [Posthumus] The only use of "chaser."

11
A comfort of retirement lives in this.
I Henry IV, iv, 1, 56. See under Home.
I beseech your majesty, make up,
Lest your retirement do amaze your friends.
I Henry IV. Act v, sc. 4, l. 4. [Prince]
In your retirement.—*Measure for Measure,* v, 1, 130.

12
Make a peaceful and a sweet retire.
Henry V. Act iv, sc. 3, l. 86. [Montjoy]
We will retire to Calais.—*Henry V,* iii, 3, 56.
Retire me to my Milan.—*Tempest,* v, 1, 310.
Retire into your trenches.—*I Henry VI,* i, 5, 33.
He is enforced to retire.—*Henry V,* iii, 6, 99.

13
Our English troops retire, I cannot stay them.
I Henry VI. Act i, sc. 5, l. 2. [Talbot]
[The] English measure back their own ground
In faint retire.
King John. Act v, sc. 5, l. 4. [Lewis]

The French fight coldly and retire themselves.
King John. Act v, sc. 3, l. 13. [Messenger]

1
If thou retire, the Dauphin, well appointed,
Stands with the snares of war to tangle thee.
I Henry VI. Act i, sc. 2, l. 21. [General]

2
Or is he but retired to make him strong?
II Henry VI. Act iv, sc. 9, l. 9. [King Henry]

Retired to ripe his growing fortunes.—*II Henry IV,* iv, 1, 13.
You are retired.—*The Winter's Tale,* iv, 4, 62.
Most retired.—*Cymbeline,* iii, 5, 36.
Much retired.—*The Winter's Tale,* iv, 2, 36.
So retired.—*The Tempest,* i, 2, 91.
Retired himself to Italy.—*Richard II,* iv, 1, 96.
Retired his power.—*Richard II,* ii, 2, 46.

3
Ne'er may he live to see a sunshine day,
That cries 'Retire,' if Warwick bid him stay.
III Henry VI. Act ii, sc. 1, l. 187. [Richard]
Forced to retire.—*III Henry VI,* ii, 5, 8.

4 With a blessed and unvex'd retire,
With unhack'd swords and helmets all unbruised,
We will bear home that lusty blood again
Which here we came to spout against your town.
King John. Act ii, sc. 1, l. 253. [King Philip] "Unhack'd" is repeated in *Antony and Cleopatra,* ii, 6, 38: "Part with unhack'd edges."

Heralds, from off our towers we might behold,
From first to last, the onset and retire
Of both your armies.
King John. Act ii, sc. 1, l. 325. [Citizen]
Sallies and retires.—*I Henry IV,* ii, 3, 54.
Make retire.—*The Rape of Lucrece,* l. 573.
Let 's retire.—*Romeo and Juliet,* iii, 1, 1.

5 Who should withhold me?
Not fate, obedience, nor the hand of Mars
Beckoning with fiery truncheon my retire.
Troilus and Cressida. Act v, sc. 3, l. 51. [Troilus]

Thou dost miscall retire: I do not fly.
Troilus and Cressida. Act v, sc. 4, l. 21. [Diomedes]

Achilles: Hark! a retire upon our Grecian part.
Myrmidon: The Trojan trumpets sound the like.
Troilus and Cressida. Act v, sc. 8, l. 15.
Back retires.—*Venus and Adonis,* l. 906.

6
You must retire yourself Into some covert.
The Winter's Tale. Act iv, sc. 4, l. 662. [Camillo]
Retire thee.—*Othello,* ii, 3, 386.
I must . . . not retire.—*The Merry Wives of Windsor,* iii, 4, 86.

RETREAT

7
In a retreat he outruns any lackey.
All's Well that Ends Well. Act iv, sc. 3, l. 323. [Parolles] See under COWARDICE.

For a retreat, how swiftly will this Feeble the woman's tailor run off.
II Henry IV. Act iii, sc. 2, l. 287. [Falstaff]

8
Let us make an honourable retreat.
As You Like It, iii, 2, 169. [Touchstone]

9
Lancaster: Now, have you left pursuit?
Westmoreland: Retreat is made and execution stay'd.
II Henry IV. Act iv, sc. 3, l. 77.

10
Here sound retreat, and cease our hot pursuit.
I Henry VI. Act ii, sc. 2, l. 3. [Bedford]

The trumpet sounds retreat, the day is ours.
I Henry IV. Act v, sc. 4, l. 163. [Prince]
The trompet sound the retreat.—*Henry V,* iii, 2, 94. Macmorris always says "trompet."

Dare any be so bold to sound retreat or parley, when I command them kill?
II Henry VI. Act iv, sc. 8, l. 4. [Cade]

11
Whose warlike ears could never brook retreat.
III Henry VI. Act i, sc. 1, l. 5. [York]

RETRIBUTION

12
But, sirrah, you shall buy this sport as dear
As all the metal in your shop will answer.
The Comedy of Errors. Act iv, sc. 1, l. 81. [Antipholus of Ephesus]

13
You shall answer me with your sword.
Cymbeline. Act i, sc. 4, l. 174. [Posthumous]

A heavy reckoning for you, sir. But the comfort is, you shall be called to no more payments, fear no more tavern-bills; which are often the sadness of parting, as the procuring of mirth.
Cymbeline. Act v, sc. 4, l. 159. [Gaoler] The only use of "tavern-bills" and "procuring."

14 'Tis the sport to have the enginer
Hoist with his own petar: and 't shall go hard
But I will delve one yard below their mines,
And blow them at the moon.
Hamlet. Act iii, sc. 4, l. 206. [Hamlet] "Enginer" occurs again in *Troilus and Cressida,* ii, 3, 8. The only use of "petar." "Delve" is repeated in *Cymbeline,* i, 1, 28.

Why, as a woodcock to mine own springe;
I am justly kill'd with mine own treachery.
Hamlet. Act v, sc. 2, l. 317. [Laertes]
Springes to catch woodcocks.—*Hamlet,* i, 3, 115.
If the springe hold, the cock's mine.—*The Winter's Tale,* iv, 3, 36. The only uses of "springe" and "springes."

15
The foul practice Hath turn'd itself on me.
Hamlet. Act v, sc. 2, l. 328. [Laertes]

He is justly served;
It is a poison temper'd by himself.
Hamlet. Act v, sc. 2, l. 338. [Laertes]

So shall you hear
Of carnal, bloody, and unnatural acts,
Of accidental judgements, casual slaughters,
Of deaths put on by cunning and forced cause,
And, in this upshot, purposes mistook
Fall'n on the inventors' heads.
Hamlet. Act v, sc. 2, l. 391. [Horatio] "Carnal" occurs again in *Cymbeline,* i, 4, 100; and "upshot" in *Twelfth Night,* iv, 2, 76.

1
I know not whether God will have it so,
For some displeasing service I have done,
That, in his secret doom, out of my blood
He 'll breed revengement and a scourge for me.

I Henry IV. Act iii, sc. 2, l. 4. [King Henry] The only use of "revengement."

2
He 'll call you to so hot an answer of it,
That caves and womby vaultages of France
Shall chide your trespass and return your mock
In second accent of his ordnance.

Henry V. Act ii, sc. 4, l. 123. [Exeter] The only use of "womby" or "vaultages."

3
'Tis but Quid for Quo.

I Henry VI. Act v, sc. 3, l. 109. [Margaret] The only use of the phrase.

4
When we saw our sunshine made thy spring,
And that thy summer bred us no increase,
We set the axe to thy usurping root.

III Henry VI. Act ii, sc. 2, l. 163. [George]

The edge hath something hit ourselves.

III Henry VI. Act ii, sc. 2, l. 166. [George]

If you ever chance to have a child,
Look in his youth to have him so cut off
As, deathsmen, you have rid this sweet young prince!

III Henry VI. Act v, sc. 5, l. 65. [Queen Margaret] The only use of "deathsmen." "Deathsman" occurs twice.

5
Heat not a furnace for your foe so hot
That it do singe yourself.

Henry VIII. Act i, sc. 1, l. 140. [Norfolk] "Singe" occurs again in *King Lear*, iii, 2, 6.

I told ye all,
When we first put this dangerous stone a-rolling,
'Twould fall upon ourselves.

Henry VIII. Act v, sc. 3, l. 103. [Suffolk] The only use of "a-rolling."

In seeking tales and informations
Against this man, whose honesty the devil
And his disciples only envy at,
Ye blew the fire that burns ye.

Henry VIII. Act v, sc. 3, l. 110. [Cromwell] The only use of "disciples." "Discipled" occurs in *All's Well that Ends Well*, i, 2, 28.

6
'Tis his own blame; hath put himself from rest,
And must needs taste his folly.

King Lear. Act ii, sc. 4, l. 293. [Goneril]

The wheel is come full circle.

King Lear. Act v, sc. 3, l. 174. [Edmund] The only use of this phrase in the plays.

7
Sow'd cockle reap'd no corn.

Love's Labour's Lost, iv, 3, 383. [Biron]

Cockle of rebellion.—*Coriolanus*, iii, 1, 70. The only uses of "cockle" in this sense. *The Taming of the Shrew*, iv, 3, 66, has, "'Tis a cockle or a walnut-shell"; and *Pericles*, iv, 4, 2, has, "Sail seas in cockles."

8
If it were done when 'tis done, then 'twere well
It were done quickly: if the assassination
Could trammel up the consequence, and catch
With his surcease success; that but this blow
Might be the be-all and the end-all here,
But here, upon this bank and shoal of time,
We 'ld jump the life to come. But in these cases
We still have judgement here; that we but teach
Bloody instructions, which, being taught, return
To plague the inventor: this even-handed justice
Commends the ingredients of our poison'd chalice
To our own lips.

Macbeth. Act i, sc. 7, l. 1. [Macbeth] The only use of "assassination," "trammel," "be-all," "end-all," and "even-handed justice." "Shoal" is repeated in *Henry VIII*, iii, 2, 436: "Shoals of honour"; and "inventor" is used again in *Hamlet*, v, 2, 396.

9
It will have blood; they say, blood will have blood.

Macbeth. Act iii, sc. 4, l. 122. [Macbeth]

Friend or brother,
He forfeits his own blood that spills another.

Timon of Athens, iii, 5, 87. [Senator]

10
Not for their own demerits, but for mine,
Fell slaughter on their souls.

Macbeth. Act iv, sc. 3, l. 226. [Macduff]

11
She hath eaten up all her beef, and she is herself in the tub.

Measure for Measure. Act iii, sc. 2, l. 58. [Pompey]

12 For your brother's life,—
The very mercy of the law cries out
Most audible, even from his proper tongue,
'An Angelo for Claudio, death for death!'

Measure for Measure. Act v, sc. 1, l. 411. [Duke] "Audible" occurs again in *Coriolanus*, iv, 5, 238.

13
O, I were damn'd beneath all depth in hell,
But that I did proceed upon just grounds
To this extremity.

Othello. Act v, sc. 2, l. 137. [Othello]

14 Blood, like sacrificing Abel's, cries,
Even from the tongueless caverns of the earth,
To me for justice and rough chastisement.

Richard II. Act i, sc. 1, l. 104. [Bolingbroke] Abel is mentioned again in *I Henry VI*, i, 3, 40. "Tongueless" is repeated in *Henry V*, i, 2, 232: "Tongueless mouths"; in *Richard III*, iii, 7, 42: "Tongueless blocks"; and in *The Winter's Tale*, i, 2, 92: "Dying tongueless."

He that hath suffer'd this disorder'd spring
Hath now himself met with the fall of leaf.

Richard II. Act iii, sc. 4, l. 48. [Gardener]

15
That high All-Seer that I dallied with
Hath turn'd my feigned prayer on my head

And given in earnest what I begg'd in jest.
Thus doth he force the swords of wicked men
To turn their own points on their masters' bosoms.

Richard III. Act v, sc. 1, l. 20. [Buckingham] The only use of "All-Seer."

1 For which foul deed
The powers, delaying, not forgetting, have
Incensed the seas and shores, yea, all the creatures,
Against your peace.

The Tempest. Act iii, sc. 3, l. 72. [Ariel]

2 What I have done, as best I may,
Answer I must and shall do with my life.

Titus Andronicus. Act i, sc. 1, l. 411. [Bassianus]

They shall be ready at your highness' will
To answer their suspicion with their lives.

Titus Andronicus. Act ii, sc. 3, l. 297. [Titus]

I shall never come to bliss
Till all these mischiefs be return'd again
Even in their throats that have committed them.

Titus Andronicus. Act iii, sc. 1, l. 273. [Titus]

There 's meed for meed, death for a deadly deed!

Titus Andronicus. Act v, sc. 3, l. 66. [Lucius]

3 If one jot beyond
The bound of honour, or in act or will
That way inclining, harden'd be the hearts
Of all that hear me, and my near'st of kin
Cry fie upon my grave!

The Winter's Tale. Act iii, sc. 2, l. 51. [Hermione]

REVELRY

4 He fishes, drinks, and wastes
The lamps of night in revel; is not more manlike
Than Cleopatra; nor the queen of Ptolemy
More womanly than he.

Antony and Cleopatra. Act i, sc. 4, l. 5. [Octavius Cæsar] The only use of "manlike."

Alexandrian revels.—*Antony and Cleopatra,* v, 2, 218.

Fairy revel.—*The Merry Wives of Windsor,* iv, 4, 58.

Moonlight revels.—*A Midsummer-Night's Dream,* ii, 1, 141.

5
Fall into our rustic revelry.

As You Like It. Act v, sc. 4, l. 183. [Duke senior] The only use of "revelry."

6
I will make my very house reel to-night.

Coriolanus. Act ii, sc. 1, l. 121. [Menenius]

They will out of their burrows, like conies after rain, and revel.

Coriolanus. Act iv, sc. 5, l. 226. [Servant] The only use of "burrows."

7
The king doth wake to-night and takes his rouse,
Keeps wassail, and the swaggering up-spring reels;
And, as he drains his draughts of Rhenish down,
The kettle-drum and trumpet thus bray out
The triumph of his pledge.

Hamlet. Act i, sc. 4, l. 8. [Hamlet] The only use of "up-spring" and "kettle-drum." "Rhenish" is mentioned again in v, 1, 197, and in *Merchant of Venice,* i, 2, 104, and iii, 1, 44.

With wine and wassail.—*Macbeth,* i, 7, 64. "Wassail" is used once again in *II Henry IV,* i, 2, 179: "A wassail candle."

Wakes and wassails.—*Love's Labour 's Lost,* v, 2, 318.

Lascivious wassails.—*Antony and Cleopatra,* i, 4, 56. The only uses of "wassails."

8
This heavy-headed revel east and west
Makes us traduced and tax'd of other nations:
They clepe us drunkards, and with swinish phrase
Soil our addition.

Hamlet. Act i, sc. 4, l. 17. [Hamlet] The only use of "heavy-headed." "Swinish" occurs again in *Macbeth,* i, 7, 67, and "clepe" in *Venus and Adonis,* l. 995.

9 Command the citizens make bonfires
And feast and banquet in the open streets.

I Henry VI. Act i, sc. 6, l. 12. [Reignier]

Some to dance, some to make bonfires, each man to what sport and revels his addiction leads him.

Othello. Act ii, sc. 2, l. 5. [Herald]

His addiction was to courses vain.

Henry V, i, 1, 54. Only uses of "addiction."

Burn, bonfires, clear and bright.—*II Henry VI,* v, 1, 3.

Nothing but bonfires.—*Winter's Tale,* v, 2, 24.

Bonfires in France.—*I Henry VI,* i, 1, 153. The only uses of "bonfires." "Bonfire" occurs in *Macbeth,* ii, 3, 22: "Everlasting bonfire."

10
Was 't you that revell'd in our parliament?

III Henry VI. Act i, sc. 4, l. 71. [Queen Margaret]

Revell'd in the heart of France.—*III Henry VI,* ii, 2, 150.

Revell'd in the night.—*Richard II,* iii, 2, 48. The only uses of "revell'd."

11 Masquers
To revel it with him and his new bride.

III Henry VI. Act iii, sc. 3, l. 224; iv, 1, 95. [King Lewis] The only use of "masquers."

A masker and a reveller!

Julius Cæsar. Act v, sc. 1, l. 62. [Cassius]

For revels, dances, masks and merry hours
Forerun fair Love, strewing her way with flowers.

Love's Labour 's Lost, iv, 3, 379. [Biron]

Sir Andrew: I delight in masques and revels sometimes altogether.

Sir Toby: Art thou good at these kickshawses, knight?

Twelfth Night. Act i, sc. 3, l. 120. The only use of "kickshawses." "Kickshaws" occurs in *II Henry IV,* v, 1, 29.

This harness'd masque and unadvised revel.

King John. Act v, sc. 2, l. 132. [Bastard] "Harness'd" is repeated in *Troilus and Cressida,* i, 2, 8: "Harness'd light."

12
Now what rests but that we spend the time
With stately triumphs, mirthful comic shows,

Such as befits the pleasure of the court?
III Henry VI. Act v, sc. 7, l. 42. [King Edward] The only use of "mirthful." "Comic" is repeated only once, in *I Henry VI,* ii, 2, 45: "Comic sport."

Revelling like lords.—*II Henry VI,* i, 1, 224.

1 See! Antony, that revels long o' nights,
Is notwithstanding up.
Julius Cæsar. Act ii, sc. 2, l. 116. [Cæsar]

Moonshine revellers.—*The Merry Wives of Windsor,* v, 5, 42.

2 What revels are in hand?
A Midsummer-Night's Dream. Act v, sc. 1, l. 36. [Theseus]

Shall we set about some revels?
Twelfth Night, i, 3, 144. [Sir Andrew]

3 I know we shall have revelling to-night.
Much Ado about Nothing. Act i, sc. 1, l. 322. [Don Pedro]

'Tis a night of revels.
Othello. Act i, sc. 3, l. 45. [Iago]

4 What pageantry, what feats, what shows,
What minstrelsy, and pretty din,
The regent made in Mytilene
To greet the king.
Pericles. Act v, sc. 2, l. 6. [Gower]

5 We will have rings and things and fine array.
The Taming of the Shrew. Act ii, sc. 1, l. 325. [Petruchio]

Revel it as bravely as the best,
With silken coats and caps and golden rings,
With ruffs and cuffs and fardingales and things;
With scarfs and fans and double change of bravery,
With amber bracelets, beads and all this knavery.
The Taming of the Shrew. Act iv, sc. 3, l. 54. [Petruchio] The only use of "fardingales."

6 When all our offices have been oppress'd
With riotous feeders, when our vaults have wept
With drunken spilth of wine, when every room
Hath blazed with lights and bray'd with minstrelsy,
I have retired me to a wasteful cock,
And set mine eyes at flow.
Timon of Athens. Act ii, sc. 2, l. 167. [Flavius] The only use of "spilth" and "bray'd."

7 Our revels now are ended.
The Tempest, iv, 1, 148. See under Vision.

REVENGE

See also Vengeance

8 Both my revenge and hate
Loosing upon thee, in the name of justice,
Without all terms of pity.
All's Well that Ends Well. Act ii, sc. 3, l. 171. [King] The only use of "loosing."

My revenges were high bent upon him,
And watch'd the time to shoot.
All's Well that Ends Well. Act v, sc. 3, l. 10. [King]

9 Now, darting Parthia, art thou struck: and now
Pleased fortune does of Marcus Crassus' death
Make me revenger.
Antony and Cleopatra. Act iii, sc. 1, l. 1. [Ventidius] "Revenger" occurs again in ii, 6, 11, and in no other play.

10 For thy revenge
Wrench up thy power to the highest.
Coriolanus. Act i, sc. 8, l. 10. [Marcius]

Revenge as spacious as between
The young'st and oldest thing.
Coriolanus. Act iv, sc. 6, l. 67. [Messenger]

Think to front his revenges with the easy groans of old women, the virginal palms of your daughters.
Coriolanus. Act v, sc. 2, l. 44. [Sentinel]

Thirst for revenge.—*Coriolanus,* i, 1, 25.

11 Be revenged;
Or she that bore you was no queen, and you
Recoil from your great stock.
Cymbeline. Act i, sc. 6, l. 126. [Iachimo]

I 'll be revenged Most throughly.
Hamlet. Act iv, sc. 5, l. 135. [Laertes]

We 'll be revenged on him.
I Henry IV. Act i, sc. 3, l. 291. [Hotspur]

I could tear her: I 'll be revenged of her.
II Henry IV. Act ii, sc. 4, l. 168. [Pistol]

I 'll be revenged as I may.
Much Ado about Nothing. Act ii, sc. 1, l. 217. [Benedick]

I will in, to be revenged for this villany.
The Taming of the Shrew. Act v, sc. 1, l. 139. [Vincentio]

Worse than Progne will I be revenged.
Titus Andronicus. Act v, sc. 2, l. 196. [Titus] The only mention of Progne (or Procnē), wife of Tereus, who, to revenge herself for his rape of Philomela, served him his own son for dinner.

I 'll be revenged on the whole pack of you.
Twelfth Night. Act v, sc. 1, l. 386. [Malvolio]

I 'll be revenged.—*The Taming of the Shrew,* ii, 1, 29; *Merry Wives of Windsor,* v, 1, 30.

We will be revenged.—*Julius Cæsar,* iii, 2, 207.

I fear 'twill be revenged.—*Cymbeline,* iv, 2, 154.

Suddenly revenged.—*Rape of Lucrece,* l. 1683.

Revenged home.—*King Lear,* iii, 3, 13.

Revenged on Eglamour.—*The Two Gentlemen of Verona,* v, 2, 51.

Revenged on Falstaff.—*The Merry Wives of Windsor,* ii, 2, 326.

Revenged on Rome.—*Titus Andronicus,* iii, 1, 301.

12 She hath despised me rejoicingly, and I 'll be merry in my revenge.
Cymbeline. Act iii, sc. 5, l. 149. [Cloten] The only use of "rejoicingly."

He will drive you out of your revenge and turn all to a merriment.
II Henry IV. Act ii, sc. 4, l. 323. [Poins]

1
Ghost: Pity me not, but lend thy serious hearing
To what I shall unfold.
Hamlet: Speak; I am bound to hear.
Ghost: So art thou to revenge, when thou shalt hear.
Hamlet. Act i, sc. 5, l. 5.
Haste me to know 't, that I, with wings as swift
As meditation or the thoughts of love,
May sweep to my revenge.
Hamlet. Act i, sc. 5, l. 29. [Hamlet]
2 So he goes to heaven;
And so am I revenged. That would be scann'd:
A villain kills my father; and for that,
I, his sole son, do this same villain send
To heaven.
O, this is hire and salary, not revenge.
Hamlet. Act iii, sc. 3, l. 74. [Hamlet] The only use of "salary."
Am I then revenged,
To take him in the purging of his soul,
When he is fit and season'd for his passage?
No!
Up, sword; and know thou a more horrid hent.
Hamlet. Act iii, sc. 3, l. 84. [Hamlet]
My revenge will come.
Hamlet. Act iv, sc. 7, l. 29. [Laertes]
Revenge should have no bounds.
Hamlet. Act iv, sc. 7, l. 129. [King]
3 Time serves wherein you may . . .
Revenge the jeering and disdain'd contempt
Of this proud king.
I Henry IV. Act i, sc. 3, l. 180. [Hotspur]
Revenge this spite.—*A Midsummer-Night's Dream,* iii, 2, 420.
Revenge these woes.—*Titus Andronicus,* iii, 2, 3.
Revenge These wrongs.—*Titus Andronicus,* v, 3, 125.
4
Rouse up revenge from ebon den with fell Alecto's snake.
II Henry IV. Act v, sc. 5, l. 39. [Pistol] The only use of "ebon." "Ebon-coloured" occurs in *Love's Labour's Lost,* i, 1, 246. The only mention of Alecto, one of the Furies.
5
I am coming on, To venge me as I may.
Henry V. Act i, sc. 2, l. 291. [King Henry]
But I 'll to his majesty and crave
I may have liberty to venge this wrong.
I Henry VI. Act iii, sc. 4, l. 41. [Bastard]
Would none but I might venge my cousin's death.
Romeo and Juliet. Act iii, sc. 5, l. 87. [Juliet]
Venge my Gloucester's death.—*Richard II,* i, 2, 36.
6
I will most horribly revenge.
Henry V, v, 1, 49. See under EATING.
I take thy groat in earnest of revenge.
Henry V. Act v, sc. 1, l. 67. [Pistol]
7
They seek revenge and therefore will not yield.
III Henry VI. Act i, sc. 1, l. 190. [Exeter]
Seek revenge.—*III Henry VI,* iii, 3, 265.
8 When I am dead and gone,
Remember to avenge me.
I Henry VI. Act i, sc. 4, l. 93. [Talbot.]
Shall I not live to be avenged on her?
II Henry VI. Act i, sc. 3, l. 85. [Queen]
Well avenged.—*Julius Cæsar,* v, 1, 54.
9
It irks his heart he cannot be revenged.
I Henry VI. Act i, sc. 4, l. 105. [Talbot]
10
He did vow upon his knees he would be even with me.
II Henry VI. Act i, sc. 3, l. 203. [Horner]
You are odd, and he is even with you.
Troilus and Cressida. Act iv, sc. 5, l. 44. [Cressida]
And nothing can or shall content my soul
Till I am even'd with him.
Othello. Act ii, sc. 1, l. 308. [Iago] The only use of "even'd."
11
Let not this make thee bloody-minded.
II Henry VI. Act iv, sc. 1, l. 36. [Suffolk] "Bloody-minded" occurs again in *III Henry VI,* ii, 6, 33.
Transported . . .
To bloody thoughts and to revenge.
Winter's Tale. Act iii, sc. 2, l. 159. [Leontes]
12
Therefore, when merchant-like I sell revenge,
Broke be my sword, my arms torn and defaced,
And I proclaim'd a coward through the world!
II Henry VI. Act iv, sc. 1, l. 41. [Whitmore] The only use of "merchant-like."
Think therefore on revenge and cease to weep.
II Henry VI. Act iv, sc. 4, l. 3. [Queen]
Oft have I struck
Those that I never saw and struck them dead.
II Henry VI. Act iv, sc. 7, l. 86. [Say]
13 You both have vow'd revenge
On him, his sons, his favorites and his friends.
III Henry VI. Act i, sc. 1, l. 55. [King Henry]
Bound to revenge,
Wert thou environ'd with a brazen wall.
III Henry VI. Act ii, sc. 4, l. 3. [Richard]
14
My ashes, as the phœnix, may bring forth
A bird that will revenge upon you all.
III Henry VI. Act i, sc. 4, l. 35. [York]
To weep is to make less the depth of grief:
Tears then for babes; blows and revenge for me!
III Henry VI. Act ii, sc. 1, l. 85. [Richard]
15
Or shall we on the helmets of our foes
Tell our devotion with revengeful arms?
III Henry VI. Act ii, sc. 1, l. 163. [Richard]
Revengeful arms.—*Rape of Lucrece,* l. 1693.
Revengeful hand. —*Richard II,* v, 3, 42.
Revengeful heart.—*Richard III,* i, 2, 74.
Revengeful steel.—*Richard II,* iv, 1, 50.
Revengeful war.—*Titus Andronicus,* iv, 3, 32.
Revenging fire.—*II Henry VI,* iv, 1, 97.
Revenging gods.—*King Lear,* ii, 1, 47.

1
Withhold revenge, dear God! 'Tis not my fault,
Nor wittingly have I infringed my vow.
III Henry VI. Act ii, sc. 2, l. 7. [King Henry] "Wittingly" is repeated twice in *Hamlet,* v, 1, 11; 13.

2
And in the very pangs of death he cried,
Like to a dismal clangour heard from far,
'Warwick, revenge! brother, revenge my death!'
III Henry VI. Act ii, sc. 3, l. 17. [Richard] The only use of "clangour."

Revenge his death.—*III Henry VI,* i, 1, 100.

Revenge my death.—*I Henry VI,* iv, 5, 18; iv, 6, 30.

O God, which this blood madest, revenge his death!
O earth, which this blood drink'st, revenge his death!
Richard III. Act i, sc. 2, l. 62. [Lady Anne]

3
Revenge did paint
The fearful difference of incensed kings.
King John. Act iii, sc. 1, l. 237. [King Philip]

I do but stay behind
To do the office for thee of revenge.
King John. Act v, sc. 7, l. 70. [Bastard]

4
I will have such revenges on you both,
That all the world shall—I will do such things,—
What they are, yet I know not; but they shall be
The terrors of the earth.
King Lear. Act ii, sc. 4, l. 282. [King Lear]

I will have my revenge ere I depart his house.
King Lear. Act iii, sc. 5, l. 1. [Cornwall]

The revenges we are bound to take upon your traitorous father are not fit for your beholding.
King Lear. Act iii, sc. 7, l. 7. [Cornwall]

5
He 'll strike, and quickly too.
King Lear. Act v, sc. 3, l. 285. [King Lear]

6
Let 's make us medicines of our great revenge,
To cure this deadly grief.
Macbeth. Act iv, sc. 3, l. 214. [Malcolm]

Revenges burn in them.
Macbeth. Act v, sc. 2, l. 3. [Menteith]

Thou mayst revenge.—*Macbeth,* iii, 3, 18.

7
Revenge to your heart, And general honour.
Measure for Measure. Act iv, sc. 3, l. 140. [Duke]

Ta'en revenge.—*Measure for Measure,* iv, 5, 33.

8
It will feed my revenge.
The Merchant of Venice. Act iii, sc. 1, l. 56. [Shylock]

To diet my revenge.
Othello. Act ii, sc. 1, l. 303. [Iago]

9
Pistol: Wilt thou revenge?
Nym: By welkin and her star!
Pistol: With wit or steel?
Nym: With both the humours, I.
Merry Wives of Windsor. Act i, sc. 3, l. 100.

Let us knog our prains together to be revenge on this same scall, scurvy, cogging companion, the host of the Garter.
The Merry Wives of Windsor. Act iii, sc. 1, l. 122. [Evans] The only use of "scall."

May we, with the warrant of womanhood and the witness of a good conscience, pursue him with any further revenge?
The Merry Wives of Windsor. Act iv, sc. 2 l. 19. [Mrs. Ford]

10
Claudio: Choose your revenge yourself;
Impose me to what penance your invention
Can lay upon my sin: yet sinn'd I not
But in mistaking.
Don Pedro: By my soul, nor I:
And yet, to satisfy this good old man,
I would bend under any heavy weight
That he 'll enjoin me to.
Much Ado about Nothing. Act v, sc. 1, l. 282.

And so dies my revenge.
Much Ado about Nothing. Act v, sc. 1, l. 302. [Leonato]

Seek we no revenge.—*Henry V,* ii, 2, 174.

Cleave to no revenge.—*Titus Andronicus,* v, 2, 136.

No revenge.—*Merchant of Venice,* iii, 1, 98.

11
I follow him to serve my turn upon him.
Othello. Act i, sc. 1, l. 42. [Iago]

Let us be conjunctive in our revenge against him.
Othello. Act i, sc. 3, l. 375. [Iago] "Conjunctive" occurs again in *Hamlet,* iv, 7, 14.

A capable and wide revenge.
Othello. Act iii, sc. 3, l. 459. [Othello]

12
O, that the slave had forty thousand lives!
One is too poor, too weak for my revenge.
Othello. Act iii, sc. 3, l. 442. [Othello]

Had all his hairs been lives, my great revenge
Had stomach for them all.
Othello. Act v, sc. 2, l. 74. [Othello]

13
Revenge on him that made me stop my breath.
The Rape of Lucrece, l. 1180.

Is it revenge to give thyself a blow?
The Rape of Lucrece, l. 1823.

By this bloody knife,
We will revenge the death of this true wife.
The Rape of Lucrece, l. 1841.

14
No man but prophesied revenge for it.
Richard III. Act i, sc. 3, l. 186. [Dorset]

Whet me To be revenged.
Richard III. Act i, sc. 3, l. 332. [Gloucester]

15
O God! if my deep prayers cannot appease thee,
But thou wilt be avenged on my misdeeds,
Yet execute thy wrath in me alone.
Richard III. Act i, sc. 4, l. 69. [Clarence]

What God will have discover'd for revenge.
Titus Andronicus. Act iv, sc. 1, l. 74. [Marcus]

God will revenge it.—*Richard III,* ii, 1, 138; ii, 2, 14.

The gods revenge it!—*Pericles,* iii, 3, 24.

Heavens be revenged on me!—*III Henry VI,* i, 1, 57.
Let heaven revenge.—*Richard II,* i, 2, 40.

1 I am hungry for revenge,
And now I cloy me with beholding it.
Richard III. Act iv, sc. 4, l. 61. [Queen Margaret]

By decimation, and a tithed death—
If thy revenges hunger for that food
Which nature loathes—take thou the destined tenth.
Timon of Athens, v, 4, 31. [Senator] The only use of "decimation" and "tithed."

2
To revenge is no valour, but to bear.
Timon of Athens. Act iii, sc. 5, l. 39. [Senator]

What, madam! be dishonour'd openly,
And basely put it up without revenge?
Titus Andronicus. Act i, sc. 1, l. 432. [Saturninus]

Revenge it, as you love your mother's life,
Or be ye not henceforth call'd my children.
Titus Andronicus. Act ii, sc. 3, l. 114. [Tamora]

3
Which way shall I find Revenge's cave?
Titus Andronicus. Act iii, sc. 1, l. 271. [Titus]

If you will have Revenge from hell, you shall.
Titus Andronicus, iv, 3, 38. [Publius]

Thus, in this strange and sad habiliment,
I will encounter with Andronicus,
And say I am Revenge, sent from below
To join with him and right his heinous wrongs.
Knock at his study, where, they say, he keeps,
To ruminate strange plots of dire revenge;
Tell him Revenge is come to join with him,
To work confusion on his enemies.
Titus Andronicus. Act v, sc. 2, l. 1. [Tamora]

Tamora: I am Revenge: sent from the infernal kingdom,
To ease the gnawing vulture of thy mind,
By working wreakful vengeance on thy foes.
Come down and welcome me to this world's light;
Confer with me of murder and of death:
There 's not a hollow cave or lurking-place,
No vast obscurity or misty vale,
Where bloody murder or detested rape
Can couch for fear, but I will find them out;
And in their ears tell them my dreadful name,
Revenge, which makes the foul offender quake.
Titus: Art thou Revenge? and art thou sent to me,
To be a torment to mine enemies? . . .
Lo, by thy side where Rape and Murder stands;
Now give some surance that thou art Revenge,
Stab them, or tear them on thy chariot-wheels. . . .
Tamora: These are my ministers, and come with me.
Titus: Are these thy ministers? what are they call'd?
Tamora: Rapine and murder; therefore called so
Cause they take vengeance on that kind of men. . . .
Titus: O sweet revenge, now do I come to thee;
And if one arm's embracement will content thee,
I will embrace thee in it by and by. . . .
Tamora: Now he firmly takes me for Revenge. . . .
Chiron: Show me a villain that hath done a rape,
And I am sent to be revenged on him.
Tamora: Show me a thousand that have done thee wrong,
And I will be revenged on them all. . . .
Farewell, Andronicus: Revenge now goes
To lay a complot to betray thy foes.
Titus: I know thou dost: and, sweet Revenge, farewell.
Titus Andronicus. Act v, sc. 2, l. 30. "Wreakful" is repeated in *Timon of Athens,* iv, 3, 229. The only use of "lurking-place" and "surance." "Chariot-wheels" is repeated in *II Henry VI,* ii, 4, 13, and in *Julius Cæsar,* i, 1, 39.

Sweet revenge.—*Othello,* v, 2, 116.
Sweet as my revenge.—*Coriolanus,* v, 3, 45.
Poor revenge.—*The Rape of Lucrece,* l. 1736.
Sharp revenge.—*Titus Andronicus,* i, 1, 137.

4
Hope of revenge shall hide our inward woe.
Troilus and Cressida. Act v, sc. 10, l. 31. [Troilus]

5 As he does conceive
He is dishonour'd by a man which ever
Profess'd to him, why, his revenges must
In that be made more bitter.
The Winter's Tale. Act i, sc. 2, l. 454. [Polixenes]

She I can hook to me.
Winter's Tale. Act ii, sc. 3, l. 6. [Leontes]

The very thought of my revenges that way
Recoil upon me.
Winter's Tale. Act ii, sc. 3, l. 19. [Leontes]

REVERENCE

6 Though mean and mighty, rotting
Together, have one dust, yet reverence,
That angel of the world, doth make distinction
Of place 'tween high and low.
Cymbeline. Act iv, sc. 2, l. 246. [Belarius]

7
How may I reverently worship thee enough?
I Henry VI. Act i, sc. 2, l. 145. [Charles]

I hold thee reverently.—*III Henry VI,* ii, 2, 109.
Do it reverently.—*II Henry IV,* iv, 4, 37. The only uses of "reverently."

8 Thou art reverent
Touching thy spiritual function, not thy life.
I Henry VI. Act iii, sc. 1, l. 49. [Gloucester]

A very reverent body.—*The Comedy of Errors,* iii, 2, 91.
Reverent care.—*II Henry VI,* iii, 1, 34; *II Henry IV,* i, 2, 113.
Reverent hands.—*I Henry VI,* v, 3, 47.

9
Reverence to your calling makes me modest.
Henry VIII. Act v, sc. 3, l. 69. [Cranmer]

10
You beastly knave, know you no reverence?
King Lear. Act ii, sc. 2, l. 75. [Cornwall]

Deserve we no more reverence?—*Henry VIII,* iv, 2, 101.
Saving your reverence.—*The Merchant of Venice,* ii, 2, 24; 139; *I Henry IV,* ii, 4, 515; *Much Ado about Nothing,* iii, 4, 32; *Measure for Measure,* ii, 1, 92.

1
With a low submissive reverence.
The Taming of the Shrew. Induction, i, 53. [Lord]
Admired reverence.—*Timon of Athens,* v, 1, 54.
Holy reverence.—*Richard II,* iii, 3, 29.

REVOLT

See also Rebellion

2
Plant those that have revolted in the van.
Antony and Cleopatra. Act iv, sc. 6, l. 9. [Cæsar] The only use of "van."

3
It were fit
That all the plagues of hell should at one time
Encounter such revolt.
Cymbeline. Act i, sc. 6, l. 110. [Iachimo]
Barbarous and unnatural revolts.—*Cymbeline,* iv, 4, 6.
Gross revolt.—*Othello,* i, 1, 135.

4
Here 's fine revolution, an we had the trick to see 't.
Hamlet. Act v, sc. 1, l. 98. [Hamlet]
Full of . . . revolutions.—*Love's Labour 's Lost,* iv, 2, 70.
Revolution of the times.—*II Henry IV,* iii, 1, 46. "Revolution" is repeated in *Antony and Cleopatra,* i, 2, 129, and in *Sonnets,* lix.
All will revolt from me, and turn to him.
III Henry VI. Act i, sc. 1, l. 151. [King Henry]
Thou wilt revolt, and fly to him, I fear.
Richard III. Act iv, sc. 4, l. 478. [King Richard]
And will revolt from me to succour him.
Titus Andronicus. Act iv, sc. 4, l. 80. [Saturninus]

5
The hearts
Of all his people shall revolt from him.
King John. Act iii, sc. 4, l. 164. [Pandulph]
Pick strong matter of revolt and wrath
Out of the bloody fingers' ends of John.
King John. Act iii, sc. 4, l. 167. [Pandulph]
Our discontented counties do revolt;
Our people quarrel with obedience,
Swearing allegiance and the love of soul
To stranger blood, to foreign royalty.
This inundation of mistemper'd humour
Rests by you only to be qualified.
King John. Act v, sc. 1, l. 8. [King John] "Inundation" is repeated in v, 1, 48, and in *Romeo and Juliet,* iv, 1, 12; "mistemper'd" in *Romeo and Juliet,* i, 1, 94: "Mistemper'd weapons."
I am not glad that such a sore of time
Should seek a plaster by contemn'd revolt.
King John. Act v, sc. 2, l. 12. [Salisbury]

6
You degenerate, you ingrate revolts.
King John, v, 2, 151. See TREASON, 1561:14.
Revolts of England.—*King John,* v, 4, 7.

7
Now minutely revolts upbraid his faith-breach.
Macbeth. Act v, sc. 2, l. 18. [Angus] The only use of "minutely" and "faith-breach."
Given him the revolt.—*Macbeth,* v, 4, 12.

8
Revolt our subjects? that we cannot mend;
They break their faith to God as well as us.
Richard II. Act iii, sc. 2, l. 100. [King Richard]

REWARD

See also Compensation, Meed, Prize

9
Thy pains not used must by thyself be paid:
Proffers not took reap thanks for their reward.
All's Well that Ends Well. Act ii, sc. 1, l. 149. [King]
Here is my hand; the premises observed,
Thy will by my performance shall be served.
All's Well that Ends Well. Act ii, sc. 1, l. 204. [King] "Premises" is repeated in *The Tempest,* i, 2, 123, and in *Henry VIII,* ii, 1, 63.

10
I will reward thee
Once for thy spritely comfort, and ten-fold
For thy good valour.
Antony and Cleopatra. Act iv, sc. 7, l. 14. [Antony] "Tenfold" (unhyphenated) is used again in *Titus Andronicus,* iii, 2, 6: "Tenfold grief."

11
Oliver: Get you with him, you old dog.
Adam: Is 'old dog' my reward? Most true
I have lost my teeth in your service.
As You Like It. Act i, sc. 1, l. 85.

12
Ask me when thou wilt, and thou shalt have it.
I Henry IV. Act ii, sc. 4, l. 69. [Prince of Wales]
He that rewards me, God reward him!
I Henry IV. Act v, sc. 4, l. 166. [Falstaff]
God reward me for it!—*I Henry IV,* iii, 3, 54.
The gods reward your kindness!—*King Lear,* iii, 6, 5.
You gods, reward them.—*Timon of Athens,* ii, 2, 222.

13
Long since we were resolved of your truth,
Your faithful service and your toil in war;
Yet never have you tasted our reward,
Or been reguerdon'd with so much as thanks,
Because till now we never saw your face.
I Henry VI. Act iii, sc. 4, l. 20. [King] The only use of "reguerdon'd." "Reguerdon" occurs in the same play, iii, 1, 170, and in no other.

14
Come, follow, follow us for thy reward.
II Henry VI. Act ii, sc. 3, l. 108. [King]
I will reward you for this venturous deed.
II Henry VI. Act iii, sc. 2, l. 9. [Suffolk]
Thus will I reward thee, the Lent shall be as long again as it is.
II Henry VI. Act iv, sc. 3, l. 7. [Cade]

A thousand crowns for his reward.—*II Henry VI,* iv, 8, 70.
We give thee for reward a thousand marks.—*II Henry VI,* v, 1, 79.
Take this reward.—*II Henry VI,* i, 2, 85.
There 's thy reward: be gone.—*III Henry VI,* iii, 3, 233.

1
All things shall redound unto your good.
II Henry VI. Act iv, sc. 9, l. 47. [Buckingham] "Redound" is used in the first play and never again.

2 Promise them such rewards
As victors wear at the Olympian games.
III Henry VI. Act ii, sc. 3, l. 52. [George] "Olympian" is repeated in *Troilus and Cressida,* iv, 5, 194: "Olympian wrestling."

3
I will requite thy forwardness.
III Henry VI. Act iv, sc. 5, l. 23. [King Edward]
I will requite thy kindness.—*III Henry VI,* iv, 6, 10; iv, 7, 78.
I will requite your loves.—*Hamlet,* i, 2, 251.
I will requite you with as good a thing.
The Tempest. Act v, sc. 1, l. 169. [Prospero]
I will requite thee.—*Much Ado about Nothing,* iii, 1, 111.
I will thee requite.—*Henry V,* iii, 6, 51.
How shall I requite you?—*Timon of Athens,* v, 1, 76.
I shall never requite him.—*The Merchant of Venice,* i, 2, 70.
He will requite your wrongs.
Titus Andronicus. Act iii, sc. 1, l. 297. [Lucius]
See how he requites me!—*Richard III,* i, 4, 68.
I 'll requite it in the highest degree.
Twelfth Night. Act iv, sc. 2, l. 128. [Malvolio]

4
And am I thus rewarded?
Henry VIII. Act iii, sc. 1, l. 133. [Queen Katharine]
Lightly rewarded.—*Love's Labour 's Lost,* i, 2, 157. The only uses of "rewarded."

5
Hubert: I am much bounden to your majesty.
King John: Good friend, thou hast no cause to say so yet,
But thou shalt have; and creep time ne'er so slow
Yet it shall come for me to do thee good.
King John. Act iii, sc. 3, l. 29.

6
Armado: There is remuneration; for the best ward of mine honour is rewarding my dependents. . . .
Costard: Now will I look to his remuneration. Remuneration! O, that 's the Latin word for three farthings: three farthings—remuneration. 'What 's the price of this inkle?' 'One penny.' 'No, I 'll give you a remuneration:' why, it carries it. Remuneration! why, it is a fairer name than French crown.
Love's Labour 's Lost. Act iii, sc. 1, l. 132. "Inkle" (braid) occurs again in *The Winter's Tale,* iv, 4, 208, and *Pericles,* v, Gower, 8.
Costard: Pray you, sir, how much carnation ribbon may a man buy for a remuneration?
Biron: What is a remuneration?
Costard: Marry, sir, halfpenny farthing.
Love's Labour 's Lost. Act iii, sc. 1, l. 146.
Biron: There 's thy guerdon; go.
Costard: Gardon, O sweet gardon! better than remuneration, a 'leven-pence farthing better: most sweet gardon! I will do it, sir, in print. Gardon! Remuneration!
Love's Labour 's Lost. Act iii, sc. 1, l. 170. The only use of "'leven-pence." "Guerdon" is used only once more in the plays, in *Much Ado about Nothing,* v, 3, 5.
Is she not then beholding to the man
That brought her for this high good turn so far?
Yes, and will nobly him remunerate.
Titus Andronicus. Act i, sc. 1, l. 396. [Titus] The only use of "remunerate."

7
I desire but the reward of a villain.
Much Ado about Nothing. Act v, sc. 1, l. 250. [Borachio]
Reward me.—*Othello,* ii, 1, 317.

8
First Murderer: Remember our reward, when the deed is done.
Second Murderer: 'Zounds, he dies: I had forgot the reward.
Richard III. Act i, sc. 4, l. 126.
Say it is done,
And I will love thee, and prefer thee too.
Richard III. Act iv, sc. 2, l. 81. [King Richard]
Meantime, but think how I may do thee good,
And be inheritor of thy desire.
Richard III. Act iv, sc. 3, l. 33. [King Richard]

9
Hath any well-advised friend proclaim'd
Reward to him that brings the traitor in?
Richard III. Act iv, sc. 4, l. 517. [King Richard] "Well-advised" is used six times.
[He] shall reward you better for my life
Than Edward will for tidings of my death.
Richard III. Act i, sc. 4, l. 236. [Clarence]

10 At no slender warning,
You are like to have a thin and slender pittance.
The Taming of the Shrew. Act iv, sc. 4, l. 61. [Tranio] The only use of "pittance."

11 I 'll bring thee
To clustering filberts and sometimes I 'll get thee
Young scamels from the rock.
The Tempest. Act ii, sc. 2, l. 175. [Caliban] The only use of "filberts" and "scamels." The meaning of "scamels" has never been satisfactorily explained.

12 Let them be received
Not without fair reward.
Timon of Athens. Act i, sc. 2, l. 196. [Timon]
You . . . will find their fit rewards.—*Henry VIII,* iii, 2, 245.
Just reward.—*Pericles,* v, 3, 86.
Great rewards.—*III Henry VI,* ii, 1, 134.

High reward.—*III Henry VI,* v, 3, 10.

1 Look for thy reward
Among the nettles at the elder-tree.
Titus Andronicus. Act ii, sc. 3, l. 271. [Saturninus] "Elder-tree" occurs again in the same scene, l. 277, and nowhere else.

Look for your reward.—*Titus Andronicus,* iv, 3, 112.

Reward with love.—*Titus Andronicus,* i, 1, 82.

2
It may be worth thy pains.
Twelfth Night. Act i, sc. 2, l. 57. [Viola]

Prosper well in this,
And thou shalt live as freely as thy lord,
To call his fortunes thine.
Twelfth Night. Act i, sc. 4, l. 38. [Duke]

RHETORIC

3
Parolles: I spake but by a metaphor.
Clown: Indeed, sir, if your metaphor stink, I will stop my nose; or against any man's metaphor.
All's Well that Ends Well. Act v, sc. 2, l. 12.

What 's your metaphor?
Twelfth Night. Act i, sc. 3, l. 76. [Sir Andrew] The only uses of "metaphor."

4
Duke: Did he not moralize this spectacle?
Lord: O, yes, into a thousand similes.
As You Like It. Act ii, sc. 1, l. 44.

Thou hast the most unsavoury similes.
I Henry IV. Act i, sc. 2, l. 89. [Falstaff]

Take all these similes to your own command.
A Lover's Complaint, l. 227.

A good swift simile, but something currish.
The Taming of the Shrew. Act v, sc. 2, l. 54. [Petruchio]

Similes of comfort.—*All's Well that Ends Well,* v, 2, 26.

Want similes.—*Troilus and Cressida,* iii, 2, 183. The only uses of "simile" and "similes."

Unlike myself thou hear'st me moralize,
Applying this to that, and so to so.
Venus and Adonis, l. 712.

Come, you are too severe a moraler.
Othello. Act ii, sc. 3, l. 301. [Iago] The only use of "moraler."

5
It is a figure in rhetoric that drink, being poured out of a cup into a glass, by filling the one doth empty the other.
As You Like It. Act v, sc. 1, l. 46. [Touchstone]

6
With many holiday and lady terms.
I Henry IV. Act i, sc. 3, l. 46. [Hotspur]

He speaks holiday.
The Merry Wives of Windsor. Act iii, sc. 2, l. 69. [Host]

7
Sweet smoke of rhetoric!
Love's Labour 's Lost. Act iii, sc. 1, l. 64. [Armado]

Fie, painted rhetoric!
Love's Labour 's Lost. Act iv, sc. 3, l. 239. [Biron]

8
Taffeta phrases, silken terms precise,
Three-piled hyperboles, spruce affectation,
Figures pedantical; these summer-flies
Have blown me full of maggot ostentation.
Love's Labour 's Lost. Act v, sc. 2, l. 406. [Biron] "Three-piled" is repeated in *Measure for Measure,* i, 2, 33: "Three-piled piece." The only use of "pedantical." "Maggots" occurs twice in *Hamlet,* ii, 2, 181, and iv, 3, 24.

Terms unsquared, . . . Would seem hyperboles.
Troilus and Cressida. Act i, sc. 3, l. 159. [Ulysses] The only use of "unsquared" and the two uses of "hyperboles." "Hyperbolical" occurs twice: *Coriolanus,* i, 9, 51, and *Twelfth Night,* iv, 2, 29.

9
These are old fond paradoxes to make fools laugh in the alehouse.
Othello. Act ii, sc. 1, l. 39. [Desdemona]

Make paradoxes.—*Troilus and Cressida,* i, 3, 184. The only uses of "paradoxes."

This was sometime a paradox.
Hamlet, iii, 1, 115. See under PROOF.

You undergo too strict a paradox.
Timon of Athens, iii, 5, 24. See under DEED.

O paradox!—*Love's Labour 's Lost,* iv, 3, 254. The only uses of "paradox."

10
What strained touches rhetoric can lend.
Sonnets. No. lxxxii.

11
Balk logic with acquaintance that you have.
The Taming of the Shrew. Act i, sc. 1, l. 34. [Tranio] The only use of "logic."

Practise rhetoric in your common talk.
The Taming of the Shrew. Act i, sc. 1, l. 35. [Tranio]

RHEUM

12
That year, indeed, he was troubled with a rheum.
Antony and Cleopatra. Act iii, sc. 2, l. 57. [Enobarbus]

A salt and sorry rheum offends me.
Othello, iii, 4, 51. See under DISEASE.

I have a rheum in mine eyes.
Troilus and Cressida, v, 3, 105. See under DISEASE.

Do curse . . . the rheum.—*Measure for Measure,* iii, 1, 31.

13
A few drops of women's rheum, which are
As cheap as lies.
Coriolanus. Act v, sc. 6, l. 46. [Aufidius]

Threatening the flames With bisson rheum.
Hamlet. Act ii, sc. 2, l. 528. [First Player] "Bisson" (blinding) is repeated in *Coriolanus* ii, 1, 70, and iii, 1, 131.

Altering rheums.—*Winter's Tale,* iv, 4, 410.

Salt rheum.—*The Comedy of Errors,* iii, 2, 131.

Sleeping rheum.—*Richard II,* i, 4, 8.

14
Why holds thine eye that lamentable rheum,
Like a proud river peering o'er his bounds?
King John. Act iii, sc. 1, l. 22. [Constance]

How now, foolish rheum!
Turning dispiteous torture out of door!
I must be brief, lest resolution drop
Out at mine eyes in tender womanish tears.
King John. Act iv, sc. 1, l. 33. [Hubert] The only use of "dispiteous."

Villany is not without such rheum.
King John, iv, 3, 108. See WATER, 1637:11.

1
You, that did void your rheum upon my beard.
The Merchant of Venice, i, 3, 118. See under MONEY.

Spit and void his rheum.—*Henry V,* iii, 5, 52.

RHYME

See also Poetry, Verse

2
I 'll rhyme you so eight years together, dinners and suppers and sleeping-hours excepted: it is the right butter-women's rank to market.
As You Like It. Act iii, sc. 2, l. 101. [Touchstone] The only use of "sleeping-hours" and "butter-women." "Butter-woman" occurs in *All's Well that Ends Well,* iv, 1, 45; and "sleeping-hour" is used twice, in *A Midsummer-Night's Dream,* iii, 2, 8, and *Troilus and Cressida,* i, 3, 254.

You have put me into rhyme.
Cymbeline. Act v, sc. 3, l. 63. [Posthumus]

You might have rhymed.—*Hamlet,* iii, 2, 296. The only use of "rhymed."

3
A rhyme is but a ballad.
Henry V. Act v, sc. 2, l. 168. [King Henry]

These fellows of infinite tongue, that can rhyme themselves into ladies' favours, they do always reason themselves out again.
Henry V. Act v, sc. 2, l. 164. [King Henry]

4
How vilely doth this cynic rhyme!
Julius Cæsar. Act iv, sc. 3, l. 133. [Cassius] The only use of "cynic."

Rude, harsh-sounding rhymes.—*King John,* iv, 2, 150. The only use of "harsh-sounding."

5
Assist me, some extemporal god of rhyme, for I am sure I shall turn sonnet. Devise, wit; write, pen; for I am for whole volumes in folio.
Love's Labour 's Lost. Act i, sc. 2, l. 189. [Armado] The only use of "folio."

O, rhymes are guards on wanton Cupid's hose:
Disfigure not his slop.
Love's Labour 's Lost. Act iv, sc. 3, l. 58. [Biron] "Slop" or "slops" (loose breeches) is used four times. See under DRESS.

When shall you see me write a thing in rhyme?
Love's Labour 's Lost, iv, 3, 181. [Biron]

6
Thou hast given her rhymes.
A Midsummer-Night's Dream. Act i, sc. 1, l. 28. [Egeus]

Some love of yours hath writ to you in rhyme.
The Two Gentlemen of Verona. Act i, sc. 2, l. 79. [Julia]

Cited up in rhymes.—*Rape of Lucrece,* l. 524.

7
I can find out no rhyme to 'lady' but 'baby,' an innocent rhyme; for 'scorn,' 'horn,' a hard rhyme; for 'school,' 'fool,' a babbling rhyme; very ominous endings; no, I was not born under a rhyming planet.
Much Ado about Nothing. Act v, sc. 2, l. 36. [Benedick] "Rhyming" is repeated in *The Two Gentlemen of Verona,* ii, 1, 149.

Speak but one rhyme, and I am satisfied;
Cry but 'Ay me!' pronounce but 'love' and 'dove.'
Romeo and Juliet. Act ii, sc. 1, l. 9. [Mercutio]

8
You, born in these latter times,
When wit 's more ripe, accept my rhymes.
Pericles. Act i, Gower, l. 11.

9
Were some child of yours alive that time,
You should live twice; in it and in my rhyme.
Sonnets. No. xvii.

Not marble, nor the gilded monuments
Of princes, shall outlive this powerful rhyme.
Sonnets. No. lv.

I 'll live in this poor rhyme,
While he insults o'er dull and speechless tribes:
And thou in this shalt find thy monument,
When tyrants' crests and tombs of brass are spent.
Sonnets. No. cvii.

Barren rhyme.—*Sonnets,* xvi.

10
Rhymes
Full of protest, of oath and big compare.
Troilus and Cressida, iii, 2, 181. See under CONSTANCY.

There was never a truer rhyme.
Troilus and Cressida. Act iv, sc. 4, l. 22. [Pandarus]

II—Rhyme and Reason

11
Neither rhyme nor reason can express how much.
As You Like It. Act iii, sc. 2, l. 418. [Orlando] See under LOVE.

12
In the why and the wherefore is neither rhyme nor reason.
The Comedy of Errors. Act ii, sc. 2, l. 48. [Dromio of Syracuse]

13
Dumain: In reason nothing.
Biron: Something then in rhyme.
Love's Labour 's Lost. Act i, sc. 1, l. 99.

A dangerous rhyme, master, against the reason of white and red.
Love's Labour 's Lost. Act i, sc. 2, l. 112. [Moth]

14
In despite of the teeth of all rhyme and reason.
The Merry Wives of Windsor. Act v, sc. 5, l. 132. [Falstaff]

15
Valentine: What are you reasoning with yourself?
Speed: Nay, I was rhyming: 'tis you that have the reason.
The Two Gentlemen of Verona. Act ii, sc. 1, l. 149.

RIB

1
In a moment threw him and broke three of his ribs.
As You Like It. Act i, sc. 2, l. 135. [Le Beau]
It is the first time that ever I heard that breaking of ribs was sport for ladies.
As You Like It. Act i, sc. 2, l. 146. [Touchstone]
2
You may tell every finger I have with my ribs.
The Merchant of Venice, ii, 2, 114. See HUNGER, 736:9.
Over-weather'd ribs.—*The Merchant of Venice,* ii, 6, 18. The only use of "over-weather'd."
Fat ribs.—*King John,* iii, 3, 9.
3
I had thought to have yerk'd him under the ribs.
Othello. Act i, sc. 2, l. 5. [Iago] The only use of "yerk'd" (thrust).
4
[The wind] hath ruffian'd so upon the sea,
What ribs of oak, when mountains melt on them,
Can hold the mortise?
Othello. Act ii, sc. 1, l. 7. [Montado] The only use of "mortise."
5
Give me ribs of steel! I shall split all
In pleasure of my spleens.
Troilus and Cressida. Act i, sc. 3, l. 177. [Ulysses]
Rib of steel.—*II Henry IV,* ii, 3, 54.
Ribs of iron.—*Much Ado about Nothing,* iv, 1, 153.
Flinty ribs.—*King John,* ii, 1, 384; *Richard II,* v, 5, 20.
Rude ribs.—*Richard II,* iii, 3, 32.

RICHES

See also Poverty and Riches; Wealth

6
Such are the rich,
That have abundance and enjoy it not.
II Henry IV. Act iv, sc. 4, l. 107. [King Henry]
What call you rich?—*I Henry IV,* iii, 3, 90.
7
Make thee rich for doing me such wrong.
II Henry IV. Act i, sc. 1, l. 90. [Northumberland]
Making rich yourself.—*Timon of Athens,* iv, 3, 529.
8
Sweet hearts, we shall be rich ere we depart,
If fairings come thus plentifully in.
Love's Labour's Lost. Act v, sc. 2, l. 1. [Princess] The only use of "fairings."
Full of riches.—*II Henry VI,* iv, 7, 67.
Double riches.—*Richard III,* iv, 4, 319.
9
I'll promise thee she shall be rich
And very rich.
The Taming of the Shrew. Act i, sc. 2, l. 62. [Hortensio] "Very rich" is repeated in i, 1, 128.
Rich she shall be.—*Much Ado about Nothing,* ii, 3, 32.
Rich in beauty.—*Romeo and Juliet,* i, 1, 221.
Rich in hope.—*Sonnets,* xxix.
Rich in joy.—*Romeo and Juliet,* v, 1, 11.
Rich in matter.—*Romeo and Juliet,* ii, 6, 30.
Rich in sorrow.—*Timon of Athens,* iv, 2, 29.
Rich in titles.—*King John,* ii, 1, 491.
Rich in virtue.—*Troilus and Cressida,* i, 3, 30.
Rich with merchandise.—*Midsummer-Night's Dream,* ii, 1, 134.
10
O then, belike, you fancy riches more.
The Taming of the Shrew. Act ii, sc. 1, l. 16. [Katharina]
11
Rich, only to be wretched, thy great fortunes
Are made thy chief afflictions.
Timon of Athens. Act iv, sc. 2, l. 43. [Flavius]
Riches point to misery.—*Timon of Athens,* iv, 2, 32.
Live rich and happy.—*Timon of Athens,* iv, 3, 532.
Rich, not gaudy.—*Hamlet,* i, 3, 71. See under DRESS.
12
My riches are these poor habiliments.
The Two Gentlemen of Verona. Act iv, sc. 1, l. 13. [Valentine]
13
It was told me I should be rich by the fairies.
The Winter's Tale. Act iii, sc. 3, l. 121. [Shepherd]

RIDDLE

14
Riddle-like lives sweetly where she dies!
All's Well that Ends Well. Act i, sc. 3, l. 223. [Helena] The only use of "riddle-like."
15
This is a riddling merchant for the nonce;
He will be here, and yet he is not here:
How can these contrarieties agree?
I Henry VI. Act ii, sc. 3, l. 57. [Countess] The only use of "contrarieties." "Contrariety" occurs in *Coriolanus,* iv, 6, 73.
Riddling confession finds but riddling shift.
Romeo and Juliet, ii, 3, 56. The only uses of "riddling."
16
Let Æsop fable in a winter's night;
His currish riddles sort not with this place.
III Henry VI. Act v, sc. 5, l. 25. [Prince of Wales] The only mention of Æsop. For the other uses of "currish" see under CUR.
17
O, ho, I know the riddle.
King Lear. Act v, sc. 1, l. 37. [Goneril]
Moth: A wonder, master! here's a costard broken in a shin.
Armado: Some enigma, some riddle: come, thy l'envoy; begin.
Costard: No egma, no riddle, no l'envoy; no salve in the mail, sir: O, sir, plantain, a plain plantain!
Love's Labour's Lost. Act iii, sc. 1, l. 71.

The play of words is upon costard, meaning originally an apple (hence costermonger), and later, humorously, the head. "Enigma" occurs again in *Coriolanus,* ii, 3, 96. "L'envoy" is used five times in this scene and nowhere else. The only use of "plantain," though "plantain-leaf" occurs in *Romeo and Juliet,* i, 2, 52.

Much upon this riddle runs the wisdom of the world.

Measure for Measure. Act iii, sc. 2, l. 242. [Duke]

1
You have not the Book of Riddles about you, have you?

The Merry Wives of Windsor. Act i, sc. 1, l. 208. [Slender]

2
Lysander riddles very prettily.

A Midsummer-Night's Dream. Act ii, sc. 2, l. 53. [Hermia]

3
King Richard: What news with you?
Stanley: None good, my lord, to please you with the hearing;
Nor none so bad, but it may well be told.
King Richard: Hoyday, a riddle! neither good nor bad!

Richard III. Act iv, sc. 4, l. 458. "Hoy-day" (hyphenated) occurs also in *Timon of Athens,* i, 2, 137, and in *Troilus and Cressida,* v, 1, 73.

4
Malvolio: I may command where I adore;
But silence, like a Lucrece knife,
With bloodless stroke my heart doth gore:
M, O, A, I, doth sway my life.
Fabian: A fustian riddle!

Twelfth Night. Act ii, sc. 5, l. 115.

5
There is that in this fardel will make him scratch his beard.

The Winter's Tale. Act iv, sc. 4, l. 726. [Shepherd]

I'll hammer it out.

Richard II. Act v, sc. 5, l. 5. [King Richard]

RIDICULE

See also Mockery, Taunt

6 I must be laugh'd at,
If, or for nothing or a little, I
Should say myself offended.

Antony and Cleopatra. Act ii, sc. 2, l. 30. [Cæsar]

You'll be laughed at.

The Merry Wives of Windsor. Act i, sc. 1, l. 122. [Falstaff]

I will desire thee to laugh at my wife, that now laughs at thee.

The Merry Wives of Windsor. Act v, sc. 5, l. 180. [Page]

Camillo and Polixenes
Laugh at me, make their pastime at my sorrow.

Winter's Tale. Act ii, sc. 3, l. 23. [Leontes]

Laugh at me.—*Henry V,* v, 2, 198; *Richard II,* iii, 3, 171.

Laugh well at me.—*All's Well that Ends Well,* ii, 1, 90.

Laugh at 's.—*Antony and Cleopatra,* iii, 13, 114.

7
Man and master laugh my woes to scorn.

The Comedy of Errors. Act ii, sc. 2, l. 207. [Adriana]

Not a thing to laugh to scorn.—*As You Like It,* iv, 2, 19. See also *Macbeth,* v, 7, 12.

Laugh'st us here to scorn.—*I Henry VI,* iv, 7, 18.

Laughed to scorn.—*Venus and Adonis,* l. 4.

8
Dost thou jeer and flout me in the teeth?

The Comedy of Errors. Act ii, sc. 2, l. 22. [Antipholus of Syracuse] The only use of "jeer." For Flouting see under DEFIANCE.

Revenge the jeering.—*I Henry IV,* i, 3, 183. The only use of "jeering."

9
Brutus: You are well understood to be a perfecter giber for the table than a necessary bencher in the Capitol.
Menenius: Our very priests must become mockers if they shall encounter such ridiculous subjects as you are.

Coriolanus. Act ii, sc. 1, l. 90. The only use of "perfecter," giber," and "bencher."

Ridiculous boldness.—*Twelfth Night,* iii, 4, 40.
Ridiculous excess.—*King John,* iv, 2, 16.
Ridiculous monster.—*The Tempest,* ii, 2, 169.
Ridiculous smiling.—*Love's Labour's Lost,* iii, 1, 78.

Their rough carriage so ridiculous.

Love's Labour's Lost. Act v, sc. 2, l. 306. [Rosaline] "Ridiculous" is used sixteen times.

10
I am afeard you make a wanton of me.

Hamlet. Act v, sc. 2, l. 310. [Hamlet]

Come, you are pleasant.

Henry VIII. Act ii, sc. 3, l. 93. [Anne]

11
Scoffs and scorns and contumelious taunts.

I Henry VI. Act i, sc. 4, l. 39. [Talbot] "Contumelious" is repeated in *II Henry VI,* iii, 2, 204: "Contumelious spirit"; and in *Timon of Athens.* v, 1, 177: "Contumelious war." "Contumeliously" occurs in *I Henry VI,* i, 3, 58.

Scoff on, vile fiend and shameless courtezan!
I trust ere long to choke thee with thine own
And make thee curse the harvest of that corn.

I Henry VI. Act iii, sc. 2, l. 45. [Burgundy]

I have too long borne
Your blunt upbraidings and your bitter scoffs.

Richard III. Act i, sc. 3, l. 103. [Queen Elizabeth] "Upbraidings" is repeated in *The Comedy of Errors,* v, 1, 73.

Dry-beaten with pure scoff!—*Love's Labour's Lost,* v, 2, 263. The only use of "dry-beaten."

Scoffing his state.—*Richard II,* iii, 2, 163. The only use of "scoffing." See under KING.

Foul is most foul, being foul to be a scoffer.

As You Like It. Act iii, sc. 5, l. 62. [Rosalind] The only use of "scoffer."

12
With envious looks, laughing at thy shame.

II Henry VI. Act ii, sc. 4, l. 12. [Gloucester]

13 A wonder and a pointing-stock
To every idle rascal follower.

II Henry VI. Act ii, sc. 4, l. 46. [Duchess of Gloucester] The only use of "pointing-stock."

Let us not be laughing-stocks to other men's humours.
Merry Wives of Windsor. Act iii, sc. 1, l. 87. [Evans] The only use of "laughing-stocks."
He has made us his vlouting-stog.
Merry Wives of Windsor. Act iii, sc. 1, l. 120. [Evans] The only use of "vlouting-stog."
Full of gibes and vlouting-stocks.
Merry Wives of Windsor. Act iv, sc. 5, l. 82. [Evans] The only use of "vlouting-stocks."
Gibes and mockeries.—*The Merry Wives of Windsor,* iii, 3, 259. See under MOCKERY.
Ready in gibes.—*Cymbeline,* iii, 4, 161.

1
Had he none else to make a stale but me?
III Henry VI, iii, 3, 260. [Warwick]
I pray you, sir, is it your will
To make a stale of me amongst these mates?
The Taming of the Shrew. Act i, sc. 1, l. 57. [Katharina]

2
If I suspect without cause, why then make sport at me.
The Merry Wives of Windsor. Act iii, sc. 3, l. 159. [Ford]
Make sport at it.—*Much Ado about Nothing,* iii, 1, 58.
Make us public sport.—*The Merry Wives of Windsor,* iv, 4, 14.
Thou thinkest I am in sport.—*Much Ado about Nothing,* i, 1, 179.
Shameful sport.—*Comedy of Errors,* iv, 4, 108.
What is this? sport?—*Winter's Tale,* ii, 1, 58.
Let me for ever be your table-sport.
The Merry Wives of Windsor. Act iv, sc. 2, l. 169. [Ford] The only use of "table-sport."

3
From this day forth,
I 'll use you for my mirth, yea, for my laughter,
When you are waspish.
Julius Cæsar. Act iv, sc. 3, l. 48. [Brutus] For "waspish" see under WASP.
Cassius: Hath Cassius lived
To be but mirth and laughter to his Brutus,
When grief, and blood ill-temper'd, vexeth him?
Brutus: When I spoke that, I was ill-temper'd too.
Julius Cæsar. Act iv, sc. 3, l. 113.

4
That 's a shealed peascod.
King Lear. Act i, sc. 4, l. 219. [Fool] The only use of "shealed" (shelled).

5
A gibing spirit,
Whose influence is begot of that loose grace
Which shallow laughing hearers give to fools.
Love's Labour 's Lost, v, 2, 868. [Rosaline]
Gibing boys.—*I Henry IV,* iii, 2, 66. The only uses of "gibing."

6
A trim exploit, a manly enterprise,
To conjure tears up in a poor maid's eyes
With your derision! none of noble sort
Would so offend a virgin, and extort
A poor soul's patience, all to make you sport.
A Midsummer-Night's Dream. Act iii, sc. 2, l. 157. [Helena]
Have you conspired, have you with these contrived
To bait me with this foul derision?
A Midsummer-Night's Dream. Act iii, sc. 2, l. 196. [Helena]
Make mouths upon me when I turn my back;
Wink each at other; hold the sweet jest up.
A Midsummer-Night's Dream. Act iii, sc. 2, l. 238. [Helena]
When they next wake, all this derision
Shall seem a dream and fruitless vision.
A Midsummer-Night's Dream. Act iii, sc. 2, l. 270. [Oberon]
I have derision medicinable,
To use between your strangeness and his pride.
Troilus and Cressida. Act iii, sc. 3, l. 44. [Ulysses] "Medicinable" is repeated in i, 3, 91; in *Much Ado about Nothing,* ii, 2, 5, and *Cymbeline,* iii, 2, 33.
Scorn and derision.—*A Midsummer-Night's Dream,* iii, 2, 123. The only uses of "derision."

7
Do not believe
That, from the sense of all civility,
I thus would play and trifle with your reverence.
Othello. Act i, sc. 1, l. 131. [Othello]

8
Nor shall he smile at thee in secret thought,
Nor laugh with his companions at thy state.
The Rape of Lucrece, l. 1065.

9
Fleer and scorn at our solemnity.
Romeo and Juliet. Act i, sc. 5, l. 59. [Tybalt]
Never fleer and jest at me.
Much Ado about Nothing. Act v, sc. 1, l. 58. [Leonato] The only uses of "fleer."
And mark the fleers, the gibes, and notable scorns,
That dwell in every region of his face.
Othello. Act iv, sc. 1, l. 83. [Iago] The only use of "fleers."

10
Lucentio: I thank thee for that gird, good Tranio.
Hortensio: Confess, confess, hath he not hit you here?
Petruchio: A' has a little gall'd me, I confess.
The Taming of the Shrew. Act v, sc. 2, l. 58.
Men of all sorts take a pride to gird at me.
II Henry IV. Act i, sc. 2, l. 7. [Falstaff]
Being moved, he will not spare to gird the gods.
Coriolanus. Act i, sc. 1, l. 260. [Brutus]
Kindly gird.—*I Henry VI,* iii, 1, 131. The only uses of "gird" in this sense.

11
All our abilities, gifts, natures, shapes,
Severals and generals of grace exact,
Achievements, plots, orders, preventions,
Excitements to the field, or speech for truce,
Success or loss, what is or is not, serves
As stuff for these two to make paradoxes.
Troilus and Cressida. Act i, sc. 3, l. 179. [Ulysses] "Excitements" is repeated in *Hamlet,* iv, 4, 58.

12
If I do not gull him into a nayword, and make him a common recreation, do not think I have wit enough to lie straight in my bed.
Twelfth Night. Act ii, sc. 3, l. 145. [Maria] "Nay-word" (hyphenated) occurs also in *The Merry Wives of Windsor,* ii, 2, 131; v, 2, 5.

The most notorious geck and gull
That e'er invention play'd on.
Twelfth Night. Act v, sc. 1, l. 351. [Malvolio] See under DECEIT.
The geck and scorn O' th' other's villainy.
Cymbeline. Act v, sc. 4, l. 67. [Sicilius] The only uses of "geck."

RIGHT

1
By Hercules, I think I am i' the right.
Antony and Cleopatra. Act iii, sc. 7, l. 68. [Soldier]
Most right.—*Antony and Cleopatra,* iii, 13, 61.
He 's in the right.—*Measure for Measure,* ii, 1, 167.
He was in the right.—*Richard III,* v, 3, 275.
Am I not i' the right?—*Hamlet,* ii, 2, 429.
Thou 'rt i' the right.—*Twelfth Night,* ii, 3, 128.
You are in the right.—*Taming of the Shrew,* iv, 3, 157; *Hamlet,* i, 5, 126; *Measure for Measure,* ii, 1, 100; *Othello,* ii, 3, 339.
You are right.—*II Henry IV,* v, 2, 102.
You are not right.—*Coriolanus,* ii, 3, 54.
That 's right.—*Henry V,* v, 1, 1.

2
O God, that right should thus overcome might!
II Henry IV. Act v, sc. 4, l. 27. [Hostess]

3
With blood and sword and fire to win your right.
Henry V. Act i, sc. 2, l. 131. [Canterbury]
Win our right.—*III Henry VI,* i, 1, 37.

4
I think he held the right.
I Henry VI. Act ii, sc. 4, l. 38. [Suffolk]
Fall out right.—*I Henry VI,* ii, 3, 4.

5
God defend the right!
II Henry VI. Act ii, sc. 3, l. 55. [King Henry] *Love's Labour's Lost,* i, 1, 216; *Richard II,* i, 3, 101.
Heaven prosper the right!
The Merry Wives of Windsor. Act iii, sc. 1, l. 30. [Evans]
Pray that the right may thrive.
King Lear. Act v, sc. 2, l. 2. [Edgar]

6
Thou hast prevailed in right!
II Henry VI. Act ii, sc. 3, l. 102. [Peter]

7
I mean to take possession of my right.
III Henry VI. Act i, sc. 1, l. 44. [York]
Say, Henry, shall I have my right or no?
III Henry VI. Act ii, sc. 2, l. 126. [Edward]
Let 'em have their rights.
Henry VIII. Act iv, sc. 1, l. 9. [Gentleman]

8
Do right unto this princely Duke of York.
III Henry VI. Act i, sc. 1, l. 166. [Warwick] The only use of "do right."
Falstaff: Why, now you have done me right.
Silence: Do me right, And dub me knight.
II Henry IV. Act iv, sc. 3, l. 76.
It stands your grace upon to do me right.
Richard II. Act ii, sc. 3, l. 138. [Ross]
Do me right.—*Henry VIII,* ii, 4, 13; *Much Ado about Nothing,* v, 1, 149; *Titus Andronicus,* i, 1, 203.
Do me but right.—*III Henry VI,* iv. 1, 69.
Do me this right.—*The Taming of the Shrew,* i, 2, 239.
Do me this last right.—*Henry VIII,* iv, 2, 158.
Who would not do thee right?
King John. Act ii, sc. 1, l. 18. [Lewis]

9
For this down-trodden equity, we tread
In warlike march these greens before your town.
King John. Act ii, sc. 1, l. 241. [King Philip] The only use of "down-trodden." "Down-trod" occurs in *I Henry IV,* i, 3, 135: "The down-trod Mortimer."
There 's no equity stirring.—*I Henry IV,* ii, 2, 106.
Equity exiled.—*II Henry VI,* iii, 1, 146.
Yoke-fellow of equity.—*King Lear,* iii, 6, 39. The only uses of "equity."

10
In her right we came;
Which we, God knows, have turn'd another way,
To our own vantage.
King John. Act ii, sc. 1, l. 548. [King Philip]
You taught me how to know the face of right.
King John. Act v, sc. 2, l. 88. [Dauphin]
That right in peace which here we urge in war.
King John. Act ii, sc. 1, l. 47. [Constance]

11
Right, As snow in harvest.
Richard III. Act i, sc. 4, l. 248. [Murderer]
Right, you say true.—*Richard II,* ii, 1, 145.
Right, you have it.—*Titus Andronicus,* iv, 2, 24.
Thou hast spoke the right.—*Henry V,* ii, 1, 129.
You say not right.—*Much Ado about Nothing,* v, 1, 73.

12
I 'll win our ancient right in France again,
Or die a soldier, as I lived a king.
Richard III. Act iii, sc. 1, l. 92. [Prince]
Old right.—*King John,* v, 4, 61.

13
Your right of birth, your empery.
Richard III. Act iii, sc. 7, l. 136. [Buckingham] "Empery" is used six times.
Rights of memory.—*Hamlet,* v, 2, 400.

14
Right for right
Hath dimm'd your infant morn to aged night.
Richard III. Act iv, sc. 4, l. 15. [Queen]
O virtuous fight,
When right with right wars who shall be most right!
Troilus and Cressida, iii, 2, 178. [Troilus]

15
Here I hit it right.
Romeo and Juliet. Act ii, sc. 3, l. 41. [Friar Laurence]
Why, this hits right.—*Timon of Athens,* iii, 1, 5.
It falls right.—*Hamlet,* iv, 7, 71.
'Tis right.—*As You Like It,* ii, 1, 51; *Coriolanus,* ii, 1, 252.
'Tis my right.—*III Henry VI,* iv, 7, 65.
'Tis thy right.—*Venus and Adonis,* l. 1184.

16
Given to time your own dear-purchased right.
Sonnets. No. cxvii. The only use of "dear-purchased."
Customary rights.—*Richard II,* ii, 1, 195.
Customed right.—*II Henry VI,* v, 1, 188.
Dear rights.—*King Lear,* iv, 3, 46.

Gentle right.—*The Rape of Lucrece,* l. 545.
Great right.—*All's Well that Ends Well,* i, 1, 30.
Native right.—*III Henry VI,* iii, 3, 190.
Obedient right.—*All's Well that Ends Well,* ii, 3, 167.
True right.—*II Henry VI,* v, 2, 25; *Sonnets,* xvii.
Poor man's right.—*Pericles,* ii, 1, 123.

1
I then do most go right.
The Winter's Tale. Act iv, sc. 3, l. 18. [Autolycus]

II—Right and Wrong

2
King Henry, be thy title right or wrong,
Lord Clifford vows to fight in thy defence.
III Henry VI. Act i, sc. 1, l. 159. [Clifford]
If that be right which Warwick says is right,
There is no wrong, but every thing is right.
III Henry VI. Act ii, sc. 2, l. 131. [Prince]

3
And do him right that, answering one foul wrong,
Lives not to act another.
Measure for Measure. Act ii, sc. 2, l. 102. [Angelo]
Hooking both right and wrong to the appetite,
To follow as it draws!
Measure for Measure. Act ii, sc. 4, l. 176. [Isabella] The only use of "hooking."
Lucio: Right.
Duke: It may be right; but you are i' the wrong
To speak before your time.
Measure for Measure. Act v, sc. 1, l. 85.

4
To do a great right, do a little wrong.
The Merchant of Venice. Act iv, sc. 1, l. 216. [Bassanio]

5
Desdemona: Beshrew me, if I would do such a wrong
For the whole world.
Emilia: Why, the wrong is but a wrong i' the world; and having the world for your labour, 'tis a wrong in your own world, and you might quickly make it right.
Othello. Act iv, sc. 3, l. 78.

6
My kinsman, whom the king hath wrong'd,
Whom conscience and my kindred bids to right.
Richard II. Act ii, sc. 2, l. 114. [York]
I have had feeling of my cousin's wrongs
And labour'd all I could to do him right;
But in this kind to come, in braving arms,
Be his own carver and cut out his way,
To find out right with wrong, it may not be.
Richard II. Act ii, sc. 3, l. 141. [York] "Carver" is repeated in *The Winter's Tale,* v, 3, 30.

7
Your mother's hand shall right your mother's wrong.
Titus Andronicus. Act ii, sc. 3, l. 121. [Tamora]
Swear unto my soul to right your wrongs.
Titus Andronicus. Act iii, sc. 1, l. 279. [Titus]

8
Right and wrong,
Between whose endless jar justice resides.
Troilus and Cressida. Act i, sc. 3, l. 116. [Ulysses]
'Twixt right and wrong.—*Troilus and Cressida,* ii, 2, 171.
Right or wrong.—*Sonnets,* cxii.

RING

9
When thou canst get the ring upon my finger which never shall come off, . . . then call me husband.
All's Well that Ends Well. Act iii, sc. 2, l. 59. [Helena, reading] Repeated in v, 3, 313.
A ring the county wears,
That downward hath succeeded in his house
From son to son, some four or five descents
Since the first father wore it.
All's Well that Ends Well. Act iii, sc. 7, l. 22. [Helena]
Diana: Give me that ring. . . .
Bertram: I'll lend it thee, my dear; but have no power
To give it from me. . . .
It is an honour 'longing to our house,
Bequeathed down from many ancestors;
Which were the greatest obloquy i' the world
In me to lose.
Diana: Mine honour's such a ring. . . .
Bertram: Here, take my ring. . . .
Diana: On your finger in the night I'll put
Another ring, that what in time proceeds
May token to the future of our deeds.
All's Well that Ends Well. Act iv, sc. 2, l. 39. "Obloquy" is repeated in *I Henry VI,* ii, 5, 49.
He hath given her his monumental ring.
All's Well that Ends Well. Act iv, sc. 3, l. 21. [Lord] "Monumental" is repeated in *Othello,* v, 2, 5: "Monumental alabaster;" and in *Troilus and Cressida,* iii, 3, 153: "Monumental mockery."
Lafeu: Helen, that's dead,
Was a sweet creature: such a ring as this,
The last time e'er I took her leave at court,
I saw upon her finger.
Bertram: Hers it was not. . .
Countess: Son, on my life,
I have seen her wear it; and she reckon'd it
At her life's rate.
Lafeu. I am sure I saw her wear it.
Bertram: You are deceived, my lord; she never saw it:
In Florence was it from a casement thrown me,
Wrapp'd in a paper.
All's Well that Ends Well. Act v, sc. 3, l. 77.
Diana: O, behold this ring,
Whose high respect and rich validity
Did lack a parallel; yet for all that
He gave it to a commoner o' the camp,
If I be one.
Countess: He blushes, and 'tis it:
Of six preceding ancestors, that gem,
Conferr'd by testament to the sequent issue,
Hath it been owed and worn. This is his wife;
That ring's a thousand proofs.
All's Well that Ends Well. Act v, sc. 3, l. 191. "Preceding" is used only once again, in *Hamlet,* i, 1, 122.

1
Have you not been acquainted with goldsmiths' wives and conned them out of rings?
As You Like It. Act iii, sc. 2, l. 287. [Jaques]

2
Give me the ring of mine you had at dinner,
Or, for my diamond, the chain you promised. . . .
I pray you, sir, my ring or else the chain.
The Comedy of Errors. Act iv, sc. 3, l. 69. [Courtezan]

A ring he hath of mine worth forty ducats,
And for the same he promised me a chain:
Both one and other he denies me now. . . .
He rush'd into my house and took perforce
My ring away. This course I fittest choose;
For forty ducats is too much to lose.
The Comedy of Errors. Act iv, sc. 3, l. 84. [Courtezan]

3
Iachimo: Your ring may be stolen too. . . .
Posthumus: I do nothing doubt you have store of thieves; notwithstanding, I fear not my ring. . . .
Iachimo: I dare thereupon pawn the moiety of my estate to your ring; which, in my opinion, o'ervalues it something. . . . I will lay you ten thousand ducats to your ring. . . .
Posthumus: My ring I hold dear as my finger; 'tis part of it. . . . I dare you to this match: here 's my ring.
Cymbeline. Act i, sc. 4, l. 98. The only use of "o'ervalues."

Iachimo: The ring is won.
Posthumus: The stone 's too hard to come by.
Iachimo: Not a whit. . . . I now
Profess myself the winner of her honour,
Together with your ring. . . .
Posthumus: If you can make 't apparent
That you have tasted her in bed, my hand
And ring is yours.
Cymbeline. Act ii, sc. 4, l. 45.

Imogen: My boon is, that this gentleman may render
Of whom he had this ring. . . .
Cymbeline: That diamond upon your finger, say
How came it yours? . . .
Iachimo: By villany I got this ring.
Cymbeline. Act v, sc. 5, l. 135.

Take that light, beseech you,
Which I so often owe; but your ring first;
And here the bracelet of the truest princess
That ever swore her faith.
Cymbeline. Act v, sc. 5, l. 414. [Iachimo]

4
I have lost a seal-ring of my grandfather's worth forty mark.
I Henry IV. Act iii, sc. 3, l. 94. [Falstaff] The only use of "seal-ring."

Falstaff: He said my ring was copper.
Prince: I say 'tis copper.
I Henry IV. Act iii, sc. 3, l. 162.

5
Cranmer: By virtue of that ring, I take my cause
Out of the gripes of cruel men, and give it
To a most noble judge, the king my master.
Chamberlain: This is the king's ring.
Surrey: 'Tis no counterfeit.
Suffolk: 'Tis the right ring, by heaven.
Henry VIII. Act v, sc. 3, l. 99.

6
Crack'd many a ring of posied gold and bone,
Bidding them find their sepulchres in mud.
A Lover's Complaint, l. 45. The only use of "posied," meaning inscribed with a motto.

Breaking rings a-twain.—*The Rape of Lucrece,* l. 1495.

7
When this ring
Parts from this finger, then parts life from hence.
The Merchant of Venice. Act iii, sc. 2, l. 185. [Bassanio]

Portia: For your love, I 'll take this ring from you:
Do not draw back your hand; I 'll take no more;
And you in love shall not deny me this.
Bassanio: This ring, good sir, alas, it is a trifle!
I will not shame myself to give you this.
Portia: I will have nothing else but only this;
And now methinks I have a mind to it.
Bassanio: There 's more depends on this than on the value.
The dearest ring in Venice will I give you,
And find it out by proclamation:
Only for this, I pray you, pardon me.
Portia: I see, sir, you are liberal in offers:
You taught me first to beg; and now methinks
You teach me how a beggar should be answer'd.
Bassanio: Good sir, this ring was given me by my wife;
And when she put it on she made me vow
That I should neither sell nor give nor lose it.
Portia: That 'scuse serves many men to save their gifts.
And if your wife be not a mad-woman,
And know how well I have deserved the ring,
She would not hold out enemy for ever,
For giving it to me. Well, peace be with you.
Antonio: My lord Bassanio, let him have the ring:
Let his deservings and my love withal
Be valued 'gainst your wife's commandment.
Bassanio: Go, Gratiano, run and overtake him;
Give him the ring.
The Merchant of Venice. Act iv, sc. 1, l. 427.

Nerissa: I 'll see if I can get my husband's ring,
Which I did make him swear to keep for ever.
Portia: Thou mayest, I warrant. We shall have old swearing
That they did give the rings away to men;
But we 'll outface them, and outswear them too.
The Merchant of Venice. Act iv, sc. 2, l. 13. "Outswear" is repeated in *Love's Labour 's Lost,* i, 2, 67.

Portia: A quarrel, ho, already! what 's the matter?
Gratiano: About a hoop of gold, a paltry ring
That she did give me, whose posy was
For all the world like cutler's poetry
Upon a knife, 'Love me, and leave me not.'

Nerissa: What talk you of the posy or the value?
You swore to me, when I did give it you,
That you would wear it till your hour of death
And that it should lie with you in your grave:
Though not for me, yet for your vehement oaths,
You should have been respective and have kept it.
Gave it a judge's clerk! no, God's my judge,
The clerk will ne'er wear hair on's face that had it.
Gratiano: Now, by this hand, I gave it to a youth. . . .
Portia: You were to blame, I must be plain with you,
To part so lightly with your wife's first gift;
A thing stuck on with oaths upon your finger
And so riveted with faith unto your flesh.
I gave my love a ring and made him swear
Never to part with it; and here he stands;
I dare be sworn for him he would not leave it
Nor pluck it from his finger, for the wealth
That the world masters. . . .
Bassanio [Aside]: Why, I were best to cut my left hand off
And swear I lost the ring defending it.
Gratiano: My Lord Bassanio gave his ring away
Unto the judge that begg'd it. . . .
Portia: What ring gave you, my lord?
Not that, I hope, which you received of me.
Bassanio: If I could add a lie unto a fault,
I would deny it; but you see my finger
Hath not the ring upon it; it is gone.
Portia: Even so void is your false heart of truth.
By heaven, I will ne'er come in your bed
Until I see the ring. . . .
Bassanio: If you did know to whom I gave the ring,
If you did know for whom I gave the ring
And would conceive for what I gave the ring
And how unwillingly I left the ring,
When nought would be accepted but the ring,
You would abate the strength of your displeasure.
Portia: If you had known the virtue of the ring,
Or half her worthiness that gave the ring,
Or your own honour to contain the ring,
You would not then have parted with the ring. . . .
Nerissa teaches me what to believe:
I'll die for't but some woman had the ring.
Bassanio: No, by my honour, madam, by my soul,
No woman had it, but a civil doctor. . . .
Portia: Let not that doctor e'er come near my house:
Since he hath got the jewel that I loved,
And that which you did swear to keep for me,
I will become as liberal as you;
I'll not deny him any thing I have,
No, not my body, nor my husband's bed. . . .
Antonio: I once did lend my body for his wealth;
Which, but for him that had your husband's ring,
Had quite miscarried: I dare be bound again,
My soul upon the forfeit, that your lord
Will never more break faith advisedly.
Portia: Then you shall be his surety. Give him this
And bid him keep it better than the other.
Antonio: Here, Lord Bassanio; swear to keep this ring.
Bassanio: By heaven, it is the same I gave the doctor!
Portia: I had it of him: pardon me, Bassanio;
For, by this ring, the doctor lay with me. . . .
You are all amazed: . . . Portia was the doctor,
Nerissa there her clerk. . . .
Bassanio: Sweet doctor, you shall be my bedfellow:
When I am absent, then lie with my wife.

The Merchant of Venice. Act v, sc. 1, l. 146. "Posy," meaning the motto inscribed on the inside of a finger-ring, is used twice in this scene, and nowhere else in the plays. "Posied" occurs in *A Lover's Complaint,* l. 45 (see preceding quotation). The only use of "cutter." "Advisedly" is repeated in *I Henry IV,* v, 1, 114.

1 I pray thee, once to-night
Give my sweet Nan this ring: there's for thy pains.

The Merry Wives of Windsor. Act iii, sc. 4, l. 103. [Fenton]

Show her this ring.—*King Lear,* iii, 1, 47.

2
Gloucester: Vouchsafe to wear this ring.
Anne: To take is not to give.
Gloucester: Look, how this ring encompasseth thy finger,
Even so thy breast encloseth my poor heart;
Wear both of them, for both of them are thine.

Richard III. Act i, sc. 2, l. 202. The only use of "encompasseth."

Hold, take my ring.—*Richard II,* ii, 2, 92.

3
Give this ring to my true knight.

Romeo and Juliet. Act iii, sc. 2, l. 142. [Juliet]

Here, sir, a ring she bade me give you, sir.

Romeo and Juliet. Act iii, sc. 3, l. 163. [Nurse]

Why I descend into this bed of death,
Is partly to behold my lady's face;
But chiefly to take thence from her dead finger
A precious ring, a ring that I must use
In dear employment.

Romeo and Juliet. Act v, sc. 3, l. 28. [Romeo]

4
Rings put upon his fingers.

The Taming of the Shrew. Induction, sc. 1, l. 38. [Lord]

Upon his bloody finger he doth wear
A precious ring, that lightens all the hole,
Which, like a taper in some monument,
Doth shine upon the dead man's earthy cheeks.

Titus Andronicus. Act ii, sc. 3, l. 226. [Martius]

5 He left this ring behind him,
Would I or not: tell him I'll none of it.

Twelfth Night. Act i, sc. 5, l. 320. [Olivia]

Malvolio: Were you not even now with the Countess Olivia?
Viola: Even now, sir. . . .
Malvolio: She returns this ring to you, sir: you

might have saved me my pains to have taken it away yourself. . . . Receive it so. . . .
Viola: I left no ring with her: what means the lady? . . .
None of my lord's ring! why, he sent her none. . . .
O time! thou must untangle this, not I;
It is too hard a knot for me to untie!
Twelfth Night. Act ii, sc. 2, l. 1. The only use of "untangle." "Untangled" occurs in *Romeo and Juliet,* i, 4, 91.
I did send,
After the last enchantment you did here,
A ring in chase of you.
Twelfth Night. Act iii, sc. 1, l. 123. [Olivia] "Enchantment" is repeated in *The Winter's Tale,* iv, 4, 446.

1
Proteus: Go presently and take this ring with thee,
Deliver it to Madam Silvia:
She loved me well deliver'd it to me.
Julia: It seems you loved not her, to leave her token. . . .
Proteus: Well, give her that ring. . . .
Julia: How many women would do such a message? . . .
This ring I gave him when he parted from me,
To bind him to remember my good will.
The Two Gentlemen of Verona. Act iv, sc. 4, l. 76.
Julia: He sends your ladyship this ring.
Silvia: The more shame for him that he sends it me;
For I have heard him say a thousand times
His Julia gave it him at his departure.
Though his false finger have profaned the ring,
Mine shall not do his Julia so much wrong.
The Two Gentlemen of Verona. Act iv, sc. 4, l. 137.
Julia: O good sir, my master charged me to deliver a ring to Madam Silvia, which, out of my neglect, was never done.
Proteus: Where is that ring, boy?
Julia: Here 'tis; this is it.
Proteus: How! let me see:
Why, this is the ring I gave to Julia.
Julia: O, cry you mercy, sir, I have mistook:
This is the ring you sent to Silvia.
Proteus: But how camest thou by this ring? At my depart
I gave this unto Julia.
Julia: And Julia herself did give it me;
And Julia herself hath brought it hither.
The Two Gentlemen of Verona. Act v, sc. 4, l. 88.

RIOT

2
I wrote to you When rioting in Alexandria.
Antony and Cleopatra. Act ii, sc. 2, l. 71. [Cæsar] The only use of "rioting."
He's a sworn rioter.—*Timon of Athens,* iii, 5, 68. The only use of "rioter."

3
When that my care could not withhold thy riots,
What wilt thou do when riot is thy care?
II Henry IV. Act iv, sc. 5, l. 135. [King Henry]

4
What stir is this? what tumult's in the heavens?
I Henry VI. Act i, sc. 4, l. 98. [Talbot] See also under Noise.
What stir is this?—*The Two Gentlemen of Verona,* v, 4, 13.
King Henry: What tumult's this?
Warwick: An uproar, I dare warrant,
Begun through malice of the bishop's men.
I Henry VI. Act iii, sc. 1, l. 75.
All in uproar.—*Henry VIII,* i, 2, 36.
By uproar sever'd.—*Titus Andronicus,* v, 3, 68.
Greater uproar.—*The Rape of Lucrece,* l. 427.
Here's a goodly tumult!—*II Henry IV,* ii, 4, 219.
Civil tumult.—*King John,* iv, 2, 247.
Broach'd this tumult.—*III Henry VI,* ii, 2, 159.
This tumult to behold.—*The Rape of Lucrece,* l. 447. The only uses of "tumult."

5
And when he please to make commotion,
'Tis to be fear'd they all will follow him.
II Henry VI. Act iii, sc. 1, l. 29. [Queen]
To make commotion, as full well he can.
II Henry VI. Act iii, sc. 1, l. 358. [York]
Commotions, uproars, with a general taint
Of the whole state.
Henry VIII. Act v, sc. 3, l. 28. [Gardiner]
Consecrate commotion's bitter edge.
II Henry IV. Act iv, sc. 1, l. 93. [Westmoreland]

6
His knights grow riotous.
King Lear. Act i, sc. 2, l. 5. [Goneril]
Riotous appetite.—*King Lear,* iv, 6, 125.
Riotous feeders.—*Timon of Athens,* ii, 2, 168.
Riotous gentleman.—*Richard III,* ii, 1, 100.
Riotous head.—*Hamlet,* iv, 5, 101.
Riotous inn.—*King Lear,* i, 4, 265.
Riotous knights.—*King Lear,* ii, 1, 96.
Riotous madness.—*Antony and Cleopatra,* i, 3, 29.
Riotous tongue.—*II Henry VI,* iv, 1, 64.
Riotous youth.—*Measure for Measure,* iv, 4, 32. The only uses of "riotous."

7
Rank and not-to-be-endured riots.
King Lear. Act i, sc. 4, l. 223. [Goneril] The only use of the phrase.
There is no fear of Got in a riot.
The Merry Wives of Windsor. Act i, sc. 1, l. 37. [Evans]
Thou wouldst have plunged thyself
In general riot.
Timon of Athens. Act iv, sc. 3, l. 255. [Timon]

8
The riot of the tipsy Bacchanals.
A Midsummer-Night's Dream. Act v, sc. 1, l. 48. [Theseus, reading] Only use of "tipsy."
Egyptian Bacchanals.—*Antony and Cleopatra,* ii, 7, 110. The only uses of Bacchanals.
Too full of riot.—*Venus and Adonis,* l. 1147.

RIPENESS

9
Time shall bring to ripeness.
Henry VIII. Act v, sc. 5, l. 21. [Cranmer]
Ripeness is all.—*King Lear,* v, 2, 11. See under Death the Inevitable. Only uses of "ripeness."

We ripe and ripe.—*As You Like It,* ii, 7, 26. See under HOUR.

1
Ripe as the pomewater; who now hangeth like a jewel in the ear of caelo, the sky, the welkin, the heaven.
Love's Labour's Lost. Act iv, sc. 2, l. 4. The only use of "pomewater" (a kind of apple), and of "caelo."

Ripe to be a bride.—*Romeo and Juliet,* i, 2, 11.
Ripe for marriage-rite.—*Pericles,* iv, Gower, 17.
Ripe for stroke!—*Timon of Athens,* iv, 1, 23.

2
Macbeth Is ripe for shaking.
Macbeth. Act iv, sc. 3, l. 238. [Malcolm]

Ripe in fortune's womb.—*Richard II,* ii, 2, 10.
Ripe in mischief.—*Twelfth Night,* v, 1, 132.
Ripe in my device.—*Hamlet,* iv, 7, 65.
Full ripe.—*Henry V,* iii, 6, 130.
Reeling ripe.—*The Tempest,* v, 1, 279.

3
Stay the very riping of the time.
The Merchant of Venice. Act ii, sc. 8, l. 40. [Salarino] The only use of "riping."

4
Things growing are not ripe until their season,
So I, being young, till now ripe not to reason.
A Midsummer-Night's Dream. Act ii, sc. 2, l. 117. [Lysander]

RISING

5
Rise from thy stool.
Antony and Cleopatra. Act ii, sc. 7, l. 62. [Menenius]

I pray you, rise.—*Antony and Cleopatra,* v, 2, 115.
Willingly rise.—*III Henry VI,* i, 2, 41.
Rise again.—*III Henry VI,* ii, 6, 93.
Star-like rise.—*Henry VIII,* v, 5, 47. "Star-like" is repeated in *Timon of Athens,* v, 1, 66: "Star-like nobleness."
Rise and mutiny.—*Julius Cæsar,* iii, 2, 234.

6
The other side o' the city is risen.
Coriolanus. Act i, sc. 1, l. 48. [Citizen]

Risen up.—*I Henry VI,* i, 4, 102.
Risen from the place.—*King Lear,* ii, 4, 29.
Risen to the top.—*Pericles,* ii, 4, 23. The only uses of "risen."

7
I hope to see Romans as cheap as Volscians.
They are rising, they are rising.
Coriolanus. Act v, sc. 5, l. 249. [Servant]

Rising and cawing.—*A Midsummer-Night's Dream,* iii, 2, 22. The only use of "cawing."
Rising at thy name.—*Sonnets,* cli.
Rising in our throne.—*Richard II,* iii, 2, 50.
Rising up in arms.—*II Henry VI,* iv, 1, 93.
Still so rising.—*Henry VIII,* iv, 2, 62.

8
Hark, hark! the lark at heaven's gate sings,
And Phœbus 'gins arise,
His steeds to water at those springs
On chaliced flowers that lies;
And winking Mary-buds begin
To ope their golden eyes:
With every thing that pretty is,
My lady sweet, arise.
Cymbeline. Act ii, sc. 3, l. 21. [Cloten] The only use of "chaliced" and "Mary-buds" (marigolds).

9
I am glad I was up so late; for that 's the reason I was up so early.
Cymbeline. Act ii, sc. 3, l. 37. [Cloten]

To be up early and down late.
The Merry Wives of Windsor. Act i, sc. 4, l. 107. [Mrs. Quickly]

Is she not down so late, or up so early?
Romeo and Juliet. Act iii, sc. 5, l. 67. [Juliet]

Not to be abed after midnight is to be up betimes.
Twelfth Night. Act ii, sc. 3, l. 1. [Sir Toby]

10
Lo, here I lie, Never to rise again.
Hamlet. Act v, sc. 2, l. 329. [Laertes]

Never rise.—*I Henry IV,* i, 3, 74.

11
Rise from the ground like feather'd Mercury.
I Henry IV, iv, 1, 106. See under HORSEMANSHIP.

Why may not he rise as well as I?
I Henry IV. Act v, sc. 4, l. 128. [Falstaff]

12
An early stirrer, by the rood!
II Henry IV. Act iii, sc. 2, l. 3. [Shallow] The only use of "early stirrer." "Early stirrers" occurs in *Henry V,* iv, 1, 6.

Hector was stirring early.
Troilus and Cressida. Act i, sc. 2, l. 52. [Pandarus]

Stir with the lark to-morrow.
Richard III. Act v, sc. 3, l. 56. [King Richard]

13
Early to-morrow will we rise, and hence.
Julius Cæsar. Act iv, sc. 3, l. 230. [Cassius]

Wherefore rise you now?—*Julius Cæsar,* ii, 1, 234.

14
As from your graves rise up, and walk like spirits.
Macbeth. Act ii, sc. 3, l. 84. [Macduff]

Rise from death.—*I Henry VI,* i, 1, 64.
Now they rise again.—*Macbeth,* iii, 4, 80.

15
What is this
That rises like the issue of a king?
Macbeth. Act iv, sc. 1, l. 86. [Macbeth]

Rise from her bed.—*Macbeth,* v, 1, 5.

16
You must be so good, sir, to rise and be put to death.
Measure for Measure. Act iv, sc. 3, l. 29. [Pompey]

Rise and be hanged.—*Measure for Measure,* iv, 3, 23.

17
No doubt they rose up early to observe
The rite of May.
A Midsummer-Night's Dream. Act iv, sc. 1, l. 137. [Theseus]

Rose at an instant.—*As You Like It,* i, 3, 76.
Up he rose.—*Hamlet,* iv, 5, 52.

1
Wake my cousin Beatrice, and desire her to rise.
Much Ado about Nothing. Act iii, sc. 4, l. 1. [Hero]
Go, bid thy master rise and come to me.
Richard III. Act iii, sc. 2, l. 31. [Hastings]
Bid them rise.—*Troilus and Cressida,* v, 3, 42.
Tell him he must awake and that quickly too.
Measure for Measure. Act iv, sc. 3, l. 32. [Abhorson]
Awake, dear heart, awake! thou hast slept well; Awake!
The Tempest. Act i, sc. 2, l. 305. [Prospero]
I have been broad awake two hours and more.
Titus Andronicus. Act ii, sc. 2, l. 17. [Lavinia]

2
Do not rise yet.
Othello. Act iii, sc. 3, l. 462. [Iago]
I will not rise.—*Richard III,* ii, 1, 97.
Never rise.—*Venus and Adonis,* l. 480.
Thou shalt not rise.—*Venus and Adonis,* l. 710.

3
Rise, prithee, rise. Sit down.
Pericles. Act i, sc. 2, l. 59. [Pericles]
Arise, I pray you, rise.—*Pericles,* i, 4, 98.
Higher rise.—*Pericles,* i, 4, 9.
Gladly rise.—*Richard II,* v, 3, 105.

4
This day I 'll rise, or else add ill to ill.
Pericles. Act ii, sc. 1, l. 172. [Pericles]

5 Never will I rise up from the ground
Till Bolingbroke have pardon'd thee.
Richard II. Act v, sc. 2, l. 116. [Duchess of York]
Bolingbroke: Rise up, good aunt.
Duchess of York: Not yet, I thee beseech. . . .
Bolingbroke: Good aunt, stand up.
Duchess: Nay, do not say, 'stand up;'
Say 'pardon' first, and afterwards 'stand up.'
Richard II. Act v, sc. 3, l. 92.

6
The rest, that love me, rise and follow me.
Richard III. Act iii, sc. 4, l. 81. [Gloucester]
Rise, and lend thine ear.—*Richard III,* iv, 2, 80.
Rise and stand.—*Romeo and Juliet,* iii, 3, 89.
Rise and fall.—*Titus Andronicus,* ii, 4, 24; *Sonnets,* cli. See under FALL.
Rise up and fall.—*The Rape of Lucrece,* l. 466.

7
Young son, it argues a distemper'd head
So soon to bid good morrow to thy bed.
Romeo and Juliet. Act ii, sc. 3, l. 33. [Friar Laurence]
Thy earliness doth me assure
Thou art up-roused by some distemperature.
Romeo and Juliet. Act ii, sc. 3, l. 39. [Friar Laurence] The only use of "earliness" and "up-roused."

RITE

See also Ceremony

8
The great prerogative and rite of love.
All's Well that Ends Well, ii, 4, 42. See under LOVE.
Rites of love.—*I Henry VI,* i, 2, 113; *Richard III,* v, 3, 101.
Rites for which I love him.—*Othello,* i, 3, 258.
Love's rite.—*Sonnets,* xxiii.
True love's rite.—*Romeo and Juliet,* v, 3, 20.
Rites of tenderness.—*I Henry IV,* v, 4, 98.
Amorous rites.—*Romeo and Juliet,* iii, 2, 8.

9
Proceed, proceed: we will begin these rites,
As we do trust they 'll end, in true delights.
As You Like It. Act v, sc. 4, l. 203. [Duke]

10 Who is this they follow?
And with such maimed rites?
Hamlet. Act v, sc. 1, l. 241. [Hamlet]
The rites of war Speak loudly for him.
Hamlet. Act v, sc. 2, l. 410. [Fortinbras]
Rites of knighthood.—*Richard II,* i, 1, 75.

11 Do we all holy rites:
Let there be sung 'Non nobis' and 'Te Deum.'
Henry V. Act iv, sc. 8, l. 127. [King Henry] The only use of "Non nobis" and "Te Deum."
Holy rite.—*Much Ado about Nothing,* v, 4, 68; *The Tempest,* iv, 1, 17.

12
The rites of marriage shall be solemnized.
King John, ii, 1, 539. See under MARRIAGE.
Ceremonial rites of marriage.—*The Taming of the Shrew,* iii, 2, 6.

13 Do all rites
That appertain unto a burial.
Much Ado about Nothing. Act iv, sc. 1, l. 209. [Friar]
Rites of burial.—*Julius Cæsar,* v, 5, 77.
Funeral rite.—*Titus Andronicus,* v, 3, 196.

14
Yearly will I do this rite.
Much Ado about Nothing. Act v, sc. 3, l. 23. [Claudio]
Duty's rites.—*Richard II,* iv, 1, 210.

15 I 'll procure to come to thee
Where and what time thou wilt perform the rite.
Romeo and Juliet. Act ii, sc. 2, l. 145. [Juliet]
We have perform'd Our Roman rites.
Titus Andronicus. Act i, sc. 1, l. 142. [Lucius]
Noble rite.—*Hamlet,* iv, 5, 215.
True rites.—*Julius Cæsar,* iii, 1, 241.

16
There shall we consummate our spousal rites.
Titus Andronicus. Act i, sc. 1, l. 337. [Saturninus] "Spousal" is repeated in *Henry V,* v, 2, 390.
Nuptial rites.—*The Merchant of Venice,* ii, 9, 6.

RIVALRY

See also Emulation

17
These three world-sharers, these competitors,
Are in thy vessel.
Antony and Cleopatra. Act ii, sc. 7, l. 76. [Menas] The only use of "world-sharers."
And every hour more competitors
Flock to their aid.
Richard III, iv, 5, 506. [Messenger]
The competitors enter.—*Twelfth Night,* iv, 2, 12.
Myself in counsel, his competitor.
The Two Gentlemen of Verona. Act ii, sc. 6, l. 35. [Proteus]

Know ye not, in Rome,
How furious and impatient they be,
And cannot brook competitors in love?
Titus Andronicus. Act ii, sc. 1, l. 75. [Aaron]

Competitors in oath.—*Love's Labour's Lost,* ii, 1, 82.
Great competitor.—*Antony and Cleopatra,* i, 4, 3.
Poor competitor.—*Titus Andronicus,* i, 1, 63.
My competitor.—*Antony and Cleopatra,* v, 1, 42. The only uses of "competitor" and "competitors."

1
World, thou hast a pair of chaps, no more;
And throw between them all the food thou hast,
They 'll grind the one the other.
Antony and Cleopatra. Act iii, sc. 5, l. 14. [Enobarbus]

I must perforce
Have shown to thee such a declining day,
Or look on thine; we could not stall together
In the whole world.
Antony and Cleopatra. Act v, sc. 1, l. 37. [Cæsar]

2 Think not, Percy,
To share with me in glory any more:
Two stars keep not their motion in one sphere;
Nor can one England brook a double reign.
I Henry IV. Act v, sc. 4, l. 64. [Prince of Wales]

3
Great rivals in our youngest daughter's love,
Long in our court have made their amorous sojourn.
King Lear. Act i, sc. 1, l. 47. [King Lear]

Rivals in my love.—*The Taming of the Shrew,* i, 2, 122.
Rival of my love.—*The Taming of the Shrew,* i, 2, 142.
Rivals of my watch.—*Hamlet,* i, 1, 13.

4
We first address towards you, who with this king
Hath rivall'd for our daughter.
King Lear. Act i, sc. 1, l. 193. [Lear] The only use of "rivall'd."

5
You both are rivals, and love Hermia;
And now both rivals, to mock Helena.
A Midsummer-Night's Dream. Act iii, sc. 2, l. 156. [Helena]

'Tis thy rival.—*The Two Gentlemen of Verona,* iv, 4, 203.
Happy rivals.—*Taming of the Shrew,* i, 1, 119.
Testy rivals.—*A Midsummer-Night's Dream,* iii, 2, 358.
Rival enemies.—*A Midsummer-Night's Dream,* iv, 1, 147.

6
He is not emulous.
Troilus and Cressida, ii, 3, 242. [Nestor]

Emulous factions.—*Troilus and Cressida,* ii, 3, 79.
Emulous honour.—*Troilus and Cressida,* iv, 1, 28.
Emulous missions.—*Troilus and Cressida,* iii, 3, 189. "Emulous" is used only in this play.

RIVER

See also Current, Stream

7
The river hath thrice flow'd, no ebb between.
II Henry IV. Act iv, sc. 4, l. 125. [Clarence]

8
With plenteous rivers and wide-skirted meads.
King Lear. Act i, sc. 1, l. 66. [King Lear] The only use of "wide-skirted."

Fruitful river.—*Hamlet,* i, 2, 80.
Peculiar river.—*Measure for Measure,* i, 2, 91.
Pelting river.—*A Midsummer-Night's Dream,* ii, 1, 91.
Silver rivers.—*Richard II,* iii, 2, 107.
Slow rivers.—*The Rape of Lucrece,* l. 1738.
Tributary rivers.—*Cymbeline,* iv, 2, 36.
Wild river.—*Henry VIII,* iii, 2, 198.
River of blood.—*Titus Andronicus,* ii, 4, 22; *Coriolanus,* i, 1, 139.
Rivers of remorse.—*King John,* iv, 3, 110.

9
To shallow rivers, to whose falls
Melodious birds sings madrigals;
There will we make our peds of roses,
And a thousand fragrant posies.
The Merry Wives of Windsor. Act iii, sc. 1, l. 17. [Evans] The only use of "posies." Evans is quoting some lines by Christopher Marlowe which are included in *The Passionate Pilgrim,* l. 359.

II—Individual Rivers

10 They take the flow o' the Nile
By certain scales i' the pyramid; they know,
By the height, the lowness, or the mean, if dearth
Or foison follow: the higher Nilus swells,
The more it promises: as it ebbs, the seedsman
Upon the slime and ooze scatters his grain,
And shortly comes to harvest.
Antony and Cleopatra. Act ii, sc. 7, l. 20. [Antony] The only use of "seedsman." The Nile is mentioned five times in this play, and also in *Cymbeline,* iii, 4, 37.

E'en as the o'erflowing Nilus presageth famine.
Antony and Cleopatra. Act i, sc. 2, l. 49. [Charmian] The only use of "o'erflowing." Nilus occurs five times in this play, and in no other.

11
And Cydnus swell'd above the banks, or for
The press of boats or pride.
Cymbeline. Act ii, sc. 4, l. 71. [Iachimo]

I am again for Cydnus.—*Antony and Cleopatra,* v, 2, 228.
Upon the river of Cydnus.—*Antony and Cleopatra,* ii, 2, 192.

12
On the gentle Severn's sedgy bank.
I Henry IV. Act i, sc. 3, l. 98. [Hotspur] The only use of "sedgy."

Swift Severn's flood;
Who then, affrighted with their bloody looks,

Ran fearfully among the trembling reeds.
I Henry IV. Act i, sc. 3, l. 103. [Hotspur]
Sandy-bottom'd Severn.—*I Henry IV*, iii, 1, 66. The only use of "sandy-bottom'd."
Cross'd the Severn.—*Cymbeline*, iii, 5, 17.
From Trent to Severn.—*I Henry IV*, iii, 1, 74.

1
See how this river comes me cranking in,
And cuts me from the best of all my land
A huge half-moon, a monstrous cantle out.
I'll have the current in this place damm'd up;
And here the smug and silver Trent shall run
In a new channel, fair and evenly;
It shall not wind with such a deep indent,
To rob me of so rich a bottom here.
I Henry IV. Act iii, sc. 1, l. 98. [Hotspur] The only use of "cranking." "Indent" occurs again in i, 3, 87, and in no other play. "Cantle" is repeated in *Antony and Cleopatra*, iii, 10, 6, and "smug" in *The Merchant of Venice*, iii, 1, 49. The Trent is mentioned four times in this scene, and nowhere else.

2
Did seat the French Beyond the river Sala.
Henry V, i, 2, 62. The Sala is mentioned twice more in this scene and nowhere else. The Elbe is referred to both times in connection with the Sala, and not again.

3
'Tis certain he hath pass'd the river Somme.
Henry V. Act iii, sc. 5, l. 1. [French King] The only mention of the Somme.

4
There is a river in Macedon; and there is also moreover a river at Monmouth: it is called Wye at Monmouth; but it is out of my prains what is the name of the other river; but 'tis all one, 'tis alike as my fingers is to my fingers, and there is salmons in both.
Henry V. Act iv, sc. 7, l. 28. [Fluellen] The only use of "salmons." The Wye is mentioned again in l. 111 of the same scene, and in *I Henry IV*, iii, 1, 65.

5
Kill and knock down! throw them into Thames.
II Henry VI. Act iv, sc. 8, l. 2. [Cade]
Thames side.—*The Merry Wives of Windsor*, iii, 3, 16.
Thames water.—*The Merry Wives of Windsor*, iii, 5, 23. The Thames is mentioned five times in *The Merry Wives of Windsor*, once in *II Henry VI*, and once in *Henry V*.

6
The troubled Tiber chafing with her shores.
Julius Cæsar. Act i, sc. 2, l. 101. [Cassius] The Tiber is mentioned five times in this play.
Let Rome in Tiber melt!—*Antony and Cleopatra*, i, 1, 33.
I would they were in Tiber!—*Coriolanus*, iii, 1, 262.
Allaying Tiber.—*Coriolanus*, ii, 1, 53.

7
The Pyrenean and the river Po.
King John. Act i, sc. 1, l. 203. [Bastard] The only mention of the Po, and use of "Pyrenean."

8
Shouldst thou take the river Styx,
I would swim after.
Troilus and Cressida. Act v, sc. 4, l. 20. [Troilus]
Dreadful shore of Styx.—*Titus Andronicus*, i, 1, 88. The only mention of the Styx. "Styga" is used in *Titus Andronicus*, ii, 1, 135, and "Stygian" in *Troilus and Cressida*, iii, 2, 10.
The Avon is not mentioned by Shakespeare, but a perfect description of the river in flood, as seen from the old Clopton Bridge, erected in 1490 and still standing, is given in *The Rape of Lucrece*, ll. 1667–73.

ROAD

9
Go hie thee presently, post to the road.
The Comedy of Errors. Act iii, sc. 2, l. 152. [Antipholus of Syracuse]
I must unto the road, to disembark
Some necessaries that I needs must use.
The Two Gentlemen of Verona. Act ii, sc. 4, l. 187. [Proteus] "Disembark" is repeated in *Othello*, ii, 1, 210.
Come to road.—*The Merchant of Venice*, v, 1, 288.

10
Ready, when time shall prompt them, to make road
Upon 's again.
Coriolanus. Act iii, sc. 1, l. 5. [Coriolanus]
Make road upon us.—*Henry V*, i, 2, 138.

11
You know the very road into his kindness,
And cannot lose your way.
Coriolanus. Act v, sc. 1, l. 59. [Brutus]
I am out of the road.—*Pericles*, iv, 5, 9.

12
At last, with easy roads, he came to Leicester.
Henry VIII. Act iv, sc. 2, l. 17. [Griffith]
Common road.—*As You Like It*, ii, 3, 33.
London road.—*I Henry IV*, ii, 1, 16.
Road of casualty.—*The Merchant of Venice*, ii, 9, 30.

ROARING

13
Roaring for a chamber-pot.
Coriolanus. Act ii, sc. 1, l. 85. [Menenius] The only use of "chamber-pot."
Roaring for Troilus.—*Troilus and Cressida*, v, 5, 37.
Roaring loud.—*I Henry IV*, i, 3, 192.
Roars so loud.—*Hamlet*, iii, 4, 52.

14
How the rogue roar'd!
I Henry IV. Act ii, sc. 2, l. 118. [Poins]
Roared for mercy.—*I Henry IV*, ii, 4, 286.

15
Falstaff: Come, prick me Bullcalf till he roar again.
Bullcalf: O Lord! good my lord captain,—
Falstaff: What, dost thou roar before thou art pricked?
II Henry IV. Act iii, sc. 2, l. 187.
Is this a place to roar in?
Henry VIII. Act v, sc. 4, l. 7. [Porter]

1 Roars As doth the lion in the Capitol.
Julius Cæsar, i, 3, 74. See under NIGHT.

2 I will roar you as gently as any sucking dove; I will roar you an 'twere any nightingale.
A Midsummer-Night's Dream, i, 2, 84. See under LION.
Well roared.—*A Midsummer-Night's Dream*, v, 1, 270.

3 Nay, lay thee down and roar.
Othello. Act v, sc. 2, l. 198. [Emilia]

4 What cares these roarers for the name of king?
The Tempest. Act i, sc. 1, l. 18. [Boatswain] The only use of "roarers."

5 The fire and cracks
Of sulphurous roaring the most mighty Neptune
Seem to besiege.
The Tempest. Act i, sc. 2, l. 203. [Ariel]

6 I will plague them all, Even to roaring.
The Tempest, iv, 1, 193. See under PLAGUE.
Make thee roar.—*The Tempest*, i, 2, 370.
Hark, they roar!—*The Tempest*, iv, 1, 262.

7 How the poor souls roared, and the sea mocked them; and how the poor gentleman roared and the bear mocked him, both roaring louder than the sea or weather.
Winter's Tale. Act iii, sc. 3, l. 101. [Clown]

ROBBER

See also Thief

8 I 'll rob none but myself; and let me die, Stealing so poorly.
Cymbeline. Act iv, sc. 2, l. 15. [Imogen]
Thou art a robber, A law-breaker, a villain.
Cymbeline. Act iv, sc. 2, l. 75. [Cloten] The only use of "law-breaker."

9 Who, I rob? I a thief? not I, by my faith.
I Henry IV. Act i, sc. 2, l. 153. [Prince of Wales]
I am accursed to rob in that thief's company.
I Henry IV. Act ii, sc. 2, l. 10. [Falstaff]
Wilt thou rob this leathern jerkin, crystal-button, not-pated, agate-ring, puke-stocking, caddis-garter, smooth-tongue, Spanish-pouch?
I Henry IV. Act ii, sc. 4, l. 77. [Prince of Wales] A succession of unique phrases: "crystal-button," "not-pated," "agate-ring," "puke-stocking," "caddis-garter," "smooth-tongue," and "Spanish-pouch." An outstanding example of Shakespeare's facility in phrase-coining.

10 Sheriff: There are two gentlemen
Have in this robbery lost three hundred marks.
Prince: It may be so: if he have robb'd these men,
He shall be answerable.
I Henry IV. Act ii, sc. 4, l. 568. "Answerable" is repeated in *The Taming of the Shrew*, ii, 1, 361, and in *Othello*, i, 3, 351.
Prince: I . . . may do anything.
Falstaff: Rob me the exchequer the first thing thou doest, and do it with unwashed hands too.
I Henry IV. Act iii, sc. 3, l. 203. "Unwashed" is repeated in *King John*, iv, 2, 201, and in *Romeo and Juliet*, i, 5, 5.

11 Which pillage they with merry march bring home.
Henry V, i, 2, 195. [Westmoreland]
Pillage and robbery.—*Henry V*, iv, 1, 175. "Pillage" is used five times.

12 To be executed for robbing a church.
Henry V. Act iii, sc. 6, l. 106. [Fluellen]
I should rob the deathsman of his fee.
II Henry VI. Act iii, sc. 2, l. 217. [Warwick] "Death's-man" occurs in *King Lear*, iv, 6, 263.
Must I rob the law?—*King John*, iv, 3, 78.
Rob our passengers.—*Richard II*, v, 3, 9.

13 Nor knows he how to live but by the spoil,
Unless by robbing of your friends and us.
II Henry VI. Act iv, sc. 8, l. 41. [Clifford]

14 Where I am robb'd and bound,
There must I be unloosed.
Henry VIII. Act ii, sc. 4, l. 146. [Wolsey] The only use of "unloosed."

15 Iago: 'Zounds, sir, you 're robb'd; for shame, put on your gown. . . .
Brabantio: What tell'st thou me of robbing? this is Venice.
Othello. Act i, sc. 1, l. 85.
Robb'd and ransack'd by injurious theft.
The Rape of Lucrece, l. 838.
I am robbed, sir, and beaten.
The Winter's Tale. Act iv, sc. 3, l. 64. [Autolycus]

16 The robb'd that smiles steals something from the thief.
Othello. Act i, sc. 3, l. 208. [Duke]
He that is robb'd, not wanting what is stol'n,
Let him not know 't and he 's not robb'd at all.
Othello. Act iii, sc. 3, l. 342. [Othello]

17 We would purge the land of these drones, that rob the bee of her honey.
Pericles. Act ii, sc. 1, l. 50. [Fisherman]
Rob the Hybla bees.—*Julius Cæsar*, v, 1, 34.
Rob the bee-hives.—*II Henry VI*, iv, 1, 109.

18 When 's god's asleep, he 'll rob his bottle.
The Tempest. Act ii, sc. 2, l. 155. [Trinculo]
These three have robb'd me.—*The Tempest*, v, 1, 272.

19 Large-handed robbers your grave masters are,
And pill by law.
Timon of Athens. Act iv, sc. 1, l. 11. [Timon] The only use of "large-handed" and of "pill" in the sense of pillage.
Supporting robbers.—*Julius Cæsar*, iv, 3, 23. The only use of "supporting."

1
Rob one another. There 's more gold. Cut throats.
Timon of Athens. Act iv, sc. 3, l. 448. [Timon]
Rob in the behalf of charity.
Troilus and Cressida, v, 3, 22. See under JUSTICE.
Rob him of his fair.—*Venus and Adonis,* l. 1086.
Rob thee of a kiss.—*Venus and Adonis,* l. 723.
2
Stand, sir, and show us that you have about ye:
If not, we 'll make you sit and rifle you.
The Two Gentlemen of Verona. Act iv, sc. 1, l. 3. [Outlaw] The only use of "rifle."

ROBE

See also Dress

3
When old robes are worn out, there are members to make new.
Antony and Cleopatra, i, 2, 171. See under WIFE.
Our old robes sit easier than our new.
Macbeth. Act ii, sc. 4, l. 38. [Macduff]
Easy robes.—*I Henry IV,* v, 1, 12.
4
The intertissued robe of gold and pearl.
Henry V, iv, 1, 279. See under KING. The only use of "intertissued."
Best robes.—*Romeo and Juliet,* iv, 1, 110.
Richest robes.—*II Henry VI,* ii, 4, 108.
Sober robes.—*Taming of the Shrew,* i, 2, 132.
Sweet robe.—*I Henry IV,* i, 2, 49.
Unreverent robes.—*The Taming of the Shrew,* iii, 2, 114.
Robe pontifical.—*I Henry IV,* iii, 2, 56.
Giant's robe.—*Macbeth,* v, 2, 21.
Judge's robe.—*Measure for Measure,* ii, 2, 61.
Give me my robe.—*Antony and Cleopatra,* v, 2, 283; *Julius Cæsar,* ii, 2, 107; *Pericles,* v, 1, 224.
5 My poor soldiers tell me, yet ere night
They 'll be in fresher robes.
Henry V. Act iv, sc. 3, l. 116. [King Henry]
6
Away with these disgraceful wailing robes!
I Henry VI. Act i, sc. 1, l. 86. [Bedford]
Thy scarlet robes as a child's bearing-cloth
I 'll use to carry thee out of this place.
I Henry VI. Act i, sc. 3, l. 42. [Gloucester]
A bearing-cloth for a squire's child!
The Winter's Tale, iii, 3, 119. The only uses of "bearing-cloth."
7
Putting on so new a fashion'd robe.
King John. Act iv, sc. 2, l. 27. [Salisbury]
New robes.—*Romeo and Juliet,* iii, 2, 30.
8
What shalt thou exchange for rags? robes; for tittles? titles; for thyself? me.
Love's Labour's Lost. Act iv, sc. 1, l. 85. [Boyet] The only use of "tittles" (points or dots).
9
Why do you dress me In borrow'd robes?
Macbeth. Act i, sc. 3, l. 109. [Macbeth]
10
Finely attired in a robe of white.
The Merry Wives of Windsor. Act iv, sc. 4, l. 72. [Mrs. Page]
Pure white robes.—*Winter's Tale,* iii, 3, 22.
11
What should I don this robe, and trouble you?
Titus Andronicus. Act i, sc. 1, l. 189. [Titus] The only use of "don."
12 Sure this robe of mine
Does change my disposition.
The Winter's Tale, iv, 4, 134. [Perdita]

ROCK

13
We were encounter'd by a mighty rock.
The Comedy of Errors, i, 1, 102. [Ægeon]
Merchant-marring rocks.—*The Merchant of Venice,* iii, 2, 274. Only use of the phrase.
Dreadful rock.—*II Henry VI,* iii, 2, 91.
Gutter'd rocks.—*Othello,* ii, 1, 69. The only use of "gutter'd."
Hard rock.—*The Tempest,* i, 2, 343.
Huge rocks.—*The Rape of Lucrece,* l. 335.
A ragged, fearful-hanging rock.—*The Two Gentlemen of Verona,* i, 2, 121. The only use of "fearful-hanging."
Raging rocks.—*A Midsummer-Night's Dream* i, 2, 33.
14
He shall be thrown down the Tarpeian rock
With rigorous hands.
Coriolanus. Act iii, sc. 1, l. 266. [Sicinius] "Tarpeian rock" is repeated in iii, 2, 3, and "rock Tarpeian" in iii, 3, 103. It is not mentioned in any other play.
To the rock, to the rock with him!
Coriolanus. Act iii, sc. 3, l. 75. [Citizens]
15
He 's the rock, the oak not to be wind-shaken.
Coriolanus. Act v, sc. 2, l. 118. [Sentinel] The only use of "wind-shaken." "Wind-shaked" occurs in *Othello,* ii, 1, 13.
16
The splitting rocks cower'd in the sinking sands
And would not dash me with their ragged sides.
II Henry VI. Act iii, sc. 2, l. 97. [Queen] The only use of "cower'd."
Bestride the rock; the tide will wash you off.
III Henry VI. Act v, sc. 4, l. 31. [Queen]
17 Lo, where comes that rock
That I advise your shunning.
Henry VIII. Act i, sc. 1, l. 113. [Norfolk]
18
And I, in such a desperate bay of death,
Like a poor bark, of sails and tackling reft,
Rush all to pieces on thy rocky bosom.
Richard III. Act iv, sc. 4, l. 232. [Queen Elizabeth]
Rocky heart.—*The Rape of Lucrece,* l. 590; *A Lover's Complaint,* l. 291.
Rocky mountains.—*II Henry IV,* iv, 1, 188.
Rocky shore.—*Richard II,* ii, 1, 62.
Rocky-hard.—*The Tempest,* iv, 1, 69. The only uses of "rocky."

ROGUE

See also Knave, Rascal, Ruffian

1

The rogues are marvellous poor.
All's Well that Ends Well. Act iv, sc. 3, l. 179. [Parolles]

Poor rogues.—*All's Well that Ends Well,* iv, 3, 153; 176; *Timon of Athens,* ii, 2, 61; *King Lear,* v, 3, 13; *Othello,* iv, 1, 112.

2

O, what a rogue and peasant slave am I!
Hamlet. Act ii, sc. 2, l. 576. [Hamlet]

A pestilence on him for a mad rogue!
Hamlet. Act v, sc. 1, l. 196. [First Clown]

3

What a frosty-spirited rogue is this!
I Henry IV. Act ii, sc. 3, l. 22. [Hotspur] The only use of "frosty-spirited."

Ah, thou honey-seed rogue! thou art a honey-seed, a man-queller, and a woman-queller.
II Henry IV. Act ii, sc. 1, l. 57. [Hostess] All three phrases are unique.

It is the foul-mouthed'st rogue in England.
II Henry IV. Act ii, sc. 4, l. 77. [Doll] The only use of "foul-mouthed'st."

You blue-bottle rogue, you filthy famished correctioner.
II Henry IV. Act v, sc. 4, l. 22. [Doll Tearsheet] The only use of "blue-bottle" and "correctioner."

A whoreson, glass-gazing, superserviceable, finical rogue.
King Lear. Act ii, sc. 2, l. 19. [Kent] "Glass-gazing," "superserviceable," and "finical" are all unique.

Bastardly rogue!—*II Henry IV,* ii, 1, 55. The only use of "bastardly."

Busy and insinuating rogue.—*Othello,* iv, 2, 131.

Cuckoldly rogue.—*The Merry Wives of Windsor,* ii, 2, 286.

Damnable both-sides rogue!—*All's Well that Ends Well,* iv, 3, 251. The only use of "both-sides" as a phrase.

Dissentious rogue.—*Coriolanus,* i, 1, 168.

Drawling, affecting rogue.—*The Merry Wives of Windsor,* ii, 1, 145. The only use of "drawling."

False-hearted rogue.—*Troilus and Cressida,* v, 1, 95. The only use of "false-hearted."

Fat rogue.—*I Henry IV,* i, 2, 210.

Filthy rogue.—*Troilus and Cressida,* v, 4, 31.

Mechanical salt-butter rogue!—*The Merry Wives of Windsor,* ii, 2, 290. The only use of "salt-butter."

Mouldy rogue.—*II Henry IV,* ii, 4, 134.

Satirical rogue.—*Hamlet,* ii, 2, 198.

Tedious rogue.—*Timon of Athens,* iv, 3, 374.

Very rogues.—*The Merry Wives of Windsor,* ii, 1, 182.

4

There is nothing but roguery to be found in villanous man.
I Henry IV. Act ii, sc. 4, l. 138. [Falstaff]

Tempt me no more to . . . Roguery!
Troilus and Cressida, v, 2, 18. The only uses of "roguery."

5

Falstaff: I have peppered two of them; two I am sure I have paid, two rogues in buckram suits. . . . Four rogues in buckram let drive at me—
Prince: What four? thou saidst but two even now.
Falstaff: Four, Hal; I told thee four.
Poins: Ay, ay, he said four. . . . Four, in buckram suits.
I Henry IV. Act ii, sc. 4, l. 211.

6

Ah, you sweet little rogue, you!
II Henry IV. Act ii, sc. 4, l. 233. [Doll]

7 Such smiling rogues as these,
Like rats, oft bite the holy cords a-twain
Which are too intrinse t' unloose; smooth every passion
That in the natures of their lords rebel;
Bring oil to fire, snow to their colder moods;
Renege, affirm, and turn their halcyon beaks
With every gale and vary of their masters,
Knowing nought, like dogs, but following.
King Lear. Act ii, sc. 2, l. 79. [Kent] The only use of "intrinse." "Renege" is repeated in *Antony and Cleopatra,* i, 1, 8.

8

Hostess: A pair of stocks, you rogue!
Sly: Ye are a baggage: the Slys are no rogues; look in the chronicles.
The Taming of the Shrew. Induction, sc. 1, l. 2.

9

What 's become of the wenching rogues? I think they have swallowed one another: I would laugh at that miracle: yet, in a sort, lechery eats itself.
Troilus and Cressida. Act v, sc. 4, l. 35. [Thersites] The only use of "wenching."

10

Here 's an overweening rogue!
Twelfth Night. Act ii, sc. 5, l. 34. [Sir Toby]

Overweening cur.—*II Henry VI,* v, 1, 151.

Overweening slave.—*The Two Gentlemen of Verona,* iii, 1, 157.

Overweening traitor.—*Richard II,* i, 1, 147.

11

I know this man well: he hath been since an ape-bearer; then a process-server, a bailiff; then he compassed a motion of the Prodigal Son, and married a tinker's wife within a mile where my land and living lies; and, having flown over many knavish professions, he settled only in rogue.
The Winter's Tale. Act iv, sc. 3, l. 100. [Autolycus] "Ape-bearer," "process-server," and "bailiff" are all unique.

An old sheep-whistling rogue, a ram-tender.
The Winter's Tale. Act iv, sc. 4, l. 804. [Autolycus] The only use of "sheep-whistling" and "ram-tender."

ROME

12

Let Rome in Tiber melt, and the wide arch
Of the ranged empire fall!
Antony and Cleopatra. Act i, sc. 1, l. 33. [Antony]

13 The Roman state, whose course will on
The way it takes, cracking ten thousand curbs

Of more strong link asunder than can ever
Appear in your impediment.
Coriolanus. Act i, sc. 1, l. 71. [Menenius]

1 Rome and her rats are at the point of battle;
The one side must have bale.
Coriolanus. Act i, sc. 1, l. 166. [Menenius] The only use of "bale" (injury).

Rome must know The value of her own.
Coriolanus. Act i, sc. 9, l. 20. [Cominius]

Now the good gods forbid
That our renowned Rome, whose gratitude
Towards her deserved children is enroll'd
In Jove's own book, like an unnatural dam
Should now eat up her own!
Coriolanus. Act iii, sc. 1, l. 290. [Menenius]

Sack great Rome with Romans.—*Coriolanus,* iii, 1, 316.

The honour'd gods Keep Rome in safety!
Coriolanus. Act iii, sc. 3, l. 33. [Coriolanus]

Rome sits safe.—*Coriolanus,* iv, 6, 36.

2 Lieutenant: You think he'll carry Rome? . . .
Aufidius: I think he'll be to Rome
As is the osprey to the fish, who takes it
By sovereignty of nature.
Coriolanus. Act iv, sc. 7, l. 27. The only use of "osprey."

He will shake Rome about your ears.—*Coriolanus,* iv, 6, 99.

'Be good to Rome,' they charged him.—*Coriolanus,* v, 6, 112.

3 Rome, thou hast lost the breed of noble bloods!
Julius Cæsar. Act i, sc. 2, l. 151. [Cassius]

When could they say till now, that talk'd of Rome,
That her wide walls encompass'd but one man?
Now is it Rome indeed and room enough,
When there is in it but one only man.
Julius Cæsar. Act i, sc. 2, l. 154. [Cassius]

Poor man! I know he would not be a wolf,
But that he sees the Romans are but sheep:
He were no lion, were not Romans hinds.
. . . What trash is Rome,
What rubbish and what offal, when it serves
For the base matter to illuminate
So vile a thing as Cæsar!
Julius Cæsar. Act. i, sc. 3, l. 104. [Cassius] "Rubbish" occurs again in *Richard II,* v, 2, 6; "butcher's offal" in *The Merry Wives of Windsor,* iii, 5, 5, and "slave's offal" in *Hamlet,* ii, 2, 608. The only use of "illuminate."

Shall Rome stand under one man's awe?
Julius Cæsar. Act ii, sc. 1, l. 52. [Brutus]

4 Your statue spouting blood in many pipes,
In which so many smiling Romans bathed,
Signifies that from you great Rome shall suck
Reviving blood, and that great men shall press
For tinctures, stains, relics and cognizance.
Julius Cæsar. Act ii, sc. 2, l. 85. [Brutus] The only use of "spouting" and "tinctures." "Tincture" occurs in *Winter's Tale,* iii, 2, 206.

Here is a mourning Rome, a dangerous Rome,
No Rome of safety for Octavius yet.
Julius Cæsar. Act iii, sc. 1, l. 288. [Antony]

5 Not that I loved Cæsar less, but that I loved Rome more.
Julius Cæsar. Act iii, sc. 2, l. 23. [Brutus]

The sun of Rome is set.—*Julius Cæsar,* v, 3, 63.

6 The imperial diadem of Rome.
Titus Andronicus. Act i, sc. 1, l. 6. [Saturninus]

Hail, Rome, victorious in thy mourning weeds!
Titus Andronicus. Act i, sc. 1, l. 70. [Titus]

Kind Rome, that hast thus lovingly reserved
The cordial of mine age to glad my heart!
Titus Andronicus. Act i, sc. 1, l. 165. [Titus]

Rome, I have been thy soldier forty years,
And led my country's strength successfully.
Titus Andronicus. Act i, sc. 1, l. 193. [Titus]

Ambitious Rome.—*Titus Andronicus,* i, 1, 132.
Antique Rome.—*Henry V,* v, Prol., 26.
Burning Rome.—*Coriolanus,* v, 1, 15.
Mighty Rome.—*The Rape of Lucrece,* l. 1644.
Old Rome.—*I Henry VI,* i, 2, 56.
Stately Rome.—*Titus Andronicus,* iv, 2, 60.
Ungrateful Rome.—*Titus Andronicus,* iv, 3, 17; *Coriolanus,* iv, 5, 136.
Rome, the nurse of judgement.—*Henry VIII,* ii, 2, 94.
In Rome no justice were.—*Titus Andronicus,* iv, 4, 20.

II—The Romans

7 A Roman by a Roman
Valiantly vanquish'd.
Antony and Cleopatra. Act iv, sc. 15, l. 57. [Antony]

Courageous Roman.—*The Rape of Lucrece,* l. 1828.
Noble Roman.—*Julius Cæsar,* i, 2, 197.
Valiant Roman.—*Coriolanus,* i, 2, 14.

8 Well fought; we are come off
Like Romans, neither foolish in our stands,
Nor cowardly in retire.
Coriolanus. Act i, sc. 6, l. 1. [Cominius]

9 We are Romans and will give you that
Like beasts which you shun beastly.
Cymbeline. Act v, sc. 3, l. 26. [Posthumus]

A Roman with a Roman's heart can suffer.
Cymbeline. Act v, sc. 5, l. 81. [Lucius]

10 I am more an antique Roman than a Dane.
Hamlet. Act v, sc. 2, l. 352. [Horatio]

11 For Romans now
Have thews and limbs like to their ancestors.
Julius Cæsar. Act i, sc. 3, l. 80. [Cassius]

Show yourselves true Romans.—*Julius Cæsar,* ii, 1, 223.

12 Who is here so rude that will not be a Roman?
Julius Cæsar. Act iii, sc. 2, l. 33. [Brutus]

I would I were a Roman.—*Coriolanus,* i, 10, 4.
I would not be a Roman.—*Coriolanus,* iv, 5, 185.

1
Brutus: As you are a Roman, tell me true.
Messala: Then like a Roman bear the truth I tell.
Julius Cæsar. Act iv, sc. 3, l. 187.

This is a Roman's part.—*Julius Cæsar,* v, 3, 89.

2
Are yet two Romans living such as these?
The last of all the Romans, fare thee well!
It is impossible that ever Rome
Should breed thy fellow.
Julius Cæsar. Act v, sc. 3, l. 98. [Brutus]

This was the noblest Roman of them all.—*Julius Cæsar,* v, 5, 68.

3
Thou art a Roman; be not barbarous.
Titus Andronicus. Act i, sc. 1, l. 378. [Marcus]

Friends, Romans, countrymen.—*Julius Cæsar,* iii, 2, 78.
Romans, countrymen, and lovers!—*Julius Cæsar,* iii, 2, 13.
Romans, friends, followers!—*Titus Andronicus,* i, 1, 9.
Roman actors.—*Julius Cæsar,* ii, 1, 226.
Roman boy.—*Antony and Cleopatra,* iv, 12, 48.
Romen brethren.—*Titus Andronicus,* i, 1, 104.
Roman citizen.—*Julius Cæsar,* iii, 2, 246.
Roman conqueror.—*As You Like It,* iv, 2, 4.
Roman courtezan.—*Cymbeline,* iii, 4, 126.
Roman dames.—*Titus Andronicus,* iv, 2, 41; *The Rape of Lucrece,* ll. 51, 1628.
Roman emperor.—*Cymbeline,* iv, 2, 384; *Titus Andronicus,* v, 1, 157.
Roman fool.—*Macbeth,* v, 8, 1.
Roman gentleman.—*Cymbeline,* iv, 3, 26.
Roman host.—*Cymbeline,* iv, 2, 352; *The Rape of Lucrece,* l. 3.
Roman ladies.—*Titus Andronicus,* ii, 1, 113; *Coriolanus,* v, 4, 41.
Roman legions.—*Cymbeline,* iv, 3, 24.
Roman lord.—*Titus Andronicus,* iv, 1, 62; *The Rape of Lucrece,* l. 301.
Romish stew.—*Cymbeline,* i, 6, 152. The only use of "Romish."

4
I am incorporate in Rome,
A Roman now adopted happily.
Titus Andronicus. Act i, sc. 1, l. 462. [Tamora]

III—The Church of Rome

5
Choose him pope and carry him to Rome,
And set the triple crown upon his head.
II Henry VI. Act i, sc. 3, l. 65. [Queen Margaret]

6
I abhor
This dilatory sloth and tricks of Rome.
Henry VIII. Act ii, sc. 4, l. 236. [King] "Dilatory" is repeated in *Othello,* ii, 3, 379: "Dilatory time."

7
The church, our holy mother.
King John. Act iii, sc. 1, l. 141. [Pandulph]

King John hath reconciled
Himself to Rome; his spirit is come in,
That so stood out against the holy church,
The great metropolis and see of Rome.
King John. Act v, sc. 2, l. 69. [Pandulph]

And come ye now to tell me John hath made
His peace with Rome? What is that peace to me? . . .
Am I Rome's slave? What penny hath Rome borne,
What men provided, what munition sent,
To underprop this action?
King John. Act v, sc. 2, l. 91. [Lewis] "Underprop the land" occurs in *Richard II,* ii, 2, 82, and "munition" in *I Henry VI,* i, 1, 168.

ROOF

See also House

8
The roof o' the chamber
With golden cherubins is fretted.
Cymbeline. Act ii, sc. 4, l. 87. [Iachimo]

Roofs of gold.—*Henry V,* i, 2, 198.
Roof of heaven.—*Antony and Cleopatra,* iii, 6, 49.
Roofs of palaces.—*Cymbeline,* iii, 3, 84.

9
I tell you, madam, were the whole frame here,
It is of such a spacious lofty pitch,
Your roof were not sufficient to contain 't.
I Henry VI. Act ii, sc. 3, l. 54. [Talbot]

10
I abjure all roofs, and choose
To wage against the enmity o' the air;
To be a comrade with the wolf and owl.
King Lear. Act ii, sc. 4, l. 211. [King Lear]

11
The roof of this court is too high to be yours.
Love's Labour's Lost. Act ii, sc. 1, l. 92. [Princess]

12
Swearing till my very roof was dry.
The Merchant of Venice, iii, 2, 206. See under OATH.

Roof of my mouth.—*The Taming of the Shrew,* iv, 1, 7.
Roof within my mouth.—*Richard II,* v, 3, 31.

13
Seeking that beauteous roof to ruinate.
Sonnets. No. x. See under HATE. "Ruinate" is repeated in *III Henry VI,* v, 1, 83, in *Titus Andronicus,* v, 3, 204; and in *The Rape of Lucrece,* l. 944.

Consecrated roof.—*Twelfth Night,* iv, 3, 25.
Household roof.—*Richard II,* iv, 1, 282.
Majestical roof.—*Hamlet,* ii, 2, 313.
Radiant roof.—*Cymbeline,* v, 4, 121.

ROOM

See also Chamber

14
Withdrew To mine own room again.
Hamlet. Act v, sc. 2, l. 15. [Hamlet]

15
The room where they supped is too hot.
II Henry IV. Act ii, sc. 4, l. 14. [Drawer]

The room is grown too hot.
Romeo and Juliet. Act i, sc. 5, l. 30. [Capulet]

16
I found the prince in the next room.
II Henry IV. Act iv, sc. 5, l. 83. [Warwick]

Next room.—*Richard III,* i, 4, 161; *The Winter's Tale,* ii, 2, 47.

Neighbour room.—*Hamlet,* iii, 4, 212.
Another room.—*III Henry VI,* v, 6, 92; *Richard II,* v, 5, 108.
Other room.—*II Henry IV,* iv, 5, 4; 18.

1
Let this supply the room.
III Henry VI. Act ii, sc. 6, l. 54. [Warwick]

Take their rooms.—*III Henry VI,* iii, 2, 132.

2 We shall have
Great store of room, no doubt, left for the ladies,
When they shall press back from the christening.
Henry VIII. Act v, sc. 4, l. 76. [Chamberlain]

3
Room for the incensed Worthies!
Love's Labour's Lost. Act v, sc. 2, l. 703. [Dumain]

4
It is an open room and good for winter.
Measure for Measure. Act ii, sc. 1, l. 135. [Froth]

Dark room.—*The Comedy of Errors,* iv, 4, 97; *Twelfth Night,* iii, 4, 148.
Fat room.—*I Henry IV,* ii, 4, 2.
Little room.—*As You Like It,* iii, 3, 15; *Henry V,* Epil., 3.
Reverend room.—*Richard II,* v, 6, 25.
Sacred room.—*The Merry Wives of Windsor,* v, 5, 61.

5
Make room, and let him stand before our face.
The Merchant of Venice. Act iv, sc. 1, l. 16. [Duke]

Make room.—*King John,* i, 1, 255.
Make good room.—*Much Ado about Nothing,* ii, 1, 88.
Find room.—*Sonnets,* lv.
Give . . . room.—*All's Well that Ends Well,* i, 2, 67; *Julius Cæsar,* iv, 3, 39.
Room enough.—*I Henry IV,* iv, 4, 92; *Julius Cæsar,* i, 2, 156; *The Tempest,* i, 1, 9.

6
I was smoking a musty room.
Much Ado about Nothing. Act i, sc. 3, l. 61. [Borachio]

7
You must forsake this room, and go with us.
Othello. Act v, sc. 2, l. 330. [Lodovico]

8 Every room
Hath blazed with lights and bray'd with minstrelsy.
Timon of Athens. Act ii, sc. 2, l. 169. [Flavius]

ROOT

9
I cannot delve him to the root.
Cymbeline. Act i, sc. 1, l. 28. [Gentleman]

Myself should be the root and father
Of many kings.
Macbeth. Act iii, sc. 1, l. 5. [Banquo]

10
I'll plant Plantagenet, root him up who dares.
III Henry VI. Act i, sc. 1, l. 48. [Warwick]

Root up.—*Timon of Athens,* v, 1, 168.
Root out.—*III Henry VI,* i, 3, 32; *Henry VIII,* v, 1, 53.
Rooted out.—*Pericles,* v, 1, 93.
Blown up by the root.—*Troilus and Cressida,* iv, 4, 56.
By the roots be hewn up.—*III Henry VI,* v, 4, 69.
Pluck'd up root and all.—*Richard II,* iii, 4, 52.
Nips his root.—*Henry VIII,* iii, 2, 357.

11
We set the axe to thy usurping root.
III Henry VI, ii, 2, 165. See under RETRIBUTION.

Set his murdering knife unto the root.
III Henry VI. Act ii, sc. 6, l. 49. [Richard]

12
We should take root here where we sit.
Henry VIII. Act i, sc. 2, l. 87. [Wolsey]

It is impossible you should take root but by the fair weather that you make yourself.
Much Ado about Nothing. Act i, sc. 3, l. 24. [Conrade]

Take root.—*The Rape of Lucrece,* l. 870.

13 Have we eaten on the insane root
That takes the reason prisoner?
Macbeth, i, 3, 84. See under MADNESS.

Root of hemlock digg'd i' the dark.
Macbeth. Act iv, sc. 1, l. 25. [Witch]

14
Why grow the branches now the root is wither'd?
Richard III, ii, 2, 41. See under TREE.

Wither'd roots.—*The Tempest,* i, 2, 463.
Antique root.—*As You Like It,* ii, 1, 31.
Earth-bound root.—*Macbeth,* iv, 1, 96. The only use of "earth-bound."
Good root.—*The Merry Wives of Windsor,* iv, 1, 56.
Perishing root.—*Cymbeline,* iv, 2, 60.
Pernicious root.—*Macbeth,* iv, 3, 85.
Royal root.—*Richard II,* i, 2, 18.
Root of thine annoy.—*Titus Andronicus,* iv, 1, 49.
Root of ancient envy.—*Coriolanus,* iv, 5, 109.
Roots of shame.—*Pericles,* iv, 6, 93.
Root o' the tongue.—*Timon of Athens,* v, 1, 136.

15
Earth, yield me roots! . . . roots, you clear heavens!
Timon of Athens. Act iv, sc. 3, l. 23. [Timon]

Yield him, who all thy human sons doth hate,
From forth thy plenteous bosom, one poor root!
. . . O, a root,—dear thanks!
Timon of Athens. Act iv, sc. 3, l. 185. [Timon]

Why should you want? Behold, the earth hath roots.
Timon of Athens. Act iv, sc. 3, l. 420. [Timon]

Can you eat roots?—*Timon of Athens,* v, 1, 77.
Eat root.—*Timon of Athens,* i, 2, 72.

16
There rooted between them then such an affection, which cannot choose but branch now.
Winter's Tale. Act i, sc. 1, l. 25. [Camillo]

Rooted in him.—*Cymbeline,* iv, 2, 57.
Rooted in us.—*Henry VIII,* v, 1, 114.
Deeply rooted.—*Cymbeline,* i, 6, 164.

ROPE

See also Hanging

1
I see that men make ropes in such a scarre
That we 'll forsake ourselves.
All's Well that Ends Well. Act iv, sc. 2, l. 38. [Diana] The only use of "scarre," whose meaning has never been explained satisfactorily.

2
Antipholus of Ephesus: Buy thou a rope and bring it home to me.
Dromio of Ephesus: I buy a thousand pound a year: I buy a rope. . . .
Antipholus: Thou drunken slave, I sent thee for a rope
And told thee to what purpose and what end.
Dromio of Syracuse: You sent me for a rope's end as soon.
The Comedy of Errors. Act iv, sc. 1, l. 20. "Rope's-end" (hyphenated) is repeated in iv, 4, 16, and 46, and occurs in no other play.
God and the rope-maker bear me witness
That I was sent for nothing but a rope!
The Comedy of Errors. Act iv, sc. 4, l. 93. [Dromio of Ephesus] The only use of "rope-maker."

3
Winchester goose, I cry, a rope! a rope!
Now beat them hence.
I Henry VI. Act iii, sc. 1, l. 53. [Gloucester] "Goose of Winchester" occurs in *Troilus and Cressida,* v, 10, 55, the reference being to a swelling in the groin caused by venereal disease.

4
Within this hour my man shall be with thee,
And bring thee cords made like a tackled stair.
Romeo and Juliet, ii, 4, 200. See under LADDER.
Made of cords.—*The Two Gentlemen of Verona,* ii, 4, 182; iii, 1, 117.
Juliet: What hast thou there? the cords
That Romeo bid thee fetch?
Nurse: Ay, ay, the cords. . . .
Juliet: Take up those cords: poor ropes, you are beguiled,
Both you and I; for Romeo is exiled.
Romeo and Juliet. Act iii, sc. 2, l. 34.
O, give me cord!—*Cymbeline,* v, 5, 213.
Holy cords.—*King Lear,* ii, 2, 80.
Penny cord.—*Henry V,* iii, 6, 50; *Cymbeline,* v, 4, 170. See under HANGING. "Cord" or "cords" is used also in *The Comedy of Errors,* v, 1, 289; *Measure for Measure,* iii, 2, 42; *The Merchant of Venice,* iv, 1, 366; *King John,* iv, 3, 127; *I Henry IV,* i, 3, 166; *Romeo and Juliet,* iii, 2, 136; *Titus Andronicus,* ii, 4, 10; and *Othello,* iii, 3, 388.

5
We will not hand a rope more.
The Tempest. Act i, sc. 1, l. 25. [Boatswain]
Haling ropes.—*Pericles,* iv, 1, 55. The only use of "haling."

6
Make the rope of his destiny our cable.
The Tempest, i, 1, 33. See under DESTINY.

ROSE

7
Against the blown rose may they stop their nose
That kneel'd unto the buds.
Antony and Cleopatra, iii, 13, 39. [Cleopatra]
Roses blown.—*Love's Labour's Lost,* v, 2, 295.
Rose distill'd.—*A Midsummer-Night's Dream,* i, 1, 76.

8
He that sweetest rose will find
Must find love's prick and Rosalind.
As You Like It, iii, 2, 117. [Touchstone]
Blow like sweet roses in this summer air.
Love's Labour's Lost, v, 2, 293. [Boyet]
Sweet Rose.—*As You Like It,* i, 2, 24.
Sweet roses.—*Sonnets,* liv.
Sweet lovely rose.—*I Henry IV,* i, 3, 175.

9
Two Provincial roses on my razed shoes.
Hamlet. Act iii, sc. 2, l. 288. [Hamlet] "Provincial" is repeated in *Measure for Measure,* v, 1, 318.

10
Plantagenet: Let him that is a true-born gentleman
And stands upon the honour of his birth,
If he suppose that I have pleaded truth,
From off this brier pluck a white rose with me.
Somerset: Let him that is no coward nor no flatterer,
But dare maintain the party of the truth,
Pluck a red rose from off this thorn with me.
Warwick: I love no colours, and without all colour
Of base insinuating flattery
I pluck this white rose with Plantagenet.
Suffolk: I pluck this red rose with young Somerset
And say withal I think he held the right. . . .
Vernon: I pluck this pale and maiden blossom here,
Giving my verdict on the white rose side.
Somerset: Prick not your finger as you pluck it off,
Lest bleeding you do paint the white rose red. . . .
Plantagenet: Now, Somerset, where is your argument?
Somerset: Here in my scabbard, meditating that
Shall dye your white rose in a bloody red. . . .
Plantagenet: Hath not thy rose a canker, Somerset?
Somerset: Hath not thy rose a thorn, Plantagenet?
Plantagenet: Ay, sharp and piercing, to maintain his truth;
Whiles thy consuming canker eats his falsehood.
Somerset: Well, I'll find friends to wear my bleeding roses. . . .

And know us by these colours for thy foes,
For these my friends in spite of thee shall wear.
Plantagenet: And, by my soul, this pale and angry rose,
As cognizance of my blood-drinking hate,
Will I forever and my faction wear,
Until it wither with me to my grave
Or flourish to the height of my degree. . . .
Warwick: And here I prophesy: this brawl to-day,
Grown to this faction in the Temple-garden,
Shall send between the red rose and the white
A thousand souls to death and deadly night.

I Henry VI. Act ii, sc. 4, l. 27. "True-born" is repeated in *Richard II,* i, 3, 309: "True-born Englishman." "Blood-drinking" occurs again in *II Henry VI,* iii, 2, 63: "Blood-drinking sighs"; and in *Titus Andronicus,* ii, 3, 224: "Blood-drinking pit." The only mention of the Temple-garden.

Then will I raise aloft the milk-white rose,
With whose sweet smell the air shall be perfumed.

II Henry VI. Act i, sc. 1, l. 254. [York]

The red rose and the white are on his face,
The fatal colours of our striving houses:
The one his purple blood right well resembles;
The other his pale cheeks, methinks, presenteth:
Wither one rose, and let the other flourish;
If you contend, a thousand lives must wither.

III Henry VI. Act ii, sc. 5, l. 97. [King]

I cannot rest
Until the white rose that I wear be dyed
Even in the lukewarm blood of Henry's heart.

III Henry VI. Act i, sc. 2, l. 33. [Richard]

We will unite the white rose and the red.

Richard III. Act v, sc. 5, l. 19. [Richmond] "White rose" is used eight times in the plays and "red rose" seven times.

1 The glowing roses
That flame through water which their hue encloses.

A Lover's Complaint, l. 286.

Blushing rose.—*Venus and Adonis,* l. 590.

Crimson rose.—*A Midsummer-Night's Dream,* ii, 1, 108.

Damask roses.—*The Winter's Tale,* iv, 4, 222.

2 When I have pluck'd the rose,
I cannot give it vital growth again,
It must needs wither: I'll smell it on the tree.

Othello. Act v, sc. 2, l. 13. [Othello]

Sweet rose, fair flower, untimely pluck'd, soon vaded,
Pluck'd in the bud, and vaded in the spring!

The Passionate Pilgrim, l. 131. "Vaded" (faded) is repeated in l. 176, and, in some editions, in *Richard II,* i, 2, 20, and in *Sonnets,* liv.

But soft, but see, or rather do not see,
My fair rose wither.

Richard II. Act v, sc. 1, l. 7. [Queen]

The roses in thy lips and cheeks shall fade
To paly ashes.

Romeo and Juliet. Act iv, sc. 1, l. 99. [Friar Laurence]

3
For flesh and blood, sir, white and red, you shall see a rose; and she were a rose indeed.

Pericles. Act iv, sc. 6, l. 37. [Boult]

4 A rose
By any other name would smell as sweet.

Romeo and Juliet, ii, 2, 43. See under Name.

5
The canker-blooms have full as sweet a dye
As the perfumed tincture of the roses.

Sonnets. No. liv. The only use of "canker-blooms." "Canker-blossom" occurs in *A Midsummer-Night's Dream,* iii, 2, 282.

Fragrant rose.—*Sonnets,* xcv.

Half-blown rose.—*King John,* iii, 1, 54.

Morning roses.—*The Taming of the Shrew,* ii, 1, 174.

Natural roses.—*Pericles,* v, Gower, 7.

II—Rose and Thorn

6 This thorn
Doth to our rose of youth rightly belong.

All's Well that Ends Well. Act i, sc. 3, l. 135. [Countess]

Rose of youth.—*Antony and Cleopatra,* iii, 13, 20.

Roses of the spring.—*Twelfth Night,* iii, 1, 161.

7
I know what thorns the growing rose defends.

The Rape of Lucrece, l. 492.

Roses have thorns.—*Sonnets.* No. xxxv.

8
The roses fearfully on thorns did stand,
One blushing shame, another white despair.

Sonnets. No. xcix.

9
What though the rose have prickles, yet 'tis pluck'd.

Venus and Adonis, l. 574. The only use of "prickles."

ROTTENNESS

10
You'll be rotten ere you be half ripe.

As You Like It. Act iii, sc. 2, l. 125. [Rosalind]

And then, from hour to hour, we rot and rot.

As You Like It, ii, 7, 27. See under Hour.

11
Something is rotten in the state of Denmark.

Hamlet. Act i, sc. 4, l. 90. [Marcellus]

Hamlet: How long will a man lie i' the earth ere he rot?
First Clown: I' faith, if he be not rotten before he die—as we have many pocky corses now-a-days, that will scarce hold the laying in—he will last you some eight year or nine year: a tanner will last you nine year.
Hamlet: Why he more than another?
First Clown: Why, sir, his hide is so tanned with his trade, that he will keep out water a great while; and your water is a sore decayer of your whoreson dead body.

Hamlet. Act v, sc. 1, l. 178. "Tanner" is

used a second time in *II Henry VI*, iv, 2, 24: "The tanner of Wingham," which is also the only mention of Wingham. The only use of "pocky" and "decayer."

A man may rot even here.—*King Lear*, v, 2, 8.

1
A rotten case abides no handling.
II Henry IV. Act iv, sc. 1, l. 161. [Westmoreland]

Rotten apples.—*The Taming of the Shrew*, i, 1, 139; *Henry V*, iii, 7, 155.
Rotten bell-wether.—*The Merry Wives of Windsor*, iii, 5, 111. "Bell-wether" occurs again in *As You Like It*, iii, 3, 85.
Rotten carcass.—*King John*, ii, 1, 456.
Rotten coffin.—*III Henry VI*, i, 3, 28.
Rotten dews.—*Coriolanus*, ii, 3, 35.
Rotten diseases.—*Troilus and Cressida*, v, 1, 21.
Rotten jaws.—*Romeo and Juliet*, 4, 3, 47.
Rotten medlar.—*Measure for Measure*, iv, 3, 184.
Rotten mouth.—*Richard III*, iv, 4, 2.
Rotten opinion.—*II Henry IV*, v, 2, 128.
Rotten orange.—*Much Ado about Nothing*, iv, 1, 33.
Rotten planks.—*Anthony and Cleopatra*, iii, 7, 63.
Rotten policy.—*I Henry IV*, i, 3, 108.
Rotten privilege.—*Coriolanus*, i, 10, 23.
Rotten times.—*II Henry IV*, iv, 4, 60.
Rotten tree.—*As You Like It*, ii, 3, 63.
Rotten silk.—*Coriolanus*, v, 6, 96.
Sound rottenness!—*King John*, iii, 4, 26. "Rottenness" occurs again in *Cymbeline*, i, 6, 125.

2
Fester'd members rot but by degree,
Till bones and flesh and sinews fall away.
I Henry VI. Act iii, sc. 1, l. 192. [Exeter]
"Fester'd" is repeated in *Richard II*, v, 3, 85.

3
The sweet war-man is dead and rotten.
Love's Labour's Lost. Act v, sc. 2, l. 666. [Armado]

Dead and rotten.—*King Lear*, v, 3, 285; *The Winter's Tale*, iii, 3, 82.
As good as rotten.—*Pericles*, iv, 2, 9.
When I in earth am rotten.—*Sonnets*, lxxxi.
Go rot!—*The Winter's Tale*, i, 2, 324. See under CURSE.

ROUGHNESS, see Rudeness

ROYALTY

See also King

4
He was likely, had he been put on,
To have proved most royally.
Hamlet. Act v, sc. 2, l. 408. [Fortinbras]

Royally appointed.—*The Winter's Tale*, iv, 4, 603.
Royally attorneyed.—*The Winter's Tale*, i, 1, 30.
Royally entertained.—*Much Ado about Nothing*, i, 3, 45.

5
Falstaff: This chair shall be my state, this dagger my sceptre, and this cushion my crown.
Prince: Thy state is taken for a joined-stool, thy golden sceptre for a leaden dagger, and thy precious rich crown for a pitiful bald crown.
I Henry IV. Act ii, sc. 4, l. 415.

6
Dominations, royalties and rights.
King John, ii, 1, 176. See under USURPATION.

Royalties and rights.—*Richard II*, ii, 1, 190.
Rights and royalties.—*Richard II*, ii, 3, 120.
Lineal royalties.—*Richard II*, iii, 3, 113.
Temporal royalties.—*The Tempest*, i, 2, 110.

7
You were crown'd before,
And that high royalty was ne'er pluck'd off.
King John. Act iv, sc. 2, l. 4. [King John]
Now hear our English king;
For thus his royalty doth speak in me.
King John. Act v, sc. 2, l. 128. [Bastard]

8
Thou camest not of the blood royal.
I Henry IV. Act i, sc. 2, l. 156. [Falstaff]

Royal blood.—*Richard III*, i, 2, 7, and seven times in later plays. See under BLOOD.
His high blood's royalty.—*Richard II*, i, 1, 58; 71.
Succeeding royalty.—*Macbeth*, iv, 3, 157.

9
The royal tree hath left us royal fruit,
Which, mellow'd by the stealing hours of time,
Will well become the seat of majesty.
Richard III. Act iii, sc. 7, l. 167. [Gloucester]

Right royal.—*Richard III*, i, 2, 245; *Antony and Cleopatra*, iii, 13, 55.
Royal and gracious.—*Richard III*, iv, 4, 204.
Fair and royal.—*Cymbeline*, iii, 5, 70.

RUDENESS

See also Manners: Bad Manners

10
It is my study
To seem despiteful and ungentle to you.
As You Like It. Act v, sc. 2, l. 85. [Rosalind]

Despiteful and intolerable.—*Titus Andronicus*. iv, 4, 50.

11
You have been too rough, something too rough.
Coriolanus. Act iii, sc. 2, l. 25. [Menenius]
She's too rough for me.
The Taming of the Shrew. Act i, sc. 1, l. 55. [Gremio]

Rough and unhospitable.—*Twelfth Night*, iii, 3, 11. See JEALOUSY, 781:11. The only use of "unhospitable."
As roughly as my modesty would let me.
The Comedy of Errors. Act v, sc. 1, l. 59 [Adriana]
Jostles roughly.—*Troilus and Cressida*, iv, 4, 36
Too roughly.—*Hamlet*, i, 2, 142.

12
Why are you grown so rude?
A Midsummer-Night's Dream. Act iii, sc. 2. l. 262. [Hermia]

13
This rudeness is a sauce to his good wit,
Which gives men stomach to digest his words

With better appetite.
Julius Cæsar. Act i, sc. 2, l. 304. [Cassius]
His rudeness so with his authorized youth
Did livery falseness in a pride of truth.
A Lover's Complaint, l. 104.

1
Thou art too wild, too rude and bold of voice.
The Merchant of Venice. Act ii, sc. 2, l. 190. [Bassanio]

2 Rude am I in my speech,
And little bless'd with the soft phrase of peace.
Othello. Act i, sc. 3, l. 81. [Othello]
Rude, in sooth; in good sooth, very rude.
Troilus and Cressida. Act iii, sc. 1, l. 59. [Pandarus]

3
I, that am rudely stamp'd, and want love's majesty
To strut before a wanton ambling nymph.
Richard III. Act i, sc. 1, l. 16. [Gloucester] "Ambling" is repeated in *The Merry Wives of Windsor,* ii, 2, 319: "Ambling gelding"; and in *Romeo and Juliet,* i, 4, 11: "I am not for this ambling."
Yet you began rudely.—*Twelfth Night,* i, 5, 228.

4
The great swing and rudeness of his poise.
Troilus and Cressida. Act i, sc. 3, l. 207. [Ulysses]
The rudeness that hath appeared in me have
I learned from my entertainment.
Twelfth Night. Act i, sc. 5, l. 230. [Viola]

5
This is as uncivil as strange.
Twelfth Night. Act iii, sc. 4, l. 277. [Viola]
Ruffian, let go that rude uncivil touch.
The Two Gentlemen of Verona. Act v, sc. 4, l. 60. [Valentine]
Uncivil arms.—*Richard II,* iii, 3, 102.
Uncivil extent.—*Twelfth Night,* iv, 1, 57.
Uncivil kerns.—*II Henry VI,* iii, 1, 310.
Uncivil lady.—*Twelfth Night,* v, 1, 115.
Uncivil outrages.—*The Two Gentlemen of Verona,* v, 4, 17.
Uncivil rule.—*Twelfth Night,* ii, 3, 132. The only uses of "uncivil."

RUFFIAN

See also Villain

6
Now, neighbour confines, purge you of your scum:
Have you a ruffian that will swear, drink, dance,
Revel the night, rob, murder, and commit
The oldest sins the newest kind of ways?
II Henry IV. Act iv, sc. 5, l. 124. [King]

7
What, wilt thou on thy death-bed play the ruffian?
II Henry VI. Act v, sc. 1, l. 164. [King]
Ancient ruffian.—*King Lear,* ii, 2, 67.
Father ruffian.—*I Henry IV,* ii, 4, 500.
Old ruffian.—*Antony and Cleopatra,* iv, 1, 4.

8
This grieved count Did see her . . .
Talk with a ruffian at her chamber window;
Who hath indeed, most like a liberal villain,
Confess'd the vile encounters they have had
A thousand times in secret.
Much Ado about Nothing. Act iv, sc. 1, l. 90. [Don Pedro]

9
A mad-cap ruffian and a swearing Jack,
That thinks with oaths to face the matter out.
The Taming of the Shrew. Act ii, sc. 1, l. 290. [Katharina]

RUIN

See also Destruction; Man: Ruined Men

10 You shall see in him
The triple pillar of the world transform'd
Into a strumpet's fool.
Antony and Cleopatra. Act i, sc. 1, l. 11. [Philo]
The noble ruin of her magic.
Antony and Cleopatra, iii, 10, 19. [Scarus]
Ruins of the noblest man.—*Julius Cæsar,* iii, 1, 256.

11 Thou art so leaky,
That we must leave thee to thy sinking, for
Thy dearest quit thee.
Antony and Cleopatra. Act iii, sc. 13, l. 63. [Enobarbus] "Leaky" is repeated in *The Tempest,* i, 1, 51.

12
What ruins are in me that can be found,
By him not ruin'd?
The Comedy of Errors. Act ii, sc. 1, l. 96. [Adriana]

13
O, I warrant, how he mammocked it!
Coriolanus. Act i, sc. 3, l. 71. [Valeria] The only use of "mammocked" (to break into fragments).

14
I say they . . . fed The ruin of the state.
Coriolanus. Act iii, sc. 1, l. 117. [Coriolanus]
Ruin of your love.—*The Merchant of Venice,* iii, 2, 175.
Formless ruin of oblivion.—*Troilus and Cressida,* iv, 5, 166.
Ruin of the times.—*The Merchant of Venice,* ii, 9, 48.
Ruins of distressful times.—*Richard III,* iv, 4, 318.
Country's ruin.—*Coriolanus,* v, 3, 116.

15 The ruin speaks that sometime
It was a worthy building.
Cymbeline. Act iv, sc. 2, l. 354. [Lucius]
Then was I as a tree
Whose boughs did bend with fruit: but in one night,
A storm or robbery, call it what you will,
Shook down my mellow hangings, nay, my leaves,
And left me bare to weather.
Cymbeline. Act iii, sc. 3, l. 60. [Belarius]

16
O God, I fear all will be overturn'd!
II Henry IV. Act v, sc. 2, l. 19. [Chief Justice] The only use of "overturn'd."

17 Hereafter ages may behold
What ruin happen'd in revenge of him.
I Henry VI. Act ii, sc. 2, l. 10. [Talbot]

1
Ruin combat with their palaces!
I Henry VI. Act v, sc. 2, l. 7. [La Pucelle]
Come all to ruin.—*Coriolanus,* iii, 2, 125.
Boisterous ruin.—*Hamlet,* iii, 3, 22.
Cureless ruin.—*Merchant of Venice,* iv, 1, 142.
Utter ruin.—*III Henry VI,* i, 1, 254.
Weak ruins.—*The Rape of Lucrece,* l. 720.

2
Ruin follows us.
III Henry VI. Act ii, sc. 3, l. 10. [George]
Ye tell me what ye wish for both,—my ruin.
Henry VIII. Act iii, sc. 1, l. 98. [Queen Katharine]

3
Goodly buildings left without a roof
Soon fall to ruin.
Pericles. Act ii, sc. 4, l. 36. [Second Lord] The only use of "fall to ruin" in the plays, in a scene probably not by Shakespeare.
Time's ruin.—*The Rape of Lucrece,* l. 1451.

4
Death, desolation, ruin and decay.
Richard III. Act iv, sc. 4, l. 409. [King Richard]
Ruin and decay.—*Richard II,* iii, 2, 102.

5
Let us be lead within thy bosom, Richard,
And weigh thee down to ruin, shame, and death!
Richard III. Act v, sc. 3, l. 153. [Ghosts]

6
Ruin hath taught me thus to ruminate,
That Time will come and take my love away.
This thought is as a death, which cannot choose
But weep to have that which it fears to lose.
Sonnets. No. lxiv.

7
Is yond despised and ruinous man my lord?
Timon of Athens. Act iv, sc. 3, l. 464. [Flavius]

Myself,
Who had the world as my confectionary,
The mouths, the tongues, the eyes and hearts of men
At duty, more than I could frame employment,
That numberless upon me stuck as leaves
Do on the oak, have with one winter's brush
Fell from their boughs and left me open, bare
For every storm that blows.
Timon of Athens. Act iv, sc. 3, l. 259. [Timon] The only use of "confectionary." "Numberless" is repeated in *Henry VIII,* ii, 1, 84.

8
'Twill be his death; 'twill be his bane; he cannot bear it.
Troilus and Cressida. Act iv, sc. 2, l. 98. [Pandarus]

RULE

9
That to come Shall all be done by the rule.
Antony and Cleopatra. Act ii, sc. 3, l. 6. [Antony]
Military rules.—*II Henry IV,* ii, 3, 30.
Rules of charity.—*Richard III,* i, 2, 68.
Rule of knighthood.—*King Lear,* v, 3, 145.
Rule of nature.—*All's Well that Ends Well,* i, 1, 148.
Rule in nature.—*Henry V,* i, 2, 188.

10
A rule as plain as the plain bald pate of father Time himself.
The Comedy of Errors. Act ii, sc. 2, l. 70. [Dromio of Syracuse] The only use of the phrase "father Time" in the plays.

11
Suffer 't, and live with such as cannot rule
Nor ever will be ruled.
Coriolanus. Act iii, sc. 1, l. 40. [Coriolanus]

12
Give place: by heaven, thou shalt rule no more
O'er him whom heaven created for thy ruler.
II Henry VI. Act v, sc. 1, l. 104. [York]
Rules the roast.—*II Henry VI,* i, 1, 109. The only use of this phrase in the plays.

13 Were they to be ruled, and not to rule,
This sickly land might solace as before.
Richard III. Act ii, sc. 3, l. 29. [Citizen]

14
If this rule were true, he should be gracious.
Richard III. Act ii, sc. 4, l. 20. [Duchess]
If your own rule be true.—*II Henry IV,* iv, 2, 86.
True rule.—*I Henry IV,* iv, 3, 39; *The Taming of the Shrew,* iii, 1, 81.
Awful rule.—*Taming of the Shrew,* v, 2, 109.
Bookish rule.—*II Henry VI,* i, 1, 259.
Uncivil rule.—*Twelfth Night,* ii, 3, 132.

15
The specialty of rule hath been neglected.
Troilus and Cressida. Act i, sc. 3, l. 78. [Ulysses] The only use of "specialty." "Specialties" occurs in *Love's Labour's Lost,* ii, 1, 165, and in *Taming of the Shrew,* ii, 1, 127.

16
Leontes: What, canst not rule her?
Paulina: From all dishonesty he can: in this,
Unless he take the course that you have done,
Commit me for committing honour, trust it,
He shall not rule me.
The Winter's Tale. Act ii, sc. 3, l. 46.

II—Ruler

See also Governor

17
Sole sir o' the world.
Antony and Cleopatra. Act v, sc. 2, l. 120. [Cleopatra]

18 Our then dictator,
Whom with all praise I point at.
Coriolanus. Act ii, sc. 2, l. 93. [Cominius] The only use of "dictator."

19 Demean himself
Unlike the ruler of a commonweal.
II Henry VI, i, 1, 189. See under BEHAVIOUR.
As doth a ruler.—*I Henry VI,* v, 5, 30.
Ruler of the land.—*II Henry VI,* ii, 4, 43.
Rulers over Rouen.—*I Henry VI,* iii, 2, 11.
Lucky ruler.—*II Henry VI,* iii, 1, 291.
I am ruler.—*II Henry VI,* iii, 2, 296. The only uses of "ruler" and "rulers."

RUMOUR

See also Report

1
That pitiful rumour may report thy flight,
To consolate thine ear.
All's Well that Ends Well. Act iii, sc. 2, l. 131. [Helena] The only use of "consolate."

Belike 'tis but a rumour.—*Antony and Cleopatra,* iv, 3, 5.

It is rumour'd.—*Coriolanus,* i, 2, 11.

This have I rumour'd.—*II Henry IV,* Ind., 33.

2
They say!
They 'll sit by the fire, and presume to know
What 's done i' the Capitol; who 's like to rise,
Who thrives and who declines; side factions and give out
Conjectural marriages; making parties strong
And feebling such as stand not in their liking
Below their cobbled shoes.
Coriolanus. Act i, sc. 1, l. 194. [Caius Marcius] The only use of "feebling" and "cobbled."

Conjectural fears.—*All 's Well that Ends Well,* v, 3, 114. The only uses of "conjectural."

Let every feeble rumour shake your hearts!
Coriolanus. Act iii, sc. 3, l. 125. [Coriolanus]

Go see this rumourer whipp'd.—*Coriolanus,* iv, 6, 47. The only use of "rumourer."

3
Open your ears; for which of you will stop
The vent of hearing when loud Rumour speaks?
I, from the orient to the drooping west,
Making the wind my post-horse, still unfold
The acts commenced on this ball of earth;
Upon my tongues continual slanders ride,
The which in every language I pronounce,
Stuffing the ears of men with false reports.
I speak of peace while covert enmity
Under the smile of safety rules the world:
. . . Rumour is a pipe
Blown by surmises, jealousies, conjectures,
And of so easy and so plain a stop
That the blunt monster with uncounted heads,
The still-discordant wavering multitude,
Can play upon it. . . . The posts come tiring on,
And not a man of them brings other news
Than they have learn'd of me: from Rumour's tongues
They bring smooth comforts false, worse than true wrongs.
II Henry IV. Induction, l. 1. The only use of "uncounted" and "still-discordant."

Rumour doth double, like the voice and echo,
The numbers of the fear'd.
II Henry IV. Act iii, sc. 1, l. 97. [Warwick]

Why is Rumour here?—*II Henry IV,* Ind., 22.

4
I heard a bustling rumour, like a fray.
Julius Cæsar. Act ii, sc. 4, l. 18. [Porita] The only use of "bustling."

5
This from rumour's tongue
I idly heard; if true or false I know not.
King John. Act iv, sc. 2, l. 123. [Messenger]

Possess'd with rumours.—*King John,* iv, 2, 145.

6
Men's mouths are full of it.
King John. Act iv, sc. 2, l. 161. [Bastard]

7
We hold rumour
From what we fear, yet know not what we fear,
But float upon a wild and violent sea
Each way and move.
Macbeth. Act iv, sc. 2, l. 19. [Ross]

8
So I have strew'd it in the common ear.
Measure for Measure. Act i, sc. 3, l. 15. [Duke]

Common rumours.—*Timon of Athens,* iii, 2, 6.

9
By holy Paul, they love his grace but lightly
That fill his ears with such dissentious rumours.
Richard III. Act i, sc. 3, l. 45. [Gloucester]

Rumour it abroad.—*Richard III,* iv, 2, 51.

Does the rumour hold for true?—*Timon of Athens,* v, 1, 4.

10
To a vision so apparent rumour
Cannot be mute.
Winter's Tale. Act i, sc. 2, l. 270. [Leontes]

RUNNING

11
You shall hear I am run away: know it before the report come.
All's Well that Ends Well. Act iii, sc. 2, l. 25. [Countess, reading]

I 'll run away till I am bigger, but then I 'll fight.
Coriolanus. Act v, sc. 3, l. 128. [Young Marcius]

Now, like to whelps, we crying run away.
I Henry VI. Act i, sc. 5, l. 26. [Talbot] "Run away" is repeated in iv, 1, 23, and in iv, 5, 31, and is used frequently throughout the later plays.

Run away for fear.—*A Midsummer-Night's Dream,* ii, 2, 95.

Run away for shame.—*Love's Labour 's Lost,* v, 2, 582.

Run for life.—*The Comedy of Errors,* iii, 2, 159.

Why do they run away?—*Midsummer-Night's Dream,* iii, 1, 115.

12
Only to seem to deserve well . . . have I run into this danger.
All's Well that Ends Well. Act iv, sc. 3, l. 332. [Parolles]

Trinculo, run into no further danger.
The Tempest. Act iii, sc. 2, l. 76. [Stephano]

Run into.—*As You Like It,* i, 1, 141; ii, 4, 35; 55; *All's Well that Ends Well,* ii, 5, 39.

13
He has no pace, but runs where he will.
All's Well that Ends Well. Act iv, sc. 5, l. 70. [Countess]

Then I 'll run.—*Antony and Cleopatra,* ii, 5, 73.

Run and show their shoulders.—*Antony and Cleopatra,* iii, 11, 8.

Turn thy back and run.—*Romeo and Juliet,* i, 1, 41.

1
Where runn'st thou so fast?
The Comedy of Errors. Act iii, sc. 2, l. 73. [Antipholus of Syracuse]
Thou runn'st before me.—*Midsummer-Night's Dream,* iii, 2, 423.
Runn'st away.—*Romeo and Juliet,* i, 1, 13.
2
How have you run
From slaves that apes would beat!
Coriolanus, i, 4, 35. See under COWARDICE.
Run barefoot up and down.—*Hamlet,* ii, 2, 528.
Contrary run.—*Hamlet,* iii, 2, 221.
3
So runs the world away.
Hamlet, iii, 2, 285. See under WORLD.
4
Show it a fair pair of heels and run from it.
I Henry IV, ii, 4, 53. See under COWARDICE.
5
I would give a thousand pound I could run as fast as thou canst. You are straight enough in the shoulders, you care not who sees your back.
I Henry IV. Act ii, sc. 4, l. 162. [Falstaff] See also under COWARDICE.
Prince: You are lions too, you ran away upon instinct. . . .
Bardolph: 'Faith, I ran when I saw others run.
I Henry IV. Act ii, sc. 4, l. 331.
He will not run.—*I Henry IV,* ii, 4, 384.
We'll not run.—*The Tempest,* iii, 2, 21.
6
He runs straight and even.
I Henry IV. Act iii, sc. 1, l. 114. [Worcester]
Run even.—*King John,* ii, 1, 576.
7
I am afraid my daughter will run mad.
I Henry IV, iii, 1, 145. "Run mad" occurs frequently throughout the plays.
8
Arm in arm they both came swiftly running.
I Henry VI. Act ii, sc. 2, l. 29. [Burgundy]
Running fast.—*Comedy of Errors,* iv, 2, 30.
Running o'er.—*Henry VIII,* iii, 2, 139.
Running out.—*Love's Labour's Lost,* iii, 1, 117.
Running neither way.—*II Henry IV,* ii, 3, 64.
9
Even so must I run on, and even so stop.
King John. Act v, sc. 7, l. 67. [Prince Henry] "Run on" is repeated in v, 4, 56.
Run directly on.—*Julius Cæsar,* iv, 1, 32.
Run o'er.—*Henry VIII,* i, 1, 144; *Julius Cæsar,* v, 5, 14; *Troilus and Cressida,* i, 2, 161.
Run off.—*II Henry IV,* iii, 2, 288.
Run up.—*Merry Wives of Windsor,* iv, 2, 81.
10
You shall run a certain course.
King Lear. Act i, sc. 2, l. 88. [Edmund]
Run his course.—*Julius Cæsar,* i, 2, 4; *Henry VIII,* iii, 2, 398.
Run his compass.—*Julius Cæsar,* v, 3, 25.
11
Nay, if you get it, you shall get it with running. Sa, sa, sa, sa.
King Lear. Act iv, sc. 6, l. 206. [King Lear] The only uses of "sa."
Well run!—*Love's Labour's Lost,* v, 2, 233; *A Midsummer-Night's Dream,* v, 1, 271.
Long run.—*Measure for Measure,* i, 4, 63.
12
'Do not run; scorn running with thy heels.' Well, the most courageous fiend bids me pack: 'Via!' says the fiend; 'away!' says the fiend; 'for the heavens, rouse up a brave mind,' says the fiend, 'and run.'
The Merchant of Venice. Act ii, sc. 2, l. 9. [Launcelot] "Via" is used seven times.
My heels are at your command; I will run.
The Merchant of Venice. Act ii, sc. 2, l. 33. [Launcelot]
I will run as far as God has any ground.
The Merchant of Venice. Act ii, sc. 2, l. 117. [Launcelot]
13
Demetrius: I'll run from thee and hide me in the brakes. . . .
Helena: Run when you will.
A Midsummer-Night's Dream. Act ii, sc. 1, l. 227.
Run through fire.—*Midsummer-Night's Dream,* ii, 2, 103.
Run in here.—*The Merry Wives of Windsor,* i, 4, 38.
Run thee to the parlour.—*Much Ado about Nothing,* iii, 1, 1.
Run smoothly.—*Much Ado about Nothing,* v, 2, 33.
Run afoot.—*Richard II,* i, 1, 63.
Run the wild-goose chase.—*Romeo and Juliet,* ii, 4, 75. The only use of "wild-goose chase."
Run to wreck.—*II Henry VI,* i, 3, 127.
14
So runn'st thou after that which flies from thee.
Sonnets. No. cxliii.
15
He that runs fastest gets the ring.
The Taming of the Shrew. Act i, sc. 1, l. 144. [Hortensio]
Run more fast.—*King John,* iv, 2, 269.
16
Run upon the sharp wind of the north.
The Tempest, i, 2, 254. See under MESSENGER.
Run ourselves aground.—*The Tempest,* i, 1, 4.
17
Speed: Must I go to him?
Launce: Thou must run to him, for thou hast stayed so long that going will scarce serve the turn.
The Two Gentlemen of Verona. Act iii, sc. 1, l. 386.
18
Whether he run or fly they know not whether.
Venus and Adonis, l. 304.
Homeward through the dark laund runs apace.
Venus and Adonis, l. 813. "Laund" (glade) is repeated in *III Henry VI,* iii, 1, 2.
19
When she will take the rein I let her run;
But she'll not stumble.
The Winter's Tale, ii, 3, 51. [Antigonus]
They stumble that run fast.—*Romeo and Juliet,* ii, 3, 94.

RUST

20
I were better to be eaten to death with a rust than to be scoured to nothing with perpetual motion.
II Henry IV. Act i, sc. 2, l. 246. [Falstaff]

1
Consume away in rust.
King John. Act iv, sc. 1, l. 65. [Arthur]
2
His glittering arms he will commend to rust.
Richard II. Act iii, sc. 3, l. 116. [Northumberland]
Let his armour rust.—*Pericles,* ii, 2, 54.
Rust, rapier!—*Love's Labour's Lost,* i, 2, 187.
Rust, sword!—*All's Well that Ends Well,* iv, 3, 373.
There rust.—*Romeo and Juliet,* v, 3, 170.
Foul-cankering rust.—*Venus and Adonis,* l. 767.
The only use of the phrase.

S

SACK

See also Wine

3
Falstaff: Give me a cup of sack: I am a rogue, if I drunk to-day.
Prince of Wales: O villain! thy lips are scarce wiped since thou drunkest last.
I Henry IV. Act ii, sc. 4, l. 167.
Let a cup of sack be my poison.
The Merry Wives of Windsor. Act ii, sc. 2, l. 49. [Falstaff] "Cup of sack" is repeated in ii, 4, 129; ii, 4, 140; ii, 4, 345; in *I Henry IV,* i, 2, 8; *II Henry IV,* ii, 4, 121; and *II Henry VI,* ii, 3, 60.
Bombard of sack.—*I Henry IV,* ii, 4, 497.
Bottle of sack.—*I Henry IV,* iv, 2, 2.
A morning's draught of sack.—*The Merry Wives of Windsor,* ii, 2, 153.
Old sack.—*I Henry IV,* i, 2, 3; *II Henry IV,* i, 2, 222.
4
If sack and sugar be a fault, God help the wicked!
I Henry IV. Act ii, sc. 4, l. 516. [Falstaff]
Peto [Reading]: Item, Sack, two gallons, 5s. 8d. Item, Anchovies and sack after supper, 2s. 6d. Item, Bread, ob.
Prince: O monstrous! but one half-penny-worth of bread to this intolerable deal of sack!
I Henry IV. Act ii, sc. 4, l. 587. The only use of "gallons" and "half-penny-worth," and the only mention of anchovies.
5
Thou hast saved me a thousand marks in links and torches, walking with thee in the night betwixt tavern and tavern: but the sack that thou hast drunk me would have bought me lights as good cheap at the dearest chandler's in Europe.
I Henry IV. Act iii, sc. 3, l. 48. [Falstaff] The only use of "chandler."
A good sherris-sack hath a two-fold operation in it. It ascends me into the brain; dries me there all the foolish and dull and crudy vapours which environ it; makes it apprehensive, quick, forgetive, full of nimble fiery and delectable shapes; which, delivered o'er to the voice, the tongue, which is the birth, becomes excellent wit. The second property of your excellent sherris is, the warming of the blood; which, before cold and settled, left the liver white and pale, which is the badge of pusillanimity and cowardice; but the sherris warms it and makes it course from the inwards to the parts extreme: it illumineth the face, which as a beacon gives warning to all the rest of this little kingdom, man, to arm; and then the vital commoners and inland petty spirits muster me all to their captain, the heart, who, great and puffed up with this retinue, doth any deed of courage; and this valour comes of sherris. So that skill in the weapon is nothing without sack, for that sets it a-work; and learning a mere hoard of gold kept by a devil, till sack commences it and sets it in act and use. Hereof comes it that Prince Harry is valiant; for the cold blood he did naturally inherit of his father, he hath, like lean, sterile and bare land, manured, husbanded and tilled with excellent endeavour of drinking good and good store of fertile sherris, that he is become very hot and valiant. If I had a thousand sons the first humane principle I would teach them should be, to forswear thin potations and to addict themselves to sack.
II Henry IV. Act iv, sc. 3, l. 103. [Falstaff] The only use of "sherris-sack," "crudy," "forgetive," "warming," "pusillanimity," and "illumineth." "Potations" is used only once again, in *Othello,* ii, 3, 56; and "delectable" in *Richard II,* ii, 3, 7.
6
By the mass, I have drunk too much sack at supper.
II Henry IV. Act v, sc. 3, l. 14. [Shallow]
Leave sack.—*I Henry IV,* v, 4, 169.
7
There 's that will sack a city.
I Henry IV. Act v, sc. 3, l. 56. [Falstaff]
Our sacks shall be a means to sack the city.
I Henry VI. Act iii, sc. 2, l. 10. [Soldier]
Sack this country.—*I Henry VI,* v, 1, 62.
Sack fair Athens.—*Timon of Athens,* v, 1, 174.
Sack of Orleans.—*I Henry VI,* ii, 2, 15.
Sack great Rome.—*Coriolanus,* iii, 1, 316.
Sacked Troy.—*All's Well that Ends Well,* i, 3, 75.
Sack the hateful mansion.—*Romeo and Juliet,* iii, 3, 107.
Her house is sack'd.—*Rape of Lucrece,* l. 1170.
8
You love sack, and so do I.
The Merry Wives of Windsor. Act ii, sc. 1, l. 9. [Mrs. Page]
I 'll give you a pottle of burnt sack.
The Merry Wives of Windsor. Act ii, sc. 1, l. 222. [Ford] "Pottle" is used again in iii, 5, 29, and in *Othello,* ii, 3, 87.
I 'll go burn some sack.—*Twelfth Night,* ii, 3, 206.

Your hearts are mighty, your skins are whole, and let burnt sack be the issue.
The Merry Wives of Windsor. Act iii, sc. 1, l. 110. [Host]

1
Go fetch me a quart of sack; put a toast in 't.
The Merry Wives of Windsor. Act iii, sc. 5, l. 3. [Falstaff]
Come, let me pour in some sack to the Thames water.
The Merry Wives of Windsor. Act iii, sc. 5, l. 22. [Falstaff]
Falstaff: Go brew me a pottle of sack finely.
Bardolph: With eggs, sir?
Falstaff: Simple, of itself; I 'll no pullet-sperm in my brewage.
The Merry Wives of Windsor. Act iii, sc. 5, l. 29. The only use of "pullet-sperm" and "brewage."
Sack and wine.—*The Merry Wives of Windsor,* v, 5, 167.

2
First Servant: Will 't please your lordship
drink a cup of sack? . . .
Sly: I ne'er drank sack in my life.
Taming of the Shrew. Induction, sc. 2, l. 2.

3
My man-monster hath drown'd his tongue in sack.
The Tempest. Act iii, sc. 2, l. 14. [Stephano] The only use of "man-monster."
Was there ever man a coward that hath drunk so much sack as I to-day?
The Tempest. Act iii, sc. 2, l. 30. [Trinculo]
A pox o' your bottle! this can sack and drinking do.
The Tempest. Act iii, sc. 2, l. 87. [Trinculo]
Butt of sack.—*The Tempest,* ii, 2, 126.

SACRIFICE

See also Self-sacrifice

4
Give the gods a thankful sacrifice.
Antony and Cleopatra. Act i, sc. 2, l. 167. [Enobarbus]
Thankful sacrifice.—*Coriolanus,* i, 6, 9.

5
Let 's quit the ground,
And smoke the temple with our sacrifices.
Cymbeline. Act v, sc. 5, l. 397. [Cymbeline]
And do upon mine altar sacrifice.—*Pericles,* v, 1, 242.

6
They come like sacrifices in their trim,
And to the fire-eyed maid of smoky war
All hot and bleeding will we offer them.
I Henry IV. Act iv, sc. 1, l. 113. [Hotspur] "Fire-eyed" occurs again in *Romeo and Juliet,* iii, 1, 129.
Sweet sacrifice.—*Henry VIII,* ii, 1, 77.

7
Go bid the priests do present sacrifice,
And bring me their opinions of success.
Julius Cæsar. Act ii, sc. 2, l. 5. [Cæsar]
Let us be sacrificers, but not butchers.
Julius Cæsar. Act ii, sc. 1, l. 166. [Brutus] The only use of "sacrificers."

8
Rescue those breathing lives to die in beds,
That here come sacrifices for the field.
King John. Act ii, sc. 1, l. 419. [Citizen]

9
Upon such sacrifices, my Cordelia,
The gods themselves throw incense.
King Lear. Act v, sc. 3, l. 20. [King Lear]

10
I stand for sacrifice:
The Merchant of Venice. Act iii, sc. 2, l. 57. [Portia]
Poor sacrifices of our enmity!
Romeo and Juliet. Act v, sc. 3, l. 304. [Capulet]

11
For their brethren slain
Religiously they ask a sacrifice.
Titus Andronicus. Act i, sc. 1, l. 123. [Titus]
Love's full sacrifice.—*Troilus and Cressida,* i, 2, 308.
First sacrifice.—*Troilus and Cressida,* iv, 2, 66.

12
I 'll sacrifice the lamb that I do love,
To spite a raven's heart within a dove.
Twelfth Night. Act v, sc. 1, l. 133. [Duke]
To offer up a weak poor innocent lamb
To appease an angry god.
Macbeth. Act iv, sc. 3, l. 16. [Malcolm]

13
O, the sacrifice!
How ceremonious, solemn and unearthly
It was i' the offering!
The Winter's Tale. Act iii, sc. 1, l. 6. [Dion] The only use of "unearthly."

SADNESS

See also Grief, Melancholy, Sorrow

14
There begins my sadness.
As You Like It. Act i, sc. 1, l. 5. [Orlando]
Why, 'tis good to be sad and say nothing.
As You Like It. Act iv, sc. 1, l. 8. [Jaques]

15
This week he hath been heavy, sour, sad,
And much different from the man he was.
The Comedy of Errors. Act v, sc. 1, l. 45. [Adriana]
He did incline to sadness, and oft-times
Not knowing why.
Cymbeline. Act i, sc. 6, l. 62. [Imogen]
I never saw him sad.—*Cymbeline,* i, 6, 63.

16
I could be sad, and sad indeed too.
II Henry IV. Act ii, sc. 2, l. 45. [Prince]
Be sad, good brothers,
For, by my faith, it very well becomes you: . . .
Be sad; But entertain no more of it, good brothers,
Than a joint burden laid upon us all.
II Henry IV. Act v, sc. 2, l. 49. [King Henry]

17
Methinks your looks are sad, your cheer appall'd.
I Henry VI. Act i, sc. 2, l. 48. [Bastard] "Appall'd" is repeated in *Troilus and Cressida,* iv, 5, 4.

18
Arthur: You are sad.
Hubert: Indeed, I have been merrier.
Arthur: Mercy on me!
Methinks no body should be sad but I:
Yet, I remember, when I was in France,
Young gentlemen would be as sad as night,

Only for wantonness.
King John. Act iv, sc. 1, l. 11.
Wherefore do you droop? why look you sad?
King John. Act v, sc. 1, l. 44. [Bastard]
I did not think to be so sad to-night.
King John. Act v, sc. 5, l. 15. [Dauphin]

1 In sooth, I know not why I am so sad:
It wearies me; you say it wearies you;
But how I caught it, found it, or came by it,
What stuff 'tis made of, whereof it is born,
I am to learn;
And such a want-wit sadness makes of me,
That I have much ado to know myself.
The Merchant of Venice. Act i, sc. 1, l. 1. [Antonio] The only use of "want-wit."

Then let us say you are sad,
Because you are not merry: and 'twere as easy
For you to laugh and leap and say you are merry,
Because you are not sad.
The Merchant of Venice. Act i, sc. 1, l. 47. [Salarino]
Unmannerly sadness.—*The Merchant of Venice,* i, 2, 54.

2 Conrade: Why are you thus out of measure sad?
Don John: There is no measure in the occasion that breeds; therefore the sadness is without limit.
Much Ado about Nothing. Act i, sc. 3, l. 1.
Wherefore are you sad?
Much Ado about Nothing. Act ii, sc. 1, l. 298. [Don Pedro]

3 Madam, your majesty is much too sad.
Richard II. Act ii, sc. 2, l. 1. [Bushy]
I cannot but be sad; so heavy sad
As, though on thinking on no thought I think,
Makes me with heavy nothing faint and shrink.
Richard II. Act ii, sc. 2, l. 30. [Queen]

4 King Richard: Why look you so sad?
Surrey: My heart is ten times lighter than my looks.
Richard III. Act v, sc. 3, l. 2.
Why look'st thou sad?—*Romeo and Juliet,* ii, 5, 21.
Look sadly.—*Richard III,* v, 3, 287; *The Two Gentlemen of Verona,* ii, 1, 31; *King John,* iii, 1, 20; *Othello,* ii, 1, 32.
Sitting sadly.—*Cymbeline,* v, 5, 160.

5 Benvolio: What sadness lengthens Romeo's hours?
Romeo: Not having that, which, having, makes them short.
Romeo and Juliet. Act i, sc. 1, l. 169.

6 Too much sadness hath congeal'd your blood.
The Taming of the Shrew. Induction, sc. 2, l. 134. [Messenger]
In good sadness.—*The Taming of the Shrew,* v, 2, 63; *All's Well that Ends Well,* iv, 3, 230; *The Merry Wives of Windsor,* iii, 5, 125; 14, 2, 93.

7 First were we sad, fearing you would not come:
Now sadder, that you come so unprovided.
The Taming of the Shrew. Act iii, sc. 2, l. 100. [Baptista]
Are you sadder than you were before?
The Two Gentlemen of Verona. Act iv, sc. 2, l. 54. [Host]
Methinks you are sadder.—*Much Ado about Nothing,* iii, 2, 16. The only uses of "sadder."

8 Wherefore look'st thou sad,
When every thing doth make a gleeful boast?
Titus Andronicus. Act ii, sc. 3, l. 10. [Tamora] The only use of "gleeful."
Prithee, be not sad.—*Timon of Athens,* ii, 2, 229.

9 Thou shalt find me, sad and solitary.
The Two Gentlemen of Verona. Act iv, sc. 4, l. 94. [Proteus]
Sad and solemn.—*Henry V,* iv, 1, 318.

10 Therefore, in sadness, now I will away.
Venus and Adonis, l. 807.
Sadness of parting.—*Cymbeline,* v, 4, 162.
Sudden sadness.—*Troilus and Cressida,* i, 1, 40.

SAFETY

See also Security

11 If knife, drugs, serpents, have
Edge, sting, or operation, I am safe.
Antony and Cleopatra. Act iv, sc. 15, l. 25. [Cleopatra]
Something you can deny for your own safety.
Antony and Cleopatra. Act ii, sc. 6, l. 95. [Enobarbus]
We pray you, for your own sake, to embrace your own safety.
As You Like It. Act i, sc. 2, l. 188. [Celia]
Provide For thine own future safety.
Henry VIII. Act iii, sc. 2, l. 420. [Wolsey]

12 Devise the fittest time and safest way.
As You Like It. Act i, sc. 3, l. 137. [Celia]
Safest haste.—*As You Like It,* i, 3, 43.
Safest occasion.—*Othello,* iii, 1, 52.
Safest passage.—*I Henry VI,* iii, 2, 22.

13 I long that we were safe and sound.
The Comedy of Errors. Act iv, sc. 4, l. 154. [Antipholus of Syracuse] The only use of "safe and sound."

14 Keep your honours safe!
Coriolanus. Act i, sc. 2, l. 37. [Aufidius]
Heaven keep your honour safe!
Measure for Measure. Act ii, sc. 2, l. 157. [Isabella]
Keep this man safe.—*Julius Cæsar,* v, 4, 27.
Keep him safely.—*Richard II,* iv, 1, 153.
Keep it safe.—*King John,* v, 2, 2.
It shall safe be kept.—*Cymbeline,* i, 6, 209.
Kept safe.—*The Two Gentlemen of Verona,* iii, 1, 111.

15 Safe mayst thou wander, safe return again!
Cymbeline. Act iii, sc. 5, l. 105. [Pisanio]
Safe arrived.—*The Comedy of Errors,* i, 1, 49; *Richard II,* ii, 2, 50; *Macbeth,* v, 8, 35.

Safe convey'd.—*Comedy of Errors,* iv, 4, 125.
Safe return.—*Titus Andronicus,* i, 1, 221; *I Henry IV,* iv, 3, 109.
Comes safe home.—*Henry V,* iv, 3, 41.

1
This head of safety.
I Henry IV. Act iv, sc. 3, l. 103. [Hotspur]

What I have done my safety urged me to.
I Henry IV. Act v, sc. 5, l. 11. [Worcester]

2 Counsel every man
The aptest way for safety.
II Henry IV. Act i, sc. 2, l. 212. [Northumberland] The only use of "aptest."

3
I charge thee waft me safely cross the Channel.
II Henry VI. Act iv, sc. 1, l. 114. [Suffolk] "Channel" in this sense is used only once more, in *II Henry IV,* ii, 1, 52.

Go safely on.—*The Tempest,* ii, 1, 327.
Safely stowed.—*Hamlet,* iv, 2, 1.

4
And yet shalt thou be safe? such safety finds
The trembling lamb environed with wolves.
III Henry VI. Act i, sc. 1, l. 241. [Queen Margaret]

Let us be back'd with God and with the seas
Which He hath given for fence impregnable,
And with their helps only defend ourselves;
In them and in ourselves our safety lies.
III Henry VI. Act iv, sc. 1, l. 43. [Hastings] "Impregnable" is repeated in *Richard II,* iii, 2, 168; in *Titus Andronicus,* iv, 4, 98; and in *Sonnets,* lxv.

Safe enough.—*Julius Cæsar,* v, 4, 20.

5 Grandam, I will pray,
If ever I remember to be holy,
For your fair safety.
King John. Act iii, sc. 3, l. 14. [Bastard]

Especial safety.—*Hamlet,* iv, 3, 42.
Plenteous safety.—*Henry VIII,* i, 1, 104.
Precious safety.—*Richard II,* i, 1, 32.
Sweet safety.—*King John,* v, 2, 142.

6
Deliver him to safety.
King John. Act iv, sc. 2, l. 158. [King John]

Hold him in safety.—*Romeo and Juliet,* v, 3, 183.
In safety.—*King John,* iii, 2, 8; *Cymbeline,* i, 6, 12.

7 This murderous shaft that 's shot
Hath not yet lighted, and our safest way
Is to avoid the aim.
Macbeth. Act ii, sc. 3, l. 147. [Malcolm]

To be thus is nothing; But to be safely thus.
Macbeth. Act iii, sc. 1, l. 48. [Macbeth]

8
Ere twice the sun hath made his journal greeting
To the under generation, you shall find
Your safety manifested.
Measure for Measure. Act iv, sc. 3, l. 92. [Duke] "Journal" is repeated in *Cymbeline,* iv, 2, 10: "Journal course."

The heavens give safety to your purposes!
Measure for Measure, i, 1, 74. [Angelo]

The gods with safety stand about thee!
Troilus and Cressida, v, 3, 94. [Priam]

9 To safeguard thine own life,
The best way is to venge my Gloucester's death.
Richard II. Act i, sc. 2, l. 35. [Duchess]

Safeguard of their brood.—*III Henry VI,* ii, 2, 18.
Safeguard of your honour.—*Measure for Measure,* v, 1, 424.
Safeguard of your wives.—*Richard III,* v, 3, 259.
Safeguard necessaries.—*Henry V,* i, 2, 176.
On safe-guard he came to me.—*Coriolanus,* iii, 1, 9. The only uses of "safeguard."

10
We are not safe, Clarence; we are not safe.
Richard III. Act i, sc. 1, l. 70. [Gloucester]

Some men else, who think themselves as safe
As thou and I.
Richard III. Act iii, sc. 2, l. 68. [Hastings]

I 'll make thee safe.—*Richard II,* v, 3, 41.

11 We two, my lord,
Will guard your person while you take your rest,
And watch your safety.
The Tempest. Act ii, sc. 1, l. 196. [Antonio]

He 's safe for these three hours.
The Tempest. Act iii, sc. 1, l. 21. [Miranda]

He 's safe.—*Measure for Measure,* v, 1, 499.

12
All thy safety were remotion.
Timon of Athens, iv, 3, 345. See under BEAST. "Remotion" (keeping aloof) is repeated in *King Lear,* ii, 4, 115.

13
This maugre all the world will I keep safe.
Titus Andronicus. Act iv, sc. 2, l. 110. [Aaron]

Then is all safe, the anchor 's in the port.
Titus Andronicus. Act iv, sc. 4, l. 38. [Tamora]

SAIL

See also Ship

14
Purple the sails, and so perfumed that
The winds were love-sick.
Antony and Cleopatra, ii, 2, 198. See under SHIP.

O my lord, my lord, Forgive my fearful sails!
Antony and Cleopatra. Act iii, sc. 11, l. 54. [Cleopatra]

Hoists sails and flies.—*Antony and Cleopatra,* iii, 10, 15.
Hoisted sail and put to sea.—*The Comedy of Errors,* v, 1, 21.
Hoised sail.—*Richard III,* iv, 4, 529. The only use of "hoised." "Hoise" occurs in *II Henry VI,* i, 1, 69.

I have hoisted sail to all the winds
Which should transport me farthest from your sight.
Sonnets. No. cxvii.

Will you hoist sail, sir? here lies your way.
Twelfth Night. Act i, sc. 5, l. 215. [Maria]

15 Behold the threaden sails,
Borne with the invisible and creeping wind,
Draw the huge bottoms through the furrow'd sea.
Henry V, iii, Prol., 10. See under SHIP. The only use of "threaden" and "furrow'd."

Portly sail.—*The Merchant of Venice,* i, 1, 9.

Proud full sail.—*Sonnets,* lxxxvi.
Proudest sail.—*Sonnets,* lxxx.
Quick sail.—*Hamlet,* v, 2, 120.

1 Now Margaret
Must strike her sail and learn awhile to serve
Where kings command.
III Henry VI. Act iii, sc. 3, l. 4. [Queen Margaret]

Strike sail.—*II Henry IV,* v, 2, 18.
Bear so low a sail.—*III Henry VI,* v, 1, 52.
Slow of sail.—*The Comedy of Errors,* i, 1, 117; *Hamlet,* iv, 6, 17.

2 I desire no more delight
Than to be under sail and gone to-night.
The Merchant of Venice. Act ii, sc. 6, l. 68. [Gratiano]

Under sail.—*Love's Labour 's Lost,* v, 2, 549; *A Midsummer-Night's Dream,* i, 1, 174; *The Merchant of Venice,* ii, 8, 1; 6; *Coriolanus,* ii, 2, 110.
Clap on more sails.—*The Merry Wives of Windsor,* ii, 2, 142.

3
We have laugh'd to see the sails conceive
And grow big-bellied with the wanton wind.
A Midsummer-Night's Dream. Act ii, sc. 1, l. 128. [Titania]
Your breath of full consent bellied his sails.
Troilus and Cressida. Act ii, sc. 2, l. 74. [Troilus]

4
Gentleman: I cannot, 'twixt the heaven and the main,
Descry a sail. . . .
[A cry within] A sail, a sail, a sail!
Cassio: What noise?
Gentleman: The town is empty; on the brow o' the sea
Stand ranks of people, and they cry 'A sail.' . . .
Cassio: Great Jove, Othello guard,
And swell his sail with thine own powerful breath.
. . . But, hark! a sail.
Othello. Act ii, sc. 1, l. 3.
Romeo: Here 's goodly gear!
Mercutio: A sail, a sail!
Benvolio: Two, two; a shirt and a smock.
Romeo and Juliet. Act ii, sc. 4, l. 107.

5 Toward Ephesus
Turn our blown sails; eftsoons I 'll tell thee why.
Pericles. Act v, sc. 1, l. 256. [Pericles] The only use of "eftsoons."

Ragged sails.—*Merchant of Venice,* ii, 6, 18.

6
In feather'd briefness sails are fill'd.
Pericles. Act v, sc. 2, l. 14. [Gower] "Feather'd" is repeated in *I Henry IV,* iv, 1, 106: "Feather'd Mercury"; and in *Othello,* i, 3, 270: "Feather'd Cupid."

SAILOR

See also Sea, Ship

7 Your ships are not well mann'd;
Your mariners are muleters, reapers, people
Ingross'd by swift impress; . . .
Their ships are yare; yours, heavy.
Antony and Cleopatra. Act iii, sc. 7, l. 35. [Enobarbus] The only use of "ingross'd." "Muleters" is repeated in *I Henry VI,* iii, 2, 68: "Base muleters of France."
The mariners all under hatches stow'd.
The Tempest. Act i, sc. 2, l. 230. [Ariel]
There shalt thou find the mariners asleep
Under the hatches.
The Tempest. Act v, sc. 1, l. 98. [Prospero]

Speak to the mariners.—*The Tempest,* i, 1, 3. "Mariner" is used five times in *The Tempest,* and only twice in all the other plays: *Antony and Cleopatra,* iii, 7, 36, and *Pericles,* iii, 1, 73.

8
The sailors sought for safety by our boat,
And left the ship.
The Comedy of Errors, i, 1, 77. [Ægeon]

Seafaring men.—*The Comedy of Errors,* i, 1, 81. The only use of the phrase.
Sailors [are] but men.—*The Merchant of Venice,* i, 3, 23.
Drunken sailor.—*Richard III,* iii, 4, 101.

9
Wilt thou upon the high and giddy mast
Seal up the ship-boy's eyes?
II Henry IV. Act iii, sc. 1, l. 18. [King]
Behold
Upon the hempen tackle ship-boys climbing.
Henry V. Act iii, Prologue, l. 8. [Chorus]

This ship-boy's semblance.—*King John,* iv, 3, 4. The only uses of "ship-boy" and "ship-boys."

10
On this day let seamen fear no wreck.
King John. Act iii, sc. 1, l. 92. [Constable]
Cried 'Good seamen!' to the sailors.
Pericles. Act iv, sc. 1, l. 54. [Marina] The only use of "seamen." "Seaman" occurs in *Pericles,* iii, 1, 8: "Seaman's whistle."

11 The shipman's toil,
With whom each minute threatens life or death.
Pericles. Act i, sc. 3, l. 24. [Helicanus] "Shipman" occurs also in *Troilus and Cressida,* v, 2, 172, and *Macbeth,* i, 3, 17.

SAINT

12
Thou . . . art indeed able to corrupt a saint.
I Henry IV. Act i, sc. 2, l. 101. [Falstaff]

Corrupt my saint to be a devil.—*Sonnets,* cxliv; *The Passionate Pilgrim,* l. 21. See under ANGEL.

13
Canonized and worshipp'd as a saint.
King John. Act iii, sc. 1, l. 177. [Pandulph]

Thou shalt be canonized.—*King John,* iii, 4, 52.
Canonized saints.—*II Henry VI,* i, 3, 63.
Canonized bones.—*Hamlet,* i, 4, 47. The only uses of "canonized."

14
This earthly saint, adored by this devil,
Little suspecteth the false worshipper.
The Rape of Lucrece, l. 85.

Blessed saint.—*I Henry VI,* iii, 3, 15.
Carved saints.—*Richard II,* iii, 3, 152.
Dead saint.—*Richard III,* iv, 1, 70.
Dear saint.—*Romeo and Juliet,* i, 5, 105.

Holy saint.—*The Comedy of Errors,* iii, 2, 14; *Richard III,* v, 3, 241.
Holy Saint Francis.—*Romeo and Juliet,* ii, 3, 65.
Sweet saint.—*Richard III,* i, 2, 49.
Mortal-breathing saint.—*Merchant of Venice,* ii, 7, 40. The only use of the phrase.

1
Seem a saint, when most I play the devil.
Richard III. Act i, sc. 3, l. 338. [Gloucester]

2
I know thou worshippest Saint Nicholas as truly as a man of falsehood may.
I Henry IV. Act ii, sc. 1, l. 71. [Chamberlain] Saint Nicholas is mentioned also in *The Two Gentlemen of Verona,* iii, 1, 300, and in *I Henry IV,* ii, 1, 67.

No longer on Saint Denis will we cry,
But Joan la Pucelle shall be France's saint.
I Henry VI. Act i, sc. 6, l. 28. [Charles] Shakespeare mentions twenty-seven saints, from Saint Anne to Saint Valentine. Saint Denis is referred to twice more, in *I Henry VI,* iii, 2, 18, and *Love's Labour's Lost,* v, 2, 87. For Saint George see under ENGLAND.

3
I hold you as a thing ensky'd and sainted,
By your renouncement an immortal spirit,
And to be talk'd with in sincerity,
As with a saint.
Measure for Measure. Act i, sc. 4, l. 34. [Lucio] The only use of "ensky'd" and "renouncement."

4
O cunning enemy, that, to catch a saint,
With saints dost bait thy hook!
Measure for Measure. Act ii, sc. 2, l. 180. [Angelo]

SALT

5
The salt of most unrighteous tears.
Hamlet, i, 2, 154. See under WOMAN: HER INCONSTANCY. The only use of "unrighteous."

6
We have some salt of our youth in us.
The Merry Wives of Windsor. Act ii, sc. 3, l. 49. [Shallow]

The salt in them is hot.—*King John,* v, 7, 45.
Make use of thy salt hours.—*Timon of Athens,* iv, 3, 85.
As salt as wolves.—*Othello,* iii, 3, 404.
Salt Cleopatra.—*Antony and Cleopatra,* ii, 1, 21.

7
Salt too little which may season give
To her foul-tainted flesh!
Much Ado about Nothing, iv, 1, 144. See DISHONOUR, 357:11.

8
The cover of the salt hides the salt, and therefore it is more than the salt.
The Two Gentlemen of Verona. Act iii, sc. 1, l. 369. [Launce]

9
Tread the ooze Of the salt deep.
The Tempest. Act i, sc. 2, l. 252. [Prospero]

Salt flood.—*Romeo and Juliet,* iii, 5, 155; *Timon of Athens,* v, 1, 219.
Salt imagination.—*Measure for Measure,* v, 1, 406.
Salt rheum.—*The Comedy of Errors,* iii, 2, 132.
Salt scorn.—*Troilus and Cressida,* i, 3, 371.
Salt-sea.—*Macbeth,* iv, 1, 24.
Salt water.—*Romeo and Juliet,* ii, 3, 71, and five times in later plays.
Salt wave.—*Love's Labour's Lost,* v, 1, 61; *Twelfth Night,* iii, 4, 419.
Salt-waved.—*The Rape of Lucrece,* l. 1116.

SALVE, see under Medicine

SAMSON

10
I am not Samson, nor Sir Guy, nor Colbrand,
To mow 'em down before me.
Henry VIII. Act v, sc. 4, l. 22. [Man] The only mention of Sir Guy.

Colbrand the giant, that same mighty man.—*King John,* i, 1, 225.
Samsons and Goliases.—*I Henry VI,* i, 2, 33. See under England. The only use of "Goliases." Goliath is mentioned in *The Merry Wives of Windsor,* v, 1, 23.

11
Moth: Samson, master: he was a man of good carriage, for he carried the town gates on his back like a porter: and he was in love.
Armado: O well-knit Samson! strong-jointed Samson! . . . Who was Samson's love, my dear Moth?
Moth: A woman, master. . . .
Armado: Tell me precisely of what complexion.
Moth: Of the sea-water green, sir. . . .
Armado: Green indeed is the colour of lovers; but to have a love of that colour, methinks Samson had small reason for it. He surely affected her for her wit.
Moth: It was so, sir; for she had a green wit.
Love's Labour's Lost. Act i, sc. 2, l. 73. The only use of "well-knit," and "strong-jointed."

Yet was Samson so tempted, and he had an excellent strength.
Love's Labour's Lost. Act i, sc. 2, l. 179. [Armado]

SANCTUARY

12
He took this place for sanctuary,
And it shall privilege him from your hands.
The Comedy of Errors. Act v, sc. 1, l. 94. [Abbess]

13
I 'll hence forthwith into the sanctuary.
III Henry VI. Act iv, sc. 3, l. 31. [Queen Elizabeth]

We will to sanctuary.—*Richard III,* ii, 4, 66.
I 'll conduct you to the sanctuary.—*Richard III,* ii, 4, 73.
Go thou to sanctuary.—*Richard III,* iv, 1, 94.

14
God in heaven forbid
We should infringe the holy privilege
Of blessed sanctuary!
Richard III. Act iii, sc. 1, l. 40. [Bourchier]

You break not sanctuary in seizing him.
The benefit thereof is always granted

To those whose dealings have deserved the place,
And those who have the wit to claim the place. . . .
Oft have I heard of sanctuary men;
But sanctuary children ne'er till now.
Richard III. Act iii, sc. 1, l. 47. [Cardinal]
Taken sanctuary.—*Richard III,* iii, 1, 28.

SAND

1 Even as men wrecked upon a sand, that look to be washed off the next tide.
Henry V. Act iv, sc. 1, l. 100. [King Henry]

2 The sands are number'd that make up my life.
III Henry VI, i, 4, 25. See LIFE, 867:11.
Now our sands are almost run.—*Pericles,* v, 2, 1.
Numbering sands.—*Richard II,* ii, 2, 146.

3 Tread on the sand; why, then you quickly sink.
III Henry VI. Act v, sc. 4, l. 30. [Queen]
Sands that will not bear.—*Cymbeline,* iii, 1, 21. See under ENGLAND.
Sinking sands.—*II Henry VI,* iii, 2, 97.
Congregated sands.—*Othello,* ii, 1, 69. "Congregated" is repeated in *All's Well that Ends Well,* ii, 1, 120.

4 The angry northern wind
Will blow these sands, like Sibyl's leaves, abroad,
And where 's your lesson, then?
Titus Andronicus. Act iv, sc. 1, l. 104. [Titus]

5 Come unto these yellow sands.
The Tempest, i, 2, 376. See under DANCING.
Neptune's yellow sands.—*Midsummer-Night's Dream,* ii, 1, 126.

SATAN, see Devil

SATIETY

6 Enough, with over-measure.
Coriolanus. Act iii, sc. 1, l. 140. [Brutus] The only use of "over-measure."

7 Thou, beastly feeder, art so full of him,
That thou provokest thyself to cast him up.
II Henry IV. Act i, sc. 3, l. 95. [Archbishop of York]

8 To give satiety a fresh appetite.
Othello, ii, 1, 231. See under LUST.

9 And with satiety seeks to quench his thirst.
The Taming of the Shrew. Act i, sc. 1, l. 24. [Lucentio]

10 A mere satiety of commendations.
Timon of Athens. Act i, sc. 1, l. 166. [Timon]
Loathed satiety.—*Venus and Adonis,* l. 19. These are the only uses of "satiety." "Sate," "sated" and "satiate" are each used once.

SATIRE

See also Ridicule

11 That is some satire, keen and critical.
A Midsummer-Night's Dream. Act v, sc. 1, l. 54. [Philostrate]
Satirical rogue.—*Hamlet,* ii, 2, 198. The only use of "satirical."

12 Dost thou think I care for a satire or an epigram?
Much Ado about Nothing. Act v, sc. 4, l. 103. [Benedick] The only use of "epigram."

13 A satire against the softness of prosperity.
Timon of Athens. Act v, sc. 1, l. 37. [Poet] The only use of "softness."
A satire to decay.—*Sonnets,* c.

SATISFACTION

14 Therefore make present satisfaction,
Or I 'll attach you by this officer.
The Comedy of Errors. Act iv, sc. 1, l. 5. [Merchant]
Let him make treble satisfaction.
Titus Andronicus. Act v, sc. 1, l. 8. [Lucius]
Give me ample satisfaction.—*The Comedy of Errors,* v, 1, 252.
Full satisfaction.—*The Comedy of Errors,* v, 1, 399.
Private satisfaction.—*Julius Cæsar,* ii, 2, 73.
Worthy satisfaction!—*Troilus and Cressida,* ii, 3, 4.
Satisfaction of my mind.—*Henry V,* iii, 2, 106.
Satisfaction of my thought.—*Othello,* iii, 3, 97.

15 I give him satisfaction?
Would he had been one of my rank!
Cymbeline. Act ii, sc. 1, l. 16. [Cloten]

16 No other satisfaction do I crave.
I Henry VI. Act ii, sc. 3, l. 77. [Talbot]
What satisfaction canst thou make?—*III Henry VI,* v, 5, 14.
How canst thou make me satisfaction?—*Henry VIII,* iv, 8, 48.

17 Yet so my fancy may be satisfied.
I Henry VI. Act v, sc. 3, l. 91. [Suffolk]
Enough: my soul shall then be satisfied.
I Henry VI. Act ii, sc. 5, l. 21. [Mortimer]
But gladly would be better satisfied.
II Henry IV. Act i, sc. 3, l. 6. [Mowbray]
And yet not satisfied.—*III Henry VI,* ii, 2, 99.

18 He shall be satisfied; and, by my honour,
Depart untouch'd.
Julius Cæsar. Act iii, sc. 1, l. 141. [Brutus]
We will be satisfied; let us be satisfied.
Julius Cæsar. Act iii, sc. 2, l. 1. [Citizens]
Be satisfied.—*Richard III,* iii, 3, 21; *Measure for Measure,* ii, 2, 104; *Romeo and Juliet,* iii, 1, 75.
Let me be satisfied.—*Romeo and Juliet,* ii, 5, 37.
I cannot be thus satisfied.—*The Merry Wives of Windsor,* ii, 1, 195.
I will satisfy you.—*As You Like It,* v, 2, 125.
I am satisfied.—*Richard III,* v, 3, 72; *Antony and Cleopatra,* iii, 13, 167; *The Winter's Tale,* ii, 1, 189.
I shall be satisfied.—*Julius Cæsar,* iv, 2, 10.

I will be satisfied.—*Macbeth,* iv, 1, 104; *Richard II,* v, 2, 59.
You shall be satisfied.—*Othello,* iv, 2, 252.
You should be satisfied.—*Julius Cæsar,* iii, 1, 226.
Fully satisfied.—*Henry VIII,* ii, 4, 148.

1 We may soon our satisfaction have
Touching that point.
Measure for Measure. Act i, sc. 1, l. 83. [Angelo]
The satisfaction I would require is likewise your own benefit.
Measure for Measure. Act iii, sc. 1, l. 156. [Duke]
For my better satisfaction.—*Measure for Measure,* iv, 2, 125.
No satisfaction, no revenge.—*The Merchant of Venice,* iii, 1, 98.

2
Satisfy me once more.
The Merry Wives of Windsor. Act iv, sc. 2, l. 172. [Ford]
Satisfy me so.—*Love's Labour 's Lost,* ii, 1, 163.
Let it satisfy you.—*All's Well that Ends Well,* ii, 3, 204.
Satisfy our eyes.—*Twelfth Night,* iii, 3, 22.
Satisfy the poor woman.—*II Henry IV,* ii, 1, 143.
Satisfy her.—*King John,* ii, 1, 557.
Straight satisfy yourself.—*Othello,* i, 1, 138.

3
Othello: Would I were satisfied! . . .
Iago: You would be satisfied?
Othello: Would! nay, I will.
Iago: And may: but, how? how satisfied, my lord? . . .
Where 's satisfaction?
Othello. Act iii, sc. 3, l. 390.
If imputation and strong circumstances,
Which lead directly to the door of truth,
Will give you satisfaction, you may have 't.
Othello. Act iii, sc. 3, l. 406. [Iago]
I will seek satisfaction of you.—*Othello,* iv, 2, 203.

4
What satisfaction canst thou have to-night?
Romeo and Juliet, ii, 2, 126. See under Vow.

5 This satisfaction
The by-gone day proclaim'd.
The Winter's Tale. Act i, sc. 2, l. 31. [Hermione] "By-gone" occurs again in iii, 2, 185, and in no other play.
Satisfy! Let that suffice.
Winter's Tale. Act i, sc. 2, l. 234. [Leontes]

SAUCINESS

See also Impertinence

6
You are more saucy with lords and honourable personages than the commission of your birth and virtue gives you heraldry.
All's Well that Ends Well. Act ii, sc. 3, l. 277. [Lafeu]
Which he thinks is a patent for his sauciness.
All's Well that Ends Well. Act iv, sc. 5, l. 69. [Countess]

7
So saucy with the hand of she here.
Antony and Cleopatra. Act iii, sc. 13, l. 98. [Antony]

8
I 'll sauce her with bitter words.
As You Like It. Act iii, sc. 5, l. 69. [Rosalind]
I 'll sauce them.—*The Merry Wives of Windsor,* iv, 3, 11.

9
Is 't not enough to break into my garden,
And, like a thief, to come to rob my grounds,
Climbing my walls in spite of me the owner,
But thou wilt brave me with these saucy terms?
II Henry VI. Act iv, sc. 10, l. 35. [Iden]

10
Beldams as you are, Saucy and overbold.
Macbeth. Act iii, sc. 5, l. 2. [Hecate] The only use of "overbold."

11
What saucy merchant was this, that was so full of his ropery?
Romeo and Juliet. Act ii, sc. 4, l. 153. [Nurse] The only use of "ropery" (knavery).
Saucy bark.—*Sonnets,* lxxx.
Saucy boat.—*Troilus and Cressida,* i, 3, 42.
Saucy boy.—*Romeo and Juliet,* i, 5, 85.
Saucy doubts.—*Macbeth,* iii, 4, 25.
Saucy fellow.—*Julius Cæsar,* i, 1, 21; iv, 3, 134.
Saucy friar.—*Measure for Measure,* v, 1, 135.
Saucy jacks.—*Sonnets,* cxxviii.
Saucy lackey.—*As You Like It,* iii, 2, 314.
Saucy looks.—*Love's Labour 's Lost,* i, 1, 85.
Saucy priest.—*I Henry VI,* iii, 1, 45.
Saucy roughness.—*King Lear,* ii, 2, 103.
Saucy stranger.—*Cymbeline,* i, 6, 151.
Saucy sweetness.—*Measure for Measure,* ii, 4, 45.
Saucy tongue.—*I Henry VI,* iii, 4, 33.
Saucy walls.—*King John,* ii, 1, 404.
Saucy wrongs.—*Othello,* i, 1, 129.

12
Great reason that my noble lord be rated
For sauciness.
Titus Andronicus. Act ii, sc. 3, l. 81. [Lavinia]
Impudent sauciness.—*II Henry IV,* ii, 1, 123; 135.
Unhair'd sauciness.—*King John,* v, 2, 133. The only use of "unhair'd."

13
You were saucy at my gates, and allowed your approach rather to wonder at you than to hear you.
Twelfth Night. Act i, sc. 5, l. 209. [Olivia]
Is 't so saucy?—*Twelfth Night,* iii, 4, 159.

14
You, minion, are too saucy.
The Two Gentlemen of Verona. Act i, sc. 2, l. 92. [Julia]

SAVAGERY

15
If this uncouth forest yield any thing savage, I will either be food for it or bring it for food to thee.
As You Like It. Act ii, sc. 6, l. 6. [Orlando] "Uncouth" is repeated in *Titus Andronicus,* ii, 3, 211: "Uncouth fear."
I thought that all things had been savage here.
As You Like It. Act ii, sc. 7, l. 107. [Orlando]

1
I would they were barbarians—as they are,
Though in Rome litter'd—not Romans—as they are not,
Though calv'd i' the porch o' the Capitol.
Coriolanus. Act iii, sc. 1, l. 238. [Coriolanus] The only use of "barbarians" and "calv'd."
Erring barbarian.—*Othello,* i, 3, 365.
Barbarian slave.—*Troilus and Cressida,* ii, 1, 52. The only uses of "barbarian."

2
Savage and inhuman creature!
Henry V. Act ii, sc. 2, l. 95. [King Henry]
Grow like savages.—*Henry V,* v, 2, 59.
Like savages.—*Love's Labour 's Lost,* v, 2, 202.
Most savage and unnatural!—*King Lear,* iii, 3, 7.
I am too savage.—*Macbeth,* iv, 2, 70.

3
This is . . . the wildest savagery.
King John. Act iv, sc. 3, l. 48. [Salisbury]
Deracinate such savagery.—*Henry V,* v, 2, 47. The only uses of "savagery." "Deracinate" is repeated in *Troilus and Cressida,* i, 3, 99.

4
We will be singuled from the barbarous.
Love's Labour 's Lost, v, 1, 86. See under EDUCATION. The only use of "singuled" (singled out).
Be not barbarous.—*Titus Andronicus,* i, 1, 378.
Was every Scythia half so barbarous?—*Titus Andronicus,* i, 1, 131.
Most barbarous.—*King Lear,* iv, 2, 43.
Not enough barbarous.—*Pericles,* iv, 2, 70.
Barbarous Moor.—*Titus Andronicus,* ii, 3, 78; v, 3, 4.
Barbarous people.—*Henry V,* iii, 5, 4.
Barbarous Scythian.—*King Lear,* i, 1, 118.
Barbarous Tamora.—*Titus Andronicus,* ii, 3, 118.

5
Barbarism itself had pitied him.
Richard II. Act v, sc. 2, l. 36. [York]
I have for barbarism spoke.—*Love's Labour 's Lost,* i, 1, 112.
Barbarism, making me a precedent.—*The Winter's Tale,* ii, 1, 84.
Proclaim barbarism.—*Troilus and Cressida,* v, 4, 18. The only uses of "barbarism."

6
Savage, extreme, rude, cruel, not to trust.
Sonnets. No. cxxix.
Savage islanders.—*II Henry VI,* iv, 1, 137.
Savages and men of Ind.—*Tempest,* ii, 2, 60.
Savage man of Ind.—*Love's Labour 's Lost,* iv, 3, 222.

7
Wolves and bears, they say,
Casting their savageness aside have done
Like offices of pity.
Winter's Tale, ii, 3, 188. See under BABY.
A savageness in unreclaimed blood.
Hamlet, ii, 1, 34. See under FAULT. The only use of "unreclaimed."
She will sing the savageness out of a bear.
Othello, iv, 1, 200. The only uses of "savageness."

SAYING, see Proverb

SCANDAL

See also Gossip, Rumour

8
Not without some scandal to yourself.
The Comedy of Errors, v, 1, 15. See under SHAME.
To his own scandal.—*Hamlet,* i, 4, 36.

9
Scandal'd the suppliants for the people.
Coriolanus. Act iii, sc. 1, l. 44. [Brutus]
Scandal'd company.—*The Tempest,* iv, 1, 90. The only uses of "scandal'd."

10
You must not put another scandal on him.
Hamlet. Act ii, sc. 1, l. 29. [Polonius]
No, in despite of sense and secrecy,
Unpeg the basket on the house's top,
Let the birds fly.
Hamlet. Act iii, sc. 4, l. 192. [Hamlet] The only use of "unpeg."

11
The liberty that follows our places stops the mouth of all find-faults.
Henry V. Act v, sc. 2, l. 297. [King Henry] The only use of "find-faults." In *Troilus and Cressida,* Prol., l. 30, there is, "Like or find fault, do as your pleasures are."

12
O, what a scandal is it to our crown,
That two such noble peers as ye should jar!
I Henry VI. Act iii, sc. 1, l. 69. [King]

13
Why, yet thy scandal were not wiped away,
But I in danger for the breach of law.
II Henry VI. Act ii, sc. 4, l. 65. [Gloucester]

14
Oft have I heard his praises in pursuit,
But ne'er till now his scandal of retire.
III Henry VI. Act ii, sc. 1, l. 149. [Richard]

15
A man That is no fleering tell-tale.
Julius Cæsar. Act i, sc. 3, l. 116. [Casca] The only use of "fleering."
I do not bid the thunder-bearer shoot,
Nor tell tales of thee to high-judging Jove.
King Lear. Act ii, sc. 4, l. 230. [King Lear] The only use of "thunder-bearer" and "high-judging." See also 1488:8.
No tell-tale nor no breed-bate.
Merry Wives of Windsor, i, 4, 12. [Mistress Quickly] The only use of "breed-bate."
We are no tell-tales.—*The Merchant of Venice,* v, 1, 123.
Lie like tell-tales.—*The Two Gentlemen of Verona,* i, 2, 133.
Keep no tell-tale.—*II Henry IV,* iv, 1, 202.
Tell-tale Day.—*The Rape of Lucrece,* l. 806.
Tell-tale women.—*Richard III,* iv, 4, 149. The only uses of "tell-tale" and "tell-tales."

16
Shall we thus permit
A blasting and a scandalous breath to fall
On him so near us?
Measure for Measure, v, 1, 121. [Duke]
Scandalous to the world.—*The Winter's Tale,* ii, 3, 121. The only uses of "scandalous."

17
Your worship was the last man in our mouths.
The Merchant of Venice, i, 3, 61. [Shylock]

18
Yea, though I die, the scandal will survive,

And be an eye-sore in my golden coat.
The Rape of Lucrece, l. 204. "Eye-sore" is repeated in *Taming of the Shrew,* iii, 2, 103.

1
Ah, would the scandal vanish with my life,
How happy then were my ensuing death!
Richard II. Act ii, sc. 1, l. 67. [Gaunt]

2
Black scandal or foul-faced reproach.
Richard III. Act iii, sc. 7, l. 231. [Gloucester] The only use of "foul-faced."

3
However these disturbers of our peace
Buz in the people's ears.
Titus Andronicus, iv, 4, 6. [Saturninus]

Particular scandal.—*Measure for Measure,* iv, 4, 30.

Vulgar scandal.—*Sonnets,* cxii.

4 What care I who calls me well or ill,
So you o'er-green my bad, my good allow?
Sonnets. No. cxii. The only use of "o'er-green."

In so profound abysm I throw all care
Of others' voices, that my adder's sense
To critic and to flatterer stopped are.
Sonnets. No. cxii.

Abysm of hell.—*Antony and Cleopatra,* iii, 13, 147.

Abysm of time.—*The Tempest,* i, 2, 50. The only uses of "abysm."

5
They are scoundrels and substractors that say so of him.
Twelfth Night. Act i, sc. 3, l. 36. [Sir Toby] The only use of "scoundrels" and "substractors."

6
I fear me, it will make me scandalized.
The Two Gentlemen of Verona. Act ii, sc. 7, l. 61. [Julia]

Live scandalized.—*I Henry IV,* i, 3, 154. The only uses of "scandalized."

7
The injury of tongues.
Winter's Tale. Act i, sc. 2, l. 338. [Camillo]

Give scandal.—*The Winter's Tale,* i, 2, 330.

SCAR

See also Wound

8
His cicatrice, an emblem of war, here on his sinister cheek.
All's Well that Ends Well. Act ii, sc. 1, l. 43. [Parolles] "Emblem" is used only once again, in *Henry VIII,* iv, 1, 89.

Yet thy cicatrice looks raw and red.
Hamlet. Act iv, sc. 3, l. 62. [King]

Large cicatrices.—*Coriolanus,* ii, 1, 164. "Cicatrice" is used a fourth time in *As You Like It,* iii, 5, 23.

9
A scar nobly got, or a noble scar, is a good livery of honour.
All's Well that Ends Well. Act iv, sc. 5, l. 105. [Lafeu]

Yonder's my lord your son with a patch of velvet on's face: whether there be a scar under 't or no, the velvet knows: but 'tis a goodly patch of velvet.
All's Well that Ends Well. Act iv, sc. 5, l. 99. [Clown]

10
When I bestrid thee in the wars and took
Deep scars to save thy life.
The Comedy of Errors. Act v, sc. 1, l. 192. [Antipholus of Ephesus]

Deep scars.—*II Henry VI,* i, 1, 87.

11 Scratches with briers,
Scars to move laughter only.
Coriolanus. Act iii, sc, 3, l. 51. [Coriolanus]

Shallow scratch.—*I Henry IV,* v, 4, 11.

Unaching scars.—*Coriolanus,* ii, 2, 152. See under BOASTING.

12
Then he will strip his sleeve and show his scars,
And say 'These wounds I had on Crispin's day.'
Henry V. Act iv, sc. 3, l. 47. [King Henry]

And patches will I get unto these cudgell'd scars,
And swear I got them in the Gallia wars.
Henry V. Act v, sc. 1, l. 93. [Pistol]

13
Show me one scar character'd on thy skin:
Men's flesh preserved so whole do seldom win.
II Henry VI. Act iii, sc. 1, l. 300. [York] "Character'd" is repeated in *The Two Gentlemen of Verona,* ii, 7, 4.

14
He jests at scars that never felt a wound.
Romeo and Juliet. Act ii, sc. 2, l. 1. [Romeo]

15
My scars can witness, dumb although they are,
That my report is just and full of truth.
Titus Andronicus. Act v, sc. 3, l. 114. [Titus]

16
'Tis but a scar to scorn.
Troilus and Cressida, i, 1, 114. [Troilus]

Scars of infamy.—*Richard III,* iii, 7, 126.

SCENE

See also Acting

17 The scene
Is now transported, gentles, to Southampton; . . .
Unto Southampton do we shift our scene.
Henry V, ii, Prol., 42.

In Troy, there lies the scene.—*Troilus and Cressida,* Prol., 1.

In fair Verona, where we lay our scene.—*Romeo and Juliet,* Prol., 2.

18
Such noble scenes as draw the eye to flow
We now present.
Henry VIII, Prol., 4.

19 How many ages hence
Shall this our lofty scene be acted over
In states unborn and accents yet unknown!
Julius Cæsar. Act iii, sc. 1, l. 111. [Cassius]

20
O, what a scene of foolery have I seen,
Of sighs, of groans, of sorrow and of teen!
Love's Labour's Lost, iv, 3, 163. [Biron]

Scene of death.—*III Henry VI,* iv, 6, 10.

Scene of mirth.—*Troilus and Cressida,* i, 3, 173.

Woe's scene.—*Richard III,* iv, 4, 27.

Last scene of all.—*As You Like It,* ii, 7, 163.

1 Worthies, away! the scene begins to cloud.
Love's Labour's Lost. Act v, sc. 2, l. 731. [Biron]

2 Fat Falstaff hath a great scene.
The Merry Wives of Windsor. Act iv, sc. 6, l. 17. [Fenton]

3 That's the scene that I would see, which will be merely a dumb-show.
Much Ado about Nothing. Act ii, sc. 3, l. 225. [Don Pedro]

4 My dismal scene I needs must act alone.
Romeo and Juliet. Act iv, sc. 3, l. 19. [Juliet]

Fast-growing scene.—*Pericles,* iv, Gower, 6. "Fast-growing" is repeated in *Richard II,* iii, 4, 34: "Fast-growing sprays."
Industrious scenes.—*King John,* ii, 1, 376.
Little scene.—*Richard II,* iii, 2, 164.
Rude scene.—*II Henry IV,* i, 1, 159.
Swelling scene.—*Henry V,* Prol., 4.
Tedious brief scene.—*A Midsummer-Night's Dream,* v, 1, 56.
Unnatural scene.—*Coriolanus,* v, 3, 184.
Scene individable.—*Hamlet,* ii, 2, 418. The only use of "individable."

5 Your patience thus allowing,
I turn my glass and give my scene such growing
As you have slept between.
The Winter's Tale. Act iv, sc. 1, l. 15. [Time]

6 It shall be so my care
To have you royally appointed as if
The scene you play were mine.
The Winter's Tale. Act iv, sc. 4, l. 601. [Camillo]

SCEPTRE

7 By my sceptre and my hopes of heaven.
All's Well that Ends Well. Act ii, sc. 1, l. 195. [King]

By my sceptre and my soul to boot.
I Henry IV. Act iii, sc. 2, l. 97. [King]

By my sceptre's awe.—*Richard II,* i, 1, 118.

8 It were for me
To throw my sceptre at the injurious gods.
Antony and Cleopatra. Act iv, sc. 15, l. 74. [Cleopatra]

9 Her sceptre so fantastically borne
By a vain, giddy, shallow, humorous youth.
Henry V. Act ii, sc. 4, l. 27. [Dauphin]
"Fantastically" is repeated in *II Henry IV,* iii, 2, 334: "Fantastically carved."

10 'Tis much when sceptres are in children's hands.
I Henry VI. Act iv, sc. 1, l. 192. [Exeter]

Hold the sceptre in his childish fist.
II Henry VI. Act i, sc. 1, l. 245. [York]

11 A sceptre, or an earthly sepulchre!
III Henry VI. Act i, sc. 4, l. 17. [York]

Wring the awful sceptre from his fist.
III Henry VI. Act ii, sc. 1, l. 154. [Warwick]

Awful princely sceptre.—*II Henry VI,* v, 1, 98.
Golden sceptre.—*I Henry VI,* v, 3, 118.
Unwieldy sceptre.—*Richard II,* iv, 1, 205.
Sceptr'd isle.—*Richard II,* ii, 1, 40.
Sceptr'd office.—*Richard III,* iii, 7, 119.
Sceptred sway.—*Merchant of Venice,* iv, 1, 193. The only uses of "sceptred."

12 Thy place is fill'd, thy sceptre wrung from thee.
III Henry VI. Act iii, sc. 1, l. 16. [King]

13 Who's that that bears the sceptre?
Henry VIII. Act iv, sc. 1, l. 38. [Gentleman]

14 A sceptre snatch'd with an unruly hand
Must be as boisterously maintain'd as gain'd.
King John. Act iii, sc. 4, l. 135. [Pandulph]
The only use of "boisterously."

15 Put a barren sceptre in my gripe.
Macbeth, iii, 1, 62. See under SON.

Some I see
That two-fold balls and treble sceptres carry.
Macbeth. Act iv, sc. 1, l. 120. [Macbeth]

16 His sceptre shows the force of temporal power.
The Merchant of Venice, iv, 1, 190. See under MERCY.

17 My sceptre for a palmer's walking-staff.
Richard II, iii, 3, 151. See under GRAVE.
The only use of "walking-staff."

His high sceptre yields
To the possession of thy royal hand.
Richard II. Act iv, sc. 1, l. 109. [York]

18 A sceptre to control the world.
Titus Andronicus, i, 1, 199. See under HONOUR.

SCHOLAR

19 Thou art a scholar; speak to it, Horatio.
Hamlet. Act i, sc. 1, l. 42. [Marcellus]

Thou 'rt a scholar.—*Twelfth Night,* ii, 3, 13.

20 Wolsey: I know your majesty has always loved her
So dear in heart not to deny her that
A woman of less place might ask by law:
Scholars allow'd freely to argue for her.
King Henry: Ay, and the best she shall have; and my favour
To him that does best.
Henry VIII. Act ii, sc. 2, l. 110.

He was a scholar, and a ripe and good one;
Exceeding wise, fair-spoken, and persuading.
Henry VIII. Act iv, sc. 2, l. 51. [Griffith]
The only use of "fair-spoken."

21 Sir, I hear you are a scholar.
The Merry Wives of Windsor. Act ii, sc. 2, l. 186. [Ford]

He is a better scholar than I thought he was.
The Merry Wives of Windsor. Act iv, sc. 1, l. 82. [Mrs. Page]

A scholar and a soldier.—*The Merchant of Venice,* i, 2, 124.
A scholar, a statesman and a soldier.—*Measure for Measure,* iii, 2, 154.

1
I would to God some scholar would conjure her.
Much Ado about Nothing. Act ii, sc. 1, l. 264. [Benedick]

2
Forsooth, a great arithmetician.
Othello. Act i, sc. 1, l. 19. [Iago] The only use of "arithmetician."
This counter-caster.—*Othello,* i, 1, 31. The only use of "counter-caster," a contemptuous term for an arithmetician.

3
Never was such a sudden scholar made.
Henry V. Act i, sc. 1, l. 32. [Canterbury]
Great scholar.—*Twelfth Night,* iv, 2, 12.
Labour'd scholar.—*Pericles,* i, 3, 17.
Young scholar.—*The Taming of the Shrew,* ii, 1, 79.
Fellow-scholars.—*Love's Labour's Lost,* i, 1, 17. The only use of the phrase.

4
All scholars, lawyers, courtiers, gentlemen,
They call false caterpillars and intend their death.
II Henry VI. Act iv, sc. 4, l. 36. [Messenger]

5
Simonides: Sir, you are music's master.
Pericles: The worst of all her scholars.
Pericles. Act ii, sc. 5, l. 30.
She will be your scholar.—*Pericles,* ii, 5, 39.
I doubt not but this populous city will
Yield many scholars.
Pericles. Act iv, sc. 6, l. 197. [Marina]

6
I am no breeching scholar in the schools.
The Taming of the Shrew. Act iii, sc. 1, l. 18. [Bianca] The only use of "breeching."

SCHOOL

See also Education

7
The schools, Embowell'd of their doctrine.
All's Well that Ends Well. Act i, sc. 3, l. 226. [Countess] "Embowell'd" is repeated in *I Henry IV,* v, 4, 109, and in *Richard III,* v, 2, 10.

8
Then the whining school-boy, with his satchel
And shining morning face, creeping like snail
Unwillingly to school.
As You Like It. Act ii, sc. 7, l. 145. [Jaques]
A peevish schoolboy, worthless of such honour.
Julius Cæsar. Act v, sc. 1, l. 61. [Cassius] "Schoolboy" is used nine times.

9
He was quick mettle when he went to school.
Julius Cæsar. Act i, sc. 2, l. 300. [Brutus]
She was a vixen when she went to school.
A Midsummer-Night's Dream. Act iii, sc. 2, l. 324. [Helena]

10
We two went to school together.
Julius Cæsar. Act v, sc. 5, l. 26. [Brutus]
My two schoolfellows.—*Hamlet,* iii, 4, 202. The only use of "schoolfellows."

11
Men shall swear I have discontinued school
Above a twelvemonth.
The Merchant of Venice. Act iii, sc. 4, l. 75. [Portia] The only use of "discontinued." "Discontinue" occurs in *Much Ado about Nothing,* v, 1, 192.

12
I 'll but bring my young man here to school.
The Merry Wives of Windsor. Act iv, sc. 1, l. 8. [Mrs. Page]
Mrs. Page: How now, Sir Hugh! no school to-day?
Evans: No; Master Slender is let the boys leave to play.
Mistress Quickly: Blessing of his heart!
Merry Wives of Windsor. Act iv, sc. 1, l. 10.

13
I have some private schooling for you both.
A Midsummer-Night's Dream. Act i, sc. 1, l. 116. [Theseus] The only use of "schooling."

14
Busy yourselves in skill-contending schools.
The Rape of Lucrece, l. 1018. The only use of "skill-contending."

15
Thy school-days frightful, desperate, wild, and furious.
Richard III. Act iv, sc. 4, l. 169. [Duchess of York] "Frightful" is used only once again, in *II Henry VI,* iii, 2, 326.
In my school-days.—*The Merchant of Venice,* i, 1, 140.
School-days' friendship.—*A Midsummer-Night's Dream,* iii, 2, 202. The only uses of "school-days."

16
As willingly as ere I came from school.
The Taming of the Shrew. Act iii, sc. 2, l. 152. [Gremio]
Like a school broke up,
Each hurries toward his home.
II Henry IV. Act iv, sc. 2, l. 104. [Hastings]
As schoolboys from their books.—*Romeo and Juliet,* ii, 2, 157. See under Love.
Going back to school.—*Hamlet,* i, 2, 113.
Keeps at school.—*As You Like It,* i, 1, 6.

SCHOOLMASTER, see Teacher

SCOLD

17
So thy cheek pays shame
When shrill-tongued Fulvia scolds.
Antony and Cleopatra. Act i, sc. 1, l. 31. [Cleopatra]
Is she shrill-tongued or low?—*Antony and Cleopatra,* iii, 3, 15. The only uses of "shrill-tongued."

18
'Tis the first time that ever
I was forced to scold.
Coriolanus. Act v, sc. 6, l. 106. [Coriolanus]

19
Gloucester: For God's sake, take away this captive scold.
Prince of Wales: Nay, take away this scolding crook-back rather.
III Henry VI. Act v, sc. 5, l. 29. "Crook-back" is used twice again in the same play (i, 4, 75; ii, 2, 96) and in no other.
Scold it out of him.—*Henry VIII,* v, 1, 173.

1
We grant thou canst outscold us; fare thee well;
We hold our time too precious to be spent
With such a brabbler.
King John. Act v, sc. 2, l. 160. [Dauphin] The only use of "outscold."
Brabbler the hound.—*Troilus and Cressida,* v, 1, 99. The only uses of "brabbler."
Thou unadvised scold.—*King John,* ii, 1, 191.
2
I had rather hear them scold than fight.
Merry Wives of Windsor, ii, 1, 239. [Page]
3 To scold and raise up such a storm
That mortal ears might hardly endure the din.
The Taming of the Shrew. Act i, sc. 1, l. 177. [Tranio]
I know she is an irksome brawling scold.
The Taming of the Shrew. Act i, sc. 2, l. 188. [Petruchio]
4
Scolding would do little good upon him.
Taming of the Shrew, i, 2, 109. [Grumio]
Scolding crook-back.—*III Henry VI,* v, 5, 30.
Scolding quean.—*All's Well that Ends Well,* ii, 2, 27.
Scolding tongue.—*The Taming of the Shrew,* i, 2, 100; 254.
Scolding winds.—*Julius Cæsar,* i, 3, 5. The only uses of "scolding."

SCONCE, see Head

SCORN

See also Contempt, Ridicule

5
Sweet Phebe, do not scorn me; do not, Phebe.
As You Like It. Act iii, sc. 5, l. 1. [Silvius]
That is the way to make her scorn you still.
As You Like It. Act ii, sc. 4, l. 22. [Corin]
The red glow of scorn.—*As You Like It,* iii, 4, 57.
6
I would not spare my brother in this case
If he should scorn me so apparently.
The Comedy of Errors. Act iv, sc. 1, l. 77. [Angelo] The only use of "apparently."
Antipholus of Ephesus: Did not her kitchen-maid rail, taunt and scorn me?
Dromio of Ephesus: Certes, she did; the kitchen-vestal scorn'd you.
The Comedy of Errors. Act iv, sc. 4, l. 77. The only use of "kitchen-maid" and "kitchen-vestal." "Certes" is used five times.
To make a loathsome abject scorn of me.
The Comedy of Errors. Act iv, sc. 4, l. 106. [Antipholus of Ephesus]
7
To show . . . scorn her own image.
Hamlet. Act iii, sc. 2, l. 26. [Hamlet]
8
He scorns to say his prayers, lest a' should be a coward.
Henry V, iii, 2, 40. See Word and Deed.
Takes no scorn.—*Henry V,* iv, 7, 107.
9
Plantagenet: I scorn thee and thy fashion, peevish boy.
Suffolk: Turn not thy scorns this way, Plantagenet.
Plantagenet: Proud Pole, I will, and scorn both him and thee.
I Henry VI. Act ii, sc. 4, l. 76.
I scorn you.—*II Henry IV,* ii, 4, 132; 322.
I scorn that with my heels.
Much Ado about Nothing. Act iii, sc. 4, l. 51. [Margaret]
Scorn our courtesy.—*The Two Gentlemen of Verona,* iv, 1, 68.
Scorn death.—*Macbeth,* iii, 5, 30.
Scorns the heat.—*Venus and Adonis,* l. 311.
Scorn the match.—*I Henry VI,* v, 3, 96.
Scorn thy meat.—*Timon of Athens,* i, 2, 38.
Scorn a present.—*The Two Gentlemen of Verona,* iii, 1, 92.
Scorn running.—*The Merchant of Venice,* ii, 2, 9.
Scorns your services.—*A Midsummer-Night's Dream,* iii, 2, 331.
Scorn thy strength.—*I Henry VI,* i, 5, 15.
Scorns the sun.—*Richard III,* i, 3, 265.
Scorn the term.—*Henry V,* ii, 1, 32.
Scorn his worthless threats!—*III Henry VI,* i, 1, 101.
Scorn to fly.—*Richard III,* iii, 4, 85.
Scorn to live.—*The Taming of the Shrew,* iv, 2, 18.
Think scorn.—*II Henry VI,* iv, 2, 13; *Love's Labour's Lost,* i, 2, 66; *Cymbeline,* iv, 4, 53.
10
Take foul scorn to fawn on him.
I Henry VI. Act iv, sc. 4, l. 35. [Lucy]
With a proud majestical high scorn.
I Henry VI. Act iv, sc. 7, l. 39. [Bastard]
Idle scorn.—*Love's Labour's Lost,* i, 1, 311; v, 2, 875.
Martial scorn.—*Romeo and Juliet,* iii, 1, 166.
Notable scorns.—*Othello,* iv, 1, 83.
Salt scorn.—*Troilus and Cressida,* i, 3, 371.
Shame's scorn.—*I Henry VI,* iv, 6, 49.
11
Dare he presume to scorn us in this manner?
III Henry VI. Act iii, sc. 3, l. 178. [King Lewis]
Setting your scorns and your mislike aside.
III Henry VI. Act iv, sc. 1, l. 24. [King Edward]
12
What means this scorn, thou most untoward knave?
King John. Act i, sc. 1, l. 243. [Lady Faulconbridge] "Untoward" is used again in *The Taming of the Shrew,* iv, 5, 79.
13
How will he scorn! how will he spend his wit!
How will he triumph, leap and laugh at it!
Love's Labour's Lost. Act iv, sc. 3, l. 147. [King]
Bruise me with scorn, confound me with a flout.
Love's Labour's Lost. Act v, sc. 2, l. 397. [Biron]
14
When at your hands did I deserve this scorn?
A Midsummer-Night's Dream. Act ii, sc. 2, l. 124. [Helena]

Scorn and derision never come in tears.
A Midsummer-Night's Dream. Act iii, sc. 2, l. 123. [Lysander]

How can these things in me seem scorn to you,
Bearing the badge of faith to prove them true?
A Midsummer-Night's Dream. Act iii, sc. 2, l. 126. [Lysander]

I scorn you not: it seems that you scorn me.
A Midsummer-Night's Dream. Act iii, sc. 2, l. 221. [Hermia]

Sweet, do not scorn her so.—*A Midsummer-Night's Dream,* iii, 2, 247.

Scornful Lysander!—*A Midsummer-Night's Dream,* i, 1, 95.

1 A fixed figure for the time of scorn
To point his slow unmoving finger at!
Othello. Act iv, sc. 2, l. 54. [Othello] The only use of "unmoving."

His scorn I approve.—*Othello,* iv, 3, 52.

2 With thy scorns drew'st rivers from his eyes.
Richard III. Act i, sc. 3, l. 176. [Gloucester]

To mitigate the scorn he gives his uncle,
He prettily and aptly taunts himself.
Richard III. Act iii, sc. 1, l. 133. [Buckingham] "Mitigate" is repeated in *I Henry VI,* iii, 1, 88, and in *Merchant of Venice,* iv 1, 203.

For one that scorn'd at me, now scorn'd of me.
Richard III. Act iv, sc. 4, l. 102. [Queen Margaret]

3 Thou comest not to be made a scorn in Rome.
Titus Andronicus. Act i, sc. 1, l. 265. [Saturninus]

4 Good beauties, let me sustain no scorn.
Twelfth Night. Act i, sc. 5, l. 186. [Viola]

O, what a deal of scorn looks beautiful
In the contempt and anger of his lip!
Twelfth Night. Act iii, sc. 1, l. 157. [Olivia]

5 Scorn at first makes after-love the more.
The Two Gentlemen of Verona. Act iii, sc. 1, l. 95. [Valentine] "After-love" is repeated in *Richard II,* v, 3, 35.

6 The sun doth scorn you and the wind doth hiss you.
Venus and Adonis, l. 1084.

Hiss'd him in scorn.
Romeo and Juliet. Act i, sc. 1, l. 119. [Benvolio]

Laugh to scorn: see under RIDICULE.

SCOTLAND

7 Antipholus of Syracuse: Where Scotland?
Dromio of Syracuse: I found it by the barrenness.
The Comedy of Errors. Act iii, sc. 2, l. 122. The only use of "barrenness."

8 That ever valiant and approved Scot.
I Henry IV. Act i, sc. 1, l. 54. [Westmoreland]

That sprightly Scot of Scots.
I Henry IV. Act ii, sc. 4, l. 377. [Falstaff]

Furious Scot.—*II Henry IV,* i, 1, 126.

Hot termagant Scot.—*I Henry IV,* v, 4, 114. "Termagant" occurs again in *Hamlet,* iii, 2, 15.

Noble Scot.—*I Henry IV,* i, 3, 212; iv, 1, 1; v, 5, 17.

Proud Scot.—*I Henry IV,* v, 3, 11.

Vile Scot.—*I Henry IV,* v, 4, 39.

9 There is not such a word
Spoke of in Scotland as this term of fear.
I Henry IV. Act iv, sc. 1, l. 84. [Earl of Douglas]

10 I will resolve for Scotland: there am I,
Till time and vantage crave my company.
II Henry IV. Act ii, sc. 3, l. 67. [Northumberland]

He is retired, to ripe his growing fortunes,
To Scotland.
II Henry IV. Act iv, sc. 1, l. 14. [York]

O, fly to Scotland.—*II Henry IV,* ii, 3, 50.

From Scotland am I stol'n.—*III Henry VI,* iii, 1, 13.

11 The Scot
Who hath been still a giddy neighbour to us;
For you shall read that my great-grandfather
Never went with his forces into France
But that the Scot on his unfurnish'd kingdom
Came pouring like the tide.
Henry V. Act i, sc. 2, l. 144. [King Henry] "Great-grandfather" is repeated in i, 1, 89, and in *III Henry VI,* ii, 2, 37. "Great-grandsire" is used in *II Henry IV,* iv, 4, 128, and in *Henry V,* i, 2, 103.

'If that you will France win,
Then with Scotland first begin:'
For once the eagle England being in prey,
To her unguarded nest the weasel Scot
Comes sneaking and so sucks her princely eggs.
Henry V. Act i, sc. 2, l. 167. [Westmoreland]

12 Forced to live in Scotland a forlorn.
III Henry VI. Act iii, sc. 3, l. 26. [Queen Margaret]

Lives in Scotland at his ease.—*III Henry VI,* iii, 3, 151.

13 Scotland hath will to help.
III Henry VI. Act iii, sc. 3, l. 34. [Queen Margaret]

Scotland hath foisons to fill up your will.
Macbeth. Act iv, sc. 3, l. 88. [Macduff]

14 Macduff: Stands Scotland where it did?
Ross: Alas, poor country!
Almost afraid to know itself. It cannot
Be call'd our mother, but our grave.
Macbeth. Act iv, sc. 3, l. 164.

15 Nerissa: What think you of the Scottish lord, his neighbour?
Portia: That he hath a neighbourly charity in him, for he borrowed a box of the ear of the Englishman and swore he would pay him again when he was able.
The Merchant of Venice. Act i, sc. 2, l. 83.

Scottish power.—*I Henry IV*, iii, 1, 85.
Scottish prisoners.—*I Henry IV*, i, 3, 259. The only uses of "Scottish."

SCOURGE

1
You have been a scourge to her enemies.
Coriolanus. Act ii, sc. 3, l. 98. [Citizen]

2
I must be their scourge and minister.
Hamlet, iii, 4, 175. See under PUNISHMENT.

3 Out of my blood
He 'll breed . . . a scourge for me.
I Henry IV, iii, 2, 7. See RETRIBUTION.
Scourge of greatness.—*I Henry IV*, i, 3, 11.
Scourged with rods.—*I Henry IV*, i, 3, 239.

4
Assign'd am I to be the English scourge.
I Henry VI. Act i, sc. 2, l. 129. [La Pucelle]
England's bloody scourge!—*II Henry VI*, v, 1, 118.
Bloody scourge.—*I Henry VI*, iv, 2, 16.

5 The Frenchman's only scourge,
Your kingdom's terror and black Nemesis.
I Henry VI. Act iv, sc. 7, l. 77. [Lucy] The only mention of Nemesis.
Is this the scourge of France?—*I Henry VI*, ii, 3, 15.

6 What scourge for perjury
Can this dark monarchy afford?
Richard III. Act i, sc. 4, l. 50. [Clarence]

7
See what a scourge is laid upon your hate.
Romeo and Juliet, v, 3, 292. See LOVE, 915:6.

SCRATCH, see Wound

SCRIPTURE

8
How dost thou understand the Scripture?
The Scripture says 'Adam digged.'
Hamlet, v, 1, 41. See under ADAM.
The devil can cite Scripture.—*The Merchant of Venice*, i, 3, 99.
Piece of scripture.—*Richard III*, i, 3, 334. The only uses of "Scripture."
Scriptures of the loyal Leonatus.—*Cymbeline*, iii, 4, 83. The only use of "scriptures."

9
By God's book are adjudged to death.
II Henry VI, ii, 3, 4. See under SIN. The only use of "God's book."

10
Old odd ends stolen out of holy writ.
Richard III. Act i, sc. 3, l. 337. [Gloucester]
So holy writ in babes hath judgement shown.
All's Well that Ends Well. Act ii, sc. 1, l. 141. [Helena]
Proofs of holy writ.—*Othello*, iii, 3, 324. The only uses of "holy writ."
Sacred writ.—*II Henry VI*, i, 3, 61. The word "bible" does not occur in the plays.

SCRUPLE

11
I will not bate thee a scruple.
All's Well that Ends Well. Act ii, sc. 3, l. 234. [Lafeu]

12
There remains a scruple in that too.
I Henry VI. Act v, sc. 3, l. 93. [Suffolk]
Possess'd him with a scruple.—*Henry VIII*, ii, 1, 158.
Laid any scruple in your way.—*Henry VIII*, ii, 4, 150.
Not making any scruple.—*Troilus and Cressida*, iv, 1, 56.

13 We do lock,
Our former scruple in our strong-barr'd gates.
King John. Act ii, sc. 1, l. 369. [Citizen] The only use of "strong-barr'd."

14
Nor need you, on mine honour, have to do
With any scruple.
Measure for Measure. Act i, sc. 1, l. 64. [Duke]
Black scruples.—*Macbeth*, iv, 3, 116.
Craven scruple.—*Hamlet*, iv, 4, 40.
Smallest scruple.—*Measure for Measure*, i, 1, 38.
Uncleanly scruples!—*King John*, iv, 1, 7.
Scrupulous faction.—*Antony and Cleopatra*, i, 3, 48.
Scrupulous wit.—*III Henry VI*, iv, 7, 61. The only uses of "scrupulous."

15 The division of the twentieth part
Of one poor scruple.
The Merchant of Venice. Act iv, sc. 1, l. 329. [Portia]

SEA

See also Neptune, Ocean, Wave

16
The empire of the sea.
Antony and Cleopatra. Act i, c. 2, l. 192. [Antony]
By sea He is an absolute master.
Antony and Cleopatra. Act ii, sc. 2, l. 165. [Cæsar]
The sea is mine.—*Antony and Cleopatra*, ii, 1, 9.
Antony: We 'll fight with him by sea.
Cleopatra: By sea! what else? . . .
Enobarbus: No disgrace
Shall fall you for refusing him at sea,
Being prepared for land.
Antony: By sea, by sea. . . . I 'll fight at sea. . . .
Soldier: O noble emperor, do not fight by sea;
Trust not to rotten planks. . . . Let the Egyptians
And the Phœnicians go a-ducking.
Anotony and Cleopatra. Act iii, sc. 7, l. 29. The only use of "a-ducking."

17
The always wind-obeying deep.
The Comedy of Errors. Act i, sc. 1, l. 64. [Ægeon] The only use of "wind-obeying."
To gaze upon the secrets of the deep.
Richard III, i, 4, 35. [Brakenbury]

18 Leaves
A shallow plash to plunge him in the deep.
The Taming of the Shrew. Act i, sc. 1, l. 22. [Lucentio] The only use of "plash" (pool).
Salt deep.—*The Tempest*, i, 2, 253.
Unsounded deeps.—*The Two Gentlemen of Verona*, iii, 2, 81.
Vasty deep.—*I Henry IV*, iii, 1, 52.

1 Charming the narrow seas
To give you gentle pass.
Henry V. Act ii, Prologue, l. 38. [Chorus]
The narrow seas that part
The French and English.
The Merchant of Venice, ii, 8, 28. [Salarino]
Wrecked on the narrow seas.—*The Merchant of Venice,* iii, 1, 4.
Commands the narrow seas.—*III Henry VI,* i, 1, 239.
Pass'd in safety through the narrow seas.—*III Henry VI,* iv, 8, 3.
As if a channel should be call'd the sea.
III Henry VI. Act ii, sc. 2, l. 141. [Richard]

2
Cheerly to sea.
Henry V. Act ii, sc. 2, l. 192. [King Henry]
He is bound to sea.—*Comedy of Errors,* iv, 1, 33.
Hoisted sail and put to sea.—*The Comedy of Errors,* v, 1, 21. "Hoisted sail" is repeated in *Sonnets,* cxvii. See under Sail.
And so to sea.—*Pericles,* iii, Gower, 44.
Then to sea, boys!—*The Tempest,* ii, 2, 56.
Put forth to seas.—*Pericles,* ii, Gower, 27.
Put to sea.—*Twelfth Night,* ii, 4, 78.
Cross the seas.—*I Henry VI,* iii, 1, 180, and frequently in later plays.
Crossing the sea.—*I Henry VI,* iv, 1, 89.

3
And in that sea of blood my boy did drench.
I Henry VI. Act iv, sc. 7, l. 14. [Talbot]
Sea of care.—*The Rape of Lucrece,* l. 1100.
Sea of glory.—*Henry VIII,* iii, 2, 360.
Seas of tears.—*III Henry VI,* ii, 5, 106.
Sea of troubles.—*Hamlet,* iii, 1, 59.

4
Commit them to the fortune of the sea.
I Henry VI. Act v, sc. 2, l. 50. [King Henry]
The pageants of the sea.
The Merchant of Venice, i, 1, 11. [Salarino]

5
The sea, with such a storm as his bare head
In hell-black night endured, would have buoy'd up,
And quench'd the stelled fires.
King Lear. Act iii, sc. 7, l. 59. [Gloucester] The only use of "hell-black," "buoy'd," and "stelled." See also Storm.

6
The watery kingdom, whose ambitious head
Spits in the face of heaven.
The Merchant of Venice, ii, 7, 44. [Morocco]

7
The beached margent of the sea.
A Midsummer-Night's Dream. Act ii, sc. 1, l. 85. [Titania]
The beached verge of the salt flood.
Timon of Athens. Act v, sc. 1, l. 219. [Timon] The only uses of "beached."
Thy sea-marge, sterile and rocky-hard.
The Tempest. Act iv, sc. 1, l. 69. [Iris] The only use of "sea-marge" and "rocky-hard."
Thus we set on, Camillo, to the sea-side.
The Winter's Tale, iv, 4, 681. [Florizel]
By the sea-side.—*The Winter's Tale,* iii, 3, 68; *The Tempest,* ii, 2, 138.
Let 's to the sea-side, ho!—*Othello,* ii, 1, 36.
To the sea-side straightway.—*Antony and Cleopatra,* iii, 11, 20.
To the sea-side.—*King John,* v, 7, 91.
Toward the sea-side.—*The Winter's Tale,* iv, 4, 856. The only uses of "sea-side."
Both sea and land.—*Sonnets,* xliv.
By sea and land.—*The Taming of the Shrew,* v, 2, 148; *Julius Cæsar,* i, 3, 87; *The Winter's Tale,* iii, 3, 84; *Antony and Cleopatra,* i, 4, 78; iii, 6, 54; iv, 2, 5.
Of sea and land.—*Cymbeline,* i, 6, 34.

8 O, let the heavens
Give him defence against the elements,
For I have lost him on a dangerous sea.
Othello. Act ii, sc. 1, l. 44. [Cassio]

9 Like to the Pontic sea,
Whose icy current and compulsive course
Ne'er feels retiring ebb.
Othello, iii, 3, 453. See under Thought. Only use of "Pontic." "Compulsive" is repeated in *Hamlet,* iii, 4, 86: "Compulsive ardour."
Swelling Adriatic seas.—*The Taming of the Shrew,* i, 2, 74. The only use of "Adriatic."
Ionian sea.—*Antony and Cleopatra,* iii, 7, 23. The only use of "Ionian."

10
Alas, the sea hath cast me on the rocks,
Wash'd me from shore to shore, and left me breath
Nothing to think on but ensuing death.
Pericles. Act ii, sc. 1, l. 5. [Pericles]
Pericles: May see the sea hath cast upon your coast.
Fisherman: What a drunken knave was the sea to cast thee in our way!
Pericles. Act ii, sc. 1, l. 60.

11
The rough seas, that spare not any man.
Pericles. Act ii, sc. 1, l. 137. [Pericles]
By the rough seas reft of ships and men.
Pericles. Act ii, sc. 3, l. 84. [Pericles]
A sea That almost burst the deck.
Pericles. Act iv, sc. 1, l. 56. [Marina]
The sea works high.—*Pericles,* iii, 1, 48.

12
But sea-room, an the brine and cloudy billow kiss the moon, I care not.
Pericles. Act iii, sc. 1, l. 45. [Sailor] The only use of "sea-room."

13 How brooks your grace the air,
After your late tossing on the breaking seas?
Richard II. Act iii, sc. 2, l. 2. [Aumerle]
Boundless sea.—*Sonnets,* lxv.
Dangerous seas.—*The Merchant of Venice,* iii, 2, 98; *II Henry IV,* i, 1, 181.
The deep-mouth'd sea.—*Henry V,* v, Prol., 11 "Deep-mouth'd" is repeated in *The Taming of the Shrew,* Ind., 1, 18: "Deep-mouth'd brach"; and in *King John,* v, 2, 173: "Deep-mouth'd thunder."
Enridged sea.—*King Lear,* iv, 6, 71. The only use of "enridged."
Farthest sea.—*Romeo and Juliet,* ii, 2, 83.
Furrow'd sea.—*Henry V,* iii, Prol., 12.
Grand sea.—*Antony and Cleopatra,* iii, 12, 10.
Great seas.—*All's Well that Ends Well,* ii. 1, 143; *Pericles,* v, 1, 194.
High seas.—*Othello,* ii, 1, 68.
Imperious seas.—*Cymbeline,* iv, 2, 35.
Mighty sea.—*Richard III,* iii, 7, 162.
Multitudinous seas.—*Macbeth,* ii, 2, 62. "Multitudinous" is repeated in *Coriolanus,* iii, 1, 156: "Multitudinous tongue."

The never-surfeited sea.—*The Tempest,* iii, 3, 55. The only use of the phrase.
The pretty-vaulting sea.—*II Henry VI,* iii, 2, 94. The only use of "pretty-vaulting."
Profound seas.—*The Winter's Tale,* iv, 4, 501.
Raging sea.—*The Two Gentlemen of Verona,* i, 2, 122; *King Lear,* iii, 4, 10.
Roaring sea.—*Romeo and Juliet,* v, 3, 39.
Rude sea.—*A Midsummer-Night's Dream,* ii, 1, 152; *Richard II,* iii, 2, 54; *Twelfth Night,* v, 1, 81.
Ruthless sea.—*III Henry VI,* v, 4, 25.
Salt sea.—*Henry V,* i, 2, 209.
Silver sea.—*Richard II,* ii, 1, 46.
Terrible seas.—*Cymbeline,* iii, 1, 27.
Triumphant sea.—*Richard II,* ii, 1, 61.
Vast sea.—*Timon of Athens,* iv, 3, 440.
Vex'd sea.—*Hamlet,* iv, 4, 2.
Wayward seas.—*Pericles,* iv, 4, 10.
Wide sea.—*Much Ado about Nothing,* iv, 1, 142.
Wild sea.—*Henry VIII,* ii, 4, 200.
Wild watery seas.—*The Comedy of Errors,* ii, 1, 21.

1
Into the tumbling billows of the main.
Richard III. Act i, sc. 4, l. 20. [Clarence] See also Wave.

Swell the curled waters 'bove the main.
King Lear. Act iii, sc. 1, l. 6. [Gentleman]

2
Stanley: Richmond is on the seas.
King Richard: There let him sink, and be the seas on him! . . .
Tell me, what doth he upon the sea?
Richard III. Act iv, sc. 4, l. 463.

3
The sea, all water, yet receives rain still
And in abundance addeth to his store.
Sonnets. No. cxxxv.

4
Now would I give a thousand furlongs of sea for an acre of barren ground, long heath, brown furze, any thing.
The Tempest. Act i, sc. 1, l. 70. [Gonzalo] "Furlongs" occurs again in *The Winter's Tale,* i, 2, 95, and "furze" in *The Tempest,* iv, 1, 180, and in no other play.

Our sea-sorrow.
The Tempest. Act i, sc. 2, l. 170. [Prospero] The only use of the phrase.

The sea mocks Our frustrate search on land.
The Tempest. Act iii, sc. 3, l. 9. [Alonso]

Though the seas threaten, they are merciful.
The Tempest. Act v, sc. 1, l. 178 [Ferdinand]

The sea cannot drown me.—*Tempest,* iii, 2, 15.

5 I shall no more to sea, to sea,
Here shall I die ashore.
The Tempest. Act ii, sc. 2, l. 44. [Stephano]

I 'll never to sea again.—*The Merry Wives of Windsor,* ii, 1, 96.

6 I 'll . . .
Promise you calm seas, auspicious gales
And sail so expeditious that shall catch
Your royal fleet far off.
The Tempest. Act v, sc. 1, l. 314. [Prospero] The only use of "expeditious."

The seas wax'd calm.—*The Comedy of Errors,* i, 1, 92.

7
The sea 's a thief, whose liquid surge resolves
The moon into salt tears.
Timon of Athens, iv, 3, 442. See under Theft.

8
If the winds rage, doth not the sea wax mad,
Threatening the welkin with his big-swoln face?
Titus Andronicus. Act iii, sc. 1, l. 223. [Titus] "Big-swoln" is repeated in *III Henry VI,* ii, 2, 111.

I am the sea; hark, how her sighs do blow!
She is the weeping welkin.
Titus Andronicus. Act iii, sc. 1, l. 226. [Titus]

9 The sea being smooth,
How many shallow bauble boats dare sail
Upon her patient breast, making their way
With those of nobler bulk!
Troilus and Cressida. Act i, sc. 3, l. 34. [Nestor]

The seas and winds, old wranglers, took a truce
And did him service.
Troilus and Cressida. Act ii, sc. 2, l. 75. [Troilus] The only use of "wranglers." "Wrangler" occurs in *Henry V,* i, 2, 264.

10
I am not to say it is a sea, for it is now the sky: betwixt the firmament and it you cannot thrust a bodkin's point. . . . I would you did but see how it chafes, how it rages, how it takes up the shore!
Winter's Tale. Act iii, sc. 3, l. 85. [Clown]

I am put to sea
With her whom here I cannot hold on shore.
The Winter's Tale. Act iv, sc. 4, l. 508. [Florizel]

Unpath'd waters, undream'd shores.
The Winter's Tale. Act iv, sc. 4, l. 577. [Camillo] The only use of "unpath'd" and "undream'd."

II—Seasickness

11 If you are sick at sea,
Or stomach-qualm'd at land, a dram of this
Will drive away distemper.
Cymbeline. Act iii, sc. 4, l. 192. [Pisanio] The only use of "stomach-qualm'd."

The winds grow high; so do your stomachs, lords.
II Henry VI. Act ii, sc. 1, l. 55. [King Henry]

12
Sea-sick, I think, coming from Muscovy.
Love's Labour 's Lost. Act v, sc. 2, l. 393. [Rosaline] The only mention of Muscovy. Muscovite is used three times in *Love's Labour 's Lost,* v, 2, 121; 265; and 303.

He . . . began to be much sea-sick, and himself little better, extremity of weather continuing.
The Winter's Tale. Act v, sc. 2, l. 128. [Autolycus]

Sea-sick bark.—*Romeo and Juliet,* v, 3, 118. The only uses of "sea-sick."

SEARCH

1
Seeks not to find that her search implies.
All's Well that Ends Well. Act i, sc. 3, l. 222. [Helena] The only use of "implies."
Marry, we'll search.—*All's Well that Ends Well,* iv, 3, 229.
Seek him with candle.—*As You Like It,* iii, 1, 6.
2
Of us must Pompey presently be sought,
Or else he seeks out us.
Antony and Cleopatra. Act ii, sc. 2, l. 161. [Lepidus]
Straight let us seek, or straight we shall be sought.
King John. Act v, sc. 7, l. 79. [Bastard]
Sought every country far and near.—*I Henry VI,* v, 4, 3.
Against the thing he sought he would exclaim.
A Lover's Complaint, l. 313.
Sought with all my might.—*The Rape of Lucrece,* l. 488.
Sought a husband.—*Pericles,* i, 1, 66.
Sought her help.—*The Tempest,* v, 1, 142.
Sought my life.—*King Lear,* iii, 4, 172.
Sought my love.—*The Merchant of Venice,* iii, 4, 70.
Sought for safety.—*The Comedy of Errors,* i, 1, 77.
Sought the remedy.—*As You Like It,* v, 2, 40.
Sought their malice.—*Henry VIII,* v, 2, 15.
Sought their shame.—*Lover's Complaint,* l. 187.
Sought to live.—*The Rape of Lucrece,* l. 1051.
Sought to murder.—*Pericles,* v, 3, 9.
Sought to sleep.—*Titus Andronicus,* ii, 4, 19.
Sought to win.—*Macbeth,* iv, 3, 118.
3
Let not search and inquisition quail.
As You Like It. Act ii, sc. 2, l. 20. [Duke]
A bootless inquisition.
The Tempest. Act i, sc. 2, l. 35. [Miranda] The only uses of "inquisition."
4
I to the world am like a drop of water
That in the ocean seeks another drop.
The Comedy of Errors. Act i, sc. 2, l. 35. [Antipholus of Syracuse]
Cease your search.—*Hamlet,* v, 2, 374.
5
They are come to search the house.
I Henry IV. Act ii, sc. 4, l. 537. [Hostess]
To search his house.—*The Merry Wives of Windsor,* iii, 5, 78.
Help to search my house.—*The Merry Wives of Windsor,* iv, 2, 167.
Search his pockets.—*I Henry IV,* ii, 4, 580.
Search this bosom.—*Julius Cæsar,* v, 3, 42.
Inward search'd—*Merchant of Venice,* iii, 2, 86.
6
Ascend my chambers; search, seek, find out.
The Merry Wives of Windsor. Act iii, sc. 3, l. 173. [Ford]
On went he for a search, and away went I for foul clothes.
The Merry Wives of Windsor. Act iii, sc. 5, l. 107. [Falstaff]
I will search impossible places.
The Merry Wives of Windsor. Act iii, sc. 5, l. 151. [Ford]
Once more search with me.—*The Merry Wives of Windsor,* iv, 2, 172.
Search you out.—*Othello,* i, 2, 47.
Careful search.—*Pericles,* iii, Gower, 16.
7
You are looked for and called for, asked for and sought for.
Romeo and Juliet. Act i, sc. 5, l. 13. [Servant]
8
Lead off this ground: and let's make further search.
The Tempest. Act ii, sc. 1, l. 323. [Alonso]
Go in search.—*King John,* ii, 1, 428.
Search, seek, and know.—*Romeo and Juliet,* v, 3, 198.
Search every acre.—*King Lear,* iv, 4, 7.
The search so slow!—*Cymbeline,* i, 1, 64.
Go search like nobles.—*Pericles,* ii, 4, 50.
Search the market narrowly.—*Pericles,* iv, 2, 3.
Some others search.—*Romeo and Juliet,* v, 3, 178.
Search my wound.—*Titus Andronicus,* ii, 3, 262.
Search of eyes.—*Romeo and Juliet,* iii, 3, 73.
The searchers of the town.—*Romeo and Juliet,* v, 2, 8. The only use of "searchers."

SEASON

See also Autumn, Spring, Summer, Winter
9
The seasons change their manners.
II Henry IV, iv, 4, 123. See under OMEN.
Out of season.—*The Comedy of Errors,* i, 2, 68; ii, 2, 48; *King Lear,* ii, 1, 121.
Wait the season.—*Love's Labour's Lost,* v, 2, 63.
10
How many things by season season'd are
To their right praise and true perfection!
The Merchant of Venice. Act v, sc. 1, l. 107. [Portia]
11
And thorough this distemperature we see
The seasons alter: hoary-headed frosts
Fall in the fresh lap of the crimson rose,
And on old Hiems' thin and icy crown
An odorous chaplet of sweet summer buds
Is, as in mockery set: the spring, the summer,
The chiding autumn, angry winter, change
Their wonted liveries, and the mazed world,
By their increase, now knows not which is which.
A Midsummer-Night's Dream. Act ii, sc. 1, l. 106. [Titania] The only use of "hoary-headed" and "chaplet."
This side is Hiems, Winter, this Ver, the Spring.
Love's Labour's Lost. Act v, sc. 2, l. 901. [Armado] The only uses of "Hiems." Ver is repeated in l. 903.
12
Three beauteous springs to yellow autumn turn'd
In process of the seasons have I seen,
Three April perfumes in three hot Junes burn'd,
Since first I saw you fresh, which yet are green.
Sonnets. No. civ.

The childing autumn.—*A Midsummer-Night's Dream,* ii, 1, 112. [Titania] The only use of "childing."
The teeming autumn, big with rich increase.
Sonnets. No. xcvii.

1
Now the happy season once more fits.
Venus and Adonis, l. 327.
Happy season.—*II Henry IV,* iv, 2, 79.
Gracious season.—*Cymbeline,* v, 5, 401.
Sad and sorry seasons.—*Sonnets,* xix.
Virtuous season.—*Measure for Measure,* ii, 2, 168.
Youthful season.—*Julius Cæsar,* ii, 1, 108.

SEAT

2
Forsake thy seat, I do beseech thee, captain,
And hear me speak a word.
Antony and Cleopatra, ii, 7, 43. [Menas]
The wheel'd seat
Of fortunate Cæsar, drawn before him, branded
His baseness.
Antony and Cleopatra. Act iv, sc. 14, l. 75. [Antony] "Wheel'd" is repeated in *Richard III,* iv, 4, 105: "Wheel'd about."
Seat for baseness.—*Cymbeline,* i, 1, 142.

3
He grew into his seat.
Hamlet, iv, 7, 86. See under HORSEMANSHIP.
Keep seat.—*Macbeth,* iii, 4, 54.
Lose his seat.—*Henry V,* i, 1, 36.
Newly in the seat.—*Measure for Measure,* i, 2, 165.

4
Struck me in my very seat of judgement.
II Henry IV. Act v, sc. 2, l. 80. [Chief Justice]
Seat of Mars.—*Richard II,* ii, 1, 41.
Seat of peace.—*Richard II,* iv, 1, 140.

5
Methought I sat in seat of majesty
In the cathedral church of Westminster,
And in that chair where kings and queens are crown'd.
II Henry VI. Act i, sc. 2, l. 36. [Duchess] The only use of "cathedral." Westminster is mentioned six times. "Seat of majesty" is repeated in *Richard III,* iii, 7, 169.

6
I must take like seat unto my fortune,
And to my humble seat conform myself.
III Henry VI. Act iii, sc. 3, l. 10. [Queen Margaret] The only use of "conform."
Chiefest seat.—*Pericles,* i, Gower, 18.
Dismal seat.—*Richard III,* iii, 3, 13.
Godlike seat.—*Troilus and Cressida,* i, 3, 31.
Great seats.—*Henry V,* iii, 5, 47.
Imperial seat.—*Titus Andronicus,* i, 1, 14.
Ingrateful seat.—*Timon of Athens,* iv, 2, 45.
Low vassal seat.—*Henry V,* iii, 5, 51.
Melancholy seat.—*Richard III,* iv, 4, 32.
Pleasant seat.—*Macbeth,* i, 6, 1.
Poor seat.—*Henry V,* i, 2, 269.
Self-same seat.—*The Rape of Lucrece,* l. 289.
Supreme seat.—*Richard III,* iii, 7, 118.

7
Oft they interchange each other's seat.
The Rape of Lucrece, l. 70.
Give us some seats.—*Measure for Measure,* v, 1, 165.

8
Long mayst thou live in Richard's seat to sit!
Richard II. Act iv, sc. 1, l. 218. [King Richard]
Thy seat is up on high.—*Richard II,* v, 5, 112.

9
The seat royal of this famous isle.
Richard III. Act i, sc. 3, l. 112. [Buckingham]
Royal seat.—*II Henry VI,* v, 1, 178.
Regal seat.—*III Henry VI,* i, 1, 26; iv, 6, 2.

SECRECY

See also Mute

10
Stall this in your bosom.
All's Well that Ends Well. Act i, sc. 3, l. 131. [Countess]
Second Lord: I will tell you a thing, but you shall let it dwell darkly with you.
First Lord: When you have spoken it, 'tis dead, and I am the grave of it.
All's Well that Ends Well. Act iv, sc. 3, l. 13.

11
I 'll have this secret from thy heart, or rip
Thy heart to find it.
Cymbeline. Act iii, sc. 5, l. 86. [Cloten]

12
This to me
In dreadful secrecy impart they did.
Hamlet. Act i, sc. 2, l. 206. [Horatio]

13
And still your fingers on your lips, I pray.
Hamlet. Act i, sc. 5, l. 188. [Hamlet] See under FINGER.
So shall . . . your secrecy to the king and queen moult no feather.
Hamlet. Act ii, sc. 2, l. 304. [Hamlet] The only use of "moult." "Moulten" occurs in *I Henry IV,* iii, 1, 152.
Be thou assured, if words be made of breath,
And breath of life, I have no life to breathe
What thou hast said to me.
Hamlet. Act iii, sc. 4, l. 197. [Queen]
For secrecy, no lady closer.—*I Henry IV,* ii, 3, 112.

14
What there is else, keep close.
I Henry IV. Act ii, sc. 4, l. 593. [Prince of Wales]
Keep it close.—*The Winter's Tale,* iii, 3, 128.

15
Madam, I have a secret to reveal.
I Henry VI. Act v, sc. 3, l. 100. [Suffolk]

16
To pry into the secrets of the state.
II Henry VI. Act i, sc. 1, l. 250. [York]
Secrets of the deep.—*Richard III,* i, 4, 35.
Secrets of my prison-house.—*Hamlet,* i, 5, 14. The only use of "prison-house."

17
Seal up your lips, and give no words but mum:
The business asketh silent secrecy.
II Henry VI. Act i, sc. 2, l. 89. [Hume] See also under SILENCE.
Silent secrecy.—*II Henry VI,* ii, 2, 68.

18
And whispers to his pillow . . .
The secrets of his overcharged soul.
II Henry VI. Act iii, sc. 2, l. 375. [Vaux]

1
I have advertised him by secret means.
III Henry VI. Act iv, sc. 5, l. 9. [Gloucester]

2
This secret is so weighty, 'twill require
A strong faith to conceal it.
Henry VIII. Act ii, sc. 1, l. 144. [Gentleman]

I . . . durst commend a secret to your ear
Much weightier than this work.
Henry VIII. Act v, sc. 1, l. 17. [Lovell] "Weightier" is repeated in *Richard III,* iii, 1, 119, and in *Timon of Athens,* iii, 5, 102.

3
Is it excepted I should know no secrets
That appertain to you?
Julius Cæsar. Act ii, sc. 1, l. 281. [Portia]

And by and by thy bosom shall partake
The secrets of my heart.
Julius Cæsar. Act ii, sc. 1, l. 305. [Brutus]

4
Like a demigod here sit I in the sky,
And wretched fools' secrets heedfully o'er-eye.
Love's Labour's Lost. Act iv, sc. 3, l. 79. [Biron] The only use of "o'er-eye." "Demigod" is repeated in *Merchant of Venice,* iii, 2, 116, and in *Measure for Measure,* i, 2, 124.

I do implore secrecy.—*Love's Labour's Lost,* v, 1, 116.

5
With sleided silk feet and affectedly
Enswathed, and seal'd to curious secrecy.
A Lover's Complaint, l. 48. "Sleided" (sleaved) is repeated in *Pericles,* iv, Gower, 21: "Sleided silk." The only use of "enswathed."

6
'Tis a secret must be locked within the teeth and the lips.
Measure for Measure. Act iii, sc. 2, l. 142. [Lucio]

I would commune with you of such things
That want no ear but yours.
Measure for Measure. Act iv, sc. 3, l. 108. [Duke]

7
What secret hath held you here?
Much Ado about Nothing. Act i, sc. 1, l. 206. [Don Pedro]

I can be secret as a dumb man.
Much Ado about Nothing. Act i, sc. 1, l. 211. [Benedick]

Look where Beatrice, like a lapwing, runs
Close by the ground, to hear our conference.
Much Ado about Nothing. Act iii, sc. 1, l. 24. [Hero]

8
The subtle-shining secrecies
Writ in the glassy margents of such books.
The Rape of Lucrece, l. 101. The only use of "subtle-shining."

9
Stay and be secret.
Richard II. Act ii, sc. 1, l. 298. [Northumberland]

10
Best to do it secretly, alone.
Richard III. Act i, sc. 1, l. 100. [Gloucester]

Do it secretly.—*The Merchant of Venice,* ii, 3, 7.

Secretly and justly.—*Much Ado about Nothing,* iv, 1, 250.

11
To himself so secret and so close,
So far from sounding and discovery,
As is the bud bit with an envious worm,
Ere he can spread his sweet leaves to the air,
Or dedicate his beauty to the sun.
Romeo and Juliet. Act i, sc. 1, l. 155. [Montague] "Sounding" is repeated in iv, 5, 143, and in *Troilus and Cressida,* iv, 2, 115.

12
Thou art to me as secret and as dear
As Anna to the queen of Carthage was.
The Taming of the Shrew. Act i, sc. 1, l. 158. [Lucentio]

13
I see thou wilt not trust the air With secrets.
Titus Andronicus. Act iv. sc. 2, l. 169. [Chiron]

14
The secrets of nature
Have not more gift in taciturnity.
Troilus and Cressida. Act iv, sc. 2, l. 74. [Æneas] The only use of "taciturnity."

15
Olivia: Speak your office.
Viola: It alone concerns your ear.
Twelfth Night. Act i, sc. 5, l. 223.

What I am, and what I would, are as secret as maidenhead; to your ears, divinity, to any other's, profanation.
Twelfth Night. Act i, sc. 5, l. 231. [Viola]

You will not extort from me what I am willing to keep in.
Twelfth Night. Act ii, sc. 1, l. 13. [Sebastian]

My matter hath no voice, lady, but to your own most pregnant and vouchsafed ear.
Twelfth Night. Act iii, sc. 1, l. 99. [Viola] "Vouchsafed" is repeated in *Antony and Cleopatra,* i, 4, 8, and in *Winter's Tale,* v, 3, 4.

16
Thou shalt never get such a secret from me but by a parable.
The Two Gentlemen of Verona. Act ii, sc. 5, l. 40. [Launce] The only use of "parable."

We have some secrets to confer about.
The Two Gentlemen of Verona. Act iii, sc. 1, l. 2. [Duke]

I am to break with thee of some affairs
That touch me near, wherein thou must be secret.
The Two Gentlemen of Verona. Act iii, sc. 1, l. 59. [Duke]

17
A thousand honey secrets shalt thou know.
Venus and Adonis, l. 16.

18
Skulking in corners?
The Winter's Tale. Act i, sc. 2, l. 289. [Leontes] The only use of "skulking."

Is there not milking-time, when you are going to bed, or kiln-hole, to whistle off these secrets, but you must be tittle-tattling before all our guests?
The Winter's Tale. Act iv, sc. 4, l. 246. [Clown] The only use of "milking-time" and "tittle-tattling." "Kiln-hole" occurs again in *The Merry Wives of Windsor,* iv, 2, 59.

It becomes thy oath full well,
Thou to me thy secrets tell.
Winter's Tale. Act iv, sc. 4, l. 306. [Mopsa]

SECURITY

1
In iron walls they deem'd me not secure.
I Henry VI. Act i, sc. 4, l. 49. [Talbot]
2
We may do it as secure as sleep.
I Henry IV. Act i, sc. 2, l. 145. [Poins]
Once again we 'll sleep secure in Rouen.
I Henry VI. Act iii, sc. 2, l. 19. [Charles]
There shall I rest secure from force and fraud.
III Henry VI. Act iv, sc. 4. l. 33. [Queen Elizabeth]
I myself secure in grace and favour.
Richard III. Act iii, sc. 4, l. 93. [Hastings]
Secure in soul.—*Henry V,* iv, Prol., 17.
3
Thus have we swept suspicion from our seat
And made our footstool of security.
III Henry VI. Act v, sc. 7, l. 13. [King Edward] The only use of "footstool."
4
Security gives way to conspiracy.
Julius Cæsar. Act ii, sc. 3, l. 8. [Artemidorus]
5
Security Is mortals' chiefest enemy.
Macbeth. Act iii, sc. 5, l. 32. [Hecate]
Security enough to make fellowships accurst.
Measure for Measure. Act iii, sc. 2, l. 241. [Duke]
6
By heaven, I think there 's no man is secure.
Richard III. Act i, sc. 1, l. 71. [Clarence]
Without security.—*Timon of Athens,* iii, 1, 46.
7
I know your reverend ages love Security.
Timon of Athens. Act iii, sc. 5, l. 80. [Alcibiades]
Fair leave and large security.
Troilus and Cressida, i, 3, 222. [Æneas]
Firm security.—*Antony and Cleopatra,* iii, 7, 49.

SEDITION, see Rebellion

SEDUCTION

8
Their promises, enticements, oaths, tokens, and all these engines of lust, are not the things they go under: many a maid hath been seduced by them; and the misery is, example, that so terrible shows in the wreck of maidenhood, cannot for all that dissuade succession, but that they are limed with the twigs that threaten them.
All's Well that Ends Well. Act iii, sc. 5, l. 20. [Mariana] The only use of "enticements."
Helena: May be the amorous count solicits her
In the unlawful purpose.
Widow: He does indeed;
And brokes with all that can in such a suit
Corrupt the tender honour of a maid:
But she is arm'd for him and keeps her guard
In honestest defence.
All's Well that Ends Well. Act iii, sc. 5, l. 72. The only use of "brokes" in the sense of bargains, and of "honestest."
Ay, so you serve us
Till we serve you; but when you have our roses,
You barely leave our thorns to prick ourselves
And mock us with our bareness.
All's Well that Ends Well. Act iv, sc. 2, l. 17. [Diana]
A seducer flourishes, and a poor maid is undone.
All's Well that Ends Well. Act v, sc. 3, l. 146. [King] The only use of "seducer."
9
He hath perverted a young gentlewoman.
All's Well that Ends Well. Act iv, sc. 3, l. 17. [Second Lord] The only use of "perverted."
Would you again betray the fore-betray'd,
And new pervert a reconciled maid?
A Lover's Complaint, l. 328. The only use of "fore-betray'd." "Pervert" occurs three times.
10
This night he fleshes his will in the spoil of her honour.
All's Well that Ends Well, iv, 3, 19. [Lord]
He was whipped for getting the shrieve's fool with child,—a dumb innocent, that could not say him nay.
All's Well that Ends Well. Act iv, sc. 3, l. 212. [Parolles] The only use of "shrieve."
See also under Pregnancy.
11
With witchcraft of his wit, with traitorous gifts,—
O wicked wit and gifts, that have the power
So to seduce!—won to his shameful lust
The will of my most seeming-virtuous queen.
Hamlet. Act i, sc. 5, l. 42. [Ghost] The only use of "seeming-virtuous."
I fear'd he did but trifle,
And meant to wreck thee.
Hamlet. Act ii, sc. 1, l. 112. [Polonius]
12
Beguiling virgins with the broken seals of perjury.
Henry V. Act iv, sc. 1, l. 174. [King Henry]
13
King Edward: To tell thee plain, I aim to lie with thee.
Lady Grey: To tell you plain, I had rather lie in prison.
III Henry VI. Act iii, sc. 2, l. 69.
He will seduce the rest.
III Henry VI. Act iv, sc. 8, l. 37. [Exeter]
14
The advantage of his absence took the king
And in the mean time sojourn'd at my father's;
Where how he did prevail I shame to speak.
King John. Act i, sc. 1, l. 102. [Robert Faulconbridge]
Lady Faulconbridge: King Richard Cœur-de-lion was thy father:
By long and vehement suit I was seduced
To make room for him in my husband's bed:
Heaven lay not my transgression to my charge!
Thou art the issue of my dear offence,
Which was so strongly urged past my defence.
Bastard: Now, by this light, were I to get again,
Madam, I would not wish a better father. . . .
Who lives and dares but say thou didst not well
When I was got, I 'll send his soul to hell.
King John. Act i, sc. 1, l. 254.

SEEMING

See also Appearance, Pretence

1 My respects are better than they seem
And my appointments have in them a need
Greater than shows itself at the first view
To you that know them not.
All's Well that Ends Well. Act ii, sc. 5, l. 71. [Bertram]

2 All good seeming,
By thy revolt, O husband, shall be thought
Put on for villany; not born where 't grows,
But worn a bait for ladies.
Cymbeline. Act iii, sc. 4, l. 56. [Imogen] The only use of "good seeming."

Mine eyes
Were not in fault, for she was beautiful;
Mine ears, that heard her flattery; nor my heart,
That thought her like her seeming.
Cymbeline. Act v, sc. 5, l. 62. [Cymbeline]

This hath some seeming.—*Cymbeline,* v, 5, 452.

3
Seems, madam! nay, it is; I know not 'seems.'
'Tis not alone my inky cloak, good mother,
Nor customary suits of solemn black,
Nor windy suspiration of forced breath,
No, nor the fruitful river in the eye,
Nor the dejected 'haviour of the visage,
Together with all forms, moods, shapes of grief,
That can denote me truly: these indeed seem,
For they are actions that a man might play:
But I have that within which passeth show;
These but the trappings and the suits of woe.
Hamlet. Act i, sc. 2, l. 76. [Hamlet] The only use of "suspiration." "Trappings" occurs again in *Twelfth Night,* v, 1, 10.

4
Seems he a dove? his feathers are but borrow'd
For he 's disposed as the hateful raven:
Is he a lamb? his skin is surely lent him,
For he 's inclined as is the ravenous wolf.
Who cannot steal a shape that means deceit?
II Henry VI. Act iii, sc. 1, l. 75. [Queen Margaret]

He must seem thus to the world.
II Henry IV. Act v, sc. 5, l. 83. [Falstaff]

5
More than I seem, and less than I was born to.
III Henry VI. Act iii, sc. 1, l. 56. [King Henry]

I do profess to be no less than I seem.
King Lear. Act i, sc. 4, l. 14. [Kent]

6
It did not always seem so.
King Lear. Act i, sc. 1, l. 3. [Gloucester]

Seeming so.—*Othello,* i, 1, 60.

7 Hence shall we see,
If power change purpose, what our seemers be.
Measure for Measure. Act i, sc. 3, l. 53. [Duke] The only use of "seemers."

Seeming, seeming!
Measure for Measure. Act ii, sc. 4, l. 150. [Isabella]

Convenient seeming.—*King Lear,* iii, 2, 56.
False seeming.—*Measure for Measure,* ii, 4, 15.
Full seeming.—*Henry VIII,* ii, 4, 108.
Long seeming.—*Othello,* v, 2, 328.
Mortal seeming.—*Cymbeline,* i, 6, 171.

8
Out on thee! Seeming! I will write against it:
You seem to me, as Dian in her orb,
As chaste as is the bud ere it be blown;
But you are more intemperate in your blood
Than Venus, or those pamper'd animals
That rage in savage sensuality.
Much Ado about Nothing. Act iv, sc. 1, l. 57. [Claudio]

Hollow pamper'd jades of Asia.—*II Henry IV,* ii, 4, 178. The only uses of "pamper'd."

9
Putting on the mere form of civil and humane seeming.
Othello. Act ii, sc. 1, l. 243. [Iago]

Men should be what they seem;
Or those that be not, would they might seem none!
Othello. Act iii, sc. 3, l. 126. [Iago]

She that, so young, could give out such a seeming.
Othello. Act iii, sc. 3, l. 209. [Iago]

10
Thou art not what thou seem'st.
Rape of Lucrece, l. 600; *I Henry IV,* v, 4, 140.

11
That seeming to be most which we indeed least are.
The Taming of the Shrew. Act v, sc. 2, l. 175. [Katharina]

12
Such to-be-pitied and o'er-wrested seeming.
Troilus and Cressida. Act i, sc. 3, l. 157. [Ulysses] The only use of either phrase.

Seeming-gladness.—*Troilus and Cressida,* i, 1, 39.
Seeming knowledge.—*All's Well that Ends Well,* ii, 3, 5.
Seeming mercy.—*I Henry IV,* v, 2, 35.
Seeming sorrow.—*II Henry IV,* v, 2, 29.
Seeming truth.—*The Merchant of Venice,* iii, 2, 100; *Much Ado about Nothing,* ii, 2, 49.
Seeming-virtuous.—*Hamlet,* i, 5, 46.

13
Silvia: Servant, you are sad.
Valentine: Indeed, madam, I seem so.
Silvia: Seem you that you are not?
Valentine: Haply I do.
Silvia: So do counterfeits.
The Two Gentlemen of Verona. Act ii, sc. 4, l. 8. See also under COUNTERFEIT.

SELF

14
Let me lodge Lichas on the horns o' the moon;
And with those hands, that grasp'd the heaviest club,
Subdue my worthiest self.
Antony and Cleopatra. Act iv, sc. 12, l. 45. [Antony]

1
O, I could divide myself and go to buffets, for moving such a dish of skim milk with so honourable an action!
I Henry IV. Act ii, sc. 3, l. 36. [Hotspur]
Mine own self.—*The Comedy of Errors,* iii, 2, 61; *Sonnets,* xxxix.
My other self.—*Richard III,* ii, 2, 151.
2
I have turn'd away my former self.
II Henry IV, v, 5, 62. See under REFORMATION.
Dear self.—*The Comedy of Errors,* ii, 2, 125.
Double self.—*The Merchant of Venice,* v, 1, 245.
Great self.—*Henry VIII,* iii, 2, 336.
Humble self.—*The Two Gentlemen of Verona,* iii, 1, 226.
Innocent self.—*Macbeth,* iii, 1, 79.
Poor self.—*The Comedy of Errors,* v, 2, 35; *Measure for Measure,* iv, 3, 148; *Timon of Athens,* iv, 2, 12; *Cymbeline,* i, 1, 119; *The Rape of Lucrece,* l. 1646.
Pretty self.—*Cymbeline,* iii, 4, 160.
Second self.—*Sonnets,* lxxiii.
Seeing self.—*Henry V,* v, 2, 325.
Unsounded self.—*The Rape of Lucrece,* l. 1819.
Woeful self.—*Love's Labour's Lost,* v, 2, 818; *A Lover's Complaint,* l. 143.
Worthless self.—*The Merchant of Venice,* ii, 9, 18.
Wretched self.—*Richard III,* i, 3, 203.
Action's self.—*Henry VIII,* i, 1, 42.
3
Now mark me, how I will undo myself.
Richard II. Act iv, sc. 1, l. 203. [King Richard]
Infusing him with self.—*Richard II,* iii, 2, 166.
Myself myself confound!
Richard III. Act iv, sc. 4, l. 399. [King Richard]
4
Make thee another self, for love of me,
That beauty still may live in thine or thee.
Sonnets. No. x.
5
I have a kind of self resides with you;
But an unkind self, that itself will leave,
To be another's fool.
Troilus and Cressida. Act iii, sc. 2, l. 155. [Cressida]
6
Your high self,
The gracious mark o' the land.
The Winter's Tale. Act iv, sc. 4, l. 7. [Perdita]
Your fair self.—*Love's Labour's Lost,* ii, 1, 151.
Your gracious self.—*Richard III,* iii, 7, 131; *Romeo and Juliet,* ii, 2, 113; *The Winter's Tale,* iv, 4, 534.
Your noble self.—*Othello,* i, 2, 92; *Henry VIII,* ii, 2, 95; *Pericles,* ii, 4, 37.
Your perfect self.—*The Two Gentlemen of Verona,* iv, 2, 124.
Your precious self.—*The Winter's Tale,* i, 2, 79.
Your royal self.—*Richard III,* iii, 1, 63; iii, 7, 195.
Your sweet self.—*Love's Labour's Lost,* v, 1, 120; *King John,* v, 7, 101; *All's Well that Ends Well,* iv, 2, 10; *Sonnets,* i, iv, cxiv, cxxvi, clix.
Self-affected.—*Troilus and Cressida,* ii, 3, 250.
Self-affrighted.—*Richard II,* iii, 2, 53.
Self-bounty.—*Othello,* iii, 3, 200.
Self-charity.—*Othello,* ii, 3, 202.
Self-comparisons.—*Macbeth,* i, 2, 55.
Self-explication.—*Cymbeline,* iii, 4, 8.
Self-glorious.—*Henry V,* v, Prol., 20.
Self-gracious.—*All's Well that Ends Well,* iv, 5, 78.
Self-harming.—*Comedy of Errors,* ii, 1, 102.
Self-reproving.—*King Lear,* v, 1, 4.
Self-willed.—*Romeo and Juliet,* iv, 2, 14; *I Henry IV,* iii, 1, 198; *Troilus and Cressida,* i, 3, 188; *Sonnets,* vi.
Self-wrong.—*The Comedy of Errors,* iii, 2, 168.
It will be noted that only one of the phrases is used more than once.

II—Self-Control

7
Good madam, keep yourself within yourself.
Antony and Cleopatra. Act ii, sc. 5, l. 75. [Charmian]
I am conqueror of myself.
Antony and Cleopatra. Act iv, sc. 14, l. 62. [Antony]
Self-sovereignty.—*Love's Labour's Lost,* iv, 1, 36. The only use of the phrase.
8
Defend yourself By calmness.
Coriolanus. Act iii, sc. 2, l. 95. [Cominius]
9
Pray ye, pacify yourself, Sir John.
II Henry IV. Act ii, sc. 4, l. 87. [Hostess] The only use of "pacify."
10
I pray you, school yourself.
Macbeth. Act iv, sc. 2, l. 15. [Ross]
11
Make thine own self the conquest of thy fury.
Timon of Athens, iv, 3, 340. See under BEAST.
12
Thank the heavens, lord, thou art of sweet composure.
Troilus and Cressida. Act ii, sc. 3, l. 251. [Ulysses]
It was a strong composure.
Troilus and Cressida. Act ii, sc. 3, l. 109. [Nestor]
His composure must be rare indeed
Whom these things cannot blemish.
Antony and Cleopatra. Act i, sc. 4, l. 22. [Cæsar] The only uses of "composure."

III—Self-Interest

13
Salisbury: Then let's make haste away, and look unto the main.
Warwick: Unto the main! . . . Main chance, father, you meant.
II Henry VI. Act i, sc. 1, l. 208. See under CHANCE.
14
Commodity, the bias of the world, . . .
This bawd, this broker, this all-changing word, . . .
And why rail I on this Commodity?
But for because he hath not woo'd me yet.
King John. Act ii, sc. 1, l. 574. [Bastard] The only use of "all-changing."

1 Others there are
Who, trimm'd in forms and visages of duty,
Keep yet their hearts attending on themselves.
Othello. Act i, sc. 1, l. 49. [Iago]
Unless self-charity be sometimes a vice,
And to defend ourselves it be a sin
When violence assails us.
Othello. Act ii, sc. 3, l. 202. [Montano] The only use of "self-charity."

IV—Self-Knowledge

2
Is it possible he should know what he is, and be that he is?
All's Well that Ends Well. Act iv, sc. i, l. 48. [Lord]
3
A wisp of straw were worth a thousand crowns,
To make this shameless callet know herself.
III Henry VI. Act ii, sc. 2, l. 144. [Edward] The only use of "wisp."
4
One that, above all other strifes, contended especially to know himself.
Measure for Measure. Act iii, sc. 2, l. 246. [Escalus]

V—Self-Love

5
I loved your father, and we love ourself.
Hamlet. Act iv, sc. 7, l. 34. [King]
6
Self-love, my liege, is not so vile a sin
As self-neglecting.
Henry V. Act ii, sc. 4, l. 74. [Dauphin] The only use of "self-neglecting."
He . . . hath no self-love.—*II Henry VI,* v, 2, 38.
7
That you should love yourself, and in that love
Not unconsider'd leave your honour, nor
The dignity of your office, is the point
Of my petition.
Henry VIII. Act i, sc. 2, l. 14. [Queen Katharine] "Unconsider'd" is repeated in *Winter's Tale,* iv, 3, 26: "Unconsider'd trifles."
Love thyself last.—*Henry VIII,* iii, 2, 443.
8
I do protest I never loved myself.
King John. Act ii, sc. 1, l. 501. [Lewis]
But do not love thyself.
Love's Labour's Lost. Act iv, sc. 3, l. 38. [King]
9 She cannot love,
Nor take no shape nor project of affection,
She is so self-endeared.
Much Ado about Nothing. Act iii, sc. 1, l. 54. [Hero] The only use of "self-endeared."
10
Since I could distinguish betwixt a benefit and an injury, I never found man that knew how to love himself.
Othello. Act i, sc. 3, l. 313. [Iago]
11
Richard loves Richard; that is, I am I.
Richard III. Act v, sc. 3, l. 183. [King Richard]
Alack, I love myself. Wherefore? for any good
That I myself have done unto myself?
Richard III. Act v, sc. 3, l. 187. [King Richard]
12
For shame! deny that thou bear'st love to any,
Who for thyself art so unprovident.
Sonnets. No. x. The only use of "unprovident."
Sin of self-love possesseth all mine eye
And all my soul and all my every part;
And for this sin there is no remedy,
It is so grounded inward in my heart.
Sonnets. No. lxii.
Self so self-loving were iniquity.
Sonnets. No. lxii.
Self-loving nuns.—*Venus and Adonis,* l. 752.
13
None that I love more than myself.
The Tempest. Act i, sc. 1, l. 22. [Boatswain]
14
Love not yourselves: Rob one another.
Timon of Athens. Act iv, sc. 3, l. 447. [Timon]
15
He loves himself: is 't not strange?
Troilus and Cressida. Act ii, sc. 3, l. 171. [Nestor]
16
You are sick of self-love, Malvolio, and taste with a distempered appetite.
Twelfth Night. Act i, sc. 5, l. 97. [Olivia]
Made of self-love.—*All's Well that Ends Well,* i, 1, 157.

SEMBLANCE

See also Appearance

17 Freshly looks and over-bears attaint
With cheerful semblance.
Henry V. Act iv, Prologue, l. 39. [Chorus]
A shy semblance.—*II Henry VI,* iii, 2, 162.
Ill-beseeming semblance.—*Romeo and Juliet,* i, 5, 76.
Like semblance.—*The Rape of Lucrece,* l. 1113.
Princely semblance.—*Richard III,* ii, 2, 51.
Rare semblance.—*Much Ado about Nothing,* v, 1, 260.
Simple semblance.—*Venus and Adonis,* l. 795.
Semblance pale.—*Pericles,* i, 1, 36.
18
Repeat their semblance often on the seas.
I Henry VI. Act v, sc. 3, l. 193. [Suffolk]
19 If thou path, thy native semblance on,
Not Erebus itself were dim enough
To hide thee from prevention.
Julius Cæsar. Act ii, sc. 1, l. 83. [Brutus] The only use of "path" as a verb. Many editors consider it a misprint for "put."
Your own semblance.—*The Merry Wives of Windsor,* iv, 2, 67.
One in semblance.—*The Comedy of Errors,* v, 1, 358.
20
The bloody proclamation to escape,
That follow's me so near, . . . taught me to shift
Into a madman's rags; to assume a semblance

That very dogs disdain'd.
King Lear. Act v, sc. 3, l. 183. [Edgar]

1
She 's but the sign and semblance of her honour.
Much Ado about Nothing, iv, 1, 34. See under HONOUR.
Semblance of a devil.—*The Rape of Lucrece,* l. 1246.
Semblance of his duty.—*Henry VIII,* i, 2, 198.
Semblance of a fowl.—*The Merry Wives of Windsor,* v, 5, 11.
Semblance of a maid.—*Much Ado about Nothing,* ii, 2, 39.
Glistering semblances of piety.—*Henry V,* ii, 2, 117. "Semblances" is used a second time in *As You Like It,* i, 3, 124.
Semblance of my soul.—*The Merchant of Venice,* iii, 4, 20.
Ship-boy's semblance.—*King John,* iv, 3, 4.

2
By the semblance
Of their white flags display'd, they bring us peace,
And come to us as favourers, not as foes.
Pericles. Act i, sc. 4, l. 71. [Cleon]

3
Of what she was no semblance did remain.
The Rape of Lucrece, l. 1453.

4
Your sweet semblance to some other give.
Sonnets. No. xiii.
Sweet semblance.—*Rape of Lucrece,* l. 1759.

5
I have your own letter that induced me to the semblance I put on.
Twelfth Night. Act v, sc. 1, l. 314. [Fabian, reading] All the uses of "semblance" are cited in this section.

SENATOR

6
The senators alone of this great world,
Chief factors of the gods.
Antony and Cleopatra. Act ii, sc. 6, l. 9. [Pompey]

7
You malign our senators for that
They are not such as you.
Coriolanus. Act i, sc. 1, l. 117. [Menenius] "Malign" is repeated in *Pericles,* v, 1, 90: "Malign my state."

8
The senators of Rome are this good belly.
Coriolanus. Act i, sc. 1, l. 152. [Menenius]
Like to the senators of antique Rome.
Henry V, Prol., v, 26.
Senators of Athens.—*Timon of Athens,* i, 1, 40; iii, 6, 90; v, 1, 139.
Senators of Venice.—*Othello,* iv, 1, 230.

9
If I should tell thee o'er this thy day's work,
Thou 'ldst not believe thy deeds: but I 'll report it
Where senators shall mingle tears with smiles.
Coriolanus. Act i, sc. 9, l. 1. [Cominius]
You grave but reckless senators.
Coriolanus. Act iii, sc. 1, l. 92. [Coriolanus]
Friendly senators.—*Coriolanus,* iv, 5, 138.
Most grave senators.—*Othello,* i, 3, 230.
Worthy senators.—*Timon of Athens,* v, 1, 161.
Senators and patricians.—*Coriolanus,* iv, 7, 30; v, 4, 56.

10
Messenger: By proscription and bills of outlawry,
Octavius, Antony, and Lepidus,
Have put to death an hundred senators.
Brutus: Therein our letters do not well agree;
Mine speak of seventy senators that died
By their proscriptions, Cicero being one.
Cassius: Cicero one!
Mesenger: Cicero is dead,
And by that order of proscription.
Julius Cæsar. Act iv, sc. 3, l. 173. "Proscription" is used once more in this play (iv, 1, 17) and occurs in no other. The only use of "outlawry." Cicero is mentioned eight times in this play, and in no other.

11
Brabantio: Thou art a villain.
Iago: You are—a senator.
Othello. Act i, sc. 1, l. 119.

12
The senate-house of planets all did sit.
Pericles. Act i, sc. 1, l. 10. [Antiochus] "Senate-house" is used three times in *Coriolanus,* and three times in *Julius Cæsar.*

13
Honour, health, and compassion to the senate!
Timon of Athens, iii, 5, 5. [Alcibiades]

14
Slaves and fools
Pluck the grave wrinkled senate from the bench,
And minister in their steads.
Timon of Athens. Act iv, sc. 1, l. 4. [Timon]
Noble senate.—*Coriolanus,* i, 1, 190.
Reverend senate.—*Timon of Athens,* v, 1, 132.
Usuring senate.—*Timon of Athens,* iii, 5, 110. "Usuring" is repeated in iv, 3, 516, and occurs in no other play. "Senate" is used thirty-one times.

SENSE

15
What impossibility would slay
In common sense, sense saves another way.
All's Well that Ends Well. Act ii, sc. 1, l. 180. [King]
Things hid . . . from common sense.—*Love's Labour 's Lost,* i, 1, 57. See under STUDY.
From common sense are hid.—*Love's Labour 's Lost,* i, 1, 64.
In common sense.—*II Henry IV,* iv, 2, 33. The only uses of "common sense."

16
You take me in too dolorous a sense.
Antony and Cleopatra, iv, 2, 39. See under MEANING.

17
Indued with intellectual sense.
Comedy of Errors, ii, 1, 22. See under MAN.

18
Sense, sure, you have,
Else could you not have motion; but sure, that sense
Is apoplex'd.
Hamlet. Act iii, sc. 4, l. 71. [Hamlet] The only use of "apoplex'd."

1
He 'll wrest the sense and hold us here all day.
II Henry VI. Act iii, sc. 1, l. 186. [Buckingham]

2 How stiff is my vile sense,
That I stand up, and have ingenious feeling
Of my huge sorrows!
King Lear. Act iv, sc. 6, l. 286. [Gloucester]

Banish'd sense.—*All's Well that Ends Well,* ii, 3, 54.
Bereaved sense.—*King Lear,* iv, 4, 9.
Daintier sense.—*Hamlet,* v, 1, 78. The only use of "daintier."
Dangerous sense.—*Measure for Measure,* iv, 4, 32.
Deepest sense.—*Sonnets,* cxxx.
Fearful sense.—*Othello,* i, 3, 12.
Heavy sense.—*Measure for Measure,* i, 4, 65.
Human sense.—*The Passionate Pilgrim,* l. 108.
Ingenious sense.—*Hamlet,* v, 1, 271.
Moving sense.—*The Passionate Pilgrim,* l. 195.
Precious sense.—*King John,* iv, 1, 94.
Quick sense.—*Troilus and Cressida,* iv, 5, 54.
Ravenous sense.—*Richard II,* iii, 2, 13.
Ready sense.—*Coriolanus,* ii, 2, 120.
Right sense.—*Much Ado about Nothing,* v, 2, 56.
Steel'd sense.—*Sonnets,* cxii.
Stranger sense.—*All's Well that Ends Well,* i, 3, 114.

3
Above the sense of sense.
Love's Labour's Lost, v, 2, 259. See under TONGUE.

4
Palter with us in a double sense.
Macbeth, v, 8, 20. See PROMISE, 1213:6.

In another sense.—*III Henry VI,* iii, 2, 60; *The Taming of the Shrew,* i, 1, 220.
In all sense.—*The Merchant of Venice,* v, 1, 136.
In my sense.—*Othello,* v, 2, 290.
In no sense.—*Taming of the Shrew,* v, 2, 141.
In that sense.—*The Rape of Lucrece,* l. 1538.

5 'Tis
Such sense, that my sense breeds with it.
Measure for Measure. Act ii, sc. 2, l. 141. [Angelo]

Your sense pursues not mine.
Measure for Measure. Act ii, sc. 4, l. 74. [Angelo]

You are very sensible, and yet you miss my sense.
The Taming of the Shrew. Act v, sc. 2, l. 18. [Petruchio]

A good sensible fellow.—*The Merry Wives of Windsor,* ii, 1, 151.
A sensible lord.—*II Henry IV,* i, 2, 220.
A sensible man.—*Othello,* ii, 3, 309.

6
He speaks sense.
The Merry Wives of Windsor. Act ii, sc. 1, l. 129. [Pistol]

7
Their sense thus weak, lost with their fears thus strong,
Made senseless things begin to do them wrong.
A Midsummer-Night's Dream. Act iii, sc. 2, l. 27. [Puck]

8
As having sense of beauty.
Othello. Act ii, sc. 1, l. 71. [Cassio]

Sense of death.—*Measure for Measure,* iii, 1, 78.
Sense of duty.—*Othello,* ii, 3, 167.
Sense of fear.—*Troilus and Cressida,* ii, 2, 12.
Sense of feeling.—*Venus and Adonis,* l. 439.
Sense of pain.—*Othello,* iii, 4, 147.
Sense of reckoning.—*Henry V,* iv, 1, 308.

9
There is more sense in that.
Othello. Act ii, sc. 3, l. 268. [Iago]

10
He in the worst sense construes their denial.
The Rape of Lucrece, l. 324.

Worser sense.—*The Rape of Lucrece,* l. 249.

11
Take it in what sense thou wilt.
Romeo and Juliet. Act i, sc. 1, l. 31. [Sampson]

12 My adder's sense
To critic and to flatterer stopped are.
Sonnets. No. cxii.

13
I see no sense for 't.
Timon of Athens. Act iii, sc. 3, l. 14. [Sempronius]

Dost think I have no sense?—*Troilus and Cressida,* ii, 1, 23.

II—The Senses

14
Stupefy and dull the sense awhile.
Cymbeline. Act i, sc. 5, l. 37. [Cornelius] The only use of "stupefy."

15
Eyes without feeling, feeling without sight,
Ears without hands or eyes, smelling sans all,
Or but a sickly part of one true sense
Could not so mope.
Hamlet. Act iii, sc. 4, l. 78. [Hamlet] "Mope" occurs again in *Henry V,* iii, 7, 143.

Awake your senses.—*Julius Cæsar,* iii, 2, 17.

16 Your other senses grow imperfect
By your eyes' anguish.
King Lear. Act iv, sc. 6, l. 5. [Edgar]

O you kind gods,
Cure this great breach in his abused nature!
The untuned and jarring senses, O, wind up
Of this child-changed father!
King Lear. Act iv, sc. 7, l. 14. [Cordelia] The only use of "child-changed."

17
All senses to that sense did make their repair,
To feel only looking on fairest of fair.
Love's Labour's Lost. Act ii, sc. 1, l. 240. [Boyet]

Sense of hearing.—*Love's Labour's Lost,* iii, 1, 2; v, 2, 670. Used only in this play.
Seeing sense.—*A Midsummer-Night's Dream,* iii, 2, 179.

18 One who never feels
The wanton stings and motions of the sense.
Measure for Measure. Act i, sc. 4, l. 58. [Lucio]

The beastliest sense.—*Measure for Measure,* ii, 1, 229. The only use of "beastliest."

1
Bardolph: The gentleman had drunk himself out of his five sentences.
Evans: It is his five senses: fie, what the ignorance is!
Merry Wives of Windsor. Act i, sc. 1, l. 179.
The five best senses.—*Timon of Athens,* i, 2, 129.
Five senses.—*Sonnets,* cxli.
Apprehensive senses.—*All's Well that Ends Well,* i, 2, 60.
Gentle senses.—*Macbeth,* i, 6, 3.
Settled senses.—*The Winter's Tale,* v, 3, 72.

2
Has Page any brains? hath he any eyes? hath he any thinking? Sure, they sleep; he hath no use of them.
The Merry Wives of Windsor. Act iii, sc. 2, l. 30. [Ford]
Be not amazed; call all your senses to you.
The Merry Wives of Windsor. Act iii, sc. 3, l. 126. [Mrs. Page]

3 It eats and sleeps and hath such senses
As we have, such.
The Tempest. Act i, sc. 2, l. 412. [Prospero]
Their rising senses
Begin to chase the ignorant fumes that mantle
Their clearer reason.
The Tempest. Act v, sc. 1, l. 66. [Prospero]
Justled from your senses.
The Tempest. Act v, sc. 1, l. 158. [Prospero] The only use of "justled."
Their senses I'll restore.—*Tempest,* v, 1, 31.

4
Yet have I the benefit of my senses as well as your ladyship.
Twelfth Night. Act v, sc. 1, l. 312. [Fabian]

5
Cheering up her senses all dismay'd.
Venus and Adonis, l. 896.
Appals her senses.—*Venus and Adonis,* l. 882.
Your senses, unintelligent of our insufficience, may, though they cannot praise us, as little accuse us.
The Winter's Tale. Act i, sc. 1, l. 15. [Archidamus] The only use of '"unintelligent" and "insufficience." "Insufficiency" occurs in *A Midsummer-Night's Dream,* ii, 2, 128, and in *Sonnets,* cl.
You smell this business with a sense as cold
As is a dead man's nose.
Winter's Tale. Act ii, sc. 1, l. 151. [Leontes]

SENTENCE

See also Judgement, Speech

I—Sentence: Judgement

6
This is a dreadful sentence.
All's Well that Ends Well. Act iii, sc. 2, l. 64. [Helena]
Black sentence.—*Julius Cæsar,* iv, 1, 17.
Immediate sentence.—*Measure for Measure,* v, 1, 378.

7
Pronounce the sentence then on me.
As You Like It. Act i, sc. 3, l. 87. [Celia]
Sir, I will pronounce your sentence: you shall fast a week with bran and water.
Love's Labour's Lost. Act i, sc. 1, l. 302. [King]

8 Passed sentence may not be recall'd
But to our honour's great disparagement.
The Comedy of Errors. Act i, sc. 1, l. 148. [Duke] "Disparagement" is repeated in *The Merry Wives of Windsor,* i, 1, 31, and in *Romeo and Juliet,* i, 5, 72.

9
He's sentenced; no more hearing.
Coriolanus. Act iii, sc. 3, l. 109. [Sicinius]
He's sentenced; 'tis too late.
Measure for Measure, ii, 2, 55. [Angelo]
He hath sentenced himself.—*Measure for Measure,* iii, 2, 271.

10
I would not thy good deeds should from my lips
Pluck a hard sentence.
Cymbeline. Act v, sc. 5, l. 288. [Cymbeline]

11
Receive the sentence of the law for sins
Such as by God's book are adjudged to death.
II Henry VI. Act ii, sc. 3, l. 3. [King Henry]
Hear your sentence.—*Henry V,* ii, 2, 166.
Receive your sentence.—*Pericles,* i, 1, 90.

12
So you must be the first that gives this sentence.
Measure for Measure, ii, 2, 106. [Isabella]
Angelo: Yet he must die.
Isabella: Under your sentence?
Angelo: Yea. . . .
I, now the voice of the recorded law,
Pronounce a sentence on your brother's life.
Measure for Measure. Act ii, sc. 4, l. 36.
Give sentence.—*Merchant of Venice,* iv, 1, 205.
Pursue sentence.—*Merchant of Venice,* iv, 1, 298.

13
The gentleman had drunk himself out of his five sentences.
Merry Wives of Windsor, i, 1, 179. See under SENSES.

14 Let your sentence
Even fall upon my life.
Othello. Act i, sc. 3, l. 119. [Othello]
Let me . . . lay a sentence,
Which, as a grise or step, may help these lovers
Into your favour.
Othello. Act i, sc. 3, l. 199. [Duke] "Grise" is repeated in *Timon of Athens,* iv, 3, 16, and in *Twelfth Night,* iii, 1, 135.
He bears the sentence well.
Othello, i, 3, 212. See under PATIENCE.

15
King Richard: The hopeless word of 'never to return'
Breathe I against thee, upon pain of life.
Mowbray: A heavy sentence, my most sovereign liege,
And all unlook'd for from your highness' mouth. . . .
What is thy sentence then but speechless death,
Which robs my tongue from breathing native breath?
King Richard: It boots thee not to be compassionate:
After our sentence plaining comes too late.
Richard II. Act i, sc. 3, l. 152. The only use

of "plaining." "Plainings" occurs in *The Comedy of Errors,* i, 1, 73: "Piteous plainings"; and in *The Rape of Lucrece,* l. 559.
Sentence of dread banishment.—*Richard II,* iii, 3, 134.

1 Who pronounced
The bitter sentence of poor Clarence' death?
Richard III. Act i, sc. 4, l. 190. [Clarence]

2
Give sentence on this execrable wretch,
That hath been breeder of these dire events.
Titus Andronicus. Act v, sc. 3, l. 177. [Æmilius] The only use of "execrable."

II—Sentence: Speech

3
Write in the dust this sentence with thy blood,
'Wind-changing Warwick now can change no more.'
III Henry VI. Act v, sc. 1, l. 56. [King Edward] The only use of "wind-changing."
Pronounce this sentence then,
Women may fall, when there 's no strength in men.
Romeo and Juliet. Act ii, sc. 3, l. 79. [Friar Laurence]

4
Good sentences and well pronounced.
The Merchant of Venice, i, 2, 11. [Portia]
Sweet and honey'd sentences.—*Henry V,* i, 1, 50.
Who fears a sentence or an old man's saw
Shall by a painted cloth be kept in awe.
Rape of Lucrece, l. 244. See under PROVERB.

5
A sentence is but a cheveril glove to a good wit: how quickly the wrong side may be turned outward!
Twelfth Night. Act iii, sc. 1, l. 12. [Clown]

SEPARATION

See also Departure, Parting

6
Our separation so abides, and flies,
That thou, residing here, go'st yet with me,
And I, hence fleeting, here remain with thee.
Antony and Cleopatra, i, 3, 102. [Antony]
Such separation as may well be said
Becomes a virtuous bachelor and a maid.
A Midsummer-Night's Dream, ii, 2, 58. See under Modesty.
By this separation I may give
That due to thee which thou deservest alone.
Sonnets. No. xxxix.
Royal necessities made separation of their society.
Winter's Tale. Act i, sc. 1, l. 28. [Camillo]
Buzzing of a separation.—*Henry VIII,* ii, 1, 148. The only uses of "separation."

7
The world and my great office will sometimes
Divide me from your bosom.
Antony and Cleopatra, ii, 3, 1. [Antony]

8
Wheresoe'er thou art in this world's globe,
I 'll have an Iris that shall find thee out.
II Henry VI. Act iii, sc. 2, l. 406. [Queen]

9
He that parts us shall bring a brand from heaven,
And fire us hence like foxes.
King Lear. Act v, sc. 3, l. 22. [King Lear]

SEPULCHRE, see Grave

SEQUEL

10 O, let me say no more!
Gather the sequel by that went before.
Comedy of Errors. Act i, sc. 1, l. 95. [Ægeon]

11
Is there no sequel at the heels of his mother's admiration?
Hamlet. Act iii, sc. 2, l. 341. [Hamlet]

12
Armado; Moth, follow.
Moth: Like the sequel, I.
Love's Labour 's Lost. Act iii, sc. 1, l. 134.

13
So will you say when you have seen the sequel.
Much Ado about Nothing. Act iii, sc. 2, l. 136. [Don John]

14
Mark how well the sequel hangs together.
Richard III. Act iii, sc. 6, l. 4. [Scrivener]
Mark the sequel.—*The Merry Wives of Windsor,* iii, 5, 109.

15
There is no consonancy in the sequel; that suffers under probation.
Twelfth Night, ii, 5, 141. [Malvolio] "Consonancy" is repeated in *Hamlet,* ii, 2, 295.

16
Well, I guess the sequel.
Two Gentlemen of Verona, ii, 1, 122. [Silvia]

SERIOUSNESS

17
I 'll hence to London on a serious matter.
III Henry VI. Act v, sc. 5, l. 47. [Gloucester]
He is posted hence on serious matter.
King Lear. Act iv, sc. 5, l. 8. [Regan]
Intending other serious matters.—*Timon of Athens,* ii, 2, 219.
Serious business.—*Love's Labour 's Lost,* ii, 1, 31; *All's Well that Ends Well,* ii, 4, 41; *Othello,* i, 3, 268.
Serious designs.—*Love's Labour 's Lost,* v, 1, 105.
Serious things.—*All's Well that Ends Well,* v, 3, 61; *Richard II,* v, 3, 79; *The Winter's Tale,* iv, 4, 791.

18
He did it with a serious mind; a heed
Was in his countenance.
Henry VIII. Act iii, sc. 2, l. 80. [Cromwell]
What serious contemplation are you in?
King Lear. Act i, sc. 2, l. 150. [Edgar]
I am more serious than my custom.
The Tempest. Act ii, sc. 1, l. 219. [Antonio]

SERPENT

See also Adder, Snake

19 'Where 's my serpent of old Nile?'
For so he calls me.
Antony and Cleopatra, i, 5, 25. [Cleopatra]

You 've strange serpents there. . . . Your serpent of Egypt is bred now of your mud by the operation of your sun: so is your crocodile.
Antony and Cleopatra. Act ii, sc. 7, l. 27. [Lepidus]

This is an aspic's trail; and these fig-leaves,
Have slime upon them, such as the aspic leaves
Upon the caves of Nile.
Antony and Cleopatra. Act v, sc. 2, l. 354. [First Guard] The only use of "fig-leaves."

Have I the aspic in my lip?—*Antony and Cleopatra,* v, 2, 296.

Aspics' tongues.—*Othello,* iii, 3, 450. The only uses of "aspic."

Serpent's tongue.—*A Midsummer-Night's Dream,* v, 1, 440.

Hold a serpent by the tongue.—*King John,* iii, 1, 258. See under PEACE.

1 'Tis given out that, sleeping in my orchard,
A serpent stung me; so the whole ear of Denmark
Is by a forged process of my death
Rankly abused: but know, thou noble youth,
The serpent that did sting thy father's life
Now wears his crown.
Hamlet. Act i, sc. 5, l. 35. [Ghost] The only use of "rankly."

2 Were there a serpent seen, with forked tongue,
That slily glided toward your majesty,
It were but necessary you were waked,
Lest, being suffer'd in that harmful slumber,
The mortal worm might make the sleep eternal.
II Henry VI. Act iii, sc. 2, l. 259. [Salisbury] The only use of "glided." "Glideth" occurs in *Titus Andronicus,* ii, 1, 85, and "gliding" in *Julius Cæsar,* i, 3, 63.

Such fell serpents as false Suffolk is.
II Henry VI. Act iii, sc. 2, l. 266. [Salisbury]

This gilded serpent.—*King Lear,* v, 3, 84.

3 Who 'scapes the lurking serpent's mortal sting?
Not he that sets his foot upon her back.
III Henry VI. Act ii, sc. 2, l. 15. [Clifford]

Who sees the lurking serpent steps aside.
The Rape of Lucrece, l. 362.

4 Throw thine eye
On yon young boy: I 'll tell thee what, my friend,
He is a very serpent in my way;
And wheresoe'er this foot of mine doth tread,
He lies before me.
King John. Act iii, sc. 3, l. 59. [King John]

Think him as a serpent's egg
Which, hatch'd, would, as his kind, grow mischievous,
And kill him in the shell.
Julius Cæsar. Act ii, sc. 1, l. 32. [Brutus]

5 There the grown serpent lies; the worm that 's fled
Hath nature that in time will venom breed,
No teeth for the present.
Macbeth. Act iii, sc. 4, l. 29. [Macbeth]

6 What, wouldst thou have a serpent sting thee twice?
The Merchant of Venice. Act iv, sc. 1, l. 69. [Shylock]

7 Do thy best
To pluck this crawling serpent from my breast!
A Midsummer-Night's Dream. Act ii, sc. 2, l. 145. [Hermia]

Methought a serpent eat my heart away.
A Midsummer-Night's Dream. Act ii, sc. 2, l. 149. [Hermia]

8 And both like serpents are, who though they feed
On sweetest flowers, yet they poison breed.
Pericles. Act i, sc. 1, l. 132. [Pericles]

9 Bid me lurk Where serpents are.
Romeo and Juliet. Act iv, sc. 1, l. 79. [Juliet]

SERVANT

See also Groom; Master and Servant

10 Helena: Sir, I can nothing say,
But that I am your most obedient servant.
Bertram: Come, come, no more of that.
All's Well that Ends Well. Act ii, sc. 5, l. 76.

Your affectionate servant.—*King Lear,* iv, 6, 276. The only use of "affectionate."

Your faithful servant.—*Cymbeline,* i, 1, 174.

11 You never had a servant to whose trust
Your business was more welcome.
All's Well that Ends Well. Act iv, sc. 4, l. 15. [Widow]

12 That mine own servant should
Parcel the sum of my disgraces by
Addition of his envy.
Antony and Cleopatra. Act v, sc. 2, l. 162. [Cleopatra]

13 Here comes your man.
The Comedy of Errors. Act ii, sc. 1, l. 43. [Luciana] See also MASTER AND MAN.

14 I had rather be their servant in my way
Than sway with them in theirs.
Coriolanus. Act ii, sc. 1, l. 219. [Coriolanus]

A petty servant to the state.—*Coriolanus,* ii, 3, 186.

He was
A noble servant to them; but he could not
Carry his honours even.
Coriolanus. Act iv, sc. 7, l. 35. [Aufidius]

15 I took him;
Made him joint-servant with me.
Coriolanus. Act v, sc. 6, l. 31. [Aufidius] The only use of "joint-servant."

16 Every good servant does not all commands:
No bond but to do just ones.
Cymbeline. Act v, sc. 1, l. 6. [Posthumus]

17 Never master had
A page so kind, so duteous, diligent,
So tender over his occasions, true,

So feat, so nurse-like.
Cymbeline. Act v, sc. 5, l. 85. [Lucius] The only use of "nurse-like."

A pretty knavish page.—*Love's Labour's Lost,* v, 2, 97.
Dwarfish pages.—*Henry VIII,* i, 1, 22.
Little page.—*The Merry Wives of Windsor,* ii, 2, 120.
Scornful page.—*Cymbeline,* v, 5, 228.
Jove's own page.—*As You Like It,* i, 3, 126.

1
I will not sort you with the rest of my servants, for, to speak to you like an honest man, I am most dreadfully attended.
Hamlet. Act ii, sc. 2, l. 274. [Hamlet]

2
Let me thy servant and not sovereign be.
I Henry VI. Act i, sc. 2, l. 111. [Charles]

Let me be your servant.—*As You Like It,* ii, 3, 46.

I shall be glad to be your servant.
The Merry Wives of Windsor. Act ii, sc. 2, l. 185. [Falstaff]

'Twill make us proud to be his servant.
Troilus and Cressida. Act iii, sc. 1, l. 168. [Helen]

To be your fellow
You may deny me; but I'll be your servant,
Whether you will or no.
The Tempest. Act iii, sc. 1, l. 84. [Miranda]

3 Thus are poor servitors,
When others sleep upon their quiet beds,
Constrain'd to watch in darkness, rain and cold.
I Henry VI. Act ii, sc. 1, l. 5. [Sentinel]

Let former grudges pass,
And henceforth I am thy true servitor.
III Henry VI. Act iii, sc. 3, l. 195. [Warwick]

Your trusty and most valiant servitor.—*Othello,* i, 3, 40.
Leaden servitor.—*Richard III,* iv, 3, 52.
Rome's servitors.—*Titus Andronicus,* i, 1, 352.
Servitors to the unjust.—*The Rape of Lucrece,* l. 285. The only uses of "servitor" and "servitors."

4
Yet thus far we are one in fortunes: both
Fell by our servants, by those men we loved most;
A most unnatural and faithless service!
Henry VIII. Act ii, sc. 1, l. 121. [Buckingham]

5
The rational hind Costard.
Love's Labour's Lost. Act i, sc. 2, l. 123. [Armado] "Rational" is repeated in *All's Well that Ends Well,* i, 1, 139: "Rational increase."

Gentle hind.—*Richard III,* ii, 4, 50.
Heartless hinds.—*Romeo and Juliet,* i, 1, 73.
Mild hind.—*A Midsummer-Night's Dream,* ii, 1, 232.
Rebellious hinds.—*II Henry VI,* iv, 2, 130.
Rude unpolish'd hinds.—*II Henry VI,* iii, 2, 271.
Shallow cowardly hind.—*I Henry IV,* ii, 3, 16.

6 Your servants ever
Have theirs, themselves and what is theirs, in compt,
To make their audit at your highness' pleasure,
Still to return your own.
Macbeth. Act i, sc. 6, l. 25. [Lady Macbeth]

7
I keep his house; and I wash, wring, brew, bake, scour, dress meat and drink, make the beds, and do all myself.
The Merry Wives of Windsor. Act i, sc. 4, l. 100. [Mistress Quickly]

8
Whatever shall become of Michael Cassio,
He's never any thing but your true servant.
Othello. Act iii, sc. 3, l. 8. [Cassio]

Servants true about me, that bare eyes
To see alike mine honour as their profits,
Their own particular thrifts.
Winter's Tale. Act i, sc. 2, l. 309. [Leontes]

9
I was a pack-horse in his great affairs.
Richard III. Act i, sc. 3, l. 122. [Gloucester] "Pack-horse" is repeated in *Richard III,* i, 3, 122, and in *The Rape of Lucrece,* l. 928.

10
Look how thy servants do attend on thee,
Each in his office ready at thy beck.
The Taming of the Shrew. Induction, sc. 2, l. 35. [Lord]

11
My trusty servant, well approved in all.
The Taming of the Shrew. Act i, sc. 1, l. 7. [Lucentio]

Your ancient, trusty, pleasant servant.
The Taming of the Shrew. Act i, sc. 2, l. 47. [Hortensio]

A servant grafted in my serious trust.
Winter's Tale. Act i, sc. 2, l. 246. [Leontes]

Trusty servant.—*King Lear,* iv, 2, 18.
Bound servants.—*Timon of Athens,* iv, 1, 10.
Gentle servant.—*The Two Gentlemen of Verona,* ii, 1, 114.
Honest poor servant.—*Timon of Athens,* iv, 3, 482.
Household servants.—*Antony and Cleopatra,* iv, 2, 9; *Richard II,* ii, 2, 60.
Industrious servant.—*The Tempest,* iv, 1, 33.
Learned and well-belov'd servant.—*Henry VIII,* ii, 4, 238.
Old servant.—*Cymbeline,* iii, 5, 54.
Sworn servant.—*Henry VIII,* i, 2, 191.
Servants of your adversity.—*Romeo and Juliet,* i, 1, 113
Serving-creature.—*Romeo and Juliet,* iv, 5, 119.
Serving-man.—*The Taming of the Shrew,* iv, 1, 49, and eight times in later plays.
Justice-like serving-man.—*II Henry IV,* v, 1, 76. The only use of "justice-like."

12
His lackey, for all the world caparisoned like a horse.
The Taming of the Shrew. Act iii, sc. 2, l. 66. [Biondello]

Base lackey.—*Richard III,* v, 3, 317.
Gentleman's lackey.—*Taming of the Shrew,* iii, 2, 73.
Saucy lackey.—*As You Like It,* iii, 2, 314.
Superfluous lackeys.—*Henry V,* iv, 2, 26.

1
She will a handmaid be to his desires.
Titus Andronicus. Act i, sc. 1, l. 331. [Tamora]
Blushing handmaid.—*Henry VIII,* ii, 3, 72.
Her handmaid.—*Twelfth Night,* i, 1, 25.
Humble handmaid.—*I Henry VI,* iii, 3, 42.
Twinkling handmaids.—*Rape of Lucrece,* l. 787.
Handmaids of all women.—*Cymbeline,* iii, 4, 159. The only uses of "handmaid" and "handmaids."

2
Pandarus: Do not you follow the young Lord Paris?
Servant: Ay, sir, when he goes before me.
Troilus and Cressida. Act iii, sc. 1, l. 1.

3
Your servant's servant is your servant, madam.
Twelfth Night. Act iii, sc. 1, l. 113. [Viola]
He is sad and civil,
And suits well for a servant with my fortunes.
Twelfth Night. Act iii, sc. 4, l. 5. [Olivia]
Duke: Belong you to the Lady Olivia, friends?
Clown: Ay, sir; we are some of her trappings.
Twelfth Night. Act v, sc. 1, l. 9. "Trappings" is repeated in *Hamlet,* i, 2, 86.

4
When a man's servant shall play the cur with him, look you, it goes hard.
The Two Gentlemen of Verona. Act iv, sc. 4, l. 1. [Launce]

5
Though I am not bookish, yet I can read waiting-gentlewoman in the 'scape.
The Winter's Tale. Act iii, sc. 3, l. 73. [Shepherd] "Waiting-gentlewoman" is repeated in *I Henry IV,* i, 3, 55, and in *Much Ado about Nothing,* ii, 1, 37; ii, 2, 14.
Possesses chambermaids and waiting-women.
King Lear, iv, 1, 65. See under DEVIL. "Chambermaids" is repeated in *Romeo and Juliet,* v, 3, 109, and in *Twelfth Night,* i, 3, 54.
Diana's waiting-women.—*Troilus and Cressida,* v, 2, 91. The only uses of "waiting-women."

SERVICE

See also Fidelity, Loyalty

6
Service is no heritage.
All's Well that Ends Well. Act i, sc. 3, l. 25. [Clown]
I see things may serve long, but not serve ever.
All's Well that Ends Well, ii, 2, 60. [Clown]
I dare not say I take you; but I give
Me and my service, ever whilst I live,
Into your guiding power.
All's Well that Ends Well, ii, 3, 109. [Helena]

7
Clown: I would cozen the man of his wife and do his service.
Lafeu: So you were a knave at his service indeed.
Clown: And I would give his wife my bauble, sir, to do her service.
Lafeu: I will subscribe for thee, thou art both knave and fool.
Clown: At your service.
Lafeu: No, no, no.
Clown: Why, sir, if I cannot serve you, I can serve as great a prince as you are.
All's Well that Ends Well. Act iv, sc. 5, l. 28. "At your service" is repeated frequently throughout the plays.
At my service.—*Richard III,* iii, 5, 9; *Love's Labour's Lost,* v, 2, 276.
At thy service.—*The Two Gentlemen of Verona,* ii, 5, 63.
At your lordship's service.—*Timon of Athens,* i, 1, 115.

8
In me 'tis villany;
In thee 't had been good service.
Antony and Cleopatra. Act ii, sc. 7, l. 80. [Pompey]
If it be so to do good service, never
Let me be counted serviceable.
Cymbeline. Act iii, sc. 2, l. 14. [Pisanio]
He hath since done good service at Shrewsbury.
II Henry IV. Act i, sc. 2, l. 71. [Servant]
He hath done good service, lady, in these wars.
Much Ado about Nothing. Act i, sc. 1, l. 48. [Messenger]
By the mess, ere theise eyes of mine take themselves to slomber, ay 'll de gud service, or ay 'll lig i' the grund for it.
Henry V. Act iii, sc. 2, l. 122. [Jamy]
The Welshman did good service.—*Henry V,* iv, 7, 103.
Buckingham: So please it you, my lord, 'twere not amiss
He were created knight for his good service.
King Henry: Iden, kneel down. Rise up a knight.
II Henry VI. Act v, sc. 1, l. 76.

9
I wish I could be made so many men,
And all of you clapp'd up together in
An Antony, that I might do you service
So good as you have done.
Antony and Cleopatra. Act iv, sc. 2, l. 16. [Antony]
Bear me, good friends, where Cleopatra bides;
'Tis the last service that I shall command you.
Antony and Cleopatra. Act iv, sc. 14, l. 131. [Antony]

10
O good old man, how well in thee appears
The constant service of the antique world,
When service sweat for duty, not for meed!
As You Like It. Act ii, sc. 3, l. 56. [Orlando]
Best service.—*Hamlet,* iv, 2, 18.
Christian service.—*Richard II,* ii, 1, 54.
Dear services.—*The Winter's Tale,* ii, 3, 150.
Duteous service.—*Richard III,* ii, 1, 63.
Excellent services.—*Henry V,* iii, 6, 4.
Faithful service.—*I Henry VI,* iii, 4, 21; *King John,* v, 7, 104; *Richard II,* iii, 3, 118.
Golden service.—*Twelfth Night,* iv, 3, 8.
Honourable service.—*All's Well that Ends Well,* iii, 5, 4.
Hopeful service.—*Henry VIII,* iii, 2, 419.
Hot service.—*The Winter's Tale,* iv, 3, 71.
Inward service.—*Hamlet,* i, 3, 13.
Loyal service.—*King Lear,* iv, 2, 7.
Meritorious service.—*The Merry Wives of Windsor,* iv, 2, 218.
Noble service.—*Cymbeline,* iv, 2, 339.

1
If I last in this service, you must case me in leather.
The Comedy of Errors. Act ii, sc. 1, l. 85. [Dromio of Ephesus]

2
Well assured They ne'er did service for 't.
Coriolanus. Act iii, sc. 1, l. 121. [Coriolanus]
This kind of service Did not deserve corn gratis.
Coriolanus. Act iii, sc. 1, l. 123. [Coriolanus]

3
The warlike service he has done, consider.
Coriolanus. Act iii, sc. 3, l. 49. [Menenius]
Services . . . for his country.
Coriolanus, i, 1, 30. See under PATRIOTISM.
Coriolanus: What, do you prate of service?
Brutus: I talk of that, that know it.
Coriolanus. Act iii, sc. 3, l. 83.
What service is here! I think our fellows are asleep.
Coriolanus. Act iv, sc. 5, l. 1. [Servant]
'Tis an honester service than to meddle with thy mistress.
Coriolanus. Act iv, sc. 5, l. 52. [Coriolanus]

4
Doctor, your service for the time is ended;
Take your own way. . . . No further service, doctor,
Until I send for thee.
Cymbeline. Act i, sc. 5, l. 30. [Queen]

5
Let me my service tender on your lips.
Cymbeline. Act i, sc. 6, l. 140. [Iachimo]
Pray, do my service to his majesty.
Henry VIII. Act iii, sc. 1, l. 179. [Queen Katharine]
First mine own service to your grace.
Henry VIII. Act iv, sc. 2, l. 115. [Capucius]
Commend my service to her beauty.
Troilus and Cressida. Act v, sc. 5, l. 3. [Diomedes]
My services to your lordship.—*King Lear,* i, 1, 29.

6
He cannot choose but take this service that I have done fatherly.
Cymbeline. Act ii, sc. 3, l. 38. [Cloten] "Fatherly" is repeated in *Much Ado about Nothing,* iv, 1, 75, and in *The Taming of the Shrew,* ii, 1, 288.
This service is not service, so being done,
But being so allow'd.
Cymbeline. Act iii, sc. 3, l. 16. [Belarius]
He brags His service as if he were of note.
Cymbeline. Act v, sc. 3, l. 92. [Captain]
The service that you three have done is more
Unlike than this thou tell'st.
Cymbeline. Act v, sc. 5, l. 353. [Cymbeline]

7
I will yet do you service.
Cymbeline. Act v, sc. 5, l. 404. [Imogen]

8
For a little Follow, and do me service.
The Tempest. Act iv, sc. 1, l. 267. [Prospero]
Do me some service ere I come to thee.
Titus Andronicus. Act v, sc. 2, l. 44. [Titus]
And here, to do you service, am become
As new into the world, strange, unacquainted.
Troilus and Cressida. Act iii, sc. 3, l. 11. [Calchas]
Do thee service.—*Coriolanus,* iv, 5, 107.
Do some service.—*II Henry VI,* iii, 2, 231.

9
We coted them on the way; and hither are they coming, to offer you service.
Hamlet. Act ii, sc. 2, l. 330. [Rosencrantz] The only use of "coted" (passed).

10
It did me yeoman's service.
Hamlet. Act v, sc. 2, l. 36. [Hamlet]
Did him service.—*Troilus and Cressida,* ii, 2, 76.

11
Your day's service at Shrewsbury hath a little gilded over your night's exploit at Gad's-hill; you may thank the unquiet time for your quiet o'er-posting that action.
II Henry IV. Act i, sc. 2, l. 167. [Chief Justice] The only use of "o'er-posting."
To serve bravely is to come halting off.
II Henry IV. Act ii, sc. 4, l. 54. [Falstaff]

12
So service shall with steeled sinews toil.
Henry V. Act ii, sc. 2, l. 36. [Scroop]

13
I must leave them, and seek some better service.
Henry V. Act iii, sc. 2, l. 56. [Boy]
Better service have I never done you
Than now to bid you hold.
King Lear. Act iii, sc. 7, l. 74. [Servant]
How wouldst thou have paid my better service!
Antony and Cleopatra. Act iv, sc. 6, l. 33. [Enobarbus]
Your legs did better service.—*III Henry VI,* ii, 2, 104. The only uses of "better service."

14
Turn them out of service.
Henry V. Act iv, sc. 3, l. 119. [King Henry]
Out of service.—*As You Like It,* i, 3, 26; *The Merry Wives of Windsor,* ii, 1, 183.
I cannot get a service, no.—*The Merchant of Venice,* ii, 2, 165.

15
Thy humble servant vows obedience
And humble service till the point of death.
I Henry VI, iii, 1, 167. [Plantagenet]
Humble service.—*Twelfth Night,* iii, 1, 106.

16
Had I but served my God with half the zeal
I served my king, he would not in mine age
Have left me naked to mine enemies.
Henry VIII. Act iii, sc. 2, l. 455. [Wolsey]

17
Take him to follow thee,
That did the latest service to my master.
Julius Cæsar. Act v, sc. 5, l. 66. [Messala]

18
Did him service Improper for a slave.
King Lear. Act v, sc. 3, l. 220. [Edgar] The only use of "improper."

19
And shape his service wholly to my hests.
Love's Labour 's Lost. Act v, sc. 2, l. 65. [Rosaline] "Hests" is repeated in *The Tempest,* i, 2, 247. "Hest" occurs three times.
For my service born.—*Love's Labour 's Lost,* v, 2, 284.

20
Impose some service on me for my love.
Love's Labour 's Lost, v, 2, 850. [Biron]

21
Will your grace command me any service to the world's end? I will go on the slight-

est errand now to the Antipodes that you can devise to send me on; I will fetch you a toothpicker now from the furthest inch of Asia, bring you the length of Prester John's foot, fetch you a hair off the great Cham's beard, do you any embassage to the Pigmies, rather than hold three words' conference with this harpy.

Much Ado about Nothing. Act ii, sc. 1, l. 271. [Benedick] The only use of "toothpicker." "Toothpick" occurs in *King John,* i, 1, 190, and in *All's Well that Ends Well,* i, 1, 171. The only mention of Prester John and the great Cham.

1
None serve with him but constrained things
Whose hearts are absent too.

Macbeth. Act v, sc. 4, l. 13. [Malcolm]

2
I am famished in his service.

The Merchant of Venice. Act ii, sc. 2, l. 113. [Launcelot]

In his service perishing.—*A Midsummer-Night's Dream,* v, 1, 86.
In your service.—*As You Like It,* i, 1, 87.
Keep in service.—*The Tempest,* i, 2, 286.

3
Because we come to do you service and you think we are ruffians, you'll have your daughter covered with a Barbary horse; you'll have your nephews neigh to you; you'll have coursers for cousins and gennets for germans.

Othello. Act i, sc. 1, l. 109. [Iago] The only use of "gennets."

4
My services which I have done the signiory
Shall out-tongue his complaints.

Othello. Act i, sc. 2, l. 18. [Othello] The only use of "signiory" and "out-tongue."

I have done the state some service, and they know 't.

Othello. Act v, sc. 2, l. 339. [Othello]

5
Serve always with assured trust.

The Passionate Pilgrim, l. 329.

6
I am for other service first.

Pericles. Act v, sc. 1, l. 254. [Pericles]

7
My gracious lord, I tender you my service,
Such as it is, being tender, raw and young;
Which elder days shall ripen and confirm
To more approved service and desert.

Richard II. Act ii, sc. 3, l. 41. [Percy]

My true service shall deserve your love.

Richard II, iii, 3, 199. [Bolingbroke]

Do me true service.—*Cymbeline,* iii, 5, 110.

8
King Richard: To do what service am I sent for hither?
York: To do that office of thine own good will
Which tired majesty did make thee offer.

Richard II. Act iv, sc. 1, l. 176.

Offer service.—*King John,* v, 1, 34; *Richard II,* ii, 3, 32; *The Taming of the Shrew,* Ind., i, 78.
Pray, accept his service.—*The Taming of the Shrew,* ii, 1, 84.

9
Remember I have done thee worthy service;
Told thee no lies, made thee no mistakings, served
Without or grudge or grumblings.

The Tempest. Act i, sc. 2, l. 247. [Ariel]
See also *All's Well that Ends Well,* iii, 5, 51.

He does make our fire,
Fetch in our wood and serves in offices
That profit us.

The Tempest. Act i, sc. 2, l. 311. [Prospero]

All this service Have I done since I went.

The Tempest. Act v, sc. 1, l. 225. [Ariel]

10
Alcibiades: His service done
At Lacedæmon and Byzantium
Were a sufficient briber for his life.
Senator: What's that?
Alcibiades: I say, my lords, he has done fair service,
And slain in fight many of your enemies.

Timon of Athens. Act iii, sc. 5, l. 59. Lacedæmon is mentioned again in ii, 2, 160, and in no other play. The only mention of Byzantium, and the only use of "briber."

11
Thersites: I serve here voluntary.
Achilles: Your last service was sufferance, 'twas not voluntary: no man is beaten voluntary.

Troilus and Cressida. Act ii, sc. 1, l. 103.

12
I will be thy beadsman, Valentine.

The Two Gentlemen of Verona. Act i, sc. 1, l. 18. [Proteus] The only use of "beadsman." "Beadsmen" occurs in *Richard II,* iii, 2, 116.

I am thus early come to know what service
It is your pleasure to command me in.

The Two Gentlemen of Verona. Act iv, sc. 3, l. 9. [Eglamour]

Madam, this service I have done for you,
Though you respect not aught your servant doth.

The Two Gentlemen of Verona. Act v, sc. 4, l. 19. [Proteus]

13
I have served Prince Florizel and in my time wore three-pile; but now I am out of service.

The Winter's Tale. Act iv, sc. 3, l. 13. [Autolycus]

Three-pile the mercer.—*Measure for Measure,* iv, 3, 11. The only uses of "three-pile" and "mercer." "Three-piled" occurs twice in *Measure for Measure,* i, 2, 33 and *Love's Labour's Lost,* v, 2, 407.

14
I think You have heard of my poor services.

Winter's Tale. Act iv, sc. 4, l. 525. [Camillo]

Displeasing service.—*I Henry IV,* iii, 2, 5.
General services.—*Cymbeline,* iv, 1, 14.
Land service.—*Antony and Cleopatra,* ii, 6, 98.
Limited service.—*Macbeth,* ii, 3, 57.
Painful service.—*Coriolanus,* iv, 5, 74.
Past service.—*II Henry IV,* iii, 2, 269.
Precedent services.—*Antony and Cleopatra,* iv, 14, 83.
Revengeful services.—*Coriolanus,* iv, 5, 95.
Sick service.—*King John,* iv, 1, 52.
Unholy service.—*Pericles,* iv, 4, 50.

Tuscan service.—*All's Well that Ends Well,* i, 2, 13.
Variable service.—*Hamlet,* iv, 3, 25.

SERVILITY

See also Fawning, Humility, Knee

1
The hearts That spaniel'd me at heels.
Antony and Cleopatra. Act iv, sc. 12, l. 20. [Antony] The only use of "spaniel'd."

2
Time-pleasers, flatterers, foes to nobleness.
Coriolanus. Act iii, sc. 1, l. 45. [Brutus]
Any thing . . . but a time-pleaser.—*Twelfth Night,* ii, 3, 160. The only uses of "time-pleaser" and "time-pleasures."

3
They stand bald before him.
Coriolanus. Act iv, sc. 5, l. 206. [Servant]
What 's worse, Must court'sy at the censure.
Cymbeline. Act iii, sc. 3, l. 54. [Belarius]

4
He did comply with his dug before he sucked it. Thus has he . . . got the tune of the time and outward habit of encounter; a kind of yesty collection, which carries them through and through the most fond and winnowed opinions; and do but blow them to their trial, the bubbles are out.
Hamlet. Act v, sc. 2, l. 195. [Hamlet] "Yesty" occurs again in *Macbeth,* iv, 1, 53.

5
To dog his heels and curtsy at his frowns,
To show how much thou art degenerate.
I Henry IV. Act iii, sc. 2, l. 127. [King Henry]
This prostrate and exterior bending.
II Henry IV. Act iv, sc. 5, l. 149. [Prince of Wales]

6
Be you prostrate and grovel on the earth.
II Henry VI. Act i, sc. 4, l. 13. [Bolingbroke]
Grovel on thy face.—*II Henry VI,* i, 2, 9. "Grovel" used twice in the first play and never thereafter. "Grovelling" occurs in *King John,* ii, 1, 305.

7
Let them break your backs with burthens, take your houses over your heads, ravish your wives and daughters before your faces.
II Henry VI. Act iv, sc. 8, l. 30. [Cade]
Servile abject drudges.—*II Henry VI,* iv, 1, 105.

8
Nor will I sue, although the king have mercies
More than I dare make faults.
Henry VIII. Act ii, sc. 1, l. 70. [Buckingham]
I never sued to friend nor enemy.
Richard III. Act i, sc. 2, l. 168. [Gloucester]
One that humbly sues.—*Richard III,* iv, 4, 101; *I Henry VI,* v, 1, 4.

9
A wretched creature and must bend his body,
If Cæsar carelessly but nod on him.
Julius Cæsar. Act i, sc. 2, l. 117. [Cassius]
These couchings and these lowly courtesies
Might fire the blood of ordinary men,
And turn pre-ordinance and first decree
Into the law of children.
Julius Cæsar. Act iii, sc. 1, l. 37. [Cæsar] The only use of "pre-ordinance."
Low-crooked court'sies and base spaniel-fawning.
Julius Cæsar. Act iii, sc. 1, l. 43. [Cæsar] The only use of "low-crooked" and "spaniel-fawning."

10
I could as well be brought
To knee his throne, and squire-like, pension beg
To keep base life afoot.
King Lear. Act ii, sc. 4, l. 216. [King Lear] The only use of "squire-like."

11
Shall I bend low and in a bondman's key,
With bated breath and whispering humbleness,
Say this:
'Fair sir, you spit on me on Wednesday last;
You spurn'd me such a day; another time
You call'd me dog; and for these courtesies
I 'll lend you thus much moneys'?
The Merchant of Venice. Act i, sc. 3, l. 124. [Shylock] The only use of "spurn'd."

12
Most ignoble stooping.
The Tempest. Act i, sc. 2, l. 116. [Prospero]
Ignoble in demeanour!—*II Henry VI,* iii, 2, 210.
Ignoble of descent.—*III Henry VI,* iv, 1, 70.
Ignoble mind.—*II Henry VI,* ii, 1, 13.
Ignoble traitor.—*Richard III,* iii, 5, 22.
Ignoble wretch.—*I Henry VI,* v, 4, 7.

13
For aye thy foot-licker.
The Tempest. Act iv, sc. 1, l. 219. [Caliban] The only use of the phrase.
Let me lick thy shoe.—*The Tempest,* iii, 2, 26.
I kiss his dirty shoe.—*Henry V,* iv, 1, 47.

14
Away with slavish weeds and servile thoughts!
Titus Andronicus. Act ii, sc. 1, l. 18. [Aaron]
Basely insinuate and send us gifts.
Titus Andronicus. Act iv, sc. 2, l. 38. [Demetrius]
At the first approach you must kneel, then kiss his foot.
Titus Andronicus. Act iv, sc. 3, l. 110. [Titus]
By the waggon-wheel
Trot, like a servile footman, all day long.
Titus Andronicus. Act v, sc. 2, l. 54. [Titus] The only use of "waggon-wheel."

15
Sir Toby: Wilt thou set thy foot o' my neck?
Sir Andrew: Or o' mine either?
Sir Toby: Shall I play my freedom at tray-trip, and become thy bond-slave?
Sir Andrew: I' faith, or I either?
Twelfth Night. Act ii, sc. 5, l. 206. The only use of "tray-trip" (a dice game).

16
Yet was he servile to my coy disdain.
Venus and Adonis, l. 112.
Subject and servile.—*Venus and Adonis,* l. 1161.

SEX, see Woman: The Sex

SHADE

1
Under the shade of melancholy boughs.
As You Like It, ii, 7, 111. See under DESERT.

2
In the shade of death I shall find joy.
II Henry VI. Act iii, sc. 2, l. 54. [King Henry]
Shade of death.—*Richard III,* i, 3, 266.
Gloomy shade of death.—*I Henry VI,* v, 4, 89.

3
Let us seek out some desolate shade and there
Weep our sad bosoms empty.
Macbeth. Act iv, sc. 3, l. 1. [Malcolm]

4
Sitting in a pleasant shade
Which a grove of myrtles made.
The Passionate Pilgrim, l. 375.
Myrtle shade.—*The Passionate Pilgrim,* l. 144.
Bush's shade.—*As You Like It,* iv, 3, 114.
Cool shade.—*Love's Labour 's Lost,* v, 2, 89.
Mulberry shade.—*A Midsummer-Night's Dream,* v, 1, 149.
Fresh tree's shade.—*III Henry VI,* ii, 5, 49.

5
Dwell in solemn shades of endless night.
Richard II. Act v, sc. 6, l. 43. [Mowbray]
Shades of night.—*Richard II,* v, 6, 43.
Night's shade.—*A Midsummer-Night's Dream,* iv, 1, 101.

6
Thou, whose shadow shadows doth make bright,
How would thy shadow's form form happy show
To the clear day with thy much clearer light,
When to unseeing eyes thy shade shines so!
How would, I say, mine eyes be blessed made
By looking on thee in the living day,
When in dead night thy fair imperfect shade
Through heavy sleep on sightless eyes doth stay!
Sonnets. No. xliii.

7
Under their sweet shade, Aaron, let us sit.
Titus Andronicus. Act ii, sc. 3, l. 16. [Tamora]
Sweet shade.—*Henry V,* ii, 2, 28.
Sweeter shade.—*III Henry VI,* ii, 5, 42.

SHADOW

See also Substance and Shadow

8
I am your shadow, my lord; I 'll follow you.
II Henry IV. Act ii, sc. 2, l. 174. [Poins]
We have a number of shadows to fill up the muster-book.
II Henry IV. Act iii, sc. 2, l. 145. [Falstaff] The only use of "muster-book."

9
I am but shadow of myself.
I Henry VI. Act ii, sc. 3, l. 50. [Talbot]
Must he be then as shadow of himself?
I Henry VI. Act v, sc. 4, l. 133. [Alençon]

In her eye I find
A wonder, or a wondrous miracle,
The shadow of myself form'd in her eye;
Which, being but the shadow of your son,
Becomes a sun and makes your son a shadow.
King John. Act ii, sc. 1, l. 496. [Dauphin]

10
To course his own shadow for a traitor.
King Lear, iii, 4, 58. See ADVERSITY, 16:15.

11
Hence, horrible shadow!
Unreal mockery, hence!
Macbeth. Act iii, sc. 4, l. 106. [Macbeth]
Poor shadows of Elysium, hence, and rest
Upon your never-withering banks of flowers.
Cymbeline. Act v, sc. 4, l. 97. [Jupiter] The only use of "never-withering." For "Elysium" see under HEAVEN.

12
Come like shadows, so depart!
Macbeth. Act iv, sc. 1, l. 111. [Witches]

13
Some there be that shadows kiss;
Such have but a shadow's bliss.
The Merchant of Venice. Act ii, sc. 9, l. 66. [Prince of Arragon, reading]
Narcissus so himself forsook,
And died to kiss his shadow in the brook.
Venus and Adonis, l. 161.
When he beheld his shadow in the brook,
The fishes spread on it their golden gills.
Venus and Adonis, l. 1099. The only use of "gills."

14
The best in this kind are but shadows.
A Midsummer-Night's Dream, v, 1, 213. See under IMAGINATION.
If we shadows have offended,
Think but this, and all is mended,
That you have but slumber'd here
While these visions did appear.
A Midsummer-Night's Dream. Act v, sc. 1, l. 430. [Puck] The only use of "slumber'd."
Swift as a shadow.—*A Midsummer-Night's Dream,* i, 1, 144. See under LOVE for full quotation.

15
Discourse fustian with one's own shadow.
Othello, ii, 3, 282. For full quotation see under DRUNKENNESS.
Servant: How dost, fool?
Apemantus: Dost dialogue with thy shadow?
Timon of Athens. Act ii, sc. 2, l. 51.

16
I know he will come in our shadow, to scatter his crowns in the sun.
Pericles. Act iv, sc. 2, l. 121. [Bawd]

17
Let ghastly shadows his lewd eyes affright.
The Rape of Lucrece, l. 971.
At his own shadow let the thief run mad,
Himself himself seek every hour to kill!
The Rape of Lucrece, l. 997.
Such shadows are the weak brain's forgeries.
The Rape of Lucrece, l. 460.

18
Nought but shadows Of what it is not.
Richard II. Act ii, sc. 2, l. 23. [Bushy]

19
Let 's step into the shadow of these trees.
Richard II. Act iii, sc. 4, l. 25. [Queen]
Chequer'd shadow.—*Titus Andronicus,* ii, 3, 15.
Circling shadow.—*Titus Andronicus,* ii, 4, 19.

Mangled shadow.—*Antony and Cleopatra,* iv, 2, 27.
Poor shadow.—*Richard III,* iv, 4, 83.
Sad shadow.—*The Rape of Lucrece,* l. 1457.
Walking shadow.—*Macbeth,* v, 5, 24.
Bolingbroke: The shadow of your sorrow hath destroy'd
The shadow of your face.
King Richard: Say that again.
The shadow of my sorrow! ha! let 's see:
. . . These external manners of laments
Are merely shadows.
Richard II. Act iv, sc. 1, l. 292.

1 Shine out, fair sun, till I have bought a glass,
That I may see my shadow as I pass.
Richard III. Act i, sc. 2, l. 263. [Gloucester]

2 There came wandering by
A shadow like an angel, with bright hair
Dabbled in blood.
Richard III. Act i, sc. 4, l. 52. [Clarence] The only use of "dabbled."
Ratcliff: Be not afraid of shadows.
King Richard: By the apostle Paul, shadows to-night
Have struck more terror to the soul of Richard
Than can the substance of ten thousand soldiers
Armed in proof.
Richard III. Act v, sc. 3, l. 215.

3 Whilst that this shadow doth such substance give.
Sonnets. No. xxxvii.

4 Their groaning shadows that are gone.
Titus Andronicus. Act i, sc. 1, l. 126. [Titus]

5 Feed upon the shadow of perfection.
The Two Gentlemen of Verona. Act iii, sc. 1, l. 177. [Valentine]
Shadow of a dream.—*Hamlet,* ii, 2, 265.
Beggars' shadows.—*Hamlet,* ii, 2, 268.
Lion's shadow.—*Merchant of Venice,* v, 1, 8.
Love's shadows.—*Romeo and Juliet,* v, 1, 11.
Shadow's shadow.—*Hamlet,* ii, 2, 266.

6 Come, shadow, come, and take this shadow up.
The Two Gentlemen of Verona. Act iv, sc. 4, l. 202. [Julia]

7 Each shadow makes him stop, each murmur stay.
Venus and Adonis, l. 706.

SHALLOWNESS

8 Shallow, shallow. . . . Most shallow man!
As You Like It. Act iii, sc. 2, l. 58. [Touchstone] Repeated in l. 75.
You 're shallow, madam.—*All's Well that Ends Well,* i, 3, 45.
Feeble, shallow, weak.—*The Comedy of Errors,* iii, 2, 35.
Vain, giddy, shallow.—*Henry V,* ii, 4, 28.

9 A good shallow young fellow: a' would have made a good pantler, a' would ha' chipped bread well.
II Henry IV. Act ii, sc. 4, l. 257. [Falstaff] "Pantler" is used four times.
Idle shallow things.—*Twelfth Night,* iii, 4, 137.
Shallow fools.—*The Rape of Lucrece,* l. 1016; *Much Ado about Nothing,* v, 1, 240.
Shallow jesters.—*I Henry IV,* iii, 2, 61.

10 You are too shallow, Hastings, much too shallow,
To sound the bottom of the after-times.
II Henry IV. Act iv, sc. 2, l. 50. [Lancaster] The only use of "after-times."

11 The shallowest thick-skin of that barren sort.
A Midsummer-Night's Dream. Act iii, sc. 2, l. 13. [Puck] The only use of "shallowest."
What wouldst thou have, boor? what, thick-skin?
The Merry Wives of Windsor. Act iv, sc. 5, l. 1. [Hostess] The only uses of "thick-skin."

SHAME

See also Disgrace

12 Our own love waking cries to see what 's done,
While shame full late sleeps out the afternoon.
All's Well that Ends Well. Act v, sc. 3, l. 65. [King]

13 Rust, sword! cool, blushes! and, Parolles, live
Safest in shame!
All's Well that Ends Well. Act iv, sc. 3, l. 373. [Parolles]

14 He is unqualitied with very shame.
Antony and Cleopatra. Act iii, sc. 11, l. 44. [Iras] The only use of "unqualitied."
Past all shame.—*The Winter's Tale,* iii, 2, 85.

15 I never saw an action of such shame;
Experience, manhood, honour, ne'er before
Did violate so itself.
Antony and Cleopatra. Act iii, sc. 10, l. 22. [Scarus]
See,
How I convey my shame out of thine eyes
By looking back what I have left behind
'Stroy'd in dishonour.
Antony and Cleopatra. Act iii, sc. 11, l. 51. [Antony] The only use of "'stroy'd."
'Twas a shame no less
Than was his loss, to course your flying flags,
And leave his navy gazing.
Antony and Cleopatra. Act iii, sc. 13, l. 10. [Enobarbus]

16 Wouldst thou be window'd in great Rome and see
Thy master thus with pleach'd arms, bending down
His corrigible neck, his face subdued
To penetrative shame?
Antony and Cleopatra. Act iv, sc. 14, l. 72. [Antony] The only use of "penetrative." "Window'd" occurs again in *King Lear,* iii, 4, 31; "pleach'd" in *Much Ado about Nothing,* iii, 1, 7; "corrigible" in *Othello,* i, 3, 329.

1
We purpose her no shame.
Antony and Cleopatra. Act v, sc. 1, l. 62. [Cæsar]
O Cæsar, what a wounding shame is this!
Antony and Cleopatra. Act v, sc. 2, l. 159. [Cleopatra]
Shame—the first that ever touch'd him.
Cymbeline, iii, 1, 24. See under CÆSAR.
2
If I be foiled, there is but one shamed that was never gracious.
As You Like It. Act i, sc. 2, l. 199. [Orlando]
You have shamed me.—*Coriolanus,* i, 8, 14.
Age, thou art shamed!—*Julius Cæsar,* i, 2, 150.
3
Shame hath a bastard fame, well managed.
The Comedy of Errors. Act iii, sc. 2, l. 19. [Luciana]
4 I wonder much
That you would put me to this shame and trouble.
The Comedy of Errors. Act v, sc. 1, l. 13. [Angelo]
Why give you me this shame?—*Measure for Measure,* iii, 1, 81.
5 Never shame to hear
What you have nobly done.
Coriolanus. Act ii, sc. 2, l. 71. [Senator]
6
I am ashamed To look upon the holy sun.
Cymbeline. Act iv, sc. 4, l. 40. [Arviragus]
I am ashamed.—*The Taming of the Shrew,* v, 2, 161; *The Winter's Tale,* v, 3, 37; *Troilus and Cressida,* iii, 2, 146; *Julius Cæsar,* ii, 2, 106; *King Lear,* i, 4, 318.
Now before the gods, I am ashamed on 't.
Timon of Athens. Act iii, sc. 2, l. 19. [Lucius]
I am almost ashamed.—*King John,* iii, 3, 27.
I am much ashamed.—*The Merchant of Venice,* ii, 6, 35.
I need not to be ashamed.—*Henry V,* iv, 7, 118.
7
Be not you ashamed to show, he 'll not shame to tell you what it means.
Hamlet. Act iii, sc. 2, l. 155. [Hamlet]
Proclaim no shame
When the compulsive ardour gives the charge.
Hamlet. Act iii, sc. 4, l. 85. [Hamlet] "Compulsive" occurs again in *Othello,* iii, 3, 454.
8
O shame! where is thy blush?
Hamlet. Act iii, sc. 4, l. 82. [Hamlet]
Blush for shame.—*King John,* v, 2, 153; *The Rape of Lucrece,* l. 54.
Blush'd to see her shame.—*The Rape of Lucrece,* l. 1344.
Shame and blush.—*Titus Andronicus,* iii, 1, 15.
Blushing shame.—*Sonnets,* xcix.
Come, come, what need you blush? shame 's a baby.
Troilus and Cressida. Act iii, sc. 2, l. 42. [Pandarus]
9
Art thou not ashamed?
I Henry IV. Act i, sc. 3, l. 118. [King Henry] Repeated in iii, 3, 184; and in *II Henry IV,* ii, 4, 152; *The Two Gentlemen of Verona,* iv, 2, 111.
Fie upon thee! Art not ashamed?
Much Ado about Nothing. Act iii, sc. 4, l. 28. [Hero] Repeated in *King Lear,* ii, 4, 196.
Are you not ashamed?—*I Henry VI,* iv, 1, 125; *II Henry IV,* ii, 1, 88; *Love's Labour 's Lost,* iv, 3, 159; *The Merry Wives of Windsor,* iii, 3, 230; iv, 2, 144; 197.
10
What trick, what device, what starting-hole, canst thou now find out to hide thee from this open and apparent shame?
I Henry IV. Act ii, sc. 4, l. 290. [Prince of Wales] The only use of "starting-hole" (subterfuge). "Open shame" is repeated in *The Rape of Lucrece,* l. 890.
All-eating shame.—*Sonnets,* ii. The only use of "all-eating."
Bastard shame.—*Sonnets,* cxxvii.
Christian shame.—*Othello,* ii, 3, 172.
Divulged shame.—*All 's Well that Ends Well,* ii, 1, 174.
Lengthen'd shame.—*Cymbeline,* v, 3, 13.
Maiden shame.—*A Midsummer-Night's Dream,* iii, 2, 285.
Murderous shame.—*Sonnets,* ix.
Notorious shame.—*The Comedy of Errors,* iv, 1, 84.
Perpetual shame.—*III Henry VI,* v, 4, 51; *King John,* v, 7, 77.
Shame perpetual.—*Winter's Tale,* iii, 2, 239.
Sovereign shame.—*King Lear,* iv, 3, 44.
World's shame.—*Richard III,* iv, 4, 27.
11
For every honour sitting on his helm,
Would they were multitudes, and on my head
My shames redoubled! for the time will come,
That I shall make this northern youth exchange
His glorious deeds for my indignities.
I Henry IV. Act iii, sc. 2, l. 142. [Prince of Wales]
To my shame.—*I Henry IV,* v, 1, 93; *Much Ado about Nothing,* v, 1, 248; *Hamlet,* iv, 4, 59.
Much to our shame.—*Love's Labour 's Lost,* v, 2, 358.
12
Witness our too much memorable shame,
When Cressy battle fatally was struck,
And all our princes captive.
Henry V. Act ii, sc. 4, l. 54. [French King] The only mention of "Cressy" and the only use of "fatally."
13
'Tis shame for us all: so God sa' me, 'tis shame to stand still; it is shame, by my hand.
Henry V. Act iii, sc. 2, l. 117. [Macmorris]
'Tis a passing shame.—*The Two Gentlemen of Verona,* i, 2, 17.
'Tis a shame.—*Romeo and Juliet,* i, 5, 84.
'Tis shame.—*King John,* iv, 2, 93; *Richard II,* ii, 1, 238.
It is shame to be thought on.—*II Henry IV,* ii, 1, 38.
It were a shame.—*The Two Gentlemen of Verona,* i, 2, 51.
Is that a shame?—*Coriolanus,* iv, 2, 17.

Were 't not a shame?—*II Henry VI;* iv, 8, 43.
Ah, what a shame!—*III Henry VI,* v, 4, 12.
What a shame was this!—*Henry VIII,* v, 3, 141.

1
For your great seats now quit you of great shames.
Henry V. Act iii, sc. 5, l. 47. [French King]
Reproach and everlasting shame
Sits mocking in our plumes.
Henry V. Act iv, sc. 5, l. 4. [Dauphin]
O perdurable shame!
Henry V. Act iv, sc. 5, l. 7. [Dauphin] "Perdurable" (lasting) occurs again in *Othello,* i, 3, 343.
Shame and eternal shame, nothing but shame!
Henry V. Act iv, sc. 5, l. 10. [Bourbon] "Eternal shame" is repeated in *Love's Labour's Lost,* i, 1, 158.
Let life be short; else shame will be too long.
Henry V. Act iv, sc. 5, l. 23. [Bourbon]

2
The shame hereof will make me hide my head.
I Henry VI. Act i, sc. 5, l. 39. [Talbot]
John: If death be so apparent, then both fly.
Talbot: And leave my followers here to fight and die?
My age was never tainted with such shame.
I Henry VI. Act iv, sc. 5, l. 44.
Shame's scorn and subject of mischance!
I Henry VI, iv, 6, 49. [John Talbot]

3
Gloucester: Sweet Nell, ill can thy noble mind abrook
The abject people gazing on thy face,
With envious looks, laughing at thy shame,
That erst did follow thy proud chariot-wheels
When thou didst ride in triumph through the streets. . . .
Duchess: Come you, my lord, to see my open shame? . . .
In thy closet pent up rue my shame. . . .
Methinks I should not thus be led along,
Mail'd up in shame, with papers on my back. . . .
But be thou mild and blush not at my shame. . . .
My shame will not be shifted with my sheet:
No, it will hang upon my richest robes
And show itself, attire me how I can.
II Henry VI. Act ii, sc. 4, l. 10. The only use of "abrook."

4
Shame to thy silver hair,
Thou mad misleader of thy brain-sick son!
II Henry VI. Act v, sc. 1, l. 162. [King Henry] "Misleader" is repeated in *I Henry IV,* "Misleader of youth"; and in *II Henry IV,* v, 5, 68. "Brain-sick" is used five times and "brainsickly" once, in *Macbeth,* ii, 2, 46.
I shame to hear thee speak.—*III Henry VI,* i, 1, 231.
I shame to speak.—*King John,* i, 1, 104.

5
For shame! in duty bend thy knee to me.
II Henry VI. Act v, sc. 1, l. 173. [King Henry] "For shame" is repeated in v, 1, 213, in v, 2, 72, and twenty-two times in later plays.
Fie, for godly shame!—*Troilus and Cressida,* ii, 2, 32.
Run away for shame.—*Love's Labour's Lost,* v, 2, 583.

6
Ah, what a shame were this!
III Henry VI. Act ii, sc. 2, l. 39. [Clifford]
No more my king, for he dishonours me,
But most himself, if he could see his shame.
III Henry VI. Act iii, sc. 3, l. 184. [Warwick]
Am I guerdon'd at the last with shame?
III Henry VI. Act iii, sc. 3, l. 191. [Warwick] "Guerdon'd" is repeated in *II Henry VI,* i, 4, 49.
The shame-faced Henry.—*III Henry VI,* iv, 8, 53. The only use of "shame-faced."
A blushing shamefast spirit.—*Richard III,* i, 4, 142. The only use of "shamefast."

7
The gods defend him from so great a shame!
Julius Cæsar. Act v, sc. 4, l. 23. [Lucilius]

8
Well could I bear that England had this praise,
So we could find some pattern of our shame.
King John. Act iii, sc. 4, l. 15. [King Philip]
And bitter shame hath spoil'd the sweet world's taste,
That it yields nought but shame and bitterness.
King John. Act iii, sc. 4, l. 110. [Dauphin]
You will but make it blush
And glow with shame of your proceedings.
King John. Act iv, sc. 1, l. 113. [Arthur]
Deep shame had struck me dumb.
King John. Act iv, sc. 2, l. 235. [King John]
Deep shames.—*Comedy of Errors,* v, 1, 253.

9
This is the bloodiest shame,
The wildest savagery, the vilest stroke,
That ever wall-eyed wrath or staring rage
Presented to the tears of soft remorse.
King John. Act iv, sc. 3, l. 47. [Salisbury] The only use of "bloodiest." "Wall-eyed" occurs again in *Titus Andronicus,* v, 1, 44: "Wall-eyed slave."

10
The shame itself doth speak
For instant remedy.
King Lear. Act i, sc. 4, l. 267. [Goneril]
O lady, lady, shame would have it hid!
King Lear. Act ii, sc. 1, l. 95. [Gloucester]
Shame of ladies!—*King Lear,* iv, 3, 29.

11
Makest thou this shame thy pastime?
King Lear. Act ii, sc. 4, l. 6. [King Lear]
Let shame come when it will, I do not call it.
King Lear. Act ii, sc. 4, l. 229. [King Lear]
These things sting
His mind so venomously, that burning shame
Detains him from Cordelia.
King Lear. Act iv, sc. 3, l. 47. [Kent] "Venomously" is repeated in *Pericles,* iii, 1, 7.

12
Sweet fellowship in shame!
Love's Labour's Lost. Act iv, sc. 3, l. 49. [King Ferdinand]
Ah, you whoreson loggerhead! you were born to do me shame.
Love's Labour's Lost. Act iv, sc. 3, l. 204.

[Biron] "Loggerhead" is repeated in *I Henry IV,* ii, 4, 4, and in *Romeo and Juliet,* iv, 4, 20. "Logger-headed" occurs in *The Taming of the Shrew,* iv, 1, 128.
Do me shame.—*King John,* iv, 3, 97.
Done me shame.—*King John,* v, 6, 13.

1
King: Biron, they will shame us. . . .
Biron: We are shame-proof, my lord.
Love's Labour 's Lost. Act v, sc. 2, l. 512. The only use of "shame-proof."

2
They sought their shame that so their shame did find.
A Lover's Complaint, l. 187.

3
I do repent me, as it is an evil,
And take the shame with joy.
Measure for Measure. Act ii, sc. 3, l. 35. [Juliet]

But that her tender shame
Will not proclaim against her maiden loss,
How might she tongue me!
Measure for Measure. Act iv, sc. 4, l. 26. [Angelo]

Perchance, publicly, she 'll be ashamed.
Measure for Measure. Act v, sc. 1, l. 278. [Lucio]

No longer session hold upon my shame.
Measure for Measure. Act v, sc. 1, l. 376. [Angelo]

4
Forget the shames that you have stain'd me with.
The Merchant of Venice. Act i, sc. 3, l. 140. [Shylock]

What, must I hold a candle to my shames?
The Merchant of Venice. Act ii, sc. 6, l. 41. [Jessica]

Must yield to such inevitable shame
As to offend, himself being offended.
The Merchant of Venice. Act iv, sc. 1, l. 57. [Shylock]

I was beset with shame.
The Merchant of Venice. Act v, sc. 1, l. 217. [Bassanio]

5
I fear not mine own shame so much as his peril.
The Merry Wives of Windsor. Act iii, sc. 3, l. 129. [Mrs. Page]

Better shame than murder.
The Merry Wives of Windsor. Act iv, sc. 2, l. 46. [Mrs. Page]

6
You 're shamed, you 're overthrown, you 're undone for ever!
The Merry Wives of Windsor. Act iii, sc. 3, l. 102. [Mrs. Page]

You will be shamed for ever.
Othello. Act ii, sc. 3, l. 163. [Iago]

7
Why then you are utterly shamed.
The Merry Wives of Windsor. Act iv, sc. 2, l. 44. [Mrs. Page]

I 'll warrant they 'll have him publicly shamed: and methinks there would be no period to the jest, should he not be publicly shamed.
The Merry Wives of Windsor. Act iv, sc. 2, l. 235. [Mrs. Ford]

Public shame.—*Love's Labour 's Lost,* i, 1, 132.

8
Why, doth not every earthly thing
Cry shame upon her?
Much Ado about Nothing. Act iv, sc. 1, l. 122. [Leonato]

Cry shame against me.—*Othello,* v, 2, 222.

9
Is it a shame to get when we are old?
Pericles. Act iv, sc. 2, l. 32. [Bawd]

10
When shame assail'd, the red should fence the white.
The Rape of Lucrece, l. 63.

This blur to youth, this sorrow to the sage,
This dying virtue, this surviving shame,
Whose crime will bear an ever-during blame.
The Rape of Lucrece, l. 222. The only use of "blur" as a noun, and of "ever-during."

The shame and fault finds no excuse nor end.
The Rape of Lucrece, l. 238.

Bequeath not to their lot
The shame that from them no device can take,
The blemish that will never be forgot.
The Rape of Lucrece, l. 534.

Hast thou put on his shape to do him shame?
The Rape of Lucrece, l. 597.

How will thy shame be seeded in thine age,
When thus thy vices bud before thy spring!
The Rape of Lucrece, l. 603. "Seeded" is repeated in *Troilus and Cressida,* i, 3, 316: "Seeded pride."

Shame folded up in blind concealing night,
When most unseen, then most doth tyrannize.
The Rape of Lucrece, l. 675.

And grave, like water that doth eat in steel,
Upon my cheeks what helpless shame I feel.
The Rape of Lucrece, l. 755.

O unseen shame! invisible disgrace!
O unfelt sore! crest-wounding, private scar!
The Rape of Lucrece, l. 827. The only use of "crest-wounding."

So of shame's ashes shall my fame be bred;
For in my death I murder shameful scorn:
My shame so dead, mine honour is new-born.
The Rape of Lucrece, l. 1188.

My shame be his that did my fame confound.
The Rape of Lucrece, l. 1202.

Shame that might ensue
By that her death, to do her husband wrong.
The Rape of Lucrece, l. 1263.

Lasting shame
On thee and thine this night I will inflict,
If thou my love's desire do contradict.
Rape of Lucrece, l. 1629. "Inflict" occurs only once more, in *II Henry VI,* iii, 1, 377.

Manly shame bids him possess his breath
And live to be revenged on her death.
The Rape of Lucrece, l. 1777.

11
Myself I throw, dread monarch, at thy foot.
My life thou shalt command, but not my shame. . . .
Take but my shame And I resign my gage.
Richard II. Act i, sc. 1, l. 165. [Mowbray]

Bound in with shame,
With inky blots and rotten parchment bonds.
Richard II. Act ii, sc. 1, l. 63. [Gaunt]

From forth thy reach he would have laid thy shame.
Richard II. Act ii, sc. 1, l. 106. [Gaunt]

Wert thou regent of the world,
It were a shame to let this land by lease;

But for thy world enjoying but this land,
Is it not more than shame to shame it so?
Richard II. Act ii, sc. 1, l. 109. [Gaunt]
Live in thy shame, but die not shame with thee!
Richard II. Act ii, sc. 1, l. 135. [Gaunt]

1 Like silly beggars
Who sitting in the stocks refuge their shame,
That many have and others must sit there.
Richard II. Act v, sc. 5, l. 25. [King Richard]

2 Foul shame upon you!
Richard III. Act i, sc. 3, l. 249. [Queen Margaret]
Shame upon you!—*King John,* ii, 1, 166.
The more shame for him.—*The Two Gentlemen of Verona,* iv, 4, 138.
The more shame for you.—*Love's Labour's Lost,* v, 2, 506; *Henry VIII,* iii, 1, 102.

3 Buckingham: Have done! for shame, if not for charity.
Queen Margaret: Urge neither charity nor shame to me: . . .
My charity is outrage, life my shame;
And in that shame still live my sorrow's rage!
Richard III. Act i, sc. 3, l. 273.
Bloody thou art, bloody will be thy end;
Shame serves thy life and doth thy death attend.
Richard III. Act iv, sc. 4, l. 194. [Duchess of York]
And in record, left them the heirs of shame.
Richard III. Act v, sc. 3, l. 335. [King Richard]

4 He was not born to shame:
Upon his brow shame is ashamed to sit;
For 'tis a throne where honour may be crown'd
Sole monarch of the universal earth.
Romeo and Juliet. Act iii, sc. 2, l. 91. [Juliet]
Fie, fie, thou shamest thy shape, thy love, thy wit.
Romeo and Juliet. Act iii, sc. 3, l. 122. [Friar Laurence]

5 This shall free thee from this present shame.
Romeo and Juliet. Act iv, sc. 1, l. 118. [Friar Laurence]
[He] here is come to do some villanous shame
To the dead bodies.
Romeo and Juliet. Act v, sc. 3, l. 52. [Paris]

6 Nor can thy shame give physic to my grief;
Though thou repent, yet I have still the loss.
Sonnets. No. xxxiv.
I am shamed by that which I bring forth,
And so should you, to love things nothing worth.
Sonnets. No. lxxii.
How sweet and lovely dost thou make the shame
Which, like a canker in the fragrant rose,
Doth spot the beauty of thy budding name!
Sonnets. No. xcv.
If thou account'st it shame, lay it on me;
And therefore frolic.
The Taming of the Shrew. Act iv, sc. 3, l. 183. [Petruchio] "Frolic" is repeated in *A Midsummer-Night's Dream,* v, 1, 394.

7 I am e'en sick of shame.
Timon of Athens. Act iii, sc. 6, l. 46. [Lord]
Shame that they wanted cunning, in excess
Hath broke their hearts.
Timon of Athens. Act v, sc. 4, l. 28. [Second Senator]

8 Ah, now thou turn'st away thy face for shame!
Titus Andronicus. Act ii, sc. 4, l. 28. [Marcus]
The girl should not survive her shame.
Titus Andronicus. Act v, sc. 3, l. 41. [Saturninus]

9 With thy shame, thy father's sorrow die!
Titus Andronicus. Act v, sc. 3, l. 47. [Titus]

10 Sir Toby: Wouldst thou not be glad to have the niggardly rascally sheep-biter come by some notable shame?
Fabian: I would exult, man.
Twelfth Night. Act ii, sc. 5, l. 5. The only use of "sheep-biter." "Sheep-biting face" occurs in *Measure for Measure,* v, 1, 359. "Niggardly" is repeated in *The Comedy of Errors,* iii, 1, 27: "Niggardly host"; *Henry V,* ii, 4, 46: "Niggardly projection"; and *The Merry Wives of Windsor,* ii, 2, 205.

11 A slave, that still an end turns me to shame!
The Two Gentlemen of Verona. Act iv, sc. 4, l. 67. [Proteus]
My shame and guilt confounds me.
The Two Gentlemen of Verona. Act v, sc. 4, l. 73. [Proteus]
Be thou ashamed that I have took upon me
Such an immodest raiment, if shame live
In a disguise of love.
The Two Gentlemen of Verona. Act v, sc. 4, l. 105. [Julia]

12 He burns with bashful shame.
Venus and Adonis, l. 49.
Pure shame and awed resistance made him fret,
Which bred more beauty in his angry eyes.
Venus and Adonis, l. 69. "Pure shame" is repeated in *I Henry VI,* ii, 4, 66.
Still is he sullen, still he lours and frets,
'Twixt crimson shame and anger ashy-pale:
Being red, she loves him best; and being white,
Her best is better'd with a more delight.
Venus and Adonis, l. 75. "Ashy-pale" occurs again in *The Rape of Lucrece,* l. 1512, but nowhere in the plays.
My face is full of shame, my heart of teen.
Venus and Adonis, l. 808.

SHAPE

See also Appearance

13 Here I am Antony;
Yet cannot hold this visible shape, my knave.
Antony and Cleopatra. Act iv, sc. 14, l. 13. [Antony]

Better shape.—*Much Ado about Nothing,* iv, 1, 237.
Blessed shape.—*Sonnets,* liii.
Gentle shapes.—*Richard III,* ii, 2, 27.
Good shape.—*Troilus and Cressida,* i, 2, 275.
Goodly shape.—*The Two Gentlemen of Verona,* iv, 1, 56.
Holier shapes.—*Timon of Athens,* iv, 3, 430.
Human shape.—*The Tempest,* i, 2, 284.
Pleasing shape.—*Hamlet,* ii, 2, 629.
Proper shape.—*II Henry IV,* iv, 1, 37.

1
It is shaped, sir, like itself.
Antony and Cleopatra. Act ii, sc. 7, l. 47. See TEAR, 1501:1.
I, that am not shaped for sportive tricks.
Richard III. Act i, sc. 1, l. 14. [Gloucester]

2
You souls of geese,
That bear the shapes of men.
Coriolanus, i, 4, 35. See under COWARDICE.
Shape of man.—*The Merchant of Venice,* iii, 2, 277; *Merry Wives of Windsor,* v, 1, 23.
Shaped out a man.—*Timon of Athens,* i, 1, 43.

3
I know the shape of 's leg.
Cymbeline. Act iv, sc. 2, l. 309. [Imogen]
Shape of his leg.—*Twelfth Night,* ii, 3, 170.

4
Thou comest in such questionable shape
That I will speak to thee.
Hamlet, i, 4, 43. See under SPIRIT.
False shapes.—*The Two Gentlemen of Verona,* iv, 2, 131.
Monstrous shape.—*The Tempest,* iii, 3, 31.
Strange shapes.—*Love's Labour's Lost,* v, 2, 773.
Surmised shape.—*Troilus and Cressida,* i, 3, 17. "Surmised" is repeated in *II Henry VI,* iii, 2, 347.
Ungrateful shape.—*Timon of Athens,* iii, 2, 80.

5
Full of fiery and delectable shapes.
II Henry IV, iv, 3, 108. See under SACK.
Fiery shapes.—*I Henry IV,* iii, 1, 14.

6
York: See, how the ugly witch doth bend her brows,
As if with Circe she would change my shape!
La Pucelle: Changed to a worser shape thou canst not be.
York: O, Charles the Dauphin is a proper man;
No shape but his can please your dainty eye.
I Henry VI. Act v, sc. 3, l. 34. Circe is mentioned again in *Comedy of Errors,* v, 1, 270.
Change shapes with Proteus.—*III Henry VI,* iii, 2, 192.

7
Who cannot steal a shape that means deceit?
II Henry VI. Act iii, sc. 1, l. 79. See SEEMING, 1330:4.

8
Madam, an if my brother had my shape,
And I had his, sir Robert's his, like him; . . .
And, to his shape, were heir to all this land,
Would I might never stir from off this place,
I would give it every foot to have his face.
King John, i, 1, 138. See PLACE, 1358:17.

9
I . . . am bethought
To take the basest and most poorest shape
That ever penury, in contempt of man,
Brought near to beast.
King Lear. Act ii, sc. 3, l. 6. [Edgar]

10
Howe'er thou art a fiend,
A woman's shape doth shield thee.
King Lear. Act iv, sc. 2, l. 66. [Albany]
Shape of a woman.—*The Merry Wives of Windsor,* v, 1, 22.
Shapes of beasts.—*The Winter's Tale,* iv, 4, 27.
Shape of a camel.—*Hamlet,* iii, 2, 394.
Shapes of grief.—*Richard II,* ii, 2, 22; *Hamlet,* i, 2, 82.
Shape of heaven.—*Hamlet,* i, 5, 54.
Shape of nature.—*Twelfth Night,* i, 5, 280.
Shape of sense.—*Troilus and Cressida,* i, 3, 385.
Shape profane.—*The Merry Wives of Windsor,* iv, 4, 60.
Husband's shape.—*Sonnets,* ix.

11
Boyet: Madam, and pretty mistresses, give ear:
Immediately they will again be here
In their own shapes. . . .
Princess: Avaunt, perplexity! What shall we do,
If they return in their own shapes to woo?
Rosaline: Good madam, if by me you 'll be advised,
Let 's mock them still, as well known as disguised.
Love's Labour's Lost. Act v, sc. 2, l. 286. "Perplexity" is repeated in *The Two Gentlemen of Verona,* ii, 3, 9, and in *The Merry Wives of Windsor,* iv, 5, 85.

12
Hast thou put on his shape to do him shame?
The Rape of Lucrece, l. 597.
Put on some other shape.—*Richard III,* iv, 4, 286.

13
Fie, fie, thou shamest thy shape, thy love, thy wit:
Which, like a usurer, abound'st in all,
And useth none in that true use indeed
Which should bedeck thy shape, thy love, thy wit:
Thy noble shape is but a form of wax,
Digressing from the valour of a man.
Romeo and Juliet. Act iii, sc. 3, l. 122. [Friar Laurence]

14
Go take this shape And hither come in 't.
The Tempest. Act i, sc. 2, l. 303. [Prospero]
Thou think'st there is no more such shapes as he.
The Tempest. Act i, sc. 2, l. 478. [Prospero]
Thy shape invisible retain thou still.
The Tempest. Act iv, sc. 1, l. 185. [Prospero]

15
In all shapes that man goes up and down in from fourscore to thirteen, this spirit walks in.
Timon of Athens. Act ii, sc. 2, l. 119. [Fool]

1
Shapes and forms of slaughter.
Troilus and Cressida, v, 3, 12. See under DREAM.

Shape and form.—*Much Ado about Nothing,* v, 1, 14.

SHEEP

2
The greatest of my pride is to see my ewes graze and my lambs suck.
As You Like It. Act iii, sc. 2, l. 80. [Corin]

The ewe that will not hear her lamb when it baes will never answer a calf when he bleats.
Much Ado about Nothing. Act iii, sc. 3, l. 74. [Dogberry] "Baes" is repeated in *Coriolanus,* ii, 1, 12: "He 's a lamb indeed, that baes like a bear."

Even now, now, very now, an old black ram
Is tupping your white ewe.
Othello. Act i, sc. 1, l. 88. [Iago] The only use of "tupping."

Two hot sheeps, marry.
Love's Labour 's Lost. Act ii, sc. 1, l. 219. [Maria]

3
Speed: Saw you my master? . . . I have play'd the sheep in losing him.
Proteus: Indeed, a sheep doth very often stray,
An if the shepherd be a while away.
Speed: You conclude that my master is a shepherd then and I a sheep? . . . Why then, my horns are his horns, whether I wake or sleep.
Proteus: A silly answer and fitting well a sheep.
Speed: This proves me still a sheep.
Proteus: True; and thy master a shepherd.
Speed: Nay, that I can deny by a circumstance. . . . The shepherd seeks the sheep, and not the sheep the shepherd; but I seek my master, and my master seeks not me: therefore I am no sheep.
Proteus: The sheep for fodder follow the shepherd; the shepherd for food follows not the sheep: thou for wages followest thy master; . . . therefore thou art a sheep.
Speed: Such another proof will make me cry 'baa.'
Proteus: But, dost thou hear? gavest thou my letter to Julia?
Speed: Ay, sir, I, a lost mutton, gave your letter to her, a laced mutton, and she, a laced mutton, gave me, a lost mutton, nothing for my labour.
Proteus: Here 's too small a pasture for such store of muttons.
The Two Gentlemen of Verona. Act i, sc. 1, l. 70. The only use of "fodder."

4
The sheep are gone to fold, birds to their nest.
Venus and Adonis, l. 532.

5
They have scared away two of my best sheep, which I fear the wolf will sooner find than the master: if any where I have them, 'tis by the seaside, browsing of ivy.
The Winter's Tale. Act iii, sc. 3, l. 66. [Shepherd] The only use of "browsing."

Peevish sheep.—*Comedy of Errors,* iv, 1, 93.

Silly sheep.—*III Henry VI,* ii, 5, 43; *Love's Labour 's Lost,* v, 1, 53.

Laban's sheep.—*The Merchant of Venice,* i, 3, 72. Laban is mentioned again in l. 79, and nowhere else.

6
I 'll be with you at your sheep-shearing too: if I make not this cheat bring out another and the shearers prove sheep, let me be unrolled and my name put in the book of virtue!
The Winter's Tale. Act iv, sc. 3, l. 128. [Autolycus] "Shearers" occurs again in the same scene, l. 44, and in no other play.

Shepherd: Bid us welcome to your sheep-shearing,
As your good flock shall prosper. . . .
Perdita: Welcome to our shearing!
The Winter's Tale. Act iv, sc. 4, l. 69. "Sheep-shearing" occurs five times in this scene, and nowhere else in the plays.

SHEETS

7
You think none but your sheets are privy to your wishes.
Antony and Cleopatra, i, 2, 41. See under WISH.

8
Should he make me
Live, like Diana's priest, betwixt cold sheets,
Whiles he is vaulting variable ramps,
In your despite, upon your purse? Revenge it.
Cymbeline. Act i, sc. 6, l. 132. [Iachimo]

Between his sheets.—*Henry V,* ii, 1, 88.

'Twixt my sheets.—*Othello,* i, 3, 393.

Bloody sheet.—*Romeo and Juliet,* v, 3, 97.

Incestuous sheets.—*Hamlet,* i, 2, 157.

Lawful sheets.—*King Lear,* iv, 6, 118.

Pair of sheets.—*II Henry IV,* ii, 4, 244.

Sheets of fire.—*King Lear,* iii, 2, 46.

Sheet of paper.—*Love's Labour 's Lost,* v, 2, 7; *Much Ado about Nothing,* ii, 3, 138; 140; *Twelfth Night,* iii, 2, 50.

9
I saw him fumble with the sheets.
Henry V, ii, 3, 15. See under DEATH.

Throw off this sheet.—*II Henry VI,* ii, 4, 105.

Happiness to their sheets!—*Othello,* ii, 3, 29.

10
Prithee, to-night
Lay on my bed my wedding sheets.
Othello. Act iv, sc. 2, l. 104.

Emilia: I have laid those sheets you bade me on the bed. . . .
Desdemona: If I do die before thee, prithee, shroud me
In one of those same sheets.
Othello. Act iv, sc. 3, l. 22.

Shrouding sheet.—*Hamlet,* v, 1, 103. The only use of "shrouding."

11
Teaching the sheets a whiter hue than white.
Venus and Adonis, l. 398.

O'er the white sheet peers her whiter chin.
The Rape of Lucrece, l. 472.
Whiter than the sheets!—*Cymbeline,* ii, 2, 16.

1
The purity and whiteness of my sheets,
Which to preserve is sleep, which being spotted
Is goads, thorns, nettles, tails of wasps.
Winter's Tale. Act i, sc. 2, l. 327. [Leontes]
The white sheet bleaching on the hedge.
Winter's Tale. Act iv, sc. 3, l. 5. [Autolycus]

SHEPHERD

2 I am shepherd to another man
And do not shear the fleeces that I graze.
As You Like It. Act ii, sc. 4, l. 78. [Corin]
Here live and die a shepherd.
As You Like It. Act v, sc. 2, l. 12. [Oliver]

3
Mistress and master, you have oft inquired
After the shepherd that complain'd of love.
As You Like It. Act iii, sc. 4, l. 51. [Corin] The only use of "complain'd."
You foolish shepherd, wherefore do you follow her?
. . . Take her to thee, shepherd. . . . Ply her hard.
. . . Shepherdess, look on him better.
As You Like It. Act iii, sc. 5, l. 49. [Rosalind]
You are there followed by a faithful shepherd;
Look upon him, love him; he worships you.
As You Like It. Act v, sc. 2, l. 87. [Rosalind]
You'll give yourself to this most faithful shepherd.
As You Like It. Act v, sc. 4, l. 14. [Rosalind]

4
Praising the proud disdainful shepherdess
That was his mistress.
As You Like It. Act iii, sc. 4, l. 53. [Corin]
Shepherdess,—a fair one are you.
The Winter's Tale. Act iv, sc. 4, l. 73. [Polixenes]
No shepherdess, but Flora
Peering in April's front.
The Winter's Tale. Act iv, sc. 4, l. 2. [Florizel] The only mention of Flora.

5
So flies the reckless shepherd from the wolf;
So first the harmless sheep doth yield his fleece
And next his throat unto the butcher's knife.
III Henry VI. Act v, sc. 6, l. 7. [King Henry]

6
Sleepest or wakest thou, jolly shepherd?
Thy sheep be in the corn;
And for one blast of thy minikin mouth,
Thy sheep shall take no harm.
King Lear. Act iii, sc. 6, l. 43. [Edgar] The only use of "minikin" (small).
O, sweet shepherd, hie thee,
For methinks thou stay'st too long.
The Passionate Pilgrim, l. 167.
Fair shepherd.—*The Winter's Tale,* iv, 4, 356.
Good shepherd.—*As You Like It,* v, 2, 89; *The Winter's Tale,* iv, 4, 166.
Homely shepherd.—*Winter's Tale,* iv, 2, 43.
Phrygian shepherds.—*Rape of Lucrece,* l. 1502.
Poor shepherd.—*As You Like It,* ii, 4, 44; iv, 3, 65.
Skilful shepherd.—*Merchant of Venice,* i, 3, 85.
Shepherd of the flock.—*II Henry VI,* ii, 2, 73.
Shepherd boy.—*As You Like It,* v, 4, 26.
Shepherd swain.—*I Henry VI,* v, 4, 37.
Shepherd youth.—*As You Like It,* iv, 3, 156.

7 Your youth,
And the true blood which peepeth fairly through 't,
Do plainly give you out an unstain'd shepherd.
Winter's Tale. Act iv, sc. 4, l. 147. [Perdita]
Thou a sceptre's heir,
That thus affect'st a sheep-hook?
The Winter's Tale. Act iv, sc. 4, l. 430. [Polixenes] The only use of "sheep-hook."
If that shepherd be not in hand-fast, let him fly.
The Winter's Tale. Act iv, sc. 4, l. 795. [Autolycus] "Hand-fast" is repeated in *Cymbeline,* i, 5, 78.
The old shepherd, which stands by like a weather-bitten conduit of many kings' reigns.
The Winter's Tale. Act v, sc. 2, l. 60. [Gentleman] The only use of "weather-bitten."
Old shepherd.—*The Winter's Tale,* v, 2, 4.

SHIFT

See also Stratagem

8 Now I must
To the young man send humble treaties, dodge
And palter in the shifts of lowness.
Antony and Cleopatra. Act iii, sc. 11, l. 61. [Antony] "Lowness" is repeated in ii, 7, 22, and in *King Lear,* iii, 4, 73.
Cleanliest shift.—*As You Like It,* iv, 1, 78. The only use of "cleanliest."

9
O mistress, mistress, shift and save yourself!
The Comedy of Errors. Act v, sc. 1, l. 168. [Servant]

10
Let it alone; I'll make other shift.
II Henry IV. Act ii, sc. 1, l. 169. [Falstaff]
And now there rests no other shift but this.
I Henry VI. Act ii, sc. 1, l. 75. [La Pucelle]

11
We'll devise a mean.
II Henry VI. Act iv, sc. 8, l. 71. [Buckingham]

12
When he was made a shriver, 'twas for shift.
III Henry VI. Act iii, sc. 2, l. 108. [Clarence] The only use of "shriver."

13
I'll find a thousand shifts to get away.
King John. Act iv, sc. 3, l. 7. [Arthur]
I must cony-catch; I must shift.
The Merry Wives of Windsor. Act i, sc. 3, l. 37. [Falstaff] The only use of "cony-catch" (cheat).

14
Cursed be that heart that forced us to this shift!
Titus Andronicus. Act iv, sc. 1, l. 72. [Marcus]

It is you that puts us to our shifts.
Titus Andronicus. Act iv, sc. 2, l. 176. [Aaron]

1 I 'll go another way to work with him.
Twelfth Night. Act iv, sc. 1, l. 35. [Sir Andrew]

SHIN

2 Moth: A wonder, master! here 's a costard broken in a shin. . . .
Costard: I, Costard, running out, that was safely within,
Fell over the threshold, and broke my shin.
Armado: We will talk no more of this matter.
Costard: Till there be no more matter in the shin.
Love's Labour 's Lost. Act iii, sc. 1, l. 70. "Costard" is a humorous term for the head.
Break my shins.—*As You Like It,* ii, 4, 60.

3 I bruised my shin th' other day while playing at sword and dagger with a master of fence.
The Merry Wives of Windsor. Act i, sc. 1, l. 294. [Slender]

4 Romeo: Your plantain-leaf is excellent for that.
Benvolio: For what, I pray thee?
Romeo: For your broken shin.
Romeo and Juliet. Act i, sc. 2, l. 52. The only use of "plantain-leaf." "Plantain" is mentioned in *Love's Labour 's Lost,* iii, 1, 74, also as a remedy for a broken shin.

5 Strike their sharp shins,
And mar men's spurring.
Timon of Athens. Act iv, sc. 3, l. 151. [Timon]
Frail shins.—*The Tempest,* iv, 1, 181.

SHIP

See also Bark, Sail, Sailor, Vessel

6 The barge she sat in, like a burnish'd throne,
Burn'd on the water: the poop was beaten gold;
Purple the sails, and so perfumed that
The winds were love-sick with them; the oars were silver,
Which to the tune of flutes kept stroke, and made
The water which they beat to follow faster,
As amorous of their strokes.
Antony and Cleopatra. Act ii, sc. 2, l. 196. [Enobarbus] "Poop" occurs again in *I Henry IV,* iii, 3, 29, and "love-sick" in *Titus Andronicus,* v, 3, 82.
My barge stays.—*Henry VIII,* i, 3, 63.
They 've left their barge.—*Henry VIII,* i, 4, 54.
See the barge be ready.—*Henry VIII,* ii, 1, 98.
There 's a barge put off from Mytilene.—*Pericles,* v, 1, 3.

7 Our great navy 's rigg'd.
Antony and Cleopatra. Act iii, sc. 5, l. 20. [Enobarbus]
Bravely rigg'd.—*The Tempest,* v, 1, 224.
Not rigg'd.—*The Tempest,* i, 2, 146. The only uses of "rigg'd."

8 He lent me Some shipping unrestored.
Antony and Cleopatra. Act iii, sc. 6, l. 27. [Cæsar]
Our overplus of shipping will we burn.
Antony and Cleopatra. Act iii, sc. 7, l. 51. [Antony] "Overplus" is repeated in iv, 6, 22, and occurs in no other play.
His shipping—
Poor ignorant baubles!—on our terrible seas,
Like egg-shells moved upon their surges, crack'd
As easily 'gainst our rocks.
Cymbeline, iii, 1, 26. See under Cæsar.
Let our cares o'erlook
What shipping and what lading 's in our haven.
Pericles. Act i, sc. 2, l. 48. [Pericles]
A ship of rich lading.—*The Merchant of Venice,* iii, 1, 30.
Precious lading.—*Titus Andronicus,* i, 1, 72. The only uses of "lading."
Take, therefore, shipping.—*I Henry VI,* v, 5, 87.
God send 'em good shipping!—*Taming of the Shrew,* v, 1, 43. The only uses of "shipping."

9 Your ships are not well-mann'd; . . .
Their ships are yare, yours heavy.
Antony and Cleopatra. Act iii, sc. 7, l. 35. [Enobarbus] See under Sailor. The only use of "well-mann'd." "Yare" (nimble, brisk) occurs ten times. "Yarely" is used in *The Tempest,* i, 1, 4, and in *Antony and Cleopatra,* ii, 2, 216.
Our ship
Which, but three glasses since, we gave out split—
Is tight and yare and bravely rigg'd as when
We first put out to sea.
Tempest. Act v, sc. 1, l. 222. [Boatswain]

10 We 'll to our ship: Away, my Thetis!
Antony and Cleopatra, iii, 7, 60. [Antony]
I have a ship
Laden with gold; take it, divide it; fly.
Antony and Cleopatra, iii, 11, 4. [Antony]

11 If any ship put out, then straight away.
The Comedy of Errors. Act iii, sc. 2, l. 191. [Antipholus of Syracuse]
Dromio of Syracuse: Master, there is a bark of Epidamnum
That stays but till her owner comes aboard
And then, sir, she bears away. Our fraughtage, sir,
I have convey'd aboard and I have bought
The oil, the balsamum and aqua-vitæ.
The ship is in her trim: the merry wind
Blows fair from land: they stay for nought at all
But for their owner, master, and yourself.
Antipholus of Ephesus: How now! a madman! Why, thou peevish sheep,
What ship of Epidamnum stays for me?
Dromio: The ship you sent me to, to hire waftage.
The Comedy of Errors. Act iv, sc. 1, l. 85. "Fraughtage" (baggage, freight) is repeated in *Troilus and Cressida,* Prol., 14. The only

use of "balsamnum" (balm). "Aqua-vitæ" occurs six times in five different plays. "Waftage" is repeated in *Troilus and Cressida,* iii, 2, 11. Epidamnum is mentioned seven times in this play, and in no other.

Antipholus of Syracuse: Is there any ship puts forth to-night? may we be gone?

Dromio of Syracuse: Why, sir, I brought you word an hour since that the bark Expedition put forth to-night; and then you were hindered by the sergeant, to tarry for the hoy Delay.

Comedy of Errors. Act iv, sc. 3, l. 35. The only use of "hoy" (a small coasting vessel).

1 Behold the threaden sails,
Borne with the invisible and creeping wind,
Draw the huge bottoms through the furrow'd sea,
Breasting the lofty surge: O, do but think
You stand upon the rivage and behold
A city on the inconstant billows dancing;
For so appears this fleet majestical.

Henry V. Act iii, Prologue, l. 10. [Chorus] The only use of "threaden," "furrow'd," "breasting," and "rivage."

The most noble bottom of our fleet.

Twelfth Night. Act v, sc. 1, l. 60. [Duke]

English bottoms.—*King John,* ii, 1, 73.

2
Your ships already are in readiness.

I Henry VI. Act iii, sc. 1, l. 186. [Gloucester]

My ships are ready.—*Winter's Tale,* i, 2, 449.

Take ship.—*Henry V,* ii, Prol., 30.

3
Yourself shall steer the happy helm.

II Henry VI. Act i, sc. 3, l. 103. [Suffolk]

Prosperous helm.—*All's Well that Ends Well,* iii, 3, 7.

We will not from the helm to sit and weep,
But keep our course, though the rough wind say no,
From shelves and rocks that threaten us with wreck.

III Henry VI. Act v, sc. 4, l. 21. [Queen Margaret] "Shelves" is repeated in *Romeo and Juliet,* v, 1, 44.

4
I stood upon the hatches in the storm.

II Henry VI. Act iii, sc. 2, l. 103. [Queen]

The giddy footing of the hatches.

Richard III. Act i, sc. 4, l. 17. [Clarence]

If he come under my hatches, I 'll never to sea again.

The Merry Wives of Windsor. Act ii, sc. 1, l. 96. [Mrs. Page]

Asleep under the hatches.—*The Tempest,* v, 1, 99.

Beneath the hatches.—*Pericles,* iii, 1, 72.

Clapp'd under hatches.—*The Tempest,* v, 1, 231.

Under hatches stowed.—*The Tempest,* i, 2, 230; v, 1, 99.

Walk upon the hatches.—*Richard III,* i, 4, 13. The only uses of "hatches."

5
Like ships before the wind.

III Henry VI. Act i, sc. 4, l. 4. [York]

How swift his ship.—*Cymbeline,* i, 3, 14.

6
Waft them over with our royal fleet.

III Henry VI. Act iii, sc. 3, l. 253. [King Lewis] "Royal fleet" is repeated in *The Tempest,* v, 1, 316.

Brave fleet with silken streamers.

Henry V, iii, Prol., 5. The only use of "streamers."

Fleet majestical.—*Henry V,* iii, Prol., 16.

Turkish fleet.—*Othello,* i, 3, 8; ii, 1, 10; 17; ii, 2, 4.

7
The ship is under sail, and here she comes amain.

Love's Labour's Lost. Act v, sc. 2, l. 549. [King Ferdinand]

The ship was under sail.—*The Merchant of Venice,* ii, 8, 5.

They fly by them with their woven wings.

The Merchant of Venice. Act i, sc. 1, l. 14. [Salarino]

Well-sailing ships.—*Pericles,* v, Gower, 18. The only use of "well-sailing."

8
But ships are but boards, sailors but men.

The Merchant of Venice. Act i, sc. 3, l. 22. [Shylock]

Trust not to rotten planks.

Antony and Cleopatra. Act iii, sc. 7, l. 63. [Soldier]

9 Argosies with portly sail,
Like signiors and rich burghers.

The Merchant of Venice. Act i, sc. 1, l. 9. [Salarino]

Three of your argosies
Are richly come to harbour.

The Merchant of Venice. Act v, sc. 1, l. 276. [Portia]

My father hath no less
Than three great argosies; besides two galliases,
And twelve tight galleys.

The Taming of the Shrew. Act ii, sc. 1, l. 380. [Tranio] The only use of "galliases." "Tight" is repeated in *Antony and Cleopatra,* iv, 4, 15. The only uses of "argosies." "Argosy" occurs five times.

10
My ships come home a month before the day.

The Merchant of Venice. Act i, sc. 3, l. 183. [Antonio]

Here I read for certain that my ships
Are safely come to road.

The Merchant of Venice. Act v, sc. 1, l. 287. [Antonio]

11
Sail like my pinnace to these golden shores.

The Merry Wives of Windsor. Act i, sc. 3, l. 89. [Falstaff]

Whilst our pinnace anchors in the Downs.—*II Henry VI,* iv, 1, 9.

Captain of a pinnace.—*II Henry VI,* iv, 1, 107. The only uses of "pinnace."

12
My boat sails freely, both with wind and stream.

Othello. Act ii, sc. 3, l. 65. [Iago]

Where 's then the saucy boat
Whose weak untimber'd sides but even now
Co-rivall'd greatness? Either to harbour fled,
Or made a toast for Neptune.

Troilus and Cressida. Act i, sc. 3, l. 42. [Nestor] The only use of "untimber'd" and "co-rivalled."

Light boats sail swift, though greater hulks draw deep.
Troilus and Cressida. Act ii, sc. 3, l. 277. [Agamemnon]
Mightiest hulk.—*I Henry VI,* v, 5, 6. "Hulk" is repeated twice in *II Henry IV* (i, 1, 19; ii, 4, 70), both referring to Falstaff.
Her boat hath a leak,
And she must not speak
Why she dares not come over to thee.
King Lear. Act iii, sc. 6, l. 28. [Fool]
Dancing boat.—*Pericles,* iii, 1, 13.
Driving boat.—*Twelfth Night,* i, 2, 11.
Shallow bauble boats.—*Troilus and Cressida,* i, 3, 35.
Small boat.—*I Henry VI,* iv, 6, 33.
A rotten carcass of a boat.—*The Tempest,* i, 2, 146. See under RATS.

1
We have descried, upon our neighbouring shore,
A portly sail of ships make hitherward.
Pericles. Act i, sc. 4, l. 60. [Lord]
Let not our ships and number of our men
Be like a beacon fired to amaze your eyes.
. . . These our ships, you happily may think
Are like the Trojan horse was stuffed within
With bloody veins, expecting overthrow,
Are stored with corn to make your needy bread,
And give them life whom hunger starved half dead.
Pericles. Act i, sc. 4, l. 86. [Pericles]

2
Ariel: I boarded the king's ship: now on the beak,
Now in the waist, the deck, in every cabin.
Prospero: . . . Of the king's ship
The mariners say how thou hast disposed
And all the rest o' the fleet.
Ariel: Safely in harbour
Is the king's ship; in the deep nook, where once
Thou call'dst me up at midnight to fetch dew
From the still-vex'd Bermoothes, there she 's hid.
. . . And for the rest o' the fleet
Which I dispersed, they all have met again
And are upon the Mediterranean flote,
Bound sadly home for Naples,
Supposing that they saw the king's ship wreck'd.
The Tempest. Act i, sc. 2, l. 195. The only use of "still-vexed," "Bermoothes," "Mediterranean," and "flote" (wave). "Mediterraneum" occurs in *Love's Labour 's Lost,* v, 1, 61: "The salt wave of the Mediterraneum."
To the king's ship, invisible as thou art.
The Tempest. Act v, sc. 1, l. 97. [Prospero]

3
Our royal, good and gallant ship.
Tempest. Act v, sc. 1, l. 237. [Boatswain]
New ship.—*The Winter's Tale,* iv, 4, 790.
Proud insulting ship.—*I Henry VI,* i, 2, 138.
Tall ship.—*The Merchant of Venice,* iii, 1, 6; *Othello,* ii, 1, 79; *Richard II,* ii, 1, 286.
Tall bark.—*King Lear,* iv, 6, 18. See under BARK.

4
Leave you not a man-of-war unsearch'd.
Titus Andronicus. Act iv, sc. 3, l. 22. [Titus] The only use of "man-of-war."

5
Go, go, be gone, to save your ship from wreck.
The Two Gentlemen of Verona, i, 1, 156. See under HANGING.

6
Thou art perfect then, our ship hath touch'd upon
The deserts of Bohemia?
The Winter's Tale. Act iii, sc. 3, l. 1. [Antigonus]
Our sever'd navy too
Have knit again, and fleet, threatening most sea-like.
Antony and Cleopatra. Act iii, sc. 13, l. 170. [Antony] The only use of "sea-like."
My navy; at whose burthen
The anger'd ocean foams.
Antony and Cleopatra. Act ii, sc. 6, l. 20. [Pompey]
Our navy is address'd, our power collected.
II Henry IV. Act iv, sc. 4, l. 5. [King]
Grapple your minds to sternage of this navy.
Henry V, iii, Prol., 18. The only use of "sternage."
Puissant navy.—*Richard III,* iv, 4, 434.
Breton navy.—*Richard III,* iv, 4, 523.

SHIPWRECK

See also Storm

7
The ship, then sinking-ripe.
The Comedy of Errors. Act i, sc. 1, l. 78. [Ægeon] The only use of "sinking-ripe."
Our helpful ship was splitted in the midst.
The Comedy of Errors. Act i, sc. 1, l. 104. [Ægeon]
The ship splits on the rock,
Which industry and courage might have saved!
III Henry VI. Act v, sc. 4, l. 10. [Queen Margaret]
Our ship did split.—*Twelfth Night,* i, 2, 9.

8
My wealthy Andrew dock'd in sand,
Vailing her high-top lower than her ribs
To kiss her burial.
The Merchant of Venice. Act i, sc. 1, l. 27. [Salarino] "Vailing" occurs again in *Love's Labour's Lost,* v, 2, 297. The only use of "wealthy Andrew," "dock'd," and "high-top" in this sense.
Antonio hath a ship of rich lading wrecked on the narrow seas; the Goodwins, I think they call the place; a very dangerous flat and fatal, where the carcases of many a tall ship lie buried. . . . The end is he hath lost a ship.
The Merchant of Venice. Act iii, sc. 1, l. 3. [Salarino]
Wreck'd three nights ago on Goodwin Sands.
King John. Act v, sc. 3, l. 11. [Messenger]
Cast away and sunk on Goodwin Sands.
King John. Act v, sc. 5, l. 13. [Messenger] The only references to the Goodwins.

9
And not one vessel 'scape the dreadful touch

Of merchant-marring rocks?
The Merchant of Venice. Act iii, sc. 2, l. 273. [Bassanio] The only use of "merchant-marring."

My ships have all miscarried, my creditors grow cruel.
The Merchant of Venice. Act iii, sc. 2, l. 318. [Bassanio, reading]

1 A noble ship of Venice
Hath seen a grievous wreck and sufferance
On most part of their fleet. . . .
The ship is here put in, A Veronesa.
Othello. Act ii, sc. 1, l. 22. [Gentleman] The only use of "Veronesa."

We see the very wreck that we must suffer;
And unavoided is the danger now,
For suffering so the causes of our wreck.
Richard II. Act ii, sc. 1, l. 267. [Ross]

Methought I saw a thousand fearful wrecks;
Ten thousand men that fishes gnaw'd upon;
Wedges of gold, great anchors, heaps of pearl,
Inestimable stones, unvalued jewels,
All scatter'd in the bottom of the sea.
Richard III. Act i, sc. 4, l. 24. [Clarence] "Gnaw'd" is repeated in *The Comedy of Errors,* v, 1, 289; "inestimable" in *Troilus and Cressida,* ii, 2, 88, and in *Pericles,* ii, 4, 8, and "unvalued" in *Hamlet,* i, 3, 19.

If this be so, as yet the glass seems true,
I shall have share in this most happy wreck.
Twelfth Night. Act v, sc. 1, l. 272. [Duke]

Sad wreck.—*Cymbeline,* iv, 2, 366.

Sunken wreck.—*Henry V,* i, 2, 165.

Wreck at sea.—*Comedy of Errors,* v, 1, 359.

Wreck of sea.—*Comedy of Errors,* v, 1, 49.

2
Third Fisherman: I am thinking of the poor men that were cast away before us even now.

First Fisherman: Alas, poor souls, it grieved my heart to hear what pitiful cries they made to us to help them, when, well-a-day, we could scarce help ourselves.
Pericles. Act ii, sc. 1, l. 18.

An argosy cast away.—*The Merchant of Venice,* iii, 1, 105.

That ever I should call thee castaway!
Antony and Cleopatra, iii, 6, 40. [Cæsar]

Desperate castaway.—*Titus Andronicus,* v, 3, 75.

Hopeless castaway.—*The Rape of Lucrece,* l. 744. The only uses of "castaway."

Wretches, orphans, castaways.—*Richard III,* ii, 2, 6. The only use of "castaways."

3
Had I been any god of power, I would
Have sunk the sea within the earth or ere
It should the good ship so have swallow'd and
The fraughting souls within her.
The Tempest. Act i, sc. 2, l. 10. [Miranda] The only use of "fraughting."

We all were sea-swallow'd.
The Tempest. Act ii, sc. 1, l. 251. [Antonio] The only use of the phrase.

4
See his shipwreck and the commonweal's.
Titus Andronicus. Act ii, 1, 24. [Aaron]

My shipwreck now's no ill.—*Pericles,* ii, 1, 139.

After shipwreck driven upon this shore.—*Pericles,* ii, 3, 85.

Shipwreck'd upon a kingdom.—*Henry VIII,* iii, 1, 149.

Shipwreck'd guests.—*The Comedy of Errors,* i, 1, 115.

Shipwrecking storms.—*Macbeth,* i, 2, 46. The only use of "shipwrecking."

5
The men are not yet cold under water.
Winter's Tale. Act iii, sc. 3, l. 107. [Clown]

6
O, the most piteous cry of the poor souls! sometimes to see 'em, and not to see 'em; now the ship boring the moon with her main-mast, and anon swallowed with yest and froth, as you 'ld thrust a cork into a hogshead. . . . But to make an end of the ship, to see how the sea flap-dragoned it: but, first, how the poor souls roared, and the sea mocked them.
The Winter's Tale. Act iii, sc. 3, l. 91. [Clown] The only use of "boring," "main-mast," "yest," and "flap-dragoned." "Cork" is used only once more, in *As You Like It,* iii, 2, 213.

SHIRT

7
The shirt of Nessus is upon me.
Antony and Cleopatra. Act iv, sc. 12, l. 43. [Cleopatra] Nessus is mentioned again in *All's Well that Ends Well,* iv, 3, 281.

8
Sir, I would advise you to shift a shirt; the violence of action has made you reek as a sacrifice.
Cymbeline. Act i, sc. 2, l. 1. [Lord]

If my shirt were bloody, then to shift it.
Cymbeline. Act i, sc. 2, l. 6. [Cloten]

9
There's but a shirt and a half in all my company; and the half shirt is two napkins tacked together and thrown over the shoulders like a herald's coat without sleeves; and the shirt, to say the truth, stolen from my host at Saint Alban's, or the red-nose innkeeper of Daventry. But that's all one; they 'll find linen enough on every hedge.
I Henry IV. Act iv, sc. 2, l. 46. [Falstaff] The only use of "tacked," "red-nose," and "Daventry."

Costard: I 'll do it in my shirt. . . .
Armado: I will not combat in my shirt. . . . The naked truth of it is I have no shirt; I go woolward for penance.
Boyet: True, and it was enjoined him in Rome for want of linen: since when, I 'll be sworn, he wore none but a dishclout of Jaquenetta's, and that a' wears next his heart for a favour.
Love's Labour's Lost. Act v, sc. 2, l. 704. The only use of "woolward." "Dishclout" occurs again in *Romeo and Juliet,* iii, 5, 221.

Here's one comes in his shirt.—*Othello,* v, 1, 47.

Work in their shirt.—*II Henry VI,* iv, 7, 57.

1
Hostess: I bought you a dozen of shirts to your back.
Falstaff: Dowlas, filthy dowlas: I have given them away to bakers' wives, and they have made bolters of them.
Hostess: Now, as I am a true woman, holland of eight shillings an ell.
I Henry IV. Act iii, sc. 3, l. 77. The only use of "dowlas" (coarse English linen), and "bolters" (boxes in which flour is sifted). "Holland" occurs again in *II Henry IV*, ii, 2, 26.

Foul shirts and smocks.—*The Merry Wives of Windsor*, iii, 5, 91.

SHOE

2
I shall stay here the forehorse to a smock,
Creaking my shoes on the plain masonry,
Till honour be bought up and no sword worn
But one to dance with!
All's Well that Ends Well. Act ii, sc. 1, l. 30. The only use of "forehorse" (leader in a team), and of "masonry."

Creaking of shoes.—*King Lear*, iii, 4, 98. The only uses of "creaking."

Your shoe untied.—*As You Like It*, iii, 2, 399.

3 I thought he slept, and put
My clouted brogues from off my feet, whose rudeness
Answer'd my steps too loud.
Cymbeline. Act iv, sc. 2, l. 213. [Arviragus] The only use of "brogues."

4
Wears his boots very smooth.
II Henry IV, ii, 4, 270. See under CHARACTER.

A pair of boots that have been candle-cases.
The Taming of the Shrew, iii, 2, 45. See under DRESS. The only use of "candle-cases."

Off with my boots, you rogues!
Taming of the Shrew, iv, 1, 147. [Petruchio]

Off with your boots.—*II Henry IV*, v, 1, 61.

Pull off my boots.—*King Lear*, iv, 6, 177.

Bring me my boots.—*Richard II*, v, 2, 84.

Give me my boots.—*Richard II*, v, 2, 77.

Get on thy boots.—*II Henry IV*, v, 3, 137.

Valentine: You are over boots in love,
And yet you never swum the Hellespont.
Proteus: Over the boots? nay, give me not the boots.
Valentine: No, I will not, for it boots thee not.
Two Gentlemen of Verona. Act i, sc. 1, l. 25.

I 'll wear a boot.—*The Two Gentlemen of Verona*, v, 2, 6.

Boots and spurs and all.—*All's Well that Ends Well*, ii, 5, 39.

Look upon his boot.—*All's Well that Ends Well*, iii, 2, 6.

Whiles your boots are green.—*The Taming of the Shrew*, iii, 2, 213.

Without boots.—*I Henry IV*, iii, 1, 68.

Fishermen's boots.—*The Merry Wives of Windsor*, iv, 5, 101. The only uses of "boot" and "boots" in this sense.

5
Spare none but such as go in clouted shoon.
II Henry VI. Act iv, sc. 2, l. 194. [Cade] The only uses of "clouted."

Sandal shoon.—*Hamlet*, iv, 5, 26. The only uses of "shoon."

Cobbled shoes.—*Coriolanus*, i, 1, 200.

Dancing shoes.—*Romeo and Juliet*, i, 4, 14.

Black shoe.—*Henry V*, iv, 7, 149.

Left shoe.—*Two Gentlemen of Verona*, ii, 3, 16.

New shoes.—*Romeo and Juliet*, iii, 1, 31.

Razed shoes.—*Hamlet*, iii, 2, 288.

6
A little month, or ere those shoes were old.
Hamlet. Act i, sc. 2, l. 147. [Hamlet]

Soles of her shoe.—*Hamlet*, ii, 2, 234.

7
Your shoes is not so good.
Henry V. Act iv, sc. 8, l. 75. [Fluellen]

8
Wear nothing but high shoes.
II Henry IV. Act i, sc. 2, l. 44. [Falstaff]

9
Marullus: What trade art thou? answer me directly.
Commoner: . . . A mender of bad soles. . . . I can mend you.
Marullus: What meanest thou by that? mend me, thou saucy fellow?
Commoner: Why, sir, cobble you.
Flavius: Thou art a cobbler, art thou?
Commoner: Truly, sir, all that I live by is with the awl: I meddle with no tradesmen's matters, nor women's matters, but with awl. I am, indeed, sir, a surgeon to old shoes; when they are in great danger, I recover them. As proper men as ever trod upon neat's-leather have gone upon my handiwork. . . .
Flavius: Why dost thou lead these men about the streets?
Commoner: Truly, sir, to wear out their shoes, to get myself into more work.
Julius Cæsar. Act i, sc. 1, l. 12. The only uses of "cobble" and "cobbler," and of "awl." "Neat's-leather" is repeated in *The Tempest*, ii, 2, 73.

The shoemaker should meddle with his yard.
Romeo and Juliet, i, 2, 39. See under LABOUR. The only use of "shoemaker."

10
Standing on slippers, which his nimble haste
Had falsely thrust upon contrary feet.
King John, iv, 2, 197. See under TAILOR.

Where are my slippers?—*The Taming of the Shrew*, iv, 1, 156. The only uses of "slippers."

I do adore thy sweet grace's slipper.
Love's Labour's Lost, v, 2, 672. See under FOOT.

Put me to my slipper.—*The Tempest*, ii, 1, 277. The only uses of "slipper" in this sense. *Othello*, ii, 1, 247, has "Slipper knave."

11
Being o'er shoes in blood, plunge in the deep.
A Midsummer-Night's Dream. Act iii, sc. 2, l. 48. [Hermia]

Over shoes in grime.—*The Comedy of Errors*, iii, 2, 106.

Over shoes in love.—*The Two Gentlemen of Verona,* i, 1, 24.

Over shoes in snow.—*Richard III,* v, 3, 326.

1
Get your apparel together, good strings to your beards, new ribbons to your pumps.

A Midsummer-Night's Dream. Act iv, sc. 2, l. 37. [Bottom]

Romeo: Then is my pump well flowered.
Mercutio: Well said: follow me this jest now till thou hast worn out thy pump.

Romeo and Juliet. Act ii, sc. 4, l. 64.

Gabriel's pumps were all unpink'd in the heel.

The Taming of the Shrew. Act iv, sc. 1, l. 136. [Grumio] The only use of "Gabriel" and "unpink'd." The only references to "pump," which is used only in this sense.

2
No more shoes than feet; nay, sometime more feet than shoes, or such shoes as my toes look through the over-leather.

The Taming of the Shrew. Induction, sc. 2, l. 11. [Sly] The only use of "over-leather."

3
How does thy honour? Let me lick thy shoe.

The Tempest. Act iii, sc. 2, l. 26. [Caliban]

I kiss his dirty shoe.—*Henry V,* iv, 1, 47. See FIDELITY, 533:3.

Wipe my shoes.—*The Two Gentlemen of Verona,* ii, 1, 86.

SHOP

4
Say that I linger'd with you at your shop.

The Comedy of Errors. Act iii, sc. 1, l. 3. [Antipholus of Ephesus]

5
We for fear compell'd to shut our shops.

I Henry VI. Act iii, sc. 1, l. 85. [Mayor]

6
Wherefore art not in thy shop to-day?

Julius Cæsar. Act i, sc. 1, l. 31. [Flavius]

7
In his needy shop a tortoise hung.

Romeo and Juliet, v, 1, 42. See under DOCTOR. "Tortoise" is repeated in *The Tempest,* i, 2, 316: "Come, thou tortoise."

The beggar's shop is shut.—*Romeo and Juliet,* v, 1, 56.

Barber's shop.—*Measure for Measure,* v, 1, 323; *The Taming of the Shrew,* iv, 3, 91.

Bosom's shop.—*Sonnets,* xxiv.

Break open shops.—*Timon of Athens,* iv, 3, 450.

SHORE

8
That pale, that white-faced shore,
Whose foot spurns back the ocean's roaring tides.

King John, ii, 1, 23. See under ENGLAND. The only use of "white-faced."

England's blessed shore.—*II Henry VI,* iii, 2, 90.

9
To the extremest shore of my modesty.

Measure for Measure, iii, 2, 266. See under MODESTY.

10
I had been drowned, but that the shore was shelvy and shallow.

Merry Wives of Windsor, iii, 5, 15. See under DROWNING. The only use of "shelvy."

11
Do but stand upon the foaming shore.

Othello. Act ii, sc. 1, l. 11. [Gentleman]

Concave shores.—*Julius Cæsar,* i, 1, 51. "Concave" is repeated in *As You Like It,* iii, 4, 26.

Confining shores.—*King John,* ii, 1, 338. "Confining" is repeated in *Henry V,* Epil., 3.

Dangerous shores.—*Troilus and Cressida,* ii, 2, 64.

Discolour'd shore.—*II Henry VI,* iv, 1, 11. "Discolour'd" is repeated in *King John,* ii, 1, 306: "Discolour'd earth"; and in *Romeo and Juliet,* v, 3, 143: "Lie discolour'd."

Dividable shores.—*Troilus and Cressida,* i, 3, 105. The only use of "dividable."

Exalted shores.—*Julius Cæsar,* i, 1, 65.

Far-off shore.—*III Henry VI,* iii, 2, 136.

Galled shore.—*The Rape of Lucrece,* l. 1440.

Golden shores.—*The Merry Wives of Windsor,* i, 3, 89.

Guiled shore.—*The Merchant of Venice,* iii, 2, 97. The only use of "guiled."

Naked shore.—*I Henry IV,* iv, 3, 77.

Neighbouring shore.—*Pericles,* i, 4, 60.

Nigh shore.—*The Tempest,* i, 2, 216.

Northern shore.—*Richard II,* ii, 1, 288.

Pagan shore.—*King John,* v, 2, 36.

Pebbled shore.—*Sonnets,* lx. The only use of "pebbled."

Reasonable shore.—*The Tempest,* v, 1, 81.

Rocky shore.—*Richard II,* ii, 1, 62.

Severn shore.—*I Henry IV,* iii, 1, 76.

Sicilian shores.—*The Winter's Tale,* v, 1, 164. The only use of "Sicilian."

Undream'd shores.—*The Winter's Tale,* iv, 4, 578. The only use of "undream'd."

Unkind shore.—*II Henry VI,* iii, 2, 87.

Vast shore.—*Romeo and Juliet,* ii, 2, 83.

Western shore.—*Richard III,* iv, 4, 482.

Shores of flint.—*Pericles,* iv, 4, 43.

Shores o' the haven.—*Cymbeline,* i, 3, 1.

Shore of rock.—*Henry VIII,* i, 1, 158.

Dreadful shore of Styx.—*Titus Andronicus,* i, 1, 88.

High shore of this world.—*Henry V,* iv, 1, 282.

Varying shore o' the world.—*Antony and Cleopatra,* iv, 15, 11.

12
We 'll bring your grace e'en to the edge o' the shore.

Pericles. Act iii, sc. 3, l. 35. [Cleon]

From shore to shore.—*Pericles,* ii, 1, 6.

13
Being on shore, honouring of Neptune's triumphs.

Pericles. Act v, sc. 1, l. 17. [Lysimachus]

Come on shore.—*Othello,* ii, 1, 28; 83.

I 'll not on shore.—*Antony and Cleopatra,* ii, 7, 137.

On shore.—*The Two Gentlemen of Verona,* i, 1, 158.

14
Pericles: What country-woman?
Here of these shores?
Marina: No, nor of any shores.

Pericles. Act v, sc. 1, l. 103. "Countrywoman" is used only once again, in *Troilus and Cressida,* iv, 1, 67.

1
Shall we refresh us, sir, upon your shore?
Pericles. Act v, sc. 1, l. 257. [Pericles]
Cast on this shore.—*Pericles,* ii, 3, 89.
Thrown upon this shore.—*Pericles,* v, 3, 23.

SHOULDER

2
Run and show their shoulders.
Antony and Cleopatra, iii, 11, 8. See FLIGHT, 551:4.
You are straight enough in the shoulders, you care not who sees your back.
I Henry IV. Act ii, sc. 4, l. 164. [Falstaff]

3
God's light, with two points on your shoulder? much!
II Henry IV. Act ii, sc. 4, l. 142. [Doll]
You have hurt him, sir, i' the shoulder.
II Henry IV. Act ii, sc. 4, l. 231. [Bardolph]

4
Thou hast drawn my shoulder out of joint.
II Henry IV. Act v, sc. 4, l. 3. [Hostess]
I fear, sir, my shoulder-blade is out.
Winter's Tale. Act iv, sc. 3, l. 76. [Autolycus] The only use of "shoulder-blade."
The bear tore out his shoulder-bone.
The Winter's Tale. Act iii, sc. 3, l. 97. [Clown] The only use of "shoulder-bone."

5
Weak shoulders, overborne with burthening grief.
I Henry VI. Act ii, sc. 5, l. 10. [Mortimer] The only use of "burthening."
Guiltless shoulders.—*Richard III,* i, 2, 98.
Manly shoulders.—*II Henry VI,* v, 2, 63.
Unreverent shoulders.—*Richard II,* ii, 1, 123.
Unworthy shoulders.—*As You Like It,* ii, 7, 76.
Cupid's shoulder.—*Troilus and Cressida,* iii, 2, 15.
Shoulder of your sail.—*Hamlet,* i, 3, 56.

6
On thy shoulder will I lean.
III Henry VI. Act ii, sc. 1, l. 189. [Edward]
Lean upon my poor shoulder.—*Love's Labour's Lost,* v, 1, 108.

7
This shoulder was ordain'd so thick to heave;
And heave it shall some weight, or break my back.
III Henry VI. Act v, sc. 7, l. 23. [Gloucester]

8 Æneas, our great ancestor,
Did from the flames of Troy upon his shoulder
The old Anchises bear.
Julius Cæsar. Act i, sc. 2, l. 112. [Cassius] Æneas is mentioned fifteen times, and Anchises three.
Bear me on your shoulders.—*Richard III,* iii, 1, 131.
They took me on their shoulders.—*The Merry Wives of Windsor,* iii, 5, 102.

9
Her shoulder is with child.
Love's Labour's Lost. Act iv, sc. 3, l. 90. [Biron]

10
They clap the lubber Ajax on the shoulder,
As if his foot were on brave Hector's breast.
Troilus and Cressida. Act iii, sc. 3, l. 139. [Ulysses]
A notable lubber.—*The Two Gentlemen of Verona,* ii, 5, 47.
This great lubber.—*Twelfth Night,* iv, 1, 14. The only uses of "lubber."
Clapp'd him on the shoulder.—*Love's Labour's Lost,* v, 2, 107; *Much Ado about Nothing,* i, 1, 261; *As You Like It,* iv, 1, 48.
A back-friend, a shoulder-clapper.—*The Comedy of Errors,* iv, 2, 37. The only use of "shoulder-clapper."

11
Over one shoulder doth she hang her head.
Venus and Adonis, l. 1058.

SHOUT

12 Every man shall bear as loud
As his strong sides can volley.
Antony and Cleopatra. Act ii, sc. 7, l. 117. [Enobarbus]

13
Hark, how they shout!
II Henry IV. Act iv, sc. 2, l. 87. [Lancaster]
Hark, they shout for joy.—*Julius Cæsar,* v, 3, 32.
Didst thou not hear their shouts?—*Julius Cæsar,* v, 3, 83.
They shouted thrice.—*Julius Cæsar,* i, 2, 226.
Mine honest neighbours shouted.—*Julius Cæsar,* i, 2, 231.
And then the people fell a shouting.—*Julius Cæsar,* i, 2, 223.
Shouting plebians.—*Antony and Cleopatra,* iv, 12, 34.

14
Whose shouts and claps out-voice the deep-mouth'd sea.
Henry V. Act v, Prologue, l. 11. The only use of "out-voice." "Deep-mouth'd" is repeated in *King John,* v, 2, 173: "Deep-mouth'd thunder"; and in *The Taming of the Shrew,* Ind., 1, 18: "Deep-mouth'd brach."

15
Hark, hark, my lord! what shouts are these?
III Henry VI. Act iv, sc. 8, l. 52. [Exeter]
What shouts are these?—*Coriolanus,* i, 1, 47; v, 3, 19.
What shout is that?—*Troilus and Cressida,* v, 9, 1.
What means this shouting?—*Julius Cæsar,* i, 2, 79.

16
Have you not made an universal shout
That Tiber trembled underneath her banks?
Julius Cæsar. Act i, sc. 1, l. 49. [Marullus]
Another general shout!—*Julius Cæsar,* i, 2, 132.
Universal shout.—*The Merchant of Venice,* iii, 2, 144.
Loving shout.—*Richard III,* iii, 7, 39.

17 We'll bring him to his house
With shouts and clamours.
Julius Cæsar. Act iii, sc. 2, l. 58. [Citizen]

SHOWER

1
A man may hear this shower sing in the wind.
The Merry Wives of Windsor. Act iii, sc. 2, l. 37. [Ford]
2
Small showers last long, but sudden storms are short.
Richard II. Act ii, sc. 1, l. 35. [Gaunt]
3
Lay the summer's dust with showers of blood.
Richard II. Act iii, sc. 3, l. 43. [Bolingbroke]
Shower of gifts.—*Timon of Athens,* v, 1, 73.
Shower of gold.—*Antony and Cleopatra,* ii, 5, 45.
Showers of oaths.—*A Midsummer-Night's Dream,* i, 1, 245.
Shower of pebbles.—*Henry VIII,* v, 4, 60.
Shower of rain.—*Antony and Cleopatra,* i, 2, 156.
Showers of silver brine.—*The Rape of Lucrece,* l. 796.
Shower of tears.—*The Taming of the Shrew,* Ind., 1, 125.
4
With thy saffron wings upon my flowers
Diffusest honey-drops, refreshing showers.
The Tempest. Act iv, sc. 1, l. 78. [Ceres] The only use of "diffusest," "honey-drops," and "refreshing."
Distilling showers.—*Venus and Adonis,* l. 66.
Incessant showers.—*III Henry VI,* i, 4, 145.
Sweet-seasoned showers.—*Sonnets,* lxxv. The only use of "sweet-seasoned."
Winter showers.—*Timon of Athens,* ii, 2, 180.

SHREW

See also Scold

5
Like a shrew, you first begin to brawl.
The Comedy of Errors. Act iv, sc. 1, l. 51. [Antipholus of Ephesus]
For women are shrews, both short and tall.
II Henry IV. Act v, sc. 3, l. 36. [Silence]
Beshrew all shrews.—*Love's Labour's Lost,* v, 2, 46.
6
I have no gift at all in shrewishness.
A Midsummer-Night's Dream. Act iii, sc. 2, l. 301. [Helena] The only use of "shrewishness."
O, when she's angry, she is keen and shrewd!
She was a vixen when she went to school;
And though she be but little, she is fierce.
A Midsummer-Night's Dream. Act iii, sc. 2, l. 323. [Helena] The only use of "vixen."
While she is here, a man may live as quiet in hell as in a sanctuary; and people sin upon purpose, because they would go thither; so, indeed, all disquiet, horror and perturbation follows her.
Much Ado about Nothing. Act ii, sc. 1, l. 265. [Benedick]
7
As curst and shrewd
As Socrates' Xanthippe.
The Taming of the Shrew. Act i, sc. 2, l. 70. [Petruchio] "Curst and shrewd" occurs also in i, 1, 185. The only mention of either Socrates or Xanthippe, which is the only word beginning with X in Shakespeare.
'Tis a world to see,
How tame, when men and women are alone,
A meacock wretch can make the curstest shrew.
The Taming of the Shrew. Act ii, sc. 1, l. 313. [Petruchio] The only use of "meacock" (cowardly), and "curstest."
Is she so hot a shrew as she's reported?
The Taming of the Shrew. Act iv, sc. 1, l. 22. [Curtis]
8
He that knows better how to tame a shrew,
Now let him speak.
The Taming of the Shrew. Act iv, sc. 1, l. 213. [Petruchio]
Tranio: Ay, and he'll tame her. . . .
Faith, he is gone unto the taming-school.
Bianca: The taming-school! what, is there such a place?
Tranio: Ay, mistress, and Petruchio is the master;
That teacheth tricks eleven and twenty long,
To tame a shrew and charm her chattering tongue.
The Taming of the Shrew. Act iv, sc. 2, l. 53. The only use of "taming-school." "Chattering" occurs again in *III Henry VI,* v, 6, 48: "Chattering pies."
Your husband, being troubled with a shrew,
Measures my husband's sorrow by his woe.
The Taming of the Shrew. Act v, sc. 2, l. 28. [Widow]
Now, in good sadness, son Petruchio,
I think thou hast the veriest shrew of all.
The Taming of the Shrew. Act v, sc. 2, l. 63. [Baptista] "Veriest" is used only three more times in the plays, again in *The Taming of the Shrew,* Ind., 1, 101: "Veriest antic"; in *I Henry IV,* ii, 2, 25: "Veriest varlet"; and in *Cymbeline,* v, 3, 77: "Veriest hind."
Now, go thy ways; thou hast tamed a curst shrew.
The Taming of the Shrew. Act v, sc. 2, l. 188. [Hortensio]
9
Bless you, fair shrew.
Twelfth Night. Act i, sc. 3, l. 50. [Sir Andrew Aguecheek]

SICKNESS

See also Disease, Doctor, Illness

10
Nature and sickness
Debate it at their leisure.
All's Well that Ends Well. Act i, sc. 2, l. 74. [King]
Sick on 't.—*All's Well that Ends Well,* i, 3, 142.
11
I am sick and sullen.
Antony and Cleopatra. Act i, sc. 3, l. 13. [Cleopatra]
Sudden sick.—*Antony and Cleopatra,* i, 3, 5.
12
Not sickness should detain me.
Antony and Cleopatra. Act ii, sc. 2, l. 173. [Lepidus]
13
The more one sickens the worse at ease he is.
As You Like It. Act iii, sc. 2, l. 24. [Corin]

Sicken at the sight.—*Antony and Cleopatra,* iii, 10, 17.

1
Go bid my woman feign a sickness.
Cymbeline. Act iii, sc. 2, l. 76. [Imogen]

2
So sick I am not, yet I am not well;
But not so citizen a wanton as
To seem to die ere sick.
Cymbeline. Act iv, sc. 2, l. 7. [Imogen]

I am not very sick, Since I can reason of it.
Cymbeline. Act iv, sc. 2, l. 13. [Imogen]

Make me sick.—*Cymbeline,* i, 6, 119.

Sick at sea.—*Cymbeline,* iii, 4, 192. See SEA-SICKNESS.

3
Messenger: These letters come from your father.
Hotspur: Letters from him! why comes he not himself?
Messenger: He cannot come, my lord; he is grievous sick.
Hotspur: 'Zounds! how has he the leisure to be sick
In such a justling time? . . .
Worcester: I would the state of time had first been whole
Ere he by sickness had been visited:
His health was never better worth than now.
Hotspur: Sick now! droop now! this sickness doth infect
The very life-blood of our enterprise;
'Tis catching hither, even to our camp.
He writes me here, that inward sickness— . . .
Worcester: Your father's sickness is a maim to us.
Hotspur: A perilous gash, a very limb lopp'd off.
I Henry IV. Act iv, sc. 1, l. 14. The only use of "justling." "Life-blood" occurs six times.

4
Hostess: Sick of a calm; yea, good faith.
Falstaff: So is all her sect; an they be once in a calm, they are sick.
II Henry IV. Act ii, sc. 4, l. 40.

Your majesty hath been this fortnight ill,
And these unseason'd hours perforce must add
Unto your sickness.
II Henry IV. Act iii, sc. 1, l. 104. [Warwick]

5
My people are with sickness much enfeebled.
Henry V. Act iii, sc. 6, l. 154. [King Henry]
"Enfeebled" is repeated in *I Henry VI,* i, 4, 69.

Sick and famish'd.—*Henry V,* iii, 5, 57.

Sick and like to die.—*Richard III,* iv, 2, 52.

Sick to death.—*Love's Labour's Lost,* iv, 3, 107; *Timon of Athens,* iii, 1, 64; *Henry VIII,* iv, 2, 1.

Full sick.—*Henry VIII,* ii, 4, 204.

Grievous sick.—*Richard II,* i, 4, 54.

Sore sick.—*II Henry IV,* iv, 3, 83; *King John,* v, 4, 6.

Speechless sick.—*Love's Labour's Lost,* v, 2, 861.

Sick and bedrid.—*Love's Labour's Lost,* i, 1, 139.

Sick in fortune.—*King Lear,* i, 2, 129.

6
For suddenly a grievous sickness took him,
That made him gasp and stare and catch the air.
II Henry VI. Act iii, sc. 2, l. 370. [Vaux]

Deadly sickness.—*The Taming of the Shrew,* iv, 3, 14.

Great sickness.—*Timon of Athens,* v, 1, 31.

Green-sickness.—*Romeo and Juliet,* iii, 5, 157; *II Henry IV,* iv, 3, 100; *Antony and Cleopatra,* iii, 2, 6; *Pericles,* iv, 6, 14.

Last sickness.—*Henry VIII,* i, 2, 184.

Present sickness.—*Richard II,* ii, 1, 132.

Wayward sickness.—*Richard III,* i, 3, 29.

7
He fell sick suddenly, and grew so ill
He could not sit his mule.
Henry VIII. Act iv, sc. 2, l. 15. [Griffith]

Fell sick.—*Sonnets,* cxviii.

Fell sick and died.—*The Merchant of Venice,* iii, 4, 71.

8
Eagerly his sickness Pursued him still.
Henry VIII. Act iv, sc. 2, l. 24. [Griffith]

My sickness grows upon me.—*King Lear,* v, 3, 105.

9
What, is Brutus sick,
And will he steal out of his wholesome bed,
To dare the vile contagion of the night
And tempt the rheumy and unpurged air
To add unto his sickness?
Julius Cæsar. Act ii, sc. 1, l. 263. [Portia]
The only use of "rheumy" and "unpurged."

By all the gods that Romans bow before,
I here discard my sickness!
Julius Cæsar. Act ii, sc. 1, l. 320. [Ligarius]

10
Are you sick, Hubert? you look pale today:
In sooth, I would you were a little sick,
That I might sit all night and watch with you.
King John. Act iv, sc. 1, l. 28. [Arthur]

Salisbury: Indeed we fear'd his sickness was past cure.
Pembroke: Indeed we heard how near his death he was
Before the child himself felt he was sick.
King John. Act iv, sc. 2, l. 86.

O vanity of sickness! fierce extremes
In their continuance will not feel themselves.
King John. Act v, sc. 7, l. 13. [Prince Henry]

11
Rosaline: Is the fool sick?
Biron: Sick at the heart.
Love's Labour's Lost. Act ii, sc. 1, l. 184.
See also under HEART.

12
Bear with me, I am sick.
Love's Labour's Lost. Act v, sc. 2, l. 417. [Biron]

I am sick till I see her.
The Merry Wives of Windsor. Act iii, sc. 2, l. 28. [Mrs. Page]

Demetrius: I am sick when I do look on thee.
Helena: And I am sick when I look not on you.
A Midsummer-Night's Dream. Act ii, sc. 1, l. 212.

I am sick in displeasure to him.
Much Ado about Nothing. Act ii, sc. 2, l. 5. [Don John]

I am sick.—*King John,* iii, 1, 12; *Twelfth Night,* i, 5, 117.

I am very sick.—*The Merchant of Venice,* iv, 1, 151; *Cymbeline,* iv, 2, 5.

Say I am sick.—*King Lear,* i, 3, 8.

Say he is sick.—*Julius Cæsar,* ii, 2, 65.

1
He is sick, my lord, Of a strange fever.
Measure for Measure. Act v, sc. 1, l. 151. [Friar Peter]

He is very sick.—*Henry V,* ii, 1, 86.

2
Sickness is catching.
A Midsummer-Night's Dream. Act i, sc. 1, l. 186. [Helena]

A sickness caught of me, and yet I well!
A Winter's Tale. Act i, sc. 2, l. 398. [Polixenes]

Contagious sickness.—*Henry VIII,* v, 3, 26.

3
They swore that you were almost sick for me.
Much Ado about Nothing. Act v, sc. 4, l. 80. [Benedick]

Sick in love.—*Much Ado about Nothing,* iii, 1, 21.

Sick of welfare.—*Sonnets,* cxviii.

4
Get you to bed; faith, you 'll be sick to-morrow
For this night's watching.
Romeo and Juliet. Act iv, sc. 4, l. 7. [Nurse]

5
Many do keep their chambers are not sick.
Timon of Athens. Act iii, sc. 4, l. 74. [Servant]

6
Why, how dost thou, man? what is the matter with thee?
Twelfth Night. Act iii, sc. 4, l. 26. [Olivia]

7
'Tis hoped his sickness is discharged.
Winter's Tale. Act ii, sc. 3, l. 11. [Servant]

He straight declined, droop'd, took it deeply,
Fasten'd and fix'd the shame on 't in himself,
Threw off his spirit, his appetite, his sleep,
And downright languish'd.
Winter's Tale. Act ii, sc. 3, l. 14. [Leontes]

Languish'd for her sake.—*Sonnets,* cxlv. The only uses of "languish'd."

Even so she languisheth.
Venus and Adonis, l. 603. The only use of "languisheth."

The dank earth weeps at thy languishment.
The Rape of Lucrece, l. 1130.

Lingering languishment.—*Titus Andronicus,* ii, 1, 110.

True languishment.—*The Rape of Lucrece,* l. 114. The only uses of "languishment."

Desperate languishings.—*All's Well that Ends Well,* i, 3, 235. "Languishing" is repeated in *Cymbeline,* i, 5, 9.

SIEGE

8
Girding with grievous siege castles and towns.
Henry V. Act i, sc. 2, l. 152. [King Henry] The only use of "girding."

9
Let 's raise the siege: why live we idly here?
I Henry VI. Act i, sc. 2, l. 13. [Reignier]

This night the siege assuredly I 'll raise.
I Henry VI. Act i, sc. 2, l. 130. [La Pucelle]

Leave off delays, and let us raise the siege.
I Henry VI. Act i, sc. 2, l. 146. [Alençon]

A holy prophetess new risen up,
Is come with a great power to raise the siege.
I Henry VI. Act i, sc. 4, l. 102. [Messenger]

His powers are not yet ready
To raise so great a siege.
Henry V. Act iii, sc. 3, l. 46. [Governor]

Siege of Orleans.—*I Henry VI,* i, 1, 111.

10 Rather with their teeth
The walls they 'll tear down than forsake the siege.
I Henry VI. Act i, sc. 2, l. 39. [Charles]

11
Turn your forces from this paltry siege
And stir them up against a mightier task.
King John. Act ii, sc. 1, l. 54. [Chatillon]

All preparation for a bloody siege
And merciless proceeding by these French
Confronts your city's eyes, your winking gates.
King John. Act ii, sc. 1, l. 213. [King John]

Amiable siege.—*The Merry Wives of Windsor,* ii, 2, 243.

Envious siege.—*Richard II,* ii, 1, 62.

Paltry siege.—*King John,* ii, 1, 54.

Strong siege.—*II Henry VI,* iii, 3, 22.

Tedious siege.—*I Henry VI,* i, 2, 53.

Wanton siege.—*All's Well that Ends Well,* iii, 7, 18.

SIGH

12
With that she sighed as she stood.
All's Well that Ends Well. Act i, sc. 3, l. 78. [Clown]

13
Then shall the sighs of Octavia blow the fire up.
Antony and Cleopatra. Act ii, sc. 6, l. 135. [Enobarbus]

I have been blown out of your gates with sighs.
Coriolanus. Act v, sc. 2, l. 81. [Menenius]

14
He furnaces The thick sighs from him.
Cymbeline. Act i, sc. 6, l. 66. [Iachimo]

Sighing like furnace.—*As You Like It,* ii, 7, 148.

15 Wherefore breaks that sigh
From the inward of thee?
Cymbeline. Act iii, sc. 4, l. 5. [Imogen]

16
He raised a sigh so piteous and profound
As it did seem to shatter all his bulk.
Hamlet. Act ii, sc. 1, l. 94. [Ophelia] The only use of "shatter."

These sighs, these profound heaves.
Hamlet. Act iv, sc. 1, l. 1. [King] The only use of "heaves" in this sense.

1
A plague of sighing and grief! it blows a man up like a bladder.
I Henry IV. Act ii, sc. 4, l. 365. [Falstaff]
Swim on bladders.—*Henry VIII*, iii, 2, 359.
Bladders full of imposthume.—*Troilus and Cressida*, v, 1, 24.
Bladders and musty seeds.—*Romeo and Juliet*, v, 1, 46. The only uses of "bladder" and "bladders."

2
But in the end, to stop my ear indeed,
Thou hast a sigh to blow away this praise.
II Henry IV. Act i, sc. 1, l. 79. [Northumberland]

3
A thousand sighs are breathed for thee!
II Henry VI. Act iii, sc. 2, l. 345. [Queen]
We two, that with so many thousand sighs
Did buy each other, must poorly sell ourselves
With the rude brevity and discharge of one.
Troilus and Cressida. Act iv, sc. 4, l. 41. [Troilus]
A thousand thousand sighs.—*Twelfth Night*, ii, 4, 64.

4
Her sighs will make a battery in his breast.
III Henry VI. Act iii, sc. 1, l. 37. [King]
Stop the rising of blood-sucking sighs.
III Henry VI. Act iv, sc. 4, l. 22. [Queen Elizabeth] The only use of "blood-sucking."
Blood-consuming sighs.—*II Henry VI*, iii, 2, 61. The only use of "blood-consuming."
Blood-drinking sighs.—*II Henry VI*, iii, 2, 63. "Blood-drinking" is repeated in *I Henry VI*, ii, 4, 108: "Blood-drinking hate"; and in *Titus Andronicus*, ii, 3, 224: "Blood-drinking pet."
Heart-sore sighs.—*The Two Gentlemen of Verona*, i, 1, 30; ii, 4, 132. The only uses of "heart-sore."
Humorous sigh.—*Love's Labour 's Lost*, iii, 1, 177.
Sad sighs.—*The Two Gentlemen of Verona*, iii, 1, 230.
Soft sighs.—*Venus and Adonis*, l. 376.
Spendthrift sigh.—*Hamlet*, iv, 7, 123. "Spendthrift" is used only once more, in *The Tempest*, ii, 1, 23.
Thriftless sighs.—*Twelfth Night*, ii, 2, 40.
Windy sighs.—*Venus and Adonis*, l. 51.
Sighs of fire.—*Twelfth Night*, i, 5, 275.
Sighs of love.—*A Midsummer-Night's Dream*, iii, 2, 97.
Love's sighs.—*Love's Labour 's Lost*, iv, 3, 347.

5
By thy favour, sweet welkin, I must sigh in thy face.
Love's Labour 's Lost. Act iii, sc. 1, l. 68. [Armado]
I think scorn to sigh.—*Love's Labour 's Lost*, i, 2, 66.

6
Sighs that burning lungs did raise.
A Lover's Complaint, l. 228.
O, that sad breath his spongy lungs bestow'd.
A Lover's Complaint, l. 326.

7
What a sigh is there! The heart is sorely charged.
Macbeth. Act v, sc. 1, l. 59. [Doctor]
No sighs but of my breathing.
The Merchant of Venice. Act iii, sc. 1, l. 100. [Shylock]

8
Sigh'd his soul toward the Grecian tents,
Where Cressid lay that night.
The Merchant of Venice. Act v, sc. 1, l. 5. [Lorenzo]

9
Then sigh not so, but let them go,
And be you blithe and bonny,
Converting all your sounds of woe
Into Hey nonny, nonny.
Much Ado about Nothing. Act ii, sc. 3, l. 68. [Balthazar, singing]
Hey non nonny, nonny.—*Hamlet*, iv, 5, 165.
Ha, no, nonny.—*King Lear*, iii, 4, 103. The only uses of "nonny."

10
She gave me for my pains a world of sighs.
Othello. Act i, sc. 3, l. 159. [Othello]

11
My sighs so deep Procure to weep,
In howling wise, to see my doleful plight.
How sighs resound Through heartless ground,
Like a thousand vanquish'd men in bloody fight!
The Passionate Pilgrim, l. 275.

12
My sighs, like whirlwinds, labour.
The Rape of Lucrece, l. 586.
Three times with sighs she gives her sorrow fire.
The Rape of Lucrece, l. 1604.
His sighs, his sorrows, make a saw
To push grief on, and back the same grief draw.
The Rape of Lucrece, l. 1672.
With a sigh, as if her heart would break.
The Rape of Lucrece, l. 1716.
Her contrite sighs unto the clouds bequeathed
Her winged sprite.
The Rape of Lucrece, l. 1727. "Contrite" is used only once again, in *Henry V*, iv, 1, 313: "Contrite tears."

13
And sigh'd my English breath in foreign clouds.
Richard II. Act iii, sc. 1, l. 20. [Bolingbroke]
Never man Sigh'd truer breath.—*Coriolanus*, iv, 5, 121.

14
Adding to clouds more clouds with his deep sighs.
Romeo and Juliet. Act i, sc. 1, l. 139. [Montague]
The sun not yet thy sighs from heaven clears,
Thy old groans ring yet in my ancient ears.
Romeo and Juliet. Act ii, sc. 3, l. 73. [Friar Laurence]

15
Cooling of the air with sighs
In an odd angle of the isle and sitting,
His arms in this sad knot.
The Tempest. Act i, sc. 2, l. 222. [Ariel]
Sigh to the winds.—*The Tempest*, i, 2, 149.

16
With our sighs we 'll breathe the welkin dim,

And stain the sun with fog.

Titus Andronicus. Act iii, sc. 1, l. 212. [Titus]

1
Why sigh you so profoundly?

Troilus and Cressida. Act iv, sc. 2, l. 83. [Cressida] The only use of "profoundly."

2
And when that hour o'erslips me in the day
Wherein I sigh not, Julia, for thy sake,
The next ensuing hour some foul mischance
Torment me for my love's forgetfulness!

The Two Gentlemen of Verona. Act ii, sc. 2, l. 9. [Proteus] The only use of "o'erslips." "Overslipped" occurs in *The Rape of Lucrece,* l. 1576.

If the wind were down, I could drive the boat with my sighs.

The Two Gentlemen of Verona. Act ii, sc. 3, l. 59. [Launce]

3 Stopping the career
Of laughter with a sigh?—a note infallible
Of breaking honesty.

Winter's Tale. Act i, sc. 2, l. 286. [Leontes]

II—Sigh and Tear

4
We cannot call her winds and waters sighs and tears; they are greater storms and tempests than almanacs can report.

Antony and Cleopatra. Act i, sc. 2, l. 152. [Enobarbus] The only use of "almanacs." "Almanac" occurs in *The Comedy of Errors,* i, 2, 41,; *II Henry IV,* ii, 4, 247; and *A Midsummer-Night's Dream,* iii, 1, 54.

Sighing every minute and groaning every hour.

As You Like It. Act iii, sc. 2, l. 321. [Rosalind]

Sigh and groan.—*Much Ado about Nothing,* v, 3, 17.

Sighs and groans.—*Love's Labour's Lost,* iii, 1, 184; iv, 3, 164.

5
Behold my sighs and tears.

I Henry VI. Act iii, sc. 1, l. 107. [King]

Sighs and tears.—*As You Like It,* v, 2, 90.

6
Storming her world with sorrow's wind and rain.

A Lover's Complaint, l. 7.

7
With sighs shot through, and biggest tears o'ershower'd.

Pericles. Act iv, sc. 4, l. 26. [Gower] The only use of "biggest" and "o'ershower'd."

8
If ever man were moved with woman's moans,
Be moved with my tears, my sighs, my groans.

The Rape of Lucrece, l. 587.

Wound it with sighing, girl, kill it with groans.

Titus Andronicus. Act iii, sc. 2, l. 15. [Titus]

9
A thousand thousand sighs to save,
Lay me, O where
Sad true lover never find my grave,
To weep there!

Twelfth Night. Act ii, sc. 4, l. 64. [Clown]

Sigh and weep.—*The Two Gentlemen of Verona,* iv, 2, 123.

Sighs and weeps.—*Romeo and Juliet,* v, 3, 184.

Weep and sigh.—*Cymbeline,* iv, 2, 392.

Musing and sighing.—*Julius Cæsar,* ii, 1, 240.

10
Sorrow that friendly sighs sought still to dry;
But like a stormy day, now wind, now rain,
Sighs dry her cheeks, tears make them wet again.

Venus and Adonis, l. 964.

My sighs are blown away, my salt tears gone.

Venus and Adonis, l. 1071.

SIGHT

I—Sight: Thing Seen

See also Spectacle

11 Thy sight, which should
Make our eyes flow with joy, hearts dance with comforts,
Constrains them weep and shake with fear and sorrow;
Making the mother, wife and child to see
The son, the husband and the father tearing
His country's bowels out.

Coriolanus. Act v, sc. 3, l. 98. [Volumnia]

12 Not an eye
But is a-weary of thy common sight.

I Henry IV. Act iii, sc. 2, l. 88. [King Henry]

13
Let us look in; the sight will much delight thee.

I Henry VI. Act i, sc. 4, l. 62. [Salisbury]

Her sight did ravish.—*II Henry VI,* i, 1, 32.

See'st thou this sweet sight?—*A Midsummer-Night's Dream,* iv, 1, 51.

Here 's a goodly sight.—*The Tempest,* v, 1, 260.

Heavenly sight!—*Othello,* v, 2, 278.

14
A sight most pitiful in the meanest wretch,
Past speaking of in a king!

King Lear. Act iv, sc. 6, l. 208. [Gentleman]

O thou side-piercing sight!—*King Lear,* iv, 6, 85. The only use of "side-piercing."

15
Macbeth: This is a sorry sight.
Lady Macbeth: A foolish thought, to say a sorry sight.

Macbeth. Act ii, sc. 2, l. 21.

Bloody sight!—*Julius Cæsar,* iii, 2, 206.

Dreaded sight.—*Hamlet,* i, 1, 25.

Dreadful sights.—*The Rape of Lucrece,* l. 462.

Dull sight.—*King Lear,* v, 3, 282.

Heavy sight!—*Antony and Cleopatra,* iv, 15, 40.

Horrible sight!—*Macbeth,* iv, 1, 122.

Horrid sights.—*Julius Cæsar,* ii, 2, 16.

Pitiful sight!—*Romeo and Juliet,* v, 3, 174.

Rudest or gentlest sight.—*Sonnets,* cxiii.

Wishful sight.—*III Henry VI,* iii, 1, 14.

16 You make me strange . . .
When now I think you can behold such sights,
And keep the natural ruby of your cheeks,
When mine is blanch'd with fear.

Macbeth. Act iii, sc. 4, l. 112. [Macbeth]

1
To see sad sights moves more than hear them told.
Rape of Lucrece, l. 1324. See Eye and Ear.
2
Moan the expense of many a vanish'd sight.
Sonnets. No. xxx.
Sometime all full with feasting on your sight
And by and by clean starved for a look.
Sonnets. No. lxxv.
I feed Most hungerly on your sight.
Timon of Athens. Act i, sc. 1, l. 261. [Alcibiades] "Hungerly" is repeated in *The Taming of the Shrew,* iii, 2, 177, and in *Othello,* iii, 4, 105.
3
A fearful sight of blood and death.
Titus Andronicus. Act ii, sc. 3, l. 216. [Martius]
Be this dismal sight
The closing up of our most wretched eyes.
Titus Andronicus. Act iii, sc. 1, l. 262. [Marcus]
The sight is dismal.
Hamlet. Act v, sc. 2, l. 378. [Ambassador]
4
Ay, madam, you may say what sights you see;
I see things too, although you judge I wink.
The Two Gentlemen of Verona. Act i, sc. 2, l. 138. [Lucetta]
I have not winked since I saw these sights.
Winter's Tale. Act iii, sc. 3, l. 106. [Clown]
5
O, what a sight it was, wistly to view
How she came stealing to the wayward boy!
Venus and Adonis, l. 343. "Wistly" is repeated in *Richard II,* v, 4, 7.
6
Here 's a sight for thee.
The Winter's Tale. Act iii, sc. 3, l. 118. [Shepherd]
I have seen two such sights, by sea and by land!
Winter's Tale. Act iii, sc. 3, l. 84. [Clown]
Strange sights.—*Julius Cæsar,* i, 3, 138; *The Winter's Tale,* iv, 4, 849.
Strangest sight.—*Henry VIII,* v, 2, 20.
Ugly sights.—*Richard III,* i, 4, 3; 23.

II—Eyesight

7
Antony: Would I had never seen her!
Enobarbus: O, sir, you had then left unseen a wonderful piece of work; which not to have been blest withal would have discredited your travel.
Antony and Cleopatra. Act i, sc. 2, l. 158. "Discredited" is repeated in *Measure for Measure,* iii, 2, 261.
Then have you lost a sight, which was to be seen, cannot be spoken of.
The Winter's Tale. Act v, sc. 2, l. 46. [Gentleman]
8
To have seen much and to have nothing, is to have rich eyes and poor hands.
As You Like It. Act iv, sc. 1, l. 23. [Rosalind]
9
I cannot be out of the sight of Orlando.
As You Like It. Act iv, sc. 1, l. 221. [Rosalind]
10
Duke: If there be truth in sight, you are my daughter.
Orlando: If there be truth in sight, you are my Rosalind.
Phebe: If sight and shape be true,
Why then, my love adieu!
As You Like It. Act v, sc. 4, l. 124.
11
Gaze where you should, and that will clear your sight.
The Comedy of Errors. Act iii, sc. 2, l. 57. [Luciana]
Gaze your fill.—*Taming of the Shrew,* i, 1, 73.
Look how they gaze!—*II Henry VI,* ii, 4, 20.
Here all eyes gaze on us.—*Romeo and Juliet,* iii, 1, 56.
I should leave grazing, were I of your flock,
And only live by gazing.
The Winter's Tale. Act iv, sc. 4, l. 109. [Camillo]
12
I would have broke mine eye-strings; crack'd them, but
To look upon him, till the diminution
Of space had pointed him sharp as my needle.
Cymbeline. Act i, sc. 3, l. 17. [Imogen] The only use of "eye-strings." "Diminution" is repeated in *Antony and Cleopatra,* iii, 13, 198.
13 It shrunk in haste away,
And vanish'd from our sight.
Hamlet. Act i, sc. 2, l. 219. [Horatio]
Vanish'd out of sight.—*Sonnets,* lxiii.
14 O, woe is me,
To have seen what I have seen, see what I see!
Hamlet. Act iii, sc. 1, l. 168. [Ophelia]
Seeing, unseen.—*Hamlet,* iii, 1, 33.
You shall see anon.—*Hamlet,* iii, 2, 250.
15
You see them perspectively.
Henry V. Act v, sc. 2, l. 347. [French King] The only use of "perspectively."
16 The dusky sky began to rob
My earnest-gaping sight of thy land's view.
II Henry VI. Act iii, sc. 2, l. 105. [Queen] The only use of "earnest-gaping."
Fair sight.—*Venus and Adonis,* l. 183.
Former sight.—*Sonnets,* cxxiii.
New-appearing sight.—*Sonnets,* vii. "New-appearing" is repeated in *Richard III,* iv, 4, 19: "New-appearing sweets."
Sudden sight.—*Taming of the Shrew,* i, 1, 225.
Truest sight.—*Venus and Adonis,* l. 1144.
Wished sight.—*The Passionate Pilgrim,* l. 202.
True-love's sight.—*A Midsummer-Night's Dream,* iii, 2, 89.
Sight of death.—*Romeo and Juliet,* v, 3, 206.
Accustom'd sight of death.—*As You Like It,* iii, 5, 4.
Sights of steel.—*II Henry IV,* iv, 1, 121.
17
The sight of me is odious in their eyes.
II Henry VI. Act iv, sc. 4, l. 46. [Lord Say]

They do offend our sight.
Henry V. Act iv, sc. 7, l. 62. [King Henry]
I cannot brook thy sight.—*King John,* iii, 1, 36.

1
You know him well by sight.
Julius Cæsar. Act i, sc. 3, l. 15. [Casca]

2
Thou shalt see me at Philippi.
Julius Cæsar. Act iv, sc. 3, l. 284. [Ghost]

3
Hence, and avoid my sight!
. . Out of my sight!
King Lear. Act i, sc. 1, l. 126. [King Lear]
"Out of my sight" is repeated in *II Henry VI,* iii, 2, 48; *King John,* iv, 2, 242; *Richard III,* i, 2, 149; *Twelfth Night,* iv, 1, 53; *Othello,* iv, 1, 258.
Out, varlet, from my sight!—*King Lear,* ii, 4, 190.
Hence, from my sight!—*Cymbeline,* i, 1, 125.
Avaunt! and quit my sight!—*Macbeth,* iii, 4, 93.
Get thee from my sight!—*Cymbeline,* v, 5, 236; *Titus Andronicus,* iii, 1, 284. See also under DISMISSAL.
Ne'er return again into my sight.—*The Two Gentlemen of Verona,* iv, 4, 65.
Never come in my sight more.—*As You Like It,* iv, 1, 41.
Come no more in my sight.—*As You Like It,* iv, 1, 52.

4
Costard: Well, if ever I do see the merry days of desolation that I have seen, some shall see.
Moth: What shall some see?
Costard: Nay, nothing, Master Moth, but what they look upon.
Love's Labour's Lost. Act i, sc. 2, l. 164.

5
Approach the chamber, and destroy your sight
With a new Gorgon.
Macbeth. Act ii, sc. 3, l. 76. [Macduff]
"Gorgon" is used once again in *Antony and Cleopatra,* ii, 5, 116.

6
You shall not be admitted to his sight.
Measure for Measure. Act iv, sc. 3, l. 125. [Duke]

7
God keep him out of my sight.
Much Ado about Nothing. Act ii, sc. 1, l. 113. [Margaret]
In sight of God.—*II Henry VI,* ii, 3, 2.
In sight of heaven.—*III Henry VI,* iii, 3, 181.

8
If you dare not trust that you see, confess not that you know.
Much Ado about Nothing. Act iii, sc. 2, l. 122. [Don John]

9
Nor could she moralize his wanton sight.
The Rape of Lucrece, l. 104.
It beguiled attention, charm'd the sight.
The Rape of Lucrece, l. 1404.

10
Bring me to their sights.
Richard III. Act iv, sc. 1, l. 25. [Anne]
Fetch me to the sight of him.
The Winter's Tale. Act iii, sc. 3, l. 139. [Shepherd]

11
If I be so disgracious in your sight,
Let me march on, and not offend your grace.
Richard III. Act iv, sc. 4, l. 177. [King]
Disgracious in the city's eyes.—*Richard III,* iii, 7, 112. "Disgracious" is used in no other play.

12
At the first sight They have changed eyes.
The Tempest. Act i, sc. 2, l. 440. [Prospero]
First sight.—*As You Like It,* iii, 5, 82; *Troilus and Cressida,* v, 2, 9.

13
The dismall'st object . . .
That ever eye with sight made heart lament!
Titus Andronicus. Act ii, sc. 3, l. 204. [Martius] "Dismall'st" occurs again in i, 1, 384, and in no other play.

14
Nay, but first, let me see, let me see, let me see.
Twelfth Night. Act ii, sc. 5, l. 122. [Malvolio]
Shall we go see the reliques of this town? . . .
I pray you, let us satisfy our eyes
With the memorials and the things of fame
That do renown this city.
Twelfth Night. Act iii, sc. 3, l. 19. [Sebastian]

15
He sees his love, and nothing else he sees,
For nothing else with his proud sight agrees.
Venus and Adonis, l. 287.

16
Who mayst see
Plainly as heaven sees earth and earth sees heaven.
Winter's Tale. Act i, sc. 2, l. 314. [Leontes]

III—Imperfect Sight

17
Bleared sights Are spectacled to see.
Coriolanus. Act ii, sc. 1, l. 222. [Brutus]
The only use of "spectacled." See POPULARITY, 1176:16.
Deficient sight.—*King Lear,* iv, 6, 23.

18
My sight was ever thick.
Julius Cæsar. Act v, sc. 3, l. 21. [Cassius]
Thick sight.—*II Henry IV,* iii, 2, 336.
Weak sights.—*A Lover's Complaint,* l. 214.

19
Quintus: My sight is very dull, whate'er it bodes.
Martius: And mine, I promise you; were 't not for shame,
Well could I leave our sport to sleep awhile.
Titus Andronicus. Act ii, sc. 3, l. 195.

SIGN

See also Omen

20
She 's a good sign.
Cymbeline. Act i, sc. 2, l. 33.
It were a good sign.—*Macbeth,* iv, 2, 62. The only uses of "good sign."

21
Render to me some corporal sign about her,
More evident than this.
Cymbeline. Act ii, sc. 4, l. 119. [Posthumus]

22
Sirs, take your places and be vigilant:
If any noise or soldier you perceive

Near to the walls, by some apparent sign
Let us have knowledge at the court of guard.
I Henry VI. Act ii, sc. 1, l. 1. [Sergeant]
I 'll by a sign give notice to our friends.
I Henry VI. Act iii, sc. 2, l. 8. [La Pucelle]

1
I can express no kinder sign of love
Than this kind kiss.
II Henry VI. Act i, sc. 1, l. 18. [King Henry]
Sign of love.—*III Henry VI,* iv, 2, 9; *Richard II,* v, 5, 65; *Othello,* i, 1, 158.
From one sign of dolour to another.
The Winter's Tale, v, 2, 95. [Gentleman]
Sign of affection.—*Much Ado about Nothing,* ii, 3, 236.
Sign of battle.—*Julius Cæsar,* v, 1, 14; 23.
Signs of conquest.—*Antony and Cleopatra,* v, 2, 135.
Signs of deadly hate.—*II Henry VI,* iii, 2, 314.
Sign of dignity.—*Richard III,* iv, 4, 89.
Sign of fear.—*Coriolanus,* iv, 6, 153; *Venus and Adonis,* l. 644.
Signs of future accidents.—*I Henry VI,* v, 3, 4.
Sign of good desert.—*The Two Gentlemen of Verona,* iii, 2, 18.
Sign of peace.—*Henry VIII,* iii, 1, 66.
Sign of plighted faith.—*I Henry VI,* v, 3, 162.
Signs of rage.—*The Rape of Lucrece,* l. 1419.
Sign of truth.—*III Henry VI,* iv, 8, 26; *The Rape of Lucrece,* l. 1532.
Signs of war.—*Richard II,* ii, 2, 74; *Henry V,* ii, 2, 192.

2
Make my image but an alehouse sign.
II Henry VI. Act iii, sc. 2, l. 81. [Queen]
An alehouse' paltry sign.—*II Henry VI,* v, 2, 67.
Ye alehouse painted signs.—*Titus Andronicus,* iv, 2, 98.

3
Be these sad signs confirmers of thy words?
King John, iii, 1, 24. See under WORD. The only use of "confirmers." "Confirmer" occurs in *As You Like It,* iii, 4, 35: "Confirmer of false reckonings."
Sad signs.—*Venus and Adonis,* l. 929.
But thou didst understand me by my signs
And didst in signs again parley with sin.
King John. Act iv, sc. 2, l. 237. [King John]

4
Pick out mine eyes with a ballad-maker's pen and hang me up at the door of a brothel-house for the sign of blind Cupid.
Much Ado about Nothing. Act i, sc. 1, l. 254. [Benedick] The only use of "brothel-house."
Signs of leaping-houses.—*I Henry IV,* i, 2, 9. The only use of "leaping-houses."

5
These are no venereal signs.
Titus Andronicus. Act ii, sc. 3, l. 37. [Aaron] The only use of "venereal."
Bastard signs.—*Sonnets,* lxviii.
Bloody sign.—*Cymbeline,* iii, 4, 128.
Evil sign.—*III Henry VI,* v, 6, 44.
Frosty signs.—*Titus Andronicus,* v, 3, 77.

6
See, how with signs and tokens she can scrowl.
Titus Andronicus. Act ii, sc. 4, l. 5. [Demetrius] The only use of "scrowl."
Thus dost talk in signs!—*Titus Andronicus,* iii, 2, 12.
Her martyr'd signs.—*Titus Andronicus,* iii, 2, 36.
Make a sign.—*Titus Andronicus,* iii, 2, 43.
Marcus: What means my niece Lavinia by these signs? . . .
Titus: Give signs, sweet girl, for here are none but friends.
Titus Andronicus. Act iv, sc. 1, l. 8.

SIGNAL

7
Giving full trophy, signal and ostent
Quite from himself to God.
Henry V. Act v, Prologue, l. 21. [Chorus]

8
For God's sake, lords, give signal to the fight.
III Henry VI. Act ii, sc. 2, l. 100. [Richard]
Give signal to the fight, and to it, lords!
III Henry VI. Act v, sc. 4, l. 72. [King Edward]
Be valiant and give signal to the fight.
III Henry VI. Act v, sc. 4, l. 82. [Queen Margaret]
Stir not until the signal.—*Julius Cæsar,* v, 1, 26.

9
When I strike my foot
Upon the bosom of the ground, rush forth.
King John. Act iv, sc. 1, l. 2. [Hubert]

10
Courageously and with a free desire
Attending but the signal to begin.
Richard II. Act i, sc. 3, l. 115. [Herald]

SILENCE

See also Secret, Tongue

11
That 's off, that 's off;
I would you rather had been silent.
Coriolanus. Act ii, sc. 2, l. 64. [Menenius]
But that you shall not say I yield being silent,
I would not speak.
Cymbeline. Act ii, sc. 3, l. 99. [Imogen]
Speak, or thy silence on the instant is
Thy condemnation and thy death.
Cymbeline. Act iii, sc. 5, l. 97. [Cloten]
I 'll speak to thee in silence.—*Cymbeline,* v, 4, 29.
Dead silence.—*The Two Gentlemen of Verona,* iii, 2, 85.
Dumb silence.—*The Two Gentlemen of Verona,* iii, 1, 207.
Gracious silence.—*Coriolanus,* ii, 1, 192.
Wilful silence.—*Richard III,* iii, 7, 28.

12
Let it be tenable in your silence still.
Hamlet. Act i, sc. 2, l. 248. [Hamlet] The only use of "tenable."
Anon, as patient as the female dove,
When that her golden couplets are disclosed,
His silence will sit drooping.
Hamlet. Act v, sc. 1, l. 309. [Queen]
The rest is silence.
Hamlet. Act v, sc. 2, l. 369. [Hamlet]

13
Prince of Wales: There 's for your silence.
Bardolph: I have no tongue, sir.
Page: And for mine, sir, I will govern it.
II Henry IV. Act ii, sc. 2, l. 178.

God keep you, Master Silence: I will not use many words with you.
II Henry IV. Act iii, sc. 2, l. 308. [Falstaff]

1
With silence, nephew, be thou polite.
I Henry VI. Act ii, sc. 5, l. 101. [Mortimer]
O, hold me not with silence over-long!
I Henry VI. Act v, sc. 3, l. 13. [La Pucelle] The only use of "over-long."

2
Suffolk: Peace, headstrong Warwick!
Warwick: Image of pride, why should I hold my peace?
II Henry VI. Act i, sc. 3, l. 178.
Hold thy peace.—*I Henry VI,* iii, 2, 58; *Romeo and Juliet,* i, 3, 49; *Twelfth Night,* ii, 3, 68; 73; iii, 4, 120.
Peace, good pint-pot; peace, good tickle-brain.
I Henry IV. Act ii, sc. 4, l. 437. [Falstaff] The only use of either phrase.
Peace, chewet, peace!—*I Henry IV,* v, 1, 29. The only use of "chewet" (chatterer).
For the love o' God, peace!—*Twelfth Night,* ii, 3, 92.
I prithee, peace.—*II Henry VI,* ii, 1, 33, and five times in later plays.
Peace, I pray you.—*The Merry Wives of Windsor,* i, 1, 138; i, 4, 84.
Peace, and be still!—*Othello,* v, 2, 46.
Peace your tattlings.—*The Merry Wives of Windsor,* iv, 1, 26. The only use of "tattlings." "Tattling" occurs in iii, 3, 99: "Tattling woman"; and in *Much Ado about Nothing,* ii, 1, 11: "Evermore tattling."
Though our silence be drawn from us with cars, yet peace.
Twelfth Night. Act ii, sc. 5, l. 70. [Fabian]

3
Cade: Command silence.
Dick: Silence!
II Henry VI. Act iv, sc. 2, l. 39. "Silence," as a command, is used frequently throughout the plays.
Let silence be commanded.—*Henry VIII,* ii, 4, 2.
Silence awhile.—*A Midsummer-Night's Dream,* iv, 1, 85.
Cock's passion, silence!—*The Taming of the Shrew,* iv, 1, 121.
Put to silence.—*Julius Cæsar,* i, 2, 290.
Be you silent.—*III Henry VI,* i, 1, 122.
I will be silent.—*Troilus and Cressida,* ii, 3, 241.
Why are you silent?—*Macbeth,* iv, 3, 137.

4
Let 's on our way in silent sort.
III Henry VI. Act iv, sc. 2, l. 28. [Warwick]

5
I do beseech
You, gracious madam, to unthink your speaking
And to say so no more.
Henry VIII. Act ii, sc. 4, l. 103. [Wolsey] The only use of "unthink."
For the benefit of silence.—*Measure for Measure,* v, 1, 190.

6
I do not know of these
That therefore only are reputed wise
For saying nothing.
The Merchant of Venice. Act i, sc. 1, l. 95. [Gratiano]
Silence is only commendable
In a neat's tongue dried and a maid not vendible.
The Merchant of Venice. Act i, sc. 1, l. 111. [Gratiano] "Vendible" is used again in *All's Well that Ends Well,* i, 1, 168.

7
Then, my queen, in silence sad,
Trip we after night's shade.
A Midsummer-Night's Dream. Act iv, sc. 1, l. 99. [Oberon]

8
Silence is the perfectest herald of joy: I were but little happy, if I could say how much.
Much Ado about Nothing. Act ii, sc. 1, l. 317. [Claudio] "Perfectest" is repeated in *Macbeth,* i, 5, 2: "Perfectest report."
Your silence most offends me.
Much Ado about Nothing. Act ii, sc. 1, l. 345. [Don Pedro]
Her silence flouts me.
The Taming of the Shrew. Act ii, sc. 1, l. 29. [Katharina]

9
The citizens are mum and speak not a word.
Richard III. Act iii, sc. 7, l. 3. [Buckingham]
Give no words but mum.—*II Henry VI,* i, 2, 89.
Mum.—*Measure for Measure,* v, 1, 288.
I come to her in white, and cry 'mum.'
The Merry Wives of Windsor. Act v, sc. 2, l. 6. [Slender] Also v, 5, 209.
Well said, master; mum!—*The Taming of the Shrew,* i, 1, 73.
Mum, then, and no more.—*Tempest,* iii, 2, 59.

10
This silence for my sin you did impute,
Which shall be most my glory, being dumb;
For I impair not beauty being mute,
When others would give life and bring a tomb.
Sonnets. No. lxxxiii.

11
All 's hush'd as midnight yet.
The Tempest. Act iv, sc. 1, l. 207. [Caliban]
Silence of the night.—*The Merchant of Venice,* v, 1, 25.
The silent of the night.—*II Henry VI,* i, 4, 19.

12
After distasteful looks and these hard factions,
With certain half-caps and cold-moving nods
They froze me into silence.
Timon of Athens. Act ii, sc. 2, l. 220. [Flavius] The only use of "distasteful," "half-caps," and "cold-moving."

13
Lay thy finger on thy lips!
Troilus and Cressida. Act i, sc. 3, l. 240. [Æneas]
Your silence,
Cunning in dumbness, from my weakness draws
My very soul of counsel!
Troilus and Cressida. Act iii, sc. 2, l. 139. [Cressida]

14
What else may hap to time I will commit;
Only shape thou thy silence to my wit.
Twelfth Night. Act i, sc. 2, l. 60. [Viola]
I like your silence, it the more shows off
Your wonder.
Winter's Tale. Act v, sc. 3, l. 21. [Paulina]

The silence often of pure innocence
Persuades when speaking fails.
Winter's Tale. Act ii, sc. 2, l. 41. [Paulina]

SILVER

1
I took this for silver.
Coriolanus. Act i, sc. 5, l. 3. [Roman]
2
Or shall I think in silver she 's immured,
Being ten times undervalued to tried gold?
The Merchant of Venice. Act ii, sc. 9, l. 52. [Morocco]
3
Thou pale and common drudge
'Tween man and man.
The Merchant of Venice. Act iii, sc. 2, l. 103. [Bassanio]
Silver with her virgin hue.—*The Merchant of Venice,* ii, 7, 22.
4
Laced with silver, set with pearls.
Much Ado about Nothing, iii, 4, 20. See under Gown.
Trapp'd in silver.—*Timon of Athens,* i, 2, 189.
5
Silver hath a sweet sound.
Romeo and Juliet. Act iv, sc. 5, l. 133. [Musician]
A piece of silver.—*The Tempest,* ii, 2, 31.

SIMPLES, see under Medicine

SIMPLICITY

6
A simple countryman, that brought her figs.
Antony and Cleopatra. Act v, sc. 2, l. 342. [Guard]
Simple clown.—*Love's Labour 's Lost,* iv, 1, 142.
Simple gulls.—*Richard III,* i, 3, 328.
7
Twice-sod simplicity, bis coctus!
Love's Labour 's Lost. Act iv, sc. 2, l. 22. [Holofernes] The only use of "twice-sod" (twice-boiled, the essence of), and "bis coctus."
The shape of Love's Tyburn that hangs up simplicity.
Love's Labour 's Lost. Act iv, sc. 3, l. 54. [Biron] The only mention of Tyburn.
To prove, by wit, worth in simplicity.
Love's Labour 's Lost. Act v, sc. 2, l. 78. [Maria]
Low simplicity.—*Merchant of Venice,* i, 3, 44.
Profound simplicity.—*Love's Labour 's Lost,* v, 2, 52.
8
You see how simple and how fond I am.
A Midsummer-Night's Dream. Act iii, sc. 2, l. 317. [Helena]
In simple and pure soul I come to you.
Othello. Act i, sc. 1, l. 107. [Roderigo]
9
Never anything can be amiss,
When simpleness and duty tender it.
A Midsummer-Night's Dream. Act v, sc. 1, l. 82. [Theseus]
Love, therefore, and tongue-tied simplicity
In least speak most, to my capacity.
A Midsummer-Night's Dream. Act v, sc. 1, l. 104. [Theseus]
10
Let me find a charter in your voice,
To assist my simpleness.
Othello. Act i, sc. 3, l. 246. [Desdemona]
11
Simple, plain Clarence!
Richard III. Act i, sc. 1, l. 118. [Gloucester]
12
I am as true as truth's simplicity
And simpler than the infancy of truth.
Troilus and Cressida. Act iii, sc. 2, l. 176. [Troilus] "Simpler" is used only once again, in *Timon of Athens,* v, 1, 27: "Simpler kind of people."
Whiles others fish with craft for great opinion,
I with great truth catch mere simplicity.
Troilus and Cressida. Act iv, sc. 4, l. 105. [Troilus]
13
He 's simple and tells much.
The Winter's Tale. Act iv, sc. 4, l. 355. [Polixenes]
How blessed are we that are not simple men!
The Winter's Tale. Act iv, sc. 4, l. 771. [Autolycus]
Simple men.—*III Henry VI,* iii, 1, 83; *The Merry Wives of Windsor,* iv, 2, 182.
Simple woman.—*Henry VIII,* ii, 4, 106.

SIN

See also Crime, Evil, Guilt, Transgression, Vice, Wickedness

14
I have then sinned against his experience and transgressed against his valour; and my state that way is dangerous, since I cannot yet find in my heart to repent.
All 's Well that Ends Well. Act ii, sc. 5, l. 10. [Lafeu] See also Transgression.
I think 't no sin
To cozen him that would unjustly win.
All 's Well that Ends Well. Act iv, sc. 2, l. 75. [Diana]
15
Most mischievous foul sin, in chiding sin.
As You Like It. Act ii, sc. 7, l. 64. [Duke]
The time shall not be many hours of age
More than it is ere foul sin gathering head
Shall break into corruption.
Richard II. Act v, sc. 1, l. 57. [King Richard]
The time will come, that foul sin, gathering head,
Shall break into corruption.
II Henry IV. Act iii, sc. 1, l. 76. [King Henry, quoting King Richard]
When, pattern'd by thy fault, foul sin may say,
He learn'd to sin, and thou didst teach the way.
The Rape of Lucrece, l. 629.
Pray for your foul sin.—*Richard II,* v, 3, 82.
Base sin.—*The Rape of Lucrece,* l. 93.
Bloody sin.—*II Henry VI,* iii, 1, 131.
Cardinal sins.—*Henry VIII,* iii, 1, 104.
Deadly sin.—*Love's Labour's Lost,* ii, 1, 105; *Romeo and Juliet,* iii, 3, 24.
Detested sins.—*Richard II,* iii, 3, 44.
Grievous sin.—*I Henry VI,* iii, 1, 128; *Richard III,* i, 4, 195.
Heinous sin.—*Titus Andronicus,* i, 1, 448.
Hell-born sin.—*The Rape of Lucrece,* l. 1519. The only use of "hell-born."
Inhibited sin.—*All 's Well that Ends Well,* i, 1,

158. "Inhibited" is repeated in *Othello*, i, 2, 79.
Private sin.—*The Rape of Lucrece*, l. 1484.
Redeemed sin.—*Othello*, ii, 3, 350.
Scarlet sin.—*Henry VIII*, iii, 2, 225.
Unbegotten sin.—*King John*, iv, 3, 54.
Virtuous sin.—*Troilus and Cressida*, iv, 4, 83.
Worse sin.—*Henry VIII*, i, 3, 60.
Worst sin.—*Timon of Athens*, iv, 2, 39.
Sin of covetousness.—*Twelfth Night*, v, 1, 50.
Sin of my ingratitude.—*Macbeth*, i, 4, 15.
Sin of perjury.—*Much Ado about Nothing*, iv, 1, 175.
Sin of self-love.—*Sonnets*, lxii. See SELF-LOVE.
Sin of thought.—*King John*, iv, 3, 135.
Sins of youth.—*The Winter's Tale*, iii, 3, 124.

1
Wickedness is sin, and sin is damnation.
As You Like It. Act iii, sc. 2, l. 44. [Touchstone]
That is another simple sin in you.
As You Like It. Act iii, sc. 2, l. 83. [Touchstone]

2
Teach sin the carriage of a holy saint.
The Comedy of Errors. Act iii, sc. 2, l. 14. [Luciana]
To sin and never for to saint.
The Passionate Pilgrim, l. 342.

3
It were sin to doubt.
Coriolanus. Act i, sc. 6, l. 68. [Marcius]
You sin against obedience.—*Cymbeline*, ii, 3, 116.
If it be sin to say so.—*Cymbeline*, iv, 2, 19.

4
O, a sin in war,
Damn'd in the first beginners!
Cymbeline. Act v, sc. 3, l. 36. [Posthumus]

5
Nymph, in thy orisons
Be all my sins remember'd.
Hamlet. Act iii, sc. 1, l. 90. [Hamlet] See also under PRAYER.

6
I 'll be no longer guilty of this sin.
I Henry IV. Act ii, sc. 4, l. 267. [Prince]
'Tis no sin.—*I Henry IV*, i, 2, 117.

7
Commit
The oldest sins the newest kind of ways.
II Henry IV, iv, 5, 127. See under RUFFIAN.

8
The sin upon my head, dread sovereign!
Henry V. Act i, sc. 2, l. 97. [Canterbury]
Bear the sin upon their own heads.—*I Henry IV*, v, 4, 153.

9
So should I give consent to flatter sin.
I Henry VI. Act v, sc. 5, l. 25. [Gloucester]
'Tis sin to flatter.—*III Henry VI*, v, 6, 3.

10
Sins
Such as by God's book are adjudged to death.
II Henry VI. Act ii, sc. 3, l. 3. [King]
Then is sin struck down like an ox, and iniquity's throat cut like a calf.
II Henry VI. Act iv, sc. 2, l. 28. [Bevis]

11
It is great sin to swear unto a sin.
II Henry VI, v, 1, 182. See under OATH. The only use of "great sin."
Greater sin.—*II Henry VI*, v, 1, 183.

12
The willing'st sin I ever yet committed
May be absolved in English.
Henry VIII. Act iii, sc. 1, l. 49. [Queen Katharine] The only use of "willing'st."
Produce the grand sum of his sins.—*Henry VIII*, iii, 2, 293.

13
Some sins do bear their privilege on earth,
And so doth yours; your fault was not your folly.
King John. Act i, sc. 1, l. 261. [Bastard]
And they shall say, when Richard me begot,
If thou hadst said him nay, it had been sin:
Who says it was, he lies; I say 'twas not.
King John. Act i, sc. 1, l. 274. [Bastard]

14
Thy sins are visited in this poor child.
King John. Act ii, sc. 1, l. 179. [Constance]
He is not only plagued for her sin,
But God hath made her sin and her the plague
On this removed issue, plagued for her
And with her plague; her sin his injury,
Her injury the beadle to her sin.
King John. Act ii, sc. 1, l. 184. [Constance] "Beadle" is used eight times in the plays.
Yes, truly; for, look you, the sins of the father are to be laid upon the children.
The Merchant of Venice. Act iii, sc. 5, l. 1 [Launcelot]
So the sins of my mother should be visited upon me.
The Merchant of Venice, iii, 5, 15. [Jessica]

15
Then God forgive the sin of all those souls
That to their everlasting residence,
Before the dew of evening fall, shall fleet.
King John. Act ii, sc. 1, l. 283. [King John]
God forgive my sins!—*III Henry VI*, v, 6, 60.
God pardon sin!—*Romeo and Juliet*, ii, 3, 44.
Heaven forgive my sins at the day of judgement!
The Merry Wives of Windsor. Act iii, sc. 3, l. 226. [Evans]
Heaven forgive our sins!—*The Merry Wives of Windsor*, v, 5, 35.
Forgive us our sins!—*Othello*, ii, 3, 116.
O, forgive me my sins!—*Tempest*, iii, 2, 139.

16
There is no sin but to be rich.
King John, ii, 1, 594. See POVERTY, 1180:11.

17
Away with me, all you whose souls abhor
The uncleanly savours of a slaughter-house;
For I am stifled with this smell of sin.
King John. Act iv, sc. 3, l. 111. [Salisbury]

18
Do not call it sin in me,
That I am forsworn for thee.
Love's Labour 's Lost. Act iv, sc. 3, l. 115. [Dumain, reading]
You must be purged too, your sins are rack'd.
Love's Labour 's Lost. Act v, sc. 2, l. 828. [Rosaline]

19
Some rise by sin, and some by virtue fall.
Measure for Measure. Act ii, sc. 1, l. 38. [Angelo]

Our compell'd sins
Stand more for number than for accompt.
Measure for Measure. Act ii, sc. 4, l. 57. [Angelo]

If that be sin, I 'll make it my morn prayer
To have it added to the faults of mine.
Measure for Measure. Act ii, sc. 4, l. 71. [Isabella]

What sin you do to save a brother's life,
Nature dispenses with the deed so far
That it becomes a virtue.
Measure for Measure. Act iii, sc. 1, l. 134. [Claudio]

Sure, it is no sin;
Or of the deadly seven it is the least.
Measure for Measure. Act iii, sc. 1, l. 110. [Claudio]

It is no sin at all.—*Measure for Measure,* ii, 4, 66.

'Tis no sin.—*Measure for Measure,* iv, 1, 73.

Hold it for no sin.—*The Rape of Lucrece,* l. 209.

1 Thy sin 's not accidental, but a trade.
Measure for Measure. Act iii, sc. 1, l. 149. [Isabella]

Nay, if the devil have given thee proofs for sin,
Thou wilt prove his.
Measure for Measure. Act iii, sc. 2, l. 31. [Duke]

2 I know it is a sin to be a mocker.
The Merchant of Venice, i, 2, 61. See under MOCKERY.

You 'll make me wish a sin.—*The Merchant of Venice,* iii, 2, 13.

Now shall I sin in my wish.—*The Merry Wives of Windsor,* iii, 3, 51.

3 Renounce his baptism,
All seals and symbols of redeemed sin.
Othello. Act ii, sc. 3, l. 349. [Iago] The only use of "symbols."

4 Their best conscience
Is not to leave 't undone, but keep 't unknown.
Othello. Act iii, sc. 3, l. 203. [Iago]

And therefore would they still in darkness be,
To have their unseen sin remain untold.
The Rape of Lucrece, l. 752.

5 Think on thy sins.
Othello. Act v, sc. 2, l. 40. [Othello]

Confess thee freely of thy sin.
Othello. Act v, sc. 2, l. 53. [Othello]

Alas, what ignorant sin have I committed?
Othello. Act iv, sc. 2, l. 70. [Desdemona]

6 One sin, I know, another doth provoke.
Pericles. Act i, sc. 1, l. 137. [Pericles]

Doubting lest that he had err'd or sinn'd.
Pericles. Act i, sc. 3, l. 22. [Helicanus]

7 The blackest sin is clear'd with absolution.
The Rape of Lucrece, l. 354. The only use of "absolution."

Wilt thou be glass wherein it shall discern
Authority for sin, warrant for blame?
The Rape of Lucrece, l. 619.

O, deeper sin than bottomless conceit
Can comprehend in still imagination.
The Rape of Lucrece, l. 701.

Sin ne'er gives a fee, He gratis comes.
The Rape of Lucrece, l. 913. See under OPPORTUNITY.

My sable ground of sin I will not paint,
To hide the truth of this false night's abuses.
The Rape of Lucrece, l. 1074.

Let sin, alone committed, light alone
Upon his head that hath transgressed so.
The Rape of Lucrece, l. 1480.

8 O, God defend my soul from such deep sin!
Richard II. Act i, sc. 1, l. 187. [Bolingbroke]

Be Mowbray's sins so heavy in his bosom,
That they may break his foaming courser's back.
Richard II. Act i, sc. 2, l. 50. [Duchess of Gloucester]

Self-affrighted tremble at his sin.
Richard II. Act iii, sc. 2, l. 53. [King Richard] The only use of "self-affrighted."

9 Though some of you with Pilate wash your hands
Showing an outward pity; yet you Pilates
Have here deliver'd me to my sour cross,
And water cannot wash away your sin.
Richard II. Act iv, sc. 1, l. 239. [King Richard]

How fain, like Pilate, would I wash my hands.
Richard III, i, 4, 279. See under MURDER. The only times that Pilate is mentioned.

10 Sin, death, and hell have set their marks on him,
And all their ministers attend on him.
Richard III. Act i, sc. 3, l. 293. [Queen Margaret]

In this sin he is as deep as I.
Richard III. Act i, sc. 4, l. 220. [Clarence]

Not for all this land
Would I be guilty of so deep a sin.
Richard III. Act iii, sc. 1, l. 42. [Bourchier]

I am in
So far in blood that sin will pluck on sin.
Richard III. Act iv, sc. 2, l. 64. [King Richard]

All several sins, all used in each degree,
Throng to the bar, crying all, Guilty! guilty!
Richard III, v, 3, 198. [King Richard]

11 Now, by the stock and honour of my kin,
To strike him dead I hold it not a sin.
Romeo and Juliet. Act i, sc. 5, l. 60. [Tybalt]

My state . . . is cross and full of sin.
Romeo and Juliet. Act iv, sc. 3, l. 4. [Juliet]

Put not another sin upon my head,
By urging me to fury.
Romeo and Juliet. Act v, sc. 3, l. 62. [Romeo]

12 Excusing thy sins more than thy sins are.
Sonnets. No. xxxv.

O, in what sweets dost thou thy sins enclose!
Sonnets. No. xcv.

13 You are three men of sin.
The Tempest. Act iii, sc. 3, l. 53. [Ariel]

14 You cannot make gross sins look clear.
Timon of Athens. Act iii, 5, 38. [Senator]

Sin the faster.—*Timon of Athens,* i, 2, 246.

To sin in Lucrece' bed.—*Titus Andronicus,* iv, 1, 64.

1 I have done sin:
For which the heavens, taking angry note,
Have left me issueless.
Winter's Tale. Act v, sc. 1, l. 172. [Leontes] "Issueless" occurs again in *Sonnets,* ix.

II—Sinner

2
O, for my beads! I cross me for a sinner.
The Comedy of Errors. Act ii, sc. 2, l. 190. [Dromio of Syracuse]
A breeder of sinners.—*Hamlet,* iii, 1, 123.
3
Forbear to judge, for we are sinners all.
II Henry VI. Act iii, sc. 3, l. 31. [King Henry]
Wretched sinners.—*I Henry VI,* i, 4, 70.
4
I will be so much a sinner, to be a double-dealer.
Twelfth Night. Act v, sc. 1, l. 37. [Duke] See under DECEIT. "Double-dealer" is repeated in *Much Ado about Nothing,* v, 4, 116.
Too weak to be a sinner.—*Timon of Athens,* i, 2, 59.

SINCERITY

5
Sincere and holy in his thoughts.
II Henry IV. Act i, sc. 1, l. 202. [Mortimer]
Sincere motions.—*Henry VIII,* i, 1, 153.
Sincere verity.—*King Lear,* ii, 2, 111.
His love sincere.—*The Two Gentlemen of Verona,* ii, 7, 76. The only uses of "sincere."
Profess sincerely.—*Coriolanus,* i, 3, 24.
I speak sincerely.—*Henry VIII,* ii, 3, 59.
Most sincerely.—*Much Ado about Nothing,* v, 2, 201. The only uses of "sincerely."
6
Nor are those empty-hearted whose low sound
Reverbs no hollowness.
King Lear. Act i, sc. 1, l. 155. [Kent] The only use of "empty-hearted" and "reverbs." "Hollowness" is repeated in i, 2, 122, and in *Richard II,* i, 2, 59: "Empty hollowness."
7
A due sincerity govern'd his deeds.
Measure for Measure. Act v, sc. 1, l. 451. [Isabella]
Bashful sincerity and comely love.
Much Ado about Nothing. Act iv, sc. 1, l. 55. [Claudio]
True sincerity.—*King John,* iii, 1, 248.
Sincerity of fear.—*I Henry IV,* ii, 3, 32.
Sincerity of love.—*Othello,* ii, 3, 333.
8
Don Pedro: He is in earnest.
Claudio: In most profound earnest.
Much Ado about Nothing. Act v, sc. 1, l. 197.
How, sir! are you in earnest then?
Titus Andronicus. Act i, sc. 1, l. 277. [Titus]
Did you perceive her earnest?
The Two Gentlemen of Verona. Act ii, sc. 1, l. 163. [Speed]
In good earnest.—*As You Like It,* iv, 1, 192; *The Winter's Tale,* i, 2, 150.
In earnestness.—*Coriolanus,* ii, 1, 229.
In great earnestness.—*Coriolanus,* iv, 6, 57.
With a solemn earnestness.—*Othello,* v, 2, 227.
Earnestness of affection.—*II Henry IV,* v, 5, 17. The only uses of "earnestness."

9
There is no time so miserable but a man may be true.
Timon of Athens. Act iv, sc. 3, l. 462. [Bandit]
You that are honest, by being what you are,
Make them best seen and known.
Timon of Athens. Act v, sc. 1, l. 71. [Timon]

SINEWS

See also Strength

10 There was it:
For which my sinews shall be stretch'd upon him.
Coriolanus. Act v, sc. 6, l. 44. [Aufidius]
11
You, my sinews, grow not instant old,
But bear me stiffly up.
Hamlet, i, 5, 94. See under COURAGE.
Soft as sinews of the new-born babe!
Hamlet, iii, 3, 71. See under KNEE.
Much unsinew'd.—*Hamlet,* iv, 7, 10. The only use of "unsinew'd."
12
The noble sinews of our power.
Henry V. Act i, sc. 2, l. 223. [King Henry]
Broken sinews.—*King Lear,* iii, 6, 105.
Lusty sinews.—*Julius Cæsar,* i, 2, 108.
Greekish sinews.—*Troilus and Cressida,* iii, 1, 166.
Steeled sinews.—*Henry V,* ii, 2, 36.
13
These are his substance, sinews, arms and strength.
I Henry VI. Act ii, sc. 3, l. 63. [Talbot]
14
Strokes received, and many blows repaid,
Have robb'd my strong-knit sinews of their strength.
III Henry VI. Act ii, sc. 3, l. 3. [Warwick]
Strong-knit limbs.—*I Henry VI,* ii, 3, 21. The only uses of "strong-knit."
Knit your sinews to the strength of mine.
King John. Act v, sc. 2, l. 63. [Lewis]
15
So shalt thou sinew both these lands together.
III Henry VI. Act ii, sc. 6, l. 91. [Warwick] The only use of "sinew" as a verb.
Who was with them a rated sinew too.
I Henry IV. Act iv, sc. 4, l. 17. [Archbishop]
Sinew of her fortune.—*Measure for Measure,* iii, 1, 230.
Sinew . . . of our host.—*Troilus and Cressida,* i, 3, 143. The only uses of "sinew."
16
Well sinewed to our defence.
King John, v, 7, 88. See under DEFENCE. The only use of "sinewed."
17 Romans now
Have thews and limbs like to their ancestors.
Julius Cæsar, i, 3, 81. See under ROME.
Thews and bulk.—*Hamlet,* i, 3, 12.
Thews, . . . bulk.—*II Henry IV,* iii, 2, 276. The only uses of "thews."
18
Shorten up their sinews With aged cramps.
The Tempest, iv, 1, 260. See under PUNISHMENT.

1
A great deal of your wit, too, lies in your sinews.
Troilus and Cressida, ii, 1, 109. See under Wit.
Her own sinews.—*Troilus and Cressida,* i, 3, 136.
Through all her sinews.—*Venus and Adonis,* l. 903.
2
Bull-bearing Milo his addition yield
To sinewy Ajax.
Troilus and Cressida, ii, 3, 258. See under Vigour. The only use of "bull-bearing" and mention of "Milo."
Sinewy Charles.—*As You Like It,* ii, 2, 13.
Sinewy neck.—*Venus and Adonis,* 99.
Sinewy sword-men.—*All's Well that Ends Well,* ii, 1, 62.
Sinewy vigour.—*Love's Labour's Lost,* iv, 3, 308. The only uses of "sinewy."
3
Get his sinews to make catlings on.
Troilus and Cressida, iii, 3, 305. See under Music. The only use of "catlings" (catgut).
Strung with poets' sinews.—*The Two Gentlemen of Verona,* iii, 2, 78.
Let grow thy sinews till their knots be strong,
And tempt not yet the brushes of the war.
Troilus and Cressida. Act v, sc. 3, l. 33. [Hector] The only use of "brushes" as a noun. As a verb, it occurs in *Much Ado about Nothing,* iii, 2, 41: "A' brushes his hat o' mornings." "Brush" is used twice, in *II Henry VI,* v, 3, 3, and in *Timon of Athens,* iv, 3, 264.
4 The sinews of this leg
All Greek, and this all Troy.
Troilus and Cressida. Act iv, sc. 5, l. 126. [Hector]
Here lies . . . thy sinews.—*Troilus and Cressida,* v, 8, 12.
5
Nay, patience, or we break the sinews of our plot.
Twelfth Night. Act ii, sc. 5, l. 83. [Fabian]
Crack my sinews.—*The Tempest,* iii, 1, 26.
Stiffen the sinews.—*Henry V,* iii, 1, 7.
Sinews fall away.—*I Henry VI,* iii, 1, 193.

SINGING, see Song

SIRE

See also Father

6
His mountain sire, on mountain standing,
Up in the air, crown'd with the golden sun,
Saw his heroical seed, and smil'd to see him,
Mangle the work of nature and deface
The patterns that by God and by French fathers
Had twenty years been made.
Henry V. Act ii, sc. 4, l. 57. [French King]
7
Then follow thou thy desperate sire of Crete,
Thou Icarus.
I Henry VI, iv, 7, 54. See under Death, 306:2.
Loving sire.—*III Henry VI,* ii, 2, 22.
Old limping sire.—*Timon of Athens,* iv, 1, 14.
Poor sire.—*III Henry VI,* ii, 2, 155.
Sweet-smelling sire.—*Venus and Adonis,* l. 1178. The only use of "sweet-smelling."
But neither bended knees, pure hands held up,
Sad sighs, deep groans, nor silver-shedding tears,
Could penetrate her uncompassionate sire.
The Two Gentlemen of Verona. Act iii, sc. 1, l. 229. [Proteus] The only use of "silver-shedding" and "uncompassionate."
Butcher-sire that reaves his son of life.
Venus and Adonis, l. 766. The only use of "butcher-sire."
8 A gross and foolish sire
Blemish'd his gracious dam.
Winter's Tale. Act iii, sc. 2, l. 198. [Paulina]

SISTER

9
Thou hast a sister by the mother's side.
Antony and Cleopatra. Act ii, sc. 2, l. 120. [Agrippa]
A sister I bequeathe you, whom no brother
Did ever love so dearly.
Antony and Cleopatra. Act ii, sc. 2, l. 152. [Cæsar]
Cæsar's sister is called Octavia.—*Antony and Cleopatra,* ii, 6, 116.
10
Dearer than the natural bond of sisters.
As You Like It. Act i, sc. 2, l. 288. [Le Beau]
11
Luciana: Comfort my sister, cheer her, call her wife. . . .
Antipholus of Syracuse: Your weeping sister is no wife of mine,
Nor to her bed no homage do I owe.
The Comedy of Errors. Act iii, sc. 2, l. 26.
Luciana: Why call you me love? call my sister so.
Antipholus of Syracuse: Thy sister's sister.
Luciana: That's my sister.
Antipholus: No;
It is thyself, mine own self's better part. . . .
Luciana: All this my sister is, or else should be.
Antipholus: Call thyself sister, sweet, for I am thee. . . .
Give me thy hand.
Luciana: O, soft, sir! hold you still:
I'll fetch my sister, to get her good will.
The Comedy of Errors. Act iii, sc. 2, l. 59.
She now shall be my sister, not my wife.
The Comedy of Errors. Act v, sc. 1, l. 416. [Dromio of Syracuse]
Our sometime sister, now our queen.
Hamlet. Act i, sc. 2, l. 8. [King]
12
A sister driven into desperate terms,
Whose worth, if praises may go back again,
Stood challenger on mount of all the age
For her perfections.
Hamlet. Act iv, sc. 7, l. 26. [Laertes]
A ministering angel shall my sister be.
Hamlet. Act v, sc. 1, l. 264. [Laertes] The only use of "ministering angel."
13
France: Bid farewell to your sisters.
Cordelia: The jewels of our father, with wash'd eyes

Cordelia leaves you: I know you what you are;
And like a sister am most loath to call
Your faults as they are named.
King Lear. Act i, sc. 1, l. 270.

Your sister is the better soldier.
King Lear. Act v, sc. 1, l. 3. [Oswald]

To both these sisters have I sworn my love;
Each jealous of the other, as the stung
Are of the adder. Which of them shall I take?
Both? one? or neither? Neither can be enjoy'd,
If both remain alive.
King Lear. Act v, sc. 1, l. 55. [Edmund]

1 This day my sister should the cloister enter.
Measure for Measure. Act i, sc. 2, l. 182. [Claudio]

Had he twenty heads to tender down
On twenty bloody blocks, he 'ld yield them up,
Before his sister should her body stoop
To such abhorr'd pollution.
Measure for Measure. Act ii, sc. 4, l. 180. [Isabella] "Pollution" is repeated in *Twelfth Night*, i, 2, 49.

Is 't not a kind of incest, to take life
From thine own sister's shame?
Measure for Measure. Act iii, sc. 1, l. 139. [Isabella]

2 The Sisters Three and such branches of learning.
The Merchant of Venice. Act ii, sc. 2, l. 66. [Launcelot]

Sisters Three.—*II Henry IV*, i, 2, 166; *A Midsummer-Night's Dream*, v, 1, 343.

The weird sisters.—*Macbeth*, i, 3, 32; i, 5, 9; ii, 1, 20; iii, 4, 133; iv, 1, 136. Not used in any other play. "Weird women" occurs in iii, 1, 2.

3 Lucentio: Mistress, what 's your opinion of your sister?
Bianca: That, being mad herself, she 's madly mated.
Taming of the Shrew. Act iii, sc. 2, l. 245.

Priam: What noise? what shriek is this?
Troilus: 'Tis our mad sister, I do know her voice.
Troilus and Cressida. Act ii, sc. 2, l. 97.

Sister Cassandra.—*Troilus and Cressida*, i, 1, 47.

Sister Bona.—*III Henry VI*, iii, 3, 121.

Sister Kate.—*Taming of the Shrew*, ii, 1, 21.

Sister Katharina.—*The Taming of the Shrew*, v, 2, 6.

Sister Nell.—*II Henry IV*, ii, 2, 140.

4 How does my bounteous sister?
The Tempest. Act iv, sc. 1, l. 103. [Juno]

Beauteous sisters.—*Romeo and Juliet*, i, 2, 68.

Dear sister.—*Hamlet*, i, 3, 33; *King Lear*, iii, 7, 13.

Elder sister.—*The Taming of the Shrew*, i, 1, 185; *The Winter's Tale*, i, 2, 98.

Eldest sister.—*II Henry VI*, ii, 2, 43; *The Taming of the Shrew*, ii, 1, 94.

Fair sister.—*III Henry VI*, iii, 3, 56; *The Comedy of Errors*, iii, 2, 164; *As You Like It*, v, 2, 21; *Henry V*, v, 2, 90; *King Lear*, v, 3, 84; *Measure for Measure*, i, 4, 19.

Fierce sister.—*King Lear*, iii, 7, 57.

Gentle sister.—*Titus Andronicus*, iii, 1, 81.

Good sister.—*The Comedy of Errors*, ii, 1, 6; *Richard III*, iv, 1, 7; *The Taming of the Shrew*, ii, 1, 1.

Kind sister.—*Richard III*, iv, 1, 11; *Hamlet*. iv, 5, 158.

Noble sister.—*Titus Andronicus*, iii, 1, 293; *Coriolanus*, v, 3, 64.

Ripe sister.—*As You Like It*, iv, 3, 88.

Sweet sister.—*Measure for Measure*, iii, 1, 133; *Twelfth Night*, v, 1, 393.

Very-loving sister.—*King Lear*, v, 1, 20. The only use of "very-loving."

Widow sister.—*Richard III*, i, 1, 109.

Wronged sister.—*Antony and Cleopatra*, iii, 6. 65.

Young sister.—*Measure for Measure*, iii, 1, 152.

5 Sweet father, cease your tears; for, at your grief,
See how my wretched sister sobs and weeps.
Titus Andronicus. Act iii, sc. 1, l. 136. [Lucius]

6 Viola: They that dally nicely with words may quickly make them wanton.
Clown: I would, therefore, my sister had had no name, sir.
Viola: Why, man?
Clown: Why, sir, her name 's a word; and to dally with that word might make my sister wanton.
Twelfth Night. Act iii, sc. 1, l. 16. See under WORD.

7 I had a sister,
Whom the blind waves and surges have devour'd.
Twelfth Night. Act v, sc. 1, l. 235. [Sebastian]

Think me as well a sister as a wife.
Twelfth Night. Act v, sc. 1, l. 325. [Olivia]

SKILL

8 My father's skill, which was the greatest
Of his profession.
All's Well that Ends Well. Act i, sc. 3, l. 249. [Helena]

Skill infinite or monstrous desperate.
All's Well that Ends Well. Act ii, sc. 1, l. 187. [King]

Skill in surgery.—*I Henry IV*, v, 1, 135.

9 Let him show His skill.
Cymbeline. Act v, sc. 5, l. 433. [Posthumus]

It was to show my skill.—*Love's Labour's Lost*, iv, 1, 28.

10 I have not the skill.
Hamlet. Act iii, sc. 2, l. 378. [Guildenstern]

Lack of skill.—*Cymbeline*, ii, 4, 22.

Want of skill.—*The Rape of Lucrece*, l. 1099.

11 Your skill shall, like a star i' the darkest night,
Stick fiery off indeed.
Hamlet. Act v, sc. 2, l. 267. [Hamlet]

1
Here stand I: lady, dart thy skill at me.
Love's Labour's Lost. Act v, sc. 2, l. 396. [Biron]

2
My ancient skill beguiles me.
Measure for Measure. Act iv, sc. 2, l. 164. [Duke]

I'll use my skill.—*The Two Gentlemen of Verona,* ii, 4, 214; *Much Ado about Nothing,* i, 2, 28.
Barren skill.—*The Rape of Lucrece,* l. 81.
Better skill.—*The Rape of Lucrece,* l. 1134.
Good skill.—*The Merry Wives of Windsor,* ii, 1, 231.
Greater skill.—*Cymbeline,* ii, 5, 33.
Little skill.—*Titus Andronicus,* ii, 1, 43.
Human skill.—*A Midsummer-Night's Dream,* ii, 2, 119.
Simple skill.—*Two Gentlemen of Verona,* i, 2, 8; *A Midsummer-Night's Dream,* v, 1, 110.
Sufficient skill.—*I Henry VI,* v, 5, 13.
Utmost skill.—*Pericles,* v, 1, 76.
Wondrous skill.—*The Rape of Lucrece,* l. 1528.
Vulcan's skill.—*Troilus and Cressida,* v, 2, 170.

3
Go you with me, and I will use your skill.
Much Ado about Nothing. Act i, sc. 2, l. 27. [Leonato]

4
Drawn by your own sweet skill.
Sonnets. No. xvi.

They had not skill enough your worth to sing.
Sonnets. No. cvi.

5
Skilless as unpractised infancy.
Troilus and Cressida, i, 1, 12. [Troilus]

Skilless in these parts.—*Twelfth Night,* iii, 3, 9.
I am skilless.—*The Tempest,* iii, 1, 53.
Skilless soldier.—*Romeo and Juliet,* iii, 3, 132. The only uses of "skilless."

SKIN

6
Tear the stain'd skin off my harlot-brow.
The Comedy of Errors. Act ii, sc. 2, l. 138. [Adriana] The only use of "harlot-brow."

7
My skin hangs about me like an old lady's loose gown.
I Henry IV, iii, 3, 3. See under THINNESS.

8
The skin is good for your broken coxcomb.
Henry V. Act v, sc. 1, l. 57. [Fluellen] Referring to the leek.

9
He shall have the skins of our enemies, to make dog's-leather of.
II Henry VI. Act iv, sc. 2, l. 25. [Bevis] The only use of "dog's-leather."

10
The skin of an innocent lamb.
II Henry VI, iv, 2, 86. See under LAWYER.

Skin of our fruit trees.—*Richard II,* iii, 4, 58.
Skins of ill-shaped fishes.—*Romeo and Juliet,* v, 1, 43. The only use of "ill-shaped."
Calf's skin.—*The Comedy of Errors,* iv, 3, 18.
Lion's skin.—*Henry V,* iv, 3, 93.
Murderer's skin.—*King John,* iv, 3, 80.
Enamell'd skin.—*A Midsummer-Night's Dream,* ii, 1, 255.
Leather skin.—*As You Like It,* iv, 2, 12.
Painted skin.—*Taming of the Shrew,* iv, 3, 180.

11
His silver skin laced with his golden blood.
Macbeth, ii, 3, 118. See STAB, 1437:14.

Your skins are whole.—*The Merry Wives of Windsor,* iii, 1, 111.

12
That termless skin
Whose bare out-bragg'd the bare it seem'd to wear.
A Lover's Complaint, l. 94. See under BEARD. The only use of "termless" and "out-bragg'd."

13
That whiter skin of hers than snow,
And smooth as monumental alabaster.
Othello. Act v, sc. 2, l. 4. [Othello]

Her alabaster skin.—*Rape of Lucrece,* l. 419.

14
He'll fill our skins with pinches.
The Tempest. Act iv, sc. 1, l. 233. [Caliban]

SKULL

15
That skull had a tongue in it, and could sing once.
Hamlet. Act v, sc. 1, l. 83. [Hamlet]

Here's a skull now; this skull has lain in the earth three and twenty years.
Hamlet. Act v, sc. 1, l. 189. [First Clown]

This same skull, sir, was Yorick's skull.
Hamlet. Act v, sc. 1, l. 198. [Clown]

Dead men's skulls.—*Richard III,* i, 4, 29; *Richard II,* iv, 1, 144.
Eyeless skulls.—*Romeo and Juliet,* v, 3, 126.
Yellow chapless skulls.—*Romeo and Juliet,* iv, 1, 83.

SKY

See also Heavens, Welkin

16
Freeze, freeze, thou bitter sky.
As You Like It, ii, 7, 184. See under BENEFITS.

Clear sky.—*II Henry IV,* iv, 3, 56.
Covering sky.—*The Winter's Tale,* i, 2, 294.
Dusky sky.—*II Henry VI,* iii, 2, 104.
Empty skies.—*Venus and Adonis,* l. 1191.
Lither sky.—*I Henry VI,* iv, 7, 21. The only use of "lither" (yielding).
Pale clear-shining sky.—*III Henry VI,* ii, 1, 28. The only use of "clear-shining."
Western sky.—*The Two Gentlemen of Verona,* v, 1, 1.

17
This brave o'erhanging firmament, this majestical roof fretted with golden fire, why, it appears no other thing to me than a foul and pestilent congregation of vapours.
Hamlet. Act ii, sc. 2, l. 312. [Hamlet] The only use of "o'erhanging."

The sky that hangs above our heads.
King John. Act ii, sc. 1, l. 397. [King John]

18
This disturbed sky Is not to walk in.
Julius Cæsar. Act i, sc. 3, l. 39. [Cicero]

The wrathful skies
Gallow the very wanderers of the dark,
And make them keep their caves.
King Lear. Act iii, sc. 2, l. 43. [Kent] The only use of "gallow."

19
Cælo, the sky, the welkin, the heaven.
Love's Labour's Lost. Act iv, sc. 2, l. 5.

[Holofernes] The only use of "cælo." See also WELKIN.

Aerial blue.—*Othello,* ii, 1, 39. The only use of "aerial."

1
Let the sky rain potatoes; let it thunder to the tune of Green Sleeves, hail kissing-comfits and snow eringoes; let there come a tempest of provocation, I will shelter me here.

The Merry Wives of Windsor. Act v, sc. 5, l. 22. [Falstaff] The only use of "potatoes," "kissing-comfits," and "eringoes." A kissing-comfit is a perfumed sweet-meat made of the candied root of the sea-eryngo, supposed to be an aphrodisiac. The ballad of *The Lady Greensleeves* was included in *A Handful of Pleasant Ditties,* published in 1584.

2
Men judge by the complexion of the sky
The state and inclination of the day.

Richard II. Act iii, sc. 2, l. 194. [Scroop]

3
The sky doth frown and lour.

Richard III. Act v, sc. 3, l. 283. [King Richard]

The skies were sorry.—*The Rape of Lucrece,* l. 1524.

4
The skies look grimly
And threaten present blusters.

The Winter's Tale. Act iii, sc. 3, l. 3. [Mariner] "Grimly" is repeated in *Antony and Cleopatra,* iv, 12, 5. The only use of "blusters." "Bluster" occurs in *Timon of Athens,* v, 4, 41: "Bluster of thy wrath."

SLANDER

See also Calumny, Gossip, Rumour

5
Tax of impudence,
A strumpet's boldness, a divulged shame
Traduced by odious ballads: my maiden's name
Sear'd otherwise.

All's Well that Ends Well. Act ii, sc. 1, l. 173. [Helena]

I am
Traduced by ignorant tongues, which neither know
My faculties nor person.

Henry VIII. Act i, sc. 2, l. 71. [Wolsey]

Traduced for levity.—*Antony and Cleopatra,* iii, 7, 14.

Traduced and tax'd of other nations.—*Hamlet,* i, 4, 18.

Traduced the state.—*Othello,* v, 2, 354. The only uses of "traduced." "Traduce" does not occur.

No less than a traducement.—*Coriolanus,* i, 9, 22. The only use of "traducement."

6
Spoke scantly of me.

Antony and Cleopatra. Act iii, sc. 4, l. 6. [Antony] The only use of "scantly."

7
A vulgar comment will be made of it,
And that supposed by the common rout
Against your yet ungalled estimation
That may with foul intrusion enter in
And dwell upon your grave when you are dead;
For slander lives upon succession,
For ever housed where it gets possession.

The Comedy of Errors. Act iii, sc. 1, l. 100. [Balthazar] "Ungalled" occurs again in *Hamlet,* iii, 2, 283.

Free from these slanders and this open shame!

The Comedy of Errors, iv, 4, 70. [Adriana]

8
You slander
The helms o' the state, who care for you like fathers,
When you curse them as enemies.

Coriolanus. Act i, sc. 1, l. 78. [Menenius]

9
Thou wrong'st a gentleman, who is as far
From thy report as thou from honour, and
Solicit'st here a lady that disdains
Thee and the devil alike.

Cymbeline. Act i, sc. 6, l. 145. [Imogen]

'Tis slander,
Whose edge is sharper than the sword, whose tongue
Outvenoms all the worms of Nile, whose breath
Rides on the posting winds and doth belie
All corners of the world: kings, queens and states,
Maids, matrons, nay, the secrets of the grave
This viperous slander enters.

Cymbeline. Act iii, sc. 4, l. 35. [Pisanio] The only use of "outvenoms."

Guiderius: Fear not slander, censure rash;
Arviragus: Thou hast finish'd joy and moan.

Cymbeline. Act iv, sc. 2, l. 272.

10
Put on him What forgeries you please.

Hamlet. Act ii, sc. 1, l. 19. [Polonius]

Forgeries of jealousy.—*A Midsummer-Night's Dream,* ii, 1, 81. The only uses of "forgeries."

11
Whose whisper o'er the world's diameter,
As level as the cannon to his blank,
Transports his poison'd shot, may miss our name,
And hit the woundless air.

Hamlet. Act iv, sc. 1, l. 41. [King] The only use of "diameter" and "woundless."

[He] wants not buzzers to infect his ear
With pestilent speeches of his father's death;
Wherein necessity, of matter beggar'd,
Will nothing stick our person to arraign
In ear and ear. O my dear Gertrude, this,
Like to a murdering-piece, in many places
Gives me superfluous death.

Hamlet. Act iv, sc. 5, l. 90. [King] The only use of "buzzers" and "murdering-piece."

12
Thou dost belie him, Percy, thou dost belie him.

I Henry IV. Act i, sc. 3, l. 113. [King Henry]

Thou dost belie her.—*Othello,* v, 2, 133.

To belie him, I will not.—*All's Well that Ends Well,* iv, 3, 299.

13
Many tales devised,
Which oft the ear of greatness needs must hear,
By smiling pick-thanks and base newsmongers.

I Henry IV. Act iii, sc. 2, l. 23. [Prince] Only use of "pick-thanks" and "newsmongers."

He speaks most vilely of you, like a foul-mouthed man as he is.
I Henry IV. Act iii, sc. 3, l. 121. [Hostess] "Foul-mouthed" is repeated in *All's Well that Ends Well*, i, 3, 60: "Foul-mouthed knave."

Hostess: Thou or any man knows where to have me, thou knave, thou!
Prince of Wales: Thou sayest true, hostess; and he slanders thee most grossly.
I Henry IV. Act iii, sc. 3, l. 146.

Do me no slander, Douglas.
I Henry IV. Act iv, sc. 3, l. 8. [Vernon]
No slander.—*Antony and Cleopatra*, ii, 6, 106.

1
I dispraised him before the wicked, that the wicked might not fall in love with him.
II Henry IV. Act ii, sc. 4, l. 346. [Falstaff]
I have dispraised Cæsar.—*Antony and Cleopatra*, ii, 5, 107. "Dispraised" is used a third time in *Two Gentlemen of Verona*, iv, 4, 107.
I have spoken of you dispraisingly.
Othello, iii, 3, 72. Only use of "dispraisingly."

2
Venom of suggestion.
II Henry IV. Act iv, sc. 4, l. 45. [King Henry]

3
You must learn to know such slanders of the age, or else you may be marvellously mistook.
Henry V. Act iii, sc. 6, l. 84. [Gower]

4
So shall my name with slander's tongue be wounded,
And princes' courts be fill'd with my reproach.
II Henry VI. Act iii, sc. 2, l. 68. [Queen]
Every word you speak in his behalf
Is slander to your royal dignity.
II Henry VI. Act iii, sc. 2, l. 208. [Warwick]

5
If thou canst for blushing, view this face,
And bite thy tongue, that slanders him with cowardice
Whose frown hath made thee faint and fly e'er this!
III Henry VI. Act i, sc. 4, l. 46. [York]

6
That slander, sir,
Is found a truth now: for it grows again
Fresher than ere it was.
Henry VIII. Act ii, sc. 1, l. 153. [Gentleman]

7
Queen Elinor: Thou monstrous slanderer of heaven and earth!
Constance: Thou monstrous injurer of heaven and earth!
Call not me slanderer.
King John. Act ii, sc. 1, l. 173. The only use of "injurer."
O, fie upon thee, slanderer!
Othello. Act ii, sc. 1, l. 114. [Desdemona] "Slanderer" occurs a third time in *Troilus and Cressida*, i, 3, 150. "Slanderers" is used in *Measure for Measure*, v, 1, 259, and in *Sonnets*, cxl.

8
Perge, good Master Holofernes, perge; so it shall please you to abrogate scurrility.
Love's Labour's Lost. Act iv, sc. 2, l. 54. [Sir Nathaniel] The only use of "perge" (continue), and "abrogate."
Pleasant without scurrility.—*Love's Labour's Lost*, v, 1, 4. The only uses of "scurrility." "Scurrilous" occurs in *The Winter's Tale*, iv, 4, 215.

9
Dost thou infamonize me among potentates? thou shalt die.
Love's Labour's Lost. Act v, sc. 2, l. 684. [Armado] The only use of "infamonize."

10
Thy slanders I forgive; and therewithal
Remit thy other forfeits.
Measure for Measure, v, 1, 525. [Duke]

11
His gift is in devising impossible slanders.
Much Ado about Nothing. Act ii, sc. 1, l. 143. [Beatrice] The only use of "devising."
And, truly, I 'll devise some honest slanders
To stain my cousin with: one doth not know
How much an ill word may empoison liking.
Much Ado about Nothing. Act iii, sc. 1, l. 84. [Hero] The only use of "empoison." "Empoisoned" occurs in *Coriolanus*, v, 6, 11.
Uncovered slander.—*Much Ado about Nothing*, iv, 1, 307.

12
She is wronged, she is slandered, she is undone.
Much Ado about Nothing. Act iv, sc. 1, l. 314. [Beatrice]

13
I say thou hast belied mine innocent child;
Thy slander hath gone through and through her heart,
And she lies buried with her ancestors;
O, in a tomb where never scandal slept,
Save this of hers, framed by thy villany!
Much Ado about Nothing. Act v, sc. 1, l. 67. [Leonato]
And she is dead, slander'd to death by villains,
That dare as well answer a man indeed
As I dare take a serpent by the tongue:
Boys, apes, braggarts, Jacks, milksops!
Much Ado about Nothing. Act v, sc. 1, l. 88. [Antonio] The only use of "milksops." "Milksop" occurs in *Richard III*, v, 3, 325.

Don Pedro: What offence have these men done?
Dogberry: Marry, sir, they have committed false report; moreover, they have spoken untruths; secondarily, they are slanders; sixth and lastly, they have belied a lady; thirdly, they have verified unjust things.
Much Ado about Nothing. Act v, sc. 1, l. 217. The only use of "secondarily."

I have belied a lady,
The princess of this country, and the air on 't
Revengingly enfeebles me.
Cymbeline. Act v, sc. 2, l. 2. [Iachimo] The only use of "revengingly."

14
If thou dost slander her and torture me,
Never pray more.
Othello. Act iii, sc. 3, l. 368. [Othello]
I will be hang'd, if some eternal villain,
Some busy and insinuating rogue,
Some cogging, cozening slave, to get some office,
Have not devised this slander.
Othello. Act iv, sc. 2, l. 130. [Emilia]

15
This slander of his blood.
Richard II. Act i, sc. 1, l. 113. [Mowbray]

Slander of his wife.—*As You Like It,* iv, 1, 61.
Slander to the state!—*Measure for Measure,* v, 1, 325.
Slander her love.—*Merchant of Venice,* v, 1, 22.

1
I am disgraced, impeach'd and baffled here,
Pierced to the soul with slander's venom'd spear,
The which no balm can cure but his heart-blood
Which breathed this poison.
Richard II. Act i, sc. 1, l. 170. [Mowbray] The only use of "impeach'd."

Alas, poor fool, how have they baffled thee!
Twelfth Night. Act v, sc. 1, l. 377. [Olivia] "Baffled" is used a third time in *II Henry IV,* v, 3, 109.

2
A partial slander sought I to avoid,
And in the sentence my own life destroy'd.
Richard II. Act i, sc. 3, l. 241. [Gaunt]

3
O, do not slander him, for he is kind.
Richard III. Act i, sc. 4, l. 247. [Clarence]

4
I was provoked by her slanderous tongue.
Richard III. Act i, sc. 2, l. 97. [Gloucester]

Done to death by slanderous tongues.
Much Ado about Nothing. Act v, sc. 3, l. 3. [Claudio] "Slanderous tongues" occurs also in *Measure for Measure,* iii, 2, 199, and *The Rape of Lucrece,* l. 161.

The serpent's tongue.—*A Midsummer-Night's Dream,* v, 1, 440.

One that is as slanderous as Satan?
The Merry Wives of Windsor. Act v, sc. 5, l. 163. [Ford]

Ugly and slanderous.—*King John,* iii, 1, 44.
Slanderous coward.—*Richard II,* i, 1, 61.
Slanderous epitaph.—*Cymbeline,* iii, 3, 52.
Slanderous lips.—*Richard II,* iv, 1, 24.

5
The envious slanders of her false accusers.
Richard III. Act i, sc. 3, l. 26. [Derby]

6
Cannot a plain man live and think no harm,
But thus his simple truth must be abused
By silken, sly, insinuating Jacks?
Richard III. Act i, sc. 3, l. 51. [Gloucester]

Slander myself as false to Edward's bed.
Richard III, iv, 4, 207. See under DAUGHTER.

7
That is no slander, sir, which is a truth.
Romeo and Juliet. Act iv, sc. 1, l. 33. [Juliet]

8
Slander 's mark was ever yet the fair.
Sonnets. No. lxx.

So thou be good, slander doth but approve
Thy worth the greater.
Sonnets. No. lxx.

Slandering creation with a false esteem.
Sonnets. No. cxxvii. "Slandering" is repeated in *Measure for Measure,* v, 1, 530: "Slandering a prince deserves it" [hanging].

9
A slave whose gall coins slander like a mint,
To match us in comparisons with dirt,
To weaken and discredit our exposure,
How rank soever rounded in with danger.
Troilus and Cressida. Act i, sc. 3, l. 193. [Nestor] "Exposure" is repeated in *Macbeth,* ii, 3, 133.

10
There is no slander in an allowed fool, though he do nothing but rail.
Twelfth Night. Act i, sc. 5, l. 101. [Olivia]

11
You must undertake to slander him.
The Two Gentlemen of Verona. Act iii, sc. 2, l. 38. [Duke]

Where your good word cannot advantage him,
Your slander never can endamage him.
The Two Gentlemen of Verona. Act iii, sc. 2, l. 42. [Duke] "Endamage" is used again in *I Henry VI,* ii, 1, 77.

12
Slander
Whose sting is sharper than the sword's.
Winter's Tale. Act ii, sc. 3, l. 85. [Paulina]

SLANG

See also Familiar Phrases

A

13
Up in the air.—*Henry V,* ii, 4, 58.
Let 's along.—*The Winter's Tale,* v, 2, 121.
He 's another.—*Cymbeline,* ii, 1, 43.
You are such another!—*Troilus and Cressida,* i, 2, 297.
Come with your appendix.—*The Taming of the Shrew,* iv, 4, 104. The only use of "appendix."

B

14
You 'll bear me a bang for that, I fear.
Julius Cæsar, iii, 3, 20. The only use of "bang."

Beat it hence!—*Comedy of Errors,* ii, 1, 102.
I am . . . besides myself.—*The Comedy of Errors,* iii, 2, 79.
They must blab.—*Othello,* iv, 1, 29. "Blab" is repeated in *II Henry VI,* iii, 1, 154, and in *Twelfth Night,* i, 2, 63.
Why have I blabb'd?—*Troilus and Cressida,* iii, 2, 132. "Blabb'd" is repeated in *Titus Andronicus,* iii, 1, 83, and "blabbing" occurs in *II Henry VI,* iv, 1, 1.
Blow you up.—*All's Well that Ends Well,* i, 1, 130.
O boy.—*King John,* iii, 1, 34.
Good boy.—*Troilus and Cressida,* i, 2, 301.
I am a bunch of radish.—*I Henry IV,* ii, 4, 206. "Radish" is repeated in *II Henry IV,* iii, 2, 334.
But what though?—*As You Like It,* iii, 3, 51.
Buz, buz!—*Hamlet,* ii, 2, 412.

C

15
What cheer?
The Taming of the Shrew, iv, 3, 37; *A Midsummer-Night's Dream,* i, 1, 122; *The Winter's Tale,* i, 2, 148; *Timon of Athens,* iii, 6, 44.

Chew upon this.—*Julius Cæsar,* i, 2, 171. "Chew" is used only once more, in *Measure for Measure,* ii, 4, 5.
Cobloaf!—*Troilus and Cressida,* ii, 1, 41. The only use of the word.
I can cross it.—*Much Ado about Nothing,* ii, 2, 3.

I am custom-shrunk.—*Measure for Measure,* i, 2, 85. The only use of the phrase, meaning having fewer customers.
Cut the cable.—*Antony and Cleopatra,* ii, 7, 78.
Come cut and long-tail.—*The Merry Wives of Windsor,* iii, 4, 47. The only use of "long-tail."

D

1
What the dickens.
Merry Wives of Windsor, iii, 2, 19. The only use of "dickens."

E

2
That 's the even of it.
Henry V, ii, 1, 128.

F

3
How will this fadge?
Twelfth Night. Act ii, sc. 2, l. 34. [Viola]
If this fadge not.—*Love's Labour 's Lost,* v, 1, 154. The only uses of "fadge" (fit).
4
We will fall for it.—*Julius Cæsar,* ii, 1, 128.
Fallen flat-long.—*The Tempest,* ii, 1, 181. The only use of "flat-long."
There 's a fellow.—*Troilus and Cressida,* i, 2, 216.
A fig for Peter!—*II Henry VI,* ii, 3, 67.
5
That 's flat.
Love's Labour 's Lost, iii, 1, 102; *I Henry IV,* i, 3, 218; iv, 2, 43.
6
I am for it.—*Othello,* ii, 3, 89.
I am for thee.—*Taming of the Shrew,* iv, 3, 152.
I am for you.—*Romeo and Juliet,* i, 1, 61; iii, 1, 86; *Much Ado about Nothing,* ii, 1, 387; *Twelfth Night,* iii, 4, 350; *Othello,* i, 2, 58; *The Winter's Tale,* ii, 1, 22.
They are for you.—*The Two Gentlemen of Verona,* ii, 1, 131.
We are for you.—*As You Like It,* v, 3, 10.

G

7
I can gleek upon occasion.
A Midsummer-Night's Dream, iii, 1, 150. "Gleek" (gibe) is repeated in *I Henry VI,* iii, 2, 123, and in *Romeo and Juliet,* iv, 5, 115. "Gleeking" occurs in *Henry V,* v, 1, 78.
Hence, old goat!—*Coriolanus,* iii, 1, 177.
Not so good.—*Much Ado about Nothing,* iii, 4, 9.
If he fall in, good night!—*I Henry IV,* i, 3, 194.
Good night our part!—*The Taming of the Shrew,* ii, 1, 303.
Good night to your redress!—*Measure for Measure,* v, 1, 301.
Good night your vow!—*The Tempest,* iv, 1, 54.

H

8
You have me, have you not?
Hamlet. Act ii, sc. 1, l. 68. [Polonius]
Fain to shuffle, to hedge.—*The Merry Wives of Windsor,* ii, 2, 26. See under HONOUR for full quotation.
A hell of time.—*Sonnets,* cxx.
O hell!—*A Midsummer-Night's Dream,* iii, 2, 145
Be my hen.—*Taming of the Shrew,* ii, 1, 227.
Hob, nob, is his word; give 't or take 't. *Twelfth Night,* iii, 4, 263.
Hold hook and line, say I.—*II Henry IV,* ii, 4, 171.
Hold or cut bow-strings.—*A Midsummer-Night's Dream,* i, 2, 114.
Not too hot.—*Cymbeline,* v, 5, 321.
How goes it?—*Othello,* iv, 3, 11; *Antony and Cleopatra,* i, 5, 38; v, 2, 332; *Macbeth,* iv, 3, 180; *The Winter's Tale,* v, 2, 29.
Well, and how?—*Troilus and Cressida,* i, 3, 320.
Well, how then?—*I Henry IV,* i, 2, 24.
Hoy-day! spirits and fires!—*Troilus and Cressida,* v, 1, 74.

K

9
This is clean kam.
Coriolanus, iii, 1, 304. The only use of "kam" (quite wrong).
'Twere good you knocked him.—*The Two Gentlemen of Verona,* ii, 4, 7.

L

10
He lays it on.
The Tempest, iii, 2, 160.
She lays it on.—*The Winter's Tale,* iv, 3, 43.
That was laid on with a trowel.—*As You Like It,* i, 2, 112. The only use of "trowel."
Hard luck.—*The Winter's Tale,* v, 2, 158.

M

11
They 'll make it good.
II Henry VI, v, 1, 122.
How now! whose mare 's dead?—*II Henry IV,* ii, 1, 46.
Hold up your head, and mince.—*The Merry Wives of Windsor,* v, 1, 8.

N

12
You come near me now.
I Henry IV, i, 2, 14.
Not in 't.—*Cymbeline,* iii, 4, 141; *The Winter's Tale,* iv, 4, 336.

P

13
Be packing.
I Henry VI, iv, 1, 46.
Pauca, there 's enough.—*Henry V,* ii, 1, 83.
I 'll peach for this.—*I Henry IV,* ii, 2, 47.
A pretty peat!—*The Taming of the Shrew,* i, 1, 78.
I 'll pheeze you, in faith.—*The Taming of the Shrew,* Ind., 1, 1.
I 'll pheeze his pride.—*Troilus and Cressida,* ii, 3, 215.
Thou art pinch'd for 't now.—*The Tempest,* v, 1, 74.
Being perhaps . . . a pip out?—*The Taming of the Shrew,* i, 2, 33.
I will advise you where to plant yourselves. *Macbeth,* iii, 1, 129.
Pluck off a little.—*Henry VIII,* ii, 3, 40.
Pow wow.—*Coriolanus,* ii, 1, 157.
The prenzie Angelo!—*Measure for Measure,* iii, 1, 94.
Goodman Puff.—*II Henry IV,* v, 3, 93.
I stand the push.—*II Henry IV,* ii, 2, 40.

You have put him down.—*Much Ado about Nothing,* ii, 1, 292.

R

1 What, dear sir, Thus raps you?
Cymbeline, i, 6, 50.
It is a riot.—*Merry Wives of Windsor,* i, 1, 35.

S

2 I 'll sauce them.
The Merry Wives of Windsor, iv, 3, 11. See under SAUCINESS.
Say, when?—*The Merchant of Venice,* i, 1, 66.
Thou 'rt a good scab.—*II Henry IV,* iii, 2, 295.
Shift away.—*Macbeth,* ii, 3, 151.
Will you shog off? I would have you solus.—*Henry V,* ii, 1, 47. "Solus" is repeated in ll. 49 and 54, and occurs in no other scene.
Shall we shog?—*Henry V,* ii, 3, 47. "Shog" is used in no other play, and is spoken only by Nym.
Sneck up!—*Twelfth Night,* ii, 3, 101. The only use of the phrase, which means "Go hang!"
Soused.—*I Henry IV,* iv, 2, 12. The only use of the word, meaning "pickled."
Spread yourselves.—*A Midsummer-Night's Dream,* i, 2, 16.
Are you such fools To square for this?
Titus Andronicus, ii, 1, 99.
Square our guess.—*All 's Well that Ends Well,* ii, 1, 153. See under KNOWLEDGE for full quotation.
Square the sex.—*Troilus and Cressida,* v, 2, 132. See under WOMAN for full quotation.
Square yourselves.—*Titus Andronicus,* ii, 1, 124.
I will be squared by this.—*The Winter's Tale,* iii, 3, 41.
It grows something stale with me.—*As You Like It,* ii, 4, 63.
More than half stewed.—*The Merry Wives of Windsor,* iii, 5, 121.
I may be straight, though they themselves be bevel.—*Sonnets,* cxxi.
You strain too far.—*I Henry IV,* iv, 1, 75.

T

3 He 'll tickle it for concupy.
Troilus and Cressida. Act v, sc. 2, l. 177. [Thersites] The only use of "concupy," a contraction of concupiscence.
Tilly-fally, Sir John.—*II Henry IV,* ii, 4, 90.
Tillyvally.—*Twelfth Night,* ii, 3, 83.
O, this is trim!—*Troilus and Cressida,* iv, 5, 33.

W

4 Let them wag; trot, trot.
The Merry Wives of Windsor, i, 3, 6. Shall we wag?—ii, 1, 238. Let him wag.—ii, 3, 74. Let us wag.—ii, 3, 101. This is the only play in which "wag" is used in this sense, and in every case it is so used by mine Host of the Garter.
It is not the wear.—*Measure for Measure,* iii, 2, 77.
One by one, we 'll weed them all at last.—*II Henry VI,* i, 3, 102.
I smell it: upon my life, it will do well.—*I Henry IV,* i, 3, 277.
Where the devil should this Romeo be?—*Romeo and Juliet,* ii, 4, 1.
Wherefore, what 's the instance?—*All 's Well that Ends Well,* iv, 1, 44.
I am with you.—*II Henry VI,* ii, 1, 48.
Poor worm!—*The Tempest,* iii, 1, 31. Repeated in *Measure for Measure,* iii, 1, 17, and in *Pericles,* i, 1, 102.

SLAUGHTER

See also Murder

5 Great the slaughter is
Here made by the Roman; great the answer be
Britons must take.
Cymbeline. Act v, sc. 3, l. 78. [Posthumus]
Appeased with slaughter.—*Cymbeline,* v, 5, 72.

6 The cowardly rascals that ran from the battle ha' done this slaughter.
Henry V. Act iv, sc. 7, l. 6. [Gower]
'Twas he that made the slaughter.
II Henry VI, iii, 2, 190. See under EVIDENCE.

7 Most of the rest slaughter'd or took likewise.
I Henry VI. Act i, sc. 1, l. 147. [Messenger]
Slaughter'd by the ireful arm
Of unrelenting Clifford.
III Henry VI. Act ii, sc. 1, l. 57. [Messenger]
Slaughter'd by thy foes.—*I Henry VI,* iii, 1, 101.

8 That slaughterer . . .
Which giveth many wounds when one will kill.
I Henry VI. Act ii, sc. 5, l. 109. [Mortimer] The only use of "slaughterer."

9 The slaughter of so many peers,
So many captains, gentlemen and soldiers.
I Henry VI, v, 4, 103. See under PATRIOTISM
Such massacre
And ruthless slaughter as are daily seen.
I Henry VI. Act v, sc. 4, l. 160. [Alençon]

10 I say not, slaughter him,
For I intend but only to surprise him.
III Henry VI. Act iv, sc. 2, l. 24. [Warwick]
I 'll slaughter thee.—*Rape of Lucrece,* l. 1634.

11 Or add a royal number to the dead,
Gracing the scroll that tells of this war's loss
With slaughter coupled to the name of kings.
King John. Act ii, sc. 1, l. 347. [King Philip] The only use of "gracing."
Even before this truce, but new before,
No longer than we well could wash our hands
To clap this royal bargain up of peace,
Heaven knows, they were besmear'd and over-stain'd
With slaughter's pencil.
King John. Act iii, sc. 1, l. 233. [King Philip] The only use of "over-stain'd."

12 Not for their own demerits, but for mine,
Fell slaughter on their souls.
Macbeth. Act iv, sc. 3, l. 226. [Macduff] "Demerits" is repeated in *Coriolanus,* i, 1, 276, and in *Othello,* i, 2, 22.

1 Such a piece of slaughter
The sun and moon ne'er look'd upon!
Pericles. Act iv, sc. 3, l. 2. [Cleon]

2
Thy brother's love, our duty and thy fault,
Provoke us hither now to slaughter thee. . . .
'Tis he that sent us hither now to slaughter thee.
Richard III. Act i, sc. 4, l. 230. [Murderer]

Your carters or your waiting-vassals
Have done a drunken slaughter.
Richard III. Act ii, sc. 1, l. 121. [King Edward] "Carters" is repeated in *Hamlet,* ii, 2, 167, and in *The Winter's Tale,* iv, 4, 331. The only use of "waiting-vassals."

Bleeding slaughter.—*Richard III,* iv, 4, 209.
Casual slaughters.—*Hamlet,* v, 2, 393.
Dying slaughter.—*King John,* ii, 1, 323.
Human slaughter.—*The Merchant of Venice,* iv, 1, 134.
Unworthy slaughter.—*Richard III,* i, 2, 88.
Priam's slaughter.—*Hamlet,* ii, 2, 469.

3
One that made means to come by what he hath,
And slaughter'd those that were the means to help him.
Richard III. Act v, sc. 3, l. 248. [Richmond]

SLAUGHTER-HOUSE, see Butcher

SLAVERY

See also Bondage

I—Slavery

4
These strong Egyptian fetters I must break,
Or lose myself in dotage.
Antony and Cleopatra. Act i, sc. 2, l. 120. [Antony]

We will fetters put upon this fear.—*Hamlet,* iii, 3, 25.
Fetter strong madness.—*Much Ado about Nothing,* v, 1, 25.
Fetter him.—*Titus Andronicus,* v, 3, 6.
Fetter you till death.—*Measure for Measure,* iii, 1, 67.
Fetter'd in amorous chains.—*Titus Andronicus,* ii, 1, 15.
Fetter'd in our prisons.—*Henry V,* i, 2, 243.

5
Delight to live in slavery.
II Henry VI. Act iv, sc. 8, l. 29. [Cade]

Free us from his slavery.—*Henry VIII,* ii, 2, 44.

6 Taken by the insolent foe
And sold to slavery.
Othello. Act i, sc. 3, l. 137. [Othello]

7
Shake off our slavish yoke.
Richard II. Act ii, sc. 1, l. 291. [Northumberland]

Slavish motive.—*Richard II,* i, 1, 193.
Slavish parts.—*Merchant of Venice,* iv, 1, 92.
Slavish tribute.—*The Rape of Lucrece,* l. 299.
Slavish weeds.—*Titus Andronicus,* ii, 1, 18.
Slave-like habit.—*Timon of Athens,* iv, 3, 205. The only use of "slave-like."

8
But slave to slavery my sweet'st friend must be.
Sonnets. No. cxxxiii.

9 I . . . would no more endure
This wooden slavery than to suffer
The flesh-fly blow my mouth.
The Tempest. Act iii, sc. 1, l. 61. [Ferdinand] The only use of "flesh-fly."

II—Slaves

10
What a past-saving slave is this!
All's Well that Ends Well. Act iv, sc. 3, l. 158. [Bertram] The only use of "past-saving."

He 's quoted for a most perfidious slave,
With all the spots o' the world tax'd and debosh'd;
Whose nature sickens but to speak a truth.
All's Well that Ends Well. Act v, sc. 3, l. 205. [Bertram]

A base slave,
A hilding for a livery, a squire's cloth,
A pantler, not so eminent.
Cymbeline. Act ii, sc. 3, l. 127. [Cloten] "Hilding" (good-for-nothing) is used six times, and "pantler" (a servant in charge of the pantry) four times.

Base slave.—*II Henry VI,* iv, 1, 67; *Coriolanus,* i, 5, 8.
Abhorred slave.—*The Tempest,* i, 2, 351.
Banditto slave.—*II Henry VI,* iv, 1, 135. The only use of "banditto."
Black slave.—*Titus Andronicus,* iv, 2, 120.
Barbarian slave.—*Troilus and Cressida,* ii, 1, 52.
Cogging, cozening slave.—*Othello,* iv, 2, 132.
Cold-blooded slave.—*King John,* iii, 1, 123. The only use of "cold-blooded."
Common slave.—*Julius Cæsar,* i, 3, 15.
Cursed slave!—*Othello,* v, 2, 276.
Damn'd slave.—*Othello,* v, 2, 243; v, 2, 292.
Devilish slave.—*Richard III,* i, 2, 90.
Drunken slave.—*Comedy of Errors,* iv, 1, 96.
False deluding slave.—*The Taming of the Shrew,* iv, 3, 31. "Deluding" is repeated in *Othello,* i, 1, 141.
Hare-brain'd slaves.—*I Henry VI,* i, 2, 37. "Hare-brain'd" occurs again in *I Henry IV,* v, 2, 19.
Knee slaves.—*Timon of Athens,* iii, 6, 107.
Lying slave.—*The Tempest,* i, 2, 344.
Mechanic slaves.—*Antony and Cleopatra,* v, 2, 209.
Mindless slave.—*The Winter's Tale,* i, 2, 301.
Murderous slave!—*Othello,* v, 1, 61.
Neat slave.—*King Lear,* ii, 2, 45.
Oft-subdued slaves.—*I Henry VI,* i, 5, 32. The only use of "oft-subdued."
One-trunk-inheriting slave.—*King Lear,* ii, 2, 20. The only use of the phrase.
Overweening slave!—*The Two Gentlemen of Verona,* iii, 1, 157.
Peasant slave.—*Hamlet,* ii, 2, 576.
Pernicious slave.—*Comedy of Errors,* v, 1, 241.
Present slaves.—*Timon of Athens,* i, 1, 71.
Quarter'd slaves.—*Coriolanus,* i, 1, 203.
Rascal bragging slave!—*II Henry IV,* ii, 4, 247.
Rascally slave!—*II Henry IV,* ii, 4, 240.
Rude slaves.—*Henry VIII,* v, 4, 3.

Sad slave.—*Sonnets,* lvii.
Silken-coated slaves.—*II Henry VI,* iv, 2, 136. The only use of "silken-coated."
Thick-lipp'd slave.—*Titus Andronicus,* iv, 2, 175. The only use of "thick-lipp'd."
Transgressing slave.—*Love's Labour's Lost,* i, 2, 159. "Transgressing" is repeated in *Richard II,* v, 3, 96: "Transgressing boy."
Unhallow'd slave!—*Titus Andronicus,* v, 3, 14.
Unmanner'd slaves.—*The Taming of the Shrew,* iv, 1, 169. "Unmanner'd" is repeated in *Richard III,* i, 2, 39: "Unmanner'd dog."
Unmannerly slave.—*The Two Gentlemen of Verona,* iii, 1, 393.
Wall-eyed slave.—*Titus Andronicus,* v, 1, 44. "Wall-eyed" is repeated in *King John,* iv, 3, 49: "Wall-eyed wrath."
Warm slaves.—*I Henry IV,* iv, 2, 19.
Weak slave.—*Romeo and Juliet,* i, 1, 17.
Worthless slave.—*The Rape of Lucrece,* l. 515.
Wretched slave.—*Henry V,* iv, 1, 285.
Yellow slave.—*Timon of Athens,* iv, 3, 33. Referring to gold.

1
Cloten: What slave art thou?
Guiderius: A thing
More slavish did I ne'er than answering
A slave without a knock.
Cymbeline. Act iv, sc. 2, l. 72.

What a slave art thou!—*I Henry IV,* ii, 4, 288.

2
I to live and die her slave.
As You Like It. Act iii, sc. 2, l. 162. [Celia, reading]

3
A slave that is not twentieth part the tithe
Of your precedent lord.
Hamlet. Act iii, sc. 4, l. 97. [Hamlet]

4
Slaves as ragged as Lazarus in the painted cloth, where the glutton's dogs licked his sores.
I Henry IV. Act iv, sc. 2, l. 27. [Falstaff] The only mention of Lazarus.

5
This is a slave, whose easy-borrow'd pride
Dwells in the fickle grace of her he follows.
King Lear. Act ii, sc. 4, l. 188. [King Lear] The only use of "easy-borrow'd."

Persuade me rather to be slave and sumpter
To this detested groom.
King Lear. Act ii, sc. 4, l. 219. [Lear] The only use of "sumpter."

Here I stand, your slave.—*King Lear,* iii, 2, 19.
Throw this slave Upon the dunghill.
King Lear. Act iii, sc. 7, l. 96. [Cornwall]

6
You have among you many a purchased slave,
Which, like your asses and your dogs and mules,
You use in abject and in slavish parts,
Because you bought them.
The Merchant of Venice. Act iv, sc. 1, l. 90. [Shylock]

7
Though I am bound to every act of duty,
I am not bound to that all slaves are free to.
Othello. Act iii, sc. 3, l. 134. [Iago]

8
Like straggling slaves for pillage fighting.
The Rape of Lucrece, l. 428.

So shall these slaves be king, and thou their slave;
Thou nobly base, they basely dignified.
The Rape of Lucrece, l. 659.

Let him have time to live a loathed slave.
The Rape of Lucrece, l. 984.

9
False slave to false delight.
The Rape of Lucrece, l. 927.

Slave to memory.—*Hamlet,* iii, 2, 198.
Slave to patience.—*Romeo and Juliet,* v, 3, 221.
Slave to thousands.—*Othello,* iii, 3, 158.
Slaves of chance.—*Winter's Tale,* iv, 4, 551.
Slaves of drink.—*Macbeth,* iii, 6, 13.
Slave of life.—*I Henry IV,* v, 4, 81.
Slave of nature.—*Richard III,* i, 3, 230.
Slaves of winter.—*Cymbeline,* iv, 4, 30.
Fancy's slave.—*The Rape of Lucrece,* l. 200.
Fortune's slaves.—*Richard II,* v, 5, 24.
Passion's slave.—*Hamlet,* iii, 2, 77.
Woe's slave.—*Richard II,* iii, 2, 210.

10
Being your slave, what should I do but tend
Upon the hours and times of your desire?
I have no precious time at all to spend,
Nor services to do, till you require.
Sonnets. No. lvii.

11
Let me be a slave, to achieve that maid
Whose sudden sight hath thrall'd my wounded eye.
The Taming of the Shrew. Act i, sc. 1, l. 224. [Lucentio]

12
Thou poisonous slave, got by the devil himself
Upon thy wicked dam, come forth!
The Tempest. Act i, sc. 2, l. 319. [Prospero]

13
Peace, tawny slave, half me and half thy dam!
Did not thy hue bewray whose brat thou art,
Had nature lent thee but thy mother's look,
Villain, thou mightst have been an emperor.
Titus Andronicus. Act v, sc. 1, l. 27. [Goth]

14
Thou art a slave, whom Fortune's tender arm
With favour never clasp'd; but bred a dog.
Timon of Athens. Act iv, sc. 3, l. 250. [Timon]

Thy slave man rebels.—*Timon of Athens,* iv, 3, 391.

SLEEP

See also Repose, Rest, Slumber

15
Here he comes, to beguile two hours in a sleep.
All's Well that Ends Well. Act iv, sc. 1, l. 25. [Lord]

Sleep as soft As captain shall.—*All's Well that Ends Well,* iv, 3, 368.

1
O, such another sleep, that I might see
But such another man!
Antony and Cleopatra. Act v, sc. 2, l. 77. [Cleopatra]

Sleep a little.—*Antony and Cleopatra,* iv, 4, 1.

We must sleep.—*Antony and Cleopatra,* iv, 14, 36.

2
Rosalind: How say you now? Is it not past two o'clock? and here much Orlando!
Celia: I warrant you, with pure love and troubled brain, he hath ta'en his bow and arrows and is gone forth to sleep.
As You Like It. Act iv, sc. 3, l. 1.

3
'Faith, I 'll lie down and sleep.
Cymbeline. Act iv, sc. 2, l. 294. [Imogen]

I 'll sleep.—*As You Like It,* iv, 1, 224.

Sleep within mine inn.—*The Comedy of Errors,* i, 2, 14.

Go sleep.—*Coriolanus,* ii, 1, 239.

4
He that sleeps feels not the tooth-ache.
Cymbeline. Act v, sc. 4, l. 177. [Gaoler]

5
Sleeping within my orchard,
My custom always of the afternoon.
Hamlet. Act i, sc. 5, l. 59. [Ghost]

Sleeping upon benches after noon.
I Henry IV, i, 2, 4. See under CHARACTER.

'Tis a custom with him I' th' afternoon to sleep.
The Tempest. Act iii, sc. 2, l. 96. [Caliban]

Sleeps out the afternoon.—*All's Well that Ends Well,* v, 3, 66.

After-dinner's sleep.—*Measure for Measure,* iii, 1, 33. "After-dinner's breath" occurs in *Troilus and Cressida,* ii, 3, 121.

6
Player King: My spirits grow dull, and fain I would beguile
The tedious day with sleep.
Player Queen: Sleep rock thy brain;
And never come mischance between us twain!
Hamlet. Act iii, sc. 2, l. 236.

Rock me asleep.—*II Henry IV,* ii, 4, 211.

Let all sleep.—*Hamlet,* iv, 4, 59.

7
I fell asleep here behind the arras.
I Henry IV. Act iii, sc. 3, l. 112. [Falstaff]

Fell asleep.—*Titus Andronicus,* ii, 4, 50; *Sonnets,* cliii.

Fall asleep.—*Henry VIII,* iii, 1, 14.

Lain asleep.—*Romeo and Juliet,* iii, 1, 29.

Lie asleep.—*Romeo and Juliet,* i, 4, 58; 80.

Lulls asleep.—*Coriolanus,* iii, 2, 115.

Charm'd asleep.—*II Henry IV,* iv, 2, 39.

8
His wonted sleep under a fresh tree's shade.
III Henry VI. Act ii, sc. 5, l. 49. [King] See under KING.

9
She is asleep: good wench, let 's sit down quiet,
For fear we wake her.
Henry VIII. Act iv, sc. 2, l. 81. [Griffith]

Thou hast been all this while asleep.
Julius Cæsar. Act v, sc. 5, l. 32. [Brutus]

I think the world 's asleep.
King Lear. Act i, sc. 4, l. 52. [King Lear]

Asleep, my love?—*A Midsummer-Night's Dream,* v, 1, 331.

Half asleep.—*Othello,* iv, 2, 97. The only use of the phrase.

10
I 'll have them sleep on cushions in my tent.
Julius Cæsar. Act iv, sc. 3, l. 243. [Brutus]

Thou shalt sleep again. . . . Sleep again, Lucius.
Julius Cæsar. Act iv, sc. 3, l. 264. [Brutus]

Sleeps again.—*Romeo and Juliet,* i, 4, 88.

I 'll sleep again.—*Taming of the Shrew,* v, 2, 43.

11
A heavy summons lies like lead upon me,
And yet I would not sleep.
Macbeth. Act ii, sc. 1, l. 6. [Banquo]

12
They did say their prayers, and address'd them
Again to sleep.
Macbeth. Act ii, sc. 2, l. 25. [Macbeth]

13
Away, you rogue, away! I am sleepy.
Measure for Measure. Act iv, sc. 3, l. 31. [Bardolph] The only use of "I am sleepy."

14
While she was in her dull and sleeping hour.
A Midsummer-Night's Dream. Act iii, sc. 2, l. 8. [Puck]

It is not Agamemnon's sleeping hour:
That thou shalt know, Trojan, he is awake,
He tells thee so himself.
Troilus and Cressida. Act i, sc. 3, l. 254. [Agamemnon] The only uses of "sleeping hour."

Sleeping-hours excepted.—*As You Like It,* iii, 2, 102. The only use of "sleeping-hours."

15
Sleep, that sometimes shuts up sorrow's eye,
Steal me awhile from mine own company.
A Midsummer-Night's Dream. Act iii, sc. 2, l. 435. [Helena]

Sleep thou there.—*A Midsummer-Night's Dream,* ii, 2, 135.

16
I have an exposition of sleep come upon me.
A Midsummer-Night's Dream. Act iv, sc. 1, l. 42. [Bottom]

17
Come, my lord, and in our flight
Tell me how it came this night
That I sleeping here was found
With these mortals on the ground.
A Midsummer-Night's Dream. Act iv, sc. 1, l. 103. [Titania]

Sleeping with my ancestors.—*II Henry IV,* iv, 4, 61.

Sleeping on your beds.—*I Henry VI,* v, 3, 41.

18
We will rather sleep than talk.
Much Ado about Nothing. Act iii, sc. 3, l. 39. [Watch]

Sleep when I am drowsy.—*Much Ado about Nothing,* i, 3, 17.

19
I cannot see how sleeping should offend.
Much Ado about Nothing. Act iii, sc. 3, l. 42. [Dogberry]

20
Roderigo: What will I do, thinkest thou?
Iago: Why, go to bed, and sleep.
Othello. Act i, sc. 3, l. 304.

I have list to sleep.
Othello. Act ii, sc. 1, l. 105. [Iago]

1
There are a kind of men so loose of soul,
That in their sleeps will mutter their affairs.
Othello. Act iii, sc. 3, l. 416. [Iago]

2
Now stole upon the time the dead of night,
When heavy sleep had closed up mortal eyes.
The Rape of Lucrece, l. 162.

Bankrupt sleep.—*Midsummer-Night's Dream*, iii, 2, 85.
Common sleep.—*A Midsummer-Night's Dream*, iv, 1, 87.
Curtain'd sleep.—*Macbeth*, ii, 1, 51.
Dull sleep.—*The Rape of Lucrece*, l. 450; *Pericles*, v, 1, 63.
Midnight sleep.—*Coriolanus*, iii, 1, 85.
Pleasant sleep.—*Romeo and Juliet*, iv, 1, 106.
Sweet sleep.—*Richard III*, iv, 2, 74; *Othello*, iii, 3, 332.
Unnatural sleep.—*Romeo and Juliet*, v, 3, 152.

3
My soul is heavy, and I fain would sleep.
Richard III. Act i, sc. 4, l. 74. [Clarence]

Sleep in peace.—*Richard III*, v, 3, 155; 256; *Titus Andronicus*, i, 1, 91.
Sleep in quiet.—*Richard III*, iii, 1, 142; *Romeo and Juliet*, iii, 5, 100.
Sleep thou a quiet sleep.—*Richard III*, v, 3, 164.

4
The golden dew of sleep.
Richard III. Act iv, sc. 1, l. 84. [Anne]

Honey-heavy dew of slumber.—*Julius Cæsar*, ii, 1, 230. See under SLUMBER.
Golden sleep.—*Romeo and Juliet*, ii, 3, 38.

5
I 'll strive, with troubled thoughts, to take a nap,
Lest leaden slumber peise me down tomorrow.
Richard III. Act v, sc. 3, l. 104. [Richmond] "Peise" (weigh) is repeated in *The Merchant of Venice*, iii, 2, 22. "Peised" (poised) occurs in *King John*, ii, 1, 575.

Take a nap.—*Twelfth Night*, v, 1, 52.
A goodly nap.—*The Taming of the Shrew*, Ind., 2, 83. The only uses of "nap" in this sense. "Taken napping" occurs twice, in *Love's Labour's Lost*, iv, 3, 130, and in *The Taming of the Shrew*, iv, 2, 46.

6
Sleep for a week; for the next night, I warrant,
The County Paris hath set up his rest,
That you shall rest but little.
Romeo and Juliet. Act iv, sc. 5, l. 5. [Nurse]

7
Sleep dwell upon thine eyes, peace in thy breast!
Would I were sleep and peace, so sweet to rest!
Romeo and Juliet. Act ii, sc. 2, l. 187. [Romeo]

Sleep kill those pretty eyes,
And give as soft attachment to thy senses
As infants' empty of all thought!
Troilus and Cressida. Act iv, sc. 2, l. 4. [Troilus] The only use of "attachment."

8
Thou art inclined to sleep; 'tis a good dulness,
And give it way: I know thou canst not choose.
The Tempest. Act i, sc. 2, l. 185. [Prospero]

Alonso: What, all so soon asleep! I wish mine eyes
Would with themselves, shut up my thoughts: I find
They are inclined to do so.
Sebastian: Please you sir,
Do not omit the heavy offer of it:
It seldom visits sorrow; when it doth,
It is a comforter.
The Tempest. Act ii, sc. 1, l. 191.

Inclined to sleep.—*As You Like It*, iv, 1, 157.
Disposed to sleep.—*II Henry IV*, iv, 5, 17.

9
Within this half hour will he be asleep.
The Tempest. Act iii, sc. 2, l. 122. [Caliban]

Asleep under the hatches.—*Tempest*, v, 1, 98.

10
Hounds and horns and sweet melodious birds
Be unto us as is a nurse's song
Of lullaby to bring her babe asleep.
Titus Andronicus. Act ii, sc. 3, l. 27. [Tamora]

Philomel, with melody
Sing in our sweet lullaby;
Lulla, lulla, lullaby, lulla, lulla, lullaby. . . .
So, good night, with lullaby.
A Midsummer-Night's Dream. Act ii, sc. 2, l. 13. [Fairies' Song]

Thou 'rt like to have A lullaby too rough.
The Winter's Tale. Act iii, sc. 3, l. 54. [Antigonus]

Lullaby to your bounty.—*Twelfth Night*, v, 1, 48. The only uses of "lullaby."

11
Let 's shut our gates and sleep.
Troilus and Cressida. Act ii, sc. 2, l. 47. [Troilus]

Sleep awhile.—*Titus and Andronicus*, ii, 3, 197.
Sleep upon 't.—*Timon of Athens*, iii, 5, 43.
Wilt thou sleep?—*The Taming of the Shrew*, Ind., 2, 39.
Still let me sleep.—*Twelfth Night*, iv, 1, 67.

II—Sound Sleep

See also Snoring

12
We did sleep day out of countenance.
Antony and Cleopatra. Act ii, sc. 2, l. 181. [Enobarbus]

There let him sleep till day.
I Henry IV. Act ii, sc. 4, l. 594. [Prince]

He sleeps by day More than the wild-cat.
Merchant of Venice. Act ii, sc. 5, l. 47. [Shylock] "Wild-cat" is repeated in *Taming of the Shrew*, i, 2, 197, and in *Othello*, ii, 1, 111.

13
The one sleeps easily because he cannot study.
As You Like It. Act iii, sc. 2, l. 338. [Rosalind]

1
Sleep hath seized me wholly.
Cymbeline. Act ii, sc. 2, l. 7. [Imogen]

2
Fast asleep behind the arras, and snorting like a horse.
I Henry IV. Act ii, sc. 4, l. 577. [Peto] "Snorting" is used again in *Othello,* i, 1, 90.
They have judged me fast asleep.
Two Gentlemen of Verona, iii, 1, 25. [Duke]
By my halidom, I was fast asleep.
Two Gentlemen of Verona, iv, 2, 136. [Host]
Fast asleep.—*Julius Cæsar,* ii, 1, 229; *Macbeth,* v, 1, 23; *Titus Andronicus,* ii, 3, 194.
So fast asleep.—*The Tempest,* ii, 1, 215.

3 Drowsed and hung their eyelids down,
Slept in his face.
I Henry IV. Act iii, sc. 2, l. 81. [King Henry] The only use of "drowsed."
Droop and drowse.—*Macbeth,* iii, 2, 52. The only use of "drowse."
Speak'st drowsily.—*Julius Cæsar,* iv, 3, 240. The only use of "drowsily."
What a strange drowsiness possesses them!
The Tempest. Act ii, sc. 1, l. 199. [Sebastian] The only use of "drowsiness."

4
I would it were my fault to sleep so soundly.
Julius Cæsar. Act ii, sc. 1, l. 4. [Brutus]
Sleep so soundly.—*Henry V,* iv, 1, 285; *The Taming of the Shrew,* Ind., 1, 33.
On the ground Sleep sound.—*A Midsummer-Night's Dream,* iii, 2, 448.
Thou sleep'st so sound.—*Julius Cæsar,* ii, 1, 233.
Soundly sleeps.—*Venus and Adonis,* l. 786.
Sound sleeping.—*The Rape of Lucrece,* l. 363.
Sleep the sounder.—*Measure for Measure,* iv, 3, 50.
Sleeping sound.—*Midsummer-Night's Dream,* ii, 2, 74.

5
And, pretty child, sleep doubtless and secure.
King John. Act iv, sc. 1, l. 130. [Hubert]
Sleep secure.—*I Henry VI,* iii, 2, 19.
Sleep in security.—*II Henry IV,* i, 2, 51.
Sleeping safe.—*Richard III,* v, 3, 320.
Sure, they sleep.—*The Merry Wives of Windsor,* iii, 2, 31.

6
As fast lock'd up in sleep as guiltless labour
When it lies starkly in the traveller's bones.
Measure for Measure. Act iv, sc. 2, l. 69. [Claudio] The only use of "starkly."
A most fast sleep.—*Macbeth,* v, 1, 9.

7
I slept the next night well, was free and merry.
Othello. Act iii, sc. 3, l. 340. [Othello]
Sleep o' nights.—*Julius Cæsar,* i, 2, 193.

8
I have been long a sleeper.
Richard III. Act iii, sc. 4, l. 24. [Gloucester] The only use of "sleeper."
Wake the sleepers.—*Antony and Cleopatra,* iv, 9, 31.
Waked their sleepers.—*The Tempest,* v, 1, 49.
Sleepers of the house.—*Macbeth,* ii, 3, 88.
These sleepers.—*A Midsummer-Night's Dream,* iv, 1, 91. The only uses of "sleepers."

9
Marry, and amen, how sound is she asleep!
Romeo and Juliet. Act iv, sc. 5, l. 8. [Nurse]
Fast, I warrant her, she.—*Romeo and Juliet,* iv, 5, 1.
Sleep for a week.—*Romeo and Juliet,* iv, 5, 5.
Heavy sleep.—*Sonnets,* xliii.
Dead of sleep.—*The Tempest,* v, 1, 230.
Thralls of sleep.—*Macbeth,* iii, 6, 13.

III—Sleep and Death

10
O sleep, thou ape of death, lie dull upon her!
And be her sense but as a monument,
Thus in a chapel lying!
Cymbeline. Act ii, sc. 2, l. 31. [Iachimo]
Why, he but sleeps:
If he be gone, he 'll make his grave a bed;
With female fairies will his tomb be haunted,
And worms will not come to thee.
Cymbeline. Act iv, sc. 2, l. 216. [Guiderius]
Sleep of death.—*Hamlet,* iii, 1, 66.
Eternal sleep.—*Titus Andronicus,* i, 1, 155; ii, 4, 15.
Eternal sleeping.—*Venus and Adonis,* l. 951.
Sleep eternal.—*II Henry VI,* iii, 2, 263.

11
Is he so hasty that he doth suppose
My sleep my death?
II Henry IV. Act iv, sc. 5, l. 61. [King Henry]
Though we seemed dead, we did but sleep.
Henry V. Act iii, sc. 6, l. 127. [Montjoy]

12 In swinish sleep
Their drenched natures lie as in a death.
Macbeth. Act i, sc. 7, l. 67. [Lady Macbeth] "Swinish" is repeated in *Hamlet,* i, 4, 19.
The sleeping and the dead Are but as pictures.
Macbeth. Act ii, sc. 2, l. 53. [Lady Macbeth]
Shake off this downy sleep, death's counterfeit,
And look on death itself! up, up, and see
The great doom's image!
Macbeth. Act ii, sc. 3, l. 81. [Macduff]
After life's fitful fever he sleeps well.
Macbeth. Act iii, sc. 2, l. 23. [Macbeth] The only use of "fitful."

13 Thy best of rest is sleep,
And that thou oft provokest; yet grossly fear'st
Thy death, which is no more.
Measure for Measure. Act iii, sc. 1, l. 17. [Duke]

14
Grim death, how foul and loathsome is thine image!
The Taming of the Shrew. Induction, sc. 1, l. 35. [Lord]
Death-conterfeiting sleep.—*A Midsummer-Night's Dream,* iii, 2, 364. The only use of the phrase.

IV—Sleep and Waking

15
Sleeping or waking, 'tis no matter how,
So he be dead.
II Henry VI, iii, 1, 263. See under MURDER.
Sleeping or waking.
I Henry VI, ii, 1, 56; *The Comedy of Errors,* ii, 2, 215.

Sleeping and waking, O defend me still!
Richard III, v, 3, 117. See under PRAYER.
Waking and in my dreams.—*II Henry VI*, i, 1, 26.
Half sleep, half waking.—*A Midsummer-Night's Dream*, iv, 1, 152.
'Tween asleep and wake.—*King Lear*, i, 2, 15.

1
Turn his sleep to wake.
King Lear. Act iii, sc. 2, l. 34. [Fool]
Sleep till I waked him.—*King Lear*, i, 2, 55; 58.

2
Sleepest or wakest thou, jolly shepherd?
King Lear. Act iii, sc. 6, l. 43. [Edgar]
Thou sleep'st.—*Julius Cæsar*, ii, 1, 46; 233; *Richard II*, iii, 2, 84; *Troilus and Cressida*, iv, 5, 114. The only uses of "sleepest."

3
If thou wake, he cannot sleep.
The Passionate Pilgrim, l. 426.
Wake and sleep.—*A Lover's Complaint*, l. 123.

4
From forth dull sleep by dreadful fancy waking.
The Rape of Lucrece, l. 450.

5
Still-waking sleep, that is not what it is!
Romeo and Juliet. Act i, sc. 1, l. 187. [Romeo] The only use of "still-waking."

6
In sleep a king, but waking no such matter.
Sonnets. No. lxxxvii.

7
When you waked, so waked as if you slept.
The Taming of the Shrew. Induction, sc. 2, l. 82. [Servant]

8 Giddy for lack of sleep,
With oaths kept waking.
The Taming of the Shrew. Act iv, sc. 3, l. 10. [Katharina]
Waked after long sleep.—*Tempest*, iii, 3, 148.

V—Insomnia

9
I'll go sleep, if I can; if I cannot, I'll rail against all the first-born of Egypt.
As You Like It. Act ii, sc. 5, l. 62. [Jaques]

10
It seems his sleeps were hinder'd by thy railing,
And therefore comes it that his head is light.
The Comedy of Errors. Act v, sc. 1, l. 71. [Abbess]

11
Break not your sleeps for that.
Hamlet. Act iv, sc. 7, l. 30. [King]
Broke their sleep.—*Coriolanus*, iv, 4, 19; *II Henry IV*, iv, 5, 69.

12
Tell me, sweet lord, what is't that takes from thee
Thy stomach, pleasure, and thy golden sleep?
I Henry IV, ii, 3, 43. See under MELANCHOLY.

O sleep, O gentle sleep,
Nature's soft nurse, how have I frighted thee,
That thou no more wilt weigh my eyelids down
And steep my senses in forgetfulness?
Why rather, sleep, liest thou in smoky cribs,
Upon uneasy pallets stretching thee
And hush'd with buzzing night-flies to thy slumber,
Than in the perfumed chambers of the great,
Under the canopies of costly state,
And lull'd with sound of sweetest melody?
O thou dull god, why liest thou with the vile
In loathsome beds, and leavest the kingly couch
A watch-case or a common 'larum-bell?
II Henry IV. Act iii, sc. 1, l. 5. [King Henry] The only use of "cribs," "pallets," "night-flies," "watch-case," and "'larum-bell." "Crib" occurs in *Hamlet*, v, 2, 88.

13
To sleep but three hours in the night.
Love's Labour's Lost, i, 1, 42. See under DAY.

14
Sleep shall neither night nor day
Hang upon his pent-house lid.
Macbeth. Act i, sc. 3, l. 19. [First Witch] "Pent-house" is repeated in *The Merchant of Venice*, ii, 6, 1, and in *Much Ado about Nothing*, iii, 3, 110.

Methought I heard a voice cry 'Sleep no more!
Macbeth does murder sleep,' the innocent sleep,
Sleep that knits up the ravell'd sleave of care,
The death of each day's life, sore labour's bath,
Balm of hurt minds, great nature's second course,
Chief nourisher in life's feast.
Macbeth. Act ii, sc. 2, l. 35. [Macbeth] The only use of "ravell'd" and "nourisher." "Sleave" is repeated in *Troilus and Cressida*, v, 1, 35: "Sleave-silk."

Glamis hath murder'd sleep, and therefore Cawdor
Shall sleep no more; Macbeth shall sleep no more.
Macbeth. Act ii, sc. 2, l. 42. [Macbeth]

You lack the season of all natures, sleep.
Macbeth. Act iii, sc. 4, l. 141. [Lady Macbeth]

A great perturbation in nature, to receive at once the benefit of sleep, and do the effects of watching!
Macbeth. Act v, sc. 1, l. 10. [Doctor]

I have known those which have walked in their sleep who have died holily in their beds.
Macbeth. Act v, sc. 1, l. 66. [Doctor] "Holily" is repeated in *Macbeth*, i, 5, 22, and in *Henry VIII*, ii, 2, 24.

15 Not poppy, nor mandragora,
Nor all the drowsy syrups of the world,
Shall ever medicine thee to that sweet sleep
Which thou owedst yesterday.
Othello. Act iii, sc. 3, l. 330. [Iago] The only use of "poppy."

Give me to drink mandragora . . .
That I might sleep out this great gap of time
My Antony is away.
Antony and Cleopatra. Act i, sc. 5, l. 4. [Cleopatra] The only uses of "mandragora" (mandrake).

16
No sleep close up that deadly eye of thine,
Unless it be whilst some tormenting dream
Affrights thee with a hell of ugly devils!
Richard III. Act i, sc. 3, l. 225. [Queen Margaret]

Cannot thy master sleep these tedious nights?
Richard III. Act iii, sc. 2, l. 6. [Hastings]

1
Weary with toil, I haste me to my bed,
The dear repose for limbs with travel tired;
But then begins a journey in my head,
To work my mind, when body's work 's expired: . . .
And keep my drooping eyelids open wide,
Looking on darkness which the blind do see.
Sonnets. No. xxvii.

2
I do not sleep: I see, I hear, I speak;
I smell sweet savours and I feel soft things.
Taming of the Shrew. Induction, sc. 2, l. 72. [Sly]

I could not sleep.—*Othello,* iii, 3, 415.
I will not sleep.—*Taming of the Shrew,* i, 2, 103.
He cannot sleep.—*Passionate Pilgrim,* l. 426.
I 'll not sleep neither.—*Antony and Cleopatra,* v, 2, 51.
Drew sleep out of mine eyes.—*Pericles,* i, 2, 96.
Sleep disturbed.—*The Rape of Lucrece,* l. 454.

3
I find not Myself disposed to sleep.
Tempest. Act ii, sc. 1, l. 201. [Sebastian]

4
I have been troubled in my sleep this night.
Titus Andronicus. Act ii, sc. 2, l. 9. [Titus]

I have not slept one wink.—*Cymbeline,* iii, 4, 103.
He hath not slept to-night.—*The Winter's Tale,* ii, 3, 31.

5
Alas, poor wretch! ah, poor capocchia! hast not slept to-night? would he not, a naughty man, let it sleep?
Troilus and Cressida. Act iv, sc. 2, l. 32. [Pandarus] The only use of "capocchia" (little fool).

6
I come to bring him sleep. 'Tis such as you,
That creep like shadows by him and do sigh
At each his needless heavings, such as you
Nourish the cause of his awaking.
The Winter's Tale. Act ii, sc. 3, l. 33. [Paulina] The only use of "heavings." "Heaving" occurs in *Love's Labour 's Lost,* iii, 1, 77, and in *Troilus and Cressida,* ii, 2, 196.

Purge him of that humour
That presses him from sleep.
Winter's Tale. Act ii, sc. 3, l. 38. [Paulina]

SLIPPER, see under Shoe

SLOTH

See also Indolence

7
Let not sloth dim your honours new-begot
I Henry VI. Act i, sc. 1, l. 79. [Messenger] The only use of "new-begot."

Slothful watch.—*I Henry VI,* iii, 2, 7. The only use of "slothful."
Hog in sloth.—*King Lear,* iii, 4, 96.

8
You have ta'en a tardy sluggard here.
Richard III. Act v, sc. 3, l. 225. [Richmond]

Sluggard negligence.—*The Rape of Lucrece,* l. 1278. The only uses of "sluggard."
Dully sluggardized.—*Two Gentlemen of Verona,* i, 1, 7. The only use of "sluggardized."

9
Why, lamb! why, lady! fie, you slug-a-bed!
Romeo and Juliet. Act iv, sc. 5, l. 2. [Nurse] The only use of "slug-a-bed."

10
Ebbing men, indeed,
Most often do so near the bottom run
By their own fear or sloth.
The Tempest. Act ii, sc. 1, l. 230. [Antonio]

Hereditary sloth.—*The Tempest,* ii, 1, 223.

SLOWNESS

11
Why, one that rode to 's execution, man,
Could never go so slow.
Cymbeline. Act iii, sc. 2, l. 72. [Imogen]

He is very slow-gaited.—*Love's Labour 's Lost,* iii, 1, 56. The only use of "slow-gaited."

12
You are as slow
As hot Lord Percy is on fire to go.
I Henry IV. Act iii, sc. 1, l. 268. [Glendower]

You are slow.—*II Henry VI,* v, 2, 72.
Thou art too slow.—*Cymbeline,* iii, 4, 100.
So slack, so slow.—*Pericles,* iv, 2, 68.
Slow as the elephant.—*Troilus and Cressida,* i, 2, 21.
I am nothing slow.—*Romeo and Juliet,* iv, 1, 3.
Too slow.—*Romeo and Juliet,* ii, 6, 15; *Antony and Cleopatra,* v, 2, 324; *Tempest,* ii, 1, 249.
Dull, and slow.—*Love's Labour 's Lost,* iii, 1, 60.
Unwieldy, slow, heavy.—*Romeo and Juliet,* ii, 5, 17.
She is slow.—*The Two Gentlemen of Verona,* iii, 1, 357.
Slow in pursuit.—*A Midsummer-Night's Dream,* iv, 1, 128.
Slow in speech.—*The Taming of the Shrew,* ii, 1, 248.
Slow in words.—*The Two Gentlemen of Verona,* iii, 1, 338.
Slow of sail.—*The Comedy of Errors,* i, 1, 117; *Hamlet,* iv, 6, 17.
Slow of study.—*A Midsummer-Night's Dream,* i, 2, 69.

SLUMBER

See also Repose, Sleep

13
In which hurtling
From miserable slumber I awaked.
As You Like It. Act iv, sc. 3, l. 132. [Oliver] The only use of "hurtling."

Harmful slumber.—*II Henry VI,* iii, 2, 262.

14
Enjoy the honey-heavy dew of slumber:
Thou hast no figures nor no fantasies,
Which busy care draws in the brains of men;
Therefore thou sleep'st so sound.
Julius Cæsar. Act ii, sc. 1, l. 230. [Brutus] The only use of "honey-heavy."

Balmy slumbers.—*Othello,* ii, 3, 258.
Pleasant slumber.—*II Henry VI,* iii, 2, 390.

15
This is a sleepy tune. O murderous slumber,
Lay'st thou thy leaden mace upon my boy,
That plays thee music?
Julius Cæsar. Act iv, sc. 3, l. 267. [Brutus]

Now leaden slumber with life's strength doth fight.
The Rape of Lucrece, l. 124.
Thick slumber Hangs upon mine eyes.
Pericles. Act v, sc. 1, l. 235. [Pericles]

1
Dost thou desire my slumbers should be broken?
Sonnets. No. lxi.
Unquiet slumbers.—*Richard III*, iii, 2, 27.

2
We may, each wreathed in the other's arms,
Our pastimes done, possess a golden slumber.
Titus Andronicus. Act ii, sc. 3, l. 25. [Tamora]
Golden slumber.—*Pericles*, iii, 2, 23.

3
When will this fearful slumber have an end?
Titus Andronicus. Act iii, sc. 1, l. 253. [Titus]

SLUTTERY, see Foulness

SMELL

4
I am qualmish at the smell of leek.
Henry V. Act v, sc. 1, l. 22. [Pistol] The only use of "qualmish."
I cannot abide the smell of hot meat.
The Merry Wives of Windsor. Act i, sc. 1, l. 297. [Slender]
Smell of calumny.—*Measure for Measure*, ii, 4, 159.
Smells of mortality.—*King Lear*, iv, 6, 136.

5
They would but stink, and putrefy the air.
I Henry VI. Act iv, sc. 7, l. 90. [La Pucelle] The only use of "putrefy."
Indeed, it doth stink in some sort, sir.
Measure for Measure. Act iii, sc. 2, l. 29. [Pompey]
Stand by the fire and stink.—*King Lear*, i, 4, 126.
Burning, scalding, stench.—*King Lear*, iv, 6, 131.
Noisome stench.—*I Henry VI*, i, 5, 23.
Odoriferous stench.—*King John*, iii, 4, 26. The only uses of "stench."

6
Let him smell His way to Dover.
King Lear. Act iii, sc. 7, l. 93. [Gloucester]
Smell the air.—*King Lear*, iv, 6, 183.

7
He smells April and May.
The Merry Wives of Windsor. Act iii, sc. 2, l. 69. [Host]
Smell like Bucklersbury in simple time.
The Merry Wives of Windsor. Act iii, sc. 3, l. 79. [Falstaff] The only mention of Bucklersbury.
Smell so sweet.—*I Henry IV*, i, 3, 54; *Othello*, iv, 2, 68.
Smelling so sweetly.—*The Merry Wives of Windsor*, ii, 2, 67.
Sweet smell.—*I Henry VI*, i, 1, 255; *Sonnets*, xcviii.
Tender smell.—*The Rape of Lucrece*, l. 695.
Smells well.—*Coriolanus*, iv, 5, 5.

8
The rankest compound of villanous smell that ever offended nostril.
The Merry Wives of Windsor. Act iii, sc. 5, l. 93. [Falstaff]
Loathsome smells.—*Romeo and Juliet*, iv, 3, 46.
Rank smell.—*Sonnets*, lxix.
Rank as a fox.—*Twelfth Night*, ii, 5, 136.
Rank as any flax-wench.—*The Winter's Tale*, i, 2, 277. The only use of "flax-wench."
Smell somewhat strong.—*All's Well that Ends Well*, v, 2, 5.
Smell so strongly.—*All's Well that Ends Well*, v, 2, 8.
Smells to heaven.—*Hamlet*, iii, 3, 36.

9
What have we here? a man or a fish? dead or alive? A fish: he smells like a fish; a very ancient and fish-like smell.
The Tempest. Act ii, sc. 2, l. 25. [Trinculo] The only use of "fish-like."
Monster, I do smell all horse-piss; at which my nose is in great indignation.
The Tempest. Act iv, sc. 1, l. 199. [Trinculo] The only use of "horse-piss." "Piss" is used only once, in *The Merry Wives of Windsor*, v, 5, 16.
I, having been acquainted with the smell before, knew it was Crab.
The Two Gentlemen of Verona. Act iv, sc. 4, l. 25. [Launce]

SMILE

10
Loose now and then
A scatter'd smile, and that I'll live upon.
As You Like It, iii, 5, 103. [Silvius]
Dimpled smiles.—*Timon of Athens*, iv, 3, 119.
Enforced smiles.—*Richard III*, iii, 5, 9.
Joyless smile.—*The Rape of Lucrece*, l. 1711.
Modest smile.—*Henry V*, iv, Prol., 33.
Pleasing smiles.—*Titus Andronicus*, ii, 3, 267.
Practiced smiles.—*The Winter's Tale*, i, 2, 116.

11
The smiles of knaves Tent in my cheeks.
Coriolanus. Act iii, sc. 2, l. 115. [Coriolanus]
Smile of safety.—*II Henry IV*, Ind., 10.

12
Thus smiling, as some fly had tickled slumber,
Not as death's dart, being laugh'd at.
Cymbeline. Act iv, sc. 2, l. 210. [Arviragus]
Smile to 't.—*Cymbeline*, iii, 4, 13.
Smile once more.—*Hamlet*, ii, 2, 180.

13
Still he smiled and talk'd.
I Henry IV. Act i, sc. 3, l. 41. [Hotspur]
He smiled me in the face.—*Henry V*, iv, 6, 21.
This king of smiles.—*I Henry IV*, i, 3, 246.

14
I say little; but when time shall serve, there shall be smiles.
Henry V. Act ii, sc. 1, l. 5. [Nym]
Upon us he smiles.—*I Henry VI*, i, 2, 4.

15
Young Talbot's valour makes me smile.
I Henry VI. Act iv, sc. 7, l. 4. [Talbot]
Makes me smile.—*Richard III*, iv, 4, 115.
Make him smile.—*A Midsummer-Night's Dream*, ii, 1, 44.
That makes me smile.—*Troilus and Cressida*, i, 2, 33.

1
Thou smiling while he knit his angry brows.
III Henry VI. Act ii, sc. 2, l. 20. [Clifford]
Who durst smile when Warwick bent his brow?
III Henry VI. Act v, sc. 2, l. 22. [Warwick]

2
Smile, gentle heaven!
III Henry VI. Act ii, sc. 3, l. 6. [Edward]
Smile heaven.—*Richard III,* v, 5, 20.
So smile the heavens.—*Romeo and Juliet,* ii, 6, 1.
Smile of heaven.—*Henry VIII,* ii, 4, 187.
Smile we would aspire to.—*Henry VIII,* iii, 2, 368.

3
Why, I can smile, and murder whiles I smile.
III Henry VI. Act iii, sc. 2, l. 182. [Gloucester]
One may smile, and smile, and be a villain.
Hamlet, i, 5, 107. See under VILLAIN.
There's daggers in men's smiles: the near in blood,
The nearer bloody.
Macbeth. Act ii, sc. 3, l. 146. [Donalbain]

4
Seldom he smiles, and smiles in such a sort
As if he mock'd himself and scorn'd his spirit
That could be moved to smile at any thing.
Julius Cæsar. Act i, sc. 2, l. 205. [Cæsar]
Look, he smiles.—*Julius Cæsar,* iii, 1, 24.

5
Those that understood him smiled at one another.
Julius Cæsar. Act i, sc. 2, l. 285. [Casca]
Smiled to see him.—*Henry V,* ii, 4, 59.
He smiled at it.—*King Lear,* iv, 2, 5.

6
Some that smile have in their hearts, I fear,
Millions of mischiefs.
Julius Cæsar. Act iv, sc. 1, l. 49. [Octavius]
We shall smile.—*Julius Cæsar,* v, 1, 118.
We'll smile indeed.—*Julius Cæsar,* v, 1, 121.

7
Come, grin on me, and I will think thou smilest.
King John. Act iii, sc. 4, l. 34. [Constable]
Make him grin.—*II Henry VI,* iii, 3, 24.
Grin in vain.—*II Henry VI,* iv, 1, 77.
Grin like lions.—*Cymbeline,* v, 3, 38. "Grin" is used twice more, in *II Henry VI,* iii, 1, 18, and in *III Henry VI,* i, 4, 56. See under CUR.

8
Nay, an thou canst not smile as the wind sits, thou 'lt catch cold shortly.
King Lear. Act i, sc. 4, l. 112. [Fool]
Smile you my speeches, as I were a fool?
King Lear. Act ii, sc. 2, l. 88. [Kent]

9
The heaving of my lungs provokes me to ridiculous smiling.
Love's Labour's Lost. Act iii, sc. 1, l. 77. [Armado] "Heaving" is repeated in *Troilus and Cressida,* ii, 2, 196, and in *The Winter's Tale,* ii, 3, 35.
A kind of smile
Which ne'er came from the lungs.
Coriolanus. Act i, sc. 1, l. 111. [Menenius]

10
Do you not smile at this?
Measure for Measure. Act v, sc. 1, l. 163. [Duke]
I did but smile till now.—*Measure for Measure,* v, 1, 233.

11
He hears merry tales and smiles not.
The Merchant of Venice. Act i, sc. 2, l. 52. [Portia]
Such a one will smile and stroke his beard,
Bid sorrow wag, cry 'hem!' when he should groan.
Much Ado about Nothing. Act v, sc. 1, l. 15. [Leonato]

12
We lose it not, so long as we can smile.
Othello. Act i, sc. 3, l. 211. [Brabantio]
Ay, smile upon her, so.
Othello. Act ii, sc. 1, l. 170. [Iago]

13
Whereat she smiled with so sweet a cheer,
That had Narcissus seen her as she stood,
Self-love had never drown'd him in the flood.
The Rape of Lucrece, l. 264. Narcissus is mentioned again in *Antony and Cleopatra,* ii, 5, 96, and in *Venus and Adonis,* l. 161.
Nor shall he smile at thee in secret thought.
The Rape of Lucrece, l. 1065.

14
They smile at me that shortly shall be dead.
Richard III. Act iii, sc. 4, l. 109. [Hastings]
Smile upon my state.—*Romeo and Juliet,* iv, 3, 4.

15
If you should smile he grows impatient.
The Taming of the Shrew. Induction, sc. 1, l. 99. [Lord]

16
What thou wilt,
Thou rather shalt enforce it with thy smile
That hew to 't with thy sword.
Timon of Athens. Act v, sc. 4, l. 44. [Senator]

17
I extend my hand to him thus, quenching my familiar smile with an austere regard of control.
Twelfth Night. Act ii, sc. 5, l. 72. [Malvolio]

18
If thou entertainest my love, let it appear in thy smiling; thy smiles become thee well; therefore in my presence still smile, dear my sweet, I prithee.
Twelfth Night. Act ii, sc. 5, l. 190. [Malvolio, reading]
Bade me come smiling.—*Twelfth Night,* v, 1, 345.
Camest in smiling.—*Twelfth Night,* v, 1, 357.
Smiling at grief.—*Twelfth Night,* ii, 4, 118.
Smiling in my face.—*Macbeth,* i, 7, 56.

19
He will smile upon her, which will now be so unsuitable to her disposition, being addicted to a melancholy as she is, that it cannot turn him into a notable contempt.
Twelfth Night. Act ii, sc. 5, l. 221. [Maria] "Addicted" is repeated in *Hamlet,* ii, 1, 19.
Why, then, methinks 'tis time to smile again.
Twelfth Night. Act iii, sc. 1, l. 137. [Olivia]

He does smile his face into more lines than is in the new map with the augmentation of the Indies.
Twelfth Night. Act iii, sc. 2, l. 84. [Maria] The only use of "augmentation."

He does nothing but smile.—*Twelfth Night,* iii, 4, 11.

1 Smilest thou?
I sent for thee upon a sad occasion.
Twelfth Night. Act iii, sc. 4, l. 19. [Olivia]

Why dost thou smile so and kiss thy hand so oft?
Twelfth Night. Act iii, sc. 4, l. 35. [Olivia]

2
Pandarus: His smiling becomes him better than any man in all Phrygia.
Cressida: O, he smiles valiantly.
Pandarus: Does he not?
Cressida: O yes, an 'twere a cloud in autumn.
Troilus and Cressida. Act i, sc. 2, l. 135.

3
Bestow thy fawning smiles on equal mates.
The Two Gentlemen of Verona. Act iii, sc. 1, l. 158. [Duke]

4
A smile recures the wounding of a frown.
Venus and Adonis, l. 465. "Recures" is repeated in *Richard III,* iii, 7, 130.

Smiles as in disdain.—*Venus and Adonis,* l. 241.

II—Smile and Tear

5
Full of tears, full of smiles.
As You Like It. Act iii, sc. 2, l. 433. [Rosalind]

Mingle tears with smiles.—*Coriolanus,* i, 9, 3.

6 Nobly he yokes
A smiling with a sigh, as if the sigh
Was that it was, for not being such a smile;
The smile mocking the sigh, that it would fly
From so divine a temple, to commix
With winds that sailors rail at.
Cymbeline. Act iv, sc. 2, l. 51. [Arviragus] The only use of "commix." "Commixed" occurs in *A Lover's Complaint,* l. 28.

7 You have seen
Sunshine and rain at once: her smiles and tears
Were like a better way: those happy smilets,
That play'd on her ripe lip, seem'd not to know
What guests were in her eyes; which parted thence,
As pearls from diamonds dropp'd.
King Lear. Act iv, sc. 3, l. 19. [Gentleman] The only use of "smilets."

Tears and smiles.—*Richard II,* iii, 2, 9.

8
I have, as when the sun doth light a storm,
Buried this sigh in wrinkle of a smile.
Troilus and Cressida. Act i, sc. 1, l. 37. [Troilus]

SMOKE

9
He was first smoked by the old lord Lafeu.
All's Well that Ends Well. Act iii, sc. 6, l. 111. [Lord] "Smoked" is repeated in *Macbeth,* i, 2, 18.

10
They begin to smoke me.
All's Well that Ends Well. Act iv, sc. 1, l. 30. [Parolles]

I 'll smoke your skin-coat, an I catch you right.
King John. Act ii, sc. 1, l. 139. [Bastard] The only use of "skin-coat."

Some of you shall smoke for it.
Titus Andronicus. Act iv, sc. 2, l. 111. [Aaron]

11
Thus must I from the smoke into the smother.
As You Like It. Act i, sc. 2, l. 299. [Orlando]

12 Far as I could well discern
For smoke and dusky vapours of the night.
I Henry VI. Act ii, sc. 2, l. 26. [Burgundy]

13
I was smoking a musty room.
Much Ado about Nothing. Act i, sc. 3, l. 61. [Borachio]

Smoking with pride.—*The Rape of Lucrece,* l. 438.

Smoking in his blood.—*Richard III,* i, 2, 94.

Smoking blood.—*III Henry VI,* ii, 3, 21.

Smoking swords.—*Coriolanus,* i, 4, 11. The only uses of "smoking."

14
This helpless smoke of words doth me no right.
The Rape of Lucrece, l. 1027.

Sweet smoke of rhetoric.—*Love's Labour's Lost,* iii, 1, 64.

Smoke of war.—*Twelfth Night,* v, 1, 56.

15 Vanisheth
As smoke from Ætna, that in air consumes,
Or that which from discharged cannon fumes.
The Rape of Lucrece, l. 1042.

Now let hot Ætna cool.—*Titus Andronicus,* iii, 1, 242. The only references to Ætna.

Bright smoke.—*Romeo and Juliet,* i, 1, 186.

Dunnest smoke of hell.—*Macbeth,* i, 5, 52. The only use of "dunnest."

Foul-reeking smoke.—*The Rape of Lucrece,* l. 799. The only use of "foul-reeking."

Crooked smokes.—*Cymbeline,* v, 5, 477.

Rotten smoke.—*Sonnets,* xxxiv.

Smoky cribs.—*II Henry IV,* iii, 1, 9.

Smoky house.—*I Henry IV,* iii, 1, 161.

Smoky light.—*Cymbeline,* i, 6, 109.

Smoky muskets.—*All's Well that Ends Well,* iii, 2, 111.

Smoky ranks.—*The Rape of Lucrece,* l. 783.

Smoky war.—*I Henry IV,* iii, 1, 161. The only uses of "smoky."

SNAIL

16
A snail, . . . though he comes slowly, he carries his house on his head.
As You Like It, iv, 1, 52. See under Wooing.

Creeping like snail.—*As You Like It,* ii, 7, 146.

Snail-paced.—*Richard III,* iv, 3, 53; *Troilus and Cressida,* v, 5, 18.

Snail slow.—*The Merchant of Venice,* ii, 5, 47.

1
Fool: Canst tell how an oyster makes his shell?
King Lear: No.
Fool: Nor I neither; but I can tell why a snail has a house. . . . To put his head in.
King Lear. Act i, sc. 5, l. 26.

2
The tender horns of cockled snails.
Love's Labour's Lost, iv, 3, 338. See under LOVE.

3 The snail, whose tender horns being hit,
Shrinks backward in his shelly cave with pain,
And there, all smother'd up, in shade doth sit,
Long after fearing to creep forth again.
Venus and Adonis, l. 1033. The only use of "shelly."

SNAKE

See also Adder, Serpent

4
A green and gilded snake . . . with indented glides did slip away.
As You Like It. Act iv, sc. 3, l. 109. [Oliver] The only use of "indented," and of "glides" as a noun.

5 Where is this viper
That would depopulate the city and
Be every man himself?
Coriolanus. Act iii, sc. 1, l. 264. [Sicinius] The only use of "depopulate."
O viper vile!—*Henry V,* ii, 1, 49.
O villains, vipers!—*Richard II,* iii, 2, 129.
Why, they are vipers.—*Troilus and Cressida,* iii, 1, 146.
Where is this viper?—*Othello,* v, 2, 285.
I am no viper.—*Pericles,* i, 1, 64. The only uses of "viper" and "vipers."

6
Or as the snake roll'd in a flowering bank,
With shining checker'd slough, doth sting a child
That for the beauty thinks it excellent.
II Henry VI. Act iii, sc. 1, l. 228. [Queen Margaret] The only use of "checker'd."
I fear me you but warm the starved snake,
Who, cherish'd in your breasts, will sting your hearts.
II Henry VI. Act iii, sc. 1, l. 343. [York] "Starved snake" is repeated in *Titus Andronicus,* iii, 1, 252.
Snakes, in my heart-blood warm'd, that sting my heart!
Richard II. Act iii, sc. 2, l. 131. [King Richard]

7
We have scotch'd the snake, not kill'd it:
She 'll close and be herself, whilst our poor malice
Remains in danger of her former tooth.
Macbeth. Act iii, sc. 2, l. 13. [Macbeth] "Scotch'd" is repeated in *Coriolanus,* iv, 5, 198: "Scotched him and notched him."
Fillet of a fenny snake
In the cauldron boil and bake.
Macbeth. Act iv, sc. 1, l. 12. [Second Witch] The only use of "fenny."

8
There the snake throws her enamell'd skin,
Weed wide enough to wrap a fairy in.
A Midsummer-Night's Dream. Act ii, sc. 1, l. 255. [Oberon] "Enamell'd" is repeated in *The Comedy of Errors,* ii, 1, 109, and in *The Two Gentlemen of Verona,* ii, 7, 28.
Spotted snakes with double tongue.
A Midsummer-Night's Dream. Act ii, sc. 2, l. 9. [Fairies' Song]
Hissing snakes.—*Titus Andronicus,* ii, 3, 100.
Scaled snakes.—*Antony and Cleopatra,* ii, 5, 95.
Tame snake.—*As You Like It,* iv, 3, 71.
Alecto's snake.—*II Henry IV,* v, 5, 39. The only mention of Alecto.

9
The snake lies rolled in the cheerful sun.
Titus Andronicus, ii, 3, 13. [Tamora]

SNORING

See also Sleep

10
Snores out the watch of night.
II Henry IV. Act iv, sc. 5, l. 28. [Prince]
Snore upon a flint.—*Cymbeline,* iii, 6, 34.

11 The surfeited grooms
Do mock their charge with snores.
Macbeth. Act ii, sc. 2, l. 5. [Lady Macbeth]

12
Sleep and snore, and rend apparel out.
The Merchant of Venice. Act iii, sc. 5, l. 5. [Shylock]
Whilst the heavy ploughman snores.—*A Midsummer-Night's Dream,* v, 1, 380.

13
Now sleep yslaked hath the rout;
No din but snores the house about,
Made louder by the o'er-fed breast.
Pericles. Act iii, Gower, l. 1. The only use of "yslaked" and "o'er-fed."

14 Thou dost snore distinctly;
There 's meaning in thy snores.
The Tempest. Act ii, sc. 1, l. 217. [Sebastian]
Snoring lie.—*The Tempest,* ii, 1, 300. The only use of "snoring."

SNOW

15
Snow the pasture sheets.
Antony and Cleopatra, i, 4, 65. See under HUNGER.

16
Cold snow melts with the sun's hot beams.
II Henry VI. Act iii, sc. 1, l. 223. [Queen]
As mountain-snow melts with the midday sun.
Venus and Adonis, l. 750. The only use of "mountain-snow."
Melt the snow.—*Titus Andronicus,* iii, 1, 20; *The Rape of Lucrece,* l. 1218.
Melted snow.—*Henry V,* iii, 5, 50.

17 A little snow, tumbled about,
Anon becomes a mountain.
King John, iii, 4, 176. See under ARMY.

18
Wish a snow in May's new-fangled mirth
Love's Labour's Lost, i, 1, 106. See under DESIRE.

19
That pure congealed white, high Taurus' snow.
A Midsummer-Night's Dream. Act iii, sc. 2,

l. 141. [Demetrius] Taurus is mentioned five times in the plays.
Purest snow.—*Coriolanus,* v, 3, 66.
December snow.—*Richard II,* i, 3, 298.
Driven snow.—*The Winter's Tale,* iv, 4, 220.
New-fall'n snow.—*Venus and Adonis,* l. 354.
Unsunn'd snow.—*Cymbeline,* ii, 5, 13. The only use of "unsunn'd."
Wondrous strange snow.—*A Midsummer-Night's Dream,* v, 1, 59.

1
Right, as snow in harvest.
Richard III. Act i, sc. 4, l. 249. [Murderer]
Over shoes in snow.—*Richard III,* v, 3, 326.

2
The white cold virgin snow upon my heart
Abates the ardour of my liver.
The Tempest. Act iv, sc. 1, l. 55. [Ferdinand]
As pure as snow, see PURITY.
As white as snow, see WHITENESS.

SOCIETY

See also Company

3
I thank you too for your society.
As You Like It, iii, 2, 272. See under COMPANY.
Society—which in the boorish is company.
As You Like It. Act v, sc. 1, l. 56. [Touchstone] The only use of "boorish."
Rude society.—*I Henry IV,* iii, 2, 14.

4
Society is no comfort To one not sociable.
Cymbeline. Act iv, sc. 2, l. 12. [Imogen]
Now art thou sociable.—*Romeo and Juliet,* ii, 4, 93.
Can he not be sociable?—*Troilus and Cressida,* ii, 3, 220.
Even sociable.—*The Tempest,* v, 1, 63.
Too sociable.—*King John,* i, 1, 188.
Sociable grief.—*King John,* iii, 4, 65. The only uses of "sociable."

5
But this is worshipful society
And fits the mounting spirit like myself.
King John. Act i, sc. 1, l. 205. [Bastard]
A sweet society of fair ones.—*Henry VIII,* i, 4, 14.
Of very soft society.—*Hamlet,* v, 2, 112.

6
Society, saith the text, is the happiness of life.
Love's Labour's Lost. Act iv, sc. 2, l. 167. [Sir Nathaniel]
I beseech your society.—*Love's Labour's Lost,* iv, 2, 166.

7
To make society
The sweeter welcome, we will keep ourself
Till supper-time alone.
Macbeth. Act iii, sc. 1, l. 42. [Macbeth] "Supper-time" is used ten times.
Mingle with society.—*Macbeth,* iii, 4, 3. See under HOST.

8
He lays before me . . . my wild societies.
The Merry Wives of Windsor. Act iii, sc. 4, l. 8. [Fenton]

9
Abjure Forever the society of men.
A Midsummer-Night's Dream. Act i, sc. 1, l. 65. [Theseus]
She hath abjured the company
And sight of men.
Twelfth Night. Act i, sc. 2, l. 40. [Captain]
Shunn'd my abhorr'd society.—*King Lear,* v, 3, 210.

10
Of her society Be not afraid.
The Tempest. Act iv, sc. 1, l. 91. [Iris]

11
Their more mature dignities and royal necessities made separation of their societies.
Winter's Tale. Act i, sc. 1, l. 27. [Camillo]

SOLDIER

See also Army, Troop

12
You have some stain of soldier in you.
All's Well that Ends Well. Act i, sc. 1, l. 122. [Helena]
Mars dote on you for his novices!
All's Well that Ends Well. Act ii, sc. 1, l. 48. [Parolles]
Lafeu: But I hope your lordship thinks not him a soldier.
Bertram: Yes, my lord, and of very valiant approof.
All's Well that Ends Well. Act ii, sc. 5, l. 1.
Countess: To be a soldier?
Gentleman: Such is his noble purpose.
All's Well that Ends Well. Act iii, sc. 2, l. 72.
From courtly friends, with camping foes to live,
Where death and danger dogs the heels of worth.
All's Well that Ends Well. Act iii, sc. 4, l. 14. [Steward]

13
This very day,
Great Mars, I put myself into thy file.
All's Well that Ends Well. Act iii, sc. 3, l. 8. [Bertram]
If you have a station in the file,
Not i' the worst rank of manhood, say 't.
Macbeth. Act iii, sc. 1, l. 102. [Macbeth] See also RANK.
Are his files As full as they report?
Timon of Athens. Act v, sc. 2, l. 1. [Senator]
The muster-file, rotten and sound, upon my life, amounts not to fifteen thousand poll; half of the which dare not shake the snow from off their cassocks, lest they shake themselves to pieces.
All's Well that Ends Well. Act iv, sc. 3, l. 188. [Parolles] The only use of "muster-file" and "cassocks."
Files and musters.—*Antony and Cleopatra,* i, 1, 3.
File of all the gentry.—*Henry VIII,* i, 1, 75; *Macbeth,* v, 2, 8.
Common file.—*Coriolanus,* i, 6, 43.
Right-hand file.—*Coriolanus,* ii, 1, 26.
Valued file.—*Macbeth,* iii, 1, 95.

14
Thy father and myself in friendship
First tried our soldiership!
All's Well that Ends Well. Act i, sc. 2, l. 25. [King]
More of his soldiership I know not.
All's Well that Ends Well. Act iv, sc. 3, l. 300. [Parolles]

His soldiership is twice the other twain.
Antony and Cleopatra. Act ii, sc. 1, l. 34. [Pompey]

Put we on Industrious soldiership.
Macbeth. Act v, sc. 4, l. 15. [Macduff]

Absolute soldiership.—*Antony and Cleopatra,* iii, 7, 43. "Soldiership" is repeated in *All's Well that Ends Well,* iii, 6, 89; *II Henry IV,* i, 2, 93; and *Othello,* i, 1, 27.

1
This is Monsieur Parolles, the gallant militarist,—that was his own phrase,—that had the whole theoric of war in the knot of his scarf, and the practice in the chape of his dagger.
All's Well that Ends Well. Act iv, sc. 3, l. 160. [Lord] The only use of "militarist" and "chape" (the metal tip of a scabbard).

Nor do I as an enemy to peace
Troop in the throngs of military men.
II Henry IV. Act iv, sc. 1, l. 61. [Archbishop of York] "Military man" occurs again in *Henry V,* iii, 2, 86.

Military discipline.—*Henry V,* iii, 2, 107.
Military policy.—*All's Well that Ends Well,* i, 1, 132.
Military rules.—*II Henry IV,* ii, 3, 30.
Most military sir.—*Love's Labour's Lost,* v, 1, 38.

2 Thou, the greatest soldier of the world,
Art turn'd the greatest liar.
Antony and Cleopatra. Act i, sc. 3, l. 38. [Cleopatra]

For one to say a soldier lies, is stabbing.
Othello. Act iii, sc. 4, l. 5. [Clown]

3
All this . . .
Was borne so like a soldier, that thy cheek
So much as lank'd not.
Antony and Cleopatra. Act i, sc. 4, l. 68. [Cæsar]

Till I shall see you in your soldier's dress,
Which will become you both.
Antony and Cleopatra, ii, 4, 4. [Lepidus]

You have shown all Hectors.—*Antony and Cleopatra,* iv, 8, 7.
How farest thou, soldier?—*Antony and Cleopatra,* ii, 6, 72. "Farest" is repeated in *I Henry VI,* i, 4, 74: "How farest thou, mirror of all martial men?"
Good fortune, worthy soldier.—*Antony and Cleopatra,* iii, 2, 22. "Worthy soldier" is repeated in iii, 7, 61.
Ancient soldier.—*Cymbeline,* v, 3, 15.
Armed soldiers.—*Richard II,* iii, 2, 25.
Armipotent soldier.—*All's Well that Ends Well,* iv, 3, 265. "Armipotent" is repeated in *Love's Labour's Lost,* v, 2, 650: "Armipotent wars."
Bloody soldier.—*Henry V,* iii, 3, 34.
Chiefest soldiers.—*Coriolanus,* v, 6, 150.
Chosen soldiers.—*III Henry VI,* iii, 3, 204.
Fellow-soldier.—*III Henry VI,* iv, 7, 70. The only use of "fellow-soldier."
Improvident soldiers!—*I Henry VI,* ii, 1, 58. "Improvident" is repeated in *The Merry Wives of Windsor,* ii, 2, 302: "Improvident jealousy."
Little soldier.—*II Henry IV,* v, 3, 34.
Main soldier.—*Antony and Cleopatra,* i, 2, 198.
Old soldier.—*Cymbeline,* v, 5, 306.
Renowned soldier.—*Richard III,* iv, 5, 9.
Skilless soldier.—*Romeo and Juliet,* iii, 3, 132.
Sleeping soldiers.—*Hamlet,* iii, 4, 120.
Unspotted soldiers.—*Henry V,* iv, 1, 169.
Young soldier.—*Twelfth Night,* iv, 1, 42.
Young noble soldier.—*All's Well that Ends Well,* iv, 5, 109.

4
O, wither'd is the garland of the war,
The soldier's pole is fall'n.
Antony and Cleopatra. Act iv, sc. 15, l. 64. [Cleopatra]

5
Then a soldier,
Full of strange oaths and bearded like the pard,
Jealous in honour, sudden and quick in quarrel,
Seeking the bubble reputation
Even in the cannon's mouth.
As You Like It. Act ii, sc. 7, l. 149. [Jaques]

6
Thou wast a soldier
Even to Cato's wish, not fierce and terrible
Only in strokes; but, with thy grim looks and
The thunder-like percussion of thy sounds,
Thou madest thine enemies shake, as if the world
Were feverous and did tremble.
Coriolanus. Act i, sc. 4, l. 56. [Lartius] The only use of "thunder-like" and "percussion."

We thank the gods
Our Rome hath such a soldier.
Coriolanus. Act i, sc. 9, l. 8. [Cominius]

Thou art their soldier, and being bred in broils
Hast not the soft way.
Coriolanus. Act iii, sc. 2, l. 81. [Volumnia]

7 When a soldier was the theme, my name
Was not far off.
Cymbeline. Act iii, sc. 3, l. 59. [Belarius]

The poor soldier that so richly fought,
Whose rags shamed gilded arms, whose naked breast
Stepp'd before targes of proof.
Cymbeline. Act v, sc. 5, l. 3. [Cymbeline] "Targes" is repeated in *Love's Labour's Lost,* v, 2, 566, and in *Antony and Cleopatra,* ii, 6, 39.

The forlorn soldier, that so nobly fought,
He would have well becomed this place, and graced
The thankings of a king.
Cymbeline. Act v, sc. 5, l. 405. [Cymbeline]

Poor soldiers.—*Henry V,* iv, 3, 116; *Cymbeline,* v, 5, 3.
Poor straggling soldiers.—*Timon of Athens,* v, 1, 7. "Straggling" is repeated in *The Rape of Lucrece,* l. 428.
Ragged soldiers.—*II Henry VI,* iv, 1, 90.

8
O, farewell, honest soldier.
Hamlet. Act i, sc. 1, l. 16. [Marcellus]

For his passage,
The soldiers' music and the rites of war
Speak loudly for him.
Hamlet. Act v, sc. 2, l. 409. [Fortinbras]

9
If I not be ashamed of my soldiers, I am a soused gurnet. I have misused the king's press damnably.
I Henry IV. Act iv, sc. 2, l. 12. [Falstaff]

The only use of "soused" (pickled), "gurnet" (a fish), and "damnably."
Prince of Wales: I did never see such pitiful rascals.
Falstaff: Tut, tut; good enough to toss; food for powder, food for powder; they 'll fill a pit as well as better: tush, man, mortal men, mortal men.
I Henry IV. Act iv, sc. 2, l. 70.

1 Up, and away!
Our soldiers stand full fairly for the day.
I Henry IV. Act v, sc. 3, l. 28. [Hotspur]

2
What a maidenly man-at-arms are you become!
II Henry IV. Act ii, sc. 2, l. 82. [Bardolph]
"Man at arms" (unhyphenated) is repeated in *III Henry VI*, iv, 4, 42, and occurs nowhere else. "Maidenly" also occurs only once more, in *A Midsummer-Night's Dream*, iii, 2, 217.
He 's like to be a cold soldier.
II Henry IV. Act iii, sc. 2, l. 134. [Falstaff]
I cannot put him to a private soldier that is the leader of so many thousands.
II Henry IV. Act iii, sc. 2, l. 177. [Falstaff]
The only use of "private soldier."
Common soldiers.—*III Henry VI*, i, 1, 9.

3
A soldier is better accommodated than with a wife.
II Henry IV. Act iii, sc. 2, l. 72. [Bardolph]
A good soldier-breeder.—*Henry V*, v, 2, 219. The only use of the phrase.

4 An iron man,
Cheering a rout of rebels with your drum.
II Henry IV. Act iv, sc. 2, l. 8. [Lancaster]
A soldier, firm and sound of heart,
And of buxom valour.
Henry V. Act iii, sc. 6, l. 27. [Pistol]
"Buxom" is used only once more, in *Pericles*, i, Gower, 23—probably not by Shakespeare.
A tried and valiant soldier.
Julius Cæsar. Act iv, sc. 1, l. 28. [Octavius]
A soldier fit to stand by Cæsar.
Othello. Act ii, sc. 3, l. 127. [Iago]

5 I am a soldier,
A name that in my thoughts becomes me best.
Henry V. Act iii, sc. 3, l. 5. [King Henry]
I am a soldier and unapt to weep
Or to exclaim on fortune's fickleness.
I Henry VI. Act v, sc. 3, l. 133. [Reignier]
The only use of "fickleness." "Unapt" is repeated in *I Henry IV*, i, 3, 2: "Unapt to stir"; *Coriolanus*, v, 1, 52: "Unapt to give"; *The Taming of the Shrew*, v, 2, 166: "Unapt to toil."
I am a soldier and now bound to France.
King John. Act i, sc. 1, l. 150. [Queen Elinor]
As I am a soldier.—*Henry V*, ii, 1, 69; *Othello*, ii, 3, 69.

6
The flesh'd soldier, rough and hard of heart,
In liberty of bloody hand shall range
With conscience wide as hell, mowing like grass
Your fresh-fair virgins and your flowering infants.
Henry V. Act iii, sc. 3, l. 11. [King Henry]
The only use of "fresh-fair."
We may as bootless spend our vain command
Upon the enraged soldiers in their spoil
As send precepts to the leviathan
To come ashore.
Henry V. Act iii, sc. 3, l. 24. [King Henry]
His soldiers sick and famish'd in their march.
Henry V. Act iii, sc. 5, l. 57. [Constable]
Trail'st thou the puissant pike?—*Henry V*, iv, 1, 40.

7
Therefore should every soldier in the wars do as every sick man in his bed, wash every mote out of his conscience: and dying so, death is to him advantage; or not dying, the time was blessedly lost wherein such preparation was gained.
Henry V. Act iv, sc. 1, l. 188. [King Henry]
O God of battles! steel my soldiers' hearts;
Possess them not with fear.
Henry V. Act iv, sc. 1, l. 306. [King Henry]

8 Now, soldiers, march away:
And how thou pleasest, God, dispose the day!
Henry V. Act iv, sc. 3, l. 131. [King Henry]
Falstaff: Must we all march?
Bardolph: Yea, two and two, Newgate fashion.
I Henry IV. Act iii, sc. 3, l. 103. The only mention of Newgate.

9
King Henry: From helmet to the spur all blood he was.
Exeter: In which array, brave soldier, doth he lie,
Larding the plain.
Henry V. Act iv, sc. 6, l. 6.
Come on, brave soldiers: doubt not of the day,
And, that once gotten, doubt not of large pay.
III Henry VI. Act iv, sc. 7, l. 87. [King Edward]
Brave soldier, pardon me.—*King John*, v, 6, 13. The only uses of "brave soldier."

10 Grow like savages,—as soldiers will
That nothing do but meditate on blood,—
To swearing and stern looks, defused attire
And every thing that seems unnatural.
Henry V. Act v, sc. 2, l. 59. [Burgundy]
"Defused" is repeated in *Richard III*, i, 2, 78.

11
I speak to thee plain soldier.
Henry V. Act v, sc. 2, l. 57. [King Henry]
Thou art a soldier only: speak no more.
Antony and Cleopatra. Act ii, sc. 2, l. 109. [Antony]

12
Ten thousand soldiers with me I will take,
Whose bloody deeds shall make all Europe quake.
I Henry VI. Act i, sc. 1, l. 155. [Bedford]
Ten thousand soldiers, Armed in proof.
Richard III. Act v, sc. 3, l. 218. [King Richard]

13
A braver soldier never couched lance.
I Henry VI. Act iii, sc. 2, l. 134. [Talbot]

A stouter champion never handled sword.
I Henry VI. Act iii, sc. 4, l. 19. [King Henry] See also under CHAMPION.
God's own soldier.—*King John,* ii, 1, 566.
God's soldier.—*Macbeth,* v, 8, 47.
Pharaoh's soldiers.—*Much Ado about Nothing,* iii, 3, 143. Pharaoh is mentioned again in *I Henry IV,* ii, 4, 520.

1 Let no soldier fly.
He that is truly dedicate to war
Hath no self-love, nor he that loves himself
Hath not essentially but by circumstance
The name of valour.
II Henry VI. Act v, sc. 2, l. 36. [Young Clifford]

2 They are soldiers,
Witty, courteous, liberal, full of spirit.
III Henry VI. Act i, sc. 2, l. 42. [York]

3 I am a soldier, I,
Older in practice, abler than yourself.
Julius Cæsar. Act iv, sc. 3, l. 30. [Cassius]
I said, an elder soldier, not a better:
Did I say 'better'?
Julius Cæsar. Act iv, sc. 3, l. 56. [Cassius]
Better soldier.—*Henry V,* iii, 6, 127; *Julius Cæsar,* iv, 3, 51; *Macbeth,* iv, 3, 191; *King Lear,* iv, 5, 3.

4
The sweet war-man is dead and rotten.
Love's Labour's Lost. Act v, sc. 2, l. 665. [Armado] The only use of "war-man."
The man of war.—*II Henry IV,* v, 1, 31.

5
I will right myself like a soldier.
Love's Labour's Lost. Act v, sc. 2, l. 734. [Armado]

6
A good and hardy soldier.
Macbeth. Act i, sc. 2, l. 4. [Malcolm]
You were good soldiers and tall fellows.
The Merry Wives of Windsor. Act ii, sc. 2, l. 10. [Falstaff]
Good soldier.—*Coriolanus,* ii, 1, 188; *Much Ado about Nothing,* i, 1, 53; *Antony and Cleopatra,* ii, 7, 111.

7
Fie, my lord, fie! a soldier, and afeard?
Macbeth. Act v, sc. 1, l. 41. [Lady Macbeth]
Your son, my lord, has paid a soldier's debt.
Macbeth, v, 8, 39. See under SON.

8
There 's not a soldier of us all, that, in the thanksgiving before meat, do relish the petition well that prays for peace.
Measure for Measure. Act i, sc. 2, l. 14. [Gentleman]

9
A fellow . . . that never set a squadron in the field,
Nor the division of a battle knows
More than a spinster.
Othello. Act i, sc. 1, l. 22. [Iago]
I have served him, and the man commands
Like a full soldier.
Othello. Act ii, sc. 1, l. 35. [Montano]

10
And let me the canakin clink, clink;
And let me the canakin clink:
A soldier 's a man;
A life 's but a span;
Why, then, let a soldier drink.
Othello. Act ii, sc. 3, l. 71. [Iago] The only use of "canakin."

11
If partially affined, or leagued in office,
Thou dost deliver more or less than truth,
Thou art no soldier.
Othello. Act ii, sc. 3, l. 218. [Montano] The only use of "partially" in the plays. It occurs again in *The Rape of Lucrece,* l. 634. "Affined" is repeated in i, 1, 39, and in *Troilus and Cressida,* i, 3, 25.
'Tis the soldiers' life
To have their balmy slumbers waked with strife.
Othello. Act ii, sc. 3, l. 257. [Othello] "Balmy" is repeated in v, 2, 16, and occurs in no other play. It is used in *Sonnets,* cvii.

12
Be a soldier to thy purpose.
Pericles. Act iv, sc. 1, l. 8. [Dionyza]

13
Thou shalt have twelve thousand fighting men!
Richard II. Act iii, sc. 2, l. 70. [Salisbury] "Fighting-men" is repeated in *Henry V,* iv, 3, 3.

14
Sometime she driveth o'er a soldier's neck,
And then dreams he of cutting foreign throats,
Of breaches, ambuscadoes, Spanish blades,
Of healths five-fathom deep; and then anon
Drums in his ear, at which he starts and wakes,
And being thus frighted swears a prayer or two
And sleeps again.
Romeo and Juliet. Act i, sc. 4, l. 82. [Mercutio] The only use of "ambuscadoes" and "five-fathom."

15
Thou art a soldier, therefore seldom rich;
It comes in charity to thee: for all thy living
Is 'mongst the dead, and all the lands thou hast
Lie in a pitch'd field.
Timon of Athens. Act i, sc. 2, l. 228. [Timon]

16
'Tis honour with most lands to be at odds;
Soldiers should brook as little wrongs as gods.
Timon of Athens. Act iii, sc. 5, l. 116.

17
But when they would seem soldiers, they have galls,
Good arms, strong joints, true swords.
Troilus and Cressida. Act i, sc. 3, l. 237. [Æneas]
We are soldiers;
And may that soldier a mere recreant prove,
That means not, hath not, or is not in love!
Troilus and Cressida. Act i, sc. 3, l. 286. [Agamemnon]
He was a soldier good;
But, by great Mars, the captain of us all,
Never like thee.
Troilus and Cressida. Act iv, sc. 5, l. 197. [Nestor]

1
Beat loud the tabourines, let the trumpets blow,
That this great soldier may his welcome know.
Troilus and Cressida. Act iv, sc. 5, l. 275. [Agamemnon] "Tabourines" (military drums) is repeated in *Antony and Cleopatra,* iv, 8, 37: "Rattling tabourines."
Great soldier.—*Measure for Measure,* iii, 1, 217.
Greater soldier.—*Coriolanus,* iv, 5, 170; 176.
Greatest soldier.—*Antony and Cleopatra,* i, 3, 38.

II—Officers

See also Commander, Officer, Rank

Captain:

2 Captain I 'll be no more;
But I will eat and drink, and sleep as soft
As captain shall: simply the thing I am
Shall make me live.
All's Well that Ends Well. Act iv, sc. 3, l. 367. [Parolles]

3
Who does i' the wars more than his captain can
Becomes his captain's captain.
Antony and Cleopatra. Act iii, sc. 1, l. 21. [Ventidius]
Our great captain's captain.—*Othello,* ii, 1, 74.

4
The itch of his affection should not then
Have nick'd his captainship.
Antony and Cleopatra. Act iii, sc. 13, l. 7. [Enobarbus] The only use of "nick'd."
Take
The captainship, thou shalt be met with thanks.
Timon of Athens. Act v, sc. 1, l. 164. [Senator] The only uses of "captainship."

5
Captain! thou abominable damned cheater, art thou not ashamed to be called captain? An captains were of my mind, they would truncheon you out, for taking their names upon you before you have earned them. You a captain! you slave, for what? for tearing a poor whore's ruff in a bawdy-house? He a captain? hang him, rogue! he lives upon mouldy stewed prunes and dried cakes. A captain! God's light, these villains will make the word as odious as the word 'occupy;' which was an excellent good word before it was ill sorted: therefore captains had need look to it.
II Henry IV. Act ii, sc. 4, l. 151. [Doll] The only use of "truncheon" as a verb.

6 As I came along,
I met and overtook a dozen captains,
Bare-headed, sweating, knocking at the taverns.
II Henry IV. Act ii, sc. 4, l. 386. [Peto]
A dozen captains stay at the door for you.
II Henry IV. Act ii, sc. 4, l. 402. [Bardolph]

7
Your captain is brave.
II Henry VI. Act iv, sc. 2, l. 69. [Cade]
Brave captain.—*I Henry VI,* iii, 4, 16.
Good captain.—*Henry V,* iv, 7, 156.
Grand captain.—*Antony and Cleopatra,* iii, 1, 9.
Honourable captain.—*I Henry VI,* iv, 4, 17.
Noble captain.—*All's Well that Ends Well,* ii, 1, 47; *Antony and Cleopatra,* ii, 7, 142; iii, 13, 189.
Royal captain.—*Henry V,* iv, Prol., 29.

8
A wise stout captain, and soon persuaded!
III Henry VI. Act iv, sc. 7, l. 30. [Gloucester]

9
That in the captain's but a choleric word,
Which in the soldier is flat blasphemy.
Measure for Measure. Act ii, sc. 2, l. 130. [Isabella]

10
O, he is the courageous captain of complements.
Romeo and Juliet. Act ii, sc. 4, l. 20. [Mercutio]

11
Say ay, and be captain of us all.
The Two Gentlemen of Verona. Act iv, sc 1, l. 65. [Outlaw]
Captain of our fairy band.—*A Midsummer-Night's Dream,* iii, 2, 110.
Captain of a pinnace.—*II Henry VI,* iv, 1, 107.
Captain of the watch.—*I Henry VI,* ii, 1, 61.

Corporal:

12
My whole charge consists of ancients, corporals, lieutenants.
I Henry IV. Act iv, sc. 2, l. 26. [Falstaff]
Good corporal! good lieutenant! offer nothing here.
Henry V. Act ii, sc. 1, l. 41. [Bardolph]
Good corporal.—*Henry V,* ii, 1, 29.
Good master corporal captain.—*II Henry IV,* iii, 2, 244.
Corporal of his field.—*Love's Labour's Lost,* iii, 1, 189.

General:

13
The general of our horse thou art.
All's Well that Ends Well. Act iii, sc. 3, l. 1. [Duke]
General of the forces.—*Cymbeline,* iii, 7, 11.
General of the Goths.—*Titus Andronicus,* iv, 4, 69.
General of your woes.—*Romeo and Juliet,* v, 3, 219.

14 What miscarries
Shall be the general's fault, though he perform
To the utmost of a man.
Coriolanus. Act i, sc. 1, l. 270. [Brutus]

15
Whilst a field should be dispatch'd and fought,
You are disputing of your generals.
I Henry VI. Act i, sc. 1, l. 72. [Messenger]
A woman's general; what should we fear?
III Henry VI. Act i, sc. 2, l. 69. [Richard]

16
When that the general is not like the hive
To whom the foragers shall all repair,

What honey is expected?
Troilus and Cressida. Act i, sc. 3, l. 81. [Ulysses] The only use of "foragers."

I was advertised their great general slept,
Whilst emulation in the army crept.
Troilus and Cressida. Act ii, sc. 2, l. 211. [Hector]

Great general.—*Love's Labour 's Lost,* iii, 1, 187; *Troilus and Cressida,* ii, 3, 270.
Brother general.—*II Henry IV,* iv, 1, 94.
Dear general.—*Othello,* v, 2, 299.
Merciful general.—*All 's Well that Ends Well,* iv, 3, 144.
Noble general.—*Troilus and Cressida,* ii, 3, 237.
Noble and valiant general.—*Othello,* ii, 2, 2.
Princely general.—*II Henry IV,* iv, 1, 141.
Valiant general.—*I Henry VI,* v, 2, 8.
Worthy general.—*Othello,* iv, 1, 229.
My sometime general.—*Coriolanus,* iv, 1, 23.

1
The magnanimous and most illustrious six-or-seven-times-honoured captain-general of the Grecian army, Agamemnon et cetera.
Troilus and Cressida. Act iii, sc. 3, l. 278. [Achilles] The only use of either phrase.

Lord general.—*Coriolanus,* i, 9, 81.

2
Are you content to be our general?
The Two Gentlemen of Verona. Act iv, sc. 1, l. 61. [Outlaw]

Lieutenant:

3
He alone dealt on lieutenancy.
Antony and Cleopatra. Act iii, sc. 11, l. 38. [Antony]

Strip you out of your lieutenancy.
Othello, ii, 1, 173. The only uses of "lieutenancy."

4
Othello: Now art thou my lieutenant.
Iago: I am your own for ever.
Othello. Act iii, sc. 3, l. 478.

Stephano: Thou shalt be my lieutenant, monster, or my standard.
Trinculo: Your lieutenant, if you list; he 's no standard.
The Tempest. Act iii, sc. 2, l. 18.

Aunchient lieutenant.—*Henry V,* iii, 6, 13. "Aunchient" is used once again in iii, 2, 83, and occurs in no other play.
Good lieutenant.—*Othello,* ii, 1, 60; ii, 3, 108; 158; 315; iii, 1, 44.
Master lieutenant.—*III Henry VI,* iv, 6, 1.

Sergeant:

5
If any hour meet a sergeant, a' turns back for very fear.
The Comedy of Errors. Act iv, sc. 2, l. 56. [Dromio of Syracuse]

A sergeant in the way.—*The Comedy of Errors,* iv, 2, 61.
Hindered by the sergeant.—*The Comedy of Errors,* iv, 3, 40.
Sergeant of the band.—*The Comedy of Errors,* iv, 3, 30.
Fell sergeant.—*Hamlet,* v, 2, 374.

6 This is the sergeant
Who like a good and hardy soldier fought.
Macbeth. Act i, sc. 2, l. 3. [Malcolm]

SOLITUDE

See also Desert

7 Now I see
The mystery of your loneliness, and find
Your salt tears' head.
All's Well that Ends Well. Act i, sc. 3, l. 176. [Countess] "Loneliness" is repeated in *Hamlet,* iii, 1, 46.

8
Forswear the full stream of the world and to live in a nook merely monastic.
As You Like It. Act iii, sc. 2, l. 440. [Rosalind] The only use of "monastic."

9
We are alone; here 's none but thee and I.
II Henry VI. Act i, sc. 2, l. 69. [Duchess] I am with thee here alone.—*III Henry VI,* ii, 4, 5. These phrases, in various forms, used throughout the plays.

All alone . . . came I.—*Romeo and Juliet,* v, 3, 252.
All alone shall live.—*Hamlet,* i, 5, 102.
All alone . . . we 'll wander.—*Antony and Cleopatra,* i, 1, 52.

10 Go with speed
To some forlorn and naked hermitage,
Remote from all the pleasures of the world.
Love's Labour 's Lost. Act v, sc. 2, l. 805. [Princess] "Hermitage" is repeated in *Richard II,* iii, 3, 148.

11 I do beseech thee, grant me this,
To leave me but a little to myself.
Othello. Act iii, sc. 3, l. 84. [Othello]

12 Empty lodgings and unfurnish'd walls,
Unpeopled offices, untrodden stones.
Richard II. Act i, sc. 2, l. 68. [Duchess of Gloucester] The only use of "untrodden."

13
Thou shalt find me, sad and solitary.
The Two Gentlemen of Verona. Act iv, sc. 4, l. 94. [Proteus] "Solitary" is repeated in *As You Like It,* iii, 2, 16. "Solitude" does not occur in the plays.

14
Holding their course to Paphos, where their queen
Means to immure herself and not be seen.
Venus and Adonis, l. 1194. "Immure" is repeated in *Troilus and Cressida,* Prol., 8. Paphos is mentioned again in *Pericles,* iv, Gower, 32, and in *The Tempest,* iv, 1, 93.

SON

See also Boy; Father and Son

15
Whether I live or die, be you the sons
Of worthy Frenchmen.
All's Well that Ends Well. Act ii, sc. 1, l. 11. [King]

An they were sons of mine, I 'd have them whipped.
All's Well that Ends Well. Act ii, sc. 3, l. 92. [Lafeu]

You are too young, too happy, and too good,
To make yourself a son out of my blood.
All's Well that Ends Well. Act ii, sc. 3, l. 102. [Helena]

1
Clown: Your son will not be killed so soon as I thought he would.
Countess: Why should he be killed?
Clown: So say I, madam, if he run away, as I hear he does: the danger is in standing to 't; that 's the loss of men, though it be the getting of children. Here they come will tell you more: for my part, I only hear your son was run away.
All 's Well that Ends Well. Act iii, sc. 2, l. 39. See also under DISCRETION.
Countess: Where is my son, I pray you?
Gentleman: Madam, he 's gone to serve the duke of Florence:
We met him thitherward.
All 's Well that Ends Well. Act iii, sc. 2, l. 53. The only use of "thitherward."
He was my son;
But I do wash his name out of my blood.
All 's Well that Ends Well. Act iii, sc. 2, l. 69. [Countess]
Your son was misled with a snipt-taffeta fellow.
All 's Well that Ends Well, iv, 5, 1. See under CHARACTER. The only use of "snipt-taffeta."
My son, in whom my house's name
Must be digested.
All 's Well that Ends Well. Act v, sc. 3, l. 73. [Lafeu]

2
I would thou hadst been son to some man else.
As You Like It. Act i, sc. 2, l. 235. [Duke]
Had I before known this young man his son,
I should have given him tears unto entreaties,
Ere he should thus have ventured.
As You Like It. Act i, sc. 2, l. 249. [Rosalind]

3 Tell me where is that son
That floated with thee on the fatal raft?
The Comedy of Errors. Act v, sc. 1, l. 347. [Ægeus]

4
Had I a dozen sons, each in my love alike and none less dear than thine and my good Marcius, I had rather had eleven die nobly for their country than one voluptuously surfeit out of action.
Coriolanus. Act i, sc. 3, l. 24. [Volumnia] The only use of "voluptuously."

5
How does your little son?
Coriolanus. Act i, sc. 3, l. 56. [Valeria]
Little son.—*The Merry Wives of Windsor,* iv, 4, 47.
Young son.—*I Henry VI,* iv, 3, 40; *Richard III,* iv, 1, 14; *Romeo and Juliet,* ii, 3, 33.
Youthful sons.—*The Rape of Lucrece,* l. 1432.

6
Your son
Will or exceed the common or be caught
With cautelous baits and practice.
Coriolanus. Act iv, sc. 1, l. 31. [Coriolanus] "Cautelous" (treacherous, wily) is used again in *Julius Cæsar,* ii, 1, 129: "Cowards and men cautelous."
I would my son
Were in Arabia, and thy tribe before him,
His good sword in his hand.
Coriolanus. Act iv, sc. 2, l. 23. [Volumnia]
As far as doth the Capitol exceed
The meanest house in Rome, so far my son . . .
Whom you have banish'd, does exceed you all.
Coriolanus. Act iv, sc. 2, l. 39. [Volumnia]
Banish'd son.—*Titus Andronicus,* iii, 1, 255; *King Lear,* iv, 7, 91.

7
Two other sons, who in the wars o' the time
Died with their swords in hand.
Cymbeline. Act i, sc. 1, l. 35. [Gentleman]
Your son 's my father's friend; he takes his part.
Cymbeline, i, 1, 165. See under PART.

8
Her son gone, So needful for this present.
Cymbeline. Act iv, sc. 3, l. 7. [Cymbeline]
Her son Is gone, we know not how nor where.
Cymbeline. Act v, sc. 5, l. 272. [Cymbeline]
Here are your sons again.—*Cymbeline,* v, 5, 348.
I know not how to wish A pair of worthier sons.
Cymbeline. Act v, sc. 5, l. 356. [Cymbeline]

9
Since, Jupiter, our son is good,
Take off his miseries.
Cymbeline. Act v, sc. 4, l. 85. [Mother]
Good son.—*Romeo and Juliet,* ii, 3, 47; 55; *Troilus and Cressida,* ii, 3, 268.
The heavens have bless'd you with a goodly son.
Richard III. Act i, sc. 3, l. 9. [Lord Grey]
Goodly sons.—*The Comedy of Errors,* i, 1, 51.
Good man's son.—*King Lear,* iv, 1, 60.

10
O wonderful son, that can so astonish a mother!
Hamlet. Act iii, sc. 2, l. 340. [Hamlet]
Beloved sons.—*King Lear,* i, 1, 140.
Bold son.—*Richard II,* i, 1, 3.
Fair son.—*I Henry VI,* iv, 5, 52; *The Comedy of Errors,* v, 1, 343; *Henry V,* v, 2, 376; *King John,* iii, 4, 103; *Richard II,* v, 2, 92.
Gentle son.—*III Henry VI,* i, 1, 259; *Hamlet,* iii, 4, 122.
Great son.—*Coriolanus,* v, 3, 140.
Honest son.—*Taming of the Shrew,* iv, 5, 69.
Hopeful son.—*Twelfth Night,* ii, 3, 85.
Human sons.—*Timon of Athens,* iv, 3, 185.
Loving son.—*III Henry VI,* v, 1, 7; *Lear,* i, 1, 43.
Princely sons.—*Richard III,* iii, 3, 20; *King John,* ii, 1, 484.
Proper son.—*Othello,* i, 3, 69.
Well-deserving son.—*Richard II,* ii, 1, 194.

11
Do you not come your tardy son to chide,
That, lapsed in time and passion, lets go by
The important acting of your dread command?
Hamlet. Act iii, sc. 4, l. 106. [Hamlet]
Your son gone; and he most violent author
Of his own just remove.
Hamlet. Act iv, sc. 5, l. 80. [King]
King: Our son shall win.
Queen: He 's fat and scant of breath.
Hamlet. Act v, sc. 2, l. 298.

12
That thou art my son, I have partly thy mother's word, partly my own opinion, but chiefly a villanous trick of thine eye and a foolish hanging of thy nether lip, that doth warrant me. If then thou be son to me, here lies the point: why, being son to me, art thou so pointed at? . . . Shall the son of

England prove a thief and take purses? a question to be asked.
I Henry IV. Act ii, sc. 4, l. 446. [Falstaff]

I will redeem all this on Percy's head
And in the closing of some glorious day
Be bold to tell you that I am your son.
I Henry IV. Act iii, sc. 2, l. 132. [Prince of Wales]

It was your presurmise,
That, in the dole of blows, your son might drop.
II Henry IV. Act i, sc. 1, l. 168. [Bardolph]
The only use of "presurmise."

1 Where is his son,
The nimble-footed madcap Prince of Wales?
I Henry IV. Act iv, sc. 1, l. 94. [Hotspur]
"Nimble-footed" is repeated in *The Two Gentlemen of Verona*, v, 3, 7.

2
Morton: But, for my lord your son,—
Northumberland: Why, he is dead. . . .
Bardolph: I cannot think, my lord, your son is dead. . . .
Morton: My lord your son had only but the corpse,
But shadows and the shows of men, to fight.
II Henry IV. Act i, sc. 1, l. 83.

Thoughtful to invest
Their sons with arts and martial exercises.
II Henry IV. Act iv, sc. 5, l. 73. [King]
The only use of "thoughtful."

3
My son, the comfort of my age.
II Henry VI. Act i, sc. 1, l. 190. [Salisbury]

His son am I; deny it if you can.
II Henry VI. Act iv, sc. 2, l. 154. [Cade]

4
Hadst thou but loved him half so well as I,
Or felt that pain which I did for him once,
Or nourish'd him as I did with my blood,
Thou wouldst have left thy dearest heart-blood there,
Rather than have made that savage duke thine heir
And disinherited thine only son.
III Henry VI. Act i, sc. 1, l. 220. [Queen Margaret]

My son is disinherited.—*III Henry VI*, i, 1, 250.

5
Thou hast one son; for his sake pity me,
Lest in revenge thereof, sith God is just,
He be as miserably slain as I.
III Henry VI. Act i, sc. 3, l. 42. [Rutland]
The only use of "miserably."

My sons, God knows what hath bechanced them:
But this I know, they have demean'd themselves
Like men born to renown by life or death.
III Henry VI. Act i, sc. 4, l. 6. [York]
"Bechanced" is repeated in *The Merchant of Venice*, i, 1, 38. "Bechance" is used once, in *The Two Gentlemen of Verona*, i, 1, 61.

Where are your mess of sons to back you now?
III Henry VI. Act i, sc. 4, l. 73. [Queen Margaret]

6
Methinks, 'tis prize enough to be his son.
III Henry VI. Act ii, sc. 1, l. 20. [Richard]

By this, I hope, she hath a son for me.
III Henry VI. Act v, sc. 5, l. 90. [King Edward]

7 Her male issue
Or died where they were made, or shortly after
This world had air'd them.
Henry VIII. Act ii, sc. 4, l. 191. [King]

Male twins.—*The Comedy of Errors*, i, 1, 56.
Male child.—*King John*, iii, 4, 79; *Henry VIII*, ii, 4, 188.

8
Brave son, derived from honourable loins!
Julius Cæsar. Act ii, sc. 1, l. 322. [Ligarius]

Brave son.—*The Tempest*, 1, 2, 438.

9 I would to heaven
I were your son, so you would love me, Hubert.
King John. Act iv, sc. 1, l. 23. [Arthur]

Many a poor man's son would have lien still
And ne'er have spoke a loving word to you.
King John. Act iv, sc. 1, l. 50. [Arthur]

He talks to me who never had a son.
King John. Act iii, sc. 4, l. 91. [Constance]

10 My son
Came then into my mind; and yet my mind
Was then scarce friends with him.
King Lear. Act iv, sc. 1, l. 35. [Gloucester]

11
Upon my head they placed a fruitless crown,
And put a barren sceptre in my gripe,
Thence to be wrench'd with an unlineal hand,
No son of mine succeeding.
Macbeth. Act iii, sc. 1, l. 61. [Macbeth]
The only use of "unlineal."

12
If their sons be ingenuous, they shall want no instruction.
Love's Labour's Lost. Act iv, sc. 2, l. 80. [Holofernes] The only use of "ingenuous."

13 A wayward son,
Spiteful and wrathful, who, as others do,
Loves for his own ends.
Macbeth. Act iii, sc. 5, l. 11. [Hecate]

Accursed sons.—*Titus Andronicus*, ii, 3, 290.
Bad sons.—*The Tempest*, i, 2, 120.
Brain-sick son.—*II Henry VI*, v, 1, 163.
Changed son.—*Hamlet*, ii, 2, 36.
Common sons.—*Coriolanus*, v, 3, 52.
Corrected son.—*Coriolanus*, v, 3, 57.
Deceitful son.—*The Taming of the Shrew*, iv, 4, 83.
Digressing son.—*Richard II*, v, 3, 66.
Forward sons.—*III Henry VI*, i, 1, 203; ii, 2, 58.
Frail son.—*Henry VIII*, iii, 2, 148.
Haughty sons.—*Titus Andronicus*, i, 1, 302.
Lawless sons.—*Titus Andronicus*, i, 1, 312.
Low-laid son.—*Cymbeline*, v, 4, 103. "Low laid" (unhyphenated) is repeated in *King John*, ii, 1, 164: "Low laid in my grave."
Lustful sons.—*Titus Andronicus*, iv, 1, 79.
Old son.—*Richard II*, v, 3, 146.
Poor son.—*Richard III*, i, 3, 120.
Prodigal Son.—*The Winter's Tale*, iv, 3, 103. See ROGUE, 1298:11.
Purblind son.—*Romeo and Juliet*, ii, 1, 12.
Rude son.—*Troilus and Cressida*, i, 3, 115.

Spleenful sons.—*Titus Andronicus,* ii, 3, 191. "Spleenful" is repeated in *II Henry VI,* iii, 2, 128: "Spleenful mutiny."
Traitorous sons.—*Titus Andronicus,* i, 1, 452; iv, 4, 53.
Treacherous son.—*Richard II,* v, 3, 60.
Unfortunate son.—*All's Well that Ends Well,* iii, 2, 28.
Unhappy son.—*Richard III,* ii, 2, 4; *Titus Andronicus,* ii, 3, 240; iv, 4, 66.
Unworthy sons.—*Titus Andronicus,* i, 1, 346.
Usurping son.—*King John,* ii, 1, 121.
Waspish-headed son.—*The Tempest,* iv, 1, 99. The only use of the phrase.
Wilful sons.—*Titus Andronicus,* iv, 4, 8.
Son of utter darkness.—*I Henry IV,* iii, 3, 42.
Sons of darkness.—*I Henry IV,* ii, 4, 191.

1

Malcolm: Macduff is missing and your noble son.
Ross: Your son, my lord, has paid a soldier's debt. . . .
Siward: Had he his hurts before?
Ross: Ay, on the front.
Siward: Why then, God's soldier be he!
Had I as many sons as I have hairs,
I would not wish them to a fairer death:
And so, his knell is knoll'd.

Macbeth. Act v, sc. 8, l. 38.

Your noble son is mad.

Hamlet. Act ii, sc. 2, l. 92. [Polonius] "Noble son" is repeated in *Titus Andronicus,* iii, 1, 237; v, 3, 155.

2

You have a son, Aumerle, my noble cousin.

Richard II. Act ii, sc. 3, l. 125. [Bolingbroke]

Have we more sons? or are we like to have?
Is not my teeming date drunk up with time?
And wilt thou pluck my fair son from mine age,
And rob me of a happy mother's name?
Is he not like thee? is he not thine own?

Richard II. Act v, sc. 2, l. 90. [Duchess]

Were he twenty times my son,
I would appeach him.

Richard II. Act v, sc. 2, l. 101. [York] "Appeach" is used a second time in l. 79, and occurs in no other scene. "Appeach'd" is used in *All's Well that Ends Well,* i, 3, 197.

Can no man tell me of my unthrifty son?
'Tis full three months since I did see him last:
If any plague hang over us, 'tis he.

Richard II. Act v, sc. 3, l. 1. [Bolingbroke]

3

He is my son; yea, and therein my shame.

Richard III. Act ii, sc. 2, l. 29. [Duchess of York]

Son I dare not call; thou art too base
To be acknowledged.

The Winter's Tale, iv, 4, 428. [Polixenes]

4

My damned son, which thy two sweet sons smother'd.

Richard III. Act iv, sc. 4, l. 134. [Duchess] "Sweet son" (or sons) is repeated in *III Henry VI,* i, 1, 228; *Richard III,* iv, 4, 25; *The Taming of the Shrew,* v, 1, 115; *Coriolanus,* iii, 2, 107; *Titus Andronicus,* ii, 3, 179.

I have no moe sons of the royal blood
For thee to murder.

Richard III. Act iv, sc. 4, l. 199. [Queen]

5

Away from light steals home my heavy son,
And private in his chamber pens himself.

Romeo and Juliet. Act i, sc. 1, l. 143. [Montague]

6

So thou, thyself out-going in thy noon,
Unlook'd on diest, unless thou get a son.

Sonnets. No. vii. The only use of "outgoing."

7

Nay, I told you your son was well beloved in Padua.

The Taming of the Shrew. Act v, sc. 1, l. 26. [Petruchio]

8

Alonso: My son is lost. . . . O thou mine heir
Of Naples and of Milan, what strange fish
Hath made his meal on thee? . . .
Sebastian: We have lost your son,
I fear, for ever. . . .
Alonso: Lead off this ground; and let's make further search
For my poor son.

The Tempest. Act ii, sc. 1, l. 109.

Thee of thy son, Alonso, They have bereft.

The Tempest. Act iii, sc. 3, l. 75. [Ariel]

My son i' the ooze is bedded.

The Tempest. Act iii, sc. 3, l. 100. [Alonso]

I wish
Myself were mudded in that oozy bed
Where my son lies.

The Tempest. Act v, sc. 1, l. 150. [Alonso] The only use of "oozy."

If this prove
A vision of the Island, one dear son
Shall I lose twice.

The Tempest. Act v, sc. 1, l. 175. [Alonso]

Dear son.—*Cymbeline,* ii, 3, 65; *Much Ado about Nothing,* ii, 1, 374; *Romeo and Juliet,* iii, 3, 7; *Titus Andronicus,* iii, 1. 22.

9 Bearing his valiant sons
In coffins from the field.

Titus Andronicus. Act i, sc. 1, l. 34. [Marcus]

Of five and twenty valiant sons,
Half of the number that King Priam had,
Behold the poor remains, alive and dead!

Titus Andronicus. Act i, sc. 1, l. 79. [Titus]

And buried one and twenty valiant sons,
Knighted in field, slain manfully in arms,
In right and service of their noble country.

Titus Andronicus. Act i, sc. 1, l. 195. [Titus]

The effects of sorrow for his valiant sons,
Whose loss hath pierced him deep and scarr'd his heart.

Titus Andronicus. Act iv, sc. 4, l. 30. [Tamora]

Valiant son.—*II Henry VI,* i, 1, 115; *III Henry VI,* ii, 5, 120.

10 Unkind and careless of thine own,
Why suffer'st thou thy sons, unburied yet,
To hover on the dreadful shore of Styx?

Titus Andronicus. Act i, sc. 1, l. 86. [Titus] The Styx is mentioned only once more, in *Troilus and Cressida,* v, 4, 20.

And if thy sons were ever dear to thee,
O, think my son to be as dear to me!

Titus Andronicus. Act i, sc. 1, l. 107. [Tamora]

Must my sons be slaughter'd in the streets,
For valiant doings in their country's cause?
Titus Andronicus. Act i, sc. 1, l. 112. [Tamora]

Slaughter'd son.—*Richard III,* i, 2, 10.

1 To this your son is mark'd, and die he must.
Titus Andronicus. Act i, sc. 1, l. 125. [Titus]

I'll go fetch thy sons
To back thy quarrels, whatsoe'er they be.
Titus Andronicus. Act ii, sc. 3, l. 53. [Aaron]

Fear not my sons; they shall do well enough.
Titus Andronicus. Act ii, sc. 3, l. 305. [Tamora]

2 For two and twenty sons I never wept,
Because they died in honour's lofty bed.
Titus Andronicus. Act iii, sc. 1, l. 10. [Titus]

This way to death my wretched sons are gone.
Titus Andronicus. Act iii, sc. 1, l. 98. [Titus]

As for my sons, say I account of them
As jewels purchased at an easy price.
Titus Andronicus. Act iii, sc. 1, l. 198. [Titus]

3 Lucius: In wrongful quarrel you have slain your son.
Titus: Nor thou, nor he, are any sons of mine;
My sons would never so dishonour me.
Titus Andronicus. Act i, sc. 1, l. 293.

O, see what thou hast done!
In a bad quarrel slain a virtuous son.
Titus Andronicus. Act i, sc. 1, l. 341. [Marcus]

4 Leontes: Are you so fond of your young prince as we
Do seem to be of ours?
Polixenes: If at home, sir,
He 's all my exercise, my mirth, my matter,
Now my sworn friend and then mine enemy,
My parasite, my soldier, statesman, all:
He makes a July's day short as December,
And with his varying childness cures in me
Thoughts that would thick my blood.
The Winter's Tale. Act i, sc. 2, l. 164. July is mentioned again in *Henry VIII,* i, 1, 154. The only use of "childness."

II—Elder and Younger Sons

5 My first son, Whither wilt thou go?
Coriolanus. Act iv, sc. 1, l. 33. [Volumnia] The only use of "first son."

I am the second son of old Sir Rowland.
As You Like It. Act v, sc. 4, l. 158. [Jaques]

Third son to the third Edward King of England.
I Henry VI, ii, 4, 84; ii, 5, 75.

Third son.—*II Henry VI,* ii, 2, 34.

Fourth son.—*II Henry VI,* ii, 2, 55.

Fifth son.—*II Henry VI,* ii, 2, 45.

6 The eldest son and heir of John of Gaunt.
II Henry VI. Act ii, sc. 2, l. 22. [York] "Eldest son" is repeated in v, 1, 49; *I Henry IV,* i, 1, 71; *II Henry IV,* ii, 1, 14; *Henry VIII,* ii, 2, 21; *King John,* i, 1, 51; *All's Well that Ends Well,* iii, 5, 79; *Much Ado about Nothing,* ii, 1, 10; *The Taming of the Shrew,* Ind., 1, 84; *Titus Andronicus,* i, 1, 103; 224; *Twelfth Night,* i, 5, 121.

This is thy eld'st son's son,
Infortunate in nothing but in thee.
King John. Act ii, sc. 1, l. 177. [Constance] "Infortunate" is used only once again, in *II Henry VI,* iv, 9, 18.

Son's son.—*Richard II,* ii, 1, 105.

7 Edward's seven sons, whereof thyself art one,
Were as seven vials of his sacred blood,
Or seven fair branches springing from one root.
Richard II. Act i, sc. 2, l. 11. [Duchess of Gloucester]

Seven sons.—*II Henry VI,* ii, 2, 10.

Three sons.—*Richard III,* i, 4, 242; *As You Like It,* i, 2, 126.

Thousand sons.—*II Henry IV,* iv, 3, 133; *Troilus and Cressida,* iii, 3, 156.

8 His son is elder, sir; His son is thirty.
Romeo and Juliet. Act i, sc. 5, l. 40. [Capulet]

I have, sir, a son by order of law, some year elder than this.
King Lear. Act i, sc. 1, l. 20. [Gloucester]

9 I am his first-born son.
Titus Andronicus, i, 1, 5; i, 1, 120.

First-born infants.—*Love's Labour's Lost,* i, 1, 101.

The first-born Cain.—*II Henry IV,* i, 1, 157. Cain is mentioned six times in the plays.

You are the first-born.—*As You Like It,* i, 1, 50.

First-born of Egypt.—*As You Like It,* ii, 5, 63.

The first male child.—*King John,* iii, 4, 79. The only use of the phrase.

10 He dies upon my scimitar's sharp point
That touches this my first-born son and heir!
Titus Andronicus. Act iv, sc. 2, l. 91. [Aaron]

Son and heir to Mars.—*Coriolanus,* iv, 5, 204.

Son and heir of old Tiberio.—*Romeo and Juliet,* i, 5, 131.

Son and heir.—*King John,* i, 1, 56; *King Lear,* ii, 2, 23; *Romeo and Juliet,* v, 3, 209. See also Inheritance.

Next son.—*II Henry VI,* ii, 2, 31.

11 The youngest son of Priam, a true knight.
Troilus and Cressida. Act iv, sc. 5, l. 96. [Ulysses]

Youngest son.—*As You Like It,* i, 1, 59; i, 2, 234; 246; *Titus Andronicus,* i, 1, 418.

Youngest born.—*King Lear,* ii, 4, 216.

Younger sons.—*I Henry IV,* iv, 2, 30.

Younger princely son.—*Cymbeline,* v, 5, 360.

Younger born.—*King John,* i, 1, 71.

12 My second joy And first-fruits of my body.
The Winter's Tale. Act iii, sc. 2, l. 98. [Hermione] The only use of "first-fruits." "First-fruit" is used in *I Henry VI,* v, 4, 13, referring to a daughter.

III—Only Sons

1
Thou mightst have had the sole son of my queen.
Cymbeline. Act i, sc. 1, l. 138. [Cymbeline]

Sole son.—*Cymbeline*, i, 1, 5; *Hamlet*, iii, 3, 77.

2 Is this our foeman's face?
Ah, no, no, no, it is mine only son!
III Henry VI. Act ii, sc. 5, l. 82. [Father]

3
Juliet: What 's he that follows there? . . .
Nurse: His name is Romeo, and a Montague;
The only son of your great enemy.
Romeo and Juliet. Act i, sc. 5, l. 134.

Only son.—*II Henry VI*, ii, 2, 19; *III Henry VI*, i, 1, 225; *The Comedy of Errors*, v, 1, 309; *Coriolanus*, i, 3, 7; *A Midsummer-Night's Dream*, i, 1, 160; *The Taming of the Shrew*, v, 1, 88.

IV—Father's and Mother's Sons

4
I, the son of a dear father murder'd.
Hamlet. Act ii, sc. 2, l. 612. [Hamlet]

Show yourself your father's son.
Hamlet. Act iv, sc. 7, l. 126. [King]

Father's son.—*Antony and Cleopatra*, iii, 6, 6; *Coriolanus*, i, 3, 62; *Cymbeline*, iii, 6, 77; *King Lear*, v, 3, 169.

5
Falstaff: Shadow, whose son art thou?
Shadow: My mother's son, sir.
Falstaff: Thy mother's son! like enough, and thy father's shadow: so the son of the female is the shadow of the male: it is often so, indeed; but much of the father's substance!
II Henry IV. Act iii, sc. 2, l. 137.

6
My mother's son did get your father's heir.
King John, i, 1, 128. See HEIR, 702:10.

Mother's son.—*The Taming of the Shrew*, iv, 5, 6, and five times in later plays.

Every mother's son.—*A Midsummer-Night's Dream*, i, 2, 80; iii, 1, 75.

Woman's son.—*Sonnets*, xli; *Venus and Adonis*, l. 201.

Women's sons.—*Timon of Athens*, iv, 3, 417.

Son of a woman.—*I Henry IV*, ii, 4, 111.

Sons of women.—*The Merry Wives of Windsor*, ii, 3, 50.

7
He is but my father's brother's son.
Richard II. Act i, sc. 1, l. 117. [King Richard]

Your brother's son shall never reign our king.
Richard III. Act iii, sc. 7, l. 215. [Buckingham]

Brother's son.—*Richard III*, iii, 7, 177; 209; *Romeo and Juliet*, iii, 5, 128.

Son and brother.—*II Henry IV*, i, 1, 67.

Sons and brothers.—*III Henry VI*, i, 2, 4.

8 My father's sister's son,
A cousin-german to great Priam's seed.
Troilus and Cressida. Act iv, sc. 5, l. 120. [Hector] The only use of "cousin-german."

Sister's son.—*Julius Cæsar*, iv, 1, 5.

9
There lives a son that suck'd an earthly mother.
Venus and Adonis, l. 863.

V—Bastard Sons

See also Bastard

10
She says up and down the town that her eldest son is like you.
II Henry IV. Act ii, sc. 1, l. 115. [Falstaff]

Ha! a bastard son of the king's?
II Henry IV. Act ii, sc. 4, l. 307. [Falstaff]

11
This my mother's son was none of his;
And if he were, he came into the world
Full fourteen weeks before the course of time.
King John. Act i, sc. 1, l. 111. [Robert]

Bastard: Is it sir Robert's son that you would seek so?
Lady Faulconbridge: Sir Robert's son! Ay, thou unreverend boy,
Sir Robert's son: why scorn'st thou at sir Robert?
He is sir Robert's son, and so art thou. . . .
Bastard: Madam, I was not old sir Robert's son:
Sir Robert might have eat his part in me
Upon Good-Friday and ne'er broke his fast:
Sir Robert could do well: marry, to confess,
Could he get me? Sir Robert could not do it:
We know his handiwork: therefore, good mother,
To whom am I beholding for these limbs?
Sir Robert never holp to make this leg.
King John. Act i, sc. 1, l. 226. [Bastard]

12
Earl of Kent: Is not this your son, my lord?
Earl of Gloucester: His breeding, sir, hath been at my charge: I have so often blushed to acknowledge him, that now I am brazed to it.
Earl of Kent: I cannot conceive you.
Earl of Gloucester: Sir, this young fellow's mother could: whereupon she grew round-wombed, and had, indeed, sir, a son for her cradle ere she had a husband for her bed.
King Lear. Act i, sc. 1, l. 8. The only use of "brazed" and "round-wombed."

13
Son and heir of a mongrel bitch.
King Lear. Act ii, sc. 2, l. 23. [Kent]

Thou bitch-wolf's son.—*Troilus and Cressida*, ii, 1, 11. The only use of "bitch-wolf."

14 Gloucester's bastard son
Was kinder to his father than my daughters
Got 'tween the lawful sheets.
King Lear. Act iv, sc. 6, l. 116. [King Lear]

The bastard son of Gloucester.—*King Lear*, iv, 7, 89.

15
The son that she did litter here.
The Tempest. Act i, sc. 2, l. 282. [Prospero]

16
Thersites: What art thou?
Margarelon: A bastard son of Priam's.
Troilus and Cressida. Act v, sc. 7, l. 14. See under BASTARD.

Son of a whore.—*Troilus and Cressida*, v, 7, 21.

Natural son.—*Timon of Athens,* iv, 3, 383.

1 I'fecks! Why, that 's my bawcock.
The Winter's Tale. Act i, sc. 2, l. 120. [Leontes] The only use of "I'fecks." "Bawcock" (beau coq, fine fellow) is repeated in *Henry V,* iii, 2, 26; iv, 1, 44; and in *Twelfth Night,* iii, 4, 125.

VI—Sons of Kings and Queens

2 These boys know little they are sons to the king.
Cymbeline. Act iii, sc. 3, l. 80. [Belarius]

Son of the king.—*II Henry IV,* ii, 2, 130; *Hamlet,* iv, 2, 13; *Winter's Tale,* iv, 1, 22.
Thy sovereign's son.—*Richard III,* i, 4, 212.
Our late-deceased emperor's sons.—*Titus Andronicus,* i, 1, 184. "Late deceased" (unhyphenated) is repeated in *I Henry VI,* iii, 2, 132, and in *A Midsummer-Night's Dream,* v, 1, 53.
Prince's son.—*Richard III,* i, 4, 266.

3 The king's two sons,
Are stol'n away and fled.
Macbeth. Act ii, sc. 4, l. 25. [Macduff]

The son is fled.—*Macbeth,* iii, 3, 20.

4 The king's son took me by the hand and called me brother.
The Winter's Tale. Act v, sc. 2, l. 151. [Cloten] See under BROTHERHOOD.

King's son.—*I Henry IV,* i, 2, 109; ii, 2, 44; ii, 4, 150; *Antony and Cleopatra,* iii, 1, 3; *The Tempest,* i, 2, 212; 221.

5 He was a queen's son, boys.
Cymbeline. Act iv, sc. 2, l. 244. [Belarius] "Queen's son" is repeated in l. 153, and in *Richard III,* ii, 3, 28.

Son to the queen.—*Cymbeline,* iv, 2, 65; 93; 119.
Empress' sons.—*Titus Andronicus,* iv, 1, 115; v, 2, 64.

VII—Miscellaneous Sons

6 Cloten: A gentlewoman's son.
Lady: That 's more
Than some, whose tailors are as dear as yours,
Can justly boast of.
Cymbeline. Act ii, sc. 3, l. 83.

Shepherd's son.—*Cymbeline,* i, 1, 150; *The Winter's Tale,* iv, 4, 846; v, 2, 69.
Wise man's son.—*Twelfth Night,* ii, 3, 45.
Yeomen's sons.—*I Henry IV,* iv, 2, 17.
Son of chivalry.—*I Henry VI,* iv, 6, 29.
Son of hell.—*II Henry VI,* v, 2, 33; *Richard III,* i, 3, 230.
Sons of your progenitors.—*I Henry VI,* iv, 1, 166.
Son of Rome.—*Julius Cæsar,* i, 2, 173; *Titus Andronicus,* v, 3, 67.
Sons of Troy.—*Troilus and Cressida,* Prol., 19.
Hydra son of war.—*II Henry IV,* iv, 2, 38.
Son unto a conqueror.—*I Henry VI,* v, 5, 73.

7 Unless the fear of death doth make me dote,
I see my son Antipholus.
The Comedy of Errors. Act v, sc. 1, l. 195. [Ægeus]

Young Arthur is my son, and he is lost.
King John. Act iii, sc. 4, l. 47. [Constance]

O Lord! my boy, my Arthur, my fair son!
My life, my joy, my food, my all the world!
My widow-comfort, and my sorrows' cure!
King John. Act iii, sc. 4, l. 103. [Constance] The only use of "widow-comfort."

Son Clarence.—*III Henry VI,* iv, 8, 11.

O dear son Edgar,
The food of thy abused father's wrath!
Might I but live to see thee in my touch,
I 'ld say I had eyes again.
King Lear. Act iv, sc. 1, l. 23. [Gloucester]

My son Edgar.—*King Lear,* i, 2, 59.

I have lost . . . My dear son Ferdinand.
The Tempest. Act v, sc. 1, l. 137. [Alonso]

Son George.—*Richard III,* v, 3, 61.
Son John.—*II Henry IV,* iv, 5, 228.

8 Numa's daughter's son,
Who, after great Hostilius, here was king.
Coriolanus. Act ii, sc. 3, l. 247. [Brutus]

9 In thee thy mother dies, our household's name,
My death's revenge, thy youth, and England's fame:
All these and more we hazard by thy stay;
All these are saved if thou wilt fly away.
I Henry VI. Act iv, sc. 6, l. 38. [Talbot]

Surely, by all the glory you have won,
An if I fly, I am not Talbot's son:
Then talk no more of flight, it is no boot;
If son of Talbot, die at Talbot's foot.
I Henry VI. Act iv, sc. 6, l. 50. [John Talbot]

10 I am the son of Henry the Fifth,
Who made the Dauphin and the French to stoop
And seized upon their towns and provinces.
III Henry VI. Act i, sc. 1, l. 107. [King Henry]

I am the son of Marcus Cato, ho!
A foe to tyrants.
Julius Cæsar. Act v, sc. 4, l. 4. [Cato]

Cato's son.—*Julius Cæsar,* v, 4, 11.

11 Our son of Cornwall,
And you, our no less loving son of Albany.
King Lear. Act i, sc. 1, l. 42. [King Lear]

12 I am the last of noble Edward's sons.
Richard II. Act ii, sc. 1, l. 171. [York] "Edward's son" occurs in ll. 121, 124.

13 This little abstract doth contain that large
Which died in Geffrey, and the hand of time
Shall draw this brief into as huge a volume.
King John. Act ii, sc. 1, l. 101. [King Philip]

Geffrey's son.—*King John,* i, 1, 8.

14 Vincentio's son brought up in Florence.
The Taming of the Shrew. Act i, sc. 1, l. 14. [Lucentio] "Vincentio's son" is repeated in i, 1, 200.

Son to Vincentio.—*The Taming of the Shrew,* ii, 1, 104; iii, 1, 32.

Here 's Lucentio,
Right son to the right Vincentio.
The Taming of the Shrew. Act v, sc. 1, l. 117. [Lucentio]

O, my son, my son! Tell me, thou villain, where is my son Lucentio?
The Taming of the Shrew. Act v, sc. 1, l. 92. [Vincentio]

1
Born in Verona, old Antonio's son.
The Taming of the Shrew. Act i, sc. 2, l. 191. [Petruchio] Repeated in ii, 1, 68.

Best's son.—*II Henry VI,* iv, 2, 24.
Bohemia's son.—*The Winter's Tale,* iv, 4, 599.
Cæsar's son.—*Titus Andronicus,* i, 1, 10.
Douglas' son.—*I Henry IV,* i, 3, 261.
Wise Laertes' son.—*Titus Andronicus,* i, 1, 380.
Blessed Mary's son.—*Richard II,* ii, 1, 56.
Merops' son.—*The Two Gentlemen of Verona,* iii, 1, 153. The only mention of Merops.
Priam's sons.—*Troilus and Cressida,* ii, 2, 126.
Siward's son.—*Macbeth,* v, 2, 9.
Thetis' sons.—*Troilus and Cressida,* i, 3, 212; iii, 3, 94.

2
The unhappy son of old Andronicus.
Titus Andronicus. Act ii, sc. 3, l. 250. [Martius] Repeated in iv, 4, 66.

Son to great Antiochus.—*Pericles,* i, 1, 26.

The son of Clarence have I pent up close.
Richard III. Act iv, sc. 3, l. 36. [King Richard]

The reputed son of Cœur-de-lion.—*King John,* i, 1, 136.

The son of Duncan,
From whom this tyrant holds the due of birth.
Macbeth. Act iii, sc. 6, l. 24. [Lord]

Duncan's sons.—*Macbeth,* iii, 6, 18.

The sons of Edward sleep in Abraham's bosom.
Richard III. Act iv, sc. 3, l. 38. [King Richard]

Son of Lucius.—*Titus Andronicus,* iv, 2, 1.
Sons of brave Plantagenet.—*III Henry VI,* ii, 1, 35.
Son of Polixenes.—*The Winter's Tale,* v, 1, 86.
Son of Priam.—*Troilus and Cressida,* iii, 3, 26; iv, 5, 96.
Sons of York.—*II Henry VI,* v, 1, 119; *III Henry VI,* ii, 6, 73; *Richard III,* ii, 4, 6; iv, 1, 14.

VIII—Son-in-Law

3
I will buy me a son-in-law in a fair.
All's Well that Ends Well. Act v, sc. 3, l. 148. [Lafeu]

4
We 'll learn our freeness of a son-in-law.
Cymbeline. Act v, sc. 5, l. 421. [Cymbeline] The only use of "freeness."

5
Since you could not be any son-in-law,
Be yet my nephew.
Much Ado about Nothing. Act v, sc. 1, l. 296. [Leonato] "Nephew" occurs thirty-five times in the plays, and "niece" forty-nine times.

6
Your son-in-law is far more fair than black.
Othello. Act i, sc. 3, l. 291. [Duke]

7
And yet we hear not of our son-in-law.
The Taming of the Shrew. Act iii, sc. 2, l. 3. [Baptista]

8 Give that changing piece
To him that flourish'd for her with his sword;
A valiant son-in-law thou shalt enjoy.
Titus Andronicus. Act i, sc. 1, l. 309. [Saturninus]

A valiant son-in-law thou shalt enjoy.
Titus Andronicus. Act i, sc. 1, l. 311. [Saturninus]

Embraces his son-in-law.—*The Winter's Tale,* v, 2, 57.
This is your son-in-law.—*The Winter's Tale,* v, 3, 149.

SONG

See also Poetry, Tune

9
You corrupt the song, sirrah.
All's Well that Ends Well. Act i, sc. 3, l. 84. [Countess]

Sold a goodly manor for a song.
All's Well that Ends Well, iii, 2, 10. See under MELANCHOLY.

10 By your most gracious pardon,
I sing but after you.
Antony and Cleopatra. Act i, sc. 5, l. 72. [Charmian]

11
I do desire you to sing. Come, more; another stanzo.
As You Like It. Act ii, sc. 5, l. 18. [Jaques] The only use of "stanzo." "Stanza" does not occur in the plays, but "stanze" is used in *Love's Labour 's Lost,* iv, 2, 107.

I would sing my song without a burden: thou bringest me out of tune.
As You Like It. Act iii, sc. 2, l. 261. [Celia]

I 'll end the song.—*As You Like It,* ii, 5, 32.
Now my song is ended.—*The Passionate Pilgrim,* l. 226.

12
Have you no song, forester, for this purpose? . . .
Sing it: 'tis no matter how it be in tune, so it make noise enough.
As You Like It. Act iv, sc. 2, l. 6. [Jaques]

Touchstone: Come, sit, sit, and a song.
Second Page: We are for you: sit i' the middle.
First Page: Shall we clap to 't roundly, without hawking or spitting or saying we are hoarse, which are only the prologues to a bad voice?
Second Page: I' faith, i' faith; and both in a tune, like two gipsies on a horse.
As You Like It. Act v, sc. 3, l. 9. The only use of "hawking" in this sense, and of "spitting."

Truly, young gentlemen, though there was no great matter in the ditty, yet the note was very untuneable. . . . I count it but time lost to hear such a foolish song.
As You Like It. Act v, sc. 3, l. 35. [Touchstone] "Untuneable" is repeated in *The Two Gentlemen of Verona,* iii, 1, 208.

Worthless song.—*Sonnets,* c.

1
Sing, siren, for thyself.
The Comedy of Errors. Act iii, sc. 2, l. 47. [Antipholus of Syracuse]
I pray you, daughter, sing, or express yourself in a more comfortable sort.
Coriolanus. Act i, sc. 3, l. 1. [Volumnia]
2
How angel-like he sings!
Cymbeline. Act iv, sc. 2, l. 48. [Arviragus] "Angel-like" is used again in *The Two Gentlemen of Verona,* ii, 4, 66.
A very excellent good-conceited thing; after, a wonderful sweet air, with admirable rich words to it.
Cymbeline. Act ii, sc. 3, l. 18. [Cloten] The only use of "good-conceited."
3
We 'll say our song the whilst.
Cymbeline. Act iv, sc. 2, l. 254. [Arviragus]
4
You must sing a-down a-down,
An you call him a-down-a.
Hamlet. Act iv, sc. 5, l. 170. [Ophelia] "A-down-a" is repeated in *The Merry Wives of Windsor,* i, 4, 44.
Pious chanson.—*Hamlet,* ii, 2, 438. The only use of "chanson."
5
I would I were a weaver; I could sing psalms or any thing.
I Henry IV. Act ii, sc. 4, l. 147. [Falstaff]
Three-man-song-men all, and very good ones; but they are most of them means and bases; but one puritan amongst them, and he sings psalms to hornpipes.
The Winter's Tale. Act iv, sc. 3, l. 46. [Clown] The only use of the first phrase, of "psalms," and of "hornpipes."
The Hundredth Psalm.—*The Merry Wives of Windsor,* ii, 1, 63. The only use of "psalm." "Psalmist" occurs in *II Henry IV,* iii, 2, 41.
6 I was train'd up in the English court;
Where, being but young, I framed to the harp
Many an English ditty lovely well
And gave the tongue a helpful ornament,
A virtue that was never seen in you.
I Henry IV. Act iii, sc. 1, l. 122. [Glendower]
And this ditty, after me,
Sing, and dance it trippingly.
A Midsummer-Night's Dream. Act v, sc. 1, l. 403. [Oberon] "Trippingly" is used again in *Hamlet,* iii, 2, 2: "Trippingly on the tongue."
7 Rest your gentle head upon her lap,
And she will sing the song that pleaseth you
And on your eyelids crown the god of sleep,
Charming your blood with pleasing heaviness.
I Henry IV. Act iii, sc. 1, l. 215. [Glendower]
8
Come sing me a bawdy song; make me merry.
I Henry IV. Act iii, sc. 3, l. 15. [Falstaff]
A merry song, come.—*II Henry IV,* ii, 4, 299.
Sing The merry songs.—*Henry VIII,* v, 5, 36.
Here was he merry, hearing of a song.
As You Like It. Act ii, sc. 7, l. 4. [First Lord]
9
A French song and a fiddle has no fellow.
Henry VIII, i, 3, 41. See under WANTONNESS.
10 The choir,
With all the choicest music of the kingdom,
Together sung 'Te Deum.'
Henry VIII. Act iv, sc. 1, l. 90. [Gentleman] "Choir" is repeated in l. 64, and occurs in no other scene. The only use of "choicest" and "Te Deum."
11
He sung, in rude harsh-sounding rhymes.
King John. Act iv, sc. 2, l. 150. [Bastard] The only use of "harsh-sounding."
12
When were you wont to be so full of songs?
King Lear. Act i, sc. 4, l. 185. [King Lear]
Singing aloud.—*King Lear,* iv, 4, 2.
13
Warble, child; make passionate my sense of hearing.
Love's Labour 's Lost, iii, 1, 1. [Armado]
Come, warble, come.—*As You Like It,* ii, 5, 38.
Well-tuned warble.—*The Rape of Lucrece,* l. 1080. The only uses of "warble."
Both warbling of one song, both in one key.
A Midsummer-Night's Dream, iii, 2, 206. See under COMRADE for full quotation. "Warbling" is repeated in v, 1, 405, "warbling note," and occurs in no other play.
With an accent tuned in selfsame key.
Troilus and Cressida. Act i, sc. 3, l. 53. [Agamemnon]
14
To jig off a tune at the tongue's end, canary to it with your feet, humour it with turning up your eyelids, sigh a note and sing a note, sometime through the throat, as if you swallowed love with singing love, sometime through the nose, as if you snuffed up love by smelling love.
Love's Labour 's Lost. Act iii, sc. 1, l. 11. [Moth] The only use of "snuffed."
Dance canary.—*All 's Well that Ends Well,* ii, 1, 77.
15 Nay, he can sing
A mean most meanly.
Love's Labour 's Lost. Act v, sc. 2, l. 327. [Biron]
16
And now about the cauldron sing,
Like elves and fairies in a ring.
Macbeth. Act iv, sc. 1, l. 41. [Hecate]
Come, now a roundel and a fairy song.
A Midsummer-Night's Dream, ii, 2, 1. The only use of "roundel."
Sing me now asleep;
Then to your offices and let me rest.
A Midsummer-Night's Dream. Act ii, sc. 2, l. 7. [Titania]
And sing while thou on pressed flowers dost sleep.
A Midsummer-Night's Dream. Act iii, sc. 1, l. 162. [Titania]

1
I will sing, that they shall hear I am not afraid.
A Midsummer-Night's Dream. Act iii, sc. 1, l. 126. [Bottom]

I pray thee, gentle mortal, sing again:
Mine ear is much enamour'd of thy note.
A Midsummer-Night's Dream. Act iii, sc. 1, l. 140. [Titania]

First, rehearse your song by rote,
To each word a warbling note.
A Midsummer-Night's Dream. Act v, sc. 1, l. 404. [Titania]

Sung By an Athenian eunuch to the harp.
A Midsummer-Night's Dream. Act v, sc. 1, l. 44. [Theseus, reading]

2
In what key shall a man take you, to go in the song?
Much Ado about Nothing. Act i, sc. 1, l. 188. [Benedick]

We 'll hear that song again.—*Much Ado about Nothing,* ii, 3, 46.

Don Pedro: By my troth, a good song.
Balthazar: And an ill singer, my lord.
Don Pedro: Ha, no, no, faith; thou singest well enough for a shift.
Benedict: An he had been a dog that should have howled thus, they would have hanged him.
Much Ado about Nothing. Act ii, sc. 3, l. 77.

3
'Fore God, an excellent song.
Othello. Act ii, sc. 3, l. 77. [Cassio]

Why, this is a more exquisite song than the other.
Othello. Act ii, sc. 3, l. 101. [Cassio]

4
An admirable musician:
O! she will sing the savageness out of a bear.
Othello. Act iv, sc. 1, l. 199. [Othello]

She had a song of 'willow;'
An old thing 'twas, but it express'd her fortune,
And she died singing it: that song to-night
Will not go from my mind; I have much to do,
But to go hang my head all at one side,
And sing it like poor Barbara.
Othello. Act iv, sc. 3, l. 28. [Desdemona] The old ballad, "Willow, Willow, Willow," or more correctly, "A Lover's Complaint being Forsaken of His Love," is given in Percy's *Reliques,* series i, bk. ii, No. 8.

The poor soul sat sighing by a sycamore tree,
Sing all a green willow;
Her hand on her bosom, her head on her knee,
Sing willow, willow, willow:
The fresh streams ran by her, and murmur'd her moans;
Sing willow, willow, willow;
Her salt tears fell from her, and soften'd the stones;
. . . Sing willow, willow, willow.
Othello. Act iv, sc. 3, l. 41. [Desdemona]

What did thy song bode, lady?
Othello. Act v, sc. 2, l. 246. [Emilia]

5
Stretched metre of an antique song.
Sonnets. No. xvii.

Speechless song.—*Sonnets,* viii.

Blind harper's song.—*Love's Labour 's Lost,* v, 2, 405.

Wanton mermaid's songs.—*Venus and Adonis,* l. 777.

Songs of Apollo.—*Love's Labour 's Lost,* v, 2, 941.

Songs of death.—*Richard III,* iv, 4, 509.

Songs of woe.—*Much Ado about Nothing,* v, 3, 14.

6
To sing a song that old was sung,
From ashes ancient Gower is come;
Assuming man's infirmities,
To glad your ear, and please your eyes,
It hath been sung at festivals,
On ember-eves and holy-ales;
And lords and ladies in their lives
Have read it for restoratives.
Pericles. Act i, Gower, l. 6. The only use of "ember-eves" (the vigil of an Ember day) and "holy-ales" (a word coined by whoever wrote this scene, probably for the sake of the rhyme).

7
And crickets sing at the oven's mouth,
E'er the blither for their drouth.
Pericles. Act iii, Gower, l. 7. The only use of "blither."

The crickets sing.—*Cymbeline,* ii, 2, 11.

I heard . . . the crickets cry.—*Macbeth,* ii, 2, 16.

8
I 'll try how you can sol, fa, and sing it.
The Taming of the Shrew. Act i, sc. 2, l. 17. [Petruchio]

Peter: I will carry no crotchets: I 'll re you, I 'll fa you; do you note me?
Musician: An you re us and fa us, you note us.
Romeo and Juliet. Act iv, sc. 5, l. 119.

Fa, sol, la, mi.—*King Lear,* i, 2, 149.

Ut, re, sol, la, mi, fa.—*Love's Labour 's Lost,* iv, 2, 102.

9
She sings as sweetly as a nightingale.
The Taming of the Shrew. Act ii, sc. 1, l. 172. [Petruchio]

She sings like one immortal.—*Pericles,* v, Gower, 3.

So sweet a breath to sing.—*Twelfth Night,* ii, 3, 21.

10
Pandarus: I 'll sing you a song now.
Helen: Ay, ay, prithee now. . . . Let thy song be love.
Troilus and Cressida. Act iii, sc. 1, l. 115.

11
Sir Andrew: Now, a song.
Sir Toby: Come on; there is sixpence for you: let 's have a song. . . .
Clown: Would you have a love-song, or a song of good life?
Sir Toby: A love-song, a love-song.
Sir Andrew: Ay, ay: I care not for good life.
Twelfth Night. Act ii, sc. 3, l. 31.

Relish a love-song.—*The Two Gentlemen of Verona,* ii, 1, 20.

Shot through the ear with a love-song.—*Romeo and Juliet,* ii, 4, 15.

He has the prettiest love-songs.—*The Winter's Tale,* iv, 4, 193.

Writing love-songs.—*As You Like It*, iii, 2, 227. The only uses of "love-song" and "love-songs."

1
Sir Toby: But shall we make the welkin dance indeed? shall we rouse the night-owl in a catch that will draw three souls out of one weaver? shall we do that?
Sir Andrew: An you love me, let 's do 't: I am dog at a catch.
Twelfth Night. Act ii, sc. 3, l. 59.

Ye squeak out your coziers' catches without any mitigation or remorse of voice.
Twelfth Night. Act ii, sc. 3, l. 97. [Malvolio] The only use of "coziers" (cobblers).

Will you troll the catch
You taught me but while-ere?
The Tempest. Act iii, sc. 2, l. 126. [Caliban] The only use of "troll" and "while-ere."

2
Give me some music . . . that piece of song,
That old and antique song we heard last night:
Methought it did relieve my passion much,
More than light airs and recollected terms
Of these most brisk and giddy-paced times.
Twelfth Night. Act ii, sc. 4, l. 1. [Duke] The only use of "recollected" and "giddy-paced."

O, fellow, come, the song we had last night.
Mark it, Cesario, it is old and plain;
The spinsters and the knitters in the sun
And the free maids that weave their thread with bones
Do use to chant it: it is silly sooth,
And dallies with the innocence of love,
Like the old age.
Twelfth Night. Act ii, sc. 4, l. 43. [Duke] The only use of "knitters."

Duke: There 's for thy pains.
Clown: No pains, sir; I take pleasure in singing, sir.
Twelfth Night. Act ii, sc. 4, l. 69.

3
That I might sing it, madam, to a tune
Give me a note: your ladyship can set.
The Two Gentlemen of Verona. Act i, sc. 2, l. 80. [Lucetta]

Best sing it to the tune of 'Light o' love.'
The Two Gentlemen of Verona. Act i, sc. 2, l. 83. [Julia]

Lucetta: Ay, and melodious were it, would you sing it.
Julia: And why not you?
Lucetta: I cannot reach so high.
Two Gentlemen of Verona. Act i, sc. 2, l. 86.

Clap's into 'Light o' Love;' that goes without a burden: do you sing it, and I 'll dance it.
Much Ado about Nothing. Act iii, sc. 4, l. 44. [Margaret]

Sing her song and dance her turn.
Winter's Tale, iv, 4, 58. See under WIFE.

4
Her song was tedious and outwore the night.
Venus and Adonis, l. 841.

A nurse's song ne'er pleased her babe so well.
Venus and Adonis, l. 974.

5
Summer songs for me and my aunts,
While we lie tumbling in the hay.
Winter's Tale. Act iv, sc. 3, l. 11. [Autolycus]

He hath songs for man or woman, of all sizes; no milliner can so fit his customers with gloves: he has the prettiest love-songs for maids; so without bawdry, which is strange; with such delicate burthens of dildos and fadings, 'jump her and thump her;' and where some stretch-mouthed rascal would, as it were, mean mischief and break a foul gap into the matter, he makes the maid to answer 'Whoop, do me no harm, good man;' puts him off, slights him, with 'Whoop, do me no harm, good man.'
The Winter's Tale. Act iv, sc. 4, l. 191. [Servant] "Milliner" occurs again in *I Henry IV*, i, 3, 36. The only use of "dildos," "fadings" and "stretch-mouthed." "Whoop" is repeated in *King Lear*, i, 4, 245.

He sings several tunes faster than you 'll tell money; he utters them as he had eaten ballads and all men's ears grew to his tunes.
Winter's Tale. Act iv, sc. 4, l. 184. [Servant]

We 'll have this song out anon by ourselves.
Winter's Tale. Act iv, sc. 4, l. 315. [Clown]

SONNET

6
Good captain, will you give me a copy of the sonnet you writ to Diana in behalf of the Count Rousillon?
As You Like It. Act iv, sc. 3, l. 354. [Lord]

7
Dauphin: I once writ a sonnet in his praise and began thus: 'Wonder of nature,'—
Orleans: I have heard a sonnet begin so to one's mistress.
Dauphin: Then did they imitate that which I composed to my courser.
Henry V. Act iii, sc. 7, l. 42.

8
Did never sonnet for her sake compile.
Love's Labour 's Lost. Act iv, sc. 3, l. 134. [King] The only use of "compile."

I am sure I shall turn sonnet.—*Love's Labour 's Lost*, i, 2, 190.

9
Margaret: Will you then write me a sonnet in praise of my beauty?
Benedick: In so high a style, Margaret, that no man living shall come over it.
Much Ado about Nothing. Act v, sc. 2, l. 4.

A halting sonnet of his own pure brain.
Much Ado about Nothing. Act v, sc. 4, l. 87. [Claudio]

Deep-brain'd sonnets.—*A Lover's Complaint* l. 209. The only use of "deep-brain'd."

True sonnet.—*Twelfth Night*, iii, 4, 24.

10
By wailful sonnets, whose composed rhymes
Should be full-fraught with serviceable vows.
The Two Gentlemen of Verona. Act iii, sc. 2, l. 69. [Proteus] The only use of "wailful" and "full-fraught."

I have a sonnet that will serve the turn.
The Two Gentlemen of Verona. Act iii, sc. 2, l. 93. [Thurio]

SORROW

See also Grief; Joy and Sorrow; Melancholy, Sadness, Unhappiness, Woe

1
Countess: The tyranny of her sorrows takes all livelihood from her cheek. No more of this, Helena; go to, no more; lest it be rather thought you affect a sorrow than have it.
Helena: I do affect a sorrow indeed, but I have it too.
All's Well that Ends Well. Act i, sc. 1, l. 57. "Livelihood" does not occur again in the plays, but is repeated in *Venus and Adonis,* l. 26.

This she delivered in the most bitter touch of sorrow that e'er I heard virgin exclaim in.
All's Well that Ends Well. Act i, sc. 3, l. 122. [Steward]

2
Our size of sorrow,
Proportion'd to our cause, must be as great
As that which makes it.
Antony and Cleopatra. Act iv, sc. 15, l. 4. [Cleopatra]

3
Wherever sorrow is, relief would be:
If you do sorrow at my grief in love,
By giving love your sorrow and my grief
Were both extermined.
As You Like It. Act iii, sc. 5, l. 86. [Silvius] The only use of "extermined."

The height of heart-heaviness.
As You Like It. Act v, sc. 2, l. 50. [Orlando] The only use of "heart-heaviness."

4
I 'll utter what my sorrow gives me leave.
The Comedy of Errors. Act i, sc. 1, l. 36. [Ægeon]

5
Which of these sorrows is he subject to?
The Comedy of Errors. Act v, sc. 1, l. 54. [Abbess]

6
I am struck with sorrow.
Coriolanus. Act v, sc. 6, l. 149. [Aufidius]

Shaken with sorrows.—*Titus Andronicus,* iv, 3, 17.

7
All
Is outward sorrow, though I think the king
Be touch'd at very heart.
Cymbeline. Act i, sc. 1, l. 8. [Gentleman]

8
Is 't enough I am sorry?
So children temporal fathers do appease;
Gods are more full of mercy. Must I repent?
I cannot do it better than in gyves,
Desired more than constrain'd.
Cymbeline. Act v, sc. 4, l. 11. [Posthumus]

Escalus: I am sorry, one so learned and so wise . . .
Should slip so grossly. . . .
Angelo: I am sorry that such sorrow I procure.
Measure for Measure. Act v, sc. 1, l. 475.

I am so sorry.—*III Henry VI,* v, 1, 92, and frequently in later plays.

9
We with wisest sorrow think on him,
Together with remembrance of ourselves.
Hamlet. Act i, sc. 2, l. 6. [King]

10
When sorrows come, they come not single spies,
But in battalions.
Hamlet. Act iv, sc. 5, l. 78. [King] "Battalion" is used once again in *Richard III,* v, 3, 11.

One sorrow never comes but brings an heir,
That may succeed as his inheritor.
Pericles. Act i, sc. 4, l. 63. [Cleon]

11
I dare swear you borrow not that face
Of seeming sorrow, it is sure your own.
II Henry IV. Act v, sc. 2, l. 28. [Gloucester]

Sorrow so royally in you appears
That I will deeply put the fashion on
And wear it in my heart.
II Henry IV. Act v, sc. 2, l. 51. [Henry V]

12
Sorrow and grief have vanquish'd all my powers.
II Henry VI. Act ii, sc. 1, l. 183. [Gloucester]

Sorrow would solace and mine age would ease.
II Henry VI. Act ii, sc. 3, l. 21. [Gloucester]

Sorrow changed to solace, solace mix'd with sorrow.
The Passionate Pilgrim, l. 203.

13
Much is your sorrow; mine ten times so much.
III Henry VI. Act ii, sc. 5, l. 112. [King]

See where comes the breeder of my sorrow!
III Henry VI. Act iii, sc. 3, l. 43. [Queen Margaret]

14
No man bears sorrow better.
Julius Cæsar. Act iv, sc. 3, l. 147. [Brutus]

15
O, if thou teach me to believe this sorrow,
Teach thou this sorrow how to make me die.
King John. Act iii, sc. 1, l. 29. [Constance]

Now will canker sorrow eat my bud
And chase the native beauty from his cheek.
King John. Act iii, sc. 4, l. 82. [Constance]

16
O, how this mother swells up toward my heart!
Hysterica passio, down, thou climbing sorrow.
King Lear. Act ii, sc. 4, l. 56. [King Lear] The only use of "hysterica passio," a distension of the stomach by gas, causing suffocation and giddiness, and sometimes called "mother."

O sides, you are too tough; Will you yet hold?
King Lear. Act ii, sc. 4, l. 200. [King Lear]

Sorrow would be a rarity most beloved,
If all could so become it.
King Lear. Act iv, sc. 3, l. 25. [Gentleman]

All 's cheerless, dark, and deadly.
King Lear. Act v, sc. 3, l. 290. [Kent] The only use of "cheerless."

17
Well, set thee down, sorrow!
Love's Labour 's Lost, iv, 3, 4. [Biron]

Sit thee down, sorrow!—*Love's Labour 's Lost,* i, 1, 315. See Prosperity, 1218:9.

Not age, but sorrow, over me hath power.
A Lover's Complaint, l. 74.

1
To show an unfelt sorrow is an office
Which the false man does easy.
Macbeth. Act ii, sc. 3, l. 142. [Malcolm]
Certain sorrow.—*The Rape of Lucrece,* l. 1311.
Deadly sorrow.—*Antony and Cleopatra,* i, 2, 76.
Desperate sorrow.—*Richard III,* ii, 2, 99.
Feeling sorrows.—*King Lear,* iv, 6, 226.
Following sorrow.—*Rape of Lucrece,* l. 186.
Foolish sorrow.—*Richard III,* iv, 1, 104.
Gentle sorrow.—*Richard II,* v, 2, 31.
Great sorrow.—*III Henry VI,* i, 1, 128. *II Henry IV,* iv, 5, 85.
Heart-sorrow.—*The Tempest,* iii, 3, 81. The only use of the phrase.
Heavy sorrow.—*Romeo and Juliet,* iii, 3, 157.
Heavy sorrows of the blood.—*II Henry IV,* iv, 5, 38.
Huge sorrows.—*King Lear,* iv, 6, 288.
Infant sorrows.—*The Rape of Lucrece,* l. 1096.
Living sorrow.—*Venus and Adonis,* l. 671.
Lost sorrow.—*Richard III,* ii, 2, 11.
Nightly sorrow.—*The Rape of Lucrece,* l. 1080.
Obsequious sorrow.—*Hamlet,* i, 2, 92.
Present sorrows.—*Othello,* iii, 4, 116.
Saint-like sorrow.—*The Winter's Tale,* v, 1, 2.
Single sorrow.—*All's Well that Ends Well,* ii, 3, 313.
Strong sorrow.—*Macbeth,* ii, 3, 130.
Sweet sorrow.—*Romeo and Juliet,* ii, 2, 185.
Time-offer'd sorrow.—*Henry VIII,* iv, 1, 6. The only use of "time-offered."
Tongue-tied sorrows.—*III Henry VI,* iii, 3, 22.
Unnatural and bemadding sorrow.—*King Lear,* iii, 1, 38. The only use of "bemadding."
Our sorrows pale.—*As You Like It,* i, 3, 106.

2
Each new morn
New widows howl, new orphans cry, new sorrows
Strike heaven on the face.
Macbeth. Act iv, sc. 3, l. 4. [Macduff]
Sighs and groans and shrieks that rend the air
Are made, not mark'd; where violent sorrow seems
A modern ecstasy.
Macbeth. Act iv, sc. 3, l. 168. [Ross]

3
Canst thou not . . .
Pluck from the memory a rooted sorrow?
Macbeth, v, 3, 39. See under MIND.

4
Your cause of sorrow
Must not be measured by his worth, for then
It hath no end.
Macbeth. Act v, sc. 8, l. 44. [Ross]
He 's worth more sorrow,
And that I 'll spend for him.
Macbeth. Act v, sc. 8, l. 50. [Malcolm]

5
Your sorrow hath eaten up my sufferance.
The Merry Wives of Windsor. Act iv, sc. 2, l. 1. [Falstaff]

6
So sorrow's heaviness doth heavier grow
For debt that bankrupt sleep doth sorrow owe.
A Midsummer-Night's Dream. Act iii, sc. 2, l. 84. [Demetrius]

7
This sorrow 's heavenly;
It strikes where it doth love.
Othello. Act v, sc. 2, l. 21. [Othello]
Wear a golden sorrow.—*Henry VIII,* ii, 3, 22.

8
Paler for sorrow than her milk-white dove.
The Passionate Pilgrim, l. 119.

9
Do not
Consume your blood with sorrowing.
Pericles. Act iv, sc. 1, l. 23. [Dionyza] The only use of "sorrowing" in the plays. It is repeated in *The Passionate Pilgrim,* l. 398.
In sorrow all devour'd.—*Pericles,* iv, 4, 25.

10
True sorrow then is feelingly sufficed
When with like semblance it is sympathized.
The Rape of Lucrece, l. 1112.
Sorrow ebbs, being blown with wind of words.
The Rape of Lucrece, l. 1330.
For sorrow, like a heavy-hanging bell,
Once set on ringing, with his own weight goes;
Then little strength rings out the doleful knell.
The Rape of Lucrece, l. 1493. The only use of "heavy-hanging."
Pencill'd pensiveness and colour'd sorrow.
The Rape of Lucrece, l. 1497. The only use of "pensiveness." "Pencill'd" is repeated in *Timon of Athens,* i, 1, 159.
Thy sorrow to my sorrow lendeth
Another power.
The Rape of Lucrece, l. 1676.

11
Sorrow ends not when it seemeth done.
Richard II. Act i, sc. 2, l. 61. [Duchess of Gloucester]
Let him not come there,
To seek out sorrow that dwells every where.
Richard II. Act i, sc. 2, l. 71. [Duchess of Gloucester]
Some unborn sorrow, ripe in fortune's womb,
Is coming towards me.
Richard II. Act ii, sc. 2, l. 10. [Queen]

12
Gnarling sorrow hath less power to bite
The man that mocks at it and sets it light.
Richard II. Act i, sc. 3, l. 292. [Gaunt] "Gnarling" is repeated in *II Henry VI,* iii, 1, 192.
Fell sorrow's tooth doth never rankle more
Than when he bites, but lanceth not the sore.
Richard II. Act i, sc. 3, l. 302. [Bolingbroke]
Sorrow to sorrow join'd.—*Richard II,* ii, 2, 66.

13
Sorrow and grief of heart
Makes him speak fondly, like a frantic man.
Richard II. Act iii, sc. 3, l. 184. [Northumberland]
Give sorrow words.
Macbeth, iv, 3, 209. See under GRIEF.
Speak out thy sorrows.—*Pericles,* i, 4, 58.
Sorrow bids me speak.—*All 's Well that Ends Well,* iii, 4, 42.
The rest let sorrow say.—*Richard II,* v, 1, 102.

14
Give sorrow leave awhile to tutor me.
Richard II. Act iv, sc. 1, l. 166. [King Richard]
Come, come, in wooing sorrow let 's be brief,
Since, wedding it, there is such length in grief.
Richard II. Act v, sc. 1, l. 93. [King Richard]

1
The sorrow that I have, by right is yours,
And all the pleasures you usurp are mine.
Richard III. Act i, sc. 3, l. 172. [Queen Margaret]

He shall split thy very heart with sorrow.
Richard III. Act i, sc. 3, l. 300. [Queen Margaret] Repeated in v, 1, 26.

Sorrow breaks seasons and reposing hours,
Makes the night morning, and the noon-tide night.
Richard III. Act i, sc. 4, l. 76. [Brakenbury]

2
I am your sorrow's nurse,
And I will pamper it with lamentations.
Richard III. Act ii, sc. 2, l. 87. [Duchess of York] The only use of "pamper."

If ancient sorrow be most reverend,
Give mine the benefit of seniory,
And let my woes frown on the upper hand.
If sorrow can admit society.
Richard III. Act iv, sc. 4, l. 35. [Queen Margaret] The only use of "seniory."

Flatter my sorrows with report of it.
Richard III. Act iv, sc. 4, l. 245. [Queen Elizabeth]

3
Could we but learn from whence his sorrows grow,
We would as willingly give cure as know.
Romeo and Juliet. Act i, sc. 1, l. 160. [Montague]

What sorrow craves acquaintance at my hand,
That I yet know not?
Romeo and Juliet. Act iii, sc. 3, l. 5. [Romeo]

Dry sorrow drinks our blood.
Romeo and Juliet. Act iii, sc. 5, l. 59. [Romeo]

These sorrows make me old.—*Romeo and Juliet,* iii, 2, 89.

Her father counts it dangerous
That she doth give her sorrow so much sway.
Romeo and Juliet. Act iv, sc. 1, l. 9. [Paris]

4
But day doth daily draw my sorrows longer
And night doth nightly make grief's strength seem stronger.
Sonnets. No. xxviii.

Ah, do not, when my heart hath 'scaped this sorrow,
Come in the rearward of a conquer'd woe;
Give not a windy night a rainy morrow.
Sonnets. No. xc.

How hard true sorrow hits.
Sonnets. No. cxx.

5
Sorrow on thee and all the pack of you,
That triumph thus upon my misery!
The Taming of the Shrew. Act iv, sc. 3, l. 33. [Katharina]

6
Weigh Our sorrow with our comfort.
The Tempest. Act ii, sc. 1, l. 8. [Gonzalo]

Brimful of sorrow and dismay.
The Tempest. Act v, sc. 1, l. 14. [Ariel]

7
Sorrow concealed, like an oven stopp'd,
Doth burn the heart to cinders where it is.
Titus Andronicus. Act ii, sc. 4, l. 36. [Marcus]

An oven that is stopp'd, or river stay'd,
Burneth more hotly, swelleth with more rage:
So of concealed sorrow may be said.
Venus and Adonis, l. 331.

8
You recount your sorrows to a stone.
Titus Andronicus. Act iii, sc. 1, l. 29. [Lucius]

Therefore I tell my sorrows to the stones;
Who, though they cannot answer my distress,
Yet in some sort they are better than the tribunes,
For that they will not intercept my tale.
Titus Andronicus. Act iii, sc. 1, l. 37. [Titus]

Prepare thy aged eyes to weep;
Or, if not so, thy noble heart to break:
I bring consuming sorrow to thine age.
Titus Andronicus. Act iii, sc. 1, l. 59. [Marcus]

Sorrow flouted at is double death.
Titus Andronicus. Act iii, sc. 1, l. 246. [Marcus]

Sorrow is an enemy,
And would usurp upon my watery eyes,
And make them blind with tributary tears.
Titus Andronicus. Act iii, sc. 1, l. 268. [Titus]

9
Marcus, attend him in his ecstasy,
That hath more scars of sorrow in his heart
Than foemen's marks upon his batter'd shield.
Titus Andronicus. Act iv, sc. 1, l. 125. [Marcus]

His sorrows are past remedy.
Titus Andronicus. Act iv, sc. 3, l. 31. [Marcus]

Let not your sorrow die, though I am dead.
Titus Andronicus. Act v, sc. 1, l. 140. [Aaron]

10
Lucius: Art thou not sorry for these heinous deeds?
Aaron: Ay, that I had not done a thousand more.
Titus Andronicus. Act v, sc. 1, l. 123.

I never wish'd to see you sorry; now
I trust I shall.
The Winter's Tale. Act ii, sc. 1, l. 123. [Hermione]

11
If she be so abandon'd to her sorrow
As it is spoke, she never will admit me.
Twelfth Night. Act i, sc. 4, l. 19. [Viola]

12
A pack of sorrows which would press you down,
Being unprevented, to your timeless grave.
The Two Gentlemen of Verona. Act iii, sc. 1, l. 20. [Proteus] The only use of "unprevented."

If hearty sorrow
Be a sufficient ransom for offence,
I tender 't here.
The Two Gentlemen of Verona. Act v, sc. 4, l. 74. [Proteus]

13
The night of sorrow now is turn'd to day.
Venus and Adonis, l. 481.

This night I'll waste in sorrow,
For my sick heart commands mine eyes to watch.
Venus and Adonis, l. 583.
Every present sorrow seemeth chief.
Venus and Adonis, l. 970.
Her voice is stopt, her joints forget to bow;
Her eyes are mad that they have wept till now.
Venus and Adonis, l. 1061.

1
I never saw a vessel of like sorrow,
So fill'd and so becoming.
The Winter's Tale. Act iii, sc. 3, l. 21. [Antigonus]
All sorrowed.—*The Winter's Tale,* v, 2, 99. "Sorrowed" is used only once again, in *Timon of Athens,* v, 1, 152.

2
My lord, your sorrow was too sore laid on,
Which sixteen winters cannot blow away,
So many summers dry: scarce any joy
Did ever so long live; no sorrow
But kill'd itself much sooner.
Winter's Tale. Act v, sc. 3, l. 49. [Camillo]

SOUL

See also Body and Soul; Spirit

3
Where souls so couch on flowers, we 'll hand in hand,
And with our sprightly port make the ghosts gaze.
Antony and Cleopatra. Act iv, sc. 14, l. 51. [Antony]

4
My soul, yet I know not why, hates nothing more than he.
As You Like It, i, 1, 171. See under HATE.
My soul should sue as advocate for thee.
The Comedy of Errors, i, 1, 146. See under MERCY.

5
A wretched soul, bruised with adversity,
We bid be quiet when we hear it cry;
But were we burden'd with like weight of pain,
As much or more we should ourselves complain.
The Comedy of Errors. Act ii, sc. 1, l. 34. [Adriana]
Wretched souls.—*Macbeth,* iv, 3, 141; *Timon of Athens,* v, 4, 70.
Angry soul.—*Richard III,* iv, 4, 250.
Distracted soul.—*Timon of Athens,* iii, 4, 115.
Distressed soul.—*The Comedy of Errors,* iv, 4, 62.
Fearful soul.—*Richard III,* iv, 4, 311; v, 1, 18.
Flying soul.—*II Henry VI,* iii, 2, 397.
Fraughting souls.—*Tempest,* i, 2, 13. The only use of "fraughting" (forming the cargo).
Grieved soul.—*Richard II,* i, 1, 138.
Indigent faint souls.—*Henry V,* i, 1, 16.
Jealous souls.—*Othello,* iii, 4, 159.
New-sad soul.—*Love's Labour's Lost,* v, 2, 741. The only use of "new-sad."
Offending soul.—*Henry V,* iv, 3, 29.
Overcharged soul.—*II Henry VI,* iii, 2, 376.
Sick soul.—*Hamlet,* iv, 5, 17.
Straying souls.—*Henry VIII,* v, 3, 64.
Stubborn soul.—*Measure for Measure,* v, 1, 485.
Suffering souls.—*Julius Cæsar,* ii, 1, 130.
Timorous soul.—*I Henry VI,* iv, 2, 40.
Tortured soul.—*Richard II,* iv, 1, 298.
Unfortunate souls.—*Macbeth,* iv, 1, 152.
Unquiet soul.—*Merchant of Venice,* iii, 2, 308.
Weeping souls.—*Richard III,* iv, 4, 53.

6
My soul aches to know.
Coriolanus. Act iii, sc. 1, l. 108. [Coriolanus]

7
How slow his soul sail'd on.
Cymbeline, i, 3, 13. See under PARTING.

8
Till then sit still, my soul.
Hamlet. Act i, sc. 2, l. 257. [Hamlet]
Let not ever
The soul of Nero enter this firm bosom.
Hamlet. Act iii, sc. 2, l. 411. [Hamlet]

9
And for my soul, what can it do to that,
Being a thing immortal as itself?
Hamlet. Act i, sc. 4, l. 66. [Hamlet]
Marry, the immortal part needs a physician; but that moves not him: though that be sick, it dies not.
II Henry IV. Act ii, sc. 2, l. 112. [Poins]
Immortal souls.—*The Merchant of Venice,* v, 1, 63.

10
O limed soul, that, struggling to be free,
Art more engaged!
Hamlet. Act iii, sc. 3, l. 68. [King]
That his soul may be as damned and black
As hell whereto it goes.
Hamlet. Act iii, sc. 3, l. 94. [Hamlet]
A black soul burning in hell-fire.
Henry V, ii, 3, 44. See under FLEA.
I 'll send his soul to hell.
King John. Act i, sc. 1, l. 272. [Bastard] See THREAT, 1521:4.

11
Thou turn'st mine eyes into my very soul;
And there I see such black and grained spots
As will not leave their tinct.
Hamlet. Act iii, sc. 4, l. 89. [Queen]
O, step between her and her fighting soul.
Hamlet. Act iii, sc. 4, l. 113. [Ghost]
My soul is full of discord and dismay.
Hamlet. Act iv, sc. 1, l. 45. [King]

12 God ha' mercy on his soul!
And of all Christian souls, I pray God.
Hamlet. Act iv, sc. 5, l. 199. [Ophelia]
God have mercy upon one of our souls!
Twelfth Night. Act iii, sc. 4, l. 183. [Sir Toby]

13
We should profane the service of the dead
To sing a requiem and such rest to her
As to peace-parted souls.
Hamlet. Act v, sc. 1, l. 259. [Priest] The only use of "peace-parted." "Requiem" is repeated in *The Phœnix and the Turtle,* l. 16.

14
Jack! how agrees the devil and thee about thy soul, that thou soldest him on Good-Friday last for a cup of Madeira and a cold capon's leg?
I Henry IV. Act i, sc. 2, l. 126. [Poins]

"Good-Friday" is repeated in *King John,* i, 1, 235.

1 Let my soul
Want mercy, if I do not join with him.
I Henry IV. Act i, sc. 3, l. 131. [Hotspur]

As I have a soul.—*Henry VIII,* iv, 1, 44.
As I hold my soul.—*Hamlet,* ii, 2, 44.
Beshrew my soul.—*King John,* v, 4, 49.
By his soul.—*III Henry VI,* i, 1, 94.
By my soul.—*I Henry IV,* i, 3, 81; v, 2, 52; and nine times in later plays.
Death of my soul!—*Macbeth,* v, 3, 16.
From my soul.—*Richard III,* iv, 1, 89; iv, 4, 255.
From thy soul.—*Richard III,* iv, 4, 257.
On my soul.—*Much Ado about Nothing,* iv, 1, 148; *King John,* v, 1, 43; v, 2, 108; *Henry VIII,* i, 2, 177.
On your soul.—*Much Ado about Nothing,* iv, 1, 14.
Upon my soul.—*King John,* iv, 3, 125; *II Henry IV,* iv, 2, 60; *Henry VIII,* iii, 1, 103; *Othello,* v, 2, 181.
So thrive my soul.—*Romeo and Juliet,* ii, 2, 154.
Take 't of my soul.—*Timon of Athens,* iii, 4, 70.
With my soul.—*Richard III,* iv, 4, 262.

2
A fool go with thy soul, whither it goes!
I Henry IV. Act v, sc. 3, l. 22. [Douglas]

3 His soul
Shall stand sore charged for the wasteful vengeance.
Henry V. Act i, sc. 2, l. 182. [King Henry]

The very bottom of my soul.—*Henry V,* ii, 2, 97.

4 I can never win
A soul so easy as that Englishman's.
Henry V. Act ii, sc. 2, l. 124. [King Henry]

English soul.—*Henry VIII,* i, 1, 146.

5
Every subject's soul is his own.
Henry V, iv, 1, 187. See KING, 808:11.

Father's soul.—*Henry V,* iii, 2, 95.
Women's souls.—*Sonnets,* xx.
World's soul.—*Timon of Athens,* iii, 2, 71.

6
What is thy soul of adoration?
Henry V. Act iv, sc. 1, l. 262. [King Henry]

Soul of bounty.—*Timon of Athens,* i, 2, 215.
Soul of counsel.—*Troilus and Cressida,* iii, 2, 141.
Souls of geese.—*Coriolanus,* i, 4, 34.
Soul of goodness.—*Henry V,* iv, 1, 4.
Soul of hope.—*I Henry IV,* iv, 1, 50.
Soul of love.—*A Midsummer-Night's Dream,* ii, 1, 182.
Soul of Rome!—*Julius Cæsar,* ii, 1, 321.
Soul of sound good-fellowship.—*Troilus and Cressida,* iv, 1, 52.
Soul of state.—*Troilus and Cressida,* iii, 3, 202.
Soul of wit.—*Hamlet,* ii, 2, 90.

7
Your fair show shall suck away their souls.
Henry V. Act iv, sc. 2, l. 17. [Constable]

8
My soul shall thine keep company to heaven;
Tarry, sweet soul, for mine, then fly abreast,
As in this glorious and well-foughten field
We kept together in our chivalry!
Henry V. Act iv, sc. 6, l. 16. [Exeter] The only use of "well-foughten."

My soul shall wait on thee to heaven,
As it on earth hath been thy servant still.
King John. Act v, sc. 7, l. 72. [Bastard]

9
Straightway give thy soul to him thou servest.
I Henry VI. Act i, sc. 5, l. 7. [Talbot]

Enough: my soul shall then be satisfied.
I Henry VI. Act ii, sc. 5, l. 21. [Mortimer]

10
And peace, no war, befall thy parting soul.
I Henry VI. Act ii, sc. 5, l. 115. [Plantagenet]

Peace to his soul, if God's good pleasure be!
II Henry VI. Act iii, sc. 3, l. 26. [King]

Peace with his soul, heaven, if it be thy will!
II Henry VI. Act v, sc. 2, l. 30. [York]

Sweet peace conduct his sweet soul to the bosom
Of good old Abraham!
Richard II. Act iv, sc. 1, l. 103. [Bolingbroke]

11
Now, quiet soul, depart when heaven please,
For I have seen our enemies' overthrow.
I Henry VI. Act iii, sc. 2, l. 110. [Bedford]

And now in peace my soul shall part to heaven,
Since I have set my friends at peace on earth.
Richard III. Act ii, sc. 1, l. 5. [King Edward]

12
Come, side by side together live and die;
And soul with soul from France to heaven fly.
I Henry VI. Act iv, sc. 5, l. 54. [Talbot] The only use of "side by side."

13
Blow ten thousand souls to heaven or hell.
II Henry VI, iii, 1, 350. See under STORM.

A thousand souls.—*I Henry VI,* ii, 4, 127.
Two thousand souls.—*Hamlet,* iv, 4, 25.

14
With his soul fled all my worldly solace.
II Henry VI. Act iii, sc. 2, l. 151. [King Henry]

Give thee thy hire and send thy soul to hell.
II Henry VI. Act iii, sc. 2, l. 225. [Warwick]

Here could I breathe my soul into the air.
II Henry VI, iii, 2, 391. See under DEATH.

15
It grieves my soul to leave thee unassail'd.
II Henry VI. Act v, sc. 2, l. 18. [Warwick] The only use of "unassailed."

It grieves my soul
That I must draw this metal from my side.
King John. Act v, sc. 2, l. 15. [Salisbury]

It irks my very soul.—*III Henry VI,* ii, 2, 6.

16
Edward: Whose soul is that which takes her heavy leave?
Richard: A deadly groan, like life and death's departing.
III Henry VI. Act ii, sc. 6, l. 42.

Thy brazen gates of heaven may ope,
And give sweet passage to my sinful soul!
III Henry VI. Act ii, sc. 3, l. 40. [Edward]

Lift my soul to heaven.—*Henry VIII,* ii, 1, 78.

1
Sweet rest his soul!
III Henry VI. Act v, sc. 2, l. 48. [Warwick]

God rest his soul.—*The Merchant of Venice,* ii, 2, 75.
God rest all Christian souls!—*Romeo and Juliet,* i, 3, 18.
Rest her soul.—*Hamlet,* v, 1, 147.
God be with his soul.—*Romeo and Juliet,* i, 3, 39.
Heaven defend your good souls.—*Othello,* i, 3, 267.

2
Take good heed
You charge not in your spleen a noble person
And spoil your nobler soul.
Henry VIII. Act i, sc. 2, l. 173. [Queen Katharine]

My soul grows sad with troubles.
Henry VIII, iii, 1, 1. See under TROUBLE.

3
Ay, marry, now my soul hath elbow-room;
It would not out at windows nor at doors.
King John. Act v, sc. 7, l. 28. [King John] The only use of "elbow-room."

I have a kind soul that would give you thanks
And knows not how to do it but with tears.
King John. Act v, sc. 7, l. 108. [Prince Henry]

Kind souls.—*Julius Cæsar,* iii, 2, 199.
Believing souls.—*II Henry VI,* ii, 1, 66.
Blessed soul.—*The Two Gentlemen of Verona,* ii, 7, 38.
Christian soul.—*I Henry VI,* iv, 2, 30; *Richard III,* iv, 4, 408; *The Merry Wives of Windsor,* iii, 1, 96.
Constant soul.—*Merchant of Venice,* ii, 6, 57.
Credent soul.—*A Lover's Complaint,* l. 279. "Credent" is repeated in *Hamlet,* i, 3, 30: "Credent ear"; *Measure for Measure,* iv, 4, 29: "Credent bulk"; and *The Winter's Tale,* i, 2, 142: "'Tis very credent."
Dear souls.—*Richard II,* ii, 1, 57; *Twelfth Night,* v, 1, 393; *Hamlet,* iii, 2, 68.
Dearest soul.—*Cymbeline,* i, 6, 118.
Departed souls.—*II Henry VI,* iv, 7, 123.
Souls departed.—*Henry VIII,* iv, 2, 156.
Divine soul.—*Richard II,* i, 1, 38.
Fair soul.—*All's Well that Ends Well,* iv, 2, 3; *The Tempest,* ii, 1, 129.
Full soul.—*The Tempest,* iii, 1, 44.
Gentle souls.—*Richard III,* iv, 4, 11.
Good soul.—*Richard II,* v, 1, 17; *Romeo and Juliet,* ii, 4, 215.
Honest soul.—*Much Ado about Nothing,* iii, 5, 41.
Invisible soul.—*Troilus and Cressida,* iii, 1, 35.
Naked soul.—*King Lear,* iv, 1, 46.
Perfect soul.—*Othello,* i, 2, 31.
Pretty soul.—*A Midsummer-Night's Dream,* ii, 2, 76.
Private soul.—*Troilus and Cressida,* iv, 5, 111.
Prophetic soul.—*Hamlet,* i, 5, 40; *Sonnets,* cvii.
Proud soul.—*I Henry IV,* i, 3, 9.
Secret soul.—*Twelfth Night,* i, 4, 14.
Sleeping soul.—*The Rape of Lucrece,* l. 423.
Special soul.—*Measure for Measure,* i, 1, 18.
Spotted souls.—*Richard II,* iii, 2, 134.
Suppler souls.—*Coriolanus,* v, 1, 55.
Sweet soul.—*Love's Labour's Lost,* iii, 1, 124, and four times in later plays.
Understanding soul.—*Henry V,* i, 2, 15.
Watchful soul.—*Richard III,* iii, 7, 77.
Willing soul.—*Richard II,* iv, 1, 108.
Winged soul.—*II Henry VI,* iii, 3, 16.
Wiser souls.—*Measure for Measure,* ii, 4, 14.
Souls refined.—*Richard II,* iv, 1, 130.

4
Thou art a soul in bliss.
King Lear. Act iv, sc. 7, l. 46. [King Lear]

A soul as even as calm.—*Henry VIII,* iii, 1, 166.
Secure in soul.—*Henry V,* iv, Prol., 17.

5
That unlettered small-knowing soul.
Love's Labour's Lost. Act i, sc. 1, l. 254. [King, reading] "Unlettered" is repeated in iv, 2, 18, and in *Henry V,* i, 1, 55. The only use of "small-knowing."

All ignorant that soul that sees thee without wonder.
Love's Labour's Lost. Act iv, sc. 2, l. 117. [Sir Nathaniel]

6
A soul feminine saluteth us.
Love's Labour's Lost. Act iv, sc. 2, l. 83. [Holofernes] The only use of "feminine."

7
Mine eternal jewel
Given to the common enemy of man.
Macbeth. Act iii, sc. 1, l. 68. [Macbeth]

Eternal soul.—*Othello,* iii, 3, 361.

8
Thy soul's flight,
If it find heaven, must find it out to-night.
Macbeth. Act iii, sc. 1, l. 141. [Macbeth]

9
Why, all the souls that were were forfeit once.
Measure for Measure, ii, 2, 73. See under REMEDY.

My soul upon the forfeit.
The Merchant of Venice. Act v, sc. 1, l. 252. [Antonio]

10
An evil soul producing holy witness.
The Merchant of Venice, i, 3, 100. See under HYPOCRISY.

Even from the gallows did his fell soul fleet.
The Merchant of Venice. Act iv, sc. 1, l. 135. [Gratiano]

11
Thinkest thou I'll endanger my soul gratis?
The Merry Wives of Windsor. Act ii, sc. 2, l. 15. [Falstaff]

12
Now is his soul ravished!
Much Ado about Nothing. Act ii, sc. 3, l. 60. [Benedick]

My soul is in the sky.—*A Midsummer-Night's Dream,* v, 1, 308.

13
With free and unconstrained soul.
Much Ado about Nothing. Act iv, sc. 1, l. 25. [Claudio] "Unconstrain'd" is repeated in *III Henry VI,* i, 1, 143.

Free souls.—*Hamlet,* iii, 2, 252.
Unconquered soul.—*II Henry VI,* iv, 10, 69.

1 These fellows have some soul;
And such a one do I profess myself.
Othello. Act i, sc. 1, l. 54. [Iago]
In simple and pure soul I come to you.
Othello. Act i, sc. 1, l. 107. [Roderigo]
Pure soul.—*Richard II,* iv, 1, 92; *Henry VIII,* v, 5, 26.
Simple souls.—*II Henry VI,* iv, 4, 10.
Plain well-meaning soul.—*Richard II,* ii, 1, 128. The only use of "well-meaning."

2
There be souls must be saved, and there be souls must not be saved.
Othello. Act ii, sc. 3, l. 106. [Cassio]
Save his soul.—*I Henry IV,* i, 3, 215.
Save your souls.—*Richard III,* i, 4, 263.
Preserved souls.—*Measure for Measure,* ii, 2, 153.

3
Let thy soul be instructed.
Othello. Act ii, sc. 1, l. 223. [Iago]

4 May his pernicious soul
Rot half a grain a day.
Othello. Act v, sc. 2, l. 155. [Emilia]
Perdition catch my soul.—*Othello,* iii, 3, 90.

5
So come my soul to bliss, as I speak true.
Othello. Act v, sc. 2, l. 250. [Emilia]
Lay down my soul at stake.—*Othello,* iv, 2, 13.

6
Ensnared my soul and body.
Othello. Act v, sc. 2, l. 302. [Othello] The only use of "ensnared."
Abuse your soul.—*Pericles,* i, 1, 126.
Knit their souls.—*Cymbeline,* ii, 3, 122.

7 With a soul
Embolden'd with the glory of her praise.
Pericles. Act i, sc. 1, l. 3. [Pericles] "Embolden'd" is repeated in *The Merry Wives of Windsor,* ii, 2, 173. "Embolden" is used once, in *Timon of Athens,* iii, 5, 3.

8
Or free that soul which wretchedness hath chain'd?
The Rape of Lucrece, l. 900.

9
Sluiced out his innocent soul through streams of blood.
Richard II, i, 1, 103. See under MURDER.
The unstooping firmness of my upright soul.
Richard II. Act i, sc. 1, l. 121. [King Richard] The only use of "unstooping."
My dancing soul doth celebrate
This feast of battle with mine adversary.
Richard II, i, 3, 91. See under FIGHTING.
Since thou hast far to go, bear not along
The clogging burthen of a guilty soul.
Richard II. Act i, sc. 3, l. 199. [Bolingbroke] The only use of "clogging."

10
My inward soul With nothing trembles.
Richard II. Act ii, sc. 2, l. 11. [Queen]
My inward soul Persuades me it is otherwise
Richard II. Act ii, sc. 2, l. 28. [Queen]
Inward soul.—*King John,* iii, 1, 227; *The Rape of Lucrece,* l. 1779.

11
Now hath my soul brought forth her prodigy.
Richard II, ii, 2, 64. See under WOE.
Uncurse their souls.—*Richard II,* iii, 2, 137 The only use of "uncurse."

12
Lords, I protest, my soul is full of woe.
Richard II. Act v, sc. 6, l. 45. [Bolingbroke]
My soul is full of sorrow.
Richard III. Act ii, sc. 1, l. 96. [King Edward]
Have torn their souls by turning them from us.
Richard II. Act iii, sc. 3, l. 83. [King Richard]
The souls of men
May deem that you are worthily disposed.
Richard II. Act iv, sc. 1, l. 226. [Northumberland]
Soul of every man.—*I Henry IV,* iii, 2, 37.

13
I will shortly send thy soul to heaven.
Richard III, i, 1, 119. See under LOVE.

14 Still the envious flood
Kept in my soul, and would not let it forth
To seek the empty, vast and wandering air.
Richard III. Act i, sc. 4, l. 37. [Clarence]
By this time, had the king permitted us,
One of our souls had wander'd in the air,
Banish'd this frail sepulchre of our flesh.
Richard II. Act i, sc. 3, l. 194. [Bolingbroke]

15
O, then began the tempest to my soul.
Richard III. Act i, sc. 4, l. 44. [Clarence]

16
Hast thou that holy feeling in thy soul,
To counsel me to make my peace with God,
And art thou yet to thy own soul so blind,
That thou wilt war with God by murdering me?
Richard III. Act i, sc. 4, l. 257. [Clarence]

17
If you will live, lament; if die, be brief,
That our swift-winged souls may catch the king's.
Richard III. Act ii, sc. 2, l. 43. [Queen Elizabeth]
Swift-winged with desire to get a grave.
I Henry VI, ii, 5, 15. The only uses of "swift-winged."

18 The little souls of Edward's children
Whisper the spirits of thine enemies
And promise them success and victory.
Richard III. Act iv, sc. 4, l. 191. [Duchess of York]
Let me sit heavy on thy soul to-morrow!
Richard III. Act v, sc. 3, l. 118; 131; 139. [Ghost]
Let thy soul despair!—*Richard III,* v, 3, 141.

19 The wrong'd souls
Of butcher'd princes fight in thy behalf.
Richard III. Act v, sc. 3, l. 122. [Ghost]
Wronged souls.—*Richard III,* v, 3, 241.

20
Quiet untroubled soul, awake, awake!
Arm, fight, and conquer, for fair England's sake!
Richard III. Act v, sc. 3, l. 149. [Ghost] The only use of "untroubled."
Thou quiet soul, sleep thou a quiet sleep.
Richard III. Act v, sc. 3, l. 163. [Ghost]

1
Methought the souls of all that I had murder'd
Came to my tent; and every one did threat
To-morrow's vengeance on the head of Richard.
Richard III. Act v, sc. 3, l. 204. [King Richard]

2
I have a soul of lead
So stakes me to the ground I cannot move.
Romeo and Juliet. Act i, sc. 4, l. 15. [Romeo]

O God, I have an ill-divining soul!
Romeo and Juliet. Act iii, sc. 5, l. 54. [Juliet] The only use of "ill-divining."

God shall mend my soul!
Romeo and Juliet. Act i, sc. 5, l. 81. [Capulet]

3
It is my soul that calls upon thy name.
Romeo and Juliet. Act ii, sc. 2, l. 165. [Romeo]

Mercutio's soul
Is but a little way above our heads,
Staying for thine to keep him company.
Romeo and Juliet. Act iii, sc. 1, l. 131. [Romeo]

My betossèd soul
Did not attend him as we rode.
Romeo and Juliet. Act v, sc. 3, l. 76. [Romeo] The only use of "betossed."

4
Poor soul, the centre of my sinful earth, . . .
Why dost thou pine within and suffer dearth?
Sonnets. No. cxlvi.

Poor soul.—*II Henry VI,* ii, 1, 84, and frequently in later plays.
Poor mad soul.—*II Henry IV,* ii, 1, 113.

5
Then, soul, live thou upon thy servant's loss,
And let that pine to aggravate thy store;
Buy terms divine in selling hours of dross
Within be fed, without be rich no more.
Sonnets. No. cxlvi.

6
It goes on, I see, As my soul prompts it.
The Tempest. Act i, sc. 2, l. 419. [Prospero]

Hear my soul speak.
Tempest. Act iii, sc. 1, l. 63. [Ferdinand]

7
Empress of my soul,
Which never hopes more heaven than rests in thee.
Titus Andronicus. Act ii, sc. 3, l. 40. [Aaron]

That which gives my soul the greatest spurn,
Is dear Lavinia, dearer than my soul.
Titus Andronicus. Act iii, sc. 1, l. 101. [Titus]

Let fools do good, and fair men call for grace,
Aaron will have his soul black like his face.
Titus Andronicus. Act iii, sc. 1, l. 205. [Aaron]

8
Like a strange soul upon the Stygian banks
Slaving for waftage. O, be thou my Charon,
And give me a swift transportance to those fields
Where I may wallow in the lily-beds.
Troilus and Cressida. Act iii, sc. 2, l. 10. [Troilus] The only use of "Stygian," "Charon," "lily-beds," and "transportance." "To hire waftage" occurs in *The Comedy of Errors,* iv, 1, 95.

Stranger soul.—*Richard III,* i, 4, 48.

9
Clown: I think his soul is in hell, madonna.
Olivia: I know his soul is in heaven, fool.
Twelfth Night. Act i, sc. 5, l. 74.

This shall end without the perdition of souls.
Twelfth Night. Act iii, sc. 4, l. 317. [Sir Toby]

SOUND

See also Noise

10
The shepherd knows not thunder from a tabor
More than I know the sound of Marcus' tongue
From every meaner man.
Coriolanus. Act i, sc. 6, l. 25. Cominius]

Thou shalt not know the sound of thine own tongue.
The Merchant of Venice. Act i, sc. 1, l. 109. [Gratiano]

My ears have not yet drunk a hundred words
Of that tongue's utterance, yet I know the sound.
Romeo and Juliet. Act ii, sc. 2, l. 58. [Juliet]

Sound of your voice.—*Measure for Measure,* v, 1, 330.

11
Hark! by the sound of drum you may perceive
Their powers are marching unto Paris-ward.
I Henry VI. Act iii, sc. 3, l. 29. [La Pucelle] The only use of "Paris-ward."

Sound of shallow foppery.—*The Merchant of Venice,* ii, 5, 35.
Sound of hope.—*Venus and Adonis,* l. 976.
Sounds of music.—*The Merchant of Venice,* v, 1, 55.
Sound of the trumpet.—*King Lear,* v, 3, 114.
Trumpet's sound.—*III Henry VI,* v, 7, 9; *Timon of Athens,* iii, 6, 37. See under TRUMPET.
Sounds of woe.—*Much Ado about Nothing,* ii, 3, 70.
Sound of words.—*King John,* iii, 1, 230; iii, 3, 51.

12
Particularities and petty sounds To cease!
II Henry VI. Act v, sc. 2, l. 44. [Young Clifford] "Particularities" is repeated in *Henry V,* iii, 2, 142.

13
Gardiner: Ye are not sound.
Cromwell: Not sound?
Gardiner: Not sound, I say.
Henry VIII. Act v, sc. 3, l. 81.

Sound as a bell.—*Much Ado about Nothing,* iii, 2, 13.
Sound of heart.—*Henry V,* iii, 6, 27.

Sound, sans crack.—*Love's Labour's Lost*, v, 2, 415.

1 Every one hears that,
Which can distinguish sound.
King Lear. Act iv, sc. 6, l. 214. [Gentleman]

Momentany as a sound.—*A Midsummer-Night's Dream*, i, 1, 143. See under Love for full quotation.

2
Deep sounds make lesser noise than shallow fords.
The Rape of Lucrece, l. 1329.

Without a sound.—*Rape of Lucrece*, l. 1464.

3
If he be slain, say 'I;' or if not, no:
Brief sounds determine of my weal or woe.
Romeo and Juliet. Act iii, sc. 2, l. 50. [Juliet]

4
This is no mortal business, nor no sound
That the earth owes.
The Tempest. Act i, sc. 2, l. 406. [Ferdinand]

O heaven, O earth, bear witness to this sound.
Tempest. Act iii, sc. 1, l. 68. [Ferdinand]

5
Sounds and sweet airs, that give delight and hurt not.
Tempest. Act iii, sc. 2, l. 145. [Caliban]

Sweet sound.—*Romeo and Juliet*, iv, 5, 134; *The Merchant of Venice*, v, 1, 84; *Twelfth Night*, i, 1, 5.

Sound of sweetest melody.—*II Henry IV*, iii, 1, 14.

Sound more sweetly.—*Julius Cæsar*, iii, 1, 50.

Sound so fair.—*Macbeth*, i, 3, 52.

6
Idle sounds resembling parasites.
Venus and Adonis, l. 848.

Dulcet sounds.—*The Merchant of Venice*, iii, 2, 51.

First-conceived sound.—*II Henry VI*, iii, 2, 44. The only use of "first-conceived."

Flattering sounds.—*Richard II*, ii, 1, 17.

Frosty sound.—*I Henry IV*, iv, 1, 128.

Greatest sound.—*Henry V*, iv, 4, 74.

Heavenly sound.—*The Taming of the Shrew*, Ind., 1, 51.

Heaviest sound.—*Macbeth*, iv, 3, 202.

Lowest sound.—*Love's Labour's Lost*, iv, 3, 335.

Malicious sounds.—*Coriolanus*, iii, 3, 55.

Melodious sound.—*Passionate Pilgrim*, l. 111.

Pleasing sound.—*Sonnets*, cxxx.

Powerful sound.—*All's Well that Ends Well*, ii, 1, 179.

Rarest sounds!—*Pericles*, v, 1, 233.

Rude sounds.—*Troilus and Cressida*, i, 1, 92.

Silver sound.—*Romeo and Juliet*, iv, 5, 130; 136; 143; 144.

Threatening sound.—*III Henry VI*, ii, 6, 58.

Unprofitable sounds.—*Rape of Lucrece*, l. 1017.

Well-tuned sounds.—*Sonnets*, viii. "Well-tuned" is repeated in *Titus Andronicus*, ii, 3, 18, and in *Othello*, ii, 1, 202.

Sound asleep, see Sleep: Sound Sleep.

SOVEREIGN

See also King

7
Hath he forgot he is his sovereign?
I Henry VI. Act iv, sc. 1, l. 52. [Gloucester]

Call my sovereign yours,
And do him homage as obedient subjects.
I Henry VI. Act iv, sc. 2, l. 6. [Talbot]

8
Mine alder-liefest sovereign,
Makes me the bolder to salute my king
With ruder terms, such as my wit affords
And over-joy of heart doth minister.
II Henry VI. Act i, sc. 1, l. 30. [Queen]
The only use of "alder-liefest" (dearest) and "over-joy." "Ruder" is repeated in *Troilus and Cressida*, iii, 2, 26.

9
We are thy sovereign, Clifford, kneel again.
II Henry VI. Act v, sc. 1, l. 127. [York]

Kneel for grace and mercy at my feet;
I am thy sovereign.
III Henry VI. Act i, sc. 1, l. 75. [King Henry]

Honour me as thy king and sovereign.
III Henry VI. Act i, sc. 1, l. 198. [King Henry]

Their true sovereign, whom they must obey.
III Henry VI. Act iv, sc. 1, l. 78. [King Edward]

Dear sovereign.—*Titus Andronicus*, ii, 3, 89.

Dread sovereign.—*Henry V*, i, 2, 97; *Henry VIII*, v, 3, 114; 148; *Richard II*, i, 1, 165.

Gracious sovereign.—*Henry VI*, iii, 1, 149, and frequently in later plays.

Mighty sovereign.—*II Henry VI*, iii, 2, 122; *Richard III*, iv, 4, 446; 466; 486; 492.

Right royal sovereign.—*King John*, i, 1, 15.

Rightful sovereign.—*II Henry VI*, ii, 2, 61.

Salt sovereign. . . . A sovereign king.—*The Rape of Lucrece*, l. 650.

Sweet sovereign.—*Cymbeline*, i, 1, 154.

Sovereign's sovereign.—*Henry V*, iii, 7, 38.

My thoughts' sovereign.—*Richard III*, iii, 1, 2.

10 Your sovereign,
Is prisoner to the foe; his state usurp'd,
His realm a slaughter-house, his subjects slain,
His statutes cancell'd and his treasure spent.
III Henry VI. Act v, sc. 4, l. 76. [Queen Margaret]

11
O, let my sovereign turn away his face
And bid his ears a little while be deaf.
Richard II. Act i, sc. 1, l. 111. [Mowbray]

Lord marshal, let me kiss my sovereign's hand,
And bow my knee before his majesty.
Richard II. Act i, sc. 3, l. 46. [Bolingbroke]

II—Sovereignty

12
To show less sovereignty than they, must needs
Appear unkinglike.
Cymbeline. Act iii, sc. 5, l. 6. [Cymbeline]
The only use of "unkinglike."

13 Fed him every minute
With words of sovereignty.
Henry VIII. Act i, sc. 2, l. 149. [Surveyor]

14
The golden yoke of sovereignty.
Richard III. Act iii, sc. 7, l. 146. [Gloucester]

Put in her tender heart the aspiring flame
Of golden sovereignty.
Richard III. Act iv, sc. 4, l. 328. [King Richard]

1
Gonzalo: I' the commonwealth I would by contraries
Execute all things; . . . No sovereignty;—
Sebastian: Yet he would be king on 't.
The Tempest. Act ii, sc. 1, l. 147.

Cull'd sovereignty.—*Love's Labour 's Lost,* iv, 3, 234.
General sovereignty.—*All 's Well that Ends Well,* i, 3, 230.
Unknown sovereignty.—*Measure for Measure,* v, 1, 392.
Sovereignty of nature.—*Coriolanus,* iv, 7, 35.
Sovereignty of reason.—*Hamlet,* i, 4, 73.

SPACE

See also Distance

2
Acordo linta.
Come on; thou art granted space.
All's Well that Ends Well. Act iv, sc. 1, l. 97. [Soldier] The only use of "accordo linta." Parolles' captors have been speaking gibberish to deceive him.

3 Let Rome in Tiber melt! . . .
Here is my space.
Antony and Cleopatra. Act i, sc. 1, l. 33. [Antony]

Make space enough between you.
Antony and Cleopatra. Act ii, sc. 3, l. 23. [Soothsayer]

4
Writ with blank space for different names.
The Merry Wives of Windsor, ii, 1, 77. See under LETTER.

Coming space.—*All 's Well that Ends Well,* ii, 3, 188.
Infinite space.—*Hamlet,* ii, 2, 262.
Large spaces.—*Troilus and Cressida,* ii, 2, 162.
Little space.—*Pericles,* iv, 1, 68.
Mightiest space.—*All 's Well that Ends Well,* i, 1, 237.
Mighty space.—*Julius Cæsar,* iv, 3, 25.
Short space.—*I Henry IV,* v, 1, 46.
So short a space.—*Richard III,* iv, 1, 79.
Small space.—*As You Like It,* iv, 3, 152.
Undistinguish'd space.—*King Lear,* iv, 6, 278. The only use of "undistinguish'd."
Whole space.—*Macbeth,* iv, 3, 36.
Space of earth.—*Troilus and Cressida,* v, 10, 27.
Three days' space.—*II Henry VI,* iii, 2, 295.
Three years' space.—*Love's Labour 's Lost,* i, 1, 52; 151.

5
Space enough Have I in such a prison.
The Tempest, i, 2, 492. See under PRISON.

Sebastian: 'Tis true my brother's daughter 's queen of Tunis;
So is she heir of Naples; 'twixt which regions
There is some space.
Antonio: A space whose every cubit
Seems to cry out, 'How shall that Claribel
Measure us back to Naples?'
The Tempest. Act ii, sc. 1, l. 255.

SPARROW

6
He . . . providently caters for the sparrow.
As You Like It, ii, 3, 44. See COMFORT, 203:1.

There 's a special providence in the fall of a sparrow.
Hamlet. Act v, sc. 2, l. 230. [Hamlet]

7
Prince: He that rides at high speed and with his pistol kills a sparrow flying.
Falstaff: You have hit it.
Prince: So did he never the sparrow.
I Henry IV. Act ii, sc. 4, l. 379.

8
Sparrows must not build in the house-eaves, because they are lecherous.
Measure for Measure. Act iii, sc. 2, l. 185. [Lucio] The only use of "house-eaves."

Play with sparrows.—*The Tempest,* iv, 1, 100.

9
I will buy nine sparrows for a penny.
Troilus and Cressida, ii, 1, 77. See under BRAIN.

Now my double-henned sparrow!
Troilus and Cressida. Act v, sc. 7, l. 11 [Thersites] The only use of "double-henned."

New-ta'en sparrow.—*Troilus and Cressida,* iii, 2, 36. The only use of "new-ta'en."

SPECTACLE

See also Sight

10
O barbarous and bloody spectacle!
II Henry VI. Act iv, sc. 1, l. 144. [First Gentleman]

The saddest spectacle that e'er I view'd.
III Henry VI. Act ii, sc. 1, l. 67. [Messenger] The only use of "saddest."

Direful spectacle.—*The Tempest,* i, 2, 26.
Heart-hardening spectacles.—*Coriolanus,* iv, 1, 25. The only use of "heart-hardening."
Heinous spectacle.—*King John,* iv, 3, 56.
Piteous spectacle!—*III Henry VI,* ii, 5, 73; *Julius Cæsar,* iii, 2, 202.
Public spectacle.—*I Henry VI,* i, 4, 41.
Savage spectacle.—*Julius Cæsar,* iii, 1, 223.

Think but how vile a spectacle it were.
The Rape of Lucrece, l. 631.

11
Call'd them blind and dusty spectacles.
II Henry VI, iii, 2, 112. See under EYES.

Seek for sorrow with thy spectacles.
II Henry VI. Act v, sc. 1, l. 165. [King Henry]

With spectacles on nose.—*As You Like It,* ii, 7, 159.

12
I can see yet without spectacles.
Much Ado about Nothing. Act i, sc. 1, l. 191. [Benedick]

I shall not need spectacles.—*King Lear,* i, 2, 36.

13
Ha' not you seen, Camillo,—
But that 's past doubt, you have, or your eye-glass
Is thicker than a cuckold's horn.
The Winter's Tale. Act i, sc. 2, l. 267. [Leontes] The only use of "eye-glass."

SPECTATOR

1
Some quantity of barren spectators.
Hamlet, iii, 2, 46. See under ACTING.
Play'd to take spectators.—*The Winter's Tale,* iii, 2, 38.
Gentle spectators.—*The Winter's Tale,* iv, 1, 20.
Good repast to the spectators.—*Cymbeline,* v, 4, 158. The only uses of "spectators." "Spectatorship" occurs in *Coriolanus,* v, 2, 71.

2
One that was a woful looker-on.
III Henry VI. Act ii, sc. 1, l. 45. [Messenger]
Incertain lookers on.—*Winter's Tale,* v, 1, 29.
Reverend looker-on.—*Richard III,* iv, 1, 31.

3 My business in this state
Made me a looker on here in Vienna.
Measure for Measure. Act v, sc. 1, l. 318. [Duke]

4
All the standers-by had wet their cheeks.
Richard III. Act i, sc. 2, l. 163. [Gloucester]
You were standers by . . . when my son
Was stabb'd with bloody daggers.
Richard III. Act i, sc. 3, l. 210. [Queen Margaret]
I would not be a stander-by to hear
My sovereign mistress clouded so, without
My present vengeance taken.
Winter's Tale. Act i, sc. 2, l. 279. [Camillo]
So long could I Stand by, a looker on.
Winter's Tale. Act v, sc. 3, l. 84. [Perdita]

5
I 'll be a candle-holder, and look on.
Romeo and Juliet. Act i, sc. 4, l. 38. [Romeo] The only use of "candle-holder."

6
While idly I stood looking on.
The Taming of the Shrew, i, 1, 155.

SPEECH

See also Conversation, Discourse, Oratory, Talk, Tongue

I—Familiar Phrases

7 Be check'd for silence,
But never tax'd for speech.
All's Well that Ends Well. Act i, sc. 1, l. 76. [Countess]

8
He desires Some private speech with you.
All's Well that Ends Well. Act ii, sc. 5, l. 62. [Helena]
Speak it privately.—*The Merchant of Venice,* ii, 4, 21.

9
But what linsey-woolsey hast thou to speak to us again?
All's Well that Ends Well. Act iv, sc. 1, l. 13. [Lord] The only use of "linsey-woolsey."
Am I that or this for what he 'll utter,
That will speak any thing?
All's Well that Ends Well. Act v, sc. 3, l. 208. [Bertram]

10
Antony: Let me speak a little.
Cleopatra: No, let me speak.
Antony and Cleopatra. Act iv, sc. 15, l. 42.
I am hush'd until our city be afire,
And then I 'll speak a little.
Coriolanus. Act v, sc. 3, l. 182. [Volumnia]
Let me speak a little.—*Twelfth Night,* iii, 4, 393.

11
I speak but brotherly of him.
As You Like It. Act i, sc. 1, l. 160. [Oliver]
To speak more properly.—*As You Like It,* i, 1, 8; *King John,* ii, 1, 514.

12
Thou speakest wiser than thou art ware of.
As You Like It. Act ii, sc. 4, l. 58. [Rosalind]
Cressida: I know not what I speak.
Troilus: Well know they what they speak that speak so wisely.
Troilus and Cressida. Act iii, sc. 2, l. 158.
Speak wisely.—*As You Like It,* i, 2, 93.

13
Speakest thou in sober meanings?
As You Like It. Act v, sc. 2, l. 76. [Orlando]

14
I speak this in hunger for bread, not in thirst for revenge.
Coriolanus. Act i, sc. 1, l. 25. [Citizen]

15
I cannot speak him home.
Coriolanus. Act ii, sc. 2, l. 107. [Cominius]
He speaks home, madam.
Othello, ii, 1, 166. See under CANDOUR.
Speak to me home.—*Antony and Cleopatra,* i, 2, 109.

16
Say, and speak thick.
Cymbeline. Act iii, sc. 2, l. 58. [Imogen]
Speaking thick, which nature made his blemish,
Became the accents of the valiant;
For those that could speak low and tardily
Would turn their own perfection to abuse,
To seem like him.
II Henry IV. Act ii, sc. 3, l. 24. [Lady Percy] The only use of "tardily."

17
How you speak!
Cymbeline. Act iii, sc. 3, l. 44. [Belarius]

18 O, never say hereafter
But I am truest speaker.
Cymbeline. Act v, sc. 5, l. 375. [Imogen]
A speaker is but a prater.
Henry V. Act v, sc. 2, l. 167. [King Henry] The only use of "prater."
Stay, you imperfect speakers, tell me more.
Macbeth. Act i, sc. 3, l. 70. [Macbeth]
Rare speaker.—*Henry VIII,* i, 2, 111.

19
Stay! speak, speak! I charge thee, speak!
Hamlet. Act i, sc. 1, l. 51. [Horatio]
I 'll speak to it, though hell itself should gape.
Hamlet. Act i, sc. 2, l. 245. [Hamlet]

20
O, speak of that; that do I long to hear.
Hamlet. Act ii, sc. 2, l. 50. [King]
What he spake, though it lack'd form a little,
Was not like madness.
Hamlet. Act iii, sc. 1, l. 171. [King]

21
A knavish speech sleeps in a foolish ear.
Hamlet. Act iv, sc. 2, l. 25. [Hamlet]
Hems, and beats her heart;
Spurns enviously at straws; speaks things in doubt,

That carry but half sense: her speech is nothing,
Yet the unshaped use of it doth move
The hearers to collection.
Hamlet. Act iv, sc. 5, l. 5. [Gentleman] The only use of "enviously" and "unshaped."

She puts the period often from his place;
And midst the sentence so her accent breaks,
That twice she doth begin ere once she speaks.
The Rape of Lucrece, l. 365.

1
How absolute the knave is! we must speak by the card, or equivocation will undo us.
Hamlet. Act v, sc. 1, l. 148. [Hamlet]

Let me speak to the yet unknowing world.
Hamlet. Act v, sc. 2, l. 390. [Horatio] The only use of "unknowing."

2
I do not speak to thee in drink but in tears, not in pleasure but in passion, not in words only, but in woes also.
I Henry IV. Act ii, sc. 4, l. 457. [Falstaff]

Speak in jest.—*I Henry IV*, ii, 3, 102.

Spoke at a venture.—*II Henry IV*, i, 1, 59.

3
You speak as having power to do wrong.
II Henry IV. Act ii, sc. 1, l. 141. [Chief Justice]

4
Doll Tearsheet: What says your grace?
Falstaff: His grace says that which his flesh rebels against.
II Henry IV. Act ii, sc. 4, l. 378.

You speak . . . you know not what.
II Henry IV. Act iv, sc. 1, l. 130. [Westmoreland]

I never thought to hear you speak again.
II Henry IV. Act iv, sc. 5, l. 92. [Prince]

Have you your wits? know you what 'tis you speak?
II Henry IV. Act v, sc. 5, l. 49. [Chief Justice]

5
That what you speak is in your conscience wash'd
As pure as sin with baptism.
Henry V. Act i, sc. 2, l. 31. [King Henry]

We speak upon our cue, and our voice is imperial.
Henry V. Act iii, sc. 6, l. 130. [Montjoy] See also under PLAY.

6
What 's to say?
Henry V. Act iv, sc. 2, l. 32. [Constable]

7
Sudden and extemporal speech.
I Henry VI. Act iii, sc. 1, l. 6. [Winchester] "Extemporal" is repeated in *Love's Labour 's Lost*, i, 2, 189; iv, 2, 50.

Speak suddenly.—*III Henry VI*, iv, 2, 4; *Richard III*, iv, 2, 20.

8
Things are often spoke and seldom meant.
II Henry VI. Act iii, sc. 1, l. 268. [Suffolk]

9
He has a familiar under his tongue; he speaks not o' God's name.
II Henry VI. Act iv, sc. 7, l. 114. [Cade]

10
I shame to hear thee speak.
III Henry VI. Act i, sc. 1, l. 231. [Queen Margaret]

11
King Henry: Hear me speak.
Queen Margaret: Thou hast spoke too much already.
III Henry VI. Act i, sc. 1, l. 257.

I 'll prove the contrary, if you 'll hear me speak.
III Henry VI. Act i, sc. 2, l. 20. [Richard]

Hear me speak before I die.
III Henry VI. Act i, sc. 3, l. 18. [Rutland]

Antonio: I pray thee, hear me speak. . . .
Shylock: I will not hear thee speak. . . .
Therefore speak no more.
The Merchant of Venice. Act iii, sc. 3, l. 11.

Hear me speak.—*III Henry VI*, iii, 3, 65, and frequently in later plays.

Hear me, for I will speak.
Julius Cæsar. Act iv, sc. 3, l. 38. [Brutus]

12
'Tis love I bear thy glories makes me speak.
III Henry VI. Act ii, sc. 1, l. 158. [Richard]

I speak no more than what my soul intends.
III Henry VI. Act iii, sc. 2, l. 94. [King Edward]

Bring forth the gallant, let us hear him speak.
III Henry VI. Act v, sc. 5, l. 12. [King Edward]

13
Speak like a subject, proud ambitious York!
III Henry VI. Act v, sc. 5, l. 17. [Prince]

I speak to subjects, and a subject speaks,
Stirr'd up by God, thus boldly for his king.
Richard II. Act iv, sc. 1, l. 132. [Carlisle]

14
You speak not like yourself.
Henry VIII. Act ii, sc. 4, l. 85. [Wolsey]

Thou speakest wonders.
Henry VIII. Act v, sc. 5, l. 56. [King Henry]

Speak'st reason.—*Much Ado about Nothing*, v, 1, 41.

Speakest skilfully.—*Love's Labour 's Lost*, ii, 1, 253.

15
What say'st thou to me? speak once again.
Julius Cæsar. Act i, sc. 2, l. 22. [Cæsar]

Speak again.—*A Midsummer-Night's Dream*, iii, 2, 404.

16
You pull'd me by the cloak; would you speak with me?
Julius Cæsar. Act i, sc. 2, l. 215. [Casca]

What you have said
I will consider; what you have to say
I will with patience hear, and find a time
Both meet to hear, and answer such high things.
Julius Cæsar. Act i, sc. 2, l. 167. [Brutus]

What, thou speak'st drowsily?
Julius Cæsar. Act iv, sc. 3, l. 240. [Brutus] The only use of "drowsily."

17
He speaks plain cannon fire, and smoke and bounce.
King John. Act ii, sc. 1, l. 462. [Bastard]

'Bounce' would a' say.—*II Henry IV*, iii, 2, 304. The only uses of "bounce." "Bounced" occurs in *Pericles*, ii, 1, 26.

Hast thou not spoke like thunder on my side?
King John, iii, 1, 124. See TREASON, 1561:4.

1 I had a thing to say,
But I will fit it with some better time.
King John. Act iii, sc. 3. l. 25. [King John]
I had a thing to say, but let it go.
King John. Act iii, sc. 3, l. 33. [King John]

2
Our eldest-born, speak first.
King Lear. Act i, sc. 1, l. 55. [King Lear] The only use of "eldest-born."
Mend your speech a little,
Lest it may mar your fortunes.
King Lear. Act i, sc. 1, l. 96. [King Lear]
Past speaking of.—*King Lear,* iv, 6, 209.

3
Speak less than thou knowest.
King Lear, i, 4, 132. See under BEHAVIOUR.
Speak all thou knowest.—*All's Well that Ends Well,* v, 3, 256.

4
He speaks the mere contrary; crosses love not him.
Love's Labour's Lost. Act i, sc. 2, l. 35. [Moth]
Vir sapit qui pauca loquitur.
Love's Labour's Lost. Act iv, sc. 2, l. 82. [Holofernes] Identified by H. H. Furness as a sentence from Lyly's *Grammar:* "The man is wise who speaketh few things."
I may speak of thee as the traveller doth of Venice;
Venetia, Venetia,
Chi non ti vede non ti pretia.
Love's Labour's Lost. Act iv, sc. 2, l. 97. [Holofernes] The only use of "Venetia."

5
Speak to be understood.
Love's Labour's Lost. Act v, sc. 2, l. 294. [Princess of France]

6 Do not bid me speak;
See, and then speak yourselves.
Macbeth. Act ii, sc. 3, l. 77. [Macduff]
Be not a niggard of your speech.
Macbeth. Act iv, sc. 3, l. 180. [Macduff]

7 But I do bend my speech
To one that can my part in him advertise.
Measure for Measure. Act i, sc. 1, l. 41. [Duke]

8
Gentleman: Do I speak feelingly now?
Lucio: I think thou dost; and, indeed, with most painful feeling of thy speech.
Measure for Measure. Act i, sc. 2, l. 36.
Speak feelingly.—*Hamlet,* v, 2, 113.
Speaks advisedly.—*The Rape of Lucrece,* l. 180.
Speak audaciously.—*Love's Labour's Lost,* v, 2, 104.
Speak briefly.—*Coriolanus,* iii, 1, 285; *Romeo and Juliet,* i, 3, 96. See also under BREVITY.
Speak fondly.—*Richard II,* iii, 3, 185.
Speak masterly.—*Twelfth Night,* ii, 4, 23.
Speak mournfully.—*Coriolanus,* v, 6, 151.
Speak nobly.—*King Lear,* v, 1, 28; *Pericles,* v, 1, 189.
Not to speak it profanely.—*Hamlet,* iii, 2, 34. The only use of "profanely." See under ACTING.
Speak proudly.—*Henry V,* iv, 3, 108.
Speak seriously.—*Timon of Athens,* iii, 2, 47.
Speak sincerely.—*Henry VIII,* ii, 3, 59.
Speak sufficiently.—*Pericles,* i, 3, 14. "Sufficiently" is repeated in *I Henry VI,* i, 4, 58: "Sufficiently revenged"; and in *The Winter's Tale,* iv, 2, 16: "Sufficiently manage."
Speak unskilfully.—*Measure for Measure,* iii, 2, 156. The only use of "unskilfully."

9
To be received plain, I'll speak more gross.
Measure for Measure. Act ii, sc. 4, l. 82. [Angelo]
Speak not so grossly.—*The Merchant of Venice,* v, 1, 266.

10
You are pleasant, sir, and speak apace.
Measure for Measure. Act iii, sc. 2, l. 120. [Duke]
Speak apace. I would thou coulds stammer, that thou mightst pour this concealed man out of thy mouth, as wine comes out of a narrow-mouthed bottle, either too much at once, or none at all. I prithee, take the cork out of thy mouth that I may drink thy tidings.
As You Like It. Act iii, sc. 2, l. 208. [Rosalind] The only use of "stammer" and "narrow-mouthed."
Speak big.—*Richard II,* iii, 2, 114.
Speaks brave words.—*As You Like It,* iii, 4, 44.
Speak comfort.—*Much Ado about Nothing,* v, 1, 21.
Speak my griefs unspeakable.—*The Comedy of Errors,* i, 1, 33.
Speaks holiday.—*The Merry Wives of Windsor,* iii, 2, 69.
Speak of patience.—*Much Ado about Nothing* v, 1, 10.
Speak patience.—*Much Ado about Nothing,* v, 1, 27.
Speaks sense.—*The Merry Wives of Windsor* ii, 1, 129.
Speaking my fancy.—*Much Ado about Nothing,* iii, 1, 95.
Speaking honourably.—*Much Ado about Nothing,* iii, 4, 29.
Speaking in deeds.—*Troilus and Cressida,* iv, 5, 98. See WORD AND DEED.

11
I can speak Against the thing I say.
Measure for Measure. Act ii, sc. 4, l. 59. [Angelo]
It oft falls out,
To have what we would have, we speak not what we mean.
Measure for Measure. Act ii, sc. 4, l. 117. [Isabella]

12
Let me entreat you speak the former language.
Measure for Measure. Act ii, sc. 4, l. 140 [Isabella]
Speak our language.—*Love's Labour's Lost,* v, 2, 175.
Speak English.—*The Merry Wives of Windsor,* iv, 3, 7. See ENGLAND, 419:4.

13
To speak so indirectly I am loath.
Measure for Measure. Act iv, sc. 6, l. 1. [Isabella]

14
Duke Vincentio: You were not bid to speak.
Lucio: No, my good lord;

Nor wish'd to hold my peace.
Measure for Measure. Act v, sc. 1, l. 78.

Thou know'st not what thou speak'st.
Measure for Measure. Act v, sc. 1, l. 105. [Duke]

I spoke it but according to the trick.
Measure for Measure. Act v, sc. 1, l. 509. [Lucio]

1
I 'll end my exhortation after dinner.
The Merchant of Venice. Act i, sc. 1, l. 104. [Gratiano] The only use of "exhortation."

Gratiano speaks an infinite deal of nothing, more than any man in all Venice.
The Merchant of Venice. Act i, sc. 1, l. 113. [Bassanio]

I speak too long; but 'tis to peize the time.
The Merchant of Venice. Act iii, sc. 2, l. 22. [Portia] "Peize" (or peise, weigh down) is repeated in *Richard III,* v, 3, 105. "Peised" occurs in *King John,* ii, 1, 575.

Ay, but I fear you speak upon the rack,
Where men enforced do speak anything.
The Merchant of Venice. Act iii, sc. 2, l. 32. [Portia]

Howsoe'er thou speak'st, 'mong other things
I shall digest it.
The Merchant of Venice. Act iii, sc. 5, l. 94. [Lorenzo]

In vain thou speak'st.—*III Henry VI,* i, 3, 21.

2
It is spoke as a Christians ought to speak.
The Merry Wives of Windsor. Act i, sc. 1, l. 103. [Evans]

You must speak possitable.
The Merry Wives of Windsor. Act i, sc. 1, l. 244. [Evans] The only use of "possitable."

Positively speak.—*Richard III,* iv, 2, 25.

3
What says my bully-rook? speak scholarly and wisely.
The Merry Wives of Windsor. Act i, sc. 3, l. 2. [Host] "Bully-rook" is used four times in this play, always by the Host. The only use of "scholarly."

I have spoke; let him follow.
The Merry Wives of Windsor. Act i, sc. 3, l. 14. [Host]

4
He 'll speak like an Anthropophaginian.
Merry Wives of Windsor. Act iv, sc. 5, l. 9. [Host] The only use of Anthropophaginian. Anthropophagi occurs in *Othello,* i, 3, 44.

Speak from thy lungs military.
The Merry Wives of Windsor. Act iv, sc. 5, l. 18. [Host]

Why, that 's spoken like an honest drovier: so they sell bullocks.
Much Ado about Nothing. Act ii, sc. 1, l. 201 [Benedick] The only use of "drovier." "Bullocks" occurs again in *II Henry IV,* iii, 2, 42

You speak like an ancient and most quiet watchman.
Much Ado about Nothing. Act iii, sc. 3, l. 41. [Dogberry]

Your worship speaks like a most thankful and reverend youth; and I praise God for you.
Much Ado about Nothing. Act v, sc. 1, l. 324. [Dogberry]

Speak like a true knight, so defend thee heaven!
Richard II. Act i, sc. 3, l. 34. [Marshal]

Pardon me, If I speak like a captain.
Timon of Athens. Act iii, sc. 5, l. 40. [Alcibiades]

Speak like a king.—*I Henry IV,* ii, 4, 476.

5
Flute: Must I speak now?
Quince: Ay, marry, must you.
A Midsummer-Night's Dream. Act iii, sc. 1, l. 91.

Wherefore speaks he this To her he hates?
A Midsummer-Night's Dream. Act iii, sc. 2, l. 227. [Helena]

His speech was like a tangled chain; nothing impaired, but all disordered.
A Midsummer-Night's Dream. Act v, sc. 1, l. 125. [Theseus] The only use of "impaired." "Tangled" is repeated in *Henry VIII,* iii, 2, 35.

Would you desire lime and hair to speak better?
A Midsummer-Night's Dream. Act v, sc. 1, l. 166. [Theseus]

6
Benedick: Would you have me speak after my custom? . . .
Claudio: I pray thee speak in sober judgement.
Much Ado about Nothing. Act i, sc. 1, l. 169.

Speak you this with a sad brow? or do you play the flouting Jack, to tell us Cupid is a good hare-finder and Vulcan a rare carpenter?
Much Ado about Nothing. Act i, sc. 1, l. 185. [Benedick] The only use of "hare-finder."

I was born to speak all mirth and no matter.
Much Ado about Nothing. Act ii, sc. 1, l. 343. [Beatrice]

[He] speaks a little off the matter.
Much Ado about Nothing. Act iii, sc. 5, l. 10. [Dogberry]

I speak not like a dotard nor a fool.
Much Ado about Nothing. Act v, sc. 1, l. 59. [Leonato]

7
Upon this hint I spake.
Othello. Act i, sc. 3, l. 166. [Othello]

Why do you speak so faintly?
Othello. Act iii, sc. 3, l. 282. [Desdemona]

Why do you speak so startingly and rash?
Othello. Act iii, sc. 4, l. 79. [Desdemona] The only use of "startingly."

8
It is not honesty in me to speak
What I have seen and known.
Othello. Act iv, sc. 1, l. 288. [Iago]

Let me have leave to speak.—*Othello,* v, 2, 195.

9
What 's dumb in show I 'll plain with speech.
Pericles. Act iii, Gower, l. 14.

There was speech in their dumbness, language in their very gesture.
The Winter's Tale. Act v, sc. 2, l. 14. [Gentleman]

10
'Tis time to speak; my pains are quite forgot.
Richard III. Act i, sc. 3, l. 117. [Gloucester]

Duchess of York: O, let me speak!
King Richard: Do then; but I 'll not hear.
Duchess of York: I will be mild and gentle in my speech.
Richard III. Act iv, sc. 4, l. 159.

1
Juliet: Speakest thou from thy heart?
Nurse: And from my soul too;
Or else beshrew them both.
Romeo and Juliet. Act iii, sc. 5, l. 228.
Be not so long to speak.—*Romeo and Juliet*. iv, 1, 66.

2
I speak but as I find.
The Taming of the Shrew. Act ii, sc. 1, l. 66. [Baptista]
Speak once in thy life.—*The Tempest,* iii, 2, 24.
We speak in vain.—*Timon of Athens,* v, 1, 193.

3
Now it is my turn to speak.
Titus Andronicus. Act v, sc. 3, l. 119. [Marcus]

4
Speak, Prince of Ithaca; and be 't of less expect
That matter needless, of importless burden,
Divide thy lips, than we are confident.
Troilus and Cressida. Act i, sc. 3, l. 71. [Agamemnon] The only use of "importless."

5
Speaking is for beggars; he wears his tongue in 's arms.
Troilus and Cressida. Act iii, sc. 3, l. 270. [Thersites]
Patroclus: What say you to 't?
Thersites: God b' wi' you, with all my heart.
Troilus and Cressida. Act iii, sc. 3, l. 293.

6 Signify this loving interview
To the expecters.
Troilus and Cressida. Act iv, sc. 5, l. 155. [Hector] The only use of "expecters."
Royal interview.—*Henry V,* v, 2, 27.
Interview between England and France.—*Henry VIII,* i, 1, 180. "Interview" is repeated in i, 1, 165, and in *Love's Labour's Lost,* ii, 1, 167.

7
He speaks nothing but madman.
Twelfth Night. Act i, sc. 5, l. 114. [Olivia]
She did speak in starts distractedly.
Twelfth Night. Act ii, sc. 2, l. 22. [Viola] The only use of "distractedly."
In conclusion put strange speech upon me:
I know not what 'twas but distraction.
Twelfth Night. Act v, sc. 1, l. 70. [Officer]

8
Thy speech serves for authority.
Twelfth Night. Act i, sc. 2, l. 20. [Viola]
He 'll speak with you, will you or no.
Twelfth Night. Act i, sc. 5, l. 162. [Malvolio]
We are to speak in public.
Twelfth Night. Act ii, sc. 1, l. 197. [Leontes]
You have said, sir.
Twelfth Night. Act iii, sc. 1, l. 12. [Clown]
I am shent for speaking to you.
Twelfth Night. Act iv, sc. 2, l. 112. [Clown] "Shent" (blamed, reproved) occurs five times.

9
Why do you speak to me? I never hurt you.
Twelfth Night. Act v, sc. 1, l. 190. [Viola]
Let me hear you speak.—*Twelfth Night,* iii, 1, 133.

10
I leave my duty a little unthought of and speak out of my injury.
Twelfth Night. Act v, sc. 1, l. 318. [Fabian] "Unthought of" is used only once again, in *I Henry IV,* iii, 2, 141.

11
To speak puling, like a beggar at Hallowmas.
The Two Gentlemen of Verona, ii, 1, 26. See under LOVE.

12
All this I speak in print, for in print I found it.
The Two Gentlemen of Verona. Act ii, sc. 1, l. 175. [Speed]

13
O, that she could speak now like a wood woman!
The Two Gentlemen of Verona. Act ii, sc. 3, l. 30. [Launce]

14
It must with circumstance be spoken.
The Two Gentlemen of Verona. Act iii, sc. 2, l. 36. [Proteus]

15
He will allow no speech, which I do guess
You do purpose to him.
Winter's Tale. Act iv, sc. 4, l. 478 [Camillo]
I was about to speak.—*Winter's Tale,* iv, 4, 454.
I make a broken delivery of the business.
The Winter's Tale. Act v, sc. 2, l. 10. [Gentleman]

II—Speaking Freely

16
Speak freely, Syracusian, what thou wilt.
The Comedy of Errors. Act v, sc. 1, l. 285. [Duke] "Syracusian" is used seven times in this play, and in no other.
Speak freely.—*Henry V,* i, 2, 231; *Henry VIII,* i, 2, 131; *Cymbeline,* v, 5, 119.
Speak freely what you think.—*III Henry VI,* iv, 1, 28. See also under CANDOUR.

17
And the offender granted scope of speech.
II Henry VI. Act iii, sc. 1, l. 176. [Cardinal Beaufort]

18
Let us speak Our free hearts each to other.
Macbeth. Act i, sc. 3, l. 154. [Macbeth]
I 'll speak all.—*Measure for Measure,* v, 1, 443.

19 Give me leave
To have free speech with you.
Measure for Measure. Act i, sc. 1, l. 78. [Escalus]
Free speech.—*Othello,* iii, 4, 129.

20
I will bestow you where you shall have time
To speak your bosom freely.
Othello. Act iii, sc. 1, l. 57. [Emilia]
I peace!
No, I will speak as liberal as the north:
Let heaven and men and devils, let them all,
All, all, cry shame against me, yet I 'll speak.
Othello. Act v, sc. 2, l. 219. [Emilia]
Free of speech.—*Othello,* iii, 3, 185.

21
Since you have given me leave to speak,
Freely will I speak.
Pericles. Act i, sc. 2, l. 101. [Helicanus]

Freely speak.—*Richard II,* i, 1, 17.

1 The fair reverence of your highness curbs me
From giving reins and spurs to my free speech;
Which else would post until it had return'd
These terms of treason doubled down his throat.
Richard II. Act i, sc. 1, l. 54. [Mowbray]

Free speech and fearless I to thee allow.
Richard II. Act i, sc. 1, l. 123. [King Richard]

Be confident to speak.
Richard II. Act ii, sc. 1, l. 274. [Ross]

2 Why, sir, I trust I may have leave to speak;
And speak I will.
The Taming of the Shrew. Act iv, sc. 3, l. 73. [Katharina]

3 Let me be privileged by my place and message,
To be a speaker free.
Troilus and Cressida. Act iv, sc. 4, l. 132. [Diomedes]

Speak frankly as the wind.—*Troilus and Cressida,* i, 3, 253. See Candour.

4 Verily I speak it in the freedom of my knowledge.
The Winter's Tale. Act i, sc. 1, l. 12. [Archidamus]

Believe me, I speak as my understanding instructs me and as mine honesty puts it to utterance.
The Winter's Tale. Act i, sc. 1, l. 20. [Archidamus]

III—Speaking Sweetly

5 Entreat your captain
To soft and gentle speech.
Antony and Cleopatra. Act ii, sc. 2, l. 2. [Lepidus]

Speak you so gently?—*As You Like It,* ii, 7, 106.

6 I . . . had Most pretty things to say.
Cymbeline. Act i, sc. 3, l. 25. [Imogen]

7 God-a-mercy, old heart! thou speak'st cheerfully.
Henry V. Act iv, sc. 1, l. 34. [King Henry]

His grace speaks cheerfully.
Richard III. Act i, sc. 3, l. 34. [Buckingham]

8 When he speaks,
The air, a charter'd libertine, is still,
And the mute wonder lurketh in men's ears,
To steal his sweet and honey'd sentences.
Henry V. Act i, sc. 1, l. 47. [Archbishop of Canterbury] The only use of "charter'd" and "honey'd."

9 We,
Almost with ravish'd listening, could not find
His hour of speech a minute.
Henry VIII. Act i, sc. 2, l. 119. [King]

10 Thou art an old love-monger and speakest skilfully.
Love's Labour's Lost. Act ii, sc. 1, l. 254. [Rosaline] The only use of "love-monger" and "skilfully."

11 Who starves the ears she feeds, and makes them hungry,
The more she gives them speech.
Pericles. Act v, sc. 1, l. 113. [Pericles]

12 Speak sweetly, man, although thy looks be sour.
Richard II, iii, 2, 193. See Sweet and Sour.

13 I love to hear her speak, yet well I know
That music hath a far more pleasing sound.
Sonnets. No. cxxx.

Julia: But shall I hear him speak?
Host: Ay, that you shall.
Julia: That will be music.
Two Gentlemen of Verona. Act iv, sc. 2, l. 33.

14 When he speaks,
'Tis like a chime a-mending.
Troilus and Cressida. Act i, sc. 3, l. 158. [Ulysses] The only use of "a-mending."

I as your lover speak.
Troilus and Cressida. Act iii, sc. 3, l. 214. [Ulysses]

15 If he had spoke, the wolf would leave his prey
And never fright the silly lamb that day.
Venus and Adonis, l. 1097.

16 When you speak, sweet,
I 'ld have you do it ever: when you sing,
I 'ld have you buy and sell so, so give alms,
Pray so; and, for the ordering your affairs.
Winter's Tale. Act iv, sc. 4, l. 136. [Florizel]

IV—Speaking Bitterly

17 Alexas: His speech sticks in my heart.
Cleopatra: Mine ear must pluck it thence.
Antony and Cleopatra. Act i, sc. 5, l. 41.

Be choked with such another emphasis!
Antony and Cleopatra. Act i, sc. 5, l. 68. [Cleopatra] "Emphasis" is used again in *Hamlet,* v, 1, 278.

18 Your speech is passion:
But, pray you, stir no embers up.
Antony and Cleopatra. Act ii, sc. 2, l. 12. [Lepidus] "Embers" is repeated in *The Rape of Lucrece,* l. 5.

Speak in passion.—*I Henry IV,* ii, 4, 424.

19 Third Citizen: He flouted us downright.
First Citizen: No, 'tis his kind of speech: he did not mock us.
Coriolanus. Act ii, sc. 3, l. 168.

20 Forbear sharp speeches to her.
Cymbeline. Act iii, sc. 5, l. 39. [Queen]

1
I will speak daggers to her, but use none.
Hamlet. Act iii, sc. 2, l. 414. [Hamlet]
O, speak to me no more;
These words, like daggers, enter in mine ears.
Hamlet. Act iii, sc. 4, l. 94. [Queen]
She speaks poniards, and every word stabs.
Much Ado about Nothing. Act ii, sc. 1, l. 255. [Benedick]

2
I have a speech of fire, that fain would blaze,
But that this folly douts it.
Hamlet. Act iv, sc. 7, l. 191. [Laertes]
Dout them with superfluous courage.
Henry V, iv, 2, 11. The only uses of "dout" and "douts" in the sense of extinguish.

3 Speak not in spite,
For you shall sup with Jesu Christ tonight.
II Henry VI. Act v, sc. 1, l. 213. [Richard]

4
More he would have said, and more he spoke,
Which sounded like a clamour in a vault,
That mought not be distinguish'd.
III Henry VI. Act v, sc. 2, l. 43. [Somerset] The only use of "mought."

5
You know that you are Brutus that speak this,
Or, by the gods, this speech were else your last.
Julius Cæsar. Act iv, sc. 3, l. 13. [Cassius]

6
Angelo: She will speak most bitterly and strange.
Isabella: Most strange, but yet most truly, will I speak.
Measure for Measure. Act v, sc. 1, l. 36.

7
Don Pedro: Runs not this speech like iron through your blood?
Claudio: I have drunk poison whiles he utter'd it.
Much Ado about Nothing. Act v, sc. 1, l. 252.

8
How darkly and how deadly dost thou speak!
Richard III. Act i, sc. 4, l. 175. [Clarence]

9
Why speaks my father so ungently?
The Tempest. Act i, sc. 2, l. 444. [Miranda] "Ungently" is repeated in *Julius Cæsar,* ii, 1, 237, and in *Troilus and Cressida,* v, 3, 1.

10 Speak, and be hang'd:
For each true word, a blister! and each false
Be as a cauterizing to the root o' the tongue,
Consuming it with speaking!
Timon of Athens. Act v, sc. 1, l. 134. [Timon] The only use of "cauterizing."
He speaks very shrewishly.—*Twelfth Night,* i, 5, 169. The only use of "shrewishly."

11 'Shrew my heart,
You never spoke what did become you less
Than this; which to reiterate were sin
As deep as that, though true.
The Winter's Tale. Act i, sc. 2, l. 281. [Camillo] The only use of "reiterate."
Thou canst not speak too much; I have deserved
All tongues to talk their bitterest.
The Winter's Tale. Act iii, sc. 2, l. 216. [Leontes] "Bitterest" is repeated in *Coriolanus,* iv, 4, 18: "Bitterest enmity"; and in *Titus Andronicus,* ii, 3, 110: "Bitterest terms."
You might have spoken a thousand things that would
Have done the time more benefit and graced
Your kindness better.
The Winter's Tale. Act v, sc. 1, l. 21. [Cleomenes]

V—Speaking Loud and Low

12
Speak as loud as Mars.
Antony and Cleopatra. Act ii, sc. 2, l. 6. [Enobarbus]
Speak loud.—*Measure for Measure,* v, 1, 19.
Speak aloud.—*Romeo and Juliet,* ii, 2, 161; *Troilus and Cressida,* ii, 2, 185.
Speak not so loud.—*Troilus and Cressida,* i, 2, 201.
I speak too loud.—*Twelfth Night,* iii, 4, 4.
Speaking too loud.—*Othello,* ii, 1, 275.
You must speak louder.—*II Henry IV,* i, 2, 78.

13
Sweet prince, speak low.
II Henry IV. Act iv, sc. 5, l. 16. [Warwick]
Speak low, if you speak love.
Much Ado about Nothing. Act ii, sc. 1, l. 103. [Don Pedro]
Speak lower.—*II Henry IV,* iv, 4, 129; *Henry V,* iv, 1, 82.
Speak softly.—*I Henry VI,* i, 1, 63; *The Comedy of Errors,* v, 1, 9; *Antony and Cleopatra,* v, 2, 323; *The Tempest,* iv, 1, 206.

14
She has brown hair, and speaks small like a woman.
The Merry Wives of Windsor. Act i, sc. 1, l. 48. [Slender]
Quince: You may speak as small as you will. . . .
Bottom: I 'll speak in a monstrous little voice.
A Midsummer-Night's Dream. Act i, sc. 2, l. 52.

VI—Speaking Fair

15
You saw they speak us fair.
The Comedy of Errors. Act iv, sc. 4, l. 156. [Dromio of Syracuse]
Speak me fair in death.—*The Merchant of Venice,* iv, 1, 275.
Speak me fair.—*Taming of the Shrew,* i, 2, 180.

16 What the vengeance!
Could he not speak 'em fair?
Coriolanus. Act iii, sc. 1, l. 263. [Menenius]
Speak them fair.—*III Henry VI,* v, 4, 24.

17 Speak fair: you may salve so,
Not what is dangerous present, but the loss
Of what is past.
Coriolanus. Act iii, sc. 2, l. 70. [Menenius]
Speak fair; but speak fair words, or else be mute.
Venus and Adonis, l. 208.
Speak fair.—*The Comedy of Errors,* iii, 2, 11; *Hamlet,* iv, 1, 36.
Speak so fair.—*Richard II,* iii, 3, 128.
Fair speech.—*Coriolanus,* iii, 2, 96.

1
Speak, my fair, and fairly.
Henry V. Act v, sc. 2, l. 177. [King Henry]
Fairly spoke.—*The Merchant of Venice,* iii, 2, 180; *The Tempest,* iv, 1, 31.
Fair-spoken.—*Henry VIII,* iv, 2, 52. The only use of the phrase.

2
Entreat him, speak him fair.
II Henry VI. Act iv, sc. 1, l. 120. [Gentleman]
Didst speak him fair?—*The Comedy of Errors,* iv, 2, 16.
Speak him fair.—*Titus Andronicus,* v, 2, 140.

3
Do I entice you? do I speak you fair?
A Midsummer-Night's Dream. Act ii, sc. 1, l. 199. [Demetrius]

4
How fair the tribune speaks to calm my thoughts!
Titus Andronicus. Act i, sc. 1, l. 46. [Saturninus]

5
All that you speak shows fair.
The Winter's Tale. Act iv, sc. 4, l. 635. [Perdita]

VII—Speaking Well

6
Just, you say well; so would I have said.
All's Well that Ends Well. Act ii, sc. 3, l. 21. [Parolles]
By all the blood that ever fury breathed,
The youth says well.
King John. Act v, sc. 2, l. 127. [Bastard]
Cried I aim? said I well?—*The Merry Wives of Windsor,* ii, 3, 92.
Sir, you say well.—*The Taming of the Shrew,* i, 2, 271.
Thou hast said well.—*The Tempest,* iii, 3, 35.
You have said well.—*Henry VIII,* iii, 2, 149.
What! have I twice said well?—*The Winter's Tale,* i, 2, 90.

7
Why, that 's well said.
I Henry IV. Act i, sc. 2, l. 161. [Falstaff]
Things that are mouldy lack use: very singular good! in faith, well said, Sir John, very well said.
II Henry IV. Act iii, sc. 2, l. 119. [Shallow]
Marry, well said; very well said.
Hamlet. Act ii, sc. 1, l. 6. [Polonius]
'Fore God, my lord, well spoken, with good accent and good discretion.
Hamlet. Act ii, sc. 2, l. 488. [Polonius]
Now she sharpens: well said, whetstone!
Troilus and Cressida. Act v, sc. 2, l. 75. [Thersites] "Whetstone" is repeated in *As You Like It,* i, 2, 57, and in *Macbeth,* iv, 3, 228.
Well said, my masters.—*II Henry VI,* i, 4, 16. "Well said" is repeated twenty-eight times in the plays.

8
Thou speak'st aright.
A Midsummer-Night's Dream. Act ii, sc. 1, l. 42. [Puck]

9
Thou didst speak but well
When most the truth; which I receive much better
Than to be pitied of thee.
Winter's Tale. Act iii, sc. 2, l. 233. [Leontes]
I cannot Speak so well, nothing so well.
The Winter's Tale. Act iv, sc. 4, l. 391. [Perdita]
Speak well.—*The Merry Wives of Windsor,* iv, 5, 65; *The Tempest,* ii, 2, 94.
Speaks well.—*Pericles,* iv, 2, 51.
Thou speak'st it well.—*The Merchant of Venice,* ii, 2, 161.
Thou speakest well.—*Twelfth Night,* i, 5, 106.
Speaking well.—*Julius Cæsar,* ii, 1, 216.

VIII—Speaking False

See also Falsehood, Lie

10
Thou speak'st it falsely, as I love mine honour.
All's Well that Ends Well. Act v, sc. 3, l. 113. [King]
Speak'st false.—*Comedy of Errors,* iv, 4, 103.
Speaking false.—*Henry VIII,* ii, 4, 136.

11
If thou speak'st false,
Upon the next tree shalt thou hang alive,
Till famine cling thee: if thy speech be sooth,
I care not if thou dost for me as much.
Macbeth. Act v, sc. 5, l. 38. [Macbeth]
My first false speaking Was this upon myself.
Macbeth. Act iv, sc. 3, l. 130. [Malcolm]
He speaks not true.—*Romeo and Juliet,* iii, 1, 182.

IX—Speaking True

12
Be it art or hap, He hath spoken true.
Antony and Cleopatra. Act ii, sc. 3, l. 32. [Antony]
I had rather seal my lips, than, to my peril,
Speak that which is not.
Antony and Cleopatra. Act v, sc. 2, l. 146. [Seleucus]

13
My liege, I am advised what I say,
Neither disturbed with the effect of wine,
Nor heady-rash, provoked with raging ire.
The Comedy of Errors. Act v, sc. 1, l. 216. [Antipholus of Ephesus] The only use of "heady-rash."
I speak not out of weak surmises, but from proof as strong as my grief and as certain as I expect my revenge.
Cymbeline. Act iii, sc. 4, l. 23. [Imogen]

14
Though thou speak'st truth,
Methinks thou speak'st not well.
Coriolanus. Act i, sc. 6, l. 13. [Cominius]
I speak the truth the next way.
All's Well that Ends Well, i, 3, 63. See under PROPHET.
Speak'st truth.—*The Winter's Tale,* v, 1, 55.
Speak truth.—*II Henry VI,* iv, 3, 11, and frequently in later plays.
Speak troth.—*Cymbeline,* v, 5, 274; *A Midsummer-Night's Dream,* ii, 2, 36.

15
Let them speak: if they speak more or less than truth, they are villains and the sons of darkness.
I Henry IV. Act ii, sc. 4, l. 189. [Falstaff]

If speaking truth
In this fine age were not thought flattery.
I Henry IV. Act iv, sc. 1, l. 1. [Hotspur]

1 But what mean I to speak so true at first?
II Henry IV. Induction, l. 27. [Rumour]

2 Far truer spoke than meant.
II Henry VI. Act iii, sc. 1, l. 183. [Gloucester]

You have spoken truer than you purposed.
The Tempest. Act ii, sc. 1, l. 19. [Gonzalo]

3 I speak the truth:
When Pistol lies, do this; and fig me, like
The bragging Spaniard.
II Henry IV. Act v, sc. 3, l. 123. [Pistol]

Pistol speaks nought but truth.
II Henry IV. Act v, sc. 5, l. 40. [Pistol]

4 On my soul, I 'll speak but truth.
Henry VIII. Act i, sc. 2, l. 177. [Surveyor]

Tell me—but truly—but then speak the truth.
King Lear. Act v, sc. 1, l. 8. [Regan]

5 It is not enough to speak, but to speak true.
A Midsummer-Night's Dream. Act v, sc. 1, l. 121. [Lysander]

Speak true.—*Love's Labour 's Lost*, v, 2, 364; *The Tempest*, iii, 1, 70.
Speaking true.—*King Lear*, i, 4, 200.
True speaking.—*Much Ado about Nothing*, iii, 4, 34.

6 Leonato: Are these things spoken, or do I but dream?
Don John: Sir, they are spoken, and these things are true.
Much Ado about Nothing. Act iv, sc. 1, l. 67.

7 To speak the truth
Shall nothing wrong him.
Othello. Act ii, sc. 3, l. 223. [Iago]

So come my soul to bliss, as I speak true;
So speaking as I think, I die, I die.
Othello. Act v, sc. 2, l. 250. [Emilia]

8 Look, what I speak, my life shall prove it true.
Richard II. Act i, sc. 1, l. 87. [Bolingbroke]

What I speak
My body shall make good upon this earth,
Or my divine soul answer it in heaven.
Richard II. Act i, sc. 1, l. 36. [Bolingbroke]

9 Speak truly, on thy knighthood and thy oath.
Richard II. Act i, sc. 3, l. 14. [Lord Marshal]

Speak truly.—*All 's Well that Ends Well*, i, 3, 224; *I Henry IV*, i, 2, 105.
Truly would I speak.—*A Midsummer-Night's Dream*, iv, 1, 154.

10 Worst in this royal presence may I speak,
Yet best beseeming me to speak the truth.
Richard II. Act iv, sc. 1, l. 115. [Carlisle]

Royal speech.—*All 's Well that Ends Well*, i, 2, 51.

11 Pandarus: I speak no more than truth.
Troilus: Thou dost not speak so much.
Troilus and Cressida. Act i, sc. 1, l. 64.

X—Speaking For and Against

12 Your lordship speaks most infallibly of him.
Hamlet. Act v, sc. 2, l. 126. [Osric]

The text most infallibly concludes it.—*Love's Labour 's Lost*, iv, 2, 169. The only uses of "infallibly."

13 Whate'er Lord Harry Percy then had said
To such a person and in such a place,
At such a time, with all the rest retold,
May reasonably die and never rise
To do him wrong or any way impeach
What then he said, so he unsay it now.
I Henry IV. Act i, sc. 3, l. 71. [Blunt] The only use of "reasonably."

14 You whoreson candle-mine, you, how vilely did you speak of me even now before this honest, virtuous, civil gentlewoman!
II Henry IV. Act ii, sc. 4, l. 326. [Prince Henry] The only use of "candle-mine" (mine of tallow).

15 Lovell: Who dare speak
One syllable against him?
Gardiner: . . . I myself have ventured
To speak my mind of him.
Henry VIII. Act v, sc. 1, l. 38.

16 If they should speak, would almost damn those ears
Which, hearing them, would call their brothers fools.
The Merchant of Venice. Act i, sc. 1, l. 98. [Gratiano]

17 She speaks for you stoutly.
Othello. Act iii, sc. 1, l. 47. [Emilia]

Speak of me as I am; nothing extenuate,
Nor aught set down in malice: then must you speak
Of one that loved not wisely but too well;
Of one not easily jealous, but being wrought
Perplex'd in the extreme; of one whose hand,
Like the base Indian, threw a pearl away
Richer than all his tribe; of one whose subdued eyes,
Albeit unused to the melting mood,
Drop tears as fast as the Arabian trees
Their medicinal gum.
Othello. Act v, sc. 2, l. 342. [Othello] "Medicinal" is repeated in *The Winter's Tale*, ii, 3, 37.

18 Fool, of thyself speak well.
Richard III. Act v, sc. 3, l. 192. [King Richard]

19 Nurse: Will you speak well of him that kill'd your cousin?
Juliet: Shall I speak ill of him that is my husband?
Romeo and Juliet. Act iii, sc. 2, l. 96.

Speak ill.—*Sonnets*, cxl.

XI—Speaking One's Mind

1
Give me leave to speak my mind.
As You Like It, ii, 7, 59. See under CANDOUR.
Had I first been put to speak my mind.
II Henry VI. Act iii, sc. 1, l. 43. [Suffolk]
Freely speak my mind.—*Richard II,* iv, 1, 327.

2
I will speak my conscience of the king.
Henry V. Act iv, sc. 1, l. 123. [King Henry]
I speak my conscience.—*II Henry VI,* iii, 1, 68.

3
Say as you think, and speak it from your souls.
II Henry VI. Act iii, sc. 1, l. 247. [York]

4
The weight of this sad time we must obey;
Speak what we feel, not what we ought to say.
King Lear. Act v, sc. 3, l. 323. [Albany]

5
You speak not as you think.
A Midsummer-Night's Dream. Act iii, sc. 2, l. 191. [Hermia]

6
Claudio: You speak this to fetch me in, my lord.
Don Pedro: By my troth, I speak my thought.
Much Ado about Nothing. Act i, sc. 1, l. 225.

7
He was wont to speak plain and to the purpose.
Much Ado about Nothing, ii, 3, 19. See CANDOUR.
Hermione, my dearest, thou never spokest
To better purpose.
Winter's Tale. Act i, sc. 2, l. 88. [Leontes]
But once before I spoke to the purpose.
The Winter's Tale. Act i, sc. 2, l. 100. [Hermione]
Why, lo you now, I have spoke to the purpose twice:
The one for ever earn'd a royal husband;
The other for some while a friend.
The Winter's Tale. Act i, sc. 2, l. 106. [Hermione]

8
Nay, speak thy mind; and let him ne'er speak more
That speaks thy words again to do thee harm!
Richard II. Act ii, sc. 1, l. 230. [Northumberland]
Speak thy mind.—*Richard II,* iv, 1, 2.
Speak their mind.—*Love's Labour 's Lost,* v, 2, 589.

XII—Speaking for Oneself

9
I scarce can speak to thank you for myself.
As You Like It. Act ii, sc. 7, l. 170. [Adam]

10
Speak thou for me and tell him what I did.
III Henry VI. Act i, sc. 1, l. 16. [Richard]
Speak for yourselves.—*Love's Labour 's Lost,* v, 2, 430.
One speak for both.
The Merchant of Venice. Act ii, sc. 2, l. 150. [Bassanio]

11
My kinsman shall speak for himself.
The Merry Wives of Windsor. Act iii, sc. 4, l. 23. [Shallow]
Speak for himself.—*II Henry IV,* v, 1, 50.
Speak not you for him.—*The Tempest,* i, 2, 460.

12
Shall I speak for thee? shall I say 'tis so?
Titus Andronicus. Act ii, sc. 4, l. 33. [Marcus]

13
He who shall speak for her is afar off guilty
But that he speaks.
The Winter's Tale. Act ii, sc. 1, l. 104. [Leontes]
It is for you we speak, not for ourselves.
The Winter's Tale. Act ii, sc. 1, l. 140. [Antigonus]

XIII—Speaking a Word
See also Word

14 Another word, Menenius,
I will not hear thee speak.
Coriolanus. Act v, sc. 2, l. 98. [Coriolanus]

15
From this time forth I never will speak word.
Othello. Act v, sc. 2, l. 304. See under TORMENT.
Talk not to me, for I 'll not speak a word.
Romeo and Juliet. Act iii, sc. 5, l. 204. [Lady Capulet]
By hell and all hell's torments,
I will not speak a word!
Troilus and Cressida. Act v, sc. 2, l. 43. [Troilus]

16
Swearing, unless I took all patiently,
I should not live to speak another word.
The Rape of Lucrece, l. 1641.

17
Duchess of York: I prithee, hear me speak.
King Richard: You speak too bitterly.
Duchess of York: Hear me a word;
For I shall never speak to thee again.
Richard III. Act iv, sc. 4, l. 179.

18
Thou fond mad man, hear me but speak a word.
Romeo and Juliet. Act iii, sc. 3, l. 52. [Friar Laurence]
Good father, I beseech you on my knees,
Hear me with patience but to speak a word.
Romeo and Juliet. Act iii, sc. 5, l. 159. [Juliet]

19
Stop close their mouths, let them not speak a word.
. . . Let them not speak to me. . . .
What would you say, if I should let you speak?
Titus Andronicus. Act v, sc. 2, l. 165. [Titus]

20 One cannot speak a word,
But it straight starts you.
Troilus and Cressida. Act v, sc. 2, l. 100. [Cressida]

XIV—Want of Speech

1
Duke: How dost thou, Charles?
Le Beau: He cannot speak, my lord.
As You Like It. Act i, sc. 2, l. 232.

I cannot speak.—*As You Like It,* i, 2, 270.

You must not speak of that.—*Coriolanus,* ii, 3, 61.

Why dost not speak?—*Coriolanus,* v, 3, 153.

2 What should we speak of
When we are old as you? when we shall hear
The rain and wind beat dark December, how,
In this our pinching cave, shall we discourse
The freezing hours away?
Cymbeline. Act iii, sc. 3, l. 35. [Arviragus] The only use of "freezing." "Pinching" is repeated in *The Winter's Tale,* i, 2, 115.

Speak, man: thy tongue
May take off some extremity, which to read
Would be even mortal to me.
Cymbeline. Act iii, sc. 4, l. 16. [Imogen]

3
I dare not speak much further.
Macbeth. Act iv, sc. 2, l. 17. [Ross]

I think, but dare not speak.—*Macbeth,* v, 1, 87.

I dare not speak.—*I Henry VI,* v, 3, 65.

O, I cannot speak!—*III Henry VI,* ii, 2, 95.

I cannot stay to speak.—*II Henry VI,* ii, 4, 86.

I can scarce speak to thee.—*King Lear,* ii, 4, 138.

Speak not to me.—*II Henry VI,* iii, 2, 352; *Richard III,* iv, 1, 39.

I will not hear them speak.—*III Henry VI,* v, 5, 4.

Never speak.—*Much Ado about Nothing,* iii, 3, 188.

4
O, speak no more, for I have heard too much.
III Henry VI. Act ii, sc. 1, l. 48. [Edward]

Lay bolts upon him: let him speak no more.
Measure for Measure. Act v, sc. 1, l. 351. [Escalus]

Speak thou no more, if all the rest will speed.
Titus Andronicus. Act i, sc. 1, l. 372. [Titus]

I will speak no more.—*II Henry IV,* ii, 3, 5.

5 You must not speak with men
But in the presence of the prioress:
Then, if you speak, you must not show your face,
Or, if you show your face, you must not speak.
Measure for Measure. Act i, sc. 4, l. 10. [Francisco]

6
Desdemona: Alas, she has no speech.
Iago: In faith, too much;
I find it still when I have list to sleep.
Othello. Act ii, sc. 1, l. 103.

7
I spare speech, which something now offends me.
Othello. Act ii, sc. 3, l. 199. [Montano]

Spare speech.—*King Lear,* iv, 2, 21.

Save my speech.—*Othello,* iv, 1, 291.

8
O, I am press'd to death through want of speaking!
Richard II. Act iii, sc. 4, l. 72. [Queen]

Slow in speech.—*The Taming of the Shrew,* ii, 1, 248.

9
Pray you, speak no more to me.
Troilus and Cressida. Act i, sc. 1, l. 91. [Pandarus]

I 'll speak with nobody.—*Troilus and Cressida,* ii, 3, 75.

10
I bade you never speak again of him.
Twelfth Night. Act iii, sc. 1, l. 118. [Olivia]

11
Proteus: What said she? nothing?
Speed: No, not so much as 'Take this for your pains.'
Two Gentlemen of Verona. Act i, sc. 1, l. 150.

Speak no more of him.—*As You Like It,* i, 2, 90.

XV—Speeches

12
This was my speech, and I will speak 't again.
Coriolanus. Act iii, sc. 1, l. 62. [Coriolanus]

13 I must,
For mine own part, unfold a dangerous speech.
Cymbeline. Act v, sc. 5, l. 312. [Belarius]

14
Hamlet: We 'll have a speech straight: come, give us a taste of your quality; come, a passionate speech.
First Player: What speech, my lord?
Hamlet: I heard thee speak me a speech once, but it was never acted; or, if it was, not above once; for the play, I remember, pleased not the million; 'twas caviare to the general.
Hamlet. Act ii, sc. 2, l. 451. The only mention of "caviare."

15
If you look for a good speech now, you undo me: for what I have to say is of mine own making; and what indeed I should say will, I doubt, prove mine own marring.
II Henry IV. Epilogue, l. 4.

16 Bade the Romans
Mark him and write his speeches in their books.
Julius Cæsar. Act i, sc. 2, l. 125. [Cassius]

You shall speak
In the same pulpit whereto I am going,
After my speech is ended.
Julius Cæsar. Act iii, sc. 1, l. 249. [Brutus]

17
Sirrah, I 'll teach thee a speech.
King Lear. Act i, sc. 4, l. 128. [Fool]

This speech of yours hath moved me,
And shall perchance do good: but speak you on;
You look as you had something more to say.
King Lear. Act v, sc. 3, l. 199. [Edmund]

18
One rubb'd his elbow thus, and fleer'd and swore
A better speech was never spoke before.
Love's Labour 's Lost. Act v, sc. 2, l. 109.

[Boyet] The only use of "fleer'd." "Fleer" is used three times, and "fleering" once.

To their penn'd speech render we no grace,
But while 'tis spoke each turn away her face.

Love's Labour's Lost. Act v, sc. 2, l. 147. [Princess of France]

Construe my speeches better, if you may.

Love's Labour's Lost. Act v, sc. 2, l. 341. [King]

O, never will I trust to speeches penn'd,
Nor to the motion of a schoolboy's tongue.

Love's Labour's Lost. Act v, sc. 2, l. 402. [Biron]

1

Have you consider'd of my speeches?

Macbeth. Act iii, sc. 1, l. 76. [Macbeth]

2

One that hath spoke most villanous speeches.

Measure for Measure. Act v, sc. 1, l. 265. [Lucio]

Spoken your speech.—*A Midsummer-Night's Dream,* iii, 1, 77.
Foul speeches.—*The Tempest,* ii, 2, 96.
Pestilent speeches.—*Hamlet,* iv, 5, 91.
Speeches rank.—*A Lover's Complaint,* l. 307.

3

I am to pray you not to strain my speech
To grosser issues nor to larger reach
Than to suspicion.

Othello. Act iii, sc. 3, l. 218. [Iago]

Upon my knees, what doth your speech import?

Othello. Act iv, sc. 2, l. 31. [Desdemona]

4

Katharina: Where did you study all this goodly speech?
Petruchio: It is extempore, from my mother-wit.
Katharina: A witty mother! witless else her son.

The Taming of the Shrew. Act ii, sc. 1, l. 264. The only use of "mother-wit." "Extempore" occurs five times in the plays.

5

I would be loath to cast away my speech, for besides that it is excellently well penned, I have taken great pains to con it.

Twelfth Night. Act i, sc. 5, l. 183. [Viola]

Viola: I will on with my speech in your praise, and then show you the heart of my message.
Olivia: Come to what is important in 't: I forgive you the praise.
Viola: Alas, I took great pains to study it, and 'tis poetical.
Olivia: It is the more like to be feigned; I pray you, keep it in.

Twelfth Night. Act i, sc. 5, l. 202.

6

Gasping to begin some speech.

The Winter's Tale. Act iii, sc. 3, l. 25. [Antigonus] "Gasping" is repeated in *II Henry IV,* i, 1, 208: "Gasping for life"; and in *Richard II,* ii, 2, 65: "Gasping new-deliver'd mother."

SPEED

See also Expedition, Haste, Swiftness

7

With the swiftest wings of speed.

All's Well that Ends Well. Act iii, sc. 2, l. 76. [Gentleman]

Speed of fire.—*All's Well that Ends Well,* iii, 2, 112.
Go speedily.—*All's Well that Ends Well,* v, 3, 152.
Speed thee straight.—*Coriolanus,* iv, 5, 93.
Speed how it will.—*Coriolanus,* v, 1, 61.
Go with speed.—*Love's Labour's Lost,* v, 2, 804.

8

I will come after you with what good speed
Our means will make us means.

All's Well that Ends Well. Act v, sc. 1, l. 34. [Helena]

Make good speed.—*II Henry IV,* iii, 1, 3.

9

Repair thou to me with as much speed as thou wouldst fly death.

Hamlet. Act iv, sc. 6, l. 23. [Horatio]

10

Come yourself with speed to us again.

I Henry IV. Act i, sc. 1, l. 105. [King Henry]

How now, good Blunt? thy looks are full of speed.

I Henry IV. Act iii, sc. 2, l. 162. [King Henry]

11

Bend you with your dearest speed.

I Henry IV. Act v, sc. 5, l. 36. [King]

Greatest speed.—*II Henry IV,* i, 1, 120.
Happy speed.—*Othello,* ii, 1, 67.
High speed.—*I Henry IV,* ii, 4, 379.
Present speed.—*The Rape of Lucrece,* l. 1307.
Swift speed.—*King John,* ii, 1, 233; *Richard II,* v, 1, 54.

12

He seem'd in running to devour the way,
Staying no longer question.

II Henry IV. Act i, sc. 1, l. 47. [Travers]

Forspent with speed.—*II Henry IV,* i, 1, 37. "Forspent" is repeated in *III Henry VI,* ii, 3, 1: "Forspent with toil."

13

A' shall charge you and discharge you with the motion of a pewterer's hammer, come off and on swifter than he that gibbets on the brewer's bucket.

II Henry IV. Act iii, sc. 2, l. 281. [Falstaff] The only use of "pewterer's."

14

Do you think me a swallow, an arrow, or a bullet? have I, in my poor and old motion, the expedition of thought? I have speeded hither with the very extremest inch of possibility; I have foundered nine score and odd posts.

II Henry IV. Act iv, sc. 3, l. 35. [Falstaff] "Foundered" is repeated in *The Tempest,* iv, 1, 30.

Helter-skelter have I rode to thee.

II Henry IV. Act v, sc. 3, l. 98. [Pistol] The only use of "helter-skelter."

To ride day and night; and not to deliberate, not to remember, not to have patience to shift me.

II Henry IV. Act v, sc. 5, l. 21. [Falstaff]

15

Where is Mountjoy the herald? speed him hence.

Henry V. Act iii, sc. 5, l. 36. [French King]

Bestow yourself with speed.—*Henry V,* iv, 3, 68.
With speed.—*I Henry IV,* v, 2, 76; *II Henry IV,* i, 1, 214; iv, 2, 59; *King John,* iv, 3, 157; *Measure for Measure,* ii, 2, 17.
Dispatch us with all speed.—*Henry V,* ii, 4, 141.
With all speed.—*II Henry VI,* i, 1, 73; *I Henry IV,* iv, 3, 48; *Richard III,* iii, 2, 17; iii, 5, 103.
With all good speed.—*Richard II,* i, 2, 66.
With sober speed.—*II Henry IV,* iv, 3, 86.

1
Stay not to expostulate, make speed.
III Henry VI. Act ii, sc. 5, l. 135. [Exeter]
Make speed.—*King Lear,* iii, 1, 36.
Make all speed.—*Measure for Measure,* iv, 3, 109.
Make some speed.—*The Merchant of Venice,* ii, 8, 37.
Speed elsewhere.—*III Henry VI,* iv, 1, 58.

2
Return from France with speed.
III Henry VI. Act iv, sc. 6, l. 61. [King Henry] "With speed" is repeated frequently in later plays.
It shall be done, my sovereign, with all speed.
III Henry VI. Act iv, sc. 6, l. 64. [Clarence]

3
Let 's about it speedily.
III Henry VI. Act iv, sc. 6, l. 102. [Somerset]
Haste you speedily.—*Measure for Measure,* iii, 1, 274.
Post speedily.—*King Lear,* iii, 7, 1.
Post back with speed.—*Julius Cæsar,* iii, 1, 287.

4
Let the gods so speed me.
Julius Cæsar. Act i, sc. 2, l. 88. [Brutus]
God speed him well.—*Richard II,* i, 4, 32.
God speed.—*I Henry VI,* iii, 2, 60; *Richard III,* ii, 3, 6.
Speed well!—*Richard III,* v, 3, 102.

5
The copy of your speed is learn'd by them;
For when you should be told they do prepare,
The tidings comes that they are all arrived.
King John. Act iv, sc. 2, l. 113. [Messenger]
King John: Be Mercury, set feathers to thy heels,
And fly like thought from them to me again.
Bastard: The spirit of the time shall teach me speed.
King John. Act iv, sc. 2, l. 174.
I conjure thee but slowly; run more fast.
King John. Act iv, sc. 2, l. 269. [King John]
So hot a speed.—*King John,* iii, 4, 11.

6 Soft! whither away so fast?
A true man or a thief that gallops so?
Love's Labour 's Lost. Act iv, sc. 3, l. 186. [King]
Speeds too fast.—*Love's Labour 's Lost,* ii, 1, 120.
It shall be speeded well.—*Measure for Measure,* iv, 5, 10.

7
Bring them, I pray thee, with imagined speed
Unto the tranect, to the common ferry
With trades to Venice.
Merchant of Venice. Act iii, sc. 4, l. 52. [Portia] The only use of "tranect" and "ferry."
Madam, I go with all convenient speed.
The Merchant of Venice. Act iii, sc. 4, l. 56. [Balthasar]

8
Come you to me at night; you shall know how I speed.
The Merry Wives of Windsor. Act ii, sc. 2, l. 278. [Falstaff] Falstaff repeats the phrase in iii, 5, 137. It is used nowhere else.

9 The mild hind
Makes speed to catch the tiger; bootless speed,
When cowardice pursues and valour flies.
A Midsummer-Night's Dream. Act ii, sc. 1, l. 232. [Helena]
Cruel speeding.—*Passionate Pilgrim,* l. 269.

10
Speed more than speed but dull and slow she deems.
The Rape of Lucrece, l. 1336.
In winged speed no motion shall I know.
Sonnets. No. li.

11
Baptista: How speed you with my daughter?
Petruchio: How but well, sir? how but well?
It were impossible I should speed amiss.
Taming of the Shrew. Act ii, sc. 1, l. 283.

12 With great speed of judgement,
Ay, with celerity.
Troilus and Cressida. Act i, sc. 3, l. 329. [Nestor] See under SWIFTNESS.

13
As thou lovest thy life, make speed from hence.
The Two Gentlemen of Verona. Act iii, sc. 1, l. 169. [Duke]

14
Saint Nicholas be thy speed!
The Two Gentlemen of Verona. Act iii, sc. 1, l. 300. [Launce]
Happy be thy speed!—*The Taming of the Shrew,* ii, 1, 139.
Good manners be your speed!—*I Henry IV,* iii, 1, 190.
Hercules be thy speed!—*As You Like It,* i, 2, 222.
Saint Denis be my speed!—*Henry V,* v, 2, 194.
Saint Francis be my speed!—*Romeo and Juliet,* v, 3, 121.

15
Never Saw I men scour so on their way.
The Winter's Tale. Act ii, sc. 1, l. 34. [Lord]
Lord: Their speed Hath been beyond account.
Leontes: . . . 'Tis good speed.
The Winter's Tale. Act ii, sc. 3, l. 197.

16
Blossom, speed thee well!
The Winter's Tale. Act iii, sc. 3, l. 46. [Antigonus]
Speed well.—*All's Well that Ends Well,* iii, 6, 72.

17
The swifter speed the better.
The Winter's Tale. Act iv, sc. 4, l. 682. [Camillo]

SPELL, see Charm

SPIDER

1
Spider-like, Out of his self-drawing web.
Henry VIII. Act i, sc. 1, l. 62. [Norfolk] The only use of "spider-like" and "self-drawing."
To draw with idle spiders' strings
Most ponderous and substantial things!
Measure for Measure. Act iii, sc. 2, l. 289. [Duke]
2
Weaving spiders, come not here;
Hence, you long-legg'd spinners, hence!
A Midsummer-Night's Dream. Act ii, sc. 2, l. 20. [Fairies] The only use of "long-legg'd." "Spinners" is repeated in *Romeo and Juliet,* i, 4, 59.
Labouring spider.—*II Henry VI,* iii, 1, 339.
3
Spiders, that suck up thy venom.
Richard II. Act iii, sc. 2, l. 14. [King Richard]
4
Why strew'st thou sugar on that bottled spider,
Whose deadly web ensnareth thee about?
Richard III. Act i, sc. 3, l. 242. [Queen Margaret]
Help me curse That bottled spider.
Richard III. Act iv, sc. 4, l. 81. [Queen Elizabeth]

SPIRIT

See also Mettle

5
Methinks in thee some blessed spirit doth speak
His powerful sound within an organ weak.
All's Well that Ends Well. Act ii, sc. 1, l. 178. [King]
Eternal spirit.—*King John,* iii, 4, 18.
Immortal spirit.—*Measure for Measure,* i, 4, 35.
Prophetic spirit.—*King John,* iii, 4, 126.
Spirit of deep prophecy.—*I Henry VI,* i, 2, 55.
6
He's of a most facinerious spirit.
All's Well that Ends Well. Act ii, sc. 3, l. 34. [Parolles] The only use of "facinerious" (ferociously wicked).
7
There's a great spirit gone!
Antony and Cleopatra. Act i, sc. 2, l. 126. [Antony]
Now my spirit is going.
Antony and Cleopatra. Act iv, sc. 15, l. 58. [Antony]
A rarer spirit never Did steer humanity.
Antony and Cleopatra. Act v, sc. 1, l. 31. [Agrippa]
8 I shall show the cinders of my spirits
Through the ashes of my chance.
Antony and Cleopatra. Act v, sc. 2, l. 173. [Cleopatra]
9
The spirit of my father, which I think is within me, begins to mutiny against this servitude.
As You Like It. Act i, sc. 1, l. 23. [Orlando]
10 His doubled spirit
Re-quicken'd what in flesh was fatigate,
And to the battle came he.
Coriolanus. Act ii, sc. 2, l. 120. [Cominius] The only use of "re-quicken'd" and "fatigate."
11
Forth at your eyes your spirits wildly peep.
Hamlet. Act iii, sc. 4, l. 119. [Queen]
12
The spirit within thee hath been so at war
And thus hath so bestirr'd thee in thy sleep,
That beads of sweat have stood upon thy brow,
Like bubbles in a late-disturbed stream.
I Henry IV. Act ii, sc. 3, l. 59. [Lady Percy] The only use of "late-disturbed."
As full of spirit as the month of May.
I Henry IV. Act iv, sc. 1, l. 101. [Vernon]
13
Your spirit is too true.
II Henry IV. Act i, sc. 1, l. 92. [Morton]
True spirit.—*The Merry Wives of Windsor,* v, 5, 33; *Sonnets,* cviii.
14
Believe me, I am passing light in spirit.
II Henry IV. Act iv, sc. 2, l. 85. [York]
Thy spirits are most tall.
Henry V. Act ii, sc. 1, l. 72. [Pistol]
15
Undaunted spirit in a dying breast!
I Henry VI. Act iii, sc. 2, l. 99. [Talbot] Also in i, 1, 127.
Bold, just and impartial spirit.
II Henry IV. Act v, sc. 2, l. 116. [King Henry V] Also in *Richard II,* i, 1, 181.
Adventurous spirit.—*I Henry IV,* i, 3, 191.
Best spirits.—*King Lear,* v, 3, 139.
Best alarmed spirits.—*King Lear,* ii, 1, 55.
Better spirit.—*Sonnets,* lxxx.
Brave spirit.—*Henry V,* iv, 2, 3.
Commanding spirit.—*I Henry VI,* iv, 7, 88.
Dauntless spirit.—*King John,* ii, 1, 72; v, 1, 53.
Fair spirit.—*Timon of Athens,* iii, 5, 18.
Fiery spirits.—*King John,* v, 2, 114.
Fiery-kindled spirits.—*King John,* ii, 1, 358. The only use of the phrase.
Haughty spirit.—*III Henry VI,* i, 1, 267.
Huge spirit.—*Antony and Cleopatra,* iv, 15, 89.
Invincible spirit.—*II Henry VI,* i, 4, 9.
Manly spirit.—*Merchant of Venice,* ii, 3, 14.
Over-mounting spirit.—*I Henry VI,* iv, 7, 15. The only use of "over-mounting."
Untired spirits.—*Julius Cæsar,* ii, 1, 227.
Unconquer'd spirit.—*I Henry VI,* iv, 2, 32.
Warlike spirit.—*Henry V,* i, 2, 104.
Willing spirits.—*Cymbeline,* iv, 2, 338.
16
Raising up wicked spirits from under ground.
II Henry VI. Act ii, sc. 1, l. 174. [Buckingham]
I never had to do with wicked spirits.
I Henry VI. Act v, sc. 4, l. 42. [Joan la Pucelle]
Devilish spirits.—*II Henry VI,* iv, 7, 80.
Abhorred spirits!—*Timon of Athens,* v, 1, 63.
Damned spirits.—*Midsummer-Night's Dream,* iii, 2, 382.
Dark spirit.—*Coriolanus,* ii, 1, 177.

Savage spirit.—*King John*, v, 2, 74.
Stubborn spirits.—*Henry VIII*, iii, 1, 163.
Worser spirit.—*King Lear*, iv, 6, 222; *Sonnets*, cxliv.

1
He dares not calm his contumelious spirit.
II Henry VI. Act iii, sc. 2, l. 204. [Queen Margaret] "Contumelious" is repeated in *I Henry IV*, i, 4, 39: "Contumelious taunts"; and in *Timon of Athens*, v, 1, 177: "Contumelious war." "Contumeliously" occurs in *I Henry VI*, i, 3, 58.
Currish spirit.—*Merchant of Venice*, iv, 1, 133.
False spirits.—*Cymbeline*, v, 5, 148.
Gibing spirit.—*Love's Labour 's Lost*, v, 2, 868.
Surly spirit.—*King John*, iii, 1, 18.

2
Fie, coward woman and soft-hearted wretch!
Hast thou not spirit to curse thine enemy?
II Henry VI. Act iii, sc. 2, l. 307. [Queen Margaret] "Soft-hearted" is repeated in *III Henry VI*, ii, 3, 25.

3
Cheer up your spirits.
III Henry VI. Act ii, sc. 2, l. 56. [Queen Margaret]
Come, sisters, cheer we up his sprites,
And show the best of our delights.
Macbeth. Act iv, sc. 1, l. 127. [First Witch]
Then cheer thy spirit.
Titus Andronicus. Act iv, sc. 4, l. 88. [Tamora]
Pluck up thy spirits.
The Taming of the Shrew. Act iv, sc. 3, l. 38. [Petruchio]

4
I do lack some part
Of that quick spirit that is in Antony.
Julius Cæsar. Act i, sc. 2, l. 28. [Brutus]
Franker spirit.—*Othello*, iii, 3, 195.
Good spirits.—*Hamlet*, iii, 2, 63.
Melting spirits.—*Julius Cæsar*, ii, 1, 122.

5
Nor stony tower, nor walls of beaten brass,
Nor airless dungeon, nor strong links of iron,
Can be retentive to the strength of spirit.
Julius Cæsar. Act i, sc. 3, l. 93. [Cassius] See under SUICIDE for full quotation.
Alacrity of spirit.—*Richard III*, v, 3, 73.
Poverty of spirit.—*Richard III*, iii, 7, 159.
Quietness of spirit.—*The Merchant of Venice*, iv, 1, 12.

6
In the spirit of men there is no blood.
Julius Cæsar. Act ii, sc. 1, l. 168. [Brutus]
Thou, like an exorcist, hast conjured up
My mortified spirit.
Julius Cæsar. Act ii, sc. 1, l. 323. [Ligarius] "Exorcist" is repeated in *All's Well that Ends Well*, v, 3, 305.

7
The choice and master spirits of this age.
Julius Cæsar. Act iii, sc. 1, l. 163. [Antony]
Able spirit.—*Sonnets*, lxxxv.
Fine spirit.—*The Tempest*, i, 2, 420.
Learned spirit.—*Othello*, iii, 3, 259.

8
With my vex'd spirits I cannot take a truce,
But they will quake and tremble all this day.
King John. Act iii, sc. 1, l. 17. [Constance]

Afflicted spirits.—*Measure for Measure*, ii, 3, 4.
Drooping spirits.—*I Henry VI*, v, 2, 1.
Drowsy spirits.—*Troilus and Cressida*, ii, 2, 210.
Extincted spirits.—*Othello*, ii, 1, 81. The only use of "extincted."
Flat, unraised spirits.—*Henry V*, Prol., 9. The only use of "unraised."
O'erpressed spirits.—*Pericles*, iii, 2, 84. "O'erpressed" is repeated in *Coriolanus*, ii, 2, 97: "O'erpressed Roman."
Weary spirit.—*II Henry IV*, iv, 5, 3.

9
Flesh his spirit in a warlike soil.
King John. Act v, sc. 1, l. 71. [Bastard]

10
My best alarum'd spirits,
Bold in the quarrel's right, roused to the encounter.
King Lear. Act ii, sc. 1, l. 55. [Edmund]

11
Now, madam, summon up your dearest spirits.
Love's Labour 's Lost. Act ii, sc. 1, l. 1. [Boyet]

12
A foolish extravagant spirit, full of forms, figures, shapes, objects, ideas, apprehensions, motions, revolutions: these are begot in the ventricle of memory, nourished in the womb of pia mater, and delivered upon the mellowing of occasion.
Love's Labour 's Lost. Act iv, sc. 2, l. 68. [Holofernes] The only use of "ventricle" and "mellowing."
Such a merry, nimble, stirring spirit.
Love's Labour 's Lost. Act v, sc. 2, l. 16. [Katharine] Also in iv, 3, 306.
My spirits are nimble.
The Tempest. Act ii, sc. 1, l. 202. [Antonio]
Delighted spirit.—*Measure for Measure*, iii, 1, 121.
Jesting spirit.—*Much Ado about Nothing*, iii, 2, 60.
Mounting spirit.—*King John*, i, 1, 206.
Skipping spirit.—*Merchant of Venice*, ii, 2, 196.
Youthful spirit.—*Richard II*, i, 3, 70.
Spirit of youth.—*Sonnets*, xcviii.
Spirit of a fiend.—*Romeo and Juliet*, iii, 2, 81.
Spirit of love.—*Henry V*, v, 2, 316; *Sonnets*, lvi; *Twelfth Night*, i, 1, 9.
Spirit of mirth.—*A Midsummer-Night's Dream*, i, 1, 14.
Spirit of peace.—*II Henry IV*, iv, 1, 46; *Henry VIII*, iv, 2, 83.
Spirit of sense.—*Troilus and Cressida*, iii, 3, 106.
Invisible spirit of wine.—*Othello*, ii, 3, 283.

13
She was sought by spirits of richest coat,
But kept cold distance.
A Lover's Complaint, l. 236.

14
Hie thee hither,
That I may pour my spirits in thine ear.
Macbeth. Act i, sc. 5, l. 26. [Lady Macbeth]
Your spirits shine through you.
Macbeth. Act iii, sc. 1, l. 128. [Macbeth]

1
I have spirit to do any thing that appears not foul in the truth of my spirit.
Measure for Measure. Act iii, sc. 1, l. 212. [Isabella]
Provost: Heaven give your spirits comfort! . . .
Duke: The best and wholesomest spirits of the night
Envelope you!
Measure for Measure. Act iv, sc. 2, l. 73. The only use of "wholesomest."

2
I will not jump with common spirits.
The Merchant of Venice. Act ii, sc. 9, l. 32. [Arragon]
Petty spirits.—*II Henry IV,* iv, 3, 119; *Cymbeline,* v, 4, 93.

3 Her gentle spirit
Commits itself to yours to be directed.
The Merchant of Venice. Act iii, sc. 11, l. 165. [Portia] Also *The Two Gentlemen of Verona,* v, 4, 55.
Gentler spirit.—*Coriolanus,* ii, 1, 55.

4
How now, mad spirit!
A Midsummer-Night's Dream. Act iii, sc. 2, l. 4. [Oberon]
Forward spirit.—*II Henry IV,* i, 1, 173.
Quaint spirits.—*A Midsummer-Night's Dream,* ii, 2, 7.

5 Noble swelling spirits,
That hold their honours in a wary distance.
Othello. Act ii, sc. 3, l. 57. [Iago]
Noble spirit.—*Timon of Athens,* i, 2, 14; *Henry VIII,* i, 1, 35; i, 2, 129; iii, 1, 169.

6
Iago: I see this hath a little dash'd your spirits.
Othello: Not a jot, not a jot.
Othello. Act iii, sc. 3, l. 214.

7
Defect Of spirit, life, and bold audacity.
The Rape of Lucrece, l. 1345.
Blushing shamefast spirit.—*Richard III,* i, 4, 142. The only use of "shamefast."
Easy-yielding spirit.—*II Henry IV,* ii, 1, 126. The only use of "easy-yielding."
Weak spirit.—*The Winter's Tale,* i, 2, 72.

8
I have a thousand spirits in one breast,
To answer twenty thousand such as you.
Richard II. Act iv, sc. 1, l. 58. [Aumerle]

9
That gallant spirit hath aspired the clouds,
Which too untimely here did scorn the earth.
Romeo and Juliet. Act iii, sc. 1, l. 122. [Benvolio]

An unaccustom'd spirit
Lifts me above the ground with cheerful thoughts.
Romeo and Juliet. Act v, sc. 1, l. 4. [Romeo]

10
The earth can have but earth, which is his due;
My spirit is thine, the better part of me.
Sonnets. No. lxxiv.
The expense of spirit in a waste of shame.
Sonnets. No. cxxix.

11
For shame, thou hilding of a devilish spirit.
The Taming of the Shrew. Act ii, sc. 1, l. 26. [Baptista]
A most impatient devilish spirit.
The Taming of the Shrew. Act ii, sc. 1, l. 152. [Hortensio]

12
Thou wast a spirit too delicate.
The Tempest. Act i, sc. 2, l. 272. [Prospero]
My spirits, as in a dream, are all bound up.
The Tempest. Act i, sc. 2, l. 486. [Ferdinand]
Bring a corollary, Rather than want a spirit.
The Tempest. Act iv, sc. 1, l. 57. [Prospero] The only use of "corollary."
I do applaud thy spirit.
The Two Gentlemen of Verona. Act v, sc. 4, l. 140. [Duke]

13
I have observed thee always for a towardly prompt spirit.
Timon of Athens. Act iii, sc. 1, l. 37. [Lucullus] The only use of "towardly."

14
That codding spirit had they from their mother.
Titus Andronicus. Act v, sc. 1, l. 99. [Aaron] The only use of "codding" (wanton).
Wanton spirits.—*Troilus and Cressida,* iv, 5, 56.
Spirit of wantonness.—*The Merry Wives of Windsor,* iv, 2, 223.

II—Spirit: Apparition

See also Ghost

15 It draws near the season
Wherein the spirit held his wont to walk.
Hamlet. Act i, sc. 4, l. 5. [Horatio]
The extravagant and erring spirit hies
To his confine.
Hamlet, i, 1, 150. See under COCK.
No spirit dare stir abroad.—*Hamlet,* i, 1, 161.

16
Be thou a spirit of health or goblin damn'd,
Bring with thee airs from heaven or blasts from hell,
Be thy intents wicked or charitable,
Thou comest in such a questionable shape
That I will speak to thee.
Hamlet. Act i, sc. 4, l. 40. [Hamlet] The only use of "questionable."

Tell
Why thy canonized bones, hears'd in death,
Have burst their cerements; why the sepulchre,
Wherein we saw thee quietly inurn'd,
Hath oped his ponderous and marble jaws,
To cast thee up again.
Hamlet. Act i, sc. 4, l. 46. [Hamlet] The only use of "cerements" and "inurn'd." "Hears'd" is repeated in *The Merchant of Venice,* iii, 1, 93.
I am thy father's spirit,
Doom'd for a certain term to walk the night,
And for the day confined to fast in fires,
Till the foul crimes done in my days of nature
Are burnt and purged away.
Hamlet. Act i, sc. 5, l. 9. [Ghost]
Rest, rest, perturbed spirit!
Hamlet. Act i, sc. 5, l. 183. [Hamlet] "Perturbed" is repeated in *Cymbeline,* iii, 4, 108: "Perturb'd court."

1
Glendower: I can call spirits from the vasty
deep.
Hotspur: Why, so can I, or so can any man;
But will they come when you do call for
them?
I Henry IV. Act iii, sc. 1, l. 53.
2
Now, ye familiar spirits, that are cull'd
Out of the powerful regions under earth,
Help me this once, that France may get the
field.
I Henry VI. Act v, sc. 3, l. 10. [La Pucelle]
3
A spirit raised from depth of under-ground,
That shall make answer to such questions
As by your grace shall be propounded him.
II Henry VI. Act i, sc. 2, l. 79. [Hume]
The only use of "under-ground" and "propounded."
4
Some spirit put this paper in the packet,
To bless your eye withal.
Henry VIII. Act iii, sc. 2, l. 129. [Norfolk]
5
Brutus: Speak to me what thou art.
Ghost: Thy evil spirit, Brutus.
Julius Cæsar. Act iv, sc. 3, l. 281.
Ill spirit, I would hold more talk with thee.
Julius Cæsar. Act iv, sc. 3, l. 289. [Brutus]
See also *The Tempest,* i, 2, 458.
6
Come not in here, nuncle, here 's a spirit.
. . . A spirit, a spirit: he says his name 's
poor Tom.
King Lear. Act iii, sc. 4, l. 39. [Fool]
Visible spirits.—*King Lear,* iv, 2, 46.
7
I am a spirit of no common rate.
A Midsummer-Night's Dream. Act iii, sc. 1, l. 157. [Titania]
We are spirits of another sort.
A Midsummer-Night's Dream. Act iii, sc. 2, l. 388. [Oberon]
Heavenly spirits.—*Love's Labour 's Lost,* v, 2, 166.
8
Is it thy spirit that thou send'st from thee
So far from home into my deeds to pry?
Sonnets. No. lxi.
9
It carries a brave form. But 'tis a spirit.
The Tempest. Act i, sc. 2, l. 411. [Miranda]
Here comes a spirit of his, and to torment me.
The Tempest. Act ii, sc. 2, l. 15. [Caliban]
The spirit torments me.
The Tempest. Act ii, sc. 2, l. 66. [Caliban]
10
These be fine things, an if they be not
sprites.
The Tempest. Act ii, sc. 2, l. 120. [Caliban]
Artificial sprites.—*Macbeth,* iii, 5, 27. See also under FAIRY.
11
Ferdinand: May I be bold
To think these spirits?
Prospero: Spirits, which by mine art
I have from their confines call'd to enact
My present fancies.
The Tempest. Act iv, sc. 1, l. 119. [Prospero]
Tricksy spirit.—*The Tempest,* v, 1, 226. "Tricksy' is repeated in *The Merchant of Venice,* iii, 5, 74: "Tricksy word."
12
Viola: If spirits can assume both form and
suit
You come to fright us.
Sebastian: A spirit I am indeed;
But am in that dimension grossly clad
Which from the womb I did participate.
Twelfth Night. Act v, sc. 1, l. 242.
13 Do your best
To fright me with your sprites; you 're
powerful at it.
The Winter's Tale. Act ii, sc. 1, l. 27. [Hermione]
I have heard, but not believed, the spirits o' the
dead
May walk again.
The Winter's Tale. Act iii, sc. 3, l. 16. [Antigonus]
14
Jove send her A better guiding spirit!
The Winter's Tale, ii, 3, 127. See also under ANGEL.
15 Make her sainted spirit
Again possess her corpse, and on this stage,
Where we 're offenders now, appear soul-
vex'd.
The Winter's Tale. Act v, sc. 1, l. 57. [Leontes] The only use of "soul-vex'd."

SPITE

16 In mere spite,
To be full quit of those my banishers,
Stand I before thee here.
Coriolanus. Act iv, sc. 5, l. 88. [Coriolanus]
The only use of "banishers."
17
No more, thou thunder-master show
Thy spite on mortal flies.
Cymbeline. Act v, sc. 4, l. 30. [Sicilius]
The only use of "thunder-master."
18
The spite of man prevaileth against me.
II Henry VI. Act i, sc. 3, l. 218. [Peter]
Fie! charity, for shame! speak not in spite.
II Henry VI. Act v, sc. 2, l. 213. [Young Clifford]
Spite of spite.—*III Henry VI,* ii, 3, 5.
O spite of spites!—*The Comedy of Errors,* ii, 2, 191.
19
Let him do his spite.
Othello. Act i, sc. 2, l. 17. [Othello]
Spite of hell.—*Othello,* iv, 1, 71.
20
Sweet love, what spite hath thy fair colour
spent?
The Rape of Lucrece, l. 1600.
21
In our two loves there is but one respect,
Though in our lives a separable spite,
Which though it alter not love's sole effect,
Yet doth it steal sweet hours from love's
delight.
Sonnets. No. xxxvi. The only use of "separable."

Made lame by fortune's dearest spite.
Sonnets. No. xxxvii.
Spite of fortune.—*Sonnets,* xc.

1
'Wonder of time,' quoth she, 'this is my spite,
That, thou being dead, the day should yet be light.'
Venus and Adonis, l. 1133.
The more my spite.—*The Comedy of Errors,* iv, 2, 8.
The more his spite appears.—*The Taming of the Shrew,* iv, 3, 2.
That were some spite.—*Romeo and Juliet,* ii, 1, 27.
Cursed spite.—*Hamlet,* i, 5, 189.
Deadly spite.—*I Henry IV,* iii, 1, 192.
Poisonous spite.—*Timon of Athens,* i, 2, 144.
Rancorous spite.—*I Henry VI,* iv, 1, 185.
Spiteful and wrathful.—*Macbeth,* iii, 5, 12. "Spiteful" is repeated in *II Henry VI,* i, 3, 158, and in *Troilus and Cressida,* ii, 3, 7.
Spite a raven's heart.—*Twelfth Night,* v, 1, 134.
Spite my wife.—*Comedy of Errors,* iii, 1, 118.

SPITTING

2
Now weep for him, then spit at him.
All's Well that Ends Well. Act iii, sc. 2, l. 438. [Rosalind]
I spit at him.—*Richard II,* i, 1, 60.
They will spit.—*As You Like It,* iv, 1, 76.
Without hawking or spitting.—*As You Like It,* v, 3, 12. The only use of "spitting."

3
Wouldst thou not spit at me and spurn at me?
The Comedy of Errors. Act ii, sc. 2, l. 136. [Adriana]
Spit, and throw stones, cast mire upon me.
Cymbeline. Act v, sc. 5, l. 222 [Posthumus]

4
Spit in my face, call me horse.
I Henry IV, ii, 4, 214. See under LIE.
As she spit in his face, so she defied him.
Measure for Measure, ii, 1, 86. See under DEFIANCE.
Spits in the face of heaven.—*The Merchant of Venice,* ii, 7, 45.

5
Spit forth Their iron indignation.
King John, ii, 1, 211. See under CANNON.
Spits forth death and mountains.
King John, ii, 1, 458. See under MOUTH.
Tongues spit their duties out.—*Henry VIII,* i, 2, 61.

6
Shylock: You . . . spit upon my Jewish gabardine, . . .
'Fair sir, you spit on me on Wednesday last;
You spurn'd me such a day; another time
You call'd me dog. . . .'
Antonio: I am as like to call thee so again,
To spit on thee again, to spurn thee too.
The Merchant of Venice. Act i, sc. 3, l. 113.
Cough and spit.—*Troilus and Cressida,* i, 3, 173.
Spit and void his rheum.—*Henry V,* iii, 5, 52.
Spit forth blood.—*Coriolanus,* i, 3, 45.
Spit it bleeding.—*Richard II,* i, 1, 194.
Spit white.—*II Henry IV,* i, 2, 237.
Wilt thou spit all thyself?—*Pericles,* iii, 1, 8.

7
Spit upon him, whilst I say he lies.
Richard II, iv, 1, 75. See under LIE.

8
Gloucester: Why dost thou spit at me?
Anne: Would it were mortal poison, for thy sake!
Richard III, i, 2, 145. See under POISON.

9
Spit in the hole, man, and tune again.
The Taming of the Shrew, iii, 1, 40. See under INSTRUMENT.

10
Would thou wert clean enough to spit upon!
Timon of Athens. Act iv, sc. 3, l. 364. [Timon]

11
If you had but looked big and spit at him,
he 'ld have run.
The Winter's Tale, iv, 3, 113. See under COWARDICE.

SPLEEN

See also Anger

12
With the spleen of all the under fiends.
Coriolanus, iv, 5, 97. See FIGHTING, 536:10.

13
A weasel hath not such a deal of spleen
As you are toss'd with.
I Henry IV. Act ii, sc. 3, l. 81. [Lady Percy]
Govern'd by a spleen.—*I Henry IV,* v, 2, 19.

14
I have no spleen against you; nor injustice
For you or any.
Henry VIII. Act ii, sc. 4, l. 89. [Wolsey]

15
With swifter spleen than powder can enforce.
King John. Act ii, sc. 1, l. 448. [Citizen]

16
A thousand spleens bear her a thousand ways.
Venus and Adonis, l. 907.
Damned spleen.—*Richard III,* ii, 4, 64.
Fierce dragons' spleens.—*King John,* ii, 1, 68.
Spleen of fiery dragons.—*Richard III,* v, 3, 350.
Hasty spleen.—*King John,* iv, 3, 97.
Heated spleen.—*III Henry VI,* ii, 1, 124.
Over-merry spleen.—*Taming of the Shrew,* Ind., 1, 137. The only use of "over-merry."
Unruly spleen.—*Romeo and Juliet,* iii, 1, 162.
Weakest spleen.—*Troilus and Cressida,* ii, 2, 128.
Youthful spleen.—*I Henry VI,* iv, 6, 13.
Full of spleen.—*The Taming of the Shrew,* iii, 2, 10.
Cool his spleen.—*The Passionate Pilgrim,* l. 76.

SPOIL

17 Our spoils he kick'd at,
And look'd upon things precious as they were
The common muck of the world.
Coriolanus. Act ii, sc. 2, l. 128. [Cominius] The only use of "muck."
No less spoil than glory.—*Coriolanus,* v, 6, 44.
Our spoils we have brought home
Do more than counterpoise a full third part
The charges of the action.
Coriolanus. Act v, sc. 6, l. 77. [Coriolanus]

1
Is not this an honourable spoil?
I Henry IV, i, 1, 74. See under PRIZE.
Apparent spoil.—*I Henry VI*, iv, 2, 26.

2
I have loaden me with many spoils.
I Henry VI. Act ii, sc. 1, l. 80. [Soldier]
Laden with honour's spoils.—*Titus Andronicus*, i, 1, 36.

3
Soldiers, defer the spoil of the city until night.
II Henry VI. Act iv, sc. 7, l. 142. [Cade]
His soldiers fell to spoil.—*Julius Cæsar*, v, 3, 7.
Spoil the city.—*II Henry VI*, iv, 4, 53.

4 O Austria! thou dost shame
That bloody spoil.
King John. Act iii, sc. 1, l. 114. [Constable]
Bloody spoil.—*Richard III*, iv, 4, 290.
Perpetual spoil.—*Coriolanus*, ii, 2, 124.
Sluttish spoils.—*Troilus and Cressida*, iv, 5, 62.
Wanton spoil.—*Coriolanus*, ii, 1, 233.
Spoil of her honour.—*All's Well that Ends Well*, iv, 3, 20.
Stratagems and spoils.—*The Merchant of Venice*, v, 1, 85. See under MUSIC.

SPORT

5
We 'll make you some sport with the fox ere we case him.
All's Well that Ends Well. Act iii, sc. 6, l. 110. [Lord]
You have lost much good sport.
As You Like It. Act i, sc. 2, l. 105. [Le Beau]
I wish ye sport.—*Cymbeline*, iv, 2, 31.

6
I saw not better sport these seven years' day.
II Henry VI. Act ii, sc. 1, l. 2. [Queen]
This is excellent sport, i' faith.—*I Henry IV*, ii, 4, 430.
Very reverend sport, truly.—*Love's Labour 's Lost*, iv, 2, 1.
Here 's sport indeed!—*Antony and Cleopatra*, iv, 15, 32.
Sport royal, I warrant you.—*Twelfth Night*, ii, 3, 187.
Gentle sport.—*Sonnets*, xcvi.
Holy sport.—*The Comedy of Errors*, iii, 2, 27.
False sport.—*A Midsummer-Night's Dream*, iii, 2, 164.
Great sport.—*Henry VIII*, i, 1, 47.
Malicious sport.—*Hamlet*, ii, 2, 536.
Merry sport.—*Merchant of Venice*, i, 3, 146.
Mountain sport.—*Cymbeline*, iii, 3, 10.
Peaceful comic sport.—*I Henry VI*, ii, 2, 45.
Such-like sport.—*Venus and Adonis*, l. 844.
Willing sport.—*The Two Gentlemen of Verona*, ii, 7, 32.

7
Thou wouldst be fee'd, I see, to make me sport.
III Henry VI. Act i, sc. 4, l. 92. [Queen Margaret] "Make sport" is repeated frequently throughout the plays.
Sport myself.—*III Henry VI*, ii, 5, 34.

8 He is given
To sports, to wildness and much company.
Julius Cæsar. Act ii, sc. 1, l. 188. [Brutus]

9
There was good sport at his making.
King Lear. Act i, sc. 1, l. 23. [Gloucester]
The act of sport.—*Othello*, ii, 1, 230.
She is sport for Jove.—*Othello*, ii, 3, 17.
Sport for ladies.—*As You Like It*, i, 2, 147.

10
There 's no such sport as sport by sport o'er-thrown.
Love's Labour 's Lost. Act v, sc. 2, l. 153. [Princess of France]
That sport best pleases that doth least know how.
Love's Labour 's Lost. Act v, sc. 2, l. 517. [Princess of France]

11
Playing patient sports in unconstrained gyves.
A Lover's Complaint, l. 242.

12
I love the sport well.
The Merry Wives of Windsor. Act i, sc. 1, l. 302. [Slender]
Besides your cheer, you shall have sport.
The Merry Wives of Windsor. Act iii, sc. 2, l. 81. [Ford]
You shall see sport anon.
The Merry Wives of Windsor. Act iii, sc. 3, l. 180. [Ford]
Heaven prosper our sport!
The Merry Wives of Windsor. Act v, sc. 2, l. 14. [Page]

13
All our evening sport from us is fled.
The Passionate Pilgrim, l. 291.

14
What sport shall we devise here in this garden?
Richard II. Act iii, sc. 4, l. 1. [Queen]
What sport to-night?—*Antony and Cleopatra*, i, 1, 47.

15
This unlook'd-for sport comes well.
Romeo and Juliet. Act i, sc. 5, l. 31. [Capulet]
Away, be gone; the sport is at the best.
Romeo and Juliet. Act i, sc. 5, l. 121. [Benvolio]

16
There be some sports are painful, and their labour
Delight in them sets off.
The Tempest. Act iii, sc. 1, l. 1. [Ferdinand]
Come and sport.—*The Tempest*, iv, 1, 74.

17 I have some sport in hand
Wherein your cunning can assist me much.
The Taming of the Shrew. Ind., sc. 1, l. 91. [Lord]
We have sport in hand.
The Merry Wives of Windsor. Act ii, sc. 1, l. 204. [Shallow]
Let 's ha' some sport with them.—*Timon of Athens*, ii, 2, 48.

18
Why, she was wash'd and cut and trimm'd, and 'twas
Trim sport for them that had the doing of it.
Titus Andronicus. Act v, sc. 1, l. 95. [Aaron]

1
Hark, what good sport is out of town to-day!
Troilus and Cressida. Act i, sc. 1, l. 116. [Æneas]
But to the sport abroad: are you bound thither?
Troilus and Cressida. Act i, sc. 1, l. 118. [Troilus]
2
If I lose a scruple of this sport, let me be boiled to death with melancholy.
Twelfth Night. Act ii, sc. 5, l. 2. [Fabian]
I will not give my part of this sport for a pension of thousands to be paid from the Sophy.
Twelfth Night. Act ii, sc. 5, l. 196. [Fabian] The Sophy is mentioned again in iii, 4, 37; and in *The Merchant of Venice,* ii, 1, 25.
3
A summer's day will seem an hour but short,
Being wasted in such time-beguiling sport.
Venus and Adonis, l. 23. The only use of "time-beguiling."
Be bold to play, our sport is not in sight.
Venus and Adonis, l. 124.
Make sport of us, see under Ridicule.

SPRING

4
In the spring time, the only pretty ring time,
When birds do sing, hey ding a ding, ding:
Sweet lovers love the spring.
As You Like It. Act v, sc. 3, l. 20. [Song] The only use of "ding."
Eternal spring-time.—*Titus Andronicus,* iii, 1, 21.
Spring-time flowers.—*The Taming of the Shrew,* ii, 1, 248.
Spring-time showers.—*II Henry VI,* iii, 1, 337.
5
The spring is near when green geese are a-breeding.
Love's Labour's Lost. Act i, sc. 1, l. 97. [Biron] The only use of "a-breeding."
Now 'tis the spring.—*II Henry VI,* iii, 1, 31.
6
This [side is] Ver, the Spring. . . . Ver, begin.
Love's Labour's Lost. Act v, sc. 2, l. 901. [Armado] The only uses of "Ver."
When daisies pied and violets blue
And lady-smocks all silver-white
And cuckoo-buds of yellow hue
Do paint the meadows with delight.
Love's Labour's Lost. Act v, sc. 2, l. 904. [The Song; Spring] The only use of "lady-smocks," "silver-white," and "cuckoo-buds." "Meadows" occurs only once again in the plays, in *Titus Andronicus,* iii, 1, 125; and also in *Sonnets,* xxxiii.
When shepherds pipe on oaten straws
And merry larks are ploughmen's clocks,
When turtles tread, and rooks, and daws,
And maidens bleach their summer smocks.
Love's Labour's Lost. Act v, sc. 2, l. 912. The only use of "oaten" and "bleach."
When daffodils begin to peer,
With heigh! the doxy over the dale,
Why, then comes in the sweet o' the year;
For the red blood reigns in the winter's pale.
The Winter's Tale. Act iv, sc. 3, l. 1. [Autolycus] The only use of "doxy."
Daffodils, That come before the swallow dares.
—*The Winter's Tale,* iv, 4, 118. Daffodils are mentioned in no other play.
7
Thy hasty spring still blasts, and ne'er grows old.
The Rape of Lucrece, l. 49.
Unruly blasts wait on the tender spring.
The Rape of Lucrece, l. 869.
Tender spring.—*Titus Andronicus,* v, 3, 167; *Venus and Adonis,* l. 127.
8
Only herald to the gaudy spring.
Sonnets. No. i.
Beauteous springs.—*Sonnets,* civ.
Disorder'd spring.—*Richard II,* iii, 4, 48.
Early spring.—*II Henry IV,* i, 3, 38.
Forward spring.—*Richard III,* iii, 1, 94.
Latter spring.—*I Henry IV,* i, 2, 177.
New come spring.—*Richard II,* v, 2, 47.
Wanton springs.—*Richard II,* i, 3, 214.
Spring of year.—*Pericles,* iv, 4, 35.
9
Love's gentle spring doth always fresh remain.
Venus and Adonis, l. 801.
Love's tender spring.—*Venus and Adonis,* l. 656.
Love's spring.—*Antony and Cleopatra,* iii, 2, 43.
Spring of love.—*The Comedy of Errors,* iii, 2, 3; *The Two Gentlemen of Verona,* i, 3, 84.
10
The spring, the head, the fountain of your blood
Is stopp'd; the very source of it is stopp'd.
Macbeth. Act ii, sc. 3, l. 103. [Macbeth]
Now stops thy spring.—*III Henry VI,* iv, 8, 55.
Wanting the spring that those shrunk pipes had fed.
The Rape of Lucrece, l. 1455.
Here stands the spring whom you have stain'd with mud.
Titus Andronicus. Act v, sc. 2, l. 171. [Titus] See also Fountain.
Fresh springs.—*The Tempest,* i, 2, 338.
Native spring.—*Romeo and Juliet,* iii, 2, 102.
Purest spring.—*II Henry VI,* iii, 1, 101.

SPY

11
The prince's espials have informed me.
I Henry VI. Act i, sc. 4, l. 8. [Master Gunner]
By your espials were discovered.—*I Henry VI,* iv, 3, 6.
Lawful espials.—*Hamlet,* iii, 1, 32. The only uses of "espials."
12
Beldam, I think we watch'd you at an inch.
II Henry VI. Act i, sc. 4, l. 45. [York]
13
Spies and speculations
Intelligent of our state.
King Lear. Act iii, sc. 1, l. 24. [Kent]
Bate-breeding spy.—*Venus and Adonis,* l. 655. The only use of "bate-breeding."
God's spies.—*King Lear,* v, 3, 17.
Single spies.—*Hamlet,* iv, 5, 78.
True spies.—*The Tempest,* v, 1, 259.

1
Some carry-tale, some please-man, some slight zany,
Some mumble-news, some trencher-knight, some Dick,
That smiles his cheek in years and knows the trick
To make my lady laugh when she 's disposed,
Told our intents before.

Love's Labour's Lost. Act v, sc. 2, l. 463. [Biron] A succession of unique phrases, "carry-tale," "please-man," "zany," "mumble-news," and "trencher-knight." "Zanies" occurs in *Twelfth Night,* i, 5, 96.

2
This is one Lucio's information against us.
Measure for Measure. Act iii, sc. 2, l. 210. [Mistress Overdone]

Whip your information.—*Coriolanus,* iv, 6, 53. The only uses of "information."

Informations against this man.—*Henry VIII,* v, 3, 110. The only use of "informations."

3
Under our tents I 'll play the eaves-dropper.
Richard III. Act v, sc. 3, l. 221. [King Richard] The only use of "eaves-dropper."

4
Thou dost here usurp
The name thou owest not; and hast put thyself
Upon this island as a spy.
The Tempest. Act i, sc. 2, l. 453. [Prospero]

5
Now question me no more; we are espied.
Titus Andronicus. Act ii, sc. 3, l. 48. [Aaron]

Saucy controller of our private steps!
Titus Andronicus, ii, 3, 60. [Tamora]

Arrogant controller.—*II Henry VI,* iii, 2, 205. The only uses of "controller."

6
I have dogged him, like his murderer.
Twelfth Night. Act iii, sc. 2, l. 81. [Maria]

Dogged with two strange followers.
Troilus and Cressida, i, 3, 365. [Ulysses]

Dogged with company.—*A Midsummer-Night's Dream,* i, 2, 106.

Dogged with curses.—*Coriolanus,* v, 3, 144.

Dogged the army.—*I Henry VI,* iv, 3, 2.

Dogged spies.—*King John,* iv, 1, 129.

Dogged war.—*King John,* iv, 3, 139.

Dogged York.—*II Henry VI,* iii, 1, 158. The only uses of "dogged."

7
Paris: I spy.
Pandarus: You spy! what do you spy?
Troilus and Cressida. Act iii, sc. 1, l. 102.

8
Scout me for him at the corner of the orchard like a bum-baily.
Twelfth Night. Act iii, sc. 4, l. 193. [Sir Toby] The only use of "bum-baily" (sheriff's officer).

9
I fear I am attended by some spies.
The Two Gentlemen of Verona. Act v, sc. 1, l. 10. [Silvia]

10
The heaven sets spies upon us.
Winter's Tale. Act v, sc. 1, l. 203. [Perdita]

STAB

See also Wound

11
Snare: It may chance cost some of our lives for he will stab.
Hostess: Alas the day! take heed of him; he stabbed me in mine own house, and that most beastly.
II Henry IV. Act ii, sc. 1, l. 12.

I 'll stab thee.—*I Henry IV,* ii, 4, 160.

Stab him; . . . stab him.—*Titus Andronicus,* v, 2, 100.

Stab them.—*Timon of Athens,* v, 1, 105.

Let 's stab ourselves.—*Henry V,* iv, 5, 7.

Stab poignards in our flesh.—*III Henry VI,* ii, 1, 98.

12
Whitmore: Speak, captain, shall I stab the forlorn swain?
Captain: First let my words stab him.
II Henry VI, iv, 1, 65. See under WORD.

13
I stabb'd your fathers' bosoms, split my breast.
III Henry VI. Act ii, sc. 6, l. 30. [Clifford]

Stabb'd in my angry mood.—*Richard III,* i, 2, 242.

Stabb'd with bloody daggers.—*Richard III,* i, 3, 212.

Stabb'd me in the field.—*Richard III,* i, 4, 56.

14
His silver skin laced with his golden blood;
And his gash'd stabs look'd like a breach in nature
For ruin's wasteful entrance.
Macbeth. Act ii, sc. 3, l. 118. [Macbeth] The only use of "gash'd."

Bemock'd-at stabs.—*The Tempest,* iii, 3, 63. The only use of "bemock'd-at." "Bemock" occurs in *Coriolanus,* i, 1, 261: "Bemock the modest moon."

15
Wild Half-can that stabbed Pots, and, I think, forty more.
Measure for Measure. Act iv, sc. 3, l. 19. [Pompey] The only mention of "Half-can."

16
Second Murderer: What, shall we stab him as he sleeps?
First Murderer: No; then he will say it was done cowardly, when he wakes.
Second Murderer: When he wakes! why, fool, he shall never wake till the judgement-day.
First Murderer: Why, then he will say we stabbed him sleeping.
Richard III. Act i, sc. 4, l. 101.

This sudden stab of rancour I misdoubt.
Richard III. Act iii, sc. 2, l. 89. [Stanley]

Think, how thou stab'dst me in my prime of youth.
Richard III. Act v, sc. 3, l. 119. [Ghost] The only use of "stab'dst."

17
Stabb'd with a white wench's black eye.
Romeo and Juliet, ii, 4, 14. See under EYE.

1 A gentleman,
Who, in my mood, I stabb'd unto the heart.
The Two Gentlemen of Verona. Act iv, sc. 1, l. 50. [Outlaw]

STAGE

See also Acting, Play

2
This wooden O.
Henry V. Act i, Prologue, l. 13. [Chorus]
This great stage of fools.—*King Lear,* iv, 6, 187. See under BIRTH.
Bloody stage.—*Macbeth,* ii, 4, 6.
Common stages.—*Hamlet,* ii, 2, 358.

3
This green plot shall be our stage, this hawthorn-brake our tiring-house.
A Midsummer-Night's Dream. Act iii, sc. 1, l. 2. [Quince] The only use of "hawthorn-brake" and "tiring-house." "Hawthorn-bush" occurs in *III Henry VI,* ii, 5, 42.

4
This huge stage presenteth nought but shows
Whereon the stars in secret influence comment.
Sonnets. No. xv.

5
If this were played upon a stage now, I could condemn it as an improbable fiction.
Twelfth Night. Act iii, sc. 4, l. 140. [Fabian] The only use of "improbable." "Fiction" appears only twice more, in *Hamlet,* ii, 2, 578, and *Timon of Athens,* v, 1, 86.
The world a stage, see under WORLD.

STAIN

See also Disgrace, Shame

6
You have some stain of soldier in you.
All's Well that Ends Well, i, 1, 122. See SOLDIER.

7
We must not So stain our judgement.
All's Well that Ends Well, ii, 1, 122. See DISEASE, 351:2.
Stain her beauty.—*Richard III,* iv, 4, 206.
Stain the stone.—*Julius Cæsar,* v, 3, 262.
Stain the sun.—*Titus Andronicus,* iii, 1, 213.

8
Iachimo: You do remember
This stain upon her?
Posthumus: Ay, and it doth confirm
Another stain, as big as hell can hold,
Were there no more but it.
Cymbeline. Act ii, sc. 4, l. 138.

9
Stain'd with the variation of each soil
Betwixt that Holmedon and this seat of ours.
I Henry IV. Act i, sc. 1, l. 64. [King Henry]
Stained with travel.—*II Henry IV,* v, 5, 25.
Stain'd with this abuse.—*The Rape of Lucrece,* l. 1655.
Stain'd with blood.—*II Henry VI,* iii, 1, 259; *III Henry VI,* i, 4, 153; *A Midsummer-Night's Dream,* v, 1, 288. See under BLOOD.
Stained with gore.—*Venus and Adonis,* l. 664.
Stain'd with grief.—*The Tempest,* i, 2, 414.
Stain'd with mud.—*Titus Andronicus,* v, 2, 171.
Stain'd with revolt.—*King John,* iv, 2, 6.
Stained with salt-water.—*Tempest,* ii, 1, 64.
Unjustly stain'd.—*Rape of Lucrece,* l. 1836.
Stain'd and deflower'd.—*Titus Andronicus,* v, 3, 38.
Stain and kill.—*The Rape of Lucrece,* l. 168.

10 Leaves behind a stain
Upon the beauty of all parts besides.
I Henry IV. Act iii, sc. 1, l. 187. [Worcester]

11
Stain to thy countrymen, thou hear'st thy doom!
I Henry VI. Act iv, sc. 1, l. 45. [King Henry]

12
Do no stain to your own gracious person.
Measure for Measure. Act iii, sc. 1, l. 208. [Duke]

13
The stain upon his silver down will stay.
The Rape of Lucrece, l. 1012.
How may this forced stain be wiped from me?
The Rape of Lucrece, l. 1701.
Compelled stain.—*The Rape of Lucrece,* l. 1708.
Her body's stain her mind untainted clears.
The Rape of Lucrece, l. 1710.

14
Stain the temper of my knightly sword.
Richard II, iv, 1, 29. See under SWORD.
Stain your swords.—*King John,* ii, 1, 45.
Stain all your edges on me.—*Coriolanus,* v, 6, 113.

15
Impure blots and stains.
Richard III. Act iii, sc. 7, l. 234. [Gloucester]
Sightless stains.—*King John,* iii, 1, 45.
Stains of right.—*King John,* ii, 1, 114.

16
Here 's such ado to make no stain a stain
As passes colouring.
Winter's Tale. Act ii, sc. 2, l. 19. [Paulina]

STAIR

17
The stairs, as he treads on them, kiss his feet.
Love's Labour's Lost. Act v, sc. 2, l. 330. [Biron]

18
Shall I always keep below stairs?
Much Ado about Nothing. Act v, sc. 2, l. 10. [Margaret]
Down stairs.—*II Henry IV,* ii, 1, 107; ii, 4, 202; 204.
Up the stairs.—*Hamlet,* iv, 3, 39.
Pair of stairs.—*As You Like It,* v, 2, 41.
Tackled stair.—*Romeo and Juliet,* ii, 4, 201.
Stairs of sand.—*Merchant of Venice,* iii, 2, 84.

STALE, see Whore

STAR

19
Helena: You were born under a charitable star.
Parolles: Under Mars, I.
Helena: I especially think, under Mars.
Parolles: Why under Mars?
Helena: The wars have so kept you under that you must needs be born under Mars.

Parolles: When he was predominant.
Helena: When he was retrograde, I think, rather.
Parolles: Why think you so?
Helena: You go so much backward when you fight.
All's Well that Ends Well. Act i, sc. 1, l. 204. [Helena] See also under BIRTH. "Retrograde" is repeated in *Hamlet,* i, 2, 114.
Our Jovial star reign'd at his birth.
Cymbeline, v, 4, 105.
Truer stars did govern Proteus' birth.
The Two Gentlemen of Verona. Act ii, sc. 7, l. 74. [Julia]

1
The luckiest stars in heaven.
All's Well that Ends Well. Act i, sc. 3, l. 252. [Helena]
They wear themselves in the cap of the time, there do muster true gait, eat, speak, and move under the influence of the most received star.
All's Well that Ends Well. Act ii, sc. 1, l. 54. [Parolles]
My homely stars have fail'd
To equal my great fortune.
All's Well that Ends Well. Act ii, sc. 5, l. 80. [Helena]

2
My good stars, that were my former guides,
Have empty left their orbs, and shot their fires
Into the abysm of hell.
Antony and Cleopatra. Act iii, sc. 13, l. 145. [Antony] "Abysm" is repeated in *The Tempest,* i, 2, 50: "Abysm of time."
The star is fall'n.—*Antony and Cleopatra,* iv, 14, 106.
Our stars, unreconcilable.—*Antony and Cleopatra,* v, 1, 46. The only use of "unreconcilable."
Starr'd most unluckily.—*The Winter's Tale,* iii, 2, 100. The only use of "starr'd."

3
Yond same star that 's westward from the pole
Had made his course to illume that part of heaven
Where now it burns.
Hamlet. Act i, sc. 1, l. 36. [Bernardo] The only use of "illume."
O all you host of heaven!
Hamlet. Act i, sc. 5, l. 92. [Hamlet]

4
What! we have seen the seven stars.
II Henry IV. Act ii, sc. 4, l. 200. [Pistol]
The seven stars.—*I Henry IV,* i, 2, 16.
Fool: The reason why the seven stars are no more than seven is a pretty reason.
Lear: Because they are not eight?
King Lear. Act i, sc. 5, l. 38. Commentators differ as to whether "the seven stars" refers to the Pleiades or the Great Bear.

5
Two stars keep not their motion in one sphere.
I Henry IV. Act v, sc. 4, l. 65. [Prince of Wales]

6
Rambures: The armour that I saw in your tent to-night, are those stars or suns upon it?
Constable: Stars, my lord.
Dauphin: Some of them will fall to-morrow, I hope.
Constable: And yet my sky shall not want.
Dauphin: That may be, for you bear a many superfluously, and 'twere more honour some were away.
Henry V. Act iii, sc. 7, l. 73. The only use of "superfluously."

7
The bad revolting stars.
I Henry VI. Act i, sc. 1, l. 4. [Bedford]
O malignant and ill-boding stars!
I Henry VI. Act iv, sc. 5, l. 6. [Talbot] "Ill-boding" is repeated in *III Henry VI,* ii, 6, 59: "Ill-boding tongue."

8
What louring star now envies thy estate?
II Henry VI. Act iii, sc. 1, l. 206. [King Henry]
My thwarting stars.—*III Henry VI,* iv, 6, 22.
Inauspicious stars.—*Romeo and Juliet,* v, 3, 111. The only use of "inauspicious."

9
A far more glorious star thy soul will make
Than Julius Cæsar.
I Henry VI. Act i, sc. 1, l. 55. [Bedford]
Heavens make a star of him!—*Pericles,* v, 3, 79.

10
Few men rightly temper with the stars.
III Henry VI. Act iv, sc. 6, l. 29. [Warwick]

11
I cannot, by the progress of the stars,
Give guess how near to day.
Julius Cæsar. Act ii, sc. 1, l. 2. [Brutus]

12
The skies are painted with unnumber'd sparks,
They are all fire and every one doth shine,
But there 's but one in all doth hold his place.
Julius Cæsar. Act iii, sc. 1, l. 63. [Cæsar] "Unnumber'd" is repeated in *King Lear,* iv, 6, 21: "Unnumber'd pebbles."
To the north star.—*Much Ado about Nothing,* ii, 1, 258.
Constant as the northern star.—*Julius Cæsar,* iii, 1, 60. See under CONSTANCY.
Constant stars.—*Sonnets,* xiv.
Fixed stars.—*Richard II,* ii, 4, 9.

13
Now, now, you stars that move in your right spheres,
Where be your powers? show now your mended faiths.
King John. Act v, sc. 7, l. 74. [Bastard]
The stars above us, govern our conditions.
King Lear. Act iv, sc. 3, l. 35. [Kent]
An admirable evasion of whoremaster man, to lay his goatish disposition to the charge of a star!
King Lear. Act i, sc. 2, l. 138. [Edmund] The only use of "goatish."

14
Look, the unfolding star calls up the shepherd.
Measure for Measure, iv, 2, 219. [Duke]

That full star that ushers in the even.
Sonnets. No. cxxxii.

Bright star of Venus.—*I Henry VI,* i, 2, 144.

1 Look how the floor of heaven
Is thick inlaid with patines of bright gold.
The Merchant of Venice. Act v, sc. 1, l. 58. [Lorenzo] The only use of "inlaid" and "patines."

These blessed candles of the night.
The Merchant of Venice. Act v, sc. 1, l. 220. [Bassanio]

Those gold candles fix'd in heaven's air.
Sonnets. No. xxi.

The burning tapers of the sky.
Titus Andronicus. Act iv, sc. 2, l. 89. [Aaron]

2 There 's husbandry in heaven;
Their candles are all out.
Macbeth. Act ii, sc. 1, l. 4. [Banquo]

3 Fair Helena, who more engilds the night
Than all yon fiery oes and eyes of light.
A Midsummer-Night's Dream. Act iii, sc. 2, l. 187. [Lysander] The only use of "engilds" and "oes." "O's" occurs in *Love's Labour 's Lost,* v, 2, 45.

4 She will find him by starlight.
A Midsummer-Night's Dream. Act v, sc. 1, l. 320. [Theseus]

Spangled starlight.—*A Midsummer-Night's Dream,* ii, 1, 29.

Till starlight be out.—*The Merry Wives of Windsor,* v, 5, 106. The only uses of "starlight."

Shall star-like rise.—*Henry VIII,* v, 5, 47.

Star-like nobleness.—*Timon of Athens,* v, 1, 66. The only uses of "star-like."

5 There 's no more sailing by the star.
Much Ado about Nothing. Act iii, sc. 4, l. 58. [Margaret]

6 Feast here awhile,
Until our stars that frown lend us a smile.
Pericles. Act i, sc. 4, l. 108. [Pericles]

Yet cease your ire, you angry stars of heaven!
Pericles. Act ii, sc. 1, l. 1. [Pericles]

Her better stars brought her to Mytilene.
Pericles. Act v, sc. 3, l. 9. [Pericles] Mytilene is mentioned nine times in this play, and in no other.

7 No comfortable star did lend his light.
The Rape of Lucrece, l. 164.

The moon being clouded presently is miss'd,
But little stars may hide them when they list.
The Rape of Lucrece, l. 1007.

The skies were sorry,
And little stars shot from their fixed places,
When their glass fell wherein they view'd their faces.
The Rape of Lucrece, l. 1524.

Mortal stars.—*The Rape of Lucrece,* l. 13.

8 All of us have cause
To wail the dimming of our shining star.
Richard III. Act ii, sc. 2, l. 101. [Gloucester] The only use of "dimming."

Shining star.—*Venus and Adonis,* l. 861.

9 The right and fortune of his happy stars.
Richard III. Act iii, sc. 7, l. 172. [Gloucester]

Was 't not a happy star Led us to Rome?
Titus Andronicus. Act iv, sc. 2, l. 32. [Aaron]

Happy star reign now!—*The Winter's Tale,* i, 2, 363.

Favourable stars.—*The Taming of the Shrew,* iv, 5, 40.

10 Be opposite all planets of good luck.
Richard III. Act iv, sc. 4, l. 402. [King Richard]

There 's some ill planet reigns.
The Winter's Tale. Act ii, sc. 1, l. 105. [Hermione]

Planets of mishap.—*I Henry VI,* i, 1, 23.

Adverse planets.—*I Henry VI,* i, 1, 54.

11 Earth-treading stars that make dark heaven light.
Romeo and Juliet. Act i, sc. 2, l. 25. [Capulet] The only use of "earth-treading."

When he shall die,
Take him and cut him out in little stars,
And he will make the face of heaven so fine
That all the world will be in love with night.
Romeo and Juliet. Act iii, sc. 2, l. 21. [Juliet]

12 Not from the stars do I my judgement pluck;
And yet methinks I have astronomy,
But not to tell of good or evil luck,
Of plagues, of dearths, or seasons' quality.
Sonnets. No. xiv. The only use of "astronomy." "Astronomer" occurs twice (*Troilus and Cressida,* i, 1, 100; *Cymbeline,* iii, 2, 27), and "astronomical" once (*King Lear,* i, 2, 164).

Let those who are in favour with their stars
Of public honour and proud titles boast.
Sonnets. No. xxv.

Till whatsoever star that guides my moving
Points on me graciously with fair aspect
And puts apparel on my tatter'd loving,
To show me worthy of thy sweet respect.
Sonnets. No. xxvi.

13 I find my zenith doth depend upon
A most auspicious star, whose influence
If now I court not but omit, my fortunes
Will ever after droop.
The Tempest. Act i, sc. 2, l. 181. [Prospero] The only use of "zenith."

14 I know thy constellation is right apt
For this affair.
Twelfth Night. Act i, sc. 4, l. 35. [Duke] The only use of "constellation."

My stars shine darkly over me.
Twelfth Night. Act ii, sc. 1, l. 3. [Sebastian]

I thank my stars I am happy.
Twelfth Night. Act ii, sc. 5, l. 185. [Malvolio]

Jove and my stars be praised!
Twelfth Night. Act ii, sc. 5, l. 187. [Malvolio]

15 The star-gazers.
Venus and Adonis, l. 509. The only use of the phrase.

1
Look, how a bright star shooteth from the sky.
Venus and Adonis, l. 815.
These are stars indeed;
And sometimes falling ones.
Henry VIII. Act iv, sc. 1, l. 54. [Gentleman]
Shooting star.—*Richard II,* ii, 4, 19.
Wandering stars.—*Hamlet,* v, 1, 279.
Blazing star.—*All's Well that Ends Well,* i, 3, 91.
Bright particular star.—*All's Well that Ends Well,* i. 1, 97. See under LOVE.
Each particular star.—*Winter's Tale,* i, 2, 425.
Chaste stars.—*Othello,* v, 2, 2.
Maidenliest star.—*King Lear,* i, 2, 143. The only use of "maidenliest."
Twinkling star.—*The Two Gentlemen of Verona,* ii, 6, 9. "Twinkling" is repeated in *I Henry VI,* v, 3, 63, and in *The Merchant of Venice,* ii, 2, 177: "Twinkling of an eye."
Stars of love.—*Phoenix and the Turtle,* l. 51.

STARVATION

See also Famine, Hunger

2
No, on the barren mountains let him starve.
I Henry IV. Act i, sc. 3, l. 89. [King Henry]
On the barren mountains starve.—*I Henry IV,* i, 3, 159.
3
I 'll starve ere I 'll rob a foot further.
I Henry IV. Act ii, sc. 2, l. 23. [Falstaff]
We 'll see 'em starve first.—*King Lear,* v, 3, 25.
4
Your grace may starve perhaps before that time.
I Henry VI. Act iii, sc. 2, l. 48. [Charles]
Ready to starve.—*II Henry VI,* i, 1, 229.
5
Starve the general world.
Love's Labour's Lost, ii, 1, 11. See under GRACE.
Starve our sight.—*A Midsummer-Night's Dream,* i, 1, 221.
Starve for a merry look.—*The Comedy of Errors,* ii, 1, 88.
Thou wilt starve, sure.—*Pericles,* ii, 1, 72.
Clean starved.—*Sonnets,* lxxv.
6
Never go home; here starve we out the night.
Troilus and Cressida. Act v, sc. 10, l. 2. [Æneas]

STATE

See also Commonwealth, Government

7
He sits in his state, as a thing made for Alexander.
Coriolanus. Act v, sc. 4, l. 22. [Menenius]
Roman state.—*Coriolanus,* i, 1, 71.
Venetian state.—*Othello,* v, 2, 337.
Volscian state.—*Coriolanus,* iv, 3, 11; iv, 7, 22.
State of Denmark.—*Hamlet,* i, 4, 90.
8
Our state to be disjoint and out of frame.
Hamlet. Act i, sc. 2, l. 20. [King]
Dejected state.—*Pericles,* ii, 2, 46.
Outcast state.—*Sonnets,* xxix.
Parlous state.—*As You Like It,* iii, 2, 45.
Primal state.—*Antony and Cleopatra,* i, 4, 41. "Primal" is repeated in *Hamlet,* iii, 3, 37: "Primal eldest curse."
Woeful state.—*Sonnets,* cxlv.
Wretched state.—*Hamlet,* iii, 3, 67.
My state is desperate.—*Twelfth Night,* ii, 2, 38.
9
Falstaff: This chair shall be my state, this dagger my sceptre, and this cushion my crown.
Prince: Thy state is taken for a joined-stool, thy golden sceptre for a leaden dagger, and thy precious rich crown for a pitiful bald crown!
I Henry IV. Act ii, sc. 4, l. 415. "Joined-stool" is repeated in *Taming of the Shrew,* ii, 1, 199, and in *II Henry IV,* ii, 4, 269. "Joint-stool" is used twice, in *Romeo and Juliet,* i, 5, 7, and in *King Lear,* iii, 6, 54. A "joint-stool" was one made by a joiner, as distinguished from one made roughly of planks.
Chair of state.—*III Henry VI,* i, 1, 51; 168; *Henry VIII,* iv, 1, 67.
Royal state.—*II Henry IV,* iv, 5, 121.
10
Brave peers of England, pillars of the state.
II Henry VI. Act i, sc. 1, l. 75. [Gloucester]
Those that know the very nerves of state.
Measure for Measure. Act i, sc. 4, l. 53. [Lucio]
11
Thus stands my state, 'twixt Cade and York distress'd;
Like to a ship that, having 'scaped a tempest,
Is straightway calm'd and boarded with a pirate.
II Henry VI. Act iv, sc. 9, l. 31. [King Henry]
Rule in this realm, and the gored state sustain.
King Lear. Act v, sc. 3, l. 320. [Albany]
Tottering state.—*Richard III,* iii, 2, 37. "Tottering" is repeated in *All's Well that Ends Well,* i, 3, 129, and in *Pericles,* iii, 2, 40.
The state totters.—*The Tempest,* iii, 2, 8. The only use of "totters."
12
A statesman and a soldier.
Measure for Measure, iii, 2, 155. See REPUTATION, 1266:7.
My soldier, statesman, all.—*The Winter's Tale,* i, 2, 168. The only uses of "statesman."
Bond-slaves and pagans shall our statesmen be.
Othello, i, 2, 99. See BONDAGE, 125:3. The only use of "statesmen."
Statist though I am none, nor like to be.
Cymbeline. Act ii, sc. 4, l. 16. [Posthumus] The only use of "statist." "Statists" occurs in *Hamlet,* v, 2, 33.
13
The state,
However this may gall him with some check,
Cannot with safety cast him.
Othello. Act i, sc. 1, l. 148. [Iago]
14
Your special mandate for the state-affairs.
Othello. Act i, sc. 3, l. 72. [Brabantio]
On to the state-affairs.—*Othello,* i, 3, 190. "State-affairs" occurs in no other scene. "State-matters" is used in iii, 4, 155.

1
Wear their brave state out of memory.
Sonnets. No. xv. See under MAN.
I see a better state to me belongs
Than that which on thy humour doth depend.
Sonnets. No. xcii.
Happy state.—*The Rape of Lucrece,* l. 16.
Healthful state.—*Sonnets,* cxviii.
2 Order well the state,
That like events may ne'er it ruinate.
Titus Andronicus. Act v, sc. 3, l. 203. [Lucius] "Ruinate" is repeated in *III Henry VI,* v, 1, 83, and in *The Rape of Lucrece,* l. 944.
3
And mighty states characterless are grated
To dusty nothing.
Troilus and Cressida. Act iii, sc. 2, l. 195. [Cressida] The only use of "characterless." "Grated" is repeated in *The Merry Wives of Windsor,* ii, 2, 6. "Dusty" occurs only once again, in *Macbeth,* v, 5, 23: "Dusty death."
Enormous state.—*King Lear,* ii, 2, 176. The only use of "enormous."
Greatest state.—*The Rape of Lucrece,* l. 1006.
Monstrous state.—*Julius Cæsar,* i, 3, 71.
Stronger state.—*Comedy of Errors,* ii, 2, 177.
Warlike state.—*Hamlet,* i, 2, 9.
4
There is a mystery—with whom relation
Durst never meddle—in the soul of state;
Which hath an operation more divine
Than breath or pen can give expressure to.
Troilus and Cressida. Act iii, sc. 3, l. 201. [Ulysses] "Expressure" is repeated in *The Merry Wives of Windsor,* v, 5, 71, and in *Twelfth Night,* ii, 3, 171.

STATUE

See also Image

5 The chimney-piece
Chaste Diana bathing. Never saw I figures
So likely to report themselves: the cutter
Was as another nature, dumb; outwent her,
Motion and breath left out.
Cymbeline. Act ii, sc. 4, l. 82. [Iachimo] The only use of "chimney-piece," "bathing," "cutter," and "outwent." See also under FIGURE.
6
We'll set thy statue in some holy place,
And have thee reverenced like a blessed saint.
I Henry VI. Act iii, sc. 3, l. 14. [Alençon]
If we stand still, . . .
We should take root here where we sit, or sit
State-statues only.
Henry VIII. Act i, sc. 2, l. 85. [Wolsey] The only use of "state-statues."
7
Erect his statua and worship it,
And make my image but an alehouse sign.
II Henry VI. Act iii, sc. 2, l. 80. [Queen Margaret]
Like dumb statuas.—*Richard III,* iii, 7, 25. "Statua" is also used twice in *Julius Cæsar,* ii, 2, 76, and iii, 2, 192.
8
Give him a statue with his ancestors.
Julius Cæsar. Act iii, sc. 2, l. 55. [Citizen]
Build his statue to make him glorious.
Pericles. Act ii, Gower, l. 14.
9
I will raise her statue in pure gold.
Romeo and Juliet. Act v, sc. 3, l. 299. [Montague]
Primitive statue.—*Troilus and Cressida,* v, 1, 60. The only use of "primitive."
10
That rare Italian master, Julio Romano, who, had he himself eternity and could put breath into his work, would beguile Nature of her custom, so perfectly he is her ape: he so near to Hermione hath done Hermione that they say one would speak to her and stand in hope of answer.
The Winter's Tale. Act v, sc. 2, l. 105. [Gentleman] The only mention of Romano.
So her dead likeness, I do well believe,
Excels whatever yet you look'd upon
Or hand of man hath done; therefore I keep it
Lonely, apart. But here it is: prepare
To see the life as lively mock'd as ever
Still sleep mock'd death.
Winter's Tale. Act v, sc. 3, l. 15. [Paulina]
Does not the stone rebuke me
For being more stone than it?
Winter's Tale. Act v, sc. 3, l. 37. [Leontes]
Leontes: Would you not deem it breathed? and that those veins
Did verily bear blood?
Polixenes: Masterly done.
The very life seems warm upon her lip.
Leontes: The fixture of her eye has motion in 't,
As we are mock'd with art.
The Winter's Tale. Act v, sc. 3, l. 64.
Leontes: Still, methinks,
There is an air comes from her: what fine chisel
Could ever yet cut breath? . . .
Paulina: If you can behold it,
I'll make the statue move indeed, descend
And take you by the hand.
The Winter's Tale. Act v, sc. 3, l. 77. The only use of "chisel."

STATURE

11
Bring me word how tall she is.
Antony and Cleopatra. Act ii, sc. 5, l. 118. [Cleopatra]
Is she as tall as me?—*Antony and Cleopatra,* iii, 3, 14.
I am more than common tall.
As You Like It. Act i, sc. 3, l. 117. [Rosalind]
He is not very tall.—*As You Like It,* iii, 5, 118.
He's as tall a man as any's in Illyria.
Twelfth Night. Act i, sc. 3, l. 20. [Sir Toby]
I am not tall enough to become the function well.
Twelfth Night. Act iv, sc. 2, l. 7. [Clown]
Tall fellow.—*Richard III,* i, 4, 156, and ten times in later plays.
Tall gentleman.—*II Henry IV,* iii, 2, 67.
A very tall man.—*Romeo and Juliet,* ii, 4, 31.
12
Jaques: What stature is she of?
Orlando: Just as high as my heart.
As You Like It. Act iii, sc. 2, l. 285.

Silvia: How tall was she?
Julia: About my stature . . . about my height.
The Two Gentlemen of Verona. Act iv, sc. 4, l. 162.

1 She hath made compare
Between our statures; she hath urged her height;
And with her personage, her tall personage,
Her height, forsooth, she hath prevail'd with him.
A Midsummer-Night's Dream. Act iii, sc. 2, l. 290. [Hermia]

How low am I? I am not yet so low
But that my nails can reach unto thine eyes.
A Midsummer-Night's Dream. Act iii, sc. 2, l. 297. [Hermia]

2
Her stature to an inch; as wand-like straight.
Pericles. Act v, sc. 1, l. 110. [Pericles] The only use of "wand-like."

STATUTE

See also Law

3
Seal'd his rigorous statutes with their bloods.
The Comedy of Errors. Act 1, sc. 1, l. 9. [Duke] "Rigorous" is repeated in *The Merchant of Venice,* iv, 1, 8, and in *Coriolanus,* iii, 1, 267. "Rigorously" occurs once, in *I Henry VI,* v, 4, 52.

4
According to the statute of the town.
The Comedy of Errors. Act i, sc. 2, l. 6. [Merchant]

Against the laws and statutes of this town.
The Comedy of Errors. Act v, sc. 1, l. 126. [Merchant]

5
More piercing statutes daily, to chain up and restrain the poor.
Coriolanus. Act i, sc. 1, l. 86. [Citizen]

6
Cade: My mouth shall be the parliament of England.
Holland: Then we are like to have biting statutes, unless his teeth be pulled out.
II Henry VI. Act iv, sc. 7, l. 16.

7
You three . . . Have sworn . . . to keep those statutes
That are recorded in this schedule here.
Love's Labour's Lost. Act i, sc. 1, l. 15. [King]

8
We have strict statutes and most biting laws,
The needful bits and curbs to headstrong weeds,
Which for this nineteen years we have let slip;
Even like an o'ergrown lion in a cave,
That goes not out to prey.
Measure for Measure. Act i, sc. 3, l. 19. [Duke]

The rigour of the statute.
Measure for Measure. Act i, sc. 4, l. 67. [Lucio]

Acts, decrees, and statutes.—*Richard II,* iv, 1, 213.
Humane statute.—*Macbeth,* iii, 4, 76.
Strong statutes.—*Measure for Measure,* v, 1, 322.
Statute of thy beauty.—*Sonnets,* cxxxiv.

STEALING, see Robber, Thief

STEED

See also Horse

9
And soberly did mount an arm-gaunt steed,
Who neigh'd so high, that what I would have spoke
Was beastly dumb'd by him.
Antony and Cleopatra. Act i, sc. 5, l. 48. [Alexas] The only use of "soberly," "arm-gaunt" and "dumb'd."

10
I mean to stride your steed.
Coriolanus. Act i, sc. 9, l. 71. [Coriolanus]

11
Steed threatens steed, in high and boastful neighs
Piercing the night's dull ear.
Henry V. Act iv, Prologue, l. 10. [Chorus] The only use of "boastful."

Hark how our steeds for present service neigh!
Henry V. Act iv, sc. 2, l. 8. [Constable]

Neighing steed.—*Othello,* iii, 3, 351.

12 Their wounded steeds
Fret fetlock deep in gore and with wild rage
Yerk out their armed heels at their dead masters,
Killing them twice.
Henry V. Act iv, sc. 7, l. 81. [Montjoy] The only use of "fetlock" and "yerk." "Yerk'd" occurs in *Othello,* i, 2, 5.

Stain'd their fetlocks in his smoking blood.
III Henry VI, ii, 3, 21. The only use of "fetlocks."

13
With sleight and manhood stole to Rhesus' tents,
And brought from thence the Thracian fatal steeds.
III Henry VI. Act iv, sc. 2, l. 20. [Warwick] The only use of "sleight" and mention of Rhesus. "Sleights" occurs in *Macbeth,* iii, 5, 26: "Magic sleights."

Phrygian steed.—*Troilus and Cressida,* iv, 5, 186.

14 A hot and fiery steed
Which his aspiring rider seem'd to know.
Richard II. Act v, sc. 2, l. 8. [York]

Barbed steeds.—*Richard III,* i, 1, 10; *Richard II,* iii, 3, 117. The only uses of "barbed," having the breast and flanks armoured.
Bounding steed.—*I Henry IV,* ii, 3, 52.
Fiery steeds.—*III Henry VI,* ii, 6, 12.
Fiery-footed steeds.—*Romeo and Juliet,* iii, 2, 1. The only use of "fiery-footed."
Foaming steeds.—*III Henry VI,* ii, 1, 183.
Noble steed.—*Coriolanus,* i, 9, 61.
Proud steed.—*Richard II,* v, 2, 19.
Snow-white goodly steed.—*Titus Andronicus,* ii, 3, 76.
Strong-neck'd steed.—*Venus and Adonis,* l. 263. The only use of "strong-neck'd."

Well-doing steed.—*A Lover's Complaint,* l. 112. The only use of "well-doing."

Well-proportion'd steed.—*Venus and Adonis,* l. 290. "Well-proportion'd" is repeated in *II Henry VI,* iii, 2, 175: "Well-proportion'd beard."

1
Phœbus' steeds are founder'd.
The Tempest. Act iv, sc. 1, l. 30. [Ferdinand] Phœbus is mentioned twenty times in the plays.

I have foundered nine score and odd posts.
II Henry IV, iv, 3, 39. The only uses of "foundered."

Mars's fiery steed.—*All's Well that Ends Well,* ii, 3, 300.

2
Vouchsafe, thou wonder, to alight thy steed,
And rein his proud head to the saddle-bow.
Venus and Adonis, l. 13. The only use of "saddle-bow." "Alight" is repeated in *King Lear,* iii, 4, 127: "Bid her alight."

The steed is stall'd up.—*Venus and Adonis,* l. 39.

STEEL

See also Sword

3
Steel, if thou turn the edge, or cut not out the burly-boned clown in chines of beef ere thou sleep in thy sheath, I beseech God on my knees thou mayst be turned to hobnails.
II Henry VI. Act iv, sc. 10, l. 59. [Cade] The only use of "burly-boned" and "chines." "Hobnails" is repeated in *I Henry IV,* ii, 4, 398. "Chine" occurs in *The Taming of the Shrew,* iii, 2, 51, and in *Henry VIII,* v. 4, 26.

4
Bloody steel grasp'd in their ireful hands.
III Henry VI, ii, 5, 132. See under DANGER.

The long divorce of steel.—*Henry VIII,* ii, 1, 76.

5
His brandish'd steel,
Which smoked with bloody execution.
Macbeth. Act i, sc. 2, l. 17. [Sergeant]

6
Shall I Sir Pandarus of Troy become,
And by my side wear steel?
The Merry Wives of Windsor. Act i, sc. 3, l. 84. [Pistol]

Filed steel.—*Twelfth Night,* iii, 3, 5.

Hammer'd steel.—*The Rape of Lucrece,* l. 951; *Sonnets,* cxx.

Piercing steel.—*Romeo and Juliet,* iii, 1, 164; *Julius Cæsar,* v, 3, 76.

Shrewd steel.—*Richard II,* iii, 2, 59.

Revengeful steel.—*Richard II,* iv, 1, 50.

Stabbing steel.—*The Winter's Tale,* iv, 4, 748.

7
Pins and poking-sticks of steel.
Winter's Tale, iv, 4, 228. See under POSSESSIONS. The only use of "poking-sticks."

Clothed in steel.—*Pericles,* ii, 1, 160. See also under ARMOUR.

STEP

8
We should not step too far.
II Henry IV. Act i, sc. 3, l. 20. [Bardolph]

Step aside.—*I Henry IV,* ii, 4, 36; *Romeo and Juliet,* i, 1, 162; *The Rape of Lucrece,* l. 362.

Step forth.—*King John,* iii, 4, 151; *The Winter's Tale,* v, 1, 221.

Step you forth.—*Cymbeline,* v, 5, 130.

Step by step.—*The Tempest,* iii, 3, 78.

9
We will untread the steps of damned flight.
King John, v, 4, 52. See under OBEDIENCE. "Untread" is repeated in *The Merchant of Venice,* ii, 6, 10.

Steps of wrong.—*King John,* iv, 2, 57.

10
One step I have advanced thee.
King Lear. Act v, sc. 3, l. 28. [Edmund]

11
That is a step
On which I must fall down, or else o'erleap,
For in my way it lies.
Macbeth. Act i, sc. 4, l. 48. [Macbeth]

12
Turn two mincing steps Into a manly stride.
The Merchant of Venice. Act iii, sc. 4, l. 67. [Portia]

Delightful steps.—*Pericles,* ii, 1, 164.

Feeble steps.—*The Two Gentlemen of Verona,* ii, 7, 10.

Graver steps.—*The Winter's Tale,* i, 2, 173.

Low steps.—*Henry VIII,* ii, 4, 112.

Peaceful steps.—*Richard II,* iii, 2, 125.

Private steps.—*Titus Andronicus,* ii, 3, 60.

13
Leads discontented steps in foreign soil.
Richard III. Act iv, sc. 4, l. 312. [King Richard] See EXILE, 435:13.

Dishonour'd step.—*King Lear,* i, 1, 231.

Sad steps.—*King Lear,* v, 3, 289.

Stealing steps.—*Hamlet,* v, 1, 79.

Usurping steps.—*Richard II,* iii, 2, 17.

14
We 'll consecrate the steps that Ajax makes
When they go from Achilles.
Troilus and Cressida. Act ii, sc. 3, l. 193. [Ulysses]

15
I 'll . . . make a pastime of each weary step,
Till the last step have brought me to my love.
The Two Gentlemen of Verona. Act ii, sc. 7, l. 35. [Julia]

Weary steps.—*Love's Labour 's Lost,* v, 2, 194; 195; *Richard II,* i, 3, 265.

Many a weary step.—*As You Like It,* ii, 7, 130.

STOMACH

See also Appetite

16
Why, if you have a stomach, to 't.
All's Well that Ends Well. Act iii, sc. 6, l. 67. [Bertram]

If you have a stomach, to 't i' God's name.
The Taming of the Shrew. Act i, sc. 2, l. 195. [Gremio]

17
It goes much against my stomach.
As You Like It. Act iii, sc. 2, l. 22. [Touchstone]

18
She is so hot because the meat is cold;
The meat is cold because you come not home;

You come not home because you have no stomach;
You have no stomach having broke your fast;
But we that know what 'tis to fast and pray
Are penitent for your default to-day.
The Comedy of Errors. Act i, sc. 2, l. 47. [Dromio of Ephesus]

Methinks your maw, like mine, should be your clock
And strike you home without a messenger.
The Comedy of Errors. Act i, sc. 2, l. 66. [Dromio of Ephesus]

So thou but think
What 'tis to cram a maw.
Measure for Measure. Act iii, sc. 2, l. 23. [Duke]

Pine the maw.—*Venus and Adonis,* l. 602.
Detestable maw.—*Romeo and Juliet,* v, 3, 45.
Gluttonous maws.—*Timon of Athens,* iii, 4, 52.
Maws of kites.—*Macbeth,* iii, 4, 73.

1 Our stomachs
Will make what 's homely savoury.
Cymbeline. Act iii, sc. 6, l. 32. [Belarius]

2
They have only stomachs to eat and none to fight.
Henry V. Act iii, sc. 7, l. 165. [Constable]

Good God, these nobles should such stomachs bear!
I Henry VI. Act i, sc. 3, l. 90. [Mayor of London]

3 We may
Taste of your wine and see what cates you have;
For soldiers' stomachs always serve them well.
I Henry VI. Act ii, sc. 3, l. 78. [Talbot]

4
He hath an excellent stomach.
Much Ado about Nothing. Act i, sc. 1, l. 52. [Beatrice]

You have no stomach, signior.
Much Ado about Nothing. Act ii, sc. 3, l. 265. [Beatrice]

His queasy stomach.—*Much Ado about Nothing,* ii, 1, 399. "Queasy" is repeated in *King Lear,* ii, 1, 19: "Queasy question"; and in *Antony and Cleopatra,* iii, 6, 20: "Queasy with insolence."

Weak stomach.—*Henry V,* iii, 2, 57.

5
Come, Kate, sit down; I know you have a stomach.
The Taming of the Shrew. Act iv, sc. 1, l. 161. [Petruchio]

We have stomachs.—*The Tempest,* iii, 3, 41.

6 Which raised in me
An undergoing stomach, to bear up
Against what should ensue.
The Tempest. Act i, sc. 2, l. 156. [Prospero] The only use of "undergoing."

My stomach is not constant.
The Tempest. Act ii, sc. 2, l. 119. [Stephano]

7 Call some knight to arms
That hath a stomach.
Troilus and Cressida, ii, 1, 136. [Achilles]

STONE

See also Jewels

8
See you yond coign o' the Capitol, yond corner-stone?
Coriolanus. Act v, sc. 4, l. 1. [Menenius] The only use of "corner-stone." "Coign" is repeated in *Macbeth,* i, 6, 7: "Coign of vantage"; and in *Pericles,* iii, Gower, 17: "Opposing coigns."

9
Twinn'd stones Upon the number'd beach.
Cymbeline, i, 6, 35. See under JUDGEMENT.

10
Sparkles this stone as it was wont? or is 't not
Too dull for your good wearing?
Cymbeline. Act ii, sc. 4, l. 40. [Posthumus]

Indian stones.—*III Henry VI,* iii, 1, 63.
Precious stone.—*Richard II,* ii, 1, 46; *King Lear,* v, 3, 190.
Stones of worth.—*Sonnets,* lii.

11
Spit, and throw stones, cast mire upon me.
Cymbeline. Act v, sc. 5, l. 222.

The gods throw stones of sulphur on me!
Cymbeline. Act v, sc. 5, l. 240. [Pisanio]

12 I told ye all,
When we first put this dangerous stone a-rolling,
'Twould fall upon ourselves.
Henry VIII, v, 3, 104. The only use of "a-rolling." See under RETRIBUTION.

13 Those sleeping stones,
That as a waist doth girdle you about.
King John. Act ii, sc. 1, l. 216. [King John]

I will stand stone-still.—*King John,* iv, 1, 77. "Stone-still" is repeated in *The Rape of Lucrece,* l. 1730.

Turn to stone.—*Troilus and Cressida,* v, 10, 18; *Othello,* iv, 1, 193.

14
Thy very stones prate of my whereabout.
Macbeth. Act ii, sc. 1, l. 58. [Macbeth]

15
Evans: What is 'lapis,' William?
William: A stone.
Evans: And what is 'a stone,' William?
William: A pebble.
Evans: No, it is 'lapis:' I pray you, remember in your prain.
The Merry Wives of Windsor. Act iv, sc. 1, l. 32. The only uses of "lapis."

16 Are there no stones in heaven
But what serve for the thunder?
Othello. Act v, sc. 2, l. 234. [Othello]

Thou dost stone my heart.
Othello, v, 2, 63. See under HEART.

17
From the cold stone sparks of fire do fly.
The Rape of Lucrece, l. 177.

Cold stone.—*Macbeth,* iv, 1, 6.
Cold and senseless stone.—*Venus and Adonis,* l. 211.
Ancient stones.—*Richard III,* iv, 1, 99.
Breathing stones.—*Richard III,* iii, 7, 25.
Bruising stones.—*The Two Gentlemen of Verona,* i, 2, 111.
Cockerel's stone.—*Romeo and Juliet,* i, 3, 53.
Counterfeit stone.—*Winter's Tale,* iv, 4, 609.

Dear stone.—*The Winter's Tale,* v, 3, 24.
Enamell'd stones.—*The Two Gentlemen of Verona,* ii, 7, 28.
Philosopher's stone.—*II Henry IV,* iii, 2, 355.
Ragged stone.—*II Henry IV,* Ind., 35; *Titus Andronicus,* v, 3, 133.
Rolling restless stone.—*Henry V,* iii, 6, 31.
Spherical stone.—*Henry V,* iii, 6, 38.
Unswept stone.—*Sonnets,* lv.
Untrodden stones.—*Richard II,* i, 2, 69. The only use of "untrodden."

1
Stones dissolved to water do convert.
The Rape of Lucrece, l. 592.
Waste huge stones with little water-drops.
Rape of Lucrece, l. 959. See under WATER.
Stone at rain relenteth.—*Venus and Adonis,* l. 200.

2
A base foul stone, made precious by the foil
Of England's chair, where he is falsely set.
Richard III. Act v, sc. 3, l. 250. [Richmond]

3
The fall of every Phrygian stone will cost
A drop of Grecian blood.
Troilus and Cressida. Act iv, sc. 5, l. 203. [Hector]
Stones of Rome.—*Julius Cæsar,* iii, 2, 234.
Stones of Troy.—*Troilus and Cressida,* iii, 2, 193.

4
A stone is soft as wax,—tribunes more hard than stones;
A stone is silent, and offendeth not.
Titus Andronicus. Act iii, sc. 1, l. 45. [Titus]

5
He is a stone, a very pebble stone, and has no more pity in him than a dog.
The Two Gentlemen of Verona. Act ii, sc. 3, l. 11. [Launce]
Fill'd their pockets full of pebble stones.
I Henry VI. Act iii, sc. 1, l. 80. [Mayor]
Then let the pebbles on the hungry beach
Fillip the stars.
Coriolanus. Act v, sc. 3, l. 58. [Coriolanus]
Shower of pebbles.—*Henry VIII,* v, 4, 60.
Unnumber'd idle pebbles.—*King Lear,* iv, 6, 21.

STORM

See also Tempest

6
In cradle of the rude imperious surge
And in the visitation of the winds,
Who take the ruffian billows by the top,
Curling their monstrous heads and hanging them
With deafening clamour in the slippery clouds,
That, with the hurly, death itself awakes.
II Henry IV. Act iii, sc. 1, l. 20. [King Henry] "Hurly" is used twice more in the plays, in *The Taming of the Shrew,* iv, 1, 206, and *King John,* iii, 4, 169.

7
I will stir up in England some black storm
Shall blow ten thousand souls to heaven or hell.
II Henry VI. Act iii, sc. 1, l. 349. [York]
Black-faced storms.—*The Rape of Lucrece,* l. 1518. "Black-faced" is repeated in *Richard III,* i, 2, 159.
Boisterous storm.—*Richard III,* ii, 3, 44.
Fell storm.—*Pericles,* iii, Gower, 53.
Hideous storm.—*Henry VIII,* i, 1, 90.
Pelleted storm.—*Antony and Cleopatra,* iii, 13, 165. The only use of "pelleted."
Pitiless storm.—*King Lear,* iii, 4, 29.
Shipwrecking storms.—*Macbeth,* i, 2, 26.
Sudden storms.—*Richard II,* ii, 1, 35.

8
I am resolved to bear a greater storm
Than any thou canst conjure up to-day.
II Henry VI. Act v, sc. 1, l. 198. [Clifford]

9
Ay, now begins a second storm to rise;
For this is he that moves both wind and tide.
III Henry VI. Act iii, sc. 3, l. 47. [Queen Margaret]
Alas, the storm is come again!—*The Tempest,* ii, 2, 39.

10
Till storms be past of civil enmity.
III Henry VI. Act iv, sc. 6, l. 98. [Somerset]
Foreign storms.—*III Henry VI,* iv, 1, 38.

11
So foul a sky clears not without a storm:
Pour down thy weather.
King John. Act iv, sc. 2, l. 108. [King John]

12
Alack, the night comes on, and the bleak winds
Do sorely ruffle.
King Lear. Act ii, sc. 4, l. 303. [Gloucester]
'Twill be a storm.—*King Lear,* ii, 4, 290.
Come out o' the storm.—*King Lear,* ii, 4, 312.
Fie on this storm!—*King Lear,* iii, 1, 49.

13
Since I was man,
Such sheets of fire, such bursts of horrid thunder,
Such groans of roaring wind and rain, I never
Remember to have heard.
King Lear. Act iii, sc. 2, l. 45. [Kent]
This contentious storm invades us to the skin.
King Lear. Act iii, sc. 4, l. 6. [Lear] "Contentious" is used again in *Tempest,* ii, 1, 118.

14
Such a storm
As oft 'twixt May and April is to see.
A Lover's Complaint, l. 101.
How you storm!—*The Merchant of Venice,* i, 3, 138. See FURY, 597:14.

15
My . . . storm of fortunes
May trumpet to the world.
Othello. Act i, sc. 3, l. 250. [Desdemona]
Storms of fortune.—*Troilus and Cressida,* i, 3, 47.
Storms of state.—*Henry VIII,* iv, 2, 21.
Storm of war.—*King John,* v, 1, 20.
Storm perpetual.—*Winter's Tale,* iii, 2, 214.

16
No cloudy show of stormy blustering weather
Doth yet in his fair welkin once appear.
The Rape of Lucrece, l. 115.
These water-galls in her dim element
Foretell new storms to those already spent.
The Rape of Lucrece, l. 1588. The only use of "water-galls" (secondary rainbows).

1
Like an unseasonable stormy day,
Which makes the silver rivers drown their shores,
As if the world were all dissolved to tears.
Richard II. Act iii, sc. 2, l. 106. [Scroop]

2
Untimely storms make men expect a dearth.
Richard III. Act ii, sc. 3, l. 35. [Citizen]

3
What storm is this that blows so contrary?
Romeo and Juliet. Act iii, sc. 2, l. 64. [Juliet]

4
You do assist the storm.
The Tempest. Act i, sc. 1, l. 15. [Boatswain]

Your reason for raising this sea-storm?
The Tempest, i, 2, 177. The only use of "sea-storm."

5
The sky, it seems, would pour down stinking pitch,
But that the sea, mounting to the welkin's cheek,
Dashes the fire out.
The Tempest. Act i, sc. 2, l. 3: [Miranda]

Bedimm'd
The noontide sun, call'd forth the mutinous winds,
And 'twixt the green sea and the azured vault
Set roaring war.
The Tempest. Act v, sc. 1, l. 41. [Prospero] "Azured" is repeated in *Cymbeline,* iv, 2, 222: "Azured harebell."

Here 's neither bush nor shrub, to bear off any weather at all, and another storm brewing; I hear it sing i' the wind.
The Tempest. Act ii, sc. 2, l. 18. [Trinculo]

Is the storm overblown? I hid me under the dead moon-calf's gaberdine for fear of the storm.
The Tempest. Act ii, sc. 2, l. 115. [Trinculo]

6
Here are no storms,
No noise, but silence and eternal sleep.
Titus Andronicus, i, 1, 154. See under GRAVE.

One hour's storm will drown the fragrant meads.
Titus Andronicus, ii, 4, 54. See EYE, 448:6.

STORY

See also Tale

7
Let us from point to point this story know,
To make the even truth in pleasure flow.
All's Well that Ends Well. Act v, sc. 3, l. 325. [King]

Let me end the story.—*Cymbeline,* v, 5, 286.

8
The story is extant, and writ in choice Italian.
Hamlet. Act iii, sc. 2, l. 273. [Hamlet]

The proofs are extant.—*The Merry Wives of Windsor,* v, 5, 127.

Is there no virtue extant?—*I Henry IV,* ii, 4, 132.

Extant moment.—*Troilus and Cressida,* iv, 5, 168.

Being extant.—*Sonnets,* lxxxiii. The only uses of "extant."

9
If thou didst ever hold me in thy heart,
Absent thee from felicity awhile,
And in this harsh world draw thy breath in pain,
To tell my story.
Hamlet. Act v, sc. 2, l. 357. [Hamlet] "Felicity" is used only once more in the plays, in *Love's Labour 's Lost,* iv, 3, 249. See quotation under BLACKNESS.

Report me and my cause aright
To the unsatisfied.
Hamlet. Act v, sc. 2, l. 350. [Hamlet]

10
Our humble author will continue the story.
II Henry IV Epilogue, l. 29. [Dancer]

Thus far, with rough and all-unable pen,
Our bending author hath pursued the story,
In little room confining mighty men,
Mangling by starts the full course of their glory.
Henry V. Epilogue, l. 1. [Chorus] The only use of "all-unable."

Make me not your story.—*Measure for Measure,* i, 4, 30.

11
But all the story of the night told over,
And all their minds transfigured so together,
More witnesseth than fancy's images
And grows to something of great constancy;
But, howsoever, strange and admirable.
A Midsummer-Night's Dream. Act v, sc. 1, l. 23. [Hippolyta] The only use of "transfigured."

12
Was 't not to this end
That thou began'st to twist so fine a story?
Much Ado about Nothing. Act i, sc. 1, l. 312. [Don Pedro]

Enchanting story.—*Rape of Lucrece,* l. 1521.
Golden story.—*Romeo and Juliet,* i, 3, 92.
Noble story.—*Henry VIII,* Prol., 26.
Woman's story.—*Macbeth,* iii, 4, 65.
Story of the Prodigal.—*II Henry IV,* ii, 1, 157; *The Merry Wives of Windsor,* iv, 5, 8.

13
Her father loved me; oft invited me;
Still question'd me the story of my life,
From year to year, the battles, sieges, fortunes,
That I have pass'd.
Othello Act i, sc. 3, l. 128. [Othello]

I long
To hear the story of your life, which must
Take the ear strangely.
The Tempest. Act v, sc. 1, l. 311. [Alonso]

The story of my life.—*The Tempest,* v, 1, 304.
Here must end the story of my life.—*The Comedy of Errors,* i, 1, 138.

14
She told him stories to delight his ear.
The Passionate Pilgrim, l. 47.

Tell thy story.—*Pericles,* v, 1, 135.

15
I 'll hear you more, to the bottom of your story.
Pericles. Act v, sc. 1, l. 166. [Pericles]

16
For never was a story of more woe.
Romeo and Juliet. Act v, sc. 3, l. 309. [Prince]

Told the sad story.—*Richard III*, i, 2, 161.
Sad stories.—*Richard II*, iii, 2, 156; *Richard III*, iv, 3, 8.
Plaintful story.—*A Lover's Complaint*, l. 2. The only use of "plaintful."

1
This story Were most impertinent.
The Tempest. Act i, sc. 2, l. 137. [Prospero]
The suit is impertinent to myself.
The Merchant of Venice, ii, 2, 146. The only uses of "impertinent."

2
A most strange story.
The Tempest. Act v, sc. 1, l. 117. [Alonso]
Fabulous story.—*Henry VIII*, i, 1, 36.

3
I 'll to thy closet; and go read with thee
Sad stories chanced in the times of old.
Titus Andronicus. Act iii, sc. 2, l. 82. [Titus]
'Tis an old story.—*Henry VIII*, ii, 3, 90.

4
Valentine: Some shallow story of deep love:
How young Leander cross'd the Hellespont.
Proteus: That 's a deep story of a deeper love.
Two Gentlemen of Verona. Act i, sc. 1, l. 21.

5
'Where did I leave?' 'No matter where;' quoth he,
'Leave me, and then the story aptly ends.'
Venus and Adonis, l. 715.
Their copious stories oftentimes begun
End without audience and are never done.
Venus and Adonis, l. 845.
Be copious in exclaims.—*Richard III*, iv, 4, 135. The only uses of "copious."

STRANGENESS

See also Novelty, Wonder

6
Why do you look so strange upon your wife?
All's Well that Ends Well. Act v, sc. 3, l. 168. [Diana]
Why look you strange on me? you know me well.
The Comedy of Errors. Act v, sc. 1, l. 295. [Ægeus]
Look strange.—*Sonnets*, lxxxix. See also under LOOK.
You all look strangely on me.
II Henry IV. Act v, sc. 2, l. 63. [King Henry]
Most strangely.—*Henry VIII*, iii, 2, 29.
Very strangely.—*Hamlet*, v, 1, 172. "Strangely" is used twenty-seven times.

7
Heard you of nothing strange about the streets?
Antony and Cleopatra. Act iv, sc. 3, l. 3. [Soldier]

8
You are a pair of strange ones.
Coriolanus. Act ii, sc. 1, l. 89. [Menenius]

9
'Tis wondrous strange, the like yet never heard of.
III Henry VI. Act ii, sc. 1, l. 33. [Edward]
O day and night, but this is wondrous strange!
Hamlet. Act i, sc. 5, l. 164. [Horatio]
"Wondrous strange" occurs a third time in *A Midsummer-Night's Dream*, v, 1, 59.

10
A thing most strange and certain.
Macbeth. Act ii, sc. 4, l. 14. [Ross]
It seems to me most strange.—*Julius Cæsar*, ii, 2, 35.
This is most strange.—*King Lear*, i, 1, 216.
Most strange.—*Pericles*, iii, 2, 24; 64.
Is it not very strange?—*Hamlet*, ii, 2, 380.
'Twas very strange.—*Pericles*, ii, 4, 13.

11
This is more strange than such a murder is.
Macbeth. Act iii, sc. 4, l. 82. [Macbeth]

12
Angelo: She will speak most bitterly and strange.
Isabella: Most strange, but yet most truly, will I speak:
That Angelo 's forsworn; is it not strange?
That Angelo 's a murderer; is 't not strange?
That Angelo is an adulterous thief,
An hypocrite, a virgin-violator;
Is it not strange and strange?
Duke: Nay, it is ten times strange.
Measure for Measure. Act v, sc. 1, l. 36. The only use of "virgin-violator."
Benedick: Is not that strange?
Beatrice: As strange as the thing I know not.
Much Ado about Nothing. Act iv, sc. 1, l. 270.

13
Hippolyta: 'Tis strange, my Theseus, that these lovers speak of.
Theseus: More strange than true.
A Midsummer-Night's Dream. Act v, sc. 1, l. 1. "'Tis strange" is repeated frequently throughout the plays.
Hamlet: 'Tis very strange.
Horatio: As I do live, my honour'd lord, 'tis true.
Hamlet. Act i, sc. 2, l. 220.
'Tis strange, 'tis very strange.—*All's Well that Ends Well*, ii, 3, 33.
'Tis so strange.—*Henry V*, ii, 2, 102.
Is it not strange?—*Measure for Measure*, v, 1, 38; 39; *Much Ado about Nothing*, iv, 1, 270; *Troilus and Cressida*, ii, 3, 171; *Antony and Cleopatra*, iii, 7, 21; iv, 3, 20.
Is not this strange?—*Pericles*, iii, 2, 107.
How strange it seems.—*Venus and Adonis*, l. 985.
O strange!—*Othello*, ii, 3, 310.
Strange it is.—*All's Well that Ends Well*, ii, 3, 125; *Antony and Cleopatra*, v, 1, 28.
That 's strange.—*Othello*, iv, 2, 11.
That, methinks, is strange.—*Julius Cæsar*, iv, 3, 184.
This is strange now.—*Coriolanus*, ii, 1, 24.
This is strange to me.—*Henry VIII*, ii, 3, 88.
Why, this is strange.—*Measure for Measure*, v, 1, 280.
Yet still it 's strange.—*Cymbeline*, iv, 2, 181.

14
'Twas strange, 'twas passing strange.
Othello. Act i, sc. 3, l. 160. [Othello]

15
I should have been more strange, I must confess.
Romeo and Juliet. Act ii, sc. 2, l. 102. [Juliet]

You grow exceeding strange.—*The Merchant of Venice,* i, 1, 67.
Will you be so strange?—*The Taming of the Shrew,* i, 1, 85.
I will be strange.—*Twelfth Night,* ii, 5, 185.
He is strange and peevish.—*Cymbeline,* i, 6, 54.

1
Do not infest your mind with beating on
The strangeness of this business.
The Tempest. Act v, sc. 1, l. 246. [Prospero] The only use of "infest."

This is a strange thing as e'er I look'd on.
The Tempest. Act v, sc. 1, l. 289. [Alonso]

Something rich and strange.—*The Tempest,* i, 2, 401.
Mark, how strange it shows.—*Timon of Athens,* iii, 4, 21.

2
Here tend the savage strangeness he puts on.
Troilus and Cressida. Act ii, sc. 3, l. 135. [Agamemnon]

Put on a form of strangeness as we pass along.
Troilus and Cressida. Act iii, sc. 3, l. 51. [Agamemnon]

I prithee now, ungird thy strangeness.
Twelfth Night. Act iv, sc. 1, l. 15. [Clown] The only use of "ungird."

She puts on outward strangeness, seems unkind.
Venus and Adonis, l. 310.

Measure my strangeness with my unripe years.
Venus and Adonis, l. 524.

3
This is not strange at all.
Troilus and Cressida. Act iii, sc. 3, l. 111. [Achilles]

'Tis not strange.—*Hamlet,* iii, 2, 210.
"Strange" was a favourite adjective with Shakespeare, who used it nearly three hundred times.

STRANGER

4
I do desire we may be better strangers.
As You Like It. Act iii, sc. 2, l. 274. [Orlando]

5
In Ephesus I am but two hours old,
As strange unto your town as to your talk.
The Comedy of Errors. Act ii, sc. 2, l. 150. [Antipholus of Syracuse]

6
This worthy signior, I thank him, makes no stranger of me.
Cymbeline. Act i, sc. 4, l. 111. [Posthumus]

A saucy stranger in his court to mart.
Cymbeline. Act i, sc. 6, l. 151. [Imogen]

First Lord: Did you hear of a stranger that 's come to court to-night?
Cloten: A stranger, and I not know on 't!
Second Lord [Aside]: He 's a strange fellow himself, and knows it not.
Cymbeline. Act ii, sc. 1, l. 36.

7
A stranger, Born out of your dominions.
Henry VIII. Act ii, sc. 4, l. 15. [Queen Katharine]

She 's a stranger now again.—*Henry VIII,* ii, 3, 17.
A noble troop of strangers.—*Henry VIII,* i, 4, 53.

8
Good God, betimes
Remove the means that make us strangers!
Macbeth. Act iv, sc. 3, l. 162. [Malcolm]

Strangers to my nature.—*Macbeth,* iv, 3, 125.
Stranger to thy thoughts.—*Othello,* iii, 3, 144.

9
An extravagant and wheeling stranger
Of here and every where.
Othello. Act i, sc. 1, l. 137. [Roderigo] The only use of "wheeling" (wandering).

10
And strangers ne'er beheld but wonder'd at;
Whose men and dames so jetted and adorn'd,
Like one another's glass to trim them by.
Pericles. Act i, sc. 4, l. 25. [Cleon] The only use of "jetted."

He well may be a stranger, for he comes
To an honour'd triumph strangely furnished.
Pericles. Act ii, sc. 2, l. 52. [Lord] The only use of "furnished."

A stranger and distressed gentleman.—*Pericles,* ii, 5, 46.

Will you, not having my consent,
Bestow your love and your affections
Upon a stranger?
Pericles. Act ii, sc. 5, l. 76. [Simonides]

11
A stranger came, and on that pillow lay
Where thou wast wont to rest thy weary head.
The Rape of Lucrece, l. 1620.

12
I am a stranger here in Gloucestershire.
Richard II. Act ii, sc. 3, l. 3. [Northumberland]

Being a stranger in this city here.
The Taming of the Shrew. Act ii, sc. 1, l. 90. [Tranio]

13
But, gentle sir, methinks you walk like a stranger.
The Taming of the Shrew. Act ii, sc. 1, l. 86. [Baptista]

Thus strangers may be haled and abused: O monstrous villain!
The Taming of the Shrew. Act v, sc. 1, l. 111. [Vincentio]

We are but strangers to him.—*Timon of Athens,* iii, 2, 4.

14
He hath known you but three days, and already you are no stranger.
Twelfth Night. Act i, sc. 4, l. 3. [Valentine]

STRATAGEM

See also Policy, Shift

15
He says he has a stratagem for 't.
All's Well that Ends Well. Act iii, sc. 6, l. 37. [Lord]

Say it was a stratagem.—*All's Well that Ends Well,* iv, 1, 55.

16
Every minute now
Should be the father of some stratagem.
II Henry IV. Act i, sc. 1, l. 7. [Northumberland]

Coin a stratagem.—*Titus Andronicus,* ii, 3, 5.

17
Saint Denis bless this happy stratagem!
I Henry VI. Act iii, sc. 2, l. 18. [Charles]

It will be an excellent stratagem.—*II Henry IV,* ii, 4, 22.
Stratagems of war.—*I Henry VI,* iv, 5, 2.

1
It were a delicate stratagem, to shoe
A troop of horse with felt.
King Lear. Act iv, sc. 6, l. 188. [King Lear]

STRAW

2
Greatly to find quarrel in a straw.
Hamlet, iv, 4, 55. See under GREATNESS.
Spurns enviously at straws.—*Hamlet,* iv, 5, 6.

3
Give me your doublet and stuff me out with straw.
II Henry IV. Act v, sc. 5, l. 87. [Shallow]

4
Those that with haste will make a mighty fire
Begin it with weak straws.
Julius Cæsar, i, 3, 108. See under FIRE.
As straw with fire flameth.
Passionate Pilgrim, l. 97. See under LOVE.
Burn the straw.—*Titus Andronicus,* ii, 3, 123.

5 Where is this straw, my fellow?
The art of our necessities is strange,
That can make vile things precious.
King Lear, iii, 2, 69. See under NECESSITY.
What art thou that dost grumble there i' the straw?
King Lear. Act iii, sc. 4, l. 43. [Kent]
He is coming; I hear his straw rustle.
Measure for Measure. Act iv, sc. 3, l. 37. [Pompey]
Lay him in straw.—*All's Well that Ends Well,* iv, 3, 289.

6
Hovel thee with swine, and rogues forlorn,
In short and musty straw.
King Lear. Act iv, sc. 7, l. 39. [Cordelia]
Pigmy's straw.—*King Lear,* iv, 6, 171.
Oaten straws.—*Love's Labour's Lost,* v, 2, 913.
Belt of straw.—*The Passionate Pilgrim,* l. 365.
Platted hive of straw.—*A Lover's Complaint,* l. 8. The only use of "platted."
Wisp of straw.—*III Henry VI,* ii, 2, 144.

7
Tremble and start at wagging of a straw.
Richard III, iii, 5, 7. See under ACTING.
Prize it not a straw.—*Winter's Tale,* iii, 2, 111.
Force not argument a straw.—*The Rape of Lucrece,* 1021.

STREAM

See also River

8
In his proper stream o'erflows himself.
All's Well that Ends Well. Act iv, sc. 3, l. 29. [Lord]

9
The rank of osiers by the murmuring stream.
As You Like It. Act iv, sc. 3, l. 80. [Celia]
Flattering streams.—*Macbeth,* iii, 2, 33.
Full stream.—*As You Like It,* iii, 2, 439.
Gentle stream.—*The Two Gentlemen of Verona,* ii, 7, 34.
Glassy streams.—*I Henry VI,* v, 3, 62; *Hamlet.* iv, 7, 168.
Late-disturbed stream.—*I Henry IV,* ii, 3, 62. The only use of "late-disturbed."
Lowest stream.—*Julius Cæsar,* i, 1, 64.
Murmuring stream.—*As You Like It,* iv, 3, 80.
Needless stream.—*As You Like It,* ii, 1, 46.
Pale streams.—*Sonnets,* xxxiii.
Pure streams.—*The Rape of Lucrece,* l. 1078.
Rich stream.—*Henry VIII,* iv, 1, 62.
Rude stream.—*Henry VIII,* iii, 2, 364.
Salt green streams.—*A Midsummer-Night's Dream,* iii, 2, 393.
Silver stream.—*Much Ado about Nothing,* iii, 1, 27.
Suffocating streams.—*Othello,* iii, 3, 389.

10
Floating straight, obedient to the stream.
The Comedy of Errors. Act i, sc. 1, l. 87. [Ægeus]
Down the stream.—*Cymbeline,* iv, 2, 184.
How runs the stream?—*Twelfth Night,* iv, 1, 64.

11
The fresh streams ran by her, and murmur'd her moans.
Othello. Act iv, sc. 3, l. 45. [Desdemona, singing]

12
The petty streams that pay a daily debt
To their salt sovereign, with their fresh falls' haste
Add to his flow, but alter not his taste.
The Rape of Lucrece, l. 649.

13
Key-cold Lucrece' bleeding stream.
The Rape of Lucrece, l. 1774. "Key-cold" is repeated in *Richard III,* i, 2, 5.
Streams of blood.—*Richard III,* v, 5, 37; *Richard II,* i, 1, 103.
Streams of foreign gore.—*I Henry VI,* iii, 3, 55.
Stream of justice.—*Timon of Athens,* v, 4, 60.
Stream o' the people.—*Coriolanus,* ii, 3, 269.
Stream of time.—*II Henry IV,* iv, 1, 70.
Stream of virtue.—*Timon of Athens,* iv, 1, 27.

14
All in vain you strive against the stream.
Venus and Adonis, l. 772.
'Gainst the stream of virtue they may strive.
Timon of Athens, iv, 1, 27. See under YOUTH.
Swims against your stream.—*II Henry IV,* v, 2, 34.

STRENGTH

15
Sir, it is A charge too heavy for my strength.
All's Well that Ends Well. Act iii, sc. 3, l. 3. [Bertram]

16
Antony: What is his strength by land?
Cæsar: Great and increasing.
Antony and Cleopatra. Act ii, sc. 2, l. 164.
Mighty strength they carry.—*Antony and Cleopatra,* ii, 1, 17.
Grown to strength.—*Antony and Cleopatra,* i, 3, 48.

17
Antony: Thou know'st
How much we do o'er-count thee.
Pompey: At land, indeed;

Thou dost o'er-count me.
Antony and Cleopatra. Act ii, sc. 6, l. 26. The only uses of "o'er-count."

1
Our strength is all gone into heaviness.
Antony and Cleopatra. Act iv, sc. 15, l. 33. [Cleopatra]

2
I come but in, as others do, to try with him the strength of my youth.
As You Like It. Act i, sc. 2, l. 181. [Orlando]
What though she strive to try her strength?
Passionate Pilgrim, l. 317. See YIELDING.
Try his strength.—*I Henry VI,* v, 5, 32.

3
The little strength that I have, I would it were with you.
As You Like It. Act i, sc. 2, l. 207. [Orlando]
We want a little personal strength.
II Henry IV. Act iv, sc. 4, l. 8. [King Henry]
Little strength.—*The Rape of Lucrece,* l. 1495.
Small strength.—*Richard III,* v, 3, 26.
Want of strength.—*III Henry VI,* v, 2, 8.
Have no strength.—*I Henry IV,* iii, 3, 7.

4
Though I look old, yet I am strong and lusty.
As You Like It, ii, 3, 47. See under AGE.
Lusty and like to live.—*The Winter's Tale,* ii, 2, 27.
Lusty, young.—*Richard II,* i, 3, 66; *Venus and Adonis,* l. 260. "Lusty" is used thirty-six times.
Why, your dolphin is not lustier.
All's Well that Ends Well. Act ii, sc. 3, l. 31. [Lafeu]
I'll take him down, an a' were lustier than he is.
Romeo and Juliet. Act ii, sc. 4, l. 159. [Nurse]
Lustier maintenance.—*I Henry IV,* v, 4, 22. The only uses of "lustier."

5
Being strong at heart, He sent me hither.
As You Like It. Act iv, sc. 3, l. 152. [Oliver]
Strong in appetite.—*Cymbeline,* iii, 6, 37.
Strong in custom.—*Pericles,* iii, 1, 52.
More strong.—*II Henry VI,* v, 1, 31; *Coriolanus,* iii, 2, 140; *Julius Cæsar,* iii, 2, 189; *King John,* iv, 2, 41; *Cymbeline,* iv, 1, 11; *Sonnets,* lxxiii; cxix.
Most strong.—*All's Well that Ends Well,* iv, 2, 59; *The Tempest,* v, 1, 77.
Passing strong.—*Venus and Adonis,* l. 297.
Somewhat strong.—*All's Well that Ends Well,* v, 2, 5.
'Tis strong.—*Twelfth Night,* i, 3, 143.
Too strong for him.—*Macbeth,* ii, 3, 45.
Waxeth strong.—*Venus and Adonis,* l. 420.

6
Gods, put the strength o' the Leonati in me!
Cymbeline. Act v, sc. 1, l. 31. [Posthumus] "Leonati seat" is used in v, 4, 60.
Renew thy strength.—*Cymbeline,* v, 5, 150.

7
With all the strength and armour of the mind.
Hamlet. Act iii, sc. 3, l. 12. [Guildenstern]
Strength of limb.—*Much Ado about Nothing,* iv, 1, 200.
Strength of love.—*Antony and Cleopatra,* iii, 2, 62.
Strength of malice.—*Julius Cæsar,* iii, 1, 174.
Strength of speech.—*II Henry IV,* iv, 5, 218.
Strength of spirit.—*Julius Cæsar,* i, 3, 95.
Strength of will.—*Romeo and Juliet,* iv, 1, 72.
Grief's strength.—*Sonnets,* xxviii.
Life's strength.—*The Rape of Lucrece,* l. 124.
Love's strength.—*Sonnets,* xxiii.
Passion's strength.—*Rape of Lucrece,* l. 1103.

8
He should draw his several strengths together.
II Henry IV. Act i, sc. 3, l. 76. [Archbishop]
Dissever your united strengths,
And part your mingled colours once again.
King John. Act ii, sc. 1, l. 388. [Bastard] "Dissever" is repeated in *All's Well that Ends Well,* ii, 1, 125.
Bid him levy straight
The greatest strength and power he can make.
Richard III. Act iv, sc. 4, l. 448. [King Richard]
Abate your strength.—*Titus Andronicus,* i, 1, 43. Strength is used throughout the plays in the sense of army or armed force.

9
Then join you with them, like a rib of steel,
To make strength stronger.
II Henry IV. Act ii, sc. 3, l. 54. [Lady Percy]
Stronger strength.—*Venus and Adonis,* l. 111.

10
As strong As aconitum or rash gunpowder.
II Henry IV. Act iv, sc. 4, l. 47. [King Henry] The only mention of "aconitum."
As strong as any man in Illyria.
Twelfth Night. Act i, sc. 3, l. 132. [Sir Andrew]
Strong as heaven itself.—*Troilus and Cressida,* v, 2, 155.
Strong as Pluto's gates.—*Troilus and Cressida,* v, 2, 153.
Strong as a tower.—*Richard II,* i, 3, 102.

11
Where is my strength, my valour, and my force?
I Henry VI. Act i, sc. 5, l. 1. [Talbot]
I scorn thy strength.—*I Henry VI,* i, 5, 15.

12
Nor should thy prowess want praise and esteem,
But that 'tis shown ignobly and in treason.
II Henry VI. Act v, sc. 2, l. 22. [York]
By his prowess conquered.—*III Henry VI,* iii, 3, 86.
Had his prowess confirmed.—*Macbeth,* v, 8, 41. The only uses of "prowess."

13
Their power, I think, is thirty thousand strong.
III Henry VI. Act ii, sc. 1, l. 177. [Warwick] See also under POWER.
The queen is valued thirty thousand strong.
III Henry VI. Act v, sc. 3, l. 14. [Gloucester]
At the battle of Patay,
When but in all I was six thousand strong.
I Henry VI. Act iv, sc. 1, l. 20. [Talbot] The only mention of Patay.
Fifty thousand strong.—*II Henry IV,* iii, 1, 96.

Seven thousand strong.—*I Henry IV,* iv, 1, 88.
Not six and twenty strong.—*I Henry IV,* iv, 3, 56.
Two thousand strong.—*Twelfth Night,* iii, 2, 59.
His forces strong.—*King John,* ii, 1, 61.

1
Give more strength to that which hath too much.
III Henry VI. Act v, sc. 4, l. 9. [Queen Margaret]

2
Are you not stronger than you were?
Henry VIII. Act ii, sc. 3, l. 100. [Old Lady]
I grow stronger.—*Henry VIII,* v, 3, 182.
Grow stronger.—*III Henry VI,* iv, 7, 59; *II Henry IV,* iv, 1, 223.
More stronger.—*Henry VIII,* i, 1, 147.
Stronger than Achilles' arm.—*Troilus and Cressida,* i, 3, 220.
Stronger than the church.—*Hamlet,* v, 1, 54.
Stronger than thy continent.—*Antony and Cleopatra,* iv, 14, 40.
Stronger than mine eyes.—*Antony and Cleopatra,* v, 2, 224.
Stronger than Hercules.—*All 's Well that Ends Well,* iv, 2, 283.
Stronger than my sex.—*Julius Cæsar,* ii, 1, 296.
Stronger than it was before.—*Othello,* ii, 3, 331.

3
I think he will stand very strong with us.
Julius Cæsar. Act ii, sc. 1, l. 142. [Cassius]
Be strong upon my side!—*Julius Cæsar,* ii, 4, 6.
Be strong and prosperous.—*Romeo and Juliet,* iv, 1, 122.
Be strong and ready.—*Coriolanus,* iii, 3, 23.
Be strong in whore.—*Timon of Athens,* iv, 3, 141.

4
Thou ever strong upon the stronger side!
King John. Act iii, sc. 1, l. 117. [Constance]

5 O, it is excellent
To have a giant's strength; but it is tyrannous
To use it like a giant.
Measure for Measure. Act ii, sc. 2, l. 107. [Isabella]

6
Mine enemy was strong, my poor self weak,
And far the weaker with so strong a fear.
The Rape of Lucrece, l. 1646.
Strength o' the enemy.—*King Lear,* iv, 5, 14.

7
Love give me strength! and strength shall help afford.
Romeo and Juliet. Act iv, sc. 1, l. 125. [Juliet]

8
Whose strength's abundance weakens his own heart.
Sonnets. No. xxiii.
Strength by limping sway disabled.—*Sonnets,* lxvi.
Strengths by strengths do fall.—*Coriolanus,* iv, 7, 55.

9
One so strong That could control the moon.
The Tempest, v, 1, 269. See under WITCH. "So strong" is repeated frequently.
What strength I have 's mine own.
The Tempest. Epilogue, l. 2. [Prospero]

10
Wanting strength to do thee so much good,
I may be pluck'd into the swallowing womb
Of this deep pit.
Titus Andronicus. Act ii, sc. 3, l. 238. [Quintus]
Quintus: I have no strength to pluck thee to the brink.
Martius: Nor I no strength to climb without thy help.
Titus Andronicus. Act ii, sc. 3, l. 241. "Brink" is used only once again, in *Timon of Athens,* v, 1, 159.

11
Strength should be lord of imbecility.
Troilus and Cressida. Act i, sc. 3, l. 114. [Ulysses] The only use of "imbecility."

12
You are as strong, as valiant.
Troilus and Cressida, ii, 3, 158. See under COMPARISON.
You are strong and manly.—*II Henry VI,* iv, 8, 53.
Obstinately strong.—*Troilus and Cressida,* v, 2, 121.

13
Strong-tempered steel his stronger strength obey'd.
Venus and Adonis, l. 111. The only use of "strong-tempered."
Ambitious strength.—*Coriolanus,* iv, 5, 118.
Ampler strength.—*Winter's Tale,* iv, 4, 414.
Ancient strength.—*Coriolanus,* iv, 2, 7.
Holy strength.—*Troilus and Cressida,* ii, 3, 136.
Mighty strength.—*III Henry VI,* iii, 1, 49.
Noble strength.—*Macbeth,* ii, 2, 45.
True strength.—*King Lear,* v, 1, 52.
Younger strengths.—*King Lear,* i, 1, 41.

STRIDE, see Walking

STRIFE

See also Discord, Fighting, Quarrel

14 I always thought
It was both impious and unnatural
That such immanity and bloody strife
Should reign among professors of one faith.
I Henry VI. Act v, sc. 1, l. 11. [King Henry] The only use of "immanity" (savageness).
Mitigate this strife.—*I Henry VI,* iii, 1, 88.
End this strife.—*Merchant of Venice,* ii, 3, 20.
Stay your strife.—*Titus Andronicus,* iii, 1, 93.

15
I pray, my lords, let me compound this strife.
II Henry VI. Act ii, sc. 1, l. 58. [King]
I will compound this strife.
The Taming of the Shrew. Act ii, sc. 1, l. 343. [Baptista]
I would to God all strifes were well compounded.
Richard III. Act ii, sc. 1, l. 74. [Queen Elizabeth]

16
And for the peace of you I hold such strife
As 'twixt a miser and his wealth is found;
Now proud as an enjoyer and anon

Doubting the filching age will steal his treasure.
Sonnets. No. lxxv. The only use of "enjoyer."
Artificial strife.—*Timon of Athens,* i, 1, 37.
Barful strife!—*Twelfth Night,* i, 4, 41. The only use of "barful."
Black strife.—*Romeo and Juliet,* iii, 1, 183.
Civil strife.—*Julius Cæsar,* i, 3, 11; iii, 1, 263.
Civil home-bred strife.—*Venus and Adonis,* l. 764.
Continual strife.—*I Henry VI,* v, 5, 63.
Doubtful strife.—*I Henry VI,* iv, 1, 151.
Equal strife.—*The Rape of Lucrece,* l. 1791.
Further strife.—*The Rape of Lucrece,* l. 689.
Future strife.—*King Lear,* i, 1, 45.
Great strifes.—*The Rape of Lucrece,* l. 899.
Lasting strife.—*Hamlet,* iii, 2, 232.
Thwarting strife.—*The Rape of Lucrece,* l. 143.
Tumultuous strife.—*I Henry VI,* i, 3, 70.
Free from strife.—*Richard II,* v, 6, 27.
With herself at strife.—*Venus and Adonis,* l. 11.

STRUMPET

See also Whore

1
Thy mistress, Pisanio, hath played the strumpet in my bed.
Cymbeline. Act iii, sc. 4, l. 21. [Imogen]
I have heard I am a strumpet; and mine ear,
Therein false struck, can take no greater wound,
Nor tent to bottom that.
Cymbeline. Act iii, sc. 4, l. 116. [Imogen]

2
I will chastise this high-minded strumpet.
I Henry VI. Act i, sc. 5, l. 12. [Talbot]
The only use of "high-minded."

3
A housewife that by selling her desires
Buys herself bread and clothes: . . .
'Tis the strumpet's plague
To beguile many and be beguiled by one.
Othello. Act iv, sc. 1, l. 95. [Iago]
Heaven stops the nose at it and the moon winks,
The bawdy wind that kisses all it meets
Is hush'd within the hollow mine of earth,
And will not hear it. What committed!
Impudent strumpet!
Othello. Act iv, sc. 2, l. 77. [Othello]
O notable strumpet!—*Othello,* v, 1, 78.

4
Othello: Are not you a strumpet?
Desdemona: No, as I am a Christian:
If to preserve this vessel for my lord
From any other foul unlawful touch
Be not to be a strumpet, I am none.
Othello. Act iv, sc. 2, l. 82.
I am no strumpet; but of life as honest
As you that thus abuse me.
Othello. Act v, sc. 1, l. 122. [Bianca]

5
Show me the strumpet that began this stir,
That with my nails her beauty I may tear.
The Rape of Lucrece, l. 1471.
That harlot strumpet.—*Richard III,* iii, 4, 73.
Damned strumpet.—*Richard III,* iii, 4, 76.
O most unhappy strumpet!—*The Comedy of Errors,* iv, 4, 127.

6
That strumpet, your unhallow'd dam.
Titus Andronicus. Act v, sc. 2, l. 191. [Titus]

7
My self on every post
Proclaim'd a strumpet.
The Winter's Tale. Act iii, sc. 2, l. 102. [Hermione]
Strumpet Fortune.—*King John,* iii, 1, 61. See under FORTUNE.

STUBBORNNESS

See also Obstinacy

8
To persever
In obstinate condolement is a course
Of impious stubbornness.
Hamlet. Act i, sc. 2, l. 92. [King] "Certain condolements" occurs in *Pericles,* ii, 1, 156.
The stubbornest young fellow.—*As You Like It,* i, 1, 148. The only use of "stubbornest." See under CHARACTER.
Stubborn to justice.—*Henry VIII,* ii, 4, 122.

9
Stubbornly he did repugn the truth.
I Henry VI. Act iv, sc. 1, l. 94. [Basset]
The only use of "stubbornly" and "repugn."

10
Are you more stubborn-hard than hammer'd iron?
King John. Act iv, sc. 1, l. 67. [Arthur]
The only use of "stubborn-hard."

11
Sirrah, thou art said to be a stubborn soul,
That apprehends no further than this world,
And squarest thy life according.
Measure for Measure. Act v, sc. 1, l. 485. [Duke]
Stubborn ancient knave.—*King Lear,* ii, 2, 133.
Stubborn, lacking duty.—*The Two Gentlemen of Verona,* iii, 1, 69.

12
His stubbornness, his checks, his frowns.
Othello, iv, 3, 20. See under LOVE.
Stubbornness of fortune.—*As You Like It,* ii, 1, 19.

STUDY

See also Scholar

13
Tutor'd in the rudiments
Of many desperate studies.
As You Like It. Act v, sc. 4, l. 31. [Orlando]
"Rudiments" is repeated in *The Taming of the Shrew,* iii, 1, 66: "Rudiments of art."
Best studies.—*King John,* iv, 2, 51.
Painful study.—*Love's Labour's Lost,* ii, 1, 23.
Study of imagination.—*Much Ado about Nothing,* iv, 1, 227.
Slow of study.—*A Midsummer-Night's Dream,* i, 2, 69.

14
All studies here I solemnly defy.
I Henry IV. Act i, sc. 3, l. 228. [Hotspur]

15
Let your study Be to content your lord.
King Lear. Act i, sc. 1, l. 279. [Goneril]
Lear: What is your study?
Edgar: How to prevent the fiend, and to kill vermin.
King Lear. Act iii, sc. 4, l. 164. The only use of "vermin."

I 'll study how to die.—*As You Like It,* iv, 3, 63.

1
Biron: What is the end of study? let me know.
King: Why, that to know, which else we should not know.
Biron: Things hid and barr'd, you mean, from common sense?
King: Ay, that is study's god-like recompense.
Biron: Come on, then; I will swear to study so,
To know the thing I am forbid to know:
As thus,—to study where I well may dine,
When I to feast expressly am forbid.
Love's Labour's Lost. Act i, sc. 1, l. 55.

If study's gain be thus and this be so,
Study knows that which yet it doth not know.
Love's Labour's Lost. Act i, sc. 1, l. 67. [Biron]

These be the stops that hinder study quite
And train our intellects to vain delight.
Love's Labour's Lost. Act i, sc. 1, l. 70. [King]

Study is like the heaven's glorious sun
That will not be deep-search'd with saucy looks:
Small have continual plodders ever won
Save base authority from others' books.
Love's Labour's Lost. Act i, sc. 1, l. 84. [Biron] The only use of "deep-search'd" and "plodders."

And so to study, three years is but short.
Love's Labour's Lost. Act i, sc. 1, l. 181. [Longaville]

Is this such a piece of study?—*Love's Labour's Lost,* i, 2, 53.

2
So study evermore is overshot:
While it doth study to have what it would
It doth forget to do the thing it should,
And when it hath the thing it hunteth most,
'Tis won as towns with fire, so won, so lost.
Love's Labour's Lost, i, 1, 143. [Biron]

And where that you have vow'd to study, lords,
In that each of you have forsworn his book,
Can you still dream and pore and thereon look?
Love's Labour's Lost, iv, 3, 296. [Biron]

Why, universal plodding poisons up
The nimble spirits in the arteries.
Love's Labour's Lost, iv, 3, 305. [Biron] The only use of "plodding" and "arteries." "Artery" occurs in *Hamlet,* i, 4, 82.

3
Here let us breathe and haply institute
A course of learning and ingenious studies.
The Taming of the Shrew. Act i, sc. 1, l. 8. [Lucentio]

The mathematics and the metaphysics,
Fall to them as you find your stomach serves you.
The Taming of the Shrew. Act i, sc. 1, l. 37. [Tranio] The only mention of "metaphysics." "Metaphysical" is used in *Macbeth,* i, 5, 30. Mathematics occurs twice more in the same play (ii, 1, 56, ii, 1, 82), and in no other.

In brief, sir, study what you most affect.
The Taming of the Shrew, i, 1, 40. See under PHILOSOPHY.

I ever Have studied physic.—*Pericles,* iii, 2, 32.

Loosely studied.—*II Henry IV,* ii, 2, 10.

Well studied.—*The Merchant of Venice,* ii, 2, 205; *Antony and Cleopatra,* ii, 6, 48.

Studied so long.—*II Henry VI,* i, 1, 90.

4
The liberal arts . . . being all my study.
The Tempest. Act i, sc. 2, l. 73. [Prospero]

Rapt in secret studies.—*The Tempest,* i, 2, 77.

Hard at study.—*The Tempest,* iii, 1, 20. The only use of the phrase.

You make me study of that.—*The Tempest,* ii, 1, 82.

Studies day and night.—*I Henry IV,* i, 3, 184.

5
Dedicated
To closeness and the bettering of my mind.
The Tempest. Act i, sc. 2, l. 89. [Prospero] The only use of "closeness."

6
All my study be to no effect.
Titus Andronicus. Act v, sc. 2, l. 12. [Titus]

7
I am not . . . lean enough to be thought a good student.
Twelfth Night. Act iv, sc. 2, l. 7. [Clown] "Good student" is repeated in *The Merry Wives of Windsor,* iii, 1, 38.

Negligent student!—*Love's Labour's Lost,* iii, 1, 36. The only uses of "student." "Students" occurs in *Love's Labour's Lost,* ii, 1, 64.

8
And though myself have been an idle truant,
Omitting the sweet benefit of time
To clothe mine age with angel-like perfection,
Yet hath Sir Proteus, for that 's his name,
Made use and fair advantage of his days.
The Two Gentlemen of Verona. Act ii, sc. 4, l. 64. [Valentine] "Angel-like" is repeated in *Cymbeline,* iv, 2, 48.

STUPIDITY

9
Your wit will not so soon out as another man's will; 'tis strongly wedged up in a block-head.
Coriolanus. Act ii, sc. 3, l. 29. [Citizen] The only use of "block-head."

10
This her son
Cannot take two from twenty, for his heart,
And leave eighteen.
Cymbeline. Act ii, sc. 1, l. 59. [Lord]

11
You blocks, you stones, you worse than senseless things!
Julius Cæsar. Act i, sc. 1, l. 40. [Marullus]

What tongueless blocks were they!
Richard III. Act iii, sc. 7, l. 42. [Gloucester]

What a block art thou!—*The Two Gentlemen of Verona,* ii, 5, 27.

A mere lifeless block.—*As You Like It,* i, 2, 263.

Thou block!—*Pericles,* iii, 2, 90.

Blockish Ajax.—*Troilus and Cressida,* i, 3, 375. The only use of "blockish."

12
Dost think I am so muddy, so unsettled,
To appoint myself in this vexation, sully
The purity and whiteness of my sheets,

Which to preserve is sleep, which being spotted
Is goads, thorns, nettles, tails of wasps,
Give scandal to the blood o' the prince my son,
Who I do think is mine and love as mine,
Without ripe moving to 't? Would I do this?
Could man so blench?
Winter's Tale. Act i, sc. 2, l. 325. [Leontes]
He something seems unsettled.
The Winter's Tale. Act i, sc. 2, l. 147. [Hermione]

1
Is he not stupid
With age and altering rheums?
The Winter's Tale. Act iv, sc. 4, l. 409. [Polonius] The only use of "stupid." "Stupidity" does not occur in the plays.

STYLE

2
Why, 'tis a boisterous and a cruel style,
A style for challengers.
As You Like It. Act iv, sc. 3, l. 31. [Rosalind]
So quiet and so sweet a style.—*As You Like It*, ii, 1, 20. See under FORTUNE.

3
There were no sallets in the lines to make the batter savoury, nor no matter in the phrase that might indict the author of affectation; but called it an honest method, as wholesome as sweet, and by very much more handsome than fine.
Hamlet. Act ii, sc. 2, l. 462. [Hamlet] The only use of "indict." "Savoury" is repeated in *Cymbeline*, iii, 6, 33.

4
What means his grace, that he hath changed his style?
No more but, plain and bluntly, 'To the king!'
Hath he forgot he is his sovereign?
Or doth this churlish superscription
Pretend some alteration in good will?
I Henry VI. Act iv, sc. 1, l. 50. [Gloucester] "Superscription" is repeated in *Timon of Athens*, ii, 2, 81.
Here is a silly stately style indeed!
The Turk, that two and fifty kingdoms hath,
Writes not so tedious a style as this.
I Henry VI. Act iv, sc. 7, l. 72. [La Pucelle]

5
Whose large style
Agrees not with the leanness of his purse.
II Henry VI. Act i, sc. 1, l. 111. [Gloucester]

6
King: A letter from the magnificent Armado. . . .
Biron: The style shall give us cause to climb in the merriness.
Love's Labour 's Lost. Act i, sc. 1, l. 192. The only use of "merriness."
I am much deceived but I remember the style.
Love's Labour 's Lost, iv, 1, 98. [Boyet]

7
I can construe the action of her familiar style.
The Merry Wives of Windsor. Act i, sc. 3, l. 50. [Falstaff]
I will aggravate his style.
The Merry Wives of Windsor. Act ii, sc. 2, l. 296. [Falstaff]

8
This was lofty!
A Midsummer-Night's Dream. Act i, sc. 2, l. 41. [Bottom]
A pretty period!
The Two Gentlemen of Verona. Act ii, sc. 1, l. 122. [Silvia]

9
Plain and not honest is too harsh a style.
Richard III. Act iv, sc. 4, l. 360. [Queen Elizabeth]

10
Why write I still all one, ever the same,
And keep invention in a noted weed,
That every word doth almost tell my name,
Showing their birth and where they did proceed?
Sonnets. No. lxxvi.
Making his style admired every where.
Sonnets. No. lxxxiv.
Theirs for their style I 'll read.—*Sonnets*, xxxii.
Mend the style.—*Sonnets*, lxxviii.

11
In polish'd form of well-refined pen.
Sonnets. No. lxxxv. The only use of "well-refined."
Writ the style of gods.—*Much Ado about Nothing*, v, 1, 37. See under PHILOSOPHY.

12
Your idle over-handled theme.
Venus and Adonis, l. 770. The only use of "over-handled."

SUBJECT

See also King and Subject

13
Alone, it was the subject of my theme.
The Comedy of Errors. Act v, sc. 1, l. 65. [Adriana]
'Tis a subject for a sovereign to reason on.
Henry V. Act iii, sc. 7, l. 38. [Dauphin]
I will have that subject newly writ o'er.
Love's Labour 's Lost. Act i, sc. 2, l. 120. [Armado]
I pray you choose another subject.
Much Ado about Nothing. Act v, sc. 1, l. 37. [Benedick]
It is too starved a subject for my sword.
Troilus and Cressida, i, 1, 96. See ARGUMENT.

14
Our subjects, sir, will not endure his yoke.
Cymbeline. Act iii, sc. 5, l. 4. [Cymbeline]

15
How many thousand of my poorest subjects
Are at this hour asleep!
II Henry IV. Act iii, sc. 1, l. 4. [King Henry]
Base subjects.—*Sonnets*, c.
Naked subject.—*II Henry IV*, i, 3, 61.

16
I am too mean a subject for thy wrath.
III Henry VI. Act i, sc. 3, l. 19. [Rutland]
Subjects to his hate.—*Richard III*, i, 3, 302.
Subject to a beast.—*Timon of Athens*, iv, 3, 347.
Subject to his birth.—*Hamlet*, i, 3, 18.
Subjects to command.—*II Henry VI*, ii, 2, 8.

Subject to your countenance.—*Henry VIII,* ii, 4, 26.
Subject to all discontents.—*Venus and Adonis,* l. 1161.
Subject to a duke.—*II Henry VI,* i, 3, 52.
Subject to Time's love.—*Sonnets,* cxxiv. See under TIME.
Subject to a tyrant.—*The Tempest,* iii, 2, 48.
Subject to a well-wished king.—*Measure for Measure,* ii, 4, 27. The only use of "well-wished."

1
You were sworn true subjects unto me.
III Henry VI. Act iii, sc. 1, l. 78. [King Henry] "True subjects" is used eight times in later plays.

Famous true subject.—*II Henry IV,* iv, 3, 70.
Careful subject.—*Henry VIII,* i, 2, 130.
Fair subject.—*Sonnets,* lxxxii.
Faithful subject.—*Henry V,* ii, 2, 161; *King John,* i, 1, 50.
Good subject.—*Richard II,* i, 1, 10.
Loving subjects.—*King John,* ii, 1, 204.
Noble subjects.—*Pericles,* ii, 4, 50.
Sworn subjects.—*Richard II,* v, 2, 39.
Tempted subject.—*The Two Gentlemen of Verona,* ii, 6, 8.
Tributary subject.—*Venus and Adonis,* l. 1045.

2
Your subjects Are in great grievance.
Henry VIII. Act i, sc. 2, l. 19. [Queen Katharine]

Rebellious subjects.—*Romeo and Juliet,* i, 1, 88.

3
The greatest monarch now alive may glory
In such an honour: how may I deserve it,
That am a poor and humble subject to you?
Henry VIII. Act v, sc. 3, l. 164. [Cranmer]

4
We are the King of England's subjects.
King John, ii, 1, 267. See under ENGLAND.

5
I hold you but a subject of this war,
Not as a brother.
King Lear. Act v, sc. 3, l. 60. [Albany]

6
Near approaches The subject of our watch.
Macbeth. Act iii, sc. 3, l. 8. [Murderer]

Subject of the land.—*Hamlet,* i, 1, 72.
Subject of mischance.—*I Henry VI,* iv, 6, 49.
Subject of my own soul's curse.—*Richard III,* iv, 1, 81.
Finny subject of the sea.—*Pericles,* ii, 1, 52.

7
His subject am I not, Nor here provincial.
Measure for Measure. Act v, sc. 1, l. 317. [Duke] "Provincial" is repeated in *Hamlet,* iii, 2, 288: "Provincial roses."

8
I am the unhappy subject of these quarrels.
The Merchant of Venice. Act v, sc. 1, l. 238. [Antonio]

Ridiculous subjects.—*Coriolanus,* ii, 1, 94.

9
Verges: If he will not stand when he is bidden, he is none of the prince's subjects.
Dogberry: True, and they are to meddle with none but the prince's subjects.
Much Ado about Nothing. Act iii, sc. 3, l. 32.

10
And subjects punish'd that ne'er thought offence.
Pericles. Act i, sc. 2, l. 28. [Pericles]

11
He is our subject, Mowbray; so art thou.
Richard II. Act i, sc. 1, l. 122. [King Richard]

I 'll swear myself thy subject.
The Tempest. Act ii, sc. 2, l. 156. [Caliban]

I am a subject.—*Richard II,* ii, 3, 133.

12
A puny subject strikes at thy great glory.
Richard II. Act iii, sc. 2, l. 86. [King Richard]

13
Like obedient subjects, follow him
To his new kingdom of perpetual rest.
Richard III. Act ii, sc. 2, l. 45. [Queen Elizabeth]

A loyal and obedient subject is
Therein illustrated.
Henry VIII. Act iii, sc. 2, l. 181. [King Henry] The only use of "illustrated."

Loyal subject.—*III Henry VI,* iv, 7, 44; *Henry V,* i, 2, 27.
Obedient subjects.—*I Henry VI,* iv, 2, 7.
Most obedient subject.—*Richard III,* iv, 2, 68.

14
Be subject To no sight but thine and mine.
The Tempest. Act i, sc. 2, l. 301. [Prospero]

SUBMISSION

See also Servility

15
I . . . do submit me to your highness' mercy.
Henry V. Act ii, sc. 2, l. 77. [Cambridge]

Submits her to thy might.—*Antony and Cleopatra,* iii, 12, 17.
Submit thee, boy.—*King John,* ii, 1, 159.
Submit thyself.—*I Henry VI,* v, 4, 130.
He shall submit.—*I Henry VI,* iii, 1, 118.

16
Submission, Dauphin! 'tis a mere French word;
We English warriors wot not what it means.
I Henry VI. Act iv, sc. 7, l. 54. [Lucy]

17
I commend this kind submission.
II Henry VI. Act v, sc. 1, l. 54. [Buckingham]

True submission.—*I Henry IV,* iii, 2, 28.

18
In all submission and humility.
II Henry VI, v, 1, 58. See under HUMILITY.

With all submission.—*King John,* v, 7, 103.

19
Submissive fall his princely feet before.
Love's Labour's Lost. Act iv, sc. 1, l. 92. [Boyet]

20
Be not as extreme in submission
As in offence.
The Merry Wives of Windsor. Act iv, sc. 3, l. 11. [Page]

21
What must the king do now? must he submit?
Richard II. Act iii, sc. 3, l. 143. [King Richard] See under KING.

1
O calm, dishonourable, vile submission!
Romeo and Juliet. Act iii, sc. 1, l. 76. [Mercutio]

SUBORNATION, see Bribery

SUBSTANCE

See also Property

2
Thy substance, valued at the highest rate,
Cannot amount unto a hundred marks.
Comedy of Errors. Act i, sc. 1, l. 24. [Duke]

3
He hath put all my substance into that fat belly of his.
II Henry IV, ii, 1, 81. See under EATING.

4
You have sent innumerable substance—
By what means got, I leave to your own conscience—
To furnish Rome, and to prepare the ways
You have for dignities.
Henry VIII. Act iii, sc. 2, l. 326. [Surrey] The only use of "innumerable."

Light or heavy in the substance.—*The Merchant of Venice,* iv, 1, 328.
Despised substance.—*Romeo and Juliet,* iii, 2, 77.
Dull substance.—*Sonnets,* xliv.
Heavy substance.—*King Lear,* iv, 6, 52.
Noble substance.—*Hamlet,* i, 4, 37.
Seeming substance.—*King Lear,* i, 1, 201.
Sightless substances.—*Macbeth,* i, 5, 50.
Of one substance bred.—*I Henry IV,* i, 1, 11.
Substance of my speech.—*II Henry IV,* iv, 1, 32.

5
I ken the wight: he is of substance good.
The Merry Wives of Windsor. Act i, sc. 3, l. 39. [Pistol]
Great in substance.—*Richard II,* iii, 2, 35.

6
You take the sum and substance that I have.
The Two Gentlemen of Verona. Act iv, sc. 1, l. 15. [Valentine]

7
What is your substance, whereof are you made?
Sonnets. No. liii.

II—Substance and Shadow

8
The son of the female is the shadow of the male: it is often so, indeed; but much of the father's substance!
II Henry IV. Act iii, sc. 2, l. 140. [Falstaff]

9
Countess: Long time thy shadow hath been thrall to me,
For in my gallery thy picture hangs:
But now the substance shall endure the like. . . .
Talbot: I laugh to see your ladyship so fond
To think that you have aught but Talbot's shadow
Whereon to practise your severity.
Countess: Why, art not thou the man?
Talbot: I am, indeed.
Countess: Then have I substance too.
Talbot: No, no, I am but shadow of myself:
You are deceived, my substance is not here;
For what you see is but the smallest part
And least proportion of humanity.
I Henry VI. Act ii, sc. 3, l. 36.

How say you, madam? are you now persuaded
That Talbot is but shadow of himself?
These are his substance, sinews, arms and strength.
I Henry VI. Act ii, sc. 3, l. 61. [Talbot]

10
The very substance of the ambitious is merely the shadow of a dream.
Hamlet. Act ii, sc. 2, l. 264. [Guildenstern]

11
The substance
Of that great shadow I did represent.
II Henry VI. Act i, sc. 1, l. 13. [Suffolk]

12
Yet look, how far
The substance of my praise doth wrong this shadow
In underprizing it, so far this shadow
Doth limp behind the substance.
The Merchant of Venice. Act iii, sc. 2, l. 127. [Bassanio] The only use of "underprizing."

13
Each substance of a grief hath twenty shadows,
Which shows like grief itself, but is not so.
Richard II. Act ii, sc. 2, l. 14. [Bushy]

Merely shadows to the unseen grief; . . .
There lies the substance.
Richard II, iv, 1, 299. See under GRIEF.

14
Shadows to-night
Have struck more terror to the soul of Richard
Than can the substance of ten thousand soldiers.
Richard III. Act v, sc. 3, l. 216. [King Richard]

15
Whilst that this shadow doth such substance give.
Sonnets, xxxvii.

What is your substance, whereof are you made,
That millions of strange shadows on you tend?
Since every one hath, every one, a shade,
And you, but one, can every shadow lend.
Sonnets. No. liii.

16
He takes false shadows for true substances.
Titus Andronicus. Act iii, sc. 2, l. 80. [Marcus]

17
Proteus: Since the substance of your perfect self
Is else devoted, I am but a shadow;
And to your shadow will I make true love.
Julia [Aside]: If 'twere a substance, you would, sure, deceive it,
And make it but a shadow as I am.
The Two Gentlemen of Verona. Act iv, sc. 2, l. 124.

SUBSTITUTE

See also Counterfeit, Imitation

1
Our substitutes in absence well invested.
II Henry IV. Act iv, sc. 4, l. 6. [King Henry]
Our substitutes at home shall have blank charters.
Richard II. Act i, sc. 4, l. 48. [King Richard]
2 Who is substituted 'gainst the French,
I have no certain notice.
II Henry IV. Act i, sc. 3, l. 84. [Hastings]
Substituted in the place of mine.—*Titus Andronicus,* iv, 2, 159. The only uses of "substituted." "Substitution" occurs only once, in *The Tempest,* i, 2, 103.
3
You speedy helpers, that are substitutes
Under the lordly monarch of the north,
Appear and aid me in this enterprise.
I Henry VI. Act v, sc. 3, l. 5. [La Pucelle]
This devil here shall be my substitute.
II Henry VI, iii, 1, 371. See under DEVIL.
Deputy-elect.—*Richard II,* iv, 1, 126. The only use of the phrase.
4
How will you do to content this substitute?
Measure for Measure. Act iii, sc. 1, l. 192. [Duke]
Duke: Were you sworn to the duke, or to the deputy?
Provost: To him and to his substitutes.
Measure for Measure. Act iv, sc. 2, l. 196.
The new deputy now for the duke.
Measure for Measure. Act i, sc. 2, l. 161. [Claudio]
Set on this wretched woman here
Against our substitute!
Measure for Measure. Act v, sc. 1, l. 132. [Duke]
First, hath this woman
Most wrongfully accused your substitute.
Measure for Measure. Act v, sc. 1, l. 139. [Friar Peter]
5
A substitute shines brightly as a king
Until a king be by.
The Merchant of Venice. Act v, sc. 1, l. 94. [Portia]
6
We have there a substitute of most allowed sufficiency.
Othello. Act i, sc. 3, l. 224. [Duke]
I left behind an ancient substitute.
Pericles. Act v, sc. 3, l. 51. [Pericles]
7 God's substitute,
His deputy anointed in His sight.
Richard II. Act i, sc. 2, l. 37. [Gaunt]
The breath of worldly men cannot depose
The deputy elected by the Lord.
Richard II, iii, 2, 57. See under KING.
'Great deputy, the welkin's viceregent and sole dominator of Navarre.'
Love's Labour's Lost. Act i, sc. 1, l. 221. [King, reading] The only use of "viceregent." "Dominator" is repeated in *Titus Andronicus,* ii, 3, 31 and iv, 1, 81.
Great deputy.—*King John,* ii, 1, 365.
Bitter deputy.—*Measure for Measure,* iv, 2, 81.
Corrupt deputy.—*Measure for Measure,* iii, 1, 265.
Good deputy.—*Measure for Measure,* iv, 1, 27.
Outward-sainted deputy.—*Measure for Measure,* iii, 1, 89. The only use of "outward-sainted."
Pernicious caitiff deputy.—*Measure for Measure,* v, 1, 88.
Strict deputy.—*Measure for Measure,* i, 2, 186.
Unworthy deputy.—*II Henry VI,* iii, 2, 286.
Deputy for Ireland.—*Henry VIII,* iii, 2, 260.
Deputy of Ireland.—*Henry VIII,* ii, 1, 42.

SUBTLETY

8
She is too subtle for thee; and her smoothness,
Her very silence and her patience
Speak to the people.
As You Like It. Act i, sc. 3, l. 79. [Duke] "Smoothness" is repeated in *Hamlet,* iii, 2, 9.
Subtle as Sphinx.—*Love's Labour's Lost,* iv, 3, 342. The only mention of the Sphinx.
Subtle as the fox.—*Cymbeline,* iii, 3, 40.
9
In him a plenitude of subtle matter
Applied to cautels, all strange forms receives.
A Lover's Complaint. l. 302. The only use of "plenitude." "Cautel" (trickery) is repeated in *Hamlet,* i, 3, 15.
10
'Tis the king's subtlety to have my life.
Pericles. Act ii, sc. 5, l. 44. [Pericles]
11
The subtle in themselves beguiled.
The Rape of Lucrece, l. 957.
12 You do yet taste
Some subtilties o' the isle, that will not let you
Believe things certain.
The Tempest. Act v, sc. 1, l. 123. [Prospero]
The world's false subtleties.—*Sonnets,* cxxxviii.

SUCCESS

13
Well, we cannot greatly condemn our success.
All's Well that Ends Well. Act iii, sc. 6, l. 58. [Bertram]
Give me leave to try success.—*All's Well that Ends Well,* i, 3, 253.
14
Smooth success Be strew'd before your feet!
Antony and Cleopatra. Act i, sc. 3, l. 100. [Cleopatra]
15 Would I might never
O'ertake pursued success.
Antony and Cleopatra. Act v, sc. 2, l. 103. [Dolabella]
16
He looks successfully.
As You Like It. Act i, sc. 2, l. 162. [Celia]
End successfully.—*The Taming of the Shrew,* iv, 1, 192.
Led . . . successfully.—*Titus Andronicus,* i, 1, 194. The only uses of "successfully."
17
And so success of mischief shall be born
And heir from heir shall hold this quarrel up

Whiles England shall have generation.
II Henry IV. Act iv, sc. 2, l. 47. [Hastings]

1
How shall I honour thee for this success?
I Henry VI. Act i, sc. 6, l. 5. [Charles]
Success unto our valiant general!
I Henry VI. Act v, sc. 2, l. 8. [Scout]
Success and victory.—*Richard III,* iv, 4, 193; v, 3, 165.
Pray for my success.—*The Two Gentlemen of Verona,* i, 1, 19.
Admired success.—*Cymbeline,* i, 1, 32.
Assured success.—*I Henry VI,* i, 2, 82.
Good success.—*III Henry VI,* iii, 3, 146; *Coriolanus,* i, 1, 264; *King Lear,* v, 3, 194; *Antony and Cleopatra,* ii, 4, 9.
Rare success.—*I Henry VI,* iv, 7, 62.
Well-found successes.—*Coriolanus,* ii, 2, 48. "Well-found" is repeated in *All's Well that Ends Well,* ii, 1, 105.

2
Things ill-got had ever bad success.
III Henry VI. Act ii, sc. 2, l. 46. [King Henry] The only use of "ill-got."
Dangerous success.—*Richard III,* iv, 4, 236.
Vile success.—*Othello,* iii, 3, 222.

3
All hitherto goes well.
III Henry VI. Act iv, sc. 2, l. 1. [Warwick]
Yet all goes well, yet all our joints are whole.
I Henry IV. Act iv, sc. 1, l. 83. [Hotspur]
Caper'd, and cried, 'All goes well.'—*Love's Labour's Lost,* v, 2, 113. The only use of "caper'd."

4
Commend me to my brother: soon at night
I'll send him certain word of my success.
Measure for Measure. Act i, sc. 4, l. 88. [Isabella]
Earnest of success.—*Macbeth,* i, 3, 90.

5 Doubt not but success
Will fashion the event in better shape
Than I can lay it down in likelihood.
Much Ado about Nothing. Act iv, sc. 1, l. 236. [Friar Francis]

6
Wordless, so greets heaven for his success.
The Rape of Lucrece, l. 112. The only use of "wordless."

7 Happily I have arrived at the last
Unto the wished haven of my bliss.
The Taming of the Shrew. Act v, sc. 1, l. 130. [Lucentio]
Bring him to the haven.—*Cymbeline,* i, 1, 171.
Happy havens.—*Richard II,* i, 3, 276.

8
Successful in the battles that he fights.
Titus Andronicus. Act i, sc. 1, l. 66. [Captain]

9 Success,
Although particular, shall give a scantling
Of good or bad unto the general.
Troilus and Cressida. Act i, sc. 3, l. 341. [Nestor] The only use of "scantling" (specimen, sample).

10
If thou hast her not i' the end, call me cut.
Twelfth Night. Act ii, sc. 3, l. 202. [Sir Toby]

Thou art made, if thou desirest to be so.
Twelfth Night. Act ii, sc. 5, l. 168. [Malvolio]

SUFFERING

See also Misery, Woe

11
Helena: You, Diana,
Under my poor instructions yet must suffer
Something in my behalf.
Diana: Let death and honesty
Go with your impositions, I am yours
Upon your will to suffer.
All's Well that Ends Well. Act iv, sc. 4, l. 26.

12
Truly in my youth I suffered much extremity for love.
Hamlet. Act ii, sc. 2, l. 190. [Polonius]
Suffer love.—*Much Ado about Nothing,* v, 2, 65.

13 Thou hast been
As one, in suffering all, that suffers nothing.
Hamlet, iii, 2, 70. See under CHARACTER.

14
Suffer the condition of these times.
II Henry IV. Act iv, sc. 1, l. 101. [Mowbray]
Suffer alteration.—*Winter's Tale,* iv, 4, 536.
Suffer dearth.—*Sonnets,* cxlvi.
Suffer ill report.—*Antony and Cleopatra,* ii, 2, 159.
Suffer indignity.—*The Tempest,* iii, 2, 42.
Suffer lawful censure.—*Coriolanus,* iii, 3, 46.
Suffer salvation.—*Much Ado about Nothing,* iii, 3, 3.
Suffer shipwreck.—*I Henry VI,* v, 5, 8.
Suffer surfeit.—*Twelfth Night,* ii, 4, 102.
Suffer wrong.—*Richard II,* ii, 1, 164.
Suffered wrong.—*Comedy of Errors,* v, 1, 398.
Suffers under probation.—*Twelfth Night,* ii, 5, 142.

15
But God be thanked for prevention;
Which I in sufferance heartily will rejoice.
Henry V. Act ii, sc. 2, l. 158. [Cambridge]
Corporal sufferance.—*Measure for Measure,* iii, 1, 80.
Noble sufferance.—*Coriolanus,* iii, 1, 24.
Patient sufferance.—*Much Ado about Nothing,* i, 3, 10.

16 A sufferance panging
As soul and body's severing.
Henry VIII. Act ii, sc. 3, l. 15. [Anne Bullen]
Her sufferance made
Almost each pang a death.
Henry VIII. Act v, sc. 1, l. 68. [Lovell]
Sufferance of our souls.—*Julius Cæsar,* ii, 1, 115.
Tame to sufferance.—*Sonnets,* lviii.

17
Who alone suffers suffers most i' the mind,
Leaving free things and happy shows behind:
But then the mind much sufferance doth o'erskip,
When grief hath mates, and bearing fellowship.
King Lear. Act iii, sc. 6, l. 111. [Edgar] The only use of "o'erskip."

Thy nature did commence in sufferance, time
Hath made thee hard in 't.
Timon of Athens. Act iv, sc. 3, l. 268. [Timon]

1
I suffer for the truth.
Love's Labour's Lost. Act i, sc. 1, l. 313. [Costard] See under TRUTH.
I suffer for it.—*The Merry Wives of Windsor,* iii, 3, 233.
Suffer in exposure.—*Macbeth,* ii, 3, 133.

2
Falstaff: I have suffered more for their sakes, more than the villanous inconstancy of man's disposition is able to bear.
Mistress Quickly: And have not they suffered? Yes, I warrant; speciously one of them.
The Merry Wives of Windsor. Act iii, sc. 4, l. 113. "Speciously" is repeated in iv, 5, 114, and occurs in no other play.
Nay, you shall hear, Master Brook, what I have suffered to bring this woman to evil for your good.
The Merry Wives of Windsor. Act iii, sc. 5, l. 96. [Falstaff]
I suffered the pangs of three several deaths.
The Merry Wives of Windsor, iii, 5, 109. See under DEATH.
Suffer'd death.—*Julius Cæsar,* iii, 2, 44; *Troilus and Cressida,* iv, 1, 74; *The Winter's Tale,* iii, 3, 42.

3
Thou . . . perforce must suffer.
Othello. Act v, sc. 2, l. 256. [Gratiano]
O, let me suffer.—*Sonnets,* lviii.
Let him suffer.—*Measure for Measure,* ii, 4, 97.

4
That they will suffer these abominations.
The Rape of Lucrece, l. 1832.
Shall we suffer this?—*III Henry VI,* i, 1, 59.
Do not suffer it!—*Richard III,* i, 3, 271.

5 O, I have suffer'd
With those that I saw suffer.
The Tempest. Act i, sc. 2, l. 5. [Miranda]
Wisely suffer.—*Timon of Athens,* iii, 5, 31.

6
Sure as I live, he had suffer'd for 't.
The Two Gentlemen of Verona. Act iv, sc. 4, l. 17. [Launce]
I so as truly suffer As e'er I did commit.
The Two Gentlemen of Verona. Act v, sc. 4, l. 76. [Proteus]

7
Not he alone shall suffer what wit can make heavy and vengeance bitter; but those that are germane to him, though removed fifty times, shall all come under the hangman.
The Winter's Tale. Act iv, sc. 4, l. 800. [Autolycus]

SUGGESTION

8
Take the hint Which my despair proclaims.
Antony and Cleopatra. Act iii, sc. 11, l. 18. [Antony]
When the best hint was given him, he not took 't.
Antony and Cleopatra. Act iii, sc. 4, l. 9. [Antony]
Posthumus . . . took his hint.—*Cymbeline,* v, 5, 172.
It is a hint that wrings mine eyes.
The Tempest. Act i, sc. 2, l. 134. [Miranda]
Ready for this hint.—*Coriolanus,* iii, 3, 23.
It was my hint to speak.—*Othello,* i, 3, 142.
Upon this hint I spake.—*Othello,* i, 3, 166.
Hint of woe.—*The Tempest,* ii, 1, 3. The only uses of "hint."

9
I 'ld turn it all To thy suggestion.
King Lear. Act ii, sc. 1, l. 75. [Edmund]
Misled by your suggestion.—*I Henry IV,* iv, 3, 51.
On your suggestion.—*King John,* iv, 2, 166.
Giddy loose suggestions.—*King John,* iii, 1, 292.

10
Suggestions are to other as to me.
Love's Labour's Lost. Act i, sc. 1, l. 159. [Biron]

11 Why do I yield to that suggestion
Whose horrid image doth unfix my hair
And make my seated heart knock at my ribs,
Against the use of nature?
Macbeth. Act i, sc. 3, l. 134. [Macbeth] "Unfix" is repeated in iv, 1, 96, and in *II Henry IV,* iv, 1, 208.

12
They 'll take suggestion as a cat laps milk;
They 'll tell the clock to any business that
We say befits the hour.
The Tempest. Act ii, sc. 1, l. 288. [Antonio]

SUICIDE

13
There is left us Ourselves to end ourselves.
Antony and Cleopatra. Act iv, sc. 14, l. 21. [Antony]
Is it sin
To rush into the secret house of death,
Ere death dare come to us?
Antony and Cleopatra. Act iv, sc. 15, l. 80. [Cleopatra]
That self hand,
Which writ his honour in the acts it did,
Hath, with the courage which the heart did lend it,
Splitted the heart.
Antony and Cleopatra. Act v, sc. 1, l. 21. [Dercetas]
It is great
To do that thing that ends all other deeds;
Which shackles accidents and bolts up change;
Which sleeps, and never palates more the dug.
Antony and Cleopatra. Act v, sc. 1, l. 4. [Cleopatra] The only use of "palates" as a verb.
This mortal house I 'll ruin.
Antony and Cleopatra. Act v, sc. 2, l. 51. [Cleopatra]

14 You good gods, give me
The penitent instrument to pick that bolt,
Then, free for ever!
Cymbeline. Act v, sc. 4, l. 9. [Posthumus]

15 That the Everlasting had not fix'd
His canon 'gainst self-slaughter!
Hamlet. Act i, sc. 2, l. 131. [Hamlet] The only use of "Everlasting" in this sense.
Against self-slaughter
There is a prohibition so divine

That cravens my weak hand.
Cymbeline. Act iii, sc. 4, l. 78. [Imogen] The only use of "prohibition" and of "cravens" as a verb. The only uses of "self-slaughter." "Self-slaughtered" occurs in *The Rape of Lucrece,* l. 1733.

1
For who would bear the whips and scorns of time,
The oppressor's wrong, the proud man's contumely,
The pangs of despised love, the law's delay,
The insolence of office and the spurns
That patient merit of the unworthy takes,
When he himself might his quietus make
With a bare bodkin? who would fardels bear,
To grunt and sweat under a weary life,
But that the dread of something after death,
The undiscover'd country from whose bourn
No traveller returns, puzzles the will
And makes us rather bear those ills we have
Than fly to others that we know not of?
Hamlet. Act iii, sc. 1, l. 70. [Hamlet] The only use of "contumely." "Quietus" occurs again in *Sonnets,* cxxvi; "oppressor" in *The Rape of Lucrece,* l. 905, and "grunt" in *A Midsummer-Night's Dream,* iii, 1, 113.

2
The corse they follow did with desperate hand
Fordo its own life.
Hamlet. Act v, sc. 1, l. 243. [Hamlet] The only use of "fordo." "Fordoes" occurs twice.

By self and violent hands Took off her life.
Macbeth. Act v, sc. 8, l. 70. [Malcolm]

3
Cassius: I know where I will wear this dagger then;
Cassius from bondage will deliver Cassius:
Therein, ye gods, you make the weak most strong;
Therein, ye gods, you tyrants do defeat:
Nor stony tower, nor walls of beaten brass,
Nor airless dungeon, nor strong links of iron,
Can be retentive to the strength of spirit;
But life, being weary of these worldly bars,
Never lacks power to dismiss itself.
If I know this, know all the world besides,
That part of tyranny that I do bear
I can shake off at pleasure.
Casca: So can I:
So every bondman in his own hand bears
The power to cancel his captivity.
Julius Cæsar. Act i, sc. 3, l. 89. The only use of "airless." "Retentive" is repeated in *Timon of Athens,* iii, 4, 82.

She fell distract,
And, her attendants absent, swallow'd fire.
Julius Cæsar. Act iv, sc. 3, l. 155. [Brutus]

By your leave, gods:—this is a Roman's part:
Come, Cassius' sword, and find Titinius' heart.
Julius Cæsar. Act v, sc. 3, l. 89. [Titinius]

Thou know'st that we two went to school together:
Even for that our love of old, I prithee,
Hold thou my sword-hilts, whilst I run on it.
Julius Cæsar. Act v, sc. 5, l. 26. [Brutus] The only use of "sword-hilts."

4
You ever-gentle gods, take my breath from me;
Let not my worser spirit tempt me again
To die before you please!
King Lear. Act iv, sc. 6, l. 221. [Gloucester] "Ever-gentle" is used again in *Macbeth,* iv, 3, 161: "Ever-gentle cousin."

5 With blade, with bloody blameful blade,
He bravely broach'd his boiling bloody breast.
A Midsummer-Night's Dream. Act v, sc. 1, l. 147. [Quince]

6
I will incontinently drown myself.
Othello. Act i, sc. 3, l. 306. [Roderigo] The only use of "incontinently."

And even with such-like valour men hang and drown
Their proper selves.
The Tempest. Act iii, sc. 3, l. 59. [Ariel]

7 Let it not be call'd impiety,
If in this blemish'd fort I make some hole
Through which I may convey this troubled soul.
The Rape of Lucrece, l. 1174.

8 Wilt thou slay thyself?
And slay thy lady too that lives in thee,
By doing damned hate upon thyself?
Romeo and Juliet. Act iii, sc. 3, l. 116. [Friar Laurence]

Did violence on herself.
Romeo and Juliet. Act v, sc. 3, l. 264. [Friar Laurence]

9
I 'll seek him deeper than e'er plummet sounded
And with him there lie mudded.
The Tempest. Act iii, sc. 3, l. 101. [Alonso] "Mudded" is used again in v, 1, 151, and in no other play

Deeper than did ever plummet sound.
The Tempest. Act v, sc. 1, l. 56. [Prospero] "Plummet" is used a third time in *The Merry Wives of Windsor,* v, 5, 173.

10
Marcus: Fie, brother, fie! teach her not thus to lay
Such violent hands upon her tender life. . . .
Titus: What violent hands can she lay on her life?
Titus Andronicus. Act iii, sc. 2, l. 21.

And she whom mighty kingdoms court'sy to,
Like a forlorn and desperate castaway,
Do shameful execution on herself.
Titus Andronicus. Act v, sc. 3, l. 74. [Marcus]

11
Theirs whose desperate hands themselves do slay.
Venus and Adonis, l. 765.

It should be noted that the word "suicide" does not occur in the plays.

SUIT

I—Apparel

1
Orlando: What, of my suit?
Rosalind: Not out of your apparel, and yet out of your suit.
As You Like It. Act iv, sc. 1, l. 87.
It is my only suit.—*As You Like It,* ii, 7, 44.
Strange suits.—*As You Like It,* iv, 1, 34.
2
Cloten: Hast any of thy late master's garments in thy possession?
Pisanio: I have, my lord, at my lodging, the same suit he wore when he took leave of my lady.
Cloten: The first service that thou dost me, fetch that suit hither.
Cymbeline. Act iii, sc. 5, l. 125.
Suit myself As does a Briton peasant.
Cymbeline, v, 1, 23. See under WEEDS.
3
Customary suits of solemn black.
Hamlet, i, 2, 78. See under SEEMING.
Suits of woe.—*Hamlet,* i, 2, 86.
Suit of sables.—*Hamlet,* iii, 2, 138.
4
Prince: For obtaining of suits?
Falstaff: Yea, for obtaining of suits, whereof the hangman hath no lean wardrobe.
I Henry IV. Act i, sc. 2, l. 80.
Buckram suits.—*I Henry IV,* ii, 4, 213; 228.
A horrid suit of the camp.—*Henry V,* iii, 6, 81.
Fresh suits.—*Henry V,* iv, 2, 57.
Three suits to his back.—*King Lear,* iii, 4, 141.
Page's suit.—*The Merchant of Venice,* ii, 4, 33.
5
Some one be ready with a costly suit
And ask him what apparel he will wear.
The Taming of the Shrew. Induction, sc. 1, l. 59. [Lord]
Go you to Barthol'mew my page,
And see him dress'd in all suits like a lady.
Taming of the Shrew. Induction, sc. 1, l. 105. [Lord]

II—Petition

6
Merchant: Arrest him at my suit. . . .
Officer: I do arrest you, sir: you hear the suit.
The Comedy of Errors. Act iv, sc. 1, l. 69.
Adriana: What, is he arrested? Tell me at whose suit.
Dromio of Syracuse: I know not at whose suit he is arrested well;
But he 's in a suit of buff which 'rested him, that can I tell.
The Comedy of Errors. Act iv, sc. 2, l. 43.
Say now, whose suit is he arrested at?
The Comedy of Errors. Act iv, sc. 4, l. 134. [Adriana]
7
I arrest you at the suit of Mistress Quickly.
II Henry IV. Act ii, sc. 1, l. 48. [Fang]
I arrest thee at the suit of Count Orsino.
Twelfth Night. Act iii, sc. 4, l. 360. [Officer]
Arrested at my suit.—*II Henry IV,* ii, 1, 77.
8
If I had a suit to Master Shallow, I would humour his men with the imputation of being near their master.
II Henry IV. Act v, sc. 2, l. 79. [Falstaff]
9
You may not, my lord, despise her gentle suit.
I Henry VI. Act ii, sc. 2, l. 47. [Burgundy]
Your several suits
Have been consider'd and debated on.
I Henry VI. Act v, sc. 2, l. 34. [King Henry]
10
Begin your suits anew, and sue to him.
II Henry VI. Act i, sc. 3, l. 42. [Queen]
Far be it we should honour such as these
With humble suit.
II Henry VI. Act iv, sc. 1, l. 123. [Suffolk]
Humble suit.—*Love's Labour 's Lost,* v, 2, 849.
Humblest suit.—*The Merry Wives of Windsor,* iii, 4, 20.
Great suit.—*Love's Labour 's Lost,* v, 2, 749.
Holy suit.—*Love's Labour 's Lost,* v, 2, 756.
Honest suit.—*Othello,* ii, 3, 347.
Importunate suit.—*Othello,* iv, 1, 26.
Mighty suit.—*Richard III,* iii, 7, 46.
Noble suit.—*A Lover's Complaint,* l. 234.
Personal suit.—*Othello,* i, 1, 9.
Presumptuous suit.—*All's Well that Ends Well,* i, 3, 204.
Unholy suits.—*Hamlet,* i, 3, 129.
Worldly suit.—*Richard III,* iii, 7, 63.
Wrongful suit.—*The Two Gentlemen of Verona,* ii, 2, 102.
Boldest suit of mirth.—*The Merchant of Venice,* ii, 2, 211.
Suit of night.—*Love's Labour 's Lost,* iv, 3, 255.
11
Dick: I have a suit unto your lordship.
Cade: Be it a lordship, thou shalt have it for that word.
II Henry VI. Act iv, sc. 7, l. 4.
12
Gloucester: Your highness will do well to grant her suit;
It were dishonour to deny it her.
King Edward: It were no less; but yet I 'll make a pause.
Gloucester: I see the lady hath a thing to grant
Before the king will grant her humble suit. . . .
King Edward: Widow, we will consider of your suit;
And come some other time to know our mind.
III Henry VI. Act iii, sc. 2, l. 8.
My suit is at an end.—*III Henry VI,* iii, 2, 81.
13
His suit was granted Ere it was ask'd.
Henry VIII. Act i, sc. 1, l. 186. [Buckingham]
Her suit is granted.—*III Henry VI,* iii, 2, 117.
Grant my suit.—*I Henry VI,* v, 3, 19.
May it please you, lords, to grant the commons' suit.
Richard II. Act iv, sc. 1, l. 154. [Northumberland]
O, make them joyful, grant their lawful suit.
Richard III. Act iii, sc. 7, l. 203. [Catesby]

1 Half your suit
Never name to us; you have half our power:
The other moiety, ere you ask, is given;
Repeat your will and take it.
Henry VIII. Act i, sc. 2, l. 10. [King Henry]

I have a suit which you must not deny me.
Henry VIII. Act v, sc. 3, l. 161. [King Henry]

2
Portia: Thou hast some suit to Cæsar, hast thou not?
Soothsayer: That I have, lady. . . .
Portia: Brutus hath a suit
That Cæsar will not grant.
Julius Cæsar. Act ii, sc. 4, l. 27.

Decius: Trebonius doth desire you to o'er-read,
At your best leisure, this his humble suit.
Artemidorus: O Cæsar, read mine first; for mine 's a suit
That touches Cæsar nearer: read it, great Cæsar.
Cæsar: What touches us ourself shall be last served.
Julius Cæsar. Act iii, sc. 1, l. 4.

3 Let it be our suit
That you have bid us ask his liberty.
King John. Act iv, sc. 2, l. 62. [Pembroke]

4
Vouchsafe to read the purpose of my coming,
And suddenly resolve me in my suit.
Love's Labour's Lost. Act ii, sc. 1, l. 109. [Princess of France]

What 's your suit?—*Measure for Measure,* ii, 2, 28.

Your suit 's unprofitable.—*Measure for Measure,* v, 1, 460.

5
The suit is impertinent to myself.
The Merchant of Venice. Act ii, sc. 2, l. 146. [Launcelot]

Gratiano: I have a suit to you.
Bassanio: You have obtain'd it.
The Merchant of Venice. Act ii, sc. 2, l. 186.

Thou hast obtain'd thy suit.—*The Merchant of Venice,* ii, 2, 153.

6
Your answer had not been inscroll'd:
Fare you well; your suit is cold.
The Merchant of Venice. Act ii, sc. 7, l. 72. [Prince of Morocco] The only use of "inscroll'd."

Bring him where his suit may be obtain'd.
The Rape of Lucrece, l. 898.

7
I follow thus A losing suit against him.
The Merchant of Venice. Act iv, sc. 1, l. 61. [Shylock]

Of a strange nature is the suit you follow.
The Merchant of Venice. Act iv, sc. 1, l. 177. [Portia]

8
Fenton: Shall I not lose my suit?
Mistress Quickly: Troth, sir, all is in his hands above.
Merry Wives of Windsor. Act i, sc. 4, l. 153.

My suit then is desperate; you 'll undertake her no more?
The Merry Wives of Windsor. Act iii, sc. 5, l. 126. [Ford]

9
The first suit is hot and hasty.
Much Ado about Nothing, ii, 1, 78. See WEDLOCK, 1647:15.

10 Nay, when I have a suit
Wherein I mean to touch your love indeed,
It shall be full of poise and difficult weight
And fearful to be granted.
Othello. Act iii, sc. 3, l. 82. [Desdemona] The only use of "difficult."

I 'll move your suit And seek to effect it.
Othello. Act iii, sc. 4, l. 166. [Desdemona]

I will give over my suit.—*Othello,* iv, 2, 201.

In thy suit be humble true.—*The Passionate Pilgrim,* l. 330.

11 By their vehement instigation,
In this just suit come I to move your grace.
Richard III. Act iii, sc. 7, l. 139. [Buckingham]

Call them again, my lord, and accept their suit.
Richard III. Act iii, sc. 7, l. 221. [Catesby]

What say you to my suit?—*Romeo and Juliet,* i, 2, 6.

Cease thy suit.—*Romeo and Juliet,* ii, 2, 153.

12
Wilt thou be pleased to hearken once again
to the suit I made to thee?
The Tempest. Act iii, sc. 2, l. 43. [Caliban]

13
She will admit no kind of suit.
Twelfth Night. Act i, sc. 2, l. 45. [Captain]

But, would you undertake another suit,
I had rather hear you to solicit that
Than music from the spheres.
Twelfth Night. Act iii, sc. 1, l. 119. [Olivia]

14
I hope my master's suit will be but cold,
Since she respects my mistress' love so much.
The Two Gentlemen of Verona. Act iv, sc. 4, l. 186. [Julia]

SUITOR

See also Wooing

15
They say poor suitors have strong breaths: they shall know we have strong arms too.
Coriolanus. Act i, sc. 1, l. 61. [Citizen]

16
A foolish suitor to a wedded lady.
Cymbeline. Act i, sc. 6, l. 2. [Imogen]

17
My humble duty remembered, I will not be your suitor.
II Henry IV. Act ii, sc. 1, l. 137. [Falstaff]

18
No humble suitors press to speak for right.
III Henry VI. Act iii, sc. 1, l. 19. [King Henry]

I am an humble suitor to your virtues.
Timon of Athens. Act iii, sc. 5, l. 7. [Alcibiades]

Humble-visaged suitors.—*Love's Labour 's Lost,* ii, 1, 34. The only use of "humble-visaged."

Common suitors.—*Julius Cæsar,* ii, 4, 35.

Princely suitors.—*Merchant of Venice,* i, 2, 38.
Renowned suitors.—*The Merchant of Venice,* i, 1, 169.

1 Nay, we must longer kneel: I am a suitor.
Henry VIII. Act i, sc. 2, l. 9. [Queen Katharine]
I am a woeful suitor to your honour.
Measure for Measure. Act ii, sc. 2, l. 27. [Isabella]

2 Troubled with a pernicious suitor.
Much Ado about Nothing. Act i, sc. 1, l. 130. [Beatrice]

3 She will not be annoy'd with suitors.
The Taming of the Shrew. Act i, sc. 1, l. 189. [Tranio]
Suitors to her and rivals in my love.
The Taming of the Shrew. Act i, sc. 2, l. 122. [Hortensio]
Hortensio: Sir, a word ere you go;
Are you a suitor to the maid you talk of, yea or no?
Tranio: And if I be, sir, is it any offence? . . .
And were his daughter fairer than she is,
She may more suitors have and me for one,
Fair Leda's daughter had a thousand wooers;
Then well one more may fair Bianca have.
The Taming of the Shrew. Act i, sc. 2, l. 229. Leda is mentioned again in *The Merry Wives of Windsor,* v, 5, 7. Her daughter, of course, was Helen of Troy.

SUM

See also Money

4 With well-weighing sums of gold, to corrupt him.
All's Well that Ends Well. Act iv, sc. 3, l. 203. [Soldier] The only use of "well-weighing."
I did send to you
For certain sums of gold, which you denied me.
Julius Cæsar. Act iv, sc. 3, l. 69. [Brutus]
When they shall know what men are rich,
They shall subscribe them for large sums of gold.
Richard II. Act i, sc. 4, l. 49. [King Richard]
Large sums of gold.—*II Henry VI,* i, 1, 129.
Sums in sealed bags.—*The Merry Wives of Windsor,* iii, 4, 16.
Sum of age.—*As You Like It,* iii, 2, 140.
Sum of parts.—*Hamlet,* iv, 7, 74.
Sums of love and wealth.—*Timon of Athens,* v, 1, 155.
Sum of good.—*Sonnets,* cix.

5 Beg thou, or borrow, to make up the sum.
Comedy of Errors. Act i, sc. 1, l. 154. [Duke]
Merchant: You know since Pentecost the sum is due,
And since I have not much importuned you. . . .
Angelo: Even just the sum that I do owe to you
Is growing to me by Antipholus.
The Comedy of Errors. Act iv, sc. 1, l. 1. "Pentecost" is mentioned again in *Romeo and Juliet,* i, 5, 38, and in *The Two Gentlemen of Verona,* iv, 4, 163.
He owes nine thousand; besides my former sum.
Timon of Athens, ii, 1, 2. See WASTE, 1634:22.
What is the sum he owes?—*The Comedy of Errors,* iv, 4, 136.

6 What is the gross sum that I owe thee?
II Henry IV. Act ii, sc. 1, l. 91. [Falstaff]
Gross sum.—*Love's Labour's Lost,* i, 2, 49.
Entire sum.—*Love's Labour's Lost,* ii, 1, 131.
Full sum.—*The Merchant of Venice,* iii, 2, 160.

7 Levy great sums of money through the realm.
II Henry VI, iii, 1, 61. See under TAXES.
Sum of money.—*Henry V,* iv, 1, 159; *I Henry VI,* v, 1, 52.

8 This is the very sum of all.
King John. Act ii, sc. 1, l. 151. [Lewis]
The sum of all I can, I have disclosed.
Richard III. Act ii, sc. 4, l. 46. [Messenger]
The sum of all.—*II Henry IV,* i, 1, 131; *Henry V,* iii, 6, 172.

9 To your audit comes
Their distract parcels in combined sums.
A Lover's Complaint, l. 230.

10 Three thousand ducats; 'tis a good round sum.
The Merchant of Venice. Act i, sc. 3, l. 104. [Shylock]
Portia: What sum owes he the Jew?
Bassanio: For me three thousand ducats.
The Merchant of Venice. Act iii, sc. 2, l. 300.
The very sum.—*Merchant of Venice,* iii, 2, 36.

11 I cannot sum up sum of half my wealth.
Romeo and Juliet. Act ii, sc. 6, l. 34. [Juliet]
So great a sum of sums.—*Sonnets,* iv.
Such sum or sums.—*The Merchant of Venice,* i, 3, 148.

12 'Tis said he gave his steward a mighty sum.
Timon of Athens. Act v, sc. 1, l. 9. [Painter]
Mighty sum.—*Henry V,* i, 2, 133.
Grand sum.—*Henry VIII,* iii, 2, 293.
Greater sum.—*Henry V,* i, 1, 79; *The Taming of the Shrew,* iii, 2, 137.
Petty sum.—*II Henry VI,* iv, 1, 22.
Present sum.—*The Merchant of Venice,* i, 1, 179.
Utmost sum.—*Sonnets,* xlix.

13 Sum my count and make my old excuse.
Sonnets. No. ii.
Sum and substance, see under SUBSTANCE.

SUMMARY

14 This fierce abridgement
Hath to it circumstantial branches, which
Distinction should be rich in.
Cymbeline. Act v, sc. 5, l. 382. [Cymbeline] "Circumstantial" is repeated in *As You Like It,* v, 4, 85.
Look, where my abridgement comes.
Hamlet. Act ii, sc. 2, l. 439.
What abridgement have you for this evening?
A Midsummer-Night's Dream, v, 1, 39.
This brief abridgement of my will I make.
The Rape of Lucrece, l. 1198.
Brook abridgement.—*Henry V,* v, Prol., 44
The only uses of "abridgement."

1
The summary of all our griefs.
II Henry IV. Act iv, sc. 1, l. 73. [Archbishop of York]
Summ'd the account of chance.—*II Henry IV,* i, 1, 167. The only use of "summ'd."
2
The continent and summary of my fortune.
The Merchant of Venice. Act iii, sc. 2, l. 131. [Bassanio]
3
Brief abstract and record of tedious days.
Richard III, iv, 4, 28. [Duchess of York]
Abstract and brief chronicles.—*Hamlet,* ii, 2, 548.
Abstract of all faults.—*Antony and Cleopatra,* i, 4, 9.
Abstract of success.—*All's Well that Ends Well,* iv, 3, 99.
This little abstract.—*King John,* ii, 1, 101.
He hath an abstract.—*The Merry Wives of Windsor,* iv, 2, 63. The only uses of "abstract."

SUMMER

See also Seasons

4 The time will bring on summer,
When briers shall have leaves as well as thorns,
And be as sweet as sharp.
All's Well that Ends Well. Act iv, sc. 4, l. 31. [Helena]
5
To be still hot summer's tanlings.
Cymbeline. Act iv, sc. 4, l. 29. [Belarius] The only use of "tanlings."
Hot summer.—*Henry V,* v, 2, 340.
Coming summer.—*The Winter's Tale,* i, 1, 6.
Costly summer.—*Merchant of Venice,* ii, 9, 94.
Glorious summer.—*Richard III,* i, 1, 2.
Beauty's summer.—*Sonnets,* civ.
Farewell, All-hallown summer!—*I Henry IV,* i, 2, 178. The only use of "All-hallown" (All-hallows).
6 Why should proud summer boast
Before the birds have any cause to sing?
Love's Labour's Lost. Act i, sc. 1, l. 102. [Biron]
Take heed, ere summer comes or cuckoo-birds do sing.
The Merry Wives of Windsor. Act ii, sc. 1, l. 127. [Pistol] The only use of "cuckoo-birds."
7
The summer still doth tend upon my state.
A Midsummer-Night's Dream. Act iii, sc. 1, l. 158. [Titania]
The middle summer's spring.—*A Midsummer-Night's Dream,* ii, 1, 82.
Middle summer.—*The Winter's Tale,* iv, 4, 107.
8
While summer-days do last.
Pericles. Act iv, sc. 1, l. 18. [Marina] The only use of the hyphenated phrase.
A summer's day will seem an hour but short.
Venus and Adonis, l. 23.
Shall I compare thee to a summer's day?—*Sonnets,* xviii.
9
Till twice five summers have enrich'd our fields.
Richard II, i, 3, 141. [King Richard]
10
Short summers lightly have a forward spring.
Richard III. Act iii, sc. 1, l. 94. [Gloucester]
11
For never-resting time leads summer on
To hideous winter and confounds him there;
Sap check'd with frost and lusty leaves quite gone,
Beauty o'ersnow'd and bareness every where.
Sonnets. No. v. The only use of "never-resting" and "o'ersnow'd."
And summer's green all girded up in sheaves
Borne on the bier with white and bristly beard.
Sonnets. No. xii. "Girded" is repeated in *Henry V,* iii, Prol., 27.
Summer's lease hath all too short a date.
Sonnets. No. xviii.
Thy eternal summer shall not fade.
Sonnets. No. xviii.
When summer's breath their masked buds discloses.
Sonnets. No. liv.
O, how shall summer's honey breath hold out
Against the wreckful siege of battering days,
When rocks impregnable are not so stout,
Nor gates of steel so strong, but Time decays
Sonnets. No. lxv. The only use of "wreckful.
Making no summer of another's green.
Sonnets. No. lxviii.
This time removed was summer's time.
Sonnets. No. xcvii.
Yet nor the lays of birds nor the sweet smell
Of different flowers in odour and in hue
Could make me any summer's story tell.
Sonnets. No. xcviii.
Not that the summer is less pleasant now.
Sonnets. No. cii.
12
This goodly summer with your winter mix'd.
Titus Andronicus. Act v, sc. 2, l. 172. [Titus]

SUN

13 Indian-like,
Religious in mine error, I adore
The sun, that looks upon his worshipper,
But knows of him no more.
All's Well that Ends Well. Act i, sc. 3, l. 210. [Helena] The only use of "Indian-like."
14 O sun,
Burn the great sphere thou movest in! darkling stand
The varying shore o' the world.
Antony and Cleopatra. Act iv, sc. 15, l. 9. [Cleopatra]
15
To hide me from the radiant sun and solace
I' the dungeon by a snuff?
Cymbeline. Act i, sc. 6, l. 86. [Iachimo]
Afric sun.—*Troilus and Cressida,* i, 3, 370.
Almighty sun.—*Troilus and Cressida,* v, 2, 173.
All-seeing sun.—*Romeo and Juliet,* i, 2, 97. "All-seeing" is repeated in *Richard III,* ii, 1, 82: "All-seeing heaven."
Bright sun of heaven.—*Henry VIII,* v, 5, 51.
Burnish'd sun.—*The Merchant of Venice,* ii,

1, 2. "Burnish'd" is repeated in *Antony and Cleopatra,* ii, 2, 196: "Burnish'd throne."
Cheerful sun.—*Titus Andronicus,* ii, 3, 13.
Evening sun.—*The Comedy of Errors,* i, 1, 28.
Fair sun.—*The Comedy of Errors,* iii, 2, 56; *Love's Labour's Lost,* iv, 3, 69; *Richard II,* v, 1, 35; *Richard III,* i, 2, 263; *Romeo and Juliet,* ii, 2, 4; *The Rape of Lucrece,* l. 1230.
Fiery sun.—*Coriolanus,* v, 3, 60.
Garish sun.—*Romeo and Juliet,* iii, 2, 25. "Garish" is repeated in *Richard III,* iv, 4, 89: "Garish flag."
Glorious sun.—*II Henry VI,* ii, 1, 22, and eight times in later plays.
Golden sun.—*Love's Labour's Lost,* iv, 3, 26; *Henry V,* ii, 4, 58.
Half-faced sun.—*II Henry VI,* iv, 1, 98.
Holy sun.—*Cymbeline,* iv, 4, 41.
Powerful sun.—*King Lear,* ii, 4, 169.
Warm sun.—*King Lear,* ii, 2, 169.
Yonder sun.—*Hamlet,* iv, 5, 65.
Beauty's sun.—*III Henry VI,* iii, 3, 126.
Suns of glory.—*Henry VIII,* i, 1, 6.
'Twixt sun and sun.—*Cymbeline,* iii, 2, 70.

1
I am too much i' the sun.
Hamlet. Act i, sc. 2, l. 67. [Hamlet]

The sun breed maggots in a dead dog, being a god kissing carrion.
Hamlet. Act ii, sc. 2, l. 181. [Hamlet]

2
Yet herein will I imitate the sun,
Who doth permit the base contagious clouds
To smother up his beauty from the world,
That, when he please again to be himself,
Being wanted, he may be more wonder'd at,
By breaking through the foul and ugly mists
Of vapours that did seem to strangle him.
I Henry IV. Act i, sc. 2, l. 220. [Prince of Wales]

Shall the blessed sun of heaven prove a micher and eat blackberries? a question not to be asked.
I Henry IV. Act ii, sc. 4, l. 448. [Falstaff] The only use of "micher" (sneak). "Blackberries" occurs again in l. 265 of the same scene, "Plentiful as blackberries," and nowhere else. "Blackberry" is used once, in *Troilus and Cressida,* where Thersites says that Ulysses is "not worth a blackberry."

3
Gorgeous as the sun at midsummer.
I Henry IV. Act iv, sc. 1, l. 102. [Vernon]

As clear as is the summer's sun.
Henry V. Act i, sc. 2, l. 86. [Canterbury]

Clear sun.—*Henry VIII,* i, 1, 226.

4
The sun doth gild our armour; up, my lords!
Henry V. Act iv, sc. 2, l. 1. [Orleans]

The sun is high and we outwear the day.
Henry V. Act iv, sc. 2, l. 63. [Constable]

5
One eye thou hast, to look to heaven for grace:
The sun with one eye vieweth all the world.
I Henry VI. Act i, sc. 4, l. 83. [Talbot]

6
Edward: Dazzle mine eyes, or do I see three suns?
Richard: Three glorious suns, each one a perfect sun;
Not separated with the racking clouds,
But sever'd in a pale clear-shining sky.
III Henry VI. Act ii, sc. 1, l. 25. The only use of "racking" and "clear-shining."

Whate'er it bodes, henceforward will I bear
Upon my target three fair-shining suns.
III Henry VI. Act ii, sc. 1, l. 40. [Edward] The only use of "fair-shining."

What, hath the firmament more suns than one?
Titus Andronicus. Act v, sc. 3, l. 17. [Saturninus]

Now they are but one lamp, one light, one sun.
III Henry VI. Act ii, sc. 1, l. 31. [Richard]

7
Sunshine brew'd a shower for him.
III Henry VI. Act ii, sc. 2, l. 156. [Edward]

A sunshine and a hail . . . at once.—*All's Well that Ends Well,* v, 3, 33.
Sunshine and rain at once.—*King Lear,* iv, 3, 20.
Our sunshine made thy spring.—*III Henry VI,* ii, 2, 163.
Sunshine day.—*III Henry VI,* ii, 1, 187; *Richard II,* iv, 1, 121.
Sunshine of your face.—*Love's Labour's Lost,* v, 2, 201.
Sunshine of his favour.—*II Henry IV,* iv, 2, 12. The only uses of "sunshine."

8
I wonder
That such a keech can with his very bulk
Take up the rays o' the beneficial sun
And keep it from the earth.
Henry VIII. Act i, sc. 1, l. 54. [Buckingham] The only use of "keech" (a lump of fat).

No sun shall ever usher forth mine honours,
Or gild again the noble troops that waited
Upon my smiles.
Henry VIII. Act iii, sc. 2, l. 410. [Wolsey]

9
To solemnize this day the glorious sun
Stays in his course and plays the alchemist,
Turning with splendour of his precious eye
The meagre cloddy earth to glittering gold.
King John. Act iii, sc. 1, l. 77. [King Philip] The only use of "cloddy."

The sun's o'ercast with blood.
King John. Act iii, sc. 1, l. 326. [Blanch]

10
Approach, thou beacon to this under globe.
King Lear. Act ii, sc. 2, l. 170. [Kent]

Heaven's fiery eye.—*Love's Labour's Lost,* v, 2, 375.
The travelling lamp.—*Macbeth,* ii, 4, 7.

11
O, 'tis the sun that maketh all things shine.
Love's Labour's Lost. Act iv, sc. 3, l. 246. [Biron]

12
I 'gin to be aweary of the sun,
And wish the estate o' the world were now undone.
Macbeth. Act v, sc. 5, l. 49. [Macbeth]

13
Then did the sun on dunghill shine.
The Merry Wives of Windsor. Act i, sc. 3, l. 70. [Pistol]

14
Thou fair sun, that on this earth doth shine.
The Passionate Pilgrim, l. 38.

The sun look'd on the world with glorious eye.
The Passionate Pilgrim, l. 81.

Shine sun, to succour flowers!
The Passionate Pilgrim, l. 208.

1 The fair and fiery-pointed sun,
Rushing from forth a cloud, bereaves our sight.
The Rape of Lucrece, l. 372. The only use of "fiery-pointed."

Or if thou wilt permit the sun to climb
His wonted height, yet ere he go to bed,
Knit poisonous clouds about his golden head.
The Rape of Lucrece, l. 775.

Heaven's fair sun that breeds the fat earth's store.
The Rape of Lucrece, l. 1837.

2 This must my comfort be,
That sun that warms you here shall shine on me;
And those his golden beams to you here lent
Shall point on me and gild my banishment.
Richard II. Act i, sc. 3, l. 144. [Bolingbroke]

See, see, King Richard doth himself appear,
As doth the blushing discontented sun
From out the fiery portal of the east,
When he perceives the envious clouds are bent
To dim his glory and to stain the track
Of his bright passage to the occident.
Richard II. Act iii, sc. 3, l. 62. [Bolingbroke] "Portal" is used only once again, in *Hamlet,* iii, 4, 136.

From sun to sun.—*Richard II,* iv, 1, 55.

3
King Richard: Tell the clock there. Give me a calendar.
Who saw the sun to-day?
Ratcliff: Not I, my lord.
King Richard: Then he disdains to shine; for by the book
He should have braved the east an hour ago.
Richard III. Act v, sc. 3, l. 276.

The sun will not be seen to-day;
The sky doth frown and lour upon our army.
Richard III. Act v, sc. 3, l. 282. [King Richard]

The sun, for sorrow, will not show his head.
Romeo and Juliet. Act v, sc. 3, l. 306. [Prince]

4
Sitting in the sun under the dove-house wall.
Romeo and Juliet. Act i, sc. 3, l. 27. [Nurse] "Dove-house" is repeated in l. 33, and occurs in no other scene.

Now is the sun upon the highmost hill
Of this day's journey.
Romeo and Juliet. Act ii, sc. 5, l. 9. [Juliet] The only use of "highmost" in the plays. It is repeated in *Sonnets,* vii, "Highmost pitch." See below.

Mid-day sun.—*I Henry VI,* i, 1, 14; *III Henry VI,* v, 2, 17; *Venus and Adonis,* l. 750.

Noontide sun.—*The Tempest,* v, 1, 42.

5
Lo! in the orient when the gracious light
Lifts up his burning head, each under eye
Doth homage to his new-appearing sight,
Serving with looks his sacred majesty;
And having climb'd the steep-up heavenly hill,
Resembling strong youth in his middle age,
Yet mortal looks adore his beauty still,
Attending on his golden pilgrimage;
But when from highmost pitch, with weary car,
Like feeble age, he reeleth from the day,
The eyes, 'fore duteous, now converted are
From his low tract and look another way.
Sonnets. No. vii. "Steep-up hill" is used again in *The Passionate Pilgrim* l. 121; "highmost" in *Romeo and Juliet,* ii, 5, 9; and "new-appearing" in *Richard III,* iv, 4, 10: "New-appearing sweets."

Sometime too hot the eye of heaven shines,
And often is his gold complexion dimm'd.
Sonnets. No. xviii.

Even so my sun one early morn did shine
With all-triumphant splendour on my brow.
Sonnets. No. xxxiii. The only use of "all-triumphant."

Suns of the world may stain when heaven's sun staineth.
Sonnets. No. xxxiii.

The sun itself sees not till heaven clears.
Sonnets. No. cxlviii.

6
Why, so this gallant will command the sun.
The Taming of the Shrew. Act iv, sc. 3, l. 198. [Hortensio]

7
O blessed breeding sun, draw from the earth
Rotten humidity; below thy sister's orb
Infect the air!
Timon of Athens. Act iv, sc. 3, l. 1. [Timon] "Humidity" is repeated in *The Merry Wives of Windsor,* iii, 3, 43: "Unwholesome humidity."

Thou sun, that comfort'st, burn!
Timon of Athens, v, 1, 134.

Sun, hide thy beams!—*Timon of Athens,* v, 1, 226.

8
Is the sun dimm'd, that gnats do fly in it?
Titus Andronicus. Act iv, sc. 4, l. 82. [Tamora]

Here never shines the sun.—*Titus Andronicus,* ii, 3, 96.

9 Therefore is the glorious planet Sol
In noble eminence enthroned and sphered
Amidst the other; whose medicinable eye
Corrects the ill aspects of planets evil.
Troilus and Cressida. Act i, sc. 3, l. 89. [Ulysses] The only use of "Sol" in this meaning. "Sphered" is repeated in iv, 5, 8, and occurs in no other play.

10
The sun doth burn my face; I must remove.
Venus and Adonis, l. 186.

Nor sun nor wind will ever strive to kiss you. . . .
The sun doth scorn you and the wind doth hiss you.
Venus and Adonis, l. 1082.

11
The sun that shines from heaven shines but warm.
Venus and Adonis, l. 193.

The sun shines hot.—*III Henry VI,* iv, 8, 60.
See under WINTER.

12 Thou clear god, and patron of all light,
From whom each lamp and shining star doth borrow

The beauteous influence that makes him bright.
Venus and Adonis, l. 860.

Sun and sharp air
Lurk'd like two thieves, to rob him of his fair.
Venus and Adonis, l. 1085.

1
The selfsame sun that shines upon his court
Hides not his visage from our cottage but
Looks on alike.
The Winter's Tale. Act iv, sc. 4, l. 454. [Perdita]

The sun looking with a southward eye upon him.
The Winter's Tale. Act iv, sc. 4, l. 819. [Autolycus] "Southward" is used again in *Coriolanus,* ii, 3, 32.

II—Sun and Moon

2
But, soft! what light through yonder window breaks?
It is the east, and Juliet is the sun.
Arise, fair sun, and kill the envious moon,
Who is already sick and pale with grief,
That thou her maid art far more fair than she:
Be not her maid, since she is envious;
Her vestal livery is but sick and green,
And none but fools do wear it.
Romeo and Juliet. Act ii, sc. 2, l. 2. [Romeo]

3
Petruchio: Good Lord, how bright and goodly shines the moon!
Katharina: The moon! the sun: it is not moonlight now.
Petruchio: I say it is the moon that shines so bright.
Katharina: I know it is the sun that shines so bright.
Petruchio: Now, by my mother's son, and that 's myself,
It shall be moon, or star, or what I list,
Or ere I journey to your father's house. . . .
I say it is the moon.
Katharina: I know it is the moon.
Petruchio: Nay, then you lie: it is the blessed sun.
Katharina: Then, God be bless'd, it is the blessed sun:
But sun it is not, when you say it is not;
And the moon changes even as your mind.
The Taming of the Shrew. Act iv, sc. 5, l. 2.

4
Teach me how
To name the bigger light, and how the less,
That burn by day and night.
The Tempest. Act i, sc. 2, l. 334. [Caliban]

5
Alcibiades: How came the noble Timon to this change?
Timon: As the moon does, by wanting light to give:
But then renew I could not, like the moon;
There were no suns to borrow of.
Timon of Athens. Act iv, sc. 3, l. 66.

6
She framed thee in high heaven's despite,
To shame the sun by day and her by night.
Venus and Adonis, l. 731.

III—Phœbus, Phaethon, and Hyperion

7
Full thirty times hath Phœbus' cart gone round.
Hamlet. Act iii, sc. 2, l. 165. [Player King]

Holy Phœbus' car.—*Antony and Cleopatra,* iv, 8, 29.
The wheels of Phœbus.—*Much Ado about Nothing,* v, 3, 26.
Phœbus' wheel.—*Cymbeline,* v, 5, 190.
Phœbus' burning kisses.—*Coriolanus,* ii, 1, 234.
Sweats in the eye of Phœbus.—*Henry V,* iv, 1, 290.

8
Phœbus, he, 'that wandering knight so fair.'
I Henry IV. Act i, sc. 2, l. 16. [Falstaff]

Bright Phœbus.—*The Winter's Tale,* iv, 4, 124.
Flickering Phœbus.—*King Lear,* ii, 2, 114.
Golden Phœbus.—*Antony and Cleopatra,* v, 2, 320.
Young Phœbus.—*Henry V,* iii, Prol., 6.
Youthful Phœbus.—*Troilus and Cressida,* i, 3, 230.

9
O Phœbus, hadst thou never given consent
That Phaethon should check thy fiery steeds,
Thy burning car never had scorch'd the earth!
III Henry VI. Act ii, sc. 6, l. 11. [Clifford]

Phœbus' steeds are founder'd.
The Tempest. Act iv, sc. 1, l. 30. [Ferdinand]

10
Gallop apace, you fiery-footed steeds,
Towards Phœbus' lodging: such a waggoner
As Phaethon would whip you to the west,
And bring in cloudy night immediately.
Romeo and Juliet. Act iii, sc. 2, l. 1. [Juliet] The only use of "fiery-footed."

Her waggoner a small grey-coated gnat.
Romeo and Juliet. Act i, sc. 4, l. 64, [Mercutio] The only use of "grey-coated."

I 'll come and be thy waggoner.
Titus Andronicus. Act v, sc. 2, l. 48. [Titus] The only uses of "waggoner."

11
Even from Hyperion's rising in the east
Until his very downfall in the sea.
Titus Andronicus. Act v, sc. 2, l. 56. [Titus]

Help Hyperion to his horse.—*Henry V,* iv, 1, 292.
Hyperion's quickening fire.—*Timon of Athens,* iv, 3, 184.
Hyperion's curls.—*Hamlet,* iii, 4, 56.
Great Hyperion.—*Troilus and Cressida,* ii, 3, 207.
Hyperion to a satyr.—*Hamlet,* i, 2, 140.

12
Why, Phaethon,—for thou art Merops' son—
Wilt thou aspire to guide the heavenly car
And with thy daring folly burn the world?
The Two Gentlemen of Verona. Act iii, sc. 1, l. 153. [Duke, reading] The only mention of Merops.

Down, down I come, like glistering Phaethon,
Wanting the manage of unruly jades.
Richard II. Act iii, sc. 3, l. 178. [King Richard]

SUNRISE

See also Dawn, Morning

1
O sun, thy uprise shall I see no more.
Antony and Cleopatra. Act iv, sc. 12, l. 18. [Antony]

Sun's uprise.—*Titus Andronicus,* iii, 1, 159. The only uses of "uprise."

2
At length the sun, gazing upon the earth,
Dispersed those vapours.
The Comedy of Errors. Act i, sc. 1, l. 89. [Ægeon]

3
The heavenly-harness'd team
Begins his golden progress in the east.
I Henry IV. Act iii, sc. 1, l. 221. [Glendower] The only use of "heavenly-harness'd."

How bloodily the sun begins to peer
Above yon busky hill!
I Henry IV. Act v, sc. 1, l. 1. [King Henry] The only use of "busky" (bosky, bushy).

4
When the morning sun shall raise his car
Above the border of this horizon.
III Henry VI. Act iv, sc. 7, l. 80. [King Edward] The only use of "horizon."

5
Here, as I point my sword, the sun arises.
Julius Cæsar. Act ii, sc. 1, l. 106. [Casca]

6
Enter there [heaven] Ere sunrise.
Measure for Measure, ii, 2, 153. See PRAYER The only use of "sunrise."

Before sunrising.—*Richard III,* v, 3, 61. The only use of "sunrising."

7
From under this terrestrial ball
He fires the proud tops of the eastern pines.
Richard II. Act iii, sc. 2, l. 41. [King Richard] "Terrestrial" is repeated in *The Merry Wives of Windsor,* iii, 1, 108.

Who doth the world so gloriously behold
That cedar-tops and hills seem burnish'd gold.
Venus and Adonis, l. 857. The only use of "cedar-tops."

The sun no sooner shall the mountains touch,
Than we will ship him hence.
Hamlet. Act iv, sc. 1, l. 29. [King]

8
An hour before the worshipp'd sun
Peer'd forth the golden window of the east.
Romeo and Juliet. Act i, sc. 1, l. 125. [Benvolio]

9
All so soon as the all-cheering sun
Should in the furthest east begin to draw
The shady curtains from Aurora's bed.
Romeo and Juliet. Act i, sc. 1, l. 140. [Montague] The only use of "all-cheering."

Yonder shines Aurora's harbinger.—*A Midsummer-Night's Dream,* iii, 2, 380. The only uses of Aurora.

10
Ere the sun advance his burning eye,
The day to cheer and night's dank dew to dry.
Romeo and Juliet. Act ii, sc. 3, l. 5. [Friar Laurence]

11
Truly not the morning sun of heaven
Better becomes the grey cheeks of the east.
Sonnets. No. cxxxii.

12
As when the golden sun salutes the morn,
And, having gilt the ocean with his beams,
Gallops the zodiac in his glistering coach,
And overlooks the highest-peering hills.
Titus Andronicus. Act ii, sc. 1, l. 5. [Aaron] The only use of "highest-peering." "Zodiac" is repeated in *Measure for Measure,* i, 2, 172.

SUNSET

13
Ere the weary sun set in the west.
The Comedy of Errors. Act i, sc. 2, l. 7. [Merchant]

Thy sun sets weeping in the lowly west.
Richard II, ii, 4, 21. See under GLORY.

14
The sun of heaven methought was loath to set,
But stay'd and made the western welkin blush.
King John. Act v, sc. 5, l. 1. [Dauphin]

The old, feeble, and day-wearied sun.—*King John,* v, 4, 35. The only use of "day-wearied."

15
O setting sun,
As in thy red rays thou dost sink to night,
So in his red blood Cassius' day is set;
The sun of Rome is set!
Julius Cæsar. Act v, sc. 3, l. 60. [Titinius]

The setting sun.—*Richard II,* ii, 1, 12.
Descending sun.—*Venus and Adonis,* l. 190.
Ere the set of sun.—*Macbeth,* i, 1, 5.
After sunset.—*Sonnets,* lxxiii.
Ere sunset.—*III Henry VI,* ii, 2, 116; *King John,* iii, 1, 110.

16
When the sun sets, who doth not look for night?
Richard III, ii, 3, 34. See under NIGHT.

When the sun sets, the air doth drizzle dew.
Romeo and Juliet, iii, 5, 127. The only use of "drizzle." "Drizzles" occurs in *Much Ado about Nothing,* iii, 3, 111: "It drizzles rain." "Drizzled" is also used twice, in *The Comedy of Errors,* v, 1, 312: "Drizzled snow"; and in *Julius Cæsar,* ii, 2, 21: "Drizzled blood."

17
The weary sun hath made a golden set,
And, by the bright track of his fiery car,
Gives signal of a goodly day to-morrow.
Richard III. Act v, sc. 3, l. 19. [Richmond] "Track" is used only once again, in *Richard II,* iii, 3, 66.

Much about cockshut time.
Richard III. Act v, sc. 3, l. 70. [Ratcliff] A cockshut was a large net for catching woodcock, and cockshut time was twilight, when the net was commonly used to catch the woodcock as they went out to feed. The only use of the word.

18
The sun begins to set; . . .
Ugly night comes breathing at his heels.
Troilus and Cressida, v, 8, 5. [Achilles]

The sun begins to gild the western sky.
The Two Gentlemen of Verona. Act v, sc. 1, l. 1. [Eglamour]

1
Look, the world's comforter, with weary gait,
His day's hot task hath ended in the west.
Venus and Adonis, l. 529.

SUPERSTITION

See also Omen

2
Have I with all my full affections
Still met the king? loved him next heaven? obey'd him?
Been, out of fondness, superstitious to him?
Henry VIII. Act iii, sc. 1, l. 129. [Queen]
He is superstitious grown of late,
Quite from the main opinion he held once
Of fantasy, of dreams and ceremonies.
Julius Cæsar. Act ii, sc. 1, l. 195. [Cassius]
Superstitious eld.—*The Merry Wives of Windsor,* iv, 4, 36.
Superstitious girl.—*Troilus and Cressida,* v, 3, 79. The only uses of "superstitious."
Superstitiously, I will be squared.—*The Winter's Tale,* iii, 3, 40.
Superstitiously doth swear.—*Pericles,* iv, 3, 49. The only uses of "superstitiously."

3
First Sailor: The sea works high, the wind is loud, and will not lie till the ship be cleared of the dead.
Pericles: That 's your superstition.
Pericles. Act iii, sc. 1, l. 48.
Do not say 'tis superstition, that
I kneel and then implore her blessing.
The Winter's Tale. Act v, sc. 3, l. 43. [Perdita] The only uses of "superstition."

SUPPER

4
Avoid then, fiend! what tell'st thou me of supping?
The Comedy of Errors. Act iv, sc. 3, l. 66. [Antipholus of Syracuse] The only use of "supping."

5
King: Now, Hamlet, where 's Polonius?
Hamlet: At supper.
King: At supper! where?
Hamlet: Not where he eats, but where he is eaten: a certain convocation of politic worms are e'en at him.
Hamlet. Act iv, sc. 3, l. 17. "Convocation" is repeated in *Henry V,* i, 1, 76: "Spiritual convocation."

6
I have bespoke supper to-morrow night in Eastcheap.
I Henry IV. Act i, sc. 2, l. 144. [Poins]
There I 'll sup.—*I Henry IV,* i, 2, 217.
There they intend to sup.—*The Winter's Tale,* v, 2, 112.

7
I hope you 'll come to supper.
II Henry IV. Act ii, sc. 1, l. 172. [Hostess]
Will you sup with me?—*II Henry IV,* ii, 1, 201.
Invited her to supper.—*Antony and Cleopatra,* ii, 2, 225.

8
Now it is supper-time in Orleans.
I Henry VI. Act i, sc. 4, l. 59. [Salisbury]
It 's supper-time, my lord.—*Richard III,* v, 3, 47.
It is now high supper-time.—*Othello,* iv, 2, 249.
At supper-time I 'll visit you.—*The Comedy of Errors,* iii, 2, 179.
We will visit you at supper-time.—*The Merchant of Venice,* ii, 2, 215.
Slink away in supper-time.—*The Merchant of Venice,* ii, 4, 1.
'Twill be supper-time ere you come.—*The Taming of the Shrew,* iv, 3, 192.
Ere supper-time.—*The Tempest,* iii, 1, 95.
Since supper-time.—*The Taming of the Shrew,* v, 2, 128.
Till supper-time.—*Macbeth,* iii, 1, 44. The only uses of "supper-time."

9
Prince: Is your master here in London?
Bardolph: Yea, my lord.
Prince: Where sups he? doth the old boar feed in the old frank?
Bardolph: At the old place, my lord, in Eastcheap.
Prince: What company?
Page: Ephesians, my lord, of the old church.
Prince: Sup any women with him?
Page: None, my lord, but old Mistress Quickly and Mistress Doll Tearsheet.
Prince: What pagan may that be?
Page: A proper gentlewoman, sir, and a kinswoman of my master's.
Prince: Even such kin as the parish heifers are to the town bull. Shall we steal upon them, Ned, at supper?
II Henry IV, ii, 2, 157. The only use of "frank" in the sense of an enclosure for hogs. "Ephesian" (boon companion) is repeated in *The Merry Wives of Windsor,* iv, 5, 19.

10
You shall sup with Jesu Christ to-night. . . .
If not in heaven, you 'll surely sup in hell.
II Henry VI, v, 1, 214. [Richard] "Jesu Christ" is repeated in *Richard II,* iv, 1, 93.
Sup to-night with my new master.—*The Merchant of Venice,* ii, 4, 18.
Let us sup betimes.—*Richard III,* iii, 1, 199.
I do entreat that we may sup together.—*Othello,* iv, 1, 273.
We all would sup together.—*Antony and Cleopatra,* iv, 8, 33.
Sup them well.—*Taming of Shrew,* Ind., l. 28.
I have supp'd full.—*Macbeth,* v, 5, 13.
Being full of supper.—*Othello,* i, 1, 99.

11
To make a bloody supper in the Tower.
III Henry VI. Act v, sc. 5, l. 85. [Clarence]
We 'll go to supper i' the morning.
King Lear. Act iii, sc. 6, l. 90. [Lear]

12
That nourishment which is called supper.
Love's Labour 's Lost. Act i, sc. 1, l. 239. [King, reading] "Nourishment" is repeated in *Henry VIII,* v, 3, 44, and in *Pericles,* i, 2, 56.

13
To-night we hold a solemn supper, sir,
And I 'll request your presence.
Macbeth. Act iii, sc. 1, l. 14. [Macbeth]

1
Let it be so hasted that supper be ready at the farthest by five of the clock.
The Merchant of Venice. Act ii, sc. 2, l. 121. [Bassanio] The only use of "hasted."
Is supper ready?—*The Taming of the Shrew,* iv, 1, 47.
Supper served up.—*Romeo and Juliet,* i, 3, 100.
Fetch my supper in.—*The Taming of the Shrew,* iv, 1, 142.
2
Bid my old master . . . to sup to-night.
The Merchant of Venice. Act ii, sc. 4, l. 18. [Launcelot]
I am bid forth to supper.
The Merchant of Venice. Act ii, sc. 5, l. 11. [Shylock]
I will not fail him at supper.—*Much Ado about Nothing,* i, 1, 279.
3
I came yonder from a great supper: the prince your brother is royally entertained.
Much Ado about Nothing. Act i, sc. 3, l. 44. [Borachio]
Let us to the great supper.—*Much Ado about Nothing,* i, 3, 73.
This night he makes a supper, and a great one.
Henry VIII. Act i, sc. 3, l. 52. [Lord Chamberlain]
4
There 's a partridge wing saved, for the fool will eat no supper that night.
Much Ado about Nothing. Act ii, sc. 1, l. 155. [Beatrice] Partridge is mentioned only once more, in *II Henry VI,* iii, 2, 191.
5
An you 'll come to supper to-night, you may; an you will not, come when you are next prepared for.
Othello. Act iv, sc. 1, l. 166. [Bianca]
Come home with me to supper.—*Richard II,* iv, 1, 333.
6
Iago: Go know of Cassio where he supp'd to-night.
[To Bianca]: What, do you shake at that?
Bianca: He supp'd at my house, but I therefore shake not.
Iago: O, did he so?
Othello. Act v, sc. 1, l. 117.
He has almost supp'd.—*Macbeth,* i, 7, 29.
7
Come, let us sup betimes, that afterwards
We may digest our complots in some form.
Richard III. Act iii, sc. 1, l. 199. [Gloucester]
Sit at supper.—*Richard III,* ii, 4, 10.
8
Come to me, Tyrrel, soon at after supper.
Richard III. Act iv, sc. 3, l. 31. [King Richard]
After supper.—*I Henry IV,* i, 2, 3; *II Henry IV,* iii, 2, 332; *The Two Gentlemen of Verona,* iii, 2, 96.
Supper is done.—*Romeo and Juliet,* i, 4, 105.
9
She will indite him to some supper.
Romeo and Juliet. Act ii, sc. 4, l. 135. [Benvolio] The only use of "indite." "Indited" is used twice, in *Love's Labour 's Lost,* iv, 1, 96, and *II Henry IV,* ii, 1, 30: "Indited to dinner."
Come again to supper.—*Timon of Athens,* iii, 1, 26.
10
Pandarus: If the king call for him at supper, you will make his excuse. . . .
Paris: What exploit 's in hand? where sups he to-night? . . .
Pandarus: You must not know where he sups.
Paris: I 'll lay my life, with my disposer Cressida.
Troilus and Cressida. Act iii, sc. 1, l. 84. "Disposer" is repeated in l. 101, and occurs in no other scene.

SUPPLICATION, see Prayer

SURETY

See also Warranty

11
One of the greatest in the Christian world
Shall be my surety.
All 's Well that Ends Well. Act iv, sc. 4, l. 2. [Helena]
She called the saints to surety.
All 's Well that Ends Well, v, 3, 108. [King]
The jeweller that owes the ring is sent for,
And he shall surety me.
All 's Well that Ends Well. Act v, sc. 3, l. 297. [Diana] "Jeweller" is repeated in *Timon of Athens,* i, 1, 8.
You shall be his surety.—*The Merchant of Venice,* v, 1, 254.
I 'll be his surety.—*The Tempest,* i, 2, 475.
We 'll surety him.—*Coriolanus,* iii, 1, 178.
12
And divest such sarcenet surety for thy oaths,
As if thou never walk'st further than Finsbury.
I Henry IV. Act iii, sc. 1, l. 256. [Hotspur] The only mention of Finsbury. "Sarcenet" (fine soft silk material) is repeated in *Troilus and Cressida,* v, 1, 36: "Sarcenet flap for a sore eye."
Go to the king; and let there be impawn'd
Some surety for a safe return again.
I Henry IV. Act iv, sc. 3, l. 108. [Hotspur] "Impawn'd" is repeated in *The Winter's Tale,* i, 2, 436. "Impawn" occurs in *Henry V,* i, 2, 21: "Impawn our person."
13
He is a man
Who with a double surety binds his followers.
II Henry IV. Act i, sc. 1, l. 190. [Morton]
He would not take his band and yours; he liked not the security.
II Henry IV. Act i, sc. 2, l. 37. [Page]
A whoreson Achitophel! A rascally yea-forsooth knave! to bear a gentleman in hand, and then stand upon security! The whoreson smooth-pates do now wear nothing but high shoes, and bunches of keys at their girdles; and if a man is through with them in honest taking up, then they must stand upon security. I had as lief they would put ratsbane in my mouth as offer to stop it with security. I looked a' should have sent me two and twenty yards of satin, as

I am a true knight, and he sends me security.
II Henry IV. Act i, sc. 2, l. 41. [Falstaff] The only mention of Achitophel, and the only use of "yea-forsooth" and "smooth-pates." "Ratsbane" is repeated in *I Henry VI,* v, 4, 29, and in *King Lear,* iii, 4, 55.

1 The bastard boys of York
Shall be the surety for their traitor father.
II Henry VI. Act v, sc. 1, l. 115. [Queen]

2
Sirrah, call in my sons to be my bail.
I know, ere they will have me go to ward,
They 'll pawn their swords for my enfranchisement.
II Henry VI. Act v, sc. 1, l. 111. [York]

I cry bail. . . . I hope, sir, your good worship will be my bail. . . . You will not bail me, then, sir?
Measure for Measure. Act iii, sc. 2, l. 43. [Pompey]

Let me be their bail.—*Titus Andronicus,* ii, 3, 295. "Bail" is used thirteen times.

3 I 'll . . . make my vouch as strong
As shore of rock.
Henry VIII. Act i, sc. 1, l. 157. [Buckingham]

Will his vouchers vouch him no more of his purchases, and double ones too, than the length and breadth of a pair of indentures?
Hamlet. Act v, sc. 1, l. 117. [Hamlet]

Here 's a voucher.—*Cymbeline,* ii, 2, 39.

Double vouchers.—*Hamlet,* v, 1, 114. The only uses of "voucher" and "vouchers."

4
The Frenchman became his surety and sealed under for another.
The Merchant of Venice. Act i, sc. 2, l. 88. [Portia]

5
Procure your sureties for your days of answer.
Richard II. Act iv, sc. 1, l. 159. [Bolingbroke]

6
He learn'd but surety-like to write for me
Under that bond that him as fast doth bind.
Sonnets. No. cxxxiv. The only use of "surety-like."

7
What surety stronger than Achilles' arm?
Troilus and Cressida. Act i, sc. 3, l. 220. [Agamemnon]

The wound of peace is surety, Surety secure.
Troilus and Cressida. Act ii, sc. 2, l. 14. [Hector]

SURFEIT

8 Thou art too full
Of the wars' surfeits, to go rove with one
That 's yet unbruised.
Coriolanus. Act iv, sc. 1, l. 45. [Coriolanus] The only use of "rove."

Surfeit out of action.—*Coriolanus,* i, 3, 28.

9
They surfeited with honey and began
To loathe the taste of sweetness, whereof a little
More than a little is by much too much.
I Henry IV. Act iii, sc. 2, l. 71. [King]

Surfeited to death.—*Othello,* ii, 1, 50.

Surfeit-swelled.—*II Henry IV,* v, 5, 54. The only use of the phrase.

10
Surfeiting in joys of love.
II Henry VI. Act i, sc. 1, l. 251. [York]

Amorous surfeiter.—*Antony and Cleopatra,* ii, 1, 33. The only use of "surfeiter."

11
As one that surfeits thinking on a want.
II Henry VI. Act iii, sc. 2, l. 248. [Queen]

Surfeit of our own behaviour.—*King Lear,* i, 2, 130.

Full surfeits.—*Antony and Cleopatra,* i, 4, 27.

12
As surfeit is the father of much fast,
So every scope by the immoderate use
Turns to restraint.
Measure for Measure. Act i, sc. 2, l. 130. [Claudio] The only use of "immoderate." "Immoderately" occurs in *Romeo and Juliet,* iv, 1, 6.

13
They are as sick that surfeit with too much as they that starve with nothing.
The Merchant of Venice. Act i, sc. 2, l. 6. [Nerissa]

For fear I surfeit.—*The Merchant of Venice,* iii, 2, 115.

14 A surfeit of the sweetest things
The deepest loathing to the stomach brings.
A Midsummer-Night's Dream. Act ii, sc. 2, l. 137. [Lysander]

My surfeit and my heresy Of all he hated!
A Midsummer-Night's Dream. Act ii, sc. 2, l. 141. [Lysander]

15
Give satiety fresh appetite.
Othello, ii, 1, 231. See under LUST.

With satiety seeks to quench his thirst.
The Taming of the Shrew. Act i, sc. 1, l. 24. [Lucentio]

Satiety of commendations.—*Timon of Athens,* i, 1, 166.

Loathed satiety.—*Venus and Adonis,* l. 19. The only uses of "satiety."

Lust . . . will sate itself.—*Hamlet,* i, 5, 56. The only use of "sate."

Sated with his body.—*Othello,* i, 3, 356. The only use of "sated."

16
Now comes the sick hour that his surfeit made.
Richard II. Act ii, sc. 2, l. 84. [York]

By surfeit die your king!
Richard III. Act i, sc. 3, l. 197. [Queen Margaret]

17
Thus do I pine and surfeit day by day,
Or gluttoning on all, or all away.
Sonnets. No. lxxv. The only use of "gluttoning."

18
Cure thy o'er-night's surfeit.
Timon of Athens. Act iv, sc. 3, l. 227. [Apemantus]

Make me surfeit.—*The Two Gentlemen of Verona,* iii, 1, 220.

19
They surfeit, yet complain on drouth.
Venus and Adonis, l. 544.

SURGEON, see Doctor

SURMISE

1
I speak not out of weak surmises.
Cymbeline. Act iii, sc. 4, l. 24. [Imogen, reading]
Wrong surmise.—*Richard III,* ii, 1, 54.
2
Now gather, and surmise.
Hamlet. Act ii, sc. 2, l. 108. [Polonius]
Surmise Of aids incertain.—*II Henry IV,* i, 3, 23.
Smother'd in surmise.—*Macbeth,* i, 3, 141.
3 Exchange me for a goat,
When I shall change the business of my soul
To such exsufflicate and blown surmises,
Matching thy inference.
Othello. Act iii, sc. 3, l. 181. [Othello] The only use of "exsufflicate" (windy), and of "inference."
Blown by surmises.—*II Henry IV,* Ind., 16.
4
By deep surmise of others' detriment;
Losing her woes in shows of discontent.
The Rape of Lucrece, l. 1579. The only use of "detriment."
Answers with surmise.—*Rape of Lucrece,* l. 83.
Trembles by surmise.—*Titus Andronicus,* ii, 3, 219.
Condemned Upon surmises.—*The Winter's Tale,* iii, 2, 113.
'Tis but surmised.—*II Henry VI,* iii, 2, 347.
Surmised shape.—*Troilus and Cressida,* i, 3, 17. The only uses of "surmised."

SUSPICION

See also Distrust

5 I do suspect you, madam;
But you shall do no harm.
Cymbeline. Act i, sc. 5, l. 31. [Cornelius]
6
He will suspect us still and find a time
To punish this offence in other faults:
Suspicion all our lives shall be stuck full of eyes.
I Henry IV. Act v, sc. 2, l. 6. [Worcester]
7
See what a ready tongue suspicion hath!
II Henry IV. Act i, sc. 1, l. 84. [Northumberland]
8 'Tis my special hope
That you will clear yourself from all suspect.
II Henry VI. Act iii, sc. 1, l. 139. [King]
The suspect is great.—*II Henry VI,* i, 3, 139.
9
Pray God he may acquit him of suspicion!
II Henry VI. Act iii, sc. 2, l. 25. [Queen]
This breeds suspicion.—*II Henry VI,* i, 3, 210.
Branded with suspicion.—*Henry VIII,* iii, 1, 128.
Indued With some suspicion.—*Henry V,* ii, 2, 140.
10
Suspicion always haunts the guilty mind.
III Henry VI. Act v, sc. 6, l. 11. [Gloucester]
Thus have we swept suspicion from our seat.
III Henry VI. Act v, sc. 7, l. 13. [King Edward]
Never have you in suspect.—*III Henry VI,* iv, 1, 142.
11
I do suspect thee very grievously.
King John. Act iv, sc. 3, l. 134. [Bastard]
12
It will stuff his suspicion more fully.
King Lear. Act iii, sc. 5, l. 22. [Edmund]
13 When we have our naked frailties hid,
That suffer in exposure, let us meet,
And question this most bloody piece of work,
To know it further.
Macbeth. Act ii, sc. 3, l. 132. [Banquo]
The king's two sons,
Are stol'n away and fled; which puts upon them
Suspicion of the deed.
Macbeth. Act ii, sc. 4, l. 25. [Macduff]
14
Having an honest man to your husband, to give him such cause of suspicion!
The Merry Wives of Windsor. Act iii, sc. 3, l. 107. [Mrs. Page]
I think my husband has some special suspicion.
The Merry Wives of Windsor. Act iii, sc. 3, l. 200. [Mrs. Ford]
Ford: I suspect without cause, mistress, do I?
Mrs. Ford: Heaven be my witness you do, if you suspect me in any dishonesty.
Merry Wives of Windsor. Act iv, sc. 2, l. 138.
15
In faith, hath not the world one man but he will wear his cap with suspicion?
Much Ado about Nothing. Act i, sc. 1, l. 199. [Benedick]
16
Your suspicion is not without wit and judgement.
Othello. Act iv, sc. 2, l. 215. [Iago]
Made you to suspect me.—*Othello,* iv, 2, 147.
17
Yet go current from suspicion!
Richard III. Act ii, sc. 1, l. 94. [Gloucester]
He lived from all attainder of suspect.
Richard III. Act iii, sc. 5, l. 32. [Gloucester]
18
Bring forth the parties of suspicion.
Romeo and Juliet. Act v, sc. 3, l. 222. [Prince]
19
You should have fear'd false times when you did feast:
Suspect still comes where an estate is least.
Timon of Athens. Act iv, sc. 3, l. 520. [Flavius]
20
My heart suspects more than mine eye can see.
Titus Andronicus. Act ii, sc. 3, l. 213. [Quintus]
21
Bid Suspicion double-lock the door.
Venus and Adonis, l. 448. The only use of "double-lock."
Her rash suspect she doth extenuate.
Venus and Adonis, l. 1010.
22
I have too much believed mine own suspicion.
Winter's Tale. Act iii, sc. 2, l. 152. [Leontes]
Ill-ta'en suspicion.—*The Winter's Tale,* i, 2, 460.
"Ill taken" occurs in *King Lear,* ii, 2, 166

1
What! look upon my brother: both your pardons,
That e'er I put between your holy looks
My ill suspicion.
Winter's Tale. Act v, sc. 3, l. 147. [Leontes]
Deep suspicion.—*Richard III,* iii, 5, 8; *Henry VIII,* iii, 1, 53.
Great suspicion.—*Romeo and Juliet,* v, 3, 187.
Strong suspicion.—*The Winter's Tale,* v, 2, 31.
Mere suspicion.—*Othello,* i, 3, 395.

SWAN

2
So doth the swan her downy cygnets save,
Keeping them prisoner underneath her wings.
I Henry VI. Act v, sc. 3, l. 56. [Suffolk]
Cygnet's down.—*Troilus and Cressida,* i, 1, 58.

3
We bodged again; as I have seen a swan
With bootless labour swim against the tide
And spend her strength with over-matching waves.
III Henry VI. Act i, sc. 4, l. 19. [York] The only use of "bodged" (to give way), and "over-matching."

4 'Tis strange that death should sing.
I am the cygnet to this pale faint swan,
Who chants a doleful hymn to his own death,
And from the organ-pipe of frailty sings
His soul and body to their lasting rest.
King John. Act v, sc. 7, l. 20. [Prince Henry] "Organ-pipe" is repeated in *The Tempest,* iii, 3, 98: "Dreadful organ-pipe."

5
Let music sound while he doth make his choice;
Then, if he lose, he makes a swan-like end,
Fading in music.
The Merchant of Venice. Act iii, sc. 2, l. 43. [Portia] The only use of "swan-like."
I will play the swan, And die in music.
Othello. Act v, sc. 2, l. 247. [Emilia]

6
Let the priest in surplice white,
That defunctive music can,
Be the death-divining swan.
Phœnix and the Turtle, l. 13. The only use of "defunctive" (funereal), and "death-divining."

7
And now this pale swan in her watery nest
Begins the sad dirge of her certain ending.
The Rape of Lucrece, l. 1611.
Snow-white swan.—*Rape of Lucrece,* l. 1011.

8 All the water in the ocean
Can never turn the swan's black legs to white,
Although she lave them hourly in the flood.
Titus Andronicus. Act iv, sc. 2, l. 101. [Aaron]

SWEARING

See also Curse, Oath

9
A whoreson jackanapes must take me up for swearing; as if I borrowed mine oaths of him and might not spend them at my pleasure. . . . When a gentleman is disposed to swear, it is not for any standers-by to curtail his oaths, ha?
Cymbeline. Act ii, sc. 1, l. 4. [Cloten] The only use of "curtail." "Curtail'd" occurs in *Richard III,* i, 1, 18.
Foam'd at the mouth, and swore.
Cymbeline. Act v, sc. 5, l. 276. [Pisanio]

10
Fall a-cursing, like a very drab.
Hamlet. Act ii, sc. 2, l. 615. [Hamlet] The only use of "a-cursing."

11
Swearest thou, ungracious boy? henceforth ne'er look on me.
I Henry IV. Act ii, sc. 4, l. 490. [Prince of Wales]
Not yours, in good sooth! Heart! you swear like a comfit-maker's wife. 'Not you, in good sooth,' and 'as true as I live,' and 'as God shall mend me,' and 'as sure as day,' . . .
Swear me, Kate, like a lady as thou art,
A good mouth-filling oath, and leave 'in sooth,'
And such protest of pepper-gingerbread,
To velvet-guards and Sunday-citizens.
I Henry IV. Act iii, sc. 1, l. 252. [Hotspur] The only use of "comfit-maker," "mouth-filling," "pepper-gingerbread," "velvet-guards," and "Sunday-citizens."

12
Cease, gentle queen, these execrations.
II Henry VI. Act iii, sc. 2, l. 305. [Suffolk]
My spiteful execrations.
Troilus and Cressida. Act ii, sc. 3, l. 7. [Thersites] The only uses of "execrations."

13
Warwick: They mock thee, Clifford: swear as thou wast wont.
Richard: What, not an oath? nay, then the world goes hard
When Clifford cannot spare his friends an oath.
I know by that he 's dead.
III Henry VI. Act ii, sc. 6, l. 76.
He did discharge a horrible oath.
Henry VIII. Act i, sc. 2, l. 206. [Surveyor]

14
Here will be an old abusing of God's patience and the king's English.
The Merry Wives of Windsor. Act i, sc. 4, l. 5. [Mistress Quickly]

15
'Ay, by gogs-wouns,' quoth he; and swore so loud,
That, all-amazed, the priest let fall the book.
The Taming of the Shrew. Act iii, sc. 2, l. 162. [Gremio] The only use of "gogs-wouns" and "all-amazed."
He stamp'd and swore.—*The Taming of the Shrew,* iii, 2, 169.
With oaths kept waking and with brawling fed.
The Taming of the Shrew. Act iv, sc. 3, l. 10. [Katharina]

1
You taught me language; and my profit on 't
Is, I know how to curse.
The Tempest. Act i, sc. 2, l. 363. [Caliban]

2
Sir Toby: Swear horrible; for it comes to pass oft that a terrible oath, with a swaggering accent sharply twanged off, gives manhood more approbation than ever proof itself would have earned him. Away!
Sir Andrew: Nay, let me alone for swearing.
Twelfth Night. Act iii, sc. 4, l. 196. The only use of "twanged."

Fire and brimstone!—*Twelfth Night,* ii, 5, 56.
Bolts and shackles!—*Twelfth Night,* ii, 5, 62.
Mort de ma vie!—*The Winter's Tale,* i, 2, 118.
Mort Dieu!—*II Henry VI,* i, 1, 123.
Mort du vinaigre!—*All 's Well that Ends Well,* ii, 3, 50.

SWEAT

3
Why, do not your courtier's hands sweat? and is not the grease of a mutton as wholesome as the sweat of a man?
As You Like It. Act iii, sc. 2, l. 56. [Touchstone]

Smell of sweat.—*Antony and Cleopatra,* i, 4, 21.

4
She sweats; a man may go over shoes in the grime of it.
The Comedy of Errors. Act iii, sc. 2, l. 105. [Dromio of Syracuse] "Grime" is repeated in *King Lear,* ii, 3, 9.

Begrimed with sweat.—*The Rape of Lucrece,* l. 1381. "Begrimed" is repeated in *Othello,* iii, 3, 387: "Begrimed and black."

5
He sweats, Strains his young nerves.
Cymbeline. Act iii, sc. 3, l. 93. [Belarius]

Sweat of industry.—*Cymbeline,* iii, 6, 31.
Sweat Of thousand friends.—*Henry VIII,* Prol., 28.
Sweat with wrath.—*Coriolanus,* i, 4, 27.

6
Beads of sweat have stood upon thy brow,
Like bubbles in a late disturbed stream.
I Henry IV. Act ii, sc. 3, l. 61. [Lady Percy]

Pearly sweat, resembling dew of night.
The Rape of Lucrece, l. 396. The only use of "pearly."

Chilling sweat.—*Titus Andronicus,* ii, 3, 212. See under FEAR. The only use of "chilling."

7
Falstaff sweats to death,
And lards the lean earth as he walks along.
I Henry IV. Act ii, sc. 2, l. 115. [Prince of Wales]

It is the pasture lards the rother's sides.
Timon of Athens, iv, 3, 12. The only uses of "lards," and of "rother" (cow).

8
But look you pray, all you that kiss my lady Peace at home, that our armies join not in a hot day; for, by the Lord, I take but two shirts out with me, and I mean not to sweat extraordinarily.
II Henry IV. Act i, sc. 2, l. 234. [Falstaff] "Extraordinarily" is used again in ii, 4, 26, and in no other play.

Alas, poor ape, how thou sweatest! come, let me wipe thy face; come on, you whoreson chops.
II Henry IV. Act ii, sc. 4, l. 233. [Doll]

Do ye yield, sir? or shall I sweat for you? If I do sweat, they are the drops of thy lovers, and they weep for thy death.
II Henry IV. Act iv, sc. 3, l. 13. [Falstaff]

For any thing I know, Falstaff shall die of a sweat, unless already a' be killed with your hard opinions.
II Henry IV. Epilogue, l. 32.

9
The honourable captain there
Drops bloody sweat from his war-wearied limbs.
I Henry VI. Act iv, sc. 4, l. 17. [Lucy] The only use of "war-wearied."

10
He was stirr'd
With such an agony he sweat extremely.
Henry VIII. Act ii, sc. 1, l. 32. [Gentleman]

Make us sweat.—*Julius Cæsar,* v, 1, 48.

11
Who else but I . . . sweat in this business?
King John. Act v, sc. 2, l. 100. [Lewis]

12
We sweat and bleed.
King Lear. Act v, sc. 3, l. 55. [Edmund]

Grunt and sweat.—*Hamlet,* iii, 1, 77.
Sweating and blowing.—*The Merry Wives of Windsor,* iii, 3, 93.
Bare-headed, sweating.—*II Henry IV,* ii, 4, 388.
Chafed with sweat.—*The Taming of the Shrew,* i, 2, 203.

13
Have napkins enow about you; here you 'll sweat for 't.
Macbeth. Act ii, sc. 3, l. 7. [Porter]

He sweats not.—*Othello,* ii, 3, 85.

14
By this the love-sick queen began to sweat,
For where they lay the shadow had forsook them,
And Titan, tired in the mid-day heat,
With burning eye did hotly over-look them.
Venus and Adonis, l. 175.

Sweating with desire.—*II Henry IV,* v, 5, 26.

SWEETNESS

15
Sweets to the sweet: farewell!
Hamlet. Act v, sc. 1, l. 266. [Queen]

16
So sweet was ne'er so fatal.
Othello. Act v, sc. 2, l. 20. [Othello]

17
The last taste of sweets, is sweetest last.
Richard II, ii, 1, 13. See REMEMBRANCE, 1259:1.

Loathe the taste of sweetness.
I Henry IV. Act iii, sc. 2, l. 72. [King Henry]

Too sharp in sweetness.—*Troilus and Cressida,* iii, 2, 25.

18
The ladies call him sweet.
Love's Labour 's Lost. Act v, sc. 2, l. 329. [Biron]

Sweet; my sweet; gentle sweet.
Love's Labour 's Lost, iv, 1, 109; iv, 2, 145; v, 2, 373; and used as terms of endearment throughout the plays.

Sweeting.—*I Henry VI,* iii, 3, 21; and four times in later plays.
Sweet o' the night.—*II Henry IV,* v, 3, 53.
Sweet o' the year.—*The Winter's Tale,* iv, 3, 3.

1
Sweets grown common lose their dear delight.
Sonnets. No. cii. See also under SURFEIT.
For compound sweet foregoing simple savour.
Sonnets. No. cxxv.

2
Sacred and sweet was all I saw in her.
The Taming of the Shrew. Act i, sc. 1, l. 181. [Lucentio]
Sweet and twenty.—*Twelfth Night,* ii, 3, 52.
Saucy sweetness.—*Measure for Measure,* ii, 4, 45.
Sweetness of affiance.—*Henry V,* ii, 2, 127.

3
'Sweet' quoth 'a! sweet sink, sweet sewer.
Troilus and Cressida. Act v, sc. 1, l. 83. [Thersites] The only use of "sewer."

II—Sweet and Sour
See also Compensation

4
They cannot be too sweet for the king's tartness.
All's Well that Ends Well. Act iv, sc. 3, l. 95. [Lord] "Tartness" is repeated in *Coriolanus,* v, 4, 18.
All yet seems well; and if it end so meet,
The bitter past, more welcome is the sweet.
All's Well that Ends Well. Act v, sc. 3, l. 333. [King]

5
Touch you the sourest points with sweetest terms.
Nor curstness grow to the matter.
Antony and Cleopatra. Act ii, sc. 2, l. 24. [Lepidus] The only use of "curstness."

6
Sweetest nut hath sourest rind.
As You Like It. Act iii, sc. 2, l. 115. [Touchstone]

7
The sweets we wish for turn to loathed sours
Even in the moment that we call them ours.
The Rape of Lucrece, l. 867.
His taste delicious, in digestion souring,
Devours his will, that lived by foul devouring.
The Rape of Lucrece, l. 699.

8
Things sweet to taste prove in digestion sour.
Richard II. Act i, sc. 3, l. 236. [Gaunt]

9
Speak sweetly, man, although thy looks be sour.
Richard II. Act iii, sc. 2, l. 193. [King Richard]

10
Seeming sweet convert to bitter gall.
Romeo and Juliet. Act i, sc. 5, l. 94. [Tybalt]
A choking gall and a preserving sweet.
Romeo and Juliet, i, 1, 200. See under LOVE.

11
Even so, being full of your ne'er-cloying sweetness,
To bitter sauces did I frame my feeding
And, sick of welfare, found a kind of meetness
To be diseased ere that there was true needing.
Sonnets. No. cxviii. The only use of "ne'er-cloying" and "meetness." "Needing" is repeated in *The Passionate Pilgrim,* l. 268.

12
You have the honey still, but these the gall;
So to be valiant is no praise at all.
Troilus and Cressida, ii, 2, 143. [Priam]
To make a sweet lady sad is a sour offence.
Troilus and Cressida, iii, 1, 80. See OFFENCE.

SWIFTNESS
See also Haste, Speed

13
Cleopatra: Celerity is never more admired
Than by the negligent.
Antony: A good rebuke,
Which might have well becomed the best of men,
To taunt at slackness.
Antony and Cleopatra. Act iii, sc. 7, l. 25.
In motion of no less celerity
Than that of thought.
Henry V, iii, Prol., 2.
Quick celerity.—*Measure for Measure,* iv, 2, 113.
Swift celerity.—*Measure for Measure,* v, 1, 399.
Celerity in dying.—*Antony and Cleopatra,* i, 2, 149.
With celerity.—*Troilus and Cressida,* i, 3, 330. The only uses of "celerity."

14
By my faith, he is very swift and sententious.
As You Like It. Act v, sc. 4, l. 65. [Duke]
Sharp and sententious.—*Love's Labour's Lost,* v, 1, 3.
Prettiest sententious.—*Romeo and Juliet,* ii, 4, 225. The only uses of "sententious."

15
The swiftest harts have posted you by land,
And winds of all the corners kiss'd your sails,
To make your vessel nimble.
Cymbeline. Act ii, sc. 4, l. 27. [Posthumus]

16
All things thought upon
That may with reasonable swiftness add
More feathers to our wings.
Henry V. Act i, sc. 2, l. 305. [King Henry]

17
Skirr away, as swift as stones
Enforced from the old Assyrian slings.
Henry V. Act iv, sc. 7, l. 64. [King Henry] "Assyrian" is repeated in *II Henry IV,* v, 3, 105: "Assyrian knight."
Skirr the country round.—*Macbeth,* v, 3, 35. The only uses of "skirr."

18
Armado: The way is but short: away!
Moth: As swift lead, sir.
Armado: The meaning, pretty ingenious?
Is not lead a metal heavy, dull, and slow?
Moth: Minimè, honest master; or rather, master, no.
Armado: I say lead is slow.

Moth: You are too swift, sir, to say so:
Is that lead slow which is fired from a gun?
Armado: Sweet smoke of rhetoric!
He reputes me a cannon; and the bullet, that 's he:
I shoot thee at the swain.
Love's Labour's Lost. Act iii, sc. 1, l. 57. The only use of "minimè" (not at all).
She would be as swift in motion as a ball.
Romeo and Juliet. Act ii, sc. 5, l. 13. [Juliet]
Swift As breathed stags.—*The Taming of the Shrew,* Ind., 2, 49.
Swift as meditation.—*Hamlet,* i, 5, 29.
Swift as quicksilver.—*Hamlet,* i, 5, 66.
Swift as a shadow.—*A Midsummer-Night's Dream,* i, 1, 144.
Swift as swallow flies.—*Titus Andronicus,* iv, 2, 172.
Swift as thought.—*Love's Labour's Lost,* iv, 3, 330.
Swift as frenzy's thoughts.—*Troilus and Cressida,* v, 10, 29.
Swift of foot.—*Othello,* ii, 3, 232; *Macbeth,* iii, 1, 38.

1
Swifter than arrow from the Tartar's bow.
A Midsummer-Night's Dream. Act iii, sc. 2, l. 101. [Puck]
Swifter than the moon's sphere.—*Midsummer-Night's Dream,* ii, 1, 7.
Swifter than the wind.—*A Midsummer-Night's Dream,* iii, 2, 94.

2
Be swift like lightning in the execution.
Richard II. Act i, sc. 3, l. 79. [Gaunt]

3
Too swift arrives as tardy as too slow.
Romeo and Juliet. Act ii, sc. 6, l. 15. [Friar Laurence]

4
Softly and swiftly, sir.
Taming of the Shrew, v, 1, 1. [Biondello]

SWIMMING

5
Say you can swim; alas, 'tis but a while!
III Henry VI. Act v, sc. 4, l. 29. [Queen]

6
With bootless labour swim against the tide.
III Henry VI. Act i, sc. 4, l. 20. [York]
Swims against your stream.—*II Henry IV,* v, 2, 34.
Swims with fins of lead.—*Coriolanus,* i, 1, 184.
Swim a league.—*A Midsummer-Night's Dream,* ii, 1, 174.

7 Darest thou, Cassius, now
Leap in with me into this angry flood,
And swim to yonder point?
Julius Cæsar. Act i, sc. 2, l. 102. [Cassius]
The torrent roar'd, and we did buffet it
With lusty sinews, throwing it aside
And stemming it with hearts of controversy.
Julius Cæsar. Act i, sc. 2, l. 107. [Cassius] The only use of "stemming."

8
Like an unpractised swimmer plunging still,
With too much labour drowns for want of skill.
The Rape of Lucrece, l. 1098. The only use of "plunging."
As two spent swimmers, that do cling together
And choke their art.
Macbeth. Act i, sc. 2, l. 8. [Sergeant]
Leander the good swimmer.—*Much Ado about Nothing,* v, 2, 30. The only uses of "swimmer." Leander is mentioned four times.

9
I saw him beat the surges under him,
And ride upon their backs; he trod the water,
Whose enmity he flung aside, and breasted
The surge most swoln that met him; his bold head
'Bove the contentious waves he kept, and oar'd
Himself with his good arms in lusty stroke
To the shore.
The Tempest. Act ii, sc. 1, l. 114. [Francisco] The only use of "breasted" and "oar'd."

10
Trinculo: I can swim like a duck, I'll be sworn.
Stephano: Here, kiss the book. Though thou canst swim like a duck, thou art made like a goose.
The Tempest. Act ii, sc. 2, l. 132.

SWINE

11 Wast thou fain, poor father,
To hovel thee with swine?
King Lear. Act iv, sc. 7, l. 38. [Cordelia]
To hug with swine.—*King John,* v, 2, 142.

12
Thrice and once the hedge-pig whined.
Macbeth. Act iv, sc. 1, l. 2. [Witch] The only use of "hedge-pig."

13
If we grow all to be pork-eaters, we shall not shortly have a rasher on the coals for money.
The Merchant of Venice. Act iii, sc. 5, l. 27. [Launcelot] The only use of "pork-eaters" and "rasher." "Pork" occurs nowhere except in *The Merchant of Venice.*

14
Some men there are love not a gaping pig.
The Merchant of Venice. Act iv, sc. 1, l. 47. [Shylock] "Gaping pig" is repeated in l. 54.
Weke, weke! so cries a pig prepared to the spit.
Titus Andronicus, iv, 2, 146. [Aaron]
The pig is burn'd.—*Comedy of Errors,* ii, 1, 66.
The pig falls from the spit.
The Comedy of Errors, i, 2, 44. See under Cooking. The only uses of "pig."

15 'Tis old, but true,
Still swine eats all the draff.
The Merry Wives of Windsor. Act iv, sc. 2, l. 109. [Mrs. Page]
Eating draff and husks.—*I Henry IV,* iv, 2, 38. The only uses of "draff" (pig-wash).
This foul swine.—*Richard III,* v, 2, 10.

16
Thou elvish-mark'd, abortive, rooting hog!
Richard III. Act i, sc. 3, l. 228. [Queen] The only use of "elvish-mark'd" and "rooting."
Hog in sloth.—*King Lear,* iii, 4, 95. "Hog" is used twice more in *A Midsummer Night's Dream,* iii, 1, 112; 114.

Keep your hogs.—*As You Like It*, i, 1, 40.
Price of hogs.—*The Merchant of Venice,* iii, 5, 26. The only uses of "hogs."

1
With javelin's point a churlish swine . . .
Whose tushes never sheathed he whetteth still.
Venus and Adonis, l. 616. The only use of "javelin."
And whom he strikes his crooked tushes slay.
Venus and Adonis, l. 624. The only use of "tushes."
And nuzzling in his flank, the loving swine
Sheathed unaware the tusk in his soft groin.
Venus and Adonis, l. 1115. The only use of "nuzzling" and "tusk."

2
Three swine-herds, that have made themselves all men of hair.
Winter's Tale. Act iv, sc. 4, l. 332. [Servant] The only use of "swine-herds." "Swine-keeping" occurs in *I Henry IV,* iv, 2, 38.

SWOONING

See also Fainting

3
Now counterfeit to swoon; why now fall down.
As You Like It. Act iii, sc. 5, l. 17. [Phebe]
Counterfeited to swoon.—*As You Like It,* v, 2, 29.
Many will swoon when they do look on blood.
As You Like It. Act iv, sc. 3, l. 159. [Oliver]

4
Swoon for what 's to come upon thee.
Coriolanus. Act v, sc. 2, l. 72. [Menenius]
What cause, do you think, I have to swoon?
Coriolanus. Act v, sc. 2, l. 107. [Senator]

5
Doth she swoon? use means for her recovery.
III Henry VI. Act v, sc. 5, l. 45. [King Edward]
I 'll not swoon at it.—*King John,* v, 6, 22.

6
Casca: He swounded and fell down. . . .
Cassius: What, did Cæsar swound?
Casca: He fell down in the market-place, and foamed at mouth, and was speechless.
Julius Cæsar. Act i, sc. 2, l. 249.
I swound to see thee.
Timon of Athens, iv, 3, 373. [Timon]
I swounded at the sight.
Romeo and Juliet. Act iii, sc. 2, l. 56. [Nurse]
She swounds to see him bleed.
Hamlet. Act v, sc. 2, l. 319. [King] The only uses of "swound," "swounds" and "swounded."

7
Help, hold his brows! he 'll swoon!
Love's Labour 's Lost. Act v, sc. 2, l. 392. [Rosalind]
Turn white and swoon.—*A Lover's Complaint,* l. 308.

8
Speak, of all loves! I swoon almost with fear.
A Midsummer-Night's Dream. Act ii, sc. 2, l. 154. [Hermia]
I swoon with this dead-killing news.
Richard III. Act iv, sc. 1, l. 35. [Queen Elizabeth] The only use of "dead-killing."

9
She swooned almost at my pleasing tale.
Titus Andronicus. Act v, sc. 1, l. 119. [Aaron]
Some swooned, all sorrowed.—*The Winter's Tale,* v, 2, 99.

SWORD

See also Iron, Steel, Weapon

10
Noble heroes, my sword and yours are kin.
All 's Well that Ends Well. Act ii, sc. 1, l. 40. [Parolles]
Worthy fellows; and like to prove most sinewy sword-men.
All 's Well that Ends Well. Act ii, sc. 1, l. 61. [Parolles] The only use of "sword-men."

11
Purposely to take
His brother here, and put him to the sword.
As You Like It. Act v, sc. 4, l. 164. [Jaques]
Put . . . unto the sword.—*II Henry VI,* iii, 1, 284.
Threaten'd . . . with the sword.—*Cymbeline,* v, 5, 78.
Shake my sword.—*All 's Well that Ends Well,* ii, 5, 96.

12
Upon your sword sit laurel victory!
Antony and Cleopatra, i, 3, 99. See VICTORY.

13
I had as lief have a reed that will do me no service as a partisan I could not heave.
Antony and Cleopatra. Act ii, sc. 7, l. 13. [Servant]
Clubs, bills, and partisans!—*Romeo and Juliet,* i, 1, 80.
Wield old partisans.—*Romeo and Juliet,* i, 1, 101.
Strike at it with my partisan.—*Hamlet,* i, 1, 140.
Pikes and partisans.—*Cymbeline,* iv, 2, 399. The only uses of "partisan" and "partisans."

14
He at Philippi kept
His sword e'en like a dancer.
Antony and Cleopatra. Act iii, sc. 11, l. 35. [Antony]
Do you misdoubt
This sword and these my wounds?
Antony and Cleopatra. Act iii, sc. 7, l. 63. [Soldier]
I and my sword will earn our chronicle.
Antony and Cleopatra. Act iii, sc. 13, l. 175. [Antony]

15
This is his sword;
I robb'd his wound of it; behold it stain'd
With his most noble blood.
Antony and Cleopatra. Act v, sc. 1, l. 24. [Dercetas]
This sword but shown to Cæsar, with this tidings,
Shall enter me with him.
Antony and Cleopatra. Act iv, sc. 14, l. 112. [Dercetas]

16
His sword, death's stamp,
Where it did mark, it took; from face to foot
He was a thing of blood, whose every motion
Was timed with dying cries.
Coriolanus. Act ii, sc. 2, l. 111. [Cominius] The only use of "timed."

How often he had met you, sword to sword.
Coriolanus. Act iii, sc. 1, l. 13. [Lartius]
Down with that sword!—*Coriolanus,* iii, 1, 226.

1
Let him feel your sword.
Coriolanus. Act v, sc. 6, l. 56. [Conspirator]
Stain all your edges on me.
Coriolanus. Act v, sc. 6, l. 113. [Coriolanus]
Stain your swords with blood.—*King John,* ii, 1, 45.

2
Died with their swords in hand.
Cymbeline. Act i, sc. 1, l. 36. [First Gentleman]
His good sword in his hand.—*Coriolanus,* iv, 2, 25.
Good sword.—*Othello,* v, 2, 262.

3
You shall answer me with your sword.
Cymbeline, i, 4, 176. See RETRIBUTION.

Hence, vile instrument!
Thou shalt not damn my hand.
Cymbeline. Act iii, sc. 4, l. 75. [Pisanio]

4 Come hither, gentlemen,
And lay your hands again upon my sword:
Never to speak of this that you have heard,
Swear by my sword.
Hamlet. Act i, sc. 5, l. 158. [Hamlet] See under OATH.

Benedick: By my sword, Beatrice, thou lovest me.
Beatrice: Do not swear, and eat it.
Much Ado about Nothing. Act iv, sc. 1, l. 276. See LOVE, 908:4.

By that sword I swear,
Which gently laid my knighthood on my shoulder.
Richard II. Act i, sc. 1, l. 78. [Mowbray]

5
Many wearing rapiers are afraid of goose-quills.
Hamlet. Act ii, sc. 2, l. 359. [Rosencrantz] The only use of "goose-quills."
Wear thy good rapier bare, and put it home.
Othello. Act v, sc. 1, l. 2. [Iago]
Sheathed My rapier in his bosom.
Titus Andronicus. Act ii, sc. 1, l. 53. [Demetrius]
I do excel thee in my rapier.—*Love's Labour 's Lost,* i, 2, 78.
The rapier and dagger man.—*Measure for Measure,* iv, 3, 15.
Unhatched rapier.—*Twelfth Night,* iii, 4, 258.

6 His antique sword,
Rebellious to his arm, lies where it falls,
Repugnant to command: unequal match'd,
Phyrrus at Priam drives; in rage strikes wide;
But with the whiff and wind of his fell sword
The unnerved father falls. . . . Lo! his sword,
Which was declining on the milky head
Of reverend Priam, seem'd i' the air to stick.
Hamlet. Act ii, sc. 2, l. 491. [Player] The only use of "repugnant," "whiff," and "unnerved."

Thou hast hung thy advanced sword i' the air,
Not letting it decline on the declined.
Troilus and Cressida, iv, 5, 188. [Nestor]

7
My sword hacked like a hand-saw—ecce signum!
I Henry IV. Act ii, sc. 4, l. 186. [Falstaff] The only other use of "handsaw" (unhyphenated) is in the famous line in *Hamlet,* ii, 2, 397: "I know a hawk from a handsaw." The only use of "ecce signum."
What a slave art thou, to hack thy sword as thou hast done, and then say it was in fight!
I Henry IV. Act ii, sc. 4, l. 288. [Prince]
Prince: 'Faith, tell me now in earnest, how came Falstaff's sword so hacked?
Peto: Why, he hacked it with his dagger, and said he would swear truth out of England but he would make you believe it was done in fight.
I Henry IV. Act ii, sc. 4, l. 333.

8
Prince: What, stand'st thou idle here? lend me thy sword:
Many a nobleman lies stark and stiff
Under the hoofs of vaunting enemies,
Whose deaths are yet unrevenged: I prithee, lend me thy sword. . . .
Falstaff: Nay, before God, Hal, if Percy be alive, thou get'st not my sword; but take my pistol, if thou wilt.
Prince: Give it me: what, is it in the case?
Falstaff: Ay, Hal; 'tis hot, 'tis hot; there 's that will sack a city. [*The Prince draws it out, and finds it to be a bottle of sack.*]
Prince: What, is it a time to jest and dally now? [*He throws the bottle at Falstaff, and exit.*]
Falstaff: Well, if Percy be alive, I 'll pierce him.
I Henry IV. Act v, sc. 3, l. 41.
This sword hath ended him.—*I Henry IV,* v, 3, 9.
That same sword-and-buckler Prince of Wales.
I Henry IV. Act i, sc. 3, l. 230. [Hotspur] The only use of the phrase.

9 Full bravely hast thou flesh'd
Thy maiden sword.
I Henry IV. Act v, sc. 4, l. 133. [Prince]
How the young whelp of Talbot's, raging-wood,
Did flesh his puny sword in Frenchmen's blood!
I Henry VI. Act iv, sc. 7, l. 35. [Bastard] The only use of "raging-wood."

10
There is not now a rebel's sword unsheathed.
II Henry IV. Act iv, sc. 4, l. 86. [Westmoreland]

I do commit into your hand
The unstained sword that you have used to bear.
II Henry IV. Act v, sc. 2, l. 113. [King Henry V]

Ere this year expire,
We bear our civil swords and native fire
As far as France.
II Henry IV. Act v, sc. 5, l. 111. [Lancaster]

Civil swords.—*Antony and Cleopatra,* i, 3, 45.

1 Therefore take heed . . .
How you awake our sleeping sword of war.
Henry V. Act i, sc. 2, l. 21. [King Henry]

Sword of heaven.—*Measure for Measure,* iii, 2, 275.
Sword of justice.—*Winter's Tale,* iii, 2, 125.

2
His brandish'd sword did blind men with his beams.
I Henry VI. Act i, sc. 1, l. 10. [Gloucester]

When he perceived me shrink and on my knee,
His bloody sword he brandish'd over me.
I Henry VI. Act iv, sc. 7, l. 5. [Talbot]

Bended sword.—*Henry V,* v, Prol., 18.
Bleeding sword.—*Henry V,* v, 2, 383; *Hamlet,* ii, 2, 513.
Deputed sword.—*Measure for Measure,* ii, 2, 60.
Discontented sword.—*Antony and Cleopatra,* ii, 6, 6.
Dreadful swords.—*II Henry VI,* iv, 1, 92.
Fair sword.—*Troilus and Cressida,* v, 3, 41.
Helpful swords.—*Richard II,* iii, 3, 132.
Keen sword.—*Macbeth,* v, 8, 10.
Lawful sword.—*Coriolanus,* v, 6, 131.
Leaden sword.—*Love's Labour's Lost,* v, 2, 481.
Prompted sword.—*Troilus and Cressida,* v, 2, 175.
Quiet sword.—*Henry V,* iii, 2, 36.
Smoking swords.—*Coriolanus,* i, 4, 11.
Senseless sword.—*Coriolanus,* i, 4, 53.
Sharp sword.—*King Lear,* ii, 1, 40.
Sharp-pointed sword.—*Richard III,* i, 2, 175. The only use of "sharp-pointed."
Threatening sword.—*Timon of Athens,* v, 1, 169.
Trenchant sword.—*Timon of Athens,* iv, 3, 115.
Two-hand sword.—*II Henry VI,* ii, 1, 46. The only use of the phrase.
Unhack'd swords.—*King John,* i, 1, 12.
Valiant sword.—*I Henry VI,* iii, 1, 171.
Victor sword.—*King Lear,* v, 3, 132.
Well-labouring sword.—*II Henry IV,* i, 1, 127. The only use of the phrase.
Cæsar's sword.—*Cymbeline,* iii, 1, 31.
Great Hector's sword.—*Troilus and Cressida,* i, 3, 76.
Mars his sword.—*Sonnets,* lv.
Neighbours' sword.—*Richard II,* i, 3, 128.
Opposers' swords.—*Coriolanus,* i, 5, 23.
Sword of Deborah.—*I Henry VI,* i, 2, 105.

3 Here is my keen-edged sword,
Deck'd with five flower-de-luces on each side;
The which at Touraine, in Saint Katharine's churchyard,
Out of a great deal of old iron I chose forth.
I Henry VI. Act i, sc. 2, l. 98. [La Pucelle]
The only use of "keen-edged."

4
Whilst any trump did sound, or drum struck up,
His sword did ne'er leave striking in the field.
I Henry VI. Act i, sc. 4, l. 80. [Talbot]

O, turn thy edged sword another way.
I Henry VI. Act iii, sc. 3, l. 52. [La Pueclle]

Till with my warlike sword, despite of fate,
To my determined time thou gavest new date.
I Henry VI. Act iv, sc. 6, l. 8. [John Talbot]

5
Plantagenet: Now, Somerset, where is your argument?
Somerset: Here in my scabbard.
I Henry VI. Act ii, sc. 4, l. 59.

6
Claudio: Wilt thou use thy wit?
Benedick: It is in my scabbard.
Much Ado about Nothing. Act v, sc. 1, l. 124.

It seem'd they would debate with angry swords.
The Rape of Lucrece, l. 1421.

7
For, were there hope to conquer them again,
My sword should shed hot blood.
II Henry VI. Act i, sc. 1, l. 117. [Warwick]

I wear no knife to slaughter sleeping men:
But here 's a vengeful sword, rusted with ease,
That shall be scoured in his rancorous heart
That slanders me with murder's crimson badge.
II Henry VI. Act iii, sc. 2, l. 197. [Suffolk]
"Vengeful" is repeated in *Titus Andronicus,* v, 2, 51: "Vengeful waggon"; and in *Sonnets,* xcix: "Vengeful canker."

8
Get thee a sword, though made of a lath.
II Henry VI. Act iv, sc. 2, l. 1. [Bevis]

Go to; have your lath glued within your sheath
Till you know better how to handle it.
Titus Andronicus. Act ii, sc. 1, l. 41. [Demetrius]

Dagger of lath.—*I Henry IV,* ii, 4, 151; *Twelfth Night,* iv, 2, 136.

9
We will have the mayor's sword borne before us.
II Henry VI. Act iv, sc. 3, l. 16. [Cade]

Hath my sword therefore broke through London gates, that you should leave me at the White Hart in Southwark?
II Henry VI. Act iv, sc. 8, l. 23. [Cade]
Southwark is mentioned again in iv, 4, 27, and in no other play. The only reference to the White Hart.

10 God forbid so many simple souls
Should perish by the sword!
II Henry VI. Act iv, sc. 4, l. 10. [King Henry]

11
My sword make way for me, for here is no staying.
II Henry VI. Act iv, sc. 8, l. 61. [Cade]

I 'll make thee . . . swallow my sword.
II Henry VI. Act iv, sc. 10, l. 31. [Cade]

Let this my sword report what speech forbears
II Henry VI. Act iv, sc. 10, l. 57. [Iden]

Sword, I will hallow thee for this thy deed,
And hang thee o'er my tomb when I am dead:
Ne'er shall this blood be wiped from thy point;
But thou shalt wear it as a herald's coat,
To emblaze the honour that thy master got.
II Henry VI. Act iv, sc. 10, l. 72. [Iden]
The only use of "hallow" and "emblaze."

12
Sword, hold thy temper.
II Henry VI. Act v, sc. 2, l. 70. [Richard]

Here draw I
A sword, whose temper I intend to stain
With the best blood that I can meet withal
In the adventure of this perilous day.
I Henry IV. Act v, sc. 2, l. 93. [Hotspur]

To stain the temper of my knightly sword.
Richard II. Act iv, sc. 1, l. 29. [Aumerle]

1 By the swords of common soldiers slain.
III Henry VI. Act i, sc. 1, l. 9. [York]

Swords of soldiers.—*King John,* ii, 1, 353

2 See how my sword weeps for the poor king's death!
O, may such purple tears be always shed
From those that wish the downfall of our house!
III Henry VI. Act v, sc. 6, l. 63. [Gloucester]

Your swords, made rich
With the most noble blood of all this world.
Julius Cæsar. Act iii, sc. 1, l. 155. [Antony]

3 With this good sword,
That ran through Cæsar's bowels, search this bosom.
Stand not to answer: here, take thou the hilts;
And, when my face is cover'd, as 'tis now,
Guide thou the sword. [*Pindarus stabs him.*] Cæsar, thou art revenged,
Even with the sword that kill'd thee.
Julius Cæsar. Act v, sc. 3, l. 41. [Cassius]

Come, Cassius' sword, and find Titinius' heart.
Julius Cæsar. Act v, sc. 3, l. 90. [Titinius]

Brutus: Hold then my sword, and turn away thy face,
While I do run upon it. Wilt thou, Strato?
Strato: Give me your hand first. Fare you well, my lord.
Brutus: Farewell, good Strato. [*Runs on his sword.*] Cæsar, now be still:
I kill'd thee not with half so good a will.
Julius Cæsar. Act v, sc. 5, l. 47.

Why should I play the Roman fool, and die
On mine own sword? whiles I see lives, the gashes
Do better upon them.
Macbeth. Act v, sc. 8, l. 1. [Macbeth]

4 By heaven, I think my sword 's as sharp as yours.
King John. Act iv, sc. 3, l. 82. [Hubert]

His sword
Hath a sharp edge: it 's long and, 't may be said,
It reaches far, and where 'twill not extend,
Thither he darts it.
Henry VIII. Act i, sc. 1, l. 109. [Norfolk]

5 With his prepared sword, he charges home
My unprovided body.
King Lear. Act ii, sc. 1, l. 53. [Edmund]

6 Bending his sword To his great master.
King Lear. Act iv, sc. 2, l. 74. [Messenger]

Give me my sword.—*King Lear,* iii, 7, 80; *Macbeth,* ii, 1, 9.

Take my sword.—*King Lear,* v, 3, 250; *Macbeth,* ii, 1, 4.

7 That such a slave as this should wear a sword,
Who wears no honesty.
King Lear. Act ii, sc. 2, l. 78. [Kent]

Thou old unhappy traitor,
Briefly thyself remember: the sword is out
That must destroy thee.
King Lear. Act iv, sc. 6, l. 232. [Oswald]

This sword of mine shall give them instant way,
Where they shall rest for ever.
King Lear. Act v, sc. 3, l. 149. [Edmund]

8 Dare me to the desert with thy sword.
Macbeth. Act iii, sc. 4, l. 104. [Macbeth]

Seize upon Fife; give to the edge o' the sword
His wife, his babes.
Macbeth. Act iv, sc. 1, l. 151. [Macbeth]

Hold fast the mortal sword, and like good men
Bestride our down-fall'n birthdom.
Macbeth. Act iv, sc. 3, l. 3. [Macduff] The only use of "down-fall'n" and "birthdom."

Mortal sword.—*Troilus and Cressida,* iv, 5, 134.

9 Be this the whetstone of your sword.
Macbeth. Act iv, sc. 3, l. 228. [Malcolm] "Whetstone" is used also in *As You Like It,* i, 2, 57, and in *Troilus and Cressida,* v, 2, 75.

Within my sword's length set him; if he 'scape,
Heaven forgive him too!
Macbeth. Act iv, sc. 3, l. 234. [Macduff]

But swords I smile at, weapons laugh to scorn,
Brandish'd by man that 's of a woman born.
Macbeth. Act v, sc. 7, l. 12. [Macbeth]

10 I combat challenge of this latten bilbo.
Word of denial in thy labras here!
The Merry Wives of Windsor. Act i, sc. 1, l. 165. [Pistol]. The only use of "latten" (brass), and "labras" (lips). "Bilbo" (sword) is repeated in iii, 5, 112, and occurs in no other play.

11 I have a sword and it shall bite upon my necessity.
The Merry Wives of Windsor. Act ii, sc. 1, l. 135. [Nym]

What, the sword and the word! do you study them both, master parson?
The Merry Wives of Windsor. Act iii, sc. 1, l. 43. [Shallow]

We will do no harm with our swords.
A Midsummer-Night's Dream. Act iii, sc. 1, l. 19. [Bottom]

12 Leonato: Nay, never lay thy hand upon thy sword;
I fear thee not.
Claudio: Marry, beshrew my hand,
If it should give your age such cause of fear:
In faith, my hand meant nothing to my sword.
Much Ado about Nothing. Act v, sc. 1, l. 54.

I care not for thy sword.—*Othello,* v, 2, 165.

13 Keep up your bright swords, for the dew will rust them.
Othello. Act i, sc. 2, l. 59. [Othello]

I heard the clink and fall of swords.
Othello. Act ii, sc. 3, l. 234. [Iago] "Clink" is used again in ii, 3, 71, and in no other play.
Following him with determined sword.—*Othello,* ii, 3, 227.

1
'Tis but a man gone. Forth, my sword: he dies.
Othello. Act v, sc. 1, l. 10. [Roderigo]
Every puny whipster gets my sword.
Othello. Act v, sc. 2, l. 244. [Othello] The only use of "whipster."
Wrench his sword from him.—*Othello,* v, 2, 288.

2
It is a sword of Spain, the ice-brook's temper.
Othello. Act v, sc. 2, l. 253. [Othello] The only use of "ice-brook."
Grecian sword.—*Coriolanus,* i, 3, 46.
Danish sword.—*Hamlet,* iv, 3, 63.
French swords.—*Hamlet,* v, 2, 168.
Roman swords.—*Cymbeline,* iii, 3, 57.
Spanish sword.—*All's Well that Ends Well,* iv, 1, 52.
Sword Philippan.—*Antony and Cleopatra,* ii, 5, 23. The only use of Philippan.

3
And then against my heart he set his sword.
The Rape of Lucrece, l. 1640.

4
There shall your swords and lances arbitrate
The swelling difference of your settled hate.
Richard II, i, 1, 200. [King Richard]
The arbitrement of swords.
Henry V, iv, 1, 168; *Cymbeline,* i, 4, 52.
The arbitrement of bloody strokes.—*Richard III,* v, 3, 89.
The arbitrement is like to be bloody.—*King Lear,* iv, 7, 95.
Mortal arbitrement.—*Twelfth Night,* iii, 4, 286.
Strict arbitrement.—*I Henry IV,* iv, 1, 70. The only uses of "arbitrement."

5
Thy murderous falchion smoking in his blood.
Richard III. Act i, sc. 2, l. 94. [Lady Anne]
With purple falchion, painted to the hilt
In blood of those that had encounter'd him.
III Henry VI. Act i, sc. 4, l. 12. [York]
With my good biting falchion
I would have made them skip.
King Lear. Act v, sc. 3, l. 276. [King Lear] The only uses of "falchion."

6
To-morrow in the battle think on me,
And fall thy edgeless sword.
Richard III. Act v, sc. 3, l. 134; 163. [Ghost] The only use of "edgeless."
Is the sword unsway'd?—*Richard III,* iv, 4, 470.
Our . . . swords our law.—*Richard III,* v, 3, 311.

7
Capulet: Give me my long sword, ho!
Lady Capulet: A crutch, a crutch! why call you for a sword?
Capulet: My sword, I say! Old Montague is come
And flourishes his blade in spite of me.
Romeo and Juliet. Act i, sc. 1, l. 82.
Let fall thy blade on vulnerable crests.
Macbeth. Act v, sc. 8, l. 11. [Macbeth]
Come, blade, my breast imbrue.—*A Midsummer-Night's Dream,* v, 1, 351.
Bloody blameful blade.—*A Midsummer-Night's Dream,* v, 1, 147.
Spanish blades.—*Romeo and Juliet,* i, 4, 84.
Treacherous blade.—*Richard III,* i, 4, 211.
A very good blade!—*Romeo and Juliet,* ii, 4, 31.

8
What mean these masterless and gory swords
To lie discolour'd by this place of peace?
Romeo and Juliet. Act v, sc. 3, l. 142. [Friar Laurence]

9
The elements,
Of whom your swords are temper'd, may as well
Wound the loud winds, or with bemock'd-at stabs
Kill the still-closing waters, as diminish
One dowle that's in my plume: my fellow-ministers
Are like invulnerable.
The Tempest. Act iii, sc. 3, l. 61. [Ariel] The only use of "bemock'd-at," "still-closing," "dowle" (one of the filaments which make up the blade of a feather), and "fellow-ministers."
Your swords are now too massy for your strengths
And will not be uplifted.
The Tempest. Act iii, sc. 3, l. 67. [Ariel]

10
Plead my successive title with your swords.
Titus Andronicus. Act i, sc. 1, l. 4. [Saturninus]
He circumscribed with his sword,
And brought to yoke, the enemies of Rome.
Titus Andronicus. Act i, sc. 1, l. 68. [Captain] "Circumscribed" is repeated in *Hamlet,* i, 3, 22.
That my sword upon thee shall approve.
Titus Andronicus. Act ii, sc. 1, l. 35. [Chiron]
This sword shall plough thy bowels up.
Titus Andronicus. Act iv, sc. 2, l. 87. [Aaron]

11
Pandarus: There be hacks!
Cressida: Be those with swords?
Pandarus: Swords! any thing, he cares not. . . . Look you how his sword is bloodied.
Troilus and Cressida. Act i, sc. 2, l. 225.
They have . . . true swords.—*Troilus and Cressida,* i, 3, 238.
Your true sword drawn.—*Troilus and Cressida,* v, 3, 56.
True sword to sword.—*Coriolanus,* i, 10, 15.

12
You know a sword employed is perilous,
And reason flies the object of all harm:
Who marvels then, when Helenus beholds
A Grecian and his sword, if he do set
The very wings of reason to his heels?
Troilus and Cressida, ii, 2, 40. See under Discretion.

II—Drawing the Sword

1 They have entertained cause enough
To draw their swords.
Antony and Cleopatra. Act ii, sc. 1, l. 46. [Pompey]
Drew their swords with you.—*Antony and Cleopatra,* ii, 2, 48.
I did not think to draw my sword 'gainst Pompey.
Antony and Cleopatra. Act ii, sc. 2, l. 156. [Antony]
Draw that thy honest sword, which thou hast worn
Most useful for thy country.
Antony and Cleopatra. Act iv, sc. 14, l. 79. [Antony]
Eros: My sword is drawn.
Antony: Then let it do at once
The thing why thou hast drawn it. . . .
Eros: Shall I strike now?
Antony: Now, Eros.
Eros: Why, there then: thus I do escape the sorrow
Of Antony's death. [*Kills himself.*]
Antony and Cleopatra. Act iv, sc. 14, l. 88.
Draw thy sword, and give me
Sufficing strokes for death.
Antony and Cleopatra. Act iv, sc. 14, l. 117. [Antony] The only use of "sufficing."

2
Nor ever didst thou draw thy sword on me.
The Comedy of Errors. Act v, sc. 1, l. 266. [Antipholus of Ephesus]
Naked swords.—*The Comedy of Errors,* iv, 4, 148.
Drawn swords.—*Comedy of Errors,* v, 1, 151.

3
What shall I need to draw my sword?
Cymbeline. Act iii, sc. 4, l. 34. [Pisanio]
I draw the sword myself.—*Cymbeline,* iii, 4, 69.
Best draw my sword; and if mine enemy
But fear the sword like me, he 'll scarcely look on 't.
Such a foe, good heavens!
Cymbeline. Act iii, sc. 6, l. 25. [Imogen]
With his sword drawn.—*Cymbeline,* v, 5, 276.

4
We will our youth lead on to higher fields
And draw no swords but what are sanctified.
II Henry IV. Act iv, sc. 4, l. 3. [King Henry]

5
Learn this lesson, draw thy sword in right.
III Henry VI. Act ii, sc. 2, l. 62. [King]
Draw thy sword: one stroke Shall free thee.
The Tempest. Act ii, sc. 1, l. 292. [Sebastian]
Draw thy sword.—*King Lear,* v, 3, 126; *Twelfth Night,* iv, 1, 46.
Drawing my sword.—*Love's Labour's Lost,* i, 2, 62.
Draws a sword.—*I Henry VI,* iii, 4, 39; *A Midsummer-Night's Dream,* iii, 2, 411.
Unsheathe your sword.—*III Henry VI,* ii, 2, 59.
Draw thy tool.—*Romeo and Juliet,* i, 1, 37. The only use of "tool" in the sense of sword.

6
I draw a sword against conspirators;
When think you that the sword goes up again?
Never, till Cæsar's three and thirty wounds
Be well avenged; or till another Cæsar
Have added slaughter to the sword of traitors.
Julius Cæsar. Act v, sc. 1, l. 51. [Octavius]

7
If I see a sword out, my finger itches to make one.
The Merry Wives of Windsor. Act ii, sc. 3, l. 47. [Shallow]

8
Pyramus must draw a sword to kill himself; which the ladies cannot abide.
A Midsummer-Night's Dream. Act iii, sc. 1, l. 11. [Bottom]
Out, sword, and wound The pap of Pyramus;
Ay, that left pap, where heart doth hop.
A Midsummer-Night's Dream. Act v, sc. 1, l. 301. [Pyramus]
Come, trusty sword;
Come, blade, my breast imbrue.
A Midsummer-Night's Dream. Act v, sc. 1, l. 350. [Thisbe]
Out, sword, and to a sore purpose!—*Cymbeline,* iv, 1, 24.

9
Draw not thy sword to guard iniquity,
For it was lent thee all that brood to kill.
The Rape of Lucrece, l. 626.

10
What my tongue speaks my right drawn sword may prove.
Richard II. Act i, sc. 1, l. 46. [Bolingbroke]

11
Advance your standards, draw your willing swords.
Richard III. Act v, sc. 3, l. 264. [Richmond]

12
Will you pluck your sword out of his pilcher by the ears?
Romeo and Juliet. Act iii, sc. 1, l. 83. [Mercutio] The only use of "pilcher" (leathern-scabbard).

13
Patricians, draw your swords, and sheathe them not
Till Saturninus be Rome's emperor.
Titus Andronicus. Act i, sc. 1, l. 204. [Saturninus]

14
Since the first sword was drawn about this question.
Troilus and Cressida. Act ii, sc. 2, l. 18 [Hector]

15
Would thou mightst never draw sword again.
Twelfth Night. Act i, sc. 3, l. 66. [Sir Toby]
I would I might never draw sword again.
Twelfth Night. Act i, sc. 3, l. 67. [Sir Andrew]
Never draw thy sword.—*Twelfth Night,* iii, 4, 429.
You drew your sword upon me without cause.
Twelfth Night. Act v, sc. 1, l. 191. [Viola]

III—Sheathing the Sword

16
Here sheathe thy sword, I 'll pardon thee my death.
III Henry VI. Act v, sc. 5, l. 70. [Queen Margaret]

1
I ha' not since put up my sword.
Julius Cæsar. Act i, sc. 3, l. 19. [Casca]
Part, fools!
Put up your swords; you know not what you do.
Romeo and Juliet. Act i, sc. 1, l. 72. [Benvolio]
Pray, sir, put your sword up, if you please.
Twelfth Night. Act iii, sc. 4, l. 354. [Viola]
Put up your sword.—*Henry V,* ii, 1, 46; *Richard III,* i, 2, 197; *Coriolanus,* v, 6, 136.
Put up thy sword.—*Romeo and Juliet,* i, 1, 75.

2
Lay aside the sword.
King John. Act i, sc. 1, l. 12. [Chatillon]
Bastard: Your sword is bright, sir; put it up again.
Salisbury: Not till I sheathe it in a murderer's skin.
King John. Act iv, sc. 3, l. 79.

3 Either thou, Macbeth,
Or else my sword with an unbatter'd edge
I sheathe again undeeded.
Macbeth. Act v, sc. 7, l. 18. [Macduff] The only use of "unbatter'd" and "undeeded."

4
Come, lay their swords to pawn.
The Merry Wives of Windsor. Act iii, sc. 1, l. 112. [Host]

5
Here Goths have given me leave to sheathe my sword.
Titus Andronicus. Act i, sc. 1, l. 85. [Titus]

6
Rest, sword; thou hast thy fill of blood and death.
Troilus and Cressida. Act v, sc. 8, l. 4. [Hector]
My half-supp'd sword, that frankly would have fed,
Pleased with this dainty bait, thus goes to bed.
Troilus and Cressida. Act v, sc. 8, l. 19. [Achilles] The only use of "half-supp'd."

SYMPATHY

7
It is a wonderful thing to see the semblable coherence of his men's spirits and his: . . . their spirits are so married in conjunction with the participation of society that they flock together in consent, like so many wild geese.
II Henry IV. Act v, sc. 1, l. 72. [Falstaff] The only use of "coherence." "Participation" is repeated in *I Henry IV,* iii, 2, 87.

8
Had he been slaughter-man to all my kin,
I should not for my life but weep with him,
To see how inly sorrow gripes his soul.
III Henry VI. Act i, sc. 4, l. 169. [Northumberland]

9
I am pale at mine heart to see thine eyes so red.
Measure for Measure. Act iv, sc. 3, l. 157. [Lucio]

10
You are not young, no more am I; go to then, there's sympathy: you are merry, so am I; ha, ha! then there's more sympathy.
The Merry Wives of Windsor. Act ii, sc. 1, l. 6. [Mrs. Page]

11
But as the earth doth weep, the sun being set,
Each flower moisten'd like a melting eye;
Even so the maid with swelling drops gan wet
Her circle eyne, enforced by sympathy.
The Rape of Lucrece, l. 1226.

12
The senseless brands will sympathize.
Richard II. Act v, sc. 1, l. 46. [King Richard]
Let it sympathize.—*I Henry IV,* v, 1, 7.
The men do sympathize.—*Henry V,* iii, 7, 158.
We sympathize.—*Troilus and Cressida,* iv, 1, 25.
Truly sympathized.—*Sonnets,* lxxxii.
Well sympathized.—*Love's Labour's Lost,* iii, 1, 52.

13 I am not made of stones,
But penetrable to your kind entreats.
Richard III. Act iii, sc. 7, l. 224. [Gloucester]
Made of penetrable stuff.—*Hamlet,* iii, 4, 36. The only uses of "penetrable."

14
O woful sympathy! Piteous predicament!
Romeo and Juliet. Act iii, sc. 3, l. 85. [Nurse]
Solemn sympathy.—*Venus and Adonis,* l. 1057.
Sympathy in years.—*Othello,* ii, 1, 232.

15
O, what a sympathy of woe is this,
As far from help as Limbo is from bliss!
Titus Andronicus. Act iii, sc. 1, l. 148. [Titus]

T

TABLE

1
A table full of welcome makes scarce one dainty dish.
The Comedy of Errors. Act iii, sc. 1, l. 23. [Antipholus of Ephesus]

2
Set at upper end o' the table; no question asked him.
Coriolanus. Act iv, sc. 5, l. 205. [Servant]
At upper end o' the table.—*The Winter's Tale,* iv, 4, 59.

3
God be at your table!
Hamlet. Act iv, sc. 5, l. 44. [Ophelia]
Set the table on a roar.
Hamlet. Act v, sc. 1, l. 211. [Hamlet]

4
At the round table.
II Henry IV. Act ii, sc. 1, l. 95. [Hostess]
Flattering table.—*King John,* ii, 1, 503.
Marriage tables.—*Hamlet,* i, 2, 181.
Moderate table.—*Timon of Athens,* iii, 4, 117.

5
And therefore will he wipe his tables clean
And keep no tell-tale to his memory.
II Henry IV. Act iv, sc. 1, l. 201. [York]
The table wherein all my thoughts
Are visibly character'd and engraved.
The Two Gentlemen of Verona. Act ii, sc. 7, l. 3. [Julia] The only use of "visibly."
Table of my memory.—*Hamlet,* i, 5, 98.
Tables of his law.—*Richard III,* i, 4, 201.
Table of my heart.—*Sonnets,* xxiv.
In our heart's table.—*All's Well that Ends Well,* i, 1, 106.
Tables of their thoughts.—*Troilus and Cressida,* iv, 5, 60.
Thy tables, are within my brain.—*Sonnets,* cxxii.

6
Macbeth: The table 's full.
Lennox: Here 's a place reserved, sir.
Macbeth. Act iii, sc. 4, l. 46.

7
Their tables were stored full, to glad the sight.
Pericles. Act i, sc. 4, l. 28. [Cleon]

8
Turn the tables up.
Romeo and Juliet. Act i, sc. 5, l. 29. [Capulet]
Set foot under thy table.—*The Taming of the Shrew,* ii, 1, 404.

9
At Priam's royal table do I sit.
Troilus and Cressida. Act i, sc. 1, l. 29. [Troilus]

TAIL

10
This body hath a tail
More perilous than the head.
Cymbeline. Act iv, sc. 2. l. 144. [Belarius]

11
Clapp'd his tail between his legs.
II Henry VI. Act v, sc. 1, l. 154. [Richard]

12
It should seem, then, that Dobbin's tail grows backward.
The Merchant of Venice. Act ii, sc. 2, l. 102. [Launcelot] The only mention of Dobbin.
Armed tail.—*Troilus and Cressida,* v, 10, 44.
Dragon's tail.—*King Lear,* i, 2, 140.
Horse's tail.—*Troilus and Cressida,* v, 8, 21; v, 10, 4.
Salmon's tail.—*Othello,* ii, 1, 156.
Tithe-pig's tail.—*Romeo and Juliet,* i, 4, 79. The only use of "tithe-pig."
Tails of wasps.—*The Winter's Tale,* i, 2, 329. See under WASP.

13
Thereby hangs a tail.
Othello, iii, 1, 8. See under TALE.

14
Shake his tail and say nothing.
The Two Gentlemen of Verona. Act ii, sc. 5, l. 37. [Launce]

15 His tail that, like a falling plume,
Cool shadow to his melting buttock lent.
Venus and Adonis, l. 314.
Proud tails.—*Venus and Adonis,* l. 923.
Thick tail.—*Venus and Adonis,* l. 298.

TAILOR

16
Lafeu: Pray you, sir, who 's his tailor?
Parolles: Sir?
Lafeu: O, I know him well, I, sir; he, sir, 's a good workman, a very good tailor.
All's Well that Ends Well. Act ii, sc. 5, l. 18.
Tailors of the earth.—*Antony and Cleopatra,* i, 2, 170.

17
I have undone three tailors.
As You Like It. Act v, sc. 4, l. 47. [Touchstone]

18
Even now a tailor call'd me to his shop
And show'd me silks that he had bought for me
And therewithal took measure of my body.
The Comedy of Errors. Act iv, sc. 3, l. 7. [Antipholus of Syracuse]

19
Thy tailor, rascal, . . . made those clothes,
Which, as it seems, make thee.
Cymbeline. Act iv, sc. 2, l. 81. [Guiderius]
Kent: You cowardly rascal, nature disclaims in thee: a tailor made thee.
Cornwall: Thou art a strange fellow: a tailor make a man?
Kent: Ay, a tailor, sir: a stone-cutter or a painter could not have made him so ill, though he had been but two hours at the trade.
King Lear. Act ii, sc. 2, l. 59. The only use of "stone-cutter."

20
'Tis the next way to turn tailor, or be red-breast teacher.
I Henry IV. Act iii, sc. 1, l. 264. [Hotspur] The only use of "red-breast."

1
Falstaff: What trade art thou, Feeble?
Feeble: A woman's tailor, sir.
Shallow: Shall I prick him, sir?
Falstaff: You may: but if he had been a man's tailor, he 'ld ha' pricked you. Wilt thou make as many holes in an enemy's battle as thou hast done in a woman's petticoat? . . . Prick the woman's tailor.
II Henry IV. Act iii, sc. 2, l. 160.

2
I saw a smith stand with his hammer, thus,
The whilst his iron did on the anvil cool,
With open mouth swallowing a tailor's news.
King John. Act iv, sc. 2, l. 193. [Hubert]
Who, with his shears and measure in his hand,
Standing on slippers, which his nimble haste
Had falsely thrust upon contrary feet.
King John. Act iv, sc. 2, l. 196. [Hubert]
Shore with shears.—*A Midsummer-Night's Dream*, v, 1, 348.
Pair of shears.—*Measure for Measure*, i, 2, 29.
Shears of destiny.—*King John*, iv, 2, 91. The only uses of "shears."

3
Faith, here 's an English tailor come hither, for stealing out of a French hose.
Macbeth. Act ii, sc. 3, l. 16. [Porter]
Come in, tailor; here you may roast your goose.
Macbeth. Act ii, sc. 3, l. 18. [Porter]

4
This secrecy of thine shall be a tailor to thee and shall make thee a new doublet and hose.
The Merry Wives of Windsor. Act iii, sc. 3, l. 33. [Mrs. Page]

5
Now will he lie ten nights awake, carving the fashion of a new doublet.
Much Ado about Nothing. Act ii, sc. 3, l. 17. [Benedick]

6
King Stephen was a worthy peer,
His breeches cost him but a crown;
He held them sixpence all too dear,
With that he call'd the tailor lown.
Othello. Act ii, sc. 3, l. 92. [Iago] A stanza from an old ballad, *Take Thy Auld Cloak About Thee*, given in Percy's *Reliques*, Series i, bk. ii, No. 7. "Lown" may be a misprint for clown. It is repeated in *Pericles*, iv, 6, 19: "Lord and lown."
Whose tailors are as dear as yours.
Cymbeline. Act ii, sc. 3, l. 84. [Lady]

7
And entertain some score or two of tailors,
To study fashions to adorn my body.
Richard III. Act i, sc. 2, l. 257. [Gloucester]
The tailor with his last.—*Romeo and Juliet*, i, 2, 40.

8
The tailor stays thy leisure,
To deck thy body with his ruffling treasure.
The Taming of the Shrew. Act iv, sc. 3, l. 59. [Petruchio] The only use of "ruffling."

9
She loved not the savour of tar nor of pitch,
Yet a tailor might scratch her where'er she did itch.
The Tempest. Act ii, sc. 2, l. 54. [Stephano]

10
The tailor make thy doublet of changeable taffeta.
Twelfth Night. Act ii, sc. 4, l. 76. [Clown] Taffeta is mentioned five times in the plays.

TALE

See also Story

11
I could a tale unfold whose lightest word
Would harrow up thy soul, freeze thy young blood,
Make thy two eyes, like stars, start from their spheres,
Thy knotted and combined locks to part
And each particular hair to stand on end,
Like quills upon the fretful porpentine.
Hamlet. Act i, sc. 5, l. 15. [Ghost] "Lightest" is repeated in *The Merchant of Venice*, iii, 2, 91.
A sharp-quill'd porpentine.—*II Henry VI*, iii, 1, 363. The only use of "sharp-quill'd." "Porpentine" is repeated in *Troilus and Cressida*, ii, 1, 27, and is used five times as the name of an inn in *The Comedy of Errors*.
Like hedgehogs which
Lie tumbling in my barefoot way and mount
Their pricks at my footfall.
The Tempest. Act ii, sc. 2, l. 10. [Caliban]
Thorny hedgehogs.—*A Midsummer-Night's Dream*, ii, 2, 10. The only uses of "hedgehogs." "Hedgehog" occurs in *Richard III*, i, 2, 102.

12
He 's for a jig or a tale of bawdry, or he sleeps.
Hamlet. Act ii, sc. 2, l. 522. [Hamlet]
Impure tale.—*The Rape of Lucrece*, l. 1078.

13
Mark now, how a plain tale shall put you down.
I Henry IV. Act ii, sc. 4, l. 281. [Prince]
This is the strangest tale that ever I heard.
I Henry IV. Act v, sc. 4, l. 158. [Lancaster]

14
It is not well done, mark you now, to take the tales out of my mouth, ere it is made and finished.
Henry V. Act iv, sc. 7, l. 44. [Fluellen]

15
Tush, my good lord, this superficial tale
Is but a preface of her worthy praise.
I Henry VI. Act v, sc. 5, l. 11. [Suffolk] The only use of "preface." "Superficial" occurs again in *Measure for Measure*, iii, 2, 147.

16
Short tale to make.
III Henry VI. Act ii, sc. 1, l. 120. [Warwick] Repeated in *Hamlet*, ii, 2, 146.
List a brief tale.—*King Lear*, v, 3, 181.

17
The tract of every thing
Would by a good discourser lose some life,
Which action's self was tongue to.
Henry VIII. Act i, sc. 1, l. 40. [Norfolk] "Tract" occurs again in *Timon of Athens*, i, 1, 50. The only use of "discourser."
Bid him recount The fore-recited practices.
Henry VIII. Act i, sc. 2, l. 127. [King Henry] The only use of "fore-recited."

1
And down I laid to list the sad-tuned tale.
A Lover's Complaint, l. 4. The only use of "sad-tuned."
Saddest tale.—*A Midsummer-Night's Dream,* ii, 1, 51.

2
I will a round unvarnish'd tale deliver
Of my whole course of love; what drugs, what charms,
What conjuration and what mighty magic, . . .
I won his daughter.
Othello. Act i, sc. 3, l. 90. [Othello] The only use of "unvarnish'd."
I think this tale would win my daughter too.
Othello. Act i, sc. 3, l. 171. [Othello]

3
How many tales to please me hath she coined!
The Passionate Pilgrim, l. 93.
Pleasing tale.—*Titus Andronicus,* iii, 2, 47; v, 1, 119.
Tales of others' griefs.—*Pericles,* i, 4, 2.

4
I was come to the whole depth of my tale.
Romeo and Juliet, ii, 4, 104. [Mercutio]
Tedious tale.—*Romeo and Juliet,* v, 3, 230.
A tale of length.—*Troilus and Cressida,* i, 3, 136.

5
Grumio: Thereby hangs a tale.
Curtis: Let 's ha 't, good Grumio.
Grumio: Lend thine ear.
Curtis: Here.
Grumio: There. [*Strikes him.*]
Curtis: This is to feel a tale, not to hear a tale.
Grumio: And therefore 'tis called a sensible tale.
The Taming of the Shrew. Act iv, sc. 1, l. 60.
Clown: O, thereby hangs a tail.
Musician: Whereby hangs a tale, sir?
Othello. Act iii, sc. 1, l. 8.
Thereby hangs a tale.—*As You Like It,* ii, 7, 28; *The Merry Wives of Windsor,* i, 4, 159.

6
Your tale, sir, would cure deafness.
The Tempest. Act i, sc. 2, l. 106. [Miranda]
Now, forward with your tale.
The Tempest. Act iii, sc. 2, l. 91. [Stephano]
For 'tis a chronicle of day by day,
Not a relation for a breakfast.
The Tempest. Act v, sc. 1, l. 163. [Prospero]

7
This is the tragic tale of Philomel,
And treats of Tereus' treason and his rape;
And rape, I fear, was root of thine annoy.
Titus Andronicus. Act iv, sc. 1, l. 47. [Titus]
She hath been reading late The tale of Tereus.
Cymbeline. Act ii, sc. 2, l. 44. [Iachimo]

8
My tales of love were wont to weary you;
I know you joy not in a love-discourse.
The Two Gentlemen of Verona. Act ii, sc. 4, l. 126. [Proteus] The only use of "love-discourse."
Amorous tale.—*Much Ado about Nothing,* i, 1, 327.
Loving tale.—*The Rape of Lucrece,* l. 480.
Sweet tale.—*I Henry IV,* ii, 4, 135.

9
She whispers in his ears a heavy tale,
As if they heard the woeful words she told.
Venus and Adonis, l. 1025.
Heavy tale.—*Much Ado about Nothing,* iii, 2, 63.
Heavier tale.—*Richard II,* iii, 2, 197.
Hellish tale.—*Titus Andronicus,* ii, 3, 105.
Piteous tale.—*King Lear,* v, 3, 214.
Tales of iron wars.—*I Henry IV,* ii, 3, 51.

10
She trembles at his tale.
Venus and Adonis, l. 591.

11
Like an old tale still, which will have matter to rehearse, though credit be asleep and not an ear open.
The Winter's Tale. Act v, sc. 2, l. 67. [Gentleman]
That she is living,
Were it but told you, should be hooted at
Like an old tale.
The Winter's Tale. Act v, sc. 3, l. 115. [Paulina]
Old tale.—*Much Ado about Nothing,* i, 1, 218; *As You Like It,* i, 2, 128; *The Merry Wives of Windsor,* iv, 4, 28; *Winter's Tale,* v, 2, 30.

II—Telling Tales

12
A mad tale he told to-day at dinner.
The Comedy of Errors. Act iv, sc. 4, l. 89. [Courtezan]

13
I shall tell you
A pretty tale: it may be you have heard it;
But, since it serves my purpose, I will venture
To stale 't a little more.
Coriolanus. Act i, sc. 1, l. 92. [Menenius]
I can tell thee pretty tales of the duke.
Measure for Measure. Act iv, sc. 3, l. 175. [Lucio]

14
If thou wert honourable,
Thou wouldst have told this tale for virtue.
Cymbeline. Act i, sc. 6, l. 142. [Imogen]
What tales I have told you
Of courts, of princes, of the tricks in war.
Cymbeline. Act iii, sc. 3, l. 14. [Belarius]
I . . . am right glad he is not standing here
To tell this tale of mine.
Cymbeline. Act v, sc. 5, l. 296. [Guiderius]

15
And, for the time shall not seem tedious,
I 'll tell thee what befel me on a day
In this self-place where now we mean to stand.
III Henry VI. Act iii, sc. 1, l. 9. [Keeper] The only use of "self-place."

16
Be well advised, tell o'er thy tale again.
King John. Act iii, sc. 1, l. 5. [Constance]
Twice-told tale.—*King John,* iii, 4, 108. See under LIFE.

17
An ancient tale new told.
King John. Act iv, sc. 2, l. 18. [Pembroke]
My tale is told.—*Love's Labour 's Lost,* v, 2, 729.

18
Bid me tell my tale in express words.
King John. Act iv, sc. 2, l. 234. [King John]

1
Mar a curious tale in telling it.
King Lear. Act i, sc. 4, l. 35. [Kent]
Tell old tales.—*King Lear,* v, 3, 12.
Tell your tale.—*I Henry IV,* i, 3, 256
2
Come, mistress, you must tell 's another tale.
Othello. Act v, sc. 1, l. 125. [Iago]
3
And when thou comest thy tale to tell,
Smooth not thy tongue with filed talk.
The Passionate Pilgrim, l. 305.
Sad tales doth tell.—*Rape of Lucrece,* l. 1496.
4
Too well, too well thou tell'st a tale so ill.
Richard II. Act iii, sc. 2, l. 121. [King Richard]
I tell this tale vilely.—*Much Ado about Nothing,* iii, 3, 157.
5
In winter's tedious nights sit by the fire
With good old folks and let them tell thee tales
Of woeful ages long ago betid;
And ere thou bid good night, to quit their griefs,
Tell thou the lamentable tale of me
And send the hearers weeping to their beds.
Richard II. Act v, sc. 1, l. 40. [King Richard]
6
Then he was urged to tell my tale again.
Richard III. Act iii, sc. 7, l. 31. [Buckingham]
Queen Elizabeth: An honest tale speeds best being plainly told.
King Richard: Then in plain terms tell her my loving tale.
Richard III. Act iv, sc. 4, l. 358.
Why dost thou run so many mile about,
When thou mayst tell thy tale a nearer way?
Richard III. Act iv, sc. 4, l. 461. [King Richard]
7 I have seen the day
That I have worn a visor and could tell
A whispering tale in a fair lady's ear,
Such as would please.
Romeo and Juliet. Act i, sc. 5, l. 23. [Capulet]
To a pretty ear she tunes her tale.
Venus and Adonis, l. 74.
8
I will tell no tales.
The Tempest. Act v, sc. 1, l. 129. [Prospero]
Tell tales.—*King Lear,* ii, 4, 231; *Twelfth Night,* ii, 1, 43.
Tell him this tale.—*King John,* iii, 1, 152.
Tell thou the tale.—*The Taming of the Shrew,* iv, 1, 74.
Let him tell the tale.—*Titus Andronicus,* v, 3, 94.
9
Bid Æneas tell the tale twice o'er.
Titus Andronicus. Act iii, sc. 2, l. 27. [Titus]
Æneas' tale to Dido.—*Hamlet,* ii, 2, 468.
10
You shall tell me another tale.
Troilus and Cressida. Act i, sc. 2, l. 90. [Pandarus]
Hermione: Tell 's a tale.
Mamillius: Merry or sad shall 't be?
Hermione: As merry as you will.
Mamillius: A sad tale 's best for winter: I have one
Of sprites and goblins.
The Winter's Tale. Act ii, sc. 1, l. 23.

TALK

See also Conversation, Speech

11
I 'll talk with you more anon.
All's Well that Ends Well. Act i, sc. 3, l. 68. [Countess]
I told your grace they would talk anon.
Henry VIII. Act i, sc. 4, l. 49. [Sands]
12
We shall talk before we fight.
Antony and Cleopatra. Act ii, sc. 6, l. 2. [Pompey]
Let us talk in good earnest.
As You Like It. Act i, sc. 3, l. 26. [Celia]
13
I will weary you then no longer with idle talking.
Know of me then, for now I speak to some purpose.
As You Like It. Act v, sc. 2, l. 56. [Rosalind]
Idle talk.—*Antony and Cleopatra,* v, 2, 50.
14
God help, poor souls, how idly do they talk!
The Comedy of Errors. Act iv, sc. 4, l. 132. [Luciana]
How ill it follows, after you have laboured so hard, you should talk so idly!
II Henry IV. Act ii, sc. 2, l. 31. [Poins]
I talk but idly, and you laugh at me.
Richard II. Act iii, sc. 3, l. 171. [King Richard]
15
What do ye talk?
Coriolanus. Act iii, sc. 1, l. 317. [Sicinius]
I talk of you.—*Coriolanus,* iii, 2, 13.
Never talk on 't.—*Cymbeline,* ii, 4, 132.
Never talk of it.—*II Henry IV,* i, 1, 54.
We 'll talk of that hereafter.—*Cymbeline,* iii, 2, 68.
16
In private I will talk with thee apart.
I Henry VI. Act i, sc. 2, l. 69. [La Pucelle]
We must talk in secret.—*Romeo and Juliet,* i, 3, 8.
17 I 'll talk to you
When you are better temper'd to attend.
I Henry IV. Act i, sc. 3, l. 234. [Worcester]
18
Talk like the vulgar sort of market men.
I Henry VI, iii, 2, 4. See under WORD.
19
Summon a parley; we will talk with him.
I Henry VI. Act iii, sc. 3, l. 35. [La Pucelle]
This is the latest parle we will admit.
Henry V. Act iii, sc. 3, l. 2. [King Henry]
Their purpose is to parle.—*Love's Labour 's Lost,* v, 2, 122.
Break the parle.—*Titus Andronicus,* v, 3, 19.
Sound a parle.—*III Henry VI,* v, 1, 16.
Angry parle.—*Hamlet,* i, 1, 62.
Gentle parle.—*King John,* ii, 1, 205.

1
I come to talk of commonwealth affairs.
II Henry VI. Act i, sc. 3, l. 156. [Gloucester]
They 'll talk of state.—*Richard II,* iii, 4, 27.
Talk of court news.—*King Lear,* v, 3, 14.
2
He talks at random; sure, the man is mad.
I Henry VI. Act v, sc. 3, l. 85. [Margaret]
I writ at random.
The Two Gentlemen of Verona, ii, 1, 117. "At random" occurs also in *The Comedy of Errors,* i, 1, 43.
3
If I chance to talk a little wild, forgive me;
I had it from my father.
Henry VIII. Act i, sc. 4, l. 26. [Sands]
4
I have an hour's talk in store for you;
Remember that you call on me to-day.
Julius Cæsar. Act ii, sc. 2, l. 121. [Cæsar]
We have an hour's talk with you.
The Merry Wives of Windsor. Act ii, sc. 1, l. 171. [Mrs. Page]
5
I would hold more talk with thee.
Julius Cæsar. Act iv, sc. 3, l. 289. [Brutus]
Talk to you sometimes.—*Julius Cæsar,* ii, 1, 285.
We must out and talk.—*Julius Cæsar,* v, 1, 22.
6
I will talk further with you.
King Lear. Act iii, sc. 1, l. 43. [Gentleman]
7
Come, come, you talk greasily; your lips grow foul.
Love's Labour 's Lost. Act iv, sc. 1, l. 139. [Maria]
Wanton talk.—*Venus and Adonis,* l. 809.
8
To be talk'd with in sincerity.
Measure for Measure. Act i, sc. 4, l. 36. [Lucio]
Talk with respect.—*The Merchant of Venice,* ii, 2, 200.
9
Let it serve for table-talk.
The Merchant of Venice. Act iii, sc. 5, l. 93. [Lorenzo] The only use of "table-talk."
Your soldiers use him as their grace 'fore meat,
Their talk at table.
Coriolanus. Act iv, sc. 7, l. 3. [Lieutenant]
Break their talk.—*The Merry Wives of Windsor,* iii, 4, 22.
Does she talk of him?—*The Merry Wives of Windsor,* iv, 2, 30.
Talk not of her.—*Much Ado about Nothing,* ii, 1, 262.
Talk in deeds.—*The Rape of Lucrece,* l. 1348. See DEED, 315:5.
10
Let 's talk of graves, of worms, of epitaphs.
Richard II. Act iii, sc. 2, l. 145. [King Richard]
Let 's talk.—*Romeo and Juliet,* iii, 5, 25.
11
I 'll talk with this good fellow.
Richard III. Act iii, sc. 2, l. 97. [Hastings]
12
We talk here in the public haunt of men.
Romeo and Juliet. Act iii, sc. 1, l. 53. [Benvolio]
Go hence, to have more talk of these sad things.
Romeo and Juliet. Act v, sc. 3, l. 307. [Prince]
But what talk I of this?—*The Taming of the Shrew,* iv, 1, 91.
13
Thou dost talk nothing to me.
The Tempest. Act ii, sc. 1, l. 170. [Alonso]
Sit then and talk with her; she is thine own.
The Tempest. Act iv, sc. 1, l. 32. [Prospero]
14
Fie, fie, how franticly I square my talk.
Titus Andronicus. Act iii, sc. 2, l. 31. [Titus] The only use of "franticly."
Talk in signs.—*Titus Andronicus,* iii, 2, 12.
Talk at pleasure.—*Titus Andronicus,* iv, 2, 134.
I am come to talk with thee.—*Titus Andronicus,* v, 2, 16.
15
But, soft! methinks I do digress too much.
Titus Andronicus. Act v, sc. 3, l. 116. [Lucius] "Digress" is repeated in *The Taming of the Shrew,* iii, 2, 109.
16
What were you talking of when I came?
Troilus and Cressida. Act i, sc. 2, l. 48. [Pandarus]
What do you talk of?—*Troilus and Cressida,* i, 2, 45.
17
Lady, give me your hand, and, as we walk,
To our own selves bend we our needful talk.
Troilus and Cressida. Act iv, sc. 4, l. 140. [Troilus]
I profit not by thy talk.
Troilus and Cressida. Act v, sc. 1, l. 16. [Thersites]
Scarce to be worth talking of.—*Twelfth Night,* iii, 4, 328.
18
Speed: 'Item: She doth talk in her sleep.'
Launce: It 's no matter for that, so she sleep not in her talk.
The Two Gentlemen of Verona. Act iii, sc. 1, l. 333.
19
My father and the gentlemen are in sad talk, and we 'll not trouble them.
Winter's Tale. Act iv, sc. 4, l. 316. [Clown]
Sad talk.—*Two Gentlemen of Verona,* i, 3, 1.
Solemn talk.—*As You Like It,* ii, 4, 21.
Common talk.—*Taming of the Shrew,* i, 1, 35.

II—Loquacity

See also Prattle

20
He . . . talks like a knell, and his hum is a battery.
Coriolanus. Act v, sc. 4, l. 22. [Menenius]
He will be talking.—*Much Ado about Nothing,* iii, 5, 36; *The Tempest,* ii, 1, 27.
Yet he talks well.—*As You Like It,* iii, 5, 110.
Wilt thou still talk?—*The Comedy of Errors,* iv, 4, 47.
Talk thy tongue weary.—*Cymbeline,* iii, 4, 115.
21
Reignier: My lord, methinks, is very long in talk.
Alençon: Doubtless he shrives this woman to her smock;

Else ne'er could he so long protract his speech.
I Henry VI. Act i, sc. 2, l. 118. "Protract" is used again in *Cymbeline,* iv, 2, 232.

1 The red wine first must rise
In their fair cheeks, my lord; then we shall have 'em
Talk us to silence.
Henry VIII. Act i, sc. 4, l. 43. [Sands]

How you do talk!—*Henry VIII,* ii, 3, 44.

2
I 'll . . . talk till doomsday here.
Love's Labour 's Lost. Act iv, sc. 3, l. 274. [Biron]

3
I wonder that you will still be talking, Signior Benedick: nobody marks you.
Much Ado about Nothing. Act i, sc. 1, l. 117. [Beatrice]

If they were but a week married, they would talk themselves mad.
Much Ado about Nothing. Act ii, sc. 1, l. 368. [Leonato]

She has been too long a talking.
Much Ado about Nothing. Act iii, sc. 2, l. 107. [Don John]

To babble and to talk.—*Much Ado about Nothing,* iii, 3, 37.

4
I 'll . . . talk him out of patience.
Othello, iii, 3, 23. See LORD, 890:9.

Come, come, you talk.—*Othello,* iv, 3, 25.

Too much talk.—*The Rape of Lucrece,* l. 1106.

5 We will not stand to prate;
Talkers are no good doers.
Richard III. Act i, sc. 3, l. 351. [Murderer] The only use of "talkers."

Have great care I be not found a talker.
Henry VIII. Act ii, sc. 2, l. 79. [King]

I 'll grow a talker for this gear.
The Merchant of Venice. Act i, sc. 1, l. 110. [Antonio] The only uses of "talker."

6 Peace, peace, Mercutio, peace!
Thou talk'st of nothing.
Romeo and Juliet. Act i, sc. 4, l. 95. [Romeo]

A gentleman, nurse, that loves to hear himself talk, and will speak more in a minute than he will stand to in a month.
Romeo and Juliet. Act ii, sc. 4, l. 155. [Romeo]

7
What! this gentleman will out-talk us all.
The Taming of the Shrew. Act i, sc. 2, l. 248. [Gremio] The only use of "out-talk."

8
Have you not done talking yet?
Troilus and Cressida. Act iii, sc. 2, l. 109. [Pandarus]

I would somebody had heard her talk yesterday, as I did.
Troilus and Cressida. Act i, sc. 1, l. 45. [Pandarus]

9
Talks as familiarly of roaring lions.
Winter's Tale, ii, 1, 459. See under MOUTH.

Talks as familiarly of John a Gaunt.—*II Henry IV,* iii, 2, 344.

III—Taciturnity
See also Silence

10
First Citizen: Is 't a verdict?
All: No more talking on 't.
Coriolanus. Act i, sc. 1, l. 11.

11
I profess not talking.
I Henry IV. Act v, sc. 2, l. 92. [Hotspur]

I do not talk much.—*Henry VIII,* ii, 1, 146.

12
Hale him away, and let him talk no more.
II Henry VI. Act iv, sc. 1, l. 131. [Captain]

We will talk no more of this matter.
Love's Labour 's Lost. Act v, sc. 1, l. 119. [Armado]

Never talk to me.—*As You Like It,* iii, 4, 1.

Talk not to me.—*The Taming of the Shrew,* ii, 1, 35; *The Merry Wives of Windsor,* iv, 6, 1.

13
'Tis no time to talk.
III Henry VI. Act iv, sc. 5, l. 24. [Gloucester]

Forbear this talk.—*III Henry VI,* iv, 1, 6.

14
Do not talk of him, But as a property.
Julius Cæsar, iv, 1, 39. See under CHARACTER.

Do not talk to me.—*Othello,* iv, 2, 102.

Talk no more.—*Richard III,* i, 4, 90; *Romeo and Juliet,* iii, 3, 60.

Break off your talk.—*Richard III,* iii, 1, 177.

Filed talk.—*The Passionate Pilgrim,* l. 306.

15
Talk not to me, for I 'll not speak a word.
Romeo and Juliet, iii, 5, 204. See SPEECH: SPEAKING A WORD.

Talk not, I advise you.—*The Taming of the Shrew,* i, 2, 44.

16
Away, and talk not; trouble us no more.
Titus Andronicus. Act i, sc. 1, l. 478. [Saturninus] See DISMISSAL, 360:1.

Stay not to talk with them.—*Titus Andronicus,* ii, 3, 306.

TAMENESS

17
I see love hath made thee a tame snake.
As You Like It. Act iv, sc. 3, l. 70. [Rosalind]

You are a tame man, go!
A Midsummer-Night's Dream. Act iii, sc. 2, l. 259. [Demetrius]

18
I am tame, sir.
Hamlet. Act iii, sc. 2, l. 322. [Hamlet]

Be not too tame neither.—*Hamlet,* iii, 2, 18.

19
The hey-dey in the blood is tame.
Hamlet, iii, 4, 69. See under AGE. "Hey-dey" is repeated in *The Tempest,* ii, 2, 190.

Tame and dull.—*I Henry IV,* iv, 3, 23.

20
Stoop tamely to the foot of majesty.
II Henry IV, iv, 2, 42. See under OBEDIENCE.

Bear it tamely.—*King Lear,* ii, 4, 279.

Live thus tamely.—*Henry VIII,* iii, 2, 279. The only uses of "tamely."

1
He 's mad that trusts in the tameness of a wolf.
King Lear. Act iii, sc. 6, l. 19. [Fool] "Tameness" is used only once again, in *The Merry Wives of Windsor,* iv, 2, 27.

2
Though what I am I cannot avoid, yet to be what I would not shall not make me tame.
The Merry Wives of Windsor. Act iii, sc. 5, l. 153. [Ford]

Tame to fortune's blows.—*King Lear,* iv, 6, 225.

Tame to sufferance.—*Sonnets,* lviii.

3
I 'll tame you; I 'll bring you in subjection.
Pericles. Act ii, sc. 5, l. 75. [Simonides]

4
I am he born to tame you, Kate.
The Taming of the Shrew. Act ii, sc. 1, l. 278. [Petruchio]

He 'll tame her.—*The Taming of the Shrew,* iv, 2, 53.

Tame a shrew.—*The Taming of the Shrew,* iv, 1, 213; iv, 2, 58.

5
If I can recover him and keep him tame.
The Tempest. Act ii, sc. 2, l. 71. [Stephano] Repeated in l. 80.

6
You must be watched ere you be made tame, must you?
Troilus and Cressida. Act iii, sc. 2, l. 45. [Pandarus]

7
Tamed with too much handling.
Venus and Adonis, l. 560.

TAPESTRY

8
Cover'd o'er with Turkish tapestry.
The Comedy of Errors. Act iv, sc. 1, l. 104. [Antipholus of Ephesus]

Hang'd With tapestry of silk and silver.
Cymbeline. Act ii, sc. 4, l. 69. [Iachimo]

9
Hostess: By this heavenly ground I tread on, I must be fain to pawn both my plate and the tapestry of my dining-chambers.
Falstaff: Glasses, glasses, is the only drinking: and for thy walls, a pretty slight drollery, or the story of the Prodigal, or the German hunting in water-work, is worth a thousand of these bed-hangings and these fly-bitten tapestries.
I Henry IV. Act ii, sc. 1, l. 152. "Dining-chambers" is repeated in *Two Gentlemen of Verona,* iv, 4, 9. The only use of "water-work," "bed-hangings," and "fly-bitten."

Smirched worm-eaten tapestry.—*Much Ado about Nothing,* iii, 3, 146. "Worm-eaten" is repeated in *As You Like It,* iii, 4, 27: "Worm-eaten nut"; and in *II Henry IV,* Ind., 35: "Worm-eaten hold."

10
My hanging all of Tyrian tapestry.
The Taming of the Shrew. Act ii, sc. 1, l. 351. [Gremio] See under POSSESSIONS. "Tyrian" is repeated in *Pericles,* v, Gower, 18: "Tyrian ship."

Rich hangings.—*II Henry VI,* v, 3, 12.

TARDINESS, see Lateness

TARRYING

See also Delay

11
I 'll tarry no longer with you.
As You Like It. Act iii, sc. 2, l. 309. [Jaques]

12
To tarry for the hoy Delay.
The Comedy of Errors. Act iv, sc. 3, l. 40. [Dromio of Syracuse] The only use of "hoy," a small coasting vessel.

13
Poins: Tarry at home and be hanged.
Falstaff: Hear ye, Yedward; if I tarry at home and go not, I 'll hang you for going. . . .
Prince: Well, come what will, I 'll tarry at home.
I Henry IV. Act i, sc. 2, l. 147. The only use of "Yedward," a familiar form of Edward.

Tarry and be hanged.—*III Henry VI,* iv, 5, 26.

14
There is no tarrying here.
Julius Cæsar. Act v, sc. 5, l. 30. [Clitus] Repeated in *Troilus and Cressida,* ii, 3, 269.

There is nor flying hence nor tarrying here.
Macbeth. Act v, sc. 5, l. 48. [Macbeth]

Tarrying in mulberry shade.—*A Midsummer-Night's Dream,* v, 1, 149. The only uses of "tarrying."

15
Thou know'st where I will tarry.
The Merchant of Venice. Act iv, sc. 2, l. 18. [Portia]

16
By my trot, I tarry too long.
Merry Wives of Windsor. Act i, sc. 4, l. 64. [Caius] "By my trot" is repeated in iv, 5, 89.

Tarry you a little-a while.—*The Merry Wives of Windsor,* i, 4, 93.

It is not good you tarry here.—*The Merry Wives of Windsor,* i, 4, 117.

Tarry for the comfort of the day.—*A Midsummer-Night's Dream,* ii, 2, 38.

17
I will therefore tarry in despite of the flesh and the blood.
The Taming of the Shrew. Induction, sc. 2, l. 129. [Sly]

I may hardly tarry so long.—*The Taming of the Shrew,* Induction, sc. 2, l. 127. [Sly]

I cannot tarry.—*The Taming of the Shrew,* iv, 4, 99.

I will not tarry.—*Henry VIII,* ii, 4, 131.

18
Tarry with him till I turn again.
Titus Andronicus. Act v, sc. 2, l. 141. [Tamora]

19
Pandarus: He that will have a cake out of the wheat must needs tarry the grinding.
Troilus: Have I not tarried?
Pandarus: Ay, the grinding; but you must tarry the bolting.
Troilus: Have I not tarried?

Pandarus: Ay, the bolting, but you must tarry the leavening.
Troilus: Still have I tarried.
Pandarus: Ay, to the leavening; but here 's yet in the word 'hereafter' the kneading, the making of the cake, the heating of the oven and the baking; nay, you must stay the cooling too, or you may chance to burn your lips.
Troilus and Cressida. Act i, sc. 1, l. 15. The only uses of "bolting," "leavening," and "heating."
Prithee, tarry: You men will never tarry.
O foolish Cressid! I might have still held off,
And then you would have tarried.
Troilus and Cressida. Act iv, sc. 1, l. 15. [Cressida]
I pray you, tarry.—*The Merchant of Venice,* iii, 2, 1.
Nay, tarry.—*Measure for Measure,* iv, 3, 174.
1
I am impatient of my tarriance.
The Two Gentlemen of Verona. Act ii, sc. 7, l. 90. [Julia]
Cytherea, all in love forlorn,
A longing tarriance for Adonis made.
The Passionate Pilgrim, l. 74. The only uses of "tarriance."

TASK

2 The long day's task is done,
And we must sleep.
Anthony and Cleopatra. Act iv, sc. 14, l. 35. [Antony]
I have perform'd my task.—*II Henry VI,* i, 1, 9.
3 Whose sore task
Does not divide the Sunday from the week.
Hamlet. Act i, sc. 1, l. 75. [Marcellus]
4
To my task will I.
I Henry VI. Act i, sc. 1, l. 152. [Bedford]
About our task.—*III Henry VI,* ii, 1, 200.
Take thou this task in hand.—*II Henry VI,* iii, 1, 318.
5
Lady Grey: Why stops my lord? shall I not hear my task?
King Edward: An easy task; 'tis but to love a king.
III Henry VI. Act iii, sc. 2, l. 52.
Easy task.—*Richard II,* iii, 2, 191.
6
Task the free breath of a sacred king.
King John, iii, 1, 148. See under KING.
Task the earth.—*Richard II,* iv, 1, 52.
Task you to recite.—*Sonnets,* lxxii.
Task his thought.—*Henry V,* i, 2, 309.
Task our thoughts.—*Henry V,* i, 2, 6.
Task my weakness.—*Othello,* ii, 3, 43.
The gallants shall be task'd.—*Love's Labour 's Lost,* v, 2, 126.
Task'd the whole state.—*I Henry IV,* iv, 3, 92.
Task'd to mow.—*Coriolanus,* i, 3, 39.
Tasking of their minds.—*The Merry Wives of Windsor,* iv, 6, 30.
How show'd his tasking?—*I Henry IV,* v, 2, 51.
But now to task the tasker.—*Love's Labour 's Lost,* ii, 1, 20. The only use of "tasker."
7
O, these are barren tasks, too hard to keep,
Not to see ladies, study, fast, not sleep!
Love's Labour 's Lost. Act i, sc. 1, l. 47. [Biron]
8
Then be this all the task it hath to say.
The Rape of Lucrece, l. 1618.
9
Come, let us to our holy task again.
Richard III. Act iii, sc. 7, l. 246. [Gloucester]
10 O most dear mistress,
The sun will set before I shall discharge
What I must strive to do.
The Tempest. Act iii, sc. 1, l. 21. [Ferdinand]
Come, let me see what task I have to do.
Titus Andronicus. Act iii, sc. 1, l. 276. [Titus]
11
And day by day I 'll do this heavy task.
Titus Andronicus. Act v, sc. 2, l. 58. [Titus]
Nature puts me to a heavy task.
Titus Andronicus. Act v, sc. 3, l. 150. [Lucius]
Hot task.—*Venus and Adonis,* l. 530.
Mean task.—*The Tempest,* iii, 1, 4.
Sad task.—*The Rape of Lucrece,* l. 1699.
Weary task.—*A Midsummer-Night's Dream,* v, 1, 381.
Worldly task.—*Cymbeline,* iv, 2, 260.

TASTE

12
Take a taste of my finding him, and relish'd it with good observance.
As You Like It. Act iii, sc. 2, l. 246. [Celia]
Sans taste.—*As You Like It,* ii, 7, 166.
13
The great'st taste Most palates theirs.
Coriolanus. Act iii, sc. 1, l. 103. [Coriolanus]
Have we not had a taste of his obedience?
Coriolanus. Act iii, sc. 1, l. 318. [Sicinius]
14
I 'll now taste of thy drug.
Cymbeline. Act iv, sc. 2, l. 38. [Imogen]
15
Come, give us a taste of your quality.
Hamlet. Act ii, sc. 2, l. 452. [Hamlet]
Taste of danger.—*I Henry IV,* iii, 1, 175.
Taste of fears.—*Macbeth,* v, 5, 9.
Taste of madness.—*Troilus and Cressida,* v, 2, 127.
Taste of tediousness.—*The Merchant of Venice,* ii, 3, 3.
16
Come, let me taste my horse.
I Henry IV. Act iv, sc. 1, l. 119. [Hotspur]
Taste bread.—*King Lear,* v, 3, 94.
Taste grief.—*Richard II,* iii, 2, 176.
Taste our mercy.—*Henry V,* iv, 7, 68.
Taste sack—*I Henry IV,* ii, 4, 501.
Taste some wine.—*Julius Cæsar,* ii, 2, 126.
Taste of your wine.—*I Henry VI,* ii, 3, 79.
17
Do you like the taste?
I Henry VI. Act iii, sc. 2, l. 44. [La Pucelle]
18
How tastes it? is it bitter?
Henry VIII. Act ii, sc. 3, l. 89. [Lady]
Bitter taste.—*II Henry IV,* iv, 5, 79.

1
She will taste as like this as a crab does to a crab.
King Lear, i, 5, 18. See under LIKENESS.

2
We of taste and feeling are.
Love's Labour 's Lost. Act iv, sc. 2, l. 30. [Nathaniel]

Gross in taste.—*Love's Labour 's Lost,* iv, 3, 339.
He had a kind of taste.—*The Merchant of Venice,* ii, 2, 19.

3
Well, well, dear Collatine, thou shalt not know
The stained taste of violated troth.
The Rape of Lucrece, l. 1058.

Fresh taste.—*Titus Andronicus,* iii, 1, 128.
Little taste.—*II Henry IV,* ii, 3, 52.
Morning taste.—*Timon of Athens,* iv, 3, 226.
Natural taste.—*A Midsummer-Night's Dream,* iv, 1, 179.
Precious taste.—*Venus and Adonis,* l. 543.
True taste.—*Othello,* ii, 1, 283.
Wilful taste.—*Sonnets,* xl.

4
Things sweet to taste prove in digestion sour.
Richard II, i, 3, 236. See SWEET AND SOUR.

Sweet world's taste.—*King John,* iii, 4, 110.
Sweetly tastes.—*As You Like It,* iv, 3, 138.
Taste as sweet.—*The Winter's Tale,* v, 3, 76.
Taste of sweetness.—*I Henry IV,* iii, 2, 72.
Taste of sweets.—*Richard II,* ii, 1, 13.
Sour to taste.—*Venus and Adonis,* l. 528.

5
Taste of it first, as thou art wont to do.
Richard II. Act v, sc. 5, l. 99. [King Richard]

Who did taste to him?—*King John,* v, 6, 28.

6
When it did taste the wormwood on the nipple
Of my dug and felt it bitter, pretty fool,
To see it tetchy and fall out with the dug!
Romeo and Juliet. Act i, sc. 3, l. 30. [Nurse]

Bitter wormwood taste.—*Rape of Lucrece,* 893.

7
Being tasted, slays all senses with the heart.
Romeo and Juliet. Act ii, sc. 3, l. 26. [Friar Laurence] See under MEDICINE.

Tasted her in bed.—*Cymbeline,* ii, 4, 57.
Tasted her sweet body.—*Othello,* iii, 3, 346.
Tasted our reward.—*I Henry VI,* iii, 4, 22.

8
In the taste confounds the appetite.
Romeo and Juliet, ii, 6, 13. See under HONEY.

9
Will 't please your honour taste of these conserves?
The Taming of the Shrew. Induction, sc. 2, l. 3. [Servant] "Conserves" is repeated in l. 7, and occurs nowhere else.

Give a taste of it.—*Troilus and Cressida,* i, 3, 389.
In way of taste.—*Troilus and Cressida,* iii, 3, 13.

10
Taste with a distempered appetite.
Twelfth Night, i, 5, 98. See under SELF-LOVE.

Taste your legs.—*Twelfth Night,* iii, 1, 87. See under LEG.

11
The tender spring upon thy tempting lip
Shows thee unripe; yet mayst thou well be tasted.
Venus and Adonis, l. 127.

12
I know not how it tastes; though it be dish'd
For me to try how.
The Winter's Tale, iii, 2, 73. See under CONSPIRACY.

TAUNT

See also Ridicule

13
Rail thou in Fulvia's phrase; and taunt my faults
With such full license as both truth and malice
Have power to utter.
Antony and Cleopatra. Act i, sc. 2, l. 111. [Antony] See also under RAILING.

With taunts
Did gibe my missive out of audience.
Antony and Cleopatra. Act ii, sc. 2, l. 73. [Cæsar]

Taunt at slackness.—*Antony and Cleopatra,* iii, 7, 28.
Taunt, and scorn me.—*The Comedy of Errors,* iv, 4, 77.
Taunt and scorn you.—*Richard III,* iii, 1, 153.

14
Brutus: Mark'd you his lip and eyes?
Sicinius: Nay, but his taunts.
Coriolanus. Act i, sc. 1, l. 259.

Tauntingly replied.—*Coriolanus,* i, 1, 114. The only use of "tauntingly." "Taunting" occurs once, in *As You Like It,* iii, 5, 134: "Taunting letter."

15
Becomes it thee to taunt his valiant age?
I Henry VI. Act iii, sc. 2, l. 54. [Talbot]

Contumelious taunts.—*I Henry VI,* i, 4, 39.
Foul taunts.—*III Henry VI,* ii, 1, 64.
Bitter taunts.—*III Henry VI,* ii, 6, 66.
Gross taunts.—*Richard III,* i, 3, 106.

16
Have I lived to stand at the taunt of one that makes fritters of English?
The Merry Wives of Windsor, v, 5, 150. See under LANGUAGE. The only use of "fritters."

17
When I had at my pleasure taunted her.
A Midsummer-Night's Dream. Act iv, sc. 1, l. 60. [Oberon]

To be thus taunted, scorn'd, and baited at.
Richard III, i, 3, 109. See under QUEEN. The only uses of "taunted."

18
He prettily and aptly taunts himself.
Richard III. Act iii, sc. 1, l. 134. [Buckingham] See under SCORN.

19
Taunt him with the license of ink.
Twelfth Night. Act iii, sc. 2, l. 47. [Sir Toby] All the uses of "taunt" and "taunts" are given in this section.

TAVERN, see Inn

TAXATION

1
You 'll be whipped for taxation one of these days.
As You Like It. Act i, sc. 2, l. 90. [Celia]
Burthenous taxations.—*Richard II,* ii, 1, 260. The only use of "burthenous."
Taxation of homage.—*Twelfth Night,* i, 5, 225.
Tax of impudence.—*All's Well that Ends Well,* ii, 1, 173.

2
Norfolk: Upon these taxations,
The clothiers all, not able to maintain
The many to them 'longing, have put off
The spinsters, carders, fullers, weavers, who,
Unfit for other life, compell'd by hunger
And lack of other means, in desperate manner
Daring the event to the teeth, are all in uproar,
And danger serves among them.
King Henry: Taxation!
Wherein? and what taxation? My lord cardinal, . . .
Know you of this taxation? . . .
Queen Katharine: These exactions,
Whereof my sovereign would have note, they are
Most pestilent to the hearing; and to bear 'em
The back is sacrifice to the load. . . .
King Henry: Still exaction!
The nature of it? in what kind, let 's know,
Is this exaction? . . .
Queen Katharine: The subjects' grief
Comes through commissions, which compel from each
The sixth part of his substance, to be levied
Without delay. . . .
King Henry: Sixth part of each?
A trembling contribution! Why, we take
From every tree lop, bark, and part o' the timber;
And, though we leave it with a root, thus hack'd,
The air will drink the sap.
Henry VIII. Act i, sc. 2, l. 30. The only use of "carders," "fullers," and "contribution." "Clothier" is repeated in *II Henry VI,* iv, 2, 5, and in *King Lear,* iv, 6, 88.
Levy great sums of money.—*II Henry VI,* iii, 1, 61. "Levy" is used fourteen times, but in every other case refers to the levying of men for an army.
Daily new exactions are devised.
Richard II, ii, 1, 249. [Willoughby] "Exactions" is used a third time in *Henry VIII,* i, 2, 25.
Exaction of the forfeiture.—*The Merchant of Venice,* i, 3, 165. The only uses of "exaction."

3
The commons hath he pill'd with grievous taxes.
Richard II. Act ii, sc. 1, l. 246. [Ross]
Tax the needy commons.—*II Henry VI,* iii, 1, 116.
Tax our policy.—*Troilus and Cressida,* i, 3, 197.

TEACHING

4
Teach me, dear creature, how to think and speak.
The Comedy of Errors. Act iii, sc. 2, l. 33. [Antipholus of Syracuse]
Teach me how to curse.—*Richard III,* iv, 4, 123.
Teach me how you look.—*Midsummer-Night's Dream,* i, 1, 192.
Teach me speed.—*King John,* iv, 2, 176.
Teach me tyranny.—*Othello,* i, 3, 197.

5
We 'll teach you to drink deep ere you depart.
Hamlet, i, 2, 175. See under DRINKING.
I 'll teach thee another course.—*Titus Andronicus,* iv, 1, 119.
Marry, I 'll teach you.—*Hamlet,* i, 3, 105.
That you must teach me.—*Hamlet,* ii, 2, 293.
That should teach us.—*Hamlet,* v, 2, 9.
I can teach you.—*I Henry IV,* iii, 1, 56; 58.
I could teach you.—*The Merchant of Venice,* iii, 2, 10.
O, let me teach thee!—*Titus Andronicus,* ii, 3, 158.

6
They will learn you by rote.
Henry V. Act iii, sc. 6, l. 74. [Gower] The use of learn in the sense of teach occurs six times in the plays.
Toadstool, learn me the proclamation.
Troilus and Cressida. Act ii, sc. 1, l. 22. [Ajax] The only use of "toadstool."

7
Teach lavoltas high and swift corantos.
Henry V, iii, 5, 33. See under DANCING.
My royal cousin, teach you our princess English?
Henry V. Act v, sc. 2, l. 308. [Burgundy]

8
When I am forgotten, as I shall be, . . .
Say, I taught thee.
Henry VIII. Act iii, sc. 2, l. 432. [Wolsey]
My good lords, hitherto, in all the progress
Both of my life and office, I have labour'd,
And with no little study, that my teaching
And the strong course of my authority
Might go one way, and safely; and the end
Was ever, to do well.
Henry VIII. Act v, sc. 3, l. 32. [Cranmer]

9
He must be taught and train'd and bid go forth.
Julius Cæsar. Act iv, sc. 1, l. 35. [Antony]

10
Cornwall: We 'll teach you—
Kent: Sir, I am too old to learn.
King Lear. Act ii, sc. 2, l. 134.
Teach her the way.—*Measure for Measure,* ii, 4, 19.
Teach thee safety.—*King John,* iii, 1, 120.
Teach them how to war.—*Henry V,* iii, 1, 25.
Teach them to sing.—*Much Ado about Nothing,* ii, 1, 239.
Teach us some fence!—*King John,* ii, 1, 290.
Teach to fight.—*Julius Cæsar,* iv, 1, 31.

11
To teach a teacher ill beseemeth me.
Love's Labour's Lost. Act ii, sc. 1, l. 108. [Princess of France] The only use of "beseemeth."

1 I do beseech you
To learn of me, who stand i' the gaps to teach you.
Pericles. Act iv, sc. 4, l. 7. [Gower]

2
I must begin with rudiments of art;
To teach you gamut in a briefer sort,
More pleasant, pithy and effectual,
Than hath been taught by any of my trade.
The Taming of the Shrew. Act iii, sc. 1, l. 66. [Hortensio] The only use of "briefer" and "pithy." "Gamut" occurs five times in this play, and nowhere else.

The rudiments of many desperate studies.
As You Like It, v, 4, 31. The only uses of "rudiments."

Teach her fingering.—*Taming of the Shrew,* ii, 1, 151.

3 I pitied thee,
Took pains to make thee speak, taught thee each hour
One thing or other.
The Tempest. Act i, sc. 2, l. 353. [Prospero]

4
Well hast thou lesson'd us.
Titus Andronicus, v, 2, 110. [Tamora]

Lesson'd us to weep.—*Richard III,* i, 4, 246.

As you were lesson'd.—*Coriolanus,* ii, 3, 185. The only uses of "lesson'd."

I shall the effect of this good lesson keep,
As watchman to my heart.
Hamlet. Act i, sc. 3, l. 45. [Ophelia]

I 'll . . . learn my lessons as I please myself.
The Taming of the Shrew. Act iii, sc. 1, l. 20. [Bianca]

Learn this lesson.—*III Henry VI,* ii, 2, 62.

Thence I learn, and find the lesson true.
Sonnets. No. cxviii.

To lesson me.—*The Two Gentlemen of Verona,* ii, 7, 5.

The lesson is but plain.—*Venus and Adonis,* l. 407.

Where 's your lesson then?—*Titus Andronicus,* iv, 1, 106.

Hard lesson.—*Much Ado about Nothing,* i, 1, 295.

5
I have taught him, even as one would say precisely, 'thus I would teach a dog.'
The Two Gentlemen of Verona. Act iv, sc. 4, l. 5. [Launce]

Thou teachest like a fool.—*Antony and Cleopatra,* i, 3, 10.

II—The Teacher

See also Tutor

6
Thus may poor fools Believe false teachers.
Cymbeline. Act iii, sc. 4, l. 86. [Imogen]

He may furnish and instruct great teachers.
Henry VIII. Act i, sc. 2, l. 113. [King]

Well, you are a rare parrot-teacher.
Much Ado about Nothing. Act i, sc. 1, l. 139. [Benedick] The only use of "parrot-teacher."

7
He teaches boys the horn-book.
Love's Labour 's Lost. Act v, sc. 1, l. 49. [Moth] The only use of "horn-book."

8
The schoolmaster is exceeding fantastical; too too vain, too too vain.
Love's Labour 's Lost. Act v, sc. 2, l. 531. [Armado]

9
Schoolmasters will I keep within my house,
Fit to instruct her youth.
The Taming of the Shrew. Act i, sc. 1, l. 94. [Baptista]

Keep a schoolmaster.—*King Lear,* i, 4, 195.

But art thou not advised, he took some care
To get her cunning schoolmasters to instruct her?
The Taming of the Shrew. Act i, sc. 1, l. 191 [Lucentio]

A schoolmaster Well seen in music.—*The Taming of the Shrew,* i, 2, 133.

Be schoolmaster
And undertake the teaching of the maid.
The Taming of the Shrew. Act i, sc. 1, l. 197 [Tranio]

Cunning in music and the mathematics.
The Taming of the Shrew. Act ii, sc. 1, l. 56. [Petruchio]

10 Here
Have I, thy schoolmaster, made thee more profit
Than other princesses can that have more time
For vainer hours and tutors not so careful.
The Tempest. Act i, sc. 2, l. 172. [Prospero]

I am unworthy for her schoolmaster.—*Pericles.* ii, 5, 40.

11
She seems a mistress To most that teach.
Winter's Tale. Act iv, sc. 4, l. 592. [Camillo]

TEAR

See also Crying; Eye: The Weeping Eye; Laughter and Tears; Sigh and Tear; Water: Tears; Weeping

12
Fall not a tear, I say; one of them rates
All that is won and lost.
Antony and Cleopatra. Act iii, sc. 11, l. 69. [Antony]

Grace grow where those drops fall!
Antony and Cleopatra. Act iv, sc. 2, l. 38. [Antony]

Tears as sovereign as the blood of hearts.
Antony and Cleopatra. Act v, sc. 1, l. 41 [Cæsar]

Tears perchance for blood.
Hamlet. Act iii, sc. 4, l. 130. [Hamlet]

13
Almost with tears I speak it.
As You Like It. Act i, sc. 1, l. 161. [Oliver]

The big round tears
Coursed one another down his innocent nose.
As You Like It, ii, 1, 38. See under ANIMAL.

With . . . biggest tears o'ershowered.—*Pericles,* iv, 4, 26. The only use of "o'ershowered."

Great tears.—*All's Well that Ends Well,* i, 1, 91.

14
Stood on the extremest verge of the swift brook,
Augmenting it with tears.
As You Like It. Act ii, sc. 1, l. 42. [First Lord]

Tears augmenting the fresh morning's dew.
Romeo and Juliet. Act i, sc. 1, l. 138. [Montague] The only uses of "augmenting."

Draw them to Tiber banks, and weep your tears
Into the channel, till the lowest stream
Do kiss the most exalted shores of all.
Julius Cæsar. Act i, sc. 1, l. 63. [Flavius]

A river . . .
Upon whose weeping margent she was set;
Like usury, applying wet to wet.
A Lover's Complaint, l. 38.

Why, man, if the river were dry, I am able to fill it with my tears.
The Two Gentlemen of Verona. Act ii, sc. 3, l. 57. [Launce]

1 Tears do not become a man.
As You Like It. Act iii, sc. 4, l. 3. [Celia]

Tears then for babes.—*III Henry VI,* ii, 1, 86.

2 The schoolboys' tears take up
The glasses of my sight!
Coriolanus. Act iii, sc. 2, l. 116. [Coriolanus]

Thou boy of tears!—*Coriolanus,* v, 6, 101.

3 My tears that fall Prove holy water on thee!
Cymbeline. Act v, sc. 5, l. 268. [Cymbeline]

Holy tear.—*Cymbeline,* iii, 4, 62.

4 Like Niobe, all tears.
Hamlet. Act i, sc. 2, l. 149. [Hamlet]

5 Weep not, sweet queen; for trickling tears are vain.
I Henry IV. Act ii, sc. 4, l. 431. [Falstaff] The only use of "trickling."

For God's sake, lords, convey my tristful queen;
For tears do stop the flood-gates of her eyes.
I Henry IV. Act ii, sc. 4, l. 433. [Falstaff]

Tristful visage.—*Hamlet,* iii, 4, 50. The only uses of "tristful." "Flood-gates" occurs again in *Venus and Adonis,* l. 959, and "flood-gate" in *Othello,* i, 3, 56.

With tears of innocency.—*I Henry IV,* iv, 3, 63.

6 Thy due from me
Is tears and heavy sorrows of the blood.
II Henry IV. Act iv, sc. 5, l. 37. [Prince]

Washing with kindly tears his gentle cheeks.
II Henry IV. Act iv, sc. 5, l. 84. [Warwick]

He hath a tear for pity.—*II Henry IV,* iv, 4, 31.

7 Let all the tears that should bedew my hearse
Be drops of balm to sanctify thy head.
II Henry IV. Act iv, sc. 5, l. 114. [King Henry]

Bedew King Henry's hearse.—*I Henry VI,* i, 1, 104.

Bedew her pastures' grass.—*Richard II,* iii, 3, 99. The only uses of "bedew."

8 Tears,
The moist impediments unto my speech.
II Henry IV. Act iv, sc. 5, l. 139. [Prince]

He has strangled His language in his tears.
Henry VIII. Act v, sc. 1, l. 156. [King]

Nor can I utter all our bitter grief,
But floods of tears will drown my oratory.
Titus Andronicus. Act v, sc. 3, l. 89. [Marcus]

9 But Harry lives, that shall convert those tears
By number into hours of happiness.
II Henry IV. Act v, sc. 2, l. 60. [King Henry V]

10 Were our tears wanting to this funeral,
These tidings would call forth their flowing tides.
I Henry VI. Act i, sc. 1, l. 82. [Exeter]

Return thee therefore with a flood of tears,
And wash away thy country's stained spots.
I Henry VI. Act iii, sc. 3, l. 56. [La Pucelle]

With mine own tears I wash away my balm.
Richard II. Act iv, sc. 1, l. 207. [King Richard] See Pomp, 1176:15.

Shed seas of tears.—*III Henry VI,* ii, 5, 106.

11 Give me thy hand,
That I may dew it with my mournful tears:
Nor let the rain of heaven wet this place,
To wash away my woful monuments.
II Henry VI. Act iii, sc. 2, l. 339. [Queen Margaret]

And with the southern clouds contend in tears,
Theirs for the earth's increase, mine for my sorrows.
II Henry VI. Act iii, sc. 2, l. 384. [Queen Margaret]

Tears virginal
Shall be to me even as the dew to fire.
II Henry VI. Act v, sc. 2, l. 52. [Young Clifford]

Virginal fencing.—*Pericles,* iv, 6, 62.

Virginal palms.—*Coriolanus,* v, 2, 45. The only uses of "virginal."

12 These tears are my sweet Rutland's obsequies:
And every drop cries vengeance for his death.
III Henry VI. Act i, sc. 4, l. 147. [York]

This cloth thou dip'st in blood of my sweet boy,
And I with tears do wash the blood away.
III Henry VI. Act i, sc. 4, l. 157. [York]

If thou tell'st the heavy story right,
Upon my soul, the hearers will shed tears;
Yea even my foes will shed fast-falling tears,
And say 'Alas, it was a piteous deed!'
III Henry VI. Act i, sc. 4, l. 160. [York] The only use of "fast-falling."

13 Ten days ago I drown'd these news in tears.
III Henry VI. Act ii, sc. 1, l. 104. [Warwick]

My tears shall wipe away these bloody marks;
And no more words till they have flow'd their fill.
III Henry VI. Act ii, sc. 5, l. 71. [Son]

See, see what showers arise,
Blown with the windy tempest of my heart.
III Henry VI. Act ii, sc. 5, l. 85. [Father]

Her tears will pierce into a marble heart.
III Henry VI. Act iii, sc. 1, l 38. [King Henry]

Ay, ay, for this I draw in many a tear.
III Henry VI. Act iv, sc. 4, l. 21. [Queen Elizabeth]

Thy tears would wash this cold congealed blood
That glues my lips and will not let me speak.
III Henry VI. Act v, sc. 2, l. 37. [Warwick] The only use of "glues." "Glue" occurs in *King John,* iii, 4, 65. "Glued" is used three times.

1
Wet my cheek with artificial tears.
III Henry VI. Act iii, sc. 2, l. 184. [Gloucester]
Borrow'd tears.—*The Rape of Lucrece,* l. 1549.
Feigned tears.—*Venus and Adonis,* l. 425.
The tears live in an onion that should water this sorrow.
Antony and Cleopatra. Act i, sc. 2, l. 176. [Enobarbus]

2
My drops of tears I 'll turn to sparks of fire.
Henry VIII, ii, 4, 72. See under QUEEN.

3
If you have tears, prepare to shed them now.
Julius Cæsar. Act iii, sc. 2, l. 173. [Antony]
Friends, I owe more tears
To this dead man than you shall see me pay.
Julius Cæsar. Act v, sc. 3, l. 101. [Brutus]

4
Ay, with these crystal beads heaven shall be bribed
To do him justice and revenge on you.
King John. Act ii, sc. 1, l. 171. [Constance]

5
Let me wipe off this honourable dew,
That silverly doth progress on thy cheeks:
My heart hath melted at a lady's tears,
Being an ordinary inundation;
But this effusion of such manly drops,
This shower, blown up by tempest of the soul,
Startles mine eyes.
King John. Act v, sc. 2, l. 45. [Dauphin] The only use of "silverly."
What a hell of witchcraft lies
In the small orb of one particular tear!
But with the inundation of the eyes
What rocky heart to water will not wear?
A Lover's Complaint, l. 288.
The inundation of her tears.
Romeo and Juliet. Act iv, sc. 1, l. 12. [Paris]
This inundation of mistemper'd humour.
King John. Act v, sc. 1, l. 12. [King John] The only uses of "inundation."

6
With cadent tears fret channels in her cheeks.
King Lear. Act i, sc. 4, l. 307. [King Lear] The only use of "cadent" (falling).
My tears begin to take his part so much,
They 'll mar my counterfeiting.
King Lear. Act iii, sc. 6, l. 63. [Edgar]
And now and then an ample tear trill'd down
Her delicate cheek.
King Lear. Act iv, sc. 3, l. 14. [Gentleman] The only use of "trill'd."
All blest secrets,
All you unpublish'd virtues of the earth,
Spring with my tears.
King Lear. Act iv, sc. 4, l. 15. [Cordelia] The only use of "unpublish'd."
I am bound
Upon a wheel of fire, that mine own tears
Do scald like molten lead.
King Lear. Act iv, sc. 7, l. 46. [King Lear]

7
Be your tears wet? yes, 'faith. I pray, weep not.
King Lear. Act iv, sc. 7, l. 71. [King Lear]
Cease your tears.—*Titus Andronicus,* iii, 1, 136.
Come, leave your tears.—*Coriolanus,* iv, 1, 1.
Dry thy melting tears.—*III Henry VI,* i, 4, 174.
Dry up your tears.—*Romeo and Juliet,* iv, 5, 79.

8
Thou shinest in every tear that I do weep:
No drop but as a coach doth carry thee;
So ridest thou triumphing in my woe.
Do but behold the tears that swell in me,
And they thy glory through my grief will show.
Love's Labour 's Lost. Act iv, sc. 3, l. 33. [Biron]
Raining the tears of lamentation.
Love's Labour 's Lost. Act v, sc. 2, l. 819. [Princess] The only use of "raining" in the plays. It is repeated in *The Rape of Lucrece,* ll. 560, 1271, and 1677.
Tears of soft remorse.—*King John,* iv, 3, 50.
Remorseful tear.—*Richard III,* i, 2, 156.
Repentant tears.—*Richard III,* i, 2, 216; *The Rape of Lucrece,* l. 502.

9
O, that infected moisture of his eye.
A Lover's Complaint, l. 323. "Moisture" is repeated in *III Henry VI,* ii, 1, 79.

10
Our tears are not yet brew'd.
Macbeth. Act ii, sc. 3, l. 130. [Donalbain]

11
Left her in her tears and dried not one of them with his comfort.
Measure for Measure. Act iii, sc. 1, l. 234. [Duke]
He, a marble to her tears, is washed with them, but relents not.
Measure for Measure. Act iii, sc. 1, l. 239. [Duke]

12
These foolish drops do something drown my manly spirit.
The Merchant of Venice. Act ii, sc. 3, l. 13. [Launcelot]
No tears but of my shedding.
The Merchant of Venice. Act iii, sc. 1, l. 100. [Shylock]

13
Leonato: Did he break into tears?
Messenger: In great measure.
Leonato: A kind overflow of kindness; there are no faces truer than those that are so washed. How much better is it to weep at joy than to joy at weeping!
Much Ado about Nothing. Act i, sc. 1, l. 24.
Wash'd it with tears.—*Much Ado about Nothing,* iv, 1, 156.
Hear these tears!—*Pericles,* i, 4, 54.
Blinding tears.—*Richard II,* ii, 2, 16.
Broken tears.—*Troilus and Cressida,* iv, 4, 50.
Contrite tears.—*Henry V,* iv, 1, 313. "Contrite" is repeated in *The Rape of Lucrece,* l. 1727: "Contrite sighs."
Cruel tears.—*Othello,* v, 2, 21.
Crystal tears.—*Venus and Adonis,* l. 491.
Fertile tears.—*Twelfth Night,* i, 5, 274.
Gentleman-like tears.—*The Winter's Tale,* v, 2, 156.
Humble tear.—*Richard III,* i, 2, 165.
Important tears.—*King Lear,* iv, 4, 26.
Liquid tears.—*II Henry VI,* iii, 2, 60.

Natural tears.—*Henry V,* iv, 2, 13.
Nature's tears.—*Romeo and Juliet,* iv, 5, 83.
Nightly tears.—*The Two Gentlemen of Verona,* ii, 4, 132.
Prophetic tears.—*Troilus and Cressida,* ii, 2, 102.
Purple tears.—*Venus and Adonis,* l. 1054.
True tears.—*Titus Andronicus,* iii, 1, 146; v, 3, 107. The phrase occurs in no other play.
Sad unhelpful tears.—*II Henry VI,* iii, 1, 218. The only use of "unhelpful."
Silver-shedding tears.—*The Two Gentlemen of Verona,* iii, 1, 230. The only use of the phrase.
Untimely tears.—*The Rape of Lucrece,* l. 570.
Weeping tears.—*As You Like It,* ii, 4, 54.
Children's tears.—*The Rape of Lucrece,* l. 431.
Lovers' tears.—*Romeo and Juliet,* i, 1, 198.
Widows' tears.—*Henry V,* ii, 4, 106.

1

Tears harden lust, though marble wear with raining.
The Rape of Lucrece, l. 560. The only use of "harden."

Cooling his hot face in the chastest tears
That ever modest eyes with sorrow shed.
The Rape of Lucrece, l. 682. The only use of "chastest."

'My girl,' quoth she, 'on what occasion break
Those tears from thee, that down thy cheeks are raining?
If thou dost weep for grief of my sustaining,
Know, gentle wench, it small avails my mood:
If tears could help, mine own would do me good.'
The Rape of Lucrece, l. 1270.

A weeping tear,
Shed for the slaughter'd husband by the wife.
The Rape of Lucrece, l. 1375.

And with my tears quench Troy that burns so long.
The Rape of Lucrece, l. 1468.

2

King Richard: What store of parting tears were shed?
Aumerle: Faith, none for me; except the north-east wind,
Which then blew bitterly against our faces,
Awaked the sleeping rheum and so by chance
Did grace our hollow parting with a tear.
Richard II. Act i, sc. 4, l. 5. See also RHEUM. The only use of "north-east."

Stain'd the beauty of a fair queen's cheeks
With tears drawn from her eyes by your foul wrongs.
Richard II. Act iii, sc. 1, l. 14. [Bolingbroke]

3

Make dust our paper and with rainy eyes
Write sorrow on the bosom of the earth.
Richard II. Act iii, sc. 2, l. 146. [King Richard]

We'll make foul weather with despised tears;
Our sighs and they shall lodge the summer corn,
And make a dearth in this revolting land.
Or shall we play the wantons with our woes,
And make some pretty match with shedding tears?
As thus, to drop them still upon one place,
Till they have fretted us a pair of graves
Within the earth; and, therein laid,—there lies
Two kinsmen digg'd their graves with weeping eyes.
Richard II. Act iii, sc. 3, l. 161. [King Richard]

Tears show their love, but want their remedies.
Richard II. Act iii, sc. 3, l. 203. [King Richard]

4

Here did she fall a tear; here in this place
I'll set a bank of rue, sour herb of grace:
Rue, even for ruth, here shortly shall be seen,
In the remembrance of a weeping queen.
Richard II. Act iii, sc. 4, l. 104. [Gardener]

Full of tears am I, Drinking my griefs.
Richard II. Act iv, sc. 1, l. 188. [King Richard]

Yet look up, behold,
That you in pity may dissolve to dew,
And wash him fresh again with true-love tears.
Richard II. Act v, sc. 1, l. 8. [Queen]

Dissolved to tears.—*Richard II,* iii, 2, 108.

5

Alas, you three, on me, threefold distress'd,
Pour all your tears!
Richard III. Act ii, sc. 2, l. 86. [Duchess of York]

The liquid drops of tears that you have shed
Shall come again, transform'd to orient pearl,
Advantaging their loan with interest
Of ten times double gain of happiness.
Richard III. Act iv, sc. 4, l. 321. [King Richard] The only use of "advantaging."

I would these dewy tears were from the ground.
Richard III. Act v, sc. 3, l. 284. [King Richard]

6

Lo, here upon thy cheek the stain doth sit
Of an old tear that is not wash'd off yet.
Romeo and Juliet. Act ii, sc. 3, l. 75. [Friar Laurence]

7

Wash they his wounds with tears.
Romeo and Juliet. Act iii, sc. 2, l. 130. [Juliet]

Evermore weeping for your cousin's death?
What, wilt thou wash him from his grave with tears?
Romeo and Juliet. Act iii, sc. 5, l. 70. [Lady Capulet]

How now! a conduit, girl? what, still in tears?
Evermore showering?
Romeo and Juliet. Act iii, sc. 5, l. 130. [Capulet] "Showering" is repeated in *I Henry IV,* v, 1, 47.

8

With his own tears made drunk.
Romeo and Juliet. Act iii, sc. 3, l. 83. [Friar Laurence]

Tears distill'd by moans.
Romeo and Juliet. Act v, sc. 3, l. 15. [Paris]

9

Ah! but those tears are pearl which thy love sheds,
And they are rich and ransom all ill deeds.
Sonnets. No. xxxiv.

Heavy tears, badges of either's woe.
Sonnets. No. xliv.

What potions have I drunk of Siren tears,
Distill'd from limbecks foul as hell within!
Sonnets. No. cxix. The only use of "limbecks" (alembics). "Limbeck" occurs in *Macbeth,* i, 7, 67.

O cunning Love! with tears thou keep'st me blind,
Lest eyes well-seeing thy foul faults should find.
Sonnets. No. cxlviii. The only use of "well-seeing."

1 The tears that she hath shed for thee
Like envious floods o'er-run her lovely face.
The Taming of the Shrew. Induction, sc. 2, l. 66. [First Servant]

His tears run down his beard, like winter's drops
From eaves of reeds.
The Tempest. Act v, sc. 1, l. 16. [Ariel] "Eaves" is used only once again, in *All's Well that Ends Well,* iii, 7, 42.

2
To re-salute his country with his tears,
Tears of true joy for his return to Rome.
Titus Andronicus. Act i, sc. 1, l. 75. [Titus] "Re-salute" is repeated in l. 326, and occurs nowhere else.

Joyful tears.—*Antony and Cleopatra,* iv, 8, 9; *Henry VIII,* v, 3, 175.

3 Rue the tears I shed,
A mother's tears in passion for her son.
Titus Andronicus. Act i, sc. 1, l. 105. [Tamora]

Passion's solemn tears.—*Love's Labour's Lost,* v, 2, 118.

4
Lo, at this tomb my tributary tears
I render, for my brethren's obsequies;
And at thy feet I kneel, with tears of joy,
Shed on the earth, for thy return to Rome.
Titus Andronicus. Act i, sc. 1, l. 159. [Lavinia]

Back, foolish tears, back to your native spring;
Your tributary drops belong to woe,
Which you, mistaking, offer up to joy.
Romeo and Juliet. Act iii, sc. 2, l. 102. [Juliet]

Tributary tears.—*Titus Andronicus,* iii, 1, 270.

5 Let it be your glory
To see her tears.
Titus Andronicus. Act ii, sc. 3, l. 139. [Demetrius]

I pour'd forth tears in vain.
Titus Andronicus. Act ii, sc. 3, l. 163. [Tamora]

6 These bitter tears which now you see
Filling the aged wrinkles in my cheeks.
Titus Andronicus. Act iii, sc. 1, l. 6. [Titus]

In the dust I write
My heart's deep languor and my soul's sad tears:
Let my tears staunch the earth's dry appetite; . . .
O earth, I will befriend thee more with rain,
That shall distil from these two ancient urns,
Than youthful April shall with all his showers:
In summer's drought I 'll drop upon thee still;
In winter with warm tears I 'll melt the snow,
And keep eternal spring-time on thy face.
Titus Andronicus. Act iii, sc. 1, l. 12. [Titus] The only use of "languor."

Let me say, that never wept before,
My tears are now prevailing orators.
Titus Andronicus. Act iii, sc. 1, l. 25. [Titus]

If any power pities wretched tears,
To that I call!
Titus Andronicus. Act iii, sc. 1, l. 209. [Titus]

7 Fresh tears
Stood on her cheeks, as doth the honey-dew
Upon a gather'd lily almost wither'd.
Titus Andronicus. Act iii, sc. 1, l. 111. [Titus] The only use of "honey-dew."

She says she drinks no other drink but tears,
Brew'd with her sorrow, mesh'd upon her cheeks.
Titus Andronicus. Act iii, sc. 2, l. 37. [Titus] The only use of "mesh'd."

Then must my earth with her continual tears
Become a deluge, overflow'd and drown'd.
Titus Andronicus. Act iii, sc. 1, l. 229. [Titus] "Deluge" is used only once again, in *Richard III,* i, 2, 61.

8 Thou art made of tears,
And tears will quickly melt thy life away.
Titus Andronicus. Act iii, sc. 2, l. 50. [Titus]

My tears have made me blind.
Titus Andronicus. Act v, sc. 3, l. 49. [Titus]

9
Draw you near To shed obsequious tears.
Titus Andronicus. Act v, sc. 3, l. 151. [Lucius]

Obsequious tear.—*Sonnets,* xxxi.

10 Like a loving child,
Shed yet some small drops from thy tender spring,
Because kind nature doth require it so.
Titus Andronicus. Act v, sc. 3, l. 166. [Lucius]

I have not another tear to shed.
Titus Andronicus. Act iii, sc. 1, l. 267. [Titus]

11 Never more
Will I my master's tears to you deplore.
Twelfth Night. Act iii, sc. 1, l. 174. [Viola] The only use of "deplore."

12
See how I lay the dust with my tears.
The Two Gentlemen of Verona. Act ii, sc. 3, l. 35. [Launce]

Where are my tears? rain, to lay this wind, or my heart will be blown up by the root.
Troilus and Cressida. Act iv, sc. 4, l. 55. [Pandarus]

13
His tears pure messengers sent from his heart.
The Two Gentlemen of Verona. Act ii, sc. 7, l. 77. [Julia]

A sea of melting pearl, which some call tears.
The Two Gentlemen of Verona. Act iii, sc. 1, l. 224. [Proteus]

14 She with her tears
Doth quench the maiden burning of his cheeks.
Venus and Adonis, l. 49.

Her contending tears,
Which long have rain'd, making her cheeks all wet.
Venus and Adonis, l. 82.

All this dumb play had his acts made plain
With tears, which, chorus-like, her eyes did rain.
Venus and Adonis, l. 359. The only use of "chorus-like."

Dost thou drink tears, that thou provokest such weeping?
Venus and Adonis, l. 949.

15
She vail'd her eyelids, who, like sluices, stopt

The crystal tide that from her two cheeks fair
In the sweet channel of her bosom dropt;
But through the flood-gates breaks the silver rain,
And with his strong course opens them again.
Venus and Adonis, l. 956. "Sluices" is repeated in *The Rape of Lucrece,* l. 1076.

Tears in her eye.—*Venus and Adonis,* l. 961.

Tears in his eyes.—*Hamlet,* ii, 2, 543; 581.

1 Whereat her tears began to turn their tide,
Being prison'd in her eye like pearls in glass;
Yet sometimes falls an orient drop beside,
Which her cheek melts, as scorning it should pass.
Venus and Adonis, l. 979.

In pity of his tender years.
They both would strive who first should dry his tears.
Venus and Adonis, l. 1091.

2 Once a day I'll visit
The chapel where they lie, and tears shed there
Shall be my recreation: so long as nature
Will bear up with this exercise, so long
I daily vow to use it.
Winter's Tale. Act iii, sc. 2, l. 239. [Leontes]

She did, with an 'Alas,' I would fain say, bleed tears, for I am sure my heart wept blood.
Winter's Tale. Act v, sc. 2, l. 95. [Gentleman]

II—Salt Tears

3 Thy tears are salter than a younger man's,
And venomous to thine eyes.
Coriolanus. Act iv, sc. 1, l. 22. [Coriolanus] The only use of "salter."

Certain drops of salt.
Coriolanus. Act v, sc. 6, l. 93. [Aufidius]

When I have deck'd the sea with drops full salt.
The Tempest. Act i, sc. 2, l. 155. [Prospero]

4 The salt of most unrighteous tears.
Hamlet. Act i, sc. 2, l. 154. [Hamlet] The only use of "unrighteous."

O heat, dry up my brains! tears seven times salt,
Burn out the sense and virtue of mine eye!
Hamlet. Act iv, sc. 5, l. 154. [Laertes]

5 The pretty-vaulting sea refused to drown me,
Knowing that thou wouldst have me drown'd on shore,
With tears as salt as sea, through thy unkindness.
II Henry VI. Act iii, sc. 2, l. 94. [Queen Margaret] The only use of "pretty-vaulting."

To drain
Upon his face an ocean of salt tears.
II Henry VI. Act iii, sc. 2, l. 143. [King Henry]

Her salt tears fell from her, and soften'd the stones.
Othello. Act iv, sc. 3, l. 47. [Desdemona] "Salt tears" is used also in *A Midsummer-Night's Dream,* ii, 2, 94; *All's Well that Ends Well,* i, 3, 178; *I Henry VI,* i, 1, 50; *Richard III,* i, 2, 154; *Timon of Athens,* iv, 3, 443; *Venus and Adonis,* l. 1071.

6 Prince Henry: O that there were some virtue in my tears,
That might relieve you!
King John: The salt in them is hot.
King John. Act v, sc. 7, l. 44.

7 Laundering the silken figures in the brine
That season'd woe had pelleted in tears.
A Lover's Complaint, l. 17. The only use of "laundering." "Pelleted" occurs again in *Antony and Cleopatra,* iii, 13, 165.

8 Seasoning the earth with showers of silver brine.
The Rape of Lucrece, l. 796.

Jesu Maria, what a deal of brine
Hath wash'd thy sallow cheeks for Rosaline!
How much salt water thrown away in waste,
To season love, that of it doth not taste!
Romeo and Juliet. Act ii, sc. 3, l. 69. [Friar Laurence] The only use of "sallow."

Like a cloistress, she will veiled walk
And water once a day her chamber round
With eye-offending brine.
Twelfth Night. Act i, sc. 1, l. 28. [Valentine] The only use of "cloistress." "Eye-offending" is used a second time in *King John,* iii, 1, 47.

Lafeu: Your commendations, madam, get from her tears.
Countess: 'Tis the best brine a maiden can season her praise in.
All's Well that Ends Well. Act i, sc. 1, l. 53.

9 Wiped the brinish pearl from her bright eyes.
The Rape of Lucrece, l. 1213.

Brinish tears.—*III Henry VI,* iii, 1, 41.

Brinish bowels.—*Titus Andronicus,* iii, 1, 97. The only uses of "brinish."

10 Get some little knife between thy teeth,
And just against thy heart make thou a hole;
That all the tears that thy poor eyes let fall
May run into that sink, and soaking in
Drown the lamenting fool in sea-salt tears.
Titus Andronicus. Act iii, sc. 2, l. 16. [Titus] The only use of "sea-salt."

III—Women's Tears

11 She makes a shower of rain as well as Jove.
Antony and Cleopatra. Act i, sc. 2, l. 156. [Enobarbus]

Showers to bring it on.—*Antony and Cleopatra,* iii, 2, 44.

12 I forbid my tears: but yet
It is our trick; nature her custom holds,
Let shame say what it will: when these are gone,
The woman will be out.
Hamlet. Act iv, sc. 7, l. 187. [Laertes]

I did not think to shed a tear
In all my misery; but thou hast forced me,
Out of thy honest truth, to play the woman.
Henry VIII. Act iii, sc. 2, l. 428. [Wolsey]

1
If that the earth could teem with woman's tears,
Each drop she falls would prove a crocodile.
Othello. Act iv, sc. 1, l. 256. [Othello]
Lepidus: What manner o' thing is your crocodile?
Antony: It is shaped, sir, like itself; and it is as broad as it hath breadth: it is just so high as it is, and moves with it[s] own organs: it lives by that which nourisheth it; and the elements once out of it, it transmigrates. . . .
Lepidus: 'Tis a strange serpent.
Antony: 'Tis so. And the tears of it are wet.
Antony and Cleopatra. Act ii, sc. 7, l. 46.
The only use of "transmigrates."
Eat a crocodile.—*Hamlet,* v, 1, 299.
Mournful crocodile.—*II Henry VI,* iii, 1, 226.
Your crocodile.—*Antony and Cleopatra,* ii, 7, 31.
The only references to the crocodile.

2
Thy tears are womanish.
Romeo and Juliet. Act iii, sc. 3, l. 110. [Friar Laurence]
Womanish tears.—*King John,* iv, 1, 36.
A woman's tear.—*Troilus and Cressida,* i, 1, 9.

3
Surprise me to the very brink of tears:
Lend me a fool's heart and a woman's eyes.
Timon of Athens. Act v, sc. 1, l. 159. [Timon]

4
I am yet so near the manners of my mother, that upon the least occasion more mine eyes will tell tales of me.
Twelfth Night. Act ii, sc. 1, l. 41. [Sebastian]
Were you a woman, as the rest goes even,
I should my tears let fall upon your cheek.
Twelfth Night. Act v, sc. 1, l. 246. [Sebastian]

TEDIOUSNESS

5
O, thou hast damnable iteration.
I Henry IV. Act i, sc. 2, l. 101. [Falstaff]
Tired with iteration.—*Troilus and Cressida,* iii, 2, 183.
What needs this iteration?—*Othello,* v, 2, 150.
The only uses of "iteration."

6 I cried 'hum,' and 'well, go to,'
But mark'd him not a word. O he is as tedious
As a tired horse, a railing wife;
Worse than a smoky house: I had rather live
With cheese and garlic in a windmill, far,
Than feed on cates and have him talk to me
In any summer-house in Christendom.
I Henry IV. Act iii, sc. 1, l. 158. [Hotspur]
The only use of "summer-house." "Windmill" occurs again in *II Henry IV,* iii, 2, 207.

7
Speak on; but be not over-tedious.
I Henry VI. Act iii, sc. 3, l. 43. [Burgundy]
The only use of "over-tedious."
Not to be weary with you.
Measure for Measure, i, 4, 25. [Lucio]

8 Like a good thing, being often read,
Grown fear'd and tedious.
Measure for Measure, ii, 4, 8. [Angelo]

9 . I do repent
The tedious moments I with her have spent.
A Midsummer-Night's Dream. Act ii, sc. 2, l. 111. [Lysander]

10
Leonato: Neighbours, you are tedious.
Dogberry: It pleases your worship to say so; . . . but truly, for mine own part, if I were as tedious as a king, I could find it in my heart to bestow it all of your worship.
Leonato: All thy tediousness on me, ah?
Dogberry: Yea, an 'twere a thousand pound more than 'tis.
Much Ado about Nothing. Act iii, sc. 5, l. 20.

11 So tedious is this day
As is the night before some festival
To an impatient child that hath new robes
And may not wear them.
Romeo and Juliet. Act iii, sc. 2, l. 28. [Juliet]
Tedious days.—*Richard III,* iv, 4, 28; *Hamlet,* iii, 2, 237.
Tedious minutes.—*Midsummer-Night's Dream,* ii, 2, 112.
Tedious nights.—*Richard III,* iii, 2, 6; *The Two Gentlemen of Verona,* i, 1, 31; *Richard II,* v, 1, 40; *A Midsummer-Night's Dream,* iii, 2, 431; *The Rape of Lucrece,* l. 1379.

12
Tedious it were to tell, and harsh to hear.
The Taming of the Shrew. Act iii, sc. 2, l. 107. [Petruchio]
Tedious tale.—*Romeo and Juliet,* v, 3, 230.

13
Pandarus: It passed.
Cressida: So let it now; for it has been a great while going by.
Troilus and Cressida. Act i, sc. 2, l. 182.

TEETH

14
By Isis, I will give thee bloody teeth.
Antony and Cleopatra. Act i, sc. 5, l. 70. [Cleopatra]
By this hand, I will supplant some of your teeth.
The Tempest. Act iii, sc. 2, l. 56. [Stephano]

15
Bid them . . . keep their teeth clean.
Coriolanus. Act ii, sc. 3, l. 67. [Coriolanus]

16 I shall live and tell him to his teeth,
'Thus didest thou.'
Hamlet. Act iv, sc. 7, l. 57. [Laertes]
Cast into my teeth.—*Julius Cæsar,* iv, 3, 99.
Hurl we in your teeth.—*Julius Cæsar,* v, 1, 64.
Throw . . . in the devil's teeth.—*Othello,* iii, 4, 184.

17
We'll fall to it with our teeth.
I Henry VI. Act iii, sc. 1, l. 90. [Servant]

18
Teeth hadst thou in thy head when thou wast born,
To signify thou camest to bite the world.
III Henry VI. Act v, sc. 6, l. 53. [King Henry]
The midwife wonder'd and the women cried
'O, Jesus bless us, he is born with teeth!'
And so I was; which plainly signified
That I should snarl and bite and play the dog.
III Henry VI. Act v, sc. 6, l. 74. [Gloucester]
The only use of "snarl."

1
Your colt's tooth is not cast yet.
Henry VIII. Act i, sc. 3, l. 48. [Chamberlain]
2
And when my knightly stomach is sufficed,
Why then I suck my teeth.
King John. Act i, sc. 1, l. 191. [Bastard]
3
Treason's tooth bare-gnawn and canker-bit.
King Lear. Act v, sc. 3, l. 122. [Edgar] The only use of either phrase.
Tooth that poisons if it bite.
King Lear. Act iii, sc. 6, l. 70. [Edgar]
Venom tooth—*Richard III,* i, 3, 291.
4
To show his teeth as white as whale's bone.
Love's Labour's Lost, v, 2, 332. [Biron]
5
Worn in the cap of a tooth-drawer.
Love's Labour's Lost. Act v, sc. 2, l. 622. The only use of "tooth-drawer," Shakespeare's closest approach to dentist.
6
Since I am a dog, beware my fangs.
Merchant of Venice, iii, 3, 7. [Shylock]
Boarish fangs.—*King Lear,* iii, 7, 58.
Icy fang.—*As You Like It,* ii, 1, 6.
Sharp fangs.—*Venus and Adonis,* l. 663.
Fangs of malice.—*Twelfth Night,* i, 5, 196.
Destruction fang mankind.—*Timon of Athens,* iv, 3, 23. The only use of "fang" as a verb.
Swords . . . are his fangs.—*King John,* ii, 1, 353. The only uses of "fang" and "fangs," except as a proper name in *II Henry IV.*
7
Benedick: I have the toothache.
Don Pedro: Draw it.
Benedick: Hang it!
Claudio: You must hang it first, and draw it afterwards.
Don Pedro: What! sigh for the toothache?
Much Ado about Nothing. Act iii, sc. 2, l. 21.
There was never yet philosopher
That could endure the toothache patiently.
Much Ado about Nothing. Act v, sc. 1, l. 36. [Leonato]
Yet is this no charm for the toothache.
Much Ado about Nothing. Act iii, sc. 2, l. 72. [Benedick]
Being troubled with a raging tooth,
I could not sleep.
Othello. Act iii, sc. 3, l. 414. [Iago]
He that sleeps feels not the toothache.
Cymbeline, v, 4, 178. See under SLEEP. The only uses of "toothache."
8
Marry, they say my uncle grew so fast
That he could gnaw a crust at two hours old:
'Twas two full years ere I could get a tooth.
Richard III. Act ii, sc. 4, l. 27. [York]
9
Pluck the keen teeth from the fierce tiger's jaws.
Sonnets. No. xix.
10
An old trot with ne'er a tooth in her head.
Taming of the Shrew, i, 2, 80. [Grumio]
Whilst I have a tooth in my head.—*All's Well that Ends Well,* ii, 3, 48.
Speed: 'Item: She hath no teeth.'
Launce: I care not for that neither, because I love crusts.
Speed: 'Item: She is curst.'
Launce: Well, the best is, she hath no teeth to bite.
Two Gentlemen of Verona. Act iii, sc. 1, l. 344.
Sans teeth.—*As You Like It,* ii, 7, 166.
His boneless gums.—*Macbeth,* i, 7, 57. The only use of "boneless" and "gums."
11
Doth set my pugging tooth on edge.
Winter's Tale. Act iv, sc. 3, l. 7. [Autolycus] The only use of "pugging" (thieving).
Set my teeth nothing on edge.—*I Henry IV.* iii, 1, 133.
Set the teeth.—*Henry V,* iii, 1, 15; *Antony and Cleopatra,* iii, 13, 181; *Coriolanus,* i, 3, 70.
Fixed teeth.—*II Henry VI,* iii, 2, 313.
Whet his teeth.—*Venus and Adonis,* l. 1113.
12
A great man, I'll warrant; I know by the picking on's teeth.
Winter's Tale. Act iv, sc. 4, l. 778. [Clown]
Pick his teeth and sing.—*All's Well that Ends Well,* iii, 2, 8.
Pick your teeth, sir.—*King Lear,* iv, 6, 250.
He and his toothpick.—*King John,* i, 1, 190. "Toothpick" is used again in *All's Well that Ends Well,* i, 1, 171.
I will fetch you a toothpicker.—*Much Ado about Nothing,* ii, 1, 274. See SERVICE, 1340: 21. The only use of "toothpicker."

TEMPER

13
You keep a constant temper.
Coriolanus. Act v, sc. 2, l. 100. [Aufidius]
Keep me in temper.—*King Lear,* i, 5, 51.
Comfortable temper.—*Timon of Athens,* iii, 4, 71.
Good temper.—*II Henry IV,* ii, 1, 87.
Hard temper.—*Henry VIII,* ii, 3, 11.
14
He holds your temper in a high respect
And curbs himself even of his natural scope
When you come 'cross his humour.
II Henry IV. Act iv, sc. 1, l. 170. [Mortimer]
His temper, therefore, must be well observed.
II Henry IV. Act iv, sc. 4, l. 36. [King]
15
Methinks now you are in an excellent good temperality.
II Henry IV. Act ii, sc. 4, l. 24. [Hostess] The only use of "temperality."
16
I know you have a gentle noble temper.
Henry VIII. Act iii, sc. 1, l. 165. [Wolsey]
Noble temper.—*King John,* v, 2, 40; *Cymbeline,* ii, 3, 6.
17
The brain may devise laws for the blood, but a hot temper leaps o'er a cold decree.
The Merchant of Venice. Act i, sc. 2, l. 19. [Portia]
18
I am glad to be so acquit of this tinder-box.
The Merry Wives of Windsor. Act i, sc. 3, l. 27. [Falstaff] The only use of "tinder-box." "Tinder" occurs in *Othello,* i, 1, 141.

1
Nay, look not big, nor stamp, nor stare, nor fret.
The Taming of the Shrew. Act iii, sc. 2, l. 230. [Petruchio]
2
You know your father's temper.
The Winter's Tale. Act iv, sc. 4, l. 477. [Camillo]
Dauntless temper.—*Macbeth,* iii, 1, 52.
Feeble temper.—*Julius Cæsar,* i, 2, 129.

TEMPERANCE

See also Moderation

3
Though you can guess what temperance should be,
You know not what it is.
Antony and Cleopatra. Act iii, sc. 13, l. 121. [Antony]
4
He cannot temperately transport his honours.
Coriolanus. Act ii, sc. 1, l. 240. [Sicinius]
Temperately proceed.—*Coriolanus,* iii, 1, 219.
Nay, temperately.—*Coriolanus,* iii, 3, 67.
Temperately keep time.—*Hamlet,* iii, 4, 140. "Temperately" occurs only four times in the plays, three times in *Coriolanus.*
5
Ask God for temperance; that 's the appliance only
Which your disease requires.
Henry VIII. Act i, sc. 1, l. 124. [Norfolk]
6
Peace, lady! pause, or be more temperate.
King John. Act ii, sc. 1, l. 195. [King Philip]
She is not hot, but temperate as the morn.
The Taming of the Shrew. Act ii, sc. 1, l. 296. [Petruchio]
7
A gentleman of all temperance.
Measure for Measure. Act iii, sc. 2, l. 253. [Escalus]
I doubt not of his temperance.—*King Lear,* iv, 7, 24.
8
Adrian: It must needs be of subtle, tender and delicate temperance.
Antonio: Temperance was a delicate wench.
Sebastian: Ay, and a subtle; as he most learnedly delivered.
The Tempest. Act ii, sc. 1, l. 41.

TEMPEST

See also Storm, Wind

9
When tempest of commotion, like the south
Borne with black vapour, doth begin to melt
And drop upon our bare unarmed heads.
II Henry IV. Act ii, sc. 4, l. 392. [Prince]
Tempest of exclamation.—*II Henry IV,* ii, 1, 87.
Tempest of provocation.—*The Merry Wives of Windsor,* v, 5, 23.
Tempest of the soul.—*King John,* v, 2, 50.
10 In fierce tempest is he coming,
In thunder and in earthquake, like a Jove.
Henry V. Act ii, sc. 4, l. 99. [Exeter]
Hideous tempest.—*III Henry VI,* v, 6, 46.
Louring tempest.—*Richard II,* i, 3, 187.
Stiff tempest.—*Henry VIII,* iv, 1, 72.
Windy tempest.—*III Henry VI,* ii, 5, 86; *The Rape of Lucrece,* l. 1788.
11
And this fell tempest shall not cease to rage
Until the golden circuit on my head,
Like to the glorious sun's transparent beams,
Do calm the fury of this mad-bred flaw.
II Henry VI. Act iii, sc. 1, l. 351. [York] The only use of "mad-bent."
This tempest,
Dashing the garment of this peace, aboded
The sudden breach on 't.
Henry VIII. Act i, sc. 1, l. 92. [Buckingham] The only use of "aboded."
12
I have seen tempests, when the scolding winds
Have rived the knotty oaks.
Julius Cæsar. Act i, sc. 3, l. 5. [Casca] "Rived" is repeated in iv, 3, 85: "Rived my heart," and occurs in no other play.
13
So, by a roaring tempest on the flood,
A whole armado of convicted sail
Is scatter'd and disjoin'd from fellowship.
King John. Act iii, sc. 4, l. 1. [King Philip] The only use of "convicted." "Disjoin'd" is repeated in *Venus and Adonis,* l. 541.
Now happy he whose cloak and cincture can
Hold out this tempest.
King John. Act iv, sc. 3, l. 155. [Bastard] The only use of "cincture."
14
This tempest will not give me leave to ponder
On things would hurt me more.
King Lear. Act iii, sc. 4, l. 24. [King Lear] The only use of "ponder."
15
Bless thee from whirlwinds, star-blasting, and taking!
King Lear. Act iii, sc. 4, l. 60. [Edgar] The only use of "star-blasting."
Whirlwinds shake fair buds.—*The Taming of the Shrew,* v, 2, 140.
Some whirlwind bear.—*The Two Gentlemen of Verona,* i, 2, 120.
Thither in a whirlwind.—*Timon of Athens,* iv, 3, 288.
Like whirlwinds.—*The Rape of Lucrece,* l. 586.
Whirlwind of passion.—*Hamlet,* iii, 2, 7. The only uses of "whirlwind" and "whirlwinds."
16
The desperate tempest hath so bang'd the Turks,
That their designment halts.
Othello. Act ii, sc. 1, l. 21. [Gentleman] "Bang'd" occurs again *Twelfth Night,* iii, 2, 24: "Bang'd the youth into dumbness." "Designment" is repeated in *Coriolanus,* v, 6, 35.
They were parted
With foul and violent tempest.
Othello. Act ii, sc. 1, l. 33. [Gentleman]
Tempests themselves, high seas and howling winds,
The gutter'd rocks and congregated sands,—

Traitors ensteep'd to clog the guiltless keel.
Othello. Act ii, sc. 1, l. 68. [Cassio] The only use of "gutter'd" and "ensteep'd."

1 O my soul's joy!
If after every tempest come such calms,
May the winds blow till they have waken'd death!
And let the labouring bark climb hills of seas
Olympus-high and duck again as low
As hell 's from heaven!
Othello. Act ii, sc. 1, l. 186. [Othello] The only use of "Olympus-high."

2 We hear this fearful tempest sing,
Yet seek no shelter to avoid the storm.
Richard II. Act ii, sc. 1, l. 263. [Northumberland]

Such crimson tempest should bedrench
The fresh green lap of fair King Richard's land.
Richard II. Act iii, sc. 3, l. 46. [Bolingbroke] The only use of "bedrench."

Raised the tempest.—*The Tempest,* v, 1, 6.

3
To calm this tempest whirling in the court.
Titus Andronicus. Act iv, sc. 2, l. 160. [Aaron]

4 The dreadful spout
Which shipmen do the hurricano call,
Constringed in mass by the almighty sun.
Troilus and Cressida. Act v, sc. 2, l. 171. [Troilus] The only use of "constringed."

Cataracts and hurricanoes.—*King Lear,* iii, 2, 2. The only uses of "hurricano" and "hurricanoes." "Hurricane" does not occur.

5 O, if it prove,
Tempests are kind and salt waves fresh in love.
Twelfth Night. Act iii, sc. 4, l. 417. [Viola]

Tempest after sun.—*Venus and Adonis,* l. 800.

TEMPLE

See also Church

6
Here we have no temple but the wood.
As You Like It. Act iii, sc. 3, l. 49. [Touchstone]

7
The temple of virtue was she.
Cymbeline. Act v, sc. 5, l. 220. [Posthumus]

So divine a temple.—*Cymbeline,* iv, 2, 55.
Anointed temple.—*Macbeth,* ii, 3, 73.
Baser temple.—*Timon of Athens,* v, 1, 51.
Chiefest temple.—*I Henry VI,* ii, 2, 12.
Large temples.—*Coriolanus,* iii, 3, 36.
Solemn temples.—*The Tempest,* iv, 1, 153.

8
My temple stands in Ephesus: hie thee thither.
Pericles. Act v, sc. 1, l. 241. [Diana]

Diana's temple is not distant far,
Where you may abide.
Pericles. Act iii, sc. 4, l. 13. [Cerimon] "Diana's temple" is repeated in v, 3, 25.

Dian's temple.—*Coriolanus,* v, 3, 67.
Apollo's temple.—*The Winter's Tale,* ii, 1, 183.
Temple of great Jupiter.—*Cymbeline,* v, 5, 482.

9 The temple much surpassing
The common praise it bears.
The Winter's Tale. Act iii, sc. 1, l. 2. [Cleon] The only use of "surpassing."

TEMPLES

10
Adorn his temples with a coronet.
I Henry VI. Act v, sc. 4, l. 134. [Alençon]

For she his hairy temples then had rounded
With coronet of fresh and fragrant flowers.
A Midsummer-Night's Dream. Act iv, sc. 1, l. 56. [Oberon]

11
Her sunny locks Hang on her temples.
The Merchant of Venice, i, 1, 170. See under HAIR.

12
Rob his temples of the diadem.
III Henry VI. Act i, sc. 4, l. 104. [Queen Margaret]

Rub him about the temples.—*Othello,* iv, 1, 53.
Dead temples.—*Richard III,* v, 5, 5.
Mortal temples.—*Richard II,* iii, 2, 161.
Tender temples.—*Richard III,* iv, 4, 383.

TEMPTATION

13
Tempt him not so too far.
Antony and Cleopatra. Act i, sc. 3, l. 11. [Charmian]

14
Ah, Luciana, did he tempt thee so?
Mightst thou perceive austerely in his eye
That he did plead in earnest? yea or no?
The Comedy of Errors. Act iv, sc. 2, l. 1. [Adriana]

Tempt thy love.—*Comedy of Errors,* iv, 2, 13.
Tempt me not.—*Comedy of Errors,* iv, 3, 48.
Tempt me no farther.—*Julius Cæsar,* iv, 3, 36.

15 That man is not alive
Might so have tempted him as you have done,
Without the taste of danger and reproof.
I Henry IV. Act iii, sc. 1, l. 173. [Mortimer]

16
Brutus: You durst not so have tempted him. . . .
Cassius: What, durst not tempt him!
Brutus: For your life you durst not.
Julius Cæsar. Act iv, sc. 3, l. 59.

17
Th' unexperient gave the tempter place.
A Lover's Complaint, l. 318. The only use of "unexperient" (inexperienced).

The tempter or the tempted, who sins most?
Ha! Not she; nor doth she tempt: but it is I
That, lying by the violet in the sun,
Do as the carrion does, not as the flower,
Corrupt with virtuous season.
Measure for Measure. Act ii, sc. 2, l. 163. [Angelo] The only uses of "tempter."

Shrewd tempters.—*I Henry VI,* i, 2, 123.
Tempters of the night.—*Cymbeline,* ii, 2, 9. The only uses of "tempters."

18
'Tis one thing to be tempted, Escalus,
Another thing to fall.
Measure for Measure. Act ii, sc. 1, l. 17. [Angelo]

I am that way going to temptation,
Where prayers cross.
Measure for Measure. Act ii, sc. 2, l. 158. [Angelo]

Most dangerous
Is that temptation that doth goad us on
To sin in loving virtue.
Measure for Measure, ii, 2, 181. [Angelo]

1 The fiend is at mine elbow and tempts me.
The Merchant of Venice. Act ii, sc. 2, l. 2. [Launcelot]

2 I never tempted her with word too large.
Much Ado about Nothing. Act iv, sc. 1, l. 53. [Claudio]

3 Tempt not a desperate man.
Romeo and Juliet. Act v. sc. 3, l. 59. [Romeo]

4 Queen Elizabeth: Shall I be tempted of the devil thus?
King Richard: Ay, if the devil tempt thee to do good.
Richard III. Act iv, sc. 4, l. 418.

5 Before thee stands this fair Hesperides,
With golden fruit, but dangerous to be touch'd;
For death-like dragons here affright thee hard.
Pericles. Act i, sc. 1, l. 29. [Antiochus] The only use of "death-like." The Hesperides are mentioned again in *Love's Labour 's Lost,* iv, 3, 341.

6 For still temptation follows where thou art.
Sonnets. No. xli.

To temptation slow.—*Sonnets,* xciv.

7 And sometimes we are devils to ourselves,
When we will tempt the frailty of our powers,
Presuming on their changeful potency.
Troilus and Cressida. Act iv, sc. 4, l. 96. [Troilus] The only use of "changeful."

8 Temptations have since then been born to 's.
The Winter's Tale. Act i, sc. 2, l. 77. [Polixenes]

You tempt him over-much.
The Winter's Tale. Act v, sc. 1, l. 73. [Cleomenes] "Over-much" is repeated in *Richard III,* i, 1, 140.

TENDERNESS

See also Affection

9 Not of a woman's tenderness to be,
Requires nor child nor woman's face to see.
Coriolanus. Act v, sc. 3, l. 129. [Coriolanus]

10 Weep no more, lest I give cause
To be suspected of more tenderness
Than doth become a man.
Cymbeline. Act i, sc. 1, l. 94. [Posthumus]

11 Make blind itself with foolish tenderness.
I Henry IV. Act iii, sc. 2, l. 91. [King Henry]

Flowery tenderness.—*Measure for Measure,* iii, 1, 83.

12 Even in thy behalf, I 'll thank myself
For doing these fair rites of tenderness.
I Henry IV. Act v, sc. 4, l. 97. [Prince]

Filial tenderness
Shall, O dear father, pay thee plenteously.
II Henry IV. Act iv, sc. 5, l. 39. [Prince] The only use of "plenteously."

13 To be tender-minded
Does not become a sword.
King Lear. Act v, sc. 3, l. 31. [Edmund] The only use of "tender-minded."

14 Her delicate tenderness will find itself abused, begin to heave the gorge.
Othello. Act ii, sc. 1, l. 235. [Iago]

15 Well we know your tenderness of heart.
Richard III. Act iii, sc. 7, l. 210. [Buckingham]

Tenderness of her nature.—*All's Well that Ends Well,* iv, 3, 60.

Tenderness of years.—*Love's Labour 's Lost,* iii, 1, 4. See under YOUTH.

Melting with tenderness.—*Richard III,* iv, 3, 7.

16 She was as tender As infancy and grace.
The Winter's Tale. Act v, sc. 3, l. 26. [Leontes]

TENOUR

See also Intention, Meaning

17 This is the tenour of the emperor's writ.
Cymbeline. Act iii, sc. 7, l. 1. [Senator]

It bears an angry tenour.—*As You Like It,* iv, 3, 11.

18 I guess their tenour.
I Henry IV. Act iv, sc. 4, l. 7. [Sir Michael]

Their cold intent, tenour and substance.
II Henry IV. Act iv, sc. 1, l. 9. [Archbishop]

According to the tenour.—*The Merchant of Venice,* iv, 1, 235.

Tenour of my book.—*Much Ado about Nothing,* iv, 1, 169.

Tenour of thy jealousy.—*Sonnets,* lxi.

Tenour of his oracle.—*Winter's Tale,* v, 1, 38.

Tenour of her woe.—*Rape of Lucrece,* l. 1310.

Tenour of our word.—*II Henry IV,* v, 5, 75.

Selfsame tenour.—*Julius Cæsar,* iv, 3, 171.

Strange tenour.—*Measure for Measure,* iv, 2, 216.

TERMS

19 Touch you the sourest points with sweetest terms.
Antony and Cleopatra, ii, 2, 24. See SWEET AND SOUR.

When perforce he could not
But pay me terms of honour, cold and sickly
He vented them; most narrow measure lent me.
Antony and Cleopatra. Act iii, sc. 4, l. 6. [Antony]

20 In good terms, in good set terms.
As You Like It, ii, 7, 16. See under FORTUNE.

21 With many holiday and lady terms
He question'd me.
I Henry IV. Act i, sc. 3, l. 46. [Hotspur]

Festival terms.—*Much Ado about Nothing,* v, 2, 41.

1 'Tis not well
That you and I should meet upon such terms
As now we meet.
I Henry IV. Act v, sc. 1, l. 9. [King Henry]

2 What terms the enemy stood on.
Henry V. Act iii, sc. 6, l. 78. [Gower]

Thou hast given me most bitter terms.
Henry V. Act iv, sc. 8, l. 44. [King Henry]

3 Terms Such as will enter at a lady's ear
And plead his love-suit.
Henry V. Act v, sc. 2, l. 99. [King Henry] "Love-suit" is repeated in *Cymbeline,* iii, 4, 136.

In terms like bride and groom
Devesting them for bed.
Othello, ii, 3, 180. See under FRIEND. The only use of "devesting."

Loving terms.—*Romeo and Juliet,* i, 1, 218.
Terms of love.—*I Henry IV,* v, 5, 3.

4 We have consented to all terms of reason.
Henry V. Act v, sc. 2, l. 357. [French King]

Terms of death.—*Measure for Measure,* ii, 4, 100.
Term of fear.—*I Henry IV,* iv, 1, 85.
Terms of friendship.—*Julius Cæsar,* iii, 1, 203.
Terms of honour.—*Hamlet,* v, 2, 257.
Terms of manage.—*I Henry IV,* ii, 3, 52.
Terms of pity.—*All's Well that Ends Well,* ii, 3, 173.
Terms of rage.—*III Henry VI,* i, 1, 265.
Terms of treason.—*Richard II,* i, 1, 57.
Terms of zeal.—*I Henry IV,* iv, 3, 63; *The Merchant of Venice,* v, 1, 205.

5 Thou hast astonish'd me with thy high terms.
I Henry VI. Act i, sc. 2, l. 93. [Charles]

With other vile and ignominious terms.
I Henry VI. Act iv, sc. 1, l. 97. [Bastard]

Abject terms.—*II Henry VI,* v, 1, 25.
Desperate terms.—*Hamlet,* iv, 7, 26.
Sore terms.—*Pericles,* iv, 2, 37.
Wrathful terms.—*Troilus and Cressida,* v, 2, 38.
Terms compulsatory.—*Hamlet,* i, 1, 103. The only use of "compulsatory."
Terms of base compulsion.—*Troilus and Cressida,* ii, 2, 153.
Terms unsquared.—*Troilus and Cressida,* i, 3, 159. The only use of "unsquared."

6 I would invent such bitter-searching terms,
As curst, as harsh and horrible to hear,
Deliver'd strongly through my fixed teeth.
II Henry VI, iii, 2, 311. See under CURSE. The only use of "bitter-searching."

In any case, be not too rough in terms.
II Henry VI, iv, 9, 44. See under LANGUAGE.

Ruder terms.—*II Henry VI,* i, 1, 30.

7 Brave me with these saucy terms.
II Henry VI, iv, 10, 38. See SAUCINESS.

Bold in terms.—*III Henry VI,* ii, 2, 85.

8 Parted you in good terms?
King Lear. Act i, sc. 2, l. 171. [Edmund]

9 Long upon these terms I held my city.
A Lover's Complaint, l. 176.

10 I like not fair terms and a villain's mind.
The Merchant of Venice, i, 3, 181. See HYPOCRISY, 745:1.

Fair terms.—*Henry V,* ii, 1, 60; 74.
Alligant terms.—*The Merry Wives of Windsor,* ii, 2, 69. The only use of "alligant," for elegant.
Equal terms.—*Richard II,* iv, 1, 22.
Happiest terms.—*I Henry IV,* v, 4, 162.
Honourable terms.—*Love's Labour's Lost,* v, 2, 327.
Large terms.—*II Henry IV,* iv, 1, 86.
Silken terms.—*Love's Labour's Lost,* v, 2, 406.

11 Stand under the adoption of abominable terms. Terms! names!
The Merry Wives of Windsor, ii, 3, 308. See WRONG, 1748:14.

Gross terms.—*II Henry IV,* iv, 4, 73.
Term in gross.—*The Merchant of Venice,* iii, 2, 160.

12 She in mild terms begg'd my patience.
A Midsummer-Night's Dream. Act iv, sc. 1, l. 63. [Oberon]

13 He . . . spoke such scurvy and provoking terms
Against your honour.
Othello. Act i, sc. 2, l. 7. [Iago]

My lord hath . . .
Thrown such despite and heavy terms upon her,
As true hearts cannot bear. . . . A beggar in his drink
Could not have laid such terms upon his callet.
Othello, iv, 2, 115. See under WHORE.

14 May any terms acquit me from this chance?
The Rape of Lucrece, l. 1706.

15 Then in plain terms tell her my loving tale.
Richard III. Act iv, sc. 4, l. 359. [King Richard]

Setting all this chat aside,
Thus in plain terms.
The Taming of the Shrew. Act ii, sc. 1, l. 271. [Petruchio]

Plain terms.—*The Merchant of Venice,* ii, 2, 68; *Hamlet,* i, 3, 132.

16 Buy terms divine in selling hours of dross.
Sonnets. No. cxlvi.

17 Twenty such vile terms,
As she had studied to misuse me so.
The Taming of the Shrew. Act ii, sc. 1, l. 159. [Hortensio]

The bitterest terms That ever ear did hear.
Titus Andronicus. Act ii, sc. 3, l. 110. [Tamora]

18 I call thee by the most modest terms.
Twelfth Night. Act iv, sc. 2, l. 36. [Clown]

TERROR

See also Fear

1
We make trifles of terrors, ensconcing ourselves into seeming knowledge, when we should submit ourselves to an unknown fear.
All's Well that Ends Well. Act ii, sc. 3, l. 4. [Lafeu] The only use of "ensconcing."
Turn terror into sport.—*Coriolanus,* ii, 2, 109.
2
Your kingdom's terror and black Nemesis.
I Henry VI. Act iv, sc. 7, l. 78. [Lucy] The only mention of Nemesis.
A terror to our foes.—*Titus Andronicus,* i, 1, 29.
3
All the foul terrors in dark-seated hell.
II Henry VI. Act iii, sc. 2, l. 328. [Suffolk] The only use of "dark-seated."
Roaring terrors.—*Cymbeline,* iv, 2, 111.
4
Direness, familiar to my slaughterous thoughts,
Cannot once start me.
Macbeth. Act v, sc. 5, l. 14. [Macbeth] The only use of "direness" and "slaughterous."
Methinks there should be terrors in him.
The Merry Wives of Windsor. Act iv, sc. 4, l. 23. [Evans]
5
More fell than anguish, hunger, or the sea!
Othello. Act v, sc. 2, l. 362. [Lodovico]
Passing fell.—*A Midsummer-Night's Dream,* ii, 1, 20.
6
What terror 'tis! but she, in worser taking,
From sleep disturbed, heedfully doth view
The sight which makes supposed terror true.
The Rape of Lucrece, l. 453.
Trembling terror.—*Rape of Lucrece,* l. 231.
7
I would thou wert the man,
That would divorce this terror from my heart.
Richard II. Act v, sc. 4, l. 8. [Exton]
8
Come, cousin, canst thou quake, and change thy colour,
Murder thy breath in middle of a word,
And then begin again, and stop again,
As if thou wert distraught and mad with terror?
Richard III. Act iii, sc. 5, l. 1. [Gloucester] "Distraught" is repeated in *Romeo and Juliet,* iv, 3, 49.
9
The horrible conceit of death and night,
Together with the terror of the place.
Romeo and Juliet. Act iv, sc. 3, l. 37. [Juliet]
The unaccustom'd terror of this night.
Julius Cæsar. Act ii, sc. 1, l. 199. [Cassius]
10
Cold terror doth men's minds confound.
Venus and Adonis, l. 1048.
Dismal terror.—*Richard III,* i, 4, 7.

TEST, see Trial

TESTAMENT, see Will

TESTIMONY

See also Proof

11
There is too great testimony in your complexion.
As You Like It, iv, 3, 171. See under COUNTERFEIT.
Princely testimony!—*Much Ado about Nothing,* iv, 1, 318.
Sufficient testimony.—*Cymbeline,* i, 4, 161.
Warranted testimony.—*All's Well that Ends Well,* ii, 5, 5.
12
The testimonies whereof lie bleeding in me.
Cymbeline. Act iii, sc. 4, l. 22. [Imogen, reading]
13
Bear me testimony and witness.
Henry V. Act iv, sc. 8, l. 38. [Fluellen]
Testimony of his intent.—*King Lear,* i, 2, 88.
14
Done in the testimony of a good conscience.
Love's Labour's Lost, iv, 2, 2. See under CONSCIENCE.
Testimony of your own sex.—*Measure for Measure,* ii, 4, 131.
Testimony of her foul proceedings.—*Titus Andronicus,* v, 3, 8.
15
Testimonies against his worth and credit.
Measure for Measure, v, 1, 244. See under OATH.
16
The testimony on my part no other
But what comes from myself.
The Winter's Tale. Act iii, sc. 2, l. 25. [Hermione]
By good testimony.—*Winter's Tale,* ii, 3, 136.
By my testimony.—*Twelfth Night,* v, 1, 164.

TEXT

17
The text is foolish.
King Lear. Act iv, sc. 2, l. 37. [Goneril]
The text is old, the orator too green.
Venus and Adonis, l. 806.
18
Certes, the text most infallibly concludes it.
Love's Labour's Lost. Act iv, sc. 2, l. 42. [Holofernes]
Approve it with a text.—*The Merchant of Venice,* iii, 2, 79.
The text underneath.—*Much Ado about Nothing,* v, 1, 185.
Fair as text B in a copy-book.—*Love's Labour's Lost,* v, 2, 42.
19
Olivia: Now, sir, what is your text?
Viola: Most sweet lady,—
Olivia: A comfortable doctrine, and much may be said of it. Where liest your text?
Viola: In Orsino's bosom.
Olivia: In his bosom! In what chapter of his bosom?
Viola: To answer by the method, in the first of his heart.
Olivia: O, I have read it: it is heresy. Have you no more to say?
Viola: Good madam, let me see your face. . . .

Olivia: You are now out of your text.
Twelfth Night. Act i, sc. 5, l. 237. The only use of "chapter."
Holy text.—*II Henry IV*, iv, 2, 7. See under Preacher.

THANKFULNESS
See also Gratitude

1
Such thanks I give
As one near death to those that wish him live.
All's Well that Ends Well. Act ii, sc. 1, l. 133. [King]

2
I must thank him only,
Lest my remembrance suffer ill report.
Antony and Cleopatra. Act ii, sc. 2, l. 158. [Antony]
I . . . am well studied for a liberal thanks
Which I do owe you.
Antony and Cleopatra. Act ii, sc. 6, l. 47. [Antony]

3
Well then, if ever I thank any man, I'll thank you. . . . And when a man thanks me heartily, methinks I have given him a penny and he renders me the beggarly thanks.
As You Like It. Act ii, sc. 5, l. 25. [Jaques]
Hearty thanks.—*King Lear*, iv, 6, 227.

4
Dromio of Syracuse: Well, sir, I thank you.
Antipholus of Syracuse: Thank me, sir! for what?
Dromio of Syracuse: Marry, sir, for this something that you gave me for nothing.
The Comedy of Errors. Act ii, sc. 2, l. 50.

5
Sicinius: Accept my thankfulness.
Messenger: Sir, we have all
Great cause to give great thanks.
Coriolanus. Act v, sc. 4, l. 62.
Accept distracted thanks.—*Troilus and Cressida*, v, 2, 189.

6
For this relief much thanks.
Hamlet. Act i, sc. 1, l. 8. [Francisco]
Your visitation shall receive such thanks
As fits a king's remembrance.
Hamlet. Act ii, sc. 2, l. 25. [Queen]
Ambassador: Where should we have our thanks?
Horatio: Not from his mouth,
Had it the ability of life to thank you.
Hamlet. Act v, sc. 2, l. 383.

7
Sure, we thank you.
Henry V. Act i, sc. 1, l. 8. [King Henry]
We therefore have great cause of thankfulness.
Henry V. Act ii, sc. 2, l. 32. [King Henry]

8
Let me give humble thanks for all at once.
III Henry VI. Act iii, sc. 3, l. 221. [Queen Margaret]

9
Take his thanks that yet hath nothing else.
III Henry VI. Act v, sc. 4, l. 59. [Prince]
Evermore thanks, the exchequer of the poor;
Which, till my infant fortune comes to years,
Stands for my bounty.
Richard II. Act ii, sc. 3, l. 65. [Bolingbroke]
Beggar that I am, I am even poor in thanks; but I thank you: and sure, dear friends, my thanks are too dear a halfpenny.
Hamlet. Act ii, sc. 2, l. 280. [Hamlet]
The thanks I give
Is telling you that I am poor of thanks
And scarce can spare them.
Cymbeline. Act ii, sc. 3, l. 93. [Imogen]

10
Vouchsafe to speak my thanks and my obedience.
Henry VIII. Act ii, sc. 3, l. 71. [Anne]
For your great graces
Heap'd upon me, poor undeserver, I
Can nothing render but allegiant thanks.
Henry VIII. Act iii, sc. 2, l. 174. [Wolsey] The only use of "allegiant" (giving allegiance). "Undeserver" is repeated in *II Henry IV*, iii, 4, 406, and in *Julius Cæsar*, iv, 3, 12.

11
O, take his mother's thanks, a widow's thanks.
King John. Act ii, sc. 1, l. 32. [Constance]

12
I praise the Lord for you: and so may my parishioners.
Love's Labour's Lost. Act iv, sc. 2, l. 75 [Sir Nathaniel] "Parishioners" is repeated in *As You Like It*, iii, 2, 164.
I praise God for you, sir.
Love's Labour's Lost. Act v, sc. 1, l. 1 [Sir Nathaniel]

13
Thanks for your pains.
Macbeth. Act i, sc. 3, l. 117. [Macbeth]
Your pains
Are register'd where every day I turn
The leaf to read them.
Macbeth. Act i, sc. 3, l. 150. [Macbeth]
Thank you for your pains.—*The Taming of the Shrew*, iii, 2, 186. Repeated six times in later plays.

14
They encounter thee with their hearts' thanks.
Macbeth. Act iii, sc. 4, l. 9. [Macbeth]
So, thanks to all at once and to each one.
Macbeth. Act v, sc. 8, l. 74. [Malcolm]

15
He should receive his punishment in thanks.
Measure for Measure. Act i, sc. 4, l. 28. [Lucio]

16
Many and hearty thankings to you both.
Measure for Measure. Act v, sc. 1, l. 4. [Duke]
Thank me no thankings.—*Romeo and Juliet*, iii, 5, 153.
The thankings of a king.—*Cymbeline*, v, 5, 407. The only uses of "thankings."
Thanking shall be for me.—*All's Well that Ends Well*, iii, 5, 101. The only use of "thanking."

17
Gobbo: God bless your worship!
Bassanio: Gramercy!
The Merchant of Venice. Act ii, sc. 2, l. 127. "Gramercy" occurs eight times in the plays.

1
Shallow: And I thank you always with my heart, la! with my heart.
Page: Sir, I thank you.
Shallow: Sir, I thank you; by yea and no, I do.
Merry Wives of Windsor. Act i, sc. 1, l. 85.
Take from my heart all thankfulness!
Pericles. Act iii, sc. 3, l. 4. [Pericles]

2
The kinder we, to give them thanks for nothing.
A Midsummer-Night's Dream. Act v, sc. 1, l. 89. [Theseus]

3
Sweet prince, you learn me noble thankfulness.
Much Ado about Nothing. Act iv, sc. 1, l. 31. [Claudio]

4
All my treasury
Is yet but unfelt thanks, which more enrich'd
Shall be your love and labour's recompense.
Richard II. Act ii, sc. 3, l. 60. [Bolingbroke]
We thank thee, gentle Percy, for thy pains;
And to thy worth will add right worthy gains.
Richard II. Act v, sc. 6, l. 11. [Bolingbroke]

5
O upright, just, and true-disposing God,
How do I thank thee, that this carnal cur
Preys on the issue of his mother's body,
And makes her pew-fellow with others' moan!
Richard III. Act iv, sc. 4, l. 55. [Queen Margaret] The only use of "true-disposing" and "pew-fellow."

6
O, give thyself the thanks, if aught in me
Worthy perusal stand against thy sight.
Sonnets. No. xxxviii. "Perusal" is repeated in *Hamlet,* ii, 1, 90.

7
This kindness merits thanks . . .
The poorest service is repaid with thanks.
The Taming of the Shrew. Act iv, sc. 3, l. 41. [Petruchio]

8
The gods require our thanks.
Timon of Athens. Act iii, sc. 6, l. 77. [Timon]
Down on thy knees, thank the holy gods as loud
As thunder threatens us.
Pericles. Act v, sc. 1, l. 200. [Pericles]
God be thanked.—*Richard III,* iii, 7, 165, and five times in later plays.
The Lord be thanked.—*The Taming of the Shrew,* Ind., 2, 99.
Thank God.—*II Henry VI,* ii, 1, 108, and thirteen times in later plays.
Thank heaven.—*As You Like It,* iii, 5, 58, and four times in later plays.
Thank my stars.—*Twelfth Night,* ii, 5, 185.

9
Thanks to men
Of noble minds is honourable meed.
Titus Andronicus. Act i, sc. 1, l. 215. [Bassianus]
I give thee thanks in part of thy deserts,
And will with deeds requite.
Titus Andronicus. Act i, sc. 1, l. 236. [Saturninus]

10
I can no other answer make but thanks.
Twelfth Night. Act iii, sc. 3, l. 14. [Sebastian]
I multiply
With one 'We thank you' many thousands moe
That go before it.
The Winter's Tale. Act i, sc. 2, l. 7. [Polixenes] The only use of "multiply."
A thousand thanks!—*III Henry VI,* iii, 2, 56; *The Taming of the Shrew,* ii, 1, 85; *Henry V,* iv, 4, 63; *Henry VIII,* i, 4, 74.

11
I will live to be thankful to thee for 't.
Twelfth Night. Act iv, sc. 2, l. 89. [Malvolio]
To be more thankful to thee shall be my study.
The Winter's Tale. Act iv, sc. 2, l. 20. [Polixenes]
I am thankful.—*Love's Labour 's Lost,* iv, 2, 74; *Henry VIII,* i, 1, 149.
I will be thankful.—*The Two Gentlemen of Verona,* ii, 4, 52.
Yet am I thankful.—*All's Well that Ends Well,* iv, 3, 366.
I shall continue thankful.—*All's Well that Ends Well,* v, 1, 17.
Ye shall find me thankful.—*Henry VIII,* v, 5, 73.
Jove make me thankful!—*Twelfth Night,* iii, 4, 83.
Generally thankful.—*All's Well that Ends Well,* ii, 3, 44.
Thankful for good turns.—*The Taming of the Shrew,* ii, 1, 166.
Most thankful.—*Much Ado about Nothing,* v, 1, 324.
Take it thankfully.—*King Lear,* iii, 6, 2; *Cymbeline,* i, 6, 28.
More thankfully.—*Cymbeline,* i, 6, 79.
Most thankfully.—*The Merchant of Venice,* iv, 2, 9; *Timon of Athens,* i, 2, 162; v, 1, 94.

THEFT

12
Lord: There 's honour in the theft.
Parolles: Commit it, count.
All's Well that Ends Well. Act ii, sc. 1, l. 34.
There 's warrant in that theft
Which steals itself, when there 's no mercy left.
Macbeth. Act ii, sc. 3, l. 151. [Malcolm]

13
If he steal aught the whilst this play is playing,
And 'scape detecting, I will pay the theft.
Hamlet. Act iii, sc. 2, l. 94. [Horatio] The only use of "detecting."

14
Nym and Bardolph are sworn brothers in filching, and in Calais they stole a fire-shovel: I knew by that piece of service the men would carry coals.
Henry V. Act iii, sc. 2, l. 48. [Boy] The only use of "fire-shovel."
His thefts were too open; his filching was like an unskilful singer; he kept not time.
The Merry Wives of Windsor. Act i, sc. 3, l. 28. [Falstaff] The only uses of "filching."

1
Lucio: Thou concludest like the sanctimonious pirate, that went to sea with the Ten Commandments, but scraped one out of the table.
Second Gentleman: 'Thou shalt not steal'?
Lucio: Ay, that he razed.
Measure for Measure. Act i, sc. 2, l. 7. The only use of "concludest." "Ten commandments" occurs again in *II Henry VI,* i, 3, 145, but refers to the fingers. "Sanctimonious" is repeated in *The Tempest,* iv, 1, 16.

2
Flat burglary as ever was committed.
Much Ado about Nothing. Act iv, sc. 2, l. 52. [Dogberry] The only use of "burglary."

3
It 's an honourable kind of thievery.
The Two Gentlemen of Verona. Act iv, sc. 1, l. 39. [Speed]
I 'll example you with thievery.—*Timon of Athens,* iv, 3, 438.
Rich thievery.—*Troilus and Cressida,* iv, 4, 45. The only uses of "thievery."

4
We steal by line and level.
Tempest. Act iv, sc. 1, l. 239. [Trinculo]

5
Easy it is Of a cut loaf to steal a shive.
Titus Andronicus. Act ii, sc. 1, l. 86. [Demetrius] The only use of "shive" (slice), and of "loaf." "Loaves" occurs in *II Henry VI,* iv, 2, 71.
Steal a kiss.—*The Two Gentlemen of Verona,* ii, 4, 160.
Steal your thoughts.—*The Merchant of Venice,* ii, 1, 12.

6
O, theft most base,
That we have stol'n what we do fear to keep!
Troilus and Cressida. Act ii, sc. 2, l. 92. [Troilus]
Injurious theft.—*The Rape of Lucrece,* l. 838.

II—Thief

See also Robber

7
Enobarbus: You have been a great thief by sea.
Menas: And you by land.
Antony and Cleopatra. Act ii, sc. 6, l. 96.
Salt-water thief!—*Twelfth Night,* v, 1, 72.

8
If our eyes had authority, here they might take two thieves kissing.
Antony and Cleopatra. Act ii, sc. 6, l. 99. [Enobarbus]

9
Or with a base and boisterous sword enforce
A thievish living on the common road?
As You Like It. Act ii, sc. 3, l. 32. [Orlando]

10
I think he is not a pick-purse nor a horse-stealer.
As You Like It. Act iii, sc. 4, l. 24. [Celia] The only use of "horse-stealer."
At hand, quoth pick-purse.—*I Henry IV,* ii, 1, 53.
It is a pick-purse.—*The Merry Wives of Windsor,* i, 1, 163. The only uses of "pick-purse."
Pick-purses in love.—*Love's Labour 's Lost,* iv, 3. 209. The only use of "pick-purses."

11
What simple thief brags of his own attaint?
The Comedy of Errors. Act iii, sc. 2, l. 16. [Luciana]

12
I do doubt nothing you have store of thieves.
Cymbeline. Act i, sc. 4, l. 107. [Posthumus]

13
We that take purses go by the moon and the seven stars, and not by Phœbus, he, 'that wandering knight so fair.'
I Henry IV. Act i, sc. 2, l. 15. [Falstaff]
Let not us that are squires of the night's body be called thieves of the day's beauty.
I Henry IV. Act i, sc. 2, l. 27. [Falstaff]
A plague upon it when thieves cannot be true one to another! Whew! A plague upon you all!
I Henry IV. Act ii, sc. 2, l. 30. [Falstaff] The only use of "whew," indicating a whistle.

14
The thieves have bound the true men. Now could thou and I rob the thieves and go merrily to London, it would be argument for a week, laughter for a month and a good jest for ever.
I Henry IV. Act ii, sc. 2, l. 98. [Prince]

15
The thieves are all scatter'd and possess'd with fear
So strongly that they dare not meet each other;
Each takes his fellow for an officer.
I Henry IV. Act ii, sc. 2, l. 112. [Prince]
The thief doth fear each bush an officer.
III Henry VI. Act v, sc. 6, l. 12. [Gloucester] See also under SHADOW.

16
Where shall I find one that can steal well? O for a fine thief, of the age of two and twenty or thereabouts!
I Henry IV. Act iii, sc. 3, l. 210. [Falstaff]
Welcome, my little tiny thief.
II Henry IV. Act v, sc. 3, l. 60. [Shallow]

17
They will steal any thing, and call it purchase. Bardolph stole a lute-case, bore it twelve leagues, and sold it for three half-pence.
Henry V. Act iii, sc. 2, l. 44. [Boy] The only use of "lute-case."

18
I remember him now; a bawd, a cut-purse.
Henry V. Act iii, sc. 6, l. 65. [Gower]
Well, bawd, I 'll turn,
And something lean to cutpurse of quick hand.
To England will I steal, and there I 'll steal.
Henry V. Act v, sc. 1, l. 90. [Pistol]
To have an open ear, a quick eye, and a nimble hand, is necessary for a cut-purse; a good nose is requisite also, to smell out work for the other senses.
The Winter's Tale. Act iv, sc. 4, l. 683. [Autolycus]

A cutpurse of the empire.—*Hamlet,* iii, 4, 99.
Cutpurse of quick hand.—*Henry V,* v, 1, 91.
Cut-purse rascal.—*II Henry IV,* ii, 4, 137. The only uses of "cut-purse."

1
Foul felonious thief that fleeced poor passengers.
II Henry VI. Act iii, sc. 1, l. 129. [Gloucester] Shakespeare used "felonious" and "fleeced" in his first play and never after that.

Down with them; fleece them.
I Henry IV. Act ii, sc. 2, l. 89. [Falstaff] The only use of "fleece" in this sense.

2
Every true man's apparel fits your thief: if it be too little for your thief, your true man thinks it big enough; if it be too big for your thief, your thief thinks it little enough: so every true man's apparel fits your thief.
Measure for Measure. Act iv, sc. 2, l. 46. [Abhorson]

We take him to be a thief.—*Measure for Measure,* iii, 2, 17.
Thief of love.—*A Midsummer-Night's Dream,* iii, 2, 283.

3
The thief gone with so much, and so much to find the thief.
The Merchant of Venice. Act iii, sc. 1, l. 97. [Shylock]

4
Take heed, have open eyes, for thieves do foot by night.
The Merry Wives of Windsor. Act ii, sc. 1, l. 126. [Pistol]

5
If you meet a thief, you may suspect him, by virtue of your office, to be no true man.
Much Ado about Nothing. Act iii, sc. 3, l. 53. [Dogberry]

The most peaceable way for you, if you do take a thief, is to let him show himself what he is and steal out of your company.
Much Ado about Nothing. Act iii, sc. 3, l. 60. [Dogberry] "Peaceable" is repeated in *Pericles,* ii, 1, 108.

Deformed thief.—*Much Ado about Nothing,* iii, 3, 131; 140.

I know that Deformed; a' has been a vile thief this seven year; a' goes up and down like a gentleman: I remember his name.
Much Ado about Nothing. Act iii, sc. 3, l. 133. [Watchman]

6
O thou foul thief.
Othello. Act i, sc. 2, l. 62. [Brabantio]

Adulterous thief.—*Measure for Measure,* v, 1, 40.
Bloody thieves.—*Othello,* v, 1, 63.
Creeping thief.—*The Rape of Lucrece,* l. 305.
Cunning thief.—*Cymbeline,* i, 4, 100.
Desperate thieves.—*III Henry VI,* i, 4, 42.
Egyptian thief.—*Twelfth Night,* v, 1, 121.
False thief.—*I Henry IV,* ii, 1, 103; *The Rape of Lucrece,* l. 888.
Gentle thief.—*Sonnets,* xl.
Injurious thief.—*Cymbeline,* iv, 2, 86.
Petty thieves.—*Henry V,* i, 2, 177.
Poor thief.—*All's Well that Ends Well,* iii, 2, 131.
Roguing thieves.—*Pericles,* iv, 1, 97. The only use of "roguing."
Sacrilegious thief.—*Cymbeline,* v, 5, 220.
Strong thief.—*Timon of Athens,* iv, 3, 45.
Sweet thief.—*Sonnets,* xxxv; xcix.
Timorous thief.—*All's Well that Ends Well,* ii, 5, 86.
Vulgar thief.—*Sonnets,* xlviii.

7
Discomfortable cousin! know'st thou not
That when the searching eye of heaven is hid,
Behind the globe, that lights the lower world,
Then thieves and robbers range abroad unseen
In murders and in outrage?
Richard II. Act iii, sc. 2, l. 37. [King Richard] The only use of "discomfortable."

Even such, they say, as stand in narrow lanes,
And beat our watch, and rob our passengers.
Richard II. Act v, sc. 3, l. 8. [Bolingbroke]

8
Draw forth thy weapon, we are beset with thieves.
The Taming of the Shrew. Act iii, sc. 2, l. 238. [Petruchio]

9
The trumpery in my house, go bring it hither,
For stale to catch these thieves.
The Tempest. Act iv, sc. 1, l. 186. [Prospero] "Trumpery" is repeated in *The Winter's Tale,* iv, 4, 608.

10
Yet thanks I must you con
That you are thieves profess'd, that you work not
In holier shapes: for there is boundless theft
In limited professions. Rascal thieves,
Here 's gold.
Timon of Athens. Act iv, sc. 3, l. 428. [Timon]

The sun 's a thief, and with his great attraction
Robs the vast sea: the moon 's an arrant thief.
And her pale fire she snatches from the sun:
The sea 's a thief, whose liquid surge resolves
The moon into salt tears: the earth 's a thief,
That feeds and breeds by a composture stolen
From general excrement: each thing 's a thief:
The laws, your curb and whip, in their rough power
Have uncheck'd theft. . . . All that you meet are thieves:
. . . nothing can you steal,
But thieves do lose it.
Timon of Athens. Act iv, sc. 3, l. 439. [Timon] The only use of "composture."

11
Rich preys make true men thieves.
Venus and Adonis, l. 724.

THEME

12
To me she speaks; she moves me for her theme.
The Comedy of Errors. Act ii, sc. 2, l. 183. [Antipholus of Syracuse]

I am your theme.—*The Merry Wives of Windsor,* v, 5, 170.
Ay, that 's the theme.—*Twelfth Night,* ii, 4, 125.
The very theme I came to talk of.—*Romeo and Juliet,* i, 3, 63.

1
Hamlet: I will fight with him upon this theme
Until my eyelids will no longer wag.
Queen: O my son, what theme?
Hamlet: I loved Ophelia.
Hamlet. Act v, sc. 2, l. 289.

2 With your theme, I could
O'ermount the lark.
Henry VIII. Act ii, sc. 3, l. 93. [Old Lady] The only use of "o'ermount."

A theme as fluent as the sea.—*Henry V,* iii, 7, 36.
A theme for disputation.—*The Rape of Lucrece,* l. 822.
Theme of our assembly.—*Coriolanus,* ii, 2, 61.
Theme of honour's tongue.—*I Henry IV,* i, 1, 81.
Theme of woe.—*The Tempest,* ii, 1, 6.

3 This weak and idle theme,
No more yielding but a dream.
A Midsummer-Night's Dream. Act v, sc. 1, l. 434. [Puck]

Idle theme.—*Venus and Adonis,* l. 422.
Common theme.—*Hamlet,* i, 2, 103.
Imperial theme.—*Macbeth,* i, 3, 129.

4
I must ply my theme.
Titus Andronicus. Act v, sc. 2, l. 80. [Tamora]

O, handle not the theme.—*Titus Andronicus,* iii, 2, 29.

5
She is a theme of honour and renown,
A spur to valiant and magnanimous deeds.
Troilus and Cressida. Act ii, sc. 2, l. 199. [Troilus]

Name her not now, sir; she 's a deadly theme.
Troilus and Cressida. Act iv, sc. 5, l. 181. [Menelaus]

Without a theme.—*Troilus and Cressida,* v, 2, 131.

THEWS, see Sinews

THINNESS

See also Fatness

6
Do I not bate? do I not dwindle? Why, my skin hangs about me like an old lady's loose gown; I am wither'd like an old apple-john.
I Henry IV. Act iii, sc. 3, l. 2. [Falstaff] "Apple-john" is repeated in *II Henry IV,* ii, 4, 2; 5.

Dwindle, peak and pine.—*Macbeth,* i, 3, 23. The only uses of "dwindle."

7
Give me this man: he presents no mark to the enemy; the foeman may with as great aim level at the edge of a penknife. . . . O, give me the spare men, and spare me the great ones. . . . O, give me always a little, lean, old, chapt, bald shot.
II Henry IV. Act iii, sc. 2, l. 284. [Falstaff] The only use of "penknife" and "chapt." "Foeman" is repeated in *III Henry VI,* ii, 5, 82.

You might have thrust him and all his apparel into an eel-skin; the case of a treble hautboy was a mansion for him, a court.
II Henry IV. Act iii, sc. 2, l. 349. [Falstaff] The only use of "hautboy." "Eel-skin" occurs again in *King John,* i, 1, 141.

You thin man in a censer.
II Henry IV. Act v, sc. 4, l. 20. [Doll]

Come, you thin thing.—*II Henry IV,* v, 4, 34.
Thin-belly.—*Love's Labour 's Lost,* iii, 1, 19.
Thin-faced.—*Twelfth Night,* v, 1, 213. The only use of either phrase.
Skinny lips.—*Macbeth,* i, 3, 45. The only use of "skinny."
Thin and hairless.—*Richard II,* iii, 2, 112.
Thin and naked.—*Richard III,* ii, 1, 117.
Thin and wholesome.—*Hamlet,* i, 5, 70.
Thin and slender.—*The Taming of the Shrew,* iv, 4, 61.
Slender as my wit.—*Love's Labour 's Lost,* iv, 1, 49.
Straight and slender.—*The Taming of the Shrew,* ii, 1, 256.
Very slender.—*II Henry IV,* i, 2, 159.

8
Watching breeds leanness, leanness is all gaunt.
Richard II. Act ii, sc. 1, l. 78. [Gaunt] The The only uses of "leanness."

Here comes lean Jack, here comes bare-bone.
I Henry IV. Act ii, sc. 4, l. 358. [Prince Henry] The only use of "bare-bone."

Lean and hungry.—*Julius Cæsar,* i, 2, 194.
Lean, and lacking juice.—*Venus and Adonis,* l. 136.
Lean and wrinkled.—*Antony and Cleopatra,* iii, 11, 37.
Lean, rent and beggar'd.—*The Merchant of Venice,* ii, 6, 19.
Forlorn and lean.—*Titus Andronicus,* ii, 3, 94.
Lank and lean.—*II Henry VI,* i, 3. 132. "Lank" is used only once again, in *Hamlet,* ii, 2, 531: "Lank loins."

9
You 'ld be so lean, that blasts of January
Would blow you through and through.
The Winter's Tale. Act iv, sc. 4, l. 111. [Perdita]

So thin that life looks through and will break out.
II Henry IV, iv, 4, 120. See under Mind.

Lean-faced.—*II Henry VI,* iii, 2, 315; *The Comedy of Errors,* v, 1, 237.
Lean-look'd.—*Richard II,* ii, 4, 11.
Lean-witted.—*Richard II,* ii, 1, 115.

THIRST

10
Dost thou thirst, base Trojan?
Henry V. Act v, sc. 1, l. 20. [Pistol]

Thirst for blood.—*I Henry VI,* iii, 1, 117.
Thirst for revenge.—*Coriolanus,* i, 1, 25.
Thirsting after prey.—*II Henry VI,* iv, 4, 51. The only use of "thirsting."
Unstanched thirst.—*III Henry VI,* ii, 6, 83.

11
When they are thirsty, fools would fain have drink.
Love's Labour 's Lost. Act v, sc. 2, l. 372. [Rosaline] See under Fool.

Thirsty after tottering honour.—*Pericles,* iii, 2, 40.
Thirsty for that noble pledge.—*Julius Cæsar,* iv, 3, 160.
Thirsty earth.—*III Henry VI,* ii, 3, 15.
Thirsty entrance.—*I Henry IV,* i, 1, 5.
Thirsty evil.—*Measure for Measure,* i, 2, 134.
None so dry or thirsty.—*The Taming of the Shrew,* v, 2, 144. The only uses of "thirsty."
Dry with rage.—*I Henry IV,* i, 3, 31.
Hot and dry.—*Hamlet,* iv, 7, 158.

1 To all, and him, we thirst,
And all to all.
Macbeth. Act iii, sc. 4, l. 91. [Macbeth] See DRINKING HEALTHS.

Quench his thirst.—*The Taming of the Shrew,* i, 1, 24.

THORN

See also Rose and Thorn

2
When briers shall have leaves as well as thorns.
All's Well that Ends Well, iv, 4, 32. See under SUMMER.

Rosalind: O how full of briers is this working-day world!
Celia: They are but burs, cousin, thrown upon thee in holiday foolery: if we walk not in the trodden paths, our very petticoats will catch them.
Rosalind: I could shake them off my coat: these burs are in my heart.
Celia: Hem them away.
Rosalind: I would try, if I could cry 'hem' and have him.
As You Like It. Act i, sc. 3, l. 12.

Rude-growing briers.—*Titus Andronicus,* ii, 3, 199. The only use of the phrase.
Triumphant brier.—*A Midsummer-Night's Dream,* iii, 1, 96.

3
Mow down thorns that would annoy our foot.
II Henry VI. Act iii, sc. 1, l. 67. [King Henry]

But O, the thorns we stand upon!
The Winter's Tale, iv, 4, 595. [Florizel]

4
What! can so young a thorn begin to prick?
III Henry VI. Act v, sc. 5, l. 13. [King Edward]

Rent with the thorns.—*III Henry VI,* iii, 2, 175. See under ADVERSITY.
Virgin thorn.—*A Midsummer-Night's Dream,* i, 1, 77.
Thorny brambles.—*Venus and Adonis,* l. 629.

5
But, alack, my hand is sworn
Ne'er to pluck thee from thy thorn.
Love's Labour's Lost. Act iv, sc. 3, l. 111. [Dumain] Repeated in *The Passionate Pilgrim,* l. 237.

6
Briers and thorns at their apparel snatch.
A Midsummer-Night's Dream. Act iii, sc. 2, l. 29. [Puck]

Torn with briers.—*A Midsummer-Night's Dream,* iii, 2, 443.
Full of briers.—*As You Like It,* i, 3, 12.

7
There thou prickest her with a thistle.
Much Ado about Nothing. Act iii, sc. 4, l. 76. [Hero]

Rough thistles.—*Henry V,* v, 2, 52.
On the top of a thistle.—*A Midsummer-Night's Dream,* iv, 1, 12. The only uses of "thistle."

8 Against a thorn thou bear'st thy part,
To keep thy sharp woes waking.
The Rape of Lucrece, l. 1135.

9 Through
Tooth'd briers, sharp furzes, pricking goss and thorns,
Which enter'd their frail shins.
The Tempest, iv, 1, 177. See under EAR. The only use of "furzes" and "goss." "Gorse" does not occur.

Brown furze.—*The Tempest,* i, 1, 70. The only uses of "furze."
Through brake, through brier.—*A Midsummer-Night's Dream,* iii, 1, 110.
Thorough bush, thorough brier.—*A Midsummer-Night's Dream,* ii, 1, 3.

10
Each envious brier his weary legs doth scratch.
Venus and Adonis, l. 705.

Scratch'd with briers.—*The Winter's Tale,* iv, 4, 436.
Scratches with briers.—*Coriolanus,* iii, 3, 51.

THOUGHT

11
The conversation of my thoughts.
All's Well that Ends Well. Act i, sc. 3, l. 240. [Helena]

Humbly entreating from your royal thoughts
A modest one.
All's Well that Ends Well. Act ii, sc. 1, l. 130. [Helena]

Royal thoughts.—*II Henry IV,* v, 2, 91.
Regal thoughts.—*Richard II,* iv, 1, 163.

12
Make me but like my thoughts.
All's Well that Ends Well. Act iii, sc. 3, l. 10. [Bertram]

13
I am wrapp'd in dismal thinkings.
All's Well that Ends Well. Act v, sc. 3, l. 128. [King]

Ill thinking.—*Othello,* iii, 4, 29.
Unworthy thinking.—*Cymbeline,* i, 4, 157.

14
Our worser thoughts heavens mend!
Antony and Cleopatra. Act i, sc. 2, l. 64. [Charmian]

15 On the sudden
A Roman thought hath struck him.
Antony and Cleopatra. Act i, sc. 2, l. 86. [Cleopatra]

'Tis a studied, not a present thought,
By duty ruminated.
Antony and Cleopatra. Act ii, sc. 2, l. 140. [Agrippa]

16
Little thought You would have follow'd.
Antony and Cleopatra. Act iii, sc. 11, l. 55. [Cleopatra]

Little thought.—*Richard III,* i, 4, 244; *Henry VIII,* iii, 1, 183.

1
Make not your thoughts your prisons.
Antony and Cleopatra. Act v, sc. 2, l. 185. [Cæsar]

2
Take to you no hard thoughts.
Antony and Cleopatra. Act v, sc. 2, l. 117. [Cæsar]

Punish me not with your hard thoughts.
As You Like It. Act i, sc. 2, l. 195. [Orlando]

Churlish thoughts.—*King John,* ii, 1, 519.
Deceitful thoughts.—*II Henry VI,* iv, 7, 109.
Doubtful thoughts.—*The Merchant of Venice,* iii, 2, 109.
Impatient thoughts.—*Othello,* i, 3, 243.
Moody thoughts.—*III Henry VI,* iv, 6, 13.

3
Ah, but I think him better than I say.
The Comedy of Errors. Act iv, sc. 2, l. 25. [Adriana]

4
Their thoughts do hit The roofs of palaces.
Cymbeline. Act iii, sc. 3, l. 83. [Belarius]

5
In what particular thought to work I know not.
Hamlet. Act i, sc. 1, l. 67. [Horatio]

We fools of nature
So horridly to shake our disposition
With thoughts beyond the reaches of our souls.
Hamlet. Act i, sc. 4, l. 54. [Hamlet]

6
There is nothing either good or bad, but thinking makes it so.
Hamlet. Act ii, sc. 2, l. 255. [Hamlet]

O, who can hold a fire in his hand
By thinking on the frosty Caucasus?
Or cloy the hungry edge of appetite
By bare imagination of a feast?
Or wallow naked in December snow
By thinking on fantastic summer's heat?
Richard II. Act i, sc. 3, l. 294. [Bolingbroke] Caucasus is mentioned again in *Titus Andronicus,* ii, 1, 17; and "wallow" occurs in *Troilus and Cressida,* iii, 2, 13: "Wallow in the lily-beds." (Which is the only use of "lily-beds.")

I can live no longer by thinking.
As You Like It. Act v, sc. 2, l. 55. [Orlando]

But thought 's the slave of life, and life time's fool.
I Henry IV. Act v, sc. 4, l. 81. [Hotspur]

7
Our thoughts are ours, their ends none of our own.
Hamlet. Act iii, sc. 2, l. 223. [Player King]

A thought which, quarter'd, hath but one part wisdom
And ever three parts coward.
Hamlet. Act iv, sc. 4, l. 42. [Hamlet]

8
O, from this time forth,
My thoughts be bloody, or be nothing worth!
Hamlet. Act iv, sc. 4, l. 65. [Hamlet]

Like to the Pontic sea,
Whose icy current and compulsive course
Ne'er feels retiring ebb, but keeps due on
To the Propontic and the Hellespont,
Even so my bloody thoughts, with violent pace,
Shall ne'er look back, ne'er ebb to humble love.
Othello. Act iii, sc. 3, l. 453. [Othello] The only use of "Pontic" and "Propontic."

I do begin to have bloody thoughts.
Tempest. Act iv, sc. 1, l. 219. [Stephano]

Bloody thoughts.—*Richard III,* ii, 1, 92; *The Winter's Tale,* iii, 2, 160.
Mortal thoughts.—*Macbeth,* i, 5, 42.
Slaughterous thoughts.—*Macbeth,* v, 5, 14.

9
It would be every man's thought; and thou art a blessed fellow to think as every man thinks: never a man's thought in the world keeps the road-way better than thine.
II Henry IV. Act ii, sc. 2, l. 60. [Prince of Wales] The only use of "road-way."

What accites your most worshipful thought to think so?
II Henry IV. Act ii, sc. 2, l. 64. [Prince of Wales] "Accites" (excites) is repeated in l. 141, and occurs nowhere else.

10
So swift a pace hath thought.
Henry V. Act v, Prologue, l. 15. [Chorus]

Swift as thought, see under SWIFTNESS.

11
In the quick forge and working-house of thought.
Henry V. Act v, Prologue, l. 23. [Chorus] The only use of "working-house."

12
Avouch the thoughts of your heart.
Henry V. Act v, sc. 2, l. 253. [King Henry]

Thought of hearts.—*Sonnets,* lxix.
Thought of fear.—*II Henry IV,* iv, 1, 153.
Thoughts of harm.—*Much Ado about Nothing,* iv, 1, 108.
Thoughts of love.—*Hamlet,* i, 5, 30; *Sonnets,* xxxix; xlvii.
Thoughts of others.—*The Merchant of Venice,* i, 3, 164.
Frenzy's thoughts.—*Troilus and Cressida,* v, 10, 29.
Honour's thought.—*Henry V,* ii, Prol., 3.
Soul's thought.—*Sonnets,* xxvi.

13
My thoughts are whirled like a potter's wheel.
I Henry VI. Act i, sc. 5, l. 19. [Talbot] The only use of "potter."

He thought no harm.—*I Henry VI,* iv, 1, 179.

14
Banish the canker of ambitious thoughts.
II Henry VI, i, 2, 18. See under AMBITION

Thoughts tending to ambition, they do plot
Unlikely wonders.
Richard II. Act v, sc. 5, l. 18. [King Richard]

Ambitious thoughts.—*Richard II,* i, 3, 130.
High-pitch'd thoughts.—*The Rape of Lucrece* l. 41.

15
I have thought upon 't, it shall be so.
II Henry VI. Act ii, sc. 7, l. 15. [Cade]

As I thought.—*III Henry VI,* ii, 1, 113.
So I thought.—*Othello,* i, 3, 36.
I thought so.—*Othello,* v, 2, 192.
Take thought.—*Julius Cæsar,* ii, 1, 187.

1
Faster than spring-time showers comes thought on thought,
And not a thought but thinks on dignity.
II Henry VI. Act iii, sc. 1, l. 337. [York]
O Thou that judgest all things, stay my thoughts,
My thoughts, that labour to persuade my soul.
II Henry VI. Act iii, sc. 2, l. 136. [King Henry]
Unloose thy long-imprison'd thoughts,
And let thy tongue be equal with thy heart.
II Henry VI. Act v, sc. 1, l. 88. [York]
The only use of "long-imprison'd."

2
Far be the thought of this from Henry's heart.
III Henry VI. Act i, sc. 1, l. 70. [King Henry]
Bethink thee once again,
And in thy thought o'er-run my former time.
III Henry VI. Act i, sc. 4, l. 44. [York]
O miserable thought! and more unlikely
Than to accomplish twenty golden crowns!
III Henry VI. Act iii, sc. 2, l. 151. [Gloucester]

3
I hear, yet say not much, but think the more.
III Henry VI. Act iv, sc. 1, l. 83. [Gloucester]
I think of as many matters as he, but I give heaven thanks and make no boast of them.
As You Like It. Act ii, sc. 5, l. 36. [Jaques]

4
The very thought of this fair company
Clapp'd wings to me.
Henry VIII. Act i, sc. 4, l. 8. [Guildford]
Winged thoughts.—*Henry V,* v, Prol., 8.

5
Full of sad thoughts and troubles.
Henry VIII. Act ii, sc. 2, l. 16. [Chamberlain]
Sad thoughts, that work too much upon him.
Henry VIII. Act ii, sc. 2, l. 58. [Norfolk]
Despairing thoughts.—*The Two Gentlemen of Verona,* iii, 1, 247.
Drooping thoughts.—*III Henry VI,* iii, 3, 21.
Troubled thoughts.—*Richard III,* v, 3, 104.

6
I am afraid
His thinkings are below the moon, not worth
His serious considering.
Henry VIII. Act iii, sc. 2, l. 133. [King]

7
Holy and heavenly thoughts still counsel her.
Henry VIII. Act v, sc. 5, l. 30. [Cranmer]
Holy thoughts.—*Richard III,* iv, 4, 404.
Holy-thoughted.—*The Rape of Lucrece,* l. 384. The only use of the phrase.
Generous thoughts.—*Hamlet,* v, 2, 253.
Honest thought.—*Julius Cæsar,* v, 5, 71.
Human thought.—*I Henry VI,* i, 1, 121.
Noble thoughts.—*II Henry IV,* v, 5, 35.
Nobler thoughts.—*All's Well that Ends Well,* ii, 3, 178.
Ripe thoughts.—*Sonnets,* lxxxvi.
His thoughts immaculate.—*The Two Gentlemen of Verona,* ii, 7, 76.

8
This breast of mine hath buried
Thoughts of great value, worthy cogitations.
Julius Cæsar. Act i, sc. 2, l. 49. [Cassius] The only use of "cogitations."
Cogitation
Resides not in that man that does not think.
The Winter's Tale. Act i, sc. 2, l. 271. [Leontes] The only use of "cogitation."

9
I would into thy bosom pour my thoughts.
King John. Act iii, sc. 3, l. 53. [King John]
Within this bosom never enter'd yet
The dreadful motion of a murderous thought.
King John. Act iv, sc. 2, l. 254. [Hubert]

10
Sir Richard, what think you? have you beheld,
Or have you read or heard? or could you think?
Or do you almost think, although you see,
That you do see? could thought, without this object,
Form such another?
King John. Act iv, sc. 3, l. 41. [Salisbury]
Thou hast a perfect thought.
King John. Act v, sc. 6, l. 6. [Hubert]

11
Bear free and patient thoughts.
King Lear. Act iv, sc. 6, l. 80. [Edgar]
Thought is bounty's foe;
Being free itself, it thinks all others so.
Timon of Athens, ii, 2, 241. [Flavius]
Thought is free.—*Twelfth Night,* i, 3, 73; *The Tempest,* iii, 2, 132.
Freer thought.—*Antony and Cleopatra,* i, 5, 11.
Unmuzzled thoughts.—*Twelfth Night,* iii, 1, 130. The only use of "unmuzzled." "Unmuzzle" occurs in *As You Like It,* i, 2, 74: "Unmuzzle your wisdom."

12
That thought abuses you.
King Lear. Act v, sc. 1, l. 11. [Edmund]
What, in ill thoughts again?
King Lear. Act v, sc. 2, l. 9. [Edgar]
Hourly thought.—*King Lear,* iv, 6, 218.

13
Those thoughts to me were oaks.
Love's Labour's Lost. Act iv, sc. 2, l. 112. [Sir Nathaniel]
Those thoughts, to me like oaks, to thee like osiers bow'd.
The Passionate Pilgrim, l. 60.

14
To dwell with him in thoughts.
A Lover's Complaint, l. 129.

15
You do unbend your noble strength, to think
So brainsickly of things.
Macbeth. Act ii, sc. 2, l. 45. [Lady Macbeth] The only use of "brainsickly."
Be not lost So poorly in your thoughts.
Macbeth. Act ii, sc. 2, l. 71. [Lady Macbeth]
Why do you keep alone,
Of sorriest fancies your companions making,
Using those thoughts which should indeed have died
With them they think on?
Macbeth. Act iii, sc. 2, l. 8. [Lady Macbeth] The only use of "sorriest."
Foolish thought.—*Macbeth,* ii, 2, 22.

1
Let it not sound a thought upon your tongue
Against my brother's life.
Measure for Measure. Act ii, sc. 2, l. 140. [Isabella]

Thoughts are no subjects;
Intents but merely thoughts.
Measure for Measure. Act v, sc. 1, l. 458. [Isabella]

2 Shall I have the thought
To think on this, and shall I lack the thought
That such a thing bechanced would make me sad?
The Merchant of Venice. Act i, sc. 1, l. 36. [Salarino] "Bechanced" is repeated in *III Henry VI,* i, 4, 6.

Chiefest thoughts.—*The Merchant of Venice,* ii, 8, 43.

3
Fair thoughts and happy hours attend on you!
The Merchant of Venice. Act iii, sc. 4, l. 41. [Lorenzo]

Fair thoughts be your fair pillow!
Troilus and Cressida. Act iii, sc. 1, l. 49. [Pandarus]

That's a fair thought to lie between maids' legs.
Hamlet. Act iii, sc. 2, l. 125. [Hamlet]

4
Would any man have thought this?
The Merry Wives of Windsor. Act ii, sc. 2, l. 304. [Ford]

Past thought.—*Othello,* i, 1, 167.

5
Heaven make you better than your thoughts!
The Merry Wives of Windsor. Act iii, sc. 3, l. 218. [Mrs. Ford]

6
I speak my thought.
Much Ado about Nothing. Act i, sc. 1, l. 226. [Don Pedro] See also SPEAKING ONE'S MIND.

I told him what I thought.
Othello. Act v, sc. 2, l. 176. [Iago]

I think, but dare not speak.
Macbeth. Act v, sc. 1, l. 87. [Doctor]

7
An bad thinking do not wrest true speaking, I'll offend nobody.
Much Ado about Nothing. Act iii, sc. 4, l. 33. [Margaret]

I am not such a fool to think what I list, nor I list not to think what I can, nor indeed I cannot think, if I would think my heart out of thinking.
Much Ado about Nothing. Act iii, sc. 4, l. 82. [Margaret]

8 The thought whereof
Doth, like a poisonous mineral, gnaw my inwards.
Othello. Act ii, sc. 1, l. 305. [Iago]

Thou . . . didst contract and purse thy brow together,
As if thou then hadst shut up in thy brain
Some horrible conceit: if thou dost love me,
Show me thy thought.
Othello. Act iii, sc. 3, l. 112. [Othello]

I prithee, speak to me as to thy thinkings,
As thou dost ruminate, and give thy worst of thoughts
The worst of words.
Othello. Act iii, sc. 3, l. 131. [Othello]

Utter my thoughts? Why, say they are vile and false?
Othello. Act iii, sc. 3, l. 136. [Iago]

It were not for your quiet nor your good,
Nor for my manhood, honesty, or wisdom,
To let you know my thoughts.
Othello. Act iii, sc. 3, l. 152. [Iago]

Othello: By heaven, I'll know thy thoughts.
Iago: You cannot; if my heart were in your hand;
Nor shall you, whilst 'tis in my custody.
Othello. Act iii, sc. 3, l. 162.

He knows thy thought.—*Macbeth,* v, 1, 69.

9
I have this while with leaden thoughts been press'd.
Othello. Act iii, sc. 4, l. 177. [Cassio]

10
But I must tell you, now my thoughts revolt.
Pericles. Act i, sc. 1, l. 78. [Pericles]

11 Some untimely thought did instigate
His all-too-timeless speed.
The Rape of Lucrece, l. 43. The only use of "all-too-timeless." "Instigate" is repeated in *II Henry VI,* iii, 1, 51.

Unstain'd thoughts do seldom dream on evil.
The Rape of Lucrece, l. 87.

Pure thoughts are dead and still,
While lust and murder wake to stain and kill.
The Rape of Lucrece, l. 167. The only use of "pure thoughts."

Die, unhallow'd thoughts, before you blot
With your uncleanness that which is divine.
The Rape of Lucrece, l. 192.

Thy thoughts, low vassals to thy state.
The Rape of Lucrece, l. 666.

Flattering thoughts.—*The Rape of Lucrece,* l. 641.

Servile thoughts.—*Titus Andronicus,* ii, 1, 18.

12
Even in this thought through the dark night he stealeth.
Rape of Lucrece, l. 729.

13
You . . . prick my tender patience to those thoughts,
Which honour and allegiance cannot think.
Richard II. Act ii, sc. 1, l. 206. [York]

Secret thoughts.—*Richard III,* iii, 5, 28; *The Rape of Lucrece,* l. 1065.

14
Let us share thy thoughts, as thou dost ours.
Richard II. Act ii, sc. 1, l. 273. [Willoughby]

My thoughts are minutes.—*Richard II,* v, 5, 51.

15
High be our thoughts.
Richard II. Act iii, sc. 2, l. 89. [King Richard]

Fit thy thoughts To mount aloft.
Titus Andronicus. Act ii, sc. 1, l. 12. [Aaron]

Honourable thoughts,
Thoughts high for one so tender.
The Winter's Tale. Act iii, sc. 2, l. 196. [Paulina]

1 Beget
A generation of still-breeding thoughts,
And these same thoughts people this little world,
In humours like the people of this world,
For no thought is contented. The better sort,
As thoughts of things divine, are intermix'd
With scruples and do set the word itself
Against the word.
Richard II. Act v, sc. 5, l. 7. [King Richard] The only use of "still-breeding." "Intermix'd" is repeated in *The Rape of Lucrece*, l. 101.

Thoughts tending to content flatter themselves
That they are not the first of fortune's slaves,
Nor shall not be the last.
Richard II. Act v, sc. 5, l. 23. [King Richard]

In this thought they find a kind of ease.
Richard II. Act v, sc. 5, l. 28. [King Richard]

2
'Tis very grievous to be thought upon.
Richard III. Act i, sc. 1, l. 141. [Gloucester] See under GRIEF.

Well thought upon.—*Richard III*, i, 3, 344.

Far be it from my heart, the thought of it!
Richard III, i, 3, 150. See under KING.

3
Good thoughts possess thee!
Richard III. Act iv, sc. 1, l. 94. [Duchess of York]

Restore yourselves
Into the good thoughts of the world again.
I Henry IV. Act i, sc. 3, l. 182. [Hotspur]

And God forgave them that so much have sway'd
Your majesty's good thoughts away from me!
I Henry IV. Act iii, sc. 2, l. 130. [Prince Henry]

Your own good thoughts excuse me.
Love's Labour's Lost. Act ii, sc. 1, l. 176. [King]

And with good thoughts makes dispensation,
Urging the worser sense for vantage still.
The Rape of Lucrece, l. 248.

Good thoughts.—*King John*, ii, 1, 112; *Julius Cæsar*, iii, 1, 176; *Antony and Cleopatra*, iii, 6, 21.

4
Dive, thoughts, down to my soul.
Richard III. Act i, sc. 1, l. 41. [Gloucester]

My brother slew no man; his fault was thought,
And yet his punishment was cruel death.
Richard III. Act ii, sc. 1, l. 104. [King Edward]

5
My thoughts' sovereign.
Richard III. Act iii, sc. 1, l. 2. [Gloucester]

Commander of my thoughts.—*Titus Andronicus*, iv, 4, 28.

6
In the mildness of your sleepy thoughts.
Richard III. Act iii, sc. 7, l. 123. [Buckingham]

Mildest thoughts.—*Titus Andronicus*, iv, 1, 85.

7 Love's heralds should be thoughts,
Which ten times faster glide than the sun's beams.
Romeo and Juliet. Act ii, sc. 5, l. 4. [Juliet]

Cheerful thoughts.—*Romeo and Juliet*, v, 1, 5.

O, this same thought did but forerun my need.
Romeo and Juliet. Act v, sc. 1, l. 53. [Romeo]

8
O, change thy thought, that I may change my mind!
Sonnets. No. x.

Changing thoughts.—*The Two Gentlemen of Verona*, iv, 4, 124.

9
My thoughts, from far where I abide,
Intend a zealous pilgrimage to thee.
Sonnets. No. xxvii.

If the dull substance of my flesh were thought,
Injurious distance should not stop my way;
For then despite of space I would be brought,
From limits far remote, where thou dost stay.
No matter then although my foot did stand
Upon the farthest earth removed from thee;
For nimble thought can jump both sea and land
As soon as think the place where he would be.
But, ah! thought kills me that I am not thought,
To leap large lengths of miles when thou art gone,
But that so much of earth and water wrought
I must attend time's leisure with my moan,
Receiving nought by elements so slow
But heavy tears, badges of either's woe.
Sonnets. No. xliv.

A quest of thoughts, all tenants to the heart.
Sonnets. No. xlvi.

10
Thyself away art present still with me;
For thou not farther than my thoughts canst move,
And I am still with them and they with thee;
Or if they sleep, thy picture in my sight
Awakes my heart to heart's and eye's delight.
Sonnets. No. xlvii.

'My thoughts do harbour with my Silvia nightly,
And slaves they are to me that send them flying:
O, could their master come and go as lightly,
Himself would lodge where senseless they are lying!
My herald thoughts in thy pure bosom rest them;
While I, their king, that hither them importune,
Do curse the grace that with such grace hath bless'd them,
Because myself do want my servants' fortune.'
The Two Gentlemen of Verona. Act iii, sc. 1, l. 140. [Duke]

11
Nor dare I question with my jealous thought
Where you may be, or your affairs suppose,
But, like a sad slave, stay and think of nought
Save, where you are how happy you make those.
Sonnets. No. lvii.

That god forbid that made me first your slave,
I should in thought control your times of pleasure,
Or at your hand the account of hours to crave,
Being your vassal, bound to stay your leisure!
Sonnets. No. lviii.

So are you to my thoughts as food to life,
Or as sweet-season'd showers are to the ground.
Sonnets. No. lxxv. The only use of "sweet-season'd."

I think good thoughts whilst others write good words,
And like unletter'd clerk still cry 'Amen'
To every hymn that able spirit affords
In polish'd form of well-refined pen.
Hearing you praised, I say ''Tis so, 'tis true,'
And to the most of praise add something more;
But that is in my thought, whose love to you,
Though words come hindmost, holds his rank before.
Then others for the breath of words respect,
Me for my dumb thoughts, speaking in effect.
Sonnets. No. lxxxv. The only use of "well-refined."

My thoughts and my discourse as madmen's are,
At random from the truth vainly express'd.
Sonnets. No. cxlvii.

Mad thought.—*Titus Andronicus,* v, 2, 74.

1
Call home thy ancient thoughts from banishment.
The Taming of the Shrew. Induction, sc. 2, l. 33. [Lord]

2
But these sweet thoughts do even refresh my labours.
The Tempest. Act iii, sc. 1, l. 14. [Ferdinand]

Sweet silent thought.—*Sonnets,* xxx.
Divining thoughts.—*III Henry VI,* iv, 6, 69.
Loving thought.—*Sonnets,* xxxii; lxxxviii.

3
Thy thoughts I cleave to.
The Tempest. Act iv, sc. 1, l. 165. [Ariel]

Shut up my thoughts.—*The Tempest,* ii, 1, 192.

4
Speechless complainer, I will learn thy thought.
Titus Andronicus. Act iii, sc. 2, l. 39. [Titus] The only use of "complainer."

King, be thy thoughts imperious, like thy name.
Titus Andronicus. Act iv, sc. 4, l. 81. [Tamora]

Imperious thoughts.—*The Two Gentlemen of Verona,* ii, 4, 130.

5
Will you subscribe his thought?
Troilus and Cressida. Act ii, sc. 3, l. 156. [Ajax] See under COMPARISON.

6
My thoughts were like unbridled children, grown
Too headstrong for their mother.
Troilus and Cressida. Act iii, sc. 2, l. 130. [Cressida] "Unbridled" is repeated in *All 's Well that Ends Well,* iii, 2, 30: "Unbridled boy."

7
For speculation turns not to itself,
Till it hath travell'd and is mirror'd there
Where it may see itself.
Troilus and Cressida. Act iii, sc. 3, l. 109. [Achilles]

Thou hast no speculation in those eyes.
Macbeth, iii, 4, 95. See under GHOST.

Speculations intelligent of our state.
King Lear, iii, 1, 24. See under SPY.

Idle speculation.—*Henry V,* iv, 2, 31. The only uses of "speculation" and "speculations."

8
Unclasp the tables of their thoughts.
Troilus and Cressida, iv, 5, 60. See under COQUETRY.

Nor dignifies an impair thought with breath.
Troilus and Cressida. Act iv, sc. 5, l. 103. [Ulysses] The only use of "impair" (unfit) as an adjective.

9
Olivia: For him, I think not on him: for his thoughts,
Would they were blanks, rather than fill'd with me!
Viola: Madam, I come to whet your gentle thoughts
On his behalf.
Twelfth Night. Act iii, sc. 1, l. 114.

Olivia: I prithee, tell me what thou think'st of me.
Viola: That you do think you are not what you are.
Olivia: If I think so, I think the same of you.
Viola: Then think you right: I am not what I am.
Olivia: I would you were as I would have you be!
Viola: Would it be better, madam, than I am?
Twelfth Night. Act iii, sc. 1, l. 150.

10
Heart sick with thought.
The Two Gentlemen of Verona. Act i, sc. 1, l. 69. [Proteus]

Thoughts that would thick my blood.
Winter's Tale. Act i, sc. 2, l. 171. [Polixenes]

Dire thought.—*The Rape of Lucrece,* l. 972.
Fearful thoughts.—*II Henry VI,* iii, 1, 331.
Foul thoughts.—*The Rape of Lucrece,* l. 346; *Othello,* ii, 1, 265; *Antony and Cleopatra,* iv, 9, 18.
Frozen thoughts.—*The Two Gentlemen of Verona,* iii, 2, 9.
Maculate thoughts.—*Love's Labour 's Lost,* i, 2, 97. The only use of "maculate" (polluted).
Rank thoughts.—*Cymbeline,* ii, 5, 24.
Reprobate thought.—*Love's Labour 's Lost,* i, 2, 64.
Sinful thought!—*The Merchant of Venice,* ii, 7, 54.
Vile thoughts.—*Pericles,* iv, Gower, 41.
Villanous thoughts.—*Othello,* ii, 1, 266.
Vulture thought.—*Venus and Adonis,* l. 551.
Wrong thought.—*King Lear,* iii, 6, 119.
Thoughts unnatural.—*Othello,* iii, 3, 233.

11
With these forced thoughts, I prithee, darken not
The mirth o' the feast.
Winter's Tale. Act iv, sc. 4, l. 41. [Florizel]

Strangle such thoughts as these with any thing
That you behold the while.
Winter's Tale. Act iv, sc. 4, l. 47. [Florizel]

By the pattern of mine own thoughts I cut out
The purity of his.
The Winter's Tale. Act iv, sc. 4, l. 392. [Perdita]

II—Thought and Act

1
Sir, for my thoughts, you have them ill to friend
Till your deeds gain them.
All's Well that Ends Well. Act v, sc. 3, l. 182. [King]

2 Give thy thoughts no tongue,
Nor any unproportion'd thought his act.
Hamlet. Act i, sc. 3, l. 59. [Polonius] The only use of "unproportion'd."

Thought-sick at the act.
Hamlet. Act iii, sc. 4, l. 51. [Hamlet] The only use of "thought-sick."

Should . . . our drift look through our bad performance,
'Twere better not assay'd.
Hamlet. Act iv, sc. 7, l. 151. [King]

3
Therefore let every man now task his thought,
That this fair action may on foot be brought.
Henry V. Act i, sc. 2, l. 309. [King Henry]

4
Be great in act, as you have been in thought.
King John. Act v, sc. 1, l. 45. [Bastard]

My actions are as noble as my thoughts,
That never relish'd of a base descent.
Pericles. Act ii, sc. 5, l. 59. [Pericles]

5
My thought, whose murder yet is but fantastical,
Shakes so my single state of man that function
Is smother'd in surmise.
Macbeth. Act i, sc. 3, l. 139. [Macbeth]

Art thou afeard
To be the same in thine own act and valour
As thou art in desire?
Macbeth. Act i, sc. 7, l. 39. [Lady Macbeth]

From this moment
The very firstlings of my heart shall be
The firstlings of my hand. And even now,
To crown my thoughts with acts, be it thought and done.
Macbeth. Act iv, sc. 1, l. 146. [Macbeth] "Firstlings" appears again, in *Troilus and Cressida,* Prol., l. 27.

Thoughts speculative their unsure hopes relate,
But certain issue strokes must arbitrate.
Macbeth. Act v, sc. 4, l. 19. [Siward] "Speculative" is repeated in *Othello,* i, 3, 271.

6
Thoughts are but dreams till their effects be tried.
The Rape of Lucrece, l. 353.

7
By their rank thoughts my deeds must not be shown.
Sonnets. No. cxxi.

Hot thoughts beget hot deeds.—*Troilus and Cressida,* iii, 1, 142. See LOVE, 900:8.

THREAT

See also Denunciation

8
Injurious duke, that threatest where 's no cause.
II Henry VI. Act i, sc. 4, l. 51. "Threatest" is used only in the first play.

This villain here . . . threatens more
Than Bargulus the strong Illyrian pirate.
II Henry VI. Act iv, sc. 1, l. 106. [Suffolk] The only mention of Bargulus, and the only use of "Illyrian," though Illyria is referred to nine times.

This is his claim, his threatening.
Henry V. Act ii, sc. 4, l. 110. [Exeter]

Nimble in threats.—*As You Like It,* iv, 3, 110.

9 Frowns, words and threats
Shall be the war that Henry means to use.
III Henry VI. Act i, sc. 1, l. 72. [King Henry]

How I scorn his worthless threats!
III Henry VI. Act i, sc. 1, l. 101. [Warwick]

There is no terror, Cassius, in your threats,
For I am arm'd so strong in honesty
That they pass by me as the idle wind,
Which I respect not.
Julius Cæsar. Act iv, sc. 3, l. 66. [Brutus]

Thy threats have no more strength than her weak prayers.
A Midsummer-Night's Dream. Act iii, sc. 2, l. 250. [Lysander]

10 The things that threaten'd me
Ne'er look'd but on my back; when they shall see
The face of Cæsar, they are vanished.
Julius Cæsar. Act ii, sc. 2, l. 10. [Cæsar]

Threaten the threatener.—*King John,* v, 1, 49. The only use of "threatener."

Threaten'd to discover him.—*King Lear,* ii, 1, 68.

11
Menaces and maledictions against kings and nobles.
King Lear, i, 2, 159. See under OMEN. The only use of "menaces" and "maledictions."

The heavens menace.—*Julius Cæsar,* i, 3, 44.

Your eyes do menace me.—*Richard III,* i, 4, 175.

Menace me with death.—*Romeo and Juliet,* v, 3, 133. The only uses of "menace."

Harms that menaced.—*Henry VIII,* i, 1, 183.

Menaced revenge.—*Henry VIII,* i, 2, 135. "Menaced" occurs in no other play.

12
Whiles I threat, he lives.
Macbeth. Act ii, sc. 1, l. 60. [Macbeth]

Every minute of his being thrusts
Against my near'st of life.
Macbeth. Act iii, sc. 1, l. 117. [Macbeth]

13
But he hath chid me hence and threaten'd me
To strike me, spurn me, nay, to kill me too.
A Midsummer-Night's Dream. Act iii, sc. 2, l. 312. [Helena]

14
Threat the glory of my precious crown.
Richard II. Act iii, sc. 3, l. 90. [King]

1
Before I be convict by course of law,
To threaten me with death is most unlawful.
Richard III. Act i, sc. 4, l. 192. [Clarence]
I with death and with
Reward did threaten and encourage him.
Winter's Tale. Act iii, sc. 2, l. 164. [Leontes]
Bohemia stops his ears, and threatens them
With divers deaths in death.
Winter's Tale. Act v, sc. 1, l. 201. [Lord]
Threaten'd me with death.—*Romeo and Juliet,* v, 3, 276.
Threatens life or death.—*Pericles,* i, 3, 25.

2
Earth gapes, hell burns, fiends roar, saints pray,
To have him suddenly convey'd away.
Richard III. Act iv, sc. 4, l. 75. [Queen Margaret]
Threat you me?—*Richard III,* i, 3, 113.

3
Why, boy, although our mother, unadvised,
Gave you a dancing-rapier by your side,
Are you so desperate grown, to threat your friends?
Titus Andronicus. Act ii, sc. 1, l. 38. [Demetrius] The only use of "dancing-rapier."
These two heads do seem to speak to me
And threat me.
Titus Andronicus. Act iii, sc. 1, l. 272. [Titus]

4 Let these threats alone,
Till accident or purpose bring you to 't.
Troilus and Cressida. Act iv, sc. 5, l. 261. [Ajax]
Bitter threats.—*The Two Gentlemen of Verona,* iii, 1, 236.

II—Some Examples

5
Perform 't, or else we damn thee.
Antony and Cleopatra. Act i, sc. 1, l. 24. [Cleopatra]
I 'll spurn thine eyes
Like balls before me; I 'll unhair thy head:
Thou shalt be whipp'd with wire, and stew'd in brine,
Smarting in lingering pickle.
Antony and Cleopatra. Act ii, sc. 5, l. 63. [Cleopatra] The only use of "unhair" and "wire." "Wires" is used in *Sonnets,* cxxx, and "pickle" occurs again in *The Tempest,* v, 1, 281: "How camest thou in this pickle?"

6
Wert thou not my brother, I would not take this hand from thy throat till this other had pulled out thy tongue.
As You Like It. Act i, sc. 1, l. 62. [Orlando]

7
At home, upon my brother's guard, even there,
Against the hospitable canon, would I
Wash my fierce hand in 's heart.
Coriolanus. Act i, sc. 10, l. 25. [Aufidius]
Would our nobility lay aside their ruth,
And let me use my sword, I 'ld make a quarry
With thousands of these quarter'd slaves, as high
As I could pick my lance.
Coriolanus. Act i, sc. 1, l. 201. [Marcius]
I shall shake thy bones Out of thy garments.
Coriolanus. Act iii, sc. 1, l. 179. [Coriolanus]
He 'll go, he says, and sowl the porter of Rome gates by the ears: he will mow all down before him, and leave his passage polled.
Coriolanus. Act iv, sc. 5, l. 213. [Servant] The only use of "sowl" (pull), and "polled."
O, that I had her here, to tear her limb-meal!
Cymbeline. Act ii, sc. 4, l. 147. [Posthumus] The only use of "limb-meal."

8
In faith, I 'll break thy little finger, Harry,
An if thou wilt not tell me all things true.
I Henry IV. Act ii, sc. 3, l. 90. [Lady Percy]
A king's son! If I do not beat thee out of thy kingdom with a dagger of lath, and drive all thy subjects afore thee like a flock of wild-geese, I 'll never wear hair on my face more.
I Henry IV. Act ii, sc. 4, l. 150. [Falstaff]

9
Prince of Wales: Embowell'd will I see thee by and by. [*Exit*]
Falstaff [*Rising up*]: Embowelled! If thou embowel me to-day, I 'll give you leave to powder me and eat me to-morrow.
I Henry IV. Act v, sc. 4, l. 109. The only use of "embowel."
Embowell'd of their doctrine.—*All's Well that Ends Well,* i, 3, 247. See under SCHOOL.
Embowell'd bosoms.—*Richard III,* v, 2, 10. The only uses of "embowell'd."

10
I 'll thrust my knife in your mouldy chaps, an you play the saucy cuttle with me.
II Henry IV. Act ii, sc. 4, l. 138. [Doll] The only use of "cuttle."
I will toss the rogue in a blanket.
II Henry IV. Act ii, sc. 4, l. 240. [Falstaff]

11
I will cut thy throat, one time or other, in fair terms.
Henry V. Act ii, sc. 1, l. 73. [Nym]
I 'll knock his leek about his pate
Upon Saint Davy's day.
Henry V. Act iv, sc. 1, l. 54. [Pistol] The only mention of Saint Davy, who is commemorated on March 1.
I will fetch thy rim out at thy throat
In drops of crimson blood.
Henry V. Act iv, sc. 4, l. 15. [Pistol] The only use of "rim" (peritoneum, intestines).
Bid him prepare; for I will cut his throat.
Henry V. Act iv, sc. 4, l. 34. [Pistol]

12
Thy heart-blood I will have for this day's work.
I Henry VI. Act i, sc. 3, l. 83. [Bishop of Winchester] "Heart-blood" occurs seven times in the plays.
Pucelle or puzzel, dolphin or dogfish,
Your hearts I 'll stamp out with my horse's heels,
And make a quagmire of your mingled brains.
I Henry VI. Act i, sc. 4, l. 107. [Talbot] The only use of "puzzel" (a dirty drab), and "dogfish." "Quagmire" is repeated in *King Lear,* iii, 4, 54.
I 'll note you in my book of memory,
To scourge you for this apprehension.
I Henry VI. Act ii, sc. 4, l. 101. [Plantagenet]

Ere the glass, that now begins to run,
Finish the process of his sandy hour,
These eyes, that see thee now well coloured,
Shall see thee wither'd, bloody, pale and dead.

I Henry VI. Act iv, sc. 2, l. 35. [General]

1 I 'll shave your crown for this,
Or all my fence shall fail.

II Henry VI. Act ii, sc. 1, l. 51. [Gloucester]

I 'll make thee eat iron like an ostrich, and swallow my sword like a great pin, ere thou and I part.

II Henry VI. Act iv, sc. 10, l. 30. [Cade] "Ostrich" was used in the first play and never again.

If mine arm be heaved in the air,
Thy grave is digg'd already in the earth.

II Henry VI. Act iv, sc. 10, l. 54. [Iden]

Meet I an infant of the house of York,
Into as many gobbets will I cut it.

II Henry VI. Act v, sc. 2, l. 57. [Young Clifford] "Gobbets" occurs again in iv, 1, 85, and in no other play.

2 I 'll have more lives
Than drops of blood were in my father's veins.

III Henry VI. Act i, sc. 1, l. 96. [Westmoreland]

Know thou, since we have begun to strike,
We 'll never leave till we have hewn thee down,
Or bathed thy growing with our heated bloods.

III Henry VI. Act ii, sc. 2, l. 167. [George] "Hewn" is repeated in iv, 4, 69, and occurs in no other play.

3
You i' the camlet, get up o' the rail;
I 'll peck you o'er the pales else.

Henry VIII. Act v, sc. 4, l. 93. [Porter] The only use of "camlet," a fabric made of the hair of the Angora goat, and of "pales" in the sense of palings.

4
Who lives and dares but say thou didst not well
When I was got, I 'll send his soul to hell.

King John. Act i, sc. 1, l. 271. [Bastard]

To cudgel you and make you take the hatch,
To dive like buckets in concealed wells,
To crouch in litter of your stable planks,
To lie like pawns lock'd up in chests and trunks,
To hug with swine, to seek sweet safety out
In vaults and prisons.

King John. Act v, sc. 2, l. 138. [Bastard]

Salisbury: Stand by, or I shall gall you, Faulconbridge.
Bastard: Thou wert better gall the devil, Salisbury.

King John. Act iv, sc. 3, l. 94.

If thou but frown on me, or stir thy foot,
Or teach thy hasty spleen to do me shame,
I 'll strike thee dead. Put up thy sword betime;
Or I 'll so maul you and your toasting-iron,
That you shall think the devil is come from hell.

King John. Act iv, sc. 3, l. 96. [Bastard] The only use of "toasting-iron."

5
I 'll make a sop o' the moonshine of you: draw, you whoreson cullionly barber-monger, draw.

King Lear. Act ii, sc. 2, l. 34. [Kent] The only use of "cullionly" and "barber-monger."

I will tread this unbolted villain into mortar, and daub the walls of a jakes with him.

King Lear. Act ii, sc. 2, l. 70. [Kent] The only use of "unbolted," "mortar," and "jakes" (privy).

Regan: Hang him instantly.
Goneril: Pluck out his eyes.

King Lear. Act iii, sc. 7, l. 4.

6
I will knog his urinals about his knave's costard.

Merry Wives of Windsor, iii, 1, 14. [Evans]

I will knog your urinals about your knave's cogscomb.

The Merry Wives of Windsor, iii, 1, 91. [Evans] The only uses of "urinals." "Urinal" occurs in *Two Gentlemen of Verona,* ii, 1, 41.

7
My spirit and my place have in them power
To make this bitter to thee.

Othello. Act i, sc. 1, l. 103. [Brabantio]

He that stirs next to carve for his own rage
Holds his soul light; he dies upon his motion.

Othello. Act ii, sc. 3, l. 173. [Othello]

I 'll tear her all to pieces.

Othello. Act iii, sc. 3, l. 431. [Othello]

I will chop her into messes.

Othello. Act iv, sc. 1, l. 211. [Othello]

Strumpet, I come,
Forth of my heart those charms, thine eyes, are blotted;
Thy bed, lust-stain'd, shall with lust's blood be spotted.

Othello. Act v, sc. 1, l. 34. [Othello] The only use of "lust-stain'd."

8
Despitefully I mean to bear thee.

The Rape of Lucrece, l. 670. The only use of "despitefully."

9
I 'll make a corse of him that disobeys.

Richard III. Act i, sc. 2, l. 37. [Gloucester]

By heaven, I 'll make a ghost of him that lets me!

Hamlet. Act i, sc. 4, l. 85. [Hamlet]

I 'll set my teeth,
And send to darkness all that stop me.

Antony and Cleopatra, iii, 13, 181. [Antony]

10 I 'll strike thee to my foot,
And spurn upon thee, beggar, for thy boldness.

Richard III. Act i, sc. 2, l. 41. [Gloucester]

11 I will tear thee joint by joint
And strew this hungry churchyard with thy limbs.

Romeo and Juliet. Act v, sc. 3, l. 35. [Romeo]

12
If thou more murmur'st, I will rend an oak
And peg thee in his knotty entrails till
Thou hast howl'd away twelve winters.

The Tempest. Act i, sc. 2, l. 294. [Prospero]

For this, be sure, to-night thou shalt have cramps,
Side-stiches that shall pen thy breath up.

The Tempest. Act i, sc. 2, l. 326. [Prospero] The only use of "side-stitches."

I 'll rack thee with old cramps,
Fill all thy bones with aches, make thee roar
That beasts shall tremble at thy din.

The Tempest. Act i, sc. 2, l. 369. [Prospero]

It should be remembered that in Shakespeare's day "aches" was pronounced in two syllables.

I 'll manacle thy neck and feet together:
Sea-water shalt thou drink; thy food shall be
The fresh-brook muscles, wither'd roots and husks
Wherein the acorn cradled.

The Tempest. Act i, sc. 2, l. 461. [Prospero] The only use of "fresh-brook," "muscles," and "cradled."

I will plague them all, Even to roaring.

The Tempest. Act iv, sc. 1, l. 192. [Prospero]

1
Hark, wretches! how I mean to martyr you.

Titus Andronicus. Act v, sc. 2, l. 181. [Titus]

Hark, villains! I will grind your bones to dust
And with your blood and it I 'll make a paste,
And of the paste a coffin I will rear
And make two pasties of your shameful heads.

Titus Andronicus. Act v, sc. 2, l. 187. [Titus] The only use of "pasties."

Lavinia, come,
Receive the blood: and when that they are dead,
Let me go grind their bones to powder small
And with this hateful liquor temper it;
And in that paste let their vile heads be baked.

Titus Andronicus. Act v, sc. 2, l. 197. [Titus]

2
I will knead him; I 'll make him supple.

Troilus and Cressida. Act ii, sc. 3, l. 231. [Ajax] The only use of "knead." "Kneaded" appears once in *Measure for Measure,* iii, 1, 121; and "kneading" twice, in *Henry V,* i, 2, 199, and *Troilus and Cressida,* i, 1, 23. "Supple" is used six times.

Our bloods are now in calm; and, so long, health!
But when contention and occasion meet,
By Jove, I 'll play the hunter for thy life
With all my force, pursuit and policy.

Troilus and Cressida. Act iv, sc. 1, l. 15. [Diomedes]

3
He has a son, who shall be flayed alive; then 'nointed over with honey, set on the head of a wasp's nest.

The Winter's Tale. Act iv, sc. 4, l. 811. [Autolycus]

Remember 'stoned' and 'flayed alive.'

Winters' Tale. Act iv, sc. 4, l. 812. [Clown] The only uses of "flayed alive" in the plays.

THRIFT

4 I have five hundred crowns,
The thrifty hire I saved under your father,
Which I did store to be my foster-nurse
When service should in my old limbs lie lame
And unregarded age in corners thrown.

As You Like It. Act ii, sc. 3, l. 38. [Adam] "Foster-nurse" is repeated in *King Lear,* iv, 4, 12. The only use of "unregarded."

5
Thrift, thrift, Horatio! the funeral baked meats
Did coldly furnish forth the marriage tables.

Hamlet. Act i, sc. 2, l. 180. [Hamlet]

Thrift may follow fawning.

Hamlet, iii, 2, 67. See under Fawning.

Base respects of thrift.—*Hamlet,* iii, 2, 193.

6
I have a mind presages me such thrift,
That I should questionless be fortunate!

The Merchant of Venice. Act i, sc. 1, l. 175. [Bassanio] "Questionless" is used again in *Pericles,* v, 1, 45.

My well-won thrift, Which he calls interest.

The Merchant of Venice. Act i, sc. 3, l. 51. [Shylock] The only use of "well-won."

This was a way to thrive, and he was blest:
And thrift is blessing, if men steal it not.

The Merchant of Venice. Act i, sc. 3, l. 90. [Shylock]

7
French thrift, you rogues.

The Merry Wives of Windsor. Act i, sc. 3, l. 93. [Falstaff]

8 I am a man
That from my first have been inclined to thrift.

Timon of Athens. Act i, sc. 1, l. 117. [Athenian]

They are thrifty honest men.—*II Henry VI,* iv, 2, 196.

9
Let us cast away nothing, for we may live to have need of such a verse.

Troilus and Cressida. Act iv, sc. 4, l. 22. [Pandarus]

Their own particular thrifts.—*The Winter's Tale,* i, 2, 311.

THROAT

10
We have used our throats in Egypt.

Antony and Cleopatra. Act ii, sc. 6, l. 144. [Enobarbus]

11 Threats the throat of that his officer
That murder'd Pompey.

Antony and Cleopatra. Act iii, sc. 5, l. 19. [Eros]

Fall to their throats.—*Antony and Cleopatra,* ii, 7, 78.

Fisting each other's throat.—*Coriolanus,* iv, 5, 131.

12 My throat of war be turn'd
Into a pipe small as an eunuch.

Coriolanus, iii, 2, 112. See under Voice.

13 I also am
Longer to live most weary, and present
My throat to thee and to thy ancient malice.

Coriolanus. Act iv, sc. 5, l. 100. [Coriolanus]

Presented to my knife his throat.

Coriolanus. Act v, sc. 6, l. 31. [Aufidius]

Offered them his throat.—*Julius Cæsar,* i, 2, 268.

14
Our throats are sentenced and stay upon execution.

Coriolanus. Act v, sc. 4, l. 8. [Menenius]

This morning for ten thousand of your throats
I 'ld not have given a doit.

Coriolanus. Act v, sc. 4, l. 59. [Menenius]

15 Their base throats tear
With giving his glory.

Coriolanus. Act v, sc. 6, l. 53. [Conspirator]

Foul throat.—*Richard III,* i, 2, 93.

Ill-uttering throat.—*Antony and Cleopatra,* ii, 5, 35. The only use of "ill-uttering."
Lofty and shrill sounding throat.—*Hamlet,* i, 1, 151.
Outstretched throat.—*Measure for Measure,* ii, 4, 153.
Rude throats.—*Othello,* iii, 3, 355.
Sweet bird's throat.—*As You Like It,* ii, 5, 4.
Enemies' throats.—*I Henry VI,* i, 1, 98.
Throat of death.—*Richard III,* v, 4, 5; *Love's Labour's Lost,* v, 2, 865.

1
Men may sleep, and they may have their throats about them.
Henry V, ii, 1, 24. See under MURDER.

2
I took by the throat the circumcised dog.
Othello. Act v, sc. 2, l. 355. [Othello]
Take thy fingers from my throat.—*Hamlet,* v, 1, 283.

3
Ready to catch each other by the throat.
Richard III, i. 3, 189. See HATE, 678:2.

4
A pox o' your throat, you bawling, blasphemous, incharitable dog!
The Tempest. Act i, sc. 1, l. 43. [Sebastian] The only use of "bawling," "blasphemous," and "incharitable."
A pox o' your throats!—*Measure for Measure,* iv, 3, 26.

5 Their knives care not,
While you have throats to answer: for myself
There 's not a whittle in the unruly camp
But I do prize it at my love before
The reverend'st throat in Athens.
Timon of Athens. Act v, sc. 1, l. 180. [Timon] The only use of "whittle" (a small, worthless clasp-knife), and of "reverend'st."
Lie in the throat, see under LYING.

II—Throat-Cutting

6
I will cut thy throat, one time or other, in fair terms.
Henry V. Act ii, sc. 1, l. 73. [Nym]
I 'll cut thy throat.—*Troilus and Cressida,* iv, 4, 131.
Why the devil should we keep knives to cut one another's throats?
Henry V. Act ii, sc. 1, l. 96. [Bardolph]
There is throats to be cut.—*Henry V,* iii, 2, 119.

7
Caused every soldier to cut his prisoner's throat.
Henry V. Act iv, sc. 7, l. 10. [Gower]
We 'll cut the throats of those we have.
Henry V. Act iv, sc. 7, l. 66. [King Henry]

8
Iniquity's throat cut like a calf.
II Henry VI, iv, 2, 29. See under SIN.

9
Cut both the villains' throats!
II Henry VI. Act iv, sc. 1, l. 20. [Captain]
Cut the villains' throats!—*I Henry IV,* ii, 2, 88.
I will cut his throat.—*Henry V,* iv, 4, 34.
Cut his throat.—*Hamlet,* iv, 7, 127.
Cut her throat.—*Cymbeline,* iii, 4, 35.
Cut their throats.—*Timon of Athens,* iii, 5, 44.
Cut throats.—*Timon of Athens,* iv, 3, 47.
Cutting foreign throats.—*Romeo and Juliet,* i, 4, 83.

10
He . . . gave them his throat to cut.
Julius Cæsar. Act i, sc. 2, l. 268. [Casca]

11
Murderer: My lord, his throat is cut; that I did for him.
Macbeth: Thou art the best o' the cut-throats.
Macbeth. Act iii, sc. 4, l. 16.
Cut-throat dog.—*The Merchant of Venice,* i, 3, 112. The only uses of "cut-throat" and "cut-throats."

12 Out with your knives,
And cut your trusters' throats!
Timon of Athens. Act iv, sc. 1, l. 9. [Timon] "Truster" is repeated in *Hamlet,* i, 2, 172.

13
This one hand yet is left to cut your throats,
Whilst that Lavinia 'tween her stumps doth hold
The basin that receives your guilty blood. . . .
And now prepare your throats.
Titus Andronicus. Act v, sc. 2, l. 182. [Titus]

THRONE

14
Thou . . . wouldst have made my throne
A seat for baseness.
Cymbeline. Act i, sc. 1, l. 141. [Cymbeline]
Affecting one sole throne.—*Coriolanus,* iv, 6, 32.

15 Let the world take note,
You are the most immediate to our throne.
Hamlet. Act i, sc. 2, l. 108. [King]

16
May honourable peace attend thy throne.
II Henry VI. Act ii, sc. 3, l. 38. [Gloucester]
God and his angels guard your sacred throne
And make you long become it!
Henry V. Act i, sc. 2, l. 7. [Canterbury]

17 That throne
Which now the house of Lancaster usurps.
III Henry VI. Act i, sc. 1, l. 22. [Warwick]
Thou factious Duke of York, descend my throne. . . .
And shall I stand, and thou sit in my throne?
III Henry VI. Act i, sc. 1, l. 74. [King Henry]
Think'st thou that I will leave my kingly throne,
Wherein my grandsire and my father sat?
III Henry VI. Act i, sc. 1, l. 124. [King Henry]
The supreme seat, the throne majestical,
The scepter'd office of your ancestors.
Richard III. Act iii, sc. 7, l. 118. [Buckingham]

18
The next degree is England's royal throne.
III Henry VI. Act ii, sc. 1, l. 193. [Warwick]
Once more we sit in England's royal throne,
Re-purchased with the blood of enemies.
III Henry VI. Act v, sc. 7, l. 1. [King Edward] The only use of "re-purchased."
His master's son, as worshipful he terms it,
Shall lose the royalty of England's throne.
Richard III. Act iii, sc. 4, l. 41. [Gloucester]
England's throne.—*King John,* iii, 4, 130.

Augustus' throne.—*Cymbeline,* iii, 5, 101.
Edward's throne.—*Richard III,* iii, 4, 42.
King Richard's throne.—*Richard II,* i, 3, 86.
Throne of Denmark.—*Hamlet,* i, 2, 49.
Throne of France.—*Henry V,* i, 2, 275.

1 It hath been
The untimely emptying of the happy throne
And fall of many kings.
Macbeth. Act iv, sc. 3, l. 67. [Macduff]

Burning throne.—*Measure for Measure,* v, 1, 295.
Burnish'd throne.—*Antony and Cleopatra,* ii, 2, 196.
Earthly throne.—*II Henry VI,* iv, 9, 1.
Hearted throne.—*Othello,* iii, 3, 448.
Innocent and aweless throne.—*Richard III,* ii, 4, 52.
Opulent throne.—*Antony and Cleopatra,* i, 5, 46.

2
In God's name, I 'll ascend the regal throne.
Richard II. Act iv, sc. 1, l. 113. [Bolingbroke]

Regal throne.—*III Henry VI,* iv, 3, 64; iv, 6, 74.
Imperial throne.—*Henry V,* i, 2, 35.
Royal throne.—*Richard II,* ii, 1, 40.
Sovereign thrones.—*Twelfth Night,* i, 1, 38.
Fair throne.—*The Rape of Lucrece,* l. 413.

3
Pluck him headlong from the usurped throne.
Richard II. Act v, sc. 1, l. 65. [King Richard]

4
Your brother's son shall never reign our king;
But we will plant some other in the throne,
To the disgrace and downfall of your house.
Richard III. Act iii, sc. 7, l. 215. [Buckingham]

You are but newly planted in your throne.
Titus Andronicus. Act i, sc. 1, l. 444.

5
Draw our throne into a sheep-cote!
The Winter's Tale. Act iv, sc. 4, l. 808. [Autolycus]

Here is my throne.—*King John,* iii, 1, 74.

THUNDER

See also Lightning

6
To tear with thunder the wide cheeks o' the air,
And yet to charge thy sulphur with a bolt
That should but rive an oak.
Coriolanus. Act v, sc. 3, l. 151. [Volumnia]

You sulphurous and thought-executing fires,
Vaunt-couriers to oak-cleaving thunderbolts,
Singe my white head!
King Lear. Act iii, sc. 2, l. 4. [King Lear]
All three phrases are unique.

Merciful Heaven,
Thou rather with thy sharp and sulphurous bolt
Split'st the unwedgeable and gnarled oak
Than the soft myrtle.
Measure for Measure. Act ii, sc. 2, l. 114. [Isabella] The only use of "unwedgeable" and "gnarled."

To the dread rattling thunder
Have I given fire and rifted Jove's stout oak
With his own bolt.
The Tempest. Act v, sc. 1, l. 44. [Prospero]

7
Gui.: Fear no more the lightning-flash,
Arv.: Nor the all-dreaded thunder-stone.
Cymbeline. Act iv, sc. 2, l. 270. The only use of "all-dreaded." "Lightning-flash" is repeated in *Titus Andronicus,* ii, 1, 3. See 1525:6.

How dare you ghosts
Accuse the thunderer, whose bolt, you know,
Sky-planted batters all rebelling coasts?
Cymbeline. Act v, sc. 4, l. 94. [Jupiter] The only use of "thunderer" and "sky-planted."

He came in thunder; his celestial breath
Was sulphurous to smell.
Cymbeline. Act v, sc. 4, l. 114. [Sicilius]

Have bared my bosom to the thunder-stone.
Julius Cæsar. Act i, sc. 3, l. 49. [Casca] The only uses of "thunder-stone."

8
But, as we often see, against some storm,
A silence in the heavens, the rack stand still,
The bold winds speechless and the orb below
As hush as death, anon the dreadful thunder
Doth rend the region.
Hamlet. Act ii, sc. 2, l. 505. [First Player]

Dreadful thunder.—*Love's Labour's Lost,* iv, 2, 119; *The Passionate Pilgrim,* l. 67.
Amazing thunder.—*Richard II,* i, 3, 81.
Deep-mouth'd thunder.—*King John,* v, 2, 173.
Direful thunders.—*Macbeth,* i, 2, 26.
Earthly thunder.—*Hamlet,* i, 2, 128.
Heaven's thunder.—*Venus and Adonis,* l. 268.
Horrid thunder.—*King Lear,* iii, 2, 46.
Rattling thunder.—*Antony and Cleopatra,* v, 2, 86.
Sweet thunder.—*A Midsummer-Night's Dream,* iv, 1, 123.
Thunder of my cannon.—*King John,* i, 1, 26.
Thunder from the south.—*King John,* ii, 1, 411.
Thunders in the index.—*Hamlet,* iii, 4, 52.

9 Coming
In thunder and in earthquake, like a Jove.
Henry V. Act ii, sc. 4, l. 99. [Exeter]

In thunder, lightning.—*Macbeth,* i, 1, 2.
Thunder, rain and wind.—*Sonnets,* xiv.
Rain, wind, thunder.—*King Lear,* iii, 2, 15.

10 Engenders thunder in his breast
And makes him roar these accusations forth.
I Henry VI. Act iii, sc. 1, l. 39. [Winchester]

If Talbot do but thunder, rain will follow.
I Henry VI. Act iii, sc. 2, l. 59. [La Pucelle]

11
O that I were a god, to shoot forth thunder
Upon these paltry, servile, abject drudges!
II Henry VI. Act iv, sc. 1, l. 104. [Suffolk]

Thunder at a playhouse.—*Henry VIII,* v, 4, 63.

12 Thou, all-shaking thunder,
Smite flat the thick rotundity o' the world!
King Lear. Act iii, sc. 2, l. 6. [King Lear]
Only use of "all-shaking" and "rotundity."

Rumble thy bellyful! Spit, fire! spout, rain!
King Lear. Act iii, sc. 2, l. 14. [King Lear]
The only use of "rumble."

What is the cause of thunder?
King Lear. Act iii, sc. 4, l. 160. [King Lear]
A question which has never been definitely answered.

The thunder would not peace at my bidding.
King Lear. Act iv, sc. 6, l. 103. [Lear]

1 Could great men thunder
As Jove himself does, Jove would ne'er be quiet,
For every pelting, petty officer
Would use his heaven for thunder;
Nothing but thunder!
Measure for Measure. Act ii, sc. 2, l. 110. [Isabella]
Jove's thunder.—*The Winter's Tale,* iii, 1, 10.

2
Let it thunder to the tune of Green Sleeves.
The Merry Wives of Windsor. Act v, sc. 5, l. 21. [Falstaff]

3
Thunder above and deeps below.
Pericles, ii, Gower, 30.
O, still
Thy deafening, dreadful thunders; gently quench
Thy nimble sulphurous flashes!
Pericles. Act iii, sc. 1, l. 4. [Pericles]

4
They dropp'd, as by a thunder-stroke.
The Tempest. Act ii, sc. 1, l. 204. [Antonio]
I took him to be killed with a thunder-stroke.
The Tempest. Act ii, sc. 2, l. 112. [Trinculo] "Thunder-stroke" is used only in *The Tempest.*

5
If it should thunder as it did before, I know not where to hide my head.
The Tempest. Act ii, sc. 2, l. 22. [Trinculo]
The thunder, That deep and dreadful organ-pipe.
The Tempest, iii, 3, 97. See under REMORSE.
Heaven's artillery.—*The Taming of the Shrew,* i, 2, 205.

6
Secure of thunder's crack or lightning flash.
Titus Andronicus. Act ii, sc. 1, l. 3. [Aaron]

7 Jupiter forbid,
And say in thunder 'Achilles go to him.'
Troilus and Cressida. Act ii, sc. 3, l. 208. [Agamemnon]
By him that thunders!—*Troilus and Cressida,* iv, 5, 136.
By Jove that thunders!—*Antony and Cleopatra,* iii, 13, 85.
Jove for 's power to thunder.—*Coriolanus,* iii, 1, 257.
Great thunder-darter.—*Troilus and Cressida,* ii, 3, 11.
Thunder-master.—*Cymbeline,* v, 4, 30. The only use of either phrase.

TICKLING

8
I 'll tickle ye for a young prince, i' faith.
I Henry IV, ii, 4, 489. See under PRINCE.
I 'll tickle your catastrophe.
II Henry IV. Act ii, sc. 1, l. 66. [Falstaff]
He 'll tickle it for his concupy.
Troilus and Cressida. Act v, sc. 2, l. 177. [Thersites] The only use of "concupy" (concupiscence).
Tickle our noses.—*I Henry IV,* ii, 4, 340.
Tickle the senseless rushes.—*Romeo and Juliet,* i, 4, 36.
Tickles still the sore.—*Troilus and Cressida,* iii, 1, 130.
Tickle where she wounds!—*Cymbeline,* i, 1, 85.
Good tickle-brain.—*I Henry IV,* ii, 4, 438. The only use of the phrase.

9
Stands on a tickle point.
II Henry VI, i, 1, 216. See under POINT.
Stands so tickle.—*Measure for Measure,* i, 2, 177.
Tickle o' the sere.—*Hamlet,* ii, 2, 337. The only uses of "tickle" in the sense of insecure.

10
She 's tickled now; her fume needs no spurs.
II Henry VI. Act i, sc. 3, l. 153. [Buckingham]
To be so tickled, they would change their state
And situation.
Sonnets. No. cxxviii.
He would have tickled you othergates than he did.
Twelfth Night, v, 1, 198. See under DRINKING. The only use of "othergates" (in another way).
Tickled his chin.—*Troilus and Cressida,* i, 2, 150.
Tickled slumber.—*Cymbeline,* iv, 2, 210.
Tickled with good success.—*Coriolanus,* i, 1, 264. The only uses of "tickled."

11
Runs tickling up and down the veins.
King John, iii, 3, 44. See under BLOOD.
Tickling a parson's nose as a' lies asleep.
Romeo and Juliet, i, 4, 80. See under PREACHER.
Caught with tickling.—*Twelfth Night,* ii, 5, 26.
Die with tickling.—*Much Ado about Nothing,* iii, 1, 80.
Tickling beams.—*The Rape of Lucrece,* l. 1090.
Tickling Commodity.—*King John,* ii, 1, 573.
Tickling skittish spirits.—*Troilus and Cressida,* Prol., 20. The only uses of "tickling."

12
If you tickle us, do we not laugh?
The Merchant of Venice, iii, 1, 68. See under JEW.
If my hair do but tickle me, I must scratch.
A Midsummer-Night's Dream, iv, 1, 28. See under ASS.
Ticklish reader.—*Troilus and Cressida,* iv, 5, 61. The only use of "ticklish."

TIDE

13
With bootless labour swim against the tide.
III Henry VI, i, 4, 20. See under SWAN.
The tide will wash you off.
III Henry VI. Act v, sc. 4, l. 31. [Queen Margaret]

14
Porter: How got they in, and be hang'd?
Man: Alas, I know not; how gets the tide in?
Henry VIII. Act v, sc. 4, l. 17.
Enter'd tide.—*Troilus and Cressida,* iii, 3, 159.

15
There is a tide in the affairs of men.
Julius Cæsar, iv, 3, 218. See under OPPORTUNITY.
Rode on his tide.—*Troilus and Cressida,* ii, 3, 141.

16 My uncontrolled tide
Turns not, but swells the higher by this let.
The Rape of Lucrece, l. 645.

Turn the tide.—*I Henry IV,* iv, 1, 67; *Venus and Adonis,* l. 979.
The turning o' the tide.—*Henry V,* ii, 3, 14.

1 The approaching tide
Will shortly fill the reasonable shore
That now lies foul and muddy.
The Tempest. Act v, sc. 1, l. 80. [Prospero]

The tide is now: nay, not thy tide of tears:
That tide will stay me longer than I should.
The Two Gentlemen of Verona. Act ii, sc. 2, l. 14. [Proteus]

Thou 'lt lose the flood, and, in losing the flood, lose thy voyage.
The Two Gentlemen of Verona. Act ii, sc. 3, l. 47. [Panthino]

Full of tide.—*Antony and Cleopatra,* iii, 2, 49.
Blown tide.—*Coriolanus,* v, 4, 50.
Crystal tide.—*Venus and Adonis,* l. 957.
Flowing tides.—*I Henry VI,* i, 1, 83.
Next tide.—*Henry V,* iv, 1, 101.
Roaring tides.—*King John,* ii, 1, 24.
Swelling tide.—*King John,* ii, 1, 74.
Varying tide.—*Antony and Cleopatra,* i, 4, 46.
Violent roaring tide.—*Rape of Lucrece,* l. 1667.
Waxing tide.—*Titus Andronicus,* iii, 1, 95.
Tide of blood.—*II Henry IV,* v, 2, 129.
Tide of knaves.—*Timon of Athens,* iii, 4, 118.
Tide of pomp.—*Henry V,* iv, 1, 281.
Tide of woes.—*Richard II,* ii, 2, 98.
Wind and tide, see under WIND.

TIDINGS

See also News

2
Ram thou thy fruitful tidings in mine ears,
That long time have been barren.
Antony and Cleopatra. Act ii, sc. 5, l. 24. [Cleopatra]

The gods rebuke me, but it is tidings
To wash the eyes of kings.
Antony and Cleopatra. Act v, sc. 1, l. 27. [Cæsar]

3
The gods bless you for your tidings.
Coriolanus. Act v, sc. 4, l. 61. [Sicinius]

4
Northumberland: What good tidings comes with you? . . .
Travers: Joyful tidings.
II Henry IV. Act i, sc. 1, l. 33. "Good tidings" is repeated in iv, 2, 106, and in *Antony and Cleopatra,* ii, 5, 39.

Tidings do I bring and lucky joys
And golden times and happy news of price.
II Henry IV. Act v, sc. 3, l. 99. [Pistol]

Glad tidings.—*II Henry VI,* iv, 9, 7.
Happy tidings.—*III Henry VI,* ii, 1, 7.
Joyful tidings.—*Romeo and Juliet,* iii, 5, 105.
Sweet tidings.—*Titus Andronicus,* iii, 1, 159.

5
Sad tidings bring I to you out of France,
Of loss, of slaughter and discomfiture.
I Henry VI. Act i, sc. 1, l. 59. [Messenger] The only use of "discomfiture."

Douglas: That 's the worst tidings that I hear of yet.
Worcester: Ay, by my faith, that bears a frosty sound.
I Henry IV. Act iv, sc. 1, l. 127.

6 Thou hast made me giddy
With these ill tidings . . . do not seek to stuff
My head with more ill news, for it is full.
King John. Act iv, sc. 2, l. 131. [King John]

Say where, when, and how,
Camest thou by this ill tidings? speak, thou wretch.
Richard II. Act iii, sc. 4, l. 79. [Queen]

Tidings of calamity.—*Richard II,* iii, 2, 105.

7
Tidings, as swiftly as the posts could run,
Were brought me of your loss and his depart.
III Henry VI. Act ii, sc. 1, l. 109. [Warwick]

Certain tidings.—*Othello,* ii, 2, 2.

8 The tidings that I bring
Will make my boldness manners.
Henry VIII. Act v, sc. 1, l. 158. [Old Lady]

These tidings will well comfort Cassius.
Julius Cæsar. Act v, sc. 3, l. 54. [Titinius]

I dare not say
How near the tidings of our comfort is.
Richard II. Act ii, sc. 1, l. 272. [Northumberland]

9
I shall make my master glad with these tidings.
The Merry Wives of Windsor. Act iv, sc. 5, l. 57. [Simple]

10
What tidings can you tell me of my lord?
Othello. Act ii, sc. 1, l. 88. [Desdemona]

What tidings?—*I Henry VI,* v, 2, 10; *II Henry VI,* ii, 1, 65; *Titus Andronicus,* iv, 3, 78; *Macbeth,* i, 5, 31.

11 Letters came last night . . .
That tell black tidings.
Richard II. Act iii, sc. 4, l. 69. [Gardener]

Colder tidings, yet they must be told.
Richard III. Act iv, sc. 4, l. 536. [Catesby]

Despiteful tidings!—*Richard III,* iv, 1, 37.

12
These tidings nip me, and I hang the head
As flowers with frost or grass beat down with storms.
Titus Andronicus. Act iv, sc. 4, l. 70. [Saturninus]

13
And yet she hears no tidings of her love.
Venus and Adonis, l. 867.

TIGER

14
The tiger will be mild whiles she doth mourn.
III Henry VI. Act iii, sc. 1, l. 39. [King Henry]

Tame tigers.—*Troilus and Cressida,* iii, 2, 85.

15
The tiger now hath seized the gentle hind.
Richard III. Act ii, sc. 4, l. 50. [Queen Elizabeth]

The tiger that doth live by slaughter.
The Rape of Lucrece, l. 955.

Empty tigers.—*Romeo and Juliet,* v, 3, 39.
Fasting tiger.—*King John,* iii, 1, 260.
Heinous tiger.—*Titus Andronicus,* v, 3, 195.
Ravenous tiger.—*Titus Andronicus,* v, 3, 5.

Tigers of Hyrcania.—*III Henry VI,* i, 4, 155.
The Hyrcan tiger.—*Macbeth,* iii, 4, 101. The only use of "Hyrcania" and "Hyrcan." "Hyrcanian" occurs twice, in *The Merchant of Venice,* ii, 7, 41: "Hyrcanian deserts"; and in *Hamlet,* ii, 2, 472: "Hyrcanian beast."

1 Pluck the keen teeth from the fierce tiger's jaws.
Sonnets. No. xix.

2 When did the tiger's young ones teach the dam?
Titus Andronicus. Act ii, sc. 3, l. 142. [Lavinia]

Rome is but a wilderness of tigers?
Tigers must prey, and Rome affords no prey
But me and mine: how happy art thou, then,
From these devourers to be banished!
Titus Andronicus. Act iii, sc. 1, l. 54. [Titus] The only use of "devourers."

TIME

See also Future, Past, Present

I—Definitions

3 Well, Time is the old justice that examines all such offenders.
As You Like It. Act iv, sc. 1, l. 203. [Rosalind]

4 Time himself is bald and therefore to the world's end will have bald followers.
The Comedy of Errors. Act ii, sc. 2, l. 107. [Dromio of Syracuse]

Old Time the clock-setter, that bald sexton Time.
King John. Act iii, sc. 1, l. 324. [Bastard] The only use of "clock-setter."

Old time.—*Love's Labour 's Lost,* i, 2, 18; *Henry VIII,* ii, 1, 93; iv, 1, 78.

5 Time is a very bankrupt and owes more than he 's worth to season.
Nay, he 's a thief too: have you not heard men say,
That Time comes stealing on by night and day?
If Time be in debt and theft, and a sergeant in the way,
Hath he not reason to turn back an hour in a day?
The Comedy of Errors. Act iv, sc. 2, l. 58. [Dromio of Syracuse]

As if Time were in debt!
The Comedy of Errors. Act iv, sc. 2, l. 57. [Adriana]

6 Thou ceaseless lackey to eternity.
The Rape of Lucrece, l. 967. The only use of "ceaseless."

O Time, thou tutor both to good and bad,
Teach me to curse him that thou taught'st this ill!
The Rape of Lucrece, l. 995.

7 Time Goes upright with his carriage.
The Tempest. Act v, sc. 1, l. 2. [Prospero]

8 Time hath, my lord, a wallet at his back,
Wherein he puts alms for oblivion,
A great-sized monster of ingratitudes.
Troilus and Cressida. Act iii, sc. 3, l. 145. [Ulysses]

Great-sized coward.—*Troilus and Cressida,* v, 10, 26. "Great-sized" is used in no other play.

For time is like a fashionable host
That slightly shakes his parting guest by the hand,
And with his arms outstretch'd, as he would fly,
Grasps in the comer.
Troilus and Cressida. Act iii, sc. 3, l. 165. [Ulysses] "Fashionable" is used only once more in the plays, in *Timon of Athens,* v, 1, 29. "Comer" is repeated in *The Merchant of Venice,* ii, 1, 21.

That old common arbitrator, Time.
Troilus and Cressida. Act iv, sc. 5, l. 225. [Hector]

The arbitrator of despairs.—*I Henry VI,* ii, 5, 28. The only uses of "arbitrator."

9 Time is the nurse and breeder of all good.
The Two Gentlemen of Verona. Act iii, sc. 1, l. 243. [Proteus]

II—Familiar Phrases

10 At all times good.
All 's Well that Ends Well, i, 1, 9.

At all times.—*Coriolanus,* i, 9, 71; *Timon of Athens,* v, 1, 124; *Henry VIII,* ii, 4, 24.
At any time.—*Richard III,* iii, 5, 11; *Comedy of Errors,* v, 1, 8; *Measure for Measure,* ii, 2, 160; *Macbeth,* v, 1, 14; *Henry VIII,* i, 2, 146.
At more time.—*Macbeth,* i, 3, 153.
At no time.—*Macbeth,* iv, 3, 128.
At one time.—*Henry V,* i, 1, 80; i, 2, 134; *Cymbeline,* i, 6, 111.
At some time.—*Coriolanus,* ii, 1, 270.
At such a time.—*I Henry IV,* i, 3, 73; *Hamlet,* ii, 2, 162.
At such times.—*Hamlet,* i, 5, 173.
At that time.—*Richard III,* iv, 2, 103, and eleven times in later plays.
That time.—*As You Like It,* i, 3, 73; *Cymbeline,* ii, 5, 7.
At this time.—*The Comedy of Errors,* iii, 1, 93, and nine times in later plays.

11 Make the choice of thy own time.
All 's Well that Ends Well. Act ii, sc. 1, l. 206. [Helena]

Own time.—*Timon of Athens,* iii, 5, 77.

12 We must away;
Our waggon is prepared, and time revives us.
All 's Well that Ends Well. Act iv, sc. 4, l. 34. [Helena]

13 When you sued staying,
Then was the time for words.
Antony and Cleopatra. Act i, sc. 3, l. 33. [Cleopatra]

You shall have time to wrangle in when you have nothing else to do.
Antony and Cleopatra. Act ii, sc. 2, l. 106. [Enobarbus]

I will have more time.—*Measure for Measure,* iv, 3, 57.
Have time.—*Othello,* iii, 1, 57; *Henry VIII,* iii, 1, 79.

Have scarce time.—*Henry VIII*, iii, 2, 139.
Nor have I time.—*Pericles*, iii, 1, 59.
Had time.—*II Henry IV*, v, 5, 11.
Had I but time.—*Hamlet*, v, 2, 347.
Had no time.—*Romeo and Juliet*, iii, 4, 2.

1
Devise the fittest time.
As You Like It. Act i, sc. 3, l. 137. [Celia]
Fittest time.—*Coriolanus*, iv, 3, 33.
Fit time.—*Measure for Measure*, iv, 5, 1; *Othello*, i, 2, 85.
Fitter time for that.—*Measure for Measure*, v, 1, 498.
Best time.—*Macbeth*, iii, 4, 5.
Better time.—*King John*, iii, 3, 26. The only use of the phrase.

2
If you outstay the time.
As You Like It. Act i, sc. 3, l. 90. [Duke] The only use of "outstay."
I have outstood my time.
Cymbeline. Act i, sc. 6, l. 207. [Iachimo] The only use of "outstood."
I must stay his time.—*Antony and Cleopatra*, iii, 13, 155.
Before the time be out?—*The Tempest*, i, 2, 246.

3
Till that time
Come thou not near me: and when that time comes,
Afflict me with thy mocks, pity me not;
As till that time I shall not pity thee.
As You Like It. Act iii, sc. 5, l. 31. [Phebe]
Till that time.—*King John*, ii, 1, 271; *Hamlet*, v, 2, 262.
Till this time.—*King John*, iii, 1, 307.

4
Therefore take the present time.
As You Like It. Act v, sc. 3, l. 31. [Song] See under PRESENT.
Take the present time by the top.—*Much Ado about Nothing*, i, 2, 15. See under OPPORTUNITY.
Present time.—*Antony and Cleopatra*, i, 4, 79.
Take time.—*III Henry VI*, i, 4, 108.
Take the time.—*III Henry VI*, v, 1, 48.
Take time to pause.—*A Midsummer-Night's Dream*, i, 1, 83.
Take longer time.—*Hamlet*, v, 2, 207.

5
There 's a time for all things.
The Comedy of Errors. Act ii, sc. 2, l. 66. [Antipholus of Syracuse]
There is no time for all things.
The Comedy of Errors. Act ii, sc. 2, l. 102. [Antipholus of Syracuse]
There is no time.—*Comedy of Errors*, ii, 2, 106.
There was a time.—*Coriolanus*, i, 1, 99.

6
Plain as the bald pate of father Time.
The Comedy of Errors. Act ii, sc. 2, l. 71. [Dromio of Syracuse] The only use of "father Time."

7
One time will owe another.
Coriolanus. Act iii, sc. 1, l. 242. [Menenius]
Is 't possible that so short a time can alter the condition of a man?
Coriolanus. Act v, sc. 4, l. 9. [Sicinius]
The time is very short.
Romeo and Juliet. Act iv, sc. 1, l. 1. [Friar Laurence]

In short time.—*Cymbeline*, v, 5, 256.
Short time after.—*I Henry IV*, iv, 3, 90.
Shorter time.—*I Henry IV*, iii, 1, 91.

8
We stood to 't in good time.
Coriolanus. Act iv, sc. 6, l. 10. [Brutus]
In good time.—*Richard III*, ii, 1, 45; iii, 1, 95; iv, 1, 12, and ten times in later plays.
Good time.—*Timon of Athens*, iii, 2, 50; *Cymbeline*, iii, 4, 185; *Henry VIII*, v, 1, 22.
Look to 't in time.—*II Henry VI*, i, 3, 47.
Send in time.—*King Lear*, v, 3, 247.
In time.—*Measure for Measure*, i, 3, 26, and frequently throughout the plays.
In all this time.—*As You Like It*, iv, 1, 96.
In his time.—*Cymbeline*, iii, 4, 61.
In my time.—*The Taming of the Shrew*, i, 2, 201; *King Lear*, ii, 2, 99; *The Winter's Tale*, iv, 3, 13.
In such a time as this.—*Julius Cæsar*, iv, 3, 7.

9
Abide the change of time.
Cymbeline. Act ii, sc. 4, l. 4. [Posthumus]
The time inviting thee.—*Cymbeline*, iii, 4, 108.
Upon a time.—*Cymbeline*, iii, 5, 137; v, 5, 153.

10
Long is it since I saw him,
But time hath nothing blurr'd those lines of favour
Which then he wore.
Cymbeline. Act iv, sc. 2, l. 103. [Belarius]
Thy issue blurr'd.—*The Rape of Lucrece*, l. 522. The only uses of "blurr'd."
Blur our name.—*II Henry VI*, iv, 1, 39. The only use of "blur" as a verb.
This blur to youth.—*The Rape of Lucrece*, l. 222. The only use of "blur" as a noun.
Blurs the grace . . . of modesty.—*Hamlet*, iii, 4, 41. The only use of "blurs."

11
I wish my brother make good time with him.
Cymbeline. Act iv, sc. 2, l. 108. [Arviragus]
Win time.—*Cymbeline*, iii, 4, 112.

12
Let 's withdraw;
And meet the time as it seeks us.
Cymbeline. Act iv, sc. 3, l. 32. [Cymbeline]
Let the time run on To good or bad.
Cymbeline. Act v, sc. 5, l. 128. [Pisanio]

13
While one with moderate haste might tell a hundred.
Hamlet. Act i, sc. 2, l. 238. [Horatio]
The time invites you.
Hamlet. Act i, sc. 3, l. 83. [Polonius]

14
Expend your time with us awhile.
Hamlet. Act ii, sc. 2, l. 23. [Queen]
Here he means to spend his time awhile.
The Two Gentlemen of Verona. Act ii, sc. 4, l. 80. [Duke]
I am resolved that thou shalt spend some time
With Valentinus in the emperor's court.
The Two Gentlemen of Verona. Act i, sc. 3, l. 66. [Antonio]
Spend the time.—*III Henry VI*, v, 7, 42; *Coriolanus*, ii, 2, 133.

15
At our more consider'd time we 'll read,
Answer, and think upon this business.
Hamlet. Act ii, sc. 2, l. 81. [King]

1
Why day is day, night night, and time is time.
Hamlet. Act ii, sc. 2, l. 88. [Polonius]
Hath there been such a time?—*Hamlet,* ii, 2, 153.
2
The whips and scorns of time.
Hamlet. Act iii, sc. 1, l. 70. [Hamlet]
3
When time is ripe.
I Henry IV. Act i, sc. 3, l. 294. [Worcester]
Ripen'd time.—*Measure for Measure,* v, 1, 116.
4
Any time this two and twenty years.
I Henry IV. Act ii, sc. 2, l. 17. [Falstaff]
Any time these three hundred years.
The Merry Wives of Windsor. Act i, sc. 1, l. 12. [Shallow]
Any time.—*The Winter's Tale,* v, 2, 147.
5
The time itself unsorted.
I Henry IV. Act ii, sc. 3, l. 13. [Hotspur] The only use of "unsorted."
6
By that time will our book, I think, be drawn.
I Henry IV. Act iii, sc. 1, l. 224. [Mortimer]
By this time.—*The Merchant of Venice,* ii, 6, 59; *King John,* ii, 1, 219; *Much Ado about Nothing,* v, 1, 262; *Richard II,* i, 3, 194; *Henry VIII,* ii, 3, 98.
7
Let time shape, and there an end.
II Henry IV. Act iii, sc. 2, l. 358. [Falstaff]
Leave it to time.—*Othello,* iii, 3, 245.
8
'Tis more than time that I were there.
I Henry IV, iv, 2, 60. [Westmoreland]
'Tis more than time.—*II Henry IV,* i, 1, 187.
'Tis the more time.—*II Henry IV,* iii, 2, 117.
Harpier cries 'Tis time, 'tis time.
Macbeth. Act iv, sc. 1, l. 3. [Third Witch] The only use of "harpier," probably an error for harpy.
'Tis time I should inform thee farther.
The Tempest. Act i, sc. 2, l. 22. [Prospero]
'Tis time It should be look'd to.
Coriolanus. Act i, sc. 9, l. 93. [Cominius]
'Tis time we twain did show ourselves i' the field.
Antony and Cleopatra. Act i, sc. 4, l. 73. [Cæsar]
'Tis time thou wert away.—*Richard II,* v, 5, 96.
'Tis time to do 't.—*Macbeth,* v, 1, 40.
'Tis time to look about.—*King Lear,* iv, 7, 92.
'Tis time to part.—*Julius Cæsar,* ii, 1, 193; *The Winter's Tale,* iv, 4, 354.
'Tis time to speak.—*Richard III,* i, 3, 117.
'Tis time you were ready.—*Much Ado about Nothing,* iii, 4, 53.
'Tis time, I trow.—*Richard II,* ii, 1, 218.
'Tis high time.—*Comedy of Errors,* iii, 2, 162.
It is time.—*II Henry IV,* iii, 2, 128.
'Tis now the time To ask of whence you are.
Cymbeline. Act v, sc. 5, l. 13. [Cymbeline]
Now 'tis time.—*Antony and Cleopatra,* iii, 12, 26.
It is now our time.—*The Merchant of Venice,* iii, 2, 188.
Now it is time.—*Henry V,* iii, 7, 167.
'Tis time.—*The Comedy of Errors,* iii, 2, 158; iv, 2, 53; and twenty-eight times in later plays.
'Twas time.—*I Henry IV,* v, 4, 115; *Coriolanus,* ii, 1, 142; *Timon of Athens,* v, 1, 126.
'Tis no time to play now.
Romeo and Juliet. Act iv, sc. 5, l. 109. [Musician]
'Tis not a time For private stomaching.
Antony and Cleopatra. Act ii, sc. 2, l. 8. [Lepidus] The only use of "stomaching."
9
We see which way the stream of time doth run.
II Henry IV. Act iv, sc. 1, l. 70. [York]
One time or other.—*II Henry IV,* iv, 3, 32; *Henry V,* ii, 1, 73.
One time or another.—*Twelfth Night,* ii, 4, 73.
10
'Tis not the first time you were overshot.
Henry V. Act iii, sc. 7, l. 134. [Orleans]
'Tis not the first time.—*Twelfth Night,* ii, 3, 71.
'Tis the first time.—*Coriolanus,* v, 6, 105.
First time.—*As You Like It,* i, 2, 146; v, 4, 28; *Julius Cæsar,* iii, 2, 175; *King Lear,* iv, 6, 183.
One time.—*Coriolanus,* v, 1, 9.
This one time.—*The Merry Wives of Windsor,* iv, 2, 168.
Second time.—*The Comedy of Errors,* ii, 2, 47; *All's Well that Ends Well,* ii, 3, 55; *I Henry IV,* v, 2, 101; *Troilus and Cressida,* iv, 5, 237; *Hamlet,* ii, 2, 402; iii, 2, 194; *Pericles,* v, 3, 44.
Two several times.—*Julius Cæsar,* v, 5, 18.
This is the third time; I hope good luck lies in odd numbers.
The Merry Wives of Windsor, v, 1, 2. See under Luck.
Third time.—*Coriolanus,* ii, 1, 138.
Three times.—*II Henry VI,* iii, 2, 357; v, 3, 8; 18; and ten times in later plays.
Three or four times.—*I Henry IV,* iii, 3, 21; *Henry V,* ii, 3, 20; *The Merry Wives of Windsor,* v, 5, 129.
Four times.—*Othello,* i, 3, 313.
Five times.—*Coriolanus,* i, 10, 7; *Romeo and Juliet,* i, 4, 47; *Titus Andronicus,* i, 1, 33; *Cymbeline,* i, 4, 113; i, 5, 63.
Six times.—*The Taming of the Shrew,* iii, 2, 61.
Seven times.—*As You Like It,* v, 4, 71; *I Henry IV,* iii, 3, 18; *Merchant of Venice,* ii, 9, 63.
Eight times.—*I Henry IV,* ii, 4, 184.
Costard: Three times thrice, sir,—
Biron: Is not nine.
Costard: Under correction, sir, we know whereuntil it doth amount.
Biron: By Jove, I always took three threes for nine.
Love's Labour's Lost. Act v, sc. 2, l. 491. The only use of "whereuntil."
Thrice three times.—*The Merchant of Venice,* i, 3, 161.
Thrice again, to make up nine.—*Macbeth,* i, 3, 36.
Nine times.—*Macbeth,* i, 3, 22.
Nine or ten times.—*Othello,* i, 2, 4.
Ten times.—*II Henry VI,* iii, 2, 357; iv, 7, 26; and twenty-five times in later plays.
Ten times o'er.—*The Merchant of Venice,* iv, 1, 211.
Ten times strange.—*Measure for Measure,* v, 1, 42.
Ten times true.—*Measure for Measure,* v, 1, 45.
A dozen times.—*Measure for Measure,* i, 2, 21.

Twelve several times.—*Coriolanus,* iv, 5, 128.
Not once, nor twice, but twenty times.
The Comedy of Errors, iii, 2, 177. [Angelo]
Twenty times.—*II Henry VI,* ii, 4, 60; iii, 2, 268; and fifteen times in later plays.
Fifty times.—*The Winter's Tale,* iv, 4, 802.
Hundred times.—*II Henry VI,* ii, 1, 90; iii, 2, 355; *Coriolanus,* iv, 5, 114; *Othello,* iii, 3, 292.
Eight score times.—*Othello,* iii, 4, 175.
A thousand times as much.
The Two Gentlemen of Verona. Act ii, sc. 1, l. 120. [Valentine] "A thousand times" is repeated fifteen times in later plays.
Three thousand times.—*Love's Labour 's Lost,* i, 1, 151.
Ten thousand times.—*The Merchant of Venice,* iii, 2, 155.
Twenty thousand times.—*II Henry VI,* iii, 2, 206.
Twenty hundred thousand times.—*Romeo and Juliet,* iii, 3, 153.

1
Time hath worn us into slovenry.
Henry V. Act iv, sc. 3, l. 114. [King Henry] The only use of "slovenry."
Do not learn for want of time.
Henry V. Act v, sc. 2, l. 57. [Burgundy]

2
I 'll sort some other time to visit you.
I Henry VI. Act ii, sc. 3, l. 27. [Talbot]

3
To my determined time thou gavest new date.
I Henry VI, iv, 6, 9. See under SWORD.

4
Be still awhile, till time do serve.
II Henry VI. Act i, sc. 1, l. 248. [York]
The time now serves not to expostulate.
The Two Gentlemen of Verona. Act iii, sc. 1, l. 251. [Proteus]
Time serves.—*I Henry IV,* i, 3, 180.
When time shall serve.—*II Henry IV,* iv, 1, 74; *Henry V,* ii, 1, 60; iii, 6, 69; *King Lear,* v, 1, 48; *The Passionate Pilgrim,* l. 333.
Will the time serve?—*Coriolanus,* i, 6, 46.
Time will not permit.—*Richard II,* ii, 2, 121.

5
Next time I 'll keep my dreams unto myself.
II Henry VI. Act i, sc. 2, l. 53. [Duchess]
Next time.—*The Merry Wives of Windsor,* i, 4, 172; *Antony and Cleopatra,* iii, 13, 192.

6
Many a time . . . it hath served me.
II Henry VI. Act iv, sc. 10, l. 12. [Cade]
Many a time.—*Richard II,* iv, 1, 92; *Othello,* iii, 3, 71; *Titus Andronicus,* v, 3, 162; *The Tempest,* iii, 1, 40.
Many times.—*Julius Cæsar,* ii, 2, 32; iii, 1, 114; and six times in later plays.
Some little time.—*King Lear,* i, 2, 176.
Some other time.—*III Henry VI,* iii, 2, 17.

7
Of one or both of us the time is come.
II Henry VI. Act v, sc. 2, l. 13. [Warwick]
The time is come.—*I Henry VI,* v, 3, 24; *Antony and Cleopatra,* iv, 14, 67.
Now a time is come.—*II Henry IV,* iv, 5, 119.
The time will come.—*I Henry IV,* iii, 2, 144; *II Henry IV,* iii, 1, 76.

8
Time suppresseth wrongs.
III Henry VI. Act iii, sc. 3, l. 77. [Queen Margaret]

9
Many a time and oft.
Julius Cæsar, i, 1, 42. See under FAMILIAR PHRASES.

10
For this time I will leave you.
Julius Cæsar. Act i, sc. 2, l. 307. [Brutus]
For this time.—*The Comedy of Errors,* iii, 1, 43; and ten times in later plays.
For a time.—*Richard II,* i, 3, 258.
For my time.—*Measure for Measure,* iii, 2, 231.
For that time.—*Richard II,* i, 3, 259.

11
O, what a time have you chose out!
Julius Cæsar. Act ii, sc. 1, l. 314. [Brutus]

12
I shall find time, Cassius, I shall find time.
Julius Cæsar. Act v, sc. 3, l. 103. [Brutus]
We shall find a time.—*As You Like It,* v, 1, 1.
Find a time.—*I Henry IV,* v, 2, 6; *Julius Cæsar,* i, 2, 169; *Romeo and Juliet,* iii, 3, 150.
Find time.—*King Lear,* ii, 2, 175.
Find the time.—*Macbeth,* iv, 3, 10.
Found time.—*Timon of Athens,* ii, 2, 200.

13
A time unseasonable.
King John. Act iv, sc. 2, l. 20. [Pembroke]
Unseasonable instant.—*Much Ado about Nothing,* ii, 2, 16.
Unseasonable stormy day.—*Richard II,* iii, 2, 106. The only uses of "unseasonable."

14
This trice of time.
King Lear. Act i, sc. 1, l. 219. [King of France]

15
Some other time for that.
King Lear. Act ii, sc. 4, l. 135. [King Lear]
Some other time.—*Othello,* iii, 3, 55.
Some time.—*II Henry VI,* ii, 4, 42, and frequently throughout the later plays.

16
Then come the time, who lives to see 't,
That going shall be used with feet.
King Lear, iii, 2, 93. See under PROPHECY.
We will greet the time.—*King Lear,* v, 1, 54.
Grant the time.—*Macbeth,* ii, 1, 24.
Beguile the time.—*Twelfth Night,* iii, 3, 41.
Spare the time.—*Henry VIII,* ii, 4, 5.

17
Cormorant devouring Time.
Love's Labour 's Lost. Act i, sc. 1, l. 4. [King Ferdinand]
Insatiate cormorant.—*Richard II,* ii, 1, 38.
Cormorant belly.—*Coriolanus,* i, 1, 125.
Cormorant war.—*Troilus and Cressida,* ii, 2, 6. The only uses of "cormorant."

18
So much for the time when.
Love's Labour 's Lost. Act i, sc. 1, l. 240. [King Ferdinand]

19 A time, methinks, too short
To make a world-without-end bargain in.
Love's Labour 's Lost. Act v, sc. 2, l. 798. [Princess of France] The only use of "world-without-end."

1 Come what come may,
Time and the hour runs through the roughest day.
Macbeth. Act i, sc. 3, l. 146. [Macbeth] "Roughest" is used only once again, in *Antony and Cleopatra,* i, 4, 64: "Roughest berry."

2
Fill up the time 'Twixt this and supper.
Macbeth. Act iii, sc. 1, l. 25. [Banquo]
Fill the time.—*All's Well that Ends Well,* iii, 7, 33.
Fill'd the time.—*Timon of Athens,* v, 4, 3.

3
You 'll rue the time.
Macbeth. Act iii, sc. 6, l. 42. [Lord]

4
Time, thou anticipatest my dread exploits.
Macbeth. Act iv, sc. 1, l. 144. [Macbeth] The only use of "anticipatest."
The fits o' the season.
Macbeth. Act iv, sc. 2, l. 17. [Ross]

5
The time you may so hoodwink.
Macbeth. Act iv, sc. 3, l. 72. [Macduff] "Hoodwink" is repeated in *All's Well that Ends Well,* iii, 6, 26, and in *Tempest,* iv, 1, 206. "Hoodwink'd" also occurs three times.
The time is free.
Macbeth. Act v, sc. 8, l. 55. [Macduff]

6
The time is yet to come.
Measure for Measure. Act ii, sc. 1, l. 176. [Elbow]
The time is come even now.
Measure for Measure. Act iv, sc. 1, l. 21. [Duke]
Now 's a time.—*Timon of Athens,* ii, 2, 152.
Now is the time.—*Sonnets,* iii.
Now is your time.—*Measure for Measure,* v, 1, 19.
This is the time.—*The Winter's Tale,* iv, 4, 688.
This our time.—*Sonnets,* cvi.
There will come a time.—*The Merry Wives of Windsor,* ii, 2, 106.
Come in time.—*Macbeth,* ii, 3, 6.
The time has been.—*Macbeth,* iii, 4, 78; v, 5, 10.
Time hath been.—*Richard II,* iii, 3, 10.
Time was.—*All's Well that Ends Well,* iv, 4, 5; *As You Like It,* iii, 5, 92; *II Henry IV,* ii, 3, 10.

7
Much upon this time have I promised here to meet.
Measure for Measure. Act iv, sc. 1, l. 17. [Duke]
Until this time.—*Comedy of Errors,* iv, 4, 69.

8
I have seen the time.
The Merry Wives of Windsor. Act ii, sc. 1, l. 236. [Shallow]

9
Give me so much of your time.
The Merry Wives of Windsor. Act ii, sc. 2, l. 242. [Ford]
Give thee time.—*The Two Gentlemen of Verona,* iii, 1, 165.
Given him time.—*King John,* ii, 1, 58.

10
That very time I saw, but thou couldst not.
A Midsummer-Night's Dream. Act ii, sc. 1, l. 155. [Oberon]
That very time.—*Richard II,* iv, 1, 14.
The very time.—*Richard II,* iv, 1, 61.

11
We must obey the time.
Othello. Act i, sc. 3, l. 301. [Othello]
The time shall more favourably minister.
Othello. Act ii, sc. 1, l. 277. [Iago] The only use of "favourably."

12
Keep time in all.
Othello. Act iv, sc. 1, l. 93. [Iago]
Keep time.—*Romeo and Juliet,* ii, 4, 21; *Hamlet,* iii, 4, 140; *Twelfth Night,* ii, 3, 99.
He kept not time.—*Merry Wives of Windsor,* i, 3, 29. See also under MUSIC, TUNE.

13
Time that is so briefly spent.
Pericles, iii, Gower, 12.
Time so idly spent.—*Sonnets,* c.
His time is spent.—*Richard II,* ii, 1, 154.
The time is spent.—*Venus and Adonis,* l. 255.
Your time 's expired.—*Pericles,* i, 1, 89.

14
Make war against proportion'd course of time.
The Rape of Lucrece, l. 774.
The course of time.—*The Two Gentlemen of Verona,* i, 3, 23; *King John,* i, 1, 113.

15 Take from Time
His charters and his customary rights.
Richard II. Act ii, sc. 1, l. 195. [York]

16
Take advantage of the absent time.
Richard II, ii, 3, 79. See under PURPOSE.
Now with the drops of this most balmy time
My love looks fresh.
Sonnets. No. cvii.
Blessed time.—*Timon of Athens,* iv, 3, 78; *Macbeth,* ii, 3, 97.
Continuate time.—*Othello,* iii, 4, 178. "Continuate" is repeated in *Timon of Athens,* i, 1, 11: "Continuate goodness."
Curbed time.—*All's Well that Ends Well,* ii, 4, 56.
Dead time.—*Richard II,* iv, 1, 10.
Eaning time.—*The Merchant of Venice,* i, 3, 88; *Pericles,* iii, 4, 6.
Fairy time.—*Love's Labour's Lost,* v, 1, 371.
Full time.—*Measure for Measure,* iv, 2, 12.
Growing time.—*I Henry VI,* ii, 4, 99.
Last time.—*II Henry VI,* i, 3, 174; *Julius Cæsar,* v, 1, 99; *The Merry Wives of Windsor,* iv, 2, 32; 98.
Odd time.—*Othello,* ii, 3, 132.
Private time.—*Hamlet,* i, 3, 92.
Recorded time.—*Macbeth,* v, 5, 21.
Same time.—*Coriolanus,* v, 3, 21.
Small time.—*Henry V,* Epil., 5.
True time.—*Richard II,* v, 5, 46.

17
O, call back yesterday, bid time return.
Richard II. Act iii, sc. 2, l. 69. [Salisbury]
Is not my teeming date drunk up with time?
Richard II, v, 2, 91. See under SON.

18
To pass away the time.
Richard III. Act i, sc. 1, l. 25. [Gloucester]

19
Hastings: What is 't o'clock?
Messenger: Upon the stroke of four.
Richard III. Act iii, sc. 2, l. 4.

What 's o'clock?—*II Henry VI,* ii, 4, 5, and eight times in later plays.

First Lord: What time o' day is it, Apemantus?
Apemantus: Time to be honest.
First Lord: That time serves still.
Apemantus: The more accursed thou, that still omitt'st it.
Timon of Athens. Act i, sc. 1, l. 265.

Much about cock-shut time.—*Richard III,* v, 3, 70. The only use of "cock-shut."

1
You, my noble lords, may name the time.
Richard III. Act iii, sc. 4, l. 19. [Hastings]

I prithee, name the time.—*Othello,* iii, 3, 62.

2
At your meet'st advantage of the time.
Richard III. Act iii, sc. 5, l. 74. [Gloucester]

In the perfectness of time.—*II Henry IV,* iv, 4, 74. "Perfectness" is repeated in *Love's Labour 's Lost,* v, 2, 173.

3
Since that time it is eleven years.
Romeo and Juliet. Act i, sc. 3, l. 35. [Nurse]

Since her time.—*Love's Labour 's Lost,* iv, 3, 267.

Ere this time.—*Timon of Athens,* iii, 2, 133.

Time out of mind.—*Romeo and Juliet,* i, 4, 69; *Measure for Measure,* iv, 2, 17.

4
You've pass'd a hell of time.
Sonnets. No. cxx.

Against that time.—*Sonnets,* xlix.

5
But did I never speak of all that time?
The Taming of the Shrew. Induction, sc. 2, l. 84. [Sly]

All the whole time.—*Henry VIII,* i, 1, 12.

All this time.—*The Taming of the Shrew,* Ind., 2, 116; *The Rape of Lucrece,* l. 1576.

6 What seest thou else
In the dark backward and abysm of time?
The Tempest. Act i, sc. 2, l. 49. [Prospero] "Abysm" is used again in *Antony and Cleopatra,* iii, 13, 147: "Abysm of hell"; and a third time in *Sonnets,* cxii: "Profound abysm."

7
After a little time, I 'll beat him too.
The Tempest. Act iii, sc. 2, l. 93. [Caliban]

After some time.—*Othello,* i, 3, 401.

8
Another time I 'll hear thee.
Timon of Athens. Act i, sc. 2, l. 184. [Timon]

Another time.—*Julius Cæsar,* ii, 2, 98; *The Merchant of Venice,* i, 1, 100; i, 3, 128; *Sonnets,* xlviii; *The Tempest,* iii, 2, 85.

9
The time is unagreeable to this business.
Timon of Athens. Act ii, sc. 2, l. 41. [Flavius] The only use of "unagreeable."

10
Now is a time to storm; why art thou still?
Titus Andronicus. Act iii, sc. 1, l. 264. [Marcus]

Time to act.—*Hamlet,* iii, 1, 129.

11
Time must friend or end.
Troilus and Cressida. Act i, sc. 2, l. 84. [Pandarus]

When time is old and hath forgot itself.
Troilus and Cressida. Act iii, sc. 2, l. 192. [Cressida]

12
In time of action.
Troilus and Cressida. Act iii, sc. 3, l. 219. [Patroclus]

Times of business.—*Henry VIII,* ii, 2, 72.

Time of day.—*II Henry VI,* iii, 1, 14, and sixteen times in later plays.

Time of death.—*III Henry VI,* ii, 6, 67; *Richard III,* i, 4, 34.

Time of help.—*Macbeth,* iv, 3, 186.

Time of life.—*I Henry IV,* v, 2, 82; *Julius Cæsar,* v, 1, 106.

Time of moon.—*Twelfth Night,* i, 5, 213.

Time of night.—*II Henry VI,* i, 4, 20, and four times in later plays.

Time of peace.—*Richard III,* i, 1, 24.

Times of pleasure.—*Sonnets,* lviii.

Time of rest.—*Julius Cæsar,* iv, 3, 262.

Times of sacrifice.—*Coriolanus,* i, 10, 21.

Time of storm.—*III Henry VI,* iv, 7, 43.

Time of trial.—*II Henry VI,* iii, 1, 138.

Time of war.—*III Henry VI,* iv, 7, 36; *Henry VIII,* iv, 1, 78.

Time of year.—*Richard II,* iii, 4, 57; *Sonnets,* lxxiii.

Time o' the year.—*Antony and Cleopatra,* i, 5, 51.

13 This place is dangerous;
The time right deadly.
Troilus and Cressida. Act v, sc. 2, l. 38. [Ulysses]

14
Good time encounter her!
The Winter's Tale. Act ii, sc. 1, l. 20. [Lady]

She is something before her time deliver'd.
Winter's Tale. Act ii, sc. 2, l. 25. [Emilia]

Before his time.—*Romeo and Juliet,* v, 3, 268; *King Lear,* iii, 2, 95.

Before my time.—*Richard III,* i, 1, 20.

Before that time.—*I Henry VI,* iii, 2, 48.

Before the time.—*Romeo and Juliet,* iv, 3, 31.

Before their time.—*The Two Gentlemen of Verona,* v, 1, 5.

Before thy time.—*III Henry VI,* i, 1, 237; *King Lear,* i, 5, 46.

Before your time.—*Measure for Measure,* v, 1, 87; *Pericles,* i, 1, 84.

15
There 's time enough for that.
Winter's Tale. Act v, sc. 3, l. 128. [Paulina]

This wide gap of time.—*The Winter's Tale,* v, 3, 154.

III—Time: Its Power

16
Time is their master, and when they see time
They 'll go or come.
The Comedy of Errors. Act ii, sc. 1, l. 8. [Luciana]

We are time's subjects, and time bids be gone.
II Henry IV. Act i, sc. 3, l. 110. [Hastings]

17
Time calls upon 's.
Antony and Cleopatra. Act ii, sc. 2, l. 160. [Lepidus]

Our time does call upon 's.
Macbeth. Act iii, sc. 1, l. 37. [Banquo]

Time
Must wear the print of his remembrance out.
Cymbeline. Act ii, sc. 3, l. 47. [Cymbeline]

The cure whereof, my lord, 'Tis time must do.
Cymbeline. Act iii, sc. 5, l. 37. [Queen]

1
The time misorder'd doth, in common sense,
Crowd us and crush us to this monstrous form,
To hold our safety up.
II Henry IV. Act iv, sc. 2, l. 33. [Archbishop of York] The only use of "misorder'd."

2
Time shall unfold what plaited cunning hides.
King Lear. Act i, sc. 1, l. 283. [Cordelia] The only use of "plaited."

The time will bring it out.
King Lear. Act v, sc. 3, l. 163. [Edmund]

3
Time 's the king of men,
He 's both their parent, and he is their grave,
And gives them what he will, not what they crave.
Pericles. Act ii, sc. 3, l. 45. [Pericles]

4
O, hear me then, injurious, shifting Time!
Be guilty of my death, since of my crime.
The Rape of Lucrece, l. 930.

Time's office is to fine the hate of foes.
The Rape of Lucrece, l. 936.

5
Mis-shapen Time, copesmate of ugly Night,
Swift subtle post, carrier of grisly care,
Eater of youth, false slave to false delight,
Base watch of woes, sin's pack-horse, virtue's snare;
Thou nursest all and murder'st all that are.
The Rape of Lucrece, l. 925. The only use of "copesmate" (companion). "Pack-horse" is repeated in *II Henry IV,* ii, 4, 177, and in *Richard III,* i, 3, 122.

Time's glory is to calm contending kings,
To unmask falsehood and bring truth to light,
To stamp the seal of time in aged things,
To wake the morn and sentinel the night,
To wrong the wronger till he render right.
The Rape of Lucrece, l. 939.

To ruinate proud buildings with thy hours,
And smear with dust their glittering golden towers.
The Rape of Lucrece, l. 944. "Smear" is used only once again, in *Macbeth,* ii, 2, 49. "Ruinate" is repeated in *III Henry VI,* v, 1, 83, and in *Titus Andronicus,* v, 3, 204.

Let him have time to tear his curled hair,
Let him have time against himself to rave,
Let him have time of Time's help to despair,
Let him have time to live a loathed slave,
Let him have time a beggar's orts to crave,
And time to see one that by alms doth live
Disdain to him disdained scraps to give.

Let him have time to see his friends his foes,
And merry fools to mock at him resort;
Let him have time to mark how slow time goes
In time of sorrow, and how swift and short
His time of folly and his time of sport;
And ever let his unrecalling crime
Have time to wail th' abusing of his time.
The Rape of Lucrece, l. 981. The only use of "unrecalling."

6
Uncomfortable time, why camest thou now
To murder, murder our solemnity?
Romeo and Juliet. Act iv, sc. 5, l. 60. [Capulet] The only use of "uncomfortable."

7
Nothing 'gainst Time's scythe can make defence.
Sonnets. No. xii.

When I have seen by Time's fell hand defaced
The rich proud cost of outworn buried age;
When sometime lofty towers I see down-razed
And brass eternal slave to mortal rage;
When I have seen the hungry ocean gain
Advantage of the kingdom of the shore,
And the firm soil win of the watery main,
Increasing store with loss and loss with store;
When I have seen such interchange of state,
Or state itself confounded to decay;
Ruin hath taught me thus to ruminate,
That Time will come and take my love away.
This thought is as a death, which cannot choose
But weep to have that which it fears to lose.
Sonnets. No. lxiv. The only use of "down-razed."

Nor gates of steel so strong, but Time decays.
Sonnets. No. lxv.

8
Devouring Time, blunt thou the lion's paws,
And make the earth devour her own sweet brood;
Pluck the keen teeth from the fierce tiger's jaws,
And burn the long-lived phœnix in her blood;
Make glad the sorry seasons as thou fleets,
And do whate'er thou wilt, swift-footed Time,
To the wide world and all her failing sweets. . . .
Yet, do thy worst, old Time: despite thy wrong,
My love shall in my verse ever live young.
Sonnets. No. xix. The only use of "swift-footed."

Time doth transfix the flourish set on youth
And delves the parallels in beauty's brow,
Feeds on the rarities of nature's truth,
And nothing stands but for his scythe to mow.
Sonnets. No. lx. The only use of "transfix."

O fearful meditation! where, alack,
Shall Time's best jewel from Time's chest lie hid?
Or what strong hand can hold his swift foot back?
Or who his spoil of beauty can forbid?
Sonnets. No. lxv.

Reckoning time, whose million'd accidents
Creep in 'twixt vows and change decrees of kings,
Tan sacred beauty, blunt the sharp'st intents,
Divert strong minds to the course of altering things.
Sonnets. No. cxv. The only use of "million'd."

Subject to Time's love or to Time's hate.
Sonnets. No. cxxiv.
This bloody tyrant, Time.—*Sonnets,* xvi.
Time's tyranny.—*Sonnets,* cxv.
Devouring Time.—*Sonnets,* xix.
Time's injurious hand.—*Sonnets,* lxiii.

1 Now the time is flush,
When crouching marrow in the bearer strong
Cries of itself 'No more.'
Timon of Athens. Act v, sc. 4, l. 9. [Alcibiades] The only use of "crouching."

2 Feed his humour kindly as we may,
Till time beget some careful remedy.
Titus Andronicus. Act iv, sc. 3, l. 29. [Publius]

3 Beauty, wit,
High birth, vigour of bone, desert in service,
Love, friendship, charity, are subjects all
To envious and calumniating time.
Troilus and Cressida. Act iii, sc. 3, l. 171. [Ulysses] The only use of "calumniating."
Injurious time now with a robber's haste
Crams his rich thievery up.
Troilus and Cressida. Act iv, sc. 4, l. 44. [Troilus]

4
Thus the whirligig of time brings in his revenges.
Twelfth Night. Act v, sc. 1, l. 384. [Clown] The only use of "whirligig."

5
A little time will melt her frozen thoughts.
The Two Gentlemen of Verona. Act iii, sc. 2, l. 9. [Duke]
A little time, my lord, will kill that grief.
The Two Gentlemen of Verona. Act iii, sc. 2, l. 15. [Proteus]
Little time.—*Hamlet,* ii, 2, 14; *Venus and Adonis,* l. 132.

IV—Time: Its Flight

6
Ere twice the horses of the sun shall bring
Their fiery torcher his diurnal ring,
Ere twice in murk and occidental damp
Moist Hesperus hath quench'd his sleepy lamp,
Or four and twenty times the pilot's glass
Hath told the thievish minutes how they pass.
All's Well that Ends Well. Act ii, sc. 1, l. 164. [Helena] The only use of "torcher," "diurnal," "murk," "occidental," and "Hesperus."

7
The inaudible and noiseless foot of Time.
All's Well that Ends Well. Act v, sc. 3, l. 41. [King] The only use of "inaudible."
The swift course of time.—*The Two Gentlemen of Verona,* i, 3, 23.
Justling time.—*I Henry IV,* iv, 1, 18. The only use of "justling."
Winged time.—*Pericles,* iv, Gower, 47.

8
And then he drew a dial from his poke,
And, looking on it with lack-lustre eye,
Says very wisely, 'It is ten o'clock:
Thus we may see,' quoth he, 'how the world wags.'
As You Like It. Act ii, sc. 7, l. 20. [Jaques] The only use of "poke" and "lack-lustre."
By this, I think, the dial points at five.
The Comedy of Errors. Act v, sc. 1, l. 118. [Merchant]
Thou, by thy dial's shady stealth may know
Time's thievish progress to eternity.
Sonnets. No. lxxvii.
Thy dial.—*Sonnets,* lxxvii.
My dial goes not true.—*All's Well that Ends Well,* ii, 5, 6.
An hour by his dial.—*As You Like It,* ii, 7, 35.
Hourly dial.—*The Rape of Lucrece.* l. 327.
More tedious than the dial.—*Othello,* iii, 4, 175.
Bawdy hand of the dial.—*Romeo and Juliet,* ii, 4, 119.
Dial-hand.—*Sonnets,* civ. The only use of the phrase.
Dial's centre.—*Henry V,* i, 4, 210.
Dial's point.—*I Henry IV,* v, 2, 84; *Richard II,* v, 5, 53. The only uses of "dial."
Dials the signs of leaping-houses.—*I Henry IV,* i, 2, 9. The only use of "leaping-houses."
Carve out dials quaintly.—*III Henry VI,* ii, 5, 24. The only uses of "dials."
Rosalind: The lazy foot of Time . . .
Orlando: Why not the swift foot of Time? had not that been as proper?
Rosalind: By no means, sir: Time travels in divers paces with divers persons. I'll tell you who Time ambles withal, who Time trots withal, who Time gallops withal and who he stands still withal.
Orlando: I prithee, who doth he trot withal?
Rosalind: Marry, he trots hard with a young maid between the contract of her marriage and the day it is solemnized: if the interim be but a se'nnight, Time's pace is so hard that it seems the length of seven year.
Orlando: Who ambles Time withal?
Rosalind: With a priest that lacks Latin and a rich man that hath not the gout. . . .
Orlando: Who does he gallop withal?
Rosalind: With a thief to the gallows, for though he go as softly as foot can fall, he thinks himself too soon there.
Orlando: Who stays it still withal?
Rosalind: With lawyers in the vacation; for they sleep between term and term and then they perceive not how Time moves.
As You Like It. Act iii, sc. 2, l. 322. The only use of "vacation."

9 To see the minutes how they run,
How many make the hour full complete;
How many hours bring about the day;
How many days will finish up the year;
How many years a mortal man may live.
III Henry VI. Act ii, sc. 5, l. 25. [King Henry]
So many hours must I tend my flock;
So many hours must I take my rest;
So many hours must I contemplate;
So many hours must I sport myself;
So many days my ewes have been with young;
So many weeks ere the poor fools will ean;
So many years ere I shall shear the fleece:
So minutes, hours, days, months, and years,
Pass'd ever to the end they were created,

Would bring white hairs unto a quiet grave.
III Henry VI. Act ii, sc. 5, l. 31. [King] The only use of "ean" (to bring forth).

For holy offices I have a time; a time
To think upon the part of business which
I bear i' the state; and nature does require
Her times of preservation.
Henry VIII. Act iii, sc. 2, l. 144. [Wolsey]

1
The extreme parts of time extremely forms
All causes to the purpose of his speed.
Love's Labour's Lost. Act v, 2, 750. [King]

Time wears.—*Merry Wives of Windsor,* v, 1, 8.

2 We have chid the hasty-footed time
For parting us.
A Midsummer-Night's Dream, iii, 2, 200. [Helena] The only use of "hasty-footed."

Swift-footed Time.—*Sonnets,* xix. The only use of "swift-footed."

Never-resting time.—*Sonnets,* v. The only use of "never-resting."

3 My time
Runs posting on in Bolingbroke's proud joy,
While I stand fooling here, his Jack o' the clock.
Richard II. Act v, sc. 5, l. 58. [King Richard] The only mention of "Jack o' the clock," the mechanical figure on old clocks which struck the hour.

The stealing hours of time.—*Richard III,* iii, 7, 168.

The time goes by.—*Twelfth Night,* iii, 4, 398.

V—Time: Its Slowness

4
And time, that takes survey of all the world,
Must have a stop.
I Henry IV. Act v, sc. 4, l. 82. [Hotspur]

5
The weary time she cannot entertain.
The Rape of Lucrece, l. 1361.

And time doth weary time with her complaining.
The Rape of Lucrece, l. 1570.

Short time seems long in sorrow's sharp sustaining.
The Rape of Lucrece, l. 1573.

They that watch see time how slow it creeps.
The Rape of Lucrece, l. 1575.

O time, cease thou thy course and last no longer.
The Rape of Lucrece, l. 1765.

The time is long.—*Love's Labour's Lost,* v, 2, 845.

The time seems long.—*Cymbeline,* iv, 4, 53.

So long a time.—*The Two Gentlemen of Verona,* ii, 7, 17.

Long time.—*Richard II,* ii, 1, 77; *Antony and Cleopatra,* ii, 5, 25; *Henry VIII,* i, 3, 45.

Long-experienced time.—*Romeo and Juliet,* iv, 1, 60. "Long-experienced" is repeated in *The Rape of Lucrece,* l. 1820: "Long-experienced wit."

Dilatory time.—*Othello,* ii, 3, 379.

VI—Time: Its Use

6 Every time
Serves for the matter that is then born in 't.
Antony and Cleopatra. Act ii, sc. 2, l. 9. [Enobarbus]

7
Take thy fair hour, Laertes; time be thine,
And thy best graces spend it at thy will!
Hamlet. Act i, sc. 2, l. 62. [King]

8
I do not only marvel where thou spendest thy time, but also how thou art accompanied.
I Henry IV. Act ii, sc. 4, l. 441. [Falstaff]

9
He weighs time Even to the utmost grain.
Henry V. Act ii, sc. 4, l. 137. [Exeter]

10
Away, away! no time shall be omitted
That shall betime, and may by us be fitted.
Love's Labour's Lost. Act iv, sc. 3, l. 381. [King]

11
Let every man be master of his time
Till seven at night.
Macbeth. Act iii, sc. 1, l. 41. [Macbeth]

We shall not spend a large expense of time.
Macbeth. Act v, sc. 8, l. 60. [Malcolm]

12
The time shall not go dully by us.
Much Ado about Nothing. Act ii, sc. 1, l. 379. [Don Pedro]

Busy time.—*Much Ado about Nothing,* i, 2, 29; iii, 5, 6. The phrase is used in no other play.

13
Be where you list, your charter is so strong
That you yourself may privilege your time
To what you will.
Sonnets. No. lviii.

14 The time 'twixt six and now
Must by us both be spent most preciously.
The Tempest. Act i, sc. 2, l. 240. [Prospero] The only use of "preciously."

15
One that . . . canst use the time well, if the time use thee well: good parts in thee.
Timon of Athens. Act iii, sc. 1, l. 38. [Lucullus]

Make use of time.—*Venus and Adonis,* l. 129.

16
We 'll part the time between 's.
Winter's Tale. Act i, sc. 2, l. 18. [Leontes]

VII—Time: Its Loss

17
Many young gentlemen flock to him every day, and fleet the time carelessly, as they did in the golden world.
As You Like It. Act i, sc. 1, l. 123. [Charles]

Lose and neglect the creeping hours of time.
As You Like It. Act ii, sc. 7, l. 112. [Orlando]

Consumed time.—*All's Well that Ends Well,* v, 3, 38.

18 I like this place,
And willingly could waste my time in it.
As You Like It. Act ii, sc. 4, l. 94. [Celia]

They will waste their time.—*Cymbeline,* iv, 4, 20.

Waste the time together.—*The Merchant of Venice,* iii, 4, 12.

Waste no time in words.—*The Merchant of Venice,* iii, 4, 54.

1 I feel me much to blame,
So idly to profane the precious time.
II Henry IV. Act ii, sc. 4, l. 390. [Prince of Wales]
To drive away the time.—*I Henry IV,* ii, 4, 31.

2
We trifle time away.
Henry VIII. Act v, sc. 3, l. 179. [King Henry]
We trifle time.—*Merchant of Venice,* iv, 1, 298.

3
For your fair sakes have we neglected time.
Love's Labour 's Lost. Act v, sc. 2, l. 765. [Biron]
We . . . Waste the time.
Pericles. Act ii, sc. 3, l. 93. [Simonides]
Thus time we waste, and longest leagues make short.
Pericles. Act iv, sc. 4, l. 1. [Gower]
Waste time.—*Hamlet,* ii, 2, 89.
Waste these times.—*Henry VIII,* v, 1, 3.

4
I wasted time, and now doth time waste me;
For now hath time made me his numbering clock:
My thoughts are minutes; and with sighs they jar
Their watches on unto mine eyes, the outward watch,
Whereto my finger, like a dial's point,
Is pointing still, in cleansing them from tears.
Richard II. Act v, sc. 5, l. 49. [King Richard] The only use of "cleansing."
Waste of idle hours.—*Richard II,* iii, 4, 66.
My dear time 's waste.—*Sonnets,* xxx.
The chronicle of wasted time.—*Sonnets,* cvi.

5
You waste the treasure of your time.
Twelfth Night. Act ii, sc. 5, l. 85. [Malvolio]
The clock upbraids me with the waste of time.
Twelfth Night. Act iii, sc. 1, l. 141. [Olivia]
But wherefore waste I time?
The Two Gentlemen of Verona. Act i, sc. 1, l. 51. [Valentine]

6 We shall lose our time,
And all be turn'd to barnacles, or to apes
With foreheads villanous low.
The Tempest. Act iv, sc. 1, l. 248. [Caliban] The only use of "barnacles."
Lose my time.—*The Two Gentlemen of Verona,* i, 1, 67.
Loss of time.—*The Two Gentlemen of Verona,* i, 3, 19; *Troilus and Cressida,* ii, 2, 4; *Coriolanus,* iii, 1, 285.
Idle time.—*Two Gentlemen of Verona,* ii, 1, 172.

7 Of this allow,
If ever you have spent time worse ere now;
If never, yet that Time himself doth say
He wishes earnestly you never may.
Winter's Tale. Act iv, sc. 1, l. 29. [Time]

VIII—Time and Place

8
That time and place with this deceit so lawful
May prove coherent.
All's Well that Ends Well. Act iii, sc. 7, l. 38. [Widow] The only use of "coherent."
Had time cohered with place or place with wishing.
Measure for Measure. Act ii, sc. 1, l. 11. [Escalus] The only use of "cohered."
When time and place shall serve.—*Much Ado about Nothing,* v, 1, 264.
Fit in his place and time.—*Love's Labour 's Lost,* i, 1, 98.
Nor time nor place Did then adhere.
Macbeth, i, 7, 50. See under OPPORTUNITY.

9
Time and place will be fruitfully offered.
King Lear. Act iv, sc. 6, l. 269. [Edgar, reading] "Fruitfully" is repeated in *All's Well that Ends Well,* ii, 2, 73: "Most fruitfully."

10
Time and place Doth make against me.
Romeo and Juliet. Act v, sc. 3, l. 224. [Friar Laurence]

IX—Time: The Times

See also Age: The Age

11
Be a child o' the time.
Antony and Cleopatra. Act ii, sc. 7, l. 106. [Antony]
Time is at his period.
Antony and Cleopatra. Act iv, sc. 14, l. 107. [Guard]
This doth fit the time.—*The Taming of the Shrew,* iv, 3, 69.

12
Put not you on the visage of the times.
II Henry IV. Act ii, sc. 3, l. 3. [Northumberland]
Such things become the hatch and brood of time.
II Henry IV. Act iii, sc. 1, l. 86. [Warwick]
Construe the times to their necessities,
And you shall say indeed, it is the time,
And not the king, that doth you injuries.
II Henry IV. Act iv, sc. 1, l. 104. [Westmoreland]
I . . . do arm myself
To welcome the condition of the time,
Which cannot look more hideously upon me
Than I have drawn it in my fantasy.
II Henry IV. Act v, sc. 2, l. 10. [Chief Justice] The only use of "hideously."

13
How I have thought of this and of these times,
I shall recount hereafter.
Julius Cæsar. Act i, sc. 2, l. 164. [Brutus]
These times.—*II Henry IV,* iv, 1, 101; *As You Like It,* ii, 3, 59; *The Merry Wives of Windsor,* ii, 1, 233.

14
Indeed, it is a strange-disposed time.
Julius Cæsar. Act i, sc. 3, l. 33. [Cicero] The only use of "strange-disposed."
Cunning times.—*Merchant of Venice,* iii, 2, 100.
Giddy-paced times.—*Twelfth Night,* ii, 4, 6. The only use of the phrase.
Latter times.—*All's Well that Ends Well,* ii, 3, 8; *Pericles,* i, Gower, 11.
Mortal times.—*Richard II,* i, 1, 177.

Other times.—*All's Well that Ends Well,* iv, 3, 79; *II Henry IV,* iii, 1, 49.
Worn times.—*The Winter's Tale,* v, 1, 142.
Younger times.—*All's Well that Ends Well,* i, 2, 46.
Times past.—*Macbeth,* iii, 1, 77.

1
To beguile the time, Look like the time.
Macbeth. Act i, sc. 5, l. 63. [Lady Macbeth]

2
In your father's time.
The Merchant of Venice. Act i, sc. 2, l. 124. [Nerissa]

Pythagoras' time.—*As You Like It,* iii, 2, 187.
Widow Dido's time.—*The Tempest,* ii, 1, 76.
I' the olden time.—*Macbeth,* iii, 4, 75.
Times of old.—*Troilus and Cressida,* iii, 2, 83.
Antique time.—*Coriolanus,* ii, 3, 126.
Antiquary times.—*Troilus and Cressida,* ii, 3, 262.
Mature time.—*King Lear,* iv, 6, 282.
Former time.—*III Henry VI,* i, 4, 45.
Succeeding times.—*The Rape of Lucrece,* l. 525.
Unborn times.—*I Henry IV,* v, 1, 21.
In time to come.—*Sonnets,* xvii.
Time to come.—*II Henry VI,* iv, 2, 138, and eleven times in later plays.

X—Good Times

3
This is a happier and more comely time.
Coriolanus. Act iv, sc. 6, l. 27. [Sicinius]

Better times.—*Measure for Measure,* v, 1, 496. The only use of the phrase.

4
The nights are wholesome; then no planets strike,
No fairy takes, nor witch hath power to charm,
So hallow'd and so gracious is the time.
Hamlet. Act i, sc. 1, l. 162. [Marcellus]

5
Well, you are come to me in happy time.
Taming of the Shrew, Ind., 1, 90.

In happy time.—*Othello,* iii, 1, 32.
Happy time.—*Romeo and Juliet,* iii, 5, 112; *Julius Cæsar,* ii, 2, 60; *Hamlet,* v, 2, 214.
Blossoming time.—*Measure for Measure,* i, 4, 41.
Golden time.—*III Henry VI,* iii, 2, 127; *II Henry IV,* v, 3, 100; *Sonnets,* iii; *Twelfth Night,* v, 1, 391.
Inviting time.—*Sonnets,* cxxiv.
Royal time.—*Richard III,* iii, 4, 4.

6
Ere we depart, we 'll share a bounteous time
In different pleasures.
Timon of Athens. Act i, sc. 1, l. 263. [Timon]

Then was a blessed time.
Timon of Athens. Act iv, sc. 3, l. 78. [Alcibiades]

XI—Bad Times

7
The time is troublesome.
Cymbeline. Act iv, sc. 3, l. 21. [Cymbeline]

8
The time is out of joint: O cursed spite,
That ever I was born to set it right!
Hamlet. Act i, sc. 5, l. 189. [Hamlet]

Pursy times.—*Hamlet,* iii, 4, 153. "Pursy" occurs again in *Timon of Athens,* v, 4, 12: "Pursy insolence."

9
The times are wild.
II Henry IV. Act i, sc. 1, l. 9. [Northumberland]

As the times do brawl.
II Henry IV. Act i, sc. 3, l. 70. [Hastings]

The scambling and unquiet time.
Henry V. Act i, sc. 1, l. 4. [Canterbury] "Scambling" (contentious) is repeated in v, 2, 218, and in *Much Ado about Nothing,* v, 1, 94.

Unquiet time.—*II Henry IV,* i, 2, 170.

10
In this troublous time what 's to be done?
III Henry VI. Act ii, sc. 1, l. 159. [Richard]

O heavy times, begetting such events!
III Henry VI. Act ii, sc. 5, l. 63. [Son] "Begetting" is repeated in *Cymbeline,* v, 5, 331, and in *The Winter's Tale,* v, 1, 133.

O bloody times!—*III Henry VI,* ii, 5, 73.
Costermonger times.—*II Henry IV,* i, 2, 191. The only use of "costermonger." A costermonger was originally a seller of costard apples, and is here used contemptuously, in the sense of mercenary or commercial.
Despised time.—*Othello,* i, 1, 162.
Distressful times.—*Richard III,* iv, 4, 318.
Hapless time.—*I Henry VI,* iii, 1, 201.
Heavy time.—*King John,* iv, 1, 47.
Ill time.—*The Winter's Tale,* iii, 3, 3.
Luckless time.—*III Henry VI,* v, 6, 45.
Needy time.—*Romeo and Juliet,* iii, 5, 106.
Perilous time.—*King John,* iv, 3, 13.
Rotten times.—*II Henry IV,* iv, 4, 60.
Sad time.—*Richard III,* i, 2, 164; *King Lear,* v, 3, 323.
Sluttish time.—*Sonnets,* lv.
Stern time.—*King Lear,* iii, 7, 63.
Woful time!—*Romeo and Juliet,* iv, 5, 30; *Macbeth,* ii, 3, 64.
Time most accurst!—*The Two Gentlemen of Verona,* v, 4, 71.
Time of lethargy.—*Winter's Tale,* iv, 4, 626.

11
We have seen the best of our time: machinations, hollowness, treachery, and all ruinous disorders, follow us disquietly to our graves.
King Lear. Act i, sc. 2, l. 122. [Gloucester] The only use of "machinations" and "disquietly." "Machination" occurs in the same play, v, 1, 46, and nowhere else.

12
Cruel are the times.
Macbeth. Act iv, sc. 2, l. 18. [Ross]

13
O, these naughty times.
The Merchant of Venice. Act iii, sc. 2, l. 18. [Portia]

Wanton time.—*I Henry IV,* v, 1, 50.

14
Cited up a thousand fearful times, . . .
That had befall'n us.
Richard III. Act i, sc. 4, l. 14. [Clarence]

Fearfull'st time.—*Richard III,* iii, 4, 106. The only use of "fearfull'st."

TIMIDITY

1
A foolish mild man; an honest man, look you, and soon dashed.
Love's Labour's Lost, v, 2, 582. [Costard]
A shy fellow.—*Measure for Measure,* iii, 2, 138.
As shy, as grave.—*Measure for Measure,* v, 1, 54. "Shy" occurs in no other play.
2
She does so blush, and fetches her wind so short, as if she were frayed with a sprite: . . . It is the prettiest villain: she fetches her breath as short as a new-ta'en sparrow.
Troilus and Cressida, iii, 2, 32. [Pandarus] The only use of "frayed" and "new-ta'en."
Timorous accent.—*Othello,* i, 1, 75.
Timorous deer.—*I Henry VI,* iv, 2, 46.
Timorous dreams.—*Richard III,* iv, 1, 85.
Timorous hare.—*Venus and Adonis,* l. 674.
Timorous soul.—*I Henry VI,* iv, 2, 40.
Timorous thief.—*All's Well that Ends Well,* ii, 5, 86.
Timorous wretch.—*III Henry VI,* i, 1, 231.
Timorous yelping.—*Venus and Adonis,* l. 881. The only uses of "timorous." "Timorously" is used once, in *Richard III,* iii, 5, 57.
"Timidity" does not occur in the plays.

TITLES

See also Honours

3
Knighthoods and honours, borne
As I wear mine, are titles but of scorn.
Cymbeline. Act v, sc. 2, l. 6. [Iachimo]
4
A borrow'd title hast thou bought too dear.
I Henry IV. Act v, sc. 3, l. 23. [Douglas]
Crooked titles
Usurp'd from you and your progenitors.
Henry V. Act i, sc. 2, l. 94. [Canterbury]
The farced title running 'fore the king.
Henry V, iv, 1, 280. See KING, 807:5. The only use of "farced," full of pompous phrases.
Bold'st titles.—*The Winter's Tale,* ii, 1, 94.
Doting title.—*Richard III,* iv, 4, 300.
False title.—*Timon of Athens,* iv, 3, 154.
Former title.—*Macbeth,* i, 2, 65.
Glorious titles.—*II Henry VI,* i, 1, 12.
Military title.—*I Henry IV,* iii, 2, 110.
Proper title.—*Henry VIII,* i, 1, 98.
Several titles.—*King John,* i, 1, 13.
Unduteous title.—*The Merry Wives of Windsor,* v, 5, 240. The only use of "unduteous."
5
Him that thou magnifiest with all these titles
Stinking and fly-blown lies here at our feet.
I Henry VI, iv, 7, 76. [La Pucelle] The only use of "magnifiest" and of "fly-blown."
6
My title,
Which is infallible, to England's crown.
II Henry VI. Act ii, sc. 2, l. 4. [York]
York: Will you we show our title to the crown?
If not, our swords shall plead it in the field.
King Henry: What title hast thou, traitor, to the crown?
III Henry VI. Act i, sc. 1, l. 102.
We now forget Our title to the crown.
III Henry VI, v, 7, 46. [King Edward]
My title's good, and better far than his.
III Henry VI. Act i, sc. 1, l. 130. [King Henry]
I know not what to say; my title's weak.
III Henry VI. Act i, sc. 1, l. 134. [King Henry]
How grounded he his title to the crown?
Henry VIII. Act i, sc. 2, l. 144. [King Henry]
7
Write up his title with usurping blood.
III Henry VI. Act i, sc. 1, l. 169. [Warwick]
8
The title honours me and mine.
III Henry VI. Act iv, sc. 1, l. 72. [Queen Elizabeth]
9
What think you of a duchess? have you limbs
To bear that load of title?
Henry VIII. Act ii, sc. 3, l. 38. [Old Lady]
10
Rich In titles, honours, and promotions.
King John. Act ii, sc. 1, l. 492. [King John]
So great a title.—*King John,* iv, 1, 10.
11
Now does he feel his title
Hang loose about him, like a giant's robe
Upon a dwarfish thief.
Macbeth. Act v, sc. 2, l. 20. [Angus]
The devil himself could not pronounce a title
More hateful to mine ear.
Macbeth. Act v, sc. 7, l. 8. [Siward]
12
Tell me once more what title thou dost bear.
The Merchant of Venice. Act ii, sc. 9, l. 35. [Prince of Arragon]
O that I had a title good enough to keep his name company!
The Merchant of Venice. Act iii, sc. 1, l. 15. [Salanio]
13
Bolingbroke: I must find that title in your tongue,
Before I make reply to aught you say.
Berkeley: Mistake me not, my lord; 'tis not my meaning
To raze one title of your honour out.
Richard II. Act ii, sc. 3, l. 72.
14
Then I salute you with this kingly title:
Long live Richard, England's royal king.
Richard III. Act iii, sc. 7, l. 239. [Buckingham]
Kingly title.—*Richard III,* iv, 1, 20.
Regal title.—*III Henry VI,* iii, 3, 28.
Noble title.—*Henry VIII,* iii, 1, 140.
Proud titles.—*I Henry IV,* v, 4, 79; *Sonnets,* xxv.
Titles of good fellowship.—*I Henry IV,* ii, 4, 307.
Title of respect.—*I Henry IV,* i, 3, 8.

TOAD

15
Toad, that under cold stone
Days and nights has thirty one
Swelter'd venom sleeping got,
Boil thou first i' the charmed pot.
Macbeth. Act iv, sc. 1, l. 6. [First Witch]
Toads infect fair founts with venom mud.
The Rape of Lucrece, l. 850.

The toad, ugly and venomous.—*As You Like It,* ii, 1, 13. See under ADVERSITY.
Venom toads.—*III Henry VI,* ii, 2, 138.
Poisonous toad.—*Richard III,* i, 3, 246.

1
That foul bunch-back'd toad!
Richard III. Act iv, sc. 4, l. 81. [Queen Elizabeth] The only use of "bunch-back'd."

Foul toad.—*Othello,* iv, 2, 61.
Fouler toad.—*Richard III,* i, 2, 148.
Black toad.—*Timon of Athens,* iv, 3, 181.
Heavy-gaited toads.—*Richard II,* iii, 2, 15. The only use of "heavy-gaited."
Loathed toad.—*Romeo and Juliet,* iii, 5, 31.

2
Thou toad, thou toad, where is thy brother Clarence?
Richard III. Act iv, sc. 4, l. 145. [Duchess of Gloucester]

A very toad.—*Romeo and Juliet,* ii, 4, 215.
Ten thousand swelling toads.—*Titus Andronicus,* ii, 3, 101.

TO-DAY, see To-morrow

TOE

3
Menenius: What do you think,
You, the great toe of this assembly?
Citizen: I the great toe! why the great toe?
Menenius: For that, being one o' the lowest, basest, poorest,
Of this most wise rebellion, thou go'st foremost.
Coriolanus. Act i, sc. 1, l. 158.

Plays the rogue with my great toe.
II Henry IV, i, 2, 274. See under DISEASE.

4
Toes Unplagued with corns.
Romeo and Juliet, i, 5, 18. See under CORN. The only use of "unplagued."

5
Each one, tripping on his toe,
Will be here with mop and mow.
The Tempest. Act iv, sc. 1, l. 46. [Ariel]

Rises on the toe.—*Troilus and Cressida,* iv, 5, 15.
Turn o' the toe.—*Twelfth Night,* i, 3, 44.
Turn'd on the toe.—*Love's Labour's Lost,* v, 2, 114.
From toe to crown.—*The Tempest,* iv, 1, 233.
Toe of frog.—*Macbeth,* iv, 1, 14.
Toe of the peasant.—*Hamlet,* v, 1, 152.

TOIL

See also Labour, Work

6
The toil o' the war,
A pain that only seems to seek out danger
I' the name of fame and honour.
Cymbeline. Act iii, sc. 3, l. 49. [Belarius]

Toil in war.—*I Henry VI,* iii, 4, 21.
Toil of grace.—*Antony and Cleopatra,* v, 2, 351.

7
Toil'd in my affairs.
II Henry IV, iii, 1, 62. See FELLOWSHIP, 533:1.

Toil'd their unbreathed memories.—*A Midsummer-Night's Dream,* v, 1, 74. The only use of "unbreathed."
Toil'd with works of war.—*Richard II,* iv, 1, 96. "Toil'd" is used a fourth time in *Sonnets,* xxv.
Toil his wits.—*II Henry IV,* i, 1, 83.

8
Forspent with toil, as runners with a race,
I lay me down a little while to breathe.
III Henry VI. Act ii, sc. 3, l. 1. [Warwick] "Forspent" is repeated in *II Henry IV,* i, 1, 37.

9
The madams too, not used to toil.
Henry VIII, i, 1, 24. See under POMP.

Unapt to toil.—*The Taming of the Shrew,* v, 2, 166. See under WOMAN.

10
After such bloody toil, we bid good night.
King John. Act v, sc. 5, l. 6. [Lewis]

Corporal toil.—*Henry V,* i, 1, 16.
Double toil.—*Macbeth,* iv, 1, 20.
Extreme toil.—*I Henry IV,* i, 3, 31.
Heavy toil.—*Love's Labour's Lost,* iv, 3, 326.
Inward toil.—*Richard III,* i, 4, 79.
Nightly toils.—*Hamlet,* i, 1, 72.

11
This toil of ours should be a work of thine.
King John. Act ii, sc. 1, l. 93. [King Philip]

12
I am toiling in a pitch.
Love's Labour's Lost. Act iv, sc. 3, l. 3. [Biron]

Toiling desperately.—*III Henry VI,* iii, 2, 178. The only uses of "toiling."

13
Stop thy unhallow'd toil, vile Montague!
Romeo and Juliet. Act v, sc. 3, l. 54. [Paris]

Is there more toil?
The Tempest. Act i, sc. 2, l. 242. [Ariel]

14
Know by measure
Of their observant toil the enemies' weight.
Troilus and Cressida. Act i, sc. 3, l. 202. [Ulysses]

TOKEN

15
Send forth your amorous token for fair Maudlin.
All's Well that Ends Well. Act v, sc. 3, l. 68. [King] The only mention of Maudlin.

I bade her, if her fortunes ever stood
Necessitied to help, that by this token
I would relieve her.
All's Well that Ends Well. Act v, sc. 3, l. 84. [King] The only use of "necessitied."

16
Some nobler token have I kept apart
For Livia and Octavia, to induce
Their mediation.
Antony and Cleopatra. Act v, sc. 2, l. 168. [Cleopatra] "Mediation" is repeated in *II Henry IV,* iv, 4, 25.

Receive no tokens.—*Hamlet,* ii, 2, 144.

17
This token serveth for a flag of truce
Betwixt ourselves and all our followers.
I Henry VI. Act iii, sc. 1, l. 138. [Gloucester]

Suffolk: But, madam, I must trouble you again;
No loving token to his majesty?
Margaret: Yes, my good lord, a pure unspotted heart,
Never yet taint with love, I send the king.
Suffolk: And this withal. [*Kisses her.*]
Margaret: That for thyself: I will not so presume

To send such peevish tokens to a king.
I Henry VI. Act v, sc. 3, l. 180.

1
The Lord's tokens on you do I see.
Love's Labour 's Lost. Act v, sc. 2, l. 423. [Biron]

2 Are there no other tokens
Between you 'greed?
Measure for Measure. Act iv, sc. 1, l. 41. [Duke]

In token of the which.—*Coriolanus,* i, 9, 60.
In token of which duty.—*The Taming of the Shrew,* v, 2, 178. See 1702:9.
On that token.—*The Merry Wives of Windsor,* iv, 6, 44.

3 She so loves the token,
For he conjured her she should ever keep it,
That she reserves it evermore about her
To kiss and talk to.
Othello. Act iii, sc. 3, l. 293. [Emilia]

This is some token from a newer friend.
Othello. Act iii, sc. 4, l. 181. [Bianca]

This is some minx's token.
Othello. Act iv, sc. 1, l. 159. [Bianca] "Minx" is repeated in iii, 3, 475, and in *Twelfth Night,* iii, 4, 133.

I never gave him token.
Othello. Act v, sc. 2, l. 61. [Desdemona]

Antique token.—*Othello,* v, 2, 216.
Watery token.—*The Rape of Lucrece,* l. 1748.
Token of reprieve.—*King Lear,* v, 3, 249.
Token of thine honour.—*Timon of Athens,* v, 4, 50.
Signs and tokens.—*Titus Andronicus,* ii, 4, 5.

4
Pandarus: I 'll be with you, niece, by and by.
Cressida: To bring, uncle?
Pandarus: Ay, a token from Troilus.
Cressida: By the same token, you are a bawd.
Troilus and Cressida. Act i, sc. 2, l. 305.

By some token.—*Comedy of Errors,* iv, 1, 56.
By this token.—*Richard III,* iv, 2, 80; *Measure for Measure,* iv, 3, 144.
A token from her daughter.—*Troilus and Cressida,* v, 1, 45.

5
Give me some token for the surety of it.
Troilus and Cressida. Act v, sc. 2, l. 60. [Diomedes]

Give her no token but stones.—*The Two Gentlemen of Verona,* i, 1, 148.

6
It seems you loved her not, to leave her token.
The Two Gentlemen of Verona. Act iv, sc. 4, l. 79. [Julia]

TOMB

See also Grave, Monument

7
Within their chiefest temple I 'll erect
A tomb, wherein his corpse shall be interr'd:
Upon the which, that every one may read,
Shall be engraved the sack of Orleans.
I Henry VI. Act ii, sc. 2, l. 12. [Talbot] Referring to the Earl of Salisbury.

8
Regan: I am glad to see your highness. . . .
King Lear: If thou shouldst not be glad,
I would divorce me from thy mother's tomb,
Sepulchring an adultress.
King Lear. Act ii, sc. 4, l. 130. The only use of "sepulchring" and of "adultress." "Adulteress" occurs four times.

9
Gilded tombs do worms infold.
The Merchant of Venice. Act ii, sc. 7, l. 69. [Prince of Morocco, reading]

Gilded tomb.—*Sonnets,* ci.
Brazen tombs.—*Love's Labour 's Lost,* i, 1, 2.
Tombs of brass.—*Sonnets,* cvii.
Glorious tomb.—*III Henry VI,* i, 4, 16.
Tomb of orphans' tears.—*Henry VIII,* iii, 2, 399.
Honourable tomb.—*Richard II,* iii, 3, 105.

10
A tomb Must cover thy sweet eyes.
A Midsummer-Night's Dream. Act v, sc. 1, l. 335. [Thisbe]

11
Benedick: If a man do not erect in this age his own tomb ere he dies, he shall live no longer in monument than the bell rings and the widow weeps.
Beatrice: And how long is that, think you?
Benedick: Question: why, an hour in clamour and a quarter in rheum.
Much Ado about Nothing. Act v, sc. 2, l. 79.

12 That same ancient vault
Where all the kindred of the Capulets lie.
Romeo and Juliet. Act iv, sc. 1, l. 111. [Friar Laurence]

The vault,
To whose foul mouth no healthsome air breathes in.
Romeo and Juliet. Act iv, sc. 3, l. 33. [Juliet] The only use of "healthsome."

A vault, an ancient receptacle,
Where, for these many hundred years, the bones
Of all my buried ancestors are pack'd.
Romeo and Juliet. Act iv, sc. 3, l. 39. [Juliet]

13
Thou detestable maw, thou womb of death,
Gorged with the dearest morsel of the earth,
Thus I enforce thy rotten jaws to open,
And, in despite, I 'll cram thee with more food!
Romeo and Juliet. Act v, sc. 3, l. 45. [Romeo]

This palace of dim night.
Romeo and Juliet. Act v, sc. 3, l. 107. [Romeo]

That nest
Of death, contagion, and unnatural sleep.
Romeo and Juliet. Act v, sc. 3, l. 151. [Friar Laurence]

14 If thou be merciful,
Open the tomb, lay me with Juliet.
Romeo and Juliet. Act v, sc. 3, l. 72. [Paris]

Open These dead men's tombs.—*Romeo and Juliet,* v, 3, 201
Ope the tomb.—*Romeo and Juliet,* v, 3, 283.
Dead man's tomb.—*Romeo and Juliet,* v, 2, 307.

15
Stain not thy tomb with blood.
Titus Andronicus. Act i, sc. 1, l. 116. [Tamora]

Traitors, away! he rests not in this tomb.
Titus Andronicus. Act i, sc. 1, l. 349. [Titus]

1 By my father's reverend tomb.
Titus Andronicus. Act ii, sc. 3, l. 296. [Titus]

Your great-grandsire's tomb.—*Henry V,* i, 2, 103. "Great-grandsire" is repeated in *II Henry IV,* iv, 4, 128.

Gloucester's tomb.—*II Henry VI,* iii, 2, 78.

Ninus' tomb.—*A Midsummer-Night's Dream,* iii, 1, 100; v, 1, 139. Rendered "Ninny's tomb" in iii, 1, 99; v, 1, 204; 268. The only mention of Ninus.

King Richard's tomb.—*Richard II,* v, 1, 12.

2 So went he suited to his watery tomb.
Twelfth Night. Act v, sc. 1, l. 241. [Viola]

TO-MORROW

See also Future

3 Know, my hearts, I hope well of to-morrow.
Antony and Cleopatra. Act iv, sc. 2, l. 42. [Antony]

To-morrow is the day.—*Antony and Cleopatra,* iv, 3, 1.

To-morrow is the joyful day.
As You Like It. Act v, sc. 3, l. 1. [Touchstone]

To-morrow; to-day; presently.—*Coriolanus,* iv, 5, 229.

4 To-morrow, good Sir Michael, is a day
Wherein the fortune of ten thousand men
Must bide the touch.
I Henry IV. Act iv, sc. 4, l. 8. [York]

Some good thing comes to-morrow.
II Henry IV, iv, 2, 84. See under MERRIMENT.

5 To-morrow then belike shall be the day.
III Henry VI. Act iv, sc. 3, l. 7. [Watch]

6 I will come to your worship to-morrow morning.
Love's Labour 's Lost, iii, 1, 161. "To-morrow morning" occurs thirteen times.

Sup with me to-morrow night.—*II Henry VI,* i, 4, 84. "To-morrow night" is used nine times.

7 O, never Shall sun that morrow see!
Macbeth. Act i, sc. 5, l. 61. [Lady Macbeth]

8 To-morrow, and to-morrow, and to-morrow,
Creeps in this petty pace from day to day
To the last syllable of recorded time.
Macbeth. Act v, sc. 5, l. 19. [Macbeth] See PAST, 1124:8.

9 Let not to-morrow then ensue to-day.
Richard II. Act ii, sc. 1, l. 197. [York]

To-day, to-day, unhappy day, too late,
O'erthrows thy joys, friends, fortune and thy state.
Richard II. Act iii, sc. 2, l. 71. [Salisbury]

Although to-day thou fill
Thy hungry eyes even till they wink with fullness,
To-morrow see again.
Sonnets. No. lvi.

Kind is my love to-day, to-morrow kind.
Sonnets. No. cv. See under LOVE: CONSTANT.

Not to-day, O Lord,
O, not to-day, think not upon the fault
My father made in compassing the crown!
Henry V. Act iv, sc. 1, l. 309. [King Henry]

10 To-morrow, then, I judge a happy day.
Richard III. Act iii, sc. 4, l. 6. [Ely]

A goodly day to-morrow.—*Richard III,* v, 3, 21.

To-morrow or next day.—*Richard III,* iii, 7, 60.

11 Here will I lie to-night;
But where to-morrow? Well, all 's one for that.
Richard III. Act v, sc. 3, l. 8. [King Richard]

12 Let 's want no discipline, make no delay;
For, lords, to-morrow is a busy day.
Richard III. Act v, sc. 3, l. 17. [King Richard]

13 Be patient; to-morrow 't shall be mended.
The Taming of the Shrew. Act iv, sc. 1, l. 179. [Petruchio]

TONGUE

See also Heart and Tongue; Language

14 At this time His tongue obey'd his hand.
All 's Well that Ends Well, i, 2, 40. See under HONOUR.

15 Mince not the general tongue.
Antony and Cleopatra, i, 2, 109. See under CANDOUR.

An host of tongues.—*Antony and Cleopatra,* ii, 5, 87.

Sued-for tongues.—*Coriolanus,* ii, 3, 216. The only use of "sued-for."

Tongues o' the common mouth.—*Coriolanus,* iii, 1, 22.

World's large tongue.—*Love's Labour 's Lost,* v, 2, 852. See under CHARACTER.

16 Their tongues rot That speak against us!
Antony and Cleopatra. Act iii, sc. 7, l. 16. [Cleopatra]

Accursed be that tongue that tells me so,
For it hath cow'd my better part of man!
Macbeth. Act v, sc. 8, l. 17. [Macbeth]

17 Tongues I 'll hang on every tree.
As You Like It. Act iii, sc. 2, l. 135. [Celia]

18 We are to put our tongues into those wounds and speak for them.
Coriolanus. Act ii, sc. 3, l. 7. [Third Citizen]

Put a tongue in every wound of Cæsar.—*Julius Cæsar,* iii, 2, 232.

19 A beggar's tongue
Make motion through my lips.
Coriolanus. Act iii, sc. 2, l. 117. [Coriolanus]

20 By thine own tongue thou art condemn'd, and must
Endure our law.
Cymbeline. Act v, sc. 5, l. 298. [Cymbeline]

21 Forbad my tongue to speak.
I Henry IV. Act i, sc. 3, l. 220. [Hotspur]

I, that have not well the gift of tongue.
I Henry IV. Act v, sc. 2, l. 78. [Hotspur]

I have a whole school of tongues in this belly of mine, and not a tongue of them all speaks any other word but my name.
II Henry IV. Act iv, sc. 3, l. 20. [Falstaff]

1 So York must sit and fret and bite his tongue.
II Henry VI. Act i, sc. 1, l. 230. [York]

Bite thy tongue.—*III Henry VI,* i, 4, 47.

Shall we bite our tongues, and in dumb shows
Pass the remainder of our hateful days?
Titus Andronicus. Act iii, sc. 1, l. 131. [Titus]

2 This tongue hath parley'd unto foreign kings
For your behoof.
II Henry VI. Act iv, sc. 7, l. 82. [Say] The only use of "parley'd."

3 Let thy tongue be equal with thy heart.
II Henry VI, v, 1, 89. See under THOUGHT.

Let thy tongue detect thy base-born heart.
III Henry VI. Act ii, sc. 2, l. 143. [Richard]

My tongue will tell the anger of my heart,
Or else my heart concealing it will break.
The Taming of the Shrew. Act iv, sc. 3, l. 77. [Katharina]

Tongue and heart.—*Measure for Measure,* i, 1, 46.

Tongue far from heart.—*Measure for Measure,* i, 4, 33. See also HEART AND TONGUE.

4 Well I wot, thou hast thy mother's tongue.
III Henry VI. Act ii, sc. 2, l. 134. [Richard]

Mother's tongue.—*Love's Labour's Lost,* i, 2, 101.

Chapmen's tongues.—*Love's Labour's Lost,* ii, 1, 16. See under BEAUTY for definition.

Honour's tongue.—*I Henry IV,* i, 1, 81.

Rich music's tongue.—*Romeo and Juliet,* ii, 6, 27.

Neat's tongue.—*Merchant of Venice,* i, 1, 112.

Rumour's tongues.—*II Henry IV,* Ind., 39; *King John,* iv, 2, 123.

Schoolboy's tongue.—*Love's Labour's Lost,* v, 2, 403.

Shepherd's tongue.—*Passionate Pilgrim,* l. 370.

Tongues of bawds.—*I Henry IV,* i, 2, 9.

Tongue of dog.—*Macbeth,* iv, 1, 15.

Tongues of heaven.—*King John,* iii, 4, 158.

Tongue of loss.—*Twelfth Night,* v, 1, 61.

Tongue of mortal.—*Love's Labour's Lost,* iv, 3, 42.

5 Let my tongue excuse all.
Henry VIII. Act v, sc. 3, l. 149. [Chancellor]

6 Thy tongue against thy tongue.
King John, iii, 1, 265. See under OATH.

7 O, that my tongue were in the thunder's mouth!
Then with a passion would I shake the world.
King John. Act iii, sc. 4, l. 38. [Constance]

My tongue shall hush again this storm of war
And make fair weather in your blustering land.
King John. Act v, sc. 1, l. 20. [Pandulph]

8 Whose tongue soe'er speaks false,
Not truly speaks.
King John, iv, 3, 91. See LIE, 859:1.

9 He hath a witchcraft . . . in 's tongue.
Henry VIII. Act iii, sc. 2, l. 18. [Chamberlain]

10 At the tongue's end.
Love's Labour's Lost. Act iii, sc. 1, l. 12. [Moth]

11 Love's tongue proves dainty Bacchus gross in taste.
Love's Labour's Lost, iv, 3, 339. See under LOVE.

12 His tongue filed.
Love's Labour's Lost. Act v, sc. 1, l. 11. [Holofernes]

Smooth not thy tongue with filed talk.
The Passionate Pilgrim, l. 306.

13 I have ne'er a tongue in my head.
The Merchant of Venice. Act ii, sc. 2, l. 166. [Launcelot]

I have no tongue but one.
Measure for Measure. Act ii, sc. 4, l. 139. [Isabella]

I have no tongue.—*II Henry IV,* ii, 2, 179. See under SILENCE.

She hath no tongue.—*Titus Andronicus,* ii, 4, 7.

Hast not a tongue?—*I Henry VI,* v, 3, 68.

'What! canst thou talk?' quoth she, 'hast thou a tongue?
O, would thou hadst not, or I had no hearing!'
Venus and Adonis, l. 427.

14 By my soul I swear
There is no power in the tongue of man
To alter me.
The Merchant of Venice. Act iv, sc. 1, l. 240. [Shylock]

Frame thy tongue.—*A Midsummer-Night's Dream,* iii, 2, 360.

Tongue, lose thy light.—*A Midsummer-Night's Dream,* v, 1, 309.

15 Half Signior Benedick's tongue in Count John's mouth.
Much Ado about Nothing. Act ii, sc. 1, l. 12. [Leonato]

Brutus' tongue.—*Julius Cæsar,* v, 5, 39.

Tongue of Isabel.—*Measure for Measure,* iv, 3, 111.

16 I cannot endure my Lady Tongue.
Much Ado about Nothing. Act ii, sc. 1, l. 284. [Benedick]

17 I had rather have this tongue cut from my mouth
Than it should do offence.
Othello. Act ii, sc. 3, l. 221. [Iago]

Ere my tongue
Shall wound my honour with such feeble wrong,
Or sound so base a parle, my teeth shall tear
The slavish motive of recanting fear,
And spit it bleeding in his high disgrace.
Richard II. Act i, sc. 1, l. 190. [Bolingbroke]

1
Will not my tongue be mute?
The Rape of Lucrece, l. 227.
Her husband's shallow tongue.
The Rape of Lucrece, l. 78.
Care-tuned tongue.—*Richard II,* iii, 2, 92. The only use of "care-tuned."
Idle tongue.—*Hamlet,* iii, 4, 11.
Iron tongue.—*King John,* iii, 3, 38; *A Midsummer-Night's Dream,* v, 1, 370.
Lamenting tongue.—*Rape of Lucrece,* l. 1465.
Poor tongue.—*The Comedy of Errors,* v, 1, 308; *The Rape of Lucrece,* l. 1718.
Self-same tongue.—*Measure for Measure,* ii, 4, 173.
Solemn tongue.—*II Henry VI,* iii, 2, 158; *Titus Andronicus,* v, 3, 81.

2
O, but they say the tongues of dying men
Enforce attention like deep harmony.
Richard II. Act ii, sc. 1, l. 5. [Gaunt]
His tongue is now a stringless instrument.
Richard II. Act ii, sc. 1, l. 149. [Northumberland] The only use of "stringless."

3
My tongue hath but a heavier tale to say.
Richard II. Act iii, sc. 2, l. 197. [Scroop]

4
O God, O God! that e'er this tongue of mine,
That laid the sentence of dread banishment
On yon proud man, should take it off again
With words of sooth!
Richard II. Act iii, sc. 3, l. 133. [King Richard]
Tongues of soothers.—*I Henry IV,* iv, 1, 7. The only use of "soothers."

5
Whilst all tongues cried 'God save thee, Bolingbroke!'
Richard II, v, 2, 11. [Duchess of York]
All tongues speak of him.—*Coriolanus,* ii, 1, 221. See under POPULARITY.

6
No joyful tongue gave him welcome home.
Richard II. Act v, sc. 2, l. 29. [York]

7
My tongue cleave to my roof within my mouth.
Richard II. Act v, sc. 3, l. 31. [Aumerle]
My tongue [might freeze] to the roof of my mouth.
The Taming of the Shrew, iv, 1, 7. [Grumio]

8
Have I a tongue to doom my brother's death,
And shall the same give pardon to a slave?
Richard III. Act ii, sc. 1, l. 102. [Edward]

9
Tongues, the voice of souls.
Sonnets. No. lxix.

10
For she had a tongue with a tang.
The Tempest. Act ii, sc. 2, l. 52. [Stephano]
Let thy tongue tang arguments of state.
Twelfth Night, ii, 5, 164.
Let thy tongue tang with arguments of state.
Twelfth Night, iii, 4, 78. The only uses of "tang."

11
Keep a good tongue in your head.
The Tempest. Act iii, sc. 2, l. 39. [Stephano]
While thou livest, keep a good tongue in thy head.
The Tempest. Act iii, sc. 2, l. 120. [Stephano]
Good tongue.—*Coriolanus,* v, 1, 36; *Henry VIII,* iii, 1, 55.
Root o' the tongue.—*Timon of Athens,* v, 1, 136.

12
That man that hath a tongue, I say, is no man,
If with his tongue he cannot win a woman.
The Two Gentlemen of Verona. Act iii, sc. 1, l. 104. [Valentine]

II—Sweet Tongues

13
Your favour is well approved by your tongue.
Coriolanus. Act iv, sc. 3, l. 9. [Volsce]
But, sure, if you
Would be your country's pleader, your good tongue
More than the instant army we can make,
Might stop our countrymen.
Coriolanus. Act v, sc. 1, l. 35. [Menenius] "Pleader" is repeated in ii, 1, 263, and occurs in no other play.
Princely tongue.—*I Henry IV,* v, 2, 57.

14
Let the candied tongue lick absurd pomp.
Hamlet. Act iii, sc. 2, l. 65. [Hamlet] "Candied" is repeated in *Timon of Athens,* iv, 3, 226, and in *The Tempest,* ii, 1, 279.
Flattering tongue.—*As You Like It,* iv, 1, 189.
Pleading tongue.—*Venus and Adonis,* l. 217.

15
Lend me the flourish of all gentle tongues.
Love's Labour's Lost. Act iv, sc. 3, l. 238. [Biron]
Gentle tongue.—*A Midsummer-Night's Dream,* iii, 2, 287.
Fair tongue.—*Love's Labour's Lost,* ii, 1, 72.
A passing pleasing tongue.—*Richard III,* i, 1, 94.
Sugar'd tongue.—*The Rape of Lucrece,* l. 893.

16
Thy tongue some say of breeding breathes.
King Lear. Act v, sc. 3, l. 143. [Edmund]

17
Well learned is that tongue that well can thee commend.
Love's Labour's Lost. Act iv, sc. 2, l. 116. [Sir Nathaniel] Repeated in *The Passionate Pilgrim,* l. 64.

18
Biron: Pay him the due of honey-tongued Boyet.
King: A blister on his sweet tongue.
Love's Labour's Lost. Act v, sc. 2, l. 334. The only use of "honey-tongued."
Sweet tongue.—*Titus Andronicus,* ii, 4, 49.
If I prove honey-mouth'd, let my tongue blister
And never to my red-look'd anger be
The trumpet any more.
The Winter's Tale. Act ii, sc. 2, l. 33. [Paulina] The only use of "honey-mouth'd" and "red-look'd."

19
For maiden-tongued he was, and thereof free.
A Lover's Complaint, l. 100. The only use of "maiden-tongued."

1 Your tongue's sweet air
More tuneable than lark to shepherd's ear,
When wheat is green, when hawthorn buds appear.
A Midsummer-Night's Dream. Act i, sc. 1, l. 183. [Helena]

My tongue should catch your tongue's sweet melody.
A Midsummer-Night's Dream. Act i, sc. 1, l. 189. [Helena]

2
Had tongue at will and yet was never loud.
Othello, ii, 1, 150. See under CHARACTER.

3
O, love's best habit is a soothing tongue.
The Passionate Pilgrim, l. 11.

4
Soft-slow tongue, true mark of modesty.
The Rape of Lucrece, l. 1220. The only use of "soft-slow."

With soft low tongue.—*The Taming of the Shrew,* Ind., 1, 114.

A slow tongue.—*Twelfth Night,* iii, 4, 81.

5
How silver-sweet sound lovers' tongues by night,
Like softest music to attending ears!
Romeo and Juliet. Act ii, sc. 2, l. 166. [Romeo] The only use of "silver-sweet."

What early tongue so sweet saluteth me?
Romeo and Juliet. Act ii, sc. 3, l. 32. [Friar Laurence]

Every tongue that speaks
But Romeo's name speaks heavenly eloquence.
Romeo and Juliet. Act iii, sc. 2, l. 32. [Juliet]

6
You are my all the world, and I must strive
To know my shames and praises from your tongue.
Sonnets. No. cxii.

That tongue that ever sweet
Was used in giving gentle doom.
Sonnets. No. cxlv.

7 Many a time
The harmony of their tongues hath into bondage
Brought my too diligent ear.
The Tempest. Act iii, sc. 1, l. 40. [Ferdinand]

8 Knit all . . . ears
To his experienced tongue.
Troilus and Cressida. Act i, sc. 3, l. 67. [Ulysses]

9
If love have lent you twenty thousand tongues,
And every tongue more moving than your own,
Bewitching like the wanton mermaid's songs,
Yet from mine ear the tempting tune is blown.
Venus and Adonis, l. 775. The only use of "bewitching."

Whose tongue is music now?
Venus and Adonis, l. 1077.

10
There is no tongue that moves, none, none, i' the world,
So soon as yours could win me.
Winter's Tale. Act i, sc. 2, l. 20. [Polixenes]

His subduing tongue.
A Lover's Complaint, l. 120. See under ARGUMENT for full quotation.

III—Rude Tongues

11
The harsh and boisterous tongue of war.
II Henry IV, iv, 1, 49. See under WAR.

Tongue of war.—*King John,* v, 2, 164.

12
Suffolk's imperial tongue is stern and rough,
Used to command, untaught to plead for favour.
II Henry VI. Act iv, sc. 1, l. 120. [Suffolk]

Our tongue is rough, coz, and my condition is not smooth.
Henry V. Act v, sc. 2, l. 313. [King Henry]

13 Such a tongue
As I am glad I have not, though not to have it
Hath lost me in your liking.
King Lear. Act i, sc. 1, l. 234. [Cordelia]

14
How dares thy harsh rude tongue sound this unpleasing news?
Richard II. Act iii, sc. 4, l. 74. [Queen]

I know your daring tongue
Scorns to unsay what once it hath deliver'd.
Richard II. Act iv, sc. 1, l. 8. [Bagot]

15
My tongue could never learn sweet smoothing words.
Richard III. Act i, sc. 2, l. 169. [Gloucester]

16
I'll use that tongue I have: if wit flow from 't
As boldness from my bosom, let 't not be doubted
I shall do good.
Winter's Tale. Act ii, sc. 2, l. 52. [Paulina]

IV—Poisonous Tongues

17
My tongue hath wrong'd him.
As You Like It. Act ii, sc. 7, l. 84. [Jaques]

18
As poisonous-tongued as handed.
Cymbeline. Act iii, sc. 2, l. 5. [Pisanio] The only use of the phrase.

With tongue in venom steep'd.
Hamlet. Act ii, sc. 2, l. 533. [First Player]

19
The envious barking of your saucy tongue.
I Henry VI. Act iii, sc. 4, l. 33. [Orleans]

Envious carping tongue.
I Henry VI. Act iv, sc. 1, l. 90. [Bastard]

Envious tongues.—*Henry VIII,* iii, 2, 446.
Aspics' tongues.—*Othello,* iii, 3, 450.
Base tongue.—*Coriolanus,* iii, 2, 100.
Bitter tongues.—*Titus Andronicus,* iii, 1, 234; v, 1, 150.
Cloven tongues.—*The Tempest,* ii, 2, 13.
Forked tongue.—*II Henry VI,* iii, 2, 259.
Ignorant tongues.—*Henry VIII,* i, 2, 72.
Lying tongue.—*Coriolanus,* iii, 3, 72.
The serpent's tongue.—*A Midsummer-Night's Dream,* v, 1, 440.

Slander's tongue.—*II Henry VI,* iii, 2, 68.

Slanderous tongues, see under SLANDER.

1 This knave's tongue begins to double.
II Henry VI. Act ii, sc. 3, l. 94. [York]

You have a double tongue within your mask.
Love's Labour's Lost. Act v, sc. 2, l. 245. [Longaville] See also under SNAKE.

An adder did it; for with doubler tongue
Than mine, thou serpent, never adder stung.
A Midsummer-Night's Dream. Act iii, sc. 2, l. 72. [Hermia] The only use of "doubler."

Double tongue.—*A Midsummer-Night's Dream,* ii, 2, 9; *Richard II,* iii, 2, 21.

2 Whose tongue more poisons than the adder's tooth!
III Henry VI. Act i, sc. 4, l. 112. [York]

3 Tongues spit their duties out, and cold hearts freeze
Allegiance in them.
Henry VIII. Act i, sc. 2, l. 61. [Queen Katharine]

4 That tongue that tells the story of thy days,
Making lascivious comments on thy sport,
Cannot dispraise but in a kind of praise.
Sonnets. No. xcv.

V—Wagging Tongues

5 I find my tongue is too foolhardy.
All's Well that Ends Well. Act iv, sc. 1, l. 32. [Parolles] "Foolhardy" is repeated in *Richard II,* v, 3, 43.

Tongue, I must put you into a butter-woman's mouth and buy myself another of Bajazet's mule, if you prattle me into these perils.
All's Well that Ends Well. Act iv, sc. 1, l. 44. [Parolles] The only use of "butter-woman." "Butter-women" occurs in *As You Like It,* iii, 2, 103. The only mention of Bajazet. His mule has proved a troublesome beast for the critics, who have never definitely turned up the story which Shakespeare referred to.

6 Repent that e'er thy tongue
Hath so betray'd thine act.
Antony and Cleopatra. Act ii, sc. 7, l. 83. [Pompey]

Cry 'holla' to thy tongue, I prithee; it curvets unseasonably.
As You Like It. Act iii, sc. 2, l. 257. [Celia] The only use of "curvets." "Curvet" occurs in *All's Well that Ends Well,* ii, 3, 299. The only use of "unseasonably."

7 Be not thy tongue thy own shame's orator.
The Comedy of Errors. Act iii, sc. 2, l. 10. [Luciana]

8 I cannot bring My tongue to such a pace.
Coriolanus. Act ii, sc. 3, l. 56. [Coriolanus]

9 What have I done, that thou darest wag thy tongue
In noise so rude against me?
Hamlet. Act iii, sc. 4, l. 39. [Queen]

No discerner Durst wag his tongue.
Henry VIII, i, 1, 32. The only use of "discerner."

You play the spaniel,
And think with wagging of your tongue to win me.
Henry VIII. Act v, sc. 3, l. 126. [King]

10 My tongue is weary.
II Henry IV, Epil., 35.

11 He hath a killing tongue and a quiet sword; by the means whereof a' breaks words, and keeps whole weapons.
Henry V. Act iii, sc. 2, l. 35. [Boy]

Fellows of infinite tongue.—*Henry V,* v, 2, 164.

12 He used his lavish tongue
And did upbraid me with my father's death:
Which obloquy set bars before my tongue
Else with the like I had requited him.
I Henry VI. Act ii, sc. 5, l. 47. [Plantagenet] "Obloquy" is repeated in *All's Well that Ends Well,* iv, 2, 44; and *The Rape of Lucrece,* l. 523.

Chattering tongue.—*The Taming of the Shrew,* iv, 2, 58. "Chattering" is repeated in *III Henry VI,* v, 6, 48: "Chattering pies."

Eloquent tongues.—*Henry V,* iii, 7, 37.

Liberal tongue.—*Richard II,* ii, 1, 229.

Nimble tongue.—*Love's Labour's Lost,* v, 2, 747.

Rattling tongue.—*Midsummer-Night's Dream,* v, 1, 102.

Ready tongue.—*II Henry IV,* i, 1, 84.

Riotous tongue.—*II Henry VI,* iv, 1, 64.

13 Why, how now, long-tongued Warwick! dare you speak?
III Henry VI. Act ii, sc. 2, l. 102. [Queen Margaret]

Long-tongued babbling.—*Titus Andronicus,* iv, 2, 150. The only uses of "long-tongued."

14 I prithee, give no limits to my tongue.
III Henry VI. Act ii, sc. 2, l. 119. [King Henry]

I do know the scope
And warrant limited unto my tongue.
King John. Act v, sc. 2, l. 122. [Bastard]

15 Peace, wilful boy, or I will charm your tongue.
III Henry VI. Act v, sc. 5, l. 31. [King Edward]

I will charm him first to keep his tongue.
The Taming of the Shrew. Act i, sc. 1, l. 214. [Lucentio]

Iago: Go to, charm your tongue.
Emilia: I will not charm my tongue; I am bound to speak.
Othello. Act v, sc. 2, l. 183.

Rein thy tongue.—*Love's Labour's Lost,* v, 2, 662.

16 I hear a tongue, shriller than all the music,
Cry 'Cæsar!' Speak; Cæsar is turn'd to hear.
Julius Cæsar. Act i, sc. 2, l. 16. [Cæsar] The only use of "shriller."

Vouchsafe good morrow from a feeble tongue.
Julius Cæsar. Act ii, sc. 1, l. 313. [Ligarius]
This tongue had not offended so to-day,
If Cassius might have ruled.
Julius Cæsar. Act v, sc. 1, l. 46. [Cassius]

1
He gives the bastinado with his tongue;
Our ears are cudgell'd.
King John. Act ii, sc. 1, l. 463. [Bastard]
"Bastinado" is repeated in *As You Like It,* v, 1, 60, and in *I Henry IV,* ii, 4, 370.
Now I breathe again
Aloft the flood, and can give audience
To any tongue, speak it of what it will.
King John. Act iv, sc. 2, l. 138. [King John]

2
His tongue, all impatient to speak and not see,
Did stumble with haste in his eyesight to be.
Love's Labour 's Lost. Act ii, sc. 1, l. 238. [Boyet]

3 Chastise with the valour of my tongue
All that impedes thee.
Macbeth. Act i, sc. 5, l. 28. [Lady Macbeth]
The only use of "impedes."
Thou comest to use thy tongue; thy story quickly.
Macbeth. Act v, sc. 5, l. 29. [Macbeth]
Use of tongue.—*The Tempest,* iii, 3, 38.

4
I would my horse had the speed of your tongue, and so good a continuer.
Much Ado about Nothing. Act i, sc. 1, l. 142. [Benedick] The only use of "continuer."
What pace is this that thy tongue keeps?
Much Ado about Nothing. Act iii, sc. 4, l. 93. [Beatrice]
'He hath the tongues;' 'That I believe,' said she, 'for he swore a thing to me on Monday night, which he forswore on Tuesday morning; there 's a double tongue; there 's two tongues.'
Much Ado about Nothing. Act v, sc. 1, l. 167. [Don Pedro]

5
Teach my tongue to be so long.
The Passionate Pilgrim, l. 350.

6
How durst thy tongue move anger to our face?
Pericles. Act i, sc. 2, l. 54. [Pericles]

7
First, like a trumpet, doth his tongue begin
To sound a parley to his heartless foe.
The Rape of Lucrece, l. 470.
My tongue shall utter all.
The Rape of Lucrece, l. 1076.

8
This tongue that runs so roundly in thy head
Should run thy head from thy unreverent shoulders.
Richard II. Act ii, sc. 1, l. 122. [King Richard]
Unreverent roles.—*The Taming of the Shrew,* iii, 2, 114.
Unreverent Gloster!—*I Henry VI,* iii, 1, 49. The only uses of "unreverent."

9
Fie, what a spendthrift is he of his tongue!
The Tempest. Act ii, sc. 1, l. 23. [Antonio]
"Spendthrift" is repeated in *Hamlet,* iv, 7, 123.
So glib of tongue.—*Troilus and Cressida,* iv, 5, 58. See under COQUETRY.

10
Fie, fie, unreverend tongue!
The Two Gentlemen of Verona. Act ii, sc. 6, l. 14. [Proteus]
Unreverend boy.—*King John,* i, 1, 227.
Unreverend friar.—*Measure for Measure,* v, 1, 307. The only uses of "unreverend."

VI—Women's Tongues

11
Look'd black upon me; struck me with her tongue,
Most serpent-like, upon the very heart.
King Lear. Act ii, sc. 4, l. 162. [King Lear]
The only use of "serpent-like."

12
The tongues of mocking wenches are as keen
As is the razor's edge invisible,
Cutting a smaller hair than may be seen,
Above the sense of sense.
Love's Labour 's Lost. Act v, sc. 2, l. 256. [Boyet]

13
How might she tongue me! Yet reason dares her no.
Measure for Measure. Act iv, sc. 4, l. 28. [Angelo]

14 Would she give you so much of her lips
As of her tongue she oft bestows on me,
You 'ld have enough.
Othello. Act ii, sc. 1, l. 101. [Iago]
She puts her tongue a little in her heart,
And chides with thinking.
Othello. Act ii, sc. 1, l. 107. [Iago]

15
I smiling credit her false-speaking tongue.
The Passionate Pilgrim, l. 7. Repeated in *Sonnets,* cxxxviii. The only uses of "false-speaking" as an adjective.

16
With untuned tongue she hoarsely calls her maid.
The Rape of Lucrece, l. 1214. The only use of "hoarsely."

17
'Tis not the trial of a woman's war,
The bitter clamour of two eager tongues.
Richard II. Act i, sc. 1, l. 48. [Mowbray]

18
Make her bear the penance of her tongue.
The Taming of the Shrew. Act i, sc. 1, l. 89. [Gremio]
And do you tell me of a woman's tongue
That gives not half so great a blow to hear
As will a chestnut in a farmer's fire?
The Taming of the Shrew. Act i, sc. 2, l. 208. [Petruchio] See under WOOING.
Renown'd in Padua for her scolding tongue.
The Taming of the Shrew. Act i, sc. 2, l. 100. [Hortensio]
Famous for a scolding tongue.
The Taming of the Shrew. Act i, sc. 2, l. 254. [Tranio]

19
Helen's golden tongue.
Troilus and Cressida. Act i, sc. 2, l. 114. [Cressida]

1
Petruchio: Who knows not where a wasp does wear his sting? In his tail.
Katharina: In his tongue.
Petruchio: Whose tongue?
Katharina: Yours, if you talk of tails: and so farewell.
Petruchio: What, with my tongue in your tail? nay, come again.
The Taming of the Shrew. Act ii, sc. 1, l. 214.
Panthino: Why dost thou stop my mouth?
Launce: For fear thou shouldst lose thy tongue.
Panthino: Where should I lose my tongue?
Launce: In thy tale.
Panthino: In thy tail!
Two Gentlemen of Verona. Act ii, sc. 3, l. 50.

2
And, lozel, thou art worthy to be hang'd,
That wilt not stay her tongue.
The Winter's Tale. Act ii, sc. 3, l. 108. [Leontes] The only use of "lozel" (scamp).

The other, when she has obtain'd your eye,
Will have your tongue too.
The Winter's Tale. Act v, sc. 1, l. 105. [Gentleman]

VII—Holding the Tongue

3
Parolles: Why, I say nothing.
Clown: Marry, you are the wiser man; for many a man's tongue shakes out his master's undoing.
All's Well that Ends Well. Act ii, sc. 4, l. 22.

Dull of tongue.—*Antony and Cleopatra,* iii, 3, 19.

4
Pluck out The multitudinous tongue.
Coriolanus. Act iii, sc. 1, l. 155. [Coriolanus] "Multitudinous is repeated in *Macbeth,* ii, 2, 62: "Multitudinous seas."

On pain of losing her tongue.
Love's Labour's Lost. Act i, sc. 1, l. 123. [Biron]

Lose her tongue.—*Titus Andronicus,* ii, 3, 43.
Lost her tongue.—*Titus Andronicus,* ii, 4, 38.

5
Fell banning hag, enchantress, hold thy tongue!
I Henry VI. Act v, sc. 3, l. 42. [York] The only use of "banning" and "enchantress."

Hold thy tongue.—*Comedy of Errors,* iv, 4, 22.
Hold your tongue, good prudence.—*Romeo and Juliet,* iii, 5, 171.
Go to, hold your tongue.—*King John,* iv, 1, 97.
Hold your tongues.—*As You Like It,* ii, 5, 31.
Hold his tongue.—*I Henry VI,* iii, 1, 61.

Yes, forsooth, I will hold my tongue; so your face bids me, though you say nothing. Mum, mum.
King Lear. Act i, sc. 4, l. 214. [Fool]

I sometime hold my tongue
Because I would not dull you with my song.
Sonnets. No. cii.

Sweet, bid me hold my tongue,
For in this rapture I shall surely speak
The thing I shall repent.
Troilus and Cressida. Act iii, sc. 2, l. 137. [Cressida]

I must hold my tongue.—*Hamlet,* i, 2, 159.
Let me not hold my tongue.—*King John,* iv, 1, 100.

Why do we hold our tongues,
That most may claim this argument for ours?
Macbeth. Act ii, sc. 3, l. 125. [Malcolm]

6
His ill-boding tongue no more shall speak.
III Henry VI, ii, 6, 59. See under DEATH. "Ill-boding" is repeated in *I Henry VI,* iv, 5, 6: "Ill-boding stars."

Make reply Without a tongue.
King John. Act iii, sc. 3, l. 49. [King John]

7
Well, keep me company but two years moe,
Thou shalt not know the sound of thine own tongue.
The Merchant of Venice. Act i, sc. 1, l. 108. [Gratiano]

8
Within my mouth you have engaol'd my tongue,
Doubly portcullis'd with my teeth and lips.
Richard II. Act i, sc. 3, l. 166. [Mowbray] The only use of "engaol'd" and "portcullis'd."

Unwilling tongue.—*Richard II,* i, 3, 245.

9
What tongueless blocks were they!
Richard III. Act iii, sc. 7, l. 42. [Gloucester] "Tongueless" is repeated in *Henry V,* i, 2, 232: "Tongueless mouth"; *Richard II,* i, 1, 105: "Tongueless caverns"; and *The Winter's Tale,* i, 2, 92: "Dying tongueless."

10
More bitterly could I expostulate,
Save that, for reverence to some alive,
I give a sparing limit to my tongue.
Richard III. Act iii, sc. 7, l. 192. [Buckingham]

My woe-wearied tongue is mute and dumb.
Richard III. Act iv, sc. 4, l. 18. [Duchess of York] The only use of "woe-wearied."

11
No tongue! all eyes! be silent.
The Tempest. Act iv, sc. 1, l. 59. [Prospero]

Tongue, not a word.—*A Midsummer-Night's Dream,* v, 1, 349.

Clamour your tongues, and not a word more.
Winter's Tale. Act iv, sc. 4, l. 250. [Clown]

12
So, now go tell, an if thy tongue can speak,
Who 'twas that cut thy tongue and ravish'd thee.
Titus Andronicus. Act ii, sc. 4, l. 1. [Demetrius]

O, that delightful engine of her thoughts,
That blabb'd them with such pleasing eloquence,
Is torn from forth that pretty hollow cage,
Where, like a sweet melodious bird, it sung
Sweet varied notes, enchanting every ear!
Titus Andronicus. Act iii, sc. 1, l. 82. [Marcus]

Cut away her tongue.—*Titus Andronicus,* v, 3, 57.

I shall cut out your tongue.
Troilus and Cressida. Act ii, sc. 1, l. 121. [Ajax]

13
Be you his eunuch, and your mute I'll be:
When my tongue blabs, then let mine eyes not see.
Twelfth Night. Act i, sc. 2, l. 62. [Captain] The only use of "blabs." "Blab" occurs in *II Henry VI,* iii, 1, 154, and in *Othello,* iv, 1, 29.

VIII—Tongue-tied

1
Since you are tongue-tied and so loath to speak,
In dumb significants proclaim your thoughts.
I Henry VI. Act ii, sc. 4, l. 25. [Plantagenet] The only use of "significants." "Significant" occurs in *Love's Labour's Lost,* iii, 1, 131.
They vanish tongue-tied.—*Julius Cæsar,* i, 1, 67.
2
Tie up my love's tongue, bring him silently.
A Midsummer-Night's Dream. Act iii, sc. 1, l. 206. [Titania] The only use of "silently."
3
Be not tongue-tied.
Richard III, iv, 4, 132. [Duchess of York]
Tongue-tied by authority.—*Sonnets,* lxvi.
Tongue-tied, speaking of your fame!
Sonnets. No. lxxx.
4
Leontes: Tongue-tied our queen? speak you.
Hermione: I had thought, sir, to have held my peace.
The Winter's Tale. Act i, sc. 2, l. 27.
Tongue-tied ambition.—*Richard III,* iii, 7, 145.
Tongue-tied maidens.—*Troilus and Cressida,* iii, 2, 219.
Tongue-tied Muse.—*Sonnets,* lxxxv.
Tongue-tied patience.—*Sonnets.* No. cxl.
Tongue-tied simplicity.—*A Midsummer-Night's Dream,* v, 1, 104.
Tongue-tied sorrows.—*III Henry VI,* iii, 3, 22. All the uses of "tongue-tied" are given in this section.

TOOL, see Instrument

TOOTH, see Teeth

TORCH

5
Since the torch is out,
Lie down, and stray no farther.
Antony and Cleopatra, iv, 14, 46. [Antony]
6
Our lamp is spent, it's out!
Antony and Cleopatra. Act iv, sc. 15, l. 85. [Cleopatra]
My oil-dried lamp.—*Richard II,* i, 3, 221. The only use of "oil-dried."
Burning lamp.—*I Henry IV,* iii, 3, 30.
Sleepy lamp.—*All's Well that Ends Well,* ii, 1, 167.
Travelling lamp.—*Macbeth,* ii, 4, 7.
Wasting lamps.—*Comedy of Errors,* v, 1, 315.
Lamps of night.—*Antony and Cleopatra,* i, 4, 5.
7
Here dies the dusky torch of Mortimer,
Choked with ambition of the meaner sort.
I Henry VI. Act ii, sc. 5, l. 122. [Plantagenet]
8
Bastard: See, noble Charles, the beacon of our friend;
The burning torch in yonder turret stands.
Charles: Now shine it like a comet of revenge,
A prophet to the fall of all our foes!
I Henry VI. Act iii, sc. 2, l. 29. "Turret" is repeated in i, 4, 26, and occurs in no other play.
Beacon of the wise.—*Troilus and Cressida,* ii, 2, 16.
Beacon to this under globe!—*King Lear,* ii, 2, 170.
As a beacon gives warning.—*II Henry IV,* iv, 3, 117.
Like a beacon.—*Pericles,* i, 4, 87. The only uses of "beacon."
9
Behold, this is the happy wedding torch!
I Henry VI. Act iii, sc. 2, l. 26. [La Pucelle]
Hymen's torch.—*The Tempest,* iv, 1, 97.
Hymen's lamps.—*The Tempest,* iv, 1, 23.
10
Statilius show'd the torch-light.
Julius Cæsar, v, 5, 2. The only use of "torch-light."
11
We have not spoken yet of torch-bearers.
The Merchant of Venice, ii, 4, 5. "Torch-bearer" occurs four times in this scene.
To be to thee to-night a torch-bearer.
Romeo and Juliet. Act iii, sc. 5, l. 14. [Juliet]
12
A waxen torch forthwith he lighteth.
The Rape of Lucrece, l. 178.
Fair torch, burn out thy light, and lend it not.
The Rape of Lucrece, l. 190.
Burning torch.—*Pericles,* ii, 2, 32.
Flaming torch.—*The Rape of Lucrece,* l. 448.
13
What torch is yond, that vainly lends his light
To grubs and eyeless skulls?
Romeo and Juliet. Act v, sc. 3, l. 125. [Friar Laurence] The only use of "grubs." "Grub" occurs in i, 4, 68, and in *Coriolanus,* v, 4, 11.
Give me thy torch.—*Romeo and Juliet,* v, 3, 1.
More torches here.—*Romeo and Juliet,* i, 5, 127.
Torches, torches!—*King Lear,* ii, 1, 34.
14
Torches are made to light.
Venus and Adonis, l. 163.

TORMENT

See also Suffering

15
I grieve to hear what torments you endur'd.
I Henry VI. Act i, sc. 4, l. 57. [Salisbury]
16
Enough, sweet Suffolk! thou torment'st thyself.
II Henry VI. Act iii, sc. 2, l. 329. [Queen]
Who shall hinder me to . . . torment myself?
Richard III. Act ii, sc. 2, l. 35. [Queen Elizabeth]
17
The loss of those three lords torments my heart.
III Henry VI. Act i, sc. 1, l. 270. [King Henry]
Torment my soul.—*III Henry VI,* i, 3, 31.
18
And from that torment I will free myself,
Or hew my way out with a bloody axe.
III Henry VI. Act iii, sc. 2, l. 180. [Gloucester]

1
O happy torment, when my torturer
Doth teach me answers for deliverance!
The Merchant of Venice. Act iii, sc. 2, l. 37. [Bassanio]

Disnatured torment.—*King Lear,* i, 4, 305. The only use of "disnatured."

2 Thou shalt not from this grove
Till I torment thee for this injury.
A Midsummer-Night's Dream. Act ii, sc. 1, l. 146. [Oberon]

That 's her torment.—*Much Ado about Nothing,* ii, 3, 129.

3
Iago: From this time forth I never will speak word. . . .
Gratiano: Torments will ope your lips.
Othello. Act v, sc. 2, l. 304.

For this slave,
If there be any cunning cruelty
That can torment him much and hold him long,
It shall be his.
Othello. Act v, sc. 2, l. 332. [Lodovico]

4
Fiend, thou torment'st me ere I come to hell!
Richard II. Act iv, sc. 1, l. 270. [King Richard]

Seize on him, Furies, take him to your torments!
Richard III. Act i, sc. 4, l. 57. [Clarence]

5 Dost thou forget
From what a torment I did free thee?
The Tempest. Act i, sc. 2, l. 250. [Prospero]

Thou best know'st
What torment I did find thee in.
The Tempest. Act i, sc. 2, l. 287. [Prospero]

It was a torment To lay upon the damn'd.
The Tempest. Act i, sc. 2, l. 289. [Prospero]

Caliban: Do not torment me: Oh!
Stephano: What 's the matter? . . .
Caliban: The spirit torments me; Oh! . . . Do not torment me, prithee; I 'll bring my wood home faster.
The Tempest. Act ii, sc. 2, l. 58.

6
Ah, that same pale hard-hearted wench, that Rosaline,
Torments him so, that he will sure run mad.
Romeo and Juliet. Act ii, sc. 4, l. 4. [Mercutio]

A torment thrice threefold thus to be cross'd.
Sonnets. No. cxxxiii.

7
Pour'st in the open ulcer of my heart
Her eyes, her hair, her cheek, her gait, her voice.
Troilus and Cressida. Act i, sc. 1, l. 53. [Troilus] "Ulcer" is repeated in *Hamlet,* iv, 7, 124.

Instead of oil and balm,
Thou lay'st in every gash that love hath given me
The knife that made it.
Troilus and Cressida. Act i, sc. 1, l. 61. [Troilus]

O gods, how do you plague me!
Troilus and Cressida. Act i, sc. 1, l. 97. [Troilus]

Hell's torments.—*Troilus and Cressida,* v, 2, 43.

Whipp'd and tormented.—*Romeo and Juliet,* i, 2, 57. The only use of "tormented."

8
What studied torments, tyrant, hast for me?
What wheels? racks? fires? what flaying? boiling?
In leads or oils? what old or newer torture
Must I receive, whose every word deserves
To taste of thy most worst?
The Winter's Tale. Act iii, sc. 2, l. 176. [Paulina] "Flaying" is repeated in *Coriolanus,* iii, 3, 89.

TORTURE

9
With vilest torture let my life be ended.
All's Well that Ends Well. Act ii, sc. 1, l. 177. [Helena]

For now All length is torture.
Antony and Cleopatra. Act iv, sc. 14, l. 45. [Antony]

10 We 'll enforce it from thee
By a sharp torture.
Cymbeline. Act iv, sc. 3, l. 11. [Cymbeline]

Thou 'lt torture me to leave unspoken that
Which, to be spoke, would torture thee.
Cymbeline. Act v, sc. 5, l. 139. [Iachimo] The only use of "unspoken."

Death Drawn on with torture.
Cymbeline. Act iv, sc. 4, l. 13. [Belarius]

Bitter torture shall
Winnow the truth from falsehood.
Cymbeline. Act v, sc. 5, l. 133. [Cymbeline] "Winnow" is repeated in *Troilus and Cressida,* i, 3, 28.

11
York: Away with her to execution!
Warwick: And hark ye, sirs; because she is a maid,
Spare for no faggots, let there be enow:
Place barrels of pitch upon the fatal stake,
That so her torture may be shortened.
I Henry VI. Act v, sc. 4, l. 54. The reference is to Jeanne d'Arc. The only use of "barrels."

12
You go about to torture me in vain.
II Henry VI. Act ii, sc. 1, l. 146. [Simpcox]

In your protectorship you did devise
Strange tortures for offenders never heard of.
II Henry VI. Act iii, sc. 1, l. 121. [York]

O, torture me no more! I will confess.
II Henry VI. Act iii, sc. 3, l. 11. [Cardinal]

13
They will by violence tear him from your palace
And torture him with grievous lingering death.
II Henry VI. Act iii, sc. 2, l. 246. [Salisbury]

Say he be taken, rack'd and tortured,
I know no pain they can inflict upon him
Will make him say I moved him to those arms.
II Henry VI. Act iii, sc. 1, l. 376. [York]

I live upon the rack.—*The Merchant of Venice,* iii, 2, 25.

Thou hast set me on the rack.—*Othello,* iii, 3, 335.

To the rack with him!—*Measure for Measure,* v, 1, 313.

1 While we devise fell tortures for thy faults.
III Henry VI. Act ii, sc. 6, l. 72. [George]

We 'll touse you Joint by joint.
Measure for Measure. Act v, sc. 1, l. 313. [Escalus] The only use of "touse" (tear).

Torture me to death.—*Much Ado about Nothing,* iv, 1, 186.

He calls for the tortures.—*All's Well that Ends Well,* iv, 3, 137.

I 'll torture him.—*The Merchant of Venice,* iii, 1, 122.

Torture my wife.—*The Merry Wives of Windsor,* iii, 2, 41.

2 The time, the place, the torture: O, enforce it!
Othello. Act v, sc. 2, l. 369. [Lodovico]

Dispiteous torture.—*King John,* iv, 1, 34. The only use of "dispiteous."

3 That deep torture may be call'd a hell
When more is felt than one hath power to tell.
The Rape of Lucrece, l. 1287.

4 I play the torturer, by small and small
To lengthen out the worst that must be spoken.
Richard II. Act iii, sc. 2, l. 198. [Sir Stephen Scroop] "Torturer" is used a second time in *The Merchant of Venice,* iii, 2, 37.

Thou, king, send out For torturers ingenious.
Cymbeline. Act v, sc. 5, l. 214. [Posthumus] The only use of "torturers."

5 Having no more but thought of what thou wert,
To torture thee the more, being what thou art.
Richard III. Act iv, sc. 4, l. 107. [Queen Margaret]

6 On pain of torture, from those bloody hands
Throw your mistemper'd weapons to the ground.
Romeo and Juliet. Act i, sc. 1, l. 93. [Prince] "Mistemper'd" is repeated in *King John,* v, 1, 12: "Mistemper'd humour."

This torture should be roar'd in dismal hell.
Romeo and Juliet. Act iii, sc. 2, l. 44. [Juliet]

7 The curses he shall have, the tortures he shall feel, will break the back of man, the heart of monster.
The Winter's Tale. Act iv, sc. 4, l. 796. [Autolycus]

Body's torture.—*The Winter's Tale,* ii, 3, 181.

Tortured body.—*All's Well that Ends Well,* ii, 1, 36.

Torture of the mind, see under REMORSE.

TOUCH

8 Whose simple touch
Is powerful to araise King Pepin.
All's Well that Ends Well, ii, 1, 78. See under MEDICINE. The only use of "araise."

Brave touch.—*A Midsummer-Night's Dream,* iii, 2, 70.

Golden touch.—*The Two Gentlemen of Verona,* iii, 2, 79.

Little touch.—*Henry V,* iv, Prol., 47.

Noble touch.—*Coriolanus,* iv, 1, 49.

Sugar touch.—*Henry V,* v, 2, 303.

Sweet touch.—*Love's Labour's Lost,* v, 1, 62.

Sweetest touches.—*Merchant of Venice,* v, 1, 67.

9 To have the touches dearest prized.
As You Like It. Act iii, sc. 2, l. 160. [Celia]

I do remember in this shepherd boy
Some lively touches of my daughter's favour.
As You Like It. Act v, sc. 4, l. 26. [Duke]

10 Often touching will wear gold.
Comedy of Errors, ii, 1, 111. See under GOLD.

11 Touch thee to the quick.
The Comedy of Errors. Act ii, sc. 2, l. 132. [Adriana] See under QUICK.

Touch me near.—*The Two Gentlemen of Verona,* iii, 1, 60.

Touches me more nearly.—*Sonnets,* xlii.

Touch us all too near.—*Richard III,* ii, 3, 26.

It touches us not.—*Hamlet,* iii, 2, 252.

12 A touch more rare
Subdues all pangs, all fears.
Cymbeline. Act i, sc. 1, l. 135. [Imogen]

That I might touch!—*Cymbeline,* ii, 2, 16.

13 Heavens,
How deeply you at once do touch me!
Cymbeline. Act iv, sc. 3, l. 3. [Cymbeline]

14 Hamlet: Another hit; what say you?
Laertes: A touch, a touch, I do confess.
Hamlet. Act v, sc. 2, l. 295.

Bide the touch.—*I Henry IV,* iv, 4, 10.

15 Touch her soft mouth, and march.
Henry V. Act ii, sc. 3, l. 61. [Pistol]

Touch the bait.—*The Passionate Pilgrim,* l. 53.

Touch one drop.—*The Taming of the Shrew,* v, 2, 145.

Touch their ears.—*The Merchant of Venice,* v, 1, 76.

Touch no food.—*Love's Labour's Lost,* i, 1, 39.

Touch the gate.—*Pericles,* i, 1, 80.

Touch ground.—*II Henry IV,* iv, 1, 17.

Touch the ground.—*I Henry IV,* i, 3, 204.

Touch heaven.—*Othello,* i, 3, 141.

Touch the meat.—*The Taming of the Shrew,* iv, 3, 46.

Touch a pen.—*Love's Labour's Lost,* iv, 3, 346.

Touch the people.—*Coriolanus,* ii, 1, 271.

Touch pitch.—*Much Ado about Nothing,* iii, 3, 60.

Touch my point.—*Hamlet,* iv, 7, 147.

Touching that point.—*Measure for Measure,* i, 1, 84.

Touch my shoulder.—*Cymbeline,* v, 3, 78.

Touch the true prince.—*I Henry IV,* ii, 4, 300; 332.

1
I will touch thee but with reverent hands.
I Henry VI. Act v, sc. 3, l. 47. [Suffolk]

2
Their touch affrights me as a serpent's sting.
II Henry VI, iii, 2, 47. See under Hand.

Their softest touch as smart as lizards' stings!
II Henry VI, iii, 2, 325. See under Curse.

3
He wants the natural touch.
Macbeth. Act iv, sc. 2, l. 9. [Lady Macduff]

4
Ay, touch him; There 's the vein.
Measure for Measure. Act ii, sc. 2, l. 70. [Lucio]

From their abominable and beastly touches
I drink, I eat, array myself, and live.
Measure for Measure. Act iii, sc. 2, l. 25. [Duke]

Base touches.—*Sonnets,* cxli.

Dreadful touch.—*The Merchant of Venice,* iii, 2, 273.

Foul unlawful touch.—*Othello,* iv, 2, 84.

Greedy touch.—*Cymbeline,* iii, 4, 165.

Mortal touch.—*Richard II,* iii, 2, 21.

Rough touch.—*Romeo and Juliet,* i, 5, 98.

Strained touches.—*Sonnets,* lxxxii.

Urgent touches.—*Antony and Cleopatra,* i, 2, 187.

5
As free from touch or soil with her
As she from one ungot.
Measure for Measure. Act v, sc. 1, l. 141. [Friar Peter] The only use of "ungot." "Ungotten" occurs in *Henry V,* i, 2, 287.

6
To win his heart, she touch'd him here and there,—
Touches so soft still conquer chastity.
The Passionate Pilgrim, l. 49. See under Chastity.

7
And shortly mean to touch our northern shore.
Richard II. Act ii, sc. 1, l. 288. [Northumberland]

8
Touch this sparingly, as 'twere far off.
Richard III, iii, 5, 93. See under Caution. "Sparingly" is repeated in *Henry V,* i, 2, 239.

Play the touch.—*Richard III,* iv, 2, 8.

9
Such heavenly touches ne'er touch'd earthly faces.
Sonnets, xvii. See under Face.

10
Know now, upon advice, it toucheth us both.
The Taming of the Shrew. Act i, sc. 1, l. 118. [Hortensio]

Toucheth none but us.—*I Henry VI,* iv, 1, 118.

Toucheth us.—*Richard III,* iii, 2, 23; *King Lear,* v, 1, 25.

Toucheth you.—*Richard III,* i, 2, 362.

11
And here she stands, touch her whoever dare;
I 'll bring mine action on the proudest he
That stops my way in Padua. . . .
Fear not, sweet wench, they shall not touch thee.
The Taming of the Shrew. Act iii, sc. 2, l. 235. [Petruchio]

I expressly am forbid to touch it.
The Taming of the Shrew. Act iv, sc. 1, l. 174. [Petruchio]

12
Touch me and speak to me.
The Tempest. Act ii, sc. 2, l. 105. [Trinculo]

O, touch me not; I am not Stephano, but a cramp.
The Tempest. Act v, sc. 1, l. 286. [Stephano] "Cramp" is repeated in *All's Well that Ends Well,* iv, 3, 324.

Touch not, upon thy life.
Pericles. Act i, sc. 1, l. 87. [Antiochus]

Do not touch.—*All's Well that Ends Well,* iii, 2, 114.

Touch not.—*Titus Andronicus,* v, 1, 49.

Touch me not so near.—*Othello,* ii, 3, 220.

I will not touch a bit.—*As You Like It,* ii, 7, 133.

13
Painter: Here is a touch; is 't good? . . .
Poet: Artificial strife
Lives in these touches, livelier than life.
Timon of Athens. Act i, sc. 1, l. 35. See under Painting.

14
Let me touch your hand.
Troilus and Cressida. Act i, sc. 3, l. 304. [Agamemnon]

15
One touch of nature makes the whole world kin.
Troilus and Cressida, iii, 3, 175. See under Nature.

Touch of consanguinity.—*Troilus and Cressida,* iv, 2, 103. The only use of "consanguinity." "Consanguineous" occurs in *Twelfth Night,* ii, 3, 82.

So excellent a touch.—*Twelfth Night,* ii, 1, 13.

16
Didst thou but know the inly touch of love.
The Two Gentlemen of Verona, ii, 7, 18. See under Love.

Love's coy touch.—*The Rape of Lucrece,* l. 669.

Touch of holy bread.—*As You Like It,* iii, 4, 15.

Touches of sweet harmony.—*The Merchant of Venice,* v, 1, 57.

Touch of pity.—*Richard III,* i, 2, 71.

Touches of remorse.—*Troilus and Cressida,* ii, 2, 115.

Bitter touch of sorrow.—*All's Well that Ends Well,* i, 3, 122.

17
Ruffian, let go that rude, uncivil touch.
The Two Gentlemen of Verona, v, 4, 60. See under Rudeness.

Take but possession of her with a touch.
The Two Gentlemen of Verona. Act v, sc. 4, l. 130. [Valentine]

18
Yet should I be in love by touching thee.
Venus and Adonis, l. 438.

What is ten hundred touches unto thee?
Are they not quickly told and quickly gone?
Venus and Adonis, l. 519.

1
One of the prettiest touches of all.
The Winter's Tale. Act v, sc. 2, l. 89. [Gentleman]

TOWER

2
Child Rowland to the dark tower came.
King Lear, iii, 4, 187. See under ENGLAND.
3
And smear with dust their glittering golden towers.
The Rape of Lucrece, l. 945.
4
Prince: I do not like the Tower, of any place.
Did Julius Cæsar build that place, my lord?
Buckingham: He did, my gracious lord, begin that place;
Which, since, succeeding ages have re-edified.
Prince: Is it upon record, or else reported
Successively from age to age, he built it?
Buckingham: Upon record, my gracious lord.
Richard III. Act iii, sc. 1, l. 68. "Re-edified" is repeated in *Titus Andronicus,* i, 1, 351.
Julius Cæsar's ill-erected tower.
Richard II. Act v, sc. 1, l. 2. [Queen] The only use of "ill-erected." The Tower is mentioned frequently in the first four plays, and also in *Richard II.* Tower-hill is mentioned once, in *Henry VIII,* v, 4, 65.
Accursed tower!—*I Henry VI,* i, 4, 76.
Stony tower.—*Julius Cæsar,* i, 3, 93.
Tower of strength.—*Richard III,* v, 3, 12.
5
Sometime lofty towers I see down-razed.
Sonnets. No. lxiv. The only use of "down-razed."
6 The eastern tower,
Whose height commands as subject all the vale.
Troilus and Cressida. Act i, sc. 2, l. 2. [Alexander]
Yond towers, whose wanton tops do buss the clouds,
Must kiss their own feet.
Troilus and Cressida. Act iv, sc. 5, l. 220. [Ulysses]
Whose towers bore heads so high they kiss'd the clouds.
Pericles. Act i, sc. 4, l. 24. [Cleon]
Air-braving towers.—*I Henry VI,* iv, 2, 13. The only use of "air-braving."
Cloud-capp'd towers.—*The Tempest,* iv, 1, 152. The only use of "cloud-capp'd."
Great towers.—*Timon of Athens,* v, 4, 25.
Moss-grown towers.—*I Henry IV,* iii, 1, 33. The only use of "moss-grown."
Towers of Troy.—*The Rape of Lucrece,* l. 1382.
7
I nightly lodge her in an upper tower.
The Two Gentlemen of Verona. Act iii, sc. 1, l. 35. [Duke]
Hero's tower.—*The Two Gentlemen of Verona,* iii, 1, 119.

TOWN

See also City

8
A walled town is more worthier than a village.
As You Like It, iii, 3, 59. See MARRIAGE, 962:15.
Walled towns of strength.—*I Henry VI,* iii, 4, 7.
Towns of garrison.—*I Henry VI,* v, 4, 168.
9
Will you walk with me about the town?
The Comedy of Errors. Act i, sc. 2, l. 22. [Antipholus of Syracuse]
Up and down the town.—*II Henry IV,* ii, 1, 114.
Backside the town.—*Cymbeline,* i, 2, 14.
10
I will not harbour in this town to-night.
The Comedy of Errors. Act iii, sc. 2, l. 154. [Antipholus of Syracuse]
Let 's leave this town.—*I Henry VI,* i, 2, 37.
11
Your native town you enter'd like a post,
And had no welcomes home.
Coriolanus. Act v, sc. 6, l. 50. [Conspirator]
12
To line and new repair our towns of war.
Henry V. Act ii, sc. 4, l. 7. [French King]
Town of war.—*Othello,* ii, 3, 213.
13
I would have blowed up the town.
Henry V. Act iii, sc. 2, l. 97. [Macmorris]
Fluellen: What call you the town's name where Alexander the Pig was born? . .
Gower: I think Alexander the Great was born in Macedon.
Henry V. Act iv, sc. 7, l. 13.
14
Being wrong'd as we are by this peevish town.
King John, ii, 1, 402. See under CANNON.
Adverse towns.—*The Comedy of Errors,* i, 1, 15; *Twelfth Night,* v, 1, 87.
Cursed town.—*I Henry VI,* ii, 2, 6.
Detestable town.—*Timon of Athens,* iv, 1, 33.
Enemy town.—*Coriolanus,* iv, 4, 24.
Peasant towns.—*II Henry IV,* Ind., 33.
Petty towns.—*I Henry VI,* i, 1, 91.
Resisting town.—*King John,* ii, 1, 38.
Threaten'd town.—*King John,* ii, 1, 481.
15
This rich fair town We make him lord of
King John. Act ii, sc. 1, l. 552. [King John]
Flourishing peopled towns.—*The Two Gentlemen of Verona,* v, 4, 3.
Great towns.—*I Henry VI,* i, 1, 63.
16
Is not he in town?
Othello. Act i, sc. 3, l. 44. [Duke]
Out of town.—*Troilus and Cressida,* i, 1, 116.
17 The rebels have consumed with fire
Our town of Cicester.
Richard II. Act v, sc. 6, l. 2. [Bolingbroke]
Lud's town.—*Cymbeline,* iii, 1, 32.
Leicester town.—*Richard III,* v, 5, 10.
Town of Leicester.—*Richard III,* v, 2, 12.
Town of Orleans.—*I Henry VI,* i, 6, 9.
Town of York.—*III Henry VI,* i, 4, 180; ii, 2, 1.
18
Sound to this coward and lascivious town
Our terrible approach.
Timon of Athens, v, 4, 1. [Alcibiades]

1 Beguile the time . . .
With viewing of the town.
Twelfth Night. Act iii, sc. 4, l. 41. [Antonio]

2
When came he to this town?
Twelfth Night. Act v, sc. 1, l. 96. [Duke]
Come to town.—*II Henry IV*, ii, 2, 177; *The Merry Wives of Windsor*, iv, 5, 78.

TOY

3
Shall we fall foul for toys?
II Henry IV. Act ii, sc. 4, l. 183. [Pistol]
See also TRIFLE.

For a toy, a thing of no regard, . . .
Destroy'd themselves.
I Henry VI. Act iv, sc. 1, l. 145. [King Henry]

4
Gurney: Good leave, good Philip.
Bastard: Philip! sparrow: James,
There's toys abroad.
King John. Act i, sc. 1, l. 231.
All is but toys.
Macbeth, ii, 3, 99. See under LIFE.

5
Such like toys as these.
Richard III. Act i, sc. 1, l. 60. [Clarence]
Being but a toy, which is no grief to give.
Richard III. Act iii, sc. 1, l. 114. [York]
Tut, a toy.—*Taming of the Shrew*, ii, 1, 404.
A toy, my liege, a toy.—*Love's Labour's Lost*, iv, 3, 201.
Airy toys.—*Merry Wives of Windsor*, v, 5, 46.
Fairy toys.—*A Midsummer-Night's Dream*, v, 1, 3.
Idle toys.—*Love's Labour's Lost*, iv, 3, 170.
Inconstant toy.—*Romeo and Juliet*, iv, 1, 119.
Jealous toy.—*Othello*, iii, 4, 156.
Lamenting toys.—*Cymbeline*, iv, 2, 193.
Toy in blood.—*Hamlet*, i, 3, 6.
Unapt to toy.—*Venus and Adonis*, l. 34.
To toy, to wanton.—*Venus and Adonis*, l. 106.

6
Haply your eye may light upon some toy
You have desire to purchase.
Twelfth Night, iii, 3, 44. [Antonio]

TRADE

See also Business, Occupation, Profession

7
Our tradesmen singing in their shops.
Coriolanus. Act iv, sc. 6, l. 8. [Sicinius]
I meddle with no tradesman's matters.
Julius Cæsar. Act i, sc. 1, l. 25. [Commoner]
None but tradesmen.—*The Winter's Tale*, iv, 7, 745. The only uses of "tradesman" and "tradesmen."

8
Have you any further trade with us?
Hamlet. Act iii, sc. 2, l. 346. [Hamlet]

9
It is like we shall have good trading.
I Henry IV. Act ii, sc. 4, l. 401. [Falstaff] The only use of "trading."

10
Traders riding to London with fat purses.
I Henry IV. Act i, sc. 2, l. 141. [Poins]
Peruse the traders.—*The Comedy of Errors*, i, 2, 13.
Embarked traders.—*A Midsummer-Night's Dream*, ii, 1, 127.
Good traders in the flesh.—*Troilus and Cressida*, v, 10, 46. The only uses of "traders."

11
Falstaff: What trade art thou, Feeble?
Feeble: A woman's tailor, sir.
II Henry IV. Act iii, sc. 2, l. 160.

12
Flavius: Speak, what trade art thou?
Commoner: Why, sir, a carpenter.
Marullus: Where is thy leather apron and thy rule?
What dost thou with thy best apparel on?
You, sir, what trade are you?
Second Commoner: Truly, sir, in respect of a fine workman, I am but, as you would say, a cobbler.
Marullus: But what trade art thou? answer me directly.
Second Commoner: A trade, sir, that, I hope, I may use with a safe conscience; which is, indeed, sir, a mender of bad soles.
Marullus: What trade, thou knave? thou naughty knave, what trade? . . .
Flavius: Thou art a cobbler, art thou?
Julius Cæsar. Act i, sc. 1, l. 5.

13
Bad is the trade that must play fool to sorrow.
King Lear. Act iv, sc. 1, l. 40. [Edgar]

Half way down
Hangs one that gathers samphire, dreadful trade!
King Lear. Act iv, sc. 6, l. 14. [Edgar] The only use of "samphire."
Penitent trade.—*Measure for Measure*, iv, 2, 53.
Trade of danger.—*II Henry IV*, i, 1, 174.
Trade of war.—*Othello*, i, 2, 1.

14
Escalus: What trade are you of, sir?
Pompey: A tapster; a poor widow's tapster.
Measure for Measure. Act ii, sc. 1, l. 206.
A tapster is a good trade.
The Merry Wives of Windsor. Act i, sc. 3, l. 18. [Falstaff]
You need not change your trade; I'll be your tapster still.
Measure for Measure. Act i, sc. 2, l. 112. [Pompey] "Tapster" is used fourteen times.

15
Escalus: How would you live, Pompey? by being a bawd?
What do you think of the trade, Pompey? is it a lawful trade?
Pompey: If the law would allow it, sir.
Measure for Measure. Act ii, sc. 1, l. 235.
Abhorson: I will instruct thee in my trade; follow.
Pompey: I do desire to learn, sir.
Measure for Measure. Act iv, sc. 2, l. 58.

16 The trade and profit of the city
Consisteth of all nations.
The Merchant of Venice. Act iii, sc. 3, l. 30. [Antonio]

1
They shall be my East and West Indies, and I will trade to them both.
The Merry Wives of Windsor. Act i, sc. 3, l. 79. [Falstaff]

2
If there be not a conscience to be used in every trade, we shall never prosper.
Pericles. Act iv, sc. 2, l. 12. [Pandar]

Lysander: Now, pretty one, how long have you been at this trade?
Marina: What trade, sir?
Lysander: Why, I cannot name 't but I shall offend.
Marina: I cannot be offended with my trade.
Pericles. Act iv, sc. 6, l. 73. See also PROFESSION.

The hold-door trade.—*Troilus and Cressida,* v, 10, 52. Referring to pandering. The only use of "hold-door."

3
If tinkers may have leave to live,
And bear the sow-skin budget,
Then my account I well may give,
And in the stocks avouch it.
The Winter's Tale. Act iv, sc. 3, l. 19. [Autolycus] The only use of "sow-skin."

4
You have let him go
And nothing marted with him.
The Winter's Tale. Act iv, sc. 4, l. 361. [Polixenes] The only use of "marted."

TRAFFIC

5
It hath in solemn synods been decreed . . .
To admit no traffic to our adverse towns.
The Comedy of Errors. Act i, sc. 1, l. 13. [Duke]

General synod.—*Hamlet,* ii, 2, 516.
Heavenly synod.—*As You Like It,* iii, 2, 158.
Hourly synod.—*Coriolanus,* v, 2, 74.
Shining synod.—*Cymbeline,* v, 4, 89.
Whole synod.—*Antony and Cleopatra,* iii, 10, 5. The only uses of "synod" and "synods."

6
Traffic with thyself alone.
Sonnets. No. iv.

Traffic of a king.—*I Henry VI,* v, 3, 164.
Traffic of our stage.—*Romeo and Juliet,* Prol., 12.
Petty traffickers.—*The Merchant of Venice,* i, 1, 12. The only use of "traffickers."

7
Great traffic through the world.
The Taming of the Shrew, i, 1, 12. See under MERCHANT.

No kind of traffic Would I admit
Tempest, ii, 1, 148. See COMMONWEALTH, 209:7.

8
Apemantus: Traffic confound thee, if the gods will not!
Merchant: If traffic do it, the gods do it.
Apemantus: Traffic 's thy god; and thy god confound thee.
Timon of Athens. Act i, sc. 1, l. 244.

My traffic is sheets; when the kite builds, look to lesser linen.
The Winter's Tale, iv, 3, 23. [Autolycus]

For traffic's sake.—*Twelfth Night,* iii, 3, 34.

9
Peaceful commerce from dividable shores.
Troilus and Cressida. Act i, sc. 3, l. 105. [Ulysses] The only use of "dividable."

All the commerce that you have had with Troy
As perfectly is ours as yours.
Troilus and Cressida. Act iii, sc. 3, l. 205. [Ulysses]

He is now in some commerce with my lady.
Twelfth Night. Act iii, sc. 4, l. 191. [Maria]

Better commerce.—*Hamlet,* iii, 1, 110. The only uses of "commerce."

TRAGEDY

See also Comedy, Play

10
For us and for our tragedy,
Here stooping to your clemency,
We beg your hearing patiently.
Hamlet. Act iii, sc. 2, l. 155. [Prologue]

11
Accursed tower! accursed fatal hand
That hath contrived this woful tragedy!
I Henry VI. Act i, sc. 4, l. 76. [Talbot]

Plotted tragedy.—*II Henry VI,* iii, 1, 153.

12
As if the tragedy
Were play'd in jest by counterfeiting actors?
III Henry VI. Act ii, sc. 3, l. 27. [Warwick]

Play'd a tragedy.—*Henry V,* 1, 2, 106.

13
Marry, if he that writ it had played Pyramus and hanged himself in Thisbe's garter, it would have been a fine tragedy: and so it is, truly; and very notably discharged.
A Midsummer-Night's Dream. Act v, sc. 1, l. 365. [Theseus] The only use of "notably."

And tragical, my noble lord, it is.
A Midsummer-Night's Dream. Act v, sc. 1, l. 66. [Philostrate]

Very tragical.—*A Midsummer-Night's Dream,* v, 1, 57.
Bitter, black, and tragical.—*Richard III,* iv, 4, 7.
Stern and tragical.—*I Henry VI,* iii, 1, 125.

14
They who brought me in my master's hate,
I live to look upon their tragedy.
Richard III. Act iii, sc. 2, l. 58. [Hastings]

15
I can counterfeit the deep tragedian.
Richard III. Act iii, sc. 5, l. 5. [Buckingham]

English tragedians.—*All's Well that Ends Well,* iv, 3, 299.
Tragedians of the city.—*Hamlet,* ii, 2, 342. The only uses of "tragedian" and "tragedians."

16
The complot of this timeless tragedy.
Titus Andronicus. Act ii, sc. 3, l. 265. [Tamora]

Tragedies and murders fell!—*The Rape of Lucrece,* l. 766.

TRAITOR, see Treason

TRANSFORMATION

See also Change

1
I think he is transform'd into a beast;
For I can no where find him like a man.
As You Like It. Act ii, sc. 7, l. 1. [Duke]
Transformed to a boy.—*The Merchant of Venice,* ii, 6, 39.
Transform'd into a fool.—*Antony and Cleopatra,* i, 1, 12.
Transformed to a gnat.—*Love's Labour 's Lost,* iv, 3, 166.
Transformed him ape.—*II Henry IV,* ii, 2, 77.
I have been transformed.—*The Merry Wives of Windsor,* iv, 5, 98.
Transformed with their fear.—*Julius Cæsar,* i, 3, 24.
Transform us not to women.—*Antony and Cleopatra,* iv, 2, 36. See WEEPING, 1649:11.

2
Dromio of Syracuse: I am transformed, master, am I not?
Antipholus of Syracuse: I think thou art in mind, and so am I.
Dromio of Syracuse: Nay, master, both in mind and in my shape.
The Comedy of Errors. Act ii, sc. 2, l. 197.
And, I think, if my breast had not been made of faith and my heart of steel,
She had transformed me to a curtal dog and made me turn i' the wheel.
The Comedy of Errors. Act iii, sc. 2, l. 150. [Dromio of Syracuse] For "curtal dog" see *The Merry Wives of Windsor,* under HOPE.

3
Upon whose dead corpse there was such misuse,
Such beastly shameless transformation,
By those Welshwomen done as may not be
Without much shame retold or spoken of.
I Henry IV. Act i, sc. 1, l. 43. [Westmoreland] The only use of "Welshwomen."
A low transformation!—*II Henry IV,* ii, 2, 194.

4
Heavens defend me from that Welsh fairy, lest he transform me into a piece of cheese!
The Merry Wives of Windsor. Act v, sc. 5, l. 85. [Falstaff]

5
What, is my Richard both in shape and mind
Transform'd and weaken'd?
Richard II. Act v, sc. 1, l. 26. [Queen]

6
Their transformations
Were never for a piece of beauty rarer.
The Winter's Tale. Act iv, sc. 4, l. 31. [Florizel]
Goodly transformation.—*Troilus and Cressida,* v, 1, 59.

TRANSGRESSION, see Trespass

TRAP

7
I must go look my twigs: he shall be caught.
All's Well that Ends Well. Act iii, sc. 6, l. 115. [Lord]

8
Entrap thee by some treacherous device.
As You Like It. Act i, sc. 1, l. 157. [Oliver]
Sought to entrap me by intelligence.
I Henry IV. Act iv, sc. 3, l. 98. [Hotspur]
Seek not to entrap me.
Pericles. Act ii, sc. 5, l. 45. [Pericles]
Entrap the wisest.—*The Merchant of Venice,* iii, 2, 101.

9
Why do you go about to recover the wind of me, as if you would drive me into a toil?
Hamlet. Act iii, sc. 2, l. 361. [Hamlet]
They have pitched a toil.—*Love's Labour 's Lost,* iv, 3, 2.

10
Pretty traps to catch the petty thieves.
Henry V. Act i, sc. 2, l. 177. [Exeter]

11
Thou laid'st a trap to take my life.
Henry VI. Act iii, sc. 1, l. 22. [Gloucester]

12
Myself have limed a bush for her.
II Henry VI. Act i, sc. 3, l. 91. [Suffolk]
And I, the hapless male to one sweet bird,
Have now the fatal object in my eye
Where my poor young was limed, and caught and kill'd.
III Henry VI. Act v, sc. 6, l. 15. [King]
She 's limed, I warrant you: we have caught her, madam.
Much Ado about Nothing, iii, 1, 104. [Ursula]
I have limed her.
Twelfth Night. Act iii, sc. 4, l. 82. [Malvolio]
You must lay lime to tangle her.
The Two Gentlemen of Verona. Act iii, sc. 2, l. 68. [Proteus]
Fly thou how thou canst, they 'll tangle thee.
II Henry VI. Act ii, sc. 4, l. 55. [Duchess] "Tangle thee" is repeated in *I Henry VI,* iv, 2, 22.
Tangle my eyes.—*As You Like It,* iii, 5, 44. The only uses of "tangle." "Tangled" occurs three times.

13
Clifford: So strives the woodcock with the gin.
Northumberland: So doth the cony struggle in the net.
III Henry VI. Act i, sc. 4, l. 61. "Struggle" is used only once again, in *King John,* iv, 1, 77.
Now is the woodcock near the gin.
Twelfth Night. Act ii, sc. 5, l. 92. [Fabian]
Thou 'ldst never fear . . .
The pitfall nor the gin.
Macbeth. Act iv, sc. 2, l. 35. [Lady Macduff]
By gins, by snares.—*II Henry VI,* iii, 1, 262. The only uses of "gin" and "gins."

14
Protect mine innocence, or I fall into
The trap is laid for me!
Henry VIII. Act v, sc. 1, l. 141. [Cranmer]

15
Springes to catch woodcocks.
Hamlet. Act i, sc. 3, l. 115. [Polonius]
As a woodcock to mine own springe.—*Hamlet.* v, 2, 317.
If the springe hold, the cock 's mine.
Winter's Tale. Act iv, sc. 3, l. 36. [Autolycus] The only uses of "springe" and "springes."

1
A golden mesh to entrap the hearts of men.
The Merchant of Venice. Act iii, sc. 2, l. 123. [Bassanio] The only use of "mesh." "Meshes" occurs in i, 2, 22, and in no other play.

2
With as little a web as this will I ensnare as great a fly as Cassio.
Othello. Act ii, sc. 1, l. 169. [Iago]
Parca's fatal web.—*Henry V,* v, 1, 21. The only mention of Parca. "Web" occurs twelve times.

3
Here comes my noble gull-catcher.
Twelfth Night. Act ii, sc. 5, l. 205. [Fabian] The only use of "gull-catcher."

TRAVAIL, see Labour

TRAVEL

4
Thou didst make tolerable vent of thy travel.
All's Well that Ends Well. Act ii, sc. 3, l. 212. [Lafeu] "Tolerable" is repeated in *Much Ado about Nothing,* iii, 3, 37.

5
You are a vagabond and no true traveller.
All's Well that Ends Well. Act ii, sc. 3, l. 276. [Lafeu]
A sort of vagabonds.—*Richard III,* v, 3, 316.
A wandering vagabond.—*Richard II,* ii, 3, 120.
Vagabond exile.—*Coriolanus,* iii, 3, 89.
Vagabond flag.—*Antony and Cleopatra,* i, 4, 45. The only uses of "vagabond" and "vagabonds."
Vagrom men.—*Much Ado about Nothing,* iii, 3, 26.
Brave Master Shooty the great traveller.
Measure for Measure. Act iv, sc. 3, l. 18. [Pompey]
A refined traveller of Spain.—*Love's Labour's Lost,* i, 1, 164.

6
A good traveller is something at the latter end of a dinner; but one that lies three thirds and uses a known truth to pass a thousand nothings with, should be once heard and thrice beaten.
All's Well that Ends Well. Act ii, sc. 5, l. 30. [Lafeu]
Lated traveller.—*Macbeth,* iii, 3, 6. "Lated" is repeated in *Antony and Cleopatra,* iii, 11, 3.
Pleasant travellers.—*The Taming of the Shrew,* iv, 5, 72.

7
Rosalind: Well, this is the forest of Arden.
Touchstone: Ay, now am I in Arden; the more fool, I; when I was at home, I was in a better place: but travellers must be content.
As You Like It. Act ii, sc. 4, l. 15.
A traveller! By my faith, you have great reason to be sad: I fear you have sold your own lands to see other men's.
As You Like It. Act iv, sc. 1, l. 21. [Rosalind]
Farewell, Monsieur Traveller: look you lisp and wear strange suits, disable all the benefits of your own country, be out of love with your nativity and almost chide God for making you that countenance you are, or I will scarce think you have swam in a gondola.
As You Like It. Act iv, sc. 1, l. 33. [Rosalind] "Gondola" is mentioned again in *The Merchant of Venice,* ii, 8, 8. "Swam" is repeated in *The Tempest,* iii, 2, 16.

Chamberlain: What news, Sir Thomas Lovell?
Lovell: Faith, my lord,
I hear of none, but the new proclamation
That 's clapp'd upon the court gate.
Chamberlain: What 's it for?
Lovell: The reformation of our travell'd gallants,
That fill the court with quarrels, talk, and tailors.
Chamberlain: I am glad 'tis there: now I would pray our monsieurs
To think an English courtier may be wise,
And never see the Louvre.
Lovell: They must either . . . leave those remnants
Of fool and feather that they got in France, . . .
Abusing better men than they can be,
Out of a foreign wisdom, renouncing clean
The faith they have in tennis and tall stockings,
Short blister'd breeches, and those types of travel,
And understand again like honest men;
Or pack to their old playfellows: there, I take it,
They may, 'cum privilegio,' wear away
The lag end of their lewdness and be laugh'd at.
Henry VIII. Act i, sc. 3, l. 16. The only use of "renouncing." "Cum privilegio" is repeated in *The Taming of the Shrew,* iv, 4, 93.

8
With long travel I am stiff and weary.
The Comedy of Errors. Act i, sc. 2, l. 15. [Antipholus of Syracuse]
Travel-tainted as I am.
II Henry IV. Act iv, sc. 3, l. 41. [Falstaff] The only use of the phrase.
Oppress'd with travel.—*The Tempest,* iii, 3, 15.
Stained with travel.—*II Henry IV,* v, 5, 25.

9
Hamlet: How chances it they travel? their residence, both in reputation and profit, was better both ways.
Rosencrantz: I think their inhibition comes by the means of the late innovation.
Hamlet. Act ii, sc. 2, l. 343. The only use of "inhibition." "Innovation" is repeated in *I Henry IV,* v, 1, 78 (see under CHANGE), and in *Othello,* ii, 3, 42.
Haply the seas and countries different
With variable objects shall expel
This something-settled matter in his heart.
Hamlet. Act iii, sc. 1, l. 179. [King] The only use of "something-settled."

10
I have watched and travell'd hard.
King Lear. Act ii, sc. 2, l. 162. [Kent]
They have travell'd all the night?
King Lear. Act ii, sc. 4, l. 90. [King Lear]
Travell'd but two hours.—*Twelfth Night,* v, 1, 166.
Travell'd hither.—*King John,* iv, 2, 143.
Travell'd to Poland.—*Measure for Measure,* i, 3, 14.

1
A man of travel, that hath seen the world.
Love's Labour's Lost. Act v, sc. 1, l. 113. [Armado]
And so am come abroad to see the world.
Taming of the Shrew, i, 2, 58. [Petruchio]
I rather would entreat thy company
To see the wonders of the world abroad
Than, living dully sluggardised at home,
Wear out thy youth with shapeless idleness.
Two Gentlemen of Verona. Act i, sc. 1, l. 5. [Valentine] The only use of "sluggardised."

2
You may be jogging whiles your boots are green.
Taming of the Shrew. Act iii, sc. 2, l. 213. [Katharina] The only use of "jogging."

3
Go travel for a while.
Pericles. Act i, sc. 2, l. 106. [Helicanus]
He's gone to travel.
Pericles. Act i, sc. 3, l. 14. [Helicanus]
Betook himself to unknown travels.
Pericles. Act i, sc. 3, l. 35. [Thaliard]

4
Call it a travel that thou takest for pleasure.
Richard II. Act i, sc. 3, l. 262. [Gaunt]
We were wandering with the antipodes.
Richard II. Act iii, sc. 2, l. 49. [King Richard] "Antipodes" is used five times.

5
If I have ranged,
Like him that travels I return again.
Sonnets. No. cix.

6
Tranio: Travel you far on, or are you at the farthest?
Pedant: Sir, at the farthest for a week or two:
But then up farther, and as far as Rome;
And so to Tripoli, if God lend me life.
The Taming of the Shrew. Act iv, sc. 2, l. 73.
To Tarsus Intend my travel.—*Pericles,* i, 2, 116.
Will he travel higher?—*All's Well that Ends Well,* iv, 3, 50.
Further travel.—*Antony and Cleopatra,* ii, 1, 31.

7
Travellers ne'er did lie,
Though fools at home condemn 'em.
The Tempest. Act iii, sc. 3, l. 26. [Antonio]

8
My youthful travel therein made me happy,
Or else I often had been miserable.
The Two Gentlemen of Verona. Act iv, sc. 1, l. 34. [Valentine]
I was then a young traveller.—*Cymbeline,* i, 4, 47.

TREACHERY

See also Betrayal; Cunning; Deceit; Faith: Faithlessness

9
O slave, of no more trust
Than love that's hired!
Antony and Cleopatra, v, 2, 154. [Cleopatra]

10
To write and read
Be henceforth treacherous!
Cymbeline. Act iv, sc. 2, l. 316. [Imogen]
Bloody, treacherous.—*Richard III,* iv, 4, 171.
Treacherous, and full of guile.—*Richard III,* ii, 1, 38.

11
O villany! Ho! let the door be lock'd:
Treachery! Seek it out.
Hamlet. Act v, sc. 2, l. 322. [Hamlet]

12
And for thy treachery, what's more manifest?
I Henry VI. Act iii, sc. 1, l. 21. [Gloucester]
You used us so
As that ungentle gull, the cuckoo's bird,
Useth the sparrow.
I Henry IV. Act v, sc. 1, l. 59. [Worcester]
Unkind usage, dangerous countenance,
And violation of all faith and troth.
I Henry IV. Act v, sc. 1, l. 69. [Worcester]

13
Him did you leave,
Second to none, unseconded by you,
To look upon the hideous god of war
In disadvantage.
II Henry IV. Act ii, sc. 3, l. 33. [Lady Percy] The only use of "unseconded." "Disadvantage" is repeated in *Coriolanus,* i, 6, 49.
That man that sits within a monarch's heart,
And ripens in the sunshine of his favour,
Would he abuse the countenance of the king,
Alack, what mischiefs might he set abroach
In shadow of such greatness!
II Henry IV. Act iv, sc. 2, l. 11. [Lancaster]
The secret mischiefs that I set abroach.
Richard III, i, 3, 325. See under MISCHIEF.
Who set this ancient quarrel new abroach?
Romeo and Juliet, i, 1, 111. See under QUARREL. The only uses of "abroach."

14
Nay, but the man that was his bedfellow,
Whom he had dull'd and cloy'd with gracious favours,
That he should, for a foreign purse, so sell
His sovereign's life to death and treachery.
Henry V. Act ii, sc. 2, l. 8. [Exeter]

15
O monstrous treachery! can this be so,
That in alliance, amity and oaths,
There should be found such false dissembling guile?
I Henry VI. Act iv, sc. 1, l. 61. [Gloucester]
Foul guile.—*Richard III,* ii, 2, 28.
By thy guile betrayed to death.
Richard III. Act v, sc. 3, l. 133. [Ghost]
It cannot be, . . . that so much guile
. . . can lurk in such a look.
The Rape of Lucrece, l. 1534.
Full of guile.—*Richard III,* ii, 1, 38. The only uses of "guile."
Wiles and guiles.—*The Passionate Pilgrim,* l. 335. The only use of "guiles."

16
Wilt thou still be hammering treachery,
To tumble down thy husband and thyself
From top of honour to disgrace's feet?
II Henry VI. Act i, sc. 2, l. 47. [Gloucester]

17
All my followers to the eager foe
Turn back and fly, like ships before the wind
Or lambs pursued by hunger-starved wolves.
III Henry VI. Act i, sc. 4, l. 3. [York] The only use of "hunger-starved." "Hungry-starved men" occurs in *I Henry VI,* i, 5, 16.

Treacherously hast thou vanquish'd him,
For hand to hand he would have vanquish'd thee.
III Henry VI. Act ii, sc. 1, l. 72. [Edward]
The only use of "treacherously."

To plague thee for thy foul misleading me.
III Henry VI. Act v, sc. 1, l. 97. [Clarence]
The only use of "misleading."

1
This holy fox,
Or wolf, or both,—for he is equal ravenous
As he is subtle, and as prone to mischief
As able to perform 't.
Henry VIII. Act i, sc. 1, l. 158. [Buckingham]

He is composed and framed of treachery.
Much Ado about Nothing. Act v, sc. 1, l. 257. [Don Pedro]

2 I do fawn on men and hug them hard
And after scandal them.
Julius Cæsar. Act i, sc. 2, l. 75. [Cassius]

3
Paying the fine of rated treachery
Even with a treacherous fine of all your lives.
King John. Act v, sc. 4, l. 37. [Melun]

4 Look like the innocent flower,
But be the serpent under 't.
Macbeth. Act i, sc. 5, l. 66. [Lady Macbeth]

Young fry of treachery!—*Macbeth,* iv, 2, 84.

5
I think it is scurvy, and begin to find myself fopped in it.
Othello. Act iv, sc. 2, l. 196. [Roderigo]
The only use of "fopped."

Take me from this world with treachery and devise engines for my life.
Othello. Act iv, sc. 2, l. 220. [Iago]

6
God for his mercy, what treachery is here!
Richard II. Act v, sc. 2, l. 75. [York]

Some known ground of treachery.
Richard II. Act i, sc. 1, l. 11. [King Richard]

7
I am subtle, false and treacherous.
Richard III. Act i, sc. 1, l. 37. [Gloucester]

8
We'll show thee Io as she was a maid,
And how she was beguiled.
The Taming of the Shrew. Induction, sc. 2, l. 56. [Lord] The only mention of Io.

Beguiled, divorced, wronged, spited, slain!
Romeo and Juliet. Act iv, sc. 5, l. 55. [Paris]
The only use of "spited."

Ay me, detested! how am I beguiled!
Twelfth Night. Act v, sc. 1, l. 142. [Olivia]

Treacherous man! Thou hast beguiled my hopes.
The Two Gentlemen of Verona. Act v, sc. 4, l. 63. [Valentine]

Treacherous coward.—*III Henry VI,* ii, 2, 114.
Treacherous son.—*Richard II,* v, 3, 60.
Treacherous villain.—*Hamlet,* ii, 2, 609; *King Lear,* iii, 7, 87; *Othello,* v, 1, 58.

9
I have sworn thee fair and thought thee bright,
Who art as black as hell, as dark as night.
Sonnets. No. cxlvii.

10
The fellow that sits next him now, parts bread with him, pledges the breath of him in a divided draught, is the readiest man to kill him.
Timon of Athens. Act i, sc. 2, l. 47. [Apemantus]

11
I cannot now prove constant to myself,
Without some treachery used to Valentine.
The Two Gentlemen of Verona. Act ii, sc. 6, l. 31. [Proteus]

Base treachery.—*The Two Gentlemen of Verona,* iv, 1, 29.

TREASON

12
For treason is but trusted like the fox,
Who, ne'er so tame, so cherish'd and lock'd up,
Will have a wild trick of his ancestors.
I Henry IV. Act v, sc. 2, l. 9. [Worcester]

13
I do arrest thee, traitor, of high treason:
And you, lord archbishop, and you, lord Mowbray,
Of capital treason I attach you both.
II Henry IV. Act iv, sc. 2, l. 107. [Westmoreland]

O monstrous traitor! I arrest thee, York,
Of capital treason 'gainst the king and crown:
Obey, audacious traitor; kneel for grace.
II Henry VI. Act v, sc. 1, l. 106. [Somerset]
"Monstrous traitor" is repeated in iv, 10, 71.

I arrest thee On capital treason.
King Lear. Act v, sc. 3, l. 82. [Albany]

Of capital treason we arrest you here.
Richard II. Act iv, sc. 1, l. 151. [Northumberland]

14
Treason and murder ever kept together,
As two yoke-devils sworn to either's purpose.
Henry V. Act ii, sc. 2, l. 105. [King Henry]
The only use of "yoke-devils."

All other devils that suggest my treasons
Do botch and bungle up damnation
With patches, colours, and with forms being fetch'd
From glistering semblances of piety;
But he that temper'd thee bade thee stand up,
Gave thee no instance why thou shouldst do treason,
Unless to dub thee with the name of traitor.
Henry V. Act ii, sc. 2, l. 114. [King Henry]
The only use of "bungle." "Dub" is repeated in *II Henry IV,* v, 3, 78, and in *III Henry VI,* ii, 2, 59. See under KNIGHT.

You would have sold your king to slaughter,
His princes and his peers to servitude,
His subjects to oppression and contempt
And his whole kingdom into desolation.
Henry V. Act ii, sc. 2, l. 170. [King Henry]

15
Since God so graciously hath brought to light
This dangerous treason lurking in our way.
Henry V. Act ii, sc. 2, l. 185. [King Henry]

Here is . . . a most contagious treason come to light, look you, as you shall desire in a summer's day.
Henry V. Act iv, sc. 8, l. 22. [Fluellen]

Thy heinous, manifest, and many treasons.
King Lear. Act v, sc. 3, l. 92. [Albany]
Bloody treason.—*Julius Cæsar,* iii, 2, 196.
Close-tongued treason.—*The Rape of Lucrece,* l. 770. The only use of "close-tongued."
Dangerous treason.—*Henry V,* ii, 2, 162.
Detested treason.—*Richard II,* ii, 3, 109.
Flat treason.—*Love's Labour 's Lost,* iv, 3, 293.
Foul treason!—*Richard II,* v, 2, 72.
Manifest treason!—*Coriolanus,* iii, 1, 172.
Traitor's treason.—*The Rape of Lucrece,* l. 877.

1 Was not thy father, Richard Earl of Cambridge,
For treason executed in our late king's days?
And, by this treason, stand'st thou not attainted?
I Henry VI. Act ii, sc. 4, l. 90. [Somerset]
Treason is not inherited, my lord.
As You Like It. Act i, sc. 3, l. 63. [Rosalind]

2 Thou shalt rue this treason with thy tears.
I Henry VI. Act iii, sc. 2, l. 36. [Talbot]
Let him perceive how ill we brook his treason
And what offence it is to flout his friends.
I Henry VI. Act iv, sc. 1, l. 74. [King]
Thou mayst not wander in that labyrinth;
There Minotaurs and ugly treasons lurk.
I Henry VI. Act v, sc. 3, l. 188. [Suffolk]
The only mention of the Minotaur. "Labyrinth" is repeated in *Troilus and Cressida,* ii, 3, 2.

3 Here is a man accused of treason: . . .
This is the man
That doth accuse his master of high treason.
II Henry VI. Act i, sc. 3, l. 180. [Suffolk]
I confess, I confess treason.—*II Henry VI,* ii, 3, 97.

4 In his simple show he harbours treason.
II Henry VI. Act iii, sc. 1, l. 54. [Suffolk]
Treason's secret knife and traitors' rage.
II Henry VI. Act iii, sc. 1, l. 174. [Beaufort]

5 And neither by treason nor hostility
To seek to put me down.
III Henry VI. Act i, sc. 1, l. 199. [King Henry]
Thou and my brother both shall buy this treason
Even with the dearest blood your bodies bear.
III Henry VI. Act v, sc. 1, l. 68. [Gloucester]
To search the secret treasons of the world.
III Henry VI. Act v, sc. 2, l. 18. [Warwick]

6 A kind of puppy To the old dam, treason.
Henry VIII. Act i, sc. 1, l. 175. [Buckingham]
And point by point the treasons of his master
He shall again relate.
Henry VIII. Act i, sc. 2, l. 7. [King]
Corrupt and treasonous.—*Henry VIII,* i, 1, 156. [Buckingham]

7 O heavens! that this treason were not, or not I the detector!
King Lear. Act iii, sc. 5, l. 13. [Edmund]
The only use of "detector."
Back do I toss these treasons to thy head.
King Lear. Act v, sc. 3, l. 146. [Edmund]

8 Treasons capital, confess'd and proved,
Have overthrown him.
Macbeth. Act i, sc. 3, l. 115. [Angus]
Very frankly he confess'd his treasons.
Macbeth. Act i, sc. 4, l. 5. [Malcolm]

9 Treason has done his worst.
Macbeth. Act iii, sc. 2, l. 24. [Macbeth]

10 Portia: Upon the rack, Bassanio! then confess
What treason there is mingled with your love.
Bassanio: None but that ugly treason of mistrust,
Which makes me fear the enjoying of my love.
There may as well be amity and life
'Tween snow and fire, as treason and my love.
The Merchant of Venice. Act iii, sc. 2, l. 26.

11 Some treason, masters: yet stand close.
Much Ado about Nothing. Act iii, sc. 3, l. 113. [Watch]
O, 'tis treason!—*Antony and Cleopatra,* i, 5, 7.

12 By . . . private treason
Will take away your life.
Pericles. Act i, sc. 2, l. 104. [Helicanus]
Thus treason works ere traitors be espied.
The Rape of Lucrece, l. 361.

13 All the treasons for these eighteen years
Complotted and contrived in this land
Fetch from false Mowbray their first head and spring.
Richard II. Act i, sc. 1, l. 95. [Bolingbroke]
The only use of "complotted."
Confess thy treasons ere thou fly the realm.
Richard II. Act i, sc. 3, l. 198. [Bolingbroke]
His treasons will sit blushing in his face,
Not able to endure the sight of day.
Richard II. Act iii, sc. 2, l. 51. [King Richard]
Every stride he makes upon my land
Is dangerous treason.
Richard II. Act iii, sc. 3, l. 92. [King Richard]
Shall I for love speak treason to thy face?
Richard II. Act v, sc. 3, l. 44. [York]
Peruse this writing here, and thou shalt know
The treason that my haste forbids me show.
Richard II. Act v, sc. 3, l. 49. [York]

14 We would have had you heard
The traitor speak, and timorously confess
The manner and the purpose of his treason.
Richard III. Act iii, sc. 5, l. 56. [Gloucester]
The only use of "timorously."
We speak no treason, man.
Richard III. Act i, sc. 1, l. 90. [Gloucester]
Let them not live to taste this land's increase
That would with treason wound this fair land's peace!
Richard III. Act v, sc. 5, l. 38. [Richmond]

1
What treason were it to the ransack'd queen,
Disgrace to your great worths and shame to me,
Now to deliver her possession up
On terms of base compulsion!
Troilus and Cressida. Act ii, sc. 2, l. 150. [Paris]

II—The Traitor

2
A traitor you do look like; but such traitors
His majesty seldom fears.
All's Well that Ends Well. Act ii, sc. 1, l. 99. [Lafeu]
First Lord: As we are ourselves, what things are we!
Second Lord: Merely our own traitors.
All's Well that Ends Well. Act iv, sc. 3, l. 24.
A counsellor, a traitress, and a dear.
All's Well that Ends Well, i, 1, 184. The only use of "traitress." See under LOVE.

3
Traitorously discovered the secrets of your army.
All's Well that Ends Well, iv, 3, 339. See PUNISHMENT, 1220:17.
Murder'd traitorously.—*II Henry VI,* ii, 2, 27.
Traitorously is murder'd.—*II Henry VI,* iii, 2, 123.
Traitorously corrupted.—*II Henry VI,* iv, 7, 35. The only uses of "traitorously."

4 Let the world rank me in register
A master-leaver and a fugitive.
Antony and Cleopatra. Act iv, sc. 9, l. 21. [Enobarbus] The only use of "master-leaver."

5
Duke: Thus do all traitors:
If their purgation did consist in words,
They are as innocent as grace itself:
Let it suffice thee that I trust you not.
Rosalind: Yet your mistrust cannot make me a traitor.
As You Like It. Act i, sc. 3, l. 54.
If she be a traitor, Why so am I.
As You Like It. Act i, sc. 3, l. 74. [Celia]

6
Hath almost made me traitor to myself.
The Comedy of Errors. Act iii, sc. 2, l. 167. [Antipholus of Syracuse]

7
Has spoken like a traitor, and shall answer
As traitors do.
Coriolanus. Act iii, sc. 1, l. 162. [Sicinius]
A traitorous innovator, A foe to the public weal.
Coriolanus. Act iii, sc. 1, l. 175. [Sicinius] The only use of "innovator."
We are peremptory to dispatch
This viperous traitor.
Coriolanus. Act iii, sc. 1, l. 286. [Sicinius] "Viperous" is repeated in *I Henry VI,* iii, 1, 72: "Viperous worm"; and in *Cymbeline,* iii, 4, 41: "Viperous slander."

8
Call me their traitor! Thou injurious tribune!
Within thine eyes sat twenty thousand deaths,
In thy hands clutch'd as many millions, in
Thy lying tongue both numbers, I would say
'Thou liest' unto thee with a voice as free
As I do pray the gods.
Coriolanus. Act iii, sc. 3, l. 69. [Coriolanus]
Tell the traitor, in the high'st degree
He hath abused your powers.
Coriolanus. Act v, sc. 6, l. 85. [Aufidius]

9 Though those that are betray'd
Do feel the treason sharply, yet the traitor
Stands in worse case of woe.
Cymbeline. Act iii, sc. 4, l. 87. [Imogen]
Belarius: Thou hadst, great king, a subject who
Was call'd Belarius.
King: What of him? he is
A banish'd traitor. . . .
Belarius: Indeed a banish'd man;
I know not how a traitor.
Cymbeline. Act v, sc. 5, l. 316.
I am no traitor.—*Henry V,* iv, 8, 16.

10
I 'll be a traitor then, when thou art king.
I Henry IV. Act i, sc. 2, l. 164. [Falstaff]
What traitors have we here?—*I Henry VI,* i, 3, 15.
What a brood of traitors have we here?—*II Henry VI,* v, 1, 141.

11 Shall our coffers, then,
Be emptied to redeem a traitor home?
Shall we buy treason?
I Henry IV. Act i, sc. 3, l. 85. [King Henry] "Emptied" is repeated in *A Lover's Complaint,* l. 255.
He calls us rebels, traitors; and will scourge
With haughty arms this hateful name in us.
I Henry IV. Act v, sc. 2, l. 40. [Worcester]
Ha! you shall see now in very sincerity of fear and cold heart, will he to the king and lay open all our proceedings.
I Henry IV. Act ii, sc. 3, l. 33. [Hotspur]

12
Some guard these traitors to the block of death,
Treason's true bed and yielder up of breath.
II Henry IV. Act iv, sc. 2, l. 121. [Lancaster] "Yielder" is repeated in *I Henry IV,* v, 3, 11, and in *A Midsummer-Night's Dream,* iii, 2, 30.

13 Thou cruel,
Ingrateful, savage and inhuman creature!
Thou that didst bear the key of all my counsels,
That knew'st the very bottom of my soul,
That almost mightst have coin'd me into gold,
Wouldst thou have practised on me for thy use!
Henry V. Act ii, sc. 2, l. 94. [King Henry]

14
An arrant traitor as any is in the universal world.
Henry V. Act iv, sc. 8, l. 10. [Fluellen]
Blind traitor.—*King Lear,* iv, 5, 37.

Dangerous consorted traitors.—*Richard II*, v, 6, 15.
Disloyal traitor.—*Macbeth*, i, 2, 52.
False-heart traitor.—*II Henry VI*, v, 1, 143. The only use of "false-heart" as an adjective.
Filthy traitor.—*King Lear*, iii, 7, 32.
Graceless traitor.—*The Taming of the Shrew*, v, 2, 160.
Horrible traitors.—*Timon of Athens*, iv, 3, 118.
Inhuman traitors.—*Titus Andronicus*, v, 2, 178.
Love's traitor.—*King John*, ii, 1, 507.
Overweening traitor.—*Richard II*, i, 1, 147.
Proclaimed traitor.—*Richard II*, ii, 3, 30.
Publish'd traitor.—*King Lear*, iv, 6, 236.
Revolted faction traitors.—*Richard II*, ii, 2, 57.
Sanctified and holy traitors.—*As You Like It*, ii, 3, 13.
Unhappy traitor.—*King Lear*, iv, 6, 232.
Vile traitor.—*I Henry VI*, iv, 3, 33.
Traitors all!—*King Lear*, v, 3, 269.

1
Condemn'd to die for treason, but no traitor.
I Henry VI. Act ii, sc. 4, l. 97. [Plantagenet]
Pronounced a traitor.—*III Henry VI*, iv, 6, 54.

2
I am lowted by a traitor villain.
I Henry VI. Act iv, sc. 3, l. 13. [York] The only use of "lowted" (made a lowt or fool of).

Mad ire and wrathful fury makes us weep,
That thus we die, while remiss traitors sleep.
I Henry VI. Act iv, sc. 3, l. 28. [York]

3
Lay hands upon these traitors and their trash.
II Henry VI. Act i, sc. 4, l. 44. [York]

Go, take hence that traitor from our sight.
II Henry VI. Act ii, sc. 3, l. 103. [King]

His fortunes I will weep and 'twixt each groan
Say 'Who 's a traitor?'
II Henry VI. Act iii, sc. 1, l. 221. [King Henry]

4
I do arrest thee of high treason here.
II Henry VI. Act iii, sc. 1, l. 197. [Suffolk] Also *Henry V*, ii, 2, 145, 147, 149; *Henry VIII*, i, 1, 201.
Arraigned of high treason.—*The Winter's Tale*, iii, 2, 14.
Guilty of high treason.—*Henry VIII*, ii, 1, 27.

Appeal each other of high treason.
Richard II. Act i, sc. 1, l. 27. [King Richard]

5
A subtle traitor needs no sophister.
II Henry VI. Act v, sc. 1, l. 191. [Queen Margaret] "Sophister" is used in the first play and never again.

6
For a thousand causes
I would prolong awhile the traitor's life.
III Henry VI. Act i, sc. 4, l. 51. [Queen Margaret]

7
Off with the traitor's head!
III Henry VI. Act ii, sc. 6, l. 85. [Warwick]

Thou art a traitor; Off with his head!
Richard III. Act iii, sc. 4, l. 77. [Gloucester]

Here is the head of that ignoble traitor.
Richard III, iii, 5, 22. See under HEAD.

Let not a traitor live!
Julius Cæsar. Act iii, sc. 2, l. 209. [Mob]

8
Ha! durst the traitor breathe out so proud words?
III Henry VI. Act iv, sc. 1, l. 112. [King Edward]

Take the great-grown traitor unawares.
III Henry VI. Act iv, sc. 8, l. 63. [Gloucester] The only use of "great-grown."

9
We 'll quickly rouse the traitors.
III Henry VI. Act v, sc. 1, l. 65. [King Edward]

O passing traitor, perjured and unjust!
III Henry VI. Act v, sc. 1, l. 106. [Warwick]

I am your better, traitors as ye are.
III Henry VI. Act v, sc. 5, l. 36. [Prince]

10
So Judas kiss'd his master,
And cried 'all hail!' when as he meant all harm.
III Henry VI. Act v, sc. 7, l. 33. [Gloucester]

Holofernes: Judas I am,—
Dumain: A Judas!
Holofernes: Not Iscariot, sir.
Judas I am, ycliped Maccabæus.
Dumain: Judas Maccabæus clipt is plain Judas.
Biron: A kissing traitor.
Love's Labour's Lost. Act v, sc. 2, l. 601. The only mention of Iscariot. The only use of "ycliped." "Ycleped" occurs in i, 1, 242. Neither form appears in any other play. Judas is mentioned twelve times in this scene. "Judas Maccabæus" is repeated in v, 1, 134, and "poor Maccabæus" occurs in v, 2, 634, being the only uses of "Maccabæus."

Three Judases, each one thrice worse than Judas!
Richard II. Act iii, sc. 2, l. 132. [King Richard] The only use of "Judases."

Yet I well remember
The favours of these men: were they not mine?
Did they not sometime cry, 'all hail!' to me?
So Judas did to Christ: but he, in twelve,
Found truth in all but one; I, in twelve thousand, none.
Richard II, iv, 1, 167. [King Richard]

11
By day and night,
He 's traitor to the height.
Henry VIII. Act i, sc. 2, l. 213. [King]

Thou art a proud traitor, priest.
Henry VIII. Act iii, sc. 2, l. 252. [Surrey]
A giant traitor!—*Henry VIII*, i, 2, 199.

12
I have this day received a traitor's judgement,
And by that name must die.
Henry VIII, ii, 1, 58. [Buckingham]

The tribulation of Tower-hill.
Henry VIII. Act v, sc. 4, l. 65. [Porter] The only use of "tribulation" and "Tower-hill."

13
Myself have to mine own turn'd enemy.
Julius Cæsar. Act v, sc. 3, l. 2. [Cassius]

14
Hast thou not spoke like thunder on my side,
Been sworn my soldier, bidding me depend

Upon thy stars, thy fortune and thy strength,
And dost thou now fall over to my foes?
King John. Act iii, sc. 1, l. 124. [Constance]

You degenerate, you ingrate revolts,
You bloody Neroes, ripping up the womb
Of your dear mother England, blush for shame.
King John. Act v, sc. 2, l. 151. [Bastard] The only use of "ripping."

1
So white, and such a traitor.
King Lear. Act iii, sc. 7, l. 37. [Regan]

Maugre thy strength, youth, place, and eminence,
Despite thy victor sword and fire-new fortune,
Thy valour and thy heart, thou art a traitor;
False to thy gods, thy brother and thy father; . . .
And, from the extremest upward of thy head
To the descent and dust below thy foot,
A most toad-spotted traitor.
King Lear. Act v, sc. 3, l. 131. [Edgar] The only use of "toad-spotted." "Maugre" (in spite of) is repeated in *Titus Andronicus,* iv, 2, 110: "Maugre all the world"; and in *Twelfth Night,* iii, 1, 163: "Maugre all thy pride." "Fire-new" is used four times.

2
Walk aside the true folk, and let the traitors stay.
Love's Labour's Lost. Act iv, sc. 3, l. 213. [Costard]

3 We are traitors
And do not know ourselves.
Macbeth. Act iv, sc. 2, l. 18. [Ross]

Son: What is a traitor?
Lady Macduff: Why, one that swears and lies.
Macbeth. Act iv, sc. 2, l. 46.

4
Thou art a traitor and a miscreant,
Too good to be so and too bad to live.
Richard II. Act i, sc. 1, l. 39. [Bolingbroke]

Once more, the more to aggravate the note,
With a foul traitor's name stuff I thy throat.
Richard II. Act i, sc. 1, l. 43. [Bolingbroke] "Foul traitor" is repeated in iv, 1, 135.

Thou art a traitor.—*The Merry Wives of Windsor,* iii, 3, 65.

5
And when I mount, alive may I not light,
If I be traitor or unjustly fight!
Richard II. Act i, sc. 1, l. 82. [Mowbray]

Like a false traitor and injurious villain.
Richard II. Act i, sc. 1, l. 91. [Bolingbroke]

A recreant and most degenerate traitor.
Richard II. Act i, sc. 1, l. 144. [Mowbray]

6
A traitor to my God, my king, and me.
Richard II. Act i, sc. 3, l. 24. [Mowbray]

A traitor to his God, his king and him.
Richard II. Act i, sc. 3, l. 108. [First Herald]

Traitor to the crown.—*III Henry VI,* i, 1, 79; 80.

Traitor to the name of God.—*Richard III,* i, 4, 210.

Traitor to the people.—*Coriolanus,* iii, 3, 66.

7
He is a traitor, foul and dangerous.
Richard II. Act i, sc. 3, l. 39. [Bolingbroke]

If ever I were traitor,
My name be blotted from the book of life,
And I from heaven banish'd as from hence!
Richard II. Act i, sc. 3, l. 201. [Mowbray]

Nay, if I turn mine eyes upon myself,
I find myself a traitor with the rest;
For I have given here my soul's consent.
Richard II. Act iv, sc. 1, l. 247. [King Richard]

8
My liege, beware; look to thyself;
Thou hast a traitor in thy presence there.
Richard II. Act v, sc. 3, l. 39. [York]

Thou kill'st me in his life; giving him breath,
The traitor lives, the true man 's put to death.
Richard II. Act v, sc. 3, l. 72. [York]

Thou frantic woman, what dost thou make here?
Shall thy old dugs once more a traitor rear?
Richard II. Act v, sc. 3, l. 89. [York]

9
Well, well, he was the covert'st shelter'd traitor
That ever lived.
Richard III. Act iii, sc. 5, l. 33. [Buckingham] The only use of "covert'st" and "shelter'd."

The subtle traitor
This day had plotted, in the council-house
To murder me.
Richard III. Act iii, sc. 5, l. 37. [Buckingham] "Council-house" is repeated in *II Henry VI,* i, 1, 90.

Warn false traitors from the like attempts.
Richard III. Act iii, sc. 5, l. 49. [Mayor]

False traitors.—*Richard II,* i, 1, 91; *The Two Gentlemen of Verona,* iv, 4, 110.

10
We must be brief when traitors brave the field.
Richard III. Act iv, sc. 3, l. 57. [King Richard]

What traitor hears me, and says not amen?
Richard III. Act v, sc. 5, l. 22. [Richmond]

Abate the edge of traitors, gracious Lord.
Richard III. Act v, sc. 5, l. 35. [Richmond]

11
Speak not you for him; he 's a traitor.
The Tempest. Act i, sc. 2, l. 460. [Prospero]

He 's a traitor.—*Macbeth,* iv, 2, 82.

12 Put thy sword up, traitor;
Who makest a show but darest not strike, thy conscience
Is so possess'd with guilt.
The Tempest. Act i, sc. 2, l. 469. [Prospero]

13
Traitors, avaunt! where is the emperor's guard?
Treason, my lord!
Titus Andronicus. Act i, sc. 1, l. 283. [Titus]

14
More, she 's a traitor and Camillo is
A federacy with her.
The Winter's Tale. Act ii, sc. 1, l. 89. [Leontes] The only use of "federacy."

A nest of traitors!—*The Winter's Tale,* ii, 3, 81.

15
But what talk we of these traitorly rascals, whose miseries are to be smiled at, their offences being so capital?
The Winter's Tale. Act iv, sc. 4, l. 820. [Autolycus] The only use of "traitorly."

TREASURE

See also Riches, Wealth

1
I have . . . casketed my treasure.
All's Well that Ends Well, ii, 5, 26. The only use of "casketed."

This is my treasurer.—*Antony and Cleopatra,* v, 2, 142. The only use of "treasurer."

2 Thou hast uphoarded in thy life
Extorted treasure in the womb of earth,
For which, they say, you spirits oft walk in death.
Hamlet. Act i, sc. 1, l. 136. [Horatio] The only use of "uphoarded."

Hidden treasure.—*Venus and Adonis,* l. 767.
Precious treasure.—*Romeo and Juliet,* i, 1, 239.
Purest treasure.—*Richard II,* i, 1, 177.
Rich treasure.—*Venus and Adonis,* l. 552.
Rarest treasure.—*Cymbeline,* iii, 4, 163.

3
Ambassador: The prince our master . . .
Therefore sends you, meeter for your spirit,
This tun of treasure. . . .
King Henry: What treasure, uncle?
Exeter: Tennis-balls, my liege.
King Henry: We are glad the Dauphin is so pleasant with us;
His present and your pains we thank you for:
When we have matched our rackets to these balls,
We will, in France, by God's grace, play a set
Shall strike his father's crown into the hazard.
Tell him he hath made a match with such a wrangler
That all the courts of France will be disturb'd
With chaces.
Henry V. Act i, sc. 2, l. 249. The only use of "rackets" in this sense, and of "chaces," a term in tennis. "Meeter" is repeated in *Antony and Cleopatra,* v, 1, 49: "Some meeter season." "Tennis-balls" occurs again in *Much Ado about Nothing,* iii, 2, 47, and "wrangler" in *Troilus and Cressida,* ii, 2, 75.

4
Thy sumptuous buildings and thy wife's attire
Have cost a mass of public treasury.
II Henry VI. Act i, sc. 3, l. 133. [Somerset]

Silken treasury.—*The Winter's Tale,* iv, 4, 361.
Lavinia's treasury.—*Titus Andronicus,* ii, 1, 131.
Sumless treasuries.—*Henry V,* i, 2, 165. The only use of "treasuries" and of "sumless."
Treasury of everlasting joy.—*II Henry VI,* ii, 1, 18.
Treasury of life.—*King Lear,* iv, 6, 43. The only uses of "treasury."
Silver treasure-house.—*Merchant of Venice,* ii, 9, 34. The only use of "treasure-house."

5
Unlock'd the treasure of his happy state.
The Rape of Lucrece, l. 16.

Treasures of your body.—*Measure for Measure,* ii, 4, 96.
Treasure of thy heart.—*II Henry VI,* ii, 1, 20.
Treasure of thy love.—*Sonnets,* cxxxvi.
Treasure of an oyster.—*Antony and Cleopatra,* i, 5, 44.
Treasure of the realm.—*II Henry VI,* iv, 1, 74.
Treasure of his spring.—*Sonnets,* lxiii.
Treasure of your time.—*Twelfth Night,* ii, 5, 85.
My soul's treasure.—*II Henry VI,* iii, 2, 382.
England's treasure.—*II Henry VI,* iii, 3, 2.

6
Who fears sinking where such treasure lies?
The Rape of Lucrece, l. 280.

7
So am I as the rich, whose blessed key
Can bring him to his sweet up-locked treasure.
Sonnets. No. lii. The only use of "up-locked."

8 The gods out of my misery
Have sent thee treasure.
Timon of Athens. Act iv, sc. 3, l. 532. [Timon]

9
We'll . . . show thee all the treasure we have got;
Which, with ourselves, all rest at thy dispose.
The Two Gentlemen of Verona. Act iv, sc. 1, l. 75. [Outlaw]

10
Alas, poor world, what treasure hast thou lost!
Venus and Adonis, l. 1075.

TREATY, see Alliance

TREE

11
Thou prunest a rotten tree.
As You Like It. Act ii, sc. 3, l. 63. [Orlando]

12
Under the greenwood tree
Who loves to lie with me,
And turn his merry note
Unto the sweet bird's throat.
As You Like It. Act ii, sc. 5, l. 1. [Amiens] The only use of "greenwood."

Celia: I found him under a tree, like a dropped acorn.
Rosalind: It may well be called Jove's tree, when it drops forth such fruit.
As You Like It. Act iii, sc. 2, l. 247.

Jove's spreading tree.—*III Henry VI,* v, 2, 14.
Arabian trees.—*Othello,* v, 2, 350; *The Phœnix and Turtle,* l. 2.
Celestial tree.—*Pericles,* i, 1, 21.
Fresh tree.—*III Henry VI,* ii, 5, 49.
Senseless trees.—*Passionate Pilgrim,* l. 393.
Sturdy trees.—*Venus and Adonis,* l. 152.

13 These trees shall be my books
And in their barks my thoughts I'll character.
As You Like It. Act iii, sc. 2, l. 5. [Orlando]

I pray you, mar no more trees with writing love-songs in their barks.
As You Like It. Act iii, sc. 2, l. 276. [Jaques]

14
The tree may be known by the fruit, as the fruit by the tree.
I Henry IV. Act ii, sc. 4, l. 471. [Falstaff] A proverb whose first appearance in English was in William Bullein's *Dialogue against the Fever Pestilence,* published in 1564.

1
Come, you 're a young foolish sapling, and must be bowed as I would have you.
Pericles. Act iv, sc. 2, l. 92. [Bawd]
Blasted sapling.—*Richard III,* iii, 4, 71.
Tender sapling.—*Titus Andronicus,* iii, 2, 50. The only uses of "sapling."

2
Why grow the branches now the root is wither'd?
Why wither not the leaves the sap being gone?
Richard III. Act ii, sc. 2, l. 41. [Queen]
Why, we take
From every tree lop, bark, and part o' the timber;
And, though we leave it with a root, thus hack'd,
The air will drink the sap.
Henry VIII. Act i, sc. 2, l. 95. [King] The only use of "lop" in the sense of twigs. "Timber" is used again in *As You Like It,* iii, 3, 90.

3
Will these moss'd trees,
That have outlived the eagle, page thy heels,
And skip where thou point'st out?
Timon of Athens. Act iv, sc. 3, l. 223. [Apemantus] "Moss'd" is repeated in *As You Like It,* iv, 3, 105: "Moss'd with age."
I have a tree, which grows here in my close,
That mine own use invites me to cut down,
And shortly must I fell it: tell my friends,
Tell Athens, in the sequence of degree
From high to low throughout, that whoso please
To stop affliction, let him take his haste,
Come hither, ere my tree hath felt the axe,
And hang himself. I pray you, do my greeting.
Timon of Athens. Act v, sc. 1, l. 208. [Timon]

4
The trees, though summer, yet forlorn and lean,
O'ercome with moss and baleful mistletoe.
Titus Andronicus. Act ii, sc. 3, l. 94. [Tamora] The only mention of mistletoe.

II—Individual Trees

See also Oak, Pine

5
The bay-trees in our country are all wither'd.
Richard II, ii, 4, 8. See under OMEN.

6
We have some old crab-trees here at home that will not
Be grafted to your relish.
Coriolanus. Act ii, sc. 1, l. 205. [Menenius]
Graft with crab-tree slip.
II Henry VI. Act iii, sc. 2, l. 214. [Suffolk] "Graft" is repeated in *Richard III,* iii, 7, 127: "Graft with ignoble plants." "Grafting" occurs in *II Henry IV,* v, 3, 3.
Crab-tree staves.—*Henry VIII,* v, 4, 3.

7
Their sweetest shade a grove of cypress trees!
II Henry VI. Act iii, sc. 2, l. 323. [Suffolk]
Cypress grove.—*Coriolanus,* i, 10, 30.
In sad cypress let me be laid.
Twelfth Night. Act ii, sc. 4, l. 53. [Clown]
A cypress, not a bosom, hideth my heart.
Twelfth Night. Act iii, sc. 1, l. 132. [Olivia]
Cypress chests.—*The Taming of the Shrew,* ii, 1, 353.

8
Among the nettles at the elder-tree.
Titus Andronicus. Act ii, sc. 3, l. 272. [Saturninus, reading] Elder-tree is used again in l. 277, and occurs in no other scene.

9
Thou art an elm, my husband, I a vine.
The Comedy of Errors, ii, 2, 176. [Adriana]
The female ivy so
Enrings the barky fingers of the elm.
A Midsummer-Night's Dream. Act iv, sc. 1, l. 46. [Titania] The only use of "enrings" and "barky."
Answer, thou dead elm.—*II Henry IV,* ii, 4, 358.

10
The line-grove that weather-fends your cell.
The Tempest. Act v, sc. 1, l. 10. [Ariel] Line-grove, i. e., lime-grove. Lime is not used in the plays as referring to the tree. The only use of "weather-fends."

11
Touchstone: Truly, the tree yields bad fruit. . . .
Rosalind: I shall graff it with a medlar: then . . . you 'll be rotten ere you be half ripe, and that 's the right virtue of the medlar.
As You Like It. Act iii, sc. 2, l. 122. Shakespeare is referring to the fact that the fruit of the medlar, which is like a small brown-skinned apple, is not eaten until it has decayed into a soft pulpy state. "Graff" is repeated in *Pericles,* v, 1, 60.
The rotten medlar.—*Measure for Measure,* iv, 3, 184.
There 's a medlar for thee, eat it.—*Timon of Athens,* iv, 3, 305.
Now will he sit under a medlar tree.—*Romeo and Juliet,* ii, 1, 34.

12
Under the cool shade of a sycamore.
Love's Labour 's Lost. Act v, sc. 2, l. 89. [Princess]
Underneath the grove of sycamore.—*Romeo and Juliet,* i, 1, 128.
Sighing by a sycamore tree.—*Othello,* iv, 3, 41.

13
There is a willow grows aslant a brook,
That shows his hoar leaves in the glassy stream.
Hamlet. Act iv, sc. 7, l. 167. [Queen] The only use of "aslant." The willow is mentioned twelve times.

14
Under yond yew-trees lay thee all along.
Romeo and Juliet. Act v, sc. 3, l. 3. [Paris]
I did sleep under this yew-tree here.
Romeo and Juliet. Act v, sc. 3, l. 137. [Balthasar] The yew-tree is mentioned in no other scene.

TREMBLING, see Fear

TRESPASS

See also Fault

15
His trespass yet lives guilty in thy blood.
I Henry VI. Act ii, sc. 4, l. 94. [Somerset]
I am so sorry for my trespass made.
III Henry VI. Act v, sc. 1, l. 92. [Clarence]

1
Your son and daughter found this trespass worth
The shame which here it suffers.
King Lear. Act ii, sc. 4, l. 44. [Kent]

2
Wilt thou make a trust a transgression?
The transgression is in the stealer.
Much Ado about Nothing. Act ii, sc. 1, l. 232. [Don Pedro]

Heaven lay not my transgression to my charge!
King John. Act i, sc. 1, l. 256. [Lady Faulconbridge]

Needs must I under my transgression bow,
Unless my nerves were brass or hammer'd steel.
Sonnets. No. cxx.

He puts transgression to 't.
Measure for Measure. Act iii, sc. 2, l. 101. [Lucio]

False transgression.—*The Two Gentlemen of Verona,* ii, 4, 197.

Flat transgression.—*Much Ado about Nothing,* ii, 1, 229.

Rude transgression.—*Love's Labour 's Lost,* v, 2, 431.

Love's transgression.—*Romeo and Juliet,* i, 1, 191. The only uses of "transgression."

Their own transgressions partially they smother.
The Rape of Lucrece, l. 634. The only use of "transgressions."

3
His trespass in our common reason . . .
To incur a private check.
Othello. Act iii, sc. 3, l. 64. [Desdemona]

Trespass 'gainst his love.—*Othello,* iv, 2, 152.

4
My digression is so vile, so base,
That it will live engraven in my face.
The Rape of Lucrece, l. 202. "Digression" is repeated in *II Henry IV,* iv, 1, 140, and in *Love's Labour 's Lost,* i, 2, 121.

5
Thou . . .
Shalt have thy trespass cited up in rhymes,
And sung by children in succeeding times.
The Rape of Lucrece, l. 523.

Trespass of thine eye.—*The Rape of Lucrece,* l. 1476.

Common trespasses.—*King Lear,* ii, 2, 151.

Loathsome trespass.—*Rape of Lucrece,* l. 812.

Present trespass.—*The Rape of Lucrece,* l. 632.

6
Wilt thou not hide the trespass of thine own?
Richard II, v, 2, 89. [Duchess of York]

7
But that your trespass now becomes a fee;
Mine ransoms yours, and yours must ransom me.
Sonnets. No. cxx.

O trespass sweetly urged!—*Romeo and Juliet,* i, 5, 111.

8
But, beseech your grace,
Be plainer with me; let me know thy trespass
By its own visage.
Winter's Tale. Act i, sc. 2, l. 264. [Camillo]

Poor trespasses, More monstrous standing by.
Winter's Tale. Act iii, sc. 2, l. 190. [Paulina]

Trespass of the queen.—*Winter's Tale,* ii, 2, 63.

TRIAL

9
What I can do can do no hurt to try.
All's Well that Ends Well. Act ii, sc. 1, l. 137. [Helena]

10
If any man doubt that, let him put me to my purgation.
As You Like It. Act v, sc. 4, l. 44. [Touchstone]

Put him to his purgation.—*Hamlet,* iii, 2, 318.

Now you will be my purgation.—*Love's Labour 's Lost,* iii, 1, 128.

Trial, And fair purgation.—*Henry VIII,* v, 3, 152. "Purgation" is repeated in *As You Like It,* 1, 3, 55, and in *The Winter's Tale,* iii, 2, 7.

11
Only make trial what your love can do
For Rome.
Coriolanus. Act v, sc. 1, l. 40. [Brutus]

Make a trial of her love.—*I Henry VI,* v, 3, 76.

Trials of thy love.—*The Tempest,* iv, 1, 6.

Trial of a woman's war.—*Richard II,* i, 1, 48.

12
Too weak to wage an instant trial.
I Henry IV. Act iv, sc. 4, l. 20. [York]

Join in trial.—*I Henry IV,* v, 1, 85.

13
Galling the gleaned land with hot assays.
Henry V. Act i, sc. 2, l. 151. [King Henry]

Bid herself assay him: I have great hope in that.
Measure for Measure. Act i, sc. 2, l. 186. [Claudio]

He hath made an assay of her virtue.
Measure for Measure. Act iii, sc. 1, l. 164. [Duke]

Let us make the assay upon him.
Timon of Athens. Act iv, sc. 3, l. 406. [Bandit] "Assay" is used nineteen times.

She hath assay'd as much as may be proved.
Venus and Adonis, l. 608.

14
Call him to present trial: if he may
Find mercy in the law, 'tis his; if none,
Let him not seek 't of us.
Henry VIII. Act i, sc. 2, l. 211. [King Henry]

I had my trial, And, must needs say, a noble one.
Henry VIII. Act ii, sc. 1, l. 118. [Buckingham]

Must now confess . . . The trial just and noble.
Henry VIII. Act ii, sc. 2, l. 91. [Wolsey]

'Tis his highness' pleasure, . . . for better trial of you,
From hence you be committed to the Tower.
Henry VIII. Act v, sc. 3, l. 52. [Gardiner]

15
I . . . am right glad to catch this good occasion
Most throughly to be winnow'd, where my chaff
And corn shall fly asunder.
Henry VIII. Act v, sc. 1, l. 109. [Cranmer]

16
Let there be some more test made of my metal,
Before so noble and so great a figure
Be stamp'd upon it.
Measure for Measure. Act i, sc. 1, l. 49. [Angelo]

Bring me to the test.—*Hamlet*, iii, 4, 142.
Overt test.—*Othello*, i, 3, 107.
Stood the test.—*The Tempest*, iv, 1, 39. The only uses of "test."

1
He hath made trial of you only.
Measure for Measure, iii, 1, 202. [Duke]
Put your trial in the villain's mouth
Which here you come to accuse.
Measure for Measure, v, 1, 304. [Duke]

2
Mistress Quickly: With trial-fire touch me his finger-end:
If he be chaste, the flame will back descend
And turn him to no pain; but if he start,
It is the flesh of a corrupted heart.
Pistol: A trial, come.
Evans: Come, will this wood take fire?
[*They burn Falstaff with their tapers*]
Falstaff: Oh, Oh, Oh!
The Merry Wives of Windsor. Act v, sc. 5, l. 88. The only use of "trial-fire" and "finger-end." "Fingers' ends" occurs four times.
Hot trial.—*King John*, ii, 1, 342.

3
Then let us teach our trial patience,
Because it is a customary cross.
A Midsummer-Night's Dream. Act i, sc. 1, l. 152. [Hermia] See under Love.
Bear this trial.—*Love's Labour 's Lost*, v, 2, 813.

4
O God defend me! how am I beset!
Much Ado about Nothing, iv, 1, 78. [Hero]
He was beset.—*Twelfth Night*, v, 1, 88.
Beset with shame.—*The Merchant of Venice*, v, 1, 217.
Beset with thieves.—*The Taming of the Shrew*, iii, 2, 238.
Dreadfully beset.—*The Rape of Lucrece*, l. 444.
Hard beset.—*The Two Gentlemen of Verona*, ii, 4, 49.
The thicket is beset.—*The Two Gentlemen of Verona*, v, 3, 11. The only uses of "beset."

5
But all these poor forbiddings could not stay him;
He in the worst sense construes their denial;
The doors, the wind, the glove, that did delay him,
He takes for accidental things of trial.
The Rape of Lucrece, l. 323. The only use of "forbiddings."

6 There is my honour's pawn;
Engage it to the trial if thou darest.
Richard II. Act iv, sc. 1, l. 55. [Lord]
Order the trial, marshal.—*Richard II*, i, 3, 99.
Bloody trial.—*Richard III*, v, 2, 16.
Knightly trial.—*Richard II*, i, 1, 81.

7 Now do I play the touch,
To try if thou be current gold indeed.
Richard III, iv, 2, 8. [King Richard]

8
Make not too rash a trial of him.
The Tempest. Act i, sc. 2, l. 467. [Miranda]

9
Every action that hath gone before,
Whereof we have record, trial did draw
Bias and thwart, not answering the aim,
And that unbodied figure of the thought
That gave 't surmised shape. Why then you princes,
Do you with cheeks abash'd behold our works,
And call them shames? which are indeed nought else
But the protractive trials of great Jove
To find persistive constancy in men.
Troilus and Cressida. Act i, sc. 3, l. 13. [Agamemnon] The only use of "unbodied," "abash'd," "protractive," and "persistive."
Days of trial.—*Richard II*, iv, 1, 106; 153.
Time of trial.—*II Henry VI*, iii, 1, 138.

10 As she hath
Been publicly accused, so shall she have
A just and open trial.
Winter's Tale. Act ii, sc. 3, l. 203. [Leontes]

TRIBUTE

11
Come, there 's no more tribute to be paid.
Cymbeline. Act iii, sc. 1, l. 34. [Cloten]
Penny tribute.—*Cymbeline*, ii, 4, 20.
Neglected tribute.—*Hamlet*, iii, 1, 178.
Slavish tribute.—*The Rape of Lucrece*, l. 299.
Wonted tribute.—*Cymbeline*, v, 5, 462.

12
The proudest peer in the realm shall not wear a head on his shoulders, unless he pay me tribute.
II Henry VI. Act iv, sc. 7, l. 127. [Cade]

13
The virgin tribute paid by howling Troy
To the sea-monster.
The Merchant of Venice. Act iii, sc. 2, l. 56. [Portia] The reference is to Ovid, *Metamorphoses*, bk. xi, l. 199 *et seq*. "Sea-monster" is repeated in *King Lear*, i, 4, 283.

14
Give him annual tribute, do him homage.
The Tempest. Act i, sc. 2, l. 113. [Prospero]

15
Receive them then, the tribute that I owe,
Mine honour's ensigns humbled at thy feet.
Titus Andronicus. Act i, sc. 1, l. 251. [Titus]

TRICK

See also Cunning, Deceit

16
Lafeu: Let my horses be well looked to, without any tricks.
Clown: If I put any tricks upon 'em, sir, they shall be jades' tricks.
All 's Well that Ends Well. Act iv, sc. 5, l. 61.
You always end with a jade's trick.
Much Ado about Nothing. Act i, sc. 1, l. 145. [Beatrice]
A red murrain o' thy jade's tricks!
Troilus and Cressida. Act ii, sc. 1, l. 20. [Thersites]
A murrain on 't.—*Coriolanus*, i, 5, 3.
A murrain on your monster!—*The Tempest*, iii, 2, 88. "Murrain": plague.

17
'Tis one of those odd tricks which sorrow shoots

Out of the mind.
Antony and Cleopatra. Act iv, sc. 2, l. 14. [Enobarbus]

1
Is 't not your trick?
Antony and Cleopatra. Act v, sc. 2, l. 75. [Cleopatra]

It is our trick.—*Hamlet,* iv, 7, 188.

2
You are never without your tricks.
Coriolanus. Act ii, sc. 3, l. 38. [Citizen]

Some trick not worth an egg.—*Coriolanus,* iv, 4, 21.

The very trick on 't.—*Coriolanus,* iv, 6, 70.

3
It is a fetch of wit.
Hamlet. Act ii, sc. 1, l. 38. [Polonius]

Mere fetches.—*King Lear,* ii, 4, 90. The only use of "fetch" and "fetches" in the sense of trick.

4
Horridly trick'd with blood of fathers.
Hamlet. Act ii, sc. 2, l. 479. [Hamlet] The only use of "tricked." "Horridly" occurs again in i, 4, 55, and in no other play.

5
There 's tricks i' the world.
Hamlet. Act iv, sc. 5, l. 5. [Gentleman]

Tricks in war.—*Cymbeline,* iii, 3, 15.

Tricks of custom.—*Othello,* iii, 3, 122.

Trick of face.—*King John,* i, 1, 85.

Trick of fame.—*Hamlet,* iv, 4, 61.

Trick of frown.—*The Winter's Tale,* ii, 3, 100.

Trick of melancholy.—*All's Well that Ends Well,* iii, 2, 9.

Trick of state.—*Henry VIII,* ii, 1, 44.

Trick of singularity.—*Twelfth Night,* ii, 5, 164; iii, 4, 79. "Singularity" is repeated in *Coriolanus,* i, 1, 282, and "singularities" is used once, in *The Winter's Tale,* v, 3, 12.

Trick of voice.—*King Lear,* iv, 6, 108.

Tricks and toys.—*Passionate Pilgrim,* l. 337.

6
I know a trick worth two of that.
I Henry IV. Act ii, sc. 1, l. 40. [Carrier]

What trick hast thou now?
I Henry IV. Act ii, sc. 4, l. 294. [Poins]

7
What a plague mean you to colt me thus?
I Henry IV. Act ii, sc. 2, l. 39. [Falstaff] The only use of "colt" with this meaning, to befool.

8
At this instant
He bores me with some trick.
Henry VIII, i, 1, 127. [Buckingham]

A speeding trick to lay down ladies.
Henry VIII. Act i, sc. 3, l. 40. [Lovell]

He coasts
And hedges his own way. But in this point
All his tricks founder.
Henry VIII, iii, 2, 38. [Chamberlain]

9
These are unsightly tricks.
King Lear. Act ii, sc. 4, l. 159. [Regan] The only use of "unsightly."

Popish tricks.—*Titus Andronicus,* v, 1, 76. The only use of "popish."

Scornful tricks.—*Venus and Adonis,* l. 501.

Villanous trick.—*I Henry IV,* ii, 4, 446.

10
I see the trick on 't.
Love's Labour's Lost. Act v, sc. 2, l. 460. [Biron]

I smell the trick on 't.
The Winter's Tale. Act iv, sc. 4, l. 655. [Autolycus]

11
If it were damnable, he being so wise,
Why would he for the momentary trick
Be perdurably fined?
Measure for Measure. Act iii, sc. 1, l. 113. [Claudio] The only use of "perdurably."

It was a mad fantastical trick of him.
Measure for Measure. Act iii, sc. 2, l. 98. [Lucio]

Fantastic tricks.—*Measure for Measure,* ii, 2, 121.

12
I have within my mind
A thousand raw tricks of these bragging Jacks,
Which I will practise.
The Merchant of Venice. Act iii, sc. 4, l. 76. [Portia]

13
That were a trick indeed!
The Merry Wives of Windsor. Act ii, sc. 2, l. 117. [Mistress Quickly]

We will yet have more tricks with Falstaff.
The Merry Wives of Windsor. Act iii, sc. 3, l. 203. [Mrs. Page]

If I be served such another trick, I 'll have my brains ta'en out and buttered, and give them to a dog for a new year's gift.
The Merry Wives of Windsor. Act iii, sc. 5, l. 6. [Falstaff] "Buttered" is used again in *King Lear,* ii, 4, 127: "Buttered his hay." The only use of "new year's gift."

14
This can be no trick.
Much Ado about Nothing. Act ii, sc. 3, 228. [Benedick]

15
This is a trick to put me from my suit.
Othello. Act iii, sc. 4, l. 87. [Desdemona]

How comes this trick upon him?
Othello. Act iv, sc. 2, l. 129. [Iago]

16
I that am not made for sportive tricks.
Richard III. Act i, sc. 1, l. 14. [Richard]

Wanton tricks.—*The Rape of Lucrece,* l. 320.

17
This trick may chance to scathe you.
Romeo and Juliet. Act i, sc. 5, l. 86. [Capulet]

18
Do you put tricks upon 's with savages and men of Ind, ha?
The Tempest. Act ii, sc. 2, l. 60. [Stephano]

As good a trick as ever hangman served thief.
Timon of Athens. Act ii, sc. 2, l. 99. [Apemantus]

19
Is it your trick to make me ope the door,
That so my sad decrees may fly away,
And all my study be to no effect?
Titus Andronicus. Act v, sc. 1, l. 10. [Titus]

20
What need these tricks?
Troilus and Cressida. Act v, sc. 1, l. 14. [Patroclus]

Cressida: What would you have me do?
Thersites: A juggling trick,—to be secretly open.
Troilus and Cressida. Act v, sc. 2, l. 23.

1 I 'll quickly cross
By some sly trick blunt Thurio's dull proceeding.
The Two Gentlemen of Verona. Act ii, sc. 6, l. 40. [Proteus]

Nay, I remember the trick you served me when I took my leave.
The Two Gentlemen of Verona. Act iv, sc. 4, l. 38. [Launce]

An' you serve me such another trick, never come in my sight more.
As You Like It. Act iv, sc. 1, l. 40. [Rosalind]

2 Come, I 'll question you
Of my lord's tricks and yours when you were boys.
Winter's Tale. Act i, sc. 2, l. 60. [Hermione]

He has discover'd my design, and I
Remain a pinch'd thing; yea, a very trick
For them to play at will.
Winter's Tale. Act ii, sc. 1, l. 50. [Leontes]

TRIFLE

See also Toy

3
He that of greatest works is finisher
Oft does them by the weakest minister: . . .
. . . great floods have flown
From simple sources, and great seas have dried
When miracles have by the greatest been denied.
All's Well that Ends Well. Act ii, sc. 1, l. 139. [Helena] The only use of "finisher."

4 I some lady trifles have reserved,
Immoment toys.
Antony and Cleopatra. Act v, sc. 2, l. 165. [Cleopatra] The only use of "immoment."

5
A trifle, some eight-penny matter.
I Henry IV. Act iii, sc. 3, l. 119. [Prince of Wales] The only use of "eight-penny matter."

Away, you trifler!—*I Henry IV,* ii, 3, 93. The only use of "trifler."

6 Let us not forego
That for a trifle that was bought with blood!
I Henry VI. Act iv, sc. 1, l. 149. [King Henry]

7
Small things make base men proud.
II Henry VI. Act iv, sc. 1, l. 106. [Suffolk]

8
Many strokes, though with a little axe,
Hew down and fell the hardest-timber'd oak.
III Henry VI. Act ii, sc. 1, l. 54. [Messenger] The only use of "hardest-timber'd."

Blunt wedges rive hard knots.
Troilus and Cressida. Act i, sc. 3, l. 316. [Ulysses]

9
Oftentimes, to win us to our harm,
The instruments of darkness tell us truths,
Win us with honest trifles, to betray 's
In deepest consequence.
Macbeth. Act i, sc. 3, l. 123. [Banquo]

10
Hang the trifle, woman! take the honour. . . . Dispense with trifles.
The Merry Wives of Windsor. Act ii, sc. 1, l. 46. [Mrs. Page]

That 's but a trifle here.—*King Lear,* v, 3, 295.
But a trifle.—*All's Well that Ends Well,* ii, 2, 36.
Careless trifle.—*Macbeth,* i, 4, 11.
Enchanted trifle.—*The Tempest,* v, 1, 112.
Small trifle.—*Merchant of Venice,* ii, 2, 170.

11 Trifles light as air
Are to the jealous confirmations strong
As proofs of holy writ.
Othello. Act iii, sc. 3, l. 322. [Iago]

12
Come, gentlemen, we sit too long on trifles.
Pericles. Act ii, sc. 3, l. 92. [Simonides]

13
It is a matter of small consequence.
Richard II. Act v, sc. 2, l. 61. [Aumerle]

14
The respects thereof are nice and trivial.
Richard III, iii, 7, 175. [Buckingham]

It had been pity you should have been put together with so mortal a purpose as then each bore, upon importance of so slight and trivial a nature.
Cymbeline. Act i, sc. 4, l. 43. [Frenchman]

Trivial argument.—*II Henry VI,* iii, 1, 241.
Trivial difference.—*Antony and Cleopatra,* ii, 2, 21.
Trivial motion.—*Coriolanus,* ii, 1, 55.
Trivial price.—*All's Well that Ends Well,* v, 3, 61.
Trivial records.—*Hamlet,* i, 5, 99. The only uses of "trivial."

15
But this is trifling.
The Tempest. Act iii, sc. 1, l. 79. [Miranda]

16
Trifles, unwitnessed with eye or ear,
Thy coward heart with false bethinking grieves.
Venus and Adonis, l. 1023. The only use of "unwitnessed" and "bethinking."

17
A snapper-up of unconsidered trifles.
Winter's Tale. Act iv, sc. 3, l. 26. [Autolycus] The only use of "snapper-up." "Unconsidered" is repeated in *Henry VIII,* i, 2, 15.

TRIUMPH

See also Victory

18 Set thee on triumphant chariots and
Put garlands on thy head.
Antony and Cleopatra. Act iii, sc. 1, l. 10. [Silius]

Triumphant garlands.—*Richard III,* iv, 4, 333.

19
Thou didst ride in triumph through the streets.
II Henry VI. Act ii, sc. 4, l. 14. [Gloucester]

Still ride in triumph over all mischance.
III Henry VI. Act iii, sc. 3, l. 18. [King Lewis]

1
I 'll throw thy body in another room
And triumph, Henry, in thy day of doom.
III Henry VI. Act v, sc. 6, l. 93. [Gloucester]
Triumphs in their death.—*III Henry VI,* ii, 4, 8.

2
How will he triumph, leap and laugh.
Love's Labour's Lost. Act iv, sc. 3, l. 148. [King]
Would I might triumph so!—*Love's Labour's Lost,* iv, 3, 110.

3
What, at the wheels of Cæsar? art thou led in triumph?
Measure for Measure. Act iii, sc. 2, l. 46. [Lucio]
Be thou sorry to follow Cæsar in his triumph.
Antony and Cleopatra. Act iii, sc. 13, l. 136. [Antony]
Cleopatra: He 'll lead me, then, in triumph?
Dolabella: Madam, he will.
Antony and Cleopatra. Act v, sc. 2, l. 109.
You are contented to be led in triumph
Through the streets of Rome?
Julius Cæsar. Act v, sc. 1, l. 109. [Cassius]
Stately triumphs.—*III Henry VI,* iv, 7, 43.

4
Do you triumph, Roman? do you triumph?
Othello. Act iv, sc. 1, l. 121. [Othello]
Bring him with triumph home.—*Julius Cæsar,* iii, 2, 54.

5
Think you, but that I know our state secure,
I would be so triumphant as I am?
Richard III. Act iii, sc. 2, l. 83. [Hastings]
Triumphing at mine enemies.—*Richard III,* iii, 4, 91.
Triumphing in my woe.—*Love's Labour's Lost,* iv, 3, 36.
Triumph not in my woes!
Richard III, iv, 4, 59. See under WOE.

6
We have not yet set down this day of triumph.
Richard III. Act iii, sc. 4, l. 44. [Derby]

7
Long live Lord Titus, my beloved brother,
Gracious triumpher in the eyes of Rome!
Titus Andronicus. Act i, sc. 1, l. 169. [Marcus Andronicus] The only use of "triumpher."
Great triumphers.—*Timon of Athens,* v, 1, 199. The only use of "triumphers."

TROOP

8 Tarry, holy pilgrim,
But till the troops come by.
All's Well that Ends Well. Act iii, sc. 5, l. 43. [Widow]
The troop is past.—*All's Well that Ends Well,* iii, 5, 96.
Yonder comes the troop.—*Troilus and Cressida,* iv, 5, 64.

9
The troops are all scattered, and the commanders very poor rogues.
All's Well that Ends Well. Act iv, sc. 3, l. 152. [Parolles]

10
Our English troops retire, I cannot stay them;
A woman clad in armour chaseth them.
I Henry VI. Act i, sc. 5, l. 2. [Talbot]
Troops of English.—*I Henry VI,* iii, 3, 32.
Troop of Florentines.—*All's Well that Ends Well,* iii, 6, 23.
Troops of armed men.—*I Henry VI,* ii, 2, 24.
Troops of cares.—*The Rape of Lucrece,* l. 720.
Troops of citizens.—*Richard III,* iii, 7, 85.
Troop of fairies.—*The Merry Wives of Windsor,* v, 3, 12.
Troops of friends.—*Macbeth,* v, 3, 25.
Troop of horse.—*King Lear,* iv, 6, 189.
Troops of horsemen.—*I Henry VI,* iv, 1, 165.
Troop of kerns.—*II Henry VI,* iii, 1, 361.
Troops of ladies.—*II Henry VI,* i, 3, 80.
Troops of soldiers.—*III Henry VI,* i, 1, 68.
Noble troop of strangers.—*Henry VIII,* i, 4, 53.
Noble troops.—*Henry VIII,* iii, 2, 411.
Blessed troop.—*Henry VIII,* iv, 2, 87.
Boyish troops.—*King John,* v, 2, 133.
Discontented troops.—*Timon of Athens,* iii, 5, 115.
Infectious troop.—*Comedy of Errors,* v, 1, 81.
Jolly troop.—*King John,* ii, 1, 321.
Plumed troop.—*Othello,* iii, 3, 349.
Populous troops.—*Antony and Cleopatra,* iii, 6, 50.
Puissant troop.—*III Henry VI,* v, 1, 6.
Well-beseeming troop.—*Titus Andronicus,* ii, 3, 56. "Well-beseeming" is repeated in *I Henry IV,* i, 1, 14: "Well-beseeming ranks."

11 Let us all together to our troops,
And give them leave to fly that will not stay;
And call them pillars that will stand to us.
III Henry VI. Act ii, sc. 3, l. 49. [George]

12
Our troops set forth to-morrow.
King Lear. Act iv, sc. 5, l. 16. [Regan]

13
Where be the thronging troops that follow'd thee?
Richard III, iv, 4, 96. See under QUEEN.
In troops I have dispersed them 'bout the isle.
The Tempest. Act i, sc. 2, l. 220. [Ariel]

TROUBLE

See also Pains

14 Cheer your heart:
Be not troubled with the time.
Antony and Cleopatra, iii, 6, 81. [Cæsar]
I will not long be troubled with you.
As You Like It. Act i, sc. 1, l. 81. [Orlando]
Troubled in sleep.—*Titus Andronicus,* ii, 2, 9.
Troubled with the lampass.—*The Taming of the Shrew,* iii, 2, 52. See under HORSE.
Troubled with a raging tooth.—*Othello,* iii, 3, 414. See under TEETH.
Troubled with a rheum.—*Antony and Cleopatra,* iii, 2, 57. See under DISEASE.
Troubled with a shrew.—*The Taming of the Shrew,* v, 2, 28. See under SHREW.
Troubled with the green sickness.—*Antony and Cleopatra,* iii, 2, 5. See under ENVY.
Troubled with thick-coming fancies.—*Macbeth,* v, 3, 38. See under FANCY.

1
Now thou 'rt troublesome.
Coriolanus. Act iv, sc. 5, l. 17. [Coriolanus]
You are strangely troublesome.
Henry VIII. Act v, sc. 3, l. 94. [Gardiner]
I 'll rather be unmannerly than troublesome.
The Merry Wives of Windsor. Act i, sc. 1, l. 325. [Slender]
Be . . . troublesome.—*II Henry IV,* ii, 3, 4.
How troublesome.—*II Henry IV,* iv, 5, 187.
So troublesome.—*II Henry IV,* iv, 5, 22.
The time is troublesome.—*Cymbeline,* iv, 3, 21.
The only uses of "troublesome."

2 You lay out too much pains
For purchasing but trouble.
Cymbeline. Act ii, sc. 3, l. 92. [Imogen]

3
Indeed, indeed, sirs, but this troubles me.
Hamlet. Act i, sc. 2, l. 224. [Hamlet]
Sea of troubles.—*Hamlet,* iii, 1, 59.

4
There was no need to trouble himself.
Henry V. Act ii, sc. 3, l. 22. [Hostess]
Nor build yourself a trouble.
Othello. Act iii, sc. 3, l. 150. [Iago]
Trouble not yourself.—*Merry Wives of Windsor,* iii, 4, 92; *Troilus and Cressida,* iv, 2, 1.
Trouble yourself no further.—*Othello,* iv, 3, 1; *Antony and Cleopatra,* ii, 4, 1.

5
Madam, I have been bold to trouble you.
I Henry VI. Act ii, sc. 3, l. 25. [Talbot]
Madam, I must trouble you again.
I Henry VI. Act v, sc. 3, l. 180. [Suffolk]

6
I would his troubles likewise were expired,
That so he might recover what was lost.
I Henry VI. Act ii, sc. 5, l. 31. [Mortimer]

7
All the trouble thou hast turn'd me to!
III Henry VI. Act v, sc. 5, l. 16. [King Edward]
Exceeding trouble.—*II Henry VI,* v, 1, 70.

8
Take thy lute, wench: my soul grows sad with troubles;
Sing, and disperse 'em, if thou canst.
Henry VIII. Act iii, sc. 1, l. 1. [Queen Katharine]
Full of . . . troubles.—*Henry VIII,* ii, 2, 16.
In trouble.—*The Merchant of Venice,* iii, 2, 293.

9 His long trouble now is passing
Out of this world.
Henry VIII. Act iv, sc. 2, l. 162. [Katharine]

10 If I have veil'd my look,
I turn the trouble of my countenance
Merely upon myself.
Julius Cæsar. Act i, sc. 2, l. 37. [Brutus]

11 I know this is a joyful trouble to you;
But yet 'tis one.
Macbeth. Act ii, sc. 3, l. 53. [Macduff]
Double, double toil and trouble.—*Macbeth,* iv, 1, 10. See under CHARM. Repeated in l. 20.
Present trouble.—*Twelfth Night,* iii, 4, 377.
Unnatural troubles.—*Macbeth,* v, 1, 80.
Troubles of the brain.—*Macbeth,* v, 3, 42. See under MIND.

12
Don Pedro: Good Signior Leonato, you are come to meet your trouble: the fashion of the world is to avoid cost, and you encounter it.
Leonato: Never came trouble to my house in the likeness of your grace: for trouble being gone, comfort should remain: but when you depart from me, sorrow abides and happiness takes his leave.
Much Ado about Nothing. Act i, sc. 1, l. 96.

13
Take I your wish, I leap into the seas,
Where 's hourly trouble for a minute's ease.
Pericles. Act ii, sc. 4, l. 44. [Helicanus]

14
Troubler of the poor world's peace.
Richard III. Act i, sc. 3, l. 221. [Queen Margaret]
Troubler of your peace.—*Pericles,* v, 1, 153.
The only uses of "troubler."

15
Balthasar: I will be gone, sir, and not trouble you.
Romeo: So shalt thou show me friendship.
Romeo and Juliet. Act v, sc. 3, l. 40.
I 'll not trouble thee.—*III Henry VI,* v, 5, 5; *King Lear,* ii, 4, 222.
I will not trouble you.—*As You Like It,* ii, 7, 171.
We 'll not trouble them.—*The Winter's Tale,* iv, 4, 317.
Trouble him no further.—*Timon of Athens,* v, 1, 216.
Trouble you no further.—*Coriolanus,* ii, 3, 117.
Trouble him no more.—*King Lear,* iv, 7, 81.
Trouble me no more.—*I Henry IV,* i, 2, 91.
Trouble us no more.—*I Henry VI,* iii, 1, 144; *II Henry VI,* iii, 1, 324; *Titus Andronicus,* i, 1, 367; 478.
Trouble you no more.—*II Henry IV,* iv, 5, 128; *Richard II,* iv, 1, 303; *The Two Gentlemen of Verona,* ii, 1, 125.
Trouble him not.—*King Lear,* iii, 6, 94.
Trouble us not.—*Richard III,* i, 2, 50; *The Tempest,* i, 1, 19.

16
Alack, what trouble was I then to you!
The Tempest. Act i, sc. 2, l. 151. [Miranda]
I trouble thee too much.—*Julius Cæsar,* iv, 3, 259.

17
O good Antonio, forgive me your trouble.
Twelfth Night. Act ii, sc. 1, l. 35. [Sebastian]

18 My stay
To you a charge and trouble: to save both,
Farewell.
The Winter's Tale. Act i, sc. 2, l. 25. [Polixenes]
We honour you with trouble.
Winter's Tale. Act v, sc. 3, l. 9. [Leontes]

TROY

19 Senseless Ilium,
Seeming to feel this blow, with flaming top
Stoops to his base, and with a hideous crash
Takes prisoner Pyrrhus' ear.
Hamlet. Act ii, sc. 2, l. 495. [First Player]

Ilium is used five times in the plays, once in *Hamlet* as above, and four times in *Troilus and Cressida*. The only use of "crash."

Troy must not be, nor goodly Ilion stand;
Our firebrand brother, Paris, burns us all.
Troilus and Cressida. Act ii, sc. 2, l. 109. [Cassandra]

So, Ilion, fall thou next! Now, Troy, sink down!
Troilus and Cressida. Act v, sc. 8, l. 11. [Achilles]

Cloud-kissing Ilion.—*The Rape of Lucrece,* l. 1370. The only use of the phrase.

Great Ilion.—*Troilus and Cressida,* iv, 5, 112.

Rich-built Ilion.—*The Rape of Lucrece,* l. 1524. The only use of "rich-built."

Heir of Ilion.—*Love's Labour's Lost,* v, 2, 658.

In Ilion.—*Troilus and Cressida,* iv, 4, 118; iv, 5, 216. The only uses of "Ilion."

1
Like a Sinon, take another Troy.
III Henry VI. Act iii, sc. 2, l. 190. [Gloucester]

So Priam's trust false Sinon's tears doth flatter,
That he finds means to burn his Troy with water.
The Rape of Lucrece, l. 1560. It was Sinon who persuaded Priam to admit the wooden horse made by the Greeks.

Speak, Rome's dear friend, as erst our ancestor,
When with his solemn tongue he did discourse
To love-sick Dido's sad attending ear
The story of that baleful burning night
When subtle Greeks surprised King Priam's Troy,
Tell us what Sinon hath bewitch'd our ears,
Or who hath brought the fatal engine in
That gives our Troy, our Rome, the civil wound.
Titus Andronicus. Act v, sc. 3, l. 80. [Marcus]

When he lay couched in the ominous horse.
Hamlet. Act ii, sc. 2, l. 476. [Hamlet]

Like the Trojan horse was stuff'd within
With bloody veins.
Pericles. Act i, sc. 4, l. 93. [Pericles]

2
And from the towers of Troy there would appear
The very eyes of men through loop-holes thrust,
Gazing upon the Greeks with little lust.
The Rape of Lucrece, l. 1382. The only use of "loop-holes."

Howling Troy.—*Merchant of Venice,* iii, 2, 56.

Strong-besieged Troy.—*The Rape of Lucrece,* l. 1429. The only use of the phrase.

3
Ah, thou, the model where old Troy did stand.
Richard II. Act v, sc. 1, l. 11. [Queen]

4
Bid Æneas tell the tale twice o'er,
How Troy was burnt and he made miserable.
Titus Andronicus. Act iii, sc. 2, l. 27. [Titus]

Half his Troy was burnt.—*II Henry IV,* i, 1, 73.

Burning Troy.—*II Henry VI,* iii, 2, 118.

Troy that burns so long.—*The Rape of Lucrece,* l. 1468.

5
In Troy, there lies the scene. From isles of Greece
The princes orgulous, their high blood chafed,
Have to the port of Athens sent their ships,
Fraught with the ministers and instruments
Of cruel war; sixty and nine, that wore
Their crownets regal; . . . and their vow is made
To ransack Troy, within whose regal immures
The ravish'd Helen, Menelaus' queen,
With wanton Paris sleeps; and that 's the quarrel.
Troilus and Cressida, Prol., 1. The only use of "orgulous" and "immures."

Priam's six-gated city.
Troilus and Cressida, Prol., 15. The only use of "six-gated."

6
After seven years' siege yet Troy walls stand.
Troilus and Cressida. Act i, sc. 3, l. 12. [Agamemnon]

Troy in our weakness stands, not in her strength.
Troilus and Cressida. Act i, sc. 3, l. 137. [Ulysses]

Yea, with a bridegroom's fresh alacrity,
Let us address to tend on Hector's heels:
The glory of our Troy doth this day lie
On his fair worth and single chivalry.
Troilus and Cressida. Act iv, sc. 4, l. 147. [Æneas]

7
Great Troy is ours, and our sharp wars are ended.
Troilus and Cressida. Act v, sc. 9, l. 10. [Agamemnon]

Sit, gods, upon your thrones and smile at Troy!
Troilus and Cressida. Act v, sc. 10, l. 7. [Troilus]

Go in to Troy, and say there, Hector's dead:
There is a word will Priam turn to stone;
Make wells and Niobes of the maids and wives,
Cold statues of the youth, and, in a word,
Scare Troy out of itself. But, march away:
Hector is dead; there is no more to say. . . .
Strike a free march to Troy! with comfort go:
Hope of revenge shall hide our inward woe.
Troilus and Cressida. Act v, sc. 10, l. 17. [Troilus]

II—The Trojans

8
There are other Trojans that thou dreamest not of.
I Henry IV. Act ii, sc. 1, l. 77. [Gadshill]

9
Thus he goes,
As did the youthful Paris once to Greece,
With hope to find the like event in love,
But prosper better than the Trojan did.
I Henry VI. Act v, sc. 5, l. 103. [Suffolk]

Thy heat of lust, fond Paris, did incur
This load of wrath that burning Troy doth bear.
The Rape of Lucrece, l. 1473.

Had doting Priam check'd his son's desire,
Troy had been bright with fame and not with fire.
The Rape of Lucrece, l. 1490.
Amorous Trojan.—*Troilus and Cressida,* v, 5, 4.
Base Trojan.—*Henry V,* v, 1, 20; 32.
False Troyan.—*A Midsummer-Night's Dream,* i, 1, 174.
Honest Troyan.—*Love's Labour 's Lost,* v, 2, 681.
Proud Trojan.—*Troilus and Cressida,* v, 6, 15.

1
Many Trojan mothers, sharing joy
To see their youthful sons bright weapons wield.
The Rape of Lucrece, l. 1431.
All the gallantry of Troy.—*Troilus and Cressida,* iii, 1, 149. The only use of "gallantry."
Gallant Trojan.—*Troilus and Cressida,* iv, 5, 183.

2
On one and other side, Trojan and Greek
Sets all on hazard.
Troilus and Cressida, Prol., 21.
Each Trojan that is master of his heart,
Let him to field.
Troilus and Cressida. Act i, sc. 1, l. 4. [Troilus]
This Trojan scorns us; or the men of Troy
Are ceremonious courtiers.
Troilus and Cressida. Act i, sc. 3, l. 233. [Agamemnon]
For here the Trojans taste our dear'st repute
With their finest palate.
Troilus and Cressida. Act i, sc. 3, l. 337. [Nestor]
For every scruple
Of her contaminated carrion weight,
A Trojan hath been slain.
Troilus and Cressida. Act iv, sc. 1, l. 70. [Diomedes]

TRUANT, see under Fidelity

TRUMPET

3
Hark! you may know by their trumpets.
All's Well that Ends Well. Act iii, sc. 5, l. 9. [Widow]
I know by his trumpets.—*All's Well that Ends Well,* v, 2, 55.
I know his trumpet.—*Othello,* ii, 1, 180.
Hark! the trumpets.—*Coriolanus,* ii, 1, 173.

4
Trumpeters,
With brazen din blast you the city's ear;
Make mingle with your rattling tabourines;
That heaven and earth may strike their sounds together,
Applauding our approach.
Antony and Cleopatra. Act iv, sc. 8, l. 35. [Antony] "Applauding" occurs also in *Timon of Athens,* v, 1, 200.
Beat loud the tabourines.—*Troilus and Cressida,* iv, 5, 275. The only uses of "tabourines."

5
Let the trumpets sound
The tucket sonance and the note to mount.
Henry V. Act iv, sc. 2, l. 34. [Constable] The only use of "tucket" and "sonance."
Let the trumpet sound.—*King Lear,* v, 1, 41.
Ho, bid my trumpet sound.—*Troilus and Cressida,* v, 3, 13.

6
Sound, trumpets, alarum to the combatants!
II Henry VI. Act ii, sc. 3, l. 95. [York] "Sound, trumpets" is used three times in this play; four times in *III Henry VI,* and occasionally in later plays.
The angry trumpet sounds alarum.
II Henry VI. Act v, sc. 2, l. 3. [Warwick]
Trumpets, speak!—*King Lear,* v, 3, 150.
A flourish, trumpets!—*Richard III,* iv, 4, 148.
Trumpet-clangor sounds.—*II Henry IV,* v, 5, 42. The only use of the phrase.

7
Now let the general trumpet blow his blast!
II Henry VI, v, 2, 43. See JUDGEMENT DAY.
Then, dreadful trumpet, sound the general doom!
Romeo and Juliet, iii, 2, 67.
Last trumpet.—*Hamlet,* v, 1, 253.

8
What lusty trumpet thus doth summon us?
King John. Act v, sc. 2, l. 117. [Lewis]
Braying trumpets.—*King John,* iii, 1, 303.
Brazen trumpets.—*Richard II,* iii, 3, 33.
Harsh-resounding trumpets.—*Richard II,* i, 3, 135. The only use of the phrase.
Hideous trumpet.—*Macbeth,* ii, 3, 87.
Loud trumpet.—*II Henry IV,* iv, 1, 52; 122.

9
Twice then the trumpets sounded.
King Lear. Act v, sc. 3, l. 217. [Edgar]
Twice have the trumpets sounded.
Measure for Measure. Act iv, sc. 6, l. 12. [Friar Peter]

10
Make all our trumpets speak; give them all breath,
Those clamorous harbingers of blood and death.
Macbeth. Act v, sc. 6, l. 9. [Macduff]

11
The trumpet of his own virtues.
Much Ado about Nothing. Act v, sc. 2, l. 87. [Benedick]
Be thou the trumpet of our wrath!
King John. Act i, sc. 1, l. 27. [King John]
Trumpet to his purposes.—*I Henry IV,* v, 1, 4.
Trumpeters of our intents.—*All's Well that Ends Well,* iv, 3, 32.
The tongue our trumpeter.—*Coriolanus,* i, 1, 121.
Trumpet forth my infamy.—*Pericles,* i, 1, 145.

12
Go see what trumpet 'tis that sounds.
The Taming of the Shrew. Induction, sc. 1, l. 74. [Lord]
Timon: What trumpet 's that?
Messenger: 'Tis Alcibiades, and some twenty horse,
All of his companionship.
Timon of Athens. Act i, sc. 1, l. 249.
The trumpets show the emperor is at hand.
Titus Andronicus. Act v, sc. 3, l. 16. [Lucius]

13
I bring a trumpet to awake his ear,
To set his sense on the attentive bent,
And then to speak.
Troilus and Cressida. Act i, sc. 3, l. 251. [Æneas]

Trumpet, blow loud,
Send thy brass voice through all these lazy tents.
Troilus and Cressida. Act i, sc. 3, l. 256. [Æneas]

Agamemnon: Give with thy trumpet a loud note to Troy,
Thou dreadful Ajax; that the appalled air
May pierce the head of the great combatant
And hale him thither.
Ajax: Thou, trumpet, there 's my purse.
Now crack thy lungs and split thy brazen pipe:
Blow, villain, till thy sphered bias check
Outswell the colic of puff'd Aquilon:
Come, stretch thy chest, and let thy eyes spout blood;
Thou blow'st for Hector.
Troilus and Cressida. Act iv, sc. 5, l. 3. "Sphered" is repeated in i, 3, 90, and occurs in no other play. The only use of "outswell." "Colic" is repeated in *I Henry IV,* iii, 1, 29, and in *Coriolanus,* ii, 1, 83. The only mention of Aquilon.

TRUST

See also Confidence

1
My resolution and my hands I 'll trust.
Antony and Cleopatra. Act iv, sc. 15, l. 49. [Cleopatra]

2
A man is well holp up that trusts to you.
The Comedy of Errors. Act iv, sc. 1, l. 22. [Antipholus of Ephesus]

Lightly trust.—*The Comedy of Errors,* iv, 4, 5.
Trust to 't.—*Coriolanus,* v, 3, 124; *Romeo and Juliet,* iii, 5, 197.

3
The credit that thy lady hath of thee
Deserves thy trust, and thy most perfect goodness
Her assured credit.
Cymbeline. Act i, sc. 6, l. 157. [Iachimo]

Trust me here.—*Cymbeline,* iv, 2, 14.
Trust me.—*III Henry VI,* iv, 2, 1, and sixteen times in later plays.
Give me trust.—*All's Well that Ends Well,* iii, 7, 8.
Trust to me.—*Troilus and Cressida,* i, 3, 338.
Trust us in your business.—*Henry VIII,* iii, 1, 173.
I will lay trust upon thee.—*King Lear,* iii, 5, 25.
On my trust.—*Measure for Measure,* v, 1, 147.
Left in trust.—*Pericles,* i, 3, 13.
Put me in trust.—*King Lear,* i, 4, 15.

4 Nor did he think it meet
To lay so dangerous and so dear a trust
On any soul removed but on his own.
I Henry IV. Act iv, sc. 1, l. 33. [Hotspur]

5
Natures of such deep trust we shall much need.
King Lear. Act ii, sc. 1, l. 117. [Cornwall]

Absolute trust.—*Macbeth,* i, 4, 14.
Best trust.—*Coriolanus,* i, 6, 54.
Honourable trust.—*Antony and Cleopatra,* iv, 6, 18.
Seeming trust.—*Sonnets,* cxxxviii.
Serious trust.—*The Winter's Tale,* i, 2, 246.
Sovereign trust.—*I Henry IV,* iii, 2, 161.

6
He 's here in double trust.
Macbeth. Act i, sc. 7, l. 12. [Macbeth]

7
Pyramus: Like Limander, am I trusty still.
Thisbe: And I like Helen, till the Fates me kill.
A Midsummer-Night's Dream. Act v, sc. 1, l. 198. The only mention of Limander.

Be trusty.—*Romeo and Juliet,* ii, 4, 204.
Neither true nor trusty.—*The Passionate Pilgrim,* l. 86.

8
Serve always with assured trust.
The Passionate Pilgrim, l. 330.

9
If he be credulous and trust my tale,
I 'll make him glad.
The Taming of the Shrew. Act iv, sc. 2, l. 67. [Tranio]

Trust my expectation.—*Much Ado about Nothing,* ii, 3, 220.
Trust their heels.—*Macbeth,* i, 2, 30.
Trust my honesty.—*The Winter's Tale,* i, 2, 434.
Trust my judgement.—*All's Well that Ends Well,* iii, 6, 34.

10 My trust,
Like a good parent, did beget of him
A falsehood in its contrary as great
As my trust was.
The Tempest. Act i, sc. 2, l. 93. [Prospero]

11 I have trusted thee, Camillo
With all the nearest things to my heart, as well
My chamber-councils.
Winter's Tale. Act i, sc. 2, l. 235. [Leontes] The only use of "chamber-councils."

II—Lack of Trust

12
Trust him not in matter of heavy consequence.
All's Well that Ends Well. Act ii, sc. 5, l. 49. [Lafeu]

I will never trust a man again.—*All's Well that Ends Well,* iv, 3, 165.
Let no such man be trusted.—*The Merchant of Venice,* v, 1, 88.

13
I . . . have no use for trusting.
Antony and Cleopatra. Act v, sc. 2, l. 15. [Cleopatra]

I will not trust you, sir.—*Richard III,* iv, 4, 492.
Ne'er trust me then.—*I Henry VI,* ii, 2, 48.
Never trust me.—*The Taming of the Shrew,* v, 2, 17; *Twelfth Night,* ii, 3, 79; 204; iii, 2, 62; *The Merry Wives of Windsor,* iv, 2, 209.
Never trust me else.—*Troilus and Cressida,* v, 2, 59.
Never trust me more.—*The Merchant of Venice,* ii, 2, 206.

14
Let it suffice thee that I trust thee not.
As You Like It. Act i, sc. 3, l. 57. [Duke]

15
Whom I will trust as I will adders fang'd.
Hamlet. Act iii, sc. 4, l. 203. [Hamlet]

I will no more trust him when he leers than I will a serpent when he hisses.
Troilus and Cressida. Act v, sc. 1, l. 96. [Thersites]

1
Hotspur: And so far will I trust thee, gentle Kate.
Lady Percy: How! so far?
Hotspur: Not an inch further.
I Henry IV. Act ii, sc. 3, l. 115.

Misuse the tenour of thy kinsman's trust.
I Henry IV. Act v, sc. 5, l. 5. [King Henry]

You have deceived our trust,
And made us doff our easy robes of peace,
To crush our old limbs in ungentle steel.
I Henry IV. Act v, sc. 1, l. 11. [King Henry]

We will not trust our eyes.
I Henry IV, v, 4, 139. See GHOST, 610:4.

2
What trust is in these times?
II Henry IV. Act i, sc. 3, l. 100. [York]

But in purged judgement trusting neither.
Henry V. Act ii, sc. 2, l. 136. [King Henry]

3
I 'll no longer trust thee.
I Henry VI. Act iii, sc. 3, l. 84. [Burgundy]

I will not trust you, I,
Nor longer stay in your curst company.
A Midsummer-Night's Dream. Act iii, sc. 2, l. 340. [Helena]

I 'll not trust your word.
A Midsummer-Night's Dream. Act iii, sc. 2, l. 268. [Demetrius] See also *Henry V,* iv, 1, 207.

4
Ah, what 's more dangerous than this fond affiance!
II Henry VI. Act iii, sc. 1, l. 74. [Queen Margaret]

5
Trust nobody, for fear you be betray'd.
II Henry VI. Act iv, sc. 4, l. 58. [Buckingham]

Trust none.—*Henry V,* ii, 3, 52.

Let him in nought be trusted.—*Henry VIII,* ii, 4, 135.

6
Trust not him that hath once broken faith.
III Henry VI. Act iv, sc. 4, l. 30. [Queen Elizabeth]

7
I trust I may not trust thee; for thy word
Is but the vain breath of a common man.
King John. Act iii, sc. 1, l. 7. [Constance]

8
He 's mad that trusts in the tameness of a wolf, a horse's health, a boy's love, or a whore's oath.
King Lear. Act iii, sc. 6, l. 19. [Fool] "Tameness" is repeated in *The Merry Wives of Windsor,* iv, 2, 27.

Grant I may never prove so fond,
To trust man on his oath or bond;
Or a harlot, for her weeping;
Or a dog, that seems a-sleeping.
Timon of Athens. Act i, sc. 2, l. 65. [Apemantus]

9
O, never will I trust to speeches penn'd!
Love's Labour 's Lost, v, 2, 402. See SPEECHES.

Trust no agent.—*Much Ado about Nothing,* ii, 1, 186.

Trust not my reading.—*Much Ado about Nothing,* iv, 1, 167.

10 Trust not my holy order,
If I pervert your course.
Measure for Measure. Act iv, sc. 3, l. 152. [Duke] "Pervert" is repeated in *Cymbeline,* ii, 4, 151.

11
I would scarce trust myself, though I had sworn to the contrary.
Much Ado about Nothing. Act i, sc. 1, l. 197. [Claudio]

Because I will not do them the wrong to mistrust any,
I will do myself the right to trust none.
Much Ado about Nothing. Act i, sc. 1, l. 245. [Benedick]

12
I 'll trust, by leisure, him that mocks me once;
Thee never, nor thy traitorous haughty sons.
Titus Andronicus. Act i, sc. 1, l. 301. [Saturninus]

I see thou wilt not trust the air With secrets.
Titus Andronicus, iv, 2, 169. See SECRECY.

13
Who should be trusted, when one's own right hand
Is perjured to the bosom?
The Two Gentlemen of Verona. Act v, sc. 4, l. 67. [Valentine]

'Tis no trusting to yond foolish lout.
The Two Gentlemen of Verona. Act iv, sc. 4, l. 71. [Proteus]

I am sorry I must never trust thee more,
But count the world a stranger for thy sake.
The Two Gentlemen of Verona. Act v, sc. 4, l. 69. [Valentine]

14
Than when I feel and see her no farther trust her.
The Winter's Tale. Act ii, sc. 1, l. 136. [Antigonus]

Trust, . . . a very simple gentleman!
Winter's Tale, iv, 4, 607.

Trust me not.—*The Winter's Tale,* v, 2, 185.

TRUTH

15
He 's very near the truth in this.
All's Well that Ends Well. Act v, sc. 3, l. 172. [Lord]

16
That truth should be silent I had almost forgot.
Antony and Cleopatra. Act ii, sc. 2, l. 110. [Enobarbus]

Truths would be tales,
Where now half tales be truths.
Antony and Cleopatra. Act ii, sc. 2, l. 136. [Agrippa]

Proclaim the truth.—*Antony and Cleopatra,* iv, 14, 126.

17
This to be true, I do engage my life.
As You Like It. Act v, sc. 4, l. 171. [Jaques]

Truth in sight.—*As You Like It,* v, 4, 124; 125.

1
Against my soul's pure truth why labour you
To make it wander in an unknown field?
The Comedy of Errors. Act iii, sc. 2, l. 37. [Antipholus of Syracuse]

I long to know the truth.—*The Comedy of Errors,* iv, 4, 146.

2
Virgilia: The gods grant them true!
Volumnia: True! pow, wow.
Menenius: True! I'll be sworn they are true.
Coriolanus. Act ii, sc. 1, l. 156. The only use of "pow, wow."

He did inform the truth.
Coriolanus. Act i, sc. 6, l. 42. [Marcius]

3
'Tis true 'tis pity; And pity 'tis 'tis true.
Hamlet. Act ii, sc. 2, l. 97. [Polonius]

Upon my soul, 'tis true, sir.
Timon of Athens, iii, 2, 48.

It is true.—*Othello,* ii, 1, 115.
And that's true too.—*King Lear,* v, 2, 11.
That's true.—*Troilus and Cressida,* i, 2, 174.
'Tis true.—*I Henry VI,* v, 4, 23, and frequently thereafter.
'Tis most true.—*Much Ado about Nothing,* v, 4, 23; *Othello,* i, 3, 70.
Most true.—*Timon of Athens,* iii, 4, 18; iii, 5, 4; *Julius Cæsar,* iii, 2, 244; *Hamlet,* ii, 2, 240.
'Tis too true.—*II Henry VI,* iii, 2, 130; iv, 2, 155; *Richard III,* ii, 3, 8; *Richard II,* ii, 2, 52; *Hamlet,* iii, 1, 49; *Pericles,* i, 4, 32.
True, too true.—*The Winter's Tale,* v, 1, 12.
That's very true.—*The Merchant of Venice,* iii, 1, 130; *Hamlet,* ii, 2, 180.
'Tis very true.—*The Taming of the Shrew,* Ind., 1, 89; *The Merchant of Venice,* iv, 1, 250; *Richard II,* iv, 1, 62.
Very true, sir.—*II Henry IV,* ii, 4, 313.
Very truth.—*II Henry IV,* iii, 2, 237; *Antony and Cleopatra,* ii, 3, 113.
True is it.—*As You Like It,* ii, 7, 120; *Love's Labour's Lost,* i, 1, 313; *King Lear,* iii, 1, 30; *Coriolanus,* i, 1, 134.
Right true it is.—*The Taming of the Shrew,* iv, 4, 40.
Truth it is.—*Much Ado about Nothing,* v, 4, 21.
This is the truth.—*Romeo and Juliet,* iii, 1, 180.
You know 'tis true.—*Troilus and Cressida,* iv, 5, 43.
As true as truth.—*Troilus and Cressida,* iii, 2, 176.

4
If circumstances lead me, I will find
Where truth is hid, though it were hid indeed
Within the centre.
Hamlet. Act ii, sc. 2, l. 157. [Polonius]

Hide the truth.—*The Rape of Lucrece,* l. 1075.

5
Will you ha' the truth on 't?
Hamlet. Act v, sc. 1, l. 26. [Clown]

Give me up the truth.
Hamlet. Act i, sc. 3, l. 98. [Polonius]

6
Is not the truth the truth?
I Henry IV. Act ii, sc. 4, l. 254. [Falstaff]

Nay, it is ten times true; for truth is truth
To the end of reckoning.
Measure for Measure. Act v, sc. 1, l. 44. [Isabella]

A truth's a truth.—*All's Well that Ends Well,* iv, 3, 178.
Truth is truth.—*Love's Labour's Lost,* iv, 1, 48; *King John,* i, 1, 105.

7
He . . . said he would swear truth out of England.
I Henry IV. Act ii, sc. 4, l. 337. [Peto]

8
Hotspur: Come, Kate, I'll have your song too.
Lady Percy: Not mine, in good sooth.
Hotspur: Not yours, in good sooth! Heart! you swear like a comfit-maker's wife.
I Henry IV. Act iii, sc. 1, l. 250. See under Swearing. "In good sooth" or "in sooth" is repeated frequently throughout the plays.

Sooth to say.—*The Comedy of Errors,* iv, 4, 72; *The Taming of the Shrew,* iv, 2, 99.
If I say sooth.—*Macbeth,* i, 2, 36.
To say the sooth.—*Henry V,* iii, 6, 151; *Henry VIII,* ii, 3, 30.
Silly sooth.—*Twelfth Night,* ii, 4, 47.
Very sooth.—*The Winter's Tale,* i, 2, 17.

9
God forbid, my dear and faithful lord,
That you should fashion, wrest, or bow your reading,
Or nicely charge your understanding soul
With opening titles miscreate, whose right
Suits not in native colours with the truth.
Henry V. Act i, sc. 2, l. 13. [King Henry] The only use of "miscreate."

'Tis so strange,
That, though the truth of it stands off as gross
As black and white, my eye will scarcely see it.
Henry V. Act ii, sc. 2, l. 102. [King Henry]

10
Dare no man answer in a case of truth?
I Henry VI. Act ii, sc. 4, l. 2. [Plantagenet]

Then say at once if I maintain'd the truth.
I Henry VI. Act ii, sc. 4, l. 5. [Plantagenet]

Pleaded truth.—*I Henry VI,* ii, 4, 29.
Repugn the truth.—*I Henry VI,* iv, 1, 94. The only use of "repugn" (resist).

11
The truth appears so naked on my side
That any purblind eye may find it out.
I Henry VI. Act ii, sc. 4, l. 20. [Plantagenet]

The naked truth.—*Love's Labour's Lost,* v, 2, 716.
Uttering bare truth.—*Sonnets,* lxix.

12
With my talk and tears Both full of truth.
III Henry VI. Act iii, sc. 3, l. 159. [Queen Margaret]

Full of truth.—*Titus Andronicus,* v, 3, 115.
To conclude with truth.—*III Henry VI,* ii, 1, 128.
For truth's sake.—*Henry VIII,* iii, 2, 397.

13
Out with it boldly: truth loves open dealing.
Henry VIII. Act iii, sc. 1, l. 40. [Queen Katharine]

Find truth.—*Henry VIII*, Prol., 9.
Truth o' the question.—*Henry VIII*, v, 1, 130.

1
Thy truth and thy integrity is rooted In us.
Henry VIII. Act v, sc. 1, l. 114. [King] See INTEGRITY.

The good I stand on is my truth and honesty.
Henry VIII. Act v, sc. 1, l. 122. [Cranmer] See HONESTY.

2
That 's the plain truth.
Henry VIII. Act v, sc. 3, l. 71. [Gardiner] The only use of "plain truth."

Bosom's truth.—*Coriolanus*, iii, 2, 57.
Even truth.—*All 's Well that Ends Well*, v, 3, 326.
Fair truth.—*Sonnets*, cxxxvii.
Firm truth.—*Henry V*, iv, 3, 14.
Flattering truth.—*Romeo and Juliet*, v, 1, 1.
Hateful truth.—*Troilus and Cressida*, iv, 4, 33.
Honest truth.—*Henry VIII*, iii, 2, 430.
Maiden truth.—*Much Ado about Nothing*, iv, 1, 166.
Nature's truth.—*All 's Well that Ends Well*, i, 3, 138.
Niggard truth.—*Sonnets*, lxxii.
Religious truth.—*Henry VIII*, iv, 2, 74.
Wither'd truth!—*Troilus and Cressida*, v, 2, 46.
Truth of honour.—*Measure for Measure*, iii, 1, 166.
Truth of my spirit.—*Measure for Measure*, iii, 1, 214.

3
It cannot be; thou dost but say 'tis so.
King John. Act iii, sc. 1, l. 6. [Constance]

I think it be no other but e'en so.
Hamlet. Act i, sc. 1, l. 108. [Bernardo]

Like the old tale, my lord: 'it is not so, nor 'twas not so, but, indeed, God forbid it should be so.'
Much Ado about Nothing. Act i, sc. 1, l. 218. [Benedick]

Nothing that is so is so.
Twelfth Night. Act iv, sc. 1, l. 9. [Clown]

4
Truth 's a dog must to kennel; he must be whipped out, when Lady the brach may stand by the fire and stink.
King Lear. Act i, sc. 4, l. 124. [Fool]

5
Be simple answerer, for we know the truth.
King Lear. Act iii, sc. 7, l. 43. [Regan] The only use of "answerer."

All my reports go with the modest truth;
Nor more nor clipp'd, but so.
King Lear. Act iv, sc. 7, l. 5. [Kent]

6
I suffer for the truth, sir.
Love's Labour 's Lost. Act i, sc. 1, l. 313. [Costard]

Truer than truth itself.
Love's Labour 's Lost. Act iv, sc. 1, l. 63. [Boyet]

7
Two truths are told,
As happy prologues to the swelling act
Of the imperial theme.
Macbeth. Act i, sc. 3, l. 127. [Macbeth]

Twofold truth.—*Sonnets*, xli.

8
I' the name of truth.
Macbeth. Act i, sc. 3, l. 52. [Banquo]

Show'd some truth.—*Macbeth*, ii, 1, 21.

9
Let 's go learn the truth of it.
Measure for Measure, i, 2, 82. [Lucio]

Hear the truth of it.
Merry Wives of Windsor. Act i, sc. 4, l. 80. [Mistress Quickly] Repeated in v, 5, 233.

Now you have heard the truth.
Titus Andronicus, v, 3, 128. [Marcus]

I hope here be truths.
Measure for Measure, ii, 1, 131. [Pompey]

10
Mark what I say, which you shall find
By every syllable a faithful verity.
Measure for Measure. Act iv, sc. 3, l. 130. [Duke]

'Twould prove the verity of certain words.
Henry VIII. Act i, sc. 2, l. 159. [Surveyor]

The verity of it is in strong suspicion.
The Winter's Tale. Act v, sc. 2, l. 31. [Gentleman]

Sincere verity.—*King Lear*, ii, 2, 111.
By the verities.—*Macbeth*, iii, 1, 8. The only use of "verities."
Verity in love.—*As You Like It*, iii, 4, 25.
Verity of extolment.—*Hamlet*, v, 2, 122.

Desdemona: Indeed! is 't true?
Othello: Most veritable.
Othello. Act iii, sc. 4, l. 75. The only use of "veritable."

11
Make the truth appear where it seems hid.
Measure for Measure. Act v, sc. 1, l. 66. [Isabella]

Confess the truth.—*Measure for Measure*, v, 1, 113.
Truth I must confess.—*Venus and Adonis*, l. 1001.

12
As this is true,
Let me in safety raise me from my knees;
Or else for ever be confixed here,
A marble monument!
Measure for Measure. Act v, sc. 1, l. 230. [Mariana] The only use of "confixed."

13
Truth will come to light. . . . At length the truth will out.
The Merchant of Venice. Act ii, sc. 2, l. 83. [Launcelot]

But it is true, without any slips of prolixity or crossing the plain highway of talk.
The Merchant of Venice. Act iii, sc. 1, l. 12. [Salanio] "Prolixity" is used again in *Romeo and Juliet*, i, 4, 3.

The seeming truth which cunning times put on
To entrap the wisest.
The Merchant of Venice. Act iii, sc. 2, l. 100. [Bassanio]

Seeming truth.—*Much Ado about Nothing*, ii, 2, 49.

14
When truth kills truth, O devilish-holy fray!
A Midsummer-Night's Dream. Act iii, sc. 2, l. 129. [Helena] The only use of "devilish-holy."

More strange than true.
A Midsummer-Night's Dream. Act v, sc. 1, l. 2. [Theseus]

Till truth make all things plain.
A Midsummer-Night's Dream. Act v, sc. 1, l. 129. [Quince]

1 Can this be true?
Much Ado about Nothing. Act iii, sc. 1, l. 107. [Beatrice]

May this be true?—*King John,* v, 4, 21.

How can this be true?—*Love's Labour 's Lost,* v, 2, 426.

Is 't true? can 't be?—*Timon of Athens,* ii, 2, 212.

Is 't true, is 't true?—*The Merchant of Venice,* iii, 1, 107.

Is it true, think you?—*The Winter's Tale,* iv, 4, 269.

Is that true?—*Othello,* iv, 2, 227.

Is this true?—*Taming of the Shrew,* iv, 5, 71.

Is not this true?—*Pericles,* i, 4, 50.

I know not if 't be true.—*Othello,* i, 3, 394.

In most comely truth.—*Much Ado about Nothing,* v, 2, 8. "In truth" is used throughout the plays.

In good truth.—*II Henry IV,* ii, 4, 28, and frequently in later plays.

2 Give us truth.
Othello. Act ii, sc. 1, l. 58. [Cassio]

Nought but truth.—*Othello,* iv, 2, 187.

3 For truth can never be confirm'd enough,
Though doubts did ever sleep.
Pericles. Act v, sc. 1, l. 203. [Pericles]

4 Where is truth, if there be no self-trust?
The Rape of Lucrece, l. 158. The only use of "self-trust."

Such signs of truth in his plain face she spied,
That she concludes the picture was belied.
The Rape of Lucrece, l. 1532.

5 Truth hath a quiet breast.
Richard II. Act i, sc. 3, l. 96. [Thomas Mowbray]

Little joy have I
To breathe this news; yet what I say is true.
Richard II. Act iii, sc. 4, l. 81. [Gardener]

Post you to London, and you will find it so;
I speak no more than every one doth know.
Richard II. Act iii, sc. 4, l. 90. [Gardener]

So help you truth.—*Richard II,* i, 3, 183.

6 Methinks the truth should live from age to age,
As 'twere retail'd to all posterity,
Even to the general all-ending day.
Richard III. Act iii, sc. 1, l. 76. [Prince of Wales] The only use of "retail'd" and "all-ending."

7 Thou wilt be stol'n, I fear,
For truth proves thievish for a prize so dear.
Sonnets. No. xlviii.

Simple truth miscall'd simplicity.
Sonnets. No. lxvi. The only use of "miscall'd."

Truth needs no colour, with his colour fix'd.
Sonnets. No. ci.

Most true it is that I have look'd on truth
Askance and strangely.
Sonnets. No. cx. "Askance" is repeated in *The Taming of the Shrew,* ii, 1, 249.

8 O, how much more doth beauty beauteous seem
By that sweet ornament which truth doth give!
Sonnets. No. liv.

Both truth and beauty on my love depends.
Sonnets. No. ci.

Truth in beauty dyed.
Sonnets. No. ci.

Truth may seem, but cannot be:
Beauty brag, but 'tis not she;
Truth and beauty buried be.
The Phœnix and the Turtle, l. 63.

9 The truth you speak doth lack some gentleness
And time to speak it in.
The Tempest. Act ii, sc. 1, l. 137. [Gonzalo]

10 Having sworn truth, ever will be true.
Twelfth Night, iv, 3, 33. See under FIDELITY.

The truth thou art unsure
To swear, swears only not to be forsworn;
Else what a mockery should it be to swear.
King John. Act iii, sc. 1, l. 283. [Pandulph]

11 For truth hath better deeds than words to grace it.
The Two Gentlemen of Verona. Act ii, sc. 2, l. 18. [Proteus]

One, lady, if you knew his pure heart's truth,
You would quickly learn to know him by his voice.
The Two Gentlemen of Verona. Act iv, sc. 2, l. 88. [Proteus]

12 By the honour of my parents, I
Have utter'd truth.
Winter's Tale. Act i, sc. 2, l. 442. [Camillo]

All 's true that is mistrusted.
Winter's Tale. Act ii, sc. 1, l. 48. [Leontes]

The great Apollo suddenly will have
The truth of this appear.
Winter's Tale. Act ii, sc. 3, l. 200. [Leontes]

If the good truth were known.—*The Winter's Tale,* ii, 1, 200.

13 Dorcas: Is it true too, think you?
Autolytus: Five justices' hands at it, and witnesses more than my pack will hold.
The Winter's Tale. Act iv, sc. 4, l. 287.

Most true, if ever truth were pregnant by circumstance.
The Winter's Tale. Act v, sc. 2, l. 33. [Gentleman]

II—Saying Truth

See also Speech: Speaking True

14 I will say true.
All's Well that Ends Well. Act iv, sc. 3, l. 171. [Parolles]

15 By the mass, lad, thou sayest true.
I Henry IV. Act ii, sc. 4, l. 400. [Falstaff]

Thou say'st true.—*The Taming of the Shrew,* iv, 3, 81; iii, 3, 149; *Pericles,* iv, 2, 22.

You say true.—*Othello,* ii, 1, 172.
You say very true.—*Henry V,* v, 1, 33.

1
I say no more than truth, so help me God!
II Henry VI. Act iii, sc. 1, l. 120. [Gloucester]

To say the truth, true and not true.
Troilus and Cressida. Act i, sc. 2, l. 105. [Cressida]

To say the truth.—*I Henry VI,* iv, 1, 30, and frequently thereafter.
To speak truth.—*II Henry VI,* iv, 3, 11, and frequently thereafter.

III—Telling Truth

2
Count: Tell true.
Helena: I will tell truth; by grace itself I swear.
All's Well that Ends Well. Act i, sc. 3, l. 225.

O! once tell true, tell true.
A Midsummer-Night's Dream. Act iii, sc. 2, l. 68. [Hermia]

Tell me true.—*All's Well that Ends Well,* v, 3, 234; *Julius Cæsar,* iv, 3, 187; *Measure for Measure,* ii, 1, 233; *Troilus and Cressida,* iv, 1, 51; *Timon of Athens,* iv, 3, 513; *Twelfth Night,* iv, 2, 121.

3
By my troth, sir, if I were to live this present hour, I will tell true.
All's Well that Ends Well. Act iv, sc. 3, l. 183. [Parolles]

I tell you true.—*The Comedy of Errors,* v, 1, 180; *Antony and Cleopatra,* iv, 6, 26.
I'll tell you true.—*Timon of Athens,* i, 2, 223.
I told him true.—*Much Ado about Nothing,* ii, 1, 223.
I told you true.—*The Merchant of Venice,* iii, 2, 259.

4
Who tells me true, though in his tale lie death,
I hear him as he flatter'd.
Antony and Cleopatra. Act i, sc. 2, l. 102. [Antony]

5
Ne'er may I look on day, nor sleep on night,
But she tells to your highness simple truth!
The Comedy of Errors. Act v, sc. 1, l. 210. [Luciana]

6
O, while you live, tell truth and shame the devil!
I Henry IV. Act iii, sc. 1, l. 62. [Hotspur]

Tell the truth.—*Richard III,* i, 2, 73; *The Merry Wives of Windsor,* iv, 4, 60.
Tell me for truth.—*III Henry VI,* iii, 3, 120.

7
They tell thee true.
I Henry IV. Act v, sc. 3, l. 6. [Blunt]

You tell me true.—*Timon of Athens,* ii, 2, 163.
To tell you true.—*Much Ado about Nothing,* ii, 1, 121.

8
The duke hath told the truth.
II Henry VI. Act ii, sc. 2, l. 28. [Warwick] "Told the truth" was used in the first play and never again.

9
Have I in conquest stretch'd mine arm so far,
To be afeard to tell greybeards the truth?
Julius Cæsar. Act ii, sc. 2, l. 66. [Cæsar]

10
It may be so: but if he say it is so, he is, in telling true, but so.
Love's Labour's Lost. Act i, sc. 1, l. 226. [Costard]

IV—Truth and Falsehood

11
True to thee
Were to prove false, which I will never be,
To him that is most true.
Cymbeline. Act iii, sc. 5, l. 163. [Pisanio]

Wherein I am false I am honest; not true, to be true.
Cymbeline. Act iv, sc. 3, l. 42. [Pisanio]

12
Your bait of falsehood takes this carp of truth.
Hamlet. Act ii, sc. 1, l. 63. [Polonius]

13
I am well acquainted with your manner of wrenching the true cause the false way.
II Henry IV. Act ii, sc. 1, l. 120. [Chief Justice]

14
As true as I believe you think them false
That give you cause to prove my saying true.
King John. Act iii, sc. 1, l. 27. [Salisbury]

15
Thus vainly thinking that she thinks me young,
Although she knows my days are past the best,
Simply I credit her false-speaking tongue:
On both sides thus is simple truth suppress'd.
Sonnets. No. cxxxviii. This sonnet is a review of the first part of *The Passionate Pilgrim,* written in 1599, a year previous to the *Sonnets.*

V—Lack of Truth

16
This is the first truth that e'er thine own tongue was guilty of.
All's Well that Ends Well. Act iv, sc. 1, l. 36. [Lord]

17
There is no truth in him.
As You Like It. Act iii, sc. 4, l. 22. [Celia]

No more truth in thee than in a drawn fox.
I Henry IV. Act iii, sc. 3, l. 128. [Falstaff]

18
Never knew what truth meant.
Henry VIII. Act ii, sc. 1, l. 105. [Buckingham]

Not At all a friend to truth.
Henry VIII. Act ii, sc. 4, l. 83. [Queen Katharine]

19
Thou shakest thy head and hold'st it fear or sin
To speak a truth.
II Henry IV. Act i, sc. 1, l. 95. [Morton]

1
There is scarce truth enough alive to make societies secure; but security enough to make fellowships accurst.
Measure for Measure. Act iii, sc. 2, l. 240. [Duke]
2
Do you think there is truth in them?
The Merry Wives of Windsor. Act ii, sc. 1, l. 178. [Ford]
Even so void is your false heart of truth.
The Merchant of Venice. Act v, sc. 1, l. 189. [Portia]
3
He doth but mistake the truth totally.
The Tempest. Act ii, sc. 1, l. 57. [Sebastian] The only use of "totally."
Cannot or will not relish a truth.
Winter's Tale. Act ii, sc. 1, l. 167. [Leontes]

TUNE

See also Music, Song

4
Both in a tune, like two gipsies on a horse.
As You Like It. Act v, sc. 3, l. 15. [Page]
In tune.—*The Taming of the Shrew,* iii, 1, 24; 38; 46; *Othello,* iii, 4, 123.
5
A wonderful sweet air, with admirable rich words to it.
Cymbeline, ii, 3, 19. See under AIR.
6
Which time she chanted snatches of old tunes.
Hamlet. Act iv, sc. 7, l. 178. [Queen] The only use of "chanted."
Tune of the time.—*Hamlet,* v, 2, 198.
Tune of your voices.—*Coriolanus,* ii, 3, 92.
Tune our heart-strings.—*The Rape of Lucrece,* l. 1141.
Tunes her tale.—*Venus and Adonis,* l. 74.
Tune my woes.—*The Rape of Lucrece,* l. 1465.
7
Keep not too long in one tune, but a snip and away.
Love's Labour's Lost. Act iii, sc. 1, l. 22. [Moth]
Jig off a tune.—*Love's Labour's Lost,* iii, 1, 12.
Tune a jig.—*Love's Labour's Lost,* iv, 3, 168.
Play the tune.—*Twelfth Night,* ii, 4, 14.
The tune of 'Green Sleeves.'—*The Merry Wives of Windsor,* ii, 1, 64; v, 5, 21.
The tune of 'Light o' love.'—*The Two Gentlemen of Verona,* i, 2, 83.
The tune of 'Two maids wooing a man.'—*The Winter's Tale,* iv, 4, 295.
8
What sayest thou to this tune, matter and method?
Measure for Measure. Act iii, sc. 2, l. 50. [Lucio]
This tune goes manly.
Macbeth. Act iv, sc. 3, l. 235. [Malcolm]
Better tune.—*King Lear,* iv, 3, 41.
Heavenly tune.—*Venus and Adonis,* l. 431.
Selfsame tune.—*Macbeth,* i, 3, 88.
Tempting tune.—*Venus and Adonis,* l. 778.
9
Hero: Why, how now? do you speak in the sick tune?
Beatrice: I am out of all other tune.
Much Ado about Nothing. Act iii, sc. 4, l. 41.
Out of tune.—*The Two Gentlemen of Verona,* iv, 2, 60, and eight times in later plays.
10
There we will unfold
To creatures stern sad tunes, to change their kinds.
The Rape of Lucrece, l. 1146.
Dismal tune.—*II Henry VI,* iii, 2, 41.
Doleful tune.—*The Winter's Tale,* iv, 4, 265.
Sleepy tune.—*Julius Cæsar,* iv, 3, 267.
11
This is a very scurvy tune to sing at a man's funeral.
The Tempest. Act ii, sc. 2, l. 46. [Stephano] "Scurvy tune" is repeated in l. 57.
Filthy tunes.—*I Henry IV,* ii, 2, 49.
12
Duke: How dost thou like this tune?
Viola: It gives a very echo to the seat
Where Love is throned.
Twelfth Night. Act ii, sc. 4, l. 20.
Methinks I do not like this tune.
The Two Gentlemen of Verona. Act i, sc. 2, l. 90. [Lucetta]
13
If it be aught to the old tune, my lord,
It is as fat and fulsome to mine ear
As howling after music.
Twelfth Night. Act v, sc. 1, l. 111. [Olivia]

TURK

14
Send them to the Turk to make eunuchs of.
All's Well that Ends Well, ii, 3, 94. See under EUNUCH.
She defies me, like Turk to Christian.
As You Like It. Act iv, sc. 3, l. 33. [Rosalind]
15
Go to Constantinople and take the Turk by the beard.
Henry V. Act v, sc. 2, l. 222. [King Henry] The only mention of Constantinople.
The Turk, that two and fifty kingdoms hath.
I Henry VI, iv, 7, 73. See under STYLE.
Out-paramoured the Turk.—*King Lear,* iii, 4, 94. The only use of "out-paramoured."
Turk Gregory.—*I Henry IV,* v, 3, 46.
16
An you be not turned Turk, there 's no more sailing by the star.
Much Ado about Nothing. Act iii, sc. 4, l. 57. [Margaret]
Are we turn'd Turks, and to ourselves do that
Which heaven hath forbid the Ottomites?
Othello. Act ii, sc. 3, l. 170. [Othello] "Ottomites" is repeated in i, 3, 33, and 235, and occurs in no other play.
Turn Turk.—*Hamlet,* iii, 2, 287.
17
We must not think the Turk is so unskilful
To leave that latest which concerns him first.
Othello. Act i, sc. 3, l. 27. [Senator]
So let the Turk of Cyprus us beguile.
Othello. Act i, sc. 3, l. 210. [Brabantio]
Nay, it is true, or else I am a Turk.
Othello. Act ii, sc. 1, l. 115. [Iago]

In Aleppo once,
Where a malignant and a turban'd Turk
Beat a Venetian and traduced the state,
I took by the throat the circumcised dog,
And smote him thus.

Othello. Act v, sc. 2, l. 352. [Othello] The only use of "circumcised" and "turban'd." Aleppo is mentioned again in *Macbeth*, i, 3, 7.

Base Phrygian Turk.—*The Merry Wives of Windsor*, i, 3, 97.

1
What, think you we are Turks or infidels?
Richard III. Act iii, sc. 5, l. 41. [Gloucester]

Turks and infidels.—*Richard II*, iv, 1, 139.

Turks, and Saracens.—*Richard II*, iv, 1, 95. The only use of "Saracens."

Turks and Tartars, never train'd
To offices of tender courtesy.

The Merchant of Venice. Act iv, sc. 1, l. 32. [Duke] The only use of "Tartars." "Tartar" occurs eight times.

TURN

2
Turn him out o' the band.
All's Well that Ends Well. Act iv, sc. 3, l. 227. [Parolles]

Bid him turn you out of doors.
Twelfth Night. Act ii, sc. 3, l. 78. [Maria]

Turn them out.—*Henry V*, iv, 3, 119.

3
I know not where to turn.
Coriolanus. Act ii, sc. 1, l. 198. [Volumnia]

O world, thy slippery turns!
Coriolanus. Act iv, sc. 4, l. 12. [Coriolanus]

4
I 'll fetch a turn about the garden.
Cymbeline. Act i, sc. 1, l. 81. [Queen] See under WALKING.

Never count the turns.—*Cymbeline*, ii, 4, 142.

Turn, and turn again!
I Henry VI. Act iii, sc. 3, l. 85. [La Pucelle]

Turn, And return.—*Venus and Adonis*, l. 704.

Then 'twas my turn to fly, and now 'tis thine.
III Henry VI, ii, 2, 105. [Warwick]

Thy turn is next.—*III Henry VI*, v, 6, 90.

Now it is my turn.—*Titus Andronicus*, v, 3, 119.

Take your turns.—*Titus Andronicus*, ii, 1, 129.

By due turns.—*King Lear*, i, 1, 137.

5
In God's name, Turn me away.
Henry VIII. Act ii, sc. 4, l. 42 [Queen]

He swears he 'll turn me away.
The Merry Wives of Windsor. Act iii, sc. 3, l. 32. [Robin]

I turn you not away.—*Antony and Cleopatra*, iv, 2, 30.

6
Wolsey: You turn the good we offer into envy.
Queen Katharine: Ye turn me into nothing.
Henry VIII. Act iii, sc. 1, l. 113.

7
Do my Lord of Canterbury
A shrewd turn, and he is your friend for ever.
Henry VIII. Act v, sc. 3, l. 178. [King]

Shrewd turn.—*All's Well that Ends Well*, iii, 5, 71.

8
Turn him off, Like to the empty ass.
Julius Cæsar. Act iv, sc. 1, l. 25. [Antony]

Turns you off.—*Antony and Cleopatra*, iii, 6, 94.

Turn him going.—*Julius Cæsar*, iii, 3, 38.

Turn her loose.—*The Merry Wives of Windsor*, ii, 1, 189.

Turn them together.—*The Merry Wives of Windsor*, ii, 1, 193.

Turn him about.—*The Merry Wives of Windsor*, v, 5, 105.

9
We will turn it finely off, sir.
Love's Labour's Lost. Act v, sc. 2, l. 511. [Costard]

At every turn.—*A Midsummer-Night's Dream*, iii, 1, 114.

10
A note will turn the balance.
A Midsummer-Night's Dream. Act v, sc. 1, l. 324. [Demetrius]

Turn the beam.—*Hamlet*, iv, 5, 157.

Turn the scale.—*Measure for Measure*, iv, 2, 32.

Turn the scales.—*II Henry IV*, ii, 4, 276.

11
So turns she every man wrong side out.
Much Ado about Nothing. Act iii, sc. 1, l. 68. [Hero] The only use of "wrong side out." See under PERVERSITY.

12
You did wish that I would make her turn:
Sir, she can turn, and turn, and yet go on,
And turn again.
Othello. Act iv, sc. 1, l. 263. [Othello]

Did he live now,
This sight would make him do a desperate turn.
Othello. Act v, sc. 2, l. 206. [Gratiano]

13
O gentle villain, do not turn away!
Richard III. Act i, sc. 3, l. 163. [Queen Margaret]

He turns away.—*Coriolanus*, v, 3, 168; *The Rape of Lucrece*, l. 1711.

Turn this way.—*III Henry VI*, i, 1, 189.

Turn aside.—*Antony and Cleopatra*, i, 3, 76.

Turn awry.—*Hamlet*, iii, 1, 87.

Turn from me.—*Antony and Cleopatra*, iv, 14, 85.

Turn and fly.—*Romeo and Juliet*, iii, 1, 179.

14
This I know, She is not for your turn.
The Taming of the Shrew. Act ii, sc. 1, l. 63. [Baptista]

For your turn.—*The Taming of the Shrew*, ii, 1, 274.

15
Whate'er he be,
It skills not much, we 'll fit him to our turn.
The Taming of the Shrew. Act iv, sc. 2, l. 62. [Tranio]

16
Now which way shall she turn?
Venus and Adonis, l. 253.

Turn head.—*Henry V*, ii, 4, 69. See DOG, 369: 10.

Turns pale.—*Troilus and Cressida*, v, 3, 81.

Turn to stone.—*Troilus and Cressida*, v, 10, 18.

Turn white.—*A Lover's Complaint*, l. 308.

II—Good Turn

17
Cleopatra: For what good turn?
Messenger: For the best turn i' the bed.
Antony and Cleopatra. Act ii, sc. 5, l. 58. See under MARRIAGE.

1
I am to do a good turn for them.
Hamlet. Act iv, sc. 6, l. 22. [Horatio]
For your kindness I owe you a good turn.
Measure for Measure. Act iv, sc. 2, l. 60. [Pompey]
2 I never . . . did ill turn
To any living creature.
Pericles. Act iv, sc. 1, l. 76. [Marina] The only use of "ill turn." See under KINDNESS.
She meant thee a good turn.—*Pericles,* iv, 2, 151.
3
Each doth good turns now unto the other.
Sonnets. No. xlvii.
Thankful for good turns.—*The Taming of the Shrew,* ii, 1, 166.
4
I 'll look you out a good turn.
Timon of Athens. Act iii, sc. 2, l. 67. [Lucius]
High good turn.—*Titus Andronicus,* i, 1, 397.
5
Oft good turns Are shuffled off.
Twelfth Night. Act iii, sc. 3, l. 15. [Sebastian]
6
Never did passenger in summer's heat
More thirst for drink than she for this good turn.
Venus and Adonis, l. 91.

III—Turn Back

7
Turn back and fly, like ships before the wind.
III Henry VI, i, 4, 4. See under TREACHERY.
Never once again turn back and fly.
III Henry VI, ii, 1, 185. See under LONDON.
8 Gentle my lord, turn back. . . .
Good my lord, turn back.
Measure for Measure. Act ii, sc. 2, l. 143. [Isabella]
Turn back an hour in a day.—*The Comedy of Errors,* iv, 2, 62.
Turns back for very fear.—*The Comedy of Errors,* iv, 2, 56. "Turn back" is repeated eight times in later plays.
Turn back to me.—*Sonnets,* cxliii.
Turn thee back.—*Henry V,* iii, 6, 148.
Turn not back.—*Troilus and Cressida,* ii, 2, 69.
Turns his back, see under BACK.

IV—Serving One's Turn

9
Why then, to-morrow, I cannot serve your turn.
As You Like It. Act v, sc. 2, l. 54. [Rosalind]
Aaron: Why, then, it seems, some certain snatch or so
Would serve your turns.
Chiron: Ay, so the turn was served.
Titus Andronicus. Act ii, sc. 1, l. 95.
Nay, that shall not serve your turn; that shall it not, in truth, la.
Troilus and Cressida. Act iii, sc. 1, l. 81. [Pandarus]
Serve your turn.—*Love's Labour 's Lost,* i, 1, 300; *The Merry Wives of Windsor,* v, 5, 108.
Serve thy turn.—*Coriolanus,* iv, 5, 94.
10
I have enough to serve mine own turn.
A Midsummer-Night's Dream. Act iii, sc. 1, l. 154. [Bottom]
I follow him to serve my turn upon him.
Othello. Act i, sc. 1, l. 42. [Iago]
My uses cry to me, I must serve my turn
Out of mine own.
Timon of Athens. Act i, sc. 2, l. 20. [Senator]
Serve my turn.—*Love's Labour 's Lost,* i, 1, 300; i, 2, 184; *Hamlet,* iii, 3, 52; *The Winter's Tale,* iv, 4, 520.
Serve our turn.—*Richard II,* iii, 2, 90.
Serve the turn.—*The Two Gentlemen of Verona,* iii, 1, 131; 134; 389; iii, 2, 93; *All's Well that Ends Well,* iv, 1, 51; *Titus Andronicus,* iii, 1, 165.

V—Turning

11
Turn up on your right hand at the next turning, but, at the next turning of all, on your left; marry, at the very next turning, turn of no hand, but turn down indirectly to the Jew's house.
The Merchant of Venice. Act ii, sc. 2, l. 42. [Launcelot]
I will leave them at the next turning.
Much Ado about Nothing. Act ii, sc. 1, l. 160. [Beatrice]
12
Turn giddy, and be holp by backward turning.
Romeo and Juliet. Act i, sc. 2, l. 48. [Benvolio]
Turning back.—*Julius Cæsar,* v, 3, 3.
Turning away.—*Twelfth Night,* i, 5, 21.
Fell a-turning.—*Passionate Pilgrim,* l. 100; 214.
Quick in turning.—*Venus and Adonis,* l. 140.
Turning o' the tide.—*Henry V,* ii, 3, 13.

TUTOR

See also Teacher

13 Tutor'd in the rudiments
Of many desperate studies.
As You Like It, v, 4, 31. See under STUDY.
Tutor'd in the world.—*The Two Gentlemen of Verona,* i, 3, 21.
Tutor'd by my art.—*Romeo and Juliet,* v, 3, 243.
Well tutored.—*Love's Labour 's Lost,* iv, 2, 77.
14
When thou dost hear I am as I have been,
Approach me, and thou shalt be as thou wast,
The tutor and the feeder of my riots.
II Henry IV. Act v, sc. 5, l. 64. [King Henry V]
15 I did send for thee
To tutor thee in stratagems of war.
I Henry VI. Act iv, sc. 5, l. 1. [Talbot]
16
Tutor both to good and bad!
The Rape of Lucrece, l. 995.
Tutor me from quarreling!—*Romeo and Juliet,* iii, 1, 32.
It tutors nature.—*Timon of Athens,* i, 1, 37.
17
To my daughters; and tell them both
These are their tutors: bid them use them well.
The Taming of the Shrew. Act ii, sc. 1, l. 111. [Baptista]

1
Indeed, I was their tutor to instruct them.
Titus Andronicus. Act v, sc. 1, l. 98. [Aaron]
Beauty's tutors.—*Love's Labour's Lost,* iv, 3, 323.
Tutors not so careful.—*The Tempest,* i, 2, 174.
An assinego may tutor thee.—*Troilus and Cressida,* ii, 1, 49. The only use of "assinego" (ass).
2
My master sues to her, and she hath taught her suitor,
He being her pupil, to become her tutor.
The Two Gentlemen of Verona. Act ii, sc. 1, l. 143. [Speed]
I would have thee to my tutor.
The Two Gentlemen of Verona. Act iii, sc. 1, l. 84. [Duke]
Shrewd tutor.—*Venus and Adonis,* l. 500.

TWELVEMONTH, see Year

TWIN

3
Delivered of . . . male twins, both alike.
The Comedy of Errors. Act i, sc. 1, l. 56. [Ægeon]
Pair of twins.—*Antony and Cleopatra,* iii, 10, 12.
Twin-born.—*Henry V,* iv, 1, 251. The only use of the phrase.
Twin-brother.—*The Merry Wives of Windsor,* ii, 1, 74. The only use of the phrase.
Twins of learning.—*Henry VIII,* iv, 2, 58.
4
Myself and a sister, both born in an hour.
Twelfth Night. Act ii, sc. 1, l. 20. [Sebastian]

TYRANNY

5
Best of my flesh, Forgive my tyranny.
Coriolanus. Act v, sc. 3, l. 42. [Coriolanus]
6
Tyranny, which never quaff'd but blood,
Would, by beholding him, have wash'd his knife
With gentle eye-drops.
II Henry IV. Act iv, sc. 5, l. 86. [Warwick] The only use of "eye-drops."
7
I will chain these legs and arms of thine,
That hast by tyranny these many years
Wasted our country, slain our citizens,
And sent our sons and husbands captivate.
I Henry VI. Act ii, sc. 3, l. 39. [Countess] "Captivate" is repeated in v, 3, 107, and in *III Henry VI,* i, 4, 115.
The period of thy tyranny approacheth.
I Henry VI. Act iv, sc. 2, l. 17. [General]
8
Lofty proud encroaching tyranny.
II Henry VI. Act iv, sc. 1, l. 95. [Captain] The only use of "encroaching."
Bloody tyranny.—*I Henry VI,* ii, 5, 100.
Insulting tyranny.—*I Henry VI,* iv, 7, 19.
Murderous tyranny.—*II Henry VI,* iii, 2, 49; *Titus Andronicus,* ii, 3, 267.
Very tyranny.—*Merchant of Venice,* iv, 1, 13.
Watchful tyranny.—*Macbeth,* v, 8, 67.
Winter's tyranny.—*II Henry IV,* i, 3, 62.
Tyranny of her sorrows.—*All's Well that Ends Well,* i, 1, 57.
9
So let high-sighted tyranny range on,
Till each man drop by lottery.
Julius Cæsar. Act ii, sc. 1, l. 118. [Brutus] The only use of "high-sighted."
Liberty! Freedom! Tyranny is dead!
Julius Cæsar. Act iii, sc. 1, l. 78. [Cinna]
10
I begin to find an idle and fond bondage in the oppression of aged tyranny; who sways, not as it hath power, but as it is suffered.
King Lear. Act i, sc. 2, l. 51. [Gloucester]
The tyranny of the open night's too rough
For nature to endure.
King Lear. Act iii, sc. 4, l. 2. [Kent]
11
Great tyranny! lay thou thy basis sure,
For goodness dare not check thee.
Macbeth. Act iv, sc. 3, l. 32. [Macduff]
12
Whether the tyranny be in his place,
Or in his eminence that fills it up,
I stagger in.
Measure for Measure. Act i, sc. 2, l. 167. [Claudio]
Sith 'twas my fault to give the people scope,
'Twould be my tyranny to strike and gall them
For what I bid them do. For we bid this be done,
When evil deeds have their permissive pass
And not the punishment.
Measure for Measure. Act i, sc. 3, l. 35. [Duke] The only use of "permissive."
13
Insulting tyranny begins to jet
Upon the innocent and aweless throne.
Richard III. Act ii, sc. 4, l. 51. [Queen Elizabeth]
His tyranny for trifles.
Richard III. Act iii, sc. 7, l. 9. [Buckingham]
The last was I that felt thy tyranny.
Richard III. Act v, sc. 3, l. 168. [Ghost of Buckingham]
Bruised underneath the yoke of tyranny.
Thus far into the bowels of the land
Have we march'd on without impediment.
Richard III. Act v, sc. 2, l. 2. [Richmond]
14
The milk thou suck'dst from her did turn to marble;
Even at thy teat thou hadst thy tyranny.
Titus Andronicus. Act ii, sc. 3, l. 144. [Lavinia] "Teat" is repeated in *Romeo and Juliet,* i, 3, 68.
Mine eyes are cloy'd with view of tyranny.
Titus Andronicus. Act iii, sc. 2, l. 55. [Titus]
I made thee miserable
What time I threw the people's suffrages
On him that thus doth tyrannize o'er me.
Titus Andronicus. Act iv, sc. 3, l. 18. [Titus]
Tyrannize upon my breast.—*Titus Andronicus,* iii, 2, 8. "Tyrannize" is used a third time in *King John,* v, 7, 47.

II—The Tyrant

15
She Phebes me: mark how the tyrant writes.
As You Like It. Act iv, sc. 3, l. 39. [Rosalind]
How fine this tyrant
Can tickle where she wounds!
Cymbeline. Act i, sc. 1, l. 84. [Imogen]

Beautiful tyrant!—*Romeo and Juliet,* iii, 2, 75.

1 So, as a painted tyrant, Pyrrhus stood.
Hamlet. Act ii, sc. 2, l. 502. [First Player]

Abhorred tyrant.—*Macbeth,* v, 7, 10.
Confident tyrant.—*Macbeth,* v, 4, 8.
Hard-favour'd tyrant.—*Venus and Adonis,* l. 931.
Jealous tyrant.—*The Winter's Tale,* iii, 2, 135.
Thracian tyrant.—*Titus Andronicus,* i, 1, 138.

2 We are no tyrant, but a Christian king.
Henry V. Act i, sc. 2, l. 241. [King Henry]

3 How can tyrants safely govern home,
Unless abroad they purchase great alliance?
III Henry VI. Act iii, sc. 3, l. 69. [Queen Margaret]

With some few bands of chosen soldiers,
I 'll undertake to land them on our coast
And force the tyrant from his seat by war.
III Henry VI. Act iii, sc. 3, l. 204. [Warwick]

4 A foe to tyrants, and my country's friend.
Julius Cæsar. Act v, sc. 4, l. 5. [Young Cato]

5 This tyrant, whose sole name blisters our tongues,
Was once thought honest: you have loved him well.
Macbeth. Act iv, sc. 3, l. 12. [Malcolm]

O nation miserable,
With an untitled tyrant bloody-scepter'd.
Macbeth. Act iv, sc. 3, l. 103. [Macduff] The only use of "untitled" and "bloody-scepter'd."

Live to be the show and gaze o' the time:
We 'll have thee, as our rarer monsters are,
Painted upon a pole, and underwrit,
'Here may you see the tyrant.'
Macbeth. Act v, sc. 8, l. 24. [Macduff] The only use of "underwrit."

6 Were he meal'd with that
Which he corrects, then were he tyrannous.
Measure for Measure. Act iv, sc. 2, l. 86. [Duke] The only use of "meal'd" (stained).

I knew him tyrannous; and tyrants' fears
Decrease not, but grow faster than the years.
Pericles. Act i, sc. 2, l. 84. [Pericles]

Thou art as tyrannous, so as thou art,
As those whose beauties proudly make them cruel.
Sonnets. No. cxxxi.

7 A professed tyrant to their sex.
Much Ado about Nothing. Act i, sc. 1, l. 170. [Benedick]

I 'll prove a tyrant to him.—*Measure for Measure,* ii, 4, 169.

8 Tyrants themselves wept.
Richard III. Act i, sc. 3, l. 185. [Rivers]

That excellent grand tyrant of the earth,
That reigns in galled eyes of weeping souls,
Thy womb let loose, to chase us to our graves.
Richard III. Act iv, sc. 4, l. 52. [Queen Margaret]

A bloody tyrant and a homicide;
One raised in blood, and one in blood establish'd.
Richard III. Act v, sc. 3, l. 246. [Richmond] "Bloody tyrant" is repeated in *Sonnets,* xvi.

If you so sweat to put a tyrant down,
You sleep in peace, the tyrant being slain.
Richard III. Act v, sc. 3, l. 255. [Richmond]

9 I will show myself a tyrant.
Romeo and Juliet. Act i, sc. 1, l. 25. [Sampson]

If I confess much, you will play the tyrant.
Troilus and Cressida. Act iii, sc. 2, l. 127. [Cressida]

Play the tyrant.—*Measure for Measure,* iii, 2, 207; *Sonnets,* v.

10 'Tis time to fear when tyrants seem to kiss.
Pericles. Act i, sc. 2, l. 79. [Pericles]

11 All tyrant, for thy sake.
Sonnets. No. cxlix.

12 A plague upon the tyrant that I serve!
The Tempest. Act ii, sc. 2, l. 166. [Caliban]

I am subject to a tyrant.—*Tempest,* iii, 3, 49.

Subject to the tyranny
Of mad mischances and much misery.
Venus and Adonis, l. 737.

13 Live you the marble-breasted tyrant still.
Twelfth Night. Act v, sc. 1, l. 127. [Duke] The only use of "marble-breasted." "Marble-hearted" occurs in *King Lear,* i, 4, 281: "Marble-hearted fiend."

14 I 'll not call you tyrant;
But this most cruel usage of your queen,
Not able to produce more accusation
Than your own weak-hinged fancy, something savours
Of tyranny and will ignoble make you,
Yea, scandalous to the world.
The Winter's Tale. Act ii, sc. 3, l. 116. [Paulina] The only use of "weak-hinged."

Were I a tyrant,
Where were her life? she durst not call me so,
If she did know me one.
The Winter's Tale. Act ii, sc. 3, l. 122. [Paulina]

U

UGLINESS

See also Appearance

1 Get thee hence:
Hadst thou Narcissus in thy face, to me
Thou wouldst appear most ugly.
Antony and Cleopatra, ii, 5, 103. [Cleopatra] Narcissus is mentioned again in *Venus and Adonis,* l. 161, and *Rape of Lucrece,* l. 265.

Ugly in her eyes.—*The Rape of Lucrece,* l. 459.

Ugly, meagre, lean.—*Venus and Adonis,* l. 931.

2 Ten times more ugly
Than ever they were fair.
Henry VIII, i, 2, 117. See under BENEFIT.

3
I am as ugly as a bear.
A Midsummer-Night's Dream. Act ii, sc. 2, l. 94. [Helena]

Ugly and slanderous to thy mother's womb,
Full of unpleasing blots and sightless stains,
Lame, foolish, crooked, swart, prodigious,
Patch'd with foul moles and eye-offending marks.
King John. Act iii, sc. 1, l. 44. [Constance]

Ugly and unnatural.—*Richard III,* i, 2, 23.

Ugly and venomous.—*As You Like It,* ii, 1, 13.

Ugly devils.—*Richard III,* i, 3, 227.

Ugly man.—*King John,* iii, 1, 37.

Ugly witch.—*I Henry VI,* v, 3, 34; *Henry V,* iv, Prol., 21.

UNCERTAINTY

See also Certainty, Doubt

4 Prepared I was not
For such a business; therefore am I found
So much unsettled.
All's Well that Ends Well. Act ii, sc. 5, l. 66. [Bertram]

He something seems unsettled.
The Winter's Tale, i, 2, 147. [Hermione]

Rectify what is unsettled.—*Henry VIII,* iii, 4, 64.

So unsettled.—*The Winter's Tale,* i, 2, 325.

Unsettled fancy.—*The Tempest,* v, 1, 59.

Unsettled humours.—*King John,* ii, 1, 66. The only uses of "unsettled."

5
Until I know this sure uncertainty,
I 'll entertain the offer'd fallacy.
The Comedy of Errors, ii, 2, 187. [Antipholus of Syracuse] The only use of "fallacy."

Here remain with your uncertainty!
Coriolanus. Act iii, sc. 3, l. 124. [Coriolanus]

Much uncertainty.—*I Henry IV,* i, 3, 299. The only uses of "uncertainty."

6
The people will remain uncertain whilst
'Twixt you there 's difference.
Coriolanus. Act v, sc. 6, l. 17. [Conspirator]

Uncertain of the issue.—*I Henry IV,* i, 1, 61.

7 In a theme so bloody-faced as this
Conjecture, expectation, and surmise
Of aids incertain should not be admitted.
II Henry IV. Act i, sc. 3, l. 22. [Bardolph] The only use of "bloody-faced."

The affairs of men rest still incertain.
Julius Cæsar. Act v, sc. 1, l. 96. [Cassius] "Incertain" occurs six times.

Incertainties now crown themselves assured.
Sonnets. No. cvii. "Incertainties" is repeated in *The Winter's Tale,* iii, 2, 170. "Incertainty" occurs only once, in *Sonnets,* cxv.

Be not uncertain.—*The Winter's Tale,* i, 2, 441. "Uncertain" occurs eleven times.

UNCONSTANT, see Inconstant

UNDERSTANDING

8
Understand what advice shall thrust upon thee; else thou diest in thine unthankfulness, and thine ignorance makes thee away.
All's Well that Ends Well. Act i, sc. 1, l. 224. [Parolles]

Thy casement I need not open, for I look through thee.
All's Well that Ends Well, ii, 3, 225. [Lafeu]

9
When a man's verses cannot be understood, nor a man's good wit seconded with the forward child Understanding, it strikes a man more dead than a great reckoning in a little room.
As You Like It, iii, 3, 12. [Touchstone]

Better understanding.—*As You Like It,* v, 1, 57.

Sweet understanding.—*Love's Labour 's Lost,* i, 1, 267.

10
An understanding simple and unschool'd.
Hamlet. Act i, sc. 2, l. 97. [King]

Give it an understanding, but no tongue.
Hamlet. Act i, sc. 2, l. 250. [Hamlet]

Put him
So much from the understanding of himself.
Hamlet. Act ii, sc. 2, l. 8. [King]

11
You have me, have you not?
Hamlet. Act ii, sc. 1, l. 68. [Polonius]

You understand me?—*The Taming of the Shrew,* i, 1, 240, and frequently in later plays.

O, understand my drift.—*The Merry Wives of Windsor,* ii, 2, 251.

I scarce could understand it.—*The Comedy of Errors,* ii, 1, 49; 54.

12
He apprehends a world of figures here,
But not the form of what he should attend.
I Henry IV. Act i, sc. 3, l. 209. [Worcester]

You apprehend passing shrewdly.
Much Ado about Nothing, ii, 1, 84. [Leonato]

13
I think his understanding is bereft.
III Henry VI. Act ii, sc. 6, l. 60. [Warwick]

Hast thou no understandings?—*The Merry Wives of Windsor,* iv, 1, 72.

14
What you would work me to, I have some aim.
Julius Cæsar. Act i, sc. 2, l. 163. [Brutus]

Men may construe things after their fashion,
Clean from the purpose of the things themselves.
Julius Cæsar. Act i, sc. 3, l. 34. [Cicero]

1
Who understandeth thee not, loves thee not.
Love's Labour's Lost. Act iv, sc. 2, l. 101. [Holofernes] The only use of "understandeth."

2
I understand not what you mean by this.
A Midsummer-Night's Dream, iii, 2, 236.

Speed: I understand thee not.
Launce: What a block art thou, that thou canst not! My staff understands me.
Speed: What thou sayest?
Launce: Ay, and what I do too: look thee, I 'll but lean, and my staff understands me.
Speed: It stands under thee, indeed.
Launce: Why, stand-under and under-stand is all one.
The Two Gentlemen of Verona. Act ii, sc. 5, l. 26. "I understand you not" occurs frequently throughout the plays.

Friend, we understand not one another.
Troilus and Cressida. Act iii, sc. 1, l. 29. [Pandarus]

3 You seem to understand me,
By each at once her choppy finger laying
Upon her skinny lips.
Macbeth. Act i, sc. 3, l. 43. [Banquo] The only use of "choppy" and "skinny."

Given to understand.—*The Merchant of Venice,* ii, 8, 7; *I Henry IV,* iv, 4, 11.
Men of understanding.—*Henry VIII,* v, 3, 135.

4
Sir, you say well and well you do conceive.
The Taming of the Shrew. Act i, sc. 2, l. 271. [Hortensio]

Nay, conceive me, conceive me, sweet coz.
The Merry Wives of Windsor, i, 1, 250.
Well, I conceive.—*The Tempest,* iv, 1, 50.
I cannot conceive you.—*King Lear,* i, 1, 12.

5
Their understanding Begins to swell.
The Tempest. Act v, sc. 1, l. 79. [Prospero]

6 Was this taken
By any understanding pate but thine?
Winter's Tale. Act i, sc. 2, l. 222. [Leontes]

Understanding friend.—*Henry VIII,* Prol., 22.
Understanding soul.—*Henry V,* i, 2, 15.

UNDERTAKING

7
Which holy undertaking with most austere sanctimony she accomplished.
All's Well that Ends Well. Act iv, sc. 3, l. 59. [Lord]

It is virtuous to be constant in any undertaking.
Measure for Measure, iii, 2, 239. See under CONSTANCY.

Your free undertaking cannot miss
A thriving issue.
Winter's Tale. Act ii, sc. 2, l. 45. [Emilia]

Desperate undertakings.—*Hamlet,* ii, 1, 104.

8
Better in my mind not undertook.
The Merchant of Venice. Act ii, sc. 4, l. 6. [Salanio]

I undertook it.—*All's Well that Ends Well,* v, 3, 132.

9
Let me be his undertaker.
Othello. Act iv, sc. 1, l. 244. [Iago]

If you will be an undertaker, I am for you.
Twelfth Night. Act iii, sc. 4, l. 349. [Sir Toby] The only uses of "undertaker."

10
Upon my life, my lord, I 'll undertake it.
Richard III, v, 3, 42. See under FIDELITY.

I 'll undertake 't.—*Coriolanus,* v, 1, 47.
I will undertake it.—*All's Well that Ends Well,* iii, 6, 76; *A Midsummer-Night's Dream,* i, 2, 92.

Wherefore then Didst undertake it?
Cymbeline. Act iii, sc. 4, l. 105. [Imogen]

This shall I undertake.—*Troilus and Cressida,* iii, 3, 36.

11
You 'll undertake her no more?
The Merry Wives of Windsor, iii, 5, 127. See under SUIT.

By my troth, I would not undertake her in this company.
Twelfth Night. Act i, sc. 3, l. 61. [Sir Andrew]

12
You know What you have underta'en to do.
The Winter's Tale. Act iii, sc. 2, l. 78. [Leontes] The only use of "underta'en."

UNHAPPINESS

See also Grief, Melancholy, Sadness

13 A more unhappy lady,
If this division chance, ne'er stood between,
Praying for both parts.
Antony and Cleopatra. Act iii, sc. 4, l. 12. [Octavia]

I am the most unhappy woman living.
Henry VIII. Act iii, sc. 1, l. 147. [Queen Katharine]

14
Thou seest we are not all alone unhappy.
As You Like It. Act ii, sc. 7, l. 136. [Duke]

15
She hath often dreamed of unhappiness and waked herself with laughing.
Much Ado about Nothing, ii, 1, 361. See JOLLITY, 787:8.

Heir to his unhappiness!—*Richard III,* i, 2, 25. The only uses of "unhappiness."

16
By you unhappied and disfigured clean.
Richard II, iii, 1, 10. See under GENTLEMAN. The only use of "unhappied." "Disfigured" is repeated in *King John,* iv, 2, 22.

17
Silvia: Unhappy that I am!
Proteus: Unhappy were you, madam, ere I came;
But by my coming I have made you happy.
Silvia: By thy approach thou makest me most unhappy.
Two Gentlemen of Verona. Act v, sc. 4, l. 28.

Unhappy that I am.—*King Lear,* i, 1, 93.
I am most unhappy.—*Othello,* iii, 4, 102.
Most unhappy.—*Othello,* iv, 1, 243.
I am now unhappy.—*Winter's Tale,* iii, 2, 36.
Ay me, unhappy!—*II Henry VI,* iii, 2, 70.
Unhappy me.—*Pericles,* i, 4, 69.

UNITY

1
That which combined us was most great, and let not
A leaner action rend us.
Antony and Cleopatra. Act ii, sc. 2, l. 18. [Lepidus] The only use of "leaner."

If I were bound to divine of this unity, I would not prophesy so.
Antony and Cleopatra. Act ii, sc. 6, l. 124. [Enobarbus]

2
The head is not more native to the heart,
The hand more instrumental to the mouth,
Than is the throne of Denmark to thy father.
Hamlet. Act i, sc. 2, l. 47. [King] The only use of "instrumental."

3
The united vessel of their blood.
II Henry IV. Act iv, sc. 4, l. 44. [King]

4
You peers, continue this united league.
Richard III. Act ii, sc. 1, l. 2. [King Edward]

Make me happy in your unity.
Richard III. Act ii, sc. 1, l. 31. [King Edward]

We will unite the white rose and the red.
Richard III. Act v, sc. 5, l. 19. [Richmond]

5
Why, every thing adheres together, that no dram of a scruple, no scruple of a scruple, no obstacle, no incredulous or unsafe circumstance.
Twelfth Night. Act iii, sc. 4, l. 86. [Malvolio] "Incredulous" is repeated in *II Henry IV*, iv, 5, 154: "Incredulous world."

One feast, one house, one mutual happiness.
The Two Gentlemen of Verona. Act v, sc. 4, l. 173. [Valentine]

UNKINDNESS

6
Is there any unkindness between my lord and you?
All's Well that Ends Well. Act ii, sc. 5, l. 35. [Bertram]

7
How mortal an unkindness is to them [women].
Antony and Cleopatra. Act i, sc. 2, l. 137. [Enobarbus]

8
Youth, you have done me much ungentleness.
As You Like It. Act v, sc. 2, l. 83. [Phebe] The only use of "ungentleness."

9
If voluble and sharp discourse be marr'd,
Unkindness blunts it more than marble hard.
The Comedy of Errors. Act ii, sc. 1, l. 92. [Adriana] "Voluble" is repeated in *Love's Labour's Lost,* ii, 1, 76, and in *Othello,* ii, 1, 242.

10
Grief-shot with his unkindness.
Coriolanus. Act v, sc. 1, l. 44. [Menenius] The only use of "grief-shot."

11
Henry, though he be infortunate,
Assure yourselves, will never be unkind.
II Henry VI. Act iv, sc. 9, l. 18. [King Henry] "Infortunate" is repeated in *Antony and Cleopatra,* iii, 6, 20.

12
This was the most unkindest cut of all.
Julius Cæsar. Act iii, sc. 2, l. 187. [Antony] See under INGRATITUDE.

Unkindest beast.—*Timon of Athens,* iv, 1, 36.
Unkindest tied.—Unkindest tides.—*The Two Gentlemen of Verona,* ii, 3, 42. The only uses of "unkindest."

13
Give me a bowl of wine.
In this I bury all unkindness.
Julius Cæsar. Act iv, sc. 3, l. 158. [Brutus]

Drink down all unkindness.
The Merry Wives of Windsor, i, 1, 204. See under DRINKING.

14
His own unkindness,
That stripp'd her from his benediction.
King Lear. Act iv, sc. 3, l. 44. [Kent]

Sharp-tooth'd unkindness.
King Lear. Act ii, sc. 4, l. 137. [King Lear] The only use of "sharp-tooth'd."

15
Who may I rather challenge for unkindness
Than pity for mischance!
Macbeth. Act iii, sc. 4, l. 42. [Macbeth]

16
But thy unkindness shall his death draw out
To lingering sufferance.
Measure for Measure. Act ii, sc. 4, l. 166. [Angelo]

His unjust unkindness, that in all reason should have quenched her love, hath, like an impediment in the current, made it more violent and unruly.
Measure for Measure. Act iii, sc. 1, l. 250. [Duke]

17
You are unkind, Demetrius; be not so.
A Midsummer-Night's Dream. Act iii, sc. 2, l. 162. [Lysander]

But why unkindly didst thou leave me so?
A Midsummer-Night's Dream. Act iii, sc. 2, l. 183. [Hermia]

Take it not unkindly.—*The Taming of the Shrew,* iii, 1, 57.
I take it much unkindly.—*Othello,* i, 1, 1.

18
Unkindness may do much;
And his unkindness may defeat my life,
But never taint my love.
Othello. Act iv, sc. 2, l. 159. [Desdemona]

19
And thy unkindness be like crooked age,
To crop at once a too long wither'd flower.
Richard II. Act ii, sc. 1, l. 133. [Gaunt]

20
That you were once unkind befriends me now.
Sonnets. No. cxx.

For if you were by my unkindness shaken
As I by yours, you've pass'd a hell of time,
And I, a tyrant, have no leisure taken
To weigh how once I suffer'd in your crime.
Sonnets. No. cxx.

1
Sick of man's unkindness.
Timon of Athens. Act iv, sc. 3, l. 176. [Timon]
We were not all unkind.—*Timon of Athens,* v, 4, 21.
Unnatural and unkind.—*Titus Andronicus,* v, 3, 48.
2
None can be call'd deform'd but the unkind.
Twelfth Night. Act iii, sc. 4, l. 402. [Antonio]
My lady is unkind, perdy. . . .
Alas, why is she so?
Twelfth Night. Act iv, sc. 2, l. 81. [Clown]
3
'Twixt his unkindness and his kindness; the one
He chides to hell and bids the other grow
Faster than thought or time.
The Winter's Tale. Act iv, sc. 4, l. 562. [Camillo]

UNTHANKFULNESS, see Gratitude

UNWILLINGNESS

4
Unwilling I agreed.
The Comedy of Errors. Act i, sc. 1, l. 61. [Ægeus]
For mine own part, sir, I do not care; but rather, because I am unwilling, and, for mine own part, have a desire to stay with my friends; else, sir, I did not care, for mine own part, so much.
II Henry IV. Act iii, sc. 2, l. 238. [Bullcalf]
5
Unwilling to outlive the good that did it.
Henry VIII. Act iv, sc. 2, l. 60. [Griffith]
Unwilling to proceed.
The Two Gentlemen of Verona, ii, 1, 112.
6
Dull unwillingness to repay a debt.
Richard III. Act ii, sc. 2, l. 92. [Dorset]
In all unwillingness.—*Richard III,* iv, 1, 58. The only uses of "unwillingness."

UNWORTHINESS

See also Worth

7
Why, look you now, how unworthy a thing you make of me!
Hamlet. Act iii, sc. 2, l. 379. [Hamlet]
8
Unworthily
Thou wast installed in that high degree.
I Henry VI. Act iv, sc. 1, l. 16. [Talbot] "Unworthily" is used only once again, in *The Two Gentlemen of Verona,* iii, 1, 29.
9
He left me proudly, as unworthy fight.
I Henry VI. Act iv, sc. 7, l. 43. [La Pucelle]
Unworthy though thou art, I 'll cope with thee.
II Henry VI. Act iii, sc. 2, l. 230. [Warwick]
10
Margaret: I am unworthy to be Henry's wife.
Suffolk: No, gentle madam; I unworthy am
To woo so fair a dame to be his wife
And have no portion in the choice myself.
I Henry VI. Act v, sc. 3, l. 121.
I could wish he would modestly examine himself, to see how much he is unworthy so good a lady.
Much Ado about Nothing. Act ii, sc. 3, l. 213. [Don Pedro]
11
Unworthy as I am.
A Midsummer-Night's Dream. Act ii, sc. 1, l. 207. [Helena]
Unworthy body as I am.—*The Two Gentlemen of Verona,* i, 2, 18.
Unworthy as she is.—*Romeo and Juliet,* iii, 5, 145.
I am unworthy.—*Pericles,* ii, 5, 40.
A poor unworthy brother.—*As You Like It,* i, 1, 36; *Titus Andronicus,* i, 1, 346.
Most unworthy.—*As You Like It,* iv, 1, 197.
12
I hold him to be unworthy of his place that does those things.
Othello. Act ii, sc. 3, l. 104. [Cassio]
13
Every cat and dog
And little mouse, every unworthy thing,
Live here in heaven and may look on her.
Romeo and Juliet. Act iii, sc. 3, l. 30. [Romeo]
14
If thy unworthiness raised love in me,
More worthy I to be beloved of thee.
Sonnets. No. cl.
15
Unworthy all the former favours
That I have fondly flatter'd her withal.
The Taming of the Shrew. Act iv, sc. 2, l. 30. [Hortensio]
16
Mine unworthiness that dare not offer
What I desire to give, and much less take
What I shall die to want.
The Tempest. Act iii, sc. 1, l. 77. [Miranda]
17
Worthy enough a herdsman; yes, him too,
That makes himself . . . Unworthy thee.
The Winter's Tale. Act iv, sc. 4, l. 445. [Polixenes] The only use of "herdsman." "Herdsmen" occurs in l. 344 of the same scene, and in *Coriolanus,* ii, 1, 105.

UPBRAIDING

See also Rebuke, Reproach

18
Hath often upbraided me withal.
The Comedy of Errors. Act iii, sc. 1, l. 113. [Antipholus of Ephesus]
Upbraided, chid and rated at.
II Henry VI. Act iii, sc. 1, l. 175. [Beaufort]
Upbraided it.—*II Henry IV,* iv, 5, 159.
19
Do not Upbraid 's with our distress.
Coriolanus. Act v, sc. 1, l. 35. [Sicinius]
20
I did upbraid her and fall out with her.
A Midsummer-Night's Dream, iv, 1, 55. "Fall out," in the sense of quarrel, is used ten times in the plays.

My master and mistress fallen out.
The Taming of the Shrew, iv, 1, 57. "Fallen out" in this sense is used six times.

1 Do not tempt my misery,
Lest that it make me so unsound a man
As to upbraid you with those kindnesses
That I have done for you.
Twelfth Night. Act iii, sc. 4, l. 383. [Antonio] The only use of "unsound."

He did upbraid me.—*I Henry VI,* ii, 5, 48.
Well they may upbraid me.—*I Henry VI,* iv, 1, 156.
Upbraid our course.—*The Tempest,* ii, 1, 287.
Upbraid his faith-breach.—*Macbeth,* v, 2, 18. The only use of "faith-breach."
Upbraid my falsehood!—*Troilus and Cressida,* iii, 2, 198.
Upbraid My gain.—*II Henry IV,* iv, 5, 193.

USE

2
Make your best use of this.
Antony and Cleopatra. Act v, sc. 2, l. 203. [Dolabella]

Best use.—*Timon of Athens,* v, 1, 146; *Cymbeline,* v, 4, 196.
Deadly use.—*King Lear,* iv, 2, 36.
Effectless use.—*Titus Andronicus,* iii, 1, 76. "Effectless" is repeated in *Pericles,* v, 1, 53: "All 's effectless."
Fair use.—*Romeo and Juliet,* ii, 3, 19.
Further use.—*All 's Well that Ends Well,* ii, 3, 41; *II Henry IV,* iv, 4, 72.
General use.—*Macbeth,* i, 2, 62.
Good use.—*I Henry IV,* iii, 3, 33; *II Henry IV,* v, 3, 11; *The Winter's Tale,* iv, 4, 616; *Cymbeline,* iii, 5, 64.
Hard use.—*Macbeth,* iii, 4, 143.
Honest use.—*All 's Well that Ends Well,* iv, 3, 341.
Instant use.—*King Lear,* ii, 1, 130; *Timon of Athens,* iii, 2, 41.
Mercy-lacking uses.—*King John,* iv, 1, 121. The only use of the phrase.
Right use.—*Hamlet,* v, 2, 95; *Henry VIII,* iii, 2, 386.
True use.—*Romeo and Juliet,* iii, 3, 124.
Unshaped use.—*Hamlet,* iv, 5, 8.

3
How weary, stale, flat and unprofitable,
Seem to me all the uses of this world!
Hamlet, i, 2, 133. See under WORLD.

4
Use almost can change the stamp of nature.
Hamlet. Act iii, sc. 4, l. 168. [Hamlet]

How use doth breed a habit in a man!
The Two Gentlemen of Verona. Act v, sc. 4, l. 1. [Valentine]

5
To what base uses we may return!
Hamlet. Act v, sc. 1, l. 223. [Hamlet]

6
Serve your uses both in purse and in person.
II Henry IV, ii, 1, 127. See under DECEIT.

7 If this servile usage once offend,
Go, and be free again.
I Henry VI. Act v, sc. 3, l. 58. [Suffolk]

Deserve this usage.—*King Lear,* ii, 4, 26.
Cruel usage.—*The Winter's Tale,* ii, 3, 117.
Fearful usage.—*The Winter's Tale,* v, 1, 153.
Rough usage.—*Cymbeline,* iv, 1, 22.
Stubborn usage.—*King John,* v, 1, 18.
Sinister usage.—*Twelfth Night,* i, 5, 188.
Unkind usage.—*I Henry IV,* v, 1, 69.
He hath good usage and great liberty.
III Henry VI, iv, 5, 6. [Gloucester]
Fair usage.—*Troilus and Cressida,* iv, 4, 121.
Princely shall be thy usage every way.
Titus Andronicus. Act i, sc. 1, l. 266. [Saturninus] The only uses of "usage."

8
Entreat her not the worse in that I pray
You use her well.
II Henry VI. Act ii, sc. 4, l. 81. [Gloucester]

I charge thee use her well.—*Troilus and Cressida,* iv, 4, 128.
Use him well.—*II Henry IV,* v, 1, 33; *Henry VIII,* v, 3, 155.
Use me well.—*The Merry Wives of Windsor,* iii, 3, 215; *King Lear,* iv, 6, 195; *Antony and Cleopatra,* iii, 2, 25.
Use them well.—*The Taming of the Shrew,* ii, 1, 111.
Let them use us well.—*Othello,* iv, 3, 103.
Use well our father.—*King Lear,* i, 1, 274.
Use you nobly.—*Titus Andronicus,* i, 1, 260.

9 These things are beyond all use,
And I do fear them.
Julius Cæsar. Act ii, sc. 2, l. 25. [Calpurnia]

10
Out of use and staled by other men.
Julius Cæsar. Act iv, sc. 1, l. 38. [Antony]

Out of use.—*Othello,* v, 1, 110; *Timon of Athens,* v, 1, 28; *Troilus and Cressida,* v, 6, 16.
In use.—*Julius Cæsar,* iii, 1, 265.
Not to use.—*Measure for Measure,* i, 3, 26.
Want of use.—*Pericles,* i, 4, 37.

11
I 'll use you for my mirth.
Julius Cæsar, iv, 3, 49. See under RIDICULE.

Let us use him.—*Julius Cæsar,* v, 5, 76.
Use him as he uses thee.—*All 's Well that Ends Well,* i, 1, 229.
Made use of him.—*Antony and Cleopatra,* iii, 5, 7.
Made use of me.—*Timon of Athens,* iii, 2, 89.
I must use thee.—*King John,* iv, 2, 159.

12
Why dost thou use me thus?
King Lear. Act ii, sc. 2, l. 11. [Oswald]

Why, madam, if I were your father's dog,
You would not use me so.
King Lear. Act ii, sc. 2, l. 144. [Kent]

But do you use me thus?—*II Henry IV,* ii, 2, 150.

13
They took from me the use of mine own house.
King Lear. Act iii, sc. 3, l. 3. [Gloucester]

Use of actions.—*Hamlet,* iii, 4, 163.
Use of your advice.—*King Lear,* ii, 1, 123.
Uses of adversity.—*As You Like It,* ii, 1, 12.
Use of anger.—*Coriolanus,* iii, 2, 30.
Use of arms.—*II Henry IV,* iv, 1, 155.
Use of eyes.—*Love's Labour 's Lost,* iv, 3, 310.
Use of nature.—*Macbeth,* i, 3, 137.
Use of quittance.—*Timon of Athens,* i, 1, 291.
Use of service.—*The Tempest.* ii, 1, 151.

Use of voice.—*Hamlet*, i, 1, 128.
Use of wits.—*The Comedy of Errors*, v, 1, 86.
Love's use.—*Sonnets*, xx.

1
Thou hotly lust'st to use her in that kind
For which thou whipp'st her.
King Lear, iv, 6, 166. See under HYPOCRISY.

Nurse: Thou must stand by too, and suffer every knave to use me at his pleasure?
Peter: I saw no man use you at his pleasure; if I had, my weapon should quickly have been out, I warrant you.
Romeo and Juliet. Act ii, sc. 4, l. 163.

Use her at thy pleasure.—*Pericles*, iv, 6, 150.

Use her as you will,
The worse to her, the better loved of me.
Titus Andronicus. Act ii, sc. 3, l. 166. [Tamora]

Use me as you will.—*The Merry Wives of Windsor*, v, 5, 173.

2
I do never use it.
The Merchant of Venice. Act i, sc. 3, l. 71. [Antonio]

I have use for it.—*Othello*, iii, 3, 319.
Is it his use?—*Othello*, iv, 1, 285.

3
Use me but as your spaniel, spurn me, strike me,
Neglect me, lose me; only give me leave,
Unworthy as I am, to follow you.
A Midsummer-Night's Dream. Act ii, sc. 1, l. 205. [Helena]

4
His use was to put a ducat in her clack-dish.
Measure for Measure. Act iii, sc. 2, l. 134. [Lucio] The only use of "clack-dish," a wooden dish with a lid carried by beggars, and clacked to attract attention.

5
Devise but how you'll use him when he comes.
The Merry Wives of Windsor. Act iv, sc. 4, l. 26. [Mrs. Ford]

6
I must use you In such another trick.
Tempest. Act iv, sc. 1, l. 36. [Prospero]

Put to use.—*Twelfth Night*, iii, 1, 57.
My uses cry to me.—*Timon of Athens*, ii, 1, 20.
Mine own use.—*Timon of Athens*, v, 1, 209.

7
To use as you think needful.
Titus Andronicus. Act v, sc. 1, l. 39. [Goth]

8
I'll use thee kindly for thy mistress' sake,
That used me so.
The Two Gentlemen of Verona. Act iv, sc. 4, l. 207. [Julia]

In my sight she uses thee kindly.
Twelfth Night. Act iii, sc. 4, l. 171. [Sir Toby, reading]

Pray you, without any more virginial fencing, will you use him kindly?
Pericles. Act iv, sc. 6, l. 62. [Bawd]

He used me kindly.—*Coriolanus*, i, 9, 83.
Use thee kindly.—*King Lear*, i, 5, 14.
Use us kindly.—*Richard III*, iii, 2, 33.
Use all gently.—*Hamlet*, iii, 2, 6.
Use her honourably.—*III Henry VI*, iii, 2, 123.
Frankly use.—*Timon of Athens*, ii, 2, 188.

9
Make use of time.
Venus and Adonis, l. 129. See under OPPORTUNITY.

USURPATION

10
You do more usurp
Than doth your brother that hath banish'd you.
As You Like It. Act ii, sc. 1, l. 27. [First Lord]

Swearing that we Are mere usurpers, tyrants.
As You Like It. Act ii, sc. 1, l. 60. [Lord]

11
Nor shall proud Lancaster usurp my right.
II Henry VI. Act i, sc. 1, l. 244. [York]

Proud ambitious Edward Duke of York
Usurps the regal title and the seat
Of England's true-anointed lawful king.
III Henry VI. Act iii, sc. 3, l. 27. [Queen Margaret] The only use of "true-anointed."

Thou usurp'st my father's right and mine.
III Henry VI. Act v, sc. 5, l. 37. [Prince Edward]

Usurp'd the throne.—*Henry V*, i, 2, 69.

12
Rebuke the usurpation
Of thy unnatural uncle.
King John. Act ii, sc. 1, l. 9. [Lewis]

Usurpation most unjust.—*I Henry VI*, ii, 5, 68.
Witness'd usurpation.—*II Henry IV*, i, 1, 63.

13
King John: Alack, thou dost usurp authority.
King Philip: Excuse; it is to beat usurping down.
Elinor: Who is it thou dost call usurper, France?
Constable: Let me make answer; thy usurping son.
King John. Act ii, sc. 1, l. 118.

Thou and thine usurp
The dominations, royalties and rights
Of this oppressed boy.
King John. Act ii, sc. 1, l. 175. [Constance] The only use of "dominations."

14
My fool usurps my body.
King Lear. Act iv, sc. 2, l. 28. [Goneril]

Like a foul usurper, went about
From this fair throne to heave the owner out.
The Rape of Lucrece, l. 412.

15
Thou didst usurp my place, and dost thou not
Usurp the just proportion of my sorrow?
Richard III. Act iv, sc. 4, l. 109. [Queen Margaret]

16
Viola: Are you the lady of the house?
Olivia: If I do not usurp myself, I am.
Viola: Most certain, if you are she, you do usurp yourself.
Twelfth Night. Act i, sc. 5, l. 197.

USURY

See also Covetousness

1
Make edicts for usury, to support usurers.
Coriolanus. Act i, sc. 1, l. 84. [Citizen]
Banish usury.—*Coriolanus,* iii, 5, 99.

2
Thou art a most pernicious usurer.
I Henry VI. Act iii, sc. 1, l. 17. [Gloucester]

3
The usurer hangs the cozener.
King Lear. Act iv, sc. 6, l. 167. [King Lear]

4
He was wont to call me usurer.
The Merchant of Venice, iii, 1, 50.
Antonio: Did he take interest?
Shylock: No, not take interest, not, as you would say,
Directly interest.
The Merchant of Venice. Act i, sc. 3, l. 76.

5 Like a usurer, abound'st in all,
And usest none.
Romeo and Juliet. Act iii, sc. 3, l. 123. [Friar Laurence]

6
Profitless usurer, why dost thou use
So great a sum of sums, yet canst not live?
Sonnets. No. iv. "Profitless" is repeated in *Much Ado about Nothing,* v, 1, 4, and in *Othello,* i, 3, 30.
Use is not forbidden usury
Which happies those that pay the willing loan.
Sonnets. No. vi. The only use of "happies."
Thou usurer, that put'st forth all to use,
And sue a friend came debtor for my sake.
Sonnets. No. cxxxiv.

7
Apemantus: You three serve three usurers?
Servants: Ay; would they served us!
Apemantus: So would I,—as good a trick as ever hangman served thief. . . .
Fool: I think no usurer but has a fool to his servant.
Timon of Athens. Act ii, sc. 2, l. 97.

8
Bless me from marrying a usurer!
Winter's Tale. Act iv, sc. 4, l. 271. [Dorcas]

V

VAGABOND, see Travel

VALENTINE, see Day: Special Days

VALOUR

See also Courage; Man: Valiant Men

9
I know thou 'rt valiant.
All's Well that Ends Well. Act iii, sc. 6, l. 88. [Bertram]
Thou knowest I am as valiant as Hercules
I Henry IV. Act ii, sc. 4, l. 298. [Falstaff]
He is now as valiant as Hercules that only tells a lie and swears it.
Much Ado about Nothing. Act iv, sc. 1, l. 324. [Beatrice]
Claudio: I take him to be valiant.
Don Pedro: As Hector, I assure you.
Much Ado about Nothing. Act ii, sc. 3, l. 195.
Valiant as a lion.—*I Henry IV,* iii, 1, 167; *Troilus and Cressida,* i, 2, 21.
Valiant I am.—*II Henry VI,* iv, 2, 57.
Free, learned, valiant.—*Twelfth Night,* i, 5, 279.
Gentle, strong and valiant.—*As You Like It,* ii, 3, 6.
Good, and valiant.—*Twelfth Night,* iii, 4, 164.
Hot and valiant.—*II Henry IV,* iv, 3, 132.
Noble and valiant.—*Othello,* ii, 2, 2.
Valiant, active, wealthy.—*II Henry VI,* iv, 7, 68
Valiant, and honest.—*Julius Cæsar,* iii, 1, 126.
Valiant and virtuous.—*I Henry VI,* iv, 1, 35.
Wise and valiant.—*Julius Cæsar,* iii, 1, 138.
Young, valiant, wise.—*Richard III,* i, 2, 245.
Most gentle and most valiant.—*Troilus and Cressida,* iv, 5, 227.
Most valiant.—*Henry V,* iv, 1, 46; *Othello,* i, 3, 40.
Thrice-valiant.—*Titus Andronicus,* v, 2, 112; *Henry V,* iv, 6, 1.

10 When valour preys on reason,
It eats the sword it fights with.
Antony and Cleopatra. Act iii, sc. 13, l. 199. [Enobarbus]
Not Cæsar's valour hath o'erthrown Antony,
But Antony's hath triumph'd on itself.
Antony and Cleopatra. Act iv, sc. 15, l. 14. [Antony]

11 My valour 's poison'd
With only suffering stain by him.
Coriolanus. Act i, sc. 10, l. 17. [Aufidius]
It is held
That valour is the chiefest virtue, and
Most dignifies the haver: if it be,
The man I speak of cannot in the world
Be singly counterpoised.
Coriolanus. Act ii, sc. 2, l. 87. [Cominius] The only use of "haver." "Counterpoised" is repeated in *II Henry VI,* iv, 1, 22, and in *III Henry VI,* iii, 3, 137.
Thy valiantness was mine, thou suck'dst it from me.
Coriolanus. Act iii, sc. 2, l. 129. [Coriolanus] The only use of "valiantness."

12
Our valour is to chase what flies.
Cymbeline. Act iii, sc. 3, l. 42. [Arviragus]
Thou mayst be valiant in a better cause.
Cymbeline. Act iii, sc. 4, l. 74. [Imogen]
Valour Becomes thee.—*Cymbeline,* iv, 2, 154.
Valour
That wildly grows in them, but yields a crop
As if it had been sow'd.
Cymbeline. Act iv, sc. 2, l. 179. [Belarius]

1
Finding ourselves too slow of sail,
We put on a compelled valour.
Hamlet. Act iv, sc. 6, l. 16. [Horatio]

2
There's no more valour in that Poins than in a wild-duck.
I Henry IV, ii, 2, 107. See under COWARDICE. "Wild-duck" is repeated in iv, 2, 21, and occurs in no other play.

Thou wilt be as valiant as the wrathful dove or most magnanimous mouse.
II Henry IV. Act iii, sc. 2, l. 170. [Falstaff]

Thou little valiant!—*King John*, iii, 1, 116.

3
His valour shown upon our crests to-day
Hath taught us how to cherish such high deeds
Even in the bosom of our adversaries.
I Henry IV. Act v, sc. 5, l. 29. [Prince]

4
True valour is turned bear-herd.
II Henry IV. Act i, sc. 2, l. 192. [Falstaff] "Bear-herd" is repeated in *The Taming of the Shrew*, Ind., 2, 21.

In a false quarrel there is no true valour.
Much Ado about Nothing. Act v, sc. 1, l. 120. [Benedick]

True valour still a true respect should have.
The Rape of Lucrece, l. 201. The only uses of "true valour."

5
Ah, you whoreson little valiant villain, you! . . . thou art as valorous as Hector of Troy, worth five of Agamemnon, and ten times better than the Nine Worthies: ah, villain!
II Henry IV. Act ii, sc. 4, l. 225. [Doll]

The most valorous . . . signieur of England.
Henry V. Act iv, sc. 4, l. 66. [Boy]

Valorous enemy.—*II Henry IV*, iv, 3, 43.

Valorous Hector.—*Troilus and Cressida*, iii, 3, 275. The only uses of "valorous."

6
I never knew yet but rebuke and check was the reward of valour.
II Henry IV. Act iv, sc. 3, l. 34. [Falstaff]

7
My pure and immaculate valour.
II Henry IV. Act iv, sc. 3, l. 41. [Falstaff]

Of approved valour.
Much Ado about Nothing, ii, 1, 395.

Of buxom valour.—*Henry V*, iii, 6, 28. "Buxom" is used a second time in *Pericles*, i, Gower, 23.

Abounding valour.—*Henry V*, iv, 3, 104. The only use of "abounding."

Good valour.—*Antony and Cleopatra*, iv, 7, 16.

8
Show thy valour, and put up your sword.
Henry V. Act ii, sc. 1, l. 45. [Hostess]

Orleans: It is no hidden virtue in him.
Constable: By my faith, sir, but it is; never any body saw it but his lackey: 'tis a hooded valour; and when it appears, it will bate.
Henry V. Act iii, sc. 7, l. 118.

Though it appear a little out of fashion,
There is much care and valour in this Welshman.
Henry V. Act iv, sc. 1, l. 85. [King Henry]

Let us but blow on them,
The vapour of our valour will o'erturn them.
Henry V. Act iv, sc. 2, l. 23. [Constable]

Exeter: Thou art framed of the firm truth of valour.
Bedford: He is as full of valour as of kindness;
Princely in both.
Henry V. Act iv, sc. 3, l. 14.

A memorable trophy of predeceased valour.
Henry V. Act v, sc. 1, l. 76. [Gower] The only use of "predeceased."

9
Orleans: I know him to be valiant.
Constable: I was told that by one who knows him better than you.
Orleans: What's he?
Constable: Marry, he told me so himself; and he said he cared not who knew it.
Henry V. Act iii, sc. 7, l. 112.

He is full so valiant.—*Macbeth*, i, 2, 24.

10
What valour were it, when a cur doth grin,
For one to thrust his hand between his teeth,
When he might spurn him with his foot away?
III Henry VI. Act i, sc. 4, l. 56. [Northumberland]

Ten to one is no impeach of valour.
III Henry VI. Act i, sc. 4, l. 60. [Northumberland]

11
The valiant never taste of death but once.
Julius Cæsar, ii, 2, 33. See COWARDICE, 257:8.

12
Where I could not be honest,
I never yet was valiant.
King Lear. Act v, sc. 1, l. 23. [Albany]

I am not valiant neither.—*Othello*, v, 2, 244.

Officious, and not valiant.—*Coriolanus*, i, 8, 14.

He is not valiant.—*The Tempest*, iii, 2, 27.

Less valiant than the virgin in the night.
Troilus and Cressida, i, 1, 11. See COWARDICE.

13
And these assume but valour's excrement
To render them redoubted!
The Merchant of Venice. Act iii, sc. 2, l. 87. [Bassanio] "Excrement" is used six times.

14
Host: A word, Mounseur Mockwater.
Caius: Mock-vater! vat is dat?
Host: Mock-water, in our English tongue, is valour, bully.
Caius: By gar, den, I have as mush mock-vater as de Englishman.
The Merry Wives of Windsor. Act ii, sc. 3, l. 59. The only uses of "mock-water."

Valour of my tongue.—*Macbeth*, i, 5, 28.

My body's valour.—*Richard II*, i, 3, 37.

15
You the valiant of this warlike isle.
Othello. Act ii, sc. 1, l. 43. [Cassio]

16
As full of valour as of royal blood.
Richard II. Act v, sc. 5, l. 114. [Exton]

So full of valour that they smote the air
For breathing in their faces; beat the ground
For kissing of their feet.
The Tempest. Act iv, sc. 1, l. 172. [Ariel]

How full of valour did he bear himself
In the last conflict, and made plenteous wounds!
Timon of Athens. Act iii, sc. 5, l. 65. [Alcibiades]

1
Be valiant, and speed well!
Richard III. Act v, sc. 3, l. 102. [Derby]

Be valiant and live.—*Richard II,* i, 3, 83.

2
To be valiant is to stand.
Romeo and Juliet. Act i, sc. 1, l. 11. [Gregory]

3
He 's truly valiant that can wisely suffer
The worst that man can breathe, and make his wrongs
His outsides, to wear them like his raiment, carelessly,
And ne'er prefer his injuries to his heart,
To bring it into danger.
Timon of Athens. Act iii, sc. 5, l. 31. [Senator]

4
Valour's show and valour's worth divide
In storms of fortune.
Troilus and Cressida. Act i, sc. 3, l. 46. [Nestor]

Knows his valour, and knows not his fear.
Troilus and Cressida. Act i, sc. 3, l. 268. [Æneas]

What propugnation is in one man's valour?
Troilus and Cressida. Act ii, sc. 2, l. 136. [Paris] The only use of "propugnation" (defence).

To be valiant is no praise at all.
Troilus and Cressida. Act ii, sc. 2, l. 145. [Priam]

In the extremity of great and little,
Valour and pride excel themselves in Hector;
The one almost as infinite as all,
The other blank as nothing.
Troilus and Cressida. Act iv, sc. 5, l. 78. [Æneas]

5
She did show favour to the youth in your sight only to exasperate you, to awake your dormouse valour, to put fire in your heart, and brimstone in your liver.
Twelfth Night. Act iii, sc. 2, l. 20. [Fabian] The only use of "dormouse."

Build me thy fortunes upon the basis of valour.
Twelfth Night. Act iii, sc. 2, l. 35. [Sir Toby]

There is no love-broker in the world can more prevail in man's commendation with woman than report of valour.
Twelfth Night. Act iii, sc. 2, l. 39. [Sir Toby] The only use of "love-broker."

6
Thurio: What says she to my valour?
Proteus: O, sir, she makes no doubt of that.
Julia (*Aside*): She needs not, when she knows it cowardice.
The Two Gentlemen of Verona. Act v, sc. 2, l. 19.

VALUE

See also Worth

7
He must be weighed rather by her value than his own.
Cymbeline. Act i, sc. 4, l. 15. [Iachimo]

Value of her dower.—*I Henry VI,* v, 1, 44.

8
The queen is valued thirty thousand strong.
III Henry VI. Act v, sc. 3, l. 14. [Gloucester]

Beyond what can be valued.—*King Lear,* i, 1, 58.

Valued at the highest rate.—*The Comedy of Errors,* i, 1, 24.

Valued to the money's worth.—*Love's Labour 's Lost,* ii, 1, 137.

Exactly valued.—*Antony and Cleopatra,* v, 2, 139.

9
Weigh thy value with an even hand.
The Merchant of Venice. Act ii, sc. 7, l. 25. [Prince of Morocco]

Value me Above this world.—*Love's Labour 's Lost,* v, 2, 445.

10
Wooing thee, I found thee of more value
Than stamps in gold or sums in sealed bags;
And 'tis the very riches of thyself
That now I aim at.
The Merry Wives of Windsor. Act iii, sc. 4, l. 15. [Fenton]

Great value.—*Julius Cæsar,* i, 2, 50.
Inestimable value.—*Pericles,* ii, 4, 8.
Kinder value.—*Coriolanus,* ii, 2, 63.
Needful value.—*Measure for Measure,* i, 1, 56.
Rich value.—*The Merchant of Venice,* ii, 9, 91.
Of much less value.—*Richard II,* ii, 3, 19.

11
Things of like value differing in the owners
Are prized by their masters.
Timon of Athens. Act i, sc. 1, l. 170. [Jeweller]

12
Troilus: What is aught, but as 'tis valued?
Hector: But value dwells not in particular will:
It holds his estimate and dignity
As well wherein 'tis precious of itself
As in the prizer.
Troilus and Cressida. Act ii, sc. 2, l. 52. The only use of "prizer."

VANITY

See also Boasting, Conceit, Egotism, Self-Love

13
Trouble me no more with vanity.
I Henry IV. Act i, sc. 2, l. 91. [Falstaff]

That vanity in years.—*I Henry IV,* ii, 4, 500.
Here 's no vanity.—*I Henry IV,* v, 3, 33.

14
I can no longer brook thy vanities.
I Henry IV. Act v, sc. 4, l. 74. [Hotspur]

O, I should have a heavy miss of thee,
If I were much in love with vanity!
I Henry IV. Act v, sc. 4, l. 105. [Prince]

1
And you shall find his vanities forespent
Were but the outside of the Roman Brutus.
Henry V. Act ii, sc. 4, l. 36. [Constable] "Forespent" is repeated in *Cymbeline,* ii, 3, 64.

Free from vainness and self-glorious pride.
Henry V. Act v, Prologue, l. 20. [Chorus] The only use of "self-glorious." "Vainness" is repeated in *Twelfth Night,* iii, 4, 389.

2
Gower: Why, here he comes, swelling like a turkey-cock.
Fluellen: 'Tis no matter for his swellings or his turkey-cocks.
Henry V. Act v, sc. 1, l. 15.

O, peace! Contemplation makes a rare turkey-cock of him: how he jets under his advanced plumes!
Twelfth Night. Act ii, sc. 5, l. 35. [Fabian] The only uses of "turkey-cock."

Does he not hold up his head, as it were, and strut in his gait?
The Merry Wives of Windsor. Act i, sc. 4, l. 30. [Mistress Quickly]

3
What had he
To do in these fierce vanities?
Henry VIII. Act i, sc. 1, l. 53. [Buckingham]

Empty vanities.—*Henry VIII,* ii, 3, 69.

4
Vanity the puppet's part.
King Lear. Act ii, sc. 2, l. 39. [Kent]

5
It would ill become me to be vain.
Love's Labour 's Lost, iv, 2, 31. See under Learning.

Be a little vain.—*Comedy of Errors,* iii, 2, 27.
Skipping and vain.—*Love's Labour 's Lost,* v, 2, 771.
Vain and frivolous.—*III Henry VI,* i, 2, 27.
Too too vain, too too vain.—*Love's Labour 's Lost,* v, 2, 532.
Vain man.—*II Henry IV,* v, 5, 48.

6
His general behaviour vain, ridiculous, and thrasonical.
Love's Labour 's Lost. Act v, sc. 1, l. 13. [Holofernes] "Thrasonical" (boastful) is repeated in *As You Like It,* v, 2, 34: "Cæsar's thrasonical brag."

7
O heaven, the vanity of wretched fools!
Measure for Measure. Act v, sc. 1, l. 164. [Duke]

8
Where doth the world thrust forth a vanity—
So it be new, there 's no respect how vile—
That is not quickly buzz'd into his ears?
Richard II. Act ii, sc. 1, l. 24. [York]

9
Light vanity, insatiate cormorant,
Consuming means, soon preys upon itself.
Richard II. Act ii, sc. 1, l. 38. [Gaunt] "Insatiate" is repeated in *Richard III,* iii, 7, 7: "Insatiate greediness"; and in *Titus Andronicus,* v, 1, 88: "Insatiate woman."

Some few vanities that make him light.
Richard II. Act iii, sc. 4, l. 86. [Gardener]

10
O heavy lightness! serious vanity!
Romeo and Juliet. Act i, sc. 1, l. 184. [Romeo]

A lover may bestride the gossamer
That idles in the wanton summer air,
And yet not fall; so light is vanity.
Romeo and Juliet. Act ii, sc. 6, l. 18. [Friar Laurence] "Gossamer" is used once again in *King Lear,* iv, 6, 49.

11
Methinks no face so gracious is as mine,
No shape so true, no truth of such account.
Sonnets. No. lxii.

Some glory in their birth, some in their skill,
Some in their wealth, some in their bodies' force,
Some in their garments, though new-fangled ill,
Some in their hawks and hounds, some in their horse.
Sonnets. No. xci.

12
Hoy-day, what a sweep of vanity comes this way!
Timon of Athens. Act i, sc. 2, l. 137. [Apemantus] "Hoy-day" is repeated in *Richard III,* iv, 4, 460, and in *Troilus and Cressida,* v, 1, 73.

13
In self-assumption greater
Than in the note of judgement.
Troilus and Cressida. Act ii, sc. 3, l. 133. [Agamemnon] The only use of "self-assumption."

Never suffers matter of the world
Enter his thoughts, save such as do revolve
And ruminate himself.
Troilus and Cressida. Act ii, sc. 3, l. 196. [Ulysses]

14
If Hector break not his neck i' the combat, he 'll break 't himself in vain-glory.
Troilus and Cressida. Act iii, sc. 3, l. 259. [Thersites]

It is not vain-glory for a man and his glass to confer in his own chamber.
Cymbeline. Act iv, sc. 1, l. 8. [Cloten]

Without vain-glory.—*Henry VIII,* iii, 1, 127. The only uses of "vain-glory."

What need these . . . vain-glories?—*Timon of Athens,* i, 2, 249. The only use of "vain-glories."

VANTAGE, see Advantage

VASSAL

See also Slave

15
I . . . will his vassal die.
All's Well that Ends Well. Act i, sc. 3, l. 165. [Helena]

I am his fortune's vassal.
Antony and Cleopatra. Act v, sc. 2, l. 29. [Cleopatra]

I, your vassal.—*Measure for Measure,* v, 1, 391.

Thy heroical vassal.—*Love's Labour 's Lost,* iv, 1, 65.

1
Make me as the poorest vassal is.
II Henry IV. Act iv, sc. 5, l. 176. [Prince]
Lowly vassal.—*II Henry VI,* iv, 1, 111.
Presumptuous vassals.—*I Henry VI,* iv, 1, 125.
Shallow vassal.—*Love's Labour's Lost,* i, 1, 256.
Woolen vassals.—*Coriolanus,* iii, 2, 9.
God's vassals.—*Henry V,* iii, 2, 8.
2
Thy proud heart's slave and vassal wretch to be.
Sonnets. No. cxli.

VEIN

3
You touch'd my vein at first.
As You Like It. Act ii, sc. 7, l. 94. [Orlando]
The fellow finds his vein
And yielding to him humours well his frenzy.
The Comedy of Errors. Act iv, sc. 4, l. 83. [Adriana]
Take each one in his vein.
Love's Labour's Lost. Act v, sc. 2, l. 548. [Biron]
4
This is Ercles' vein, a tyrant's vein.
Midsummer-Night's Dream. Act i, sc. 2, l. 42. [Bottom] "Ercles" is used also in l. 31.
King Cambyses' vein.—*I Henry IV,* ii, 4, 426. A hit at a bombastic play, *A Lamentable Tragedie, Mixed full of Pleasant Mirth, Containing the Life of King Cambises, King of Persia,* produced in 1570.
5
There is no following her in this fierce vein.
A Midsummer-Night's Dream. Act iii, sc. 2, l. 82. [Demetrius]
Conquering vein.—*I Henry VI,* iv, 7, 95.
Vein of chivalry.—*Troilus and Cressida,* v, 3, 32.
6
I am not in the giving vein to-day. . . .
Thou troublest me; I am not in the vein.
Richard III. Act iv, sc. 2, l. 122. [King Richard] The only use of "troublest."
7
He rubs the vein of him.
Troilus and Cressida. Act ii, sc. 3, l. 210. [Nestor]

II—Veins

8
The veins unfill'd, our blood is cold.
Coriolanus, v, 1, 51. See DINING, 344:1. "Unfill'd" is repeated in *Twelfth Night,* ii, 3, 7.
My veins are chill,
And have no more of life than may suffice
To give my tongue that heat to ask your help.
Pericles. Act ii, sc. 1, l. 76. [Pericles]
Cold and empty veins.—*Richard III,* i, 2, 59.
9
Rouse thy vaunting veins.
Henry V. Act ii, sc. 3, l. 4. [Pistol]
Azure veins.—*The Rape of Lucrece,* l. 419. "Azure" is repeated in *Cymbeline,* ii, 2, 22.
Bawdy veins.—*Troilus and Cressida,* iv, 1, 69.
Bloody veins.—*Pericles,* i, 4, 94.
Blue veins.—*The Rape of Lucrece,* l. 440.
Bluest veins.—*Antony and Cleopatra,* ii, 5, 29. The only use of "bluest."
Infant's veins.—*King John,* iii, 4, 132.
Lively veins.—*Sonnets,* lxvii.
Scorched veins.—*King John,* iii, 1, 278. "Scorched" is repeated in *III Henry VI,* ii, 6, 13.
Sickly veins.—*Henry V,* iv, 2, 20.
Small inferior veins.—*Coriolanus,* i, 1, 142.
Veins of actions.—*Troilus and Cressida,* i, 3, 6.
Veins o' the earth.—*The Tempest,* i, 2, 255.

VENGEANCE

See also Revenge

10
Aroused vengeance sets him new a-work.
Hamlet. Act ii, sc. 2, l. 510. [Player] The only use of "a-work."
Wasteful vengeance.—*Henry V,* i, 2, 283.
11
Threefold vengeance tend upon your steps!
II Henry VI. Act iii, sc. 2, l. 304. [Queen]
12 I 'll venge thy death,
Or die renowned by attempting it.
III Henry VI. Act ii, sc. 1, l. 87. [Richard]
13
Vengeance comes along with them.
III Henry VI. Act ii, sc. 5, l. 134. [Exeter]
They shall feel the vengeance of my wrath.
III Henry VI. Act iv, sc. 1, l. 82. [King Edward]
14 All vengeance comes too short
Which can pursue the offender.
King Lear. Act ii, sc. 1, l. 90. [Regan]
I shall see
The winged vengeance overtake such children.
King Lear. Act iii, sc. 7, l. 65. [Gloucester]
15
Vengeance! plague! death! confusion!
King Lear. Act ii, sc. 4, l. 96. [King Lear]
O, vengeance!—*Hamlet,* ii, 2, 610.
O, vengeance, vengeance!—*Cymbeline,* ii, 5, 8.
What the vengeance!—*Coriolanus,* iii, 1, 262.
16
Arise, black vengeance, from thy hollow cell!
Othello. Act iii, sc. 3, l. 447. [Othello]
17
Put we our quarrel to the will of heaven;
Who, when they see the hours ripe on earth,
Will rain hot vengeance on offenders' heads.
Richard II. Act i, sc. 2, l. 6. [Gaunt]
Tongues of heaven,
Plainly denouncing vengeance.
King John. Act iii, sc. 4, l. 158. [Pandulph] The only use of "denouncing."
Render vengeance.—*Richard II,* iv, 1, 67.
18 Doing worthy vengeance on thyself,
Which didst unworthy slaughter upon others.
Richard III. Act i, sc. 2, l. 87. [Lady Anne]
Clarence: Take heed; for he holds vengeance in his hands,
To hurl upon their heads that break his law.
Murderer: And that same vengeance doth he hurl on thee,
For false forswearing and for murder too.
Richard III. Act i, sc. 4, l. 204. "Forswear-

ing" is used only once again, in *I Henry IV,* v, 2, 39.

To-morrow's vengeance.—*Richard III,* v, 3, 206.

1 We will have vengeance for it, fear thou not.
Romeo and Juliet. Act iii, sc. 5, l. 88. [Lady Capulet]

Can vengeance be pursued further than death?
Romeo and Juliet. Act v, sc. 3, l. 55. [Paris]

2 A vengeance on your crafty wither'd hide!
The Taming of the Shrew. Act ii, sc. 1, l. 406. [Tranio]

3 Vengeance is in my heart, death in my hand,
Blood and revenge are hammering in my head.
Titus Andronicus. Act ii, sc. 3, l. 38. [Aaron]

Befall what may befall,
I 'll speak no more but 'Vengeance rot you all!'
Titus Andronicus. Act v, sc. 1, l. 57. [Aaron]

Wreakful vengeance.—*Titus Andronicus,* v, 2, 32. "Wreakful" is repeated in *Timon of Athens,* iv, 3, 229: "Wreakful heaven."

4 Vengeance on the traitor.
Titus Andronicus. Act iv, sc. 3, l. 34. [Marcus]

Vengeance on the whole camp!
Troilus and Cressida. Act ii, sc. 3, l. 19. [Thersites]

A vengeance on 't!
The Two Gentlemen of Verona. Act ii, sc. 3, l. 21. [Launce]

5 Weeping, cursing, vowing vengeance.
Troilus and Cressida. Act v, sc. 5, l. 31. [Ulysses]

Do some vengeance.—*Troilus and Cressida,* ii, 2, 73.

Venom'd vengeance.—*Troilus and Cressida,* v, 3, 47.

6 For present vengeance, Take it on her.
The Winter's Tale. Act ii, sc. 3, l. 22. [Leontes]

The sweet'st, dear'st creature 's dead, and vengeance for 't
Not dropp'd down yet.
The Winter's Tale. Act iii, sc. 2, l. 202. [Paulina]

VENOM

See also Poison; Tongue: Poisonous Tongues

7 Laertes: The treacherous instrument is in thy hand,
Unbated and envenom'd. . . .
Hamlet: The point envenom'd too!
Then, venom, to thy work!
Hamlet. Act v, sc. ii, l. 327. "Unbated" is repeated in iv, 7, 139, and in *The Merchant of Venice,* ii, 6, 11. "Envenom'd" occurs five times.

Envenom him with words, or get thee gone.
King John. Act iii, sc. 1, l. 63. [Constable]

Envenom with his envy.—*Hamlet,* iv, 7, 104.

What is comely envenoms him.—*As You Like It,* ii, 3, 15. The only uses of "envenom."

8 You shall digest the venom of your spleen,
Though it do split you.
Julius Cæsar. Act iv, sc. 3, l. 47. [Brutus]

9 Thou stormest venomously;
Wilt thou spit all thyself?
Pericles. Act iii, sc. 1, l. 7. [Pericles] "Venomously" is used only once again, in *King Lear,* iv, 3, 48.

Ugly and venomous.—*As You Like It,* ii, 1, 13. "Venomous" is used five times.

10 Being so applied,
His venom in effect is purified.
The Rape of Lucrece, l. 531.

11 Anointed let me be with deadly venom.
Richard III. Act iv, sc. 1, l. 62. [Anne]

VENTURE

12 I 'ld venture
The well-lost life of mine on his grace's cure.
All's Well that Ends Well. Act i, sc. 3, l. 253. [Helena] The only use of "well-lost."

I will venture . . . a little more.
Coriolanus. Act i, sc. 1, l. 94. [Menenius]

13 Diseased ventures
That play with all infirmities for gold
Which rottenness can lend nature!
Cymbeline. Act i, sc. 6, l. 123. [Iachimo] "Rottenness" is repeated in *King John,* iii, 4, 26.

Personal venture.—*Macbeth,* i, 3, 91.

Merchant's venture.—*II Henry IV,* ii, 4, 69.

14 So dare we venture thee,
Albeit considerations infinite
Do make against it.
I Henry IV. Act v, sc. 1, l. 101. [King Henry]

15 'Twas ten to one;
And yet we ventured on such dangerous seas
That if we wrought out life 'twas ten to one;
And yet we ventured, for the gain proposed
Choked the respect of likely peril fear'd;
And since we are o'erset, venture again.
Come, we will all put forth, body and goods.
II Henry IV. Act i, sc. 1, l. 180. [Bardolph] "O'erset" is repeated in *Romeo and Juliet,* iii, 5, 137.

So to the venture.—*II Henry IV,* Epil., 8.

Spoke at a venture.—*II Henry IV,* i, 1, 59.

Like an ill venture it come unluckily home.
II Henry IV, Epil., 13.

16 I am much too venturous.
Henry VIII. Act i, sc. 2, l. 54. [Queen]

Bold, and venturous.—*Richard III,* iv, 4, 170.

Venturous or desperate.—*I Henry VI,* ii, 1, 45.

Venturous deed.—*II Henry VI,* iii, 2, 9.

Venturous fairy.—*Midsummer-Night's Dream,* iv, 1, 39. The only uses of "venturous."

1
I 'll venture one have-at-him.
Henry VIII. Act ii, sc. 2, l. 85. [Suffolk] "Have at him" (unhyphenated) is repeated in *II Henry IV*, i, 2, 217.

I am afraid; and yet I 'll venture it.
King John. Act iv, sc. 3, l. 5. [Arthur]

Venture at it.—*Henry VIII,* ii, 1, 156.

Venture for me.—*The Merchant of Venice,* iii, 2, 10.

Venture in your own behalf.—*King Lear,* iv, 2, 20.

Venture madly.—*The Taming of the Shrew,* ii, 1, 329.

Venture maidenhead.—*Henry VIII,* ii, 3, 25.

Venture to depart.—*The Two Gentlemen of Verona,* iv, 3, 36.

2
My ventures are not in one bottom trusted.
The Merchant of Venice, i, 1, 42. See under MERCHANDISE.

Have all his ventures fail'd? What, not one hit?
The Merchant of Venice. Act iii, sc. 2, l. 270. [Bassanio]

In my school-days, when I had lost one shaft,
I shot his fellow of the self-same flight
The self-same way with more advised watch,
To find the other forth, and by adventuring both
I oft found both.
The Merchant of Venice. Act i, sc. 1, l. 140. [Bassanio] The only use of "adventuring." "School-days" is repeated in *Richard III,* iv, 4, 169, and in *A Midsummer-Night's Dream,* iii, 2, 202.

Other ventures he hath, squandered abroad.
The Merchant of Venice. Act i, sc. 3, l. 21. [Shylock] The only use of "squandered."

Lose our ventures.—*Julius Cæsar,* iv, 3, 224.

3
I 'll make a shaft or a bolt on 't: 'slid, 'tis but venturing.
The Merry Wives of Windsor. Act iii, sc. 4, l. 24. [Slender] The only use of "venturing."

4
I should venture purgatory for 't.
Othello. Act iv, sc. 3, l. 77. [Emilia]

Being ireful, on the lion he will venture.
Venus and Adonis, l. 628.

Desperate ventures.—*Richard III,* v, 3, 319.
See PEASANT, 1134:16.

VENUS

5
Yonder Venus in her glimmering sphere.
A Midsummer-Night's Dream, iii, 2, 61. See under MURDER. "Glimmering" is repeated in ii, 1, 77: "Glimmering night"; and in v, 1, 398: "Glimmering light." It occurs in no other play.

6
Venus smiles not in a house of tears.
Romeo and Juliet. Act iv, sc. 1, l. 8. [Paris]

7
The simplicity of Venus' doves.
A Midsummer-Night's Dream. Act i, sc. 1, l. 171. [Hermia]

Ceres: Tell me . . . If Venus or her son . . .
Do not attend the queen? Since they did plot
The means that dusky Dis my daughter got,
Her and her blind boy's scandal'd company
I have forsworn.
Iris: Of her society
Be not afraid: I met her deity
Cutting the clouds toward Paphos and her son
Dove-drawn with her.
The Tempest. Act iv, sc. 1, l. 86. Dis (Pluto) is mentioned again in *The Winter's Tale,* iv, 4, 118; and Paphos in *Pericles,* iv, Gower, 32. The only use of "dove-drawn."

8
In characters as red as Mars his heart
Inflamed with Venus.
Troilus and Cressida. Act v, sc. 2, l. 164. [Troilus]

9
Sick-thoughted Venus makes amain unto him,
And like a bold-faced suitor 'gins to woo him.
Venus and Adonis, l. 5. The only use of "sick-thoughted." "Bold-faced" is repeated in *I Henry VI,* iv, 6, 12.

Venus, with young Adonis sitting by her,
Under a myrtle shade began to woo him.
The Passionate Pilgrim, l. 143.

VERITY, see Truth

VERSE

See also Numbers, Poetry, Rhyme

10
This is the very false gallop of verses: why do you infect yourself with them?
As You Like It. Act iii, sc. 2, l. 119. [Touchstone]

Celia: Didst thou hear these verses?
Rosalind: O, yes, I heard them all, and more too; for some of them had in them more feet than the verses would bear.
Celia: That 's no matter: the feet might bear the verses.
Rosalind: Ay, but the feet were lame and could not bear themselves without the verse and therefore stood lamely in the verse.
As You Like It. Act iii, sc. 2, l. 172.

I pray you, mar no moe of my verses with reading them ill-favouredly.
As You Like It. Act iii, sc. 2, l. 278. [Orlando]

11
Nay, then, God be wi' you, an you talk in blank verse.
As You Like It. Act iv, sc. 1, l. 31. [Jaques]

The even road of a blank verse.
Much Ado about Nothing. Act v, sc. 2, l. 34. [Benedick]

The blank verse shall halt for 't.
Hamlet. Act ii, sc. 2, l. 339. [Hamlet]

12
Marry, if you would put me to verses or to dance for your sake, Kate, why you undid me.
Henry V. Act v, sc. 2, l. 137. [King Henry] "Undid" is repeated in *Antony and Cleopatra,* ii, 2, 210.

13
Cinna: I am Cinna the poet, I am Cinna the poet.
Citizen: Tear him for his bad verses, tear him for his bad verses.
Julius Cæsar. Act iii, sc. 3, l. 32.

1
Holofernes: As Horace says in his— What, my soul, verses?
Nathaniel: Ay, sir, and very learned.
Holofernes: Let me hear a staff, a stanze, a verse; lege, domine.
Love's Labour's Lost. Act iv, sc. 2, l. 104. The only use of "stanze" and "lege" (aphetic form of allege used in 16th century).
Demetrius (reading): 'Integer vitæ, scelerisque purus,
Non eget Mauri jaculis, nec arcu.'
Chiron: O, 'tis a verse in Horace; I know it well:
I read it in the grammar long ago.
Titus Andronicus. Act iv, sc. 2, l. 20. An imperfect rendering of the beginning of the twenty-second ode of the first book of Horace. These are the only references to Horace. The only use of "grammar," except for "grammar school" in *II Henry VI,* iv, 7, 37.

2
I will prove those verses to be very unlearned, neither savouring of poetry, wit, nor invention.
Love's Labour's Lost. Act iv, sc. 2, l. 164. [Holofernes] The only use of "savouring."
Some thousand verses of a faithful lover.
Love's Labour's Lost. Act v, sc. 2, l. 50. [Katharine]
He writes verses.—*The Merry Wives of Windsor,* iii, 2, 69.

3
Who will believe my verse in time to come,
If it were fill'd with your most high deserts?
Though yet, heaven knows, it is but as a tomb
Which hides your life and shows not half your parts.
Sonnets. No. xvii.
Yet, do thy worst, old Time: despite thy wrong,
My love shall in my verse ever live young.
Sonnets. No. xix.
So it is not with me as with that Muse
Stirr'd by a painted beauty to his verse,
Who heaven itself for ornament doth use
And every fair with his fair doth rehearse.
Sonnets. No. xxi.
Why is my verse so barren of new pride,
So far from variation or quick change?
Sonnets. No. lxxvi.
Your monument shall be my gentle verse,
Which eyes not yet created shall o'er-read,
And tongues to be your being shall rehearse
When all the breathers of this world are dead;
You still shall live—such virtue hath my pen—
Where breath most breathes, even in the mouths of men.
Sonnets. No. lxxxi.
Was it the proud full sail of his great verse,
Bound for the prize of all too precious you,
That did my ripe thoughts in my brain inhearse,
Making their tomb the womb wherein they grew?
Sonnets. No. lxxxvi. The only use of "inhearse." "Inhearsed" occurs in *I Henry VI,* iv, 7, 45.
For to no other pass my verses tend
Than of your graces and your gifts to tell;
And more, much more, than in my verse can sit
Your own glass shows you when you look in it.
Sonnets. No. ciii.

4
Thy verse swells with stuff so fine and smooth
That thou art even natural in thine art.
Timon of Athens. Act v, sc. 1, l. 87. [Timon]
Happy verse.—*Timon of Athens,* i, 1, 16.

5
What verse for it?
Troilus and Cressida. Act v, sc. 10, l. 40. [Pandarus]

6
Thus your verse
Flow'd with her beauty once.
Winter's Tale. Act v, sc. 1, l. 101. [Paulina]

VESSEL

See also Bark, Ship

7
The scarfs and the bannerets about thee did manifoldly dissuade me from believing thee a vessel of too great a burthen.
All's Well that Ends Well. Act ii, sc. 3, l. 214. [Lafeu] The only use of "bannerets" and "manifoldly."

8
No vessel can peep forth, but 'tis as soon
Taken as seen.
Antony and Cleopatra. Act i, sc. 4, l. 53. [Messenger]
Strike the vessels, ho!—*Antony and Cleopatra,* ii, 7, 103.

9
The empty vessel makes the greatest sound.
Henry V, iv, 4, 73. Quoted as a saying. First used by John Lyly in *Euphues,* in 1579.
Hollow vessels.—*Pericles,* i, iv, 67.

10
Let 's to the seaside, ho!
. . . to see the vessel that 's come in.
Othello. Act ii, sc. 1, l. 36. [Montano]

11
Their vessel shakes On Neptune's billow.
Pericles, iii, Gower, 44.
Our vessel is of Tyre.—*Pericles,* v, 1, 23.

12
A brave vessel,
Who had, no doubt, some noble creature in her,
Dash'd all to pieces.
The Tempest. Act i, sc. 2, l. 6. [Miranda]
A bawbling vessel . . . for shallow draught and bulk unprizable.
Twelfth Night, v, 1, 57. See under FAME. The only use of "bawbling." "Unprizable" is repeated in *Cymbeline,* i, 4, 99.
Gentle vessel.—*Merchant of Venice,* i, 1, 32.
Goodly vessel.—*Pericles,* v, 1, 18.
Mortal vessel.—*Pericles,* iv, 4, 30.
Noble vessel.—*Julius Cæsar,* v, 5, 13.
Perished vessel.—*Measure for Measure,* iii, 1, 225.
United vessel.—*II Henry IV,* iv, 4, 44.
Wide vessel.—*Henry V,* iv, Prol., 3.
Vessels of my love.—*Timon of Athens,* ii, 2, 186.
Nature's fragile vessel.—*Timon of Athens,* v, 1, 204.

13
Most opportune to our need I have
A vessel rides fast by.
The Winter's Tale. Act iv, sc. 4, l. 510.

[Florizel] "Opportune" is repeated in *The Tempest,* iv, 1, 26: "Opportune place."
Weaker vessel, see under WOMAN.

VEXATION

See also Annoyance

1
Parolles: My lord, you do me most insupportable vexation.
Lafeu: I would it were hell-pains for thy sake, and my poor doing eternal.
All's Well that Ends Well. Act ii, sc. 3, l. 243. "Hell-pains" is repeated in *Othello,* i, 1, 155; and "insupportable" in *Julius Cæsar,* iv, 3, 151, and in *Othello,* v, 2, 98.
Deserved vexation.—*Coriolanus,* iii, 3, 140.
Fierce vexation.—*Midsummer-Night's Dream,* iv, 1, 74.
Repeated Vexations.—*Cymbeline,* i, 6, 5.

2
He 's shrewdly vexed at something.
All's Well that Ends Well. Act iii, sc. 5, l. 92. [Mariana]
Norfolk: He is vex'd at something.
Surrey: I would 'twere something that would fret the string,
The master-cord on 's heart!
Henry VIII. Act iii, sc. 2, l. 104. The only use of "master-cord."

3 I beseech you, sir,
Harm not yourself with your vexation.
Cymbeline. Act i, sc. 1, l. 133. [Imogen]
Vex not yourself.—*Richard II,* ii, 1, 3.

4
I am not vexed more at any thing in the earth: a pox on 't!
Cymbeline. Act ii, sc. 1, l. 19. [Cloten]

5
Vexation almost stops my breath.
I Henry VI. Act iv, sc. 3, l. 41. [York]

6
They vex me past my patience!
Henry VIII. Act ii, sc. 4, l. 130. [Queen]
Vex him with eager words.—*III Henry VI,* ii, 6, 68.
Vex us with shot.—*I Henry VI,* i, 4, 13.
Vex a very saint.—*The Taming of the Shrew,* iii, 2, 28.

7
Full of vexation come I, with complaint.
A Midsummer-Night's Dream. Act i, sc. 1, l. 22. [Egeus]

8
The deep vexation of his inward soul
Hath served a dumb arrest upon his tongue.
The Rape of Lucrece, l. 1779.

9
I am so vexed, that every part about me quivers.
Romeo and Juliet. Act ii, sc. 4, l. 170. [Nurse]
My fingers itch.
Romeo and Juliet. Act iii, sc. 5, l. 165. [Capulet]

10
Sir, I am vex'd; Bear with my weakness.
The Tempest. Act iv, sc. 1, l. 158. [Prospero]
All thy vexations
Were but my trials of thy love, and thou
Hast strangely stood the test.
The Tempest. Act iv, sc. 1, l. 5. [Prospero]

11
It would be much vexation to your age.
The Two Gentlemen of Verona. Act iii, sc. 1, l. 16. [Proteus]

12
'Twill vex thy soul to hear what I shall speak.
Titus Andronicus. Act v, sc. 1, l. 62. [Aaron]
I will not vex your souls.
Richard II. Act iii, sc. 1, l. 2. [Bolingbroke]
Vex my grieved soul.—*Richard II,* i, 1, 138.
Vex not his ghost.—*King Lear,* v, 3, 313.
Vex not his prescience.—*Antony and Cleopatra,* i, 2, 20.

13
How vexest thou this man!
Twelfth Night. Act iv, sc. 2, l. 28. [Clown]

VIANDS, see Food

VICE

14
It is not Cæsar's natural vice to hate
Our great competitor.
Antony and Cleopatra. Act i, sc. 4, l. 2. [Cæsar]
But when we in our viciousness grow hard—
O misery on 't!—the wise gods seel our eyes.
Antony and Cleopatra. Act iii, sc. 13, l. 111. [Antony] The only use of "viciousness." "Seel" is repeated in *Othello,* i, 3, 270; iii, 3, 210.

15
Vicious, ungentle, foolish, blunt, unkind.
The Comedy of Errors, iv, 2, 21. See under CHARACTER.
Vicious in my guess.—*Othello,* iii, 3, 145.
Vicious to have mistrusted.—*Cymbeline,* v, 5, 65.

16
What he cannot help in his nature, you account a vice in him.
Coriolanus. Act i, sc. 1, l. 42. [Citizen]

17 She hath lived too long,
To fill the world with vicious qualities.
I Henry VI. Act v, sc. 4, l. 34. [York]
Corrupt and tainted with a thousand vices.
I Henry VI. Act v, sc. 4, l. 45. [La Pucelle]

18
The gods are just, and of our pleasant vices
Make instruments to plague us.
King Lear. Act v, sc. 3, l. 170. [Edgar]
Through tatter'd clothes small vices do appear.
King Lear, iv, 6, 168. See under JUSTICE.

19
All sects, all ages smack of this vice; and he
To die for 't!
Measure for Measure. Act ii, sc. 2, l. 5. [Provost]
There is a vice that most I do abhor,
And most desire should meet the blow of justice.
Measure for Measure. Act ii, sc. 2, l. 29. [Isabella]
Wilt thou be made a man out of my vice?
Measure for Measure. Act iii, sc. 1, l. 138. [Isabella]
Do thou but think
What 'tis to cram a maw or clothe a back
From such a filthy vice.
Measure for Measure, iii, 2, 22. [Duke]

Fie, these filthy vices!
Measure for Measure. Act ii, sc. 4, l. 42. [Angelo]

Twice treble shame on Angelo,
To weed my vice and let his grow!
Measure for Measure. Act iii, sc. 2, l. 283. [Duke]

1
I do confess the vices of my blood.
Othello. Act i, sc. 3, l. 123. [Othello]

Vice of lying.—*II Henry IV,* iii, 2, 326.

Vice of mercy.—*Troilus and Cressida,* v, 3, 37.

2
Did you perceive how he laughed at his vice?
Othello. Act iv, sc. 1, l. 180. [Iago]

3
Canker vice the sweetest buds doth love.
Sonnets. No. lxx.

4
Your old vice still.
The Two Gentlemen of Verona. Act iii, sc. 1, l. 283. [Speed]

I 'll be with you again
In a trice,
Like to the old Vice,
Your need to sustain;
Who, with dagger of lath,
In his rage and his wrath,
Cries, ah, ha! to the devil.
Twelfth Night. Act iv, sc. 2, l. 132. [Clown]

5 I ne'er heard yet
That any of these bolder vices wanted
Less impudence to gainsay what they did
Than to perform it first.
Winter's Tale. Act iii, sc. 2, l. 55. [Leontes]

II—Vice and Virtue

6
Apparel vice like virtue's harbinger.
The Comedy of Errors. Act iii, sc. 2, l. 12. [Luciana]

7 In the fatness of these pursy times
Virtue itself of vice must pardon beg.
Hamlet. Act iii, sc. 4, l. 153. [Hamlet] The only use of "fatness." "Pursy" is repeated in *Timon of Athens,* v, 4, 12: "Pursy insolence."

8
You nickname virtue: vice you should have spoke;
For virtue's office never breaks men's troth.
Love's Labour 's Lost. Act v, sc. 2, l. 349. [Princess of France]

9
There is no vice so simple but assumes
Some mark of virtue on his outward parts.
The Merchant of Venice. Act iii, sc. 2, l. 81. [Bassanio]

10 Do but see his vice;
'Tis to his virtue a just equinox,
The one as long as the other.
Othello. Act ii, sc. 3, l. 128. [Iago] The only use of "equinox." *Twelfth Night,* ii, 3, 24, has "equinoctial."

11
So shall my virtue be his vice's bawd.
Richard II. Act v, sc. 3, l. 67. [York]

12
So smooth he daub'd his vice with show of virtue.
Richard III. Act iii, sc. 5, l. 29. [Gloucester] The only use of "daub'd."

13
Virtue itself turns vice, being misapplied;
And vice sometimes by action dignified.
Romeo and Juliet. Act ii, sc. 3, l. 21. [Friar Laurence] The only use of "misapplied."

Virtue that transgresses is but patched with sin; and sin that amends is but patched with virtue.
Twelfth Night. Act i, sc. 5, l. 53. [Clown]

14
Speed: 'Here follow her vices.'
Launce: Close at the heels of her virtues.
The Two Gentlemen of Verona. Act iii, sc. 1, l. 324.

15
Autolycus: I cannot tell, good sir, for which of his virtues it was, but he was certainly whipped out of the court.
Clown: His vices, you would say; there 's no virtue whipped out of the court: they cherish it to make it stay there; and yet it will no more but abide.
Autolycus: Vices, I would say, sir.
The Winter's Tale. Act iv, sc. 3, l. 93.

VICTORY

See also Triumph

16
Upon your sword Sit laurel victory!
Antony and Cleopatra. Act i, sc. 3, l. 99. [Cleopatra]

We have beat them to their beds.
Antony and Cleopatra. Act iv, sc. 8, l. 19. [Antony]

17
Brings a' victory in his pocket?
Coriolanus. Act ii, sc. 1, l. 135. [Menenius]

Holding Corioli in the name of Rome,
Even like a fawning greyhound in the leash,
To let him slip at will.
Coriolanus. Act i, sc. 6, l. 37. [Marcius]

18
You have won a happy victory.
Coriolanus. Act v, sc. 3, l. 186. [Coriolanus]

Happy victory!—*Richard III,* v, 3, 165.

Happy victories.—*I Henry IV,* v, 3, 97.

Bold-faced victory.—*I Henry VI,* iv, 6, 12. The only use of "bold-faced."

Glorious victory.—*King John,* ii, 1, 394.

19
Why so sadly Greet you our victory?
Cymbeline. Act v, sc. 5, l. 23. [Cymbeline]

Dishonourable victory.—*I Henry VI,* i, 1, 20.

Small victory.—*Romeo and Juliet,* iv, 1, 30.

20
All 's done, all 's won; here breathless lies the king.
I Henry IV. Act v, sc. 3, l. 16. [Douglas]

21
God on our side, doubt not of victory.
II Henry VI. Act iv, sc. 8, l. 54. [Clifford] See also under ENGLAND.

Why, so! then am I sure of victory.
III Henry VI. Act iv, sc. 1, l. 147. [King Edward]

1
So is the equal poise of this fell war.
Here on this molehill will I sit me down.
To whom God will, there be the victory!
III Henry VI. Act ii, sc. 5, l. 13. [King Henry] "Molehill" occurs also in i, 4, 67, and in *Coriolanus,* v, 3, 30.

2
We are those which chased you from the field
And slew your fathers, and with colours spread
March'd through the city to the palace gates.
III Henry VI. Act i, sc. 1, l. 90. [Warwick]

3
Either victory, or else a grave.
III Henry VI. Act ii, sc. 2, l. 174. [Edward]
The harder match'd, the greater victory.
III Henry VI. Act v, sc. 1, l. 70. [King Edward]

4
We are graced with wreaths of victory.
III Henry VI. Act v, sc. 3, l. 2. [King Edward]
Did I not meet thy friends? and did not they
Put on my brows this wreath of victory?
Julius Cæsar. Act v, sc. 3, l. 81. [Titinius]
You, my knight and guest;
To whom this wreath of victory I give.
Pericles. Act ii, sc. 3, l. 9. [Thaisa]
With . . . wreaths of victory.—*The Rape of Lucrece,* l. 110.

5 Victory, with little loss, doth play
Upon the dancing banners of the French.
King John. Act ii, sc. 1, l. 307. [Herald]
O, bravely came we off, . . .
And wound our tattering colours clearly up,
Last in the field, and almost lords of it!
King John. Act v, sc. 5, l. 4. [Dauphin] The only use of "tattering."

6
If you have victory, let the trumpet sound
For him that brought it.
King Lear. Act v, sc. 1, l. 41. [Edgar]
The victory fell on us.
Macbeth. Act i, sc. 2, l. 58. [Ross]

7
A victory is twice itself when the achiever brings home full numbers.
Much Ado about Nothing. Act i, sc. 1, l. 8. [Leonato] The only use of "achiever."

8
To reach at victory above my head.
Richard II. Act i, sc. 3, l. 72. [Bolingbroke]

9
Fortune and victory sit on thy helm!
Richard III. Act v, sc. 3, l. 79. [Derby]
Victory sits on our helms.
Richard III. Act v, sc. 3, l. 351. [King Richard]
I should mount with wings of victory.
Richard III. Act v, sc. 3, l. 106. [Richmond]

10
The day is ours.
Richard III. Act v, sc. 5, l. 2. [Richmond]
The day is yours.—*Pericles,* ii, 3, 13.
Bound with laurel boughs.
Titus Andronicus. Act i, sc. 1, l. 74. [Titus]
A laurel crown.—*III Henry VI,* iv, 6, 34.

II—The Victor

11
Although the victor, we submit to Cæsar.
Cymbeline. Act v, sc. 5, l. 460. [Cymbeline]

12 Come to me, friend or foe,
And tell me who is victor.
III Henry VI. Act v, sc. 2, l. 5. [Warwick]
Now we are victors.—*I Henry VI,* i, 2, 4.

13
I will predominate over the peasant.
The Merry Wives of Windsor. Act ii, sc. 2, l. 294. [Falstaff] "Predominate" is repeated in *Timon of Athens,* iv, 3, 142.

14
Thus art with arms contending was victor of the day,
Which by a gift of learning did bear the maid away:
Then, lullaby, the learned man hath got the lady gay;
For now my song is ended.
The Passionate Pilgrim, l. 223.

15
A captive victor that hath lost in gain.
The Rape of Lucrece, l. 730.
Thou dead, both die, and both shall victors be.
The Rape of Lucrece, l. 1211.

16
She shall be sole victress, Cæsar's Cæsar.
Richard III. Act iv, sc. 4, l. 336. [King Richard] The only use of "victress."

17 What shall be done
To him that victory commands? or do you purpose
A victor shall be known?
Troilus and Cressida. Act iv, sc. 5, l. 65. [Æneas]

VICTUALS, see Food

VIGOUR

18
Thy nerves are in their infancy again
And have no vigour in them.
The Tempest. Act i, sc. 2, l. 484. [Prospero]

19 For thy vigour,
Bull-bearing Milo his addition yield
To sinewy Ajax.
Troilus and Cressida. Act ii, sc. 3, l. 257. [Ulysses] The only use of "bull-bearing."
Double vigour.—*Measure for Measure,* ii, 2, 184.
Mortal vigour.—*Venus and Adonis,* l. 953.
Sinewy vigour.—*Love's Labour's Lost,* iv, 3, 308.
Vigour of bone.—*Troilus and Cressida,* iii, 3, 172.

VILENESS

See also Wickedness

20 Vileness is so:
The property by what it is should go,
Not by the title.
All's Well that Ends Well. Act ii, sc. 3, l. 136. [King] The only use of "vileness."

21
This argues that her kind of life hath been
Wicked and vile.
I Henry VI. Act v, sc. 4, l. 15. [York]

Base and vile.—*A Midsummer-Night's Dream,* i, 1, 232.
Cowardly and vile.—*Julius Cæsar,* v, 1, 104.
Vile and bad.—*The Comedy of Errors,* v, 1, 67.
Vile and false.—*Othello,* iii, 3, 136.

1 'Tis vile, . . .
And better in my mind not undertook.
The Merchant of Venice. Act ii, sc. 4, l. 6. [Salanio]

O how vile!—*Twelfth Night,* iii, 4, 399.
O vile!—*Love's Labour 's Lost,* iv, 3, 280.
O vile, intolerable!—*The Taming of the Shrew,* v, 2, 93.
Make me vile.—*Pericles,* iii, 3, 21.
More vile.—*I Henry VI,* v, 3, 112.
Most vile.—*Henry V,* iv, Prol., 50.

2 'Tis better to be vile than vile esteem'd.
Sonnets. No. cxxi. See under REPUTATION.

3 No, we detest such vile base practices.
The Two Gentlemen of Verona. Act iv, sc. 1, l. 73. [Outlaw]

VILLANY

4 He hath out-villained villany so far, that the rarity redeems him.
All's Well that Ends Well. Act iv, sc. 3, l. 305. [Lord] The only use of "out-villained."

5 What villany soe'er I bid thee do, to perform it directly and truly, I would think thee an honest man.
Cymbeline. Act iii, sc. 5, l. 112. [Cloten]

In me 'tis villany.—*Antony and Cleopatra,* ii, 7, 80.
Villany of our fears.—*Cymbeline,* v, 2, 13.

6 Being thus be-netted round with villanies.
Hamlet. Act v, sc. 2, l. 29. [Hamlet] The only use of "be-netted."

7 Their villany goes against my weak stomach, and therefore I must cast it up.
Henry V. Act iii, sc. 2, l. 56. [Boy]

The filthy and contagious clouds
Of heady murder, spoil and villany.
Henry V. Act iii, sc. 3, l. 31. [King Henry]

8 There 's villany abroad.
Love's Labour 's Lost. Act i, sc. 1, l. 189. [Dull]

Black villany.—*Pericles,* iv, 4, 44.
Bloody villany.—*King John,* iv, 2, 225.

9 The villany you teach me, I will execute, and it shall go hard but I will better the instruction.
The Merchant of Venice. Act iii, sc. 1, l. 75. [Shylock]

I will consent to act any villany against him, that may not sully the chariness of our honesty.
Merry Wives of Windsor. Act ii, sc. 1, l. 101. [Mrs. Ford] The only use of "chariness."

10 Whose spirits toil in frame of villanies.
Much Ado about Nothing. Act iv, sc. 1, l. 191. [Benedick]

My villany they have upon record; which I had rather seal with my death than repeat over to my shame.
Much Ado about Nothing. Act v, sc. 1, l. 246. [Borachio]

11 O mistress, villany hath made mocks with love!
Othello. Act v, sc. 2, l. 151. [Emilia]

Villany, villany, villany!
I think upon 't, I think: I smell 't: O villany!—
I thought so then:—I 'll kill myself for grief:—
O villany, villany!
Othello. Act v, sc. 2, l. 190. [Emilia]

12 Ay, there 's the villany.
The Taming of the Shrew. Act iv, sc. 3, l. 145. [Petruchio]

13 All is oblique;
There 's nothing level in our cursed natures,
But direct villany.
Timon of Athens. Act iv, sc. 3, l. 18. [Timon] "Oblique" is repeated in *Troilus and Cressida,* v, 1, 60.

Do villany, do, since you protest to do 't.
Timon of Athens. Act iv, sc. 3, l. 437. [Timon]

14 A very excellent piece of villany.
Titus Andronicus, ii, 3, 7. See under GOLD.

O, how this villany
Doth fat me with the very thoughts of it!
Titus Andronicus. Act iii, sc. 1, l. 203. [Aaron]

Shall I endure this monstrous villany?
Titus Andronicus. Act iv, sc. 4, l. 51. [Saturninus]

II—The Villain

15 I am alone the villain of the earth.
Antony and Cleopatra. Act iv, sc. 6, l. 30. [Enobarbus]

I am a villain: yet I lie, I am not.
Richard III. Act v, sc. 3, l. 191. [King Richard]

I am a villain.—*I Henry IV,* i, 2, 108; *Much Ado about Nothing,* ii, 3, 272.
I am a villain else.—*I Henry IV,* ii, 4, 229; iii, 2, 182.
I am a very villain.—*I Henry IV,* ii, 1, 34.
I am a very villain else.—*Othello,* iv, 1, 129.
Villain that I am!—*Othello,* v, 1, 29.

16 Slave, soulless villain, dog! O rarely base!
Antony and Cleopatra. Act v, sc. 2, l. 157. [Cleopatra] The only use of "soulless."

Base dunghill villain.—*II Henry VI,* i, 3, 196.
Villain base.—*Cymbeline,* iv, 2, 80.

17 Oliver: Wilt thou lay hands on me, villain?
Orlando: I am no villain; I am the youngest son of Sir Rowland de Boys; he was my father, and he is thrice a villain that says such a father begot villains
As You Like It. Act i, sc. 1, l. 58.

There is not one so young and so villanous this day living.
As You Like It. Act i, sc. 1, l. 161. [Oliver]

Some villains of my court
Are of consent and sufferance in this.
As You Like It. Act ii, sc. 2, l. 2. [Duke]

1
Thou art a villain to impeach me thus.
The Comedy of Errors. Act v, sc. 1, l. 29. [Antipholus of Syracuse]

Brabantio: Thou art a villain.
Iago: You are—a senator.
Othello. Act i, sc. 1, l. 119.

Thou art a villain.—*Romeo and Juliet,* iii, 1, 64; *Pericles,* ii, 5, 50.

You are a villain.—*Much Ado about Nothing,* v, 1, 146.

More villain thou.—*As You Like It,* iii, 1, 15.

2
One Pinch, a hungry lean-faced villain.
The Comedy of Errors. Act v, sc. 1, l. 238. [Antipholus of Ephesus] "Lean-faced" is repeated in *II Henry VI,* iii, 2, 315: "Lean-faced Envy."

All-worthy villain!—*Cymbeline,* iii, 5, 94. "All-worthy" is repeated in l. 93, and appears nowhere else.

Barbarous villains!—*II Henry VI,* iv, 4, 15.
Close villain.—*Cymbeline,* iii, 5, 85.
Damned villain.—*Othello,* v, 2, 316.
Detestable villain!—*Titus Andronicus,* v, 1, 94.
Dissembling villain.—*The Comedy of Errors,* iv, 4, 103.
Double villain.—*Cymbeline,* iv, 2, 88.
Dull, unmindful villain.—*Richard III,* iv, 4, 444. The only use of "unmindful."
False villain.—*The Winter's Tale,* ii, 1, 48.
Fat villain.—*II Henry IV,* ii, 2, 77.
Fine villain!—*Taming of the Shrew,* v, 1, 68.
Hellish villain.—*Othello,* v, 2, 368.
Honey-suckle villain.—*II Henry IV,* ii, 1, 56. The only use of "honey-suckle" as an adjective.
Horrible villain!—*Antony and Cleopatra,* ii, 5, 63.
Injurious villain.—*Richard II,* i, 1, 91.
Insolent villain!—*Coriolanus,* v, 6, 131.
Liberal villain.—*Much Ado about Nothing,* iv, 1, 93.
Monstrous villain!—*The Taming of the Shrew,* v, 1, 112.
Murderous villains!—*Titus Andronicus,* iv, 2, 88.
Notorious villain.—*The Taming of the Shrew,* v, 1, 54; *Othello,* v, 2, 239.
Paper-faced villain.—*II Henry IV,* v, 4, 12. The only use of the phrase.
Plain-dealing villain.—*Much Ado about Nothing,* i, 3, 34.
Precious villain!—*Othello,* v, 2, 235.
Senseless villain!—*The Taming of the Shrew,* i, 2, 36.
Shag-hair'd villain!—*Macbeth,* iv, 2, 83. "Shag-hair'd" is repeated in *II Henry VI,* iii, 1, 367.
Stony-hearted villains.—*I Henry IV,* ii, 2, 29. The only use of "stony-hearted."
Sweet villain!—*The Winter's Tale,* i, 2, 136.
Treacherous villain!—*King Lear,* iii, 7, 87; *Othello,* v, 1, 58; *Hamlet,* ii, 2, 609.
Trusty villain.—*The Comedy of Errors,* i, 2, 19.
Unbolted villain.—*King Lear,* ii, 2, 71. The only use of "unbolted" (unsifted, coarse).
Wicked villain.—*Measure for Measure,* i, 2, 27.
Wretched villain.—*Othello,* v, 1, 41.

3
Two villains, whose false oaths prevail'd
Before my perfect honour.
Cymbeline. Act iii, sc, 3, l. 66. [Belarius]

Thou then look'st like a villain; now methinks
Thy favour 's good enough.
Cymbeline. Act iii, sc. 4, l. 50. [Imogen]

Some villain, ay, and singular in his art,
Hath done you both this cursed injury.
Cymbeline. Act iii, sc. 4, l. 124. [Pisanio]

Ay me, most credulous fool,
Egregious murderer, thief, any thing
That 's due to all the villains past, in being,
To come!
Cymbeline. Act v, sc. 5, l. 210. [Posthumus]

I am Posthumus,
That kill'd thy daughter:—villain-like, I lie—
That caused a lesser villain than myself,
A sacrilegious thief, to do 't. . . .
Spit, and throw stones, cast mire upon me, set
The dogs o' the street to bay me: every villain
Be call'd Posthumus Leonatus; and
Be villany less than 'twas!
Cymbeline. Act v, sc. 5, l. 217. [Posthumus] "Sacrilegious" is repeated in *Macbeth,* ii, 3, 72: "Sacrilegious murder."

4
O villain, villain, smiling, damned villain!
My tables,—meet it is I set it down,
That one may smile, and smile, and be a villain.
Hamlet. Act i, sc. 5, l. 106. [Hamlet]

Hamlet: There 's ne'er a villain dwelling in all Denmark
But he 's an arrant knave.
Horatio: There needs no ghost, my lord, come from the grave
To tell us this.
Hamlet. Act i, sc. 5, l. 123.

Ere this
I should have fatted all the region kites
With this slave's offal: bloody, bawdy villain!
Remorseless, treacherous, lecherous, kindless villain!
Hamlet. Act ii, sc. 2, l. 605. [Hamlet] The only use of "kindless." "Offal" is repeated in *Julius Cæsar,* i, 3, 109, and in *The Merry Wives of Windsor,* iii, 5, 5.

5
Call me villain and baffle me.
I Henry IV. Act i, sc. 2, l. 113. [Falstaff] "Baffle" is used only once again, in *Twelfth Night,* ii, 5, 176.

This is the most omnipotent villain that ever cried
'Stand' to a true man.
I Henry IV. Act i, sc. 2, l. 121. [Falstaff] "Omnipotent" is repeated in *Richard II,* iii, 3, 85: "Omnipotent God"; and in *The Merry Wives of Windsor,* v, 5, 8: "Omnipotent Love!"

That villanous abominable misleader of youth.
I Henry IV. Act ii, sc. 4, l. 508. [Prince] "Misleader" is repeated in *II Henry IV,* v, 5, 68, and in *II Henry VI,* v, 1, 163.

6
The villains march wide betwixt the legs, as if they had gyves on; for indeed I had the most of them out of prison.
I Henry IV. Act iv, sc. 2, l. 44. [Falstaff]

Ah, you whoreson little valiant villain, you!
II Henry IV. Act ii, sc. 4, l. 225. [Doll]

Whoreson villain.—*The Taming of the Shrew,* iv, 1, 158.

Whoreson, senseless villain!—*The Comedy of Errors,* iv, 4, 25.

Whore-masterly villain.—*Troilus and Cressida,* v, 4, 8. The only use of "whore-masterly."

1

Cut both the villains' throats; for die you shall.

II Henry VI, iv, 1, 20. See under LIFE.

Here 's a villain!—*II Henry VI,* iv, 2, 96.

2

He 's a villain and a traitor.

II Henry VI, iv, 2, 115. See under EDUCATION.

A villain and a traitor.—*Henry V,* iv, 8, 26.

Villain! traitor! slave!—*Richard II,* v, 2, 72.

Villain slave.—*Richard III,* iv, 4, 144.

Villain! larron!—*Merry Wives of Windsor,* i, 4, 71. The only use of "larron" (robber).

They were villains!—*Julius Cæsar,* iii, 2, 159.

Villains by necessity.—*King Lear,* i, 2, 132.

3

Thou slave, thou wretch, thou coward!
Thou little valiant, great in villany!

King John. Act iii, sc. 1, l. 115. [Constance]

Avaunt, thou hateful villain, get thee gone!

King John. Act iv, sc. 3, l. 77. [Salisbury]

A resolved villain,
Whose bowels suddenly burst out.

King John. Act v, sc. 6, l. 29. [Hubert]

4

O villain, villain! . . . Abhorred villain! Unnatural, detested, brutish villain! worse than brutish!

King Lear. Act i, sc. 2, l. 80. [Gloucester]

Strong and fasten'd villain!

King Lear. Act ii, sc. 1, l. 79. [Gloucester]

5

Armado: Take away this villain; shut him up.

Moth: Come, you transgressing slave; away!

Love's Labour 's Lost. Act i, sc. 2, l. 158. "Transgressing" is repeated in *Richard II,* v, 3, 96: "Transgressing boy."

6

I would not be the villain that thou think'st
For the whole space that 's in the tyrant's grasp,
And the rich East to boot.

Macbeth. Act iv, sc. 3, l. 35. [Macduff]

Thou bloodier villain
Than terms can give thee out!

Macbeth. Act v, sc. 8, l. 7. [Macduff] The only use of "bloodier."

Bloody villains.—*Titus Andronicus,* iv, 2, 17.

7

Precise villains they are, that I am sure of.

Measure for Measure. Act ii, sc. 1, l. 54. [Elbow]

In foul mouth
And in the witness of his proper ear,
To call him villain?

Measure for Measure. Act v, sc. 1, l. 309. [Escalus]

8

When rich villains have need of poor ones, poor ones may make what price they will.

Much Ado about Nothing. Act iii, sc. 3, l. 120. [Borachio]

Is he not approved in the height a villain?

Much Ado about Nothing. Act iv, sc. 1, l. 303. [Beatrice]

Which is the villain? let me see his eyes,
That, when I note another man like him,
I may avoid him.

Much Ado about Nothing. Act v, sc. 1, l. 269. [Leonato]

9

What 's he then that says I play the villain?

Othello. Act ii, sc. 3, l. 342. [Iago]

Who calls me villain?—*Hamlet,* ii, 2, 599.

10

Where is that viper? bring the villain forth.

Othello. Act v, sc. 2, l. 284. [Lodovico]

Where 's the villain?—*King Lear,* ii, 1, 39; 43.

Find out this villain.—*King Lear,* i, 2, 124.

11

The homely villain court'sies to her low.

The Rape of Lucrece, l. 1338.

12

Now by mine honour, by my life, by my troth,
I will appeach the villain.

Richard II. Act v, sc. 2, l. 78. [York] "Appeach" is repeated in l. 102 and occurs in no other scene. "Appeach'd" is used in *All 's Well that Ends Well,* i, 3, 197.

Hence, villain! never more come in my sight.

Richard II. Act v, sc. 2, l. 86. [Duchess of York]

13

Therefore, since I cannot prove a lover,
To entertain these fair well-spoken days,
I am determined to prove a villain.

Richard III. Act i, sc. 1, l. 28. [Gloucester] "Well-spoken" is repeated in i, 3, 348, and in *The Two Gentlemen of Verona,* i, 2, 10.

O gentle villain, do not turn away!

Richard III. Act i, sc. 3, l. 163. [Queen Margaret]

A murderous villain, and so still thou art.

Richard III. Act i, sc. 3, l. 134. [Queen Margaret]

14

A villain that is hither come in spite,
To scorn at our solemnity this night.

Romeo and Juliet. Act i, sc. 5, l. 64. [Tybalt]

Villain am I none;
Therefore farewell; I see thou know'st me not.

Romeo and Juliet. Act iii, sc. 1, l. 67. [Romeo]

A braggart, a rogue, a villain, that fights by the book of arithmetic!

Romeo and Juliet. Act iii, sc. 1, l. 105. [Mercutio]

Villain and he be many miles asunder.

Romeo and Juliet. Act iii, sc. 5, l. 82. [Juliet]

15

'Tis a villain, sir, I do not love to look on.

The Tempest. Act i, sc. 2, l. 309. [Miranda]

16

Your lordship 's a goodly villain.

Timon of Athens. Act iii, sc. 3, l. 28. [Servant]

Must thou needs stand for a villain in thine own work?

Timon of Athens. Act v, sc. 1, l. 40. [Timon]

Remain assured That he 's a made-up villain.

Timon of Athens. Act v, sc. 1, l. 100. [Timon] The only use of "made-up."

Each man apart, all single and alone,
Yet an arch-villain keeps him company.
Timon of Athens. Act v, sc. 1, l. 110. [Timon] "Arch-villain" is repeated in *Measure for Measure,* v, 1, 57.

1
You are both decipher'd, that 's the news,
For villains mark'd with rape.
Titus Andronicus. Act iv, sc. 2, l. 8. [Young Lucius] "Decipher'd" is repeated in *I Henry VI,* iv, 1, 184.

Go, drag the villain hither by the hair.
Titus Andronicus. Act iv, sc. 4, l. 56. [Saturninus]

O barbarous, beastly villains, like thyself!
Titus Andronicus. Act v, sc. 1, l. 97. [Lucius]

2
It is the prettiest villain.
Troilus and Cressida. Act iii, sc. 2, l. 35. [Pandarus]

Here comes the little villain.—*Twelfth Night,* ii, 5, 16.

Die I a villain, then!—*Troilus and Cressida,* iv, 4, 85.

3
These are the villains
That all the travellers do fear so much.
The Two Gentlemen of Verona. Act iv, sc. 1, l. 5. [Speed]

4
That false villain
Whom I employ'd was pre-employ'd by him.
Winter's Tale. Act ii, sc. 1, l. 48. [Leontes] The only use of "pre-employ'd."

Should a villain say so,
The most replenish'd villain in the world,
He were as much more villain.
Winter's Tale. Act ii, sc. 1, l. 78. [Hermione]

Would I knew the villain,
I would land-damn him.
The Winter's Tale. Act ii, sc. 1, l. 142. [Antigonus] The only use of "land-damn," to make a hell on earth.

VINE

5
Thou art an elm, my husband, I a vine.
The Comedy of Errors, ii, 2, 176. See under Wife: Man and Wife.

6
Her vine, the merry cheerer of the heart,
Unpruned dies; her hedges, even-pleached.
Henry V. Act v, sc. 2, l. 42. [Burgundy] The only use of "cheerer" and "even-pleached."

The vines of France and milk of Burgundy.
King Lear. Act i, sc. 1, l. 86. [King Lear]

7
Like to a wither'd vine
That droops his sapless branches.
I Henry VI, ii, 5, 11. See under Arm.

8
Every man shall eat in safety,
Under his own vine, what he plants.
Henry VIII, v, 5, 34. See Prophecy, 1215:9.

9
For one sweet grape who will the vine destroy?
The Rape of Lucrece, l. 215.

10
Vines with clustering bunches growing.
The Tempest. Act iv, sc. 1, l. 112. [Ceres]

Fruitful vines.—*Richard III,* v, 2, 8.

Increasing vine!—*Cymbeline,* iv, 2, 60.

II—Vineyard

11
Let us quit all
And give our vineyards to a barbarous people.
Henry V. Act iii, sc. 5, l. 3. [Constable]

Our vineyards . . . grow to wildness.
Henry V, v, 2, 54. See under Learning.

Tilth, vineyard, none.—*The Tempest,* ii, 1, 152. "Tilth" is repeated in *Measure for Measure,* i, 4, 44: "Tilth and husbandry."

Thy pole-clipt vineyard.—*The Tempest,* iv, 1, 68. The only use of "pole-clipt" (hedged in with poles).

With a vineyard back'd.—*Measure for Measure,* iv, 1, 29.

VIOLENCE

12
The violence of action hath made you reek as a sacrifice.
Cymbeline, i, 2, 2. See Shirt, 1355:8.

13
Pass with your best violence.
Hamlet. Act v, sc. 2, l. 309. [Hamlet]

Show of violence.—*Hamlet,* i, 1, 144.

14
They will by violence tear him from your palace.
II Henry VI, iii, 2, 246. See under Torture.

15
Offer him no violence,
Unless he seek to thrust you out perforce.
III Henry VI. Act i, sc. 1, l. 33. [Warwick]

Tyrant's violence.—*III Henry VI,* iv, 4, 29.

16
Blown with restless violence round about.
Measure for Measure, iii, 1, 125. See under Death.

Downright violence.—*Othello,* i, 3, 250.

Tragic violence.—*Richard III,* ii, 2, 39.

Untimely violence.—*Richard III,* i, 3, 201.

17
Mark me with what violence she first loved the Moor.
Othello. Act ii, sc. 1, l. 224. [Iago]

18
If you knew my parentage,
You would not do me violence.
Pericles. Act v, sc. 1, l. 100. [Marina]

Did violence on herself.—*Romeo and Juliet,* v, 3, 264. See under Suicide.

VIOLET

19
A violet in the youth of primy nature,
Forward, not permanent, sweet, not lasting,
The perfume and suppliance of a minute.
Hamlet. Act i, sc. 3, l. 7. [Laertes] The only use of "primy," "permanent," and "suppliance."

I would give you some violets, but they withered.
Hamlet, iv, 5, 184. See under Flowers.

20
To throw a perfume on the violet.
King John, iv, 2, 12. See under Excess.

21
Who are the violets now
That strew the green lap of the new come spring?
Richard II. Act v, sc. 2, l. 46. [Duchess of York]

When I behold the violet past prime.
Sonnets. No. xii.

1
These blue-vein'd violets whereon we lean
Never can blab, nor know not what we
mean.

Venus and Adonis, l. 125. The only use of "blue-vein'd."

The forward violet.—*Sonnets,* xcix.

The nodding violet.—*A Midsummer-Night's Dream,* ii, 1, 250.

Purple violets.—*Pericles,* iv, 1, 16.

2
Violets dim,
But sweeter than the lids of Juno's eyes.

The Winter's Tale, iv, 4, 120. See under FLOWERS.

Violets blue.—*Love's Labour's Lost,* v, 2, 904.

VIRGINITY

See also Chastity, Maid, Maidenhead

3
Parolles: Are you meditating on virginity?
Helena: Ay. You have some stain of soldier in you: let me ask you a question. Man is enemy to virginity; how may we barricado it against him?
Parolles: Keep him out.
Helena: But he assails; and our virginity, though valiant, in the defence yet is weak: unfold to us some warlike resistance.
Parolles: There is none: man, sitting down before you, will undermine you and blow you up.
Helena: Bless our poor virginity from underminers and blowers up! Is there no military policy, how virgins might blow up men?
Parolles: Virginity being blown down, man will quicklier be blown up: marry, in blowing him down again, with the breach yourselves made, you lose your city. It is not politic in the commonwealth of nature to preserve virginity. Loss of virginity is rational increase and there was never virgin got till virginity was first lost. That you were made of is metal to make virgins. Virginity by being once lost may be ten times found; by being ever kept, it is ever lost. . . . Virginity murders itself; and should be buried in highways out of all sanctified limit, as a desperate offendress against nature. Virginity breeds mites, much like a cheese; consumes itself to the very paring, and so dies with feeding his own stomach. Besides, virginity is peevish, proud, idle, made of self-love, which is the most inhibited sin in the canon. Keep it not; you cannot choose but lose by 't: out with 't! within ten year it will make itself ten, which is a goodly increase; and the principal itself not much the worse: away with 't!
Helena: How might one do, sir, to lose it to her own liking?
Parolles: Let me see: marry, ill, to like him that ne'er it likes. 'Tis a commodity will lose the gloss with lying; the longer kept, the less worth: off with 't while 'tis vendible; answer the time of request. Virginity, like an old courtier, wears her cap out of fashion: richly suited, but unsuitable: just like the brooch and tooth-pick, which wear not now. Your date is better in your pie and your porridge than in your cheek: and your virginity, your old virginity, is like one of our French withered pears, it looks ill, it eats drily; marry, 'tis a withered pear.

All's Well that Ends Well. Act i, sc. 1, l. 121. "Barricado" occurs again in *The Winter's Tale,* i, 2, 204: "No barricado for a belly"—amusingly in accord with Parolles' dictum. The only use of "underminers," although "undermine" is repeated in *II Henry VI,* i, 2, 98, and in *Troilus and Cressida,* ii, 3, 9. Also the only use of "blowers up," "quicklier," "drily," and "offendress." "Mite" is repeated in *Pericles,* ii, Gower, 8; "inhibited" in *Othello,* i, 2, 79; "vendible" in *The Merchant of Venice,* i, 1, 112: "A maid not vendible"; and "toothpick" in *King John,* i, 1, 190. "Toothpicker" is used in *Much Ado about Nothing,* ii, 1, 274.

Ask him upon his oath, if he does think
He had not my virginity.

All's Well that Ends Well. Act v, sc. 3, l. 185. [Diana]

4
A poor unlearned virgin.

All's Well that Ends Well. Act i, sc. 3, l. 246. [Countess]

Poor virgin.—*As You Like It,* v, 4, 60.

The best-regarded virgins.—*Merchant of Venice,* ii, 1, 10. The only use of "best-regarded."

Damosella virgin.—*Love's Labour's Lost,* iv, 2, 132. The only use of "damosella."

Fresh-fair virgins.—*Henry V,* iii, 3, 14. The only use of "fresh-fair."

Kind virgin.—*Pericles,* v, 1, 141.

Spotless virgin.—*II Henry VI,* v, 1, 186.

Sweet virgin.—*I Henry VI,* iii, 3, 16.

5
A virgin from her tender infancy,
Chaste and immaculate in very thought;
Whose maiden blood, thus rigorously effused,
Will cry for vengeance at the gates of heaven.

I Henry VI. Act v, sc. 4, l. 50. [La Pucelle] The only use of "rigorously" and "effused."

And yet, forsooth, she is a virgin pure.

I Henry VI. Act v, sc. 4, l. 83. [York]

6
A virgin,
A most unspotted lily shall she pass
To the ground, and all the world shall mourn her.

Henry VIII. Act v, sc. 5, l. 61. [Cranmer]

7
This was no damsel neither, sir; she was a virgin.

Love's Labour's Lost. Act i, sc. 1, l. 294. [Costard]

I deny her virginity.—*Love's Labour's Lost,* i, 1, 298.

1
Hail, virgin, if you be, as those cheek-roses
Proclaim you are no less!
Measure for Measure. Act i, sc. 4, l. 16. [Lucio] The only use of "cheek-roses."

I would not—though 'tis my familiar sin
With maids to seem the lapwing and to jest,
Tongue far from heart—play with all virgins so.
Measure for Measure. Act i, sc. 4, l. 31. [Lucio]

2
If I would yield him my virginity,
Thou mightst be freed.
Measure for Measure. Act iii, sc. 1, l. 98. [Isabella]

Pretty virginity.—*The Merry Wives of Windsor,* i, 1, 46.

3
Theseus: Thrice-blessed they that master so their blood,
To undergo such maiden pilgrimage;
But earthlier happy is the rose distill'd,
Than that which withering on the virgin thorn
Grows, lives and dies in single blessedness.
Hermia: So will I grow, so live, so die, my lord,
Ere I will yield my virgin patent up.
A Midsummer-Night's Dream. Act i, sc. 1, l. 74. The only use of "thrice-blessed," and "earthlier."

The rich worth of your virginity.
A Midsummer-Night's Dream. Act ii, sc. 1, l. 219. [Demetrius]

4
Leonato: If you, in your own proof,
Have vanquish'd the resistance of her youth,
And made defeat of her virginity,—
Claudio: I know what you would say: if I have known her,
You will say she did embrace me as a husband,
And so extenuate the 'forehand sin.
Much Ado about Nothing. Act iv, sc. 1, l. 46.

5
Here comes that which grows to the stalk; never plucked yet, I can assure you.
Pericles. Act iv, sc. 6, l. 45. [Bawd]

Bawd: Use her at thy pleasure: crack the glass of her virginity, and make the rest malleable.
Boult: An if she were a thornier piece of ground than she is, she shall be ploughed.
Pericles. Act iv, sc. 6, l. 150. The only use of "malleable" and "thornier."

To take from you the jewel you hold so dear.
Pericles. Act iv, sc. 6, l. 164. [Boult]

6
Young budding virgin, fair and fresh and sweet,
Whither away, or where is thy abode?
Happy the parents of so fair a child;
Happier the man, whom favourable stars
Allot thee for his lovely bed-fellow!
The Taming of the Shrew. Act iv, sc. 5, l. 37. [Katharina]

7
To general filths
Convert o' the instant, green virginity.
Timon of Athens. Act iv, sc. 1, l. 6. [Timon]

8
Let not the virgin's cheek
Make soft thy trenchant sword; for those milk-paps,
That through the window-bars bore at men's eyes,
Are not within the leaf of pity writ.
Timon of Athens. Act iv, sc. 3, l. 114. [Timon] The only use of "trenchant," "milk-paps," and "window-bars."

Giving our holy virgins to the stain
Of contumelious, beastly, mad-brain'd war.
Timon of Athens. Act v, sc. 1, l. 176. [Timon] "Mad-brain'd" is repeated in *I Henry VI,* i, 2, 15.

9
Lady, you are the cruell'st she alive,
If you will lead these graces to the grave
And leave the world no copy.
Twelfth Night. Act i, sc. 5, l. 259. [Viola] The only use of "cruell'st."

VIRTUE

See also Goodness; Vice and Virtue

10
Thy blood and virtue
Contend for empire in thee, and thy goodness
Share with thy birthright!
All's Well that Ends Well. Act i, sc. 1, l. 71. [Countess]

11
Whose virtue and whose general graces speak
That which none else can utter.
Antony and Cleopatra. Act ii, sc. 2, l. 132. [Agrippa]

O infinite virtue, comest thou smiling from
The world's great snare uncaught?
Antony and Cleopatra. Act iv, sc. 8, l. 17. [Cleopatra] "Uncaught" occurs only once more, in *King Lear,* ii, 1, 59.

12
The people praise her for her virtues.
As You Like It. Act i, sc. 2, l. 292. [Le Beau]

And thou wilt show more bright and seem more virtuous
When she is gone.
As You Like It. Act i, sc. 3, l. 83. [Duke]

Why are you virtuous?
As You Like It. Act ii, sc. 3, l. 5. [Adam]

Your virtues, gentle master,
Are sanctified and holy traitors to you.
As You Like It. Act ii, sc. 3, l. 12. [Adam]

Every eye which in this forest looks
Shall see thy virtue witness'd every where.
As You Like It. Act iii, sc. 2, l. 7. [Orlando]

Virtue is no horn-maker.
As You Like It. Act iv, sc. 1, l. 63. [Orlando] The only use of "horn-maker."

13
Our virtues
Lie in the interpretation of the time.
Coriolanus. Act iv, sc. 7, l. 49. [Aufidius]

14
She holds her virtue still and I my mind.
Cymbeline. Act i, sc. 4, l. 69. [Posthumus]

He was as calm as virtue.
Cymbeline. Act v, sc. 5, l. 174. [Iachimo]

The temple Of virtue was she.
Cymbeline. Act v, sc. 5, l. 220. [Posthumus]

1
Virtue itself 'scapes not calumnious strokes.
Hamlet. Act i, sc. 3, l. 38. [Laertes]

I hope your virtues
Will bring him to his wonted way again.
Hamlet. Act iii, sc. 1, l. 40. [Queen]

Virtue cannot so inoculate our old stock but we shall relish of it.
Hamlet. Act iii, sc. 1, l. 119. [Hamlet] The only use of "inoculate."

2
Assume a virtue, if you have it not.
Hamlet. Act iii, sc. 4, l. 160. [Hamlet]

3
Is there no virtue extant?
I Henry IV. Act ii, sc. 4, l. 132. [Falstaff]

If that man should be lewdly given, he deceiveth me; for, Harry, I see virtue in his looks.
I Henry IV. Act ii, sc. 4, l. 469. [Falstaff]

I was as virtuously given as a gentleman need to be; virtuous enough; swore little; diced not above seven times a week; went to a bawdy-house not above once in a quarter—of an hour; paid money that I borrowed, three or four times; lived well and in good compass: and now I live out of all order, out of all compass.
I Henry IV. Act iii, sc. 3, l. 16. [Falstaff]

If a man will make courtesy and say nothing, he is virtuous.
II Henry IV. Act ii, sc. 1, l. 135. [Falstaff]

4
Virtue he had, deserving to command.
I Henry VI. Act i, sc. 1, l. 9. [Gloucester]

Bethink thee on her virtues that surmount.
I Henry VI. Act v, sc. 3, l. 191. [Suffolk] "Surmount" is repeated in *Richard II,* ii, 3, 64. "Surmounted" occurs in *Love's Labour 's Lost,* v, 2, 677.

5
Virtuous, mild and too well given
To dream on evil or to work my downfall.
II Henry VI. Act iii, sc. 1, l. 72. [King Henry]

6
O miserable age! virtue is not regarded in handicrafts-men.
II Henry VI. Act iv, sc. 2, l. 11. [Bevis] The only use of "handicrafts-men."

Virtue is of so little regard in these coster-monger times that true valour is turned bear-herd.
II Henry IV. Act i, sc. 2, l. 190. [Falstaff] The only use of "costermonger." "Bear-herd" is repeated in *The Taming of the Shrew,* Ind., 2, 21.

7
'Tis but the fate of place, and the rough brake
That virtue must go through.
Henry VIII. Act i, sc. 2, l. 75. [Wolsey]

High note 's Ta'en of your many virtues.
Henry VIII. Act ii, sc. 3, l. 59. [Lord Chamberlain]

Christendom shall ever speak his virtue.
Henry VIII. Act iv, sc. 2, l. 63. [Griffith]

8
Virtue finds no friends.
Henry VIII. Act iii, sc. 1, l. 126. [Queen Katharine]

9
I know her virtuous And well deserving.
Henry VIII. Act iii, sc. 2, l. 97. [Wolsey]

10 Virtue and true beauty of the soul,
For honesty and decent carriage.
Henry VIII. Act iv, sc. 2, l. 144. [Katharine] The only use of "decent."

Saba was never
More covetous of wisdom and fair virtue
Than this pure soul shall be; all princely graces, . . .
With all the virtues that attend the good,
Shall still be doubled on her.
Henry VIII. Act v, sc. 5, l. 24. [Cranmer] The only mention of Saba.

11 Do not stain
The even virtue of our enterprise.
Julius Cæsar, ii, 1, 132. See under OATH.

My heart laments that virtue cannot live
Out of the teeth of emulation.
Julius Cæsar. Act ii, sc. 3, l. 13. [Artemidorus]

12
Fairest Cordelia, that art most rich, being poor;
Most choice, forsaken; and most loved, despised!
Thee and thy virtues here I seize upon.
King Lear. Act i, sc. 1, l. 253. [King of France]

I hope, for my brother's justification, he wrote this but as an essay or taste of my virtue.
King Lear. Act i, sc. 2, l. 46. [Edmund] The only use of "justification." "Essay" is repeated in *Sonnets,* cx.

Trust to thy single virtue.
King Lear. Act v, sc. 3, l. 103. [Albany]

Ample virtue.—*II Henry IV,* iv, 1, 163.
Best virtue.—*All 's Well that Ends Well,* iv, 3, 285; *As You Like It,* iii, 2, 302.
Chiefest virtue.—*Coriolanus,* ii, 2, 88.
Dear virtue.—*Sonnets,* cxlii.
Fair virtue.—*Love's Labour 's Lost,* ii, 1, 47; *A Midsummer-Night's Dream,* iii, 1, 143; *Troilus and Cressida,* iv, 4, 89; *Henry VIII,* v, 5, 25.
Hidden virtue.—*Henry V,* iii, 7, 118.
Knightly virtue.—*Richard III,* iv, 4, 370.
Maiden virtue.—*King John,* ii, 1, 98; *Sonnets,* lxvi.
Poor virtue.—*II Henry IV,* ii, 4, 51.
Right virtue.—*As You Like It,* iii, 2, 127.
Solid virtue.—*Othello,* iv, 1, 277.
Sweet virtue.—*The Two Gentlemen of Verona,* iii, 1, 277; *Sonnets,* xciii.
Untainted virtue.—*Richard III,* iii, 1, 7.
Whitest virtue.—*Measure for Measure,* iii, 2, 198. "Whitest" is repeated in *Henry VIII,* i, 1, 209.
Full of virtue.—*The Two Gentlemen of Verona,* iii, 1, 65.
Virtue of compassion.—*The Tempest,* i, 2, 27.
Virtue of my heart.—*A Midsummer-Night's Dream,* iv, 1, 174.

13 A well-accomplish'd youth,
Of all that virtue love for virtue loved.
Love's Labour 's Lost. Act ii, sc. 1, l. 56. [Katharine] "Well-accomplish'd" is repeated in *The Two Gentlemen of Verona,* iv, 3, 13.

1
[He] hath borne his faculties so meek, hath been
So clear in his great office, that his virtues
Will plead like angels, trumpet-tongued against
The deep damnation of his taking-off.
Macbeth. Act i, sc. 7, l. 17. [Macbeth] The only use of "trumpet-tongued." "Taking-off" is repeated in *King Lear,* v, 1, 65: "Speedy taking-off."

2 If our virtues
Did not go forth of us, 'twere all alike
As if we had them not.
Measure for Measure. Act i, sc. 1, l. 34. [Duke]

I know your virtue hath a license in 't,
Which seems a little fouler than it is,
To pluck on others.
Measure for Measure. Act ii, sc. 4, l. 145. [Isabella]

I have confess'd her and I know her virtue.
Measure for Measure. Act v, sc. 1, l. 533. [Duke]

Most strait in virtue.—*Measure for Measure,* ii, 1, 9.

3
Virtue is bold, and goodness never fearful.
Measure for Measure. Act iii, sc. 1, l. 215. [Duke]

4
We would have thrust virtue out of our hearts by the head and shoulders and have given ourselves without scruple to hell.
The Merry Wives of Windsor. Act v, sc. 5, l. 155. [Mrs. Page]

5
Can virtue hide itself?
Much Ado about Nothing. Act ii, sc. 1, l. 127. [Ursula]

Hero itself can blot out Hero's virtue.
Much Ado about Nothing. Act iv, sc. 1, l. 83. [Claudio]

Thus did she, an hour together, trans-shape thy particular virtues.
Much Ado about Nothing. Act v, sc. 1, l. 171. [Don Pedro] The only use of "trans-shape."

6
If virtue no delighted beauty lack,
Your son-in-law is far more fair than black.
Othello. Act i, sc. 3, l. 290. [Duke]

Roderigo: I confess it is my shame to be so fond; but it is not in my virtue to amend it.
Iago: Virtue! a fig! 'tis in ourselves that we are thus or thus.
Othello. Act i, sc. 3, l. 319.

Where virtue is, these are more virtuous.
Othello. Act iii, sc. 3, l. 186. [Othello]

7
I 'll show the virtue I have borne in arms.
Pericles. Act ii, sc. 1, l. 151. [Pericles]

I hold it ever,
Virtue and cunning were endowments greater
Than nobleness and riches: careless heirs
May the two latter darken and expend;
But immortality attends the former,
Making man a god.
Pericles. Act iii, sc. 2, l. 26. [Cerimon] "Immortality" is used only once again, in *The Rape of Lucrece,* l. 725.

I 'll do any thing now that is virtuous; but I am out of the road of rutting for ever.
Pericles. Act iv, sc. 5, l. 8. [Gentleman] The only use of "rutting."

Thou art a piece of virtue.
Pericles. Act iv, sc. 6, l. 118. [Lysimachus]

Although assail'd with fortune fierce and keen,
Virtue preserved from fell destruction's blast,
Led on by heaven, and crown'd with joy at last.
Pericles, v, 3, Gower, 88.

8
Virtue claims from beauty beauty's red,
Which virtue gave the golden age to gild
Their silver cheeks.
The Rape of Lucrece, l. 59.

What virtue breeds iniquity devours.
The Rape of Lucrece, l. 872.

9
Your discipline in war, wisdom in peace,
Your bounty, virtue, fair humility.
Richard III. Act iii, sc. 7, l. 16. [Buckingham]

10
He lends thee virtue and he stole that word
From thy behaviour.
Sonnets. No. lxxix.

Prove thee virtuous, though thou art forsworn.
Sonnets. No. lxxxviii.

11 For the time I study,
Virtue and that part of philosophy
Will I apply that treats of happiness
By virtue specially to be achieved.
The Taming of the Shrew. Act i, sc. 1, l. 17. [Lucentio] See under PHILOSOPHY.

12 In grateful virtue I am bound
To your free heart.
Timon of Athens. Act i, sc. 2, l. 5. [Ventidius]

13 Outlive thy father's days,
And fame's eternal date, for virtue's praise!
Titus Andronicus. Act i, sc. 1, l. 167. [Titus]

Whose virtues will, I hope,
Reflect on Rome as Titan's rays on earth,
And ripen justice in this commonweal.
Titus Andronicus. Act i, sc. 1, l. 225. [Titus]

14
He lives in fame that died in virtue's cause.
Titus Andronicus. Act i, sc. 1, l. 390. [All]

15 All his virtues, . . .
Do in our eyes begin to lose their gloss.
Troilus and Cressida. Act ii, sc. 3, l. 126. [Agamemnon]

O, let not virtue seek
Remuneration for the thing it was.
Troilus and Cressida. Act iii, sc. 3, l. 169. [Ulysses]

16 I cannot sing,
Nor heel the high lavolt, nor sweeten talk,
Nor play at subtle games; fair virtues all.
Troilus and Cressida. Act iv, sc. 4, l. 87. [Troilus]

And teach lavoltas high.—*Henry V,* iii, 5, 33.
The lavolta was a lively dance for two persons.

17
Virtue is beauty, but the beauteous evil
Are empty trunks o'erflourish'd by the devil.
Twelfth Night. Act iii, sc. 4, l. 403. [Antonio] The only use of "o'erflourish'd."

My mouse of virtue.—*Twelfth Night,* i, 5, 69.

1 To make a virtue of necessity.
The Two Gentlemen of Verona. Act iv, sc. 1, l. 62. [Outlaw]

There is no virtue like necessity.—*Richard II,* i, 3, 278.

VISAGE

See also Countenance, Face

2 The poor and untempering effect of my visage.
Henry V. Act v, sc. 2, l. 240. [King Henry] The only use of "untempering."

3 O, let me view his visage, being dead,
That living wrought me such exceeding trouble.
II Henry VI. Act v, sc. 1, l. 69. [King Henry]

To behold his visage Even to my full of view.
Troilus and Cressida. Act iii, sc. 3, l. 240. [Achilles]

4 There 's more in 't than fair visage.
Henry VIII. Act iii, sc. 2, l. 88. [Wolsey]

Lovely visage.—*Henry V,* v, 2, 37.

Silver visage.—*A Midsummer-Night's Dream,* i, 1, 210.

Visages of duty.—*Othello,* i, 1, 50.

Dian's visage.—*Othello,* iii, 3, 387.

5 A plague upon your epileptic visage!
King Lear. Act ii, sc. 2, l. 87. [Kent] The only use of "epileptic."

Monstrous visage.—*Julius Cæsar,* ii, 1, 81.

Tristful visage.—*Hamlet,* iii, 4, 50.

Wolvish visage.—*King Lear,* i, 4, 330. "Wolvish" is repeated in *The Merchant of Venice,* iv, 1, 138.

Visage of offence.—*Hamlet,* iii, 3, 47.

6 On his visage was in little drawn
What largeness thinks in Paradise was sawn.
A Lover's Complaint, l. 90. The only use of "sawn."

7 There are a sort of men whose visages
Do cream and mantle like a standing pond.
Merchant of Venice. Act i, sc. 1, l. 88. [Gratiano] The only use of "cream" as a verb.

8 Put on a more importunate aspect,
A visage of demand.
Timon of Athens. Act i, sc. 2, l. 28. [Senator]

VISION

9 Last night the very gods show'd me a vision.
Cymbeline. Act iv, sc. 2, l. 346. [Soothsayer]

The vision . . . Is full accomplish'd.
Cymbeline. Act v, sc. 5, l. 467. [Soothsayer]

10 Lo, whilst I waited on my tender lambs,
And to sun's parching heat display'd my cheeks,
God's mother deigned to appear to me
And in a vision full of majesty
Will'd me to leave my base vocation
And free my country from calamity.
I Henry VI. Act i, sc. 2, l. 76. [La Pucelle] "Vocation" is repeated in *II Henry VI,* iv, 2, 18: "Labour in thy vocation"; and in *I Henry IV,* i, 2, 116: "Labour in his vocation."

11 Saw you not, even now, a blessed troop
Invite me to a banquet; whose bright faces
Cast thousand beams upon me, like the sun?
They promised me eternal happiness.
Henry VIII. Act iv, sc. 2, l. 87. [Katharine]

A vision fair and fortunate.
Julius Cæsar, ii, 2, 84. See under DREAM.

12 What visions have I seen!
A Midsummer-Night's Dream. Act iv, sc. 1, l. 81. [Titania]

I have had a most rare vision.
A Midsummer-Night's Dream. Act iv, sc. 1, l. 210. [Bottom]

Fatal vision.—*Macbeth,* ii, 1, 36. See under DAGGER.

Fruitless vision.—*Midsummer-Night's Dream,* iii, 2, 371.

13 Pure Dian, bless thee for thy vision! I
Will offer night-oblations to thee.
Pericles. Act v, sc. 3, l. 70. [Pericles] The only use of "night-oblations."

14 These things seem small and undistinguishable,
Like far-off mountains turned into clouds.
A Midsummer-Night's Dream. Act iv, sc. 1, l. 191. [Demetrius] "Undistinguishable" is repeated in ii, 1, 100, and occurs in no other play.

15 This is a most majestic vision.
Tempest. Act iv, sc. 1, l. 118. [Ferdinand]

Our revels now are ended. These our actors,
As I foretold you, were all spirits and
Are melted into air, into thin air:
And, like the baseless fabric of this vision,
The cloud-capp'd towers, the gorgeous palaces,
The solemn temples, the great globe itself,
Yea, all which it inherit, shall dissolve
And, like this insubstantial pageant faded,
Leave not a rack behind.
The Tempest. Act iv, sc. 1, l. 148. [Prospero] The only use of "baseless," "cloud-capp'd," and "insubstantial."

A vision of the island.—*Tempest,* v, 1, 176.

VISITATION

16 Your visitation shall receive such thanks
As fits a king's remembrance.
Hamlet. Act ii, sc. 2, l. 25. [Queen]

This visitation
Is but to whet thy almost blunted purpose.
Hamlet. Act iii, sc. 4, l. 110. [Ghost]

Is it a free visitation?—*Hamlet,* ii, 2, 284.

Here make visitation.—*Henry VIII,* i, 1, 179.

1
I am made to understand that you have lent him visitation.
Measure for Measure. Act iii, sc. 2, l. 255. [Escalus]

2 Thou art infected!
This visitation shows it.
Tempest. Act iii, sc. 1, l. 30. [Prospero]

3
I take all and your several visitations
So kind to heart.
Timon of Athens. Act i, sc. 2, l. 224. [Timon]

4
I will corrupt the Grecian sentinels
To give you nightly visitation.
Troilus and Cressida. Act iv, sc. 4, l. 74. [Troilus]

Gentle visitation.—*Love's Labour 's Lost,* v, 2, 181.
Loving visitation.—*The Merchant of Venice,* iv, 1, 153.
Visitation of my friends.—*Richard III,* iii, 7, 107.
Visitation of the winds.—*II Henry IV,* iii, 1, 21.

5
Sicilia means to pay Bohemia the visitation which he justly owes him.
The Winter's Tale. Act i, sc. 1, l. 7. [Camillo] It is worth noting that, although "visit" occurs fifty-nine times in the plays and poems, it is always as a verb. The phrase "pay a visit" nowhere occurs.

'Tis not a visitation framed, but forced
By need and accident.
The Winter's Tale, v, 1, 91. See under ACCIDENT.

VISOR

See also Mask

6
Case ye, case ye; on with your vizards.
I Henry IV. Act ii, sc. 2, l. 55. [Bardolph]

I have vizards for you all.—*I Henry IV,* i, 2, 142.
Our vizards we will change.—*I Henry IV,* i, 2, 199.

7
Katharine: What, was your vizard made without a tongue?
Longaville: I know the reason, lady, why you ask.
Katharine: O for your reason! quickly, sir; I long.
Longaville: You have a double tongue within your mask,
And would afford my speechless vizard half.
Love's Labour 's Lost. Act v, sc. 2, l. 242.

Rosaline: Which of the vizards was it that you wore?
Biron: Where? when? what vizard? why demand you this?
Rosaline: There, then, that vizard; that superfluous case
That hid the worse and show'd the better face.
Love's Labour 's Lost. Act v, sc. 2, l. 385.

Never come in vizard to my friend.
Love's Labour 's Lost. Act v, sc. 2, l. 404. [Biron]

I 'll go buy them vizards.—*The Merry Wives of Windsor,* iv, 4, 70.
Mask'd and vizarded.—*The Merry Wives of Windsor,* iv, 6, 40.
Being vizarded.—*Troilus and Cressida,* i, 3, 83. The only uses of "vizarded."

8
Don Pedro: My visor is Philemon's roof; within the house is Jove.
Hero: Why, then, your visor should be thatched.
Much Ado about Nothing. Act ii, sc. 1, l. 99. Philemon is mentioned again in *Pericles,* iii, 2, 1.

My very visor began to assume life and scold with her.
Much Ado about Nothing. Act ii, sc. 1, l. 248. [Benedick]

But one visor remains.—*Much Ado about Nothing,* ii, 1, 164.

9
With a virtuous vizard hide foul guile!
Richard III, ii, 2, 28. See under DECEIT.

10
Give me a case to put my visage in:
A visor for a visor!
Romeo and Juliet. Act i, sc. 4, l. 29. [Mercutio]

I have seen the day That I have worn a visor.
Romeo and Juliet, i, 5, 23. See under TALE.

VOICE

See also Speech

11 His voice was propertied
As all the tuned spheres.
Antony and Cleopatra, v, 2, 83. See MAN, 948:4. "Propertied" is repeated in *King John,* v, 2, 79, and in *Twelfth Night,* iv, 2, 99; and "tuned" in *Taming of the Shrew,* iii, 1, 23.

12
My voice is ragged: I know I cannot please you.
As You Like It. Act ii, sc. 5, l. 15. [Amiens]

God mend your voices!
As You Like It. Act v, sc. 3, l. 42. [Touchstone]

13 His big manly voice,
Turning again towards childish treble.
As You Like It, ii, 7, 161. See MAN, 940:12.

Though now our voices
Have got the mannish crack, sing him to the ground.
Cymbeline. Act iv, sc. 2, l. 235. [Arviragus] "Mannish" is repeated in *As You Like It,* i, 3, 123, and in *Troilus and Cressida,* iii, 3, 217.

And speak between the change of boy and man
With a reed voice.
The Merchant of Venice. Act iii, sc. 4, l. 66. [Portia] The only use of "reed" as an adjective.

14 My throat of war be turn'd,
Which quired with my drum, into a pipe
Small as an eunuch, or the virgin voice
That babies lulls asleep!
Coriolanus. Act iii, sc. 2, l. 112. [Coriolanus] The only use of "quired."

Voice of unpaved eunuch.—*Cymbeline,* ii, 3, 34. The only use of "unpaved" (without stones).
I shall lack voice.—*Coriolanus,* ii, 2, 86.

1
Pray God, your voice, like a piece of uncurrent gold, be not cracked within the ring.
Hamlet. Act ii, sc. 2, l. 447. [Hamlet] "Uncurrent" is repeated in *Twelfth Night,* iii, 3, 16, and in *The Winter's Tale,* iii, 2, 50.
Crack my clear voice with sobs.
Troilus and Cressida, iv, 2, 114. See under DESPAIR.

2
Is not your voice broken?
II Henry IV, i, 2, 206. See under AGE AND YOUTH.
Broken voice.—*Hamlet,* ii, 2, 582.
Brass voice.—*Troilus and Cressida,* i, 3, 257.
Double voice.—*A Lover's Complaint,* l. 3.
Gracious voice.—*The Merchant of Venice,* iii, 2, 76.
Hardest voice.—*The Merry Wives of Windsor,* i, 3, 51.
Main voice.—*Hamlet,* i, 3, 28.
Poison'd voice.—*I Henry VI,* v, 4, 121.
Safer voice.—*Othello,* i, 3, 226.

3
For my voice, I have lost it with halloing and singing of anthems.
II Henry IV. Act i, sc. 2, l. 212. [Falstaff] "Halloing" is repeated in *The Two Gentlemen of Verona,* v, 4, 13; and "anthem" in *The Two Gentlemen of Verona,* iii, 1, 240.
My voice shall sound as you do prompt mine ear.
II Henry IV. Act v, sc. 2, l. 119. [King Henry]

4
I did never know so full a voice issue from so empty a heart: but the saying is true, 'The empty vessel makes the greatest sound.'
Henry V. Act iv, sc. 4, l. 71. [Boy]
Haply a woman's voice may do some good,
When articles too nicely urged be stood on.
Henry V. Act v, sc. 2, l. 93. [Queen Isabel]
Thy voice is music.
Henry V. Act v, sc. 2, l. 263. [King Henry]
Women's voices.—*Richard II,* iii, 2, 113.

5
Well didst thou, Richard, to suppress thy voice.
I Henry VI. Act iv, sc. 1, l. 182. [Exeter]

6
Lords, with one cheerful voice welcome my love.
II Henry VI. Act i, sc. 1, l. 36. [King]

7
Dicky your boy, that with his grumbling voice,
Was wont to cheer his dad in mutinies.
III Henry VI. Act i, sc. 4, l. 76. [Queen Margaret] The only use of "Dicky."

8
What warlike voice . . . is this?
Henry VIII. Act i, sc. 4, l. 50. [Wolsey]

9
Methinks thy voice is alter'd.
King Lear. Act iv, sc. 6, l. 7. [Gloucester]
Changed voices.—*Romeo and Juliet,* iii, 5, 32.

10 Her voice was ever soft,
Gentle, and low, an excellent thing in woman.
King Lear. Act v, sc. 3, l. 272. [King Lear]
Cleopatra: Didst hear her speak? is she shrill-tongued or low?
Messenger: Madam, I heard her speak; she is low-voiced.
Antony and Cleopatra. Act iii, sc. 3, l. 15. The only use of "low-voiced." "Shrill-tongued" is repeated in i, 1, 32, and in no other play.

11
My voice is in my sword.
Macbeth, v, 8, 7. See WORD AND DEED.

12
I 'll speak in a monstrous little voice.
A Midsummer-Night's Dream. Act i, sc. 2, l. 55. [Bottom]
I will aggravate my voice.
A Midsummer-Night's Dream. Act i, sc. 2, l. 83. [Bottom]
He is a very paramour for a sweet voice.
A Midsummer-Night's Dream. Act iv, sc. 2, l. 11. [Quince]
Most sweet voices!—*Coriolanus,* ii, 3, 119.
Silver-voiced.—*Pericles,* v, 1, iii. The only use of the phrase.

13 Tax not so bad a voice
To slander music any more than once.
Much Ado about Nothing. Act ii, sc. 3, l. 46. [Balthazar]
I pray God his bad voice bode no mischief.
Much Ado about Nothing. Act ii, sc. 3, l. 83. [Benedick]
Harsh in voice.—*Venus and Adonis,* l. 134.

14
With her own white fleece her voice controll'd
Entombs her outcry in her lips' sweet fold.
The Rape of Lucrece, l. 678.

15
Clarence: Thy voice is thunder, but thy looks are humble.
Murderer: My voice is now the king's, my looks mine own.
Richard III. Act i, sc. 4, l. 173.
Thine eye Jove's lightning seems, thy voice his dreadful thunder,
Which, not to anger bent, is music and sweet fire.
The Passionate Pilgrim, l. 67.
The ear-deafening voice o' the oracle,
Kin to Jove's thunder.
Winter's Tale. Act iii, sc. 1, l. 9. [Cleomenes] The only use of "ear-deafening."

16 O, for a falconer's voice,
To lure this tassel-gentle back again!
Romeo and Juliet. Act ii, sc. 2, l. 159. [Juliet] The only use of "tassel-gentle."

17
His forward voice now is to speak well of his friend; his backward voice is to utter foul speeches and to detract.
Tempest. Act ii, sc. 2, l. 94. [Stephano] "Detract" is repeated in *I Henry VI,* v, 4, 142.

Voices

That, if I then had waked after long sleep,
Will make me sleep again.
The Tempest. Act iii, sc. 2, l. 147. [Caliban]

1
Crowns With an imperial voice.
Troilus and Cressida. Act i, sc. 3, l. 186. [Nestor]
Our voice is imperial.—*Henry V,* iii, 6, 131.
Monarch's voice.—*Julius Cæsar,* iii, 1, 272.

2
If the dull brainless Ajax come safe off,
We 'll dress him up in voices.
Troilus and Cressida. Act i, sc. 3, l. 381. [Ulysses] The only use of "brainless."
In second voice we 'll not be satisfied:
We come to speak with him.
Troilus and Cressida. Act ii, sc. 3, l. 149. [Agamemnon]

3
Thy small pipe
Is as the maiden's organ, shrill and sound,
And all is semblative a woman's part.
Twelfth Night. Act i, sc. 4, l. 32. [Duke] The only use of "semblative."
A mellifluous voice, as I am true knight.
Twelfth Night. Act ii, sc. 3, l. 54. [Sir Andrew] The only use of "mellifluous."

4
Thy mermaid's voice hath done me double wrong.
Venus and Adonis, l. 429.
Her voice is stopt.—*Venus and Adonis,* l. 1061.
Adonis' voice.—*Venus and Adonis,* l. 978.
Actor's voice.—*Troilus and Cressida,* Prol., 24.
Voice of Christendom.—*Henry VIII,* ii, 2, 88.
Voice of the recorded law.—*Measure for Measure,* ii, 4, 61.
Voice of lions.—*Troilus and Cressida,* iii, 2, 95.
Voice of a nightingale.—*King Lear,* iii, 6, 32.
Voice of occupation.—*Coriolanus,* iv, 6, 97.
Voice of souls.—*Sonnets,* xlix.

II—Knowing the Voice

5
But tell me yet, dost thou not know my voice?
The Comedy of Errors. Act v, sc. 1, l. 300. [Ægeon]
Not know my voice! O time's extremity,
Hast thou so crack'd and splitted my poor tongue
In seven short years, that here my only son
Knows not my feeble key of untuned cares?
The Comedy of Errors, v, 1, 307. [Ægeon]
Knows he not thy voice?—*All 's Well that Ends Well,* iv, 1, 11.
I do know her voice.—*Troilus and Cressida,* ii, 2, 98.
I know his voice.—*I Henry IV,* ii, 2, 53.
I know that voice.—*King Lear,* iv, 6, 96.
I should know that voice.—*Tempest,* ii, 2, 90.

6
The snatches in his voice,
And burst of speaking, were as his.
Cymbeline. Act iv, sc. 2, l. 105. [Belarius]
Hear thy voice.—*Henry V,* iii, 6, 48.

7
The trick of that voice I do well remember.
King Lear. Act iv, sc. 6, l. 108. [Gloucester]
I remember you, sir, by the sound of your voice.
Measure for Measure, v, 1, 330. [Duke]

8
He knows me as the blind man knows the cuckoo,
By the bad voice.
The Merchant of Venice, v, 1, 112. [Portia]
That is the voice,
Or I am much deceived, of Portia.
The Merchant of Venice. Act v, sc. 1, l. 356. [Lorenzo]

9
The voice of Cassio: Iago keeps his word.
Othello. Act v, sc. 1, l. 28. [Othello]
Alas! that was my lady's voice.
Othello. Act v, sc. 2, l. 119. [Emilia]
The voice of dead Thaisa!—*Pericles,* v, 3, 34.

10
This, by his voice, should be a Montague.
Romeo and Juliet. Act i, sc. 5, l. 56. [Tybalt]
This same should be the voice of Friar John.
Romeo and Juliet. Act v, sc. 5, l. 2. [Friar Laurence]

11
Nor know I you by voice or any feature.
Twelfth Night. Act iii, sc. 4, l. 387. [Viola]
Voice and favour!—*Pericles,* v, 3, 13.

III—Voices: Votes

12
Are you all resolved to give your voices?
Coriolanus. Act ii, sc. 3, l. 41. [Citizen]
Worthy voices!—*Coriolanus,* ii, 3, 145.
Coriolanus: Your good voice, sir; what say you?
Citizen: You shall ha 't, worthy sir.
Coriolanus: A match, sir. There 's in all two worthy voices begged. I have your alms: adieu.
Coriolanus. Act ii, sc. 3, l. 84.
Citizen: We . . . give you our voices heartily. . . .
Coriolanus: I will make much of your voices, and so trouble you no further.
Coriolanus. Act ii, sc. 3, l. 112.
Here come moe voices.
Your voices: for your voices I have fought;
Watch'd for your voices; for your voices bear
Of wounds two dozen odd; battles thrice six
I have seen and heard of; for your voices have
Done many things, some less, some more: your voices.
Coriolanus. Act ii, sc. 3, l. 132. [Coriolanus]
The tribunes
Endue you with the people's voice.
Coriolanus. Act ii, sc. 3, l. 146. [Menenius] "Endue" is used only once more, in *Twelfth Night,* i, 5, 105. "Endued" occurs once, in *The Two Gentlemen of Verona,* v, 4, 153.
Sicinius: Have you chose this man?
Citizen: He has our voices, sir.
Coriolanus. Act ii, sc. 3, l. 163.
Yield your voices.—*Coriolanus,* ii, 3, 184.
I 'll have five hundred voices of that sound.
Coriolanus. Act ii, sc. 3, l. 219. [Citizen]
Must these have voices, that can yield them now,
And straight disclaim their tongues?
Coriolanus. Act iii, sc. 1, l. 34. [Coriolanus]
Have you a catalogue
Of all the voices that we have procured
Set down by the poll?
Coriolanus. Act iii, sc. 3, l. 8. [Sicinius] "Catalogue" is repeated in *All 's Well that Ends Well,* i, 3, 149; *Macbeth,* iii, 1, 92; *Cymbeline,* i, 4, 5. "Cate-log" occurs in *The Two Gentlemen of Verona,* iii, 1, 273.
I do demand
If you submit you to the people's voices?
Coriolanus. Act iii, sc. 3, l. 43. [Sicinius]

What is the matter
That being pass'd for consul with full voice,
I am so dishonour'd that the very hour
You take it off again?
Coriolanus. Act iii, sc. 3, l. 58. [Coriolanus]

Suffer'd me by the voice of slaves to be
Whoop'd out of Rome.
Coriolanus. Act iv, sc. 5, l. 83. [Coriolanus] The only use of "whoop'd."

Ye 're goodly things, you voices!
Coriolanus. Act iv, sc. 6, l. 147. [Cominius]

1
You have the voice of the king himself for your succession.
Hamlet. Act iii, sc. 2, l. 355. [Rosencrantz]

He has my dying voice.
Hamlet. Act v, sc. 2, l. 367 [Hamlet]

2
I have no further gone in this than by
A single voice.
Henry VIII. Act i, sc. 2, l. 69. [Wolsey]

All the clerks,
I mean the learned ones, in Christian kingdoms
Have their free voices.
Henry VIII. Act ii, sc. 2, l. 92. [Wolsey]

3
Is there no voice more worthy than my own?
Julius Cæsar. Act iii, sc. 1, l. 49. [Metellus]

Your voice shall be as strong as any man's
In the disposing of new dignities.
Julius Cæsar. Act iii, sc. 1, l. 177. [Cassius]

You . . . took his voice who should be prick'd to die,
In our black sentence and proscription.
Julius Cæsar. Act iv, sc. 1, l. 16. [Octavius]

4
Let me have thy voice in my behalf.
The Merry Wives of Windsor. Act i, sc. 4, l. 167. [Fenton]

Let her have your voices.—*Othello,* i, 3, 261.

5
Be assured of this,
That the magnifico is much beloved,
And hath in his office a voice potential.
Othello. Act i, sc. 1, l. 11. [Iago] "Magnifico" is repeated in *Merchant of Venice,* iii, 2, 282.

6
I 'll give my voice on Richard's side.
Richard III. Act iii, sc. 2, l. 53. [Hastings]

In the duke's behalf I 'll give my voice.
Richard III. Act iii, sc. 4, l. 20. [Hastings]

You have my voice to it.
Timon of Athens. Act iii, sc. 5, l. 1. [Senator]

7
They answer, in a joint and corporate voice.
Timon of Athens. Act ii, sc. 2, l. 213. [Flavius]

General voice.—*II Henry IV,* iv, 1, 136.

8
I ask your voices and your suffrages.
Titus Andronicus. Act i, sc. 1, l. 218. [Titus]

Forbear your suffrages.—*Pericles,* ii, 4, 41.

Give their suffrage.—*Coriolanus,* ii, 2, 142.

People's suffrages.—*Titus Andronicus,* iv, 3, 19. The only uses of "suffrage" and "suffrages."

9
For well I know
The common voice do cry it shall be so.
Titus Andronicus. Act v, sc. 3, l. 139. [Æmilius]

By common voice.—*Titus Andronicus,* i, 1, 21.

With one voice.—*Troilus and Cressida,* i, 3, 221.

VOTARY

10
Who are the votaries, my loving lords,
That are vow-fellows with this virtuous duke?
Love's Labour's Lost. Act ii, sc. 1, l. 37. [Princess of France] The only use of "vow-fellows."

I am a votary.—*Love's Labour's Lost,* v, 2, 892.

11
His mother was a votaress of my order.
A Midsummer-Night's Dream. Act ii, sc. 1, l. 123. [Titania]

The imperial votaress passed on.
A Midsummer-Night's Dream, ii, 1, 163. See under Moon.

Unto Diana there a votaress.
Pericles, iv, Gower, l. 4. The only uses of "votaress."

12
I am no idle votarist.
Timon of Athens. Act iv, sc. 3, l. 27. [Timon] "Votarist" is repeated in *Measure for Measure,* i, 4, 5, and in *Othello,* iv, 2, 190.

13
That art a votary to fond desire.
The Two Gentlemen of Verona. Act. i, sc. 1, l. 52. [Valentine]

You are already Love's firm votary.
The Two Gentlemen of Verona. Act iii, sc. 2, l. 58. [Duke]

VOW

See also Oath

14
I prithee, do not strive against my vows.
All's Well that Ends Well. Act iv, sc. 2, l. 14. [Bertram]

'Tis not the many paths that makes the truth,
But the plain single vow that is vow'd true.
All's Well that Ends Well. Act iv, sc. 2, l. 21. [Diana]

His vows are forfeited to me, and my honour 's paid to him.
All's Well that Ends Well. Act v, sc. 3, l. 142. [King]

I dare vow for her.—*All's Well that Ends Well,* i, 3, 113.

15
He . . . vows, if he can take you,
To scorch your face and to disfigure you.
The Comedy of Errors. Act v, sc. 1, l. 182. [Servant] "Scorch" is repeated in *The Merry Wives of Windsor,* i, 3, 74. See under Coquetry.

16
When the blood burns, how prodigal the soul
Lends the tongue vows.
Hamlet. Act i, sc. 3, l. 116. [Polonius]

Suck'd the honey of his music vows.
Hamlet. Act iii, sc. 1, l. 164. [Ophelia]

1 I will die a hundred thousand deaths
Ere break the smallest parcel of this vow.
I Henry IV. Act iii, sc. 2, l. 158. [Prince]
Entertain my vows!—*II Henry VI*, iv, 9, 14.
Fulfil my vow.—*The Winter's Tale*, iv, 4, 497.
Keep thy vow.—*Henry V*, iv, 7, 151.

2
Now have I paid my vow unto his soul;
For every drop of blood was drawn from him
There hath at least five Frenchmen died to-night.
I Henry VI. Act ii, sc. 2, l. 7. [Talbot]
My vows are equal partners with thy vows.
I Henry VI. Act iii, sc. 2, l. 85.
That great vow
Which did incorporate and make us one.
Julius Cæsar. Act ii, sc. 1, l. 272. [Portia]
Let our reciprocal vows be remembered.—*King Lear*, iv, 6, 267. The only use of "reciprocal." "Reciprocally" occurs in *Henry VIII*, i, 1, 162.

3
Before I see thee seated in that throne, . . .
I vow by heaven these eyes shall never close.
III Henry VI. Act i, sc. 1, l. 22. [Warwick]
Warwick: Here on my knee I vow to God above,
I 'll never pause again, never stand still,
Till either death hath closed these eyes of mine
Or fortune given me measure of revenge.
Edward: O Warwick, I do bend my knee with thine;
And in this vow do chain my soul to thine!
III Henry VI. Act ii, sc. 3, l. 29.
Vow to God.—*I Henry IV*, iv, 3, 60.
Vow to heaven.—*Titus Andronicus*, i, 1, 474.

4
And here, to pledge my vow, I give my hand.
III Henry VI. Act iii, sc. 3, l. 250. [Prince]
He hath made a solemn vow
Never to lie and take his natural rest.
III Henry VI. Act iv, sc. 3, l. 4. [Watch]
Made a vow.—*Love's Labour 's Lost*, ii, 1, 22.
The vow is made.—*Titus Andronicus*, iii, 1, 280.

5
My vows and prayers Yet are the king's.
Henry VIII. Act ii, sc. 1, l. 88. [Buckingham]

6 O, let thy vow
First made to heaven, first be to heaven perform'd.
King John. Act iii, sc. 1, l. 265. [Pandulph]
Thy later vows against thy first
Is in thyself rebellion to thyself.
King John. Act iii, sc. 1, l. 288. [Pandulph]

7
Kneeling before this ruin of sweet life,
And breathing to his breathless excellence
The incense of a vow, a holy vow.
King John. Act iv, sc. 3, l. 65. [Salisbury]
With almost all the holy vows of heaven.
Hamlet. Act i, sc. 3, l. 114. [Ophelia]
Be not of my holy vows afraid.
A Lover's Complaint, l. 179.
My vow was earthly.—*Love's Labour 's Lost*, iv, 3, 66; *The Passionate Pilgrim*, l. 35.

8
O, we have made a vow to study, lords,
And in that vow we have forsworn our books.
Love's Labour 's Lost. Act iv, sc. 3, l. 318. [Biron]
Vow, alack, for youth unmeet,
Youth so apt to pluck a sweet!
Love's Labour 's Lost. Act iv, sc. 3, l. 113. [Dumain] Repeated in *The Passionate Pilgrim*, l. 239.
Vows and consecrations.—*A Lover's Complaint*, l. 263. The only use of "consecrations."

9
I have vow'd to Jaquenetta to hold the plough for her sweet love three years.
Love's Labour 's Lost. Act v, sc. 2, l. 892. [Armado]
This by the eye of Cynthia hath she vow'd.
Pericles. Act ii, sc. 5, l. 11. [Simonides]
Vow'd revenge.—*III Henry VI*, i, 1, 55.
Vow'd to study.—*Love's Labour 's Lost*, iv, 3, 296.
Vow'd with integrity.—*Love's Labour 's Lost*, v, 2, 356.
Divinely vow'd.—*King John*, ii, 1, 237.

10
I have toward heaven breathed a secret vow
To live in prayer and contemplation.
The Merchant of Venice. Act iii, sc. 4, l. 27. [Portia]
A vow of single life.—*A Midsummer-Night's Dream*, i, 1, 121.
The vow of mine order.—*Measure for Measure*, iv, 2, 180.

11
Look, when I vow, I weep; and vows so born,
In their nativity all truth appears.
A Midsummer-Night's Dream. Act iii, sc. 2, l. 124. [Lysander]

12
If sanctimony and a frail vow betwixt an erring barbarian and a super-subtle Venetian be not too hard for my wits and all the tribe of hell, thou shalt enjoy her.
Othello. Act i, sc. 3, l. 362. [Iago] The only use of "super-subtle."
If souls guide vows, if vows be sanctimonies,
If sanctimony be the gods' delight,
If there be rule in unity itself,
This is not she.
Troilus and Cressida. Act v, sc. 2, l. 139. [Troilus] The only use of "sanctimonies." "Sanctimony" occurs a third time in *All's Well that Ends Well*, iv, 3, 59: "Austere sanctimony."

13
Now, by yond marble heaven,
In the due reverence of a sacred vow
I here engage my words.
Othello. Act iii, sc. 3, l. 460. [Othello]
Sacred vows.—*King John*, iii, 1, 229; *Measure for Measure*, iv, 3, 149.
Sainted vow.—*All's Well that Ends Well*, iii, 4, 7.

14
Witness, you ever-burning lights above,
You elements that clip us round about,
Witness that here Iago doth give up
The execution of his wit, hands, heart,

To wrong'd Othello's service!
Othello. Act iii, sc. 3, l. 463. [Iago] "Ever-burning" is repeated in *Titus Andronicus,* iii, 1, 243: "Ever-burning hell."

1
That deep vow, which Brutus made before,
He doth again repeat.
The Rape of Lucrece, l. 1847.

2 By the glorious worth of my descent,
This arm shall do it, or this life be spent.
Richard II. Act i, sc. 1, l. 107. [Bolingbroke]

Now, by my sceptre's awe, I make a vow.
Richard II. Act i, sc. 1, l. 118. [King Richard]

3
A pleasing cordial, princely Buckingham,
Is this thy vow unto my sickly heart.
Richard III. Act ii, sc. 1, l. 41. [King Edward]

4
To breathe such vows as lovers use to swear.
Romeo and Juliet. Act ii, Prologue, l. 10. [Chorus]

Vows of love.—*Richard III,* v, 3, 98.

5
Romeo: O, wilt thou leave me so unsatisfied?
Juliet: What satisfaction canst thou have to-night?
Romeo: The exchange of thy love's faithful vow for mine.
Juliet: I gave thee mine before thou didst request it:
And yet I would it were to give again.
Romeo: Wouldst thou withdraw it? for what purpose, love?
Juliet: But to be frank, and give it thee again.
Romeo and Juliet. Act ii, sc. 2, l. 125.

Made exchange of vow.—*Romeo and Juliet,* ii, 3, 62.

6
This I do vow and this shall ever be;
I will be true.
Sonnets. No. cxxiii.

7
Hortensio: Here I firmly vow
Never to woo her more. . . .
Tranio: Here I take the like unfeigned oath,
Never to marry with her. . . .
Hortensio: Would all the world but he had quite forsworn!
The Taming of the Shrew. Act iv, sc. 2, l. 28. "Unfeigned" is repeated in *III Henry VI,* iii, 3, 51: "Unfeigned love"; and in the same play, iii, 3, 202: "Unfeigned friend."

8
Their vow is made To ransack Troy.
Troilus and Cressida, Prol., 8. The only use of "ransack."

We vow to weep seas, live in fire, eat rocks, tame tigers.
Troilus and Cressida. Act iii, sc. 2, l. 84. [Troilus]

Vow debate.—*Sonnets,* lxxxix.

Vows a league.—*The Rape of Lucrece,* l. 287.
Vows of obedience.—*I Henry VI,* iii, 1, 167.
Vows reformation.—*II Henry VI,* iv, 2, 70.
Vows revenge.—*Coriolanus,* iv, 6, 67.
Vows to crown himself.—*II Henry VI,* iv, 4, 31.
Vows to fight.—*III Henry VI,* i, 1, 160.

9 Strangles our dear vows
Even in the birth of our own labouring breath.
Troilus and Cressida. Act iv, sc. 4, l. 39. [Troilus]

Fail fame; honour or go or stay;
My major vow lies here, this I 'll obey.
Troilus and Cressida. Act v, sc. 1, l. 48. [Achilles]

Hector: The gods have heard me swear.
Cassandra: The gods are deaf to hot and peevish vows:
They are polluted offerings, more abhorr'd
Than spotted livers in the sacrifice.
Troilus and Cressida. Act v, sc. 3, l. 15. "Polluted" is repeated in *I Henry VI,* v, 4, 43: "Polluted with your lusts."

10
Pardon me, sweet one, even for the vows
We made each other but so late ago.
Twelfth Night. Act v, sc. 1, l. 221. [Sebastian]

11
You put me off with limber vows.
The Winter's Tale. Act i, sc. 2, l. 47. [Hermione] The only use of "limber."

Serviceable vows.—*The Two Gentlemen of Verona,* iii, 2, 70.

Truant vows.—*Troilus and Cressida,* i, 3, 270.

II—Broken Vows

12 Riotous madness,
To be entangled with those mouth-made vows,
Which break themselves in swearing!
Antony and Cleopatra. Act i, sc. 3, l. 29. [Cleopatra] The only use of "mouth-made."

Violated vows
'Twixt the soul of friend and friend.
As You Like It. Act iii, sc. 2, l. 141. [Celia, reading]

Vows made in wine.—*As You Like It,* iii, 5, 73.

13
The time was once when thou unurged wouldst vow
That never words were music to thine ear,
That never object pleasing in thine eye,
That never touch well welcome to thy hand,
That never meat sweet-savour'd in thy taste,
Unless I spake, or look'd, or touch'd, or carved to thee.
The Comedy of Errors. Act ii, sc. 2, l. 115. [Adriana] The only use of "sweet-savour'd." "Unurged" is repeated in *King John,* v, 2, 10: "Unurged faith."

14
Shall I be tempted to infringe my vow
In the same time 'tis made?
Coriolanus. Act v, sc. 2, l. 20. [Coriolanus]

1
Men's vows are women's traitors!
Cymbeline. Act iii, sc. 4, l. 56. [Imogen]

Vows of women.—*Cymbeline,* ii, 4, 110. See under WOMAN.

2
Do not believe his vows; for they are brokers,
Not of that dye which their investments show,
But mere implorators of unholy suits,
Breathing like sanctified and pious bawds,
The better to beguile.
Hamlet. Act i, sc. 3, l. 127. [Polonius] "Investments" is used only once again in the plays, in *II Henry IV*, iv, 1, 45. The only use of "implorators."

3
Marriage-vows as false as dicers' oaths.
Hamlet. Act iii, sc. 4, l. 44. [Hamlet] The only use of "marriage-vows" and "dicers." "Marriage-vow" occurs in *The Merry Wives of Windsor,* ii, 2, 258.

Holy wedlock vow.—*Rape of Lucrece,* l. 809.
Nuptial vow.—*Titus Andronicus,* ii, 3, 125.
Deep-divorcing vow.—*The Comedy of Errors,* ii, 2, 140. The only use of "deep-divorcing."

4
Thou hast sought to make us break our vow,
Which we durst never yet.
King Lear. Act i, sc. 1, l. 171. [King Lear]

5
Vows for thee broke deserve not punishment.
Love's Labour's Lost. Act iv, sc. 3, l. 63. [Longaville] Repeated in *The Passionate Pilgrim,* l. 32.

Vows are but breath, and breath a vapour is.
Love's Labour's Lost. Act iv, sc. 3, l. 68. [Longaville] Repeated in *The Passionate Pilgrim,* l. 37.

I, that am honest; I, that hold it sin
To break the vow I am engaged in.
Love's Labour's Lost. Act iv, sc. 3, l. 177. [Biron]

6
Vows were ever brokers to defiling.
A Lover's Complaint, l. 173. "Defiling" is repeated in *Pericles,* i, 1, 131.

7
Swallowed his vows whole.
Measure for Measure. Act iii, sc. 1, l. 235. [Duke]

8
Stealing her soul with many vows of faith
And ne'er a true one.
The Merchant of Venice. Act v, sc. 1, l. 19. [Jessica]

9
By all the vows that ever men have broke,
In number more than ever women spoke.
A Midsummer-Night's Dream. Act i, sc. 1, l. 175. [Hermia]

10
God keep all vows unbroke that swear to thee!
Richard II. Act iv, sc. 1, l. 215. [King Richard] The only use of "unbroke."

Like a traitor to the name of God,
Didst break that vow.
Richard III. Act i, sc. 4, l. 210. [Murderer]

Good night your vow!—*The Tempest,* iv, 1, 54.

11
Leave their false vows with him,
Like empty purses pick'd.
Timon of Athens. Act iv, sc. 2, l. 11. [Servant]

12
Unheedful vows may heedfully be broken.
Two Gentlemen of Verona. Act ii, sc. 6, l. 11. [Proteus] The only use of "unheedful."

That hast deceived so many with thy vows.
The Two Gentlemen of Verona. Act iv, sc. 2, l. 98. [Silvia]

Dismiss your vows.—*Venus and Adonis,* l. 25.

VOYAGE

13
Thy loving voyage
Is but for two months victuall'd.
As You Like It. Act v, sc. 4, l. 197. [Jaques] The only use of "victuall'd."

Hard voyages.—*Cymbeline,* v, 3, 44.
Late voyage.—*Henry VIII,* i, 3, 6.
Prosperous voyages.—*The Comedy of Errors,* i, 1, 41.

14
Arm you, I pray you, to this speedy voyage.
Hamlet. Act iii, sc. 3, l. 24. [King]

15
If he should intend this voyage towards my wife,
I would turn her loose to him.
The Merry Wives of Windsor. Act ii, sc. 1, l. 188. [Page]

16
I 'll make a voyage to the Holy Land,
To wash this blood off from my guilty hand.
Richard II. Act v, sc. 6, l. 49. [Bolingbroke]

He will repent the breath of his great voyage.
Pericles. Act iv, sc. 1, l. 37. [Dionyza]

Life's uncertain voyage.—*Timon of Athens,* v, 1, 205.

17
In one voyage
Did Claribel her husband find at Tunis.
The Tempest. Act v, sc. 1, l. 208. [Gonzalo]

18
My determinate voyage is mere extravagancy.
Twelfth Night. Act ii, sc. 1, l. 11. [Sebastian] The only use of "extravagancy."

I am bound to your niece, sir; I mean, she is the list of my voyage.
Twelfth Night. Act iii, sc. 1, l. 85. [Viola]

Lose thy voyage.—*The Two Gentlemen of Verona,* ii, 3, 47.

VULGARITY

See also People

19
King: I think thee now some common customer.
Diana: By Jove, if ever I knew man, 'twas you.
All's Well that Ends Well. Act v, sc. 3, l. 287.

Prince: This Doll Tearsheet should be some road.
Poins: I warrant you, as common as the way between Saint Alban's and London.
II Henry IV. Act ii, sc. 2, l. 182.

As common as the stairs
That mount the Capitol.
Cymbeline. Act i, sc. 6, l. 105. [Imogen]
As common
As any the most vulgar thing to sense.
Hamlet. Act i, sc. 2, l. 99. [King]
So common-hackney'd in the eyes of men,
So stale and cheap to vulgar company.
I Henry IV. Act iii, sc. 2, l. 40. [King Henry] The only use of "common-hackney'd."
Why thy odour matcheth not thy show,
The solve is this, that thou dost common grow.
Sonnets. No. lxix. The only use of "solve."
Base, common and popular.—*Henry V,* iv, 1, 38.
1
Abandon—which is in the vulgar leave.
As You Like It. Act v, sc. 1, l. 53. [Touchstone]
2
Be thou familiar, but by no means vulgar.
Hamlet. Act i, sc. 3, l. 61. [Polonius]
3
So do our vulgar drench their peasant limbs
In blood of princess.
Henry V. Act iv, sc. 7, l. 80. [Montjoy]
Vulgar sort of market-men.—*I Henry VI,* iii, 2, 4. "Market-men" is repeated in v, 5, 54, and occurs in no other play.
4
I 'll about
And drive away the vulgar from the streets.
Julius Cæsar. Act i, sc. 1, l. 75. [Flavius]
5
O base and obscure vulgar!
Love's Labour 's Lost. Act iv, sc. 1, l. 70. [Boyet, reading]
The base vulgar.—*Love's Labour 's Lost,* i, 2, 51.
Most sure and vulgar.—*King Lear,* iv, 6, 214.
Vulgar air.—*King John,* ii, 1, 387.
Vulgar comment.—*The Comedy of Errors,* iii, 1, 100.
Vulgar fame.—*Antony and Cleopatra,* iii, 13, 119.
Vulgar groom.—*II Henry VI,* iv, 1, 128.
Vulgar proof.—*Twelfth Night,* iii, 1, 135.
Vulgar scandal.—*Sonnets,* cxii.
Vulgar station.—*Coriolanus,* ii, 1, 231.
Vulgar wit.—*Love's Labour 's Lost,* iv, 1, 144.
Vulgar wisdoms.—*Coriolanus,* i, 1, 219.
Vulgarly accused.—*Measure for Measure,* v, 1, 160. The only use of "vulgarly."
6
Vulgars give bold'st titles.
Winter's Tale. Act ii, sc. 1, l. 94. [Leontes]

W

WAGER

See also Gaming, Match, Odds

7
Marcius: Yonder comes news. A wager they have met.
Lartius: My horse to yours, no.
Marcius: 'Tis done. . . . Say, has our general met the enemy?
Messenger: They lie in view; but have not spoken as yet.
Lartius: So, the good horse is mine.
Marcius: I 'll buy him of you.
Lartius: No, I 'll nor sell nor give him: lend him you I will
For half a hundred years.
Coriolanus. Act i, sc. 4, l. 1.
8
The description
Of what is in her chamber nothing saves
The wager you have laid.
Cymbeline. Act ii, sc. 4, l. 93. [Posthumus]
I have lost my wager.—*Cymbeline,* i, 6, 18.
9
We 'll make a solemn wager on your cunnings.
Hamlet. Act iv, sc. 7, l. 156. [King] The only use of "cunnings."
The king, sir, hath wagered with him six Barbary horses: against the which he has imponed, as I take it, six French rapiers and poniards.
Hamlet. Act v, sc. 2, l. 155. [Osric] "Imponed" (impawned) is repeated in l. 171, and occurs in no other scene.
King: Cousin Hamlet, You know the wager?
Hamlet: Very well, my lord;
Your grace hath laid the odds o' the weaker side.
Hamlet. Act v, sc. 2, l. 270.
10
I 'll lay my head to any good man's hat,
These oaths and laws will prove an idle scorn.
Love's Labour 's Lost. Act i, sc. 1, l. 310. [Biron]
My hat to a halfpenny.
Love's Labour 's Lost, v, 2, 563. [Biron]
11
My wretchedness unto a row of pins,
They 'll talk of state.
Richard II. Act iii, sc. 4, l. 26. [Queen] "Row" is used only once again, in *Hamlet,* ii, 2, 438.
12
Petruchio: He whose wife is most obedient
To come at first when he doth send for her,
Shall win the wager which we will propose.
Hortensio: Content. What is the wager?
Lucentio: Twenty crowns.
Petruchio: Twenty crowns!
I 'll venture so much of my hawk or hound,
But twenty times so much upon my wife.
Lucentio: A hundred then.
Hortensio: Content.
Petruchio: A match! 'tis done.
The Taming of the Shrew. Act v, sc. 2, l. 67.
The wager thou hast won.
The Taming of the Shrew. Act v, sc. 2, l. 112. [Baptista]

Nay, I will win my wager better yet.
The Taming of the Shrew. Act v, sc. 2, l. 116. [Petruchio]
'Twas I won the wager, though you hit the white;
And, being a winner, God give you good night!
The Taming of the Shrew. Act v, sc. 2, l. 186. [Petruchio]

1
Condition, I had gone barefoot to India.
Troilus and Cressida. Act i, sc. 2, l. 80. [Pandarus]

2
It 's four to one she 'll none of me.
Twelfth Night. Act i, sc. 3, l. 113. [Sir Andrew]
Twenty to one.—*The Two Gentlemen of Verona,* i, 1, 72.

3
I dare lay any money 'twill be nothing yet.
Twelfth Night. Act iii, sc. 4, l. 432. [Sir Toby]

WAIST

4
Chief Justice: Your means are very slender, and your waste is great.
Falstaff: I would it were otherwise; I would my means were greater, and my waist slenderer.
II Henry IV. Act i, sc. 2, l. 159. The only use of "slenderer."
When I was about thy years, Hal, I was not an eagle's talon in the waist.
I Henry IV. Act ii, sc. 4, l. 363. [Falstaff]
Falstaff: My honest lads, I will tell you what I am about.
Pistol: Two yards, and more.
Falstaff: No quips now, Pistol! Indeed, I am in the waist two yards about; but I am now about no waste; I am about thrift.
Merry Wives of Windsor. Act i, sc. 3, l. 42.
Buckle in a waist most fathomless.
Troilus and Cressida, ii, 2, 30. See under KING. The only use of "fathomless."

5
Girdled with a waist of iron.
I Henry VI. Act iv, sc. 3, l. 20. [Lucy]

6
Down from the waist they are Centaurs.
King Lear, iv, 6, 126. See WOMAN, 1702:2.
A German from the waist downward.
Much Ado about Nothing, iii, 2, 35.

7
An your waist, mistress, were as slender as my wit,
One o' these maids' girdles for your waist should be fit.
Love's Labour's Lost. Act iv, sc. 1, l. 49. [Costard]

WAKING, see Sleep and Waking

WALKING

8
Walk not in the trodden paths.
As You Like It, i, 3, 14. See under THORN.

9
Will you walk with me about the town,
And then go to my inn and dine with me?
The Comedy of Errors. Act i, sc. 2, l. 22. [Antipholus of Syracuse]
Pleaseth you walk with me down to his house.
The Comedy of Errors. Act iv, sc. 1, l. 12. [Angelo]

10
When he walks, he moves like an engine, and the ground shrinks before his treading.
Coriolanus. Act v, sc. 4, l. 19. [Menenius]

11
I 'll fetch a turn about the garden.
Cymbeline. Act i, sc. 1, l. 81. [Queen]
Come, you and I must walk a turn together.
Henry VIII. Act v, sc. 1, l. 93. [King]
A turn or two I 'll walk
To still my beating mind.
Tempest. Act iv, sc. 1, l. 162. [Prospero]

12
With solemn march
Goes slow and stately by them: thrice he walk'd
By their oppress'd and fear-surprised eyes.
Hamlet. Act i, sc. 2, l. 20. [Horatio] The only use of "fear-surprised."
How he looks, and how he goes!
Troilus and Cressida. Act i, sc. 2, l. 254. [Pandarus]

13
Will you walk out of the air, my lord?
Hamlet. Act ii, sc. 2, l. 208. [Polonius]
I will walk here in the hall.
Hamlet. Act v, sc. 2, l. 180. [Hamlet]
Walk i' the sun.—*Hamlet,* ii, 2, 185.
Walk you here.—*Hamlet,* iii, 1, 43.

14
If I travel but four foot by the squier further afoot,
I shall break my wind.
I Henry IV. Act ii, sc. 2, l. 12. [Falstaff] "By the squier" (square, foot-rule) is repeated in *Love's Labour 's Lost,* v, 2, 474, and in *The Winter's Tale,* iv, 4, 348.
'Sblood, I 'll not bear mine own flesh so far afoot again for all the coin in thy father's exchequer.
I Henry IV. Act ii, sc. 2, l. 37. [Falstaff]
We 'll walk afoot awhile, and ease our legs.
I Henry IV. Act ii, sc. 2, l. 83. [First Traveller]
Walked ten mile a-foot.—*Much Ado about Nothing,* ii, 3, 16. See under ARMOUR.
Walk on foot.—*Taming of the Shrew,* iv, 3, 188.
We walk invisible.—*I Henry IV,* ii, 1, 96.

15
His lordship is walk'd forth into the orchard.
II Henry IV. Act i, sc. 1, l. 4. [Porter]
Walk in the orchard.—*Much Ado about Nothing,* iii, 1, 5.

16
I do here walk before thee like a sow that hath overwhelmed all her litter but one.
II Henry IV. Act i, sc. 2, l. 12. [Falstaff]

17
He 's walked the way of nature.
II Henry IV, v, 2, 4. See under DEATH.

18
Walk'd about the streets.
Julius Cæsar, i, 3, 46. See under NIGHT.
Walk'd about.—*Julius Cæsar,* ii, 1, 239.
Walk abroad.—*Romeo and Juliet.* Act i, sc. 1, l. 127. [Benvolio] Also *Julius Cæsar,* iii, 2, 256.

Walk along.—*The Two Gentlemen of Verona,* v, 4, 162.
Walk aside.—*Love's Labour's Lost,* iv, 3, 213; *Much Ado about Nothing,* iii, 2, 73; *Measure for Measure,* iv, 1, 59.
Walk awhile.—*Cymbeline,* i, 1, 176.
Walk before.—*Love's Labour's Lost,* iv, 1, 147.
Walk by.—*Othello,* v, 2, 30.
Walked barefoot.—*Othello,* iv, 3, 39.
Walk forth.—*Julius Cæsar,* ii, 2, 8.
Walk we forth.—*Julius Cæsar,* iii, 1, 108.
Walk'd hand in hand.—*Troilus and Cressida,* iv, 5, 203.
Walk hence.—*The Two Gentlemen of Verona,* iii, 1, 246.
Walk hereabout.—*Othello,* iii, 4, 165.
Walk in.—*The Comedy of Errors,* v, 1, 419; *The Merry Wives of Windsor,* i, 1, 292.
Will you walk in?—*Troilus and Cressida,* iii, 2, 64; 107.
Walk into her house.—*Troilus and Cressida,* iv, 3, 5.
Walk in thievish ways.—*Romeo and Juliet,* iv, 1, 79.
Walk near.—*Timon of Athens,* ii, 2, 132.
Walk off.—*Henry V,* ii, 1, 61; *Troilus and Cressida,* iii, 2, 7.
Walk this way.—*Cymbeline,* i, 1, 103.
Walk thither.—*Henry VIII,* iv, 1, 116.
Walk upon the beach.—*King Lear,* iv, 6, 17.
Walk Upon the hatches.—*Richard III,* i, 4, 12.
Walk upon my knees.—*Richard II,* v, 3, 93. See under Joy.
Walk with me.—*Cymbeline,* v, 5, 119.
Walk like sprites.—*Macbeth,* ii, 3, 84.
Walked like a private man.—*Titus Andronicus,* iv, 4, 75.

1
Is it physical to walk unbraced?
Julius Cæsar, ii, 1, 262. See MORNING.

2
Here walk I in the black brow of night
To find you out.
King John. Act v, sc. 6, l. 17. [Hubert]
Walk by night.—*King John,* i, 1, 172.
Walk the night.—*Hamlet,* i, 5, 10.

3
Will 't please your highness walk?
King Lear. Act iv, sc. 7, l. 83. [Cordelia]
Tybalt, you rat-catcher, will you walk?
Romeo and Juliet. Act iii, sc. 1, l. 78. [Mercutio] The only use of "rat-catcher."
Will you walk, sir?—*Othello,* iv, 3, 4.
Come, we will walk.—*Measure for Measure,* iv, 5, 12.
Prithee, let 's walk.—*Henry VIII,* v, 1, 116.
Betook myself to walk.—*Love's Labour's Lost,* i, 1, 237. "Betook" is repeated in *Pericles,* i, 3, 35.

4
The right-valiant Banquo walk'd too late;
. . . men must not walk too late.
Macbeth. Act iii, sc. 6, l. 5. [Lennox]
Right valiant father.—*III Henry VI,* ii, 1, 10.
Right valiant lord.—*Troilus and Cressida,* ii, 3, 200. The only uses of "right valiant."

5
When was it she last walked?
Macbeth. Act v, sc. 1, l. 3. [Doctor]
I have known those which have walked in their sleep.
Macbeth. Act v, sc. 1, l. 66. [Doctor]

6
You must walk by us on our other hand.
Measure for Measure. Act v, sc. 1, l. 17. [Duke]

7
Turn two mincing steps Into a manly stride.
The Merchant of Venice. Act iii, sc. 4, l. 67. [Portia]
I mean to stride your steed.
Coriolanus, i, 9, 71. See under STEED.
Stride a limit.—*Cymbeline,* iii, 3, 35.
The strides they victors made.—*Cymbeline,* v, 3, 43. See under RETIREMENT.
Every stride he makes upon my land
Is dangerous treason.
Richard II, iii, 3, 92. [King Richard]
On the moment Follow his strides.
Timon of Athens. Act i, sc. 1, l. 80. [Poet]
A stride and a stand.—*Troilus and Cressida,* iii, 3, 252.
Tarquin's ravishing strides.—*Macbeth,* ii, 1, 55.
Tedious stride.—*Richard II,* i, 3, 268. The only uses of "stride" and "strides."

8
We should hold day with the Antipodes,
If you would walk in absence of the sun.
The Merchant of Venice. Act v, sc. 1, l. 127. [Bassanio] "Antipodes" is used five times in as many different plays.

9
There want not many that do fear
In deep of night to walk by this Herne's oak.
The Merry Wives of Windsor. Act iv, sc. 4, l. 39. [Page]
Walk round about an oak.—*The Merry Wives of Windsor,* iv, 4, 31.
Walk in the park.—*The Merry Wives of Windsor,* iii, 3, 240.
Walk by the Counter-gate.—*The Merry Wives of Windsor,* iii, 3, 85. The only mention of the Counter-gate, the gate of the Counter, a name for debtors' prisons.

10
I will walk up and down here.
A Midsummer-Night's Dream, iii, 1, 126. See under SONG.
Walk up and down.—*Julius Cæsar,* i, 3, 25; *King John,* iii, 4, 94.

11
Hop in his walks and gambol in his eyes.
A Midsummer-Night's Dream. Act iii, sc. 1, l. 168. [Titania]
Go, hop me over every kennel home,
For you shall hop without my custom, sir.
The Taming of the Shrew. Act iv, sc. 3, l. 98. [Petruchio]
Hop as light as bird.—*A Midsummer-Night's Dream,* v, 1, 401.
Hop forty paces.—*Antony and Cleopatra,* ii, 2, 234.
Hop without thy head.—*II Henry VI,* i, 3, 140.
Where heart doth hop.—*A Midsummer-Night's Dream,* v, 1, 304. The only uses of "hop."
Where be . . . your gambols?
Hamlet. Act v, sc. 1, l. 207. [Hamlet] "Gambol" is repeated in iii, 4, 144.
Other gambol faculties a' has.
II Henry IV. Act ii, sc. 4, l. 273. [Falstaff]

Gallimaufry of gambols.—*The Winter's Tale,* iv, 4, 335. "Gallimaufry" (medley) is repeated in *Merry Wives of Windsor,* ii, 1, 119.
Wanton gambols.—*Merchant of Venice,* iii, 2, 93. The only uses of "gambol" and "gambols."

1
Don Pedro: Lady, will you walk about with your friend?
Hero: So you walk softly and look sweetly and say nothing, I am yours for the walk.
Much Ado about Nothing. Act ii, sc. 1, l. 89. "Will you walk?" is repeated in ii, 3, 218.
Pray, walk softly, do not heat your blood.
Pericles. Act iv, sc. 1, l. 49. [Dionyza]
Pray you, tread softly, that the blind mole may not
Hear a foot fall.
The Tempest. Act iv, sc. 1, l. 194. [Caliban]

2
I will be walking on the works.
Othello. Act iii, sc. 2, l. 3. [Othello]
Walking in a thick-pleached alley in mine orchard.
Much Ado about Nothing. Act i, sc. 2, l. 9. [Antonio] The only use of "thick-pleached," bordered with close hedges of intertwined shrubs.
Walking in the garden.—*Antony and Cleopatra,* iii, 5, 17.
Early walking.—*Romeo and Juliet,* i, 1, 130.
Wary walking.—*Julius Cæsar,* ii, 1, 15.

3
'Twill do me good to walk.
Othello. Act iv, sc. 3, l. 2. [Othello]

4
Walk half an hour, Leonine, at the least.
Pericles. Act iv, sc. 1, l. 46. [Dionyza]

5
I am not for this ambling.
Romeo and Juliet. Act i, sc. 4, l. 11. [Romeo] "Ambling" is repeated in *Richard III,* i, 1, 17, and in *Merry Wives of Windsor,* ii, 2, 319.

6
Trudge about Through fair Verona.
Romeo and Juliet. Act i, sc. 2, l. 34. [Capulet]
'Twas no need, I trow, To bid me trudge.
Romeo and Juliet. Act i, sc. 3, l. 33. [Nurse]
Trudge, plod away o' the hoof.
The Merry Wives of Windsor. Act i, sc. 3, l. 91. [Falstaff]
'Tis time, I think, to trudge.—*The Comedy of Errors,* iii, 2, 158. See under DEPARTURE.
Trudge . . . in all haste.—*The Merry Wives of Windsor,* iii, 3, 13.
That trudge betwixt the king.—*Richard III,* i, 1, 73. The only uses of "trudge."

7
How now, my headstrong! where have you been gadding?
Romeo and Juliet. Act iv, sc. 2, l. 16. [Capulet] The only use of "gadding."
Waddled all about.—*Romeo and Juliet,* i, 3, 37. The only use of "waddled."

8
I grant I never saw a goddess go;
My mistress, when she walks, treads on the ground.
Sonnets. No. cxxx.

9
Say thou wilt walk; we will bestrew the ground.
The Taming of the Shrew. Induction, sc. 2, l. 42. [Lord] "Bestrew" is repeated in *The Tempest,* iv, 1, 20.
O, let me see thee walk: thou dost not halt. . . .
Did ever Dian so become a grove
As Kate this chamber with her princely gait?
The Taming of the Shrew. Act ii, sc. 1, l. 258. [Petruchio]
You may go walk.—*The Taming of the Shrew,* iii, 1, 59.

10
When wert thou wont to walk alone?
Titus Andronicus. Act i, sc. 1, l. 339. [Titus]
Walks, like contempt, alone.—*Timon of Athens,* iv, 2, 15.
To walk alone, like one that had the pestilence.
The Two Gentlemen of Verona, ii, 1, 21. See under LOVE.

11
The forest walks are wide and spacious.
Titus Andronicus. Act ii, sc. 1, l. 114. [Aaron]

12
And so let 's leave her to her silent walks.
Titus Andronicus. Act ii, sc. 4, l. 8. [Demetrius]
Close walk.—*II Henry VI,* ii, 2, 3.
Glorious walk.—*Pericles,* i, 2, 4.
Quiet walks.—*II Henry VI,* iv, 10, 19.
Royal walks.—*A Midsummer-Night's Dream,* v, 1, 31.

13
Like a cloistress, she will veiled walk.
Twelfth Night, i, 1, 28. See under TEAR. The only use of "cloistress."
Do not let them walk too open.
Twelfth Night. Act iii, sc. 3, l. 37. [Sebastian]

14
When you walked, to walk like one of the lions.
The Two Gentlemen of Verona, ii, 1, 28. See under LOVE.

15 We two will walk, my lord,
And leave you to your graver steps.
Winter's Tale. Act i, sc. 2, l. 172. [Polixenes]

II—Walking: Gait

16
With his lion gait walk the whole world.
Henry V. Act ii, sc. 2, l. 122. [King Henry]

17
I do know him by his gait.
Julius Cæsar. Act i, sc. 3, l. 132. [Casca]
I know his gait, 'tis he.—*Othello,* v, 1, 23.
I know her by her gait.—*Tempest,* iv, 1, 102.
Go your gait.—*Julius Cæsar,* iv, 6, 242.

18
Methought thy very gait did prophesy
A royal nobleness.
King Lear. Act v, sc. 3, l. 175. [Albany]
His gait majestical.—*Love's Labour 's Lost,* v, 1, 12.

19
Does he not . . . strut in his gait?
The Merry Wives of Windsor. Act i, sc. 4, l. 31. [Mistress Quickly]

1
With pretty and with swimming gait.
A Midsummer-Night's Dream. Act ii, sc. 1, l. 130. [Titania]
Walk with gentle gait.—*Sonnets,* cxxviii.

2
'Tis he, I ken the manner of his gait;
He rises on the toe: that spirit of his
In aspiration lifts him from the earth.
Troilus and Cressida. Act iv, sc. 5, l. 14. [Ulysses] The only use of "aspiration."

WALL

3
We 'll break our walls,
Rather than they shall pound us up.
Coriolanus. Act i, sc. 4, l. 15. [Senator]
Within your walls.—*Coriolanus,* i, 4, 13.

4
The heavens hold firm
The walls of thy dear honour!
Cymbeline, ii, 1, 68. See under HONOUR.

5
They of those marches, gracious sovereign,
Shall be a wall sufficient to defend
Our inland from the pilfering borderers.
Henry V. Act i, sc. 2, l. 140. [Canterbury] The only use of "pilfering."
Girdled with maiden walls that war hath never entered.
Henry V. Act v, sc. 2, l. 349. [French King] "Girdled" is repeated in *I Henry VI,* v, 3, 20.

6
Let 's get us from the walls.
I Henry VI. Act iii, sc. 2, l. 71. [La Pucelle]

7
Here will I sit before the walls of Rouen
And will be partner of your weal or woe.
I Henry VI. Act iii, sc. 2, l. 91. [Bedford]
The walls of strong-besieged Troy.
The Rape of Lucrece, l. 1429. The only use of "strong-besieged."
Troy walls.—*Troilus and Cressida,* i, 3, 12.
Troyan walls.—*The Merchant of Venice,* v, 1, 4.
Walls of Troy.—*Troilus and Cressida,* i, 1, 2; i, 3, 278.
Walls of Athens.—*Timon of Athens,* v, 1, 170.
Corioli walls.—*Coriolanus,* i, 8, 8.
Pisa walls.—*Taming of the Shrew,* ii, 1, 369.
Verona walls.—*Romeo and Juliet,* iii, 3, 17.

8
On a brick wall have I climbed into this garden.
II Henry VI. Act iv, sc. 10, l. 7. [Cade]
Stone walls.—*Coriolanus,* i, 1, 210.
Climbing my walls in spite of me the owner.
II Henry VI. Act iv, sc. 10, l. 37. [Iden]

9
See how the surly Warwick mans the wall!
III Henry VI. Act v, sc. 1, l. 17. [Gloucester]
Keep the walls.—*I Henry VI,* iii, 2, 69.
O'erlook the walls.—*Richard III,* iii, 5, 17.

10
The wall is high, and yet I will leap down.
King John. Act iv, sc. 3, l. 1. [Arthur]
Leap o'er the walls.—*I Henry VI,* ii, 2, 25.

11
'Tis not the roundure of your old-faced walls
Can hide you from our messengers of war,
Though all these English and their discipline
Were harbour'd in their rude circumference.
King John. Act ii, sc. 1, l. 259. [King Philip] The only use of "roundure" and "harbour'd." "Old-faced" is repeated in *I Henry IV,* iv, 2, 34; and "circumference" in *The Merry Wives of Windsor,* iii, 5, 113, and in *Midsummer-Night's Dream,* v, 1, 247.
Beauteous wall.—*Twelfth Night,* i, 2, 48.
Brazen wall.—*III Henry VI,* ii, 4, 4.
Castle walls.—*I Henry VI,* v, 3, 129; *Richard II,* iii, 2, 170.
City walls.—*King John,* ii, 1, 234; *Titus Andronicus,* i, 1, 26.
Consecrated wall.—*The Rape of Lucrece,* l. 723.
Crystal walls.—*The Rape of Lucrece,* l. 1251.
Dove-house wall.—*Romeo and Juliet,* i, 3, 27. "Dove-house" is used only in this scene, repeated in l. 33.
Ivory wall.—*The Rape of Lucrece,* l. 464.
Prison walls.—*Richard II,* v, 5, 21.
Saucy walls.—*King John,* ii, 1, 404.
Unfurnish'd walls.—*Richard II,* i, 2, 68.
White-limed walls!—*Titus Andronicus,* iv, 2, 98. The only use of "white-limed."
Wide walls.—*Julius Cæsar,* i, 2, 155.
Wall of flesh.—*King John,* iii, 3, 20.
Walls of glass.—*Sonnets,* v.
Walls of a jakes.—*King Lear,* ii, 2, 72. The only use of "jakes" (privy).

12
Quince: We must have a wall in the great chamber; for Pyramus and Thisby, says the story, did talk through the chink of a wall.
Snout: You can never bring in a wall. What say you, Bottom?
Bottom: Some man or other must present Wall: and let him have some plaster, or some loam, or some rough-cast about him, to signify wall.
A Midsummer-Night's Dream. Act iii, sc. 1, l. 63. "Loam" is repeated in *Richard II,* i, 1, 179, and in *Hamlet,* v, 1, 233.
This man, with lime and rough-cast, doth present
Wall, that vile Wall which did these lovers sunder;
And through Wall's chink, poor souls, they are content
To whisper. At the which let no man wonder.
A Midsummer-Night's Dream. Act v, sc. 1, l. 132. [Quince, as Prologue] "Rough-cast" is used a third time in l. 162, and occurs in no other play. "Vile wall" is repeated in l. 202.
In this same interlude it doth befall
That I, one Snout by name, present a wall;
And such a wall, as I would have you think,
That had in it a crannied hole or chink,
Through which the lovers, Pyramus and Thisby,
Did whisper often very secretly.
A Midsummer-Night's Dream. Act v, sc. 1, l. 156. [Snout] The only use of "crannied."
And thou, O wall, O sweet, O lovely wall,
That stand'st between her father's ground and mine!

Thou wall, O wall, O sweet and lovely wall,
Show me thy chink, to blink through with mine eyne!
A Midsummer-Night's Dream. Act v, sc. 1, l. 175. [Pyramus]

Theseus: Now is the mural down between the two neighbours.
Demetrius: No remedy, my lord, when walls are so wilful to hear without warning.
A Midsummer-Night's Dream. Act v, sc. 1, l. 208. The only use of "mural."

The wall is down.—*A Midsummer-Night's Dream,* v, 1, 357.

1 All the walls
With painted imagery had said at once
'Jesu preserve thee!'
Richard II. Act v, sc. 2, l. 15. [York] The only use of "imagery."

2
Sampson: I will take the wall of any man or maid of Montague's.
Gregory: That shows thee a weak slave; for the weakest goes to the wall.
Sampson: True; and therefore women, being the weaker vessels, are ever thrust to the wall: therefore I will push Montague's men from the wall, and thrust his maids to the wall.
Romeo and Juliet. Act i, sc. 1, l. 15.

Juliet: The orchard walls are high and hard to climb. . . .
Romeo: With love's light wings did I o'erperch these walls.
Romeo and Juliet. Act ii, sc. 2, l. 63. See under LOVE. The only use of "o'er-perch."

Orchard wall.—*Romeo and Juliet,* ii, 1, 5.

3
Painting thy outward walls so costly gay.
Sonnets. No. cxlvi.

Outward wall.—*Merchant of Venice,* ii, 9, 29.

4 O thou wall,
That girdlest in those wolves, dive in the earth,
And fence not Athens!
Timon of Athens. Act iv, sc. 1, l. 1. [Timon] The only use of "girdlest."

These walls of ours
Were not erected by their hands from whom
You have received your griefs; nor are they such
That these great towers, trophies and schools should fall
For private faults in them.
Timon of Athens. Act v, sc. 4, l. 22. [Senator]

5
Yonder walls, that pertly front your town.
Troilus and Cressida. Act iv, sc. 5, l. 219. [Ulysses] "Pertly" is repeated in *The Tempest,* iv, 1, 58.

WANDERING

6
To-night we 'll wander through the streets and note
The qualities of people.
Antony and Cleopatra. Act i, sc. 1, l. 53. [Antony]

He gives them good leave to wander.
As You Like It. Act i, sc. 1, l. 109. [Charles]

7 I will go lose myself
And wander up and down to view the city.
The Comedy of Errors. Act i, sc. 2, l. 30. [Antipholus of Syracuse]

8
I may wander From east to occident.
Cymbeline, iv, 2, 371. See under MASTER. "Occident" is repeated in *Richard II,* iii, 3, 67.

Safe mayst thou wander.—*Cymbeline,* iii, 5, 105.

9
Wander o'er this bloody field.
Henry V. Act iv, sc. 7, l. 75. [Montjoy]

Wander in an unknown field.—*The Comedy of Errors,* iii, 2, 38.

10
You wander from the good we aim at.
Henry VIII. Act iii, sc. 1, l. 138. [Wolsey]

11
I have no will to wander forth of doors,
Yet something leads me forth.
Julius Cæsar. Act iii, sc. 3, l. 3. [Cinna]

Whither wander you?—*A Midsummer-Night's Dream,* ii, 1, 1; *As You Like It,* i, 2, 59.

I do wander every where.—*A Midsummer-Night's Dream,* ii, 1, 6.

12
I am that merry wanderer of the night.
Midsummer-Night's Dream. Act ii, sc. 1, l. 43. [Puck]

Wanderers of the dark.—*King Lear,* iii, 2, 44.

Welcome, wanderer.—*A Midsummer-Night's Dream,* ii, 1, 247. The only uses of "wanderer" and "wanderers."

13
'Wander,' a word for shadows like myself,
As take the pain, but cannot pluck the pelf.
The Passionate Pilgrim, l. 191.

14
Now, for my life, she 's wandering to the Tower,
On pure heart's love, to greet the tender princes.
Richard III. Act iv, sc. 1, l. 3. [Duchess of York]

Wandering in the wood.—*A Midsummer-Night's Dream,* ii, 2, 35.

Wandering with the antipodes.—*Richard II,* iii, 2, 49.

Wandering here and there.—*A Midsummer-Night's Dream,* iii, 2, 381.

And when I wander here and there,
I then do most go right.
The Winter's Tale. Act iv, sc. 3, l. 17. [Autolycus]

15 He himself wander'd away alone,
No man knows whither.
Richard III. Act iv, sc. 4, l. 514. [Messenger]

Wander'd forth.—*Comedy of Errors,* ii, 2, 3.

Wander'd in the air.—*Richard II,* i, 3, 195.

Wander'd through the forest.—*The Two Gentlemen of Verona,* v, 2, 38.

Faulty wander'd.—*I Henry IV,* iii, 2, 27.

16
Wander we to see thy honest son.
The Taming of the Shrew. Act iv, sc. 5, l. 69. [Petruchio]

WANT

1
Want will perjure The ne'er-touched vestal.
Antony and Cleopatra, iii, 12, 30. See under WOMAN. The only use of "ne'er-touched."

2
His present want
Seems more than we shall find it.
I Henry IV. Act iv, sc. 1, l. 44. [Hotspur]
Desperate want.—*Timon of Athens,* iv, 3, 469.

3
If thou wantest any thing, and wilt not call, beshrew thy heart.
II Henry IV. Act v, sc. 3, l. 58. [Shallow]

4
And she again wants nothing, to name want,
If want it be not that she is not he.
King John. Act ii, sc. 1, l. 435. [Citizen]
Where nothing wants that want itself doth seek.
Love's Labour 's Lost. Act iv, sc. 3, l. 237. [Biron]
Let them want nothing that my house affords.
Taming of the Shrew. Induction, sc. 1, l. 104. [Lord]
She . . . wants nothing i' the world.
All's Well that Ends Well. Act ii, sc. 4, l. 4. [Clown]
He wants nothing.—*Coriolanus,* v, 4, 24.
Want nothing.—*Sonnets,* xlix.
Nothing wants.—*Venus and Adonis,* l. 1459.

5
He that keeps nor crust nor crum,
Weary of all, shall want some.
King Lear. Act i, sc. 4, l. 217. [Fool] The only use of "crum." "Crums" occurs in *Twelfth Night,* ii, 3, 129.

6
He wants the natural touch.
Macbeth. Act iv, sc. 2, l. 9. [Lady Macduff]

7
Such a want-wit sadness makes of me.
The Merchant of Venice, i, 1, 6. See under SADNESS. The only use of "want-wit" as a hyphenated phrase.
Want wit.—*The Comedy of Errors,* ii, 2, 153; *The Two Gentlemen of Verona,* ii, 6, 12; *Titus Andronicus,* ii, 1, 26.
Want of wit.—*Romeo and Juliet,* iii, 5, 74; *The Rape of Lucrece,* l. 153.
Wants her wits.—*Coriolanus,* iv, 2, 44.

8
The ripe wants of my friend.
The Merchant of Venice. Act i, sc. 3, l. 64. [Antonio]
I would . . . Supply your present wants.
The Merchant of Venice. Act i, sc. 3, l. 139. [Shylock]
Send them after to supply our wants.
Richard II. Act i, sc. 4, l. 51. [King Richard]

9
Ford: Want no money, Sir John; you shall want none.
Falstaff: Want no Mistress Ford, Master Brook; you shall want none.
Merry Wives of Windsor. Act ii, sc. 2, l. 268.
He wants money.—*Much Ado about Nothing,* iii, 2, 20.
Want for money.—*Timon of Athens,* iii, 2, 10.
Want of money.—*The Two Gentlemen of Verona,* ii, 1, 31.
Want the best.—*All's Well that Ends Well,* i, 1, 81.
Want conceit.—*The Passionate Pilgrim,* l. 51.
Want countenance.—*I Henry IV,* i, 2, 175.
Want credit.—*The Tempest,* iii, 3, 25.
Want eyes.—*Cymbeline,* v, 4, 192.
Wanteth food.—*Pericles,* i, 4, 11.
Want gold.—*Timon of Athens,* ii, 1, 5.
Want of gold.—*Timon of Athens,* iv, 3, 401.
Want guilders.—*The Comedy of Errors,* iv, 1, 4.
Wants hard use.—*Macbeth,* iii, 4, 143.
Want love.—*Coriolanus,* i, 3, 90.
Wants matter.—*The Merry Wives of Windsor,* v, 5, 144.
Want Spirits.—*The Tempest,* Epil., 13.
Wants not spirit.—*Coriolanus,* iii, 1, 95.
Want treasure.—*Timon of Athens,* ii, 2, 214.
Want troops.—*Antony and Cleopatra,* iv, 14, 53.
Want true colour.—*Macbeth,* iii, 4, 130.

10
What I have been I have forgot to know;
But what I am, want teaches me to think on.
Pericles. Act ii, sc. 1, l. 74. [Pericles]

11
For what I have I need not to repeat;
And what I want it boots not to complain.
Richard II. Act iii, sc. 4, l. 17. [Queen]
Feel want.—*Richard II,* iii, 2, 175.

12
Scarcity and want shall shun you.
The Tempest, iv, 1, 116. See under BLESSING.
Take what I shall die to want.—*The Tempest,* iii, 1, 79.

13
Banditti: We are not thieves, but men that much do want.
Timon: Your greatest want is, you want much of meat.
Why should you want? Behold, the earth hath roots;
Within this mile break forth a hundred springs;
The oaks bear mast, the briers scarlet hips;
The bounteous housewife, nature, on each bush
Lays her full mess before you. Want! Why want?
Timon of Athens. Act iv, sc. 3, l. 418. The only use of "mast" and of "hips" in this sense.
Want of meat.—*Cymbeline,* v, 4, 163.
Want of breeding.—*Cymbeline,* iv, 4, 26.
Want of company.—*The Merry Wives of Windsor,* iii, 2, 14.
Want of conscience.—*Sonnets,* cli.
Want of government.—*I Henry IV,* iii, 1, 184.
Want of husbandry.—*II Henry VI,* iii, 1, 33.
Want of language.—*All's Well that Ends Well,* iv, 1, 77.
Want of linen.—*Love's Labour 's Lost,* v, 2, 719.
Want of love.—*Venus and Adonis,* l. 202.
Want of means.—*Richard III,* v, 3, 331.
Want of men.—*I Henry VI,* i, 1, 69.
Want of pity.—*Titus Andronicus,* v, 3, 200.
Want of rain.—*A Midsummer-Night's Dream,* i, 1, 130.
Want of resolution.—*II Henry VI,* iv, 8, 65.
Want of skill.—*The Rape of Lucrece,* l. 1099.
Want of strength.—*III Henry VI,* v, 2, 8.
Want of time.—*Henry V,* v, 2, 57.

Want of idle time.—*The Two Gentlemen of Verona,* ii, 1, 172.
Want of use.—*Pericles,* i, 4, 37.
Want of wisdom.—*King Lear,* i, 4, 366; *Henry VIII,* v, 3, 13.

WANTONNESS

See also Adultery; Lechery; Lewdness; Love and Lust; Whore

1 Certain it is I liked her,
And boarded her i' the wanton way of youth.
All's Well that Ends Well. Act v, sc. 3, l. 210. [Bertram] See also under WOOING.

2 If he fill'd
His vacancy with his voluptuousness,
Full surfeits, and the dryness of his bones,
Call on him for 't.
Antony and Cleopatra. Act i, sc. 4, l. 25. [Cæsar] The only use of "dryness."

There 's no bottom, none,
In my voluptuousness: your wives, your daughters,
Your matrons and your maids, could not fill up
The cistern of my lust.
Macbeth. Act iv, sc. 3, l. 60. [Malcolm] The only uses of "voluptuousness." "Voluptuously" occurs once, in *Coriolanus,* i, 3, 27. "Cistern" is repeated in *Othello,* iv, 2, 61, and in *Antony and Cleopatra,* ii, 5, 95.

We have willing dames enough; there cannot be
That vulture in you, to devour so many
As will to greatness dedicate themselves,
Finding it so inclined.
Macbeth. Act iv, sc. 3, l. 73. [Macduff]

3 But all the charms of love,
Salt Cleopatra, soften thy waned lip!
Let witchcraft join with beauty, lust with both!
Tie up the libertine in a field of feasts,
Keep his brain fuming.
Antony and Cleopatra. Act ii, sc. 1, l. 20. [Pompey] The only use of "fuming." "Waned" is repeated in *III Henry VI,* iv, 7, 4: "Waned state."

To wanton with this queen.—*Titus Andronicus,* ii, 1, 21.

4 I did not think
This amorous surfeiter would have donn'd his helm.
Antony and Cleopatra. Act ii, sc. 1, l. 32. [Pompey] The only use of "surfeiter."

5
You have tasted her in bed.
Cymbeline. Act ii, sc. 4, l. 57. [Posthumus]

Perchance he spoke not, but,
Like a full-acorn'd boar, a German one,
Cried 'O!' and mounted.
Cymbeline. Act ii, sc. 5, l. 15. [Posthumus] The only use of "full-acorn'd."

6
Thou didst accuse him of incontinency.
Cymbeline. Act iii, sc. 4, l. 49. [Imogen] "Incontinency" is repeated in ii, 4, 127, and in *Hamlet,* ii, 1, 30.

Incontinent before marriage.—*As You Like It,* iv, 2, 42.

Turn incontinent.—*Timon of Athens,* iv, 1, 3. "Incontinent" in this sense is used a third time in *Troilus and Cressida,* v, 1, 106: "Incontinent varlets."

7
You jig, you amble, and you lisp, and nick-name God's creatures, and make your wantonness your ignorance.
Hamlet. Act iii, sc. 1, l. 150. [Hamlet] "Nick-name" is repeated in *Love's Labour's Lost,* v, 2, 349, and in *Romeo and Juliet,* ii, 1, 12.

You make a wanton of me.
Hamlet. Act v, sc. 2, l. 310. [Hamlet]

A wightly wanton with a velvet brow.
Love's Labour's Lost. Act iii, sc. 1, l. 198. [Biron] The only use of "wightly" (nimble).

An approved wanton.—*Much Ado about Nothing,* iv, 1, 45.
A cocker'd silken wanton.—*King John,* v, 1, 70. The only use of "cocker'd" (pampered).
Rash wanton.—*A Midsummer-Night's Dream,* ii, 1, 63.

8
Wanton as youthful goats, wild as young bulls.
I Henry IV. Act iv, sc. 1, l. 103. [Vernon]

Wanton as a child.—*Love's Labour's Lost,* v, 2, 771.
Wanton and effeminate.—*Richard II,* v, 3, 10.
All too wanton.—*King John,* iii, 3, 36.

9
I 'll canvass thee between a pair of sheets.
II Henry IV, ii, 4, 243. [Doll] "Canvass thee" is repeated in *I Henry IV,* i, 3, 36.

And it is thought abroad that 'twixt my sheets
He has done my office.
Othello. Act i, sc. 3, l. 393. [Iago]

10
Lascivious, wanton, more than well beseems
A man of thy profession and degree.
I Henry VI. Act iii, sc. 1, l. 19. [Gloucester]

The loose encounters of lascivious men.
Two Gentlemen of Verona, ii, 7, 41. [Julia]

Leave thy lascivious wassails.
Antony and Cleopatra, i, 4, 56. [Cæsar]

That 's a lascivious apprehension.
Timon of Athens. Act i, sc. 1, l. 211. [Timon]

Lascivious boy.—*All's Well that Ends Well,* iv, 3, 248; 333.
Lascivious comments.—*Sonnets,* xcv.
Lascivious Edward.—*III Henry VI,* v, 5, 34.
Lascivious Goth.—*Titus Andronicus,* ii, 3, 110.
Lascivious grace.—*Sonnets,* xl.
Lascivious metres.—*Richard II,* ii, 1, 19.
Lascivious Moor.—*Othello,* i, 1, 127.
Lascivious pleasing of a lute.—*Richard III,* i, 1, 13.
Lascivious town.—*Timon of Athens,* v, 4, 1.
Lascivious turtles.—*Merry Wives of Windsor,* ii, 1, 82. The only uses of "lascivious."

11
She and the Dauphin have been juggling.
I Henry VI. Act v, sc. 4, l. 68. [York]

York: Why, here 's a girl! I think she knows not well,
There were so many, whom she may accuse.
Warwick: It 's sign she hath been liberal and free.
I Henry VI. Act v, sc. 4, l. 80.

She is too liberal.
The Two Gentlemen of Verona. Act iii, sc. 1, l. 355. [Speed]
I will become as liberal as you.
The Merchant of Venice, v, 1, 226. [Portia]

1 The sly whoresons
Have got a speeding trick to lay down ladies;
A French song and a fiddle has no fellow.
Henry VIII. Act i, sc. 3, l. 39. [Lovell] The only use of "fiddle."
When the brown wench
Lay kissing in your arms.
Henry VIII. Act iii, sc. 2, l. 295. [Surrey]

2
I am doubtful that you have been conjunct
And bosom'd with her.
King Lear. Act v, sc. 1, l. 12. [Regan] "Conjunct" is repeated in ii, 2, 125, and occurs in no other play.

3
If she had been a woman cardinally given, might have been accused in fornication, adultery, and all uncleanliness.
Measure for Measure. Act ii, sc. 1, l. 80. [Elbow] The only use of "cardinally," for carnally, and of "uncleanliness."
Duke: Know you this woman?
Lucio: Carnally, she says.
Measure for Measure. Act v, sc. 1, l. 214. The only use of "carnally."
Carnal acts.—*Hamlet,* v, 2, 392.
Carnal cur.—*Richard III,* iv, 4, 56.
Carnal stings.—*Othello,* i, 3, 335. The only uses of "carnal."

4
See you the fornicatress be removed.
Measure for Measure. Act ii, sc. 2, l. 23. [Angelo] The only use of "fornicatress."

5
Condemn'd upon the act of fornication
To lose his head.
Measure for Measure. Act iv, sc. 1, l. 70. [Isabella]
Accuses him of fornication.—*Measure for Measure,* v, 1, 195; ii, 1, 80. See No. 3 above.
Given to fornications.—*The Merry Wives of Windsor,* v, 5, 166.
Bless me, what a fry of fornication is at door?
Henry VIII. Act v, sc. 4, l. 36. [Porter] The only uses of "fornication" and "fornications."

6
Lord, Lord! your worship 's a wanton!
The Merry Wives of Windsor. Act ii, sc. 2, l. 57. [Mistress Quickly]
The spirit of wantonness is, sure, scared out of him.
The Merry Wives of Windsor. Act iv, sc. 2, l. 223. [Mrs. Page]
I rather will suspect the sun with cold
Than thee with wantonness.
The Merry Wives of Windsor. Act iv, sc. 4, l. 7. [Ford]

7
He hath not yet made wanton the night with her; and she is sport for Jove . . .
I 'll warrant her, full of game.
Othello. Act ii, sc. 3, l. 15. [Iago]
O, 'tis the spite of hell, the fiend's arch-mock,
To lip a wanton in a secure couch,
And to suppose her chaste!
Othello. Act iv, sc. 1, l. 71. [Iago] The only use of "arch-mock."

8
All the impure blots and stains thereof.
Richard III. Act iii, sc. 7, l. 234. [Gloucester] The only use of "impure" in the plays. It appears in *Venus and Adonis,* l. 766, and in *The Rape of Lucrece,* l. 1078. "Impurity" does not appear in the plays, but once in *The Rape of Lucrece,* l. 854.

9 Her wanton spirits look out
At every joint and motive of her body.
Troilus and Cressida. Act iv, sc. 5, l. 56. [Ulysses]
Wanton air.—*The Passionate Pilgrim,* l. 230.
Wanton dalliance.—*I Henry VI,* v, 1, 23.
Wanton sight.—*The Rape of Lucrece,* l. 104.
Wanton talk.—*Venus and Adonis,* l. 809.
Wanton tricks.—*The Rape of Lucrece,* l. 320.

10 You 'ld wanton with us,
If we would have you.
The Winter's Tale. Act ii, sc. 1, l. 18. [Lady]
Play the wantons.—*Richard II,* iii, 3, 164.

WAR

See also Army, Battle, Soldier

11 It may well serve
A nursery to our gentry, who are sick
For breathing and exploit.
All 's Well that Ends Well. Act i, sc. 2, l. 15. [Lord]
O, 'tis brave wars!
Most admirable: I have seen those wars.
All 's Well that Ends Well. Act ii, sc. 1, l. 26. [Parolles]
Expertness in wars.—*All 's Well that Ends Well,* iv, 3, 202. "Expertness" is repeated in iv, 3, 296, and occurs in no other play.

12
To the wars, my boy, to the wars!
All 's Well that Ends Well. Act ii, sc. 3, l. 295. [Parolles]
We must all to the wars.
I Henry IV. Act ii, sc. 4, l. 595. [Prince]
Some to the wars, to try their fortunes there.
The Two Gentlemen of Verona, i, 3, 8. See under HOME.
She 'll to the wars.—*I Henry IV,* iii, 1, 195.
Go to war.—*Troilus and Cressida,* ii, 3, 145; *Othello,* i, 3, 257; *Antony and Cleopatra,* ii, 2, 66.

13 O you leaden messengers,
That ride upon the violent speed of fire,
Fly with false aim; move the still-peering air,
That sings with piercing; do not touch my lord.
All 's Well that Ends Well. Act iii, sc. 2, l. 111. [Helena] The only use of "still-peering."
Write, write, that from the bloody course of war
My dearest master, your dear son, may hie.
All 's Well that Ends Well. Act iii, sc. 4, l. 8. [Steward]
Bloody courses.—*II Henry IV,* i, 1, 159.

14 Many hot inroads
They make in Italy; the borders maritime

Lack blood to think on 't.
Antony and Cleopatra. Act i, sc. 4, l. 50. [Messenger] The only use of "inroads," and "maritime."

You were the word of war.
Antony and Cleopatra. Act ii, sc. 2, l. 44. [Cæsar]

That magical word of war.
Antony and Cleopatra. Act iii, sc. 1, l. 31. [Ventidius] The only use of "magical."

The brave squares of war.—*Antony and Cleopatra,* iii, 11, 40.

The front of war.—*Antony and Cleopatra,* v, 1, 44.

Prepared for war.—*Antony and Cleopatra,* iii, 6, 58.

1 Wars 'twixt you twain would be
As if the world should cleave, and that slain men
Should solder up the rift.
Antony and Cleopatra. Act iii, sc. 4, l. 30. [Octavia] The only use of "solder." "Solder'st" occurs in *Timon of Athens,* iv, 3, 388: "Solder'st close impossibilities."

A charge we bear i' the war,
And, as the president of my kingdom, will
Appear there for a time.
Antony and Cleopatra. Act iii, sc. 7, l. 17. [Cleopatra] The only use of "president."

O love,
That thou couldst see my wars to-day, and knew'st
The royal occupation! thou shouldst see
A workman in 't.
Antony and Cleopatra. Act iv, sc. 4, l. 15. [Antony]

You shall see
How hardly I was drawn into this war.
Antony and Cleopatra. Act v, sc. 1, l. 73. [Cæsar]

2
Were half to half the world by the ears and he
Upon my party, I 'ld revolt, to make
Only my wars with him.
Coriolanus. Act i, sc. 1, l. 237. [Coriolanus]

The present wars devour him.
Coriolanus. Act i, sc. 1, l. 262. [Brutus]

Present wars.—*Othello,* i, 3, 235; *Cymbeline,* iv, 3, 43.

3 Mend and charge home,
Or, by the fires of heaven, I 'll leave the foe
And make my wars on you.
Coriolanus. Act i, sc. 4, l. 38. [Marcius]

He has been bred i' the wars
Since he could draw a sword.
Coriolanus. Act iii, sc. 1, l. 320. [Menenius]

Honour and policy, like unsever'd friends,
I' the war do grow together.
Coriolanus. Act iii, sc. 2, l. 42. [Volumnia] The only use of "unsever'd."

The end of war 's uncertain.
Coriolanus. Act v, sc. 3, l. 141. [Volumnia]

Pouring war
Into the bowels of ungrateful Rome,
Like a bold flood o'er-bear.
Coriolanus. Act iv, sc. 5, l. 135. [Aufidius]

You are to know
That prosperously I have attempted and
With bloody passage led your wars even to
The gates of Rome.
Coriolanus. Act v, sc. 6, l. 74. [Coriolanus] "Prosperously" occurs again in *Hamlet,* ii, 2, 214.

4 I do believe,
Statist though I am none, nor like to be,
That this will prove a war.
Cymbeline. Act ii, sc. 4, l. 15. [Posthumus] "Statist," which Shakespeare uses in the sense of statesman, is repeated in *Hamlet,* v, 2, 33.

War and confusion
In Cæsar's name pronounce I 'gainst thee: look
For fury not to be resisted.
Cymbeline. Act iii, sc. 1, l. 66. [Lucius]

5
Fearful wars point at me.
Cymbeline. Act iv, sc. 3, l. 7. [Cymbeline]

Fearful war.—*II Henry IV,* iv, 1, 63.
Brief wars.—*Coriolanus,* i, 3, 112.
Contumelious, beastly, mad-brain'd war.—*Timon of Athens,* v, 1, 177.
Cruel war.—*Troilus and Cressida,* Prol., 5; *Coriolanus,* i, 3, 15.
Dangerous wars.—*Titus Andronicus,* iii, 1, 3.
Dreadful war.—*III Henry VI,* i, 1, 187.
Fell war.—*III Henry VI,* ii, 5, 13.
Inward wars.—*II Henry IV,* iii, 1, 107.
Just and charitable war.—*King John,* ii, 1, 36.
Lasting war.—*Richard III,* iv, 4, 344.
Mortal war.—*Sonnets,* xlvi.
Needful war.—*III Henry VI,* ii, 1, 147.
None-sparing war.—*All's Well that Ends Well,* iii, 2, 108. The only use of the phrase.
Open war.—*III Henry VI,* i, 2, 19.
Pelting wars.—*Troilus and Cressida,* iv, 5, 267.
Petty war.—*Antony and Cleopatra,* ii, 1, 34.
Public war.—*Pericles,* i, 2, 104.
Revengeful war.—*Titus Andronicus,* iv, 3, 32.
Roaring war.—*The Tempest,* v, 1, 44.
Smoky war.—*I Henry IV,* iv, 1, 114.
Successful wars.—*Titus Andronicus,* i, 1, 172.
Wasteful war.—*Sonnets,* lv.
Weary wars.—*Titus Andronicus,* i, 1, 28.
Cupid's wars.—*Pericles,* i, 1, 38.
Morning's war.—*III Henry VI,* ii, 5, 1.

6
No more shall trenching war channel her fields,
Nor bruise her flowerets with the armed hoofs
Of hostile paces.
I Henry IV. Act i, sc. 1, l. 7. [King Henry] The only use of "trenching." "Flowerets" occurs again in *A Midsummer-Night's Dream,* iv, 1, 60.

The edge of war, like an ill-sheathed knife,
No more shall cut his master.
I Henry IV. Act i, sc. 1, l. 17. [King Henry] The only use of "ill-sheathed."

7
In thy faint slumbers I by thee have watch'd,
And heard thee murmur tales of iron wars;
Speak terms of manage to thy bounding steed;
Cry 'Courage! to the field!' And thou hast talk'd

Of sallies and retires, of trenches, tents,
Of palisadoes, frontiers, parapets,
Of basilisks, of cannon, culverin,
Of prisoners' ransom and of soldiers slain,
And all the currents of a heady fight.
I Henry IV. Act ii, sc. 3, l. 50. [Lady Percy] The only use of "sallies," "palisadoes," "parapets," and "culverin." "Heady" is repeated in *Henry V,* i, 1, 34, and iii, 3, 32.

He doth fill fields with harness in the realm,
Turns head against the lion's armed jaws,
And, being no more in debt to years than thou,
Leads ancient lords and reverend bishops on
To bloody battles and to bruising arms.
I Henry IV. Act iii, sc. 2, l. 101. [King Henry]

At war.—*I Henry IV,* ii, 3, 59; *II Henry IV,* iii, 1, 60; *Measure for Measure,* ii, 2, 33.

1 The mailed Mars shall on his altar sit
Up to the ears in blood.
I Henry IV. Act iv, sc. 1, l. 116. [Hotspur]

Will you again unknit
This churlish knot of all-abhorred war?
I Henry IV. Act v, sc. 1, l. 15. [King Henry] The only use of "all-abhorred."

You cast the event of war.
II Henry IV. Act i, sc. 1, l. 166. [Morton]

This Hydra son of war.
II Henry IV. Act iv, sc. 2, l. 38. [Archbishop of York]

2 O yet, for God's sake, go not to these wars!
II Henry IV. Act ii, sc. 3, l. 9. [Lady Percy]

Is there not wars?—*II Henry IV,* i, 2, 85.

3 Let us sway on and face them in the field.
II Henry IV. Act iv, sc. 1, l. 24. [Mowbray]

Their neighing coursers daring of the spur,
Their armed staves in charge, their beavers down,
Their eyes of fire sparkling through sights of steel
And the loud trumpet blowing them together.
II Henry IV. Act iv, sc. 1, l. 119. [Mowbray]

4 We doubt not of a fair and lucky war.
Henry V. Act ii, sc. 2, l. 184. [King Henry]

The signs of war advance.
Henry V. Act ii, sc. 2, l. 192. [King Henry]

Never war advance
His bleeding sword 'twixt England and fair France.
Henry V. Act v, sc. 2, l. 382. [French King]

5 This hungry war Opens his vasty jaws.
Henry V. Act ii, sc. 4, l. 104. [Exeter]

What is it then to me, if impious war,
Array'd in flames like to the prince of fiends,
Do, with his smirch'd complexion, all fell feats
Enlink'd to waste and desolation?
Henry V. Act iii, sc. 3, l. 15. [King Henry] The only use of "enlink'd."

Look to see
The blind and bloody soldier with foul hand
Defile the locks of your shrill-shrieking daughters;
Your fathers taken by the silver beards,
And their most reverend heads dash'd to the walls,
Your naked infants spitted upon pikes.
Henry V. Act iii, sc. 3, l. 33. [King Henry] The only use of "shrill-shrieking" and "spitted."

Blood and destruction shall be so in use
And dreadful objects so familiar
That mothers shall but smile when they behold
Their infants quarter'd with the hands of war.
Julius Cæsar. Act iii, sc. 1, l. 265. [Antony]

6 Rush on his host, as doth the melted snow
Upon the valleys, whose low vassal seat
The Alps doth spit and void his rheum upon.
Henry V. Act iii, sc. 5, l. 50. [French King]

It is the greatest admiration in the universal world, when the true and aunchient prerogatifes and laws of the wars is not kept: . . . There is no tiddle taddle nor pibble pabble in Pompey's camp; I warrant you, you shall find the ceremonies of the wars, and the cares of it, and the forms of it, and the sobriety of it, and the modesty of it, to be otherwise.
Henry V. Act iv, sc. 1, l. 66. [Fluellen] The only use of "tiddle taddle" and "pibble pabble." "Aunchient" is repeated in iii, 2, 83: "Aunchient wars," and occurs in no other play.

7 One would have lingering wars with little cost.
I Henry VI. Act i, sc. 1, l. 74. [Messenger]

8 Nor men nor money hath he to make war.
I Henry VI. Act i, sc. 2, l. 17. [Reignier]

Make war.—*III Henry VI,* ii, 2, 31; *Richard II,* iii, 2, 133; *Antony and Cleopatra,* ii, 2, 50; iv, 12, 15; *Pericles,* i, 2, 45.

Making war.—*The Comedy of Errors,* iii, 2, 127.

Make war upon themselves.—*Richard III,* ii, 4, 62.

Make War with mankind.—*Macbeth,* ii, 4, 18.

Make no wars.—*Antony and Cleopatra,* ii, 1, 13.

I made these wars for Egypt and the queen,—
Whose heart I thought I had, for she had mine.
Antony and Cleopatra. Act iv, sc. 14, l. 15. [Antony]

Made wars.—*Antony and Cleopatra,* ii, 2, 95; iii, 5, 4.

9 Nay, then, I see our wars
Will turn unto a peaceful comic sport,
When ladies crave to be encounter'd with.
I Henry VI. Act ii, sc. 2, l. 45. [Burgundy] "Comic" is repeated in *III Henry VI,* v, 7, 43: "Mirthful comic shows."

10 You tempt the fury of my three attendants,
Lean famine, quartering steel, and climbing fire;
Who in a moment even with the earth
Shall lay your stately and air-braving towers.
I Henry VI. Act iv, sc. 2, l. 10. [Talbot] The only use of "quartering" and "air-braving."

We will plague thee with incessant wars.
I Henry VI. Act v, sc. 4, l. 154. [York]

11 Wilt thou go dig a grave to find out war,

And shame thine honourable age with blood?
II Henry VI. Act v, sc. 1, l. 169. [King Henry]

O war, thou son of hell,
Whom angry heavens do make their minister,
Throw in the frozen bosoms of our part
Hot coals of vengeance!
II Henry VI. Act v, sc. 2, l. 33. [Clifford]

1
First shall war unpeople this my realm.
III Henry VI. Act i, sc. 1, l. 126. [King Henry]

It is war's prize to take all vantages.
III Henry VI. Act i, sc. 4, l. 59. [Northumberland]

Dreadful war shall answer his demand.
III Henry VI. Act iii, sc. 3, l. 259. [Warwick]

We shall have more wars before 't be long.
III Henry VI. Act iv, sc. 6, l. 91. [Somerset]

2
With himself at war.
Julius Cæsar. Act i, sc. 2, l. 46. [Brutus]

Why should I war without the walls of Troy,
That find such cruel battle here within?
Troilus and Cressida. Act i, sc. 1, l. 2. [Troilus]

3
The proud control of fierce and bloody war.
King John. Act i, sc. 1, l. 17. [Chatillon]

Here have we war for war and blood for blood,
Controlment for controlment.
King John. Act i, sc. 1, l. 19. [King John]

Now the manage of two kingdoms must
With fearful bloody issue arbitrate.
King John. Act i, sc. 1, l. 37. [Queen Elinor]

Blood hath bought blood and blows have answer'd blows;
Strength match'd with strength, and power confronted power.
King John. Act ii, sc. 1, l. 329. [Citizen]

Then defy each other, and pell-mell
Make work upon ourselves, for heaven or hell.
King John. Act ii, sc. 1, l. 406. [Bastard] "Pell-mell" is used five times.

Cry 'havoc,' kings!—*King John,* ii, 1, 357. See Havoc.

4
Away, and glister like the god of war,
When he intendeth to become the field.
King John. Act v, sc. 1, l. 54. [Bastard]

The stern and direful god of war,
Whose sinewy neck in battle ne'er did bow.
Venus and Adonis, l. 98.

The god of war.—*Titus Andronicus,* iv, 2, 95.

5
Your breath first kindled the dead coal of wars
Between this chastised kingdom and myself,
And brought in matter that should feed this fire;
And now 'tis far too huge to be blown out
With that same weak wind which enkindled it.
King John. Act v, sc. 2, l. 83. [Dauphin] "Enkindled" is repeated in *Julius Cæsar,* ii, 1, 249, and in *Troilus and Cressida,* ii, 2, 63.

Maintain this war.—*King John,* v, 2, 102.

This gallant head of war.
King John. Act v, sc. 2, l. 113. [Pandulph]

This dwarfish war, these pigmy arms.
King John. Act v, sc. 2, l. 135. [Bastard]

Strike up the drums; and let the tongue of war
Plead for our interest and our being here.
King John. Act v, sc. 2, l. 164. [Dauphin]

Leave this war.—*King John,* v, 7, 86.

6
Have you heard of no likely wars toward?
King Lear. Act ii, sc. 1, l. 11. [Edmund]

7 Bellona's bridegroom, lapp'd in proof,
Confronted him with self-comparisons,
Point against point rebellious, arm 'gainst arm,
Curbing his lavish spirit.
Macbeth. Act i, sc. 2, l. 54. [Ross] The only use of "Bellona" and "self-comparisons."

He Prepares for some attempt of war.
Macbeth. Act iii, sc. 6, l. 38. [Lord]

8
There is a kind of merry war betwixt Signior Benedick and her.
Much Ado about Nothing. Act i, sc. 1, l. 62. [Leonato]

9
Follow thou the wars.
Othello. Act i, sc. 3, l. 345. [Iago]

The wars must make examples Out of their best.
Othello. Act iii, sc. 3, l. 65. [Desdemona]

10
Go to the wars, would you? where a man may serve seven years for the loss of a leg, and have not money enough in the end to buy him a wooden one?
Pericles. Act iv, sc. 6, l. 180. [Boult] The only use of "wooden."

11 A woman's war,
The bitter clamour of two eager tongues.
Richard II, i, 1, 48. See under Tongue.

12 With boisterous untuned drums,
With harsh-resounding trumpets' dreadful bray,
And grating shock of wrathful iron arms.
Richard II. Act i, sc. 3, l. 134. [King Richard] The only use of "harsh-resounding." "Grating" is repeated in *Hamlet,* iii, 1, 3; and "untuned" in *The Comedy of Errors,* v, 1, 310, and in *King Lear,* iv, 7, 16.

With eight tall ships, three thousand men of war.
Richard II. Act ii, sc. 1, l. 286. [Northumberland] See under Ship.

Why have they dared to march
So many miles upon her peaceful bosom,
Frighting her pale-faced villages with war
And ostentation of despised arms?
Richard II. Act ii, sc. 3, l. 92. [York]

He is come to open
The purple testament of bleeding war.
Richard II. Act iii, sc. 3, l. 93. [King Richard]

13
Grim-visaged war hath smooth'd his wrinkled front.
Richard III. Act i, sc. 1, l. 9. [Gloucester] The only use of "grim-visaged."

Soon that war had end.—*Antony and Cleopatra,* i, 2, 95.

Our wars are done.—*Othello,* ii, 1, 20.
Our sharp wars are ended.—*Troilus and Cressida,* v, 9, 10.

1
During the wars of York and Lancaster.
Richard III. Act i, sc. 4, l. 15. [Clarence]
Cyprus wars.—*Othello,* i, 1, 151.
Gallia wars.—*Henry V,* v, 1, 94.
Irish wars.—*Richard II,* i, 4, 62; ii, 1, 259; *I Henry IV,* iv, 3, 88; v, 1, 53.
Polack wars.—*Hamlet,* v, 2, 387. "Polack" is used five times in *Hamlet,* and in no other play.
Tuscan wars.—*All's Well that Ends Well,* ii, 3, 290.
Wars in France.—*Henry VIII,* i, 2, 60.
War with God.—*Richard III,* i, 4, 260.

2
Dangerous success of bloody wars.
Richard III. Act iv, sc. 4, l. 236. [King Richard]
Bloody war.—*II Henry VI,* iv, 4, 12.

3 Put thy fortune to the arbitrement
Of bloody strokes and mortal-staring war.
Richard III. Act v, sc. 3, l. 89. [Derby] The only use of "mortal-staring."
The arbitrement is like to be bloody.
King Lear. Act iv, sc. 7, l. 95. [Gentleman]

4 Wherefore do not you a mightier way
Make war upon this bloody tyrant, Time?
Sonnets. No. xvi.
Greater war.—*Antony and Cleopatra,* ii, 7, 10.

5
Such war of white and red within her cheeks!
The Taming of the Shrew, iv, 5, 30. See under CHEEK.
War of white and damask.—*Coriolanus,* ii, 1, 232.

6 Time it is, when raging war is done,
To smile at scapes and perils overblown.
The Taming of the Shrew. Act v, sc. 2, l. 2. [Lucentio]
Offer war.—*Taming of the Shrew,* v, 2, 162.

7
Now good or bad, 'tis but the chance of war.
Troilus and Cressida, Prol., 31.
The chance of war.—*I Henry IV,* i, 3, 95; *Titus Andronicus,* i, 1, 264; *Cymbeline,* v, 5, 75.
Fortuna de la guerra.
Loves Labour's Lost. Act v, sc. 2, l. 533. [Armado] Quoted as a proverb.
State of war.—*Troilus and Cressida,* i, 3, 191; ii, 3, 271.
The stroke of war.—*I Henry VI,* v, 3, 155; *Timon of Athens,* v, 4, 22.
The trade of war.—*Othello,* i, 2, 1.

8 Like as there were husbandry in war,
Before the sun rose he was harness'd light,
And to the field goes he; where every flower
Did, as a prophet, weep what it foresaw.
Troilus and Cressida. Act i, sc. 2, l. 7. [Alexander] The only use of "foresaw."
Consumed
In hot digestion of this cormorant war.
Troilus and Cressida. Act ii, sc. 2, l. 5. [Priam] Shakespeare used "cormorant" as an adjective four times.
In that I'll war with you.
Troilus and Cressida. Act iii, sc. 2, l. 178. [Cressida]
My little stomach to the war.
Troilus and Cressida. Act iii, sc. 3, l. 220. [Patroclus]

9
I bring no overture of war, no taxation of homage.
Twelfth Night. Act i, sc. 5, l. 224. [Viola]

10
O, what a war of looks was there between them!
Venus and Adonis, l. 355. See under EYE.

II—Civil War

11 The intestine shock
And furious close of civil butchery.
I Henry IV. Act i, sc. 1, l. 12. [King Henry] "Intestine" is used a second time in *The Comedy of Errors.* i, 1, 11: "Intestine jars."

12
Cease this civil war.
III Henry VI. Act i, sc. 1, l. 197. [King Henry]
Such civil war is in my love and hate.
Sonnets. No. xxxv.
Civil war.—*III Henry VI,* ii, 5, 77; *Henry V,* v, 2, 243; *King John,* iii, 1, 264; *Love's Labour's Lost,* ii, 1, 226.

13
Domestic fury and fierce civil strife
Shall cumber all the parts of Italy.
Julius Cæsar. Act iii, sc. 1, l. 263. [Antony] "Cumber" is repeated in *Timon of Athens,* iii, 6, 52.

14 For our eyes do hate the dire aspect
Of civil wounds plough'd up with neighbours' sword.
Richard II. Act i, sc. 3, l. 127. [King Richard]

15
March on, march on, since we are up in arms;
If not to fight with foreign enemies,
Yet to beat down these rebels here at home.
Richard III. Act iv, sc. 4, l. 530. [King Richard]

16
With man's blood paint the ground, gules, gules:
Religious canons, civil laws are cruel;
Then what should war be?
Timon of Athens. Act iv, sc. 3, l. 59. [Timon]
Head to foot, now is he total gules.
Hamlet, ii, 2, 479. The only uses of "gules."

17 Like a boar too savage, doth root up
His country's peace.
Timon of Athens, v, 1, 168. [Senator]

18
Civil home-bred strife.
Venus and Adonis, l. 764. "Home-bred" is repeated in *Richard II,* i, 3, 187: "Home-bred hate"; and in *III Henry VI,* iv, 1, 38: "Home-bred marriage."

III—War and Peace

1 What would you have, you curs,
That like nor peace nor war? the one affrights you,
The other makes you proud.
Coriolanus. Act i, sc. 1, l. 172. [Marcius]

If it be honour in your wars to seem
The same you are not, which, for your best ends,
You adopt your policy, how is it less or worse,
That it shall hold companionship in peace
With honour, as in war, since that to both
It stands in like request?
Coriolanus. Act iii, sc. 2, l. 46. [Volumnia]

Second Servant: This peace is nothing, but to rust iron, increase tailors, and breed ballad-makers.
First Servant: Let me have war, say I; it exceeds peace as far as day does night; it 's sprightely, waking, audible, and full of vent. Peace is a very apoplexy, lethargy; mulled, deaf, sleepy, insensible; a getter of more bastard children than war 's a destroyer of men.
Second Servant: 'Tis so: and as war, in some sort, may be said to be a ravisher, so it cannot be denied but peace is a great maker of cuckolds.
First Servant: Ay, and it makes men hate one another.
Third Servant: Reason; because they then less need one another. The wars for my money.
Coriolanus. Act iv, sc. 5, l. 234. "Audible" is repeated in *Measure for Measure,* v, 1, 413, and "ravisher" in *Titus Andronicus,* v, 2, 103. The only use of "mulled."

Nature,
Not to be other than one thing, not moving
From the casque to the cushion, but commanding peace
Even with the same austerity and garb
As he controll'd the war.
Coriolanus. Act iv, sc. 7, l. 41. [Aufidius] "Austerity" is repeated in *A Midsummer-Night's Dream,* i, 1, 90, and in *The Taming of the Shrew,* iv, 4, 7.

Though I cannot make true wars,
I 'll frame convenient peace.
Coriolanus. Act v, sc. 3, l. 190. [Coriolanus]

Never was a war did cease,
Ere bloody hands were wash'd, with such a peace.
Cymbeline. Act v, sc. 5, l. 484. [Cymbeline]

2 You, lord archbishop,
Whose see is by a civil peace maintain'd,
Whose beard the silver hand of peace hath touch'd,
Whose learning and good letters peace hath tutor'd,
Whose white investments figure innocence,
The dove and very blessed spirit of peace,
Wherefore do you so ill translate yourself
Out of the speech of peace that bears such grace,
Into the harsh and boisterous tongue of war;
Turning your books to graves, your ink to blood,
Your pens to lances and your tongue divine
To a loud trumpet and a point of war?
II Henry IV. Act iv, sc. 1, l. 41. [Westmoreland] "Investments" is repeated in *Hamlet,* i, 3, 128.

War, or peace, or both at once, may be
As things acquainted and familiar to us.
II Henry IV. Act v, sc. 2, l. 138. [King Henry V]

3
Peace itself should not so dull a kingdom,
Though war nor no known quarrel were in question,
But that defences, musters, preparations,
Should be maintain'd, assembled and collected,
As were a war in expectation.
Henry V. Act ii, sc. 4, l. 16. [Dauphin]

Once more unto the breach, dear friends, once more;
Or close the wall up with our English dead.
In peace there 's nothing so becomes a man
As modest stillness and humility:
But when the blast of war blows in our ears,
Then imitate the action of the tiger.
Henry V. Act iii, sc. 1, l. 1. [King Henry]

Making the wars their bulwark, that have before gored the gentle bosom of peace with pillage and robbery.
Henry V. Act iv, sc. 1, l. 175. [King Henry]

4
One that still motions war and never peace,
O'ercharging your free purses with large fines.
I Henry VI. Act i, sc. 3, l. 64. [Winchester] The only use of "o'ercharging."

To ease your country of distressful war,
And suffer you to breathe in fruitful peace.
I Henry VI. Act v, sc. 4, l. 126. [Beaufort]

5
Thus war hath given thee peace, for thou art still.
Peace with his soul, heaven, if it be thy will!
II Henry VI. Act v, sc. 2, l. 29. [York]

6
Smooth the frowns of war with peaceful looks.
III Henry VI. Act ii, sc. 6, l. 32. [Edward]

7
From a resolved and honourable war,
To a most base and vile-concluded peace.
King John. Act ii, sc. 1, l. 585. [Bastard] The only use of "vile-concluded."

The grappling vigour and rough frown of war
Is cold in amity and painted peace.
King John. Act iii, sc. 1, l. 104. [Constance] The only use of "grappling."

War! war! no peace! peace is to me a war.
King John. Act iii, sc. 1, l. 113. [Constance]

Therefore thy threatening colours now wind up:
And tame the savage spirit of wild war,
That, like a lion foster'd up at hand,
It may lie gently at the foot of peace.
King John. Act v, sc. 2, l. 73. [Pandulph]

Now for the bare-pick'd bone of majesty
Doth dogged war bristle his angry crest
And snarleth in the gentle eyes of peace.
King John. Act iv, sc. 3, l. 148. [Bastard] The only use of "bare-pick'd."

1
Welcome is peace, if he on peace consist;
If wars, we are unable to resist.
Pericles. Act i, sc. 4, l. 83. [Cleon]

2
Peace shall go sleep with Turks and infidels,
And in this seat of peace tumultuous wars
Shall kin with kin and kind with kind confound;
Disorder, horror, fear and mutiny
Shall here inhabit, and this land be call'd
The field of Golgotha and dead men's skulls.
Richard II. Act iv, sc. 1, l. 139. [Bishop of Carlisle]

Memorize another Golgotha.
Macbeth. Act i, sc. 2, l. 40. [Sergeant] The only reference to Golgotha.

3
In God's name, cheerly on, courageous friends,
To reap the harvest of perpetual peace
By this one bloody trial of sharp war.
Richard III. Act v, sc. 2, l. 14. [Richmond]

Make war breed peace, make peace stint war, make each
Prescribe to other as each other's leech.
Timon of Athens. Act v, sc. 4, l. 83. [Alcibiades] The only use of "leech."

WARBLE, see Song

WARNING

4
Our hearts receive your warnings.
All's Well that Ends Well. Act ii, sc. 1, l. 22. [Lords]

God warn us!—*As You Like It,* iv, 1, 77.

5
You were fore-advised.
Coriolanus. Act ii, sc. 3, l. 199. [Sicinius] The only use of "fore-advised."

6
Look to it well and say you are well warn'd.
I Henry VI. Act ii, sc. 4, l. 103. [Plantagenet]

But say, I warn'd ye;
Take heed, for heaven's sake, take heed.
Henry VIII. Act iii, sc. 1, l. 109. [Queen Katharine]

Be warned by me.—*Henry V,* iii, 7, 60.

7
Thy grave admonishments prevail with me.
I Henry VI. Act ii, sc. 5, l. 98. [Plantagenet]

When was my lord so much ungently temper'd,
To stop his ears against admonishment?
Troilus and Cressida. Act iv, sc. 3, l. 1. [Andromache] The only uses of "admonishment" and "admonishments."

8
Somewhat too sudden, sirs, the warning is.
I Henry VI. Act v, sc. 3, l. 14. [Charles]

I think he had a very fair warning.
II Henry VI. Act iv, sc. 6, l. 12. [Smith]

9
Well, I will arm me, being thus forewarn'd.
III Henry VI. Act iv, sc. 1, l. 113. [King Edward]

We were forewarned of your coming.
III Henry VI. Act iv, sc. 7, l. 17. [Mayor of York] The only uses of "forewarned." "Forewarn" appears but once, in *The Winter's Tale,* iv, 4, 215.

You might
The better arm you to the sudden time,
Than if you had at leisure known of this.
King John. Act v, sc. 6, l. 25. [Hubert]

10
Beware the ides of March.
Julius Cæsar. Act i, sc. 2 ,l. 18. [Soothsayer]

Cæsar: The ides of March are come.
Soothsayer: Ay, Cæsar; but not gone.
Julius Cæsar. Act iii, sc. 1, l. 1.

Remember March, the ides of March remember.
Julius Cæsar. Act iv, sc. 3, l. 18. [Brutus]

11 Warnings, and portents,
And evils imminent.
Julius Cæsar. Act ii, sc. 2, l. 80. [Cæsar]

Do not presume too much upon my love;
I may do that I shall be sorry for.
Julius Cæsar. Act iv, sc. 3, l. 63. [Cassius]

12
Who is it that hath warn'd us to the walls?
King John. Act ii, sc. 1, l. 201. [Citizen]

I would not have you, lord, forget yourself,
Nor tempt the danger of my true defence;
Lest I, by marking of your rage, forget
Your worth, your greatness and nobility.
King John. Act iv, sc. 3, l. 83. [Hubert]

13
I have told you what I have seen and heard; but faintly, nothing like the image and horror of it.
King Lear. Act i, sc. 2, l. 190. [Edmund]

14
He has given him warning.
Measure for Measure. Act iii, sc. 2, l. 36. [Elbow]

I give thee warning.—*Timon of Athens,* i, 2, 33.

He would . . . take no warning.—*Timon of Athens,* iii, 1, 28.

15
Double and treble admonition.
Measure for Measure. Act iii, sc. 2, l. 205. [Escalus]

Frozen admonition.—*Richard II,* ii, 1, 118. The only uses of "admonition."

16
And I to Ford shall eke unfold
How Falstaff, varlet vile,
His dove will prove, his gold will hold,
And his soft couch defile.
The Merry Wives of Windsor. Act i, sc. 3, l. 105. [Pistol]

17
Cough, or cry 'hem,' if any body come.
Othello. Act iv, sc. 2, l. 29. [Othello]

18
I charge you, as you hope to have redemption
By Christ's dear blood shed for our grievous sins,
That you depart and lay no hands on me.
Richard III. Act i, sc. 4, l. 194. [Clarence]

19
The boy gives warning something doth approach.
Romeo and Juliet. Act v, sc. 3, l. 18. [Paris]

20
Now let me see if I can construe it: 'Hic ibat Simois,' I know you not, 'hic est Sigeia

tellus,' I trust you not; 'Hic steterat Priami,' take heed he hear us not, 'regia,' presume not, 'celsa senis,' despair not.
The Taming of the Shrew. Act iii, sc. 1, l. 41. [Bianca] The Latin is from Ovid's *Heroides,* Bk. i, ll. 33, 34: "Here flowed the Simois; this is the Sigeian land; here stood the lofty palace of the ancient Priam."
Slender warning.—*The Taming of the Shrew,* iv, 4, 60.
At an hour's warning.—*Coriolanus,* iv, 3, 50.

WARRANT

See also Surety

1 A doubtful warrant of immediate death.
Comedy of Errors, i, 1, 69. See LIGHT, 870:4.
Upon warrant of bloody affirmation.
Cymbeline. Act i, sc. 4, l. 63. [Frenchman]

2 Upon thy princely warrant, I descend
To give thee answer of thy just demand.
I Henry VI. Act v, sc. 3, l. 143. [Reignier]
Christian warrant.—*Henry VIII,* iii, 2, 244.
External warrants.—*Measure for Measure,* ii, 4, 137.
Further warrant.—*Much Ado about Nothing,* iii, 2, 115.
Good warrant.—*The Tempest,* iii, 3, 49.
Lively warrant.—*Titus Andronicus,* v, 3, 44.
Modest warrant.—*Coriolanus,* iii, 1, 276.
Strong warrant.—*Richard II,* iv, 1, 235.
Warrant, quittance.—*The Merry Wives of Windsor,* i, 1, 10.

3 I 'll warrant they 'll make it good.
II Henry VI. Act v, sc. 1, l. 122. [York] "I 'll warrant," or "I warrant" is repeated frequently throughout the plays.
I 'll not warrant that.—*Measure for Measure,* ii, 4, 59.
I warrant thee.—*II Henry VI,* iv, 3, 19, and ten times in later plays.
I warrant you.—*I Henry VI,* i, 4, 21, and forty-two times in later plays.

4 Here is a warrant from The king.
Henry VIII. Act i, sc. 1, l. 216. [Brandon]

5 I hope your warrant will bear out the deed.
King John. Act iv, sc. 1, l. 6. [Executioner]
Give us warrant.—*King John,* v, 2, 66.
Here 's the warrant.—*Measure for Measure,* iv, 2, 66.
Showed him a seeming warrant.—*Measure for Measure,* iv, 2, 160.
The warrant 's come.—*Measure for Measure,* iv, 3, 44.
The warrant 's for yourself.—*Measure for Measure,* v, 1, 83.

6 Had you a special warrant for the deed?
Measure for Measure. Act v, sc. 1, l. 464. [Duke]
Warrant for blame.—*Rape of Lucrece,* l. 620.
Warrant of my note.—*King Lear,* iii, 1, 18.
Warrant of her virginity.—*Pericles,* iv, 2, 63.
Warrant of womanhood.—*The Merry Wives of Windsor,* iv, 2, 220.
Wisdom's warrant.—*Love's Labour 's Lost,* v, 2, 71.
God warrant us.—*Midsummer-Night's Dream,* v, 1, 326.
Lord warrant us!—*As You Like It,* iii, 3, 5.

7 I give thee warrant of thy place.
Othello. Act iii, sc. 3, l. 20. [Desdemona]
Out of warrant.—*Othello,* i, 2, 79.

8 With such general warranty of heaven.
Othello. Act v, sc. 2, l. 60. [Desdemona]
As far . . . As we have warranty.
Hamlet, v, 1, 250. See under FUNERAL.
I have a warranty.—*The Merchant of Venice,* i, 1, 132. The only uses of "warranty."
Having a warrant for it.—*Richard III,* i, 4, 112.
Having no warrant.—*Winter's Tale,* ii, 2, 58.

9 Such strength and warrantize of skill.
Sonnets. No. cl.
I 'll be your warrantize.—*I Henry VI,* i, 3, 13. The only uses of "warrantize."

WARRIOR

See also Soldier

10 That most famous warrior,
Duke Menaphon, your most renowned uncle.
The Comedy of Errors. Act v, sc. 1, l. 368. [Antipholus of Ephesus] The only mention of Menaphon.

11 Thou art my warrior; I holp to frame thee.
Coriolanus. Act v, sc. 3, l. 62. [Volumnia]
Flower of warriors.—*Coriolanus,* i, 6, 32.
O my fair warrior!—*Othello,* ii, 1, 184.

12 This Hotspur, Mars in swathling clothes,
This infant warrior.
I Henry IV. Act iii, sc. 2, l. 112. [King Henry] The only use of "swathling clothes." "Swathing-clothes" occurs in *Cymbeline,* i, 1, 59.
I saw him hold Lord Percy at the point
With lustier maintenance than I did look for
Of such an ungrown warrior.
I Henry IV. Act v, sc. 4, l. 21. [King] The only use of "ungrown."

13 We are but warriors for the working-day;
Our gayness and our gilt are all besmirch'd
With rainy marching in the painful field.
Henry V. Act iv, sc. 3, l. 109. [King Henry] The only use of "gayness." "Gaiety" does not occur at all.
Bastard warriors.—*Henry V,* iii, 5, 31.

14 Honoured
To feast so great a warrior in my house.
I Henry VI. Act ii, sc. 3, l. 81. [Count]

15 And when the hardiest warriors did retire,
Richard cried 'Charge! and give no foot of ground!'
III Henry VI. Act i, sc. 4, l. 14. [York]
Approved warriors.—*Titus Andronicus,* v, 1, 1.
Brave warriors.—*III Henry VI,* i, 4, 66; ii, 1, 209; iv, 8, 64.
Gallant warriors.—*I Henry IV,* iv, 4, 26.
Warriors all.—*Henry V,* iv, 3, 10.

1
Women and children of so high a courage,
And warriors faint! why, 'twere perpetual shame.
III Henry VI. Act v, sc. 4, l. 50. [Oxford]
2
Fierce fiery warriors fought upon the clouds.
Julius Cæsar, ii, 2, 19. See under OMEN.
3
Unhandsome warrior that I am.
Othello. Act iii, sc. 4, l. 151. [Desdemona]
4
The painful warrior famoused for fight,
After a thousand victories once foil'd,
Is from the book of honour razed quite,
And all the rest forgot for which he toil'd.
Sonnets. No. xxv. The only use of "famoused."
5
I 'll make you feed on berries and on roots,
And feed on curds and whey, and suck the goat,
And cabin in a cave, and bring you up
To be a warrior, and command a camp.
Titus Andronicus. Act iv, sc. 2, l. 177. [Aaron] The only use of "whey." "Curds" occurs five times.
6 Let an old man embrace thee;
And, worthy warrior, welcome to our tents.
Troilus and Cressida. Act iv, sc. 5, l. 199. [Nestor]

WASHING

See also Cleanliness

7
Wash your liver as clean as a sound sheep's heart.
As You Like It. Act iii, sc. 2, l. 442. [Rosalind]
Washes all the air.—*A Midsummer-Night's Dream,* ii, 1, 104.
Wash the blood away.—*III Henry VI,* i, 4, 158.
Wash this cold congealed blood.—*III Henry VI,* v, 2, 37.
Wash my brain.—*Antony and Cleopatra,* ii, 7, 105.
Washes bucks.—*II Henry VI,* iv, 2, 51.
Wash the eyes of kings.—*Antony and Cleopatra,* v, 1, 28.
8
I have not wash'd My nose that bled.
Coriolanus. Act i, sc. 9, l. 47. [Marcius]
I will go wash.—*Coriolanus,* i, 9, 63.
9 Bid them wash their faces
And keep their teeth clean.
Coriolanus. Act ii, sc. 3, l. 66. [Coriolanus]
Go, wash thy face, and draw the action.
II Henry IV. Act ii, sc. 1, l. 162. [Falstaff]
When was he wont to wash his face?
Much Ado about Nothing. Act iii, sc. 2, l. 56. [Claudio]
He swears
Never to wash his face, nor cut his hairs.
Pericles. Act iv, sc. 4, l. 27. [Gower]
Wash the foul face of the sluttish ground.
Venus and Adonis, l. 983.
10
Wash it white as snow.
Hamlet, iii, 3, 46. See under HAND.
Wash her clean.—*Much Ado about Nothing,* iv, 1, 143.
11
Washing with kindly tears his gentle cheeks.
II Henry IV, iv, 5, 84. See under TEAR.
Washing thy wound.—*II Henry IV,* ii, 1, 99.
Wash'd his knife.—*II Henry IV,* iv, 5, 87.
Wash'd in Lethe.—*II Henry IV,* v, 2, 72.
Wash'd As pure as sin.—*Henry V,* i, 2, 31.
Not wash'd to-day—*Love's Labour 's Lost,* iv, 3, 273.
Washed and cudgelled.—*The Merry Wives of Windsor,* iv, 5, 99.
Wash'd it with tears.—*Much Ado about Nothing,* iv, 1, 156.
Wash'd to death.—*Richard III,* v, 3, 132.
Wash'd with the farthest sea.—*Romeo and Juliet,* ii, 2, 83.
Wash'd thy sallow cheeks.—*Romeo and Juliet,* ii, 3, 70.
Wash'd with dew.—*The Taming of the Shrew,* ii, 1, 174.
12 Go get some water,
And wash this filthy witness from your hand.
Macbeth. Act ii, sc. 2, l. 46. [Macbeth]
Wash your blood From off my hands.
Richard II, iii, 1, 5. See under BLOOD.
Wash this blood from off my guilty hand.
Richard II, v, 6, 50. See under BLOOD.
How fain, like Pilate, would I wash my hands.
Richard III. Act i, sc. 4, l. 279. [Murderer]
Some of you with Pilate wash your hands.
Richard II, iv, 1, 239. See under SIN.
Will 't please your mightiness to wash your hands?
The Taming of the Shrew. Induction, sc. 2, l. 78. [Servant]
Go home, call for sweet water, wash thy hands.
Titus Andronicus, ii, 4, 6. See under HAND.
Wash my fierce hand.—*Coriolanus,* i, 10, 27.
Wash our hands.—*King John,* iii, 1, 234.
Wash their hands.—*Titus Andronicus,* ii, 3, 45.
Wash your hands.—*Richard II,* iv, 1, 239; *Macbeth,* v, 1, 68.
Washes his hands.—*I Henry IV,* ii, 4, 116.
Washing her hands.—*Macbeth,* v, 1, 33.
Bloody hands were wash'd.—*Cymbeline,* v, 5, 485.
How prettily the young swain seems to wash
The hand was fair before!
The Winter's Tale. Act iv, sc. 4, l. 376. [Polixenes]
13
I wash, wring, brew.
The Merry Wives of Windsor. Act i, sc. 4, l. 101. See under SERVANT.
Wash myself.—*The Merry Wives of Windsor,* iii, 3, 167.
14
I am half afraid he will have need of washing.
The Merry Wives of Windsor. Act iii, sc. 3, l. 193. [Mrs. Ford]
15
Wash me in steep-down gulfs of liquid fire!
Othello, v, 2, 280. See REMORSE, 1260:8.

1
A plague on them, they ne'er come but I look to be washed.
Pericles. Act ii, sc. 1, l. 28. [Fisherman]

2
Wash the balm off from an anointed king.
Richard II, iii, 2, 55. See under KING.

Wash away my balm.—*Richard II,* iv, 1, 207.
Thy balm wash'd off.—*III Henry VI,* iii, 1, 17.
Wash you off.—*III Henry VI,* v, 4, 31.
Wash'd off.—*Henry V,* iv, 1, 101.

3
Wash him fresh again with true-love tears.
Richard II, v, 1, 10. See under TEAR.

4
Shall I have some water?
Come, Kate, and wash.
The Taming of the Shrew. Act iv, sc. 1, l. 156. [Petruchio]

Wash dish.—*The Tempest,* ii, 2, 187.

5
Why, she was wash'd and cut and trimm'd.
Titus Andronicus, v, 1, 95. See under SPORT.

6
I will wash off gross acquaintance.
Twelfth Night, ii, 5, 176. See under BEHAVIOUR. "Wash off" is repeated in iii, 2, 27.

Wash'd off.—*Romeo and Juliet,* ii, 3, 76.
Wash away.—*Richard II,* iv, 1, 240.
Wash'd away.—*I Henry IV,* iii, 2, 137; *Love's Labour's Lost,* iv, 3, 271.

7
Speed: 'She can wash and scour.'
Launce: A special virtue; for then she need not be washed and scoured.
The Two Gentlemen of Verona. Act iii, sc. 1, l. 313.

WASP

8
There be moe wasps that buzz about his nose
Will make this sting the sooner.
Henry VIII. Act iii, sc. 2, l. 55. [Suffolk]

9
In thy weak hive a wandering wasp hath crept,
And suck'd the honey which thy chaste bee kept.
The Rape of Lucrece, l. 839.

Injurious wasps, to feed on such sweet honey
And kill the bees that yield it with your stings.
The Two Gentlemen of Verona. Act i, sc. 2, l. 106. [Julia]

10
Petruchio: Come, come, you wasp; i' faith, you are too angry.
Katharina: If I be waspish, best beware my sting.
Petruchio: My remedy is then, to pluck it out.
Katharina: Ay, if the fool could find it where it lies.
Petruchio: Who knows not where a wasp does wear his sting? In his tail.
The Taming of the Shrew. Act ii, sc. 1, l. 210.

Waspish action.—*As You Like It,* ii, 3, 132.
When you are waspish.—*Julius Cæsar,* iv, 3, 50. The only uses of "waspish."
Tails of wasps.—*The Winter's Tale,* i, 2, 329.

11
But when ye have the honey ye desire,
Let not this wasp outlive, us both to sting.
Titus Andronicus. Act ii, sc. 3, l. 131. [Tamora]

WASTE

12
Your means are very slender, and your waste is great.
II Henry IV, i, 2, 160. See under WAIST.

Waste and desolation.—*Henry V,* iii, 3, 18.

13
So shall he waste his means.
Julius Cæsar, iv, 3, 200. See under ENEMY.

Waste of his revenues.—*King Lear,* ii, 1, 102.
By inches waste you.—*Cymbeline,* v, 5, 52.
Waste inwardly.—*Much Ado about Nothing,* iii, 1, 78.

14
You but waste your words.
Measure for Measure, ii, 2, 72. See under WORD.

15
Help to waste His borrow'd purse.
The Merchant of Venice, ii, 5, 50. See under PURSE.

Made waste.—*The Merchant of Venice,* i, 1, 157.

16
Waste no time in words.
The Merchant of Venice, iii, 4, 54. For "wasting time" see TIME: ITS LOSS.

Waste night, day and time.—*Hamlet,* ii, 2, 89.
Thou among the wastes of time must go.
Sonnets. No. xii.
Waste of shame.—*Sonnets,* cxxix.

17
I am now about no waste; I am about thrift.
The Merry Wives of Windsor, i, 3, 47. See under WAIST.

He will never, I think, in the way of waste, attempt us again.
The Merry Wives of Windsor. Act iv, sc. 2, l. 226. [Mrs. Page]

18
I have wasted myself out of my means.
Othello, iv, 2, 187. See under PRODIGALITY.

19
The waste is no whit lesser than thy land.
Richard II. Act ii, sc. 1, l. 103. [Gaunt]

20
We waste our lights in vain.
Romeo and Juliet, i, 4, 45. See under DELAY.

Huge waste.—*Romeo and Juliet,* i, 1, 224.

21
Makest waste in niggarding.
Sonnets. No. i. The only use of "niggarding."

22
He owes nine thousand; besides my former sum,
Which makes it five and twenty. Still in motion
Of raging waste? It cannot hold; it will not.
Timon of Athens. Act ii, sc. 1, l. 2. [Senator]

Wast'd, thaw'd, and done.—*Venus and Adonis,* l. 749.

WATCHING

See also Spy

1
I 'll watch him
Till he be dieted to my request.
Coriolanus. Act v, sc. 1, l. 56. [Menenius]
I 'll watch him tame.—*Othello,* iii, 3, 23.
Well worth watching.—*Cymbeline,* ii, 4, 68.

2
Break we our watch up.
Hamlet. Act i, sc. 1, l. 168. [Horatio]
Give her good watch.—*Hamlet,* iv, 5, 75.
Kept the watch.—*Hamlet,* i, 2, 208.

3
Hold you the watch to-night?
Hamlet. Act i, sc. 2, l. 225. [Hamlet]
I will watch to-night.—*Hamlet,* i, 2, 242.
I have watch'd the night.—*II Henry VI,* iii, 1, 110.
For all the frosty nights that I have watch'd.
Titus Andronicus. Act iii, sc. 1, l. 5. [Titus]
She shall watch all night.—*The Taming of the Shrew,* iv, 1, 208.
To watch the night.—*The Taming of the Shrew,* v, 2, 150.
The watch of night.—*II Henry IV,* iv, 5, 28.
Watch to-night, pray to-morrow.—*I Henry IV,* ii, 4, 306.
Watch'd the winter's night.—*III Henry VI,* v, 7, 17.
Watch you to-night.—*Othello,* ii, 1, 271.
This odd-even and dull watch o' the night.
Othello. Act i, sc. 1, l. 124. [Roderigo] The only use of "odd-even."
Ten nights' watchings.—*Much Ado about Nothing,* ii, 1, 387.

4
Our watch-word was 'Hem boys!'
II Henry IV. Act iii, sc. 2, l. 231. [Shallow] The only use of "watch-word."
Whan I give the watch-'ords, do as I pid you.
The Merry Wives of Windsor. Act v, sc. 4, l. 3. [Evans] The only use of "watch-words."

5
Even these three days have I watch'd.
I Henry VI. Act i, sc. 4, l. 16. [Gunner]
I have two nights watched with you.
Macbeth. Act v, sc. 1, l. 1. [Doctor]
I have watch'd and travell'd hard.
King Lear. Act ii, sc. 2, l. 162. [Kent]

6
Now do thou watch, for I can stay no longer.
I Henry VI. Act i, sc. 4, l. 18. [Gunner]
Constrain'd to watch in darkness, rain, and cold.
I Henry VI. Act ii, sc. 1, l. 7. [Sentinel]
Watch your pleasure.—*Julius Cæsar,* iv, 3, 249.
Stand my watch.—*Macbeth,* v, 5, 33.

7
The special watchman of our English weal.
I Henry VI. Act iii, sc. 1, l. 66. [King]
An ancient and most quiet watchman.—*Much Ado about Nothing,* iii, 3, 42.
Play the watchman.—*Sonnets,* lxi.
Watchman to my heart.—*Hamlet,* i, 3, 46. The only uses of "watchman." "Watchmen" occurs in *Antony and Cleopatra,* iv, 3, 18.

8
Watch thou and wake when others be asleep.
II Henry VI. Act i, sc. 1, l. 249. [York]
For some must watch, and some must sleep.
Hamlet, iii, 2, 284. See under WORLD.

9
Be heedful: hence, and watch.
King John. Act iv, sc. 1, l. 5. [Hubert]

10
Watch me like Argus.
The Merchant of Venice. Act v, sc. 1, l. 230. [Portia]
Though Argus were her eunuch.—*Love's Labour's Lost,* iii, 1, 201.
Purblind Argus.—*Troilus and Cressida,* i, 2, 31. The only references to Argus.
To watch, like one that fears robbing.
The Two Gentlemen of Verona, ii, 1, 25. See under LOVE.

11
I think we have watched you now.
The Merry Wives of Windsor. Act v, sc. 5, l. 107. [Page]

12
We must to the watch.
Othello. Act ii, sc. 3. l. 12. [Cassio]
I must to the watch.—*Othello,* ii, 3, 340.
Let 's set the watch.—*Othello,* ii, 3, 125.
Here 's a goodly watch indeed!—*Othello,* ii, 3, 160.

13
Watch the horologe a double set.
Othello, ii, 3, 135. See under DRINKING. The only use of "horologe" (clock).
Watch the clock.—*Sonnets,* lvii.

14
Watching breeds leanness, leanness is all gaunt.
Richard II. Act ii, sc. 1, l. 78. [Gaunt]

15
Use careful watch, choose trusty sentinels.
Richard III. Act v, sc. 3, l. 54. [King Richard]
Careful watch.—*Antony and Cleopatra,* iv, 3, 7.
Advised watch.—*Merchant of Venice,* i, 1, 142.
Catlike watch.—*As You Like It,* iv, 3, 116. The only use of "catlike."
Monstrous watch.—*I Henry IV,* ii, 4, 530.
Most observant watch.—*Hamlet,* i, 1, 71.
Outward watch.—*Richard II,* v, 5, 52.
Slothful watch.—*I Henry VI,* iii, 2, 7.

16
He and I Will watch thy waking.
Romeo and Juliet. Act iv, sc. 1, l. 115. [Friar Laurence]
I have watch'd ere now
All night for lesser cause.
Romeo and Juliet. Act iv, sc. 4, l. 9. [Capulet]
I will watch you from such watching now.
Romeo and Juliet. Act iv, sc. 4, l. 12. [Capulet]
I 'll watch you better yet.—*The Taming of the Shrew,* iii, 1, 50.

17
I must wait, and watch withal.
The Taming of the Shrew. Act iii, sc. 1, l. 61. [Lucentio]
Watch . . . narrowly.—*The Taming of the Shrew,* iii, 2, 141.
Watch our vantage.—*The Taming of the Shrew,* iii, 2, 146.
Watch your safety.—*The Tempest,* ii, 1, 198.

18
Another way I have to man my haggard,
To make her come and know her keeper's call,

That is, to watch her, as we watch these kites
That bate and beat and will not be obedient.
The Taming of the Shrew. Act iv, sc. 1, l. 196. [Petruchio] "Haggard" (wild female hawk, caught when in aduly plumage) is used five times in the plays.

You watch'd her well.—*II Henry VI,* i, 4, 58.

1
Cressida: At all these wards I lie, at a thousand watches.
Pandarus: Say one of your watches.
Cressida: Nay, I 'll watch you for that; and that 's one of the chiefest of them too: if I cannot ward what I would not have hit, I can watch you for telling how I took the blow; unless it swell past hiding, and then it 's past watching.
Troilus and Cressida. Act i, sc. 2, l. 287.

What, are you gone again? you must be watched ere you be made tame, must you?
Troilus and Cressida. Act iii, sc. 2, l. 45. [Pandarus]

2
Perchance wind up my watch.
Twelfth Night, ii, 5, 66. See under FROWN.

Winding up the watch of his wit.
The Tempest, ii, 1, 12. See under WIT.

Watchers of mine own heart's sorrow.
The Two Gentlemen of Verona, ii, 4, 135. See under LOVE.

Show us to be watchers.—*Macbeth,* ii, 2, 71. The only uses of "watchers."

WATER

See also Fire and Water

3
Too much of water hast thou, poor Ophelia.
Hamlet. Act iv, sc. 7, l. 186. [Laertes]

Your water is a sore decayer of your whoreson dead body.
Hamlet. Act v, sc. 1, l. 188. [Clown] The only use of "decayer."

Water swells a man.—*The Merry Wives of Windsor,* iii, 5, 16.

Will she hold out water?—*I Henry IV,* ii, 1, 93.

Full of water.—*Richard II,* iv, 1, 187.

4
Falstaff: Sirrah, you giant, what says the doctor to my water?
Page: He said, sir, the water itself was a good healthy water; but, for the party that owed it, he might have more diseases than he knew for.
II Henry IV. Act i, sc. 2, l. 1.

Carry his water to the wise woman.
Twelfth Night. Act iii, sc. 4, l. 114. [Fabian]

I would not so much as make water but in a sink-a-pace.
Twelfth Night. Act i, sc. 3, l. 139. [Sir Toby] The only use of "sink-a-pace" (cinquepace).

When didst thou see me heave up my leg and make water against a gentlewoman's farthingale? didst thou ever see me do such a trick?
Twe Gentlemen of Verona. Act iv, sc. 4, l. 41. [Launce] "Farthingale" is repeated in ii, 7, 51, and in *Merry Wives of Windsor,* iii, 3, 69.

It is certain that when he makes water his urine is congealed ice.
Measure for Measure. Act iii, sc. 2, l. 117. [Lucio]

Others, when the bagpipe sings i' the nose,
Cannot contain their urine.
The Merchant of Venice. Act iv, sc. 1, l. 49. [Shylock] "Urine" is used a third time in *Macbeth,* ii, 3, 32.

5
By water shall he die and take his end.
II Henry VI. Act i, sc. 4, l. 34. [Spirit] Repeated in l. 68.

A cunning man did calculate my birth
And told me that by water I should die.
II Henry VI. Act iv, sc. 1, l. 34. [Suffolk]

6
Smooth runs the water where the brook is deep.
II Henry VI. Act iii, sc. 1, l. 53. [Suffolk]

Deep sounds make lesser noise than shallow fords.
The Rape of Lucrece, l. 1329.

7
Much rain wears the marble.
III Henry VI, iii, 2, 50. [Gloucester]

Waste huge stones with little water-drops.
The Rape of Lucrece, l. 959.

When waterdrops have worn the stones of Troy.
Troilus and Cressida. Act iii, sc. 2, l. 193. [Cressida] "Water-drop" is repeated in *Richard II,* iv, 1, 262, and in *King Lear,* ii, 4, 280.

Stone at rain relenteth.—*Venus and Adonis,* l. 200.

8
Court holy-water in a dry house is better than this rain-water out o' door.
King Lear. Act iii, sc. 2, l. 10. [Fool] The only use of "rain-water."

Holy water.—*Titus Andronicus,* i, 1, 323; *Cymbeline,* v, 5, 269.

9
Drinks the green mantle of the standing pool.
King Lear. Act iii, sc. 4, l. 138. [Edgar]

Sebastian: Well, I am standing water.
Antonio: I 'll teach you how to flow.
The Tempest. Act ii, sc. 1, l. 221.

Standing water.—*Twelfth Night,* i, 5, 168.

10
A little water clears us of this deed.
Macbeth, ii, 2, 67. See under DEED.

Go get some water.—*Macbeth,* ii, 2, 46.

Shall I have some water?—*The Taming of the Shrew,* iv, 1, 156.

11
Now will I raise the waters.
The Merchant of Venice. Act ii, sc. 2, l. 51. [Launcelot]

12
Throw cold water.
The Merry Wives of Windsor. Act ii, sc. 3, l. 89. [Host]

Cold water.—*Timon of Athens,* v, 1, 77.

Luke-warm water.—*Timon of Athens,* iii, 6, 99. "Lukewarm" (unhyphenated) is repeated in *III Henry VI,* i, 2, 34: "Lukewarm blood."

Best water.—*Coriolanus,* ii, 3, 250.

Curled waters.—*King Lear,* iii, 1, 6.

Distilled waters.—*The Taming of the Shrew,* Ind., 1, 48.

Fresh water.—*The Tempest,* i, 2, 160.

Frozen water.—*Titus Andronicus,* iii, 1, 252.
Humming water.—*Pericles,* iii, 1, 64. "Humming" is repeated in *The Tempest,* ii, 1, 317.
Interrupted waters.—*Coriolanus,* iii, 1, 249.
Roaring waters.—*The Merchant of Venice,* i, 1, 34; *Cymbeline,* iii, 1, 20.
Salt water.—*Richard II,* iv, 1, 245; *Romeo and Juliet,* ii, 3, 71; *The Tempest,* ii, 1, 64.
Sodden water.—*Henry V,* iii, 5, 18. "Sodden" is repeated in *Troilus and Cressida,* iii, 1, 44, and in *Pericles,* iv, 2, 21.
Still-closing waters.—*The Tempest,* iii, 3, 64. The only use of "still-closing."
Sweet water.—*Romeo and Juliet,* v, 3, 14; *Titus Andronicus,* ii, 4, 6.
Thames water.—*The Merry Wives of Windsor,* iii, 5, 23.
Unpath'd waters.—*The Winter's Tale,* iv, 4, 578. The only use of "unpath'd."
Weeping water.—*A Lover's Complaint,* l. 304.
Wild waters.—*The Tempest,* i, 2, 2.
Yielding water.—*Richard II,* iii, 3, 58.

1
Water cannot wash away your sin.
Richard II, iv, 1, 242. See under Sin.

2
The waters swell before a boisterous storm.
Richard III. Act ii, sc. 3, l. 44. [Citizen]
The bounded waters
Should lift their bosoms higher than the shores
And make a sop of all this solid globe.
Troilus and Cressida. Act i, sc. 3, l. 111. [Ulysses]

3
Love's fire heats water, water cools not love.
Sonnets. No. cliv.

4
Here 's that which is too weak to be a sinner, honest water, which ne'er left man i' the mire.
Timon of Athens. Act i, sc. 2, l. 58. [Apemantus]

5 More water glideth by the mill
Than wots the miller of.
Titus Andronicus. Act ii, sc. 1, l. 85. [Demetrius] First published in John Heywood's *Proverbs,* in 1546.

6
Nay, I am for all waters.
Twelfth Night. Act iv, sc. 2, l. 68. [Clown]
Above water.—*The Winter's Tale,* iv, 4, 281.

II—Water: Tears

See also Tear

7
Where be the sacred vials thou shouldst fill
With sorrowful water?
Antony and Cleopatra. Act i, sc. 3, l. 63. [Cleopatra]

8 There will be a world of water shed
Upon the parting of your wives and you.
I Henry IV. Act iii, sc. 1, l. 94. [Glendower]

9
The pretty and sweet manner of it forced
Those waters from me which I would have stopp'd;
But I had not so much of man in me,
And all my mother came into mine eyes
And gave me up to tears.
Henry V. Act iv, sc. 6, l. 28. [Exeter]
Let not women's weapons, water-drops,
Stain my man's cheeks!
King Lear. Act ii, sc. 4, l. 280. [King Lear]

10 What I should say
My tears gainsay; for every word I speak,
Ye see, I drink the water of mine eyes.
III Henry VI. Act v, sc. 4, l. 73. [Queen Margaret]

11
Trust not those cunning waters of his eyes,
For villany is not without such rheum;
And he, long traded in it, makes it seem
Like rivers of remorse and innocency.
King John. Act iv, sc. 3, l. 107. [Salisbury] "Traded" is repeated in *Troilus and Cressida,* ii, 2, 64.

12
Command these fretting waters from your eyes
With a light heart.
Measure for Measure. Act iv, sc. 3, l. 151. [Duke]

13
How much salt water thrown away in waste!
Romeo and Juliet, ii, 3, 71. See under Tear.

WAVE

See also Sea

14
As good to chide the waves as speak them fair.
III Henry VI. Act v, sc. 4, l. 24. [Queen Margaret]
Stem the waves.—*III Henry VI,* ii, 6, 36.

15 Though the yesty waves
Confound and swallow navigation up.
Macbeth. Act iv, sc. 1, l. 53. [Macbeth] "Yesty" is repeated in *Hamlet,* v, 2, 199.

16
The chidden billow seems to pelt the clouds;
The wind-shaked surge, with high and monstrous mane,
Seems to cast water on the burning bear,
And quench the guards of the ever-fixed pole.
Othello. Act ii, sc. 1, l. 12. [Second Gentleman] "Pelt" is used again in *I Henry VI,* iii, 1, 82. The only use of "wind-shaked." "Wind-shaken" occurs in *Coriolanus,* v, 2, 117; and "ever-fixed" again in *Sonnets,* cxvi.
I never saw so huge a billow.
Pericles. Act iii, sc. 2, l. 58. [Servant]
Tumbling billows of the main.
Richard III, i, 4, 20. See under Sea.
Billows of the sea.—*Henry VIII,* iii, 1, 10.
Cloudy billow.—*Pericles,* iii, 1, 46.
Inconstant billows.—*Henry V,* iii, Prol., 15.
Ruffian billows.—*II Henry IV,* iii, 1, 22.
Neptune's billow.—*Pericles,* iii, Gower, 45.

17
By waves from coast to coast is tost.
Pericles, ii, Gower, 34.
Never was waves nor wind more violent;
And from the ladder-tackle washes off

A canvas-climber.
Pericles. Act iv, sc. 1, l. 60. [Marina] The only use of "ladder-tackle" and "canvas-climber."

1 Like Arion on the dolphin's back,
I saw him hold acquaintance with the waves.
Twelfth Night. Act i, sc. 2, l. 15. [Captain] The only mention of Arion.

The wild waves . . .
Whose ridges with the meeting clouds contend.
Venus and Adonis, l. 819.

Wild waves.—*The Tempest,* i, 2, 379.
Bold waves.—*The Tempest,* i, 2, 205.
Contentious waves.—*The Tempest,* ii, 1, 118.
Over-matching waves.—*III Henry VI,* i, 4, 21. The only use of "over-matching."
Ruthless waves.—*III Henry VI,* v, 4, 36.
Salt wave.—*Love's Labour's Lost,* v, 1, 61; *Twelfth Night,* iii, 4, 419.
Silver waves.—*The Comedy of Errors,* iii, 2, 48.
Waves of Tiber.—*Julius Cæsar,* i, 2, 114.
Wave o' the sea.—*The Winter's Tale,* iv, 4, 141.

WAVERING, see Indecision

WAX

2
I nor wax nor honey can bring home.
All's Well that Ends Well, i, 2, 65. See under Death.

Our thighs pack'd with wax.—*II Henry IV,* iv, 5, 77.
Bee's wax.—*II Henry VI,* iv, 2, 89.

3
He waxed like a sea.
Coriolanus, ii, 2, 103. See under Growth.

Wax'd calm.—*The Comedy of Errors,* i, 1, 92.
Waxed pale.—*The Two Gentlemen of Verona,* iii, 1, 228.
Wax'd shorter.—*Timon of Athens,* iii, 4, 11. The only uses of "waxed."
Waxeth strong.—*Venus and Adonis,* l. 420. The only use of "waxeth."

4 Good wax, thy leave. Blest be
You bees that make these locks of counsel!
Cymbeline. Act iii, sc. 2, l. 35. [Imogen]

Leave, gentle wax; and, manners, blame us not.
King Lear. Act iv, sc. 6, l. 264. [Edgar]

By your leave, wax. Soft! and the impressure her Lucrece, with which she uses to seal.
Twelfth Night. Act ii, sc. 5, l. 102. [Malvolio]

Break the neck of the wax.—*Love's Labour's Lost,* iv, 1, 59.

5 Set this up with wax
Upon old Brutus' statue.
Julius Cæsar. Act i, sc. 3, l. 145. [Cassius]

Take with wax.—*Timon of Athens,* v, 3, 6.
With wax.—*Timon of Athens,* v, 4, 68.

6
That was the way to make his godhead wax.
Love's Labour's Lost, v, 2, 10. See under Growth.

The elder I wax the better I shall appear.
Henry V, v, 2, 247. See under Age.

Old I do wax.—*Henry V,* v, 1, 89.
Wax dim.—*I Henry VI,* ii, 5, 9.
Wax great.—*II Henry VI,* iv, 10, 22.
Wax hollow.—*Henry V,* v, 2, 170.
Wax mad.—*Titus Andronicus,* iii, 1, 223.
Wax poor.—*Hamlet,* iii, 1, 101.
He waxes desperate.—*Hamlet,* i, 4, 87.
It waxes late.—*Romeo and Juliet,* i, 5, 128.

7
No more than wax shall be accounted evil
Wherein is stamp'd the semblance of a devil
The Rape of Lucrece, l. 1245.

8 Steel my lance's point,
That it may enter Mowbray's waxen coat.
Richard II. Act i, sc. 3, l. 74. [Bolingbroke]

Waxen epitaph.—*Henry V,* i, 2, 233.
Waxen hearts.—*Twelfth Night,* ii, 2, 31.
Waxen image.—*The Two Gentlemen of Verona,* ii, 4, 201.
Waxen tapers.—*The Merry Wives of Windsor,* iv, 4, 50.
Waxen thighs.—*A Midsummer-Night's Dream,* iii, 1, 172.
Waxen torch.—*The Rape of Lucrece,* l. 178.
Waxen minds.—*The Rape of Lucrece,* l. 1240.
Waxen deaf.—*II Henry VI,* iii, 2, 76.
Waxen in their mirth.—*A Midsummer-Night's Dream,* ii, 1, 56. The only uses of "waxen."

9
What wax so frozen but dissolves with tempering?
Venus and Adonis, l. 565. "Tempering" is repeated in *II Henry IV,* iv, 3, 140, and in *Romeo and Juliet,* ii, Prol., 14.

Be as wax.—*Hamlet,* iii, 4, 84.
Her wax must melt.—*III Henry VI,* iii, 2, 51.
Soft as wax.—*Titus Andronicus,* iii, 1, 45.
Softer than wax.—*Passionate Pilgrim,* l. 88.
Wrought . . . like wax.—*III Henry VI,* ii, 1, 171.
A form in wax.—*A Midsummer-Night's Dream,* i, 1, 49.
A form of wax.—*King John,* v, 4, 24; *Romeo and Juliet,* iii, 3, 126.
A man of wax.—*Romeo and Juliet,* i, 3, 76.
A wide sea of wax.—*Timon of Athens,* i, 1, 47.

WAY

See also Course, Method, Path, Road

10 This drivest me to entreat you
That presently you take your way for home.
All's Well that Ends Well. Act ii, sc. 5, l. 68. [Helena]

You know the way home again.
Coriolanus. Act v, sc. 2, l. 103. [Senator]

The next way home.—*Winter's Tale,* iii, 3, 131.
Next way.—*I Henry IV,* ii, 1, 10; iii, 1, 264; *All's Well that Ends Well,* i, 3, 63; *Othello,* i, 3, 205.
Direct way.—*Coriolanus,* ii, 3, 25.
Downright way.—*Measure for Measure,* iii, 2, 112.
Nearer way.—*Richard III,* iv, 4, 462.
Nearer this ways.—*The Merry Wives of Windsor,* ii, 2, 46.
Nearest way.—*Macbeth,* i, 5, 19.

Which is the readiest way To the house?
The Taming of the Shrew. Act i, sc. 2, l. 220. [Tranio]

Readiest way.—*Richard III,* i, 1, 155.

1
Helena: Is this the way?
Widow: Ay, marry, is 't.
All's Well that Ends Well. Act iii, sc. 5, l. 40.
This is the way.—*Titus Andronicus,* iv, 3, 1.
'Tis the way.—*Romeo and Juliet,* i, 1, 234.
That 's the way.—*Love's Labour 's Lost,* v, 1, 147; v, 2, 868; *Measure for Measure,* v, 1, 280; *Othello,* ii, 3, 393; *Antony and Cleopatra,* v, 2, 224.
I think it is our way.—*Richard III,* i, 1, 78.
That 's not your way.—*Othello,* iv, 1, 197.
This is not the way.—*Twelfth Night,* iii, 4, 121.
Was 't not the way?—*Macbeth,* iii, 3, 19.
That was the way.—*Love's Labour 's Lost,* v, 2, 10.

2
Let him have his way.
All's Well that Ends Well. Act iii, sc. 6, l. 2. [Lord]
Have his way.—*III Henry VI,* iii, 2, 139.
Let me have way.—*Measure for Measure,* v, 1, 238.

3
He can come no other way but by this hedge-corner.
All's Well that Ends Well. Act iv, sc. 1, l. 1. [Lord] "Hedge-corner" is repeated in *The Taming of the Shrew,* Ind., 1, 20.
Yonder he is coming, this way.
The Merry Wives of Windsor. Act iii, sc. 1, l. 27. [Simple]
I am glad I came this way so happily.
Henry VIII. Act v, sc. 2, l. 8. [Butts]
Come this way.—*II Henry VI,* i, 3, 2; *The Comedy of Errors,* v, 1, 120; *All's Well that Ends Well,* iii, 5, 40; *Timon of Athens,* i, 2, 137; *Twelfth Night,* i, 5, 324.
Come on your ways.—*The Tempest,* ii, 2, 85.
Come thy ways.—*As You Like It,* ii, 3, 66; *Twelfth Night,* ii, 5, 1.
Come your ways.—*As You Like It,* i, 2, 221; *Hamlet,* i, 3, 135; *King Lear,* ii, 2, 42; *Troilus and Cressida,* iii, 2, 47.
Step this way.—*The Merry Wives of Windsor,* iii, 3, 175.
That way are they coming.—*Macbeth,* v, 2, 6.

4
The flowery way that leads to the broad gate and the great fire.
All's Well that Ends Well. Act iv, sc. 5, l. 57. [Clown]
The primrose way to the everlasting bonfire.
Macbeth. Act ii, sc. 3, l. 21. [Porter]
Steep and thorny way to heaven.
Hamlet. Act i, sc. 3, l. 48. [Ophelia] See PREACHER, 1190:13.

5
In each thing give him way, cross him in nothing.
Antony and Cleopatra, i, 3, 9. [Charmian]
Gave him way In all his own desires.
Coriolanus, v, 6, 32. See under DESIRE.
It is not good to cross him; give him way.
Pericles. Act v, sc. 1, l. 232. [Lysimachus]
'Tis best to give him way.
King Lear. Act ii, sc. 4, l. 301. [Cornwall]
Give it way.—*The Tempest,* i, 2, 186.
Give me way.—*Coriolanus,* iv, 4, 25.
Give them way.—*Twelfth Night,* iii, 4, 217.
Give them instant way.—*King Lear,* v, 3, 149.
Fie! you must give way.—*Cymbeline,* i, 1, 158.
Give way.—*Richard III,* i, 3, 196, and fifteen times in later plays.
Given way.—*Much Ado about Nothing,* iv, 1, 158; *King Lear,* iii, 6, 5.
Yields him way.—*The Rape of Lucrece,* l. 309.

6
I am so lated in the world, that I
Have lost my way for ever.
Antony and Cleopatra. Act iii, sc. 11, l. 4. [Antony] "Lated" is repeated in *Macbeth,* iii, 3, 6.
You . . . cannot lose your way.
Coriolanus, v, 1, 60. See ROAD, 1295:11.
Lose my way.—*King John,* iv, 3, 140.

7
Forego The way that promises assurance.
Antony and Cleopatra. Act iii, sc. 7, l. 47. [Enobarbus]
Show me the way.—*Antony and Cleopatra,* iii, 10, 35.
Show me which way.—*Antony and Cleopatra,* iii, 7, 75.
Show us the way.—*Antony and Cleopatra,* ii, 6, 83.

8
I will seek Some way to leave him.
Antony and Cleopatra. Act iii, sc. 13, l. 201. [Enobarbus]

9
Bravest at the last,
She levell'd at our purposes, and, being royal,
Took her own way.
Antony and Cleopatra. Act v, sc. 2, l. 338. [Cæsar] "Levell'd" is repeated in *Much Ado about Nothing,* iv, 1, 239, and in *Timon of Athens,* i, 1, 47.
Take your own way.—*Cymbeline,* i, 5, 31.
Take the instant way.—*Troilus and Cressida,* iii, 3, 153.

10
Second Citizen: Which way do you judge my wit would fly?
Third Citizen: . . . If it were at liberty, 'twould, sure, southward.
Second Citizen: Why that way?
Third Citizen: To lose itself in a fog.
Coriolanus. Act ii, sc. 3, l. 27. "Southward" is repeated in *The Winter's Tale,* iv, 4, 819.

11
If you will pass
To where you are bound, you must inquire your way.
Coriolanus. Act iii, sc. 1, l. 53. [Sicinius]

12
The very way to catch them.
Coriolanus, iii, 1, 80. See under DISEASE.
This is the way to kindle, not to quench.
Coriolanus. Act iii, sc. 1, l. 197. [Menenius]
That is the way to lay the city flat.
Coriolanus, iii, 1, 204. See under CITY.
It is the humane way.—*Coriolanus,* iii, 1, 327.
We 'll proceed In our first way.
Coriolanus. Act iii, sc. 1, l. 334. [Sicinius]

13
To this day no guess is knowledge
Which way they went.
Cymbeline. Act i, sc. 1, l. 60. [Gentleman]
You know not which way you shall go.
Cymbeline. Act v, sc. 4, l. 181. [Gaoler]
Go all which way it will!
Richard II. Act ii, sc. 2, l. 87. [York]

Let it go which way it will.
II Henry IV, iii, 2, 254. See under DEATH.
Send him word by me which way you go.
King John. Act v, sc. 3, l. 7. [Messenger]
Which way would Hector have it?
Troilus and Cressida. Act iv, sc. 5, l. 71. [Agamemnon]
Now which way shall she turn?
Venus and Adonis, l. 253.
Which way?—*Romeo and Juliet,* v, 3, 168.
Which way hast thou been?—*Julius Cæsar,* ii, 4, 21.
Which way ran he?—*Romeo and Juliet,* iii, 1, 142; 143.
He ran this way.—*Romeo and Juliet,* ii, 1, 5.
This way she runs.—*Venus and Adonis,* l. 905.
Which is the way?—*Measure for Measure,* iii, 2, 53; *Cymbeline,* iv, 2, 291.
How or which way.—*I Henry VI,* ii, 1, 71; *Richard II,* ii, 2, 109.

1 Two beggars told me
I could not miss my way.
Cymbeline. Act iii, sc. 6, l. 8. [Imogen]
The only use of "miss my way."
He could not miss 't.—*The Tempest,* ii, 1, 40.

2
They must sweep my way.
Hamlet. Act iii, sc. 4, l. 204. [Hamlet]
Sweep your way.—*Antony and Cleopatra,* iii, 11, 17.

3
Give even way unto my rough affairs.
II Henry IV. Act ii, sc. 3, l. 2. [Northumberland]
Even way.—*Much Ado about Nothing,* iv, 1, 265.

4
I knew there was but one way.
Henry V, ii, 3, 16. See under DEATH.
One way.—*Antony and Cleopatra,* ii, 5, 116.

5
I will trot to-morrow a mile, and my way shall be paved with English faces.
Henry V. Act iii, sc. 7, l. 86. [Dauphin]

6
This way, . . . that way.
III Henry VI, ii, 5, 5. See under BATTLE.
Go you down that way towards the Capitol;
This way will I.
Julius Cæsar. Act i, sc. 1, l. 68. [Flavius]
You that way: we this way.
Love's Labour's Lost. Act v, sc. 2, l. 941. [Armado]
You that way and you this.
Timon of Athens. Act v, sc. 1, l. 109. [Timon]
That way, I'll this.—*King Lear,* iii, 1, 54.
Each his several way.—*Much Ado about Nothing,* v, 3, 29.
Several ways.—*I Henry VI,* ii, 1, 30.
Sundry ways.—*Macbeth,* iv, 3, 48.
Thousand ways.—*Venus and Adonis,* ll. 477, 907.

7
Let 's on our way.
III Henry VI. Act iv, sc. 2, l. 28. [Warwick]
She is two months on her way.
Love's Labour's Lost. Act v, sc. 2, l. 679. [Costard]
We will bring you on your way.
Love's Labour's Lost. Act v, sc. 2, l. 883. [King]
Blanca: I pray you, bring me on the way a little,
And say if I shall see you soon at night.
Cassio: 'Tis but a little way that I can bring you.
Othello. Act iii, sc. 4, l. 197.
I'll bring thee on thy way.
Richard II. Act i, sc. 3, l. 304. [Gaunt]
Meet you on the way.—*Richard III,* iv, 1, 51.
On your way.—*II Henry IV,* ii, 1, 73.
On my way.—*Pericles,* iv, Gower, 50.
On the way.—*Hamlet,* ii, 2, 330; iii, 1, 17; *King Lear,* iv, 2, 14; *Sonnets,* l.

8
This way, my lord; for this way lies the game.
III Henry VI, iv, 5, 14. See GAME, 600:6.
This way the king will come, this is the way
To Julius Cæsar's ill-erected tower.
Richard II. Act v, sc. 1, l. 1. [Queen]
This way, or not at all, stand you in hope.
Titus Andronicus. Act ii, sc. 1, l. 119. [Aaron]

9
In the way of loyalty and truth.
Henry VIII. Act iii, sc. 2, l. 272. [Wolsey]
Way of argument.—*Henry V,* iii, 2, 104.
Way of bargain.—*I Henry IV,* iii, 1, 139.
Way of blindness.—*Cymbeline,* v, 4, 197.
Way of caution.—*Hamlet,* i, 3, 95.
Way of flattery.—*Coriolanus,* iii, 2, 137.
Way of honesty.—*King John,* i, 1, 181; *The Merry Wives of Windsor,* ii, 2, 75; *Antony and Cleopatra,* v, 2, 253.
Perfect ways of honour.—*Henry VIII,* v, 5, 38.
Way of life.—*Macbeth,* v, 3, 22.
Way of life or death.—*Pericles,* i, 1, 54.
Way of nature.—*II Henry IV,* v, 2, 4.
Way of our profession.—*Henry VIII,* iii, 1, 157.
Way of taste.—*Troilus and Cressida,* iii, 3, 13.
Way of truth.—*Troilus and Cressida,* ii, 2, 189.
Way of winking.—*Cymbeline,* v, 4, 198.
Wanton way of youth.—*All's Well that Ends Well,* v, 3, 211.
Indirect crook'd ways.—*II Henry IV,* iv, 5, 185.
Way to death.—*Titus Andronicus,* iii, 1, 98.
Way to dusty death.—*Macbeth,* v, 5, 23.

10
Found thee a way, out of his wreck, to rise in;
A sure and safe one, though thy master miss'd it.
Henry VIII. Act iii, sc. 2, l. 437. [Wolsey]
Safest way.—*As You Like It,* i, 3, 137; *Macbeth,* ii, 3, 148.

11
Ye shall go my way.
Henry VIII. Act iv, sc. 1, l. 114. [Gentleman]
Go one way.—*Henry VIII,* v, 3, 36.
Go thy ways.—*The Taming of the Shrew,* iv, 5, 23, and twelve times in later plays.
Go your way.—*As You Like It,* iv, 3, 69, and three times in later plays.
He is gone this way.—*II Henry IV,* iv, 5, 56.

12 I know
A way, if it take right, in spite of fortune
Will bring me off again.
Henry VIII. Act iii, sc. 2, l. 218. [Wolsey]
Find a way.—*Henry VIII,* v, 4, 88.
Find his way.—*Hamlet,* ii, 1, 98.
Find the way.—*As You Like It,* ii, 4, 81.

Fled this way.—*King Lear,* ii, 1, 44.
Pass this way.—*The Winter's Tale,* iv, 4, 20.
Prepare the ways.—*Henry VIII,* iii, 2, 328.
Stop my way.—*Sonnets,* xliv.
Stop our way.—*Macbeth,* i, 3, 77.
Teach the way.—*The Rape of Lucrece,* l. 630.
Turn this way.—*III Henry VI,* i, 1, 189.
Work my way.—*The Rape of Lucrece,* l. 513.

1
Make way there for the princess.
Henry VIII. Act v, sc. 4, l. 91. [Porter]
Make way, unruly woman!—*Richard II,* v, 2, 110.
Make way.—*II Henry VI,* iv, 8, 62; *Coriolanus,* ii, 2, 40; *Titus Andronicus,* i, 1, 64; ii, 2, 24.
Make cruel way.—*Troilus and Cressida,* iv, 5, 184.
Come, I will make you way.
Hamlet. Act iv, sc. 6, l. 32. [Horatio]
Make his way.—*III Henry VI,* iv, 5, 10; *Henry VIII,* i, 1, 64.
Make my way long.—*Cymbeline,* iv, 2, 149.
Make thy way.—*King Lear,* v, 3, 29.

2
The way was made, And paved with gold.
Henry VIII. Act i, sc. 1, l. 187. [Buckingham]
I have made my way.—*Othello,* v, 2, 263.

3
Out of my way.
Julius Cæsar. Act iii, sc. 1, l. 46. [Cæsar]
Out of our way.—*The Tempest,* i, 1, 29.
Out of the way.—*Julius Cæsar,* iii, 1, 26; *Othello,* i, 3, 366; iii, 1, 40; iii, 4, 80; iv, 2, 7.

4
I have a way to win their loves again.
King John. Act iv, sc. 2, l. 168. [King John]

5
That way madness lies.
King Lear, iii, 4, 21. See under MADNESS.

6
Old Man: Alack, sir, you cannot see your way.
Gloucester: I have no way, and therefore want no eyes.
King Lear. Act iv, sc. 1, l. 19.
See his way.—*The Two Gentlemen of Verona,* ii, 4, 94.

7
Gloucester: Know'st thou the way to Dover?
Edgar: Both stile and gate, horse-way, and foot-path.
King Lear. Act iv, sc. 1, l. 58. The only use of "horse-way."
Foot-path way.—*The Winter's Tale,* iv, 3, 132. The only uses of "foot-path."

8
One way I like this well; . . .
Another way, The news is not so tart.
King Lear. Act iv, sc. 2, l. 83. [Goneril] "Tart" (grievous) is repeated in *Antony and Cleopatra,* ii, 5, 38.
I must another way.
Romeo and Juliet. Act ii, sc. 5, l. 74. [Nurse] "Another way" is used eight times.
Some one way, some another.
Othello. Act i, sc. 1, l. 177. [Brabantio]
One way or other.—*Troilus and Cressida,* iii, 3, 297.
One way or the other.—*The Merry Wives of Windsor,* iii, 1, 89.
Other way.—*Antony and Cleopatra,* ii, 5, 117.
Some other way.—*Much Ado about Nothing,* iv, 1, 329.
Many other ways.—*Antony and Cleopatra,* iv, 1, 5.
Many ways.—*Macbeth,* iv, 3, 97.
Both ways.—*Hamlet,* ii, 2, 345.
Neither way.—*Hamlet,* v, 2, 312; *Antony and Cleopatra,* ii, 5, 50.
Newer way.—*The Rape of Lucrece,* l. 1365.

9
The ways are dangerous.
King Lear. Act iv, sc. 5, l. 17. [Regan]
The way is but short.—*Love's Labour's Lost,* iii, 1, 57.
Your way is shorter.—*Antony and Cleopatra,* ii, 4, 7.

10
In my way it lies.
Macbeth. Act i, sc. 4, l. 50. [Macbeth]
Being in the way.—*The Two Gentlemen of Verona,* i, 2, 39.
Stands in my way.—*Henry V,* v, 2, 346.
Stand in our way.—*Henry V,* iii, 6, 167.
Stood in the way.—*Henry V,* v, 2, 355.

11
Thou marshall'st me the way that I was going.
Macbeth. Act ii, sc. 1, l. 42. [Macbeth]

12
He did show me The way twice o'er.
Measure for Measure, iv, 1, 41. See under PRECEPT.

13
By God's sonties, 'twill be a hard way to hit.
The Merchant of Venice. Act ii, sc. 2, l. 47. [Gobbo] The only use of "sonties" (saints).
Hard way.—*Richard II,* ii, 3, 7.

14
Evans: I pray you now, good Master Slender's serving-man, and friend Simple by your name, which way have you looked for Master Caius, that calls himself doctor of physic?
Simple: Marry, sir, the pittie-ward, the park-ward, every way; old Windsor way, and every way but the town way.
Evans: I most fehemently desire you you will also look that way.
The Merry Wives of Windsor. Act iii, sc. 1, l. 1. The only use of "pittie-ward" (unexplained), and "park-ward."
Every way makes my gain.
Othello. Act v, sc. 1, l. 14. [Iago] "Every way" is used eight times.
Each way.—*Coriolanus,* iii, 1, 49; *Macbeth,* iv, 2, 22.

15
Have you any way then to unfool me again?
The Merry Wives of Windsor. Act iv, sc. 2, l. 120. [Ford] The only use of "unfool."
Any way.—*King Lear,* iii, 3, 6; *Pericles,* ii, 2, 49.

16
To speak troth, I have forgot our way.
A Midsummer-Night's Dream. Act ii, sc. 2, l. 36. [Lysander]

Fallen am I in dark uneven way.
A Midsummer-Night's Dream. Act iii, sc. 2, l. 417. [Lysander]
Rough uneven ways.—*Richard II,* ii, 3, 7.

1
Keep your way, i' God's name.
Much Ado about Nothing. Act i, sc. 1, l. 144. [Benedick]
Keep your way.—*The Merry Wives of Windsor,* iii, 2, 1; *Henry VIII,* ii, 4, 128.
Keep on your way.—*Coriolanus,* iv, 2, 10.

2
There are ways to recover the general again.
Othello. Act ii, sc. 3, l. 272. [Iago]

3
We are half way there.
Pericles. Act i, sc. 4, l. 78. [Cleon]
Half way.—*The Taming of the Shrew,* i, 1, 62; *King Lear,* iv, 6, 14.

4
There 's no way to be rid on 't but by the way to the pox.
Pericles. Act iv, sc. 6, l. 16. [Bawd]
Will you not go the way of woman-kind?
Pericles, iv, 6, 149. See under CHASTITY.

5
King Richard: We did observe. Cousin Aumerle,
How far brought you high Hereford on his way?
Aumerle: I brought high Hereford, if you call him so,
But to the next highway, and there I left him.
Richard II. Act i, sc. 4, l. 1.
On the highway.—*The Winter's Tale,* iv, 3, 29.
King's highway.—*Richard II,* iii, 3, 156. The only use of this phrase.
Plain highway.—*Merchant of Venice,* iii, 1, 13.
Highway to my bed.—*Romeo and Juliet,* iii, 2, 134. The only uses of "highway." "Highways" occurs in *All 's Well that Ends Well,* i, 1, 152, and in *Merchant of Venice,* v, 1, 263.

6
King Richard: Go, count thy way with sighs; I mine with groans.
Queen: So longest way shall have the longest moans.
King Richard: Twice for one step I 'll groan, the way being short,
And piece the way out with a heavy heart.
Richard II. Act v, sc. 1, l. 89.

7
By the way, I 'll sort occasion.
Richard III, ii, 2, 148. See OCCASION, 1090: 15. "By the way" is repeated in iv, 5, 15, and eleven times in later plays.

8
Gloucester: The weary way hath made you melancholy.
Prince: No, uncle; but our crosses on the way
Have made it tedious, wearisome, and heavy.
Richard III. Act iii, sc. 1, l. 3.
Alas, the way is wearisome and long!
Two Gentlemen of Verona, ii, 7, 8. [Lucetta]
A weary way.—*Richard II,* ii, 3, 8.
Bad ways.—*Julius Cæsar,* iii, 1, 192.
Cold ways.—*Coriolanus,* iii, 1, 220.
False way.—*II Henry IV,* ii, 1, 121; *The Winter's Tale,* iv, 4, 151.
Foul way.—*I Henry IV,* ii, 1, 93; *The Taming of the Shrew,* iv, 1, 2; *Twelfth Night,* ii, 3, 201.
Little way.—*Romeo and Juliet,* iii, 1, 132.
Tedious ways.—*I Henry IV,* iii, 1, 48.
Thievish ways.—*Romeo and Juliet,* iv, 1, 79.
Uncertain way.—*Richard III,* iv, 2, 64.

9
King Richard: Come, come, you mock me; this is not the way
To win your daughter.
Queen Elizabeth: There is no other way;
Unless thou couldst put on some other shape.
Richard III. Act iv, sc. 4, l. 283.
There is no other way.—*Macbeth,* iii, 4, 107; *The Winter's Tale,* iv, 4, 704.
No other way.—*Measure for Measure,* ii, 4, 88; *Henry VIII,* v, 3, 92.
No way but this.—*Othello,* v, 2, 358; *Twelfth Night,* iii, 2, 42.
No way can I stray.—*Richard II,* i, 3, 206.
No way to fly.—*III Henry VI,* ii, 6, 24.
In no way.—*Coriolanus,* i, 1, 43.

10
It is you that have chalk'd forth the way
Which brought us hither.
The Tempest. Act v, sc. 1, l. 203. [Gonzalo] The only use of "chalk'd."

11
Make a clear way to the gods.
Timon of Athens, iii, 4, 77. See under DEBT.
Clear way.—*Pericles,* iv, 6, 113.
Beaten way.—*Hamlet,* ii, 2, 277.
Bold way.—*II Henry IV,* v, 2, 82.
Cheaper way.—*Measure for Measure,* ii, 4, 105.
Delicate way.—*Othello,* i, 3, 360.
Easy ways.—*Antony and Cleopatra,* v, 2, 359.
Fair way.—*Antony and Cleopatra,* iii, 2, 66.
General way.—*Timon of Athens,* ii, 2, 209.
Great way.—*All 's Well that Ends Well,* i, 1, 112; *Julius Cæsar,* ii, 1, 107.
Mightier way.—*Sonnets,* xvi.
Peaceable way.—*Much Ado about Nothing,* iii, 3, 61.
Self-same way.—*Merchant of Venice,* i, 1, 142.
Soft way.—*Coriolanus,* iii, 2, 82.
Sweet way.—*Richard II,* iii, 2, 205.
Wonted way.—*Hamlet,* iii, 1, 41.
Worthier way.—*King Lear,* i, 1, 214.

12
Barr'st me my way in Rome?
Titus Andronicus, i, 1, 291. See under BOY.

13
I will lead the way.
Troilus and Cressida. Act iii, sc. 3, l. 54. [Agamemnon]
Lead the way.—*II Henry VI,* ii, 4, 110, and seven times in later plays.
Lead 's the way.—*Pericles,* v, 3, 84.

14
Olivia: There lies your way, due west.
Viola: Then westward-ho!
Twelfth Night. Act iii, sc. 1, l. 145. The only use of "westward-ho."
Here lies our way.—*Troilus and Cressida,* iv, 1, 79.
Here lies your way.—*Twelfth Night,* i, 5, 216.

15
The best way is to slander Valentine.
The Two Gentlemen of Verona, iii, 2, 31.

Best way.—*Richard II,* i, 2, 36; *Merry Wives of Windsor,* ii, 1, 67; *Tempest,* ii, 2, 39.
There is no better way than that.
Merry Wives of Windsor, iv, 4, 17. [Ford]
Any of these ways are yet better than this.
Pericles. Act iv, sc. 6, l. 188. [Marina]
Better way.—*King Lear,* iv, 3, 21.
Yea, marry, that 's the eftest way.
Much Ado about Nothing. Act iv, sc. 2, l. 38. [Dogberry] The only use of "eftest" (easiest).
Aptest way.—*II Henry IV,* i, 1, 213.

WEAKNESS

1
Strong Enobarb Is weaker than the wine.
Antony and Cleopatra, ii, 7, 130. See under Drinking.
Far the weaker.—*The Rape of Lucrece,* l. 1646.
Much weaker.—*The Tempest,* v, i, 146.
Something weaker.—*As You Like It,* i, 2, 272.
2
Out of my weakness and my melancholy, . . .
Abuses me to damn me.
Hamlet. Act ii, sc. 2, l. 630. [Hamlet]
3
And, weakling, Warwick takes his gift again.
III Henry VI. Act v, sc. 1, l. 37. [Warwick]
Myself a weakling.—*The Rape of Lucrece,* l. 584. The only uses of "weakling."
4
Weakness possesseth me, and I am faint.
King John. Act v, sc. 3, l. 17. [King John]
Weak and faint.—*I Henry VI,* i, 1, 158.
Weak and cold.—*Passionate Pilgrim,* l. 163.
Weak, and despised.—*King Lear,* iii, 2, 20.
Weak, and melancholy.—*Richard III,* i, 1, 136.
Weak and sickly.—*Henry V,* iii, 6, 164.
Weak and silly.—*Venus and Adonis,* l. 1016.
Weak and unserviceable.—*All's Well that Ends Well,* iv, 3, 151. The only use of "unserviceable."
Weak and wearied.—*II Henry IV,* ii, 4, 385.
Weak and worthless.—*Henry V,* iii, 6, 141.
Weak and writhled.—*I Henry VI,* ii, 3, 23. The only use of "writhled" (wrinkled).
5
I pray you, father, being weak, seem so.
King Lear. Act ii, sc. 4, l. 204. [Regan]
Weak with age.—*Richard II,* ii, 2, 83.
Mine age is weak.—*All's Well that Ends Well,* iii, 4, 41.
Weak with toil.—*Cymbeline,* iii, 6, 37.
Weak of courage.—*III Henry VI,* iv, 1, 12.
Full weak.—*Cymbeline,* iii, 7, 5.
More weak.—*II Henry VI,* v, 1, 31.
Most weak, most weak.—*Antony and Cleopatra,* iii, 4, 29; *Venus and Adonis,* l. 1145.
Too weak.—*Timon of Athens,* i, 2, 59; *King Lear,* v, 3, 197; *Othello,* iii, 3, 443; *Henry VIII,* ii, 3, 43; *The Rape of Lucrece,* l. 865.
Weak in seeming.—*Sonnets,* cii.
6
All matter else seems weak.
Much Ado about Nothing, iii, 1, 54. See under Wit.
All 's too weak.—*Macbeth,* i, 2, 15.
Feeble, shallow, weak.—*The Comedy of Errors,* iii, 2, 35.
Soft and weak.—*The Taming of the Shrew,* v, 2, 165.
7
Bear with her weakness, which, I think, proceeds
From wayward sickness, and no grounded malice.
Richard III. Act i, sc. 3, l. 28. [Derby]
Bear with my weakness.—*Tempest,* iv, 1, 159.
Blame my weakness.—*All's Well that Ends Well,* ii, 1, 88.
See his weakness.—*Henry V,* iii, 6, 132.
8
The weakest goes to the wall.
Romeo and Juliet. Act i, sc. 1, l. 17. [Gregory]
9
With mine own weakness being best acquainted.
Sonnets. No. lxxxviii.
The weakness which I feel.
The Tempest, i, 2, 487. See under Prison.
Weakness of mine eyes.—*Julius Cæsar,* iv, 3, 276.
10
I am weaker than a woman's tear.
Troilus and Cressida. Act i, sc. 1, l. 9. [Troilus]
All my powers do their bestowing lose,
Like vassalage at unawares encountering
The eye of majesty.
Troilus and Cressida. Act iii, sc. 2, l. 39. [Troilus] The only use of "vassalage."
11
With cold-pale weakness numbs each feeling part.
Venus and Adonis, l. 892. The only use of "cold-pale."
12 It is but weakness
To bear the matter thus; mere weakness.
Winter's Tale. Act ii, sc. 3, l. 1. [Leontes]
Childish weakness.—*III Henry VI,* v, 4, 38.
O noble weakness!—*Antony and Cleopatra,* v, 2, 347.

WEALTH

See also Riches

13
I am not worthy of the wealth I owe,
Nor dare I say 'tis mine, and yet it is;
But, like a timorous thief, most fain would steal
What law does vouch mine own.
All's Well that Ends Well. Act ii, sc. 5, l. 84. [Helena]
14 Let 's away
And get our . . . wealth together.
As You Like It, i, 3, 136. See under Jewel.
15 Our wealth increased
By prosperous voyages I often made.
The Comedy of Errors. Act i, sc. 1, l. 40. [Ægeon]
16
Have I affected wealth or honour? speak.
II Henry VI. Act iv, sc. 7, l. 104. [Say]
Gather wealth.—*II Henry VI,* iv, 10, 23.
17
I have not been desirous of their wealth,
Nor much oppress'd them with great subsidies.
III Henry VI. Act iv, sc. 8, l. 44. [King Henry] The only use of "subsidies." "Subsidy" occurs in *II Henry VI,* iv, 7, 25.

1
What piles of wealth hath he accumulated
To his own portion! How, i' the name of thrift,
Does he rake this together!
Henry VIII. Act iii, sc. 2, l. 107. [King]
The only use of "accumulated."
That world of wealth I have drawn together
For mine own ends; indeed, to gain the popedom,
And fee my friends in Rome.
Henry VIII. Act iii, sc. 2, l. 212. [Wolsey]
The only use of "popedom."

2 Hubert, for the wealth of all the world,
Will not offend thee.
King John. Act iv, sc. 1, l. 131. [Hubert]
For all the wealth that ever I did see,
I would not have him know so much by me.
Love's Labour's Lost. Act iv, sc. 3, l. 149. [King]
I would not, for the wealth of Athens, I had done 't now.
Timon of Athens. Act iii, sc. 2, l. 57. [Lucius]
Wealth of all the town.—*Romeo and Juliet,* i, 5, 71.
Wealth of Windsor Castle.—*The Merry Wives of Windsor,* iii, 3, 232.
Wealth That the world masters.—*The Merchant of Venice,* v, 1, 173.

3 By the power that made me,
I tell you all her wealth.
King Lear. Act i, sc. 1, l. 210. [King Lear]

4 Thy wealth being forfeit to the state,
Thou hast not left the value of a cord.
The Merchant of Venice. Act iv, sc. 1, l. 365. [Gratiano]

5
The wealth I have waits on my consent.
The Merry Wives of Windsor, iii, 2, 78. See under CONSENT.

6
It is all the wealth that he has left.
Much Ado about Nothing, i, 1, 70. See under REASON.
All my wealth.—*Titus Andronicus,* ii, 4, 13.
Half my wealth.—*Coriolanus,* iv, 6, 160.

7
What priceless wealth the heavens had him lent.
The Rape of Lucrece, l. 17.

8
O, him she stores, to show what wealth she had
In days long since, before these last so bad.
Sonnets. No. lxvii.
Richer than wealth.—*Sonnets,* xci.

9
Wealth is burden of my wooing dance.
The Taming of the Shrew. Act i, sc. 2, l. 68. [Petruchio]
Wealth enough.—*The Taming of the Shrew,* i, 2, 86.
Incomparable wealth.—*The Taming of the Shrew,* iv, 2, 98.

10
Who cannot keep his wealth must keep his house.
Timon of Athens. Act iii, sc. 3, l. 42. [Servant]
Who would not wish to be from wealth exempt,
Since riches point to misery and contempt?
Timon of Athens. Act iv, sc. 2, l. 31. [Flavius]
Lay out their wealth.—*Timon of Athens,* i, 2, 241.

11 Good fellows all,
The latest of my wealth I 'll share amongst you.
Timon of Athens. Act iv, sc. 2, l. 22. [Flavius]
Hadst thou wealth again Rascals should have 't.
Timon of Athens. Act iv, sc. 3, l. 217. [Apemantus]
Were all the wealth I have shut up in thee,
I 'ld give thee leave to hang it.
Timon of Athens. Act iv, sc. 3, l. 279. [Timon]
Take wealth and lives together.
Timon of Athens. Act iv, sc. 3, l. 436. [Timon]
Poor wealth.—*Timon of Athens,* iv, 3, 495.
Heaps and sums of . . . wealth.—*Timon of Athens,* v, 1, 155.

12
The learned pate Ducks to the golden fool.
Timon of Athens. Act iv, sc. 3, l. 17. [Timon]

13
Speed: She hath . . . more wealth than faults.
Launce: Why, that word makes the faults gracious.
The Two Gentlemen of Verona. Act iii, sc. 1, l. 376.

14
Then know that I have little wealth to lose.
The Two Gentlemen of Verona. Act iv, sc. 1, l. 11. [Valentine]
Lost much wealth.—*Comedy of Errors,* v, 1, 49.

WEAPON

See also Arms, Sword

15
Masters, lay down your weapons.
Coriolanus. Act iii, sc. 1, l. 331. [Sicinius]
Lay your weapons down.—*II Henry VI,* iv, 2, 131.
Beat down their weapons.—*Romeo and Juliet,* iii, 1, 89.

16
Osric: You are not ignorant of what excellence Laertes is— . . . I mean, sir, for his weapon. . . .
Hamlet: What 's his weapon?
Osric: Rapier and dagger.
Hamlet: That 's two of his weapons: but, well.
Hamlet. Act v, sc. 2, l. 143.
The rapier and dagger man.—*Measure for Measure,* iv, 3, 16. The only use of "dagger man."

17 Their weapons only
Seem'd on our side; but for their spirits and souls,
This word, rebellion, it had froze them up.
II Henry IV. Act i, sc. 1, l. 197. [Morton]

18
Alas, alas! put up your naked weapons, put up your naked weapons.
II Henry IV. Act ii, sc. 4, l. 222. [Hostess]
My naked weapon is out.
Romeo and Juliet. Act i, sc. 1, l. 39. [Sampson]

1
Using no other weapon but his name.
Henry V, ii, 1, 81. See under NAME.
His weapons holy saws of sacred writ.
II Henry VI, i, 3, 61. See under HOLINESS.

2
The bishop and the Duke of Gloucester's men,
Forbidden late to carry any weapon,
Have fill'd their pockets full of pebble stones.
I Henry VI. Act iii, sc. 1, l. 78. [Mayor]

3
Be well assured
You put sharp weapons in a madman's hands.
II Henry VI. Act iii, sc. 1, l. 346. [York]
Take away his weapon.—*II Henry VI,* ii, 3, 98.

4
Why, how now, lords! your wrathful weapons drawn
Here in our presence! dare you be so bold?
II Henry VI. Act iii, sc. 2, l. 237. [King]
Draw forth thy weapon.
The Taming of the Shrew. Act iii, sc. 2, l. 238. [Petruchio]
Let 's draw our weapons.—*Tempest,* ii, 1, 322.
I saw their weapons drawn.—*The Tempest,* ii, 1, 320.
Wherefore stand'st thou with thy weapon drawn?
Titus Andronicus. Act iii, sc. 1, l. 48. [Titus]
My weapon drawn.—*Titus Andronicus,* v, 1, 37.

5
Their weapons like to lightning came and went;
Our soldiers, like the night-owl's lazy flight,
Or like an idle thresher with a flail,
Fell gently down, as if they struck their friends.
III Henry VI. Act ii, sc. 1, l. 129. [Warwick] The only use of "thresher" and "flail."

6
We put a sting in him,
That at his will he may do danger with.
Julius Cæsar. Act ii, sc. 1, l. 16. [Brutus]

7
Weapons! arms! what 's the matter here?
King Lear. Act ii, sc. 2, l. 50. [Gloucester]
Get weapons, ho!—*Othello,* i, 1, 182.
Women's weapons.—*King Lear,* ii, 4, 280.
Weapon to wear.—*King Lear,* iii, 4, 142.

8
Evans: What weapons is he?
Simple: No weapons, sir.
Merry Wives of Windsor. Act iii, sc. 1, l. 30.
Nay, good master parson, keep in your weapon.
The Merry Wives of Windsor. Act iii, sc. 1, l. 76. [Page]

9
Get your weapons in your hand.
A Midsummer-Night's Dream. Act iv, sc. 1, l. 11. [Bottom]

10
They are dangerous weapons for maids.
Much Ado about Nothing. Act v, sc. 2, l. 22. [Benedick]
Bright weapons.—*The Rape of Lucrece,* l. 1432.
Broken weapons.—*Othello,* i, 3, 174.
Red weapons.—*Julius Cæsar,* iii. 1, 109.
Mistemper'd weapons.—*Romeo and Juliet,* i, 1, 94. "Mistemper'd" is repeated in *King John,* v, 1, 12: "mistemper'd humour."

11
Montano: Take you this weapon,
Which I have here recover'd from the Moor:
Come, guard the door without. . . .
Othello: I have another weapon in this chamber;
It is a sword of Spain, the ice-brook's temper:—
O, here it is. Uncle, I must come forth.
Gratiano: If thou attempt it, it will cost thee dear:
Thou hast no weapon, and perforce must suffer.
Othello: . . . Behold, I have a weapon;
A better never did itself sustain
Upon a soldier's thigh. . . .
Be not afraid, though you do see me weapon'd.
Othello. Act v, sc. 2, l. 239. The only use of "ice-brook" and "weapon'd."

12
What, would you have my weapon, little lord?
Richard III. Act iii, sc. 1, l. 122. [Gloucester]

13
Come from thy ward,
For I can here disarm thee with this stick
And make thy weapon drop.
The Tempest. Act i, sc. 2, l. 471. [Prospero]

14
My grandsire, well advised, hath sent by me
The goodliest weapons of his armoury
To gratify your honourable youth.
Titus Andronicus. Act iv, sc. 2, l. 10. [Lucius] "Armoury" is repeated in iv, 1, 113, and occurs in no other play.

15
Empale him with your weapons round about.
Troilus and Cressida. Act v, sc. 7, l. 5. [Achilles] The only use of "empale."

WEARINESS

16
Rosalind: O Jupiter, how weary are my spirits!
Touchstone: I care not for my spirits, if my legs were not weary.
As You Like It. Act ii, sc. 4, l. 1.
I pray you, bear with me; I cannot go no further.
As You Like It. Act ii, sc. 4, l. 9. [Celia]
I found him under a tree, like a dropped acorn.
As You Like It. Act iii, sc. 2, l. 248. [Celia]
I am weary of you.
As You Like It. Act iii, sc. 2, l. 302. [Orlando]

17
Weariness
Can snore upon the flint, when resty sloth
Finds the down pillow hard.
Cymbeline. Act iii, sc. 6, l. 33. [Belarius] "Resty" is repeated in *Sonnets,* c.

1
How weary, stale, flat and unprofitable,
Seem to me all the uses of this world!
Hamlet. Act i, sc. 2, l. 133. [Hamlet]

2
Prince Henry: Before God, I am exceeding weary.
Poins: Is 't come to that? I had thought weariness durst not have attached one of so high blood.
Prince Henry: Faith, it does me; though it discolours the complexion of my greatness to acknowledge it.
II Henry IV. Act ii, sc. 2, l. 1. The only use of "discolours." "Discolour" occurs in *Henry V*, iii, 6, 171.
I shall be weary.—*I Henry IV*, ii, 3, 87.
Journey-bated and brought low.—*I Henry IV*, iv, 3, 26. The only use of "journey-bated."
Stiff and weary.—*Comedy of Errors*, i, 2, 15.
Wearied and out-breathed.—*II Henry IV*, i, 1, 108. The only use of "out-breathed."
Weary and o'erwatch'd.—*King Lear*, ii, 2, 177. "O'erwatch'd" is repeated in *Julius Cæsar*, iv, 3, 241, and in *A Midsummer-Night's Dream*, v, 1, 373.
Weary and old.—*Henry VIII*, iii, 2, 363.
Weary for the staleness.—*Pericles*, v, 1, 58.
Never so weary.—*A Midsummer-Night's Dream*, iii, 2, 442.
So weary.—*The Rape of Lucrece*, l. 1542.

3
I stay too long by thee, I weary thee.
II Henry IV. Act iv, sc. 5, l. 94. [King]
Shepherd: I know, sir, we weary you.
Polixenes: You weary those that refresh us.
The Winter's Tale. Act iv, sc. 4, l. 341.
I will weary you no longer.—*As You Like It*, v, 2, 56.
Not to be weary with you.—*Measure for Measure*, i, 4, 25.

4
Art thou not weary, John? how dost thou fare?
I Henry VI. Act iv, sc. 6, l. 27. [Talbot]
They are weary?—*King Lear*, ii, 4, 89.

5
It wearies me; you say it wearies you.
The Merchant of Venice, i, 1, 2. See under SADNESS.

6
And still, as you are weary of the weight,
Rest you.
Richard III. Act i, sc. 2, l. 31. [Anne]
I 'm weary of this charge, the gods can witness.
Timon of Athens. Act iii, sc. 4, l. 25. [Hortensius]
Weary of all.—*King Lear*, i, 4, 218.
Weary of dainty . . . grievances.—*II Henry IV*, iv, 1, 197.
Weary of his life.—*I Henry VI*, i, 2, 26.
Weary of their lives.—*Richard III*, v, 3, 329.
Weary of rest.—*Venus and Adonis*, l. 853.
Weary of solid firmness.—*II Henry IV*, iii, 1, 48.
Weary of the world.—*Venus and Adonis*, l. 1189.
Weary of these worldly bars.—*Julius Cæsar*, i, 3, 96.
Weary with disasters.—*Macbeth*, iii, 1, 112.
Weary with toil.—*Sonnets*, xxvii.

7
Besides, of weariness he did complain him,
And talk'd of virtue.
The Rape of Lucrece, l. 845.

8
Was ever man so beaten? was ever man so ray'd? was ever man so weary?
The Taming of the Shrew. Act iv, sc. 1, l. 2. [Grumio] "Ray'd" (dirtied, fouled) is repeated in iii, 2, 54: "Ray'd with the yellows," and occurs in no other play.
I have watch'd so long That I am dog-weary.
The Taming of the Shrew. Act iv, sc. 2, l. 60. [Biondello] The only use of "dog-weary."
I am thoroughly weary.—*Cymbeline*, iii, 6, 36.

9
You look wearily.
The Tempest. Act iii, sc. 1, l. 32. [Miranda] The only use of "wearily."
Old lord, I cannot blame thee,
Who am myself attach'd with weariness,
To the dulling of my spirits.
The Tempest. Act iii, sc. 3, l. 4. [Alonso] The only use of "dulling."

10
I am not weary, and 'tis long to night.
Twelfth Night. Act iii, sc. 3, l. 21. [Sebastian]
Ne'er be weary.—*Timon of Athens*, i, 2, 227.

WEATHER

11
I am not a day of season,
For thou mayst see a sunshine and a hail
In me at once: but to the brightest beams
Distracted clouds give way; so stand thou forth;
The time is fair again.
All 's Well that Ends Well. Act v, sc. 3, l. 32. [King]

12
I must make fair weather yet a while.
II Henry VI. Act v, sc. 1, l. 30. [York]
Make fair weather in your blustering land.
King John, v, 1, 21. See under TONGUE.
Fair weather after you!
Love's Labour 's Lost. Act i, sc. 2, l. 149. [Jaquenetta]
It is impossible you should take true root but by the fair weather that you make yourself.
Much Ado about Nothing. Act i, sc. 3, l. 25. [Conrade]

13
This is hot weather, gentlemen.
II Henry IV. Act iii, sc. 2, l. 101. [Falstaff]
Hot weather.—*II Henry VI*, iv, 10, 10.

14
Pour down thy weather.
King John. Act iv, sc. 2, l. 109. [King John]

15
What plume of feathers is he that indited this letter?
What vane? what weathercock?
Love's Labour 's Lost. Act iv, sc. 1, l. 96. [Princess of France]
A vane blown with all winds.—*Much Ado about Nothing*, iii, 1, 66.
The vane on the house.—*Much Ado about Nothing*, iii, 3, 138. The only uses of "vane."
Where had you this pretty weathercock?
The Merry Wives of Windsor. Act iii, sc. 2, l. 18. [Ford]

Weathercock on a steeple.—*The Two Gentlemen of Verona,* ii, 1, 142. The only uses of "weathercock."

1
Many can brook the weather that love not the wind.
Love's Labour's Lost. Act iv, sc. 2, l. 34. [Sir Nathaniel]

2
Considering the weather, a taller man than I will take cold.
The Taming of the Shrew. Act iv, sc. 1, l. 10. [Grumio] "Taller" is repeated in *Love's Labour's Lost,* v, 2, 846.
The weather being cold.—*Venus and Adonis,* l. 402.
Cold weather.—*Henry VIII,* i, 4, 22.
Winter weather.—*Passionate Pilgrim,* l. 159.

3
It is foul weather in us all, good sir,
When you are cloudy.
The Tempest. Act ii, sc. 1, l. 141. [Gonzalo]
We'll make foul weather.—*Richard II,* iii, 3, 161. "Foul weather" is repeated in six later plays.
Blustering weather.—*Rape of Lucrece,* l. 115.
Rough weather.—*As You Like It,* ii, 5, 47.

4
'Tis like to be loud weather.
The Winter's Tale. Act iii, sc. 3, l. 11. [Mariner]
Extremity of weather continuing.—*The Winter's Tale,* v, 2, 129. The only use of "continuing."
Endured all weathers.—*Winter's Tale,* v, 1, 195.

WEDLOCK

See also Marriage, Match, Nuptial

5
I have wedded her, not bedded her; and sworn to make the 'not' eternal.
All's Well that Ends Well. Act iii, sc. 2, l. 23. [Countess reading] "Bedded" is repeated in *Hamlet,* iii, 4, 121, and in *The Tempest,* iii, 3, 100.
If you ever wed.—*All's Well that Ends Well,* ii, 3, 98.
Think to wed.—*All's Well that Ends Well,* i, 1, 98.

6
Let your wedding be to-morrow.
As You Like It. Act v, sc. 2, l. 15. [Orlando]
The wedding being there to-morrow, there is a great coil to-night.
Much Ado about Nothing. Act iii, sc. 3, l. 99. [Dogberry]
Intended wedding.—*Much Ado about Nothing,* ii, 2, 46.
Happy wedding.—*I Henry VI,* iii, 2, 26.

7
Wedding is great Juno's crown:
O blessed bond of board and bed!
'Tis Hymen peoples every town;
High wedlock then be honoured:
Honour, high honour and renown,
To Hymen, god of every town!
As You Like It. Act v, sc. 4, l. 147. [Song]
Hymen's lamps shall light you.
The Tempest. Act iv, sc. 1, l. 23. [Prospero] "Hymen" is mentioned ten times in the plays.

8
Were you wedded, you would bear some sway.
The Comedy of Errors. Act ii, sc. 1, l. 28. [Adriana]
If you did wed my sister for her wealth,
Then for her wealth's sake use her with more kindness.
The Comedy of Errors. Act iii, sc. 2, l. 5. [Luciana]

9
What is wedlock forced but a hell,
An age of discord and continual strife?
Whereas the contrary bringeth bliss,
And is a pattern of celestial peace.
I Henry VI. Act v, sc. 5, l. 62. [Suffolk]

10
Wedded be thou to the hags of hell.
II Henry VI. Act iv, sc. 1, l. 79. [Captain]
Wedded to calamity.—*Romeo and Juliet,* iii, 3, 3.

11
I'll join mine eldest daughter and my joy
To him forthwith in holy wedlock bands.
III Henry VI. Act iii, sc. 3, l. 242. [Warwick]

12
Biron: Is she wedded or no?
Boyet: To her will, sir, or so.
Love's Labour's Lost. Act ii, sc. 1, l. 211.
She's wedded.—*Cymbeline,* i, 1, 7.

13
For you shall hence upon your wedding-day.
The Merchant of Venice. Act iii, sc. 2, l. 314. [Portia] "Wedding-day" occurs fourteen times in the plays.
Wedding-bed.—*Romeo and Juliet,* i, 5, 137; iii, 2, 136.
Wedding cheer.—*The Taming of the Shrew,* iii, 2, 188; *Romeo and Juliet,* iv, 5, 87.
Wedding-dower.—*The Two Gentlemen of Verona,* iii, 1, 78.
Wedding-garment.—*The Taming of the Shrew,* iv, 1, 51.
Wedding-ring.—*Comedy of Errors,* ii, 2, 139.

14
I will wed thee in another key,
With pomp, with triumph and with revelling.
A Midsummer-Night's Dream. Act i, sc. 1, l. 18. [Theseus]
Your warrior love
To Theseus must be wedded.
A Midsummer-Night's Dream. Act ii, sc. 1, l. 71. [Titania]
There shall the pairs of faithful lovers be
Wedded, with Theseus, all in jollity.
A Midsummer-Night's Dream. Act iv, sc. 1, l. 95. [Oberon]

15
Wooing, wedding, and repenting, is as a Scotch jig, a measure, and a cinque pace: the first suit is hot and hasty, like a Scotch jig, and full as fantastical; the wedding, mannerly-modest, as a measure, full of state and ancientry; and then comes repentance and with his bad legs, falls into the cinque pace faster and faster, till he sink into his grave.
Much Ado about Nothing. Act ii, sc. 1, l. 76.

[Beatrice] The only uses of "cinque pace," "Scotch," and "mannerly-modest." "Ancientry" occurs again in *Winter's Tale,* iii, 3, 63.

1
She tells me here, she 'll wed the stranger knight,
Or never more to view nor day nor light.
Pericles. Act ii, sc. 5, l. 16. [Simonides]

Wed his daughter.—*The Two Gentlemen of Verona,* ii, 6, 39.
Wed this shepherd.—*As You Like It,* v, 4, 22.
Wed unto a woman.—*The Comedy of Errors,* i, 1, 37.
Wed woman.—*As You Like It,* v, 4, 130.
Wed to one half lunatic.—*The Taming of the Shrew,* ii, 1, 289.

2
The impious breach of holy wedlock vow.
The Rape of Lucrece, l. 809.

False to wedlock.—*Othello,* v, 2, 142.
True to wedlock.—*The Winter's Tale,* v, 1, 124.

3
If you love her then, to-morrow wed her; but it would better fit your honour to change your mind.
Much Ado about Nothing. Act iii, sc. 2, l. 118. [Don John]

4
When thou wed'st, let sorrow haunt thy bed!
Richard III. Act iv, sc. 1, l. 74. [Anne] The only use of "wed'st."

5
Hortensio: Were my state far worser than it is, I would not wed her for a mine of gold.
Petruchio: Hortensio, peace! thou know'st not gold's effect.
The Taming of the Shrew. Act i, sc. 2, l. 91.

Deny to wed.—*Taming of the Shrew,* ii, 1, 180.
Refuse to wed.—*A Midsummer-Night's Dream,* i, 1, 64.
I 'll not wed.—*Romeo and Juliet,* iii, 5, 187.

6
Yet never means to wed where he hath woo'd.
The Taming of the Shrew, iii, 2, 17. See under Wooing.

Wed at leisure.—*The Taming of the Shrew,* iii, 2, 11.

WEED

See also Flower and Weed

7
We bring forth weeds
When our quick minds lie still.
Antony and Cleopatra, i, 2, 113. See under Fault.

8
Do not spread the compost on the weeds,
To make them ranker.
Hamlet. Act iii, sc. 4, l. 151. [Hamlet] The only use of "compost."

Fat weed.—*Hamlet,* i, 5, 32.
Midnight weeds.—*Hamlet,* iii, 2, 268.
Headstrong weeds.—*Measure for Measure,* i, 3, 20.
Unwholesome weeds.—*Rape of Lucrece,* l. 870.

9
Her fallow leas
The darnel, hemlock and rank fumitory
Doth root upon.
Henry V. Act v, sc. 2, l. 45. [Burgundy] The only use of "fumitory" (fumaria).

Crown'd with rank fumiter and furrow-weeds,
With bur-docks, hemlock, nettles, cuckoo-flowers,
Darnel, and all the idle weeds that grow
In our sustaining corn.
King Lear. Act iv, sc. 4, l. 3. [Cordelia] The only use of "fumiter," "furrow-weeds," "bur-docks," and "cuckoo-flowers." "Darnel" occurs a third time in *I Henry VI,* iii, 2, 44, and "hemlock" a third time in *Macbeth,* iv, 1, 25.

10
Now 'tis the spring, and weeds are shallow-rooted;
Suffer them now, and they 'll o'ergrow the garden
And choke the herbs for want of husbandry.
II Henry VI. Act iii, sc. 1, l. 31. [Queen Margaret] The only use of "shallow-rooted" and "o'ergrow."

Most subject is the fattest soil to weeds.
II Henry IV. Act iv, sc. 4, l. 54. [King Henry]

11
What doth cherish weeds but gentle air?
III Henry VI. Act ii, sc. 6, l. 21. [Clifford]

12
He 's a rank weed, . . .
And we must root him out.
Henry VIII. Act v, sc. 1, l. 52. [Gardiner]

13
He weeds the corn and still lets grow the weeding.
Love's Labour 's Lost. Act i, sc. 1, l. 96. [Longaville] The only use of "weeding."

Weed this wormwood from your fruitful brain.
Love's Labour 's Lost, v, 2, 857. See under Bitterness.

Weed your better judgements.—*As You Like It,* ii, 7, 45.
Weed this land.—*II Henry IV,* iv, 1, 205.
Weed her love.—*The Two Gentlemen of Verona,* iii, 2, 49.
Weed my vice.—*Measure for Measure,* iii, 2, 284.
Weed up thyme.—*Othello,* i, 3, 326.

14
O thou weed,
Who art so lovely fair and smell'st so sweet
That the sense aches at thee, would thou hadst ne'er been born!
Othello. Act iv, sc. 2, l. 67. [Othello]

15
The weeds which his broad-spreading leaves did shelter.
Richard II. Act iii, sc. 4, l. 50. [Gardener] "Broad-spreading" is repeated in *I Henry VI,* i, 2, 135.

O'ergrown by weeds.—*Rape of Lucrece,* l. 281.

16
Small herbs have grace, great weeds do grow apace.
Richard III. Act ii, sc. 4, l. 13. [York]

They are not herbs, you knave; they are nose-herbs.
All's Well that Ends Well. Act iv, sc. 5, l. 20. [Lafeu] The only use of "nose-herbs."

Such wither'd herbs as these
Are meet for plucking up.
Titus Andronicus. Act iii, sc. 1, l. 178. [Titus]

Enchanted herbs.—*Merchant of Venice,* v, 1, 13.

Wholesome herbs.—*Richard II,* iii, 4, 46.

1
Idle weeds are fast in growth.
Richard III. Act iii, sc. 1, l. 103. [York]

II—Weeds: Dress

See also Dress

2
With a proud heart he wore his humble weeds.
Coriolanus. Act ii, sc. 3, l. 161. [Brutus] The only use of "humble weeds." "Humble weed" occurs in l. 229.

3
I 'll disrobe me
Of these Italian weeds and suit myself
As doth a Briton peasant.
Cymbeline. Act v, sc. 1, l. 22. [Posthumus]

Weeds of Athens he doth wear.
Midsummer-Night's Dream, ii, 2, 71. [Puck]

4
His sables and his weeds,
Importing health and graveness.
Hamlet. Act iv, sc. 7, l. 81. [King] "Sables" is used only once again, in iii, 2, 138: "Suit of sables."

Grave weeds.—*Titus Andronicus,* iii, 1, 43.

Mourning weeds.—*III Henry VI,* iii, 3, 229; *Titus Andronicus,* i, 1, 70; v, 3, 197.

5
Be better suited:
These weeds are memories of those worser hours:
I prithee, put them off.
King Lear. Act iv, sc. 7, l. 6. [Cordelia]

Come, let us hence, and put on other weeds.
Much Ado about Nothing. Act v, sc. 3, l. 30. [Don Pedro]

6
A tatter'd weed, of small worth held.
Sonnets, ii. See under AGE.

Tatter'd weeds.—*Romeo and Juliet,* v, 1, 39.

Thin weeds.—*Love's Labour 's Lost,* v, 2, 811.

Away with slavish weeds!—*Titus Andronicus,* ii, 1, 18.

7
Gentle Lucetta, fit me with such weeds
As may beseem some well-reputed page.
The Two Gentlemen of Verona. Act ii, sc. 7, l. 42. [Julia] "Well-reputed" is repeated in *Julius Cæsar,* ii, 1, 295.

8
Let me see thee in thy woman's weeds.
Twelfth Night. Act v, sc. 1, l. 280. [Duke]

Maiden weeds.—*Twelfth Night,* v, 1, 262.

9
These your unusual weeds to each part of you
Do give a life.
Winter's Tale. Act iv, sc. 4, l. 1. [Florizel]

WEEPING

See also Crying; Eye: The Weeping Eye; Laughter and Tears; Tear

10
He weeps like a wench that had shed her milk.
All's Well that Ends Well, iv, 3, 123. [Lord]

To weep, like a young wench that had buried her grandam.
The Two Gentlemen of Verona. Act ii, sc. 1, l. 23. [Speed] See under LOVE.

11
Look, they weep;
And I, an ass, am onion-eyed! for shame,
Transform us not to women.
Antony and Cleopatra. Act iv, sc. 2, l. 34. [Enobarbus] The only use of "onion-eyed."

Dissolve, thick cloud, and rain; that I may say,
The gods themselves do weep!
Antony and Cleopatra. Act v, sc. 2, l. 302. [Charmian]

12
Rosalind: But have I not cause to weep?
Celia: As good cause as one would desire; therefore weep.
As You Like It. Act iii, sc. 4, l. 4.

I will weep for nothing, like Diana in the fountain.
As You Like It. Act iv, sc. 1, l. 154. [Rosalind]

I will weep a while longer.
Much Ado about Nothing. Act iv, sc. 1, l. 258. [Beatrice]

I will go sit and weep.
The Taming of the Shrew. Act ii, sc. 1, l. 35. [Katharina]

Sit still and weep.—*Pericles,* v, 1, 191.

13
The incessant weepings of my wife,
Weeping before for what she saw must come,
And piteous plainings of the pretty babes,
That mourn'd for fashion, ignorant what to fear.
The Comedy of Errors. Act i, sc. 1, l. 71. [Ægeon] The only use of "plainings." "Plaining" occurs in *Richard II,* i, 3, 175.

No longer will I be a fool,
To put the finger in the eye and weep.
The Comedy of Errors, ii, 2, 206. [Adriana]

14
O lady, weep no more, lest I give cause
To be suspected of more tenderness
Than doth become a man.
Cymbeline. Act i, sc. 1, l. 93. [Posthumus]

Cease to weep.—*II Henry VI,* iv, 4, 3.

Weep not.—*I Henry IV,* ii, 4, 431; *King Lear,* iv, 7, 71; *Antony and Cleopatra,* iv, 14, 21.

Unapt to weep.—*I Henry VI,* v, 3, 133.

15
I cannot sing: I 'll weep, and word it with thee;
For notes of sorrow out of tune are worse
Than priests and fanes that lie.
Cymbeline. Act iv, sc. 2, l. 240. [Guiderius] The only use of "fanes." "Fane" occurs in *Coriolanus,* i, 10, 20.

Lady: Madam, I 'll sing.
Queen: 'Tis well that thou hast cause;
But thou shouldst please me better, wouldst thou weep.
Lady: I could weep, madam, would it do you good,
Queen: And I could sing, would weeping do me good,
And never borrow any tear of thee.
Richard II. Act iii, sc. 4, l. 19.

1
He weeps for what is done.
Hamlet. Act iv, sc. 1, l. 27. [Queen]
He weeps on.—*The Two Gentlemen of Verona,* ii, 3, 29.
Poor boy, he weeps.—*King John,* ii, 1, 166.
Poor girl! she weeps.—*The Taming of the Shrew,* ii, 1, 24.
Haply she will weep.—*Richard III,* iv, 4, 273.

2
Thou 'lt set me a-weeping.
II Henry IV. Act ii, sc. 4, l. 301. [Doll] The only use of "a-weeping."
Blind with weeping.—*II Henry VI,* iii, 2, 62.

3
Weep over his country's wrongs.
I Henry IV. Act iv, sc. 3, l. 81. [Hotspur]

4
Wouldst have me weep? why, now thou hast thy will.
III Henry VI. Act i, sc. 4, l. 144. [York]
I 'll bear thee hence, where I may weep my fill.
III Henry VI. Act ii, sc. 5, l. 113. [Son]

5
What, weeping-ripe, my Lord Northumberland?
Think but upon the wrong he did us all,
And that will quickly dry thy melting tears.
III Henry VI. Act i, sc. 4, l. 172. [Queen Margaret]
The king was weeping-ripe for a good word.
Love's Labour's Lost. Act v, sc. 2, l. 274. [Rosaline] The only uses of "weeping-ripe."

6
I cannot weep; for all my body's moisture
Scarce serves to quench my furnace-burning heart.
III Henry VI. Act ii, sc. 1, l. 79. [Richard] The only use of "furnace-burning."
I cannot weep; nor answer have I none,
But what should go by water.
Othello. Act iv, sc. 2, l. 103. [Desdemona]

7
I, that did never weep, now melt with woe
That winter should cut off our spring-time so.
III Henry VI. Act ii, sc. 3, l. 46. [Richard]
Weep, wretched man, I 'll aid thee tear for tear;
And let our hearts and eyes, like civil war,
Be blind with tears, and break o'ercharged with grief.
III Henry VI. Act ii, sc. 5, l. 76. [King]

8 If you can be merry then, I 'll say
A man may weep upon his wedding-day.
Henry VIII, Prol., 31.

9
O, now you weep; and, I perceive, you feel
The dint of pity: these are gracious drops.
Julius Cæsar. Act iii, sc. 2, l. 197. [Antony]
O, I could weep My spirit from mine eyes!
Julius Cæsar. Act iv, sc. 3, l. 99. [Cassius]

10 I must withdraw and weep
Upon the spot of this enforced cause.
King John. Act v, sc. 2, l. 29. [Salisbury]

11
You think I 'll weep; No, I 'll not weep:
I have full cause of weeping; but this heart
Shall break into a hundred thousand flaws,
Or ere I 'll weep.
King Lear. Act ii, sc. 4, l. 285. [King Lear]

12
Let us seek out some desolate shade, and there
Weep our sad bosoms empty.
Macbeth. Act iv, sc. 3, l. 1. [Malcolm]

13
Then down upon her knees she falls, weeps, sobs, beats her heart, tears her hair, prays, curses.
Much Ado about Nothing. Act ii, sc. 3, l. 152. [Claudio]
Sob and weep.—*Richard III,* i, 2, 162; *Titus Andronicus,* iii, 1, 137.
Sighs, and weeps.—*Romeo and Juliet,* v, 3, 184; *The Two Gentlemen of Verona,* iv, 2, 123.

14
She wept heartily and said she cared not.
Much Ado about Nothing. Act v, sc. 1, l. 175. [Claudio]

15
I must weep, But they are cruel tears.
Othello. Act v, sc. 2, l. 20. [Othello]
Weep'st thou for him to my face?
Othello. Act v, sc. 2, l. 77. [Othello]
Thou weep'st.—*Cymbeline,* v, 5, 352.
Weeps upon me.—*Othello,* iv, 1, 143.

16
I weep for thee, and yet no cause I have.
The Passionate Pilgrim, l. 137.
I will weep for thee.—*Henry V,* ii, 2, 140.
Weep for her.—*Hamlet,* ii, 2, 586.
Weep for him.—*As You Like It,* iii, 2, 437; *Julius Cæsar,* iii, 2, 26; *Macbeth,* iv, 2, 62.
Weep for thy death.—*II Henry IV,* iv, 3, 15.
Weep for my pardon.—*Antony and Cleopatra,* iv, 14, 45.

17
To weep that you live as you do makes pity in your lovers: seldom but that pity breeds you a good opinion, and that opinion a mere profit.
Pericles. Act iv, sc. 2, l. 129. [Bawd]
Why do you weep?—*Pericles,* v, 1, 178.

18
Which makes the maid weep like the dewy night.
The Rape of Lucrece, l. 1232.
Makes me weep.—*I Henry VI,* iv, 3, 28; *Love's Labour's Lost,* iv, 3, 40.
Make one weep.—*Othello,* iv, 2, 127.
Make us weep.—*Pericles,* iii, 2, 104.
Made me weep.—*Pericles,* v, 1, 187.

19
A pretty while these pretty creatures stand,
Like ivory conduits coral cisterns filling:
One justly weeps; the other takes in hand
No cause, but company, of her drops spilling.
The Rape of Lucrece, l. 1233. "Spilling" is repeated in *Richard II,* ii, 1, 131.
Here feelingly she weeps Troy's painted woes.
The Rape of Lucrece, l. 1492.
Then son and father weep with equal strife
Who should weep most, for daughter or for wife.
The Rape of Lucrece, l. 1791.

20
Weep thou for me in France, I for thee here;

Better far off than near, be ne'er the near.
Richard II. Act v, sc. 1, l. 87. [King Richard]
Weep the fire out.—*Richard II,* v, 1, 48.

1
Weeping made you break the story off.
Richard II. Act v, sc. 2, l. 2. [Duchess]

2
Clarence: He will weep.
Murderer: Ay, millstones; as he lesson'd us to weep.
Richard III. Act i, sc. 4, l. 245.
Your eyes drop millstones, when fools' eyes drop tears.
Richard III. Act i, sc. 3, l. 354. [Gloucester]
Pandarus: Queen Hecuba laughed until that her eyes ran o'er.
Cressida: With mill-stones.
Troilus and Cressida. Act i, sc. 2, l. 156. The only uses of "millstones."

3
Good aunt, you wept not for our father's death;
How can we aid you with our kindred tears?
Richard III. Act ii, sc. 2, l. 62. [Boy]
She for an Edward weeps, and so do I;
I for a Clarence weep, so doth not she:
These babes for Clarence weep, and so do I;
I for an Edward weep, so do not they.
Richard III. Act ii, sc. 2, l. 82. [Duchess of York]
Weep their gain and loss.—*Richard III,* ii, 4, 59.
Weep their dust.—*All's Well that Ends Well,* v, 3, 64.

4
So dear I loved the man, that I must weep.
Richard III. Act iii, sc. 5, l. 24. [Gloucester]
Although they were flesh'd villains, bloody dogs,
Melting with tenderness and kind compassion
Wept like two children in their deaths' sad stories.
Richard III. Act iv, sc. 3, l. 6. [Tyrrel]

5
Blubbering and weeping, weeping and blubbering.
Romeo and Juliet. Act iii, sc. 3, l. 87. [Nurse] The only uses of "blubbering."
O, she says nothing, sir, but weeps and weeps.
Romeo and Juliet. Act iii, sc. 3, l. 99. [Nurse]
Wail and weep.—*Richard III,* ii, 2, 34.
Weep and wail.—*King Lear,* iii, 6, 74.
Weeping and wailing.—*Romeo and Juliet,* iii, 2, 128.

6
Weep afresh love's long since cancell'd woe.
Sonnets. No. xxx.
Cannot choose but weep.—*Sonnets,* lxiv.

7
I am a fool To weep at what I am glad of.
The Tempest. Act iii, sc. 1, l. 73. [Miranda]
Weep for joy.—*Richard II,* iii, 2, 4. See PATRIOTISM, 1130:4.
Weep with laughing.—*Timon of Athens,* iv, 3, 493. See LAUGHTER AND TEARS.

8
I have inly wept.
The Tempest. Act v, sc. 1, l. 200. [Gonzalo]

9
What, dost thou weep? Come nearer. Then I love thee,
Because thou art a woman, and disclaim'st
Flinty mankind; whose eyes do never give
But thorough lust and laughter.
Timon of Athens. Act iv, sc. 3, l. 489. [Timon]

10
When I do weep, they humbly at my feet
Receive my tears and seem to weep with me.
Titus Andronicus. Act iii, sc. 1, l. 41. [Titus]
To weep with them that weep doth ease some deal.
Titus Andronicus. Act iii, sc. 1, l. 245. [Marcus]
O Lord, I cannot speak to him for weeping;
My tears will choke me, if I ope my mouth.
Titus Andronicus. Act v, sc. 3, l. 174. [Lucius]

11
Pandarus: He will weep you, an 'twere a man born in April.
Cressida: And I 'll spring up in his tears, an 'twere a nettle against May.
Troilus and Cressida. Act i, sc. 2, l. 188.
Weep seas.—*Troilus and Cressida,* iii, 2, 84.

12
Nay, 'twill be this hour ere I have done weeping.
The Two Gentlemen of Verona. Act ii, sc. 3, l. 1. [Launce]
My mother weeping, my father wailing, my sister crying, our maid howling, our cat wringing her hands, and all our house in a great perplexity, yet did not this cruel-hearted cur shed one tear.
The Two Gentlemen of Verona. Act ii, sc. 3, l. 7. [Launce] The only use of "cruel-hearted."

13
To think upon her woes I do protest
That I have wept a hundred several times.
The Two Gentlemen of Verona. Act iv, sc. 4, l. 149. [Julia]
Weep at woes.—*A Lover's Complaint,* l. 307.
Weeping at my woes.—*Titus Andronicus,* iii, 1, 100.

14
Julia: And at that time I made her weep agood,
For I did play a lamentable part:
Madam, 'twas Ariadne passioning
For Theseus' perjury and unjust flight;
Which I so lively acted with my tears
That my poor mistress, moved therewithal
Wept bitterly; and would I might be dead
If I in thought felt not her very sorrow! . . .
Silvia: I weep myself to think upon thy words.
The Two Gentlemen of Verona. Act iv, sc. 4, l. 170. The only use of "agood" and "passioning." Ariadne is mentioned again in *A Midsummer-Night's Dream,* ii, 1, 80.

15
And now she weeps, and now she fain would speak,

And now her sobs do her intendments break.
Venus and Adonis, l. 222.

1
I am not prone to weeping, as our sex
Commonly are; the want of which vain dew
Perchance shall dry your pities: but I have
That honourable grief lodged here which burns
Worse than tears drown.
The Winter's Tale. Act ii, sc. 1, l. 108. [Hermione]

Do not weep, good fools;
There is no cause: when you shall know your mistress
Has deserved prison, then abound in tears
As I come out.
The Winter's Tale. Act ii, sc. 1, l. 118. [Hermione]

This dream of mine,—
Being now awake, I 'll queen it no inch farther,
But milk my ewes and weep.
Winter's Tale. Act iv, sc. 4, l. 458. [Perdita]

Clown: We wept, and there was the first gentleman-like tears that ever we shed.
Shepherd: We may live, son, to shed many more.
The Winter's Tale. Act v, sc. 2, l. 155.

WEIGHT

See also Burden

2
We, poising us in her defective scale,
Shall weigh thee to the beam.
All's Well that Ends Well. Act ii, sc. 3, l. 161. [King] The only use of "poising."

Weigh too light.—*All's Well that Ends Well,* iii, 4, 31.
Weigh it lightly.—*Richard III,* iii, 1, 121.

3
Burdened
With lesser weight but not with lesser woe.
The Comedy of Errors. Act i, sc. 1, l. 108. [Ægeon]

4
He must be weighed rather by her value than his own.
Cymbeline. Act i, sc. 4, l. 15. [Iachimo]

5
God keep lead out of me! I need no more weight than mine own bowels.
I Henry IV. Act v, sc. 3, l. 34. [Falstaff]

6
I hope he that looks upon me will take me without weighing.
II Henry IV. Act i, sc. 2, l. 188. [Falstaff]

7
Weigh this well.
II Henry IV. Act v, sc. 2, l. 102. [King]

Weigh him well.—*Troilus and Cressida,* iv, 5, 81.

8
Thou art no Atlas for so great a weight.
III Henry VI. Act v, sc. 1, l. 36. [Warwick] The only mention of Atlas.

Great weight.—*Antony and Cleopatra,* i, 4, 25.

9
There was the weight that pull'd me down.
Henry VIII. Act iii, sc. 2, l. 407. [Wolsey]

10
You weigh equally; a feather will turn the scale.
Measure for Measure. Act iv, sc. 2, l. 31. [Provost]

The weight of a hair will turn the scales between their avoirdupois.
II Henry IV. Act ii, sc. 4, l. 280. [Falstaff] The only use of "avoirdupois."

In equal balance justly weigh'd.
II Henry IV. Act iv, sc. 1, l. 67. [Archbishop of York] "Justly weigh'd" is repeated in *Twelfth Night,* v, 1, 375, and in *Pericles,* v, 1, 89.

In equal scale weighing delight and dole.
Hamlet, i, 2, 13. See JOY AND SORROW.

Each weighs nor less nor more.
Troilus and Cressida, iv, 1, 65. See under COMPARISON.

Weigh equal.—*King John,* ii, 1, 486.
Even weigh.—*Midsummer-Night's Dream,* iii, 2, 133.
Weigh so even.—*King John,* ii, 1, 332.
You will nothing weigh.—*A Midsummer-Night's Dream,* iii, 2, 131.

11
An there be any matter of weight chances, call up me.
Much Ado about Nothing. Act iii, sc. 3, l. 91. [Dogberry]

Matter of weight.—*Antony and Cleopatra,* i, 2, 71.
Point of weight.—*Henry VIII,* iii, 1, 71.
Things of weight.—*Henry V,* i, 2, 5.
Weights of baseness.—*Cymbeline,* iii, 5, 88.
Weight of carrion flesh.—*The Merchant of Venice,* iv, 1, 41.
Carrion weight.—*Troilus and Cressida,* iv, 1, 71.
Weight of government.—*III Henry VI,* iv, 6, 51.

12
To satisfy this good old man,
I would bend under any heavy weight
That he 'll enjoin me to.
Much Ado about Nothing. Act v, sc. 1, l. 286. [Don Pedro] "Enjoin" is repeated in *The Winter's Tale,* ii, 3, 173.

13
Full of . . . difficult weight.
Othello. Act iii, sc. 3, l. 82. [Desdemona]

Full weight.—*As You Like It,* i, 2, 9.

14
Weary of the weight.
Richard III. Act i, sc. 2, l. 31. [Anne]

Weigh thee down.—*Richard III,* v, 3, 153.
Weigh down.—*Timon of Athens,* v, 1, 154.

15
Too light for such a swain as you to catch;
And yet as heavy as my weight should be.
The Taming of the Shrew. Act ii, sc. 1, l. 205. [Katharina]

WELCOME

16
We 'll be before our welcome.
All's Well that Ends Well. Act iv, sc. 4, l. 14. [Helena]

17
Welcome shall they be.
All's Well that Ends Well. Act iii, sc. 1, l. 19. [Duke]

And in my voice most welcome shall you be.
As You Like It. Act ii, sc. 4, l. 87. [Corin]
Most welcome.—*Coriolanus,* iv, 5, 153; *Othello,* iv, 3, 4; *Romeo and Juliet,* i, 2, 23; *Cymbeline,* iii, 6, 72.
More welcome.—*All's Well that Ends Well,* iv, 4, 16; *Richard II,* iii, 1, 31.
Fairly welcome.—*Timon of Athens,* i, 2, 182.
Kindly welcome.—*Cymbeline,* i, 6, 14.
Ever welcome.—*Antony and Cleopatra,* iii, 6, 90.
Passing welcome.—*The Taming of the Shrew,* ii, 1, 113.
Very welcome.—*Measure for Measure,* iii, 1, 49.

1
Thou art right welcome as thy master is.
As You Like It. Act ii, sc. 7, l. 198. [Duke]
Your lordship is right welcome back to Denmark.
Hamlet. Act v, sc. 2, l. 81. [Osric]
Your graces are right welcome.
King Lear. Act ii, sc. 1, l. 131. [Gloucester]
Right welcome.—*Richard II,* iii, 3, 122; *Timon of Athens,* i, 1, 262.

2
My master is of churlish disposition
And little recks to find the way to heaven
By doing deeds of hospitality.
As You Like It. Act ii, sc. 4, l. 80. [Corin]
Reward not hospitality
With such black payment as thou hast pretended.
The Rape of Lucrece, l. 575. The only uses of "hospitality."

3
O my dear niece, welcome thou art to me!
Even daughter, welcome, in no less degree.
As You Like It. Act v, sc. 4, l. 153. [Duke]

4
Gave healthful welcome to their shipwreck'd guests.
The Comedy of Errors. Act i, sc. 1, l. 115. [Ægeon]
Balthazar: I hold your dainties cheap, sir, and your welcome dear.
Antipholus of Ephesus: O, Signior Balthazar, either at flesh or fish,
A table full of welcome makes scarce one dainty dish.
Balthazar: Good meat, sir, is common; that every churl affords.
Antipholus of Ephesus: And welcome more common; for that 's nothing but words.
Balthazar: Small cheer and great welcome makes a merry feast.
The Comedy of Errors. Act iii, sc. 1, l. 21.
Fit welcome.—*King Lear,* ii, 4, 236.
Good welcome.—*The Comedy of Errors,* iii, 1, 20; *Henry VIII,* i, 4, 6.
Sweeter welcome.—*Macbeth,* iii, 1, 43.

5
Here is neither cheer, sir, nor welcome.
The Comedy of Errors. Act iii, sc. 1, l. 66. [Angelo]
You do not give the cheer: the feast is sold
That is not often vouch'd, while 'tis a-making,
'Tis given with welcome.
Macbeth. Act iii, sc. 4, l. 33. [Lady Macbeth] "A-making" is repeated in *Hamlet,* i, 3, 119.
Bid your friends welcome, show a merry cheer.
The Merchant of Venice. Act iii, sc. 2, l. 315. [Portia]
She securely gives good cheer
And reverend welcome to her princely guest.
The Rape of Lucrece, l. 89.

For Good Cheer see under Eating.

6
Volumnia: I know not where to turn: O, welcome home:
And welcome, general and ye 're welcome all.
Menenius: A hundred thousand welcomes.
Coriolanus. Act ii, sc. 1, l. 198.
A thousand welcomes!—*Coriolanus,* iv, 5, 151.
Five thousand welcomes.—*The Two Gentlemen of Verona,* ii, 5, 10.

7
A curse begin at very root on 's heart,
That is not glad to see thee!
Coriolanus. Act ii, sc. 1, l. 202. [Menenius]

8
Call all your tribes together, praise the gods,
And make triumphant fires; strew flowers before them:
Unshout the noise that banish'd Marcius,
Repeal him with the welcome of his mother;
Cry 'Welcome, ladies, welcome!'
Coriolanus. Act v, sc. 5, l. 2. [Senator] The only use of "unshout."

9
You are as welcome, worthy sir, as I
Have words to bid you.
Cymbeline. Act i, sc. 6, l. 29. [Imogen]
I 'll love him as my brother:
And such a welcome as I 'ld give to him
After long absence, such is yours: most welcome!
Cymbeline. Act iii, sc. 6, l. 72. [Arviragus]
The night to the owl and the morn to the lark less welcome.
Cymbeline. Act iii, sc. 6, l. 94. [Arviragus]
All the remain is 'Welcome!'—*Cymbeline,* iii, 1, 87.

10
Gentlemen, you are welcome to Elsinore.
Hamlet. Act ii, sc. 2, l. 387. [Hamlet] Repeated in l. 573.
Welcome, my lord, to this brave town of York.
III Henry VI. Act ii, sc. 2, l. 1. [Queen Margaret]
You are welcome to Cyprus.—*Othello,* iv, 1, 274.
Welcome to London.—*II Henry IV,* ii, 4, 316; *Richard III,* iii, 1, 1.
Welcome to Milan!—*The Two Gentlemen of Verona,* ii, 5, 1.
Welcome to Rome.—*Coriolanus,* ii, 1, 184; *Titus Andronicus,* i, 1, 147; *Antony and Cleopatra,* ii, 2, 28; iii, 6, 85.
Welcome to Troy!—*Troilus and Cressida,* iv, 1, 21.
Welcome from Egypt.—*Antony and Cleopatra,* ii, 2, 174.
Welcome to our table.—*As You Like It,* ii, 7, 105.
Welcome us to town.—*The Taming of the Shrew,* i, 1, 47.
Welcome them ashore.—*Richard III,* iv, 4, 439.

1
The appurtenance of welcome is fashion and ceremony.
Hamlet. Act ii, sc. 2, l. 388. [Hamlet] The only use of "appurtenance."
And ceremoniously let us prepare
Some welcome for the mistress of the house.
The Merchant of Venice. Act v, sc. 1, l. 37. [Lorenzo] The only use of "ceremoniously."

2
Thou whoreson mad compound of majesty, by this light flesh and corrupt blood, thou art welcome.
II Henry IV. Act ii, sc. 4, l. 319. [Falstaff]
He is welcome.—*I Henry VI,* ii, 3, 14.
He shall be welcome.—*I Henry IV,* iv, 1, 94.
Welcome, by my soul.—*I Henry IV,* iv, 1, 86.
Thrice welcome!—*I Henry VI,* i, 2, 47; *Twelfth Night,* v, 1, 248.

3
Now welcome more, and ten times more beloved,
Than if thou never hadst deserved our hate.
III Henry VI. Act v, sc. 1, l. 103. [King Edward]

4
Ladies, a general welcome from his grace
Salutes you all.
Henry VIII. Act i, sc. 4, l. 1. [Guildford]
You 're welcome, my fair guests.
Henry VIII. Act i, sc. 4, l. 35. [Wolsey]
Once more
I shower a welcome on ye; welcome all.
Henry VIII. Act i, sc. 4, l. 63. [Wolsey]

5
Once more in mine arms I bid him welcome.
Henry VIII. Act ii, sc. 2, l. 99. [King]
Bid him welcome.—*As You Like It,* v, 4, 40; *Cymbeline,* iii, 6, 69.
Bid her welcome.—*Coriolanus,* i, 3, 47; *The Merchant of Venice,* iii, 2, 240.
Bid it welcome.—*The Winter's Tale,* iv, 4, 496.
Bid us welcome.—*Macbeth,* i, 4, 57.
Bid you welcome.—*The Merchant of Venice,* iii, 2, 225; *Much Ado about Nothing,* i, 1, 156; *Cymbeline,* iii, 1, 78.
Bid welcome.—*Timon of Athens,* iv, 3, 215.

6
Embrace him, love him, give him welcome hither.
King John. Act ii, sc. 1, l. 11. [Dauphin]
I give you welcome with a powerless hand,
But with a heart full of unstained love.
King John. Act ii, sc. 1, l. 15. [Arthur] The only use of "powerless."
Go, give 'em welcome.—*Henry VIII,* i, 4, 57.
Give it welcome.—*Hamlet,* i, 5, 165.
Let them be welcome.—*King John,* ii, 1, 83.

7
Whose welcome, I perceived, had poison'd mine.
King Lear. Act ii, sc. 4, l. 39. [Kent]

8
Meantime receive such welcome at my hand
As honour without breach of honour may
Make tender of to thy true worthiness.
Love's Labour 's Lost. Act ii, sc. 1, l. 169. [King]
I will . . . undertake your ben venuto.
Love's Labour 's Lost. Act iv, sc. 2, l. 162. [Holofernes]
'Alla nostra casa ben venuto.'
The Taming of the Shrew. Act i, sc. 2, l. 25. [Hortensio] The only use of the phrase, "Welcome to our house."
I shall be your ben venuto.
The Taming of the Shrew. Act i, sc. 2, l. 282. [Hortensio] The only uses of "ben venuto."

9
Biron: You are welcome, sir: adieu.
Boyet: Farewell to me, sir, and welcome to you.
Love's Labour 's Lost. Act ii, sc. 1, l. 213.
Baptista: You are welcome, sir.
Petruchio: And yet I come not well.
The Taming of the Shrew. Act iii, sc. 2, l. 90. "You are welcome" is used fifteen times.

10
Welcome, pure wit! thou partest a fair fray.
Love's Labour 's Lost. Act v, sc. 2, l. 484. [Biron]
Welcome, all.—*Titus Andronicus,* v, 3, 28.
Welcome, ass.—*Twelfth Night,* ii, 3, 18.
Welcome, wanderer.—*A Midsummer-Night's Dream,* ii, 1, 247.

11
To beguile the time,
Look like the time; bear welcome in your eye,
Your hand, your tongue.
Macbeth. Act i, sc. 5, l. 64. [Lady Macbeth]
Sleek o'er your rugged looks;
Be bright and jovial among your guests to-night.
Macbeth. Act iii, sc. 2, l. 27. [Lady Macbeth] The only use of "sleek" as a verb. As an adjective it is used twice, in *A Midsummer-Night's Dream,* iv, 1, 3: "Sleek smooth head"; and in *Henry VIII,* iii, 2, 241: "Sleek and wanton."
At first And last the hearty welcome. . . .
Our hostess keeps her state, but in best time
We will require her welcome.
Macbeth. Act iii, sc. 4, l. 1. [Macbeth]
My heart speaks they are welcome.
Macbeth. Act iii, sc. 4, l. 8. [Lady Macbeth]

12
Bassanio: By your leave,
I bid my very friends and countrymen,
Sweet Portia, welcome.
Portia: So do I, my lord:
They are entirely welcome.
The Merchant of Venice. Act iii, sc. 2, l. 225.
Portia: You are welcome home, my lord.
Bassanio: I thank you, madam. Give welcome to my friend. . . .
Portia: Sir, you are very welcome to our house:
It must appear in other ways than words,
Therefore I scant this breathing courtesy:
The Merchant of Venice. Act v, sc. 1, l. 132.
Welcome home.—*Richard III,* v, 3, 260, and nine times in later plays.

1
As I am a true spirit, welcome!
The Merry Wives of Windsor. Act v, sc. 5, l. 33. [Falstaff]

2
Where I have come, great clerks have purposed
To greet me with premeditated welcomes;
Where I have seen them shiver and look pale,
Make periods in the midst of sentences,
Throttle their practised accent in their fears
And in conclusion dumbly have broke off,
Not paying me a welcome. Trust me, sweet,
Out of this silence yet I picked a welcome;
And in the modesty of fearful duty
I read as much as from the rattling tongue
Of saucy and audacious eloquence.
A Midsummer-Night's Dream. Act v, sc. 1, l. 93. [Theseus] "Premeditated" is repeated in *Henry V,* iv, 1, 170: "Premeditated murder"; and in *I Henry VI,* iii, 1, 1: "Premeditated lines." The only use of "shiver." "Shivers" occurs in *Richard II,* iv, 1, 289, and in *Troilus and Cressida,* ii, 1, 42. The only use of "throttle." "Dumbly" is repeated in *Richard II,* v, 1, 95.

3
The worser welcome.
Othello. Act i, sc. 1, l. 95. [Brabantio]
Hollow welcomes.—*Timon of Athens,* i, 2, 16.

4
To say you 're welcome were superfluous.
Pericles. Act ii, sc. 3, l. 2. [Simonides]

5
To them say,
My house and welcome on their pleasure stay.
Romeo and Juliet. Act i, sc. 2, l. 36. [Capulet]

6
Go, sirrah, take them to the buttery,
And give them friendly welcome every one.
Taming of the Shrew. Induction, sc. 1, l. 102. [Lord] The only use of "buttery." "Buttery-bar" occurs in *Twelfth Night,* i, 3, 74.

7
To thee and thy company I bid
A hearty welcome.
The Tempest. Act v, sc. 1, l. 110. [Prospero]
Welcome heartily.—*The Taming of the Shrew,* iv, 1, 157.

8
You shall not make me welcome:
I come to have thee thrust me out of doors.
Timon of Athens, i, 2, 24. [Apemantus]
To nothing are they welcome.
Timon of Athens, iii, 6, 94. See under FRIEND.

9
They 're welcome all; let 'em have kind admittance:
Music, make their welcome!
Timon of Athens. Act i, sc. 2, l. 134. [Timon]
When there is nothing living but thee, thou shalt be welcome.
Timon of Athens. Act iv, sc. 3, l. 360. [Timon]
None so welcome.—*Timon of Athens,* i, 2, 223.
Respectively welcome.—*Timon of Athens,* iii, 1, 7. The only use of "respectively."

10
Yourself shall feast with us before you go
And find the welcome of a noble foe.
Troilus and Cressida. Act i, sc. 3, l. 308. [Agamemnon]

Faith and troth,
Strain'd purely from all hollow bias-drawing,
Bids thee, with most divine integrity,
From heart of very heart, great Hector, welcome.
Troilus and Cressida. Act iv, sc. 5, l. 168. [Agamemnon] The only use of "bias-drawing."
Most gentle and most valiant Hector, welcome.
Troilus and Cressida. Act iv, sc. 5, l. 227. [Ulysses]
Welcome to our tents.—*Troilus and Cressida,* iv, 5, 200.

11
Welcome ever smiles,
And farewell goes out sighing.
Troilus and Cressida. Act iii, sc. 3, l. 168. [Ulysses]

12
I fear We shall be much unwelcome.
Troilus and Cressida. Act iv, sc. 1, l. 44. [Paris] "Unwelcome" is used five times, three times in the phrase "unwelcome news."

13
Agamemnon: Most dearly welcome to the Greeks, sweet lady.
Nestor: Our general doth salute you with a kiss.
Troilus and Cressida. Act iv, sc. 5, l. 18.
Most dearly welcome!—*The Winter's Tale,* v, 1, 130.

14
Methinks I see
Leontes opening his free arms and weeping
His welcome forth.
Winter's Tale. Act iv, sc. 4, l. 557. [Camillo]

15
Welcome hither,
As is the spring to the earth.
Winter's Tale. Act v, sc. 1, l. 151. [Leontes]
Welcome hither.—*The Two Gentlemen of Verona,* ii, 4, 102, and twelve times in later plays.

WELFARE

16
Take heed, my lord; the welfare of us all
Hangs on the cutting short that fraudful man.
II Henry VI. Act iii, sc. 1, l. 181. [Queen] The only use of "fraudful."

17
Study for the people's welfare.
III Henry VI. Act iv, sc. 3, l. 39. [Warwick]

18
Until her husband's welfare she did hear.
The Rape of Lucrece, l. 263.

19
Sick of welfare, found a kind of meetness
To be diseased.
Sonnets. No. cxviii.

20
I am the turned forth, be it known to you,
That have preserved her welfare in my blood.
Titus Andronicus. Act v, sc. 3, l. 109. [Lucius]

WELKIN

See also Sky

1
By welkin and her star.
The Merry Wives of Windsor. Act i, sc. 3, l. 101. [Nym]
Starry welkin.—*A Midsummer-Night's Dream,* iii, 2, 356.
Fair welkin.—*The Rape of Lucrece,* l. 116.
Sweet welkin.—*Love's Labour's Lost,* iii, 1, 68.
Weeping welkin.—*Titus Andronicus,* iii, 1, 227.
Western welkin.—*King John,* v, 5, 2.
The welkin, the heaven.—*Love's Labour's Lost,* iv, 2, 5.

2
Amaze the welkin with your broken staves!
Richard III. Act v, sc. 3, l. 341. [King Richard]

3
Shall we make the welkin dance indeed?
Twelfth Night, ii, 3, 59. See under SONG.
Make the welkin answer.—*The Taming of the Shrew,* Ind., 2, 47.
Let the welkin roar.—*II Henry IV,* ii, 4, 182.
Out of my welkin.—*Twelfth Night,* iii, 1, 65. See under WORD.

WENCH

4
Dost thou conjure for wenches, that thou call'st for such store?
The Comedy of Errors. Act iii, sc. 1, l. 34. [Dromio of Syracuse]
I know a wench of excellent discourse,
Pretty and witty, wild and yet, too, gentle.
The Comedy of Errors. Act iii, sc. 1, l. 109. [Antipholus of Ephesus]

5
She's the kitchen wench and all grease; I know not what use to put her to but to make a lamp of her and run from her by her own light. I warrant her rags and the tallow in them will burn a Poland winter.
The Comedy of Errors. Act iii, sc. 2, l. 96. [Dromio of Syracuse]
But a kitchen-wench.—*Romeo and Juliet,* ii, 4, 42.
Kitchen-maid.—*Comedy of Errors,* iv, 4, 77.
Kitchen-malkin.—*Coriolanus,* ii, 1, 224.
Kitchen-trull.—*Cymbeline,* v, 5, 177.
Kitchen-vestal.—*Comedy of Errors,* iv, 4, 78.

6
Here she comes in the habit of a light wench: and thereof comes that the wenches say 'God damn me;' that's as much to say 'God make me a light wench.' It is written, they appear to men like angels of light: light is an effect of fire, and fire will burn; ergo, light wenches will burn.
The Comedy of Errors. Act iv, sc. 3, l. 52. [Dromio of Syracuse] The only use of "God damn me."
And that's great marvel, loving a light wench.
Love's Labour's Lost. Act i, sc. 2, l. 129. [Moth]
Light wenches may prove plagues to men forsworn.
Love's Labour's Lost. Act iv, sc. 3, l. 385. [Biron]
You are a light wench
Love's Labour's Lost. Act v, sc. 2, l. 25. [Katharine]

7
An 'twere not for thy humours, there's not a better wench in England.
II Henry IV. Act ii, sc. 1, l. 160. [Falstaff]

8
Prince of Wales: Must I marry your sister?
Poins: God send the wench no worse fortune!
II Henry IV. Act ii, sc. 2, l. 151.

9
Young Talbot was not born
To be the pillage of a giglot wench.
I Henry VI. Act iv, sc. 7, l. 40. [La Pucelle] "Giglot" is repeated in *Measure for Measure,* v, 1, 352, and in *Cymbeline,* iii, 1, 31.

10
Sir, I confess the wench.
Love's Labour's Lost. Act i, sc. 1, l. 285. [Costard]

11
A wench full grown,
Even ripe for marriage-rite.
Pericles, iv, Gower, 16. The only use of "marriage-rite."

12
That same pale hard-hearted wench.
Romeo and Juliet. Act ii, sc. 4, l. 4. [Mercutio]

13
That wench is stark mad or wonderful froward.
The Taming of the Shrew. Act i, sc. 1, l. 69. [Tranio]

14
Now, by the world, it is a lusty wench.
The Taming of the Shrew. Act ii, sc. 1, l. 161. [Petruchio]
Why, there's a wench!—*The Taming of the Shrew,* v, 2, 180.

15
Sir Andrew: Before me, she's a good wench.
Sir Toby: She's a beagle, true-bred, and one that adores me: what o' that?
Sir Andrew: I was adored once too.
Twelfth Night. Act ii, sc. 3, l. 194. "Beagle" is repeated in *Timon of Athens,* iv, 3, 175.
Angry wenches.—*The Taming of the Shrew,* ii, 1, 250.
Base wench.—*Love's Labour's Lost,* i, 2, 62.
Brown wench.—*Henry VIII,* iii, 2, 295.
Delicate wench.—*The Tempest,* ii, 1, 43.
Excellent wench.—*Twelfth Night,* ii, 5, 120.
False wench.—*Troilus and Cressida,* v, 2, 70.
Foolish wench!—*The Tempest,* i, 2, 479.
Gentle wench.—*The Rape of Lucrece,* l. 1273.
Good wench.—*The Merchant of Venice,* ii, 2, 175; *II Henry IV,* ii, 4, 407; *Henry VIII,* iv, 2, 81; 167; *Othello,* iii, 3, 313.
Hot wench.—*I Henry IV,* i, 2, 11.
Ill-starred wench.—*Othello,* v, 2, 272. The only use of "ill-starred."
Little wench.—*Love's Labour's Lost,* iv, 1, 126.
Poor wench.—*Love's Labour's Lost,* v, 2, 682; *Henry VIII,* iii, 1, 148.
Mad wenches.—*Love's Labour's Lost,* ii, 1, 256; v, 2, 264.

Mocking wenches.—*Love's Labour's Lost,* v, 2, 256.
Sullen wench.—*Romeo and Juliet,* iii, 3, 143.
Sweet wench.—*The Taming of the Shrew,* iii, 2, 240; *Titus Andronicus,* iii, 1, 283.
Unstanched wench.—*The Tempest,* i, 1, 51. "Unstanched" is repeated in *III Henry VI,* ii, 6, 83: "Unstanched thirst."
White wench.—*Romeo and Juliet,* ii, 4, 14.
Young wench.—*The Two Gentlemen of Verona,* ii, 1, 24.

WHINING, see under Complaint

WHIPPING

See also Beating, Scourge

1
Countess: You were lately whipped, sir, as I think.
Clown: O Lord, sir! spare not me.
Countess: Do you cry, 'O Lord, sir!' at your whipping, and 'spare not me'? Indeed your 'O Lord, sir!' is very sequent to your whipping: you would answer very well to a whipping, if you were but bound to 't.
All's Well that Ends Well. Act ii, sc. 2, l. 52.

He was whipped for getting the shrieve's fool with child.
All's Well that Ends Well. Act iv, sc. 3, l. 212. [Parolles] The only use of "shrieve."

He shall be whipped through the army with this rhyme in 's forehead.
All's Well that Ends Well. Act iv, sc. 3, l. 262. [Bertram]

I 'd have them whipped.—*All's Well that Ends Well,* ii, 3, 93.

2
Thou shalt be whipp'd with wire.
Antony and Cleopatra, ii, 5, 65. See THREAT, 1520:5.

You will be whipped.—*Antony and Cleopatra,* iii, 13, 88.

3
Take hence this Jack, and whip him. . . .
Whip him. . . . Whip him, fellows,
Till, like a boy, you see him cringe his face,
And whine aloud for mercy.
Antony and Cleopatra. Act iii, sc. 13, l. 93. [Antony] The only use of "cringe."

Antony: Is he whipp'd?
Attendant: Soundly, my lord.
Antony: Cried he? and begg'd a' pardon?
Attendant: He did ask favour.
Antony and Cleopatra. Act iii, sc. 13, l. 131.

Whipped for taxation.—*As You Like It,* i, 2, 91.

4
Go whip him 'fore the people's eyes.
Coriolanus. Act iv, sc. 6, l. 60. [Sicinius]

Go see this rumourer whipp'd.—*Coriolanus,* iv, 6, 47. The only use of "rumourer."

5
Use every man after his desert, and who would 'scape whipping?
Hamlet, ii, 2, 556. See under DESERVING. "'Scape whipping" is repeated in *Pericles,* ii, 1, 93.

Deserves . . . To be whipped.—*Love's Labour's Lost,* i, 2, 125.

Worthy to be whipped.—*Much Ado about Nothing,* ii, 1, 227.

6
Why, look you, I am whipp'd and scourged with rods,
Nettled and stung with pismires.
I Henry IV. Act i, sc. 3, l. 239. [Hotspur] The only mention of pismires.

Thou gavest them the rod, and putt'st down thine own breeches.
King Lear. Act i, sc. 4, l. 189. [Fool]

Come, thou child,
I 'll whip thee with a rod: he is defiled
That draws a sword on thee.
A Midsummer-Night's Dream. Act iii, sc. 2, l. 409. [Puck]

Whipp'd with rods.—*Antony and Cleopatra,* iv, 1, 3.

7
She shall have whipping-cheer enough, I warrant her.
II Henry IV. Act v, sc. 4, l. 5. [Beadle] The only use of "whipping-cheer."

8
Gloucester: My masters of Saint Alban's, have you not beadles in your towns, and things called whips?
Mayor: Yes, my lord, if it please your grace.
Gloucester: Then send for one presently. . . . Now fetch me a stool hither by and by. Now, sirrah, if you mean to save yourself from whipping, leap me over this stool and run away.
Simpson: Alas, master, I am not able to stand alone:
You go about to torture me in vain.
Gloucester: Well, sir, we must have you find your legs. Sirrah beadle, whip him till he leap over that same stool.
II Henry VI. Act ii, sc. 1, l. 135.

I have seen him whipped three market-days together.
II Henry VI. Act iv, sc. 2, l. 62. [Dick] The only use of "market-days."

Let them be whipped through every market-town, till they come to Berwick, from whence they came.
II Henry VI. Act ii, sc. 1, l. 159. [Gloucester] "Market-town" is repeated in *King Lear,* iii, 6, 78.

Nay, whip me then.—*III Henry VI,* iii, 2, 28.

9
Take heed, sirrah; the whip.
King Lear. Act i, sc. 4, l. 123. [King Lear]

He must be whipp'd out.
King Lear, i, 4, 125. See under TRUTH.

Let him be whipped.—*King Lear,* i, 4, 180.

10
King Lear: An you lie, sirrah, we 'll have you whipped.
Fool: I marvel what kin thou and thy daughters are. They'll have me whipped for speaking true, thou 'lt have me whipped for lying; and sometimes I am whipped for holding my peace.
King Lear. Act i, sc. 4, l. 197.

Whipped from tithing to tithing, and stock-punished, and imprisoned.
King Lear. Act iii, sc. 4, l. 139. [Edgar] The only use of "tithing" and "stock-punished."

1
Then shall Hector be whipped for Jaquenetta that is quick by him.
Love's Labour 's Lost. Act v, sc. 2, l. 687. [Costard]

Love's whip.—*Love's Labour 's Lost,* iii, 1, 176.

2
Holofernes: Go, whip thy gig. . . .
Moth: I will whip about your infamy circum circa,—a gig of a cuckold's horn.
Love's Labour 's Lost. Act v, sc. 1, l. 69. The only use of "circum circa" (round and round).

Whipping a gig.—*Love's Labour 's Lost,* iv, 3, 167.

Whipped top.—*The Merry Wives of Windsor,* v, 1, 27.

3
Whip to our tents, as roes run o'er land.
Love's Labour 's Lost. Act v, sc. 2, l. 309. [Princess of France]

Whips out his rapier.—*Hamlet,* iv, 1, 10.

4
You 'll find good cause to whip them all.
Measure for Measure. Act ii, sc. 1, l. 142. [Angelo]

You shall have . . . an unpitied whipping.
Measure for Measure. Act iv, sc. 2, l. 14. [Provost]

5
Escalus: In plain dealing, Pompey, I shall have you whipt. . . .
Pompey: Whip me? No, no; let carman whip his jade:
The valiant heart 's not whipt out of his trade.
Measure for Measure. Act ii, sc. 1, l. 264. See under Beating. The only use of "carman." "Carmen" occurs in *II Henry IV,* iii, 2, 341.

Lucio: I had rather it would please you I might be whipt.
Duke: Whipt first, sir, and hanged after. . . .
Let him be whipt and hanged.
Measure for Measure. Act v, sc. 1, l. 512.

I whipt me behind the arras.—*Much Ado about Nothing,* i, 3, 63. These are the only uses of "whipt."

6
I 'll whip you from your foining fence.
Much Ado about Nothing. Act v, sc. 1, l. 84. [Antonio]

7
Whip me such honest knaves.
Othello, i, 1, 49. See under Knave.

Whip me, ye devils.—*Othello,* v, 2, 277.

Whip thee, gosling.—*Pericles,* iv, 2, 91. "Gosling" is repeated in *Coriolanus,* v, 3, 35.

8
Let 's whip these stragglers o'er the seas again;
Lash hence these overweening rags of France.
Richard III. Act v, sc. 3, l. 327. [King Richard] The only use of "stragglers."

Put in every honest hand a whip
To lash the rascals naked through the world.
Othello, iv, 2, 142. See under Knave.

Why dost thou lash that whore?
King Lear, iv, 6, 165. See under Hypocrisy.

Her whip of cricket's bone, the lash of film.
Romeo and Juliet, i, 4, 63. See under Fairy.

How smart a lash.—*Hamlet,* iii, 1, 50. The only uses of "lash."

Lash'd with woe.—*The Comedy of Errors,* ii, 1, 15. The only use of "lash'd."

9
Whipped at the high cross every morning.
The Taming of the Shrew, i, 1, 136. See under Dowry.

Whipp'd and tormented.—*Romeo and Juliet,* i, 2, 57.

10
Not all the whips of heaven are large enough.
Timon of Athens, v, 1, 64. See under Friend.

Whips and scorns of time.—*Hamlet,* iii, 1, 70.

Keen whips.—*Measure for Measure,* ii, 4, 101.

11
He was certainly whipped out of the court.
Winter's Tale, iv, 3, 95. See Vice, 1599:15.

Whipped out of the court.—*The Winter's Tale,* iv, 3, 97.

Whips me out of the chamber.—*The Two Gentlemen of Verona,* iv, 4, 31.

Whip him out.—*The Two Gentlemen of Verona,* iv, 4, 23.

Whip the dog.—*The Two Gentlemen of Verona,* iv, 4, 27.

Whip you to the west.—*Romeo and Juliet,* iii, 2, 3.

Whip your information.—*Coriolanus,* iv, 6, 53.

Whip hypocrisy.—*Love's Labour 's Lost,* iv, 3, 151.

Whip this dwarfish war.—*King John,* v, 2, 135.

WHISPER

12
I 'll whisper with the general, and know his pleasure.
All 's Well that Ends Well. Act iv, sc. 3, l. 329. [Soldier]

13
Never admitted A private whisper.
Coriolanus. Act v, sc. 3, l. 6. [Aufidius]

Secret whispers.—*Henry V,* iv, Prol., 7.

14
At least, the whisper goes so.
Hamlet. Act i, sc. 1, l. 80. [Horatio]

15
Why whisper you, my lords, and answer not?
III Henry VI. Act i, sc. 1, l. 149. [Exeter]

16
Mark, how they whisper.
King John. Act ii, sc. 1, l. 475. [Queen Elinor]

And when they talk of him, they shake their heads
And whisper one another in the ear;
And he that speaks doth gripe the hearer's wrist,
Whilst he that hears makes fearful action,
With wrinkled brows, with nods, with rolling eyes.
King John. Act iv, sc. 2, l. 188. [Hubert]

1
What did you whisper in your lady's ear?
Love's Labour 's Lost. Act v, sc. 2, l. 436. [Princess]
What did the Russian whisper in your ear?
Love's Labour 's Lost. Act v, sc. 2, l. 443. [Princess]
Whisper her ear.—*Much Ado about Nothing,* iii, 1, 4.
Tell a whispering tale in a fair lady's ear.
Romeo and Juliet. Act i, sc. 5, l. 25. [Capulet]
She whispers in his ear a heavy tale.
Venus and Adonis, l. 1125.
Whispers in mine ear.—*Venus and Adonis,* l. 659.
Rain sacrificial whisperings in his ear.
Timon of Athens. Act i, sc. 1, l. 81. [Poet] The only use of "sacrificial."
Hark in thine ear.—*The Tempest,* i, 2, 318.

2
Foul whisperings are abroad.
Macbeth. Act v, sc. 1, l. 79. [Doctor]

3
They 're here with me already, whispering, rounding
'Sicilia is a so-forth:' 'tis far gone,
When I shall gust it last.
The Winter's Tale. Act i, sc. 2, l. 217. [Leontes] The only use of "rounding" and of "gust" in the sense of taste or understand.
And so forth.—*Love's Labour 's Lost,* iv, 2, 96; *II Henry IV,* v, 3, 4; *Twelfth Night,* i, 5, 267; iii, 4, 82.
Or so forth.—*Hamlet,* ii, 1, 61.

4
Is whispering nothing?
Winter's Tale. Act i, sc. 2, l. 284. [Leontes]
Your followers I will whisper to the business.
Winter's Tale. Act i, sc. 2, l. 437. [Camillo]
'Tis well they are whispering.
Winter's Tale. Act iv, sc. 4, l. 249. [Clown]

WHISTLING

5
Whistling to the air.
Antony and Cleopatra. Act ii, sc. 2, l. 221. [Enobarbus]
Hollow whistling.—*I Henry IV,* v, 1, 5. See under WIND.

6
Hear the shrill whistle which doth order give
To sounds confused.
Henry V. Act iii, Prologue, l. 9. [Chorus]
The boatswain whistles, and The master calls.
Pericles. Act iv, sc. 1, l. 64. [Marina]
The master's whistle.—*The Tempest,* i, 1, 8.
The seaman's whistle.—*Pericles,* iii, 1, 8.
Pipes and whistles.—*As You Like It,* ii, 7, 163.

7
Some time I shall sleep out, the rest I 'll whistle.
King Lear. Act ii, sc. 2, l. 163. [Kent]
Worth the whistle.—*King Lear,* iv, 2, 29.

8 Whistle then to me
As signal that thou hear'st something approach.
Romeo and Juliet. Act v, sc. 3, l. 7. [Paris]

9 If I do prove her haggard,
Though that her jesses were my dear heart-strings,
I 'ld whistle her off and let her down the wind,
To prey at fortune.
Othello. Act iii, sc. 3, l. 260. [Othello] The only use of "jesses," the straps fastened around the legs of a trained hawk.

WHITENESS

10 Thou wilt lie upon the wings of night
Whiter than new snow on a raven's back.
Romeo and Juliet. Act iii, sc. 2, l. 18. [Juliet]
White his shroud as the mountain snow.
Hamlet. Act iv, sc. 5, l. 35. [Ophelia]
White as driven snow.—*The Winter's Tale,* iv, 4, 220.
White as snow.—*Hamlet,* iii, 3, 46; iv, 5, 195.
Whiter than snow.—*Othello,* v, 2, 4.
White as lawn.—*The Rape of Lucrece,* l. 259.
White as milk.—*The Merchant of Venice,* iii, 2, 86; *Pericles,* iv, Gower, 22.
White as whale's bone.—*Love's Labour 's Lost,* v, 2, 332.
Turn white.—*A Lover's Complaint,* l. 308.

11
O'er the white sheet peers her whiter chin,
The reason of this rash alarm to know.
The Rape of Lucrece, l. 472.
Teaching the sheets a whiter hue than white.
Venus and Adonis, l. 398. See under LOVE.
Whiter than the sheets.—*Cymbeline,* ii, 2, 16.
Pure white.—*A Midsummer-Night's Dream,* iii, 2, 144.
Silver white.—*The Rape of Lucrece,* l. 56; 1405.
White and spotless.—*Titus Andronicus,* i, 1, 81.
Whiter than the paper.—*The Merchant of Venice,* ii, 4, 13.

12
Nor did I wonder at the lily's white.
Sonnets. No. xcviii.
Lily white.—*Venus and Adonis,* l. 1053.
White as a lily.—*The Two Gentlemen of Verona,* ii, 3, 22.

WHORE

13
If it lay in their hands to make me a cuckold, they would make themselves whores, but they 'ld do 't!
Antony and Cleopatra, i, 2, 80. [Alexas]
He hath given his empire Up to a whore.
Antony and Cleopatra, iii, 6, 66. [Cæsar]
Have I my pillow left unpress'd in Rome,
Forborne the getting of a lawful race,
And by a gem of women, to be abused
By one that looks on feeders?
Antony and Cleopatra. Act iii, sc. 13, l. 106. [Antony] The only use of "unpress'd" and "forborne."
Triple-turn'd whore! 'tis thou
Hast sold me to this novice.
Antony and Cleopatra. Act iv, sc. 12, l. 13. [Antony] The only use of "triple-turn'd."
Boy my greatness I' the posture of a whore.
Antony and Cleopatra. Act v, sc. 2, l. 220. [Cleopatra]

14
'I saw him enter such a house of sale,'
Videlicet, a brothel.
Hamlet. Act ii, sc. 1, l. 60. [Polonius] "Videlicet" is used four times in as many different plays.

Thy mistress is o' the brothel.—*Timon of Athens,* iv, 1, 13.
Keep thy foot out of brothels.—*King Lear,* iii, 4, 99.
More like a brothel.—*King Lear,* i, 4, 266.
The brothel 'scapes.—*Pericles,* v, Gower, 1. The only uses of "brothel" and "brothels."
Brothel-house.—*Much Ado about Nothing,* i, 1, 256. The only use of the phrase.
Bawdy-house, see under BAWD.
Leaping-houses.—*I Henry IV,* i, 2, 9.

1
That he is, saving your reverence, a whoremaster, that I utterly deny.
I Henry IV. Act ii, sc. 4, l. 515. [Falstaff]
The deputy cannot abide a whoremaster: if he be a whoremonger, and comes before him, he were as good go a mile on his errand.
Measure for Measure. Act iii, sc. 2, l. 36. [Elbow] The only use of "whoremonger."
Apemantus: We may account thee a whoremaster and a knave; which notwithstanding, thou shalt be no less esteemed.
Servant: What is a whoremaster, fool?
Fool: A fool in good clothes, and something like thee. 'Tis a spirit: sometime 't appears like a lord; sometime like a lawyer; sometime like a philosopher, with two stones moe than 's artificial one: he is very often like a knight; and, generally, in all shapes that man goes up and down in from fourscore to thirteen, this spirit walks in.
Timon of Athens. Act ii, sc. 2, l. 110.
Whoremaster man.—*King Lear,* i, 2, 137. The only uses of "whoremaster." "Whoremasterly" occurs in *Troilus and Cressida,* v, 4, 7.

2
The whores call him mandrake.
II Henry IV, iii, 2, 338. See under CHARACTER.
Thou that givest whores indulgences to sin.
I Henry VI. Act i, sc. 3, l. 35. [Gloucester]
Leave thy drink and thy whore.
King Lear, i, 4, 137. See under BEHAVIOUR.
Arrant whore.—*King Lear,* ii, 4, 52.
Common whore.—*Timon of Athens,* iv, 3, 42.
Villanous whore!—*Othello,* v, 2, 229.
Rebel's whore.—*Macbeth,* i, 2, 15.
Whore of Babylon.—*Henry V,* ii, 3, 41. See under WOMAN.
Whores and knaves.—*The Tempest,* ii, 1, 166.
A very good whore!—*Romeo and Juliet,* ii, 4, 32.

3
Ever your fresh whore and your powdered bawd.
Measure for Measure. Act iii, sc. 2, l. 61. [Lucio] The only use of "powdered." See also BAWD.
Your whores, sir, . . . using painting.
Measure for Measure, iv, 2, 39. See under HANGING.
I beseech your highness, do not marry me to a whore.
Measure for Measure, v, 1, 520. [Lucio]

4
Evans: What is your genitive case plural, William? . . .
William: Genitive,—horum, harum, horum.
Mistress Quickly: Vengeance of Jenny's case! fie on her! never name her, child, if she be a whore.
Evans: For shame, 'oman.
Mistress Quickly: You do ill to teach the child . . . to call 'horum:' fie upon you!
Evans: 'Oman, art thou lunatics? hast thou no understanding for thy cases and the numbers of the genders?
Merry Wives of Windsor. Act iv, sc. 1, l. 60. The only uses of "genitive." "Plural" is repeated in *Two Gentlemen of Verona,* v, 4, 52.

5
Leonato's Hero, your Hero, every man's Hero.
Much Ado about Nothing. Act iii, sc. 2, l. 109. [Don John]

6
Villain, be sure thou prove my love a whore,
Be sure of it; give me the ocular proof;
Or, by the worth of man's eternal soul,
Thou hadst been better have been born a dog
Than answer my waked wrath!
Othello. Act iii, sc. 3, l. 359. [Othello] The only use of "ocular."
O, the world hath not a sweeter creature: she might lie by an emperor's side and command him tasks.
Othello. Act iv, sc. 1, l. 194. [Othello]
This is a subtle whore,
A closet lock and key of villanous secrets:
And yet she'll kneel and pray.
Othello. Act iv, sc. 2, l. 21. [Othello]
Othello: Was this fair paper, this most goodly book,
Made to write 'whore' upon? . . .
Desdemona: By heaven, you do me wrong. . . .
Othello: What, not a whore?
Desdemona: No, as I shall be saved. . . .
Othello: I cry you mercy, then:
I took you for that cunning whore of Venice
That married with Othello.
Othello. Act iv, sc. 2, l. 71.
I cannot say 'whore:'
It does abhor me now I speak the word;
To do the act that might the addition earn
Not the world's mass of vanity could make me.
Othello. Act iv, sc. 2, l. 161. [Desdemona]

7
She turn'd to folly, and she was a whore.
Othello. Act v, sc. 2, l. 132. [Othello]
This is the fruit of whoring.
Othello. Act v, sc. 1, l. 116. [Iago] The only use of "whoring."

8
He call'd her whore: a beggar in his drink
Could not have laid such terms upon his callet.
Othello. Act iv, sc. 2, l. 120. [Emilia]
My lord hath so bewhored her,
Thrown such despite and heavy terms upon her,
As true hearts cannot bear.
Othello. Act iv, sc. 2, l. 115. [Emilia] The only use of "bewhored."
Hath she forsook so many noble matches,
Her father and her country and her friends,
To be call'd whore? would it not make one weep?
Othello. Act iv, sc. 2, l. 125. [Emilia]

Why should he call her whore? who keeps her
company?
What place? what time? what form? what
likelihood?
Othello. Act iv, sc. 2, l. 137. [Emilia]

1
Pandar: Search the market narrowly: Mytilene is full of gallants. We lost too much money this mart by being too wenchless.
Bawd: We were never so much out of creatures. We have but poor three, and they can do no more than they can do; and they with continual action are even as good as rotten.
Pericles. Act iv, sc. 2, l. 3. The only use of "wenchless."
Neither is our profession any trade; it 's no calling.
Pericles. Act iv, sc. 2, l. 43. [Pandar]
Lysander: How long have you been of this profession?
Marina: E'er since I can remember.
Lysander: Did you go to 't so young? Were you a gamester at five or at seven?
Marina: Earlier too, sir, if now I be one.
Lysander: Why, the house you dwell in proclaims you to be a creature of sale. . . . Come, bring me to some private place: come, come.
Pericles. Act iv, sc. 6, l. 77.

2 This fell whore of thine
Hath in her more destruction than thy
sword,
For all her cherubin look.
Timon of Athens. Act iv, sc. 3, l. 61. [Timon]
Be a whore still: they love thee not that use
thee;
Give them diseases, leaving with thee their lust.
Make use of thy salt hours: season the slaves
For tubs and baths; bring down rose-cheeked
youth
To the tub-fast and the diet.
Timon of Athens. Act iv, sc. 3, l. 83. [Timon] The only use of "tubs" and "tub-fast," referring to the use of the sweating cure. "Tub" occurs in *Measure for Measure,* iii, 2, 59, and in *Cymbeline,* i, 6, 48. "Rose-cheeked" is repeated in *Venus and Adonis,* l. 3.
Be whores still;
And he whose pious breath seeks to convert you,
Be strong in whore, allure him, burn him up;
Let your close fire predominate his smoke,
And be no turncoats.
Timon of Athens. Act iv, sc. 3, l. 139. [Timon] The only use of "turncoats." "Turncoat" occurs in *Much Ado about Nothing,* i, 1, 125; and "predominate" in *Merry Wives of Windsor,* ii, 2, 294.
Make curl'd-pate ruffians bald;
And let the unscarr'd braggarts of the war
Derive some pain from you: plague all;
That your activity may defeat and quell
The source of all erection.
Timon of Athens. Act iv, sc. 3, l. 160. [Timon] The only use of "curl'd-pate." "Unscarr'd" is repeated in *Richard III,* iv, 4, 209.

3
The heavier for a whore.
Troilus and Cressida, iv, 1, 66. See under COMPARISON.
The heavier for a husband.—*Much Ado about Nothing,* iii, 4, 35. See under HUSBAND.

4
Thersites: Thou art thought to be Achilles' male varlet.
Patroclus: Male varlet, you rogue! what 's that?
Thersites: Why, his masculine whore.
Troilus and Cressida. Act v, sc. 1, l. 17.

5
Ulysses: She will sing any man at first sight.
Thersites: And any man may sing her, if he can take her cliff; she 's noted.
Troilus and Cressida. Act v, sc. 2, l. 9.
A proof of strength she could not publish more,
Unless she said 'My mind is now turn'd whore.'
Troilus and Cressida, v, 2, 113. [Thersites]
If the son of a whore fight for a whore, he tempts judgement.
Troilus and Cressida, v, 7, 21. [Thersites]
The lazar kite of Cressid's kind.
Henry V. Act ii, sc. 1, l. 80. [Pistol] The only use of "lazar kite."

II—Whore: Some Synonyms

See also Bawd, Strumpet

Callet:

6 A callet
Of boundless tongue, who late hath beat
her husband
And now baits me.
Winter's Tale. Act ii, sc. 3, l. 90. [Leontes]
Contemptuous, base-born callet.—*II Henry VI,* i, 3, 86.
Shameless callet.—*III Henry VI,* ii, 2, 145.
"Callet" is used a fourth time in *Othello,* iv, 2, 121, given above.

Courtezan:

7
This is a brave night to cool a courtezan.
King Lear. Act iii, sc. 2, l. 79. [Fool]
Roman courtezan.—*Cymbeline,* iii, 4, 126.
Shameless courtezan!—*I Henry VI,* iii, 2, 45.
A brace of courtezans.—*Richard III,* iii, 7, 74.
Give to courtezans.—*II Henry VI,* i, 1, 223.
The only uses of "courtezan."

Drab:

8
They say he keeps a Trojan drab, and uses the traitor Calchas' tent.
Troilus and Cressida, v, 1, 104. [Thersites]
The parrot will not do more for an almond than he for a commodious drab.
Troilus and Cressida, v, 2, 195. The only use of "almond" and "commodious."
Take this drab away.—*II Henry VI,* ii, 1, 156.
Cursed drab.—*I Henry VI,* v, 4, 32.
Luxurious drab.—*Troilus and Cressida,* v, 4, 9.
Drabs and knaves.—*Measure for Measure,* ii, 1, 247.
A very drab.—*Hamlet,* ii, 2, 615. The only uses of "drab."
Quarrelling, Drabbing.—*Hamlet,* ii, 1, 26. The only use of "drabbing."

Harlot:

1
She with harlots feasted in my house.
The Comedy of Errors. Act v, sc. 1, l. 205. [Antipholus of Ephesus]

2
Portia is Brutus' harlot, not his wife.
Julius Cæsar. Act ii, sc. 1, l. 287. [Portia]

3
He sups to-night with a harlotry.
Othello. Act iv, sc. 2, l. 239. [Iago]

A peevish self-will'd harlotry.
Romeo and Juliet. Act iv, sc. 2, l. 14. [Capulet]

Harlotry players.—*I Henry IV,* ii, 4, 437. The only uses of "harlotry."

4
Held with a brace of harlots.
Timon of Athens. Act iv, sc. 3, l. 79. [Timon]

Dissembling harlot.—*The Comedy of Errors,* iv, 4, 104.

Hildings and harlots.—*Romeo and Juliet,* ii, 4, 45.

Punk:

5
This punk is one of Cupid's carriers.
The Merry Wives of Windsor. Act ii, sc. 2, l. 141. [Pistol]

Duke: Neither maid, widow, nor wife?
Lucio: My lord, she may be a punk; for many of them are neither maid, widow, nor wife.
Measure for Measure. Act v, sc. 1, l. 176. The only uses of "maid, widow, nor wife."

Marrying a punk.—*Measure for Measure,* v, 1, 528.

Taffeta punk.—*All's Well that Ends Well,* ii, 2, 24. The only uses of "punk."

Stale:

6
I stand dishonour'd, that have gone about
To link my dear friend to a common stale.
Much Ado about Nothing. Act iv, sc. 1, l. 65. [Don Pedro]

Poor I am but his stale.—*The Comedy of Errors,* ii, 1, 101.

Is it your will
To make a stale of me amongst these mates?
The Taming of the Shrew. Act i, sc. 1, l. 56. [Katharina]

Make a stale.—*III Henry VI,* iii, 3, 260; *Titus Andronicus,* i, 1, 304.

Bully stale.—*The Merry Wives of Windsor,* ii, 3, 30.

A contaminated stale.—*Much Ado about Nothing,* ii, 2, 26. The only uses of "stale" in this sense.

Miscellaneous:

7
O thou public commoner!
Othello. Act iv, sc. 2, l. 73. [Othello]

'Tis such another fitchew! marry, a perfumed one.
Othello. Act iv, sc. 1, l. 150. [Cassio] "Fitchew" is repeated in *Troilus and Cressida,* v, 1, 67, and in *King Lear,* iv, 6, 124.

Scurvy knave! I am none of his flirt-gills; I am none of his skains-mates.
Romeo and Juliet. Act ii, sc. 4, l. 161. [Nurse] The only use of "flirt-gills" and "skains-mates."

Throw the quean in the channel.
II Henry IV. Act ii, sc. 1, l. 51. [Falstaff] "Quean" is repeated in *All's Well that Ends Well,* ii, 2, 27, and in *The Merry Wives of Windsor,* iv, 2, 180.

Like an Amazonian trull.
III Henry VI, i, 4, 114. See under WOMAN. "Amazonian" is repeated in *Coriolanus,* ii, 2, 95. "Trull" is used four times.

WHY AND WHEREFORE, see under Cause

WICKEDNESS

See also Badness, Sin, Vileness

8
I have been, madam, a wicked creature, as you and all flesh and blood are.
All's Well that Ends Well, i, 3, 37. [Clown]

Wicked creatures.—*King Lear,* ii, 4, 259.
Wicked bastard.—*As You Like It,* iv, 1, 216.
Wicked bawd.—*Measure for Measure,* iii, 2, 20.
Wicked beast.—*Timon of Athens,* iii, 2, 49.
Wicked caitiff.—*Measure for Measure,* ii, 1, 193; *Timon of Athens,* v, 4, 71.
Wicked fiend.—*Romeo and Juliet,* iii, 5, 235.
Wicked foe.—*The Rape of Lucrece,* l. 1035.
Wicked men.—*Richard III,* v, 1, 23.
Wicked spirits.—*I Henry VI,* v, 4, 42; *II Henry VI,* ii, 1, 174.
Wicked varlet.—*Measure for Measure,* ii, 1, 174; 199.
Wicked villain.—*Measure for Measure,* i, 2, 27.

9
Wickedness is sin.
As You Like It, iii, 2, 44. See under SIN.

10
Now am I . . . little better than one of the wicked.
I Henry IV. Act i, sc. 2, l. 106. [Falstaff]

Is she of the wicked? is thine hostess here of the wicked? or is thy boy of the wicked?
II Henry IV. Act ii, sc. 4, l. 355. [Prince of Wales]

God help the wicked!—*I Henry IV,* ii, 4, 517.

11
What rein can hold licentious wickedness
When down the hill he holds his fierce career?
Henry V. Act iii, sc. 3, l. 22. [King Henry]

12
Such is thy audacious wickedness,
Thy lewd, pestiferous and dissentious pranks,
As very infants prattle of thy pride.
I Henry VI. Act iii, sc. 1, l. 14. [Gloucester] "Pestiferous" is repeated in *All's Well that Ends Well,* iv, 3, 340: "Pestiferous reports." "Dissentious" is used four times.

13
O God, what mischiefs work the wicked ones,
Heaping confusion on their own heads thereby!
II Henry VI. Act ii, sc. 1, l. 186. [King]

By wicked means to frame our sovereign's fall.
II Henry VI. Act iii, sc. 1, l. 52. [Suffolk]

14
I'll never care what wickedness I do,
If this man come to good.
King Lear. Act iii, sc. 7, l. 99. [Servant]

1
As wicked as his wife.
The Merry Wives of Windsor. Act v, sc. 5, l. 165. [Ford]
Wicked wife.—*Pericles,* v, 1, 173.

2
Into the chamber wickedly he stalks,
And gazeth on her yet unstained bed.
The Rape of Lucrece, l. 365. The only use of "wickedly."

WIDOW

See also Wife and Widow

3
I am a poor widow of Eastcheap.
II Henry IV. Act ii, sc. 1, l. 76. [Hostess]
Are you not ashamed to enforce a poor widow to so rough a course to come by her own?
II Henry IV. Act ii, sc. 1, l. 88. [Chief Justice]
Poor widow.—*Measure for Measure,* ii, 1, 207.

4 Many a thousand widows
Shall this his mock mock out of their dear husbands.
Henry V. Act i, sc. 2, l. 284. [King Henry]

5
I and ten thousand in this luckless realm
Had left no mourning widows for our death.
III Henry VI. Act ii, sc. 6, l. 18. [Clifford]

6
The widow likes him not, she knits her brows.
III Henry VI. Act iii, sc. 2, l. 82. [Gloucester]
The widow likes it not, for she looks very sad.
III Henry VI. Act iii, sc. 2, l. 110. [Gloucester]

7
In hope he 'll prove a widower shortly,
I'll wear the willow garland for his sake.
III Henry VI. Act iii, sc. 3, l. 227. [Bona]
Great Marc Antony Is now a widower.
Antony and Cleopatra. Act ii, sc. 2, l. 121. [Agrippa] "Widower" is repeated in *All's Well that Ends Well,* v, 3, 70; 142; and in *The Tempest,* ii, 1, 79, as given below.

8
How may we content This widow lady?
King John. Act ii, sc. 1, l. 547. [King Philip] The only use of "widow lady."
Lady widow.—*Romeo and Juliet,* i, 2, 69.

9
A widow, husbandless, subject to fears.
King John. Act iii, sc. 1, l. 14. [Constance] The only use of "husbandless."

10
Each new morn New widows howl.
Macbeth. Act iv, sc. 3, l. 5. [Macduff]

11
Neither maid, widow, nor wife.
Measure for Measure, v, 1, 178. See under Maid.

12
Made her widow to a woful bed?
Richard III. Act i, sc. 2, l. 249. [Gloucester]
Your widow-dolour likewise be unwept!
Richard III. Act ii, sc. 2, l. 65. [Girl] The only use of "widow-dolour" and "unwept."
'Be thou,' quoth I, 'accursed,
For making me, so young, so old a widow!'
Richard III. Act iv, sc. 1, l. 72. [Anne]

13
A beauty-waning and distressed widow,
Even in the afternoon of her best days,
Made prize and purchase of his lustful eye,
Seduced the pitch and height of all his thoughts
To base declension and loathed bigamy.
Richard III. Act iii, sc. 7, l. 185. [Buckingham] The only use of "beauty-waning" and "bigamy."
Jealous o'erworn widow.—*Richard III,* i, 1, 81. "Over-worn" occurs in *Twelfth Night,* iii, 1, 66.
Mourning widow.—*Henry V,* i, 2, 58.
Wappen'd widow.—*Timon of Athens,* iv, 3, 38. The only use of "wappen'd" (fatigued).

14
The world will be thy widow and still weep
That thou no form of thee hast left behind,
When every private widow well may keep
By children's eyes her husband's shape in mind.
Sonnets. No. ix.

15
I 'll assure her of her widowhood.
The Taming of the Shrew. Act ii, sc. 1, l. 125. [Petruchio] The only use of "widowhood."

16
I will be married to a wealthy widow,
Ere three days pass, which hath as long loved me.
The Taming of the Shrew. Act iv, sc. 2, l. 37. [Hortensio]
I' faith, he 'll have a lusty widow now,
That shall be woo'd and wedded in a day.
The Taming of the Shrew. Act iv, sc. 2, l. 50. [Tranio]
Have to my widow! and if she be froward,
Then hast thou taught Hortensio to be untoward.
The Taming of the Shrew. Act iv, sc. 5, l. 78. [Hortensio]
Good widow.—*Taming of the Shrew,* v, 2, 25.
Loving widow.—*Taming of the Shrew,* v, 2, 7.
Sweet widow.—*III Henry VI,* iii, 2, 93.

17
Adrian: Tunis was never graced before with such a paragon to their queen.
Gonzalo: Not since widow Dido's time.
Antonio: Widow! a pox o' that! How came that widow in? widow Dido!
Sebastian: What if he had said 'widower Æneas' too? Good Lord, how you take it!
The Tempest. Act ii, sc. 1, l. 74.
Sebastian: Bate, I beseech you, widow Dido.
Antonio: O, widow Dido! ay, widow Dido.
The Tempest. Act ii, sc. 1, l. 100.

18 Milan and Naples have
Moe widows in them of this business' making
Than we bring men to comfort them.
The Tempest. Act ii, sc. 1, l. 132. [Sebastian]

WIFE

See also under Lady

1
Helena: This is the man.
King: Why, then, young Bertram, take her; she's thy wife.
Bertram: My wife, my liege! I shall beseech your highness,
In such a business give me leave to use
The help of mine own eyes. . . .
A poor physician's daughter for my wife! Disdain
Rather corrupt me ever!
All's Well that Ends Well. Act ii, sc. 3, l. 111.
War is no strife
To a dark house and a detested wife.
All's Well that Ends Well. Act ii, sc. 3, l. 308. [Bertram]
'Tis a hard bondage to become the wife
Of a detesting lord.
All's Well that Ends Well. Act iii, sc. 5, l. 67. [Diana] The only use of "detesting."
I would he loved his wife.
All's Well that Ends Well. Act iii, sc. 5, l. 82. [Diana]
He has much worthy blame laid upon him for shaking off so good a wife and so sweet a lady.
All's Well that Ends Well. Act iv, sc. 3, l. 7. [First Lord]
His wife some two months since fled from his house.
All's Well that Ends Well. Act iv, sc. 3, l. 56. [Lord]
Buried a wife, mourned for her.
All's Well that Ends Well. Act iv, sc. 3, l. 101. [Bertram]

2
I wonder, sir, sith wives are monsters to you,
And that you fly them as you swear them lordship,
Yet you desire to marry.
All's Well that Ends Well. Act v, sc. 3, l. 155. [King]
You, that have turn'd off a first so noble wife,
May justly diet me.
All's Well that Ends Well. Act v, sc. 3, l. 220. [Diana]
First wife.—*All's Well that Ends Well,* v, 3, 280. The only use of "first wife."
New wife.—*III Henry VI,* iv, 1, 57.
New-married wife.—*Henry V,* v, 2, 190.

3
At that time he got his wife with child.
All's Well that Ends Well, v, 3, 302. See under PREGNANCY.
'Tis but the shadow of a wife you see,
The name and not the thing.
All's Well that Ends Well. Act v, sc. 3, l. 308. [Helena]

4
Here comes my clog.
All's Well that Ends Well. Act ii, sc. 5, l. 58. [Bertram]
With his clog at his heels.
The Winter's Tale. Act iv, sc. 4, l. 693. [Autolycus]
Come with your appendix.—*The Taming of the Shrew,* iv, 4, 104. The only use of "appendix."

5
In Syracusa was I born, and wed
Unto a woman, happy but for me,
And by me, had not our hap been bad.
With her I lived in joy.
Comedy of Errors. Act i, sc. 1, l. 37. [Ægeon]
The great care of goods at random left
Drew me from kind embracements of my spouse.
Comedy of Errors. Act i, sc. 1, l. 43. [Ægeon]
O hound of Crete, think'st thou my spouse to get?
Henry V. Act ii, sc. 1, l. 77. [Pistol]
Commit not with man's sworn spouse.
King Lear. Act iii, sc. 4, l. 84. [Edgar]
So qualified as may beseem
The spouse of any noble gentleman.
The Taming of the Shrew. Act iv, sc. 5, l. 66. [Petruchio] The only uses of "spouse."

6
My wife is shrewish when I keep not hours.
The Comedy of Errors. Act iii, sc. 1, l. 2. [Antipholus of Ephesus] The only use of "shrewish."
My wife—but, I protest, without desert—
Hath oftentimes upbraided me withal.
The Comedy of Errors. Act iii, sc. 1, l. 112. [Antipholus of Ephesus]
My wife is in a wayward mood to-day.
The Comedy of Errors. Act iv, sc. 4, l. 4. [Antipholus of Ephesus]

7
As from a bear a man would run for life,
So fly I from her that would be my wife.
The Comedy of Errors. Act iii, sc. 2, l. 159. [Dromio of Syracuse]
She that would be your wife now ran from you.
The Comedy of Errors. Act iv, sc. 4, l. 152. [Dromio of Syracuse]
No wife of mine.—*Comedy of Errors,* iii, 2, 42.

8
Volumnia: But, O, thy wife!
Coriolanus: My gracious silence, hail!
Coriolanus. Act ii, sc. 1, l. 192.
My wife comes foremost.—*Coriolanus,* v, 3, 22.

9
Why did you throw your wedded lady from you?
Cymbeline. Act v, sc. 5, l. 261. [Imogen] "Wedded lady" is repeated in i, 6, 2.
Wedded mistress.—*Coriolanus,* iv, 5, 123.
Wedded lord.—*Pericles,* iii, 4, 9.

10
An I could get me but a wife in the stews,
I were manned, horsed, and wived.
II Henry IV. Act i, sc. 2, l. 59. [Falstaff]
Like an offensive wife
That hath enraged him on to offer strokes,
As he is striking, holds his infant up
And hangs resolved correction in the arm
That was uprear'd to execution.
II Henry IV. Act iv, sc. 1, l. 210. [Archbishop of York] "Offensive" is repeated in *King Lear,* iv, 2, 11.
Lewd-tongued wife.
The Winter's Tale. Act ii, sc. 3, l. 172. [Leontes] The only use of "lewd-tongued."
Makeless wife.—*Sonnets,* ix. Only use of "makeless."

Railing wife.—*I Henry IV,* iii, 1, 160.
Unworthy wife.—*The Rape of Lucrece,* l. 1304.
Wicked wife.—*Pericles,* v, 1, 173.
Wretched wife.—*The Rape of Lucrece,* l. 1826.

1
Thy wife is proud; she holdeth thee in awe.
I Henry VI. Act i, sc. 1, l. 39. [Bishop of Winchester]

Fond man, remember that thou hast a wife.
I Henry VI. Act v, sc. 3, l. 81. [Suffolk]

Married wife.—*II Henry VI,* ii, 4, 28; *Richard II,* v, 1, 73.

2
Not whom we will, but whom his grace affects,
Must be companion of his nuptial bed.
I Henry VI. Act v, sc. 5, l. 57. [Suffolk]

3
Suffolk: What woman is this?
Wife: His wife, an 't like your worship.
II Henry VI. Act ii, sc. 1, l. 79.

My wife desired some damsons,
And made me climb, with danger of my life.
II Henry VI. Act ii, sc. 1, l. 102. [Simpcox]
The only mention of damsons.

Cade: My wife descended of the Lacies,—
Dick [*Aside*]: She was, indeed, a pedler's daughter, and sold many laces.
II Henry VI. Act iv, sc. 2, l. 47.

We charge and command that their wives be as free as heart can wish or tongue can tell.
II Henry VI. Act iv, sc. 7, l. 131. [Cade]

4 When he took a beggar to his bed,
And graced thy poor sire with his bridal-day,
Even then that sunshine brew'd a shower for him.
III Henry VI. Act ii, sc. 2, l. 154. [Edward]
The only use of "bridal-day."

How will my wife for slaughter of my son
Shed seas of tears and ne'er be satisfied!
III Henry VI. Act ii, sc. 5, l. 105. [Father]

5 Is it for a wife
That thou art malcontent? I will provide thee.
III Henry VI. Act iv, sc. 1, l. 59. [King Edward]

Nor how to be contented with one wife.
III Henry VI. Act iv, sc. 3, l. 37. [Warwick]

6 No man living
Could say 'This is my wife' there; all were woven
So strangely in one piece.
Henry VIII. Act iv, sc. 1, l. 79. [Gentleman]

7
Me, yourself, your half.
Julius Cæsar. Act ii, sc. 1, l. 274. [Portia]
"Better half," as referring to a wife, does not occur in the plays.

Am I yourself
But, as it were, in sort of limitation,
To keep with you at meals, comfort your bed,
And talk to you sometimes?
Julius Cæsar. Act ii, sc. 1, l. 282. [Portia]
"Limitation" occurs only once more, in *Coriolanus,* ii, 3, 146.

8
Since that respects of fortune are his love,
I shall not be his wife.
King Lear. Act i, sc. 1, l. 251. [Cordelia]

I must change arms at home, and give the distaff
Into my husband's hands.
King Lear. Act iv, sc. 2, l. 17. [Goneril]

9
Boyet: Do not curst wives hold that self-sovereignty
Only for praise sake, when they strive to be
Lords o'er their lords?
Princess of France: Only for praise: and praise we may afford
To any lady that subdues a lord.
Love's Labour 's Lost. Act iv, sc. 1, l. 36.
The only use of "self-sovereignty."

My lord, be ruled by me.
Titus Andronicus. Act i, sc. 1, l. 442. [Tamora]

10
What, I! I love! I sue! I seek a wife!
Love's Labour's Lost. Act iii, sc. 1, l. 191. [Biron]

Dumain: But what to me, my love? but what to me?
A wife? . . .
Katharine: Not so, my lord; . . .
Come when the king doth to my lady come;
Then if I have much love, I 'll give you some.
Love's Labour 's Lost. Act v, sc. 2, l. 833.

11
My dearest partner of greatness.
Macbeth. Act i, sc. 5, l. 12. [Lady Macbeth]

Partner of your bed.—*Winter's Tale,* iv, 4, 558.
Partner of your weal or woe.—*I Henry VI,* iii, 2, 92.
Partner of his fortune.—*The Two Gentlemen of Verona,* i, 3, 59.
Partner in this action.—*Coriolanus,* v, 3, 2.
Partners in the business.—*Cymbeline,* i, 6, 184
Equal partners.—*I Henry VI,* iii, 2, 85.
Good partner.—*Much Ado about Nothing,* iii, 5, 62.
Fellow partner.—*Measure for Measure,* iv, 2, 19.
Noble partners.—*Henry VIII,* v, 3, 168; v, 5, 6; *Macbeth,* i, 3, 54; *Antony and Cleopatra,* ii, 2, 22.
Present partner.—*The Winter's Tale,* iv, 2, 58.
Sweet partner.—*Henry VIII,* i, 4, 103.

12 She is fast my wife,
Save that we do the denunciation lack.
Measure for Measure. Act i, sc. 2, l. 151. [Claudio] The only use of "denunciation."

But Tuesday night last gone in 's garden-house
He knew me as a wife.
Measure for Measure. Act v, sc. 1, l. 229. [Mariana]

This is the body
That . . . did supply thee at thy garden-house.
Measure for Measure. Act v, sc. 1, l. 212. [Mariana] "Garden-house" occurs in no other scene.

Look that you love your wife; her worth worth yours.
Measure for Measure. Act v, sc. 1, l. 502. [Duke]

1 The lottery of my destiny
Bars me the right of voluntary choosing:
But if my father had not scanted me
And hedged me by his wit, to yield myself
His wife who wins me by that means I told you,
Yourself, renowned prince, then stood as fair
As any comer I have look'd on yet
For my affection.
The Merchant of Venice. Act ii, sc. 1, l. 15. [Portia]

If thou keep promise, I shall end this strife,
Become a Christian and thy loving wife.
The Merchant of Venice. Act ii, sc. 3, l. 20. [Jessica]

Take what wife you will to bed,
I will ever be your head.
The Merchant of Venice. Act ii, sc. 9, l. 70. [Arragon, reading]

2
Here 's a small trifle of wives: alas, fifteen wives is nothing! eleven widows and nine maids is a simple coming-in for one man.
The Merchant of Venice. Act ii, sc. 2, l. 170. [Launcelot] The only use of "coming-in" as a hyphenated phrase.

When you shall please to play the thieves for wives,
I 'll watch as long for you then.
The Merchant of Venice. Act ii, sc. 6, l. 23. [Lorenzo]

The rest aloof are the Dardanian wives,
With bleared visages, come forth to view
The issue of the exploit.
The Merchant of Venice. Act iii, sc. 2, l. 58. [Portia] The only use of "Dardanian."

3
First go with me to church and call me wife,
And then away to Venice to your friend;
For never shall you lie by Portia's side
With an unquiet soul.
The Merchant of Venice. Act iii, sc. 2, l. 306. [Portia]

Antonio: Commend me to your honourable wife. . . .
Bassanio: Antonio, I am married to a wife
Which is as dear to me as life itself;
But life itself, my wife, and all the world,
Are not with me esteem'd above thy life;
I would lose all, ay, sacrifice them all
Here to this devil, to deliver you.
Portia: Your wife would give you little thanks for that,
If she were by, to hear you make the offer.
Gratiano: I have a wife, whom, I protest, I love:
I would she were in heaven, so she could
Entreat some power to change this currish Jew.
Nerissa: 'Tis well you offer it behind her back;
The wish would else make an unquiet house.
Shylock: These be Christian husbands.
The Merchant of Venice. Act iv, sc. 1, l. 273.

4
Our revolted wives share damnation together.
The Merry Wives of Windsor. Act iii, sc. 2, l. 40. [Ford]

Should all despair
That have revolted wives, the tenth of mankind
Would hang themselves.
Winter's Tale. Act i, sc. 2, l. 198. [Leontes]

5
I will deliver his wife into your hand.
The Merry Wives of Windsor. Act v, sc. 1, l. 31. [Falstaff]

Money buys lands, and wives are sold by fate.
The Merry Wives of Windsor. Act v, sc. 5, l. 246. [Ford]

6
A fellow almost damn'd in a fair wife.
Othello. Act i, sc. 1, l. 21. [Iago]

Fair wife.—*The Rape of Lucrece,* l. 1824.
Dear wife.—*Coriolanus,* iii, 3, 114; *Macbeth,* iii, 2, 36.
Good wife.—*Merry Wives of Windsor,* ii, 2, 35.
Sweet wife.—*Coriolanus,* iv, 1, 48; *II Henry IV,* ii, 3, 7.

7
Montano: What is she?
Cassio: She that I spake of, our great captain's captain.
Othello. Act ii, sc. 1, l. 73.

Our general's wife is now the general.
Othello. Act ii, sc. 3, l. 320. [Iago]

General's wife.—*Othello,* iii, 1, 27.

8
Bring him jump where he may Cassio find
Soliciting his wife.
Othello. Act ii, sc. 3, l. 393. [Iago]

To see how he prizes the foolish woman your wife!
Othello. Act iv, sc. 1, l. 185. [Iago]

9
If she come in, she 'll sure speak to my wife:
My wife! my wife! what wife? I have no wife!
Othello. Act v, sc. 2, l. 96. [Othello]

The woman falls; sure, he hath kill'd his wife. . . .
He 's gone, but his wife 's kill'd.
Othello. Act v, sc. 2, l. 236. [Gratiano]

Wife for wife.—*Othello,* ii, 1, 308.

10
My dearest wife was like this maid.
Pericles. Act v, sc. 1, l. 108. [Pericles]

Cerimon: This is your wife.
Pericles: Reverend appearer, no;
I threw her overboard with these very arms.
Pericles. Act v, sc. 3, l. 18. The only use of "appearer."

11
If ever he have wife, let her be made
As miserable by the death of him
As I am made by my poor lord and thee!
Richard III. Act i, sc. 2, l. 26. [Anne]

O, spare my guiltless wife!
Richard III. Act i, sc. 4, l. 72. [Clarence]

Thy adversary's wife doth pray for thee.
Richard III. Act v, sc. 3, l. 166. [Ghost]

12
My wife hath bid the world good night.
Richard III. Act iv, sc. 3, l. 39. [King Richard]

For happy wife, a most distressed widow.
Richard III. Act iv, sc. 4, l. 98. [Queen Margaret]

Neither maid, widow, nor wife.
Measure for Measure, v, 1, 178. See under MAID.

1
If you do fight in safeguard of your wives,
Your wives shall welcome home the conquerors.
Richard III. Act v, sc. 3, l. 259. [Richmond]

You having lands, and blest with beauteous wives,
They would restrain the one, distain the other.
Richard III. Act v, sc. 3, l. 321. [King Richard] "Distain" is repeated in *Troilus and Cressida,* i, 3, 241 and in *Pericles,* iv, 3, 31.

2
Paris: Happily met, my lady and my wife!
Juliet: That may be, sir, when I may be a wife.
Paris: That may be must be, love, on Thursday next.
Romeo and Juliet. Act iv, sc. 1, l. 18.

Alas, my liege, my wife is dead to-night;
Grief of my son's exile hath stopp'd her breath.
Romeo and Juliet. Act v, sc. 3, l. 210. [Montague]

Three hours wife.—*Romeo and Juliet,* iii, 2, 99.

3
Sly: Where is my wife?
Page: Here, noble lord: what is thy will with her?
Sly: Are you my wife and will not call me husband?
My men should call me 'lord:' I am your good-man.
Page: My husband and my lord, my lord and husband;
I am your wife in all obedience. . . .
Sly: Servants, leave me and her alone.
Madam, undress you and come now to bed.
Page: Thrice-noble lord, let me entreat of you
To pardon me yet for a night or two.
The Taming of the Shrew. Induction, sc. 2, l. 104. The only use of "undress" and of "good-man" as a hyphenated phrase meaning husband.

4
This is a way to kill a wife with kindness.
The Taming of the Shrew. Act iv, sc. 1, l. 211. [Petruchio]

5
I am your wife, if you will marry me;
If not, I'll die your maid.
The Tempest. Act iii, sc. 1, l. 83. [Miranda]

She's your wife.—*Richard III,* i, 3, 22.
Ask'd her for his wife.—*Pericles,* i, Gower, 37.
Will you be my wife?—*The Taming of the Shrew,* i, 1, 56.

6
Not to be his wife,
That is another's lawful promised love.
Titus Andronicus. Act i, sc. 1, l. 297. [Lucius]

7
How may I avoid,
Although my will distaste what it elected,
The wife I chose?
Troilus and Cressida. Act ii, sc. 2, l. 65. [Troilus]

Your quondam wife swears still by Venus' glove:
She's well, but bade me not commend her to you.
Troilus and Cressida. Act iv, sc. 5, l. 179. [Hector]

8
When wit and youth is come to harvest,
Your wife is like to reap a proper man.
Twelfth Night. Act iii, sc. 1, l. 143. [Olivia]

9
I now am full resolved to take a wife.
The Two Gentlemen of Verona. Act iii, sc. 1, l. 76. [Duke]

I take to-day a wife.
Troilus and Cressida. Act ii, sc. 2, l. 61. [Troilus]

A woman that Lord Brutus took to wife.
Julius Cæsar. Act ii, sc. 1, l. 293. [Portia]
The only use of the phrase, "took to wife."

10
Leontes: He dreads his wife.
Paulina: So I would you did.
The Winter's Tale. Act ii, sc. 3, l. 79.

Thou ne'er shalt see Thy wife Paulina more.
The Winter's Tale. Act iii, sc. 3, l. 35. [Antigonus]

When my old wife lived, upon
This day she was both pantler, butler, cook,
Both dame and servant; welcomed all, served all;
Would sing her song and dance her turn; now here,
At upper end o' the table, now i' the middle.
Winter's Tale. Act iv, sc. 4, l. 55. [Shepherd]

No more such wives; therefore, no wife.
Winter's Tale. Act v, sc. 1, l. 56. [Leontes]

II—True Wives

11
He lost a wife
Whose beauty did astonish the survey
Of richest eyes, whose words all ears took captive,
Whose dear perfection hearts that scorn'd to serve
Humbly call'd mistress.
All's Well that Ends Well. Act v, sc. 3, l. 15. [Lafeu]

My wife The nonpareil.—*Cymbeline,* ii, 5, 7.

12
I have been to you a true and humble wife,
At all times to your will conformable;
Ever in fear to kindle your dislike,
Yea, subject to your countenance, glad or sorry
As I saw it inclined.
Henry VIII. Act ii, sc. 4, l. 23. [Queen Katharine] "Conformable" is repeated in *The Taming of the Shrew,* ii, 1, 280.

I have been your wife, in this obedience,
Upward of twenty years, and have been blest
With many children by you.
Henry VIII. Act ii, sc. 4, l. 35. [Queen Katharine]

That man i' the world who shall report he has
A better wife, let him in nought be trusted,
For speaking false in that: thou art, alone,
If thy rare qualities, sweet gentleness,
Thy meekness saint-like, wife-like government,
Obeying in commanding, and thy parts

Sovereign and pious else, could speak thee out.
Henry VIII. Act ii, sc. 4, l. 134. [King] "Wife-like" is repeated in *Cymbeline,* iii, 2, 8.

When I am dead, good wench,
Let me be used with honour: strew me over
With maiden flowers, that all the world may know
I was a chaste wife to my grave.
Henry VIII. Act iv, sc. 2, l. 167. [Katharine]

1
You are my true and honourable wife,
As dear to me as are the ruddy drops
That visit my sad heart.
Julius Cæsar. Act ii, sc. 1, l. 288. [Brutus] The only use of "ruddy."

O ye gods,
Render me worthy of this noble wife!
Julius Cæsar. Act ii, sc. 1, l. 302. [Brutus]

Constant wife.—*Cymbeline,* v, 5, 449.
Gentle wife.—*Love's Labour's Lost,* v, 2, 836.
Humble wife.—*The Taming of the Shrew,* Ind., 1, 116.
Loving wife.—*II Henry IV,* ii, 3, 1.
True wife.—*The Rape of Lucrece,* l. 1841.

2
She 's as fartuous a civil modest wife, and one, I tell you, that will not miss you morning nor evening prayer, as any is in Windsor, whoe'er be the other.
The Merry Wives of Windsor. Act ii, sc. 2, l. 100. [Mistress Quickly] The only use of "fartuous," Mistress Quickly's attempt at "virtuous."

Never a wife in Windsor leads a better life than she does.
The Merry Wives of Windsor. Act ii, sc. 2, l. 122. [Mistress Quickly]

Your wife is as honest a 'omans as I will desires among five thousand, and five hundred too.
The Merry Wives of Windsor. Act iii, sc. 3, l. 236. [Evans]

Wives may be merry, and yet honest too:
We do not act that often jest and laugh.
The Merry Wives of Windsor. Act iv, sc. 2, l. 107. [Mrs. Page]

The honest woman, the modest wife, the virtuous creature, that hath the jealous fool to her husband!
The Merry Wives of Windsor. Act iv, sc. 2, l. 135. [Ford]

3
What priceless wealth the heavens had him lent
In the possession of his beauteous mate;
Reckoning his fortune at such high-proud rate,
That kings might be espoused to more fame,
But king nor peer to such a peerless dame.
The Rape of Lucrece, l. 17. The only use of "priceless."

Unkind mate.—*The Comedy of Errors,* ii, 1, 38.
Warlike mate.—*I Henry VI,* i, 2, 92.

I was a loyal wife:
So am I now: O no, that cannot be;
Of that true type hath Tarquin rifled me.
The Rape of Lucrece, l. 1048. "Rifled" is repeated in l. 692 and occurs nowhere else. "Rifle" is used in *The Two Gentlemen of Verona,* iv, 1, 4.

4
To live an unstain'd wife to my sweet love.
Romeo and Juliet. Act iv, sc. 1, l. 88. [Juliet]

Othello: Why, what art thou?
Desdemona: Your wife, my lord; your true
And loyal wife.
Othello. Act iv, sc. 2, l. 34.

This most patient, sweet and virtuous wife.
The Taming of the Shrew. Act iii, sc. 2, l. 197. [Petruchio]

III—False Wives

5
He that kisses my wife is my friend.
All's Well that Ends Well. Act i, sc. 3, l. 49. [Clown] See under FRIEND.

I would cozen the man of his wife and do his service.
All's Well that Ends Well. Act iv, sc. 5, l. 28. [Clown]

6
O, let him marry a woman that cannot go, sweet Isis, I beseech thee! and let her die too, and give him a worse! and let worse follow worse, till the worst of all follow him laughing to his grave, fifty-fold a cuckold!
Antony and Cleopatra. Act i, sc. 2, l. 65. [Charmian] The only use of "fifty-fold."

As it is a heart-breaking to see a handsome man loose-wived, so it is a deadly sorrow to behold a foul knave uncuckolded.
Antony and Cleopatra. Act i, sc. 2, l. 74. [Iras] The only use of "heart-breaking," "loose-wived," and "uncuckolded."

7 Draw within the compass of suspect
The unviolated honour of your wife.
The Comedy of Errors. Act iii, sc. 1, l. 87. [Balthazar] The only use of "unviolated."

8
The fittest time to corrupt a man's wife is when she 's fallen out with her husband.
Coriolanus. Act iv, sc. 3, l. 33. [A Roman]

9 How many
Must murder wives much better than themselves
For wrying but a little!
Cymbeline. Act v, sc. 1, l. 3. [Posthumus] The only use of "wrying."

10
Our madams mock at us, and plainly say
Our mettle is bred out and they will give
Their bodies to the lust of English youth
To new-store France with bastard warriors.
Henry V. Act iii, sc. 5, l. 28. [Dauphin] The only use of "new-store."

11
Noble she is, but if she have forgot
Honour and virtue and conversed with such
As, like to pitch, defile nobility,
I banish her my bed and company
And give her as a prey to law and shame.
II Henry VI. Act ii, sc. 1, l. 194. [Gloucester]

12
Briefly, I do mean to make love to Ford's wife: I spy entertainment in her.
The Merry Wives of Windsor. Act i, sc. 3, l. 48. [Falstaff]

He loves your wife.—*The Merry Wives of Windsor,* ii, 1, 136; 139.

See the hell of having a false woman!
The Merry Wives of Windsor. Act ii, sc. 2, l. 305. [Ford]

I will rather trust a Fleming with my butter, Parson Hugh the Welshman with my cheese, an Irishman with my aqua-vitæ bottle, or a thief to walk my ambling gelding, than my wife with herself: then she plots, then she ruminates, then she devises; and what they think in their hearts they may effect, they will break their hearts but they will effect.
The Merry Wives of Windsor. Act ii, sc. 2, l. 316. [Ford] The only use of "Fleming."

1 I will make him tell the tale anew,
Where, how, how oft, how long ago, and when
He hath, and is again to cope your wife.
Othello. Act iv, sc. 1, l. 85. [Iago]

I think my wife be honest and think she is not.
Othello. Act iii, sc. 3, l. 384. [Othello]

It is a common thing . . . To have a foolish wife.
Othello. Act iii, sc. 3, l. 302. [Iago]

Wife, thou art a fool.—*Richard II,* v, 2, 68.

Emilia: He says thou told'st him that his wife was false. . . .
Iago: I told him what I thought, and told no more
Than what he found himself was apt and true.
Othello. Act v, sc. 2, l. 173.

Look to your wife.—*Richard III,* iv, 2, 95; *Othello,* iii, 3, 197.

2 My wife is slippery.
Winter's Tale. Act i, sc. 2, l. 273. [Leontes]

My wife 's a hobby-horse, deserves a name
As rank as any flax-wench that puts to
Before her troth-plight.
The Winter's Tale. Act i, sc. 2, l. 276. [Leontes] The only use of "flax-wench." "Troth-plight" is repeated in v, 3, 151, and in *Henry V,* ii, 1, 21.

Were my wife's liver
Infected as her life, she would not live
The running of one glass.
Winter's Tale. Act i, sc. 2, l. 304. [Leontes]

IV—Individual Wives

Antony's Wife:

3 Fulvia thy wife first came into the field.
Antony and Cleopatra. Act i, sc. 2, l. 92. [Messenger]

Fulvia thy wife is dead.—*Antony and Cleopatra,* i, 2, 122.

When it pleaseth their deities to take the wife of a man from him, it shows to man the tailors of the earth; comforting therein, that when old robes are worn out, there are members to make anew.
Antony and Cleopatra. Act i, sc. 2, l. 168. [Enobarbus]

What says the married woman? You may go:
Would she had never given you leave to come!
Let her not say 'tis I that keep you here:
I have no power upon you; hers you are.
Antony and Cleopatra. Act i, sc. 3, l. 20. [Cleopatra] The only use of "married woman."

Antony: As for my wife,
I would you had her spirit in such another:
The third o' the world is yours; which with a snaffle
You may pace easy, but not such a wife.
Enobarbus: Would we had all such wives, that the men might go to wars with the women!
Antony and Cleopatra. Act ii, sc. 2, l. 61. The only use of "snaffle."

Enobarbus: Cæsar's sister is call'd Octavia.
Menenius: True, sir; she was the wife of Caius Marcellus.
Enobarbus: But she is now the wife of Marcus Antonius.
Antony and Cleopatra. Act ii, sc. 6, l. 115.

Enobarbus: Octavia is of a holy, cold, and still conversation.
Menas: Who would not have his wife so?
Enobarbus: Not he that himself is not so.
Antony and Cleopatra. Act ii, sc. 6, l. 131.

Prove such a wife As my thoughts make thee.
Antony and Cleopatra. Act iii, sc. 2, l. 25. [Cæsar]

The wife of Antony
Should have an army for an usher.
Antony and Cleopatra. Act iii, sc. 6, l. 43. [Cæsar]

Your wife Octavia, with her modest eyes
And still conclusion, shall acquire no honour
Demuring upon me.
Antony and Cleopatra. Act iv, sc. 15, l. 27. [Cleopatra] The only use of "demuring."

Elbow's Wife:

4 Escalus: What was done to Elbow's wife, that he hath cause to complain of? . . . What was done to Elbow's wife, once more?
Pompey: Once, sir? there was nothing done to her once.
Elbow: I beseech you, sir, ask him what this man did to my wife.
Pompey: I beseech your honour, ask me.
Escalus: Well, sir; what did this gentleman to her? . . .
Pompey: How could Master Froth do the constable's wife any harm? . . . By this hand, sir, his wife is a more respected person than any of us all.
Elbow: Varlet, thou liest; thou liest, wicked varlet! the time is yet to come that she was ever respected with man, woman or child.
Pompey: Sir, she was respected with him before he married with her. . . .
Elbow: O thou caitiff! O thou varlet! O thou wicked Hannibal! I respected with her before I was married to her! If ever I was respected with her, or she with me, let not your worship think me the poor duke's officer.
Measure for Measure. Act ii, sc. 1, l. 120.

Petruchio's Wife:

5 Petruchio, shall I then come roundly to thee

And wish thee to a shrewd ill-favour'd wife?
The Taming of the Shrew. Act i, sc. 2, l. 59. [Hortensio]
One rich enough to be Petruchio's wife.
The Taming of the Shrew. Act i, sc. 2, l. 67. [Petruchio]
I can, Petruchio, help thee to a wife,
With wealth enough and young and beauteous.
The Taming of the Shrew. Act i, sc. 2, l. 84. [Hortensio]
Your father hath consented
That you shall be my wife. . . .
Never make denial;
I must and will have Katharine to my wife.
The Taming of the Shrew. Act ii, sc. 1, l. 271. [Petruchio]
Now must the world point at poor Katharine,
And say, 'Lo, there is mad Petruchio's wife,
If it would please him come and marry her!'
The Taming of the Shrew. Act iii, sc. 2, l. 18. [Katharina]
She is my goods, my chattels; she is my house,
My household stuff, my field, my barn,
My horse, my ox, my ass, my any thing.
The Taming of the Shrew. Act iii, sc. 2, l. 232. [Petruchio]

Miscellaneous:

1
How dost thou like the Lord Bassanio's wife?
The Merchant of Venice. Act iii, sc. 5, l. 77. [Lorenzo]
She were an excellent wife for Benedick.
Much Ado about Nothing. Act ii, sc. 1, l. 366. [Don Pedro]
Cæsar's wife.—*Julius Cæsar,* ii, 2, 99.
Doctor Caius' wife.—*The Merry Wives of Windsor,* v, 5, 186.
Cleon's wife, with envy rare,
A present murderer does prepare.
Pericles, iv, Gower, 37.
This is Edward's wife, that monstrous witch.
Richard III. Act iii, sc. 4, l. 72. [Gloucester]
The thane of Fife had a wife: where is she now?
Macbeth. Act v, sc. 1, l. 47. [Lady Macbeth]

2
Has Ford's wife and Page's wife acquainted each other how they love me?
The Merry Wives of Windsor. Act ii, sc. 2, l. 114. [Falstaff]
I was Geffrey's wife.—*King John,* iii, 4, 46.
Gonzago's wife.—*Hamlet,* iii, 2, 275.

3
I hoped thou shouldst have been my Hamlet's wife.
Hamlet. Act v, sc. 1, l. 267. [Queen]
Harry's wife.—*Richard III,* iv, 4, 59.
Harry Percy's wife.—*I Henry IV,* ii, 3, 111.
Hortensio's wife.—*The Taming of the Shrew,* v, 2, 101.
I am Duke Humphrey's wife.—*II Henry VI,* ii, 4, 42.
She 's like to be Lucentio's wife.—*The Taming of the Shrew,* iv, 4, 66.

4
Art thou not second woman in the realm,
And the protector's wife, beloved of him?
II Henry VI. Act i, sc. 2, l. 43. [Gloucester]
Not all these lords do vex me half so much
As that proud dame, the lord protector's wife.
She sweeps it through the court with troops of ladies,
More like an empress than Duke Humphrey's wife:
Strangers in court do take her for the queen:
She bears a duke's revenues on her back,
And in her heart she scorns our poverty.
II Henry VI. Act i, sc. 3, l. 78. [Queen]
Romeo's faithful wife.—*Romeo and Juliet,* v, 3, 232.

5
We say that Shore's wife hath a pretty foot.
Richard III, i, 1, 93. See under APPEARANCE.
Shore's wife.—*Richard III,* iii, 5, 31.

6
York's wife, and queen of sad mischance.
Richard III. Act iv, sc. 4, l. 114. [Queen]

7
Thy wife, that wretched Anne thy wife,
That never slept a quiet hour with thee,
Now fills thy sleep with perturbations.
Richard III. Act v, sc. 3, l. 159. [Ghost of Lady Anne] The only use of "perturbations." "Perturbation" occurs three times.
Anne, my wife.—*Richard III,* iv, 2, 52.
Anne, wife to thy Edward.—*Richard III,* i, 2, 10.
Wife to Cornwall.—*King Lear,* i, 1, 69.

8
Bona shall be wife to the English King.
III Henry VI. Act iii, sc. 3, l. 139. [King Lewis]
Dame Eleanor Cobham, Gloucester's wife.—*II Henry VI,* ii, 3, 1.

9
Tell me some reason why the Lady Grey
Should not become my wife and England's queen.
III Henry VI. Act iv, sc. 1, l. 25. [King Edward]

10
Helen . . . wife to Sparta's king.
Troilus and Cressida. Act ii, sc. 2, l. 183. [Hector]

11
Did not goodwife Keech, the butcher's wife, come in then?
II Henry IV. Act ii, sc. 1, l. 102. [Hostess] The only use of "goodwife."
Brother's wife.—*Richard II,* i, 2, 54; *Henry VIII,* ii, 4, 181.
Comfit-maker's wife.—*I Henry IV,* iii, 1, 253. The only use of "comfit-maker."
Deputy's wife.—*I Henry IV,* iii, 3, 130.
Husband's brother's wife.—*Hamlet,* iii, 4, 15.
Neighbour's wife.—*Richard III,* i, 4, 141.
Sailor's wife.—*The Tempest,* ii, 1, 4.
Wife of Jupiter.—*The Tempest,* iv, 1, 77.

V—Man and Wife

12
This unworthy husband of his wife.
All's Well that Ends Well. Act iii, sc. 4, l. 30. [Countess]

13
Celia: Will you, Orlando, have to wife this Rosalind?
Orlando: I will.
Rosalind: Ay, but when?

Orlando: Why now; as fast as she can marry me.
Rosalind: Then you must say 'I take thee, Rosalind, for wife.'
Orlando: I take thee, Rosalind, for wife. . . .
Rosalind: I do take thee, Orlando, for my husband.
As You Like It. Act iv, sc. 1, l. 130.

1
Thou art an elm, my husband, I a vine,
Whose weakness married to thy stronger state
Makes me with thy strength to communicate:
If aught possess thee from me it is dross,
Usurping ivy, brier, or idle moss:
Who, all for want of pruning, with intrusion
Infect thy sap and live on thy confusion.
The Comedy of Errors. Act ii, sc. 2, l. 176. [Adriana] The only use of "pruning."

The female ivy so
Enrings the barky fingers of the elm.
A Midsummer-Night's Dream. Act iv, sc. 1, l. 48. [Titania] The only use of "enrings" and "barky."

2
Thou hast no husband yet nor I no wife.
The Comedy of Errors. Act iii, sc. 2, l. 69. [Antipholus of Syracuse]

She that doth call me husband, even my soul
Doth for a wife abhor.
The Comedy of Errors. Act iii, sc. 2, l. 163. [Antipholus of Syracuse]

Ill it doth beseem your holiness
To separate the husband and the wife.
The Comedy of Errors. Act v, sc. 1, l. 110. [Adriana]

3
Man and wife is one flesh.
Hamlet. Act iv, sc. 3, l. 54. [Hamlet]

Man and wife, being two, are one in love.
Henry V. Act v, sc. 2, l. 389. [Queen Isabel]

Man and wife: . . .
It pleaseth me so well, that I will see you wed;
And then with what haste you can get you to bed.
Pericles. Act ii, sc. 5, l. 84. [Simonides]

4
I am an honest man's wife.
I Henry IV. Act iii, sc. 3, l. 136. [Hostess]

5
Even such a husband
Hast thou of me as she is for a wife.
The Merchant of Venice. Act iii, sc. 5, l. 88. [Lorenzo]

Let me give light, but let me not be light;
For a light wife doth make a heavy husband.
The Merchant of Venice. Act v, sc. 1, l. 129. [Portia]

6
And when I lived, I was your other wife:
And when you loved, you were my other husband.
Much Ado about Nothing. Act v, sc. 4, l. 60. [Hero]

7
I do think it is their husbands' faults
If wives do fall: say that they slack their duties,
And pour our treasures into foreign laps,
Or else break out in peevish jealousies,
Throwing restraint upon us; or say they strike us,
Or scant our former having in despite;
Why, we have galls, and though we have some grace,
Yet have we some revenge. Let husbands know
Their wives have sense like them: they see and smell
And have their palates both for sweet and sour,
As husbands have. What is it that they do
When they change us for others? Is it sport?
I think it is: and doth affection breed it?
I think it doth: is 't frailty that thus errs?
It is so too: and have not we affections,
Desires for sport, and frailty, as men have?
Then let them use us well: else let them know,
The ills we do, their ills instruct us so.
Othello. Act iv, sc. 3, l. 87. [Emilia]

8
There stays a husband to make you a wife.
Romeo and Juliet. Act ii, sc. 5, l. 71. [Nurse]

9
What nearer debt in all humanity
Than wife is to the husband?
Troilus and Cressida. Act ii, sc. 2, l. 175. [Hector]

WILDERNESS, see Desert

WILDNESS

10
He 's very wild; Addicted so and so.
Hamlet. Act ii, sc. 1, l. 18. [Polonius] "Addicted" is repeated in *Twelfth Night,* ii, 5, 223.

He is given . . . to wildness.
Julius Cæsar, ii, 1, 189. See under SPORT.

11
And for your part, Ophelia, I do wish
That your good beauties be the happy cause
Of Hamlet's wildness.
Hamlet. Act iii, sc. 1, l. 38. [Queen]

12
This same starved justice hath done nothing but prate of the wildness of his youth.
II Henry IV. Act iii, sc. 2, l. 327. [Falstaff]

Our youths and wildness shall no whit appear.
Julius Cæsar, ii, 1, 148. See under GRAVITY.

13
Let me in my present wildness die.
II Henry IV, iv, 5, 153. See under PRETENCE.

The breath no sooner left his father's body,
But that his wildness, mortified in him,
Seem'd to die too.
Henry V. Act i, sc. 1, l. 25. [Canterbury]

Grow to wildness.—*Henry V,* v, 2, 55.

14
Thou art too wild, too rude and bold of voice.
The Merchant of Venice, ii, 2, 190. See under RUDENESS.

Desperate, wild, and furious.—*Richard III,* iv, 4, 169.

Wild and yet, too, gentle.—*The Comedy of Errors,* iii, 1, 110.
Wild in nature.—*Macbeth,* ii, 4, 16.
Wild in their attire.—*Macbeth,* i, 3, 40.
Gone wild.—*II Henry IV,* v, 2, 123.
Make me wild.—*Antony and Cleopatra,* v, 2, 154.

1 Her spirits are as coy and wild
As haggerds of the rock.
Much Ado about Nothing. Act iii, sc. 1, l. 35. [Hero]
Wild as young bulls.—*I Henry IV,* iv, 1, 103.

2
I am wild in my beholding.
Pericles. Act v, sc. 1, l. 224. [Pericles]
'Twere most piteous to be wild.
The Winter's Tale, ii, 1, 182. See under ACT.

WILL

See also Woman: Her Will

3
Obey our will, which travails in thy good.
All's Well that Ends Well, ii, 3, 165. See under OBEDIENCE.
I shall obey his will.—*All's Well that Ends Well,* ii, 5, 62.

4
To come thus was I not constrain'd, but did it
On my free will.
Antony and Cleopatra. Act iii, sc. 6, l. 56. [Octavia] The only use of "free will."
I did suppose it should be on constraint;
But, heaven be thank'd, it is but voluntary.
King John. Act v, sc. 1, l. 28. [King John]

5
His will hath in it a more modest working.
As You Like It. Act i, sc. 2, l. 214. [Orlando]

6
O, know he is the bridle of your will.
The Comedy of Errors. Act ii, sc. 1, l. 13. [Luciana]
Then let your will attend on their accords.
The Comedy of Errors. Act ii, sc. 1, l. 25. [Luciana]

7
Prithee now, say you will, and go about it.
Coriolanus. Act iii, sc. 2, l. 98. [Volumnia]
Do your best wills,
And make me blest to obey!
Cymbeline. Act v, sc. 1, l. 16. [Posthumus]
Best will.—*Timon of Athens,* iv, 2, 49.

8 Blest be those,
How mean soe'er, that have their honest wills,
Which seasons comfort.
Cymbeline. Act i, sc. 6, l. 7. [Imogen]
Honest will.—*Taming of the Shrew,* v, 2, 158.

9
After your will, have cross'd the sea.
Cymbeline. Act iv, sc. 2, l. 334. [Captain]
At will.—*Othello,* ii, 1, 150.
At thy will.—*Hamlet,* i, 2, 63.
At your will.—*Cymbeline,* iv, 3, 13.
Do your will.—*Coriolanus,* iii, 2, 137.
You may do your will.—*Julius Cæsar,* iv, 1, 27.

10 No soil nor cautel doth besmirch
The virtue of his will.
Hamlet. Act i, sc. 3, l. 15. [Laertes] The only use of "besmirch." "Cautel" (treachery) is repeated in *A Lover's Complaint,* l. 303.
His will is not his own.—*Hamlet,* i, 3, 17.

11
Our wills and fates do so contrary run
That our devices still are overthrown.
Hamlet. Act iii, sc. 2, l. 221. [Player King]

12
Now, master sheriff, what is your will with me?
I Henry IV. Act ii, sc. 4, l. 555. [Prince]
What 's your will, sir? what 's your will?
Love's Labour 's Lost. Act iv, sc. 1, l. 52. [Princess of France]
Here, noble lord: what is thy will with her?
The Taming of the Shrew. Induction, sc. 2, l. 105. [Page]
What is your will, sir, that you send for me?
The Taming of the Shrew. Act v, sc. 2, l. 100. [Katharina]
Sailor: What is your will?
Helicanus: That he have his.
Pericles. Act v, sc. 1, l. 5. "What is your will?" is used twelve times in the plays.
What 's your grace's will?—*Macbeth,* iv, 1, 135.
What are their wills?—*Timon of Athens,* i, 2, 123.

13
Ill will never said well.
Henry V, iii, 7, 123. See under PROVERB.
Ill will.—*All's Well that Ends Well,* v, 3, 265; *As You Like It,* iii, 5, 71; *Richard III,* i, 3, 69.

14
Warder: We do no otherwise than we are will'd.
Gloucester: Who willed you? or whose will stands but mine?
I Henry VI. Act i, sc. 3, l. 10.
As will the rest, so willeth Winchester.
I Henry VI. Act iii, sc. 1, l. 162. [Winchester]
What wills Lord Talbot pleaseth Burgundy.
I Henry VI. Act iii, sc. 2, l. 130. [Burgundy]

15
I danced attendance on his will.
II Henry VI. Act i, sc. 3, l. 174. [York]
He stays upon your will.—*Antony and Cleopatra,* i, 2, 119.

16
If it be thy will!
II Henry VI. Act v, sc. 2, l. 30. [York]
If it be your will.—*Coriolanus,* iv, 4, 7.
If thy will be so.—*Richard III,* v, 5, 32.
If you will.—*King John,* ii, 1, 513.
An't be thy will.—*Twelfth Night,* i, 5, 35; *The Winter's Tale,* iii, 3, 70.
An he will.—*Twelfth Night,* i, 5, 136.
Is it your will?—*The Taming of the Shrew,* i, 1, 56; *King Lear,* i, 4, 280.
'Tis our will.—*Love's Labour 's Lost,* v, 2, 175.

17 Like rich hangings in a homely house,
So was his will in his old feeble body.
II Henry VI. Act v, sc. 3, l. 12. [Richard]

18
I . . . must have my will.
III Henry VI. Act iv, sc. 1, l. 15. [King Edward]
You shall have some part of your will.
As You Like It. Act i, sc. 1, l. 82. [Oliver]
Now thou hast thy will.—*III Henry VI,* i, 4, 144.
Have his will.—*Comedy of Errors,* iv, 2, 18.

If I might have my will.—*Titus Andronicus,* v, 3, 188.
When you will.—*II Henry VI,* iii, 3, 8.

1 It was my will and grant;
And for this once my will shall stand for law.
III Henry VI. Act iv, sc. 1, l. 49. [King Edward]

2
His will is most malignant.
Henry VIII. Act i, sc. 2, l. 141. [Wolsey]

3
Cannot, is false, and that I dare not, falser:
I will not come to-day.
Julius Cæsar. Act ii, sc. 2, l. 63. [Cæsar]

4
My uncle's will in this respect is mine.
King John. Act ii, sc. 1, l. 510. [Blanch]
All and every part of what we would
Doth make a stand at what your highness will.
King John. Act iv, sc. 2, l. 38. [Salisbury]

5
[I] am fall'n out with my more headier will.
King Lear, ii, 4, 111. See MIND AND BODY. The only use of "headier."

Benumbed wills.—*Troilus and Cressida,* ii, 2, 179.
Cloyed will.—*Cymbeline,* i, 6, 47.
Constant will.—*King Lear,* i, 1, 44.
Hot burning will.—*The Rape of Lucrece,* l. 247. The only use of "hot-burning."
Incensed will.—*Henry VIII,* i, 2, 65.
Particular will.—*Troilus and Cressida,* ii, 2, 53.
Rebel will.—*The Rape of Lucrece,* l. 625.
Resolved will.—*The Two Gentlemen of Verona,* ii, 6, 12.
Rude will.—*Romeo and Juliet,* ii, 3, 28.
Will to help.—*III Henry VI,* iii, 3, 34.
Force of his will.—*Much Ado about Nothing,* i, 1, 239.
Strength of will.—*Romeo and Juliet,* iv, 1, 72.
Too blunt a will.—*Love's Labour's Lost,* ii, 1, 49.

6 We attend,
Like humble-visaged suitors, his high will.
Love's Labour's Lost. Act ii, sc. 1, l. 33. [Princess] The only use of "humble-visaged."
High will.—*Richard II,* v, 2, 38; *Romeo and Juliet,* iv, 5, 95.

7
Princess: Our Lady help my lord! he'll be forsworn.
King: Not for the world, fair madam, by my will.
Princess: Why, will shall break it; will and nothing else.
Love's Labour's Lost. Act ii, sc. 1, l. 98.
By my will.—*II Henry IV,* iv, 1, 159; *Troilus and Cressida,* ii, 3, 202.
By thy will.—*Venus and Adonis,* l. 639.

8
Consents bewitch'd, ere he desire, have granted;
And dialogued for him what he would say,
Ask'd their own wills, and made their wills obey.
A Lover's Complaint, l. 132. The only use of "dialogued."

9 Being unprepared,
Our will became the servant to defect;
Which else should free have wrought.
Macbeth. Act ii, sc. 1, l. 17. [Macbeth]

10
Always obedient to your grace's will.
Measure for Measure. Act i, sc. 1, l. 26. [Angelo]
Obedient to his honest will.
The Taming of the Shrew, v, 2, 158. See HUSBAND, 743:6.

11
At war 'twixt will and will not.
Measure for Measure, ii, 2, 33. See under INDECISION.
Look, what I will not, that I cannot do.
Measure for Measure. Act ii, sc. 2, l. 52. [Angelo]

12
So is the will of a living daughter curbed by the will of a dead father.
The Merchant of Venice. Act i, sc. 2, l. 26. [Portia]
Curb this cruel devil of his will.
The Merchant of Venice. Act iv, sc. 1, l. 217. [Bassanio]

13
He hath studied her will, and translated her will, out of honesty into English.
The Merry Wives of Windsor. Act i, sc. 3, l. 54. [Pistol]
Do what she will, say what she will, take all, pay all, go to bed when she list, rise when she list, all is as she will.
The Merry Wives of Windsor. Act ii, sc. 2, l. 123. [Mistress Quickly]
Got's will!—*Merry Wives of Windsor,* iii, 1, 62.
Od's plessed will!—*The Merry Wives of Windsor,* i, 1, 273.
Od's my will!—*As You Like It,* iv, 3, 17.

14
The will of man is by his reason swayed.
A Midsummer-Night's Dream. Act ii, sc. 2, l. 115. [Lysander]
His will Lord of his reason.
Antony and Cleopatra. Act iii, sc. 13, l. 3. [Enobarbus]

15
I will overbear your will.
A Midsummer-Night's Dream. Act iv, sc. 1, l. 184. [Theseus]

16
Against her will, as it appears.
Much Ado about Nothing. Act v, sc. 4, l. 5. [Leonato]
Against his will.—*III Henry VI,* v, 1, 30; *Much Ado about Nothing,* iii, 3, 88; *King Lear,* i, 4, 116.
Against my will.—*The Two Gentlemen of Verona,* iii, 2, 26.
Against their will.—*The Winter's Tale,* i, 2, 198; v, 1, 46.

17
Our bodies are our gardens, to the which our wills are gardeners; so that if we will plant nettles, or sow lettuce, set hyssop and weed up thyme, supply it with one gender of herbs, or distract it with many, either to have it sterile with idleness, or manured with industry, why, the power

and corrigible authority of this lies in our wills.

Othello. Act i, sc. 3, l. 323. [Iago] The only mention of "lettuce" and "hyssop." "Thyme" occurs again in *A Midsummer-Night's Dream,* ii, 1, 249; "manured" in *II Henry IV,* iv, 3, 129; and "corrigible" in *Antony and Cleopatra,* iv, 14, 74.

One may smell in such a will most rank,
Foul disproportion, thoughts unnatural.

Othello. Act iii, sc. 3, l. 232. [Iago] "Disproportion" is repeated in *III Henry VI,* iii, 2, 160.

Her will, recoiling to her better judgement,
May fall to match you with her country forms
And happily repent.

Othello. Act iii, sc. 3, l. 236. [Iago] The only use of "recoiling."

1 To her will frame all thy ways.

The Passionate Pilgrim, l. 323.

Frame Your will to mine.

Pericles. Act ii, sc. 5, l. 82. [Simonides]

What they will.—*Pericles,* i, 4, 76.

What you will.—*Sonnets,* lviii; *Twelfth Night,* i, 5, 117.

2 My will is strong, past reason's weak removing.

The Rape of Lucrece, l. 243.

My will is back'd with resolution.

The Rape of Lucrece, l. 352.

Thou with patience must my will abide;
My will that marks thee for my earth's delight.

The Rape of Lucrece, l. 486.

Will is deaf and hears no heedful friends.

The Rape of Lucrece, l. 495.

Yoke thy liking to my will.

The Rape of Lucrece, l. 1633.

3 Like a jade Self-will himself doth tire.

The Rape of Lucrece, l. 707. The only use of "self-will." "Self-willed" occurs three times.

4 Your will be done: this must my comfort be.

Richard II. Act i, sc. 3, l. 144. [Bolingbroke]

Their sacred wills be done!

The Winter's Tale. Act iii, sc. 3, l. 7. [Antigonus]

5 It is my will, the which if thou respect,
Show a fair presence and put off these frowns.

Romeo and Juliet. Act i, sc. 5, l. 74. [Capulet]

Attend our will.—*Romeo and Juliet,* iii, 1, 201.

Forestall their will.—*Rape of Lucrece,* l. 728.

Oppose my will.—*Macbeth,* iv, 3, 65.

6 I myself am mortgaged to thy will.

Sonnets. No. cxxxiv. The only use of "mortgaged."

Whoever hath her wish, thou hast thy 'Will,'
And 'Will' to boot, and 'Will' in overplus;
More than enough am I that vex thee still,
To thy sweet will making addition thus.
Wilt thou, whose will is large and spacious,
Not once vouchsafe to hide my will in thine?
Shall will in others seem right gracious,
And in my will no fair acceptance shine?
The sea, all water, yet receives rain still
And in abundance addeth to his store;
So thou, being rich in 'Will,' add to thy 'Will'
One will of mine to make my large 'Will' more.
Let no unkind, no fair beseechers kill;
Think all but one, and me in that one 'Will.'

Sonnets. No. cxxxv. "Overplus" is repeated in *Antony and Cleopatra,* iii, 7, 51, and iv, 6, 22. The only use of "beseechers."

If thy soul check thee that I come so near,
Swear to thy blind soul that I was thy 'Will,'
And will, thy soul knows, is admitted there;
Thus far for love my love-suit, sweet, fulfil.
'Will' will fulfil the treasure of thy love,
Ay, fill it full with wills, and my will one. . . .
Make but my name thy love, and love that still,
And then thou lovest me, for my name is 'Will.'

Sonnets. No. cxxxvi. "Love-suit" is repeated in *Henry V,* v, 2, 101, and in *Cymbeline,* iii, 4, 136.

So will I pray that thou mayst have thy 'Will,'
If thou turn back, and my loud crying still.

Sonnets. No. cxliii.

7 Till now you have gone on and fill'd the time
With all licentious measure, making your wills
The scope of justice.

Timon of Athens. Act v, sc. 4, l. 3. [Alcibiades]

These are my mates, that make their wills their law.

The Two Gentlemen of Verona. Act v, sc. 4, l. 14. [Valentine]

8 The will dotes that is attributive
To what infectiously itself affects,
Without some image of the affected merit.

Troilus and Cressida. Act ii, sc. 2, l. 58. [Hector] The only use of "attributive" and "infectiously."

In will peculiar and in self-admission.

Troilus and Cressida, ii, 3, 176. [Ulysses] The only use of "self-admission."

The will is infinite.—*Troilus and Cressida,* iii, 2, 88.

9 My will is something sorted with his wish.
Muse not that I thus suddenly proceed;
For what I will, I will, and there an end.

The Two Gentlemen of Verona. Act i, sc. 3, l. 63. [Antonio]

My will is even this.—*The Two Gentlemen of Verona,* iv, 2, 93.

Will of God: see under God.

Will of heaven: see under Heaven.

II—Will: Good Will

10 I do beg your good will in this case.

All's Well that Ends Well. Act i, sc. 3, l. 23. [Clown]

I hope I have your good will.—*The Merry Wives of Windsor,* iii, 2, 62.

Let me have your good will.—*The Merry Wives of Windsor,* iii, 4, 86.

He hath my good will.—*The Merry Wives of Windsor,* iv, 4, 84.

I tell you for good will.—*The Merry Wives of Windsor,* iv, 5, 82.
With all good will.—*A Midsummer-Night's Dream,* iii, 2, 164.

1
I will do my good will, sir: you can have no more.
II Henry IV. Act iii, sc. 2, l. 167. [Feeble]

2
But, for my will, my will is your good will
May stand with ours.
Much Ado about Nothing. Act v, sc. 4, l. 28. [Benedick]

Arm'd With his good will.—*The Taming of the Shrew,* i, 1, 6.

3
My good will is to it,
And yours it is against.
The Tempest. Act iii, sc. 1, l. 30. [Miranda]

My good will is great.—*Pericles,* iii, 4, 18.
"Good will" is used thirty-six times in the plays.

III—Will: Testament

4
He hath . . . made his will and read it
To public ear.
Antony and Cleopatra. Act iii, sc. 4, l. 3. [Antony]

I ne'er made my will yet, I thank heaven; I am not such a sickly creature, I give heaven praise.
The Merry Wives of Windsor. Act iii, sc. 4, l. 60. [Slender]

Bid a sick man in sadness make his will.
Romeo and Juliet. Act i, sc. 1, l. 208. [Romeo]

Some two months hence my will shall here be made.
Troilus and Cressida. Act v, sc. 10, l. 53. [Pandarus]

5
'Poor deer,' quoth he, 'thou maketh a testament
As worldlings do, giving thy sum of more
To that which had too much.'
As You Like It. Act ii, sc. 1, l. 47. [Lord]
"Worldlings" is repeated in *II Henry IV,* v, 3, 103: "Worldlings base."

Make his testament.—*I Henry VI,* i, 5, 17.
Purple testament.—*Richard II,* iii, 3, 94.

6
Antony: Here 's a parchment with the seal of Cæsar;
I found it in his closet, 'tis his will:
Let but the commons hear this testament—
Which, pardon me, I do not mean to read—
And they would go and kiss dead Cæsar's wounds. . . .
Citizen: We 'll hear the will: read it, Marc Antony.
All: The will, the will! we will hear Cæsar's will.
Antony: Have patience, gentle friends, I must not read it;
It is not meet you know how Cæsar loved you.
You are not wood, you are not stones, but men;
And, being men, hearing the will of Cæsar,
It will inflame you, it will make you mad. . . .
Citizen: Read the will; we 'll hear it, Antony;
You shall read us the will, Cæsar's will. . . .
All: The will! the testament! . . .
Citizen: The will! read the will!
Antony: You will compel me, then, to read the will?
Then make a ring about the corpse of Cæsar,
And let me show you him that made the will. . . .
Wherein hath Cæsar thus deserved your loves?
Alas, you know not: I must tell you, then:
You have forgot the will I told you of.
All: Most true. The will! Let 's stay and hear the will.
Antony: Here is the will, and under Cæsar's seal.
Julius Cæsar. Act iii, sc. 2, l. 133.

Fetch the will hither, and we shall determine
How to cut off some charge in legacies.
Julius Cæsar. Act iv, sc. 1, l. 8. [Antony]

Mention it within their wills.—*Julius Cæsar,* iii, 2, 140.
Will of Cæsar.—*Julius Cæsar,* iii, 2, 148.

7
Robert: Shall then my father's will be of no force
To dispossess that child which is not his?
Bastard: Of no more force to dispossess me, sir,
Than was his will to get me, as I think.
King John. Act i, sc. 1, l. 130.

Elinor: I can produce
A will that bars the title of thy son.
Constable: Ay, who doubts that? a will! a wicked will;
A woman's will; a canker'd grandam's will!
King John. Act ii, sc. 1, l. 191.

8
Thou left'st me nothing in thy will.
The Passionate Pilgrim, l. 138.

By will bequeath'd.—*King John,* i, 1, 109.

9
Let 's choose executors and talk of wills.
Richard II. Act iii, sc. 2, l. 148. [King Richard]

WILLINGNESS

10
Most willing spirits,
That promise noble service.
Cymbeline. Act iv, sc. 2, l. 338. [Captain]

Willing bondman.—*Julius Cæsar,* i, 3, 113.
Willing soul.—*Richard II,* iv, 1, 108.

11
My staff? here, noble Henry, is my staff:
As willingly do I the same resign
As e'er thy father Henry made it mine;
And even as willingly at thy feet I leave it
As others would ambitiously receive it.
II Henry VI. Act ii, sc. 3, l. 32. [Gloucester]

1
Willingness rids way.
III Henry VI. Act v, sc. 3, l. 21. [King Edward]
With all willingness.—*II Henry VI,* iii, 1, 150.
2
I was as willing to grapple as he was to board.
Love's Labour's Lost. Act ii, sc. 1, l. 218. [Boyet]
Thou art willing.—*Julius Cæsar,* iv, 3, 259.
Most willing.—*Henry VIII,* iv, 2, 130.
God willing.—*Hamlet,* i, 5, 187.
3
We have willing dames enough.
Macbeth, iv, 3, 73. See under WANTONNESS.
She is very willing.—*Twelfth Night,* ii, 3, 108.
4
You embrace your charge too willingly.
Much Ado about Nothing. Act i, sc. 1, l. 103. [Don Pedro]
Willingly I go.—*Love's Labour's Lost,* ii, 1, 35.
5
I do agnize A natural and prompt alacrity.
Othello. Act i, sc. 3, l. 232. [Othello] The only use of "agnize" (confess).
Alacrity of spirit.—*Richard III,* v, 3, 73.
Alacrity in sinking.—*The Merry Wives of Windsor,* iii, 5, 13.
Fresh alacrity.—*Troilus and Cressida,* iv, 4, 147. The only uses of "alacrity."
6
As willingly as e'er I came from school.
The Taming of the Shrew. Act iii, sc. 2, l. 152. [Gremio]
As willingly as one would kill a fly.
Titus Andronicus, v, 1, 142. See under DEED.
7
Me shall you find ready and willing.
The Taming of the Shrew. Act iv, sc. 4, l. 34. [Pedant]
You shall find me yare.
Measure for Measure. Act iv, sc. 2, l. 61. [Pompey]
8
Lord: The swallow follows not summer more willing than we your lordship.
Timon: Nor more willingly leaves winter.
Timon of Athens. Act iii, sc. 6, l. 31.
More willingly.—*Hamlet,* ii, 2, 220; *Measure for Measure,* v, 1, 481.
Most willingly.—*Coriolanus,* ii, 2, 66; *Measure for Measure,* iii, 2, 257.
How willingly.—*King John,* iv, 2, 45; *The Two Gentlemen of Verona,* iii, 2, 22.
Very willingly.—*I Henry IV,* v, 2, 34.

WIND

See also Storm, Tempest

9
The icy fang
And churlish chiding of the winter's wind,
Which, when it bites and blows upon my body,
Even till I shrink with cold, I smile and say
'This is no flattery.'
As You Like It. Act ii, sc. 1, l. 6. [Duke senior]
Blow, blow, thou winter wind.
As You Like It, ii, 7, 174. See under INGRATITUDE.
Winter's powerful wind.—*III Henry VI,* v, 2, 15.
10
Carried with more speed before the wind.
The Comedy of Errors. Act i, sc. 1, l. 110. [Ægeon]
Against the wind.—*Coriolanus,* i, 4, 34; iii, 2, 104.
11
An if the wind blow any way from shore,
I will not harbour in this town to-night.
The Comedy of Errors. Act iii, sc. 2, l. 153. [Antipholus of Syracuse]
The merry wind Blows fair from land.
The Comedy of Errors. Act iv, sc. 1, l. 90. [Dromio of Syracuse]
12
The wind sits in the shoulder of your sail.
Hamlet. Act i, sc. 3, l. 56. [Polonius]
Now sits the wind fair.—*Henry V,* ii, 2, 12.
The wind sits fair.—*Richard II,* ii, 2, 123.
We see the wind sit sore upon our sails,
And yet we strike not, but securely perish.
Richard II, ii, 1, 265. [Northumberland]
13
There is something in the wind.
The Comedy of Errors. Act iii, sc. 1, l. 69. [Antipholus of Ephesus]
How now, lad! is the wind in that door, i' faith?
I Henry IV. Act iii, sc. 3, l. 102. [Falstaff]
Sits the wind in that corner?
Much Ado about Nothing. Act ii, sc. 3, l. 102. [Benedick]
14
Both wind and tide stays for this gentleman.
The Comedy of Errors, iv, 1, 46. [Angelo]
Wind and tide.—*III Henry VI,* iii, 3, 48; iv, 3, 59; v, 1, 53.
15
Let the mutinous winds
Strike the proud cedars 'gainst the fiery sun.
Coriolanus. Act v, sc. 3, l. 59. [Coriolanus]
Mutinous winds.—*The Tempest,* v, 1, 42.
16
The contrarious winds that held the king so long.
I Henry IV. Act v, sc. 1, l. 52. [Worcester] "Contrarious" is repeated in *Measure for Measure,* iv, 1, 62: "Contrarious quests."
17
Was I for this nigh wreck'd upon the sea
And twice by awkward wind from England's bank
Drove back again unto my native clime? . . .
What did I then, but cursed the gentle gusts
And he that loosed them forth their brazen caves;
And bid them blow towards England's blessed shore.
II Henry VI. Act iii, sc. 2, l. 83. [Queen]
Gentle gust.—*The Rape of Lucrece,* l. 549.
Conveying gusts.—*Coriolanus,* i, 6, 5.
Extreme gusts.—*The Taming of the Shrew,* ii, 1, 136.
Extremest gust.—*Timon of Athens,* iii, 5, 54.

Fretting gust.—*III Henry VI,* ii, 6, 35.
Greater gust.—*III Henry VI,* iii, 1, 88.
Stormy gusts.—*Sonnets,* xiii.
Tempestuous gusts.—*I Henry VI,* v, 5, 5; *Titus Andronicus,* v, 3, 69.
Allay the gust.—*Twelfth Night,* i, 3, 33.
Gusts and foul flaws.—*Venus and Adonis,* l. 456.
Gusts of heaven.—*Merchant of Venice,* iv, 1, 77. The only uses of "gust" and "gusts" in this sense. It is used in the sense of taste in *The Winter's Tale,* i, 2, 219, and in *Sonnets,* cxiv.

1
Making the wind my post-horse.
II Henry IV. Induction, l. 4. [Rumour]
The winds,
Who take the ruffian billows by the top.
II Henry IV, iii, 1, 21. See STORM, 1446:6.

2
We shall be winnow'd with so rough a wind
That even our corn shall seem as light as chaff
And good from bad find no partition.
II Henry IV. Act iv, sc. 1, l. 194. [Mowbray]
Rough winds do shake the darling buds of May.
Sonnets, xviii.
Rough wind.—*III Henry VI,* v, 4, 22.
Foul wind.—*Much Ado about Nothing,* v, 2, 53.
Howling winds.—*Othello,* ii, 1, 68.
Loud winds.—*The Tempest,* iii, 3, 63.
Raging wind.—*III Henry VI,* i, 4, 145.
Roaring wind.—*King Lear,* iii, 2, 47.
Rude wind.—*King Lear,* iv, 2, 30.
Scolding winds.—*Julius Cæsar,* i, 3, 5.
Warring winds.—*King Lear,* iv, 7, 32. The only use of "warring."
Whistling wind.—*Midsummer-Night's Dream,* ii, 1, 86.

3
Yet, by your leave, the wind was very high.
II Henry VI. Act ii, sc. 1, l. 3. [Queen]
The winds grow high.—*II Henry VI,* ii, 1, 55.
High winds.—*The Rape of Lucrece,* l. 335; *Venus and Adonis,* l. 305.

4
Falstaff: What wind blew you hither, Pistol?
Pistol: Not the ill wind which blows no man to good.
II Henry IV. Act v, sc. 3, l. 89. The only use of "ill wind."
Hortensio: And tell me now, sweet friend, what happy gale
Blows you to Padua here from old Verona?
Petruchio: Such wind as scatters young men through the world
To seek their fortunes farther than at home
Where small experience grows.
The Taming of the Shrew. Act i, sc. 2, l. 48.
Auspicious gales.—*The Tempest,* v, 1, 314.
Little gale.—*III Henry VI,* v, 3, 10.
With every gale.—*King Lear,* ii, 2, 85. The only uses of "gale" and "gales."

5
Calm the fury of this mad-bred flaw.
II Henry VI, iii, 1, 354. See under TEMPEST.
I do not fear the flaw.—*Pericles,* iii, 1, 39.
Standing every flaw.—*Coriolanus,* v, 3, 74.
Foul flaws.—*Venus and Adonis,* l. 456.
Winter's flaw.—*Hamlet,* v, 1, 238. The only uses of "flaw" and "flaws" in the sense of a sudden squall of wind.

6
And thou that smiledst at good Duke Humphrey's death
Against the senseless winds shalt grin in vain,
Who in contempt shall hiss at thee again.
II Henry VI. Act iv, sc. 1, l. 76. [Captain]
The wind doth hiss you.—*Venus and Adonis,* l. 1084.

7
Ill blows the wind that profits nobody.
III Henry VI. Act ii, sc. 5, l. 55. [Son]

8
The adverse winds,
Whose leisure I have stay'd.
King John. Act ii, sc. 1, l. 57. [Chatillon]
Opposed winds.—*The Winter's Tale,* i, 1, 34.

9
Bids the wind blow the earth into the sea,
Or swell the curled waters 'bove the main,
That things might change or cease.
King Lear. Act iii, sc. 1, l. 5. [Gentleman]
Blow, winds, and crack your cheeks!
King Lear. Act iii, sc. 2, l. 1. [King Lear]
Blow wind!—*Julius Cæsar,* v, 1, 67; *Macbeth,* v, 5, 51.

10
Through the sharp hawthorn blows the cold wind.
King Lear. Act iii, sc. 4, l. 47. [Edgar]
Still through the hawthorn blows the cold wind.
King Lear. Act iii, sc. 4, l. 102. [Edgar]
Cold wind.—*All's Well that Ends Well,* i, 1, 115.
Bleak winds.—*King John,* v, 7, 40.

11
Through the velvet leaves the wind,
All unseen, can passage find.
Love's Labour's Lost, iv, 3, 105. [Dumain]
Repeated in *The Passionate Pilgrim,* l. 231.
The invisible and creeping wind.—*Henry V,* iii, Prol., 11.
Viewless winds.—*Measure for Measure,* iii, 1, 124.

12
When winds breathe sweet, unruly though they be.
A Lover's Complaint, l. 103.
Unruly wind.—*I Henry IV,* iii, 1, 30.

13
Though you untie the winds and let them fight
Against the churches.
Macbeth. Act iv, sc. 1, l. 52. [Macbeth]
I'll give thee a wind.—*Macbeth,* i, 3, 11.

14
My wind cooling my broth
Would blow me to an ague, when I thought
What harm a wind too great at sea might do.
The Merchant of Venice, i, 1, 22. [Salarino]

15
When the sweet wind did gently kiss the trees.
The Merchant of Venice, v, 1, 2. [Lorenzo]
The wind is come about.—*The Merchant of Venice,* ii, 6, 64.
Gentle wind.—*Venus and Adonis,* l. 189.
The gentlest winds of heaven.—*Pericles,* iii, 3, 37. The only use of "gentlest."

16
Methinks the wind hath spoke aloud at land;

A fuller blast ne'er shook our battlements.
If it hath ruffian'd so upon the sea,
What ribs of oak, when mountains melt on them,
Can hold the mortise?
Othello. Act ii, sc. 1, l. 5. [Montano] The only use of "ruffian'd," and "mortise." "Mortised" occurs in *Hamlet*, iii, 3, 20.

Blow me about in winds!—*Othello*, v, 2, 279.

1
The bawdy wind that kisses all it meets.
Othello, iv, 2, 78. See STRUMPET, 1453:3.

Strumpet wind.—*Merchant of Venice*, ii, 6, 16.

Wandering wind.—*Pericles*, i, 1, 96.

Wanton wind.—*A Midsummer-Night's Dream*, ii, 1, 129.

2
The stuff we have, a strong wind will blow it to pieces.
Pericles. Act iv, sc. 2, l. 19. [Bawd]

Bounteous winds have brought
This king to Tarsus.
Pericles. Act iv, sc. 4, l. 17. [Gower]

Driven before the wind.—*Pericles*, v, Gower, 14.

3
The wind wars with his torch to make him stay.
The Rape of Lucrece, l. 311.

4
Blow, till thou burst thy wind, if room enough!
The Tempest. Act i, sc. 1, l. 8. [Boatswain]

I shall break my wind.—*I Henry IV*, ii, 2, 14.

Break his wind.—*Timon of Athens*, v, 4, 12.

5
The winds whose pity, sighing back again,
Did us but loving wrong.
The Tempest. Act i, sc. 2, l. 150. [Prospero]

Mountain winds.—*The Tempest*, i, 2, 499.

6
The green leaves quiver with the cooling wind
And make a chequer'd shadow on the ground.
Titus Andronicus. Act ii, sc. 3, l. 14. [Tamora]

The cool and temperate wind.—*Henry V*, iii, 3, 30.

7
My son and I will have the wind of you.
Titus Andronicus. Act iv, sc. 2, l. 133. [Aaron]

You were as good to shoot against the wind.
Titus Andronicus. Act iv, sc. 3, l. 57. [Titus]

8
The splitting wind
Makes flexible the knees of knotted oaks.
Troilus and Cressida. Act i, sc. 3, l. 49. [Nestor] "Flexible" is repeated in *III Henry VI*, i, 4, 141.

Wind and tempest.—*Troilus and Cressida*, i, 3, 26.

The ruffian Boreas.—*Troilus and Cressida*, i, 3, 38. The only mention of Boreas.

9
She . . . fetches her wind so short.
Troilus and Cressida, iii, 2, 33.

Is not . . . your wind short?—*II Henry IV*, i, 2, 206.

10
'Twill endure wind and weather.
Twelfth Night, i, 5, 255. See under BEAUTY.

Even as the wind is hush'd before it raineth.
Venus and Adonis, l. 458.

Wind and rain, see under RAIN.

11 The wind, imprison'd in the ground,
Struggling for passage, earth's foundation shakes.
Venus and Adonis, l. 1046.

12
May blow No sneaping winds at home.
Winter's Tale. Act i, sc. 2, l. 12. [Polixenes] "Sneaping" (nipping) is repeated in *Love's Labour's Lost*, i, 1, 100: "Sneaping frost."

Each wind that blows.—*The Winter's Tale*, ii, 3, 154.

Every wind that blows.—*The Winter's Tale*, iv, 4, 552.

Winds of March.—*Winter's Tale*, iv, 4, 120.

II—The Four Winds

13
For the four winds blow in from every coast.
The Merchant of Venice. Act i, sc. 1, l. 168. [Bassanio]

Plucking the grass, to know where sits the wind.
The Merchant of Venice. Act i, sc. 1, l. 18. [Salanio]

The wind is come about.—*The Merchant of Venice*, ii, 6, 64.

14
Eastern wind.—*A Midsummer-Night's Dream*, iii, 2, 142.

North-east wind.—*Richard II*, i, 4, 6.

15 The tyrannous breathing of the north
Shakes all our buds from growing.
Cymbeline. Act i, sc. 3, l. 36. [Imogen]

The angry northern wind.—*Titus Andronicus*, iv, 1, 104.

The sharp wind of the north.—*The Tempest*, i, 2, 254.

The wind is northerly.—*Hamlet*, v, 2, 98. The only use of "northerly."

16 The southern wind
Doth play the trumpet to his purposes,
And by his hollow whistling in the leaves
Foretells a tempest and a blustering day.
I Henry IV. Act v, sc. 1, l. 3. [King Henry]

A prosperous south-wind friendly.
The Winter's Tale. Act v, sc. 1, l. 161. [Florizel] The only use of "south-wind."

Like foggy south puffing with wind and rain.
As You Like It. Act iii, sc. 5, l. 50. [Rosalind]

The dew-dropping south.—*Romeo and Juliet*, i, 4, 103. The only use of "dew-dropping."

17
Marina: Is this wind westerly that blows?
Leonine: South-west.
Marina: When I was born, the wind was north.
Pericles. Act iv, sc. 1, l. 51. The only use of "westerly."

A south-west blow on ye
And blister you all o'er!
The Tempest. Act i, sc. 2, l. 323. [Caliban] The only uses of "south-west."

WINDOW

1
So, my good window of lattice, fare thee well; thy casement I need not open, for I look through thee.
All's Well that Ends Well. Act ii, sc. 3, l. 224. [Lafeu]
Clamber not you up to the casements then.
The Merchant of Venice. Act ii, sc. 5, l. 31. [Shylock] The only use of "clamber."
But stop my house's ears, I mean my casements.
The Merchant of Venice, ii, 5, 34. [Shylock]
You would have thought the very windows spake,
So many greedy looks of young and old
Through casements darted their desiring eyes.
Richard II. Act v, sc. 2, l. 12. [York]
Go to the casement.—*The Merry Wives of Windsor,* i, 4, 2.
Leave a casement . . . open.—*A Midsummer-Night's Dream,* iii, 1, 57.
Look through a casement.—*Cymbeline,* ii, 4, 34.
Out at the casement.—*As You Like It,* iv, 1, 163.
Out of a casement.—*All's Well that Ends Well,* v, 3, 230.
From a casement thrown.—*All's Well that Ends Well,* v, 3, 93.
Casement of my closet.—*King Lear,* i, 2, 65.
The only uses of "casement" and "casements."

2
Thy crystal window ope; look out.
Cymbeline. Act v, sc. 4, l. 81. [Sicilius]
Why pry'st thou through my window? leave thy peeping.
The Rape of Lucrece, l. 1089.
That hath his windows glazed with thine eyes.
Sonnets, xxiv.
Her two blue windows faintly she up-heaveth.
Venus and Adonis, l. 482.
Windows of thine eyes.—*Richard III,* v, 3, 116.
Windows to my breast.—*Sonnets,* xxiv.
Eyes' windows.—*Romeo and Juliet,* iv, 1, 100.
Downy windows.—*Antony and Cleopatra,* v, 3, 319.
Window of the heart, see under EYE.

3
Our windows are broke down in every street
And we for fear compell'd to shut our shops.
I Henry VI. Act iii, sc. 1, l. 84. [Mayor]

4
Go but with me to-night, you shall see her chamber-window entered, even the night before her wedding-day.
Much Ado about Nothing. Act iii, sc. 2, l. 114. [Don John] "Chamber-window" is repeated six times in this play; three times in *The Two Gentlemen of Verona,* and once in *All's Well that Ends Well.*
Visit by night your lady's chamber-window.
Two Gentlemen of Verona, iii, 2, 83. [Proteus]

5
These windows that let forth thy life.
Richard III, i, 2, 12. See under WOUND.

6
Then, window, let day in.
Romeo and Juliet, iii, 5, 41. See under DAY.
Golden window of the east.—*Romeo and Juliet,* i, 1, 126.
Windows of thine age.—*Sonnets,* iii.

7
See where he looks out of the window.
The Taming of the Shrew. Act v, sc. 1, l. 57. [Vincentio] See also v, 1, 32; *The Merchant of Venice,* ii, 5, 41.
Out at your window.—*Much Ado about Nothing,* iv, 1, 85; 311.

8
What lets but one may enter at her window?
The Two Gentlemen of Verona. Act iii, sc. 1, l. 113. [Valentine]
Now must we to her window.—*The Two Gentlemen of Verona,* iii, 1, 113.
Compassed window.—*Troilus and Cressida,* i, 2, 120.
Bay windows.—*Twelfth Night,* iv, 2, 40. See HOUSE, 732:9.

WINE

See also Drinking, Sack

9
There's one grape yet; I am sure thy father drunk wine.
All's Well that Ends Well. Act ii, sc. 3, l. 105. [Lafeu]

No more
The juice of Egypt's grape shall moist this lip.
Antony and Cleopatra. Act v, sc. 2, l. 284. [Cleopatra]
The wine she drinks is made of grapes.
Othello. Act ii, sc. 1, l. 256. [Iago]

Go, suck the subtle blood o' the grape,
Till the high fever seethe your blood to froth,
And so 'scape hanging.
Timon of Athens. Act iv, sc. 3, l. 432. [Timon]

10
Wine enough Cleopatra's health to drink.
Antony and Cleopatra, i, 2, 11. See under DRINKING: DRINKING HEALTHS.
Till that the conquering wine hath steep'd our sense
In soft and delicate Lethe.
Antony and Cleopatra, ii, 7, 113. [Antony]

Tonight I'll force
The wine peep through their scars.
Antony and Cleopatra, iii, 13, 190. [Antony]

11
Come, thou monarch of the vine,
Plumpy Bacchus with pink eyne!
In thy fats our cares be drown'd,
With thy grapes our hairs be crown'd:
Cup us, till the world go round.
Antony and Cleopatra, ii, 7, 120. [Song]
Dainty Bacchus.—*Love's Labour's Lost,* iv, 3, 339. Bacchus is mentioned only twice.

12
Give me some wine, and let me speak a little.
Antony and Cleopatra. Act iv, sc. 15, l. 42. [Antony]
Some wine, within there!—*Antony and Cleopatra,* iii, 11, 73.

13
Good wine needs no bush.
As You Like It, Epil., 4. Quoting a proverb deriving from Publilius Syrus (*Sententiæ,* No. 968), and first appearing in English in Richard Taverner's *Proverbs,* in 1539.

Yet to good wine they do use good bushes.
As You Like It, Epil., 5.
Good wine is a good familiar creature, if it be well used: exclaim no more against it.
Othello. Act ii, sc. 3, l. 313. [Iago]
Good wine.—*Henry VIII,* i, 4, 6.

1
A cup of hot wine with not a drop of allaying Tiber in 't.
Coriolanus. Act ii, sc. 1, l. 52. [Menenius]
A cup of wine that 's brisk and fine,
And drink unto the leman mine.
II Henry IV. Act v, sc. 3, l. 48. [Silence] "Leman" is repeated in *The Merry Wives of Windsor,* iv, 2, 172, and in *Twelfth Night,* ii, 3, 26.
Fill me a bowl of wine.—*Richard III,* v, 3, 63.
Give me a bowl of wine.—*Richard III,* v, 3, 72.
Fill me some wine.—*Timon of Athens,* iii, 1, 8.

2
Wine, wine, wine! What service is here!
Coriolanus. Act iv, sc. 5, l. 1. [Servant]
Have we no wine here?—*Coriolanus,* i, 9, 92.

3
Set me the stoups of wine upon that table.
Hamlet. Act v, sc. 2, l. 278. [King]
Come, lieutenant, I have a stoup of wine.
Othello. Act ii, sc. 3, l. 30. [Iago]
Marian, I say! a stoup of wine!
Twelfth Night. Act ii, sc. 3, l. 14. [Sir Toby]
Fetch me a stoup of liquor.
Hamlet. Act v, sc. 1, l. 68. [Clown] The only uses of "stoup" and "stoups."

4
You have drunk too much canaries; and that 's a marvellous searching wine, and it perfumes the blood ere one can say 'What 's this?'
II Henry IV. Act ii, sc. 4, l. 29. [Hostess]
Thou lackest a cup of canary.
Twelfth Night. Act i, sc. 3, l. 85. [Sir Toby]
Drink canary.—*The Merry Wives of Windsor,* iii, 2, 89. The only use of "canary" and "canaries" in this sense.
Milk of Burgundy.—*King Lear,* i, 1, 86.
Claret wine.—*II Henry VI,* iv, 6, 4. The only use of "claret."
Greekish wine.—*Troilus and Cressida,* v, 1, 1.
A flagon of Rhenish.—*Hamlet,* v, 1, 197. The only use of "flagon."
Draughts of Rhenish.—*Hamlet,* i, 4, 10.
Rhenish wine.—*Merchant of Venice,* i, 2, 104.
Red wine and Rhenish.—*The Merchant of Venice,* iii, 1, 44. The only uses of Rhenish.

5
Give Master Bardolph some wine, Davy.
II Henry IV. Act v, sc. 3, l. 26. [Shallow]

6
A man cannot make him laugh; but that 's no marvel, he drinks no wine.
II Henry IV. Act iv, sc. 3, l. 95. [Falstaff]

7
It was excess of wine that set him on.
Henry V. Act ii, sc. 2, l. 42. [King Henry]
Disturbed with the effect of Wine.—*The Comedy of Errors,* v, 1, 215.

8
Good friends, go in, and taste some wine with me.
Julius Cæsar. Act ii, sc. 2, l. 126. [Cæsar]
Fill, Lucius, till the wine o'erswell the cup;
I cannot drink too much of Brutus' love.
Julius Cæsar. Act iv, sc. 3, l. 161. [Cassius] "O'erswell" is repeated in *Henry V,* ii, 1, 97, and in *King John,* ii, 1, 337.

9
Wine loved I deeply.
King Lear. Act iii, sc. 4, l. 94. [Edgar]
Wine and wassail.—*Macbeth,* i, 7, 64.

10
The wine of life is drawn.
Macbeth, ii, 3, 100. See under LIFE.

11
We shall have all the world drink brown and white bastard.
Measure for Measure. Act iii, sc. 2, l. 4. [Elbow] "Bastard" was the name given a sweet Spanish wine, resembling muscadel; or, more generally, any sweetened wine.
Your brown bastard is your only drink.
I Henry IV. Act ii, sc. 4, l. 82. [Prince]
Score a pint of bastard in the Half-moon.
I Henry IV. Act ii, sc. 4, l. 31. [Prince] "Pint" is used only once again, in *Othello,* ii, 3, 68. The only uses of "bastard" in this sense.

12
Carry the wine in; we 'll drink within.
The Merry Wives of Windsor. Act i, sc. 1, l. 195. [Page]
Drink some wine ere you go.
Much Ado about Nothing, iii, 5, 57. [Leonato]

13
O thou invisible spirit of wine, if thou hast no name to be known by, let us call thee devil!
Othello. Act ii, sc. 3, l. 283. [Cassio]
Some wine, boys!—*Othello,* ii, 3, 76.

14
Clarence: Give me a cup of wine.
Murderer: You shall have wine enough, my lord, anon.
Richard III. Act i, sc. 4, l. 167.
I, that was wash'd to death with fulsome wine.
Richard III. Act v, sc. 3, l. 132. [Ghost of the Duke of Clarence]
I 'll drown you in the malmsey-butt within.
Richard III. Act i, sc. 4, l. 277. [Murderer] "Malmsey-butt" is repeated in l. 161.
Metheglin, wort, and malmsey.—*Love's Labour 's Lost,* v, 2, 233. The only use of "malmsey." "Metheglin" is repeated in *The Merry Wives of Windsor,* v, 5, 167, and "worts" in the same play, i, 1, 123.

15
Come and crush a cup of wine.
Romeo and Juliet. Act i, sc. 2, l. 85. [Servant]

16
'Scape being drunk for want of wine.
Tempest, ii, 1, 146. See under DRUNKENNESS.

17
He shall taste of my bottle; if he have never drunk wine afore, it will go near to remove his fit.
The Tempest. Act ii, sc. 2, l. 77. [Stephano]
If all the wine in my bottle will recover him, I will help his ague.
The Tempest. Act ii, sc. 2, l. 96. [Stephano]
Trinculo: O Stephano, hast any more of this?
Stephano: The whole butt, man: my cellar is in a rock by the sea-side where my wine is hid.
The Tempest. Act ii, sc. 2, l. 137. The only use of "cellar."

Hogshead of wine.—*The Tempest,* iv, 1, 252.

1
To see . . . wine heat fools.
Timon of Athens. Act i, sc. 1, l. 271. [Apemantus]

Drunken spilth of wine.—*Timon of Athens,* ii, 2, 169. The only use of "spilth."

WING

2
Another would fly swift, but wanteth wings.
I Henry VI. Act i, sc. 1, l. 75. [Messenger]

Would I had wings!—*Cymbeline,* iii, 5, 161.
On the wing.—*Hamlet,* ii, 2, 132.

3
Protected
Under the wings of our protector's grace.
II Henry VI. Act i, sc. 3, l. 40. [Queen]

Stir a wing.—*III Henry VI,* i, 1, 47.

4
The wing of all occasions.
The Merry Wives of Windsor, ii, 2, 209. See under Wooing.

Airy wings.—*Richard III,* iv, 4, 13.
Batty wings.—*A Midsummer-Night's Dream,* iii, 2, 365. The only use of "batty."
Blessed wings.—*Henry VIII,* v, 1, 161.
Chaste wings.—*The Phœnix and the Turtle,* l. 4.
Coal-black wings.—*Rape of Lucrece,* l. 1009.
Drowsy, slow, and flagging wings.—*II. Henry VI,* iv, 1, 5. The only use of "flagging."
Feather'd wings.—*Venus and Adonis,* l. 306.
Gilded wings.—*Titus Andronicus,* iii, 2, 61.
Leathern wings.—*Midsummer-Night's Dream,* ii, 2, 4.
Mealy wings.—*Troilus and Cressida,* iii, 3, 79. The only use of "mealy."
Nimble wing.—*I Henry IV,* v, 1, 64.
Painted wings.—*Troilus and Cressida,* iii, 2, 15.
Saffron wings.—*The Tempest,* iv, 1, 78.
Swiftest wing.—*Macbeth,* i, 4, 17.
Trustless wings.—*The Rape of Lucrece,* l. 2. The only use of "trustless."
Tyrant wing.—*Phœnix and the Turtle,* l. 10.
Woven wings.—*Merchant of Venice,* i, 1, 14.
Dragon's wings.—*I Henry VI,* i, 1, 11; *Troilus and Cressida,* v, 8, 17.
Howlet's wing.—*Macbeth,* iv, 1, 17. The only use of "howlet" (owl).
Love's light wings.—*Romeo and Juliet,* ii, 2, 66.
Ravens' wings.—*The Rape of Lucrece,* l. 949.
Swallow's wings.—*Richard III,* v, 2, 23.
Wings of grasshoppers.—*Romeo and Juliet,* i, 4, 60.
Wings of war.—*King John,* ii, 1, 14.
Lend me wings.—*The Two Gentlemen of Verona,* ii, 6, 42.
Shaking her wings.—*Venus and Adonis,* l. 57.
Use my wings.—*The Winter's Tale,* iv, 1, 4.

WINKING

5
If I had play'd the desk or table-book,
Or given my heart a winking mute and dumb,
Or look'd upon this love with idle sight;
What might you think?
Hamlet. Act ii, sc. 2, l. 136. [Polonius] "Table-book" (note-book) is repeated in *The Winter's Tale,* iv, 4, 610.

Her winks, and nods.—*Hamlet,* iv, 5, 11.

6
King Henry: Teach your cousin to consent winking.
Burgundy: I will wink on her to consent.
Henry V. Act v, sc. 2, l. 331.

I will wink.—*Henry V,* ii, 1, 8.
I 'll wink and couch.—*The Merry Wives of Windsor,* v, 5, 52.
Wink now.—*II Henry VI,* ii, 1, 105.

7
Wink at the Duke of Suffolk's insolence.
II Henry VI. Act ii, sc. 2, l. 327. [York]

The winking of authority.—*King John,* iv, 2, 211.

8
And moody Pluto winks while Orpheus plays.
The Rape of Lucrece, l. 553.

9
You saw my master wink and laugh upon you?
The Taming of the Shrew. Act iv, sc. 4, l. 75. [Biondello]

Not be seen to wink.—*Love's Labour 's Lost,* i, 1, 43.

10
The eye wink at the hand.
Macbeth, i, 4, 52. See under Desire.

11
Here 's three solidares for thee. Good boy, wink at me, and say thou sawest me not.
Timon of Athens. Act iii, sc. 1, l. 47. [Lucullus] The only use of "solidares."

Wink each at other.—*A Midsummer-Night's Dream,* iii, 2, 239.

12
I had rather wink than look on them.
The Two Gentlemen of Verona. Act v, sc. 2, l. 14. [Julia]

Wink again,
And I will wink; so shall the day seem night.
Venus and Adonis, l. 121.

Lasting wink.—*The Winter's Tale,* i, 2, 317.
Perpetual wink.—*The Tempest,* ii, 1, 285. See under Death.

WINNING

See also Gain and Loss

13
Will you be mine, now you are doubly won?
All's Well that Ends Well. Act v, sc. 3, l. 315. [Helena]

14
As I my poor self did exchange for you,
To your so infinite loss, so in our trifles
I still win of you.
Cymbeline. Act i, sc. 1, l. 119. [Posthumus]

What I have lost to-day at bowls I 'll win to-night of him.
Cymbeline. Act ii, sc. 1, l. 53. [Cloten]

15
I will win for him an I can; if not, I will gain nothing but my shame.
Hamlet. Act v, sc. 2, l. 184. [Hamlet]

I shall win at the odds.—*Hamlet,* v, 2, 222.

16
Then with the losers let it sympathize,
For nothing can seem foul to those that win.
I Henry IV. Act v, sc. 1, l. 7. [King Henry]

But mine I am sure thou art, who e'er thou be,
And thus I win thee.
I Henry IV. Act v, sc. 4, l. 37. [Douglas]

1
Anjou and Maine! myself did win them both.
II Henry VI. Act i, sc. 1, l. 119. [Warwick]

2
Brother, I go; I 'll win them, fear it not.
III Henry VI. Act i, sc. 2, l. 60. [Montague]

Win the day.—*III Henry VI,* ii, 1, 136; *Richard III,* v, iii, 145; *King John,* v, 4, 30; 39.
Won the day.—*III Henry VI,* iv, 4, 15.

3
I was fain to draw mine honour in, and let 'em win the work.
Henry VIII. Act v, sc. 4, l. 60. [Porter]

Win the battle.—*Antony and Cleopatra,* ii, 3, 36.
Win a crown.—*Richard II,* iv, 1, 24.
Win your daughter.—*Richard III,* iv, 4, 283.
Win immortal fame.—*Henry V,* iii, 2, 11.
Win my favour.—*Love's Labour 's Lost,* iii, 1, 153.
Win grace.—*Love's Labour 's Lost,* ii, 1, 60.
Win your grace.—*Richard II,* ii, 3, 163.
Win The hearts of all.—*I Henry IV,* iv, 3, 83.
Win my love.—*The Taming of the Shrew,* Ind., 1, 109; iv, 2, 42.
Win their loves.—*King John,* iv, 2, 168.
Win your love.—*Love's Labour 's Lost,* iii, 1, 8.
Win the match.—*King John,* v, 2, 106.
Win our own.—*Richard II,* iii, 2, 191.
Win a paradise.—*Love's Labour 's Lost,* iv, 3, 73.
Win the prize.—*Taming of the Shrew,* ii, 1, 344.
Win our purpose.—*Coriolanus,* i, 6, 50.
Win our right.—*III Henry VI,* i, 1, 37; *Richard III,* iii, 1, 92.
Win your right.—*Henry V,* i, 2, 131.
Win renown.—*King John,* v, 2, 115.
Win A soul.—*Henry V,* ii, 2, 124.
Win time.—*Cymbeline,* iii, 4, 112.
Win the wager.—*The Taming of the Shrew,* v, 2, 69; 116.
Win a woman.—*The Two Gentlemen of Verona,* iii, 1, 105.
Win any woman.—*Much Ado about Nothing,* ii, 1, 17.
Win a woman's heart.—*King John,* i, 1, 269.

4
I shall . . .
Win you this city without stroke or wound.
King John. Act ii, sc. 1, l. 417. [Citizen]

He that wins of all.—*King John,* ii, 1, 569.

5
Husband, I cannot pray that thou mayst win.
King John. Act iii, sc. 1, l. 331. [Blanch]

What he hath won, that hath he fortified.
King John. Act iii, sc. 4, l. 10. [Dauphin]

6
We shall ne'er win at that sport.
The Merchant of Venice. Act iii, sc. 2, l. 220. [Gratiano]

He may win.—*Merchant of Venice,* iii, 2, 47.

7
We are the Jasons, we have won the fleece.
The Merchant of Venice. Act iii, sc. 2, l. 244. [Gratiano]

Many Jasons come in quest of her.
The Merchant of Venice, i, 1, 172. Jason is mentioned in no other play.

8
They laugh that win.
Othello. Act iv, sc. 1, l. 125. [Othello]

What shall I do to win my lord again?
Good friend, go to him; for, by this light of heaven,
I know not how I lost him.
Othello. Act iv, sc. 2, l. 149. [Desdemona]

9
Sure, I fear, we shall ne'er win him to it.
Richard III, iii, 7, 80. [Buckingham]

This wins him, liver and all.
Twelfth Night. Act ii, sc. 5, l. 106. [Fabian]

10
Gremio: Provided that he win her.
Grumio: I would I were as sure of a good dinner.
The Taming of the Shrew. Act i, sc. 2, l. 217.

Truly, sir, I think you 'll hardly win her.
The Two Gentlemen of Verona. Act i, sc. 1, l. 141. [Speed]

Win a lady.—*Henry V,* v, 2, 142.

11
Troilus: Why was my Cressid then so hard to win?
Cressida: Hard to seem won: but I was won, my lord,
With the first glance.
Troilus and Cressida. Act iii, sc. 2, l. 124.

II—The Winner

12
The event Is yet to name the winner.
Cymbeline. Act iii, sc. 5, l. 14. [Lucius]

Winner of her honour.—*Cymbeline,* ii, 4, 53.
Winner and loser.—*Hamlet,* iv, 5, 143.

13
The gentler gamester is the soonest winner.
Henry V, iii, 6, 120. See GENTLENESS, 608:7.

Beshrew the winners, for they play'd me false!
II Henry VI, iii, 1, 184. See under Loss.

14
Being a winner, God give you good night!
The Taming of the Shrew, v, 2, 187. See under WAGER.

15
Go together,
You precious winners all; your exultation
Partake to every one.
The Winter's Tale. Act v, sc. 3, l. 130. [Paulina] The only use of "exultation."

WINTER

See also Seasons, Summer

16
Quake in the present winter's state and wish
That warmer days would come.
Cymbeline. Act ii, sc. 4, l. 5. [Posthumus] "Warmer" is repeated in *The Winter's Tale,* iii, 3, 76.

17
The winter coming on and sickness growing.
Henry V. Act iii, sc. 3, l. 55. [King Henry]

18
The sun shines hot; and, if we use delay,
Cold biting winter mars our hoped-for hay.
III Henry VI. Act iv, sc. 8, l. 60. [King Edward] "Hoped-for" occurs again in v, 4, 35: "Hoped-for mercy," and in no other play.

Barren winter, with his wrathful nipping cold.
II Henry VI, ii, 4, 3. See under COMPENSATION. "Nipping" is repeated in *Hamlet,* i, 4, 2.
Angry winter.—*A Midsummer-Night's Dream,* ii, 1, 112.
Churlish winter.—*II Henry IV,* i, 3, 62.
Deepest winter.—*Timon of Athens,* iii, 4, 14.
Frozen winters.—*Richard II,* i, 3, 211.
Furious winter.—*Cymbeline,* iv, 2, 259.
Hideous winter.—*Sonnets,* v.
Lagging winters.—*Richard II,* i, 3, 214. The only use of "lagging."
Limping winter.—*Romeo and Juliet,* i, 2, 28. "Limping" is repeated in *Timon of Athens,* iv, 1, 14: "Limping sire."
Lusty winter.—*As You Like It,* ii, 3, 52.
A Poland winter.—*Comedy of Errors,* iii, 2, 99.
Rough winter.—*The Two Gentlemen of Verona,* ii, 4, 163.
Sap-consuming winter.—*Comedy of Errors,* v, 1, 312. The only use of "sap-consuming."
Trembling winter.—*Winter's Tale,* iv, 4, 81.

1
And none of you will bid the winter come
To thrust his icy fingers in my maw.
King John. Act v, sc. 7, l. 36. [King John]

2
Winter 's not gone yet, if the wild-geese fly that way.
King Lear. Act ii, sc. 4, l. 46. [Fool]

3
When icicles hang by the wall
And Dick the shepherd blows his nail
And Tom bears logs into the hall
And milk comes frozen home in pail,
When blood is nipp'd and ways be foul,
Then nightly sings the staring owl.
Love's Labour 's Lost, v, 2, 922.
The only use of "nipp'd."

Roping icicles.—*Henry V,* iii, 5, 23. The only use of "roping" (hanging).

When all aloud the wind doth blow
And coughing drowns the parson's saw,
And birds sit brooding in the snow
And Marian's nose looks red and raw,
And roasted crabs hiss in the bowl,
Then nightly sings the staring owl.
Love's Labour 's Lost, v, 2, 930. The only use of "brooding." "Roasted crab" occurs in *A Midsummer-Night's Dream,* ii, 1, 48.

4
The human mortals want their winter here.
A Midsummer-Night's Dream. Act ii, sc. 1, l. 101. [Titania]

5
No man inveigh against the wither'd flower,
But chide rough winter that the flower hath kill'd.
Not that devour'd, but that which doth devour,
Is worthy blame.
The Rape of Lucrece, l. 1254. The only use of "inveigh."

6
When great leaves fall, the winter is at hand.
Richard III. Act ii, sc. 3, l. 33. [Citizen]

Winter of our discontent.
Richard III, i, 1, 1. See under DISCONTENT.

7
Winter, which being full of care,
Makes summer's welcome thrice more wish'd, more rare.
Sonnets. No. lvi.

Yet seem'd it winter still.—*Sonnets,* xcviii.

8
Three winters cold
Have from the forests shook three summers' pride.
Sonnets. No. civ.

What is six winters? they are quickly gone.
Richard II. Act i, sc. 3, l. 260. [Gaunt]
Six or seven winters.—*Measure for Measure,* iii, 1, 76.
Twelve winters.—*The Tempest,* i, 2, 296.
Sixteen winters.—*The Winter's Tale,* v, 3, 50.
Forty winters.—*Sonnets,* ii.
Five-score winters.—*Love's Labour 's Lost,* iv, 3, 242. "Five-score" is repeated in iv, 2, 41, and occurs in no other play.

9
Winter tames man, woman and beast.
The Taming of the Shrew. Act iv, sc. 1, l. 24. [Grumio]

10
I 'll take that winter from your lips, fair lady.
Troilus and Cressida. Act iv, sc. 5, l. 24. [Achilles]

WISDOM

See also Learning

11
I leave you to your wisdom.
All's Well that Ends Well. Act ii, sc. 5, l. 76. [Bertram]

12
Parolles: Well, I shall be wiser.
Lafeu: Even as soon as thou canst, for thou hast to pull at a smack o' the contrary.
All's Well that Ends Well. Act ii, sc. 3, l. 235.

The wiser, the waywarder.
As You Like It. Act iv, sc. 1, l. 162. [Rosalind] The only use of "waywarder."
You are afraid, and therein the wiser.
Cymbeline. Act i, sc. 4, l. 146. [Iachimo]
He is the wiser man.
The Merry Wives of Windsor. Act ii, sc. 3, l. 39. [Shallow]

The felon
Loaden with irons wiser than the judge,
If wisdom be in suffering.
Timon of Athens. Act iii, sc. 5, l. 49. [Alcibiades] "Felon" is repeated in *II Henry VI,* iii, 1, 132, and in *Romeo and Juliet,* v, 3, 69.

13
Wisdom and fortune combating together,
If that the former dare but what it can,
No chance may shake it.
Antony and Cleopatra. Act iii, sc. 13, l. 79. [Thyreus]

I approve Your wisdom.—*Antony and Cleopatra,* v, 2, 150.

14
Unmuzzle your wisdom.
As You Like It. Act i, sc. 2, l. 74. [Rosalind] The only use of "unmuzzle." "Unmuzzled" occurs in *Twelfth Night,* iii, 1, 130.

1
Thus men may grow wiser every day.
As You Like It. Act i, sc. 2, l. 145. [Touchstone]

2
Master, be wise.
The Comedy of Errors. Act iv, sc. 3, l. 76. [Dromio of Syracuse]
Nay, but be wise.—*Othello,* iii, 3, 432.
Be wise.—*Othello,* v, 2, 223.

3
Your better wisdoms, which have freely gone
With this affair along.
Hamlet. Act i, sc. 2, l. 15. [King]
Foreign wisdom.—*Henry VIII,* i, 3, 29.
Vulgar wisdoms.—*Coriolanus,* i, 1, 219.
Wholesome wisdom.—*Othello,* iii, 1, 49.

4
You shall do marvellous wisely.
Hamlet. Act ii, sc. 1, l. 3. [Polonius]
We must do it wisely.—*Much Ado about Nothing,* iii, 5, 65.
Wisely done.—*Romeo and Juliet,* iii, 5, 234.
Then wisely, good sir.—*The Tempest,* ii, 1, 8.
Wisely, wisely.—*Romeo and Juliet,* ii, 4, 132.
Wisely and slow.—*Romeo and Juliet,* ii, 3, 94.
Wisely and truly.—*Julius Cæsar,* iii, 3, 17.
Not wisely but too well.—*Othello,* v, 2, 344.
Wisely definite.—*Cymbeline,* i, 6, 43.
Wisely suffer.—*Timon of Athens,* iii, 5, 31.
Most wisely.—*Troilus and Cressida,* i, 3, 138.
So wisely.—*II Henry IV,* iv, 5, 181.
Very wisely.—*As You Like It,* ii, 7, 53; *Julius Cæsar,* v, 1, 38.

5
Wisdom cries out in the streets, and no man regards it.
I Henry IV. Act i, sc. 2, l. 99. [Prince]
I marked him not; and yet he talked very wisely, but I regarded him not; and yet he talked wisely, and in the street too.
I Henry IV. Act i, sc. 2, l. 96. [Falstaff]
Wisely was it said.—*Hamlet,* iii, 3, 30.

For speaking wisely, see under SPEECH.

6
Divorce not wisdom from your honour.
II Henry IV. Act i, sc. 1, l. 162. [Bardolph]
Your wisdom be your guide.
II Henry IV. Act ii, sc. 3, l. 6. [Lady Northumberland]

7 What to your wisdoms seemeth best,
Do or undo.
II Henry VI. Act iii, sc. 1, l. 195. [King]
Be it as your wisdom will.—*Measure for Measure,* ii, 1, 32.

8
Whose wisdom was a mirror to the wisest.
III Henry VI. Act iii, sc. 3, l. 84. [Oxford]
Your grace hath still been famed for virtuous;
And now may seem as wise as virtuous.
III Henry VI. Act iv, sc. 6, l. 26. [Warwick]
I doubt not of your wisdom.—*Julius Cæsar,* iii, 1, 183.

9
I would you would make use of that good wisdom,
Whereof I know you are fraught.
King Lear. Act i, sc. 4, l. 240. [Goneril]
I pray, desire her call her wisdom to her.
King Lear. Act iv, sc. 5, l. 35. [Regan]

10
Lord, how wise you are!
Love's Labour's Lost. Act i, sc. 2, l. 143. [Jaquenetta]
Sapient sir.—*King Lear,* iii, 6, 24. The only use of "sapient."

11 To your huge store
Wise things seem foolish and rich things but poor.
Love's Labour's Lost. Act v, sc. 2, l. 377. [Biron]
Your wit makes wise things foolish.
Love's Labour's Lost, v, 2, 374. See under WIT.

Vouchsafe
In your rich wisdom to excuse or hide
The liberal opposition of our spirits.
Love's Labour's Lost. Act v, sc. 2, l. 741. [Princess]

12
He hath a wisdom that doth guide his valour.
Macbeth, iii, 1, 53. See under BOLDNESS.
Wisdom! to leave his wife, to leave his babes,
His mansion and his titles in a place
From whence himself does fly?
Macbeth. Act iv, sc. 2, l. 6. [Lady Macduff]

13
Thus wisdom wishes to appear most bright
When it doth tax itself.
Measure for Measure. Act ii, sc. 4, l. 78. [Angelo]
Show your wisdom, daughter,
In your close patience
Measure for Measure. Act iv, sc. 3, l. 122. [Duke]
Pace your wisdom
In that good path that I would wish it go.
Measure for Measure. Act iv, sc. 3, l. 137. [Duke]

14
Thou art as wise as thou art beautiful.
A Midsummer-Night's Dream. Act iii, sc. 1, l. 151. [Titania]
You are wise and full of gibes and vlouting-stocks.
The Merry Wives of Windsor. Act iv, sc. 5, l. 82. [Evans] The only use of "vlouting-stocks."

15
Before God! and, in my mind, very wise.
Much Ado about Nothing. Act ii, sc. 3, l. 192. [Claudio]

16
'Nay,' said I, 'the gentleman is wise:' 'Certain,' said she, 'a wise gentleman.'
Much Ado about Nothing. Act v, sc. 1, l. 165. [Don Pedro]
Wise burgher.—*Measure for Measure,* i, 2, 103. The only use of "burgher." "Burghers" occurs twice, in *As You Like It,* ii, 1, 23: "Native burghers"; and *The Merchant of Venice,* i, 1, 10: "Rich burghers."
Wise father.—*The Merchant of Venice,* ii, 2, 80.
Wise girls.—*Love's Labour's Lost,* v, 2, 58.
Wise gods.—*Antony and Cleopatra,* iii, 13, 112.
Wise man (men).—*III Henry VI,* iii, 1, 25, and twenty-five times in later plays.
Wise mother.—*The Merchant of Venice,* i, 3, 74.
Wise ones.—*Othello,* ii, 1, 143.
Wise people.—*Antony and Cleopatra,* v, 2, 267.

Wise physician.—*The Merry Wives of Windsor,* ii, 3, 56.
Wise prince.—*III Henry VI,* iii, 3, 85.
Wise woman.—*Twelfth Night,* iii, 4, 114; *The Merry Wives of Windsor,* iv, 5, 27; 59.

1
She that in wisdom never was so frail
To change the cod's head for the salmon's tail.
Othello. Act ii, sc. 1, l. 155. [Iago] The only use of "cod." "Cods" occurs in *As You Like It,* ii, 4, 53.

2
To wisdom he 's a fool that will not yield.
Pericles. Act ii, sc. 4, l. 54. [Lord]

3
Sad pause and deep regard beseem the sage.
The Rape of Lucrece, l. 277.
Be sage.—*Pericles,* iv, 6, 102.
Sage counsellors.—*II Henry IV,* iv, 5, 121.
Sage, grave men.—*Richard III,* iii, 7, 227.
Sage saws.—*Twelfth Night,* iii, 4, 413.
Sorrow to the sage.—*The Rape of Lucrece,* l. 222. The only uses of "sage."

4
It is a point of wisdom.
Richard III. Act i, sc. 4, l. 99. [Murderer]
Wisdom in peace.—*Richard III,* iii, 7, 16.
Wisdom of their choice.—*Coriolanus,* ii, 3, 104.
Wisdom of the world.—*Measure for Measure,* iii, 2, 242.

5
Be wise as thou art cruel.
Sonnets. No. cxl.

6
Hark, Tranio! thou may'st hear Minerva speak.
The Taming of the Shrew. Act i, sc. 1, l. 84. [Lucentio] Minerva is mentioned again in *Cymbeline,* v, 5, 164.
Though he be blunt, I know him passing wise.
The Taming of the Shrew. Act iii, sc. 2, l. 24. [Tranio]

7
You have taken it wiselier than I meant you should.
The Tempest. Act ii, sc. 1, l. 21. [Sebastian] The only use of "wiselier."

8 I will not praise thy wisdom,
Which, like a bourn, a pale, a shore, confines
Thy spacious and dilated parts.
Troilus and Cressida. Act ii, sc. 3, l. 259. [Ulysses] "Dilated" is repeated in *All's Well that Ends Well,* ii, 1, 59.
Instructed by the antiquary times,
He must, he is, he cannot but be wise.
Troilus and Cressida. Act ii, sc. 3, l. 262. [Ulysses] The only use of "antiquary."
Let thy fair wisdom, not thy passion, sway
In this uncivil and unjust extent
Against thy peace.
Twelfth Night. Act iv, sc. 1, l. 56. [Olivia]

9
What wisdom stirs amongst you?
The Winter's Tale. Act ii, sc. 1, l. 21. [Hermione]
Very wisely, puppies!
The Winter's Tale, iv, 4, 725. [Autolycus]

II—Wisdom and Folly

See also Fool and Wise Man

10 Full oft we see
Cold wisdom waiting on superfluous folly.
All's Well that Ends Well. Act i, sc. 1, l. 115. [Helena]

11
Herein lives wisdom, beauty and increase;
Without this, folly, age and cold decay.
Sonnets. No. xi.

12
Well, God give them wisdom that have it; and those that are fools, let them use their talents.
Twelfth Night. Act i, sc. 5, l. 14. [Clown]
This fellow is wise enough to play the fool;
And to do that well craves a kind of wit:
He must observe their mood on whom he jests,
The quality of persons, and the time,
And, like the haggard, check at every feather
That comes before his eye. This is a practice
As full of labour as a wise man's art:
For folly that he wisely shows is fit;
But wise men, folly-fall'n, quite taint their wit.
Twelfth Night. Act iii, sc. 1, l. 67. [Viola] The only use of "folly-fall'n."

WISH

See also Desire

13
Wishers were ever fools.
Antony and Cleopatra. Act iv, sc. 15, l. 37. [Cleopatra]
Lysander: Here is my bed: sleep give thee all his rest!
Hermia: With half that wish the wisher's eyes be press'd!
Midsummer-Night's Dream. Act ii, sc. 2, l. 64. The only uses of "wisher" and "wishers."

14
You think none but your sheets are privy to your wishes.
Antony and Cleopatra. Act i, sc. 2, l. 41. [Alexas]
Made of wishes.—*As You Like It,* v, 2, 101.

15
Thy wish was father, Harry, to that thought.
II Henry IV. Act iv, sc. 5, l. 93. [King Henry] The epigram derives from Cæsar, *De Bello Gallico,* iii, 18, but Shakespeare coined the phrase.

16
If wishes would prevail with me,
My purpose should not fail with me.
Henry V. Act iii, sc. 2, l. 16. [Pistol]

17
He comes upon a wish.
Julius Cæsar. Act iii, sc. 2, l. 271. [Antony]

18
Our wishes on the way May prove effects.
King Lear. Act iv, sc. 2, l. 15. [Goneril]

19
Would all were well!
Richard III. Act i, sc. 3, l. 40. [Queen Elizabeth]
Would yet he had lived!—*Measure for Measure,* iv, 4, 35.
Would I knew his mind.—*The Two Gentlemen of Verona,* i, 2, 33.

Would to God.—*Richard III,* i, 3, 140; *Much Ado about Nothing,* ii, 1, 264; *Richard II,* ii, 2, 100; *II Henry IV,* i, 2, 243.
Would to Heaven!—*Measure for Measure,* ii, 2, 67.
We would, and we would not.
Measure for Measure, iv, 4, 37. See under GRACE.
What would thou more?—*The Merry Wives of Windsor,* ii, 2, 31.
What would you?—*Love's Labour 's Lost,* v, 2, 178; *The Merchant of Venice,* ii, 2, 150; *The Two Gentlemen of Verona,* iv, 4, 115.

1 O, that she were
An open et cætera, thou a poperin pear!
Romeo and Juliet. Act ii, sc. 1, l. 37. [Mercutio] The only use of "et cætera," "poperin" (from Poperinge, a town of West Flanders).
And are etceteras nothing?—*II Henry IV,* ii, 4, 198. The only use of "et cæteras."

2
Blister'd be thy tongue For such a wish!
Romeo and Juliet. Act iii, sc. 2, l. 90. [Juliet] "Blister'd" is repeated in *Measure for Measure,* ii, 3, 12, and in *Henry VIII,* i, 3, 31.

3 I say no more,
Nor wish no less; and so, I take my leave.
Titus Andronicus. Act i, sc. 1, l. 401. [Bassianus]

4
Antonio: And how stand you affected to his wish?
Proteus: As one relying on your lordship's will
And not depending on his friendly wish.
The Two Gentlemen of Verona. Act i, sc. 3, l. 60. The only use of "relying."
High wish.—*Timon of Athens,* iv, 3, 245.
Inward wish.—*Henry V,* i, 1, 39.
Next wish.—*Taming of the Shrew,* i, 1, 244.
Noble wish.—*Coriolanus,* iii, 3, 38.
Virtuous wish.—*Sonnets,* xvi.

II—Good Wishes

5
Madam, I desire your holy wishes.
All's Well that Ends Well. Act i, sc. 1, l. 68. [Bertram]
The best wishes that can be forged in your thoughts be servants to you!
All's Well that Ends Well. Act i, sc. 1, l. 84. [Bertram] The only use of the phrase, "best wishes."
Better wishes.—*Henry VIII,* v, 1, 26.

6 He is one . . .
That I wish well. 'Tis pity—
That wishing well had not a body in 't,
Which might be felt; that we, the poorer born,
Whose baser stars do shut us up in wishes,
Might with effects of them follow our friends.
All's Well that Ends Well. Act i, sc. 1, l. 191. [Helena]
I wish him well.—*Measure for Measure,* iii, 2, 97.
I wish you well.—*The Merchant of Venice,* iv, 1, 420.
I wish your worship well.—*Much Ado about Nothing,* v, 1, 333.
You wish me well.—*Pericles,* v, 1, 16.
My wish receive, Which great Love grant!
All's Well that Ends Well. Act ii, sc. 3, l. 90. [Helena]

7
Let your fair eyes and gentle wishes go with me to my trial.
As You Like It. Act i, sc. 2, l. 198. [Orlando]
O, a good wish upon you!
As You Like It. Act i, sc. 3, l. 24. [Celia]
Good wishes, praise and prayers.—*I Henry VI,* v, 3, 173.
My good wishes.—*Twelfth Night,* ii, 5, 102.
Joy and good wishes!—*Henry V,* v, 2, 3.

8
Thy own wish wish I thee in every place!
Love's Labour 's Lost. Act ii, sc. 1, l. 179. [King]

9
It is the king's most sweet pleasure and affection to congratulate the princess.
Love's Labour 's Lost. Act v, sc. 1, l. 92. [Armado] The only use of "congratulate."
To gratulate the gentle princes there.
Richard III. Act iv, sc. 1, l. 10. [Queen Elizabeth]
Come freely To gratulate thy plenteous bosom.
Timon of Athens. Act i, sc. 2, l. 129. [Cupid]
Gratulate his safe return.—*Titus Andronicus,* i, 1, 221.
There 's more behind that is more gratulate.
Measure for Measure. Act v, sc. 1, l. 535. [Duke] The only uses of "gratulate."

10
Isabella: Peace here; grace and good company!
Provost: Who 's there? come in: the wish deserves a welcome.
Measure for Measure. Act iii, sc. 1, l. 44.

11 It is now our time,
That have stood by and seen our wishes prosper,
To cry, good joy: good joy, my lord and lady!
The Merchant of Venice. Act iii, sc. 2, l. 189. [Nerissa]
I wish him joy.—*Much Ado about Nothing,* ii, 1, 200.
I thank you for your wish, and am well pleased
To wish it back on you.
The Merchant of Venice. Act iii, sc. 4, l. 43. [Portia]

12
Take from my mouth the wish of happy years.
Richard II. Act i, sc. 3, l. 94. [Mowbray]

13
Look, what is best, that best I wish in thee:
This wish I have; then ten times happy me!
Sonnets, xxxvii.

14
To your wishes' height advance you both.
Titus Andronicus. Act ii, sc. 1, l. 125. [Aaron]
A charitable wish and full of love.
Titus Andronicus. Act iv, sc. 2, l. 43. [Chiron]

1
Recking as little what betideth me
As much I wish all good befortune you.
The Two Gentlemen of Verona, iv, 3, 40. The only use of "recking" and "befortune."

III—Getting One's Wish

2
He will fill thy wishes to the brim.
Antony and Cleopatra. Act iii, sc. 13, l. 18. [Antony]

I shall think my brother happy in having what he wishes for.
As You Like It. Act v, sc. 2, l. 51. [Orlando]

3
Every thing lies level to our wish.
II Henry IV. Act iv, sc. 4, l. 7. [King Henry]

4
You shall have . . . every thing you wish.
II Henry VI. Act v, sc. 1, l. 47. [York]

5
Why, now thou hast thy wish.
III Henry VI. Act i, sc. 4, l. 143. [York]

Hath her wish.—*Sonnets,* cxxxv.

6
May you be happy in your wish, my lord!
For, I profess, you have it.
Henry VIII. Act iii, sc. 2, l. 43. [Suffolk]

You have your wish.—*The Two Gentlemen of Verona,* iv, 2, 93.

7
Bear witness, Heaven, I have my wish for ever.
The Two Gentlemen of Verona, v, 4, 119. [Proteus]

I have my wish!—*Love's Labour 's Lost,* iv, 3, 81; *Romeo and Juliet,* i, 3, 62.

O that I had my wish!—*Love's Labour 's Lost,* iv, 3, 92.

Let me obtain my wish.—*Pericles,* v, 1, 35.

WIT

8
He had the wit which I can well observe
To-day in our young lords.
All 's Well that Ends Well. Act i, sc. 2, l. 32. [King]

9
Nay, I shall ne'er be ware of mine own wit till I break my shins against it.
As You Like It. Act ii, sc. 4, l. 59. [Touchstone]

He that hath learned no wit by nature nor art may complain of good breeding or comes of a very dull kindred.
As You Like It. Act iii, sc. 2, l. 30. [Corin]

You have too courtly a wit for me.
As You Like It. Act iii, sc. 2, l. 72. [Corin]

You have a nimble wit: I think 'twas made of Atalanta's heels.
As You Like It. Act iii, sc. 2, l. 293. [Jaques] Atalanta is mentioned again in the same scene, l. 155, and nowhere else.

10
Rosalind: Make the doors upon a woman's wit and it will out at the casement; shut that and 'twill out at the key-hole; stop that, 'twill fly with the smoke out at the chimney.
Orlando: A man that had a wife with such a wit, he might say, 'Wit, whither wilt?'
Rosalind: Nay, you might keep that check for it till you met your wife's wit going to your neighbour's bed.
Orlando: And what wit could wit have to excuse that?
As You Like It. Act iv, sc. 1, l. 162. The only use of "key-hole."

11
Touchstone: Art thou wise?
William: Ay, sir, I have a pretty wit.
As You Like It. Act v, sc. 1, l. 31.

I thank your pretty sweet wit for it.
II Henry IV. Act i, sc. 2, l. 231. [Falstaff]

12
He uses his folly like a stalking-horse and under the presentation of that he shoots his wit.
As You Like It. Act v, sc. 4, l. 111. [Duke senior] The only use of "stalking-horse." "Presentation" occurs again in *Richard III,* iv, 4, 84.

13
Are my discourses dull? barren my wit?
The Comedy of Errors. Act ii, sc. 1, l. 91. [Adriana]

Shallow wit.—*Henry V,* i, 2, 295.
Weak wit.—*Henry VIII,* iii, 1, 72.
Lacking wit.—*Henry VIII,* iii, 1, 177.
Of small wit.—*Henry VIII,* v, 4, 49.
Want of wit.—*The Rape of Lucrece,* l. 153.

14
I 'll try whether my old wit be in request
With those that have but little.
Coriolanus. Act iii, sc. 1, l. 251. [Menenius]

Little tiny wit.—*King Lear,* iii, 2, 74.

15
I believe, it is a fetch of wit.
Hamlet. Act ii, sc. 1, l. 38. [Polonius]

Ophelia: You are keen, my lord, you are keen.
Hamlet: It would cost you a groaning to take off my edge.
Hamlet. Act iii, sc. 2, l. 258.

My wit 's diseased.
Hamlet. Act iii, sc. 2, l. 333. [Hamlet]

I like thy wit well, in good faith.
Hamlet. Act v, sc. 1, l. 51. [Clown]

16
I am not only witty in myself, but the cause that wit is in other men.
II Henry IV. Act i, sc. 2, l. 11. [Falstaff]

As witty a piece of Eve's flesh as any in Illyria.
Twelfth Night. Act i, sc. 5, l. 30. [Clown]

You must be witty now.
Troilus and Cressida. Act iii, sc. 2, l. 32. [Pandarus]

The deep-revolving witty Buckingham.
Richard III. Act iv, sc. 2, l. 42. [King Richard] The only use of "deep-revolving."

17
A good wit will make use of any thing.
II Henry IV. Act i, sc. 2, l. 277. [Falstaff]

Doll: They say Poins has a good wit.
Falstaff: He a good wit? hang him, baboon! his wit 's as thick as Tewksbury mustard.
II Henry IV. Act ii, sc. 4, l. 260. "Tewksbury" is mentioned seven times in the plays.

Yet was Solomon so seduced, and he had a very good wit.
Love's Labour 's Lost, i, 2, 180. [Armado]

Profound Solomon.—*Love's Labour 's Lost,* iv, 3, 168. "Solomon" is mentioned in no other play. "Sultan Solyman" occurs in *The Merchant of Venice,* ii, 1, 26.

Herein I judge mine own wit good.
II Henry VI. Act iii, sc. 1, l. 232. [Queen Margaret]

Good wit.—*As You Like It,* iii, 3, 13; *Julius Cæsar,* i, 2, 304; *Much Ado about Nothing,* ii, 1, 135; *Twelfth Night,* iii, 1, 13.

1
Pregnancy is made a tapster, and hath his quick wit wasted in giving reckonings.
II Henry IV. Act i, sc. 2, l. 192. [Falstaff] The only use of "pregnancy." "Pregnant" is used fourteen times in the plays, always in the sense of full of meaning.

I would you had but the wit: 'twere better than your dukedom.
II Henry IV. Act iv, sc. 3, l. 92. [Falstaff]

2
My wit untrain'd in any kind of art.
I Henry VI, i, 2, 73. See under DAUGHTER.

3
I 'll try this widow's wit.
III Henry VI. Act iii, sc. 2, l. 33. [King Edward]

Away with scrupulous wit!
III Henry VI. Act iv, sc. 7, l. 61. [Hastings]

4
There is such disorder in my wit.
King John. Act iii, sc. 4, l. 102. [Constance]

5
Let me, if not by birth, have lands by wit.
King Lear. Act i, sc. 2, l. 199. [Edmund]

Thou hadst little wit in thy bald crown.
King Lear. Act i, sc. 4, l. 177. [Fool]

Thou hast pared thy wit o' both sides, and left nothing i' the middle.
King Lear, i, 4, 205. See under FOOL.

Thy wit shall ne'er go slip-shod.
King Lear. Act i, sc. 5, l. 11. [Fool] The only use of "slip-shod."

Armado: He surely affected her for her wit.
Moth: It was so, sir; for she had a green wit.
Love's Labour 's Lost. Act i, sc. 2, l. 92.

She hath Dian's wit.
Romeo and Juliet. Act i, sc. 1, l. 215. [Romeo] Diana was Shakespeare's favourite goddess; he mentions her forty-nine times.

Angry wit.—*Timon of Athens,* i, 1, 241.
Love's fine wit.—*Sonnets,* xxiii.
Nature's wit.—*As You Like It,* i, 2, 53.
Man's wit.—*Othello,* iii, 4, 22.
Wit of man.—*A Midsummer-Night's Dream,* iv, 1, 211.

6
My father's wit and mother's tongue, assist me!
Love's Labour 's Lost. Act i, sc. 2, l. 101. [Moth]

7
I am less proud to hear you tell my worth
Than you much willing to be counted wise
In spending your wit in the praise of mine.
Love's Labour 's Lost. Act ii, sc. 1, l. 17. [Princess of France]

The only soil of his fair virtue's gloss,
If virtue's gloss will stain with any soil,
Is a sharp wit match'd with too blunt a will;
Whose edge hath power to cut, whose will still wills
It should none spare that come within his power.
Love's Labour 's Lost. Act ii, sc. 1, l. 47. [Maria]

For he hath wit to make an ill shape good,
And shape to win grace though he had no wit.
Love's Labour 's Lost. Act ii, sc. 1, l. 59. [Katharine]

His eye begets occasion for his wit;
For every object that the one doth catch
The other turns to a mirth-moving jest,
Which his fair tongue, conceit's expositor,
Delivers in such apt and gracious words
That aged ears play truant at his tales
And younger hearings are quite ravished;
So sweet and voluble is his discourse.
Love's Labour 's Lost. Act ii, sc. 1, l. 69. [Rosaline] The only use of "mirth-moving" and "expositor." "Voluble" is repeated in *The Comedy of Errors,* ii, 1, 92, and in *Othello,* ii, 1, 242.

8
Your wit 's too hot, it speeds too fast, 'twill tire.
Love's Labour 's Lost. Act ii, sc. 1, l. 120. [Biron]

Repair thy wit, good youth, or it will fall
To cureless ruin.
The Merchant of Venice. Act iv, sc. 1, l. 141. [Shylock]

9
O' my troth, most sweet jests! most incony vulgar wit!
When it comes so smoothly off, so obscenely, as it were, so fit.
Love's Labour 's Lost. Act iv, sc. 1, l. 144. [Costard] "Incony" (fine, delicate) occurs again in iii, 1, 136, and in no other play. "Smoothly" is repeated in *Much Ado about Nothing,* v, 2, 33, and "obscenely" in *A Midsummer-Night's Dream,* i, 2, 111.

And his page o' t' other side, that handful of wit!
Ah, heavens, it is a most pathetical nit!
Love's Labour 's Lost. Act iv, sc. 1, l. 149. [Costard] "Handful" is repeated in *A Midsummer-Night's Dream,* iv, 1, 41; "pathetical" in *Love's Labour 's Lost,* i, 2, 103, and in *As You Like It,* iv, 1, 96; and "nit" in *The Taming of the Shrew,* iv, 3, 110.

A sweet touch, a quick venue of wit! snip, snap, quick and home! it rejoiceth my intellect: true wit!
Love's Labour 's Lost. Act v, sc. 1, l. 62. [Armado] The only use of "venue."

Well bandied both; a set of wit well play'd.
Love's Labour 's Lost. Act v, sc. 2, l. 29. [Princess of France] The only use of "bandied."

They never meet but there 's a skirmish of wit between them.
Much Ado about Nothing. Act i, sc. 1, l. 63. [Leonato] "Skirmish" is repeated in *I Henry VI,* i, 2, 34 and i, 4, 69.

10
Thou halfpenny purse of wit.
Love's Labour 's Lost. Act v, sc. 1, l. 77. [Costard]

None are so surely caught, when they are catch'd,
As wit turn'd fool.
Love's Labour 's Lost. Act v, sc. 2, l. 69. [Princess of France]

11
This fellow pecks up wit as pigeons pease,
And utters it again when God doth please:

He is wit's pedler, and retails his wares
At wakes and wassails, meetings, markets,
fairs.
Love's Labour's Lost. Act v, sc. 2, l. 315. [Biron] "Pease" is repeated in *The Tempest,* iv, 1, 69. "Pease" is also used twice, in *I Henry IV,* ii, 1, 9, and in *A Midsummer-Night's Dream,* iv, 1, 42.

Your wit makes wise things foolish.
Love's Labour's Lost. Act v, sc. 2, l. 374. [Biron]

Thrust thy sharp wit quite through my ignorance;
Cut me to pieces with thy keen conceit.
Love's Labour's Lost. Act v, sc. 2, l. 398. [Biron]

My wit is at an end.—*Love's Labour's Lost,* v, 2, 430.

1
Rosalind: Your task shall be,
With all the fierce endeavor of your wit
To enforce the pained impotent to smile.
Biron: To move wild laughter in the throat of death?
It cannot be; it is impossible:
Mirth cannot move a soul in agony.
Love's Labour's Lost. Act v, sc. 2, l. 862.

2
Thou speak'st with all thy wit; and yet, i' faith,
With wit enough for thee.
Macbeth. Act iv, sc. 2, l. 42. [Lady Macduff]

Goodly Lord, what a wit-snapper are you!
The Merchant of Venice. Act iii, sc. 5, l. 55. [Lorenzo] The only use of "wit-snapper."

Wilt thou show the whole wealth of thy wit in an instant?
The Merchant of Venice. Act iii, sc. 5, l. 61. [Lorenzo]

3
One that hath taught me more wit than ever I learned before in my life.
The Merry Wives of Windsor. Act iv, sc. 5, l. 60. [Falstaff]

My admirable dexterity of wit.
The Merry Wives of Windsor. Act iv, sc. 5, l. 120. [Falstaff]

See now how wit may be made a Jack-a-lent, when 'tis upon ill employment!
The Merry Wives of Windsor. Act v, sc. 5, l. 134. [Falstaff] "Jack-a-lent" (a figure set up to be pelted) occurs again in iii, 3, 27, and in no other play.

4
If I had wit enough to get out of this wood, I have enough to serve mine own turn.
A Midsummer-Night's Dream. Act iii, sc. 1, l. 152. [Bottom]

He hath simply the best wit of any handicraft man in Athens.
A Midsummer-Night's Dream. Act iv, sc. 2, l. 9. [Flute] The only use of "handicraft." "Handicrafts-men" occurs in *II Henry VI,* iv, 2, 12.

It is the wittiest partition that ever I heard discourse, my lord.
A Midsummer-Night's Dream. Act v, sc. 1, l. 167. [Demetrius] The only use of "wittiest."

5
If he have wit enough to keep himself warm, let him bear it for a difference between himself and his horse.
Much Ado about Nothing. Act i, sc. 1, l. 68. [Beatrice]

Leonato: Hath the fellow any wit that told you this?
Antonio: A good sharp fellow.
Much Ado about Nothing. Act i, sc. 2, l. 17.

He doth indeed show some sparks that are like wit.
Much Ado about Nothing. Act ii, sc. 3, l. 193. [Don Pedro]

6
Do you think I do not know you by your excellent wit?
Much Ado about Nothing. Act ii, sc. 1, l. 126. [Ursula]

Excellent wit.—*II Henry IV,* iv, 3, 110.

High-day wit.—*The Merchant of Venice,* ii, 9, 98. The only use of "high-day."

Tender wit.—*The Two Gentlemen of Verona,* i, 1, 47.

Wit incomparable.—*III Henry VI,* iii, 2, 85.

7
I may chance have some odd quirks and remnants of wit broken on me.
Much Ado about Nothing. Act ii, sc. 3, l. 244. [Benedick]

8
Her wit
Values itself so highly that to her
All matter else seems weak.
Much Ado about Nothing. Act iii, sc. 1, l. 52. [Hero]

Margaret: Doth not my wit become me rarely?
Beatrice: It is not seen enough, you should wear it in your cap.
Much Ado about Nothing. Act iii, sc. 4, l. 69.

9
We will spare for no wit, I warrant you; here 's that shall drive some of them to a noncome.
Much Ado about Nothing. Act iii, sc. 5, l. 66. [Dogberry] The only use of "noncome," usually considered to be a nonsensical abbreviation for "noncompos (mentis)," but perhaps a Dogberry substitute for "nonplus."

10
Claudio: Wilt thou use thy wit?
Benedick: It is in my scabbard: shall I draw it?
Don Pedro: Dost thou wear thy wit by thy side?
Claudio: Never any did so, though very many have been beside their wit.
Much Ado about Nothing. Act v, sc. 1, l. 124.

11
Sir, I shall meet your wit in the career, an you charge it against me.
Much Ado about Nothing. Act v, sc. 1, l. 135. [Benedick]

Benedick: Sir, your wit ambles well; it goes easily.
Don Pedro: . . . I said, thou hadst a fine wit: 'True,' said she, 'a fine little one.' 'No,' said I, 'a great wit:' 'Right,' says she, 'a great gross one.' 'Nay,' said I, 'a good wit:' 'Just,' said she, 'it hurts nobody.'
Much Ado about Nothing. Act v, sc. 1, l. 158.

Benedick: Thy wit is as quick as the greyhound's mouth; it catches.
Margaret: And yours as blunt as the fencer's foils, which hit, but hurt not.
Benedick: A most manly wit, Margaret; it will not hurt a woman.
Much Ado about Nothing. Act v, sc. 2, l. 11.

Proteus: Beshrew me, but you have a quick wit.
Speed: And yet it cannot overtake your slow purse.
Two Gentlemen of Verona. Act i, sc. 1, l. 132.

Quick wit.—*Much Ado about Nothing*, ii, 1, 399.

1
Thou know'st we work by wit, and not by witchcraft;
And wit depends on dilatory time.
Othello. Act ii, sc. 3, l. 378. [Iago] "Dilatory" occurs again in *Henry VIII*, ii, 4, 237: "Dilatory sloth."

Bear some charity to my wit; do not think it so unwholesome.
Othello. Act iv, sc. 1, l. 123. [Cassio]

Of so high and plenteous wit and invention.
Othello. Act iv, sc. 1, l. 201. [Othello]

[He] turn'd your wit the seamy side without.
Othello. Act iv, sc. 2, l. 146. [Emilia] The only use of "seamy."

2
Lending him wit that to bad debtors lends.
The Rape of Lucrece, l. 964.

What wit sets down is blotted straight with will;
This is too curious-good, this blunt and ill.
The Rape of Lucrece, l. 1299. The only use of "curious-good."

Began to clothe his wit in state and pride.
The Rape of Lucrece, l. 1809.

3
With what a sharp-provided wit he reasons!
Richard III. Act iii, sc. 1, l. 132. [Buckingham] The only use of "sharp-provided."

4
Thy wit is a very bitter sweeting; it is a most sharp sauce.
Romeo and Juliet. Act ii, sc. 4, l. 83. [Mercutio]

O, here 's a wit of cheveril, that stretches from an inch narrow to an ell broad!
Romeo and Juliet. Act ii, sc. 4, l. 87. [Mercutio] Cheveril is kidskin, used especially for gloves in Shakespeare's time because of its flexibility.

Thy wit, that ornament to shape and love,
Mis-shapen in the conduct of them both,
Like powder in a skilless soldier's flask,
Is set a-fire by thine own ignorance.
Romeo and Juliet. Act iii, sc. 3, l. 130. [Friar Laurence] "Flask" is used only once again, in *Love's Labour 's Lost*, v, 2, 619.

5
Musician: Put up your dagger, and put out your wit.
Peter: Then have at you with my wit! I will dry-beat you with an iron wit, and put up my iron dagger.
Romeo and Juliet. Act iv, sc. 5, l. 123. "Drybeat" is used again in iii, 1, 82, and in no other play.

6
Look, he 's winding up the watch of his wit; by and by it will strike.
The Tempest. Act ii, sc. 1, l. 12. [Sebastian]

Wit shall not go unrewarded while I am king of this country. 'Steal by line and level' is an excellent pass of pate.
The Tempest. Act iv, sc. 1, l. 242. [Stephano] The only use of "unrewarded."

7
Upon her wit doth earthly honour wait.
Titus Andronicus. Act ii, sc. 1, l. 10. [Aaron]

Her sacred wit
To villany and vengeance consecrate.
Titus Andronicus. Act ii, sc. 1, l. 120. [Aaron]

Thy years want wit, thy wit wants edge.
Titus Andronicus. Act ii, sc. 1, l. 26. [Demetrius]

He that had wit would think that I had none.
Titus Andronicus, ii, 3, 1. See under GOLD.

8
Pandarus: Hector shall not have his wit this year.
Cressida: He shall not need it, if he have his own.
Troilus and Cressida. Act i, sc. 2, l. 92.

He has a shrewd wit, I can tell you.
Troilus and Cressida. Act i, sc. 2, l. 206. [Pandarus]

What modicums of wit he utters!
Troilus and Cressida. Act ii, sc. 1, l. 74. [Thersites] The only use of "modicums."

This Ajax . . . has not so much wit . . . as will stop the eye of Helen's needle.
Troilus and Cressida. Act ii, sc. 1, l. 83. [Thersites]

Achilles: Will you set your wit to a fool's?
Thersites: No, I warrant you; for a fool's will shame it.
Troilus and Cressida. Act ii, sc. 1, l. 94.

A great deal of your wit, too, lies in your sinews, or else there be liars.
Troilus and Cressida. Act ii, sc. 1, l. 108. [Thersites]

Whose wit was mouldy ere your grandsires had nails on their toes.
Troilus and Cressida. Act ii, sc. 1, l. 114. [Thersites]

9
I will keep where there is wit stirring and leave the faction of fools.
Troilus and Cressida. Act ii, sc. 1, l. 129. [Thersites]

Take not that little little less than little wit from them that they have! which short-armed ignorance itself knows is so abundant scarce, it will not in circumvention deliver a fly from a spider, without drawing their massy irons and cutting the web.
Troilus and Cressida. Act ii, sc. 3, l. 14. [Thersites] The only use of "short-armed." "Circumvention" is repeated in *Coriolanus*, i, 2, 6.

Ajax: An all men were o' my mind,—
Ulysses: Wit would be out of fashion.
Troilus and Cressida. Act ii, sc. 3, l. 225.

10
Where is my wit? I know not what I speak.
Troilus and Cressida. Act iii, sc. 2, l. 158. [Cressida]

Bites his lip with a politic regard, as who should say 'There were wit in this head, an 'twould out;' and so there is, but it lies as coldly in him as fire in a flint, which will not show without knocking.
Troilus and Cressida. Act iii, sc. 3, l. 254. [Thersites]

Fear not my truth: the moral of my wit
Is 'plain and true;' there's all the reach of it.
Troilus and Cressida. Act iv, sc. 4, l. 109. [Troilus]

Wit larded with malice and malice forced with wit.
Troilus and Cressida. Act v, sc. 1, l. 64. [Thersites]

1
Methinks sometimes I have no more wit than a Christian or an ordinary man has: but I am a great eater of beef and I believe that does harm to my wit.
Twelfth Night. Act i, sc. 3, l. 88. [Sir Andrew]

Wit, an't be thy will, put me into good fooling! Those wits, that think they have thee, do very oft prove fools; and I, that am sure I lack thee, may pass for a wise man: for what says Quinapalus? 'Better a witty fool than a foolish wit.'
Twelfth Night. Act i, sc. 5, l. 35. [Clown] The only mention of Quinapalus, an invention of Shakespeare.

Thou most excellent devil of wit!
Twelfth Night. Act ii, sc. 5, l. 226. [Sir Toby]

Have you no wit?—*Twelfth Night,* ii, 3, 94.

2
Made wit with musing weak.
The Two Gentlemen of Verona. Act i, sc. 1, l. 69. [Proteus]

Sir Thurio borrows his wit from your ladyship's looks, and spends what he borrows kindly in your company.
The Two Gentlemen of Verona. Act ii, sc. 4, l. 38. [Valentine]

Sir, if you spend word for word with me, I shall make your wit bankrupt.
The Two Gentlemen of Verona. Act ii, sc. 4, l. 41. [Thurio]

3
And he wants wit that wants resolved will
To learn his wit to exchange the bad for better.
The Two Gentlemen of Verona. Act ii, sc. 6, l. 12. [Proteus]

4
Fair fall the wit that can so well defend her!
Venus and Adonis, l. 472.

Wit waits on fear.—*Venus and Adonis,* l. 690.

II—Wits

See also Mind

5
We that have good wits have much to answer for.
As You Like It. Act v, sc. 1, l. 12. [Touchstone]

Good wits will be jangling.
Love's Labour's Lost. Act ii, sc. 1, l. 225. [Princess of France]

6
I knew he was not in his perfect wits.
The Comedy of Errors, v, 1, 42. [Angelo]

Why stay we to be baited
With one that wants her wits?
Coriolanus. Act iv, sc. 2, l. 43. [Sicinius]

7
Our wits are so diversely coloured.
Coriolanus. Act ii, sc. 3, l. 22. [Citizen] The only use of "diversely."

8
Leaving their wits with their wives.
Henry V, iii, 7, 160. See under England.

Being in his right wits and his good judgements.
Henry V. Act iv, sc. 7, l. 49. [Fluellen]

I have labour'd With all my wits.
Henry V. Act v, sc. 2, l. 24. [Burgundy]

9
My wits begin to turn.
King Lear. Act iii, sc. 2, l. 67. [King Lear]

His wits begin to unsettle.
King Lear. Act iii, sc. 4, l. 167. [Kent] The only use of "unsettle."

Trouble him not, his wits are gone.
King Lear. Act iii, sc. 6, l. 94. [Kent]

Her wits, I fear me, are not firm.
Measure for Measure. Act v, sc. 1, l. 33. [Angelo]

10
Such short-lived wits do wither as they grow.
Love's Labour's Lost. Act ii, sc. 1, l. 54. [Princess of France] "Short-lived" is repeated in iv, 1, 15: "Short-lived pride," and occurs in no other play.

And spend his prodigal wits in bootless rhymes.
Love's Labour's Lost. Act v, sc. 2, l. 64. [Rosaline]

Fantastic wits.—*Venus and Adonis,* l. 850.

Homely wits.—*The Two Gentlemen of Verona,* i, 1, 2.

Rash bavin wits.—*I Henry IV,* iii, 2, 61. The only use of "bavin" (faggots, soon ablaze).

Simple wits.—*Love's Labour's Lost,* v, 2, 264.

11
Muster your wits; stand in your own defence;
Or hide your heads like cowards, and fly hence.
Love's Labour's Lost. Act v, sc. 2, l. 85. [Boyet]

Are these the breed of wits so wonder'd at?
Love's Labour's Lost. Act v, sc. 2, l. 266. [Princess of France]

Rosaline: Well-liking wits they have; gross, gross; fat, fat.
Princess: O poverty in wit, kingly-poor flout!
Love's Labour's Lost. Act v, sc. 2, l. 268. The only use of "well-liking" and "kingly-poor."

Well, better wits have worn plain statute-caps.
Love's Labour's Lost. Act v, sc. 2, l. 281. [Rosaline] The only use of "statute-caps" (woollen caps ordered by Parliament in 1571).

12
They would whip me with their fine wits till I were as crestfallen as a dried pear.
The Merry Wives of Windsor. Act iv, sc. 5, l. 101. [Falstaff] "Crest-fallen" is repeated in *II Henry VI,* iv, 1, 59, and in *Richard II,* i, 1, 188.

Finest wits.—*The Two Gentlemen of Verona,* i, 1, 44.

Fright the ladies out of their wits.
A Midsummer-Night's Dream. Act i, sc. 2, l. 82. [Bottom]

Here's a fellow frights English out of his wits.
The Merry Wives of Windsor. Act ii, sc. 1, l. 143. [Page]

Scared out of his good wits.
King Lear. Act iv, sc. 1, l. 60. [Edgar]

I will stare him out of his wits.
The Merry Wives of Windsor. Act ii, sc. 2, l. 291. [Falstaff]

Out o' your wits and hearing too?
The Tempest. Act iii, sc. 2, l. 86. [Trinculo]

1
In our last conflict four of his five wits went halting off, and now is the whole man governed with one.
Much Ado about Nothing. Act i, sc. 1, l. 65. [Beatrice]

Nay, if thy wits run the wild-goose chase, I have done, for thou hast more of the wild-goose in one of thy wits than, I am sure, I have in my whole five.
Romeo and Juliet. Act ii, sc. 4, l. 75. [Mercutio] The only use of "wild-goose chase."

Clown: Alas, sir, how fell you besides your five wits?
Malvolio: Fool, there was never man so notoriously abused: I am as well in my wits, fool, as thou art.
Clown: But as well? then you are mad indeed, if you be no better in your wits than a fool.
Twelfth Night. Act iv, sc. 2, l. 92.

Bless thy five wits!—*King Lear,* iii, 4, 59; iii, 6, 60.

Five wits.—*Romeo and Juliet,* i, 4, 47; *Sonnets,* cxli.

2
What, have you lost your wits?
Othello. Act i, sc. 1, l. 92. [Brabantio]

Are his wits safe? is he not light of brain?
Othello. Act iv, sc. 1, l. 280. [Lodovico]

3
Arm'd his long-hid wits.
The Rape of Lucrece, l. 1816. The only use of "long-hid."

4
This keen encounter of our wits.
Richard III. Act i, sc. 2, l. 115. [Gloucester]

5
O, how we joy to see your wit restored!
The Taming of the Shrew. Induction, sc. 2, l. 79. [Servant]

6
His wits
Are drown'd and lost in his calamities.
Timon of Athens. Act iv, sc. 3, l. 88. [Alcibiades]

7
And what an if
His sorrows have so overwhelm'd his wits,
Shall we be thus afflicted in his wreaks,
His fits, his frenzy, and his bitterness?
Titus Andronicus. Act iv, sc. 4, l. 9. [Saturninus]

8
Maria: Sure, the man is tainted in 's wits.
Olivia: Go call him hither. I am as mad as he,
If sad and merry madness equal be.
Twelfth Night. Act iii, sc. 4, l. 13. See also under MADNESS.

I am as well in my wits as any man in Illyria.
Twelfth Night. Act iv, sc. 2, l. 95. [Malvolio]

Malvolio, Malvolio, thy wits the heavens restore! endeavor thyself to sleep, and leave thy vain bibble babble.
Twelfth Night. Act iv, sc. 2, l. 103. [Clown] The only use of "bibble babble."

Olivia: Prithee, read i' thy right wits.
Clown: So I do, madonna; but to read his right wits is to read thus.
Twelfth Night. Act v, sc. 1, l. 305.

WITCH AND WITCHCRAFT

See also Charm, Conjuring, Magic

I—Witch

9
Out, fool! O forgive thee for a witch.
Antony and Cleopatra. Act i, sc. 2, l. 40. [Charmian]

The witch shall die.
Antony and Cleopatra. Act iv, sc. 12, l. 47. [Cleopatra]

10
There's none but witches do inhabit here.
The Comedy of Errors. Act iii, sc. 2, l. 161. [Antipholus of Syracuse]

Soul-killing witches that deform the body.
The Comedy of Errors, i, 2, 100. See under MAGIC. The only use of "soul-killing."

I see these witches are afraid of swords.
The Comedy of Errors. Act iv, sc. 4, l. 151. [Antipholus of Syracuse]

Avaunt, thou witch!—*The Comedy of Errors,* iv, 3, 80.

Turn witch.—*The Comedy of Errors,* iv, 4, 160.

11
Devil or devil's dam, I'll conjure thee:
Blood will I draw on thee, thou art a witch.
I Henry VI. Act i, sc. 5, l. 5. [Talbot]

That witch, that damned sorceress.—*I Henry VI,* iii, 2, 38.

12
See, how the ugly witch doth bend her brows.
I Henry VI. Act v, sc. 3, l. 34. [York]

Like a foul and ugly witch.—*Henry V,* iv, Prol., 21.

Foul wrinkled witch, what makest thou in my sight?
Richard III. Act i, sc. 3, l. 164. [Gloucester]

Cunning witch.—*II Henry VI,* i, 2, 75.

13
Wizards know their times:
Deep night, dark night, the silent of the night,
The time of night when Troy was set on fire;
The time when screech-owls cry and ban-dogs howl
And spirits walk and ghosts break up their graves,
That time best fits the work we have in hand.
II Henry VI. Act i, sc. 4, l. 18. [Bolingbroke] The only use of "ban-dog" (chained mastiff).

Made the wizard famous.—*II Henry VI,* v, 2, 69.

A wizard told him.—*Richard III,* i, 1, 56.
Doting wizard.—*The Comedy of Errors,* iv, 4, 61. The only uses of "wizard."

1 Dealing with witches and with conjurers.
II Henry VI. Act ii, sc. 1, l. 172. [Buckingham]

2 'Aroint thee, witch!' the rump-fed ronyon cries.
Macbeth. Act i, sc. 3, l. 6. [First Witch] The only use of "rump-fed," fed on scraps or offal. "Ronyon" (a scurvy person) occurs again in *Merry Wives of Windsor,* iv, 2, 195.

He met the night-mare, and her nine-fold;
Bid her alight,
And her troth plight,
And, aroint thee, witch, aroint thee!
King Lear. Act iii, sc. 4, l. 126. [Edgar] The only use of "night-mare" and "nine-fold." These two are the only uses of "aroint."

3 What are these
So wither'd and so wild in their attire,
That look not like the inhabitants o' the earth,
And yet are on 't?
Macbeth. Act i, sc. 3, l. 39. [Banquo]

4 Ford: A witch, a quean, an old cozening quean! . . . You witch, you hag, you baggage. . . .
Evans: By yea and no, I think the 'oman is a witch indeed: I like not when a 'oman has a great peard.
Merry Wives of Windsor. Act iv, sc. 2, l. 180.

Witch of Brentford.—*The Merry Wives of Windsor,* iv, 2, 100; iv, 5, 120.

5 The foul witch Sycorax, who with age and envy
Was grown into a hoop? hast thou forgot her?
The Tempest. Act i, sc. 2, l. 258. [Prospero]

This damn'd witch Sycorax,
For mischiefs manifold and sorceries terrible.
The Tempest. Act i, sc. 2, l. 263. [Prospero]

His mother was a witch, and one so strong
That could control the moon, make flows and ebbs,
And deal in her command without her power.
The Tempest. Act v, sc. 1, l. 269. [Prospero]

6 A mankind witch! Hence with her, out o' door:
A most intelligencing bawd!
The Winter's Tale. Act ii, sc. 3, l. 67. [Leontes] The only use of "intelligencing."

II—Witchcraft

7 Witchcraft celebrates
Pale Hecate's offerings.
Macbeth. Act ii, sc. 1, l. 51. [Macbeth] "Hecate" is mentioned seven times.

Juggling witchcraft.—*King John,* iii, 1, 168.
Witchcraft in your lips.—*Henry V,* v, 2, 301.
Witchcraft of his wit.—*Hamlet,* i, 5, 43.

8 This is the only witchcraft I have used.
Othello. Act i, sc. 3, l. 169. [Othello]

9 See how I am bewitch'd.
Richard III. Act iii, sc. 4, l. 70. [Gloucester]

Pray God, he be not bewitched!
Twelfth Night. Act iii, sc. 4, l. 112. [Maria]

You witch me in it.
Timon of Athens. Act v, sc. 1, l. 158. [Timon]

10 This is Edward's wife, that monstrous witch,
Consorted with that harlot strumpet Shore,
That by their witchcraft thus have marked me.
Richard III. Act iii, sc. 4, l. 72. [Gloucester]

I pray you all, tell me what they deserve
That do conspire my death with devilish plots
Of damned witchcraft, and that have prevail'd
Upon my body with their hellish charms?
Richard III. Act iii, sc. 4, l. 61. [Gloucester]

11 A witchcraft drew me hither.
Twelfth Night. Act v, sc. 1, l. 79. [Antonio]

Fresh piece Of excellent witchcraft.
The Winter's Tale. Act iv, sc. 4, l. 432. [Polixenes]

WITNESS

12 God and the rope-maker bear me witness.
The Comedy of Errors. Act iv, sc. 4, l. 93. [Dromio of Ephesus] The only use of "rope-maker."

God is my witness.—*II Henry VI,* i, 3, 192.
God witness with me.—*Richard III,* iv, 4, 60; *II Henry IV,* iv, 5, 150.
Heaven bear witness.—*Henry VIII,* ii, 1, 59; ii, 4, 22.
Take the High'st to witness.—*All's Well that Ends Well,* iv, 2, 24.

13 You shall bear
A better witness back than words, which we,
On like conditions, will have counter-seal'd.
Coriolanus. Act v, sc. 3, l. 203. [Coriolanus] The only use of "counter-seal'd."

14 If you will make 't an action, call witness to 't.
Cymbeline. Act ii, sc. 3, l. 156. [Imogen]

15 You cannot witness for me, being slain.
I Henry VI. Act iv, sc. 5, l. 43. [John Talbot]

Having no witness to confirm my speech.
Macbeth. Act v, sc. 1, l. 21. [Gentlewoman]

16 He hath witness of his servant's malice.
II Henry VI. Act i, sc. 3, l. 213. [Gloucester]

I have good witness.—*II Henry VI,* i, 3, 204.
Good witness.—*Much Ado about Nothing,* iv, 2, 82.

17 I shall not want false witness to condemn me,
Nor store of treasons to augment my guilt.
II Henry VI. Act iii, sc. 1, l. 168. [Gloucester] "False witness" was never used after the first play.

Perjured witness.—*Henry VIII,* v, 1, 136.
Suborn'd the witness.—*Othello,* iii, 4, 153.

1
No witness Would come against you.
Henry VIII. Act v, sc. 1, l. 107. [King Henry]

Dearly witness.—*Henry VIII,* v, 3, 30.

2 Give me thy hand, Messala:
Be thou my witness.
Julius Cæsar. Act v, sc. 1, l. 75. [Cassius]

Thyself art witness.—*The Two Gentlemen of Verona,* iv, 2, 110.

You are my witnesses.—*Much Ado about Nothing,* iii, 2, 132.

3
O, when the last account 'twixt heaven and earth
Is to be made, then shall this hand and seal
Witness against us to damnation!
King John. Act iv, sc. 2, l. 116. [King John]

4
Wash this filthy witness from your hand.
Macbeth. Act ii, sc. 2, l. 47. [Lady Macbeth]

5 Lorenzo here
Shall witness I set forth as soon as you.
The Merchant of Venice. Act v, sc. 1, l. 271. [Portia]

6
The witness of a good conscience.
The Merry Wives of Windsor. Act iv, sc. 2, l. 220. [Mrs. Ford]

Witness of his proper ear.—*Measure for Measure,* v, 1, 310.

Witnesses of true experience.—*Titus Andronicus,* v, 3, 78.

Witness of this ill.—*Richard III,* iii, 4, 69.

Witness of her lightness.—*The Taming of the Shrew,* iv, 2, 24.

Witness of my love.—*As You Like It,* iii, 2, 1.

Witness to that vow.—*Richard III,* iii, 7, 180.

7
I can bear them witness.
Much Ado about Nothing. Act ii, sc. 3, l. 240. [Benedick]

Bear witness.—*The Comedy of Errors,* iv, 4, 80; *The Two Gentlemen of Verona,* v, 4, 110; *Much Ado about Nothing,* v, 2, 89; *The Merry Wives of Windsor,* ii, 3, 36; *The Winter's Tale,* iv, 4, 395; v, 1, 72; *The Tempest,* iii, 1, 68; *Henry VIII,* ii, 1, 59.

Bear me witness.—*The Comedy of Errors,* iv, 4, 93; *Henry V,* v, 2, 385; *Antony and Cleopatra,* iv, 9, 5.

Witness bear.—*Sonnets,* cxxxi.

8
You can witness with me this is true.
Richard II. Act iv, sc. 1, l. 63. [Fitzwater]

Witness this is true.—*Titus Andronicus,* v, 3, 124.

9
A dire induction am I witness to.
Richard III. Act iv, sc. 4, l. 5. [Queen Margaret]

I am witness with her.—*The Comedy of Errors,* iv, 4, 92.

Thus far I witness with him.—*The Comedy of Errors,* v, 1, 254.

That can I witness.—*II Henry VI,* i, 3, 176.

To this I witness.—*Sonnets,* cxxiv.

Witness most truly.—*As You Like It,* ii, 7, 193.

Sufficient honest witnesses.—*The Taming of the Shrew,* iv, 4, 95.

10
This is a witness that I am thy son.
Titus Andronicus. Act ii, sc. 3, l. 116. [Demetrius]

Bleeding witness.—*Richard III,* i, 2, 234.

In witness whereof.—*Troilus and Cressida,* iii, 2, 61.

WOE

See also Grief, Misery, Sorrow

11 When your words are done,
My woes end likewise with the evening sun.
The Comedy of Errors. Act i, sc. 1, l. 27. [Ægeon]

Lash'd with woe.—*Comedy of Errors,* ii, 1, 15.

Laugh my woes to scorn.—*The Comedy of Errors,* ii, 2, 207.

In mine own woe charm'd.—*Cymbeline,* v, 3, 68.

12 It us befitted
To bear our hearts in grief and our whole kingdom
To be contracted in one brow of woe.
Hamlet. Act i, sc. 2, l. 2. [King]

But I have that within which passeth show;
These but the trappings and the suits of woe.
Hamlet. Act i, sc. 2, l. 85. [Hamlet] See SEEMING, 1330:3, for full quotation.

We pray you, throw to earth
This unprevailing woe.
Hamlet. Act i, sc. 2, l. 106. [King] The only use of "unprevailing."

Bitter woes.—*Titus Andronicus,* iii, 2, 3.

Client woes.—*Richard III,* iv, 4, 127. The only use of "client" as an adjective. "Clients" occurs in *Measure for Measure,* i, 2, 110, and in *Pericles,* iv, 6, 6.

Conquer'd woe.—*Sonnets,* xc.

Constant woe.—*Venus and Adonis,* l. 967.

Feeling woe.—*Pericles,* i, 1, 48.

General woe.—*King Lear,* v, 3, 318.

Guilty woe.—*The Rape of Lucrece,* l. 1482.

Inward woe.—*Troilus and Cressida,* v, 10, 31.

Kingly woe.—*Richard II,* iii, 2, 210.

Lesser woe.—*The Comedy of Errors,* i, 1, 109.

Living woe.—*Richard III,* iv, 4, 119.

Mortal woe.—*Richard II,* ii, 1, 152.

Nameless woe.—*Richard II,* ii, 2, 40.

Never-ending woes.—*The Rape of Lucrece,* l. 935. The only use of "never-ending."

Painted woes.—*The Rape of Lucrece,* l. 1492.

Speechless woe.—*The Rape of Lucrece,* l. 1674.

True old woe.—*Pericles,* iv, 4, 24.

Season'd woe.—*A Lover's Complaint,* l. 18.

Second woe.—*Measure for Measure,* ii, 1, 298.

Sharp woes.—*The Rape of Lucrece,* l. 1136.

Unprofitable woe!—*Pericles,* iv, 1, 26.

A very woe.—*Sonnets,* cxxix.

Dole and woe.—*Pericles,* iii, Gower, 42.

Beldam's woes.—*The Rape of Lucrece,* l. 1458.

English woes.—*Richard III,* iv, 4, 115.

Lucrece' woes.—*The Rape of Lucrece,* l. 1747.

Subjects' woe.—*III Henry VI,* ii, 5, 111.

13
One woe doth tread upon another's heel,
So fast they follow.
Hamlet. Act iv, sc. 7, l. 164. [Queen]

1
Nothing so heavy as these woes of mine.
II Henry VI. Act v, sc. 2, l. 65. [Young Clifford]

2
And now, to add more measure to your woes,
I come to tell you things sith then befall'n.
III Henry VI. Act ii, sc. 1, l. 105. [Warwick]

Would I were dead! if God's good will were so;
For what is in this world but grief and woe?
III Henry VI. Act ii, sc. 5, l. 19. [King Henry]

Woe above woe! grief more than common grief!
III Henry VI. Act ii, sc. 5, l. 94. [King Henry]

Woe, woe are we, sir, you may not live to wear
All your true followers out.
Antony and Cleopatra. Act iv, sc. 14, l. 133. [Guard]

Woe, woe, for England! not a whit for me.
Richard III. Act iii, sc. 4, l. 82. [Hastings]

Woe is me to think upon thy woes.
Titus Andronicus. Act iii, sc. 1, l. 240. [Messenger]

Woe is me!—*II Henry VI,* iii, 2, 72; *Hamlet,* iii, 1, 168; iii, 2, 173; *Lover's Complaint,* l. 78.
Woe is my heart!—*Cymbeline,* v, 5, 2.
Woe, woe!—*The Rape of Lucrece,* l. 1802.
O woe!—*Romeo and Juliet,* v, 3, 13.
O, treble woe.—*Hamlet;* v, 1, 269.
Alack for woe!—*Love's Labour's Lost,* iv, 1, 15; *Richard II,* iii, 3, 70.
Alas, and woe!—*Antony and Cleopatra,* iv, 14, 107.
Woe, alas!—*Macbeth,* ii, 3, 92.
Woe and heavy well-a-day!—*Pericles,* iv, 4, 49.
Woe enough.—*Romeo and Juliet,* iii, 2, 115.
Woe me!—*Measure for Measure,* i, 4, 26.
Woe the while!—*Henry V,* iv, 7, 78; *Julius Cæsar,* i, 3, 82; *The Winter's Tale,* iii, 2, 173.
Woe 'tis so!—*Antony and Cleopatra,* iv, 15, 17.

3
Ay, marry, There will be woe indeed.
Henry VIII. Act i, sc. 3, l. 38. [Lovell]

Full of woe.—*Henry VIII,* Prol., 3; ii, 1, 140.

4
Woe to the hand that shed this costly blood!
Julius Cæsar, iii, 1, 258. See under HAND.

Woe to my lord chief-justice!—*II Henry IV,* v, 3, 145.
Woe unto the birds.—*Venus and Adonis,* l. 455.
Woe upon thy life!—*Othello,* iii, 3, 366.
Woe upon ye!—*Henry VIII,* iii, 1, 114.

5 Leave those woes alone which I alone
Am bound to under-bear.
King John. Act iii, sc. 1, l. 64. [Constance] The only use of "under-bear."

6
Woe, that too late repents.
King Lear. Act i, sc. 4, l. 279. [King Lear]

When we our betters see bearing our woes,
We scarcely think our miseries our foes.
King Lear. Act iii, sc. 6, l. 109. [Edgar]

Woes by wrong imaginations lose
The knowledge of themselves.
King Lear, iv, 6, 290. See under GRIEF.

7
If there be more, more woful, hold it in;
For I am almost ready to dissolve,
Hearing of this.
King Lear. Act v, sc. 3, l. 202. [Albany]

I am as woful as Virginius was,
And have a thousand times more cause.
Titus Andronicus. Act v, sc. 3, l. 50. [Titus] "Virginius" is mentioned a second time in l. 36, and in no other scene.

'Tis woful.—*Henry VIII,* ii, 1, 167.

8 Shrieking undistinguish'd woe,
In clamours of all size, both high and low.
A Lover's Complaint, l. 20. "Undistinguish'd" is repeated in *King Lear,* iv, 6, 278.

Never so in woe.—*A Midsummer-Night's Dream,* iii, 2, 442.

9
Measure his woe the length and breadth of mine.
Much Ado about Nothing. Act v, sc. 1, l. 11. [Leonato]

Let my woes frown on the upper hand.
If sorrow can admit society,
Tell o'er your woes again by viewing mine.
Richard III, iv, 4, 37. See under SORROW.

10
I'll then disclose our woes, felt several years.
Pericles. Act i, sc. 4, l. 18. [Cleon]

I am great with woe, and shall deliver weeping.
Pericles. Act v, sc. 1, l. 107. [Pericles]

11
Fellowship in woe doth woe assuage,
As palmers' chat makes short their pilgrimage.
The Rape of Lucrece, l. 790.

Sour woe delights in fellowship.
Romeo and Juliet. Act iii, sc. 2, l. 116. [Juliet]

So two, together weeping, make one woe.
Richard II. Act v, sc. 1, l. 86. [King Richard]

12
Old woes, not infant sorrows, bear them mild.
The Rape of Lucrece, l. 1096.

Deep woes roll forward like a gentle flood,
Who, being stopp'd, the bounding banks o'erflows.
The Rape of Lucrece, l. 1118.

My woes are tedious, though my words are brief.
The Rape of Lucrece, l. 1309.

Woe hath wearied woe.
The Rape of Lucrece, l. 1363.

Though woe be heavy, yet it seldom sleeps.
The Rape of Lucrece, l. 1574.

In me moe woes than words are now depending.
The Rape of Lucrece, l. 1615.

My woe too sensible thy passion maketh
More feeling-painful: let it then suffice
To drown one woe, one pair of weeping eyes.
The Rape of Lucrece, l. 1679. The only use of "feeling-painful."

Such emulation in their woe.
The Rape of Lucrece, l. 1808.

Is woe the cure for woe?
The Rape of Lucrece, l. 1821.

13 Woe doth the heavier sit,
Where it perceives it is but faintly borne.
Richard II. Act i, sc. 3, l. 280. [Gaunt]

Thou art the midwife to my woe.
Richard II. Act ii, sc. 2, l. 62. [Queen]

1
Now hath my soul brought forth her prodigy,
And I, a gasping new-deliver'd mother,
Have woe to woe, sorrow to sorrow join'd.
Richard II. Act ii, sc. 2, l. 64. [Queen] "New-deliver'd" is repeated in *Richard III,* i, 1, 21: "New-deliver'd Hastings."
And where 's that valiant crook-back prodigy?
III Henry VI. Act i, sc. 4, l. 75. [Queen]

2
God for his mercy! what a tide of woes
Comes rushing on this woeful land at once!
Richard II. Act ii, sc. 2, l. 98. [York]
My lord, wise men ne'er sit and wail their woes.
Richard II. Act iii, sc. 2, l. 178. [Carlisle]
Woe is forerun with woe.
Richard II. Act iii, sc. 4, l. 28. [Queen]
Abbot of Westminster: A woeful pageant have we here beheld.
Bishop of Carlisle: The woe 's to come; the children yet unborn
Shall feel this day as sharp to them as thorn.
Richard II. Act iv, sc. 1, l. 321.

3
You live that shall cry woe for this hereafter.
Richard III. Act iii, sc. 3, l. 7. [Vaughan]
Triumph not in my woes!
God witness with me, I have wept for thine.
Richard III. Act iv, sc. 4, l. 59. [Duchess of York]

4
This but begins the woe.
Romeo and Juliet. Act iii, sc. 1, l. 125. [Romeo]
All these woes shall serve
For sweet discourses in our time to come.
Romeo and Juliet. Act iii, sc. 5, l. 52. [Romeo]
We see the ground whereon these woes do lie;
But the true ground of all these piteous woes
We cannot without circumstance descry.
Romeo and Juliet. Act v, sc. 3, l. 179. [Watch]
What further woe conspires against my age?
Romeo and Juliet. Act v, sc. 3, l. 212. [Montague]
And then will I be general of your woes,
And lead you even to death.
Romeo and Juliet. Act v, sc. 3, l. 219. [Prince]

5
With old woes new wail my dear time's waste.
Sonnets, xxx. See REMEMBRANCE, 1259:5.
Weep afresh love's long since cancell'd woe.
Sonnets, xxx.
Other strains of woe, which now seem woe,
Compared with loss of thee will not seem so.
Sonnets, xc.
Tired with my woe.—*Sonnets,* l.
Make you woe.—*Sonnets,* lxxi.

6
Our hint of woe
Is common; every day some sailor's wife,
The masters of some merchant and the merchant
Have just our theme of woe.
The Tempest. Act ii, sc. 1, l. 3. [Gonzalo]
I am woe for 't, sir.
The Tempest. Act v, sc. 1, l. 139. [Prospero]

7
They have nursed this woe, in feeding life.
Titus Andronicus. Act iii, sc. 1, l. 74. [Titus]
My bowels cannot hide her woes,
But like a drunkard must I vomit them.
Titus Andronicus. Act iii, sc. 1, l. 231. [Titus]
The wofull'st man that ever lived in Rome.
Titus Andronicus. Act iii, sc. 1, l. 290. [Lucius]
Thou map of woe.
Titus Andronicus. Act iii, sc. 2, l. 12. [Titus]
Woe betide thee evermore!
Titus Andronicus. Act iv, sc. 2, l. 56. [Nurse]
Wipe away her woe!—*Titus Andronicus,* v, 3, 148.
Have done with woes.—*Titus Andronicus,* v, 3, 176.

8
O, I have fed upon this woe already,
And now excess of it will make me surfeit.
The Two Gentlemen of Verona. Act iii, sc. 1, l. 219. [Valentine]
Waxed pale for woe.—*The Two Gentlemen of Verona,* iii, 1, 228.

9
Her heavy anthem still concludes in woe.
Venus and Adonis, l. 839. "Anthem" is repeated in *II Henry IV,* i, 2, 213, and in *The Two Gentlemen of Verona,* iii, 1, 240.
Her woes the more increasing.—*Venus and Adonis,* l. 254.

10
O lords, When I have said, cry 'woe!'
The Winter's Tale. Act iii, sc. 2, l. 200. [Paulina]
Who was most marble there changed colour; some swooned, all sorrowed: if all the world could have seen 't, the woe had been universal.
The Winter's Tale. Act v, sc. 2, l. 97. [Gentleman]

WOLF

11
A wolf, nay, worse, a fellow all in buff.
The Comedy of Errors. Act iv, sc. 2, l. 36. [Dromio of Syracuse]
He 's in a suit of buff.—*The Comedy of Errors,* iv, 2, 45.
Buff jerkin.—*I Henry IV,* i, 2, 48; 52. The only uses of "buff."

12
Thou wolf in sheep's array.
I Henry VI. Act i, sc. 3, l. 55. [Gloucester]
See also under APPEARANCE.

13
Thus is the shepherd beaten from thy side
And wolves are gnarling who shall gnaw thee first.
II Henry VI. Act iii, sc. 1, l. 191. [Gloucester] "Gnarling" is repeated in *Richard II,* i, 3, 292: "Gnarling sorrow."
And now loud-howling wolves arouse the jades
That drag the tragic melancholy night;
Who, with their drowsy, slow and flagging wings,
Clip dead men's graves and from their misty jaws
Breathe foul contagious darkness in the air.
II Henry VI. Act iv, sc. 1, l. 3. [Captain] The only use of "loud-howling," "arouse," and "flagging."

Belly-pinched wolf.—*King Lear,* iii, 1, 13. The only use of "belly-pinched."
Hunger-starved wolves.—*III Henry VI,* i, 4, 5. The only use of "hunger-starved."
Irish wolves.—*As You Like It,* v, 2, 119.
Universal wolf.—*Troilus and Cressida,* i, 3, 121.

1
She-wolf of France, but worse than wolves
of France.
III Henry VI. Act i, sc. 4, l. 111. [York]
The only use of "she-wolf."

2 Single out some other chase;
For I myself will hunt this wolf to death.
III Henry VI. Act ii, sc. 4, l. 12. [Richard]
Yonder is the wolf that makes this spoil.
III Henry VI. Act v, sc. 4, l. 80. [Queen Margaret]

3
The wolf behowls the moon.
A Midsummer-Night's Dream. Act v, sc. 1, l. 379. [Puck] The only use of "behowls."
The wolves have prey'd.—*Much Ado about Nothing,* v, 3, 25.

4
The wolf doth grin before he barketh.
Venus and Adonis, l. 459.
Affable wolves.—*Timon of Athens,* iii, 6, 105.

II—Wolf and Lamb

5
Menenius: Pray you, who does the wolf love?
Sicinius: The lamb.
Coriolanus. Act ii, sc. 1, l. 8.

6
When thou didst keep my lambs a-field,
I wish some ravenous wolf had eaten thee!
I Henry VI. Act v, sc. 4, l. 30. [Shepherd]

7
The wolf hath seized his prey, the poor
lamb cries.
The Rape of Lucrece, l. 677.

8
Wilt thou, O God, fly from such gentle
lambs,
And throw them in the entrails of the
wolf?
Richard III. Act iv, sc. 4, l. 22. [Queen Elizabeth]

9
How many lambs might the stern wolf
betray,
If like a lamb he could his looks translate!
Sonnets. No. xcvi.

WOMAN

See also Character: Woman's Character; Dame; Fear: Women's Fears; Housewife; Lady; Man and Woman; Tears: Women's Tears; Tongue: Women's Tongues; Wrong: Women's Wrongs

I—Familiar Phrases

10
This woman's an easy glove, my lord; she goes off and on at pleasure.
All's Well that Ends Well. Act v, sc. 3, l. 278. [Lafeu]

11
As well a woman with an eunuch play'd
As with a woman.
Antony and Cleopatra. Act ii, sc. 5, l. 5. [Cleopatra]
Were kisses all the joys in bed,
One woman would another wed.
The Passionate Pilgrim, l. 345.
Two women placed together makes cold
weather.
Henry VIII. Act i, sc. 4, l. 22. [Lord Chamberlain]
What says the married woman?—*Antony and Cleopatra,* i, 3, 20. See under Wife.

12
The bountiful blind woman doth most mistake in her gifts to women.
As You Like It. Act i, sc. 2, l. 38. [Rosalind]

13
I must comfort the weaker vessel, as doublet and hose ought to show itself courageous to petticoat.
As You Like It. Act ii, sc. 4, l. 5. [Rosalind]
Hostess: You are the weaker vessel, as they say, the emptier vessel.
Doll: Can a weak empty vessel bear such a huge full hogshead?
II Henry IV. Act ii, sc. 4, l. 65.
Women, being the weaker vessels, are ever thrust to the wall.
Romeo and Juliet. Act i, sc. 1, l. 19. [Sampson]
The weaker vessel.—*Love's Labour's Lost,* i, 1, 275.

14
Do you not know I am a woman? when I think, I must speak.
As You Like It. Act iii, sc. 2, l. 263. [Rosalind] See also Tongue: Women's Tongues.
Woman of the world.—*As You Like It,* v, 3, 5. See under World.

15
You have simply misused our sex in your love-prate: we must have your doublet and hose plucked over your head, and show the world what the bird hath done to her own nest.
As You Like It. Act iv, sc. 1, l. 205. [Celia]
The only use of "love-prate."
Our sex.—*A Midsummer-Night's Dream,* iii, 2, 218; *Antony and Cleopatra,* v, 2, 124; *The Winter's Tale,* ii, 1, 108.
Their gentle sex to weep are often willing.
The Rape of Lucrece, l. 1237.
I do not know
One of my sex, no woman's face remember.
The Tempest. Act iii, sc. 1, l. 48. [Miranda]
So much against the mettle of your sex.
Twelfth Night. Act v, sc. 1, l. 330. [Duke]
"Sex" is used twenty times in the plays and poems, always with reference to women.

16
You clown, abandon,—which is in the vulgar leave,—the society,—which in the boorish is company,—of this female,—which in the common is woman; which together is, abandon the society of this female, or, clown, thou perishest.
As You Like It. Act v, sc. 1, l. 52. [Touchstone]
Men . . . Are masters to their females.
The Comedy of Errors, ii, 1, 24.

A child of our grandmother Eve, a female; or, for thy more sweet understanding, a woman.
Love's Labour's Lost. Act i, sc. 1, l. 266. [King Ferdinand]

Curses all Eve's daughters, of what complexion soever.
The Merry Wives of Windsor. Act iv, sc. 2, l. 24. [Mrs. Page]

Poor females.—*A Midsummer-Night's Dream,* iii, 2, 441.

1
'Tis said, a woman's fitness comes by fits.
Cymbeline. Act iv, sc. 1, l. 6. [Cloten]

O most delicate fiend!
Who is 't can read a woman?
Cymbeline. Act v, sc. 5, l. 47. [Cymbeline]

2
One that was a woman, sir; but, rest her soul, she 's dead.
Hamlet. Act v, sc. 1, l. 146. [First Clown]

3 Constant you are,
But yet a woman: and for secrecy,
No lady closer; for I well believe
Thou wilt not utter what thou dost not know.
I Henry IV. Act ii, sc. 3, l. 111. [Hotspur]

Go to, you are a woman, go.
I Henry IV. Act iii, sc. 3, l. 70. [Falstaff]

4
We knew where the bona-robas were and had the best of them all at commandment.
II Henry IV. Act iii, sc. 2, l. 26. [Shallow]
Shallow uses "bona-roba" (showy wanton) a second time in line 217, and it does not occur again in the plays.

5
No woman shall succeed in Salique land.
Henry V, i, 2, 39. See under Law.

6
Art thou not second woman in the realm?
II Henry VI. Act i, sc. 2, l. 43. [Gloucester]

Are not you the chief woman?—*Love's Labour's Lost,* iv, 1, 51.

A woman of less place.—*Henry VIII,* ii, 2, 112.

7 Thou art an Amazon
And fightest with the sword of Deborah.
I Henry VI. Act i, sc. 2, l. 104. [Charles]
The only mention of Deborah.

How ill-beseeming is it in thy sex
To triumph, like an Amazonian trull,
Upon their woes whom fortune captivates!
III Henry VI. Act i, sc. 4, l. 113. [York]
"Amazonian" is repeated in *Coriolanus,* ii, 2, 95: "Amazonian chin."

Belike she minds to play the Amazon.
III Henry VI. Act iv, sc. 1, l. 106. [Edward]

Like Amazons.—*King John,* v, 2, 155.

Bouncing Amazon.—*A Midsummer-Night's Dream,* ii, 1, 70. The only use of "bouncing." The only uses of "Amazon" and "Amazons."

8
Wilt thou be daunted at a woman's sight?
I Henry VI. Act v, sc. 3, l. 69. [Suffolk]

Tush, women have been captivate ere now.
I Henry VI. Act v, sc. 3, l. 107. [Margaret]

9
She 's beautiful and therefore to be woo'd;
She is a woman, therefore to be won.
I Henry VI. Act v, sc. 3, l. 78. [Suffolk]

She is a woman, therefore may be woo'd;
She is a woman, therefore may be won.
Titus Andronicus, ii, 1, 82. [Demetrius]

10
Why stand we like soft-hearted women here,
Wailing our losses, whiles the foe doth rage?
III Henry VI. Act ii, sc. 3, l. 25. [Warwick]

Soft-hearted wretch.—*II Henry VI,* iii, 2, 307. The only uses of "soft-hearted."

11 Great-bellied women,
That had not half a week to go.
Henry VIII. Act iv, sc. 1, l. 76. [Gentleman]
"Great-bellied" is repeated in *Measure for Measure,* ii, 1, 102.

12
How hard it is for women to keep counsel!
Julius Cæsar. Act ii, sc. 4, l. 9. [Portia]

Tell-tale women.—*Richard III,* iv, 4, 149.

13
I am yet Unknown to woman.
Macbeth, iv, 3, 126. See under Chastity.

I never saw a woman.—*The Tempest,* iii, 2, 108.

14
O, I could play the woman!
Macbeth, iv, 3, 230. See under Play.

Transform us not to women.—*Antony and Cleopatra,* iv, 2, 36.

15
Was he not born of woman?
Macbeth, v, 3, 4. See under Birth.

What 's he
That was not born of woman? Such a one
Am I to fear, or none.
Macbeth. Act v, sc. 7, l. 2. [Macbeth]

Came of women.—*Henry V,* ii, 1, 122.

Of no woman bred.—*Venus and Adonis,* l. 214

16
I never heard the absent duke much detected for women; he was not inclined that way.
Measure for Measure. Act iii, sc. 2, l. 128. [Duke]

17
Simple: There 's an old woman, a fat woman, gone up into his chamber. . . .
Host: Ha! a fat woman! . . . Let her descend, bully, let her descend; my chambers are honourable: fie! privacy? fie!
The Merry Wives of Windsor. Act iv, sc. 5, l. 12. "Fat woman" is used five times in this act, and occurs nowhere else. "Privacy" is repeated in *Troilus and Cressida,* iii, 3, 190.

Old woman.—*The Merry Wives of Windsor,* iv, 2, 87, and four more times in later scenes. The phrase occurs in no other play. "Young woman" is not used at all.

Old women.—*Henry V,* iii, Prol., 20; *Coriolanus,* v, 2, 45; *Measure for Measure,* iv, 3, 9.

Living women.—*Coriolanus,* v, 3, 97.

Sad women.—*Coriolanus,* iv, 1, 25.

Weird women.—*Macbeth,* iii, 1, 2.

Wise woman.—*The Merry Wives of Windsor,* iv, 5, 27; 59; *Twelfth Night,* iii, 4, 114.

Wretched woman.—*Measure for Measure,* v, 1, 132.

Athenian woman.—*A Midsummer-Night's Dream,* iii, 2, 39.

1
I . . . think it no addition, nor my wish,
To have him see me woman'd.
Othello. Act iii, sc. 4, l. 193. [Cassio] The only use of "woman'd."

2
Women grow by men.
Romeo and Juliet, i, 3, 95. See under MAN AND WOMAN.

3
Women are made to bear, and so are you.
The Taming of the Shrew. Act ii, sc. 1, l. 201. [Petruchio]

Women are more valiant
That stay at home, if bearing carry it.
Timon of Athens. Act iii, sc. 5, l. 47. [Alcibiades]

4
I see a woman may be made a fool,
If she had not a spirit to resist.
The Taming of the Shrew. Act iii, sc. 2, l. 222. [Katharina]

5
Flout 'em and scout 'em
And scout 'em and flout 'em.
The Tempest. Act iii, sc. 2, l. 130. [Stephano]

6
Æneas: How now, Prince Troilus! wherefore not afield?
Troilus: Because not there: this woman's answer sorts,
For womanish it is to be from thence.
Troilus and Cressida. Act i, sc. 1, l. 108.

He never was so womanish.
Henry VIII. Act ii, sc. 1, l. 38. [First Gentleman]

Cowardly and womanish.—*Richard III,* i, 4, 264.

Womanish fear.—*Romeo and Juliet,* iv, 1, 119.

Womanish tears.—*King John,* iv, 1, 36.

Thy tears are womanish.—*Romeo and Juliet,* iii, 3, 110. See under TEAR.

Show us womanish.—*Julius Cæsar,* i, 3, 84. The only uses of "womanish."

7
To be slow in words is a woman's only virtue.
The Two Gentlemen of Verona. Act iii, sc. 1, l. 338. [Launce]

8
Thou wert as witty a piece of Eve's flesh as any in Illyria.
Twelfth Night. Act i, sc. 5, l. 30. [Clown] See also under FLESH.

9
Duke: Then let thy love be younger than thyself,
Or thy affection cannot hold the bent;
For women are as roses, whose fair flower
Being once display'd, doth fall that very hour.
Viola: And so they are: alas, that they are so;
To die, even when they to perfection grow!
Twelfth Night. Act ii, sc. 4, l. 37.

10
He . . . will not use a woman 'awlessly.
Two Gentlemen of Verona. Act v, sc. 4, l. 14. [First Outlaw] The only use of "lawlessly."

He will not manage her, although he mount her.
Venus and Adonis, l. 598.

11
Lady: Who taught you this?
Mamillius: I learnt it out of women's faces.
The Winter's Tale. Act ii, sc. 1, l. 11.

II—Woman: Her Virtues

12
Age cannot wither her, nor custom stale
Her infinite variety: other women cloy
The appetites they feed; but she makes hungry
Where most she satisfies: for vilest things
Become themselves in her; that the holy priests
Bless her when she is riggish.
Antony and Cleopatra. Act ii, sc. 2, l. 240. [Enobarbus] The only use of "riggish" (wanton). "Variety" does not occur again in the plays, but is repeated in *Venus and Adonis,* l. 21.

13
You are an honest woman, and well thought on.
II Henry IV. Act ii, sc. 4, l. 99. [Hostess]

A very honest woman, but something given to lie;
As a woman should not do.
Antony and Cleopatra. Act v, sc. 2, l. 252. [Clown]

Charge an honest woman with picking thy pocket!
I Henry IV. Act iii, sc. 3, l. 176. [Prince]

Marina: Are you a woman?
Bawd: What would you have me be, an I be not a woman?
Marina: An honest woman, or not a woman.
Bawd: Marry, whip thee, gosling: I think I shall have something to do with you.
Pericles. Act iv, sc. 2, l. 87.

An honest woman of her word.—*The Merchant of Venice,* iii, 1, 7.

Evans: As honest a 'omans as I will desires among five thousand. . . .
Caius: By gar, I see 'tis an honest woman.
The Merry Wives of Windsor. Act iii, sc. 3, l. 236. See under WIFE.

The honest woman, the modest wife.—*The Merry Wives of Windsor,* iv, 2, 136.

If she be less than an honest woman, she is indeed more than I took her for.
The Merchant of Venice, iii, 5, 45. See under CHASTITY.

Honest woman.—*Measure for Measure,* ii, 1, 73; *The Merchant of Venice,* ii, 2, 17.

Honest women.—*Pericles,* iv, 6, 205.

14
Her valiant courage and undaunted spirit,
More than in women commonly is seen.
I Henry VI. Act v, sc. 5, l. 70. [Suffolk]

I have heard her reported to be a woman of an invincible spirit.
II Henry VI. Act i, sc. 4, l. 8. [Bolingbroke]

Methinks a woman of this valiant spirit
Should, if a coward heard her speak these words,
Infuse his breast with magnanimity
And make him, naked, foil a man at arms.
III Henry VI. Act v, sc. 4, l. 39. [Prince of Wales] The only use of "magnanimity."

1
By heaven, she is a dainty one.
Henry VIII. Act i, sc. 4, l. 94. [King Henry]
A woman, I dare say without vain-glory,
Never yet branded with suspicion.
Henry VIII. Act iii, sc. 1, l. 127. [Queen Katharine]
Believe me, sir, she is the goodliest woman
That ever lay by man.
Henry VIII. Act iv, sc. 1, l. 69. [Gentleman]

2
I grant I am a woman; but withal
A woman that Lord Brutus took to wife:
I grant I am a woman; but withal
A woman well-reputed, Cato's daughter,
Think you I am no stronger than my sex,
Being so father'd and so husbanded?
Julius Cæsar. Act ii, sc. 1, l. 292. [Portia]
"Well-reputed" is repeated in *The Two Gentlemen of Verona,* ii, 7, 43.
What a woman are you!—*The Merry Wives of Windsor,* iv, 2, 44.

3
A fine woman! a fair woman! a sweet woman!
Othello. Act iv, sc. 1, l. 189. [Othello]
Fair woman.—*Richard II,* v, 1, 16; *The Merry Wives of Windsor,* ii, 2, 43; *King Lear,* iii, 2, 35; *Antony and Cleopatra,* ii, 6, 104.
Sweet woman.—*The Merry Wives of Windsor,* ii, 2, 92.

4
Divine perfection of a woman.
Richard III. Act i, sc. 2, l. 75. [Gloucester]
Deserving woman.—*Othello,* ii, 1, 146.
Noble woman.—*Coriolanus,* iii, 2, 31.
True woman.—*I Henry IV,* iii, 3, 82.

5
A woman's face with Nature's own hand painted
Hast thou, the master-mistress of my passion;
A woman's gentle heart, but not acquainted
With shifting change, as is false woman's fashion;
An eye more bright than theirs, less false in rolling,
Gilding the object whereupon it gazeth;
A man in hue, all 'hues' in his controlling,
Which steals men's eyes and women's souls amazeth.
And for a woman wert thou first created;
Till Nature, as she wrought thee, fell a-doting,
And by addition me of thee defeated,
By adding one thing to my purpose nothing.
But since she prick'd thee out for woman's pleasure,
Mine be thy love and thy love's use their treasure.
Sonnets. No. xx. The only use of "master-mistress" and "a-doting."

6
For several virtues
Have I liked several women; never any
With so full soul, but some defect in her
Did quarrel with the noblest grace she owned
And put it to the foil: but you, O you,
So perfect and so peerless, are created
Of every creature's best!
The Tempest. Act iii, sc. 1, l. 42. [Ferdinand]

7
A woman of quick sense.
Troilus and Cressida. Act iv, sc. 5, l. 54. [Nestor]
Women of good carriage.—*Romeo and Juliet,* i, 4, 94.
Good woman.—*All's Well that Ends Well,* i, 3, 86; 90; *Henry VIII,* ii, 3, 55; Epil., 10. Although Shakespeare used the word "woman" nearly seven hundred times, he used "good woman" only four times, and in only two of his plays.

8
If not divine,
Yet let her be a principality,
Sovereign to all creatures on the earth.
The Two Gentlemen of Verona. Act ii, sc. 4, l. 151. [Valentine]
Falsehood, cowardice and poor descent,
Three things that women highly hold in hate.
The Two Gentlemen of Verona. Act iii, sc. 2, l. 32. [Proteus]

III—Woman: Her Faults

9
One good woman in ten, madam; . . . One in ten, quoth a'! An we might have a good woman born but one every blazing star, or at an earthquake, 'twould mend the lottery well: a man may draw his heart out, ere a' pluck one.
All's Well that Ends Well. Act i, sc. 3, l. 86. [Clown]

10
Under a compelling occasion, let women die: it were pity to cast them away for nothing; though, between them and a great cause, they should be esteemed nothing.
Antony and Cleopatra. Act i, sc. 2, l. 141. [Enobarbus] The only use of "compelling."
Women are not
In their best fortunes strong; but want will perjure
The ne'er-touch'd vestal.
Antony and Cleopatra. Act iii, sc. 12, l. 29. [Cæsar] The only use of "ne'er-touch'd."
You must not think I am so simple but I know the devil himself will not eat a woman: I know that a woman is a dish for the gods, if the devil dress her not. But, truly, these same whoreson devils do the gods great harm in their women; for in every ten that they make, the devils mar five.
Antony and Cleopatra. Act v, sc. 2, l. 273. [Clown]

11
What woman in the city do I name,
When that I say the city-woman bears
The cost of princes on unworthy shoulders?
As You Like It. Act ii, sc. 7, l. 74. [Jaques]
The only use of "city-woman."
Dost thou think, though I am caparisoned like a man, I have a doublet and hose in my disposition?
As You Like It. Act iii, sc. 2, l. 204. [Rosa-

lind] "Caparisoned" is repeated in *The Taming of the Shrew,* iii, 2, 67.

Rosalind: I thank God I am not a woman, to be touched with so many giddy offences as he hath generally taxed their whole sex withal.
Orlando: Can you remember any of the principal evils that he laid to the charge of women?
Rosalind: There were none principal; they were all like one another as half-pence are.

As You Like It. Act iii, sc. 2, l. 365.

Women still give the lie to their consciences.

As You Like It. Act iii, sc. 2, l. 410. [Rosalind]

O, that woman that cannot make her fault her husband's occasion, let her never nurse her child herself, for she will breed it like a fool!

As You Like It. Act iv, sc. 1, l. 177. [Rosalind]

Wilt thou love such a woman? What, to make thee an instrument and play false strains upon thee!

As You Like It. Act iv, sc. 3, l. 67. [Rosalind]

1 The vows of women
Of no more bondage be, to where they are made,
Than they are to their virtues; which is nothing.

Cymbeline. Act ii, sc. 4, l. 110. [Posthumus]

O perjured woman!—*The Comedy of Errors,* v, 1, 212; *Othello,* v, 2, 63.

2 Could I find out
The woman's part in me! For there 's no motion
That tends to vice in man, but I affirm
It is the woman's part: be it lying, note it,
The woman's; flattering, hers; deceiving, hers;
Lust and rank thoughts, hers, hers; revenges, hers;
Ambitions, covetings, change of prides, disdain,
Nice longing, slanders, mutability,
All faults that may be named, nay, that hell knows,
Why, hers, in part or all; but rather, all;
For even to vice
They are not constant, but are changing still
One vice, but of a minute old, for one
Not half so old as that. I 'll write against them,
Detest them, curse them: yet 'tis greater skill
In a true hate, to pray they have their will:
The very devils cannot plague them better.

Cymbeline. Act ii, sc. 5, l. 19. [Posthumus] "Mutability" is repeated in *Henry V,* iii, 6, 36.

3
For women's fear and love holds quantity;
In neither aught, or in extremity.

Hamlet. Act iii, sc. 2, l. 177. [Player Queen]

O most pernicious woman!—*Hamlet,* i, 5, 105.
Thou pernicious woman.—*Measure for Measure,* v, 1, 241.

4
Women are shrews, both short and tall.

II Henry IV, v, 3, 36. See under Shrew.

5
Boy: A' said once, the devil would have him about women.
Hostess: A' did in some sort, indeed, handle women; but then he was rheumatic, and talked of the whore of Babylon.

Henry V. Act ii, sc. 3, l. 37. "Babylon" is mentioned again in *Twelfth Night,* ii, 3, 84.

Devils incarnate.—*Henry V,* ii, 3, 34. "Incarnate" is repeated in *Titus Andronicus,* v, 1, 40.

6
These women are shrewd tempters with their tongues.

I Henry VI. Act i, sc. 2, l. 123. [Alençon]

7
Foul fiend of France, and hag of all despite!

I Henry VI. Act iii, sc. 2, l. 52. [Talbot]

This is the hag, when maids lie on their backs,
That presses them and learns them first to bear,
Making them women of good carriage.

Romeo and Juliet. Act i, sc. 4, l. 92. [Mercutio]

You witch, you hag, you.—*The Merry Wives of Windsor,* iv, 2, 187; 194.
Blue-eyed hag.—*The Tempest,* i, 2, 269. The only use of "blue-eyed."
Gross hag!—*The Winter's Tale,* ii, 3, 108.
Fell banning hag!—*I Henry VI,* 5, 3, 42.
Hateful wither'd hag!—*Richard III,* i, 3, 215.
Filthy hags!—*Macbeth,* iv, 1, 115.
Secret, black, and midnight hags!—*Macbeth,* iv, 1, 48.
Unnatural hags!—*King Lear,* ii, 4, 281.
Hags of hell.—*II Henry VI,* iv, 1, 79. The only uses of "hag" and "hags."

8
I . . . which am a silly woman.

III Henry VI. Act i, sc. 1, l. 243. [Queen Margaret]

Silly women.—*The Two Gentlemen of Verona,* iv, 1, 72.
Wrangling woman.—*III Henry VI,* ii, 2, 176.

9
'Tis beauty that doth oft make women proud;
But, God he knows, thy share thereof is small:
'Tis virtue that doth make them most admired;
The contrary doth make thee wonder'd at;
'Tis government that makes them seem divine;
The want thereof makes thee abominable:
Thou art as opposite to every good
As the Antipodes are unto us,
Or as the south to the septentrion.
O tiger's heart wrapt in a woman's hide!
How couldst thou drain the life-blood of the child,
To bid the father wipe his eyes withal,
And yet be seen to bear a woman's face?
Women are soft, mild, pitiful and flexible;
Thou stern, obdurate, flinty, rough, remorseless.

III Henry VI. Act i, sc. 4, l. 128. [York] The only use of "septentrion" (the north). "Antipodes" occurs five times. "Flexible" is repeated in *Troilus and Cressida,* i, 3, 50; and "remorseless" in *II Henry VI,* iii, 1, 213, and in *Hamlet,* ii, 2, 609.

1 All my glories
In that one woman I have lost for ever.

Henry VIII. Act iii, sc. 2, l. 408. [Wolsey]

2
There was never yet fair woman but she made mouths in a glass.

King Lear. Act iii, sc. 2, l. 35. [Fool]

Let not the creaking of shoes nor the rustling of silks betray thy poor heart to woman.

King Lear. Act iii, sc. 4, l. 98. [Edgar] "Rustling" is repeated in *Cymbeline,* iii, 3, 24.

If she live long,
And in the end meet the old course of death,
Women will all turn monsters.

King Lear. Act iii, sc. 7, l. 100. [Servant]

Proper deformity seems not in the fiend
So horrid as in woman.

King Lear. Act iv, sc. 2, l. 60. [Albany]

Howe'er thou art a fiend,
A woman's shape doth shield thee.

King Lear. Act iv, sc. 2, l. 66. [Albany]

Down from the waist they are Centaurs,
Though women all above:
But to the girdle do the gods inherit,
Beneath is all the fiends';
There 's hell, there 's darkness, there 's the sulphurous pit,
Burning, scalding, stench, consumption.

King Lear. Act iv, sc. 6, l. 126. [King Lear] "Scalding" is repeated in *III Henry VI,* v, 7, 18. The Centaurs are referred to again in *Titus Andronicus,* v, 2, 204. In *The Comedy of Errors* there is an inn called the Centaur, which is mentioned six times.

3
A woman, that is like a German clock,
Still a-repairing, ever out of frame,
And never going aright, being a watch,
But, being watch'd that it may still go right!

Love's Labour's Lost. Act iii, sc. 1, l. 192. [Biron] The only use of "a-repairing."

4
These poor informal women are no more
But instruments of some more mightier member
That sets them on.

Measure for Measure. Act v, sc. 1, l. 236. [Angelo] The only use of "informal."

5
That a woman conceived me, I thank her; that she brought me up, I likewise give her most humble thanks: but that I will have a recheat winded in my forehead, or hang my bugle in an invisible baldrick, all women shall pardon me.

Much Ado about Nothing. Act i, sc. 1, l. 240. [Benedick] The only use of "recheat," "winded," and "baldrick."

One woman is fair, yet I am well; another is wise, yet I am well; another virtuous, yet I am well; but till all graces be in one woman, one woman shall not come in my grace.

Much Ado about Nothing. Act ii, sc. 3, l. 28. [Benedick]

6 You are pictures out of doors,
Bells in your parlours, wild-cats in your kitchens,
Saints in your injuries, devils being offended,
Players in your housewifery, and housewives in your beds.

Othello. Act ii, sc. 1, l. 110. [Iago] See also HOUSEWIFE. The only use of "wild-cats." "Wild-cat" occurs in *The Merchant of Venice,* ii, 5, 48, and in *The Taming of the Shrew,* i, 2, 197.

7
The wiles and guiles that women work,
Dissembled with an outward show,
The tricks and toys that in them lurk,
The cock that treads them shall not know.

The Passionate Pilgrim, l. 335.

If he be addict to vice,
Quickly him they will entice;
If to women he be bent,
They have at commandement.

The Passionate Pilgrim, l. 415. "Addict" is repeated in *II Henry IV,* iv, 3, 135.

8
Then call them not the authors of their ill,
No more than wax shall be accounted evil
Wherein is stamp'd the semblance of a devil.

The Rape of Lucrece, l. 1244.

Their smoothness, like a goodly champaign plain,
Lays open all the little worms that creep.

The Rape of Lucrece, l. 1247. The only use of "champaign."

Weak-made women.—*The Rape of Lucrece,* l. 1260. The only use of "weak-made."

Bad woman.—*Measure for Measure,* ii, 1, 64.

Foolish woman.—*Richard II,* v, 2, 80; *The Merry Wives of Windsor,* iii, 5, 42; *Othello,* iv, 1, 186; *The Winter's Tale,* iii, 2, 228.

Thou fond mad woman.—*Richard II,* v, 2, 95. "Fond mad" is repeated in *Romeo and Juliet,* iii, 3, 52: "Thou fond mad man."

Fond woman.—*Richard II,* v, 2, 101; *Titus Andronicus,* ii, 3, 172.

Thou frantic woman.—*Richard II,* v, 3, 89.

Jealous woman.—*Comedy of Errors,* v, 1, 69.

Unruly woman!—*Richard II,* v, 2, 110.

9
Petruchio: Katharine, I charge thee, tell these headstrong women
What duty they do owe their lords and husbands.
Widow: Come, come, you 're mocking: we will have no telling. . . .
Katharina: Fie, fie! unknit that threatening unkind brow,
And dart not scornful glances from those eyes,
To wound thy lord, thy king, thy governor:
It blots thy beauty as frosts do bite the meads,
Confounds thy fame as whirlwinds shake fair buds,
And in no sense is meet or amiable.
A woman moved is like a fountain troubled,
Muddy, ill-seeming, thick, bereft of beauty;

And while it is so, none so dry or thirsty
Will deign to sip or touch one drop of it. . . .
I am ashamed that women are so simple
To offer war where they should kneel for peace,
Or seek for rule, supremacy and sway,
When they are bound to serve, love and obey.
Why are our bodies soft and weak and smooth,
Unapt to toil and trouble in the world,
But that our soft conditions and our hearts
Should well agree with our external parts?
Come, come, you froward and unable worms!
My mind hath been as big as one of yours,
My heart as great, my reason haply more,
To bandy word for word, and frown for frown;
But now I see our lances are but straws,
Our strength as weak, our weakness past compare,
That seeming to be most which we indeed least are.
Then vail your stomachs, for it is no boot,
And place your hands below your husband's foot:
In token of which duty, if he please,
My hand is ready; may it do him ease.

The Taming of the Shrew. Act v, sc. 2, l. 130. The only use of "ill-seeming."

A harsh hearing when women are froward.

The Taming of the Shrew. Act v, sc. 2, l. 183. [Lucentio]

1
No grace? no womanhood? Ah, beastly creature!
The blot and enemy to our general name!

Titus Andronicus. Act ii, sc. 3, l. 182. [Lavinia]

Aaron: I begot him on the empress.
Lucius: O most insatiate and luxurious woman!

Titus Andronicus. Act v, sc. 1, l. 87. "Insatiate" is repeated in *Richard II,* ii, 1, 38: "Insatiate cormorant"; and in *Richard III,* iii, 7, 7: "Insatiate greediness."

2
Let it not be believed for womanhood!
Think, we had mothers; do not give advantage
To stubborn critics, apt, without a theme,
For depravation, to square the general sex
By Cressid's rule.

Troilus and Cressida. Act v, sc. 2, l. 129. [Troilus] The only use of "depravation."

IV—Woman: Her Brain

3
Women's gentle brain
Could not drop forth such giant-rude invention.

As You Like It. Act iv, sc. 3, l. 33. [Rosalind] The only use of "giant-rude."

Rosalind: A woman's thought runs before her actions.
Orlando: So do all thoughts; they are winged.

As You Like It. Act iv, sc. 1, l. 140.

4
A woman that
Bears all down with her brain.

Cymbeline. Act ii, sc. 1, l. 58. [Lord]

You must forget to be a woman; change
Command into obedience: fear and niceness—
The handmaids of all women, or, more truly,
Woman it pretty self—into a waggish courage;
Ready in gibes, quick-answer'd, saucy.

Cymbeline. Act iii, sc. 4, l. 157. [Pisanio] The only use of "niceness" and "quick-answer'd." "Waggish" is repeated in *A Midsummer-Night's Dream,* i, 1, 240.

5
You know I am a woman, lacking wit.

Henry VIII. Act iii, sc. 1, l. 177. [Queen Katharine]

You are a very simplicity 'oman.

The Merry Wives of Windsor. Act iv, sc. 1, l. 31. [Evans]

6
Let mild women to him lose their mildness,
Wilder to him than tigers in their wildness.

The Rape of Lucrece, l. 979.

V—Woman: Her Heart

7
No more, but e'en a woman, and commanded
By such poor passion as the maid that milks
And does the meanest chares.

Antony and Cleopatra. Act iv, sc. 15, l. 75. [Cleopatra] The only use of "chares" (chores). "Chare" occurs in v, 2, 231, and in no other play.

8
Alas, poor women! make us but believe,
Being compact of credit, that you love us;
Though others have the arm, show us the sleeve;
We in your motion turn and you may move us.

The Comedy of Errors. Act iii, sc. 2, l. 21. [Luciana]

9
You, that have so fair parts of woman on you,
Have too a woman's heart.

Henry VIII. Act ii, sc. 3, l. 27. [Lady]

10
Ay me, how weak a thing
The heart of woman is!

Julius Cæsar. Act ii, sc. 4, l. 39. [Portia]

Women's waxen hearts.—*Twelfth Night,* ii, 2, 31. See under APPEARANCE for full quotation.

11
Escalus: I will go darkly to work with her.
Lucio: That's the way; for women are light at midnight.

Measure for Measure. Act v, sc. 1, l. 279.

Earthly women.—*Merchant of Venice,* iii, 5, 85.

12
Duke: There is no woman's sides
Can bide the beating of so strong a passion
As love doth give my heart; no woman's heart
So big, to hold so much; they lack retention.

Alas, their love may be call'd appetite,
No motion of the liver, but the palate,
That suffer surfeit, cloyment and revolt;
But mine is all as hungry as the sea,
And can digest as much: make no compare
Between that love a woman can bear me
And that I owe Olivia.
Viola: Ay, but I know—
Duke: What dost thou know?
Viola: Too well what love women to men may owe:
In faith, they are as true of heart as we.
Twelfth Night. Act ii, sc. 4, l. 96. The only use of "cloyment." "Retention" is repeated in v, 1, 84, and in *King Lear,* v, 3, 47.

VI—Woman: Her Inconstancy

1 Frailty, thy name is woman!—
A little month, or ere those shoes were old
With which she followed my poor father's body,
Like Niobe, all tears:—why she, even she—
. . . married with my uncle,
My father's brother, but no more like my father
Than I to Hercules: within a month:
Ere yet the salt of most unrighteous tears
Had left the flushing in her galled eyes,
She married. O, most wicked speed, to post
With such dexterity to incestuous sheets!
It is not nor it cannot come to good.
Hamlet. Act i, sc. 2, l. 146. [Hamlet] The only use of "unrighteous."

Angelo: Nay, women are frail too.
Isabella: Ay, as the glasses where they view themselves. . . .
Women! Help Heaven! men their creation mar
In profiting by them. Nay, call us ten times frail;
For we are soft as our complexions are,
And credulous to false prints.
Angelo: I think it well: . . . Be that you are,
That is, a woman; if you be more, you 're none;
If you be one, as you are well express'd
By all external warrants, show it now,
By putting on the destined livery.
Measure for Measure. Act ii, sc. 4, l. 124.

I do perceive
These poor informal women are no more
But instruments of some more mightier member
That sets them on.
Measure for Measure. Act v, sc. 1, l. 235. [Angelo] The only use of "informal."

False woman.—*III Henry VI,* ii, 2, 149; *The Merry Wives of Windsor,* ii, 2, 305; *Troilus and Cressida,* iii, 2, 211; *Sonnets,* xx.

False-boding woman!—*Richard III,* i, 3, 247. The only use of "false-boding."

2
Bring me a constant woman to her husband,
One that ne'er dream'd a joy beyond his pleasure;
And to that woman, when she has done most,
Yet will I add an honour, a great patience.
Henry VIII. Act iii, sc. 1, l. 134. [Queen Katharine]

3
Relenting fool, and shallow, changing woman!
Richard III. Act iv, sc. 4, l. 431. [King Richard]

O despiteful love! unconstant woman-kind!
The Taming of the Shrew. Act iv, sc. 2, l. 14. [Tranio] The only use of "woman-kind." "Women-kind" occurs in *Pericles,* iv, 6, 159.

4
O that I thought it could be in a woman . . .
To feed for aye her lamp and flames of love;
To keep her constancy in plight and youth;
Outliving beauty's outward, with a mind
That doth renew swifter than blood decays! . . .
How were I then uplifted!
Troilus and Cressida. Act iii, sc. 2, l. 165. [Troilus] The only use of "outliving."

Pandarus: You are such a woman! one knows not at what ward you lie.
Cressida: Upon my back, to defend my belly; upon my wit, to defend my wiles; upon my secrecy, to defend mine honesty; my mask, to defend my beauty.
Troilus and Cressida. Act i, sc. 2, l. 282.

VII—Woman: Her Will

5
She 'll hamper thee, and dandle thee like a baby:
Though in this place most master wear no breeches.
II Henry VI. Act i, sc. 3, l. 148. [Duchess of Gloucester] The only use of "hamper." "Dandle" is repeated in *Titus Andronicus,* iv, 2, 161.

That you might still have worn the petticoat,
And ne'er have stol'n the breech from Lancaster.
III Henry VI. Act v, sc. 5, l. 23. [Gloucester] The only use of "breech."

6 A will! a wicked will;
A woman's will; a canker'd grandam's will!
King John. Act ii, sc. 1, l. 193. [Constance]

O undistinguish'd space of woman's will!
King Lear. Act iv, sc. 6, l. 278. [Edgar] The only use of "undistinguish'd."

7
Why, this it is, when men are ruled by women.
Richard III. Act i, sc. 1, l. 62. [Gloucester]

VIII—A Woman's "No"

8
Make denials Increase your services.
Cymbeline. Act ii, sc. 3, l. 53. [Queen]

9
Have you not heard it said full oft,
A woman's nay doth stand for nought?
The Passionate Pilgrim, l. 339.

1 Play the maid's part, still answer nay, and take it.
Richard III. Act iii, sc. 7, l. 51. [Buckingham]

2 Maids, in modesty, say 'no' to that
Which they would have the profferer construe 'ay.'
The Two Gentlemen of Verona. Act i, sc. 2, l. 55. [Julia] The only use of "profferer."

A woman sometimes scorns what best contents her.
The Two Gentlemen of Verona. Act iii, sc. 1, l. 93. [Valentine]

IX—Poor, Lone Woman

3 For she 's a woman to be pitied much.
III Henry VI. Act iii, sc. 1, l. 36. [King Henry]

A poor lone woman.—*II Henry IV,* ii, 1, 35.

I am a most poor woman, and a stranger,
Born out of your dominions.
Henry VIII. Act ii, sc. 4, l. 15. [Queen Katharine]

4 I am a simple woman, much too weak
To oppose your cunning.
Henry VIII. Act ii, sc. 4, l. 106. [Queen Katharine]

A poor weak woman, fall'n from favour.
Henry VIII. Act iii, sc. 1, l. 20. [Queen Katharine]

Alas, I am a woman, friendless, hopeless! . . .
A woman lost among ye, laugh'd at, scorn'd.
Henry VIII. Act iii, sc. 1, l. 80. [Queen Katharine] The only use of "friendless."

What will become of me now, wretched lady?
I am the most unhappy woman living.
Henry VIII. Act iii, sc. 1, l. 146. [Queen Katharine]

WOMB

See also Pregnancy

5 My womb, my womb, my womb, undoes me.
II Henry IV. Act iv, sc. 3, l. 24. [Falstaff]

O my accursed womb, the bed of death!
Richard III. Act iv, sc. 1, l. 54. [Duchess of York]

Womb of death.—*Romeo and Juliet,* v, 3, 45.
Womb of earth.—*Hamlet,* i, 1, 137.
Womb of pia mater.—*Love's Labour 's Lost,* iv, 2, 71. See under SPIRIT.
Womb of time.—*Othello,* i, 3, 337.
Cannon's womb.—*Romeo and Juliet,* v, 1, 65.
Daughter's womb.—*Richard III,* iv, 4, 423.
Earth's dark womb.—*Rape of Lucrece,* l. 549.
My mother's womb.—*I Henry VI,* iv, 5, 35; *III Henry VI,* iii, 2, 153; *King John,* iii, 1, 44.
Thy mother's heavy womb.—*Richard III,* i, 3, 231; *Coriolanus,* v, 3, 124.
Swallowing womb.—*Titus Andronicus,* ii, 3, 239.

6 Murder not then the fruit within my womb.
I Henry VI. Act v, sc. 4, l. 63. [La Pucelle]

Fruit of her womb.—*II Henry IV,* v, 4, 15.
Her womb's increase.—*Coriolanus,* iii, 3, 114.

7 Commanded nature, that my lady's womb,
If it conceived a male child by me, should
Do no more offices of life to 't than
The grave does to the dead.
Henry VIII. Act ii, sc. 4, l. 188. [King]

Into her womb convey sterility.
King Lear. Act i, sc. 4, l. 300. [King Lear] The only use of "sterility."

8 Your brother and his lover have embraced:
As those that feed grow full, as blossoming time
That from the seedness the bare fallow brings
To teeming foison, even so her plenteous womb
Expresseth his full tilth and husbandry.
Measure for Measure. Act i, sc. 4, l. 40. [Lucio] The only use of "seedness." "Tilth" occurs again in *The Tempest,* ii, 1, 152.

For where is she so fair whose unear'd womb
Disdains the tillage of thy husbandry?
Sonnets. No. iii. The only use of "unear'd" and "tillage."

9 Her womb then rich with my young squire.
A Midsummer-Night's Dream. Act ii, sc. 1, l. 131. [Titania]

10 All love the womb that their first being bred.
Pericles. Act i, sc. 1, l. 107. [Pericles]

11 From forth the kennel of thy womb hath crept
A hell-hound that doth hunt us all to death.
Richard III. Act iv, sc. 4, l. 47. [Queen Margaret]

Thy womb let loose.—*Richard III,* iv, 4, 54.

12 Like widow'd wombs after their lords' decease.
Sonnets. No. xcvii.

Concave womb.—*A Lover's Complaint,* l. 1.
Hollow womb.—*Richard II,* ii, 1, 83; *Venus and Adonis,* l. 268.
Teeming womb.—*Richard II,* ii, 1, 51.

13 Good wombs have borne bad sons.
The Tempest. Act i, sc. 2, l. 120. [Miranda]

14 Ensear thy fertile and conceptious womb,
Let it no more bring out ingrateful man!
Go great with tigers, dragons, wolves, and bears;
Teem with new monsters.
Timon of Athens. Act iv, sc. 3, l. 187. [Timon] The only use of "ensear" and "conceptions."

Sin-conceiving womb.—*King John,* ii, 1, 182. The only use of "sin-conceiving."

15 From that womb where you imprison'd were
He is enfranchised.
Titus Andronicus. Act iv, sc. 2, l. 124. [Aaron]

WONDER

See also Admiration, Marvel, Miracle, Strangeness

1 Nay, I 'll speak that
Which you will wonder at.
All's Well that Ends Well. Act iv, sc. 1, l. 94. [Parolles]
Thou speakest wonders.—*Henry VIII,* v, 5, 56.

2
Kneel down, kneel down, and wonder.
Antony and Cleopatra. Act iii, sc. 2, l. 19. [Enobarbus]
Look pale and wonder.—*As You Like It,* i, 1, 164.
Be still and wonder.—*Coriolanus,* iii, 2, 11.
Cast yourself in wonder.—*Julius Cæsar,* i, 3, 60.
Wonder greatly.—*Titus Andronicus,* ii, 3, 266.

3
O wonderful, wonderful, and most wonderful wonderful! and yet again wonderful, and after that, out of all hooping!
As You Like It. Act iii, sc. 2, l. 201. [Celia] The only use of "hooping" (shouting with amazement).
A wonderful piece of work.
Antony and Cleopatra. Act i, sc. 2, l. 159. [Enobarbus]

4
Saw you anything more wonderful?
Julius Cæsar. Act i, sc. 3, l. 14. [Cicero]
I tell thee, Licio, this is wonderful.
The Taming of the Shrew. Act iv, sc. 2, l. 15. [Tranio]
O wonderful!—*Richard III,* i, 2, 73; *Hamlet,* i, 5, 118; iii, 2, 340.
Most wonderful!—*Much Ado about Nothing,* ii, 3, 98; *Twelfth Night,* v, 1, 232.
'Tis wonderful!—*Henry V,* iv, 8, 117; *King John,* iii, 4, 178.

5
Rosalind: Did your brother tell you how I counterfeited to swoon when he showed me your handkercher?
Orlando: Ay, and greater wonders than that.
As You Like It. Act v, sc. 2, l. 28.

6
Our earth's wonder, more than earth divine.
The Comedy of Errors. Act iii, sc. 2, l. 32. [Antipholus of Syracuse]
Navarre shall be the wonder of the world.
Love's Labour's Lost. Act i, sc. 1, l. 12. [King]
Wonders of the world.—*The Two Gentlemen of Verona,* i, 1, 6. See under TRAVEL.
Gallia's wonder.—*I Henry VI,* iv, 7, 48.

7
This I wonder at.
The Comedy of Errors. Act iv, sc. 2, l. 47. [Adriana] "I wonder" is used frequently throughout the plays, beginning with *III Henry VI,* i, 1, 1.
I do much wonder.—*Much Ado about Nothing,* ii, 3, 8.
I wonder at it.—*Much Ado about Nothing,* iii, 3, 123.
I should wonder.—*Measure for Measure,* iii, 1, 191.
I wonder in my soul.—*Othello,* iii, 3, 68.
Yet let me wonder.—*I Henry IV,* iii, 2, 29.

8 Men of heart
Look'd wondering each at other.
Coriolanus. Act v, sc. 6, l. 99. [Aufidius]

9 You are made
Rather to wonder at the things you hear
Than to work any.
Cymbeline. Act v, sc. 3, l. 53. [Posthumus]
A mark of wonder.—*Cymbeline,* v, 5, 365.

10
It harrows me with . . . wonder.
Hamlet. Act i, sc. 1, l. 44. [Hamlet]
Feeds on his wonder, keeps himself in clouds.
Hamlet. Act iv, sc. 5, l. 89. [King]

11
By being seldom seen, I could not stir
But like a comet I was wonder'd at.
I Henry IV. Act iii, sc. 2, l. 46. [King Henry] "Wondered at" occurs nine times in the plays.
To lay apart their particular functions and wonder at him.
Henry V. Act iii, sc. 7, l. 40. [Dauphin]

12 Sometime he angers me
With telling me of the moldwarp and the ant,
Of the dreamer Merlin and his prophecies,
And of a dragon and a finless fish,
A clip-wing'd griffin and a moulten raven,
A couching lion and a ramping cat,
And such a deal of skimble-skamble stuff
As puts me from my faith.
I Henry IV. Act iii, sc. 1, l. 148. [Hotspur] The only use of "moldwarp" (mole), "finless," "clip-wing'd," "moulten," and "skimble-skamble." Merlin is mentioned again in *King Lear,* iii, 2, 95, and the griffin in *A Midsummer-Night's Dream,* ii, 1, 232.

13
Mute wonder lurketh in men's ears.
Henry V. Act i, sc. 1, l. 49. [Canterbury]
But thou, 'gainst all proportion, didst bring in
Wonder to wait on treason and on murder.
Henry V. Act ii, sc. 2, l. 109. [King Henry]

14 Valiant Talbot above human thought
Enacted wonders with his sword and lance.
I Henry VI. Act i, sc. 1, l. 121. [Messenger]
Thou mayst bereave him of his wits with wonder.
I Henry VI. Act v, sc. 3, l. 195. [Suffolk]
Because you want the grace that others have,
You judge it straight a thing impossible
To compass wonders but by help of devils.
I Henry VI. Act v, sc. 4, l. 46. [La Pucelle]

15
These few days' wonder will be quickly worn.
II Henry VI. Act ii, sc. 4, l. 69. [Gloucester]
Gloucester: That would be ten days' wonder at the least.
Clarence: That 's a day longer than a wonder lasts.
Gloucester: By so much is the wonder in extremes.
III Henry VI. Act iii, sc. 2, l. 113.
I was seven of the nine days out of wonder before you came.
As You Like It, iii, 2, 184. [Rosalind]

1
Leave off to wonder why I drew you hither,
Into this chiefest thicket of the park.
III Henry VI. Act iv, sc. 5, l. 2. [Gloucester]

2
I stood rapt in the wonder of it.
Macbeth. Act i, sc. 5, l. 6. [Lady Macbeth]

For my part, I am so attired in wonder,
I know not what to say.
Much Ado about Nothing. Act iv, sc. 1, l. 146. [Benedick]

3 Can such things be,
And overcome us like a summer's cloud,
Without our special wonder?
Macbeth. Act iii, sc. 4, l. 110. [Macbeth]

4
By heaven, the wonder in a mortal eye!
Love's Labour 's Lost, iv, 3, 85. See under EYE.

Silent wonder of still-gazing eyes.
The Rape of Lucrece, l. 84. The only use of "still-gazing."

Wonder of his eye.—*The Rape of Lucrece,* l. 95.

This composed wonder of your frame.
Sonnets. No. lix.

5
Be you in the Park about midnight, at Herne's oak, and you shall see wonders.
The Merry Wives of Windsor. Act v, sc. 1, l. 11. [Falstaff]

Former wonders.—*Henry VIII,* i, 1, 18.

General wonder.—*Pericles,* iv, Gower, 11.

Unlikely wonders.—*Richard II,* v, 5, 19. "Unlikely" is repeated in *III Henry VI,* iii, 2, 151, and in *Coriolanus,* iv, 6, 71.

6
Masters, I am to discourse wonders: but ask me not what; for if I tell you, I am no true Athenian.
A Midsummer-Night's Dream. Act iv, sc. 2, l. 29. [Bottom]

Gentles, perchance you wonder at this show;
But wonder on, till truth makes all things plain.
A Midsummer-Night's Dream. Act v, sc. 1, l. 128. [Quince]

7
At the which let no man wonder.
A Midsummer-Night's Dream. Act v, sc. 1, l. 135. [Quince]

Let wonder seem familiar.
Much Ado about Nothing. Act v, sc. 4, l. 70. [Friar Francis]

8
It gives me wonder great as my content
To see you here before me.
Othello. Act ii, sc. 1, l. 185. [Othello]

Sure, there 's some wonder in this handkerchief.
Othello. Act iii, sc. 4, l. 101. [Desdemona]

9 The heavens,
Through you, increase our wonder.
Pericles. Act iii, sc. 2, l. 96. [Gentleman]

Beyond all wonder.—*Pericles,* i, 2, 75.

10
Make it no wonder.
The Taming of the Shrew. Act iii, sc. 2, l. 193. [Petruchio]

No wonder!—*Cymbeline,* iii, 6, 11.

11
Here is a wonder, if you talk of a wonder.
The Taming of the Shrew. Act v, sc. 2, l. 106. [Lucentio]

Is that a wonder?—*Troilus and Cressida,* iii, 3, 195.

And that 's a wonder.—*The Taming of the Shrew,* ii, 1, 411.

'Tis a wonder.—*The Taming of the Shrew,* v, 2, 189; *King Lear,* iv, 7, 41.

A wonder, lady!—*King John,* ii, 1, 50.

A wonder, master!—*Love's Labour 's Lost,* iii, 1, 71.

Which is a wonder.—*Henry V,* i, 1, 53.

12 I will . . .
At least bring forth a wonder.
The Tempest. Act v, sc. 1, l. 170. [Prospero]

O you wonder.—*The Tempest,* i, 2, 426.

13 I 'll show thee wondrous things,
That highly advantage thee to hear.
Titus Andronicus. Act v, sc. 1, l. 55. [Aaron]

14
I could not with such estimable wonder overfar believe that.
Twelfth Night. Act ii, sc. 1, l. 28. [Sebastian] The only use of "overfar." "Estimable" occurs once again in *The Merchant of Venice,* i, 3, 167.

Though 'tis wonder that enwraps me thus,
Yet 'tis not madness.
Twelfth Night. Act iv, sc. 3, l. 3. [Sebastian] The only use of "enwraps."

15
Wonder not, nor admire not in thy mind.
Twelfth Night. Act iii, sc. 4, l. 165. [Sir Toby, reading]

Wonder not.—*The Taming of the Shrew,* iv, 5, 63; *Much Ado about Nothing,* iii, 2, 115.

16
Please you, I 'll tell you as we pass along,
That you will wonder what hath fortuned.
The Two Gentlemen of Verona. Act v, sc. 4, l. 168. [Valentine] The only use of "fortuned."

I will tell thee wonders.—*Love's Labour 's Lost,* i, 2, 144.

17
If thou 'lt see a thing to talk on when thou art dead and rotten, come hither.
Winter's Tale. Act iii, sc. 3, l. 81. [Shepherd]

Enough then for your wonder.
Winter's Tale. Act iv, sc. 4, l. 395. [Florizel]

I lost a couple, that 'twixt heaven and earth
Might thus have stood begetting wonder as
You, gracious couple.
Winter's Tale. Act v, sc. 1, l. 132. [Paulina]

A notable passion of wonder appeared in them.
Winter's Tale. Act v, sc. 2, l. 17. [Gentleman]

Such a deal of wonder is broken out within this hour that ballad-makers cannot be able to express it.
Winter's Tale. Act v, sc. 2, l. 25. [Gentleman]

WOOD

See also Forest

18 Are not these woods
More free from peril than the envious court?
As You Like It. Act ii, sc. 1, l. 3. [Duke]

Rooky wood.—*Macbeth,* iii, 2, 51. The only use of "rooky."

Wild wood.—*As You Like It,* v, 4, 165.

Wood of Crete.—*Midsummer-Night's Dream,* iv, 1, 118.

1

You, Polydore, have proved best woodman and
Are master of the feast.

Cymbeline. Act iii, sc. 6, l. 28. [Belarius]

He's a better woodman than thou takest him for.

Measure for Measure. Act iv, sc. 3, l. 170. [Lucio]

Am I a woodman, ha? Speak I like Herne the hunter?

The Merry Wives of Windsor. Act v, sc. 4, l. 30. [Falstaff]

He is no woodman that doth bend his bow
To strike a poor unseasonable doe.

The Rape of Lucrece, l. 580. The only uses of "woodman."

2

Brave followers, yonder stands the thorny wood,
Which, by the heavens' assistance and your strength,
Must by the roots be hewn up yet ere night.

III Henry VI. Act v, sc. 4, l. 67. [King Edward]

Like one lost in a thorny wood.

III Henry VI. Act iii, sc. 2, l. 174. [Gloucester]

Roaming through a thorny wood.

The Taming of the Shrew. Induction, sc. 2, l. 59. [Servant]

3

Apparition: Macbeth shall never vanquish'd be until
Great Birnam wood to high Dunsinane hill
Shall come against him.
Macbeth: That will never be:
Who can impress the forest, bid the tree
Unfix his earth-bound root? Sweet bodements! good!
Rebellion's head, rise never till the wood
Of Birnam rise.

Macbeth. Act iv, sc. 1, l. 92. The only use of "earth-bound." "Bodements" is repeated in *Troilus and Cressida,* v, 3, 80.

Till Birnam wood remove to Dunsinane,
I cannot taint with fear.

Macbeth. Act v, sc. 3, l. 2. [Macbeth]

Messenger: As I did stand my watch upon the hill,
I look'd toward Birnam, and anon, methought,
The wood began to move.
Macbeth: Liar and slave!
Messenger: Let me endure your wrath, if 't be not so:
Within this three mile may you see it coming;
I say, a moving grove.

Macbeth. Act v, sc. 5, l. 33.

4 In the wood, where often you and I
Upon faint primrose-beds were wont to lie,
Emptying our bosoms of their counsel sweet.

A Midsummer-Night's Dream. Act i, sc. 1, l. 214. [Hermia] The only use of "primrose-beds."

Thou told'st me they had stolen unto this wood;
And here am I, and wode within this wood.

A Midsummer-Night's Dream. Act ii, sc. 1, l. 191. [Demetrius] The only use of "wode" (wood).

He was ware of me
And stole into the covert of the wood.

Romeo and Juliet. Act i, sc. 1, l. 131. [Benvolio]

5

Out of this wood do not desire to go.

A Midsummer-Night's Dream. Act iii, sc. 1, l. 155. [Titania]

Get out of this wood.—*A Midsummer-Night's Dream,* iii, 1, 153.

6

And, like a forester, the groves may tread.

A Midsummer-Night's Dream. Act iii, sc. 2, l. 390. [Oberon]

Grove of cypress trees.—*II Henry VI,* iii, 2, 323.

Cypress grove.—*Coriolanus,* i, 10, 30.

Grove of myrtles.—*Passionate Pilgrim,* l. 376.

Myrtle grove.—*Venus and Adonis,* l. 865.

Grove of sycamore.—*Romeo and Juliet,* i, 1, 128.

Haunted grove.—*Midsummer-Night's Dream,* iii, 2, 5.

Holy groves.—*Titus Andronicus,* ii, 3, 58.

Moving grove.—*Macbeth,* v, 5, 37.

Rough-grown grove.—*The Rape of Lucrece,* l. 1249. The only use of "rough-grown."

7

Whilst you have fed upon my signories,
Dispark'd my parks and fell'd my forest woods.

Richard II. Act iii, sc. 1, l. 23. [Bolingbroke] The only use of "dispark'd."

Blasted woods.—*Timon of Athens,* iv, 3, 538.

8

Timon will to the woods.

Timon of Athens, iv, 1, 35. See under MAN.

9

The woods are ruthless, dreadful, deaf, and dull.

Titus Andronicus. Act ii, sc. 1, l. 128. [Aaron]

The woods are green.—*Titus Andronicus,* ii, 2, 2.

The ruthless, vast, and gloomy woods.

Titus Andronicus. Act iv, sc. 1, l. 53. [Titus]

Mistrustful wood.—*Venus and Adonis,* l. 826.

10 Unfrequented woods
I better brook than flourishing peopled towns.

The Two Gentlemen of Verona, v, 4, 2. See under SOLITUDE.

Unfrequented plots.—*Titus Andronicus,* ii, 1, 115. The only uses of "unfrequented."

11

As they were mad, unto the wood they hie them,
Out-stripping crows that strive to over-fly them.

Venus and Adonis, l. 323. The only use of "out-stripping" and "over-fly."

II—Wood: Timber

1
He talks of wood: it is some carpenter.
I Henry VI. Act v, sc. 3, l. 90. [Margaret]
O wood divine!—*Love's Labour's Lost,* iv, 3, 248.
Blessed wood.—*Sonnets,* cxxviii.
Dead wood.—*Sonnets,* cxxviii.

2
We take
From every tree . . . part o' the timber.
Henry VIII, i, 2, 96. See under Tree.
Green timber.—*As You Like It,* iii, 3, 90. The only uses of "timber."

3
Come, will this wood take fire?
The Merry Wives of Windsor. Act v, sc. 5, l. 92. [Evans]

4
Burn sweet wood to make the lodging sweet.
The Taming of the Shrew. Induction, sc. 1, l. 49. [Lord]

5
I'll bring my wood home faster.
The Tempest. Act ii, sc. 2, l. 75. [Caliban]
Bringing wood.—*The Tempest,* ii, 2, 16.
Fetch in our wood.—*The Tempest,* i, 2, 312.
Get thee wood enough.—*The Tempest,* ii, 2, 165.
There's wood enough within.—*The Tempest,* i, 2, 314.
Pile of wood.—*Titus Andronicus,* i, 1, 128.

WOOING

See also Suit

6 The count he wooes your daughter,
Lays down his wanton siege before her beauty,
Resolved to carry her.
All's Well that Ends Well. Act iii, sc. 7, l. 17. [Helena]
Every night he comes
With musics of all sorts and songs composed
To her unworthiness.
All's Well that Ends Well. Act iii, sc. 7, l. 39. [Widow]
My mother told me just how he would woo,
As if she sat in 's heart; she says all men
Have the like oaths.
All's Well that Ends Well. Act iv, sc. 2, l. 69. [Diana]

7
Leave me alone to woo him.
As You Like It. Act i, sc. 3, l. 135. [Celia]
I remember the wooing of a peascod instead of her, from whom I took two cods and giving her them again, said with weeping tears 'Wear these for my sake.'
As You Like It. Act ii, sc. 4, l. 51. [Touchstone] The only use of "cods." "Cod" occurs in *Othello,* ii, 1, 156: "Cod's head."

8
I set him every day to woo me.
As You Like It. Act iii, sc. 2, l. 429. [Rosalind]
Come every day to my cote and woo me.
As You Like It. Act iii, sc. 2, l. 448. [Rosalind] "Cote" is repeated in ii, 4, 83, and occurs in no other play.
Rosalind: I had as lief be wooed of a snail.
Orlando: Of a snail?
Rosalind: Ay, of a snail; for though he comes slowly, he carries his house on his head; a better jointure, I think, than you make a woman.
As You Like It. Act iv, sc. 1, l. 52. See also under Dowry.
Come, woo me, woo me, for now I am in a holiday humour and like enough to consent.
As You Like It. Act iv, sc. 1, l. 68. [Rosalind]
Whiles the eye of man did woo me,
That could do no vengeance to me.
As You Like It. Act iv, sc. 3, l. 47. [Rosalind]

9
Thee will I love and with thee lead my life:
Thou hast no husband yet nor I no wife.
Give me thy hand.
The Comedy of Errors. Act iii, sc. 2, l. 67. [Antipholus of Syracuse]
Mightst thou perceive austerely in his eye
That he did plead in earnest? yea or no?
The Comedy of Errors. Act iv, sc. 2, l. 2. [Adriana] "Austerely" is repeated in *The Tempest,* iv, 1, 1.
Adriana: With what persuasion did he tempt thy love?
Luciana: With words that in an honest suit might move.
The Comedy of Errors. Act iv, sc. 2, l. 13.

10 Were you a woman, youth,
I should woo hard but be your groom.
Cymbeline. Act iii, sc. 6, l. 69. [Guiderius]
Woo me oft For my confections.—*Cymbeline,* i, 5, 14.

11
'Tis told me, he hath very oft of late
Given private time to you; and you yourself
Have of your audience been most free and bounteous.
Hamlet. Act i, sc. 3, l. 91. [Polonius]
Woo for leave to do him good.
Hamlet. Act iii, sc. 4, l. 155. [Hamlet]

12
Will you vouchsafe to teach a soldier terms
Such as will enter at a lady's ear
And plead his love-suit to her gentle heart?
Henry V. Act v, sc. 2, l. 99. [King Henry]
Whose love-suit hath been to me
As fearful as a siege.
Cymbeline, iii, 4, 136. [Imogen] "Love-suit" is used a third time in *Sonnets,* cxxxvi.

13
My wooing is fit for thy understanding.
Henry V. Act v, sc. 2, l. 125. [King Henry]
I know no ways to mince it in love, but directly to say 'I love you;' and if you urge me farther than to say 'do you in faith?' I wear out my suit. . . . What sayest thou then to my love? speak, my fair, and fairly, I pray thee.
Henry V. Act v, sc. 2, l. 129. [King Henry]
If I could win a lady at leap-frog, or by vaulting into my saddle with my armour on my back, under the correction of bragging be it spoken, I should quickly leap into a wife.
Henry V. Act v, sc. 2, l. 142. [King Henry] The only use of "leap-frog."

14
You took occasion to be quickly woo'd.
I Henry IV, v, 1, 56. See Occasion, 1090:1.
Sudden wooing.—*As You Like It,* v, 2, 8.

1
I 'll make my heaven in a lady's lap,
And deck my body in gay ornaments,
And witch sweet ladies with my words and looks.
III Henry VI. Act iii, sc. 2, l. 148. [Gloucester]

I am commanded, with your leave and favour,
Humbly to kiss your hand and with my tongue
To tell the passion of my sovereign's heart;
Where fame, late entering at his heedful ears,
Hath placed thy beauty's image and thy virtue.
III Henry VI. Act iii, sc. 3, l. 60. [Warwick]

2
What shall we do,
If they return in their own shapes to woo?
Love's Labour's Lost. Act v, sc. 2, l. 298. [Princess of France]

Nor woo in rhyme, like a blind harper's song!
Love's Labour's Lost. Act v, sc. 2, l. 405. [Biron] The only use of "harper."

Our wooing doth not end like an old play;
Jack hath not Jill.
Love's Labour's Lost. Act v, sc. 2, l. 884. [Biron]

3
For feasts of love I have been call'd unto,
Till now did ne'er invite, nor never woo.
A Lover's Complaint, l. 181.

4
I would outstare the sternest eyes that look,
Outbrave the heart most daring on the earth,
Pluck the young sucking cubs from the she-bear,
Yea, mock the lion when he roars for prey,
To win thee, lady.
The Merchant of Venice. Act ii, sc. 1, l. 27. [Morocco] The only use of "cubs" and "she-bear." "Cub" occurs in *Twelfth Night,* v, 1, 167; "sternest" is repeated in *Macbeth,* ii, 2, 4; "outstare" in *Antony and Cleopatra,* iii, 13, 195, and in *Henry VIII,* i, 1, 129; and "outbrave" in *Sonnets,* xciv.

Wooing here until I sweat again.
The Merchant of Venice. Act iii, sc. 2, l. 205. [Gratiano]

5
Woo a maid in way of marriage.
The Merchant of Venice. Act ii, sc. 9, l. 13. [Arragon]

Woo another wife.—*Cymbeline,* i, 1, 113.
Woo contrary.—*Love's Labour's Lost,* v, 2, 135.
Woo honour.—*All's Well that Ends Well,* ii, 1, 15.
Woo in other places.—*Henry V,* v, 2, 163.
Woo my daughter.—*Pericles,* v, 1, 263.
Woo my queen.—*The Winter's Tale,* iii, 2, 157.
Woo your company.—*As You Like It,* ii, 7, 10.
Woo your own destruction.—*Henry VIII,* v, 1, 140.

6
'To her, boy,' say I.
The Merry Wives of Windsor. Act i, sc. 3, l. 61. [Pistol]

Mrs. Page: Unless he know some strain in me, that I know not myself, he would never have boarded me in this fury.
Mrs. Ford: 'Boarding,' call you it? I 'll be sure to keep him above deck.
Mrs. Page: So will I: if he come under my hatches, I 'll never to sea again.
The Merry Wives of Windsor. Act ii, sc. 1, l. 90. The only use of "boarding."

I would he had boarded me.
Much Ado about Nothing. Act ii, sc. 1, l. 148. [Beatrice]

For I will board her, though she chide as loud
As thunder when the clouds in autumn crack.
The Taming of the Shrew. Act i, sc. 2, l. 95. [Petruchio]

Accost, Sir Andrew, accost. . . .
Front her, board her, woo her, assail her.
Twelfth Night. Act i, sc. 3, l. 52. [Sir Toby]

I liked her And boarded her.—*All's Well that Ends Well,* v, 3, 211.

7
He wooes both high and low, both rich and poor,
Both young and old, one with another, Ford;
He loves the gallimaufry.
The Merry Wives of Windsor. Act ii, sc. 1, l. 117. [Pistol] "Gallimaufry" (promiscuous assemblage) is repeated in *The Winter's Tale,* iv, 4, 335.

Yet there has been knights, and lords, and gentlemen, with their coaches, I warrant you, coach after coach, letter after letter, gift after gift; smelling so sweetly, all musk, and so rushling, I warrant you, in silk and gold; and in such alligant terms; and in such wine and sugar of the best and the fairest, that would have won any woman's heart; and, I warrant you, they could never get an eye-wink of her.
Merry Wives of Windsor. Act ii, sc. 2, l. 64. [Mistress Quickly] The only use of "musk," "rushling," "alligant," and "eye-wink."

I have pursued her as love hath pursued me; which hath been on the wing of all occasions.
The Merry Wives of Windsor. Act ii, sc. 2, l. 208. [Ford]

Use your art of wooing; win her to consent to you: if any man may, you may as soon as any.
The Merry Wives of Windsor. Act ii, sc. 2, l. 244. [Ford]

Anne Page is at a farm-house a-feasting; and thou shalt woo her.
The Merry Wives of Windsor. Act ii, sc. 3, l. 92. [Host] The only use of "farm-house" and "a-feasting."

She will die, if he woo her.—*The Merry Wives of Windsor,* ii, 3, 183.

We shall have the freer wooing.
The Merry Wives of Windsor. Act iii, sc. 2, l. 86. [Shallow]

8
Good Mistress Page, for that I love your daughter
In such a righteous fashion as I do,
Perforce, against all checks, rebukes and manners,
I must advance the colours of my love
And not retire: let me have your good will.
The Merry Wives of Windsor. Act iii, sc. 4, l. 82. [Fenton]

I will never mistrust my wife again, till thou art able to woo her in good English.
The Merry Wives of Windsor. Act v, sc. 5, l. 141. [Ford]

1 I woo'd thee with my sword,
And won thy love, doing thee injuries.
A Midsummer-Night's Dream. Act i, sc. 1, l. 16. [Theseus]

Thou hast by moonlight at her window sung
With feigning voice verses of feigning love,
And stolen the impression of her fantasy
With bracelets of thy hair, rings, gawds, conceits,
Knacks, trifles, nosegays, sweetmeats, messengers
Of strong prevailment in unharden'd youth.
A Midsummer-Night's Dream. Act i, sc. 1, l. 30. [Egeus] The only use of "unharden'd" and "prevailment." "Nosegays" is repeated in *The Winter's Tale,* iv, 3, 44; and "sweetmeats" in *Romeo and Juliet,* i, 4, 76.

Playing on pipes of corn and versing love
To amorous Phillida.
A Midsummer-Night's Dream. Act ii, sc. 1, l. 67. [Titania] The only use of "versing," and the only reference to Phillida.

Then will two at once woo one;
That must needs be sport alone;
And those things do best please me
That befal preposterously.
A Midsummer-Night's Dream. Act iii, sc. 2, l. 118. [Puck] "Preposterously" is used four times.

2
We cannot fight for love, as men may do;
We should be woo'd and were not made to woo.
A Midsummer-Night's Dream. Act ii, sc. 1, l. 241. [Helena]

But, though I loved you well, I woo'd you not:
And yet, good faith, I wish'd myself a man,
Or that we women had men's privilege
Of speaking first.
Troilus and Cressida. Act iii, sc. 2, l. 134. [Cressida]

3
Good troth, you do me wrong, good sooth, you do,
In such disdainful manner me to woo.
A Midsummer-Night's Dream. Act ii, sc. 2, l. 129. [Helena]

Why should you think that I should woo in scorn?
A Midsummer-Night's Dream. Act iii, sc. 2, l. 122. [Lysander]

4 In her bosom I 'll unclasp my heart
And take her hearing prisoner with the force
And strong encounter of my amorous tale.
Much Ado about Nothing. Act i, sc. 1, l. 325. [Don Pedro]

With a good leg and a good foot, uncle, and money enough in his purse, such a man would win any woman in the world, if a' could get her good-will.
Much Ado about Nothing. Act ii, sc. 1, l. 15. [Beatrice]

The fault will be in the music, cousin, if you be not wooed in good time.
Much Ado about Nothing. Act ii, sc. 1, l. 72. [Beatrice]

5
I cannot woo in festival terms.
Much Ado about Nothing. Act v, sc. 2, l. 41. [Benedick]

Thou and I are too wise to woo peaceably.
Much Ado about Nothing. Act v, sc. 2, l. 73. [Benedick] "Peaceably" is repeated in *II Henry VI,* iii, 3, 25: "Let him pass peaceably."

6
[He] came a-wooing with you.
Othello. Act iii, sc. 3, l. 71. [Desdemona]

Lucentio that comes a-wooing.
The Taming of the Shrew, iii, 1, 35. The only uses of "a-wooing."

7
But plainly say thou lovest her well,
And set thy person forth to sell.
The Passionate Pilgrim, l. 309.

8
You have heard something of my power, and so stand aloof for more serious wooing.
Pericles. Act iv, sc. 6, l. 93. [Lysimachus]

9
Queen Elizabeth: How canst thou woo her?
King Richard: That would I learn of you,
As one that are best acquainted with her humour.
Richard III. Act iv, sc. 4, l. 268.

Under what title shall I woo for thee?
Richard III. Act iv, sc. 4, l. 340. [Queen Elizabeth]

10
She is the hopeful lady of my earth:
But woo her, gentle Paris, get her heart,
My will to her consent is but a part.
Romeo and Juliet. Act i, sc. 2, l. 15. [Capulet]

If thou dost love, pronounce it faithfully:
Or if thou think'st I am too quickly won,
I 'll frown and be perverse and say thee nay,
So thou wilt woo.
Romeo and Juliet. Act ii, sc. 2, l. 94. [Juliet]

When and where and how
We met, we woo'd and made exchange of vow,
I 'll tell thee as we pass.
Romeo and Juliet. Act ii, sc. 3, l. 61. [Romeo]

I wonder at this haste; that I must wed
Ere he, that should be husband, comes to woo.
Romeo and Juliet. Act iii, sc. 5, l. 119. [Juliet]

11
They live unwoo'd and unrespected fade.
Sonnets. No. liv. The only use of "unwoo'd."

12
Gremio: But will you woo this wild-cat?
Petruchio: Will I live?
Grumio: Will he woo her? ay, or I 'll hang her.
Petruchio: Why came I hither but to that intent?
Think you a little din can daunt mine ears?
Have I not in my time heard lions roar?
Have I not heard the sea puff'd up with winds
Rage like an angry boar chafed with sweat?
Have I not heard great ordnance in the field,

And heaven's artillery thunder in the skies?
Have I not in a pitched battle heard
Loud 'larums, neighing steeds, and trumpets' clang?
And do you tell me of a woman's tongue,
That gives not half so great a blow to hear
As will a chestnut in a farmer's fire?
The Taming of the Shrew. Act i, sc. 2, l. 197. The only use of "clang." "Wild-cat" is repeated in *Merchant of Venice,* ii, 5, 48, and in *Othello,* ii, 1, 111; and "chestnut" in *As You Like It,* iii, 4, 12, and in *Macbeth,* i, 3, 4.

I promised we would be contributors
And bear his charge of wooing, whatsoe'er.
The Taming of the Shrew. Act i, sc. 2, l. 215. [Hortensio] The only use of "contributors."

You will curse your wooing.
The Taming of the Shrew, ii, 1, 75. [Gremio]

This liberty is all that I request,
That, upon knowledge of my parentage,
I may have welcome 'mongst the rest that woo
And free access and favour as the rest.
The Taming of the Shrew. Act ii, sc. 1, l. 95. [Tranio]

My business asketh haste,
And every day I cannot come to woo.
The Taming of the Shrew. Act ii, sc. 1, l. 115. [Petruchio]

I am rough and woo not like a babe.
The Taming of the Shrew. Act ii, sc. 1, l. 138. [Petruchio]

1 I will attend her here,
And woo her with some spirit when she comes,
Say that she rail; why then I 'll tell her plain
She sings as sweetly as a nightingale:
Say that she frown; I 'll say she looks as clear
As morning roses newly wash'd with dew:
Say she be mute and will not speak a word;
Then I 'll commend her volubility,
And say she uttereth piercing eloquence:
If she do bid me pack, I 'll give her thanks,
As though she bid me stay by her a week:
If she deny to wed, I 'll crave the day
When I shall ask the banns and when be married.
The Taming of the Shrew. Act ii, sc. 1, l. 169. [Petruchio] "Volubility" is repeated in *All 's Well that Ends Well,* iv, 3, 284.

2 To be noted for a merry man,
He 'll woo a thousand, 'point the day of marriage,
Make feasts, invite friends, and proclaim the banns;
Yet never means to wed where he hath woo'd.
The Taming of the Shrew. Act iii, sc. 2, l. 14. [Katharina]

Asked twice on the banns.—*I Henry IV,* iv, 2, 18.

I contradict your banns.—*King Lear,* v, 3, 87.

3
Hearing thy mildness praised in every town,
Thy virtues spoke of, and thy beauty sounded,
Yet not so deeply as to thee belongs,
Myself am moved to woo thee for my wife.
The Taming of the Shrew. Act ii, sc. 1, l. 192. [Petruchio]

She hung about my neck; and kiss on kiss
She vied so fast, protesting oath on oath,
That in a twink she won me to her love.
The Taming of the Shrew. Act ii, sc. 1, l. 310. [Petruchio] The only use of "vied." "Twink" is repeated in *The Tempest,* iv, 1, 43: "Ay, with a twink."

I must, forsooth, be forced
To give my hand opposed against my heart
Unto a mad-brain rudesby full of spleen;
Who woo'd in haste and means to wed at leisure.
The Taming of the Shrew. Act iii, sc. 2, l. 8. [Katharina] The only use of "mad-brain."

Rudesby, be gone.—*Twelfth Night,* iv, 1, 55. The only uses of "rudesby."

4
Grant I may ever love, and rather woo
Those that would mischief me than those that do!
Timon of Athens, iv, 3, 474. See under ENEMY.

So did we woo
Transformed Timon to our city's love
By humble message and by promised means.
Timon of Athens. Act v, sc. 4, l. 18. [Senator]

5 He 's as tetchy to be woo'd to woo,
As she is stubborn-chaste against all suit.
Troilus and Cressida. Act i, sc. 1, l. 99. [Troilus] The only use of "stubborn-chaste."

Words, vows, gifts, tears, and love's full sacrifice,
He offers in another's enterprise.
Troilus and Cressida. Act i, sc. 2, l. 308. [Cressida]

6
Olivia: Why, what would you?
Viola: Make me a willow cabin at your gate,
And call upon my soul within the house;
Write loyal cantons of contemned love
And sing them loud even in the dead of night;
Halloo your name to the reverberate hills
And make the babbling gossip of the air
Cry out 'Olivia'!
Twelfth Night. Act i, sc. 5, l. 287. The only use of "cantons" (songs). "Halloo" is repeated in *King Lear,* iii, 4, 79; and "reverberate" in *King John,* v, 2, 170, and *Troilus and Cressida,* iii, 3, 120.

Get thee to yond same sovereign cruelty:
Tell her, my love, more noble than the world,
Prizes not quantity of dirty lands;
The parts that fortune hath bestow'd upon her,
Tell her, I hold as giddily as fortune;
But 'tis that miracle and queen of gems
That nature pranks her in attracts my soul.
Twelfth Night. Act ii, sc. 4, l. 83. [Duke] "Giddily" is repeated in *Much Ado about Nothing,* iii, 3, 140.

1
I 'll woo you like a soldier, at arms' end,
And love you 'gainst the nature of love,—force ye.
The Two Gentlemen of Verona. Act v, sc. 4, l. 57. [Proteus]

2
Sick-thoughted Venus makes amain unto him,
And like a bold-faced suitor 'gins to woo him.
Venus and Adonis, l. 5. The only use of "sick-thoughted." See also SUITOR.

I have been woo'd, as I entreat thee now,
Even by the stern and direful god of war.
Venus and Adonis, l. 97.

Being proud, as females are, to see him woo her,
She puts on outward strangeness, seems unkind,
Spurns at his love and scorns the heat he feels.
Venus and Adonis, l. 309.

3
With wisdom I might fear, my Doricles,
You woo'd me the false way.
Winter's Tale. Act iv, sc. 4, l. 150. [Perdita]

O, thus she stood,
Even with such life of majesty, warm life,
As now it coldly stands, when first I woo'd her!
Winter's Tale Act v, sc. 3, l. 34. [Leontes]

When she was young you woo'd her; now in age
Is she become the suitor?
Winter's Tale. Act v, sc. 3, l. 108. [Paulina]

II—Wooed and Won

4
Men are April when they woo, December when they wed.
As You Like It. Act iv, sc. 1, l. 147. [Rosalind]

Women are angels, wooing:
Things won are done; joy's soul lies in the doing.
That she beloved knows nought that knows not this:
Men prize the thing ungain'd more than it is:
That she was never yet that ever knew
Love got so sweet as when desire did sue.
Therefore this maxim out of love I teach:
Achievement is command; ungain'd, beseech:
Then though my heart's content firm love doth bear,
Nothing of that shall from mine eyes appear.
Troilus and Cressida. Act i, sc. 2, l. 312. [Cressida] The only use of "maxim."

5
Fain would I woo her, yet I dare not speak;
I 'll call for pen and ink, and write my mind.
Fie, de la Pole! disable not thyself;
Hast not a tongue? is she not here? . . .
How canst thou tell she will deny thy suit,
Before thou make a trial of her love? . . .
She 's beautiful and therefore to be woo'd;
She is a woman, therefore to be won.
I Henry VI. Act v, sc. 3, l. 65. [Suffolk]

She is a woman, therefore may be woo'd.
Titus Andronicus. Act ii, sc. 1, l. 82. See WOMAN, 1698:9.

6
Whom I with pain have woo'd and won.
I Henry VI. Act v, sc. 3, l. 138. [Suffolk]

7
Longaville: Shall we resolve to woo these girls of France?
King Ferdinand: And win them too.
Love's Labour 's Lost. Act iv, sc. 3, l. 371.

Win me and wear me.
Much Ado about Nothing. Act v, sc. 1, l. 82. [Antonio]

8
Was ever woman in this humour woo'd?
Was ever woman in this humour won?
Richard III. Act i, sc. 2, l. 228. [Gloucester]

And I nothing to back my suit at all,
But the plain devil and dissembling looks,
And yet to win her, all the world to nothing!
Richard III. Act i, sc. 2, l. 236. [Gloucester]

9
Gentle thou art and therefore to be won,
Beauteous thou art, therefore to be assailed;
And when a woman woos, what woman's son
Will sourly leave her till she have prevailed?
Sonnets. No. xli. "Sourly" is repeated in *Sonnets,* xxxv. It does not occur in the plays.

10
Woo her, wed her and bed her.
The Taming of the Shrew. Act i, sc. 1, l. 149. [Gremio]

Wooing, wedding and repenting.
Much Ado about Nothing, ii, 1, 76. See under WEDLOCK. The only use of "repenting."

11
Though they be long ere they are wooed, they are constant being won.
Troilus and Cressida, iii, 2, 117. See under CONSTANCY.

III—Wooing for Oneself

12
Let him woo for himself.
The Merry Wives of Windsor. Act iii, sc. 4, l. 51. [Anne]

The prince wooes for himself.—*Much Ado about Nothing,* ii, 1, 181.

13
Therefore all hearts in love use their own tongues;
Let every eye negotiate for itself
And trust no agent.
Much Ado about Nothing. Act ii, sc. 1, l. 184. [Claudio]

Have you any commission from your lord to negotiate with any face?
Twelfth Night, i, 5, 250. The only uses of "negotiate." "Negotiation" occurs in *Troilus and Cressida,* iii, 3, 24.

14
I have wooed in thy name, and fair Hero is won.
Much Ado about Nothing. Act ii, sc. 1, l. 309. [Don Pedro]

15
Be the attorney of my love to her:
Plead what I will be, not what I have been;
Not my deserts, but what I will deserve.
Richard III. Act iv, sc. 4, l. 413. [King Richard]

1
She . . . bade me, if I had a friend that loved her,

I should but teach him how to tell my story,
And that would woo her.
Othello. Act i, sc. 3, l. 164. [Othello]

2 I 'll do my best
To woo your lady: yet, a barful strife!
Whoe'er I woo, myself would be his wife.
Twelfth Night. Act i, sc. 4, l. 40. [Viola] The only use of "barful" (hindering).

Yet will I woo for him, but yet so coldly
As, heaven it knows, I would not have him speed.
The Two Gentlemen of Verona. Act iv, sc. 4, l. 111. [Julia]

3
Can thy right hand seize love upon thy left?
Then woo thyself, be of thyself rejected.
Venus and Adonis, l. 158.

IV—The Wooer

4
He is the bluntest wooer in Christendom.
III Henry VI. Act iii, sc. 2, l. 83. [Clarence] The only use of "bluntest."

A twelvemonth and a day
I 'll mark no words that smooth-faced wooers say.
Love's Labour 's Lost. Act v, sc. 2, l. 837. [Katharine] "Smooth-faced" is repeated in *Richard III,* v, 5, 33: "Smooth-faced peace"; and in *King John,* ii, 1, 573.

I am glad this parcel of wooers are so reasonable.
The Merchant of Venice. Act i, sc. 2, l. 118. [Portia]

Whiles we shut the gates upon one wooer, another knocks at the door.
The Merchant of Venice. Act i, sc. 2, l. 147. [Portia]

Other wooers.—*The Merry Wives of Windsor,* i, 4, 173.

5
She mocks all her wooers out of suit.
Much Ado about Nothing, ii, 1, 365. See under Mockery.

Don Pedro: I pray thee, sing, and let me woo no more.
Balthazer: Because you talk of wooing, I will sing;
Since many a wooer doth commence his suit
To her he thinks not worthy, yet he wooes,
Yet will he swear he loves.
Much Ado about Nothing. Act ii, sc. 3, l. 50.

6
To her I go, a jolly thriving wooer.
Richard III. Act iv, sc. 3, l. 43. [King Richard] "Thriving" is repeated in *The Winter's Tale,* ii, 2, 45: "Thriving issue."

Prepare her ears to hear a wooer's tale.
Richard III. Act iv, sc. 4, l. 327. [King]

7
Make one among these wooers.
The Taming of the Shrew. Act i, sc. 1, l. 252. [Lucentio]

Fair Leda's daughter had a thousand wooers.
The Taming of the Shrew. Act i, sc. 2, l. 244. [Tranio] See under Helen.

But thou with mildness entertain'st thy wooers,
With gentle conference, soft and affable.
The Taming of the Shrew, ii, 1, 252. See under Character.

WORD

See also Speech

I—Familiar Phrases

8
He words me, girls, he words me.
Antony and Cleopatra. Act v, sc. 2, l. 191. [Cleopatra]

Words him, I doubt not, a great deal from the matter.
Cymbeline. Act i, sc. 4, l. 16. [Iachimo]

9
Rosalind: Answer me in one word. . . .
Celia: 'Tis a word too great for any mouth of this age's size.
As You Like It. Act iii, sc. 2, l. 237.

In a word.—*Coriolanus,* iv, 5, 100; *Cymbeline,* iii, 5, 82; *The Merchant of Venice,* i, 1, 35; iii, 2, 99; *Troilus and Cressida,* v, 10, 20; *The Two Gentlemen of Verona,* ii, 4, 71.

At a word.—*Coriolanus,* i, 3, 122; *The Merry Wives of Windsor,* i, 1, 109; i, 3, 15; ii, 2, 16; *Much Ado about Nothing,* ii, 1, 118.

At the next word.—*Cymbeline,* iii, 5, 96.

Of my word.—*Titus Andronicus,* iv, 3, 59.

Upon the word.—*Julius Cæsar,* i, 2, 104.

10
Who, every word by all my wit being scann'd,
Want wit in all one word to understand.
The Comedy of Errors. Act ii, sc. 2, l. 152. [Antipholus of Syracuse]

Holofernes: Via, goodman Dull! thou hast spoken no word all this while.
Dull: Nor understood none neither, sir.
Love's Labour 's Lost. Act v, sc. 1, l. 156.

Dost understand the word?—*Othello,* v, 2, 153.

11 Even her very words
Didst thou deliver to me on the mart.
The Comedy of Errors. Act ii, sc. 2, l. 165. [Antipholus of Syracuse]

These were his very words.
III Henry VI. Act iv, sc. 1, l. 92. [Post] Also *Richard II,* v, 4, 3.

'Nearest his heart:' those are the very words.
The Merchant of Venice. Act iv, sc. 1, l. 254. [Shylock]

These very words I heard him utter.
Henry VIII. Act i, sc. 2, l. 135. [Surveyor]

The very words.—*The Merry Wives of Windsor,* ii, 1, 85.

The selfsame words.—*III Henry VI,* v, 5, 20; *Macbeth,* i, 3, 88.

12
When spake I such a word?
The Comedy of Errors. Act ii, sc. 2, l. 13. [Dromio of Syracuse]

King: Say, man, were these thy words?
Horner: Hang me, if ever I spake the words.
II Henry VI. Act i, sc. 3, l. 189.

13
Words are but wind.
The Comedy of Errors. Act iii, sc. 1, l. 75. [Dromio of Ephesus] A proverb dating back, in English, to about 1200, when the unknown author of *Ancrene Riwle,* l. 122, asked, "Hwat is word bute wind?" Alexander Barclay, in his *Shyp of Folys,* i, 207 (1508), has the exact form which Shakespeare used eighty five years later.

Beatrice: Foul words is but foul wind, and foul wind is but foul breath, and foul breath is noisome; . . .
Benedick: Thou hast frighted the word out of his right sense, so forcible is thy wit.
Much Ado about Nothing. Act v, sc. 2, l. 52. "Foul words" is repeated in *Love's Labour 's Lost,* iv, 1, 19.

Words are easy, like the wind.
The Passionate Pilgrim, l. 405. See under Friend for full quotation.

So shall my lungs coin words.
Coriolanus. Act iii, sc. 1, l. 77. [Coriolanus]

Words to little purpose.—*Coriolanus,* iii, 2, 89.

1 I shall short my word
By lengthening my return.
Cymbeline. Act i, sc. 6, l. 201. [Iachimo] The only use of "lengthening."

Do not play in wench-like words with that
Which is so serious.
Cymbeline. Act iv, sc. 2, l. 230. [Guiderius] The only use of "wench-like."

Think on my words.—*Cymbeline,* i, 5, 75.

2
These are but wild and whirling words.
Hamlet. Act i, sc. 5, l. 133. [Horatio] "Whirling" is repeated in *Titus Andronicus,* iv, 2, 160.

Words like wildfire.—*The Rape of Lucrece,* l. 1523.

3
Polonius: What do you read, my lord?
Hamlet: Words, words, words.
Hamlet. Act ii, sc. 2, l. 193.

Words, words, mere words, no matter from the heart.
Troilus and Cressida. Act v, sc. 3, l. 108. [Troilus]

4
Like a whore, unpack my heart with words.
Hamlet. Act ii, sc. 2, l. 614. [Hamlet] The only use of "unpack."

These words are not mine.
Hamlet. Act iii, sc. 2, l. 102. [King]

How in my words soever she be shent,
To give them seals never, my soul, consent!
Hamlet. Act iii, sc. 2, l. 416. [Hamlet]

5
My words fly up, my thoughts remain below:
Words without thoughts never to heaven go.
Hamlet. Act iii, sc. 3, l. 97. [King]

Botch the words up fit to their own thoughts.
Hamlet. Act iv, sc. 5, l. 10. [Gentleman]

'Twas my word.—*Hamlet,* iii, 4, 30.

6 I cried 'hum,' and 'well, go to,'
But mark'd him not a word.
I Henry IV, iii, 1, 159. See under Tediousness.

7
Make him eat twenty of his words.
II Henry IV. Act ii, sc. 2, l. 149. [Prince]

Beatrice: Will you not eat your word?
Benedick: With no sauce that can be devised to it.
Much Ado about Nothing. Act iv, sc. 1, l. 280.

I will not eat my word.—*As You Like It,* v, 4, 155.

8
Go to; I have spoke at a word.
II Henry IV. Act iii, sc. 2, l. 319. [Shallow]

'Tis needful that the most immodest word
Be look'd upon and learn'd.
II Henry IV, iv, 4, 70. See under Companion.

A good soldier-like word.—*II Henry IV,* iii, 2, 73. See under Phrase.

What are his words?—*Henry V,* iv, 4, 46.

9 Believe my words,
For they are certain and unfallible.
I Henry VI. Act i, sc. 2, l. 58. [Bastard] The only use of "unfallible." "Infallible" occurs five times.

I 'll send him certain word.—*Measure for Measure,* i, 4, 89.

Certain words.—*Measure for Measure,* v, 1, 129; *Henry VIII,* i, 2, 159.

10
This day, in argument upon a case,
Some words there grew 'twixt Somerset and me.
I Henry VI. Act ii, sc. 5, l. 45. [Plantagenet]

Have some words.—*Julius Cæsar,* v, 1, 25.

11
My fainting words do warrant death.
I Henry VI. Act ii, sc. 5, l. 95. [Mortimer]

Airy word.—*Romeo and Juliet,* i, 1, 96.

Broad words.—*Macbeth,* iii, 6, 21.

Deliberate word.—*Measure for Measure,* iii, 1, 90.

Empty words.—*Measure for Measure,* ii, 4, 2. The only use of the phrase.

Express words.—*King John,* iv, 2, 234.

Household words.—*Henry V,* iv, 3, 52.

Latest words.—*Troilus and Cressida,* i, 3, 33.

Latin word.—*Love's Labour 's Lost,* iii, 1, 138.

Lightest word.—*Hamlet,* i, 5, 15.

12
When Gloucester says the word, King Henry goes.
I Henry VI. Act iii, sc. 1, l. 184. [King Henry]

Say but the word.—*II Henry VI,* iii, 1, 272.

Brutus gave the word too early.
Julius Cæsar. Act v, sc. 3, l. 5. [Titinius]

Give the word.—*Henry V,* iv, 6, 38; *King Lear,* iv, 6, 93.

Give the word, ho!—*Julius Cæsar,* iv, 2, 2.

Speak the word along.—*Julius Cæsar,* iv, 2, 33.

13
Speak, Pucelle, and enchant him with thy words.
I Henry VI. Act iii, sc. 3, l. 40. [Charles]

She hath bewitch'd me with her words.
I Henry VI. Act iii, sc. 3, l. 58. [Burgundy]

Let not his smoothing words
Bewitch your hearts.
II Henry VI. Act i, sc. 1, l. 156. [Cardinal Beaufort]

My troupe could never learn sweet smoothing words.
Richard III, i, 2, 169. The only uses of "smoothing words."

Heavens grant that Warwick's words bewitch him not!
III Henry VI. Act iii, sc. 3, l. 112. [Queen Margaret]

1 These haughty words of hers
Have batter'd me like roaring cannon-shot.
I Henry VI. Act iii, sc. 3, l. 78. [Burgundy] The only use of "cannon-shot."

Strumpet, thy words condemn thy brat and thee.
I Henry VI. Act v, sc. 4, l. 84. [York]

2
Her words y-clad with wisdom's majesty.
II Henry VI. Act i, sc. 1, l. 33. [King Henry] The only use of "y-clad."

Her words do show her wit incomparable.
III Henry VI. Act iii, sc. 2, l. 85. [King Edward]

3
Ignominious words, though clerkly couch'd.
II Henry VI. Act iii, sc. 1, l. 179. [Suffolk]

Ignominious terms.—*I Henry VI,* iv, 1, 97.

Ignominious treasons.—*II Henry VI,* iv, 8, 66. The only uses of "ignominious."

Lowly words were ransom for their fault.
II Henry VI, iii, 1, 127. See under PITY.

Such abominable words as no Christian ear can endure to hear.
II Henry VI, iv, 7, 44. See under EDUCATION.

4
I thank thee, Meg; these words content me much.
II Henry VI. Act iii, sc. 2, l. 26. [King Henry]

O, Clifford, how thy words revive my heart!
III Henry VI. Act i, sc. 1, l. 163. [King Henry]

His words do take possession of my bosom.
King John. Act iv, sc. 1, l. 32. [Hubert]

These words, these looks, infuse new life in me.
Titus Andronicus. Act i, sc. 1, l. 461. [Titus] "Infuse" is repeated in *III Henry VI,* v, 4, 41, and in *The Merchant of Venice,* iv, 1, 132.

5
Thy words move rage and not remorse in me.
II Henry VI. Act iv, sc. 1, l. 112. [Suffolk]

And will you credit this base drudge's words,
That speaks he knows not what?
II Henry VI. Act iv, sc. 2, l. 159. [Stafford]

6
Tell me their words as near as thou canst guess them.
III Henry VI. Act iv, sc. 1, l. 90. [King Edward]

7
By heaven, brat, I'll plague ye for that word.
III Henry VI. Act v, sc. 5, l. 27. [Gloucester]

These words hereafter thy tormentors be!
Richard II. Act ii, sc. 1, l. 136. [Gaunt] The only use of "tormentors."

8
I am glad that my weak words
Have struck but thus much show of fire from Brutus.
Julius Cæsar. Act i, sc. 2, l. 176. [Cæsar]

But yesterday the word of Cæsar might
Have stood against the world.
Julius Cæsar, iii, 2, 123. See under CÆSAR.

Mark'd ye his words?—*Julius Cæsar,* iii, 2, 177.

9
And bid me say to you by word of mouth.
Julius Cæsar. Act iii, sc. 1, l. 280. [Servant]

I'll deliver thy indignation to him by word of mouth.
Twelfth Night. Act ii, sc. 3, l. 141. [Sir Toby]

I will deliver his challenge by word of mouth.
Twelfth Night. Act iii, sc. 4, l. 209. [Sir Toby] The only uses of the phrase, "By word of mouth."

10 Thy word
Is but the vain breath of a common man.
King John. Act iii, sc. 1, l. 7. [Constable]

Be these sad signs confirmers of thy words?
Then speak again; not all thy former tale,
But this one word, whether thy tale be true.
King John. Act iii, sc. 1, l. 24. [Constance] The only use of "confirmers." "Confirmer" occurs in *As You Like It,* iii, 4, 35.

Repeats his words.—*King John,* iii, 4, 95.

11
If I would stand against thee, would the reposal
Of any trust, virtue, or worth in thee
Make thy words faith'd?
King Lear. Act ii, sc. 1, l. 72. [Edmund] The only use of "reposal" and "faith'd."

12
'Tis not in thee . . . To bandy hasty words.
King Lear. Act ii, sc. 4, l. 178. [King Lear] "Hasty words" is repeated in *The Taming of the Shrew,* iv, 3, 169.

To bandy word for word and frown for frown.
The Taming of the Shrew. Act v, sc. 2, l. 172. [Katharina] See under WOMAN for full quotation.

This factious bandying.—*I Henry VI,* iv, 1, 190. "Bandying" is repeated in *Romeo and Juliet,* iii, 1, 92.

13
We arrest your word.
Love's Labour's Lost. Act ii, sc. 1, l. 160. [Princess of France]

I do arrest your words.
Measure for Measure. Act ii, sc. 4, l. 134. [Angelo]

14
The word is well culled, chose, sweet and apt.
Love's Labour's Lost. Act v, sc. 1, l. 98. [Holofernes]

They have lived long on the alms-basket of words. I marvel thy master hath not eaten thee for a word; for thou art not so long by the head as honorificabilitudinitatibus: thou art easier swallowed than a flap-dragon.
Love's Labour's Lost. Act v, sc. 1, l. 41. [Costard] The only use of "alms-basket," and "honorificabilitudinitatibus," a stock example of the longest Latin word, which is said to have first appeared in 1548 in a volume entitled *The Complaynt of Scotland.* It was used by Thomas Nashe in *Lenten Stuff,* and by Beaumont and Fletcher in *The Mad Lover.* "Flap-dragon" occurs again in *II Henry IV,* ii, 4, 267. "Flap-dragoned" is used in *The Winter's Tale,* iii, 3, 100.

It were a fault to snatch words from my tongue.
Love's Labour's Lost. Act v, sc. 2, l. 382. [Rosaline]

1
Honest plain words best pierce the ear of grief.
Love's Labour 's Lost. Act v, sc. 2, l. 763. [Biron]
True plain words.—*Sonnets,* lxxxii.
2
The words of Mercury are harsh after the songs of Apollo.
Love's Labour 's Lost. Act v, sc. 2, l. 940. [Armado]
3
So well thy words become thee as thy wounds;
They smack of honour both.
Macbeth. Act i, sc. 2, l. 43. [Duncan]
First Senator: That 's well spoke. . . .
These words become your lips as they pass through them.
Second Senator: And enter in our ears like great triumphers
In their applauding gates.
Timon of Athens. Act v, sc. 1, l. 196.
Gracious triumpher.—*Titus Andronicus,* i, 1, 170. The only uses of "triumpher" and "triumphers."
4
There would have been a time for such a word.
Macbeth. Act v, sc. 5, l. 18. [Macbeth]
5 I, that do speak a word,
May call it back again.
Measure for Measure. Act ii, sc. 2, l. 57. [Isabella] See also SPEECH: SPEAKING A WORD.
6
You but waste your words.
Measure for Measure. Act ii, sc. 2, l. 72. [Angelo]
Waste no time in words.—*The Merchant of Venice,* iii, 4, 54.
7
The friar and you Must have a word anon.
Measure for Measure. Act v, sc. 1, l. 363. [Duke]
Hast thou or word, or wit, or impudence,
That yet can do thee office?
Measure for Measure. Act v, sc. 1, l. 368. [Duke]
8
Madam, you have bereft me of all words.
The Merchant of Venice. Act iii, sc. 2, l. 177. [Bassanio]
How every fool can play upon the word!
The Merchant of Venice. Act iii, sc. 5, l. 48. [Lorenzo]
9
O dear discretion, how his words are suited!
The fool hath planted in his memory
An army of good words.
The Merchant of Venice. Act iii, sc. 5, l. 70. [Lorenzo] "Good words" occurs fifteen times in later plays.
Speak a good word . . . for my master.
The Merry Wives of Windsor. Act i, sc. 4, l. 88. [Simple]
10
I would have sworn his disposition would have gone to the truth of his words; but they do no more adhere and keep place together than the Hundredth Psalm to the tune of 'Green Sleeves.'
The Merry Wives of Windsor. Act ii, sc. 1, l. 60. [Mrs. Ford] The only reference to the Hundredth Psalm (Old Hundredth).
11
How much an ill word may empoison liking.
Much Ado about Nothing. Act iii, sc. 1, l. 87. [Hero] The only use of "ill word" and "empoison."
Envenom him with words.—*King John,* iii, 1, 63.
12
I have studied eight or nine wise words to speak to you, which these hobby-horses must not hear.
Much Ado about Nothing. Act iii, sc. 2, l. 73. [Benedick]
13
A word in your ear.
Much Ado about Nothing. Act iv, sc. 2, l. 29. [Dogberry]
One word in your ear.
Troilus and Cressida. Act v, sc. 2, l. 34. [Cressida]
I pray you, let-a me speak a word with your ear.
Merry Wives of Windsor, iii, 1, 31. [Caius]
Shall I speak a word in your ear?
Much Ado about Nothing. Act v, sc. 1, l. 144. [Benedick]
14
I will but spend a word here in the house,
And go with you.
Othello. Act i, sc. 2, l. 48. [Othello]
15
These sentences, to sugar, or to gall,
Being strong on both sides, are equivocal:
But words are words.
Othello. Act i, sc. 3, l. 216. [Brabantio] "Equivocal" is repeated in *All's Well that Ends Well,* v, 3, 250.
Word for word.—*Twelfth Night,* i, 3, 28.
16 I know thou . . .
Weigh'st thy words before thou givest them breath.
Othello. Act iii, sc. 3, l. 118. [Othello]
It is not words that shake me thus.
Othello. Act iv, sc. 1, l. 42. [Othello]
I understand a fury in your words,
But not the words.
Othello. Act iv, sc. 2, l. 32. [Desdemona]
17
Out, idle words, servants to shallow fools!
Unprofitable sounds, weak arbitrators!
The Rape of Lucrece, l. 1016. The only use of "arbitrators." "Arbitrator" occurs in *I Henry VI,* ii, 5, 28, and in *Troilus and Cressida,* iv, 5, 225.
Idle words.—*Taming of the Shrew,* Ind., 2, 85.
18
This helpless smoke of words doth me no right.
The Rape of Lucrece, l. 1027.
Pawn'd honest looks, but laid no words to gage.
The Rape of Lucrece, l. 1351.
19
How long a time lies in one little word!
Four lagging winters and four wanton springs

End in a word: such is the breath of kings.
Richard II. Act i, sc. 3, l. 213. [Bolingbroke] The only use of "lagging."

1
Three words, dear Romeo, and good night indeed.
Romeo and Juliet. Act ii, sc. 2, l. 142. [Juliet]
Three words, conference.—*Much Ado about Nothing,* ii, 1, 278.

2
What say'st thou? hast thou not a word of joy?
Romeo and Juliet. Act iii, sc. 5, l. 213. [Juliet]
Words of heaven.—*Measure for Measure,* i, 2, 126.
Word of peace.—*II Henry IV,* iv, 2, 87.
Word of promise.—*Macbeth,* v, 8, 21.
Words of sovereignty.—*Henry VIII,* i, 2, 150.
Word of a tapster.—*As You Like It,* iii, 4, 34.
Word of war.—*Antony and Cleopatra,* iii, 1, 31; ii, 2, 44.

3
So all my best is dressing old words new,
Spending again what is already spent.
Sonnets. No. lxxvi.
The dedicated words which writers use.
Sonnets. No. lxxxii. See under WRITING.
Words come hindmost.—*Sonnets,* lxxxv. "Hindmost" is repeated in *II Henry VI,* iii, 1, 2, and in *Troilus and Cressida,* iii, 3, 160.

4
Sir, you seem a sober ancient gentleman by your habit, but your words show you a madman.
The Taming of the Shrew. Act v, sc. 1, l. 75. [Tranio]
Thy words are madness.
Twelfth Night. Act v, sc. 1, l. 101. [Duke]

5
For both our sakes, I would that word were true.
The Taming of the Shrew. Act v, sc. 2, l. 15. [Hortensio]
True word.—*Timon of Athens,* v, 1, 135.

6
Silence! one word more
Will make me chide thee, if not hate thee.
The Tempest. Act i, sc. 2, l. 476. [Prospero]
You cram these words into mine ears against
The stomach of my sense.
The Tempest. Act ii, sc. 1, l. 106. [Alonso]

7
Their words are natural breath.
The Tempest, v, 1, 156. See under AMAZEMENT.
Words be made of breath.—*Hamlet,* iii, 4, 197.

8
Will you befriend me so far, as to use mine own words to him?
Timon of Athens. Act iii, sc. 2, l. 64. [Lucius]

9
They that dally nicely with words may quickly make them wanton.
Twelfth Night. Act iii, sc. 1, l. 16. [Viola]
But indeed words are very rascals since bonds disgraced them . . . words are grown so false, I am loath to prove reason with them.
Twelfth Night. Act iii, sc. 1, l. 24. [Clown]
Mistake the word.—*The Two Gentlemen of Verona,* iii, 1, 284.

10
Mark thou my words.
The Winter's Tale. Act iv, sc. 4, l. 441. [Polixenes]

II—One Word

See also Speech: Speaking a Word

11
Good sparks and lustrous, a word, good metals.
All's Well that Ends Well. Act ii, sc. 1, l. 41. [Parolles]
Parolles: I beseech your honour to hear me one single word.
Lafeu: You beg a single penny more: come, you shall ha't; save your word.
All's Well that Ends Well. Act v, sc. 2, l. 37.
Hear me one word; . . . hear me but a word.
If, by the tribunes' leave, and yours, good people,
I may be heard, I would crave a word or two.
Coriolanus. Act iii, sc. 1, l. 215. [Menenius]
Hear me but one word.—*III Henry VI,* i, 1, 170, and with variations twenty-three times in later plays.

12
Let me have audience for a word or two.
As You Like It. Act v, sc. 4, l. 157. [Jaques de Boys]

13
I would crave a word or two.
Coriolanus. Act iii, sc. 1, l. 283. [Menenius]
Madam, your mother craves a word with you.
Romeo and Juliet. Act i, sc. 5, l. 113. [Nurse]

14
Vouchsafe me speak a word.
The Comedy of Errors. Act v, sc. 1, l. 282. [Ægeon]
Guildenstern: Good my lord, vouchsafe me a word with you.
Hamlet: Sir, a whole history.
Hamlet. Act iii, sc. 2, l. 307.
Dumain: Will you vouchsafe with me to change a word?
Maria: Name it.
Love's Labour's Lost. Act v, sc. 2, l. 238.
Vouchsafe a word, young sister, but one word.
Measure for Measure. Act iii, sc. 1, l. 152. [Duke]
Mistress Quickly: Shall I vouchsafe your worship a word or two?
Falstaff: Two thousand, fair woman: and I'll vouchsafe thee the hearing.
Merry Wives of Windsor. Act ii, sc. 2, l. 41.
I beseech your honour, vouchsafe me a word.
Timon of Athens. Act i, sc. 2, l. 183. [Flavius]
Will you vouchsafe me a word?
Troilus and Cressida. Act iii, sc. 1, l. 64. [Pandarus] Shakespeare was fond of "vouchsafe" and used it no less than fifty-two times.

15
Shall I entreat a word?
Julius Cæsar. Act ii, sc. 1, l. 100. [Cassius]
List a word.—*Julius Cæsar,* v, 5, 15.
I'll talk a word with this same learned Theban. . . .
Let me ask you one word in private.
King Lear. Act iii, sc. 4, l. 162. [King Lear]
A word, good sir; . . . a word.
The Tempest. Act i, sc. 2, l. 442. [Prospero]

Thou fellow, a word.—*Love's Labour's Lost,* iv, 1, 102.
A word, I pray you.—*Macbeth,* i, 3, 127.
Pray you, a word.—*Troilus and Cressida,* iii, 1, 1.
Hark, a word with you.—*Troilus and Cressida,* v, 2, 7.

1
Claudio: One word, good friend. Lucio, a word with you.
Lucio: A hundred, if they 'll do you any good.
Measure for Measure. Act i, sc. 2, l. 146.
A word or two with Claudio.—*Measure for Measure,* iii, 1, 48.

2
Duke: Provost, a word with you.
Provost: As many as you please.
Measure for Measure. Act iii, sc. 1, l. 50.
A word with you.—*Richard III,* iii, 4, 37, and seven times in later plays.
One word more.—*II Henry IV,* Epil., 29, and eight times in later plays.
One word, sir.—*Much Ado about Nothing,* iii, 5, 49.

3
Master Slender would speak a word with you.
The Merry Wives of Windsor. Act iii, sc. 4, l. 30. [Mistress Quickly]
I would speak a word with you!—*Othello,* v, 2, 90.
Hear me speak a word.—*Antony and Cleopatra,* ii, 7, 42.

4
A word or two before you go.
Othello. Act v, sc. 2, l. 338. [Othello]
A word ere you go.—*The Taming of the Shrew,* i, 2, 229.

5
O my friends, I have one word to say to you.
Timon of Athens. Act i, sc. 2, l. 174. [Timon]

III—Sending and Bringing Word

6
I brought you word an hour since.
The Comedy of Errors. Act iv, sc. 3, l. 37. [Dromio of Syracuse]
Brought word.—*II Henry IV,* ii, 4, 20.

7
Send them word you will not come.
Julius Cæsar. Act ii, sc. 2, l. 95. [Decius]
Send him (you) word.—*II Henry VI,* iii, 2, 243, and frequently in later plays.
Sends word.—*Pericles,* ii, Gower, 22.

8 Bring us word unto Octavius' tent
How everything is chanced.
Julius Cæsar. Act v, sc. 5, l. 31. [Antony]
Bring me word.—*Antony and Cleopatra,* ii, 5, 118.
Brings word.—*The Merchant of Venice,* i, 2, 138; v, 1, 28; *Troilus and Cressida,* iii, 3, 34.

9
I must carry her word quickly.
The Merry Wives of Windsor. Act iii, sc. 5, l. 48. [Mistress Quickly]

10
He sent me word to stay within.
The Merry Wives of Windsor. Act iii, sc. 5, l. 59. [Falstaff]
He sent me word.—*As You Like It,* v, 4, 74.
I sent him word.—*As You Like It,* v, 4, 76.
Sent word.—*I Henry IV,* iii, 2, 164.

11
Achilles shall have word of this intent.
Troilus and Cressida. Act i, sc. 3, l. 306. [Agamemnon]

IV—Sweet Words

12 His plausive words
He scatter'd not in ears, but grafted them,
To grow there and to bear.
All's Well that Ends Well. Act i, sc. 2, l. 53. [King] "Plausive" is repeated in iv, 1, 29: "Plausive invention"; and in *Hamlet,* i, 4, 30: "Plausive manners."
Whose words all ears took captive.
All's Well that Ends Well. Act v, sc. 3, l. 17. [Lafeu]
Alone she was, and did communicate to herself her own words to her own ears.
All's Well that Ends Well. Act i, sc. 3, l. 111. [Steward]

13
What care I for words? yet words do well
When he that speaks them pleases those that hear.
As You Like It. Act iii, sc. 5, l. 111. [Phebe]

14
Never words were music to thine ear, . . .
Unless I spake.
The Comedy of Errors. Act ii, sc. 2, l. 116. [Adriana]

15
Take in a town with gentle words.
Coriolanus. Act iii, sc. 2, l. 59. [Volumnia]
Gentle words will not prevail.
II Henry VI. Act iv, sc. 2, l. 184. [Stafford]
Speak gentle words and humbly bend thy knee.
III Henry VI. Act v, sc. 1, l. 22. [King Edward]
Let 's fight with gentle words
Till time lend friends and friends their helpful swords.
Richard II. Act iii, sc. 3, l. 131. [Aumerle]

16
Each word thou hast spoke hath weeded from my heart
A root of ancient envy.
Coriolanus. Act iv, sc. 5, l. 108. [Aufidius] The only use of "weeded."

17 Words of so sweet breath composed
As made the things more rich.
Hamlet. Act iii, sc. 1, l. 98. [Ophelia]
His purse is empty already; all 's golden words are spent.
Hamlet. Act v, sc. 2, l. 136. [Horatio]
Golden words.—*The Rape of Lucrece,* l. 1430.

18
Rare words! brave world!
I Henry IV. Act iii, sc. 3, l. 229. [Falstaff]
Admirable rich words.—*Cymbeline,* ii, 3, 20.
Charming words.—*Cymbeline,* i, 3, 35.
Comfortable words.—*Richard II,* ii, 2, 76.
Earnest words.—*II Henry VI,* iii, 2, 316.
Heart-easing words.—*The Rape of Lucrece,* l. 1782. The only use of "heart-easing."
Loving words.—*The Two Gentlemen of Verona,* i, 2, 105; *King John,* iv, 1, 51.
Moving words.—*III Henry VI,* iii, 1, 34; *The Two Gentlemen of Verona,* v, 4, 55.

Successful words.—*The Taming of the Shrew,* i, 2, 158.
Words of sooth.—*Richard II,* iii, 3, 136.

1
A' uttered as prave words at the pridge as you shall see in a summer's day.
Henry V. Act iii, sc. 6, l. 66. [Fluellen]
Brave words.—*As You Like It,* iii, 4, 44.

2
Words sweetly placed and modestly directed.
I Henry VI. Act v, sc. 3, l. 179. [Suffolk]

3
Those gracious words revive my drooping thoughts
And give my tongue-tied sorrows leave to speak.
III Henry VI. Act iii, sc. 3, l. 21. [Queen Margaret]
Gracious words.—*Love's Labour's Lost,* ii, 1, 73.

4
Your words,
Domestics to you, serve your will as 't please
Yourself pronounce their office.
Henry VIII. Act ii, sc. 4, l. 113. [Queen Katharine]

5
Cassius: But for your words, they rob the Hybla bees,
And leave them honeyless.
Antony: Not stingless too.
Brutus: O, yes, and soundless too;
For you have stol'n their buzzing, Antony,
And very wisely threat before you sting.
Julius Cæsar. Act v, sc. 1, l. 34. The only use of "honeyless" and "stingless." "Soundless" is repeated in *Sonnets,* lxxx. "Buzzing" occurs five times.

My woman's heart
Grossly grew captive to his honey words.
Richard III. Act iv, sc. 1, l. 79. [Anne]
Words more sweet, and yet more dangerous,
Than baits to fish, or honey-stalks to sheep.
Titus Andronicus. Act iv, sc. 4, l. 90. [Tamora] The only use of "honey-stalks."

6
Biron: White-handed mistress, one sweet word with thee.
Princess of France: Honey, and milk, and sugar; there is three.
Biron: Nay, then, two treys, and if you grow so nice,
Metheglin, wort, and malmsey.
Love's Labour's Lost. Act v, sc. 2, l. 230. The only use of "white-handed," "treys," "metheglin" (a spiced drink made from wort and honey), "wort," and "malmsey." "Metheglins" occurs in *The Merry Wives of Windsor,* v, 5, 167: "Given to . . . metheglins."
Biron: One word in secret.
Princess: Let it not be sweet.
Love's Labour's Lost. Act v, sc. 2, l. 236.
Sweet words.—*Julius Cæsar,* iii, 1, 42; *Cymbeline,* v, 3, 72.

7
They did not bless us with one happy word.
Love's Labour's Lost. Act v, sc. 2, l. 370. [Rosaline] The only use of "happy word."

I implore so much expense of thy royal sweet breath as will utter a brace of words.
Love's Labour's Lost. Act v, sc. 2, l. 523. [Armado]

8
She has here spoken holy words.
Pericles. Act iv, sc. 6, l. 142. [Boult]
Close our hands with holy words.—*Romeo and Juliet,* ii, 6, 6. See under MARRIAGE.
Holy word.—*King John,* v, 1, 5.

9
For God's sake, entertain good comfort,
And cheer his grace with quick and merry words.
Richard III. Act i, sc. 3, l. 4. [Grey]
Your grace attended to their sugar'd words,
But look'd not on the poison of their hearts.
Richard III. Act iii, sc. 1, l. 13. [Gloucester] "Sugar'd words" occurs also in *I Henry VI,* iii, 3, 18, and *II Henry VI,* iii, 2, 45. "Sugar'd game" is used in *Timon of Athens,* iv, 3, 259.

10
Pandarus: Fair be to you, my lord, and to all this fair company! fair desires, in all fair measure, fairly guide them! especially to you, fair queen! fair thoughts to your fair pillow!
Helen: Dear lord, you are full of fair words.
Troilus and Cressida. Act iii, sc. 1, l. 46.
Fair words.—*II Henry IV,* iv, 4, 104; *Coriolanus,* iii, 3, 91; *Romeo and Juliet,* ii, 1, 11; *Antony and Cleopatra,* ii, 6, 67; *Venus and Adonis,* l. 208.
Guileful fair words.—*I Henry VI,* i, 1, 77. "Guileful" is repeated in *Titus Andronicus,* v, 1, 104.

11
My words are as full of peace as matter.
Twelfth Night. Act i, sc. 5, l. 226. [Viola]
Peaceful words.—*II Henry VI,* i, 1, 122.

12
I Do come with words as medicinal as true,
Honest as either.
Winter's Tale. Act ii, sc. 3, l. 36. [Paulina] "Medicinal" is repeated in *Othello,* v, 2, 351.

V—Bitter Words

13
Ah, what sharp stings are in her mildest words!
All's Well that Ends Well. Act iii, sc. 4, l. 18. [Countess]

14
As fast as she answers thee with frowning looks, I 'll sauce her with bitter words.
As You Like It. Act iii, sc. 5, l. 68. [Rosalind]
These are very bitter words.
II Henry IV. Act ii, sc. 4, l. 184. [Hostess]
Bitter words to ban her cruel foes.
The Rape of Lucrece, l. 1460.
And in the breath of bitter words let 's smother
My damned son, which thy two sweet sons smother'd.
Richard III. Act iv, sc. 4, l. 133. [Duchess of York]
When did she cross thee with a bitter word?
The Taming of the Shrew. Act ii, sc. 1, l. 28. [Baptista]

1 Ethiope words, blacker in their effect
Than in their countenance.
As You Like It. Act iv, sc. 3, l. 35. [Rosalind]

2
Brutus: Sir, I hope
My words disbench'd you not.
Coriolanus: No, sir; yet oft,
When blows have made me stay, I fled from words.
Coriolanus. Act ii, sc. 2, l. 74. The only use of "disbench'd" (causing a person to leave his seat).

Such words that are but roted in
Your tongue, though but bastards and syllables
Of no allowance to your bosom's truth.
Coriolanus. Act iii, sc. 2, l. 55. [Volumnia] The only use of "roted" (learned by rote).

3
Have you given him any hard words of late?
Hamlet. Act ii, sc. 1, l. 107. [Polonius] The only use of "hard words."

These words, like daggers, enter in mine ears.
Hamlet. Act iii, sc. 4, l. 95. [Queen]

I have words to speak in thine ear will make thee dumb.
Hamlet. Act iv, sc. 6, l. 24. [Horatio]

4
These words of yours draw life-blood from my heart.
I Henry VI. Act iv, sc. 6, l. 43. [John Talbot]

5
Whitmore: Speak, captain, shall I stab the forlorn swain?
Captain: First let my words stab him, as he hath me.
Suffolk: Base slave, thy words are blunt and so art thou.
II Henry VI. Act iv, sc. 1, l. 65.

Every word stabs.—*Much Ado about Nothing,* ii, 1, 255.

6 If we should recount
Our baleful news, and at each word's deliverance
Stab poniards in our flesh till all were told,
The words would add more anguish than the wounds.
III Henry VI. Act ii, sc. 1, l. 96. [Richard]

These words will cost ten thousand lives this day.
III Henry VI. Act ii, sc. 2, l. 177. [Edward]

7
And now, instead of bullets wrapp'd in fire,
To make a shaking fever in your walls,
They shoot but calm words folded up in smoke,
To make a faithless error in your ears.
King John. Act ii, sc. 1, l. 227. [King John]

O, that a man should speak those words to me!
King John. Act iii, sc. 1, l. 130. [Austria]

8 I have words
That would be howl'd out in the desert air,
Where hearing should not latch them.
Macbeth. Act iv, sc. 3, l. 193. [Ross]

Choleric word.—*Measure for Measure,* ii, 2, 130.

Dangerous words.—*Much Ado about Nothing,* v, 1, 97.

9
Here are a few of the unpleasant'st words
That ever blotted paper!
The Merchant of Venice. Act iii, sc. 2, l. 254. [Bassanio] The only use of "unpleasant'st."

A tricksy word.—*The Merchant of Venice,* iii, 5, 74. "Tricksy" is repeated in *The Tempest,* v, 1, 226: "Tricksy spirit."

10
What he gets more of her than sharp words, let it lie on my head.
The Merry Wives of Windsor. Act ii, sc. 1, l. 190. [Page]

11
I am amazed at your passionate words.
A Midsummer-Night's Dream. Act iii, sc. 2, l. 220. [Hermia]

Methinks his words do from such passion fly,
That he believes himself: so do not I.
Twelfth Night. Act iii, sc. 4, l. 407. [Viola]

12
Queen Elizabeth: My words are dull; O, quicken them with thine!
Queen Margaret: Thy woes will make them sharp, and pierce like mine.
Richard III. Act iv, sc. 4, l. 124.

Her words are done, her woes the more increasing.
Venus and Adonis, l. 254.

Woeful words.—*Venus and Adonis,* l. 1126.

Word of woe.—*The Rape of Lucrece,* l. 1605.

13
Ah, word ill urged to one that is so ill!
Romeo and Juliet. Act i, sc. 1, l. 209. [Romeo]

14
Be thou arm'd for some unhappy words.
The Taming of the Shrew. Act ii, sc. 1, l. 140. [Baptista]

15
Lips, let sour words go by and language end:
What is amiss plague and infection mend!
Timon of Athens. Act v, sc. 1, l. 223. [Timon]

16
O monstrous! what reproachful words are these?
Titus Andronicus. Act i, sc. 1, l. 308. [Titus]

These words are razors to my wounded heart.
Titus Andronicus. Act i, sc. 1, l. 314. [Titus] The only use of "razors." "Razor" occurs in *Love's Labour's Lost,* v, 2, 257, and in *Pericles,* v, 3, 75.

Let them hear what fearful words I utter.
Titus Andronicus. Act v, sc. 2, l. 169. [Titus]

17
Go in to Troy, and say there, Hector's dead:
There is a word will Priam turn to stone.
Troilus and Cressida, v, 10, 17. [Troilus]

18
She gave me none, except an angry word.
The Two Gentlemen of Verona. Act ii, sc. 1, l. 164. [Valentine]

Foul words and frowns must not repel a lover.
Venus and Adonis, l. 573.

19
Forewarn him that he use no scurrilous words.
The Winter's Tale. Act iv, sc. 4, l. 216. [Perdita] The only use of "forewarn" and "scurrilous."

VI—Few Words

1
What needs more words?
Antony and Cleopatra. Act ii, sc. 7, l. 132. [Cæsar]

2
Celia: Not a word?
Rosalind: Not one to throw at a dog.
Celia: No, thy words are too precious to be cast away upon curs; throw some of them at me.
As You Like It. Act i, sc. 3, l. 2.

What, not a word?—*Romeo and Juliet,* iv, 5, 4. "Not a word" is repeated eight times in later plays.

3
Not one word more of the consumed time.
All's Well that Ends Well. Act v, sc. 3, l. 38. [King]

Not one word more.—*Love's Labour's Lost,* v, 2, 262; *Timon of Athens,* iv, 2, 28.
Not a word more.—*Winter's Tale,* iv, 4, 251.

4
If their purgation did consist in words,
They are as innocent as grace itself.
As You Like It. Act i, sc. 3, l. 55. [Duke]

Hoping to purge himself with words.—*Coriolanus,* v, 6, 9.

5
No more words, we beseech you.
Coriolanus. Act iii, sc. 1, l. 75. [Senator]

No more words.—*III Henry VI,* ii, 5, 72; *Measure for Measure,* iii, 2, 218; *Much Ado about Nothing,* ii, 1, 115; *Troilus and Cressida,* ii, 1, 124.

6
That ever this fellow should have fewer words than a parrot, and yet the son of a woman!
I Henry IV. Act ii, sc. 4, l. 110. [Prince]

Take heed, be wary how you place your words;
Talk like the vulgar sort of market men
That come to gather money for their corn.
I Henry VI. Act iii, sc. 2, l. 3. [La Pucelle]

7
Seal up your lips, and give no words but mum.
II Henry VI, i, 2, 89. See under SECRECY.

No word to your master that I am yet come to town.
II Henry IV. Act ii, sc. 2, l. 177. [Prince]

No words!—*Love's Labour's Lost,* i, 1, 231; *A Midsummer-Night's Dream,* ii, 2, 152.

8
Have done with words, my lords.
III Henry VI. Act ii, sc. 2, l. 117. [King Henry]

Ha' done with words.—*The Taming of the Shrew,* iii, 2, 118.

9
Few words,
But such as I, without your special pardon,
Dare not relate.
III Henry VI. Act iv, sc. 1, l. 86. [Post]

Few words, but, to effect.
King Lear. Act iii, sc. 1, l. 52. [Kent]

'Twixt such friends as we Few words suffice.
The Taming of the Shrew. Act i, sc. 2, l. 66. [Petruchio]

Few words to fair faith.
Troilus and Cressida. Act iii, sc. 2, l. 103. [Troilus]

Few words.—*Macbeth,* iii, 2, 4.
In few words.—*III Henry VI,* iv, 7, 53; *Timon of Athens,* iii, 5, 97.

10
I 'll not trouble thee with words.
III Henry VI. Act v, sc. 5, l. 5. [Oxford]

11
I have not yet made known to Mariana
A word of this.
Measure for Measure. Act iv, sc. 1, l. 49. [Duke]

Come, no more words of it.—*II Henry IV,* ii, 1, 150.
Let 's have no words of this.—*Hamlet,* iv, 5, 46.

12
Evans: Pauca verba, Sir John, goot worts.
Falstaff: Good worts! good cabbage.
The Merry Wives of Windsor. Act i, sc. 1, l. 123. The only use of "cabbage," and of "worts." "Wort" occurs in *Love's Labour 's Lost,* v, 2, 233. "Pauca verba" is repeated in *Love's Labour 's Lost,* iv, 2, 171.

Pauca loquitur.—*Love's Labour 's Lost,* iv, 2, 83. The only use of the phrase.
My words are brief.—*The Rape of Lucrece,* l. 1309.

13
Gaunt: O, to what purpose dost thou hoard thy words,
That thou return'st no greeting to thy friends?
Bolingbroke: I have too few to take my leave of you,
When the tongue's office should be so prodigal
To breathe the abundant dolour of the heart.
Richard II. Act i, sc. 3, l. 253.

Where words are scarce, they are seldom spent in vain,
For they breathe truth that breathe their words in pain.
Richard II. Act ii, sc. 1, l. 7. [Gaunt]

Wanting words.—*Sonnets,* xxvi.

14
Maintain no words with him, good fellow.
Twelfth Night. Act iv, sc. 2, l. 107. [Clown]

Without more words.—*The Taming of the Shrew,* i, 2, 232.

VII—Many Words

15
I love not many words.
All's Well that Ends Well. Act iii, sc. 6, l. 91. [Parolles]

I am not of many words.
Much Ado about Nothing. Act i, sc. 1, l. 158. [Don John]

16
It is not a confident brow, nor the throng of words that come with such more than impudent sauciness from you, can thrust me from a level consideration.
II Henry IV. Act ii, sc. 1, l. 122. [Chief Justice]

17
Why should she live, to fill the world with words?
III Henry VI. Act v, sc. 5, l. 44. [Gloucester]

Vex him with eager words.—*III Henry VI,* ii, 6, 68.

1 Not a word of his
But buffets better than a fist of France:
Zounds! I was never so bethump'd with words
Since I first call'd my brother's father dad.
King John. Act ii, sc. 1, l. 464. [Bastard] The only use of "bethump'd."

This all-changing word.—*King John,* ii, 1, 582. The only use of "all-changing."

2
A man of fire-new words.
Love's Labour's Lost. Act i, sc. 1, l. 179. [Biron] "Fire-new" is used four times.

How low soever the matter, I hope in God for high words.
Love's Labour's Lost. Act i, sc. 1, l. 194. [Biron] The only use of "high words."

High-born words.—*Love's Labour's Lost,* i, 1, 173. "High-born" is repeated in *King John,* v, 2, 79.

3
Thou wilt be like a lover presently
And tire the hearer with a book of words.
Much Ado about Nothing. Act i, sc. 1, l. 308. [Don Pedro]

Now is he turned orthography; his words are a very fantastical banquet, just so many strange dishes.
Much Ado about Nothing. Act ii, sc. 3, l. 21. [Benedick]

Rackers of orthography.—*Love's Labour's Lost,* v, 1, 22. The only uses of "orthography."

4 Through his lips do throng
Weak words, so thick come in his poor heart's aid,
That no man could distinguish what he said.
The Rape of Lucrece, l. 1783.

Sportive words.—*The Rape of Lucrece,* l. 1813.

5 Impute his words
To wayward sickliness and age in him.
Richard II. Act ii, sc. 1, l. 141. [York] The only use of "sickliness."

His words come from his mouth, ours from our breast.
Richard II. Act v, sc. 3, l. 102. [Duchess of York]

6
Duchess of York: Why should calamity be full of words?
Queen Elizabeth: Windy attorneys to their client woes,
Airy succeeders of intestate joys,
Poor breathing orators of miseries!
Let them have scope: though what they do impart
Help not at all, yet do they ease the heart.
Richard III. Act iv, sc. 4, l. 126. The only use of "intestate." "Succeeders" is repeated in v, 5, 30, and occurs in no other play.

7
To what end are all these words?
The Taming of the Shrew. Act i, sc. 2, l. 250. [Petruchio]

I will be free
Even to the uttermost, as I please, in words.
The Taming of the Shrew. Act iv, sc. 3, l. 79. [Katharina]

8
A fine volley of words, gentlemen, and quickly shot off.
The Two Gentlemen of Verona. Act ii, sc. 4, l. 33. [Silvia]

You have an exchequer of words.
The Two Gentlemen of Verona. Act ii, sc. 4, l. 43. [Valentine]

9
Free vent of words love's fire doth assuage.
Venus and Adonis, l. 334.

VIII—Keeping One's Word

See also Bond

10
Many a man would take you at your word.
The Comedy of Errors. Act i, sc. 2, l. 17. [Dromio of Syracuse]

I'll take the ghost's word for a thousand pound.
Hamlet. Act iii, sc. 2, l. 297. [Hamlet]

Archbishop of York: I take your princely word for these redresses.
Lancaster: I give it you, and will maintain my word.
II Henry IV. Act iv, sc. 2, l. 66.

Take the word of a king and a bachelor.
Henry V. Act v, sc. 2, l. 229. [King Henry]

It was well done of you to take him at his word.
Love's Labour's Lost. Act ii, sc. 1, l. 217. [Princess of France]

You may take my word, my lord.—*Timon of Athens,* i, 2, 220.

I take thee at thy word.—*Romeo and Juliet,* ii, 2, 49.

I will take thy word.—*Romeo and Juliet,* ii, 2, 91.

I'll take thy word for faith.—*Pericles,* i, 2, 120.

11
His word might bear my wealth at any time.
The Comedy of Errors. Act v, sc. 1, l. 8. [Angelo]

I to thee engaged a prince's word.
The Comedy of Errors. Act v, sc. 1, l. 162. [Duke]

12
Each word made true and good.
Hamlet. Act i, sc. 2, l. 210. [Horatio]

13
O, but she'll keep her word.
Hamlet. Act iii, sc. 2, l. 241. [Hamlet]

I judge
By his blunt bearing he will keep his word.
Henry V. Act iv, sc. 8, l. 184. [King Henry]

Had I but said, I would have kept my word.
II Henry VI, iii, 2, 293. See under OATH.

Senators: 'Tis most nobly spoken.
Alcibiades: Descend, and keep your words.
Timon of Athens. Act v, sc. 4, l. 63.

Now keep your holy word.
King John. Act v, sc. 1, l. 5. [King John]

Keep thy word justly.—*King Lear,* iii, 4, 83.

Keep my word.—*The Taming of the Shrew,* iii, 2, 108; *A Midsummer-Night's Dream,* iii, 2, 226.

Keep thy word.—*I Henry IV,* i, 2, 135; *Henry V,* iv, 1, 238.

Keep you your word.—*As You Like It*, v, 4, 19.
Keep your word.—*As You Like It*, v, 4, 21; 23.
Keep his word.—*I Henry IV*, v, 2, 5; *Henry V*, iv, 7, 185; *Troilus and Cressida*, v, 1, 102.
Keep word, Lysander.—*A Midsummer-Night's Dream*, i, 1, 222.
Keeping thy word.—*I Henry IV*, i, 2, 135.

1
I will engage my word to thee.
I Henry IV. Act ii, sc. 4, l. 563. [Prince]

2
Darest thou be as good as thy word now?
I Henry IV. Act iii, sc. 3, l. 163. [Prince]
Sir, I will be as good as my word.
II Henry IV. Act v, sc. 5, l. 90. [Falstaff]
I have been as good as my word.
Henry V. Act iv, sc. 8, l. 33. [Williams]
I 'll be as good as my word.
The Merry Wives of Windsor, iii, 4, 112; *Twelfth Night*, iii, 4, 357.

3
Nay, task me to my word.
I Henry IV. Act iv, sc. 1, l. 9. [Hotspur]
Better than my word I am.—*I Henry IV*, i, 2, 234.

4 Be it your charge, my lord,
To see perform'd the tenour of our word.
II Henry IV. Act v, sc. 5, l. 74. [King Henry]

5
Rescued is Orleans from the English:
Thus Joan la Pucelle hath perform'd her word.
I Henry VI. Act i, sc. 6, l. 2. [La Pucelle]

6
Darest thou maintain the former words thou spakest?
I Henry VI. Act iii, sc. 4, l. 31. [Vernon]
By him that made me, I 'll maintain my words
On any plot of ground in Christendom.
I Henry VI. Act ii, sc. 4, l. 88. [Somerset]
Sir John stands to his word.—*I Henry IV*, i, 2, 130.

7 The noble lord
Most honourably doth uphold his word.
Love's Labour's Lost. Act v, sc. 2, l. 448. [Princess]

8
You yet shall hold your word.
The Merry Wives of Windsor. Act v, sc. 5, l. 258. [Ford]
O' my word.—*Coriolanus*, i, 3, 62; *Romeo and Juliet*, i, 1, 1; *Taming of the Shrew*, i, 2, 108.
On my word.—*The Merry Wives of Windsor*, iv, 2, 61; 79.

9 Your grace's word shall serve,
As well as I had seen and heard him speak.
Richard III. Act iii, sc. 5, l. 62. [Mayor]
Rest on my word.—*Titus Andronicus*, i, 1, 267.
I have pass'd My word.—*Titus Andronicus*, i, 1, 469.
Pass his word.—*Twelfth Night*, i, 5, 87.

10
Troilus: You know now your hostages; your uncle's word and my firm faith.
Pandarus: Nay, I 'll give my word for her too.
Troilus and Cressida. Act iii, sc. 2, l. 115.

11
His words are bonds.
The Two Gentlemen of Verona. Act ii, sc. 7, l. 75. [Julia] See under BOND.

IX—Breaking One's Word

12
The time was, father, that you broke your word,
When you were more endear'd to it than now.
II Henry IV. Act ii, sc. 3, l. 10. [Lady Percy]
I break my warlike word.
I Henry VI. Act iv, sc. 3, l. 31. [York]
The regent hath with Talbot broke his word.
I Henry VI. Act iv, sc. 6, l. 2. [Talbot]
Breaks words.—*Henry V*, iii, 2, 37.

13
They are not men o' their words.
King Lear. Act iv, sc. 6, l. 106. [King Lear]

14
It is prodigious, there will come some change; the sun borrows of the moon, when Diomed keeps his word.
Troilus and Cressida. Act v, sc. 1, l. 100. [Thersites]
I will not keep my word.
Troilus and Cressida. Act v, sc. 2, l. 98. [Cressida]

X—Individual Words

15 Our courteous Antony,
Whom ne'er the word of 'No' woman heard speak.
Antony and Cleopatra. Act ii, sc. 2, l. 227. [Enobarbus]

16 Now to my word;
It is 'Adieu, adieu! remember me.'
Hamlet. Act i, sc. 5, l. 110. [Hamlet]
The words that follow'd
Should be 'Remember mine.'
The Winter's Tale, v, 1, 66. See under EYE.

17 There is not such a word
Spoke of in Scotland as this term of fear.
I Henry IV, iv, 1, 84. See under SCOTLAND.
What is honour? a word.—*I Henry IV*, v, 1, 136. See under HONOUR.

18
God's light, these villains will make the word as odious as the word 'occupy'; which was an excellent good word before it was ill sorted.
II Henry IV. Act ii, sc. 4, l. 160. [Doll Tearsheet] "Occupy" is repeated in *Romeo and Juliet*, ii, 4, 105.
This word 'sallet' was born to do me good.
II Henry VI. Act iv, sc. 10, l. 11. [Cade] "Sallet" (salad) is used three times in this scene, and also in *Hamlet*, ii, 2, 462, and *King Lear*, iii, 4, 137.

19
'Couple a gorge!' That is the word.
Henry V. Act ii, sc. 1, l. 76. [Pistol]
'Cover' is the word.—*The Merchant of Venice*, iii, 5, 57.
Death 's the word.—*Antony and Cleopatra*, i, 2, 139.
Hanging is the word.—*Cymbeline*, v, 4, 155.
Slaying is the word.—*Julius Cæsar*, v, 5, 4.

O me, the word 'choose!'—*The Merchant of Venice,* i, 2, 24.
The word 'farewell.'—*Richard II,* i, 4, 16.
That word 'judgement.'—*Richard III,* i, 4, 109.
That same word, rebellion.—*II Henry IV,* i, 1, 194.
With this word 'Stand, stand.'—*Cymbeline,* v, 3, 31.

1 The word is 'Pitch and Pay.'
Henry V. Act ii, sc. 3, l. 51. [Pistol]
Hob, nob, is his word: give 't or take 't.
Twelfth Night, iii, 4, 263. [Sir Toby]

2 Submission, Dauphin! 'tis a mere French word.
I Henry VI, iv, 7, 54. See under SUBMISSION.

3 This word 'love,' which greybeards call divine.
III Henry VI, v, 6, 81. See under LOVE.
Fine word,—legitimate!
King Lear. Act i, sc. 2, l. 18. [Edmund]
His word was still,—Fie, foh and fum,
I smell the blood of a British man.
King Lear. Act iii, sc. 4, l. 188. [Edgar]

4 Remuneration! . . . I will never buy and sell out of this word.
Love's Labour 's Lost. Act iii, sc. 1, l. 143. [Costard]
Defile! a foul word.
Love's Labour 's Lost. Act iv, sc. 3, l. 3. [Biron]

5 He clepeth a calf, cauf; half, hauf; neighbour vocatur nebour; neigh abbreviated ne.
Love's Labour 's Lost. Act v, sc. 1, l. 24. [Holofernes] The only use of "clepeth."

6 His words were 'Farewell, mistress;' nothing else.
The Merchant of Venice. Act ii, sc. 5, l. 45. [Jessica]
The words expressly are 'a pound of flesh.'
The Merchant of Venice. Act iv, sc. 1, l. 307. [Portia]
A Daniel, still say I, a second Daniel!
I thank thee, Jew, for teaching me that word.
The Merchant of Venice. Act iv, sc. 1, l. 340. [Gratiano]

7 Evans: What is he, William, that does lend articles?
William: Articles are borrowed of the pronoun, and be thus declined, Singulariter, nominativo, hic, hæc, hoc. . . .
Mistress Quickly: You do ill to teach the child such words: he teaches him to hick and to hack, . . . and to call 'horum:' fie upon you.
The Merry Wives of Windsor. Act iv, sc. 1, l. 39. The only use of "singulariter," of "hic, hæc, hoc," and of "hick." "Pronoun" occurs again in the same scene, l. 77, "nominativo" in l. 44, and "horum" in l. 63. None is used in any other scene.

8 'Wander,' a word for shadows like myself.
The Passionate Pilgrim, l. 191.

9 The hopeless word of 'never to return'
Breathe I against thee.
Richard II, i, 3, 152. See under BANISHMENT.
The word 'grace'
In an ungracious mouth is but profane.
Richard II, ii, 3, 88. See under GRACE.

10 An if I were thy nurse, thy tongue to teach,
'Pardon' should be the first word of thy speech.
Richard II, v, 3, 113. See under PARDON.
Pardon 's the word to all.—*Cymbeline,* v, 5, 422.

11 Our ancient word of courage, fair Saint George.
Richard III, v, 3, 349. See under ENGLAND.

12 I stretch it out for that word 'broad.'
Romeo and Juliet. Act ii, sc. 4, l. 89. [Romeo]
Some word there was, worser than Tybalt's death,
That murder'd me: I would forget it fain;
But, O, it presses to my memory,
Like damned guilty deeds to sinners' minds:
'Tybalt is dead, and Romeo—banished;'
That 'banished,' that one word 'banished,'
Hath slain ten thousand Tybalts. . . .
There is no end, no limit, measure, bound,
In that word's death; no words can that woe sound.
Romeo and Juliet. Act iii, sc. 2, l. 108. [Juliet]
Friar Laurence: The kind prince hath . . .
Turn'd that black word death to banishment.
Romeo: . . . 'Banished'?
O friar, the damned use that word in hell;
Howlings attend it: how hast thou the heart,
Being a divine, a ghostly confessor,
A sin-absolver, and my friend profess'd,
To mangle me with that word 'banished'?
Friar Laurence: Thou fond mad man, hear me but speak a word. . . .
I 'll give thee armour to keep off that word.
Romeo and Juliet. Act iii, sc. 3, l. 25. The only use of "sin-absolver."

13 I will construe to them whence you come; who you are and what you would are out of my welkin, I might say 'element,' but the word is over-worn.
Twelfth Night. Act iii, sc. 1, l. 63. [Clown]
Vent my folly! he has heard that word of some great man and now applies it to a fool.
Twelfth Night. Act iv, sc. 1, l. 12. [Clown]

XI—Word and Deed

14 If thou proceed
As high as word, my deed shall match thy meed.
All's Well that Ends Well, ii, 1, 212. [King]

15 Ill deeds are doubled with an evil word.
The Comedy of Errors, iii, 2, 20. [Luciana]

16 Let deeds express
What 's like to be their words.
Coriolanus. Act iii, sc. 1, l. 132. [Coriolanus]
Hadst thou foxship
To banish him that struck more blows for Rome
Than thou hast spoken words? . . .

More noble blows than ever thou wise words;
And for Rome's good.
Coriolanus. Act iv, sc. 2, l. 18. [Volumnia] The only use of "foxship" (ingratitude).

1
Thy words, I grant, are bigger, for I wear not
My dagger in my mouth.
Cymbeline. Act iv, sc. 2, l. 78. [Guiderius]

2 If he says he loves you,
It fits your wisdom so far to believe it
As he in his particular act and place
May give his saying deed.
Hamlet. Act i, sc. 3, l. 24. [Laertes]

The harlot's cheek, beautied with plastering art,
Is not more ugly to the thing that helps it
Than is my deed to my most painted word.
Hamlet. Act iii, sc. 1, l. 51. [King] The only use of "beautied" and "plastering."

Suit the action to the word, the word to the action.
Hamlet. Act iii, sc. 2, l. 19. [Hamlet]

What would you undertake,
To show yourself your father's son in deed
More than in words?
Hamlet. Act iv, sc. 7, l. 125. [King]

3
Turning the word to sword and life to death.
II Henry IV. Act iv, sc. 2, l. 10. [Lancaster]

4
He hath heard that men of few words are the best men; and therefore he scorns to say his prayers, lest a' should be thought a coward: but his few bad words are matched with as few good deeds.
Henry V. Act iii, sc. 2, l. 38. [Boy]

Dare not avouch in your deeds any of your words?
Henry V. Act v, sc. 1, l. 77. [Gower]

5
I will not answer thee with words, but blows.
I Henry VI. Act i, sc. 3, l. 69. [Gloucester]

By words or blows here let us win our right.
III Henry VI. Act i, sc. 1, l. 37. [York]

Brutus: Words before blows: is it so, countrymen?
Octavius: Not that we love words better, as you do.
Brutus: Good words are better than bad strokes, Octavius.
Antony: In your bad strokes, Brutus, you give good words.
Julius Cæsar. Act v, sc. 1, l. 27.

Tybalt: Gentlemen, good den: a word with one of you.
Mercutio: And but one word with one of us? couple it with something; make it a word and a blow.
Romeo and Juliet. Act iii, sc. 1, l. 41.

6
O, let no words, but deeds, revenge this treason!
I Henry VI. Act iii, sc. 2, l. 49. [Bedford]

7
As for words, whose greatness answers words,
Let this my sword report what speech forbears.
II Henry VI. Act iv, sc. 10, l. 56. [Iden]

I cannot give due action to my words,
Except a sword or sceptre balance it.
II Henry VI. Act v, sc. 1, l. 8. [York]

Queen: His sons, he says, shall give their words for him.
York: Will you not, sons?
Edward: Ay, noble father, if our words will serve.
Richard: And if words will not, then our weapons shall.
II Henry VI. Act v, sc. 1, l. 137.

8
'Tis better said than done.
III Henry VI. Act iii, sc. 2, l. 90. [Lady Grey] The only use of the phrase.

So said, so done, is well.—*The Taming of the Shrew,* i, 2, 186.

That I had said and done!—*II Henry VI,* i, 4, 31.

Said or done.—*Othello,* ii, 3, 201.

9
Wolsey: And ever may your highness yoke together,
As I will lend you cause, my doing well
With my well saying!
King Henry: 'Tis well said again;
And 'tis a kind of good deed to say well:
And yet words are no deeds.
Henry VIII. Act iii, sc. 2, l. 150.

With his deed did crown His word upon you.
Henry VIII. Act iii, sc. 2, l. 155. [King]

10
Your large speeches may your deeds approve,
That good effects may spring from words of love.
King Lear. Act i, sc. 1, l. 187. [Kent]

A tardiness in nature
Which often leaves the history unspoke
That it intends to do.
King Lear. Act i, sc. 1, l. 238. [King of France] The only use of "tardiness."

11
Words to the heat of deeds too cold breath gives.
Macbeth. Act ii, sc. 1, l. 61. [Macbeth]

I have no words: My voice is in my sword.
Macbeth. Act v, sc. 8, l. 6. [Macduff]

12
My words express my purpose.
Measure for Measure. Act ii, sc. 4, l. 148. [Angelo]

I endow'd thy purposes
With words that made them known.
The Tempest. Act i, sc. 2, l. 357. [Prospero]

13
Your words and performances are no kin together.
Othello. Act iv, sc. 2, l. 185. [Roderigo]

14 She would not blot the letter
With words, till action might become them better.
The Rape of Lucrece, l. 1322.

15
Let not my cold words here accuse my zeal.
Richard II. Act i, sc. 1, l. 47. [Mowbray]

1 I will pay thy graces
Home both in word and deed.
The Tempest. Act v, sc. 1, l. 70. [Prospero]
Awful both in deed and word.—*Pericles,* ii, Gower, 4.

2 Foul-spoken coward, that thunder'st with thy tongue,
And with thy weapon nothing darest perform!
Titus Andronicus. Act ii, sc. 1, l. 59. [Chiron] The only use of "foul-spoken" and "thunder'st."
There speak and strike, brave boys, and take your turns.
Titus Andronicus. Act ii, sc. 1, l. 129. [Aaron]

3 Troilus: You have bereft me of all words, lady.
Pandarus: Words pay no debts, give her deeds: but she 'll bereave you o' the deeds too.
Troilus and Cressida. Act iii, sc. 2, l. 58.
Matchless, firm of word,
Speaking in deeds and deedless in his tongue.
Troilus and Cressida. Act iv, sc. 5, l. 97. [Ulysses] The only use of "deedless." "Matchless" is repeated in *Love's Labour 's Lost,* ii, 1, 17.
I 'll endeavour deeds to match these words.
Troilus and Cressida. Act iv, sc. 5, l. 259. [Hector]
Go, wind, to wind, there turn and change together.
My love with words and errors still she feeds;
But edifies another with her deeds.
Troilus and Cressida. Act v, sc. 3, l. 110. [Troilus] The only use of "edifies."

WORK

See also Employment, Labour, Toil

4 I have done my work ill, friends.
Antony and Cleopatra. Act iv, sc. 14, l. 105. [Antony]
What work is here!—*Antony and Cleopatra,* v, 2, 328.

5 This is not Fortune's work neither, but Nature's.
As You Like It. Act i, sc. 2, l. 54. [Celia]
Work of nature.—*Richard III,* iv, 3, 18; *Henry V,* ii, 4, 60.
Work of heaven.—*Romeo and Juliet,* v, 3, 261.
Works of war.—*Richard II,* iv, 1, 96.

6 What work 's, my countrymen, in hand? where go you
With bats and clubs?
Coriolanus. Act i, sc. 1, l. 56. [Menenius]
There 's other work in hand.
Cymbeline. Act v, sc. 5, l. 103. [Imogen]
The work we have in hand,
Most bloody, fiery and most terrible.
Julius Cæsar. Act i, sc. 3, l. 129. [Cassius]
Come on, Nerissa; I have work in hand.
The Merchant of Venice. Act iii, sc. 4, l. 57. [Portia]

7 Make us quick in work.
Coriolanus. Act i, sc. 4, l. 10. [Marcius]
My work hath yet not warm'd me.
Coriolanus. Act i, sc. 5, l. 18. [Marcius]

8 Here 's goodly work!
Coriolanus. Act iii, sc. 1, l. 261. [Menenius]
O, you have made good work!
Coriolanus. Act iv, sc. 6, l. 80. [Cominius] Also v, 1, 15.
You have made good work,
You and your apron-men.
Coriolanus. Act iv, sc. 6, l. 95. [Menenius] The only use of "apron-men" (mechanics).
Great work.—*II Henry IV,* i, 3, 48.
Greatest works.—*All 's Well that Ends Well,* ii, 1, 139.
Worthy work.—*Coriolanus,* ii, 2, 49.
Gentle work.—*Sonnets,* v.

9 You have made fair work!
Coriolanus. Act iv, sc. 6, l. 100. [Menenius]
Knew you of this fair work?
King John. Act iv, sc. 3, l. 116. [Bastard]

10 Having work
More plentiful than tools to do 't.
Cymbeline, v, 3, 8. See under Enemy.
To thy work.—*Hamlet,* v, 2, 333.
I want work!—*I Henry IV,* ii, 4, 118.

11 My old dame will be undone now for one to do her husbandry and her drudgery.
II Henry IV. Act iii, sc. 2, l. 125. [Mouldy] The only use of "drudgery."

12 The work ish given over. . . . By my hand, I swear, and my father's soul, the work ish ill done.
Henry V. Act iii, sc. 2, l. 93. [Macmorris]

13 There is not work enough for all our hands.
Henry V. Act iv, sc. 2, l. 19. [Constable]
Out of work.—*Henry V,* i, 2, 114.
Lack of work.—*All 's Well that Ends Well,* i, 1, 24.
Lacks work.—*Troilus and Cressida,* v, 5, 21.
Do no work to-day!—*Henry V,* iv, 3, 18.
Do my work.—*Pericles,* iv, 1, 71.
Do our work.—*The Tempest,* iii, 2, 158.
Do their work.—*A Midsummer-Night's Dream,* ii, 1, 41.

14 Your honours shall perceive how I will work
To bring this matter to the wished end.
I Henry VI. Act iii, sc. 3, l. 27. [La Pucelle]

15 I am sick with working.
I Henry VI. Act v, sc. 5, l. 86. [King Henry]
Working so grossly in a natural cause.
Henry V. Act ii, sc. 2, l. 107. [King Henry]
Leave working.—*Henry VIII,* iii, 1, 2.
Fell working.—*II Henry IV,* iv, 5, 207.
Modest working.—*As You Like It,* i, 2, 215.
Working-days.—*Much Ado about Nothing,* ii, 1, 341; *Henry V,* i, 2, 277; *As You Like It,* i, 3, 12.

1
Let us to our work.
II Henry VI. Act i, sc. 4, l. 15. [Bolingbroke]
Awhile to work, and after holiday.
Richard II. Act iii, sc. 1, l. 44. [Bolingbroke]
Well, to our work.—*Julius Cæsar,* iv, 3, 196.
Well then, to work.—*King John,* ii, 1, 37.
Set at work.—*Henry VIII,* iii, 1, 74.

2
Work in their shirt too; as myself, for example, that am a butcher.
II Henry VI. Act iv, sc. 7, l. 57. [Dick]
Work against him.—*All 's Well that Ends Well,* iv, 2, 29.
Work confusion.—*Titus Andronicus,* v, 2, 8.
Work contrariously.—*Henry V,* i, 2, 206. The only use of "contrariously."
Works a miracle.—*The Merchant of Venice,* iii, 2, 90.
Work exceeding miracles.—*I Henry VI,* v, 4, 41.
Work for bread.—*Midsummer-Night's Dream,* ii, 2, 10.
Work for tears.—*King John,* ii, 1, 303.
Work in Athens.—*Midsummer-Night's Dream,* v, 1, 72.
Work mine end.—*The Tempest,* v, 1, 53.
Work my downfall.—*II Henry VI,* iii, 1, 73.
Work my way.—*The Rape of Lucrece,* l. 513.
Work upon his blood.—*Othello,* iv, 1, 286.

3
It is the shameful work of Hubert's hand.
King John. Act iv, sc. 3, l. 62. [Pembroke]
Rough work.—*Timon of Athens,* i, 1, 43. See under MAN.
Ruthful work.—*Troilus and Cressida,* v, 3, 48.

4
If it be a man's work, I 'll do it.
King Lear. Act v, sc. 3, l. 39. [Captain]
Men's works.—*Timon of Athens,* v, 1, 225.

5
You rise to play and go to bed to work.
Othello. Act ii, sc. 1, l. 116. [Iago]
Amorous works.—*Othello,* v, 2, 213.
The work of generation.—*The Merchant of Venice,* i, 3, 83.

6
Look on the tragic loading of this bed;
This is thy work.
Othello. Act v, sc. 2, l. 363. [Lodovico] The only use of "loading."
A most miraculous work.—*Macbeth,* iv, 3, 147.

7
Tell me how it works.
Pericles. Act iii, sc. 2, l. 10. [Cerimon]
Does it work?—*Twelfth Night,* ii, 5, 214.
Will this work?—*Henry VIII,* iii, 2, 37.
It works.—*The Tempest,* i, 2, 493.
Now it begins to work.—*The Taming of the Shrew,* iii, 2, 220.
Now let it work.—*Julius Cæsar,* iii, 2, 265; *Hamlet,* iii, 4, 205.
Let me work.—*Julius Cæsar,* ii, 1, 209.

8
Much imaginary work was there.
The Rape of Lucrece, l. 1422.

9
Now have I done a good day's work.
Richard III. Act ii, sc. 1, l. 1. [King Edward] "Day's work" is repeated in *I Henry VI,* i, 3, 83; *Henry V,* iv, 3, 97; *Coriolanus,* i, 9, 1; *Cymbeline,* i, 5, 57.
Now is my day's work done; I 'll take good breath.
Troilus and Cressida. Act v, sc. 8, l. 3. [Hector]

10
Come, come with me, and we will make short work.
Romeo and Juliet. Act ii, sc. 6, l. 35. [Friar Laurence]

11
'Tis a very excellent piece of work.
The Taming of the Shrew. Act i, sc. 1, l. 258. [Sly]
A very good piece of work, I assure you, and a merry.
A Midsummer-Night's Dream. Act i, sc. 2, l. 14. [Bottom]
What a piece of work in a man!
Hamlet, ii, 2, 316. See under MAN.
Will the king hear this piece of work?
Hamlet. Act iii, sc. 2, l. 52. [Hamlet]
A wonderful piece of work.
Antony and Cleopatra. Act i, sc. 2, l. 160. [Enobarbus]
A piece of work
So bravely done, so rich, that it did strive
In workmanship and value.
Cymbeline. Act ii, sc. 4, l. 72. [Iachimo]
'Tis a knavish piece of work: but what o' that?
Hamlet. Act iii, sc. 2, l. 250. [Hamlet]
This most bloody piece of work.
Macbeth. Act ii, sc. 3, l. 134. [Banquo]
Filthy piece of work.—*Timon of Athens,* i, 1, 202.
Bloody work.—*King John,* iv, 3, 57.

12
There 's more work.
The Tempest. Act i, sc. 2, l. 238. [Prospero]
Work you then.—*The Tempest,* i, 1, 45.
Work not so hard.—*The Tempest,* iii, 1, 16.
Our work should cease.—*The Tempest,* v, 1, 5.

13
You are rapt, sir, in some work.
Timon of Athens. Act i, sc. 1, l. 19. [Painter]
You have work'd for me.—*Timon of Athens,* v, 1, 116. The only use of "work'd."
Last work.—*Timon of Athens,* i, 1, 228.
Shriving work.—*Richard III,* iii, 2, 116. The only use of "shriving."

14
I like your work;
And you shall find I like it.
Timon of Athens. Act i, sc. 1, l. 160. [Timon]
I like the work well.—*Othello,* iii, 4, 189.

15
How earnestly are you set a-work!
Troilus and Cressida. Act v, sc. 10, l. 38. [Pandar]

16
Did not I say he would work it out?
Twelfth Night. Act ii, sc. 5, l. 139. [Fabian]

17
She can spin for her living.
The Two Gentlemen of Verona, iii, 1, 318.
Get your living by reckoning.—*Love's Labour 's Lost,* v, 2, 498.
My land and living.—*Winter's Tale,* iv, 3, 104.

1
Every lane's end, every shop, church, session, hanging, yields a careful man work.
The Winter's Tale. Act iv, sc. 4, l. 700. [Autolycus]

II—The Workman

2
He, sir, he 's a good workman.
All's Well that Ends Well, ii, 5, 21. See under TAILOR.
Excellent workman!—*Timon of Athens,* v, 1, 32.
Fine workman.—*Julius Cæsar,* i, 1, 10.
3
Thou shouldst see A workman in 't.
Antony and Cleopatra, iv, 4, 17. See under WAR.
Therein I must play the workman.
Cymbeline. Act iv, sc. 1, l. 7. [Cloten]
Do 't Like workmen.—*Timon of Athens,* iv, 3, 438.
4
The king's council are no good workmen.
II Henry VI. Act iv, sc. 2, l. 16. [Bevis]
5
When workmen strive to do better than well,
They do confound their skill in covetousness.
King John. Act iv, sc. 2, l. 28. [Pembroke]
6
The well-skill'd workman this mild image drew.
The Rape of Lucrece, l. 1520. The only use of "well-skill'd."

WORLD

See also Earth

7
Wilt thou be lord of the whole world? . . .
Though thou think me poor, I am the man
Will give thee all the world.
Antony and Cleopatra. Act ii, sc. 7, l. 67. [Menas]
The whole world shall not save him.
Cymbeline. Act v, sc. 5, l. 321. [Cymbeline]
The whole world.—*The Comedy of Errors,* iii, 2, 102, and twelve times in later plays.
The universal world.—*Henry V,* iv, 1, 67; iv, 8, 11.
The versal world.—*Romeo and Juliet,* ii, 4, 219. The only use of "versal."
The universal earth.—*Romeo and Juliet,* iii, 2, 94.
8
The third o' the world is yours.
Antony and Cleopatra, ii, 2, 63. See under WIFE.
Enobarbus: A' bears the third part of the world, man; see'st not?
Menas: The third part, then, is drunk: would it were all,
That it might go on wheels!
Antony and Cleopatra. Act ii, sc. 7, l. 96.
9
Darkling stand
The varying shore o' the world.
Antony and Cleopatra, iv, 14, 10. See under SUN. "Darkling" is repeated in *A Midsummer-Night's Dream,* ii, 2, 86, and in *King Lear,* i, 4, 327.
10
If thus thou vanishest, thou tell'st the world
It is not worth leave-taking.
Antony and Cleopatra. Act v, sc. 2, l. 300. [Cleopatra]
Let me tell the world.
I Henry IV. Act v, sc. 2, l. 66. [Vernon]
11
I shall . . . do the world no injury, for in it I have nothing; only in the world I fill up a place, which may be better supplied when I have made it empty.
As You Like It. Act i, sc. 2, l. 202. [Orlando]
12
Duke Senior: This wide and universal theatre
Presents more woeful pageants than the scene
Wherein we play in.
Jaques: All the world 's a stage,
And all the men and women merely players.
As You Like It. Act ii, sc. 7, l. 137. See under LIFE for full quotation.
Let this world no longer be a stage.
II Henry IV, 1, 1, 155. See under CHAOS.
I hold the world but as the world, Gratiano;
A stage where every man must play a part,
And mine a sad one.
The Merchant of Venice. Act i, sc. 1, l. 77. [Antonio]
13
The poor world is almost six thousand years old.
As You Like It. Act iv, sc. 1, l. 94. [Rosalind]
Poor world.—*Richard III,* i, 3, 221.
Ah, how the poor world is pestered with such waterflies, diminutives of nature!
Troilus and Cressida, v, 1, 37. [Thersites]
Dost know the water-fly?—*Hamlet,* v, 2, 84.
Let the water-flies Blow me.—*Antony and Cleopatra,* v, 2, 59. The only uses of "water-fly" and "water-flies."
14
How the world is changed with you
The Comedy of Errors. Act ii, sc. 2, l. 154. [Luciana]
Is 't possible the world should so much differ,
And we alive that lived?
Timon of Athens. Act iii, sc. 1, l. 49. [Flaminius]
15
Bring me word thither
How the world goes, that to the pace of it
I may spur on my journey.
Coriolanus. Act i, sc. 10, l. 31. [Aufidius]
Thou seest the world, Volumnius, how it goes.
Julius Cæsar. Act v, sc. 5, l. 22. [Brutus]
King Lear: You see how this world goes.
Gloucester: I see it feelingly. . . .
King Lear: A man may see how this world goes with no eyes.
King Lear. Act iv, sc. 6, l. 150.
How goes the world with thee?
Richard III. Act iii, sc. 2, l. 98. [Hastings]
Poet: How goes the world?
Painter: It wears, sir, as it grows.
Timon of Athens. Act i, sc. 1, l. 2.

How goes the world?—*Macbeth,* ii, 4, 21; *The Taming of the Shrew,* iv, 1, 36; *Timon of Athens,* ii, 2, 37.

As this world goes.—*Hamlet,* ii, 2, 179; *The Winter's Tale,* ii, 3, 72.

How the world wags.—*As You Like It,* ii, 7, 23. See under TIME.

1
There is a world elsewhere.
Coriolanus. Act iii, sc. 3, l. 135. [Coriolanus]

A better world than this.—*As You Like It,* i, 2, 296.

The world to come.—*Troilus and Cressida,* iii, 2, 180. The only use of the phrase.

2
This twenty years
This rock and these demesnes have been my world;
Where I have lived at honest freedom, paid
More pious debts to heaven than in all
The fore-end of my time.
Cymbeline. Act iii, sc. 3, l. 69. [Belarius] The only use of "fore-end."

3
Let the world take note.
Hamlet. Act i, sc. 2, l. 108. [King]

The world hath noted.—*Othello,* ii, 3, 192.

4
Why, let the stricken deer go weep,
The hart ungalled play;
For some must watch, while some must sleep:
So runs the world away.
Hamlet. Act iii, sc. 2, l. 282. [Hamlet] "Ungalled" is repeated in *The Comedy of Errors,* iii, 1, 102.

5
This is no world
To play with mammets and to tilt with lips:
We must have bloody noses and crack'd crowns,
And pass them current too.
I Henry IV. Act ii, sc. 3, l. 94. [Hotspur]

A whining mammet.—*Romeo and Juliet,* iii, 5, 186. The only uses of "mammet" and "mammets" (doll, puppet).

Daff'd the world aside, And bid it pass.
I Henry IV. Act iv, sc. 1, l. 96. [Hotspur] "Daff'd" (thrust) is repeated in *Much Ado about Nothing,* ii, 3, 176, with the meaning of doffed.

6
Let . . . all the world repine.
I Henry VI. Act v, sc. 2, l. 20. [La Pucelle]

Let all the world say no, I 'll keep my own.
The Taming of the Shrew. Act iii, sc. 2, l. 143. [Lucentio]

You are my all the world.—*Sonnets,* cxii.

You in my respect are all the world.
A Midsummer-Night's Dream. Act ii, sc. 1, l. 224. [Helena] Also *Titus Andronicus,* ii, 1, 71; *The Tempest,* i, 2, 69.

My life, my joy, my food, my all the world!
King John. Act iii, sc. 4, l. 104. [Constance]

For all the world like cutler's poetry.
The Merchant of Venice. Act v, sc. 1, l. 149. [Gratiano]

All the world was of my father's mind.
As You Like It. Act i, sc. 2, l. 248. [Rosalind]

All the world well knows.—*King Lear,* ii, 2, 160. "All the world" is repeated frequently throughout the plays.

All this the world well knows.—*Sonnets,* cxxix.

7
Till then, think of the world.
Julius Cæsar. Act i, sc. 2, l. 311. [Cassius]

Either there is a civil strife in heaven,
Or else the world, too saucy with the gods,
Incenses them to send destruction.
Julius Cæsar. Act i, sc. 3, l. 11. [Casca]

O world, thou wast the forest to this hart;
And this, indeed, O world, the heart of thee.
Julius Cæsar. Act iii, sc. 1, l. 207. [Antony]

8
The world, who of itself is peised well,
Made to run even upon even ground.
King John. Act ii, sc. 1, l. 575. [Bastard] The only use of "peised" (poised). "Peise" (weigh) occurs in *Richard III,* v, 3, 105, and *The Merchant of Venice,* iii, 2, 22.

9
Strives in his little world of man to out-scorn
The to-and-fro-conflicting wind and rain.
King Lear. Act iii, sc. 1, l. 10. [Gentleman] The only use of "out-scorn" and "to-and-fro-conflicting."

World of men.—*I Henry VI,* ii, 2, 48; *Richard III,* i, 4, 186.

10
O you mighty gods!
This world I do renounce.
King Lear. Act iv, sc. 6, l. 34. [Gloucester]

O ruin'd piece of nature! This great world
Shall so wear out to nought.
King Lear. Act iv, sc. 6, l. 137. [Gloucester]

Great world.—*The Merchant of Venice,* i, 2, 2; *Othello,* i, 3, 86; *Antony and Cleopatra,* ii, 6, 9.

11
Is the world as it was, man? Which is the way? Is it sad, and few words? or how? The trick of it?
Measure for Measure. Act iii, sc. 2, l. 52. [Lucio]

12
You have too much respect upon the world:
They lose it that do buy it with much care.
The Merchant of Venice. Act i, sc. 1, l. 74. [Gratiano]

13
The world must be peopled.
Much Ado about Nothing. Act ii, sc. 3, l. 251. [Benedick]

14
Leave the world tor me to bustle in.
Richard III. Act i, sc. 1, l. 152. [Gloucester]

Come, bustle, bustle.—*Richard III,* v, 3, 289. "Bustle" occurs only in this play.

15
Would you enforce me to a world of care?
Richard III. Act iii, sc. 7, l. 223. [Gloucester]

World of restless cares.—*Richard III,* i, 4, 81.

World of curses.—*I Henry IV,* i, 3, 164.

World of earthly blessings.—*II Henry VI,* i, 1, 22.

World of happy days.—*Richard III,* i, 4, 6.

World of sighs.—*Othello,* i, 3, 159.

World of torments.—*Love's Labour's Lost,* v, 2, 353.

World of water.—*I Henry IV,* iii, 1, 94.

What world is this?—*Pericles,* iii, 2, 106.
This breathing world.—*Richard III,* i, 1, 21.
The incredulous world.—*II Henry IV,* iv, 5, 154. "Incredulous" is repeated in *Twelfth Night,* iii, 4, 88: "Incredulous circumstance."

1
King Richard: Now, by the world—
Queen Elizabeth: 'Tis full of thy foul wrongs.
Richard III. Act iv, sc. 4, l. 374.

By the world.—*Love's Labour's Lost,* iv, 3, 18; v, 1, 107; 111; *The Taming of the Shrew,* ii, 1, 161; *Othello,* iii, 3, 383.
Throughout the world.—*Romeo and Juliet,* ii, 2, 148.

2
I would not for the world they saw thee here.
Romeo and Juliet. Act ii, sc. 2, l. 74. [Juliet]

Not for the world.—*Romeo and Juliet,* ii, 2, 97, and six times in later plays.
You will not do 't for all the world, I hope.
Pericles. Act iv, sc. 1, l. 85. [Marina]
For all the world.—*The Taming of the Shrew,* iii, 2, 66, and six times in later plays.
Before all the world.—*Titus Andronicus,* iv, 2, 109.
Nothing in the world.—*The Merchant of Venice,* iii, 2, 248.
All the world to nothing.—*Richard III,* i, 2, 238; *Romeo and Juliet,* iii, 5, 215.

3
The world will wail thee, like a makeless wife;
The world will be thy widow.
Sonnets. No. ix. The only use of "makeless" (husbandless).

But let your love even with my life decay,
Lest the wise world should look into your moan
And mock you with me after I am gone.
Sonnets. No. lxxi.

The world is bent my deeds to cross.
Sonnets. No. xc.

4
Let the world slide: sessa!
Taming of the Shrew. Induction, sc. 1, l. 6. [Sly] "Sessa," a word of doubtful meaning, occurs twice in *King Lear,* iii, 4, 104; iii, 6, 77.

Let the world slip.
The Taming of the Shrew. Induction, sc. 2, l. 146. [Sly]

Bid the world good night.—*Richard III,* iv, 3, 39.

A man
Whom this beneath world doth embrace and hug.
Timon of Athens. Act i, sc. 1, l. 44. [Poet]

Lower world.—*Richard II,* iii, 2, 38; *The Tempest,* v, 1, 173.
Christian world.—*All's Well that Ends Well,* iv, 4, 2.
General world.—*Love's Labour's Lost,* ii, 1, 11; *As You Like It,* ii, 7, 69.
Such another world.—*Othello,* v, 2, 144.

5
O my good lord, the world is but a word:
Were it all yours to give it in a breath,
How quickly were it gone!
Timon of Athens. Act ii, sc. 2, l. 161. [Flavius]

Timon: What wouldst thou do with the world, Apemantus, if it lay in thy power?
Apemantus: Give it the beasts, to be rid of the men.
Timon of Athens. Act iv, sc. 3, l. 321.

6
Is this the Athenian minion, whom the world
Voiced so regardfully?
Timon of Athens. Act iv, sc. 3, l. 80. [Timandra] See also under REPUTATION. The only use of "regardfully."

Myself, Who had the world as my confectionary.
Timon of Athens, iv, 3, 260. See under RUIN. The only use of "confectionary."

7
This before all the world do I prefer;
This maugre all the world will I keep safe.
Titus Andronicus. Act iv, sc. 2, l. 109. [Aaron]

8
Is it a world to hide virtues in?
Twelfth Night. Act i, sc. 3, l. 140. [Sir Toby]

I am afraid this great lubber, the world, will prove a cockney.
Twelfth Night. Act iv, sc. 1, l. 14. [Clown] "Cockney" is used only once more in the plays, in *King Lear,* ii, 4, 123. "Lubber" occurs four times.

9
Set the world at nought.
The Two Gentlemen of Verona. Act i, sc. 1, l. 68. [Proteus]

Then may I set the world on wheels.
The Two Gentlemen of Verona. Act iii, sc. 1, l. 317. [Launce]

Count the world a stranger for thy sake.
The Two Gentlemen of Verona, v, 4, 70. See under TRUST.

10
They looked as they had heard of a world ransomed, or one destroyed.
The Winter's Tale. Act v, sc. 2, l. 16. [Gentleman]

II—The Good World

11
The world goes well.
Coriolanus. Act iv, sc. 6, l. 5. [Sicinius]

12
The world may laugh again.
II Henry VI. Act ii, sc. 4, l. 82. [Gloucester]

Merry world.—*II Henry VI,* iv, 2, 9; *Measure for Measure,* iii, 2, 6; *Twelfth Night,* iii, 1, 109.

13
Here 's a good world the while!
Richard III. Act iii, sc. 6, l. 10. [Scrivener]

Here 's a good world!—*King John,* iv, 3, 116.
Calm world.—*I Henry IV,* iv, 2, 32.
Fair world.—*Hamlet,* iii, 2, 185.
Golden world.—*As You Like It,* i, 1, 125.
Majestic world.—*Julius Cæsar,* i, 2, 130.
Stirring world.—*Coriolanus,* iv, 5, 234.
Sweet world.—*King John,* iii, 4, 110.

14 O brave new world
That has such people in 't!
The Tempest. Act v, sc. 1, l. 183. [Miranda]

Brave world!—*I Henry IV,* iii, 3, 229.
New world.—*Richard II,* iv, 1, 78; v, 1, 24.

III—The Bad World

1
O, how full of briers is this working-day world!
As You Like It. Act i, sc. 3, l. 12. [Rosalind] "Working-day" is used four times.
O, what a world is this, when what is comely
Envenoms him that bears it!
As You Like It. Act ii, sc. 3, l. 14. [Adam]
All-seeing heaven, what a world is this!
Richard III. Act ii, sc. 1, l. 82. [Queen Elizabeth] "All-seeing" is repeated in *Romeo and Juliet,* i, 2, 97: "All-seeing sun."
Ay me! what is this world!—*II Henry VI,* iii, 2, 380.

2
I will through and through
Cleanse the foul body of the infected world,
If they will patiently receive my medicine.
As You Like It. Act ii, sc. 7, l. 59. [Jaques]

3
O world, thy slippery turns!
Coriolanus. Act iv, sc. 4, l. 12. [Coriolanus]

4
How weary, stale, flat and unprofitable,
Seem to me all the uses of this world!
Fie on 't! ah fie! 'tis an unweeded garden,
That grows to seed; things rank and gross in nature
Possess it merely.
Hamlet. Act i; sc. 2, l. 133. [Hamlet] The only use of "unweeded."

5
God help the while! a bad world, I say.
I Henry IV. Act ii, sc. 4, l. 146. [Falstaff]
The world is grown so bad,
That wrens make prey where eagles dare not perch.
Richard III. Act i, sc. 3, l. 70. [Gloucester]
Now this ill-wresting world is grown so bad,
Mad slanderers by mad ears believed be.
Sonnets. No. cxl. The only use of "ill-wresting."
Bad is the world.—*Richard III,* iii, 6, 13.
Bad world the while!—*King John,* iv, 2, 100.

6
A world of odds.
I Henry VI. Act iv, sc. 4, l. 25. [Lucy]

7
O let the vile world end!
II Henry VI, v, 2, 40. See under JUDGEMENT DAY.
Vile world.—*Sonnets,* lxxi; *Antony and Cleopatra,* v, 2, 317.
All-hating world.—*Richard II,* v, 5, 66. The only use of "all-hating."
Dull world.—*Antony and Cleopatra,* iv, 14, 61.
Earthly world.—*Macbeth,* iv, 2, 75.
Fangled world.—*Cymbeline,* v, 4, 134. The only use of "fangled" (fond of foppery).
Forlorn world.—*Sonnets,* xxxiii.
Hard world.—*Richard II,* v, 5, 21.
Harsh world.—*Hamlet,* v, 2, 359.
Injurious world!—*Measure for Measure,* iv, 3, 127.
Loathsome world.—*Romeo and Juliet,* v, 1, 81.
Mad world!—*King John,* ii, 1, 561.
Mazed world.—*A Midsummer-Night's Dream,* ii, 1, 113.
Monstrous world!—*Othello,* iii, 3, 377.
Naughty world.—*The Merchant of Venice,* v, 1, 91.
Poor rude world.—*The Merchant of Venice,* iii, 5, 87.
Tough world.—*King Lear,* v, 3, 314.
Wicked, wicked world!—*The Merry Wives of Windsor,* ii, 1, 20.
Wild world.—*The Comedy of Errors,* ii, 1, 21.

8
Smile, gentle heaven! or strike, ungentle death!
For this world frowns, and Edward's sun is clouded.
III Henry VI. Act ii, sc. 3, l. 6. [Edward]
The world goes hard.—*III Henry VI,* ii, 6, 77.
Account this world but hell.—*III Henry VI,* iii, 2, 169.

9
Cassius is aweary of the world.
Julius Cæsar. Act iv, sc. 3, l. 95. [Cassius]
My little body is aweary of this great world.
Merchant of Venice. Act i, sc. 2, l. 2. [Portia]
Weary of the world.—*Venus and Adonis,* l. 1189.

10
World, world, O world!
But that thy strange mutations make us hate thee,
Life would not yield to age.
King Lear. Act iv, sc. 1, l. 10. [Edgar] The only use of "mutations." "Mutation" occurs in *Cymbeline,* iv, 2, 133.
O world! world! world!—*Troilus and Cressida,* v, 10, 36.

11
'Twas never merry world since, of two usuries, the merriest was put down.
Measure for Measure, iii, 2, 6. [Pompey]
'Twas never merry world
Since lowly feigning was call'd compliment.
Twelfth Night, iii, 1, 109. See under PRETENCE.

12
God help us! it is a world to see.
Much Ado about Nothing. Act iii, sc. 5, l. 38. [Dogberry]

13
This world to me is like a lasting storm,
Whirring me from my friends.
Pericles. Act iv, sc. 1, l. 20. [Marina] The only use of "whirring."
A world of harms.—*The Rape of Lucrece,* l. 28.

14
The world is full of rubs.
Richard II. Act iii, sc. 4, l. 4. [Queen]

15
I fear, I fear 'twill prove a troublous world.
Richard III. Act ii, sc. 3, l. 5. [Second Citizen] "Troublous world" is repeated in the same scene, l. 9, and in *III Henry VI,* v, 5, 7.

16
The world is not thy friend nor the world's law;
The world affords no law to make thee rich;
Then be not poor, but break it, and take this.
Romeo and Juliet. Act v, sc. 1, l. 72. [Romeo]

17
Why does the world report that Kate doth limp?
O slanderous world!
The Taming of the Shrew. Act ii, sc. 1, l. 254. [Petruchio]

A cold world, Curtis.
The Taming of the Shrew. Act iv, sc. 1, l. 37. [Grumio]

1
This is the world's soul; and just of the same piece
Is every flatterer's spirit.
Timon of Athens. Act iii, sc. 2, l. 71. [Stranger]

I am sick of this false world, and will love nought
But even the mere necessities upon 't.
Timon of Athens. Act iv, sc. 3, l. 376. [Timon]

2
It is a bawdy planet.
Winter's Tale. Act i, sc. 2, l. 201. [Leontes]

Ill planet.—*The Winter's Tale,* ii, 1, 105. See under STAR.

IV—The World: Its Size and Shape

3 The round world
Should have shook lions into civil streets.
Antony and Cleopatra. Act v, sc. 1, l. 15. [Cæsar]

The thick rotundity o' the world.
King Lear. Act iii, sc. 2, l. 7. [King Lear] The only use of "rotundity."

This world's globe.—*II Henry VI,* iii, 2, 406.

4
Does the world go round?
Cymbeline. Act v, sc. 5, l. 232. [Cymbeline]

It is a reeling world, indeed, my lord.
Richard III. Act iii, sc. 2, l. 38. [Catesby]

He that is giddy thinks the world turns round.
The Taming of the Shrew. Act v, sc. 2, l. 20. [Widow]

5
The world's a huge thing: it is a great price
For a small vice.
Othello. Act iv, sc. 3, l. 69. [Emilia]

And little of this great world can I speak,
More than pertains to feats of broil and battle.
Othello. Act i, sc. 3, l. 86. [Othello]

This great world Shall so wear out to nought.
King Lear. Act iv, sc. 6, l. 137. [Gloucester]

Great world.—*The Merchant of Venice,* i, 2, 2; *Antony and Cleopatra,* ii, 6, 9.

Giant world.—*King John,* v, 2, 57.

Vast world.—*Coriolanus,* iv, 1, 42.

6
The four opposing coigns
Which the world together joins.
Pericles. Act iii, Gower, l. 17.

All corners of the world.—*Cymbeline,* iii, 4, 39.

The three corners of the world.—*King John,* v, 7, 116.

The three-nook'd world.—*Antony and Cleopatra,* iv, 6, 6. The only use of "three-nook'd," consisting of Europe, Asia, and Africa.

The three-fold world.—*Julius Cæsar,* iv, 1, 14.

7
Friar Laurence: The world is broad and wide.
Romeo: There is no world without Verona walls,
But purgatory, torture, hell itself.
Romeo and Juliet. Act iii, sc. 3, l. 16. "Purgatory" is repeated in *Othello,* iv, 3, 77.

The world's large spaces.—*Troilus and Cressida,* ii, 2, 162.

This spacious world.—*Richard III,* i, 2, 246; *Pericles,* iv, 3, 5.

The wide world.—*The Merchant of Venice,* i, 1, 167; *Much Ado about Nothing,* iv, 1, 291; *As You Like It,* i, 3, 134; *Troilus and Cressida,* ii, 2, 206; *Titus Andronicus,* i, 1, 248; *Sonnets,* xix, cvii, cxxxvii.

A world too wide.—*As You Like It,* ii, 7, 160.

This little world.—*Richard II,* ii, 1, 45; v, 5, 9; *King Lear,* iii, 1, 10.

The narrow world.—*Julius Cæsar,* i, 2, 135.

The pendent world.—*Measure for Measure,* iii, 1, 126.

V—The World: Its Beginning and End

8
To the end o' the world.
Coriolanus. Act iii, sc. 1, l. 304. [Menenius]

To the world's end.—*Much Ado about Nothing,* ii, 1, 272.

The world's end.—*Troilus and Cressida,* iii, 2, 209. See also JUDGEMENT DAY.

This brief world.—*Timon of Athens,* iv, 3, 253.

This mortal world.—*II Henry VI,* i, 2, 21.

9
As the world were now but to begin.
Hamlet, iv, 5, 103. See under CUSTOM.

Since first the world begun.—*Romeo and Juliet,* i, 2, 98.

10
A great while ago the world begun.
Twelfth Night. Act v, sc. 1, l. 414. [Clown]

Antique world.—*As You Like It,* ii, 3, 57.

This old world!—*King John,* iii, 4, 145; *Sonnets,* lix.

VI—Knowing the World

11
I hope it is no dishonest desire to desire to be a woman of the world.
As You Like It. Act v, sc. 3, l. 3. [Audrey]

Falstaff: Deliver them like a man of this world.
Pistol: A foutre for the world and worldlings base!
II Henry IV. Act v, sc. 3, l. 101.

A foutre for thine office.—*II Henry IV,* v, 3, 121. "Foutre" is used in no other scene.

12
The world, familiar to us and unknown.
Henry V. Act iii, sc. 7, l. 40. [Dauphin]

Our known world.—*Hamlet,* i, 1, 85.

The yet unknowing world.—*Hamlet,* v, 2, 390.

13
I 'll look upon the world.
II Henry VI. Act ii, sc. 4, l. 38. [Duchess]

14
A blusterer, that the ruffle knew
Of court, of city.
A Lover's Complaint, l. 58. The only use of "blusterer."

A man . . . that hath seen the world.—*Love's Labour 's Lost,* v, 1, 114.

Men . . . Who know the world.—*Pericles,* i, 1, 48.

Know the world.—*The Merry Wives of Windsor,* ii, 2, 136.

Know the whole world.—*Troilus and Cressida,* ii, 3, 243.

Witness the world.—*King Lear,* v, 3, 77; 97.

1
Why, then the world 's mine oyster.
Which I with sword will open.
The Merry Wives of Windsor. Act ii, sc. 2, l. 2. [Pistol]

2
I will catechize the world for him.
Othello. Act iii, sc. 4, l. 16. [Clown] "Catechize" is repeated in *King John,* i, 1, 192, and in *Twelfth Night,* i, 5, 68.

3
Come abroad to see the world.
The Taming of the Shrew, i, 2, 58. See under TRAVEL.

'Tis a world to see.—*The Taming of the Shrew,* ii, 1, 313.

4
I have consider'd well his loss of time
And how he cannot be a perfect man,
Not being tried and tutor'd in the world.
The Two Gentlemen of Verona. Act i, sc. 3, l. 20. [Antonio]

WORM

5
Cleopatra: Hast thou the pretty worm of Nilus there,
That kills and pains not?
Clown: Truly, I have him. But I would not be the party that should desire you to touch him, for his biting is immortal; those that do die of it do seldom or never recover.
Cleopatra: Rememberest thou any that have died on 't?
Clown: Very many, men and women too. I heard one of them no longer than yesterday: a very honest woman, but something given to lie; as a woman should not do, but in the way of honesty: how she died of the biting of it, what pain she felt: truly, she makes a very good report o' the worm: . . . the worm 's an odd worm. . . . I wish thee all joy of the worm.
Cleopatra: Farewell.
Clown: You must think this, look you, that the worm will do his kind.
Cleopatra: Ay, ay; farewell.
Clown: Look you, the worm is not to be trusted but in the keeping of wise people; for, indeed, there is no goodness in the worm. . . .
Cleopatra: Well, get thee gone; farewell.
Clown: Yes, forsooth: I wish you joy o' the worm.
Antony and Cleopatra. Act v, sc. 2, l. 243.

The worms of Nile.—*Cymbeline,* iii, 4, 37.

Viperous worm.—*I Henry VI,* iii, 1, 72.

The eyeless venom'd worm.—*Timon of Athens,* iv, 3, 182.

6
King: Now, Hamlet, where 's Polonius?
Hamlet: At supper.
King: At supper! where?
Hamlet: Not where he eats, but where he is eaten; a certain convocation of politic worms are e'en at him. Your worm is your only emperor for diet; we fat all creatures else to fat us, and we fat ourselves for maggots.
Hamlet. Act iv, sc. 3, l. 20. [Hamlet] "Convocation" is repeated again in *Henry V,* i, 1, 76: "Spiritual convocation." "Maggots" is repeated in ii, 2, 181, and "maggot ostentation" occurs in *Love's Labour 's Lost,* v, 2, 409.

A man may fish with the worm that hath eat of a king, and eat of the fish that hath fed of that worm.
Hamlet. Act iv, sc. 3, l. 28. [Hamlet]

Now my Lady Worm's; chapless, and knocked about the mazzard with a sexton's spade.
Hamlet. Act v, sc. 1, l. 97. [Hamlet] "Mazzard" (head) is repeated in *Othello,* ii, 3, 155: "Knock you o'er the mazzard."

Chapless skulls.—*Romeo and Juliet,* iv, 1, 83. The only uses of "chapless."

7
Worm-eaten hold of ragged stone.
II Henry IV, Ind., 35. See under CASTLE.

Worm-eaten nut.—*As You Like It,* iii, 4, 27.

Worm-eaten tapestry.—*Much Ado about Nothing,* iii, 3, 145. The only uses of "worm-eaten."

8
Only compound me with forgotten dust;
Give that which gave thee life unto the worms.
II Henry IV. Act iv, sc. 5, l. 116. [King Henry]

Food for worms.—*I Henry IV,* v, 4, 87. See under DEATH.

A prey for worms.—*Richard III,* iv, 4, 386.

The prey of worms.—*Sonnets,* lxxiv.

Worms have eaten them.—*As You Like It,* iv, 1, 108. See under LOVE.

Worms will not come to thee.—*Cymbeline,* iv, 2, 218.

9
The worm-holes of long vanish'd days.
Henry V, ii, 4, 86.

To fill with worm-holes stately monuments.
The Rape of Lucrece, l. 946. The only uses of "worm-holes."

10
The smallest worm will turn being trodden on.
III Henry VI. Act ii, sc. 2, l. 17. [Clifford] From Heywood's *Proverbs* (Pt. ii, ch. 4): "Tread a woorme on the tayle, and it must turne agayne." (1546)

I trod upon a worm against my will,
But I wept for it.
Pericles, iv, 1, 79. See under KINDNESS for full quotation.

11
When I shall dwell with worms.
Henry VIII. Act iv, sc. 2, l. 126. [Katharine]

Ring these fingers with thy household worms.
King John, iii, 4, 31. See under DEATH.

Little worms.—*The Rape of Lucrece,* l. 1248.

12 Thou 'rt by no means valiant;
For thou dost fear the soft and tender fork
Of a poor worm.
Measure for Measure. Act iii, sc. 1, l. 15. [Duke]

Poor worm.—*The Tempest,* iii, 1, 31; *Pericles,* i, 1, 102.

1
Vile worm, thou wast o'erlook'd even in thy birth.
The Merry Wives of Windsor. Act v, sc. 5, l. 87. [Pistol]
Vilest worms.—*Sonnets,* lxxi.
2
Worm nor snail, do no offence.
A Midsummer-Night's Dream, ii, 2, 23.
3
The worms were hallow'd that did breed the silk.
Othello, iii, 4, 73. See under MAGIC.
Thou owest the worm no silk.—*King Lear,* iii, 4, 108.
4
Why should the worm intrude the maiden bud?
The Rape of Lucrece, l. 848.
The bud bit with an envious worm.
Romeo and Juliet. Act i, sc. 1, l. 157. [Montague]
A worm i' the bud.—*Twelfth Night,* ii, 4, 114.
5
The worm of conscience still begnaw thy soul!
Richard III. Act i, sc. 3, l. 222. [Queen Margaret] The only use of "begnaw."
Don Worm, his conscience.—*Much Ado about Nothing,* v, 2, 86.
6
They have made worms' meat of me.
Romeo and Juliet. Act iii, sc. 1, l. 112. [Mercutio]
Thou worms-meat!—*As You Like It,* iii, 2, 67. The only uses of "worms-meat."
She made him roast-meat for worms.
Pericles. Act iv, sc. 2, l. 25. [Boult] The only use of "roast-meat."
7
Here will I remain
With worms that are my chamber-maids.
Romeo and Juliet, v, 3, 109. See under DEATH.
8
Shall worms, inheritors of this excess,
Eat up thy charge? is this thy body's end?
Sonnets. No. cxlvi.
Make worms thine heir.—*Sonnets,* vi.
9
Come, come, you froward and unable worms!
The Taming of the Shrew. Act v, sc. 2, l. 169. [Katharina]
Earth's worm.—*Venus and Adonis,* l. 933.

WORSHIP

10
The worship of the whole world.
Antony and Cleopatra. Act iv, sc. 14, l. 86. See COUNTENANCE, 243:16.
He worships you.—*As You Like It,* v, 2, 88.
Give me worship.—*III Henry VI,* iv, 3, 16.
I will worship thee.—*King John,* ii, 1, 598.
To thee be worship!—*Timon of Athens,* v, 1, 55.
11
All adoration, duty, and observance.
As You Like It, v, 2, 102. See under LOVE.
With adorations, fertile tears.
Twelfth Night, i, 5, 274. See under LOVE.
What is thy soul of adoration?
Henry V, iv, 1, 262. See under CEREMONY.
I profess myself her adorer.
Cymbeline, i, 4, 74. The only use of "adorer."
Sir Toby: One that adores me: what o' that?
Sir Andrew: I was adored once too.
Twelfth Night. Act ii, sc. 3, l. 197.
I do adore thee.—*The Tempest,* ii, 2, 143.
I do adore thee so.—*Twelfth Night,* ii, 1, 48.
I do adore thy sweet grace's slipper.—*Love's Labour's Lost,* v, 2, 672.
Honour and adore.—*Titus Andronicus,* i, 1, 42.
12
Seal what I end withal! This double worship,
Where one part does disdain the cause, the other
Insult without all reason.
Coriolanus. Act iii, sc. 1, l. 142. [Coriolanus]
13
How may I reverently worship thee enough?
I Henry VI, i, 2, 145. See under REVERENCE.
Worship me their lord.—*II Henry VI,* iv, 2, 81.
An't like your worship.—*II Henry VI,* ii, 1, 80; *The Winter's Tale,* iv, 4, 736; v, 2, 167.
An't please your worship.—*Richard III,* i, 1, 88; *II Henry IV,* v, 3, 84; *The Merry Wives of Windsor,* ii, 2, 35. "Your worship," as a form of salutation, is used throughout the plays.
14
I would she had bestowed this dotage on me.
Much Ado about Nothing. Act ii, sc. 3, l. 175. [Don Pedro]
Her dotage now I do begin to pity.
A Midsummer-Night's Dream. Act iv, sc. 1, l. 52. [Oberon]
Banish your dotage.—*Timon of Athens,* iii, 5, 99.
Lose myself in dotage.—*Antony and Cleopatra,* i, 2, 121.
Voluntary dotage.—*Othello,* iv, 1, 27.
This dotage of our general's.—*Antony and Cleopatra,* i, 1, 1. "Dotage" in the sense of excessive fondness is used again in *Much Ado about Nothing,* ii, 3, 224. In the sense of feebleness of mind it occurs in only one play, *King Lear,* where it is used three times, i, 4, 315; 349; ii, 4, 200. For "dote" see under LOVE.
15
Shall he be worshipp'd
Of that we hold an idol more than he?
Troilus and Crsesida. Act ii, sc. 3, l. 198. [Ulysses]
Thou shalt be worshipp'd, kiss'd, loved and adored!
The Two Gentlemen of Verona. Act iv, sc. 4, l. 204. [Julia]
Worshipp'd as a saint.—*King John,* iii, 1, 177. See also under SAINT.
Worshipp'd with a waxen epitaph.—*Henry V,* i, 2, 233.
Lord worshipped might he be!—*The Merchant of Venice,* ii, 2, 98.
16
All the Greeks begin to worship Ajax.
Troilus and Cressida. Act iii, sc. 3, l. 182. [Ulysses]
17
At first I did adore a twinkling star,
But now I worship a celestial sun.
The Two Gentlemen of Verona. Act ii, sc. 6,

l. 9. [Proteus] "Twinkling" is repeated in *I Henry VI*, v, 3, 63, and in *The Merchant of Venice*, ii, 2, 177: "The twinkling of an eye."
Worship shadows and adore false shapes.
The Two Gentlemen of Verona. Act iv, sc. 2, l. 131. [Silvia]
Worship dirty gods.—*Cymbeline*, iii, 6, 56. See under GOLD.

1 Thou,
His cupbearer,—whom I from meaner form
Have bench'd and rear'd to worship.
The Winter's Tale. Act i, sc. 2, l. 312. [Leontes] "Cup-bearer" (this time hyphenated) occurs again in *Winter's Tale*, i, 2, 313.

WORTH

See also Unworthiness, Value

I—Worth

2
Let every word weigh heavy of her worth
That he does weigh too light.
All's Well that Ends Well. Act iii, sc. 4, l. 31. [Countess]
Weigh What it is worth.—*Antony and Cleopatra*, ii, 6, 33.
And worth it, with addition!—*All's Well that Ends Well*, iv, 2, 3.

3
Her worth, being mounted on the wind,
Through all the world bears Rosalind.
As You Like It. Act iii, sc. 2, l. 95. [Rosalind, reading]
Her worth worth yours.—*Measure for Measure*, v, 1, 502.

4
Worth all your predecessors since Deucalion.
Coriolanus. Act ii, sc. 1, l. 101. [Menenius] Deucalion is mentioned again in *The Winter's Tale*, iv, 4, 442.
Worth six on him.—*Coriolanus*, iv, 5, 174.
Worth five of Agamemnon.—*II Henry IV*, ii, 4, 237.
Worth ten on 't.—*Much Ado about Nothing*, iii, 4, 23.
Worth five thousand of you.—*Measure for Measure*, i, 2, 61.
Worth all the rest.—*Macbeth*, ii, 1, 45.
Twenty times his worth.—*II Henry VI*, iii, 2, 268.
Men of great worth.—*As You Like It*, v, 4, 161.
Their worth is great.—*The Taming of the Shrew*, ii, 1, 102.
Great worth.—*The Two Gentlemen of Verona*, i, 2, 44; *Troilus and Cressida*, ii, 2, 151.

5
If this be worth your hearing, Mark it.
Cymbeline. Act i, sc. 1, l. 57. [Gentleman]
Worth the eating.—*Julius Cæsar*, i, 2, 296.
Worth keeping.—*Troilus and Cressida*, ii, 2, 81.
Worth the listening to.—*I Henry IV*, ii, 4, 235. See under ATTENTION.
Worth the looking on.—*Measure for Measure*, v, 1, 208.
Worth naming.—*Othello*, ii, 3, 330.
Worth the noting.—*Much Ado about Nothing*, ii, 3, 57.
Well worth the seeing.—*Henry VIII*, iv, 1, 61.
Worth seizure.—*As You Like It*, iii, 1, 10.
Worth your vengeance.—*Cymbeline*, v, 1, 11.
Worth the viewing.—*Venus and Adonis*, l. 1076.
Well worth watching.—*Cymbeline*, ii, 4, 68.
Worth your breeding.—*Henry V*, iii, 1, 28. See under ANCESTRY.

6
A score of good ewes may be worth ten pounds.
II Henry IV. Act iii, sc. 2, l. 56. [Silence]
A wisp of straw were worth a thousand crowns.
III Henry VI, ii, 2, 144. See SELF-KNOWLEDGE.
Worth forty ducats.—*The Comedy of Errors*, iv, 3, 84.
Worth forty mark.—*I Henry IV*, iii, 3, 95.
Worth a million.—*I Henry IV*, iii, 3, 156.
Worth a noble.—*Richard III*, i, 3, 82.
Worth a thousand.—*II Henry IV*, ii, 1, 158.
Worth gold.—*II Henry IV*, ii, 4, 35.
Worth a monarchy.—*II Henry VI*, iv, 10, 21.
Worth all our mundane cost.—*Pericles*, iii, 2, 71. The only use of "mundane."
A thing of worth.—*II Henry VI*, iii, 2, 410.
Money's worth.—*Love's Labour's Lost*, ii, 1, 137.

7 What were 't worth to know
The secret of your conference?
Henry VIII. Act ii, sc. 3, l. 50. [Chamberlain]

8
Him and his worth and our great need of him
You have right well conceited.
Julius Cæsar. Act i, sc. 3, l. 161. [Cassius]

9 You have obedience scanted,
And well are worth the want that you have wanted.
King Lear. Act i, sc. 1, l. 281. [Goneril]

10
He that helps him take all my outward worth.
King Lear. Act iv, sc. 4, l. 10. [Cordelia]
Inward worth.—*Sonnets*, lxvi.
Adventurous worth.—*Pericles*, ii, 4, 51.
Better worth.—*I Henry IV*, iv, 1, 27.
Fair worth.—*Troilus and Cressida*, iv, 4, 150.
Kingdom's worth.—*III Henry VI*, iii, 3, 94.
Sea's worth.—*Othello*, i, 2, 28.
Worth and credit.—*Measure for Measure*, v, 1, 244.

11
Your worth is very dear in my regard.
The Merchant of Venice. Act i, sc. 1, l. 62 [Antonio]
Nor is the wide world ignorant of her worth,
For the four winds blow in from every coast
Renowned suitors.
The Merchant of Venice. Act i, sc. 1, l. 167. [Bassanio]

12
The rich worth of your virginity.
A Midsummer-Night's Dream, ii, 1, 219. See under VIRGINITY.
The longer kept, the less worth.—*All's Well that Ends Well*, i, 1, 167. Referring to VIRGINITY.

13
There 's some of worth would come aboard.
Pericles. Act v, sc. 1, l. 9. [Helicanus]

The worth that learned charity aye wears.
Pericles. Act v, sc. 3, l. 94. [Gower]

1 They are but beggars that can count their worth.
Romeo and Juliet. Act ii, sc. 6, l. 32. [Juliet]

2 Your worth, wide as the ocean is.
Sonnets. No. lxxx.

Finding thy worth a limit past my praise.
Sonnets. No. lxxxii.

I never saw that you did painting need
And therefore to your fair no painting set;
I found, or thought I found, you did exceed
The barren tender of a poet's debt;
And therefore have I slept in your report,
That you yourself being extant well might show
How far a modern quill doth come too short,
Speaking of worth, what worth in you doth show.
Sonnets. No. lxxxiii.

3 Worth What 's dearest to the world!
Tempest. Act iii, sc. 1, l. 38. [Ferdinand]

4 You have added worth unto 't and lustre.
Timon of Athens. Act i, sc. 2, l. 154. [Timon]

5 Imagined worth
Holds in his blood such swoln and hot discourse
That 'twixt his mental and his active parts
Kingdom'd Achilles in commotion rages
And batters down himself.
Troilus and Cressida. Act ii, sc. 3, l. 182. [Ulysses] The only use of "kingdom'd."

6 To her own worth She shall be prized.
Triolus and Cressida. Act iv, sc. 4, l. 135. [Diomedes]

7 If it be worth stooping for, there it lies in your eye; if not, be it his that finds it.
Twelfth Night. Act ii, sc. 2, l. 15. [Malvolio]

But, were my worth as is my conscience firm,
You should find better dealing.
Twelfth Night. Act iii, sc. 3, l. 17. [Sebastian]

8 I know the gentleman
To be of worth and worthy estimation
And not without desert so well reputed.
The Two Gentlemen of Verona. Act ii, sc. 4, l. 55. [Valentine]

9 Far behind his worth
Come all the praises that I now bestow.
The Two Gentlemen of Verona. Act ii, sc. 4, l. 71. [Valentine]

10 Welcome him then according to his worth.
The Two Gentlemen of Verona. Act ii, sc. 4, l. 83. [Duke]

His worth is warrant for his welcome hither.
The Two Gentlemen of Verona. Act ii, sc. 4, l. 102. [Silvia]

Worth a welcome.—*I Henry IV*, iv, 1, 87.

11 The gentleman
Is full of virtue, bounty, worth.
The Two Gentlemen of Verona. Act iii, sc. 1, l. 64. [Valentine]

A youthful gentleman of worth.
The Two Gentlemen of Verona. Act iii, sc. 1, l. 107. [Duke]

All I can is nothing
To her whose worth makes other worthies nothing.
The Two Gentlemen of Verona. Act ii, sc. 4, l. 165. [Valentine]

12 Come, Camillo,
And take her by the hand, whose worth and honesty
Is richly noted and here justified
By us, a pair of kings.
Winter's Tale. Act v, sc. 3, l. 143. [Leontes]

She was more worth such gazes
Than what you look on now.
Winter's Tale. Act v, sc. 1, l. 226. [Paulina]

II—Worthiness

13 Even to the utmost syllable of your worthiness.
All's Well that Ends Well. Act iii, sc. 6, l. 74. [Bertram]

I know your worthiness.—*Henry V*, ii, 2, 69.

14 There was never a worthier man.
Coriolanus. Act ii, sc. 3, l. 43. [Citizen]

He 's a worthy man.—*Coriolanus*, ii, 2, 39; 126; iii, 3, 35.

A worthy fellow.—*Coriolanus,* v, 2, 116; *Timon of Athens*, i, 1, 229; *Cymbeline*, ii, 3, 60; *Henry VIII*, iii, 2, 72.

The worthy thane of Ross.—*Macbeth*, i, 2, 45. The phrase "worthy thane" occurs twenty-seven times in *Macbeth,* and in no other play.

He 's worthy of it.—*Henry VIII*, v, 3, 155.

Thou art worthy of it.—*All's Well that Ends Well,* ii, 3, 231.

Yes, he is worthy of thee.—*Timon of Athens,* i, 1, 231.

Most worthy.—*The Winter's Tale,* iv, 4, 384.

15 Marcius is worthy of present death.
Coriolanus. Act iii, sc. 1, l. 211. [Brutus]

Worthy death.—*II Henry VI*, iii, 1, 242; *Coriolanus,* iii, 1, 298.

Worthy blame.—*III Henry VI*, v, 5, 54; *Rape of Lucrece*, l. 1257; *Passionate Pilgrim,* 301.

Worthy to be hang'd.—*Winter's Tale*, ii, 3, 109.

Worthy to be judge.—*I Henry VI*, iv, 1, 42.

Worthy to be whipped.—*Much Ado about Nothing,* ii, 1, 227.

Thrice-worthy.—*Love's Labour's Lost,* v, 1, 151; *Henry V*, iv, 4, 66; *Troilus and Cressida*, ii, 3, 200.

16 That 's worthily As any ear can hear.
Coriolanus. Act iv, sc. 1, l. 55. [Menenius]

17 The worthiest sir that ever
Country call'd his! and you his mistress, only
For the most worthiest fit!
Cymbeline. Act i, sc. 6, l. 160. [Iachimo]

The best feather of our wing.
Cymbeline. Act i, sc. 6, l. 186. [Iachimo]

Worthy To inlay heaven with stars.
Cymbeline. Act v, sc. 5, l. 351. [Belarius] The only use of "inlay."

Worthy his goodness.—*The Winter's Tale,* v, 1, 176.

Worthy to live.—*II Henry VI,* iv, 7, 50.

1
Whether your grace be worthy, yea or no,
Dispute not that: York is the worthier.
II Henry VI. Act i, sc. 3, l. 110. [Warwick]

2 Thou art worthy of the sway,
To whom the heavens in thy nativity
Adjudged an olive branch and laurel crown,
As likely to be blest in peace and war.
III Henry VI. Act iv, sc. 6, l. 32. [Clarence]

3
Till you compound whose right is worthiest,
We for the worthiest hold the right from both.
King John. Act ii, sc. 1, l. 281. [Citizen]

Worthiest To have command obey'd.—*Anthony and Cleopatra,* iii, 13, 87.

4
Bold of your worthiness, we single you
As our best-moving fair solicitor.
Love's Labour 's Lost. Act ii, sc. 1, l. 29. [Princess of France] The only use of "best-moving." "Solicitor" is repeated in *Othello,* iii, 3, 27.

5
Holofernes: Sir, you shall present before her the Nine Worthies. . . .
Nathaniel: Where will you find men worthy enough?
Love's Labour 's Lost. Act v, sc. 1, l. 125. The Nine Worthies were commonly said to be three Gentiles: Hector, Alexander, Julius Cæsar; three Jews: Joshua, David, Judas Maccabæus; and three Christians: Arthur, Charlemagne, and Godfrey of Bouillon. Here Pompey and Hercules are reckoned among the nine.

Ten times better than the Nine Worthies.
II Henry IV. Act ii, sc. 4, l. 238. [Doll]

6
Worthy the owner, and the owner it.
The Merry Wives of Windsor. Act v, sc. 5, l. 64. [Mistress Quickly]

7
The other must be held the worthier.
A Midsummer-Night's Dream. Act i, sc. 1, l. 55. [Theseus]

Reason says you are the worthier maid.
A Midsummer-Night's Dream. Act ii, sc. 2, l. 116. [Lysander]

8
That she is worthy, I know.
Much Ado about Nothing. Act i, sc. 1, l. 231. [Don Pedro]

The lady is very well worthy.—*Much Ado about Nothing,* i, 1, 224.

Worthy of thy praise.—*The Merchant of Venice,* i, 2, 133.

Worthy of thy sweet respect.—*Sonnets,* xxvi.

9
He is a good one, and his worthiness
Does challenge much respect.
Othello. Act ii, sc. 1, l. 212. [Othello]

Great worthiness.—*Love's Labour 's Lost,* ii, 1, 63.

True worthiness.—*Love's Labour 's Lost,* ii, 1, 171.

O worthiness of nature!—*Cymbeline,* iv, 2, 25.

10
O, how thy worth with manners may I sing,
When thou art all the better part of me?
Sonnets. No. xxxix.

Blessed are you, whose worthiness gives scope,
Being had, to triumph, being lack'd, to hope.
Sonnets. No. lii.

11 Worthier than himself
Here tend the savage strangeness he puts on, . . .
And underwrite in an observing kind
His humorous predominance.
Troilus and Cressida. Act ii, sc. 3, l. 134. [Agamemnon] The only use of "underwrite."

The worthiest of them tell me name by name.
Troilus and Cressida. Act iv, sc. 5, l. 160. [Hector]

12
He is as worthy for an empress' love
As meet to be an emperor's counsellor.
The Two Gentlemen of Verona. Act ii, sc. 4, l. 76. [Duke]

And think me worthy of an empress' love.
The Two Gentlemen of Verona. Act v, sc. 4, l. 141. [Duke]

III—Worthlessness

13
I have now found thee; when I lose thee again, I care not: yet art thou good for nothing but taking up; and that thou 'rt scarce worth.
All's Well that Ends Well. Act ii, sc. 3, l. 216. [Lafeu] The only use of "good for nothing."

You are not worth another word.
All's Well that Ends Well. Act ii, sc. 3, l. 280. [Lafeu]

It is not worth the wagging of your beards.
Coriolanus. Act ii, sc. 1, l. 96. [Menenius]

She is not worth what she doth cost.
Troilus and Cressida. Act ii, sc. 2, l. 51. [Hector]

That same dog-fox, Ulysses, is not proved worth a blackberry.
Troilus and Cressida. Act v, sc. 4, l. 12. [Thersites] The only use of "dog-fox" and "blackberry."

Timon: What dost thou think 'tis worth?
Apemantus: Not worth my thinking.
Timon of Athens. Act i, sc. 1, l. 219.

Not worth His serious considering.—*Henry VIII,* iii, 2, 134.

Not worth our debate.—*Cymbeline,* i, 4, 173.

Not worth an egg.—*Coriolanus,* iv, 4, 21.

Not worth the enjoying.—*II Henry VI,* iii, 1, 334.

Not worth the feeding.—*Antony and Cleopatra,* v, 2, 271.

Not worth a gooseberry.—*II Henry IV,* i, 2, 196. The only use of "gooseberry."

Not worth the hanging.—*Cymbeline,* i, 5, 20.

Not worth leave-taking.—*Antony and Cleopatra,* v, 2, 301.

Not worth a pin.—*The Two Gentlemen of Verona,* ii, 7, 55.

Not worth the search.—*The Merchant of Venice,* i, 1, 118.
Not worth The splinter of a lance.—*Troilus and Cressida,* i, 3, 282.
Not worth sun-burning.—*Henry V,* v, 2, 154. See under FACE.
Not worth the time of day.—*Pericles,* iv, 3, 35.
Poor in worth.—*Troilus and Cressida,* iii, 3, 130.
Scarce to be worth talking of.—*Twelfth Night,* iii, 4, 328.

1 In argument of praise, or to the worth
Of the great count himself, she is too mean
To have her name repeated.
All's Well that Ends Well. Act iii, sc. 5, l. 62. [Helena]
She is not worth thee.—*Twelfth Night,* ii, 4, 28.

2 Owes more than he 's worth.
Comedy of Errors, iv, 2, 58. See under DEBT.

3 Holding a weak supposal of our worth.
Hamlet. Act i, sc. 2, l. 18. [King] The only use of "supposal."

4 All that I can do is nothing worth.
Henry V. Act iv, sc. 1, l. 320. [King Henry]
Nothing worth.—*Venus and Adonis,* l. 418; *Sonnets,* lxxii; *Hamlet,* iv, 4, 66.
Little worth.—*I Henry VI,* v, 3, 151.
Of small worth.—*Sonnets,* ii.

5 Worthless of such honour.
Julius Cæsar. Act v, sc. 1, l. 61. [Cassius]
My worthless self.—*The Merchant of Venice,* ii, 9, 18.
You are worthless.—*The Two Gentlemen of Verona,* i, 1, 161.

6 I would that I were low laid in my grave:
I am not worth this coil that 's made for me.
King John. Act ii, sc. 1, l. 164. [Arthur] "Low laid" is repeated in *Cymbeline,* v, 4, 103.
Goneril: I have been worth the whistle. . . .
Albany: You are not worth the dust which the rude wind
Blows in your face.
King Lear. Act iv, sc. 2, l. 29.
No worthier than the dust.—*Julius Cæsar,* iii, 1, 116.

7 Now worth this, And now worth nothing.
The Merchant of Venice. Act i, sc. 1, l. 35. [Salarino]
Not so much worth.—*Love's Labour 's Lost,* v, 2, 561.

8 Not worthy to touch Fortune's fingers.
Twelfth Night. Act ii, sc. 5, l. 170. [Malvolio]

9 There is none worthy,
Respecting her that 's gone.
Winter's Tale. Act v, sc. 1, l. 34. [Paulina]

10 A man not worth her pains, much less
The adventure of her person.
Winter's Tale. Act v, sc. 1, l. 155. [Leontes]
Worth the pains.—*The Merchant of Venice,* ii, 6, 33; *Twelfth Night,* i, 2, 57. See also under PAINS.

WOUND

See also Hurt, Injury, Scar, Stab

11 Alas, poor shepherd! searching of thy wound,
I have by hard adventure found mine own.
As You Like It. Act ii, sc. 4, l. 44. [Rosalind]
Now to the bottom dost thou search my wound.
Titus Andronicus. Act ii, sc. 3, l. 262. [Saturninus]

12 Phebe: Now show the wound mine eye hath made in thee. . . .
Silvius: If ever,—as that ever may be near,—
You meet in some fresh cheek the power of fancy,
Then shall you know the wounds invisible
That love's keen arrows make.
As You Like It. Act iii, sc. 5, l. 20.
Love's wound.—*A Midsummer-Night's Dream,* ii, 1, 167.
Love-wounded Proteus.—*The Two Gentlemen of Verona,* i, 2, 114. The only use of "love-wounded."
Wound me not with thine eye but with thy tongue.
Sonnets. No. cxxxix.

13 Brief, I recover'd him, bound up his wound.
As You Like It. Act iv, sc. 3, l. 151. [Oliver]
Bind up my wounds.—*Richard III,* v, 3, 177.

14 Antony: Thou bleed'st apace.
Scarus: I had a wound here that was like a T,
But now 'tis made an H. . . .
We 'll beat 'em into bench-holes: I have yet
Room for six scotches more.
Antony and Cleopatra. Act iv, sc. 7, l. 6. The only use of "bench-holes" (privies) and "scotches" (gashes).

With joyful tears
Wash the congealment from your wounds, and kiss
The honour'd gashes whole.
Antony and Cleopatra. Act iv, sc. 8, l. 9. [Antony] The only use of "congealment."
A perilous gash, a very limb lopp'd off.
I Henry IV. Act iv, sc. 1, l. 43. [Hotspur]

The gashes
That bloodily did yawn upon his face.
Henry V. Act iv, sc. 6, l. 13. [Exeter]
But I am faint, my gashes cry for help.
Macbeth. Act i, sc. 2, l. 42. [Sergeant]

Safe in a ditch he bides,
With twenty trenched gashes on his head;
The least a death to nature.
Macbeth. Act iii, sc. 4, l. 26. [Murderer] "Trenched" is repeated in *The Two Gentlemen of Verona,* iii, 2, 7.
Each new day a gash Is added to her wounds.
Macbeth. Act iv, sc. 3, l. 40. [Malcolm]
Give me a gash, put me to present pain.
Pericles, v, 1, 193. See under JOY.

1
I have some wounds upon me, and they smart
To hear themselves remember'd.
Coriolanus. Act i, sc. 9, l. 28. [Marcius]
Menenius: Where is he wounded? . . . Marcius is coming home: he has more cause to be proud. Where is he wounded?
Volumnia: I' the shoulder and i' the left arm: there will be large cicatrices to show the people. . . . He received in the repulse of Tarquin seven hurts i' the body.
Menenius: One i' the neck, and two i' the thigh —there 's nine that I know.
Volumnia: He had, before this last expedition, twenty-five wounds upon him.
Menenius: Now it 's twenty-seven: every gash was an enemy's grave.
Coriolanus. Act ii, sc. 1, l. 59.
Menenius: Is he not wounded? he was wont to come home wounded. . . .
Volumnia: O, he is wounded; I thank the gods for 't.
Menenius: So do I too, if it be not too much: . . . the wounds become him.
Coriolanus. Act ii, sc. 1, l. 130.

2
I had rather have my wounds to heal again
Than hear say how I got them.
Coriolanus. Act ii, sc. 2, l. 73. [Coriolanus]
Look, sir, my wounds!
I got them in my country's service.
Coriolanus. Act ii, sc. 3, l. 57. [Coriolanus]
I have wounds to show you, which shall be yours in private.
Coriolanus. Act ii, sc. 3, l. 83. [Coriolanus]
You have received many wounds for your country.
Coriolanus. Act ii, sc. 3, l. 113. [Citizen]
Of wounds two dozen odd.
Coriolanus. Act ii, sc. 3, l. 135. [Coriolanus]
Wounds received for 's country.
Coriolanus. Act ii, sc. 3, l. 172. [Citizen]
He said he had wounds, which he could show in private.
Coriolanus. Act ii, sc. 3, l. 174. [Citizen]
Good man, the wounds that he does bear for Rome!
Coriolanus. Act iv, sc. 2, l. 28. [Volumnia]

3
Menenius: The wounds his body bears, which show
Like graves i' the holy churchyard.
Coriolanus: Scratches with briers,
Scars to move laughter only.
Coriolanus. Act iii, sc. 3, l. 50.
And God forbid a shallow scratch should drive
The Prince of Wales from such a field as this,
Where stain'd nobility lies trodden on,
And rebels' arms triumph in massacres!
I Henry IV. Act v, sc. 4, l. 11. [Prince]
Benvolio: What, art thou hurt?
Mercutio: Ay, ay, a scratch, a scratch; marry, 'tis enough.
Romeo and Juliet. Act iii, sc. 1, l. 95. See under Hurt.
'Zounds, a dog, a rat, a mouse, a cat, to scratch a man to death!
Romeo and Juliet. Act iii, sc. 1, l. 104. [Mercutio]

4
Having found the back-door open
Of the unguarded hearts, heavens, how they wound!
Cymbeline. Act v, sc. 3, l. 45. [Posthumus]
"Back-door" is repeated in *The Merry Wives of Windsor,* iii, 3, 25.

5
All smarting with my wounds being cold.
I Henry IV. Act i, sc. 3, l. 49. [Hotspur]
"Smarting" is repeated in *Antony and Cleopatra,* ii, 5, 66.
All those wounds, Those mouthed wounds.
I Henry IV. Act i, sc. 3, l. 96. [Hotspur]
They wound my thoughts worse than thy sword my flesh.
I Henry IV. Act v, sc. 4, l. 79. [Hotspur]

6
Therefore, sirrah, with a new wound in your thigh, come you along with me.
I Henry IV. Act v, sc. 4, l. 130. [Falstaff]
I 'll take it upon my death, I gave him this wound in the thigh; if the man were alive and would deny it, 'zounds, I would make him eat a piece of my sword.
I Henry IV. Act v, sc. 4, l. 154. [Falstaff]
Giving myself a voluntary wound
Here, in the thigh.
Julius Cæsar. Act ii, sc. 1, l. 300. [Portia]

7
The king is almost wounded to the death.
II Henry IV. Act i, sc. 1, l. 14. [Bardolph]
Wounded to death.—*King John,* v, 4, 9.
Wounded dangerously.—*III Henry VI,* i, 1, 11.
Wounded with disdain.—*The Passionate Pilgrim,* l. 221.
Deep-sore wounding.—*Venus and Adonis,* l. 432. The only use of "deep-sore."

8
I am loath to gall a new-healed wound.
II Henry IV. Act i, sc. 2, l. 166. [Chief Justice]
The new-heal'd wound of malice.
Richard III, ii, 2, 125. The only uses of "new-healed."

9
Why, then, let grievous, ghastly, gaping wounds
Untwine the Sisters Three!
II Henry IV. Act ii, sc. 4, l. 212. [Pistol]
"Untwine" is repeated in *Cymbeline,* iv, 2, 59.
Gaping wound.—*The Merchant of Venice,* iii, 2, 268.

10
Behold the wounds, the most unnatural wounds,
Which thou thyself hast given her woful breast.
I Henry VI. Act iii, sc. 3, l. 50. [La Pucelle]

11
That bears so shrewd a maim; two pulls at once.
II Henry VI. Act ii, sc. 3, l. 41. [Queen]
Your father's sickness is a maim to us.
I Henry IV. Act iv, sc. 1, l. 42. [Worcester]
So deep a maim.—*Richard II,* i, 3, 156. The only uses of "maim" as a noun. As a verb it occurs once, in *A Lover's Complaint,* l. 312.
Maims of shame.—*Coriolanus,* iv, 5, 92. The only use of "maims."
I am maim'd forever!—*Othello,* v, 1, 27.

Maim'd you two outright.—*The Taming of the Shrew,* v, 2, 62.
Maim'd the jurisdiction.—*Henry VIII,* iii, 2, 312.
Maim'd and most imperfect.—*Othello,* i, 3, 99.
Maimed rites.—*Hamlet,* v, 1, 242. The only uses of "maimed."

1
Send succours, lords, and stop the rage betime,
Before the wound do grow uncurable;
For, being green, there is great hope of help.
II Henry VI. Act iii, sc. 1, l. 285. [Post] "Uncurable" is repeated in v, 2, 86, "uncurable discomfit," and occurs in no other play. "Incurable" is used five times.

A green wound.—*II Henry IV,* ii, 1, 106; *Henry V,* v, 1, 44.

2 The wound that bred this meeting here
Cannot be cured by words.
III Henry VI. Act ii, sc. 2, l. 121. [Clifford]

Cureless are my wounds.—*III Henry VI,* ii, 6, 23. "Cureless" is repeated in *The Merchant of Venice,* iv, 1, 42.

With a wound I must be cured.
Antony and Cleopatra. Act iv, sc. 14, l. 78. [Antony]

Unrecuring wound.—*Titus Andronicus,* iii, 1, 90. The only use of "unrecuring."

3
The air hath got into my deadly wounds,
And much effuse of blood doth make me faint.
III Henry VI. Act ii, sc. 6, l. 27. [Clifford] The only use of "effuse."

Deadly wounds.—*I Henry IV,* i, 3, 109.
Deathful wound.—*II Henry VI,* iii, 2, 404.
Deep wound.—*Sonnets,* cxxxiii.
Destroying wound.—*Richard II,* iii, 2, 139.
Long-grown wounds.—*I Henry IV,* iii, 2, 156. The only use of "long-grown."
Reeking wounds.—*Macbeth,* i, 2, 39.
Unadvised wounds.—*Rape of Lucrece,* l. 1488.
Wide wound.—*Venus and Adonis,* l. 1052.

4 Thy wounds . . .
Which, like dumb mouths, do ope their ruby lips.
Julius Cæsar. Act iii, sc. 1, l. 259. [Antony]

Show you sweet Cæsar's wounds, poor poor dumb mouths,
And bid them speak for me.
Julius Cæsar. Act iii, sc. 2, l. 229. [Antony]

5
And heal the inveterate canker of one wound
By making many.
King John. Act v, sc. 2, l. 14. [Salisbury]

6
He pricks and wounds.
King John, v, 7, 17. See under DEATH.

Prick and sting.—*Hamlet,* i, 5, 88.
Shall I prick him down?—*II Henry IV,* iii, 2, 153.
Prick him down.—*Julius Cæsar,* iv, 1, 3.
Prick not your finger.—*I Henry VI,* ii, 4, 49.
Prick their finger.—*II Henry IV,* ii, 2, 121.
Prick thy finger.—*III Henry VI,* i, 4, 55.
Pin prick.—*King Lear,* iv, 7, 56.
Pins, wooden pricks.—*King Lear,* ii, 3, 16.
Small pricks.—*Troilus and Cressida,* i, 3, 343.
Love's prick.—*As You Like It,* iii, 2, 118.

7
What wound did ever heal but by degrees?
Othello. Act ii, sc. 3, l. 377. [Iago]

I thought you had received some bodily wound.
Othello. Act ii, sc. 3, l. 267. [Iago]

8
'Once,' quoth she, 'did I see a fair sweet youth
Here in these brakes deep-wounded with a boar,
Deep in the thigh, a spectacle of ruth!
See, in my thigh,' quoth she, 'here was the sore,'
She showed hers; he saw more wounds than one,
And blushing fled, and left her all alone.
The Passionate Pilgrim, l. 125. The only use of "deep-wounded."

9 The wound that nothing healeth,
The scar that will, despite of cure, remain.
The Rape of Lucrece, l. 731.

To see the salve doth make the wound ache more.
The Rape of Lucrece, l. 1116. See under MEDICINE.

My wounds ache at you.—*Timon of Athens,* iii, 5, 95.

10 Through her wounds doth fly
Life's lasting date from cancell'd destiny.
The Rape of Lucrece, l. 1728.

Do wounds help wounds, or grief help grievous deeds?
The Rape of Lucrece, l. 1822.

11
He in peace is wounded, not in war.
The Rape of Lucrece, l. 831.

12
Lo, in these windows that let forth thy life,
I pour the helpless balm of my poor eyes.
Richard III. Act i, sc. 2, l. 12. [Anne]

13
O, gentlemen, see, see! dead Henry's wounds
Open their congeal'd mouths and bleed afresh!
Richard III. Act i, sc. 2, l. 55. [Lady Anne]

Look, how thy wounds do bleed at many vents!
Troilus and Cressida. Act v, sc. 3, l. 82. [Cassandra]

14 It had upon its brow
A bump as big as a young cockerel's stone;
A parlous knock.
Romeo and Juliet. Act i, sc. 3, l. 52. [Nurse] The only use of "bump." "Cockerel" is repeated in *The Tempest,* ii, 1, 31.

I saw the wound, I saw it with mine eyes,—
God save the mark!—here on his manly breast.
Romeo and Juliet. Act iii, sc. 2, l. 52. [Nurse]

15 He that wounded her
Hath hurt me more than had he kill'd me dead.
Titus Andronicus. Act iii, sc. 1, l. 91. [Titus]

Ah, that this sight should make so deep a wound,
And yet detested life not shrink thereat!
Titus Andronicus. Act iii, sc. 1, l. 247. [Lucius]

1 Who hath brought the fatal engine in
That gives our Troy, our Rome, the civil wound.
Titus Andronicus. Act v, sc. 3, l. 86. [Marcus]
Civil wounds.—*Richard III,* v, 5, 40; *Richard II,* i, 3, 128.

2
Those wounds heal ill that men do give themselves.
Troilus and Cressida. Act iii, sc. 3, l. 229. [Patroclus]
The private wound is deepest.
The Two Gentlemen of Verona. Act v, sc. 4, l. 71. [Valentine]

3
That I may give the local wound a name
And make distinct the very breach whereout
Hector's great spirit flew: answer me, heavens!
Troilus and Cressida. Act iv, sc. 1, l. 244. [Achilles] The only use of "whereout."
Patroclus' wounds have roused his drowsy blood,
Together with his mangled Myrmidons,
That noseless, handless, hack'd and chipp'd come to him.
Troilus and Cressida. Act v, sc. 5, l. 34. [Ulysses] The only use of "noseless."
Cæsar's three and thirty wounds.—*Julius Cæsar,* v, 1, 53.
Lucrece' wound.—*The Rape of Lucrece,* l. 1810.
Priam's wounds.—*The Rape of Lucrece,* l. 1448.
Priam's painted wound.—*The Rape of Lucrece,* l. 1466.

4 Another licking of his wound,
'Gainst venom'd sores the only sovereign plaster.
Venus and Adonis, l. 915. The only use of "licking."
The wide wound that the boar had trench'd
In his soft flank; whose wonted lily white
With purple tears, that his wound wept, was drench'd.
Venus and Adonis, l. 1052. "Flank" occurs again in l. 1115, and nowhere else.

WRATH

See also Anger, Fury, Rage

5
They are in the very wrath of love.
As You Like It, v, 2, 44. See under LOVE.

6
Wrath o'erwhelm'd my pity.
Coriolanus. Act i, sc. 9, l. 86. [Coriolanus]
Sweat with wrath.—*Coriolanus,* i, 4, 27.
Roasted in wrath and fire.—*Hamlet,* ii, 2, 483.
Passing fell and wrath.—*A Midsummer-Night's Dream,* ii, 1, 20.
Highly moved to wrath.—*Titus Andronicus,* i, 1, 419.

7
The good gods assuage thy wrath, and turn the dregs of it upon this varlet here.
Coriolanus. Act v, sc. 2, l. 82. [Menenius]

8
I something fear my father's wrath.
Cymbeline. Act i, sc. 1, l. 86. [Imogen]
I am senseless of your wrath; a touch more rare
Subdues all pangs, all fears.
Cymbeline. Act i, sc. 1, l. 135. [Imogen]
Let 's follow him, and pervert the present wrath
He hath against himself.
Cymbeline. Act ii, sc. 4, l. 151. [Philario]
Tasting of our wrath.—*Cymbeline,* v, 5, 308.

9
No more, I say: if thou dost plead for him,
Thou wilt but add increase unto my wrath.
II Henry VI. Act iii, sc. 2, l. 291. [King Henry]

10
Angry, wrathful, and inclined to blood.
II Henry VI. Act iv, sc. 2, l. 134. [Brother]
Be wrathful still.—*II Henry VI,* v, 2, 70.
Spiteful and wrathful.—*Macbeth,* iii, 5, 12.

11
Wrath makes him deaf.
III Henry VI. Act i, sc. 4, l. 53. [Queen Margaret]

12
Be thou the trumpet of our wrath.
King John. Act i, sc. 1, l. 27. [King John]
I am burn'd up with inflaming wrath;
A rage whose heat hath this condition,
That nothing can allay, nothing but blood,
The blood, and dearest-valued blood, of France.
King John. Act iii, sc. 1, l. 340. [King John] The only use of "dearest-valued."

13
Let me endure your wrath.
Macbeth. Act v, sc. 5, l. 36. [Messenger]
Thou hadst been better have been born a dog
Than answer my waked wrath!
Othello. Act iii, sc. 3, l. 362. [Othello]

14 Testy wrath
Could never be her mild companion.
Pericles. Act i, sc. 1, l. 17. [Pericles]

15
Exeute thy wrath in me alone.
Richard III, i, 4, 71. See under REVENGE.
Put in their hands thy bruising irons of wrath!
Richard III, v, 3, 110. See under PRAYER.

16
All this from my remembrance brutish wrath
Sinfully pluck'd.
Richard III. Act ii, sc. 1, l. 118. [King Edward] "Sinfully" is repeated in *Henry V,* iv, 1, 155.
Cloudy wrath.—*Richard III,* i, 3, 268.
Hot wrath.—*A Lover's Complaint,* l. 293.
Flaming wrath.—*II Henry VI,* v, 2, 55.
Swift wrath.—*II Henry IV,* Ind., 30.
Wall-eyed wrath.—*King John,* iv, 3, 49. "Wall-eyed" is used once again in *Titus Andronicus,* v, 1, 44: "Wall-eyed slave."
The devil wrath.—*Othello,* ii, 3, 298. See under FAULT.

17
I 'll teach them to prevent wild Alcibiades' wrath.
Timon of Athens. Act v, sc. 1, l. 206. [Timon]
Hector's wrath.—*Troilus and Cressida,* i, 2, 11.

18
O, why should wrath be mute, and fury dumb?
Titus Andronicus. Act v, sc. 3, l. 184. [Aaron]

1
By heaven! my wrath shall far exceed the love
I ever bore my daughter or thyself.
The Two Gentlemen of Verona. Act iii, sc. 1, l. 166. [Duke]
Come not within the measure of my wrath.
The Two Gentlemen of Verona. Act v, sc. 4, l. 127. [Valentine]

2
If thou . . . wilt encounter with my wrath, say so.
Winter's Tale. Act ii, sc. 3, l. 138. [Leontes]

WRECK, see Shipwreck

WREN

3
The poor wren,
The most diminutive of birds, will fight,
Her young ones in her nest, against the owl.
Macbeth. Act iv, sc. 2, l. 9. [Lady Macduff]
The wren goes to 't.—*King Lear,* iv, 6, 114. See under LOVE AND LUST.
The wren with little quill.—*A Midsummer-Night's Dream,* iii, 1, 131. See under BIRD.
Petty wrens.—*Pericles,* iv, 3, 22.
The chirping of a wren.—*II Henry VI,* iii, 2, 42. See under COMFORT.

4
Wrens make prey where eagles dare not perch.
Richard III, i, 3, 71. See under WORLD.

5
Look, where the youngest wren of mine comes.
Twelfth Night. Act iii, sc. 2, l. 70. [Sir Toby]

WRETCH

6
A needy, hollow-eyed, sharp-looking wretch.
The Comedy of Errors, v, 1, 240. See under CHARACTER.
Base wretch.—*Cymbeline,* ii, 3, 118.
Base ignoble wretch!—*I Henry VI,* v, 4, 7.
Basest and contemned'st wretches.—*King Lear,* ii, 2, 150.
Bloody wretch.—*Richard III,* v, 5, 5.
Caitiff wretch.—*Romeo and Juliet,* v, 1, 52.
Cursed wretch.—*The Winter's Tale,* iv, 4, 469.
Damned wretch.—*II Henry VI,* iv, 10, 83.
Debile wretch.—*Coriolanus,* i, 9, 48. "Debile" is repeated in *All's Well that Ends Well,* ii, 3, 39: "Debile minister."
Dew-bedabbled wretch.—*Venus and Adonis,* l. 703. The only use of the phrase.
Dishonest wretch!—*Measure for Measure,* iii, 1, 137.
Disobedient wretch!—*Romeo and Juliet,* iii, 5, 161.
Execrable wretch.—*Titus Andronicus,* v, 3, 177.
Hated wretch.—*Richard III,* i, 2, 17. See under CURSE.
Inhuman wretch.—*Merchant of Venice,* iv, 1, 4.
Meacock wretch.—*The Taming of the Shrew,* ii, 1, 315. See under SHREW. The only use of "meacock" (cowardly).
Meanest wretch.—*King Lear,* iv, 6, 208.
Mortal wretch.—*Antony and Cleopatra,* v, 2, 306.
Profane wretch.—*Othello,* i, 1, 115.
Rude wretch.—*Measure for Measure,* iv, 3, 85.
Vassal wretch.—*Sonnets,* cxli.

7
Wretch more worth your vengeance.
Cymbeline. Act v, sc. 1, l. 11. [Posthumus]
Wretches fettered in our prisons.
Henry V. Act i, sc. 2, l. 243. [King Henry]
Wretch that lies in woe.—*A Midsummer-Night's Dream,* v, 1, 384.

8
A wretch whose natural gifts were poor
To those of mine!
Hamlet. Act i, sc. 5, l. 51. [Ghost]

9
Be these the wretches that we play'd at dice for?
Henry V. Act iv, sc. 5, l. 8. [Dauphin]

10
Ah, timorous wretch!
Thou hast undone thyself, thy son and me.
III Henry VI. Act i, sc. 1, l. 231. [Queen]

11
She, poor wretch, for grief can speak no more.
III Henry VI, iii, 1, 47. "Poor wretch" occurs seven times in the plays and twice in the poems.
Excellent wretch!—*Othello,* iii, 3, 90.
Fond wretch.—*Measure for Measure,* v, 1, 105.
Pretty wretch.—*Romeo and Juliet,* i, 3, 44.
Soft-hearted wretch!—*II Henry VI,* iii, 2, 307. "Soft-hearted" is repeated in *III Henry VI,* ii, 3, 25: "Soft-hearted women."

12
A wretch whom nature is ashamed
Almost to acknowledge hers.
King Lear. Act i, sc. 1, l. 215. [King Lear]

13
Poor naked wretches, wheresoe'er you are,
That bide the pelting of this pitiless storm,
How shall your houseless heads and unfed sides,
Your loop'd and window'd raggedness, defend you
From seasons such as these?
King Lear. Act iii, sc. 4, l. 28. [King Lear] The only use of "unfed," "loop'd," and "raggedness." "Window'd" occurs again in *Antony and Cleopatra,* iv, 14, 72, and "houseless" is repeated in l. 26 of the same scene, "Houseless poverty," and nowhere else.
Poor miserable wretches.—*Henry V,* ii, 2, 178.

14
Never saw I
Wretches so quake: they kneel, they kiss the earth.
The Winter's Tale. Act v, sc. 1, l. 198. [Lord]
Groaning wretches.—*Love's Labour's Lost,* v, 2, 862.

15
Sly frantic wretch, that holp'st to make me great,
In hope thyself should govern Rome and me.
Titus Andronicus. Act iv, sc. 4, l. 59. [Saturninus]

16
Ungracious wretch,
Fit for the mountains and the barbarous caves,
Where manners ne'er were preach'd! out of my sight!
Twelfth Night. Act iv, sc. 1, l. 51. [Olivia]

WRETCHEDNESS

See also Man: Wretched Man; Misery

1 O Jove! I think
Foundations fly the wretched.
Cymbeline. Act iii, sc. 6, l. 6. [Imogen]

2
I, of ladies most deject and wretched.
Hamlet. Act iii, sc. 1, l. 163. [Hamlet]

What will become of me now, wretched lady?
Henry VIII. Act iii, sc. 1, l. 146. [Queen] "Wretched lady" is repeated in l. 102, and occurs nowhere else.

3
Sick in the world's regard, wretched and low,
A poor unminded outlaw sneaking home.
I Henry IV. Act iv, sc. 3, l. 57. [Hotspur] The only use of "unminded."

4
King: Ah, woe is me for Gloucester, wretched man!
Queen: Be woe for me, more wretched than he is.
II Henry VI. Act iii, sc. 2, l. 72.

5 What can happen
To me above this wretchedness? all your studies
Make me a curse like this.
Henry VIII. Act iii, sc. 1, l. 122. [Queen Katharine]

Spirits of peace, where are ye? are ye all gone,
And leave me here in wretchedness behind ye?
Henry VIII. Act iv, sc. 2, l. 83. [Katharine]

Full of wretchedness.—*Romeo and Juliet,* v, 1, 68.

Fierce wretchedness.—*Timon of Athens,* iv, 2, 30.

True wretchedness.—*Cymbeline,* iii, 4, 63.

6
I' the last night's storm I such a fellow saw;
Which made me think a man a worm.
King Lear. Act iv, sc. 1, l. 34. [Gloucester]

That I am wretched Makes thee the happier.
King Lear. Act iv, sc. 1, l. 68. [Gloucester]

Is wretchedness deprived that benefit,
To end itself by death?
King Lear. Act iv, sc. 6, l. 61. [Gloucester]

7
I love not to see wretchedness o'ercharged
And duty in his service perishing.
A Midsummer-Night's Dream. Act v, sc. 1, l. 85. [Hippolyta]

Free that soul which wretchedness hath chain'd.
The Rape of Lucrece, l. 900.

8
My wretchedness unto a row of pins.
Richard II. Act iii, sc. 4, l. 26. [Queen]

Whilst that my wretchedness doth bait myself.
Richard II. Act iv, sc. 1, l. 238. [King Richard] All the uses of "wretchedness" are given in this section.

9
Wretched in this alone, that thou mayst take
All this away and me most wretched make.
Sonnets. No. xci.

WRINKLE

10
The wrinkles in my brows, now fill'd with blood,
Were liken'd oft to kingly sepulchres.
III Henry VI. Act v, sc. 2, l. 19. [Warwick] The only use of "liken'd."

11
Let it stamp wrinkles in her brow of youth.
King Lear. Act i, sc. 4, l. 306. [King Lear]

Wrinkled brow.—*The Merchant of Venice,* iv, 1, 270.

Wrinkled brows.—*King John,* iv, 2, 192.

Wrinkled front.—*Richard III,* i, 1, 9.

Wrinkled eld.—*Troilus and Cressida,* ii, 2, 104.

12
With mirth and laughter let old wrinkles come.
The Merchant of Venice. Act i, sc. 1, l. 80. [Gratiano]

Wrinkle of a smile.—*Troilus and Cressida,* i, 1, 38.

Aged wrinkles.—*Titus Andronicus,* iii, 1, 7.

Frowning wrinkle.—*King John,* ii, 1, 505.

Necessary wrinkles.—*Sonnets,* cviii.

Remorseless wrinkles.—*The Rape of Lucrece,* l. 562.

Wrinkles strange.—*Sonnets,* xciii.

13
Thou canst help time to furrow me with age,
But stop no wrinkle in his pilgrimage.
Richard II. Act i, sc. 3, l. 229. [Gaunt] The only use of "furrow" as a verb. It is used as a noun in *The Tempest,* iv, 1, 135.

No deeper wrinkles yet? hath sorrow struck
So many blows upon this face of mine,
And made no deeper wounds?
Richard II. Act iv, sc. 1, l. 277. [King Richard]

14
So thou through windows of thine age shalt see
Despite of wrinkles this thy golden time.
Sonnets. No. iii.

O, carve not with thy hours my love's fair brow,
Nor draw no lines there with thine antique pen.
Sonnets. No. xix.

Time's furrows.—*Sonnets,* xxii.

Lines and wrinkles.—*Sonnets,* lxiii.

15
Thus is his cheek the map of days outworn.
Sonnets. No. lxviii.

The wrinkles which thy glass will truly show
Of mouthed graves will give thee memory.
Sonnets. No. lxxvii. The only use of "mouthed."

A pox of wrinkles.—*Timon of Athens,* iv, 3, 148.

Wrinkles forbid!—*Antony and Cleopatra,* i, 2, 19.

16
Witness these trenches made by grief and care.
Titus Andronicus. Act v, sc. 2, l. 23. [Titus]

17
Thou canst not see one wrinkle in my brow.
Venus and Adonis, l. 139.

WRITING

1
If he should write,
And I not have it, 'twere a paper lost,
As offer'd mercy is.
Cymbeline. Act i, sc. 3, l. 2. [Imogen]

2
I 'll call for pen and ink, and write my mind.
I Henry VI. Act v, sc. 3, l. 66. [Suffolk]
See also INK, PEN.

Her maid is gone, and she prepares to write.
The Rape of Lucrece, l. 1296.

Write, pen.—*Love's Labour 's Lost,* i, 2, 191.

Look you how he writes.—*II Henry IV,* ii, 2, 117.

I will write against it.—*Much Ado about Nothing,* iv, 1, 57.

3
These numbers will I tear, and write in prose.
Love's Labour 's Lost. Act iv, sc. 3, l. 57. [Longaville]

When shall you see me write a thing in rhyme?
Love's Labour 's Lost, iv, 3, 181. See under RHYME.

Writ in rhyme.—*The Two Gentlemen of Verona,* i, 2, 79.

He writes brave verses.—*As You Like It,* iii, 4, 43.

Writing love-songs.—*As You Like It,* iii, 2, 277.

4
Writ o' both sides the leaf, margent and all.
Love's Labour 's Lost. Act v, sc. 2, l. 8. [Princess of France]

Writ in the glassy margents of such books.
The Rape of Lucrece, l. 102.

5
There is a written scroll! I 'll read the writing.
The Merchant of Venice. Act ii, sc. 7, l. 64. [Morocco]

What 's here? A scroll; and written round about?
Titus Andronicus. Act iv, sc. 2, l. 18. [Demetrius]

6
Live still and write mine epitaph.
The Merchant of Venice. Act iv, sc. 1, l. 118. [Antonio]

Writing of my epitaph.—*Timon of Athens,* v, 1, 188.

Write me a prologue.—*A Midsummer-Night's Dream,* iii, 1, 18. See under PROLOGUE.

Write a ballad.—*A Midsummer-Night's Dream,* iv, 1, 220.

I 'll write it straight.—*As You Like It,* iii, 5, 136.

It will soon be writ.—*Rape of Lucrece,* l. 1295.

It is written.—*The Comedy of Errors,* iv, 3, 55; *Romeo and Juliet,* i, 2, 38.

Writ in choice Italian.—*Hamlet,* iii, 2, 274.

7
To write and read comes by nature.
Much Ado about Nothing, iii, 3, 12. See under EDUCATION.

8
Eleven hours I spent to write it over.
Richard III. Act iii, sc. 6, l. 5. [Scrivener]

I will write again.—*Romeo and Juliet,* v, 2, 28.

Took some pains in writing.—*The Merchant of Venice,* v, 1, 182.

9
O, let me, true in love, but truly write.
Sonnets. No. xxi.

O, know, sweet love, I always write of you,
And you and love are still my argument.
Sonnets. No. lxxvi.

For who 's so dumb that cannot write to thee,
When thou thyself dost give invention light?
Sonnets. No. xxxviii.

Lean penury within that pen doth dwell
That to his subject lends not some small glory;
But he that writes of you, if he can tell
That you are you, so dignifies his story,
Let him but copy what in you is writ,
And such a counterpart shall fame his wit,
Making his style admired everywhere.
Sonnets. No. lxxxiv. The only use of "counterpart."

O, blame me not, if I no more can write!
Sonnets. No. ciii.

10
There is enough written upon this earth
To stir a mutiny in the mildest thoughts
And arm the minds of infants to exclaims.
Titus Andronicus. Act iv, sc. 1, l. 84. [Marcus]

And, come, I will go get a leaf of brass,
And with a gad of steel will write these words.
Titus Andronicus. Act iv, sc. 1, l. 102. [Titus]

All this done Upon the gad!—*King Lear,* i, 2, 26. The only uses of "gad."

11
Valentine: Last night she enjoined to write some lines to one she loves. . . .
Speed: Are they not lamely writ?
Valentine: No, boy, but as well as I can do them.
Two Gentlemen of Verona. Act ii, sc. 1, l. 93.

Valentine: She hath not writ to me?
Speed: What need she, when she hath made you write to yourself?
Two Gentlemen of Verona. Act ii, sc. 1, l. 157.

Or fearing else some messenger that might her mind discover,
Herself hath taught her love himself to write unto her lover.
The Two Gentlemen of Verona. Act ii, sc. 1, l. 173. [Speed]

12
I thank you, gentle servant: 'tis very clerkly done.
The Two Gentlemen of Verona. Act ii, sc. 1, l. 114. [Silvia]

Clerkly couch'd.—*II Henry VI,* iii, 1, 179.

Thou art clerkly, thou art clerkly.
The Merry Wives of Windsor. Act iv, sc. 5, l. 58. [Host] The only uses of "clerkly."

13
I writ at random, very doubtfully.
The Two Gentlemen of Verona. Act ii, sc. 1, l. 117. [Valentine]

The lines are very quaintly writ.
The Two Gentlemen of Verona. Act ii, sc. 1, l. 128. [Silvia]

'Twas well writ.—*Twelfth Night,* iii, 4, 43.

I would have had them writ more movingly.
The Two Gentlemen of Verona. Act ii, sc. 1, l. 134. [Silvia] The only use of "movingly."

1
Things known betwixt us three, I 'll write you down.
The Winter's Tale. Act iv, sc. 4, l. 570. [Camillo]
Write down.—*Much Ado about Nothing,* iv, 2, 17; 20; 43; 73; 78.
Written down.—*Much Ado about Nothing,* iv, 2, 80; *King John,* v, 2, 4; *II Henry IV,* i, 2, 202.
Write down thy mind.—*Titus Andronicus,* ii, 4, 3.
2
Sir, you yourself
Have said and writ so, but your writing now
Is colder than that theme.
Winter's Tale. Act v, sc. 1, l. 98. [Paulina]

II—The Writer

3
All your writers do consent that ipse is he.
As You Like It. Act v, sc. 1, l. 47. [Touchstone] The only use of "ipse."
Their writers do them wrong.
Hamlet, ii, 2, 366. See under CRITICISM.
Ancient writers.—*I Henry IV,* ii, 4, 455.
Learned writer.—*Much Ado about Nothing,* iii, 5, 68.
Writers say.—*The Two Gentlemen of Verona,* i, 1, 42; i, 1, 45; *Henry V,* i, 2, 64.
4
If you be not too much cloyed with fat meat, our humble author will continue the story.
II Henry IV, Epil., 26.
With rough and all-unable pen,
Our bending author hath pursued the story.
Henry V, Epil., 2. The only use of "all-unable."
Any author in the world.—*Love's Labour 's Lost,* iv, 3, 312.
5
I tell you what mine authors say.
Pericles, i, Gower, 20.
I will read politic authors.
Twelfth Night, ii, 5, 176. See under READING.
The author's drift.
Troilus and Cressida. Act iii, sc. 3, l. 113. [Ulysses]
6
I grant thou wert not married to my Muse
And therefore mayst without attaint o'erlook
The dedicated words which writers use
Of their fair subject, blessing every book.
Sonnets. No. lxxxii.
7
My boy shall fetch the scrivener presently.
The Taming of the Shrew. Act iv, sc. 4, l. 59. [Tranio] The only use of "scrivener."

III—Handwriting

8
If skin were parchment and the blows you gave were ink,
Your own handwriting would tell you what I think.
The Comedy of Errors. Act iii, sc. 1, l. 13. [Dromio of Ephesus] The only use of "handwriting."
9
O, learn'd indeed were that astronomer
That knew the stars as I his characters.
Cymbeline. Act iii, sc. 2, l. 27. [Imogen]
Laertes: Know you the hand?
King: 'Tis Hamlet's character.
Hamlet. Act iv, sc. 7, l. 52.
Gloucester: You know the character to be your brother's? . . .
Edmund: It is his hand, my lord; but I hope his heart is not in the contents.
King Lear. Act i, sc. 2, l. 66.
You know the character.—*Measure for Measure,* iv, 2, 208.
Cerimon: Know you the character?
Thaisa: It is my lord's.
Pericles. Act iii, sc. 4, l. 3.
Know to be his character.—*The Winter's Tale,* v, 2, 38.
Thou didst produce my very character.
King Lear. Act ii, sc. 1, l. 72. [Edmund]
Perfect me in the characters!
Pericles. Act iii, sc. 2, l. 67. [Cerimon]
Golden characters.—*Pericles,* iv, 3, 44.
10
I once did hold it, as our statists do,
A baseness to write fair and labour'd much
How to forget that learning.
Hamlet. Act v, sc. 2, l. 33. [Hamlet] The only use of "statists" (statesmen). "Statist" occurs in *Cymbeline,* ii, 4, 16.
Hubert: Can you not read it? is it not fair writ?
Arthur: Too fairly, Hubert, for so foul effect.
King John. Act iv, sc. 1, l. 37.
There it is in writing, fairly drawn.
Taming of the Shrew, iii, 1, 70. [Lucentio]
Wrote it fair.—*Hamlet,* v, 2, 32.
11
He can . . . write court-hand.
II Henry VI, iv, 2, 100. The only use of "court-hand."
12
Rackers of orthography.
Love's Labour 's Lost. Act v, sc. 1, l. 21. [Holofernes] The only use of "rackers."
Now he is turned orthography.—*Much Ado about Nothing,* ii, 3, 21. The only uses of "orthography."
13
Claudio: Here 's a paper written in his hand. . . .
Hero: Here's another
Writ in my cousin's hand.
Much Ado about Nothing. Act v, sc. 4, l. 86.
Let me see the writing.—*Richard II,* v, 2, 57.
14
I can write very like my lady your niece: on a forgotten matter we can hardly make distinction of our hands.
Twelfth Night. Act ii, sc. 3, l. 173. [Maria]
By my life, this is my lady's hand: these be her very C's, her U's and her T's; and thus makes she her great P's. It is, in contempt of question, her hand.
Twelfth Night. Act ii, sc. 5, l. 95. [Malvolio]
Go, write it in a martial hand; . . . though you write with a goose-pen, no matter.
Twelfth Night. Act iii, sc. 2, l. 45. [Sir Toby] The only use of "goose-pen."
I think we do know the sweet Roman hand.
Twelfth Night. Act iii, sc. 4, l. 30. [Malvolio]

You must not now deny it is your hand:
Write from it, if you can, in hand or phrase.
Twelfth Night. Act v, sc. 1, l. 339. [Malvolio]
Alas, Malvolio, this is not my writing,
Though, I confess, much like the character:
But out of question 'tis Maria's hand.
Twelfth Night. Act v, sc. 1, l. 353. [Olivia]

WRONG

See also Harm; Injury; Right and Wrong

1
I most unfeignedly beseech your lordship to make some reservation of your wrongs.
All's Well that Ends Well. Act ii, sc. 3, l. 259. [Parolles]
Do it unfeignedly.—*Richard III,* ii, 1, 22.
Most unfeignedly.—*King John,* ii, 1, 526. The only uses of "unfeignedly."

2
Men's reports Give him much wrong'd.
Antony and Cleopatra. Act i, sc. 4, l. 39. [Messenger]
Most mighty duke, behold a man much wrong'd.
The Comedy of Errors. Act v, sc. 1, l. 330. [Abbess]
Never was man thus wronged.
Twelfth Night. Act iv, sc. 2, l. 32. [Malvolio]

3
Be it my wrong you are from me exempt,
But wrong not that wrong with a more contempt.
The Comedy of Errors. Act ii, sc. 2, l. 173. [Adriana]

4
'Tis double wrong, to truant with your bed
And let her read it in thy looks at board.
The Comedy of Errors. Act iii, sc. 2, l. 17. [Luciana]
He does me double wrong.—*Richard II,* iii, 2, 215.
You do me double wrong.—*The Taming of the Shrew,* iii, 1, 16.
Double wrong.—*Venus and Adonis,* l. 429.
Treble wrong.—*Venus and Adonis,* l. 329.

5
Antipholus of Ephesus: You wrong me much to say so.
Angelo: You wrong me more, sir, in denying it.
The Comedy of Errors. Act iv, sc. 1, l. 65.
You wrong me, sir.—*The Two Gentlemen of Verona,* iii, 4, 73; *The Taming of the Shrew,* ii, 1, 46; *Twelfth Night,* v, 1, 310.
You wrong this presence.—*Antony and Cleopatra,* ii, 2, 111.
This wrongs you.—*The Two Gentlemen of Verona,* iv, 2, 161.

6
Beside the charge, the shame, imprisonment,
You have done wrong to this my honest friend.
The Comedy of Errors. Act v, sc. 1, l. 18. [Angelo]
Beyond imagination is the wrong
That she this day hath shameless thrown on me.
The Comedy of Errors. Act v, sc. 1, l. 201. [Antipholus of Ephesus]
My wrongs might make one wiser mad.
The Comedy of Errors. Act v, sc. 1, l. 217. [Antipholus of Ephesus]
Suffer'd wrong.—*Comedy of Errors,* v, 1, 398.
Suffer wrong.—*Richard II,* ii, 1, 164.

7
We were i' the wrong.
Coriolanus. Act iv, sc. 6, l. 156. [Citizen]
You are i' the wrong.—*Measure for Measure,* v, 1, 86.
Quite in the wrong.—*Othello,* iv, 1, 104.

8
Think'st thou it honourable for a noble man
Still to remember wrongs?
Coriolanus. Act v, sc. 3, l. 154. [Volumnia]

9
You will not pocket up wrong.
I Henry IV. Act iii, sc. 3, l. 184. [Prince]
I must pocket up these wrongs.
King John. Act iii, sc. 1, l. 200. [Austria]
It is plain pocketing up of wrongs.
Henry V. Act iii, sc. 2, l. 54. [Boy] The only use of "pocketing."

10
Broke oath on oath, committed wrong on wrong.
I Henry IV. Act iv, sc. 3, l. 101. [Hotspur]
Bitter wrong.—*A Midsummer-Night's Dream,* iii, 2, 361.
Bloody wrongs.—*Titus Andronicus,* i, 1, 141.
Enforced wrong.—*The Merchant of Venice,* v, 1, 240.
Feeble wrong.—*Richard II,* i, 1, 191.
Foul wrongs.—*Richard III,* iv, 4, 374; *Richard II,* iii, 1, 15; *Measure for Measure,* ii, 2, 103.
Heinous wrongs.—*Titus Andronicus,* v, 2, 4.
Perfect wrong.—*King John,* iii, 1, 189.
True wrongs.—*II Henry IV,* Ind., 40.

11
I have in equal balance justly weigh'd
What wrongs our arms may do, what wrongs we suffer,
And find our griefs heavier than our offences.
II Henry IV. Act iv, sc. 1, l. 67. [Archbishop of York]
When we are wrong'd and would unfold our griefs,
We are denied access unto his person
Even by those men that most have done us wrong.
II Henry IV. Act iv, sc. 1, l. 77. [Archbishop of York]

12
Go to; I say he shall have no wrong.
II Henry IV. Act v, sc. 1, l. 58. [Shallow]

13
Whose wrongs give edge unto the swords
That make such waste in brief mortality.
Henry V. Act i, sc. 2, l. 27. [King Henry]

14
Thou know'st little of my wrongs.
I Henry VI. Act i, sc. 3, l. 59. [Gloucester]
Now, by God's will, thou wrong'st him, Somerset.
I Henry VI. Act ii, sc. 4, l. 82. [Warwick]
Poor gentleman! his wrong doth equal mine.
I Henry VI. Act ii, sc. 5, l. 22. [Mortimer]
And for those wrongs, those bitter injuries,
Which Somerset hath offer'd to my house,

I doubt not but with honour to redress.
I Henry VI. Act ii, sc. 5, l. 124. [Plantagenet]
So shall his father's wrongs be recompensed.
I Henry VI. Act iii, sc. 1, l. 161. [Warwick]

1
Prick'd on by public wrongs sustain'd in France.
I Henry VI. Act iii, sc. 2, l. 78. [Talbot]
Private wrongs.—*Richard II,* ii, 1, 166.

2
Bastard: Hew them to pieces, hack their bones asunder,
Whose life was England's glory, Gallia's wonder.
Charles: O, no, forbear! for that which we had fled
During the life, let us not wrong it dead.
I Henry VI. Act iv, sc. 7, l. 47.

3
I will subscribe and say I wrong'd the duke.
II Henry VI. Act iii, sc. 1, l. 38. [Queen]
How much thou wrong'st me, heaven be my judge.
II Henry VI. Act iv, sc. 10, l. 82. [Iden]
That 's some wrong, indeed.—*II Henry VI,* i, 3, 22.

4
Thou never didst them wrong nor no man wrong.
II Henry VI. Act iii, sc. 1, l. 209. [King Henry]
Never wrong'd you.—*A Midsummer-Night's Dream,* iii, 2, 308.

5
What wrong is this unto the prince your son!
III Henry VI. Act i, sc. 1, l. 176. [Clifford]
King Edward: Therein thou wrong'st thy children mightily.
Lady Grey: Herein your highness wrongs both them and me.
III Henry VI. Act iii, sc. 2, l. 74.

6 Though usurpers sway the rule awhile,
Yet heavens are just, and time suppresseth wrongs.
III Henry VI. Act iii, sc. 3, l. 76. [Queen Margaret]

7
I will revenge his wrong to Lady Bona
And replant Henry in his former state.
III Henry VI. Act iii, sc. 3, l. 197. [Warwick] The only use of "replant."
If Lucius live, he will requite your wrongs.
Titus Andronicus. Act iii, sc. 1, l. 297. [Lucius]

8
O masters, if I were disposed to stir
Your hearts and minds to mutiny and rage,
I should do Brutus wrong, and Cassius wrong, . . .
I will not do them wrong; I rather choose
To wrong the dead, to wrong myself and you,
Than I will wrong such honourable men.
Julius Cæsar. Act iii, sc. 2, l. 126. [Antony]
I fear I wrong the honourable men
Whose daggers have stabb'd Cæsar; I do fear it.
Julius Cæsar. Act iii, sc. 2, l. 156. [Antony]

9
That you have wrong'd me doth appear in this.
Julius Cæsar. Act iv, sc. 3, l. 1. [Cassius]
You wrong me every way; you wrong me, Brutus.
Julius Cæsar. Act iv, sc. 3, l. 55. [Cassius]

10
It must go wrong with you and me.
King John. Act i, sc. 1, l. 41. [Elinor]
We go wrong, we go wrong.
Troilus and Cressida. Act v, sc. 1, l. 74. [Agamemnon]
Choose wrong.—*Merchant of Venice,* ii, 1, 40.
Choosing wrong.—*Merchant of Venice,* iii, 2, 2.

11
Oppress'd with wrongs.
King John. Act iii, sc. 1, l. 13. [Constance]
The oppressor's wrong.—*Hamlet,* iii, 1, 71.
Possessed with a thousand wrongs.—*King John,* iii, 3, 41.

12
By day and night he wrongs me.
King Lear. Act i, sc. 3, l. 3. [Goneril]

13
And, for my love, I pray you wrong me not.
The Merchant of Venice. Act i, sc. 3, l. 171. [Shylock]

14
Shallow: He hath wronged me, Master Page.
Page: Sir, he doth in some sort confess it.
Merry Wives of Windsor. Act i, sc. 1, l. 105.
He hath wronged me; indeed he hath; at a word, he hath, believe me: Robert Shallow, esquire, saith, he is wronged.
The Merry Wives of Windsor. Act i, sc. 1, l. 107. [Shallow]
He hath wronged me in some humours.
The Merry Wives of Windsor. Act ii, sc. 1, l. 133. [Nym]
My bed shall be abused, my coffers ransacked, my reputation gnawn at; and I shall not only receive this villanous wrong, but stand under the adoption of abominable terms, and by him that does me this wrong.
The Merry Wives of Windsor. Act ii, sc. 2, l. 306. [Ford] The only use of "gnawn."

15
If you would know your wronger, look on me.
Much Ado about Nothing. Act v, sc. 1, l. 272. [Borachio]
Wrong the wronger till he render right.
The Rape of Lucrece, l. 943.
The wronger Of her or you.—*Cymbeline,* ii, 4, 54. The only uses of "wronger."

16 The duke himself,
Or any of my brothers of the state,
Cannot but feel this wrong as 'twere their own.
Othello. Act i, sc. 2, l. 95. [Brabantio]
Such noble sense of thy friend's wrong!
Othello. Act v, sc. 1, l. 32. [Othello]

17
Celestial as thou art, O do not love that wrong,
To sing heaven's praise with such an earthly tongue.
The Passionate Pilgrim, l. 69.

1
What wrong, what shame, what sorrow I shall breed.
The Rape of Lucrece, l. 499.
Thou wrong'st his honour, wound'st his princely name.
The Rape of Lucrece, l. 599.

2
O, sit my husband's wrongs on Hereford's spear,
That it may enter butcher Mowbray's breast!
Richard II. Act i, sc. 2, l. 47. [Duchess of Gloucester]
Now, afore God, 'tis shame such wrongs are borne
In him, a royal prince, and many moe
Of noble blood in this declining land.
Richard II. Act ii, sc. 1, l. 238. [Northumberland]
Wrong not your prince you love.
Pericles. Act ii, sc. 4, l. 25. [Helicanus]

3
Look on my wrongs with an indifferent eye: . . .
Will you permit that I shall stand condemn'd
A wandering vagabond; my rights and royalties
Pluck'd from my arms perforce and given away
To upstart unthrifts?
Richard II. Act ii, sc. 3, l. 116. [Bolingbroke] "Upstart" is repeated in *I Henry VI,* iv, 7, 87.
To rouse his wrongs and chase them to the bay.
Richard II. Act ii, sc. 3, l. 128. [Bolingbroke]

4
Uncharitably with me have you dealt,
And shamefully by you my hopes are butcher'd.
Richard III. Act i, sc. 3, l. 275. [Queen Margaret] The only use of "uncharitably."
So in the Lethe of thy angry soul
Thou drown the sad remembrance of those wrongs
Which thou supposest I have done to thee.
Richard III. Act iv, sc. 4, l. 250. [King Richard]

5
God's wrong is most of all.
Richard III. Act iv, sc. 4, l. 377. [Queen Elizabeth]
Wrong hath but wrong, and blame the due of blame.
Richard III. Act v, sc. 1, l. 29. [Buckingham]
Awake, and think our wrongs in Richard's bosom
Will conquer him! awake, and win the day!
Richard III. Act v, sc. 3, l. 144. [Ghosts]
Wronged souls.—*Richard III,* v, 3, 241.

6
Thou wrong'st it, more than tears, with that report.
Romeo and Juliet. Act iv, sc. 1, l. 32. [Paris]

7
Those pretty wrongs that liberty commits.
Sonnets. No. xli.
Then need I not to fear the worst of wrongs,
When in the least of them my life hath end.
Sonnets. No. xcii.
O, call not me to justify the wrong
That thy unkindness lays upon my heart.
Sonnets. No. cxxxix.

8
Good sister, wrong me not, nor wrong yourself,
To make a bondmaid and a slave of me.
The Taming of the Shrew. Act ii, sc. 1, l. 1. [Bianca] The only use of "bondmaid."
Why dost thou wrong her that did ne'er wrong thee?
The Taming of the Shrew. Act ii, sc. 1, l. 27. [Baptista]
The more my wrong, the more his spite appears.
The Taming of the Shrew. Act iv, sc. 3, l. 2. [Katharina]

9
With their high wrongs I am struck to the quick.
The Tempest. Act v, sc. 1, l. 25. [Prospero]
Thy dukedom I resign and do entreat
Thou pardon me my wrongs.
The Tempest. Act v, sc. 1, l. 118. [Alonso]

10
If wrongs be evils and enforce us kill,
What folly 'tis to hazard life for ill!
Timon of Athens. Act iii, sc. 5, l. 36. [Senator]
Now breathless wrong
Shall sit and pant in your great chairs of ease.
Timon of Athens. Act v, sc. 4, l. 10. [Alcibiades]

11
Wrung with wrongs more than our backs can bear.
Titus Andronicus. Act iv, sc. 3, l. 48. [Titus]
Despiteful and intolerable wrongs!
Titus Andronicus. Act iv, sc. 4, l. 50. [Saturninus]
Wrongs, unspeakable, past patience,
Or more than any living man could bear.
Titus Andronicus. Act v, sc. 3, l. 126. [Marcus]
What wrongs are these!—*Titus Andronicus,* iv, 4, 1.
What wrongs were theirs.—*Timon of Athens,* v, 1, 156.

12
To persist
In doing wrong extenuates not wrong,
But makes it much more heavy.
Troilus and Cressida. Act ii, sc. 2, l. 186. [Hector]

13
Art thou not ashamed
To wrong him with thy importunacy?
The Two Gentlemen of Verona. Act iv, sc. 2, l. 112. [Silvia]
Your importunacy cease till after dinner.
Timon of Athens, ii, 2, 42. The only uses of "importunacy."

14
You offer him, if this be so, a wrong
Something unfilial.
The Winter's Tale. Act iv, sc. 4, l. 415. [Polixenes] The only use of "unfilial."

II—Do Wrong

1
Be not afraid that I your hand should take;
I 'll never do you wrong for your own sake.
All 's Well that Ends Well. Act ii, sc. 3, l. 95. [Helena]

Do you wrong.—*Measure for Measure,* ii, 1, 280.

He does me wrong.—*All 's Well that Ends Well,* v, 3, 189.

2 I never do him wrong,
But he does buy my injuries, to be friends;
Pays dear for my offences.
Cymbeline. Act i, sc. 1, l. 104. [Queen]

The wrongs he did me Were nothing prince-like.
Cymbeline. Act v, sc. 5, l. 292. [Guiderius]
The only use of "prince-like."

3
We do it wrong, being so majestical,
To offer it the show of violence.
Hamlet. Act i, sc. 1, l. 143. [Marcellus]

4
Certainly she did you wrong.
Henry V. Act ii, sc. 1, l. 20. [Bardolph]

5
Thou dost then wrong me, as that slaughterer doth
Which giveth many wounds when one will kill.
I Henry VI. Act ii, sc. 5, l. 109. [Mortimer]
The only use of "slaughterer."

6
It shall advantage more than do us wrong.
Julius Cæsar. Act iii, sc. 1, l. 242. [Brutus]

I will not do thee so much wrong to wake thee.
Julius Cæsar. Act iv, sc. 3, l. 270. [Brutus]

7
All things that you should use to do me wrong
Deny their office.
King John. Act iv, sc. 1, l. 118. [Arthur]

8
You do me wrong to take me out o' the grave.
King Lear. Act iv, sc. 7, l. 45. [King Lear]
"Do me wrong" is repeated nine times.

By yonder moon I swear you do me wrong.
The Merchant of Venice. Act v, sc. 1, l. 142. [Gratiano]

Do him wrong.—*King John,* i, 3, 75; *Measure for Measure,* iii, 2, 137.

Do them wrong.—*Hamlet,* ii, 2, 367.

9
You do the king my father too much wrong
And wrong the reputation of your name.
Love's Labour 's Lost. Act ii, sc. 1, l. 154. [Princess of France]

10 You do me now more wrong
In making question of my uttermost
Than if you had made waste of all I have.
The Merchant of Venice. Act i, sc. 1, l. 155. [Antonio]

11
Truly, la! I will not do you that wrong.
The Merry Wives of Windsor. Act i, sc. 1, l. 322. [Slender]

Do no wrong.—*A Midsummer-Night's Dream,* ii, 2, 11.

Do the world no wrong.—*Measure for Measure,* ii, 2, 53.

Doing no wrong.—*The Merchant of Venice,* iv, 1, 89.

Do wrong to none.—*All 's Well that Ends Well,* i, 1, 74.

12
Marry, thou dost wrong me; thou dissembler, thou.
Much Ado about Nothing. Act v, sc. 1, l. 53. [Leonato]

13
Cassio did some little wrong to him.
Othello. Act ii, sc. 3, l. 242. [Iago]

14
They do me wrong, and I will not endure it.
Richard III. Act i, sc. 3, l. 42. [Gloucester]

I do the wrong, and first begin to brawl.
Richard III. Act i, sc. 3, l. 324. [Gloucester]

Who does do you wrong?—*The Taming of the Shrew,* v, 1, 143.

15
He doth me wrong to feed me with delays.
Titus Andronicus. Act iv, sc. 3, l. 42. [Titus]

Come, come, you 'll do him wrong ere you 're ware.
Troilus and Cressida. Act iv, sc. 2, l. 56. [Æneas]

16
Now, as thou lovest me, do him not that wrong
To bear a hard opinion of his truth.
The Two Gentlemen of Verona. Act ii, sc. 7, l. 80. [Julia]

'You do him the more wrong,' quoth I.
The Two Gentlemen of Verona. Act iv, sc. 4, l. 29. [Launce]

III—Done Wrong

17
It cannot be that she hath done thee wrong.
The Comedy of Errors. Act v, sc. 1, l. 135. [Duke]

'Tis he, foul creature, that hath done thee wrong.
Venus and Adonis, l. 1005.

Done you wrong.—*All 's Well that Ends Well,* ii, 3, 317.

18
He hath done me wrong.
I Henry VI. Act iv, sc. 1, l. 85. [Vernon]
Also *III Henry VI,* iii, 3, 231.

19
Cassius: Most noble brother, you have done me wrong.
Brutus: Judge me, you gods! wrong I mine enemies?
And, if not so, how should I wrong a brother?
Julius Cæsar. Act iv, sc. 2, l. 37.

20
Some villain hath done me wrong.
King Lear. Act i, sc. 2, l. 180. [Edgar]

Your sisters
Have, as I do remember, done me wrong.
King Lear. Act iv, sc. 7, l. 73. [King Lear]

Madam, you have done me wrong,
Notorious wrong.
Twelfth Night. Act v, sc. 1, l. 336. [Malvolio]

Done me wrong.—*The Merchant of Venice,* ii, 2, 141.

Done him wrong.—*Rape of Lucrece,* l. 1467.

Done us wrong.—*II Henry IV,* iv, 1, 79.

1
We then have done you bold and saucy wrongs.
Othello. Act i, sc. 1, l. 129. [Roderigo]

2 The wrongs I have done thee stir
Afresh within me.
Winter's Tale. Act v, sc. 1, l. 148. [Leontes]

IV—Self-Wrong

3
Do not yourself such wrong, who are in this
Relieved, but not betray'd.
Antony and Cleopatra. Act v, sc. 2, l. 40. [Proculeius]

Do not yourself wrong.
II Henry IV. Act iii, sc. 2, l. 272. [Shallow]

4 And took some pride
To do myself this wrong.
Coriolanus. Act v, sc. 6, l. 37. [Aufidius]

5
You wrong'd yourself to write in such a case.
Julius Cæsar. Act iv, sc. 3, l. 6. [Brutus]

Thou wrong'st thyself.—*All's Well that Ends Well,* ii, 3, 153.

6
I think I have done myself wrong, have I not?
Measure for Measure. Act i, sc. 2, l. 41. [Gentleman]

7
You do yourself wrong, indeed, la!
The Merry Wives of Windsor. Act i, sc. 1, l. 326. [Slender]

Good Master Ford, be contented: you wrong yourself too much.
The Merry Wives of Windsor. Act iii, sc. 3, l. 177. [Page]

You do yourself mighty wrong.
The Merry Wives of Windsor. Act iii, sc. 3, l. 221. [Mrs. Page]

Do myself wrong.—*Much Ado about Nothing,* ii, 1, 214.

8
But you gave leave to my unwilling tongue
Against my will to do myself this wrong.
Richard II. Act i, sc. 3, l. 245. [Gaunt]

9
I fear you have done yourself some wrong.
The Tempest. Act i, sc. 2, l. 443. [Prospero]

You do yourselves Much wrong.—*Timon of Athens,* i, 2, 212.

You do yourselves but wrong.—*Timon of Athens,* iii, 4, 53.

The wrongs I did myself.—*The Winter's Tale,* v, 1, 9.

V—Women's Wrongs

10
Unless a woman should be made an ass and a beast, to bear every knave's wrong.
II Henry IV. Act ii, sc. 1, l. 40. [Hostess]

Wrong this virtuous gentlewoman.
II Henry IV. Act ii, sc. 4, l. 353. [Prince Henry]

11
She had the wrong.
III Henry VI. Act iv, sc. 1, l. 102. [King Edward]

Believe me, she has had much wrong.
Henry VIII. Act iii, sc. 1, l. 48. [Queen Katharine]

Why should we, good lady,
Upon what cause, wrong you?
Henry VIII. Act iii, sc. 1, l. 155. [Wolsey]

12
Say you have wrong'd her, sir.
King Lear. Act ii, sc. 4, l. 154. [Regan]

13
Relate your wrongs; in what? by whom? be brief.
Measure for Measure. Act v, sc. 1, l. 26. [Duke]

Heaven shield your grace from woe,
As I, thus wrong'd, hence unbelieved go!
Measure for Measure. Act v, sc. 1, l. 118. [Isabella] The only use of "unbelieved."

Proclaim it, provost, round about the city,
Is any woman wrong'd by this lewd fellow,
As I have heard him swear himself there 's one
Whom he begot with child, let her appear,
And he shall marry her: the nuptial finish'd,
Let him be whipt and hang'd.
Measure for Measure. Act v, sc. 1, l. 514. [Duke]

She, Claudio, that you wrong'd, look you restore.
Measure for Measure. Act v, sc. 1, l. 531. [Duke]

14
Your wrongs do set a scandal on my sex.
A Midsummer-Night's Dream. Act ii, sc. 1, l. 240. [Helena]

15
She is much wronged by you.
Much Ado about Nothing. Act ii, sc. 1, l. 245. [Don Pedro]

Wrong her honour.—*Much Ado about Nothing,* iv, 1, 193.

Wronged his honour.—*Much Ado about Nothing,* ii, 2, 23.

16
Benedick: Surely I do believe your fair cousin is wronged.
Beatrice: Ah, how much might the man deserve of me that would right her!
Much Ado about Nothing. Act iv, sc. 1, l. 261.

17
The niggard prodigal that praised her so,—
In that high task hath done her beauty wrong,
Which far exceeds his barren skill to show.
The Rape of Lucrece, l. 79.

He did her wrong.—*Rape of Lucrece,* l. 1462.

I did her wrong.—*King Lear,* i, 5, 25.

18
And what wrong else may be imagined
By foul enforcement might be done to me,
From that, alas, thy Lucrece is not free.
The Rape of Lucrece, l. 1622.

Plight your honourable faiths to me
With swift pursuit to venge this wrong of mine.
The Rape of Lucrece, l. 1690.

1 By God's holy mother,
She hath too much wrong.
Richard III. Act i, sc. 3, l. 306. [Gloucester]

But you have all the vantage of her wrong.
Richard III. Act i, sc. 3, l. 310. [Gloucester]

Loving wrong.—*The Tempest*, i, 2, 151.

2
They ravish'd her, and cut away her tongue;
And they, 'twas they, that did her all this wrong.
Titus Andronicus. Act v, sc. 3, l. 57. [Titus]

Ravish'd and wrong'd.—*Titus Andronicus*, iv, 1, 52. See also under RAPE.

Y

YEAR

3
Like to the time o' the year between the extremes
Of hot and cold.
Antony and Cleopatra. Act i, sc. 5, l. 51. [Alexas]

Time of year.—*Richard II*, iii, 4, 57; *Sonnets*, lxxiii.

4
The big year, swoln with some other grief,
Is thought with child by the stern tyrant war.
II Henry IV. Induction, l. 13. [Rumour]

Bounteous year.—*Timon of Athens*, iii, 3, 39.
Ever-running year.—*Henry V*, iv, 1, 293. The only use of "ever-running."
Fair year.—*As You Like It*, iv, 1, 101.
First year.—*II Henry VI*, iv, 6, 5.
Merry year.—*II Henry IV*, v, 3, 19.
Next year.—*All's Well that Ends Well*, ii, 1, 28.
Present year.—*Merchant of Venice*, i, 1, 44.
This year.—*II Henry IV*, iii, 2, 254; v, 5, 111; iv, 4, 691; *Troilus and Cressida*, i, 2, 92.
The year of our redemption.—*Henry V*, i, 2, 60.

5
There stay until the twelve celestial signs
Have brought about the annual reckoning.
Love's Labour's Lost. Act v, sc. 2, l. 807. [Princess of France]

A twelvemonth and a day.—*Love's Labour's Lost*, v, 2, 837; 887.
Twelvemonth term.—*Love's Labour's Lost*, v, 2, 860.
Above a twelvemonth.—*The Merchant of Venice*, iii, 4, 76.
A twelve-month hence.—*Richard III*, iii, 2, 57.
A twelvemonth longer.—*Pericles*, ii, 4, 45.
Some twelvemonth since.—*Twelfth Night*, i, 2, 37.
Within this twelvemonth.—*As You Like It*, iii, 1, 7. "Twelvemonth" is used fifteen times.

6
Compound with him by the year.
Measure for Measure. Act iv, sc. 2, l. 25. [Provost]

By the year.—*The Taming of the Shrew*, ii, 1, 371; 374.
A year since.—*Much Ado about Nothing*, ii, 2, 12.
From year to year.—*Othello*, i, 3, 130.

7 The year growing ancient,
Not yet on summer's death.
Winter's Tale. Act iv, sc. 4, l. 79. [Perdita]

II—Years

See also Age

8
Cleopatra: Guess at her years, I prithee. . . .
Messenger: I do think she 's thirty.
Antony and Cleopatra. Act iii, sc. 3, l. 29.

9
Thou hast years upon thee.
Coriolanus. Act iv, sc. 1, l. 45. [Coriolanus]

I have seen more years, I 'm sure, than ye.
Julius Cæsar. Act iv, sc. 4, l. 132. [Poet]

I have years on my back forty eight.
King Lear. Act i, sc. 4, l. 42. [Kent] The only use of "forty eight."

My years be past the best.—*The Passionate Pilgrim*, l. 6.
His full and ripen'd years.—*Richard III*, ii, 3, 14.
Happy years.—*Richard II*, i, 3, 94; *Twelfth Night*, i, 4, 30.
Mellow'd years.—*III Henry VI*, iii, 3, 104. "Mellow'd" is repeated in *Richard III*, iii, 7, 169.
Infirm and choleric years.—*King Lear*, i, 1, 302.
Wretched years.—*I Henry VI*, i, 1, 48.

10
When I was about thy years.
I Henry IV. Act ii, sc. 4, l. 363. [Falstaff]

11
You . . . bear your years very well.
II Henry IV. Act iii, sc. 2, l. 92. [Shallow]

12
My years are young!
I Henry VI. Act v, sc. 1, l. 21. [King Henry]

Young years.—*I Henry VI*, ii, 5, 107.

13
How many years a mortal man may live.
III Henry VI. Act ii, sc. 5, l. 28. [King Henry]

So many years ere I shall shear the fleece.
III Henry VI. Act ii, sc. 5, l. 37. [King Henry] See under TIME. "Shear the fleece" is repeated in *As You Like It*, ii, 4, 79.

Many years of happy days befal
My gracious sovereign, my most loving liege!
Richard II. Act i, sc. 1, l. 20. [Bolingbroke]

Thou hast many years to live.
Richard II. Act i, sc. 3, l. 225. [King Richard] See under LIFE.

God save King Harry, unking'd Richard says,
And send him many years of sunshine days!
Richard II. Act iv, sc. 1, l. 220. [King Richard] "Unking'd" is repeated in v, 5, 37, and occurs in no other play.

These many years.—*I Henry VI,* ii, 3, 40; *Cymbeline,* iv, 2, 66.
Many years.—*Cymbeline,* iv, 4, 22; v, 4, 142; v, 5, 439; 456.
Several years.—*Pericles,* i, 4, 18.

1
Misgraffed in respect of years.
A Midsummer-Night's Dream. Act i, sc. 1, l. 137. [Lysander] The only use of "misgraffed."

2
Pleasing to her tender years.
Richard III. Act iv, sc. 4, l. 342. [Queen Elizabeth] See under YOUTH.
Tender years.—*Venus and Adonis,* l. 1091.
Unripe years.—*The Passionate Pilgrim,* l. 51; *Venus and Adonis,* l. 524.
Lack of years.—*Merchant of Venice,* iv, 1, 162.

3
And since that time it is eleven years.
Romeo and Juliet. Act i, sc. 3, l. 35. [Nurse]
Ten years are spent since first he undertook
This cause of Rome.
Titus Andronicus. Act i, sc. 1, l. 31. [Marcus Andronicus]
For seven long year.—*King Lear,* iii, 4, 145.
The length of seven year.—*As You Like It,* iii, 2, 335.
Seven short years.—*The Comedy of Errors,* vi, i, 309.
Three years is but short.—*Love's Labour's Lost,* i, 1, 181.

4
O, by this count I shall be much in years
Ere I again behold my Romeo.
Romeo and Juliet. Act iii, sc. 5, l. 46. [Juliet]

5
Myself am struck in years.
The Taming of the Shrew. Act ii, sc. 1, l. 362. [Gremio]
Well struck in years.—*Richard III,* i, 1, 92.

6
Duke: What years, i' faith?
Viola: About your years, my lord.
Duke: Too old, by heaven.
Twelfth Night. Act ii, sc. 4, l. 28.

YEOMAN

7
It did me yeoman's service.
Hamlet, v, 2, 36. See under SERVICE.

8
Where's your yeoman? Is't a lusty yeoman?
II Henry IV. Act ii, sc. 1, l. 4. [Hostess]

9
Good yeomen,
Whose limbs were made in England, show us here
The mettle of your pasture.
Henry V. Act iii, sc. 1, l. 25. [King Henry]
Bold yeomen.—*Richard III,* v, 3, 338.
English yeoman.—*III Henry VI,* i, 4, 123.
Yeoman of the wardrobe.—*Twelfth Night,* ii, 5, 45.

10
Somerset: We grace the yeoman by conversing with him. . . .
Warwick: Spring crestless yeomen from so deep a root?
I Henry VI. Act ii, sc. 4, l. 81. The only use of "crestless."
Till thou be restored, thou art a yeoman.
I Henry VI. Act ii, sc. 4, l. 95. [Somerset]

11
Fool: Prithee, nuncle, tell me whether a madman be a gentleman or a yeoman?
King Lear: A king, a king!
Fool: No, he's a yeoman that has a gentleman to his son; for he's a mad yeoman that sees his son a gentleman before him.
King Lear. Act iii, sc. 6, l. 10.

YIELDING

12
I yield thee up my life.
Antony and Cleopatra. Act v, sc. 1, l. 12. [Dercetas]
Yield the ghost.—*I Henry VI,* i, 1, 67; *Richard III,* i, 4, 37.

13
All places yield to him ere he sits down.
Coriolanus. Act iv, sc. 7, l. 28. [Aufidius]

14
Cloten: Thou art a robber,
A law-breaker, a villain: yield thee, thief.
Guiderius: To who? to thee? What art thou? Have not I
An arm as big as thine? a heart as big? . . .
Why I should yield to thee?
Cymbeline. Act iv, sc. 2, l. 77. The only use of "law-breaker."

15
Do ye yield, sir? or shall I sweat for you?
II Henry IV. Act iv, sc. 3, l. 13. [Falstaff]
What say you? will you yield, and this avoid,
Or, guilty in defence, be thus destroy'd?
Henry V. Act iii, sc. 3, l. 42. [King Henry]
Yield thee to my hand.—*King John,* ii, 1, 156.

16
Warwick: Yield, my lord protector; yield, Winchester;
Except you mean with obstinate repulse
To slay your sovereign and destroy the realm. . . .
Winchester: He shall submit, or I will never yield.
Gloucester: Compassion on the king commands me stoop;
Or I would see his heart out, ere the priest
Should ever get that privilege of me. . . .
Winchester: Well, Duke of Gloucester, I will yield to thee;
Love for thy love and hand for hand I give.
I Henry VI. Act iii, sc. 1, l. 112.
And made me almost yield upon my knees.
I Henry VI. Act iii, sc. 3, l. 80. [Burgundy]

17
And, vanquish'd as I am, I yield to thee,
Or to the meanest groom.
II Henry VI. Act ii, sc. 1, l. 184. [Gloucester]
I will yield to him.—*II Henry VI,* i, 3, 109.

18
Hercules himself must yield to odds.
III Henry VI. Act ii, sc. 1, l. 53. [Messenger]
I humbly yield.—*III Henry VI,* iii, 1, 101.

1
First Soldier: Yield, or thou diest.
Lucilius: Only I yield to die.
Julius Cæsar. Act v, sc. 4, l. 12.
Yield or die.—*II Henry VI,* iv, 2, 135.

2
I see a yielding in the looks of France.
King John. Act ii, sc. 1, l. 474. [Queen Elinor]
How well this yielding rescues thee from shame!
Love's Labour's Lost. Act i, sc. 1, l. 118. [King Ferdinand]

3
Macduff: Yield thee, coward. . .
Macbeth: I will not yield,
To kiss the ground before young Malcolm's feet.
Macbeth. Act v, sc. 8, l. 23.
I will never yield.—*I Henry VI,* iii, 1, 118.
I would not yield.—*Love's Labour's Lost,* v, 2, 354.
Yield not.—*Midsummer-Night's Dream,* i, 1, 69.

4
You press me far, and therefore I will yield.
The Merchant of Venice. Act iv, sc. 1, l. 425. [Portia]

5
Relent, sweet Hermia: and, Lysander, yield
Thy crazed title to my certain right.
A Midsummer-Night's Dream. Act i, sc. 1, l. 91. [Demetrius]
I yield you up my part.—*A Midsummer-Night's Dream,* iii, 2, 165.
Yields you up.—*A Midsummer-Night's Dream,* i, 1, 119.
Yield them up.—*A Lover's Complaint,* l. 221.
Yielding of her up.—*Troilus and Cressida,* ii, 2, 25.
Yields him way.—*The Rape of Lucrece,* l. 309.
Yields at last.—*Venus and Adonis,* l. 566.

6
I yield upon great persuasion; and partly to save your life.
Much Ado about Nothing. Act v, sc. 4, l. 95. [Beatrice]
I yield all this.—*The Winter's Tale,* iv, 4, 421.

7
What though she strive to try her strength,
And ban and brawl, and say thee nay,
Her feeble force will yield at length,
When craft hath taught her thus to say,
'Had women been so strong as men,
In faith, you had not had it then.'
The Passionate Pilgrim, l. 317.
So I to her and so she yields to me.
The Taming of the Shrew. Act ii, sc. 1, l. 137. [Petruchio]

8
I cannot nor I will not yield to you.
Richard III. Act iii, sc. 7, l. 207. [Gloucester]
I cannot yield.—*All's Well that Ends Well,* iii, 1, 10.

9 Therefore pardon me,
And not impute this yielding to light love,
Which the dark night hath so discovered.
Romeo and Juliet. Act ii, sc. 2, l. 104. [Juliet]
Yield to my love.—*The Rape of Lucrece,* l. 668.
Yield to my hand.—*Rape of Lucrece,* l. 1210.

10
Yield to his humour, smooth and speak him fair.
Titus Andronicus. Act v, sc. 2, l. 140. [Tamora]

YOKE

11
Never . . . yoke with him for tribune.
Coriolanus. Act iii, sc. 1, l. 57. [Sicinius]

12 Against all colour here
Did put the yoke upon 's; which to shake off
Becomes a warlike people.
Cymbeline. Act iii, sc. 1, l. 51. [Cymbeline]
Our subjects, sir, Will not endure the yoke.
Cymbeline. Act iii, sc. 5, l. 5. [Cymbeline]

13
Yoke-fellow to his honour-owing wounds.
Henry V. Act iv, sc. 6, l. 9. [Exeter] The only use of "honour-owing."
Yoke-fellows in arms.—*Henry V,* ii, 3, 56.
Yoke-fellow of equity.—*King Lear,* iii, 6, 39. The only uses of "yoke-fellow" and "yoke-fellows."

14
He yoketh your rebellious necks.
I Henry VI. Act ii, sc. 3, l. 64. [Talbot] See also under NECK. The only use of "yoketh."

15
Can I bear this shameful yoke?
II Henry VI. Act ii, sc. 4, l. 37. [Duchess]
Bearing yoke.—*The Rape of Lucrece,* l. 409.
Burthen'd yoke.—*Richard III,* iv, 4, 111.

16 'Twere pity
To sunder them that yoke so well together.
III Henry VI, iv, 1, 23. See under MARRIAGE.
We 'll yoke together like a double shadow.
III Henry VI. Act iv, sc. 6, l. 49. [Warwick]

17
Groaning underneath this age's yoke.
Julius Cæsar. Act i, sc. 2, l. 61. [Cassius]
O Cassius, you are yoked with a lamb.
Julius Cæsar, iv, 3, 110. See under ANGER.

18
These that accuse him of his intent towards our wives are a yoke of his discarded men.
The Merry Wives of Windsor. Act ii, sc. 1, l. 180. [Page]
Yoke of bullocks.—*II Henry IV,* iii, 2, 42. "Bullocks" is repeated in *Much Ado about Nothing,* ii, 1, 202.
Yoke you like draught-oxen.—*Troilus and Cressida,* ii, 1, 116. The only use of "draught-oxen."

19 Do not these fair yokes
Become the forest better than the town?
The Merry Wives of Windsor. Act v, sc. 5, l. 111. [Mrs. Page]

20 His lordship, whose unwished yoke
My soul consents not to give sovereignty.
A Midsummer-Night's Dream. Act i, sc. 1, l. 81. [Hermia]

21
An thou wilt needs thrust thy neck into a yoke, wear the print of it and sigh away Sundays.
Much Ado about Nothing. Act i, sc. 1, l. 103. [Benedick]

1
I shall with aged patience bear your yoke.
Pericles, ii, 4, 48. See under PATIENCE.
Bear the yoke.—*Much Ado about Nothing,* i, 1, 263.

2
Shake off our slavish yoke.
Richard II. Act ii, sc. 1, l. 291. [Northumberland]

Shake the yoke of inauspicious stars
From this world-wearied flesh.
Romeo and Juliet, v, 3, 111. See under DEATH. The only use of "inauspicious" and "world-wearied."

3
Bear the golden yoke of sovereignty.
Richard III. Act iii, sc. 7, l. 146. [Gloucester]
Yoke of government.—*II Henry IV,* iv, 4, 10.
Yoke of love.—*Merchant of Venice,* iii, 4, 13.
Yoke of tyranny.—*Richard III,* v, 2, 2.
Fortune's yoke.—*III Henry VI,* iii, 3, 17.

4
Brought to yoke the enemies of Rome.
Titus Andronicus. Act i, sc. 1, l. 69. [Captain]
Roman yoke.—*Titus Andronicus,* i, 1, 111.
Yoke of Rome.—*Titus Andronicus,* iv, 1, 109.

YOUTH

See also Age and Youth

5
Even so it was with me when I was young.
All's Well that Ends Well. Act i, sc. 3, l. 134. [Countess]
When I was young.—*The Winter's Tale,* iv, 4, 358; *I Henry VI,* iii, 4, 17.

6
To be young again, if we could.
All's Well that Ends Well. Act ii, sc. 2, l. 40. [Countess]
If I were young again.—*The Merry Wives of Windsor,* i, 1, 40.

7
I 'ld give bay Curtal and his furniture,
My mouth no more were broken than these boys',
And writ as little beard.
All's Well that Ends Well. Act ii, sc. 3, l. 65. [Lafeu]

8
She is young, wise, fair.
All's Well that Ends Well. Act ii, sc. 3, l. 138. [King]
Young and fair.—*As You Like It,* ii, 7, 37.
Young and handsome.—*Henry VIII,* ii, 2, 3.
Young and light.—*The Taming of the Shrew,* ii, 1, 204.
Young and rose-lipp'd.—*Othello,* iv, 2, 61. The only use of "rose-lipp'd."
Young and simple.—*Lover's Complaint,* l. 320.
Young, valiant, wise.—*Richard III,* i, 2, 245.

9
The staggers and the careless lapse
Of youth and ignorance.
All's Well that Ends Well. Act ii, sc. 3, l. 170. [King]

10
If I were but two hours younger, I 'ld beat thee.
All's Well that Ends Well. Act ii, sc. 3, l. 268. [Lafeu]
He looks younger than he did.
Much Ado about Nothing. Act iii, sc. 2, l. 48. [Leonato]
We shall ne'er be younger.
The Taming of the Shrew. Induction, sc. 2, l. 146. [Sly]

11
My salad days,
When I was green in judgement.
Antony and Cleopatra. Act i, sc. 5, l. 73. [Cleopatra]
His greener days.—*Henry V,* ii, 4, 136.

12
He wears the rose Of youth upon him.
Antony and Cleopatra. Act iii, sc. 13, l. 20. [Antony]
Our rose of youth.—*All's Well that Ends Well,* i, 3, 136.
Rose-cheeked youth.—*Timon of Athens,* iv, 3, 86. The only use of "rose-cheeked."
Prime of youth.—*III Henry VI,* ii, 1, 23; *Richard III,* v, 3, 119.
Most rich in youth.—*Sonnets,* xv.
The vaward of our youth.—*II Henry IV,* i, 2, 200. See under AGE AND YOUTH.

13
Three proper young men, of excellent growth and presence.
As You Like It. Act i, sc. 2, l. 129. [Le Beau]
"Young men" or "young man" is used thirty-seven times in the plays.
What, ye knaves! young men must live.
I Henry IV. Act ii, sc. 2, l. 95. [Falstaff]
Young gentleman, your spirits are too bold for your years.
As You Like It. Act i, sc. 2, l. 183. [Celia]
"Young gentleman (or gentlemen)" occurs nine times.

14
Thou art a gallant youth.
As You Like It. Act i, sc. 2, l. 241. [Duke]
Gallant youth.—*Henry V,* iii, 5, 25.
Valiant youth.—*Cymbeline,* v, 5, 289.
It is a pretty youth: not very pretty:
But, sure, he 's proud, and yet his pride becomes him:
He 'll make a proper man: the best thing in him
Is his complexion.
As You Like It. Act iii, sc. 5, l. 113. [Phebe]
Pretty youth.—*The Two Gentlemen of Verona,* iv, 2, 58; *As You Like It,* iii, 2, 352; iv, 1, 1.
I see by you I am a sweet-faced youth.
The Comedy of Errors. Act v, sc. 1, l. 418. [Dromio of Ephesus]
The fairest youth That ever made eye swerve.
Winter's Tale. Act iv, sc. 4, l. 384. [Florizel]
Beauteous and lovely youth.—*Sonnets,* liv.
Delicate youth.—*Othello,* i, 2, 74.
Fair youth.—*As You Like It,* iii, 2, 404; iv, 3, 6; *Cymbeline,* iii, 6, 64; 90.
Fair sweet youth.—*Passionate Pilgrim,* l. 125.
Flowering youth.—*I Henry VI,* ii, 5, 56.
Fresh and stainless youth.—*Twelfth Night,* i, 5, 278.
Gentle youth.—*The Two Gentlemen of Verona,* iv, 4, 178; *Romeo and Juliet,* v, 3, 59.
Most thankful and reverend youth.—*Much Ado about Nothing,* v, 1, 325.
Noble youth.—*II Henry IV,* ii, 3, 22; *Hamlet,* i, 5, 38; v, 1, 247.
Sweet youth.—*The Two Gentlemen of Verona,* ii, 5, 3; *A Midsummer-Night's Dream,* v, 1,

145; *As You Like It,* iii, 5, 64; *Much Ado about Nothing,* iii, 2, 52.

1
I was too young that time to value her.
As You Like It. Act i, sc. 3, l. 73. [Celia]
You are too young in this.—*As You Like It,* i, 1, 57.

2
All 's brave that youth mounts and folly guides.
As You Like It. Act iii, sc. 4, l. 48. [Celia]

3
When yet he was but tender-bodied and the only son of my womb, when youth with comeliness plucked all gaze his way.
Coriolanus. Act i, sc. 3, l. 8. [Volumnia] The only use of "tender-bodied" and "comeliness."

His pupil age
Man-entered thus, he waxed like a sea.
Coriolanus, ii, 2, 102. See under GROWTH. "Pupil age" is repeated in *I Henry IV,* ii, 4, 106. The only use of "man-entered."

4 Briefly die their joys
That place them on the truth of girls and boys.
Cymbeline. Act v, sc. 5, l. 106. [Lucius]

5
Thou 'rt my good youth, my page.
Cymbeline. Act v, sc. 5, l. 118. [Cymbeline]
Good youth.—*As You Like It,* iii, 2, 454; iv, 1, 103; *The Merchant of Venice,* iv, 1, 141; *Twelfth Night,* i, 4, 15; iii, 1, 142; *Cymbeline,* iv, 2, 374; 394.

6
The canker galls the infants of the spring,
Too oft before their buttons be disclosed,
And in the morn and liquid dew of youth
Contagious blastments are most imminent.
Hamlet. Act i, sc. 3, l. 39. [Laertes] The only use of "blastments."
Youth to itself rebels, though none else near.
Hamlet. Act i, sc. 3, l. 44. [Laertes]

7 He is young,
And with a larger tether may he walk
Than may be given you.
Hamlet. Act i, sc. 3, l. 124. [Polonius] The only use of "tether."

Polonius: Such wanton, wild and usual slips
As are companions noted and most known
To youth and liberty.
Reynaldo: As gaming, my lord.
Polonius: Ay, or drinking, fencing, swearing, quarrelling,
Drabbing.
Hamlet. Act ii, sc. 1, l. 22. The only use of "drabbing."
My leaping-time.
Cymbeline. Act iv, sc. 2, l. 200. [Arviragus] The only use of "leaping-time."

8
To flaming youth let virtue be as wax.
Hamlet. Act iii, sc. 4, l. 84. [Hamlet]
Blown youth.—*Hamlet,* iii, 1, 167.
Burning youth.—*Measure for Measure,* i, 3, 6.
Flush youth.—*Antony and Cleopatra,* i, 4, 52.
Hot youth.—*Richard II,* ii, 3, 99.
Straying youth.—*Sonnets,* xli.
Ungovern'd youth.—*Richard III,* iv, 4, 392; *The Two Gentlemen of Verona,* iv, 1, 45.
Unstaid youth.—*Richard II,* ii, 1, 2.
Wilful youth.—*Merchant of Venice,* i, 1, 146.

9
Which makes him prune himself, and bristle up
The crest of youth against your dignity.
I Henry IV. Act i, sc. 1, l. 98. [Westmoreland]
They hate us youth.
I Henry IV. Act ii, sc. 2, l. 89. [Falstaff]

10
For though the camomile, the more it is trodden on the faster it grows, yet youth, the more it is wasted the sooner it wears.
I Henry IV. Act ii, sc. 4, l. 440. [Falstaff] The only mention of camomile. Shakespeare derived the saying from John Lyly's *Euphues,* p. 46.
My youth Hath faulty wander'd and irregular.
I Henry IV. Act iii, sc. 2, l. 26. [Prince]
My nephew's trespass may be well forgot;
It hath the excuse of youth and heat of blood.
I Henry IV. Act v, sc. 2, l. 16. [Worcester]
O, Harry, thou hast robb'd me of my youth!
I Henry IV. Act v, sc. 4, l. 77. [Hotspur]

11
The happiest youth, viewing his progress through,
What perils past, what crosses to ensue,
Would shut the book, and sit him down and die.
II Henry IV. Act iii, sc. 1, l. 54. [King Henry]

12 In the very May-morn of his youth,
Ripe for exploits and mighty enterprises.
Henry V. Act i, sc. 2, l. 120. [Bishop of Ely] The only use of "May-morn."

Our master
Says that you savour too much of your youth,
And bids you be advised there 's nought in France
That can be with a nimble galliard won.
Henry V. Act i, sc. 2, l. 249. [Ambassador]
A vain, giddy, shallow, humorous youth.
Henry V. Act ii, sc. 4, l. 28. [Dauphin]

13
Now all the youth of England are on fire,
And silken dalliance in the wardrobe lies.
Henry V. Act ii, Prologue, l. 1. [Chorus]
English youth.—*Henry V,* iii, 5, 30.
Youth of the realm.—*II Henry VI,* iv, 7, 36.

14
And shall my youth be guilty of such blame?
I Henry VI. Act iv, sc. 5, l. 47. [John Talbot]

My years are young!
And fitter is my study and my books
Than wanton dalliance with a paramour.
I Henry VI. Act v, sc. 1, l. 21. [King Henry]

15
My tender youth was never yet attaint
With any passion of inflaming love.
I Henry VI. Act v, sc. 5, l. 81. [King Henry]
Tender youth is soon suggested.
The Two Gentlemen of Verona. Act iii, sc. 1, l. 34. [Duke]
Tender years.—*I Henry VI,* iii, 1, 71; iv, 1, 149; *Richard III,* iv, 4, 342.
Tenderness of years.—*Love's Labour 's Lost,* iii, 1, 4.

Tender, raw, and young.—*Richard II,* ii, 3, 42.
Young and tender.—*As You Like It,* i, 1, 135.
His years but young.—*The Two Gentlemen of Verona,* ii, 4, 69.

1
Ay, good leave have you; for you will have leave,
Till youth take leave and leave you to the crutch.
III Henry VI. Act iii, sc. 2, l. 34. [Gloucester]
Lose thy youth.—*II Henry VI,* v, 2, 46.
Spend his youth.—*II Henry VI,* i, 1, 78.

2
These are the youths that thunder at a playhouse, and fight for bitten apples; that no audience, but the tribulation of Tower-hill, or the limbs of Limehouse, their dear brothers, are able to endure.
Henry VIII. Act v, sc. 4, l. 63. [Porter] The only use of "bitten," "tribulation," "Tower-hill," and "Limehouse."
I know young bloods look for a time of rest.
Julius Cæsar. Act iv, sc. 3, l. 262. [Brutus]
The sea will ebb and flow, heaven show his face;
Young blood doth not obey an old decree.
Love's Labour's Lost. Act iv, sc. 3, l. 216. [Biron]
Rouse up thy youthful blood, be valiant and live.
Richard II. Act i, sc. 3, l. 83. [Gaunt]

3
King Lear: So young, and so untender?
Cordelia: So young, my lord, and true.
King Lear. Act i, sc. 1, l. 108.
A look untender.—*Cymbeline,* iii, 4, 12. The only uses of "untender."

4
The younger rises when the old doth fall.
King Lear. Act iii, sc. 3, l. 26. [Edmund]

5
A most acute juvenal; volable and free of grace!
Love's Labour's Lost. Act iii, sc. 1, l. 67. [Armado] The only use of "volable" (quick-witted).
The juvenal, the prince, your master, whose chin is not yet fledged.
II Henry IV. Act i, sc. 2, l. 22. [Falstaff]
Most brisky juvenal.
A Midsummer-Night's Dream. Act iii, sc. 1, l. 97. [Flute] The only use of "brisky."
Tender juvenal.—*Love's Labour's Lost,* i, 2, 8. Four times repeated. See under AGE AND YOUTH. The only uses of "juvenal."

6
Youth so apt to pluck a sweet!
Love's Labour's Lost. Act iv, sc. 3, l. 113. [Dumain, reading] Repeated in *The Passionate Pilgrim,* l. 240.
The kingly state of youth.
Love's Labour's Lost. Act iv, sc. 3, l. 293. [Biron]

7
Gentle maid,
Have of my suffering youth some feeling pity.
A Lover's Complaint, l. 177

8
Many unrough youths that even now
Protest their first of manhood.
Macbeth. Act v, sc. 2, l. 10. [Lennox] The only use of "unrough."

He only lived but till he was a man;
The which no sooner had his prowess confirm'd
In the unshrinking station where he fought,
But like a man he died.
Macbeth. Act v, sc. 8, l. 40. [Ross] The only use of "unshrinking."
He should have lived,
Save that his riotous youth, with dangerous sense,
Might in the times to come have ta'en revenge,
By so receiving a dishonour'd life
With ransom of such shame.
Measure for Measure. Act iv, sc. 4, l. 31. [Angelo]
Bragging youth.—*Merchant of Venice,* iii, 4, 69.
Disdainful youth.—*A Midsummer-Night's Dream,* ii, 1, 261.
Foolish youth!—*II Henry IV,* iv, 5, 97.
Moonish youth.—*As You Like It,* iii, 2, 430. The only use of "moonish."
Slaughter'd youth.—*Romeo and Juliet,* v, 3, 84.
Truant youth.—*I Henry IV,* v, 2, 63.
Unbaked and doughy youth.—*All's Well that Ends Well,* iv, 5, 4. The only use of "unbaked" and "doughy."
Unhappy youth!—*As You Like It,* ii, 3, 16.
Unharden'd youth.—*A Midsummer-Night's Dream,* i, 1, 35. The only use of "unharden'd."

9
In her youth
There is a prone and speechless dialect,
Such as move men.
Measure for Measure. Act i, sc. 2, l. 87. [Claudio] "Dialect" is repeated in *King Lear,* ii, 2, 115.

10
Such a hare is madness the youth, to skip o'er the meshes of good counsel the cripple.
The Merchant of Venice. Act i, sc. 2, l. 21. [Portia]
A cripple soon can find a halt.
The Passionate Pilgrim, l. 308.
Chide the cripple.—*Henry V,* iv, Prol., 20.
Restore this cripple.—*II Henry VI,* ii, 1, 133.
Tardy cripple.—*Richard III,* ii, 1, 89. The only uses of "cripple" as a noun. As a verb it is used once, in *Timon of Athens,* iv, 1, 24: "Cripple our senators."

11
Would I were young for your sake, Mistress Anne!
The Merry Wives of Windsor. Act i, sc. 1, l. 268. [Shallow]
You are not young; no more am I.
The Merry Wives of Windsor. Act ii, sc. 1, l. 6. [Mrs. Page]

12
We have some salt of our youth in us.
The Merry Wives of Windsor, ii, 3, 50. See under SALT.
And youthful still! in your doublet and hose this raw rheumatic day!
The Merry Wives of Windsor. Act iii, sc. 1, l. 46. [Page]
He capers, he dances, he has eyes of youth, he writes verses, he speaks holiday, he smells April and May.
The Merry Wives of Windsor. Act iii, sc. 2, l. 68. [Host]

His May of youth and bloom of lustihood.
Much Ado about Nothing. Act v, sc. 1, l. 76. [Leonato] "Lustihood" is repeated in *Troilus and Cressida,* ii, 2, 50.

1
Had we fought, I doubt we should have been too young for them.
Much Ado about Nothing. Act v, sc. 1, l. 118. [Don Pedro]
Here is a thing too young for such a place.
Pericles. Act iii, sc. 1, l. 15. [Lychorida]
I am too young.—*Romeo and Juliet,* iii, 5, 188.

2
Is there not charms
By which the property of youth and maidhood
May be abused?
Othello. Act i, sc. 1, l. 172. [Brabantio]
The gravity and stillness of your youth
The world hath noted.
Othello. Act ii, sc. 3, l. 191. [Othello]

3
Untutor'd youth,
Unskilful in the world's false forgeries.
The Passionate Pilgrim, l. 3.
Untutor'd youth
Unlearned in the world's false subtleties.
Sonnets. No. cxxxviii.
Untutor'd lad.—*III Henry VI,* v, 5, 32.
Untutor'd churl.—*II Henry VI,* iii, 2, 213.
Untutor'd to repeat.—*Pericles,* i, 4, 74. The only uses of "untutor'd."

4
Youth is full of pleasance.
The Passionate Pilgrim, l. 157.

5
Not sick, although I have to do with death,
But lusty, young, and cheerly drawing breath.
Richard II. Act i, sc. 3, l. 65. [Bolingbroke]

6
Deal mildly with his youth;
For young hot colts being raged do rage the more.
Richard II. Act ii, sc. 1, l. 69. [York]

7
Oh, he is young, and his minority
Is put into the trust of Richard Gloucester.
Richard III. Act i, sc. 3, l. 11. [Queen]
I am young.—*Macbeth,* iv, 3, 14.
You are young.—*Henry VIII,* i, 4, 9.
Young in days.—*Timon of Athens,* v, 3, 8.
The young days.—*Love's Labour's Lost,* i, 2, 15. See under AGE.
Young in deed.—*Macbeth,* iii, 4, 144.
Young in limbs.—*Merchant of Venice,* ii, 7, 71.
Ever young.—*Timon of Athens,* iv, 3, 385.
So young.—*Othello,* iii, 3, 209.
Not so young.—*King Lear,* i, 4, 40.

8
He was the wretched'st thing when he was young,
So long a-growing and so leisurely.
Richard III. Act ii, sc. 4, l. 19. [Duchess] The only use of "wretched'st" and "a-growing." "Leisurely" is repeated in *The Winter's Tale,* v, 3, 152.
So wise so young, they say, do never live long.
Richard III. Act iii, sc. 1, l. 79. [Gloucester]

9
A virtuous and well govern'd youth.
Romeo and Juliet. Act i, sc. 5, l. 70. [Capulet]
Virtuous youth.—*All's Well that Ends Well,* i, 3, 216.
A well-accomplished youth.—*Love's Labour's Lost,* ii, 1, 56. "Well-accomplished" is repeated in *Two Gentlemen of Verona,* iv, 3, 13.
Home-keeping youth.—*The Two Gentlemen of Verona,* i, 1, 2. See under HOME. The only use of "home-keeping."

10
Where unbruised youth with unstuff'd brain
Doth couch his limbs, there golden sleep doth reign.
Romeo and Juliet. Act ii, sc. 3, l. 37. [Friar Laurence] The only use of "unstuff'd."

11
Stealing away the treasure of his spring.
Sonnets. No. lxiii.
Thou hast pass'd by the ambush of young days.
Sonnets. No. lxx.
In my young days.—*Titus Andronicus,* iv, 3, 91.
Being of so young days.—*Hamlet,* ii, 2, 11.

12
A proper stripling and an amorous!
The Taming of the Shrew. Act i, sc. 2, l. 144. [Grumio]
A handsome stripling.—*Richard III,* i, 3, 101.
Two striplings.—*Cymbeline,* v, 3, 19. The only uses of "stripling" and "striplings."

13
Well aim'd of such a young one.
The Taming of the Shrew, ii, 1, 237. "Young one" is used nine times in the plays.
Youngling, thou canst not love.
The Taming of the Shrew, ii, 1, 339. "Youngling" is repeated in *Titus Andronicus,* ii, 1, 73; iv, 2, 93.
A youngster proud and wild.
The Passionate Pilgrim, l. 120. The only use of "youngster."
What, will you make a younker of me?
I Henry IV. Act iii, sc. 3, l. 92. [Falstaff]
How like a younker!—*The Merchant of Venice,* ii, 6, 14.
Trimm'd like a younker!—*III Henry VI,* ii, 1, 24. The only uses of "younker."

14
She is young and apt:
Our own precedent passions do instruct us
What levity 's in youth.
Timon of Athens. Act i, sc. 1, l. 132. [Athenian]
Lust and liberty
Creep in the minds and marrows of our youth,
That 'gainst the stream of virtue they may strive,
And drown themselves in riot!
Timon of Athens. Act iv, sc. 1, l. 25. [Timon]

15
My youth can better spare my blood than you.
Titus Andronicus. Act iii, sc. 1, l. 166. [Lucius]
And would not, but in fury, fright my youth.
Titus Andronicus. Act iv, sc. 1, l. 24. [Lucius]
The vigour and the picture of my youth.
Titus Andronicus. Act iv, sc. 2, l. 108. [Aaron]

16
Pandarus: Why, he is very young: and yet will he, within three pound, lift as much as his brother Hector.

Cressida: Is he so young a man and so old a lifter?
Troilus and Cressida. Act i, sc. 2, l. 125. The only use of "lifter." Referring to Troilus.
O admirable youth! he ne'er saw three and twenty.
Troilus and Cressida. Act i, sc. 2, l. 255. [Pandarus]
One that knows the youth Even to his inches.
Troilus and Cressida. Act iv, sc. 5, l. 110. [Ulysses]
1
The Grecian youths are full of quality.
Troilus and Cressida, iv, 4, 78. See under GREECE.
Greekish youth.—*Troilus and Cressida,* iv, 5, 185.
Athenian youth.—*Midsummer-Night's Dream,* i, 1, 13.
Northern youth.—*I Henry IV,* iii, 2, 145.
Shepherd youth.—*As You Like It,* iv, 3, 156.
2
Not yet old enough for a man, nor young enough for a boy; as a squash is before 'tis a peascod, or a codling when 'tis almost an apple: 'tis with him in standing water, between boy and man.
Twelfth Night. Act i, sc. 5, l. 165. [Malvolio] The only use of "codling" (green apple).
How shall I feast him? what bestow of him?
For youth is bought more oft than begg'd or borrow'd.
Twelfth Night. Act iii, sc. 4, l. 2. [Olivia]
I have persuaded him the youth 's a devil.
Twelfth Night. Act iii, sc. 4, l. 321. [Sir Toby]
3
Youth 's a stuff will not endure.
Twelfth Night. Act ii, sc. 3, l. 53. [Clown]
4
To be fantastic may become a youth.
The Two Gentlemen of Verona. Act ii, sc. 7, l. 47. [Julia]
I have need of such a youth
That can with some discretion do my business.
The Two Gentlemen of Verona. Act iv, sc. 4, l. 69. [Proteus]
5
Young, and so unkind?
Venus and Adonis, l. 187.
6
Measure my strangeness with my unripe years.
Venus and Adonis, l. 524.
Unripe years did want conceit.
The Passionate Pilgrim, l. 51.
7
I would there were no age between sixteen and three-and-twenty, or that youth would sleep out the rest; for there is nothing in the between but getting wenches with child, wronging the ancientry, stealing, fighting.
The Winter's Tale. Act iii, sc. 3, l. 59. [Shepherd] "Ancientry" is repeated in *Much Ado about Nothing,* ii, 1, 80. The only use of "wronging."
With young.—*III Henry VI,* ii, 5, 35. See TIME, 1534:9.
8
Remember since you owed no more to time
Than I do now.
Winter's Tale. Act v, sc. 1, l. 219. [Florizel]

Z

ZEAL

9
This doth infer the zeal I had to see him.
II Henry IV. Act v, sc. 5, l. 13. [Falstaff]
10 An upright zeal to right prevails
More than the nature of a brother's love!
III Henry VI. Act v, sc. 1, l. 78. [Warwick]
Ardent zeal.—*Timon of Athens,* iii, 3, 33.
Christian zeal.—*Richard III,* iii, 7, 103.
Hospitable zeal.—*King John,* ii, 1, 244.
True zeal.—*Richard II,* v, 3, 108.
Bright in zeal.—*Troilus and Cressida,* iv, 4, 28.
11 Urge them while their souls
Are capable of this ambition,
Lest zeal, now melted by the windy breath
Of soft petitions, pity and remorse,
Cool and congeal again to what it was.
King John. Act ii, sc. 1, l. 476. [Queen Elinor] The only use of "congeal."
Methinks my zeal to Valentine is cold.
The Two Gentlemen of Verona. Act ii, sc. 4, l. 203. [Proteus]
Cold in zeal.—*Richard III,* ii, 1, 40.
Freeze up their zeal.—*King John,* iii, 4, 150.
12
Whom zeal and charity brought to the field.
King John. Act ii, sc. 1, l. 565. [Bastard]
A voluntary zeal and an unurged faith.
King John. Act v, sc. 2, l. 10. [Salisbury] "Unurged" is used a second time in *The Comedy of Errors,* ii, 2, 115.
13
What zeal, what fury hath inspired thee now?
Love's Labour 's Lost. Act iv, sc. 3, l. 229. [King]
Where zeal strives to content, and the contents
Dies in the zeal of that which it presents.
Love's Labour 's Lost. Act v, sc. 2, l. 518. [Princess of France]
14
Intend a kind of zeal both to the prince and Claudio.
Much Ado about Nothing. Act ii, sc. 2, l. 36. [Borachio]
Counterfeited zeal.—*II Henry IV,* iv, 2, 27.

INDEX AND CONCORDANCE

SUGGESTIONS FOR THE USE OF THE CONCORDANCE

The CONCORDANCE is a word-index to all the quotations in the book, with the entries grouped alphabetically by leading words, and followed by a reference not only to the page on which the quotation appears, but also to its number on the page, so that it may be turned to instantly. The first entry in the index is "A B C: lost his A B C, 901:1," which means that the quotation in which this phrase occurs will be found in the first section on page 901.

Identifying words and phrases are generously given, in order that a quotation which is not exactly remembered may be traced through any one of a number of channels. For such simple phrases as "Caviare to the general," or "Ears of the groundlings," either of the principal words may be consulted, for an entry will be found under each of them, "Caviare," "General," "Ears," and "Groundlings." The selection from the longer passages is also unusually full. For example, Macbeth's famous

> "To-morrow, and to-morrow, and to-morrow,
> Creeps in this petty pace from day to day
> To the last syllable of recorded time,
> And all our yesterdays have lighted fools
> The way to dusty death,"

will be found entered under "To-morrow," "Pace," "Day," "Syllable," "Time," "Yesterdays," "Way," "Dusty," and "Death." Occasionally it may be necessary to consult a second word when no entry is found under the first one looked for, but usually, if only one important word of a quotation is correctly remembered, the quotation will be found entered there.

The word selected for the index entry is always the noun—if there is a noun—which is the subject of the sentence, but many others are thrown in for good measure, as in the lines from *Macbeth* quoted above. Where there is no noun, the principal adjective or verb is used. "Be able for thine enemy" will be found under both "Able" and "Enemy." An effort has been made to include all unusual words and phrases by which a quotation might stick in the memory, and all unique words are also indexed, however unimportant they may be.

The only exception to this detailed indexing is when the subject is a very short one. The black-letter lines in the CONCORDANCE indicate subject-headings in the body of the book, and where the subject contains only a few entries, such as "Abstinence," the quotations under this subject carrying this word are not indexed separately, unless they are unusually important, and the reader should turn at once to the subject itself and run through the entries under it—a matter of a moment. This system is followed throughout the book, in order to keep the CONCORDANCE free from unnecessary entries and to hold it within manageable proportions. Where the same key-word occurs in quotations under other headings it is, of course, indexed. In the case of "Abstinence" this is not necessary, because Shakespeare used the word only four times and all its uses are grouped under the subject in the text, but in the case of another short subject, "Adder," there are four entries from quotations on other pages. Three of these are from quotations which do not appear under "Adder," and one from a quotation which appears there only as a phrase, "The adder blue," but which is given at length on page 1056:15. Where a phrase occurs twice, once simply as a phrase and again as part of a longer quotation, the entry is always from the latter.

When no phrase or key-word is exactly remembered by the reader, but only the general tenour of the quotation, it is necessary for him to turn to the text and look through the quotations under the appropriate subject-heading. Perhaps he wishes to find Hamlet's advice to the players, but remembers none of the lines. In that case, he will naturally look first under "Players" (p. 1164), where he will find a cross-reference to "Acting and Actor," under which, in the second entry (10:11), is the quotation sought. Where the search is not for a special quotation, but to ascertain what Shakespeare has to say on any particular subject, the text is, of course, consulted at once, without reference to the CONCORDANCE. In such cases, the cross-references should not be overlooked.

Some niceties of the alphabetical arrangement should, perhaps, be explained. Under each subject the singular noun comes first ("Air," for example), then the singular possessive ("Air's"), then the hyphenated compounds ("Air-braving," "Air-drawn"), and finally the plural and the plural possessive. Proper nouns precede common nouns, and all foreign-language quotations follow the English ones, even if the key-words are identical, as in the case of "Air," where a French quotation occurs. Where a word is used in the text in both hyphenated and unhyphenated form (as bedfellow), the modern usage is followed in the INDEX. It should also be remembered that a word is sometimes spelled in different ways, as "blessed" and "blest." Cross-references call attention to this, and both spellings should be consulted.

All entries necessarily are very brief, but an effort has been made to give sufficient context to enable the reader to identify the quotation readily. It should be pointed out, however, that the mind of the reader will not always run exactly in accord with the mind of the indexer and so the phrase which springs to the reader's memory may not be the exact one which the indexer has chosen for his entry, in which case a little perseverance may be required to turn up the quotation desired.

No one can get the full benefit of this book without understanding thoroughly the use of the CONCORDANCE, and if the reader will take the time to familiarize himself with the suggestions given above, he will find the book far more useful and satisfactory then it could otherwise be.

INDEX AND CONCORDANCE

Accidents, *continued*
particular a. 5:5
rare a. 5:8
shackles a. 1460:13
this night's a. 5:11
unpurposed 5:3
with mortal a. oppressed 5:5
Accites to think so 1514:9
Acclamations hyperbolical 1183:14
Accommodated 1150:10
Accommodations that thou bear'st 868:19
Accommodo: comes of "a." 1150:10
Accompanying his foot 590:6
Accomplice 5
Accomplices: happiness to his a. 5:16
Accomplish as you may 1269:11
Accomplished in himself 633:6
with what we lack 44:7
Accomplishing the knights 54:7
Accomplishment of years 313:7
so hotly chased 313:7
Accompt 392:14
cast a. 402:4
Accord 26:11
with full a. 1134:7
Accost, Sir Andrew, a. 1710:6
Accosting: give a. welcome 237:1
Account: beggarly a. of empty boxes 369:4
call him to so strict a. 616:4
jump not on a just a. 765:3
last a. 'twixt heaven 1694:3
my a. I well may give 1554:3
of hours to crave 1517:11
sent to my a. 1035:8
Accountant for as great a sin 920:10
Accoutred like young men 355:9
Accoutrement: outward a. 1088:17
Accoutrements: poor a. 379:6
Accrue: profits will a. 1210:18
Accumulated to his portion 1644:1
Accumulation of renown 1260:15
Accursed in being so blest 276:9
Accusation 6
false a. 767:10
public a. 6:17
thought his a. true 6:17
villain's a. 6:7
your a. overweigh 1050:3
Accusations: roar these a. forth 1524:10
Accuse 6
false a. 6:10
him home and home 6:15
I should a. myself 333:14
many dare a. you 6:13
some innocent 7:3
these men 7:6
Accused: accuser and the a. 7:7
falsely a. 7:1
him all this while 6:3
him strongly 6:13
in true report 1263:17
publicly a. 1566:10
wrongfully a. 7:1
Accuser 7
Accusers: false a. 1377:5
Accusing wrongfully 7:1
Ace: turned up a. 894:2
Ache: charm a. with air 179:8
in his shoulders 783:2
in my bones 352:10
Acheron 834:5
black as A. 557:17
Aches contract and starve 278:8
Achieve: bid them a. me 124:14
you cannot as you would a. 1269:11
Achievement 313:1
is command 1713:4
Achievements: how my a. mock me 313:1
of no less account 313:1
takes from our a. 313:1
Achiever brings home full numbers 1600:7
Achilles go to him 1525:7
if not A., nothing 1054:1
kingdom'd A. 1737:5
Achitophel: whoreson A. 1471:13
Aconitum: as strong as a. 1451:10
Acordo linta 1416:3

Acorn 560:14
dropped a. 1563:12
wherein the a. cradled 1521:12
Acorn-cups: creep into a. 463:2
Acquaintance 7
desire you of more a. 8:5
desire your more a. 331:10
face me out of his a. 270:7
hold a. with the waves 143:6
how creeps a. 7:12
how her a. grew 8:6
I will a. strangle 1086:6
lending me this a. 852:7
lies little amongst them 8:7
like old a. in a trance 978:1
new a. of thy mind 981:12
of our old a. tell 1049:2
old a. 7:14
old a. in a trance 376:16
on so little a. 912:2
small a. 7:11
true a. of mine ear 4:16
upon better a. 906:5
wash off gross a. 91:7
Acquainted: art not a. 7:8
be a. 7:13; 812:13
be better a. 7:12; 8:5
make a. 8:8
well a. 7:9
with tapsters 87:5
with these answers 43:9
Acquisition: thine own a. 290:8
Acquit 767:7
him of suspicion 1473:9
Acquittance 767:7
so the a. follows 665:7
Acquittances: produce a. 767:7
Acquitted 767:7
Acre of barren ground 1325:4
search every a. 1326:8
Acres: bosky a. 1238:11
throw millions of a. on us 1031:4
Act 8
a slave to limit 921:4
arch a. of piteous massacre 1038:2
be the same in thine own a. 1519:5
betray'd thine a. 1545:6
bodily a. 9:9
bound to every a. of duty 1381:7
cried up for our best a. 627:16
cruel a. 8:12
did the a. of darkness 926:7
do the a. 1660:6
dreaded a. 8:12
esteem no a. but that of hand 10:5
finished his mortal a. 10:6
foul a. 9:12
further this a. of grace 143:8
hath three branches 387:6
his a. did not o'ertake his bad intent 9:5
holy a. 9:14
horrid a. of the divorce 367:11
impious a. 9:12
in safety 10:5
loathsome a. of lust 926:7
monstrous a. 8:12
my woes 10:5
no a. of common passage 8:16
noble a. 9:13
of fear, grace, etc. 9:9
of fornication 1625:5
of hares 921:4
of shame 920:10
of sport 927:1
of this importance 10:8
of tragic violence 9:12
particular a. and place 1726:2
seest that a. afoot 1161:6
sleep an a. or two 1162:5
some a. that has no relish of salvation in 't 703:8
swelling a. 1576:7
that roars so loud 9:1
that very chance doth throw 10:3
the deed 10:5
the woman 10:5
this a. is as an ancient tale 9:6
this a. shows horrible 9:10
this a. so evilly born 9:6
this a. will be my fame 9:12
this heavy a. with heavy heart relate 9:10

Act, *continued*
to a., to do, and to perform 387:6
wholesome a. 9:14
Acted ere they be scann'd 1169:10
so lively a. with my tears 1651:14
well a. 10:9
Acting 10
important a. of your command 1397:11
of a dreadful thing 9:5
resolute a. of your blood 110:6
Action 8
and accent 5:1
body's a. 9:9
bring mine a. 1551:11
continual a. 1661:1
dangerous a. 10:7; 284:11
draw the a. 1633:9
dumb a. 1043:1
every a. that hath gone 1566:9
fair a. 1519:3
fearful a. 1658:16
give due a. to my words 1726:7
glorious 10:2
graceless a. 9:6
here the a. lies 794:11
honourable a. 10:2
imitate the a. of the tiger 1630:3
in a. all of precept 1191:12
in a. how like an angel 941:1
instant a. 9:4
is eloquence 451:13
it is an accustomed a. 662:1
kindred a. like to this 9:6
let not leaner a. rend us 1586:1
make 't an a. 1693:14
making such sober a. 659:18
might become them 1726:14
no unchaste a. 357:9
of battery 844:13
of slander 844:13
of such shame 1344:15
outward a. 9:10
pious a. 744:1
pretty a. 8:17
rarer a. is in virtue 572:5
ridiculous and awkward a. 1108:7
so honourable an a. 1331:1
suit the a. to the word 10:11
till a., lust is perjured 927:7
waspish a. 145:4
Action-taking knave 816:6
Actions blacker than night 947:8
fair and good 280:5
her a. shall be holy 709:3
her private a. 168:16
his a. show like to madness 931:11
his a. were not visible 1263:9
most ridiculous 898:10
my a. noble as my thoughts 1519:4
necessary a. 9:4
outward a. 678:2
that a man might play 1330:3
thousand a., once afoot 9:3
unnecessary a. 1137:12
would grow single 312:13
your a. are my dreams 377:6
Active: most a. 9:2
Active-valiant: more a. 606:2
Activity: doing is a. 313:9
may defeat and quell 1661:2
Actor 11
accounted a good a. 12:3
after a well-graced a. 12:7
as an unperfect a. 12:1
earthly a. 11:7
I 'll prove a busy a. 12:1
let go by the a. 516:11
like a dull a. now 12:1
may plead pardon 11:8
Actors are at hand 12:6
best a. in the world 12:3
counterfeiting a. 1554:12
our a. were all spirits 1609:15
Roman a. 1300:3
Acts: all your a. are queens 315:11
brave a. 9:13
carnal, bloody, and unnatural a. 1273:15
decrees and statutes 1443:8
of black night 10:4
so much applauded 48:1
thy wild a. denote 10:1
Acutely: answer thee a. 147:5

B

Beard, *continued*
he hath but a little b. 74: 9
his b. grew thin 74:11
his b. was grizzled 73: 7
I have a b. coming 1164: 9
I will b. him 321: 8
in palm of hand 74:10
is more than a youth 74: 7
is turned white 73: 7
little yellow b. 74: 9
look upon this b. 74: 3
make him scratch his b. ...146: 8
meet him b. to b. 73: 5
neglected 900: 5
of formal cut 940:12
of the general's 73: 3
plucks off my b. 256: 1
silver b. 73: 7
takes him by the b. 73:13
thee to thy face 73:10
usurped b. 74: 7
was white as snow 73: 7
wear a b. upon your chin ..74:10
well-proportioned b. 1443:14
what a b. hast thou got 74: 5
white and bristly b. 1465:11
white b. 21:9; 25:7; 73: 7
whose b. the silver hand of
peace hath touch'd ...1630: 2
whose b. they have singed ..73: 4
woman has a great b. 1693: 4
writ as little b. 1755: 7
you had more b. 73: 6
Bearded like the pard 1392: 5
to my face 73:10
Beardless boy 74:10
vain comparative 806: 9
Beardlessness 74
Beards of Hercules 256: 9
old men have grey b. 23: 4
silver b. 1627: 5
swear by your b. 815: 3
'tis merry in hall when b.
wag all 73:12
your b. forbid me 74: 4
Bearing: blunt b. 1723:13
brave b. 413: 2
discreet and stable b. 91: 8
valour in the b. 411:12
Bearing-cloth: child's b. ..1297: 6
Bears i' the town 72:13
meek b. 548:14
my two brave b. 72:10
roaring b. 72:12
tied by the neck 850:12
will not bite one another ...72:13
with glasses 548: 3
Beast 75
adulterate b. 75: 5
bonny b. he loved 967: 1
familiar b. to man 75:10
for Perseus 722: 2
gentle b. 880:10
give it the b. 1731: 5
grisly b., which Lion hight 879: 1
Hyrcanian b. 1526:15
ill-beseeming b. 954:10
let a b. be lord of beasts ...75: 6
little better than a b. 176:10
makes a b. a man 899: 3
making b. with two backs ..926:13
many a b. then in a city ..267: 9
meaning me a b. 76: 2
no b. so fierce 1157: 8
O monstrous b. 76: 2
play the noble b. 1164: 6
presently a b. 386: 5
remain a b. with beasts 76: 4
rough b. that knows no right 75:15
rude b. will profit 238:10
sick-fall'n b. 224: 1
strange b. makes a man ...419: 3
that bears me 722:11
the more b., I say 76: 2
thou art a b. 75: 7
transform'd into a b. 1555: 1
unkindest b. more kinder ..948: 2
what a b. am I 75:11
what a b. art thou 76: 4
what a b. was I 185: 6
what a wicked b. was I 715:10
what b. couldst thou be 76: 4
what b. was 't, then 75: 9
with many heads 1034:13
without a heart 152:10

Beast-like: life was b. 865:13
Beastliest sense 1334:18
Beastliness: bolting-hutch of
b. 174: 5
Beastly: how b. she doth
court 254:10
we are b. 174: 3
Beasts and birds and fishes ..75:14
did leap 75:14
let b. bear gentle minds 75:15
may have the world in em-
pire 625: 1
shall tremble 1521:12
that meet me run 1019: 1
transform ourselves into b. 386: 5
very strange b. 562: 3
Beat down 76: 9
every man should b. thee ..76: 6
from his best ward 78: 6
he has b. my bones 124:11
him most pitifully 77:10
I could b. forty of them 77: 3
I 'ld b. him like a dog 177: 3
I 'll b. him too 78: 3
it hence 1377:14
me at the mart 77: 1
me because her horse stumbled 78: 2
me grievously 77:10
me to death 78: 2
more you b. me 370: 6
now b. them hence 77: 6
them to their beds 1599:16
them to their wives 77: 2
thou hast b. me out 77: 3
us out of it 77: 4
you to your tent 76: 7
Beated and chopp'd 25:18
Beaten 76:8
are we not b. 320: 5
black and blue 77:10
I 'ld have thee b. 77: 8
into all the colours of the
rainbow 77:10
let us be b. 538:11
like a dog 78: 5
Beating 76
and hanging are terrors ...668:16
heats me with b. 77: 1
Beatrice: wake my cousin
B. 1293: 1
Beauteous and swift 722: 6
thou art 1713: 9
thou art b. 81: 7
Beautied with plastering
art 1726: 2
Beauties: examine other b. ..81: 9
one who composed your b. .509: 8
richest b. on the earth 81: 5
those whose b. proudly
make 1583: 6
your good b. be the happy
cause 1671:11
'Beautified' is a vile phrase 1150: 8
with goodly shape 79: 4
Beautiful: mild and b. 993:11
of many accounted b. 82: 6
she was b. 1330: 2
she 's b. and therefore to
be woo'd 1713: 5
still I see her b. 82: 7
Beautify 78:12
Beauty 78
alluring b. 24: 8
and her brain go not to-
gether 80: 7
and honour in her 81: 4
arched b. of the brow 145: 1
be her wedding-dower 375: 1
blemish'd once 80: 9
blots thy b. as frosts 1702: 9
brag, but 'tis not she 1577: 8
breedeth b. 80:13
cannot please his eye 80: 6
chase the b. from his cheek 1407:15
claims no worse a husband 740: 2
could b. have better com-
merce than with honesty 80: 5
daily b. in his life 78:11
dedicate his b. to the sun .1328:11
delighted b. 1608: 6
done her b. wrong 1751:17
doom'd this b. to a grave ..636:15
doth b. lack 102:11
doth varnish age 79:11

Beauty, *continued*
exquisite, unmatchable b. ...82: 5
fed upon fresh b. 921: 7
first he did praise my b. ..1183:13
fresh b. for the use 80:13
gorgeous b. 81: 4
hath deform'd us 79:11
hath his power and will ...822:13
hath made me effeminate ...79:15
her b. is exquisite 46:12
her b. makes this vault 637:13
herself is black 216: 1
his b. in these black lines .1171: 7
I ne'er saw true b. 82: 1
I saw sweet b. 82: 2
I see thy b. 82: 2
if b. have a soul 79: 3
impair not b. being mute .1367:10
in b., education 81: 6
inward b. and invisible ...452: 5
is a flower 79: 1
is a witch 79:12
is bought by judgement 82:11
is but a doubtful good 80: 9
is proposed my fee 79:14
itself doth of itself persuade 79:13
let her b. look 80: 7
like a dial-hand 80:10
lives with kindness 801: 6
making beautiful old rhyme 80: 1
more doth b. beauteous
seem 1577: 8
my b. as the spring 82: 8
my b., though but mean 82:11
my love's sweet b. 981:12
my poor b. had purloin'd
his eyes 927: 4
O fairest b. 81: 4
of a fair queen's cheeks ..1498: 2
of a woman's face 460:10
of blessed marriage 780:13
of brow, cheek, etc. 78:10
of the world 941: 1
of this sinful dame 85: 4
of thy mind 997:11
of your eyes 460:14
o'ersnow'd 1465:11
Proserpina's b. 422:20
provoketh thieves 78: 8
purchased by the weight ...80: 8
pure and princely b. 1036: 9
rich in b. 1284: 9
right arched b. 78:10
sees Helen's b. in a brow
of Egypt 922:12
shiver'd all b. of my glass .749:14
should look so 450:12
should not be wasted 80:13
shows all the b. of the sun 896: 2
slander'd with a bastard
shame 103: 2
smother up his b. 1466: 2
spot the b. of thy name ...1348: 6
stain her b. 290: 4
starved with severity 181: 9
stirr'd by a painted b. to
his verse 1597: 3
such b. as a woman's eye ..448:12
such seems your b. still 24:11
summer b. 881: 2
sweet b. hath no name 80:10
tainted b. 80: 9
tan sacred b. 1533: 8
that is born here 82: 5
that made barren the boast .81: 3
that the tyrant oft reclaims .79: 8
thick, bereft of b. 1702: 9
thy b. hath ensnared thee ..79:13
thy b. sounded 1712: 3
thy unused b. must be
tomb'd with thee 80:12
till now I never knew thee .661: 2
'tis b. that doth oft make
women proud 1701: 9
'tis b. truly blent 82: 6
to her b. I commend my
vows 82: 7
too rich for use 81:11
true b. of the soul 739:12
turn all b. into thoughts of
harm 908: 5
'twas thy b. that provoked me 79:14
unmask her b. to the moon 934: 7
upon my mask, to defend
my b. 1704: 4

Bribe: hark how I 'll b. you . 140: 2
to pay my sword 139: 9
Bribed the Destinies 335: 5
Briber: sufficient b. 1341:10
Bribery 139
Bribes: base b. 140: 1
Brick-wall: against a b. 293: 4
Bricklayer 828:11
Bricks are alive 428:18
Bridal-day: graced thy poor
sire with his b. 1665: 4
Bride 140
be b. to you 140:10
brought the b. to bed 85: 4
encounter darkness as a b. . 305: 8
gallant b. 140:13
in b. bury brotherhood 140: 5
joyful b. 140: 7
lead espoused my b. 962: 3
lovely b. 140:8; 140:12
loving b. 140: 8
mistress b. 140:10
new b. 1275:11
new-made b. 140: 4
new untrimmed b. 337:14
obey the b. 140:11
practise how to b. it 140:10
ripe to be a b. 1292: 1
took the b. about the neck . 812:13
wait upon this b. 140:11
youngest for a b. 290: 9
Bride-bed: to best b. will we . 83: 1
to have decked 934: 8
Bridegroom 141
in my death 305: 8
mad-brain'd b. 1200:10
Brides and bridegrooms all . 141: 5
Bridge: London b. . . 542:6; 884: 4
take the b. away 1074: 7
what need the b. much
broader than the flood . 875: 1
Bridget, Cicely, Gillian . . . 1051: 2
does B. paint still 1110: 2
Bridle: I 'll b. it 1260: 1
of your will 1672: 6
Brief and tedious of it 493: 3
as the lightning 895: 5
as woman's love 903: 7
be b. 139:6; 801: 1
be b. when traitors brave . 1562:10
better b. than tedious 139: 6
how b. the life of man 864:14
I must be b. 1282:14
I will be b. 139: 1
now-born b. 958: 5
only to be b. 139: 3
sweet verbal b. 138:14
tedious and b. 1003:11
this is the b. of money . . . 1177: 8
Briefer sort 1495: 2
Briefest end 1268: 4
Briefness 139:4
in feather'd b. 1313: 6
Brier 1513:9; 1513:10
like the red rose on tri-
umphant b. 201: 6
Briers and thorns 1513: 6
how full of b. is this working-day world 1513: 2
rude-growing b. 1513: 2
scarlet hips 1623:13
scratch'd with b. 1513:10
shall have leaves 1465: 4
tooth'd b. 1041: 7
torn with b. 1513: 6
Bright as heaven's beauties . 445: 8
be b. and jovial 1654:11
darkly b. are b. in dark . . . 446: 2
in zeal 1759: 9
too b. to be looked against . . 81: 7
Bright-burning Troy 565: 1
Bright-shining day 196:13
Brighten: God of heaven b. it 713: 8
Brighter than glass 178: 2
Brightness of her cheek 183:11
Brim: pleasure drown the b. 919: 9
Brimful of sorrow 1409: 6
Brimstone: fire and b. 543:17
in your liver 1592: 5
Brinded cat 161: 9
Brine 1500:8
drink nought but b. 384: 4
stew'd in b. 1520: 5
Brine-pit with our tears 580: 4
Bring me off again 1640:12

Bringer: comprehends some
b. 751: 1
first b. of unwelcome news
hath but a losing office 1063:14
Bringing: good b. up 457:15
Bringings-forth: his own b. . . 44: 9
Brinish bowels, pearl 1500: 9
tears 1260: 2
Brink: to the b. 1452:10
very b. of tears 1501: 3
Brisky juvenal 1757: 5
Bristle up 1756: 9
Bristled hair 655: 6
lips 21: 4
Bristol castle 160:14
Britain: hath B. all the sun . 417: 1
in your duller B. 778:17
is a world by itself 415: 1
British 415:9
Briton 417:7
here comes the B. 420: 9
Britons strut with courage . . 417: 7
valiant B. 417: 7
Brittle as the glory 457:12
Broach this business 150: 1
Broached in jest 784: 1
Broad and general as air . . 1143: 2
as b. as it hath breadth . . 1501: 1
that word 'b.' 1725:12
Broad-fronted Cæsar 1015: 6
Broad-spreading leaves . . . 1648:15
Broadsides: fear we b. 321: 9
Brock: hang thee, b. 667: 5
Brogues: clouted b. 1356: 3
Broil 538:7
Broiled and eaten him 1221: 2
Broiling: where been b. . . . 1141:10
Broils: being bred in b. . . . 1392: 6
civil b. 1245:17
furious raging b. 1123: 2
in loud applause 48: 6
root out the work 981:12
tumultuous b. 538: 7
Brokenly: confess it b. 906: 2
Broker: play the b. 792:14
that b., that still breaks . . 1144:14
this bawd, this b. 1331:14
Brokers: they are b. 1616: 2
to defiling 1616: 6
Brokers-between, Pandars . 1112:14
Brokes with all 1329: 8
Broking pawn 264:12
Brooch and gem 172:11
and tooth-pick 1605: 3
of lead 845: 8
Brood: bring forth brave b. 188: 6
her own sweet b. 398: 4
of traitors 1560:10
Brooded watchful day 295:11
Brooding in the snow 1683: 3
Brook 141
by a running b. 623: 3
drowned in the b. 562: 3
I cannot b. thy sight 1064: 5
where Adon used 885: 1
Brooks: books in the run-
ning b. 866:10
small b. to flow 579:13
Broom-groves 963: 3
Broth: my wind cooling my
b. 1677:14
Brothel 1659:14
Brothel-house: door of a b. 1366: 4
Brother 141
banish'd b. 142: 4
bare-foot b. 142: 9
better a b. dies 142: 8
blasting his wholesome b. . . 741: 1
blindly shed the b.'s blood . 417: 5
bloody b. 141:15
by the mother's side 142: 5
by the surer side 143: 5
called me b. 144: 6
commend me to my b. . . . 1459: 4
dear b. 143: 3
elder b. 141:13
eldest b. 141:13
embrace thy b. there 142: 1
find out thy b. 141:16
firebrand b., Paris, burns
us all 1570:19
for in that name doth na-
ture plead 143: 3
gentle b. 143: 3
good b. 143: 3

Brother, *continued*
he is your b. 143: 5
he must be my b. 286:15
here lies your b. 143: 2
how fares my b. 142: 6
hurt my b. 5: 7
I am a second b. 142:14
I have a b. 142: 7
I my b. know 143: 6
I never had a b. 142: 4
I should call you b. 507: 7
if my b. had my shape . . . 1349: 8
like a b. toil'd 533: 1
like b. and b. 143: 9
look upon my b. 1474: 1
love him as my b. 1653: 9
loved thee as a b. 905:10
my b. had but justice 795:15
my b. he is in Elysium 700: 6
my b. is amorous 897: 8
my b. slew no man 1517: 4
ne'er a b. like you 142:10
new sworn b. 210: 3
noble b. 143: 3
of gracious order 142: 9
of my blood 143: 6
own b. 143: 3
poor b. 142:7; 143: 6
poor unworthy b. 746:11
puff'd his own b. 157: 3
rather my b. die by the law 142: 8
redeem your b. 142: 8
reft of his b. 142: 4
should a b. dare 167: 3
should be perfidious 143: 2
stood out against your b. . . 142:10
sweet b. 143: 3
sworn b. to a leash of
drawers 1051: 6
sworn b. to grim Neces-
sity 1058: 2
unworthy b. 1587:11
valiant b. 143: 5
weigh our b. with ourself . 142: 8
will you kill your b. 143: 5
worthy b. 143: 3
wrong a b. 1750:19
yielding up thy b. 142: 8
you call'd me b. 142: 1
your b. cannot live 142: 7
your b. is but young 141:14
your b. is legitimate 142: 5
your b. kindly greets you . . 642:16
Brother-in-law 143:7
Brother-like: this is b. 142: 2
Brother-love 143: 4
Brotherhood 143; 144:4
Brotherly 142:3
Brothers: all the b. too 291: 2
are we not b. 144: 1
blind b. and sisters 370:15
call their b. fools 1425:16
forty thousand b. 142: 2
redeem my b. 143: 4
sworn b. in filching 1509:14
to make you b. 33:13
twinn'd b. of one womb . . . 142:11
younger b. 141:14
Broths: sauced our b. 236: 8
Brought low 475: 4
Brow 144
angry b. 145: 4
bare b. of a bachelor 962:15
beauty's b. 1533: 8
bent his b. 1388: 1
black b. of night 1619: 2
chaste unsmirched b. 144: 7
dangerous b. 230: 5
frowning b. to b. 1194:15
gentle b. of true sincerity . 755:14
he knits his b. 38: 9
his bloody b. 107: 5
let the b. o'erwhelm it . . . 145: 6
lift up thy b. 247:11
living b. 183:13
my love's fair b. 1744:14
not a confident b. 1722:16
o' the sea 1313: 4
of bragging horror 121:13
of Egypt 144:14
of much distraction 365:12
of progeny 186: 7
of woe 1694:12
of youth 1744:11
prepare thy b. to frown . . . 145: 5

Cleanliest shift is to kiss ..810:14
Cleanly: live c. as a noble .1254:14
not neat, but c. 1057: 7
Cleansing them from tears 1536: 4
Clear as day 440: 6
as morning roses 1712: 1
from treason 766:14
got c. 482: 7
in his great office 1608: 1
Clear-shining sky 1466: 6
Clearest gods 622: 1
Clearstores toward the south 732: 9
Cleave the general ear 10: 9
Clef: one c., two notes 1074:11
Cleitus 30: 5
Clemency: stooping to your
c. 1554:10
Clement: more c. than vile
men 309: 7
Clement's Inn 250:14
Cleopatra a gypsy 213: 6
from Antony win C. 1212: 3
salt C. 1624: 3
she was C. 1050:10
Clepe us drunkards 1275: 8
Clepeth a calf, cauf 1725: 5
Clept all by the name 941: 7
Clergyman 1191:1
Clerk: unletter'd c. 1517:11
will ne'er wear hair 1289: 7
Clerk-like experienced 608: 4
Clerkly 1745:12
Clerks in Christian king-
doms 1613: 2
great c. have purposed ..1655: 2
learned c. 612: 5
Saint Nicholas' c. 668: 4
Clew: wound a goodly c. ..1168:13
Client breaks, as desperate 696:12
woes 1694:12
Clients: lack no c. 243:11
Cliff: take her c. 1661: 5
whose high and bending
head 707: 8
Clifford: black-faced C. 1066: 8
unrelenting C. 1379: 7
Cliffs: chalky c. 707: 9
Climate: Christian c. 318: 9
in a fertile c. dwell 556: 5
is delicate 29: 8
that they point upon 1099: 8
their c. foggy 417: 1
this c. overlooks 1084:12
whilst you do c. here 760: 1
Climatures and country men 1098:14
Climber-upward 33: 6
Clime: fresher c. 1148:13
native c. 1676:17
pines the c. 1073: 1
Clink and fall of swords ..1481:13
Clinking of pewter 383: 6
Clinquant: all c. 582:12
Clip: let me c. ye 1077:10
Clip-winged griffin 1706:12
Clipper: be a c. 582: 7
Clippeth thee about 416: 2
Clipping her 291: 5
Cloak 195
get on your c. 481: 2
I have night's c. to hide ..1065: 6
not alone my inky c. 1330: 3
of night being pluck'd 1037:10
old c. makes a new jerkin ..87: 5
pull'd me by the c. 1418:16
scarlet c. 382:14
take thine auld c. about
thee 1198: 7
travel without my c. 197: 3
Cloak-bag of guts 174: 5
Cloaks: wise men put on c. 197: 3
Clock 196
by the c., 'tis day 296:11
German c. 1702: 3
hath strucken twelve 196: 6
no c. in the forest 196: 5
now c. strikes one 726: 9
numbering c. 1536: 4
tell the c. 1460:12; 1467: 3
unhappy was the c. 196: 7
upbraids me 196:10
watch the c. 196: 9
Clock-setter: old Time the c. 1527: 4
Clocks do toll 199: 5
ploughmen's c. 1436: 6
wishing c. more swift 237: 3
Clod: kneaded c. 304: 9
Cloddy: meagre c. earth ..1466: 9
Clodpole: from a c. 855: 1
Clog: enfranchised with a c. 1205: 1
here comes my c. 1664: 4
of conscience 637: 7
the foot of a flea 108: 2
with his c. at his heels ..1664: 4
Clogging burthen 1413: 9
Clogs: hang c. on them 188: 3
me with this answer 42: 6
Cloister: in shady c. mew'd 1077: 9
Cloistered flight 552: 4
Cloistress: like a c. 1500: 8
Close: keep it c. 1327:14
she 'll c. and be herself ..1390: 7
still c. as sure 19: 6
Close-stool: fortune's c. ..1112:15
on a c. 878:13
Close-tongued treason 1068: 3
Closeness: dedicated to c. ..1454: 5
Closest kept 543:18
Closet: I 'll to thy c. 1448: 3
in thy c. pent up 1346: 3
Closet-war: mappery, c. 999:14
Closing of some glorious day 1397:12
of the lips 880: 9
Closure 135:12
guilty c. of thy walls 1205: 5
Cloten, be thy name 1051: 5
Cloth: by a painted c. 1219: 1
in the painted c. 1381: 4
patch'd with c. of any
colour 1256:15
squire's c. 1380:10
Cloth-of-gold 44:6; 631:4
Clotharius 1073:11
Clothed in steel 54: 6
Clothes 379:4
are after such a pagan cut 382: 9
dress'd! and in your c. 379:10
drown my c. 387: 4
excellent good c. 1227: 7
familiarity with fresher c. 499:17
foul c. 1326: 6
see you these c. 608: 5
stinking c. 300: 7
take up your wife's c. 380: 5
these c. are good enough ..381: 6
through tatter'd c. small
vices do appear 795:10
what honest c. 380: 5
which make thee 1485:19
Clothier means to dress 209: 5
Clothiers all 1494: 2
Clothing me 1016:11
Clotpoles: like c. 666:15
Clotpoll: call the c. back ..565: 8
Cloud 196
an 'twere a c. in autumn 1389: 2
dissolve, thick c. 1649:11
every c. engenders not a
storm 197: 1
hath brightest day a c. 214: 3
he has a c. in 's face 978: 7
my c. of dignity 342: 9
of sorrow 895: 1
of winter showers 1185:11
summer's c. 1707: 3
takes all away 896: 2
threatening c. 196:13
yond same black c. 197: 4
Cloud-capped towers 1609:15
Cloud-eclipsed so 447:13
Cloud-kissing Ilion 1570:19
Cloudiness: storm and c. 459: 5
Clouds: above the c. 196:12
adding to c. more c. 1362:14
and eclipses stain 753:13
base contagious c. 1466: 2
blessed are c. 460:10
break the c. 759: 5
coal-black c. 197: 1
curl'd c. 534: 4
cutting c. toward Paphos .1596: 7
dews and dangers come ..292:11
distracted c. give way 1646:11
dying c. contend 291: 7
envious c. 1467: 2
filthy and contagious c. ..1601: 7
foreign c. 1362:13
fret the c. 585: 6
give way, dull c. 276: 1
invulnerable c. of heaven ..157: 1
keeps himself in c. 1706:10
Clouds, *continued*
kiss'd the c. 194:12
knit poisonous c. above his
golden head 1467: 1
let base c. o'ertake 197: 3
looks in the c. 33: 6
many c. consulting 197: 3
methought would open 377:12
racking c. 1466: 6
slippery c. 1446: 6
southern c. 1496:11
still hang on you 978: 6
weeping c. 1006: 6
when c. appear, wise men
put on their cloaks 197: 3
when c. in autumn crack 1710: 6
Clout: hit the c. 483:22
upon his head 382: 6
Clouted shoon 1356: 5
Cloven: how it came c. 343: 6
Clover: green c. 553:12
Cloves: stuck with c. 612: 7
Clown 197
bore it 563: 6
burly-boned c. 1444: 3
simple c. 1368: 6
sweet c. 563: 6
you c., abandon 1697:16
Clownish fool 561: 5
Clowns: play your c. 10:10
Cloy the edge of appetite ..1514: 6
Cloyed with fat meat 1746: 4
with long continuance 1201: 7
Cloyless sauce 47: 1
Cloyment and revolt 1703:12
Club: cleft his c. 706:13
grasp'd the heaviest c. ...1330:14
Hercules' c. 271: 7
whose c. kill'd Cerberus ..370: 4
Clubs, bills and partisans ..1478:13
cannot part them 912: 2
cried out 'C.' 484: 1
Clucked thee to the wars ..1026:15
Clyster-pipes 540:11
Co-equal with the crown ..1199:10
Co-heirs: they are c. 702:18
Co-join with something 1075:15
Co-mates and brothers 217: 5
Co-partners in my claim 210: 3
Co-rivall'd greatness 1353:12
Coach after c. 1710: 7
glistering c. 1469:12
Coachmakers: fairies' c. 463: 4
Coactive art 1075:15
Coagulate gore 112: 3
Coal 197
burn us all into one c. 197: 8
dead c. of wars 1628: 5
dying c. 198: 1
like a c. of fire 1073: 9
quench the c. 197:13
Coal-black as jet 201: 9
is better 103: 3
Coals: add c. to Cancer 197:15
carry c. 1509:14
dead c. 197:12
dying c. burnt out 453: 6
hot c. of vengeance 1627:11
kindling c. that fires 696: 7
make c. cheap 197: 9
of glowing fire 197:11
that fires all my breast 197:11
we 'll not carry c. 197:14
Coarse metal 422:13
Coarsely: reports but c. 831: 2
Coast 198
cast upon your c. 1324:10
from c. to c. is tost 1637:17
it is your native c. 415: 6
see the c. clear'd 327: 9
Coasteth to the cry 725:10
Coasts and hedges 1567: 8
rebelling c. 1524: 7
Coat 198
golden c. 442: 6
green velvet c. 133: 3
herald's c. without sleeves 1355: 9
his c. is of proof 524: 4
horseman's c. 198:16
leathern c. 39: 9
long motley c. 1162: 5
motley c. 562: 1
my c. is better 198:11
spoil his c. with scanting ..198: 7
waxen c. 1638: 8

Coats: gay new c. 198: 9
glittering in golden c., like images 198: 6
gold c. 553:12
I would not be in some of your c. for two pence ..198:15
in heraldry 198: 9
lined their c. 140: 3
of steel 1032: 1
silken c. and caps 1276: 5
Cobble you 1356: 9
Cobbled shoes 1307: 2
Cobbler: am but a c. 1553:12
thou art a c., art thou 1356: 9
Cobloaf 1377:15
Cobweb: good Master C. ..1053: 3
Cock 199
and capon too 199: 2
by c. 920: 3
by c. and pie 1084:11
crow like a c. 199: 8
diminish'd to her c. 364:14
early village c. 199: 5
first c. 199: 6
is mine 1555:15
morning c. crew loud 199: 3
ousel c. so black 98: 4
Pistol's c. is up 199: 4
retired to a wasteful c. ..1276: 6
second c. hath crow'd 199: 6
since the first c. 549:12
that is the trumpet 199: 3
that treads them 1702: 7
Cock-a-diddle-dow 199: 8
Cock-a-hoop: set c. 476:13
Cock-pigeon: Barbary c. 780: 9
Cock-shut time 1531:19
Cock-sure 476:13
Cockatrice 454:13
Cockatrices: kill by the look, like c. 167:11
Cockered silken wanton 132: 2
Cockerel 199: 8
Cockerel's: young c. stone .1741:14
Cockle of rebellion 1250: 4
or a walnut-shell 1274: 7
sow'd c. reap'd no corn ..1274: 7
Cockled snails 894:14
Cockles: sail seas in c. 1274: 7
Cockney: as the c. did 402: 8
prove a c. 1731: 8
Cockpit: can this c. hold ..199: 9
Cocks: country c. do crow ..199: 5
drown'd the c. 1238: 4
his c. do win the battle 199: 1
Codding spirit 1432:14
Codling almost an apple 1759: 2
Codpiece 199
as massy as his club 504:11
geld a c. of a purse 1225: 4
Cods: took two c. 1709: 7
Cœur-de-lion: by C. knighted 822: 5
was thy father 1329:14
Coffer: empty c. 612:15
of her friends 375: 5
rich jewel'd c. of Darius ..981: 6
there 's half my c. 366:11
Coffer-lids that close eyes ..453: 9
Coffers: ivory c. 1178:13
my c. ransacked 1748:14
shall our c. be emptied ..1560:11
Coffers-up his gold 255: 4
Coffin: black c. 555: 1
of paste a c. I will rear ..1522: 1
Coffined: come c. home 841: 1
Coffins: rotten c. 677: 5
Cog 182:5
I cannot c. 155: 8
their hearts 310: 7
Cogging companion 642: 4
slave 642: 4
Cogitation resides not 1515: 8
worthy c. 1515: 8
Cognition: have c. 1128:13
Cognizance of incontinency 926: 5
relics and c. 1299: 4
Cogscomb: knave's c. 1521: 6
Cohere and jump 193:16
Cohered with place 1536: 8
Coherence: semblable c. ..1484: 7
Coherent: prove c. 1536: 8
Cohorts: dissipation of c. ..1099:11
Coign o' the Capitol 1445: 8
of vantage 98: 1
Coigns: four opposing c. ..1733: 6
Coil: great c. to-night 1647: 6
not worth this c. 1739: 6
reason for this c. 1249:12
shuffled off this mortal c. ..304: 6
this c. would not infect ..1249:12
with protestation 1218:18
Coin: far as my c. would stretch 260:11
false c. 373:15
his c. may be a coward's ..999:15
in thy father's exchequer 1618:14
king's c. 805: 4
let out their c. 557:12
molten c. 593:14
stamped c. 860: 6
that bears the figure 37: 6
Coinage: answer the c. 1016: 8
very c. of your brain 750: 8
Coiner with his tools 69:11
Coistrel: every c. that 372:12
Col: appelez-vous le c. 1058:12
Colbrand the giant 1314:10
Cold and numb 200:10
and sickly 199:13
as a snowball 199:13
as any stone 200:11
as c. as can be 199:13
as is a dead man's nose ..1335: 5
biting c. would never let grass grow 275: 4
blood 112: 6
catch c. and curse 352: 9
catch c. on 's feet 200: 2
comfort me with c. 203: 9
death's eternal c. 732: 4
endure the winter's c. 213: 4
found her wondrous c. 199:13
freezing c. 3:9; 328:16
hot and c. 697: 5
I am c. myself 200: 6
I have caught extreme c. ..352: 9
in blood 112: 6
in great affairs 200: 5
in zeal 1759:11
indifferent c. 200: 3
it is very c. 29: 7
like thy chastity 180: 6
nipping c. 200: 3
of an earthly c. 200:10
shivering c. and sickness .1073: 1
straight is c. again 38:14
take c. 495:13
thou 'lt catch c. shortly ..1388: 8
'tis bitter c. 691:10
'tis very c. 697: 3
too c. for hell 200: 7
too c. in thinking of it 752:12
whoreson c. 352: 7
winter's c. 200: 4
wrapp'd in repentant c. ...927: 3
wrathful nipping c. 214: 3
you are c. and stern 199:13
Cold-blooded slave 1380:10
Cold-hearted toward me 200: 1
Cold-moving nods 1367:12
Cold-pale weakness 1643:11
Coldest: most c. 894: 2
Coldly 200:12
plead so c. 929: 6
Coldness 200:8
and delay 323: 6
Colevile kissing my foot 64:14
Coleville of the dale 1051:10
Colic of puff'd Aquilon 1572:13
pinched with c. ...353:11; 841:10
with a kind of c. pinch'd ..398:10
Collateral 792:8; 916:15
Collatine: wail'd by C. 1032: 8
Colleagued with the dream ...15: 3
Collied judgement, night ...895: 5
Collier 197:14
Colliers counted bright 102:11
Collop: my c. 896:11
of my flesh 287:10
Collusion holds in exchange 1022: 6
Coloquintida: bitter as c. ...560: 9
Colossus: like a C. 640: 1
nothing but a c. 593: 2
Colossus-wise: stands c. 118:13
Colour 200
against all c. here 1754:12
change thy c. 1507: 8
changed c. 1696:10
dissembling c. 364: 7
cast thy nighted c. off 444: 3
Colour, *continued*
do you change c. 171:10
excellent c. 656:14
for his death 299: 3
for my visitation 200:13
for your going 1119: 5
give c. to my cheek 107: 8
hath forsook his cheeks 888: 3
having c. enough 216: 4
her lively c. kill'd 201:15
holds not c. with the time ..90: 1
in thy face 215: 8
just of his c. 201:13
lose some c. 789: 6
of c. like red rose 201: 6
of her hair 656:13
of his beard 312: 8
of that c. 476: 3
of the king 756:11
of the nutmeg 722: 2
put c. in thy cheek 183: 1
sanguine c. of the leaves ..183: 5
scorn'd a fair c. 232: 7
self-same c. 476: 3
show no c. 200:13
steals the c. 201:14
that may please the eye 1250: 7
'tis a c. she abhors 505: 7
turned his c. 10: 9
'twas indeed his c. 201:13
under the c. of commending 200:13
under the c. of his usual game 600: 8
what c. is this cloak 201: 9
what I have to do will want true c. 200:13
Colourable colours 201:12
Coloured: well c. 201: 3
Colours: add c. to chameleon 269:11
advance our waving c. 547: 3
advance the c. of my love 1710: 8
cheerful c. 547: 5
fatal c. of our houses 1302:10
fear no c. 201:7; 525: 4
hopeful c. 547: 5
I love no c. 201: 7
idly spread 547: 6
in his true c. 201: 5
know us by these c. 547: 3
let our bloody c. wave 547: 5
native c. 1575: 9
of the rainbow 77:10; 381:10
of their trade 1038:13
our c. do return 547: 6
part your mingled c. 1451: 8
prosper our c. 1218: 8
should be wash'd away 215:10
tattering c. 1600: 5
their c., often borne 547: 4
threatening c. 1630: 7
unacquainted c. 547: 6
under whose c. he had fought so long 823: 5
with c. spread 1600: 2
Colt 723:9
me thus 1567: 7
there 's a c. indeed 1201:10
Colted by him 920: 3
Colts: unbacked c. 1041: 7
unhandled c. 1039:12
young hot c. 1758: 6
Columbine: that c. 554: 3
Columbines 553:10
Comb: crow with your c. on 199: 2
leave her c. 86: 8
Combat 201
beauteous c. 202: 7
dared to the c. 201:16
grant me the c. 202: 1
long was c. doubtful 202: 6
noble c. 791: 1
personal c. 201:16
single c. 202: 1
sportful c. 202: 7
what a noble c. 202: 4
Combatant: great c. 1572:13
Combatants 202:3
Combed: sleekly c. 681:16
Combinate husband 741: 9
Combination and a form 44:13
solemn c. 962: 4
Combined by a sacred vow ...2:13
Combless cock 199: 7
Combustion: dire c. 1100: 1
Combustious matter 900: 4

Conceit ... 218
and grief a combat fight ... 219: 3
bottomless c. ... 1370: 7
deceitful ... 219: 3
dull c. ... 218:15
earthy-gross c. ... 218:13
fair c. ... 218:16
forged quaint c. ... 218:17
his c. is false ... 219: 2
horrible c. of death ... 1507: 9
how c. may rob treasury ... 218:19
in weakest bodies ... 218:14
is deeper than you think ... 219: 6
keen c. ... 1688:11
more rich in matter ... 219: 5
no more c. in him ... 218:15
noble and a true c. ... 34: 3
of good c. ... 218:12
of very liberal c. ... 218:18
press'd down with c. ... 218:13
profound c. ... 219: 1
ravish any dull c. ... 1142: 9
rich c. taught me ... 219: 7
some c. or other ... 184: 8
some good c. of thine ... 393: 6
some horrible c. ... 1516: 8
thy c. is nearer death ... 218:12
'tis nothing but c. ... 219: 4
vain c. ... 808: 2
want c. ... 1623: 9
Conceited: right well c. ... 1736: 8
Conceitless: so c. ... 549: 1
Conceits are poisons ... 219: 2
their c. have wings ... 218:20
Conceive ... 1585:4
I cannot c. you ... 1401:12
plainly c., I love you ... 907: 6
she will c., I hope ... 1192: 2
thus I c. by him ... 1192: 2
Conception ... 219
choke the strong c. ... 223: 3
Conceptions proper to myself 219:10
Conceptious womb ... 1705:14
Concernings: dear c. hide ... 1230:10
time and our c. ... 853:11
Conclave: holy c. ... 192:11
Conclude, c. ... 900: 8
and be agreed ... 572: 8
to c. ... 219:17
Concluded ... 219:16
Concludes: his fault c. but what the law should end 515: 6
Conclusion ... 219
bald c. ... 657: 7
Christian-like c. ... 1189:12
foregone c. ... 477: 6
lame and impotent c. ... 220: 1
merciless c. ... 1028: 8
read the c. ... 220: 3
shall be crowned ... 219:19
this is my c. ... 219:19
vile c. I begin to utter ... 219:18
Conclusions: preposterous c. 64:12
to be as kisses ... 592: 2
try c. ... 219:15
Concord: gentle c. ... 677:10
jarring c. ... 347:11
mar the c. ... 347:15
of my state ... 1040:12
of sweet sounds ... 1039:12
of this discord ... 347:11
of well-tuned sounds ... 1041: 2
wiry c. ... 881: 6
Concubine: be your c. ... 1231: 6
Concupiscible lust ... 926:10
Concupy: tickle it for his c. 1525: 8
Concurring both in name ... 1134: 4
Condemn them to her service 912: 1
Condemnation ... 220
is pronounced ... 95:14
or approof ... 1034: 3
Condemned by course of law 220: 8
by the king's own mouth ... 220:14
generally c. ... 220:10
stand c. ... 220:10
to burn ... 220: 4
Condemning some to death ... 220: 5
Condescend ... 705:5
Condign praise ... 1184: 8
punishment ... 1221:11
Condition ... 220
alter the c. of a man ... 220:16
assured of my c. ... 58: 9
demand of him my c. ... 220:15
forget c. of my estate ... 220:15

Condition, *continued*
full of most blessed c. ... 220:18
gentle c. ... 221: 1
hard c. ... 220:16; 807: 5
hot c. of their blood ... 1039:12
in my c. a prince ... 221: 4
light c. in a beauty dark ... 220:18
mark his c. ... 221: 2
my c. is not smooth ... 1544:12
of a saint ... 960: 5
of so quick c. ... 674:12
of the time ... 1536:12
of the worst degree ... 221: 2
of these times ... 1459:14
of what c. are you ... 1051:10
on good c.; on like c. ... 221: 5
shall our c. stand ... 221: 7
they account gentle ... 1140: 5
unhoused free c. ... 962: 8
upon c. ... 221: 5
Conditionally ... 264: 2
Conditions: gentle thy c. ... 221: 8
I embrace these c. ... 221: 6
make c. ... 221: 8
no c. of our peace ... 1134: 4
of a friendly peace ... 1134:12
slight c. ... 221: 8
soft c. ... 1702: 9
we shall stand upon ... 221: 6
with fair c. ... 221: 7
Condole: I will c. ... 11: 1
Condolement: obstinate c. ... 1453: 8
Condolements: certain c. ... 1453: 8
Conduce ... 1249:14
Conduct: give courteous c. 253:11
impartial c. of my soul ... 713: 8
Conductor of his people ... 846:10
Conduit: as from a c. ... 893:13
how now! a c. ... 1498: 7
weather-bitten c. ... 1351: 7
with three issuing spouts ... 115:12
Conduits: ivory c. ... 1650:19
of my blood ... 22: 4
Confection: that c. ... 801:12
Confectionary: had the world as my c. ... 1306: 7
Confections: for my c. ... 801:12
Confederacy ... 1169:1
Confer with me of murder 1038: 8
Conference ... 221
break off your c. ... 221:13
forbear your c. ... 221:18
free and friendly c. ... 253: 5
gentle c., soft and affable ... 178: 3
harsh ... 150: 1
have private c. ... 221:17
have some c. ... 221:16
hear our c. ... 1328: 7
hold three words' c. ... 1340:21
I will overhear their c. ... 221:14
in sad c. ... 221:15
love's c. ... 899: 7
not willing longer c. ... 221:12
she urged c. ... 221:10
was sadly borne ... 221:15
Confess and live ... 222:12
here on my knee ... 222: 4
I am in love ... 906: 8
I c. nothing ... 223: 1
I c. that I am old ... 23: 8
I must needs c. ... 982:14
most freely I c. ... 336: 5
not that you know ... 1365: 8
the wilful abuse ... 4: 6
thee freely ... 223: 3
who set thee up ... 1130:10
you 'll not c. ... 223: 1
yourself freely ... 223: 3
yourself to heaven ... 222: 4
Confessed: hath c. ... 222: 5
it is not redressed ... 222:13
Confession ... 222
fell to a large c. ... 223: 7
finds but riddling shift ... 1284:15
his c. is taken ... 222: 5
holy c. ... 223: 4
in your looks ... 222: 3
make c. and be absolved ... 223: 4
she did intend c. ... 223: 4
strange c. in thine eye ... 222: 3
Confessions: his c. justify 222:10
Confessor ... 223:5
to one or two ... 1139: 5
Confidence ... 223
with all c. he swears ... 14:14

Confident ... 223:8
all too c. ... 55: 3
be c. to speak ... 1422: 1
from foreign purposes ... 416: 2
Confidently undertake ... 223: 9
Confine: hies to his c. ... 1432:15
of blood and breath ... 1260: 4
Confineless harms ... 175: 4
Confines: neighbour c. ... 1305: 6
quiet c. ... 1136: 9
wards and dungeons ... 1204: 1
Confining shores ... 1357:11
Confirmation ... 1214:1
Confirmations: jealous c. ... 1214: 1
strong ... 1568:11
Confirmer of false reckonings ... 1079: 6
Confirmers of thy words ... 1716:10
Confiscation: by c. ... 741: 9
Confixed here ... 1576:12
Conflict of her hue ... 115: 6
such as was supposed ... 921: 3
though c. be sore ... 923: 9
Confluence: see this c. ... 1142: 3
Conflux of meeting sap ... 825: 5
Conformable: to your will c. 1667:12
Confound: myself myself c. 1331: 3
them by some course ... 250: 6
you ... 477: 7
Confounded in the dark she lay ... 32: 4
Confusion ... 223
come to great c. ... 1216: 4
heaping c. on their heads 1662:13
how soon c. may enter ... 60: 7
I bar c. ... 223:13
let c. live ... 172: 5
make large c. ... 224: 5
musical c. ... 725: 7
of their cries ... 224: 3
swallow'd in c. ... 224: 3
there begins c. ... 422:12
thick ... 1272:10
vast c. waits ... 224: 1
work c. on his enemies ... 1279: 3
Confusions: try c. with him 311: 5
Confutation: in c. ... 1264:13
Confutes: nothing c. me ... 440: 1
Congeal: cool and c. ... 1759:11
Congealed your blood ... 112: 8
Congealment: wash the c. 1739:14
Conger: eats c. and fennel ... 174: 5
muddy c. ... 667:12
Congied with the duke ... 327: 2
Congratulate the princes ... 1686: 9
Congreeing in a full close ... 630: 1
Congreeted: you have c. ... 1096:16
Congregate: where merchants most do c. ... 983: 7
Congregation of vapours ... 1374:17
Congruent epitheton ... 21: 9
Congruing to that effect ... 853: 3
Conies: like c. after rain ... 590: 9
Conjectural fears ... 467:13
marriages ... 1307: 2
Conjecture ... 750:9
Conjoin together ... 961: 5
Conjoins with my disease ... 351: 9
Conjunct and bosom'd with her ... 920: 7
and flattering ... 362: 6
Conjunction ... 30:11
this year in c. ... 31: 5
trace the c. ... 789: 3
Conjunctive in our revenge 1278:11
to my life ... 905: 8
Conjuration: earnest c. ... 224:10
mock not my senseless c. ... 1012:14
what c. ... 1487: 2
Conjurations: buz these c. ... 629: 7
I do defy thy c. ... 224:10
Conjure ... 224:6
I 'll learn to c. ... 225: 1
nay, I 'll c. too ... 224:10
thee but slowly ... 1429: 5
Conjured me beyond them ... 224:11
to attend ... 129:15
Conjurer ... 224:7
Conjurers and sorcerers ... 933: 1
dealing with c. ... 1693: 1
Conjures: she c. ... 224: 8
Conjuring ... 224
Conned them out of rings 1289: 1
Connive at us ... 622:12
Conqueror ... 225

Content, *continued*
to spend the time ... 233:13
well c. ... 234: 2
with any choice ... 190: 7
Contented: none c. ... 11: 3
to be what they are ... 958: 4
with what I most enjoy c. least ... 347: 7
Contention ... 235
and occasion meet ... 879: 8
no quarrel, but a slight c. .1228:14
of the sea and skies ... 532: 8
Contentious storm ... 1446:13
Contentless: best state, c. .. 347: 9
Contents: calm c. ... 699:10
o' the story ... 776: 4
Continence and nobility ... 358: 3
Continency: unpeople with c. 181:11
Continent and summary .. 1465: 2
as c., as chaste ... 181:11
my c. of beauty ... 81: 5
orbed c. ... 1082: 9
stronger than thy c. ... 1452: 2
to hide the slain ... 305:11
Continents: concealing c. .. 653:14
Continually ... 870:12
Continuate goodness ... 627: 6
time ... 1531:16
Continuer: so good a c. ... 1546: 4
Continuing: extremity c. .. 1647: 4
Contract: dispense with c. .. 96:14
mark our c. ... 368: 2
of eternal bond of love ... 97: 1
of her marriage ... 1534: 8
of true love ... 958: 5
true c. ... 97: 1
us 'fore these witnesses ... 97: 1
vow'd c. ... 97: 1
you pretend ... 97: 1
Contracted: long since c. ... 97: 1
to a maid ... 97: 1
to them both ... 963: 7
to this woman ... 97: 1
Contracting: old c. ... 355: 8
Contraction: body of c. ... 317: 7
Contradict thyself ... 235:10
Contradicted your desire .. 331: 6
Contradiction ... 235
without c. ... 1226: 7
Contraries: by c. execute .. 209: 7
confounding c. ... 172: 5
such unity do hold ... 235: 9
Contrarieties agree ... 1284:15
Contrarious quests ... 640: 5
winds ... 1676:16
Contrariously: work c. ... 235: 9
Contrary: hear to the c. ... 483:11
prove the c. ... 1418:11
speaks the mere c. ... 1419: 4
you must c. me ... 1265:12
Contribution: trembling c. 1494: 2
Contributors: be c. ... 1711:12
Contrite sighs, tears ... 1362:12
Contriver ... 269:12
close c. of all harms ... 179: 3
secret and villanous c. ... 173:12
Contriving of lust ... 926: 8
Controller ... 1437:5
Controlment for c. ... 1628: 3
without c. ... 1230: 3
Controversy: despite of all c. 633: 8
dismiss the c. bleeding ... 841:10
here is the strangest c. ... 235: 7
tarre them to c. ... 370: 1
Contumelious spirit ... 1431: 1
taunts ... 420:12
Contumeliously break peace 1134: 9
Contumely: proud man's c. 1461: 1
Contusions: aged c. ... 1090: 4
Convenience: good c. ... 712: 8
of time and means ... 1102: 6
Conveniency: plain c. ... 793: 9
Convented upon a treaty ... 31: 1
Conversation ... 235
cold, and still c. ... 1669: 3
coped withal ... 172:11
of my thoughts ... 1513:11
Converse with him that is wise 90: 7
Conversed together ... 217:11
Conversing with him ... 236: 1
Conversion so sweetly tastes 1254:12
Converted: be c. ... 1254:12
become c. ... 908: 4
from the world ... 1254:12
how you may be c. ... 441:12

Converted, *continued*
may I be so c. ... 441:12
Convertite ... 1254:13
Convey the wise it call ... 1151: 4
Conveyance: madest quick c. 1038: 4
thy sly c. ... 311: 1
Conveyances of his lands .. 762:14
of our blood ... 344: 1
Conveyed: safe c. ... 1311:15
Conveyers are you all ... 844: 4
Convict by course of law .. 1520: 1
Convicted sail ... 1503:13
Convocation ... 1470:5
of politic worms ... 1734: 6
spiritual c. ... 1734: 6
Convoy and our bark ... 719:15
be my c. ... 830:11
is assistant ... 853: 3
Convulsions: dry c. ... 1222: 8
Cony: so doth the c. struggle 320: 4
Cony-catch: I must c. ... 1351:13
Cony-catched in business ... 182: 8
Cony-catching: full of c. .. 784: 3
rascals ... 1241:11
Cook: play the c. ... 1164: 1
rascal c. ... 236: 9
'tis an ill c. that cannot lick his own fingers ... 236:11
to honest creatures ... 377: 8
were of my mind ... 236:10
Cooked: you are well c. ... 665: 7
Cookery ... 236
Cooks: cunning c. ... 236:11
Epicurean c. ... 47: 1
Cool: have things c. ... 314:10
let it c. the while ... 1220: 9
Cooled glowing hot ... 697: 6
Cooling: stay the c. ... 1128:12
the air with sighs ... 1362:15
Cooped here for defence ... 321: 1
Coops from other lands ... 416: 2
Copatain hat ... 382:14
Cope: I 'll c. with thee ... 1587: 9
under the c. ... 181: 5
Copesmate of ugly Night .. 1533: 5
Cophetua: King C. ... 64:16
King C. loved ... 272: 4
let King C. know the truth 1061:13
Copies: takes virtuous c. .. 891: 6
Copious: be c. in exclaims .. 432: 7
stories ... 1448: 5
Copped hills ... 1103:13
Copper ... 991:11
Copulation: let c. thrive ... 919:11
of cattle ... 71: 8
Copulatives: country c. ... 919:11
Copy ... 873:12
and book, that fashion'd others ... 430:11
be c. now to men ... 430:11
leave the world no c. ... 1606: 9
not let that c. die ... 188: 5
of my child ... 873: 7
of the sonnet ... 1406: 6
of your speed ... 1429: 5
to these younger times ... 430:11
what in you is writ ... 1745: 9
Copy-book: text B in a c. ... 82:11
Coquetry ... 236
Coragio: bravely, c. ... 551: 3
Coral ... 881:7
Coram ... 797: 3
Coranto: come home in a c. 192:10
lead her a c. ... 1: 7
Corantos: swift c. ... 282:12
Cord ... 1302:4
give me c., or knife ... 1259:14
want'st a c. ... 666: 5
Corded ladder ... 830:12
Cordial and not poison ... 1175: 2
of mine age ... 1299: 6
pleasing c. ... 1615: 3
that ye bring ... 203: 7
Cords: gnaw'd in two my c. 124: 1
holy c. ... 1302: 4
if there be c., or knives .. 1222: 5
made of c. ... 1302: 4
take up those c. ... 1302: 4
Core: in my heart's c. ... 945:11
most putrefied c. ... 46: 7
thou c. of envy ... 422:20
Corinthian, lad of mettle ... 176: 4
Coriolanus: Caius Marcius C. 13: 6
he would not answer to .. 1045: 7
renowned C. ... 1045: 7

Cork: take the c. out of thy mouth ... 1419:10
thrust a c. into a hogshead 1355: 6
Corky arms ... 52: 8
Cormorant ... 1530:17
insatiate c. ... 1593: 9
war ... 1629: 8
Corn ... 237
at our own price ... 237: 4
autumn's c. ... 557: 6
bladed c. be lodged ... 398:12
come to sell their c. ... 958: 2
deserve c. gratis ... 1340: 2
he weeds the c. ... 1648:13
like to the summer's c. ... 74: 1
lodge the summer c. ... 1498: 3
not c. for rich men only .. 1219: 3
o'ergrown with weeds ... 927: 3
of a c. cry woe ... 237: 7
our c. is to reap ... 673: 6
over-ripen'd c. ... 682: 7
shall seem as light as chaff 1677: 2
stored with c. ... 1354: 1
sustaining c. ... 1648: 9
want ye c. for bread ... 237: 5
Corn-field: green c. ... 237: 5
Cornelia never read ... 1245:11
Corner ... 237
at every c. have them kiss 811: 8
deserves a c. ... 329:11
sits the wind in that c. .. 1676:13
utmost c. of the west ... 416: 2
Corner-cap of society ... 238: 1
Corner-stone: yond c. ... 1445: 8
Corners: all c. else o' the earth ... 1205: 8
belie all c. of the world ... 1375: 9
four c. of the earth ... 332: 1
skulking in c. ... 1328:18
three c. of the world ... 416: 8
Corns: she hath c. ... 237: 7
unplagued with c. ... 1539: 4
Cornuto: peaking C. ... 742: 1
Corollary: bring a c. ... 1432:12
Coronation ... 263:9
determine of the c. ... 164:14
Coronation-day ... 352: 7
Coronet ... 263:8
of fragrant flowers ... 1504:10
of gold ... 1118:12
Corporal ... 1395
what seem'd c. melted ... 610: 1
Corpse ... 118:13
See also Corse
cold c. ... 1240: 2
dead c. ... 1555: 3
of Cæsar ... 1675: 6
poor c. ... 592:16
possess her c. ... 1433:15
Corpulent: goodly man and c. ... 945:13
Correct him for his fault .. 516: 9
Corrected son ... 392: 4
Correction ... 238
dread c. wait on us ... 1251:16
resolved c. ... 1664:10
strong c. ... 464: 7
take thy c. mildly ... 993: 5
under c. ... 477: 8
under the c. of bragging .. 1709:13
Correctioner: famished c. .. 1298: 3
Correspondence with true sight ... 449:15
Correspondent to command 1087: 9
Corresponding: well c. ... 866:12
Corrigible authority ... 1673:17
neck ... 1344:16
Corrivals: moe c. ... 950: 8
Corroborate: fracted and c. 694:13
Corrosive: fretful c. ... 1119:14
rather c. ... 159:10
Corrupt: able to c. a saint ... 1: 7
and tainted ... 1598:17
and treasonous ... 1559: 6
the Grecian sentinels ... 139:13
Corrupted by spells ... 239: 4
she is c., changed ... 239: 4
through affection ... 844:11
traitorously c. ... 1560: 3
Corrupter ends ... 565: 5
her c. of words ... 565: 5
Corrupters of my faith ... 238:14
Corruptibly: touch'd c. ... 239: 3
Corruption ... 238
break into c. ... 1368:15

Discoloured earth, shore ...1357:11
Discolours the complexion .1646: 2
Discomfit: uncurable d. 346:11
Discomfited 346:11
Discomfiture: slaughter, d. 1526: 5
Discomfort 346
swells 203:11
you, it nothing must 366: 7
Discomfortable cousin 1511: 7
Discommend so much 837: 5
Disconsolate: all d. 979: 4
Discontent 346
attired in d. 347: 5
big d. 877: 1
brawling d. 347: 2
content you in my d. 347: 8
heart's d. 277:6; 346:15
let not d. daunt 347:10
thy d. thou didst bequeath .347: 5
what 's more miserable than d. 346:15
worst of d. 346:14
wrought out of their d. ...347: 1
Discontenting father 512: 8
Discontents at home 347: 1
dissemble your d. 347:10
poor d. 170: 9
Discontinue your company .211:11
Discontinued school 1320:11
Discord 347
armed d. 295:11
concord of this d. 347:11
doth afflict my soul 347:13
fall to some d. 347:12
hark, what d. follows 322:14
his d. dulcet 347:11
in countries, d. 1099:11
in the spheres 347:11
melodious d. 347:15
restless d. loves no stops ...347:13
so musical a d. 725: 7
Discords: hear nothing but d. 1000:13
in dismal d. sung 99: 9
straining harsh d. 838: 6
Discourse 348
admirable d. 348:10
bid me d. 349: 1
brief d. 348: 4
enchanting d. 349: 1
excellent dumb d. 348:12
grow commendable in none 348: 8
his d. peremptory 176: 7
how likes she my d. 348:15
I prithee 348: 5
is heavy, fasting 348: 2
it is no time to d. 348: 4
large d. 348: 4
list his d. of war 348: 4
no d., except it be of love ..896: 3
of disability 348:14
of excellent d. 349: 1
of good d. 177: 7
of love and peace 348:15
of my dear faith 911: 1
of reason 111:11
of the state of things 348: 6
of thought 533:16
our d. is all of her 348: 9
passionate d. 348: 6
put your d. into some frame 348: 3
smooth d. 348:10
so sweet and voluble his d. 1688: 7
sweet d. 1696: 4
swoln and hot d. 1737: 5
the freezing hours away .1427: 2
voluble and sharp d. 1586: 9
wants d. of reason 75: 5
with air do hold d. 348: 3
your fair d. as sugar 348:10
Discoursed: at large d. 348: 1
Discourser: good d. 1486:17
Discourses: are my d. dull 1687:13
Discourtesy: unfold equal d. 800: 8
Discover a thing to you.....349: 5
Discoverers: send d. forth ..349: 3
Discoveries: deal of d. 349: 6
escape d. 425:14
of dishonour 349: 6
preposterous d. 353:15
Discovery 349
be not aimed at 270: 8
diligent d. 349: 6
fair d. of her way 32: 4
South-sea of d. 349: 2

Discredited your travel ...1364: 7
Discretion 349
adventure my d. 350: 3
best d. 349:12
better part of valour is d. 1116:10
covering d. with a coat of folly 349:10
good d. 349:12; 1424: 7
lack d. 21:7; 255: 8
led by some d. 349:11
let your d. be your tutor ...10:10
O dear d. 1717: 9
old folks have d. 350: 1
safe d. 1177: 3
use thy d. 349: 8
was it d., lords 349:11
with great d. 1229: 3
with some d. 1759: 4
Discretions can persuade ...349:11
brings goot d. 336: 2
Discuss: speak, breathe, d. .675: 2
Disdain 350
and scorn ride sparkling ..350: 8
believe not thy d. 350: 4
cold d. 332: 7
corrupt me ever 1664: 1
dishonour to d. him 357:13
in a dull d. 116: 3
my dear Lady D. 350: 8
proud d. 1108: 2
servile to my coy d. 1342:16
they do d. us much 350: 4
torments me with d. 450:12
wounded with d. 1740: 7
Disdained of all 155: 9
Disdainful: she is too d. ...350: 8
Disdainfully did sting 422:17
greet him not, or else d. ...350:11
Disdaining 350:5
Disease 351
dissolute d. 351:12
foul d. 351: 5
hang upon him like a d. ...351:13
have d., and feel 't not 352: 2
I cannot name the d. 352: 2
I 'll tell thee my d. 351: 9
mourns at his d. 351:13
of all-shunn'd poverty 590: 7
of not listening 59:15
that must be cut away 351: 4
that 's in my flesh 288: 8
the d. is incurable 1225: 2
this d. is beyond my practice 351:12
thou d. of a friend 593:14
Diseased: be d. 1476:11
we are all d. 351: 9
Diseases are grown so catching 1151:11
as many d. as two and fifty horses 24: 9
bequeath you my d. 352: 1
caught, as men take d. 210:12
desperate grown 351: 6
dulcet d. 562:13
figuring d. in me 351: 8
give them d. 1661: 2
have been sold dearer 936: 5
help to make d. 351: 8
lance d. in our bodies 351: 3
may d. lick up bloods 1003:18
may d. only work upon 't ..278: 8
more d. than he knew 1636: 4
of the world 66: 1
purchased many d. 351: 8
rheumatic d. do abound ...353:14
rotten d. of the south 353:15
subject to the same d. 785: 3
turn d. to commodity 351: 7
what rank d. grow 809:15
Disedged by her 1259:14
Disembark some necessaries 1295: 9
Disfigure not his slop 380: 4
so d. her 540: 3
Disfigured clean 1585:16
much d. 1191: 4
Disfurnish myself 715:10
she 'll d. us 1240: 5
Disgorge into the world 429: 3
Disgrace 354
and horror 354: 2
brook such d. well 354: 3
deep d. in brotherhood 144: 4
even to a full d. 12: 1
high d. 1542:17

Disgrace, *continued*
his d. is to be called boy ...271: 7
in d. with fortune 355: 1
invisible d. 1347:10
of death 470: 7
sound not my d. 354:11
stately Rome's d. 354:15
take it as a sweet d. 1215: 5
to your great worth 1560: 1
we have digested 1239: 9
what a d. is it 1046: 6
Disgraced by inkhorn mate 1202: 2
part away d. 842:10
stands d. 354:14
Disgraceful wailing robes .1031:13
Disgraces have of late 354: 1
sustain moe new d. 354:10
Disgracing of these colours 354: 7
Disgracious in the city's eyes 1094:14
Disguise 355
of love 355:11
to sound Falstaff 355:10
us at my lodging 218: 1
wild d. 385: 7
Disguised: as well known as d. 1349:11
to get your love 355:11
to myself d. 355: 4
you were d. 355: 6
Disguiser: death 's a great d. 300: 5
Disguises: strange d. 355:10
Dish 355
chameleon's d. 28:20
dainty d. 1653: 4
fit for the gods 798: 7
for a king 30: 2
here 's a d. I love not 356: 5
his Egyptian d. 355:15
my d. of chastity 181: 5
nor wash d. 966:15
of skim milk 1331: 1
of some three-pence 356: 4
take away this d. 356: 5
that I do love 356: 6
thou full d. of fool 564: 7
velvet d., fie, fie 158: 2
Dishabited: been d. 84: 5
Dishclout: Romeo 's a d. to him 607:12
wore but a d. 1355: 9
Dished for me to try 230:13
Dishes: covered d. 355:15
feed on nourishing d. 528: 2
foster'd with cold d. 97: 1
so many strange d. 1723: 3
two d., but to one table 808: 6
Dishonest: you grow d. 356: 9
Dishonestly afflicted 356: 7
most d. 356: 7
Dishonesty 356
from all d. 1306:16
no d. shall appear 356: 8
Dishonour 356
amazed at his d. 357:10
base d. blur our name 357: 7
foul d. to my grave 357:13
in thine age 357: 7
it is my more d. 357: 1
mangles judgement 356:13
pronounce d. of her 831: 3
so d. me 357: 6
some d. we had 1252:19
suffer not d. to approach ..358: 3
to deny it her 357: 8
traffics with man's nature 1110: 8
Dishonoured: be d. openly 1279: 2
by a man 1279: 5
so d. 357: 2
Dishonours: he d. me 1346: 6
Disinherited thine only son 1398: 4
Disjoins remorse from power 640: 1
Disjoint and out of frame .1441: 8
things d. 524:11
Dislike 358
feed on this d. 358:10
of our proceedings 358: 4
what most he should d. seems pleasant 1148: 7
your d. doth cloud my joys 358: 7
Disliken the truth 355:14
Dislikes: it d. me 358: 7
Disliking eye 443:13
Dislimns: the rack d. 196:11

Espoused: I was e. 962: 3
to death 921:10
Essay of my virtue 1607:12
Essence: glassy e. 941: 8
she is my e. 911: 4
Essential vesture 936: 3
Essentially am not in madness 269: 7
mad 930:10
not e. but by circumstance 1394: 1
Estate: came to man's e. ..817: 7
contemptible e. 287:10
disabled mine e. 1177: 6
know our own e. 145:10
my e. be fallen 34: 5
my e. is very low 261: 4
o' the world 1466:12
of great e. 173:10
of my poor queen 1188: 8
of seven years' health 853: 1
preposterous e. 925: 1
sin against our own e. 838: 8
unspeakable e. 650: 9
Estates, degrees and offices ..986:17
sicken'd their e. 1210: 2
Esteem: evidence of good e. ..428:17
false e. 1377: 8
of good e. 1266: 3
our e. was made the poorer 785: 6
she is of good e. 375: 7
so high in his e. 1266: 3
world's e. 1266: 4
Esteeming: rich e. 913:12
Estimable: not so e. 550: 8
wonder 1707:14
Estimate: dear wife's e. 185:10
thou know'st thy e. 503: 4
Estimation: beggar the e. ..319: 4
earn a dearer e. 1140: 5
make head against my e. 16:14
of a hair 656: 2
of no e. in the world 1266: 3
speak not this in e. 825:11
ungalled e. 1375: 7
worthy e. 1737: 8
Estranged from thyself 929: 1
thus e. 929: 1
Estridge: dove will peck e. 597: 1
Estridges: plumed like e. 53: 6
Et tu, Brute 152: 4
Etcætera: open e. 1686: 1
Etceteras: are e. nothing ..1172: 5
Eternal: brass e. slave 1533: 7
Eternally be knit 960:10
Eterne: nature's copy 's not e. 1026: 8
proof e. 1259:15
Eternity 426
divide e. in twain 366:13
passing through nature to e. 303: 4
to e. doth rest 300:11
wish'd this world's e. 302: 7
Eternized in all age 71: 3
Ethiope: black E. reaching 822:13
Ethiopes of their sweet complexion crack 102:11
Ethiopian 426
Eunuch 426
be you his e. 1547:13
made it an e. 209: 5
small as an e. 1610:14
sung by Athenian e. 1405: 1
voice of unpaved e. 1039: 7
would I were an e. 181:12
Eunuchs: make e. of 1579:14
Europa 145:14
Europe: make all E. quake 1393:12
Evade: if he e. us 427: 4
Evades: he e. them 427: 4
Evasion 427:9
admirable e. 1439:13
there can be no e. 715:12
wing'd thus swift 49: 6
Evasions: his e. have ears ..427: 9
Eve: grandmother E. 1697:16
he had tempted E. 13: 1
what E., what serpent 13: 1
Eve's daughters 287: 8
Even: be e. and direct 155: 2
be e. in our government ..630: 9
be e. with me 1277:10
bear ourselves as e. as we can 309: 8
give e. or give none 967: 4
good e. 642: 9

Even, *continued*
he is e. with you 967: 4
I will be e. with thee 373: 7
or odd 1092: 6
that 's the e. of it 1378: 2
Even-handed justice 1274: 8
Even-pleached: hedges e. ..1604: 6
Evened with him 1277:10
Evening 427
about e. come 427:12
how still the e. is 428: 2
present e. 1195: 1
summer's e. 428: 1
this e. 427:11
Evenly 35:11
Event 428
as the e. stamps them 428:13
cast the e. of war 428: 8
customed e. 1099:10
daring the e. to the teeth 1494: 2
ill e. 428: 5
obscene and most preposterous e. 428: 9
see the e. 428:14
unborn e. I do commend 428:11
Events can never fall out good 428:13
confused e. new hatch'd ..1100: 1
dire e. 428: 5
fierce e. 428: 5
high e. as these 428: 4
leave him to his e. 428:10
not natural e. 428: 3
strange and terrible e. 202:13
strange e. are welcome 428: 3
these most strange e. 219:14
Ever and anon 472: 7
for e. and a day ..426:10; 901: 4
for e. and for e. 502: 7
Ever-burning hell 690: 5
lights above 1614:14
Ever-during blame 1347:10
Ever-esteemed duty 393:10
Ever-fixed mark 902:11
pole 1637:16
Ever-gentle 1461:4
Ever-harmless looks 1078:16
Ever-preserved love 155: 2
Ever-running year 807: 5
Everlasting had not fix'd ..1460:15
Everlastingly: hate him e. ..677:13
love her e. 902: 6
make rough winter e. 717:13
Everything includes itself in power 1182: 2
Evidence 428
bear e. against my soul 319: 1
bring in the e. 429: 2
give in e. 794:11
modest e. 428:17
to swear 927: 4
true e. 428:17
where are the e. 429: 2
Evident: so e. 381: 8
to any formal capacity 156: 1
Evil 429
beauteous e. are empty trunks o'erflourish'd ..1608:17
dared to do that e. 1222: 1
disease call'd the e. 353:13
do good against e. 628: 6
dream on e. 1607: 5
ensuing e. 429: 9
forget your e. 572: 9
greater in e. 627:11
my female e. tempteth 37: 4
no e. lost is wail'd 429: 4
no man means e. but the devil 338: 6
purposed e. 5: 7
strong and swelling e. 429:13
that men do lives after them 627:17
that thou causest 429:13
thirsty e. 1512:11
thou dost e. 429:11
too true an e. 429:15
unlook'd-for e. 338:13
your e. quits you well 429:13
Evil-eyed unto you 1027: 1
Evilly bestowed 319: 2
born 319: 2
Evils: accidental e. 1149:18
bear my e. alone 430: 5
build their e. on the graves of great men 1005: 6

Evils, *continued*
cave-keeping e. 941:11
enow to darken 627:12
fix'd e. sit so fit 627:11
future e. 429: 7
imminent 1631:11
oppress'd with two weak e. 1103:11
principal e. laid to women .1700:11
repent the e. I have done 1262: 2
she hatch'd 429: 5
that take leave 429:10
these e. thou repeat'st 429:12
turning past e. to advantages 1201: 6
when e. are most free 230: 5
Evitate and shun 311: 6
Ewe bleat for the lamb 692:12
that will not hear 1350: 2
whereof the e. not bites 463: 2
Ewer: bear the e. 1144: 1
silver basin and e. 663: 7
Ewers to lave her hands ..663: 7
Ewes being rank 100:12
fulsome e. 100:12
good e. 1736: 6
have been with young 1534: 9
milk my e. and weep 1652: 1
see my e. graze 1350: 2
Exacting: pay false e. 355: 8
Exaction 1494:2
of the forfeiture 598:18
Exactions: new e. 1494: 2
Exalt: he doth e. himself ..633: 2
Examine him upon that point 1173: 1
Example 430
Christian e. 431: 2
find e. of thousands 319: 4
gave the clergy ill e. 430:16
hang'd up for e. 666: 4
he has given e. 430: 6
he 'll be made an e. 430:14
lest e. breed 430:13
make him an e. 430:14
my digression 1191: 5
rare e. 430: 7
stale e. 431: 1
that so terrible shows 1329: 8
there is e. for 't 431: 4
want e. 430:17
you with thievery 1510: 3
Exampled 430:12
Examples gross as earth 430: 9
make e. 430:14
of every minute's instance 430:10
out of late e. 1220: 5
set here for e. 430:15
three e. of the like 430: 7
Exasperate: why art thou e. ..39:15
Exceedingly well aim'd 479: 7
well read 479: 7
Excellence 431
breathless e. 1614: 7
fair divided e. 954: 2
his e. did earn it 1050: 1
in a galliard 284: 2
our carver's e. 431:10
praise your e. 431: 5
study's e. 431:10
that e. that angels love 901: 8
Excellencies: crammed with e. 177: 3
Excellency 431:8
of her honour 716:10
Excellent: comes off e. 431: 7
so e. in art 470: 2
that will be e. 431: 7
to have a giant's strength 1452: 5
Excelling: Silvia is e. 431: 9
Excels each mortal thing ..431: 9
Except not any 431:14
Excepted: only you e. 431:14
Excepting none 431:14
Exception 431
bid him speak 712: 4
Exceptions: take e. ..127:4; 495:13
takes e. at your person 851:10
takes e. to your ill hours ..431:13
took e. at this badge 63:10
Exceptless rashness 1242:13
Excess 431
give me e. of it 1042: 1
giving of e. 127:11
of laughter....................840: 9
of wine set him on 1680: 7

Excess, *continued*
scant this e. 902: 8
wasteful and ridiculous e. 432: 1
where e. begs all 432: 2
will make me surfeit 1696: 8
Exchange: made e. of vow 1711:10
Exchequer: father's e. 1618:14
his e. is too poor 1239: 9
king's e. 1016: 7
of the poor 1508: 9
of words 1723: 8
rob me the e. 1296:10
Exchequers: they shall be e. 182: 6
Excitements to the field ..1286:11
Exclaim no more against it 1679:13
what makes you thus e. ..432: 4
Exclaims: be copious in e. 1448: 5
deep e. 398: 2
Exclamation 432
Exclamations: drown your e. 1128: 5
Excommunicate: cursed and e. 275: 8
Excrement: dally with my e. 74: 3
general e. 1511:10
pocket up my pedlar's e. .1138: 4
so plentiful an e. 657: 8
valour's e. 1591:13
Excusable: that was e. 432: 8
Excuse 432
fair e. 222:11
give me e. 432:10
good e. for me hereafter ...958:11
hath the e. of youth 1756:10
hear my e. 432:11
himself 6: 9
I will not e. you 432:11
I will not have e. 432:11
make his e. 1471:10
make my old e. 188: 5
make no e. current 667:14
make your e. wisely 432:15
me 432:14
no e. shall serve 432:11
remember your brother's e. 1259: 9
strange e. 921: 7
this admits no e. 432:11
to work upon his wife 589:12
what cannot be amended ..432:10
why should e. be born 432:13
you must e. us 432:14
Excused: stand e. 333:14
you shall not be e. 432:11
you 're e. 432:14
Excuses for thy faults 432:15
patch'd up your e. 1125: 6
shall not be admitted 432:11
Excusez-moi 432:14
Excusing of a fault 514:12
Execrable wretch 1336: 2
Execrations: cease these e. 1474:12
spiteful e. 1474:12
Execute all things 314: 3
thou shalt e. 314: 3
Executed: be e. 798: 9
Execution 434
away with her to e. 1549:11
bloody e. 434: 7
carry him to e. 434: 5
deliver'd over to e. 434: 2
do e. on my flesh 188: 7
do e. on the watch 434: 6
do shameful e. on herself 1461:10
do some fatal e. 13: 4
his e. sworn 220:14
hopeful e. 434: 4
is e. done 434: 5
mad and fantastic e. 434: 7
of his wit, hands, heart ..1614:14
prepare for your e. 220: 6
present e. 434: 1
put it in e. 1223: 6
rode to 's e. 1386:11
sorry e. 665: 5
sudden e. of my will 434: 1
Executioner 434
call your e. 684: 3
common e. 434: 8
I will not be the e. 434:12
I 'll provide his e. 434: 9
judge and e. 791: 8
then thou art an e. 434:10
Executioners: here come my e. 434:13
Executor 434:14

Executors: let 's choose e. 1675: 9
Exempt from envy 912: 9
from public haunt 866:10
themselves from fear 317: 3
you are from me e. 1747: 3
Exercise 434
arts and e. 55:12
bear up with this e. 1500: 2
devout 695:17
for art and e. 389: 5
gentle e. and proof of arms 167: 3
hath been too violent 434:15
he 's all my e. 1400: 4
holy e. 709: 1
hunting was his daily e. ..737: 5
Exercises: arts and martial e. 1398: 2
Exhalation: natural e. 1099:10
Exhalations: behold these e. 1099: 2
whizzing in the air 870: 9
Exhale: therefore e. 636:12
Exhaust their mercy 62: 2
Exhibition: petty e. 318: 7
Exhortation: end my e. 1420: 1
Exigent: cross me in this e. 1230: 5
drawing to their e. 440: 9
Exile 435
hath more terror in his look 66:11
vagabond e. 984: 2
wilfully e. themselves 870:13
world's e. is death 66:11
Exion: my e. is entered 41: 4
Exits and their entrances ..940:12
Exorciser: no e. harm thee ..179: 1
Exorcist: is there no e. 441:16
like an e. 1431: 6
Expect: be 't of less e. 1421: 4
Expectance from both sides ..436: 5
Expectancy and rose 995: 3
of more arrivance 435:19
Expectation 435
better bettered e. 436: 2
fainted, longing for what ..435:17
fresh e. troubled not 435:22
full of e. 1168:16
hath made us forward 435:18
hath this day on end 435:21
mock the e. of the world ..435:20
never trust my e. 921:12
now sits E. in the air 435:21
of our prosperity 436: 3
of plenty 503:10
of thy time 466: 2
oft e. fails 435:17
patient e. 1127: 4
sets all on hazard 436: 5
trust my e. 1573: 9
whirls me round 436: 5
you stand in coldest e. 435:20
Expectations and comforts ..436: 3
Expected of my friends 587:10
when it is least e. 436: 1
Expecters of our Trojan part 436: 5
Expecting 436:4
Expedience 436:11
Expedient 436:10
for the wise 1186: 7
Expediently: do this e. 436: 6
Expedition 436
fiery e. be my wing 436:12
good e. be my friend 436:13
great e. 436: 8
hasten on this e. 436: 8
intercepts my e. 436: 8
Irish e. 436: 8
last e. 436: 8
of my violent love 916: 8
of thought 1428:14
promises approach 436: 8
speediest e. 436:13
stubborn and boisterous e. .149: 5
swiftest e. 436:13
who intercepts my e. 1028:12
Expeditious: sail so e. 1325: 6
Expense 437
cost me some e. 239:14
gall'd with my e. 599: 7
large e. of time 1535:11
of many a vanish'd sight 1364: 2
of spirit in a waste of shame 927: 7
without e. at all 1134: 8
Expenses: for your e. 437: 8
there 's e. for thee 437: 8
Experience 437
give e. tongue 437:18

Experience, *continued*
is by industry achieved 438: 1
make bold her bashful years with your e. 1028:12
makes you sad 437:10
manhood, honour 1344:15
manifest e. 975:10
many bulwarks builded 437:15
old and want'st e. 25: 2
pawn their e. 437: 9
purchased this e. 437:14
sinned against his e. 1368:14
small e. grows 1677: 4
so much e. for my pains ..437:16
true e. 1694: 6
unless e. be a jewel 976:14
Experienced 437:14
Experiences: guided by others' e. 437:11
Experiment 438
Experimental seal 425: 4
Expert in his drinking 418: 8
Expertness in wars 1625:11
Expiate 304:1
Explication: in way of e. ..498: 8
Exploit 438
close e. of death 139:13
night's e. at Gad's-hill 1340:11
trim e. 1286: 6
what e. 's in hand 1471:10
worthy e. 419:11
Exploits: anticipatest my dread e. 1531: 4
do more e. with his mace .1098: 1
high e. and honourable deeds 762: 7
Exposition of sleep 1382:16
your e. hath been most sound 791: 9
your e. on the holy text ..1190:14
Expositor: conceit's e. 1688: 7
Expostulate 1264:19
bitterly could I e. 1547:10
stay not to e. 1429: 1
what majesty should be 49:13
Expostulation: use e. kindly 1264:19
Exposture to each chance 1211:15
wild e. to each chance 248: 7
Exposure: discredit our e. 1377: 9
suffer in e. 1473:13
Expressed: and not e. 789: 5
Expressing: past all e. 874:10
Expressive: be more e. 479: 8
Expressure: give e. to 1442: 4
of his eye 312: 8
Expulsed from France 581:12
Exquisite 568:17
call hers e. 81: 9
very e. friend 589: 1
Exsufflicate surmises 1473: 3
Extant 1447:8
Extemporal speech 1418: 7
Extemporally will stage us 12: 9
Extempore 988:3
do any thing e. 622:12
do it e. 878:14
it is e. 1428: 4
Extent: uncivil and unjust e. 1685: 8
Extenuate his offence 1094: 2
nothing e. 1425:17
Extenuated: his glory not e. 306: 5
Extenuation let me beg 432:12
Exteriorly: rude e. 572:16
Exteriors: course o'er my e. 236:13
Extermined: both e. 1407: 3
Extinct in both 44:12
Extincted spirits 543: 7
Extinguish art 632:13
Extirp: impossible to e. 849:11
Extirpate me and mine 849:11
Extirped from our provinces 581:12
Extol 1186:2
you e. me thus 329:14
Extolled: as 'tis e. 1133: 5
Extolment: verity of e. 176: 3
Extract one spark of evil .429: 8
Extracted from many objects 978: 8
Extracting frenzy 929: 8
Extraordinarily: beats as e. 696:14
sweat e. 1475: 8
Extraordinary 639:10
something e. in thee 907:10
Extravagancy: mere e. 1616:18
Extravagant 199:3

Feather, *continued*
raven's f. ... 278: 7
stirring of a f. ... 479:19
this f. stirs ... 169:22
was ever f. so lightly blown 1034:14
will turn the scale ... 1652:10
Feather-bed: edge of a f. ... 426: 4
Feathered briefness ... 1313: 6
Cupid ... 150: 4
Mercury ... 150: 4
Feathers: add more f. to our wings ... 1476:16
added f. to the learned's wing ... 527: 2
are more beautiful ... 381: 4
growing f. ... 527: 1
his f. are but borrow'd ... 1330: 4
most courteous f. ... 527: 1
pluck'd from Cæsar's wing 152: 7
set f. to thy heels ... 1429: 5
soar with his light f. ... 272: 3
Featly: foot it f. ... 283:10
she dances f. ... 284: 6
Feats: fell f. ... 1627: 5
he hath done ... 316: 4
high f. ... 316: 4
of a lion ... 600: 2
of broil and battle ... 1733: 5
tell them your f. ... 316: 4
these f., so crimeful ... 317: 8
warlike f. ... 316: 4
what f. he did that day ... 316: 3
what f., what shows ... 1276: 4
wondrous f. ... 316: 4
Feature ... 527
cheated of f. ... 322: 7
complete in mind and f. ... 259: 8
done good f. shame ... 527:13
of blown youth ... 401:11
peerless f. approves her fit . 288: 2
shapes them to your f. ... 444:14
Featured like him ... 347: 7
how rarely f. ... 1148: 8
Featureless and rude ... 188: 5
Features are abroad ... 527:12
February face ... 459: 5
Fed: both have f. as well ... 213: 3
highly f. and lowly taught . 954:14
within be f. ... 1414: 5
Federacy with her ... 1562:14
Fee bestow upon thy disease 351: 5
death 's my f. ... 305: 7
golden f. for which I plead 1104:11
honey f. of parting ... 813:11
more f. than hate ... 916: 1
pin's f. ... 867: 1
Fee-farm: kiss in f. ... 813: 3
Fee-grief: is it a f. ... 645: 6
Fee-simple: have him in f. ... 338: 6
of his salvation ... 139: 8
of my life ... 1229:10
rivelled f. of the tetter ... 353:15
Feeble: most forcible F. ... 480:15
Feeble: help the f. up ... 605: 8
shallow, weak ... 1643: 6
Feebling such as stand not . 1307: 2
Feebly: utter'd f. ... 315:12
Feed ... 528:2; 528:12
and clothe thee ... 549: 4
and regard him not ... 528: 4
cannot f. mine eye ... 898: 7
I f. most hungerly ... 528: 7
it will f. my revenge ... 1278: 8
like oxen at a stall ... 1107: 9
on your lips ... 880:10
please your highness f. ... 528: 7
rest ourselves and f. ... 420: 8
sit down and f. ... 559: 9
stand to and f. ... 528: 7
those that f. grow full ... 1705: 8
thou wouldst be f. ... 1435: 7
to f. were best at home ... 528: 3
too much on this dislike ... 528:10
where thou wilt ... 136: 7
Feeder ... 528
Feeders digest it ... 526:14
looks on f. ... 1659:13
riotous f. ... 1276: 6
Feedest: where f. thou ... 528: 8
Feeding ... 527
full of high f. ... 235: 5
not worth the f. ... 1738:13
on that which doth ... 528: 6
with eager f. food doth choke the feeder ... 528:14

Feel: how dost thou f. ... 529: 3
I do f. it and see 't ... 529: 8
I f. this pin prick ... 529: 1
we cannot f. too little ... 529: 2
what 'tis to love ... 918: 7
what wretches f. ... 1176:14
Feeler's soul ... 660: 1
Feeling ... 528
hast thou a touch, a f. ... 529: 6
have ingenious f. ... 1334: 2
holy f. in thy soul ... 1413:16
love's f. is more soft ... 894:14
no f. of his business ... 528:15
not by our f. ... 529: 4
of her passion ... 1123:13
painful f. of thy speech ... 1419: 8
some f. of the sport ... 985: 5
tender f., to base touches prone ... 529: 5
thou hast no f. ... 528:15
without sight ... 1334:15
Feeling-painful: more f. ... 1695:12
Fees: pay your f. ... 1131: 8
Feet: at thy f. I kneel ... 1499: 4
blessed f. were nail'd ... 192: 1
churlish f. ... 568: 2
contrary f. ... 568: 2
cut my tender f. ... 552:12
direct thy f. where thou . 1121: 2
disgrace's f. ... 1557:16
have my old f. stumbled ... 567:11
her f. were much too dainty 567:15
humbled at thy f. ... 1566:15
kiss their own f. ... 1552: 6
kissing Cæsar's f. ... 813: 1
kissing of their f. ... 1591:16
might bear the verses ... 1596:10
more f. than shoes ... 380: 9
more f. than the verses ... 1596:10
princely f. ... 1456:19
sleided silk f. ... 1328: 5
thrust upon contrary f. ... 1486: 2
treacherous f. ... 568: 2
were lame ... 1596:10
with printless f. do chase ... 463: 2
yet are these f. unable ... 567: 7
Feign: if I do f. ... 1196: 2
Feigned: like to be f. ... 1428: 5
Feigning ... 1196:2
Felicitate: alone f. ... 906: 7
Felicity: absent thee from f. 1447: 9
Fell as death ... 591:15
more f. than anguish ... 1507: 5
my f. of hair ... 524:12
passing f. ... 1507: 5
right as it f. out ... 222: 6
shortly must I f. it ... 1564: 3
they f. together ... 467: 7
Fell-lurking curs ... 72:10
Fellies from her wheel ... 577: 8
Fellow ... 529
admirable conceited f. ... 531:13
all in buff ... 535: 7
art thou mad, old f. ... 928:11
bearded f. ... 530:14
blunt f. ... 155: 1
brave f. ... 531:13
breed thy f. ... 1300: 2
by hand of nature mark'd . 530:13
dangerous f., hence ... 1173:11
foolish f. ... 531:11
gallant f. ... 600: 3
good blunt f. ... 530:12
good f.; good limbed f. ... 531: 3
good sensible f. ... 1334: 5
good shallow young f. ... 1344: 9
good sharp f. ... 1689: 3
half-faced f. ... 458: 8
he 's a strange f. ... 1449: 6
hilding f. that had stolen ... 530: 7
honest f. ... 530:17
hook-nosed f. of Rome ... 225: 5
I am a poor f. ... 1180: 8
in a long motley coat ... 530:10
is distract ... 365: 6
is not this a rare f. ... 530: 1
is not this a strange f. ... 313: 4
is the f. mad ... 931: 3
kind f. ... 530:17
lewd f. ... 1751:13
little quiver f. ... 529:11
mad f. ... 530: 5
mad f. of the north ... 1072:14
many a good tall f. ... 156:17
marvellous witty f. ... 531: 1

Fellow, *continued*
melancholy f. ... 978: 8
most active f. in Europe ... 94: 5
naked f. ... 530:14
ne'er see such a f. ... 530: 9
noble f., I warrant him ... 530: 3
notable f. ... 1199: 8
o' the strangest mind ... 531: 9
of a good respect ... 530:12
of infinite jest ... 530: 4
of no mark nor likelihood 1100: 9
of no merits ... 986:11
of the royal bed ... 531:12
of the self-same colour ... 530:14
old fat f. ... 977:10
old f. ... 530:14
paltry, insolent f. ... 531: 8
poor f. ... 530:15
prettier f. of the two ... 355: 9
proper f. of my hands ... 530: 9
rich f. enough ... 531: 1
saucy f. ... 530:11
scurvy f. ... 531:10
shy f. ... 1538: 1
sneaking f. ... 531: 8
snipt-taffeta f. ... 1397: 1
some scurvy f. ... 817: 2
spoke like a tall f. ... 1266:12
strange f. ... 530: 2
strong f. ... 529:13
sweet f. to 't ... 963:14
tall f. ... 1442:11
tall f. of thy hands ... 532: 1
that f. is a f. of much licence ... 530:16
that hath had losses ... 531: 1
that never had the ache ... 530: 9
there 's a f. ... 1378: 4
this is a respected f. ... 1270: 2
thou art a merry f. ... 531: 9
thou art a strange f. ... 1485:19
'tis a most gallant f. ... 529:12
to be your f. you may deny me ... 1338: 2
turn yon f. in his grave ... 637: 9
very scurvy f. ... 1199: 8
very tainted f. ... 529:11
what a monstrous f. ... 1237:12
what f. is that ... 530: 2
what muffled f. is that ... 530:16
whoreson mad f. ... 930: 7
with the great belly ... 530: 7
world hath not her f. ... 213: 5
worthy f. ... 530:3; 531:6; 1478:10
young f. ... 530: 8
Fellow-fault ... 513: 9
Fellow-ministers ... 1482: 9
Fellow-scholars ... 1320: 3
Fellow-servant ... 1009: 8
Fellow-soldier ... 1392: 3
Fellow-student ... 1011:12
Fellowly drops ... 448: 5
Fellows: good f. all ... 1644:11
he hath lost his f. ... 531: 4
in arms ... 531: 4
learned and authentic f. ... 529: 9
mock poor f. thus ... 1011:16
of infinite tongue ... 1545:11
our f. are asleep ... 1340: 3
tall f. ... 1394: 6
there be good f. in world ... 531: 3
these f. have some soul ... 1413: 1
we are but plain f. ... 860: 6
we are f. still ... 531: 7
Fellowship ... 532
bearing f. ... 1459:17
disjoin'd from f. ... 1503:13
good f. come to you ... 532: 4
great men's f. ... 949: 9
half-faced f. ... 458: 8
in woe doth woe assuage . 1695:11
royal f. of death ... 306: 1
sweet f. in shame ... 1346:12
to die with us ... 306: 1
Fellowships: make f. accurst 1579: 1
Felon loaden with irons ... 1683:12
Felonious thief ... 1511: 1
Felony to drink small beer . 416: 6
treason, f., sword ... 1137: 1
Female ... 1697:16
to my soul ... 134: 1
Feminine: soul f. ... 1412: 6
Fen: his f. makes fear'd ... 375: 8
unwholesome f. ... 278: 7
Fen-sucked fogs ... 277:10

Groom, *continued*
ordinary g. 1131: 9
poor g. of thy stable 648:10
this detested g. 1381: 5
'tis a g. indeed 141: 7
vulgar g. 682: 9
Grooms: dunghill g. 321:10
poor g. are sightless night .809: 2
sleepy g. 648: 8
surfeited g. 1390:11
unpolish'd g. 326: 5
you are gallant g. 535: 6
Groping for trouts 1192: 6
Gross as a mountain 858: 5
as black and white 1575: 9
as ever touch'd conjecture 499:17
come to him by the g. 1179: 1
in taste 1493: 2
most g. 357:12
not g. to sink 896: 4
sell by g. 633: 5
so g. in his jealousy 781: 3
Grosser 648:12
Grossly: so g. 648:14
Grossness 648; 649:1
hiding the g. with fair ornament 1256:10
little characters sum up ..1224:14
of the foppery 92: 4
of this age 26: 3
Ground 649
affect the very g. 906: 8
beat the g. 1591:16
bestrew the g. 1620: 9
bleeding g. 1028: 3
by this heavenly g. 127: 8
dank and dirty g. 935:10
disdain'd the g. 1198:10
England's g., farewell 419: 1
follow me to plainer g. 649:19
gave you some g. 835:15
get g. and vantage 15: 7
give g. 649:15
God's g. and his earth ...1266: 2
good g., be pitiful 649:16
heavenly g. I tread on 1491: 9
hollow g. 395: 3
indeed is tawny 635:15
is bloody 649:21
kiss the g. 1754: 3
kisses the base g. 811:16
known g. of treachery ...1558: 6
lay him i' the cold g. 636: 8
lead off this g. 1399: 8
let 's quit the g. 1310: 5
look not to the g. 649:20
looks upon the g. 133:10
made the g. my bed 649: 7
may that g. gape 508: 9
measured the g. 649:13
methinks the g. is even ...649:11
now for the g. which 649:17
of study's excellence 460:10
on the g. sleep sound 1384: 4
plod I the cold g. 918: 8
rise from the g. 724: 3
rock the g. 283: 3
run even upon even g. 1730: 8
sable g. of sin 1370: 7
shrinks before his treading 1618:10
sing him to the g. 1610:13
sink in the g. 649:14
slippery g. 260:12
sluttish g. 1633: 9
stakes me to the g. 1414: 2
sweep the g. 880: 6
tawny g. 108: 3
that gave them first 649:10
that I am banish'd from ..275: 4
to root upon 649:12
to the g. 731: 9
touch g. 718: 5
treads on the g. 1620: 8
true g. of all these piteous woes 1696: 4
under g. 649:10
uneven g. 649:11
unsanctified 146:10
we 'll shift our g. 1079: 9
Grounded: so g. inward 1332:12
Groundlings: split the ears of the g. 10:11
Grounds: come to rob my g. 1316: 9
proceed upon just g. 1274:13
Grove 1708:6
Grovel 1342:6
Grovelling lies 741: 5
Groves: abandoned her holy g. 738: 1
Growing: bathed thy g. ...1521: 2
Grown: avoid what 's g. ..1220:12
to strength 1450:16
Growth 650
gain nothing but g. 650: 1
give full g. 650: 7
give it vital g. again 1303: 2
of excellent g. 1755:13
overta'en him in his g. 650: 6
Grubbed up now 596: 4
Grubs and eyeless skulls ..1548:13
Grudge 650
from ancient g. break 1043: 7
or grumblings 1341: 9
Grudged us contribution ...650:12
Grudges: here grow no damned g. 638: 5
let former g. pass 533: 5
Grudging 650:15
Gruel: make the g. thick ...560: 2
Grumble there i' the straw 1450: 5
what, do you g. 215: 5
Grumblest and railest 215: 5
thou g. 1237:18
Grumbling 215:5
Grumblings: grudge or g. .1341: 9
Grund: lig i' the g. 1339: 8
Grunt and roar 611: 2
and sweat under a weary life 1461: 1
Guard 650
beat down Edward's g. ...651: 4
betake you to your g. 390: 2
emperor's g. 1562:13
have some g. 651:11
have you had quiet g. 650:18
henceforth g. thee well ...798: 1
of chosen shot 651: 2
of patience 1128:13
out of his g. 651:10
she keeps her g. 650:17
stand upon our g. 651: 9
stands at a g. with envy ..175: 5
too wanton 157:10
Guardage: run from her g. .936: 3
Guardant: angry g. 651: 2
Jock g. 779: 7
Guarded: strongly g. 651: 7
weakly g. 651: 7
Guardian 651:6
of their bones 637: 2
Guardian Angel 37
Guardians: made you my g. 651: 6
Guards of the ever-fixed pole 1637:16
shook off my sober g. 524:10
you heavenly g. 37: 3
Gud-day 643: 2
Gudgeon: fool g. 1101:10
Guerdon of her wrongs 470: 8
there 's thy g. 1281: 6
Guerdoned with shame 1346: 6
Guess 651
as I g. 651:18
as you g. 652: 6
by g. 652: 6
by this what you are 652: 3
by thy g. 651:18
canst thou not g. 652: 7
give a likely g. 652: 7
giving themselves to g. ...652: 4
I cannot g. 651:16
I g. at it 652: 3
I partly g. 651:13
near g. of my memory 652: 3
no g. is knowledge 1639:13
of their true strength 652: 2
perfect g. 651:15
ready g. 651:15
square our g. by shows ...825: 9
thou the rest 651:18
you cannot g. 652: 5
you may g. quickly 652: 1
Guessed: often as I g. 651:17
that it was she 651:17
well g., believe me 651:17
Guesses: vile g. 652: 4
Guessingly set down 853: 8
Guest 652
alehouse g. 652:18
forward g. 652:18
Guest, *continued*
I appear not like a g. 525: 9
invited many a g. 652:17
keen g. 89:13
look to the g. 652: 9
make yourself my g. 652: 8
master g. 965: 8
not like a g. 1207: 1
princely g. 1653: 5
sad distemper'd g. 274: 3
shakes his parting g. 1527: 8
sour unwelcome g. 782: 2
strange g. 652: 8
such a g. as grief 645:13
that best becomes table 512: 8
this g. of summer 98: 1
we are your g. to-night ...652:14
you are my g. 653: 1
your house's g. 652:13
Guest-cavaleire 652:15
Guest-wise sojourn'd 694: 2
Guests: bid the g. 526: 9
cherish thy g. 89:18
fair g. 1654: 4
merry g. 725: 5
shipwreck'd g. 1653: 4
so many g. invite 652:17
unbidden g. are often welcomest when gone 652:11
what g. were in her eyes ..1389: 7
ye shall be my g. 652:12
you are my g. 652:12
your g. approach 1003:17
Guiana: region in G. 1225: 5
Guide 846:6
Guided by thee hitherto ...269: 9
Guider: our g., come 846: 6
Guides: former g. 846: 6
safer g. 846: 6
Guidon: my g. 547: 1
Guilders for my voyage ...1016:10
want g. 1623: 9
Guildhall: towards G. 970: 1
Guile 1557:15
dissembling g. 364: 7
foul g. 1610: 9
full of g. 589:13
Guiled shore 1106: 3
Guileful fair words 1134: 8
Guiles that women work ..1702: 7
Guilt 653
apparent g. 793:12
bear the g. 654: 1
being great 654: 4
double g. of this opportunity 1103: 1
his g. but idly posted over .653: 8
is plain 654:10
murderous g. shows not ...913:11
my g. be on my head 654: 7
of conscience 227: 5
of murder 653:10
of murder bucklers thee ..322: 3
stronger g. defeats 653: 5
within their bosoms lie ...654: 6
your g. is great 653: 7
Guiltier than him 794: 5
than my guiltiness 654: 2
Guiltily awake 654: 8
Guiltiness 653:12
I know not 523: 1
of my mind 92: 4
Guiltless 766:14
of the meaning 971: 4
Guilty 653:3; 653:10
because he 's g. 6: 3
bloody and g. 654: 8
confess me much g. 653:15
he pleaded still not g. 6:12
in defence 1753:15
is he found g. 653:11
make mad the g. 10: 9
not g. 654:11; 766:14
of my death 1533: 4
not g. of his own death ...387: 6
of a several bastardy 1213: 4
of high treason 1561: 4
of so deep a sin 1370:10
of this sin 1369: 6
pleaded still not g. 653:11
wherein am I g. 653: 8
Guilty-like: so g. 654: 3
Guinea-hen: love of a g. ...387: 6
Guise o' the world 504: 4
this time's g. 414:11

H

Hearts, *continued*
makes old h. fresh 189: 1
more proof than shields ...536: 9
move your h. to pity 1157: 8
O you hard h. 266: 3
of all his people 1280: 5
of controversy 1477: 7
of gold 532: 4
of most hard temper 691: 7
of old gave hands 695:17
of princes kiss obedience ..1202: 6
old h. 691:14
our h. are in the trim 690: 7
our h. of brothers' temper 689:10
our h. receive your warnings 1631: 4
our h. wear Timon's livery 531: 7
our h. you see not 661: 4
quite lost their h. 688:11
rob me of the people's h. 1142: 4
rough h. of flint 1157: 1
scarcely have the h. 688:14
severed in religion 267: 3
speak our free h. 1421:18
steal away your h. 687:14
steel my soldiers' h. 1393: 7
steel'd the h. of men 692:11
sting your h. 1390: 6
stir these daughters' h. 288: 9
stir your h. and minds ..1748: 8
stone him with harden'd h. 692:10
subdues all sorts of h. 579: 3
sweet h. 693: 9
that makes these hard h. ..693: 1
that scorn'd to serve 1667:11
that spaniel'd me 1342: 1
their h. were yours 686:17
they steal h. 460: 8
thousand h. are great 688:15
true h. cannot bear 1660: 8
twice fifteen thousand h. of England's breed 418: 7
unguarded h. 1740: 4
unrelenting h. 692: 8
where are these h. 830: 7
whose h. are absent 1341: 1
win the h. of all 744: 2
women's waxen h. 46: 8
your h. are mighty 1309: 8
your h. I 'll stamp out 1520:12

Heat 697
by your h. you burn 38: 3
fantastic summer's h. 1514: 6
farewell, h. 828:12
fear no more the h. o' the sun 303: 3
freezes the h. of life 523: 5
he 's of the h. of ginger ..722: 2
I have from thence 697:12
i' the h. 674: 7
in h. of action 9: 4
made in h. of blood 1096: 1
measures the h. of our livers 21: 9
mid-day h. 1475:14
my blood 38:3; 697: 8
neither h., affection 23:10
O h., dry up my brains ..1500: 4
of a luxurious bed 85: 1
of blood 112:12; 1756:10
of deeds 1726:11
of his displeasure 697: 8
of lust 1571: 9
of this descending sun 137:13
one h. another h. expels ..919: 6
outwardly, or breath within 308: 7
parching h. 328:16
Promethean h. 871: 2
rash false h. 927: 3
retort that h. again 761: 8
scorns the h. he feels 1713: 2
seven years' h. 404: 9
summer's parching h. 200: 4
summer's scalding h. 264: 6
sun's parching h. 1609:10
who struck this h. up 38: 3
your blood 112:12

Heat-oppressed brain 281: 1
Heath: blasted h. 772: 8
long h. 1325: 4
Heathen: art a h. 12:12
Heathenish: most h. 649: 4
Heating of the blood 112:12
of the oven 1128:12
Heaved thence 214: 6
to head 525:11
Heaved-up hand 789: 8

Heaven 697
afore H. 698: 1
alack, that h. should practise stratagems 699:11
all-seeing h., what a world 1732: 1
an 't please h. 698: 1
and earth 1257:17
and earth may strike 1572: 4
and fortune bar 577:17
and honour be witness 701:14
and yourself had part 700: 5
ascend to h. 700: 2
be judge 911: 4
be my judge 1748: 3
be my witness 1473:14
be the record 699: 8
bear witness 533: 5
before high h. 222:4; 904:6; 941: 8
below crisp h. 1056:15
bless thee 697:13
bound to h. in daily thanks 698:15
brightest h. of invention ..775: 9
by H. 698: 1
by h. and earth 700: 7
by yond marble h. 1614:13
can h. be so envious 699:11
come from h. 700:14
come to h. 700: 2
comfort her 699: 2
defend me 699: 4
defend me h. 539: 2
defend your good souls 150: 4
did h. look on 698:19
doth with us as we with torches do 698:20
dropp'd from h. 699:14
either in h. or hell 700:13
figures some event 1099: 7
fled to h. 700: 2
for h. or hell 1628: 3
forbid 699: 5
forgive him 572: 2
forgive him too 1481: 9
forgive my sins 1369:15
from h. banish'd 1562: 7
from h. to earth 266: 9
from h. to hell is flown away 678: 6
gentle h., pity 1156: 6
get you to h. 936: 1
give h. countless eyes 1182:11
give h. praise 1675: 4
give thee moving graces ...632:13
give your spirits comfort ..699: 2
gone to h. 300: 6
grant us its peace 1136: 3
guide thy pen 699:17
hail, thou fair h. 701: 4
has an end in all 698:12
hath a hand in these events 699:10
hath an end in all 241:13
hath infused them 698:17
hath my empty words 1187:16
hath pleased it so 1221: 4
have mercy on me 798:14
he is in h. 700: 4
help him 698: 5
I am in h. for him 698: 6
I 'll make my h. to dream ..701: 1
if h. will take the present at our hands 909: 5
in h. or in earth 700: 8
in h. or in hell 1031:11
in my mouth 744:11
in your cheek 82: 5
inlay h. with stars 1737:17
is above all 791: 5
is here, where Juliet lives ..698: 2
itself doth frown 698:18
itself for ornament doth use 1597: 3
keep me from such counsel 241:13
keep your honour 699:12
keeps his part in eternal life 700: 5
knows how dearly 288: 3
knows how I love you 907:10
knows your hearts 698:13
leave her to h. 1259:15
led on by h. 1608: 7
let h. kiss earth 700: 8
let h. revenge 699: 9
let h. see the pranks 1187: 1
live here in h. 698: 2
lock thy h. from thee 699:15
loved him next h. 906: 3

Heaven, *continued*
make a h. of hell 917:11
make dark h. light 1440:11
make h. drowsy with the harmony 894:14
make my h. in a lady's lap 1710: 1
make thee free of it 699: 4
may decrease it 906: 5
meet in h. 502: 6
mend all 698: 6
merciful H. 985:10; 1524: 6
my h. to dream 264: 5
my sole earth's h. 905: 4
nearer to h. than when I saw you last 650: 3
neither looks upon the h. nor earth 700:10
never hopes more h. 1414: 7
new h., new earth 904: 8
next my h. the best 135:13
nor h. nor earth at peace 1135: 8
nor of h. nor earth 1262: 5
now h. hath all 700: 5
now h. walks on earth 700:11
O h., O earth 910: 5
of her brow 449: 1
of his thought 698: 2
on earth 698: 2
one of you does not serve h. well 699: 3
pack'd with post-horse up to h. 700: 4
pardon him 1114:13
plainly as h. sees earth ..1365:16
praise h. for it 1184: 9
pray h. 1190: 6
preserve you 699: 4
prosper the right 1287: 5
rain grace 699: 4
rest them now 1272: 1
restore thee 699: 4
see what h. can do 699: 6
self-same h. that frowns ..701: 9
set ope thy everlasting gates 700: 2
shall be bribed 1497: 4
shall hear our prayers 1190: 6
shall we serve h. 699: 1
she 's not in h. 700: 1
shield your grace 1751:13
show his face 1757: 2
shun the h. that leads men 927: 7
smile, gentle h. 1732: 8
so defend thee h. 1420: 4
so he goes to h. 1277: 2
so help me H. 698: 5
so speed me 699: 3
spite of wreakful h. 260: 7
still guards the right 36:11
stops the nose at it 1453: 3
strike at h. with your staves 597:18
strong as h. itself 768:18
such grace did lend her 207:11
summons thee to h. or to hell 820: 9
sweet h. 931: 7
take my soul 120:13
thank h. 1509: 8
then h. mocks itself 468:14
they tempt h. 672: 1
thy h. is on earth 33: 4
'tis so set down in h. 700: 8
to earth 253: 1
to h. I do appeal 698:10
to kiss the turrets bow'd ..699: 7
to throne in 621: 7
touch h. 1550:15
trouble deaf h. with my bootless cries 1188:13
turn'd a h. unto a hell 899: 6
'twixt h. and earth 700:7; 1707:17
unfolds both h. and earth ..895: 5
until we meet in h. 1120: 1
use his h. for thunder 1525: 1
vaulty h. so high 838: 6
vouch with me, h. 699: 8
vow to h. 1614: 3
wash both h. and hell 620: 8
when h. doth weep 700: 9
when h. please 1165:15
will direct it 698: 7
wisheth you in h. 700:13
with lightning strike 397:13
withhold thine indignation, mighty h. 698:18
would in little show 698: 4

I

J

K

Kiss, *continued*
like native things 1054:15
long as my exile 811: 1
long may they k. 881:10
loving k. for k. 814:11
me hard 812: 6
me through the hole 812: 3
men will k. 813:10
murders with a k. 813: 9
not half a k. to choose 901: 2
on k. she vied so fast 1712: 3
one gentle k. the more 812:10
one k. shall stop our mouths 812: 9
one poor k. 881:10
one sweet k. 813: 9
ride 's with one soft k. ..1186: 4
rob thee of a k. 813:11
salute you with a k. 813: 5
seal with a righteous k. ..1120: 9
search it with a sovereign k. 811:15
single famish'd k. 813: 4
so sweet a k. 449: 1
steal a k. 1510: 5
steal a k. and die 882: 1
take this warm k. on thy pale cold lips 814:11
tender k. 881: 3
that k. is comfortless 813: 2
that k. which is my heaven 810:11
the book 1079:10
the rod 238:11
then come k. me, sweet and twenty 896: 1
this is a soldier's k. 810:11
this k., if it durst speak ..811:14
thus with a k. I die 812: 7
thy royal finger 814: 7
'tis but a k. I beg 813:10
to k. in private 812: 5
true love's k. 812:10
unauthorized k. 812: 5
witness the loving k. 811:10
you k. by the book 812:12
you shall have a k. 813:11
you take is better than you give 813: 5
you twenty with a breath ..811:11
Kissed thee ere I kill'd thee 812: 7
well k. 812: 5
Kisses: Cassio's k. 812: 5
doubled k. 810:10
gave me twenty k. 813: 2
his k. are Judas's children .811:10
I understand thy k. 811: 3
is twenty hundred k. such a trouble 813:10
many thousand k. 810:12
memorial dainty k. 1259:10
my k. bring again 812: 1
pair of reechy k. 806: 8
Phœbus' burning k. 183: 3
pluck'd up k. by the roots 812: 6
rain'd k. 810:11
smother thee with k. 813: 9
straight on k. dream 376: 3
tempting k. 811: 9
ten k. short as one 813: 9
thinking their own k. sin ..881: 3
thousand k. buys 813:10
twenty thousand k. 811: 8
were k. all the joys in bed 1697:11
Kissing: his k. is as full of sanctity 811:10
in k., do you render or receive 813: 5
in your arms 1625: 1
kindle with continual k. ..813:11
made for k. 880:18
quicken with k. 810:12
with golden face 1025:13
with inside lip 237: 3
with k. him I should have kill'd him 813:11
Kissing-comfits: hail k. 1375: 1
Kitchen-maid: her k. 1321: 6
Kitchen-malkin 1656: 5
Kitchen-trull 1656: 5
Kitchen-trulls: crack'd of k. 1152: 3
Kitchen-vestal scorn'd you 1321: 6
Kitchen-wench: but a k. ...1077: 2
Kitchened me for you 585:12
Kitchens: for our k. we kill the fowl 580: 8
Kite: hungry k. 394: 1
lazar k. 1661: 5

Kite, *continued*
soar with unbloodied beak ..428:18
when the k. builds 1554: 8
Kites and buzzards 394: 3
and ravens 62: 3
Kitten: be a k. and cry mew .64:15
Knack 613:6
a toy, a trick 158: 2
see this k. 614:10
Knacks: load my she with k. 613: 6
trifles, nosegays 613: 6
Knapped 'em o' the coxcombs 402: 8
ginger 629: 9
Knave 814
and fool 565: 7
at his service 1339: 7
base notorious k. 817: 2
beastly k. 1279:10
both k. and fool 1339: 7
calumnious k. 814:13
counterfeits well 245: 7
cowardly k. 816: 1
crafty k. does need no broker 816: 2
cuckoldy k. 816: 9
devilish k. 817: 2
doth court my love 254:10
drunken k. was the sea ..1324:10
false disloyal k. 817: 2
fantastical k. 1210: 9
first k. that madest a duke .816: 8
foolish prating k. 815: 5
foolish, rascally k. 814:13
foul-mouthed k. 814:13
gallant k. 600: 3
good k. and well fed 814:13
he 's an arrant k. 1602: 4
he 's but Fortune's k. 151: 7
is handsome, young 817: 2
jealous k. 816: 9
jealous rascally k. 742: 1
jealous wittolly k. 1180: 3
lousy k. 815:4; 815: 7
lunatic k. 925: 6
lyingest k. in Christendom 816: 3
mad k. 817: 5
make a k. of thee 513: 8
more k. than fool 565: 8
muddy k. 815: 6
naughty k. 1553:12
of common hire 651: 8
pestilent complete k. 817: 2
plain k. 816: 6
play the k. 1164: 5
played the k. with fortune 576: 5
prating k. 1187: 4
pretty k. 816: 5
scauld k. 815: 7
scurvy k. 815: 7
scurvy, lousy k. 400: 4
scurvy railing k. 1242: 2
shrewd k. and an unhappy 814:13
stubborn ancient k. 816: 6
thank God you are rid of a k. 817: 1
that mightily deceives 817: 6
thou 'rt a k. 814:13
'tis the base k. that jars ..817: 5
unthrifty k. 3: 3
untoward k. 1321:12
villanous k. 817: 2
what pestilent k. is this ..817: 4
where 's my k. 565: 8
yea-forsooth k. 1471:13
Knaveries: fery honest k. 1167: 9
full of k. 818: 2
make such k. yours 1: 1
Knavery 818
beads and all this k. 1276: 5
by my k. 815: 3
I see their k. 57: 4
Knaves: crafty k. 816: 2
drunken k. 385:11
false k. 817: 1
foul-mouthed k. 947: 9
half a score k. or so 817: 5
lazy k. 816: 4
lying k. 816: 3
misbegotten k. 815: 6
sweet k. 254: 2
that smell of sweat 385: 7
these kind of k. I know ..744: 7
untaught k., unmannerly ..118:13
verier k. desire to live 816: 7
whip me such honest k. ...817: 2
you serve k. 43: 7

Knead: I will k. him 1522: 2
Kneaded clod 304: 9
Kneading of the cake 1491:19
up the honey 86: 9
Knee 818
beggar's k. 818:14
bend my k. 818:16
bend my k. with thine 1614: 3
bended k. 818:16
bow a k. to man 819:13
bow my k. before his majesty 1415:11
danced thee on his k. 634:13
debase your princely k. ...819: 6
drops down the k. 819: 8
fair knighthood's bending k. 818:16
hath thy k. forgot to bow 818:16
he should bow his k. 803: 5
hinge thy k. 818:11
humbly bend thy k. 733: 9
humbly on thy k. 733: 9
in duty bend thy k. 25:15
most humbly on my k. 847: 2
my k., made hard 819: 1
my k. shall bow 818: 8
no bending k. will call thee Cæsar now 153: 3
sawest thine own k. 818:13
sink, my k., i' the earth 392: 4
stiff unbowed k. 38: 9
the way into his mercy 733: 7
upon my bended k. 733: 9
upon my feeble k. 127: 6
will you not lend a k. 819: 3
with his k. the door he opens 373: 1
Knee-crooking knave 817: 2
Knee-deep: inch-thick, k. ...682: 2
Kneel before him 820: 2
bootless k. 820: 1
do yet but k. by me 820: 3
down, k. down 819:14
for grace 819:13; 1558:13
for grace and mercy 1415: 9
to him with thanks 819:11
we must longer k. 1464: 1
wilt thou k. with me 820: 5
yet she 'll k. and pray 1660: 6
you shall not k. 819:11
Kneeled: would you had k. 819:10
Kneeling 819
at our feet 819:10
Knees: arm'd k. 818: 9
bow, stubborn k. 818:12
courtiers' k. 819: 5
down on thy k. 1509: 8
down on your k., and thank heaven fasting 896: 6
down upon her k. she falls 1650:13
for ever may my k. grow to the earth 819: 6
for ever will I walk upon my k. 789: 9
go to your k. 819: 2
his k. knocking each other 522: 9
humbled on your k. 1115: 6
lend me your k. 819: 3
let her have your k. 106: 3
my k. grow to the earth ..1114:14
of knotted oaks 1678: 8
oftener upon her k. 819: 1
on his k. at meditation ..1203: 3
on my k. 818:15
on their k. and hands 590: 6
on your k. for pardon 1115: 2
our k. shall kneel 819: 6
raise me from my k. 1576:12
shame him with our k. 818: 9
supple k. feed arrogance ...819: 5
upon her k. she falls 467: 2
with his k. he kiss'd the Cretan strand 734: 3
yield upon my k. 1753:16
your k. to me 392: 4
Knell 820
hear his k. rung out 793: 2
his k. is knoll'd 1399: 1
ring fancy's k. 501: 2
rings doleful k. 93:14
rings out the doleful k. ..1408:10
Knew: an you k. how 827: 9
before I k. thee, I k. nothing 826: 9
but what you are 827: 8
I k. not what I did 1114: 6
I would I k. 825:10
would I k. thy heart 688:13

Leisure, *continued*
stay your l. ... 851:14
to make good ... 378: 9
to make love ... 851:13
to repent ... 851:13
wait for no man's l. ... 155: 9
your l. serves you not ... 851:17
Leisurely: do it l. ... 315: 5
so l. ... 1758: 8
Leisures: we 'll make our l. to attend on yours ... 851:14
Leman: drink unto the l. mine ... 1680: 1
his wife's l. ... 781: 2
sixpence for thy l. ... 613: 2
Lemon ... 612: 7
Lend aid ... 27:10
I will not l. thee a penny . 1139:12
I 'll l. you something ... 852: 9
less than thou owest ... 90: 8
let him l. me the money ... 22: 4
me arms and aid ... 1082:14
neither l. nor borrow ... 127:11
nothing for God's sake ... 127:12
to each man enough ... 127:14
Lender ... 852:6
neither borrower nor l. be . 127:10
Lending ... 852
borrowing and l. ... 127:10
me this acquaintance ... 8: 2
Lendings: in name of l. ... 852: 7
off, off, you l. ... 380: 3
Lends: she l. to those are free ... 1056:13
Length: all l. is torture ... 1549: 9
and breadth of a pair ... 1472: 3
and breadth of mine ... 1695: 9
such l. in grief ... 1408:14
sword's l. ... 1481: 9
whole head's l. ... 684: 5
Lengthening my return ... 1715: 1
Lengths: large l. of miles .. 1517: 9
of seas and shores ... 69:14
Lenity ... 984:12
away to heaven, respective l. 597:10
this too much l. must be laid aside ... 1156: 5
use l., sweet chuck ... 1236: 9
Lent shall be as long again . 1280:14
Lenten entertainment ... 43:10
good l. answer ... 43:10
Lenten-pie ... 43:10
Leo-natus ... 1045: 8
Leonati ... 1451: 6
Leonatus ... 706:14
Leper: I am no loathsome l. 455:15
Leperous distilment ... 1173:12
Leprosy: general l. ... 278: 8
make hoar l. adored ... 624:17
no l. thou speak'st ... 278: 8
whom l. o'ertake ... 551: 4
Less: by hoping more, have l. ... 255: 4
greater hides the l. ... 641:13
ne'er the l. ... 910: 4
no l. than fame bruited ... 470: 3
no l. than I seem ... 1330: 5
than I was born to ... 803: 6
Lesser is my fear ... 520:10
than my name ... 640: 7
Lesson ... 1495:4
find the l. true ... 975: 6
is but plain ... 903: 4
learn any hard l. ... 908: 3
learn this l. ... 1483: 5
where 's your l., then ... 1315: 4
Lessoned: as you were l. .. 1495: 4
us to weep ... 1651: 2
well has he l. us ... 1495: 4
Lessons: I 'll learn my l. .. 1166: 5
Let ... 486:5; 486:6
ah, l. be, l. be ... 486: 6
Let-alone lies not in your good will ... 486: 5
Lethargied: discernings l. .. 745:13
Lethargy ... 352:12
Lethe ... 570:10
crimson'd in thy l. ... 1036: 7
let fancy still my sense in L. steep ... 377: 3
of the angry soul ... 1749: 4
soft and delicate L. ... 1679:10
wash'd in L. ... 1633:11
Lethe'd dulness ... 47: 1
Lets: these l. attend time .. 1255:18

Letter ... 852
after l., gift after gift ... 1710: 7
bear a l. to him ... 723: 6
blot the l. with words ... 1726:14
for l. ... 854: 2
from your friends ... 855: 4
given you a l. ... 855: 4
her l. now is seal'd ... 854: 6
here 's your l. ... 852:12
humoured l. ... 854: 1
I 'll write a very taunting l. 852:11
if this l. move him not ... 855: 1
is too long by half a mile . 853: 9
my golden l. ... 201: 6
of the oracle ... 1103:16
of your own device ... 852:12
read in the bitter l. ... 844: 2
shall have a rare l. ... 854:13
steep this l. in sack ... 853: 4
thou unnecessary l. ... 853: 7
what l. are you reading ... 855: 3
your l. is with Jupiter ... 854: 9
Lettered: are you not l. ... 849: 4
Letters came last night ... 1526:11
forged l. ... 683: 4
full of love ... 853:10
golden l. ... 295:11
know the l. ... 1245: 8
of commendations ... 206:16
of commission ... 208: 4
of good credit ... 260:15
sadly penn'd in blood ... 853:13
should not be known ... 209: 7
these l. come from your father ... 1360: 3
thy l. may be here ... 855: 5
Letters-patent: tied it by l. . 854: 7
Lettuce: sow l. ... 1673:17
Level as the cannon ... 1375:11
at my abuses ... 4:11
at the edge of a penknife . 1512: 7
deadly l. of a gun ... 1049: 1
nothing l. in our natures . 1601:13
now with men ... 21: 4
of mine aim ... 28: 3
of your frown ... 595: 1
to your judgement ... 792: 8
Levelled at our purposes .. 1639: 9
false ... 28:10
'Leven-pence farthing ... 1281: 6
Levers to lift me up ... 395: 3
Leviathan: ere l. can swim . 675: 3
send precepts to the l. ... 1393: 6
Leviathans: huge l. ... 1039:12
Levity ... 855
hide their l. ... 782: 4
more l. to lechery ... 849:11
traduced for l. ... 1375: 5
what l. 's in youth ... 1758:14
Levy ... 1494:2
foreign l. ... 302: 9
Lewd ... 855:14
'tis l. and filthy ... 158: 2
you have been so l. ... 855:11
Lewd-tongued wife ... 1664:10
Lewdly: be l. given ... 945:13
bent ... 855:11
Lewdly-inclined ... 855:11
Lewdness ... 855
though l. court it ... 926: 4
Lewdsters: such l. ... 855:13
Liable: apt, l. to be employ'd 285: 9
Liar ... 860
and slave ... 1708: 3
common l. ... 477: 5
infinite and endless l. ... 173:12
measureless l. ... 691: 2
turn'd the greatest l. ... 1392: 2
Liars and adulterers ... 860:12
and swearers are fools ... 666: 7
be burnt for l. ... 707: 7
there be l. ... 1213:11
you 're l. all ... 860:14
Libbard's head on knee ... 682: 4
Libelling against the senate 765: 6
Libels and dreams ... 1168:16
Liberal: be most l. ... 856: 2
become as l. as you ... 1289: 7
been l. and free ... 1624:11
full of spirit ... 856: 1
of your loves ... 241:13
she is too l. ... 1624:11
something too l. ... 1117: 9
to mine own children ... 856: 5
you are l. in offers ... 1289: 7

Liberality ... 856
fair looks and l. ... 254:11
virtue, youth, l. ... 942: 1
Liberté: la l. ... 856:15
Liberties: lose your l. ... 856:14
such-like l. of sin ... 933: 1
take their l. ... 856:14
Libertine ... 856
charter'd l. ... 1422: 8
tie up the l. ... 1624: 3
Libertines: none but l. ... 856: 9
Liberty ... 856
at l. ... 857: 3
bid us ask his l. ... 1463: 3
delivered him to his l. ... 856:17
freedom, and enfranchisement ... 857: 2
gain your l. ... 856:17
gain'd thy daughter princely l. ... 288: 1
gave their country l. ... 857: 2
give thee thy l. ... 856:17
go we in content to l. ... 856:12
he brings me l. ... 856:17
headstrong l. is lash'd with woe ... 856:13
I must have l. withal ... 856:12
is all that I request ... 857: 7
loss of l. ... 893:13
lost my l. ... 856:14
ne'er look on l. ... 442: 3
of bloody hand ... 1393: 6
of flight ... 551: 8
of gazing ... 856:17
of the prison ... 856:17
plucks justice by the nose . 857: 4
put me into everlasting l. .. 857: 5
this l. is all I request ... 1711:12
to venge this wrong ... 1277: 5
turn'd my captive state to l. 856:17
why should their l. than ours be more ... 150: 2
Library ... 126:15
License ... 857
of free foot ... 429: 3
of ink ... 765:10
such full l. ... 516: 7
Licentious ... 855:10
Licking of his wound ... 1742: 4
Lid: by God's l. ... 687: 3
Lids of Juno's eyes ... 555: 5
vailed l. ... 507:14
Lie ... 857
add a l. unto a fault ... 1289: 7
and cog and flout ... 132: 8
and do no harm ... 858: 2
by an emperor's side ... 1660: 6
Circumstantial ... 857:16
devise some virtuous l. ... 858: 1
Direct ... 857:16
either we or they must lower l. ... 836: 2
fain learn to l. ... 859: 2
falsely doth he l. ... 858:10
full low ... 302:10
give me the l. ... 608: 5
give me the l. another time 860: 5
give the l. ... 860: 3
give the l. to their consciences ... 1700:11
gives me the l. ... 256: 1
giving him the l. ... 386: 6
giving itself the l. ... 939: 7
I aim to l. with thee ... 920: 6
I l. with her and she with me ... 912:11
I love to hear him l. ... 859: 5
I will l. for you ... 859:12
I will not l. to you ... 859: 7
i' the throat ... 860: 4
in your throat ... 860: 7
may do thee grace ... 858: 6
nay, then you l. ... 1468: 3
odious, damned l. ... 859: 9
on her ... 859:13
rather l. in prison ... 1329:13
requited him for his l. ... 386: 6
seven times removed ... 857:16
shall I tell you a l. ... 859: 7
something given to l. ... 1734: 5
swallow down that l. ... 859:10
tell a monstrous l. ... 859:14
tells a l. and swears it ... 857:11
that l. shall l. so heavy ... 859:11
there you l. ... 301:11

Lie, *continued*
therefore I 'll l. with him .963: 5
they l. deadly 458: 3
thou dost l. in 't 858: 4
'tis a quick l. 858: 4
upon my soul, a l., wicked l. 859: 9
will poor folks l. 858: 2
with a slight oath 783: 2
with her or on her 859:13
you told a l.; an odious, damned l. 859: 9
you 'll l. like dogs 859:14
Lie-giver: thou the l. 859:11
Lief: as l. have been myself 210: 8
I had as l. 486: 7
had as l. not be 866: 5
I had as l. be wooed 1709: 8
Liefest: my l. liege 413: 2
Liege: most loving l. 1752:13
my liefest l. 413: 2
of all loiterers 271: 8
sovereign l. 309:14
Lies: as cheap as l. 1282:13
by l. we flatter'd be 912:11
disdain'd in the reporting ..708: 1
forged l. 857:11
he l., and l., and l. 859:11
he l. to the heart 859: 9
incomprehensible l. 858: 5
one that l. three thirds ...1556: 6
puny l. I 'll tell 859: 6
swear the l. he forges 857:11
tell quaint l. 921:11
telling her fantastical l. ...116: 9
these l. are like their father 858: 5
though I know she l. 859:13
told thee no l. 1341: 9
two or three probable l. 775: 6
villain-like he l. 859: 3
wanton l. 860: 1
well steel'd 859:12
what l. I have heard 858: 2
why should I carry l. 860: 2
Liest: thou l. 858:7; 858: 8
Lieu: in l. thereof 486: 8
in l. whereof 486: 8
Lieutenancy 1396:3
Lieutenant 1396
good l. 1395:12
Life 860
abridge thy l. 867:20
all my l. to come 751:19
all that l. can rate 865:14
and being 35: 8
and liberty 861:17
answer my l. my judgement 793: 4
answer with my l. 1275: 2
as if his l. lay on 't 1145:13
austere insociable l. 865: 6
bad l. reft me 1:12
baser l. 404: 2
bear a charmed l. 861:15
being weary of these bars 1461: 3
better l., past fearing death 868:19
borne l. away 868:11
breathe l. into a stone 973:13
breathed such l. with kisses 812:12
brittle l. 1265:18
by my l. 862:10
by my l., my troth 1081: 4
chaste l. 181:11
come to l. 476:17
consist of the four elements 861: 1
cost thy l. 239:11
dare my l. lay down 1233: 1
dead l., poor mortal ghost..611: 4
dear l. 864: 3
defend my innocent l. 865: 4
deprived him of his l. 867: 9
detested l. 1741:15
dispatch his nighted l. 866: 7
end a hapless l. 867:19
end l. when I end loyalty .923: 9
end my l. to-day 868: 1
eternal l. 861:14
even as my l. my blood ...909: 3
every man holds dear 715:12
evil l. 865: 9
expect victorious l. 868: 4
farewell l. with thee 1119:15
feed on l. 528: 2
feverous l. entertain 868:19
fie upon this quiet l. 117: 7
for further l. I ne'er hope ..867:12
for l., I prize it 867: 5

Life, *continued*
for l. or death 870: 3
for my l. 862:10
for your l. you durst not .1504:16
full of l. 751: 2
gasping for l. 1428: 6
gave thee l. too soon 132: 1
give over this l. 1254:14
give them l. 1354: 1
given me l. and living 861:17
God lend my l. 864:12
God save your l. 861: 2
good l. 865: 8
hapless l. 924: 7
haply this l. is best 866:12
happy l. 865:16
hateful l. 865:10
hazard l. 862:14
hazard l. for ill 1749:10
hazard thy l. for dinner 76: 4
hear me breathe my l. 862: 7
Hector's l. is done 868: 2
her l. is only safest 99: 3
here my l. must end 867:11
his l. was gentle 946: 6
hold l. at any price 390: 2
how long fairly shall her sweet l. last 867:21
I bear a charmed l. 179: 5
I cannot tell what you think of this l. 866: 5
I care not for good l. 1405:11
I did give that l. 867:19
I do engage my l. 1574:17
I do not set my l. at a pin's fee 867: 1
I gave thee l. 1267: 9
I hold my l. as dear 864:12
I know my l. so even 866:13
I love long l. better than figs 864: 6
I shall have such a l. 1013: 3
I 'll amend my l. 982: 6
I 'll lay my l. 1471:10
if of l. you keep a care 864:13
immortal l. 861:14
in death 868:13
in l. but double death 868:13
in my l. what comfort 740: 7
in print o' l. 65: 1
in this l. lie hid moe thousand deaths 868:19
is a shuttle 860:17
is alter'd now 170:14
is as tedious as a twice-told tale 866: 6
is but a span 1394:10
is but a walking shadow ..860:16
it is a l. in death 922: 5
jump the l. to come 1274: 8
keep base l. afoot 1342:10
lead a private l. 340: 3
lead an upright l. 865: 6
let l. be short 1346: 1
let my old l. be sacrificed ..844: 8
like l. in excrements 655: 6
live a second l. on second head 656:15
lived in death 869: 3
long l. 864: 6
long weary l. 727: 6
longer l. and able means ..867:12
looks through 999: 8
lose his l. 862:16
loss of l. 893:13
lost his l. 863: 1
make a l. of jealousy 781: 8
make away my guiltless l. .863:12
man's l. as cheap as beast's 861:12
man's l. is a tedious one ...866: 6
man's l. is no more than to say 'One' 864:15
married l. 862: 4
mild may be thy l. 993: 6
monstrous l. 307: 1
my l., be thine 604:11
my l. I never held 867: 3
my l., in any case 864: 5
my l. is my foe's debt 862: 2
my l. is run his compass ...867:13
my l. is spann'd 864:14
my l. is yours 862: 8
my l., my joy, my food .1402: 7
my l. shall prove it true ..1425: 8
my l. sinks down to death ..980: 4

Life, *continued*
my l. stands in the level ..867: 5
my l. thou shalt command 1347:11
my l. upon her faith 464: 6
my l. upon 't 862: 9
my l. were better ended ...915: 6
my only l. 188: 4
my poor l. must answer ...861:19
no certain l. achieved 868:16
no l. to ours 865:15
no longer than thy love ...862: 6
noble l. before a long 861: 2
not for my l. 862:10
not l., but love in death ..922: 2
nothing in his l. became him like the leaving it .306: 8
nurse the l. with honour ...28:12
o' the building 1038: 5
o' the need 255:11
'od's my little l. 1085: 2
of majesty 1713: 3
of our design 1211:16
of passion 865:11
of purity 865: 6
on my l. 862:10
on wholesome l. usurp ...1173:13
our little l. is rounded with a sleep 865: 2
pardon thee thy l. 1114: 4
pass upon his l. 1181: 8
pawn down my l. 862: 9
pay thy l. thou owest me ..862:15
practised on man's l. 1183: 4
preferr'st l. before honour ..714: 2
preserved with infamy 1026: 4
prolong the traitor's l. ...1561: 6
promise of his l. 1213: 8
prosperous be thy l. 718: 7
prosperous l., long 866: 1
put on a religious l. 1256: 4
reason thus with l. 868:19
receiving a dishonour'd l. .1757: 8
reclusive and religious l. ..866:14
remember your bold l. ...1258: 7
resign thy l. 867:20
safeguard thine own l. ...1312: 9
save a paltry l. 470: 5
save his l. 863:2; 863: 3
save my l. 863:4; 863: 5
save this bastard's l. 863: 6
save your l. 1754: 6
see the l. as lively mock'd 1442:10
seek your l. 863:13
sell every man his l. as dear as mine 861: 5
sell his sovereign's l. 1557:14
set my l. on any chance ..1006: 9
set my l. upon a cast 679:12
shamed l. a hateful 868:19
shamed l. in his dishonour .715: 4
shamefully bereft of l. 867: 9
she render'd l. 1045: 2
shepherd's l. 866:11
shorten Harry's happy l. ..861: 6
shorten thy l. one week ...667: 9
shortens not his own l. 387: 6
single l. 862: 4
sought my l. 1326: 2
stretch'd-out l. 22:11
strike at thy l. 863:14
such a l. were strange 862: 4
sweat under weary l. 866: 4
sweet l. 861:7; 1614: 7
take away a l. true made ..867:17
take away her l. 864: 2
take l. from thine own sister's shame 1373: 1
take my l. 864: 3
tender l. 1461:10
that I have desired 864: 9
that late I led 862: 3
that l. was mine 867:19
there 's l. in 't 861:13
this gives l. to thee 1171: 7
this l. is most jolly 787: 5
this l. is nobler 865:15
thy l. and wits at once ...867:15
thy l. is dear 865:14
thy l. to me is sweet 306: 2
thy l. 's a miracle 1001:12
'tide l., 'tide death 977:15
time's fool 1514: 6
'tis a l.; you coin'd it 864: 3
'tis the soldiers' l. 1394:11
to come 751:19; 861:14

Lord, *continued*
merry mocking l. 890: 6
mongrel beef-witted l. 891: 7
my bosom's l. sits lightly .. 690: 7
my dear l. is he 966: 8
my l. and husband 1667: 3
my l. and lady 891:15
my l. and master 965: 6
my l. and sovereign 890: 1
my l. is not my l. 890: 9
my l. shall never rest 890: 9
my l. the king 890: 1
no l. of thine 891: 2
O L. 892:5; 1657: 1
o' the feast 736:14
of folded arms 271: 8
of his fortunes 889: 3
of his reason 889: 3
of hosts 71: 1
of my life 534: 4
of my love, to whom 393: 6
of such a spirit 889: 3
of the soil 889: 3
of the whole world 1729: 7
of this fair mansion 1178: 9
of thy presence 836: 6
of Trojan blood 889: 7
of weak remembrance 891: 5
old l. 890: 4
praise the L. 1184: 9
praise the L. for you 1508:12
precedent l. 1381: 3
preserve thy good grace ... 892: 5
protect him 889:9; 892: 5
proud l. 891: 8
return, thou wandering l. .. 889:10
right valiant l. 889: 6
Roman l. 1300: 3
Rome's imperial l. 1195: 5
scurvy, old, filthy, scurvy l. 888:14
see the l. the prologue ... 891:10
sensible l. 1334: 5
sodden-witted l. 891: 7
sweet l. 890: 9
take him for thy l. 891:12
this is a l. 889: 5
thou art a l. 891:17
thrice-gracious l. 1231: 4
thrice-noble l. 1667: 3
unworthy and unnatural l. . 888:14
warrant us 892: 5
wedded l. 1664: 9
who is thy l. 891:15
worship me their l. 1735:13
worthy l. of unworthy wife 891: 1
you are l. of duty 509: 9
Lord-protectorship 874: 7
Lordliness: honour of thy l. 977: 3
Lordling's daughter 290: 1
Lordlings, farewell 1215: 6
Lordly **889:9**
Lords: ancient l. 1626: 7
are you l. o' the field 534: 7
four of their l. I 'll change 889: 7
Got's l. and his ladies 891:13
I eat not l. 892: 1
o'er their l. 1665: 9
of the wide world 953: 8
officious l. 973:12
revelling like l. 1275:12
Lordship: his l. 890: 2
his l. knows me well 534: 2
Lorenzo swear he loved 1067: 4
Lose: I will go l. myself .. 1622: 7
itself in a fog 557:14
nothing by custom 280: 9
they l. it that do buy it .. 1730:12
thou art sure to l. 600: 5
thou shalt l. nothing 525: 6
we l. it not, so long as we
can smile 1388:12
what have we to l. 864: 3
Loser **892:11**
winner and l. 1682:12
Losers: thus l. part 892:11
will have leave 892:11
with the l. sympathise ... 1681:16
Loses: who l. and who wins 894: 7
Losing of our prayers 1187:10
of this day 292: 9
Loss **892**
all this l. of blood 115:12
assured l. 894: 6
exposed to l. 517: 3
great l. 892:10

Loss, *continued*
her maiden l. 1347: 3
history his l. 1258: 3
hour's poor l. 727: 9
I have still the l. 1348: 6
in love that touches me 646: 6
insupportable and touching l. 893: 1
light l. of England 342: 1
make not your l. your sport 892: 9
my l. is my love's gain 893: 9
no l. is known to me 892:10
no l. shall touch her 996:10
of a leg 1628:10
of liberty 856:14
of maidenhead 938: 1
of such a lord 672: 4
of those great towns 298:13
of time 1536: 6
of virginity is rational .. 1605: 3
of what is past 1423:17
our hap is l. 669: 1
recover all our l. 1253: 2
repent the l. 1261:10
so dear a l. 893: 7
so great and little l. 70:14
stand in assured l. 323: 7
upon l. 893: 4
what l. is it to be rid
of care 160: 6
what l. your honour may
sustain 180: 9
with store 1533: 7
worst is worldly l. 893: 6
your l. is as yourself 892:10
your l. is great 892: 9
your so infinite l. 1681:14
Losses: all l. are restored .. 588: 1
give l. their remedies 893: 2
wailing our l. 1698:10
we have borne 1239: 9
Lost a dearer thing than
life 181: 7
all is l. 95:12
all together l. 601: 6
and recover'd in a day ... 1253: 2
by lack of stooping 1197: 3
recover what was l. 1570: 6
sooner l. and worn 501: 7
Lot: paid me scot and l. 245: 1
Lots: draw l. 601:1; 736:10
it is l. to blanks 1051: 3
Lottery **601:7**
blessed l. to him 1208: 1
mend the l. well 1700: 9
of my destiny 1666: 1
Loud: as l. as thunder 1509: 8
so l. and so melancholy ... 980: 1
speak l. 1423:12
speak not so l. 1423:12
yet was never l. 177: 8
Loud-howling wolves 1696:13
Lour: frown and l. 594:18
Lourest: if thou l. on me .. 595: 1
Lours and frets 1348:12
Louses: dozen white l. 198:10
Lousy: he is l. 815: 7
Lout: gross l. 678:11
so vile a l. as he 917: 8
sweet l. 257:10
yond foolish l. 1574:13
Louvre: never see the L. .. 1556: 7
Love **894**
adds a precious seeing 449:10
admits no qualifying dross 646:11
all in l. forlorn 1492: 1
all my fond l. thus do I
blow to heaven 919: 3
all our l. is lost 922: 2
all that l. is gone 903:11
alters not with his brief
hours and weeks 902:11
ambitious l. hath so 918: 8
ambitious sought a match . 906: 4
an you l. me 897: 9
and am beloved 902: 7
and amity 33:13
and be silent 913:10
and honour thee 715:11
and meekness 1199:11
and quiet life 1136:16
are we not all in l. 907: 3
as much l. in rhyme 900: 7
bade me swear 913: 2
beat l. down 76: 9

Love, *continued*
because I l. him, I must pity 916: 6
belike you thought our l.
would last too long 918:10
bestow your l. upon a
stranger 1449:10
between them like the palm
might flourish 901: 6
blunt not his l. 917: 6
boy L. is perjured 271:11
boy's l. 1574: 8
breaks through and picks
them all at last 80: 3
but l., first learned 894:14
by heart you l. her 693:11
by heaven, I do l. 900: 7
by looks reviveth 887: 4
by l. that thunders 518: 1
call me but l., and I 'll be
new baptized 1048: 7
can comment upon every
woe 896: 4
can you l. the gentleman .. 906: 5
can you l. this lady 906: 5
carry half my l. 962: 6
cast my l. on him 914: 2
chameleon L. can feed on
air 561: 2
choice l. of Signior Gremio . 910: 4
choose l. by another's eyes 895: 5
come in perfect l. 909: 5
comely l. 1371: 7
comforteth like sunshine .. 921: 7
contemned l. 920: 1
cools, friendship falls off . 1099:11
counsel me to fall in l. 897:16
course of true l. never did
run smooth 895: 5
cunning l. 903: 9
dead l. 919: 6
dear l. 909: 7
death-marked l. 1122: 8
delights in praises 896: 3
deny that thou bear'st l. .. 1332:12
deserve my l. by loving ... 898: 1
desire all good men's l. 414: 5
distempering gentle L. 782: 2
do it for ancient l. 899:12
doth approach disguised .. 895: 1
doth l. on fortune tend 903: 8
doth to her eyes repair 450: 3
dress'd him with our l. ... 403:16
due to l. as thoughts 895: 5
dying l. lives still 899:13
embrace each other's l. ... 66: 7
entertain my l. 260: 3
entertainest my l. 1388:18
erring l. 920: 1
eternal l. in l.'s fresh case . 902:11
even of pure l. 1130: 2
everlasting l. 34: 1
extremity of l. 439: 2
fair l. 902: 1
fall deep in l. 575:14
fall in l. 467:5; 897:16
fall in l. with what she
fear'd 915: 2
fallen in l. with your foulness 579: 5
falling in l. 897:16
false l. 904: 2
father's l. is enough 507:10
first best l. 902: 1
for l. allow 904: 3
for l. of God 896: 5
for the l. of God 620:13
for the l. of laughter 896: 5
for the l. of L. 150: 1
for the l. of mockery 1089: 4
for thy l. 1753:16
forswore me 917: 7
free l. 920: 1
from my heart's l. 909: 6
get thee to thy l. 921: 1
give me l. 907: 6
give me strength 1452: 7
goes toward l. 895: 6
got so sweet 1713: 4
grant I may ever l. 1712: 4
great l. 902: 1
great l., sharp as his spur . 724: 7
groans for l. 648: 6
hath chased sleep 896: 3
hath l. in thy old blood no
living fire 918: 2

M

Man, *continued*
whom both waters and wind
have made the ball 952: 8
whom fortune hath cruelly
scratched 576: 5
whoremaster m. 1439:13
whoreson round m. 512:12
whose blood is warm 951: 3
why should a m. be proud 1198:15
wise m. 943:11; 1684:16
wise m. and a fool 199:10
wise m. knows himself fool 566: 1
wiser m. 943:11
wish'd myself a m. 954: 7
woeful m. 892: 3
wofull'st m. 1696: 7
woman's m. 953: 9
worse m. 945: 8
worthy m. 1737:14
would any m. have thought 1516: 4
wretched m. 508:9; 1744: 4
wretched ragged m. 952: 2
yond m. is ever angry 39: 7
you are a merry m. 987:12
you are a tame m. 1490:17
you are the wiser m. 1547: 3
you were the very m. 245: 4
you 'll be the m. 476:13
you 're a made old m. 626: 2
your 're an odd m. 967: 4
young m. 952:12; 1755:13
young m. married is a m.
that 's marr'd 958: 6
Man-at-arms 951:1
maidenly m. 1393: 2
Man-child: he was a m. 942:10
Man-entered thus 650: 2
Man-monster: my m. 1310: 3
Man-of-war unsearch'd ...1354: 4
Man-queller and a woman-
queller 1298: 3
Manacle of love 1205:14
thy neck 1521:12
Manacles 1205:14
of the all-building law 843: 7
put you in m. 1246:10
Manage: expedient m. must
be made 852: 3
of two kingdoms 1628: 3
spur 'em till they obey m. 724: 5
sufficiently m. 1419: 8
taught their m. 721: 7
unlucky m. 924: 8
wanting his m. 149:13
work her to your m. 1107:14
Manager: usual m. of mirth 1003:11
your m. is in love 906: 8
Managing of quarrels 1229: 3
Manakin: dear m. to you ..945: 8
Mandate for the state-af-
fairs 1441:14
Mandragora 1385:15
Mandrake: whores called
him a m. 174: 5
whoreson m. 131: 9
Mane: high and monstrous
m. 1637:16
thin m. 723: 8
Manes: ad m. fratrum 1206:13
per m. vehor 1206:13
Manfully: slew him m. in
fight 799: 6
Mangling by starts 1447:10
reprehends her m. eye 449: 5
Mangy: issue of a m. dog ..278: 8
Manhood 944:5
as m. shall compound 389: 9
gives m. more approbation 1475: 2
if m. be not forgot 953: 4
is melted into courtesies ...954: 7
much against my m. 1170:17
shake my m. thus 868:17
Manhoods: hold their m.
cheap 616: 7
saving your m. 944: 5
Manifoldly dissuade me ...1597: 7
Mankind: destruction fang
m. 335:11
fain would I have hated all
m. 276: 7
flinty m. 1651: 9
how beauteous m. is 944:18
rails against married m. ..1237:12
Manlike: not more m. than
Cleopatra 1275: 4

Manly: be m. 290: 3
Manna: drop m. in the way 560: 3
Manned, horsed, and wived 1664:10
Manner: as the m. of our
country is 280: 3
cunning m. of our flight ..552:10
hideous and dreadful m. ..338: 6
in the roundest m. 42: 3
in this m. accused 7: 1
of a man 954: 3
of his gait 312: 8
of his speech 968: 3
of these world's delights ..648:12
of your garments 602:13
pretty and sweet m. 1637: 9
such disdainful m. 1711: 3
to the m. born 280: 3
what m. of man 945:13
what m. of man is he 942:16
Mannered as she is born ...759: 8
he is one the truest m. 172:10
Mannerly 956:6
Mannerly-modest 1647:15
Manners 954
blame us not 1638: 4
country m. give our betters
way 955:11
dishonest m. of their life ..609:12
excuse my m. 955:13
extend my m. 955:13
external m. of laments 646: 2
forget a lady's m. 955: 4
frame your m. to the time .956: 2
good m. 955: 1
good m. at the court 250:11
good m. be your speed ...1429:14
good m. shall lie all 955: 1
I 'll corrupt her m. 290: 4
judge by m. 287: 3
lavish m. 955: 1
lent a man any m. 250:11
men's evil m. live in brass .955:10
more than m. will 211: 2
never sawest good m. 250:11
no m. left among maids ...956: 7
of my mother 1501: 4
of the town 955: 3
plausive m. 955: 1
public m. 956: 1
she says that I lack m. 955: 2
stand upon our m. 956: 7
their m. are so apish 566: 5
their m. more gentle-kind .956: 3
thou dost affect my m. 956: 4
thy m. must be wicked 250:11
use your m. discreetly ...956: 2
what m. is in this 637:13
where m., ne'er were
preach'd 1743:16
Manning-tree ox 174: 5
Mannish cowards 44: 7
got the m. crack 1610:13
impudent and m. 954:12
Manor of Pickt-hatch 766: 7
sold a goodly m. for a song 978: 6
Manors: laying m. on 'em ..63: 2
my m. that I had 1178: 4
Mansion 956
bought the m. of a love ...910: 1
everlasting m. 638: 3
for him, a court 1512: 7
her m. batter'd 956: 8
innocent m. of my love 691: 3
sack the hateful m. 1049: 1
so long tenantless 3:10
what a m. have those vices
got 46: 4
Mansionry: loved m. 98: 1
Manslaughter: bring m.
into form 1230: 2
Mantle: in russet m. clad .1024: 5
night's black m. 1065: 6
of the standing pool 1636: 9
pitchy m. 291: 7
Mantled in your own 838: 8
Manure the ground 9:12
Manured, husbanded 1309: 5
with industry 1673:17
Manus: strangle serpents in
his m. 706:10
Many: mutable, rank-
scented m. 1034:10
O thou fond m. 47:11
Many-coloured messenger ..990:13
Many-headed multitude ...1034:13

Map 956
I see, as in a m. 410:11
of days outworn 183:13
of death 869: 3
of honour, truth 457: 8
of woe 1696: 7
which deep impression 459: 6
Mapped it truly 1158: 6
Mappery, closet-war 999:14
Maps of the 'orld 956:12
peering in m. for ports ...956:13
Mar: make and m. 11: 1
oft we m. what 's well 487:11
that which God made 746:11
what m. you then 487:12
Marble to her tears 1497:11
turn to m. 1582:14
wear with raining 1498: 1
Marble-breasted tyrant ...1583:13
Marble-constant: I am m. .231: 3
Marble-hearted fiend 762: 1
Marbled mansion 956: 9
March: ides of M. ..31:6; 1631:10
is wasted fourteen days ..1020: 9
remember M. 1020: 9
March: expedient m. 436:10
must we all m. 1393: 8
step after a stranger m. ...346: 2
strike a free m. to Troy ..1571: 7
to-morrow for the m. 652:10
tread in warlike m. 1287: 9
triumphant m. 884: 7
with solemn m. goes slow .1618:12
March-chick: forward M. .1195:12
Marches: dreadful m. 1136:10
his m. are expedient 436:10
Marching: rainy m. 1632:13
Marchpane: piece of m. 560:11
Mare 721:6
have his m. again 779:15
ride thee like the m. 400: 3
whose m.' s dead 1378:11
Mares would bear a soldier 721: 6
Margaret my name 1052: 3
Margent and all 1745: 4
beached m. of the sea 1324: 7
of his eyes 457:13
weeping m. 1495:14
Margents: glassy m. 1328: 8
Margery is my mother 1028: 6
Marian, Cicely, Gillian 1051: 2
Mariana: dejected M. 488: 6
Marigold at the sun's eye ..1202: 6
that goes to bed wi' the
sun 555: 6
Marigolds: her eyes, like m. 449: 4
shall as a carpet hang 637: 6
Marina: call'd M. 1053: 5
my gentle babe M. 62: 5
Mariner 1313:7
gentle m. 248:10
Mariners under hatches ...1313: 7
speak to the m. 1313: 7
your m. are muleters 1313: 7
Maritime: borders m. 1625:14
Marjoram: savory, m. 555: 6
Mark 956
he was the m. and glass ...430:11
ay, and m. thee too 59:15
bless the m. 957:12
but that m. 957: 7
but this 957: 3
do you m. me 487:14
ever-fixed m. 902:11
fair m. is soonest hit 957: 9
God bless the m. 620:11
God save the m. ..620:11; 1741:14
golden m. I seek to hit 264: 1
gracious m. o' the land ..1331: 6
hast thou a m. to thyself ..402: 4
hit the m. 487:15
hits the m. 130: 7
I know you level at 957: 4
marvellous well shot 957: 7
no drowning m. upon him .667: 6
of favour 957: 6
of modesty 1544: 4
of mouldy muskets 956:14
of my shoulder 956:16
of wonder 1014: 9
presents no m. to the
enemy 1512: 7
prodigious 187:10
scornful m. of every eye ..742: 9
set a m. so bloody 957:11

Milk, *continued*
innocent m. in its most innocent mouth 994: 4
mother's m. 133: 2
of Burgundy 1604: 6
of human kindness 800:14
she can m. 994: 3
skim m. 994: 2
sweet m. of concord 172: 3
take my m. for gall 993:13
thou suck'dst from her ..1582:14
white as m. 1659:10
Milk-livered man 256: 9
Milk-paps: those m. 1606: 8
Milk-sop: a m. 258: 6
Milk-sops: Jacks, m. 1376:13
Milk-white 994:3
before m. 554: 6
both m. 35:10
Milked: chopt hands had m. .810:13
Milking-time: is there not m. 1328:18
Milkmaid 994:3
'tis a m. 937: 9
Milky 994:3; 608:9
Mill-sixpences 1225: 4
Mill-wheels: fast as m. 648: 4
Milliner: no m. can so fit his customers 1406: 5
perfumed like a m. 889: 8
Million: attest a m. 539:11
of manners 955:11
once, and a m. 51: 2
worth a m. 1736: 6
Millioned accidents 1533: 8
Millions: clutch'd as many m. 1560: 8
mighty ones and m. 78: 7
of mischiefs 1388: 6
of strange shadows 1457:15
Millstones 1651:2
Milo: bull-bearing M. 1600:19
Mimic: forth my m. comes 751:11
Mince it sans remorse 62: 2
know no ways to m. it ..1709:13
not the general tongue 154: 8
this matter 488: 5
Minced man 942: 1
Mincing with his sword ..740: 8
Mind 994
all of one m. 994: 6
base and humble m. 995: 9
base ignoble m. 995: 9
be my m. 1126: 8
be not of that m. 997: 7
bear a base m. 995: 9
bear you it in m. 995: 6
beastly m. 994: 5
beating in my m. 1234: 9
bend your m. 997: 3
better to change your m. .1648: 3
bloody m. 997: 8
body fill'd and vacant m. 807: 5
bore a m. that envy 994:11
bore the m. that I do 994: 6
bounteous m. indeed 1199:11
break thy m. to me 999: 2
but one m. in all 994: 6
call to m. 982: 1
call we to m. 957: 3
came into my m. 997: 9
canst thou not minister to a m. diseased 996: 9
change my m. 1517: 8
change the m. 998: 5
change your m. 171: 9
come into my m. 1036: 8
commons' m. 995:10
complete in m. 527:14
corrupted m. 997: 3
disturbed m. 997:10
enchant the m. 444:12
ever serve his m. 997:15
every minute you do change a m. 1140: 2
farewell the tranquil m. ..502: 9
fit his m. to death 996:10
frame your m. to mirth ..202: 9
furnish'd with a m. so rare 80: 7
gentle m. 995:13
golden m. stoops not 996:13
good m. 995: 2
greases his pure m. 948: 3
growing once corrupt 94: 9
guilty m. 997:4; 1473:10
Mind, *continued*
haughty m. 607: 9
have in m. 996:12
have no m. 996:12
have you a m. to sink ..997:14
he bears an honourable m. .998: 3
he will not m. me 997:14
heavy m. 996:14
henceforth my wooing m. shall be express'd 996: 6
her m. untainted 1438:13
his m. is bent to holiness 708:16
honest m. and plain 744: 7
I am not in my perfect m. 931: 9
I have a man's m. 954: 1
I have a m. presages me 1522: 6
I know your m. 998:12
I sway by 374: 1
I 'll hold my m. 426:16
I 'll show my m. 999: 6
if your m. dislike 995: 4
ignoble m. 1342:12
ill can thy noble m. abrook 1346: 3
inward m. he doth debate 997: 4
keep in that m. 996:16
keep your m. peaceful ...204: 7
kept in m. 994: 8
knew his m. 43:13
know my m. 918: 5
know the lady's m. 833: 9
know'st thou his m. 998:10
let thy dauntless m. 247: 8
let your m. be coupled with your words 997:17
lives in thy m. 997:14
mock the m. 682:14
month's m. to them 998: 3
move a woman's m. 613: 4
much sufferance doth o'erskip 1459:17
my great m. most kingly 548:11
my m. as generous 70: 1
my m. exceeds the compass 995:12
my m. hath been as big 1702: 9
my m. is changed 998: 8
my m. is heavy 996:14
my m. is troubled 997:10
my m. is turn'd whore ..1661: 5
my m. misgives 995:15
my m. she has mated 31:12
my m. was never yet more mercenary 996:13
my m. 's not on 't 1162: 6
my most true m. 444:14
never m. was so unwise ..997:15
no m. that 's honest 996: 8
no m. to hunt this day ..737: 2
noble m. 995: 3
noblest m. he carries 995: 3
not in the m. 958:11
now I know thy m. 678: 6
of a m. 994: 6
of an old father's m. 996: 5
of my father's m. 1730: 6
o'er-rule my m. for once 997: 9
perceive my m. 995:10
pure m. 997: 6
put in m. 995: 6
rancorous m. 1238:15
refresh the m. of man 1041: 5
right noble m. 995: 3
rouse up a brave m. 1308:12
say her m. 999: 2
say my m. 154:10
seal up thy m. 994: 9
serious m. 1336:18
shall banquet 999:11
show a weak m. 174: 5
show'd a mounting m. ...804: 7
since m. at first in character was done 749:16
so his m. cankers 24:12
so pure a m. 696: 1
speak my m. 154:10; 999:3; 1426: 1
speak thy m. 1426: 8
speaking the m. 1426: 1
still my beating m. 1618:11
taint not thy m. 1027: 3
tell him my m. 198: 8
tell me your m. 990:16
that doth renew swifter 997:17
that fears him much 520: 9
that is a virtuous m. 996:15
Mind, *continued*
that 's my m. too 994: 6
thou hast a m. that suits 997:18
thrifty m. 995:13
thy m. is a very opal 997:18
thy m. is now as low ..994:12
'tis the m. that makes the body rich 999:13
'tis with my m. as with the tide 756: 9
to ease my m. 1237:17
to be honest 711:13
told his m. upon mine ear 659:17
troubled m. drave me ...997:10
unclean m. 177: 5
unmatched m. 995:11
vacant m. 995: 8
vex me with inconstant m. 756: 3
villain's m. 1506:10
weak and silly m. 563: 7
weak m. and able body ..999: 8
wear a m. dark 994:12
what a noble m. is here o'erthrown 995: 3
what is in thy m. 995: 1
when m. is quicken'd 995: 8
when the m. 's free, the body 's delicate 999:10
wicked m. 994: 5
wiped it from my m. 995: 4
with a m. that doth renew 1704: 4
wooing m. 996: 6
would I knew his m. ...1685:19
write down thy m. 971: 8
write my m. 1713: 5
yet have I a m. 995:15
you bear a gentle m. 608: 9
your m. is all as youthful 996: 1
your m. is the clearer ...1198:15
your m. is tossing 996:11
your m. of love 123: 3
Mind's eye 444:10; 444:11
Minded: how you stand m. 998:13
like the weather 996: 3
so m. 996: 3
Mindful messenger 990:12
Minds: all their m. transfigured 1447:11
arm the m. of infants ...1745:10
bring noblest m. to basest ends 589:15
busy giddy m. 1228: 7
corrupt m. 842:11
diet rank m. 974: 5
divert strong m. 1533: 8
fathers' m. are dead 257: 7
fearful m. 995:15
fearless m. climb soonest 995:11
great m. 844:11; 995:16
green m. look after 817: 2
hurt m. 996: 8
I have frequent been with unknown m. 997:12
infected m. to their deaf pillows will discharge ..996: 8
labour'd in their m. 828:14
men's m. are wild 1004:10
men's m. mistrust 286: 1
noble m. keep ever with their likes 1070:10
our m. we will unfold ...999: 4
quick m. lie still 1648: 7
rest your m. in peace ...1228:10
shown their royal m. 194: 4
sinners' m. 1725:12
strong m. 995:13
sway'd by eyes 444:14
their m. may change 998: 6
troubled m., that wake ..1271: 6
waxen m. 954: 8
whose m. are dedicate ...935: 6
Mine: as you are m., I am yours 908: 2
dearer than Plutus' m. ..689:11
hollow m. of earth 1453: 3
I am sure thou art 1681:16
me and m. 875: 3
of gold 1648: 5
she is m. own 787: 3
she was m. and not m. ..1178:16
that I was proud on 1178:14
thou m. of bounty 129: 9
'tis m. and I will have it .550: 8
what is m. 1178:14

Offend: I 'll o. nobody 1516: 7
no further o. you 1092:15
none does o., none 1093:13
none o. where all alike do dote 430:17
to o. and judge 791: 8
'twould o. him 1092:14
we come not to o. 1094: 7
Offended: all have not o. ..1093:13
be not o. 1093: 6
him I have o. 1093:10
how have I o. ..1093:13; 1211: 5
I am o. with you 1094:17
in what have I o. 1093: 9
make me not o. 366: 6
offend, himself being o. ..1347: 4
wherein have I o. most ..1093: 7
wherein have I o. you 1094:14
with my trade 1554: 2
Offendendo: se o. 387: 6
Offender **1095**
for the fault's love is the o. friended 985: 3
Offenders: foul o. 1095: 9
late o. 1095: 6
loving o., I will excuse ye 1095:10
other o. we will pause upon 1095: 5
such o. so cut off 1095: 7
we 're o. now 1095:10
which are the o. 1095: 8
Offending: import o. 1207: 1
Offendress: desperate o. 1605: 3
Offensive wife 1664:10
Offer **1095**
an o., that we will accept 1096: 3
change not your o. 1096: 1
embrace this gentle o. 1095:17
embrace your o. ..405:16; 1095:17
gentle o. 1095:17
gentleman-like o. 607: 3
heaven's o. we refuse 1255: 9
her this from me 1096: 4
made an o. 1095:15
take this o. 1095:11
this o. comes from mercy 1095:14
up 1095:16
we o. fair 1095:14
your o. is the best 1096: 3
Offered: fairly o. 1095:14
Offerings: faithfull'st o. ..1095:13
Hecate's o. 1693: 7
polluted o. 1615: 9
rich o. 1095:13
Offers: gracious o. 1095:17
make no more o. 1096: 1
these o. he shakes off 1095:12
Office **1096**
all men's o. to speak patience 1127:15
and affairs of love 593:10
and custom 1105:15
attend mine o. 1096: 5
becomes a woman best ..1097:16
choose what o. thou wilt ..1096:15
courteous o. 1097: 7
declare thine o. 1096: 5
deny their o. 1750: 7
did him a desired o. 1096: 6
do any modest o. 739:12
do me this courteous o. ..1095: 1
do the o. of revenge 1278: 3
do thee o. 1717: 7
do your o. 1096:13
dog 's obeyed in o. 60:12
done me a charitable o. 178:15
done my o. 1624: 9
each one to his o. 1097:10
enforce mine o. on you ...1096: 5
forgot a husband's o. 740: 4
fortune's o. 1097: 4
good o. 1096: 6
great o. 1096: 7
hath but a losing o. 1063:14
high o. 1096: 7
I do hold of you 1263:16
I do not like the o. 1097: 6
ill o. 1097:14
ill o. for a gentleman 608: 3
is indifferent 1097:15
it is my o. 740: 5
leagued in o. 1394:11
let the high o. go 1096: 7
man's o., but not yours 943: 1
modest o. 1014: 1
morning's holy o. 603:11

Office, *continued*
not an o. for a friend 1096:20
of a fowl 552: 1
of a warming pan 1097: 7
of God and devil 618:16
of great worth 1097:15
of love 1097: 7
of my heart 533:16
of our hand 329: 9
of the gods 1096: 9
opposite to Saint Peter 704: 7
princely o. 1097: 9
pronounce their o. 1720: 4
put out of o. 1097:13
scepter'd o. of ancestors ..1523:17
season'd o. 1096: 8
simple o. of love 907:10
speak your o. 1328:15
stolen both mine o. 1045: 6
take mine o. 1097: 5
this is my o. 1097:12
thou dost thy o. fairly 1096:13
time's o. is to fine 1533: 4
'tis an ill o. 1097:14
'tis an o. of discovery 1088: 2
tongue's o. 1722:13
trust o. of mine eyes 441:16
villain's o. or a fool's 1097:14
virtue's o. never breaks men's troth 1599: 8
you have shown your father a child-like o. 1097: 1
you know your o. 1097:10
Office-badge in court 378: 2
Officed instruments 150: 4
Officer **1097**
arrest me with an o. 1098: 1
art thou o., or art thou base 1098: 5
be you as the people's o. ..1098: 3
fee me an o. 1098: 7
filthy o. he is 1097:17
fit for the place 1097:15
here 's a wise o. 1098: 6
leave him to the o. 1098: 1
mortal o. 621: 7
never more be o. of mine .1098:11
of state 1098: 2
peevish o. 1098: 1
pelting, petty o. 1525: 1
poor o. of mine 1097:17
prince's o. 1098: 9
so indiscreet an o. 1098: 6
spoke like an o. 1097:12
sweet grace's o. 1098: 9
takes his fellow for an o. ..1510:15
that murder'd Pompey ...1522:11
worthy o. in the war 1098: 3
Officers **1395**
all the o. in Windsor 1098: 8
pluck down my o. 1098: 4
poor duke's o. 1098: 9
special o. of night 1098:12
spongy o. 833:13
of sorts 1098: 2
of the town 1098: 2
wilt thou kill God's o. 1098: 4
Offices: all o. are open 1097:10
do your o. 1096:13
for holy o. I have a time ..1534: 9
mart your o. for gold 140: 1
noble o. of mediation 216:10
of nature 635:20
of life 1705: 7
of tender courtesy 253:10
that profit us 1341: 9
then to your o. 1404:16
these o. shall profit thee ..1097:11
unpeopled o. 1396:12
what are your o. 1096: 8
Officious **973:12**
so tenderly o. 863: 6
to make this banquet 526:11
Offspring **187:13**
Oft: many a time and o. ...1530: 9
Oft-subdued slaves 257: 2
Oil and balm 1549: 7
and fire too strong 1250: 3
and flax 79: 8
as smooth as o. 1269:14
bring o. to fire 1298: 7
Oil-dried lamp 303:12
Old and fond of issue 507:12
and merry 22: 4
and reverend 25: 3
and rich 23:10

Old, *continued*
and sere 174: 1
and yet not wise 25: 3
as o. as Sibyl 933: 7
before thy time 77: 8
how o. are you 25: 8
I am o., I am o. 905: 9
I do wax 1638: 6
in judgement 22: 4
too o., by heaven 1753: 6
too o. to be engaged 895: 5
too o. to learn 1494:10
wrinkled, faded 23: 9
you are too o. 952:10
you never can be o. 24:11
Old-faced walls 1621:11
Olden time 1037: 2
Oldest hath borne most 21: 6
Oldness cannot relish them ..23: 7
Olive: bear the o. freely ...1133:14
hold the o. in my hand 1133:14
Olives of endless age 1133:14
Olympian games 1281: 2
like an O. wrestling 1131: 5
Olympus: blue O. 1234:14
huge as high O. 514:11
to a molehill 1026:15
wilt thou lift up O. 754: 5
Olympus-high 1504: 1
Omen **1098**
Ominous to noble peers 1205: 5
Omission to do 315: 9
Omit him not 90: 5
nothing we 'll o. 1253: 6
Omittance is no quittance ..489: 4
Omnipotent **1602:5**
On: off and on 489: 3
or shall we on 589:10
set on to this 761: 2
Once **489:5**
all at o. 471: 8
not o., nor twice 1529:10
Once-commended beauty 79: 9
One: all for o. we gage 601: 6
all 's o. for that 1541:11
all 's o. to me 471:12
but o., poor o. 188: 4
fairest o. of three 290: 1
great gross o. 649: 2
is o. too many 489: 7
is o. too much 188: 3
is reckon'd none 1077: 4
it 's all o. 339: 7
not o. before another 143: 9
say 'O.' 864:15
ten to o. 471:12
that I loved not wisely 1425:17
that 's all o. 1163:7; 1355: 9
thou and I am o. 217: 5
'tis all o. 1295: 4
too much by thee 188: 3
'twere all o. 916:15
we are o. in fortunes 1338: 4
One-half: this o. year 305:13
One-trunk-inheriting slave ..816: 6
Ones: wise o. 1684:16
Oneyers: great o. 210:11
Ongles: les o. 1044: 3
Onion will do well 448: 4
Onion-eyed: I am o. 1649:11
Onions: eat no o. 137:16
mine eyes smell o. 448: 4
Only **489:8**
Onset and retire 1273: 4
still expecting 436: 4
Ooze and bottom of the sea 1184: 4
find the o. 978:10
of the salt deep 990:13
Oozy: mudded in o. bed ..1399: 8
Opal: sapphire and o. blend .786: 6
thy mind is a very o. 997:18
Open **489:10**
be secretly o. 1567:20
we are too o. here 1207: 5
Open-eyed conspiracy 230:11
Opener and intelligencer ..1190:14
Opening of the gorgeous east 291: 8
Openness: deliver with more o. your answers 40:13
Operant poison 398: 5
powers 398: 5
Operation more divine 1442: 4
of the orbs 1085: 1
two-fold o. 1309: 5
Operative: simples o. 974: 8

Opinion 1100
ask my o. too 1101:10
base o. 1101: 4
better o. 1101:13
craving your o. 1101: 2
cured of this diseased o. ..1102: 2
dress'd in an o. 219: 1
false o. 1101: 8
foul o. 716: 7
go we under our o. still ..1101:16
good o. 1101:5; 1650:17
good o. of my knowledge ..826: 2
great o. 1101: 5
hard o. of his truth 1750:16
Hector's o. is this 1101:17
hideous o. of his rage 167:11
his own o. was his law ...1101: 3
his very o. 1101: 8
hold o. with Pythagoras ..1226:12
ill o. 1101: 4
in my o. 1101: 1
is but a fool 1101:14
learned without o. 848: 8
let loose my o. 1101:15
main o. be held once 1470: 2
maintain my o. 1101:15
makes sound o. sick 1101: 7
my own o. 1101:1; 1397:12
of Pythagoras 1226:13
put off my o. 1101:11
raze out rotten o. 435:20
rear the higher our o. 1100: 8
redeem'd thy lost o. 1100: 9
rich o. 1101: 5
right o. 1100:12
satisfy my o. 1100:11
shall be surgeon 1100:12
sovereign mistress of effects 1101:13
steel a strong o. 1101:16
stick the small'st o. 1101:13
that did help me 1100: 9
that fire cannot melt 1101:11
that o. of yourself 1101: 6
that so sticks 1100: 8
there 's an ill o. spread ...1101: 4
this is mine o. 1101: 1
true o. 165:15
what 's your o. of sister ..1373: 3
Opinioned: let them be o. ..1101:12
Opinions: deliver our just o. 1100:10
golden o. from all sorts of people 1101: 9
hard o. 1101: 4
have your express o. 1100:10
in our o. 1101: 1
killed with your hard o. ..1475: 8
men's o. 607: 7
most fond and winnowed o. 1342: 4
new o., divers and dangerous 1101: 3
return'd in his o. 1101: 3
speak plainly your o. 1100:10
Opportune place 927: 8
to our need 1597:13
Opportunities: good o. 1102: 8
many o. to cut him off 1102:10
to meet her 1102:12
Opportunity 1102
cannot attain it 1102:12
embrace this o. 1102: 8
find like o. 1102: 8
give thee o. 1102: 5
had I o. 1102: 5
ill-annexed o. 1102:13
in vain I rail at O. 1102:13
ne'er meet with O. 1102:13
O O., thy guilt is great ...1102:13
of night 1013:15
of sharp revenge 622: 8
omit no o. 643: 4
that o. we have again 1102: 5
thy servant, O. 1102:13
vile O. 1102:13
Oppose: I o. not myself ...1103: 6
Opposed: they shall be well o. 1103: 4
we stand o. 1103: 5
we were o. 1103: 7
you are potently o. 940: 3
Opposeless wills 1228:16
Opposer: great o. 1103: 3
Opposite: be o. with a kinsman 91: 6
bloody and fatal o. 177: 4

Opposite, *continued*
each o. that blanks the face of joy 740: 9
so o. to marriage 936: 3
to every good 1701: 9
Opposites: mighty o. 641: 8
of such repairing nature ..556:14
of this day's strife 158: 9
Opposition 1103
disobedient o. 361: 9
he found no o. 1103: 3
in o. bloody 591: 8
in single o. 537: 3
of our spirits 1684:11
peevish o. 506: 6
Oppositions: single o. 1103: 3
Oppressed: nor much o. them 1103:11
with wrongs 1748:11
Oppressing and betraying ...96:10
Oppression 1103
counterfeit o. of such grief 502:10
day's o. is not eased 297: 4
earth is throng'd by man's o. 1103:13
free from o. 584: 5
of aged tyranny 1582:10
Oppressor: while the o. feeds 1106: 9
Opulency: youth and o. 548:15
Oracle 1103
believe it against an o. 91:17
gave hope 1104: 8
hear an o. 60: 1
I am Sir O. 219: 1
in Apollo's name, his o. ..1104: 7
is fulfilled 1104: 8
my o., my prophet 1217: 5
seal'd-up o. 1104: 7
some o. must rectify 1104: 4
was fulfilled 442:14
wert thou an o. 1104: 5
yet shall the o. give rest ..1103: 6
Oracles are hardly attain'd 1103:17
may they not be my o. ...1104: 2
Orange: civil as an o. 781: 1
give not this rotten o. to your friend 586:16
Orange-tawny beard 74: 6
bill 98: 4
Orange-wife 841:10
Oration: deliver an o. 632: 9
drest to some o. 1104:16
fold it in the o. 821: 4
serve for your o. 1104:15
Orator 1104
how quaint an o. 1104:12
I am no o., as Brutus is ...176: 6
naughty o. 1104: 9
play the o. 1104:11; 1164: 6
shame's o. 1545: 7
subtle o. 1104:12
too green 1507:17
Orators are dumb when beauty pleadeth 79:13
breathing o. of miseries ..1723: 6
good o., when they are out, thy will spit 1104: 9
prevailing o. 1499: 6
Oratory 1104:14
drown my o. 1496: 8
to her o. adds more grace ..404:13
Orb as hush as death 1524: 8
circled o. 1023: 5
of one particular tear 1497: 5
smallest o. which thou behold'st 1040: 6
this o. o' the earth 470: 4
Orbs: empty left their o. ..1439: 2
fiery o. 793: 1
Orchard: sleeping in my o. 1337: 1
sleeping within my o. 1382: 5
walk in the o. 1618:15
walk'd forth into the o. ..1618:15
Orchard-end: at the o. 390: 2
Ordain: devise, o. 1105: 5
Ordained: for this was I o. ..334:14
Ordaining he should be a cuckold 267: 7
Order 1104
according to our o. 1105: 8
blest o. 1105: 2
by o. of law 631:2; 842: 8
devil take o. now 1104:19
gave everything view 1105: 4

Order, *continued*
give o. for my funeral 596: 7
hadst thou not o. 1105: 9
high o. in this solemnity ..1104:18
holy o. 1105:2; 1574:10
honourable o. 1105: 2
I gave him no o. 631: 6
I have given o. 1105:14
I will take o. 1104:17
impose some gentle o. 1105: 5
in o. 1105: 3
let o. die 172: 2
noble o. of Saint George .1105: 2
of his funeral 1105: 7
of my fingering 770:14
of proscription 1333:10
of the course 249: 9
of the field 1105: 7
of their fight 1105: 7
out of o. 1105: 3
outward o. 326:10
such temperate o. 430:16
stand not upon the o. of your going 360: 5
take o. for his burial 147: 2
take o. for mine own affairs 1105: 1
take some o. in the town ..1105: 1
take some privy o. 1105:12
there is o. ta'en for you ..1105: 1
there shall be o. for 't 1105: 9
three-fold o. ta'en 956:11
yourselves in o. set 1105:10
Ordering: mutual o. 1041: 2
on 't 894: 8
of the mind 1105: 6
of this present time 1105: 6
your affairs 1422:16
Orderless: order o. 1105: 5
Orderly 1105:13
make it o. and well 505: 5
to end 89:10
Orders: pretty o. beginning 1105: 9
send fair-play o. 216:12
take due o. for a priest ...1200: 2
Ordinance: God's fair o. ...961: 5
God's just o. 304: 2
let o. come 334:11
Ordinant: heaven o. 698: 7
Ordinaries: two o. 529:10
Ordinary: for his o. pays his heart 686: 9
Ordnance 157:5
great o. 1711:12
Ordure: with o. hide those roots 349:10
Organ: every lovely o. of her life 751: 2
maiden's o., shrill 1612: 3
most miraculous o. 1035: 7
Organ-pipe: dreadful o. ...1260:12
of frailty 1474: 4
Organs: its own o. 1501: 1
of her fantasy 935: 9
of increase 277:10
Orgulous: princes o. 1571: 5
Orient: from the o. to the drooping west 1307: 3
lo! in the o. 1467: 5
Orifex: admits no o. 367: 8
Origin and commencement .917: 4
my o. and ender 89:15
Original: it hath its o. 352: 6
we are their o. 1115:12
Orisons 1188:6
Orleans: rescued is O. 1724: 5
Ornament 1106
is but the guiled shore ...1106: 3
of beauty is suspect 79: 2
of his cheek 73: 6
of knighthood 1106: 1
of life 257:11
Rome's rich o. 1106: 1
sweet o. that decks 1106: 1
sweet o. which truth doth give 1577: 8
this o. makes me look dismal 1106: 4
to shape and love 1690: 4
world is still deceived with o. 1106: 3
world's fresh o. 1106: 1
Ornaments: deck my body in gay o. 1710: 1
grave o. 1016:11

Ornaments, *continued*
grave beseeming o. 194: 6
help me sort needful o. 1106: 5
of household 1178: 5
of praise 1184: 8
our mistress' o. are chaste .617:15
profaned their scarlet o. ..881: 6
those sweet o. 663:11
true o. to know a holy man 709: 1
Orphan **1106**
reave the o. of his patrimony 1080: 7
Orphans: new o. cry 1408: 2
were never o. had so dear a loss 893: 7
Orpheus drew trees 1039:12
while O. plays 1681: 8
with his lute made trees ..1039:12
Ort: some slender o. 625: 3
Orthography: now is he turned o. 1723: 3
rackers of o. 1746:12
Orts and imitations 528: 2
beggar'd o. to crave 1533: 5
of her love 756: 4
one that feeds on o. 175: 2
Osier: under an o. 885: 1
Osiers: like o. bow'd 1515:13
Osprey to the fish 1299: 2
Ossa: make O. like a wart 1031: 4
Ostent: in a sad o. 90:10
Ostentare, to show 755: 6
Ostentation: all o. of sorrow 210:13
delightful o. 1108: 3
formal o. 596: 6
maggot o. 1282: 8
mourning o. 1032: 4
of despised arms 1628:12
of our love 913: 9
Ostents: fair o. of love 254: 7
Ostler: bid the o. 721:10
Ostlers trade-fallen 815: 6
Ostrich: eat iron like an o. 1521: 1
Othello: black O. 972: 1
Othello's occupation 's gone 1091: 7
Other: no o. than I appear ..45:15
one or the o. 489: 7
Othergates: tickled you o. ..387: 2
Otherwise: do no o. 1086: 6
Otter: why, an o. 75: 7
Ottoman: enemy O. 413:11
Ottomites 1579:16
Ounce of civet 750:14
sweet o. of man's flesh 550: 7
Ouphes: strew good luck, o. 924: 3
urchins, o., and fairies 462: 6
Ours: France being o. 581: 8
Ourself thou didst abuse 4: 7
Ourselves: end o. 1460:13
sorry for o. 571: 8
think o. perfect 670: 7
'tis in o. that we are thus and thus 1608: 6
we are not o. 999:10
we do remember 1257:13
Out **489:11**
be not o. with me 489:11
brief candle 154: 1
fall o. 1228: 6
falls o. 479:12
fell o. 480: 1
giving o. 1196: 4
keep him o. 1605: 3
Launcelot and I are o. 489:11
this will o. 489:11
'twill o., 'twill o. 1136: 6
upon ye 241:14
Out-bragged the web 75: 2
Out-breathed: wearied and o. 440: 2
Out-burneth: as straw o. ...919: 4
Out-craftied him 778:17
Out-dared dastard 524:16
Out-dwells his hour 963:17
Out-face the winds 1044:12
Out-faced infant state 264: 8
them all 244: 7
Out-frown fortune's frown .594:15
Out-go his father 509: 1
my thinking on you 1257:11
Out-going in thy noon 1399: 6
Out-Herods Herod 1145: 5
Out-jest: labours to o. 563: 5
Out-night you 1067: 4
Out-paramoured the Turk ..926: 8
Out-peer these twain 948: 6

Out-pray: our prayers do o. his 1189:10
Out-rode me 721:13
Out-scorn wind and rain ..1730: 9
Out-shining beams 302:11
Out-speaks possession 1178: 5
Out-stripping crows 1708:11
Out-swear Cupid 271: 6
we 'll o. them too 271: 6
Out-sweetened not thy breath 553: 7
Out-talk us all 1490: 7
Out-tongue his complaints 1341: 4
Out-villained villany 1601: 4
Out-voice the sea 1358:14
Out-wall: my o. 45: 6
Outbrave the heart 1710: 4
Outbreak of a fiery mind ...514: 4
Outcry: entombs her o. 1611:14
Outdare: boldly did o. 121: 8
Outdared 121: 8
Outdares: sensibly o. 121: 8
Outdone his former deeds 8:15
Outface it with semblances ..44: 7
me with thy looks 440: 7
we 'll o. them 1289: 7
Outfacing me 455: 8
Outfly our apprehensions ...49: 6
Outgoes the heart of kindness 509: 1
Outgrown me far 650: 6
Outlaw in a castle 1199: 6
poor unminded o. 1744: 3
Outlawed from my blood 512: 4
Outlive thy father's days ..1608:13
Outliving beauty's outward 1704: 4
Outlook: to o. conquest 16: 5
Outprized by a trifle 1009: 3
Outrage **1106**
darest do such o. 122: 3
do a desperate o. 401:12
do o. to himself 324: 2
peace, ho! no o. 1136: 6
rancorous o. 1238:15
Outrages: do no o. 1106:15
known to commit o. 174: 6
pardon thee these o. 1114: 8
uncivil o. 1305: 5
Outscold: thou canst o. us .1321: 1
Outsell her gift 8:17
Outside: martial o. 44: 7
my o. have not charm'd 46: 8
of the Roman Brutus 1593: 1
of this work 45: 6
stubborn o. 508: 3
thy o. looks so fair 45: 6
what a goodly o. 468: 4
Outsport discretion 350: 2
Outstare: follow and o. him .871: 8
the lightning 871: 8
the sternest eyes 1710: 4
Outstay the time 1528: 2
Outstood my time 1528: 2
Outstretched his span 864:14
Outstrike thought 694:11
Outstrip **300:15**
Outstripped by every pen ..1172: 1
Outswear them too 1289: 7
Outswell the colic 1572:13
Outvenoms worms of Nile .1375: 9
Outward: outliving beauty's o. 1704: 4
so fair an o. 1142: 7
they show well o. 45: 7
with o. praise is crown'd .1185: 9
Outward-sainted deputy 744:11
Outwards: nature's o. 45: 7
Outwent her 1442: 5
Outwork: fancy o. nature ...44: 6
Outworths a noble's blood ...88: 7
Oven: like an o. stopp'd ..1409: 7
that is stopp'd 1409: 7
Over and beside 489:12
and o. 489:12
give o. 481: 5
told them o. and o. 345:10
Over-awe: may o. 1202: 1
Over-blown: clean o. 191:12
Over-boldly borne ourselves 121:15
Over-canopied with woodbine 544: 7
Over-careful **489:13**
foolish o. fathers 508: 2
Over-cool their blood 353: 8
Over-credulous haste 674:11
Over-daring Talbot 16: 3
Over-earnest with your Brutus 1028: 1

Over-eyeing of his odd behaviour 91: 4
Over-fed 489:13
Over-fly them 1708:11
Over-fond of the shepherd's daughter 898: 6
Over-full 489:13
Over-goes my invention 457:14
Over-greedy love 918:13
Over-handled theme 1455:12
Over-happy: not o. 669: 7
Over-joy of heart 1415: 8
Over-kind 489:13
Over-kindness: your o. doth wring tears from me ...800:16
Over-leather: through the o. 1357: 2
Over-long: hold me o. 1367: 1
Over-lusty at legs 850:12
French 582: 8
Over-matching waves 1474: 3
Over-measure: enough, with o. 1315: 6
Over-merry spleen 438:10
Over-mounting spirit 108: 6
Over-much: tempt him o. ..1505: 8
Over-partial looks 452: 9
Over-pay and pay again ..1131: 7
Over-proud in sap 1220:10
think him o. 1198:15
Over-reach the greybeard ..1170: 1
Over-reaching: gross o. 270: 4
Over-red thy fear 256: 9
Over-ripened corn 682: 7
Over-roasted rather 665: 7
Over-running: lose by o. ..1242: 8
Over-shine the earth 870: 7
Over-stained: besmear'd and o. 1379:11
Over-swear: all those sayings will I o. 1082: 9
Over-tedious: be not o. 1501: 7
Over-topping: trash for o. ..252: 7
Over-veiled the earth 291: 7
Over-view: betray'd to thy o. 96: 5
Over-wash'd with woe 183: 8
Over-weathered ribs 68: 3
Over-ween **1195:14**
Over-weens too much 1195:14
Overboard: I threw her o. .1666:10
Overbold: saucy and o. ...1316:10
Overbulk us all 430: 4
Overfar believe that 1707:14
Overflow: kind o. of kindness 1497:13
of good converts to bad ...628: 5
Overflowed and drown'd ...398: 7
fearing to be o. 398: 7
Overglance the superscript .440: 5
Overgo thy plaints 1032: 9
Overgone with care 159: 7
Overgorged with gobbets .1027: 9
Overhasty marriage 959:11
Overhear **221:14**
Overheard him and his practices 1183: 2
what you shall overhear ...686: 2
Overhold his price 1196:18
Overlive the hazard 1188: 2
Overlooking: bequeathed to my o. 185: 9
Overpassed thy days 1204: 5
Overpays all I can do 1131: 7
Overpeered: top-branch o. ..165: 6
Overpeering of his list 673:14
Overplus of shipping 1352: 8
'Will' is o. 1674: 6
Overscutched huswives 174: 5
Oversights: ancient o. 835: 2
Overstep not the modesty of nature 10:10
Overt test 1214:11
Overthrow **1106**
expecting o. 1354: 1
incurable ensues 974: 7
most assured o. 1239: 9
our glory's o. 1004: 7
seen our enemies' o. 1411:11
Overthrown **1106:19**
Overthrows: piteous o. 922:13
Overtopped them all 1154:12
Overture: made the o. 40: 4
of peace 1133:12
of war 1629: 9
without more o. 793:16
Overturned: all will be o. .1305:16

Patience, *continued*
I know your p. ... 1053: 3
I of him will gather p. ... 1127:15
in p. our proceeding be ... 1235: 3
is for poltroons ... 1127: 1
is quite beaten from her breast ... 1123:14
is sottish ... 1126: 4
is stale ... 1128: 3
keep me in p. ... 429:13
laugh'd him out of p. ... 839:11
lend me p. to forbear ... 1129: 3
lend your p. to us ... 1126:10
linger your p. on ... 1126:14
more than savages would suffer ... 1126: 3
my p. here is touch'd ... 1127:10
of poor p. borrow ... 1128: 1
oppose my p. to his fury ... 1127:11
out of p. ... 1127:14
past p. ... 1749:11
persuade me p. ... 1127: 2
poor soul's p. ... 1286: 6
pray your p. ... 1126:13
preaches p. to him ... 1126: 6
prick my tender p. ... 1516:13
quite beside his p. ... 1126:11
sat like p. on a monument 911: 3
says it is past her cure ... 893:12
seem'd to scorn his woes ... 993: 9
she begg'd my p. ... 1506:12
show'd a most noble p. ... 1127: 3
speak p. ... 1127:15
sprinkle cool p. ... 1126:10
stoop with p. to my fortune 577: 5
strengthen your p. ... 1126:10
take p. to you ... 1129: 5
take your p. to you ... 1127: 3
talk him out of p. ... 1490: 4
tame p. boast ... 1128: 3
tempting of your p. ... 1127: 3
that p., p. I need ... 1127: 8
think upon p. ... 1126: 3
thou young cherubin ... 1128: 1
though p. be a tired mare 1126:15
to endure ... 1006: 6
to endure all this ... 1128:11
to endure it now ... 303: 9
to endure the load ... 577:17
tongue-tied p. ... 350:14
tread upon my p. ... 1126:11
urging helpless p. ... 1126: 6
use your p. ... 1126:16
vex me past my p. ... 1598: 6
wake your p. ... 1127:15
where is the p. now ... 1127: 6
whose p. is, as a virtue ... 1128:13
will with p. hear ... 1418:16
with aged p. bear yoke ... 1128: 8
with p. calm the storm ... 1127: 2
your humble p. pray ... 1211:19
your p. so predominant ... 1127: 9
Patient as a gentle stream ... 250: 9
as the female dove ... 1129: 1
as the midnight sleep ... 1126: 8
be p. outwardly ... 1129: 1
be your p. ... 976: 1
dies while physician sleeps 369: 2
he is more p. ... 1127: 5
held me p. ... 1128: 4
how long shall I be p. ... 393: 4
I must be p. ... 1129: 4
poor as Job, but not so p. 1126:12
'tis for me to be p. ... 16:11
too careless p. ... 369: 3
we must be p. ... 636: 8
willing p. ... 975: 5
yourself, madam ... 1128: 5
Patiently: sit p. ... 1126:14
took all p. ... 1426:16
Patines of bright gold ... 1440: 1
Patrician ... 1129
humorous p. ... 1129: 6
Patricians: great p. ... 14: 1
Patrimony ... 763:5
Patriotism ... 1129
Patron ... 1130
of all light ... 1467:12
Patronage his theft ... 1199: 6
Patroness ... 1130:12
Patrons of my right ... 1129: 7
Patrum: Limbo P. ... 1204: 4
Pattern ... 1191:8
as a p. or a measure ... 1201: 6
beauty's p. ... 79: 1

Pattern, *continued*
cunning'st p. of excelling nature ... 871: 2
in himself to know ... 791: 7
of all patience ... 1127: 6
of celestial peace ... 1647: 9
of mine own thoughts ... 1518:11
of the worn-out age ... 886: 4
some p. of our shame ... 1346: 8
to all princes ... 1215: 9
you p. of all those ... 573: 5
Patterned by that ... 1160: 3
Patterns: deface the p. ... 1372: 6
one of the p. of love ... 896: 7
Pauca ... 389:11
loquitur ... 1722:12
there 's enough ... 1378:13
verba ... 1722:12
Paul: by holy P. ... 1307: 8
by the apostle P. ... 1344: 2
Paulina: thy wife P. ... 1667:10
Paunch ... 513:3
fat p. ... 256: 4
him with a stake ... 1038: 7
Paunches: fat p. have lean pates ... 513: 3
Pause ... 1130
awhile ... 242: 6
coldly p. for thee ... 1131: 1
give us p. ... 304: 6
I p. for a reply ... 1262:11
I stand in p. ... 756: 8
I 'll make a p. ... 1462:12
I 'll never p. again ... 1614: 3
made a p. ... 1131: 2
must give us p. ... 377:18
peace, lady! p. ... 1503: 6
sad p. and deep regard ... 1685: 3
too long a p. ... 1131: 3
twenty times made p. ... 1032: 7
Pauser: outrun the p., reason 916: 8
Paved with English faces ... 1640: 5
with gold ... 1641: 2
Pavement: lie there for p. ... 723: 4
Pavilion: out of his p. ... 538:10
Pavilioned in the fields of France ... 417: 9
Pavilions: brave p. ... 641:17
Paw: bear's fell p. ... 272: 9
Pawn both my plate ... 127: 8
broking p. ... 264:12
her honour's p. ... 1082:10
me to this your honour ... 714: 3
mine honour's p. ... 167: 8
my honour's p. ... 1566: 6
the little blood ... 863: 6
their experience ... 131: 4
to wage against thy enemies 867: 3
Pawned with the other ... 213: 5
Pawns: like p. lock'd up ... 1521: 4
Paws: blunt the lion's p. ... 1533: 8
devouring p. ... 878: 6
princely p. pared ... 879: 7
Pay and yet p. still ... 252:13
dear ... 1133: 9
doubt not of large p. ... 1393: 9
forget to p. ourselves ... 570: 8
full dearly ... 1133: 9
have in yearly p. ... 1179:14
he means to p. ... 1132: 2
he shall p. for him ... 1133: 4
he shall p. for this ... 1132:11
heavenly p. ... 36:11
him again when he was able ... 1322:15
I 'll make them p. ... 1132:11
I 'll p. thy pleasure ... 1168: 7
let them have p. ... 1132: 5
make us p. down ... 60:14
me all together ... 1132: 4
more than he owes ... 1017:15
present p. ... 144: 2
the debt ... 309:13
them at thy leisure ... 813:10
they 'll p. for it ... 1132:11
too dear ... 1133: 9
we shall p. for all ... 1131:11
when he was able ... 1:10
you shall p. well ... 1132:11
Pay-word ... 998:16
Paying for them honestly ... 1132:10
I do not like that p. back ... 1016: 7
Payment ... 1131
black p. ... 1653: 2
downright p. ... 984:10

Payment, *continued*
fair p. for foul words ... 1131: 9
give him his p. ... 1131: 9
give worse p. ... 1133:10
prays your speedy p. ... 1131: 9
that were but light p. ... 282:11
there 's p. for you ... 625: 5
too little p. for so great a debt ... 743: 6
Payments: called to no more p. ... 1273:13
Pays: fool who p. before ... 1131: 8
he p. the whole ... 1131:11
he p. you as surely ... 390: 2
himself with being proud ... 1197: 3
Pax: he hath stolen a p. ... 665:11
Peace ... 1133; 1367:2
above all earthly dignities ... 226:10
and plenty ... 1218:12
and prosperity ... 1218:12
and quietness ... 1134:10
ascend to heaven ... 1135:11
base and vile-concluded p. 1630: 7
be at p. ... 1135: 8
be at your labour ... 545: 6
be to France ... 1135:11
be with him ... 1134: 6
bequeath happy p. to you ... 1136: 7
break the p. ... 1136: 4
breed this present p. ... 1109: 6
call him to long p. ... 510:10
cannot make your p. ... 321: 2
celestial p. ... 1647: 9
Christian p. to souls ... 588: 7
civil p. maintained ... 1630: 2
command a p. ... 364: 9
conclude effeminate p. ... 1134:12
conduct his soul ... 128: 8
continue p. and love ... 1134:10
depart in p. ... 327:10
drawn, and talk of p. ... 1136:15
entertain a solemn p. ... 1135: 1
entreat him to a p. ... 1136:12
entreat true p. of you ... 1136:12
eternal p. ... 541: 1
fair England's p. ... 31: 2
flourish in p. and plenty ... 416: 6
for the love o' God, p. ... 1367: 2
frame convenient p. ... 1630: 1
freedom and liberty ... 857: 2
fright fair p. ... 1136: 9
fright our native p. ... 1224:10
frighted p. to pant ... 1134: 3
fruitful p. ... 1630: 4
get you hence in p. ... 1135: 3
glooming p. this morning with it brings ... 1025:12
go in p. ... 1135: 3
God's p. ... 1135: 5
happy p. ... 1136: 7
have a godly p. ... 1134:11
have they made ... 1133:15
heaven's p. be with him ... 1135: 5
hold thy p. ... 89:8; 817:7; 1367: 2
hold your p. ... 348:15; 484:2; 1136: 6
honourable p. attend thy throne ... 1523:16
I prithee, p. ... 1367: 2
implored a general p. ... 1134:12
in p. is wounded ... 1741:11
in p. there 's nothing so becomes a man ... 1630: 3
in this prison ... 1205:10
in thy breast ... 1383: 7
is a great maker of cuckolds ... 1630: 1
is a very apoplexy ... 1630: 1
is nothing but to rust iron 1630: 1
is of the nature of a conquest ... 1134: 5
is to me a war ... 1630: 7
itself should not so dull ... 1630: 3
keep p. ... 485: 9
keep the p. ... 24:3; 658:6; 1136:14
kiss my lady P. ... 1475: 8
kneel for p. ... 1702: 9
leave you in p. ... 1135:10
like nor p. nor war ... 1630: 1
litigious p. ... 1136: 8
live at p. ... 487: 1
live in p. ... 487: 1
live in p. abandon'd ... 277: 9
lives again ... 1136:13
made p. ... 1133:15

Pride, *continued*
smoking with p. 662: 8
so their p. doth grow 1198: 8
strain'd p. 1198: 2
this p. hath drawn my love 1199: 2
three summers' p. 1683: 8
'tis p. that pulls the country down 1198: 7
went before 1197: 5
who cries out on p. 1197: 1
Priest **1199**
and holy water 962: 3
both p. and clerk 1200: 7
coward Jack p. 1200: 6
delicate and tender p. 1201: 1
down fell p. and book 1200:10
go with sir p. 992: 8
great Apollo's p. 1104: 7
have a good p. 958:11
I will be his p. 1200: 2
in surplice white 1474: 6
kill de Jack p. 798:11
learned p. 848:10
let fall the book 1200:10
live like Diana's p. 1350: 8
meddling p. 1200: 4
no Italian p. shall tithe .. 1200: 4
no p. shovels in dust 668: 8
now I want the p. 1200: 8
old p. of Saint Luke's 1200:10
presumptuous p. 1200: 1
saucy p. 1199: 6
scurvy jack-a-nape p. 1200: 6
scurvy jack-dog p. 1200: 6
that lacks Latin 1534: 8
this p. has no pride 1200: 3
visited by a p. 1205:10
was good enough 958:11
you shall be the p. 1199: 4
you shall not lack a p. 1200: 7
Priest-like fasts 344: 1
thou hast cleansed my bosom 1255: 6
Priesthood **1199:11**
Priestly farewell to her 502: 9
Priests and fanes that lie 1649:15
and friars 1199: 8
are more in word 1200: 5
bid the p. do sacrifice 1310: 7
god Bel's p. 504:11
holy p. bless her when she is riggish 1699:12
in holy vestments 54:12
must become mockers 1199: 5
pray for enemies 413: 2
sad and solemn p. 1199: 7
swear p. and cowards 1080:10
when p. are more in word than matter 1216: 4
Prig, for my life 856:11
Primal eldest curse 275: 1
state 639: 4
Prime: as p. as goats 927: 2
of youth 1024:10; 1755:12
stab'dst me in p. of youth . 1437:16
thy p. of manhood daring . 951: 4
Primer: no p. business 148: 6
Primero: forswore at p. .. 1083: 7
Primest creature 1142: 9
Primitive statue 1442: 9
Primo, secundo, tertio 390: 3
Primogenitive and due of birth 101: 5
Primrose: pale p. 553: 7
path of dalliance treads .. 1190:13
Primrose-beds: faint p. ... 1708: 4
Primroses: pale p. 555: 5
Primy nature 1604:19
Prince **1200**
alias, the p. of darkness .. 1200:11
as he is a p. 1082: 2
begging p. what beggar pities not 1203: 2
black p. 336:8; 1200:11
brave young p. 634:10
bury him as a p. 556:11
but studies his companions 1201: 6
by fortune of my birth 764:15
dread p. of plackets 271: 8
effeminate p. 1202: 1
fine new p. 1203: 7
fond of your young p. 1203: 7
God send the p. a better companion 209:11
greatest p. o' the world .. 1200:12
he was a p. 1200:13

Prince, *continued*
he 's a gallant p. 1201: 8
hopeful p. 719:11
how fares the p. 1203: 3
knew'st this was the p. 1203: 7
makest a p. thy servant 243:13
most gracious p. 1203: 3
Neapolitan p. 1201:10
of Arragon 1201:10
of cats 161:11
of chivalry 189:12
of darkness 1201: 8
of dumbness 1043: 1
of fiends 1627: 5
of Ithaca 1201:10
of Morocco 1201:10
of palfreys 722: 2
of the blood 1201: 8
of the world 336: 8
of Wales 1201: 4
perish, base p. 1202: 2
renowned p. 1666: 1
royal p. 1749: 2
serve as great a p. 1339: 7
slandering a p. 1377: 8
such a p. 1201: 8
sweet young p. 1274: 4
this p. is not an Edward .. 1203: 3
thou no more art p. 1202: 5
tickle ye for a young p. .. 1525: 8
to p. it much 1055: 5
touch the true p. 1550:15
true p. may prove a thief . 1201: 5
wandering p. and Dido 921: 3
welcome, high p. 1202: 2
wise p. 1684:16
wisest p. that there had reign'd 1201: 8
wrong not your p. 1749: 2
young p. 1201: 3
Prince-like: nothing p. 1750: 2
Princes: all our p. captive 1345:12
are a model 1202: 9
are the glass, the school .. 1202: 9
butcher'd p. 1413:19
cloudy p. 884: 1
gratulate the gentle p. ... 1686: 9
greet the tender p. 1622:14
have but their titles 1203: 1
of the Goths 1201:10
should be free 1202: 3
should live like gods 1202: 9
show them p. born 1200:13
sometimes famous p. 1202: 8
Princess **1203**
fresh p. 814: 6
high and mighty p. 1052: 5
most virtuous p. 290: 2
of pure white 664:11
of this country 1376:13
teach our p. English 419: 6
the p. my sister 144: 6
truest p. that ever swore 1289: 3
Principal itself not much the worse 1605: 3
of all the deer 319: 7
Principality: let her be a p. 1700: 8
Princox: you are a p. 754: 9
Print: although the p. be little 873:12
he will p. them 854: 2
in p. I found it 1421:12
of goodness 628: 9
of his remembrance 1532:17
with your p. impress'd 693:11
Printed in her blood 814: 4
in thy hand 814: 4
Printing: cause p. to be used 402: 4
Printless foot 463: 2
Prints: false p. 1704: 1
Priority and place 322:14
Priscian a little scratched .. 837:11
Prison **1203**
away with him to p. 1204: 7
bear me to p. 1204: 8
cast in p. 1205: 2
commend me to the p. 1204: 8
compare this p. where I live 1205: 4
contagious p. 1204: 3
deserved more than a p. 330: 9
deserved p. 1652: 1
earthly p. of their bones .. 638: 4
for a debtor 866:12
from hence to p. 1204: 7
he shall not go to p. 1205: 7

Prison, *continued*
hollow p. of my flesh 691:14
I long to see my p. 1204: 8
in p. hast thou spent a pilgrimage 1204: 5
let me live in p. 1204: 8
let p. swallow 'em 1204: 7
let 's away to p. 1205: 1
out of p. and kept sheep .. 988: 9
rather lie in p. 920: 6
roughly send to p. 1204: 7
shut up in p. 1206:10
take him to p. 1204: 7
thou bloody p. 1205: 5
to p. 1204: 7
vaulty p. 1068: 3
vile p. of afflicted breath .. 120: 7
wall'd p. 1205: 1
what dost thou in p. 1204: 1
yield myself to p. 1130: 1
Prison-house: secrets of my p. 1327:16
Prisoned bird 1205: 1
in her eye 1500: 1
Prisoner **1205**
close p. rest 1206: 9
he is my p. 309: 5
is a prince 1206: 3
like a poor p. 1206:11
liquid p. pent 1206:12
my chamber's p. 1206: 5
my p.? or my guest 653: 2
nine years old 1206: 8
poor p. in his twisted gyves 1120: 8
proudest p. of the Goths .. 1206:13
taken p. 495:13; 1206: 2
then art thou p. 1206: 2
this p. freely give I 1206: 3
to the palsy 51:16
to the Tower 1205: 5
you 're my p. 1205:12
Prisoners: for p. ask'st thou 1206: 2
it is not for p. to be too silent 1206: 6
let out the p. 1206: 4
Scottish p. 1322:15
set our p. free 1206: 4
what p. thou hast ta'en .. 1206: 2
Prisonment: safe in his p. . 1204: 2
Prisons: fetter'd in our p. . 1380: 4
let p. swallow 'em 1003:18
Pristine health 685: 8
wars 685: 8
Prithee **1188:4**
Privacy **1207**
fie! p.? fie 1698:17
of this my p. 1207: 6
Private: I left him p. 1207: 4
in his chamber 1399: 5
let me enjoy my p. 361: 3
Privately **1207:7**
speak it p. 1417: 8
Privates: her p. we 577: 8
Privilege **1207**
ancient p. of Athens 1207:11
child-bed p. denied 1207:16
get that p. of me 1753:16
he bears him on place's p. . 1207:10
holy p. of sanctuary 1207:16
lost thy princely p. 1207: 9
men's p. 1207:16
never to see me 1207:11
nothing p. him 1207:12
of a private man 1207:10
of age 22: 6
of antiquity 22: 6
of blessed sanctuary 1314:14
of mine honours 1207:16
of nature 1207:16
of speaking first 1711: 2
plead your honourable p. . 1207: 8
presuming on an ague's p. 1207:12
rotten p. and custom 677: 2
you break no p. 1207:13
your beauty bears 116: 1
Privileged by age 22: 6
by my place 1422: 3
to speak 809: 6
Privilegio: cum p. 855:12
Privily **1207:2**
Privity o' the king 48: 9
Privy **1207:3**
to the plot 1170: 4
to thy country's fate 506: 6
Privy-kitchen: Lucifer's p. . 458: 4

Prize 1208
a p., a p. 1208: 4
a p. no less 1208: 6
contending in a p. 1208: 7
gallant p. 1208: 2
goodly p., fit for the devil's grace 1208: 3
he brought home noble p. ..1208: 3
he is my p. 1208: 8
is that my p. 330: 1
it not a straw 1450: 7
lawful p. 961: 2
laying the p. aboard 453:13
made p. and purchase 1663:13
me at her worth 991:10
of all too precious you ...1597: 3
play'd your p. 1208:11
proclaim'd p. 1208: 3
she is my p. 1208: 8
'tis p. enough to be his son 1398: 6
triumphant p. 1208: 9
war's p. to take all vantages 1628: 1
wicked p. itself buys out the law 794:11
win the p. 1682: 3
you yourselves 211: 6
Prized by their masters ...1592:11
Prizer: in the p. 1592:12
Prizes of accident 717:12
Probable 1208:12
Probal to thinking 18: 1
Probation of a sisterhood ..1077: 6
suffers under p. 1336:15
Proceed no further 148:16
Proceeded well 1208:17
Proceeders: quick p. 674:10
Proceeding 1208
I like this fair p. 1208:15
is this p. just 1208:15
merciless p. 1361:11
on your just p. 361:10
plain p. is more plain 1208:16
stop all good p. 1208:17
Proceedings: contrary p. ...367:14
foul p. 1208:15
inform them of our p. 1208:14
just p. 1208:14
lay open all our p. 1560:11
of a drunken brain 1208:18
violent p. 1208:18
Process 1209
forged p. of my death 1337: 1
hear the p. 1209: 2
of this sandy hour 1520:12
of this time 248: 9
of thy kindness 801: 1
proceed by p. 1209: 1
such was the p. 1209: 6
Process-server: then a p. ..1298:11
Proclaim was madness 930: 9
Proclamation 1209
bloody p. to escape 1332:20
did you hear the p. 1209:11
find out by p. 1289: 7
give a better p. 1266: 7
I heard the p. 1209: 7
learn me the p. 1209:12
make open p. 1209: 8
new p. that 's clapp'd upon the court gate 1556: 7
of thy passion 775: 6
that you are vanished 1209:13
Proclamations: chosen with p. to-day 403:18
Proconsul: creates Lucius p. 208: 1
Procrastinate his end 720: 8
Procreants: leave p. alone ..360: 6
Procreation, residence 142:11
Procuring of mirth 1273:13
Prodigal: be p. 1210: 7
fool and a p. 1210: 5
how like the p. 68: 3
how p. the soul 1613:16
I was no p. 1210: 5
if that one be p. 1210: 4
killed for the P. 12:11
niggard p. that prais'd her so 1751:17
of all dear grace 633: 3
ye have been too p. 1210: 2
Prodigality 1209
of nature 607: 8
Prodigally gave them all ...633: 3
Prodigals: tattered p. 1209:15

Prodigies and signs 1099:10
disturb'd with p. on earth 1100: 7
do so conjointly meet 1099: 8
Prodigious and untimely ...187:15
grown, and fearful 949: 7
Prodigiously be cross'd ...1192: 5
Prodigy: crook-back p. 1696: 1
of fear 1099: 1
unusual p. 1021: 8
Proface 383: 8
Profanation: foul p. 641:10
void of all p. 192: 6
Profane: so old and so p. ..378: 1
too much p. 1049: 2
Profanely: not to speak it p. .10:10
Profaneness 'gainst oracle .1104: 8
Profaners of this steel 1251: 3
Profess sincerely 1371: 5
Professes not answering 43: 8
not keeping of oaths 1082:14
Profession 1210
charmed me from my p. ..1210:16
constant to my p. 1210:16
do the p. some grace 1210:10
high p. spiritual 714: 7
hold up Adam's p. 12:12
makes our p. to stink 1210:15
my p. 's sacred 480:19
neither is our p. any trade 1661: 1
of fortune-telling 933: 5
Professions: knavish p. ...1298:11
limited p. 1511:10
some of all p. 1210:13
Professors 1210:11
of one faith 1452:14
Profferer construe 'ay' 1705: 2
Proffers not took reap thanks 1280: 9
Proficient: so good a p. ...383: 6
Profit 1210
common p. of his country 1130: 1
despise p. where most gain 1211: 5
do yourself a p. 1211: 4
draws us a p. from all ...1088: 1
find p. by losing of our prayers 1187:10
from all things we see ...1210:17
I p. not by thy talk 1489:17
is yet to come 1211: 4
made thee more p. 1495:10
my p. on 't 1475: 1
no p. but the name 649: 9
no p. grows where is no pleasure ta'en 1150: 2
not my p. that does lead mine honour 712: 9
of excess is surfeit 255: 4
of their shining nights ...1047: 3
should hardly draw me ..1211: 2
thank you for this p. 1211: 4
yield thee so much p. 1211: 5
Profitably: answer thee p. ..43: 6
Profitless: danger p. 285:16
falls into mine ears as p. ..242: 7
usurer 1590: 6
Profits: high p. might come 129:11
of my death 1211: 1
of the mind 505:13
will accrue 144: 2
Profound in his art 932:14
Profoundest pit 121: 5
Profoundly: why sigh so p. 1363: 1
Progenitors 35:1
Progeny 186:7
Progne: worse than P. 290:10
Prognosticate: this I p. 410:10
Prognostication: fruitful p. 1112: 2
hottest day p. proclaims ...293: 4
Progress 1211
golden p. in the east 1469: 3
of the stars 1439:11
Time's thievish p. 1534: 8
Progression: way of p. 853: 9
Prohibit: God p. it 977:17
Prohibition so divine 1460:15
Project 1211
of a power 1182:16
Projection: niggardly p. ..1348:10
Prolixious blushes 115: 7
Prolixity: slips of p. 1576:13
Prologue 1211
index and obscure p. 849:13
is this a p. 1211:18
of our comedy 811: 9
rid his p. like a rough colt 1212: 1

Prologue, *continued*
to an egg and butter 632: 9
to his sleep 384: 2
to my brains 1211:18
to some great amiss 1098:14
to the omen 1098:14
to their play 1211:20
vilely penn'd 1211:20
what 's past is p. 10: 3
write me a p. 1212: 1
Prologue-like your humble patience pray 1211:19
Prologues: happy p. 1576: 7
to a bad voice 1403:12
Promethean fire 448:11
heat 448:11
Prometheus tied to Caucasus 450: 2
Promise 1212
aid 27:11
and performance 1213:14
beyond the p. of his age ...600: 2
break an hour's p. 923: 1
break p. with him 1213:11
come now, your p. 1213:10
do not keep your p. 1212: 4
excuse his broken p. 1212: 5
foolish woman's p. 1213: 9
is this your p. 1212: 7
keep p., love 1212: 4
keep the word of p. 1213: 6
keep your p. 485: 9
knows at what time to p. ..802: 3
nothing of that wonderful p. 177: 4
of high pay 1213: 3
of satisfaction 84: 9
of their mettle 947: 5
passed my word and p. ...1212: 9
performed my p. 1212: 3
register'd in p. 95: 9
remember thy p. pass'd ..1213:10
such a beauteous day 197: 3
this I p. here 1212: 9
to p. is most courtly 1213:15
what do you p. 1212: 9
what she requires 1212: 3
you made your mother ...1212: 7
Promise-breaker: hourly p. .173:12
worse than a p. 677: 2
Promise-breech 261:11
Promise-crammed: eat air p. .28:20
Promise-keeping: precise in p. 1213: 7
Promised is the charity of age 1213: 5
you p. me to wed 920: 2
Promises: deceiving p. 1212: 7
fill his ear with golden p. 1213:13
his p. fly so beyond state .1213:15
his p. were mighty 1213:14
if p. be kept 1212: 4
keep your p. in love 1212: 4
these p. are fair 1212: 8
thy p. are like Adonis' gardens 1213: 2
Promiseth 1212:10
Promising is the very air o' the time 1213:15
Promotion follows 319: 4
Promotions are daily given 1071: 1
high p. 342:11
Promontory: blue p. 196:11
highest p. top 370:13
sat upon a p. 987: 9
stands upon a p. 377: 9
sterile p. 397:10
strong-based p. have I made shake 1154:15
Prompted by your trouble ..852: 9
to my revenge 511: 8
Prompter: after the p. 1212: 2
without a p. 538:15
Prompting eyes 449: 1
Prompture of the blood 926:13
Prone: not p. to weeping ..1652: 1
to mischief 1558: 1
Pronounce but 'love' and 'dove' 1283: 7
Proof 1214
add p. unto mine armour .1189: 8
against their enmity 887: 6
armed in p. 1344: 2
as strong as my grief 1424:13
blast in p. 1211:11

Publicly: he doth it p. 620:10
proclaim it p. 489: 6
Publisher of this pretence ..916: 1
Publishing a truth 859:15
Pucelle: excellent P. 431: 6
hath bravely played 1118:12
or puzzel 1520:12
what 's that P. 934:11
Puck a liar call 432: 9
sweet P. 462: 8
Pudding: as p. to his skin ..40: 2
blessed p. 220:18
in his belly 174: 5
yield the crow a p. 262: 7
Puddings he hath stolen ...593:17
Puddle 834:6
gilded p. 277: 7
kennel, p., sink 277: 7
Puddled his clear spirit 39: 3
Pudency so rosy 1013: 9
Puff: goodman P. 1378:13
Puffs away from thence 39: 5
Pugging tooth 1502:11
Puisny tilter 189:11
Puissance 1220
deliver our p. 436: 9
make imaginary p. 366:13
Puke-stocking 1296: 9
Puking: mewling and p. 940:12
Puling 835:10
Pull all about mine ears ..1268: 5
Puller down of kings 803: 7
Pullet-sperm: I 'll no p. ...1310: 1
Pulls: two p. at once 1740:11
Pulpit: speak in same p. ..1427:16
Pulpiter: gentle p. 1190:12
Pulse 696
ere your p. twice beat 675:14
feeling my p. 439:10
feverous p. 692: 2
have you a working p. 463: 3
let me feel your p. 659:17
my p., as yours, does temperately keep time 696:14
strive upon your p. 286:15
Pulsidge: your p. beats 696:14
Pump 1357:1
Pumpion: gross watery p. ..513: 4
Pumps: Gabriel's p. 1357: 1
Pun thee into shivers 546: 8
Punched full of deadly holes 1038: 5
Punish: I will p. home 1221:13
me for what you make me do 1221: 1
me with this 1221: 4
you by the heels 59:15
Punished: heavily p. 1221:14
let me be p. 1222:10
too austerely p. you 214: 7
Punishment 1220
foulness is the p. 579: 9
his p. was cruel death 1517: 4
I never gave them condign p. 1221:11
judicious p. 288: 9
more in policy than malice 1222: 4
or trial 858: 2
out-run native p. 619: 4
pleasing p. that women bear 1192: 1
receive his p. in thanks ..1508:15
received the p. 1221: 3
too good for them 1222: 2
Punishments: brave p. 1222: 2
Punk 1662
Punto: pass thy p. 389:11
reverso 390: 1
Pupil: being her p. 1582: 2
too far in years to be a p. now 22: 8
Pupil-like, take correction ..805: 1
Puppet: exceeding p. 774:13
make a p. of me 491:11
marry him to a p. 962:13
you p., you 245: 3
Puppets: see the p. dallying 774: 8
Puppies: blind bitch's p. 1260: 7
have oceans, p. 835:15
very wisely, p. 1685: 9
Puppy 370:15
kind of p. to old dam 1559: 6
Puppy-dog 370:15
Puppy-dogs 1033:11
Puppy-headed monster 1019: 5

Purblind 107:1
Purchase: call it p. 1510:17
no p. in money 458: 4
of a glorious beauty 300:10
with still lasting war 31: 2
Purchased at an infinite rate 437:14
Pure: as p. as snow 1222:14
as the unsullied lily 716: 9
be they as p. as grace 320: 8
be thou as p. as snow 153:13
for his love 340: 7
innocent and p. 1222:14
seem as p. as snow 175: 4
so p. a mind 997: 6
wash'd as p. as sin 1633:11
Purgation 1565:10
did consist in words 1560: 5
guilt or the p. 796:11
put him to his p. 801:14
Purgatory, torture, hell 66:11
venture p. for 't 318: 7
Purge by any desperate change 1235: 5
find her disease and p. it ..351:12
him of that humour 1386: 6
himself with words 1722: 4
I 'll p. and leave sack 1254:14
our country's p. 974: 9
Purged and deposed 524: 8
you must be p. too 1369:18
Purgers, not murderers ...1038:12
Purging of his soul 1277: 2
Purifies itself 468:12
Puritan 177:3
Purity 1222
all p. 894:10
impious p. 1222:12
in p. of manhood 548:14
so strain'd a p. 910: 8
such a winnow'd p. 1222:12
Purled up the sky 138:12
Purlieus of this forest 570: 2
Purloined his eyes 927: 4
Purple with love's wound ..554: 6
Purple-coloured face 738: 2
Purple-hued maltworms 210:11
Purple-in-grain beard 74: 6
Purpled hands 418: 7
Purples: long p. 553:11
Purport: in p. 888: 5
Purpose 1223
a p. more grave 1224: 5
acquainted with your p. ..1224: 9
assist me in my p. 1224: 6
before this p. cool 314:10
better for our p. 474: 3
better shall my p. work ..1224: 8
brain'd my p. 302: 2
but to the p. 139: 2
change this p. 1224:17
do not forego the p. 1224:12
drive his p. on 1223:10
fated to the p. 992:17
fell p. 1260: 5
flighty p. never is o'ertook 1224: 4
for what p., love 1615: 5
full of p. 54:14
good p. 1223:14
haste her to the p. 833:14
hold that p. 1223: 6
I knew of your p. 1224: 6
is but the slave to memory 1223:10
it hath to climb 322:14
it serves my p. 1487:13
knows our p. 1169:11
make my p. swift 898: 1
make our p. necessary 1223:17
make your own p. 1224: 1
makes strong the vow 1224:14
mistaking his p. 1008: 8
must weigh the folly 1223:12
my p. was for Tarsus 1224: 9
my p. should not fail 1685:16
my p. would prove well ..1223: 9
never by advised p. meet .1169: 3
no p. in them 1224: 1
not to sell 1185: 9
not to the p. 213: 6
nothing of my p. 1095: 1
of his speed 1535: 1
of his treason 1559:14
of my coming 1463: 4
of unkindness 1060: 3
on p. 1223: 8
on p. trimm'd up 240: 9

Purpose, *continued*
our p. is discovered 1223:17
our p. is twelve month old 1223:11
our p. may hold 1173:13
outran my p. 1224: 8
self-same p. 820:14
so mortal a p. 1568:14
speak to some p. 1488:13
spoke to the p. 1426: 7
strongly in my p. bred ...1060: 7
such is his noble p. 1391:12
suspend thy p. 277:10
tell me all his p. 1224: 6
their p. is to parle 254: 6
think nothing to any p. ..1224: 7
thy p. marriage 961: 7
to a sore p. 1483: 8
to marry 961: 1
to my p. nothing 1700: 5
to the p. 490:19; 1223: 3
'twas not my p. 1223:16
'twas not my p., thus to beg a kiss 813: 4
unchaste p. 716: 8
unlawful p. 1329: 8
we had a p. of defence 321: 2
whet thy blunted p. 1609:16
win our p. 1682: 3
you the p. cherish 1224:12
you undertake is dangerous 284:10
your p. is both good and reasonable 1223:14
Purpose-changer: that p. ..1144:14
Purposes: ask him his p. .1224: 2
better act of p. mistook ..1008: 6
endow'd thy p. with words 1726:12
fulfilled their secret p. ...1223:18
levell'd at our p. 1639: 9
mistook fall'n on the inventors' heads 1273:15
my p. do draw me 1223: 4
our p. God hath discover'd 1223:13
recount their p. 1224: 3
sound the p. of all hearts .696: 8
studied p. 1223:14
understand my p. aright .1224: 1
written p. 1223:14
Purposing to destroy 1267: 9
Purr of fortune's 814:13
Purse 1225
and brain both empty 972:10
fill thy p. with money 1225: 6
foreign p. 1557:14
had my p. as if the strings were thine 1225: 6
halfpenny p. of wit 1688:10
he cannot creep into a halfpenny p. 218: 7
here 's my p. 1225: 8
his p. is empty 1719:17
in p. and in person 310:11
keep your p. 1225: 8
of gold 1225: 1
of rich prosperity 1218: 6
open your p. 1225:10
overtake your show p. 1689:11
pick Master Slender's p. .1225: 4
prodigal's p. 1225: 1
she bears the p. 1225: 5
take this p. of gold 1131: 7
the ducats straight 1017: 5
there is my p. to cure 114:11
there 's my p. 1572:13
waste his borrow'd p. 1225: 3
who steals my p. steals trash 1050: 2
your p. is not hot 1225:11
Purse-bearer: be your p. ...1225: 8
Purse-taking: praying to p. 982: 5
Pursed up his heart 693: 6
Purses: cold p. 1099: 2
empty p. 1225: 1
fat p. 1553:10
free p. 1225: 1
like empty p. pick'd 590: 7
our p. shall be proud 999:13
picked their festival p. 1225: 4
picking of p. 345: 6
prove thief and take p. ...1397:12
stuff your p. full 265: 8
Pursue it with a soul of love 1226: 6
me not 917:11
Pursuing that that flies, and flying what pursues 897: 1

Queen, *continued*
teach me to be your q. ... 393: 5
tell the q. these news ... 1061:10
that bore thee ... 1232: 4
this q. will live ... 1232: 6
thrice-crowned q. of night 1022: 1
thrice-gracious q. ... 1231: 4
to be a q. in bondage ... 1231: 3
wanton with this q. ... 1624: 3
weep not, sweet q. ... 1496: 5
weeping q. ... 1498: 4
woo my q. ... 1710: 5
worth many babes ... 305: 9
would not be a q. ... 1231: 7
wrangling q. ... 1230: 8
Queens: weeping q. ... 290: 4
Quell: our great q. ... 654: 1
Quenched: what hath q. them 121:16
Quenchless fury ... 321:12
Quern: labour in the q. ... 462: 8
Quest: go in q. of beauty .. 906: 4
of thoughts, all tenants ... 1517: 9
what lawful q. have given their verdict up ... 429: 2
Questant: bravest q. ... 469: 7

Question ... 1233
ask you a q. ... 1233: 3
ask'st me such a q. ... 1233: 7
call in q. ... 1233: 8
decline the whole q. ... 1234:10
did so stagger me ... 1234: 2
hear some q. ... 1233:13
left us yet to prove ... 903: 8
let me q. more in particular 1233: 8
make no q. of that ... 1234:10
make so slight a q. ... 1233:12
making q. of my uttermost 1750:10
me no more ... 1234: 9
more should I q. thee ... 1233: 3
no q. ... 947: 3
no q. asked him ... 1485: 2
no q. of that ... 1233:13
not to be asked ... 1233:11
of this straw ... 308: 9
one q. to your daughter .. 1234: 7
out of our q. wipe him ... 341:10
out of q. ... 400:4; 1233:13
out of q. so it is ... 616:14
put another q. ... 1233: 9
queasy q. ... 1445: 4
sans q. ... 402: 5
so the q. stands ... 1233:12
stay no longer q. ... 1234: 4
staying no longer q. ... 1428:12
such fair q. as soul ... 937: 7
suffer q. for your residence 361:10
that is not the q. ... 1233: 6
that is the q. ... 756: 8
that q. 's out of my part .. 1234:11
that 's a q. ... 1233: 6
there 's the q. ... 1056:1; 1233: 6
to be asked ... 1397:12
what a q. 's that ... 954: 4
yond man ... 736: 4
Questionable shape ... 1432:16
Questioned by my fears ... 522: 5
Questioning: with q. ... 1233: 5
Questionless be fortunate .. 1522: 6
with her sweet harmony .. 936: 5
Questions: ask q. and sing 978: 6
spur me with such q. ... 1234: 3
Quests: contrarious q. ... 1676:16
Queubus: equinoctial of Q. . 566:19

Quick ... 1234
and dead ... 1234:14
and in mine arms ... 1234:14
be buried q. with her .. 1234:14
be q. ... 1235: 1
be q., thou 'rt best ... 149:11
by him ... 1658: 1
for the dead, not for the q. 858: 4
how q. and fresh art thou 896: 1
how q. is love ... 912: 6
in answers ... 41: 4
make us q. in work ... 1727: 7
not be so q. ... 674:10
of ear ... 396: 5
set q. i' the earth ... 1234:14
she 's q. ... 1192: 4
snip, snap, q. ... 1235: 1
struck to the q. .. 491:15; 1749: 9
tent him to the q. ... 491:15
touch thee to the q. ... 855:10
wound to the q. ... 877: 7
you must not be so q. ... 1235: 1
Quick-answered, saucy ... 1703: 4
Quick-conceiving discontents 125:15
Quick-raised power ... 1182:15
Quick-shifting antics ... 564:10
Quick-witted folks ... 564:12
Quickening in his eye ... 441: 6
Quicker for a fray ... 850: 9
Quicklier be blown up ... 1605: 3
Quickly: told and q. gone .. 1551:18
Quicksand of deceit ... 311: 1
Quicksands: these q., Lepidus 284: 8
swift as q. it courses ... 1173:12
Quid for Quo ... 1274: 3
Quiddities: in thy quips and thy q. ... 379: 8
where be his q. ... 844:15

Quiet ... 1235
as a lamb ... 834:12
be q. ... 1235: 4
be q. and depart ... 327: 6
come to start my q. ... 386: 2
glad he is so q. ... 1235: 7
her q. interrupted ... 956: 8
I can be q. ... 1127: 7
keep q. in his conscience .. 226: 6
let 's sit down q. ... 1382: 9
never at q. ... 1235: 9
no q. find ... 1235: 9
she is much out of q. ... 366: 5
Quietness: give me q. ... 1235: 5
grown sick of rest ... 1235: 5
of spirit ... 1127:11
stablish q. ... 1235: 5
Quietus: he himself might his q. make ... 1461: 1
Quill: modern q. ... 1737: 2

Quillets ... 182:4
do not stand on q. ... 1035:15
his q., his cases ... 844:15
sharp q. of the law ... 842: 6
sound his q. shrilly ... 844:15
Quills: like q. upon the fretful porpentine ... 1486:11
Quinapalus: what says Q. 1691: 1
Quintain: but a q. ... 1116:10
Quintessence of dust ... 941: 1
of every sprite ... 1244: 7
Quip Modest ... 867:16

Quips ... 782:8
all her sudden q. ... 911: 4
thy q. and thy quiddities .. 379: 8
Quire hold their hips ... 840: 6
Quired with my drum ... 1610:14
Quiring: still q. ... 1040: 6
Quirk: she has her q. ... 1249: 4

Quirks ... 177:2
and remnants of wit ... 1689: 7
of blazoning pens ... 936: 3
of joy and grief ... 790: 5
Quit: he q. being ... 299: 6
here I q. him ... 670:12
Quittance of desert ... 329: 9
or obligation ... 797: 3
rendering faint q. ... 440: 2
warrant, q. ... 1632: 2
Quiver: why dost thou q. .. 522:13
Quivering thigh ... 224:10
Quo: Quid for Q. ... 1274: 3
Quoif: thou sickly q. ... 651: 1
Quoit him down ... 1162: 9
Quoits: golden q. ... 1179: 1
plays at q. well ... 174: 5
Quondam day ... 293: 1
queen ... 1231: 6
Quoted and sign'd ... 318: 1
joint by joint ... 442:10
Quotidian tertian ... 352: 3
of love ... 900: 5

R

R; both with an R. ... 853: 7
Rabbit: like a r. on a spit ... 52:10
whoreson upright r. ... 360: 1
Rabbit-sucker ... 1221: 5

Rabble ... 1235
trim r. ... 588: 7
Rabblement hooted ... 1235:13

Race ... 1236
drowsy r. of night ... 93: 5
fiery r. ... 332:10
give my sensual r. the rein 856: 8
happy r. of kings ... 805: 5
or two of ginger ... 1236: 4
whole r. of mankind ... 678: 8

Rack ... 1549:13
haled from the r. ... 875:15
leave not a r. behind ... 1609:15
of this tough world ... 302: 9
stand still ... 1524: 8
thee in their fancies ... 640: 5
thee with old cramps ... 1521:12
then we r. the value ... 893: 5
upon the r., Bassanio ... 1559:10
Racked and tortured ... 1549:13
Rackers of orthography .. 1746:12
Rackets: match'd our r. to these balls ... 600: 7
Racking clouds ... 1466: 6
Radiance: bright r. ... 916:15
sacred r. of the sun ... 1085: 1
sickly r. do amend ... 786: 6
Radish: like a forked r. ... 174: 5
Raft: fatal r. ... 1397: 3
Rag: away, thou r. ... 360: 1
not a r. of money ... 1016: 4
poor r. ... 360: 1
thou r. of honour ... 713: 6
Ragamuffins: led my r. ... 537: 4

Rage ... 1236
abate thy manly r. ... 1236: 9
and hot blood ... 19: 8
appertaining r. ... 1249: 7
barren r. of death's eternal cold ... 732: 4
be his ... 978: 2
bid'st thou me r. ... 1236:10
extremity of r. ... 439: 2
eyeless r. ... 657: 4
fall in r. ... 14:16
fawn on r. ... 734: 1
fell battle's r. ... 1237: 3
fire's extreme r. ... 900: 3
Frenchmen's r. ... 25:15
full battle's r. ... 601: 6
great r. of heart ... 597: 6
hard-favour'd r. ... 1236: 9
heaven's fell r. ... 24:10
impatiently doth r. ... 274:16
in r. sent out ... 1237: 4
in r. strikes wide ... 1479: 6
incensed r. ... 1236:13
leave without thy r. ... 1239: 4
my r. was blind ... 527:10
moves in him more r. ... 1237: 4
must be withstood ... 1237: 5
of lust ... 927: 3
pernicious r. ... 111: 5
pious r. ... 1236:15
present harsh r. ... 517: 8
put not your worthy r. .. 1236: 6
raged do r. the more ... 1758: 6
replete with too much r. .. 1237: 6
roused with r. ... 1237: 7
shamed gilded arms ... 1392: 7
shift into a madman's r. .. 1332:20
staring r. ... 1346: 9
stop the r. betime ... 1741: 1
swelleth with more r. ... 1409: 7
that was in thy r. ... 1237: 6
thy r. shall burn thee ... 1236:12
tiger-footed r. ... 1236: 6
to r. the city turn ... 1237: 2
traitor's r. ... 1559: 4
ungovern'd r. ... 1236:14
whose heat hath ... 1742:12
Rages: allay my r. ... 1246:11
furious winter's r. ... 303: 3
give thy r. balm ... 65: 6
his r. and his furies ... 1236: 9
how it r. ... 1325:10
murder's r. ... 1102:13
Ragged: dishonourable r. .. 815: 6
old, and beggarly ... 89: 2
Raggedest hour ... 727: 5
Raggedness: window'd r. .. 1743:13
Raging of the sea ... 172: 6
Raging-mad: be r. ... 900: 4
Raging-wood ... 1479: 9
Rags: ensconce your r. ... 714:15
guarded with r. ... 1250: 8
her r. and the tallow ... 1656: 5
in r. thou knowest none .. 439: 2
more r. to lay on thee ... 383: 2
overweening r. of France .. 583: 2
what shalt thou exchange for r. ... 1297: 8
Rail against great buildings 1180: 6
come in and r. ... 1237:18
I r. at him ... 78: 4

Sick, *continued*
that surfeit with too much 1472:13
these news made me s. ...1064: 2
to death 278:8; 1360: 5
with civil blows 809:15
with groans 557: 1
with working of my thoughts 364: 9
would you were a little s. 1360:10
would you were not s. 438: 7
yet am I s. with fear 521:10
you are so s. of late 366: 7
you 'll be s. to-morrow ...1361: 4
Sick-fallen beast 224: 1
Sick-thoughted Venus 1596: 9
Sicken at the sight 1359:13
Sickens: more one s. 1359:13
Sicker: I the s. be 548: 8
Sickle: his s., hour 728:17
Sicklemen: sunburnt s. 673:11
Sicklied o'er with the pale cast of thought 756: 8
Sickliness: wayward s. 1723: 5
Sickness 1359
add unto his s. 1360: 9
by s. had been visited 1360: 3
caught of me 1361: 2
contagious s. 759:11
deadly s. 1360: 6
denying thee any thing 326: 4
diet his s. 740: 5
feign a s. 1360: 1
freely die 684:10
full of s. and diseases 351:10
great s. 1360: 6
grievous s. took him 1360: 6
growing 1682:17
he hath the falling s. 152: 8
his s. is discharged 1361: 7
his s. pursued him 1360: 8
his s. was past cure 1360:10
I here discard my s. 1360: 9
inward s. 1360: 3
is catching 46:10
it warms the very s. in my heart 6: 6
last s. 1360: 6
long s. of health 1075:14
my s. grows upon me 1360: 8
not s. should detain me 210: 7
present s. 1360: 6
sicken to shun s. when we purge 975: 6
this s. doth infect the very life-blood 1360: 3
wayward s. 1643: 7
with s. much enfeebled ...1360: 5
your father's s. is a maim to us 1360: 3
Side by s. together live 1411:12
come thou on my s. 1203: 2
long-boat's s. 683:10
of the offering s. 1095:13
one s. will mock another ..1012: 6
seamy s. without 1690: 1
sever'd from your s. 533: 4
strong upon stronger s. ...1452: 4
tender s. 541: 1
Thames s. 1295: 5
turn'd almost the wrong s. out 899: 8
turns she every man the wrong s. out 1148: 8
windy s. of care 690:16
windy s. of the law 844:12
wrong s. out 499: 8
wrong s. turned outward ..1336: 5
Side-piercing sight 1363:14
Side-stitches that shall pen .1521:12
Sided in his behalf 705: 1
Sides: both s. the leaf 1745: 4
breaks the s. of loyalty ...1250:13
keep my s. to myself 763: 7
no woman's s. can bide the beating of so strong a passion 1703:12
O, can my s. hold 839:14
O s., you are too tough ..1407:16
o' the world may danger ..1226:15
rother's s. 1475: 7
stretch the s. o' the world ..153: 5
strong s. can volley 1358:12
that 's s. and heart 283: 7
unfed s. 1743:13
weak untimber'd s. 1353:12

Siege 1361
as fearful as a s. 1709:12
assuredly I 'll raise 1361: 9
forsake the s. 1361:10
grievous s. 1361: 8
his s. is now against the mind 304: 8
laugh a s. to scorn 161: 1
lays down his wanton s. ..1709: 6
lays strong s. 535:13
of loving terms 1014: 5
of Orleans 1361: 9
paltry s. 1361:11
raise the s. 1361: 9
raise this tedious s. 934:11
seven years' s. 1571: 6
unrespective s. 559:15
very s. of justice 795:15
wreckful s. of days 1465:11
Sieve: in a s. I 'll thither sail 313: 5
intensible s. 916:15
Sift him on that argument ..50:11
this matter further 493: 5
Sigeia: hic est S. tellus 1631:20
Sigh 1361
and say 'amen' 90:10
and weep 1363: 9
buried this s. in wrinkle of a smile 1389: 8
for the toothache 1502: 7
help us to s. and groan 992:15
humorous s. 1362: 4
I must s. in thy face 1362: 5
like a schoolboy 901: 1
raised a s. so piteous 1361:16
spendthrift s. 1362: 4
stopping laughter with a s. 1363: 3
then s. not so 1362: 9
think scorn to s. 1362: 5
to blow away this praise ..1362: 2
to the winds 1362:15
wedged with a s. 695: 3
what a s. is there 1362: 7
wherefore breaks that s. ..1361:15
why s. you so profoundly .1363: 1
with a rising s. he wisheth 700:13
with a s., as if her heart would break 1362:12
with a s. like Tom o' Bedlam 979: 6
Sighed and kiss'd 850:15
she s. as she stood 1361:12
Sighing every minute 1363: 4
like furnace 940:12
wound it with s. 1363: 8
Sighs: all made of s. and tears 894:10
and groans 1363: 4
and groans and shrieks ..1408: 2
and groans and tears 354:14
and tears 1363: 5
and tears and groans 648: 1
and weeps 1650:13
blood-consuming s. 1362: 4
blood-drinking s. 1031:14
blood-sucking s. 1362: 4
call her winds and waters s. and tears 1363: 4
consume away in s. 1012:12
contrite s. 1362:12
daily heart-sore s. 896: 3
deep s. 1362:14
dry her cheeks 1363:10
friendly s. sought to dry ..1363:10
furnaces the thick s. 1361:14
her s. will make a battery in his breast 1362: 4
his s., his sorrows 1362:12
how her s. do blow 1325: 8
how s. resound 1362:11
love's s. 1362: 4
my s. are blown away 1363:10
my s., like whirlwinds 1362:12
my s. so deep 1362:11
no s. but of my breathing .1362: 7
of fire 911: 1
of love, that costs dear 900: 6
of Octavia blow the fire ..1361:13
sad s., deep groans 1372: 7
saw s. reek from you 1123: 7
so many thousand s. 1362: 3
soft s. 1362: 4
that burning lungs raise ..1362: 6
thousand s. are breathed .1362: 3
thousand thousand s. 1363: 9
thriftless s. 911: 2

Sighs, *continued*
thy s. from heaven clears .1362:14
windy s. 1362: 4
with s. she gives her sorrow fire 1362:12
with s. shot through 1363: 7
with s. they jar 1536: 4
Sight 1363
accustomed s. of death 434: 8
admitted to his s. 1365: 6
avaunt! and quit my s. 359:12
avoid my s. 1365: 3
blind s., dead life 611: 4
bloody s. 1363:15
charm'd the s. 659:18
come no more in my s. ...1365: 3
common s. 1363:12
daunted at a woman's s. ..1698: 8
deficient s. topple down ...364:14
destroy your s. 1365: 5
disgracious in your s. 1365:11
dismal s. 1364: 3
dreaded s. 1363:15
dull s. 1363:15
earnest-gaping s. 1364:16
endure the s. of day 1559:13
endure your s. 411: 5
fearful s. of blood 1364: 3
fed them with his s. 528:12
feed her s. 528:12
first s. 1365:12
forswear it, s. 82: 1
get thee from my s. .359:9; 360: 4
glad the s. 1485: 7
heavenly s. 1363:13
heavy s. 1363:15
her s. did ravish 1363:13
here 's a goodly s. 442: 5
here 's a s. for thee 1364: 6
hence, from my s. 359: 9
horrible s. 1363:15
I cannot brook thy s. 1364:17
idle s. 1681: 5
if s. and shape be true 1364:10
in s. of God 1365: 7
in s. of heaven 1365: 7
is dismal 1364: 3
keep him out of my s. 1365: 7
many an old man's s. 1215: 4
moralize his wanton s. 446: 9
most pitiful 1363:14
my s. is very dull 1365:18
my s. was ever thick 1365:18
never more come in my s. .1603:12
new-appearing s. 1467: 5
now my s. fails 748:14
of death 1364:16
of lovers feedeth those in love 922: 8
of me is odious 1364:17
offend our s. 1364:17
out of my s. .66:1; 360:8; 1365: 3
out of the s. of Orlando ..1364: 9
pitiful s. 1363:15
proud s. 1365:15
rudest or gentlest s. 444:14
see'st thou this sweet s. ..1363:13
side-piercing s. 1363:14
starve our s. from lovers' food 1120: 5
strange s. 495: 3
strangest s. 1364: 6
subject to no s. 776:11
such a s. will blind 510:13
that will clear your s. 1364:11
then have you lost a s. 1364: 7
thick s. 1365:18
this is a sorry s. 1363:15
thy s. is young 1245:11
vanish'd from our s. 1364:13
vanish'd s. 1364: 2
what a s. it was 1364: 5
who ever loved that loved not at first s. 912: 2
will much delight thee 1363:13
wishful s. 1363:15
Sight-holes: stop all s. 453:12
Sightly: lies as s. 878:11
Sights: behold such s. 1363:16
bleared s. are spectacled ..1176:16
bring me to their s. 1365:10
dreadful s. 1363:15
horrid s. 1363:15
of steel 1627: 3
seen two such s. 1364: 6

Slough: cast thy humble s. ..171: 6
casted s. 995: 8
shining checker'd s. 1390: 6
Slovenly unhandsome corse .118:13
Slovenry: worn us into s. .1530: 1
Slow as the elephant 177: 1
I am nothing s. 1386:12
I am s. of study 878:14
in speech 1427: 8
of sail 1313: 1
snail s. 1389:16
so s. 1386:11
thou art too s. 1386:12
though s., deadly 1173:10
too s. 1386:12
too s. of sail 1591: 1
you are s. 1386:12
Slow-gaited: very s. 1386:11
Slow-winged turtle 374: 6
Slowed: should be s. 675:13
Slowness **1386**
cross'd with s. 214: 8
my s. that I do not 214: 8
Slubber: content to s. 149: 5
not business 149: 5
Slug: thou s., thou sot 326: 5
Slug-a-bed: you s. 1386: 9
Sluggard **1386:8**
Sluggardized: dully s. 1557: 1
Sluggish crare 978:10
Sluiced in 's absence 268: 3
out his innocent soul 110:13
Sluices: like s. 1499:15
Slumber **1386**
from miserable s. I awaked 1386:13
golden s. of repose 728: 6
harmful s. 1337: 2
leaden s. peise me down ..1383: 5
leaden s. with life's stream 1386:15
O murderous s. 1386:15
pleasant s. in thy lap 327:10
shake off s. 864:13
thick s. hangs upon mine eyes 1386:15
tickled s. 1525:10
when will this fearful s. have an end 1387: 3
Slumbered: but s. here 1343:14
Slumbers: balmy s. waked 1394:11
faint s. 1626: 7
my s. should be broken ...1387: 1
unquiet s. 1387: 1
Slut **579:6**
Sluts and sluttery 579: 6
hold up, you s. 381: 5
Sluttery **579:6**
Sluttishness may come 579: 6
Slys are no rogues 1298: 8
Smack: clamorous s. 812:13
o' the contrary 1683:12
of honour both 1717: 3
of neighbouring languages .836:11
of observation 1088:17
of this vice 1598:19
some s. of age 21: 9
whether I s. or no 1088:17
Smacking of every sin 175: 4
Smacks it not something ...242: 2
Small **882:4**
as a wand 82: 7
as an eunuch 426:18
by s. and s. 1550: 4
speak as s. as you will ...1423:14
things s. as nothing 641:14
Small-knowing soul 1412: 5
Smaller than the smallest .1182:16
Smallness of a gnat 618: 6
Smart as lizards' stings 277: 6
ease thy s. 1222: 3
made me s. 1222: 3
some of us will s. for it ..1222: 3
they s. to hear themselves 1740: 1
Smarting in lingering pickle 1520: 5
with my wounds 1740: 5
Smarts: guess at others' s. .695: 6
Smatch: some s. of honour .714:10
Smatter with your gossips ..629:13
Smear with dust 1533: 5
Smeared all with dust 391:11
Smell **1387**
acquainted with the s. 370:15
ancient and fish-like s. ...1387: 9
here 's the s. of blood 662: 1
him out by that 900: 8
his way to Dover 1387: 6

Smell, *continued*
I cannot s. 936: 1
I s. it 1379: 4
loseth thy old s. 1239: 5
of calumny 1050: 3
of hot meat 1387: 4
of sweat 1475: 3
rank s. of weeds 555: 9
so strongly 1387: 8
so sweet 1387: 7
somewhat strong 576: 5
stifled with s. of sin 1369:17
sweet s. 1387: 7
sweet s. of different flowers 1465:11
tender s. 1387: 7
to the violet 137:13
villanous s. 1387: 8
what a man cannot s. out, he may spy into 1073:12
Smellest so sweet 1648:14
Smelling sans all 1334:15
so sweet 1710: 7
so sweetly 1387: 7
Smells from the general weal 1074: 7
it s. most sweetly 1143:16
it s. to heaven 1093: 1
loathsome s. 1387: 8
of mortality 1387: 4
Smelt 'em out 493:14
Smile **1387**
and stroke his beard 1388:11
as the wind sits 1388: 8
at no man's jests 155: 9
at thee in secret thought ..1388:13
ay, s. upon her, so 1388:12
do not s. at me 117:11
do you not s. at this 1388:10
does nothing but s. 1388:19
enforce it with thy s. 1388:16
he will s. upon her 1388:19
I can s., and murder whiles I s. 1388: 3
I did but s. till now 1388:10
if you should s. he grows impatient 1388:15
in men's faces 549: 9
in my presence still s. 1388:18
joyless s. 1387:10
kind of s. which ne'er came from the lungs 1388: 9
loose a scatter'd s. 1387:10
make him s. 1387:15
makes me s. 1387:15
modest s. 144: 3
moved to s. at any thing .1388: 4
nor shall he s. at thee 1286: 8
of heaven 698:11
of safety 1387:11
once more 1387:12
one may s., and s., and be a villain 1602: 4
quenching my familiar s. .1388:17
recures the wounding of a frown 1389: 4
so s. the heavens 9:14
to 't 1387:12
some that s. have in their hearts, millions of mischiefs 1388: 6
sweetly did she s. 1120: 6
they s. at me that shortly shall be dead 1388:14
we shall s. 502: 7
we would aspire to 1202: 6
we 'll s. indeed 1388: 6
why dost thou s. so 1389: 1
Smiled at one another 1388: 5
he s. at it 1388: 5
he s. me in the face 1387:13
still he s. and talk'd 1387:13
to see him 1388: 5
with so sweet a cheer 1388:13
Smiles and tears 1389: 7
as in disdain 350:16
dimpled s. 62: 2
enforced s. 11: 3
fawning s. 1389: 3
full of s. 175:11
he s. valiantly 1389: 2
in such a sort as if he mock'd himself 1388: 4
making practised s. 421: 4
of knaves 1387:11
pleasing s. 745: 5

Smiles, *continued*
robb'd that s. steals something from the thief ...1296:16
seldom he s. 1388: 4
there shall be s. 1387:14
thy s. become thee well ..1388:18
upon us he s. 1387:14
waited upon my s. 1466: 8
Smilets: happy s. 1389: 7
Smiling at grief 911: 3
bade me come s. 1388:18
camest in s. 1388:18
his s. becomes him 1389: 2
mocking the sigh 1389: 6
ridiculous s. 1388: 9
yokes a s. with a sigh 1389: 6
Smilingly revolt 747:11
Smirched thus 758:18
Smith: I saw a s. stand ...1486: 2
Smock **379:5**
were a she-angel 1179: 1
Smocks: foul s. 379: 5
summer s. 1436: 6
Smoke **1389**
and bounce 1418:17
and dusky vapours 1389:12
bright s. 1389:15
dunnest s. of hell 1068: 1
foul-reeking s. 1068: 3
from the s. into the smother 342:15
helpless s. of words 1389:14
like incense 1144: 2
of war 1389:14
rotten s. 197: 3
sweet s. of rhetoric 1476:18
they begin to s. me 1389:10
vanish as s. from Ætna ..1389:15
you shall s. for it 1389:10
Smoked: first s. 1389: 9
with bloody execution 1444: 5
Smokes: crooked s. 621:11
Smoking **1389:13**
Smoky **1389:15**
Smooth, deceive and cog 549: 9
how s. and even 744: 4
with mine enemy 1175: 6
Smooth-faced **456:4**
Smooth-pates: whoreson s. 1471:13
Smooth-tongue 1296: 9
Smoothly: comes so s. off .1688: 9
Smoothness: her s. 1458: 8
Smother: from the smoke into the s. 342:15
Smothered in surmise 1473: 2
Smothering of the sense ...394:11
Smug and silver Trent 1295: 1
come so s. 88: 3
Smutched thy nose 1074: 9
Snaffle: with a s. pace 1669: 3
Snail **1389**
carries his house on his head 1389:16
creeping like s. 940:12
shrinks backward 1390: 3
thou drone, thou s. 746:15
why a s. has a house 1390: 1
wooed of a s. 1709: 8
Snail-paced beggary 323: 9
Snail-slow in profit 1211: 3
Snake **1390**
fell Alecto's s. 1277: 4
green and gilded s. 1390: 4
made thee a tame s. 1490:17
roll'd in a flowering bank 1390: 6
rolled in the cheerful sun 1390: 9
scotch'd the s., not kill'd it 1390: 7
strangling a s. 706:10
throws her enamell'd skin 1390: 8
warm the starved s. 1390: 6
Snakes in my heart-blood warm'd 1390: 6
scaled s. 1390: 8
spotted s. with double tongue 1390: 8
thousand hissing s. 721: 4
Snaky: crisped, s. 656:15
Snap: short, quick, s. 675: 2
Snapper-up of unconsidered trifles 1568:17
Snare: virtue's s. 1533: 5
world's great s. 1606:11
Snares of war 1273: 1
tedious s. 133: 9
Snarl and bite 1501:18
Snarling all before I came .678: 2

Solicitor: fair s. 1738: 4
thy s. shall rather die 162: 9
Solidares: three s. for thee 1681:11
Solitary: sad and s. 1396:13
Solitude 1396
Solomon 1687:17
Solon's happiness 596: 9
Solus: have you s. 1379: 2
Solve: the s. is this 1616:19
Solyman: Sultan S. 1687:17
Something: every s. 789: 5
in the wind 1676:13
that nature gave me 244: 1
there was s. in him 459:10
there 's s. in 't 494: 1
this s. that you gave me for nothing 1508: 4
to remember me by 1258: 6
too much of this 494: 1
Something-settled matter ..1556: 9
Somme: river S. 1295: 3
Son 1396
and brother 1401: 7
and heir 1400:10
art thou a woman's s. 918: 7
art thou my s. 512: 5
banish'd s. 1397: 6
bastard s. 1401:10; 1401:14
bastard s. of Priam's 1401:16
be unlawfully born 142: 8
Best's s. 1403: 1
bitch-wolf's s. 1401:13
blessed Mary's s. 192: 1
blest with a goodly s. 511:13
Bohemia's s. 1403: 1
bold s. 1397:10
brain-sick s. 1346: 4
brave s. 1398: 8
brother's s. 1401: 7
but woman's s. 438: 3
by my mother's s. 1468: 3
by order of law 1400: 8
Cæsar's s. 1403: 1
Cato's s. 1402:10
changed s. 1398:13
dear s. 1399: 8
deceitful s. 1398:13
digressing s. 1398:13
disinherited thine only s. ..1398: 4
Douglas' s. 1403: 1
Edward's s. 1402:12
eldest s. 1400: 6
eldest s. is like you 1401:10
every mother's s. 665: 8
fair s. 1397:10; 1402: 7
father's brother's s. 1401: 7
father's sister's s. 1401: 8
father's s. 1401: 4
fifth s. 1400: 5
first s. 1400: 5
first-born s. 1400: 9
forward s. 822: 4
fourth s. 1400: 5
frail s. 1398:13
from s. to s. 1288: 9
Geffrey's s. 1402:13
gentle s. 1397:10
gentlewoman's s. 1402: 6
get a s. 1399: 6
good man's s. 1397: 9
good s. 1397: 9
goodly s. 1397: 9
great s. 1397:10
had a s. for her cradle ere husband for her bed 1401:12
he is my s. 1399: 3
he was my s. 1397: 1
her s. gone 1397: 8
his s. am I 1398: 3
his s. is elder 1400: 8
honest s. 1622:16
hopeful s. 719:11
I am your s. 1397:12
I dare not call 1399: 3
I, his sole s. 1277: 2
I will not call him s. 511: 4
is fled 1402: 3
is not this your s. 1401:12
kill a s. of mine 1195:11
king's s. 1402: 4
like the prodigious s. 1218: 4
little s. 1397: 5
loss you have is but a s. ..893:12
love you my s. 904: 6
loving s. 1397:10

Son, *continued*
loving s. of Albany 1402:11
low-laid s. 1398:13
make yourself a s. 1396:15
makes your s. a shadow ..1343: 9
Merops' s. 1403: 1
mine only s. 1401: 2
mother's s. 1401: 6
my lord your s. 890: 1
my mother's s. 1401: 5
my s. came into my mind 1398:10
my s. i' the ooze is bedded 1399: 8
my s. is disinherited 1398: 4
my s. is lost 1399: 8
my s. profits nothing 1245: 9
natural s. and sire 625: 1
neighbour shepherd's s. ..287: 1
never borne thee s. 508: 9
never had a s. 1398: 9
next s. 1400:10
no s. of mine succeeding ..1398:11
noble s. 1399: 1
Numa's daughter's s. 1402: 8
O, my s., my s. 1402:14
of a dear father 511: 8
of a whore 1661: 5
of a woman 1722: 6
of Clarence 1403: 2
of Cœur-de-lion 1403: 2
of Duncan 1403: 2
of hell 704:12; 1627:11
of Henry the Fifth 1402:10
of Lucius 1403: 2
of Marcus Cato 1402:10
of my grandfather 634:14
of Polixenes 1403: 2
of Priam 1403: 2
of Rome 1402: 6
of Talbot 1402: 9
of the female is the shadow of the male 1401: 5
of the king 1402: 2
of thy abused father's wrath 1402: 7
of utter darkness 458: 4
of your great enemy 1048: 7
old Antonio's s. 1403: 1
old s. 1398:13
only s. 1401: 3
only s. of my womb 1756: 3
our s. is good 1397: 9
our s. of Cornwall 1402:11
our s. shall win 1397:11
poor man's s. 1398: 9
poor s. 1398:13; 1399: 8
prince's s. 1402: 2
princely s. 1397:10
Prodigal S. 1298:11
proper s. 1397:10
purblind s. and heir 272: 4
queen's s. 1402: 5
respects me as her s. 1270:13
right s. 1402:14
rude s. 512: 7
seal'd the s. of chivalry ..189:12
second s. 1400: 5
shall the s. of England prove a thief 1397:12
she hath a s. for me 1398: 6
shepherd's s. 1402: 6
Sir Robert's s. 1401:11
sister's s. 1401: 8
Siward's s. 1403: 1
slain a virtuous s. 1400: 3
slaughter'd s. 1399:10
smother my damned s. ..1720:14
sole s. 1401: 1
son's s. 1400: 6
spare my first-born s. 863:11
steals home my heavy s. ..1399: 5
sweet s. 1399: 4
Talbot's s. 1402: 9
tardy s. 1397:11
tell me of my unthrifty s. 1399: 2
that she did litter here ..1401:15
that suck'd an earthly mother 1401: 9
that well deserves 511: 9
thee of thy s. they have bereft 1399: 8
there 's s. against father ..512: 2
think my s. to be as dear 1399:10
third s. 1400: 5
this Hydra s. of war 1627: 1
thou art my s. 1397:12

Son, *continued*
thou hast one s. 1398: 5
thy mother's s. 511:10
thy sovereign's s. 1402: 2
to great Antiochus 1403: 2
to some man else 1397: 2
to the queen 1402: 5
treacherous s. 509:10
twenty times my s. 1399: 2
unfortunate s. 1007: 4
unhappy s. 1398:13
unhappy s. of old Andronicus 1403: 2
unto a conqueror 225:12
usurping s. 1589:13
Vincentio's s. 1402:14
was ever s. so rued 511:13
wayward s., spiteful 1398:13
well-deserving s. 702:12
where is his s. 1398: 1
where is my s. 1397: 1
where is that s. 1397: 3
who is the theme 511: 9
who should succeed the father but the s. 511:13
whose s. art thou 1401: 5
why, being s. to me, art thou so pointed at 1172: 6
wise Laertes' s. 1403: 1
wise man's s. 1402: 6
witless else her s. 1428: 4
woman's s. 1401: 6
wonderful s. 1397:10
would my s. were in Arabia 1397: 6
would to heaven I were your s. 1398: 9
you have a s. 1399: 2
you have slain your s. 1400: 3
young s. 1397: 5
youngest s. 1400:11
your brother's s. shall never reign 1524: 4
your noble s. is mad 929:10
your s. gone 1397:11
your s. is mark'd 1400: 1
your s. shall have my daughter 375: 7
your s. that is 132: 4
your s. was misled 1397: 1
your s. was run away 1397: 1
your s. was well beloved 1399: 7
your s. will not be killed 1397: 1
your s. 's my father's friend 1118:20
Son-in-law 1403
Sonance: tucket s. 1572: 5
Song 1403
antique s. 1405: 5
blind harper's s. 1710: 2
by my troth, a good s. 1405: 2
dull you with my s. 1547: 5
fairy s. 1404:16
foolish s. 1403:12
'fore God, an excellent s. 1405: 3
French s. and a fiddle has no fellow 1625: 1
have you no s., forester ..1403:12
her s. was tedious 1406: 4
I 'll end the s. 1403:11
I 'll have your s. too 1575: 8
let thy s. be love 899:13
let 's have a s. 1405:11
mermaid's s. 987: 8
merry s. 1404: 8
more exquisite s. 1405: 3
now my s. is ended 1600:14
nurse's s. ne'er pleased ..1406: 4
nurse's s. of lullaby 1383:10
of good life 1405:11
rehearse your s. by rote ...1405: 1
say our s. the whilst ...1404: 3
she had a s. of 'willow' ..1405: 4
sing a s. that old was sung 1405: 6
sing her s. and dance 1667:10
sing me a bawdy s. 1404: 8
sing s. without a burden ..1403:11
sing the s. that pleaseth ..1404: 7
sing you a s. now 1405:10
sit, and a s. 1403:12
sold a goodly manor for a s. 978: 6
speechless s. 1405: 5
that old and antique s. ...1406: 2
that s. to-night will not go from my mind 1405: 4

Speak, *continued*
all thou knowest 1419: 3
all your part at once 11: 4
and be hang'd 1423:10
and look back 11: 3
and purpose not 744: 7
apace 1419:10
as liberal as the north ...1421:20
as loud as Mars 1423:12
as my understanding instructs me 1422: 4
audaciously 1419: 8
before your time 1288: 3
best unto the purpose 73:12
better s. of you than you deserve 330: 5
bid him s. of patience 1127:15
briefly 139: 7
but brotherly 1417:11
by the card 1418: 1
comfort 204: 4
dare not s. 1427: 3
didst hear her s. 1611:10
do not bid me s. 1419: 6
do not s. to me 1155: 9
fair 1423:17
feelingly 1419: 8
fondly 1419: 8
for yourselves 1426:10
frankly as the wind 156: 2
freely 1421:16
freely s. 1421:21
freely what you think 155: 3
from thy lungs military ...925:11
he cannot s. 1427: 1
he 'll s. with you 1421: 8
hear me s. 685:13; 1418:11; 1426:17
hear me s. a word 1327: 2
hear me s. indifferently ...757:12
him fair 1424:2; 1754:10
his very heart 128: 5
how deadly dost thou s. ..1423: 8
how you s. 1417:17
I cannot s., nor think 827:13
I charge thee, s. 1417:19
I dare not s. 1427:3; 1713: 5
I love to hear her s. 1422:13
I must s. in passion 11: 1
I only s. right on 404:11
I s. but as I find 1421: 2
I s. from certainties 166: 8
I s. my conscience 226: 6
I s. sincerely 1371: 5
I s. too long 1420: 1
I was about to s. 1421:15
I will not hear her s. 360: 1
I will s., that so my heart may burst 695: 2
I will s. to thee 1349: 4
I 'll s. a little 1417:10
I 'll s. more gross 648:14
I 'll s. to it 1417:19
I 'll s. with nobody 1427: 9
if we list to s. 427:10
ill 1425:19
in jest 1418: 2
in passion 1422:18
in public 1421: 8
in sober judgement 1420: 6
it to my shame 189: 8
know not what I s. 1417:12
less than thou knowest 90: 8
let him s. no more 1033:12
let me s. a little 1417:10
let them not s. a word 1033:12
let them s. 1424:15
like a subject 1418:13
like a wood woman 1421:13
look you s. justly 794:10
low 1423:13
low and tardily 1417:16
low, if you s. love 1423:13
made us s. like friends 899:12
masterly 1419: 8
me fair 1423:15
me fair in death 298:10
more in a minute 1490: 6
more properly 1417:11
most bitterly and strange .1423: 6
most truly will I s. 1423: 6
mournfully 1419: 8
must I s. now 1420: 5
my mind 999: 3
never s. again of him 1427:10

Speak, *continued*
no harm 671: 5
no more 1418:11; 1427: 4
no more of him 1427:11
no more than truth 1425:11
no more to me 1427: 9
nobly 1419: 8
not as you think 1426: 5
not bid to s. 1419:14
not enough to s., but to s. true 1425: 5
not, reply not 43: 4
not so grossly 648:14
not to me 1427: 3
not to s. it profanely 10:10
not to s. of 1200: 3
not you for him 1562:11
now she fain would s. 1651:15
O, let me s. 1420:10
O, s. of that 1417:20
of horrors 888: 5
of me as I am 940: 8
of nothing but despair 346:13
of patience 1419:10
of thee as the traveller doth of Venice 1419: 4
once again 1418:15
once in thy life 1421: 2
one s. for both 1426:10
or die 307: 2
out of my injury 1421:10
plain and to the purpose ..155:13
positively s. 1420: 2
proudly 1419: 8
say, and s. thick 1417:16
scholarly and wisely 1420: 3
seriously 1419: 8
shall I hear him s. 1422:13
shall I s. for thee 1426:12
she must not s. 1353:12
sincerely 1419: 8
so faintly 1420: 7
so startingly 1420: 7
so true at first 1425: 1
so wide 890: 8
so wisely 1417:12
so wisely under arrest 261: 3
softly 1423:13
suddenly 139:6; 1418: 7
sufficiently 1419: 8
sweetly, man 1476: 9
that which is not 1424:12
them fair 1637:14
there s. and strike 1727: 2
they s. us fair 1423:15
this I s. in print 1421:12
thou canst not s. too much .330:13
thou for me 1426:10
thus must thou s. 5: 1
thy mind 1426: 8
to be understood 1419: 5
to me home 154: 8
to me no more 1423: 1
to some purpose 1488:13
to s. puling, like a beggar ..901: 1
to s. so fair 69: 5
to s. so indirectly I am loath 1419:13
to the business 148:10
to thee in drink 1418: 2
truly 1425: 9
unbonneted 35: 8
unskilfully 1419: 8
we s. in vain 1421: 2
we s. not what we mean ..1419:11
we s. upon our cue 1418: 5
well 1424: 9
well of him 1425:19
what I know 825:11
what should we s. of 1427: 2
what we feel 1426: 4
why do you s. to me 1421: 9
why dost not s. 1427: 1
will s. any thing 1417: 9
would you s. with me 1418:16
you must not s. of that ..1427: 1
you must not s. with men 1427: 5
you must s. louder 297:13
you on 1427:17
you so gently 1422: 5
you s. as having power ...1418: 3
you s. him far 1184: 1
you s. not as you think ...311: 7
you s. not like yourself ..1418:14
you s. too bitterly 1426:17

Speak, *continued*
you s. upon the rack 1420: 1
you s. you know not what 1418: 4
you this with a sad brow .1420: 6
your fair pleasure 1168: 6
Speaker 1417:18
be a s. free 1422: 3
in his parliament 1190:14
most rare s. 848: 8
no other s. of my actions ..714: 7
Speakers: imperfect s. 753: 9
Speakest: in vain thou s. ..1420: 1
skilfully 1418:14
thou s. it falsely 1424:10
thou s. not well 1424:14
wiser than thou art ware of 1417:12
Speaking: burst of s. 1612: 6
false 1424:10
false s. 1424:11
honourably 1419:10
in deeds 1419:10
is for beggars 1421: 5
little s. shows his love but small 914: 2
past s. of 1363:14
persuades when s. falls ..1367:14
senseless s., or a s. such as sense cannot unite 377:17
so s. as I think 1425: 7
too loud 1423:12
true 1425: 5
true s. 1516: 7
Speaks a little off 1420: 6
advisedly 1419: 8
cheerfully 1422: 7
for you stoutly 1425:17
he knows not what 1716: 5
he s. but for his friend 586:14
he s. home 154:13
he s. most vilely of you ..1375:13
he s. not o' God's name ..1418: 9
he s. not true 20: 5
he s. very shrewishly 1423:10
she s., yet says nothing 445: 2
small like a woman 1423:14
things in doubt 1417:21
what 's in his heart 154:13
wherefore s. he this 1420: 5
who s. not truly, lies 859: 1
Spear: Achilles' s. 806:10
gored with Mowbray's s. ..448: 1
slander's venom'd s. 1377: 1
Spear-grass 1073: 5
Specialty of rule 1306:15
Speciously one of them ...1460: 2
Spectacle 1416
else were this a savage s. .1247:16
heinous s. 1036: 9
how vile a s. 1416:10
moralize this s. 1282: 4
of ruth 1741: 8
piteous s. 878: 7
saddest s. e'er I view'd 684: 1
to be a public s. 420:12
Spectacled to see 1365:17
Spectacles: blind and dusty s. 452: 6
heart-hardening s. 1416:10
I shall not need s. 1416:12
pair of s. 494: 6
see without s. 1416:12
so precious 793: 1
with s. on nose 940:12
Spectator 1417
Spectators: barren s. 10:11
gentle s. 1417: 1
play'd to take s. 1417: 1
Spectatorship: long in s. ...665: 6
Speculation 1518:7
thou hast no s. in those eyes 610:13
Speculations intelligent ...1518: 7
Speculative instruments 150: 4
thoughts s. 1519: 5
Sped: I am s. 739: 6
you two are s. 86: 2
Speech 1417
affect s. and discourse 630: 6
better s. was never spoke 1427:18
cast away my s. 1428: 5
cleave the general ear with horrid s. 10:10
common s. gives him a worthy pass 1265:13
extemporal s. 1418: 7

Staff, *continued*
is quickly found to beat a dog 369:12
my s.? here is my s. 1675:11
my s. understands me 1585: 2
no s. more reverend 267: 8
of honour for mine age 715:11
of my age 132: 4
of office did I break 532:13
or a prop 45:10
we have no s. 705: 7
Stag 319:5
Stage 1438
all the world 's a s. 940:12
black s. for tragedies 1068: 3
me to their eyes 1177: 3
this great s. of fools 100: 9
this huge s. presenteth 1438: 4
where every man must play a part 1729:12
Staged: be s. to the show 151: 6
Stages: common s. 1438: 2
Stagger in 1582:12
in this attempt 59: 3
Staggering: without any s. 1131: 4
Staggers and careless lapse 1755: 9
how come these s. on me 31: 8
spoiled with s. 723: 1
Stags: breathed s. 726: 3
desperate s. 418: 5
Staider senses 522: 7
Stain 1438
and kill 1438: 9
another s., as big as hell 1438: 8
compelled s. 580: 2
do no s. to your person 1438:12
her body's s. her mind untainted clears 999:12
how may this forced s. be wiped from me 1438:13
leaves behind a s. 1438:10
make no s. a s. 1438:16
remember this s. upon her 1438: 8
some s. of soldier in you 1605: 3
to thy countrymen 1438:11
upon his silver down 262:12
upon thy cheek s. doth sit 1498: 6
Stained and deflower'd 1438: 9
unjustly s. 1438: 9
with blood 109: 2
Staining act 1265:14
Stainless maidenhoods 893: 8
youth 893: 8
Stains of right 1438:15
sightless s. 1584: 3
Stair 1438
like a tackled s. 830:11
Stair-work: some s. 921: 8
Stairs: down s. 1438:18
keep below s. 1438:18
kiss his feet 1438:17
of sand 1438:18
pair of s. to marriage 912: 2
that mount the Capitol 1616:19
Stake: die in it at the s. 1101:11
fatal s. 1549:11
I am tied to the s. 334:17
rich s. drawn 565: 6
we are at the s. 413: 6
Stale 1662
drink the s. of horses 277: 7
it a little more 1487:13
make a s. of me 1286: 1
none else to make a s. 1286: 1
poor I am but his s. 755:11
poor I am s. 95:13
so s. and cheap 1616:19
something s. and hoar 670:10
something s. with me 1379: 2
'tis s. to sigh 1032: 5
to catch these thieves 1511: 9
Staled by other men 175: 2
Staleness: weary for the s. 800:17
Stalk about her door 373: 5
grows to the s. 1606: 5
on, s. on 580:10
she crops the s. 555: 3
Stalking-horse: like a s. 1687:12
Stalks up and down 1197: 2
Stall this in your bosom 1327:10
we could not s. together 1294: 1
Stalled in mine 278: 6
Stalling of an ox 605:11
Stammer: would thou couldst s. 1419:10
Stamp and swear 116: 9
death's s. 299:10
fire-new s. of honour 715: 7
hanging a golden s. about their necks 351:12
of merit 986:17
of nature 1588: 4
of nobleness 1070: 9
of one defect 320: 8
rave, and fret 38:10
Stamped and swore 1474:15
rudely s. 1305: 3
Stamps in gold 1592:10
that are forbid 926:10
Stanchless avarice 255: 3
Stand 494:9
alone 2: 7
aloof 494:9; 1711: 8
as one upon a rock 286: 3
betwixt you and danger 286: 6
fast 77:2; 494: 9
grace to s. 634: 8
I will s. for 't 494: 9
let him s., and rave 1222: 9
make a s. 1673: 4
never s. still 1614: 3
now doth thy honour s. as firm as faith 714:15
observe her; s. close 1089: 4
only that I s. for 716: 2
rise and s. 1293: 6
stride and a s. 1619: 7
this word 's., s.' 1724:19
thou must s. by 1168: 2
to and do as we 751:12
to answer thee 41: 8
to our authority 60: 7
up 1293: 5
very strong with us 5:17
Stand-under and under-stand 1585: 2
Standard: he 's no s. 1396: 4
Standards: advance your s. 1483:11
Stander-by: be a s. 1417: 4
Standers: slippery s. 467: 9
Standers-by 1417:4
Standing-bed and truckle-bed 731:12
Standing-bowl of wine 385: 2
Standing-tuck: vile s. 326: 8
Stanze: hear a staff, a s. 1597: 1
Stanzo: another s. 1403:11
Staple of his argument 50: 5
Star 1438
adore a twinkling s. 1735:17
attending s., scarce seen 1009: 6
blazing s., or earthquake 1700: 9
born under a charitable s. 1438:19
bright particular s. 916:15
bright s. of Venus 1439:14
each particular s. 559: 5
far more glorious s. thy soul will make 1439: 9
fortune's s. 320: 8
full s. that ushers in the even 1439:14
give a name to every fixed s. 1047: 3
happy s. led us to Rome 1440: 9
happy s. reign now 1440: 9
heavens make a s. of him 1439: 9
how a bright s. shooteth 1441: 1
is fall'n 1439: 2
maidenliest s. 334:16
moist s. 1022: 2
most auspicious s. 1440:13
moves not but in his sphere 905: 8
no comfortable s. did lend his light 1440: 7
north s. 759:12
northern s. 231: 7
of a galliard 851: 8
our Jovial s. reign'd 1438:19
sanguine s. 1014: 9
shining s. 1440: 8
shining s. doth borrow 1467:12
shooting s. 1441: 1
there was a s. danced 99: 3
to every wandering bark 902:11
unfolding s. calls shepherd 1439:14
watery s. 1022: 2
what louring s. now envies 1439: 8
whatsoever s. that guides 1440:12
worship a celestial s. 1735:17
Star-blasting and taking 1503:15
Star-chamber matter 843:10
Star-crossed lovers 922:13
Star-gazers 1440:15
Star-like nobleness 1071: 3
rise, as great in fame 1215: 9
Stare, and stand an end 655: 6
him out of his wits 1691:12
in this strange s. 32: 2
Stared: they s. 365: 7
Stark and stiff 1479: 8
mad 928:10
Starkly: lies s. 1384: 6
Starlight 1440:4
Starred most unluckily 1439: 2
Starry welkin 557:17
Stars above us, govern our conditions 1439:13
angry s. of heaven 1440: 6
are those s. or suns 1439: 6
ashamed of day 445:11
bad revolting s. 1439: 7
baser s. do shut us up 1686: 6
certain s. shot madly 987: 9
chaste s. 164:11
conjures the wandering s. 644: 5
constant s. 445:10
cut him out in little s. 1440:11
depend upon thy s. 1561:14
dishonour my fair s. 357:14
do spangle heaven 445:10
earth-treading s. 1440:11
favourable s. 1606: 6
fixed s. 1439:12
good s., that were my former guides 1439: 2
happy s. 1440: 9
her better s. brought her to Mytilene 1440: 6
hide your fires 331: 8
I thank my s. 1440:14
in my s. I am above thee 640:10
in secret influence 1438: 4
inauspicious s. 1755: 2
knew the s. as I his characters 1746: 9
let the s. give light 104:11
little s. may hide them 1440: 7
little s. shot 1440: 7
luckiest s. in heaven 1439: 1
malignant and ill-boding s. 1439: 7
mortal s., as bright 445: 8
my homely s. have fail'd 1439: 1
my s. be praised 1440:14
my s. shine darkly 1440:14
not from the s. do I my judgement pluck 1440:12
of love 1441: 1
our s. that frown 1440: 6
our s., unreconcilable 1439: 2
pour the s. down plagues 1145: 2
seven s. 1439:4; 1510:13
temper with the s. 1439:10
thank my s. 1509: 8
these are s. indeed 1441: 1
thwarting s. 1439: 8
truer s. did govern 1438:19
two of the fairest s. 183:11
two s. keep not their motion in one sphere 1294: 2
will kiss the valleys 1092:11
wilt thou reach s. 33:12
with trains of fire 1098:14
you s. that move in your right spheres 1439:13
Start: get the s. 1111:14
take the s., run away 850: 9
why do you s. 522:15
Start-up: young s. 616:15
Starting-hole: what s. 1345:10
Startingly: speak so s. 1420: 7
Starvation 1441
Starve before that time 1441: 4
for a merry look 887:11
here s. we out the night 1441: 6
I 'll s. ere I 'll rob 1441: 3
on barren mountains s. 1441: 2
ready to s. 1155: 4
see 'em s. first 447:12
thou wilt s. 1441: 5
with feeding 38: 1
with nothing 1472:13
Starved: clean s. for a look 1364: 2
for want of exercise 1034: 4
Starveling: Robin S. 1164: 9
Starveling: he is no S. 512:12
you s. 326: 8

Sun, *continued*
crown'd with the golden s. 1372: 6
descending s. 1469:15
doth burn my face 1467:10
doth gild our armour 1466: 4
doth scorn you 1467:10
doubt that the s. doth move 905: 7
Edward's s. is clouded ..1732: 8
ere the s. advance 1469:10
evening s. 1694:11
fair s. 1465:15
fair s. that on this earth 1466:14
feeble and day-wearied s. 1067: 9
fiery s. 1676:15
from s. to s. 1467: 2
garish s. 1465:15
gaudy s. would peep 676:13
gazing upon the earth 1469: 2
'gins his reflection 203:11
glorious s. 1465:15
glorious s. reflex his beams 277: 5
glorious s. stays in his course 1466: 9
golden s. gives not 449: 1
golden s. salutes the morn 1469:12
good morrow to the s. 603:11
gorgeous as the s. 1466: 3
half-faced s. 458: 8
have no s. to ripe 132: 2
heaven's fair s. 1467: 1
heaven's glorious s. 1454: 1
heaven's s. staineth 1467: 5
heavenly and earthly s. ...868: 3
here never shines the s. 328:16
here the s. arises 1469: 5
herein will I imitate the s. 1466: 2
hide the s. with a blanket ..152: 5
hide thy beams 1467: 7
how bloodily the s. begins 1469: 3
I adore the s. 1465:13
is daily new and old 910: 2
is high 1466: 4
is in heaven 294:14
is o'ercast with blood 1466: 9
is the s. dimm'd, that gnats do fly in it 1467: 8
it is the blessed s. 1468: 3
it is the s. that shines 1468: 3
itself sees not till heaven clears 1467: 5
like the s. 'gainst glass 275: 4
like the s., it shines every where 567: 1
look upon the holy s. 1088: 1
look'd on the world 1466:14
looks pale 417: 1
make the s. dance 1039: 6
melts with midday s. 1390:16
mid-day s. 1467: 4
mid-day s. fierce bent 443: 1
morning s. of heaven 1469:11
morning s. shall raise 1469: 4
never shall s. morrows see 1541: 7
no sooner shall the mountains touch 1469: 7
no s. shall ever usher 1466: 8
noontide s. 1467: 4
now is the s. upon the highmost hill 1467: 4
O s., thy uprise 1469: 1
of heaven was loath to set 1469:14
of Rome is set 1469:15
one early morn did shine .1467: 5
permit the s. to climb 1467: 1
powerful s. 1465:15
radiant s. 1465:15
scorns the s. 1321: 9
selfsame s. that shines ..1468: 1
setting s., and music 1259: 1
shall greet them 469:13
shine out, fair s. 1344: 1
shine s., to succour flowers 1466:14
shines hot 1682:18
sitting in the s. 1467: 4
stain the s. with fog 1362:16
summer's s. 1466: 3
suspect the s. with cold ..1625: 6
that shines from heaven ..1467:11
that s. may never set 804: 2
that s., thine eye 442: 4
that warms you here shall shine on me 1467: 2
the s. 's a thief 1511:10
then did the s. on dunghill shine 1466:13

Sun, *continued*
then no s. must shine 293: 6
thou s., that comfort'st ..1467: 7
thy s. sets weeping 617: 2
'tis the s. that maketh all things shine 1466:11
to shame the s. by day 1468: 6
too much i' the s. 1466: 1
turn the s. to ice 754: 5
'twixt s. and s. 1465:15
unless the s. were post 853:14
walk i' the s. 287: 5
warm s. 105: 7
was not so true 533:14
weary s. hath made a golden set 1469:17
weary s. set in the west ..983: 4
when the s. sets, the air doth drizzle dew 1469:16
when the s. sets, who doth not look for night 1064:14
where he was born 781: 6
who saw the s. to-day 1467: 3
will not be seen to-day ..1467: 3
will not show his head ..1467: 3
will set before 1492:10
with one eye vieweth 1466: 5
worshipp'd s. peer'd forth 1469: 8
Sun-bright eye 445: 5
Sun-burning: not worth s. .458: 7
Sun-expelling mask 964:10
Sun-like majesty 445:13
Sunbeams: vanish'd in s. ..393:13
Sunburnt 642:3
Sunday: divide the S. from the week 1492: 3
Sunday-citizens 1474:11
Sundays: sigh away S. 1754:21
Sunder: pity to s. them ..1119: 7
Sundered: shall we be s. ..1119: 7
Sunken: blue eye and s. 900: 5
Sunrise 1469
enter there ere s. 1188:12
Sunrising: before s. 1469: 6
Suns: do I see three s. 1466: 6
fair-shining s. 1466: 6
no s. to borrow of 1468: 5
of glory 1465:15
of the world 1467: 5
three glorious s. 1466: 6
Sunset 1469
after s. 1469:15
ere s. 295:11; 1469:15
fadeth in the west 25:18
Sunshine 1466:7
after rain 921: 7
and rain at once 1389: 7
brew'd a shower 1665: 4
of his favour 1557:13
of your face 460:10
our s. made thy spring ..1274: 4
see a s. and a hail 1646:11
Sup: I s. upon myself 38: 1
I will not s. to-night 765: 9
let us s. betimes 1471: 7
them well 1470:10
there I 'll s. 1470: 6
there they intend to s. ..1470: 6
we all would s. together ..506: 5
will you s. with me 1470: 7
you 'll surely s. in hell ..1470:10
Super-dainty Kate 1053: 8
Super-subtle Venetian 1614:12
Superficial tale 1486:15
very s. 175: 6
Superficially: faith, sir, s. ..827:10
glozed, but s. 50:14
Superfluity comes sooner by white hairs 1013: 6
one for s. 776: 5
Superfluous: be so s. 729: 9
in poorest thing s. 1059: 7
to say you 're welcome were s. 1655: 4
Superfluously: bear s. 1439: 6
Superflux: shake the s. 1176:14
Supernal judge 791: 5
Supernatural and causeless 1001: 7
Superpraise my parts 311: 7
Superscript: overglance s. ..440: 5
Superscription: churlish s. 1455: 4
read me the s. 1245:10
Superserviceable rogue 816: 6
Superstition 1470
Superstitious 1470:2

Superstitiously doth swear 1470: 2
Supervise: on the s. 683: 5
the canzonet 1077: 1
Supervisor: you, the s. 927: 2
Supped: he has almost s. ..1471: 6
he s. at my house 1471: 6
I have s. full 1470:10
with sorrow 502: 8
Supper 1470
after s. 1471: 8
at s. 1470: 5
being full of s. 386: 2
bespoke s. to-morrow night 1470: 6
bid forth to s. 1471: 2
come again to s. 1471: 9
come to s. 1470:7; 1471: 5
draws toward s. 1234: 5
eat no s. that night 1471: 4
fetch my s. in 1471: 1
go to s. i' the morning ...1072:12
hold a solemn s. 1470:13
I came from a great s. 1471: 3
invited her to s. 1470: 7
is done 838: 8
is s. ready 1471: 1
make a bloody s. 1470:11
served up 1471: 1
this night he makes a s. ..1471: 3
Supper-time 1470:8
Supping: tell'st thou me of s. 1470: 4
Supple and courteous 1140: 3
I 'll make him s. 1522: 2
joints 278: 8
Suppler souls 344: 1
Suppliance of a minute ...1604:19
Suppliant 1189:9
Suppliants for the people .1189: 9
scandal'd the s. 1317: 9
Supplicant: humble s. 586:17
Supplication 1190:7
Supplications: deliver our s. 1190: 7
to his lordship 1190: 7
Supply: find s. immediate .1059:11
Supplying every stage 642: 7
Supplyment: beginning nor s. 532:11
Support him by the arm 51: 5
Supportable to make the loss 893:12
Supportance of his vow 390: 3
Supporting robbers 1296:19
Supposal: weak s. 1739: 3
Suppose: vain s. 587: 4
Supposes: counterfeit s. 312: 3
Supposition: glorious s. 987: 8
Supremacy: great s. 1181: 7
right s. 1136:16
thy full s. 761: 1
Supreme: imperious s. 304: 3
Sups: where s. he ..116:5; 1471:10
Sur-addition Leonatus 616: 3
Sur-reigned jades 112: 9
Surance: give some s. 1279: 3
Surcease: catch with his s. success 1274: 8
no pulse, but s. 697: 2
to honour 999: 7
Sure as bark on tree 166:12
as I live 495:10
as s. a card 159: 4
as s. as day 1474:11
he 'll come 495:10
I have made him s. 1131:15
it is no sin 495:10
most s. and vulgar 71: 5
nothing so s. 907: 3
of a good dinner 1682:10
of foot 722: 6
so s. as this beard 's grey ..70: 7
thou art s. of me 533:15
very s., very s. 303: 6
Surely as feet hit ground 1133:10
Surer: no s. than is fire upon the ice 1140: 2
Surest way to get 330: 4
Sureties: procure your s. ..1472: 5
Surety 1471
be his s.; be my s. 1471:11
became his s. 1472: 4
double s. 1471:13
for their traitor father ..1472: 1
he shall s. me 1471:11
of the world 808: 1
sarcenet s. for thy oaths ..1471:12
we 'll s. him 1471:11

Sword, *continued*
rebel's s. unsheathed 1479:10
rest, s., thou hast thy fill .1484: 6
rust, s., cool, blushes 1344:13
see how my s. weeps 1481: 2
senseless s. 1480: 2
shake my s. or hear drum ..709: 5
shall I need to draw my s. 1112:16
sharp-pointed s. 1480: 2
sheathe my s. 1484: 5
sheathe thy s. 1483:16
should end it 389:11
sleeping s. of war 1480: 1
Spanish s. 1482: 2
strip your s. stark naked ...390: 2
swallow my s. like a pin ..1521: 1
take my s. 1481: 6
this is his s. 1478:14
this s. but shown to Cæsar
shall enter me 1478:15
this s. hath ended him 1479: 8
this s. of mine 1481: 7
threaten'd with the s. 1478:11
threatening s. 1480: 2
true s. 1482:11
trusty s. 1483: 8
turn thy edged s. 1480: 4
two-hand s. 1480: 2
unbated 770: 2
unsheathe your s. ..408:17; 822: 4
unstained s. that you 1479:10
up, s. 1277: 2
upon your s. sit laurel victory 1599:16
valiant s. 1480: 2
victor s. 1562: 1
warlike s. 1480: 4
well-labouring s. 1480: 2
why call you for a s. 1482: 7
with his s. drawn 1483: 3
wooed thee with my s. ...1711: 1
wounds like a leaden s. 450:10
wrench his s. from him 1482: 1
you drew your s. upon me ..739:10
your s. is bright 1484: 2
your true s. drawn 1482:11
Sword-and-buckler Prince ..1201: 4
Sword-hilts: hold my s. 1461: 3
Sword-men: sinewy s. 1478:10
Sworder: against a s. 151: 6
Roman s. and banditto slave 307: 2
Swords and lances arbitrate 1482: 4
be those with s. 1482:11
bear our civil s. 1479:10
debate with angry s. 1480: 6
died with their s. in hand .1479: 2
draw no s. but what are
sanctified 1483: 4
draw your willing s. 1483:11
drawn s. 1483: 2
dreadful s. 1480: 2
eat s. first 1198:17
French s. 1482: 2
helpful s. 1719:15
I smile at 100:10
in your country's service
drew your s. 575: 5
keep up your bright s. 1481:13
lay their s. to pawn 1484: 4
masterless and gory s. ...1482: 8
naked s. 1483: 2
of common soldiers 1481: 1
of soldiers are his teeth 304: 8
of wicked men 1274:15
our s. our law 1482: 6
our s. shall plead it 1538: 6
pawn their s. 1472: 2
put up your s. 1484: 1
rather see the s. 131: 4
Roman s. 1482: 2
sheathed their s. for lack
of argument 49:15
smoking s. 1389:13
stain your s. with blood ..1479: 1
they have true s. 1482:11
true s. 1394:17
unhack'd s. and helmets ..1135:12
we measured s. and parted .857:16
your s. are now too massy 1482: 9
your s., made rich 1481: 2
Swore by his honour 1084: 9
I s. in jest 783: 8
Sworn: be but s. my love ...909: 7
I have s. an oath 1081:7; 1083: 7
I have s. thee fair 1558: 9

Sworn, *continued*
I have s. to do it 314: 2
my love to be 912: 1
on a book 1079:10
to do amiss 314: 8
to give him aid 27:18
to marry me 963: 5
to the contrary 1574:11
with a solemn tongue 1080: 1
Swound: I s. to see thee 278: 8
Swounded and fell down ..1478: 6
I s. at the sight 1478: 6
Swounds, I should take it ..256: 1
she s. to see him 1478: 6
Swum ashore, like a duck ...426: 7
you never s. the Hellespont 897:14
Sycamore 1564:12
Sycorax: foul witch S. 1693: 5
Sylla: ambitious S. 1027: 9
Syllable: believe you by the s. 92: 7
every s. that here was spoke 981:15
last s. of recorded time ...1124: 8
least s. of thy addition 816: 6
speak one s. 1425:15
to the s. 1087: 9
utmost s. of worthiness .1737:13
Syllables of no allowance ..1721: 2
Syllogism: simple s. 1219: 9
Sylvia is myself 67: 2
who is S. 207:11
Symbols of redeemed sin ...1370: 3
Sympathize 1484:12
Sympathized: truly s. 1484:12
well s. 1484:12
Sympathy 1484
in choice 895: 5
in years 927: 1
of love 457: 8
solemn s. 1484:14
there 's s. 1484:10
what a s. of woe 1484:15
woful s. 1484:14
Synod 1554:5
in general s. 577: 8
sit in hourly s. 1218: 5
whole s. of them 621: 4
Synods: solemn s. 1554: 5
Syracusa: in S. was I born 1664: 5
Syracusian merchant 2: 3
speak freely, S. 1421:16
Syrups: drowsy s. of the
world 1385:15
wholesome s. 974: 1

T

Table 1485
at the round t. 1485: 4
cover the t. 344: 5
divorce myself both from
thy t., and thy bed 367:12
flattering t. of her eye 917: 8
full of welcome 1653: 4
have a fairer t. 575:21
have a t. by himself 212: 3
in our heart's t. 1257:10
moderate t. 1485: 4
of my heart 452: 8
of my memory 981: 2
Priam's royal t. 1485: 9
set the t. on a roar 880: 3
the t. 's full 1485: 6
welcome to our t. 559: 9
wherein all my thoughts ..1485: 5
Table-book: play'd the t. ...1681: 5
Table-sport: be your t. 1286: 2
Table-talk: serve for t. 1489: 9
Tabled by his side 14: 2
Tables: clasp young Cupid's
t. 1187:14
furnish forth marriage t. .1522: 5
of his law 1037:12
plays at t. 601: 5
thy t. are within my brain 1485: 5
turn the t. up 1485: 8
unclasp the t. of their
thoughts 237: 1
were stored full 194:12
wipe his t. clean 1258: 3
Tabor and the pipe 1040: 8
dost live by thy t. 193: 6
play on the t. 282:13
then I beat my t. 1041: 7
Tabourines: beat loud the t. 1395: 1
rattling t. 1572: 4

Taciturnity 1490
gift in t. 1328:14
Tacked together 1355: 9
Tackle: hempen t. 1313: 9
nor t., sail, nor mast 1242:19
of my heart is crack'd 695: 4
silken t. swells with the
touches of those hands .659:12
though thy t. is torn 44:11
Tackled stair 830:11
Tadpole: I 'll broach the t. ...62: 2
toad, the t. 400: 6
Taffeta: changeable t. 1486:10
flame-coloured t. 851: 8
rich t. 81: 5
Tag: before the t. return ..1140: 8
Tag-rag people 1140: 8
Tail 1485
clapp'd his t. between his
legs 272: 9
Dobbin's t. grows backward 1485:12
in his t. 1547: 1
salmon's t. 1685: 1
shake his t. and say nothing 967:13
thereby hangs a t. 770: 7
thick t., broad buttock 723: 8
this body hath a t. 1485:10
under the dragon's t. 334:16
Tailor 1485
call'd the t. lown 1486: 6
even now a t. call'd me ..1485:18
fall out with a t. 380: 7
here 's an English t. 1486: 3
made thee 1485:19
make a man 1485:19
make thy doublet 1486:10
man's t. 1486: 1
next way to turn t. 1485:20
see the t. paid 1133: 3
stays thy leisure 1486: 8
thy t. made those clothes,
which, as it seems, make
thee 1485:19
very good t. 1485:16
who 's his t. 1485:16
with his last 829: 5
woman's t. 1486: 1
yet a t. might scratch her .1486: 9
Tailors are as dear as yours 1402: 6
I have undone three t. ...1485:17
increase t. 1630: 1
of the earth 1669: 3
score or two of t. 1486: 7
Tails of wasps 1454:12
proud t. 1485:15
talk of t. 1547: 1
Taint: any t. of vice 762: 9
fall'n into t. 19:11
I cannot t. with fear 521: 4
of our best man 1101:16
of the whole state 1291: 5
Tainting of my love 911: 3
Taints and blames 104: 3
his t. and honours 627:12
of liberty 514: 4
Tainture of thy nest 514: 6
Take 495:13
her by the arm 51: 5
how you t. it 1663:17
I 'll t. him down 1451: 4
knew not what to t. 738:18
no harm 671: 5
to t. is not to give 1290: 2
vantage 15: 9
what I shall die to want ..1587:16
Take One's Part 1118
Taker: life-weary t. 1175: 2
make the t. mad 927: 7
runs presently mad 351:13
Takes: it t. him off 386: 6
tell me how he t. it 918: 5
Taking: honest t. up 1471:13
in worser t. 1507: 6
Taking-off 1608:1
Talbot: if T. do but thunder,
rain will follow 1524:10
is but shadow of himself ..1457: 9
is my name T. 1046:11
young T. 1656: 9
Tale 1486
a mad t. he told 929: 2
Æneas' t. to Dido 1488: 9
amorous t. 1711: 4
ancient t. new told 9: 6
every t. condemns me 227: 8

Tarrying ... 1491
nor flying hence nor t. ... 285:13
Tarsus: this T. ... 194:12
to T. intend my travel ... 1557: 6
Tart: so t. a favour ... 1062: 5
Tartar: out, tawny T. ... 360: 8
Tartars: Turks and T. ... 1580: 1
Tartly: how t. looks ... 887: 2
Tartness: king's t. ... 1476: 4
of his face ... 458: 2
Task ... 1492
about our t. ... 316: 6
be this all the t. ... 1492: 8
day's t. is done ... 1492: 2
easy t. to love a king ... 1492: 5
easy t. to win our own ... 1177: 9
heavier t. could not ... 644: 1
heavy t. ... 1492:11
his day's hot t. hath ended 1470: 1
I have perform'd my t. ... 1492: 2
me to my word ... 1724: 3
sad t. hath not said ... 1218:17
shall I not hear my t. ... 1492: 5
sore t. does not divide ... 1492: 3
take thou this t. in hand ... 1492: 4
thy worldly t. hast done ... 303: 3
to my t. will I ... 1492: 4
to our holy t. ... 1492: 9
weary t. fordone ... 1170:13
what t. I have to do ... 1492:10
you to recite ... 1492: 6
Tasked to mow ... 1492: 6
Tasker: task the t. ... 1492: 6
Tasking: how show'd his t. 1492: 6
of their minds ... 1492: 6
Tasks: command him t. ... 1660: 6
easy t. ... 185: 6
these are barren t. ... 1492: 7
Tassel of a prodigal's purse .327: 1
Tassel-gentle: lure this t. ... 1611:16
Taste ... 1492
as like this as a crab ... 872: 4
as sweet ... 1493: 4
bitter wormwood t. ... 1102:13
confounds the appetite ... 712: 2
delight the t. ... 324: 7
do you like the t. ... 1492:17
forgot the t. of fears ... 524:12
fresh t. ... 1493: 3
give a t. of it ... 1493: 9
give us a t. of your quality 1427:14
great'st t. most palates ... 1492:13
had a kind of t. ... 509: 7
his t. delicious ... 1476: 7
last t. of sweets ... 1259: 1
little t. ... 1493: 3
loathe the t. of sweetness .1472: 9
Lord Timon's bounty ... 129:15
morning t. ... 1493: 3
my natural t. ... 47: 7
of danger and reproof ... 1504:15
of his obedience ... 1085:10
of it first ... 1493: 5
of madness ... 1492:15
of much correction ... 238: 7
of my bottle ... 1680:17
of my finding him ... 1492:12
of tediousness ... 731:13
of thy drug ... 1492:14
of thy most worst ... 1549: 8
of your wine ... 1445: 3
our comfort ... 203: 3
precious t. ... 1493: 3
sans t., sans every thing ... 940:12
sour to t. ... 595:13
stained t. of violated troth 1493: 3
sweet world's t. ... 1346: 8
this bitter t. ... 102: 5
we of t. and feeling are ... 1493: 2
who did t. to him ... 1493: 5
wilful t. ... 1493: 9
with a distempered appetite 1332:16
Tasted her in bed ... 1289: 3
mayst thou well be t. ... 1493:11
praise us as we are t. ... 1186: 1
Tastes: how t. it ... 1492:18
know not how it t. ... 1493:12
Tasting of our wrath ... 1742: 8
Tattering colours ... 1600: 5
Tatters: tear a passion to t. ... 10:11
Tattle what they please ... 830: 1
Tattling: evermore t. ... 629:11
Tattlings: peace your t. ... 629:11
Taught and train'd ... 1494: 9
highly fed and lowly t. ... 954:14

Taught, *continued*
me first to beg ... 88:10
say I t. thee ... 1494: 8
thee each hour ... 1495: 3
who t. you this ... 1699:11
Taunt ... 1493
and scorn me ... 1321: 6
at slackness ... 1476:13
Taunted ... 1493:17
Taunting letter ... 852:11
Tauntingly replied ... 1493:14
Taunts: aptly t. himself ... 1322: 2
bitter t. ... 1493:15
contumelious t. ... 420:12
gross t. ... 1493:15
many foul t. ... 684: 1
Taurus: born under T. ... 283: 7
Taurus': high T. snow ... 1390:19
Tavern ... 765:15
betwixt t. and t. ... 1309: 5
like a t. or a brothel ... 175: 3
wish this t. were my drum .400: 2
Tavern-bills: no more t. ... 1273:13
Tavern-reckonings ... 1170:16
Taverns: given to t. ... 765:15
knocking at the t. ... 1395: 6
Tawdry-lace and gloves ... 618: 1
Tawny-finned fishes ... 545: 3
Tax any private party ... 1197: 1
I t. not you ... 1264:12
of impudence ... 1375: 5
she 'll t. him home ... 1264:12
they t. our policy ... 258:10
Taxation ... 1494
know you of this t. ... 1494: 2
of homage ... 1629: 9
whipped for t. ... 1657: 3
Taxations: burthenous t. ... 1494: 1
upon these t. ... 1494: 2
Taxed and debosh'd ... 1380:10
of other nations ... 1275: 8
Taxes: grievous t. ... 1494: 3
Taxing like a wild-goose flies 261:17
Te Deum ... 1404:10
Teach ... 1494:5; 1494:10
me how a beggar should be answer'd ... 88:10
me how to curse ... 276: 4
me how to flatter ... 548:10
the children behaviours ... 91: 1
thee another course ... 250: 7
thou didst t. the way ... 1368:15
young babes ... 185: 6
Teacher ... 1495
be red-breast t. ... 1485:20
teach a t. ... 1494:11
Teachers: instruct great t. .1495: 6
Teachest like a fool ... 561: 7
Teaching ... 1494
follow mine own t. ... 431: 2
of the maid ... 1495: 9
Team: he that ears my land spares my t. ... 267: 3
of horse ... 484: 7
Tear ... 1495
aid thee t. for t. ... 1650: 7
ample t. trill'd down ... 1497: 6
did not think to shed a t. .1500:12
do not t. away thyself ... 1119: 9
draw in many a t. ... 1496:13
fall not a t. ... 1495:12
he hath a t. for pity ... 178: 6
her all to pieces ... 1521: 7
here did she fall a t. ... 1498: 4
him to pieces ... 230: 6
holy and obsequious t. ... 897: 5
holy t. ... 1496: 3
let fall a t. ... 1162: 5
never borrow any t. ... 1649:15
never shed remorseful t. ... 448: 3
not a t. can fall ... 687: 9
not another t. to shed ... 1499:10
old t. not wash'd off yet ... 1498: 6
profane a t. ... 448: 1
scorn an humble t. ... 448: 3
thee joint by joint ... 1521:11
weeping t. shed ... 1498: 1
woman's t. ... 1501: 2
Tear-disdained eye ... 447:13
Tear-falling pity ... 1157: 9
Tear-stain'd eyes ... 447: 3
Tearful eyes ... 447: 4
Tears: abound in t. ... 1652: 1
aid you with our kindred t. 1651: 3
and heavy sorrows ... 1496: 6

Tears, *continued*
artificial t. ... 1497: 1
as salt as sea ... 1500: 5
as sovereign as blood ... 1495:12
back, foolish t. ... 1499: 4
be moved with my t. ... 1363: 8
be your t. wet ... 1497: 7
behind him he leaves t. ... 1071: 9
bid him shed t. ... 448: 4
big round t. ... 39: 9
biggest t. o'ershower'd ... 1363: 7
bitter t. ... 1499: 6
blind with t. ... 1650: 7
blind with tributary t. ... 1409: 8
blinding t. ... 1497:13
borrow'd t. ... 1497: 1
break into t. ... 1497:13
brinish t. ... 1260: 2
broken t. ... 1497:13
cadent t. fret channels ... 1497: 6
cease your t. ... 1373: 5
chastest t. that ever modest eyes with sorrow shed 1498: 1
children's t. ... 1497:13
combating with t. and smiles ... 459: 8
commanded t. ... 448: 4
conjure t. up ... 1286: 6
contending t. ... 1499:14
continual t. ... 1499: 7
convert those t. ... 1496: 9
cruel t. ... 1650:15
crystal t. gave light ... 445: 4
despised t. ... 1498: 3
dew it with mournful t. 1032:11
dissolved to t. ... 1498: 4
distill'd by moans ... 1498: 8
do not become a man ... 1496: 1
do stop the flood-gates ... 1496: 5
dost thou drink t. ... 1499:14
drawn from her eyes ... 1498: 2
drawn salt t. ... 448: 3
drop t. as fast ... 1425:17
drown the stage with t. ... 10: 9
dry his t. ... 1500: 1
dry thy melting t. ... 1650: 5
dry up your t. ... 1497: 7
exhibit my tongue ... 502: 6
fast-falling t. ... 1496:12
feigned t., your flattery ... 549: 2
fertile t. ... 911: 1
fill it with my t. ... 1495:14
for his love ... 153: 5
fresh t. stood on her cheeks 1499: 7
full of t. am I ... 1498: 4
full of t., of smiles ... 175:11
gave me up to t. ... 1637: 9
gentleman-like t. ... 1652: 1
given him t. unto entreaties 1397: 2
great t. grace remembrance 507: 8
harden lust ... 1498: 1
has t. in 's eyes ... 10: 9
hear these t. ... 195: 2
heavy t., badges of woe ... 1517: 9
her salt t. fell from her ... 1405: 4
her t. began to turn ... 1500: 1
her t. will pierce ... 1496:13
his t. pure messengers ... 1499:13
his t. run down his beard 1499: 1
hot t. which break ... 868:17
I forbid my t. ... 1500:12
I owe more t. ... 1497: 3
I would these dewy t. were from the ground ... 1498: 5
if you have t., prepare to shed them now ... 1497: 3
important t. ... 1497:13
in her eye ... 448: 8
in his eyes ... 10: 9
joyful t. ... 1499: 2
joyful t. show heart ... 689: 9
kindred t. ... 1651: 3
leave your t. ... 1497: 7
left her in her t. ... 1497:11
let my t. staunch the earth's dry appetite ... 1499: 6
like Niobe, all t. ... 1704: 1
liquid t. ... 557: 1
live in an onion ... 1497: 1
lovers' t. ... 1497:13
made of t. ... 1499: 8
many t. to wash ... 1124: 9
master's t. to you deplore 1499:11
melt at my t. ... 213:11
mingle t. with smiles ... 1333: 9

Time 1527
aboding luckless t. 99: 9
about cockshut t. 1469:17
after a little t. 1532: 7
after some t. 1532: 7
against that t. 1532: 4
all this t. 1532: 5
ambles withal 1534: 8
and case requireth haste ... 674: 4
and our concernings 853:11
and place 1536: 8
and the hour 1531: 1
another t. 1532: 8
anticipating t. 48:14
antique t. 1537: 2
any t. 1529: 4
are as the time is 943:15
as if T. were in debt 1527: 5
at any (no, one, some) t. .. 1527:10
at such a t. 1425:13
at that (this) t. 1527:10
bald sexton T. 1527: 4
balmy t. 1531:16
be thine 1535: 7
before her t. 1532:14
before the t. be out 1528: 2
beguile the t. 827:12
besmear'd with sluttish t. 1021: 7
best t., better t. 1528: 1
bid t. return 1531:17
bids be gone 1532:16
blessed t. 1531:16; 1537: 6
blossoming t. 1705: 8
breathing t. of day 1253:14
busy t. 1535:12
by that (this) t. 1529: 6
by t., by means and place 1102: 6
calls upon 's 1532:17
calumniating t. 1534: 3
come before their t. 923: 1
come stealing on 1527: 5
consumed t. 1722: 3
continuate t. 1531:16
cormorant devouring T. 1530:17
creep t. ne'er so slow 1281: 5
curbed t. 919: 9
dead t. 1531:16
dead t. of night 721: 4
decays 1465:11
despised t. 1537:10
devise the fittest t. 1311:12
devouring T., blunt thou .. 1533: 8
dilatory t. 1690: 1
do thy worst, old T. 1533: 8
doth transfix the flourish .. 1533: 8
dream away the t. 376: 7
drink with any t. 383: 6
drive away the t. 1536: 1
drugs fit, and t. agreeing 1102: 6
eaning t. 100:12
enough to mourn 1031:10
envious, calumniating t. .. 1534: 3
ere this t. 1532: 3
every t. serves 1535: 6
expend your t. with us ... 1528:14
fair t. of day 293: 6
father T. 1306:10
fearfull'st t. 1537:14
fill up the t. 1531: 2
find t. 1530:12
first t. 1529:10
fit it with some better t. 1419: 1
fit t. 1528: 1
fit t. of law 1205: 3
fitter t. for that 1528: 1
fleet the t. carelessly 570: 1
for all things 1528: 5
for such a word 1717: 4
for this t. 1530:10
for words 1527:13
force, and death 899:14
from t. to t. 496:10
from this t. forth 1514:8; 1549: 3
full t. 1531:16
gallops withal 1534: 8
give me so much of your t. 1531: 9
give the t. of day 1024: 9
give thee t. 1531: 9
given private t. to you ... 1709:11
goes by, away 752:12
goes on crutches 919: 9
goes upright 1527: 7
good t. encounter her 1192:11
good t. of day 293: 6
grant the t. 1530:16

Time, *continued*
growing t. 1531:16
had not scythed 24:10
had t. cohered 1536: 8
hapless t. 292:11
happier and more comely t. 1537: 3
happy t. 1537: 5
has been 610:13
hasty-footed t. 1535: 2
hath a wallet at his back .. 1527: 8
hath been 1531: 6
hath made thee hard 1459:17
hath not yet so dried 1:12
hath nothing blurr'd 1528:10
hath rooted out my parentage 1115: 7
hath there been such a t. 1529: 1
hath worn us into slovenry 1530: 1
have t. 1527:13
he keeps his t. well 385: 5
he kept not t. 1509:14
heavy t. 1537:10
hereafter t. 1124: 9
high t. 496:10
himself is bald 657: 7
his t. is spent 1531:13
hold our t. too precious ... 1321: 1
how long a t. lies in one
little word 1717:19
how slow it creeps 1535: 5
I have seen the t. 1531: 8
I must stay his t. 1528: 2
I wasted t. 1536: 4
idle t. 1536: 6
if T. be in debt 1527: 5
ill t. 1537:10
in good t. 972:8; 1528: 8
in our t. to come 1696: 4
in spring t. 894:10
in such a t. as this 1093:10
in t. 1528: 8
in t. to come 598: 7
in your father's t. 1537: 2
injurious, shifting T. 1533: 4
injurious t., now 1534: 3
invites you 1528:13
inviting thee 1528: 9
inviting t. 1537: 5
is a very bankrupt 1527: 5
is at his period 1536:11
is come 1530: 7
is come even now 1531: 6
is come round 867:13
is fair again 1646:11
is free 1531: 5
is it a t. to jest and dally 1479: 8
is kept with tears 366: 3
is like a fashionable host .. 1527: 8
is long 1535: 5
is out of joint 1537: 8
is the king of men 1533: 3
is the nurse 1527: 9
is the old justice 1527: 3
is their master 1532:16
is troublesome 1537: 7
is unagreeable 1532: 9
is very short 1528: 7
is yet to come 1270: 2
it is now our t. 1686:11
itself unsorted 1529: 5
keep t. 1531:12
keeps t., distance 390: 1
large expense of t. 437: 3
last syllable of recorded t. 1124: 8
last t. 1531:16
leave it to t. 1529: 7
let him have t. 1533: 5
let the t. run on 1528:12
let t. shape 1529: 7
let 's not confound the t. .. 150: 1
long t. 1535: 5
long-experienced t. 1535: 5
lose my t. 393: 9
lose our t. 1536: 6
loss of t. 893:13
make good t. 1528:11
make use of t. 1103: 2
many a t. 1530: 6
many a t. and oft 725:2;
.... 1017:4; 1127: 4
mark how slow t. goes 1533: 5
mature t. 1537: 2
meet the t. 1528:12
mis-shapen T. 1533: 5
misorder'd doth crowd us 1533: 1

Time, *continued*
mock the t. with fairest
show 459:12
more consider'd t. 1528:15
most accurst 1537:10
much upon this t. 1531: 7
must friend or end 1532:11
must have a stop 1535: 4
my t. runs posting 1535: 3
name the t. 1532: 1
needy t. 1537:10
neglected t. 1536: 3
never-resting t. 1535: 2
next t. 1530: 5
no t. for all things 657: 7
no t. shall be omitted 1535:10
no t. so miserable 1371: 9
no t. to chide you 185: 6
no t. to lend money 852: 8
nor t. nor place did then
adhere 1102:11
now doth t. waste me 1536: 4
now is a t. to storm 1532:10
now is the t. 1531: 6
now is the t. of help 705: 9
now it is t. 1529: 8
now serves not .. 581:12; 1264:19
now the t. is flush 1534: 1
never-resting t. 1465:11
O t., cease thou 1535: 5
O t. most accurst 592: 3
O t.! thou must untangle
this, not I 1290: 5
o' day 1531:19
odd t. 1531:16
o'er-run my former t. 1515: 2
o'erpast 1124: 9
of action 1532:12
of day 643: 2
of death 1532:12
of folly 1533: 5
of help 1532:12
of lethargy 1537:10
of life 861:10
of life is short 864:16
of moon 1532:12
of night 1532:12; 1692:13
of peace 1532:12
of preservation 1534: 9
of rest 1757: 2
of sorrow 1533: 5
of sport 1533: 5
of storm 1532:12
of the night 1066: 2
of thy nativity 278: 3
of trial 1566: 9
of war 1532:12
of year 1532:12
old T. the clock-setter 1527: 4
olden t. 1537: 2
one at a t. 489: 7
one t. or another 472: 8
one t. or other 1529: 9
one t. will owe another .. 1528: 7
only pretty ring t. 1436: 4
our t. does call upon 's .. 1532:17
our t. of stay is short ... 1120: 7
out of mind 1532: 3
outstay the t. 1528: 2
outstood my t. 1528: 2
own t. 1527:11
part the t. between 's 1535:16
pass away the t. 1531:18
pay the t. but needful woe 645: 2
perilous t. 1537:10
piping t. of peace 1136:10
present t. doth boast 1124: 5
present t. 's so sick 974: 7
privilege your t. 1535:13
profane the precious t. 1536: 1
Pythagoras' t. 1537: 2
qualifies the spark 918:11
redeeming t. 1093: 3
revives us 1527:12
right deadly 286: 5
royal t. 1537: 5
sad t. 1537:10
same t. 1531:16
second t. 1529:10
seems long 1535: 5
sent before my t. 100: 1
serves 1530: 4
shall bring to ripeness ... 1215: 9
shall favourably minister 1531:11
shall not go dully 1535:12

Tongue, *continued*
his t. sounds ever after as a sullen bell ... 1063:14
hold my (thy) t. ... 1547: 5
hold your t. ... 484: 2
honour's t. ... 1512: 2
how durst thy t. move anger to our face ... 1546: 6
how might she t. me ... 1347: 3
husband's shallow t. ... 1543: 1
I can speak thy t. ... 836:12
I cannot bring my t. to such a pace ... 1545: 8
I do know your t. ... 837: 2
I have no t. but one ... 837: 2
I have no t., sir ... 1366:13
I hear a t. cry 'Cæsar' ... 1545:16
I must hold my t. ... 696: 5
if thy t. can speak ... 1547:12
imperial t. is stern ... 1544:12
iron t. and brazen mouth ... 93: 5
iron t. of midnight ... 992: 9
it hath no t. to vex you ... 1152:17
keep a good t. in your head 1543:11
killing t. and quiet sword . 1545:11
knave's t. begins to double 1545: 1
know'st my t. so well ... 837: 2
let me not hold my t. ... 452:15
let my t. blister ... 1543:18
let my t. excuse all ... 1542: 5
let thy t. be equal with thy heart ... 1515: 1
let thy t. detect thy base-born heart ... 1542: 3
let thy t. tang ... 1543:10
let t. of war plead ... 1628: 5
liberal t. ... 1545:12
like a strange t. ... 1201: 6
like a trumpet doth his t. begin ... 1546: 7
lolling t. with slaughtering 412: 7
lose her t. ... 1547: 4
lose thy light ... 1542:14
lose thy t. ... 1547: 1
love's t. proves dainty Bacchus gross in taste ... 894:14
lying t. ... 1560: 8
many a man's t. shakes out his master's undoing ... 1547: 3
mince not the general t. ... 1541:15
mine own t. splits ... 385: 7
mother's t. ... 1542: 4
multitudinous t. ... 1547: 4
my t. cannot express my grief ... 647: 3
my t. cleave to my roof ... 1114:14
my t. could never learn ... 1544:15
my t. hath heavier tale ... 1543: 3
my t. hath wrong'd him ... 1544:17
my t. is too foolhardy ... 1545: 5
my t. is weary ... 1545:10
my t. shall hush again ... 1542: 7
my t. shall utter all ... 1546: 7
my t. should catch your t.'s sweet melody ... 1544: 1
my t. should stumble ... 277: 6
my t., though not my heart 696: 5
my t. to the roof of my mouth ... 543:13
my t. will tell the anger ... 1542: 3
neat's t. dried ... 1367: 6
nimble t. ... 1545:12
no joyful t. gave welcome 1543: 6
no t.! all eyes ... 1547:11
no t. hath power ... 275: 8
no t. that moves ... 1544:10
nor can my t. unload my heart's great burthen ... 696: 7
nor heart cannot conceive . 721: 1
nor t. of mortal tell ... 1231: 9
not a t. of them all ... 1541:21
not a word ... 1547:11
O, that my t. were in the thunder's mouth ... 1542: 7
of dog ... 1542: 4
of him that makes ... 783:10
of Isabel ... 1542:15
of loss cried fame ... 470:14
of mortal ... 1542: 4
one and the self-same t. ... 1034: 3
our t. is rough ... 1544:12
owner's t. doth publish ... 913:12
passing pleasing t. ... 46: 1
pleading t. ... 1543:14
pluck out multitudinous t. 1547: 4

Tongue, *continued*
poor tired t. ... 835: 7
poor t. ... 1543: 1
pray God his t. be hotter ... 277: 4
princely t. ... 1184: 3
pulled out thy t. ... 1520: 6
put a t. in every wound ... 1043: 6
puts her t. a little in her heart ... 1546:14
question with a wicked t. . 1233: 8
rattling t. of saucy and audacious eloquence ... 1655: 2
ready t. ... 1545:12
rein thy t. ... 1545:15
rich music's t. ... 789:12
robs my t. from breathing 1335:15
rumour's t. I idly heard ... 1307: 5
saucy t. ... 1544:19
schoolboy's t. ... 1427:18
scolding t. ... 1321:4; 1546:18
serpent's t. ... 1544:19
she but lost her t. ... 1070: 7
she hath no t. ... 662: 1
shepherd's t. ... 1542: 4
Signior Benedick's t. ... 1542:15
slanderous t. ... 153:14
slow t. ... 1544: 4
smooth not thy t. with filed talk ... 1488: 2
soft low t. ... 254: 1
soft-slow t. ... 1544: 4
solemn t. ... 1543: 1
soothing t. ... 1544: 3
speak the French t. ... 583: 4
speaking of my t. ... 837: 2
speaks the common t. ... 837: 2
speak'st with every t. ... 625: 1
splitted my poor t. ... 1612: 5
stay her t. ... 1547: 2
strange t. makes my cause . 419: 7
struck me with her t. ... 1546:11
subduing t. ... 50: 6
such a t. ... 1544:13
such an earthly t. ... 907: 3
sugar'd t. to bitter wormwood taste ... 1102:13
sweet t. ... 1543:18
talk thy t. weary ... 1489:20
teach my t. to be so long . 1546: 5
that his t. must vent ... 154:13
that skull had a t. ... 1374:15
that t. that ever sweet ... 1544: 6
that t. that tells the story . 1545: 4
the t. our trumpeter ... 1572:11
the world's large t. ... 176: 7
there 's a double t. ... 1546: 4
thine own t. ... 1578:16
this t. had not offended ... 1545:16
this t. hath parley'd ... 1542: 2
this t. of mine ... 1543: 4
this t. that runs so roundly 1546: 8
thunder'st with thy t. ... 1727: 2
thy t. against thy t. ... 1081: 1
thy t. makes Welsh as sweet 837: 1
thy t. may take off some extremity ... 1427: 2
thy t. of breeding breathes 1543:16
thy t. will not confess ... 424:14
tie up my love's t. ... 1548: 2
to doom my brother's death 1543: 8
torment you with bitter t. ... 339: 7
trippingly on the t. ... 1404: 6
try with t. too ... 1039: 7
tune thy woes to thy lamenting t. ... 770:11
understand in another t. ... 837: 2
unreverend t. ... 1546:10
untuned t. ... 1546:16
unwilling t. ... 1751: 8
use that t. I have ... 1544:16
use thy t. ... 1546: 3
wag his t. in censure ... 165:11
wag thy t. ... 496:16
well learned is that t. ... 1543:17
what a ready t. suspicion hath ... 1473: 7
what my t. dares not, that my heart shall say ... 696:10
what my t. speaks ... 1483:10
what t. shall smooth thy name ... 1049: 1
when my t. blabs ... 1547:13
which I know will not lie ... 453: 1
whose t. is music now ... 1544: 9
whose t. more poisons ... 1545: 2

Tongue, *continued*
whose t. outvenoms all the worms of Nile ... 1375: 9
whose t. shall ask me ... 1139: 9
whose t. soe'er speaks false 859: 1
will not my t. be mute ... 1260: 9
with a tang ... 1543:10
with his t. he cannot win a woman ... 1543:12
with mine own t. deny ... 1176:15
with my t. in your tail ... 1547: 1
with my t. to tell the passion ... 1710: 1
with slander's t. be wounded ... 1376: 4
with t. in venom steep'd ... 1544:18
without her t. ... 43:13
woe-wearied t. ... 1006:12
you have a double t. ... 1610: 7
your t. divine ... 1630: 2

Tongue-tied ... 1548

Tongueless ... 1274:14; 1547:9

Tongues: all t. cried ... 1543: 5
all t. give thee that due ... 1185: 9
all t. speak of him ... 1176:16
all t. to talk bitterest ... 330:13
bestowed that time in the t. 837: 2
bite our t. ... 1542: 1
bitter t. ... 1544:19
calumnious t. ... 814:13
chapmen's t. ... 1542: 4
clamour your t. ... 1547:11
clocks the t. of bawds ... 729: 9
cloven t. do hiss ... 13: 3
deserved all t. to talk ... 1423:11
disclaim their t. ... 1612:12
eager t. ... 1546:17
eloquent t. ... 1545:12
full of t., of eyes ... 1111: 6
gentle t. ... 1543:15
have you the t. ... 837:13
he hath the t. ... 1546: 4
hold our (your) t. ... 1547: 5
I 'll hang on every tree ... 1541:17
in trees ... 866:10
lack t. to praise ... 453: 3
lovers' t. ... 1544: 5
o' the common mouth ... 1541:15
of dying men ... 242:10
of heaven denouncing ... 1594:17
of men full of deceits ... 310:11
of mocking wenches ... 1546:12
of soothers ... 549: 5
of the common mouth ... 60: 7
put our t. into those wounds ... 1541:18
Rumour's t. ... 1307: 3
silence envious t. ... 1135: 6
slanderous t. ... 796:3; 1377: 4
speechless t. ... 1042:14
spit their duties out ... 1545: 3
sued-for t. ... 1541:15
the voice of souls ... 1543: 9
their t. rot ... 1541:16
there 's two t. ... 1546: 4
'tis of aspics' t. ... 1173: 6
to be your being shall rehearse ... 1597: 3
traduced by ignorant t. ... 1375: 5
twenty thousand t. ... 1544: 9
us, that have our t. ... 336: 4
when t. speak sweetly ... 1047: 4
To-night: let me live t. ... 798:14
or never ... 969: 4

Tool, Tools ... 770:10

with the great t. ... 757:10
Tooth: adder's t. ... 1545: 2
by treason's t. bare-gnawn 1052: 8
chewed with a t. ... 1254:14
colt's t. ... 1502: 1
Ethiopian's t. ... 664:15
fell sorrow's t. ... 1408:12
flesh his t. on every innocent 857: 9
fortune's t. ... 919: 5
have a t. in my head ... 934: 1
his venom t. will rankle ... 370: 8
in danger of her former t. 1390: 7
mad dog's t. ... 780:11
ne'er a t. in her head ... 24: 9
of time and razure ... 329:14
serpent's t. ... 187: 4
set my pugging t. on edge 1502:11
that poisons if it bite ... 370: 2
thy t. is not so keen ... 761:10
troubled with a raging t. . 1502: 7

Toys: airy t. 1553: 5
all is but t. 866: 9
any t. for your head 1018: 3
fairy t. 455: 3
fall foul for t. 1553: 3
idle t. 1553: 5
immoment t. 1568: 4
lamenting t. is jollity 787: 6
of desperation 334: 6
such like t. as these 1553: 5
there 's t. abroad 1553: 4
tricks and t. that in them lurk 1702: 7
Track of his fiery car 1469:17
stain the t. of his passage .1467: 2
Tract: leaving no t. behind .394: 3
low t. 1467: 5
of every thing 1486:17
Tractable 1087:4
Trade 1553
and profit of the city 1553:16
bad is the t. that must play fool to sorrow 1553:13
change your t. 1553:14
dreadful t. 364:14
further t. with us 1553: 8
good t. 1553:14
hold-door t. 1112:14
how long have you been at this t. 1554: 2
I will t. to them both 757:11
instruct thee in my t. 1553:15
is it a lawful t. 1553:15
more penitent t. than your bawd 668: 6
of danger ranged 246:12
of moe preferments 1191:14
of war 1037: 5
to t. and traffic 179: 3
what t. are you of 1553:14
what t. art thou ..1356:9; 1486: 1
Trade-fallen: ostlers t.......815: 6
Traded: long t. in it 1637:11
pilots 1154: 1
Traders 1553:10
Trades: beloved of all the t. 310: 7
Tradesman 1553:7
Trading: good t. 1553: 9
Tradition: mock at ancient t. 1011:16
Traditional: too t. 1089:15
Traduced 1375:5
Traducement: less than a t. 1375: 5
to hide your doings 218: 2
Traffic 1554
admit no t. 1554: 5
confound thee 1554: 8
great t. through the world 1554: 7
is thy god 1554: 8
my t. is sheets 877:16
no kind of t. would I admit 209: 7
of a king 802:10
of our stage 1554: 6
with thyself alone 1554: 6
Traffickers: petty t. 1554: 6
Tragedian: deep t. 11: 3
Tragedians: English t. 12: 2
of the city 12: 2
Tragedies and murders fell 1554:16
Tragedy 1554
comedy, history 12: 3
conclude their plotted t. ..1211:20
it would have been a fine t. 1554:13
play'd a t. 1554:12
plotted t. 1554:11
timeless t. 1554:16
woful t. 1554:11
Tragical 1554:13
merry and t. 1003:11
Trail of policy 133: 7
on the false t. they cry 737: 3
this is an aspic's t. 1336:19
Train: honour's t. is longer 714: 6
you t. me to offend you ...1094:17
Train'd thee to my house ..1206: 2
Training: give her princely t. 759: 8
Traitor 1560
accuse York for a t. 6: 9
an arrant t. as any is 1560:14
audacious t. 1558:13
banish'd t. 1560: 9
blind t. 1191:15
call me their t. 1560: 8
covert'st shelter'd t. 1562: 9

Traitor, *continued*
disloyal t. 1560:14
durst the t. breathe 1561: 8
false t. and villain 1562: 5
false t. to myself 966:17
false-heart t. 1560:14
filthy t. 1560:14
find myself a t. 1562: 7
foul t. 1562: 4
giant t. 1561:11
graceless t. 743: 6
great-grown t. 1561: 8
he is a t. ..583:4; 1562:7; 1562:11
himself love's t. 917: 8
I am no t. 1560: 9
I 'll be a t. then 1560:10
if she be a t., why so am I 1560: 5
ignoble t. 684: 6
kissing t. 1561:10
let not a t. live 1561: 7
lives, the true man 's put to death 1562: 8
make me t. to myself 1560: 6
O monstrous t., I arrest thee 1558:13
O passing t., perjured ...1561: 9
old unhappy t. 1481: 7
overweening t. 1298:10
proclaimed t. 1560:14
pronounced a t. 1561: 1
publish'd t. 1560:14
recreant and most degenerate t. 1562: 5
redeem a t. home 1560:11
she 's a t. 1562:14
spoken like a t. 1560: 7
stands in worse case 1560: 9
subtle t. has plotted 1562: 9
subtle t. needs no sophister 1561: 5
take hence that t. 1561: 3
thou art a proud t. 1561:11
thou art a t. 1561:7; 1562:1; 1562: 4
thou hast a t. in thy presence 1562: 8
thou t., thou false thief ..1102:13
to my God, my king 1562: 6
to the crown 1562: 6
to the height 1561:11
to the name of God 1616:10
to the people 1562: 6
toad-spotted t. 1562: 1
unhappy t. 1560:14
vile t. 1560:14
viperous t. 1560: 7
what is a t. 1562: 3
what t. hears me 1562:10
who 's a t. 1561: 3
you do look like 1560: 2
Traitorly rascals 1562:15
Traitorously 1560:3
Traitors all 1560:14
as ye are 1561: 9
avaunt 1562:13
dangerous consorted t. 1560:14
ensteep'd to clog 1503:16
false t. 1562: 9
guard these t. to the block of death 1560:12
horrible t. 1560:14
inhuman t. 1560:14
let the t. stay 1562: 2
men's vows are women's t. 1616: 1
merely our own t. 1560: 2
overweening t. 1560:14
proclaim them t. 430:14
quickly rouse the t. 194:13
remiss t. sleep 1561: 2
revolted faction t. 1560:14
sanctified and holy t. 1606:12
take deep t. for thy dearest friends 591:12
thus do all t. 1560: 5
we are t. and do not know ourselves 1562: 3
what t. have we here 1071:12
Traitress and a dear 903: 6
Trammel up the consequence 1274: 8
Trampling contemptuously ..350:16
Trance: stir him from his t. 376:16
Tranced: I left him t. 376:16
Trances: restless t. 1271: 7
Tranect: bring them unto the t. 1429: 7

Tranio: his name is T. 1053: 8
Tranquil mind 234:11
Tranquillity: nobility and t. .210:11
Trans-shape thy virtues ...1608: 5
Transcendence: great t. 1180:17
Transcends: that praise t. ..1186: 1
Transferred: now t. 452: 9
Transfigured: their minds t. 1447:11
Transfix the flourish 1533: 8
Transformation 1555
a low t. 355: 5
beastly shameless t. 1555: 3
goodly t. of Jupiter 145:13
Hamlet's t. 1267:11
Transformations: their t. were never rarer 1555: 6
Transformed 1555:1
and weaken'd 1555: 5
him ape 44: 1
I am t., am I not 1555: 2
with their fear 1099: 8
Transgressing boy 130:14
slave 1603: 5
Transgression 1565:2
Transgressions: their own t. partially they smother .515: 4
Translate thy life into death 798: 1
you must t. 968: 7
Translated: thou art t. 171: 4
Translation of hypocrisy ...744: 9
Transmigrates: it t. 1501: 1
Transmutation: by t. a bear-herd 745:14
Transparent as barricadoes .732: 9
Helena 694: 2
Transportance: swift t. 1414: 8
Transpose to form and dignity 899: 7
Transylvanian is dead 64: 6
Trap 1555
is laid for me 1555:14
say 'marry t.' with you ...734:12
to take my life 1555:11
Trapped in silver 723: 2
Trappings: some of her t. .1339: 3
these but the t. and the suits of woe 1330: 3
Traps: pretty t. 1555:10
Trash for over-topping 252: 7
for so much t. 140: 1
I do suspect this t. 764:13
it is but t. 497: 4
'tis t. 497: 4
vile t. 311: 3
what t. is Rome 1299: 3
who steals my purse steals t. 1050: 2
Travail: fall in t. 829:11
gentle t., to the gladding ..100: 5
gone in t. 828: 8
is all our t. turn'd 828: 8
of a worthier pen 50:13
on this t. look for greater birth 829:10
Travailed in the shower 828: 8
Travails in thy good 1672: 3
Travel 1556
but four foot 1618:14
discredited your t. 1364:17
further t. 1557: 6
go t. for a while 1557: 2
he 's gone to t. 208:13
how chances it they t. 1556: 9
my youthful t. made me happy 1557: 8
not able to t. 2: 8
oppress'd with t. 1103:11
stained with t. 533: 1
that thou takest for pleasure 1557: 4
will he t. higher 1557: 6
with long t. I am stiff 1556: 8
with t. much oppress'd 934: 2
with t. tired 1386: 1
you far on 1557: 6
Travel-tainted as I am 1556: 8
Travelled all the night 1556:10
but two hours 1556:10
Traveller 1556:7
good t. is something 1556: 6
I was then a young t. 1557: 8
no true t. 1556: 5
now spurs lated t. apace ...766: 4
refined t. of Spain 1556: 5
Shooty the great t. 1556: 5

U

Violence, *continued*
of action has made you reek 1355: 8
of either grief or joy 790: 8
offer him no v. 1604:15
when v. assails us 1332: 1
you would not do me v. ..1115: 7
Violenteth in a sense 646:11
Violet 1604
lying by the v. in the sun 1504:17
nodding v. grows 554: 7
smells to him as to me 807: 4
Violets blue 1436: 6
blue-vein'd v. 1605: 1
dim, but sweeter 555: 5
I would give you some v. ..553:10
purple v. and marigolds ...637: 6
who are the v. now 1604:21
Viper 1390:5
Viperous 1560:7
Vipers: O villains, v. 1390: 5
they are v. 1390: 5
Vir sapit qui pauca loquitur 1419: 4
Virgin 1605:4
from her tender infancy ..1605: 5
he that hangs himself is a v. 667:10
most kind v. 1053: 5
never v. got till virginity was first lost 1605: 3
she is a v. pure 1605: 5
she was a v. 1209:11
so offend a v. 1286: 6
young budding v. 1606: 6
Virgin-knot 938:2
Virgin-like: look'st so v. 5:15
Virgin-violator: a v. 1448:12
Virginal 1496:11
Virginalling upon his palm 1112: 8
Virgined it e'er since 811: 1
Virginity 1605
being blown up 1605: 3
breeds mites 1605: 3
by being once lost may be ten times found 1605: 3
green v. 1606: 7
he had not my v. 1605: 3
I deny her v. 937: 4
is peevish proud 1605: 3
loss of v. 893:13
meditating on v. 1605: 3
murders itself 1605: 3
pretty v. 1606: 2
wears her cap out of fashion 1605: 3
yield him my v. 868:19
Virginius: as woful as V. ..1695: 7
rash V. 290:10
Virgins: beguiling v. 1329:12
best-regarded v. 1605: 4
fresh-fair v. 1393: 6
giving our holy v. to the stain of mad-brain'd war 1606: 8
might blow up men 1605: 3
play with all v. so 1606: 1
Virtue 1606
according to his v. let us use him 1269:16
ample v. 1607:12
and cunning were endowments 1608: 7
and she is her own dower ..934: 1
and that part of philosophy 1150: 2
and true beauty 1607:10
as it never will be moved ..926: 4
assume a v., if you have it not 1607: 2
best v. 1607:12
bethink thee on her v. ...1607: 4
by v. of that ring 1289: 5
calls v. hypocrite 8:19
can v. hide itself 1608: 5
cannot so inoculate our old stock 1607: 1
chiefest v. 1607:12
claims from beauty beauty's red 1608: 8
dear v. 1607:12
dislikest of v. 287: 1
even v. of our enterprise ..1080:10
fair v. 1607:12
finds no friends 1607: 8
for v. loved 1607:13
forgive me my v. 571:13
full of v., bounty 1737:11
he had, deserving 1607: 4

Virtue, *continued*
he lends thee v. 1608:10
her sober v., years 163: 4
Hero's v. 1608: 5
I have borne in arms 1608: 7
I know her v. 1608: 2
I see v. in his looks 945:13
if v. no beauty lack 1608: 6
in grateful v. I am bound 1608:12
in my tears 1500: 6
is beauty 1608:17
is bold 1608: 3
is but patched with sin 1125:11
is choked with foul ambition 33: 5
is her own dower 375: 1
is no horn-maker 1606:12
is not regarded 1607: 6
is of so little regard 1607: 6
is profaned 338:13
is there no v. extant 1447: 8
itself of vice must pardon beg 1599: 7
itself 'scapes not calumnious strokes 1607: 1
itself turns vice 1599:13
let not v. seek remuneration 1608:15
maiden v. of the crown ...264: 8
maiden v. rudely strumpeted 180:10
make a v. of necessity ...1609: 1
my poor v. 351: 8
new-built v. and obedience 1087: 8
no hidden v. in him 1591: 8
no man's v. to be so moral 1127:15
no v. like necessity 1058: 1
no v. whipped out of court 1599:15
O infinite v. 1606:11
of a good wing 349: 7
of compassion 1607:12
of his will 1672:10
of mine eye 1500: 4
of my heart 1607:12
of the ring 1289: 7
of this jest 858: 5
of your eye 450: 9
of your office 1511: 5
pawn'd his knightly v. 358: 1
preserved from destruction 1608: 7
rich in v. 1284: 9
right v. of the medlar 1564:11
rough brake that v. must go through 1607: 7
see thy v. witness'd 1606:12
see v. in his looks 1607: 3
she holds her v. still 1606:14
show v. her own feature 10:10
simple v. 115: 8
so shall my v. be his vice's bawd 1599:11
solid v. 176:11
some by v. fall 1369:19
special v. 1634: 7
such v. hath my pen 1597: 3
sweet v. answer not 80:10
sweet v. in a maid 994: 3
that possession would not show us 893: 5
that transgresses 1599:13
that was never seen in you 1404: 6
this dying v. 1347:10
thrust v. out of our hearts 1608: 4
'tis v. that doth make them most admired 1701: 9
to v. consecrate 358: 3
trust to thy single v. 1607:12
turn her v. into pitch 1169:14
untainted v. of your years 312: 2
we do admire this v. 14: 9
what v. breeds iniquity devours 1608: 8
whitest v. 767: 2
with valour couched 444: 7
would stain that o'er with silver white 460:12
yon dame that minces v. ..744: 8
you nickname v. 1599: 8
your v. hath a license in 't 1608: 2
your v. well deserves it 329: 4
Virtues and traitors too 177: 5
cardinal v. 475:16
cherished by our v. 261: 5
fair v. all 1608:16
for many v. excellent 398: 3

Virtues, *continued*
for several v. have I liked several women 1700: 6
graced with external gifts 899: 1
his v. plead like angels ..1608: 1
if our v. did not go forth 1608: 2
our v. would be proud 860:15
praise her for her v. 1606:12
shining upon others 761: 8
stuffed with honourable v. ..173: 7
that attend the good 1215: 9
their v. we write in water 955:10
thy v. here I seize upon ..1607:12
thy v. spoke of 1712: 3
unpublish'd v. of the earth 1497: 6
your v. are traitors 1606:12
your v. the fairer 1198:15
Virtuous and fair 290: 4
and holy, be thou conqueror 225:17
and holy; chosen from above 708:16
be v. to be obstinate 1089: 8
enough; swore little 1607: 3
famed for v. 469: 6
he would needs be v. 563: 1
I know her v. 1607: 9
I suppose him v. 173:10
mild and too well given ..1607: 5
mild and v. 993:11
offend none but the v. ...1251: 5
out of all suspicion, she is v. 832: 9
prove thee v. 1608:10
seem more v. 1606:12
to lie as to live chastely ...858: 1
why are you v. 1606:12
Virtuously given 1607: 3
Visage 1609
all his v. wann'd 10: 9
behold her silver v. 1022: 6
behold his v. 1609: 3
confront the v. of offence ..984: 4
devotion's v. 744: 1
flay thy wolfish v. 1044: 5
fortified her v. 676: 9
hides not his v. 1468: 1
I saw Othello's v. in his mind 997: 2
let me view his v. 1609: 3
mask thy monstrous v. 230: 5
more in 't than fair v. 1609: 4
of offence 1609: 5
of the times 1536:12
plough thy v. up 1044: 5
put on a v. of demand 1609: 8
settled v. 744:11
show your knave's v. 459: 1
tristful v. 1496: 5
with an importing v. 147: 8
Visages: bleared v. 1666: 2
do cream and mantle 1609: 7
of duty 1609: 4
Visibly character'd 1485: 5
Vision 1609
dream and fruitless v. 1286: 6
fair and fortunate 377:11
fatal v., sensible to feeling 281: 1
full of majesty 1609:10
is full accomplish'd 1609: 9
is this a v. 376:15
most majestic v. 1609:15
most rare v. 1609:12
of the island 1399: 8
sent to her from heaven ..934:11
touching this v. 610: 3
Visions: what v. have I seen 1609:12
Visitation 1609
gentle v. 1610: 4
give you nightly v. 1610: 4
here make v. 1609:16
is it a free v. 755: 1
loving v. 1610: 4
of my friends 588:12
of the winds 1446: 6
this v. shows it 760: 9
'tis not a v. framed 5:13
which he justly owes 1610: 5
you have lent him v. 1610: 1
Visitings: compunctious v. of nature 1260: 5
Visitors: flood of v. 553: 6
Visor 1610
a v. for a v. 1610:10
but one v. remains 1610: 8
I have worn a v. 1488: 7
is an arrant knave 815: 4
my v. began to assume life 1610: 8

Wife, *continued*
leave his w. 1684:12
lewd-tongued w. 1664:10
lie with his neighbour's w. .227: 7
lie with my w. 368:11
light w. doth make a heavy husband 1671: 5
like a makeless w. 1731: 3
like an offensive w. that hath enraged him 1664:10
live an unstain'd w. 1668: 4
look to your w. 1669: 1
love your w. 1665:12
loving w. 1666:1; 1668: 1
make love to Ford's w. 1668:12
make you a w. 1671: 8
man and w. are one in love 1671: 3
man and w. is one flesh ..1671: 3
married a tinker's w. 1298:11
married to a w. 1666: 3
married w. 1665: 1
modest w. 1014: 1
my w. can speak no English 419: 5
my w. comes foremost 1664: 8
my w. desired some damsons 1665: 3
my w. hath bid the world good night 1666:12
my w. is dead to-night 1667: 2
my w. is in a wayward mood 1664: 6
my w. is nothing 1075:15
my w. is shrewish 1664: 6
my w. is slippery 1669: 2
my w.! my w.! what w. ..1666: 9
my w. the nonpareil 1667:11
my w. 's a hobby-horse ...1669: 2
myself would be his w. ...1714: 2
neither maid, widow, nor w. 937: 5
never a w. in Windsor leads a better life 1668: 2
never mistrust my w. 1710: 8
new w. 1664: 2
new-married w. 583: 3
no w. of mine 1372:11
of a detesting lord 1664: 1
of Caius Marcellus 1669: 3
of Hercules 706: 4
offensive w. 1664:10
please your w. 1165: 9
prove such a w. as my thoughts make thee ...1669: 3
quickly leap into a w. 1709:13
quondam w. 1667: 7
railing w. 1501: 6
resolved to take a w. 1667: 9
Romeo's faithful w. 1670: 4
sailor's w. 1696: 6
say my w. is fair 781: 5
shaking off so good a w. ..1664: 1
she is fast my w. 1665:12
she 's thy w. 1664: 1
she 's your w. 1667: 5
shrewd ill-favour'd w. 1669: 5
so noble w. 1664: 2
soliciting his w. 1666: 8
spare my guiltless w. 1666:11
spite my w. 1434: 1
sweet and virtuous w. 1668: 4
take the w. from him 1669: 3
take what w. you will to bed 1666: 1
then lie with my w. 1289: 7
this is a way to kill a w. with kindness 1667: 4
this is his w. 1214: 2
this is my w. 1665: 6
this is your w. 1666:10
this noble w. 1668: 1
this unworthy w. 891: 1
thou hadst a w. once 99: 5
thou hast a w. 1665: 1
thou kep'st a w. herself 740: 1
thy w. hath dream'd 376:15
thy w. is proud 1665: 1
three-hours w. 1049: 1
to Sparta's king 1670:10
to your place 914:13
took to w. 1667: 9
torture my w. 1550: 1
true and honourable w. ...1668: 1
true and humble w. 1667:12
true and loyal w. 1668: 4
usurer's w. 65: 1
where is my w. 1667: 3

Wife, *continued*
wicked w. 1664:10
will you be my w. 1667: 5
with w. enough 1669: 5
woo another w. 1710: 5
would he loved his w. 1664: 1
wretched w. 1664:10
yield myself his w. 1666: 1
'you are my true and honourable w. 1668: 1
you shall be my w. 1669: 5
your husband's brother's w. 1230:10
your quondam w. swears still by Venus' glove ..1667: 7
your w. in all obedience ..1667: 3
your w. is as honest 1668: 2
your w. upward of twenty years 1667:12
Wife-like government 1667:12
more goddess-like than w. .1221: 3
Wight: base Hungarian w. ..87: 6
furious w. 636:12
I ken the w. 1178:10
of high renown 322:10
she was a w. 177: 8
Wightly wanton 1624: 7
Wights: venomous w. 1069: 1
Wild and yet, too, gentle ..1656: 4
as young bulls 1624: 8
gone w. 1671:14
he 's very w. 1671:10
make me w. 1671:14
too w., too rude 1117: 9
turn'd w. in nature 722: 6
Wild-boars roasted whole ...559: 6
Wild-cat: more than the w. 1383:12
woo this w. 1711:12
Wild-cats in your kitchens 1702: 6
Wild-duck 256:3
Wild-fowl: fearful w. 878:14
Wild-geese fly that way ...1683: 2
Wild-goose chase 737: 4
more of the w. 1692: 1
Wild-mare: rides the w. 174: 5
Wilderness 328:13
is populous enough 906: 3
of monkeys 1018: 8
of tigers 1527: 2
Wildfire: ball of w. 458: 4
Wildly: start not so w. 348: 3
Wildness 1671
ere w. vanquish my senses 522: 7
given to w. 1435: 8
grow to w. 848: 7
Hamlet's w. 1671:11
his w., mortified 1671:13
let me in my present w. die 1196: 2
of his youth 1671:12
wilder than tigers in their w. 1703: 6
Wilds: vasty w. of wide Arabia 328:14
Wiles and guiles that women work 1702: 7
upon my wit, to defend my w. 1704: 4
Wilful-blame: too w. 261:17
Wilful-negligent 1060:13
Wilful-opposite: too w. ...1089:13
Wilfulness: book my w. 425: 8
Hydra-headed w. 1089:10
Will: mayst have thy 'W.' ..1674: 6
my name is 'W.' 1051: 1
thou hast thy 'W.' 1674: 6
Will 1672
after your w. 1672: 9
against his w. 1673:16
against my w. ...1057:9; 1751: 8
all is as she w. 1673:13
an 't be thy w. 1672:16
as w. the rest 1672:14
asking my good w. 290: 7
at war 'twixt w. and w. not 1673:11
at w., at thy w. 1672: 9
attend our w. 1674: 5
best w. 1672: 7
by God's w. 619:12
by my w. 1673: 7
by w. bequeath'd 1675: 8
canker'd grandam's w. ...1675: 7
cloyed w. 331:15
command thy rebel w. 205:18
constant w. 1673: 5

Will, *continued*
do my good w. 313: 6
do what you w. ...486:11; 813: 7
do your w. 1672: 9
dotes that is attributive ...1674: 8
fetch the w. hither 1675: 6
fleshes his w. in the spoil of her honour 1329:10
forestall their w. 1674: 5
frame your w. to mine ...1674: 1
free w. 1672: 4
God's good w. 1695: 2
God's w. 619:12
God's w. be done 619:12
good w. 1674:10
hath a w. to die 305:10
have my w. 1672:18
he hath made his w. 1675: 4
he hath my good w. 1674:10
he, nill he 387: 6
headier w. 999:10
heaven's w. 698:12
her w., recoiling 1673:17
hide my w. in thine 1674: 6
high w. 1673: 6
his w. is most malignant ..1673: 2
his w. is not his own 640:14
his w. Lord of his reason .1673:14
honest w. 1672: 8
hot-burning w. 1673: 5
I am fall'n out with my more headier w. 999:10
I do beg your good w. 1674:10
I w. not come to-day 1673: 3
if e'er my w. did trespass ..533:16
if it be thy w. 1411:10
if it be your w. 1672:16
ill w. never said well 1219: 3
in w. peculiar 1674: 8
incensed w. 1673: 5
into appetite 47: 9
is deaf 1674: 2
is infinite 921: 4
is large and spacious 1674: 6
it is my w. 1674: 5
it was against our w. 228: 1
leads the w. to desperate undertakings 894:11
let me have your good w. .1710: 8
let your w. attend 1672: 6
make his w. his act 641:12
most incorrect to heaven ..644: 3
my father's w. 1675: 7
my good w. is great 1252: 8
my uncle's w. is mine 1673: 4
my w. enkindled 452: 4
my w. is back'd with resolution 1674: 2
my w. is even this 1674: 9
my w. is something sorted 1674: 9
my w. is strong 1674: 2
my w. is your good w. 1675: 2
my w. shall stand for law 1673: 1
no w. to wander forth ..1622:11
obedient to his w. 1673:10
obedient to your grace's w. 1086: 8
obey our w. 1086: 6
'od's my w. 1085: 2
of a dead father 1673:12
of a living daughter 1673:12
of God 619: 2
of heaven 1594:17
of heaven be done 698:12
of man is by his reason swayed 1673:14
oppose my w. 1103: 6
our w. became the servant 1673: 9
overbear your w. 1673:15
particular w. 1673: 5
pray they have their w. ..1701: 2
puzzles the w. 1461: 1
resolved w. 1673: 5
rude w. 1673: 5
say you w., and go 1672: 7
shall break it 1673: 7
so was his w. in his old feeble body 508: 8
stays upon your w. 1672:15
stubborn w. to please 561: 8
studied her w. 1673:13
such a w. most rank 1673:17
sweet w. 1674: 6
that bars the title 1675: 7
their law 's their w. 809:10
thou hast thy w. 1650: 4

Winds, *continued*
contrarious w. that held the king so long 1676:16
did sing it to me 1260:12
four w. blow in 1736:11
free as mountain w. 584:11
gentlest w. of heaven 1677:15
grow high 1325:11
high w. 983:8; 1677: 3
howling w. 1677: 2
if the w. rage 1325: 8
make his bleak w. kiss ..1072:15
may the w. blow till they have waken'd death ..1504: 1
of all the corners 1476:15
of March 555: 5
opposed w. 217:12
piping to us 557:17
rough w. do shake 1677: 2
scolding w. have rived ..1503:12
senseless w. 1677: 6
sneaping w. 1678:12
untie the w. 1677:13
viewless w. 304: 9
warring w. 456: 5
were love-sick 1352: 6
wound the loud w. 1482: 9
Windsor: born at W. 101:10
castle 160:14
forest 570: 3
Wine 1679
carry the w. in 1680:12
claret w. 1680: 4
conquering w. hath steep'd our sense in Lethe 1679:10
drink some w. ere you go 1680:12
enough to drink 1679:10
fill, Lucius, till the w. o'er-swell the cup 1680: 8
fill me some w. 1680: 1
force the w. peep through 1679:10
give me some w. ..385:1; 1679:12
good w. is a good familiar creature 1679:13
good w. needs no bush 1679:13
Greekish w. 112:12
have we no w. here 1680: 2
have w. enough anon 1680:14
he calls for w. 385: 3
he drinks no w. 1680: 6
is made of grapes 1679: 9
loved I deeply 1680: 9
marvellous searching w. ..1680: 4
of life is drawn 866: 9
red w. and rhenish 107: 2
red w. first must rise 1490: 1
sack and w. 1310: 1
some w., boys 1680:13
some w., within there 1679:12
such w. and sugar 1710: 7
taste some w. with me ..1680: 8
to good w. they do use good bushes 1679:13
to see w. heat fools 526:10
wash'd to death with fulsome w. 1680:14
with w. and wassail 1275: 7
Wing 1681
country's broken w. 246: 2
dragon w. of night 1065: 4
hold a w. quite from flight ..19: 8
howlet's w. 1681: 4
imagined w. our scene flies 1029:14
of all occasions 1710: 7
on the w. of occasions 1090:12
on w. soaring aloft 393:13
partridge w. 1471: 4
prunes the immortal w. 97: 6
stir a w. 1681: 3
stoop with the like w. 19: 8
swiftest w. of recompense 1252: 5
wherewith we fly to heaven 747:17
with nimble w. we were enforced to fly 551: 7
Wings and no eyes figure unheedy haste 913: 6
as swift as meditation 1277: 1
borrow Cupid's w. 272: 3
chaste w. obey 98: 7
clapp'd w. to me 1515: 4
coal-black w. 262:12
flies with swallow's w. 719:10
follow us with w. 551:11
from Cupid's shoulder pluck his painted w. ..272: 7

Wings, *continued*
he has w. 650: 2
lend me w. 898: 1
love's light w. 899:10
mount with w. of victory 1600: 9
no w. to fly from God 619: 4
of night 1659:10
of our protector's grace ..1681: 3
of war 1681: 4
ravens' w. 1681: 4
saffron w. upon my flowers 1359: 4
set the very w. of reason to his heels 349: 7
shaking her w. 1681: 4
slender gilded w. 556: 9
slow and flagging w. 1696:13
swallow's w. 1681: 4
swiftest w. of speed 1428: 7
use my w. 1681: 4
wanteth w. 1681: 2
with what w. shall his affection fly 19: 8
would I had w. 1681: 2
woven w. 1353: 7
Wink again, and I will w. 1681:12
and laugh upon you 1681: 9
as good to w. 1064:15
at insolence 1681: 7
do w. and yield 934:10
each at other 1286: 6
every w. of an eye 634: 9
give enemy lasting w. 1175: 4
I have not slept one w. ..1386: 4
I will w. and hold out 777: 3
I 'll w. and couch 462: 7
not be seen to w. 296:10
on her to consent 1681: 6
perpetual w. 301: 9
rather w. than look 1681:12
such as w. 445:12
when most I w. 446: 2
while one would w. 270: 7
with fullness 1541: 9
you judge I w. 1364: 4
Winked: I have not w. since I saw these sights 1364: 4
Winkest whiles thou art waking 575: 1
Winking 1681
at your discords 1222: 7
leap'd into destruction ..1182:16
mute and dumb 1681: 5
of authority 808: 1
to consent w. 1681: 6
Winks: he w. and turns 881:10
her w., and nods 1681: 5
Winner 1682
and loser 892:11; 894: 4
being a w., God give you 1617:12
name the w. 428: 6
of her honour 1289: 3
Winners: beshrew the w. ..892:11
Winning 1681
hazard the w. 679: 6
light w. make prize light 1208:10
will put any man into courage 894: 2
Winnow the truth from falsehood 1549:10
Winnowed: throughly to be w. 1565:15
with so rough a wind 1677: 2
Winnows the light away ..365: 4
Wins: he that w. of all 935: 1
this w. him, liver and all 1682: 9
whoever w., on that side shall I lose 894: 6
Winter 1682
and rough weather 412: 3
angry w. 1326:11
as w. to foul weather 901: 4
barren w., with his cold ..214: 3
being full of care 1683: 7
bid the w. come 1683: 1
burn a Poland w. 1656: 5
chide rough w. 1683: 5
churlish w. 1682:18
cold biting w. mars 1682:18
coming on 1682:17
deepest w. in Timon's purse 1225: 7
dreading the w. near 3: 9
fall the w. long 553:10
frozen w. 1682:18
furious w. 1682:18
hideous w. 1465:11

Winter, *continued*
how like a w. hath my absence been 3: 9
I 'll take that w. from your lips, fair lady 813: 5
is at hand 1683: 6
is not gone yet 1683: 2
limping w. 204: 9
lust's w. comes 921: 7
lusty w. 1682:18
make rough w. everlastingly 717:13
of our discontent 347: 6
present w. 1195: 1
sap-consuming w. 1682:18
should cut off spring-time 1650: 7
still w. in storm perpetual 819: 9
tames man, woman and beast 1683: 9
trembling w. 555: 5
yet seem'd it w. still 3: 9
Winter-time: all the w. 338: 6
Winterly: if w. 1062:12
Winters: howl'd away twelve w. 1521:12
five-score w. worn 449: 1
four lagging w. 1717:19
six frozen w. spent 66: 7
six or seven w. 868:19
sixteen w. cannot blow ..1410: 2
three w. cold 1683: 8
what is six w. 790:14
when forty w. shall besiege thy brow 24:11
worn so many w. out 1048: 3
Wire: whipp'd with w. 1520: 5
Wires: black w. grow on her head 656: 5
Wiry concord 881: 6
friends 655: 8
Wis: I w. your grandam ..961: 5
Wisdom 1683
and blood combating 110: 8
and fortune combating 1683:13
and goodness to the vile seem vile 628: 1
as your w. will 1684: 7
by their wit to lose 563: 9
call her w. to her 1684: 9
cries out in the streets ..1684: 5
divorce not w. from your honour 367:16
doubt not of your w. 1684: 8
fair w., not thy passion ..1685: 8
foreign w. 1684: 3
herein lives w., beauty ..1685:11
his w. be not tainted 931:11
I approve your w. 1683:13
I will not praise thy w. ..1685: 8
if w. be in suffering 1683:12
in peace, your bounty 1608: 9
in w. hatch'd 100:11
in w. never was so frail ..177: 8
in your rich w. 1684:11
is consumed in confidence ..223:10
leave you to your w. 1683:11
made use of that good w. 1684: 9
modern w. plucks me 674:11
modest w. 1014: 1
of nature can reason 1099:11
of the world 1284:17
of their choice 1685: 4
of w. and of reach 269: 6
pace your w. 1684:13
see cold w. waiting 1685:10
show your w. 1684:13
suck'd w. from thy teat ..961: 6
that doth guide his valour 121:17
'tis w. to conceal our meaning 970:11
to leave his wife 1684:12
to w. he 's a fool that will not yield 1685: 2
unmuzzle your w. 1515:11
what w. stirs 1685: 9
wholesome w. 1255:13
whose w. was a mirror ..1684: 8
wishes to appear most bright 1684:13
your own proper w. 712: 8
your w. be your guide 1684: 6
Wisdoms: better w. 1684: 3
vulgar w. 1684: 3
your w. could not discover 566: 7
Wise and full of gibes 1684:14
and valiant 1590: 9

Womb, *continued*
fatal cannon's w. 1175: 2
foul w. of night 1067: 6
from her w. children 398: 3
from his mother's w. untimely ripp'd 100: 1
from that w. where you imprison'd were 102: 1
from the w. I did participate 1433:12
her w. then rich 1705: 9
hollow w. inherits 637: 7
hollow w. resounds 723: 8
if wishes had a w. 185:11
in the w. he stay'd 131: 7
into her w. convey sterility 1705: 7
my lady's w. 1705: 7
my mother's w. 1705: 5
my w. undoes me 94: 5
of death 1540:13
of earth 1563: 2
of pia mater 1431:12
of time 428:12
offspring in my w. 186:11
her plenteous w. expresseth 1705: 8
ripe in fortune's w. 1408:11
ripping up the w. 1561:14
shame my mother's w. 1027: 8
sin-conceiving w. 1705:14
slanderous to thy mother's w. 1584: 3
strangling thee in her accursed w. 1028:12
swallowing w. of this deep pit 1452:10
teeming w. 1705:12
that bed, that w. 142:11
thy mother's heavy w. 187:15
thy w. let loose 1583: 8
tread on mother's w. 245:10
uneared w. 1705: 8
unmeasurable 1056:15
wherein they grew 1597: 3
within a puddle's w. 834: 6
your daughter's w. 188: 2
Wombs: good w. have borne bad sons 1705:13
like widow'd w. 1705:12
Womby vaultages 1274: 2
Women: a' did handle w. ..1701: 5
alas, poor w.! make us but believe 1703: 8
are angels, wooing 1713: 4
are as roses 1699: 9
are light at midnight 1703:11
are made to bear 1699: 3
are more valiant 411:12
are not in their best fortunes strong 1700:10
are shrewd tempters 1701: 6
are shrews, both short and tall 1701: 4
are soft, mild 1701: 9
ashamed that w. are so simple 1702: 9
being the weaker vessels ..1622: 2
bigger, w. grow by men ...954: 9
came of w. 1698:15
cannot love where they 're beloved 917: 1
detected for w. 755: 7
disdain the German w. 609:12
do abuse their husbands ...742: 8
earthly w. 1703:11
for several virtues have I liked several w. 1700: 6
ghastly w., transformed ..1099: 8
great-bellied w. 1192: 7
had w. been so strong as men 1754: 7
have been captivate 1698: 8
headstrong w. 1702: 9
honest w. 1699:13
how hard it is for w. to keep counsel 1698:12
how many w. would do such a message 1291: 1
let mild w. lose their mildness 1703: 6
living w. 1698:17
make one of her w. lawyer .844:14
make our w. fight 760:20
may fall, when there 's no strength in men 954: 9
nay, w. are frail too 1704: 1

Women, *continued*
none but w. left to wail ..1179: 3
of all fashion 1207:16
of good carriage 937: 8
other w. cloy the appetites 1699:12
poor informal w. 1702: 4
sad w. 1698:17
say so, that will say anything 874: 1
set the w. on 215: 1
silly w. 1106:15
still give the lie to their consciences 1700:11
sup any w. with him 1470: 9
tell-tale w. rail 809: 8
to change their shapes 998: 9
to w. he be bent 1702: 7
transform us not to w. ...1649:11
two w. placed together makes cold weather ...1697:11
weak-made w. 1702: 8
weird w. 1698:17
why stand we like soft-hearted w. here 1698:10
will all turn monsters 1702: 2
will love her 903: 5
wise w. 1698:17
wish'd w. had men's privilege 1711: 2
you should be w. 74: 4
Won: gentle thou art and therefore to be w. 1713: 9
hard to seem w. 1682:11
in this humour w. 1713: 8
she is a woman, therefore to be w. 1713: 5
so fairly w. 294:12
things w. are done 1713: 4
well w. is still well shot ..1147:13
with blood 111: 1
with the first glance 1682:11
you are doubly w. 1681:13

Wonder 1706
a w., master 1352: 2
and amazement 32: 3
and that 's a w. 1707:11
at the things you hear 1706: 9
at this haste 675:13
attired in w. 1707: 2
be still and w. 1706: 2
begetting w. 1707:17
bring forth a w. 1707:12
bring in w. to wait on treason 1706:13
cast yourself in w. 522:14
enough for your w. 1707:17
feeds on his w. 1706:10
few days' w. 1706:15
Gallia's w. 1748: 2
general w. 1707: 5
gives me w. 1707: 8
greatly 1706: 2
harrows me with w. 1706:10
here is a w. 1707:11
I am bound to w. 1155:12
I do much w. 1706: 7
I w. in my soul 1234: 8
in a mortal eye 440:14
increase our w. 1707: 9
is that a w. 1707:11
kneel down, and w. 151: 6
leave off to w. 1707: 1
let no man w. 1621:12
let w. seem familiar 1707: 7
make it no w. 1707:10
mute w. lurketh in men's ears 1422: 8
no w. 1707:10
not 1707:15
O you w. 937: 1
of good deeds 319: 2
of nature 1406: 7
of the world 1706: 6
of time 1434: 1
of your frame 1707: 4
our earth's w. 1706: 6
out of w. 1706:15
rapt in the w. of it 1707: 2
shows off your w. 1367:14
silent w. of still-gazing eyes 1707: 4
special w. 1707: 3
spend our w. too 13:14
such estimable w. 1707:14
ten days' w. 1706:15

Wonder, *continued*
there 's some w. in this handkerchief 1707: 8
this I w. at 1706: 7
'tis a w. 1707:11
'tis w. that enwraps me ..1707:14
too much w. of his eye ...446: 9
white w. of Juliet's hand ..664:14
yet let me w. 1706: 7
you will w. at 1706: 1
Wonder-wounded hearers ...644: 5
Wondered: be more w. at ..1466: 2
I was wondered at 1706:11

Wonderful 1706:3; 1706:4
O w., when devils tell the truth 339: 1
Wondering each other's chance 978: 1
grace equal with w. 634: 9
look'd w. each at other 255: 8
not w. at the present 1124: 5
Wonders: compass w. 1706:14
discourse w. 1707: 6
enacted w. 1706:14
enroll'd 'mongst w. 949: 6
former w. 1707: 5
greater w. than that 1706: 5
his w. and his praises do contend 1184:10
I will tell thee w. 1707:16
see the w. of the world 1557: 1
they do plot unlikely w. ..1514:14
thou speakest w. 1418:14
you shall see w. 1707: 5
Wondrously: leans w. 347: 9
Woo: cannot come to w. ...1711:12
cannot w. in festival terms 1711: 5
come, w. me, w. me 1709: 8
contrary 1710: 5
fain would I w. her 1713: 5
for leave to do him good ..1709:11
he 'll w. a thousand 1712: 2
her, wed her and bed her ..1713:10
her with some spirit 1712: 1
how canst thou w. her 1711: 9
I set him every day to w. me 1709: 8
I should w. hard 1709:10
in other places 231: 5
just how he would w. 1709: 6
leave me alone to w. him .1709: 7
let him w. for himself 1713:12
let me w. no more 1714: 5
nor w. in rhyme 1710: 2
not like a babe 1711:12
rather w. those that would mischief me 1712: 4
thee for my wife 1712: 3
then w. thyself 1714: 3
two at once w. one 1711: 1
vow never to w. her 254:10
we were not made to w. ..1711: 2
when I come to w. ladies, I fright them 508: 3
yet will I w. for him 1714: 2
you like a soldier 1713: 1
your own destruction 335: 6

Wood 1707
began to move 1708: 3
Birnam w. 1708: 3
blessed w. whose motion ...881: 6
burn sweet w. 1144: 1
fetch in our w. 1341: 9
get out of this w. 1708: 5
get thee w. enough 545: 9
he talks of w. 828: 7
I 'll bring my w. home 1549: 5
in some mistrustful w. 32: 4
in the w. where often 1708: 4
lost in a thorny w. 16:12
making dead w. more blest 881: 6
nor doth this w. lack worlds of company 211: 3
O w. divine 907: 1
of Birnam 1251: 1
of Crete 1707:18
out of this w. do not desire to go 1708: 5
Priam's painted w. 65: 6
rooky w. 1707:18
stolen unto this w. 1708: 4
there 's w. enough within .1709: 5
unto the w. they hie 1708:11
wandering in the w. 1622:14
wild w. 1707:18

Yielder: not born a y. 256: 6
up of breath 1560:12
Yielding 1753
'gainst some reason 1248: 5
I see a y. 1754: 2
impute this y. to light love 1754: 9
this y. rescues thee 1754: 2
Yieldings: accessary y. 755: 5
Yields: she y. to me 1754: 7
you up 1754: 5
Yoke 1754
and sufferance 257: 7
bear the y. 145:12
bear your y. 1128: 8
brought to y. the enemies .1482:10
endure the y. 1754:12
equal y. of love 210: 2
fortune's y. 247: 8
golden y. of sovereignty ..1755: 3
my burthen'd y. 146: 6
never y. with him 1754:11
no bearing y. they knew ...136: 4
of bullocks 1754:18
of government 1251: 7
of his discarded men 1754:18
of inauspicious stars 302:12
of love 1755: 3
of Rome 1755: 4
of tyranny 1582:13
put the y. upon 's 1754:12
Roman y. 158:13
shake off our slavish y. ...1380: 7
shameful y. 1754:15
sinks beneath the y. 245:14
so well together 959:12
this age's y. 26: 4
unwished y. 1754:20
we 'll y. together 217: 7
will not endure his y. 1455:14
Yoke-devils: two y. 1558:14
Yoke-fellow 217:7
Yoke-fellows in arms 1754:13
Yoked: so y. by a fool 566:13
with a lamb 38:14
Yokes: fair y. 1754:19
Yoketh your rebellious necks 1754:14
Yoking arms 52: 9
York is the worthier 1738: 1
welcome to Y. 1653:10
You: all too precious y. 1208: 9
alone are y. 1185: 9
but y., O y. 1700: 6
how wise y. are 1684:10
tell that y. are y. 1745: 9
Young and fair, handsome, light, etc. 1755: 8
and rose-lipp'd 1755: 8
and simple 1755: 8
and so unkind 1759: 5
and tender 1756:15
feed their y. 528:12
he is very y. 1758:16
I am too y. 918: 3
I doubt we should have been too y. for them ..1758: 1
if I were y. again 1755: 6
in days 1758: 7
in limbs 21:11
make the y. old 900: 4
noble and y. 1071: 4
poor y. was limed 1555:12
she is y. and apt 1758:14
she is y., wise, fair 712: 5
so y., and true 1757: 3
such a y. one 1758:13
thou ever y., fresh 625: 1
to be y. again 1755: 6
too y. for such a place 1758: 1
too y. in this 1756: 1
too y. to value her 1756: 1
too y., too happy 1396:15
valiant, wise 1590: 9
we that are y. 21: 6
when I was y. 1755: 5
with y. 1759: 7
would I were y. 1757:11
yet but y. in deed 314:13
you are not y. 1484:10
you are y. 1758: 7
Young-eyed cherubins 1040: 6
Younger: looks y. than he did 73: 6
the y. rises 1757: 4
we shall ne'er be y. 1755:10
Youngest for a bride 936: 9
Youngling, learn thou 191: 7
thou canst not love 910: 4
Youngly thou best owest ...111: 9
Youngster proud and wild .1758:13
Younker 1758:13
or a prodigal 68: 3
trimm'd like a y. 1024:10
Yours: I am y. for ever 97: 2
take upon you what is y. .1178: 8
this same myself are y. ...1178: 9
to you and y. 1178: 9
what is y. is mine 1178: 9
what 's mine is y. 498:14
Yourself: am I y. 1665: 7
be to y. as you would to your friend 586: 5
do not y. such wrong 1751: 3
hang y. 667:12
keep y. within y. 1331: 7
know y. 896: 6
making y. no less 1178:12
me, y., your half 1665: 7
praise y. 1186: 5
prepare y. 1193: 7
straight satisfy y. 1316: 2
vex not y. 242:10
you cannot shun y. 212: 4
you forget y. 570:12
you may thank y. 892:10
you will kill y. 798:13
Yourselves: cursing y. 274:17
go hang y. 667:16
love not y. 1332:14
Youth 1755
abused her delicate y. 179: 9
and ease 21: 6
and liberty 1756: 7
authorized y. did livery falseness 1304:13
bang'd the y. into dumbness 1503:16
beauteous and lovely y. ..1755:14
blown y. 1756: 8
bring down rose-cheeked y. 1661: 2
burning y. 1224: 5
chid his truant y. 222: 8
commit his y. to your direction 345: 9
corrupted the y. of the realm 402: 4
deal mildly with his y. ...1758: 6
die in his y. 307: 6
disdainful y. 832:17
English y. 1756:13
fair y. 1755:14
fairest y. that ever made eye swerve 912: 1
fine bragging y. 583: 7
flaming y. 1756: 8
flowering y. 164: 3
flush y. 1756: 8
foolish y. 1757: 8
fresh and stainless y. 173:10
fright my y. 1758:15
gallant y. 600:3; 1755:14
gentle y. 1755:14
good y. 1756: 5
Greekish y. 1759: 1
happiest y., viewing his progress 1756:11
home-keeping y. have ever homely wits 710: 2
honourable y. 1645:14
hot y. 1756: 8
humorous y. 734: 6
I do adore thee 21:12
in art 56: 2
in my y. I never did apply ..22: 4
in y., when I did love 905: 8
is a devil 1759: 2
is a rare courtier 252: 8
is a stuff will not endure ..896: 1
is bought more oft than begg'd or borrow'd 1759: 2
is full of pleasance 21:12
is full of sport 21:12
is hot and bold 21:12
is nimble 21:12
is wild 21:12
it is a pretty y. 1755:14
know of your y. 332: 3
led on by bloody y. 1250: 8
like summer morn 21:12
lose thy y. in peace 508: 6
maiden y. 934:12
Youth, *continued*
melted down thy y. 927: 9
moonish y. 1757: 8
more than a y. 742: 5
my tender y. was never yet attaint 1756:15
my y. can better spare my blood 1758:15
my y. hath faulty wander'd 1756:10
nips y. i' the head 744:11
no less becomes the livery ..21: 7
noble y. 1755:14
noble y. did dress 1002: 3
not clean past your y. 21: 9
O admirable y. 1758:16
of England 1756:13
of primy nature 1604:19
pretty y. 1755:14
resembling strong y. in his middle age 1467: 5
riotous y. 1757: 8
robb'd me of my y. 1756:10
shall my y. be guilty 1756:14
shallow, humorous y. 1319: 9
shepherd y. 1351: 6
slaughter'd y. 637:13
so apt to pluck a sweet ...1614: 8
spend his y. 1757: 1
spend his y. at home 710: 2
stir up Athenian y. 988:13
straying y. 1756: 8
suffering y. 1757: 7
sweet y. 1755:14
sweet y. is in love 900: 8
sweet-faced y. 872: 6
tell this y. what 'tis to love .894:10
tender y. is soon suggested 1756:15
thankful and reverend y. .1420: 4
that flourisheth 22: 2
that means to be of note ..1024: 4
the more it is wasted 1756:10
they hate us y. 1756: 9
this northern y. 1345:11
thou art a gallant y. 1755:14
thou hast nor y. nor age ..868:19
till y. take leave 1757: 1
to flaming y. let virtue be as wax 1756: 8
to itself rebels 1756: 6
unbaked and doughy y. ...1757: 8
unbruised y. with unstuff'd brain 1758:10
ungovern'd y. 1756: 8
unhappy y. 1757: 8
unharden'd y. 1711: 1
unstaid y. 242:10
untutor'd y. 912:11; 1758: 3
valiant y. 1755:14
virtuous y. 1758: 9
we will our y. lead on 847: 1
wear out thy y. with shapeless idleness 1557: 1
well govern'd y. 1758: 9
well-accomplished y. 1607:13
what levity 's in y. 855: 8
wilful y. 1756: 8
Youthful still 1757:12
Youths: Grecian y. are full of quality 642: 4
our y. and wildness 638:14
that fight for bitten apples 1757: 2
unrough y. that protest their first of manhood .1757: 8
Yslaked: sleep y. 1390:13

Z

Zanies: fools' z. 566:12
Zany: some slight z. 1437: 1
Zeal 1759
accuse my z. 1726:15
and charity brought to the field 582: 1
burns in his nose 1073: 9
had I but served my God with half the z. 1340:16
hot ardent z. 891: 6
infer the z. I had 1759: 9
more bright in z. 910: 8
of all professors 1210:11
quench the z. of professors .80: 4
right Christian z. 340: 6
true z. and deep integrity 1189:10
upright z. to right prevails 1759:10
with what z. 148: 6